Lane Cooper,
Ithaca, Jan. 12, 1916.

from his friend and comrade,
Charles G. Osgood

MacKellar

A CONCORDANCE

TO THE

POEMS OF EDMUND SPENSER

EDMOND SPENCER
A·1596·ÆT·86·

Edmund Spenser
From a reputed portrait in the possession of
the Right Honorable Lewis Harcourt, of Nuneham Park

A CONCORDANCE

TO THE

POEMS OF EDMUND SPENSER

COMPILED AND EDITED

BY

CHARLES GROSVENOR OSGOOD

PROFESSOR OF ENGLISH IN PRINCETON UNIVERSITY

PUBLISHED BY

THE CARNEGIE INSTITUTION OF WASHINGTON

1915

CARNEGIE INSTITUTION OF WASHINGTON

Publication No. 189

PRESS OF J. B. LIPPINCOTT COMPANY
PHILADELPHIA

PREFACE

SPENSER is not a popular poet. He has never been in any marked degree even fashionable. Milton, content with fit audience though few, ranked in Pope's and Johnson's time with Shakespeare and the musical glasses. Ladies read his poetry in their boudoirs, and chatted about its beauties in company—absurdly enough no doubt. But such admiration could never befall Spenser. His materials, quality, and intention forbid that a multitude of readers should ever gather about him.

Yet his is a peculiar glory. From the appearance of the *Shepherd's Calendar* to this day he has been neither ignored nor neglected. An ardent and undying appreciation, glowing round about his poetry, has given constant proof of the abundant vitality within. In steadiness of appreciation from his first signal performance, and in absence of strong disapproval at any time, he seems to be distinguished above all other English poets.

But if this appreciation has been fairly constant in degree, it has further distinguished Spenser by its variety. Each generation of critics has discovered new things in him, and each has admired him for a different quality. And though all these qualities are actual, the sum of all is not the sum of his poetry. A new generation, with new knowledge and philosophies, will correct and enlarge the critical measure of the man and his work. Spenser is like a landscape of rugged mountain or restless sea, qualified with glimpses of more genial and intimate details—sunlit meadow, or human habitation. Viewed in the changing lights of history and opinion, by interpreters of varying temper and judgment, he changes in significance, and indeed in total appearance, though essentially ever the same. While this is the case in the history of any great artist, it is peculiarly so with Spenser. To the classicist he is classic; to the romanticist, romantic. To Milton he is "sage and serious," a higher teacher than Scotus or Aquinas, one in whose rapturous song more is meant than meets the ear; to a man of the senses his imagination teems with loveliness, and riots in a boundless paradise of beautiful things. To the mystic he is a seer, to the moralist an expositor of ethics. For the historian he embodies and illustrates in essence the noblest traits of the two great cultures from which his work drew its sustenance. He is lyric or epic, satiric or philosophical, naïve or sophisticated. To all men of finer perceptions and sensibilities he is all things. He is the poet's poet.

Viewed historically, all great art is of two kinds. Especially so is poetry. Either its creative influence is not exerted much beyond itself, and its glory is primarily its own; or it reveals the power to propagate itself through succeeding generations, to found a school, to poetize material and language for artists in ages

v

to come, to exert subtle and pervading influences in creating and shaping new artists, new mediums, new art. Of the first kind is the art of Dante and Shakespeare and Beethoven. For, though these have unquestionably influenced successors, yet in proportion to their greatness their power in this respect is small. Of the second kind is the poetry of the Greeks, whose material, drawn from ordinary sources in life common to all men, is refined, heightened, transmuted by their touch, and handed down to singers of later ages already filled with the sublimer meaning essential to poetry. Thus a roving and unscrupulous adventurer, with a talent for sensation, was so transformed by Homer and others that Dante employs him to express, in one of its purest and earliest forms, the energy and aspiration of the Renaissance, and in Tennyson he symbolizes the heroic curiosity of science that marks the later age. So also the language of the Greek poets was in essence the common speech of men in their times; but it too has been purged and elevated by their use of it in poetry until it has become a quickening, purifying, and ennobling influence in the poetic language of all other tongues upon which it has breathed. In this sense Greek poetry is normalizing and standard; in this sense especially it is classic.

In much the same sense Milton and Spenser are classic. Though usually ranked in English poetry fourth among the sons of light, Spenser is in this respect perhaps the first of them all. From his contemporary, Marlowe, to the present day, virtually all great poets of whatever manner or school bear witness, conscious or unconscious, to his power. Works consciously imitated from Spenser—*The Purple Island*, *The Castle of Indolence*, *Childe Harold*—though numerous enough, represent but a more superficial and less significant phase of it. In subtler and more essential ways Spenser's power exerts itself in Marlowe, Shakespeare, the Fletchers, Jonson, Milton, Dryden, Pope, Gray, Collins, Goldsmith, Chatterton, Burns, Wordsworth, Coleridge, Scott, Shelley, Keats, Tennyson, and a host of minor writers. Here it is seen in the metrical form, there in the fable or matter, now in the style, now in the single phrase or word; it appears even in the transformed aspect of things which Spenser has helped his successors to perceive. Indeed, much of the traditional language and idiom of our poetry has been made poetical by Spenser, and begins with him.

As yet the just measure of this far-reaching power in Spenser is undetermined. In truth the exact appraisal and description of the poet's work as a whole is but begun. Criticism of his poetry, however appreciative, has been hitherto almost entirely impressionistic and variable, and we are still far from the whole truth concerning him. We are told by various writers that he is gentle, or coarse, or saccharine, or formless, or artificial, or excessive, or recondite, or obvious. One who reads Spenser thoughtfully, and continues to read him, readily grows sceptical of the generalizations vainly repeated from critic to critic. But Spenser can yet be known. He is discoverable in the use which he made of all the materials ready to his hand, in the services which he rendered to the English language, in his daring and exquisite manipulation of words, in the beauty and the meaning of story, picture, song, idea that constitute his poetry, and in their structural relation to each other. A concordance to his poems, whatever its minor uses, is content to justify itself as a means to the discovery of these real values in Spenser, that his cultural and spiritualizing power may be enlarged among readers who are by nature capable of his influence.

The first of many questions to confront the maker of a concordance is the choice of a text. In 1907, at the inception of the work, the text of Morris [1] (cited as M.), then the best, was adopted for this concordance. Work was well under way when, in 1908, was published a new and more accurate text by Professor R. E. Neil Dodge [2] (cited as D.). D., like M., is founded upon all the first editions; but it is more nearly free from misprints, and is on the whole more judicious and consistent in its readings from later editions. It therefore is, to my mind, the best text. In 1909 appeared an edition of the *Faery Queen* by Mr. J. C. Smith, and in 1910 an edition of the Minor Poems by Professor Ernest de Sélincourt; the two constitute a complete edition in three volumes,[3] which is here cited as Oxf.

D., since it is founded upon the same originals as M., has served to correct numerous misprints, inaccuracies, and inconsistencies of M. To this end I have collated the two editions nearly throughout. Oxf., where it is based upon the same originals as M. and D., has often served to settle a difference between them. For Books I–III of the *Faery Queen*, however, it follows the edition of 1596, where the others follow that of 1590. Where Oxf. differs in vocabulary from the others, I have recorded the variants that the word-list of the poet might be as nearly complete as possible. A few errors in Oxf. have been disregarded, such as "chased" for "chafed," *Hub.* 6; "runes" for "tunes," *Mui.* 412 (corrected in the one-volume reprint, 1912); "Coloffes" for "Colosses," *Ti.* 409; "loves" for "Joves," *Epith.* 99.

Here it may be remarked that the diæresis used occasionally in the original text, and more frequently by M., to indicate the pronunciation of a syllable otherwise silent, and the accent used by M. for the same purpose, have been regularly omitted.

The concordance, then, is based upon M. corrected by D., and includes the variants of vocabulary in Oxf. All these quotations from Oxf. are designated by an asterisk (*).

The text of Spenser, for whatever reason, was left by the poet in much disorder. It was inaccurately printed during his life, and deteriorated through subsequent editions, so that a complete restoration will never be possible. In fact it does not seem reasonable to expect great improvement upon what we now have,

---

[1] The so-called Globe edition, ed. Richard Morris and John W. Hales, Macmillan, 1869. It has frequently been reprinted without revision of the text.

[2] Cambridge Poets, Houghton Mifflin Company.

[3] Oxford University Press. It has been issued in one volume, with certain corrections of errors, but the words are often so crowded as to make it in places almost illegible.

though a concordance, among other uses, may serve to determine the correct reading in a considerable number of cases. This imperfection of the text presents many difficulties to the editor of a concordance which cannot arise from the more exact and consistent text of a later poet.

One of these is the distinguishing of compounds. Spenser sparingly used the hyphen to designate a compound, nor was he consistent in his practice. Thus "sea god" (III. iv. 43. 9), "sea-god" (IV. xi. 8. 2), and "seagod" (IV. xi. 6. 6). This confusion is further confounded by M.'s only partial endeavor to bring about uniformity. Where the original has "steeleheaded" once, and "steele-headed" twice, M. alters only one "steeleheaded" to "steele-headed." The original reads "over all" consistently; M., in two thirds of the instances, reads "over-all," but leaves the others unaltered. In following M., therefore, the concordance does not always show the use or disuse of the hyphen in the original text. This can be correctly observed in D. and Oxf. Similar is the case of such words as *afresh, as well, awhile, instead*, which the original printed sometimes as one word, sometimes as two, but which M. does not accurately reproduce in this respect. Then, too, it is often hard to tell whether two words are essentially compound or distinct, such as "loving lays" (*T. M.* 413), "heavie wounded" (I. viii. 14. 5), "mad man" (in which the position of the stress is a criterion). Many words in Spenser may seem compound to the modern ear which perhaps were not so to him. The most numerous of doubtful cases are the combinations of adverb and participle, made more doubtful by the poet's habit of placing the adverb, in form often the same as the adjective, before the verb. Such are "sad amazed" (I. v. 32. 5), "soft growing" (IV. vii. 33. 4), "sweete smyling" (IV. Pr. 5. 7), and combinations with *out*—"out boastes" (II. v. 33. 9), "out budding" (I. vii. 17. 4), "out crying" (II. iii. 34. 8), "out find," "out showe" (*S. C.* Ap. 78). In deciding questions of compounds, including those of an adverb and a participle, I have appealed to the *New English Dictionary*. When this has failed, I have usually listed such combinations as compounds where they are clearly attributive. Particularly numerous are combinations of *half* and *well*, for which useful rules may be found in the *New English Dictionary*, vol. 5, p. 32, middle column, s. v. *half-* "in comb."; and in the *Concise Oxford Dictionary*, p. 1013, top of the first column. When all is done, a few doubtful cases remain.

The compound adjective in a predicate use found in other Elizabethans appears in Spenser; for example, "Still solemne sad, or still disdainefull coy" (II. vi. 37. 5; cf. I. ii. 2. 8), "cruell kynde" (IV. vii. 30. 5), "greedie fiers" (IV. ii. 21. 5), "mellow ripe" (*S. C.* D. 107), "sullein sad" (III. xii. 18. 2). Such compounds were of course less subject to custom than to individual choice. In Spenser they are not hyphened, and in these, as in all doubtful cases, I have classified them as they were printed in the first editions.

The distinction between the possessive singular and the possessive plural is sometimes difficult, since the apostrophe is almost never used. Doubtful instances are "lives" (VI. iii. 31. 9), "others" (*Gn.* 408), "spirits" (VI. xi. 44. 5), and certain cases under *heaven's* and *heavens'*. Cases in translations were decided by consulting the originals; certain others by considering Spenser's practice in the use of the word; but a few, when other means failed, by arbitrary judgment.

The poems indexed in the concordance are all found in M., D., and Oxf., except a slightly variant version of *Am.* i, which was published by Professor Gollancz in *Proceedings of the British Academy*, 1907–8, p. 100.

I have omitted *The Doleful Lay of Clorinda*, *The Mourning Muse of Thestylis*, and other poems originally printed with *Astrophel*, because they are obviously not Spenser's. It is hard to see why editors continue religiously to include them in every edition. I have included two stanzas which form an interlude between *The Doleful Lay of Clorinda* and *The Mourning Muse of Thestylis*. They are unmistakably Spenser's.

The numbering of references applies to all editions except in the cases of the *Dedicatory Sonnets to the Faery Queen* and the *Amoretti*. The following table gives the corresponding numbers of the *Dedicatory Sonnets* in M. and Oxf.:

M.	Oxf.	M.	Oxf.	M.	Oxf.
1	1	7	10	13	12
2	6	8	14	14	13
3	3	9	2	15	15
4	4	10	5	16	16
5	7	11	9	17	17
6	8	12	11		

The last of the *Amoretti* are numbered as follows:

M.	Oxf.	M.	Oxf.
82	82	86	87
83	84	87	88
84	85	88	89
85	86		

The sonnet numbered 83 in Oxf. is a slight variant of 35.

The order of words is strictly alphabetical. The inflected forms of all words are separately listed. The possessive singular precedes the nominative and objective plural form, and the possessive plural follows it.

The varied and often whimsical spelling in Spenser is no doubt chiefly owing to the poet's intention or indifference, but in many cases to the printer's carelessness. The word *afraid*, for example, appears as *affraid*, *affraide*, *affrayd*, *afraid*, *afrayd*, *afrayde*. To make a manageable concordance it is necessary to marshal such variants under a normal spelling, and I have, with a few necessary exceptions, indexed all quotations under the modern spelling, in general using the index-form found in the *New English Dictionary*. Numerous cross-references should obviate all difficulty in finding a word, but in any case the reader has only to recall its modern spelling to find its place in the concordance. There are apparent exceptions to this rule, as in unfamiliar proper names and obsolete words or forms. For the unfamiliar names from British history I have sought the forms in Miss Harper's study of *The Sources of the British Chronicle History in Spenser's Faerie Queene.* Names invented by Spenser I have indexed under the most frequent spelling (*Artegall*, rather than *Arthegall*). An exception to my practice is furnished by the preterites of several verbs of the third ablaut class, such as *begon, dronk, rong, song, spon.* Where by rhyme or grammar it is clear that the form is equivalent to the *u*-form, it is listed thereunder. If in any case this is not clear, a separate list of the *o*-forms is made.

Homographs are not distinguished. *Read*, pres. and pret., are in one list; so *bear*, v., and *bear*, n.; *wind*, v., and *wind*, n.

Certain words which are distinct in modern English were evidently identical to Spenser, with two not always distinct meanings. Such are *fain, feign* (cf. II. iv. 1. 8; vii. 61. 6; V. i. 22. 8; vi. 3. 8; *Am.* lxxxvi. 10); *throe*, n., "pain," *throw*, n., "cast," which sometimes merge in the sense "blow causing pain" (cf. *Mui.* 414); *travail, travel* (cf. IV. x. 3. 1; VI. iii. 9. 9). *Read* and *rede* are not distinguished in spelling by Spenser. In the sense "advise" I list the word under *rede*, in other senses under *read*, though the participle at V. viii. 13. 6, properly classified under *rede* (cf. *N. E. D.*, s. v., 1. 3), is for convenience listed under *read*. *Lea* and *lee* are uncertain. The word which occurs at *Ti.* 135, 603; V. ii. 19. 1; *Proth.* 38, 115 surely has a meaning different from any given in *N. E. D.*, though this meaning is not altogether clear. Dr. Henry Bradley in a letter to the editor suggests: "Perhaps 'watercourse' or 'river-bed' might do, but even that seems to yield an awkward tautology in connexion with *channell*. It looks as if Spenser took the word to mean the 'descending tract traversed by a river.' How he got this notion it would be difficult to say." Even these explanations do not wholly satisfy *Proth.* 38 and 115–18. No doubt here is another case of Spenser's vague use of a musical word. The classification of *race*, "scratch, demolish," *raced, rast, rased*, presented difficulty. *Race, rase, raze*, are variants of one verb, though *race* was doubtless pronounced differently from the others in Spenser's time, as it is now. In the sense "demolish" he evidently distinguished it by the spelling and the unvoiced pronunciation, for he spells it *race, raced;* his spellings *rast, ras't, raste*, indicate the same pronunciation. In *rased*, "scratched" (III. i. 65. 7), he apparently understands a different word. Therefore I have followed his spelling and classified the instances meaning "demolish" under *race*, and the instance meaning "scratch" under *rase*, with cross-reference from *raze*.

Past participles with the prefix *y-*, which serves in Spenser only a metrical purpose, are listed not under Y, but with the simple form of the participle. Under Y, however, they are all given with cross-references, so that the reader can at a glance see what words were so used. In one or two instances the prefix *y-* appears in another form of the verb. Such instances are of course recorded under Y.

When the work of compilation began, I purposed to follow, as nearly as possible, a chronological order in citing the quotations. In general the reasons for so doing are obvious; in Spenser's case, however, it has proved impracticable, since the chronology of his works must ever remain in many details doubtful. His practice of postponing publication for years, and of revising at publication, or during the preceding interval, greatly complicates the problem. I have departed from the usual order of the editions, however, and made some rearrangement of the Minor Poems, guided in part by Professor Dodge's opinions in his prefaces to them. If the work were to be done over, the order of texts would be that of his edition, which at any rate is an improvement over the traditional one.

I have endeavored to represent every word in Spenser's verse by at least one quotation. There are, of course, many common words of which a complete list of instances would be too long for convenience. For these I have followed the example of Professor Cooper in his *Concordance to Wordsworth*, and given partial lists. They are:

A	Canst	Hither	Ours	Till
About	Could	How	Ourselves	To
Above	Couldst	I	Out	Toward (*prep.*)
Adown	Did (*aux.*)	If	Over	Towards
After	Didst (*aux.*)	I'll	Own (*pron.*)	Twixt
Again	Do (*aux.*)	In	Quite	Under
Against	Does (*aux.*)	Indeed	Same	Until
Ah	Dost (*aux.*)	Is	Shalbe	Unto
Alas	Doth (*aux.*)	Lest	Shall	Up
All	Down (*adv.* and *prep.*)	Lo	Since	Us
Also	Each	Many	Sith	Was
Am	Either (*conj.*)	May (*aux.*)	So	Wast
Among	Eke (*adv.*)	Me	Soon as	We
Amongst	Else	Might (*aux.*)	Such	Were
An	Ere	Mightest	Than	When
Any	Ever	Mongst	That	Whenas
Are	For	More (*adv.*)	The	Whence
Art (*vb.*)	Forth	Most (*adv.*)	Thee	Where
As	For to	Mote	Their	Whether (*conj.*)
As if	Fro	Much (*adv.*)	Theirs	Which
At	From	My	Them	Whose
Aught	Full (*adv.*)	Myself	Themselves	Why
Be	Gainst	Ne	Then	Will (*aux.*)
Because	Had (*aux.*)	Neither (*conj.*)	Thence	With
Been	Has (*aux.*)	Nis	There	Within
Before	Hast (*aux.*)	No	These	Would
Behind	Have (*aux.*)	Nor	They	Wouldst
Being (*part.*)	He	Not	Thine	Ye
Beside	Hence	Now	This	Yet
Between	Her	O	Those	You
Betwixt	Here	Of	Thou	Your
Both	Hers	On	Though	Yours
But	Herself	Or	Through	Yourself
By	Him	Other	Thus	Yourselves
Can	Himself	Ought	Thy	
Cannot	His	Our	Thyself	

In compiling these lists some care has been taken to include peculiar or significant instances of each word. Thus the lists for *as, as if, than,* include all similes introduced by these words. By consulting these and the complete list s. v. *like*, the reader is enabled quickly to consider this very interesting and important element in the poet's art. For *I, me, my*, all cases are retained in which "Spenser" is the antecedent. The varied uses of preposition, conjunction, or modal auxiliary, I have tried to illustrate in each case. But if these lists do not satisfy a reader's curiosity, he may easily consult various monographs, such as K. Boehm, *Spensers Verbalflexion;* R. Liese, *Die Flexion des Verbums bei Spenser;* H. Boehm, *Spensers Relativsatz;* H. Düring, *Uber die Pronomina bei Spenser;* H. Brendel, *Über die Konjunctionen bei Spenser;* Steininger, *Der Gebrauch der Präposition bei Spenser.* Instances have often been retained because of the peculiar part which the word, insignificant in itself, plays in the cadence or alliteration of a line, or for the value of the instances in determining, either through rhyme or metre, the Spenserian pronunciation of the word. As it is, most of the partial lists are sufficiently long—perhaps in some cases too long.

This work was begun, and has in large part gone forward, under the auspices of the Concordance Society. The burden of compilation has been much relieved by the help of many collaborators, a number of them volunteers. Not only was my wife's share in the mere labor very heavy, but to her the book owes many a device by which the task was shortened, and the detection of many an inaccuracy which would have impaired its usefulness. I would particularly make acknowledgments to Mr. Alain C. White, who paid for nearly all the transcription, and took part in the earlier stages of the work. To Professor Lane Cooper I am indebted for expert advice, as well as for an actual share in the labor. Others who have given generously of their time and strength are Miss Mary Hollingsworth Beach, Miss Sylvia Woodbridge Beach, Miss Mildred Emily Cook, Miss Elsie Lydia Croll, Miss Natalie Merrill, Miss Margaretta Paxton, and Miss Adeline Mitchill Scott. Acknowledgment is also due the Right Honorable Lewis Harcourt for permission to reproduce the portrait of Spenser in his possession. Finally, I would acknowledge the liberal facilities which the Carnegie Institution of Washington has provided for the publication of this work.

Doctor Johnson good-humoredly defined a lexicographer as "a harmless drudge," and concordance-making, which is but a lower form of lexicography, surely escapes none of its drudgery. But for this drudgery the labor yields compensations, if only in handling from day to day bright ravelings from the rich fabric of Spenser's poetry, or in hearing, until their cadence falls familiarly upon the ear, snatches of his incomparable music in all the changes of instrument and voice of which he is preëminently the master.

PRINCETON, *August 7, 1915.*

¶ *Quotations marked with an asterisk (*) record variant readings in the Oxford Edition.*

¶ *Following is a list of Abbreviations, with titles to which they refer in order of citation and their page numbers in various editions.*

(References without designation of title are to book, canto, stanza, and line, of the *Faery Queen*.)

Abbreviations	Titles	Globe (M.)	Cambridge (D.)	Smith and de Sélincourt (Oxf.)	
				3 vols.	1 vol.
Bel.[1]	First version of *The Visions of Bellay*, in the *Theatre for Worldlings*	700	765	1.490	606
Pet.[1]	First version of *The Visions of Petrarch*, in the *Theatre for Worldlings*	702	765	1.484	606
Rev.	Four visions from Revelation, in the *Theatre for Worldlings*	701	767	1.501	608
Bel.	Readings common to both versions of *The Visions of Bellay*	538	125	1.274	523
Pet.	Readings common to both versions of *The Visions of Petrarch*	541	128	1.282	525
Bel.[2]	Second version of *The Visions of Bellay*	538	125	1.274	523
Pet.[2]	Second version of *The Visions of Petrarch*	541	128	1.282	525
Ro.	*Ruins of Rome*	526	108	1.235	509
Van.	*Visions of the World's Vanity*	536	122	1.268	521
To his Booke	Prelude to *Shepherd's Calendar*	440	4	1.2	416
S. C.	*Shepherd's Calendar*	446	9	1.14	421
S. C. Env.	Envoy to *Shepherd's Calendar*	486	56	1.121	467
Frag.	Two lines quoted in E. K.'s gloss on the October Eclogue	479	47	1.103	459
Gn.	*Vergil's Gnat*	504	79	1.172	486
Hub.	*Prosopopoia: or Mother Hubbard's Tale*	512	90	1.197	495
T. M.	*Tears of the Muses*	497	70	1.153	480
U. V.	*Iambicum Trimetrum*, in Spenser's first letter to Harvey	707	769	1.505	636
Tetrasticon, Ex tempore	Two fragments, in Spenser's second letter to Harvey	709	771,2	1.505	611
Com. Son. i.	Commendatory Sonnet i	607	762	1.480	603
Ti.	*Ruins of Time*	489	59	1.128	471
Mui.	*Muiopotmos*	531	116	1.255	516
D.	*Daphnaida*	542	678	1.289	528
As.	*Astrophel*	559	699	1.337	547
As. Int.	The last two stanzas of *Clorinda's Lay*	563	704	1.346	550
Col.	*Colin Clout's Come Home Again*	549	687	1.309	536
Ded. Son.	*Verses addressed by the Author of the Faery Queen to Various Noblemen*	7	140	3.492	410
III. xii. 43–47 *or.*	Stanzas originally at the conclusion of the Third Book of the *Faery Queen*, afterward rejected	692	767	2.517	210
Am.	*Amoretti*	572	717	1.372	562
Am.[1]i	Variant of *Am.* i, published in *Proceedings of the British Academy*, 1907–8, p. 100				
Epig.	*Epigrams*	586	734	1.417	577
Epith.	*Epithalamion*	587	735	1.422	580
Com. Son. ii-iv	Commendatory Sonnets ii-iv	608	762	1.480	603
H. L.	*Hymn in Honor of Love*	592	742	1.437	586
H. B.	*Hymn in Honor of Beauty*	596	746	1.446	590
H. H. L.	*Hymn of Heavenly Love*	599	750	1.455	593
H. H. B.	*Hymn of Heavenly Beauty*	602	754	1.464	596
Proth.	*Prothalamion*	605	759	1.474	601

A (*partial list*). *See* **Abed, Aloft, An, Aright, Arights, Asleep, Aslumbering, Asunder, Awhile, Now-a-days.**	
Then did *a* ghost appeare	*Bel.*[1] i. 5
I cast to goe *a* shooting.	*S.C.* Mar. 63
let them gange alone *a* Gods name;	*S.C.* S. 100
(*a* Gods name)	*Hub.* 111
Adventure which might them *a* working set;	*Hub.* 224
none, except *a* God, or God him guide,	*Mui.* 222
Hast wandred through the world now long *a* day,	I. x. 9. 6
which she in *a* earthen Pot did poure,	III. ii. 49. 7
When one so oft *a* night did ring his matins bell.	III. x. 48. 9
For he had been *a* fatting hogs of late,	VII. vii. 40. 3
Aaron's. Resembling *Aarons* glorie in his place:	*Hub.* 463
Aback. They drewe *abacke,* as halfe with shame	*S.C.* Jun. 63
All suddenly dismaid, . . . He fled *abacke*	*Gn.* 298
and flood from mouth, Did fly *abacke,*	II. vii. 58. 7
each *abacke* rebowndes With roaring rage;	IV. i. 42. 3
From his revengefull purpose shronke *abacke,*	IV. vi. 21. 4
forst him flie *abacke,* himselfe to save:	IV. vii. 28. 4
ne once *abacke* did flit,	IV. ix. 29. 8
turn'd *abacke,* and to retyre him hasted	VI. vi. 28. 3
bet *abacke,* threatning in vaine to bite,	VI. xii. 29. 4
Aband. Vortiger have forst the kingdome to *aband.*	II. x. 65. 9
Abandon. *Abandon,* then, the base and viler clowne;	*S.C.* O. 37
Abandon quiet home to seeke for it,	*Col.* 686
Abandon this forestalled place at erst,	II. iv. 39. 3
Abandon soone, I read, the caytive spoile	II. viii. 12. 4
shameful . . . t' *abandon* noble chevisaunce	III. xi. 24. 6
rather then my love *abandon* so,	IV. vii. 16. 8
As to *abandon* that which doth containe Your honours stile,	V. xi. 55. 5
Abandoned. her knight . . . Had her *abandond.*	I. iii. 3. 7
thee *abandond* wholy do possesse,	III. ii. 46. 3
when he wrapped found Th' *abandond* spoyle,	VI. xii. 9. 5
Thence-forth *abandond* her delicious brooke,	VII. vi. 54. 2
the siege by you *abandon'd* quite.	*Am.* xiv. 2
Abandoning. by *abandoning* his sword,	V. v. 17. 7
Abase. that warriour gan *abace* His threatned speare,	II. i. 26. 7
lowly did *abase* their lofty crests	II. ii. 32. 4
Thus lowly to *abase* thy beautie bright,	II. iv. 25. 8
low *abase* the high heroicke spright,	II. vii. 10. 6
his speare he gan *abase* And voide his course:	IV. vi. 3. 4
misfortune, which did me *abase* Unto this shame,	VI. i. 12. 7
He stayd his second strooke, and did his hand *abase.*	VI. vi. 31. 9
did his head for bashfulnesse *abase,*	VI. viii. 5. 5
Abased. have thy pride so much *abaced,*	*Ro.* xiii. 12
Abash. Nothing might *abash* the villein bold,	II. vii. 42. 8
Those tidings sad Did much *abash* Sir Artegall to heare,	V. xi. 40. 7
Abashed. And be not *abasht:*	*S.C.* Ap. 83
The tydings straunge did him *abashed* make,	I. xii. 29. 2
The man was much *abashed* at his boast;	II. iii. 17. 1
nathemoe Was he *abashed* now,	II. iv. 8. 5
abasht he was Through fear and wonder	II. viii. 7. 1
more *abasht* for shame	II. ix. 43. 1
Abasht that her a straunger did avise;	II. xii. 66. 4
seeing her selfe descryde, Was all *abasht,*	III. iii. 20. 2
boastfull men so oft *abasht* to heare?	III. iv. 1. 7
All suddeinly *abasht* shee chaunged hew,	III. v. 30. 5
The wretched man . . . Was all *abasht,*	III. x. 25. 2
Therewith the Gyant much *abashed* sayd,	V. ii. 44. 1
she turn'd her head, as halfe *abashed,*	V. v. 30. 1
abasht with secrete shame	V. vii. 38. 3
Abasht at his rebuke, that bit her neare,	V. xi. 64. 3
Much was the Knight *abashed* at that word	VI. i. 26. 1
approaching nye, . . . Then much *abasht,*	VI. iii. 21. 3
therewith much *abashed* and affrayd,	VI. vii. 22. 1
The Goddesse, all *abashed* with that noise,	VII. vi. 47. 1
abashed to behold So many gazers	*Epith.* 159
Abashment. fild his senses with *abashment* great;	III. viii. 16. 7
all her sences with *abashment* quite were quayld.	III. viii. 34. 9
Abate. miserie doth bravest mindes *abate,*	*Hub.* 256
'The Lyon, . . . his princely puissance doth *abate,*	I. iii. 7. 2
Her piteous wordes might not *abate* his rage,	I. iii. 38. 1
Let now *abate* the terrour of your might,	I. v. 14. 4
In ashes . . . array His daintie corse, proud humors to *abate;*	I. x. 26. 2
th' others pleasing service to *abate,*	II. ii. 19. 5
T' *abate* all spasme, and soke the swelling bruze;	III. v. 33. 7
at the last his fiercenes gan *abate,*	III. vii. 35. 3
Ne ought your burning fury mote *abate;*	III. viii. 28. 7
Mote not mislike you also to *abate* Your zealous hast,	III. viii. 51. 6
both full liefe his boasting to *abate:*	III. ix. 14. 4
They gan *abate* the rancour of their rage,	IV. ii. 28. 2
her besought . . . rigour to *abate,*	IV. ii. 50. 2
for want of breath gan to *abate,*	IV. iii. 26. 6
when as he saw her hastie heat *Abate,*	IV. vi. 16. 2
sufferaunce soft, which rigour can *abate,*	IV. viii. 1. 7
her inburning wrath she gan *abate,*	IV. viii. 17. 8
Him selfe he bent their furies to *abate,*	IV. ix. 34. 6
Gins to *abate* the brightnesse of his beme,	V. ix. 35. 3
Which when as Zele perceived to *abate,*	V. ix. 46. 7
Abate—*Continued.*	
one evill, which doth . . . all our blisse *abate;*	VI. iv. 30. 7
Cryde mercie, to *abate* the extremitie of law.	VI. vii. 36. 9
I would *abate* the sternenesse of my stile,	VII. vi. 37. 3
Abated. Her bountie she *abated,* and his cheare empayrd.	II. x. 30. 9
Abating. Nought *abating* of his former spight,	VI. vii. 10. 5
Abear. So did the Faerie knight himselfe *abeare,*	V. xii. 19. 1
Thus did the gentle knight himselfe *abeare*	VI. ix. 45. 1
Abed. mightie manhode brought *a bedde* of ease,	*S.C.* O. 68
Delight is layd *abedde;*	*S.C.* D. 137
that goodly glee, . . . Is layd *abed,*	*T.M.* 183
Abessa. *Abessa,* daughter of Corceca slow,	I. iii. 18. 4
Abet. *Abett* that virgins cause disconsolate,	I. x. 64. 2
All arm'd to point, his chalenge to *abet:*	IV. iii. 6. 2
The meede of thy mischalenge and *abet.*	IV. iii. 11. 2
were he here, that would it with his sword *Abett,*	VI. i. 28. 4
To reskue him, and his weake part *abet,*	VI. v. 22. 4
Abhominably. *See* **Abominably.**	
Abhor. wordes, and lookes, and sighes she did *abhore;*	I. vi. 4. 4
wretched world he gan for to *abhore,*	I. x. 21. 4
gan *abhorre* her broods unkindly crime,	II. x. 9. 4
Such as by nature men *abhorre* and hate;	II. xii. 36. 3
The hevens such crueltie *abhorre.'*	III. viii. 48. 9
ungodly trade The heavens *abhorre,*	IV. vii. 12. 4
He now t' *abhorre* and loath her person had procured.	V. ix. 39. 9
Whom Gods doe hate, and heavens *abhor* to see;	VI. vi. 10. 2
Abhorred. never was *abhord* The simple shepheards kynd.	*S.C.* Jul. 139
hatefull heresies, of God *abhor'd:*	*Hub.* 389
why hath he me *abhord?'*	I. iii. 7. 9
Much feared I to have bene quite *abhord,*	I. iii. 27. 3
many mischiefes follow cruell Wrath: *Abhorred* bloodshed,	I. iv. 35. 2
her *abhorred* face, so filthy and so fowle.	I. v. 30. 9
Tounge hates to tell the rest that eye to see *abhord.'*	II. i. 11. 9
That had almost committed crime *abhord,*	II. i. 27. 3
Mortal vengeaunce joyne to crime *abhord?*	II. ii. 30. 4
Abhorred bloodshed, and vile felony,	III. iv. 58. 3
loathsom life, of God and man *abhord,*	III. x. 51. 2
ten thousand monsters foule *abhor'd*	IV. xi. 3. 8
So great her pride that she such basenesse much *abhord.*	V. v. 27. 9
brought he forth with griesly grim aspect *Abhorred* Murder,	V. ix. 48. 2
Sith which she hath me ever since *abhord,*	V. xi. 50. 7
Such cruelty she would have soone *abhord*	*Am.* xxxi. 14
Abid. *See* **Abide, Abode.**	
Eftesoones the roaring billowes still *abid,*	III. iv. 32. 7
Abide. *See* **Abid.**	
that is flitting doth *abide* and stay.	*Ro.* iii. 14
Nor prince, nor peere, nor kin, they would *abide.*	*Ro.* xxiii. 14
No blame to thee, whosoever dost *abide* By Nyle,	*Ro.* xxxi. 3
The least of thousands which on earth *abide,*	*Van.* iii. 8
by your flocks on Kentish downes *abyde,*	*S.C.* N. 63
While here on earth she did *abyde.*	*S.C.* N. 199
in the woods of Astery *abide;*	*Gn.* 20
'There next the utmost brinck doth he *abide,*	*Gn.* 385
All things doo change that under heaven *abide,*	*Ti.* 206
what can long *abide* above this ground	*Ti.* 568
please his fancie, nor him cause t' *abide:*	*Mui.* 158
what on earth can long *abide* in state,	*Mui.* 217
so . . . hot That living creature mote it not *abide;*	I. ii. 29. 6
Infinite sorts of people did *abide* There waiting long,	I. iv. 6. 7
many skilfull leaches him *abide* To salve his hurts,	I. v. 17. 2
forth she rose, ne lenger would *abide,*	I. v. 19. 3
Abyde, till I have told the message which I have.'	I. v. 21. 9
late repentance which shall long *abyde,*	I. vii. 23. 7
No . . . deceiptfull traine, Might once *abide* the terror	I. viii. 4. 6
blisse may not *abide* in state of mortall men.	I. viii. 44. 9
Una faire, Did in that castle afterwards *abide,*	I. viii. 50. 7
nor for gold nor glee will I *abyde* By you,	I. ix. 32. 7
With sacred rites and vowes for ever to *abyde.*	I. xii. 36. 9
be ye sure, he dearely shall *abyde,*	II. i. 20. 3
we far off will *abide* to vew.'	II. i. 25. 7
wakefull watches ever to *abide;*	II. iii. 41. 6
'*Abide* the fortune of thy present fate;	II. vii. 60. 2
the while that Guyon did *abide* in Mamons house,	II. viii. 3. 1
breake the launce and let the head *abyde.*	II. viii. 36. 7
other some could not *abide* to toy;	II. ix. 35. 4
was not so hardy to *abide* That bitter stownd,	II. xi. 25. 4
none mote it *abyde;*	III. i. 66. 6
in this thraldome Britons shall *abide;*	III. iii. 44. 2
At least eternall meede shall you *abide.'*	III. v. 11. 5
In which full many lovely Nymphes *abyde;*	III. vi. 16. 5
In faithfull love, t' *abide* for evermore;	III. vi. 53. 4
choosing solitarie to *abide* Far from all neighbours,	III. vii. 6. 6
she list not the batteill to *abide,*	III. vii. 44. 3
did *abide* for ever chaste and sownd.'	III. vii. 56. 7
firmely fixed did *abide* In contemplation	III. ix. 24. 3
With them as housewife ever to *abide,*	III. x. 36. 7
it would not on none of them *abide,*	IV. v. 17. 8
Her list no longer in that place *abide;*	IV. v. 29. 2
the same for whom they did *abyde.*	IV. vi. 9. 5

Abide—*Continued.*
it is too long here to *abide*, ... IV. vii. 47. 8
yet with him as relickes did *abide* . . . . IV. viii. 6. 3
Whereas that wofull man in languor did *abide*. . . . IV. viii. 11. 9
entring in found none therein *abide*, ... IV. viii. 23. 4
did in safe securitie *abide*, ... IV. viii. 31. 4
in the Porch did evermore *abide* An hideous Giant, ... IV. x. 16. 5
Durst not the sternnesse of his looke *abide*; . . . . IV. x. 18. 3
There did this lucklesse mayd seven months *abide*, ... IV. xi. 4. 6
maketh him *abide* Till . . . on his backe he ride, ... IV. xii. 13. 4
By that same carefull Squire did then *abide*, ... V. i. 23. 2
So ye will sweare my judgement to *abide*.' . . . . V. i. 25. 7
by that Bridge whereas he doth *abide*: . . . . V. ii. 10. 7
his faint foe no longer could *abide* His puissance, ... V. ii. 17. 7
In which the Paynims daughter did *abide*, ... V. ii. 20. 2
In which it doth immoveable *abide*, ... V. ii. 35. 6
Ne would within his ballaunce well *abide*: . . . . V. ii. 45. 2
Ne any token doth thereof *abide*: . . . . V. iii. 25. 7
how far hence does she *abide*?' . . . . V. iv. 33. 2
arrowes haild so thicke, that they could not *abide*. . . . . V. iv. 38. 9
The more she rag'd, the more he did *abide*; . . . . V. v. 6. 8
t' *abide* the balefull stowre . . . . V. v. 18. 7
greater shame t' *abide* so great misprize, ... V. v. 48. 4
Ne would *abide*, till she had aunswere made, ... V. vi. 17. 7
Yet being forst to *abide* the daies returning, ... V. vi. 31. 3
Yet mote he algates now *abide*, and answere make. . . . . V. viii. 5. 9
Ne after him did Artigall *abide*, ... V. x. 17. 8
like a bulwarke firmely did *abyde*, ... V. x. 35. 4
Durst not *abide*, but fled away for feare, ... V. x. 38. 3
Nought may *abide* the tempest of his yre; . . . . V. xi. 58. 8
Calidore did with her there *abyde* . . . . VI. i. 30. 2
For he durst not *abide* with Calidore to fight. . . . . VI. iii. 25. 9
Where she in safe assuraunce mote *abide*, ... VI. iii. 28. 8
He bad him stand t' *abide* the bitter stoure . . . . VI. iii. 48. 4
Durst not the furie of his force *abyde*, ... VI. vi. 28. 2
bootelesse thing him seemed to *abide* So mighty blowes, ... VI. vii. 46. 8
'*Abide*, ye caytive treachetours untrew, ... VI. viii. 7. 4
Abide, and from them lay your loathly hands, ... VI. viii. 7. 8
Or else *abide* the death that hard before you stands.' . . . . VI. viii. 7. 9
doth litle crave contented to *abyde*. . . . . VI. ix. 17. 9
Ne durst *abide* the daunger of the end; . . . . VI. x. 35. 4
Ne durst *abide* behind, for dread of worse effort. . . . . VI. xi. 42. 9
none his daunger daring to *abide* . . . . VI. xi. 49. 6
In that still happy state for ever to *abide*. . . . . VII. vi. 5. 9
The harder wonne, the firmer will *abide*. . . . . *Am.* vi. 4
Too feeble I t' *abide* the brunt so strong, ... *Am.* xii. 9
all the woes and wrecks which I *abide*, ... *Am.* xxv. 11

Abides. *Abides* in highest place above the best, ... *Gn.* 614

Abiding. Which not *abiding*, but more scornfully Scoffing . . . . II. xii. 16. 7
Never *abiding* in their stedfast plights: . . . . VII. vii. 21. 3

Abie. *See* **Aby.**

Ability. of lesse livelood and *hability*, ... VI. iii. 7. 7

Abject. letting him arise like *abject* thrall, ... VI. vii. 26. 6
like a most demisse And *abject* thrall, ... *H.H.L.* 137

Abjected. upon the soyle Having her selfe in wretched wize *abjected*, ... V. ix. 9. 8

Abjecting. downe againe himselfe disdainfully *Abjecting*, ... III. xi. 13. 7

Able. *See* **War-able.**
At last, not *able* to beare so great weight, ... *Ro.* xx. 12
Should *able* be so great an one to wring. . . . . *Van.* ix. 14
The same was *able* with like lovely lay . . . . *Gn.* 461
So much as they were *able* well to beare, ... *Hub.* 1157
They *able* are with power of mightie spell . . . . *Ti.* 374
Nor better *hable*, . . . her name to glorifie. . . . . *Col.* 378
Hable to melt the hearers heart unweeting, ... *Col.* 598
A worke of wondrous grace, and *hable* (**able*) soules to save. I. ix. 19. 9
she was *hable* with her wordes to kill, . . . the hart . . . . I. x. 19. 8
to the rest more *hable* he might bee; . . . . I. x. 45. 2
hardy fowle above his *hable* might, ... I. xi. 19. 6
tall young men, all *hable* armes to sownd; . . . . I. xii. 5. 7
His deare delights were *hable* to annoy: . . . . I. xii. 41. 4
Hable to heale the sicke, and to revive the ded. . . . . II. iii. 22. 9
Both horse and man nigh *able* for to choke; . . . . II. v. 3. 5
with paine Or powre, be *hable* it to remedy, ... III. iii. 40. 4
So long as breath and *hable* puissaunce . . . . III. vii. 3. 1
Three such as *able* were to match a puissant host? . . . . IV. iii. 24. 9
Which neither *able* were to wag, or once to weld. . . . . IV. iv. 18. 9
none his force were *able* to withstond, ... IV. iv. 23. 8
Gainst whom none *able* was to stand on ground; . . . . IV. iv. 28. 3
able was weake harts away to steal. . . . . IV. v. 10. 5
able was all daungers to withstond: . . . . IV. ix. 18. 4
Ne any *able* was him to withstand, ... V. xii. 7. 6
So long as these two armes were *able* to be wroken. . . . . VI. ii. 7. 9
was not *able* up him selfe to reare, ... VI. viii. 25. 6
better *able* it to guide alone; . . . . VII. vi. 11. 4
scarse his loosed limbes he *hable* was to weld. . . . . VII. vii. 31. 9

Abler. They mote the *abler* be to passe unto the rest. . . . . VI. iv. 15. 9

Ablest. *hablest* wit of most I know this day. . . . . *Col.* 383

Aboard. foord Which . . . doth beare *aboord* The ploughmans hope *Ro.* xiv. 3
yron bands *abord* The Pontick sea . . . . *Gn.* 46
They were in doubt, and flatly set *abord*. . . . . *Hub.* 324
The same *aboord* us gently did receave, ... *Col.* 224
He lowdly cald to such as were *abord* . . . . II. vi. 4. 2
him selfe she tooke *aboord*, ... II. vi. 19. 6
Tho him she brought *abord*, ... II. vi. 38. 1
They goe *abord*, And he eftsoones gan launch . . . . II. xi. 4. 3
till he her layd *abord*. . . . . III. x. 6. 4

Abode. *See* **Abid.**
beholde the bright *abode* Of God and men. . . . . *Rev.* iv. 5
they . . . liken theyr *abode*; . . . . *S.C.* Jul. 108

Abode—*Continued.*
Since round about us it doth make *aboad!* . . . . *As.* 90
there *abode*, whylst any beast of name Walkt . . . . I. vi. 29. 3
Here she a while may make her safe *abode*, ... I. xii. 42. 5
unto the place Where he *abode*, ... II. ii. 20. 2
To make there lenger sojourne and *abode*; . . . . III. i. 1. 6
Emongst the shady leaves, their sweet *abode*, ... III. vi. 42. 8
with her fled away without *abode*. . . . . III. viii. 19. 5
Found it the fittest soyle for their *abode*, ... III. ix. 49. 5
with stedfast eye and courage stout *Abode*, ... III. xii. 37. 6
those two Ladies late, Aemylia and Amoret, *abode*, ... IV. viii. 19. 3
wherein make *abode* So many learned impes, ... IV. xi. 26. 4
prayd the place of her *abode* to learne; . . . . V. xi. 21. 3
To make *abode* that night he greatly was besought. . . . . VI. iii. 2. 9
there was this wights *abode*. . . . . VI. iv. 13. 9
unable were . . . To move one foote, but there must make *abode*: VI. vi. 19. 7
In these wylde deserts where she now *abode*, ... VI. viii. 35. 1

Abode's. When my *abodes* prefixed time is spent, ... *Am.* xlvi. 1

Abodes. all their sundry kinds, and all their hid *abodes*. . . . IV. xi. 10. 9

Abolish. with thy blood *abolish* so reprochfull blott.' . . . . II. iv. 45. 9

Abominably. her sowre breath *abhominably* smeld; . . . . I. viii. 47. 5

Abound. may *abound* in riches above measure. . . . . *Gn.* 128
yong plants, which wont with fruit t' *abound*, ... *T.M.* 251
wee that earst in joyance did *abound*, ... *T.M.* 307
In riotous excesse doth there *abound*. . . . . *Mui.* 168
where salvage beasts do most *abound*, ... *As.* 82
much more . . . *abound* in that same land then this: . . . *Col.* 309
Cynthia doth in sciences *abound*, ... *Col.* 745
all within . . . did with store of every thing *abound*, ... I. viii. 35. 3
sydes with blood, did all *abownd*. . . . . II. iv. 3. 9
she in pleasaunt purpose did *abound*, ... II. vi. 6. 3
Fountaines of gold and silver to *abownd*, ... II. vii. 17. 5
all the sinnes wherewith his lewd life did *abound*. . . . . II. viii. 45. 9
After their hives with honny do *abound*. . . . . II. ix. 51. 5
With which the world did in those dayes *abound*: . . . . II. x. 63. 6
made there to *abound* with lavish affluence. . . . . II. xii. 42. 9
In which all pleasures plenteously *abownd*, ... II. xii. 58. 3
every Satyre first did give a busse . . . so busses did *abound*. III. x. 46. 4
What time the dayes with scorching heat *abound*, ... IV. i. 13. 7
whereas all the plagues and harmes *abound* . . . . IV. i. 20. 2
love with gall and hony doth *abound*; . . . . IV. x. 1. 2
the world with goodnesse did *abound*: . . . . V. Pr. 9. 2
when the world with sinne gan to *abound*, ... V. i. 11. 1
From seeking favour where it doth *abound*; . . . . V. v. 42. 2
it there most useth to *abound*; . . . . VI. i. 1. 2
through the wealth wherein he did *abound*, ... VI. xii. 4. 4
Of woods and forrests which therein *abound*, ... VII. vi. 38. 8
Doth to this day with Wolves and Thieves *abound*: . . . . VII. vi. 55. 8
Liv'd here on earth, and plenty made *abound*; . . . . VII. vii. 37. 7
let your bed with pleasures chast *abound*, ... *Proth.* 103

Aboundance, Aboundant. *See* **Abundance,** *etc.*

Abounded. Paridell, in whom a kindly pride . . . *Abounded*, . . III. ix. 32. 8

Aboundeth. Love most *aboundeth* there. . . . . *Col.* 775

Abounding. A pleasant bowre with all delight *abounding* . . *Gn.* 187
Each place *abounding* with fowle injuries, ... *Hub.* 1305
The utmost rowme *abounding* with all precious store: . . . . III. xi. 27. 9
Abounding all with delices most rare, ... IV. x. 6. 2

Abounds. in my carrion carcas *abounds*.' . . . . *S.C.* May 258
Where ease *abownds* yt's eath to doe amis: . . . . II. iii. 40. 5

About (*partial list*). *See* **Abouts, Bout, Round about, Thereabout.**
I sawe, an hundred pillers eke *about*, ... *Bel.*[1] ii. 2
hundred Nymphes sate side by side *about*; . . . . *Bel.* xii. 10
head with Lawrell garnisht was *about*. . . . . *Bel.*[2] ix. 12
darkned was the welkin all *about*, ... *Pet.* iii. 10
our flockes do graze *about* in sight, ... *S.C.* Ap. 31
bigge Bulles of Basan brace hem *about*, ... *S.C.* S. 124
Manie great bandogs which her gird *about*: . . . . *Gn.* 540
sitting all in seates *about* me round, ... *Hub.* 25
high time their wits *about* to geather. . . . . *Hub.* 570
manie Nymphes *about* them flocking round, ... *Mui.* 295
A cruell Satyre . . . ranging all *about*, ... *D.* 157
sound yshrilled far *about*, ... *Col.* 62
path . . . like to lead the labyrinth *about*; . . . . I. i. 11. 4
hurling her hideous taile *About* her cursed head; . . . . I. i. 16. 3
She lookt *about*, and seeing one in mayle, ... I. i. 16. 5
Gathred themselves *about* her body round, ... I. i. 25. 4
He cast *about*, and searcht his baleful bokes againe. . . . . I. ii. 2. 9
all the poison ran *about* his chaw; . . . . I. iv. 30. 4
he brandisheth *about* his hed: . . . . I. iv. 33. 4
his waste is girt *about*. . . . . I. vi. 14. 9
Flocke all *about* to see her lovely face; . . . . I. vi. 18. 4
while equal destinies Did ronne *about*, ... I. vii. 43. 5
every coast that heaven walks *about* . . . . I. vii. 45. 3
His sparkling blade *about* his head he blest, ... I. viii. 22. 3
all *about* it wandring ghostes did wayle . . . . I. ix. 33. 9
all *about* old stockes and stubs of trees, ... I. ix. 34. 1
hong *about* his shoulders round, ... I. ix. 35. 5
A multitude of babes *about* her hong, ... I. x. 31. 1
the ayre about with smoke and stench did fill. . . . . I. xi. 13. 9
The wrathfull beast *about* him turned . . . . I. xi. 16. 7
about him soared round; . . . . I. xi. 18. 7
His hideous tayle then hurled he *about*, ... I. xi. 23. 1
gan his sturdy sterne *about* to weld, ... I. xi. 28. 8
looked all *about*, ... I. xi. 33. 6
blowes *about* him stoutly laid, ... I. xi. 42. 4
noble crew *about* them waited rownd . . . . I. xii. 5. 4
lookt *about*, but nowhere could espye . . . . II. iii. 19. 6
the skirt *about* Was hemd . . . . II. iii. 26. 8
turned her *about*, and fled . . . . II. iii. 42. 9
his dreadfull blade *about* he cast, ... II. v. 12. 3

About—*Continued.*
he rudely flasht The waves *about,* . . . II. vi. 42. 7
Whom all that folke . . . Doe flock *about,* . . . II. vii. 48. 6
flow'd *about* it round. . . . II. vii. 56. 7
skirt with gold Was fretted all *about,* . . . II. ix. 37. 2
His chamber all was hangd *about* with rolls . . . II. ix. 57. 6
with lively jollitee To fly *about,* . . . II. xii. 60. 8
displayd The clothes *about* her round . . . III. ii. 47. 5
the Nymphes sitt all *about* him rownd, . . . III. iv. 44. 1
He flyes *about,* and with his flaggy winges . . . III. vi. 39. 7
all *about* grew every sort of flowre, . . . III. vi. 45. 1
all *about* the glistring walles were hong . . . III. xi. 52. 1
her wel-pointed wepons did *about* her dresse. . . . III. xi. 55. 9
Such when those Knights and Ladies all *about* Beheld her, . . . IV. i. 14. 1
weedes, Which she her selfe had sowen all *about,* . . . IV. i. 25. 3
And rash provoking perils all *about,* . . . IV. ii. 46. 8
The field with listes was all *about* enclos'd, . . . IV. iii. 4. 1
beaten were and chased all *about.* . . . IV. iv. 43. 4
about her middle small . . . IV. v. 16. 3
dogs did barke and howle *About* the house, . . . IV. v. 41. 7
Which he in store *about* him kept alway, . . . IV. viii. 20. 7
filthy lockes *about* her scattered wide, . . . IV. viii. 23. 7
evermore his eyes *about* him went, . . . IV. x. 12. 7
With all my might I gan to lay *about:* . . . IV. x. 19. 7
High reared mounts, the lands *about* to vew; . . . IV. x. 24. 5
all *about* her necke and shoulders . . . IV. x. 42. 1
all *about* her altar scattered lay . . . IV. x. 43. 1
ten thousand monsters . . . Did waite *about* it, . . . IV. xi. 3. 9
with meet service waited him *about,* . . . IV. xi. 30. 4
ambrosiall odours forth did throw To all *about,* . . . IV. xi. 46. 4
all *about* that rocke the sea did flow: . . . IV. xii. 15. 5
An hundred times *about* the pit side fares . . . IV. xii. 17. 8
Didst cast *about* by sleight . . . V. i. 24. 9
he began to lay *about* . . . V. vi. 30. 1
tempest . . . all *about* did blow The holy fire, . . . V. vii. 14. 4
Priestes she found full busily *About* their holy things . . . V. vii. 17. 8
Full fiercely layde the Amazon *about,* . . . V. vii. 31. 1
fenst himselfe *about* with many a flaming brand. . . . V. viii. 35. 9
scattred all *about,* and strow'd upon the greene. . . . V. viii. 42. 9
She was *about* affaires of common-wele, . . . V. ix. 36. 3
running unto them . . . Fell straight *about* their neckes . . . V. x. 20. 2
With his huge flaile began to lay *about;* . . . V. xi. 47. 7
And cast his shield *about* to be in readie plight. . . . V. xii. 16. 9
he therewith the knight drew all *about:* . . . V. xii. 22. 3
Lords and Ladies which *about* you dwell, . . . VI. Pr. 7. 8
About him flockt, . . . VI. i. 24. 2
having soone his armes *about* him dight, . . . VI. i. 32. 6
Turned his steede *about* another way, . . . VI. iii. 37. 2
wary watch *about* her . . . keepe. . . . VI. iii. 44. 9
when he lookt *about* on every syde, . . . VI. iv. 24. 3
all *about* did close the compasse of his eye. . . . VI. iv. 24. 9
At last, *about* the setting of the Sunne, . . . VI. iv. 26. 1
looking all *about* where he mote fynd . . . VI. iv. 26. 4
put them all *about* himselfe unfit, . . . VI. v. 8. 6
beat *about* him round; . . . VI. v. 19. 4
whom they full busie found *About* the sad Serena things to dight, VI. v. 25. 3
To goe *about* to salve such kynd of sore, . . . VI. vi. 13. 2
To fight with many foes *about* him ment, . . . VI. vi. 27. 5
Turnes him *about* with fell avengement: . . . VI. vi. 27. 7
environed *about* With slaughtred bodies . . . VI. vi. 38. 1
weapons . . . With which he layd *about,* . . . VI. vi. 38. 9
He gaz'd *about* and stared horriblie, . . . VI. vii. 42. 8
his locks, . . . Were bound *about* . . . VI. vii. 43. 8
went *about* Him to have bound and thrald . . . VI. viii. 11. 6
with his club him all *about* so blist, . . . VI. viii. 13. 4
With all the Gods *about* him congregate: . . . VII. vi. 19. 5
Cupid selfe *about* her fluttred all in greene. . . . VII. vii. 34. 9
about him dight His wanton wings . . . *Am.* iv. 7
breaking forth, did thick *about* me throng. . . . *Am.* xii. 8
In angry wize he flyes *about,* . . . *Epig.* iv. 9
To which the people standing all *about,* . . . *Epith.* 143
daunce *about* them, and *about* them sing, . . . *Epith.* 276
walkes *about* high heaven al the night? . . . *Epith.* 375
wag his eyas wings *About* that mightie bound . . . *H.H.L.* 25
About him wait, and on his will depend, . . . *H.H.L.* 65
all *about* him sheddeth glorious light: . . . *H.H.B.* 161
Gan flock *about* these twaine, . . . *Proth.* 120

Abouts. The which his naked sides he wrapt *abouts;* . . . I. ix. 36. 3

Above (*partial list*). *See* **Bove.**
above all moniments Seven Romane Hils, . . . *Ro.* ii. 13
Gods of love, . . . Looke from *above,* . . . *S.C.* Ja. 15
and eke to love, Is graunted scarce to Gods *above,* . . . *S.C.*Mar.Emb.2
(As garments doen, which wexen old *above,*) . . . *S.C.* Jun. 39
For it was a perilous beast *above* all, . . . *S.C.* S. 214
His creste *above,* . . . did shine . . . *Gn.* 260
Ye gentle Spirits, breathing from *above,* . . . *T.M.* 361
'Most gentle spirite, breathed from *above* . . . *Ti.* 281
freed from . . . death, they live for aye *above,* . . . *Ti.* 396
Above the reach of ruinous decay, . . . *Ti.* 422
The beame of beautie sparkled from *above,* . . . *Col.* 468
bred *above* in Venus bosome deare: . . . *Col.* 840
praise her worth, though far my wit *above.* . . . *Col.* 942
swell With timely pride *above* the Aegyptian vale . . . I. i. 21. 2
mightie causes wrought in heaven *above,* . . . I. i. 51. 3
calles to you *above* From wandring Stygian shores, . . . I. iv. 48. 8
Monarch layd Low under all, yet *above* all in pride, . . . I. v. 48. 6
renowmed make *Above* all knights . . . I. xi. 2. 9
Long he them bore *above* the subject plaine, . . . I. xi. 19. 1
contend With hardy fowle *above* his hable might, . . . I. xi. 19. 6
advaunce his broad discoloured brest *Above* his wonted pitch, I. xi. 31. 8

Above—*Continued.*
The same advauncing high *above* his head, . . . I. xi. 38. 1
hevens just . . . Vouchsafed to behold us from *above.* . . . II. i. 50. 4
Kindled *above* at th' hevenly makers light, . . . II. iii. 23. 2
all *above* besprinckled was throughout . . . II. iii. 26. 6
that *above* were added to that under grownd . . . II. vii. 31. 9
one *above* the rest in speciall . . . II. xii. 86. 6
The fayrest vertue, far *above* the rest: . . . III. Pr. 1. 2
ykindled first *above* Emongst th' eternall spheres . . . III. iii. 1. 2
him he loved *above* all mankinde, . . . III. v. 12. 7
left her blisfull bowre of joy *above:* . . . III. vi. 11. 5
Fashiond *above* within their inmost part, . . . III. vi. 44. 7
virgin that . . . *above* all Dames is deemd, . . . III. vii. 52. 4
crowne of heavenly prayse with Saintes *above,* . . . III. viii. 42. 7
thy sweete smyling mother from *above,* . . . IV. Pr. 5. 7
slyde Over his horses taile *above* a stryde; . . . IV. iv. 44. 5
Began to peepe *above* this earthly masse, . . . IV. v. 45. 4
the band Of noble minds derived from *above,* . . . IV. vi. 31. 8
Ne wist whether *above* she were or under ground. . . . IV. vii. 9. 9
above a score Of Knights and Squires . . . IV. ix. 8. 4
such grace is given them from *above,* . . . IV. x. 2. 1
layd up in heaven *above,* . . . IV. xi. 10. 3
Inachus, renowmd *above* the rest; . . . IV. xi. 15. 5
layd *above,* Like ruefull ghost, . . . IV. xii. 20. 8
Above the earth upreard his flaming head, . . . VI. i. 31. 2
placed high *above* Or low beneath, . . . VI. ii. 1. 5
whilest he thus was setling things *above,* . . . VI. vi. 37. 1
Above a launces length him forth did beare, . . . VI. vii. 11. 3
fire, Kindled *above* unto the Maker neere; . . . *Am.* viii. 2
woven all *above* With woodbynd flowers . . . *Am.* lxxi. 9
How chearefully thou lookest from *above,* . . . *Epith.* 291
Where thou doest sit in Venus lap *above,* . . . *H.L.* 24
up aloft *above* my strength . . . *H.B.* 6
Farre *above* feeble reach of earthly sight, . . . *H.H.L.* 5
to increase *Above* the fortune of their first condition, . . . *H.H.L.* 81
fell from *above* Through pride, . . . *H.H.L.* 94
With heavenly thoughts farre *above* humane skil, . . . *H.H.L.* 282
love, Kindled through sight of those faire things *above.* . . . *H.H.L.* 287
For farre *above* these heavens, which here we see, . . . *H.H.B.* 64
Above that Idole of his fayning thought, . . . *H.H.B.* 223

Abraid. *See* **Abray.**
For feare least her unwares she should *abrayd,* . . . III. i. 61. 2
Out of his quiet slomber him *abrade,* . . . III. xi. 8. 4

Abray. *See* **Abraid.**
when as I did out of sleepe *abray,* . . . IV. vi. 36. 5

Abrayed. *See* **Abraid, Abray.**
At last with irkesom trouble she *abrayd;* . . . III. x. 50. 1
Sir Satyrane *abraid* Out of the swowne, . . . IV. iv. 22. 1
So oftentimes he out of sleepe *abrayd,* . . . IV. v. 42. 8
Scudamour, who now *abrayd,* Beheld, . . . IV. vi. 24. 1

Abridge. doo in darknesse not *abridge* my breath, . . . *D.* 445
T' *abridg* their journey long, and lingring day; . . . III. ii. 4. 3
Thy daies *abridge* through proofe of puissaunce, . . . III. viii. 18. 2

Abridged. Their days mote be *abridged* through their corage stout. IV. ii. 46. 9
his *abridged* dayes in dolour wast, . . . V. v. 46. 6

Abridgment. she desyrd th' *abridgement* of her fate, . . . III. viii. 2. 3

Abroad. Threw forth *abrode* a thousand . . . leames, . . . *Bel.*[1] ix. 10
raunge *abroad* to seeke her food, . . . *Bel.*[2] vi. 5
dart *abroad* the thunder bolts of warre, . . . *Ro.* xi. 10
Cedar . . . That farre *abroad* her daintie odours threwe; . . . *Van.* vii. 3
Love still sleepeth not, But is *abroad* . . . *S.C.* Mar. 27
Yode forth *abroade* unto the greene wood, . . . *S.C.* May 178
if he chaunce come when I am *abroade,* . . . *S.C.* May 223
balk the right way, and strayen *abroad.* . . . *S.C.* S. 93
To feede *abroad* where pasture best befalls. . . . *Gn.* 72
Spread themselves farre *abroad* . . . *Gn.* 77
seeke Their fortunes farre *abroad,* . . . *Hub.* 48
Abroad, where change is, . . . *Hub.* 101
for eare-marked beasts *abroad* be bruted. . . . *Hub.* 188
now in other state *abroad* to range: . . . *Hub.* 356
lost their time in wandring loose *abroad;* . . . *Hub.* 399
Novices, new come *abroad,* . . . *Hub.* 405
tidings you *abroad* doo heare? . . . *Hub.* 605
do them any torte There or *abroad;* . . . *Hub.* 1079
to range *abroad* in fresh attire, . . . *Mui.* 37
did his beames *abroad* dispred, . . . *Mui.* 52
Clarion . . . did cast *abroad* to fare: . . . *Mui.* 55
Walking *abroad* with all her Nymphes . . . *Mui.* 115
I walkt *abroade* to breath the freshing ayre . . . *D.* 26
whose praises wide Were spred *abroad;* . . . *D.* 145
To seek *abroad,* . . . His mistresse name, . . . *As.* 87
What needeth perill to be sought *abroad,* . . . *As.* 89
Hereof when tydings far *abroad* did passe, . . . *As.* 199
The shepheards there *abroad* may safely lie, . . . *Col.* 316
straunge adventures, which *abroad* did pas. . . . I. i. 30. 4
trees, that faire did spred Their armes *abroad,* . . . I. ii. 28. 4
pillage severall, Which he had got *abroad* . . . I. iii. 16. 9
He had in armes *abroad* wonne muchell fame, . . . I. vi. 20. 5
far *abroad* for straunge adventures sought; . . . I. vi. 29. 7
To weete of newes that did *abroad* betide, . . . I. vi. 34. 5
heard *abroad* of that her champion trew, . . . I. vi. 36. 5
then againe *abroad* . . . Well may she speede, . . . I. xii. 42. 7
famous far *abroad* for warlike gest, . . . II. ii. 16. 7
Abroad in armes, at home in studious kynd, . . . II. iii. 40. 8
still as *abroad* he strew His wicked arrowes, . . . II. xi. 28. 1
From seeking praise and deeds of armes *abrode,* . . . III. i. 1. 8
spred *Abroad* thy fresh youths fayrest flowre, . . . III. ii. 31. 7
Speed thee to spred *abroad* thy beames bright, . . . III. iv. 60. 4
in the countrey she *abroad* him sought, . . . III. vi. 15. 1
their trew loves without suspition tell *abrode.* . . . III. vi. 42. 9

Abroad—*Continued.*
raungd *abrode* to seeke adventures wilde, . . . III. vii. 30. 2
To wander through the world *abroad* at will, . . . III. vii. 54. 4
yet three yeares I now *abrode* have strayd, . . . III. vii. 57. 4
Proteus *abrode* did rove, . . . III. viii. 29. 8
Gan first inquire of tydings farre *abrode,* . . . III. viii. 45. 8
far *abroad* his mightie braunches threw . . . III. ix. 47. 8
they, seeking farre *abrode,* . . . III. ix. 49. 4
gan to treate of deeds of armes *abrode,* . . . IV. iv. 5. 4
His weapons which lay scattered all *abrode,* . . . IV. iv. 23. 2
fame . . . Flew first *abroad,* . . . IV. x. 4. 2
So many learned impes, that shoote *abrode,* . . . IV. xi. 26. 5
walkt *abrode,* and round about did rome . . . IV. xii. 4. 5
to tell *abrode* your shame.' . . . V. i. 28. 9
I heard report that farre *abrode* did fly, . . . V. iv. 29. 4
Then gan the other further to devize Of things *abrode,* . . . V. vi. 20. 8
her keepers had forsaken . . . and scattered were *abrode.* . . . V. xi. 60. 3
Did spred *abroad* and throw in th' open wynd: . . . V. xii. 33. 7
they mote treat of things *abrode* at leasure, . . . VI. iii. 22. 4
Upon a day he cast *abrode* to wend, . . . VI. iv. 17. 2
wend *abrode,* though feeble and forlorne, . . . VI. v. 7. 3
One day, as he did raunge the fields *abroad,* . . . VI. x. 5. 1
The trustie damzell bearing it *abrode* . . . VI. xii. 7. 1
raunged farre *abroad* in every border, . . . VII. vii. 4. 8
Abrode. *See* **Abroad.**
Abruptly. There *abruptly* it did end, . . . II. x. 68. 2
Absence. the wight whose *absence* is our carke; . . . *S.C.* N. 66
too long *absence* him had sore annoyd, . . . III. xii. 44. *or.* 3
What did betide to the faire Pastorell During his *absence,* . . . VI. xii. 14. 4
So I her *absens* will my penaunce make, . . . *Am.* lii. 13
Sits mourning for the *absence* of her mate; . . . *Am.* lxxxviii. 2
Mourne to my selfe the *absence* of my love; . . . *Am.* lxxxviii. 6
Absent. To which whiles *absent* he his mind did sett, . . . II. x. 60. 3
Out of his sight her selfe once to *absent:* . . . III. x. 3. 8
Ne thence the Irishe Rivers *absent* were, . . . IV. xi. 40. 1
Ne any Knight was *absent* that brave courage bore. . . . V. iii. 2. 9
To his owne *absent* love to be untrew: . . . V. v. 56. 3
Absolute. To make his worke more *absolute,* desird . . . the vew. *Ded. Son.* xvii. 3
Abstain. Could not *abstaine* mine eyes with teares to steepe; . . . *D.* 171
Oft from those grave affaires were wont *abstaine,* . . . *Ded. Son.* i. 5
Sir Guyon could uneath From teares *abstayne;* . . . II. i. 56. 6
They gan *abstaine* from dint of direfull stroke, . . . II. ii. 28. 8
learne from pleasures poyson to *abstaine;* . . . II. ii. 45. 4
who can *abstaine,* when Rancor rife Kindles Revenge, . . . II. iv. 44. 4
she better can *abstaine:* . . . II. vi. 1. 7
counseld him *abstaine* from perilous fight; . . . II. vii. 42. 7
Dernly unto her called to *abstaine* . . . III. xii. 34. 4
Why doth mine hand from thine avenge *abstaine,* . . . IV. i. 52. 7
More hard for hungry steed t' *abstaine* from pleasant lare. . . . IV. viii. 29. 9
Abstaine from pleasure, and restraine your will; . . . VI. vi. 14. 5
'Stay, stay, Sir Knight! for love of God *abstaine* . . . VI. viii. 17. 5
being checkt he did *abstaine* streightway, . . . VI. viii. 29. 4
Onely let her *abstaine* from cruelty. . . . *Am.* xlii. 13
Abundance. th' *aboundance* of an ydle braine Will judged be, . . . II. Pr. 1. 3
through great *abundance* of her smart. . . . IV. xii. 11. 9
that the blood ensew'd In great *aboundance,* . . . VI. iii. 50. 8
some, that hath *abundance* at his will, . . . VI. ix. 30. 3
Abundant. Out of her fruitfull lap *aboundant* flowres; . . . IV. x. 45. 2
To count the seas *abundant* progeny, . . . IV. xii. 1. 2
hardned more with my *aboundant* teares: . . . IV. xii. 7. 5
Of which he had with him *abundant* store . . . V. viii. 34. 2
Abundantly. Pouring forth streames of teares *abundantly;* . . . *T.M.* 230
Abus. River that whylome was hight The ancient *Abus,* . . . II. x. 16. 3
Abuse. though envie it *abuse:* . . . *Gn.* 6
false Reynold would *abuse* The simple Suter, . . . *Hub.* 883
Was led away of them that did *abuse* her. . . . *Mui.* 136
Arachne figur'd how Jove did *abuse* Europa . . . *Mui.* 277
gracelesse men them greatly do *abuse.'* . . . *Col.* 327
bad him . . . with false shewes *abuse* his fantasy, . . . I. i. 46. 4
So every good to bad he doth *abuse;* . . . I. iv. 32. 5
in al *abuse* thou hast thy selfe defild? . . . I. ix. 46. 9
Or ever gentle Damzell so *abuse:* . . . II. i. 19. 3
would *abuse* so gentle Dame! . . . II. iv. 20. 9
For suffering such *abuse* as knighthood sham'd, . . . II. v. 21. 5
With such vaine shewes thy worldlinges vyle *abuse;* . . . II. vii. 39. 5
If ought amis her liking may *abuse:* . . . III. Pr. 5. 4
ignorant of servants bad *abuse* . . . III. ix. 18. 6
with thy charmes . . . to thy will *abuse?* . . . III. x. 4. 6
To sell her borrowed beautie to *abuse:* . . . IV. i. 31. 4
Her nature is all goodnesse to *abuse,* . . . IV. viii. 25. 1
Unto *abuse* of lawlesse lust was lent, . . . IV. viii. 32. 3
she it with foule *abuse* did marre; . . . V. ix. 38. 3
was bent her to *abuse;* . . . VI. vii. 40. 7
could no lenger beare so great *abuse* . . . VI. vii. 45. 4
He from you take that chiefedome which ye doe *abuse.* . . . VI. viii. 1. 9
theirs that do *abuse* it unto ill: . . . *H.B.* 156
Abused. How fowlie they their offices *abus'd,* . . . *Hub.* 563
with her gealous termes his open eares *abusd:* . . . I. v. 37. 9
an Enchaunter bad His sence *abusd,* . . . I. vii. 49. 4
Guyon, by Archimage *abusd,* . . . II. i. Arg.
drive me to withdraw my blind *abused* love. . . . II. iv. 24. 9
Abusd her plenty and fat swolne encreace . . . II. vii. 16. 7
Which ever after they *abusd* to ill, . . . II. xii. 31. 8
The virgin whom he had *abusde* so sore; . . . III. viii. 36. 6
How to avenge himselfe so sore *abusd,* . . . III. ix. 12. 8
For fault of few that have *abusd* the same; . . . IV. Pr. 2. 5
how that Hag his love *abused* had . . . IV. vi. 28. 3
her error I *abusd* To my friends good . . . IV. viii. 60. 7
with how great vaunt of braverie He them *abused* . . . V. iii. 39. 8
In vaine complayning to be so *abused;* . . . VI. ii. 22. 7

Abused—*Continued.*
to be so fowle *abused* Of a rude churle, . . . VI. iii. 33. 4
with such scornefull pryde Had him *abusde* . . . VI. iii. 47. 6
So lewdly had *abusde,* as ye did lately heare. . . . VI. vi. 17. 9
Yond Lady and her Squire with foule despight *Abusde,* . . . VI. viii. 6. 4
That goodly beautie . . . Is foule *abusd,* . . . *H.B.* 150
Commend to you by loves *abused* name, . . . *H.B.* 172
He was revyld, disgrast, and foule *abused;* . . . *H.H.L.* 242
Abuser. Whom he had feignd th' *abuser* of my love to bee. . . . II. iv. 27. 9
Abuses. foule *abuses* both in realme and raine; . . . *Hub.* 1276
Avenge thy selfe on them for their *abuses.* . . . *Col.* 794
avenge th' *abuses* of that proud And shamefull Knight . . . VI. v. 34. 3
Abusing. *Abusing* manie through their cloaked guile, . . . *Hub.* 344
Abusion. turne the name of Souldiers to *abusion,* . . . *Hub.* 220
T' excuse his former treason and *abusion,* . . . *Hub.* 1363
Through fine *abusion* of that Briton mayd; . . . IV. i. 7. 2
with unmanly guile And foule *abusion,* . . . V. xii. 40. 4
Abusions. Foolish delights, and fond *abusions,* . . . II. xi. 11. 8
Aby. *See* **Buy.**
Both pype and Muse shall sore the while *abye.'* . . . *S.C.* Ja. 71
manie often did *abie* full sore; . . . *Ti.* 101
to him that mindes his chaunce t' *abye?'* . . . II. iv. 40. 4
His life for dew revenge should deare *abye?* . . . II. viii. 28. 8
That direfull stroke thou dearely shalt *aby:'* . . . II. viii. 33. 4
Who dyes, the utmost dolor doth *abye;* . . . III. iv. 38. 5
he dearly shall *abye:* . . . III. vi. 24. 8
nought that wanteth rest can long *aby:* . . . III. vii. 3. 5
abie What fortune and his fate on him will lay; . . . III. x. 3. 1
Yet thou, false Squire, his fault shalt deare *aby,* . . . IV. i. 53. 8
The which ere long full deare he shall *abie:* . . . IV. vi. 8. 5
To have him slaine, or dearely doen *aby:* . . . V. iii. 36. 4
She death shall sure *aby.'* (*shall by) . . . V. xi. 40. 6
perhaps he mote it deare *aby.'* . . . VI. i. 28. 4
Ne time would give, nor any termes *aby,* . . . VI. ii. 19. 7
But th' utmost end perforce for to *aby,* . . . VI. iii. 44. 3
quickely thence avaunt, Or deare *aby;* . . . VI. vi. 21. 3
who so hardie hand on her doth lay, It dearely shall *aby,* . . . VI. xi. 15. 9
Jove, all fearlesse, forc't them to *aby;* . . . VII. vi. 24. 6
Whatever ill before he did *aby:* . . . *H.L.* 242
Abysm. dredd darknes of the deepe *Abysmé,* . . . *T.M.* 189
Abyss. His wide *Abysse* him forced forth to spewe, . . . *Van.* v. 10
Borne in the bosome of the black *Abysse,* . . . *T.M.* 260
downe hee fell into the deepe *Abisse,* . . . *Ti.* 545
into his darke *abysse* all ravin fell. . . . I. xi. 12. 9
In th' huge *abysse* of his engulfing grave, . . . II. xii. 5. 8
Downe in the bottome of the deepe *Abysse,* . . . IV. ii. 47. 6
Abysses. let those deep *Abysses* open rive, . . . *Ro.* i. 7
Accent. thy *accent* will excell in Tragick plaints . . . *Col.* 426
with her dolefull *accent* beare with him a part. . . . IV. viii. 3. 9
Accents. The dreadfull *accents* of their outcries shrill. . . . *T.M.* 286
deadly *accents,* which like swords Did wound my heart, . . . *D.* 297
to the waters fall tuning their *accents* fit. . . . VI. x. 7. 9
Let none of these theyr drery *accents* sing; . . . *Epith.* 351
gentle Eccho . . . Their *accents* did resound, . . . *Proth.* 113
Accept. driven T' *accept* a Benefice in peeces riven. . . . *Hub.* 540
excuse, that mote ye please Well to *accept,* . . . I. iii. 29. 7
Accept therefore My simple selfe, . . . I. viii. 27. 4
well *accept,* as well it did behove, . . . IV. viii. 60. 3
to *accept* her to his wedded wife: . . . IV. ix. 15. 6
So praying him t' *accept* her service evermore. . . . V. v. 54. 9
It gladly did *accept,* as he did say: . . . VI. ii. 38. 7
She gladly did of that same babe *accept,* . . . VI. iv. 37. 6
vouchsafe, O goddesse, to *accept,* . . . *Am.* xxii. 13
Let her *accept* me as her faithfull thrall; . . . *Am.* xxix. 10
Accepting. Which he *accepting* well, as he could weete, . . . V. iv. 51. 4
Which she *accepting,* he so neare her drew . . . V. vii. 16. 4
All which *accepting,* and with faithfull oth Bynding himselfe . . . VI. i. 44. 1
Accepts. his service . . . she *accepts* with thankes . . . I. v. 16. 4
Access. to have *accesse* Unto the Prince, . . . *Hub.* 1201
That none mote have *accesse,* . . . IV. x. 6. 4
Accident. By other *accident,* that earst befell, . . . II. ii. 11. 8
other *accident* which him aghast; . . . III. v. 3. 5
By what straunge *accident* faire Chrysogone Conceiv'd these infants, . . . III. vi. 5. 2
by what *accident* she there arriv'd? . . . III. vii. 14. 4
For marveill of that *accident* extreame: . . . III. viii. 22. 4
Which sodaine *accident* him much dismaid, . . . IV. viii. 7. 8
all the *accident* there hapned plaine, . . . IV. viii. 46. 7
To be disordred by some *accident,* . . . V. v. 10. 3
There chaunst to them a dangerous *accident:* . . . VI. x. 34. 3
This fatall chaunce, this dolefull *accident,* . . . VI. xi. 31. 2
Accidents. To commun *accidents* stil open layd, . . . III. v. 36. 7
times comparing with their *accidents,* . . . VI. xii. 20. 2
cutting off through hasty *accidents,* . . . *Epith.* 429
Accloyeth. The mouldie mosse, which thee *accloieth,* . . . *S.C.* F. 135
Accloys. with uncomely weedes the gentle wave *accloyes.* . . . II. vii. 15. 9
Accoasting. *See* **Accosting.**
Accoied. *See* **Accoyed.**
Accoil. *See* **Bel-accoil.**
Accoiled. About the Caudron many Cookes *accoyld* . . . II. ix. 30. 6
Accompanied. Whom als *accompanied* the Oke, . . . *Gn.* 204
with whome, as once I rode *accompanyde,* . . . I. ii. 35. 6
Him als *accompanyd* upon the way A comely Palmer, . . . II. i. 7. 1
Accompanyde with Phaedria the faire: . . . II. vi. 28. 2
of none *accompanyde;* . . . II. vii. 2. 3
With whom as they thus rode *accompanide,* . . . IV. ii. 4. 1
So as he rode with them *accompanide,* . . . IV. iv. 7. 6
Save that she algates him a while *accompanide.* . . . IV. vi. 44. 9
Accompanyde with angelick delightes. . . . *Am.* lxxxiii. 8

Accompany. My selfe would offer you t' *accompanie* . . . *Hub.* 97
She might in equall armes *accompany,* . . . III. iii. 61. 4
each the other vow'd t' *accompany:* . . . VI. vi. 16. 1
Accompanyd, -yde. *See* **Accompanied.**
Accomplish. *See* **Complishing.**
The marriage to *accomplish* vowd betwixt you twayn. . . . I. xii. 19. 9
They should *accomplish* both a knightly deed, . . . VI. vii. 4. 8
By which he mote *accomplish* his request, . . . VI. xi. 5. 6
Accomplished. when the terme is full *accomplishid,* . . . III. iii. 48. 1
eke in blood *Accomplished,* . . . III. ix. 42. 7
Accomplishment. th' *accomplishment* of it Sufficient worke . *Am.* xxxiii. 6
Accompt, -ed, *etc.* *See* **Account,** *etc.*
Accorage. *See* **Accourage.**
Accord. sweetly in *accord* (*accorde* [1]) did tune their voyce . . *Pet.* iv. 6
with his vitall notes *accord,* . . . *Ro.* xxv. 6
Age and Winter *accord* full nie, . . . *S.C.* F. 27
Accorde not with thy Muses meriment, . . . *S.C.* N. 34
in sweet *accord* All places . . . to fill, . . . *T.M.* 241
were not better fayre it to *accord* . . . II. ii. 30. 2
So happy peace they made and faire *accord.* . . . II. iii. 9. 1
Accord of friendes, consent of Parents sought, . . . II. iv. 21. 3
dore, Which to them opened of his owne *accord,* . . . II. vii. 31. 3
Forth passed on their way in fayre *accord,* . . . II. ix. 2. 4
Received is to grace and new *accord,* . . . II. x. 66. 4
In which *accord* the Prince was also plaste, . . . III. i. 12. 7
of their owne *accord* All things . . . doe grow, . . . III. vi. 34. 2
of her owne *accord,* This gentle Damzell, . . . III. viii. 1. 3
With perfect peace and bandes of fresh *accord,* . . . III. x. 51. 4
Fell softly forth, as of his owne *accord,* . . . III. xii. 38. 2
hard t' *accord* two things so far in dout. . . . IV. i. 11. 9
So did they all their former strife *accord;* . . . IV. i. 15. 5
to *accord* them all this meanes deviz'd: . . . IV. v. 25. 3
to Braggadochio selfe alone She came of her *accord,* . . . IV. v. 26. 9
Till they with mariage meet might finish that *accord.* . . . IV. vi. 41. 9
An happie life with grace and good *accord,* . . . IV. viii. 18. 2
at last *accord* To joyne in one, . . . IV. xi. 43. 7
'Certes, your strife were easie to *accord,* . . . V. iv. 16. 2
to her yeelded of his owne *accord;* . . . V. v. 17. 2
Yet would she not thereto yeeld free *accord* . . . V. v. 27. 6
this proude Dame, disdayning all *accord,* . . . V. viii. 22. 3
Entyced her to him for to *accord.* . . . V. xi. 50. 5
All this *accord* to which he Crudor had compeld. . . . VI. i. 44. 9
Her selfe acknowledg'd bound for that *accord,* . . . VI. i. 45. 8
joyning joy with her in one *accord,* . . . VI. xii. 22. 3
did she know how ill these two *accord* . . . *Am.* xxxi. 13
Let endlesse Peace your steadfast hearts *accord,* . . . *Proth.* 101
Accordance. I list none *accordaunce* make . . . *S.C.* May 164
taught in such *accordance* to agree? . . . *Col.* 846
the third time shall fayre *accordaunce* make: . . . III. iii. 30. 7
them selves full eath perswade To faire *accordaunce,* . . . V. viii. 14. 5
Accorded. when they were *accorded* from the fray, . . . III. ix. 17. 3
Paridell for her strives: They are *accorded:* . . . IV. ii. Arg.
So, well *accorded,* forth they rode together . . . IV. ii. 29. 1
Thus when they all *accorded* goodly were, . . . IV. iii. 51. 1
now so well *accorded* all anew, . . . IV. ix. 40. 5
According. *according* to occasion. . . . *Hub.* 652
I will pay Penance to her, *according* their decree, . . . *D.* 370
I cannot thinke *according* to her worth: . . . *Col.* 627
To shew it to this knight, *according* his desire.' . . . I. x. 50. 9
Discourst his voyage long, *according* his request. . . . I. xii. 15. 9
T' adorne thy forme *according* thy desart, . . . II. iv. 26. 2
Therefore a Fay he her *according* hight, . . . II. x. 71. 8
All shap't *according* their conditions: . . . II. xi. 11. 6
According to their mindes like monstruous.' . . . II. xii. 85. 5
According to their kynds. . . . III. vi. 30. 6
according to each wit: . . . IV. i. 14. 4
all three *according* to their kynd: . . . IV. ii. 53. 4
nought *according* to his mind He could out-learne, . . . IV. viii. 22. 5
To which when he *according* did repaire, . . . IV. viii. 51. 2
I them all *according* their degree Cannot recount, . . . IV. xi. 40. 7
According their degrees disposed well. . . . IV. xii. 3. 5
According to the line of conscience, . . . V. i. 7. 4
According to the custome of their law: . . . V. ii. 11. 7
found No easie meanes *according* to his mind: . . . V. viii. 42. 3
according to the former token . . . VI. vi. 18. 1
He staide his hand *according* her desire, . . . VI. viii. 18. 1
(*according* as they had decreed) . . . VII. vi. 52. 1
According to their sundry kinds of features, . . . VII. vii. 4. 3
According as thy selfe doest see and heare, . . . VII. vii. 56. 7
According as the heavens have her graced, . . . *H.B.* 116
According to an heavenly patterne wrought, . . . *H.H.L.* 108
Accordingly. Who, being askt, *accordingly* confessed all. . . IV. v. 23. 9
So it more faire *accordingly* it makes, . . . *H.B.* 45
Accords. manie *accords* (*accordes* [1]) more sweete . . . *Bel.* xii. 8
Accost. all the shores, which to the sea *accoste,* . . . V. xi. 42. 6
Accosting. Whether high towring or *accoasting* low, . . . VI. ii. 32. 2
Account. what *account* both these will make; . . . *S.C.* May 51
When great Pan *account* of shepeherdes shall aske. . . . *S.C.* May 54
make like *account* of his brother. . . . *S.C.* Au. 43
Giving *accompt* of th' annuall increce . . . *Hub.* 301
They shall him make an ill *accompt* of thrift. . . . *Hub.* 307
Of all the rest that I am tyde t' *account:* . . . *Ded. Son.* vii. 10
a gentle Lady of great sway And high *accompt* . . . III. v. 4. 6
Here to *account* the endlesse progeny . . . III. vi. 30. 7
Causde me be called to *accompt* therefore; . . . VI. viii. 22. 2
Why then should I *accoumpt* of little paine, . . . *Am.* xxvi. 13
Accounted. *accounted* heretofore The learneds meed . . . *T.M.* 411
How ever now *accompted* Elfins sonne, . . . I. x. 60. 2
she in tract of time *accompted* was his owne. . . . VI. ix. 14. 9
Accounts. *Accoumpts* my self her captive quite forlorne. . . *Am.* xxix. 4

Accourage. that same froward twaine would *accorage,* . . . II. ii. 38. 7
Her to recomfort, and *accourage* bold, . . . III. viii. 34. 2
Accourting. *Accourting* each her frend with lavish fest: . . . II. ii. 16. 5
Accoutrements. he was clad in strange *accoutrements,* . . . *Hub.* 672
Accoyed. Then is your carelesse corage *accoied,* . . . *S.C.* F. 47
with kind words *accoyd,* vowing great love to mee. . . . IV. viii. 59. 9
Accrew, -ed. *See* **Accrue,** *etc.*
Accrue. Doo ye not feele your torments to *accrewe,* . . . *Ro.* xv. 11
such wealth might unto thee *accrew;* . . . *Col.* 655
though powre faild, her courage did *accrew;* . . . V. v. 7. 4
Accrued. Having his forces all in one *accrewed,* . . . IV. vi. 18. 7
Accursed. He now hath placed his *accursed* brood, . . . *T.M.* 315
shame and sorrow and *accursed* case . . . *T.M.* 514
A cruell beast of most *accursed* brood . . . *As.* 116
th' unkindly Impes, of heaven *accurst,* . . . I. i. 26. 2
When those *accursed* messengers of hell, . . . Came . . . I. ii. 2. 1
Into the hands of hys *accursed* fone, . . . I. ii. 23. 8
Accursed usury was all his trade, . . . I. iv. 27. 8
grace, . . . that *accurst* hand-writing doth deface. . . . I. ix. 53. 8
to *accursed* fate, The guilt I doe ascribe: . . . III. iv. 37. 8
that *accursed* Hag, her hostesse late, . . . III. viii. 2. 1
Entrenched deep with knyfe *accursed* keene, . . . III. xii. 20. 6
Well worthie thou to be of Jove *accurst,* . . . IV. ii. 49. 8
Of this *accursed* Carle of hellish kind, . . . IV. vii. 18. 4
Thereto they usde one most *accursed* order, . . . VI. viii. 36. 1
made them all *accurst* That God had blest, . . . VII. vi. 5. 7
Upon thee fall for thine *accursed* hyre . . . *Am.* lxxxv. 6
Seeing him lie like creature long *accurst* . . . *H.H.L.* 129
Accuse. Such as Dame Pallas, . . . Could not *accuse.* . . . *Mui.* 303
Least that the world thee dead *accuse* of guilt, . . . *D.* 82
Shall I *accuse* the hidden cruell fate, . . . I. i. 51. 2
His almes for want of faith he doth *accuse.* . . . I. iv. 32. 4
thing refused doe not afterward *accuse.'* . . . II. vii. 18. 9
With which she guiltlesse persons may *accuse,* . . . IV. viii. 25. 3
if men you of cruelty *accuse,* . . . VI. viii. 1. 8
The heavens of their fortunes fault *accuse,* . . . VI. ix. 29. 2
T' *accuse* of pride, or rashly blame for ought. . . . *Am.* lxi. 4
Accused. them of crimes and heresies *accus'd,* . . . *Hub.* 564
him before His father fierce of treason false *accusd,* . . . I. v. 37. 8
sore *accus'd* His falshood, . . . III. vi. 13. 3
evermore the Carle of courtesie *accusd.* . . . III. ix. 12. 9
lewd Impietie, that her *accused* sore. . . . V. ix. 48. 9
refused To take me up . . . for no just cause *accused,* . . . VI. ii. 22. 4
a rude churle, . . . *accused* Of fowle discourtesie, . . . VI. iii. 33. 5
He taken was, betrayd, and false *accused;* . . . *H.H.L.* 240
Accusements. new *accusements* to produce in place: . . . V. ix. 47. 2
Accuser. giving hastie credit to th' *accuser,* . . . *Mui.* 135
his *accuser* thereuppon defide; . . . V. i. 23. 7
Accusing. her *accusing* of dishonesty, . . . I. iii. 23. 4
As heven *accusing* guilty of her death, . . . II. i. 49. 2
Accusing fortune and too cruell fate, . . . II. i. 56. 8
Accusing highest Jove and gods ingrate; . . . II. vii. 60. 7
Such was this Ladies fit in her loves fond *accusing.* . . . V. vi. 14. 9
Accustomed. with fell tooth *accustomd* to blood, . . . *As.* 118
Then we poore shepheards are *accustomd* here, . . . *Col.* 785
The martiall brood *accustomed* to fight: . . . III. i. 13. 5
As the proud Persian Queenes *accustomed.* . . . III. i. 41. 4
Achates. Did order all th' *Achates* in seemely wise, . . . II. ix. 31. 4
Ache. thy joynts benomd with *ache?* . . . *S.C.* Au. 4
Acheron. They pas the bitter waves of *Acheron,* . . . I. v. 33. 1
Achieve. vertuous deeds, . . . they care not to *atchive.* . . . *T.M.* 96
Devizing how that . . . turnament With greatest honour he *atchieven* might: . . . I. v. 1. 8
many hard adventures did *atchieve;* . . . III. i. 3. 6
t' *atchieve* an hard emprize; . . . III. iii. 53. 7
honor which thou didst *atchive.* . . . III. v. 26. 9
Could that *atchieve* whereto he did aspire, . . . IV. vi. 43. 6
hard t' *atchieve* (*atchive*) and bring to end. . . . *Am.* li. 8
happy he! that can at last *achyve* . . . so sweet a rest; . . . *Am.* lxiii. 9
Achieved. *Atcheived* the golden Fleece in Colchid land, . . . *Ro.* x. 2
had *atchievde* so great a conquest by his might. . . . I. xi. 55. 9
Was never man, who most conquestes *atchiev'd,* . . . II. v. 15. 3
Which he *atchiev'd* to his great ornament; . . . IV. ii. 39. 4
she wondrous deeds of arms *atchieved,* . . . IV. iv. 46. 6
sundry battels, which she hath *atchieved* . . . V. iv. 33. 6
Atchiev'd so hard a quest, as few before; . . . VI. i. 5. 8
Which he *atchieved* to his owne great gaines, . . . VI. ix. 2. 8
till he had it *attchieved?* . . . VI. x. 1. 6
Achievement. Virgin which beheld . . . The whole *atchievement* I. viii. 26. 3
Of late most hard *atchiev'ment* by you donne, . . . II. i. 32. 2
'His be the praise that this *atchiev'ment* wrought, . . . II. i. 33. 2
many hard *Atchievement* wrought, . . . II. xi. 15. 4
By his sole manhood and *atchievement* stout Dismay'd, . . . IV. iv. 43. 2
he had far'd In that *atchievement,* . . . IV. ix. 41. 6
in *atchievement* of her high behest I should no creature joyne VI. ii. 37. 7
To his *atchievement* of the Blatant Beast: . . . VI. xii. 2. 7
resolving to returne in hast Unto so great *atchievement,* . . . VI. xii. 13. 2
Achievements. purchas Through brave *atcheivements* from his enemies; . . . *Ti.* 655
with . . . bold *atchievements* her did entertaine. . . . *As.* 70
famous harde *atchievements* still pursew; . . . I. vii. 45. 5
that seeke with warlike spoyle, And great *atchiev'ments,* . . . II. i. 8. 8
I in armes, and in *atchievements* brave, . . . II. vii. 33. 6
Where be the brave *atchievements* doen by some? . . . III. iv. 1. 3
Achilles. *Achilles* preassing through the Phrygian glaives, . . *H.L.* 233
Achilles'. to sheild *Achilles* life from fate of Troyan field. . . *Mui.* 64
Achilles armes, which Arthegall did win: . . . III. ii. 25. 6
Achyve. *See* **Achieve.**
Acidale. Therefore it rightly cleeped was mount *Acidale.* . . . VI. x. 8. 9

Acidalian. in her secret bowre On *Acidalian* mount, ... IV. v. 5. 5
With bathing in the *Acidalian* brooke. . . . . *Epith.* 310
Acknowledge. (as ye all *acknowledge* must) . . . . VII. vi. 27. 1
Acknowledged. Her selfe *acknowledg'd* bound for that accord, VI. i. 45. 8
Acknowledg'd for his owne faire Pastorell. . . . . VI. xii. 22. 4
Acontius. fruit, With which *Acontius* got his lover trew, . . II. vii. 55. 2
Acorns. The Oke, whose *Acornes* were our foode, ... *Gn.* 206
having beene with *Acorns* alwaies fed, ... *T.M.* 590
Acquaintance. Ne in this new *acquaintaunce* could delight; I. vi. 32. 3
Where shortly they in great *acquaintance* grew, ... VI. xi. 41. 3
Acquainted. well *acquainted* with that commune plight, . . . I. x. 23. 2
never had *acquainted* beene With such queint usage, ... VI. ix. 35. 1
Acquit. how t' *acquite* themselves unto their Lord . . . . . *Hub.* 323
till I have *acquitt* your captive knight, ... I. vii. 52. 6
Were not that . . . stedfast truth *acquite* him out of all. . . . I. viii. 1. 4
did *acquite* a murdrer felonous; . . . . II. vii. 62. 7
(God doe us well *acquight!*) . . . . II. xii. 3. 3
Which had himselfe so stoutly well *acquit,* . . . . VI. ii. 24. 2
Him selfe thereof he labourd to *acquite,* . . . . VI. iii. 21. 7
how thereof her selfe she did *acquite,* . . . . VI. vi. 17. 2
I will them soone *acquite,* and both of blame assoile.' . . . . VI. viii. 6. 9
To be *acquit* fro my continual smart; . . . . *Am.* xlii. 6
Radigund . . . from her direfull doome *acquit,* . . . . V. iv. 39. 2
Acrasia. where vile *Acrasia* does wonne; . . . . II. i. 51. 2
Acrasia, a false enchaunteresse, ... II. i. 51. 3
Till I that false *Acrasia* have wonne; . . . . II. ii. 44. 6
The vyle *Acrasia,* that with vaine delightes, ... II. v. 27. 2
For thou to serve *Acrasia* thy selfe doest vaunt. . . . . . . II. vi. 9. 9
false *Acrasia,* and her wicked wiles; . . . . II. ix. 9. 6
Doth overthrow the Bowre of blis, And *Acrasy* defeat. . . . . II. xii. Arg.
Here wonnes *Acrasia,* whom we must surprise, ... II. xii. 69. 8
the captived *Acrasia* he sent, ... III. i. 2. 1
Acrates. The sonnes of old *Acrates* and Despight; . . . . . . II. iv. 41. 6
Acrates, sonne of Phlegeton and Jarre; . . . . II. iv. 41. 7
Those were the two sonnes of *Acrates* old, ... II. viii. 10. 6
Acrates'. What is become of great *Acrates* sonne? . . . . . . II. v. 35. 6
Sir Guyon, . . . is by *Acrates* sonne despoyld; . . . . II. viii. Arg.
Acres. To prove how many *acres* he did spred of land. . . . . . I. xii. 11. 9
Act. Ah heavens! that doe this hideous *act* behold, ... I. vi. 5. 6
'And lives he yet . . . that wrought this *act?* . . . . II. i. 12. 2
She was empassiond at that piteous *act,* . . . . III. ix. 38. 4
Actaea. Speedy Hippothoe, and chaste *Actea,* . . . . IV. xi. 50. 1
Action. every *action* doth them much commend, ... VI. ii. 2. 3
Actions. all his *actions* frame, ... II. v. 1. 2
all their *actions* to direct aright: . . . . III. iii. 2. 4
By lively *actions* he gan bewray Some argument . . . . . . III. xii. 4. 5
to God all mortall *actions* here, . . . do plaine appeare; . . . *H.H.B.* 172
Activity. living him in all *activity* To thee shall represent. . . III. iii. 29. 3
Actors. th' *actours* won the meede meet for their crymes. . . V. ix. 42. 5
Acts. wont the world with famous *acts* to fill; . . . . *T.M.* 430
So brave a Trompe, thy noble *acts* to sound! . . . . *Ti.* 434
Though now their *acts* be no where to be found, ... IV. ii. 32. 5
Thy *acts,* O Scanderbeg, this volume tels. *Com.Son.*iii.14
I should enabled be thy *actes* to sing. . . . . *H.L.* 21
Adam. That Paradise hast found whych *Adam* lost: . . . . . . *S.C.* Jun. 10
Adamant. Hewen out of *Adamant* rocke with engines keene, . I. vii. 33. 7
As if in *Adamant* rocke it had beene pight. . . . . I. xi. 25. 5
her in chaines of *adamant* he tyde; . . . . II. xii. 82. 6
Tempred with *Adamant* amongst the same, ... V. i. 10. 2
bynd with *adamant* chayne: . . . . *Am.* xlii. 10
Adamantine. in th' *Adamantine* mould Of his true hart . . . V. vi. 2. 6
th' *Adamantine* shield which he did beare . . . . V. xi. 10. 7
Together linkt with *Adamantine* chaines; . . . . *H.L.* 89
First, th' Earth, on *adamantine* pillers founded . . . . . . *H.H.B.* 36
Adamants. his *Adamants* with which he shines And glisters wide, IV. xi. 31. 7
Adam's. from wretched *Adams* line To purge away . . . . . . II. x. 50. 3
Adaw. The sight whereof did greatly him *adaw,* . . . . III. vii. 13. 4
haughtie spirits meekely to *adaw,* . . . . IV. vi. 26. 8
fervour of his flames somewhat *adaw* . . . . V. ix. 35. 4
Adawed. yeelded, with shame and greefe *adawed,* . . . . . . *S.C.* F. 141
As one *adaw'd,* and halfe confused stood; . . . . V. v. 45. 5
Like one *adawed* with some dreadfull spright: . . . . V. vii. 20. 8
Adays. *See* **Now-a-days.**
That dewly *adayes* counts mine. . . . . *S.C.* Mar. 42
Add. *Add* faith unto your force, and be not faint; . . . . . . I. i. 19. 3
of her plenty *adde* unto their need: . . . . II. ii. 38. 8
now he strength gan *adde* unto his will, ... III. viii. 26. 6
But to the rest, . . . My labour *adde,* . . . . III. viii. 50. 9
He would be there, and honor to her spousall *ad.* . . . . . V. ii. 3. 9
Thereto *adde* art, even womens witty trade, ... V. v. 49. 5
some hope your words unto me *add.'* . . . . VI. i. 10. 5
adde more brightnesse to your goodly hew, ... *H.B.* 178
Added. O vainesse! to be *added* to the rest, ... *Ti.* 459
thereto *added* wordes of wondrous might. . . . . I. x. 24. 6
added grace unto her excellence: . . . . I. xii. 24. 4
added flame unto his former fire, ... II. v. 8. 4
that above were *added* to that under grownd. . . . . II. vii. 31. 9
There *added* was by goodly ordinaunce . . . . II. ix. 30. 3
New matter *added* to his former fire; . . . . IV. vi. 11. 2
Addeem. So unto him they did *addeeme* the prise . . . . . . V. iii. 15. 2
Addeemed. *Addeem'd* me to endure this penaunce sore; . . . VI. viii. 22. 5
Adder. like an *Adder* lurking in the weedes, ... II. v. 34. 1
Adder's. Venemous toung, tipt with vile *adders* sting, ... *Am.* lxxxv. 1
Adders. lockes uncombed cruell *adders* be. . . . . *Gn.* 344
Curled with thousand *adders* venemous, ... I. v. 34. 3
Adding. *adding* new Feare to his first amazment, ... I. ix. 24. 1
adding more impetuous forse, ... II. iv. 6. 3
adding anguish to the bitter wound . . . . IV. vii. 1. 7
To which he *adding* comely guize withall . . . . VI. i. 2. 5
Addoom. unto me *addoom* that is my dew; . . . . VII. vii. 56. 8

Address. thither they themselves meant to *addresse,* . . . . . *Hub.* 657
to have accesse . . . but by his owne *addresse,* . . . . *Hub.* 1202
Unto his journey did himselfe *addresse,* . . . . *Mui.* 146
She . . . bad her knight *addresse* him to the fray, ... I. ii. 14. 5
A shrilling trompett . . . unto battaill bad them selves *addresse:* I. v. 6. 2
streight against that knight his speare he did *addresse.* . . . II. i. 25. 9
unto batteil doe your selves *addresse;* . . . . II. viii. 18. 2
on his arme *addresse* his goodly shield . . . . III. i. 4. 8
Sir Satyrane him towardes did *addresse,* . . . . III. viii. 45. 1
They all agree, and forward them *addresse:* . . . . III. x. 40. 1
gan their shields *addresse* them selves afore: . . . . IV. iv. 4. 8
Did to the Faery Queene her way *addresse,* . . . . V. i. 4. 2
To deedes of armes . . . They gan themselves *addresse,* . . . . V. iii. 4. 4
'Goe, damzell, quickly, doe thy selfe *addresse* . . . . V. iv. 48. 4
Gan her *addresse* unto her former way. . . . . V. vi. 36. 3
gan with courage fierce *addresse* him to the fight. . . . . . V. x. 31. 9
he gan him selfe streightway Thereto *addresse,* . . . . V. xi. 21. 5
Gan freshly him *addresse* unto his former way. . . . . . . VI. iii. 13. 9
Which that nights fortune would for him *addresse.* . . . . . VI. iii. 44. 4
gan himselfe *addresse* to take her part. . . . . VI. v. 8. 3
He wist not to which side him to *addresse:* . . . . VI. vi. 26. 5
cruell warriour, doth herselfe *addresse* To battell, ... *Am.* xi. 3
Addressed. many an auncient Trophee was *addrest,* . . . . . *Bel.*[2] v. 5
So weren his under-songs well *addrest.* . . . . *S.C.* Au. 128
With dolefull layes unto the time *addrest:* . . . . *As.* Interl. 226
like a goodly beacon high *addrest,* . . . . *Col.* 562
Full jolly knight he seemde, and wel *addrest;* . . . . I. ii. 11. 7
his mightie shild Upon his manly arme he soone *addrest,* . . . I. viii. 6. 7
Whom when the Prince, to batteill new *addrest* . . . did see, I. viii. 22. 1
this good knight his way with me *addrest,* . . . . I. x. 11. 3
fresh encounter towardes him *addrest;* . . . . I. xi. 17. 2
Her greeting sends in these sad lines *addrest* . . . . I. xii. 26. 2
him *addrest* Unto the journey . . . . II. iii. 1. 6
He to Cordelia him selfe *addrest,* . . . . II. x. 31. 5
Him selfe *addrest* to that adventure hard: . . . . II. xi. 3. 8
He to the Carle him selfe agayn *addrest,* . . . . II. xi. 37. 2
to the sea-coast at length she her *addrest.* . . . . III. iv. 6. 9
with his scyth *addrest* Does mow the flowring herbes . . . . III. vi. 39. 3
Her selfe to fight *addrest,* and threw her lode aside. . . . . III. vii. 38. 9
Her dreadfull weapon she to him *addrest,* . . . . III. vii. 42. 2
he him selfe so busily *addrest,* . . . . III. viii. 35. 5
To her this song most fitly is *addrest,* . . . . IV. Pr. 4. 8
The warlike Britonesse her soone *addrest,* . . . Her fayned Paramour, ... IV. i. 36. 1
His foe was soone *addrest:* . . . . IV. iii. 14. 9
Against Cambello fiercely him *addrest;* . . . . IV. iii. 22. 8
Gainst whom Sir Paridell himselfe *addrest,* . . . . IV. iv. 6. 8
addrest his maiden-headed shield, ... IV. iv. 17. 4
after him Sir Douglas him *addrest,* . . . . IV. iv. 21. 4
her *addrest* With ready hand . . . . IV. viii. 10. 5
Eftsoones him selfe he to their aide *addrest,* . . . . IV. ix. 32. 5
streight him selfe unto the fight *addrest,* . . . . V. ii. 12. 2
Towards which coast her love his way *addrest:* . . . . V. vi. 7. 5
His dwelling was, to which he him *addrest:* . . . . V. vi. 22. 5
to his former journey him *addrest;* . . . . V. xi. 35. 8
Himselfe *addrest* unto this new debate, ... VI. viii. 13. 3
himselfe *addrest* In shepheards weed; . . . . VI. ix. 36. 3
other daintie thing for her *addrest,* . . . . VI. x. 40. 4
Addressing. her goodly shield *addressing* fayre, ... III. iv. 14. 1
Adicia. They . . . drive his wife *Adicia* to despaire. . . . . . V. viii. Arg.
stird up . . . By his bad wife that hight *Adicia;* . . . . V. viii. 20. 3
Fit for *Adicia* there to build her wicked bowre. . . . . . . V. ix. 1. 9
Adieu. '*Adieu,* delightes, that lulled me asleepe; . . . . . . *S.C.* D. 151
Adieu, my deare, whose love I bought so deare; . . . . *S.C.* D. 152
Adieu, my little Lambes and loved sheepe; . . . . *S.C.* D. 153
Adieu, ye Woodes, that oft my witnesse were: . . . . *S.C.* D. 154
Adieu, good Hobbinoll, that was so true, ... *S.C.* D. 155
Tell Rosalind, her Colin bids her *adieu.'* . . . . *S.C.* D. 156
Thus, deare! *adieu,* whom I expect ere long." . . . . *D.* 292
Ne gave him leave to bid that aged sire *Adieu;* . . . . II. vi. 20. 6
New yeare, . . . bidding th' old *Adieu,* . . . . *Am.* iv. 3
Adin. the king of Louthiane, Hight *Adin,* . . . . III. iii. 37. 6
Adjoined. She lightly unto him *adjoyned* syde to syde; . . . III. vii. 42. 9
Adjoining. Built on a rocke *adjoyning* to the seas: . . . . . II. ii. 12. 7
To losse of love *adjoyning* losse of frend, ... II. iv. 31. 2
That to the gate of Hell, . . . Was next *adjoyning,* . . . . . II. vii. 24. 7
Out of the rockes and caves *adjoyning* nye; . . . . II. ix. 13. 3
Adjudged. To her therefore The fayrest Ladie was *adjudgd* . IV. v. 8. 9
she her selfe *adjudged* to the Knight . . . . V. iv. 20. 4
Tho unto Satyran she was *adjudged,* . . . . IV. v. 22. 1
whose The honour of the prize should be *adjudg'd* . . . . . V. iii. 13. 9
adjudged so by law; . . . . V. ix. 25. 3
Adjured. I am *adjur'd* best counsell to impart . . . . V. vii. 19. 8
Admetus. The servant of *Admetus,* cowheard vile, ... III. xi. 39. 4
Admirable. knowne . . . To have done much more *admirable* deedes. . . . . I. vii. 36. 3
That Turrets frame most *admirable* was, ... II. ix. 45. 1
seemd a worke of *admirable* witt; . . . . II. xii. 44. 2
Where I may see those *admirable* things . . . . *H.H.L.* 3
And all with *admirable* beautie deckt. . . . . *H.H.B.* 35
In which they see such *admirable* things, ... *H.H.B.* 260
Admirance. With great *admiraunce* inwardly was moved, . . V. x. 39. 4
Admiration. *admiration* of that heavenly light, ... *H.B.* 13
With *admiration* of their passing light, ... *H.H.L.* 279
Admire. How I *admire* ech turning of thy verse! . . . . *S.C.* Au. 194
Such immortal mirrhor, as he doth *admire,* . . . . *S.C.* O. 93
he nothing can *admire,* . . . . *Hub.* 610
grace, That men *admire* in goodlie womankinde, ... *D.* 212
Gan her *admire,* and her sad sorrowes rew, ... I. vi. 31. 4
ne let him then *admyre,* . . . . II. Pr. 4. 3

Admire—*Continued.*
That mortall men her glory should *admyre.* . . . . III. v. 52. 6
Whose great assembly they did much *admire,* . . . . V. ii. 29. 6
Her wisedome did *admire,* and hearkned to her loring. . . . V. vii. 42. 9
Much did Sir Calidore *admyre* his speach . . . . VI. ii. 13. 1
Him much more now then earst he gan *admire* . . . . VI. ii. 34. 2
all men did her person much *admire,* . . . . VI. vii. 28. 6
him did oft embrace, and oft *admire,* . . . . VI. viii. 27. 8
all this worlds gay showes, which we *admire,* . . . . VI. ix. 27. 4
That as a Goddesse men might her *admire,* . . . . VII. vi. 4. 3
The soverayne beauty which I doo *admyre,* . . . . *Am.* iii. 1
The thing which I doo most in her *admire,* . . . . *Am.* v. 3
I honor and *admire* the Makers art. . . . . *Am.* xxiv. 4
many now much worship and *admire!* . . . . *Am.* xxvii. 8
The beame of light, whom mortal eyes *admyre;* . . . . *Am.* lxi. 10
admire such worlds rare wonderment; . . . . *Am.* lxix. 12
All that they know not envy or *admyre;* . . . . *Am.* lxxxiv. 6
Admire their statues, their Colossoes great: . . . . *Com. Son.* iii. 6
robs the harts of those which it *admyre;* . . . . *H.B.* 61
men the more *admyre* their fountaine may; . . . . *H.B.* 186
The mirrour of his owne thought doth *admyre.* . . . . *H.B.* 224
which fondly here *admyre* Faire seeming shewes, ... *H.H.B.* 16
Enough is me t' *admyre* so heavenly thing, ... *H.H.B.* 236

Admired. *Alla Turchesca,* much the more *admyr'd;* . . . . *Hub.* 677
of the world *admired* ev'rie where, ... *Ti.* 122
Admir'd of base-borne men from farre away: . . . . *Ti.* 424
That all the Gods *admir'd:* . . . . *Mui.* 327
Such as the world *admyr'd,* . . . . *Col.* 191
Admyr'd of all, yet envied of none, ... *Col.* 550
Made by the Maker selfe to be *admired;* . . . . *Col.* 561
Ne bene so much *admir'd* of later age. . . . . *Ded. Son.* xiii. 6
that victorious man, Whom all *admired* as from heaven sent, . I. xii. 9. 4
all the Gods *admird* his lofty note. . . . . II. x. 3. 5
many one *Admyrd* her goodly haveour, ... III. vi. 52. 8
Admir'd of all the people and much glorifide. . . . . IV. iii. 51. 9
much *admired* The manner of their worke . . . . IV. v. 38. 1
oft *admir'd* his monstrous shape, ... IV. vii. 32. 7
Their like resemblaunce much *admired* there, ... IV. ix. 11. 2
all men much *admyrde* her change, and spake her praise. . . IV. ix. 16. 9
Admyr'd her beautie much, ... IV. xii. 33. 4
simple Truth did rayne, and was of all *admyred.* . . . . V. Pr. 3. 9
men *admyr'd* his over-ruling might; . . . . V. i. 8. 5
Yet was *admired* much of fooles, women, and boys. . . . . V. ii. 30. 9
He much *admired* both his heart and hew, ... V. viii. 12. 8
Admyr'd of many, honoured of all; . . . . V. ix. 33. 2
Admyr'd of all the rest in presence there, ... V. x. 15. 7
Sir Calidore . . . more *admyr'd* the stroke . . . . VI. ii. 13. 2
He praysd it much, and much *admyred* it; . . . . VI. ii. 24. 5
The more it is *admir'd* of many a wight, ... VI. vii. 29. 8
much *admyr'd* the Beast, but more *admyr'd* the Knight. . . . VI. xii. 37. 9
your bright beams, of my weak eies *admyred,* . . . . *Am.* vii. 11
Such mercy shall you make *admyr'd* to be; . . . . *Am.* xlix. 13
The more of stedfast mynds to be *admyred,* . . . . *H.L.* 171
make it more *admyr'd* of foe and frend; . . . . *H.B.* 264
those Idees . . . which Plato so *admyred,* . . . . *H.H.B.* 83
That all posteritie *admyred* it, ... *H.H.B.* 213

Admirer. with his Squire, th' *admirer* of his might, ... I. viii. 3. 1

Admirers. *Admirers* of her glorious excellence; . . . . *T.M.* 584

Admires. Which the late world *admyres* for wondrous monuments. . . . . III. iii. 2. 9
Admires the mirrour of so heavenly light. . . . . *H.L.* 196

Admiring. much *admyring* that so goodly frame, ... IV. x. 31. 1
her *admiring* as some heavenly wight, ... VI. ix. 9. 6

Admit. Both that the Bishop may *admit* of thee, ... *Hub.* 533
so soone as life did me *admitt* Into this world, ... I. ix. 3. 5
Atin by no way She would *admit,* . . . . II. vi. 4. 9

Admitted. to the seates of happie soules *admitted:* . . . . *Gn.* 478
He as a Knight might justly be *admitted;* . . . . IV. i. 12. 8
Talus mote not be *admitted* to her part. . . . . V. vii. 3. 9

Admyre, *etc. See* **Admire.**

Ado. flat refusd to have *adoe* with mee, ... III. vii. 58. 3
By which I hardly past with much *adoe:* . . . . IV. x. 57. 7
ye have much *adoe* to deale withall.' . . . . VI. i. 10. 8
they to it fell With small *adoe,* . . . . VI. ix. 17. 8

Adonis. in the gardens of *Adonis* nurst: . . . . *Col.* 804
Did in the gardins of *Adonis* fynd . . . . II. x. 71. 4
The fayre *Adonis,* turned to a flowre; . . . . III. i. 34. 5
Gardins of *Adonis* fraught With pleasures . . . . III. vi. Arg.
The Gardin of *Adonis,* far renowmd by fame. . . . . III. vi. 29. 9
That in the Gardin of *Adonis* springs, ... III. vi. 39. 2
with faire *Adonis* playes his wanton partes. . . . . III. vi. 49. 9

Adonis'. to enjoy Her deare *Adonis* joyous company, ... III. vi. 46. 2

Adore. make all wights *adore* The beast, ... *Rev.* i. 13
rayse His heavenly Muse, th' Almightie to *adore.* . . . . *Ro.* Env. 12
I reverence and *adore:* . . . . *S.C.* Jul. 114
their high steppes *adore:* . . . . *S.C.* Env. 11
him dead thou dost *adore* As living, ... *Ti.* 249
Will honour heaven, or heavenlie powers *adore,* . . . . *D.* 198
t' *adore,* with humble mind, The image . . . . *Col.* 350
so we him *adore* With humble hearts . . . . *Col.* 815
Bids me, . . . to *adore* His goodly image, ... *Ded. Son.* xv. 8
That would compell all nations to *adore,* . . . . I. v. 47. 2
Una . . . Whom salvage nation does *adore,* . . . . I. vi. Arg.
Whom highly he did reverence and *adore,* . . . . I. x. 49. 5
Doe her *adore* with sacred reverence, ... II. ii. 41. 8
his deare hart the picture gan *adore;* . . . . II. viii. 43. 5
Dying her serve, and living her *adore;* . . . . III. v. 46. 7
thought her to *adore* with humble spright: . . . . III. vii. 11. 8
T' *adore* thing so divine as beauty were but right. . . . . III. vii. 11. 9
Yet tried did *adore.* . . . . III. ix. 25. 6

Adore—*Continued.*
for his worth, that all men did *adore,* . . . . IV. i. 39. 5
All other Idoles which the heathen *adore,* . . . . IV. x. 40. 2
Congealed litle drops which doe the morne *adore.* . . . . IV. xi. 46. 9
Much did that Squire Sir Artegall *adore* . . . . V. i. 30. 1
That Gods and men doe equally *adore,* . . . . V. vii. 1. 2
Those Nations farre thy justice doe *adore;* . . . . V. x. 3. 8
The more would wretched lovers her *adore.* . . . . VI. vii. 30. 4
So dying live, and living do *adore* her. . . . . *Am.* xiv. 14
perfect Beautie, which all men *adore;* . . . . *H.B.* 40
Adore the powre of thy great Majestie, ... *H.B.* 271

Adored. Yet of the devout people is *ador'd,* . . . . *Ro.* xxviii. 10
dead, as living, ever him *ador'd:* . . . . I. i. 2. 4
ever most *adord* As the God of my life? . . . . I. iii. 7. 8
her *ador'd* by honorable name, ... I. xii. 8. 4
noble knights . . . Which her *ador'd,* . . . . III. viii. 47. 8
young Knight, . . . doubly overcommen, her *ador'd.* . . . . IV. i. 15. 4
Justice sate high *ador'd* with solemne feasts, ... V. Pr. 9. 8
her *adored* with due humblenesse . . . . V. xii. 24. 7

Adoring. as a Goddesse her *adoring,* . . . . V. vii. 42. 8
him *adoring* as her lives deare Lord, ... VI. i. 45. 6

Adorn. Was wont this auncient Citie to *adorne,* . . . . *Ro.* xxix. 7
To *adorne* her grace: . . . . *S.C.* Ap. 130
dauncing all in companie, *Adorne* that God: . . . . *Gn.* 28
chieflie doth each noble minde *adorne,* . . . . *Hub.* 831
The Stage with Tragick buskin to *adorne,* . . . . *T.M.* 152
With some few silver-dropping teares t' *adorne;* . . . . *Ti.* 683
with remembraunce of your gracious name, . . . *adorne* these verses . . . . *Ded. Son.* xvi. 5
T' *adorne* thy forme according thy desart, ... II. iv. 26. 2
Fitt to *adorne* the dead, ... II. vii. 51. 9
Of all Gods workes which doe this worlde *adorne,* . . . . II. ix. 1. 1
like a pompous bride . . . too lavishly *adorne,* . . . . II. xii. 50. 8
This Gardin to *adorne* with all variety. . . . . II. xii. 59. 9
Thy Grandsire Nereus promist to *adorne?* . . . . III. iv. 36. 5
The girlond of her honour did *adorne:* . . . . III. v. 51. 3
Adorne the world with like to heavenly light, ... III. v. 53. 2
Phœbus with faire beames did her *adorne,* . . . . III. vi. 2. 8
Without *adorne* of gold or silver bright, ... III. xii. 20. 2
Doest fayrest shine, and most *adorne* thy place; . . . . IV. x. 44. 3
as with a Crowne He doth *adorne,* . . . . IV. xi. 34. 8
goodly seem'd t' *adorne* her royall state; . . . . V. ix. 31. 3
doe *adorne* your Court where courtesies excell. . . . . VI. Pr. 7. 9
And lost the crowne which should my head by right *adorne,*). VI. ii. 27. 9
valour the which did *adorne* His meanesse much, ... VI. iii. 7. 8
To make a garland to *adorne* her hed, ... VI. iii. 23. 8
shame is to *adorne* . . . one so basely borne: . . . . VI. vi. 36. 4
this to *adorne,* she all the rest did pill. . . . . VI. x. 5. 9
Besides a thousand more which ready bee Her to *adorne,* . . VI. x. 21. 8
decke the body or *adorne* the mynde, ... VI. x. 23. 2
Princes bowres *adorne* with painted imagery. . . . . VII. vii. 10. 9
appeare t' *adorne* her beauties grace? . . . . *Am.* xxi. 4
they therewith doe Poetes heads *adorne,* . . . . *Am.* xxix. 7
Each of which did her with theyr guifts *adorne;* . . . . *Am.* lxi. 8
when as day the heaven doth *adorne,* . . . . *Am.* lxxxvi. 5
Beene to me ayding, others to *adorne,* . . . . *Epith.* 2
doe still *adorne* her beauties pride, ... *Epith.* 104
Helpe to *addorne* my beautifullest bride: . . . . *Epith.* 105
all the postes *adorne* as doth behove, ... *Epith.* 206
doth the world with her delight *adorne,* . . . . *H.B.* 151

Adorned. an Elephant, *Adorn'd* with bells and bosses . . . . *Van.* viii. 2
Adornd with purest golde and precious stone; . . . . *Ti.* 86
Nor alive nor dead be of the Muse *adorned!* . . . . *Ti.* 455
Adorned all with costly cloth of gold, ... *Ti.* 632
Adorn'd with wisedome and with chastitie, ... *D.* 215
with . . . her deare favours dearly well *adorned;* . . . . *As.* 154
Upon a virgin brydes *adorned* head, ... *Col.* 338
Adorned with all honourable parts: . . . . *Col.* 529
Adorned all with gold and girlonds gay, ... I. iv. 17. 2
Duessa, . . . *Adornd* with gold and jewels . . . . I. v. 21. 2
a tyre of gold, *Adornd* with gemmes . . . . I. x. 31. 6
hill, . . . *Adornd* with fruitfull Olives . . . . I. x. 54. 2
Like Phœbus face *adornd* with sunny rayes, ... II. viii. 5. 6
her *adorned* hed . . . forth to advaunce, ... II. xii. 1. 2
Goodly *adorned* and exceeding faire: . . . . III. xii. 14. 5
is *adorn'd* of it With many a gentle Muse . . . . IV. xi. 34. 8
Adorn'd with all divine perfection, ... IV. xii. 34. 2
both *adorn'd* with lampes of flaming light; . . . . V. iii. 19. 4
Ador'd with honor and all comely grace: . . . . V. iii. 23. 2
Her selfe *adorn'd* with gems and jewels manifold. . . . . V. vii. 13. 9
Adorned all with gemmes of endlesse price, ... V. ix. 27. 6
Like to the Evening starre *adorn'd* with deawy ray. . . . . VI. vii. 19. 9
Adornd with goodly gifts of beauties grace, ... VI. viii. 2. 2
Her mind *adornd* with vertues manifold. . . . . *Am.* xv. 14
Adorn'd with honour, love, and chastity! . . . . *Am.* lxix. 8
Adornd with beautyes grace and vertues store? . . . . *Epith.* 170
Adornd with thousand lamps of burning light, ... *H.H.L.* 59
all with gemmes and jewels gorgeously *Adornd,* . . . . *H.H.B.* 188
meades *adornd* with daintie gemmes . . . . *Proth.* 14

Adorning. *adorning* it with spoyle Of th' heavenly riches . . . *H.B.* 118

Adorns. Yet so as him their terrour more *adornes.* . . . . *Mui.* 88
Adornes the person of her Majestye; . . . . II. ii. 41. 5
adornes rich Waterford; . . . . IV. xi. 43. 2

Adown *(partial list).*
Till it by fatall doome *adowne* did fall. . . . . *Ro.* xvi. 14
Thou then *adowne* might'st fall more horriblie. . . . . *Ro.* xxxi. 14
stremes the trickling teares *Adowne* thy cheeke, ... *S.C.* Ap. 8
Medway, that trickling stremis *Adowne* the dales of Kent, . . *S.C.* Jul. 82
Adowne whose necke, in terrible array, ... *Gn.* 347
All these through fained crimes he thrust *adowne,* . . . . *Hub.* 1186

Adown—*Continued.*
adowne the Lee I sawe an Harpe . . . Swimming, . . . *Ti.* 603
carelesse locks . . . Hong long *adowne,* . . . *D.* 44
adowne his coursers side The red bloud trickling . . . I. ii. 14. 8
floods of blood *adowne* their sides did raile, . . . I. vi. 43. 7
Thrise did she sinke *adowne* in deadly swownd, . . . I. vii. 24. 3
High over hills, and lowe *adowne* the dale, . . . I. vii. 28. 8
scaly tayle was stretcht *adowne* his back full low. . . . I. vii. 31. 9
hong *adowne* his side . . . I. viii. 3. 6
Doth roll *adowne* the rocks, . . . I. viii. 22. 9
snowy lockes *adowne* his shoulders shed; . . . I. x. 48. 2
adowne he looked to the grownd To have returnd; . . . I. x. 67. 5
thick entangled knots *adown* does slack, . . . I. xi. 11. 4
ne once *adowne* would lay Her dainty limbs . . . I. xi. 32. 7
Ne weene my right with strength *adowne* to tread, . . . I. xii. 28. 5
saw the red blood rayle *Adowne* so fast, . . . II. viii. 37. 4
Adowne the rolling river she did poure, . . . II. x. 19. 7
doth throw *Adowne* the streame, . . . II. xi. 18. 8
adowne he kest The lumpish corse . . . II. xi. 42. 5
Adowne he kest it with so puissant wrest, . . . II. xi. 42. 7
Did bow *adowne* as overburdened. . . . II. xii. 55. 6
Low his lascivious armes *adown* did creepe, . . . II. xii. 61. 6
she low *adowne* did lose, . . . II. xii. 67. 3
like pure Orient perles *adowne* it trild; . . . II. xii. 78. 5
She with her Nourse *adowne* to sleepe did lye; . . . III. ii. 28. 4
Til thou in open fielde *adowne* be smott: . . . III. ii. 46. 5
seeking him *adowne* to tread, . . . III. iii. 39. 7
Shall tread *adowne,* and doe him fowly dye; . . . III. iii. 39. 8
adowne Upon the grassy ground her selfe she layd . . . III. vi. 7. 1
at last perforce *adowne* did ly, . . . III. vii. 3. 7
adowne out of her christall eyne . . . III. vii. 9. 1
Dropped *adowne* upon her yvory brest: . . . III. viii. 35. 4
did them selves *adowne* display . . . III. ix. 20. 5
terrify To looke *adowne,* or upward to the hight: . . . III. x. 56. 6
hong *adowne* his head as he did dreame; . . . III. xi. 41. 7
that mightie chaine, . . . *adowne* gan fall, . . . III. xii. 37. 8
streames of bloud did rayle *Adowne,* . . . IV. ii. 18. 4
Adowne their sides like litle rivers stremed, . . . IV. iii. 28. 7
Into the Martian field *adowne* descended . . . IV. v. 6. 8
Her feeble joynts layd eke *adowne* to rest; . . . IV. v. 39. 7
glaunst *Adowne* her backe . . . IV. vi. 13. 4
thence forth glaunst *Adowne* in vaine, . . . IV. vi. 19. 4
all *adowne* their riven sides did ronne. . . . IV. ix. 27. 5
raught full low *adowne.* . . . IV. x. 31. 9
Her goodly lockes *adowne* her backe did flow . . . IV. xi. 46. 1
Over the Castle wall *adowne* her cast, . . . V. ii. 27. 3
By a false trap was let *adowne* to fall . . . V. vi. 27. 7
with such monstrous poise *adowne* descended, . . . V. xii. 21. 3
Compeld him soone the spoyle *adowne* to lay. . . . VI. iv. 20. 4
Upon the grasse her selfe *adowne* she layd; . . . VI. viii. 34. 3
even as his right hand *adowne* descends, . . . VI. viii. 49. 2
adowne They prayd him sit, . . . VI. ix. 7. 2
As from a limbeck did *adown* distill. . . . VII. vii. 31. 5
Birdes did passe along, *Adowne* the Lee, . . . *Proth.* 115

Adrad. That antique horror, which made heaven *adredd.* . . . *Ro.* xvii. 8
hardie will he had . . . that made him lesse *adrad.* . . . *Gn.* 304
of daunger nought *ydrad,* (**y'drad*) . . . *As.* 87
They marched fayrly forth, of nought *ydred.* . . . II. xii. 38. 7
the whole family, therewith *adredd,* . . . III. i. 62. 7
the bold Britonesse was nought *ydred,* . . . III. xii. 2. 8
Yet nought thereof was Triamond *adredde,* . . . IV. iii. 25. 1
mightie kingdomes of his force *adred;* . . . IV. viii. 47. 5
The sight whereof the Lady sore *adrad,* And fain'd to fly . . . V. i. 22. 7
Upon him set, of perill nought *adrad,* . . . VI. v. 16. 3

Adread. *See* **Adrad.**

Adred, -d(e). *See* **Adrad.**

Adrian. in frayle wood on *Adrian* gulf doth fleet, . . . II. vii. 14. 4

Adultery. Even foule *Adulterie* her face before, . . . V. ix. 48. 8

Advance. did her courage to the heavens *advaunce.* . . . *Ro.* vi. 14
Seem'd above heavens powre it selfe to *advaunce;* . . . *Ro.* xi. 4
So vainely *tadvaunce* thy headlesse hood; . . . *S.C.* F. 86
Advaunce the worthy whome shee loveth best, . . . *S.C.* O. 47
Whether thee list thy loved lasse *advaunce,* . . . *S.C.* N. 7
balefull boughes of Cypres doen *advaunce;* . . . *S.C.* N. 145
none whom fortune freely doth *advaunce.* . . . *Gn.* 555
vertue to *advaunce,* and vice deride, . . . *Hub.* 812
All his care was himselfe how to *advaunce,* . . . *Hub.* 845
them for ever highly to *advaunce,* . . . *Hub.* 961
Such followes those whom fortune doth *advaunce.* . . . *Hub.* 1136
Didst to the type of honour earst *advaunce:* . . . *T.M.* 70
That him to highest honour shall *advaunce.* . . . *Ti.* 271
when she list *advance* her heavenly voyce, . . . *D.* 313
to what course thou please thy selfe *advance:* . . . *Col.* 425
and next unto her selfe *advance,* . . . *Col.* 501
she saw the knight his speare *advaunce,* . . . I. ii. 14. 3
he forward gan *advaunce* His faire enchaunted steed, . . . I. iii. 25. 8
he gan *advaunce* With huge force . . . I. vii. 11. 1
How to *advaunce* with favourable hands, . . . I. ix. 1. 8
Eftsoones he gan *advance* his haughty crest, . . . I. xi. 15. 5
advaunce his broad discoloured brest Above his wonted pitch, I. xi. 31. 7
to his mistresse each himselfe strove to *advaunce.* . . . II. ii. 16. 9
to court he cast t' *advaunce* (**avaunce*) his first degree. . . II. iii. 5. 9
towards gan a deadly shafte *advaunce,* . . . II. iii. 34. 5
do *advaunce* Mine auncestry from famous Coradin, . . . II. iv. 36. 7
she may thee *advance* for works and merits just.' . . . II. vii. 49. 9
Doth blesse her servaunts, and them high *advaunce.* . . . II. ix. 5. 5
Did high *advaunce* the crowne of Faery: . . . II. x. 75. 5
To pricke of highest prayse forth to *advaunce,* . . . II. xii. 1. 3
to *advaunce* his name and glory more, . . . III. iv. 21. 6
His pace he freshly forward did *advaunce,* . . . III. vii. 3. 3

Advance—*Continued.*
t' *advance* thy goodly chastitee . . . III. viii. 43. 3
much he did *advaunce* In all his speach, . . . III. ix. 48. 1
goodly well *advaunce* that goodly well was tryde.' . . . III. xii. 39. 9
Soone after did the brethren three *advance* In brave aray . . IV. iii. 5. 4
Each labouring t' *advance* the others gest, . . . IV. iv. 36. 7
Hercules, that did *advance* To vanquish all the world . . . IV. xi. 16. 5
True vertue to *advance,* . . . V. iii. 3. 9
ere his readie speare He could *advance,* . . . V. viii. 33. 6
Ne lesse the Lady did *advaunce.* . . . VI. iii. 19. 5
he gan aloft t' *advance* his arme, . . . VI. viii. 45. 8
Advance the banner of thy conquest hie, . . . *H.B.* 268
loud *advaunce* her laud; . . . *Epith.* 145

Advanced. *See* **High-advanced.**
still I hoped to be up *advaunced,* . . . *Hub.* 63
vertues bare regard *advaunced* bee, . . . *Hub.* 638
how that shepheard strange thy cause *advanced.'* . . . *Col.* 357
For high desert, *advaunst* to that degree. . . . *Col.* 527
Mecænas, . . . it first *advaunst* . . . *Ded. Son.* xiii. 4
turning fierce her speckled taile *advaunst,* . . . I. i. 17. 6
Antiochus, the which *advaunst* His cursed hand gainst God, . . I. v. 47. 8
Sir Terwin . . . well himselfe *advaunst* . . . I. ix. 27. 3
with wonted rage he him *advaunced* neare. . . . I. xi. 52. 9
lewd rybauld, with vyle lust *advaunst,* . . . II. i. 10. 3
To see the Redcrosse thus *advaunced* hye; . . . II. i. 23. 6
to be *advaunced* hye: . . . II. iii. 10. 7
advaunst his shield atweene, . . . II. iv. 46. 6
was *advaunced* hye A stately siege . . . II. vii. 44. 4
Fiercely *advaunst* his valorous right arme, . . . II. xi. 34. 7
'He should *advaunced* bee to high regard,' . . . III. i. 27. 8
So shall your glory bee *advaunced* much, . . . III. x. 28. 6
As Jove will have *advaunced* to the skie, . . . IV. iii. 44. 2
Thy love is there *advaunst* to be another Grace. . . . VI. x. 16. 9
striving . . . To be *advanced* highest in degree. . . . *Com. Son.* ii. 8

Advancement. Hunt after honour and *advauncement* vaine, . . *Ti.* 51
Proud of such glory and *advancement* vayne, . . . I. iv. 9. 5
Ne ought that did to his *advauncement* tend; . . . II. xii. 80. 6
Is this thine high *advauncement?* . . . III. iv. 36. 3

Advancing. *Advancing* vertue and suppressing vice. . . . *Col.* 323
Greatly *advauncing* his gay chevalree: . . . I. v. 16. 5
high *advauncing* his blood-thirstie blade, . . . I. viii. 16. 1
The same *advauncing* high above his head, . . . I. xi. 38. 1
had ye then him forth *advauncing* seene, . . . IV. iii. 23. 4
advauncing that enchaunted shield, . . . IV. x. 19. 6

Advantage. the Knight him at *advantage* (**avantage*) fownd; I. viii. 10. 3
Taking *advantage* of his open jaw, . . . I. xi. 53. 6
Misfortune waites *advantage* to entrap The man . . . II. iv. 17. 4
closely did awayt *Avauntage,* . . . II. v. 9. 7
Making *advauntage,* to revenge their spight, . . . II. viii. 25. 2
That in *advauntage* would his puissaunce bost: . . . II. viii. 26. 4
at last, when he *advantage* spyde, . . . II. viii. 36. 2
of the time doth dew *advauntage* take. . . . III. iii. 52. 4
That least *avantage* mote to him afford, . . . III. x. 6. 2
Waiting *advauntage* on the pray to sease, . . . III. x. 30. 6
by slight And foule *advantage* this good Knight dismayd, . IV. i. 44. 3
Through which *advantage,* in his strength he rose, . . . IV. iii. 30. 1
Now hurtling round *advantage* for to take: . . . IV. iv. 29. 7
Still as *advantage* they espyde thereto: . . . IV. vi. 18. 3
for *advantage* ground unto him gave, . . . IV. vii. 28. 7
the Paynim . . . great *advantage* had, . . . V. ii. 13. 6
Weening at last to win *advantage* new; . . . V. v. 7. 2
Having by chaunce espide *advantage* neare, . . . V. vii. 32. 2
of her widowhed Taking *advantage,* . . . V. x. 12. 2
Thereto a great *advauntage* eke he has . . . V. xi. 6. 1
watch *advauntage* how to worke his care, . . . V. xi. 13. 4
Ne for *advantage* terme to entertaine, . . . V. xi. 56. 4
when as fit *advantage* he did spy, . . . V. xii. 20. 1
following that faire *advantage* fast, . . . VI. i. 39. 2
meant to make *advantage* of his misery. . . . VI. iii. 46. 9
Having by chaunce a close *advantage* vew'd, . . . VI. iii. 50. 4
To spy where he may some *advauntage* get, . . . VI. vii. 47. 5
at *advantage* him at last he tooke, . . . VI. vii. 48. 2
wayt *advantage* when they downe did light. . . . VI. viii. 14. 5
sold for most *advantage,* . . . VI. xi. 10. 9

Adventer. *See* **Adventure.**

Adventure. a strange *adventure,* that betided . . . *Hub.* 37
the Ape, beginning well to wey This hard *adventure,* . . . *Hub.* 113
Adventure which might them a working set; . . . *Hub.* 224
Loath was the Ape, though praised, to *adventer,* . . . *Hub.* 1005
In salvage forrest by *adventure* slew, . . . *Mui.* 67
she doth new bands *adventure* dread;— . . . *Col.* 567
Durst not *adventure* such unknowen wayes, . . . *Col.* 670
Upon a great *adventure* he was bond, . . . I. i. 3. 1
Your first *adventure:* many such I pray, . . . I. i. 27. 8
He passed forth, and new *adventure* sought: . . . I. i. 28. 8
to seeke *adventure* in straunge place; . . . I. iii. 29. 2
By straunge *adventure* as it did betyde, . . . I. vi. 21. 2
what *adventure* . . . Hath brought you hither into Faery land, I. ix. 6. 3
Of her *adventure* myndfull for to bee. . . . I. x. 68. 8
did enterpris Th' *adventure* of the Errant damozell; . . . II. i. 19. 8
whither now on new *adventure* bownd: . . . II. ii. 39. 6
Through fortune of his first *adventure* fayre, . . . II. iii. 7. 2
long he yode, yet no *adventure* found, . . . II. vii. 2. 6
hard *adventure* which I have in hand, . . . II. ix. 8. 8
What straunge *adventure* doe ye now pursew? . . . II. ix. 9. 2
Him selfe addrest to that *adventure* hard: . . . II. xi. 3. 8
So hard a workemanship *adventure* darre, . . . III. Pr. 2. 8
Whom straunge *adventure* did from Britayne sett . . . III. i. 8. 7
Great hazard were it, and *adventure* fond, . . . III. i. 10. 8
Dare not *adventure* on the stubborne pray, . . . III. i. 22. 3

Adventure—*Continued.*
Ne durst *adventure* rashly in to wend, . . . III. iii. 14. 2
That suddein chaunge she straunge *adventure* thought. . . . III. vi. 20. 5
by *adventure* brought Unto your dwelling, . . . III. vii. 8. 7
As if he were on some *adventure* bent, . . . III. viii. 44. 8
afterwardes on what *adventure* now he rode. . . . III. viii. 45. 9
on *adventure* by the way he past. . . . III. x. 35. 5
wander wide At wilde *adventure*, . . . III. x. 36. 3
forth he rode as his *adventure* fell; . . . III. x. 38. 4
By great *adventure* travelled that way; . . . IV. ii. 20. 3
Which faire *adventure* when Cambello spide, . . . IV. iii. 20. 1
Upon her first *adventure* forth did ride, . . . IV. v. 29. 4
bound Upon an hard *adventure* yet in quest, . . . IV. vi. 42. 3
All that *adventure* which ye did assay . . . IV. ix. 40. 8
on that hard *adventure* forth I went, . . . IV. x. 5. 1
An hard *adventure*, which did then befall, . . . V. i. 3. 4
wend with him on his *adventure* hard; . . . V. i. 30. 5
We on his first *adventure* may him forward send. . . . V. iii. 40. 9
That battells utmost triall to *adventer*. . . . V. v. 5. 5
Uppon his first *adventure* which him forth did call. . . . V. vii. 43. 9
by *adventure* found them faring so, . . . V. viii. 15. 6
did to them bewray A straunge *adventure*, . . . V. ix. 4. 5
To graunt him that *adventure* for his former feat. . . . V. x. 15. 9
on his first *adventure* forward forth did ride. . . . V. x. 17. 9
Uppon an hard *adventure* sore bestad, . . . VI. i. 4. 2
prayd that he with him might goe On his *adventure*, . . . VI. ii. 36. 4
And heare th' *adventure* of her late mischaunce; . . . VI. iii. 19. 2
An hard *adventure* with unhappie end, . . . VI. iv. 17. 7
Ne wight with him on that *adventure* went, . . . VI. vi. 18. 6
Were glad to heare of that *adventure* new, . . . VI. vii. 5. 3
A great *adventure*, which did him from them devide. . . . VI. viii. 30. 9

Adventured. he it oft *adventur'd* to invade. . . . I. xi. 49. 4
as I late *adventured* for your sake, . . . IV. i. 40. 3
That could her purchase with his lives *adventur'd* gage. . . . IV. iii. 4. 9
The which I earst *adventur'd* for your sake: . . . VI. vii. 15. 4

Adventurer. 'He is a great *adventurer*,' . . . II. iii. 12. 5

Adventure's. In this *adventures* chauncefull jeopardie: . . . *Hub.* 98
pant with hope of that *adventures* hap: . . . IV. x. 9. 2
To follow his *adventures* first intent, . . . V. iv. 3. 6
Consisted much in that *adventures* priefe: . . . V. vii. 44. 5

Adventures. full of fortunes, and *adventures* straunge, . . . *Hub.* 91
passing foorth, as their *adventures* fell, . . . *Hub.* 359
The rest of thine *adventures*, that betyded.' . . . *Col.* 329
straunge *adventures*, which abroad did pas. . . . I. i. 30. 4
far abroad for straunge *adventures* sought; . . . I. vi. 29. 7
After long labours and *adventures* spent, . . . I. vi. 30. 2
Tidings of warre, and of *adventures* new; . . . I. vi. 36. 2
warres, nor new *adventures*, none he herd. . . . I. vi. 36. 3
forward fare as their *adventures* fell: . . . I. ix. 2. 5
areedes . . . of *adventures* rare: . . . I. ix. 28. 7
Of straunge *adventures*, and of perils sad . . . I. xii. 15. 4
they his pittifull *adventures* heard; . . . I. xii. 16. 3
The brave *adventures* of this faery knight, . . . II. Pr. 5. 7
As wont ye knightes to seeke *adventures* wilde, . . . II. i. 50. 6
he by many rash *adventures* wan, . . . II. ii. 17. 4
to heare of straunge *adventures* to be told. . . . II. ii. 42. 9
Seeking for daunger and *adventures* vaine? . . . II. vi. 17. 5
seek *adventures* as he with Prince Arthure went. . . . III. i. 2. 9
many hard *adventures* did atchieve; . . . III. i. 3. 6
Seeking *adventures* hard, to exercise Their puissaunce, . . . III. i. 14. 3
To hunt out perilles and *adventures* hard, . . . III. ii. 7. 2
many straunge *adventures* to bee fond, . . . III. ii. 8. 3
To seeke *adventures* which mote him befall, . . . III. iv. 4. 7
great *adventures* by him donne: . . . III. iv. 20. 6
raungd abrode to seeke *adventures* wilde, . . . III. vii. 30. 2
A long discourse of his *adventures* vayne, . . . III. viii. 44. 2
many fortunes prov'd . . . And great *adventures* found, . . . III. ix. 48. 9
of their loves did treat, And hard *adventures*, . . . IV. i. 16. 2
Seeking *adventures* in the salvage wood, . . . IV. ii. 45. 2
Seeking *adventures* where they anie knew. . . . IV. ii. 46. 5
deeds of armes abrode, And strange *adventures*, . . . IV. iv. 5. 5
The hard *adventures* and strange haps to tell, . . . IV. v. 28. 8
when on *adventures* they did ride, . . . IV. vi. 44. 8
Seeking *adventures* where he mote heare tell; . . . IV. vii. 42. 3
Through hard *adventures* deedes of armes to try, . . . V. iv. 29. 2
Through other great *adventures* hethertoo Had it forslackt: . . . V. xii. 3. 5
adventures, which had . . . to him befallen late. . . . VI. iii. 22. 5
His long *adventures* gan to him relate, . . . VI. iii. 22. 8
did inquire After *adventures*, . . . VI. v. 11. 6
ere I doe his *adventures* tell . . . VI. xii. 14. 1

Adventurest. Thy life and honor late *adventurest*, . . . I. xii. 29. 8

Adventuring. Them to disable from revenge *adventuring*. . . . V. iv. 31. 9

Adventurous. 'Full many knights, *adventurous* and stout, . . . I. vii. 45. 1
Those be the riches fit for an *advent'rous* knight.' . . . II. vii. 10. 9
have full many feats *adventurous* Performd, . . . III. iii. 54. 5
Advent'rous knighthood on her selfe to don; . . . III. iii. 57. 6
Unto those knights *adventurous*, . . . III. ix. 32. 3
Like knight *adventurous* in outward vew, . . . IV. i. 33. 3
Had him misfalne in his *adventurous* quest; . . . V. vi. 4. 2
All noble Knights, which were *adventurous*, . . . V. vi. 32. 8
by *adventrous* marchandize to thrive,) . . . VI. viii. 35. 7
What puissant conquest, what *adventurous* paine, . . . *H.L.* 221

Adversity. Blew up a bitter storme of foule *adversity*. . . . VI. x. 38. 9

Advice. to restraine The lust . . . with good *advice*, . . . *S.C.* O. 22
Mishaps are maistred by *advice* discrete, . . . I. vii. 40. 7
'let be thy deepe *advise*: . . . II. iii. 16. 1
by whose *advise* old Priams cittie fell, . . . II. ix. 48. 6
With temperate *advice* discounselled, . . . II. xii. 34. 2
By their *advice*, and her owne wicked wit, . . . III. viii. 5. 1

Adviceful. Britomart with sharpe *avizefull* eye . . . IV. vi. 26. 1

Adviewed. *See* **Aviewed.**

Advise. *See* **Advice.**
the Ape, . . . thus began t' *advise*. . . . *Hub.* 113
Thus therefore I *advize* upon the case, . . . *Hub.* 129
With that the husbandman gan him *avize*, . . . *Hub.* 281
Us to *advise*, which forth but lately moved, . . . *Hub.* 410
The Lion looking up gan him *avize*, . . . what had . . . *Hub.* 1324
'the way to win Is wisely to *advise*; . . . I. i. 33. 6
He . . . gan himselfe *advise* To prove his sense, . . . I. i. 50. 5
He would no lenger stay him to *advize*, . . . I. iii. 19. 4
would him *advise* The angry beastes not rashly to despise, . . . I. vi. 25. 4
That when the carefull knight gan well *avise*, . . . I. viii. 15. 5
your daughter can ye well *advize*, . . . I. xii. 18. 5
let that man with better sence *advize*, . . . II. Pr. 2. 1
mote I wisely you *advise* to doon, . . . II. iii. 15. 3
Gan him *avize*, howe ill did him beseme . . . II. vi. 27. 4
Of that seas nature did him not *avise*: . . . II. vi. 46. 5
Avise thee well, and chaunge thy wilfull mood, . . . II. vii. 38. 8
in your selfe doe not the same *advise*? . . . II. ix. 38. 3
The next could of thinges present best *advize*; . . . II. ix. 49. 2
antique Regesters for to *avise*, . . . II. ix. 59. 4
The wretched man gan then *avise* too late, . . . II. x. 31. 1
He gan *avize* to follow him no more, . . . II. xi. 27. 6
Forthy he gan some other wayes *advize*, . . . II. xi. 44. 6
'Here now behoveth us well to *avyse*, . . . II. xii. 17. 6
Abasht that her a straunger did *avise*; . . . II. xii. 66. 4
thus the Palmer: 'Now, Sir, well *avise*; . . . II. xii. 69. 6
They stayd not to *avise* who first should bee, . . . III. i. 18. 3
She gan *avize* where els he mote him hyde: . . . III. vi. 16. 2
as he better did their shape *avize*, . . . III. x. 21. 2
advise ye well Before ye enterprise that way to wend: . . . III. x. 40. 7
the flore to shrinke he did *avyse*; . . . III. xi. 10. 7
not to depart Till morrow next shee did her selfe *avize*, . . . III. xii. 28. 4
gan *advize* with her old Squire, . . . III. xii. 45. 6
then better doe *advise*: . . . IV. viii. 15. 6
He gan *advise* how best he mote darrayne That enterprize . . . IV. ix. 4. 4
he gan him selfe *advise* To stay his hand, . . . IV. ix. 35. 5
gan *avise* To winne me honour . . . IV. x. 4. 3
It's late in death of daunger to *advize*, . . . IV. xii. 28. 6
Whom ever as he did the more *avize*, . . . V. iii. 18. 8
showre of arrowes, which them staid, And better bad *advise*, . . . V. iv. 38. 5
well thy wits *advise*, . . . V. v. 34. 6
She stayd not to *advise* which way to take, . . . V. vi. 39. 1
Gan to *advize* what best were to be done. . . . V. ix. 8. 5
Which cruell outrage when as Artegall Did well *avize*, . . . V. xii. 18. 2
gan t' *advize* How great a hazard she at earst had made . . . VI. iii. 8. 6
He stayed not t' *advize* which way were best . . . VI. iv. 5. 1
'The best' (sayd he) 'that I can you *advize*, . . . VI. vi. 14. 1
entyrely prayd T' *advize* him better . . . VI. vii. 22. 4
did *advize* To dare not to pollute so sacred threasure . . . VI. viii. 43. 7
Tho gan Sir Calidore him to *advize* Of his first quest, . . . VI. xii. 12. 1
to *advise* What way is best . . . VII. vi. 21. 6
gan now *advise* What course were best to take . . . VII. vi. 22. 8
in your choice of Loves, this well *advize*, . . . *H.B.* 190

Advised. *See* **Ill-advised, Well-advised.**
if by me thou list *advised* be, . . . *S.C.* Jun. 17
'Right well, deere Gossip, ye *advized* have, . . . *Hub.* 193
'Right well, Sir knight, ye have *advised* bin.' . . . I. i. 33. 4
Such wondrous science . . . When Jove *avizd*, . . . I. v. 40. 2
bids thee be *advized* for the best, . . . I. xii. 26. 5
Sith him in Faery court he late *avizd*; . . . II. i. 31. 6
adviz'd him to refraine From chase of greater beastes, . . . III. i. 37. 6
At last she her *avisde*, . . . III. iii. 6. 1
when that villayn he *aviz'd*, . . . III. v. 23. 1
had not her thereof before *aviz'd*, . . . III. vi. 19. 4
ill they seemed sure *avizd* to bee, . . . III. vii. 57. 8
Certes, me seemes, bene not *advised* well; . . . IV. ii. 24. 5
Which troublous stirre when Satyrane *aviz'd*, . . . IV. v. 25. 1
he him knew not, ne *aviz'd* at all, . . . IV. vii. 43. 6
I with better reason him *aviz'd*, . . . IV. viii. 58. 1
the Prince, when as he them *avized*, . . . IV. ix. 11. 1
Be well *adviz'd* that he stand stedfast still; . . . V. vi. 1. 7
She was by him *adviz'd* to send me . . . VI. ii. 30. 2

Advisement. afterwards with grave *advizement* said: . . . *Hub.* 176
manly courage, Tempred with . . . *advizement* sage, . . . *Ded. Son.* xiv. 9
strong *advizement* of six wisards old, . . . I. iv. 12. 8
With goodly counsell and *advisement* right; . . . I. x. 23. 5
Tempring the passion with *advizement* slow, . . . II. v. 13. 2
my succour or *advizement* meete . . . II. ix. 9. 3
The best *advizement* was, of bad, to let her Sleepe . . . VI. viii. 38. 1

Advising. But, him *avizing*, he that dreadfull deed Forbore, . . . *Hub.* 1238
him *avizing* better, . . . II. xii. 28. 4
her *avizing* of the vertues rare . . . III. ii. 22. 7
Of which her selfe *avising* readily, . . . III. iii. 59. 5
her well *avizing* hee perceiv'd To be no vision . . . III. viii. 23. 1
avizing right Her goodly personage . . . III. ix. 23. 5
He looked backe, and her *avizing* (**advizing*) well, . . . IV. ii. 22. 7
Which well *avizing*, streight she gan to cast . . . VI. xii. 16. 1

Advocates. Rose many *advocates* for her to plead: . . . V. ix. 45. 2

Adward. *See* **Award.**

Aeacid. th' one *Aeacide* did his fame extend; . . . *Gn.* 525
Thetis wedding with *Aeacidee*, . . . VI. x. 22. 5

Aeacus. 'There be the two stout sonnes of *Aeacus*, . . . *Gn.* 481

Aegean. Amid th' *Aegaean* sea long time did stray, . . . II. xii. 13. 2
Fled fearfull Daphne on th' *Aegaean* strond, . . . III. vii. 26. 4
Through the *Agaean* (**Aegaean*) seas from Pirates vew, . . . IV. xi. 23. 7

Aegeria. As was *Aegerie* that Numa tought: . . . II. x. 42. 8

Aegid. to her selfe she gives her *Aegide* shield, . . . *Mui.* 321

Aegina. like a fire, when he *Aegin'* assayd: . . . III. xi. 35. 2

Aegle. *See* **Eagle.**

Aemathian. *See* **Emathian.**
Aemilia. I rest his wretched thrall, the sad *Aemylia.'* . . . IV. vii. 18. 9
'Ah, sad *Aemylia!'* (then sayd Amoret) . . . IV. vii. 19. 1
forth the sad *Aemylia* issewed, . . . IV. vii. 34. 1
those two Ladies late, *Aemylia* and Amoret, abode, . . . IV. viii. 19. 3
instead of his *Aemylia* faire, This Gyants sonne, . . . IV. viii. 51. 4
Aemylia well he lov'd, . . . IV. viii. 57. 8
soone as sad *Aemylia* did espie . . . IV. viii. 63. 1
'He lives,' (quoth he) 'and his *Aemylia* loves.' . . . IV. viii. 63. 6
The Squire of low degree, releast, *Aemylia* takes to wife: . . . IV. ix. Arg.
soone as faire *Aemylia* beheld . . . IV. ix. 9. 1
Aemilia's. mine and his *Aemylias* libertie. . . . IV. viii. 57. 7
Aemuled, Aemuling. *See* **Emuled,** *etc.*
Aeneas. I would to heare desyre What to *Aeneas* fell; . . . III. ix. 40. 7
stout *Aeneas* in the Trojane fyre, . . . *H.L.* 232
Aeolus. blustring *Aeolus* his boasted syre; . . . I. vii. 9. 2
all his windes Dan *Aeolus* did keepe . . . III. viii. 21. 6
Dan *Aeolus,* in great displeasure . . . IV. ix. 23. 1
Aeolus'. some ungracious blast, out of the gate Of *Aeoles* raine, *Mui.* 420
Nor *Aeolus* sharp blast could worke them any wrong. . . . III. vi. 44. 9
Aeolus faire daughter, Arne hight, . . . III. xi. 42. 2
Aerie, Aery. *See* **Airy.**
Aesculapius. sad *Aesculapius* far apart Emprisond was . . . I. v. 36. 7
Aesculape . . . by his art Did heale them all againe, . . . I. v. 39. 8
To *Aesculapius* brought the wounded knight: . . . I. v. 41. 3
Aeson. As that brave sonne of *Aeson,* . . . *Ro.* x. 1
Aetion. last not least, is *Aetion,* . . . *Col.* 444
Aetna. As burning *Aetna* from his boyling stew . . . I. xi. 44. 5
it in flames of *Aetna* wrought apart, . . . II. viii. 20. 7
More whott then *Aetn',* or flaming Mongiball . . . II. ix. 29. 7
Like an huge *Aetn'* of deepe engulfed gryefe, . . . III. ii. 32. 6
Aetnean. Then doo the *Aetnean* Cyclops him affray, . . . *Gn.* 541
Afar. Whom when the Briton Prince *afarre* beheld . . . IV. ix. 32. 1
Afear. As ghastly bug, does greatly them *affeare:* . . . II. iii. 20. 5
Afeard. streightway of death *afeard,* . . . *Hub.* 1360
Him all amazd, and almost made *afeard:* . . . I. xi. 26. 5
I hid my selfe from it, as one *affeard;* . . . II. iii. 45. 8
them of drowning made *affeard.* . . . II. xii. 2. 9
much I am *affeard* . . . III. vi. 23. 3
flyes away of her owne feete *afeard,* . . . III. vii. 1. 3
of each noyse *affeard,* . . . III. vii. 19. 3
ne of death *afeard.* . . . III. x. 52. 5
woxe *afeard* Of outrage for the words . . . IV. i. 50. 3
halfe *affeard* Of th' uncouth sight, . . . IV. iii. 31. 5
faire Amoret, of nought *affeard,* . . . IV. vii. 4. 1
Against him stoutly ran, as nought *afeard,* . . . VI. i. 19. 3
Nether of envy nor of chaunge *afeard:* . . . VI. v. 12. 5
afeard Of villany to be to her inferd: . . . VI. viii. 31. 4
He, much *affeard,* to her confessed short . . . VII. vi. 51. 7
griesly vultures, make us once *affeard:* . . . *Epith.* 348
Afeared. *See* **Afeard.**
Affairs. ye doo weld th' *affaires* of earthlie creature; . . . *Ro.* ix. 4
they so ill Did order their *affaires,* . . . *Hub.* 560
simple men, which never came in place Of worlds *affaires,* . . . *Hub.* 835
that ye ruled bee In all *affaires,* . . . *Hub.* 1052
Oft from those grave *affaires* were wont abstaine, . . . *Ded. Son.* i. 5
To menage of most grave *affaires* is bent; . . . *Ded. Son.* ix. 2
well himselfe advaunst In all *affayres,* . . . I. ix. 27. 4
wondrous wit to menage high *affayres,* . . . II. x. 37. 2
discoursed diversly Of straunge *affaires,* . . . III. ix. 53. 2
Welds kingdomes causes and *affaires* of state, . . . IV. Pr. 1. 2
She was about *affaires* of common-wele, . . . V. ix. 36. 3
great *affaires* in mynd Would not permit . . . VI. v. 41. 1
Affamished. *See* **Love-affamished.**
Affear. *See* **Afear.**
Affeared, Affeard. *See* **Afeard.**
Affect. Your stubborne hart t' *affect* with fraile infirmity. . . . II. xii. 28. 9
To sincke into his sence, nor mind *affect,* . . . II. xii. 53. 3
with infinite *affect* For his exceeding courtesie, . . . VI. i. 45. 2
His dear *affect* with silence did restraine, . . . VI. v. 24. 4
your tongue, your talk restraine From that they most *affect,* . . . VI. vi. 7. 9
From that day forth she gan him to *affect,* . . . VI. x. 37. 1
lust, Whose base *affect* through cowardly distrust . . . *H.L.* 180
Affected. As diverse wits *affected* divers beene. . . . IV. v. 11. 5
Ne lesse was she in secret hart *affected,* . . . IV. xii. 35. 6
as if great griefe had her *affected.* . . . V. ix. 9. 9
from those outward sences, ill *affected,* . . . VI. vi. 8. 1
Affection. With inward ruth and deare *affection,* . . . Van. xii. 3
A servant to the vile *affection* . . . *Hub.* 817
Deare unto all that true *affection* beare: . . . *Ti.* 243
drizling teares did shed for pure *affection.* . . . I. iii. 6. 9
(Entire *affection* hateth nicer hands) . . . I. viii. 40. 3
fraile *affection* did constraine His stout courage to stoupe, . . . II. i. 42. 8
more *affection* to increace, . . . II. i. 60. 8
glad t' embosome his *affection* vile, . . . II. iv. 25. 3
His hart with great *affection* was embayd, . . . II. viii. 55. 2
with entyre *affection* him receav'd, . . . II. x. 31. 6
Through goodly temperaunce and *affection* chaste; . . . III. i. 12. 2
this *affection* nothing straunge I finde; . . . III. ii. 40. 5
with entire *Affection* I doe languish . . . III. ii. 44. 5
Lodestarre of all chaste *affection* . . . III. vi. 52. 5
conceiv'd *affection* bace, And cast to love her . . . III. vii. 15. 7
He ween'd that his *affection* entire She should aread; . . . III. vii. 16. 7
overcommen quight Of huge *affection,* . . . III.xii.45.*or.*6
Ne naturall *affection* faultlesse blame . . . IV. Pr. 2. 4
More franke *affection* did to her afford. . . . IV. i. 15. 7
Albee in heart he like *affection* fond, . . . IV. i. 34. 3
Ne ever was with fond *affection* moved, . . . IV. ii. 36. 3
with so firme *affection* were allyde, . . . IV. ii. 43. 2
t' increase *affection* naturall, . . . IV. ii. 54. 4

Affection—*Continued.*
Profest to her true friendship and *affection* sweet. . . . IV. iii. 50. 9
friendship, which a faint *affection* breeds . . . IV. iv. 1. 8
Ne thinke th' *affection* of her hart to draw . . . IV. vi. 33. 2
Her graunted love, but with *affection* cold, . . . IV. viii. 53. 5
The deare *affection* unto kindred sweet, . . . IV. ix. 1. 5
naturall *affection* soone doth cesse, . . . IV. ix. 2. 1
The course of loose *affection* to forstall, . . . IV. ix. 19. 3
gan thenceforth to cast *affection,* . . . V. v. 43. 7
touched with intire *affection* nigh him drew; . . . V. viii. 12. 9
For deare *affection* and unfayned zeale . . . VI. ii. 26. 5
And deare *affection* of so dolefull dreare, . . . VI. iii. 4. 5
with entire *affection* and appearaunce plaine. . . . VI. v. 38. 9
From things that stirre up fraile *affection;* . . . VI. vi. 7. 7
him bewayling with *affection* base, . . . VI. vii. 18. 3
Move such *affection* in the inward mynd, . . . *H.B.* 76
That in light wits did loose *affection* move; . . . *H.H.L.* 11
that deare Lord with so entyre *affection,* . . . *H.H.L.* 157
by signes his glad *affection* show, . . . *Proth.* 117
Affectionate. well *affectionate,* Friendship professed . . . III. iii. 62. 7
Each others griefe with zeale *affectionate,* . . . VI. iii. 12. 5
Affection's. Shoot out his darts to base *affections* wound; . . . *Am.* viii. 6
Affections. to *affections* does the bridle lend! . . . II. iv. 34. 2
that which strong *affections* doe apply . . . II. xi. 1. 2
as the one stird up *affections* bace, . . . III. i. 46. 3
Let not her fault your sweete *affections* marre, . . . III. i. 49. 3
doth base *affections* move In brutish mindes, . . . III. iii. 1. 5
loose *affections* streightly to restraine; . . . IV. v. 4. 8
pure *affections* bred in spotlesse brest, . . . *Am.* lxxxiii. 5
The which the base *affections* doe obay, . . . *Epith.* 196
base *affections,* which your eares would bland . . . *H.B.* 171
loves, with which the world doth . . . stirre up *affections* base, *H.H.L.* 263
Affects. With chast *affects* that naught but death can sever; . . . *Am.* vi. 12
Affiance. *Affyaunce* made, my happinesse begonne, . . . II. iv. 21. 4
Affianced. He was *affyaunced* long time before, . . . I. xii. 27. 2
Affied. though *affide* unto a former love, . . . IV. viii. 53. 1
was unto him *affide,* . . . V. iii. 2. 2
turn'd the trust which was in her *affyde,* . . . V. v. 53. 6
ever he to Lady was *affyde,* To spare her Knight, . . . VI. iii. 49. 8
Affix. Looke thou no further, but *affixe* thine eye . . . *H.H.B.* 50
Affixed. she *affixed* had Her hart on knight . . . III. ii. 11. 3
with firme eyes *affixt* the ground still viewed. . . . VII. vii. 57. 3
Upon the lowly ground *affixed* are; . . . *Epith.* 161
Thereon his mynd *affixed* wholly is, . . . *H.L.* 204
Afflict. Starres conspiring wretched men t' *afflict,* . . . *T.M.* 482
as to *afflict* so sore The innocent, . . . *D.* 200
double griefs *afflict* concealing harts, . . . I. ii. 34. 5
T' *afflict* the creatures which therein did dwell; . . . II. xii. 51. 6
All night *afflict* thy naturall repose; . . . III. ii. 31. 2
T' *afflict* the other Saxons unsubdewd; . . . III. iii. 38. 2
secretly *afflict* with jealous feare, . . . V. vi. 4. 6
inly did *afflict* her pensive thought . . . VI. iii. 6. 8
wreckes, and wicked enmitie Doe them *afflict,* . . . VI. ix. 19. 7
Thou doest *afflict* as well the not-deserver, . . . *H.L.* 159
sullein care, . . . did *afflict* (*aflict) my brayne,) . . . *Proth.* 9
Afflicted. *See* **Sad-afflicted.**
Our life *afflicted* with incessant paine, . . . *D.* 275
The argument of mine *afflicted* stile: . . . I. Pr. 4. 8
Lowde shriking, him *afflicted* to the very sowle. . . . IV. v. 41. 9
whom he list reserve to be *afflicted* more. . . . IV. viii. 54. 9
to *afflicted* minds sweet rest and quiet sends. . . . IV. x. 34. 9
The which *afflicted* his engrieved mind; . . . IV. xii. 25. 8
To whom complayning her *afflicted* plight, . . . V. i. 4. 3
Else should *afflicted* wights oftimes despeire: . . . V. iii. 1. 5
Her selfe there close *afflicted* long in vaine, . . . V. vi. 15. 2
with meeke humblesse and *afflicted* mood, . . . *Am.* ii. 11
Afflicting. Him still reviling and *afflicting* sore, . . . VI. viii. 4. 2
Affliction. all this worlds *affliction* . . . *T.M.* 129
in *affliction* wast my better age: . . . *D.* 374
long *affliction* which I have endured: . . . *Col.* 944
Should plonged be in such *affliction* . . . III. viii. 1. 5
whilome did attend On faire Irene in her *affliction,* . . . V. xi. 37. 7
ever more and more her owne *affliction* wrought. . . . VI. v. 6. 9
Without *affliction* or disquietnesse . . . VI. xi. 1. 2
Afflicts. day and night *afflicts* with mortall paine, . . . III. xi. 17. 2
Affluence. made there to abound with lavish *affluence.* . . . II. xii. 42. 9
Afford. Which might it you in pitie please t' *afford,* . . . *Hub.* 251
thereby willing to *affoord* them aide; . . . *Hub.* 414
favourable times did us *afford* Free libertie . . . *T.M.* 243
Till please the heavens *affoord* me remedy. . . . *T.M.* 294
whilest the fates *affoord* me vitall breath, . . . *Ti.* 309
doen the heavens *afford* him vitall food?' . . . II. i. 12. 3
affoord To ferry that old man over . . . II. vi. 19. 8
afford Which he had brought for Braggadochio vaine. . . . II. viii. 19. 3
Of that faire Castle to *affoord* them vew: . . . II. ix. 20. 8
but if remedee Thou her *afford,* . . . III. iii. 16. 9
yet mote they well Thus much *afford* me, . . . III. iv. 39. 3
Would me refuse their pledges to *afford,* . . . III. vii. 56. 6
That least avantage mote to him *afford,* . . . III. x. 6. 2
Amoret, . . . More franke affection did to her *afford.* . . . IV. i. 15. 7
what good fortune did to him *afford;* . . . IV. viii. 18. 7
Ne other end their fury would *afford,* . . . V. iv. 6. 3
To bide that judgement ye shall us *afford.'* . . . V. iv. 16. 5
To be her thrall and service her *afford:* . . . V. v. 17. 5
'All times have wont safe passage to *afford* . . . V. viii. 22. 1
Through promise to *afford* her timely aide, . . . V. xi. 41. 4
to the shamefull doer it *afford.* . . . VI. i. 26. 3
to me such curtesie *afford,* . . . VI. iii. 39. 6
if they would *afford* him ayde at need . . . VI. vii. 4. 6

Afford—*Continued.*
To graunt him favour or *afford* him love: VI. xi. 5. 4
That fruitfull issue may to you *afford,* *Proth.* 104
Afforded. the dore To him did open and *affoorded* way: II. vii. 26. 2
Affraid, Affrayd. *See* **Afraid.**
Affrap. They bene ymett, both ready to *affrap,* II. i. 26. 6
to *affrap* The warlike ryder to his most mishap: III. ii. 6. 4
Affray. I thus mazed was with great *affray,* *Bel.*[2] xv. 11
Marry, Diggon, what should him *affraye* *S.C.* S. 208
flocking Persians did the Greeks *affray;* *Gn.* 50
snakes . . . hang in heapes, that horridly *affray,* *Gn.* 349
Then doo the Aetnean Cyclops him *affray,* *Gn.* 541
Nor outlawes fell *affray* the forest raunger. *Col.* 319
full of . . . cold *affray,* Gan shut the dore. I. iii. 12. 7
both . . . souce so sore that they the heavens *affray;* I. v. 8. 7
th' unwonted sound, . . . did them *affray,* I. v. 30. 4
when the flying heavens he would *affray;* I. vii. 34. 4
corage fierce that all men did *affray,* II. x. 15. 2
Shee, that base Braggadochio did *affray,* III. v. 27. 7
did nigh *affray* That Capons corage: III. viii. 15. 5
afterwardes *affray* with cruell threat, III. ix. 9. 3
When as he saw the mercilesse *affray* IV. iv. 22. 4
The feare whereof seem'd much her to *affray;* IV. vi. 45. 4
Full many did *affray,* IV. x. 16. 9
The dreadfull sight did them so sore *affray,* V. viii. 40. 5
with unwonted terror halfe *affray,* V. ix. 24. 4
through *affray,* Had hid themselves, V. x. 19. 3
As if that there were some tumultuous *affray.* V. xi. 43. 9
made to fly like doves whom the Eagle doth *affray.* V. xii. 5. 9
well approv'd in batteilous *affray,* VI. i. 2. 8
comming forth yet full of late *affray* VI. i. 44. 7
Without tempestuous storms or sad *afray:* *Epith.* 327
Affret. with the terrour of their fierce *affret* III. ix. 16. 3
with the furie of their owne *affret* IV. ii. 15. 6
Carelesse of perill in their fiers *affret,* IV. iii. 6. 7
passing forth with furious *affret,* IV. iii. 11. 7
Affriended. deadly foes so faithfully *affrended,* IV. iii. 50. 5
Affright. sate long time in sencelesse sad *affright,* *Ti.* 475
gan threaten hellish paine, . . . them to *affright:* I. ii. 2. 7
with love revokt from vaine *affright,* I. vi. 28. 3
Againe she stricken was with sore *affright,* I. xi. 50. 7
off-shaking vaine *affright* She nigher drew, I. xi. 55. 6
As one out of a deadly dreame *affright,* II. i. 45. 6
dead through great *affright* II. iii. 19. 7
with horrible *affright* And hellish fury II. iv. 30. 1
As one *affright* With hellish feends, II. v. 37. 6
in great *affright* And haste he rose II. vii. 6. 1
him that walkes in feare and sad *affright.* II. vii. 29. 9
Gan her recomfort from so sad *affright,* II. xi. 16. 5
Thereat he smitten was with great *affright,* II. xi. 39. 1
That all their sences filled with *affright;* II. xii. 2. 7
As one with vew of ghastly feends *affright:* III. ii. 29. 7
sore *affright,* Wondred to see her belly so upblone, III. vi. 9. 7
all that could not from *affright* her hold, III. viii. 34. 5
as if suddein great *affright* Had them surprizd. III. ix. 23. 4
fild with new *affright.* III. xii. 44. 9
gan shun his dreadfull sight, . . . in daungerous *affright.* IV. iv. 41. 9
Are rapt with wonder and with rare *affright.* V. iii. 19. 7
broken with some fearefull dreames *affright,* V. vi. 14. 2
She was dismayd, or faynted through *affright,* V. viii. 45. 7
through sudden strange *affright* V. x. 19. 5
backe she would have turnd for great *affright:* V. xi. 26. 5
Their cruell strokes and terrible *affright;* VI. i. 36. 7
Staide not to succour her in that *affright,* VI. iii. 26. 4
And his sad Ladie left in pitifull *affright:* VI. iv. 1. 9
Gan cry aloud with horrible *affright,* VI. iv. 8. 8
with great *affright* She starting up VI. vi. 31. 1
the cowheard, deaded with *affright,* VI. vii. 25. 7
faire Pastorell through great *affright* Was almost dead, VI. xi. 43. 7
Was troubled much at their so strange *affright,* VII. vi. 15. 7
Mongst wretched men (dismaide with her *affright*) VII. vi. 32. 7
Affrighted. *Affrighted* had the fairest Florimell, III. v. 23. 2
even the hellish fiends *affrighted* bee At sight thereof, VI. vi. 10. 4
Affrights. Make sudden sad *affrights:* *Epith.* 339
Affronted. Duessa, full of . . . fiers disdaine to be *affronted* so, I. viii. 13. 2
him *affronted* with impatient might: II. v. 20. 7
the fast earth *affronted* them so sore, III. iv. 7. 7
Affronting. him *affronting* soone, to fight was readie prest. IV. iii. 22. 9
Affy. sought her to *affy* To a great pere; VI. iii. 7. 2
Affyaunce, Affyde. *See* **Affiance, Affied.**
Afloat. bathing all the creakie shore *aflot,* *Bel.*[2] ix. 7
Afoord. *See* **Afford.**
Afore. the good hap of th' oldest times *afore,* *Ro.* xix. 6
wonne from all the world *afore,* *Ro.* xxii. 7
Such cause of mourning never hadst *afore;* *S.C.* N. 54
'Dido is gone *afore;* *S.C.* N. 193
not as I wont *afore,* *S.C.* D. 61
us, which living loved thee *afore,* *Ti.* 339
gentle kinde as ever Fowle *afore;* *Ti.* 591
layes forth her threatfull pikes *afore* The engines *Mui.* 85
much *afore* I feard, *Col.* 266
doth all *afore* him far surpasse; *Col.* 417
unto his Lord, where he him left *afore.* I. i. 44. 9
They him saluted, standing far *afore,* I. x. 49. 7
he reared high *afore* His body monstrous, I. xi. 8. 6
Ne ought his sturdy strokes might stand *afore,* I. xi. 37. 8
The which *afore* is fayrly to be kend, I. xii. 1. 4
Her lockes, . . . Grew all *afore,* II. iv. 4. 6
Did follow that ensample which he blam'd *afore.* II. vi. 45. 9
with his dreadfull hornes them drives *afore,* II. viii. 42. 4

Afore—*Continued.*
made him twise to reele, that never moov'd *afore.* II. viii. 44. 9
nathemore Would they once turne, but kept on as *afore:* II. xii. 15. 5
of their comming well he wist *afore;* III. iii. 15. 2
Betweene the nations different *afore,* III. iii. 49. 2
For his great vertues proved long *afore:* III. iii. 60. 5
the faire flowres that decked him *afore:* III. iv. 17. 8
that way in which that Damozell Was fledd *afore,* III. iv. 47. 9
For all the damage which he had him doen *afore.* III. v. 18. 9
when charmes had closed it *afore.* III. xii. 27. 9
of fayned friendship which they vow'd *afore.* IV. ii. 18. 9
They sent that Squire *afore,* IV. ii. 31. 3
those two other Knights espide Marching *afore,* IV. iv. 2. 7
gan their shields addresse them selves *afore:* IV. iv. 4. 8
with no better fortune then the rest *afore.* IV. iv. 45. 9
all the rest which had the best *afore,* IV. v. 8. 6
all *afore* that seemed fayre and bright, IV. v. 14. 1
her angels face, unseene *afore,* IV. vi. 19. 5
their lives thou lanchedst long *afore,* IV. vii. 1. 8
The signe whereof yet stain'd his bloudy lips *afore.* IV. vii. 5. 9
knottie snags were sharpned all *afore,* IV. vii. 7. 5
fast she flies, and farre *afore* him goes, IV. vii. 21. 8
Soone as they thence departed were *afore,* IV. viii. 35. 1
'Ne was he ever vanquished *afore,* IV. viii. 48. 1
Knights and Squires to him unknowne *afore:* IV. ix. 8. 5
The Prince yet being fresh untoucht *afore;* IV. ix. 34. 2
covered with a slender veile *afore;* IV. x. 40. 7
These marched farre *afore* the other crew: IV. xi. 12. 1
seem'd to stoupe *afore* With bowed backe, IV. xi. 26. 1
as ye heard *afore.* V. iii. 13. 5
buskins . . . laced close *afore;* V. v. 3. 3
So both agreed to send that mayd *afore,* V. ix. 8. 6
Then gan she cry much louder then *afore,* V. xi. 30. 1
forth issuing with his scouts *afore,* V. xii. 6. 8
He gan at him let drive more fiercely then *afore.* V. xii. 22. 9
as he past *afore* withouten dread, V. xii. 39. 8
of none *afore* . . . I have had; VI. i. 10. 3
Did issue forth to meete his foe *afore;* VI. i. 32. 7
So wondrously now chaung'd from that she was *afore.* VI. i. 46. 9
Came to the place whereas ye heard *afore* VI. ii. 40. 4
a straunge knight, that neare *afore* him went, VI. vii. 4. 4
'He rides' (said Turpine) 'there not farre *afore,* VI. vii. 6. 1
Which I to others did inflict *afore,* VI. viii. 22. 4
Although his quest were farre *afore* him gon: VI. ix. 12. 3
one still towards shew'd her selfe *afore;* VI. x. 24. 8
The which the Faery Queene had long *afore* Bequeath'd to him, VI. xii. 12. 4
Aforehand. As he himselfe hath lov'd us *afore-hand,* *H.H.L.* 186
Afraid. I was with so dreadfull sight *afrayde,* *Bel.*[1] xi. 11
Therewith *affrayd,* I ranne away; *S.C.* Mar. 94
I weene thou be *affrayd* *S.C.* Jul. 71
the Ape was sore *afrayde,* *Hub.* 955
Afraid of everie leafe that stir'd him by, *Hub.* 1007
What frayes ye, that were wont to comfort me *affrayd?* I. i. 52. 9
She, of nought *affrayd,* . . . him daily sought; I. iii. 3. 7
Affraid least to themselves the like mishappen might. I. iii. 20. 9
Ne yet of present perill be *affraid,* I. iv. 49. 3
of that proud Paynim sore *afrayd.* I. vi. 47. 9
of him selfe he seemd to be *affrayd;* I. ix. 23. 4
the stiffe beame quaked as *affrayd,* I. xi. 20. 5
of shame *affrayd,* She set her downe to weepe II. ii. 8. 2
The Palmer . . . Woxe sore *affraid,* II. viii. 9. 3
The clowdes, as thinges *affrayd,* before him flye; II. viii. 48. 3
all the three thereat woxe much *afrayd,* II. xii. 22. 6
Of every finest fingers touch *affrayd;* III. i. 61. 5
Of much more uncouth thing I was *affrayd,* III. ii. 40. 3
affraid of him as feend of hell. III. iv. 47. 9
no lesse *afrayd* Then of wilde beastes III. iv. 51. 3
of her safety greatly grew *afrayd.* III. vii. 25. 3
he was much *afraid* him selfe alone to fynd. III. x. 41. 9
all his many it *affraide* did make: III. xii. 23. 8
watcht on every side, of secret foes *affrayd,* IV. ii. 36. 9
Whereat she sore *affrayd,* yet her besought IV. ii. 50. 1
lightly started up as one *affrayd,* IV. v. 42. 6
Its best to hope the best, though of the worst *affrayd.'* IV. vi. 37. 9
no man was *affrayd* Of force, V. Pr. 9. 3
like as one whom feends had made *affrayd,* V. iii. 18. 4
when the villaine saw her so *affrayd,* V. ix. 12. 4
she, *afrayd* of nought, By guilefull treason V. xi. 39. 6
As he of some misfortune were *afrayd;* VI. v. 3. 4
therewith much abashed and *affrayd,* VI. vii. 22. 1
affrayd of every chaunges dread. VI. ix. 27. 9
who sees not would be *affrayd* to heare: VI. xi. 17. 8
Calidore, thereof no whit *afrayd,* VI. xii. 29. 1
Were much *afraid,* and wondred at that sight; VII. vi. 14. 5
Doth make both Gods and hellish fiends *affraid:* VII. vi. 18. 3
Great shame it is to leave, like one *afrayd,* *Am.* xiv. 3
is of nought *affrayd.* *Am.* lviii. 4
Affrayd of every dangers least dismay. *Am.* lxxxvii. 4
Afray. *See* **Affray.**
Afresh. Therewith he gan *afresh* to waile *D.* 169
grow *afresh,* as they had never seene Fleshly corruption, III. vi. 33. 3
'*afresh* appeard The glory of the later world III. ix. 44. 1
Would afterwards *afresh* the sleeping evill reare. IV. i. 34. 9
charging him *afresh* thus felly him bespake. IV. iii. 10. 9
He then *afresh* with new encouragement Did him assayle, IV. iii. 26. 7
fiercely each assayling gan *afresh* to fight. IV. iii. 35. 9
all *afresh* gan former fight renew. IV. ix. 26. 6
She gan *afresh* thus to renew her wretched case. IV. xii. 8. 9
She gan *afresh* to chafe, IV. xii. 27. 9
To set *afresh* on all the other crew: V. iii. 12. 4

Afresh—*Continued.*
There he him courst *a-fresh,* . . . V. ix. 16. 8
They turne *afresh,* and oft renew their former threat. . . . V. xi. 45. 9
Those knights began *afresh* them to assayle, . . . V. xi. 59. 2
courage chill Kindling *afresh,* gan battell to renew, . . . VI. i. 35. 8
laying yet *afresh,* . . . Upon the rest . . . VI. vi. 38. 3
now gan *afresh* to rancle sore, . . . VI. x. 31. 3
Comes forth *afresh* out of their late dismay, . . . *Am.* xl. 11
Afric. *See* **Africa.**
hundred steps of *Afrike* golds enchase: . . . *Bel.*[2] ii. 8
though beyond the *Africk* Ismael . . . he were, . . . III. iii. 6. 7
Africa. Pyrrhus and the puissaunce Of *Afrike* could not tame, . . . *Ro.* xxi. 2
Which mear'd her rule with *Africa,* and Byze, . . . *Ro.* xxii. 2
All that which *Afrike* ever brought forth strange; . . . *Ro.* xxix. 10
Ne *Afrike* thereof guiltie is, . . . *Ro.* xxxi. 5
Africanus. So Ennius the elder *Africane,* . . . *Ded. Son.* i. 7
After (*partial list*).
But I the ship saw *after* rais'd againe. . . . *Bel.*[2] xiii. 14
After, at sea a tall ship did appeare, . . . *Pet.* ii. 1
After th' Ionicke, Atticke, Doricke guise; . . . *Ro.* xxix. 3
and *after* hasted Thy sommer prowde, . . . *S.C.* Ja. 21
Yt chaunced *after* upon a day, . . . *S.C.* F. 143
It was not long, *after* shee was gone, . . . *S.C.* May 235
Renne *after* hastely thy silver sound; . . . *S.C.* Jun. 61
But *after* vertue gan for age to stoope, . . . *S.C.* O. 67
The wiser Muses *after* Colin ranne. . . . *S.C.* D. 48
In some straunge habit, *after* uncouth wize; . . . *Hub.* 84
And *after* askt an almes . . . *Hub.* 363
That *after* we may favour seeke to win?' . . . *Hub.* 644
Did ever *after* scorne on foote to goe. . . . *Hub.* 752
never *after* anie Should of his race . . . *Hub.* 1241
That *after* Tityrus first sung his lay, . . . *Col.* 2
Now, *after* Astrofell is dead and gone: . . . *Col.* 449
long while *after* I am dead and rotten, . . . *Col.* 640
shortly *after,* . . . *Col.* 859
He strowd an *Ave-Mary after* and before. . . . I. i. 35. 9
huntest *after* fame, . . . I. iv. 1. 2
after that he had faire Una lorne, . . . I. iv. 2. 1
ever *after* in most wretched case, . . . I. iv. 3. 5
lusted *after* all that he did love; . . . I. iv. 26. 2
Soone *after* comes the cruell Sarazin, . . . I. v. 4. 1
assembled . . . *after* their wofull falles, . . . I. v. 51. 3
the lad n'ould *after* joy, . . . I. vi. 17. 8
dronke with blood, yet thristed *after* life: . . . I. vi. 38. 8
Both hongred *after* death; . . . I. vi. 43. 9
he comes fast *after* mee.' . . . I. ix. 25. 2
Who first us greets, and *after* fayre areedes . . . I. ix. 28. 6
Sleepe *after* toyle, port *after* stormie seas, . . . I. ix. 40. 8
now *after* death and buriall done, . . . I. x. 43. 1
Which *after* all to heaven shall thee send; . . . I. x. 61. 2
And *after* to his Pallace he them bringes, . . . I. xii. 13. 1
I bownden am streight *after* this emprize, . . . I. xii. 18. 4
That *after* soone I dearely did lament; . . . II. iv. 29. 5
I, poursewing my fell purpose, *after* went. . . . II. iv. 31. 9
And *after* spent with pride and lavishnesse, . . . II. vii. 12. 4
After the Paynim brethren conquer'd were, . . . II. ix. 2. 1
And *after* all an army strong she leav'd, . . . II. x. 31. 8
Whom to poursue the Infant *after* hide . . . II. xi. 25. 7
Which ever *after* they abusd to ill, . . . II. xii. 31. 8
After long wayes and perilous paines endur'd, . . . III. i. 1. 2
all spurd *after,* fast as they mote fly, . . . III. i. 18. 4
Not that she lusted *after* any one, . . . III. ii. 23. 7
And, *after* having whispered a space . . . III. ii. 50. 4
Then ever him before, or *after,* living wight: . . . III. iii. 11. 9
First ill, and *after* ruled wickedly; . . . III. iii. 46. 3
After that they againe returned beene, . . . III. vi. 33. 1
Long *after* she from perill was releast: . . . III. vii. 1. 7
And *after* gan inquire his parentage, . . . III. vii. 46. 7
'So liv'd they ever *after* in like sin, . . . III. vii. 49. 1
And *after* cast him up upon the shore; . . . III. viii. 36. 8
Who, *after* Greekes did Priams realme destroy, . . . III. ix. 36. 7
He up remounted light, and *after* faind to wend. . . . III. x. 38. 9
Next *after* him went Doubt, . . . III. xii. 10. 1
alwaies flitting . . . *After* each beautie . . . IV. ii. 5. 3
Which vertue it for ever *after* did retaine. . . . IV. v. 4. 9
Shall breath it selfe awhile *after* so long a went. . . . IV. v. 46. 9
looking *after* long did mark which away she straid. . . . IV. viii. 7. 9
Whom *after* did a mightie man pursew, . . . IV. viii. 38. 6
And *after* promist large amends to make. . . . IV. viii. 60. 6
In which he long time *after* did remaine . . . IV. xi. 7. 5
after she had wept and wail'd a space, . . . IV. xii. 8. 8
streight he *after* sent His yron page, . . . V. i. 20. 1
after that the utmost date assynde . . . V. vi. 3. 6
After that them in battell he had wonne: . . . V. x. 30. 6
As thicke as doth the seede *after* the sowers hand: . . . V. xii. 7. 9
Ran *after* fast to reskue the distressed mayde. . . . VI. iii. 24. 9
ne did the other stay, But *after* went directly . . . VI. iii. 37. 5
did inquire *After* adventures, . . . VI. v. 11. 5
After that Timias had againe recured . . . VI. v. 12. 1
Still looking *after* him that did him chace, . . . VI. vi. 29. 8
And *after* all, for greater infamie, . . . VI. vii. 27. 1
After his rusticke wise, . . . Offred him drinke . . . VI. ix. 6. 7
long while *after,* whilest him list remaine, . . . VI. ix. 34. 2
After that he had labourd long in vaine . . . VI. xii. 32. 3
Albe that, long time *after* Calidore, . . . VI. xii. 39. 5
many of their stemme long *after* did survive: . . . VII. vi. 2. 9
They *after* follow'd all with shrill out-cry, . . . VII. vi. 52. 6
after Wrong was lov'd, and Justice solde, . . . VII. vii. 37. 8
Ne any then shall *after* it inquire, . . . *Am.* xxvii. 9
soone *after,* fresh againe enured His former cruelty. . . . *Epig.* iv. 53

After—*Continued.*
Twixt sleepe and wake, *after* she weary was, . . . *Epith.* 309
Weakely at first, but *after* with desyre Lifted . . . *H.L.* 67
at first Made of meere love, and *after* liked well, . . . *H.H.L.* 128
And *after,* when we fared had amisse, . . . *H.H.L.* 192
Afterclaps. For feare of *afterclaps,* for to prevent: . . . *Hub.* 332
After-send. To *after-send* his foe, that him may overtake? . . . I. v. 10. 9
Afterward. 'His blessed body . . . Was *afterward* . . . convaid, I. ii. 24. 2
thing refused doe not *afterward* accuse.' . . . II. vii. 18. 9
Who *afterward* was Emperour of Rome, . . . II. x. 60. 2
afterward both sea and land possest; . . . IV. xi. 18. 4
Afterwards. *afterwards* with grave advizement said: . . . *Hub.* 176
at first him credit gaine, Which *afterwards* . . . *Hub.* 690
afterwards I handled her so fayre, . . . *D.* 120
in that castle *afterwards* abide, . . . I. viii. 50. 7
afterwardes them to his Dame he leades, . . . I. x. 8. 1
afterwards he in his stead did raigne, . . . II. x. 58. 4
Did *afterwards* make shipwrack violent . . . II. xii. 7. 8
afterwards did rule the night and day: . . . II. xii. 13. 7
afterwardes they gan . . . To stirre up strife, . . . III. i. 64. 4
thou *afterwardes* did rayse Most famous fruites . . . III. iii. 3. 6
Least *afterwards* it be too late to take thy flight.' . . . III. iv. 14. 9
afterwardes on what adventure now he rode. . . . III. viii. 45. 9
afterwardes affray with cruell threat, . . . III. ix. 9. 3
afterwardes, close creeping as he might, . . . III. x. 44. 1
Would *afterwards* afresh the sleeping evill reare. . . . IV. i. 34. 9
afterwards did for her loves first hire Give it to her, . . . IV. v. 4. 5
afterwardes themselves doth cruelly devoure. . . . IV. vii. 12. 9
all his life, which *afterwards* he lad, . . . IV. viii. 2. 4
long time *afterwards* did lead An happie life . . . IV. viii. 18. 1
afterwards continu'd there a while . . . IV. ix. 12. 6
seeking often entraunce *afterwards* in vaine. . . . IV. x. 13. 9
afterwards she gan him soft to shrieve, . . . IV. xii. 26. 5
Where many years it *afterwards* remayned, . . . V. ii. 19. 5
afterwards a sonne to him shalt beare, . . . V. vii. 23. 7
So there a while they *afterwards* remained, . . . V. vii. 42. 1
afterwards thus to him saide. . . . VI. i. 11. 9
Whom *afterwards* my selfe with many a wound Did slay . . . VI. vii. 16. 8
afterwards of all her rich array; . . . VI. viii. 41. 3
afterwards to cheare with speaches kind; . . . VI. viii. 50. 7
many of them *afterwards* obtain'd Great power . . . VII. vi. 3. 1
Agaean. *See* **Aegaean.**
Again (*partial list*).
A twinne of forked trees send forth *againe.* . . . *Bel.* v. 14
For no such shadow shalbe had *againe.* . . . *Pet.* iii. 14
The Giants old should once *again* uprise, . . . *Ro.* iv. 6
Cooling *agaïne* his former kindled heate, . . . *Ro.* xi. 5
mounting up *againe* from whence he came, . . . *Ro.* xx. 5
Colin them gives to Rosalind *againe.* . . . *S.C.* Ja. 60
That, once sea-beate, will to sea *againe:* . . . *S.C.* F. 34
Such an one would make thee younge *againe.* . . . *S.C.* F. 68
Little him aunswered the Oake *againe,* . . . *S.C.* F. 140
The Axes edge did oft turne *againe,* . . . *S.C.* F. 203
That seeing, I levelde *againe* . . . *S.C.* Mar. 85
Ne durst *againe* his fyrye face out showe: . . . *S.C.* Ap. 78
The time was once, and may *againe* retorne, . . . *S.C.* May 103
Driven for neede to come home *agayne.* . . . *S.C.* S. 67
Which when they thinken *agayne* to quench, . . . *S.C.* S. 88
as it sprong, it wither must *agayne:* . . . *S.C.* O. 77
For that I thee restor'd to life *againe,* . . . *Gn.* 354
To cut the ships from turning home *againe* . . . *Gn.* 522
'*Againe* great dole on either partie grewe, . . . *Gn.* 529
what he toucht came not to light *againe;* . . . *Hub.* 702
Her back *againe* to life sent for his sake. . . . *Ti.* 392
My thought returned greeved home *againe,* . . . *Ti.* 478
Yet stayed not, till I *againe* did call: . . . *D.* 60
That us, late dead, has made *againe* alive: . . . *Col.* 31
Record to us that lovely lay *againe:* . . . *Col.* 97
move to take him to her grace *againe.* . . . *Col.* 175
So proudly, that she made them roare *againe.* . . . *Col.* 223
to make the dead *againe* alive. . . . *Col.* 599
sought backe to turne *againe;* . . . I. i. 16. 6
but he *againe,* Shooke him so hard, . . . I. i. 42. 5
With that misformed spright he backe returnd *againe.* . . . I. i. 55. 9
to her snowy Palfrey got *agayne,* . . . I. iii. 8. 8
And fates expired could renew *again,* . . . I. v. 40. 3
Or ever hope recover her *againe:* . . . I. vi. 33. 6
The knight her lightly reared up *againe,* . . . I. vi. 37. 5
downe *againe* she fell unto the ground, . . . I. vii. 24. 1
he her quickly reared up *againe:* . . . I. vii. 24. 2
Ecchoes three aunswer'd it selfe *againe:* . . . I. viii. 4. 4
That all the fieldes rebellowed *againe.* . . . I. viii. 11. 4
Againe his wonted angry weapon proov'd, . . . I. viii. 21. 3
him smot *againe* so sore, . . . I. viii. 24. 2
Again he askt, . . . I. viii. 32. 6
againe he sayde, *He could not tell;* . . . I. viii. 32. 8
againe he answered. . . . I. viii. 33. 2
of passed feare Is to be . . . ware of like *agein.* . . . I. viii. 44. 6
Him yett *againe,* and yett *againe,* bespake . . . I. ix. 24. 6
He lov'd . . . a Lady gent, That him *againe* lov'd . . . I. ix. 27. 7
Did not he all create To die *againe?* . . . I. ix. 42. 3
to kill, And rayse *againe* to life . . . I. x. 19. 9
Not unto such as could him feast *againe,* . . . I. x. 37. 6
turne *againe* Backe to the world, . . . I. x. 63. 1
smot *againe* . . . But backe *againe* the sparcling steele recoyld, I. xi. 25. 2, 3
reare *againe* The senceless corse . . . I. xi. 48. 7
Ye then shall hither backe retourne *agayne,* . . . I. xii. 19. 8
then *againe* abroad On the long voiage . . . I. xii. 42. 7
He shall you doe dew recompence *agayne,* . . . II. i. 14. 8
re-echoed *againe;* . . . II. i. 38. 2

Again—*Continued.*
thrise she sunck *againe,* . . . . II. i. 46. 3
He maketh warre, he maketh peace *againe,* . . . . II. ii. 26. 7
Throughout the wood that ecchoed *againe,* . . . . II. iii. 20. 8
his foe fettred would release *agayne,* . . . . II. v. 24. 8
groning deepe, thus answerd him *againe;* . . . . II. vii. 59. 3
Againe he heard a more efforced voyce, ... II. viii. 4. 3
who nought *againe* Him answered, ... II. viii. 23. 2
We would, and would *againe,* if that we could; . . . . . . II. ix. 12. 5
soone retournd *againe* With greater fury . . . . II. ix. 15. 1
backe *againe* faire Alma led them right, ... II. ix. 33. 5
to his crowne she him restord *againe;* . . . . II. x. 32. 1
Who shortly it to him restord *agayne,* . . . . II. x. 44. 7
twise they were repulsed backe *againe,* . . . . II. x. 48. 1
He is *againe* unto his rule restord; . . . . II. x. 66. 2
Remounts *againe* into the open ayre, ... II. xi. 36. 8
backe *againe* it did alofte rebownd, ... II. xi. 42. 8
A second fall redoubling backe *agayne.* . . . . II. xi. 43. 5
none of them himselfe could reare *againe:* . . . . III. i. 29. 2
she gan *againe* Her to bethinke . . . . III. ii. 22. 8
Ne ever to his worke returnd *againe:* . . . . III. iii. 11. 3
doen they onely sleepe, and shall *againe* reverse? . . . . . III. iv. 1. 9
Shee should not then have bene relyv'd *againe;* . . . . . . III. iv. 35. 4
with his speare requited him *againe,* . . . . III. v. 21. 7
Till they *agayn* returne . . . . III. vi. 32. 9
sent into the chaungefull world *agayne,* . . . . III. vi. 33. 7
Troy *againe* out of her dust was reard . . . . III. ix. 44. 3
Once to me yold, not to be yolde *againe:* . . . . III. xi. 17. 4
Againe, when as the Trojane boy so fayre He snatcht . . . . III. xi. 34. 4
made the sparkling waves to smoke *agayne,* . . . . III. xi. 41. 3
hee Which wrought it could the same recure *againe.* . . . . III. xii. 34. 7
Againe he drove at him with double might, ... IV. iii. 10. 2
softly askt *againe* What mister wight it was . . . . IV. vii. 10. 4
when he to himselfe returnd *againe,* . . . . IV. viii. 44. 1
Oft listening if he mote her heare *againe,* . . . . IV. xii. 17. 4
By which it's easie him to know *againe,* . . . . V. i. 19. 7
And, as they were, them equalize *againe.* . . . . V. ii. 38. 5
backe *againe* they homeward turnd their feete; . . . . . . V. iv. 51. 7
with her shield she warded it *againe,* . . . . V. v. 10. 8
lerne So fond a lesson as to love *againe:* . . . . V. v. 46. 4
She fayn'd to count the time *againe* anew, ... V. vi. 5. 4
To make new warre against the Gods *againe.* . . . . V. vii. 11. 6
them repaide *againe* with double more. . . . . V. vii. 31. 4
Against him made *againe.* . . . . V. viii. 9. 5
Againe the Pagan threw another dart, ... V. viii. 34. 1
sodainely, t' avenge him selfe *againe* . . . . V. xi. 8. 3
Againe . . . He did him smite . . . . V. xii. 23. 5
all the aire rebellowed *againe,* . . . . V. xii. 41. 6
to your selfe doe it returne *againe.* . . . . VI. Pr. 7. 3
Refused hath to yeeld her love *againe,* . . . . VI. i. 15. 3
He now *againe* is on his former way . . . . VI. ii. 3. 5
'loth were I . . . yet breake it should *againe,* . . . . . . VI. ii. 7. 7
And me in lieu thereof revil'd *againe,* . . . . VI. ii. 11. 8
I . . . backe returned His scornefull taunts unto his teeth *againe,* VI. ii. 12. 2
the faint sprite he did revoke *againe* . . . . VI. iii. 28. 2
And with mad moode *againe* upon him flew, ... VI. iv. 6. 3
from his steed him nigh he drew *againe:* . . . . VI. iv. 7. 5
backe return'd *againe* With speede . . . . VI. iv. 9. 3
Recured well, and made him whole *againe;* . . . . VI. iv. 16. 7
having all his bands *againe* uptyde, ... VI. iv. 24. 1
He with him thought backe to returne *againe;* . . . . VI. iv. 24. 2
All is in time like to returne *againe* To that foule feend, . . VI. iv. 31. 7
Vowing that never he in bed *againe* . . . . VI. iv. 40. 6
To whom the Squire nought aunswered *againe,* . . . . VI. v. 24. 2
to requite him with the like *againe,* . . . . VI. viii. 9. 1
all is now repayd with interest *againe.* . . . . VI. viii. 21. 9
turne *againe* my teme, ... VI. ix. 1. 1
Whom by no meanes thou canst recall *againe;* . . . . VI. x. 20. 3
Mongst which the theeves them questioned *againe,* . . . . . VI. xi. 39. 5
revive That long had lyen dead, and made *again* alive. . . . VI. xi. 50. 9
closing it *againe* like as before, ... VI. xii. 8. 3
forst him turne *againe:* Sternely he turnd *againe,* . . . . VI. xii. 26. 2, 3
woods and dales, . . . Did ring *againe,* . . . . VII. vi. 52. 9
turning to themselves at length *againe,* . . . . VII. vii. 58. 6
Retourne *agayne,* my forces late dismayd, ... *Am.* xiv. 1
back *again* doth chace Their looser lookes . . . . *Am.* xxi. 7
The same at night she did *againe* unreave: . . . . *Am.* xxiii. 4
Will shine *again,* and looke on me at last, ... *Am.* xxxiv. 11
love thee for the same *againe;* . . . . *Am.* lxviii. 10
none can call *againe* the passed time. . . . . *Am.* lxx. 14
Agayne, I wrote it with a second hand; . . . . *Am.* lxxv. 3
They ydly back returne to me *agayne:* . . . . *Am.* lxxviii. 10
againe enured His former cruelty. . . . . *Epig.* iv. 53
Had he required life of us *againe,* . . . . *H.H.L.* 179
Of that selfe mould, . . . and to the same *againe* shall fade, . *H.H.L.* 199
their points rebutted backe *againe* Are duld, ... *H.H.B.* 122

Against (*partial list*). *See* **Gainst.**
I bent my bolt *against* the bush, ... *S.C.* Mar. 70
Agaynst his cruell scortching heate, ... *S.C.* Jul. 25
it to maintaine *Against* vile Zoilus backbitings *Ded.Son.*xii.14
Sisyphus an huge round stone did reele *Against* an hill, . . . I. v. 35. 4
'will ryde *Against* my liking backe . . . . I. ix. 32. 6
What justice can but judge *against* thee right, ... I. ix. 37. 8
Against the day of wrath . . . . I. ix. 46. 5
to fight *Against* spirituall foes, ... I. x. 1. 4
To tell were as to strive *against* the streame: . . . . I. xii. 23. 3
Against his praise to stirre up enmitye . . . . II. i. 23. 8
eldest did *against* the youngest goe, And both *against* the
middest . . . . II. ii. 13. 8, 9
Do arme yourself *against* that day, ... II. iii. 15. 9

Against—*Continued.*
her Javelin bright *Against* him bent, ... II. iii. 42. 8
Against him turning all his fell intent, ... II. iv. 6. 6
ready dight . . . *Against* the viaundes should be ministred. . II. ix. 27. 4
lov'd their native flesh *against* al kynd, ... III. ii. 41. 3
Makes the huge element, *against* her kinde, To move . . . . III. ix. 15. 5
That almost had *against* you trespassed this day.' . . . . . IV. vi. 3. 9
hath in this Ladie wrought *Against* the course of kind, . . . IV. vi. 30. 5
'Then have they all themselves *against* me bent: . . . . . . IV. viii. 16. 4
Against the stones and trees did rayle anew, ... IV. viii. 36. 8
And her *against* sate comely Curtesie, ... IV. x. 51. 3
Her silver feet, faire washt *against* this day: . . . . V. xi. 47. 6
With inward griefe and malice did *against* them swell. . . . V. vii. 10. 9
To make new warre *against* the Gods againe. . . . . V. vii. 11. 6
leveld all *against* one certaine place, ... V. x. 34. 7
found no more T' oppose *against* his powre . . . . V. x. 38. 6
blasphemies forth threw *Against* his Gods, ... V. xi. 12. 4
to reskue her *against* a Knight, ... VI. i. 29. 6
inly wroth *Against* her Knight, ... VI. iii. 33. 2
Did shut the gate *against* him . . . . VI. iii. 38. 2
Did front him, face to face *against* him bent: . . . . VI. v. 20. 8
both with equall might *Against* him ran; . . . . VI. vii. 7. 6
much griev'd *against* that straunger knight, ... VI. vii. 20. 6
Abusde, *against* all reason and all law, ... VI. viii. 6. 4
nought *against* their wils might countervaile: . . . . VII. vi. 49. 7
The which my selfe *against* my selfe doe make; . . . . *Am.* xliv. 6
fresh *against* my selfe to fight. . . . . *Am.* xliv. 12
Against the Brydale day, ... *Proth.*17,35,143
Against their Brydale day, ... *Proth.*53,89,179
this Lay, Prepar'd *against* that Day, ... *Proth.* 88
Against their wedding day, ... *Proth.* 125

Agamemnon. 'There also goodly *Agamemnon* bosts, ... *Gn.* 545

Aganippus. the wise Cordelia Was sent to *Agganip* (**Aganip*)
of Celtica. . . . . II. x. 29. 5

Agape. *Agape* Doth lengthen her sonnes lives. . . . . IV. ii. Arg.
Her name was *Agape,* . . . . IV. ii. 41. 7

Agast. *See* **Aghast.**

Agave. Cruell *Agave,* flying vengeance sore . . . . *Gn.* 172
Wondred *Agave,* Poris, and Nesaea, ... IV. xi. 49. 6

Agdistes. a God . . . Did wisely make, and good *Agdistes* call; II. xii. 48. 2

Age. *See* **Quietage.**
Ne rust of *age* hating continuance, ... *Ro.* xiii. 6
posteritie Of *age* ensuing shall you ever read? . . . . *Ro.* xxxii. 2
this *age,* in which all good is geason, ... *Van.* i. 5
Age and Winter accord full nie, ... *S.C.* F. 27
stoope-gallaunt *Age,* the hoste of Greevaunce. . . . . *S.C.* F. 90
Of my old *age* have this one delight, ... *S.C.* May 202
ryper *age* such pleasures doth reprove: . . . . *S.C.* Jun. 36
after vertue gan for *age* to stoope, ... *S.C.* O. 67
my *age,* now passed youngthly pryme, ... *S.C.* D. 75
That was the golden *age* of Saturne old, ... *Hub.* 151
lanterne unto late succeeding *age,* . . . . *Ti.* 170
Whose praises I to future *age* doo sing; . . . . *Ti.* 277
Their names shall of the later *age* be heard, ... *Ti.* 348
Nor *age,* nor envie, shall them ever wast. . . . . *Ti.* 406
To be a wonder to all *age* ensuing, ... *Ti.* 552
'No *age* hath bred . . . more vertue in a wight; . . . . . . *D.* 218
For *age* to dye is right, but youth is wrong; . . . . *D.* 243
in affliction wast my better *age:* . . . . *D.* 374
ensample to the present *age* Of th' old Heroes, ... *Ded. Son.* vi. 3
In the first season of my feeble *age,* . . . . *Ded. Son.* vii. 4
Ne bene so much admir'd of later *age.* . . . . *Ded. Son.* xiii. 6
That are the great Mecaenas of this *age,* . . . . *Ded. Son.* xiii. 9
Moste noble Lord, the honor of this *age,* . . . . *Ded. Son.* xiv. 6
in the first flowre of my freshest *age,* . . . . I. ii. 23. 1
when he sees his *age,* And hoarie head of Archimago old, . . . I. iii. 38. 3
Feare, sicknesse, *age,* losse, labour, sorrow, strife, ... I. ix. 44. 6
She was a woman in her freshest *age,* . . . . I. x. 30. 1
eien . . . through great *age* had lost their kindly sight, . . . I. x. 47. 4
Which to late *age* were never mentioned. . . . . II. Pr. 2. 5
fiers fate did crop the blossome of his *age.* . . . . II. i. 41. 9
'It was my fortune, commune to that *age,* . . . . II. iv. 19. 1
Weake handes, but counsell is most strong in *age.'* . . . . . II. vi. 48. 5
leave the rudenesse of that antique *age* . . . . II. vii. 18. 2
with thy brutenesse shendst thy comely *age,* . . . . II. viii. 12. 3
in the flowre now of her freshest *age;* . . . . II. ix. 18. 7
rype of *age,* And in demeanure sober, ... II. ix. 27. 8
There sate a man of ripe and perfect *age,* . . . . II. ix. 54. 2
ripe *age* bad him surrender late His life, ... II. x. 13. 8
feeble *age* Nigh to his utmost date . . . . II. x. 27. 6
Three sones he dying left, all under *age;* . . . . II. x. 64. 1
soone comes *age* that will her pride deflowre; . . . . II. xii. 75. 7
As if that *age* badd him that burden spare, ... III. i. 4. 5
Let later *age* that noble use envy, ... III. i. 13. 8
ne her unguilty *age* Did weene, ... III. ii. 26. 3
The comfort of her *age* and weary dayes, ... III. vii. 12. 2
Now in the blossome of his freshest *age.* . . . . III. vii. 46. 5
*In stead thereof sweet peace and quiet *age* . . . . IV. iii. 43. 5
That needed much her weake *age* to desire, ... IV. v. 39. 8
eke that *age* despysed nicenesse vaine, ... IV. viii. 27. 5
antique *age,* yet in the infancie Of time, ... IV. viii. 30. 1
know the moniments of passed *age:* . . . . IV. xi. 17. 6
Eione well in *age,* . . . . IV. xi. 50. 7
When as mans *age* was in his freshest prime, ... V. Pr. 1. 3
from the golden *age,* that first was named, ... V. Pr. 2. 1
in former *age* A Ladie of great worth . . . . V. x. 7. 1
Of which though present *age* doe plenteous seeme, ... VI. Pr. 4. 6
But now weake *age* had dimd his candle-light: . . . . VI. iii. 3. 4
So long as *age* enabled him thereto, ... VI. v. 37. 2
being now attacht with timely *age,* . . . . VI. vi. 4. 6

Age—*Continued.*
Wasting the strength of her immortal *age:* VI. vi. 11. 6
when thy glory shall be farre displayd To future *age,* VI. x. 28. 9
Lo! one, whom later *age* hath brought to light, *Com. Son.* iii. 9
Aged. Lifting to heaven her *aged* hoarie head, *Ro.* xxviii. 3
There grewe an *aged* Tree on the greene, *S.C.* F. 102
bends what ever power his *aged* yeares Him lent, *Gn.* 646
broad spreading like an *aged* tree, *Ti.* 452
With fruitfull hope his *aged* breast he fed *Mui.* 25
good Harpalus, now woxen *aged* *Col.* 380
An *aged* Sire, in long blacke weedes yclad, I. i. 29. 2
Quoth then that *aged* man: I. i. 33. 5
he . . . hardly was restreined of that *aged* sire. I. ii. 5. 9
Weary of *aged* Tithones saffron bed, I. ii. 7. 2
bowing downe her *aged* backe, she kist The wicked witch, I. v. 27. 1
governing . . . *aged* limbs on cypresse stadle stout, I. vi. 14. 8
downe he tombled; as an *aged* tree, I. viii. 22. 5
He was an *aged* syre, all hory gray, I. x. 5. 5
them to his Dame he leades, That *aged* Dame, I. x. 8. 2
Then said the *aged* Caelia, 'Deare dame, I. x. 17. 1
Wherein an *aged* holy man did lie, I. x. 46. 5
There they doe finde that godly *aged* Sire, I. x. 48. 1
'Most trew,' then said the holy *aged* man; I. x. 59. 1
Fayre ympe of Phoebus and his *aged* bryde, I. xi. 5. 7
It could . . . *aged* long decay Renew, I. xi. 30. 4
the deawy bed Of *aged* Tithone I. xi. 51. 3
That *aged* Syre, the Lord of all that land, I. xii. 3. 2
aged Queene, Arayd in antique robes I. xii. 5. 1
Least his long way his *aged* limbes should tire: II. i. 7. 5
his *aged* Guide in presence came; II. i. 31. 3
that same Hag, his *aged* mother, hight Occasion; II. iv. 10. 8
Unto an *aged* woman, poore and bare, II. v. 17. 3
Ne gave him leave to bid that *aged* sire Adieu; II. vi. 20. 5
them beside an *aged* Sire did trace, II. viii. 10. 3
Crav'd leave of Alma and that *aged* sire II. ix. 60. 8
Their *aged* Syre, thus eased of his crowne, II. x. 29. 6
Till *aged* Hely by dew heritage it gaynd. II. x. 45. 9
him beside an *aged* Squire there rode, III. i. 4. 3
Her *aged* Nourse, whose name was Glauce hight, III. ii. 30. 2
th' *aged* Nourse, her calling to her bowre, III. ii. 49. 4
Then it had lighted on an *aged* Oke, III. vii. 41. 3
An *aged* sire with head all frory hore, III. viii. 30. 3
forgot that whylome I heard tell From *aged* Mnemon; III. ix. 47. 4
The *aged* Dame, him seeing so enraged, IV. i. 54. 1
Through that false witch, and that foule *aged* drevill; IV. ii. 3. 8
that old *aged* Dame, his faithfull Squire, IV. v. 39. 6
with him eke that *aged* Squire attone; IV. v. 46. 3
In which old Styx her *aged* bones alway . . . doth lay. IV. xi. 4. 4
the *aged* Ocean and his Dame Old Tethys, IV. xi. 18. 1
much more *aged* was his wife then he, IV. xi. 24. 6
seem'd full *aged* by his outward sight, IV. xi. 25. 7
he met An *aged* wight wayfaring all alone, V. xi. 37. 2
being *aged* now, and weary to Of warres delight VI. v. 37. 5
Then came to them a good old *aged* syre, VI. ix. 13. 6
welcom'd of that honest syre And of his *aged* Beldame VI. ix. 17. 2
him beside His *aged* wife, VI. xi. 18. 5
there sate an hory Old *aged* Sire, VII. vi. 8. 6
on Themmes brode *aged* backe *Proth.* 133
Agenor. Great Belus, Phoeax, and *Agenor* best; IV. xi. 15. 7
Age's. What recked I of wintrye *ages* waste?— *S.C.* D. 29
One onelie lives, her *ages* ornament, *T.M.* 571
'She fell away in her first *ages* spring, *D.* 239
pourtrahed With natures pen, in *ages* grave degree, I. viii. 33. 8
later *ages* pride, like corn-fed steed, II. vii. 16. 6
Florimell, in her first *ages* flowre, IV. v. 5. 7
Ages. Through the worlds endles *ages* to survive. *Gn.* 56
succeeding *ages* have no light Of things forepast, *T.M.* 103
in *ages* past none might professe *T.M.* 559
'Looke backe, who list, unto the former *ages,* *Ti.* 57
have from wisest *ages* hidden beene; II. Pr. 3. 2
The wisest men, I weene, that lived in their *ages.* II. ix. 47. 9
Three *ages,* such as mortall men contrive, II. ix. 48. 5
things foregone through many *ages* held, II. ix. 56. 2
Of warlike puissaunce in *ages* spent, III. ii. 3. 1
who so list looke backe to former *ages,* IV. Pr. 3. 1
It hath bene through all *ages* ever seene, IV. v. 1. 1
that they should endure through many *ages,* *Am.* li. 3
may sing To *ages* following. *Proth.* 160
Agganip. *See* **Aganippus.**
Aggrace. Of kindnesse and of courteous *aggrace;* II. viii. 56. 8
that which all faire workes doth most *aggrace,* II. xii. 58. 8
Aggraced. that knight so much *agraste,* That she him taught I. x. 18. 7
Aggrate. Doth borrow grace, the fancie to *aggrate;* *T.M.* 406
strove with most delights Him to *aggrate,* II. v. 33. 2
each one sought his Lady to *aggrate:* II. ix. 34. 5
that may dayntest fantasy *aggrate,* II. xii. 42. 7
Palmer, if it mote thee so *aggrate,* II. xii. 85. 8
Pleasure, that doth both gods and men *aggrate,* III. vi. 50. 8
to *aggrate* The virgin whom he had abusde III. viii. 36. 5
She litle answer'd him, but lightly did *aggrate.* IV. ii. 23. 9
The more t' *aggrate* his God with such his blouddy guize. V. xi. 19. 9
What ever thing he did her to *aggrate,* VI. x. 33. 2
Aggravate. hardly finde to *aggravate* her griefe; III. viii. 1. 8
aggravate the horror of her blame: V. ix. 43. 4
Aggrieve. with rehearsing would me more *agreeve.* *Ti.* 91
Aggrieved. At their first presence grew *agrieved* sore, I. x. 49. 2
Which Guyon marking said; 'Be nought *agriev'd,* II. v. 15. 1
all those stranger knights full sore *agrieved,* IV. iv. 46. 8
Right sore *agrieved* at her sharpe reproofe, IV. vii. 37. 2
him the more *agreev'd* I found thereby: IV. viii. 57. 5
Aggrieves. Which yet *aggreeves* (*agreves* [1]) my hart *Pet.* iv. 12
Aghast. Greatly *aghast* with this piteous plea, *S.C.* F. 157
forth shee yode, thereat halfe *aghast:* *S.C.* May 233
All *agast,* lowdly she gan to call *S.C.* May 296
I in minde remained sore *agast,* *Ti.* 578
nought *aghast,* his mightie hand enhaunst: I. i. 17. 8
As one *aghast* with feends or damned sprights, I. ii. 4. 5
The fearefull shepheard, often there *aghast,* Under them never sat, I. ii. 28. 7
damned sprights sent forth to make ill men *aghast.* I. v. 31. 9
his chacing steedes *aghast* Both charett swifte and huntsman overcast: I. v. 38. 4
other griesly thing that him *aghast.* I. ix. 21. 4
There him he findes all sencelesse and *aghast,* I. ix. 23. 3
which sight at first him sore *aghast.* II. viii. 4. 9
At sight whereof the people stand *aghast;* III. i. 16. 7
other accident which him *aghast;* III. v. 3. 5
To move and tremble as it were *aghast,* III. ix. 15. 6
Nether of ydle showes, nor of false charmes *aghast.* III. xii. 29. 9
Carried with wings of feare, like fowle *aghast,* V. viii. 4. 7
made him stagger and stand halfe *agast,* V. xi. 28. 7
full sore *aghast* He staggered to and fro V. xii. 23. 3
from the wall him seeing so *aghast,* VI. i. 23. 1
forst him gape and gaspe, with dread *aghast,* VI. iii. 26. 8
found, . . . the Ladie fearefully *aghast,* VI. iv. 9. 7
the Squire, now nigh *aghast,* Revived was, VI. v. 21. 8
He lightly started up like one *aghast,* VI. viii. 47. 8
lookt up like one *aghast.* VI. xi. 22. 9
In dreadfull darknesse dreadfully *aghast;* VI. xi. 32. 5
so sore him dread *aghast.* VII. vi. 52. 5
Aglaia. Next faire *Aglaia,* last Thalia merry; VI. x. 22. 8
Aglaura. So having said, *Aglaura* him bespake: *Col.* 584
Aglets. besprinckled was throughout With golden *aygulets,* II. iii. 26. 7
on his head an hood with *aglets* sprad, VI. ii. 5. 8
Ago. *See* **Agone.**
Sicker this morrowe, no lenger *agoe,* *S.C.* May 19
they han sold thilk same long *agoe,* *S.C.* S. 98
Chaunced to Roffynn not long *ygoe?* *S.C.* S. 171
great Augustus long *ygoe* is dead, *S.C.* O. 62
Nowe is time to dye: Nay, time was long *ygoe:* *S.C.* N. 81
calamities, That long *agoe* did grieve *Ti.* 443
not long *agoe* Her sonne . . . love did beare, *Mui.* 130
Dead long *ygoe,* I wote, thou haddest bin, I. ii. 18. 3
his eye sight him fayled long *ygo;* I. viii. 30. 5
restore To native crowne and kingdom late *ygoe;* II. i. 2. 7
the Palmer, whom he long *ygoe* Had lost, II. viii. 53. 5
his mother long *ygoe* Did him, they say, forwarne III. v. 9. 6
great chaine, wherewith not long *ygoe* He bound that . . . Lady III. xii. 41. 6
Which long *agoe* he taken had in hond: V. iv. 3. 7
with the rest they tooke not long *agoe;* VI. xi. 11. 7
long *ygo,* Whilest ye in durance dwelt, VI. xii. 17. 5
Agone. th' antique faith of Justice long *agone* *Gn.* 359
Dee, which Britons long *ygone* Did call divine, IV. xi. 39. 3
Can tell things doen in heaven so long *ygone,* VII. vii. 2. 8
Agonies. When oblique Saturne sate in th' house of *agonyes.* II. ix. 52. 9
Agony. Heare, then, my paine and inward *agonie.* *Hub.* 58
With shrikes and groanes and grievous *agonie.* *T.M.* 358
I . . . Feele my hart perst with so great *agony,* I. iii. 1. 8
Him to beguile of griefe and *agony;* I. v. 17. 8
In this distressed doubtfull *agony,* I. x. 22. 6
death were better then such *agony,* II. iv. 33. 3
great sorrow and sad *agony* II. xii. 27. 7
Full of sad feare and doubtfull *agony* III. vii. 32. 1
Ne stayd his flight nor fearefull *agony,* III. x. 56. 2
Agree. Tway things doen ill *agree.* *S.C.* Jul. 152
The Foxe was glad, and quickly did *agree:* *Hub.* 102
with his glistring armes does ill *agree;* I. ix. 22. 8
So both *agree* their bodies to engrave: II. i. 60. 1
They soone *agree:* So to his steed he gott, II. iii. 46. 2
Whereto he drew in hast it to *agree.* II. iv. 3. 4
Birdes, voices, instruments, windes, waters, all *agree:* II. xii. 70. 9
So well they both *agree:* III. x. 11. 8
Him seemed more their maner did *agree;* III. x. 21. 3
They all *agree,* and forward them addresse: III. x. 40. 1
(The harder it to make them well *agree*) IV. ii. 38. 4
true friendships bond Doth their long strife *agree.* IV. iii. Arg.
So mortall foes so friendly to *agree,* IV. iii. 49. 7
did secretly *agree* To overthrow my state IV. vii. 15. 4
over-ruld at last, he did to me *agree.* IV. viii. 58. 9
Why should they not likewise in love *agree,* IV. xi. 40. 4
whether with truth or falshood they *agree.* V. ii. 47. 9
with this present treatise doth *agree,* V. iii. 3. 8
they overcommen *Agree* to goe with her; V. ix. 4. 2
To see her Ladie, as they did *agree;* V. ix. 20. 2
all in spight and malice did *agree;* VI. i. 9. 4
they all *agree* That Colin Clout should pipe, VI. ix. 41. 5
all the Gods in councell did *agree* *Am.* xxiv. 9
mercy doth with beautie best *agree,* *Am.* liii. 13
taught in such accordance to *agree?* *Col.* 846
So goodly all *agree,* with sweet consent, *Epith.* 83
well *agree* withouten breach or jar. *Epith.* 132
made out of one mould the more t' *agree;* *H.B.* 207
with his spirits proportion to *agree,* *H.B.* 227
(for pride and love may ill *agree*) *H.H.L.* 95
Agreeably. The which were armed both *agreeably,* VI. vii. 3. 7
Both clad in shepheards weeds *agreeably,* VI. xi. 36. 2
Agreed. Well *agreed,* Willie: *S.C.* Au. 49
The dowre *agreed,* the day assigned plaine, *Col.* 126
So hard the discord was to be *agreede.* I. ii. 37. 7
they to peace *agreed.* II. x. 51. 9

Agreed—*Continued.*
diff'ring both in willes *agreed* in fine: II. xii. 59. 7
all *agreed*, through sweete diversity, II. xii. 59. 8
So goodly all *agreed* they forth yfere did ryde. III. i. 12. 9
At last they both *agreed* her . . . not to awake III. vi. 27. 7
They beene *agreed;* and to the gates they goe III. ix. 17. 6
Agreed to travell, and their fortunes try. IV. iv. 6. 4
They all *agreed:* IV. iv. 13. 1
thereto well *agreed* His word, IV. iv. 39. 7
This being ended thus, and all *agreed*, IV. v. 9. 7
They all *agreed:* and then that snowy Mayd Was in the middest plast IV. v. 26. 1
So both to wreake their wrathes on Britomart *agreed*. IV. vi. 8. 9
I with that Squire *agreede* away to flit, IV. vii. 17. 6
Betwixt the Medway and the Thames *agreed*. IV. xi. 8. 4
both *agreed* that this their bridale feast IV. xi. 9. 1
have *agreed* To thrall my looser life, V. v. 29. 8
So both *agreed* to send that mayd afore, V. ix. 8. 6
yet to his aide *agreed*, V. xi. 57. 7
There he remaind with them right well *agreed*, VI. i. 47. 7
The knight full gladly soone *agreed* thereto, VI. ix. 16. 8
Thereto they all attonce *agreed* well; VI. xi. 20. 7
faire bespoke with words, that he at last *agreed*. VI. xi. 35. 9
To whom they both *agreed* to take their way, VI. xi. 36. 8
Thereto they soone *agreed*, VI. xi. 40. 6
most *agreed*, and did this sentence give, VII. vi. 50. 7
at the time that was before *agreed*, VII. vii. 3. 1

Agreeing. though not all *agreeing* With some *Ro.* ix. 12
Her name is Munera, *agreeing* with her deedes. V. ii. 9. 9
Agreeing in bad will and cancred kynd; V. xii. 33. 2
Agreeing well both with the place and season, VI. iv. 37. 5

Agreement. With whome king Coyll made an *agreement*, II. x. 59. 3
make *agreement* with her thrilling eyes; *Am.* xxxvi. 6

Agreeve, Agrieve, -d. *See* **Aggrieve,** *etc.*

Agrise. Engrost with mud which did them fowle *agrise*, II. vi. 46. 7
His manly face, that did his foes *agrize*, III. ii. 24. 4
any yron eyes to see it would *agrize*. V. x. 28. 9

Agrised. Like ghost late risen from his grave *agryz'd*, IV. viii. 12. 7
From mortall eyes that should be sore *agrized;* VII. vii. 6. 3

Aguise. How for the Court themselves they might *aguize;* *Hub.* 656
her head she fondly would *aguize* With gaudy girlonds, II. vi. 7. 3

Aguised. To be her Squire, and do her service well *aguisd*. II. i. 21. 9
Wherewith above all knights ye goodly seeme *aguizd!* II. i. 31. 9
A looking glasse, right wondrously *aguiz'd*, III. ii. 18. 8
full rich *aguiz'd* As each one had his furnitures deviz'd. V. iii. 4. 4

Ah (*partial list*).
Ah, God! that love *S.C.* Ja. 54
Ah for pittie! *S.C.* F. 1
Ah, foolish Boy! that is with love yblent: *S.C.* Ap. 155
But *ah!* false Fortune *S.C.* May. 198
Ah! God shield, man, that I *S.C.* Jul. 9
Ah! where were ye this while *As.* 127
Ah, wretched world! *T.M.* 121, 123, 125
Our pleasant Willy, *ah!* is dead of late: *T.M.* 208
Ah! my loves queene, *Col.* 170
'*Ah* far be it (quoth Colin Clout) fro me, *Col.* 464
'*Ah!* shepheards, (then said Colin) ye ne weet *Col.* 927
'*Ah* Sir, my liege Lord, and my love, I. i. 51. 1
'*Ah* me! that is a double death,' (she said) I. iv. 51. 6
'*Ah* Lady deare,' quoth then the gentle knight, I. vii. 40. 1
He is not, *ah!* he is not such a foe, II. iv. 10. 4
Ah! see, whoso fayre thing doest faine to see, II. xii. 74. 2
'*Ah!*' (said she then) 'now may ye all see plaine, III. i. 29. 7
But *ah!* my rymes too rude and rugged arre, III. ii. 3. 6
'*Ah!* my deare daughter, *ah!* my dearest dread, III. ii. 30. 6
'*Ah!* read,' (quoth Britomart) 'how is she hight?' III. iii. 56. 1
But *ah!* who can deceive his destiny, III. iv. 27. 1
Ah God! what other could he do at least, III. v. 43. 8
ah, farre be such reproch fro mee! III. v. 46. 3
But *ah* for pittie! that I have thus long IV. xi. 1. 1
Who her despysd (*ah!* who would her despyse?) IV. xi. 5. 2
'*Ah!* woe is me, and well-away!' V. i. 15. 1
'*Ah* wellaway!' (sayd then the yron man) V. vi. 16. 1
'*Ah* gentle Knights! what meane ye V. viii. 11. 2
'*Ah!* Sir, but mote ye please, V. xi. 18. 2
'*Ah* mercie, Sir! doe me not slay, VI. i. 39. 8
'*Ah!* nay, Sir Knight,' (said she) 'it may not be, VI. viii. 30. 1
'*Ah*, well-away!' (sayd he VI. xi. 29. 1
'But *ah!* if Gods should strive with flesh yfere, VII. vi. 31. 7
Ah! when will this long weary day have end, *Epith.* 278
Ah, Gods! that ever ye that monster placed *H.L.* 271
Ah! whither, Love! wilt thou now carrie mee? *H.B.* 1
But *ah!* here fits not well Olde woes, *Proth.* 141

Ahead. *See* **Head.**

Aid. With your *ayd* to fore-stall my neere decay.' *S.C.* May 273
Of *ayde* or counsell in my decaye. *S.C.* S. 247
in *ayde* of that fierce fight, *Gn.* 505
No Muses *aide* me needes heretoo to call; *Hub.* 43
thereby willing to affoord them *aide;* *Hub.* 414
tyrannie is with strange *ayde* supported. *Hub.* 1121
Did lend her secret *aide*, *Mui.* 127
her play-fellowes *aide* to call, *Mui.* 282
This lowly Muse, . . . Flies for like *aide* *Ded. Son.* xiii. 8
with thy mother mylde come to mine *ayde;* I. Pr. 3. 6
grove . . . That promist *ayde* the tempest to withstand; I. i. 7. 3
their service . . . To *aide* his friendes, or fray his enimies. I. i. 38. 5
'My weaker yeares, . . . Fly to your fayth for . . . sure *ayde:* I. i. 52. 6
Having both found a new friend you to *aid*, I. ii. 27. 2
my secret *aide* Shall follow you.' I. iv. 51. 8
for thine *ayd*, Here take thy lovers token I. vi. 47. 6

Aid—*Continued.*
will to might gives greatest *aid*.' I. vii. 41. 4
Unto his *aide* she hastily did draw Her dreadfull beast; I. viii. 12. 3
to *ayde* his frend, Againe his wonted angry weapon proov'd, I. viii. 21. 2
O heare, how piteous he to you for *ayd* does call!' I. viii. 28. 9
none did . . . *aid* envy to him in need that stands; I. ix. 1. 6
Poore prisoners to relieve with gratious *ayd*, I. x. 40. 2
the tender Orphans of the dead And wydowes *ayd*, I. x. 43. 3
To *aide* a virgin desolate, foredonne; I. x. 60. 4
His trusty sword he cald to his last *aid*, I. xi. 42. 2
to Diana calling lowd for *ayde*, II. ii. 8. 4
rushed in on foot to *ayd* her ere she dyde. II. iii. 3. 9
Gave him great *ayd*, II. iii. 4. 7
Atin to Cymochles for *ayd* flyes. II. v. Arg.
Into the lake he lept his Lord to *ayd*, II. vi. 46. 1
So evill thing to seeke unto their *ayd*, II. vii. 14. 8
Against fowle feendes to *ayd* us militant! II. viii. 2. 5
thy faithfull *aide* in hard assay, II. viii. 7. 4
by whose most gratious *ayd* I live this day, II. viii. 55. 5
'Fortune . . . Seldom' (said Guyon) 'yields to vertue *aide*, II. ix. 8. 2
He sent to Germany straunge *aid* to reare; II. x. 64. 7
the villein, comming to their *ayd*, II. xi. 29. 4
eke the Redcrosse knight gave her good *ayd*, III. i. 66. 7
displayd The clothes about her round with busy *ayd;* III. ii. 47. 5
Strongly to *ayde* his countrey III. iii. 27. 8
'Great *ayd* thereto his mighty puissaunce . . . shall give III. iii. 28. 1
desire No service but thy safety and *ayd;* III. v. 36. 4
gives ye so good *ayd* To your disports: III. vi. 21. 4
ne her need implore Lucinaes *aide:* III. vi. 27. 4
To call them all in order to her *ayde*, III. viii. 4. 6
The wretched man hearing her call for *ayd*, III. x. 14. 1
Ne canst her *ayde*, ne canst her foe dismay; III. xi. 11. 7
Thence to depart for further *aide* t' enquire: III. xii. 45. 8
For pitie that ye want a fellow for your *ayd*.' IV. i. 33. 9
They to his succour ran with readie *ayd;* IV. i. 37. 2
love and friendly *aid* Mongst gentle knights to nourish IV. i. 46. 3
He pricked forth in *ayd* of Satyran; IV. iv. 19. 2
To hasten greatly to his parties *ayd*, IV. iv. 20. 2
Ne living *aide* for her on earth appeares, IV. vii. 23. 2
few plants, preserv'd through heavenly *ayd*, IV. viii. 33. 3
all the way full loud for *aide* did crie, IV. viii. 38. 4
with unwilling *ayd*, To guide the beast IV. ix. 5. 3
she cald to him for *aide;* IV. ix. 7. 2
each one taking part in others *aide* IV. ix. 24. 7
Eftsoones him selfe he to their *aide* addrest, IV. ix. 32. 5
Whose glorie is to *aide* all suppliants pore, V. i. 4. 6
Him for to *aide*, if *aide* he chaunst to neede, V. i. 13. 2
Your *aide* to guide me out of errour blind.' V. vii. 19. 5
for their so noble *ayd* V. viii. 23. 8
gave him great *ayde:* V. ix. 5. 3
when as foes enforst, or friends sought *ayde*, V. ix. 30. 8
unto gratious great Mercilla call For *ayde* V. x. 14. 4
Through promise to afford her timely *aide*, V. xi. 41. 4
Assure your selfe, Sir Knight, she shall have *ayd*, V. xi. 43. 3
holding up her wretched hands To him for *aide*, V. xi. 44. 9
They drew unto his *aide;* V. xi. 47. 2
yet to his *aide* agreed, V. xi. 57. 7
Artegall doth Sir Burbon *aide*, V. xii. Arg.
maintayne That Tyrants part with close or open *ayde*, V. xii. 25. 6
him called to his *aide:* VI. i. 11. 6
Ladies *ayde* in every stead and stound.' VI. i. 42. 9
I should no creature joyne unto mine *ayde:* VI. ii. 37. 8
and calling oft for *ayde;* VI. iii. 24. 6
stone Which lay thereby (so fortune him did *ayde*) VI. iv. 21. 3
if they would afford him *ayde* at need VI. vii. 4. 6
Ne powre had to withstand, ne hope of any *ayd*. VI. vii. 48. 9
He left his lofty steede to *aide* him neare; VI. viii. 12. 7
Calidore soone comming to her *ayde*, VI. x. 35. 6
unable it to *ayd:* VI. xii. 16. 5
Mov'd by your might and ordered by your *ayde*, VII. vii. 49. 7
reposeth In her owne powre, and scorneth others *ayde;* *Am.* lviii. 2
With secret *ayde* doest succour and supply, *Epith.* 402

Aiding. Beene to me *ayding*, others to adorne, *Epith.* 2

Ail. She wist not, silly Mayd, what she did *aile*, III. ii. 27. 7
Ran hastily, to weete what did him *ayle*. IV. i. 43. 4

Aim. The onely upshot whereto he doth *ayme:* *Hub.* 770
To *ayme* their counsels to the fairest scope, *Hub.* 960
seeing him ryde so ranck, And *ayme* at him, II. iii. 6. 8
knowes her port, and thither sayles by *ayme*, II. vi. 10. 3
the end, To which al men doe *ayme*, II. vii. 32. 8
her false eies, that at her hart did *ayme*, III. i. 50. 7
Ne by inquirie learne, nor ghesse by *ayme;* VI. iv. 24. 7
creatures which by name Thou canst not count, much lesse their natures *aime;* *H.H.B.* 33

Aimed. *See* **Nigh-aimed.**
of all his drifte the *aymed* end: II. i. 3. 4
the *aymed* marke which he had eyde: II. iv. 7. 5
The quivering steele his *aymed* end wel knew, II. iv. 46. 3
ere the stroke could seize his *aymed* place, III. vii. 40. 3
at him his beam-like speare he *aimed*, IV. iv. 24. 1
With dreadfull weapon *aymed* at his head, IV. viii. 41. 7
ere they come unto their *aymed* scope, VI. iii. 5. 3

Aiming. th' other, *ayming* better, did him smite Full in the shield VI. vi. 8. 1
Ayming his arrow at my very hart: *Am.* xvi. 10

Air. With Balmelike odor did perfume the *aire*. *Bel.*[1] ix. 4
birdes from *aire* descending downe *Rev.* iii. 9
tumbling through the *ayre* (*aire*[1]) *Bel.* vii. 10
with black horror did the *ayre* appall: *Bel.*[2] viii. 4
With balmie odours fil'd th' *ayre* farre and nie. *Bel.*[2] xi. 4
sperst in the *aire* The weake foundations *Bel.*[2] xiv. 13

Air—*Continued.*
sudden storme did so turmoyle the *aire*, . . . *Pet.* ii. 7
sharped steeples high shot up in *ayre;* . . . *Ro.* ii. 2
earthly vapours gathered in the *ayre*, . . . *Ro.* xx. 2
The simple *ayre*, the gentle warbling wynde, . . . *S.C.* Jun. 4
with gentle murmure of the breathing *ayre*, . . . *Gn.* 186
With brandisht tongue the emptie *aire* did gride, . . . *Gn.* 254
A litle noursling of the humid *ayre*, . . . *Gn.* 282
tost in th' *ayre* with everie windie blast: . . . *Gn.* 334
made him meat for wild foules of the *ayre*. . . . *Gn.* 380
let the flitting *aire* my vaine words sever.' . . . *Gn.* 638
Corrupted had th' *ayre* with his noysome breath, . . . *Hub.* 7
as a thistle-downe in th' *ayre* doth flie, . . . *Hub.* 634
Pierce the dull heavens and fill the *ayer* wide, . . . *T.M.* 118
monstrous error, flying in the *ayre*, . . . *T.M.* 257
doo possesse the Empire of the *aire*, . . . *Mui.* 18
In the wide *aire* to make her wandring flight; . . . *Mui.* 139
To raine in th' *aire* from th' earth to highest skie, . . . *Mui.* 212
The sea, the *aire*, the fire, the day, the night, . . . *Mui.* 228
In bloodie streames foorth fled into the *aire*, . . . *Mui.* 439
I walkt abroade to breath the freshing *ayre* . . . *D.* 26
'What man henceforth that breatheth vitall *ayre* . . . *D.* 197
th' *ayre* be filled with noyse of dolefull knells, . . . *D.* 335
I hate the *Ayre*, because sighes of it be; . . . *D.* 405
Shot her sharp pointed beames through purest *aire*. . . . *As.* 58
He, making speedy way through spersed *ayre*, . . . I. i. 39. 1
fram'd of liquid *ayre* her tender partes, . . . I. i. 45. 3
he spred A seeming body of the subtile *aire*, . . . I. ii. 3. 3
Morning . . . Had spred her purple robe through deawy *aire*, I. ii. 7. 3
Or guilefull spright wandring in empty *aire*, . . . I. ii. 32. 6
forth they marchen . . . To take the solace of the open *aire*, I. iv. 37. 2
Phoebus . . . hurld his glistring beams through gloomy *ayre*. . I. v. 2. 5
Through widest *ayre* making his ydle way, . . . I. v. 8. 4
all the *ayre* it fills, . . . I. v. 16. 9
Through mirkesome *aire* her ready way she makes; . . . I. v. 28. 3
their noise which through the *aire* was thrown, . . . I. vi. 45. 8
This nymph, quite tyr'd with heat of scorching *ayre*, . . . I. vii. 5. 3
all the *ayre* doth choke, That none can breath, . . . I. vii. 13. 6
steed . . . under him did trample as the *aire*, . . . I. vii. 37. 7
scourging th' emptie *ayre* with his long trayne, . . . I. viii. 17. 3
The light . . . Such blazing brightnesse through the *ayer* threw, I. viii. 19. 4
all the *ayre* with terror filled wyde, . . . I. xi. 4. 2
whenas him list the *ayre* to beat, . . . I. xi. 10. 6
all the *ayre* about with smoke and stench did fill. . . . I. xi. 13. 9
The yielding *ayre*, which nigh too feeble found Her flitting parts, . . . I. xi. 18. 4
therewith scourge the buxome *aire* so sore, . . . I. xi. 37. 6
none that breatheth living *aire* does know . . . II. Pr. 1. 6
shee gan to breath out living *aire*. . . . II. i. 43. 9
Gan cleare the deawy *ayre* . . . II. iii. 1. 4
Unworthie of the commune breathed *ayre*, . . . II. iii. 7. 5
for heat of scorching *aire*, . . . II. iii. 26. 3
Sometimes she song as lowd as larke in *ayre*, . . . II. vi. 3. 3
how the fowles in *aire* Doe flocke, . . . II. vi. 28. 7
One with great bellowes gathered filling *ayre*, . . . II. vii. 36. 1
Gan sucke this vitall *ayre* into his brest, . . . II. vii. 66. 6
in the *aire* their clustring army flies, . . . II. ix. 16. 4
Remounts againe into the open *ayre*, . . . II. xi. 36. 8
the milde *ayre* with season moderate . . . II. xii. 51. 7
do not in th' *ayre* more lightly flee. . . . II. xii. 77. 9
the cleare *ayre* engroste, . . . III. iv. 13. 2
through the raine Of the wide *ayre* . . . III. iv. 49. 5
All suddeinly dim wox the dampish *ayre*, . . . III. iv. 52. 1
soone as calmed was the christall *ayre*, . . . III. v. 51. 8
with plumy wings doth sheare The subtile *ayre* . . . III. vii. 39. 4
th' open freshnes of the gentle *aire*, . . . III. viii. 11. 4
th' *ayre* was milde and cleared was the skie, . . . III. viii. 21. 5
through the persant *aire* shoote forth their azure streames. . . III. ix. 20. 9
as a thonder bolt Perceth the yielding *ayre*, . . . III. xi. 25. 7
with wide winges to beat the buxome *ayre:* . . . III. xi. 34. 2
On whom he got faire Pegasus that flitteth in the *ayre*. . . III. xi. 42. 9
in the ydle *ayre* he mov'd still here and theare. . . . III. xii. 8. 9
Ne into *ayre* did vanish presently, . . . IV. iii. 13. 4
Through the wide region of the wastfull *aire*, . . . IV. viii. 8. 8
fire devoure the *ayre*, and hell them quight, . . . IV. x. 35. 6
queene of th' *ayre*, . . . IV. x. 47. 7
of the fire one ballaunce make, And one of th' *ayre*, . . . V. ii. 31. 4
so did the fire the *aire;* . . . V. ii. 32. 4
they with *aire*, that not a drop can slide: . . . V. ii. 35. 8
Her goodly bow, which paints the liquid *ayre*, . . . V. iii. 25. 3
Soring through his wide Empire of the *aire* . . . V. iv. 42. 2
through the *aire* doth beare; . . . V. vi. 40. 5
the change of *aire* and place Would change her paine, . . . V. vii. 45. 3
lends unto it leave the emptie *ayre* to beat. . . . V. xii. 18. 9
all the *aire* rebellowed againe, . . . V. xii. 41. 6
To take the *ayre* and heare the thrushes song, . . . VI. iv. 17. 3
glyding through the *ayre* lights all the heavens darke. . . . VI. vii. 7. 9
did the *ayre* with terror fill, . . . VI. viii. 46. 3
she past the region of the *ayre* And of the fire, . . . VII. vi. 7. 6
'Next is the *Ayre;* . . . VII. vii. 22. 1
On thing so tickle as th' unsteady *ayre*, . . . VII. vii. 22. 6
Fire to *Ayre*, and th' *Ayre* to Water sheere, . . . VII. vii. 25. 6
Water fights With Fire, and *Ayre* with Earth, . . . VII. vii. 25. 8
Juno, of the *ayre;* . . . VII. vii. 26. 6
Not *ayre;* for she is not so light or rare: . . . *Am.* lv. 7
Like a vaine bubble blowen up with *ayre:* . . . *Am.* lviii. 6
The earth, the *ayre*, the water, and the fyre, . . . *H.L.* 78
Ayre hated earth, and water hated fyre, . . . *H.L.* 83
Then th' *Aire* still flitting, but yet firmely bounded . . . *H.H.B.* 38
Ayre more then water . . . appeares more pure and fayre. . . *H.H.B.* 48

Air—*Continued.*
fire much more then *ayre* . . . appeares more pure and fayre. . *H.H.B.* 48
enlumineth the darke And dampish *aire*, whereby al things are red; . . . *H.H.B.* 165
through the trembling *ayre* Sweete-breathing Zephyrus did softly play . . . *Proth.* 1

Air-cutting. With his *aire-cutting* wings he measured wide, . . *Mui.* 154

Airy. All which the *ayrie* Echo did resound. . . . *Gn.* 232
Through the wide compas of the *ayrie* coast; . . . *Mui.* 38
an Eagle, . . . His *aery* plumes doth rouze, . . . I. xi. 9. 6
From off the earth take his *aerie* flight. . . . II. iii. 19. 5
fixed at his backe to cut his *ayery* wayes. . . . II. viii. 5. 9
aery spirite under false pretence, . . . II. xi. 39. 8
Was from her fled as flit as *ayery* Dove, . . . III. vi. 11. 4
nothing left but like an *aery* Spright, . . . III. x. 57. 4
guyded through th' *ayrie* wyde By some bad spirit . . . V. viii. 34. 6
ayry Towers upraised much more high. . . . *Com. Son.* iv. 4

Alabaster. The chapters *Alablaster* (*Alabaster*[1]), . . . *Bel.* iv. 3
Alabaster throughly taught In all this skill, . . . *Col.* 400
In whose white *alabaster* brest did stick . . . II. i. 39. 5
Ascending by ten steps of *Alablaster* wrought. . . . II. ix. 44. 9
hid no whit her *alablaster* skin, . . . II. xii. 77. 5
Her *alablaster* brest she soft did kis, . . . III. ii. 42. 7
Her yvorie neck; her *alablaster* brest; . . . VI. viii. 42. 1

Alack. layd him downe, and groned, '*Alack! Alack!* . . . *S.C.* May 246

Aladine. And Aldus was his name; and his sonnes, *Aladine*. . VI. iii. 3. 9
The lusty *Aladine*, though meaner borne . . . VI. iii. 7. 6
The gentle *Aladine* did earst invade, . . . VI. iii. 8. 4
Of which occasion *Aldine* taking hold . . . VI. iii. 15. 1

Alaid. *See* **Allayed.**

Alanus. it transferd to *Alane*, . . . VII. vii. 9. 6
Go seek he out that *Alane* where he may be sought. . . . VII. vii. 9. 9

Alarm. *See* **Larum-bell.**
So both together give a new *allarme*, . . . IV. iv. 35. 4
Did them assault with terrible *allarme;* . . . V. xi. 58. 3
Whereat they shouted all, and made a loud *alarme*. . . . VI. viii. 45. 9

Alarms. love does give his sweet *Alarmes* Without bloodshed, . II. vi. 34. 7
With which he wont to stirre up battailous *alarmes*. . . . V. v. 21. 9
being waked with these loud *alarmes*, . . . VI. viii. 47. 7
doth sound on hie Warres and *allarums* . . . VII. vi. 3. 8
al the world, fil'd with thy wide *Alarmes*, . . . *Proth.* 158

Alas (*partial list*).
Alas, this world doth nought but grievance hold! . . . *Bel.* iii. 12
where she, *alas*, opprest, Fell . . . *Pet.* i. 11
she (*alas*) Strake on a rock, . . . *Pet.* ii. 8
Phoenix there *alas*, Spying the tree destroid, . . . *Pet.* v. 8
Alas! by little ye to nothing flie, . . . *Ro.* vii. 7
pale and wanne he was, (*alas* the while!) . . . *S.C.* Ja. 8
And yet, *alas!* but now my spring begonne, And yet, *alas!* yt is already donne. . . . *S.C.* Ja. 29, 30
(*alas!* why doe I love?) . . . (*alas!* why am I lorne?) . . *S.C.* Ja. 61, 62
'Sicke, sicke, *alas!* and . . . *S.C.* May 264
Dido, my deare, *alas!* is dead, . . . *S.C.* N. 58
(small joy to him, *alas!*) . . . *Ti.* 652
Both wise and hardie, (too hardie, *alas!*) . . . *As.* 72
'how should, *alas!* Silly old man, . . . I. i. 30. 5
from his wound yet welled fresh, *alas!* . . . I. ix. 36. 7
'I Pilate am, the falsest Judge, *alas!* . . . II. vii. 62. 3
'Long lackt, *alas!* Hath bene . . . II. viii. 7. 3
(love far sought *alas!*) . . . III. i. 8. 8
'*Alas!* for pittie that so faire a crew, . . . IV. v. 18. 3
slaine her children ruefully, *alas!* . . . V. x. 6. 9
'Die? out *alas!*' then Calidore did cry, . . . VI. xi. 29. 5
alasse, he cryde, and wel-away! . . . *Epig.* iv. 27

Alba. in long *Alba* plast his throne apart; . . . III. ix. 43. 7

Albanactus. *Albanact* had all the Northerne part, . . . II. x. 14. 2

Albanese-wise. sleeves dependaunt *Albanese-wyse:* . . . III. xii. 10. 4

Albania. part, Which of himselfe *Albania* he did call; . . . II. x. 14. 3
A private life ledd in *Albania* With Gonorill, . . . II. x. 29. 7
This of *Albany* newly nominate, . . . II. x. 38. 4
Twede, the limit betwixt Logris land And *Albany:* . . . IV. xi. 36. 7

Albany. *See* **Albania.**

Albe. *Albee* my love he seeke with dayly suit; . . . *S.C.* Ja. 56
albee rude Pan thou please, . . . *S.C.* Ja. 67
Albee forswonck and forswatt I am. . . . *S.C.* Apr. 99
I am a poore sheepe, *albe* my coloure donne, . . . *S.C.* May 266
I play to please myselfe, *all be* it ill. . . . *S.C.* Jun. 72
Albe he envie at my rustick quill: . . . *Col.* 393
Albe of love I alwayes humbly deemed, . . . *Col.* 828
albee his woundes wyde . . . unready were to ryde. . . . I. v. 45. 4
Albe Charissa were their chiefest founderesse. . . . I. x. 44. 9
albe the knight her much did pray. . . . II. vi. 4. 9
albe his drowsy den were next; . . . II. vii. 25. 6
The trespass still doth live, *albee* the person dye.' . . . II. viii. 28. 9
their praises speake, *all be* they loth, . . . II. x. 40. 7
Albe her guiltlesse conscience her cleard, . . . III. vi. 10. 2
All be he subject to mortalitie, . . . III. vi. 47. 4
eke my selfe, *albee* I simple such, . . . III. x. 28. 8
Albe the wound were nothing deepe imprest, . . . III. xii. 33. 7
albee in face And outward shew faire semblance they did beare; IV. i. 17. 5
Albee in heart he like affection fond, . . . IV. i. 34. 3
Albee untrue she wist them by assay. . . . IV. i. 50. 5
Albee his turne were next; . . . IV. iv. 20. 3
Albe that Hatred was thereto full loth, . . . IV. x. 33. 3
Albe they endlesse seeme in estimation, . . . IV. xii. 1. 6
albee he rich or poore, . . . V. ii. 6. 3
albe all love of men she scorne, . . . V. v. 40. 7
albe he wanted sence And sorrowes feeling, . . . V. vi. 9. 4
left his love, *albe* her strong request, . . . V. viii. 3. 4

Albe—*Continued.*
Albe that it most safety to him gave, . . . V. xi. 46. 5
albe he earst did wyte His wavering mind, . . . V. xi. 57. 6
Albe his Lady, . . . did reprove, . . . VI. iii. 42. 6
Albe that Dame, by all the meanes she might, . . . VI. iv. 39. 5
Albe the wyld-man hardly would refraine. . . . VI. v. 27. 5
Albe the stroke so strong and puissant were, . . . VI. viii. 16. 2
Albe with all their might those Brigants her did keepe. . . . VI. xi. 23. 9
albe he saw them all asleepe. . . . VI. xi. 37. 9
Albe that . . . The good Sir Pelleas him tooke in hand, . . . VI. xii. 39. 5
Albe they worthy blame, or cleare of crime: . . . VI. xii. 40. 6
what ye do, *albe* it good or ill. . . . *Epith.* 367
beautie, *albe* heavenly borne, Is foule abusd, . . . *H.B.* 149
Albeit. I play to please myselfe, *all be it* ill. . . . *S.C.* Jun. 72
albeit his owne deare Squire he were, . . . IV. vii. 43. 5
Albion. namd it ALBION: . . . II. x. 6. 7
that huge sonne of hideous *Albion,* . . . II. x. 11. 6
Albion had conquered first by warlike feat.' . . . III. ix. 46. 9
mightie *Albion,* father of the bold And warlike people . . . IV. xi. 15. 8
Albion the sonne of Neptune was, . . . IV. xi. 16. 1
Out of his *Albion* did on dry-foot pas Into old Gall, . . . IV. xi. 16. 3
Alcestis. 'There chast *Alceste* lives inviolate, . . . *Gn.* 425
Alcides. Thinke him *Alcides* with the Lyons skin, . . . *Mui.* 71
the Lyon, which with toyle *Alcides* slew, . . . *D.* 166
that renowmed Snake Which great *Alcides* in Stremona slew, . I. vii. 17. 2
t' Olympick Jove, And to his sonne *Alcides,* . . . II. v. 31. 4
lad, . . . so deare To great *Alcides,* . . . III. xii. 7. 6
torne in pieces by *Alcides* great; . . . V. viii. 31. 4
That great *Alcides* whilome overthrew, . . . VI. xii. 32. 2
Alcides'. may emongst *Alcides* labours stand.' . . . III. vii. 61. 4
under great *Alcides* furie fell; . . . IV. i. 23. 5
after that his monstrous father fell Under *Alcides* club, . . . V. x. 11. 3
Alcluid. from *Alcluid* to Panwelt did that border bownd. . . II. x. 63. 9
Alcmena. As when his Syre with *Alcumena* lay. . . . *Hub.* 1299
the puissant brood Of golden girt *Alcmena,* . . . *Ti.* 380
faire *Alcmena* better match did make, . . . III. xi. 33. 6
Lyke as when Jove with fayre *Alcmena* lay, . . . *Epith.* 328
Alcon. there is pleasing *Alcon,* . . . *Col.* 394
Alcon's. Imagery of Baetus or of *Alcons* vanity . . . *Gn.* 104
Alcumena. *See* **Alcmena.**
Alcyon. Even sad *Alcyon,* whose empierced brest . . . *D.* 6
Most like *Alcyon* seeming at a glaunce; . . . *D.* 53
Alcyon he, the jollie Shepheard swaine . . . *D.* 54
I softlie sayd, *Alcyon!* . . . *D.* 58
Then stay, *Alcyon,* gentle shepheard! . . . *D.* 68
'Certes, *Alcyon,* painfull is thy plight, . . . *D.* 174
"*Alcyon!* ah, my first and latest love! . . . *D.* 263
Ah! why does my *Alcyon* weepe and mourne, . . . *D.* 264
Why should *Alcyon* then so sore lament . . . *D.* 271
sad *Alcyon* dyde in lifes disdaine. . . . *D.* 525
there is sad *Alcyon* bent to mourne, . . . *Col.* 384
Aldeboran. when *Aldeboran* was mounted hye . . . I. iii. 16. 1
Alder. A yong *alder* hard beside him pight, . . . *Gn.* 299
Alders. the cooly shade Of the greene *alders* . . . *Col.* 59
Aldine. *See* **Aladine.**
Aldus. And *Aldus* was his name; . . . VI. iii. 3. 9
Alebion. *See* **Alebius.**
Alebius. *Alebius,* that know'th The waters depth, . . . IV. xi. 14. 7
Alege. *See* **Allege.**
Alemaine. *See* **Almain.**
Alew. *See* **Halloo.**
Alexander. which *Alexander* did confound; . . . II. ix. 45. 7
Of *Alexander,* and his Princes five . . . IV. i. 22. 8
Alexis. *Alexis* broke his tale asunder, . . . *Col.* 352
(said *Alexis* then) . . . *Col.* 368
Algate. *See* **Algates.**
Algates. But if thou *algate* lust light virelayes, . . . *S.C.* N. 21
either (*algates*) would be Lords alone; . . . *Hub.* 1025
Sith Una now he *algates* must forgoe . . . II. i. 2. 5
algates mote he soft himselfe appease, . . . II. ii. 12. 2
he would *algates* with Pyrochles fight, . . . II. v. 20. 2
for he would *algates* fight: . . . II. v. 37. 9
him restor'd to helth that would have *algates* dyde. . . . II. vi. 51. 9
she mote *algates* dye: . . . III. i. 53. 6
they for love of him would *algates* dy: . . . III. iv. 26. 8
that Squyre unknowne Mote *algates* passe: . . . III. v. 17. 6
on foot mote *algates* fare . . . III. vii. 4. 1
would have *algates* riv'd The hart out of his brest: . . . III. viii. 3. 5
if ought *algate* Might fayrer be. . . . III. viii. 9. 5
May her perhaps containe, that else would *algates* fleet.' . . III. ix. 7. 9
Mercie . . . give, That he mote *algates* dye, . . . III. x. 7. 9
to alight on foote her *algates* did compell: . . . IV. vi. 13. 9
Save that she *algates* him a while accompanide. . . . IV. vi. 44. 9
Guyon would him *algates* have perforse, . . . V. iii. 30. 4
Yet mote he *algates* now abide, . . . V. viii. 5. 9
if ye *algates* covet to assay This simple sort of life . . . VI. ix. 33. 7
Algrind. (as *Algrind* used to say) . . . *S.C.* May 75
(as I have heard Old *Algrind* often sayne) . . . *S.C.* Jul. 126
Sike one (sayd *Algrind*) Moses was, . . . *S.C.* Jul. 157
say me, what is *Algrind,* (*Algrin) . . . *S.C.* Jul. 213
Ah! good *Algrind!* his hap was ill, . . . *S.C.* Jul. 229
Algrind's. I am taught, by *Algrinds* (*Algrins) ill, . . . *S.C.* Jul. 219
Alight. There they *alight,* in hope themselves to hide . . . I. ii. 29. 8
From her unhastie beast she did *alight;* . . . I. iii. 4. 2
The heavie hap which on them is *alight;* . . . I. iii. 20. 8
Night arriving did *alight* From her nigh weary wayne, . . . I. v. 41. 1
I did *alight* From loftie steed, . . . I. ix. 13. 1
fast before the king he did *alight;* . . . I. xii. 25. 5
forst t' *alight,* on foot mote algates fare . . . III. vii. 4. 1
the Boaster from his loftie sell Faynd to *alight,* . . . III. x. 38. 6
to *alight* on foote her algates did compell: . . . IV. vi. 13. 9
to *alight* on foote her algates did compell: . . . IV. vi. 13. 9
both wearie of the way We did *alight,* . . . IV. vi. 36. 3
T' *alight,* and rest their wearie limbs awhile. . . . IV. vii. 3. 6
The Lady to *alight* did eft require, . . . V. i. 21. 3
he bad me by and by For to *alight:* . . . VI. ii. 17. 6
on foote *alight* To justifie thy fault . . . VI. iii. 35. 8
did *alite* Upon the fruitfull earth, . . . VII. vi. 20. 8
Alighted. The noble knight *alighted* . . . From loftie steed, . I. viii. 2. 7
Now had the Carle *Alighted* from his Tigre, . . . II. xi. 33. 7
alighted from her light-foot beast, . . . III. iv. 7. 1
Alighting. Is now no more seen flying, nor *alighting.* . . . *Ro.* xvii. 14
There she *alighting* fell before her feet, . . . IV. viii. 9. 5
There they *alighting* by that Damzell were Directed in, . . V. ix. 22. 1
Alike. both milder beasts and fiercer foes *Alike* . . . devoure. *Bel.*[2] viii. 8
Ylike to my flocke and thine; . . . *S.C.* Mar. 39
Ylike as others, girt in gawdy greene? . . . *S.C.* May 4
live *ylike* as men of the laye. . . . *S.C.* May 76
Ylike as a Monster of many heads; . . . *S.C.* S. 121
ylike to me was libertee and lyfe. . . . *S.C.* D. 36
all be brethren *ylike* dearly bought: . . . *Hub.* 142
when both *alike* are dedd; . . . *T.M.* 448
all mens states *alike* unstedfast be. . . . *D.* 518
right and wrong *ylike* in equall balaunce waide. . . . I. iv. 27. 9
'what oddes can ever bee, Where both doe fight *alike,* . . . I. iv. 50. 4
both *alike,* when death hath both suppress, . . . II. i. 59. 5
Both slow and swift *alike* do serve my tourne; . . . II. vi. 10. 6
light *ylike* is loth'd of them and thee; . . . III. iv. 58. 8
fled Ever *alike,* . . . III. vii. 2. 5
nets dispred, With which he . . . many had *ylike* misled: . . III. x. 9. 8
For her, that each of you *alike* doth loth, . . . IV. i. 47. 4
Triamond was stout and strong *alike:* . . . IV. ii. 42. 3
So all *alike* did love, and loved were, . . . IV. iii. 52. 8
So both together, *ylike* felly bent, Like fiercely met. . . V. viii. 7. 5
Of good and bad *alike,* of low and hie, . . . VI. xii. 28. 6
heaven and earth I both *alike* do deeme, . . . VII. vii. 15. 6
Sith heaven and earth are both *alike* to thee, . . . VII. vii. 15. 7
Alimeda. *See* **Halimede.**
Alite. *See* **Alight.**
Alive. shrilling voyce of wight *alive* . . . *Ro.* i. 5
yet *alive* art founde? . . . *S.C.* D. 96
Yet manie Poets honourd him *alive.* . . . *Ti.* 224
'What booteth it to have been rich *alive?* . . . *Ti.* 351
whilome was *alive* the wisest wight: . . . *Ti.* 445
Nor *alive* nor dead be of the Muse adorned! . . . *Ti.* 455
Of all *alive* did seeme the fairest wight. . . . *Mui.* 24
(I weene), the wofulst man *alive,* . . . *D.* 5
To plague th' unrighteous which *alive* remaine; . . . *D.* 359
To whom *alive* was nought so deare as hee: . . . *As.* 128
That us, late dead, has made againe *alive:* . . . *Col.* 31
eke to make the dead againe *alive.* . . . *Col.* 599
Be witnesse of her bountie here *alive,* . . . *Col.* 646
He, tumbling downe *alive,* . . . his mother earth did kis, . I. ii. 19. 5
he is one the truest knight *alive,* . . . I. iii. 37. 6
unto hell did thrust him downe *alive,* . . . I. v. 40. 5
calles to mind his pourtraiture *alive,* . . . I. vi. 17. 3
resolving him to find *Alive* or dead; . . . I. vii. 28. 3
Old Timon, . . . In warlike feates th' expertest man *alive,* . I. ix. 4. 3
Archimago . . . The falsest man *alive:* . . . I. xii. 34. 9
Great and most glorious virgin Queene *alive,* . . . II. ii. 40. 3
the best and noblest knight *alive* Prince Arthur is, . . . II. iii. 18. 3
'That am, I weene, most wretched man *alive;* . . . II. vi. 45. 2
yonder comes the prowest knight *alive,* . . . II. viii. 18. 3
may not hope by flight to scape *alive,* . . . II. viii. 50. 3
By Phoebus doome the wisest thought *alive,* . . . II. ix. 48. 2
Proofe be thou, Prince, the prowest man *alyve,* . . . II. xi. 30. 6
gaping wide to swallow them *alyve* . . . II. xii. 5. 7
A place pickt out by choyce of best *alyve,* . . . II. xii. 42. 3
Most goodly meede, the fairest Dame *alive:* . . . III. i. 18. 8
fairest knight *alive,* when armed was her brest. . . . III. ii. 4. 9
alive The dreary image of sad death appeares: . . . III. iv. 57. 6
she is the fairest wight *alive,* I trow.' . . . III. v. 5. 9
Till him *alive* or dead she did invent. . . . III. v. 10. 4
alive Out of that forest should escape their might: . . . III. v. 16. 7
Now God thee keepe, thou gentlest squire *alive,* . . . III. v. 26. 6
I enjoyd the gentlest Dame *alive;* . . . III. x. 27. 2
'Ah! gentlest knight *alive,*' . . . III. xi. 19. 1
best is lov'd of all *alive,* . . . IV. Pr. 4. 7
shar'd to him the spoiles that he had got *alive.* . . . IV. i. 22. 9
Whose like *alive* on earth he weened not: . . . IV. ii. 8. 5
none *alive* but joy'd in Florimell, . . . IV. ii. 23. 2
That none durst ever whilest thou wast *alive,* . . . IV. ii. 34. 4
vassall to the vilest wretch *alive,* . . . IV. vii. 12. 2
Ne ever thing so well was doen *alive,* . . . IV. viii. 25. 8
lov'd me deare, as dearest thing *alive.* . . . IV. viii. 56. 6
made it so to ride as it *alive* was found. . . . IV. ix. 4. 9
save all us three *alive.*' . . . IV. xii. 31. 9
she rather should with him remaine *Alive,* . . . V. i. 27. 6
'Clarinda, whom of all I trust *alive,* . . . V. v. 29. 4
The justest man *alive* and truest did appeare. . . . V. vii. 2. 9
else he sure had left not one *alive,* . . . V. vii. 36. 8
The fayrest kyne *alive,* but of the fiercest kynd: . . . V. x. 9. 9
'Haile, good Sir Sergis, truest Knight *alive,* . . . V. xi. 38. 2
they the mildest man *alive* would make Forget his patience, . V. xii. 42. 3
alive or dead Her foe deliver up . . . VI. i. 31. 5
whether he *alive* be to be found, . . . VI. v. 28. 7
few of them he left *alive,* . . . VI. vi. 24. 2
If yet he were *alive,* or to destruction brought. . . . VI. vi. 37. 9
Upon the rest that did *alive* remaine; . . . VI. vi. 38. 4
Pastorell, were she *alive* or slaine: . . . VI. xi. 39. 4

All—*Continued.*
all he did was to deceive good knights, . . . II. i. 23. 1
Wherewith above *all* knights ye goodly seeme aguizd! . . . II. i. 31. 9
all I did, I did but as I ought. . . . II. i. 33. 5
spred his glory through *all* countryes wide. . . . II. i. 35. 4
That *all* her goodly garments staind arownd, . . . II. i. 39. 8
armour *all* with blood besprincled was; . . . II. i. 41. 3
all his sences seemd berefte attone: . . . II. i. 42. 4
all in bright armour clad, . . . II. i. 45. 4
Have not *all* seized on your frozen hart, . . . II. i. 46. 6
all I seeke is but to have redrest . . . II. i. 48. 4
so far *all* sence they pas. . . . II. i. 49. 6
(*all* flesh doth frayltie breed) . . . II. i. 52. 6
ended *all* her woe in quiet death. . . . II. i. 56. 4
For *all* so great shame after death I weene, . . . II. i. 59. 8
he cutt a lock of *all* their heare, . . . II. i. 61. 2
nought they beene For *all* his washing cleaner. . . . II. ii. 3. 6
be for *all* chaste Dames an endlesse moniment.' . . . II. ii. 10. 9
all this while were at their wanton rest, . . . II. ii. 16. 4
was, for terrour more, *all* armd in shyning bras. . . . II. ii. 17. 9
all to lawlesse lust encouraged . . . II. ii. 18. 5
all on uprore . . . II. ii. 20. 6
The house was raysd, and *all* that in did dwell. . . . II. ii. 20. 7
All for their Ladies froward love to gaine, . . . II. ii. 26. 4
pleasd them *all* with meete satiety. . . . II. ii. 39. 2
Drawing to him the eies of *all* arownd, . . . II. ii. 39. 8
All Faery lond does peaceably sustene. . . . II. ii. 40. 5
over *all* the earth it may be seene, . . . II. ii. 40. 7
In her the richesse of *all* heavenly grace . . . II. ii. 41. 1
all, that els this worlds enclosure bace Hath great . . . II. ii. 41. 3
That may this day in *all* the world be found. . . . II. ii. 42. 5
all knights of worth and courage bold . . . II. ii. 42. 8
Me, *all* unfitt for so great purpose, . . . II. ii. 43. 9
all that gentle noriture ensu'th; . . . II. iii. 2. 5
Now gan his hart *all* swell in jollity, . . . II. iii. 5. 1
all suddeinly he seemd enragd, . . . II. iii. 14. 1
Should neede of *all* his armes him to defend, . . . II. iii. 17. 4
All good and honour might therein be red, . . . II. iii. 24. 5
All in a silken Camus lilly whight, . . . II. iii. 26. 4
all above besprinckled was . . . II. iii. 26. 6
all the skirt about Was hemd with golden fringe. . . . II. iii. 26. 8
All bard with golden bendes, . . . II. iii. 27. 4
therein entrayld The ends of *all* the knots, . . . II. iii. 27. 8
all the people decke with girlands greene, . . . II. iii. 28. 3
Where *all* the Nymphes have her unwares forlore, . . . II. iii. 31. 3
well may thee befall, As *all* the like, . . . II. iii. 37. 7
All vertue merits praise, but such the most of *all.'* . . . II. iii. 37. 9
Therein I have spent *all* my youthly daies, . . . II. iii. 38. 4
happy blis And *all* delight does raigne, . . . II. iii. 39. 5
her dores to *all* stand open wide. . . . II. iii. 41. 9
her sweete words that *all* his sence dismayd, . . . II. iii. 42. 3
all might see He had not trayned bene . . . II. iii. 46. 4
Grew *all* afore, and loosely hong unrold; . . . II. iv. 4. 6
all behinde was bald, . . . II. iv. 4. 7
all on fire streight way, . . . II. iv. 6. 5
Against him turning *all* his fell intent, . . . II. iv. 6. 6
Knitt *all* his forces, . . . II. iv. 9. 7
Occasion; the roote of *all* wrath and despight. . . . II. iv. 10. 9
all his power was utterly defaste, . . . II. iv. 14. 3
all soild with blood and myre: . . . II. iv. 16. 4
Of *all* my sorrow and of these sad teares, . . . II. iv. 18. 2
Of *all* my love and *all* my privitie; . . . II. iv. 20. 2
he now had boulted *all* the floure, . . . II. iv. 24. 2
Did *all* she might more pleasing to appeare. . . . II. iv. 25. 4
That it should not deface *all* others lesser light? . . . II. iv. 25. 9
faire Claribell with *all* her art, . . . II. iv. 26. 5
My hart, my handes, mine eies, and *all* assayd! . . . II. iv. 28. 7
chawing vengeaunce *all* the way I went, . . . II. iv. 29. 2
What bootes it *al* to have, and nothing use? . . . II. vi. 17. 6
'What art thou, man, (if man at *all* thou art) . . . II. vii. 7. 1
of my plenty poure out unto *all,* . . . II. vii. 8. 3
Honour, estate, and *all* this worldes good, . . . II. vii. 8. 6
At thy commaund lo! *all* these mountaines bee: . . . II. vii. 9. 2
All these may not suffise, . . . II. vii. 9. 4
Sheilds, steeds, and armes, and *all* things for thee meet, . . . II. vii. 11. 3
'*All* otherwise' (saide he) 'I riches read, . . . II. vii. 12. 1
deeme thee roote of *all* disquietnesse; . . . II. vii. 12. 2
Abusd her plenty . . . To *all* licentious lust, . . . II. vii. 16. 8
Take what thou please of *all* this surplusage; . . . II. vii. 18. 7
powre of *al* which them poursew.' . . . II. vii. 19. 9
All these before the gates of Pluto lay, . . . II. vii. 24. 1
with wonder *all* the way Did feed his eyes, . . . II. vii. 24. 3
Both roofe, and floore, and walls, were *all* of gold, . . . II. vii. 29. 1
In *all* that rowme was nothing to be seene . . . II. vii. 30. 1
All bard with double *bends,* . . . II. vii. 30. 3
all the grownd with sculs was scattered, . . . II. vii. 30. 6
all the wealth which is, or was of yore, . . . II. vii. 31. 7
Could gathered be through *all* the world arownd, . . . II. vii. 31. 8
the end, To which *al* men doe ayme, . . . II. vii. 32. 8
hundred fournaces *all* burning bright: . . . II. vii. 35. 5
To weet whence *all* the wealth . . . Proceeded, . . . II. vii. 38. 4
all thine ydle offers I refuse. . . . II. vii. 39. 2
All that I need I have: . . . II. vii. 39. 3
he himselfe was *all* of golden mould, . . . II. vii. 40. 7
made him scorne *all* creatures great and small, . . . II. vii. 41. 7
with his pride *all* others powre deface: . . . II. vii. 41. 8
that *all* men might it see: . . . II. vii. 45. 3
all that preace did rownd about her swell . . . II. vii. 46. 5
all by wrong waies for themselves prepard: . . . II. vii. 47. 5
Whom *all* that folke . . . Doe flock about, . . . II. vii. 48. 5

All—*Continued.*
all this worldes blis, For which ye men doe strive; . . . II. vii. 48. 8
loaden *all* with fruit as thick as it might bee. . . . II. vii. 53. 9
tree, So fayre and great that shadowed *all* the ground, . . . II. vii. 56. 2
'Most cursed of *all* creatures under skye, . . . II. vii. 59. 4
unto *all* that live in high degree, . . . II. vii. 60. 3
All which he did to do him deadly fall . . . II. vii. 64. 1
if he inclyned had at *all,* . . . II. vii. 64. 3
he was wary wise in *all* his way, . . . II. vii. 64. 6
But *all* so soone as his enfeebled spright . . . II. vii. 66. 5
all his sences were with deadly fit opprest. . . . II. vii. 66. 9
all his workes with mercy doth embrace, . . . II. viii. 1. 7
all for love, and nothing for reward. . . . II. viii. 2. 8
all the fields resounded with the ruefull cry. . . . II. viii. 3. 9
Two Paynim knights *al* armd as bright as skie, . . . II. viii. 10. 2
gold *al* is not that doth golden seeme; . . . II. viii. 14. 5
Ne *all* good knights that shake well speare and shield. . . . II. viii. 14. 6
The worth of *all* men by their end esteeme, . . . II. viii. 14. 7
Is sacrilege, and doth *all* sinnes exceed: . . . II. viii. 16. 5
all his sences drowned in deep sencelesse wave: . . . II. viii. 24. 9
all his seede the curse doth often cleave, . . . II. viii. 29. 4
Through *all* those foldes the steelehead passage wrought, . . . II. viii. 32. 7
all his armour steepe, . . . II. viii. 37. 4
all the forest quakes to heare him rore: . . . II. viii. 42. 7
quite disparted *all* the linked frame, . . . II. viii. 44. 7
all the sinnes wherewith his lewd life did abound. . . . II. viii. 45. 9
stony feare . . . *all* his sence dismayd, . . . II. viii. 46. 2
With that *all* desperate, as loathing light, . . . II. viii. 47. 1
Assembling *all* his force and utmost might, . . . II. viii. 47. 3
all attonce their malice forth do poure: . . . II. viii. 48. 7
casting wronges, and *all* revenge behind, . . . II. viii. 51. 3
all thy wronges will wipe out of my sovenaunce.' . . . II. viii. 51. 9
left his headlesse body bleeding *all* the place. . . . II. viii. 52. 9
Are not *all* knightes by oath bound . . . II. viii. 56. 4
Of *all* Gods workes which doe this worlde adorne, . . . II. ix. 1. 1
To serve that Queene with *al* my powre and might. . . . II. ix. 7. 4
I labour would to guide you through *al* Faery land.' . . . II. ix. 8. 9
gan Sir Guyon *all* the story shew, . . . II. ix. 9. 5
All threatning death, *all* in straunge manner armd; . . . II. ix. 13. 5
all so faire and fensible withall; . . . II. ix. 21. 3
All which compacted made a goodly Diapase. . . . II. ix. 22. 9
The one before, by which *all* in did pas, . . . II. ix. 23. 2
all armed bright In glistring steele, . . . II. ix. 26. 2
in the midst of *all* There placed was . . . II. ix. 29. 4
all things one, and one as nothing was, . . . II. xii. 34. 8
The gentle warbling wind low answered to *all.* . . . II. xii. 71. 9
All had he lost much blood . . . III. i. 21. 5
Al holding crosses in their hands on hye, . . . III. iii. 38. 6
Abode, to weet what end would come of *all.* . . . III. xii. 37. 6
All is his justly that *all* freely dealth. . . . IV. i. 6. 5
Might be my lucky lot; sith *all* by lot we hold. . . . IV. x. 4. 9
Al which the heavens containe, and in their courses guide. . . V. ii. 35. 9
To chalenge *all* in right of Florimell, . . . V. iii. 4. 8
to pay him with that one for *all:* . . . V. xi. 8. 6
Knights ought be true, and truth is one in *all:* . . . V. xi. 56. 8
running *all* with greedie joyfulnesse To faire Irena, . . . V. xii. 24. 5
Whose nature is to grieve and grudge at *all* . . . V. xii. 31. 2
Now *al* is done: bring home the bride againe; . . . *Epith.* 242
Poure out to *all* that wull, . . . *Epith.* 252
this worlds great frame, in which *al* things . . . *H.H.L.* 22
Wherewith he hath encompassed this *All.* . . . *H.H.B.* 42
through *all* Spaine did thunder, . . . *Proth.* 147
name may ring Through *al* the world, . . . *Proth.* 158
Allan. Gnats . . . Out of the fennes of *Allan* doe arise, . . . II. ix. 16. 2
All and some. th' armies of their creatures *all and some* . . . *Mui.* 229
they streight were vanisht *all and some;* . . . III. xii. 30. 4
Alla Turchesca. his behavior altogether was *Alla Turchesca,* *Hub.* 677
Allay. *See* **Allege.**
So Maro oft did Caesars cares *allay.* . . . *Ded. Son.* i. 8
sorrow . . . to *allay,* and calme her storming paine, . . . I. vii. 38. 5
Whose wrathfull wreakes them selves doe now *alay;* . . . I. viii. 43. 4
Did heale his woundes, and scorching heat *alay;* . . . I. xi. 50. 6
ought *allay* the storme of your despight, . . . II. viii. 27. 5
At length *allay,* and stint thy stormy strife, . . . III. iv. 8. 8
She bath'd her brest the boyling heat t' *allay;* . . . III. vi. 6. 7
Allayed. the anguish of his spright Some deale *alaid,* . . . *D.* 173
After his murdrous spoyles and bloudie rage *allayd.* . . . I. Pr. 3. 9
ever when his passion *allayd,* . . . IV. ii. 12. 6
soone *allayd* that Knights conceiv'd displeasure, . . . VI. iii. 22. 2
All be. *See* **Albe.**
All-concealing. Carried in clowdes of *all-concealing* night. . . *Hub.* 340
Allectus. him *Allectus* treacherously slew, . . . II. x. 57. 7
Allege. *See* **Allay.**
That shall *alegge* this bitter blast, . . . *S.C.* Mar. 5
With hope of thing that may *alegge* his smart; . . . III. ii. 15. 4
Allegeance. Of sorrow and despeyre without *aleggeaunce!* . . . III. v. 42. 9
Allegiance. *alleageance,* and fast fealty, Which I do owe unto
all womankynd, . . . I. iii. 1. 6
'Live, and *alleagaunce* owe To him . . . II. v. 13. 5
Alleluia. Sing, ye sweet Angels, *Alleluya* sing, . . . *Epith.* 240
Alleys. all within were pathes and *alleies* wide, . . . I. i. 7. 7
walkes and *alleyes* dight With divers trees . . . IV. x. 25. 1
All for. *All for* their Maister is lustlesse and old. . . . *S.C.* F. 84
All for thou lackest somedele their delight. . . . *S.C.* May 56
All for her shepheards bene beastly and blont. . . . *S.C.* S. 109
All for they holden shame of theyr cote: . . . *S.C.* S. 111
All for they casten too much of worlds care, . . . *S.C.* S. 114
All for they nould be buxome and bent. . . . *S.C.* S. 149
All for he did his devoyr belive! . . . *S.C.* S. 227
All for she Scudamore will not denay. . . . III. xi. 11. 5

All hail. *'All haile,* Sir knight! . . . II. iii. 37. 6
pacing fairely forth did bid *all haile,* . . . IV. iii. 46. 5
Cupid humbly came, And sayd to her; *'All hayle,* my mother!' *Epig.* iii. 3
Alliance. high *alliance* unto forren powre; . . . V. ix. 45. 6
Allied. noble mindes of yore *allyed* were, . . . I. ix. 1. 3
to him *allide* His daughter Genuiss' in marriage: . . . II. x. 52. 3
with so firme affection were *allyde,* . . . IV. ii. 43. 2
Allide with bands of mutuall couplement; . . . IV. iii. 52. 3
Allies. Ruddoc and proud Stater, both *allyes,* . . . II. x. 38. 3
likewise Should handle as the rest of her *allies,* . . . VII. vi. 30. 5
Allo. *Allo* hight, Broad-water called farre; . . . *Col.* 123
Or unto *Allo,* or to Mulla cleare: . . . *Col.* 302
Strong *Allo* tombling from Slewlogher steep, . . . IV. xi. 41. 8
Allot. Whom fortune for her husband would *allot:* . . . III. ii. 23. 6
her in mynde did to him selfe *allot.* . . . VI. xi. 4. 5
doe the seasons of the yeare *allot,* . . . *Epith.* 100
Allotted. To whom but little dowre *allotted* was: . . . V. iv. 9. 3
Allowance. with how small *allowaunce* . . . II. vii. 15. 3
Allowed. That to strange knight no better countenance *allowd.* I. iv. 15. 9
that first fayre Amoret Might be to her *allow'd,* . . . IV. i. 12. 3
Allthing. what thing on earth, that *all thing* breeds, . . . *T.M.* 43
Allure. bigger notes, that may thy sense *allure,* . . . *Gn.* 11
allure Chast Ladies eares to fantasies impure. . . . *Hub.* 819
The noble hearts to pleasures they *allure,* . . . *T.M.* 331
may *allure* the senses to delight, . . . *D.* 324
That may thy Muse and mates to mirth *allure.* . . . *Col.* 391
with delight Doth man *allure* for to enlarge his kynd; . . . *Col.* 872
sweetnesse doth *allure* the weaker sence . . . II. vi. 1. 3
For to *allure* fraile mind to carelesse ease: . . . II. vi. 13. 6
mote the passengers thereto *allure;* . . . II. xii. 12. 6
T' *allure* weake traveillers, . . . II. xii. 31. 9
offered faire guiftes t' *allure* her sight; . . . III. viii. 38. 7
She did *allure* with gifts and speaches milde . . . V. i. 6. 5
Did cast for to *allure* into her trap to fall. . . . V. v. 52. 9
Nought under heaven so strongly doth *allure* The sence of man, . . . V. viii. 1. 1
The peoples great compassion unto her *allure.* . . . V. ix. 38. 9
to *allure* such fondlings . . . unto their owne decay: . . . VI. vi. 42. 3
her to his love *allure,* . . . VI. x. 32. 8
t' *allure* me to thy side, . . . VII. vi. 34. 8
She to her love doth lookers eyes *allure;* . . . *Am.* xxi. 6
Mote soften it and to his will *allure:* . . . *Am.* li. 10
She doth *allure* me to mine owne decay, . . . *Am.* liii. 7
Allured. Whether *allured* with my pipes delight, . . . *Col.* 61
when thereto they might not be *allur'd,* . . . III. i. 1. 7
allur'd with close delight, . . . IV. iv. 16. 4
to disloyalty she will not be *allured.* . . . IV. x. 2. 9
those, whom she to pitie had *allured,* . . . V. ix. 39. 8
ne would unto his lore *Allured* be . . . V. xi. 61. 7
by slights *allur'd,* and to their purpose lad. . . . V. xii. 37. 9
Allur'd with myldnesse of the gentle wether . . . VI. iii. 23. 3
red Cherries from the tree, With which he her *allured,* . . . VII. vi. 43. 7
Allur'd a Dolphin him from death to ease. . . . *Am.* xxxviii. 4
That nether will for better be *allured,* . . . *Am.* lix. 3
Allurement. Through false *allurement* of that pleasing baite, . IV. Pr. 1. 7
sweet *allurement* of her lovely hew; . . . *Am.* xxxi. 10
Allurements. all her vaine *allurements* did forsake; . . . II. xii. 17. 4
with what sleights and sweet *allurements* she Entyst the Boy, III. i. 35. 1
Allurements'. by his false *allurements* wylie draft . . . IV. ii. 10. 4
Allures. to his part *allures,* and bribeth under hand. . . . V. viii. 18. 9
Alluring. *See* **Bees-alluring.**
a noyse *alluring* sleepe . . . *Bel.* xii. 7
Powres forth sweete odors and *alluring* sights; . . . *Mui.* 164
All were. none, *all were* it Jove his sire, Should boast . . . *Ro.* xi. 13
be envied, *All were* it of my foe, . . . *S.C.* May 58
All were they lustye as thou didst see, . . . *S.C.* S. 64
All were Elisa one of thilke same ring; . . . *S.C.* O. 53
All were my spirite heavie and diseased, . . . *Hub.* 40
All were I drown'd in carelesse quiet . . . *D.* 136
All were my self, through griefe, in deadly drearing. . . . *D.* 189
All were my notes but rude and roughly dight; . . . *Col.* 363
All were his earthly eien both blunt and bad, . . . I. x. 47. 3
All were she daily with himselfe in place, . . . I. xii. 23. 7
when Sir Guyon saw, *all were* he wroth, Yet algates . . . II. ii. 12. 1
Came with them eke, *all were* they wondrous loth, . . . II. ii. 34. 2
All were they borne of her owne native slime: . . . II. x. 9. 5
All were the wownd so wide and wonderous . . . II. xi. 38. 2
all were she loth; . . . II. xii. 57. 8
All were it Zeuxis or Praxiteles, . . . III. Pr. 2. 3
All were he wearie of his former paine; . . . III. i. 29. 4
that vile Hag, *all were* her whole delight In mischiefe, . . . III. vii. 9. 8
All were the beame in bignes like a mast, . . . III. vii. 40. 6
them dislodge, *all were* they liefe or loth; . . . III. ix. 13. 8
Sir Paridell, *all were* he deare; . . . III. x. 37. 2
ever were on earth, *all were* they set together . . . IV. x. 29. 9
all were he much renound For noble courage . . . V. viii. 36. 7
All which he did assault . . . *All were* they nigh an hundred V. viii. 50. 6
All were it to his mortall enemie, . . . VI. vii. 23. 4
all were they cleanest From blamefull blot, . . . VI. xii. 41. 3
All were she fraught with pride and impudence, . . . VII. vi. 25. 2
All were it, as the rest, but rudely writ? . . . *Am.* xxxiii. 8
pay the price, *all were* his debt extreeme. . . . *H.H.L.* 133
Ally. *See* **Re-ally.**
vertues like mote unto him *allye.* . . . II. i. 23. 9
Alma. in which Doth sober *Alma* dwell, . . . II. ix. Arg.
Alma she called was; a virgin bright, . . . II. ix. 18. 1
as *Alma* passed with her guestes, . . . II. ix. 26. 6
backe againe faire *Alma* led them right, . . . II. ix. 33. 5
Soone as the gracious *Alma* came in place, . . . II. ix. 36. 1
Till *Alma* him bespake: . . . II. ix. 43. 6

Alma—*Continued.*
counselled faire *Alma* how to governe well. . . . II. ix. 48. 9
Whom *Alma* having shewed to her guestes, . . . II. ix. 53. 1
Alma thence them led . . . II. ix. 54. 9
Crav'd leave of *Alma* and that aged sire . . . II. ix. 60. 8
gentle *Alma,* seeing it so late, . . . II. x. 77. 5
Alma, like a virgin Queene most bright, . . . II. xi. 2. 6
The Ferriman, as *Alma* had behight, . . . II. xi. 4. 2
eke the fayrest *Alma* mett him there . . . II. xi. 49. 3
Of the faire *Alma* greatly were procur'd . . . III. i. 1. 5
Almain. the brave warlicke brood of *Alemaine,* . . . *Ro.* xxxi. 7
Almighty. rayse His heavenly Muse, th' *Almightie* to adore. *Ro. Env.* 12
high Jove, in whose *almightie* hand . . . *Hub.* 1225
almightie Jove, . . . Hurles forth his thundring dart . . . I. viii. 9. 1
'Who life did limit by *almightie* doome,' . . . I. ix. 41. 6
Almightie God her gave such powre and puissaunce great. . I. x. 20. 9
Great God it planted . . . With his *Almighty* hand, . . . I. xi. 46. 8
Merlin made by his *almightie* art . . . II. viii. 20. 2
Eternall God, in his *almightie* powre, . . . III. v. 52. 1
first was spoken by th' *Almighty* Lord, . . . III. vi. 34. 5
even th' *Almightie* selfe she did maligne, . . . IV. i. 30. 2
As their *Almightie* maker first ordained, . . . IV. x. 35. 3
to praise th' *Almighty* that doth send it! . . . VI. ix. 21. 9
Hecate, in whose *almighty* hand He plac't all rule . . . VII. vi. 3. 3
Most wise, most holy, most *almightie* Spright! . . . *H.H.L.* 39
Th' *Almighty,* seeing their so bold assay, . . . *H.H.L.* 85
Vouchsafe then, O thou most *Almightie* Spright! . . . *H.H.B.* 8
Almighty's. th' *Almighties* bosome, where he nests; . . . *T.M.* 389
Angels waighting on th' *Almighties* chayre. . . . *T.M.* 510
As where th' *Almighties* lightning brond does light, . . . I. viii. 21. 8
By righteous sentence of th' *Almighties* law. . . . I. ix. 50. 4
to be th' *Almighties* see; . . . IV. x. 30. 7
Goddesse, that doest highest sit . . . in th' *Almighties* stead, V. Pr. 11. 2
Sith in th' *Almighties* everlasting seat She first was bred, . V. x. 1. 7
She commeth in, before th' *Almighties* view; . . . *Epith.* 211
Almond. an *almond* tree ymounted hye On top of greene Selinis I. vii. 32. 5
Almoner. The second was as *Almner* of the place: . . . I. x. 38. 1
Almost. When Winters wastful spight was *almost* spent, . . *S.C.* Ja. 2
almost sterv'd did much lament and mourne. . . . *Hub.* 580
for feare now *almost* ded; . . . *Hub.* 1374
It *almost* drowned was, . . . *Ti.* 622
I for dole was *almost* like to die. . . . *Ti.* 672
it in me breeds *almost* equall paine. . . . *D.* 175
through long wars left *almost* waste, . . . *Ded. Son.* v. 3
almost rent her tender hart in tway, . . . I. vii. 27. 4
Him all amazd, and *almost* made afeard: . . . I. xi. 26. 5
had *almost* committed crime abhord, . . . II. i. 27. 3
almost it did haynous violence . . . II. i. 28. 6
Sabrina, *almost* dead with feare, . . . II. x. 19. 3
Belphebe findes him *almost* dead, . . . III. v. Arg.
Panting for breath, and *almost* out of hart, . . . III. v. 4. 1
almost in the backe he oft her strake; . . . III. vii. 44. 6
He fainted, and was *almost* dead with feare, . . . III. x. 37. 7
when the second watch was *almost* past, . . . III. xii. 29. 6
His mighty heart did *almost* rend in tway, . . . IV. iv. 22. 7
That *almost* had against you trespassed this day.' . . . IV. vi. 3. 9
She *almost* fell againe into a swound, . . . IV. vii. 9. 8
almost dead and desperate Through her late hurts, . . . IV. viii. 19. 7
almost blind through eld, . . . IV. xi. 24. 9
And *almost* would his balances have broken; . . . V. ii. 47. 2
death, the which them *almost* overtooke, . . . V. ii. 54. 4
As if the prize she gotten had *almost,* . . . V. v. 10. 3
quake For very ruth, which did it *almost* rive, . . . V. vii. 36. 6
So that he now has *almost* spent his spright, . . . VI. v. 17. 5
with one fall his necke he *almost* brake; . . . VI. ix. 44. 3
Pastorell through great affright Was *almost* dead, . . . VI. xi. 43. 8
That made him *almost* mad for fell despight: . . . VI. xii. 31. 7
with the sight thereof was *almost* queld; . . . VII. vi. 25. 3
Alms. askt an *almes* for Gods deare love. . . . *Hub.* 363
His *almes* for want of faith he doth accuse. . . . I. iv. 32. 4
godly worke of *Almes* and charitee, . . . I. x. 45. 4
Of which he dealt large *almes,* as did befall: . . . IV. iv. 32. 4
Aloft. Waving *aloft* with triple point to skie, . . . *Bel.*[2] xi. 2
Whether they fare on foote, or flie *aloft,* . . . *Ro.* xxiv. 3
Tho gan shepheards swaines to looke *aloft,* . . . *S.C.* May 124
learne to looke *alofte;* . . . *S.C.* Jul. 10
tread *aloft* in buskin fine, . . . *S.C.* O. 113
I lifted am *aloft* . . . *Gn.* 33
with proud vaunt his head *aloft* doth holde; . . . *Gn.* 259
teach the warbling pipe to sound *aloft,* . . . *T.M.* 290
From hence we mount *aloft* unto the skie, . . . *T.M.* 505
Fame with golden wings *aloft* doth flie, . . . *Ti.* 421
mount *aloft* unto the Cristall skie, . . . *Mui.* 44
My Muse, . . . With bolder wing shall dare *alofte* to sty . . *Ded. Son.* ii. 9
his hideous club *aloft* he dites, . . . I. viii. 18. 4
Forelifting up *a-loft* his speckled brest, . . . I. xi. 15. 2
gan he tosse *aloft* his stretched traine, . . . I. xi. 37. 5
the last deadly smoke *aloft* did steeme, . . . I. xii. 2. 4
To climbe *aloft,* and others to excell: . . . II. vii. 46. 7
Or flings *aloft,* or treades downe in the flore, . . . II. viii. 42. 5
backe againe it did *alofte* rebownd, . . . II. xi. 42. 8
on the rocke the waves breaking *aloft* . . . II. xii. 33. 3
her two lilly paps *aloft* displayd, . . . II. xii. 66. 6
standing high *aloft* low lay thine eare, . . . III. iii. 9. 1
vapour thin and light Reeking *aloft* . . . III. vii. 5. 3
when she saw *aloft* appeare The Trojane flames . . . III. x. 12. 7
Nine times he heard him come *aloft* ere day, . . . III. x. 48. 5
The same *aloft* he hung in open vew, . . . IV. vi. 16. 1
friskt, and flong *aloft,* and louted low on knee. . . . V. iii. 34. 9
At an Herneshaw, that lyes *aloft* on wing, . . . VI. vii. 9. 2

Aloft—*Continued.*
Sometimes *aloft* he layd, sometimes alow, . . . VI. viii. 13. 6
His dreadfull hand he heaved up *aloft,* . . . VI. viii. 15. 1
being up he lookt againe *aloft,* . . . VI. viii. 26. 1
he gan *aloft* t' advance his arme, . . . VI. viii. 45. 8
my fraile spirit . . . Lift up *aloft,* . . . VII. vii. 1. 5
I *aloft* should reare My Trophee, . . . VII. vii. 56. 4
The merry Larke hir mattins sings *aloft;* . . . *Epith.* 80
with desyre Lifted *aloft,* . . . *H.L.* 68
up *aloft* above my strength . . . *H.B.* 6
From thence to mount *aloft,* by order dew, . . . *H.H.B.* 24
Mount up *aloft* through heavenly contemplation, . . . *H.H.B.* 136
Alone. In God *alone* my confidence do stay. . . . *Bel.* i. 14
Being one day at my window all *alone,* . . . *Pet.* i. 1
I saw a Phoenix in the wood *alone,* . . . *Pet.* v. 1
to the field *alone* he speedeth, . . . *S.C.* F. 197
Now stands the Brere like a lord *alone,* . . . *S.C.* F. 222
we close shrowded in thys shade *alone.* . . . *S.C.* Ap. 32
letten them runne at randon *alone:* . . . *S.C.* May 46
Tripping over the dale *alone,* . . . *S.C.* Au. 63
To him be the wroughten mazer *alone.* . . . *S.C.* Au. 134
let hem gange *alone* . . . *S.C.* S. 100
he satte in secreate shade *alone,* . . . *S.C.* D. 5
either (algates) would be Lords *alone;* . . . *Hub.* 1025
Eftsones by counsell of the Foxe *alone,* . . . *Hub.* 1112
confidence The which the Ape repos'd in him *alone,* . . . *Hub.* 1165
Playing *alone* carelesse on hir heavenlie Virginals. . . . *U.V.* 6
I in languor left there all *alone.* . . . *Ti.* 644
seeke *alone* to weepe, and dye *alone.'* . . . *D.* 77
To die *alone,* unpitied, unplaind; . . . *D.* 79
To you *alone* I sing this mournfull verse, . . . *As.* Pr. 7
For one *alone* he cared, . . . *As.* 53
Her he did love, her he *alone* did honor, . . . *As.* 59
Ne her with ydle words *alone* he wowed, . . . *As.* 67
I weened sure he was our God *alone,* . . . *Col.* 773
she fayre *alone,* when none was faire in place. . . . I. ii. 38. 9
Alone he, wandring, thee too long doth want: . . . I. v. 13. 3
The gentle virgin, left behinde *alone,* . . . I. vi. 33. 3
On top of greene Selinis all *alone,* . . . I. vii. 32. 6
The force, . . . In one *alone* left hand he now unites, . . . I. viii. 18. 2
Where sate a gentle Lady all *alone,* . . . II. i. 13. 5
His Palmer now shall foot no more *alone.* . . . II. iii. 3. 5
Wandreth *alone* with bow and arrowes keene, . . . II. iii. 31. 4
bide *alone* behinde; . . . II. iii. 32. 4
Making sweet solace to herselfe *alone:* . . . II. vi. 3. 2
gnawing Gealosy . . . Sitting *alone,* . . . II. vii. 22. 5
Honour and dignitie from her *alone* Derived are, . . . II. vii. 48. 7
Then did he raigne *alone,* . . . II. x. 33. 9
now *alone* he conquerour remaines: . . . II. xi. 48. 1
Upon a milkwhite Palfrey all *alone,* . . . III. i. 15. 2
wreake your wronges wrought to this knight *alone,* . . . III. i. 28. 5
Is not enough that I *alone* doe dye, . . . III. ii. 35. 3
Huge hostes of men he could *alone* dismay, . . . III. iii. 12. 5
through this forrest wandreth thus *alone?* . . . III. v. 7. 8
In this wilde forrest wandring all *alone,* . . . III. vi. 5. 4
To be th' ensample of true love *alone,* . . . III. vi. 52. 4
To savegard her ywandred all *alone:* . . . III. viii. 46. 8
Alone he rode without his Paragone; . . . III. x. 35. 6
her up he cast . . . and lett her fly *alone:* . . . III. x. 35. 8
Straying *alone* withouten groome or guide: . . . III. x. 36. 5
he was much afraid him selfe *alone* to fynd. . . . III. x. 41. 9
now the hevens obey to me *alone,* . . . III. xi. 35. 8
there stood an Image all *alone* . . . III. xi. 47. 4
of their loves did treat . . . twixt themselves *alone,* . . . IV. i. 16. 2
that he *alone* That lost faire Ladies ornament should weare, . . . IV. ii. 26. 3
Gainst all those knights, . . . save they *alone.* . . . IV. ii. 28. 9
That men on him the more might gaze *alone.* . . . IV. iv. 14. 6
Sweete is the love that comes *alone* with willingnesse. . . . IV. v. 25. 9
to Braggadochio selfe *alone* She came of her accord, . . . IV. v. 26. 8
now no more for him but I *alone,* . . . IV. vii. 13. 6
spredding over all the flore *alone,* . . . IV. vii. 20. 7
She syre and mother is her selfe *alone,* . . . IV. x. 41. 8
let him live unlov'd, or love him selfe *alone.* . . . IV. xii. 9. 9
languisht, and *alone* did weepe, . . . IV. xii. 19. 9
right sate in the middest of the beame *alone.* . . . V. ii. 48. 9
So were they left Lords of the field *alone:* . . . V. iii. 12. 8
Where she might sit nigh to the den *alone,* . . . V. ix. 8. 7
unto those *alone* The which unto him sacrificed bee: . . . V. x. 29. 5
he met An aged wight wayfaring all *alone,* . . . V. xi. 37. 2
Whiles she *alone* is left, and thou here found? . . . V. xi. 38. 6
a Ladie faire he saw Standing *alone* . . . VI. ii. 4. 2
Being unhable else *alone* to ride, . . . VI. iii. 46. 3
But Calepine, now being left *alone* . . . VI. iv. 39. 1
He would not suffer her *alone* to fare, . . . VI. v. 8. 2
Why have ye me *alone* thus long yleft? . . . VI. v. 23. 6
In which he liv'd *alone,* like carelesse bird in cage. . . . VI. vi. 4. 9
must proceede *alone* From your owne will to cure your maladie. . . . VI. vi. 7. 2
Now left *alone* in great extremity; . . . VI. vi. 16. 3
Would not her leave *alone* in her great need. . . . VI. vi. 16. 5
Whereas his love was sitting all *alone,* . . . VI. vi. 30. 2
Whereas the Prince himselfe lay all *alone,* . . . VI. vii. 18. 7
In th' open fields an Infant left *alone;* . . . VI. ix. 14. 6
Now seeing Calidore left all *alone,* . . . VI. ix. 16. 2
Was she to whom that shepheard pypt *alone;* . . . VI. x. 15. 8
her *alone* he for his part desired . . . VI. xi. 4. 3
'But what could he gainst all them doe *alone?* . . . VI. xi. 32. 1
better able it to guide *alone;* . . . VII. vi. 11. 4
thou *alone* That art yborne of heaven . . . VII. vii. 2. 6
Phoebus selfe, who lightsome is *alone,* . . . VII. vii. 51. 7
Leaves, lines, and rymes, seeke her to please *alone,* . . . *Am.* i. 13

Alone—*Continued.*
stormes, which she *alone* on me doth raine. . . . *Am.* xlvi. 14
Long-while *alone* in languor to remaine. . . . *Am.* lii. 8
a tree *alone* all comfortlesse, . . . *Am.* lvi. 7
I *alone,* now left disconsolate, . . . *Am.* lxxxviii. 5
So I unto my selfe *alone* will sing; . . . *Epith.* 17
vertue . . . giveth lawes *alone,* . . . *Epith.* 195
leave my love *alone,* . . . *Epith.* 312
yet not best, but to be lov'd *alone;* . . . *H.L.* 250
Along. *Along* the bankes of the Italian ([2]Ausonian) streame. . . . *Bel.*[1] v. 4
Ran flowing all *along* the creekie shoare . . . *Bel.*[1] vii. 7
he spide, Lying *along* before him . . . *Gn.* 267
Drawing in teemes *along* the starrie skie; . . . *Gn.* 458
slide In silver channell, downe *along* the Lee, . . . *Ti.* 135
he *along* would flie Upon the streaming rivers, . . . *Mui.* 46
with her went *along,* as a strong gard . . . I. iii. 9. 2
His three deformed heads did lay *along,* . . . I. v. 34. 2
Drew by the heare *along* upon the grownd . . . II. iv. 3. 6
all *along* Drew him through durt and myre . . . II. v. 23. 3
did swim *Along* the shore . . . II. vi. 2. 6
On every side they placed were *along;* . . . II. vii. 30. 5
raunges reard *along* the wall, . . . II. ix. 29. 2
all *along* the Southerne sea-coast . . . II. x. 6. 4
the light bubles daunced all *along,* . . . II. xii. 10. 4
Whose lignage from this Lady I derive *along.* . . . III. iv. 3. 9
kept her ready way *Along* the strond; . . . III. iv. 18. 3
swim *Along* the margent of the fomy shore, . . . III. iv. 34. 4
the same *along* did trace By tract of blood, . . . III. v. 28. 3
In endlesse rancke *along* enraunged were, . . . III. vi. 35. 8
as he led the Beast *along* the way, . . . III. vii. 37. 1
who that was which chaced her *along* the lands. . . . III. vii. 46. 9
saw his drover drive *along* the streame, . . . III. viii. 22. 2
Along the fomy waves driving his finny drove. . . . III. viii. 29. 9
with the waves Of wealthy Thamis washed is *along,* . . . III. ix. 45. 2
flancked both the bridges sides *along,* . . . IV. x. 7. 4
Tyne, *along* whose stony bancke . . . IV. xi. 36. 1
equitie to measure out *along* . . . V. i. 7. 3
His corps was carried downe *along* the Lee, . . . V. ii. 19. 1
So him they led through all their streetes *along* . . . V. xi. 34. 5
may no Knight nor Lady passe *along* That way . . . VI. i. 13. 5
to his first quest he passed forth *along.* . . . VI. i. 47. 9
He him preventing layes on earth *along,* . . . VI. viii. 49. 3
Therewith he mured up his mouth *along,* . . . VI. xii. 34. 4
Be strewed with fragrant flowers all *along,* . . . *Epith.* 50
Loe! where she comes *along* with portly pace, . . . *Epith.* 148
Along the shoare of silver streaming Themmes; . . . *Proth.* 11
softly swimming downe *along* the Lee, . . . *Proth.* 38
When downe *along* by pleasant Tempes shore, . . . *Proth.* 79
those joyous Birdes did passe *along,* . . . *Proth.* 114
Aloof. Then badd the knight his Lady yede *aloof,* . . . I. xi. 5. 1
stood *aloofe,* unweeting what to doe; . . . III. x. 22. 3
He durst not nigh approch, but kept *aloofe,* . . . IV. vii. 37. 4
staying nought to question from *aloofe,* . . . IV. x. 9. 8
kept *aloofe* for dread to be descryde, . . . VI. vii. 3. 3
Aloud. One cride *aloude.* . . . *Rev.* i. 9
With thondring voice cride out *aloude,* . . . *Rev.* ii. 13
the Foxe *alowd* did cry, . . . *Hub.* 1070
he roar'd *alowd,* as he were wood, . . . *Hub.* 1352
when they list to blow Their pipes *aloud,* . . . *Col.* 379
with death opprest He ror'd *aloud,* . . . I. iii. 42. 9
The Elfe him calls *alowd,* . . . I. v. 13. 8
'Lo! yonder he,' cryde Archimage *alowd,* . . . II. i. 25. 1
began these words *aloud* to sownd. . . . II. ii. 39. 9
Chaunted *alowd* their chearefull harmonee, . . . II. v. 31. 7
Then gan the cursed wretch *alowd* to cry, . . . II. vii. 60. 6
Did shrieke *alowd,* that through the hous it rong, . . . III. i. 62. 6
Alowd to her he oftentimes did call, . . . III. iv. 48. 6
to him did cry And call *alowd* for helpe, . . . III. x. 13. 7
She heard a shrilling Trompet sound *alowd,* . . . III. xii. 1. 5
offred that to justifie *alowd.* . . . IV. i. 10. 4
They all gan shout *aloud,* . . . IV. iii. 49. 9
Then would he laugh *aloud,* . . . IV. vii. 26. 9
He cald to him *aloud* his case to rew, . . . IV. viii. 40. 7
howld *aloud* to see his Lord there slaine, . . . IV. viii. 46. 4
'Thereat he shriekt *aloud,* . . . IV. viii. 62. 1
To whom I cald *aloud,* halfe angry therewithall. . . . IV. x. 11. 9
for helpe *aloud* in earnest cride: . . . V. ix. 12. 3
Crying for helpe *aloud:* . . . V. ix. 14. 6
Called *aloud* unto the watchfull ward . . . V. x. 31. 3
He brayd *aloud* for very fell despight; . . . V. xi. 8. 2
With that *aloude* she gan to bray and yell, . . . V. xi. 28. 1
Gan shout *aloud,* that unto heaven it rong; . . . V. xi. 34. 2
At him began *aloud* to barke and bay . . . V. xii. 41. 2
Crying *aloud* (*in vaine) to shew her sad misfare . . . VI. iii. 24. 5
Gan cry *aloud* with horrible affright, . . . VI. iv. 8. 8
aloude the faire Serena cryde Unto the Knight, . . . VI. v. 27. 1
She starting up began to shrieke *aloud;* . . . VI. vi. 31. 2
Then one of them *aloud* unto him cryde, . . . VI. vii. 7. 1
Cryde out *aloud* for mercie, . . . VI. vii. 12. 2
Then out *aloud* she cries, . . . VI. viii. 40. 7
to shrill And shrieke *aloud,* . . . VI. viii. 46. 2
in their lower braunches sung *aloud;* . . . VI. x. 6. 7
Gan cry to them *aloud* to helpe her . . . VI. x. 34. 9
gan *aloud* for Pastorell to call, . . . VI. xi. 44. 2
no more Him liberty was left *aloud* to rore: . . . VI. xii. 36. 5
Gan call to him *aloud* with all their might . . . VII. vi. 15. 4
how the Minstrils gin to shrill *aloud* . . . *Epith.* 129
Crying *aloud* with strong confused noyce, . . . *Epith.* 138
Alow. Sometimes aloft he layd, sometimes *alow,* . . . VI. viii. 13. 6
Alpheus. Swift Rhene, and *Alpheus* still immaculate, . . . IV. xi. 21. 4

Al Portugese. *Al Portugese,* loose like an emptie gut; . . . . *Hub.* 212
Already. yt is *already* donne. . . . . *S.C.* Ja. 30
His name is worne *alreadie* out of thought, ... *Ti.* 222
alreadie dead with feare, ... *Col.* 205
Already harnessed for journey new, ... I. v. 20. 7
he *already* plighted his right hand Unto another love, ... I. xii. 26. 8
hardly could bee hurt who was *already* stong. . . . . II. i. 3. 9
trouble of renewing fight *Already* fought, ... II. v. 25. 3
loe! *already* how the fowles in aire Doe flocke, ... II. vi. 28. 7
Whom fortune hath *already* laid in lowest seat.' . . . . II. viii. 27. 9
Alreadie seemes that fortunes headlong wheele . . . . V. x. 20. 7
her he deemes *already* but a damned ghoste.' . . . . V. xi. 42. 9
Being *alreadie* dead with fearefull fright: . . . . VI. viii. 45. 3
His trompet shrill hath thrise *already* sounded, ... *Am.* xix. 2
Als. *See* **Also.**
Also (*partial list*).
Ten hornes *also* the stately beast did beare. . . . . *Rev.* ii. 5
Then did I see the beast and Kings *also* . . . . *Rev.* iii. 11
It *als* will end the paine which I endure. . . . . *Ro.* vii. 14
Then *also* marke how Rome, from day to day, ... *Ro.* xxvii. 9
Where gathering *also* filth . . . . *Van.* iv. 11
Als my budding braunch thou wouldest cropp; . . . . *S.C.* F. 58
For *als* at home I have a syre, ... *S.C.* Mar. 40
And *also* who, and whence that he were? . . . . *S.C.* May 261
Better is . . . *Als* for thy flocke and thee. . . . . *S.C.* Jul. 8
That *als* we mought doe soe. . . . . *S.C.* Jul. 120
Als Colin Cloute she would not once disdayne; . . . . *S.C.* N. 101
Als of their maisters hast no lesse regarde . . . . *S.C.* D. 11
Also (*All so) my age, now passed youngthly pryme, ... *S.C.* D. 75
I learned *als* the signes of heaven to ken, ... *S.C.* D. 83
Here *also* playing on the grassy greene, ... *Gn.* 177
Whom *als* accompanied the Oke, ... *Gn.* 204
'There *also* those two Pandionian maides, ... *Gn.* 401
there lives *also* the immortall praise Of womankinde, ... *Gn.* 428
And *also* him that false Ulysses slewe, ... *Gn.* 531
'There *also* goodly Agamemnon bosts, ... *Gn.* 545
For which *also* I claime my selfe more fit . . . . *Hub.* 1038
all joy and jolly meriment Is *also* deaded, ... *T.M.* 210
'There *also,* where the winged ships were seene . . . . *Ti.* 148
thou thy selfe herein shalt *also* live: . . . . *Ti.* 258
layes of love he *also* could compose: . . . . *As.* 35
There *also* is (ah no, he is not now!) . . . . *Col.* 432
And *also* for the love which thou doest beare . . . . *Ded. Son.* iii. 10
Upon his shield the like was *also* scor'd, ... I. i. 2. 5
wanting rest, will *also* want of might? . . . . I. i. 32. 7
And *also* nigh consumed is the lingring day. . . . . I. iv. 3. 9
With drery shriekes did *also* her bewray; . . . . I. v. 30. 7
There *also* was king Croesus, ... I. v. 47. 6
There *also* was that mightie Monarch layd . . . . I. v. 48. 5
Als Una earnd her traveill to renew. . . . . I. ix. 18. 5
Als flew his steed . . . . I. ix. 21. 7
Him *als* accompanyd upon the way . . . . II. i. 7. 1
Als in her lap a lovely babe did play. . . . . II. i. 40. 5
Both loosers lott, and victours prayse *alsoe:* . . . . II. v. 15. 8
Here *also* sprong that goodly golden fruit, ... II. vii. 55. 1
Als when his brother saw the red blood . . . . II. viii. 37. 3
Als his faire Leman . . . She overhent, ... II. x. 18. 8
He *also* gave to fugitives . . . . II. x. 41. 6
In which accord the Prince was *also* plaste, ... III. i. 12. 7
Where *also* proofe of thy prow valiaunce . . . . III. iii. 28. 3
in the seas, That raignest *also* in the Continent, ... III. iv. 10. 2
Mote not mislike you *also* to abate . . . . III. viii. 51. 6
And *also* far unlike conditions has; . . . . III. ix. 4. 7
Shee *also* dofte her heavy haberjeon, ... III. ix. 21. 1
Also to win Deucalions daughter bright, ... III. xi. 42. 5
Those dreadfull flames she *also* found delayd . . . . III. xii. 42. 7
There *also* was the name of Nimrod strong; . . . . IV. i. 22. 7
cursed seedes doe *also* serve To her for bread, ... IV. i. 26. 1
Als as she double spake, ... IV. i. 28. 1
Where I with sound of trompe will *also* rest a whyle. . . . . IV. iv. 48. 9
Als of his owne rash hand one wound was to be seene. . . . . IV. vii. 35. 9
Which losse her made like passion *also* prove: . . . . IV. viii. 3. 5
And *also* of their private loves beguyled, ... IV. ix. 36. 5
did me *also* friend in my retrate. . . . . IV. x. 57. 9
There *also* some most famous founders were . . . . IV. xi. 15. 1
Proud of his Adamants . . . as *als'* of wondrous Bath, ... IV. xi. 31. 8
There *also* was the wide embayed Mayre; . . . . IV. xi. 44. 1
And *also* those which wonne in th' azure sky: . . . . IV. xii. 1. 4
That powre he *also* doth to Princes lend, ... V. Pr. 10. 6
thether *also* came in open sight . . . . V. iii. 14. 1
eke of powre . . . And *als'* of princely grace . . . . V. v. 41. 9
So *also* did that great Oetean Knight . . . . V. viii. 2. 4
Als at his backe a great wyde net he bore, ... V. ix. 11. 6
He *also* gan uplooke . . . . VI. iii. 11. 2
And *also* for the sharpnesse of her rankling wound: . . . . VI. iv. 9. 9
brought them *also* ease, ... VI. v. 40. 3
Both of . . . And *also* of the object of his vew, ... VI. ix. 26. 6
With them *also* was taken Coridon, ... VI. x. 41. 1
Als Claribell Ne lesse did tender the faire Pastorell, ... VI. xii. 11. 4
also quite forsooke All those faire forrests . . . . VII. vi. 54. 5
thither *also* came all other creatures, ... VII. vii. 4. 1
the clouds are *also* tost and roll'd, ... VII. vii. 20. 8
Yet in his hand a spade he *also* hent, ... VII. vii. 32. 6
them we gods do rule, and in them *also* thee. . . . . VII. vii. 48. 9
And *also* to sustayne thy selfe with food. . . . . *Am.* ii. 8
let them *also* with them bring in hand . . . . *Epith.* 41
Be *also* present heere, ... *Epith.* 71
Hymen *also* crowne with wreathes of vine; . . . . *Epith.* 256
Which *also* were with selfe-same price redeemed . . . . *H.H.L.* 202
Alsoon. *Alsoone* may shepheard clymbe to skye . . . . *S.C.* Jul. 101

Altar. Placed on high upon an *Altare* faire, ... *Ti.* 492
th' *Altare,* on the which this Image staid, ... *Ti.* 498
there beside of marble stone was built An *Altare,* . . . . I. viii. 36. 2
There was an *Altar* built of pretious stone . . . . III. xi. 47. 2
an *altar* of some costly masse, ... IV. x. 39. 2
all about her *altar* scattered lay . . . . IV. x. 43. 1
from the *Altar* all about did blow The holy fire, ... V. vii. 14. 4
an *Altar* framed Of costly Ivory, ... V. x. 28. 2
The Monster underneath the *Altar* lay: . . . . V. xi. 21. 7
like an *Altar* did itselfe uprere . . . . VI. viii. 42. 5
an *altar* shortly they erected To slay her on. . . . . VI. viii. 44. 3
Of few greene turfes an *altar* soone they fayned, ... VI. viii. 44. 8
The Damzell was before the *altar* set, ... VI. viii. 45. 2
Whom by the *Altar* he doth sitting find . . . . VI. viii. 50. 2
Will builde an *altar* to appease her yre; . . . . *Am.* xxii. 10
Bring her up to th' high *altar,* . . . . *Epith.* 215
whiles she before the *altar* stands, ... *Epith.* 223
About the sacred *Altare* doe remaine, ... *Epith.* 230
Altar's. odours rising from the *altars* flame. . . . . IV. x. 37. 3
by the *altars* side her selfe to slumber plaste. . . . . V. vii. 8. 9
forth isswed from under th' *Altars* smooke A dreadfull feend V. xi. 22. 4
Altars. with a sheepe, The *Altars* hallowing. . . . . *S.C.* Jul. 136
Hath powred forth for thee, and th' *altars* sprent: . . . . *Mui.* 239
mourning *altars,* purgd with enimies life, ... I. iii. 36. 7
proud Antiochus . . . on his *altares* daunst. . . . . I. v. 47. 9
Witnesse the burning *Altars,* which he swore, ... I. xii. 27. 5
What hevens? what *altars?* . . . . I. xii. 30. 3
th' *altars* fume with frankincense arownd, ... III. iv. 17. 4
Altars defyld, and holy things defast; . . . . IV. i. 21. 5
'An hundred *Altars* round about were set, ... IV. x. 38. 1
altars unto him and temples lent, ... V. vii. 2. 3
Altars fouled, and blasphemy spoke, ... VI. xii. 25. 3
decke with floures thy *altars* well beseene. . . . . *H.L.* 293
Altar-stone. Under that cursed Idols *altar-stone* . . . . V. x. 29. 2
Alter. least mishap the most blisse *alter* may? . . . . *Mui.* 220
(which none yet durst Of Gods or men *alter* . . . . VII. vi. 5. 6
he his course doth *alter* every yeare, ... VII. vii. 51. 3
it can *alter* all the course of kynd. . . . . *Am.* xxx. 14
Alteration. Bold *Alteration* pleades Large Evidence: . . . . VII. vii. Arg.
What is the same but *alteration* plaine? . . . . VII. vii. 55. 4
Altered. her white streight legs were *altered* . . . . *Mui.* 349
chaunged is and often *altred* to and froe. . . . . III. vi. 37. 9
The substaunce is not chaungd nor *altered,* . . . . III. vi. 38. 1
that they may *altred* bee, And chaung'd . . . . IV. ii. 51. 6
all the worlds faire frame . . . She *alter'd* quite; . . . . VII. vi. 5. 7
Which every howre is chang'd and *altred* cleane . . . . VII. vii. 22. 7
Although. *Although* the compast world were sought around. . *Ti.* 567
Whose lives *although* decay'd, yet loves decayed never. . . . IV. x. 27. 9
scracht Her cursed head, *although* it itched naught: . . . . V. xii. 30. 4
although good Fortune me befall, ... VI. i. 6. 6
Yet would he not him hurt *although* he might; . . . . VI. i. 34. 3
Although Blandina did with all her arts . . . . VI. v. 33. 5
Although his quest were farre afore him gon: . . . . VI. ix. 12. 3
Knowing his voice, *although* not heard long sin, ... VI. xi. 44. 3
Altogether. his behaviour *altogether* was *Alla Turchesca* . . *Hub.* 676
dayes Had in rude fields bene *altogether* spent, ... *Col.* 669
head was *altogether* bald, ... I. viii. 47. 1
Alway. deep waters which her drownd *alway:* . . . . *Col.* 858
with chaste heart to honor him *alway:* . . . . *Col.* 888
from a sacred fountaine welled forth *alway.* . . . . I. i. 34. 9
alway Are wont to cleave unto the lowly clay, ... III. v. 1. 4
makes him *alway* Suspect her truth, ... III. ix. 5. 3
She *alway* smyld, ... III. xii. 13. 5
Which he in store about him kept *alway,* . . . . IV. viii. 20. 7
In which old Styx her aged bones *alway* . . . doth lay. . . . IV. xi. 4. 4
Deawed with silver drops that trickled downe *alway.* . . . . IV. xi. 25. 9
Now ye have made my heart to wake *alway,* . . . . V. vi. 25. 7
joyous peace and quietnesse *alway* . . . . V. ix. 24. 7
that which yeeldeth vertues meed *alway?* . . . . V. xi. 17. 8
He foot by foot him followed *alway,* . . . . VI. vi. 28. 6
Always. *alwayes* flow to quench his thirstie heate. . . . . *Gn.* 120
where soules doo *alwaies* mourne; . . . . *Gn.* 620
others *alwayes* have before me stept, ... *Hub.* 77
with Acorns *alwaies* fed, ... *T.M.* 590
Nowe doe I *alwayes* dye, ... *U.V.* 18
happie there I maie thee *alwaies* see. . . . . *Ti.* 308
of love I *alwayes* humbly deemed, ... *Col.* 828
The sacred Muses have made *alwaies* clame . . . . *Ded. Son.* iv. 1
he did *alwaies* strive . . . . I. v. 40. 7
Mercie, that his steps upbare And *alwaies* led, ... I. x. 44. 5
sad horror with grim hew Did *alwaies* sore, ... II. vii. 23. 2
wife, though *alwaies* faithful prov'd. . . . . II. x. 17. 9
the Heavens *alwayes* joviall Lookte on them lovely, ... II. xii. 51. 1
Nothing on earth mote *alwaies* happy beene: . . . . III. i. 10. 7
love does *alwaies* bring forth bounteous deeds, ... III. i. 49. 8
Which *alwaies* of his paines he made the chiefest meed. . . . III. iv. 4. 9
stretched forth in ydlenesse *alwayes,* . . . . III. vii. 12. 4
so her selfe did *alwaies* to him tell; . . . . III. viii. 19. 8
alwayes did their dread encounter fly: . . . . III. xi. 6. 4
Gainst whom he *alwayes* bent a brasen shield, ... III. xii. 12. 8
alwaies in her hand two clewes of silke she twynd. . . . . III. xii. 14. 9
Was *alwaies* flitting as the wavering wind . . . . IV. ii. 5. 2
Yet victors both them selves *alwayes* esteemed: . . . . IV. iii. 28. 5
with her *alwaies* ride, till he another get.' . . . . IV. iv. 9. 9
alwaies wept and wailed night and day, ... IV. viii. 2. 8
Blandamour, whom *alwaies* he envide; . . . . IV. ix. 26. 4
The same to all stood *alwaies* open wide; . . . . IV. x. 16. 4
Alwayes to execute her stedfast doome, ... V. i. 12. 3
alwaies doe their powre within just compasse pen. . . . . V. ii. 19. 9
what on earth can *alwayes* happie stand? . . . . V. iii. 9. 1

Always—*Continued.*
my most delight hath *alwaies* been To hunt VI. ii. 31. 6
he grace and glory wonne *alwaies,* VI. vi. 4. 4
On which his hungry eye was *alwayes* bent; VI. ix. 26. 7
sayling *alwaies* in the port. VI. x. 2. 9
Frequented of these gentle Nymphes *alwayes,* VI. x. 19. 4
'Therefore they *alwaies* smoothly seeme to smile, VI. x. 24. 1
the thicke shrubs, which did them *alwaies* shade VI. x. 42. 3
His target *alwayes* over her pretended; VI. xi. 19. 4
his high head, that seemeth *alwayes* hore VII. vii. 11. 3
alwayes seeme as one, VII. vii. 51. 2

Am (*partial list*).
my poore wretched ghost . . . too and fro *am* tost. *Gn.* 339
I beyond all these *am* carried *Gn.* 419
'I, that do seeme not I, Duessa *ame,*' I. v. 26. 6
High God be witnesse that I guiltlesse *ame;* I. xii. 30. 6
Yet *am* I glad that here I now in safety *ame.* III. viii. 23. 9
in great doubt I *ame,* III. x. 39. 7

Amain. The Sarazin, this hearing, rose *amain,* I. vi. 41. 7
her way does cut *amaine,* III. iv. 49. 5
His seahorses did seeme to snort *amayne,* III. xi. 41. 1
he thus began *amaine:* IV. i. 52. 5
teares gan shed *amaine,* IV. iii. 47. 5
eke the breathfull bellowes blew *amaine,* IV. v. 38. 7
A streame of coleblacke bloud thence gusht *amaine,* IV. vii. 27. 8
coucht his speare, and ran at him *amaine.* VI. i. 33. 4
layd at him *amaine* with all his will and might. VI. vi. 27. 9
Let drive at him so dreadfully *amaine,* VI. vii. 46. 4
Which when the Lady saw, she cryde *amaine;* VI. viii. 17. 4
ran at him *amaine* With open mouth, VI. xii. 26. 4

Amaranth. Red *Amaranthus,* lucklesse Paramour; *Gn.* 677
Sad *Amaranthus,* made a flowre but late, III. vi. 45. 6
Sad *Amaranthus,* in whose purple gore III. vi. 45. 7

Amarous. *See* **Amorous.**

Amaryllis. Having his *Amaryllis* left to mone. *Col.* 435
Helpe *Amaryllis* this her losse to mourne: *Col.* 437
Phyllis, Charillis, and sweet *Amaryllis.* *Col.* 540
Amaryllis, whether fortunate Or else unfortunate *Col.* 564

Amate. the blind God that doth me thus *amate,* I. i. 51. 4
never knight . . . More luckless dissaventures did *amate:* I. ix. 45. 4
That cheard his friendes, and did his foes *amate:* II. i. 6. 4
The which them did in modest wise *amate,* II. ix. 34. 4
him soonest doth *amate,* And findeth dew effect III. iv. 27. 4
him he held, and did through might *amate.* III. vii. 35. 1
in the Porch, that did them sore *amate,* III. xi. 21. 5
when she saw, it did her much *amate* IV. ii. 50. 7
Did him assayle, and mightily *amate,* IV. iii. 26. 8
all the warders it did sore *amate,* V. ii. 21. 3
ne let you *amate* Your misery, V. iv. 28. 4
It did them all exceedingly *amate,* VII. vi. 19. 7

Amated. 'Ye bene right hard *amated,* II. ii. 5. 3
Stood long amaz'd as she *amated* weare: V. xi. 64. 5

Amavia. Guyon . . . Fyndes Mordant and *Amavia* slaine II. i. Arg.
Mordant and *Amavia* did rew, II. ii. 45. 8

Amaze. It did him *amaze.* *S.C.* Ap. 76
All in *amaze* he suddenly up start I. ii. 5. 1
Her glorious glitterand light doth all mens eies *amaze.* I. iv. 16. 9
strove for to *amaze* the weaker sights: I. vii. 30. 5
Halfe in *amaze* with horror hideous, II. xi. 38. 4
Ne had one word to speake for great *amaze,* III. vii. 7. 8
At length they both upstarted in *amaze,* IV. ii. 17. 1
All which by nature made did nature selfe *amaze.* IV. x. 24. 9
Not with *amaze,* as women wonted bee, V. vii. 25. 2
Straunge there to see, it did them much *amaze,* V. ix. 24. 3
These marchants fixed eyes did so *amaze,* VI. xi. 13. 6
they suddaine all arose In great *amaze,* VII. vi. 24. 5
my stonisht hart stood in *amaze,* *Am.* xvi. 3
to *amaze* weake mens confused skil, *Am.* xvii. 2
Why stand ye still ye virgins in *amaze,* *Epith.* 181
it doth much *amaze* The greatest wisards *H.H.B.* 167

Amazed. Her stombling steppe some what her *amazed,* *S.C.* May 231
That detestable sight him much *amazde,* I. i. 26. 1
Their steeds doe stagger, and *amazed* stand; I. ii. 15. 6
with the sight *amazd,* forgat his furious forse, I. iii. 5. 9
forth they ran, like two *amazed* deare, I. iii. 22. 7
His hasty hand he doth *amased* hold, I. iii. 38. 5
the virgin . . . who all this while *Amased* stands, I. iii. 40. 2
whose glorious vew Their frayle *amazed* senses did confound: I. iv. 7. 3
The wise Southsayer . . . Th' *amazed* vulgar telles of warres I. v. 8. 9
He standes *amazed* how he thence should fade: I. v. 15. 5
She greatly grew *amazed* at the sight, I. v. 21. 3
The trembling ghosts with sad *amazed* mood, I. v. 32. 5
The Marriner yet halfe *amazed* stares At perill past, I. vi. 1. 4
All stand *amazed* at so uncouth sight, I. vi. 9. 6
She, more *amazd,* in double dread doth dwell; I. vi. 10. 1
The doubtfull Damzell . . . *amazd* does sitt, I. vi. 12. 3
The God himselfe, . . . Stood long *amazd,* I. vi. 15. 7
amazd At flashing beames of that sunshiny shield, I. viii. 20. 1
flowre of chevalrie, That with your worth the world *amazed* make, I. viii. 26. 8
Which when the knights beheld *amazd* they were, I. viii. 49. 1
all the hevens stood still *amazed* with his threat. I. xi. 10. 9
Him all *amazd,* and almost made afeard: I. xi. 26. 5
All in the open hall *amazed* stood I. xii. 25. 1
when the Pesaunt saw, *amazd* he stood, II. iii. 43. 1
Sterne was their looke; like wild *amazed* steares, II. ix. 13. 8
That sonnes of men *amazd* their sternnesse to behold. II. x. 7. 9
Nigh his wits end then woxe th' *amazed* knight, II. xi. 44. 1
Great Neptune stoode *amazed* at their sight, III. iv. 32. 1
So stared he on her, and stood long while *amaz'd.* III. vii. 13. 9

Amazed—*Continued.*
That wondrous sight faire Britomart *amazd,* III. xi. 49. 6
Do greatly stand *amaz'd* at such unwonted wonder. IV. ii. 16. 9
They . . . Were much *amaz'd* the headlesse tronke to see Stand up IV. iii. 21. 2
Stood still *amaz'd,* holding his idle sweard; IV. iii. 31. 7
all the rest it did *amazed* make, IV. iv. 29. 4
all men stood *amaz'd,* and at his might did wonder. V. iii. 8. 9
Stood long *amaz'd* as she amated weare: V. xi. 64. 5
was so far from being ought *amazed,* VI. viii. 26. 8
Whereat the knight *amaz'd* yet did not rest, VI. xi. 28. 7
All beeing with so bold attempt *amazed,* VII. vi. 13. 8
I stand *amazed* At wondrous sight *Am.* iii. 7
they stood *amazed* still, *Proth.* 58

Amazement. adding new Feare to his first *amazment,* I. ix. 24. 2
In which *amazement* when the Miscreaunt Perceived I. ix. 49. 1
him into great *amaz'ment* drove, II. ii. 3. 8
with *amazement* great Did rend the ratling skyes II. ii. 20. 8
great *amazement* of so wondrous sight; III. ix. 23. 2
the bosters hart did thrill With such *amazment,* III. x. 43. 6
all were with *amazement* smit, IV. i. 14. 2
too and fro in great *amazement* reel'd; IV. iii. 9. 7
found himselfe on ground in great *amazement.* IV. vi. 11. 9
With great *amazement* they were stupefide; V. iii. 17. 5
his hart was inly child With great *amazement,* VI. ii. 4. 9
In their *amazement* lyke Narcissus vaine, *Am.* xxxv. 7

Amazon. The *Amazon* huge river, now found trew? II. Pr. 2. 8
a proud *Amazon* did late defy All the brave Knights V. iv. 29. 5
'How hight that *Amazon?*' V. iv. 33. 1
to guide the way Unto the dwelling of that *Amazone:* V. iv. 35. 6
th' *Amazon,* as best it likt her selfe to dight. V. v. 1. 9
Then tooke the *Amazon* this noble knight, V. v. 20. 1
the warlike *Amazon* . . . Gan cast a secret liking V. v. 26. 7
seeking thus to salve the *Amazon,* V. v. 43. 5
Which when the cruell *Amazon* perceived, V. v. 47. 1
The warlike *Amazon* out of her bowre did peepe. V. vii. 26. 9
the *Amazone* Began the streight conditions to propound, V. vii. 28. 1
Full fiercely layde the *Amazon* about, V. vii. 31. 1
Whom that proud *Amazon* subdewed had, V. vii. 41. 6

Amazon's. *The *Amazons* huge river now found trew? II. Pr. 2. 8
There bound t' obay that *Amazons* proud law, V. v. 22. 3

Amazons. as that famous Queene Of *Amazons,* II. iii. 31. 6
doth beare his name Of warlike *Amazons,* IV. xi. 21. 9
Queene of *Amazons,* in armes well tride V. iv. 33. 5
With which those *Amazons* his love still craved, V. vi. 2. 4
Unto the land of *Amazons,* as she was bent. V. vii. 24. 9

Ambassage. as on *ambassage* sent Both too and fro, *Hub.* 472

Amber. Gold, *amber,* yvorie, perles, owches, rings, III. iv. 23. 5

Ambition. *Ambition* is engendred easily; *Ro.* xxiii. 10
Blinde through *ambition,* and with vengeance wood, *Gn.* 411
Through prowd *ambition* and hart-swelling hate, *Mui.* 5
That was *Ambition,* rash desire to sty, II. vii. 46. 8
Through proud *ambition* against her rebeld, II. x. 32. 7
through *ambition* downe themselves doe drive VI. ix. 22. 4
Now loath great Lordship and *ambition;* VI. ix. 28. 5
Did puffe them up with greedy bold *ambition,* *H.H.L.* 79

Ambitious. (As most usen *Ambitious* folke:) *S.C.* F. 161
Such was thend of this *Ambitious* brere, *S.C.* F. 237
he kindleth his *ambitious* sprights *Hub.* 768
th' Ape was stryfull, and *ambicious;* *Hub.* 1021
And taught *ambitious* Rome to tyrannise *Ded. Son.* i. 3
two rams, stird with *ambitious* pride, I. ii. 16. 1
Ambitious Sylla, and sterne Marius; I. v. 49. 8
his *ambitious* sonnes unto them twayne Arraught the rule, II. x. 34. 7
this land was tributarie made T' *ambitious* Rome, II. x. 49. 7
Serving th' *ambitious* will of Augustine, III. iii. 35. 3
O sacred hunger of *ambitious* mindes, V. xii. 1. 1
She gan to cast in her *ambitious* thought VII. vi. 7. 3
She gan to burne in her *ambitious* spright, VII. vi. 10. 5

Ambitiously. Arrogate to themselves *ambitiously:* VII. vii. 16. 4

Amble. Hard is to teach an old horse *amble* trew: III. viii. 26. 3

Ambling. a trotting Stalion get An *ambling* Colt, VI. iii. 1. 7

Ambrosia. There drincks she Nectar with *Ambrosia* mixt, *S.C.* N. 195
On Nectar and *Ambrosia* do feede. *Ti.* 399
a pledge I leave with thee . . . My yong *Ambrosia;* *D.* 290
were with sweet *Ambrosia* all besprinckled light. III. vi. 18. 9

Ambrosial. that *Ambrosiall* hew, Which wonts to decke the Gods *Hub.* 1267
ambrosiall odours from them threw, II. iii. 22. 7
with *ambrosiall* kisses bathe his eyes; III. i. 36. 4
Deawd with *ambrosiall* kisses, IV. Pr. 5. 6
The which *ambrosiall* odours forth did throw IV. xi. 46. 3
More sweet than Nectar, or *Ambrosiall* meat, *Am.* xxxix. 13
Bathing thy wings in her *ambrosiall* kisse, *H.L.* 25

Ambrosius. *Ambrose* and Uther, did ripe yeares attayne, II. x. 67. 2
coosen unto king *Ambrosius;* III. iii. 13. 8

Ambush. Out of their *ambush* broke, and gan him to invade. VI. v. 17. 9
A wicked *ambush* which lay hidden long *Am.* xii. 6

Ambushment. Drawne into danger through close *ambushment;* *Gn.* 532
Lyes in *ambushment* of his hoped pray, *Mui.* 404
lay in *ambushment* there, IV. x. 20. 7

Amearst. *See* **Amerced.**

Ameled. full fayre *aumayld:* II. iii. 27. 5

Amenage. must first begin, and well her *amenage:* II. iv. 11. 2

Amenance. Whether for Armes and warlike *amenaunce,* *Hub.* 781
kend him . . . by his armes and *amenaunce,* II. viii. 17. 8
By faithfull service and meete *amenaunce,* II. ix. 5. 7
Without regard of grace or comely *amenaunce.* III. i. 41. 9
In brave aray and goodly *amenance,* IV. iii. 5. 5

Amend. *See* **Amended.**
The world is well *amend,* *S.C.* Jul. 170
My piteous plight and losse to *amend?* *S.C.* S. 245

Amend—*Continued.*
Light not on some that may our state *amend;* . . . *Hub.* 171
I must stay; I may it not *amend,* . . . *D.* 453
thy daintie pen may . . . oversights *amend.* . . . *Ded.Son.*xii.12
Yet no'te the same *amend,* ne yet withstond, . . . II. xii. 57. 7
She wist not how t' *amend,* nor how it to withstond. . . . III. ii. 52. 9
their decayed kingdomes shall *amend:* . . . III. iii. 23. 5
ryde he could not, till his hurts he did *amend.* . . . III. x. 1. 9
thought in mind it shortly to *amend:* . . . IV. iv. 45. 7
Good hart in evils doth the evils much *amend.* . . . V. x. 22. 9
began to assay T' *amend* what was amisse, . . . VI. v. 10. 9
it booteth not to weene . . . It ever to *amend:* . . . VI. vi. 9. 6
my flockes father daily doth *amend* it. . . . VI. ix. 21. 8
Chaunge eke our mynds, and former lives *amend;* . . . *Am.* lxii. 6
Amended. *See* **Amend.**
had so great dismay so well *amended:* . . . IV. iii. 50. 7
his scarse diet somewhat was *amended,* . . . V. v. 57. 2
By means whereof, that mote not be *amended,* . . . VI. xi. 19. 5
nought may be *amended* any wheare. . . . *H.B.* 35
Amendment. *Amendment* readie still at hand did wayt, . . . I. x. 26. 7
make you good *amendment* for the same: . . . II. i. 20. 4
Amends. made *amends* to her with treble praise. . . . *Col.* 924
All wrongs have mendes, but no *amends* of shame. . . . II. i. 20. 5
Till he had made *amends,* and full restore . . . III. v. 18. 8
promist large *amends* to make. . . . IV. viii. 60. 6
They drew their swords, in mind to make *amends* . . . V. viii. 10. 2
Yeeld for *amends* my selfe yours evermore, . . . V. viii. 13. 5
Amends may for the trespasse soone be made, . . . V. viii. 14. 2
how could her love make half *amends* therefore? . . . VI. vii. 38. 9
Could make *amends* to God for mans misguyde, . . . *H.H.L.* 144
Amerced. Shall be by him *amearst* with penance dew. . . . *Am.* lxx. 12
Americ. From th' utmost brinke of the *Americke* shore . . . V. x. 3. 6
America. all that now *America* men call: . . . II. x. 72. 6
Amiable. A sweet regard and *amiable* grace, . . . II. xii. 79. 5
shee was full of *amiable* grace . . . III. i. 46. 1
therein sat an *amiable* Dame, . . . IV. x. 31. 3
with *amiable* grace To laugh at me, . . . IV. x. 56. 3
Her wand did move with *amiable* looke, . . . V. vii. 8. 2
A goodly youth of *amiable* grace, . . . VI. ii. 5. 2
Mark when she smiles with *amiable* cheare, . . . *Am.* xl. 1
chearefull grace and *amiable* sight; . . . *H.B.* 131
But in his sweet and *amiable* sight. . . . *H.H.L.* 273
Amice. Arayd in habit blacke, and *amis* thin, . . . I. iv. 18. 8
Amid (*partial list*). *Amidde* the yong greene wood; . . . *Pet.*[1] iii. 3
raunge *amydde* the mazie thickette, . . . *S.C.* D. 25
Floting *amid* the sea in jeopardie, . . . *Col.* 273
seemd *amid* the surges for to fleet, . . . *Col.* 286
Amid the thickest woods. . . . I. i. 11. 7
Amid the bowels of the earth . . . I. i. 39. 4
Amid the ocean waves, . . . II. x. 5. 6
Isle of Delos . . . *Amid* th' Aegaean sea . . . II. xii. 13. 2
when *amid* the thickest woodes they were, . . . III. x. 43. 1
doe both together smite *Amid* their shields, . . . V. x. 32. 3
th' Earth, . . . founded *Amid* the Sea, . . . *H.H.B.* 37
Amidas. my younger brother, *Amidas,* . . . V. iv. 9. 1
'Now tell me, *Amidas,* if that ye may, . . . V. iv. 17. 2
So, *Amidas,* the land was yours first hight; . . . V. iv. 19. 8
Both *Amidas* and Philtra were displeased; . . . V. iv. 20. 2
Amiddes, Amids. *See* **Amidst.**
Amidst. *Amidst* the yong greene wood; . . . *Pet.*[2] iii. 3
a gulph most hideous *Amidst* the Towne. . . . *Gn.* 605
there *amiddes* His magick bookes, . . . I. i. 36. 7
amidst her rayling, she did pray . . . I. iii. 23. 6
Amidst a flock of Damzelles . . . II. v. 32. 4
His speare *amids* her sun-brode shield arriv'd: . . . III. vii. 40. 4
Amidst the bridale feast, . . . IV. i. 3. 3
amidst the billowes beating of her, . . . V. iv. 10. 6
as a precious gemme *Amidst* a ring . . . VI. x. 12. 8
which there *amidst* them traced, . . . VI. x. 25. 2
a rocke *amidst* the raging floods; . . . *Am.* lvi. 10
Amintas. *Amyntas* quite is gone, . . . *Col.* 434
Her losse is yours, your losse *Amyntas* is, . . . *Col.* 438
Amyntas, floure of shepheards pride forlorne: . . . *Col.* 439
Amintas'. Me seemes I see *Amintas* wretched fate, . . . III. vi. 45. 8
Amiss. on thy corbe shoulder it leanes *amisse.* . . . *S.C.* F. 56
things lightly done *amis* Knew how to pardon, . . . *Gn.* 475
Which pardon me, if I *amisse* have pend; . . . *Hub.* 1386
begot *amisse* By yawning Sloth . . . *T.M.* 262
not mine; *amisse* I mine did say: . . . *D.* 234
leave their lambes to losse, misled *amisse.* . . . *Col.* 687
all the rest do most-what fare *amis,* . . . *Col.* 757
wonted feare of doing ought *amis,* . . . I. i. 49. 2
Whither the soules doe fly of men that live *amis.* . . . I. ii. 19. 9
In stead of foe to wound my friend *amis?'* . . . I. iii. 39. 5
slew with glauncing dart *amisse* A gentle Hynd, . . . I. vi. 17. 5
How that same knight should doe so fowle *amis,* . . . II. i. 19. 2
shonne The cursed land where many wend *amis,* . . . II. i. 51. 8
yt's eath to doe *amis:* . . . II. iii. 40. 5
He wist him selfe *amisse,* and angry said; . . . II. vi. 22. 6
when thinges were lost, or laid *amis,* . . . II. ix. 58. 6
Of her fond favorites so nam'd *amis,* . . . II. xii. 69. 5
If ought *amis* her liking may abuse: . . . III. Pr. 5. 4
certes seemes bestowed not *amis:* . . . III. ii. 42. 4
So be ye pleasd to pardon all *amis.* . . . III. vii. 53. 5
mov'd *amisse* with massy mucks unmeet regard. . . . III. x. 31. 9
something *amisse* to mend; . . . III. x. 38. 6
them that love, and do not live *amisse.* . . . IV. Pr. 2. 9
punish wicked men that walke *amisse:* . . . IV. i. 20. 3
on her waited things *amisse* to mend, . . . IV. xi. 47. 3
most she thought *amis,* . . . IV. xii. 22. 4

Amiss—*Continued.*
once *amisse* growes daily wourse and wourse: . . . V. Pr. 1. 9
this world with them *amisse* doe move. . . . V. Pr. 6. 7
most is Mars *amisse* . . . V. Pr. 8. 8
To shew that clemence oft, in things *amis,* . . . V. vii. 22. 8
Ne none can backe returne that once are gone *amis.* . . . V. ix. 6. 9
began to assay T' amend what was *amisse,* . . . VI. v. 10. 9
Lyke sacred priests that never thinke *amisse!* . . . *Am.* xxii. 8
And after, when we fared had *amisse,* . . . *H.H.L.* 192
Amity. lovely peace, and gentle *amity,* . . . II. vi. 35. 3
Ammon's. would as *Ammons* sonne be magnifide, . . . I. v. 48. 8
Among (*partial list*). I will part them all you *among.'* . . . *S.C.* Ap. 153
shrowde *Emong* the bushes rancke? . . . *S.C.* Jul. 4
sike mischiefe graseth hem *emong,* . . . *S.C.* S. 113
As if a Woolfe were *emong* the sheepe: . . . *S.C.* S. 192
in preace *emong* the learned troupe: . . . *S.C.* O. 70
Emong the shepeheards swaines . . . *S.C.* N. 6
The fayrest floure our gyrlond all *emong* . . . *S.C.* N. 75
a goddesse now *emong* the saintes, . . . *S.C.* N. 175
dewed with teares they han be ever *among.* . . . *S.C.* D. 112
Much do I feare *among* such fiends to sit; . . . *Gn.* 381
snares the subtill loupes *among;* . . . *Mui.* 429
And ever sprinckle brackish teares *among,* . . . *D.* 530
place my dolefull plaint your plaints *emong.* . . . *As.* Pr. 6
the sports that shepheards are *emong.* . . . *As.* 76
lost *emong* those rocks . . . *Col.* 154
I *among* the rest, of many least, . . . *Col.* 252
Of which *among* you many yet remaine, . . . *Col.* 739
baite his steedes the Ocean waves *emong.* . . . I. i. 32. 9
chose an halter from *among* the rest, . . . I. ix. 54. 4
On every side floting the floodes *emong:* . . . II. xii. 10. 7
Some litle life his feeble sprites *emong;* . . . III. iv. 41. 8
Eglantine and Caprifole *emong,* . . . III. vi. 44. 6
there *among* Stood gazing, . . . IV. iii. 37. 3
Emong the living, or *emong* the dead? . . . IV. vii. 11. 2
And still *among* most bitter wordes they spake, . . . V. xii. 42. 1
the streight, and rocks *among*) . . . VI. i. 13. 7
mixed threats *among,* and much unto her vowed. . . . VI. xi. 4. 9
dwell In much delight, and many joyes *among,* . . . VI. xii. 11. 8
the birds love-learned song, The deawy leaves *among!* . . . *Epith.* 89
Amongst (*partial list*). *See* **Mongst.**
Emongst themselves with cruell furie striving, . . . *Ro.* x. 11
did joy *amongst* my peeres: . . . *S.C.* Jun. 35
emongste the meaner sorte: . . . *S.C.* Env. 8
Emongst the rest the clambring Yvie grew, . . . *Gn.* 217
amongst Cymerian shades, . . . *Gn.* 370
Emongst the rest a wicked maladie Raign'd *emongst* men, . . . *Hub.* 9, 10
Amongst the rest a good old woman was, . . . *Hub.* 33
if we (*emongst* so manie) . . . *Hub.* 170
Beg *amongst* those that beggers doe defie.' . . . *Hub.* 192
boldlie doth *amongst* the boldest go; . . . *Hub.* 666
A Bases part *amongst* their consorts . . . *T.M.* 28
Charlemaine *amongst* the Starris seaven. . . . *T.M.* 462
Emongst the rest a gentle Nymph was found, . . . *Mui.* 118
Emongst these leaves she made a Butterflie, . . . *Mui.* 329
amongst those blessed ones. . . . *D.* 287
Emongst the shepheards in their shearing feast; . . . *As.* 32
them to vouchsafe *emongst* his rimes to name, . . . *As.* 38
Wide wounds *emongst* them many one he made, . . . *As.* 107
as he rag'd *emongst* that beastly rout, . . . *As.* 115
Keeping my sheepe *amongst* the cool shade . . . *Col.* 58
emongst the learned throng.' . . . *Col.* 367
Amongst all these was none his paragone. . . . *Col.* 451
Emongst the seats of Angels . . . *Col.* 614
Amongst the shepheards daughters . . . *Col.* 641
Emongst those wretches which I there descryde.' . . . *Col.* 675
shepheards daughters which *emongst* you bee, . . . *Col.* 932
To blazon broade *emongst* her learned throng: . . . I. Pr. 1. 8
Emongst the rest rode that false Lady faire, . . . I. iv. 37. 4
Emongst wild beastes and woods, . . . I. vi. 23. 9
Hesperus *emongst* the lesser lights, . . . I. vii. 30. 4
Emongst that bounch to open it withall; . . . I. viii. 37. 5
high *emongst* all knights hast hong thy shield, . . . I. x. 60. 6
thou, *emongst* those Saints whom thou doest see, . . . I. x. 61. 6
faire Medina . . . *emongst* them ran; . . . II. ii. 27. 4
when the winde *emongst* them did inspyre, . . . II. iii. 30. 3
Emongst thine equall peres, . . . II. iii. 39. 4
Mingled *emongst* loose Ladies . . . II. v. 28. 9
when myld Zephyrus *emongst* them blew, . . . II. v. 29. 8
wave did play *Emongst* the pumy stones, . . . II. v. 30. 3
made *emongst* them selves a sweete consort, . . . II. v. 31. 8
land, *Emongst* wide waves sett, . . . II. vi. 12. 2
oftentimes *emongst* them beare a part, . . . II. vi. 25. 2
More fitt *emongst* black fiendes then men to have his place. . . II. vii. 41. 9
The which *emongst* the gods false Ate threw; . . . II. vii. 55. 5
Emongst the rest of those same ruefull sightes, . . . II. vii. 57. 7
them *amongst* some . . . did themselves *emongst* the heaves
enfold, . . . II. xii. 55. 1, 3
Cupid still *emongest* them kindled lustfull fyres. . . . III. i. 39. 9
Emongst the Roses grow some wicked weeds: . . . III. i. 49. 6
Emongst th' eternall spheres and lamping sky, . . . III. iii. 1. 3
Emongst the woody hiles of Dynevowre: . . . III. iii. 8. 6
Emongst his young ones shall divide . . . III. iii. 47. 9
emongst the which was seene A goodly Armour, . . . III. iii. 58. 6
Amongst her watry sisters by a pond, . . . III. iv. 29. 7
sweete love gentle fitts *emongst* them throwes, . . . III. vi. 41. 5
Emongst the shady leaves, . . . III. vi. 42. 8
she does joy to play *emongst* her peares, . . . III. ix. 4. 8
that straunger knight *emongst* the rest . . . III. ix. 20. 1
Whereas his lovely wife *emongst* them lay, . . . III. x. 48. 2

Amongst—*Continued.*
chose *emongst* the jolly Satyres still to wonne. . . . III. x. 51. 9
Emongst them was sterne Strife, . . . III. xii. 25. 3
Amongst all which was none more faire then shee, . . . IV. i. 9. 5
Amongst the rest there was a jolly Knight, . . . IV. i. 10. 1
The which *amongst* the Lapithees befell; . . . IV. i. 23. 2
Amongst those famous ympes of Greece, . . . IV. ii. 1. 8
Amongst her teares immixing prayers meeke, . . . IV. iii. 47. 6
Amongst the lesser starres in evening cleare. . . . IV. v. 14. 4
With blistred hands *emongst* the cinders brent, . . . IV. v. 35. 3
Amongst the rest some one, . . . IV. x. 43. 7
With silver streames *amongst* the linnen stray'd; . . . IV. x. 52. 5
amongst the wanton Nymphs to sport and toy. . . . IV. xi. 19. 9
there, *amongst* the rest, . . . IV. xi. 53. 6
Amongst the rest was faire Cymodoce . . . IV. xii. 3. 6
Did march *amongst* the many all the way, . . . IV. xii. 18. 8
So farre he past *amongst* his enemies band . . . V. iii. 9. 3
That in these woods *amongst* the Nymphs dost wonne, . . . VI. ii. 25. 2
For love *amongst* the woodie Gods to dwell) . . . VI. ii. 26. 3
To hunt the salvage chace, *amongst* my peres, . . . VI. ii. 31. 7
And borne great sway in armes *amongst* his peares; . . . VI. iii. 3. 3
Amongst wilde beastes in desert forrests bred, . . . VI. v. 29. 7
Amongst so many foes, . . . VI. vi. 37. 6
what gladfull glee They made *amongst* them selves; . . . VI. viii. 37. 2
with helping hands did strive, *Amongst* themselves, . . . VI. ix. 15. 7
set his rest *amongst* the rusticke sort, . . . VI. x. 2. 6
which doe grow *Amongst* poore hyndes, . . . VI. x. 3. 6
Amongst the rest, the which they then did pray, . . . VI. x. 40. 1
That worldly chaunces doe *amongst* them cast, . . . VI. xi. 1. 3
Were troubled, and *amongst* themselves at ods, . . . VII. vi. 23. 3
Amongst thy deerest relicks to be kept. . . . *Am.* xxii. 14
amongst themselves did jar, . . . *Am.* xliv. 2
To wayt on Love *amongst* his lovely crew; . . . *Am.* lxx. 10
Prepare your selves to march *amongst* his host, . . . *H.L.* 40

Amoret. birth of fayre Belphoebe and Of *Amorett* . . . III. vi. Arg.
she bore in like cace Fayre *Amoretta* . . . III. vi. 4. 5
Her *Amoretta* cald, to comfort her dismayd. . . . III. vi. 28. 9
Why then is *Amoret* in caytive band, . . . III. xi. 10. 2
Faire *Amorett* must dwell in wicked chaines, . . . III. xi. 24. 3
redeemes faire *Amoret* through charmes decayd. . . . III. xii. Arg.
was stonisht sore; But most faire *Amoret,* . . . III. xii. 44. 6
Fayre Britomart saves *Amoret:* . . . IV. i. Arg.
Amoret right fearefull was and faint . . . IV. i. 5. 4
avow'd That fairest *Amoret* was his by right, . . . IV. i. 10. 3
that first fayre *Amoret* Might be to her allow'd, . . . IV. i. 12. 2
eke fayre *Amoret,* now freed from feare, . . . IV. i. 15. 6
'I saw him have your *Amoret* at will; . . . IV. i. 49. 1
Her lovely *Amoret* did open shew; . . . IV. v. 13. 2
the gentle *Amoret* Likewise assayd . . . IV. v. 19. 2
Ne her owne *Amoret* forgoe so light . . . IV. v. 20. 7
taking with her lovely *Amoret,* . . . IV. v. 29. 3
Amoret, companion of her care: . . . IV. v. 30. 5
Desiring of his *Amoret* to heare . . . IV. vi. 34. 3
request you tydings of my love, My *Amoret,* . . . IV. vi. 34. 7
she went to seeke faire *Amoret,* . . . IV. vi. 46. 6
Amoret rapt by greedie lust Belphebe saves . . . IV. vii. Arg.
The lovely *Amoret,* whose gentle hart Thou martyrest . . . IV. vii. 2. 4
faire *Amoret,* of nought affeard, . . . IV. vii. 4. 1
(then sayd *Amoret*) 'Thy ruefull plight I pitty . . . IV. vii. 19. 1
when as fearefull *Amoret* perceived, . . . IV. vii. 21. 1
She left the gentle Squire with *Amoret:* . . . IV. vii. 35. 2
those two Ladies late, Aemylia and *Amoret,* abode, . . . IV. viii. 19. 3
Amoret, so neare unto decay, . . . IV. viii. 20. 4
great feeblesse, which did oft assay Faire *Amoret* . . . IV. viii. 37. 4
with him did beare Faire *Amoret,* . . . IV. ix. 17. 7
his conquest tell Of vertuous *Amoret:* . . . IV. x. Arg.
Whose ever be the shield, faire Amoret be his. . . . IV. x. 8. 9
That same was fayrest *Amoret* in place, . . . IV. x. 52. 8

Amoret's. that of *Amorets* hart-binding chaine, . . . IV. i. 1. 4

Amorous. with their beauties *amorous* reflexion, . . . *Col.* 546
Working belgardes and *amorous* retrate; . . . II. iii. 25. 3
To steale a snatch of *amorous* conceipt, . . . II. v. 34. 6
th' *amarous* sweet spoiles to greedy eyes revele. . . . II. xii. 64. 9
Grew pensive through that *amarous* discourse, . . . III. iv. 5. 3
with *amorous* delights And pleasing toyes . . . III. x. 8. 1
Long were to tell the *amorous* assayes, . . . III. xi. 44. 1
him beside marcht *amorous* Desyre, . . . III. xii. 9. 1
To bath in joy and *amorous* desire, . . . IV. x. 38. 7
diving deepe through *amorous* insight, . . . *Am.* lxxvi. 7
Thence to the soule darts *amorous* desyre, . . . *H.B.* 60
they see, through *amorous* eye-glaunces, . . . *H.B.* 239

Amounted. up he rose, and thence *amounted* streight. . . . I. ix. 54. 1

Amours. in *Amours* the passing howrs to spend, . . . II. vi. 35. 4

Amove. she well pleased was thence to *amove* him farre. . . . II. vi. 37. 9

Amoved. *Amooved* him out of his stonie swound, . . . *D.* 545
At her so pitteous cry was much *amoov'd* Her champion . . . I. viii. 21. 1
sore *amoved* with so puissaunt push, . . . I. xi. 16. 6
Therewith *amoved* from his sober mood, . . . II. i. 12. 1
none of all them her thereof *amov'd* . . . III. ix. 24. 8
the shady damp Out of the goodly heven *amoved* quight, . . . III. x. 1. 4
stouping downe she him *amoved* light; . . . III. xi. 13. 1

Amoves. him *amoves* with speaches seeming fitt: . . . I. iv. 45. 3
sad remembraunce now the Prince *amoves* . . . I. ix. 18. 3

Amphion's. that I had *Amphions* instrument, . . . *Ro.* xxv. 5

Amphisa. The daughter of *Amphisa,* who by race A Faerie was, III. vi. 4. 2

Amphitrite. Faire *Amphitrite,* most divinely faire, . . . IV. xi. 11. 6
Joyous Thalia, goodly *Amphitrite,* . . . IV. xi. 49. 2

Amphitryonid. till th' *Amphytrionide* Him slew . . . VII. vii. 36. 6

Ample. Judge, by these *ample* ruines vew, the rest . . . *Ro.* xxvii. 5
Fro me do flow into an *ample* flood, . . . II. vii. 8. 8

Ample—*Continued.*
That stretcht itselfe into an *ample* playne; . . . II. vii. 21. 2
More *ample* spirit then hitherto was wount . . . II. x. 1. 6
And eke that *ample* Pitt, . . . II. x. 11. 1
it was a great And *ample* volume, . . . II. x. 70. 3
The which into an *ample* laver fell, . . . II. xii. 62. 3
Her *ample* shield she threw before her face, . . . III. xi. 25. 2
all the people in that *ample* hous . . . III. xi. 49. 3

Ampler. In *ampler* wise it selfe will forth display. . . . *Ded.Son.*xvi.14

Amplify. Thus gan her plaintif Plea with words to *amplifie:* . . . VII. vii. 13. 9

Amyas. The Dwarfe cald at the doore of *Amyas* . . . IV. viii. 59. 2
'And lives yet *Amyas?*' . . . IV. viii. 63. 5

An (*partial list*). *See* **And, And if, Another.**
a frame *an* hundred cubites hie . . . *an* hundred pillers eke . . . *Bel.*[1] ii. 1, 2
An high headland . . . Like to *an* horne, . . . *Col.* 281, 2
an heap of coine he told; . . . I. iv. 27. 5
an huge round stone did reele Against *an* hill, . . . I. v. 35. 3, 4
An heard of Bulles, . . . I. viii. 11. 6
an whole Regiment . . . V. i. 30. 9
An house of auncient fame: . . . *Proth.* 131

Anamnestes. he *Anamnestes* cleped is; . . . II. ix. 58. 8

Ancestors. Rome, in the time of her great *ancesters,* . . . *Ro.* xix. 7

Ancestries. the famous *auncestryes* Of my most dreaded Soveraigne . . . II. x. 1. 7

Ancestry. onely boast of Armes and *Auncestrie,* . . . *T.M.* 94
the *auncestrie* Of th' old Heroes . . . *T.M.* 439
th' antique glory of thine *auncestry* . . . *Ded. Son.* iii. 6
in this antique ymage thy great *auncestry.* . . . II. Pr. 4. 9
advaunce Mine *auncestry* from famous Coradin, . . . II. iv. 36. 8
Their countreys *auncestry* to understond, . . . II. ix. 60. 7
My glorious Soveraines goodly *auncestrye,* . . . III. iii. 4. 7
Both shew their *auncestry.* . . . III. ix. Arg.
titles vaine, Derived farre from famous *Auncestrie:* . . . *Com. Son.* ii. 4

Anchises'. *'Anchyses* sonne, begott of Venus fayre,' . . . III. ix. 41. 1

Anchor. Upon her arme a silver *anchor* lay, . . . I. x. 14. 6
take assured hold Upon her silver *anchor,* . . . I. x. 22. 3

Ancient. many *auncient* Trophees . . . *Bel.*[1] v. 5
auncient glory of the Romaine peares (lordes[1]). . . . *Bel.* iv. 8
the great (*om.*[1]) glorie and the *auncient* praise, . . . *Bel.* x. 6
many an *auncient* Trophee . . . *Bel.*[2] v. 5
The which this *auncient* Citie whilome made! . . . *Ro.* xxv. 4
th' *auncient* Plot of Rome, displayed plaine, . . . *Ro.* xxvi. 13
Was wont this *auncient* Citie to adorne, . . . *Ro.* xxix. 7
it had bene an *auncient* tree, . . . *S.C.* F. 207
Matching the wealth of th' *auncient* Frankincence; . . . *Gn.* 674
Were forst their *auncient* houses to let lie, . . . *Hub.* 1178
th' *auncient* Genius of that Citie brent: . . . *Ti.* 19
For being borne an *auncient* Lions haire, . . . *D.* 122
auncient truth confirm'd with credence old. . . . *Col.* 103
It giveth name unto that *auncient* Cittie, . . . *Col.* 112
Royall lynage . . . Of *ancient* Kinges and Queenes, . . . I. i. 5. 4
'O! thou most *auncient* Grandmother of all, . . . I. v. 22. 2
auncient Night arriving did alight . . . I. v. 41. 1
By vew of her he ginneth to revive His *ancient* love, . . . I. vi. 17. 2
To see his syre and ofspring *auncient.* . . . I. vi. 30. 4
This was the *auncient* keeper of that place, . . . I. viii. 31. 7
There was an *auncient* house not far away, . . . I. x. 3. 1
The *auncient* Dame Him goodly greeted . . . I. x. 11. 5
An *auncient* matrone she to her does call, . . . I. x. 34. 2
thou springst from *ancient* race Of Saxon kinges, . . . I. x. 65. 1
Of *auncient* time there was a springing well, . . . I. xi. 29. 3
Forth came that *auncient* Lord, and aged Queene, . . . I. xii. 5. 1
That *auncient* Lord gan fit occasion finde, . . . I. xii. 15. 3
It was an *auncient* worke of antique fame, . . . II. ii. 12. 8
Lo! to that shore one in an *auncient* gowne, . . . II. vi. 47. 4
old records from *auncient* times derivd, . . . II. ix. 57. 7
An *auncient* booke, hight *Briton moniments,* . . . II. ix. 59. 6
River that whylome was hight The *ancient* Abus, . . . II. x. 16. 3
no moniment of Brutus, nor of Britons glorie *auncient.* . . . II. x. 36. 9
out of the *auncient* Trojan blood, . . . III. iii. 22. 6
comprovinciall In *auncient* times unto great Britainee, . . . III. iii. 32. 7
As whylome was the custome *ancient* . . . IV. vi. 44. 7
Sprung of the *auncient* stocke of Princes straine, . . . IV. viii. 33. 7
That was a temple faire and *auncient,* . . . IV. x. 5. 3
to maintaine that castels *ancient* rights . . . IV. x. 7. 9
Therein resembling Janus *auncient* . . . IV. x. 12. 5
Ancient Ogyges, even th' auncientest; . . . IV. xi. 15. 4
His *auncient* parents, namely th' *auncient* Thame. . . . IV. xi. 24. 5
auncient heavy burden which he bore . . . IV. xi. 26. 3
Of which the *auncient* Lincolne men doe call: . . . IV. xi. 39. 8
Saturnes *ancient* raigne . . . V. Pr. 9. 1
the heyre of *ancient* kings And mightie Conquerors, . . . V. ix. 29. 7
In which a worthy *auncient* Knight did wonne: . . . VI. ii. 48. 8
Yet did that *auncient* matrone all she might, . . . VI. xii. 14. 6
Her antique race and linage *ancient,* . . . VII. vi. 2. 2
ancient monuments of mightie peeres, . . . *Com. Son.* iii. 2
An house of *auncient* fame: . . . *Proth.* 131

Ancientest. Ancient Ogyges, even th' *auncientest;* . . . IV. xi. 15. 4

Anciently. Brutus, *anciently* deriv'd From roiall stocke . . . II. x. 9. 6
In sort as they were formed *auncientły,* . . . V. ii. 32. 8

And (*co-ord. conj. omitted*).
Shall twentie have, *and* twentie thou hast wonne: . . . *Hub.* 530

And for. *And for* the deawie night now doth nye, . . . *S.C.* May 316
And, for he was but slowe, did slowth off shake . . . *Gn.* 309

And if. *and if* foxes bene so crafty as so, . . . *S.C.* May 313
and if in rymes with me thou dare strive, . . . *S.C.* Au. 21
And if for gracelesse greefe I dye, . . . *S.C.* Au. 113
That waketh *and if* but a leafe sturre. . . . *S.C.* S. 183
And if that any buddes of Poesie, . . . *S.C.* O. 73
And if one could, it were . . . *Hub.* 512

And if—*Continued.*
And if I waste, who will bewaile . . . *U.V.* 19
And if I starve, who will record my cursed end? . . . *U.V.* 20
And if I dye, who will saye: . . . *U.V.* 21
And if in him found pity ever place, . . . *As.* Pr. 17
Androgeus. *Androgeus* and Tenantius, pictures of his might. . II. x. 46. 9
Androgeus, false to native soyle, . . . II. x. 48. 6
Andromeda. The faire *Andromeda* from perill freed: . . . *Ti.* 649
Anew. *See* **New, Of.**
this hydra new, . . . budding monstrous crimes *anew,* . . . *Bel.*[2] x. 12
then the next *anew,* Began . . . *T.M.* 113
auncestrie Of th' old Heroes memorizde *anew;* . . . *T.M.* 440
His Eliseis would be redde *anew.* . . . *Col.* 403
wretched we, . . . Must now *anew* begin . . . II. i. 32. 7
gan Carausius tirannize *anew,* . . . II. x. 57. 5
still *anew* With wonder of her beauty . . . III. ix. 23. 8
Therewith their dulled sprights they edgd *anew,* . . . IV. ii. 17. 6
Then, turning to those Knights, he gan *anew:* . . . IV. ii. 24. 1
In whom he liv'd *anew,* of former life deprived. . . . IV. iii. 13. 9
he now begunne To challenge her *anew,* . . . IV. iv. 8. 6
gan the part of Chalengers *anew* To range the field, . . . IV. iv. 25. 3
The morrow next the Turney gan *anew:* . . . IV. iv. 26. 1
Hath conquered you *anew* in second fight: . . . IV. vi. 31. 3
He wilfully did cut and shape *anew;* . . . IV. vii. 40. 2
unto strength restor'd her soone *anew.* . . . IV. viii. 20. 9
Against the stones and trees did rayle *anew,* . . . IV. viii. 36. 8
their courses change *anew.* . . . IV. ix. 26. 9
now so well accorded all *anew,* . . . IV. ix. 40. 5
gan he make him tread his steps *anew,* . . . IV. xii. 13. 8
'Thou that presum'st to weigh the world *anew,* . . . V. ii. 34. 1
To call to count, or weigh his workes *anew,* . . . V. ii. 42. 6
Whom having quickly arm'd againe *anew,* . . . V. iii. 12. 2
She fayn'd to count the time againe *anew,* . . . V. vi. 5. 4
when as she him *anew* had clad, . . . V. vii. 41. 8
He gan t' efforce the evidence *anew,* . . . V. ix. 47. 1
He gan devize to be aveng'd *anew* . . . VI. vii. 2. 6
therewith flesht upon him set *anew,* . . . VI. viii. 9. 7
The new begins his compast course *anew:* . . . *Am.* lxii. 2
Out of my prison I will breake *anew;* . . . *Am.* lxxx. 6
Angel. An *Angell* then descending downe from Heaven, . . . *Rev.* ii. 12
Then cried a shining *Angell* . . . *Rev.* iii. 8
Living on earth like *Angell* new divinde, . . . *D.* 214
Much like an *Angell* in all forme and fashion.' . . . *Col.* 615
either Spright, Or *Angell,* . . . II. x. 71. 7
To send thine *Angell* from her bowre of blis . . . III. v. 35. 3
Angell, or Goddesse doe I call thee right? . . . III. v. 35. 5
'Ah! gentle Squire, Nor Goddesse I, nor *Angell;* . . . III. v. 36. 2
Like a sweet *Angell* twixt two clouds uphild; . . . VI. xi. 21. 3
Some *angell* she had beene. . . . *Epith.* 153
The brightest *Angell,* even the Child of Light, . . . *H.H.L.* 83
Nor spirit, nor *Angell,* though they man surpas, . . . *H.H.L.* 143
Angela. 'Fayre *Angela'* (quoth she) 'men do her call, . . . III. iii. 56. 2
Which long'd to *Angela,* the Saxon Queene, . . . III. iii. 58. 8
Angelic. 'Tell me, have ye seene her *angelick* face, . . . *S.C.* Ap. 64
Accompanyde with *angelick* delightes. . . . *Am.* lxxxiii. 8
Angelical. Th' *Angelicall* soft trembling voyces . . . II. xii. 71. 3
Angel-like. She, *Angel-like,* the heyre of ancient kings . . . V. ix. 29. 7
Angel's. since I saw that *Angels* blessed eie, . . . *Col.* 40
Her *angels* face, . . . shyned bright, . . . I. iii. 4. 6
an *Angels* voice Singing before th' eternall majesty, . . . I. xii. 39. 3
hevenly pourtraict of bright *Angels* hew, . . . II. iii. 22. 2
The heavenly pourtraict of bright *Angels* hew. . . . IV. v. 13. 4
her *angels* face, unseene afore, . . . IV. vi. 19. 5
soone as he beheld that *angels* face . . . IV. xii. 34. 1
When ye behold that *Angels* blessed looke, . . . *Am.* i. 11
The glorious pourtraict of that *Angels* face, . . . *Am.* xvii. 1
Angels. *Angels* waighting on th' Almighties chayre. . . . *T.M.* 510
To sing with *Angels* her immortall praize. . . . *T.M.* 588
Two *Angels,* downe descending with swift flight, . . . *Ti.* 625
Saints and *Angels* in celestiall thrones . . . *D.* 285
Emongst the seats of *Angels* . . . *Col.* 614
From flocks and fields, to *angels* and to skie.' . . . *Col.* 619
hevenly throne, where thousand *Angels* shine . . . I. x. 51. 6
he might see The blessed *Angels* . . . I. x. 56. 2
blessed *Angels* he sends to and fro, . . . II. viii. 1. 8
indewd With heavenly powre, and by *Angels* reskewd, . . . III. iii. 38. 5
Such as the *Angels* weare before Gods tribunall! . . . III. v. 53. 9
Fit song of *Angels* caroled to bee! . . . III. viii. 43. 1
in heven, . . . Emongst the *Angels,* . . . III. ix. 2. 7
like to *Angels* playing heavenly toyes, . . . IV. x. 42. 5
Mongst which crept litle *Angels* through the glittering gleames. V. ix. 28. 9
Seemed those litle *Angels* did uphold The cloth of state, . . . V. ix. 29. 1
But *Angels* come to lead fraile mindes to rest . . . *Am.* viii. 7
of the brood of *Angels* hevenly borne; . . . *Am.* lxi. 6
even th' *Angels* . . . Forget their service . . . *Epith.* 229
Sing, ye sweet *Angels,* Alleluya sing, . . . *Epith.* 240
An heavenly Hymne, such as the *Angels* sing, . . . *H.L.* 302
An infinite increase of *Angels* bright, . . . *H.H.L.* 55
Sith purest *Angels* fell to be impure? . . . *H.H.L.* 98
No lesse then *Angels* whom he did ensew, . . . *H.H.L.* 121
Angels and Archangels, which attend On Gods owne person, . *H.H.B.* 97
That th' *Angels* selves can not endure his sight. . . . *H.H.B.* 119
For she . . . *Angels* eke, in beautie doth excell, . . . *H.H.B.* 206
Angels, which her goodly face behold . . . *H.H.B.* 232
not seeme . . . of any earthly Seede, But rather *Angels,* . . . *Proth.* 66
Angels'. She did excell, and seem'd of *Angels* race, . . . *D.* 213
this bright *Angels* towre quite dims that towre of glas.' . . . I. x. 58. 9
Like *Angels* life was then mens happy cace; . . . II. vii. 16. 5
seemed borne of *Angels* brood, . . . IV. iii. 39. 7
emptie place . . . through those *Angels* fall, . . . *H.H.L.* 102

Angels'—*Continued.*
Angels, or of *Angels* breede; . . . *Proth.* 66
Anger. *Anger* nould let him speake to the tree, . . . *S.C.* F. 199
a courser . . . the sharpe yron did for *anger* eat, . . . I. iii. 33. 5
To frett for *anger,* or for griefe to mone? . . . II. iii. 3. 4
Outrageous *anger,* and woe-working jarre, . . . II. v. 16. 3
full of *anger* fiersly to him cryde; . . . II. viii. 31. 5
sterne Strife, and *Anger* stout; . . . III. xii. 25. 3
for the present did her *anger* shrowd, . . . IV. i. 10. 7
nought but dire revenge his *anger* mote defray. . . . IV. v. 31. 9
strife and warre and *anger* does subdew; . . . IV. x. 34. 7
They doe his *anger* calme, and cruell vengeance stay. . . . V. ix. 31. 9
Angered. she repented sore to have him *angered.* . . . III. vi. 20. 9
Phoebe therewith sore was *angered,* . . . III. vi. 24. 1
Anger's. Ne once to breath awhile their *angers* tempest ceast. . VI. i. 36. 9
Angle. Into the utmost *Angle* of the world he knew, . . . III. ix. 47. 9
Angles. themselves of her name *Angles* call. . . . III. iii. 56. 7
Angrily. She threw away her burden *angrily;* . . . III. vii. 44. 2
snatching from her hand halfe *angrily* The belt . . . IV. v. 19. 8
Angry. Through his faire hide his *angrie* sting did threaten, . *Van.* ii. 11
cruell fate And *angry* Gods pursue . . . *S.C.* Jun. 15
hath his jawes with *angrie* spirits rent, . . . *Gn.* 278
His *angry* steede did chide his foming bitt, . . . I. i. 1. 6
angry Jove an hideous storme of raine Did poure . . . I. i. 6. 6
Threatning her *angrie* sting, him to dismay; . . . I. i. 17. 7
Halfe *angrie* asked him, for what he came. . . . I. i. 43. 5
Before that *angry* heavens list to lowre, . . . I. ii. 22. 4
With pittie calmd downe fell his *angry* mood. . . . I. iii. 8. 5
Him litle answerd th' *angry* Elfin knight; . . . I. iv. 42. 8
would him advise The *angry* beastes not rashly to despise, . . I. vi. 25. 5
all that might his *angry* passage stay; . . . I. viii. 9. 8
Then tooke the *angrie* witch her golden cup, . . . I. viii. 14. 1
Againe his wonted *angry* weapon proov'd, . . . I. viii. 21. 3
his *angry* needle shott Quite through his shield, . . . I. xi. 38. 5
Both knightes and ladies forth right *angry* far'd, . . . II. ii. 19. 8
He wist him selfe amisse, and *angry* said; . . . II. vi. 22. 6
Guyons *angry* blade so fiers did play . . . II. vi. 31. 5
a Beare, whom *angry* curres have touzd, . . . II. xi. 33. 3
So is his *angry* corage fayrly pacifyde. . . . III. i. 11. 9
she with *angry* scorne did him withstond, . . . III. viii. 25. 8
with the *angry* working of the wave . . . III. viii. 37. 4
angry Gods and cruell skie . . . III. ix. 33. 4
an *angry* Waspe th' one in a viall had, . . . III. xii. 18. 7
'Fond Squire,' full *angry* then sayd Paridell, . . . IV. ii. 22. 5
Her *angrie* teame breaking their bonds of peace . . . IV. iii. 41. 3
Throwne out by *angry* Jove in his vengeance, . . . IV. vi. 14. 2
fayned still her former *angry* mood, . . . IV. vi. 29. 8
halfe *angry* therewithall. . . . IV. x. 11. 9
that *angry* foole Which follow'd her, . . . VI. vii. 39. 6
the Captaine in full *angry* wize Made answere, . . . VI. xi. 12. 1
Cynthia's selfe, more *angry* then the rest, . . . VII. vi. 51. 1
she wants to temper *angry* Jove, . . . *Am.* xxxix. 3
In *angry* wize he flyes about, . . . *Epig.* iv. 9
Anguish. tell the *anguish* of my inward smart, . . . *T.M.* 422
mitigates the *anguish* of the minde. . . . *Ti.* 161
I felt such *anguish* wound my feeble heart, . . . *Ti.* 482
the huge *anguish,* which dooth multiplye My dying paines, . . *D.* 73
the *anguish* of his spright Some deale alaid, . . . *D.* 172
My bread shall be the *anguish* of my mind, . . . *D.* 375
With inward *anguish* and great griefe opprest: . . . *As.* 206
waste the wearie night In secret *anguish* . . . I. i. 53. 3
And bitter *anguish* of his guilty sight, . . . I. ii. 6. 2
For *anguish* great they gan to rend their heare, . . . I. iii. 22. 4
the lad . . . pynd away in *anguish* . . . I. vi. 17. 9
her deare heart with *anguish* did torment, . . . I. vi. 32. 4
sad Una fraught with *anguish* sore, . . . I. vi. 45. 7
you intrete, For to unfold the *anguish* of your hart: . . . I. vii. 40. 6
wondrous *anguish* in his hart it wrought, . . . I. viii. 15. 8
hellish *anguish* did his soule assaile; . . . I. ix. 49. 4
whether dread did dwell Or *anguish* in her hart, . . . I. x. 14. 5
prickt with *anguish* of his sinnes so sore, . . . I. x. 21. 7
For pitty of his payne and *anguish* sore; . . . I. x. 28. 7
full of griefe and *anguish* vehement, . . . I. xi. 26. 1
this wretched woman overcome Of *anguish,* . . . II. i. 58. 7
'The gnawing *anguish,* and sharp gelosy, . . . II. iv. 23. 1
Whence foorth it breakes in sighes and *anguish* ryfe, . . . III. ii. 32. 8
In restlesse *anguish* and unquiet paine; . . . III. iv. 61. 2
did consume his gall with *anguish* sore: . . . III. x. 18. 2
through long *anguish* and selfe-murdring thought, . . . III. x. 57. 1
In wilfull *anguish* and dead heavinesse, . . . III. xii. 43. *or.* 7
His chaunge of cheere that *anguish* did bewray, . . . IV. i. 50. 7
stirs up *anguish* and contentious rage: . . . IV. iii. 43. 4
The signes of *anguish* one mote plainely read, . . . IV. v. 45. 8
pyning *anguish* hid in gentle hart, . . . IV. vi. 1. 2
adding *anguish* to the bitter wound . . . IV. vii. 1. 7
Full of sad *anguish* and in heavy case: . . . IV. vii. 38. 4
As one with griefe and *anguishe* overcum, . . . IV. vii. 44. 4
In wretched *anguishe* and incessant woe, . . . IV. ix. 39. 6
So much the greater still her *anguish* grew, . . . V. v. 28. 1
She parted thence her *anguish* to appease. . . . V. vii. 45. 5
all the night for bitter *anguish* weepe, . . . VI. iii. 10. 4
The *anguish* of his paine to overpasse: . . . VI. iii. 14. 7
And there all night himselfe in *anguish* tost, . . . VI. iv. 40. 5
The bitter *anguish* of their sharpe disease . . . VI. v. 32. 5
it forth doth bring Sorrow, and *anguish,* . . . VI. vi. 8. 6
more increast the *anguish* of his paine: . . . VI. xi. 26. 3
His hart quite deaded was with *anguish* great, . . . VI. xi. 33. 2
To utter forth the *anguish* of his hart: . . . *Am.* xlviii. 10
My pining *anguish* to appease. . . . *Epig.* iv. 60
to augment the *anguish* of my smart, . . . *H.L.* 145

Animate. Stole fire from heven to *animate* His worke, II. x. 70. 7
Annex. to faire semblaunce doth light faith *annexe:* III. i. 54. 7
thereto she did *annexe* False crimes and facts, IV. viii. 35. 5
Annexed. his house is unto his *annext:* II. vii. 25. 8
both their lives may likewise be *annext* Unto the third, IV. ii. 52. 8
Annoy. griefe, that dothe our hearts *anoy.* *Pet.*[1] vi. 12
bitter griefe and sorrowfull *annoy:* *Pet.*[2] vi. 12
So weakest may *anoy* the most of might! *Van.* x. 14
With mortall cares and cumbrous worlds *anoy!* *Ti.* 305
O sad joy, made of mourning and *anoy!* *Ti.* 322
When ye doo heare my sorrowfull *annoy,* *D.* 514
She spoyld thereof, and filled with *annoy.* *As.* 162
The staie whereof shall nought these eares *annoy,* *Col.* 98
still are wont most happie states t' *annoy:* *Col.* 663
cryes, As still are wont t' *annoy* the walled towne, I. i. 41. 7
Fore-casting how his foe he might *annoy;* I. iv. 45. 2
pynd away in anguish and selfe-wild *annoy.* I. vi. 17. 9
His deare delights were hable to *annoy:* I. xii. 41. 4
her sweet peace and pleasures did *annoy,* II. vi. 37. 7
All pleasaunce was to them griefe and *annoy:* II. ix. 35. 5
whose sad *annoy* The Gods doe dread, III. vi. 24. 7
sloth that oft doth noble mindes *annoy.* IV. vii. 23. 9
with bootlesse paine *Annoy* this noble Knight, V. v. 15. 9
joy . . . now turnd to sad *annoy?* VI. iii. 4. 9
Far from all neighbourhood the which *annoy* it may. VI. v. 34. 9
chaunge old yeares *annoy* to new delight. *Am.* lxii. 14
annoy The safety of our joy; *Epith.* 324
Annoyance. *See* **Noyance.**
Were wont to play, from all *annoyance* free, *Ti.* 138
but more *annoiaunce* breed: III. ii. 37. 2
'Night! thou foule Mother of *annoyaunce* sad, III. iv. 55. 1
Annoyed. Your carefull heards with cold bene *annoied:* *S.C.* F. 48
same so sore *annoyed* has the knight, I. i. 22. 1
their quiet government *annoyd;* II. x. 14. 8
oft *annoyd* with sondry bordragings, II. x. 63. 4
sore *annoyed,* groping in that griesly night, II. xii. 35. 9
glauncing fel to ground, but him *annoyed* naught. III. v. 24. 9
that wilde Bore, the which him once *annoyd,* III. vi. 48. 5
too long absence him had sore *annoyd,* III. xii. 44. *or.* 3
sore *annoyd* The Prince on foot, IV. viii. 37. 5
So many monsters which the world *annoyed,* V. v. 24. 6
often hath *annoyd* Good Knights VI. i. 7. 8
most of all Defetto him *annoyde,* VI. v. 20. 4
Annoyeth. My Sinamon smell too much *annoieth:* *S.C.* F. 136
Annoys. devisd redresse for such *annoyes:* II. ii. 43. 8
mucky filth his braunching armes *annoyes,* II. vii. 15. 8
for those Picts *annoyes,* II. x. 64. 6
Such as the troubled Theatres oftimes *annoyes.* IV. iii. 37. 9
Annual. Giving accompt of th' *annuall* increce *Hub.* 301
Anon. I thought *anone,* That *Pet.* v. 3
he will come, without calling, *anone.* *S.C.* May 153
the false Foxe came to the dore *anone:* *S.C.* May 236
gainst whom appeard *anon* Hector, *Gn.* 515
(said the Foxe *anon*) *Hub.* 124
the Ape *anon* Himselfe had cloathed *Hub.* 659
all the gates he found fast lockt *anon,* *Hub.* 1350
ever and *anon,* . . . He cryed out, *Col.* 168
In mighty armes he was yclad *anon,* I. ii. 11. 3
They do arrive *anone* II. i. 13. 4
Of deadly drugs I gave him drinke *anon,* II. iv. 30. 8
fly this fearefull stead *anon,* II. iv. 42. 8
passing by, forth ledd her guestes *anone* II. ix. 28. 8
ever and *anone* with rosy red II. ix. 41. 3
of him was slaine *anon.* II. x. 11. 9
sweet Love *anone* Taketh his nimble winges, III. i. 25. 8
ever and *anone* the rosy red Flasht through her face, III. ii. 5. 6
bad her all things put in readinesse *anon.* III. iii. 57. 9
Anone one sent out of the thicket neare A cruell shaft, III. v. 20. 3
Sate downe upon the dusty ground *anon;* III. vii. 10. 8
ever and *anone,* when none was ware, III. ix. 28. 1
which ever and *anon* Threates . . . him to fall upon, III. x. 58. 4
Anon she gan perceive the house to quake, III. xii. 37. 1
All unawares he started up *anon,* IV. iii. 31. 3
Unto his lofty steede he clombe *anone,* IV. v. 46. 1
So both *anon* Together met, V. viii. 9. 5
walkt about them ever and *anone* V. x. 10. 5
he knew *anone* That it was he V. xi. 37. 5
There did the Prince him overtake *anone,* VI. vi. 30. 4
all which I put in fals out *anon,* VI. viii. 24. 7
lighting candles new, gan search *anone,* VI. xi. 20. 8
The simple mayd did yield to him *anone;* VII. vi. 45. 1
Most dainty trees, that, shooting up *anon,* VII. vii. 8. 7
Another. *See* **One another.**
He blusht to see *another* Sunne belowe, *S.C.* Ap. 77
shepheard must walke *another* way, *S.C.* May 81
Of all my flocke there nis sike *another,* *S.C.* Au. 38
The whiles *another* high doth overlooke *Gn.* 87
They forg'd *another,* as for Clerkes booke-redd. *Hub.* 358
Then must thou thee dispose *another* way: *Hub.* 504
he usde *another* slipprie slight, *Hub.* 859
another swaine Of gentle wit *As.* Interl. 217
From thence *another* world of land we kend, *Col.* 272
in *another* corner wide were strowne I. v. 49. 3
himselfe doth hate, To love *another:* I. vi. 47. 6
to tell her lamentable cace, . . . will need *another* place. I. vi. 48. 9
Another like faire tree eke grew thereby, I. xi. 47. 6
Another saide, that in his eyes did rest . . . fyre, I. xii. 10. 7
Another said, he saw him move his eyes indeed. I. xii. 10. 9
Unto *another* love, and to *another* land. I. xii. 26. 9
Another her out boastes, and all for tryall strips. II. v. 33. 9

Another—*Continued.*
Another warre, and other weapons, I Doe love, II. vi. 34. 6
Another blis before mine eyes I place, II. vii. 33. 3
Another happines, *another* end. II. vii. 33. 4
Him to entrap unwares *another* way he wist. II. vii. 34. 9
shortly brought Unto *another* rowme, II. vii. 35. 2
Another did the dying bronds repayre II. vii. 36. 3
espyde *Another* wretch, II. vii. 61. 2
in *another* great rownd vessell plaste, II. ix. 32. 3
Another seemed envious or coy, II. ix. 35. 7
Another in her teeth did gnaw a rush; II. ix. 35. 8
Another Damsell of that gentle crew, II. ix. 40. 2
Sir Guyon chaunst eke on *another* booke, II. ix. 60. 1
he *another* and *another* did expell. II. xi. 24. 9
he came unto *another* gate; II. xii. 53. 6
he him selfe betooke *another* way, III. i. 2. 7
To chaunge my liefe, and love *another* Dame; III. i. 24. 3
Another arrow hath your lovers hart to hit.' III. ii. 35. 9
Another harnesse which did hang thereby III. iii. 61. 2
heales up one, and makes *another* wound! III. v. 42. 2
The like that mine may be your paine *another* tide. III. vi. 21. 9
at that berth *another* Babe she bore; III. vii. 48. 1
To make *another* like the former Dame, III. viii. 5. 7
Another Florimell, in shape and looke III. viii. 5. 8
Another knight, whom tempest thither brought, III. ix. 12. 2
Hath fownd *another* partner of your payne; III. ix. 40. 2
Another plant, that raught to wondrous hight, III. ix. 47. 7
from her went to seeke *another* lott, III. x. 37. 3
at that rowmes upper end *Another* yron dore, III. xi. 54. 7
That she, your love, list love *another* knight, IV. i. 46. 6
each of you alike doth loth, And loves *another,* IV. i. 47. 5
The other breathing now *another* spright, IV. iii. 35. 8
with her alwaies ride, till he *another* get.' IV. iv. 9. 9
if to match that Lady they had sought *Another* like, IV. iv. 10. 8
So that the doome was to *another* day differd. IV. iv. 36. 9
after him *another* Knight, IV. v. 40. 8
Shall for *another* canticle be spared: IV. v. 46. 7
Her second care, though in *another* kind: IV. vi. 46. 7
I here will stay Untill *another* tyde IV. vi. 47. 9
Selfe to forget to mind *another* is over-sight.' IV. vii. 10. 9
I will deferre the end untill *another* tide. IV. vii. 47. 9
Exchanged out of one into *another* feare. IV. ix. 17. 9
First from one coast, . . . And then *another,* IV. ix. 33. 8
I will them in *another* tell. IV. ix. 41. 9
another sort Of lovers IV. x. 26. 3
Unto *an other* Canto I will overpas. IV. xi. 53. 9
Which to *another* place I leave to be perfected. IV. xii. 35. 9
die guiltie of the blame The which *another* did, V. i. 15. 9
Is with the tide unto *another* brought: V. ii. 39. 8
Another, that would seeme to have more wit, V. iii. 33. 6
in *an other* Canto will be best contayned. V. v. 57. 9
One while she blam'd her selfe; *another* whyle She V. vi. 5. 1
That for *another* Canto will more fitly fall. V. vii. 45. 9
Soone after these he saw *another* Knight, V. viii. 5. 1
Againe the Pagan threw *another* dart, V. viii. 34. 1
fit matter for *another* song. V. viii. 51. 9
This knight, . . . had wounded sore *Another* knight VI. ii. 40. 6
So fare on foote till thou *another* gayne, VI. iii. 32. 2
Turned his steede about *another* way, VI. iii. 37. 2
in *another* Canto shall to end be brought. VI. iii. 51. 9
Was wandred in the wood *another* way, VI. vii. 19. 6
The end whereof Ile keepe untill *another* cast. VI. viii. 51. 9
drawing thence his speach *another* way, VI. ix. 18. 7
Another while I baytes and nets display VI. ix. 23. 5
Another time, when as they did dispose To practice games VI. ix. 43. 1
Another quest, *another* game in vew He hath, VI. x. 2. 3
was placed *Another* Damzell, VI. x. 12. 7
Thy love is there advaunst to be *another* Grace. VI. x. 16. 9
graced her so much to be *another* Grace. VI. x. 26. 9
'*Another* Grace she well deserves to be, VI. x. 27. 1
Will in *another* Canto better be begonne. VI. x. 44. 9
of their Winter spring *another* Prime, VII. vii. 18. 7
with *another* doth it streight recure; *Am.* xxi. 11
How then should I, without *another* wit, *Am.* xxxiii. 9
lend you me *another* living brest. *Am.* xxxiii. 14
another Element inquire Whereof she mote be made; *Am.* lv. 9
bring in hand *Another* gay girland, *Epith.* 42
Though from *another* place I take my name, *Proth.* 130
Another's. 'I saw *anothers* fate approaching fast, *Gn.* 361
Ill mynd so much to mynd *anothers* ill, *As.* 111
mindes *an others* (**anothers*) cares. I. v. 18. 9
Anothers wrongs to wreake upon thy selfe: I. vi. 42. 3
Your court'sie takes on you *anothers* dew offence.' II. i. 28. 9
Him ill beseemes *anothers* fault to name, II. ix. 38. 4
seekes to know *anothers* griefe in vaine, IV. vii. 10. 7
Upon your selves *anothers* wrong to wreake? V. viii. 11. 3
in *anothers* losse great pleasure take, V. xii. 32. 8
Answer. he nould *answere* at all: *S.C.* May 297
Ne wist what *answere* unto him to frame, *Hub.* 313
Respite till morrow t' *answere* his desire; *Hub.* 326
none vouchsafes to *answere* to our call; *T.M.* 352
The Elfe him calls alowd, But *answer* none receives; I. v. 13. 9
To warde the same, nor *answere* commers call. I. viii. 3. 4
no man car'd to *answere* to his crye: I. viii. 29. 7
ne ever other *answere* made. I. viii. 32. 9
His *answere* likewise was, *he could not tell:* I. viii. 34. 1
Whose *aunswere* bad me still assured bee, I. ix. 5. 7
the Redcrosse knight this *answere* sent: I. xii. 31. 1
Great favour I thee graunt for *aunswere* thus to stay.' II. iii. 7. 9
this *answere* forth he threw: II. iii. 33. 1

Answer—*Continued.*
simple *answere,* wanting colours fayre . . . . II. x. 28. 6
Whereto that single knight did *answere* frame: . . . . III. i. 24. 1
ne ready *answere* make, ... III. ii. 5. 2
Staid not to *answer;* . . . . IV. i. 52. 2
answere for thy wrong as shall fall out in fight.' . . . . IV. ii. 13. 9
gan this bitter *answere* to him make: . . . . IV. ii. 14. 2
seemeth well to *answere* to your weede, ... IV. vi. 5. 3
unto every thing did *aunswere* mum: . . . . IV. vii. 44. 5
of him no *aunswere* she received, ... IV. ix. 7. 3
with sterne countenance and indignant pride Did *aunswere,* . V. i. 23. 6
too weake To *aunswere* his defiaunce in the field, ... V. i. 24. 2
With proud disdaine did scornefull *answere* make, ... V. iii. 16. 2
To whom the elder did this *aunswere* frame: . . . . V. iv. 7. 1
Both which to barre he with this *answere* met her: . . . . V. v. 37. 6
Ne would abide, till she had *aunswere* made, ... V. vi. 17. 7
Yet mote he algates now abide, and *answere* make. . . . . V. viii. 5. 9
The Prince staid not his *aunswere* to devize, ... V. xi. 4. 1
Ne ought to *answere* thereunto did find; . . . . V. xi. 64. 3
The Dwarfe . . . Brought *aunswere* backe, ... VI. i. 31. 4
Yet for the time this *answere* he to him behight. . . . . VI. ii. 36. 9
Which *answer* when the groome returning brought . . . . VI. iii. 43. 3
To whom the Prince . . . Mylde *answer* made, ... VI. vi. 20. 6
she thereto nould plead, nor *answere* ought, ... VI. vii. 36. 3
The villaine stayd not *aunswer* to invent, ... VI. viii. 8. 1
answere him awhit thereto. . . . . VI. viii. 50. 9
the Captaine in full angry wize Made *answere,* . . . . VI. xi. 12. 2
The woods shall to me *answer,* . . . . *Epith.* 18
That all the woods may *answer,* . . . . *Epith.* 36
The woods shall to you *answer,* . . . . *Epith.* 55
That all the woods may *answer,* . . . . *Epith.* 73
That all the woods them *answer,* . . . . *Epith.* 91
The whiles the woods shal *answer,* . . . . *Epith.* 109
all the woods shal *answer,* . . . . *Epith.* 128
al the woods them *answer,* . . . . *Epith.* 147
That all the woods may *answer,* . . . . *Epith.* 166
To which the woods did *answer,* . . . . *Epith.* 184
al the woods should *answer,* . . . . *Epith.* 203
That al the woods may *answere,* . . . . *Epith.* 222
That all the woods may *answere,* . . . . *Epith.* 241
To which the woods shall *answer,* . . . . *Epith.* 260
That all the woods may *answer,* . . . . *Epith.* 277
That all the woods them *answer,* . . . . *Epith.* 295
The woods no more shall *answere,* . . . . *Epith.* 314
Ne let the woods them *answer* . . . . *Epith.* 333
Ne let the woods them *answer,* . . . . *Epith.* 352
Ne will the woods now *answer,* . . . . *Epith.* 371
Ne let the woods us *answere,* . . . . *Epith.* 389
Ne any woods shall *answer,* . . . . *Epith.* 408
The woods no more us *answer,* . . . . *Epith.* 426
Answerable. Most *answerable* to his wyld disguize . . . . IV. iv. 42. 5
Answered. Little him *aunswered* the Oake againe, ... *S.C.* F. 140
answerd his mother, all should be done. . . . . *S.C.* May 228
(*answer'd* then the Ape) . . . . *Hub.* 71
With lowd laments her *answered* . . . . *T.M.* 418
oft she cald to him, who *answerd* nought, ... *As.* 167
To whom the shepheard gently *answered* thus; . . . . *Col.* 36
'True (*answered* he) . . . . *Col.* 620
the rude wench her *answerd* nought at all: . . . . I. iii. 11. 3
He *answered* nought, but in a traunce still lay, ... I. iii. 39. 6
Him litle *answerd* th' angry Elfin knight; . . . . I. iv. 42. 8
answerd he then ferce, 'I no whitt reck; . . . . I. iv. 50. 8
Ecchoes three *aunswer'd* it selfe againe: . . . . I. viii. 4. 4
Who *answerd* him full soft, ... I. viii. 32. 5
He could not tell, againe he *answered.* . . . . I. viii. 33. 2
He *answerd* nought at all; . . . . I. ix. 24. 1
him *answered* the Redcrosse knight, ... II. i. 33. 1
Yet mildly him to purpose *answered;* . . . . II. iv. 39. 8
In great disdaine he *answerd:* . . . . II. vii. 7. 6
Him Mammon *answered;* 'That goodly one, ... II. vii. 48. 4
groning deepe, thus *answerd* him againe; . . . . II. vii. 59. 3
lifting up his head, him *answerd* thus; . . . . II. vii. 62. 2
To whom the Palmer fearlesse *answered:* . . . . II. viii. 13. 1
nought againe Him *answered,* as courtesie became; . . . . II. viii. 23. 3
The Palmer . . . Him *answered:* . . . . II. viii. 54. 4
gently *answered,* They entraunce did desire. . . . . II. ix. 11. 9
It *answered* was, ... II. ix. 39. 8
She *answerd* nought, but more abasht for shame . . . . II. ix. 43. 1
In his big base them fitly *answered;* . . . . II. xii. 33. 2
The gentle warbling wind low *answered* to all. . . . . II. xii. 71. 9
At last, the passion past, she thus him *answered.* . . . . III. ii. 5. 9
Her shortly *answered:* 'Faire martiall Mayd, ... III. ii. 9. 4
The Dwarfe him *answerd;* . . . . III. v. 4. 2
everie one her *answerd,* . . . . III. vi. 14. 3
To whom halfe weeping she thus *answered;* . . . . III. vi. 20. 6
Her mildly *answer'd:* 'Beldame, be not wroth . . . . III. vii. 8. 6
With nought but ghastly lookes him *answered;* . . . . III. vii. 14. 6
Him *answered,* that all were now retyrd . . . . III. ix. 10. 3
with the like him *aunswerd* evermore. . . . . III. ix. 28. 7
answered; 'Sir, him wise I never held, ... IV. i. 34. 7
He little *answer'd,* but . . . did forbeare; . . . . IV. i. 45. 1
She litle *answer'd* him, but lightly did aggrate. . . . . IV. ii. 23. 9
To whom thus *aunswer'd* was: 'Ah, wretched wight! . . . . IV. vii. 10. 6
'Unhappy mayd' (then *answer'd* she), ... IV. vii. 11. 5
to his speach he *aunswered* no whit, ... IV. vii. 44. 1
no man *aunswred* me by name; . . . . IV. x. 11. 4
no man *answred* to my clame: . . . . IV. x. 11. 5
who still her *answered,* there was nought. . . . . IV. xii. 24. 9
To whom she *answer'd:* . . . . IV. xii. 31. 1
he *aunswerd* wroth, 'Loe! there thy hire;' . . . . V. ii. 11. 8

Answered—*Continued.*
Then *answered* the righteous Artegall, ... V. ii. 39. 2
He *answered* that he would try it streight; . . . . V. ii. 44. 7
many things demaund, to which she *answer'd* light. . . . . V. vi. 20. 9
Thus *answer'd:* 'Lewdly thou my love depravest, ... V. vii. 32. 8
He boldly *aunswerd* him, ... V. xi. 4. 8
(Then *answered* he) 'which often hath annoyd . . . . VI. i. 7. 8
To whom he *answered* thus: . . . . VI. i. 12. 5
Yet *answer'd* thus: 'Not unto me the shame, ... VI. i. 26. 2
the other . . . Yet boldly *answer'd,* . . . . VI. ii. 18. 7
to him *aunswer'd,* that there was no place . . . . VI. iii. 38. 7
To whom the Squire nought *aunswered* againe, ... VI. v. 24. 2
Fortune *aunswerd* not unto his call; . . . . VI. viii. 10. 1
They *answer'd* him that no such beast they saw, ... VI. ix. 6. 1
'Surely, my sonne,' (then *answer'd* he againe) . . . . VI. ix. 20. 1
answerd then that swaine, ... VI. x. 20. 1
they *aunswer'd* . . . That they were poore heardgroomes, . . . VI. xi. 39. 7
did sternely lower, And stoutly *answer'd,* . . . . VII. vi. 18. 5
Him boldly *answer'd* thus to his demaund: . . . . VII. vi. 26. 3
Answering. all her Sisters, thereto *answering,* . . . . *T.M.* 171
Who thereto *answering* said: . . . . III. viii. 46. 1
answering their wearie turnes around, ... IV. v. 33. 8
Answers. when he heard her *answers* loth, ... I. vii. 38. 3
neede, that *answers* not to all requests, ... IV. viii. 27. 3
hearing th' *answeres* of his pregnant wit, ... VI. ii. 24. 4
Ant. a little *Ant,* a silly worme, ... *Van.* viii. 9
Antelope. The *Antelope,* and Wolfe both fiers and fell; . . . **I. vi. 26. 5**
Anthem. Wayting when as the *Antheme* should be sung on hye. . IV. x. 48. 9
The Choristers the joyous *Antheme* sing, ... *Epith.* 221
Anthems. At morne and even, besides their *Anthemes* sweete, . *Hub.* 451
Their *anthemes* sweet, devized of loves prayse, ... *Am.* xix. 6
Antics. entayld With curious *antickes,* . . . . II. iii. 27. 5
Woven with *antickes* and wyld ymagery; . . . . II. vii. 4. 6
Wrought with wilde *Antickes,* . . . . III. xi. 51. 5
Antidote. With salve, or *antidote,* or other mene, ... VI. vi. 9. 5
Antiochus. *Antiochus,* the which advaunst His cursed hand gainst God, ... I. v. 47. 8
Antiope. In Satyres shape *Antiopa* he snatcht; . . . . III. xi. 35. 1
Antique. for your *antique* furie here doo call, ... *Ro.* i. 12
The *antique* Rhodian will likewise set forth The great Colosse, *Ro.* ii. 9
Upon her bellie th' *antique* Palatine, ... *Ro.* iv. 10
That *antique* horror, which made heaven adredd. . . . . *Ro.* xvii. 8
Under these *antique* ruines yet remaine. . . . . *Ro.* xix. 14
Those *antique* Caesars, sleeping long in darke, ... *Ro.* xxv. 3
The *antique* pride which menaced the skie, ... *Ro.* xxvii. 2
th' *antique* faith of Justice long agone . . . . *Gn.* 359
here the *antique* fame of stout Camill Doth ever live; . . . . *Gn.* 601
Where be those learned wits and *antique* Sages, ... *Ti.* 59
all my *antique* moniments defaced? . . . . *Ti.* 179
th' *antique* glory of thine auncestry . . . . *Ded. Son.* iii. 6
whose famous ofspring The *antique* Poets wont . . . to sing; *Ded. Son.* vi. 5
Lay forth . . . The *antique* rolles, ... I. Pr. 2. 4
The *Antique* ruins of the Romanes fall: . . . . I. v. 49. 4
that great Champion of the *antique* world, ... I. xi. 27. 1
aged Queene, Arayd in *antique* robes downe to the grownd, . . I. xii. 5. 2
th' *antique* world excesse and pryde did hate: . . . . I. xii. 14. 8
all this famous *antique* history . . . . II. Pr. 1. 2
in this *antique* ymage thy great auncestry. . . . . II. Pr. 4. 9
It was an auncient worke of *antique* fame, ... II. ii. 12. 8
The *antique* shapes of kings and kesars straunge and rare. . II. vii. 5. 9
'The *antique* world . . . Fownd no defect . . . . II. vii. 16. 1
leave the rudenesse of that *antique* age . . . . II. vii. 18. 2
that, which *antique* Cadmus whylome built In Thebes, ... II. ix. 45. 6
antique Regesters for to avise, ... II. ix. 59. 4
In *antique* times was salvage wildernesse, ... II. x. 5. 3
The noble braunch from th' *antique* stocke was torne . . . . II. x. 36. 4
Semiramis, Whom *antique* history so high doth rayse, ... II. x. 56. 3
antique praises unto present persons fitt. . . . . III. Pr. 3. 9
O! goodly usage of those *antique* tymes, ... III. i. 13. 1
As whylome was the *antique* worldes guize, ... III. i. 39. 3
by record of *antique* times I finde . . . . III. ii. 2. 1
all his armour seemd of *antique* mould, ... III. ii. 25. 2
the sleeping memoree Of those same *antique* Peres, ... III. iii. 22. 8
The royall seed, the *antique* Trojan blood, ... III. iii. 42. 8
Where is the *Antique* glory now become, ... III. iv. 1. 1
As it in *antique* bookes is mentioned. . . . . III. vi. 6. 3
of the *antique* Trojan stocke there grew Another plant, . . . III. ix. 47. 6
all the *antique* Worthies merits far did passe. . . . . III. ix. 50. 9
There was the signe of *antique* Babylon; . . . . IV. i. 22. 1
as *antique* stories tellen us, ... IV. ii. 32. 1
After the Persian Monarks *antique* guize, ... IV. iii. 38. 8
antique age, yet in the infancie Of time, ... IV. viii. 30. 1
(as *antique* fathers tell) . . . . IV. xi. 37. 2
the *antique* wisards well invented . . . . IV. xii. 2. 1
present time The image of the *antique* world compare, . . . V. Pr. 1. 2
But to the *antique* use which was of yore, ... V. Pr. 3. 5
Well therefore did the *antique* world invent . . . . V. vii. 2. 1
Her *antique* race and linage ancient, ... VII. vi. 2. 2
famous warriors of *anticke* world . . . . *Am.* lxix. 1
antique Babel, Empresse of the East, ... *Com. Son.* iv. 1
Antiquities. Cease not to sound these olde *antiquities;* . . . *Ro.* xxxii. 10
vouch *antiquities,* which no body can know. . . . . II. Pr. 1. 9
So long they redd in those *antiquities,* . . . . II. x. 77. 3
Antiquity. 'Cambden! the nourice of *antiquitie,* . . . . *Ti.* 169
Antiquitee of Faery lond: . . . . II. ix. 60. 2
wonder of *antiquity* long stopt his speach. . . . . II. x. 68. 9
a God him sage *Antiquity* Did wisely make, ... II. xii. 48. 1
Well did *Antiquity* a God thee deeme, ... III. iii. 2. 1
The warlike Worthies, from *antiquitye,* . . . . III. iii. 4. 4
records of *antiquitie* appeare, ... IV. xi. 10. 4

Antiquity—*Continued.*
being matcht with plaine *Antiquitie*, . . . VI. Pr. 4. 7
in all *Antiquity* So faire a patterne finde, . . . VI. Pr. 6. 1
doth vaine *antiquitie* so vaunt Her ancient monuments . . . *Com. Son.* iii. 1
Antonius. High Caesar, great Pompey, and fiers *Antonius.* . . . I. v. 49. 9
Antony. so did warlike *Antony* neglect The worlds whole rule V. viii. 2. 6
Anvil. As sparkles from the *Andvile* use to fly, . . . I. xi. 42. 6
Like sparke of fire that from the *andvile* glode, . . . IV. iv. 23. 5
About the *Andvile* standing evermore . . . IV. v. 36. 2
So dreadfully he did the *andvile* beat, . . . IV. v. 37. 5
As if she had an yron *andvile* beene, . . . V. v. 8. 2
beat on th' *andvile* (**andvyle*) of her stubberne wit . . . *Am.* xxxii. 8
Any (*partial list*).
not in *anie* wise . . . *Pet.* iv. 3
spirite might not *anie* moe Be vext . . . *Pet.*[2] vii. 7
If under heaven *anie* endurance were, . . . *Ro.* xxxii. 5
Ne suffred him in *anie* place to rest, . . . *Van.* iv. 9
'Ye Gods of love, . . . (If *any* gods . . . *S.C.* Ja. 14
Well mought it beseme *any* harvest Queene. . . . *S.C.* Au. 36
uneth may I stand *any* more: . . . *S.C.* S. 48
prive or pert yf *any* bene, . . . *S.C.* S. 162
Reliven not for *any* good. . . . *S.C.* N. 89
greene as *any* goord. . . . *Gn.* 164
anie would have smarted. . . . *Gn.* 640
ere that *anie* way I doo betake, . . . *Hub.* 69
To *anie* service, or to *anie* place? . . . *Hub.* 121
not be of *anie* occupation; . . . *Hub.* 155
uncontrol'd of *anie:* . . . *Hub.* 169
take what paines may *anie* living wight; . . . *Hub.* 271
Nor on us taken *anie* state of life, . . . *Hub.* 407
But readie are of *anie* to make preife. . . . *Hub.* 408
Ne let thy learning question'd be of *anie.* . . . *Hub.* 524
I for my selfe must care before els *anie.* . . . *Hub.* 1196
Ne would he *anie* let . . . *Hub.* 1201
never after *anie* Should . . . be voyd . . . *Hub.* 1241
nor cared for of *anie*, . . . *T.M.* 225
neither you nor we shall *anie* more . . . *T.M.* 409
'Name have I none . . . nor *anie* being, . . . *Ti.* 34
Nor ever ship shall saile there *anie* more. . . . *Ti.* 154
Nor *anie* lives that . . . *Ti.* 164
Scarse *anie* left to close his eylids neare; Scarse *anie* left . . . *Ti.* 194, 195
as white as *anie* milke, . . . *Ti.* 561
Above the reach of *anie* living sight: . . . *Ti.* 628
might for *anie* Princes couche . . . *Ti.* 633
might *anie* in his trap betray. . . . *Mui.* 248
Nor *anie* skil'd in workmanship . . . Nor *anie* skil'd in loupes. *Mui.* 365, 366
Ne *anie* noyse, ne *anie* motion made. . . . *Mui.* 400
I care that *any* should bemone . . . or *any* weepe . . . *D.* 75, 76
No toong can tell, nor *any* forth can set, . . . *As.* 171
As fairly formd as *any* star . . . *As.* 188
as skilfull in that art as *any*. . . . *Col.* 75
not *any* gentle wit of name . . . *Col.* 733
Ne *any* there . . . *Col.* 779
Not perceable with power of *any* starr: . . . I. i. 7. 6
plain none might her see, nor she see *any* plaine, . . . I. i. 16. 9
thrise three times did fast from *any* bitt; . . . I. iii. 14. 4
if that *any* else did Jove excell; . . . I. iv. 11. 7
Unfit he was for *any* worldly thing, . . . I. iv. 23. 1
death it was, when *any* good he saw; . . . I. iv. 30. 7
He hated . . . him no lesse, that *any* like did use; . . . I. iv. 32. 2
death ensewd if *any* him descryde. . . . I. v. 52. 9
there abode, whylst *any* beast of name Walkt . . . I. vi. 29. 3
it would pitty *any* living eie. . . . I. vi. 43. 6
steed . . . chauft that *any* on his backe should sitt: . . . I. vii. 37. 8
never *any* could that girlond win, . . . I. vii. 45. 6
Each dore he opened without *any* breach, . . . I. viii. 34. 8
If *any* strength we have, it is to ill, . . . I. x. 1. 8
any other wight, That hither turnes his steps. . . . I. x. 10. 2
left not *any* marke where it did light, . . . I. xi. 25. 4
Ne lets her waves with *any* filth be dyde; . . . II. ii. 9. 8
Ne *any* evill meanes she did forbeare, . . . II. iv. 5. 8
more sweete then *any* bird . . . II. vi. 25. 1
Lives *any* that you hath thus ill apayd? . . . II. ix. 37. 7
slaine, ere *any* thereof thought: . . . II. x. 51. 4
That never entraunce *any* durst pretend, . . . II. xi. 15. 8
from vew of *any* which them eyd. . . . II. xii. 63. 9
never *any* mote with her compayre: . . . III. i. 26. 5
softely felt if *any* member moov'd, . . . III. i. 60. 7
Ne *any* noise she made, . . . III. i. 61. 6
that *any* doth confownd Them . . . III. ii. 14. 7
Ne braver proofe in *any* of thy powre . . . III. iii. 3. 2
dare thou not, I charge, in *any* cace . . . III. iii. 8. 7
quake when *any* him to them does name. . . . III. iii. 12. 9
lenger here then ever *any* stood?' . . . III. iii. 42. 9
gentle Sleepe envyde him *any* rest: . . . III. iv. 54. 1
fresh in face and guize As *any* Nimphe; . . . III. vi. 23. 8
ne *any* does envy Their goodly meriment . . . III. vi. 41. 8
never *any* knight Is suffred here . . . III. ix. 6. 3
Of knights and ladies *any* meetings were; . . . III. x. 19. 8
tell thy griefe, if *any* hidden lye: . . . III. x. 26. 2
long, and swift as *any* Roe, . . . III. xi. 5. 8
Ne yet by *any* meanes remov'd away; . . . III. xi. 23. 8
construe it By *any* ridling skill, . . . III. xi. 54. 5
Seeking adventures where they *anie* knew. . . . IV. ii. 46. 5
Ne ever for rebuke or blame of *any* balkt. . . . IV. x. 25. 9
if *any* Gods at all Have care . . . IV. xii. 9. 1
Nor unto *any* meaner to complaine; . . . IV. xii. 29. 3
Ne *any* liv'd on ground that durst withstand . . . V. i. 8. 6
Ne *any* armoure could his dint out-ward; . . . V. i. 10. 8
Ne ever *any* asketh reason why. . . . V. ii. 41. 2

Any—*Continued.*
he stood as still as *any* stake, . . . V. iii. 34. 5
mad For *any* death to chaunge life, . . . V. iv. 11. 5
Not wronging *any* other by my will, . . . V. iv. 14. 4
Any her proud observaunce will withstand, . . . V. iv. 32. 2
if thou canst win him *any* way . . . V. v. 33. 6
Least *any* should betray his Lady . . . V. vi. 26. 9
nor *any* could she spie: . . . V. vi. 35. 7
Serves her as *any* Princesse under sky, . . . V. viii. 18. 7
For *any* brybes, or threates of *any* to be wroken. . . . V. ix. 24. 9
Yet glad . . . life enjoy for *any* composition: . . . V. x. 27. 5
To which they had no right, nor *any* wrongfull state. . . . V. xi. 3. 9
For guiftes of gold or *any* worldly glee, . . . V. xi. 63. 3
Ne *any* able was him to withstand, . . . V. xii. 7. 6
Ne ever *any* found his match . . . V. xii. 15. 4
That had to *any* happily betid, . . . V. xii. 32. 2
ill that *any* did, Or harme that *any* had, . . . V. xii. 32. 5, 6
whatsoever good by *any* sayd . . . V. xii. 34. 1
if that *any* ill she heard of *any*, . . . V. xii. 35. 1
by no art, nor *any* leaches might, . . . VI. vi. 1. 5
Ne lodging would to *any* of them graunt; . . . VI. vi. 21. 5
So as he could not weld him *any* way: . . . VI. viii. 11. 5
Did care a whit, ne *any* liking lend: . . . VI. ix. 10. 8
Impatient of *any* paramoure: . . . VI. ix. 39. 5
sore her payn'd, by *any* to be drest. . . . VI. xi. 24. 7
ne *any* him doth spare; . . . VI. xi. 48. 7
shund to match with *any* forrein fere. . . . VI. xii. 4. 9
Ne ever *any* durst till then impose; . . . VI. xii. 36. 3
Ne ever could, by *any*, more be brought . . . VI. xii. 39. 3
ne maystred *any* more: . . . VI. xii. 39. 4
if that *any* were on earth belowe . . . VII. vi. 16. 5
(Beeing of stature tall as *any* there . . . VII. vi. 28. 3
beautifull of face As *any* of the Goddesses . . . VII. vi. 28. 5
close might view That never *any* saw, . . . VII. vi. 45. 3
fled more fast Then *any* Deere, . . . VII. vi. 52. 5
more tall of stature Then *any* of the gods . . . VII. vii. 5. 4
richer seem'd then *any* tapestry, . . . VII. vii. 10. 8
Unseene of *any*, yet of all beheld; . . . VII. vii. 13. 4
Injurie, Which *any* of thy creatures do . . . VII. vii. 14. 6
Ne *any* Lake, . . . Ne Poole so small, . . . VII. vii. 20. 5
Ne *any* then shall after it inquire, Ne *any* mention . . . *Am.* xxvii. 9, 10
Fondnesse it were for *any*, being free, . . . *Am.* xxxvii. 13
Ne let the same of *any* be envide: . . . *Epith.* 15
By *any* service I might do to thee, . . . *H.L.* 6
sweeter farre then *any* Nectar is; . . . *H.L.* 26
That whole remaines scarse *any* little part; . . . *H.L.* 144
more then *any* tongue can tell, . . . *H.L.* 264
wrong it were that *any* other twaine . . . *H.B.* 204
See more then *any* other eyes can see, . . . *H.B.* 234
Beseeming well the bower of *anie* Queene, . . . *Proth.* 170
Any one. Her match in beautie was not *anie one.* . . . *Van.* vii. 5
that *anie one* should dare To come . . . *Gn.* 273
Nor *anie one* doth care to call us in, . . . *T.M.* 343
Ne *any one* himselfe doth ought esteeme, . . . *Col.* 781
Yet was there not with her else *any one*, . . . II. vi. 3. 5
Not that she lusted after *any one*, . . . III. ii. 23. 7
hearke what *any one* did good report, . . . V. xii. 34. 8
As *any one* that lived in his daies, . . . VI. vi. 4. 2
doe not *any one* envy, Nor am envyde of *any one* . . . VI. ix. 21. 1, 2
Any's. to backbite *Anies* good name . . . *Hub.* 720
Anything. Listening if *any thing* did rushe, . . . *S.C.* Mar. 71
that *anie thing* could please Fell Cerberus, . . . *Gn.* 439
So long as *any thing* it in the caudron gott. . . . II. ix. 29. 9
Ne ever Artegall his griple strong For *any thing* wold slacke, V. ii. 14. 9
Anywhere. nought may be amended *any wheare.* . . . *H.B.* 35
Aon. Phoenix, and *Aon*, and Pelasgus old; . . . IV. xi. 15. 6
Apace. the Welkin thicks *apace*, . . . *S.C.* Mar. 115
Ye shepheards daughters, . . . Hye you there *apace:* . . . *S.C.* Ap. 128
Then ryse, ye blessed Flocks, and home *apace*, . . . *S.C.* Jun. 118
flye backe to heaven *apace*. . . . *S.C.* O. 84
Brave Impe of Bedford! grow *apace* in bountie, . . . *Ti.* 272
Then do they cry and call to love *apace*, . . . *Col.* 879
Her to behold do thither runne *apace;* . . . I. vi. 18. 2
He left his stond, and her pursewd *apace*, . . . I. vi. 48. 6
Fled to the wastfull wildernesse *apace*, . . . I. viii. 50. 3
after fly *apace*. . . . II. iii. 28. 9
turned her about, and fled away *apace*. . . . II. iii. 42. 9
so he me poursewd *apace*, . . . II. iv. 32. 5
The whiles false Archimage and Atin fled *apace*. . . . II. viii. 56. 9
shot at him *apace*. . . . II. xi. 26. 9
Apace he shot, and yet he fled *apace*, . . . II. xi. 27. 1
their yellow heare Christalline humor dropped downe *apace*. II. xii. 65. 6
she ran *apace* Unto his reskew, . . . III. i. 22. 7
tombling downe *apace* Emongst the woody hilles . . . III. iii. 8. 5
Shall to the utmost mountaines fly *apace*. . . . III. iii. 34. 4
Through thicke and thin her to poursew *apace*, . . . III. vii. 23. 2
lefte his love to losse, and fled him selfe *apace*. . . . III. viii. 18. 9
the great waters gin *apace* to swell, . . . III. viii. 24. 2
the Gyaunt saw, . . . and from them fled *apace:* . . . III. xi. 5. 4
His dewy lockes did drop with brine *apace* . . . IV. xi. 11. 3
They round about him gan to swarme *apace*, . . . V. iv. 23. 7
Yet Talus after them *apace* did plie, . . . V. vi. 30. 4
after those two former rode *apace* . . . V. viii. 5. 2
he followd him *apace;* . . . V. ix. 16. 5
All arm'd to point, issuing forth *apace*, . . . V. x. 34. 2
Into the wood was bearing her *apace* . . . VI. iii. 25. 2
Phoebus . . . Unto his Inne began to draw *apace;* . . . VI. iii. 29. 2
Pursuing him *apace* with greedy speede; . . . VI. iii. 46. 7
after him the wyld man ran *apace*, . . . VI. iv. 8. 1
Playing on pipes and caroling *apace*, . . . VI. ix. 5. 3

Apace—*Continued.*
He pypt *apace,* whilest they him daunst about. . . . VI. x. 16. 5
Pype, jolly shepheard, pype thou now *apace* . . . VI. x. 16. 6
She made me often pipe, and now to pipe *apace*. . . . VI. x. 27. 9
Whose harvest seemd to hasten now *apace,*) . . . *Am.* lxxvi. 10
Begin his witlesse note *apace* to clatter. . . . *Am.* lxxxiv. 4
Apaid. *See* **Ill-apaid, Well-apaid.**
Lives any that you hath thus ill *apayd?* . . . II. ix. 37. 7
ill mote ye bene *apayd.'* . . . III. vi. 21. 5
lay musing long on that him ill *apayd*. . . . IV. v. 42. 9
Apart. Here will I dwell *apart* In gastfull grove . . . *S.C.* Au. 169
my nightly cryes Ye heare *apart,* . . . *S.C.* Au. 190
to be In this or that praysd diversly *apart,* . . . *Col.* 569
Lay now thy deadly Heben bowe *apart,* . . . I. Pr. 3. 5
put feare *apart,* And tel both who ye be, . . . I. ii. 21. 8
sad Aesculapius far *apart* Emprisond was . . . I. v. 36. 7
drowne in dissolute delights *apart,* . . . II. vi. 25. 7
these rich hils of welth doest hide *apart* . . . II. vii. 7. 3
it in flames of Aetna wrought *apart,* . . . II. viii. 20. 7
nothing he from her reserv'd *apart,* . . . III. ii. 22. 3
in long Alba plast his throne *apart;* . . . III. ix. 43. 7
when *apart* (if ever her *apart*) . . . III. x. 7. 1
at the Idoles feet *apart* . . . IV. x. 48. 7
his sharpe sword he threw from him *apart,* . . . V. v. 13. 3
calling her *apart,* Gan to demaund of her some tydings good, V. v. 45. 1
Whose fellow he before had sent *apart;* . . . VI. ii. 6. 5
taking them *apart* into his cell, . . . VI. vi. 6. 1
Apay. what thee dooth so ill *apay.'* . . . *D.* 70
past perils well *apay.'* . . . IV. ix. 40. 9
with gratefull service me right well *apay*. . . . V. v. 33. 9
Apayed. *See* **Apaid.**
Ape. the Foxe and th' *Ape* by him misguided; . . . *Hub.* 38
The Foxe and th' *Ape,* disliking of their evill . . . *Hub.* 46
'Neighbour *Ape,* and my Gossip eke beside, . . . *Hub.* 53
(answer'd then the *Ape*) . . . *Hub.* 71
'Surely (said th' *Ape*) . . . *Hub.* 95
the *Ape,* beginning well to wey This hard adventure, . . . *Hub.* 112
Well seemd the *Ape* to like this ordinaunce; . . . *Hub.* 173
The *Ape* clad Souldierlike, . . . *Hub.* 204
bad the *Ape* him dight To play his part, . . . *Hub.* 233
Eftsoones the *Ape* himselfe gan up to reare, . . . *Hub.* 237
To whom the *Ape,* 'I am a Souldiere, . . . *Hub.* 246
Whenas the *Ape* him hard so much to talke . . . *Hub.* 267
Thus is this *Ape* become a shepheard swaine, . . . *Hub.* 303
The Foxe then counsel'd th' *Ape* . . . *Hub.* 325
th' *Ape* a cassocke sidelong hanging downe; . . . *Hub.* 354
'Ah! (said the *Ape,* as sighing wondrous sad) . . . *Hub.* 368
'Ah! but (said th' *Ape*) . . . *Hub.* 431
th' *Ape* and Foxe ere long so well them sped, . . . *Hub.* 552
th' *Ape* his Parish Clarke procur'd to bee. . . . *Hub.* 557
tell us (said the *Ape*) . . . *Hub.* 615
(said the *Ape*) how shall we first come in, . . . *Hub.* 643
the *Ape* anon Himselfe had cloathed like a Gentleman, . . . *Hub.* 659
the fond *Ape,* himselfe uprearing hy . . . *Hub.* 663
Thus did the *Ape* at first him credit gaine, . . . *Hub.* 689
unto such the *Ape* lent not his minde: . . . *Hub.* 794
there came a secret fee, To th' *Ape,* . . . *Hub.* 876
none but such as this bold *Ape,* unblest, . . . *Hub.* 915
now the *Ape* wanting his huckster man, . . . *Hub.* 925
the *Ape* was sore afrayde, . . . *Hub.* 955
Scarse could the *Ape* yet speake, . . . *Hub.* 964
(sayd the *Ape*) . . . *Hub.* 973
'Fond *Ape!* (sayd then the Foxe) . . . *Hub.* 977
The *Ape,* that earst did nought but chill and quake, . . . *Hub.* 993
Loath was the *Ape,* though praised, to adventer, . . . *Hub.* 1005
th' *Ape* was stryfull, and ambicious; . . . *Hub.* 1021
'I am most worthie, (said the *Ape*) . . . *Hub.* 1027
Sir *Ape,* you are astray: . . . *Hub.* 1033
Man is not like an *Ape* In his chiefe parts, . . . *Hub.* 1042
The *Ape* was glad to end the strife so light, . . . *Hub.* 1056
Themselves to humble to the *Ape* prostrate, . . . *Hub.* 1083
the *Ape* in wondrous stomack woxe, . . . *Hub.* 1103
The *Ape,* thus seized of the Regall throne, . . . *Hub.* 1111
Nought suffered he the *Ape* to give or graunt, . . . *Hub.* 1143
confidence The which the *Ape* repos'd in him alone, . . . *Hub.* 1165
What time the *Ape* the kingdome first did gaine, . . . *Hub.* 1207
an usurping *Ape,* with guile suborn'd, . . . *Hub.* 1233
th' *Ape* himselfe, as one whose wits were reft, . . . *Hub.* 1356
th' *Ape* still flying he no where might get: . . . *Hub.* 1372
Thus was the *ape* . . . put into Malbeccoes cape. . . . III. ix. 31. 8
Apelles'. *Apelles* wit, or Phidias his skill, . . . *Ro.* xxix. 6
Ape's. to the *Apes* folish care, . . . *S.C.* May 96
slaine to serve the *Apes* beheasts: . . . *Hub.* 1308
turning all unto the *Apes* confusion, . . . *Hub.* 1364
th' *Apes* long taile . . . he quight Cut off, . . . *Hub.* 1381
Apes. all *Apes* but halfe their eares have left, . . . *Hub.* 1383
Apes, Lyons, Aegles, Owles, . . . II. ix. 50. 9
some like to *Apes,* dismayd, . . . II. xi. 11. 4
Apish. As that same *Apish* crue is wont to doo: . . . *Hub.* 731
Apollo. O thou far renowmed sonne Of great *Apollo!* . . . I. v. 43. 7
thence *Apollo,* King of Leaches, brought. . . . IV. xii. 25. 4
Apollo came; . . . IV. xii. 25. 5
Apollo's. The golden brood of great *Apolloes* wit, . . . *T.M.* 2
for *Apolloes* temple highly herried.' . . . II. xii. 13. 9
skill In leaches craft, by great *Apolloes* lore, . . . III. iv. 41. 3
Appall. with black horror did the ayre *appall:* . . . *Bel.*[2] viii. 4
you to see doth th' heaven it selfe *appall;* . . . *Ro.* vii. 6
what payne doth thee so *appall;* . . . *S.C.* Au. 15
raging Love dothe *appall* the weake stomacke: . . . *U.V.* 11
when him list the raskall routes *appall,* . . . I. vii. 35. 5

Appall—*Continued.*
her misshaped parts did them *appall:* . . . I. viii. 46. 7
Her gracious words their rancour did *appall,* . . . II. ii. 32. 1
her great words did *appall* My feeble corage, . . . II. iii. 44. 5
trembling terror did his hart *apall;* . . . II. xi. 39. 2
if these did the knight *appall;* . . . II. xii. 25. 6
So th' other did mens rash desires *apall,* . . . III. i. 46. 4
Would make to melt, or pitteously *appall;* . . . III. vii. 9. 7
he fownd, that did him sore *apall*. . . . III. vii. 31. 9
might Did all that youthly rout so much *appall,* . . . IV. ii. 40. 3
Therewith her wrathfull courage gan *appall,* . . . IV. vi. 26. 7
An huge great Lyon lay, that mote *appall* An hardie courage, . V. ix. 33. 4
Therewith Grandtorto selfe I did *appall,* . . . V. xi. 53. 8
As if such pride the other could *apall;* . . . VI. viii. 26. 7
Appalled. all things seem'd *appalled* at his sight. . . . *Gn.* 256
with the suddein shrill I was *appalled*. . . . *Ti.* 581
with deepe dismay Was much *appald,* . . . *D.* 187
could the stoutest corage have *appald;* . . . III. vii. 22. 3
it much *appald* her troubled spright: . . . V. viii. 45. 5
no whit more *appalled* for the same, . . . VI. i. 32. 3
griesly wounds that him *appalled* sore; . . . VI. vii. 14. 5
This their request the Captaine much *appalled,* . . . VI. xi. 10. 6
Appareled. the tall trees with leaves *appareled* . . . II. xii. 12. 4
appareiled With costly clothes of Arras . . . III. i. 34. 1
her therein *appareled* Well as she might, . . . III. iii. 59. 8
Fury was full ill *appareiled* In rags, . . . III. xii. 17. 1
Apparent. *See* **Heir apparent.**
Of which, *apparaunt* proofe was to be seene, . . . *Ded. Son.* xi. 8
Apparition. What shape he list in *apparition*. . . . *Hub.* 1290
Appeach. oft of error did himselfe *appeach:* . . . II. xi. 40. 3
hoste n'ote him *appeach* Of vile ungentlenesse, . . . III. x. 6. 8
least she him sought t' *appeach* Of treason, . . . V. v. 37. 3
Did her *appeach;* and, to her more disgrace, . . . V. ix. 47. 7
Appeached. the fowle reproch, Which them *appeached,* . . . II. viii. 44. 2
Appeal. Thrice unto you with lowd voyce I *appeale,* . . . *Ro.* i. 11
their praiers to *appele* With great devotion, . . . III. ii. 48. 4
Hath hither brought for succour to *appele;* . . . III. iii. 19. 8
thought t' *appeale* from that which was decreed . . . IV. v. 22. 7
He gan that Ladie strongly to *appele* . . . V. ix. 39. 5
to the highest . . . I *appeale.'* . . . VII. vi. 35. 6
And to his soveraine mercie doe *appeale;* . . . *H.H.L.* 257
Appear. did a ghost *appeare* before mine eyes . . . *Bel.*[1] i. 5
Then did *appeare* to me a sharped spire . . . *Bel.*[1] iii. 1
truely doth *appeare* unto our eyes, . . . *Bel.*[1] xi. 2
Then did a Ghost before mine eyes *appeare,* . . . *Bel.*[2] i. 5
a sharped spyre . . . *appeare* to mee, . . . *Bel.*[2] iii. 2
did to that sad Florentine *appeare,* . . . *Bel.*[2] xiii. 2
trulie doth unto our eyes *appeare,* . . . *Bel.*[2] xv. 2
at sea a tall ship did *appeare* (*appere*[1]), . . . *Pet.* ii. 1
Doo make her Idole through the world *appeare*. . . . *Ro.* v. 14
in Porphyre and Marble doo *appeare,* . . . *Ro.* xxxii. 7
the shepheard, seeing day *appeare,* . . . *Gn.* 70
'Well may *appeare* by proofe of their mischaunce, . . . *Gn.* 553
because your griefe doth great *appeare,* . . . *Hub.* 73
That before God we may *appeare* more gay, . . . *Hub.* 462
to *appeare* The morrow next at Court, . . . *Hub.* 1098
Man without understanding doth *appeare;* . . . *T.M.* 128
Like tragicke Pageants seeming to *appeare*. . . . *Ti.* 490
So now in heaven a signe it doth *appeare,* . . . *Ti.* 615
When as the land she saw no more *appeare,* . . . *Mui.* 286
Water doth within his bancks *appeare.'* . . . *Col.* 95
of their passage doth *appeare* no token, . . . *Col.* 143
nought but sea and heaven to us *appeare*. . . . *Col.* 227
most goodly rivers there *appeare,* . . . *Col.* 300
all that therein wondrous doth *appeare* . . . *Col.* 842
gan heaven out of darknesse dread For to *appeare,* . . . *Col.* 856
Perhaps not vaine they may *appeare* to you. . . . *Ded. Son.* ix. 12
Who rough, and blacke, and filthy, did *appeare,* . . . I. iv. 24. 5
he no where doth *appeare,* But vanisht is. . . . I. v. 13. 7
never did such brightnes there *appeare;* . . . I. v. 21. 5
As, when just time expired, should *appeare*. . . . I. ix. 14. 4
both sweet and brave They might *appeare,* . . . I. x. 42. 5
see on the walles *appeare,* . . . I. xi. 3. 4
as an Eagle, seeing pray *appeare,* . . . I. xi. 9. 5
trickling blood, and gobbets raw . . . did *appeare,* . . . I. xi. 13. 4
The morrow next gan earely to *appeare,* . . . I. xi. 33. 1
The joyous day gan early to *appeare;* . . . I. xi. 51. 1
As bright as doth the morning starre *appeare* . . . I. xii. 21. 5
neither silke nor silver therein did *appeare,* . . . I. xii. 22. 9
such to some *appeare*. . . . II. Pr. 3. 9
great rule of Temp'raunce goodly doth *appeare* . . . II. Pr. 5. 9
drery death . . . made darke clouds *appeare:* . . . II. i. 45. 3
in her face faire peace and mercy doth *appeare*. . . . II. ii. 40. 9
Did all she might more pleasing to *appeare,* . . . II. iv. 25. 4
Ne thenceforth life ne corage did *appeare;* . . . II. viii. 46. 3
of yeares yet fresh, as mote *appere,* . . . II. ix. 52. 3
By whom a little skippet floting did *appeare*. . . . II. xii. 14. 9
not one puffe of winde there did *appeare,* . . . II. xii. 22. 5
'Lo! where does *appeare* The sacred soile . . . II. xii. 37. 7
Such wondrous powre did in that staffe *appeare,* . . . II. xii. 40. 8
as the Cyprian goddesse . . . did first *appeare:* . . . II. xii. 65. 4
The secrete signes of kindled lust *appeare,* . . . II. xii. 68. 6
grace, Mixed with manly sternesse, did *appeare,* . . . II. xii. 79. 6
Did sparckle forth great light, and glorious did *appeare*. . . III. i. 32. 9
so did let her goodly visage to *appere*. . . . III. i. 42. 9
Her tender babe, it seeing safe *appeare,* . . . III. ii. 11. 8
Tell me some markes by which he may *appeare,* . . . III. ii. 16. 3
To let the secret of her hart to her *appeare*. . . . III. ii. 34. 9
one that worthy may perhaps *appeare;* . . . III. ii. 42. 3
was loth to let her purpose plaine *appeare;* . . . III. iii. 17. 9

Appear—*Continued.*
That whylome wont in wemen to *appeare?* . . . . III. iv. 1. 2
shortly he a great Lord did *appeare,* . . . . III. iv. 23. 8
in that monstrous wise did to the world *appere.* . . . . . . III. vii. 48. 9
The furthest North that did to them *appeare:* . . . . III. ix. 49. 3
when she saw aloft *appeare* The Trojane flames . . . . . . III. x. 12. 7
bad before his soveraine Lord *appere.* . . . . III. x. 23. 7
love in thousand monstrous formes doth oft *appeare.* . . . . III. xi. 51. 9
living creature none she saw *appeare.* . . . . III. xi. 55. 2
That by his gate might easily *appeare;* . . . . III. xii. 8. 6
naked nigh she did *appeare,* . . . . III. xii. 17. 2
mote to none but to the warie wise *appeare* . . . . IV. i. 17. 9
some part Thereof did in his frouning face *appeare:* . . . . IV. i. 45. 4
Deeming them doughtie, as they did *appeare,* . . . . IV. ii. 31. 2
these rimes, so rude as doth *appeare,* . . . . IV. ii. 33. 7
Ne lesse his skill in weapons did *appeare;* . . . . IV. iii. 7. 4
Made her to change her hew, and hidden love t' *appeare.* . . . IV. iii. 46. 9
So many Ladies sought, as shall *appeare;* . . . . IV. v. 6. 4
to the last unconquer'd did *appeare;* . . . . IV. v. 8. 7
Now base and contemptible did *appeare,* . . . . IV. v. 14. 2
Full blacke and griesly did his face *appeare,* . . . . IV. v. 34. 6
The things, that day most minds, at night doe most *appeare.* . IV. v. 43. 9
Like to a golden border did *appear,* . . . . IV. vi. 20. 3
Where this same cursed caytive did *appeare* . . . . IV. vii. 24. 4
A foule and lothsome creature, did *appeare,* . . . . IV. vii. 34. 4
as shall *appeare* by his event. . . . . IV. viii. 64. 9
they so like in person did *appeare,* . . . . IV. ix. 10. 8
some ill whose cause did not *appeare.* . . . . IV. x. 12. 9
all his former parts did earst *appere:* . . . . IV. x. 20. 5
The waters play, and pleasant lands *appeare,* . . . . IV. x. 44. 8
in her cheekes made roses oft *appeare:* . . . . IV. x. 50. 5
records of antiquitie *appeare,* . . . . IV. xi. 10. 4
glittering spangs that did like starres *appeare,* . . . . . . IV. xi. 45. 5
The which in floods and fountaines doe *appere,* . . . . . . IV. xi. 52. 8
then plaine it did *appeare,* . . . . V. ii. 48. 7
Some blisfull houres at last must needes *appeare;* . . . . . V. iii. 1. 4
As when two sunnes *appeare* in the azure skye, ... V. iii. 19. 1
'By which that glorie gotten doth *appeare.* . . . . V. iii. 22. 4
Within his mouth a blacke spot doth *appeare,* . . . . V. iii. 32. 8
Which well I prove, as shall *appeare* by triall, ... V. iv. 15. 6
How that three warlike persons did *appeare,* . . . . V. iv. 36. 3
that his guilt the greater may *appeare,* . . . . V. v. 48. 6
The justest man alive and truest did *appeare.* . . . . V. vii. 2. 9
There did *appeare* unto her heavenly spright A wondrous vision, V. vii. 12. 7
Whose porch, that most magnificke did *appeare,* . . . . . . V. ix. 22. 3
Yet did *appeare* rare beautie in her face, ... V. ix. 38. 4
sith he heard but one that did *appeare,* . . . . V. xi. 2. 8
if that no champion doe *appeare,* . . . . V. xi. 40. 2
is ought so bright And beautifull as glories beames *appeare,* . V. xi. 62. 8
from close friends, that dar'd not to *appeare,* . . . . V. xii. 10. 8
Soone as he did within the listes *appeare,* . . . . V. xii. 16. 1
Did underneath him like a pond *appeare,* . . . . V. xii. 20. 7
The one of them, that elder did *appeare,* . . . . V. xii. 29. 1
I never saw in any greater hope *appeare.'* . . . . VI. ii. 26. 9
Make their welcome to them well *appeare.* . . . . VI. iii. 6. 4
That forth out of an hill fresh gushing did *appere.* . . . . . VI. iii. 50. 9
Yet in his bodie made no wound nor bloud *appeare.* . . . . . VI. iv. 5. 9
by rude tokens made to her *appeare* His deepe compassion . . VI. iv. 11. 3
Like troubled ghost, did dreadfully *appeare,* . . . . VI. vi. 32. 8
(yet did no bloud *appeare,*) . . . . VI. viii. 16. 5
being naked . . . The goodly threasures of nature *appeare:* . . VI. viii. 41. 7
thighes, whose glorie did *appeare* Like a triumphal Arch, . . . VI. viii. 42. 7
this sweet peace, whose lacke did then *appeare,* . . . . . . VI. ix. 25. 6
whose pleasaunce did *appere* To passe all others . . . . . . VI. x. 5. 4
The playnes all waste and emptie did *appeare;* . . . . VI. xi. 26. 7
In which what filth and ordure did *appeare,* . . . . VI. xii. 24. 5
that to all may better yet *appeare,* . . . . VII. vi. 1. 6
In which faire beames of beauty did *appeare* . . . . VII. vi. 31. 2
Before great Natures presence should *appeare,* . . . . VII. vi. 36. 3
hanging downe his head, did like a Mome *appeare.* . . . . . VII. vi. 49. 9
Onely th' infernall Powers might not *appeare;* . . . . VII. vii. 3. 6
Her head and face was hid that mote to none *appeare.* . . . . VII. vii. 5. 9
Shall to your eyes *appeare* incontinent. . . . . VII. vii. 17. 5
Yet all are in one body, and as one *appeare.* . . . . VII. vii. 25. 9
by his plough-yrons mote right well *appeare.* . . . . VII. vii. 35. 4
though he lesse *appeare* To change his hew, ... VII. vii. 51. 1
ne other can *appeare.* . . . . VII. vii. 53. 9
Nothing doth firme and permanent *appeare,* . . . . VII. vii. 56. 2
appeare t' adorne her beauties grace? . . . . *Am.* xxi. 4
sweetly doe *appeare* An hundred Graces . . . . *Am.* xl. 3
The goodly ymage . . . would therein *appere.* . . . . *Am.* xlv. 12
So weake my powres, so sore my wounds, *appeare,* . . . . . . *Am.* lvii. 5
which doth longer unto me *appeare,* . . . . *Am.* lx. 7
your light . . . in my darknesse, greater doth *appeare,* . . . . *Am.* lxvi. 12
Appeare out of the East. . . . . *Epith.* 287
in their place doth now a third *appeare,* . . . . *Com. Son.* iv. 9
The Sunne more bright and glorious doth *appeare;* . . . . . . *H.L.* 277
now so faire and seemely they *appeare,* . . . . *H.B.* 34
to make your beautie more *appeare,* . . . . *H.B.* 183
By view whereof it plainly may *appeare,* . . . . *H.H.B.* 43
Fairer then all the rest which there *appeare,* . . . . *H.H.B.* 102
to God . . . even the thoughts of men, do plaine *appeare;* . . *H.H.B.* 173
gemmes and jewels, . . . that brighter then the starres *appeare,* *H.H.B.* 188
Nor Jove himselfe, . . . whiter did *appeare;* . . . . *Proth.* 43
they *appeare,* . . . Like a Brydes Chamber flore. . . . . . . *Proth.* 81
Appearance. Did use to hide, and plaine *apparaunce* shonne) . III. i. 52. 8
with entire affection and *appearaunce* plaine. . . . . VI. v. 38. 9
Appeared. a Hynde *appear'd* (*appearde*[1]) to mee, ... *Pet.* i. 4
some quicke, Whose shape *appeared* not; . . . . *S.C.* Mar. 75
The Image of that Gnat *appeard* to him, ... *Gn.* 324

Appeared—*Continued.*
gainst whom *appeard* anon Hector, ... *Gn.* 515
So soone as day *appeard* to peoples vewing, ... *Hub.* 104
Appeared in their native propertis, ... *Ti.* 284
Next unto this a statelie Towre *appeared,* . . . . *Ti.* 505
in minde to slipp away, Soone as *appeard* safe opportunitie: . I. ii. 41. 7
From top to toe no place *appeared* bare, ... I. vii. 29. 6
from his head no place *appeared* to his feete. . . . . II. i. 5. 9
their natures bad *appeard* in both; . . . . II. ii. 34. 5
Soone as my loathed love *appeard* in sight, ... II. iv. 29. 3
nayles like clawes *appeard.* . . . . II. vii. 3. 9
appeared to have beene of old . . . . II. vii. 4. 4
Ne drop of blood *appeared* shed to bee, ... II. xi. 38. 1
when *appeared* the third Morrow bright . . . . II. xii. 2. 4
The art which all that wrought *appeared* in no place. . . . . II. xii. 58. 9
through the christall waves *appeared* plaine: . . . . II. xii. 64. 7
ere the dawning day *appear'd,* . . . . III. vii. 19. 1
more fresh And fierce he still *appeard,* . . . . III. vii. 32. 9
in his port *appeared* manly hardiment. . . . . III. viii. 44. 9
'afresh *appeard* The glory of the later world . . . . III. ix. 44. 1
she mervaild that no footings trace Nor wight *appeard,* . . . III. xi. 53. 6
The morrowe next *appeard* with joyous cheare, ... III. xii. 28. 6
Bellona in that warlike wise To them *appear'd,* . . . . IV. i. 14. 7
After each beautie that *appeard* in sight, ... IV. ii. 5. 3
Him dead behight, as he to all *appeard,* . . . . IV. iii. 31. 2
through both sides the wound *appeard.* . . . . IV. iii. 33. 9
the hardy Satyrane *Appear'd* in place, ... IV. iv. 26. 3
charg'd his spere At him that first *appeared* . . . . IV. iv. 40. 2
an hundred Ladies moe *Appear'd* in place, ... IV. v. 11. 9
Like to the ruddie morne *appeard* in sight, ... IV. vi. 19. 6
Right plaine *appeard,* though she it would dissemble, ... IV. vi. 29. 7
Ne in his face or bloud or life *appeard;* . . . . IV. vi. 37. 3
close *appeard* in that rude brutishnesse, ... IV. vii. 45. 5
Under the which her feet *appeared* plaine, ... IV. xi. 47. 5
the Lady forth *appeared* Uppon the Castle wall; . . . . V. ii. 22. 1
none *appear'd* of all that raskall rout, ... V. ii. 54. 8
so soone as morrow light *Appear'd* in heaven, ... V. iii. 7. 2
if the least *appear'd,* her eyes she streight reprieved: . . . V. vi. 24. 9
Of all that vision which to her *appeard,* . . . . V. vii. 20. 2
On th' other side her foe *appeared* soone in sight. . . . . . V. vii. 27. 9
of his shape *appear'd* no litle moniment. . . . . V. viii. 43. 9
The morrow next *appear'd* with purple hayre . . . . V. x. 16. 5
Appear'd like Aspis sting that closely kils, ... V. xii. 36. 4
For the rare hope which in his yeares *appear'd,* . . . . . . VI. ii. 34. 3
So fresh the image of her former dread . . . to her *appeard,* . VI. viii. 31. 7
soone as he *appeared* to their vew, ... VI. x. 18. 1
no way *Appeard* for people in nor out to pas, ... VI. x. 41. 8
Appeareth. pleasant spring *appeareth:* . . . . *S.C.* Mar. 9
'Whose borrowed beautie now *appeareth* plaine . . . . I. ii. 39. 2
Honour is least where oddes *appeareth* most. . . . . II. viii. 26. 5
As outward it *appeareth* to the eye, ... *H.B.* 226
That darknesse there *appeareth* never none; . . . . *H.H.L.* 73
Appearing. Through their thin coverings *appearing* fayre, . . . *Gn.* 286
Appearing well in that well tuned song, ... *Col.* 418
By miracle, not yet *appearing* playne, ... IV. xi. 1. 7
Appearing like the mouth of Orcus griesly grim: . . . . . . VI. xii. 26. 9
Appears. death . . . to them *appeares* In thousand formes, . . *Gn.* 583
Even as new occasion *appeares?* . . . . *Hub.* 119
no footing now on earth *appeares?* . . . . *Ti.* 65
of that brightnes now *appeares* no shade, ... *Ti.* 124
in the midst thereof a star *appeares,* . . . . *As.* 187
Where none *appeares* can make her selfe a way, ... I. vi. 7. 2
Then first the cole of kindly heat *appeares* . . . . I. ix. 9. 3
Nor drop of blood in all his face *appeares,* . . . . I. ix. 22. 4
The dreary image of sad death *appeares:* . . . . III. iv. 57. 7
That well (me seemes) *appeares,* . . . . IV. iv. 2. 1
Ne living aide for her on earth *appeares,* . . . . IV. vii. 23. 2
like a pined ghost he soone *appeares:* . . . . IV. vii. 41. 4
They all are wandred much; that plaine *appeares:* . . . . . . V. Pr. 5. 5
the one *appeares* But like a little Mount . . . . V. iv. 7. 6
way betwixt them none *appeares* in sight; . . . . V. vi. 40. 3
That well in courteous Calidore *appeares;* . . . . VI. ii. 3. 1
some Heroicke sead, That in thy face *appeares* . . . . VI. ii. 25. 9
this my cause of griefe to you *appeares;* . . . . VI. iv. 33. 8
That well *appears* in this discourteous knight, ... VI. vii. 2. 1
when the rose in her red cheekes *appeares;* . . . . *Am.* lxxxi. 3
heaven then fire, *appeares* more pure and fayre. . . . . *H.H.B.* 49
Appease. Stygian powres *appease:* . . . . *Gn.* 440
T' *appease* the powers; . . . . *Gn.* 606
we will *appease* our jarre; . . . . *Hub.* 1048
From heaven descending to *appease* their strife, ... *Ti.* 667
nought on earth may lessen or *appease;* . . . . *D.* 276
seemd she to *appease* Her mournefull plaintes, beguiled of her art, ... I. i. 54. 6
Now then, your plaint *appease.'* . . . . I. iii. 29. 9
untill Dayes enemy Did him *appease;* . . . . I. v. 34. 7
appease your griefe and heavy plight, ... II. i. 14. 5
she gan *appease* Her voluntarie paine, ... II. i. 16. 8
Yet algates mote he soft himselfe *appease,* . . . . II. ii. 12. 2
ne sweete entreaties, might *Appease* his heat, ... II. v. 38. 4
t' *appease* the stormy winde Of malice . . . . II. vi. 8. 8
So pleased did his wrathfull purpose faire *appease.* . . . . . II. vi. 13. 9
halfe discontent, mote nathelesse Himselfe *appease,* . . . . . II. vi. 24. 2
secrete powre t' *appease* inflamed rage: . . . . II. viii. 26. 8
jeopardy Which in his land he lately did *appease,* . . . . . . II. x. 17. 4
yet may it nought *appease* My raging smart, ... III. ii. 43. 3
Besought him his great corage to *appease,* . . . . III. x. 30. 8
did not seeke t' *appease* their deadly hate, ... IV. ii. 20. 8
He gan to cast how to *appease* the same, ... IV. v. 25. 2
Whereby to seeke some meanes it to *appease.* . . . . IV. xii. 22. 3

Appease—*Continued.*
In waylfull plaints that none was to *appease;* . . . V. vi. 26. 2
with thy bloud thou shalt *appease* the spright . . . V. vi. 37. 8
She parted thence her anguish to *appease.* . . . V. vii. 45. 5
I . . . strove to *appease* him, . . . VI. ii. 21. 8
the Prince sought to *appease* The bitter anguish . . . VI. v. 32. 4
were not that the Prince did him *appeaze,* . . . VI. vi. 40. 7
which no man can *appease;* . . . VI. ix. 19. 7
Will builde an altar to *appease* her yre; . . . *Am.* xxii. 10
The dreadfull tempest of her wrath *appease,* . . . *Am.* xxxviii. 7
seeke first to *appease* The inward languor . . . *Am.* l. 9
My pining anguish to *appease.* . . . *Epig.* iv. 60
Appeased. the outragious passion nigh *appeased,* . . . *D.* 555
Ne might his rancling paine with patience be *appeasd.* . . . I. xi. 38. 9
during life will never be *appeasd!'* . . . II. iv. 33. 6
so her she soone *appeasd* With sugred words . . . III. vi. 25. 3
she for the present was *appeased,* . . . IV. vi. 44. 1
So was their discord by this doome *appeased,* . . . V. iv. 20. 5
Appeaze. *See* **Appease.**
Appele. *See* **Appeal.**
Appellation. bade Dan Phoebus scribe her *Appellation* seale. . VII. vi. 35. 9
Appere. *See* **Appear.**
Appertain. a girdle . . . Well knowne to *appertaine* to Florimell, IV. ii. 25. 8
I ween'd did *appertaine* To none . . . IV. xii. 30. 4
To whom they aunswer'd, as did *appertaine,* . . . VI. xi. 39. 7
Appertained. So that it to the looker *appertaynd:* . . . III. ii. 19. 4
to her selfe that threasure *appertained;* . . . V. iv. 13. 5
Appetite. A jolly yeoman . . . Whose name was *Appetite:* . . II. ix. 28. 3
they slaked had the fervent heat Of *appetite* . . . III. i. 52. 2
Appetites. Their fervent *appetites* they quenched had, . . . I. xii. 15. 2
When all men had . . . their *appetites* suffiz'd . . . V. iii. 4. 2
Applaud. As in approvance, doe thereto *applaud,* . . . *Epith.* 144
Apple. Here eke that famous golden *Apple* grew, . . . II. vii. 55. 4
The golden *Apple,* cause of all their wrong, . . . IV. i. 22. 5
What time the golden *apple* was unto him brought. . . . VI. ix. 36. 9
Apples. *See* **Queen-apples.**
Loaden with fruit and *apples* rosy redd, . . . I. xi. 46. 2
Their fruit were golden *apples* glistring bright, . . . II. vii. 54. 1
fruitfull *apples* to have borne awhile, . . . IV. iii. 29. 5
Twoo golden *apples* of unvalewd price; . . . *Am.* lxxvii. 6
Her cheekes lyke *apples* which the sun hath rudded, . . . *Epith.* 173
Applied. To thinges of ryper season selfe *applyed,* . . . *S.C.* D. 76
(so well he him *applyde*) . . . *Hub.* 1014
Like as a warlike Brigandine, *applyde* To fight, . . . *Mui.* 84
With like conditions to their kindes *applyde:* . . . I. iv. 18. 4
Whose flying feet so fast their way *applyde,* . . . II. iv. 37. 3
he balmes and herbes thereto *applyde,* . . . II. vi. 51. 6
his busy paines *applyde* To melt the golden metall, . . . II. vii. 35. 8
Their pleasaunt tunes they sweetly thus *applyde:* . . . II. xii. 32. 2
counsell sage in steed thereof to him *applyde.* . . . II. xii. 82. 9
sweet birdes thereto *applide* Their daintie layes . . . III. i. 40. 3
Eftsoones her steps she thereunto *applyd,* . . . III. vii. 5. 6
to their senses vyld Her gentle speach *applyde,* . . . III. vii. 15. 4
wondrous gladnes to her hart *applyde.* . . . III. viii. 2. 9
thereto all his power and might *applide:* . . . IV. iv. 24. 2
with good thewes and speaches well *applyde* . . . IV. ix. 14. 6
To whom his course he hastily *applide,* . . . V. iv. 21. 4
Yet was the stroke so forcibly *applide,* . . . V. xi. 11. 1
all his powre *applyed* thereunto, . . . V. xii. 22. 2
she so well *applyde* Her pleasing tongue, . . . VI. vi. 43. 4
Then all their helpes they busily *applyde* . . . VI. xi. 22. 3
all the playnts which to her be *applyde.* . . . *Am.* xxxii. 12
Applies. Awaite whereto their service he *applyes,* . . . I. i. 38. 4
him to a tree *applyes,* . . . II. v. 10. 4
Apply. none fitter then this to *applie.* . . . *S.C.* F. 100
Nor anie man, we should our selves *applie;* . . . *Hub.* 131
Then to some Noble-man your selfe *applye,* . . . *Hub.* 489
To some of these thou must thy selfe *apply;* . . . *Hub.* 633
thereto doth his Courting most *applie:* . . . *Hub.* 784
applie The faithfull service of my learned skill, . . . *T.M.* 427
Awake, and to his Song a part *applie:* . . . *Ti.* 236
to his wicked worke each part *applie.* . . . *Mui.* 253
This same he did *applie* For to entrap . . . *Mui.* 374
they list not their mery pipes *applie?* . . . *Col.* 373
Unlesse to please it selfe it can *applie;* . . . *Col.* 708
he gan *apply* relief . . . I. x. 24. 4
he meant his corrosives to *apply,* . . . I. x. 25. 8
Ne other worldly busines did *apply:* . . . I. x. 46. 7
sweete Musicke did *apply* Her curious skill . . . I. xii. 38. 6
Who ever doth to temperaunce *apply* His stedfast life, . . . II. v. 1. 1
Ne cared she her course for to *apply;* . . . II. vi. 5. 7
to them does the steddy helme *apply,* . . . II. vii. 1. 8
did *apply* Their mindes to prayse . . . II. x. 22. 5
that which strong affections doe *apply* . . . II. xi. 1. 2
They all that charge did fervently *apply* . . . II. xi. 7. 6
old Syre, thy course doe thereunto *apply.'* . . . II. xii. 10. 9
As diverse witts to diverse things *apply;* . . . III. i. 57. 3
though no reason may *apply* Salve to your sore, . . . III. ii. 36. 4
to *apply* Salves to his wounds, . . . III. iv. 43. 7
His steed eke seemd t' *apply* his steps to his intent. . . . III. iv. 61. 9
costly Cordialles she did *apply,* . . . III. v. 50. 4
Forthy she thither cast her course t' *apply,* . . . III. vi. 16. 8
apply His nimble feet to her conceived feare, . . . III. vii. 24. 5
now so fast his feet he did *apply,* . . . III. xi. 6. 5
gan *apply* Fit medcine to his griefe, . . . III. xi. 13. 8
At least it faire endevour will *apply.'* . . . III. xi. 15. 6
spare thy happy daies, and them *apply* To better boot; . . . III. xi. 19. 5
Of love full manie lessons did *apply,* . . . IV. Pr. 3. 8
did his yron brond so fast *applie,* . . . IV. iii. 25. 7
toward them his course seem'd to *apply:* . . . IV. vi. 6. 7

Apply—*Continued.*
many salves did to his sore *applie,* . . . IV. xi. 6. 2
Whereby she might *apply* some medicine; . . . IV. xii. 21. 5
all the powre she did *apply* . . . V. iv. 41. 8
he did *apply* His mightie hands . . . V. v. 24. 3
all his powre doth thereunto *apply:* . . . V. viii. 18. 5
Behinde, beside, before, as he it list *apply.* . . . V. xi. 6. 9
To the sea-shore he gan his way *apply,* . . . V. xii. 3. 8
wisely use, and well *apply,* . . . VI. i. 3. 6
Ne could her liking to his love *apply,* . . . VI. iii. 7. 4
Unto his first exploite he did him selfe *apply.* . . . VI. iii. 19. 9
So well he did his busie paines *apply,* . . . VI. iii. 28. 1
that wyld man did *apply* His best endevour . . . VI. iv. 16. 1
Whatever formes ye list thereto *apply,* . . . VI. iv. 35. 6
in vaine doe salves to you *applie;* . . . VI. vi. 6. 9
evermore his speach he did *apply* To th' heards, . . . VI. ix. 12. 8
He daily did *apply* him selfe to donne All dewfull service, . . VI. x. 32. 5
he gan his hundred tongues *apply,* . . . VI. xii. 33. 2
fashion to what he it list *apply.* . . . *Am.* xxxii. 4
a leach, that would *apply* Fit medicines . . . *Am.* l. 3
Applying. Which speaches she *applying* to the scope Of her intent, . . . V. v. 39. 8
Appoint. He did *appoint* a warlike equipage . . . *Hub.* 1118
did *appoynt* To lodge the warlike maide, . . . III. i. 60. 3
Appointed. *See* **Pointed.**
Observ'd th' *appointed* way, as her behooved, . . . *Gn.* 467
The place *appointed* where it should be doone. . . . *Col.* 127
The fourth *appointed* by his office was . . . I. x. 40. 1
The sencelesse corse *appointed* for the grave: . . . I. xi. 48. 8
he came unto th' *appointed* place, . . . II. iv. 28. 1
upon th' *appointed* day . . . they came; . . . IV. iv. 13. 5
Within a grove *appointed* him to meete; . . . IV. vii. 17. 8
From the first point of his *appointed* sourse; . . . V. Pr. 1. 8
Bound like a beast *appointed* to the stall: . . . V. i. 22. 6
To doe those workes to them *appointed* dew; . . . V. v. 22. 7
bringing them to their *appointed* place, . . . V. viii. 27. 1
presuming on th' *appointed* tyde, . . . Did thither come; . . V. xi. 39. 1
Appointed by that mightie Faerie Prince, . . . V. xii. 3. 3
the dismall day *Appointed* for Irenas death . . . V. xii. 11. 2
appointed have her place Mongst rocks and caves, . . . VI. vi. 11. 3
Appointed to attend her dewly day and night. . . . VI. xii. 14. 9
Eftsoones the time and place *appointed* were, . . . VII. vi. 36. 1
at th' *appointed* tyde, Each one did make his Bryde . . . *Proth.* 177
Appose. Then gan Authority her to *appose* . . . V. ix. 44. 1
Apprentice. How then shall I, *Apprentice* to the skill . . . III. Pr. 3. 1
Approach. eftsones Winter gan to *approche;* . . . *S.C.* F. 225
when *approchen* the stormie stowres, . . . *S.C.* May 156
Next did the Myrtle tree to her *approach,* . . . *Gn.* 223
with vile cloaths *approach* Gods majestie, . . . *Hub.* 465
Gods majestie, Whom no uncleannes may *approachen* nie. . . *Hub.* 466
in highest place, t' *approach* him nigh, . . . *Hub.* 470
Let those three fatall Sisters . . . *Approach* hereto; . . . *D.* 19
Nor suffer solace to *approach* him nie, . . . *D.* 548
faine have fled, ne durst *approchen* neare; . . . I. ix. 34. 8
the ever damned Beast Durst not *approch,* . . . I. xi. 49. 2
Durst not *approch* for dread which she misdeemd; . . . I. xi. 55. 4
Ne durst *approch* him nigh to touch, or once assay. . . . I. xii. 9. 9
Ne should faire Claribell . . . *approch* thee neare: . . . II. iv. 26. 6
suffer Sleepe once thither-ward *Approch,* . . . II. vii. 25. 6
he fiercely gan *approch,* . . . II. viii. 44. 3
the Squire gan nigher to *approch,* . . . II. ix. 11. 3
labour lost it was to weene *approch* him neare. . . . II. xi. 25. 9
To which nor fish nor fowle did once *approch,* . . . II. xii. 8. 3
to him beckned to *approch* more neare, . . . II. xii. 68. 8
None of them rashly durst to her *approch,* . . . III. i. 64. 7
she gan *approch* to the sea shore, . . . III. vii. 25. 4
Ne suffreth he resort of living wight *Approch* to her, . . . III. ix. 5. 7
durst not for dread *approchen* nie, . . . III. x. 22. 2
Ne none can suffer to *approchen* neare: . . . III. xi. 22. 5
Scudamour was shortly well aware Of his *approch,* . . . IV. i. 41. 5
He durst not nigh *approch,* but kept aloofe, . . . IV. vii. 37. 4
none . . . did darre Him to assault, nor once *approach* him nie; V. iv. 44. 6
seeing her *approch* gan forward set . . . V. viii. 6. 8
Still when he sought t' *approch* unto him ny . . . V. viii. 36. 1
To which when now then gan *approch* in sight, . . . V. x. 30. 7
Yet would not neare *approch* in daungers eye, . . . VI. vii. 3. 2
ne mote the ruder clowne, Thereto *approch;* . . . VI. x. 7. 5
she would not him permit Once to *approch* to her . . . VI. xi. 8. 2
when no more could nigh to him *approch,* . . . VI. xi. 47. 1
let no thought of joy, . . . Dare to *approch,* . . . *Am.* lii. 10
pride dare not *approch,* . . . *Am.* lxv. 9
Thereto *approch* to tempt her mind to ill. . . . *Epith.* 199
striveth still T' *approch* more neare, . . . *H.L.* 248
As to the Highest they *approch* more neare, . . . *H.H.B.* 100
Approached. Wherto *approched* not in anie wise . . . *Pet.* iv. 3
When as they nigh *approached,* . . . *Hub.* 243
darke night fast *approched,* . . . *D.* 557
The first, to which we nigh *approched,* . . . *Col.* 280
His Lady, . . . *Approcht* in hast to greet his victorie; . . . I. i. 27. 2
they now *approched* neare, . . . I. xi. 1. 4
He soone *approched,* panting, breathlesse, . . . II. iv. 37. 6
he in hast *approched* to the shore, . . . II. vi. 48. 9
approched neare Where Guyon lay . . . II. viii. 3. 5
Their visages imprest when they *approched* neare. . . . II. xi. 5. 9
they nigh *approched* to the sted . . . II. xii. 30. 1
soone as they *approcht* with deadly threat, . . . II. xii. 40. 1
to the Castle gate *approcht* in quiet wise. . . . III. ix. 9. 9
as they now *approched* nigh at hand . . . IV. ii. 31. 1
Him weening, ere he nigh *approcht,* to have represt. . . . IV. iv. 6. 7
Whom, when they nigh *approcht,* they plaine descryde . . . IV. vi. 9. 4

Approached—*Continued.*
when she nigh *approcht*, the Dove Would flit . . . IV. viii. 11. 1
ere that it to him *approched* neare, . . . IV. viii. 44. 7
to his castle they *approched* neare; . . . IV. ix. 5. 5
Unto the porch *approcht* which open stood; . . . IV. x. 31. 2
To whom as they *approched*, . . . V. i. 14. 1
To whom when he *approched* neare in sight, . . . V. iv. 21. 6
when he nigh *approcht*, shee mote arede That it was Talus, . V. vi. 8. 5
So forth they past, till they *approched* ny . . . V. ix. 8. 1
To which when she *approched*, thus she sayd: . . . V. ix. 20. 3
Till nigh unto the place at length *approcht* he has. . . . V. xi. 36. 9
To whom as he *approcht*, . . . V. xi. 37. 5
as they *approcht* the cause to know, . . . V. xi. 44. 1
whenas he *approched* nigh in vew, . . . VI. iii. 47. 3
when he nigh *approcht*, . . . VI. vii. 20. 4
as they *approcht*, they gan augment Their cruelty, . . . VI. viii. 4. 6
Unto this place when as the Elfin Knight *Approcht*, . . . VI. x. 10. 2
as he unto him *approched* nye, . . . VI. xi. 27. 7
to the place when they *approched* nye, . . . VI. xi. 36. 5
he him fast pursuing soone *approched* neare. . . . VI. xii. 25. 9
Approacheth. Ne that *approcheth* nigh the wyde descent, . II. xii. 6. 8
Approaching. 'I saw anothers fate *approaching* fast, . . . *Gn.* 361
Approaching nigh, his face I vewed nere, . . . *D.* 50
The Messenger *approching* to him spake; . . . I. i. 42. 1
approching she to her gan call, . . . I. iii. 11. 1
Approaching nigh she wist it was the same, . . . I. iii. 26. 8
The knight, *approching* nigh, of him inquerd . . . I. vi. 36. 1
The witch *approching* gan him fayrely greet, . . . I. vii. 3. 6
when these two *approching* he aspide, . . . I. x. 49. 1
Approching nigh, he reared high afore . . . I. xi. 8. 6
To them *approching*, thus the knight bespake; . . . II. i. 8. 6
The knight, *approching* nigh, thus to her said: . . . II. i. 14. 1
the sad pang *approching* shee does feele, . . . II. i. 38. 8
Approching, first the Hag did thrust away; . . . II. iv. 6. 2
Approching nigh, he never staid to greete, . . . II. v. 3. 1
Fiercely *approching* to him lowdly cryde, . . . II. v. 35. 3
to her bed *approching*, . . . III. i. 60. 5
The knight, *approching*, sternely her bespake: . . . III. iv. 14. 4
Whom when as nigh *approching* she espyde, . . . III. vii. 44. 1
To whom *approching*, well he mote perceive . . . III. vii. 46. 1
nigh *Approching*, with bold words and bitter threat . . . III. viii. 16. 2
shrieking Hububs them *approching* nere, . . . III. x. 43. 3
Approching nigh, eftsoones his wanton hart Was tickled . . . IV. i. 33. 5
when as Blandamour *approching* nie . . . IV. i. 38. 7
Yet nigh *approching* he them fowle bespake, . . . IV. iv. 4. 1
Whereto *approaching* nigh they heard the sound . . . IV. v. 33. 6
soone as them *approaching* he descride, . . . IV. vi. 2. 7
as th' other nigh *approaching* vewed The armes . . . IV. vi. 3. 3
soone as she him saw *approching* neare . . . IV. vi. 10. 3
espies that griesly wight *Approching* nigh, . . . IV. vii. 22. 6
when that theefe *approching* nigh espide . . . IV. vii. 29. 5
were from *approaching* scard; . . . IV. x. 17. 7
Approching nigh unto him, cheeke by cheeke, . . . V. ii. 49. 7
soone as they him nigh *approching* spide, . . . V. ii. 53. 1
the terme, *approching* fast, required speed. . . . V. xi. 65. 9
doth reed A storme *approching* . . . V. xii. 18. 6
when they nigh *approching* had espyde Sir Artegall, . . . V. xii. 38. 2
him called to his aide; To whom *approching*, . . . VI. i. 11. 7
To whom Sir Calidore *approaching* nye, . . . VI. iii. 21. 1
An armed Knight *approaching* to the place . . . VI. iii. 30. 7
To whom *approching*, when as she perceived . . . VI. iv. 27. 1
Eftsoones he spide a Knight *approching* nye; . . . VI. v. 22. 1
Approching to him neare, his hand he stayd, . . . VI. vi. 39. 2
approching thus he gan to say: . . . VI. viii. 7. 3
approaching neare he plainely found . . . VI. viii. 27. 5
the Priest with naked armes full net *Approching* nigh, . . . VI. viii. 45. 5
the moystie night *approching* fast . . . VI. ix. 13. 1
Water fights With Fire. . . . *approaching* neere: . . . VII. vii. 25. 8
Approvance. As in *approvaunce* of his pleasing wordes. . . II. xii. 76. 3
In *approvance* of thy wrong, . . . VI. vi. 35. 1
As in *approvance*, doe thereto applaud, . . . *Epith.* 144
Approve. which better to *approve*, . . . II. iv. 24. 6
She hath ordaind this law, which we *approve*, . . . III. i. 26. 6
by dint of sword *approve*, That she is fairer . . . III. i. 27. 3
T' *approve* the unknowen purpose of eternall fate. . . . III. iv. 28. 9
to *approve* his right with speare and shield, . . . V. i. 24. 4
it *approve* upon his carrion corse. . . . V. iii. 30. 5
did not his demaund *approve*, . . . VI. iii. 42. 4
'Which to *approven* true, as I have told, . . . VII. vii. 27. 1
mercy . . . Unto us taught, and to *approve* it trew, . . . *H.H.L.* 212
to *approve* How much, himselfe that loved us, we love. . . . *H.H.L.* 216
Approved. *approoved* The feends to be too cruell and severe, . *Gn.* 465
for to make his powre *approved* more, . . . I. vi. 26. 1
Which had *approved* bene in uses manifold. . . . I. viii. 3. 9
oft *approv'd* in many hard assay; . . . II. iii. 15. 7
Full oft *approved* in many a cruell warre; . . . II. iv. 41. 4
his *approved* skill, to ward, Or strike, . . . II. v. 8. 6
Hengist and Horsus, well *approv'd* in warre, . . . II. x. 65. 2
noble prowesse, which they had *approv'd*, . . . III. ix. 24. 6
courage . . . *Approved* oft in perils manifold, . . . IV. ii. 39. 3
Ne lesse *approved* was Cambelloes might, . . . IV. iii. 7. 3
Approved oft in many a perlous fight. . . . IV. iv. 40. 5
in this storie find *approved* plaine; . . . IV. ix. 3. 2
That I too true by triall have *approved*; . . . IV. x. 1. 6
Approv'd that day that she all others did excell. . . . V. iii. 15. 9
as well *approv'd* in many a doubt; . . . V. xi. 47. 5
well *approv'd* in batteilous affray, . . . VI. i. 2. 8
Which never yet they had *approv'd* in fight, . . . VI. vii. 5. 5
With such huge strokes, *approved* oft in fight, . . . VI. viii. 14. 2
Approving. spectacle, *approving* trew The wofull tale . . . I. ix. 37. 1

Approving—*Continued.*
Approving dayly to their noble eyes . . . V. x. 5. 5
April. Like *April* shoure so stremes the trickling teares . . . *S.C.* Ap. 7
fresh *Aprill*, full of lustyhed, And wanton as a Kid . . . VII. vii. 33. 1
Apron. put before his lap a *napron* white, . . . V. v. 20. 8
Aptly. As they doe know each can most *aptly* use: . . . VI. ix. 29. 5
Aptness. through kindly *aptnes* of his joynts. . . . *Hub.* 695
Arabian. 'Not so th' *Arabian* Myrrhe did set her mynd, . . . III. ii. 41. 1
Araby. They bring them wines of Greece and *Araby*, . . . I. v. 4. 5
Through boyling sands of *Arabie* . . . I. vi. 35. 6
Arachne. *Arachne*, by his means was vanquished . . . *Mui.* 261
Arachne figur'd how Jove did abuse Europa . . . *Mui.* 277
Which when *Arachne* saw, . . . *Mui.* 337
Arachne high did lifte Her cunning web, . . . II. vii. 28. 7
More subtile web *Arachne* cannot spin; . . . II. xii. 77. 7
Aragnoll. *Aragnoll* (so his foe was hight) . . . *Mui.* 385
So to his worke *Aragnoll* him prepares. . . . *Mui.* 408
Araught. his ambitious sonnes unto them twayne *Arraught* the rule, . . . II. x. 34. 8
Aray, Arayd, Arayed, *etc. See* **Array, Arrayed,** *etc.*
Arbor. Whiles old Sylvanus slept in shady *arber* sownd: . . . I. vi. 7. 9
did an *Arber* greene dispred, . . . II. v. 29. 2
a thick *Arber* goodly over-dight, . . . II. vii. 53. 3
There was a pleasaunt *Arber*, . . . III. vi. 44. 2
Arboret. No *arborett* with painted blossomes drest . . . II. vi. 12. 7
Arbors. *arbors* sweet, in which the Shepheards swaines . . . *T.M.* 279
With boughes and *arbours* woven cunningly, . . . II. vi. 2. 8
deckt with flowers and *herbars* daintily: . . . II. ix. 46. 2
their gardins did deface; Their *arbers* spoyle . . . II. xii. 83. 7
Sitting in covert shade of *arbors* sweet, . . . IV. viii. 9. 2
here and there were pleasant *arbors* pight, . . . IV. x. 25. 3
Arc. The double front of a triumphall *Arke*: . . . *Bel.* iv. 4
Arcadian. To runne thy shrill *Arcadian* Pipe to heare: . . . *Ti.* 328
Arcady. A gentle shepheard borne in *Arcady*, . . . *As.* 1
Arch. that great *Arche*, which Trajan edifide, . . . *Ti.* 551
thighes, whose glorie did appeare Like a triumphal *Arch*, . . VI. viii. 42. 8
Archangels. Angels and *Archangels*, which attend On Gods owne person, . . . *H.H.B.* 97
Archdeacons. To Deanes, to *Archdeacons*, to Commissaries. . . *Hub.* 421
Arched. Eftsoones in compas *arch't*, . . . *Ro.* xx. 3
Above the compasse of the *arched* skie; . . . *T.M.* 370
like the coloured Rainbowe *arched* wide: . . . *Ti.* 550
The roofe hereof was *arched* over head, . . . II. ix. 46. 1
Archt over head with an embracing vine, . . . II. xii. 54. 2
arched all with porches, . . . IV. x. 6. 8
all dispred With shining gold, and *arched* over hed, . . . V. vii. 5. 5
Archer. hie as mought an *Archer* reache with sight. . . . *Bel.*[1] iii. 4
far as *Archer* might his level see: . . . *Bel.*[2] iii. 4
the blindfoulded pretie God, that feathered *Archer*, . . . *Tetrasticon* 1
The *Archer* God, the sonne of Cytheree, . . . *Mui.* 98
the false *Archer*, which that arrow shot . . . III. ii. 26. 7
Archers. One of those *archers* closely did I spy, . . . *Am.* xvi. 9
Arches. These same olde walls, olde *arches*, which thou seest, . *Ro.* iii. 3
Archigald. Next *Archigald*, who for his proud disdayne . . . II. x. 44. 4
Archimago. 'Hether' (quoth he,) 'me *Archimago* sent, . . . I. i. 43. 6
subtill *Archimago*, . . . praisd his divelish arts, . . . I. ii. 9. 1
subtill *Archimag*, that Una sought . . . I. iii. 24. 6
Archimago said, a felon strong To many knights did . . . worke disgrace; . . . I. iii. 29. 3
when he sees his age, And hoarie head of *Archimago* old, . . . I. iii. 38. 4
'Why *Archimago*, lucklesse syre, What doe I see? . . . I. iii. 39. 1
Being in deed old *Archimage*, did stay . . . I. vi. 48. 2
The subtile traines of *Archimago* old; . . . I. vii. 26. 2
Ye shall him *Archimago* find, I ghesse, . . . I. xii. 34. 8
Guyon, by *Archimage* abusd, . . . II. i. Arg.
whenas *Archimago* them did view, . . . II. i. 8. 1
So had false *Archimago* her disguysd, . . . II. i. 21. 6
'Lo! yonder he,' cryde *Archimage* alowd, . . . II. i. 25. 1
at length with *Archimage* they meet: . . . II. iii. 11. 2
lowdly cald; 'Help, helpe! O *Archimage!* . . . II. vi. 48. 2
Which when as *Archimago* heard, . . . II. vi. 51. 1
meeting earst with *Archimago* slie . . . II. viii. 10. 7
False *Archimage* provokte their corage prowd, . . . II. viii. 11. 3
Archimage besought, him that afford Which . . . II. viii. 19. 3
The whiles false *Archimage* and Atin fled apace. . . . II. viii. 56. 9
Yet did false *Archimage* her still pursew, . . . III. iv. 45. 1
Archimago's. after *Archimagoes* fowle defeat, . . . I. vi. 3. 1
Architect. That conning *Architect* of cancred guyle, . . . II. i. 1. 1
Arcs. Triumphant *Arcks*, spyres, neighbours to the skie, . . . *Ro.* vii. 5
These wals, these *arcks*, these baths, . . . *Ro.* xxvii. 4
Admire . . . Their rich triumphall *Arcks* which they did raise, *Com. Son.* iii. 7
Ardennes. Nor famous *Ardeyn*, nor fowle Arlo, is. . . . *As.* 96
then that same water of *Ardenne*, . . . IV. iii. 45. 2
Ardeyn. *See* **Ardennes.**
Are (*partial list*). *See* **They're.**
all things which beneath the Moone have being *Are* temporall, *Ro.* ix. 11
manie sundrie colours *arre* In Iris bowe; . . . *Mui.* 92
'that thou *are* bent To die alone, . . . *D.* 78
nought my praises of her needed *arre*, . . . *Col.* 533
though nobly ye inclined *are*, . . . *Ded. Son.* x. 7
so in they entred *ar*. . . . I. i. 7. 9
al that in the wide deepe wandring *arre* . . . I. ii. 1. 5
they the woods *are* past, and come now to the plaine. . . . I. vi. 33. 9
And at the point two stinges in fixed *arre*, . . . I. xi. 11. 8
each of other worthy *are*.' . . . III. ii. 10. 9
all which fifty *are*, All which she . . . IV. xi. 48. 5
oddes I finde twixt those, and these which *are*, . . . V. Pr. 1. 5
Aread. *Areede* uprightly who has the victorye. . . . *S.C.* Au. 130
if thou this song *areede*; . . . *S.C.* Au. 146
areede who has thee so dight? . . . *S.C.* S. 7

Aread—*Continued.*
to me, my trustie friend, *aread* Thy councell: . . . *Hub.* 81
Can rightfully *aread* so dolefull lay. . . . *T.M.* 52
Therefore more plaine *areade* this doubtfull case.' . . . *D.* 182
gan thus to him *areed.* . . . *Col.* 15
whether fortunate Or else unfortunate may I *aread,* . . . *Col.* 565
His name Ignaro did his nature right *aread.* . . . I. viii. 31. 9
Aread in graver wise what I demaund of thee.' . . . I. viii. 33. 9
what high intent, Hath brought you hither . . . *Aread,* . . . I. ix. 6. 5
'Sir knight, *aread* who hath ye thus arayd, . . . I. ix. 23. 7
His name was meeke Obedience, rightfully *aredd.* . . . I. x. 17. 9
Who better can the way to heaven *aread* . . . I. x. 51. 4
But now *aread,* old father, . . . I. x. 64. 5
Withhold . . . I you *aread;* . . . I. xii. 28. 4
if by lookes one may the mind *aread,* . . . II. i. 7. 6
thou certeinly to mee *areed,* . . . II. iii. 14. 8
Of courtesie to mee the cause *aread* . . . II. v. 16. 8
'Therefore *aread,* Sir, if thou have a love.' . . . III. i. 28. 1
All which the Redcrosse knight to point *aredd,* . . . III. ii. 16. 8
vauntage made of that which Merlin had *ared;* . . . III. iii. 20. 9
his large bountie rightly doth *areed:* . . . III. iv. 59. 4
Dwarfe, *aread* what is that Lady bright . . . III. v. 7. 7
He ween'd that his affection entire She should *aread;* . . . III. vii. 16. 8
him *aredd* To turne his steede about, . . . III. viii. 17. 8
thou maist *aread* . . . Florimell to bee; . . . III. viii. 47. 5
Aread what course of you is safest dempt, . . . III. xi. 23. 3
'*Aread,* thou Squire, that I the man may learne, . . . IV. ii. 25. 3
So hard this Idole was to be *ared,* . . . IV. v. 15. 7
'Then this, Sir Salvage Knight,' (quoth he) '*areede:* . . . IV. vi. 5. 1
I can not unto you *aread* a right: . . . IV. vi. 35. 3
Shall death be th' end, or ought else worse, *aread?*' . . . IV. vii. 11. 4
whereby she might *aread* What mister wight he was, . . . IV. viii. 13. 5
nathemore his meaning she *ared,* . . . IV. viii. 14. 1
as he gan the same to him *aread,* . . . IV. viii. 41. 5
to thy people righteous doome *aread,* . . . V. Pr. 11. 4
'*Aread*' (sayd he) 'which way then did he make? . . . V. i. 19. 1
Thereby Sir Artegall did plaine *areed* . . . V. iii. 35. 1
shee mote *arede* That it was Talus, . . . V. vi. 8. 5
aread, Sir Sergis, how long space . . . V. xi. 42. 1
time and place convenient to *areed,* . . . V. xii. 9. 3
aread, . . . wherefore Betwixt you two began this strife . . . VI. ii. 8. 8
Please it you, Ladie, to us to *aread* . . . VI. ii. 15. 2
But yet *aread* to me, how hight thy Lord, . . . VI. iii. 39. 8
That which your selfe have earst *ared* so right? . . . VI. iv. 28. 2
'*Aread,* good Sire, some counsell that may us sustaine.' . . . VI. vi. 13. 9
he mote *aread* Plaine signes in him of life . . . VI. vii. 20. 4
our rudenesse to your selfe *aread.*' . . . VI. ix. 33. 9
Who can *aread* what creature mote she bee, . . . VI. x. 25. 3
Areed, ye sonnes of God, as best ye can devise.' . . . VII. vi. 21. 9
wouldest needs thine owne conceit *areed!* . . . VII. vi. 46. 8
Lodwick, this of grace to me *aread;* . . . *Am.* xxxiii. 5
thy victorious conquests to *areed,* . . . *H.L.* 11

Areads. Me . . . the sacred Muse *areeds* To blazon broade . . . I. Pr. 1. 7
fayre *areedes* Of tydinges straunge, . . . I. ix. 28. 6
Nature soone Her righteous Doome *areads.* . . . VII. vii. Arg.

Areare. *See* **Arrear.**

Ared, Aredd, Arede. *See* **Aread.**

Arere. *See* **Arrear.**

Aret. 'The charge which God doth unto me *arrett,* . . . II. viii. 8. 1
unto each a Bulwarke did *arrett,* . . . II. xi. 7. 3
And a quicke moving Spirit did *arret* To stirre and roll them . . . VII. vii. 7. 3
the judges did *arret* her Unto the second best . . . IV. v. 21. 4

Arew. *See* **Arow.**

Argante. 'That Geauntesse *Argante* is behight, . . . III. vii. 47. 2
that *Argante* vile and vitious, . . . III. xi. 3. 7

Argo. The wondred *Argo,* which . . . through the Euxine . . . II. xii. 44. 8

Argoan. The great *Argoan* ships brave ornament, . . . *Gn.* 210

Argolic. from th' *Argolick* ships with furious yre . . . *Gn.* 495
'Th' *Argolicke* power returning home againe, . . . *Gn.* 561
Europa floting through th' *Argolick* fluds: . . . VII. vii. 33. 4

Argonauts. did drive The noble *Argonauts* to outrage fell; . . . IV. i. 23. 7

Argos. To cut the ships from turning home againe To *Argos;* . . . *Gn.* 523

Argue. that doth *argue* you To be divine, . . . *Am.* lxxix. 9

Argument. Thou onely fit this *Argument* to write, . . . *Ded. Son.* viii. 5
The *argument* of mine afflicted stile: . . . I. Pr. 4. 8
Argument worthy of Maeonian quill; . . . II. x. 3. 1
This odious *argument* my rymes should shend, . . . III. ix. 1. 4
too long thought Every discourse, and every *argument,* . . . III. ix. 53. 7
he gan bewray Some *argument* . . . III. xii. 4. 6
Whose lofty *argument,* uplifting me, . . . *Am.* lxxxii. 13

Arguments. Be *arguments* of a vile donghill mind, . . . VI. vii. 1. 6

Argus. Well-eyed, as *Argus* was, . . . *S.C.* Jul. 154
Roffy is wise, and as *Argus* eyed,) . . . *S.C.* S. 203
womans subtiltyes Can guylen *Argus,* . . . III. ix. 7. 3

Argus'. wondren at bright *Argus* blazing eye; . . . *S.C.* O. 32
fayre Pecocks, . . . full of *Argus* eyes their tayles dispredden . . . I. iv. 17. 9

Ariadne. the crowne, which *Ariadne* wore . . . VI. x. 13. 1

Aright. So thought I eke of him, and think I thought *aright.* . . . I. vii. 49. 9
'to read *aright* The course of heavenly cause, . . . I. ix. 6. 6
To leade *aright,* that he should never fall . . . I. x. 34. 7
my name and nation redd *aright,* . . . I. x. 67. 3
(Their Chiefetain Humber named was *aright,*) . . . II. x. 16. 7
sonnes, too young to rule *aright,* . . . II. x. 46. 8
'Palmer, stere *aright,* And keepe an even course; . . . II. xii. 3. 1
all their actions to direct *aright:* . . . III. iii. 2. 4
whence it sprong, I can not read *aright:* . . . III. iii. 16. 7
in each point her selfe informd *aright,* . . . III. iv. 4. 3
'father, I note read *aright* . . . III. viii. 23. 7
'From him my linage I derive *aright,* . . . III. ix. 36. 1

Aright—*Continued.*
He did the better counterfeite *aright:* . . . III. x. 47. 7
none That to their willes could them direct *aright,* . . . IV. i. 16. 8
pledges pawnd the same to keepe *aright:* . . . IV. iii. 3. 4
excuse Me from discovering you my name *aright,* . . . IV. vi. 4. 7
somewhat redder then beseem'd *aright,* . . . IV. vi. 19. 8
I can not unto you aread *a right:* . . . IV. vi. 35. 3
when your pleasure is to deeme *aright,* . . . IV. viii. 17. 4
Corflambo was he cald *aright,* . . . IV. viii. 49. 1
her footing to direct *aright,* . . . IV. xi. 25. 4
where he ought rise *aright:* . . . V. Pr. 8. 7
each of either take his share *aright:* . . . V. i. 26. 5
'Of things unseene how canst thou deeme *aright,*' . . . V. ii. 39. 1
the least word . . . he could way *aright.* . . . V. ii. 44. 4
vaine it is to deeme of things *aright,* . . . V. iv. 1. 6
'Sayd I not then' (quoth shee), 'erwhile *aright,* . . . V. vi. 16. 6
witnesse forth *aright* in forrain land, . . . V. ix. 37. 5
Though also those mote question'd be *aright,* . . . V. ix. 40. 7
Whether withheld from me . . . I cannot read *aright.* . . . V. xi. 49. 9
to beare themselves *aright* To all of each degree . . . VI. ii. 1. 3
rather seem'd . . . Gotten by spoyle then purchaced *aright:* . . . VI. v. 9. 5
Withouten guide her to conduct *aright,* . . . VI. v. 7. 8
when they went astray, He could . . . them reduce *aright,* . . . VI. vi. 3. 8
could not weigh of worthinesse *aright;* . . . VI. vii. 29. 6
What could the Gods doe more, but doe it more *aright?* . . . VI. vii. 31. 9
when as all things readie were *aright,* . . . VI. viii. 45. 1
keepes her course *aright;* . . . *Am.* lix. 6
If ever I did honour thee *aright,* . . . *Epith.* 122
of both them deem *aright,* . . . *Com. Son.* ii. 10

Arights. When they had seene and heard her doome *a-rights* . . . V. x. 4. 3

Arimathea. Hither came Joseph of *Arimathy,* . . . II. x. 53. 7

Arion. that was *Arion* crownd; . . . IV. xi. 23. 3
Arion, when . . . He forth was thrown . . . *Am.* xxxviii. 1

Arise. Out of hir ashes as a worme *arise.* . . . *Bel.*[1] vi. 14
Out of her dust like to a worm *arise.* . . . *Bel.*[2] vii. 14
branches did I see *arise* Out of the . . . tree, . . . *Pet.* iii. 1
towards heaven freshly to *arise* . . . *Ro.* xvii. 11
they which see the dawning day *arize;* . . . *Ro.* xxii. 4
what might *arise* of the bare sheepe, . . . *S.C.* May 107
A thrilling throbbe from her hart did *aryse,* . . . *S.C.* May 208
What good thereof to Cuddie can *arise?* . . . *S.C.* O. 18
Out of the lowly vallies did *arise,* . . . *Gn.* 191
From whence *arise* diversitie of sects, . . . *Hub.* 388
How manie honest men see ye *arize* Daylie thereby, . . . *Hub.* 419
Might unto some of those in time *arise?* . . . *Hub.* 426
if the living yerely doo *arise* To fortie pound, . . . *Hub.* 528
'*Arise,* (said Mercurie) thou sluggish beast, . . . *Hub.* 1327
Arise, and doo thyself redeeme from shame, . . . *Hub.* 1331
Ne other grace vouchsafed them to showe . . . scarse them bad *arise.* . . . I. iv. 14. 4
So from the ground she fearelesse doth *arise,* . . . I. vi. 13. 3
How with that pensive Maid he best might thence *arise.* . . . I. vi. 32. 9
'*Arise,* thou cursed Miscreaunt, . . . I. vi. 41. 1
Arise, and . . . maintain Thy guilty wrong . . . I. vi. 41. 5
Arise, sir Knight; *arise,* and leave this cursed place.' . . . I. ix. 53. 9
as thought From heaven to come, or thither to *arise;* . . . I. x. 4. 2
Him hasty to *arise.* . . . II. v. 37. 6
Infinite mischiefes of them doe *arize,* . . . II. vii. 12. 6
At the well-head the purest streames *arise;* . . . II. vii. 15. 7
Gnats . . . Out of the fennes of Allan doe *arise,* . . . II. ix. 16. 2
it doth, as cloud from sea, *aryse.* . . . II. ix. 42. 5
no time nor reason could *arize,* . . . II. ix. 49. 4
My lowly verse may loftily *arise,* . . . II. x. 1. 4
freshly to *arize* From th' earth, . . . II. xi. 44. 8
thother rather higher did *arise,* . . . II. xii. 66. 5
Betwixt two shady mountaynes doth *arize:* . . . III. ii. 24. 7
Proud Etheldred shall from the North *arise,* . . . III. iii. 35. 2
Unable to *arise,* or foote or hand to styre. . . . III. vii. 45. 9
Paridell . . . Could not *arise* the counterchaunge to scorse, . . . III. ix. 16. 7
a third kingdom yet is to *arise* . . . III. ix. 44. 6
When that same Maske againe should forth *arize.* . . . III. xii. 28. 5
Whence neither greatly hasted to *arise,* . . . IV. vi. 10. 8
did *arize* On stately pillours . . . IV. x. 6. 8
In order as it did to him *arize.* . . . VI. i. 5. 5
by discovering my estate, Harme may *arise* . . . VI. ii. 27. 3
the cause, whence evill doth *arize,* . . . VI. vi. 14. 3
letting him *arise* like abject thrall, . . . VI. vii. 26. 6
Yet nathemore him suffred to *arize;* . . . VI. viii. 18. 2
Then suffred he Disdaine up to *arise,* . . . VI. viii. 25. 5
She at his bidding meekely did *arise,* . . . VI. ix. 15. 1
if any grace chaunst to *arize* To him, . . . VI. x. 33. 8
We daily see new creatures to *arize,* . . . VII. vii. 18. 6
And as these heavens still by degrees *arize,* . . . *H.H.B.* 71

Arising. *Arysing* forth to run her mighty race, . . . *Epith.* 150

Arive. *See* **Arrive.**

Ark. Lastly I saw an *Arke* of purest golde . . . *Ti.* 659
The *Arke* did beare with him above the skie, . . . *Ti.* 668
Bearing that precious relicke in an *arke* Of gold, . . . IV. iv. 15. 2

Arke. *See* **Arc.**

Arlo. Nor famous Ardeyn, nor fowle *Arlo,* is. . . . *As.* 96
highest hights Of *Arlo*-hill (Who knowes not *Arlo*-hill?) . . . VII. vi. 36. 6
tell how *Arlo* . . . Was made the most unpleasant . . . VII. vi. 37. 5
She chose this *Arlo;* . . . VII. vi. 39. 6
All those faire forrests about *Arlo* hid; . . . VII. vi. 54. 6
The gods assembled all on *Arlo* Hill; . . . VII. vii. 3. 2
Arlo scarsly could them all containe, . . . VII. vii. 4. 4
this same day when she on *Arlo* sat, . . . VII. vii. 7. 2

Arm. Her power it selfe against it selfe did *arme;* . . . *Ro.* xxi. 10
Didst *arme* thy hand against thy proper hart; . . . *Ro.* xxxi. 11
had the use of his right *arme* bereaved. . . . *Hub.* 208

Arm—*Continued.*
his mightie shild Upon his manly *arme* . . . I. viii. 6. 7
He smott off his left *arme*, . . . I. viii. 10. 6
He downe let fall his *arme*, . . . I. viii. 19. 7
on his *arme* a bounch of keyes he bore, . . . I. viii. 30. 6
from his *armo* did reach Those keyes, . . . I. viii. 34. 6
who most trustes in *arme* of fleshly might, . . . I. ix. 11. 6
Ylinked *arme* in *arme* in lovely wise: . . . I. x. 12. 3
Upon her *arme* a silver anchor lay, . . . I. x. 14. 6
the force of fleshly *arme*, Ne molten mettall, . . . I. xi. 36. 6
Do *arme* your self against that day, . . . II. iii. 15. 9
that stroke of living *arme* Should him dismay, . . . II. v. 7. 2
hurling high his yron braced *arme*, . . . II. v. 7. 5
Fiercely advaunst his valorous right *arme*, . . . II. xi. 34. 7
on his *arme* addresse his goodly shield . . . III. i. 4. 8
her soft *arme* lay underneath his hed, . . . III. i. 36. 3
So feeble is the powre of fleshly *arme*. . . . III. iv. 27. 6
Forthwith themselves . . . they gan *arme* bylive, . . . III. v. 16. 2
shield gins to untye From her lefte *arme*, . . . III. ix. 22. 9
His powrelesse *arme*, benumbd with secret feare, . . . IV. vi. 21. 3
away with him did beare Under his *arme*, . . . IV. vii. 24. 8
not that *arme*, nor thou the man, I reed, . . . V. iii. 21. 3
this the *arme* the which that shield did beare, . . . V. iii. 22. 2
Let him feele hardnesse of thy heavie *arme*: . . . V. v. 49. 8
quite smit off his *arme* as he it up did lift. . . . V. xi. 7. 9
your victorious *arme* will not yet cease, . . . V. xi. 18. 5
he gan aloft t' advance his *arme*, . . . VI. viii. 45. 8
with the selfe same wound Launcht through the *arme*, . . . VI. xi. 19. 9

Armed. Hir head full bravely with a morian *armed*, . . . *Bel.*[1] xi. 5
the stout hynde *arm'd* his right hand with steele: . . . *Ro.* xviii. 6
with stout courage *arm'd* against mischaunce, . . . *Ro.* xxi. 3
or *armed* be with clawes, or scalie creasts, . . . *Ro.* xxiv. 4
backe was *arm'd* against the dint of speare . . . *Van.* vi. 2
throughly *arm'd* against such coverture, . . . *Hub.* 683
armd with blindnesse and with boldnes stout, . . . *T.M.* 265
A Knight all *arm'd*, upon a winged steed; . . . *Ti.* 646
one in mayle, *Armed* to point, . . . I. i. 16. 6
A faithlesse Sarazin, all *armde* to point, . . . I. ii. 12. 6
One . . . Full strongly *armd*, and on a courser free . . . I. iii. 33. 3
cruell Sarazin, In woven maile all *armed* warily; . . . I. v. 4. 2
his dreadfull club . . . All *armd* with ragged snubbes . . . I. viii. 7. 4
With griping talaunts *armd* to greedy fight, . . . I. viii. 48. 7
Ne fleshly brest can *armed* be so sownd, . . . I. ix. 11. 2
An *armed* knight towards them gallop fast, . . . I. ix. 21. 2
over all with brasen scales was *armd*, . . . I. xi. 9. 1
his more hardned crest was *armd* so well, . . . I. xi. 24. 5
steele . . . that erst him *armd;* That erst him goodly *armd*, . I. xi. 27. 8, 9
A goodly knight, all *armd* in harnesse meete, . . . II. i. 5. 8
The dead corse of an *armed* knight was spred, . . . II. i. 41. 2
direfull chaunce, *armd* with avenging fate, . . . II. i. 44. 6
all *armd* in shyning bras. . . . II. ii. 17. 9
armd with fire more hardly he mote him withstond. . . . II. v. 22. 9
An *armed* knight that towardes him fast ran; . . . II. vi. 41. 2
Two Paynim knights al *armd* as bright as skie, . . . II. viii. 10. 2
An *armed* knight, of bold and bounteous grace, . . . II. viii. 17. 5
at his feet . . . an *armed* corse did lye, . . . II. viii. 23. 8
againe he *armed* felt his hond: . . . II. viii. 40. 6
All threatning death, all in straunge manner *armd;* . . . II. ix. 13. 5
all *armed* bright In glistring steele, . . . II. ix. 26. 2
Armed with dartes of sensuall Delight, . . . II. xi. 13. 6
arm'd with raging flame. . . . II. xi. 23. 9
Bright Scolopendraes *arm'd* with silver scales; . . . II. xii. 23. 8
Both firmely *armd* for every hard assay, . . . II. xii. 38. 8
Halfe *armd* and halfe unarmd, . . . III. i. 63. 3
fairest knight alive, when *armed* was her brest. . . . III. ii. 4. 9
A comely knight, all *arm'd* in complete wize, . . . III. ii. 24. 2
weening to have *arm'd* him, she did quite disarme. . . . III. iv. 27. 9
He was all *armd* in rugged steele unfilde, . . . III. vii. 30. 4
An *armed* knight upon a courser strong, . . . III. viii. 15. 3
th' one was *armed* all in warlike wize, . . . III. x. 21. 4
Armd with his thunderbolts and lightning fire, . . . III. xi. 33. 4
Feare, all *arm'd* from top to toe, . . . III. xii. 12. 1
Two *armed* Knights that toward them did pace, . . . IV. i. 17. 2
With murdrous weapons *arm'd* to cruell fight, . . . IV. ii. 16. 2
All *arm'd* to point, his chalenge to abet: . . . IV. iii. 6. 2
all unawares espide An *armed* Knight . . . IV. vi. 2. 5
She *arm'd* her tongue, and thought at him to scold; . . . IV. vi. 27. 7
Streight forth issewd a Knight all *arm'd* to proofe, . . . IV. x. 9. 6
Both strongly *arm'd*, as fearing one another; . . . IV. x. 32. 2
on the Bridge he ready *armed* saw The Sarazin, . . . V. ii. 11. 2
Whom having quickly *arm'd* againe anew, . . . V. iii. 12. 2
the one him seem'd a Knight all *armed*, . . . V. iv. 36. 4
came Artegall . . . All *arm'd* to point, . . . V. v. 5. 2
the sound Of *armed* men comming . . . V. vi. 28. 7
Two Knights all *armed* ready for to fight; . . . V. vi. 29. 2
Both *armed* Knights and eke unarmed rout; . . . V. vi. 30. 3
(With yron wheeles and hookes *arm'd* dreadfully, . . . V. viii. 28. 5
gainst all that warlike rout Of knights and *armed* men, . . . V. viii. 50. 3
when it hath *arm'd* it selfe with might? . . . V. ix. 1. 3
Whose top was *arm'd* with many an yron hooke, . . . V. ix. 11. 2
The *armed* knights stopping his passage by, . . . V. ix. 14. 8
for the *armed* knight To thinke to follow him . . . V. ix. 15. 8
three knights he spyde, All *arm'd* to point, . . . V. x. 34. 2
Nathelesse him selfe he *armed* all in hast, . . . V. xi. 3. 1
The *armed* Prince with shield so blazing bright . . . V. xi. 26. 2
All *armed* in a cote of yron plate . . . V. xii. 14. 3
Fighting on foot, . . . Against an *armed* knight . . . VI. ii. 3. 9
that youth had kild That *armed* knight, . . . VI. ii. 4. 7
great blame . . . For *armed* Knight a wight unarm'd to wrong: VI. ii. 8. 7
he nigh espyde An *armed* Knight approaching . . . VI. iii. 30. 7

Armed—*Continued.*
He goth on foote all *armed* by her side, . . . VI. iii. 46. 1
chaunst far off an *armed* Knight to spy . . . VI. iii. 46. 6
All *arm'd* to point came ryding thetherward; . . . VI. v. 11. 3
Himselfe in hast he *arm'd*, . . . VI. vii. 2. 9
The which were *armed* both agreeably, . . . VI. vii. 3. 7
Calidore Had, underneath, him *armed* privily. . . . VI. xi. 36. 4
Sir Calidore him *arm'd* as he thought best, . . . VI. xi. 42. 4
terrifide his foes, and *armed* him, . . . VI. xii. 26. 8
with brows full sternly bent And *armed* strongly, . . . VII. vii. 32. 4

Armeddan. The fift *Armeddan*, skild in lovely layes; . . . V. iii. 5. 7

Armeric. *See* **Americ.**

Armest. With which thou *armest* his resistlesse hand. . . . *H.L.* 230

Armies. th' *armies* of their creatures all and some . . . *Mui.* 229
daunt unequall *armies* of his foes, . . . I. vii. 34. 3
Nations captived, and huge *armies* slaine: . . . IV. i. 21. 8
Armies of lovely lookes, and speeches wise, . . . V. v. 34. 8
Armies of Loves still flying too and fro, . . . *H.B.* 240

Arming. Holding in hand a goodly *arming* sword, . . . II. vi. 47. 6
arming him withall Eftsoones forth pricked proudly . . . V. x. 31. 7

Armor. *See* **Coat-armor.**
doubted Knights, whose woundlesse *armour* rusts, . . . *S.C.* O. 41
his glistring *armor* made A litle glooming light, . . . I. i. 14. 4
That in his *armour* bare a croslet red? . . . I. vi. 36. 6
ere he could his *armour* on him dight, . . . I. vii. 8. 1
His mightie *Armour*, missing most at need; . . . I. vii. 19. 5
His glitterand *armour* shined far away, . . . I. vii. 29. 4
Both shield and sword, and *armour* all he wrought . . . I. vii. 36. 6
as the clashing of an *Armor* bright, . . . I. xi. 9. 8
through his *armour* all his body seard, . . . I. xi. 26. 7
armour all with blood besprincled was; . . . II. i. 41. 3
all in bright *armour* clad, . . . II. i. 45. 4
seeing one, that shone in *armour* fayre, . . . II. iii. 11. 3
all his *armour* sprinckled was with blood, . . . II. vi. 41. 6
all his *armour* swept, That all the blood . . . II. vi. 42. 7
why should a dead dog be deckt in *armour* bright?' . . . II. viii. 15. 9
all his *armour* steepe, . . . II. viii. 37. 4
Sir Guyon, in bright *armour* clad, . . . II. xi. 3. 5
Ah! gentlest knight, that ever *armor* bore, . . . III. i. 7. 5
all his *armour* seemd of antique mould, . . . III. ii. 25. 2
A goodly *Armour*, and full rich aray, . . . III. iii. 58. 7
one, all in *armour* bright, . . . III. iv. 12. 2
Each gan . . . weary *armour* free, . . . III. ix. 19. 7
with shield and *armour* fit; . . . IV. i. 14. 7
These warlike Champions, all in *armour* shine, . . . IV. iii. 3. 8
streames of blood his *armour* all bedide. . . . IV. iv. 24. 7
starting up streight for his *armour* sought: . . . IV. iv. 33. 3
For all his *armour* was like salvage weed . . . IV. iv. 39. 4
in his *armour* layd him down to rest: . . . IV. v. 39. 2
when he saw the Prince in *armour* bright, . . . IV. viii. 40. 6
Ne any *armour* could his dint out-ward; . . . V. i. 10. 8
all these knights, which that day *armour* bore, . . . V. iii. 13. 7
broke his sword in twaine, and all his *armour* sperst. . . . V. iii. 37. 9
streight her selfe did dight, and *armor* don, . . . V. vi. 17. 8
Him clad in th' *armour* of a Pagan knight, . . . V. viii. 26. 2
Kept himselfe still in his straunge *armour* dight: . . . V. viii. 27. 5
Commaunded straight his *armour* to be brought; . . . V. viii. 28. 3
Onely his shield and *armour*, which there lay, . . . V. viii. 44. 1
seeing all in *armour* bright as day, . . . V. ix. 24. 2
gan hew So hideously uppon his *armour* bright, . . . V. xi. 5. 4
all his *armour* did with purple dye: . . . V. xii. 20. 8
He wore no *armour*, ne for none did care, . . . VI. vii. 43. 1

Armoric. Them closely into *Armorick* did beare: . . . II. x. 64. 5
Armoricke, where long in wretched cace He liv'd, . . . III. iii. 41. 4

Armors. all their *armours* staynd with bloudie gore; . . . IV. ii. 18. 6
Whereof there was great store, and *armors* bright, . . . V. vii. 41. 4
all his *armours* readie dight that day, . . . V. x. 16. 3
With those brave *armours* lying on the ground, . . . VI. v. 25. 4

Armory. Well worthie be you of that *Armory*, . . . I. i. 27. 5
that same *Armory* Downe taking, . . . III. iii. 59. 7

Armpit. Stroke him . . . In th' *arm-pit* full, . . . IV. iii. 33. 9

Arms. Folding hir *armes* with thousand sighs . . . *Bel.*[1] viii. 2
Their *armes* in shamefull wise bounde . . . *Bel.*[1] xi. 10
Folding her *armes* to Heaven . . . *Bel.*[2] x. 2
With *armes* bound at their backs . . . *Bel.*[2] xv. 10
Through *armes* and vassals Rome the world subdu'd, . . . *Ro.* viii. 1
Out of the earth engendred men of *armes* . . . *Ro.* x. 3
Had all the world in *armes* against her bent, . . . *Ro.* xxi. 6
All that the Ocean graspes in his long *armes;* . . . *Ro.* xxvi. 6
Shewing her wreathed rootes, and naked *armes*, . . . *Ro.* xxviii. 6
With *armes* full strong and largely displayd, . . . *S.C.* F. 104
Whose naked *Armes* stretch unto the fyre, . . . *S.C.* F. 171
Knitting his wanton *armes* with grasping hold, . . . *Gn.* 218
ere that unto *armes* I me betooke, . . . *Hub.* 291
Now his bright *armes* assaying, now his speare, . . . *Hub.* 741
(large breath in *armes* most needfull) . . . *Hub.* 745
his stiffe *armes* to stretch with Eughen bowe, . . . *Hub.* 747
Whether for *Armes* and warlike amenaunce, . . . *Hub.* 781
Desire of honor or brave thought of *armes* . . . *Hub.* 825
the wilde beasts whom *armes* did glorifie, . . . *Hub.* 1184
Of men of *armes* he had but small regard, . . . *Hub.* 1189
with their spredding *armes* Do beat their buds, . . . *T.M.* 77
onely boast of *Armes* and Auncestrie, . . . *T.M.* 94
did those *Armes* first give To their Grandsyres, . . . *T.M.* 95
She *armes* the brest with constant patience . . . *T.M.* 133
men of *armes* doo wander unrewarded. . . . *Ti.* 441
twixt their blessed *armes* it carried . . . *Ti.* 627
Drawne into *armes* . . . Through prowd ambition . . . *Mui.* 4
in their *armes* then softly did him reare: . . . *As.* 146
had it *armes* and wings, . . . *Col.* 218

Arms—*Continued.*

To all that *armes* professe and chevalry. . . . *Ded. Son.* iv. 4
Moste noble Lord, the . . . Precedent of all that *armes* ensue? . *Ded. Son.* xiv. 7
Ycladd in mightie *armes* and silver shielde, ... I. i. 1. 2
Yet *armes* till that time did he never wield. . . . . I. i. 1. 5
Without regard of *armes* and dreaded fight: . . . . I. ii. 3. 6
In mighty *armes* he was yclad anon, ... I. ii. 11. 3
two goodly trees, that faire did spred Their *armes* abroad, . . I. ii. 28. 4
A knight her mett in mighty *armes* embost, ... I. iii. 24. 4
feates of *armes* did wisely understand. . . . . I. iii. 42. 5
Young knight whatever, that dost *armes* professe, ... I. iv. 1. 1
an errant knight in *armes* ycled, . . . they new arrived find: . I. iv. 38. 4
I feare the . . . oddes of *armes* in field.' . . . . I. iv. 50. 2
'he beares . . . enchaunted *armes,* that none can perce; . . . I. iv. 50. 6
He . . . did him selfe prepayre In sunbright *armes,* . . . . I. v. 2. 8
oth . . . T' observe the sacred lawes of *armes* . . . . I. v. 4. 9
armes . . . Into a pure vermillion now are dyde. . . . . I. v. 9. 5
in her *armes* To Aesculapius brought the wounded knight: . I. v. 41. 2
Whome having softly disaraid of *armes,* . . . . I. v. 41. 4
He had in *armes* abroad wonne muchell fame, ... I. vi. 20. 5
whelpes she saw how he did . . . lull in rugged *armes* . . . . I. vi. 27. 9
had he beene where earst his *armes* were lent, ... I. vi. 42. 7
So willingly she came into his *armes,* . . . . I. vii. 15. 3
wrought For this young Prince, when first to *armes* he fell; . I. vii. 36. 7
His rawbone *armes,* . . . Were clene consum'd; . . . . I. viii. 41. 6
with his glistring *armes* does ill agree; . . . . I. ix. 22. 8
he of rope or *armes* has now no memoree. . . . . I. ix. 22. 9
a Groome, . . . gan despoile Of puissant *armes,* . . . . I. x. 17. 8
deeds of *armes* must I at last be faine . . . to leave, ... I. x. 62. 5
'What need of *armes,* where peace doth ay remaine,' . . . . I. x. 62. 7
prove thy puissant *armes,* . . . . I. x. 66. 9
Those glistring *armes* that heven with light did fill, ... I. xi. 4. 8
I this man of God his godly *armes* may blaze. . . . . I. xi. 7. 9
thought his *armes* to leave, and helmet to unlace. . . . . I. xi. 26. 9
With heat, toyle, wounds, *armes,* smart, and inward fire, . . I. xi. 28. 2
tall young men, all hable *armes* to sownd; . . . . I. xii. 5. 7
by the faith which I to *armes* have plight, ... I. xii. 18. 3
I present was . . . When *armes* he swore, ... II. i. 19. 7
His warlike *armes* about him gan embrace, ... II. i. 26. 2
That decks and *armes* your shield with faire defence: . . . . II. i. 28. 8
he his *armes* about her sides gan fold, ... II. i. 46. 4
with bold furie *armes* the weakest hart: . . . . II. i. 57. 8
The litle babe up in his *armes* he hent; . . . . II. ii. 1. 4
his sad fathers *armes* with blood defilde, ... II. ii. 11. 3
Since errant *armes* to sew he first began: . . . . II. ii. 17. 5
they mingled were in furious *armes,* . . . . II. ii. 27. 1
Is this the joy of *armes?* . . . . II. ii. 29. 5
made to spoile Themselves of soiled *armes,* . . . . II. ii. 33. 8
His puissant *armes* about his noble brest, ... II. iii. 1. 8
Should neede of all his *armes* him to defend, ... II. iii. 17. 4
Through deeds of *armes* and prowesse martiall. . . . . II. iii. 37. 8
Abroad in *armes,* at home in studious kynd, ... II. iii. 40. 8
Thought in his bastard *armes* her to embrace. . . . . II. iii. 42. 6
As feates of *armes,* and love to entertaine: . . . . II. iv. 1. 6
fayre defence and goodly menaging Of *armes* . . . . II. iv. 8. 4
In his strong *armes* he stifly him embraste, ... II. iv. 14. 1
One in bright *armes* embatteiled full strong, ... II. v. 2. 3
Therby thine *armes* seem strong, ... II. v. 5. 6
That he in ods of *armes* was conquered: . . . . II. v. 14. 6
hong their conquerd *armes* . . . On gallow trees, ... II. v. 26. 8
His prickling *armes,* entrayld with roses red, ... II. v. 29. 5
called for his *armes,* for he would algates fight: . . . . II. v. 37. 9
noise of *armes,* or vew of martiall guize, ... II. vi. 25. 8
nor these *armes* Are meet, ... II. vi. 34. 2
Of love they ever greater glory bore Then of their *armes;* . . II. vi. 35. 7
Delighting all in *armes* and cruell warre, ... II. vi. 37. 6
with his raging *armes* he rudely flasht The waves about, . . . II. vi. 42. 6
in der-doing *armes* . . . my vowed daies do spend, ... II. vii. 10. 1
Faire shields, gay steedes, bright *armes* be my delight; . . . II. vii. 10. 8
Sheilds, steeds, and *armes,* and all things for thee meet, . . . II. vii. 11. 3
mucky filth his braunching *armes* annoyes, ... II. vii. 15. 8
I in *armes,* and in atchievements brave, ... II. vii. 33. 6
Glistring in *armes* and battailous aray, ... II. vii. 37. 2
Soone as those glitterand *armes* he did espye, ... II. vii. 42. 1
With him in bloody *armes* they rashly did debate. . . . . II. viii. 11. 9
I will him reave of *armes,* . . . . II. viii. 15. 7
kend him . . . by his *armes* and amenaunce, ... II. viii. 17. 8
thou broken hast The law of *armes* . . . . II. viii. 31. 7
Twixt his two mighty *armes* engrasped fast, ... II. viii. 49. 6
withstond Oppressours powre by *armes* and puissant hond? . . II. viii. 56. 5
sith I *armes* and knighthood first did plight, ... II. ix. 7. 2
Both in his *armes* and crowne, ... II. x. 51. 7
taking *armes* the Britons to her drew; . . . . II. x. 54. 7
Eftsoones himselfe in glitterand *armes* he dight, ... II. xi. 17. 1
Glistring in *armes* and warlike ornament, ... II. xi. 24. 2
in his *armes* Snatcht first the one, and then the other . . . . II. xi. 31. 1
Twixt his two mighty *armes* him up he snatcht, ... II. xi. 42. 1
of his *armes* despoyled easily . . . . II. xi. 49. 7
Over the waves his rugged *armes* doth lift, ... II. xii. 4. 4
strongly forth did stretch His brawnie *armes,* . . . . II. xii. 21. 2
to bayt His tyred *armes* for toylesome wearinesse, ... II. xii. 29. 8
art in mightie *armes* most magnifyde . . . . II. xii. 32. 4
Sir knight, your ready *arms* about you throw.' . . . . II. xii. 37. 9
He hearkned, and his *armes* about him tooke, ... II. xii. 38. 1
dilate Their clasping *armes* in wanton wreathings intricate: . II. xii. 53. 9
Low his lascivious *armes* adown did creepe, ... II. xii. 61. 6
His warlike *Armes,* the ydle instruments . . . . II. xii. 80. 1
From seeking praise and deeds of *armes* abrode, ... III. i. 1. 8
sith warlike *armes* he bore . . . . III. i. 7. 2
Ne *armes* to beare against the others syde: . . . . III. i. 12. 6

Arms—*Continued.*

yett in *armes* Noctante greater grew: . . . . III. i. 45. 7
to the troubled chamber all in *armes* did throng. . . . . III. i. 62. 9
her bright *armes* about her body dight. . . . . III. i. 67. 3
To whom no share in *armes* and chevalree They doe impart, . III. ii. 1. 4
sith they warlike *armes* have laide away, ... III. ii. 2. 7
'All my delight on deedes of *armes* is sett, ... III. ii. 7. 1
What shape, what shield, what *armes,* what steed, what stedd, III. ii. 16. 6
Achilles *armes,* which Arthegall did win: . . . . III. ii. 25. 6
Betwixt her feeble *armes* her quickly keight, ... III. ii. 30. 4
her twixt her *armes* twaine Shee streightly straynd, ... III. ii. 34. 1
Long time ye both in *armes* shall beare great sway, ... III. iii. 28. 5
civile *armes* to exercise no more: . . . . III. iii. 49. 5
now all Britany doth burne in *armes* bright. . . . . III. iii. 52. 9
Let us in feigned *armes* our selves disguize, ... III. iii. 53. 2
great desire Of warlike *armes* . . . . III. iii. 57. 3
Beside those *armes* there stood a mightie speare, ... III. iii. 60. 1
She might in equall *armes* accompany, ... III. iii. 61. 4
Ne ever dofte her *armes,* . . . . III. iv. 5. 2
till he became A mighty man at *armes,* . . . . III. iv. 20. 5
none in equall *armes* him matchen might: . . . . III. iv. 24. 3
His uncouth shield and straunge *armes* her dismayd, ... III. v. 51. 1
Ill weares he *armes,* that nill them use for Ladies sake.' . . . III. v. 11. 9
in martiall law And deedes of *armes* . . . . III. vii. 52. 4
fast her clipping twixt his *armes* twayne, ... III. viii. 10. 1
deedes of *armes* had ever in despaire, ... III. viii. 11. 7
All the brave knightes that doen in *armes* excell . . . . III. viii. 46. 7
deeds of *armes* which unto them became, ... III. ix. 32. 4
my dayes to spend In seewing deeds of *armes,* . . . . III. ix. 37. 9
ran into her lovers *armes* right fast; . . . . III. x. 13. 5
To prove some deeds of *armes* upon an equall pere?' . . . . III. x. 24. 9
al good knights, that *armes* doe bear this day, ... III. x. 27. 8
His *armes,* which he had vowed to disprofesse, ... III. xi. 20. 4
nould she d'off her weary *armes,* . . . . III. xi. 55. 5
his owne *armes* when glittering he did spy . . . . III. xii. 12. 4
Lightly he clipt her twixt his *armes* twaine, ... III. xii. 45. *or.* 1
Was then assembled deeds of *arms* to see: . . . . IV. i. 9. 4
bore great sway in *armes* and chivalrie, ... IV. i. 32. 2
one . . . That did those *armes* and that same scutchion weld, . IV. i. 34. 5
oft for her in bloudie *armes* they fought. . . . . IV. ii. 37. 5
They loved *armes,* and knighthood did ensew, ... IV. ii. 46. 4
To view and deeme the deedes of *armes* that day: . . . . IV. iii. 4. 4
Sir Priamond, with equall worth And equall *armes,* . . . . IV. iii. 6. 4
their *armes* away to rend; . . . . IV. iii. 35. 4
gan to treate of deeds of *armes* abrode, ... IV. iv. 5. 4
One in bright *armes,* with ready speare in rest, ... IV. iv. 6. 6
A Painim knight that well in *armes* was skild, ... IV. iv. 17. 7
The shield and *armes,* well knowne to be the same . . . . IV. iv. 27. 5
For to have rent his shield and *armes* away, ... IV. iv. 31. 2
Cambelloes *armes* therefore he on him threw, ... IV. iv. 33. 6
their deedes of *armes* to shew. . . . . IV. iv. 37. 2
Ne was there Knight that ever thought of *armes,* . . . . IV. iv. 38. 1
she wondrous deeds of *armes* atchieved, ... IV. iv. 46. 6
with the praise of *armes* and chevalrie . . . . IV. v. 1. 2
vewed The *armes* he bore, ... IV. vi. 3. 4
That rather seemes, sith knowen *armes* ye shonne.' . . . . IV. vi. 5. 5
Attyr'd in forraine *armes* and straunge aray: . . . . IV. vi. 9. 3
shun his mightie strokes, gainst which no *armes* avayled. . IV. vi. 12. 9
This ugly creature in his *armes* her snatcht, ... IV. vii. 8. 1
in his *armes* her bearing Ran, ... IV. vii. 8. 6
Whilest he in *armes* her bore; . . . . IV. vii. 9. 2
Traind up in feats of *armes* and knightlinesse; . . . . IV. vii. 45. 7
heavie *armes* which sore annoyd The Prince . . . . IV. viii. 37. 5
Wherein the honor both of *Armes* ye shame, ... IV. ix. 37. 4
I, having *armes* then taken, ... IV. x. 4. 3
did in noble deedes of *armes* excell, ... IV. xi. 37. 4
blame it is to him, that *armes* profest, ... IV. xii. 8. 4
brawney *armes* had lost their knowen might, ... IV. xii. 20. 4
Expert in battell and in deedes of *armes;* . . . . V. ii. 5. 4
both in *armes* well traind, and throughly tride: . . . . V. ii. 17. 4
They rose in *armes,* and all in battell order stood. . . . . V. ii. 51. 9
To deedes of *armes* and proofe of chevalrie . . . . V. iii. 4. 3
All sixe well-seene in *armes,* and prov'd in many a fight. . . V. iii. 5. 9
Full many deeds of *armes* that day were donne, ... V. iii. 6. 5
There Marinell great deeds of *armes* did shew, ... V. iii. 8. 4
rather had to lose then trie in *armes* his right. . . . . V. iii. 31. 9
By law of *armes* there neede ones right to trie, ... V. iii. 32. 2
blotted out his *armes* with falshood blent, ... V. iii. 37. 7
himselfe baffuld, and his *armes* unherst, ... V. iii. 37. 8
armes dishonour with base villanie, ... V. iii. 38. 7
Through hard adventures deedes of *armes* to try, ... V. iv. 29. 2
she doth them of warlike *armes* despoile, ... V. iv. 31. 3
Queene of Amazons, in *armes* well tride . . . . V. iv. 33. 5
Out of her steely *armes* were flashing seene, ... V. v. 8. 4
she causd his warlike *armes* Be hang'd on high, ... V. v. 21. 6
Ne doffe her *armes,* though he her much besought: . . . . V. vi. 23. 5
armes had borne, but little good could finde, ... V. vi. 32. 4
with lone Of *armes* hast knighthood stolne, ... V. vi. 37. 5
in queint disguise Of British *armes* doest maske . . . . V. vii. 21. 2
As glad to heare of *armes,* . . . . V. vii. 25. 5
both their skill forgot, And practicke use in *armes;* . . . . V. vii. 29. 5
gushed through their *armes,* that all in gore They trode, . . V. vii. 31. 7
In glistering *armes* right goodly well-beseene, ... V. viii. 29. 4
th' *armes* and legs of three to succour him in fight. . . . . V. x. 8. 9
When one in *armes* she saw, ... V. x. 19. 6
he streight Cals for his *armes,* . . . . V. x. 31. 7
two more of his *armes* did fall away, ... V. xi. 11. 7
long since aside had set The use of *armes,* . . . . V. xi. 37. 4
when he gave me *armes* in field to fight, ... V. xi. 53. 3
clasping twixt his *armes,* her up did reare . . . . V. xi. 64. 7

Arms—*Continued.*
no Knight at all, But scorne of *armes* VI. i. 25. 2
Both noble *armes* and gentle curtesie VI. i. 26. 8
having soone his *armes* about him dight, VI. i. 32. 6
court'sie doth as well as *armes* professe, VI. i. 41. 2
By thee no knight; which *armes* impugneth plaine?' VI. ii. 7. 5
'loth were I to have broken The law of *armes:* VI. ii. 7. 7
So long as these two *armes* were able to be wroken VI. ii. 7. 9
he me . . . Assayld, not knowing what to *armes* doth long.' VI. ii. 8. 5
Or stay till he his *armes,* . . . Might lightly fetch VI. ii. 19. 5
since the day that *armes* I first did reare, VI. ii. 26. 8
Onely the use of *armes,* . . . I have not tasted yet; VI. ii. 32. 6
I may beare *armes,* VI. ii. 33. 6
These goodly gilden *armes* which I have won VI. ii. 33. 9
the high desire To love of *armes,* VI. ii. 34. 5
with so unknightly breach Of *armes,* VI. ii. 42. 5
of stature large, Clad all in gilden *armes,* VI. ii. 44. 7
And borne great sway in *armes* amongst his peares; VI. iii. 3. 3
And loved all that did to *armes* incline; VI. iii. 3. 6
His warlike *armes* he had from him undight, VI. iii. 20. 5
in his tender *armes* her forced up to stay VI. iii. 27. 9
Then up he tooke her twixt his *armes* twaine, VI. iii. 28. 4
Not wont on foote with heavy *armes* to trace, VI. iii. 29. 5
blot of all that *armes* uppon them take, VI. iii. 35. 2
that thou for ever doe those *armes* forsake, VI. iii. 35. 5
armes or weapon had he none to fight, VI. iv. 4. 1
Well then him chaunst his heavy *armes* to want, VI. iv. 19. 1
Then tooke he up betwixt his *armes* twaine VI. iv. 23. 1
Withouten *armes* or steede to ride upon, VI. iv. 39. 3
And offred him . . . both horse and *armes* VI. iv. 39. 8
Those warlike *armes* which Calepine whyleare Had left behind VI. v. 8. 4
streight his cumbrous *armes* aside did lay VI. v. 10. 6
him embracing twixt his *armes* entire, VI. v. 23. 4
Renowmed much in *armes* and derring doe; VI. v. 37. 4
hanging up his *armes* and warlike spoyle, VI. v. 37. 8
thou dost of *arms* despoile, VI. vi. 34. 6
Ne ever *armes* ne ever knighthood dare Hence to professe; VI. vi. 36. 3
having from his craven bodie torne Those goodly *armes,* VI. vi. 36. 8
Having his *armes* and warlike things undight, VI. vii. 19. 3
the Priest with naked *armes* full net Approching nigh, VI. viii. 45. 4
Had traveld still on foot in heavie *armes,* VI. viii. 47. 2
catching up his *arms,* streight to the noise forth past VI. viii. 47. 9
doffing his bright *armes* VI. ix. 36. 3
holding fast twixt both his *armes* extended Fayre Pastorell, VI. xi. 19. 7
in his *armes* the dreary dying mayd, VI. xi. 21. 2
her embracing twixt her *armes* twaine, VI. xii. 19. 6
Despoyld of warlike *armes* and knowen shield *Am.* lii. 4
through thy prowesse, and victorious *armes,* *Proth.* 155
Armulla. the Northside of *Armulla* dale) *Col.* 105
Armulla yields None fairer, *Col.* 278
Army. on horses white, A puissant *armie* *Rev.* iii. 7
his *army* dry-foot through them yod, I. x. 53. 5
in the aire their clustring *army* flies; II. ix. 16. 4
after all an *army* strong she leav'd, II. x. 31. 8
An *army* brought, and with him batteile fought, II. x. 51. 2
all that dreadfull *Armie* fast gan flye II. xii. 26. 8
Arne. Aeolus faire daughter, *Arne* hight, III. xi. 42. 2
Arose. Thereout a strange beast . . . *arose,* *Bel.*[2] viii. 5
suddenly *arose* a tempest great, *Bel.*[2] xiii. 5
from the Northerne coast a storme *arose,* *Bel.*[2] xiv. 10
Arose, and homeward drove his sonned sheepe, *S.C.* Ja. 77
till mickle woe Thereof *arose,* *Mui.* 133
At last . . . *Arose* the virgin, borne of heavenly brood, I. iii. 8. 7
In haste Duessa from her place *arose,* I. v. 14. 1
from thence *arose* away The mother I. v. 44. 4
when fervent sorrow slaked was, She up *arose,* I. vii. 28. 2
she up *arose* with seemely grace, I. x. 8. 4
freshly up *arose* the doughty knight, I. xi. 52. 1
They all attonce out of their seates *arose,* II. ix. 36. 2
up *arose* a man of matchlesse might, II. x. 37. 1
stout Bunduca up *arose,* II. x. 54. 6
the villeine overthrowne Out of his swowne *arose,* II. xi. 35. 4
the other likewise up *arose,* II. xii. 67. 1
Lightly *arose* out of her wearie bed, III. i. 59. 6
shee up out of her deadly fitt *Arose,* III. iv. 31. 2
He up *arose,* as halfe in great disdaine, III. iv. 61. 5
an hideous storme of winde *arose,* III. xii. 2. 1
The trumpets sounded, and they all *arose* IV. iii. 51. 2
He seeing her depart *arose* up light, IV. vii. 37. 1
Then up *arose* a person of deepe reach, V. ix. 39. 1
Would have the passion hid, and up *arose* withall V. ix. 50. 9
They both *arose,* and at him loudly cryde, V. xii. 38. 4
He up *arose,* however liefe or loth, VI. i. 44. 3
At sight of her they suddaine all *arose* VII. vi. 24. 4
Around. the fountaine, where they sat *around,* *S.C.* Jun. 60
grashoppers chirped them *around;* *Gn.* 231
With mumming and with masking all *around,* *Hub.* 802
Although the compast world were sought *around* *Ti.* 567
her faire damzels, flocking her *arownd,* *Mui.* 116
Twelve Gods doo sit *around* in royall state, *Mui.* 307
sitting then *around,* One of those groomes, *Col.* 11
wrapping up her wrethed sterne *arownd,* I. i. 18. 5
the Graces . . . dauncing all *around;* I. i. 48. 8
his mates him pledg *around* I. iii. 31. 9
Teaching the Satyres, which her sat *around,* I. vi. 30. 8
Three miles it might be easy heard *arownd,* I. viii. 4. 3
The neighbor woods *arownd* with hollow murmur ring I. viii. 11. 9
overflowed all the field *arownd,* I. viii. 16. 8
The light-foot Squyre her quickly turnd *around,* I. viii. 25. 7
hill, . . . Adornd with fruitfull Olives all *arownd,* I. x. 54. 2

Around—*Continued.*
That all her goodly garments staind *arownd,* II. i. 39. 8
Drawing to him the eies of all *arownd,* II. ii. 39. 8
The day that first doth lead the yeare *around,* II. ii. 42. 7
throwe her sweete smels al *arownd* II. vi. 12. 9
nought but desert wildernesse shewed all *around* II. vii. 2. 9
with dread and horror compassed *arownd* II. vii. 20. 9
Could gathered be through all the world *arownd,* II. vii. 31. 8
Like highest heaven compassed *around,* II. ix. 45. 2
they behold *arownd* A large and spacious plaine, II. xii. 50. 1
flowing low and thick her cloth'd *arownd,* II. xii. 67. 4
Lyons, and Buls, which romed them *arownd* III. i. 14. 9
sore beset on every side *arownd,* III. i. 21. 2
About their Ladye first they flockt *arownd;* III. i. 64. 1
restlesse walketh all the world *arownd,* III. ii. 14. 4
th' altars fume with frankincense *arownd,* III. iv. 17. 4
So, like a wheele, *arownd* they ronne from old to new III. vi. 33. 9
wald with sods *around;* III. vii. 6. 3
with like labour walke the world *arownd,* III. vii. 56. 2
drawne upon the waves that fomed him *arownd* III. viii. 30. 9
he gan to gather up *around* His weapons IV. iv. 23. 1
answering their wearie turnes *around,* IV. v. 33. 8
'Thus sate they all *around* in seemely rate: IV. x. 52. 1
Chasing the gentle Calepine *around,* VI. iv. 2. 8
And every little limbe he searcht *around,* VI. iv. 23. 6
did keepe His fleecie flock upon the playnes *around,* VI. xii. 9. 2
Environd with tenne thousand starres *around* VII. vi. 9. 3
Thieves should rob and spoile that Coast *around:* VII. vi. 55. 6
throwing flowres out of her lap *around:* VII. vii. 34. 3
dainty odours from them threw *around,* *Am.* lxiv. 3
And carrie all the rest with him *around;* *H.H.B.* 74
His throne is all encompassed *around,* *H.H.B.* 177
all the rest *around* To her redoubled *Proth.* 109
Arow. all her teeth *arew,* V. xii. 29. 5
Arraigned. brought Unto the barre whereas she was *arrayned;* VI. vii. 36. 2
Arranged. So both to batteill fierce *arraunged* arre, I. ii. 36. 5
two knights, . . . *arraung'd* in batteill new, I. vi. 38. 4
Arras. which was on every side With . . . costly *arras* dight. I. iv. 6. 6
all within full rich arayd he found, With royall *arras,* I. viii. 35. 2
Parlour . . . with royall *arras* richly dight, II. ix. 33. 7
With costly clothes of *Arras* and of Toure; III. i. 34. 2
the walls yclothed were With goodly *arras* of great majesty, III. xi. 28. 2
All which in that faire *arras* was most lively writ III. xi. 39. 9
not with *arras* made in painefull loome, III. xi. 51. 3
odourd sheetes, and *Arras* coverlets *Epith.* 304
Araught. *See* **Araught.**
Array. *See* **Ray.**
Elisa, decked as thou art In royall *aray;* *S.C.* Ap. 146
When love-lads masken in fresh *aray?* *S.C.* May 2
their flockes fleeces them to *araye:* *S.C.* May 116
Adowne whose necke, in terrible *array,* *Gn.* 347
with the finest silkes us to *aray,* *Hub.* 461
The Mule all deckt in goodly rich *aray,* *Hub.* 582
the false Foxe him helped to *array* *Hub.* 1063
To gather flowres her forhead to *array:* *Mui.* 117
which was on every side With rich *array* . . . dight I. iv. 6. 6
most brave embellished With royall robes and gorgeous *array,* I. iv. 8. 4
to match, in roiall rich *array,* Great Junoes golden chayre, I. iv. 17. 4
him selfe prepayre In sunbright armes, and battailous *array;* I. v. 2. 8
In ashes and sackcloth he did *array* His daintie corse, I. x. 26. 1
naked nature seemely to *aray;* I. x. 39. 5
all the house did sweat with great *aray:* I. xii. 38. 5
Aray thyselfe in her most gorgeous geare, II. iv. 26. 8
Glistring in armes and battailous *aray,* II. vii. 37. 2
never earthly Prince in such *aray* His glory did enhaunce, II. vii. 44. 8
match his brother proud in battailous *aray* II. viii. 22. 9
the sumptuous *aray* Of that great chamber III. i. 32. 1
A goodly Armour, and full rich *aray,* III. iii. 58. 7
Her lovers shape and chevalrous *aray:* III. iv. 5. 5
bestrowed all with rich *aray* Of pearles III. iv. 18. 4
A teme of Dolphins raunged in *aray* III. iv. 33. 1
wandred in the world in straunge *aray,* III. vi. 11. 8
the maskers marched forth in trim *aray* III. xii. 6. 9
the sunburnt Indians do *aray* Their tawney bodies III. xii. 8. 3
in warlike fresh *aray* Them found IV. ii. 53. 3
on the other side, in fresh *aray,* Fayre Canacee IV. iii. 4. 5
In brave *aray* and goodly amenance, IV. iii. 5. 5
before them found in fresh *aray* Manie a brave knight IV. iv. 13. 7
Attyr'd in forraine armes and straunge *aray:* IV. vi. 9. 3
Both clad in colours like, and like *array,* IV. xi. 47. 8
fowly did *array* Withouten pitty of her goodly hew, V. ii. 25. 7
t' inquire The cause of their *array,* V. ii. 52. 9
The bridegromes state, the brides most rich *aray,* V. iii. 3. 3
They were an hundred knights of that *array,* V. iii. 11. 5
Came forth into the rout, and them t' *array* began V. iv. 36. 9
Sixe of thy fellowes of the best *array,* V. iv. 49. 7
round about him preace in riotous *aray* V. vi. 29. 9
that Sir Artegall should him *array* V. viii. 25. 4
Presenting him with all the rich *array* V. viii. 51. 4
never saw they there the like *array;* V. ix. 24. 5
her cause in battailous *array* Against him justifie, V. xi. 40. 3
Flocking together in confusde *array;* V. xi. 43. 8
in battailous *array* Wayting his foe, V. xii. 12. 7
When Artegall she saw in that *array,* V. xii. 13. 8
a Ladie faire . . . on foot in foule *array;* VI. ii. 4. 2
in batteilous *array* I may beare armes, VI. ii. 33. 5
Calidore in seemly good *array* VI. iii. 9. 7
He passed forth with her in faire *array,* VI. iii. 16. 4
T' amend what was amisse, and put in right *aray* VI. v. 10. 9
Seeing his royall usage and *array* VI. v. 41. 7

Array—*Continued.*
Met her in such misseeming foule *array;* VI. vii. 39. 3
in this wize, and this unmeete *array,* VI. viii. 22. 6
they spoile her . . . of all her rich *array;* VI. viii. 41. 3
in beautyfull *array* Above all other lasses VI. x. 26. 3
doffing her *array,* She bath'd her lovely limbes, VII. vi. 45. 8
All her *array* and vestiments to tell, VII. vii. 9. 2
assembled were On Haemus hill in their divine *array,* VII. vii. 12. 3
Him slew, and with his hide did him *array.* VII. vii. 36. 7
as ye her *array,* *Epith.* 106
Set all your things in seemely good *aray,* *Epith.* 114
gan to raunge them selves in huge *array,* *H.L.* 79
in what rags, and in how base *aray,* *H.H.L.* 228
The earth did fresh *aray;* *Proth.* 69
The which presenting all in trim *Array,* *Proth.* 85
Arrayed. Mart, In loves and gentle jollities *arraid,* I. Pr. 3. 8
sluggish Idlenesse, . . . *Arayd* in habit blacke, I. iv. 18. 8
in garments gilt And gorgeous gold *arayd,* I. v. 26. 8
A goodly knight . . . Together with his Squyre, *arayed* meet: I. vii. 29. 3
There all within full rich *arayd* he found, I. viii. 35. 1
'Sir knight, aread who hath ye thus *arayd,* I. ix. 23. 7
She was *araied* all in lilly white, I. x. 13. 1
all in yellow robes *arayed* still. I. x. 30. 9
aged Queene, *Arayd* in antique robes downe to the grownd, I. xii. 5. 2
rich *arayd,* and yet in modest guize, II. ii. 14. 6
soone her selfe *arayd,* II. iv. 27. 2
with him brought Pryene, rich *arayd,* II. iv. 28. 2
In robe of lilly white she was *arayd,* II. ix. 19. 1
In a long purple pall . . . she was *arayd;* II. ix. 37. 2
Puttockes, all in plumes *arayd;* II. xi. 11. 5
an hideous hoast *arrayd* Of huge Sea monsters, II. xii. 22. 8
was *arayd,* or rather disarayd, II. xii. 77. 3
The noble Britomartis her *arayd,* III. i. 67. 2
fayre Britomartis, thus *arayd,* III. iii. 19. 5
Thus when she had the virgin all *arayd,* III. iii. 61. 1
'What mister wight,' (saide he) 'and how *arayd?*' III. v. 5. 1
richlier by many partes *arayd;* III. xi. 51. 2
In silken samite she was light *arayd,* III. xii. 13. 3
which erst She saw so rich and royally *arayd,* III. xii. 42. 2
The which was all in lilly white *arayd,* IV. x. 52. 4
Old Cybele, *arayd* with pompous pride, IV. xi. 28. 4
As he with golden saddle is *arayd,* V. iii. 35. 4
this, that seem'd so faire And royally *arayd,* V. ix. 40. 2
what cruell hand hath thus *arayd* This knight VI. ii. 42. 3
jolly June, *arrayd* All in greene leaves, VII. vii. 35. 1
rich *arrayd* In garment all of gold VII. vii. 37. 1
In goodly colours gloriously *arrayd;* *Am.* lxx. 4
lie like Gods in yvorie beds *arayd,* *H.L.* 285
arayd with much more orient hew, *H.B.* 79
Arrays. the fleece, which him *arayes,* *Gn.* 97
Arrear. Ne ever did her ey-sight turne *arere,* *Gn.* 468
grownd he gave, and lightly lept *areare:* II. xi. 36. 5
when his force gan faile his pace gan wex *areare* III. vii. 24. 9
Malbecco . . . would have fled *arere,* III. x. 23. 5
That forst him backe recoyle and reele *areare,* VI. iv. 5. 8
eeke this wallet at your backe *arreare,* VI. viii. 23. 8
Arrest. her former dred Were hard behind, her ready to *arrest;* III. vii. 2. 6
all his senses did full soone *arrest:* IV. v. 43. 5
arrest The Author, and him bring before his presence prest. VII. vi. 16. 8
Arrested. whenas Morpheus had . . . *Arrested* all that courtly company, I. iv. 44. 7
Arresting. there *arresting,* readie way did yield For bloud IV. iii. 9. 4
Arrett. *See* **Aret.**
Arrival. at his first *arrivall* them began . . . to pacifie, II. ii. 21. 8
came tydings to the Tyrants eare . . . Of their *arrival:* V. xii. 6. 6
none tydings bore Of Artegals *arryvall* V. xii. 11. 6
Arrive. Faine would *arive,* but cannot for the storme, *Ro.* xxi. 12
when ye *arrive* in that same place; I. ix. 32. 8
They do *arrive* anone Where sate a gentle Lady II. i. 13. 4
Untill they nigh unto that Gulfe *arryve,* II. xii. 5. 2
they shortly doe *arryve* Whereas the Bowre of Blisse II. xii. 42. 1
'At last in Latium he did *arryve,* III. ix. 42. 1
Till they *arrive* at their last ruinous decay. V. Pr. 6. 9
none can there *arrive* without an hoste: V. xi. 42. 8
I hope ere long for to *arryve:* *Am.* lxiii. 6
till they at last *arive* To the most faire, *H.H.B.* 76
Arrived. here *arriv'd,* to see if like he found. *Hub.* 688
He soft *arrived* on the grassie plaine. *Hub.* 1263
the drerie stownd is now *arrived,* *Mui.* 415
Arrived there, the little house they fill, I. i. 35. 1
By this *arrived* there Dame Una, I. iii. 12. 8
Arrived there, they passed in forth right; I. iv. 6. 1
an errant knight in armes ycled, . . . they new *arrived* find: I. iv. 38. 6
The wyld woodgods, *arrived* in the place, I. vi. 9. 1
Arriv'd wher they in erth their fruitles blood had sown. I. vi. 45. 9
Arrived there, That bare-head knight I. ix. 34. 6
Arrived there, the dore they find fast lockt, I. x. 5. 1
There when the Elfin knight *arrived* was, I. x. 44. 1
that hoarie king, with all his traine, Being *arrived* I. xii. 12. 3
well *arrived* are, (high God be blest!) I. xii. 17. 8
As wetherbeaten ship *arryv'd* on happie shore. II. i. 2. 9
arrived where that sad pourtraict Of death II. i. 39. 3
Where when the knight *arriv'd,* II. ii. 14. 1
in that place straunge knight *arrived* late, II. ii. 19. 7
Till they *arrived* in that pleasaunt Ile, II. vi. 22. 3
soone *arrived* on the shallow sand, II. vi. 38. 4
So soon as Mammon there *arrivd,* II. vii. 26. 1
ere the point *arrived* where it ought, II. viii. 32. 4
now *arrived* in his fatall howre, II. viii. 43. 8
Driven by fatall error here *arriv'd,* II. x. 9. 8

Arrived—*Continued.*
arrived here three hoyes Of Saxons, II. x. 64. 8
Till they *arrived* where they lately had Charm'd II. xii. 84. 4
They beene ymett, and both theyr points *arriv'd;* III. i. 6. 1
Soone as they bene *arriv'd* upon the brim III. iv. 34. 1
He on the bancke *arryvd* with mickle payne, III. v. 21. 2
arryv'd, As did Belphoebe, in the bloody place, III. v. 37. 2
where their Lady was *arrived* at the last. III. v. 37. 9
till they *arrived* were In that same shady covert III. vi. 26. 5
by what accident she there *arriv'd?* III. vii. 14. 4
As shee *arrived* on the roring shore, III. vii. 27. 2
His speare amids her sun-brode shield *arriv'd:* III. vii. 40. 4
Paridell . . . now by fortune was *arrived* here, III. x. 37. 4
Till they *arriv'd* whereas their purpose they did plott. III. xi. 20. 9
when the Victoresse *arrived* there III. xii. 44. 1
in case it had *arrived* Where it was ment, IV. iii. 18. 1
Staid not till it *arrived* in his side, IV. iv. 24. 5
that same gentle Squire *arriv'd* in place IV. vii. 24. 3
Artegall, *arriv'd* in place, V. iv. 23. 5
now the Knights, being *arrived* neare, V. iv. 37. 1
Unto whose temple when as Britomart *Arrived,* V. vii. 3. 7
Soone after whom the Prince *arrived* there, V. viii. 27. 6
'Loe! now, right noble knights, *arriv'd* ye bee V. ix. 20. 4
When these two stranger knights *arriv'd* in place, V. ix. 36. 2
till that the Prince *arrived* Within the land V. x. 18. 1
Ere that huge stroke *arrived* on him neare, V. xi. 10. 5
there *arriv'd* again whence forth he set, V. xii. 28. 2
So now they be *arrived* both in sight Of this wyld man, VI. v. 25. 1
Whenas these Knights *arriv'd,* they wist not where nor how. VI. v. 35. 9
night *arrived* hard at hand, VI. ix. 16. 3
Arrived in this Isle, though bare and blunt, VI. xi. 9. 5
how those marchants were *Arriv'd* in place VI. xi. 10. 2
Arriving. There he *arriving* round about doth flie, *Mui.* 169
auncient Night *arriving* did alight I. v. 41. 1
The pointed steele, *arriving* rudely theare, I. xi. 16. 3
the sharpe steele, *arriving* forcibly On his broad shield, II. v. 4. 3
Atin, *arriving* there, when him he spyde II. v. 35. 1
here *arriving,* strongly challenged The crowne II. x. 67. 3
The Squyre *arriving* fiercely in his armes Snatcht II. xi. 31. 1
They, here *arriving,* staid awhile without, III. iii. 14. 1
a straunger king, from unknowne soyle *Arriving,* III. iii. 33. 4
The Damzell there *arriving* entred in; III. vii. 7. 1
soone *arryving* they restrained were Of ready entraunce, III. viii. 52. 3
At last *arriving* by the listes side, IV. iii. 46. 1
There this faire crewe *arriving* did divide IV. iv. 14. 1
in his nape *arriving,* through it thrild IV. vii. 31. 6
Arriving there he found this wretched man IV. vii. 43. 1
Artegall, *arriving* happily, V. iv. 6. 7
Where they *arriving* by the watchman were Descried streight; V. iv. 36. 1
Where soone *arriving* they received were In seemely wise, V. vi. 22. 6
all strangers, in that region *Arryving,* V. x. 9. 8
There he *arriving* boldly did present VI. iii. 18. 1
arriving with the fall of day VI. iii. 37. 7
Arriving there, . . . He found the gate wyde ope, VI. vi. 19. 1
Shee there *arriving* boldly in did pass; VII. vi. 24. 1
Arrogance. sdeignfull pride, and wilfull *arrogaunce:* *Hub.* 1135
Arrogant. *arrogant* delight Of th' high descent whereof he was yborne, I. vii. 10. 1
Arrogate. *Arrogate* to themselves ambitiously: VII. vii. 16. 4
Arrow. Hasting to raunch the *arrow* out, *S.C.* Au. 97
Hey, ho, the *arrowe!* *S.C.* Au. 102
stouping, like an *arrowe* from a bowe, *Hub.* 1262
in my heart his yron *arrow* steep, I. vii. 39. 5
Whose right haunch earst my stedfast *arrow* strake? II. iii. 32. 8
Drew out a deadly bow and *arrow* keene, III. i. 65. 2
the false Archer, which that *arrow* shot III. ii. 26. 7
Another *arrow* hath your lovers hart to hit.' III. ii. 35. 9
therewith shott an *arrow* at the lad; III. v. 24. 7
whom late their ladies *arrow* ryv'd: III. v. 37. 5
through his soule like poysned *arrow* perst, IV. v. 31. 4
The *arrow* to his deadly marke desynde. IV. vii. 30. 4
She sent an *arrow* forth with mighty draught, IV. vii. 31. 4
that selfe *arrow* which the Carle had kild; IV. vii. 36. 5
Ayming his *arrow* at my very hart: *Am.* xvi. 10
thou pointest thy Sons poysned *arrow,* *H.B.* 62
Arrow's. Whom having slain through luckles *arrowes* glaunce, III. ix. 48. 3
Arrows. could both Phoebus *arrowes* ward, *Mui.* 79
he shootes his *arrowes* every where *Col.* 811
Wandreth alone with bow and *arrowes* keene, II. iii. 31. 4
yonder is no game For thy fiers *arrowes,* II. iii. 35. 2
mortall *arrowes,* wherewith he doth fill The world II. viii. 6. 3
every one did bow and *arrowes* beare. II. xi. 8. 7
Their fluttring *arrowes,* thicke as flakes of snow, II. xi. 18. 2
many *arrowes* under his right side, II. xi. 21. 2
still as abroad he strew His wicked *arrowes,* II. xi. 28. 2
which with her *arrowes* keene She wounded had, III. v. 28. 2
turne his *arrowes* to their exercize. III. vi. 23. 5
broken bowes and *arrowes* shivered short; III. xi. 46. 7
A mortall bow and *arrowes* keene did hold, III. xi. 48. 2
With bow in hand and *arrowes* ready bent, IV. vii. 29. 6
With fell despight her cruell *arrowes* tynde IV. vii. 30. 7
Her mortall *arrowes* she at him did threat, IV. vii. 37. 8
With a sharpe showre of *arrowes,* which them staid, V. iv. 38. 4
arrowes haild so thicke, that they could not abide. V. iv. 38. 9
Darting their deadly *arrowes,* fyry bright, *Am.* xvi. 7
The sweet eye-glaunces, that like *arrowes* glide; *Am.* xvii. 9
thousand *arrowes,* which your eies have shot: *Am.* lvii. 8
Art (*partial list of vb.*).
arte and nature strived to joyne *Bel.*[1] x. 5
Art and Nature had assembled *Bel.*[2] xii. 5

Art—*Continued.*
what ever nature, *arte,* And heaven could doo, . . . *Ro.* v. 1
All that Lysippus practike *arte* could forme, . . . *Ro.* xxix. 5
Thou onely cause, O Civill furie! *art,* . . . *Ro.* xxxi. 9
Thou *art* a fon . . . *S.C.* F. 69
Shepheard to see them in theyr *art* outgoe. . . . *S.C.* Jun. 64
That *art* the roote of all this ruthfull woe! . . . *S.C.* Jun. 116
Made me by *arte* more cunning in the same. . . . *S.C.* D. 42
thou *art* he whom . . . *Gn.* 630
there (said the Priest) is *arte* indeed: . . . *Hub.* 483
whatsoever mother-wit or *arte* Could worke, . . . *Hub.* 1138
Without vaine *art* or curious complements, . . . *T.M.* 542
it by *arte* was framed to endure . . . *Mui.* 61
Arte, with her contending, doth aspire . . . *Mui.* 165
Himselfe as skilfull in that *art* as any. . . . *Col.* 75
A filed toung, furnisht with tearmes of *art,* . . . *Col.* 701
No *art* of schoole, but Courtiers schoolery. . . . *Col.* 702
thee, that *art* the sommers Nightingale, . . . *Ded. Son.* viii. 1
she to appease Her mournefull plaintes, beguiled of her *art,* . I. i. 54. 7
a Cave ywrought by wondrous *art,* . . . I. v. 36. 5
Aesculape that by his *art* Did heale them all againe, . . . I. v. 39. 8
all things els the which his *art* did teach: . . . I. v. 44. 3
Great maistresse of her *art* was that false Dame, . . . I. vii. 1. 8
never rest, Till I that treachours *art* have heard . . . I. ix. 32. 2
whether *art* it were or heedlesse hap, . . . II. iii. 30. 6
faire Claribell with all her *art,* . . . II. iv. 26. 5
art, stryving to compayre With nature, . . . II. v. 29. 1
passe . . . Their native musicke by her skilful *art:* . . . II. vi. 25. 4
wrought by *art* and counterfetted shew, . . . II. vii. 45. 5
Merlin made by his almightie *art* . . . II. viii. 20. 2
He built by *art* upon the glassy See . . . II. x. 73. 8
best alyve, That natures worke by *art* can imitate: . . . II. xii. 42. 4
her mother *Art,* as halfe in scorne . . . II. xii. 50. 6
So made by *art* to beautify the rest, . . . II. xii. 55. 2
The *art* which all that wrought appeared in no place. . . . II. xii. 58. 9
nature had for wantonesse ensude *Art,* . . . II. xii. 59. 4
and that *Art* at nature did repine; . . . II. xii. 59. 4
If pourtrayd it might bee by any living *art.* . . . III. Pr. 1. 9
living *art* may not least part expresse, . . . III. Pr. 2. 1
as well that *art* she knew, . . . III. i. 35. 2
pleasing wordes are like to Magick *art,* . . . III. ii. 15. 5
to their purpose used wicked *art:* . . . III. ii. 41. 4
Which Bladud made by Magick *art* of yore, . . . III. iii. 60. 2
every thing consumes, and calcineth by *art.* . . . III. v. 48. 9
not by *art* But of the trees owne inclination made, . . . III. vi. 44. 2
by her wicked *art* Late foorth she sent, . . . III. viii. 2. 5
her Sprightes to entertaine, The maisters of her *art:* . . . III. viii. 4. 5
For all that *art* he learned had of yore; . . . III. ix. 28. 4
So perfect in that *art* was Paridell, . . . III. x. 5. 1
there sleights and *art* She cast to use, . . . III. xii. 28. 1
Figuring straunge characters of his *art:* . . . III. xii. 31. 2
So great a mistresse of her *art* she was, . . . IV. ii. 10. 1
Which she by *art* could use unto her will, . . . IV. ii. 44. 3
Such as the maker selfe could best by *art* devize. . . . IV. iii. 38. 9
understanding by her mightie *art* . . . IV. iii. 40. 6
What medicine can any Leaches *art* Yeeld such a sore, . . . IV. vi. 1. 5
with womanish *art* To hide her wound, . . . IV. vi. 40. 7
Vaine is the *art* that seekes it selfe for to deceive. . . . IV. vi. 40. 9
by wit or *art* Could that atchieve . . . IV. vi. 43. 5
Art, playing second natures part, supplyed it. . . . IV. x. 21. 9
Thereto adde *art,* even womens witty trade, . . . V. v. 49. 5
The *art* of mightie words that men can charme; . . . V. v. 49. 6
least by that *art* He should his purpose misse, . . . V. vi. 24. 2
Some Clarkes doe doubt in their devicefull *art* . . . V. x. 1. 1
So much more, then, is that of powre and *art* . . . V. x. 2. 5
by no *art,* nor any leaches might, . . . VI. vi. 1. 5
As he the *art* of words knew wondrous well, . . . VI. vi. 6. 3
learn'd the *art* to please, . . . VI. vi. 43. 3
no skill of Leaches *art* Mote him availe, . . . VI. x. 31. 5
Cannot expressed be by any *art.* . . . *Am.* xvii. 12
when I sigh, she sayes, I know the *art;* . . . *Am.* xviii. 11
the worke of Nature or of *Art,* . . . *Am.* xxi. 1
Such *art* of eyes I never read in bookes! . . . *Am.* xxi. 14
I honor and admire the Makers *art.* . . . *Am.* xxiv. 4
Expressing all thy mothers powrefull *art.* . . . *Am.* xxxix. 2
Sweet is thy vertue, as thy selfe sweet *art.* . . . *Am.* xxxix. 5
such sweet cordialls passe Physitions *art.* . . . *Am.* l. 12
eeke for comfort often called *art* . . . *Epith.* 394
we nature see of *art* Exceld, . . . *H.B.* 83
How then dare I, the novice of his *Art,* . . . *H.H.B.* 225

Artegall. As *Arthegall* and Sophy now beene honored.' . . . II. ix. 6. 9
to Britomart Describeth *Artegall:* . . . III. ii. Arg.
donne Late foule dishonour . . . and *Arthegall* he hight.' . . . III. ii. 8. 9
The noble *Arthegall* hath ever borne the name. . . . III. ii. 9. 9
Achilles armes, which *Arthegall* did win: . . . III. ii. 25. 6
bewrayes to Britomart The state of *Arthegall;* . . . III. iii. Arg.
ordaynd to bee The spouse of Britomart, is *Arthegall:* . . . III. iii. 26. 2
of *Arthegall* and his estate. . . . III. iii. 62. 5
She learned had th' estate of *Arthegall,* . . . III. iv. 4. 2
Britomart winnes the prize from all, And *Artegall* doth quell. . IV. iv. Arg.
knowne to few, that *Arthegall* he hight, . . . IV. iv. 42. 8
charg'd his powrefull speare At *Artegall,* . . . IV. iv. 44. 2
thereat greatly grudged *Arthegall,* . . . IV. v. 9. 1
Both Scudamour and *Arthegall* Doe fight with Britomart: . . IV. vi. Arg.
Artegall, beholding his mischaunce, . . . IV. vi. 11. 1
Sir *Arthegall* renewed His strength still more, . . . IV. vi. 18. 4
Beheld the lovely face of *Artegall* . . . IV. vi. 26. 2
Him thus bespake: 'Certes, Sir *Artegall,* . . . IV. vi. 28. 6
Soone as she heard the name of *Artegall,* . . . IV. vi. 29. 1
Sir *Artegall,* the salvage knight, . . . IV. vi. 31. 1

Artegall—*Continued.*
Artegall close smyling joy'd in secret hart. . . . IV. vi. 32. 9
All being guided by Sir *Artegall:* . . . IV. vi. 39. 5
In all which time Sir *Artegall* made way . . . IV. vi. 40. 1
Sir *Artegall,* who . . . was bound Upon an hard adventure . IV. vi. 42. 2
loe! here thy *Artegall.* . . . V. Pr. 11. 9
Artegall trayn'd in Justice lore . . . V. i. Arg.
The Champion of true Justice, *Artegall:* . . . V. i. 3. 2
Chose *Artegall* to right her to restore; . . . V. i. 4. 8
Artegall in justice was upbrought . . . V. i. 5. 1
willed him with *Artegall* to wend, . . . V. i. 12. 4
'Who was it then,' (sayd *Artegall*) . . . V. i. 16. 1
Artegall By that same carefull Squire did then abide, . . . V. i. 23. 1
Artegall by signes perceiving plaine . . . V. i. 24. 6
Whom when so willing *Artegall* perceaved; . . . V. i. 28. 1
Much did that Squire Sir *Artegall* adore . . . V. i. 30. 1
Artegall heares of Florimell, . . . V. ii. Arg.
of her health when *Artegall* did heare, . . . V. ii. 3. 5
Ne was Sir *Artegall* behinde: . . . V. ii. 12. 3
Which oddes when as Sir *Artegall* espide, . . . V. ii. 14. 1
Ne ever *Artegall* his griple strong . . . wold slacke, . . . V. ii. 14. 8
So *Artegall* at length him forst forsake His horses backe . . V. ii. 16. 1
Artegall in swimming skilfull was, . . . V. ii. 16. 6
Artegall was better breath'd beside, . . . V. ii. 17. 5
Artegall pursewd him still so neare . . . V. ii. 18. 1
Artegall him selfe her seemelesse plight did rew. . . . V. ii. 25. 9
Sir *Artegall* undid the evill fashion, . . . V. ii. 28. 7
All which when *Artegall* did see and heare, . . . V. ii. 33. 6
Then answered the righteous *Artegall,* . . . V. ii. 39. 2
'Well then,' sayd *Artegall,* 'let it be tride: . . . V. ii. 45. 4
'Now take the right likewise,' sayd *Artegale,* . . . V. ii. 46. 1
Artegall him fairely gan asswage, . . . V. ii. 47. 3
In warlike wise when *Artegall* did vew, . . . V. ii. 52. 2
To *Artegall* he turn'd and went with him throughout. . . . V. ii. 54. 9
Sir *Artegall* into the Tilt-yard came, . . . V. iii. 10. 2
for Sir *Artegall* Came Braggadochio, . . . V. iii. 14. 7
All which when *Artegall* . . . well advewed, . . . V. iii. 20. 1
Artegall that golden belt uptooke, . . . V. iii. 27. 1
Which troublous stirre when *Artegall* perceived, . . . V. iii. 30. 6
Which *Artegall* well hearing, . . . V. iii. 32. 1
Thereby Sir *Artegall* did plaine areed . . . V. iii. 35. 1
So did he mitigate Sir *Artegall;* . . . V. iii. 37. 1
when as time to *Artegall* shall tend, . . . V. iii. 40. 8
Artegall dealeth right betwixt Two brethren . . . V. iv. Arg.
this of *Artegall,* which here we have to say. . . . V. iv. 2. 9
Artegall, arriving happily, . . . V. iv. 6. 7
Then *Artegall* thus to the younger sayd: . . . V. iv. 17. 1
Then *Artegall* . . . Departed on his way, . . . V. iv. 20. 6
Artegall, arriv'd in place, . . . V. iv. 23. 5
'How hight that Amazon?' (sayd *Artegall*) . . . V. iv. 33. 1
Whom when as *Artegall* in that distresse By chaunce beheld, . V. iv. 41. 1
Artegall him selfe to rest did dight, . . . V. iv. 51. 8
Artegall fights with Radigund, . . . V. v. Arg.
Then forth came *Artegall* out of his tent. . . . V. v. 5. 1
So did Sir *Artegall* upon her lay, . . . V. v. 8. 1
Thus there long while continu'd *Artegall,* . . . V. v. 26. 1
gan thenceforth to cast affection, . . . To *Artegall,* . . . V. v. 43. 9
Some men, I wote, will deeme in *Artegall* Great weaknesse, . V. vi. 1. 1
it was Talus, *Artegall* his groome: . . . V. vi. 8. 6
The eldest of which was slaine erewhile By *Artegall,* . . . V. vi. 33. 5
he weend that this his present guest Was *Artegall,* . . . V. vi. 34. 2
Which still was wont with *Artegall* remaine; . . . V. vi. 34. 4
On which Pollente with *Artegall* did fight. . . . V. vi. 36. 7
She fights with Radigund . . . And *Artegall* thence frees. . V. vii. Arg.
Made them sweare fealty to *Artegall;* . . . V. vii. 43. 6
her noble Lord, sir *Artegall,* . . . V. vii. 45. 6
Prince Arthure and Sir *Artegall* Free Samient from feare: . V. viii. Arg.
Yet could it not sterne *Artegall* retaine, . . . V. viii. 3. 1
at length she did before her spie Sir *Artegall;* . . . V. viii. 6. 5
Artegall was stronger, And better skild in Tilt . . . V. viii. 7. 6
finding there ready prest Sir *Artegall,* . . . V. viii. 9. 2
when as *Artegall* did Arthure vew, . . . V. viii. 12. 6
Then *Artegall* gan of the Prince enquire, . . . V. viii. 15. 1
that Sir *Artegall* should him array . . . V. viii. 25. 4
Sir *Artegall* Him clad in th' armour . . . V. viii. 26. 1
kept as prisonere By *Artegall,* . . . V. viii. 46. 6
Artegall, being thereof aware, . . . V. viii. 48. 1
Then *Artegall,* himselfe discovering plaine, . . . V. viii. 50. 1
Where righteous *Artegall* her late exyled; . . . V. ix. 2. 2
with Sir *Artegall* a space Well solast . . . V. ix. 3. 1
Artegall him after did pursew, . . . V. ix. 15. 1
to his Lord Sir *Artegall* it lent, . . . V. ix. 18. 2
Artegall . . . was against her bent: . . . V. ix. 49. 4
The noble Prince and righteous *Artegall,* . . . V. x. 4. 2
leaving *Artegall* to his owne care, . . . V. x. 17. 4
Ne after him did *Artigall* (**Artegall*) abide, . . . V. x. 17. 8
turne we now to noble *Artegall;* . . . V. xi. 36. 1
Those tidings sad Did much abash Sir *Artegall* to heare, . . V. xi. 40. 7
'Now turne againe,' (Sir *Artegall* then sayd) . . . V. xi. 43. 1
Of whom Sir *Artegall* gan then enquire . . . V. xi. 48. 6
why have ye' (said *Artegall*) 'forborne Your own good shield . V. xi. 52. 1
To whom thus *Artegall:* 'Certes, Sir knight, . . . V. xi. 55. 1
'Fie on such forgerie!' (sayd *Artegall*) . . . V. xi. 56. 6
Sir *Artegall* . . . to his aide agreed, . . . V. xi. 57. 6
Sayd *Artegall:* 'What foule disgrace is this . . . V. xi. 62. 1
Artegall, seeing his cruell deed, . . . V. xi. 65. 6
Artegall doth Sir Burbon aide, . . . V. xii. Arg.
Sir *Artegall,* long having since Taken in hand th' exploit, . . V. xii. 3. 1
Sir *Artegall* with that old knight Did forth descend, . . . V. xii. 6. 1
Artegall him seeing so to rage Willd him to stay, . . . V. xii. 8. 1

Artegall—*Continued.*
Sir *Artegall* did cause his tent There to be pitched . . . V. xii. 10. 1
comming to the place, and finding there Sir *Artegall*, . . . V. xii. 12. 7
When *Artegall* she saw in that array, . . . V. xii. 13. 8
With dreadfull looke he *Artegall* beheld, . . . V. xii. 16. 2
Which cruell outrage when as *Artegall* Did well avize, . . . V. xii. 18. 1
Which *Artegall* perceiving strooke no more, . . . V. xii. 22. 6
linckt together gainst Sir *Artegall;* . . . V. xii. 37. 2
when they nigh approching had espyde Sir *Artegall*, . . . V. xii. 38. 3
If her Sir *Artegall* had not preserved, . . . V. xii. 43. 4
Artegall, returning yet halfe sad . . . VI. i. 4. 4
To whom Sir *Artegall* gan to expresse . . . VI. i. 5. 3
'What is that quest,' (quoth then Sir *Artegall*) . . . VI. i. 6. 8
Sayd *Artegall*, 'I such a Beast did see, . . . VI. i. 9. 2
'Now God you speed,' (quoth then Sir *Artegall*) . . . VI. i. 10. 6
Artegall's. Talus brings newes . . . of *Artegals* mishap: . . . V. vi. Arg.
gan enquire . . . The certaine cause of *Artegals* detaine, . . . V. vi. 15. 7
none tydings bore Of *Artegals* arryvall . . . V. xii. 11. 6
Arthur. Prince *Arthure* meets with Una . . . I. vii. Arg.
Faire virgin, . . . Brings *Arthure* to the fight: . . . I. viii. Arg.
His loves and lignage *Arthure* tells: . . . I. ix. Arg.
Prince *Arthure*, crowne of Martiall band?' . . . I. ix. 6. 5
Prince *Arthur* gave a boxe of Diamond sure, . . . I. ix. 19. 1
Arthur on his way To seeke his love, . . . I. ix. 20. 1
Sith her Prince *Arthur* of proud ornaments . . . spoyld. . . . II. i. 22. 6
the best and noblest knight alive Prince *Arthur* is, . . . II. iii. 18. 4
Sir Guyon, . . . Whom *Arthure* soone hath reskewed, . . . II. viii. Arg.
Prince *Arthur*, flowre of grace and nobilesse, . . . II. viii. 18. 4
So rag'd Prince *Arthur* twixt his foemen twaine, . . . II. viii. 42. 8
So did Prince *Arthur* beare himselfe in fight, . . . II. viii. 48. 8
Arthur all that reckoning defrayd: . . . II. x. 49. 8
Prince *Arthure* them repelles, . . . II. xi. Arg.
seek adventures as he with Prince *Arthure* went. . . . III. i. 2. 9
Florimell of *Arthure* is Long followed, . . . III. iv. Arg.
Prince *Arthur* heares of Florimell: . . . III. v. Arg.
from Prince *Arthure* fled with winges of idle feare. . . . III. vi. 54. 9
His owne deare Lord Prince *Arthure* came that way, . . . IV. vii. 42. 2
Corflambo chaseth Placidas, And is by *Arthure* slaine. . . . IV. viii. Arg.
Prince *Arthur* stints their strife. . . . IV. ix. Arg.
Prince *Arthur* graunted had To yeeld . . . IV. ix. 4. 1
Prince *Arthure* and Sir Artegall Free Samient from feare: . . . V. viii. Arg.
when as Artegall did *Arthure* vew, . . . V. viii. 12. 6
Prince *Arthur* takes the enterprize . . . V. x. Arg.
Prince *Arthure* overcomes the great Gerioneo . . . V. xi. Arg.
Till she Prince *Arthure* fynd; . . . VI. v. Arg.
Prince *Arthur* and young Timias, . . . VI. v. 11. 8
sib to great Orgolio, which was slaine By *Arthure*, . . . VI. vii. 41. 9
Prince *Arthure* overcomes Disdaine; . . . VI. viii. Arg.
They met Prince *Arthure* with Sir Enias, . . . VI. viii. 4. 3
Arthure with the rest went onward still . . . VI. viii. 30. 7
Artillery. planted there their huge *artillery*, . . . II. xi. 7. 8
Of his sharpe dartes and whot *artilleree:* . . . III. vi. 14. 5
Arts. the God of goodly *Arts:* . . . *T.M.* 58
they that scorne the schoole of *arts* divine, . . . *T.M.* 520
In learned *artes*, and goodlie governaunce, . . . *Ti.* 270
There learned *arts* do florish in great honor, . . . *Col.* 320
arts of schoole have there small countenance, . . . *Col.* 703
for profession of all learned *arts*, . . . *Col.* 754
Mecaenas . . . to al that civil *artes* professe, . . . *Ded.Son.*xiii.10
amiddes His magick bookes, and *artes* of sundrie kindes, . . . I. i. 36. 8
all this while, with charmes and hidden *artes*, . . . I. i. 45. 1
he praisd his divelish *arts*, . . . I. ii. 9. 4
'by whose mischievous *arts* Art thou misshaped thus, . . . I. ii. 34. 2
when he saw his flatt'ring *artes* to fayle, . . . I. vi. 5. 1
No magicke *arts* hereof had any might, . . . I. vii. 35. 1
her golden cup, . . . replete with magick *artes;* . . . I. viii. 14. 2
by her wicked *arts* and wylie skill, . . . I. xii. 32. 6
His *artes* he moves, and . . . Himselfe he frees . . . II. i. 1. 7
Greece, the Nourse of all good *arts*, . . . II. ix. 48. 1
All *artes*, all science, all Philosophy, . . . II. ix. 53. 8
in *artes* Exceld at Athens . . . II. x. 25. 6
Tryde all her *arts* and all her sleights thence out to wrest. . . II. xii. 81. 9
They have exceld in *artes* and pollicy, . . . III. ii. 2. 8
her divelish deedes And hellish *arts* . . . III. vii. 6. 8
by her divelish *arts* thought to prevaile . . . III. vii. 21. 8
all the *artes*, that subtill wits discover, . . . IV. iii. 40. 2
ye double noursery Of *Arts!* . . . IV. xi. 26. 9
with all her *arts* Him otherwise perswade . . . VI. v. 33. 5
Arts'. when her face is staynd with magicke *arts* constraint. I. vii. 34. 9
Arvirage. *Arvirage* his brothers place supplyde . . . II. x. 51. 6
never king more highly magnifide . . . then was *Arvirage;* . . II. x. 52. 2
As (*partial list, except in similes*). *See* **As for, As if, As then, As though, As when, As yet, Ever as, Like as, Soon as, Whenas, Whereas, Whileas.**
seene so faire a thing *as* this, . . . *Bel.*[1] iv. 13
Out of hir ashes *as* a worme arise. . . . *Bel.*[1] vi. 14
Even by an hundred such *as* Hercules, . . . *Bel.*[1] viii. 12
Descendeth garnisht *as* a loved spouse. . . . *Rev.* iv. 4
So far *as* Archer might his level see: . . . *Bel.* iii. 4
As cleare *as* Christall gainst the Sunnie beames, . . . *Bel.* xii. 2
The seates and benches shone *as* yvorie, . . . *Bel.* xii. 9
short *as* thought, . . . *Bel.*[2] viii. 13
So faire *as* mote the greatest god delite; . . . *Pet.* i. 5
So great riches *as* like cannot be found! . . . *Pet.* ii. 14
As snowe and golde together had been wrought: . . . *Pet.* vi. 6
Wherewith she languisht *as* the gathered floure; . . . *Pet.* vi. 9
Such *as* the Berecynthian Goddesse bright, . . . *Ro.* vi. 1
As that brave sonne of Aeson, . . . *Ro.* x. 1
Like *as* whilome the children of the earth . . . *Ro.* xii. 1
As men in Summer fearles passe the foord . . . *Ro.* xiv. 1

As—*Continued.*
And *as* the coward beasts use to despise . . . *Ro.* xiv. 5
as at Troy most dastards of the Greekes . . . *Ro.* xiv. 9
Like *as* ye see the wrathfull Sea from farre . . . *Ro.* xvi. 1
Like *as* ye see fell Boreas with sharpe blast . . . *Ro.* xvi. 5
as ye see huge flames spred diverslie, . . . *Ro.* xvi. 9
As waves, *as* winde, *as* fire, spred over all, . . . *Ro.* xvi. 13
So long *as* Joves great Bird did make his flight, . . . *Ro.* xvii. 1
Long *as* her ship, tost with so manie freakes, . . . *Ro.* xxi. 5
As he that having long in tempest sailed, . . . *Ro.* xxi. 11
As, in a vicious bodie, grose disease . . . *Ro.* xxiii. 11
Like *as* the seeded field greene grasse first showes, . . . *Ro.* xxx. 1
as in season due the husband mowes . . . *Ro.* xxx. 5
As they which gleane, the reliques use to gather, . . . *Ro.* xxx. 13
a Bull *as* white *as* driven snowe, . . . *Van.* ii. 2
did beare (*as* batteilant) A gilden towre, . . . *Van.* viii. 3
she did seeme to daunce, *as* in delight, . . . *Van.* ix. 7
As child whose parent is unkent, . . . *To his Booke* 2
'*As* shee that feeles the deepe delight . . . *Frag.*
as the Sheepe, such was the shepeheards looke, . . . *S.C.* Ja. 7
'Such rage *as* winters reigneth in my heart, . . . *S.C.* Ja. 25
As on your boughes the ysicles depend. . . . *S.C.* Ja. 42
Shepheards devise she hateth *as* the snake, . . . *S.C.* Ja. 65
All *as* I were through the body gryde: . . . *S.C.* F. 4
shake, *As* doen high Towers . . . *S.C.* F. 6
Perke *as* a Peacock; . . . *S.C.* F. 8
as the lowring Wether lookes downe, . . . *S.C.* F. 29
His hornes bene *as* broad *as* Rainebowe bent, . . . *S.C.* F. 73
His dewelap *as* lythe *as* lasse of Kent: . . . *S.C.* F. 74
As halfe unwilling to cutte the graine; . . . *S.C.* F. 204
sytten we soe, *As* weren overwent with woe, . . . *S.C.* Mar. 2
A stepdame eke, *as* whott *as* fyre, . . . *S.C.* Mar. 41
As thicke *as* it had hayled. . . . *S.C.* Mar. 87
bowe and shafts *as* then none had, . . . *S.C.* Mar. 113
we here sitten *as* drownd in a dreme. . . . *S.C.* May 16
Crowned *as* king: . . . *S.C.* May 30
Will doe *as* did the Foxe by the Kidde . . . *S.C.* May 171
The false Foxe, *as* he were starke lame: . . . *S.C.* May 279
and if foxes bene so crafty *as* so, . . . *S.C.* May 312
So calme, so coole, *as* no where else . . . *S.C.* Jun. 5
time in passing weares, (*As* garments doen, . . . *S.C.* Jun. 39
losse of her, whose love *as* lyfe I wayd, . . . *S.C.* Jun. 47
As messengers of this my painfull plight, . . . *S.C.* Jun. 98
meeke he was, *as* meeke mought be, . . . *S.C.* Jul. 129
Simple *as* simple sheepe; . . . *S.C.* Jul. 130
Well-eyed, *as* Argus was, . . . *S.C.* Jul. 154
stoute *as* steede of brasse. . . . *S.C.* Jul. 156
gazd on her *as* they were wood, . . . *S.C.* Au. 75
As cleare *as* the christall glasse; . . . *S.C.* Au. 80
All *as* the Sunnye beame so bright, . . . *S.C.* Au. 81
as the thonder cleaves the cloudes, . . . *S.C.* Au. 85
as Dame Cynthias silver raye, . . . *S.C.* Au. 89
say it, Cuddie, *as* thou art a ladde: . . . *S.C.* Au. 143
tune your pypes *as* ruthful *as* ye may. . . . *S.C.* Au. 150
With sight of such *as* (*a) chaunge my restlesse woe. . . . *S.C.* Au. 172
They looken bigge *as* Bulls . . . *S.C.* S. 44
As cocke on his dunghill crowing . . . *S.C.* S. 46
as the bright starre Seemeth ay greater . . . *S.C.* S. 76
as a Monster of many heads; . . . *S.C.* S. 121
wise, and *as* Argus eyed,) . . . *S.C.* S. 203
All *as* the shepheard that did fetch his dame . . . *S.C.* O. 28
did sing . . . So *as* the Heavens did quake . . . *S.C.* O. 60
mount *as* high, and sing *as* soote *as* Swanne. . . . *S.C.* O. 90
flowe *as* fast *as* spring doth ryse. . . . *S.C.* O. 108
our pypes, that shrild *as* lowde *as* Larke; . . . *S.C.* N. 71
floureth fresh, *as* it should never fayle? . . . *S.C.* N. 86
hang theyr heads *as* they would learne to weepe; . . . *S.C.* N. 134
With doleful pleasaunce, so *as* I ne wotte . . . *S.C.* N. 204
'Then *as* the springe gives place to elder time, . . . *S.C.* D. 73
Whose ranckling wound *as* yet does rifelye bleede. . . . *S.C.* D. 94
withered, *as* they had bene gathered long; . . . *S.C.* D. 110
Sike follies nowe have gathered *as* too ripe, . . . *S.C.* D. 117
cast hem out *as* rotten . . . *S.C.* D. 118
fresh springing wells, *as* christall neate, . . . *Gn.* 119
sings *As* merrie notes . . . *As* that Ascraean bard, . . . *Gn.* 148, 149
and leads *as* joyfull life; . . . *Gn.* 150
As the great Ocean doth himselfe divide. . . . *Gn.* 160
mosse *as* greene *as* any goord. . . . *Gn.* 164
As that faire troupe . . . Staied thee, . . . *Gn.* 182
As in avengement of his heedles smart, . . . *Gn.* 291
As the great clap of thunder . . . *Gn.* 519
'Them therefore *as* bequeathing to the winde, . . . *Gn.* 633
As well of worldly livelode *as* of life, . . . *Hub.* 147
he leaned, *as* one farre in elde. . . . *Hub.* 218
me trust *as* your owne ghostly father.' . . . *Hub.* 280
seeme *as* Saintlike *as* Saint Radegund: . . . *Hub.* 497
Courtiers, *as* the tide, doo rise and fall.' . . . *Hub.* 614
Els *as* a thistle-downe in th' ayre doth flie, . . . *Hub.* 634
keepe this *as* a lawe: . . . *Hub.* 1054
As when his Syre with Alcumena lay. . . . *Hub.* 1299
As one late in a traunce, . . . *Hub.* 1325
roar'd alowd, *as* he were wood, . . . *Hub.* 1352
as one whose wits were reft, . . . *Hub.* 1356
the rest, *as* borne of salvage brood, . . . *T.M.* 589
And, *as* one carelesse of suspition, . . . *Com. Son.* i. 5
Doth *as* a vapour vanish, . . . *Ti.* 56
of the whole world *as* thou wast the Empresse, . . . *Ti.* 83
greislie shades, such *as* doo haunt in hell . . . *Ti.* 125
Forgotten quite *as* they were never borne. . . . *Ti.* 182
die, *as* one Of the meane people, . . . *Ti.* 190

As—*Continued.*

That as a glasse upon the water shone, *Ti.* 220
And dead is now, as living, counted deare, *Ti.* 242
His bodie, as a spotles sacrifise; *Ti.* 298
Die . . . as the thing Which never was, *Ti.* 346
as things wipt out with a sponge *Ti.* 361
thoughts of men do as themselves decay; *Ti.* 401
As with each storme does fall away, *Ti.* 514
Such as on earth man could not more devize, *Ti.* 521
two Beares, as white as anie milke, *Ti.* 561
haire as soft as silke, *Ti.* 563
gentle kinde as ever Fowle afore; *Ti.* 591
his shinie wings as silver bright, *Mui.* 89
as each had been a Dove; *Mui.* 291
As in their Syres new love both triumphing: *Mui.* 294
Such as Dame Pallas, such as Envie pale, *Mui.* 301
in good order as he could devise. *Mui.* 388
As he that did all daunger quite despise, *Mui.* 390
Downe . . . eyes were throwne, As loathing light; *D.* 47
lookt aside as in disdainefull wise, *D.* 59
White as the native Rose *D.* 108
As the least lamb in all my flock *D.* 126
As stubborne steed, that is with curb restrained, *D.* 194
was by them as thing impure rejected; *D.* 209
fell she not as one enforst to dye, *D.* 253
as one toyld with travaile downe doth lye, *D.* 255
as a speedie post that passeth by. *D.* 413
as the mother of the Gods, *D.* 463
As one disposed wilfullie to die, *D.* 552
As Somers larke that with her song doth greet *As.* 33
As faire as Venus *As.* 56
so waste as this, Nor famous Ardeyn, . . . is. *As.* 95
bright and long, As Sunny beames *As.* 158
As fairly formd as any star *As.* 188
As fittest flowres to deck his mournfull hearse. *As.* Interl. 228
jolly groome was he, As ever piped. *Col.* 13
long As water doth within his bancks appeare.' *Col.* 95
a daughter fresh as floure of May, *Col.* 106
As men use most to covet forreine thing.' *Col.* 162
In whose brave mynd, as in a golden cofer, *Col.* 488
shyneth as the morning cleare, *Col.* 506
as the trees do grow, her name may grow: *Col.* 633
As base, or blunt, unmeet for melodie. *Col.* 710
measured by his weed, As harts by hornes, *Col.* 712
many worthie ones . . . As ever else in Princes Court *Col.* 738
But as Exuls out of his court be thrust.' *Col.* 894
Deare as thou art unto thy selfe, *Ded. Son.* iii. 13
As the wide compasse of the firmament *Ded. Son.* ix. 5
dead, as living, ever him ador'd: I. i. 2. 4
As one that inly mournd, so was she sad, I. i. 4. 6
So pure and innocent, as that same lambe, I. i. 5. 1
lept As Lyon fierce upon the flying pray, I. i. 17. 2
As when old father Nilus gins to swell I. i. 21. 1
monsters, fowle, and blacke as inke, I. i. 22. 7
As gentle shepheard in sweete eventide, I. i. 23. 1
knockt his brest, as one that did repent. I. i. 29. 9
faire him quited, as that courteous was; I. i. 30. 2
could file his tongue as smooth as glas: I. i. 35. 7
As messenger of Morpheus, I. i. 36. 3
As one then in a dreame, I. i. 42. 7
Remounted up as light as chearefull Larke; I. i. 44. 7
For all so deare as life is to my hart, I. i. 54. 2
As one aghast with feends I. ii. 4. 5
her he hated as the hissing snake, I. ii. 9. 8
As many formes . . . As ever Proteus I. ii. 10. 3, 4
As when two rams, stird with ambitious pride, I. ii. 16. 1
Astonied, both stand sencelesse as a blocke, I. ii. 16. 5
unmoved as a rocke, I. ii. 16. 7
the flashing fier flies, As from a forge, I. ii. 17. 8
languish, as the striken hind. I. ii. 24. 9
As raging flames who striveth to suppresse.' I. ii. 34. 6
shine as the Morning starre. I. ii. 36. 4
Fraelissa was as faire as faire mote bee, I. ii. 37. 8
As all unweeting of that well she knew; I. ii. 45. 2
Though true as touch, I. iii. 2. 5
faire as ever living wight was fayre, I. iii. 2. 6
Far from all peoples preace, as in exile, I. iii. 3. 3
As the great eye of heaven, shyned bright, I. iii. 4. 7
As he her wronged innocence did weet. I. iii. 6. 3
adord As the God of my life? I. iii. 7. 9
should as death unto my deare heart light: I. iii. 27. 5
Much like, as when the beaten marinere, I. iii. 31. 1
he was strong, . . . As ever wielded speare I. iii. 42. 4
a rich throne, as bright as sunny day; I. iv. 8. 2
A mayden Queene that shone as Titans ray, I. iv. 8. 5
As envying her selfe, I. iv. 8. 9
she was wondrous faire, as any living wight. I. iv. 10. 9
As faire Aurora in her purple pall I. iv. 16. 4
seemd as fresh as Flora in her prime; I. iv. 17. 3
As ashes pale of hew, and seeming ded; I. iv. 33. 7
Phoebus, fresh as brydegrome to his mate, I. v. 2. 3
As when a Gryfon, seized of his pray, I. v. 8. 2
As when a wearie traveiler, that strayes I. v. 18. 1
on their rusty bits did champ as they were wood. I. v. 20. 9
twyfold Teme, of which two blacke as pitch, I. v. 28. 4
did never cease to bay, As giving warning I. v. 30. 3
A ruefull sight as could be seene I. v. 46. 1
As when a ship . . . An hidden rocke escaped. I. vi. 1. 1
As rock of Diamond stedfast evermore. I. vi. 4. 5
gan her beautie shyne as brightest skye, I. vi. 4. 8

As—*Continued.*

As when a greedy Wolfe, I. vi. 10. 3
They, all as glad as birdes of joyous Pryme, I. vi. 13. 5
the which the lovely boy Did love as life, I. vi. 17. 7
his beheast they feared as a tyrans law. I. vi. 26. 9
all tand . . . As he had traveild many a sommers day I. vi. 35. 5
As when two Bores, with rancling malice mett, I. vi. 44. 4
the streame, as cleare as christall glas: I. vii. 6. 3
pouldred all as thin as flowre: I. vii. 12. 4
As when that divelish yron Engin, I. vii. 13. 1
Such one it was, as that renowmed Snake I. vii. 17. 1
his eyes did shine as glas. I. vii. 17. 9
prowdly threw to ground, as things of naught; I. vii. 18. 5
As when a cloud his beames doth over-lay; I. vii. 34. 7
As when her face is staynd I. vii. 34. 9
steed . . . Who under him did trample as the aire, I. vii. 37. 7
With staring countenance sterne, as one astownd, I. viii. 5. 7
As when almightie Jove, in wrathfull mood, I. viii. 9. 1
as when in Cymbrian plaine An heard of Bulles, I. viii. 11. 5
As where th' Almighties lightning brond does light, I. viii. 21. 8
tombled; as an aged tree, High growing I. viii. 22. 5
Or as a Castle, reared high and round, I. viii. 23. 1
globe of earth, as it for feare did quake. I. viii. 23. 9
old man, with beard as white as snow, I. viii. 30. 2
were slaine as sheepe out of the fold, I. viii. 35. 7
a deepe descent, as darke as hell, I. viii. 39. 8
as in hate of honorable eld, Was overgrowne I. viii. 47. 2
Her wrizled skin, as rough as maple rind, I. viii. 47. 8
the river Dee, as silver cleene, I. ix. 4. 7
flew his steed as he his bandes had brast, I. ix. 21. 7
tread the wynd, As he had beene a fole of Pegasus I. ix. 21. 9
stood, as one that had aspyde Infernall furies I. ix. 24. 4
not so happy as mote happy bee: I. ix. 27. 5
creeping close, as Snake in hidden weedes, I. ix. 28. 8
stared as astound; I. ix. 35. 7
shronke into his jawes, as he did never dyne. I. ix. 35. 9
as a swords poynt through his hart did perse, I. ix. 48. 2
As he were charmed with inchaunted rimes; I. ix. 48. 8
As it a ronning messenger had beene. I. ix. 51. 7
As in a swowne: I. ix. 52. 3
mortall life gan loath as thing forlore, I. x. 21. 5
Cupids wanton snare As hell she hated; I. x. 30. 6
thrust them forth still as they wexed old: I. x. 31. 4
As carefull Nourse her child from falling I. x. 35. 9
Which as a stocke he left unto his seede. I. x. 38. 7
For as the tree does fall, so lyes it ever low. I. x. 41. 9
As Eagles eie that can behold the Sunne. I. x. 47. 6
As hoary frost with spangles doth attire I. x. 48. 3
Mount, Such one as that same mighty man of God, I. x. 53. 2
as it were for endlesse memory Of that deare Lord I. x. 54. 3
As commonly as frend does with his frend. I. x. 56. 5
in like cace, As wretched men, I. x. 62. 4
As for loose loves, they' are vaine, I. x. 62. 9
as deare as ever knight was deare, I. xi. 1. 7
As mountaine doth the valley overcaste. I. xi. 8. 5
as an Eagle, seeing pray appeare, I. xi. 9. 5
as the clashing of an Armor bright, I. xi. 9. 8
Bespotted as with shieldes of red and blacke, I. xi. 11. 5
as sure as death in deed, I. xi. 12. 3
As two broad Beacons, sett in open fieldes, I. xi. 14. 3
far within, as in a hollow glade, I. xi. 14. 8
As for great joyance I. xi. 15. 4
As chauffed Bore his bristles doth upreare; I. xi. 15. 6
As bidding bold defyaunce I. xi. 15. 9
So far as Ewghen bow a shaft may send, I. xi. 19. 2
As hagard hauke, I. xi. 19. 5
the stiffe beame quaked as affrayd, I. xi. 20. 5
He cryde, as raging seas are wont to rore I. xi. 21. 1
As they the earth would shoulder from her seat; I. xi. 21. 4
gulfe does gape, as he would eat I. xi. 21. 5
As did this knight twelve thousand dolours daunt, I. xi. 27. 7
Renew, as one were borne that very day. I. xi. 30. 5
clapt his yron wings as victor he did dwell. I. xi. 31. 9
As Eagle, fresh out of the ocean wave, I. xi. 34. 3
marveiles at himselfe stil as he flies: I. xi. 34. 8
As hundred ramping Lions seemd to rore, I. xi. 37. 3
to the earth him drove, as stricken dead; I. xi. 38. 3
As sparkles from the Andvile use to fly, I. xi. 42. 6
As burning Aetna from his boyling stew I. xi. 44. 5
As they in pure vermilion had been dide, I. xi. 46. 3
forth flowd, as from a well, I. xi. 48. 1
As it had deawed bene with timely raine: I. xi. 48. 5
lay, as in a dreame of deepe delight, I. xi. 50. 4
rosy cheekes, for shame as blushing red: I. xi. 51. 4
him rencountring fierce, as hauke in flight, I. xi. 53. 4
downe he fell, as an huge rocky clift, I. xi. 54. 5
all the people, as in solemne feast, I. xii. 4. 6
As fresh as flowres in medow greene I. xii. 6. 7
As fayre Diana in fresh sommers day I. xii. 7. 7
all admired as from heaven sent, I. xii. 9. 4
As that your daughter can ye well advize, I. xii. 18. 5
As bright as doth the morning starre appeare I. xii. 21. 5
faire and fresh, as freshest flowre in May; I. xii. 22. 1
To tell were as to strive against the streame: I. xii. 23. 3
As chained beare whom cruell dogs doe bait, I. xii. 35. 7
Like as it had bene many an Angels voice I. xii. 39. 3
As wetherbeaten ship II. i. 2. 9
faire and sheene As on the earth . . . was never seene II. i. 10. 6
as sure as hound The stricken Deare II. i. 12. 8
false Duessa . . . As a chaste Virgin II. i. 21. 5

As—*Continued.*

As gentle Hynd, whose sides with cruell steele . . . . II. i. 38. 6
Pitifull spectacle, *as* ever eie did vew! . . . . II. i. 40. 9
His hart gan wexe *as* starke *as* marble stone, ... II. i. 42. 2
grone, *As* Lion, grudging . . . . II. i. 42. 6
death did sitt *as* sad *As* lump of lead, ... II. i. 45. 2, 3
As one out of a deadly dreame affright, ... II. i. 45. 6
herselfe . . . threw to ground, *as* hating life . . . . II. i. 45. 9
As heven accusing guilty . . . . II. i. 49. 2
slyding soft, *as* downe to sleepe her layd, ... II. i. 56. 3
Gan smyle on them, . . . *As* carelesse of his woe, ... II. ii. 1. 7
As budding braunch rent from the native tree, ... II. ii. 2. 6
As hynd from her, so she fled . . . . II. ii. 7. 9
from whose two heads, *As* from two weeping eyes, ... II. ii. 9. 2
it is chaste and pure *as* purest snow, ... II. ii. 9. 7
As when a Beare and Tygre, being met . . . . II. ii. 22. 5
As a tall ship tossed in troublous seas, ... II. ii. 24. 1
As ever of their loves they would be glad: . . . . II. ii. 28. 4
as doth an hidden moth The inner garment frett, ... II. ii. 34. 7
As morning Sunne her beames dispredden . . . . II. ii. 40. 8
As Peacocke that his painted plumes doth pranck, ... II. iii. 6. 4
The Miser threw him selfe, *as* an Offall, ... II. iii. 8. 7
As ghastly bug, does greatly them affeare: . . . . II. iii. 20. 5
made the forrest ring, *as* it would rive . . . . II. iii. 20. 9
Her face so faire *as* flesh it seemed not, ... II. iii. 22. 1
Her face . . . Cleare *as* the skye, ... II. iii. 22. 3
Or *as* that famous Queene Of Amazons, ... II. iii. 31. 5
shake, and rowze *as* comming late from rest. . . . . II. iii. 35. 9
As fearfull fowle, that long in secret cave . . . . II. iii. 36. 1
I hid my selfe from it, *as* one affeard; . . . . II. iii. 45. 8
gan to ride *As* one unfitt therefore, ... II. iii. 46. 4
as a blindfold Bull, at randon fares, ... II. iv. 7. 8
as the Sunny beames do glaunce and glide . . . . II. v. 2. 4
As one affright With hellish feends, ... II. v. 37. 6
as swift *as* glaunce of eye, A litle Gondelay, ... II. vi. 2. 6
Sometimes she song *as* lowd *as* larke in ayre, ... II. vi. 3. 3
Sometimes she laught, *as* merry *as* Pope Jone; . . . . II. vi. 3. 4
dull billowes thicke *as* troubled mire, ... II. vi. 20. 7
helmett, which *as* Titan shone, ... II. vi. 31. 6
still he stood *as* sencelesse stone. . . . . II. vi. 31. 9
bitter rate, *As* Shepheardes curre, that in darke . . . . . . II. vi. 39. 4
As Pilot well expert in perilous wave, ... II. vii. 1. 1
His hand that trembled *as* one terrifyde; . . . . II. vii. 6. 7
uncertein light: Such *as* a lamp, ... II. vii. 29. 7
uncertein light: . . . *as* the Moone, ... II. vii. 29. 8
such exceeding store, *As* eie of man did never see . . . . . . II. vii. 31. 5
whose dore . . . did open, *as* it had beene taught. . . . . . II. vii. 35. 3
wyde, *As* it some Gyeld or solemne Temple weare. . . . . . . II. vii. 43. 4
There, *as* in glistring glory she did sitt, ... II. vii. 46. 1
loaden all with fruit *as* thick *as* it might bee. . . . . . . II. vii. 53. 9
Gaz'd after him, *as* fowle escapt by flight. . . . . II. viii. 9. 4
courd it tenderly, *As* chicken newly hatcht, ... II. viii. 9. 9
knights al armd *as* bright *as* skie, ... II. viii. 10. 2
'no knight so rude . . . *As* to doen outrage . . . . II. viii. 26. 2
make his carkas *as* the outcast dong? . . . . II. viii. 28. 5
as thicke *as* stormie showre, Their strokes did raine: . . . . II. viii. 35. 5
as a stedfast towre, Whom foe . . . doth assaile, ... II. viii. 35. 7
a large lukewarme flood, Red *as* the Rose, ... II. viii. 39. 2
As salvage Bull, whom two fierce mastives bayt, ... II. viii. 42. 1
as a man whom hellish feendes have frayd, ... II. viii. 46. 4
all desperate, *as* loathing light, ... II. viii. 47. 1
As when a windy tempest bloweth hye, ... II. viii. 48. 1
The clowdes, *as* thinges affrayd, before him flye; . . . . . . II. viii. 48. 3
as in scorne . . . their malice forth do poure: . . . . II. viii. 48. 6
as a Bittur in the Eagles clawe, ... II. viii. 50. 2
As one that loathed life, and yet despysd to dye. . . . . . II. viii. 50. 9
Whose glory shineth *as* the morning starre, ... II. ix. 4. 6
it shooke *as* it would fall. . . . . II. ix. 11. 5
As when a swarme of Gnats at eventide . . . . II. ix. 16. 1
as a cloud doth seeme to dim the skies; . . . . II. ix. 16. 5
faire *as* faire mote ever bee, ... II. ix. 18. 6
so high *as* foe might not it clime, ... II. ix. 21. 2
Lady . . . right faire and fresh *as* morning rose, ... II. ix. 36. 7
blood her snowy cheekes did dye . . . *as* polisht yvory . . . . II. ix. 41. 5
it doth, *as* cloud from sea, aryse. . . . . II. ix. 42. 5
so wisely *as* I may.' . . . . II. ix. 42. 9
survewd *as* hils doen lower ground; . . . . II. ix. 45. 4
all that fained is, *as* leasings, tales, ... II. ix. 51. 9
flying fast *as* Roebucke . . . . II. x. 7. 5
dreadful wights *As* far exceeded men . . . . II. x. 8. 9
fluttring arrowes, thicke *as* flakes of snow, ... II. xi. 18. 2
him fell before; *As* withered leaves drop . . . . II. xi. 19. 4
a Tygre . . . That *as* the winde ran . . . . II. xi. 20. 5
Those could he well direct and streight *as* line, ... II. xi. 21. 6
As pale and wan *as* ashes . . . . II. xi. 22. 1
His body leane and meagre *as* a rake, ... II. xi. 22. 2
as cold and drery *as* a snake, ... II. xi. 22. 4
as swift on foot *as* chased Stags; . . . . II. xi. 23. 5
as the winged wind his Tigre fled, ... II. xi. 26. 1
(*As* wonts the Tartar by the Caspian lake, ... II. xi. 26. 7
As one awakte out of long slombring shade, ... II. xi. 31. 7
as a Beare, whom angry curres have touzd, ... II. xi. 33. 3
fierce retourning, *as* a faulcon fayre, ... II. xi. 36. 6
As when Joves harnesse-bearing Bird . . . . II. xi. 43. 1
the Carle *as* fast Gan heap huge strokes . . . . II. xi. 43. 8
Gan heap huge strokes on him, *as* ere he down was cast. . . . II. xi. 43. 9
Rocke of Reproch, and it *as* death to dred!' . . . . II. xii. 9. 9
'*As* th' Isle of Delos whylome, ... II. xii. 13. 1
bravely furnished *as* ship might bee, ... II. xii. 19. 3
the great sea . . . *As* threatning to devoure . . . . II. xii. 21. 9

As—*Continued.*

The waves . . . *as* they enraged were, ... II. xii. 22. 2
all . . . we dreadfull hold, Be but *as* bugs . . . . II. xii. 25. 8
Art, *as* halfe in scorne Of niggard Nature, ... II. xii. 50. 6
bounches hanging . . . *As* freely offering to be gathered; . . . II. xii. 54. 6
deepe empurpled *as* the Hyacine, ... II. xii. 54. 7
as the Rubine laughing sweetely red, ... II. xii. 54. 8
emongst the leaves enfold, *As* lurking from the vew . . . . . II. xii. 55. 4
downe againe Her plong, *as* over-maystered . . . . II. xii. 64. 3
as through a vele, So through the christall waves . . . . . . II. xii. 64. 6
As that faire Starre, the messenger of morne, ... II. xii. 65. 1
Or *as* the Cyprian goddesse, newly borne . . . . II. xii. 65. 3
Such *as* attonce might not . . . be heard elsewhere: . . . . . II. xii. 70. 3
made him stagger, *as* he were not well: . . . . III. i. 6. 5
Whose face did seeme *as* cleare *as* Christall stone, ... III. i. 15. 4
And eke, through feare, *as* white *as* whales bone: . . . . . . III. i. 15. 5
as a blazing starre doth farre outcast His hearie beames, . . . III. i. 16. 5
As the proud Persian Queenes accustomed. . . . . III. i. 41. 4
As when fayre Cynthia, in darkesome night, ... III. i. 43. 1
As hee that hath espide a vermeill Rose, ... III. i. 46. 6
as a cole to kindle fleshly flame, ... III. i. 50. 2
as it had beene a flake Of lightning . . . . III. ii. 5. 7
The loving mother . . . not so much rejoyce *as* she . . . . . III. ii. 11. 9
Lookt foorth, *as* Phoebus face out of the east . . . . III. ii. 24. 6
As one with vew of ghastly feends affright: . . . . III. ii. 29. 7
As one in wilfull bale for ever buried. . . . . III. ii. 31. 9
As smoke and sulphure mingled with confused stryfe. . . . . III. ii. 32. 9
languish, *as* the leafe faln from the tree, ... III. ii. 39. 8
As it an Earth-quake were: . . . . III. ii. 42. 9
As fayre Aurora, rysing hastily, ... III. iii. 20. 4
As, when a foggy mist hath overcast The face of heven, . . . III. iv. 13. 1
lay *as* in a swowne, ... III. iv. 30. 6
As swifte *as* swallowes on the waves they went, ... III. iv. 33. 5
fled, *as* light-foot hare . . . . III. iv. 46. 4
affraid of him *as* feend of hell. . . . . III. iv. 47. 9
bold, *as* ever Squyre that waited . . . . III. v. 12. 9
as faire *as* Phoebus sunne. . . . . III. v. 27. 9
As it an earthly Paradize had beene: . . . . III. v. 40. 5
mightie ill, Which, *as* a victour proud, gan ransack . . . . . III. v. 48. 4
drye up and blast; *As* percing levin, ... III. v. 48. 8
wasted, *as* the snow congeald When the bright sunne . . . . III. v. 49. 5
Such *as* the Angels weare before Gods tribunall! . . . . III. v. 53. 9
shund dishonor which *as* death she feard: . . . . III. vi. 10. 5
from her fled *as* flit *as* ayery Dove, ... III. vi. 11. 4
fresh in face and guize *As* any Nimphe; . . . . III. vi. 23. 8
blandishment, Which *as* a fountaine from her sweete lips went. III. vi. 25. 5
as faire *as* springing day, ... III. vi. 26. 9
So faire a place *as* Nature can devize: . . . . III. vi. 29. 3
beautie fades away, *As* doth the lilly . . . . III. vi. 38. 9
Stared . . . *as* one astound, ... III. vii. 7. 7
As glad of that small rest *as* Bird of tempest gon. . . . . . III. vii. 10. 9
as one, which hath gaz'd On the bright Sunne . . . . III. vii. 13. 6
she, *as* one nigh of her wits depriv'd, ... III. vii. 14. 5
in bands, *as* conquered To be her thrall, ... III. vii. 17. 7
mone, *as* they had been undonne. . . . . III. vii. 19. 9
feeds on wemens flesh *as* others feede on gras. . . . . III. vii. 22. 9
swifte *as* word that from her went, ... III. vii. 23. 6
Lightly she leaped, *as* a wight forlore, ... III. vii. 25. 7
As Florimell fled from that Monster . . . . III. vii. 26. 5
As he that strives to stop a suddein flood, ... III. vii. 34. 1
As white seemes fayrer macht with blacke attone; . . . . . . III. ix. 2. 4
His money, which he lov'd *as* living breath; . . . . III. x. 2. 8
As Hellene, when she saw . . . The Trojane flames . . . . . . III. x. 12. 7
I loath *as* doung, ne deeme my dew reward: . . . . III. x. 31. 6
As one out of a dreame not waked well . . . . III. x. 49. 7
That, *as* a Snake, still lurked . . . . III. x. 55. 9
That was *as* trew in love *as* Turtle to her make. . . . . III. xi. 2. 9
he was long, and swift *as* any Roe, ... III. xi. 5. 8
implore *As* gentle Ladyes helplesse misery: . . . . III. xi. 18. 6
Foolhardy *as* th' Earthes children, ... III. xi. 22. 8
as a thonder bolt Perceth the yielding ayre, ... III. xi. 25. 6
As faining to be hidd from envious eye; . . . . III. xi. 28. 5
playd In the rich metall *as* they living were. . . . . III. xi. 51. 6
As it with mighty levers had bene tore; . . . . III. xii. 3. 4
as on the readie flore Of some Theatre, ... III. xii. 3. 5
as to heare a play, ... III. xii. 4. 4
As those same plumes so seemd he vaine and light, ... III. xii. 8. 5
For still he far'd *as* dauncing in delight, ... III. xii. 8. 7
nycely trode, *as* thornes lay in his way, ... III. xii. 10. 6
As ashes pale of hew, ... III. xii. 12. 6
As a dismayd Deare in chace embost, ... III. xii. 17. 8
Her brest all naked, *as* nett yvory . . . . III. xii. 20. 1
she, *as* morrow fresh, her selfe did reare . . . . III. xii. 28. 8
Fell softly forth, *as* of his owne accord, ... III. xii. 38. 2
Was closed up, *as* it had not beene bor'd, ... III. xii. 38. 5
vanisht quite, *as* it were not the same, ... III. xii. 43. 5
So seemd those two, *as* growne together quite, ... III. xii. 46. *or.* 5
as thing reserv'd from stealth. . . . . IV. i. 6. 7
Like *as* the shining skie in summers night, ... IV. i. 13. 6
was, *as* it were, her baude . . . . IV. i. 31. 3
As fresh and fragrant *as* the floure-deluce . . . . IV. i. 31. 7
As when two billowes . . . Do meete together, ... IV. i. 42. 1
as when in chace The Parthian strikes a stag . . . . IV. i. 49. 7
a God or godlike man . . . Such *as* was Orpheus, ... IV. ii. 1. 7
Or such *as* that celestiall Psalmist was, ... IV. ii. 2. 1
wise words, . . . Such *as* that prudent Romane well . . . . . IV. ii. 2. 7
flitting *as* the wavering wind After each beautie . . . . IV. ii. 5. 2
As when two warlike Brigandines at sea, ... IV. ii. 16. 1
As men awaked rashly out of dreme, ... IV. ii. 17. 2
To see their thrids so thin *as* spiders frame, ... IV. ii. 50. 8

As—*Continued.*
As when two Tygers prickt with hungers rage . . . IV. iii. 16. 1
As when a Vulture greedie of his pray, . . . IV. iii. 19. 1
As one whose inner parts had bene ythrild . . . IV. iii. 22. 4
As thicke *as* hayle forth poured from the skie: . . . IV. iii. 25. 5
As fast *as* water-sprinkles gainst a rocke are dasht. . . . IV. iii. 25. 9
And tribute eke withall, *as* to his Soveraine. . . . IV. iii. 27. 9
fell *as* dead . . . Yet dead he was not, . . . IV. iii. 30. 5
As one that had out of a dreame bene reard, . . . IV. iii. 31. 4
halfe affeard . . . *as* he some ghost had seene, . . . IV. iii. 31. 6
As one in feare the Stygian gods t' offend, . . . IV. iii. 32. 2
Such *as* the troubled Theatres oftimes . . . IV. iii. 37. 9
Such famous men, . . . *As* Jove will have advaunced . . . IV. iii. 44. 2
Canacee, *as* fresh *as* morning rose, . . . IV. iii. 51. 7
as life were to each other liefe. . . . IV. iii. 52. 7
As two fierce Buls, . . . IV. iv. 18. 3
As one that seemed doubtfull . . . IV. iv. 20. 4
As two wild Boares together grapling go, . . . IV. iv. 29. 8
As when two greedy Wolves doe breake . . . IV. iv. 35. 6
as her life by her esteemed deare . . . IV. v. 6. 2
daz'd the eyes of all *as* with exceeding light. . . . IV. v. 10. 9
shone *as* Phebes light Amongst the lesser starres . . . IV. v. 14. 3
As guilefull Goldsmith that by secret skill . . . IV. v. 15. 1
as thing deviz'd her to defame. . . . IV. v. 17. 5
faire a crew, *As* like can not be seene . . . IV. v. 18. 4
their words *as* wind esteemed light. . . . IV. v. 27. 7
started up *as* one affrayd, . . . IV. v. 42. 6
in his face, *as* in a looking glasse, . . . IV. v. 45. 7
Did leape to her, *as* doth an eger hound . . . IV. vi. 12. 3
Heaping huge strokes *as* thicke *as* showre of hayle, . . . IV. vi. 16. 5
He blest himselfe *as* one sore terrifide: . . . IV. vi. 24. 7
trussing me, *as* Eagle doth his pray, . . . IV. vii. 18. 6
as swift *as* wind . . . IV. vii. 18. 7
with her body, *as* a buckler, . . . IV. vii. 26. 4
winged feete *as* nimble *as* the winde, . . . IV. vii. 30. 2
As when Latonaes daughter, . . . IV. vii. 30. 5
As one with griefe and anguishe overcum, . . . IV. vii. 44. 4
As blasted bloosme through heat doth languish . . . IV. viii. 2. 9
flew away *as* lightly *as* the wind: . . . IV. viii. 7. 7
as one daunted with her presence dread, . . . IV. viii. 13. 7
As messengers of his true meaning . . . IV. viii. 13. 9
steps so soft *as* foot could stryde, . . . IV. viii. 37. 2
So faire *as* ever yet saw living eie; . . . IV. viii. 49. 5
as faire *as* any under skie: . . . IV. viii. 49. 7
I to him *as* to my soule did beare, . . . IV. viii. 55. 3
lov'd me deare, *as* dearest thing alive. . . . IV. viii. 56. 6
as the soule doth rule the earthly masse, . . . IV. ix. 2. 6
though Poeana were *as* faire *as* morne, . . . IV. ix. 3. 6
so to ride *as* it alive was found. . . . IV. ix. 4. 9
as he captive were, . . . IV. ix. 5. 2
minde did travell *as* with chylde . . . IV. ix. 17. 3
She was *as* safe *as* in a Sanctuary, . . . IV. ix. 19. 6
As when Dan Aeolus, in great displeasure . . . IV. ix. 23. 1
As when two Barkes . . . contrary courses sew, . . . IV. ix. 26. 7
Against those two let drive, *as* they were wood: . . . IV. ix. 29. 5
As when an eager mastiffe once doth prove The tast of bloud . IV. ix. 31. 5
the ground was strow'd with flowres *as* fresh *as* May. . . . IV. x. 37. 9
As with a robe, . . . IV. xi. 11. 8
made the rockes to roare *as* they were rent. . . . IV. xi. 12. 5
that upon them goth *As* on the ground, . . . IV. xi. 14. 6
it encompast round *as* with a golden fret. . . . IV. xi. 27. 9
whom *as* with a Crowne He doth adorne, . . . IV. xi. 34. 7
flowres . . . all her shoulders spred *As* a new spring; . . . IV. xi. 46. 5
As withered weed through cruell winters tine, . . . IV. xii. 34. 6
A sorie sight *as* ever seene . . . V. i. 14. 2
so light, *As* that it seem'd above the ground he went; . . . V. i. 20. 3
he was swift *as* swallow in her flight, . . . V. i. 20. 4
strong *as* Lyon in his lordly might. . . . V. i. 20. 5
As rated Spaniell takes his burden up for feare. . . . V. i. 29. 9
As when a Dolphin and a Sele are met . . . V. ii. 15. 1
As when a Faulcon hath with nimble flight . . . V. ii. 54. 1
As when two sunnes appeare in the azure skye, . . . V. iii. 19. 1
As roses did with lilies interlace; . . . V. iii. 23. 5
Her snowy substance melted *as* with heat, . . . V. iii. 24. 7
As when the daughter of Thaumantes faire . . . V. iii. 25. 1
as the death he hated such despight, . . . V. iii. 31. 8
he stood *as* still *as* any stake, . . . V. iii. 34. 5
As when a Beare hath seiz'd her cruell clawes . . . V. iv. 40. 6
quilted upon sattin white *as* milke; . . . V. v. 2. 3
As the faire Moone in her most full aspect . . . V. v. 3. 8
flakes of fire, bright *as* the sunny ray, . . . V. v. 8. 3
As one that would confesse, yet faine would it denie. . . . V. v. 31. 9
As one adaw'd, and halfe confused . . . V. v. 45. 5
As a bad Nurse, which, fayning to receive . . . V. v. 53. 1
There *as* she looked long, at last she spide . . . V. vi. 8. 1
mute, *as* one in great suspence; . . . V. vi. 9. 7
As when the flashing Levin haps to light . . . V. vi. 40. 1
Her seem'd, *as* she was doing sacrifize . . . V. vii. 13. 1
As when a Tygre and a Lionesse Are met . . . V. vii. 30. 1
all they, *as* a Goddesse her adoring, . . . V. vii. 42. 8
So ran they all, *as* they had bene at bace, . . . V. viii. 5. 4
Serves her *as* any Princesse under sky, . . . V. viii. 18. 7
shone *as* bright *as* doth the heaven sheene: . . . V. viii. 29. 5
As when the firie-mouthed steedes, . . . V. viii. 40. 1
as that madding mother, mongst the rout Of Bacchus . . . V. viii. 47. 5
As a mad bytch, . . . V. viii. 49. 1
dreadfull wight he was *as* ever went . . . V. ix. 10. 4
all his bones *as* small *as* sandy grayle He broke, . . . V. ix. 19. 4
Whom seeing all in armour bright *as* day, . . . V. ix. 24. 2
like a cloud, *as* likest may be told, . . . V. ix. 28. 4

As—*Continued.*
As a faire stoupe of her high soaring thought, . . . V. ix. 34. 7
As the bright sunne, what time his fierie teme . . . V. ix. 35. 1
To see if entrance there *as* yet obtaine he might, . . . V. x. 33. 9
As three great Culverings for battrie bent, . . . V. x. 34. 6
As fast *as* feete could carry them . . . V. x. 36. 2
trembling joynts, *as* he for terrour shooke; . . . V. xi. 28. 8
As when the Mast of some well-timbred hulke . . . V. xi. 29. 1
makes her ribs to cracke *as* they were torne; . . . V. xi. 29. 4
ye promist, *as* ye were a Knight, . . . V. xi. 39. 2
flocking round about them, *as* a swarme Of flyes . . . V. xi. 58. 1
As when the wrathfull Boreas doth bluster, . . . V. xi. 58. 7
As thicke *as* doth the seede after the sowers hand: . . . V. xii. 7. 9
As when a skilfull Marriner doth reed A storme approching . V. xii. 18. 5
pleasure take, *As* she had got thereby . . . V. xii. 32. 9
loudly cryde, *As* it had bene two shepheards curres . . . V. xii. 38. 5
In whose pure minde, *as* in a mirrour sheene, . . . VI. Pr. 6. 5
tribute backe repay *as* to their King: . . . VI. Pr. 7. 5
'A shamefull use *as* ever I did heare,' . . . VI. i. 14. 1
As doth a Steare, in heat of sommers day, . . . VI. i. 24. 4
plates asunder brake, *As* they had potshares bene; . . . VI. i. 37. 5
Calidore rising up *as* fresh *as* day . . . VI. iii. 13. 8
as a well it were That . . . gushing did appere. . . . VI. iii. 50. 8
he was swift *as* any Bucke in chace) . . . VI. iv. 8. 3
showes, *as* fitter beene For courting fooles . . . VI. v. 38. 7
As doth the poysnous sting, which infamy . . . VI. vi. 1. 3
a doughty Knight, *As* any one . . . VI. vi. 4. 2
still did lie *as* dead, . . . VI. vi. 32. 3
As one that had no life him left through former feare. . . VI. vi. 32. 9
As when a cast of Faulcons make their flight . . . VI. vii. 9. 1
his locks, *as* blacke *as* pitchy night, . . . VI. vii. 43. 7
As when a sturdy ploughman with his hynde . . . VI. viii. 12. 1
rest her selfe *as* in a gladsome port, . . . VI. x. 9. 4
Another Damzell, *as* a precious gemme . . . VI. x. 12. 7
made him pipe so merrily, *as* never none. . . . VI. x. 15. 9
'So farre, *as* doth the daughter of the day . . . VI. x. 26. 1
Like *as* a sort of hungry dogs, ymet . . . VI. xi. 17. 1
lustie knight *as* ever wielded speare, . . . VI. xii. 3. 6
as a girlond seemes to deck the locks . . . VII. vi. 41. 3
Shouting *as* they the heavens would have brast; . . . VII. vi. 52. 7
Not such *as* Craftes-men by their idle skill . . . VII. vii. 8. 3
knittest each to each, *as* brother unto brother. . . . VII. vii. 14. 9
even the gods to thee, *as* men to gods, do seeme. . . . VII. vii. 15. 9
'*As* for her tenants, that is, man and beasts, . . . VII. vii. 19. 1
Autumne all in yellow clad, *As* though he joyed . . . VII. vii. 30. 2
As from a limbeck did adown distill. . . . VII. vii. 31. 5
wanton *as* a Kid whose horne new buds: . . . VII. vii. 33. 2
All in greene leaves, *as* he a Player were; . . . VII. vii. 35. 2
backward yode, *as* Bargemen wont to fare . . . VII. vii. 35. 7
full grosse and fat *As* fed with lard, . . . VII. vii. 40. 2
Such *as* they faine Dan Cupid to have beene, . . . VII. vii. 46. 7
'*as* changefull *as* the Moone' men use to say. . . . VII. vii. 50. 7
she *as* steele and flint doth still remayne. . . . *Am.* xviii. 14
My soule was ravisht quite *as* in a traunce; . . . *Am.* xxxix. 10
kill with looks *as* Cockatrices doo: . . . *Am.* xlix. 10
cruell and unkind, *As* is a Tygre, . . . *Am.* lvi. 2
proud and pittilesse, *As* is a storme, . . . *Am.* lvi. 6
hard and obstinate, *As* is a rocke . . . *Am.* lvi. 10
As Mars in three-score yeares doth run his spheare. . . . *Am.* lx. 4
as a steed refreshed after toyle, . . . *Am.* lxxx. 5
I wander *as* in darkenesse of the night, . . . *Am.* lxxxvii. 3
Behold your faces *as* the christall bright, . . . *Epith.* 64
And, *as* ye use to Venus, to her sing, . . . *Epith.* 108
There vertue raynes *as* Queene in royal throne, . . . *Epith.* 194
Yet so, *as* that . . . They mixe themselves, . . . *H.L.* 90
As after stormes, . . . The Sunne . . . *H.L.* 276
An heavenly Hymne, such *as* the Angels sing, . . . *H.L.* 302
As plaine *as* light discovers dawning day. . . . *H.B.* 238
And *as* these heavens still by degrees arize, . . . *H.H.B.* 71
And shew himselfe . . . *As* in a looking-glasse, . . . *H.H.B.* 115
And in the same, *as* in a brasen booke, . . . *H.H.B.* 130
As each had bene a Bryde; . . . *Proth.* 23
shone *as* heavens light, . . . *Proth.* 52
So fresh they seem'd *as* day, . . . *Proth.* 70
Even *as* their Brydale day, which was not long: . . . *Proth.* 71
murmurde low, *As* he would speake, . . . *Proth.* 116

Ascend. Though meane her lot, yet higher did her mind *ascend*, VI. ix. 10. 9
To Joves high Palace straight cast to *ascend*, . . . VII. vi. 23. 8
till to his perfect end Of purest beautie it at last *ascend*; . . *H.H.B.* 47

Ascending. *Ascending* did his beames abroad dispred, . . . *Mui.* 52
Ascending by ten steps of Alablaster wrought. . . . II. ix. 44. 9
Ascending up, with many a stately stayre, . . . *Epith.* 179

Ascertain. which none *ascertaine* may. . . . *D.* 504

Asclepiodate. *Asclepiodate* him overcame, . . . II. x. 58. 1

Ascraean. that *Ascraean* bard, whose fame now rings . . . *Gn.* 149

Ascribe. Ne let the man *ascribe* it to his skill, . . . I. x. 1. 6
to accursed fate, The guilt I doe *ascribe*: . . . III. iv. 37. 9

Ash. the *Ash* for nothing ill; . . . I. i. 9. 7

Ashamed. manie beg which are thereof *ashamed*. . . . *Hub.* 352
Cupid selfe of them *ashamed* is, . . . *Col.* 768
halfe *ashamed* wondred at the sight: . . . I. iii. 38. 6
ashamd that stroke of living arme Should him dismay, . . . II. v. 7. 2
as yet *ashamd* how rude Pan did her dight. . . . II. ix. 40. 9
Whereof she seemes *ashamed* inwardly: . . . III. iii. 20. 7
She was *asham'd* to be so loose surpriz'd; . . . III. vi. 19. 2
those two Ladies much *asham'd* did wexe: . . . IV. viii. 35. 7
The Squire him selfe . . . Was much *asham'd* . . . VI. viii. 5. 3
Asham'd to thinke how he that enterprize . . . forslacked had . VI. xii. 12. 3

Ashes. Out of hir *ashes* as a worme arise. . . . *Bel.*[1] vi. 14
The *ashes* of a mightie Emperour: . . . *Bel.* iii. 8

Ashes—*Continued.*
her bodie turn'd to *ashes* colde. . . . *Bel.*[2] vii. 12
shall never die . . . ne in *ashes* rest; . . . *Ro.* i. 4
The corpes of Rome in *ashes* is entombed, . . . *Ro.* v. 9
The honour yet in *ashes* doo maintaine; . . . *Ro.* vii. 4
Olde Rome out of her *ashes* to revive, . . . *Ro.* Env. 5
all the Rhetaean shore to *ashes* turne, . . . *Gn.* 511
lye in mine owne *ashes*, . . . *Ti.* 40
low in *ashes* lay, . . . *Ti.* 502
Which th' *ashes* seem'd of some great Prince to hold, . . . *Ti.* 661
Whether should of those *ashes* keeper bee. . . . *Ti.* 665
to those *ashes* gave a second life, . . . *Ti.* 669
And crownes their *ashes* with immortall baies. . . . *Ded. Son.* iv.12
Thrise every weeke in *ashes* shee did sitt, . . . I. iii. 14. 2
As *ashes* pale of hew, and seeming ded; . . . I. iv. 33. 7
sacred *ashes* over it was strowed new. . . . I. viii. 35. 9
wasted life doe lye in *ashes* low: . . . I. ix. 8. 5
blow the fire which them to *ashes* brent: . . . I. ix. 10. 6
In *ashes* and sackcloth he did array His daintie corse, . . . I. x. 26. 1
in dead parents balefull *ashes* bred, . . . II. ii. 2. 2
Vile is the vengeaunce on the *ashes* cold, . . . II. viii. 13. 6
As pale and wan as *ashes* was his looke, . . . II. xi. 22. 1
in his *ashes* raked up and hid, . . . III. iii. 48. 3
in thine *ashes* buried low dost lie, . . . III. ix. 33. 2
Troynovant was built of old Troyes *ashes* cold. . . . III. ix. 38. 9
he fast away did fly, As *ashes* pale of hew, . . . III. xii. 12. 6
burning all to *ashes* powr'd it downe the brooke. . . . V. ii. 27. 9
This lower world nigh all to *ashes* brent, . . . V. viii. 40. 8
That other swayne, like *ashes* deadly pale, . . . VI. vii. 17. 8
Nought leaving but their barren *ashes* without seede. . . . VII. vii. 24. 9
What then remaines but I to *ashes* burne, . . . *Am.* xxxii. 13
buried now in their own *ashes* ly; . . . *Com. Son.* iv. 7
And in her *ashes* shrowd my dying shame; . . . *H.H.L.* 19
Ashore. put us all *ashore* on Cynthias land. . . . *Col.* 289
Ashy. spirites, whose *ashie* cinders lie Under deep ruines, . . . *Ro.* i. 1
Now on these *ashie* tombes shew boldnesse vaine, . . . *Ro.* xiv. 13
Ye pallid spirits, and ye *ashie* ghoasts, . . . *Ro.* xv. 1
those pallid cheekes and *ashy* hew, . . . *D.* 302
Asia. All that which *Asie* ever had of prise, . . . *Ro.* xxix. 11
of all *Asie* bore the soveraine crowne, . . . III. ix. 39. 4
which all *Asia* sought with vowes prophane, . . . IV. x. 30. 3
Asian. Greeke and *Asian* rivers stayned with their blood. . . . III. iii. 22. 9
Aside. suddenly casting *aside* his vew, . . . *Gn.* 294
from him Laertes sonne his vewe Doth turne *aside*, . . . *Gn.* 534
borne *aside* Into a secret corner . . . *Hub.* 1017
Looking *aside* I saw a stately Bed, . . . *Ti.* 631
He lookt *aside* as in disdainefull wise, . . . *D.* 59
To turne *aside* unto my Cabinet, . . . *D.* 558
And the dim vele . . . *aside* he layd, . . . *Ded. Son.* ix.11
And layd her stole *aside*. . . . I. iii. 4. 6
Their frowning forheades, . . . all *asyde* doe lay; . . . I. vi. 11. 6
he them spying gan to turne *aside* . . . I. vi. 34. 7
Til breathlesse both themselves *aside* retire, . . . I. vi. 44. 6
crowned mitre rudely threw *asyde:* . . . I. viii. 25. 3
forst him lay his hevenly thoughts *aside;* . . . I. x. 49. 3
herselfe withdraw *asyde;* . . . I. xi. 5. 2
Fayre Goddesse, lay that furious fitt *asyde*. . . . I. xi. 7. 1
She had layd her mournefull stole *aside*, . . . I. xii. 22. 2
this misseeming discord meekely lay *aside*.' . . . II. ii. 31. 9
He slips *aside;* . . . II. v. 10. 6
he rose for to remove *aside* Those pretious hils . . . II. vii. 6. 2
horse and man it made to reele *asyde;* . . . II. viii. 31. 2
turning soft *aside*, . . . II. ix. 39. 6
turning quicke *aside* His light-foot beast, . . . II. xi. 25. 5
to his starting steed that swarv'd *asyde*, . . . III. i. 11. 6
turning him *aside*, . . . III. v. 34. 6
laying his sad dartes *Asyde*, . . . III. vi. 49. 9
threw her lode *aside*. . . . III. vii. 38. 9
drew her selfe *aside* in sickernesse, . . . III. xi. 55. 8
seeing it at hand, he swary'd *asyde*, . . . IV. iii. 18. 6
layd *aside* when so she usd her looser sport. . . . IV. v. 3. 9
whereas he stood not farre *aside*, . . . IV. vi. 24. 2
swarv'd *aside*, and there againe did stay: . . . IV. viii. 10. 8
he was forced to withdraw *aside*, . . . V. ii. 20. 7
First in one ballance set the true *aside*.' . . . V. ii. 45. 5
set the truth and set the right *aside*, . . . V. ii. 48. 1
turn'd *aside* for shame to heare what he did tell. . . . V. iii. 16. 9
All suddenly, ere one can looke *aside*, . . . V. iii. 25. 5
in rage she turn'd from him *aside*, . . . V. vi. 11. 7
ne ever lookt *aside*, But still right downe; . . . V. vi. 18. 4
She turnd her head *aside*, . . . V. vii. 38. 4
from his saddle swarved nought *asyde*, . . . V. x. 35. 2
long since *aside* had set The use of armes, . . . V. xi. 37. 3
That bloudie scutchin, being battered sore, I layd *aside*, . . . V. xi. 54. 5
'Therefore, faire Lady, lay *aside* this griefe, . . . VI. ii. 46. 1
streight his cumbrous armes *aside* did lay . . . VI. v. 10. 6
Ne would him suffer once to shrinke *asyde*, . . . VI. vi. 28. 7
So humbly taking leave she turnd *aside;* . . . VI. viii. 30. 6
Unto a litle grove not farre *asyde*, . . . VI. viii. 44. 2
when they mov'd the carcases *aside*, . . . VI. xi. 22. 1
laying feare *aside* to doe his charge, . . . VII. vi. 17. 6
Now lay those sorrowfull complaints *aside;* . . . *Epith.* 12
As if (*partial list*).
As if my yeare were wast . . . *S.C.* Ja. 28
As if a Woolfe were emong the sheepe: . . . *S.C.* S. 192
As if it the old man selfe had bene: . . . *S.C.* S. 218
As if some evill were to her betight? . . . *S.C.* N. 174
barke out flames, as *if* on fire he fed; . . . *Gn.* 346
Did move, *as if* they could him understand; . . . *Gn.* 454
as if that he had shedd Much blood . . . *Hub.* 206

As if—*Continued.*
as if he aspyr'd To dignitie, . . . *Hub.* 678
Pallace quaked . . . *As if* it quite were riven . . . *Hub.* 1354
As if her eyes had beene two springing wells; . . . *T.M.* 536
As if shee all to water would have gone; . . . *T.M.* 596
As if his daies for ever should remaine? . . . *Ti.* 54
'Wasted it is, *as if* it never were; . . . *Ti.* 120
as if it shold Be for some bride, . . . *Ti.* 634
As if his heart in peeces would have rent. . . . *D.* 49
So lay she downe, *as if* to sleepe she went, . . . *D.* 256
As if to me had chanst some evill tourne! . . . *D.* 266
As if that death he in the face had seene, . . . *D.* 565
As if it scornd the daunger of the same; . . . *Col.* 215
As if the way she perfectly had knowne. . . . *Col.* 269
As if his godhead thou didst present see.' . . . *Col.* 834
As if her life upon the wager lay; . . . I. iii. 12. 2
As if his feare still followed him behynd: . . . I. ix. 21. 6
As if in Adamant rocke it had beene pight. . . . I. xi. 25. 5
As if late fight had nought him damnifyde, . . . I. xi. 52. 7
As if her hart with sorrow had transfixed beene: . . . II. i. 15. 9
as if some new mishap, Had him betide, . . . II. i. 26. 8
As if their lives had in his hand beene gagd; . . . II. iii. 14. 3
plott of fertile land, . . . *As if* it had by Natures . . . II. vi. 12. 3
as if in lucklesse warre His forlorne steed . . . II. vi. 41. 3
As if the highest God defy he would: . . . II. vii. 40. 5
As if the rest some wicked hand did rend, . . . II. x. 68. 4
As if that hungers poynt or Venus sting . . . II. xii. 39. 3
As if it had to him bene sacrifide, . . . II. xii. 49. 4
she sighed soft, *as if* his case she rewd. . . . II. xii. 73. 9
As if that age badd him that burden spare, . . . III. i. 4. 5
Which in that cloth was wrought *as if* it lively grew. . . . III. i. 38. 9
As if she had a fever fitt, did quake, . . . III. ii. 5. 4
as if that he were wood, . . . III. iii. 47. 7
as if her former dred Were hard behind, . . . III. vii. 2. 5
As if he did a dogge in kenell rate . . . III. ix. 14. 7
as if suddein great affright Had them surprizd. . . . III. ix. 23. 4
As if they lay in wait, . . . III. x. 20. 9
As if he could have kild him with his looke, . . . III. x. 24. 2
As if the word so spoken were halfe donne, . . . III. x. 33. 2
As if he heaven and hell would over-ronne, . . . III. x. 33. 7
As if no trespas ever had beene donne: . . . III. x. 51. 6
As if the wind him on his winges had borne; . . . III. x. 55. 2
As if he had beene slombring in the shade; . . . III. xi. 8. 2
as if his hart were peeces made, . . . III. xi. 8. 7
As if his dayes were come to their last reach: . . . III. xi. 12. 5
as if it streight would lose The worlds foundations . . . III. xii. 2. 3
As if in minde he somewhat had to say; . . . III. xii. 4. 2
As if he had in prison long bene pent: . . . IV. v. 34. 5
as if one him suddenly did call: . . . IV. v. 42. 7
Fell downe to ground; *as if* the steele had sence, . . . IV. vi. 21. 6
stood still mute, *as if* he had beene dum, . . . IV. vii. 44. 2
As if but then the battell had begonne; . . . IV. ix. 27. 2
As if some proved perill he did feare, . . . IV. x. 12. 8
As if some blame of evill she did feare, . . . IV. x. 50. 4
gnashed with his teeth, *as if* he band High God, . . . V. ii. 18. 7
As if she had an yron andvile beene, . . . V. v. 8. 2
As if the prize she gotten had almost, . . . V. v. 10. 3
In sencelesse swoune, *as if* her life forsooke, . . . V. v. 11. 4
As if before she had not counted trew: . . . V. vi. 5. 5
As if that by his silence he would make . . . V. vi. 9. 8
As if him selfe to solace he were faine: . . . V. vi. 19. 5
Which they now hackt and hewd *as if* such use they hated. . . . V. vii. 29. 9
As if she did some great calamitie deplore. . . . V. ix. 8. 9
wayle, *as if* great griefe had her affected. . . . V. ix. 9. 9
as if that there were some . . . V. ix. 23. 4
As if that it she would in peeces rend, . . . V. xi. 27. 4
As if that there were some tumultuous affray. . . . V. xi. 43. 9
as if he fearelesse were, . . . V. xii. 14. 2
As if he would have daunted him with feare; . . . V. xii. 16. 3
As if that long she had not eaten ought; . . . V. xii. 30. 7
As if that he attonce would me devoure: . . . VI. i. 9. 6
as if against his will, . . . VI. i. 35. 2
As if his cry did meane for helpe to call . . . VI. iv. 18. 3
As if they would have slaine them presently: . . . VI. vi. 23. 5
As if he would in peeces him have rent: . . . VI. vi. 40. 6
As if he would have passed through him quight; . . . VI. vii. 10. 7
as if his enemies He scorned . . . VI. vii. 42. 3
As if he with his lookes would all men terrifie. . . . VI. vii. 42. 9
As if he never had received fall, . . . VI. viii. 26. 2
As if he would have daunted him withall: . . . VI. viii. 26. 4
As if such pride the other could apall; . . . VI. viii. 26. 7
As if some miracle of heavenly hew . . . VI. ix. 8. 8
as if her heart in twaine Had riven bene . . . VI. xi. 22. 7
As if he did from late daunger fly, . . . VI. xi. 27. 5
As if he learned had obedience long, . . . VI. xii. 37. 2
As if the love of some new Nymph, late seene, . . . VII. vii. 11. 6
As if ye please it into parts divide, . . . VII. vii. 17. 3
As if it were one voyce, . . . *Epith.* 139
Ask. if that any *aske* thy name, . . . *To his Booke* 13
Nought *aske* I, but onely to hold my right; . . . *S.C.* F. 186
When great Pan account of shepeherdes shall *aske*. . . . *S.C.* May 54
aske hem therefore what they han paund: . . . *S.C.* S. 95
Thilke sollein sadder plight doth *aske*, . . . *S.C.* N. 17
the worse despise; I *aske* no more. . . . *S.C.* Env. 12
Twixt them that *aske*, and them that asked bee. . . . *Hub.* 374
Una gan to *aske*, if ought he knew, . . . I. vi. 36. 4
When houre of death is come, let none *aske* whence, nor why. I. ix. 42. 9
To *aske* this Briton Maid, what uncouth wind . . . III. ii. 4. 5
everie one did *aske*, did he him see? . . . III. vi. 14. 2
Softly at last he gan his mother *aske*, . . . III. vii. 14. 1

Ask—*Continued.*
Did *aske* me, how I could her love deserve, ... III. vii. 53. 8
the cause . . . He did them *aske,* . . . . IV. ix. 35. 9
Did *aske* what cause brought that man to decay, ... V. iv. 23. 6
Ne stayd to *aske* if it were he by name, ... VI. i. 33. 3
let me *aske* you this withouten blame; . . . . VII. vii. 53. 4
Had it beene wrong to *aske* his owne with gaine? . . . . . . *H.H.L.* 180
Askance. Lettice . . . That scornefully lookes *askaunce;* . . . *S.C.* Mar. 21
with staring eyes fixed *askaunce,* . . . . II. vii. 7. 5
askaunce Her wanton eyes . . . Did roll too lightly, ... III. i. 41. 6
looking still *askaunce* Gainst Britomart, ... III. ix. 27. 3
Under his eiebrowes looking still *askaunce;* . . . . III. xii. 15. 2
Asked. *asked* who thee forth did bring, ... *To his Booke* 8
Asked the cause of his great distresse, ... *S.C.* May 260
Askt if in husbandrie he ought did knowe, ... *Hub.* 262
asked him, if he could willing bee . . . . *Hub.* 284
after *askt* an almes for Gods deare love. . . . . *Hub.* 363
askt what license, or what Pas they had? . . . . *Hub.* 367
Or *asked* for their pas by everie squib, ... *Hub.* 371
Twixt them that aske, and them that *asked* bee. . . . . *Hub.* 374
he *askt* how good might growe . . . . *Hub.* 965
Asked why? say: Waking Love suffereth no sleepe: . . . . . *U.V.* 10
I (to her calling) *askt* what her so vexed. . . . . *Ti.* 21
Whom when I *asked* from what place he came, ... *Col.* 64
asked him, if he did know Of straunge adventures, ... I. i. 30. 3
Halfe angrie *asked* him, for what he came. . . . . I. i. 43. 5
he *askt* her, what the Lyon ment; . . . . I. iii. 32. 8
The knight . . . gently *askt,* where all the people bee, ... I. viii. 32. 3
he *askt,* where that same knight was layd, ... I. viii. 32. 6
Then *asked* he, which way he in might pas? . . . . I. viii. 33. 1
Him oft and oft I *askt* in privity, ... I. ix. 5. 5
asked to what end they clomb that tedious hight? . . . . . . I. x. 49. 9
Askt who he was, and what he ment thereby? . . . . II. vii. 59. 2
The knight him calling *asked* who he was? . . . . II. vii. 62. 1
Then Guyon *askt,* what meant those beastes . . . . II. xii. 84. 9
Of whom he *asked,* whence he lately came, ... III. v. 3. 6
shortly *asked* her, what cause her brought . . . . III. vi. 20. 2
She *askt,* what devill had her thither brought, ... III. vii. 8. 2
rudely *askte* her, how she thither came? . . . . III. viii. 23. 6
asked him for Hellenore: . . . . III. x. 38. 1
a jolly knight, Who, being *asked* for his love, ... IV. i. 10. 2
Who, being *askt,* accordingly confessed all. . . . . IV. v. 23. 9
softly *askt* againe What mister wight it was . . . . IV. vii. 10. 4
With that she *askt,* what ghosts there under ground . . . . . IV. vii. 33. 5
He *askt* who had that Dame so fouly dight, ... V. i. 14. 8
askt him where . . . her bridale cheare Should be solemniz'd; V. ii. 3. 7
He *askt* what privie tokens he did beare? . . . . V. iii. 32. 6
asked her what were those two her fone, ... V. viii. 16. 2
asked him, if that he were the same, ... V. xi. 4. 4
in rude wise him *asked,* what he was . . . . VI. vi. 20. 2
askt where were the rest? . . . . VI. xi. 28. 2
askt againe, what ment that rufull hew: . . . . VI. xi. 28. 8
Askt her, how mote her words be understood, ... VI. xii. 17. 3
Askest. Yet nought thou *ask'st* in lieu of all this love, ... *H.H.L.* 176
Asketh. Ne ever any *asketh* reason why. . . . . V. ii. 41. 2
Askew. he on it lookt scornefully *askew,* . . . . III. x. 29. 3
He lookt *askew* with his mistrustfull eyes, ... III. xii. 10. 5
With her dull eyes did seeme to looke *askew,* . . . . V. xii. 29. 2
Glauncing *askew,* as if his enemies He scorned . . . . VI. vii. 42. 3
that sunne-shine that makes them looke *askew:* . . . . VI. x. 4. 5
when ye lowre, or looke on me *askew,* . . . . *Am.* vii. 7
Asking. To have thy *asking,* yet waite manie yeeres; . . . . *Hub.* 902
to leave The Court, not *asking* any passe or leave; . . . . . *Hub.* 936
Tho further *asking* her of sondry things, ... VI. xii. 20. 1
Asks. anie other place you have, Which *askes* small paines, . . *Hub.* 278
other, that hath litle, *askes* no more, ... VI. ix. 30. 5
Aslake. mourning altars, . . . The black infernall Furies doen
aslake: . . . . I. iii. 36. 8
No skill can stint, nor reason can *aslake.* . . . . *Am.* xliv. 8
seeking to *aslake* thy raging fyre, ... *H.B.* 4
Asleep. I chaunst to fall *asleepe* (**a sleepe*) with sorowe . . *S.C.* Mar. 47
Thou, pleasaunt spring, hast luld me oft *asleepe* (**a sleepe*), . *S.C.* Au. 155
Lulled *a sleepe* through loves misgovernaunce. . . . . *S.C.* N. 4
where the chaunting birds luld me *asleepe* (**a sleepe*), . . . *S.C.* D. 71
'Adieu, delightes, that lulled me *asleepe;* . . . . *S.C.* D. 151
hir pleasures were wonte to lull me *asleepe:* . . . . *U.V.* 13
yrockt *asleepe* (**a sleepe*) his irkesome spright, ... I. i. 55. 5
To lull him soft *asleepe* (**a sleepe*) that by it lay: . . . . . II. v. 30. 4
By this she had him lulled fast *asleepe* (**a sleepe*), ... II. vi. 18. 1
Finding the Nymph *asleepe* (**a sleepe*) in secret wheare, . . III. iv. 19. 7
To seeke if he perchance *asleepe* (**a sleepe*) were layd, . . VI. v. 3. 7
albe he saw them all *asleepe.* . . . . VI. xi. 37. 9
Aslope. His wicked fortune that had turnd *aslope,* . . . . . . III. iv. 52. 8
Aslumbering. These she had him now laid *aslombering* . . . II. xii. 72. 5
Asonder. *See* **Asunder.**
Asopus. sad *Asopus,* comely with his hoarie head. . . . . . IV. xi. 14. 9
Aspect. Of milde *aspect,* and haire as soft as silke, ... *Ti.* 563
the fayre *aspect* Of that sweet place, ... II. xii. 53. 1
Looking with myld *aspect* upon the earth . . . . III. vi. 2. 3
The house of goodly formes and faire *aspect,* . . . . III. vi. 12. 2
An hideous beast of horrible *aspect,* . . . . III. vii. 22. 2
Fansy, like a lovely Boy Of rare *aspect,* . . . . III. xii. 7. 2
she was gentle and of milde *aspect,* . . . . III. xii. 14. 3
Pure in *aspect,* and like to christall glasse, ... IV. x. 39. 7
there came Stoure with terrible *aspect,* . . . . IV. xi. 32. 1
As the faire Moone in her most full *aspect* . . . . V. v. 3. 8
Such wondrous powre hath wemens faire *aspect* . . . . V. viii. 2. 8
with more myld *aspect* those two to entertake. . . . . V. ix. 35. 9
brought he forth with griesly grim *aspect* Abhorred Murder, . V. ix. 48. 1
Of horrible *aspect* and dreadfull mood, ... V. x. 8. 7

Aspect—*Continued.*
grim Sir Saturne oft doth spare His sterne *aspect,* . . . . . VII. vii. 52. 8
Yet field and bowre are full of her *aspect:* . . . . *Am.* lxxviii. 3
Whose sweet *aspect* both God and man can move, ... *Am.* lxxxviii. 11
sole *aspect* he counts felicitye. . . . . *H.L.* 217
Cures all their sorrowes with one sweete *aspect.* . . . . . . *H.B.* 245
But in th' *aspect* of that felicitie, ... *H.H.B.* 284
Aspects. corrupt envyes, And covetous *aspects,* . . . . II. xi. 8. 9
Most ugly shapes and horrible *aspects,* . . . . II. xii. 23. 1
*The house of goodly formes and faire *aspects,* . . . . III. vi. 12. 2
Aspen. The *Aspine* good for staves; . . . . I. i. 8. 9
like a leafe of *Aspin* greene, ... I. ix. 51. 4
Aspied. *See* **Espied.**
Astonisht stood, as one that had *aspyde* Infernall furies . . . I. ix. 24. 4
when these two approching he *aspide,* . . . . I. x. 49. 1
Far off *aspyde* a young man, ... III. xi. 3. 3
Aspine. *See* **Aspen.**
Aspire. So whilom did this Monarchie *aspyre,* . . . . *Ro.* xvi. 12
Unto such tyrannie doth *aspire;* . . . . *S.C.* F. 172
cause a caytive corage to *aspire;* . . . . *S.C.* O. 95
How to a Benefice he might *aspire?* . . . . *Hub.* 482
aspire Unto so loftie pitch of perfectnesse, ... *T.M.* 393
unto heaven let your high minde *aspire,* . . . . *Ti.* 685
aspire T' excell the naturall with made delights; . . . . . . *Mui.* 165
to the highest she did still *aspyre,* . . . . I. iv. 11. 8
till to ryper yeares he gan *aspyre,* . . . . I. vi. 23. 7
what she was that did so high *aspyre?* . . . . II. vii. 48. 3
hope ever to *aspire* . . . Unto such blisse? . . . . II. ix. 5. 6
by well doing sought to honour to *aspyre.* . . . . II. ix. 39. 9
to all high desert and honour doth *aspire.* . . . . III. v. 1. 9
His caytive thought durst not so high *aspire:* . . . . III. vii. 16. 5
Could that atchieve whereto he did *aspire,* . . . . IV. vi. 43. 6
might not *aspire* To match so high, ... IV. viii. 50. 3
Brave thoughts and noble deeds did evermore *aspire.* . . . . IV. x. 26. 9
rould in clouds to heaven did *aspire,* . . . . IV. x. 38. 4
the high desire . . . which in you doth *aspire,* . . . . . . VI. ii. 34. 5
So likewise did this Titanesse *aspire* . . . . VII. vi. 4. 1
doth *aspire* To thrust faire Phoebe from her silver bed, . . . VII. vi. 21. 2
'Will never mortall thoughts ceasse to *aspire* . . . . VII. vi. 29. 2
'Cease therefore, daughter, further to *aspire,* . . . . VII. vii. 59. 1
and makes his flames to heaven *aspire.* . . . . *Am.* vi. 8
to the heaven her haughty lookes *aspire:* . . . . *Am.* lv. 11
Base things, that to her love too bold *aspire!* . . . . *Am.* lxi. 12
But not to deeme of her desert *aspyre.* . . . . *Am.* lxxxiv. 8
Unto like goodly semblant to *aspyre;* . . . . *H.L.* 109
no higher dare *aspyre,* . . . . *H.L.* 184
From heavens hight, to which they did *aspyre,* . . . . *H.H.L.* 88
pompe to which proud minds *aspyre* By name of honor, . . . *H.H.B.* 277
Aspired. his lookes loftie, as if he *aspyr'd* To dignitie, . . . *Hub.* 678
with Pyramides to heaven *aspired,* . . . . *Ti.* 408
how for to depryve Mercilla of her crowne, by her *aspyred,* . V. ix. 41. 7
Aspiring. *See* **High-aspiring.**
Nor the swift furie of the flames *aspiring,* . . . . *Ro.* xiii. 1
make thee winges of thine *aspyring* wit, ... *S.C.* O. 83
Through thoughts *aspyring* to eternall fame: . . . . IV. ix. 2. 5
Asp's. Cleopatra, . . . with stroke Of *Aspes* sting her selfe did
stoutly kill; . . . . I. v. 50. 8
Appear'd like *Aspis* sting that closely kils, ... V. xii. 36. 4
Asps. like the stings of *aspes* that kill with smart, ... IV. viii. 26. 8
Ass. The Sheepe and th' *Asse,* . . . . *Hub.* 1068
A lovely Ladie . . . Upon a lowly *Asse* . . . . I. i. 4. 2
Upon a slouthfull *Asse* he chose to ryde, ... I. iv. 18. 7
they her *Asse* would worship fayn. . . . . I. vi. 19. 9
Whom late we left ryding upon an *Asse,* . . . . VI. vii. 27. 8
Betweene the toylefull Oxe and humble *Asse,* . . . . *H.H.L.* 227
Assaid. *See* **Assayed.**
Assail. gan *assaile* this ship with dreadfull threat, ... *Bel.*[2] xiii. 7
oft faining to retire And oft him to *assaile,* . . . . *Gn.* 307
With greedy force each other doth *assayle,* . . . . I. v. 6. 6
With greedy force he gan the fort *assayle,* . . . . I. vi. 5. 3
they gan, . . . fiersly to *assaile* Each other, ... I. vi. 43. 2
crudled cold his corage gan *assayle,* . . . . I. vii. 6. 7
hellish anguish did his soule *assaile;* . . . . I. ix. 49. 4
he fiersly did his foe *assaile,* . . . . I. xi. 42. 3
him *assayle* on everie side. . . . . II. ii. 22. 9
towre, Whom foe with double battry doth *assaile,* . . . . . . II. viii. 35. 8
Fiersly at first those knights they did *assayle,* . . . . II. ix. 14. 1
That castle to *assaile* on every side, ... II. xi. 5. 4
T' *assayle* with open force or hidden guyle, ... II. xi. 7. 4
All those this sences Fort *assayle* incessantly. . . . . II. xi. 12. 9
then *assayle* him fresh, ere he could shift for more. . . . . II. xi. 27. 9
with sharpe threates her often did *assayle;* . . . . III. viii. 40. 8
So furiously each other did *assayle,* . . . . IV. ii. 18. 1
with new encouragement Did him *assayle,* . . . . IV. iii. 26. 8
Rose in his strength, and gan her fresh *assayle,* . . . . . . IV. vi. 16. 4
Whilest trembling horrour did his sense *assayle,* . . . . . . IV. vi. 22. 8
made way for his maister to *assaile;* . . . . V. ii. 24. 4
Her ready to *assaile,* . . . . V. xi. 26. 3
Them also gan *assaile* with outrage bold, ... V. xi. 47. 3
Those knights began afresh them to *assayle,* . . . . V. xi. 59. 2
which way were best His foe t' *assayle,* . . . . VI. iv. 5. 2
Sharpely they all attonce did him *assaile,* . . . . VI. v. 18. 1
With dreadfull force they all did him *assaile,* . . . . VI. vi. 26. 1
do him *assayle* on every side, ... VI. xi. 48. 6
Sought to *assaile* the heavens eternall towers, ... VII. vi. 20. 3
Assailed. this new Hydra mete to be *assailde* . . . . *Bel.*[1] viii. 11
Yet was she foyld, when as she me *assailed.* . . . . *Ti.* 112
She found her selfe *assayld* with great perplexity; . . . . . I. x. 22. 9
with fresh onsett he *assayld,* . . . . II. v. 11. 3
with importune outrage him *assayld;* . . . . II. vi. 29. 2

Assailed—_Continued._
*Cruelly they _assayled_ that fift Fort, . . . II. xi. 13. 5
with his naked hands him forcibly _assayld_. . . . II. xi. 41. 9
Assayld the flame; the which . . . gave place, . . . III. xi. 25. 4
Triamond . . . sharpely him _assayld_, . . . IV. iii. 25. 3
he started up anon, . . . And fresh _assayld_ his foe: . . . IV. iii. 31. 5
With such fell greedines he her _assayled_, . . . IV. vi. 12. 6
Whom he _assayld_ with dreadlesse hardiment, . . . V. iii. 11. 3
But he me first . . . _Assayld_, . . . VI. ii. 8. 5
with huge resistlesse might The dores _assayled_, . . . VI. xi. 43. 3
Assailing. him _assayling_ sore his carkas teare, . . . III. x. 53. 7
fiercely each _assayling_ gan afresh to fight. . . . IV. iii. 35. 9
There her _assayling_ fiercely fresh, . . . V. iv. 41. 4
without weapon him _assayling_ neare, . . . VI. iv. 20. 3
fierce _assayling_ him, with all their might . . . VI. xi. 47. 8
fierce _assailing_ forst him turne againe: . . . VI. xii. 26. 2
Assails. him _assailes_ with all the might he may; . . . IV. vii. 25. 4
Assaracus. old _Assaracus_, and Inachus divine. . . . II. ix. 56. 9
Assaracus'. roiall stocke of old _Assaracs_ line, . . . II. x. 9. 7
Assault. With horrible _assault_, and fury fell, . . . II. ii. 20. 4
Their sharp _assault_ right boldly did rebut, . . . II. ii. 23. 2
His rude _assault_ and rugged handeling . . . II. iv. 8. 1
T' avoide the rash _assault_ . . . II. v. 10. 3
strong siege and battailous _assault_, . . . II. xi. 9. 2
that old leachour, which with bold _assault_ . . . III. viii. 36. 1
Resolv'd him to _assault_ with manhood stout, . . . IV. x. 19. 4
still continu'd his _assault_ the more, . . . V. ii. 24. 1
none . . . did darre Him to _assault_, . . . V. iv. 44. 6
With fresh _assault_ upon him she did fly, . . . V. v. 14. 3
All which he did _assault_ with courage stout, . . . V. viii. 50. 5
Did them _assault_ with terrible allarme; . . . V. xi. 58. 3
Who ever thinkes . . . To wrong the weaker, oft falles in his owne _assault_.' . . . VI. ii. 23. 9
Seeing his sharpe _assault_ and cruell stoure, . . . VI. iv. 3. 3
His first _assault_ full warily did ward, . . . VI. iv. 5. 5
their _assault_ withstood so mightily, . . . VI. vi. 23. 7
Assay. With feeble wings _assay_ to mount on hight; . . . _Bel._^{2} vii. 2
O, how great ruth, and sorrowfull _assay_, . . . _Pet._^{2} ii. 11
the Giaunts did the Gods _assay_; . . . _Ro._ xvii. 4
I would _assay_ with that which in me is, . . . _Ro._ xxv. 12
should _assay_ Those royall ornaments to steale away? . . . _Hub._ 997
with vertuous deeds _assay_ To mount to heaven, . . . _Ti._ 425
Purfled with gold and pearle of rich _assay_; . . . I. ii. 13. 3
her bright blazing beautie did _assay_ To dim the brightnesse . I. iv. 8. 7
She . . . strove to maister sorrowfull _assay_, . . . I. vii. 27. 2
Therefore, deare Sir, your mightie powres _assay_.' . . . I. viii. 2. 6
The sad earth, wounded with so sore _assay_, . . . I. viii. 8. 7
Great woe and sorrow did her soule _assay_, . . . I. xi. 32. 2
His newly-budded pineons to _assay_, . . . I. xi. 34. 7
thrise in vaine to draw it did _assay_; . . . I. xi. 41. 8
Ne durst approch him nigh to touch, or once _assay_. . . . I. xii. 9. 9
her on either side doe sore _assay_, . . . II. ii. 24. 5
Ne thought of honour ever did _assay_ His baser brest, . . . II. iii. 4. 3
hath his sword through hard _assay_ forgone, . . . II. iii. 12. 6
oft approv'd in many hard _assay_; . . . II. iii. 15. 7
With beastly brutish rage gan him _assay_, . . . II. iv. 6. 7
To overthrow him strongly did _assay_, . . . II. iv. 8. 8
A knight of wondrous powre and great _assay_, . . . II. iv. 40. 6
she would _assay_ To laugh . . . II. vi. 7. 6
Till season serve new passage to _assay_: . . . II. vi. 23. 7
tempt his guest to take thereof _assay_; . . . II. vii. 34. 4
thy faithfull aide in hard _assay_, . . . II. viii. 7. 4
So ready dight fierce battaile to _assay_, . . . II. viii. 22. 8
stoutly he withstood their strong _assay_; . . . II. viii. 36. 1
assay To ease you of that ill, . . . II. ix. 42. 8
I would _assay_ Thy name, O soveraine Queene! . . . II. x. 3. 8
sacked Rome too dearely did _assay_, . . . II. x. 40. 3
Through great bloodshed and many a sad _assay_, . . . II. x. 49. 2
Provoked them the breaches to _assay_, . . . II. xi. 14. 7
th' utmost meanes of victory _assay_, . . . II. xi. 41. 4
Flying from Junoes wrath and hard _assay_, . . . II. xii. 13. 5
Both firmely armd for every hard _assay_, . . . II. xii. 38. 8
for witnes of his hard _assay_ . . . III. i. 2. 5
none of all the six before him durst _assay_. . . . III. i. 21. 9
Of pearles and pretious stones of great _assay_, . . . III. iv. 18. 5
assay To bring her sonne unto his last decay. . . . III. iv. 28. 4
each to _assay_ Whether more happy were . . . III. iv. 46. 8
through the ford to passen did _assay_; . . . III. v. 18. 4
the third brother him did sore _assay_, . . . III. v. 21. 3
Ne durst _assay_ to wade the perlous seas, . . . III. vii. 28. 3
assay With burning charet wheeles it nigh to smite; . . . III. vii. 41. 6
he likewise gan _assay_ . . . III. xi. 26. 2
From twentie Knights that did him all _assay_; . . . IV. i. 2. 4
though spite did oft _assay_ To blot her with dishonor . . . IV. i. 4. 8
too late his manhood and his might I did _assay_, . . . IV. i. 35. 2
Albee untrue she wist them by _assay_. . . . IV. i. 50. 5
thought againe it to _assay_. . . . IV. viii. 10. 9
great feeblesse, which did oft _assay_ Faire Amoret . . . IV. viii. 37. 3
All which who list by tryall to _assay_ . . . IV. ix. 3. 1
did Britomart _assay_ To speake to them, . . . IV. ix. 31. 1
All that adventure which ye did _assay_ . . . IV. ix. 40. 8
stones of rich _assay_, . . . IV. x. 15. 5
They gan with all their weapons him _assay_, . . . V. ii. 53. 2
to have wrought unwares some villanous _assay_. . . . V. iv. 23. 9
To try her Fortune, and his force _assay_, . . . V. iv. 47. 7
he would not once _assay_ To reskew his owne Lord, . . . V. v. 19. 8
So cunningly she wrought her crafts _assay_, . . . V. v. 52. 5
Whereby his strengthes _assay_ he might him teach. . . . V. viii. 37. 5
Wherewith full wroth he fiercely gan _assay_ . . . V. xi. 11. 4
For great desire that Monster to _assay_, . . . V. xi. 21. 2

Assay—_Continued._
he gan her with courage fierce _assay_, . . . V. xi. 26. 6
now they doe so sharpely him _assay_, . . . V. xi. 46. 1
I long in vaine have bent . . . and daily meanes _assay_; . . . V. xi. 51. 4
did _assay_ To make them both as merry . . . VI. iii. 9. 4
loth t' _assay_ The proofe of battell now . . . VI. iii. 41. 3
misguyde His former malice to some new _assay_, . . . VI. iii. 47. 8
Such were this Ladies pangs and dolorous _assay_. . . . VI. v. 5. 9
began to _assay_ T' amend what was amisse, . . . VI. v. 10. 8
doe him sharpe _assay_ On every side, . . . VI. v. 19. 3
To thrust him out of dore doing his worst _assay_. . . . VI. vi. 21. 9
hornes doe threat Desperate daunger, if he them _assay_, . . . VI. vii. 47. 3
Ne list the Knight the powre thereof _assay_, . . . VI. viii. 8. 7
covet to _assay_ This simple sort of life . . . VI. ix. 33. 7
he did _assay_ In his strong hand their rugged teats to hold, . . VI. ix. 37. 7
All on confused heapes themselves _assay_, . . . VI. xi. 17. 5
how they mote best _assay_. . . . VI. xi. 36. 9
Disdayne to yield unto the first _assay_. . . . _Am._ xiv. 8
long stormes and tempests sad _assay_, . . . _Am._ lxiii. 1
after long pursuit and vaine _assay_, . . . _Am._ lxvii. 5
assay A mortall thing so to immortalize; . . . _Am._ lxxv. 5
Th' Almighty, seeing their so bold _assay_, . . . _H.H.L._ 85
Assayed. _See_ **Ill-assayed.**
Of hundred Hercules to be _assaide_, . . . _Bel._^{2} x. 11
Where no such troublous tydes han us _assayde_; . . . _S.C._ O. 117
once _assai'd_ to burne this world so wide. . . . _Gn._ 376
th' other was with Thetis love _assaid_, . . . _Gn._ 491
O, how great sorrow my sad soule _assaid_! . . . I. ii. 24. 5
Such fearefull fitt _assaid_ her trembling hart, . . . I. vi. 11. 1
assayd In his bras-plated body to embosse, . . . I. xi. 20. 2
Thrise he _assayd_ it from his foote to draw, . . . I. xi. 41. 7
his lustfull fyre To kindle oft _assayd_, . . . II. iii. 23. 7
My hart, my handes, mine eies, and all _assayd_! . . . II. iv. 28. 7
Of that third troupe was cruelly _assayd_; . . . II. xi. 11. 2
Cruelly they _assayed_ that fift Fort, . . . II. xi. 13. 5
full hardly was _assayd_ Of deadly daunger, . . . III. v. 13. 1
That stratageme had oftentimes _assayd_ This crafty Paramoure, III. x. 10. 8
daunger vaine it were to have _assayd_ That cruell element, . . III. xi. 22. 3
like a fire, when he Aegin' _assayd_: . . . III. xi. 35. 2
With which so sore he Ferramont _assaid_, . . . IV. iv. 20. 7
Likewise _assayd_ to prove that girdles powre; . . . IV. v. 19. 3
when in vaine to fight she oft _assayd_, . . . IV. vi. 27. 6
The warlike Dame was on her part _assaid_ . . . IV. ix. 30. 1
Full many Ladies often had _assayd_ . . . V. iii. 28. 1
ere they _assaid_ Unknowen perill . . . V. iv. 38. 5
Which Burbon seeing her againe _assayd_; . . . V. xi. 64. 6
by vow, which I profest . . . when I it _assayd_, . . . VI. ii. 37. 6
Whence he _assayd_ to rise, but could not for his hurt. . . . VI. viii. 16. 9
So her with flattering words he first _assaid_; . . . VII. vi. 43. 4
never ought was excellent _assayde_ Which was not hard . . . _Am._ li. 7
Assaying. Now his bright armes _assaying_, now his speare, . . _Hub._ 741
Assays. he is fit to use in all _assayes_, . . . _Hub._ 780
As goodlie well ye shew'd in late _assaies_, . . . _Ded. Son._ x. 8
they traveild long yfere, Through many hard _assayes_ . . . II. i. 35. 2
Assayes the house of Busyrane, . . . III. xi. Arg.
Long were to tell the amorous _assayes_, . . . III. xi. 44. 1
in hard _assaies_ Were cowards knowne, . . . IV. x. 18. 6
there _assaies_ His foe . . . V. ii. 8. 6
A noble Knight, and tride in hard _assayes_; . . . V. iii. 5. 2
time his speach To all _assayes_; . . . V. ix. 39. 4
but terrible and stearne In all _assaies_ . . . VI. iii. 40. 4
past through many perillous _assayes_, . . . VI. vi. 3. 4
who so list the like _assayes_ to ken, . . . _H.B._ 88
His paines, his povertie, his sharpe _assayes_, . . . _H.H.L._ 235
Assemblance. To weete the cause of their _assemblaunce_ wide: V. iv. 21. 5
Assemble. How soone would yee _assemble_ many a fleete, . . . III. viii. 28. 3
themselves gan there _assemble_; . . . IV. vi. 29. 5
Gan into one _assemble_ all the might Of all his hands, . . . V. xi. 8. 4
Resolved in one t' _assemble_ all his force, . . . VI. viii. 14. 8
Assembled. Faunes With hideous cry _assembled_ . . . _Bel._^{1} x. 12
Art and Nature had _assembled_ All pleasure . . . _Bel._^{2} xii. 5
all the beasts he caus'd _assembled_ bee, . . . _Hub._ 1377
In her thou maist them all _assembled_ see, . . . _Col._ 570
thralles . . . thither were _assembled_ day by day . . . I. v. 51. 2
To him _assembled_ with one full consort, . . . I. xii. 4. 7
A route of people there _assembled_ were, . . . II. vii. 44. 1
Like many swarmes of Bees _assembled_ round, . . . II. ix. 51. 4
Was then _assembled_ deeds of armes to see: . . . IV. i. 9. 4
wooers _Assembled_ were to weet whose she should bee, . . . IV. ii. 38. 2
Assembled were in field the chalenge to define. . . . IV. iii. 3. 9
Assembled for to get the honour of that game. . . . IV. iv. 13. 9
full many a warlike swaine _Assembled_ were, . . . IV. iv. 26. 5
when all those knightes againe _Assembled_ were . . . IV. iv. 37. 2
Assembled in one place: . . . IV. v. 12. 6
all those Nymphes, which then _assembled_ were . . . IV. xi. 10. 7
sonnes of Neptune, now _assembled_ here: . . . IV. xi. 15. 3
The gods _assembled_ all on Arlo Hill: . . . VII. vii. 3. 2
since the day That all the gods whylome _assembled_ were . . VII. vii. 12. 2
Assemblies. Bred in _assemblies_ of the vulgar sort, . . . IV. i. 28. 4
Assembling. _Assembling_ all his force and utmost might, . . . II. viii. 47. 3
unto him _assembling_ forreigne might, . . . II. x. 35. 4
Assembly. the whole _assembly_ of those heards Moov'd at his speech, . . . _Col._ 648
Whose great _assembly_ they did much admire, . . . V. ii. 29. 6
Then was that whole _assembly_ quite dismist, . . . VII. vii. 59. 8
Assent. Let never Ladie to his love _assent_, . . . IV. v. 18. 8
Britomart would not thereto _assent_, . . . IV. v. 20. 6
Unto my choise by no meanes would _assent_, . . . IV. vii. 16. 3
Assented. The Prince _assented_; . . . VI. viii. 7. 1
Asses. measured by his weed, As . . . _asses_ by their eares: . _Col._ 712

Asses—*Continued.*
asses been not all whose eares exceed, . . . *Col.* 713
Assieged. th' *assieged* Castles ward . . . II. xi. 15. 1
Assigned. The dowre agreed, the day *assigned* plaine, . . . *Col.* 126
Have in the Ocean charge to me *assignd;* . . . *Col.* 253
the sacred lawes of armes that are *assynd.* . . . I. v. 4. 9
the Dwarfe the way to her *assynd;* . . . I. vii. 28. 4
That Lady, whom I had to me *assynd,* . . . II. iv. 22. 6
Keeping that slombred corse to him *assind:* . . . II. viii. 11. 7
The rest had severall offices *assynd;* . . . II. ix. 31. 6
To him *assigned* for his worthy lott, . . . II. x. 12. 3
unto them what destinie was *assynd,* . . . she did not tell; . IV. ii. 53. 5
Are by the Gods to drinck thereof *assynd;* . . . IV. iii. 43. 8
have the sea in charge to them *assinde,* . . . IV. xi. 52. 2
the utmost date *assynde* For his returne . . . V. vi. 3. 6
to his kyne for food *assynd;* . . . V. x. 9. 8
To him *assynd* her high beheast to doo, . . . V. xii. 3. 7
therein hath a Seneschall *assynd,* . . . VI. i. 15. 7
had to her that soveraigne seat By highest Jove *assign'd,* . . . VII. vi. 12. 2
Then thinkes what punishment were best *assign'd,* . . . VII. vi. 48. 8
Assignment. Gainst which the second troupe *assignment* makes; II. xi. 10. 2
Assind(e). *See* **Assigned.**
Assist. What God or Fortune would *assist* his might. . . . *Gn.* 301
to *assist* the Britons fone. . . . III. iii. 33. 9
None can have tidings to *assist* her side: . . . V. xi. 42. 5
'to *assist* me now at need . . . V. xi. 57. 2
Assistance. Ne wight with him for his *assistance* went, . . . V. iv. 3. 8
she did th' *assistance* need Of this her groome; . . . VI. v. 10. 4
Assize. An hundred cubits high by just *assize,* . . . *Bel.*[2] ii. 2
Assoil. Till that you come where ye your vowes *assoyle,* . . . *D.* 535
carefull thoughts did quite *assoile.* . . . III. i. 58. 9
I will their sweatie yokes *assoyle* . . . III. xii. 47. *or.* 5
In seeking him that should her paine *assoyle;* . . . IV. v. 30. 3
Well weeting how their errour to *assoyle,* . . . IV. vi. 25. 2
did her passed paines in quiet rest *assoyle.* . . . IV. vii. 3. 9
From all this worlds incombraunce did himselfe *assoyle.* . . . V. v. 37. 9
I will them soone acquite, and both of blame *assoile.'* . . . VI. viii. 6. 9
waights, with which he did *assoyle* Both more and lesse, . . . VII. vii. 38. 7
my poore life, all sorrowes to *assoyle,* . . . *Am.* xi. 9
stoutly will that second worke *assoyle,* . . . *Am.* lxxx. 7
friendships faultie guile For ever to *assoile.* . . . *Proth.* 100
Assoiled. soule *assoyld* from sinfull fleshlinesse. . . . *D.* 259
Till from her bands the spright *assoiled* is, . . . I. x. 52. 8
Before her sonne could well *assoyled* bee, . . . II. v. 19. 2
her from so infamous fact *assoyld,* . . . III. viii. 32. 7
His wearie ghost *assoyld* from fleshly band . . . IV. iii. 13. 1
she that wrongfull challenge soone *assoyled,* . . . IV. ix. 36. 7
Assoiling. Their heavenly vertues from these woes *assoyling,* . *Ro.* xix. 11
Assot. That monstrous error, which doth some *assott,* . . . II. x. 8. 3
Assote. Willye, I wene thou bee *assot;* . . . *S.C.* Mar. 25
Assotted. some extasye *Assotted* had his sence, . . . III. viii. 22. 9
Assuage. her thirst for to *asswage.* . . . *Bel.*[2] vi. 8
rage These bitter blasts never ginne *tasswage?* . . . *S.C.* F. 2
to *aswage* The ranckorous rigour of his might, . . . *S.C.* F. 184
is hard to *asswage:* . . . *S.C.* May 137
nought their kindled corage may *aswage:* . . . I. xi. 6. 5
That forward paire she ever would *asswage,* . . . II. ii. 38. 5
It's eath his ydle fury to *aswage,* . . . II. iv. 11. 7
better reason will *aswage* The rash revengers heat. . . . II. viii. 26. 6
Th' infernall feends with it he can *asswage,* . . . II. xii. 41. 6
His wrathfull will with reason to *aswage;* . . . III. i. 11. 4
'doe nought *aswage* My stubborne smart, . . . III. ii. 37. 1
Asswage the fury which his entrails teares: . . . III. vii. 21. 4
No living creature could his cruelty *asswage.* . . . III. viii. 28. 9
with their honours . . . The furious flames of malice to *asswage.* IV. ii. 28. 4
spoyle, On which they weene their famine to *asswage,* . . . IV. iii. 16. 3
Devized by the Gods, for to *asswage* Harts grief, . . . IV. iii. 43. 2
instantly desired T' *asswage* his wrath, . . . IV. ix. 35. 4
with her least word can *asswage* The surging seas, . . . IV. xi. 50. 4
Artegall him fairely gan *asswage,* . . . V. ii. 47. 3
By all meanes seeking to *asswage* their ires; . . . V. iv. 4. 7
'That Knight shall all the troublous stormes *asswage* . . . V. vii. 23. 1
asswage Their forces furie, and their terror slake; . . . V. xii. 8. 3
With such faire words she did their heat *asswage,* . . . VI. v. 30. 6
Makes th' heavens . . . him with vowes *asswage.* . . . VI. vi. 11. 9
sought by making signes him to *asswage;* . . . VI. vi. 39. 3
ye high hevens, . . . *Aswage* your storms; . . . *Am.* xlvi. 11
now t' *asswage* the force of this new flame, . . . *H.L.* 8
Assuaged. His bloody rage *aswaged* with remorse, . . . I. iii. 5. 8
much *aswag'd* the passion of his plight, . . . I. x. 24. 8
His flaming furie sought to have *assuaged* With sober words, . IV. i. 54. 3
from revenge their willes they scarce *asswag'd:* . . . IV. v. 27. 3
Yet he with strong perswasions her *asswaged,* . . . IV. vi. 43. 1
Assuagement. some *asswagement* of their painefull plight. . . V. v. 40. 4
Without hope of *aswagement* or release? . . . *Am.* xxxvi. 4
Assumed. Which it *assumed* of some stubborne grownd, . . . *H.B.* 145
Assurance. *See* **Self-assurance.**
in their might repose their most *assurance,* . . . *Van.* xi. 13
nys on earth *assuraunce* to be sought; . . . *S.C.* N. 157
meane estate In safe *assurance,* . . . *Hub.* 910
Gan to provide for all things in *assurance,* . . . *Hub.* 1113
in ought under heaven repose *assurance,* . . . *D.* 499
'Henceforth in safe *assuraunce* may ye rest, . . . I. ii. 27. 1
boasts of . . . vaine *assuraunce* of mortality, . . . I. x. 1. 2
in *assuraunce* it may never stand, . . . II. xi. 30. 4
fortune, Boteswaine, no *assurance* knowes; . . . III. iv. 9. 7
for his more *assuraunce,* she inquir'd One day of Proteus . . . III. iv. 25. 1
found right safe *assurance* theare. . . . IV. i. 15. 9
shake the safe *assuraunce* of their state: . . . IV. ix. 16. 4
for *assurance* to my doome to stand, . . . V. iv. 16. 6

Assurance—*Continued.*
Yet in my truthes *assurance* I rest fixed fast.' . . . V. v. 38. 9
With safe *assuraunce* and establishment: . . . V. xi. 35. 4
Where she in safe *assuraunce* mote abide, . . . VI. iii. 28. 8
which mote pervart His safe *assurance,* . . . *Am.* xlii. 12
Weake is th' *assurance* that weake flesh reposeth . . . *Am.* lviii. 1
fayleth, trusting on his owne *assurance;* . . . *Am.* lviii. 10
That sacred Peace may in *assurance* rayne, . . . *Epith.* 354
Assurd(e). *See* **Assured.**
Assure. By more and more she gan her wings t' *assure* . . . *Bel.*[2] vii. 3
tidings there is none, I you *assure,* . . . *Hub.* 612
his life from yron death *assure,* . . . *Mui.* 59
who can him *assure* of happie day, . . . *Mui.* 218
Assure your selfe, it fell not all to ground; . . . I. i. 54. 1
Assure your selfe I will you not forsake.' . . . I. vii. 52. 7
to observe in word of knights they did *assure.* . . . II. ii. 32. 9
his Lordes life did *assure.* . . . II. viii. 30. 9
Uneath is to *assure;* . . . II. x. 8. 2
A signe which did to him the victorie *assure.* . . . IV. iii. 32. 9
Assure your selfe, Sir Knight, she shall have ayd, . . . V. xi. 43. 3
all the bands Which may a Knight *assure* . . . V. xii. 2. 2
or might myselfe *assure* . . . *H.L.* 297
How then can sinfull flesh itselfe *assure,* . . . *H.H.L.* 97
Assured. well *assur'd* (*assurde*[1]), she mounted up to joy. . . . *Pet.* vi. 10
I warne thee now *assured* sitt, . . . I. ii. 18. 5
danger great, if not *assurd* decay, I saw before mine eyes, . I. ii. 41. 8
aunswere bad me still *assured* bee, . . . I. ix. 5. 7
Ne yet *assur'd* of life by you, Sir knight, . . . I. ix. 30. 7
Speranza . . . taught him how to take *assured* hold . . . I. x. 22. 2
with solemne oath and plighted hand *Assurd,* . . . II. iv. 23. 9
wondrous massy and *assured* sownd, . . . III. ii. 25. 3
with unwearied powre his party still *assured.* . . . IV. iv. 37. 9
the gentle hart should most *assured* bind. . . . IV. ix. 1. 9
of my love at length I rest *assured,* . . . IV. x. 2. 8
her well *assured* That it was no old sore . . . IV. xii. 23. 8
Till we may be *assur'd* they shall their course retaine.' . . . V. ii. 36. 9
that of him she mote *assured* stand, . . . VI. i. 31. 8
of her grace did stand againe *assured,* . . . VI. v. 12. 3
By her that is most *assured* to her selfe. . . . *Am.* lviii. Title
when as she most supposeth Her selfe *assurd,* . . . *Am.* lviii. 4
to your selfe ye most *assured* arre! . . . *Am.* lviii. 14
assured Unto her selfe, and setled so in hart, . . . *Am.* lix. 1
Most happy she, that most *assur'd* doth rest; . . . *Am.* lix. 13
Assynd(e). *See* **Assigned.**
Assyrian. Be not twice steeped in *Assyrian* dye; . . . *Gn.* 98
after he had wonne th' *Assyrian* foe, . . . *Hub.* 751
'What nowe is of th' *Assyrian* Lyonesse, . . . *Ti.* 64
th' *Assyrian* tyrant would have made . . . *Ti.* 496
Astart. No daunger there the shepheard can *astert;* . . . *S.C.* N. 187
oft out of her bed she did *astart,* . . . III. ii. 29. 6
Astate. *See* **Estate.**
Asteria. *See* **Astery.**
Astert. *See* **Astart.**
Astery. in the woods of *Astery* abide; . . . *Gn.* 20
a gentle Nymph was found, Hight *Astery,* . . . *Mui.* 119
when he with *Asterie* did scape; . . . III. xi. 34. 3
Astond. *See* **Astoned.**
Astoned. all *astonned* with this nightly ghost, . . . *Bel.*[1] vii. 1
Astond he stood, and up his heare did hove; . . . I. ii. 31. 8
Astonied. all *astonied* with this mighty ghoast, . . . *Bel.*[2] ix. 1
astonied with the stroke, . . . *S.C.* Jul. 227
She stood *astonied* long, . . . *Mui.* 339
Astonied with the stroke of their owne hand, . . . I. ii. 15. 8
with the terror of the shocke, *Astonied,* both stand . . . I. ii. 16. 5
All stand *astonied* at her beautie bright, . . . I. vi. 9. 8
Stood all *astonied;* . . . VII. vi. 28. 6
Astonish. it did *astonish* him long space. . . . IV. viii. 43. 9
Astonished. *astonisht* dost behold The antique pride . . . *Ro.* xxvii. 1
all *astonished* with deepe dismay, . . . *Ti.* 473
stand *astonisht* at his curious skill, . . . *Col.* 8
stood awhile *astonisht* at his words, . . . *Col.* 650
Astonisht stood, as one that had aspyde Infernall furies . . . I. ix. 24. 4
still he sate long time *astonished,* . . . I. xii. 29. 3
astonisht, still he stood as sencelesse stone. . . . II. vi. 31. 9
She was *astonisht* at her heavenly hew, . . . III. vii. 11. 5
She was *astonisht* with exceeding dreed, . . . III. x. 50. 5
The beast *astonisht* stands in middest of his smart. . . . IV. i. 49. 9
with the sudden stroke *astonisht* sore, . . . IV. ii. 7. 1
they, like men *astonisht,* still did stand. . . . IV. iii. 48. 5
All looking on, and like *astonisht* staring, . . . IV. x. 56. 8
Stood still by him *astonisht* at his lore, . . . IV. xi. 23. 8
He long *astonisht* stood, ne ought he sayd, . . . V. iii. 18. 5
all *astonisht* he him selfe did find, . . . V. iv. 27. 3
Downe streight to ground fell his *astonisht* steed, . . . V. xi. 9. 1
standing long *astonished* in spright, . . . VI. x. 17. 3
to the ground *astonished* he fell; . . . VI. x. 36. 4
wonder at that sight, And stand *astonisht* . . . *Epith.* 189
Astonishment. *See* **Stonishment.**
all the forrest with *astonishment* Thereof did tremble, . . . *Hub.* 1346
of his cruell rage Nigh dead with . . . faint *astonishment,* . I. iii. 13. 4
never in this straunge *astonishment.'* . . . II. vi. 49. 4
Awhile he stood in this *astonishment,* . . . II. xi. 41. 1
suddein strook with great *astonishment;* . . . III. vii. 3. 9
Fell streight to ground in great *astonishment.* . . . III. viii. 12. 7
her out of *astonishment* he wrought; . . . III. viii. 35. 6
Malbecco stopt in great *astonishment,* . . . III. x. 41. 1
They stricken were with great *astonishment,* . . . V. iii. 26. 2
his senses straunge *astonishment,* . . . V. v. 12. 2
Through great *astonishment* of that strange sight; . . . V. vii. 20. 6
Not so great wonder and *astonishment* . . . V. vii. 39. 1

Astonishment—*Continued.*
makes the wals to stagger with *astonishment:* . . . . V. x. 34. 9
There he him found in great *astonishment,* . . . . VI. vii. 14. 3
to knowe The cause of this so strange *astonishment,* . . . . . VII. vi. 16. 3
It stopped is with thoughts *astonishment;* . . . . *Am.* iii. 10
this the worke of harts *astonishment.* . . . . *Am.* lxxxi. 14
Astonned. *See* **Astoned.**
Astonying. Doe hide themselves from her *astonying* looke . . V. ii. 54. 5
Astound. Both Nymphes and Muses nigh she made *astownd,* . *D.* 314
Th' Elfe, therewith *astownd,* Upstarted. . . . . I. vii. 7. 7
With staring countenance sterne, as one *astownd,* . . . . . . I. viii. 5. 7
his hollow eyne . . . stared as *astound;* . . . . I. ix. 35. 7
scared nations doest with horror sterne *astownd.* . . . . . . I. xi. 6. 9
with mortall stroke *astownd,* . . . . III. iv. 17. 5
Stared on her awhile, as one *astound,* . . . . III. vii. 7. 7
the Squire, in her defense, her sore *astound.* . . . . IV. viii. 19. 9
He thereat wext exceedingly *astound,* . . . . VI. viii. 27. 7
Astraea. (since fayre *Astraea* left The sinfull world) . . . *D.* 218
was taught By faire *Astraea* with great industrie, ... V. i. 5. 4
Astraea here mongst earthly men did dwell, ... V. i. 5. 8
Astraea loathing lenger here to space . . . . V. i. 11. 2
Astraeus. *Astraeus,* that did shame Himselfe . . . . IV. xi. 13. 7
Astray. Sir Ape, you are *astray:* . . . . *Hub.* 1033
Will was his guide, and griefe led him *astray.* . . . . I. ii. 12. 4
whether right he went, or else *astray.* . . . . I. iv. 19. 9
bones of men whose life had gone *astray.* . . . . I. iv. 36. 9
With many rather for to goe *astray,* . . . . I. x. 10. 6
That never leads the traveiler *astray,* . . . . I. x. 52. 4
Of the poore traveiler that went *astray* . . . . III. i. 43. 6
with his staffe, that drives his heard *astray,* . . . . III. viii. 31. 8
I found her golden girdle cast *astray,* . . . . III. viii. 49. 8
A womans will, which is disposd to go *astray.* . . . . III. ix. 6. 9
she so farre *astray,* as none can tell?' . . . . IV. ii. 22. 4
thought she wandred was, or gone *astray:* . . . . IV. vi. 36. 7
did inly mourne, like one *astray.* . . . . IV. xii. 18. 9
his creatures from their course *astray,* . . . . V. Pr. 6. 8
his owne love left *astray.* . . . . V. iv. 9. 9
That ye were runne so fondly far *astray* . . . . V. iv. 26. 8
leading th' ever-burning lampe *astray,* . . . . V. viii. 40. 7
with sage counsell, when they went *astray,* He could enforme, VI. vi. 3. 7
this Lady, like a sheepe *astray,* . . . . VI. viii. 36. 8
Whose course is often stayd, yet never is *astray.* . . . . . VI. xii. 1. 9
Out of her course doth wander far *astray!* . . . . *Am.* xxxiv. 4
my frayle thoughts too rashly led *astray!* . . . . *Am.* lxxvi. 6
was wont to lead my thoughts *astray;* . . . . *Am.* lxxxvii. 2
Astrofell. *See* **Astrophel.**
Astrophel. Feede ye hencefoorth on bitter *Astrofell,* . . . . . *D.* 346
With dolours dart for death of *Astrophel.* . . . . *As.* Pr. 10
Astrophel he hight. . . . . *As.* 6
Young *Astrophel,* the pride of shepheards praise, ... *As.* 7
Young *Astrophel,* the rusticke lasses love: . . . . *As.* 8
When *Astrophel* so ever was away. . . . . *As.* 30
The dolefulst beare that ever man did see, Was *Astrophel,* . *As.* 150
Like *Astrophel,* which thereinto was made. . . . . *As.* 186
From this day forth do call it *Astrophel:* . . . . *As.* 196
Whom *Astrophel* full deare did entertaine, ... *As.* Interl. 219
after *Astrofell* is dead and gone: . . . . *Col.* 449
while as *Astrofell* did live and raine, ... *Col.* 450
Urania, sister unto *Astrofell,* . . . . *Col.* 487
Asunder. That Romane Eagle seene to cleave *asunder,* . . . . *Ro.* xvii. 10
So cleaves thy soule *asonder:* . . . . *S.C.* Au. 88
clap of thunder . . . cloudes *asunder* dryve. . . . . *Gn.* 520
Alexis broke his tale *asunder,* . . . . *Col.* 352
he snatcht the wood, And quite *a sunder* broke. . . . . I. xi. 22. 3
his huge taile he quite *a sonder* clefte; . . . . I. xi. 39. 8
hart of flint *asonder* could have rifte; . . . . II. vii. 23. 8
Which hewing quite *asunder,* . . . . II. viii. 38. 6
flockes, Which fled *asonder,* and him fell before; . . . . . . II. xi. 19. 3
nathemore the steele *asonder* riv'd, ... III. vii. 40. 5
Their wooden ribs are shaken nigh *asonder.* . . . . IV. ii. 16. 6
eke thy childrens thrids to be *asunder* burst!' . . . . IV. ii. 49. 9
the staffe *asunder* brake, ... IV. iii. 10. 6
Therewith *asunder* in the midst it brast, ... IV. iii. 12. 1
rived were like rotten wood *asunder;* . . . . IV. iii. 15. 6
did divide Them selves *asunder:* . . . . IV. iv. 14. 2
it would loose, or else *asunder* teare. . . . . IV. v. 3. 5
a rocke of Diamond it could rive And rend *asunder* . . . . . . IV. v. 37. 9
full oft she both of them had seene *Asunder,* . . . . IV. ix. 10. 4
Rashing off helmes, and ryving plates *asonder,* . . . . V. iii. 8. 6
with their troupes did far *asunder* cast; . . . . V. iv. 43. 8
his owne waight his necke *asunder* broke, ... V. viii. 8. 3
seem'd a marble rocke *asunder* could have rive. . . . . V. xi. 5. 9
Did quake to heare, and nigh *asunder* brast: . . . . V. xi. 28. 5
cleft his head *asunder* to his chin. . . . . VI. i. 23. 5
They hew'd their helmes, and plates *asunder* brake, ... VI. i. 37. 4
As if his lungs and lites were nigh *asunder* brast. . . . . . VI. iii. 26. 9
So did that Squire his foes disperse and drive *asonder.* . . . VI. v. 19. 9
Yet did so streightly them *asunder* keepe, ... VI. xii. 5. 8
Aswage, *etc.* *See* **Assuage.**
At (*partial list*). *See* **At once, At one, Whereat.**
kings gronde *at* hir feete, Their armes . . . bounde *at* their backes. . . . . *Bel.*[1] xi. 9, 10
At length, even *at* the time, when Morpheus . . . . *Bel.* xv. 1
Jove *at* them his thunderbolts let flie, ... *Ro.* xii. 4
the good man *at* him did laye. . . . . *S.C.* F. 214
To feede theyr flocks *at* will, ... *S.C.* Jul. 66
they han the devill *at* commaund, ... *S.C.* S. 94
when it is *at* best. . . . . *S.C.* S. 241
wondren *at* bright Argus blazing eye; . . . . *S.C.* O. 32
stretch her selfe *at* large from East to West; . . . . *S.C.* O. 44

At—*Continued.*
when as *at* last he spide, ... *Gn.* 266
thus *at* point prepared, ... *Gn.* 281
walke about the world *at* pleasure . . . . *Hub.* 159
Till *at* the length he published . . . . *Hub.* 568
At sound whereof, they all . . . . *Col.* 246
my Cynthia serve *At* sea, ... *Col.* 261
stroke *at* her with more then manly force, ... I. i. 24. 6
At last faire Hesperus in highest skie . . . . I. ii. 6. 6
But that the Knight him *at* advantage fownd; . . . . I. viii. 10. 3
let him die *at* ease, that liveth here uneath? . . . . I. ix. 38. 9
He lefte his captive Beast *at* liberty, ... III. vii. 38. 2
'tell *at* one word, How many fownd'st thou . . . . III. vii. 56. 8
loudly barkt *at* mee, ... VI. i. 9. 5
Atalanta. with which th' Euboean young man wan Swift *Atalanta,* . . . . II. vii. 54. 9
apples . . . which *Atalanta* did entice; . . . . *Am.* lxxvii. 8
Atcheived, Atchieve, Atchive, *etc.* *See* **Achieve,** *etc.*
Ate. by his side his steed the grassy forage *ate.* . . . . . . I. vii. 2. 9
Apple . . . emongst the gods false *Ate* threw; . . . . II. vii. 55. 5
Her name was *Ate,* mother of debate . . . . IV. i. 19. 1
So false Duessa; but vile *Ate* thus: . . . . IV. i. 47. 1
Ate soone discovering his desire, ... IV. ii. 11. 6
So Florimell with *Ate* forth was brought, ... IV. iv. 10. 2
Ate eke provokt him privily . . . . IV. iv. 11. 6
Thereto him *Ate* stird, new discord to maintaine. . . . . . . IV. v. 22. 9
The crime which cursed *Ate* kindled earst, ... IV. v. 31. 2
through lewd upbraide Of *Ate* and Duessa, ... IV. ix. 24. 6
that old hag of hellish hew, The cursed *Ate,* . . . . V. ix. 47. 4
Athenians. th' unjust *Atheniens* made to dy Wise Socrates; . II. vii. 52. 6
Athens. All that which *Athens* ever brought forth wise; . . . *Ro.* xxix. 9
Which she with Neptune did for *Athens* trie: . . . . *Mui.* 306
Exceld at *Athens* all the learned preace, ... II. x. 25. 7
Athos. how mount *Athos* . . . Was digged downe, ... *Gn.* 45
Athwart. *Athwart* his brest a bauldrick . . . . I. vii. 29. 8
bauldricke, which forelay *Athwart* her snowy brest, ... II. iii. 29. 6
Sometimes *athwart,* sometimes he strook him strayt, ... II. v. 9. 8
With wanton yvie twine entrayld *athwart,* . . . . III. vi. 44. 5
Lying *athwart* her horse in great distresse, ... III. vii. 37. 7
in gilden armes, with azure band Quartred *athwart,* . . . . VI. ii. 44. 8
Atin. His am I *Atin,* his in wrong and right, ... II. iv. 42. 5
Atin to Cymochles for ayd flyes. . . . . II. v. Arg.
rash Pyrochles varlett, *Atin* hight, ... II. v. 25. 4
There *Atin* fownd Cymochles sojourning, ... II. v. 28. 1
Atin, arriving there, when him he spyde . . . . II. v. 35. 1
Atin ay him pricks with spurs of shame . . . . II. v. 38. 9
The wrath which *Atin* kindled in his mind, ... II. vi. 2. 3
Atin by no way She would admit, ... II. vi. 4. 8
Upon that shore he spyed *Atin* stand, ... II. vi. 38. 7
Atin drew nigh to weet what it mote bee, ... II. vi. 43. 1
O *Atin!* helpe to me last death to give.' . . . . II. vi. 45. 5
Him *Atin* spying knew right well of yore, ... II. vi. 48. 1
stryful *Atin* in their stubborne mind . . . . II. viii. 11. 4
The whiles false Archimage and *Atin* fled apace. . . . . . . II. viii. 56. 9
Atlas. the moist daughters of huge *Atlas* . . . . III. i. 57. 8
Atlas'. On *Atlas* mighty shoulders is upstayd, ... *Ded. Son.* ix. 6
those which Hercules . . . Got from great *Atlas* daughters, . II. vii. 54. 6
At once. You deemen the Spring is come *attonce;* . . . . . . *S.C.* F. 38
Mought her necke bene joynted *attonce,* . . . . *S.C.* Mar. 53
all *attonce* her beastly bodie raizd . . . . I. i. 18. 3
To have *attonce* devourd her tender corse; . . . . I. iii. 5. 6
Of all *attonce* he cast avengd to be, ... I. v. 12. 6
increasing more Their puissant force, and cruell rage *attonce,* I. vi. 45. 3
all *atonce* to kill, ... I. xi. 13. 6
He cast *at once* him to avenge for all; . . . . I. xi. 40. 6
He thought *attonce* him to have swallowed . . . . I. xi. 53. 2
both with greedy forse *Attonce* upon him ran, ... II. ii. 22. 2
Attonce he wards and strikes; . . . . II. ii. 25. 6
Both fled *attonce,* . . . . II. iii. 19. 9
With whom . . . *Attonce* I was upbrought; . . . . II. iv. 18. 4
Both of them high *attonce* their handes enhaunst, ... II. vi. 31. 1
both *attonce* their huge blowes down did sway. . . . . II. vi. 31. 2
him *attonce* disarm'd; . . . . II. vi. 51. 2
both *attonce* him charge on either syde . . . . II. viii. 35. 1
Them both *atonce* compeld with courage bold . . . . II. viii. 41. 7
all *attonce* their malice forth do poure: . . . . II. viii. 48. 7
They all *attonce* out of their seates arose, ... II. ix. 36. 2
attonce at him let fly Their fluttring arrowes, ... II. xi. 18. 1
all *attonce,* gaping full greedily, ... II. xii. 39. 7
Such as *attonce* might not on living ground, ... II. xii. 70. 3
they all *attonce* upon him laid, ... III. i. 21. 1
all *attonce* discovered her desire . . . . III. i. 53. 1
Redcrosse knight ran to the stownd, . . . with them *attons:* III. i. 63. 3
the raine Of Britons eke with him *attonce* shall dye; . . . . III. iii. 40. 2
Love and despight *attonce* her courage kindled hath. . . . . III. iv. 12. 9
Bad eke *attonce* their charetts to be sought: . . . . III. iv. 31. 4
two great champions did *attonce* pursew . . . . III. iv. 46. 2
both *attonce* on both sides him bestad, ... III. v. 22. 8
eke *attonce* the heavy trees they clyme, ... III. vi. 42. 5
Such laesinesse both lewd and poore *attonce* him made. . . . III. vii. 12. 9
Into his hart *attonce:* . . . . III. viii. 31. 5
did eke beguyle, Both eyes and hart *attonce,* . . . . III. x. 5. 5
all the passions . . . Did him *attonce* oppresse, ... III. x. 17. 9
death and life *attonce* unto him gives, ... III. x. 60. 3
As if their soules they would *attonce* have rent . . . . IV. ii. 18. 2
fild the lookers on *attonce* with ruth and wonder. . . . . . IV. iii. 15. 9
So both *at once* fell dead upon the field, ... IV. iii. 34. 8
all *at once* at him gan fiercely flie, ... IV. ix. 33. 2
at once both head and helmet to have raced. . . . . V. v. 11. 9
eke the knight *attonce* she did betray; . . . . V. v. 52. 7

At once—*Continued.*
Pelmell with them *attonce* did enter in. . . . V. vii. 35. 4
Did all their speares *attonce* on him enchace. . . . V. x. 34. 5
Doe all *attonce* their thunders rage forth rent, . . . V. x. 34. 8
all *attonce* they on the Prince did thonder, . . . V. x. 35. 1
Through all three bodies he him strooke *attonce,* . . . V. xi. 14. 1
all the three *attonce* fell on the plaine, . . . V. xi. 14. 2
As if that he *attonce* would me devoure: . . . VI. i. 9. 6
both their hands on hie *At once* did heave . . . VI. i. 38. 2
as he would devoure His life *attonce;* . . . VI. iii. 48. 8
Sharpely they all *attonce* did him assaile, . . . VI. v. 18. 1
they both *at once* . . . Did bend their speares, . . . VI. vii. 7. 4
then her eate *attonce,* or many meales to make. . . . VI. viii. 37. 9
all *attonce* upstart, And round about her flocke, . . . VI. viii. 40. 1
Thereto they all *attonce* agreed well; . . . VI. xi. 20. 7
Bade her *attonce* from heavens coast to pack, . . . VII. vi. 12. 8
Then all *attonce* their hands upon Molanna laid. . . . VII. vi. 51. 9
better were *attonce* to let me die, . . . Am. xxv. 5
which her made *attonce* so cruell faire. . . . Am. lv. 4
At one. his Queene *attone* Was Lady Flora, . . . S.C. May 30
With lowd laments her answered all *at one.* . . . T.M. 418
how should else things so far from *attone,* . . . Col. 843
So beene they both *at one,* . . . II. i. 29. 1
all his sences seemd berefte *attone:* . . . II. i. 42. 4
They both *attone* Did dewty to their Lady, . . . II. ix. 28. 6
fro me reft both life and light *attone.* . . . III. v. 7. 6
white seemes fayrer macht with blacke *attone;* . . . III. ix. 2. 4
The knights in couples marcht with ladies linckt *attone.* . . . IV. iv. 14. 9
with him eke that aged Squire *attone;* . . . IV. v. 46. 3
linckt with me in the same chaine *attone?'* . . . IV. vii. 14. 7
assaid Of Claribell and Blandamour *attone;* . . . IV. ix. 30. 2
let me die and end my daies *attone,* . . . IV. xii. 9. 8
Whether of them the greater were *attone;* . . . V. ii. 48. 8
With sodaine stounds of wrath and griefe *attone;* . . . V. vi. 17. 6
pursu'd of them *attone.* . . . V. viii. 16. 5
backeward he *attone* with him did wend: . . . V. xi. 43. 5
thrust it all *attone* Into his gaping throte, . . . VI. iv. 21. 4
Atonement. Of finall peace and faire *attonement* . . . V. viii. 21. 8
Atropos. That cruell *Atropos* eftsoones undid, . . . IV. ii. 48. 7
To whom fierce *Atropos:* 'Bold Fay, . . . IV. ii. 49. 6
Attach. a Capias Should issue forth t' *attach* that scornefull lasse. . . . VI. vii. 35. 5
Him to *attache,* and downe to hell to throwe; . . . VII. vi. 16. 7
Attached. the Gard . . . *Attacht* that faytor false, . . . I. xii. 35. 5
The faire Sabrina . . . She there *attached,* . . . II. x. 19. 4
the sharpe hauke which her *attached* neare, . . . III. viii. 33. 4
He her unwares *attacht,* and captive held by might. . . . IV. ix. 6. 9
Terpine . . . She caused to be *attacht,* . . . V. v. 18. 6
the stound which mortally *attacht* him. . . . VI. iii. 10. 9
Being now *attacht* with timely age, . . . VI. vi. 4. 6
The damzell was *attacht,* and shortly brought Unto the barre VI. vii. 36. 1
Attaching. her *attaching* thought her hands to tye; . . . II. xi. 28. 6
Attain. Ne other knowledge ever did *attaine,* . . . Hub. 837
To seeke her strayed Champion if she might *attayne.* . . . I. iii. 8. 9
high heaven to *attaine?* . . . I. x. 50. 3
How dare I thinke such glory to *attaine?'* . . . I. x. 62. 2
Unto her happy mansion *attaine:* . . . II. iii. 41. 4
Ye well may hope, and easely *attaine?* . . . II. ix. 6. 4
Ambrose and Uther, did ripe yeares *attayne,* . . . II. x. 67. 2
by the ransack of that peece they should *attayn.* . . . II. xi. 14. 9
In hope her to *attaine* by hooke or crooke, . . . III. i. 17. 6
hopelesse ever to *attaine* My Ladies love . . . III. vii. 60. 6
at the last he did himselfe *attaine,* . . . IV. vii. 27. 6
eke pursew, if he *attaine* it may.' . . . V. v. 39. 7
others . . . Though they enforce themselves, cannot *attaine;* VI. ii. 2. 6
he . . . dyde, before I did *attaine* Ripe yeares . . . VI. ii. 28. 4
Till to some place of rest they mote *attaine,* . . . VI. iii. 28. 7
Till that his Ladies sight he mote *attaine,* . . . VI. iv. 40. 8
The which my selfe could never yet *attayne.* . . . Am. lxxxiii. 10
t' *attaine,* Unto the type of true Nobility; . . . Com. Son. ii. 1
Ne thinks on ought but how it to *attaine;* . . . H.L. 205
Attained. 'These, that have it *attaynd,* were in like cace, . . I. x. 62. 3
Till her he had *attaind* and brought in place, . . . III. vii. 23. 4
He wilfull lost that he before *attayned:* . . . V. v. 17. 8
ere his stroke *attayned* his intent, . . . VI. viii. 15. 6
Ere he *attain'd* the point by him intended, . . . VI. ix. 46. 8
Attaint. Phoebus golden face it did *attaint,* . . . I. vii. 34. 6
Lest she with blame her honor should *attaint,* . . . IV. i. 5. 5
him to touch with falshoods fowle *attaint,* . . . V. vi. 12. 3
Attchieved. *See* **Achieved.**
Attemper. To the waters fall their tunes *attemper* . . . S.C. Jun. 8
Attempered. bene thine eyes *attempred* to the yeare, . . . S.C. Ap. 5
Thus fairely shee *attempered* her feast, . . . II. ii. 39. 1
Attempred goodly well for health and for delight. . . . II. xi. 2. 9
Gently *attempred,* and disposd so well, . . . II. xii. 51. 8
Their notes unto the voice *attempred* sweet; . . . II. xii. 71. 2
Attempt. in avengement of their bold *attempt,* . . . Gn. 577
was content to *attempt* that enterprise, . . . Hub. 995
With like *attempt* to like end to renew. . . . I. v. 42. 4
'Daunger without discretion to *attempt* Inglorious, . . . III. xi. 23. 1
with so strong *attempt* I had begonne. . . . IV. x. 53. 5
forced to forgoe th' *attempt* remedilesse.' . . . V. xi. 51. 9
us drave To this *attempt* to wreake his hid despight, . . . VI. vii. 12. 8
T' *attempt* the empire of the heavens hight, . . . VII. vi. 7. 4
All beeing with so bold *attempt* amazed, . . . VII. vi. 13. 8
Attempt to work her gentle mindes unrest: . . . Am. lxxxiii. 4
Attempted. *See* **Late-attempted.**
Such as she was when Pallas she *attempted,* . . . Mui. 346
will ye, fond Dame, *attempted* bee Unto a strangers love, . . V. xi. 63. 1
Attend. on whom did *attend* A fayre flocke of Faeries, . . . S.C. May 31

Attend—*Continued.*
To keep his sheep, or to *attend* his swyne, . . . Hub. 285
When that was done, he might *attend* his playes: . . . Hub. 394
In the mean-time upon the King t' *attend.* . . . Hub. 1100
doo still *attend* To wash faire Cynthiaes sheep, . . . Col. 257
The fifth had charge sick persons to *attend,* . . . I. x. 41. 1
to *attend* awhile their forward steps they stay. . . . II. i. 35. 9
Unto thy bounteous baytes . . . to *attend;* . . . II. vii. 10. 4
a covetous Spright . . . thereby did *attend,* . . . II. vii. 32. 2
A little boy did on him still *attend* To reach, . . . II. ix. 58. 4
th' Author selfe could not at least *attend* To finish it: . . . II. x. 68. 5
as her Squyre *attend* her carefully. . . . III. iii. 61. 5
A thousand thousand naked babes *attend* About him . . . III. vi. 37. 3
attend Him selfe from deadly daunger to defend: . . . III. vii. 32. 4
Ne wight him to *attend,* or way to guide, . . . IV. vi. 44. 6
in order seemly good Did on the Thamis *attend,* . . . IV. xi. 44. 8
On her two pretty handmaides did *attend,* . . . IV. xi. 47. 1
weeping day and night did him *attend,* . . . IV. xii. 21. 6
An yron man, which did on her *attend* . . . V. i. 12. 2
to his doome with listfull eares did both *attend.* . . . V. i. 25. 9
duely did *attend* Uppon the rites and daily sacrifize, . . . V. vii. 4. 2
by his stirrup Talus did *attend,* . . . V. viii. 29. 6
Those did upon Mercillaes throne *attend,* . . . V. ix. 32. 5
Ne day nor night did sleepe t' *attend* them on, . . . V. x. 10. 4
whilome did *attend* On faire Irene . . . V. xi. 37. 6
that foule feend, who dayly doth *attend* . . . VI. iv. 31. 8
he did her *attend* most carefully, . . . VI. v. 9. 6
Without my care, but onely to *attend* it; . . . VI. ix. 21. 6
all the day to what I list I doe *attend.* . . . VI. ix. 22. 9
those three in the midst doe chiefe on her *attend.* . . . VI. x. 21. 9
Appointed to *attend* her dewly day and night. . . . VI. xii. 14. 9
my thoughts doo day and night *attend,* . . . Am. xxii. 7
he, that would *attend,* Mote soften it . . . Am. li. 9
All night therefore *attend* your merry play, . . . Epith. 368
Thy handmaides be, which do on thee *attend,* . . . H.B. 261
on his owne dread presence to *attend,* . . . H.H.L. 68
Angels and Archangels, which *attend* On Gods owne person, H.H.B. 97
So they . . . Did on those two *attend,* . . . Proth. 123
Attendance. The rest upon her person gave *attendance* great. III. vi. 17. 9
slacke *attendaunce* unto straungers call. . . . III. ix. 18. 7
With dayly service and *attendance* dew, . . . VI. xii. 5. 2
Attended. Yet Britomart *attended* duly on her, . . . IV. i. 8. 8
many a pretty Page *Attended* duely, . . . IV. xi. 29. 2
They all on him this day *attended* well, . . . IV. xi. 30. 3
duly her *attended* day and night; . . . VII. vi. 9. 4
Attendement. *See* **Attendment.**
Attendeth. wretched end which still *attendeth* on her.' . . . VI. vi. 25. 7
Attending. All which she there on her *attending* had: . . . IV. xi. 48. 6
her *attending* in full seemly sort, . . . IV. xii. 18. 7
Attendment. Would he restrayned be from his *attendement.* VI. vi. 18. 9
Attent. With vigilant regard and dew *attent,* . . . III. ix. 52. 3
Hong still upon his melting mouth *attent;* . . . VI. ix. 26. 2
kept her sheepe with diligent *attent,* . . . VI. ix. 37. 3
Attention. With strong endevour and *attention* dew. . . . Am. lxxx. 8
Attentive. her beholding with *attentive* eye, . . . IV. viii. 10. 1
Attest. Which that brave races greatnes did *attest,* . . . Bel.² v. 7
to thy mother dead *attest* That cleare she dide . . . II. i. 37. 6
Attic. After th' Ionicke, *Atticke,* Doricke guise; . . . Ro. xxix. 3
the East . . . Burnt th' *Attick* towres, . . . Gn. 44
Attire. his rich *attire* and goodly forme, . . . Van. viii. 6
joy'd to range abroad in fresh *attire,* . . . Mui. 37
lavish Nature, in her best *attire,* . . . Mui. 163
plaine *attire* such glorious gallantry Disdaines . . . Col. 729
others trimly dight Their gay *attyre;* . . . I. iv. 14. 9
a gentle Squyre, . . . clad in comely sad *attyre;* . . . I. x. 7. 3
frost with spangles doth *attire* The mossy braunches . . . I. x. 48. 3
A comely Palmer, clad in black *attyre,* . . . II. i. 7. 2
disguising both in straunge And base *atyre,* . . . III. iii. 7. 2
her Maides *attyre* To turne into a massy habergeon, . . . III. iii. 57. 7
That he with fleshly weeds would them *attire:* . . . III. vi. 32. 5
Upon the ground in ragged rude *attyre,* . . . V. viii. 23. 6
Of men disguiz'd in womanishe *attire,* . . . V. vi. 37. 7
seemed, by their portance and *attire,* . . . VI. v. 11. 4
a woman spoyld of all *attire* . . . VI. viii. 48. 5
With shepheards hooke in hand, and fit *attyre,* . . . VI. ix. 13. 8
To follow sheepe and shepheards base *attire:* . . . VI. ix. 24. 4
She should it cause to be fostred under straunge *attyre.* . . . VI. xii. 6. 9
Did deck himselfe in freshest faire *attire;* . . . VII. vii. 11. 2
made him change his gray *attire* to greene: . . . VII. vii. 11. 8
Shall doffe her fleshes borrowd fayre *attyre,* . . . Am. xxvii. 6
proud mayd, whom now those leaves *attyre* . . . Am. xxviii. 8
her golden tresses She doth *attyre* under a net of gold; . . . Am. xxxvii. 2
Doe lyke a golden mantle her *attyre:* . . . Epith. 156
He downe descended, . . . in fleshes fraile *attyre,* . . . H.H.L. 137
Attired. in handsome wise Your selfe *attyred,* . . . Hub. 488
Attyr'd in forraine armes and straunge aray: . . . IV. vi. 9. 3
'Thereto she is full faire, and rich *attired,* . . . V. ii. 10. 1
Attires. the Faeries and their strange *attires;* . . . Hub. 30
so goodly and so gay In your *attyres,* . . . Hub. 591
Attonce, Attone, Attones, Attons. *See* **At once, At one.**
Attrapped. all his steed With oaken leaves *attrapt,* . . . IV. iv. 39. 6
Attribute. More then goodwill to me *attribute* nought; . . . II. i. 33. 4
To *attribute* their folly unto fate, . . . V. iv. 28. 2
Ye may *attribute* to your selves as Kings, . . . VII. vii. 49. 3
Attune. To sadder times thou mayst *attune* thy quill, . . . S.C. N. 35
Their diverse notes t' *attune* unto his lay, . . . II. xii. 76. 2
Attuned. *See* **Well-attuned.**
Atween. him thus *atweene* bespake: . . . Col. 81
fares them both *atweene!* . . . II. i. 58. 5
advaunst his shield *atweene,* . . . II. iv. 46. 6

Atween—*Continued.*
Phaedria . . . *atweene* them ran; . . . II. vi. 32. 2
atweene her lilly handes . . . the juice thereof did scruze; . III. v. 33. 3
two other Knights *atweene:* . . . IV. iv. 34. 5
kissing them *atweene,* . . . IV. vii. 35. 6
thrown his shield *atween,* . . . V. xi. 30. 9
Atwene that Ladie myld and recreant knight, . . . VI. vi. 37. 2
Did cast his shield *atweene;* . . . VI. xii. 30. 2
Sprinckled with perle, and perling flowres *atweene,* . . . *Epith.* 155
seemst to laugh *atweene* thy twinkling light, . . . *Epith.* 292
Atwixt. the way *atwixt* them twaine. . . . I. viii. 13. 9
With dreadfull thunder and lightning *atwixt,* . . . III. xii. 2. 2
Atyre. *See* **Attire.**
Aubrian. The sandy Slane, the stony *Aubrian,* . . . IV. xi. 41. 2
Audience. voyd of speech in that drad *audience,* . . . VII. vi. 25. 5
Aught (*partial list*).
Ne *ought* save Tyber hastning to his fall . . . *Ro.* iii. 11
ought may happen, that hath bene beforne) . . . *S.C.* May 104
ought of the gotten good . . . *S.C.* S. 129
Ne *ought* the whelky pearles esteemeth hee, . . . *Gn.* 105
how to pardon, when *ought* is omitted; . . . *Gn.* 476
Nor *ought* cald mine or thine: . . . *Hub.* 149
Askt if in husbandrie he *ought* did knowe, . . . *Hub.* 262
Regard of honour harbours more than *ought,* . . . *Hub.* 718
nor *ought* like the same. . . . *Hub.* 868
when he *ought* would bring to pas, . . . *Hub.* 1167
when he *ought* not pleasing would put by . . . *Hub.* 1169
Who of the Grecian Libbard now *ought* heares, . . . *Ti.* 68
Ne *ought* to me remaines, . . . *Ti.* 156
Ne of so brave a building *ought* remained, . . . *Ti.* 559
If *ought* against thine honour I have tolde; . . . *Mui.* 103
She stood astonied long, ne *ought* gainesaid; . . . *Mui.* 339
Of *ought* that framed is of mortall moulde, . . . *D.* 493
Or in *ought* under heaven repose assurance, . . . *D.* 499
Found *ought* in him, that she could say was ill. . . . *As.* 24
Unmeet for man, in whom was *ought* regardfull . . . *Col.* 185
Such greatnes I cannot compare to *ought:* . . . *Col.* 335
if I her like *ought* on earth might read, . . . *Col.* 336
ought could fynd Worth harkening to, . . . *Col.* 366
ought in them blameworthie thou doest spie.' . . . *Col.* 679
Ne any one himselfe doth *ought* esteeme, . . . *Col.* 781
The . . . Knight could not for *ought* be staide; . . . I. i. 14. 2
Long way he traveiled before he heard of *ought.* . . . I. i. 28. 9
wonted feare of doing *ought* amis, . . . I. i. 49. 2
If that of such a Lady shee could tellen *ought.* . . . I. iii. 24. 9
ought have done, that ye displeasen might, . . . I. iii. 27. 4
ne *ought* he feares To be partaker of her wandring woe; . . . I. iii. 44. 7
if *ought* higher were than that, did it desyre. . . . I. iv. 11. 9
Una gan to aske, if *ought* he knew, . . . I. vi. 36. 4
Ne wanted *ought* to shew her bounteous or wise. . . . I. x. 11. 9
Ne *ought* the powre of mighty men did dread . . . I. x. 43. 5
Ne *ought* his sturdy strokes might stand afore, . . . I. xi. 37. 8
Ne *ought* he car'd whom he endamaged . . . II. ii. 18. 7
Ne *ought* the praise of prowesse more doth marre . . . II. ii. 30. 8
ne *ought* would eat, . . . II. ii. 35. 2
Ne *ought* would speake, . . . II. ii. 35. 3
that *ought* those puissant hands may marre: . . . II. vi. 44. 8
Ne *ought* mote ever sinck downe to the bottom there. . . . II. vi. 46. 9
ne them parted *ought:* . . . II. vii. 24. 7
Or *ought* that els your honour might maintaine; . . . II. viii. 19. 7
Mote *ought* allay the storme of your despight, . . . II. viii. 27. 5
Not good nor serviceable elles for *ought,* . . . II. ix. 32. 2
Ne *ought,* I weene, are ye therein behynd, . . . II. ix. 38. 8
if *ought* else that I mote not devyse, . . . II. ix. 42. 7
when ever he for *ought* did send; . . . II. ix. 58. 5
Lives *ought* that to her linage may compaire; . . . II. x. 2. 3
ceased not the bloody fight for *ought;* . . . II. x. 51. 5
Ne *ought* save perill still as he did pas: . . . II. xii. 2. 3
if *ought* with Eden mote compayre. . . . II. xii. 52. 9
Ne *ought* that did to his advauncement tend; . . . II. xii. 80. 6
Ne *ought* their goodly workmanship might save Them . . . II. xii. 83. 3
Ne *ought* the more their mightie strokes surceasse. . . . III. i. 23. 2
The noble corage never weeneth *ought* . . . III. ii. 10. 4
Therein discovered was, ne *ought* mote pas, . . . III. ii. 19. 6
Ne *ought* in secret from the same remaynd; . . . III. ii. 19. 7
ne *ought* my flame relent, . . . III. ii. 43. 4
Ne *ought* it mote the noble Mayd avayle, . . . III. ii. 52. 1
As if *ought* in this world . . . Were from him hidden, . . . III. iii. 15. 4
Ne *ought* ye want but skil, . . . III. iii. 53. 8
ne her right course for *ought* forsooke. . . . III. iv. 44. 9
When she for *ought* him sharpely did reprove, . . . III. vi. 11. 7
least *ought* did ill betide To that faire Maide, . . . III. vii. 31. 4
if *ought* algate Might fayrer be. . . . III. viii. 9. 5
Ne *ought* your burning fury mote abate; . . . III. viii. 28. 7
ought your goodly patience offend, . . . III. ix. 1. 5
Ne ever is he wont on *ought* to feed But todes and frogs, . . III. x. 59. 1
as bad as she, and worse, if worse *ought* were. . . . III. xi. 3. 9
Ne *ought* but deare Bisaltis ay could make him glad. . . . III. xi. 41. 9
if that *ought* doe death exceed; . . . III. xii. 35. 3
if *ought* he did offend. . . . III. xii. 36. 9
old and crooked and not good for *ought.* . . . IV. ii. 3. 5
That chaleng'd *ought* in Florimell, . . . IV. ii. 28. 9
For *ought* that Glauce could or doe or say. . . . IV. v. 31. 6
This hand may helpe, or succour *ought* supplie, . . . IV. vi. 8. 7
Shall death be th' end, or *ought* else worse, aread?' . . . IV. vii. 11. 4
Ne *ought* mote make him change his wonted tenor, . . . IV. vii. 47. 3
Ne *ought* mote ease or mitigate his paine, . . . IV. vii. 47. 4
For *ought* will from his greedie pleasure spare: . . . IV. viii. 29. 8
ne would for *ought* Consent . . . IV. viii. 58. 5
Ne lend an eare to *ought* that might behove. . . . IV. ix. 31. 4

Aught—*Continued.*
For *ought* that ever she could doe or say; . . . IV. x. 15. 2
Ne ever *ought* but of their true loves talkt, . . . IV. x. 25. 8
Ne *ought* on earth that merry is and glad, . . . IV. x. 47. 3
Ne *ought* on earth that lovely is and fayre, . . . IV. x. 47. 4
ought more hard, then thinke to reckon right. . . . IV. xi. 53. 3
If *ought* lay hidden in his grieved thought, . . . IV. xii. 24. 8
Ne would for *ought* obay, as did become, . . . V. i. 29. 3
Ne *ought* the water cooled their whot bloud, . . . V. ii. 13. 3
make him cease for *ought.* . . . V. ii. 22. 9
If *ought* he had the same to counterpoys; . . . V. ii. 30. 6
Ne is the earth the lesse, or loseth *ought,* . . . V. ii. 39. 6
nought they could him hurt, ne *ought* dismay: . . . V. ii. 53. 4
ne *ought* he sayd, Ne *ought* he did, . . . V. iii. 18. 5, 6
Ne of that goodly hew remayned *ought,* . . . V. iii. 24. 8
he ne would For *ought* or nought be wonne . . . V. iv. 30. 6
'Can dread of *ought* your dreadlesse hart withhold, . . . V. v. 31. 2
to talke of *ought,* Or *ought* to heare . . . V. vi. 21. 1, 2
ne would undressed be for *ought,* . . . V. vi. 23. 4
Ne feed on *ought* the which . . . V. vii. 10. 2
Can from th' immortall Gods *ought* hidden bee? . . . V. vii. 21. 6
Could *ought* on earth so wondrous change . . . V. vii. 40. 6
Could so great courage stouped have to *ought?* . . . V. vii. 40. 8
Ne once for *ought* . . . V. viii. 6. 3
Ne *ought* avayled . . . V. ix. 15. 8
Nor of *ought* else . . . V. ix. 28. 3
Is *ought* on earth so pretious . . . V. xi. 62. 6
is *ought* so bright And beautifull . . . V. xi. 62. 7
Ne *ought* dismayed was Sir Calidore, . . . VI. i. 32. 4
for feare Of . . . *ought* that might befall: . . . VI. ii. 35. 4
Fearlesse who *ought* did thinke or ought did say, . . . VI. iii. 16. 5
When *ought* he did, that did their lyking gaine. . . . VI. iv. 16. 5
ne marvaile *ought,* For that same beast was bred . . . VI. vi. 9. 6
she thereto nould plead, nor answere *ought,* . . . VI. vii. 36. 3
far from being *ought* amazed, . . . VI. viii. 26. 8
Fearelesse of *ought* that mote . . . VI. viii. 34. 7
Ne *ought* was tyred . . . Ne *ought* was feared . . . VI. viii. 47. 3, 4
With which none had to doe, ne *ought* partake, . . . VI. xi. 12. 4
Would not for *ought* be drawne . . . VI. xi. 35. 6
Ne yielded *ought* for favour or for feare; . . . VII. vi. 12. 4
Ne *ought* he said, what ever he did heare, . . . VII. vi. 49. 8
never *ought* was excellent assayde Which was not hard. . . . *Am.* li. 7
Ne *ought* so hard, but he, . . . Mote soften it . . . *Am.* li. 9
Ne *ought* for tempest doth from it depart, . . . *Am.* lix. 7
Ne *ought* for fayrer weathers false delight. . . . *Am.* lix. 8
T' accuse of pride, or rashly blame for *ought.* . . . *Am.* lxi. 4
Ne *ought* so strong that may his force withstand, . . . *H.L.* 229
Ne *ought* demaunds but that we loving bee, . . . *H.H.L.* 185
Ne can on earth compared be to *ought.* . . . *H.H.B.* 210
Ne *ought* on earth can want unto the wight . . . *H.H.B.* 244
Augment. Whose streames my tricklinge teares did ofte *augment.* *S.C.* Au. 156
'Resort of people doth my greefs *augment,* . . . *S.C.* Au. 157
all that may *augment* My doole, . . . *S.C.* Au. 164
so shall I not *augment* With sight of such . . . *S.C.* Au. 171
so let your yrksome yells *augment.* . . . *S.C.* Au. 178
the more *taugment* The memory of hys misdeede . . . *S.C.* Au. 185
breake your sounder sleepe, And pitie *augment.'* . . . *S.C.* Au. 192
daylie more *augment* Through his fine feates . . . *Hub.* 691
rather seekes my sorrow to *augment* . . . *T.M.* 425
Which daily more and more he did *augment,* . . . *As.* 19
to *augment* her painefull penaunce more, . . . I. iii. 14. 1
to *augment* the glorie of his guile, His dearest love, . . . I. iv. 42. 1
She wilfully her sorrow did *augment,* . . . II. i. 15. 2
more to *augment* his spight, . . . II. v. 22. 5
rather doth my helpelesse griefe *augment;* . . . III. ii. 43. 5
So striving each did other more *augment,* . . . III. v. 55. 6
did the more *augment* His mighty rage, . . . III. xi. 26. 6
Till thou cam'st hither to *augment* our mone; . . . IV. vii. 13. 8
evermore their malice did *augment;* . . . IV. ix. 25. 6
He gan his earnest fervour to *augment,* . . . V. ix. 46. 8
their disgraces Did much the more *augment,* . . . V. xii. 28. 9
gan t' *augment* her bitternesse much more; . . . VI. i. 32. 2
outward salves that may *augment* it more.' . . . VI. vi. 13. 4
much *augment* her doole . . . VI. vii. 39. 9
they gan *augment* Their cruelty, . . . VI. viii. 4. 6
Which she did more *augment* with modest grace . . . VI. ix. 9. 3
ne wish for more it to *augment,* . . . VI. ix. 20. 4
So for to quench his fire he did it more *augment.* . . . VI. ix. 34. 9
daily more her favour to *augment;* . . . VI. x. 37. 2
The more t' *augment* her price through praise of comlinesse. . VI. xi. 11. 9
dayly more *augment* my miseryes? . . . *Am.* xxxvi. 8
Then doe I more *augment* my foes despight; . . . *Am.* xliv. 10
to *augment* the anguish of my smart, . . . *H.L.* 145
Augmented. all the rest her dolefull din *augmented* . . . *T.M.* 357
Trebly *augmented* was his furious mood . . . I. xi. 22. 7
that *augmented* all her other prayse, . . . IV. ii. 35. 7
much *augmented* all their other praise; . . . IV. ii. 54. 3
the seas by her are most *augmented:* . . . IV. xii. 2. 3
'Likewise the earth is not *augmented* more . . . V. ii. 40. 1
The more she still *augmented* her owne smart, . . . V. v. 28. 4
she sternely bade His miserie to be *augmented* more, . . . V. v. 54. 6
feele my flames *augmented* manifold! . . . *Am.* xxx. 8
Augmenteth. all the more my sorrow it *augmenteth,* . . . *Am.* xlii. 3
August. The sixt was *August,* being rich arrayd . . . VII. vii. 37. 1
Augustine. Serving th' ambitious will of *Augustine,* . . . III. iii. 35. 3
Augustus. great *Augustus* long ygoe is dead, . . . *S.C.* O. 62
We now have playde (*Augustus*) wantonly, . . . *Gn.* 1
Augustus'. Mecaenas, . . . It first advaunst to great *Augustus* grace, . . . *Ded. Son.* xiii. 4
Aumayld. *See* **Ameled.**

Aurelius. Thenceforth *Aurelius* peaceably did rayne, ... II. x. 67. 7
Aurora. fayre *Aurora,* with her rosie heare, ... *Gn.* 68
As faire *Aurora* . . . the dawning day doth call. . . . . . I. iv. 16. 4
fayre *Aurora* from the deawy bed Of aged Tithone . . . . . I. xi. 51. 2
As fayre *Aurora,* rysing hastily, ... III. iii. 20. 4
fresh *Aurora* had the shady damp . . . amoved . . . . . III. x. 1. 3
Ausonian. Along the bancks of the *Ausonian* streame: . . . . *Bel.*[2] v. 4
th' *Ausonian* light might be restor'd! . . . . . *Ro.* xxv. 8
Authentical. Under the Sea-gods seale *autenticall,* . . . . . IV. xii. 32. 2
Author. Phoebus, shall be the *author* of my song, ... *Gn.* 15
To be the *author* of her ill unwares, ... *Gn.* 631
The Foxe, first *Author* of that treacherie, ... *Hub.* 1379
The foe of faire things, th' *author* of confusion, ... *Mui.* 244
To patronize the *authour* of their praise, ... *Ded. Son.* iv. 10
'The *author* then,' . . . 'of all my smarts, Is one Duessa, . . . I. ii. 34. 7
The *authour* of this fact we here behold, ... I. ix. 37. 7
His owne woes *author,* who so bound it findes, ... II. v. 1. 8
That am the *authour* of this hainous deed, ... II. vi. 33. 8
As *author* of unjustice, there to let him dye. . . . . . II. vii. 60. 9
th' *Author* selfe could not at least attend To finish it: . . . . II. x. 68. 5
the first *author* of all Elfin kynd; . . . . . II. x. 71. 2
th' *authour* of all woman kynd; . . . . . II. x. 71. 7
their chiefe and th' *authour* of that strife: . . . . . II. xi. 16. 8
th' *authour* of life and light; . . . . . III. vi. 9. 2
The enimy of peace, and *authour* of all strife. . . . . . III. vi. 14. 9
heaven, first *author* of my languishment, ... IV. viii. 16. 5
That was the *author* of her punishment; . . . . . IV. xii. 16. 3
on his Lady, th' *author* of that wrong, ... V. viii. 24. 8
As th' onely *author* of her wofull tine; . . . . . VI. viii. 33. 3
the *author* of thy bale to be, ... VI. x. 29. 4
to arrest The *Author,* and him bring before his presence prest. VII. vi. 16. 9
th' *author* of my blisse, ... *Am.* xxii. 9
the *author* of their balefull bane: . . . . . *H.L.* 128
Lift up thy mind to th' *Author* of thy weale, ... *H.H.L.* 256
Authority. Then gan *Authority* her to appose . . . . . V. ix. 44. 1
obtain'd Great power of Jove, and high *authority:* . . . . . VII. vi. 3. 2
Author's. deedes ought not be scand By th' *authors* manhood, . V. xi. 17. 4
Authors. His chiefest letts and *authors* of his harmes, ... II. xi. 31. 3
Autonoe. Cymodoce, and stout *Autonoe,* . . . . . IV. xi. 50. 6
Autumn. Then came the *Autumne* all in yellow clad, ... VII. vii. 30. 1
Avail. the welked Phoebus gan *availe* His weary waine; . . . . *S.C.* Ja. 73
froward fortune doth ever *availe:* . . . . . *S.C.* S. 251
thing on earth that is of most *availe,* . . . . . *S.C.* N. 87
would he further none but for *availe;* (**a vaile*) *Hub.*1204
rip up griefe where it may not *availe:* . . . . . I. vii. 39. 8
litle may such guile thee now *avayl,* . . . . . II. v. 5. 8
bids them nought *availe.* . . . . . II. viii. 35. 9
Ne ought it mote the noble Mayd *avayle,* . . . . . III. ii. 52. 1
Ne shall *availe* the wicked sorcery . . . . . III. iii. 36. 3
Where force might not *availe,* there sleights . . . . . III. xii. 28. 1
nought did then *availe* . . . . . V. ii. 24. 5
Life, freedome, grace, and gifts of great *availe,* . . . . . V. v. 49. 3
Gainst which no flight nor rescue mote *avayle,* . . . . . V. xi. 59. 5
Ne ought it mote *availe* her to entreat . . . . . VI. vii. 40. 1
no skill of Leaches art Mote him *availe,* . . . . . VI. x. 31. 6
when the Beast saw he mote nought *availe* By force, ... VI. xii. 33. 1
Availe. *See* **Avale.**
Availed. pumie stones I . . . threwe; but nought *availed:* . . . *S.C.* Mar. 90
his bright shield that nought him now *avayld;* . . . . . II. xi. 41. 8
shun his mightie strokes, gainst which no armes *avayled.* . . IV. vi. 12. 9
Ne ought *avayled* for the armed knight To thinke to follow him V. ix. 15. 8
Availeth. O! what now *availeth* that I was? . . . . . I. ii. 22. 6
Avails. 'O! what *availes* it of immortall seed To beene ybredd . III. iv. 38. 1
He to them calles and speakes, yet nought *avayles;* . . . . . V. viii. 39. 7
Avale. when his later spring gins to *avale,* . . . . . I. i. 21. 5
from their sweaty Coursers did *avale,* . . . . . II. ix. 10. 7
Ruffed of love, gan lowly to *availe;* . . . . . III. ii. 27. 2
Eftsoones out of her Coch she gan *availe,* . . . . . IV. iii. 46. 4
the glaive . . . He gan forthwith t' *avale,* . . . . . IV. x. 19. 9
could so meekly make proud hearts *avale,* . . . . . VI. viii. 25. 3
Avales. but now it *avales.* . . . . . *S.C.* F. 8
Avantage, Avauntage. *See* **Advantage.**
Avarice. greedy *Avarice* by him did ride, ... I. iv. 27. 1
Such one was *Avarice,* the fourth of this faire band. . . . . I. iv. 29. 9
avarice gan through his veines inspire . . . . . II. vii. 17. 8
Through *avarice,* or powre, or guile, or strife, ... V. xi. 1. 3
Avaunt. backstarting with disdainefull yre Bad him *avaunt,* . V. xi. 61. 6
Sternely did bid him quickely thence *avaunt,* . . . . . VI. vi. 21. 2
Avaunting. To him *avaunting* in great bravery, ... II. iii. 6. 3
Ave Mary. He strowd an *Ave-Mary* after and before. . . . . . I. i. 35. 9
Avenge. chose with scornfull shame Him to *avenge,* . . . . . *Hub.* 1240
In great *avenge* did roll downe from his hill . . . . . *Col.* 149
Avenge thy selfe on them for their abuses. . . . . . *Col.* 794
Whom to *avenge* she had this Knight from far compeld. . . . I. i. 5. 9
Or else goe them *avenge,* . . . . . I. v. 24. 3
shame t' *avenge* so weake an enimy; . . . . . I. viii. 45. 8
Him to *avenge* before his blood were cold, ... I. ix. 37. 5
boystrous battaile make, each other to *avenge.* . . . . . I. xi. 21. 9
He cast at once him to *avenge* for all; . . . . . I. xi. 40. 6
them conjure t' *avenge* this shamefull injury. . . . . . I. xii. 27. 9
Which to *avenge* he to this place me led, ... II. i. 30. 7
taught T' *avenge* his Parents death . . . . . II. iii. 2. 9
Which to *avenge* on him they dearly vowd, ... II. viii. 11. 1
Which to *avenge* the Palmer him forth drew . . . . . II. ix. 9. 7
Whose death t' *avenge,* his mother mercilesse, ... II. x. 35. 6
Avenge his fathers losse with speare and shield, ... III. iii. 31. 8
on their Paynim foes *avenge* their ranckled ire. . . . . . III. iii. 36. 9
with fell cruelty In their *avenge* . . . . . III. iii. 46. 9
cast t' *avenge* him of that fowle despight . . . . . III. v. 15. 3
to *avenge* his divelish despight, ... III. vii. 28. 7
Avenge—*Continued.*
to *avenge* the implacable wrong . . . . . III. vii. 35. 5
How to *avenge* himselfe so sore abusd, ... III. ix. 12. 8
Why doth mine hand from thine *avenge* abstaine, ... IV. i. 52. 7
both were bent t' *avenge* his usage base, ... IV. iv. 4. 7
Which to *avenge* Sir Devon him did dight, ... IV. iv. 21. 1
cast t' *avenge* his friends indignity. . . . . . IV. iv. 28. 5
cast t' *avenge* the shame doen to his freend: . . . . . IV. vi. 45. 2
to that *avenge* by you decreed . . . . . IV. vi. 8. 6
He doth *avenge* on Sanglier His Ladies bloud . . . . . V. i. Arg.
T' *avenge* that shame they did on him commit, ... V. iv. 39. 4
whose untimely fate For to *avenge,* . . . . . V. vi. 33. 7
With full intent t' *avenge* that villany . . . . . V. vi. 35. 4
t' *avenge* him selfe againe . . . . . V. xi. 8. 3
Will it *avenge,* and pay thee with thy right; . . . . . VI. i. 25. 8
as it were t' *avenge* his wrath on mee, ... VI. ii. 22. 1
I may *avenge* him of so foule despight.' . . . . . VI. ii. 42. 6
greedy to *avenge* that vile despight, ... VI. iii. 45. 7
him *avenge* of that so villenous despight. . . . . . VI. iv. 3. 9
avenge th' abuses of that proud And shamefull Knight . . . VI. v. 34. 3
For to *avenge* in time convenient, ... VI. vii. 4. 7
this wrongfull deed, That we may it *avenge,* . . . . . VI. vii. 5. 9
Thought sure t' *avenge* his grudge, ... VI. ix. 43. 9
make the matter to *avenge* her yre: . . . . . *Am.* xlviii. 2
Avenged. be *aveng'd* on those that breed thy blame.' . . . . *Hub.* 1332
with harts on edge To be *aveng'd* each on his enimy. . . . . I. iv. 43. 4
Of all attonce he cast *avengd* to be, ... I. v. 12. 6
To be *avenged* of so great despight; . . . . . I. xi. 17. 6
till he *avenged* bee Of that despight, ... II. iii. 12. 7
For he has vowd to beene *avengd* that day . . . . . II. v. 38. 5
To be *avenged* of that shot whyleare; . . . . . II. xi. 25. 3
To bene *avenged* of the shame he did . . . . . III. v. 13. 5
Fit time t' awaite *avenged* for to bee. . . . . . IV. v. 9. 6
started up *avenged* for to be . . . . . IV. v. 44. 6
Brutus warlicke sonne, Locrinus, them *aveng'd,* . . . . . IV. xi. 38. 2
To be *avenged* for so fowle a deede, ... V. vi. 31. 2
gan eftsoones devize to be *aveng'd* for it. . . . . . V. viii. 45. 9
be *aveng'd* of their unknightly play. . . . . . V. x. 36. 4
That he could not thereof *avenged* bee; . . . . . VI. iii. 43. 6
To be *aveng'd* on him and to devoure his corse. . . . . . VI. iv. 20. 9
He gan devize to be *aveng'd* anew . . . . . VI. vii. 2. 6
Avengeful. through Joves *avengefull* wrath, ... *T.M.* 8
Frame thunderbolts for Joves *avengefull* threate. . . . . . IV. v. 37. 4
With curses vaine in his *avengefull* ire; . . . . . IV. viii. 40. 3
The piercing points of his *avengefull* darts; . . . . . *H.L.* 30
From the just wrath of his *avengefull* threate . . . . . *H.H.B.* 150
Avengement. As in *avengement* of his heedles smart, ... *Gn.* 291
in *avengement* of his pride . . . . . *Gn.* 389
in *avengement* of their bold attempt, ... *Gn.* 577
the *avengement* for this shame . . . . . *Hub.* 1317
Nought may thee save from heavens *avengement.* . . . . . *Mui.* 240
Ne car'd for blood in his *avengement:* . . . . . I. iv. 34. 5
strife, and blood-shed, and *avengement,* . . . . . I. ix. 43. 4
did he wist not what in his *avengement.* . . . . . II. iv. 6. 9
hid His shamefull head from his *avengement* strong, ... III. v. 13. 8
The fearefull end of his *avengement* sad, ... III. v. 24. 4
In your *avengement* and despiteous rage, ... III. viii. 28. 6
enhaunce His haughtie courage to *avengement* (**advengement*) IV. iii. 8. 8
right hand In full *avengement* heaved up on hie, ... IV. viii. 43. 2
To fierce *avengement* of that womans pride, ... V. vi. 18. 7
With all their force to worke *avengement* strong . . . . . V. viii. 24. 6
Souldan . . . Sought onely slaughter and *avengement;* . . . . V. viii. 30. 5
slaine . . . by just *avengement* Of noble Tristram, ... VI. iii. 17. 3
greedily him griping his *avengement* stayd. . . . . . VI. v. 26. 9
Turnes him about with fell *avengement:* . . . . . VI. vi. 27. 7
Avenger. Him to the mercy of th' *avenger* lent. . . . . . *Mui.* 432
Avengeress. that cruell Queene *avengeresse,* . . . . . III. viii. 20. 6
Avenger's. He nigh them drew to stay th' *avengers* forse, . . V. iii. 30. 7
Avenge's. Did beare them both to fell *avenges* end, ... IV. ii. 15. 2
Avenging. You, whom my hard *avenging* destinie Hath made judge . . . . . I. i. 51. 8
O, how can . . . simple truth subdue *avenging* wrong! . . . . I. iii. 6. 5
ghosts . . . Have felt the bitter dint of his *avenging* blade. . I. vii. 47. 9
prouder vaunt that proud *avenging* boy Did soone pluck downe, I. ix. 12. 3
his *avenging* wrath to clemency incline. . . . . . I. x. 51. 9
To worken mischiefe, and *avenging* woe, ... II. i. 2. 2
direfull chaunce, armd with *avenging* fate, ... II. i. 44. 6
Threatning the point of her *avenging* blaed; . . . . . III. i. 63. 8
The instruments of his *avenging* yre. . . . . . *H.H.B.* 182
Aventine. Mount Viminall and *Aventine* doo meete. . . . . *Ro.* iv. 14
Aventred. her mortall speare She mightily *aventred* . . . . . III. i. 28. 7
his poynant speare he fierce *aventred* . . . . . IV. iii. 9. 1
Aventring. eft *aventring* his steele-headed launce, ... IV. vi. 11. 3
Avernus'. yawning gulfe of deepe *Avernus* hole. . . . . . I. v. 31. 3
Aves. thrise nine hundred *Aves* she was wont to say. . . . . I. iii. 13. 9
Aveugle's. If old *Aveugles* sonnes so evill heare? . . . . . I. v. 23. 7
let stay *Aveugles* sonne there . . . . . I. v. 44. 6
Aviewed. All which when Artegall . . . well *advewed,* . . . . V. viii. 20. 2
Avisd, Avise, Avizd, *etc.* *See* **Advise,** *etc.*
Avizefull. *See* **Adviceful.**
Avoid. May them *avoyde,* or remedie provide. . . . . . *Mui.* 224
Did fayre *avoide* the violence him nere: . . . . . I. viii. 7. 8
T' *avoide* the rash assault . . . . . II. v. 10. 3
Vyle rancor to *avoid* and cruel surquedry. . . . . . III. i. 13. 9
weene by warning to *avoyd* his fate? . . . . . III. iv. 27. 2
warily he did *avoide* the blow, ... III. v. 21. 6
That her sweet love his malice mote *avoyd,* . . . . . III. vi. 48. 7
to *avoyde* th' intollerable stowre, ... III. ix. 13. 1
to *avoide* the occasion of the ill: . . . . . VI. vi. 14. 2
Avoided. no'te *avoyded* be by earthly skill or powre. . . . . II. viii. 43. 9

Avoided—*Continued.*
was *avoided* quite, and throwne out privily. . . . . II. ix. 32. 9
when the Britonesse saw all the rest *Avoided* . . . . III. i. 58. 6
they *avoyded* were, and vainely by did slyde. . . . . IV. iii. 7. 9
Or warded, or *avoyded* and let goe, ... IV. iii. 17. 4
Did shun the proofe thereof, and it *avoyded* light. . . . . IV. viii. 44. 9
When all his strokes he saw *avoyded* quite, ... VI. viii. 14. 7
Avoids. The warie fowle . . . *avoydes* it, shunning light, ... IV. iii. 19. 6
Avon. *Avon* marched in more stately path, ... IV. xi. 31. 6
Avouch. 'That word shall I,' (said he) '*avouchen* good, ... I. x. 64. 8
Avoud. *See* **Avowed.**
Avoure. to make *avoure* Of the lewd words and deedes . . . . VI. iii. 48. 5
Avow. I *avow* to thee, Such wounded beast . . . I did not see, . II. iii. 33. 4
'Certes,' (then said the Prince) 'I God *avow*, ... II. ix. 7. 1
Then I *avow*, by this most sacred head . . . . III. ii. 33. 5
I *avow* to thee, by wrong or right . . . . III. ii. 46. 8
A table . . . I *avow* to hallow unto thee!' . . . . III. iv. 10. 9
I here *avow* thee never to forsake. . . . . III. v. 11. 8
Avowed. fie on Fortune, mine *avowed* foe, ... I. viii. 43. 3
The hasty heat of his *avowd* revenge delayd. . . . . II. vi. 40. 9
love *avowd* to other Lady late, ... II. vii. 50. 7
avow'd That fairest Amoret was his by right, ... IV. i. 10. 2
Nor hold from suite of his *avowed* quest, ... V. viii. 3. 2
avoud . . . He would avenge th' abuses . . . . VI. v. 34. 1
Avowing. In death *avowing* th' innocence of her sonne. . . . . I. v. 39. 3
Avyse. *See* **Advise.**
Await. thousand perills lie in close *awaite* . . . . *Mui.* 221
lurking closely, in *awayte* now lay, ... *Mui.* 247
Awaite whereto their service he applyes, ... I. i. 38. 4
death him did *awaite* in daily wretchednesse. . . . . I. xii. 33. 9
closely did *awayt* Avauntage, ... II. v. 9. 6
Forgets with wary warde them to *awayt*, ... II. viii. 42. 3
To thinke how supper did them long *awaite*: . . . . II. x. 77. 7
They battred day and night, and entraunce did *awate*. . . . . II. xi. 6. 9
for your ruine at the last *awayt*.' . . . . II. xii. 29. 4
themselves they set There in *await* . . . . III. v. 17. 7
thousand perills which them still *awate*, ... IV. iii. 1. 5
Fit time t' *awaite* avenged for to bee. . . . . IV. v. 9. 6
Delay in close *awaite* . . . . IV. x. 14. 5
drew him on with hope fit leasure to *awayt*. . . . . V. v. 42. 9
Yet to *awayt* fit time she weened best, ... V. v. 44. 8
The Briton Prince him readie did *awayte*, ... V. viii. 29. 3
They in *awayt* would closely him ensnarle, ... V. ix. 9. 3
He watcht in close *awayt* with weapons prest, ... VI. vi. 44. 3
the foole, which did that end *awayte*, Came running in; . . . VI. viii. 11. 1
the Spyder, that doth lurke In close *awayt*, ... *Am.* lxxi. 4
at her chamber dore *awayt*, ... *Epith.* 52
T' *awayt* the comming of your joyous make, ... *Epith.* 87
Let all the virgins therefore well *awayt*: . . . . *Epith.* 111
Awaited. him *awaited* still with pensive mynd. . . . . I. x. 68. 3
occasion . . . he long *awaited* had in vayne, ... II. i. 5. 3
warily *awaited* day and night, ... II. vii. 32. 3
them *awaited* ready at the ford The Ferriman, ... II. xi. 4. 1
them *awayted* there a certaine space, ... III. i. 19. 4
Awayted there for Britomarts returne, ... III. xii. 45. 2
Where groomes *awayted* her to have undrest; . . . . V. vi. 23. 3
Awaiting. the hot Syrian Dog on him *awayting*, ... *Hub.* 5
early foe *awaiting* him beside To have devourd, ... I. xi. 52. 4
awaiting shortly to obtayn Thy carcas . . . . II. vi. 28. 8
Awaiting passage which him late did faile; . . . . II. vi. 40. 7
Awayting to entrap the warelesse wight . . . . IV. x. 20. 8
The Sarazin, *awayting* for some spoile: . . . . V. ii. 11. 3
Awaits. Guyon . . . The Redcrosse knight *awaytes*; . . . . II. i. Arg.
Awake. *See* **Wake.**
For to *awake* out of th' infernall shade . . . . *Ro.* xxv. 2
Tho will we little Love *awake*, ... *S.C.* Mar. 22
My courage earnd it to *awake*, ... *S.C.* Mar. 77
Warnd him *awake*, from death himselfe to keep. . . . . *Gn.* 288
If he *awake*, yet is not death the next, ... *Hub.* 987
out of dust their memories *awake*? . . . . *T.M.* 450
shepheards boy, at length *awake* for shame! . . . . *Ti.* 231
Awake, and to his Song a part applie: . . . . *Ti.* 236
my sleepie Muse, *awake*; . . . . *Col.* 48
He bad *awake* blacke Plutoes griesly Dame; . . . . I. i. 37. 4
So sound he slept, that nought mought him *awake*. . . . . I. i. 42. 3
the dreadfull passion Was overpast, and manhood well *awake*, I. ii. 32. 2
Whom broad *awake* she findes, in troublous fitt, ... I. iv. 45. 1
Out of his swowning dreame he gan *awake*; . . . . I. v. 12. 2
ere he could out of his swowne *awake*, ... I. vii. 15. 7
'Dear Dame,' (quoth he) 'you sleeping sparkes *awake*, ... I. ix. 8. 1
The sparke of noble corage now *awake*, ... I. xi. 2. 6
The God of warre . . . Thou doest *awake*, ... I. xi. 6. 8
That nothing should him hastily *awake*. . . . . II. vi. 18. 4
Out of her quiet slomber did *awake*, ... III. i. 61. 8
O let them soone *awake*! . . . . III. iv. 2. 2
Out of her heavie swowne not to *awake* . . . . III. vi. 27. 8
the good Sir Satyrane gan *awake* . . . . III. vii. 45. 1
To gin *awake*, and stir his frosen spright: . . . . III. viii. 23. 5
none him durst *awake* out of his dreme; . . . . III. ix. 10. 6
her for to *awake* he did the more constraine. . . . . III. x. 49. 9
With busie care they strove him to *awake*, ... IV. i. 43. 6
Seem'd to *awake* in horrible dismay, ... V. vii. 15. 3
Love, that long hath slept . . . Wils him *awake*, ... *Am.* iv. 7
griefe renew, and passions doe *awake* . . . . *Am.* xliv. 11
in her winters bowre not well *awake*; . . . . *Am.* lxx. 6
Doe ye *awake*; . . . . *Epith.* 22
Bid her *awake*; for Hymen is *awake*, ... *Epith.* 25
Bid her *awake* therefore, ... *Epith.* 30
Wake now, my love, *awake*! . . . . *Epith.* 74
When meeter were that ye should now *awake*, ... *Epith.* 86

Awake—*Continued.*
My love is now *awake* out of her dreames, ... *Epith.* 92
Awaked. Who, with the noyse *awaked*, commeth out . . . . I. vi. 14. 6
Sir Guyon from his traunce *awakt*, ... II. viii. 53. 1
As one *awakte* out of long slombring shade, ... II. xi. 31. 7
thought he yet did dreame Not well *awakte*; . . . . III. viii. 22. 8
upstarted . . . As men *awaked* rashly out of dreme, ... IV. ii. 17. 2
he was soone *awaked* therewithall, ... IV. v. 42. 5
Awaking. her *awaking* bad her quickly dight, ... *Ti.* 639
now *awaking*, fierce at them gan fly, ... II. xii. 84. 6
awaking, well they kent That their fayre guest was gone, . . III. vii. 19. 7
Whereat the Prince *awaking*, ... VI. vii. 25. 1
the theefe *awaking* light Unto the entrance ran; . . . . VI. xi. 43. 4
Award. terrifie from Fortunes faire *adward*: . . . . IV. x. 17. 5
death t' *adward* I ween'd did appertaine . . . . IV. xii. 30. 4
Aware. Thereby to coosin men not well *aware*: . . . . *Hub.* 874
ere ye be *aware* will flit away; . . . . *D.* 502
'Be well *aware*,' quoth then that Ladie milde, ... I. i. 12. 1
ere one be *aware*, by secret stealth His powre is reft, ... I. ix. 31. 7
right well *aware* To shonne the engin . . . . II. xi. 36. 2
ere well he was *aware*, ... III. i. 6. 6
downe him smot ere well *aware* he weare; . . . . III. i. 28. 8
Therefore, faire Damzell, be ye well *aware*, ... III. ii. 10. 6
Scudamour was shortly well *aware* Of his approch, ... IV. i. 41. 4
But he was well *aware*, and leapt before his fall. . . . . V. ii. 12. 9
he was soone *aware* of their ill minde, ... V. iv. 24. 1
never yet was wight so well *aware*, ... V. vi. 1. 8
Artegall, being thereof *aware*, ... V. viii. 48. 1
Whereof when as the Gyant was *aware*, ... V. xi. 9. 5
onely wexed now the more *aware* . . . . V. xi. 13. 2
Ere they were well *aware* of living wight, ... VI. iii. 21. 2
Whereof whenas the Prince was well *aware*, ... VI. vi. 27. 1
Be well *aware* how ye the same doe use, ... VI. viii. 1. 6
he, right well *aware*, his rage to ward . . . . VI. xii. 30. 1
weaker harts, which are not wel *aware*? . . . . *Am.* xxxvii. 8
Awarned. bird and beast *awarned* made To shrowd themselves, III. x. 46. 8
Awate. *See* **Await.**
Away. *See* **Wela-way.**
all their teares he shall wipe cleane *away*. . . . . *Rev.* iv. 7
Sudden both Palme and Olive fell *away*, ... *Bel.*[2] ix. 13
Threw down the seats, and drove the Nymphes *away*. . . . *Bel.*[2] xii. 14
each thing at last we see Doth passe *away*: . . . . *Pet.* v. 8
That which is firme doth flit and fall *away*, ... *Ro.* iii. 13
Forst with the filth his egs to fling *away*: . . . . *Van.* iv. 12
That winde nor tide could move her thence *away*. . . . . *Van.* ix. 12
With breathed sighes is blowne *away* . . . . *S.C.* Ja. 40
Therewith affrayd, I ranne *away*; . . . . *S.C.* Mar. 94
ranne *awaye* with him in all hast. . . . . *S.C.* May 293
Those weary wanton toyes *away* dyd wype, ... *S.C.* Jun. 48
For liker bene they to pluck *away* more, ... *S.C.* S. 128
when as Lowder was farre *awaye*, ... *S.C.* S. 196
One bitter blast blewe all *away*. . . . . *S.C.* N. 119
'Thus is my sommer worne *away* . . . . *S.C.* D. 97
my hope *away* dyd wipe. . . . . *S.C.* D. 108
All was blowne *away* of the wavering wynd. . . . . *S.C.* D. 126
Which are from Indian seas brought far *away*; . . . . *Gn.* 106
holding guilefully *away* Ulysses men, ... *Gn.* 194
Out of the land is fled *away* . . . . *Gn.* 360
from my beard the fat *away* have swept; . . . . *Hub.* 78
They stole *away*, and tooke their hastie flight, ... *Hub.* 339
Now all those needlesse works are laid *away*; . . . . *Hub.* 455
ran *away* by night. . . . . *Hub.* 574
Now the nigh aymed ring *away* to beare. . . . . *Hub.* 742
with his wicked charmes . . . he would it drive *away*, . . . *Hub.* 827
Whose part once past all men bid take *away*: . . . . *Hub.* 932
But ran *away* in his rent rags by night, ... *Hub.* 937
And bad him put all cowardize *away*: . . . . *Hub.* 958
Those royall ornaments to steale *away*? . . . . *Hub.* 998
He all those royall signes had stolne *away*, ... *Hub.* 1016
For though to steale the Diademe *away* . . . . *Hub.* 1034
At sight of him, gan fast *away* to flye; . . . . *Hub.* 1069
So went the Sheepe *away* with heavie hart: . . . . *Hub.* 1222
From underneath his head he tooke *away*, ... *Hub.* 1322
Fled fast *away* from that so dreadfull din. . . . . *Hub.* 1348
He did uncase, and then *away* let flie: . . . . *Hub.* 1380
And his sweete waters *away* with him led. . . . . *Ti.* 147
That everie shower will wash and wipe *away*; . . . . *Ti.* 205
to bring *awaie* Out of dread darkenesse . . . . *Ti.* 375
Ne may with storming showers be washt *away*, ... *Ti.* 404
Admir'd of base-borne men from farre *away*: . . . . *Ti.* 424
With dolefull shrikes shee vanished *away*, ... *Ti.* 471
With showres of heaven and tempests worne *away*; . . . . *Ti.* 501
As with each storme does fall *away*, ... *Ti.* 514
I heard a voyce that called farre *away*, ... *Ti.* 638
From him would steale them privily *away*, ... *Mui.* 111
Was led *away* of them that did abuse her. . . . . *Mui.* 136
Grewe in this Gardin, fetcht from farre *away*, ... *Mui.* 202
snatcheth quite *away* One of the litle yonglings . . . . *Mui.* 406
Let him be banisht farre *away* from hence; . . . . *D.* 10
Like to some Pilgrim come from farre *away*. . . . . *D.* 42
And brought *away* fast bound with silver chaine. . . . . *D.* 119
'Out of the world thus was she reft *awaie*, ... *D.* 162
Revoked life, that would have fled *away*, ... *D.* 188
And through untimely tempest fall *away*! . . . . *D.* 238
'She fell *away* in her first ages spring, ... *D.* 239
She fell *away* against all course of kinde. . . . . *D.* 242
She fel *away* like fruit blowne downe with winde. . . . . *D.* 244
The whiles soft death *away* her spirit hent, ... *D.* 258
So having said, *away* she softly past: . . . . *D.* 293
'The good and righteous he *away* doth take, ... *D.* 358

Away—*Continued.*

my Daphne they have tane *away*; . . . *D.* 365
They tarrie not, but flit and fall *away*, . . . *D.* 397
because, all times doo flye So fast *away*, . . . *D.* 412
And pine *away* in selfe-consuming paine! . . . *D.* 436
But ere ye be aware will flit *away*; . . . *D.* 502
all mens hearts . . . He stole *away*, . . . *As.* 22
When Astrophel so ever was *away*. . . . *As.* 30
every field and forest far *away* . . . *As.* 81
In forreine soyle pursued far *away*, . . . *As.* 92
From her red cheeks the roses rent *away*; . . . *As.* 160
without harme us farre *away* did beare, . . . *Col.* 225
Nought else but smoke, and fumeth soone *away*. . . . *Col.* 720
Behind her farre away a Dwarfe did lag, . . . I. i. 6. 1
A shadie grove not farr *away* they spide, . . . I. i. 7. 2
That nigh his manly hart did melt *away*, . . . I. i. 47. 5
so both *away* do fly. . . . I. ii. 6. 9
her knight, who far *away* was fled, . . . I. ii. 7. 7
for feare would quake, And oft would flie *away*. . . . I. ii. 10. 8
The true Saint George, was wandred far *away*, . . . I. ii. 12. 2
from him fled *away* with all her powre; . . . I. ii. 20. 4
to bring *away* The Sarazins shield, . . . I. ii. 20. 6
who perforce me led With him *away*, . . . I. ii. 25. 3
fly, ah! fly far hence *away*, . . . I. ii. 31. 4
in minde to slipp *away*, . . . I. ii. 41. 6
her pitcher downe she threw, And fled *away*: . . . I. iii. 11. 7
Whose needlesse dread for to remove *away*, . . . I. iii. 14. 6
Which doen *away*, He left him lying so, . . . I. iii. 39. 8
Have reft *away* with his sharp rending clawes: . . . I. iii. 41. 6
Beares her *away* upon his courser light: . . . I. iii. 43. 8
that still did flitt And fall *away*, . . . I. iv. 5. 6
from him snacht *away*: . . . I. iv. 39. 6
chace *away* sweet sleepe from sluggish eye, . . . I. iv. 44. 4
maid, *away* with him he bare, . . . I. iv. 47. 7
To drive *away* the dull melancholy; . . . I. v. 3. 5
That would his rightfull ravine rend *away*: . . . I. v. 8. 5
The creeping deadly cold *away* did shake: . . . I. v. 12. 4
Did softly swim *away*, . . . I. v. 28. 6
from thence arose *away* The mother. . . . I. v. 44. 4
Good cause he had to hasten thence *away*; . . . I. v. 45. 6
Led her *away* into a forest wilde; . . . I. vi. 3. 2
Satyres far *away* Within the wood . . . I. vi. 7. 7
fast *away* gan ryde. . . . I. vi. 8. 9
feare to put *away*, . . . I. vi. 11. 8
pynd *away* in anguish . . . I. vi. 17. 9
fly *away* for feare of fowle disgrace; . . . I. vi. 18. 7
children deare, whom he *away* had wonne: . . . I. vi. 27. 7
turning backe gan fast to fly *away*; . . . I. vi. 28. 2
He led *away* with corage stout . . . I. vi. 33. 4
'Not far *away*,' (quoth he) . . . I. vi. 39. 7
the royall Mayd Fledd farre *away*, . . . I. vi. 47. 9
when he saw the Damsell passe *away*, . . . I. vi. 48. 5
His glitterand armour shined far *away*, . . . I. vii. 29. 4
leaving all behind her fled *away*: . . . I. viii. 25. 6
Ne let that wicked woman scape *away*; . . . I. viii. 28. 5
Duessa, when her borrowed light Is laid *away*, . . . I. viii. 49. 6
slombring soft my hart did steale *away*, . . . I. ix. 13. 6
would faine have runne *away*; . . . I. ix. 25. 3
Fledd fast *away*, halfe dead . . . I. ix. 30. 6
A dreary corse, whose life *away* did pas, . . . I. ix. 36. 5
'Come; come *away*, . . . I. ix. 53. 1
There was an auncient house not far *away*, . . . I. x. 3. 1
themselves to beare *away*, . . . I. x. 20. 7
The filthy blottes of sin to wash *away*. . . . I. x. 27. 7
To put *away* out of his carefull brest. . . . I. x. 29. 6
Which still before him she remov'd *away*, . . . I. x. 35. 4
clothes meet to keepe keene cold *away*, . . . I. x. 39. 4
The feeble soule departing hence *away*. . . . I. x. 41. 5
beare them quite *away*. . . . I. xi. 18. 9
guilt of sinfull crimes cleane wash *away*; . . . I. xi. 30. 2
That feared chaunce from her to turne *away*: . . . I. xi. 32. 5
To reave by strength the griped gage *away*: . . . I. xi. 41. 6
Whose false foundacion waves have washt *away*, . . . I. xi. 54. 6
wynd and weather call her thence *away*. . . . I. xii. 1. 9
widow-like sad wimple throwne *away*, . . . I. xii. 22. 3
precious odours fetcht from far *away*, . . . I. xii. 38. 4
To drive *away* the dull Melancholy; . . . I. xii. 38. 8
away is quickly gone To seeke that knight, . . . II. i. 13. 2
Of which he honour still *away* did beare, . . . II. i. 35. 3
take *away* this long lent loathed light: . . . II. i. 36. 7
Take not *away*, now got, which none would give to me.' . . . II. i. 47. 9
and ran *away* full light. . . . II. iii. 4. 9
but *away* Was suddein vanished . . . II. iii. 19. 1
Or fly *away*, or bide alone behinde; . . . II. iii. 32. 4
So turned her about, and fled *away* apace. . . . II. iii. 42. 9
all behinde was bald, and worne *away*, . . . II. iv. 4. 7
Approching, first the Hag did thrust *away*; . . . II. iv. 6. 2
he that last left helpe *away* did take, . . . II. iv. 13. 4
to flye Full fast *away*, . . . II. iv. 13. 7
washt *away* his guilt with guilty potion. . . . II. iv. 30. 9
She fled *away* with ghastly dreriment, . . . II. iv. 31. 8
The drops dry up, and filth wipe cleane *away*: . . . II. iv. 35. 8
far *away* they spyde A varlet ronning . . . II. iv. 37. 1
Eftsoones he fled *away*, . . . II. iv. 46. 9
marge Of his sevenfolded shield *away* it tooke, . . . II. v. 6. 3
So him *away* he drew . . . II. v. 25. 1
Fledd fast *away* to tell his funerall . . . II. v. 25. 8
and wypt *away* his toilsom sweat. . . . II. v. 30. 9
her shallow ship *away* did slide, . . . II. vi. 5. 1
It cut *away* upon the yielding wave, . . . II. vi. 5. 6
thereof nigh one quarter sheard *away*; . . . II. vi. 31. 4
all the blood and filth *away* was washt; . . . II. vi. 42. 8
a lamp, whose life does fade *away*, . . . II. vii. 29. 7
Had he so doen, he had him snatcht *away*, . . . II. vii. 34. 5
The life did flit *away* out of her nest, . . . II. vii. 66. 8
having laid his cruell bow *away* . . . II. viii. 6. 2
dread of death and dolor doe *away*; . . . II. viii. 7. 7
and vanisht quite *away*. . . . II. viii. 8. 9
That vertuous steele he rudely snatcht *away*, . . . II. viii. 22. 6
Resolv'd to put *away* that loathly blame, . . . II. viii. 44. 4
good knights,' (said he) 'fly fast *away*, . . . II. ix. 12. 1
blow them quite *away*, and in the Ocean cast. . . . II. ix. 16. 9
Others to beare the same *away* did mynd; . . . II. ix. 31. 8
turnd his face *away*, . . . II. ix. 44. 2
that great Lady thence *away* them sought . . . II. ix. 44. 6
to blazon far *away*. . . . II. x. 3. 9
overflowd all countries far *away*, . . . II. x. 15. 4
did *away* that blame . . . II. x. 23. 4
light goes out, and weeke is throwne *away*: . . . II. x. 30. 2
To purge *away* the guilt of sinfull crime. . . . II. x. 50. 4
Was by Maximian lately ledd *away*, . . . II. x. 62. 2
fast the land behynd them fled *away*. . . . II. xi. 4. 6
fled fast *away* for feare: . . . II. xi. 25. 6
That other Hag did far *away* espye . . . II. xi. 28. 8
His owne good sword . . . he lightly threw *away*, . . . II. xi. 41. 7
An hideous roring far *away* they heard, . . . II. xii. 2. 6
Throwing *away* her broken chaines . . . II. xi. 47. 4
all the seas for feare doe seeme *away* to fly. . . . II. xii. 3. 9
whom we must surprise, Els she will slip *away*, . . . II. xii. 69. 9
see soone after how she fades and falls *away*. . . . II. xii. 74. 9
Fled all *away* for feare of fowler shame. . . . II. xii. 81. 7
Then led they her *away*, . . . II. xii. 84. 1
A stately Castle far *away* she spyde, . . . III. i. 20. 2
and soone *away* is gone.' . . . III. i. 25. 9
So did she steale his heedelesse hart *away*, . . . III. i. 37. 1
With her soft garment wipes *away* the gore . . . III. i. 38. 5
Tho were the tables taken all *away*; . . . III. i. 56. 6
Of which they still the girlond bore *away*; . . . III. ii. 2. 4
sith they warlike armes have laide *away*: . . . III. ii. 2. 7
But sleepe full far *away* from her did fly: . . . III. ii. 28. 5
men their weary cares Do lay *away*, . . . III. ii. 32. 2
Therefore *away* doe dread; . . . III. ii. 33. 7
To doe the frosen cold *away* to fly; . . . III. ii. 34. 5
whylome by false Faries stolne *away*, . . . III. iii. 26. 6
And his last fate him from thee take *away*; . . . III. iii. 28. 7
Where far *away* one, all in armour bright, . . . III. iv. 12. 2
flowres and girlonds far *away* Shee flong, . . . III. iv. 30. 1
They softly wipt *away* the gelly blood . . . III. iv. 40. 6
To doe *away* vaine doubt . . . III. iv. 48. 7
chace *away* this too long lingring night; . . . III. iv. 60. 5
Chace her *away*, from whence she came, to hell: . . . III. iv. 60. 6
Carried *away* with wings of speedy feare.' . . . III. v. 6. 6
that fierce foster, which late fled *away*, . . . III. v. 18. 5
(So from her often he had fled *away*, . . . III. vi. 11. 6
Venus hers thence far *away* convayd, . . . III. vi. 28. 6
that faire flowre of beautie fades *away*, . . . III. vi. 38. 8
Yet flyes *away* of her owne feete afeard, . . . III. vii. 1. 3
No need to bid her fast *away* to flie: . . . III. vii. 24. 2
From peril free he *away* her (*her *away*) did beare; . . . III. vii. 24. 8
Hurling his sword *away* . . . III. vii. 33. 6
She bore him fast *away*. . . . III. vii. 43. 6
She threw *away* her burden angrily; . . . III. vii. 44. 2
made her selfe more light *away* to fly: . . . III. vii. 44. 4
I will *away* her beare.' . . . III. viii. 12. 9
without reskew led her quite *away*. . . . III. viii. 13. 5
To steale *away* that I with blowes have wonne, . . . III. viii. 17. 2
And with her fled *away* without abode. . . . III. viii. 19. 5
But Florimell her selfe was far *away*, . . . III. viii. 20. 1
both renowmed far *away*; . . . III. ix. 51. 2
away her wondring eye . . . her weake hart from her bore; . . . III. ix. 52. 6
To weet how he her love *away* did steale, . . . III. x. 5. 8
The which she meant *away* with her to beare; . . . III. x. 12. 5
he far *away* espide A couple, . . . III. x. 20. 6
Through open outrage he her bore *away*, . . . III. x. 27. 6
Hence farre *away* we will blyndfolded ly, . . . III. x. 42. 7
That hardly he with life *away* does fly, . . . III. x. 53. 8
And ran *away*, ran with his selfe *away*; . . . III. x. 54. 6
O! let him far be banished *away*, . . . III. xi. 2. 1
Ne yet by any meanes remov'd *away*; . . . III. xi. 23. 8
Which doen, he backe retyred soft *away*, . . . III. xii. 4. 7
That their report did far *away* rebound; . . . III. xii. 6. 7
he fast *away* did fly, . . . III. xii. 12. 5
Which first it opened, and bore all *away*. . . . III. xii. 27. 3
And put *away* remembrance of late teene; . . . III. xii. 40. 7
eke the Ladie selfe he brought *away*, . . . IV. i. 2. 7
Conveyed quite *away* to living wight unknowen. . . . IV. i. 3. 9
which sent *away* So many Centaures . . . IV. i. 23. 3
That one did reach the other pusht *away*; . . . IV. i. 29. 2
The whiles his love *away* the other bore, . . . IV. ii. 7. 3
Whom to thy selfe thou takest quite *away*? . . . IV. ii. 13. 7
To barre the prease of people farre *away*; . . . IV. iii. 4. 2
Broke up the listes, their armes *away* to rend; . . . IV. iii. 35. 4
Harts grief, and bitter gall *away* to chace, . . . IV. iii. 43. 3
Are washt *away* quite from their memorie. . . . IV. iii. 44. 7
Sternly stept forth and raught *away* his speare, . . . IV. iv. 20. 6
Or went *away* sore wounded . . . IV. iv. 21. 9
For to have rent his shield and armes *away*, . . . IV. iv. 31. 2
Cambello it *away* before had got. . . . IV. iv. 33. 5
Leading his friend *away*, . . . IV. iv. 33. 9

Away—*Continued.*

bore The prayse of prowesse from them all *away*. . . . . . . IV. iv. 48. 4
brought with her from thence that goodly belt *away*. . . . . IV. v. 5. 9
able was weake harts *away* to steale. . . . . IV. v. 10. 5
That she should surely beare the bell *away;* . . . . IV. v. 13. 6
it loos'd And fell *away,* . . . . IV. v. 16. 7
secretly from thence that night her bore *away*. . . . . IV. v. 27. 9
Not farre *away,* . . . They spide . . . . IV. v. 32. 8
farre *away* A Knight . . . they spyde, ... IV. vi. 9. 1
Her ventayle shard *away,* . . . . IV. vi. 19. 3
Fearing least she your loves *away* should woo: . . . . IV. vi. 30. 8
And stolne *away* from her beloved mate, ... IV. vi. 47. 7
through the forrest bore her quite *away,* . . . . IV. vii. 8. 2
I with that Squire agreede *away* to flit, ... IV. vii. 17. 6
now he her *away* with him did beare . . . . IV. vii. 24. 7
But fled *away* with ghastly dreriment, ... IV. vii. 29. 8
turnd her face, and fled *away* for evermore. . . . . IV. vii. 36. 9
weapons all he broke And threw *away,* . . . . IV. vii. 39. 2
Having espide this Cabin far *away,* . . . . IV. vii. 42. 5
have the sterne remembrance wypt *away* . . . . IV. viii. 1. 8
And pensive sorrow pind and wore *away,* . . . . IV. viii. 2. 6
flew *away* as lightly as the wind: . . . . IV. viii. 7. 7
With ready hand it to have reft *away;* . . . . IV. viii. 10. 6
And still from her escaping soft *away:* . . . . IV. viii. 11. 5
A litle cotage farre *away* they spide, ... IV. viii. 23. 2
And steale *away* the crowne of their good name: . . . . . . IV. viii. 25. 4
Shooting forth farre *away* two flaming streames, ... IV. viii. 39. 3
and killeth farre *away*. . . . . IV. viii. 39. 9
(so fast *away* he flew) . . . . IV. viii. 40. 4
snatcht him up and with me bore *away*. . . . . IV. viii. 61. 9
But have perforce him hether brought *away*.' . . . . IV. viii. 62. 5
farre *away* from these, ... IV. x. 26. 3
turn'd his face *away,* . . . . IV. x. 33. 4
The whilest their eldest brother was *away,* . . . . IV. x. 42. 6
to steale her thence *away,* . . . . IV. xii. 15. 1
He wist not how her thence *away* to bere, ... IV. xii. 15. 8
His cheared heart eftsoones *away* gan chace . . . . IV. xii. 34. 3
Out of their proper places farre *away,* . . . . V. Pr. 6. 6
Fro me reft mine *away* by lawlesse might, ... V. i. 17. 8
Not so to leave her, nor *away* to cast, ... V. i. 18. 3
So he my love *away* with him hath borne, ... V. i. 18. 8
Nor tooke *away* his love, ... V. i. 23. 9
Else he doth hold him backe or beat *away*. . . . . V. ii. 6. 5
That sure they ween'd she was escapt *away;* . . . . V. ii. 25. 2
the streame washt *away* her guilty blood. . . . . V. ii. 27. 5
He gives to this, from that he takes *away,* . . . . V. ii. 41. 8
But he the right from thence did thrust *away,* . . . . V. ii. 49. 1
Where they were leading Marinell *away;* . . . . V. iii. 11. 2
The glorious picture vanisheth *away,* . . . . V. iii. 25. 6
The whiles his guilefull groome was fled *away,* . . . . V. iii. 38. 1
The most part of my land hath washt *away,* . . . . V. iv. 8. 3
my land he first did winne *away,* . . . . V. iv. 14. 6
layd Unto your part, and pluckt from his *away,* . . . . . . V. iv. 17. 4
he spide A rout of many people farre *away;* . . . . V. iv. 21. 3
The badges of reproch, he threw *away,* . . . . V. iv. 35. 4
Her from the quarrey he *away* doth drive, ... V. iv. 42. 8
When thus the field was voided all *away,* . . . . V. iv. 46. 1
Halfe of her shield he shared quite *away,* . . . . V. v. 9. 2
they were fayne to let him scape *away,* . . . . V. v. 19. 3
Not farre *away,* . . . His dwelling was, ... V. vi. 22. 4
talk't of pleasant things the night *away* to weare. . . . . . V. vi. 22. 9
dawning light Bad doe *away* the dampe . . . . V. vii. 26. 8
loth to loose her right *away,* Doth . . . stoutly stond. . . . V. vii. 30. 5
Who still from him as fast *away* did flie, ... V. viii. 6. 2
From whom she earst so fast *away* did flie: . . . . V. viii. 16. 3
turne *away* From her unto the miscreant . . . . V. viii. 19. 5
him did beare So fast *away* that, ... V. viii. 33. 5
with their ryder ranne perforce *away:* . . . . V. viii. 38. 4
He up did take, and with him brought *away,* . . . . V. viii. 44. 3
to see her Ladie thence not farre *away*. . . . . V. ix. 3. 9
Which wonned in a rocke not farre *away,* . . . . V. ix. 4. 7
To turne her eyes from his intent *away;* . . . . V. ix. 13. 7
Ran with her fast *away* unto his mew, ... V. ix. 14. 5
He threw his burden downe, and fast *away* did fly. . . . . . V. ix. 14. 9
prickt him so that he *away* it threw: . . . . V. ix. 18. 6
Then ganne it runne *away* incontinent, ... V. ix. 18. 7
Seeking to drive *away* deepe-rooted dreede . . . . V. x. 22. 4
As fast as feete could carry them *away;* . . . . V. x. 36. 2
Streight th' other fled *away,* . . . . V. x. 37. 7
Durst not abide, but fled *away* for feare, ... V. x. 38. 3
That two more of his armes did fall *away,* . . . . V. xi. 11. 7
Her Lions clawes he from her feete *away* did wipe. . . . . . V. xi. 27. 9
farre *away,* . . . They spide a Lady . . . . V. xi. 44. 6
forced him to throw it quite *away,* . . . . V. xi. 46. 3
Like scattred chaffe the which the wind *away* doth fan. . . . V. xi. 47. 9
By open force to fetch her quite *away:* . . . . V. xi. 51. 2
bore her quite *away,* . . . . V. xi. 64. 9
whence he them chast *away,* . . . . V. xii. 5. 8
those which earst did fly *away* for feare, ... V. xii. 6. 5
sounded the retraite, and drew his folke *away*. . . . . V. xii. 9. 9
called was *away* To Faerie Court, ... V. xii. 27. 2
did steale mens hearts *away:* . . . . VI. i. 2. 6
they that Ladies lockes doe shave *away,* . . . . VI. i. 13. 8
With his long taile the bryzes brush *away*. . . . . VI. i. 24. 5
Therefore he wild her doe *away* all dread; . . . . VI. i. 31. 7
put *away* proud looke and usage sterne, ... VI. i. 40. 8
enchantment, that . . . did steale the hart *away*. . . . . . . VI. ii. 3. 4
A tall young man, from thence not farre *away,* . . . . VI. ii. 3. 7
'The widow Queene . . . Thought best *away* me to remove . VI. ii. 29. 7
to frolicke, and to put *away* The pensive fit . . . . VI. iii. 9. 2
And drove *away* the stound . . . . VI. iii. 10. 9

Away—*Continued.*

by outragious force *away* did beare: . . . . VI. iii. 18. 7
in his wide great mouth *away* her bare . . . . VI. iii. 24. 4
His weapons soone from him he threw *away,* . . . . VI. iii. 27. 6
and fled himselfe *away* for feare. . . . . VI. iv. 7. 9
From his soft eyes the teares he wypt *away,* . . . . VI. iv. 23. 4
Sir Calepine himselfe *away* had hidden it. . . . . VI. v. 8. 9
and sad dispaire *away* did cast. . . . . VI. v. 21. 9
Hath you thus long *away* from me bereft? . . . . VI. v. 23. 8
in all battels bore *away* the baies: . . . . VI. vi. 4. 5
therefore lightly bad him packe *away,* . . . . VI. vi. 21. 6
flying still did ward, and warding fly *away*. . . . . VI. vi. 28. 9
Those goodly armes, he them *away* did give, ... VI. vi. 36. 8
Thence he him brought *away,* . . . . VI. vi. 39. 7
The gentle Prince not farre *away* they spyde, ... VI. vii. 6. 7
Thence passing forth, not farre *away* he found . . . . VI. vii. 18. 6
they were *away* convayd? . . . . VI. vii. 34. 6
fled *away* with all the speede she mought, ... VI. vii. 50. 4
fled fast *away,* afeard . . . . VI. viii. 31. 4
Ne any will had thence to move *away,* . . . . VI. ix. 12. 2
the fayre mayd the table ta'ne *away,* . . . . VI. ix. 18. 2
I hunt the Fox, . . . and him dislodge *away;* . . . . VI. ix. 23. 2
did thrust it farre *away,* . . . . VI. ix. 33. 2
to drive the ravenous Wolfe *away,* . . . . VI. ix. 37. 4
Keeping all noysome things *away* from it, ... VI. x. 7. 8
They vanisht all *away* out of his sight, ... VI. x. 18. 2
why, when I them saw, fled they *away* from me?' . . . . . . VI. x. 19. 9
thence he had no will *away* to fare, ... VI. x. 30. 8
Through cowherd feare he fled *away* as fast, ... VI. x. 35. 3
And drove *away* their flocks; . . . . VI. x. 39. 9
And all his people captive led *away;* . . . . VI. x. 40. 3
this lucklesse mayd *away* was lad, ... VI. x. 40. 4
carried captive by those theeves *away;* . . . . VI. x. 41. 2
flyes *away* as fast as he can hye, ... VI. xi. 18. 8
And his love reft *away,* . . . . VI. xi. 25. 3
Whose whelpes are stolne *away,* . . . . VI. xi. 25. 9
doe feare *away,* and tell.' . . . . VI. xi. 29. 9
upon an hill not farre *away,* . . . . VI. xi. 36. 6
and take the spoyle *away;* . . . . VI. xi. 38. 6
So drove them all *away,* . . . . VI. xi. 51. 9
seeing Calidore, *away* he flew, ... VI. xii. 25. 7
past *away,* his doings to relate . . . . VII. vi. 19. 2
all his garments he had cast *away*. . . . . VII. vii. 36. 2
wrapped well . . . to keep the cold *away;* . . . . VII. vii. 42. 2
did softly slyde And swim *away:* . . . . VII. vii. 43. 5
love of things so vaine to cast *away;* . . . . VII. viii. 1. 7
her frowne me drives *away*. . . . . *Am.* xxi. 12
wast and weare *away* in termes unsure, ... *Am.* xxv. 3
when a dreadfull storme *away* is flit, ... *Am.* xl. 7
Is prisoner led *away* with heavy hart, ... *Am.* lii. 3
Shall turne to caulmes, and tymely cleare *away*. . . . . . . *Am.* lxii. 12
Seeing the game from him escapt *away,* . . . . *Am.* lxvii. 2
bring *away* Captivity thence captive, ... *Am.* lxviii. 3
But came the waves, and washed it *away:* . . . . *Am.* lxxv. 2
that cloud of pryde . . . with smiles she drives *away*. . . . *Am.* lxxxi. 8
joyous houres doe fly *away* too fast. . . . . *Am.* lxxxvi. 14
He tooke his wings and *away* did fly. . . . . *Epig.* i. 6
One of his shafts she stole *away*. . . . . *Epig.* ii. 4
Ring ye the bels, to make it weare *away,* . . . . *Epith.* 274
To filch *away* sweet snatches of delight, ... *Epith.* 362
Doing *away* the drosse which dims the light . . . . *H.B.* 48
And passe *away,* like to a sommers shade; . . . . *H.B.* 68
shall fade and fall *away* To that they were, ... *H.B.* 95
with His onely breath them blew *away* . . . . *H.H.L.* 87
idle hopes, which still doe fly *away,* . . . . *Proth.* 8

Aways. farre *awayes* A rulesse rout . . . . *Gn.* 430

Awe. *See* **Overawe.**

Sterne face, and front full of Saturnlike *awe* . . . . *Bel.*² ix. 4
Departed to his home in dreadfull *awe,* . . . . *Hub.* 1109
her fiers servant, full of kingly *aw* And high disdaine, ... I. iii. 41. 1
sturdie courage tame with dreadfull *aw,* . . . . I. vi. 26. 8
He sett the false Duessa, for more *aw* and dread. . . . . . . I. vii. 18. 9
waytes for death with dread and trembling *aw;* . . . . II. viii. 50. 4
with terrour and with *aw* So inly smot, ... III. vii. 13. 5
So goodly grave, and full of princely *aw,* . . . . IV. vi. 33. 5
Held vertue for it selfe in soveraine *awe:* . . . . IV. viii. 30. 6
He thought her to compell by crueltie and *awe*. . . . . . . IV. xi. 2. 9
tost the Paynim without feare or *awe;* . . . . V. viii. 41. 7
His name was *Awe;* . . . . V. ix. 23. 1
Bate somewhat of that Majestie and *awe* . . . . V. ix. 35. 7
Glad to be quit from that proud Tyrants *awe,* . . . . V. xii. 24. 3
falling downe with humble *awe,* . . . . VI. vii. 36. 8
Without regard of pitty or of *awe?* . . . . VI. viii. 6. 5

Awful. those that weld the *awful* crowne, ... *S.C.* O. 40
Jove in midst with *awfull* Majestie, ... *Mui.* 308
peoples hartes with *awfull* terror tye, ... I. vii. 16. 7
with dredd Majestie and *awfull* yre, ... II. iii. 23. 8
awfull terror deepe into him strooke, ... III. x. 24. 4
use of *awfull* Majestie remove. . . . . IV. Pr. 5. 4
filles with *awful* dread, ... V. Pr. 11. 5
even wilde beasts did feare his *awfull* sight, ... V. i. 8. 4
His snaky-wreathed Mace, whose *awfull* power . . . . VII. vi. 18. 2
Myld humblesse, mixt with *awfull* majesty. . . . . *Am.* xiii. 5
with *awful* might The lawes of wedlock still dost patronize; *Epith.* 390
Humbled with feare and *awfull* reverence, ... *H.H.B.* 141

Awhape. Deeply doo your sad words my wits *awhape,* . . . . *Hub.* 72
could *awhape* An hardy hart; . . . . IV. vii. 5. 4

Awhaped. any man would nigh *awhaped* make: . . . . V. xi. 32. 5

Awhile. *See* **While.**

Now listen *a while* and hearken the end. . . . . *S.C.* F. 101
Hearken *awhile* . . . The rurall song . . . . *S.C.* D. 17

Awhile—*Continued.*
the Pilgrim that the Ploughman playde *awhyle;* . . . . . . *S.C.* Env. 10
As pausing in great doubt, *awhile* he staid, ... *Hub.* 175
shedding teares *a while,* I still did rest, ... *Ti.* 32
Not mine, but His, which mine *awhile* her made; . . . . . . *D.* 235
stood *awhile* astonisht at his words, ... *Col.* 650
But, sith thou maist not so, give leave *a while* . . . . . . *Ded. Son.* xii. 9
The which to heare vouchsafe . . . *a-while!* . . . . I. Pr. 4. 9
to the Dwarfe *a while* his needlesse spere he gave. . . . . . I. i. 11. 9
Returne from whence ye came, and rest *a while,* . . . . . . I. iv. 51. 3
With fawning wordes he courted her *a while;* . . . . I. vi. 4. 1
Would not *a while* her forward course pursew, ... I. ix. 20. 6
a whyle I read you rest, ... I. x. 17. 4
she *awhile* him stayes, himselfe to rest, ... I. x. 45. 1
now *a while* lett downe that haughtie string, ... I. xi. 7. 7
There eke my feeble barke *a while* may stay, ... I. xii. 1. 8
Here she *a while* may make her safe abode, ... I. xii. 42. 5
attend *awhile* their forward steps . . . . II. i. 35. 9
Into her lodging to repaire *awhile,* . . . . II. ii. 33. 4
here *a while* ye may in safety rest, ... II. vi. 23. 6
They stayd *a while,* and forth she gan proceede: . . . . . . II. vi. 33. 6
cloudes . . . *A while* his heavy eylids cover'd have, ... II. viii. 24. 8
A while they fled, but soone retournd againe . . . . II. ix. 15. 1
they *awhile* with court and goodly game . . . . II. ix. 44. 4
here I *a while* must stay, To see a cruell fight . . . . . . II. xi. 4. 8
Awhile he stood in this astonishment, ... II. xi. 41. 1
turne thy rudder hitherward *awhile* . . . . II. xii. 32. 6
both *awhile* would covered remaine, ... II. xii. 64. 4
Gazing *awhile* at his unwonted guise; . . . . II. xii. 66. 2
So as they gazed after her *a whyle,* . . . . III. i. 17. 1
Therewith *a while* she her flit fancy fedd, ... III. i. 56. 1
no powre To speake *a while,* ne ready answere make, ... III. ii. 5. 2
Her selfe *awhile* therein she vewd in vaine: . . . . III. ii. 22. 6
They, here arriving, staid *awhile* without, ... III. iii. 14. 1
the Prophet still *awhile* did stay, ... III. iii. 21. 4
'All which his sonne Careticus *awhile* Shall well defend, . . . III. iii. 33. 1
having vewd *awhile* the surges hore . . . . III. iv. 7. 4
He rested him *awhile;* . . . . III. v. 41. 3
Stared on her *awhile,* as one astound, ... III. vii. 7. 7
to rest her faint And wearie limbes *awhile.* . . . . III. vii. 10. 5
each *awhile* lay like a sencelesse corse. . . . . III. ix. 16. 5
sighing soft *awhile,* at last she thus: . . . . III. ix. 39. 1
for her sake her cattell fedd *awhile,* . . . . III. xi. 39. 2
His blindfold eies he bad *awhile* unbinde, ... III. xii. 22. 6
Upon the ground *awhile* in slomber lay; . . . . IV. ii. 7. 2
lying still *awhile,* both did forget . . . . IV. ii. 15. 8
To stay their hands, till he *awhile* had spoken; . . . . . . IV. ii. 21. 2
Stood still *awhile,* and his fast footing kept, ... IV. iii. 20. 8
fruitfull apples to have borne *awhile,* . . . . IV. iii. 29. 8
Where I with sound of trompe will also rest *a whyle.* . . . . IV. iv. 48. 9
Shall breath it selfe *awhile* after so long a went. . . . . . IV. v. 46. 9
To graunt unto those warriours truce *a whyle;* . . . . IV. vi. 25. 7
Save that she algates him *a while* accompanide. . . . . . . IV. vi. 44. 9
rest their wearie limbs *awhile.* . . . . IV. vii. 3. 6
He bowed low, and so *a while* did lie: . . . . IV. viii. 43. 5
when *awhile* they had together beene, ... IV. ix. 10. 1
continu'd there *a while* To rest him selfe, ... IV. ix. 12. 6
Did stay *a while* their greedy bickerment, ... V. iv. 6. 8
a while doth pause To heare the piteous beast . . . . V. iv. 40. 8
she star'd *A while* about her with confused eye; . . . . . . V. v. 13. 8
I will *a while* with his first folly beare, ... V. v. 48. 8
A while she walkt, and chauft; *a while* she threw Her selfe . V. vi. 13. 6
So there *a while* they afterwards remained, ... V. vii. 42. 1
at the sight of these those were *awhile* debard. . . . . . . V. ix. 36. 9
There he with Belgae did *awhile* remaine . . . . V. xi. 35. 1
did *a while* asswage Their forces furie, ... V. xii. 8. 3
awhile he rested still: . . . . VI. i. 35. 5
Ne once to breath *awhile* their angers tempest ceast. . . . . VI. i. 36. 9
his mortall hand *a while* he stayd; . . . . VI. i. 40. 1
Whom Calidore *awhile* well having vewed . . . . VI. ii. 7. 1
There to their fortune leave we them *awhile,* . . . . VI. ii. 40. 1
Compelled were themselves *awhile* to rest, ... VI. iv. 15. 6
having there their wounds *awhile* redrest, ... VI. iv. 15. 8
now West he went *awhile,* Then North, ... VI. iv. 25. 2
There they *awhile* some gracious speaches spent, ... VI. v. 24. 6
I must *awhile* forbeare to you to tell; . . . . VI. vi. 17. 3
if ye please to lend me leave *awhile,* . . . . VI. viii. 6. 8
awhile she stayd; Till the sharpe passion being overpast, . . VI. viii. 19. 2
sitting downe, her selfe *awhile* bethought . . . . VI. viii. 32. 7
Give leave *awhyle,* good father, in this shore To rest my barcke, VI. ix. 31. 3
A while on her they greedily did gaze, ... VI. xi. 13. 8
when the Shepheard breathed had *awhyle,* . . . . VI. xi. 30. 1
after griefe *awhile* had had his course, ... VI. xi. 34. 1
There they *a while* together thus did dwell . . . . VI. xii. 11. 7
'Harken to mee *awhile,* yee heavenly Powers! . . . . VII. vi. 20. 1
having pauz'd *awhile,* Jove thus bespake: . . . . VII. vi. 29. 1
gather to myselfe new breath *awhile.* . . . . *Am.* lxxx. 4
faulcon . . . That flags *awhile* her fluttering wings beneath, . *H.H.B.* 27

Awhit. *See* **Whit.**

Awniduff. Swift *Awniduff,* which of the English man Is cal'de
Blacke-water, ... IV. xi. 41. 5

Awoke. *See* **Awook.**
How kenst thou that he is *awoke?* . . . . *S.C.* Mar. 28
'When I *awoke,* and found her place devoyd, ... I. ix. 15. 1
out of his delightfull dreame The man *awoke,* . . . . II. v. 37. 2
he *awoke* out of his ydle dreme; . . . . II. vi. 27. 2
Who, long before *awoke,* . . . Was to the battell . . . . . . V. vii. 27. 3

Awook. *See* **Awoke.**
Like one that out of deadly dreame *awooke:* . . . . VI. iii. 11. 3
ne out of swoune *awooke,* . . . . VI. vii. 48. 5

Awry. his embrodered Bonet sat *awry:* . . . . III. xii. 9. 6
wrong redresse in such as wend *awry:* . . . . V. ii. 1. 4
so were realmes and nations run *awry.* . . . . V. ii. 32. 6
Like to a rancke of piles that pitched are *awry.* . . . . . . V. xi. 9. 9
suffers not one looke to glaunce *awry,* . . . . *Epith.* 236

Ax. *See* **Pole-ax.**
heav'd his murdrous *axe* at him . . . . IV. iii. 17. 9
with his *axe* him smote in evill hower, ... IV. iii. 20. 5
with his huge great yron *axe* gan hew . . . . V. xi. 5. 3
Eftsoones againe his *axe* he raught on hie, ... V. xi. 10. 1
did his yron *axe* so nimbly wield, ... V. xii. 19. 7
His *axe* he could not from his shield undoe; . . . . V. xii. 22. 5

Axes. with their *axes* both so sorely bet, ... IV. iii. 15. 3

Ax's. The *Axes* edge did oft turne againe, ... *S.C.* F. 203

Ay. thereto *aye* wonned to repayre The shepheards daughters . *S.C.* F. 119
(*Ay* little helpe to harme there needeth!) . . . . *S.C.* F. 198
it ranckleth, *ay* more and more, ... *S.C.* Au. 101
Seemeth *ay* greater when it is farre: . . . . *S.C.* S. 77
ay deeper and deeper sinck. . . . . *S.C.* S. 133
loftie verse of hem was loved *aye.* . . . . *S.C.* O. 66
whose endles sovenaunce . . . may *aye* remaine, ... *S.C.* N. 6
'*Ay* me! that dreerie Death . . . . *S.C.* N. 123
The fieldes *ay* fresh, the grasse *ay* greene. . . . . *S.C.* N. 189
Ay, francke shepheard, how bene thy verses meint . . . . . . *S.C.* N. 203
'*Ay* me! that thankes so much should faile . . . . *Gn.* 353
'*Ay* me! . . . whom evill hap . . . . *Hub.* 601
Ay me! what thing on earth, ... *T.M.* 43
they live for *aye* above, ... *Ti.* 396
Recorded by the Muses, live for *ay;* . . . . *Ti.* 403
to be His, with him to live for *ay.* . . . . *D.* 236
Calling to me (*ay* me!) this wise bespake; . . . . *D.* 262
Ay wont in desert darknes to remaine, ... I. i. 16. 8
the chastest flowre that *aye* did spring . . . . I. i. 48. 4
Ay me! . . . well may I rew . . . . I. vi. 36. 7
Remedilesse for *aie* he doth him hold. . . . . I. vii. 51. 8
Ay me! how many perils . . . . I. viii. 1. 1
Ay wont to laugh when them I heard to cry, ... I. ix. 10. 5
On top whereof *ay* dwelt the ghastly Owle, ... I. ix. 33. 6
That *ay* thereof her babes might sucke their fill; . . . . . . I. x. 30. 8
that pleasaunt Mount, that is for *ay* . . . . I. x. 54. 6
where peace doth *ay* remaine,' . . . . I. x. 62. 7
let me heare for *aie* in peace remaine, ... I. x. 63. 3
'*Ay* me! deare Lady, ... II. i. 44. 4
(*ay* the while, that he is not so now!) . . . . II. i. 50. 1
Bynempt a sacred vow, which none should *ay* releace. . . . . II. i. 60. 9
thyselfe my captive yield for *ay.* . . . . II. iii. 7. 8
'*Ay* wretch, . . . thy destinies withstand . . . . II. iii. 8. 3
aye with foe In fayre defence . . . was wont to fight; . . . II. iv. 8. 2
in Stygian lake, *ay* burning bright, Had kindled: . . . . . . II. v. 22. 7
Atin *ay* him pricks with spurs of shame . . . . II. v. 38. 9
my trew liegeman yield thy selfe for *ay,* . . . . II. viii. 51. 7
all that in the world was *ay* thought wittily. . . . . II. ix. 53. 9
Donwallo dyde, (for what may live for *ay?*) . . . . II. x. 40. 1
Ay caroling of love and jollity, ... III. i. 40. 5
aye the cups their bancks did overflow; . . . . III. i. 51. 6
aye betweene the cups she did prepare . . . . III. i. 51. 7
Ay joyning foot to foot, and syde to syde; . . . . III. i. 66. 8
Ay doing thinges that to his fame redownd, ... III. ii. 14. 5
'*Ay* me! how much I feare . . . . III. ii. 33. 1
who with reason can you *aye* reprove . . . . III. ii. 40. 6
tell me, Britomart, If *ay* more goodly creature . . . . III. iii. 32. 2
I deeme that counsel *aye* most fit, ... III. iii. 52. 3
usd the same in batteill *aye* to beare; . . . . III. iii. 60. 3
She firmely hath emprisoned for *ay,* . . . . III. vi. 48. 6
aie more fresh And fierce he still appeard, ... III. vii. 32. 8
'*Ay* me!' (said Paridell) . . . . III. viii. 50. 1
Ay when to him she cryde, to her he turnd, ... III. x. 15. 1
Ne ought but deare Bisaltis *ay* could make him glad. . . . . . III. xi. 41. 9
aye the more that she the same reherst, ... IV. v. 31. 7
'*Aye* me!' (said she) 'where am I, ... IV. vii. 11. 1
Aye me, to see that gentle maide so tost!' . . . . IV. ix. 38. 5
'*Ay* me,' (quoth she) 'what wicked destinie! . . . . V. vi. 10. 8
'*Ay* me!' (sayd she) . . . . V. x. 23. 1
Ay me, that ever guyle in wemen was invented! . . . . V. xi. 50. 9
liberty I leave to you for *aye* me to disgrace . . . . VI. i. 28. 8
swore to him true fealtie for *aye.* . . . . VI. i. 44. 4
aie me! is this the timely joy, ... VI. iii. 4. 8
'*Aye* me!' (sayd then Serena, sighing sore) . . . . VI. vi. 13. 5
Aie me! how could her love make half amends . . . . VI. vii. 38. 9
For *aye* the more that she did them entreat, ... VI. viii. 3. 8
But *aye,* the more he rag'd, the more his powre increast. . . VI. xii. 32. 9
damned ghosts which dwell For *aye* in darkenesse, ... VI. xii. 35. 8
Hast sumd in one, and cancelled for *aye:* . . . . *Epith.* 318
So hast thou often done (*ay* me, the more!) To me . . . . . . *H.L.* 141
Ay me! deare Lord! that ever I might hope, ... *H.L.* 294
oft it falles, (*aye* (**ay*) me, the more to rew!) . . . . . . *H.B.* 148
Ay me! what can us lesse than that behove? . . . . *H.H.L.* 178

Ayery, Ayrie, *etc.* *See* **Airy.**

Aygulets. *See* **Aglets.**

Azure. with his *azure* wings he cleav'd The liquid clowdes, . . *Hub.* 1258
with brave plumes doth beate the *azure* skie, ... *Ti.* 423
Betwixt the centred earth and *azure* skies, ... *Mui.* 19
deckt the *azure* field with her fayre pouldred skin. . . . . . III. ii. 25. 9
He up gan lifte toward the *azure* skies, ... III. v. 34. 4
through the persant aire shoote forth their *azure* streames. . . III. ix. 20. 9
also those which wonne in th' *azure* sky: . . . . IV. xii. 1. 4
As when two sunnes appeare in the *azure* skye, ... V. iii. 19. 1
in gilden armes, with *azure* band Quartred athwart, ... VI. ii. 44. 7

B

Babblers. *Bablers* of folly, and blazers of cryme: II. ix. 25. 6
Babblers unworthy been of so divine a meed. VII. vi. 46. 9
Babbling. his *babling* tongue did yet blaspheme IV. viii. 45. 6
Babe. her litle *babe* revyld, I. xii. 11. 3
sweete *Babe,* . . . Long maist thou live, II. i. 37. 1
in her lap a lovely *babe* did play II. i. 40. 5
So deare thee, *babe,* I bought; II. i. 53. 8
The litle *babe* up in his armes he hent; II. ii. 1. 4
'Ah! lucklesse *babe,* borne under cruell starre, II. ii. 2. 1
The bloody-handed *babe* unto her truth Did earnestly committ, II. iii. 2. 2
the Nimphe that bore A gyaunt *babe* II. xii. 52. 3
nine monethes did beare . . . Her tender *babe,* III. ii. 11. 8
everlasting woe, Be to the Briton *babe* III. iii. 42. 2
Up they them tooke; each one a *babe* uptooke, III. vi. 28. 1
Dame Phoebe to a Nymphe her *babe* betooke III. vi. 28. 3
at that berth another *Babe* she bore; III. vii. 48. 1
About that wofull couple . . . And their young bloodie *babe* V. iii. 31. 3
The litle *babe* did loudly scrike and squall, VI. iv. 18. 1
The litle *babe,* sweet relickes of his pray; VI. iv. 23. 2
This litle *babe,* of sweete and lovely face, VI. iv. 35. 4
She gladly did of that same *babe* accept, VI. iv. 37. 6
She forth gan lay unto the open light The litle *babe,* VI. xii. 7. 5
Babel. king Nine whilome built *Babell* towre. II. ix. 21. 6
antique *Babel,* Empresse of the East, *Com. Son.* iv. 1
second *Babell* . . . Her ayry Towers upraised much more high. *Com. Son.* iv. 3
Babe's. *Babes* bloody handes may not be clensd: II. ii. Arg.
this *babes* bloody hand May not be clensd II. ii. 10. 1
Babes. suck . . . To two young *babes:* *Bel.* ix. 10
bells, and *babes,* and glasses, in hys packe: *S.C.* May 240
So praysen *babes* the Peacoks spotted traine, *S.C.* O. 31
With bitter woundes her owne deere *babes* to slay, *Gn.* 399
With blood of guiltlesse *babes,* and innocents I. viii. 35. 6
ay thereof her *babes* might sucke their fill; I. x. 30. 8
A multitude of *babes* about her hong, I. x. 31. 1
bugs to fearen *babes* withall, II. xii. 25. 8
Wordes fearen *babes.* III. iv. 15. 3
nor with commune food, As other wemens *babes,* III. vi. 5. 9
two *babes,* as faire as springing day. III. vi. 26. 9
from her loving side the tender *babes* to take. III. vi. 27. 9
A thousand thousand naked *babes* attend About him III. vi. 32. 3
These three so noble *babes* to bring forth at one clap. IV. ii. 43. 9
Got these three lovely *babes,* that prov'd three champions bold. IV. ii. 45. 9
Babler, Babling. *See* **Babbler,** *etc.*
Baby. The blynd boy, Venus *baby,* *Epig.* i. 2
Babylon. great *Babylon* is fallen. *Rev.* ii. 14
Great *Babylon* her haughtie walls will praise, *Ro.* ii. 1
There was that great proud king of *Babylon,* I. v. 47. 1
There was the signe of antique *Babylon;* IV. i. 22. 1
Bacchante. fierce *Bacchante* seemd too fell and keene; III. i. 45. 6
Bacchus. *Bacchus* and Hercules I raisd to heaven, *T.M.* 461
"So soone as *Bacchus* with the Nymphe does lincke!" II. i. 55. 6
Such first was *Bacchus,* V. i. 2. 1
Crowne ye God *Bacchus* with a coronall, *Epith.* 255
Bacchus'. *Bacchus* fruite is frend to Phoebus wise; *S.C.* O. 106
Bacchus merry fruit they did invent, I. vi. 15. 2
Bacchus fruit out of the silver plate III. ix. 30. 3
mongst the rout Of *Bacchus* Priests, V. viii. 47. 6
Bace. *See* **Base.**
Bachelor. many a *bachelor* to waite on him, *Epith.* 28
Back. shall *backe* reverse To their first discord, *Ro.* xxii. 11
Whose *backe* was arm'd against the dint of speare *Van.* vi. 2
on his *backe* did beare . . . A gilden towre, *Van.* viii. 3
His gylden quiver at his *backe,* *S.C.* Mar. 82
Bearing a trusse of tryfles at hys *backe,* *S.C.* May 239
whence thou camst, flye *backe* to heaven *S.C.* O. 84
his heard *back* from that water foord Drave, *Gn.* 166
The scalie *backe* of that most hideous snake *Gn.* 305
back to them to repayre, *Gn.* 382
sad Eurydice . . . For looking *back,* *Gn.* 435
Backe to be borne, though it unlawfull were. *Gn.* 464
Bett *back* the furie of the Trojan fyre. *Gn.* 496
Fled *back* to heaven, *Hub.* 3
To speed to day, to be put *back* to morrow; *Hub.* 899
on his *backe* the skin he did, *Hub.* 1062
backe go to their wofull toomb. *Ti.* 49
'Looke *backe* . . . unto the former ages, *Ti.* 57
Fled *back* too soone unto his native place; *Ti.* 291
Her *back* againe to life sent *Ti.* 392
spredding all his *backe,* with dreadfull view *Mui.* 69
on his *backe* Her through the sea did beare; *Mui.* 278
She seem'd still *backe* unto the land to looke, *Mui.* 281
The silken downe with which his *backe* is dight, *Mui.* 334
turning *back,* he saide, *D.* 61
first since thy turning *backe* *Col.* 19
Dauncing upon the waters *back* to lond, *Col.* 214
back returnedst to this barrein soyle, *Col.* 656
chose *back* to my sheep to tourne, *Col.* 672
her bag Of needments at his *backe.* I. i. 6. 4
backe returne with foule disgrace, I. i. 13. 3
backe to turne againe; I. i. 16. 6
her boldly kept From turning *backe,* I. i. 17. 4
from her turne him *backe.* I. i. 20. 5
He, *backe* returning I. i. 44. 6
he *backe* returnd againe. I. i. 55. 9
Doe *backe* rebutte, and ech to other yealdeth I. ii. 15. 9
Shee turning *backe,* I. ii. 21. 1
on his *backe* a heavy load he bare I. iii. 16. 7

Back—*Continued.*
Shee *backe* retourned I. iii. 24. 2
true love hath no powre To looken *backe;* I. iii. 30. 8
hee . . . both from *backe* and belly still did spare, I. iv. 28. 4
They *backe* retourned to the princely Place; I. iv. 38. 3
backe retyred to her cave, I. v. 21. 6
bowing downe her aged *backe,* she kist The wicked witch, I. v. 27. 1
turning *backe* in silence I. v. 31. 1
backe retourned I. v. 31. 7
backe retourning, took her wonted way I. v. 44. 7
turning *backe* gan fast to fly away; I. vi. 28. 2
backe to fight againe, new breathed I. vi. 44. 9
An yron brest, and *back* of scaly bras, I. vii. 17. 8
scaly tayle was stretcht adowne his *back* full low. I. vii. 31. 9
steed . . . chauft that any on his *backe* should sitt: I. vii. 37. 8
brought not *backe* the balefull body I. vii. 50. 5
looking *back* would faine have runne away; I. ix. 25. 3
Against my liking *backe* to doe you grace: I. ix. 32. 6
lifted up his hand, that *backe* againe did start. I. ix. 51. 9
turne againe *Backe* to the world, I. x. 63. 2
back returne unto this place, I. x. 64. 3
To Una *back* he cast him to retyre, I. x. 68. 2
Does overspred his long bras-scaly *back,* I. xi. 11. 2
th' ydle stroke yet *backe* recoyld I. xi. 17. 3
backe againe the sparcling steele recoyld, I. xi. 25. 3
Behynd his *backe,* unweeting, where he stood, I. xi. 29. 2
the knight *back* overthrowen fell. I. xi. 30. 9
Who him rencountring fierce, . . . Perforce rebutted *backe.* I. xi. 53. 5
back retyrd, his life blood forth I. xi. 53. 9
Backe to retourne to that great Faery Queene, I. xii. 18. 6
Ye then shall hither *backe* retourne agayne, I. xii. 19. 8
Unto his Faery Queene *backe* to retourne; I. xii. 41. 8
call *backe* life to her forsaken shop. II. i. 43. 7
with redoubled buffes them *backe* did put: II. ii. 23. 4
ne ever *backe* retourned eye; II. iii. 19. 9
at her *backe* a bow and quiver gay, II. iii. 29. 2
low behinde her *backe* were scattered: II. iii. 30. 5
she, swarving *backe,* her Javelin II. iii. 42. 7
pluckt him *backe;* II. iv. 6. 5
both his hands fast bound behind his *backe,* II. iv. 14. 8
Behind his *backe* he bore a brasen shield, II. iv. 38. 1
backe rebownding left the forckhead keene: II. iv. 46. 8
being entred might not *backe* retyre; II. vi. 20. 2
Back to the strond retyrd, II. vi. 40. 6
Into the world to guyde him *backe,* II. vii. 65. 9
backe againe him brought to living light. II. vii. 66. 4
fixed at his *backe* to cut his ayery wayes. II. viii. 5. 9
dreadfull Death behynd thy *backe* doth stond.' II. viii. 37. 9
backe againe turning his busie hond, II. viii. 41. 6
backe againe faire Alma led them right, II. ix. 33. 5
Into the which retourning *backe* he fell: II. x. 11. 4
repulsed *backe* againe, And twise renforst *backe* II. x. 48. 1, 2
halfe the steele behind his *backe* did rest; II. xi. 37. 5
the steele . . . Which drawing *backe,* II. xi. 37. 6
backe againe it did alofte rebownd, II. xi. 42. 8
A second fall redoubling *backe* agayne. II. xi. 43. 5
ghosts doen often creepe *Backe* to the world, II. xii. 6. 6
nought that falles . . . May *backe* retourne, II. xii. 6. 9
neither toyle nor traveill might her *backe* recoyle. II. xii. 19. 9
Ne did the other *backe* his foote returne, III. i. 5. 7
To weet if they would turne *backe* to that place; III. i. 19. 5
hold them *backe* that would in error fall: III. i. 46. 5
The worde gone out she *backe* againe would call, III. ii. 9. 1
To this his native soyle thou *backe* shalt bring, III. iii. 27. 7
Shall *backe* repulse the valiaunt Brockwell twise, III. iii. 35. 5
Least *back* againe the kingdom he from them should beare. III. iii. 45. 9
through *back* waies, that none might them espy, III. iii. 61. 7
Whiles on his broad rownd *backe* they softly slid, III. iv. 32. 2
So with the Dwarfe he *back* retourn'd againe, III. v. 12. 1
Soone as she Venus saw behinde her *backe,* III. vi. 19. 1
they agayn returne *backe* by the hinder gate. III. vi. 32. 9
She turnd her selfe *backe* to her wicked leares; III. vii. 21. 7
bringe her *backe* againe, III. vii. 21. 9
all his *backe* was spect With thousand spots III. vii. 22. 4
almost in the *backe* he oft her strake; III. vii. 44. 6
Thence *backe* returning to the former land, III. vii. 61. 5
she *backe* retourning III. viii. 2. 6
retourned *back* againe To his first way. III. viii. 44. 5
backe agayne To turne your course, III. ix. 40. 5
folke, which sought him *backe* to drive, III. ix. 42. 3
whenas Malbecco spyed clere, He turned *backe,* III. x. 23. 5
thy wife shall *backe* be sent: III. x. 32. 2
Ne ever looked *back* for good or ill; III. x. 43. 7
She turnd her, and returned *backe* againe; III. x. 49. 8
turning *backe* to Scudamour, III. xi. 22. 6
backe retire, all scorcht and pittifully brent. III. xi. 26. 9
Through the greene gras his long bright burnisht *back* declares. III. xi. 28. 9
he *backe* retyred soft away, III. xii. 4. 7
at his *backe* a brode Capuccio had, III. xii. 10. 3
from her *backe* her garments she did teare, III. xii. 17. 4
his charmes *back* to reverse. III. xii. 36. 2
Returning *back,* those goodly rowmes, III. xii. 42. 1
who so list looke *backe* to former ages, IV. Pr. 3. 1
About her *backe* and all her bodie wound: IV. i. 13. 5
The other *backe* retired and contrarie trode. IV. i. 28. 9
thrise he drew it *backe;* IV. i. 54. 9
He looked *backe,* and, her avizing well, IV. ii. 22. 7

Back—*Continued.*
with such furie *backe* at him it heft, ... IV. iii. 12. 5
from daunger of the throwes *Backe* to retire, ... IV. iii. 26. 4
Drives *backe* the current of his kindly course, ... IV. iii. 27. 4
when the floud is spent, then *backe* againe, ... IV. iii. 27. 6
Who *backe* returning told, as he had seene, ... IV. iv. 3. 1
tombling *backe* he downe did slyde . . . . . IV. iv. 44. 4
thence it glaunst Adowne her *backe,* . . . . . IV. vi. 13. 4
it chynd his *backe* behind the sell, ... IV. vi. 13. 8
backe returned with right heavie mind . . . . . IV. vi. 46. 4
Backe to that desert forrest they retyred, ... IV. vi. 47. 1
behind her *backe* she heard One rushing forth . . . . . IV. vii. 4. 3
ere she *backe* could turne to taken heed, ... IV. vii. 4. 5
looking *backe* espies . . . . . IV. vii. 22. 5
forst him *backe* . . . to retreat. . . . . . IV. vii. 37. 9
Unto those woods he turned *backe* againe, ... IV. vii. 38. 3
hard behind his *backe* his foe was prest, ... IV. viii. 41. 6
bet the others *backe;* . . . . . IV. ix. 25. 2
seem'd to stoupe afore With bowed *backe,* . . . . . IV. xi. 26. 2
Her goodly lockes adowne her *backe* did flow . . . . . IV. xi. 46. 1
Till like a victor on his *backe* he ride, ... IV. xii. 13. 5
Backe to him selfe he gan returne the blame, ... IV. xii. 16. 2
backe he came . . . . . IV. xii. 23. 7
He bad him stay, and *backe* with him retire, ... V. i. 21. 1
Else he doth hold him *backe* or beat away. . . . . . V. ii. 6. 5
whiles he his *backe* bestrad. . . . . . V. ii. 13. 9
him forst forsake His horses *backe* . . . . . V. ii. 16. 2
So *backe* he brought Sir Marinell againe; . . . . . V. iii. 12. 1
backe againe To Braggadochio did his shield restore, ... V. iii. 13. 1
Talus by the *backe* the boaster hent, ... V. iii. 37. 2
drawing *backe* deceived their intent: . . . . . V. iv. 24. 2
backe againe they homeward turnd their feete; . . . . . V. iv. 51. 7
backe returning where his Dame did lie, ... V. vi. 30. 7
the Goddesse with her rod him *backe* did beat. . . . . . V. vii. 15. 9
yet neither has forgon His horses *backe,* . . . . . V. viii. 9. 8
made him *backe* againe as fast to fly; . . . . . V. viii. 36. 3
backe againe upon themselves they turned, ... V. viii. 38. 3
backe with both his hands unto him hayles The resty raynes, V. viii. 39. 5
misween'd for her owne Knight, That brought her *backe:* . . V. viii. 46. 7
Ne none can *backe* returne that once are gone amis. . . . . . V. ix. 6. 9
on his *backe* an uncouth vestiment . . . . . V. ix. 10. 7
at his *backe* a great wyde net he bore, ... V. ix. 11. 6
ere he could his weapon *backe* repaire, ... V. xi. 13. 7
backe she would have turnd for great affright: . . . . . V. xi. 26. 5
ere that it she *backe* againe had borne, ... V. xi. 29. 7
soone as he their outrage *backe* doth beat, ... V. xi. 45. 8
forced them . . . *Backe* to recule; . . . . . V. xi. 47. 6
forst at first those knights *backe* to retyre: . . . . . V. xi. 58. 6
by no meanes it *backe* againe he forth could wrast. . . . . . V. xii. 21. 9
he *backe* returned from that land, ... V. xii. 28. 1
tribute *backe* repay as to their King: . . . . . VI. Pr. 7. 5
The Dwarfe . . . Brought aunswere *backe,* . . . . . VI. i. 31. 4
I . . . *backe* returned His scornefull taunts . . . . . VI. ii. 12. 1
After long search and chauff he turned *backe* . . . . . VI. ii. 21. 2
turning *backe* unto that gentle boy, ... VI. ii. 24. 1
And turne we *backe* to good Sir Calidore; . . . . . VI. ii. 40. 2
To beare this burden on your dainty *backe;* . . . . . VI. ii. 47. 8
Whom on his *backe* he bore, ... VI. iii. 2. 6
Or beare her on thy *backe* with pleasing payne, ... VI. iii. 32. 4
refuge was still Behind his Ladies *back;* . . . . . VI. iii. 49. 6
That forst him *backe* recoyle and reele areare, ... VI. iv. 5. 8
backe return'd againe With speede. . . . . . VI. iv. 9. 3
He with him thought *backe* to returne againe; . . . . . VI. iv. 24. 2
backe returning to that sorie Dame, ... VI. v. 4. 1
his *backe* for best safegard He lent against a tree, ... VI. v. 18. 8
soone as he returned *backe* againe, ... VI. v. 34. 2
he did repell And beat them *back,* . . . . . VI. vi. 23. 9
that craven cowherd Knight Was at his *backe* . . . . . VI. vi. 26. 7
descending *backe* in haste he sought If yet he were alive, ... VI. vi. 37. 8
from his horses *backe* . . . him forth did beare, ... VI. vii. 11. 2
Backe to the place where Turpine late he lore; . . . . . VI. vii. 14. 2
He would have *backe* retyred from that sight, ... VI. vii. 20. 8
out of the wood issew'd *Backe* to the place, ... VI. vii. 23. 9
turne we now *backe* to that Ladie free, ... VI. vii. 27. 7
maugre all his might *backe* to relent: . . . . . VI. vii. 45. 8
His mindes sad message *backe* unto him sent; . . . . . VI. viii. 8. 3
with his club bet *backe* his brondyron bright . . . . . VI. viii. 10. 4
Rebeaten *backe* upon himselfe againe, ... VI. viii. 10. 6
eeke this wallet at your *backe* arreare, ... VI. viii. 23. 8
Then turning *backe* unto that captive thrall, ... VI. viii. 27. 1
returning to that Ladie *backe,* . . . . . VI. viii. 50. 1
Backe to the furrow which I lately left. . . . . . VI. ix. 1. 2
from the country *back* to private fames he scorsed. . . . . . VI. ix. 3. 9
backe returning to my sheepe againe, ... VI. ix. 25. 7
to retrate . . . or *backe* to turne againe, ... VI. ix. 31. 8
He *backe* returned to his rusticke wonne, ... VI. x. 32. 2
bringeth *backe* againe. . . . . . VI. xi. Arg.
To call the soule *backe* to her home againe; . . . . . VI. xi. 22. 4
turne we *backe* to Calidore where we him found. . . . . . VI. xi. 24. 9
when he *backe* returned from the wood, ... VI. xi. 25. 1
backe returning to his dearest deare, ... VI. xi. 50. 1
Yet durst he not draw *backe,* . . . . . VI. xii. 36. 6
Bending her horned browes, did put her *back;* . . . . . VII. vi. 12. 6
back returning to Molann' againe, ... VII. vi. 53. 2
Behinde his *back* a sithe, . . . he bore . . . . . VII. vii. 36. 8
all the woods theyr ecchoes *back* rebounded, ... *Am.* xix. 7
back again doth chace Their looser lookes . . . . . *Am.* xxi. 7
all your tempests cannot hold me *backe,* . . . . . *Am.* xlvi. 10
Drawne with sweet pleasures bayt, it *back* doth fly, ... *Am.* lxxii. 7
my hart . . . flyes *backe* unto your sight. . . . . . *Am.* lxxiii. 8

Back—*Continued.*
They ydly *back* returne to me agayne: . . . . . *Am.* lxxviii. 10
When once the Crab behind his *back* he sees. . . . . . *Epith.* 269
backe againe they go, ... *H.B.* 242
their points rebutted *backe* againe Are duld, ... *H.H.B.* 122
on Themmes brode aged *backe* . . . . . *Proth.* 133
Backbite. to *backbite* Anies good name for envie . . . . . *Hub.* 719
the verse of famous Poets witt He does *backebite,* . . . . . I. iv. 32. 7
lewdly did miscall And wickedly *backbite:* . . . . . IV. viii. 24. 9
after them did barke, and still *backbite,* . . . . . IV. viii. 36. 3
some wicked tongues did it *backebite,* . . . . . VI. xii. 41. 5
Backbitings. Against vile Zoilus *backbitings* vaine. . . . . . *Ded.Son.* xii. 14
Leasinges, *backbytinges,* and vain-glorious crakes, ... II. xi. 10. 7
Back-gate. close convaid, and to the *backgate* brought, . . II. ix. 32. 7
Backs. Their armes . . . bounde at their *backes.* . . . . . *Bel.*[1] xi. 10
With armes bound at their *backs* . . . . . *Bel.*[2] xv. 10
with the weight their *backs* nigh broken were: . . . . . *Hub.* 1158
Buls he would him make To tame, and ryde their *backes,* . . I. vi. 24. 7
Does ride on both their *backs,* . . . . . II. ii. 24. 9
stone; Such as behind their *backs* . . . Were throwne . . . . V. Pr. 2. 6
Back-starting. *backstarting* with disdainefull yre . . . . . V. xi. 61. 5
Backward. now stept, now crept, now *backward* drew, ... *Hub.* 1012
with the Lady *backward* sought to wend. . . . . . I. i. 28. 2
Their *backward* bent knees teach her humbly to obay. . . . . I. vi. 11. 9
So *backward* still was turnd his wrincled face: . . . . . I. viii. 31. 4
as he fledd his eye was *backward* cast, ... I. ix. 21. 5
Sunne to stay, Or *backward* turne his course . . . . . I. x. 20. 3
forst him to retire A little *backeward* . . . . . I. xi. 45. 3
As he recoiled *backeward,* . . . . . I. xi. 45. 7
yet did he never quaile, Ne *backward* shrinke, ... II. viii. 35. 7
Him *backeward* overthrew, and downe him stayd . . . . . II. xi. 29. 2
Still as she fledd her eye she *backward* threw, ... III. i. 16. 1
oft looking *backward,* . . . . . III. iv. 50. 6
th' head fell *backeward* on the Continent; . . . . . III. v. 25. 7
with sterne horror *backward* gan to start; . . . . . III. v. 30. 6
when againe he *backeward* cast his eye, ... III. x. 14. 4
Still fled he forward, looking *backward* still; . . . . . III. x. 56. 1
as she *backward* cast her busie eye . . . . . III. xi. 50. 1
with the force it *backward* forced him to bow. . . . . . IV. iii. 11. 9
As fast as forward erst now *backward* to retrate. . . . . . IV. iii. 26. 9
she him forced *backward* to retreat, ... IV. vi. 15. 3
th' other *backeward* bent, ... IV. x. 12. 4
I did *backeward* looke, ... IV. x. 20. 1
Such as behind their backs (so *backward* bred) . . . . . V. Pr. 2. 6
Nought could he do but . . . *backward* still retyre; . . . . . V. v. 16. 2
ever as she rode her eye was *backeward* bent. . . . . . V. viii. 4. 9
Ere to his den he *backward* could recoyle, ... V. ix. 9. 4
Talus soone him overtooke, and *backward* drew. . . . . . V. ix. 18. 9
So *backeward* he attone with him did wend: . . . . . V. xi. 43. 5
He lent against a tree, that *backeward* onset bard. . . . . . VI. v. 18. 9
The warie foule his bill doth *backward* wring; . . . . . VI. vii. 9. 4
backeward he enforced him to fall; . . . . . VI. xii. 30. 4
backward yode, as Bargemen wont to fare . . . . . VII. vii. 35. 7
Bad. *See* **Bade.**
From good to *badd,* and from *badde* to worse, ... *S.C.* F. 12
Badde is the best; . . . . . *S.C.* S. 105
the *bad* daughter of old Cadmus brood, ... *Gn.* 171
Better a short tale than a *bad* long shriving: . . . . . *Hub.* 543
bad her tongue that it so bluntly tolde. . . . . . *Hub.* 1388
Through their *bad* dooings, or base slothfulnesse, ... *T.M.* 99
Simple in shew and voide of malice *bad;* . . . . . I. i. 29. 7
A bold *bad* man, that dar'd to call . . . Gorgon, ... I. i. 37. 7
all three bred Of one *bad* sire, ... I. ii. 25. 8
with their counsels *bad,* her kingdome did uphold. . . . . . I. iv. 12. 9
So every good to *bad* he doth abuse; . . . . . I. iv. 32. 5
To make one great by others losse is *bad* excheat. . . . . . I. v. 25. 9
an Enchaunter *bad* His sence abusd, ... I. vii. 49. 3
what evill starre On you hath . . . pourd his influence *bad,* . I. viii. 42. 7
All were his earthly eien both blunt and *bad,* . . . . . I. x. 47. 3
On them she workes her will to uses *bad:* . . . . . II. i. 52. 4
'death is an equall doome To good and *bad,* . . . . . II. i. 59. 2
As selfe to dyen *bad,* unburied *bad* to beene.' . . . . . II. i. 59. 9
their natures *bad* appeard in both; . . . . . II. ii. 34. 5
Mortall Samnitis, and Cicuta *bad,* . . . . . II. vii. 52. 5
Bad therefore I him deeme . . . . . II. viii. 14. 9
'Good or *bad,'* gan his brother fiers reply, ... II. viii. 15. 1
what doth his *bad* death now satisfy . . . . . II. viii. 15. 3
Bad counsels, prayses, and false flatteries: . . . . . II. xi. 10. 8
ghosts doen often creepe . . . *bad* livers to torment: . . . . II. xii. 6. 6
for thy *bad* And brutish shape . . . . . III. iv. 55. 3
the dew reward Of his *bad* deedes, ... III. v. 14. 7
Unweeting of their wile and treason *bad,* . . . . . III. v. 18. 3
for that spectacle *bad* . . . their cruell vengeaunce blin, . . . III. v. 22. 6
he follow should his brethren *bad,* . . . . . III. v. 24. 5
'The tydinges *bad,* Which now in Faery court . . . . . III. viii. 46. 1
never let th' ensample of the *bad* Offend the good; . . . . . III. ix. 2. 1
ignorant of servants *bad* abuse . . . . . III. ix. 18. 6
purloyned for his maister *bad)* . . . . . III. x. 54. 4
This all as *bad* as she, and worse, if worse ought were. . . III. xi. 3. 9
Of the *bad* issue of his counsell vaine, ... IV. ii. 6. 2
For evill deedes may better then *bad* words be bore. . . . . . IV. iv. 4. 9
that *bad* eyes might it not prophane: . . . . . IV. iv. 15. 3
rather wholly dead . . . then in so *bad* a stead. . . . . . IV. iv. 22. 9
wearie limmes recur'd after late usage *bad.* . . . . . IV. vi. 39. 9
Whose *bad* condition yet it doth retaine, ... IV. xi. 38. 8
both to good and *bad* he dealeth right, ... V. Pr. 10. 4
For any death to chaunge life, though most *bad:* . . . . . V. iv. 11. 5
As a *bad* Nurse, which, fayning to receive . . . . . V. v. 53. 1
tell what ever it be, good or *bad,* . . . . . V. vi. 10. 2
'Cease, thou *bad* newes-man! . . . . . V. vi. 11. 4

Bad—*Continued.*
never word did say Nor good nor *bad*, . . . V. vi. 18. 4
To have beheld a spectacle so *bad;* . . . V. vii. 38. 5
stird up . . . By his *bad* wife that hight Adicia; . . . V. viii. 20. 3
guyded through th' ayrie wyde By some *bad* spirit . . . V. viii. 34. 7
the bold title of a poet *bad* He on himselfe had ta'en, . . . V. ix. 25. 8
forth he far'd with all his many *bad*, . . . V. xi. 3. 2
Fallen into that Tyrants hand and usage *bad*. . . . V. xi. 40. 9
those villens through their usage *bad* Them fouly rent, . . . V. xi. 60. 8
Agreeing in *bad* will and cancred kynd; . . . V. xii. 33. 2
in *bad* maner they did disagree, . . . V. xii. 33. 3
what so Envie good or *bad* did fynd . . . V. xii. 33. 4
faynes to weave false tales and leasings *bad*, . . . V. xii. 36. 8
their *bad* Stuard neither plough'd nor sowed, . . . VI. iv. 14. 7
his tongue doth whet Gainst all, both good and *bad*, . . . VI. vi. 12. 4
ywroken Of all the vile demeane and usage *bad*, . . . VI. vi. 18. 4
The best advizement was, of *bad*, to let her Sleepe . . . VI. viii. 38. 1
day, that doth discover *bad* and good, . . . VI. viii. 51. 7
Now made the spoile of theeves and Brigants *bad*, . . . VI. x. 40. 7
Of good and *bad* alike, of low and hie, . . . VI. xii. 28. 6
all other creatures her *bad* dooings rewed. . . . VII. vi. 4. 9
wrong of right, and *bad* of good did make . . . VII. vi. 6. 3
'Of that *bad* seed is this bold woman bred, . . . VII. vi. 21. 1
before that *bad* occasion, . . . VII. vi. 54. 3
From good to *bad*, from *bad* to worst of all: . . . VII. vii. 19. 6
so *bad* end for hereticks ordayned; . . . *Am.* xlviii. 6
Bade. He *bade* me upwarde unto heaven looke. . . . *Bel.*[1] i. 8
bad me to reare My lookes to heaven . . . *Bel.*[2] i. 7
bad defiance to his enemie. . . . *Van.* vi. 6
bad him battaile even to his jawes: . . . *Van.* x. 8
badde the Brere in his plaint proceede. . . . *S.C.* F. 159
thwarting his huge shield, Them battell *bad*, . . . *Gn.* 515
bad the Ape him dight To play his part, . . . *Hub.* 233
bad next day that all should readie be: . . . *Hub.* 329
bad him put all cowardize away: . . . *Hub.* 958
in the Kings name *bad* them both to stay, . . . *Hub.* 1071
dreadles *bad* them come to Corte, . . . *Hub.* 1077
bad him flie with never-resting speed . . . *Hub.* 1247
he *bad* the Lyon be remitted Into his seate, . . . *Hub.* 1254
bad him stay at ease till further preeving. . . . *Hub.* 1366
it *bad* me, to the other side To cast mine eye, . . . *Ti.* 587
her awaking *bad* her quickly dight, . . . *Ti.* 639
Bad her faire damzels, flocking her arownd, . . . *Mui.* 116
My Daphne hence departing *bad* me so; . . . *D.* 454
She *bad* me stay, till she for me did send. . . . *D.* 455
He *bad* awake blacke Plutoes griesly Dame; . . . I. i. 37. 4
Unto that Elfin knight he *bad* him fly, . . . I. i. 46. 2
She . . . *bad* her knight addresse him to the fray, . . . I. ii. 14. 5
Her soone he overtooke, and *bad* to stay; . . . I. ii. 20. 8
Thether Duessa *badd* him bend his pace, . . . I. iv. 3. 7
Ne other grace vouchsafed . . . scarse them *bad* arise. . . . I. iv. 14. 4
bad say on the secrete of her hart: . . . I. iv. 46. 2
trompet . . . unto battaill *bad* them selves addresse: . . . I. v. 6. 2
wonne from death, she *bad* him tellen plaine . . . I. vi. 37. 7
sternely *bad* him other business plie . . . I. vi. 46. 7
badd the waters, . . . Be such as she her selfe was . . . I. vii. 5. 6
The noble knight . . . *badd* the Ladie stay, . . . I. viii. 2. 8
So, as she *bad*, that witch they disaraid, . . . I. viii. 46. 1
Whose aunswere *bad* me still assured bee, . . . I. ix. 5. 7
She . . . *badd* me love her deare; . . . I. ix. 14. 2
bad him choose what death he would desire; . . . I. ix. 50. 8
Then *badd* the knight his Lady yede aloof, . . . I. xi. 5. 1
He *badd* to open wyde his brasen gate, . . . I. xii. 3. 6
badd thereof take heed; . . . I. xii. 10. 8
Bad on that Messenger rude hands to reach. . . . I. xii. 35. 3
badd tell on the tenor of his playnt: . . . II. i. 9. 2
bad me call Lucina to me neare. . . . II. i. 53. 5
both their champions *bad* Pursew the end . . . II. ii. 28. 2
each *bad* other flye: . . . II. iii. 19. 8
bad him stay till time the tide renewd. . . . II. vi. 26. 9
voyce, That *bad* him come in haste. . . . II. viii. 4. 4
As him the Steward *badd*. . . . II. ix. 28. 6
ripe age *bad* him surrender late His life, . . . II. x. 13. 8
his Palmer *bad* To stere the bote . . . II. xii. 28. 1
he the boteman *bad* row easily, . . . II. xii. 33. 8
As if that age *badd* him that burden spare, . . . III. i. 4. 5
Badd those same six forbeare that single enimy. . . . III. i. 22. 9
He *bad* tell on; . . . III. iii. 16. 1
bad her all things put in readinesse anon. . . . III. iii. 57. 9
Badd her old Squyre unlace her lofty creast: . . . III. iv. 7. 3
Bad her from womankind to keepe him well, . . . III. iv. 25. 7
His mother *bad* him wemens love to hate, . . . III. iv. 27. 7
shee *bad* her charett to be brought; . . . III. iv. 31. 2
Bad eke attonce their charetts to be sought: . . . III. iv. 31. 4
eies . . . I mote have closed, and him *bed* farewell, . . . III. iv. 39. 5
Him boldly *bad* his passage there to stay, . . . III. v. 18. 7
did bite The bitter earth, and *bad* to lett him in . . . III. v. 22. 2
bad them to increase and multiply: . . . III. vi. 34. 6
Badd her commaund my life to save or spill. . . . III. vii. 54. 2
Eftsoones she *badd* me, . . . To wander through the world . . . III. vii. 54. 3
Bad that same boaster, as he mote, on high, . . . III. viii. 16. 3
bad that none their joyous treason should reveale, . . . III. x. 5. 9
bad before his soveraine Lord appere. . . . III. x. 23. 7
They after both, and boldly *bad* him bace, . . . III. xi. 5. 5
bad the stubborne flames to yield him way: . . . III. xi. 26. 4
His blindfold eies he *bad* awhile unbinde, . . . III. xii. 22. 6
bad them leave their labours and long toyle . . . IV. iv. 48. 6
bad him rise, or surely he should die. . . . IV. vi. 23. 6
bad them, if so be they were not bound, . . . IV. vii. 33. 7
Bad them not looke for better entertayne; . . . IV. viii. 27. 4

Bad—*Continued.*
She *bad* to lighten my too heavie band, . . . IV. viii. 61. 3
He *bad* him stay, and backe with him retire, . . . V. i. 21. 1
bad his servant Talus to invent Which way . . . V. ii. 20. 8
he *bad* them Florimell forth call. . . . V. iii. 22. 9
She *bad* that streight the gates should be unbard, . . . V. iv. 37. 8
showre of arrowes, which them staid, And better *bad* advise, . . . V. iv. 38. 5
she sternely *bade* His miserie to be augmented more, . . . V. v. 54. 5
mounting to her steede *bad* Talus guide her on. . . . V. vi. 17. 9
But fild with courage . . . she *bad* to open bold, . . . V. vii. 25. 6
she *bad* them forth to hold. . . . V. vii. 25. 9
Bad doe away the dampe of drouzie sleepe, . . . V. vii. 26. 8
would no lenger treat, but *bad* them sound; . . . V. vii. 28. 7
bad Deliver him his owne, . . . V. xi. 3. 7
backstarting with disdainefull yre *Bad* him avaunt, . . . V. xi. 61. 6
Bad him to flie with all the speed he could . . . VI. i. 29. 4
he *bad* me by and by For to alight: . . . VI. ii. 17. 5
He *bad* him stand t' abide the bitter stoure . . . VI. iii. 48. 4
therefore lightly *bad* him packe away, . . . VI. vi. 21. 6
He *bad* his eyes to be unblindfold both, . . . VI. vii. 33. 8
Bad them be still; . . . VI. xi. 14. 8
Boldly him *bad* such injurie forbeare; . . . VI. xi. 15. 2
Bade her attonce from heavens coast to pack, . . . VII. vi. 12. 8
At last he *bade* her (with bold stedfastnesse) . . . VII. vi. 17. 7
bade Dan Phoebus scribe her Appellation seale. . . . VII. vi. 35. 9
Bade Order call them all before her Majesty. . . . VII. vii. 27. 9
streame, . . . *bad* his billowes spare . . . *Proth.* 48
Badge. Unlesse that some gay Mistresse *badge* he beares: . . . *Col.* 780
For whose sweete sake that glorious *badge* he wore, . . . I. i. 2. 3
cursed steele against that *badge* I bent, . . . II. i. 27. 5
The sacred *badge* of my Redeemers death, . . . II. i. 27. 6
To loose the *badge* that should his deedes display.' . . . V. xi. 52. 5
in which he did endosse His deare Redeemers *badge* . . . V. xi. 53. 5
Which is the *badge* of honour and of fame, . . . VI. iii. 35. 3
it is the *badge* which I doe beare, . . . *Am.* xxviii. 3
Badger. Into the hole, the which the *Badger* swept. . . . *Ti.* 217
Badges. The *badges* of reproch, he threw away, . . . V. iv. 35. 4
to adorne With so brave *badges* . . . VI. vi. 36. 5
Badly. 'Seest not how *badly* all things present bee, . . . V. ii. 37. 2
badly doest thou hide Thy maisters shame, . . . V. vi. 11. 4
hearing how his people *badly* sped, . . . VI. vi. 24. 4
Baetus'. Imagery Of *Baetus* or of Alcons vanity. . . . *Gn.* 104
Baffled. himselfe *baffuld*, and his armes unherst, . . . V. iii. 37. 8
Turpine is *baffuld;* . . . VI. vii. Arg.
him hung upon a tree, And *baffuld* so, . . . VI. vii. 27. 3
Bag. her fine corpes to a *bag* of venim grewe. . . . *Mui.* 352
wearied with bearing of her *bag* . . . I. i. 6. 3
Unfitly furnisht with thy *bag* and booke, . . . III. x. 24. 7
in this *bag*, which I behinde me don, . . . VI. viii. 24. 4
Yet is the bottle leake, and *bag* so torne, . . . VI. viii. 24. 6
in a *bag* all sorts of seeds ysame, . . . VII. vii. 32. 7
Bagpipe. Or is thy *Bagpype* broke, that soundes so sweete? . . . *S.C.* Ap. 3
How can *Bagpipe* or joynts be well apayd? . . . *S.C.* Au. 6
Care now his idle *bagpipe* up to raise, . . . *Ti.* 226
'Let *Bagpipe* never more be heard to shrill, . . . *D.* 323
broke his *bag-pipe* quight, . . . VI. x. 18. 5
Bagpipes. bene thy *Bagpypes* renne farre out of frame? . . . *S.C.* Au. 3
They heard a noyse of many *bagpipes* shrill, . . . III. x. 43. 2
Then gan the *bagpypes* and the hornes to shrill . . . VI. viii. 46. 1
Bags. Thy Ewes, that wont to have blowen *bags*, . . . *S.C.* F. 81
from backe and belly still did spare, To fill his *bags*, . . . I. iv. 28. 5
Baid. *See* **Bayed.**
Baies. *See* **Bays.**
Bail. now nill be quitt with *baile* nor borrowe. . . . *S.C.* May 131
though my *bale* with death I bought, . . . *S.C.* Au. 105
Ne none there was to reskue her, ne none to *baile*. . . . IV. ix. 7. 9
Use silly Faunus, now within their *baile:* . . . VII. vi. 49. 2
Bailiff-errant. A *Baylieffe-errant* forth in post did passe, . . . VI. vii. 35. 7
Bains. *See* **Banns.**
Bait. *See* **Bate.**
beautie is the *bayt* which . . . Doth man allure . . . *Col.* 871
The Sunne, . . . doth *baite* his steedes the Ocean waves emong. I. i. 32. 9
thousand other waies to *bait* his fleshly hookes. . . . I. iv. 25. 9
As chained beare whom cruell dogs doe *bait*, . . . I. xii. 35. 7
The fish that once was caught new *bait* wil hardly byte. . . . II. i. 4. 9
falsed oft his blowes t' illude him with such *bayt*. . . . II. v. 9. 9
so glorious *bayte* Would tempt his guest . . . II. vii. 34. 3
In frayle intemperaunce through sinfull *bayt;* . . . II. vii. 64. 2
salvage Bull, whom two fierce mastives *bayt*, . . . II. viii. 42. 1
her guilefull *bayt* She will embosome deeper in your mind, . . . II. xii. 29. 2
Unwares the hidden hooke with *baite* I swallowed. . . . III. ii. 38. 9
Through false allurement of that pleasing *baite*, . . . IV. Pr. 1. 7
made the *baite* of bestiall delight: . . . IV. viii. 32. 4
feeling him thus bite upon the *bayt*, . . . V. v. 42. 6
notwithstanding all the subtill *bait* . . . V. vi. 2. 3
Nought under heaven so strongly doth allure . . . As beauties lovely *baite*, . . . V. viii. 1. 3
Gan forth to lay his *bayte* her to beguyle, . . . V. ix. 12. 8
They sent that Blatant Beast to be a *baite* . . . VI. v. 15. 3
feeding on the *bayt* of his owne bane: . . . VI. ix. 34. 4
Barking and biting all that him doe *bate*, . . . VI. xii. 40. 5
Is but a *bayt* such wretches to beguile, . . . *Am.* xli. 10
To make the *bayte* her gazers to embrew: . . . *Am.* liii. 11
Drawne with sweet pleasures *bayt*, . . . *Am.* lxxii. 7
the *bait* of sinne, and sinners scorne, . . . *H.B.* 152
with false beauties flattring *bait* misled, . . . *H.H.B.* 290
Baited. *See* **Bate.**
Under blacke stole hyding her *bayted* hooke; . . . I. i. 49. 6
bayted every word, . . . III. x. 6. 7
Is *bayted* of a mastiffe and a hound . . . VI. v. 19. 2

Baiting. After the chafed Lyons cruell *bayting*, ... *Hub.* 6
Baits. layen *baytes* to beguile her brother; . . . . *S.C.* S. 39
fish, which they with *baits* usde to betraie, ... *Ti.* 152
Mordant and Amavia slaine With pleasures poisoned *baytes*. . II. i. Arg.
thy bounteous *baytes* and pleasing charmes, ... II. vii. 10. 3
luring *baytes* oftimes doe heedlesse harts entyse. . . . . . . IV. x. 49. 9
Another while I *baytes* and nets display . . . . VI. ix. 23. 5
hookes, That from the foolish fish theyr *bayts* doe hyde: . . . *Am.* xlvii. 4
Bake. *bake* their sides uppon the cold hard stone, ... V. vii. 9. 3
Balance. seeing . . . The doubtfull *ballaunce* equally to sway, I. ii. 38. 2
right and wrong ylike in equall *ballaunce* waide. . . . . . . I. iv. 27. 9
in true *ballaunce* thou wilt weigh thy state; . . . . I. ix. 45. 2
His credit now in doubtfull *ballaunce* hong: . . . . II. i. 3. 8
Whilst thus the case in doubtfull *ballance* hong, ... IV. iii. 37. 1
Whether shall weigh the *balance* downe; . . . . IV. ix. 1. 4
to weigh both right and wrong In equall *ballance* . . . . . . V. i. 7. 2
next her selfe her righteous *ballance* hanging bee. . . . . . V. i. 11. 9
An huge great paire of *ballance* in his hand, ... V. ii. 30. 3
fild his *ballaunce* full of idle toys: . . . . V. ii. 30. 8
So would he of the fire one *ballaunce* make, ... V. ii. 31. 3
Then would he *ballaunce* heaven and hell together, ... V. ii. 31. 5
take thy *ballaunce*, if thou be so wise, ... V. ii. 43. 1
the least word that ever could be layd Within his *ballaunce* . V. ii. 44. 4
So he the words into his *ballaunce* threw, ... V. ii. 44. 8
streight the winged words out of his *ballaunce* flew. . . . . V. ii. 44. 9
Ne would within his *ballaunce* well abide: . . . . V. ii. 45. 2
First in one *ballance* set the true aside.' . . . . V. ii. 45. 5
said, 'Be not upon thy *balance* wroken, ... V. ii. 47. 4
The eare must be the *ballance*, ... V. ii. 47. 8
Balances. weighed out in *ballaunces* so nere, ... V. ii. 35. 3
almost would his *balances* have broken; . . . . V. ii. 47. 2
His battred *ballances* in peeces lay, ... V. ii. 50. 7
Bald. shortly *balde* and bared she became. . . . . *Van.* vii. 12
His toppe was *bald*, and wasted with wormes, ... *S.C.* F. 113
Her crafty head was altogether *bald*, ... I. viii. 47. 1
all behinde was *bald*, and worne away, ... II. iv. 4. 7
Baldric. Athwart his brest a *bauldrick* brave he ware, ... I. vii. 29. 8
Knit with a golden *bauldricke*, ... II. iii. 29. 5
with brave *bauldrick* garnished. . . . . III. iii. 59. 9
The heavens bright-shining *baudricke* to enchace; . . . . . . V. i. 11. 7
Which decke the *Bauldricke* of the Heavens bright; . . . . . *Proth.* 174
Bale. *See* **Bail.**
lyeth buryed long in Winters *bale;* . . . . *S.C.* N. 84
the sweete Cypresse, signe of deadly *bale*. . . . . *Gn.* 216
Into this bitter *bale* I am outcast, ... *Gn.* 330
Let now your blisse be turned into *bale*, ... *D.* 320
To slaughter them, and worke their finall *bale*, ... *As.* 105
light she hated as the deadly *bale*, ... I. i. 16. 7
She fedd her wound with fresh renewed *bale*. . . . . I. vii. 28. 6
Soone as I thinke upon my bitter *bale*. . . . . I. vii. 39. 6
Th' eternall *bale* of heavie wounded harts: . . . . I. viii. 14. 5
still he strove to cloke his inward *bale*, ... I. ix. 16. 3
when he . . . felt our feeble harts Embost with *bale*, ... I. ix. 29. 2
we may pitty such unhappie *bale*, ... II. ii. 45. 3
Her faultie Handmayd, which that *bale* did breede, ... II. iv. 29. 8
thee to endlesse *bale* captived lead. . . . . II. v. 16. 6
which doe men in *bale* to sterve, ... II. vi. 34. 3
A song of *bale* and bitter sorrow sings, ... II. vii. 23. 7
As one in wilfull *bale* for ever buried. . . . . III. ii. 31. 9
bringe her backe againe, or worke her finall *bale*. . . . . . . III. vii. 21. 9
poysnous *bale* did breede To all that on him lookt . . . . . IV. viii. 39. 4
Of their vaine prowesse turned to their proper *bale*. . . . . V. iv. 24. 9
my last *bale* to breed.' . . . . V. v. 29. 9
bring us *bale* and bitter sorrowings, ... VI. iii. 5. 5
Lay in the lap of death, rewing his wretched *bale*. . . . . . VI. vii. 17. 9
thence to banish *bale*, ... VI. x. 8. 6
the author of thy *bale* to be, ... VI. x. 29. 4
th' inward *bale* of my love-pined hart; . . . . *Am.* ii. 2
Baleful. Such stormy stoures do breede my *balefull* smart, . . *S.C.* Ja. 27
balefull barking bringes in hast Pyne, ... *S.C.* Jul. 23
did fetch his dame From Plutoes *balefull* bowre . . . . . . *S.C.* O. 29
balefull boughes of Cypres doen advaunce; . . . . *S.C.* N. 145
Winter is come, that blowes the *balefull* breath, ... *S.C.* D. 149
That *balefull* sorrow he no longer beares . . . . *Gn.* 644
he at last laid forth on *balefull* beare. . . . . *T.M.* 162
For the Shriche-owle to build her *balefull* bowre: . . . . . . *Ti.* 130
The bit of *balefull* steele and bitter stownd, ... *Mui.* 62
He cast about, and searcht his *baleful* bokes againe. . . . . . I. ii. 2. 9
But few returned, having scaped hard, With *balefull* beggery, . I. iv. 3. 4
powres . . . Have borne him hence to Plutoes *balefull* bowres: I. v. 14. 8
Begin, and end the bitter *balefull* stound; . . . . I. vii. 25. 8
brought not backe the *balefull* body dead: . . . . I. vii. 50. 5
Yet live perforce in *balefull* darkenesse bound? . . . . I. viii. 38. 5
the ghastly Owle, Shrieking his *balefull* note, ... I. ix. 33. 7
bitter doome of death and *balefull* mone . . . . I. x. 53. 8
thereby dead that *balefull* Beast did deeme, ... I. xii. 2. 7
in dead parents *balefull* ashes bred, ... II. ii. 2. 2
balefull speare he fiercely bent . . . . II. viii. 32. 1
of the battell *balefull* end had made, ... II. xi. 29. 7
First did it shew the bitter *balefull* stowre, ... III. i. 34. 7
To enter into that same *balefull* Bowre, ... III. iii. 8. 8
Into the *balefull* house of endlesse night, ... III. v. 22. 3
In *balefull* night where all thinges are forgot: . . . . III. vi. 47. 3
Brought unto *balefull* ruine, ... III. ix. 34. 4
Resolv'd to build his *balefull* mansion . . . . III. x. 58. 2
Brought thee from *balefull* house of Proserpine, ... III. xi. 1. 2
Full dreadfull thinges out of that *balefull* booke He red, . . . III. xii. 36. 3
To ward his bodie from the *balefull* stound, ... IV. viii. 45. 2
Like to the *balefull* house of lowest hell, ... IV. xi. 4. 3
balefull Oure, late staind with English blood, ... IV. xi. 44. 5

Baleful—*Continued.*
t' abide the *balefull* stowre . . . . V. v. 18. 7
sad tydings of his *balefull* smart . . . . V. vi. 3. 3
lowre Upon their blisse, and *balefull* fortune frowne: . . . . V. x. 26. 7
from her *balefull* minde all care he banished. . . . . V. x. 39. 9
Of butchers *balefull* hand to ground is feld, ... VI. xii. 30. 8
bitter stormes, and *balefull* countenance . . . . VII. vii. 23. 5
when I feele the bitter *balefull* smart, ... *Am.* xxiv. 5
the author of their *balefull* bane: . . . . *H.L.* 128
Balefulness. Because they breed sad *balefulnesse* in mee; . . *D.* 410
their blisse he turn'd to *balefulnesse*. . . . . II. xii. 83. 5
Bales. T' entrap unwary fooles in their eternall *bales*. . . . VI. x. 3. 9
Balk. *balk* the right way, and strayen abroad. . . . . *S.C.* S. 93
labour, that did from his liking *balke*, ... *Hub.* 268
Her list in stryfull termes with him to *balke*, ... III. ii. 12. 3
Not sparing wight, ne leaving any *balke*, ... VI. xi. 16. 4
Balked. Ne ever for rebuke or blame of any *balkt*. . . . . . IV. x. 25. 9
Ball. *See* **Bawl.**
thy *Ball* is a bold bigge curre, ... *S.C.* S. 164
Ballads. Bransles, *Ballads*, virelayes, and verses vaine; . . III. x. 8. 5
Ballance, -aunce. *See* **Balance.**
Balliards. *See* **Billiards.**
Balm. Embathed *Balme*, and chearfull Galingale, ... *Mui.* 194
A trickling streame of *Balme*, most soveraine . . . . I. xi. 48. 2
Balme, whose vertuous might Did heale his woundes, ... I. xi. 50. 5
With *balme*, and wine, and costly spicery, ... II. xi. 49. 4
They pourd in soveraine *balme* and Nectar good, ... III. iv. 40. 8
And powring *balme*, . . . Into his wounds, ... VI. ii. 48. 3
Balm-like. With *Balmelike* odor did perfume the aire. . . *Bel.*[1] ix. 4
Balms. he *balmes* and herbes thereto applyde, ... II. vi. 51. 6
Balmy. With *balmie* odours fil'd th' ayre . . . . *Bel.*[2] xi. 4
Ban. *See* **Bann, Banns, Bans.**
Gan both to envy, and bitterly to *ban;* . . . . IV. ix. 9. 7
There gan he me to curse and *ban*, ... VI. ii. 21. 4
Banck(e). *See* **Bank.**
Banckett(s). *See* **Banquet(s).**
Band. *See* **Banned.**
beside the honourable *band* Of great Heroes . . . . *Gn.* 479
Such one was Avarice, the fourth of this faire *band*. . . . . I. iv. 29. 9
Huge routs of people did about them *band*, ... I. iv. 36. 5
Phoebe fayre With all her *band* was following the chace, . . I. vii. 5. 2
Prince Arthure, crowne of Martiall *band?*' . . . . I. ix. 6. 5
thou slepst in tender swadling *band*, ... I. x. 65. 7
far before did march a goodly *band* Of tall young men, . . . I. xii. 5. 6
since that *band* ye cannot now release, ... I. xii. 19. 5
thy daughter linck, in holy *band* Of wedlocke, ... I. xii. 26. 6
By breaking of the *band* betwixt us twaine; . . . . I. xii. 34. 4
seeming sorely chauffed at his *band*, ... I. xii. 35. 6
The usuall joyes at knitting of loves *band*. . . . . I. xii. 40. 5
by that same sacred *band* Betwixt us both, ... II. iv. 23. 6
thy remembraunce and perpetuall *band* . . . . II. x. 69. 4
That wicked *band* of villeins . . . . II. xi. 5. 3
that fourth *band* which cruell battry bent . . . . II. xi. 12. 1
Till it dissolved be from earthly *band*. . . . . II. xi. 30. 5
firmely bound with faithfull *band*, ... III. iii. 27. 6
A *band* of Britons, ryding on forray . . . . III. iii. 58. 4
For great despight of that unwonted *band*, ... III. vii. 36. 4
he had broke his *band*, And was returnd . . . . III. vii. 61. 7
Why then is Amoret in caytive *band*, ... III. xi. 10. 2
vertue is the *band* that bindeth harts most sure. . . . . . . IV. ii. 29. 9
His wearie ghost assoyld from fleshly *band* . . . . IV. iii. 13. 1
mighty spirites bound with mightier *band*, ... IV. iii. 48. 7
vauncing forth from all the other *band* Of knights, ... IV. iv. 17. 3
Thus was Sir Satyrane with all his *band* . . . . IV. iv. 43. 1
that late weaker *band* of chalengers relieved. . . . . IV. iv. 46. 9
Having through stirring loosd their wonted *band*, ... IV. vi. 20. 2
the *band* Of noble minds derived from above, ... IV. vi. 31. 7
She bad to lighten my too heavie *band*, ... IV. viii. 61. 3
the *band* of vertuous mind, ... IV. ix. 1. 8
Unwilling to behold that lovely *band*. . . . . IV. x. 33. 5
many a *band* of Scots and English both, ... IV. xi. 36. 8
Ne loose that he hath bound with stedfast *band*. . . . . . . V. ii. 42. 4
being freed from Proteus cruell *band* . . . . V. iii. 2. 1
So farre he past amongst his enemies *band*, ... V. iii. 9. 3
put to that base service of her *band*, ... V. iv. 32. 7
When they have shaken off the shamefast *band*, ... V. v. 25. 2
her good Knights, of which so brave a *band* Serves her . . . V. viii. 18. 6
He sent to her his basenet as a faithfull *band*. . . . . VI. i. 31. 9
in gilden armes, with azure *band* Quartred athwart, ... VI. ii. 44. 7
whether free with him she now were, or in *band?* . . . . . . V. vii. 27. 9
Such was the beauty of this goodly *band*, ... VI. x. 14. 1
Yet none of them could ever bring him into *band*. . . . . . . VI. xii. 39. 9
your hand, The pledge of all our *band!* . . . . *Epith.* 239
Eternally bind thou this lovely *band*, ... *Epith.* 396
Should in loves gentle *band* combyned bee . . . . *H.B.* 205
And bound thereto with an eternall *band*, ... *H.H.L.* 187
Banderol. lastly to despoyle of knightly *bannerall*. . . . . VI. vii. 26. 9
Bandogs. We han great *Bandogs* will teare their skinne. . . . *S.C.* S. 163
Manie great *bandogs* which her gird about: . . . . *Gn.* 540
Bandon. The pleasaunt *Bandon* crownd with many a wood; IV. xi. 44. 2
Band's. she doth new *bands* adventure dread;— . . . . *Col.* 567
Bands. *See* **Swathbands.**
The *bands* of th' elements shall backe reverse . . . . *Ro.* xxii. 11
yron *bands* abord The Pontick sea . . . . *Gn.* 46
(Both two sure *bands* in friendship to be tide) . . . . *Hub.* 54
so tame . . . And buxome to his *bands*, ... *Hub.* 626
freed from *bands* of impacable fate, ... *Ti.* 395
in their wrath breake off the vitall *bands*, ... *D.* 18
when as death these vitall *bands* shall breake, ... *Col.* 630
soone to loose her wicked *bands* did her constraine. . . . . . I. i. 19. 9

Bands—*Continued.*
That was in sacred *bandes* of wedlocke tyde To Therion, . . . I. vi. 21. 5
So oft as he, . . . is to sinfull *bands* made thrall: . . . I. viii. 1. 7
Els should this Redcrosse knight in *bands* have dyde, . . . I. viii. 1. 8
nether darkenesse fowle, nor filthy *bands,* . . . his purpose could withhold, . . . I. viii. 40. 1
The knights knitt friendly *bands:* . . . I. ix. Arg.
this good Prince redeemd the Redcrosse knight from *bands.* . I. ix. 1. 9
Als flew his steed as he his *bandes* had brast, . . . I. ix. 21. 7
why they in *bands* were layd; . . . I. x. 40. 7
Till from her *bands* the spright assoiled is, . . . I. x. 52. 8
Himselfe in streighter *bandes* too rash implyes, . . . I. xi. 23. 5
My conscience cleare with guilty *bands* would bynd? . . . I. xii. 30. 5
Whom Princes late displeasure left in *bands,* . . . II. i. 1. 2
gan to breake the *bands* of their captivitee. . . . II. v. 18. 9
him she tooke And threw in *bands,* . . . II. x. 18. 7
broke his caytive *bands;* . . . II. xi. 33. 2
The lothfull life, now loosd from sinfull *bands,* . . . II. xi. 46. 3
Throwing away her broken chaines and *bands,* . . . II. xi. 47. 4
both them strongly bound In captive *bandes,* . . . II. xii. 82. 5
Sweete love such lewdnes *bands* from his faire companee. . . . III. ii. 41. 9
Proud of his dying honor and deare *bandes,* . . . III. iv. 17. 3
in *bands,* as conquered To be her thrall, . . . III. vii. 17. 7
He reard him up and loosd his yron *bands,* . . . III. vii. 46. 6
It is not yron *bandes,* nor hundred eyes, . . . III. ix. 7. 4
With perfect peace and *bandes* of fresh accord, . . . III. x. 51. 4
her small waste girt rownd with yron *bands* . . . III. xii. 30. 8
Witnesse their broken *bandes* there to be seene, . . . IV. i. 24. 6
Allide with *bands* of mutuall couplement; . . . IV. iii. 52. 3
tyde In *bands* of friendship, . . . IV. x. 27. 8
bound them with inviolable *bands;* . . . IV. x. 35. 4
To let faire Florimell in *bands* remayne, . . . IV. xi. 1. 4
In *bands* of love, . . . IV. xi. 1. 5
now they doe with captive *bands* him bind; . . . V. iii. 9. 7
for joy he brake His *bands,* . . . V. iii. 34. 8
Fast bound on every side with iron *bands,* . . . V. iv. 5. 2
'Bound unto me but not with such hard *bands* . . . V. v. 33. 1
many yron *bands* on him to lade: . . . V. v. 54. 7
farre away, amid their rakehell *bands,* . . . V. xi. 44. 6
bands of nature, that wilde beastes restraine, . . . V. xii. 1. 5
all the *bands* Which may a Knight assure . . . V. xii. 2. 1
they that breake *bands* of civilitie, . . . VI. i. 26. 6
He him by all the *bands* of love besought, . . . VI. iii. 15. 6
having all his *bands* againe uptyde, . . . VI. iv. 24. 1
kept in *bands,* or from their loves exyled, . . . VI. vii. 33. 4
These two, unworthy of your wretched *bands,* . . . VI. viii. 7. 6
He from those *bands* weend him to have unwound; . . . VI. viii. 27. 4
in subtile *bands* Of the blynd boy; . . . VI. ix. 11. 6
doth the Blatant Beast Subdew, and bynd in *bands.* . . . VI. xi. Arg.
Thus long continu'd . . . Bellamour in *bands;* . . . VI. xii. 10. 2
Yet greatly did the Beast repine at those Straunge *bands,* . . VI. xii. 36. 2
brought Into like *bands,* ne maystred any more: . . . VI. xii. 39. 4
hold in loves soft *bands,* Lyke captives . . . *Am.* i. 3
Have ever since me kept in cruell *bands.* . . . *Am.* xii. 12
Out of her *bands* ye by no meanes shall get. . . . *Am.* xxxvii. 12
Sweet be the *bands,* the which true love doth tye . . . *Am.* lxv. 5
In whose streight *bands* ye now captived are . . . *Am.* lxxi. 7
My hart (whom none with servile *bands* can tye, . . . *Am.* lxxiii. 2
th' Earth, . . . engirt with brasen *bands;* . . . *H.H.B.* 37

Bandy. *See* **Bands.**
To *bandie* Crownes, and Kingdoms to bestowe: . . . VII. vi. 32. 8

Bane. such sight hath bred my *bane.* . . . *S.C.* Ja. 53
commen to his reskew, ere his bitter *bane.* . . . II. xi. 29. 9
It never rests till it have wrought his finall *bane.* . . . VI. vi. 8. 9
feeding on the bayt of his owne *bane:* . . . VI. ix. 34. 4
The more I love and doe embrace my *bane.* . . . *Am.* xlii. 4
O mighty charm! which makes men love theyr *bane,* . . . *Am.* xlvii. 13
the author of their balefull *bane:* . . . *H.L.* 128

Baneful. Helpe me, ye *banefull* byrds, . . . *S.C.* Au. 173
a deepe descent, . . . breathed ever forth a filthie *banefull* smell. . . . I. viii. 39. 9
bit them with his *banefull* teeth of injury. . . . VI. xii. 28. 9

Bangor. *Bangor* with massacred Martyrs fill, . . . III. iii. 35. 6

Banish. The which to *banish* with faire exercise . . . *Hub.* 737
Why doo they *banish* us, . . . *T.M.* 147
banish me, which do professe the skill . . . *T.M.* 521
dogges . . . Watching to *banish* Care their enimy, . . . I. i. 40. 5
To *banish* cowardize and bastard feare: . . . I. vi. 24. 2
Her sisters, . . . Strive her to *banish* cleane. . . . II. ii. Arg.
To *banish* sloth that oft doth noble mindes annoy. . . . IV. vii. 23. 9
with guilefull words her to perswade To *banish* feare; . . . V. ix. 12. 6
to *banish* all remorse, . . . V. ix. 43. 3
naught may boot to *banishe* them from thence; . . . V. xi. 45. 7
thence to *banish* bale, . . . VI. x. 8. 6

Banished. Out of the Court for ever *banished.* . . . *Hub.* 924
me have *banished,* with all the rest . . . *T.M.* 195
Banisht by those that Love with leawdnes fill. . . . *T.M.* 384
Let him be *banisht* farre away from hence; . . . *D.* 10
banisht had my selfe, like wight forlore, . . . *Col.* 182
Banisht from living wights, our wearie daies we waste.' . . . I. ii. 42. 9
Banisht from princely bowre to wastefull wood! . . . III. iii. 42. 6
O! let him far be *banished* away, . . . III. xi. 2. 1
From all brave knights be *banisht* with defame; . . . V. iii. 38. 8
into moores and marshes *banisht* had, . . . V. x. 18. 4
from her balefull minde all care he *banished.* . . . V. x. 39. 9
full glad That he had *banisht* hunger, . . . VII. vii. 30. 4

Banishment. With fowle reproach, and cruell *banishment?* . *T.M.* 426

Bank. On that great rivers *banck* (*banke*[1]), . . . *Bel.* i. 6
by a rivers *bancke* that swift downe slidd, . . . *Bel.*[2] xv. 7
Upon a sunnie *banke* outstretched lay, . . . *Van.* iii. 2

Bank—*Continued.*
sittes on yonder *bancke,* . . . *S.C.* Jul. 2
Where on a sunnie *banke* the Lambes doo play, . . . *Mui.* 402
that long hath stood Upon the *bancke,* . . . I. ix. 39. 9
In wine and meats she flowd above the *banck,* . . . II. ii. 36. 6
One sitting ydle on a sunny *banck,* . . . II. iii. 6. 2
to behold he clomb up to the *bancke,* . . . II. vii. 57. 1
Upon the *banck* they sitting did espy . . . II. xii. 14. 7
both over *banck* and bush, . . . III. i. 17. 5
by no meanes the high *banke* he could sease, . . . III. v. 19. 8
He on the *bancke* arryvd with mickle payne, . . . III. v. 21. 2
Ne *banck* nor bush could stay him, . . . III. x. 55. 3
the mouldred earth had cav'd the *banke;* . . . IV. v. 33. 2
along whose stony *bancke* . . . IV. xi. 36. 1
Bursting forth teares like springs out of a *banke*), . . . V. i. 15. 2
Stood on the further *bancke* beholding him; . . . VI. iii. 34. 2
Whose rutty *Bancke,* . . . Was paynted all with variable flowers, . . . *Proth.* 12

Banket, -s. *See* **Banquet, -s.**

Banks. Along the *bankes* of the Italian streame. . . . *Bel.*[1] v. 4
Along the *bancks* of the Ausonian streame: . . . *Bel.*[2] v. 4
Enclosing it with *banks* on everie side, . . . *Gn.* 658
along the Lee, About whose flowrie *bankes* . . . *Ti.* 136
flowrie *bancks* with silver liquor steepe; . . . *D.* 102
About the grassie *bancks* of Haemony . . . *As.* 3
water doth within his *bancks* appeare.' . . . *Col.* 95
The *bankes* are overflowne . . . II. iv. 11. 9
Nor bounds nor *banks* his headlong ruine may sustayne. . . . II. xi. 18. 9
aye the cups their *bancks* did overflow; . . . III. i. 51. 6
in strong *bancks* his violence enclose, . . . III. vii. 34. 2
Xanthus sandy *bankes* with blood all overflowne. . . . III. ix. 35. 9
shadie seates, and sundry flowring *bankes,* . . . IV. x. 25. 4
within strong *bancks* is pent, . . . VI. i. 21. 2
Nymphes and Faeries by the *bancks* did sit . . . VI. x. 7. 6

Bann. The pleasant Boyne, the fishy fruitfull *Ban,* . . . IV. xi. 41. 4

Banned. as if he *band* High God, . . . V. ii. 18. 7
curst, and *band,* and blasphemies forth threw . . . V. xi. 12. 3
Free that was thrall, and blessed that was *band;* . . . *H.H.L.* 184

Banner. comming forth shall spred his *banner* brave . . . III. iii. 30. 3
with black dishonor . . . decke thy bloudy *baner?* . . . VI. vi. 25. 5
her faire countenance, like a goodly *banner,* . . . *Am.* v. 11
Advance the *banner* of thy conquest hie, . . . *H.B.* 268

Bannerall. *See* **Banderol.**

Banners. A goodly ship with *banners* bravely dight, . . . *Van.* ix. 2
With scutchins gilt and *banners* broad displayd; . . . IV. iii. 5. 6
Ne hostes of men with *banners* brode dispred, . . . IV. viii. 47. 7

Banning. Swearing and *banning* most blasphemously, . . . V. viii. 28. 2

Banns. *See* **Bans.**
He gan renew the late forbidden *bains,* . . . I. xii. 36. 7

Banquet. to her guestes doth bounteous *banket* dight, . . . II. xi. 2. 8
then his bloudy *banket* should beginne. . . . IV. vii. 20. 9
that great *banquet* of the watry Gods, . . . IV. xi. 10. 8
The manner of the Gods when they at *banquet* be. . . . IV. xii. 3. 9
Ne with th' eternall Gods to *bancket* come; . . . IV. xii. 4. 4
like one unto a *banquet* bid, . . . V. xii. 32. 7

Banquet-houses. Their *banket houses* burne; their buildings race; . . . II. xii. 83. 8

Banquets. did the *bankets* of the Gods bewray, . . . *Gn.* 386
In beds, in bowres, in *banckets,* and in feasts: . . . III. vi. 22. 4
The royall *banquets,* and the rare delights, . . . V. iii. 3. 5
Like Gods with Nectar in their *bankets* free; . . . *H.B.* 249

Bans. *See* **Banns.**
with blasphemous *bannes* high God in peeces tare. . . . III. vii. 39. 9
In vaine the Pagan *bannes,* and sweares, and rayles, . . . V. viii. 39. 4

Baptized. his *baptized* hands now greater grew, . . . I. xi. 36. 4

Bar. *See* **Outbar.**
There was no *barre* to stop, nor foe him to empeach. . . . I. viii. 34. 9
Duessa, it to *barre,* Her false sleightes doe imploy. . . . I. xii. Arg.
To *barre* the prease of people farre away; . . . IV. iii. 4. 2
to *barre* the rout From rudely pressing to the middle center; V. v. 5. 6
Both which to *barre* he with this answere met her: . . . V. v. 37. 6
brought, as prisoner to the *barre,* . . . V. ix. 38. 1
brought Unto the *barre* whereas she was arrayned; . . . VI. vii. 36. 2
She found no meanes to *barre* him, . . . VI. xi. 7. 7
Pealing from Jove to Nature's *bar,* . . . VII. vii. Arg.
Orpheus with his harp theyr strife did *bar.* . . . *Am.* xliv. 4

Barbarian. Till that *Barbarian* hands it quite did spill, . . . *Ro.* xxx. 10

Barbarism. him beside sits ugly *Barbarisme,* . . . *T.M.* 187
With brutish *barbarisme* is overspredd: . . . *Ded. Son.* v. 4

Barbarous. *barbarous* villaines in disordred heape, . . . *Bel.*[1] v. 10
a *barbarous* troupe of clownish fone . . . *Bel.*[2] v. 10
committ Her single person to their *barbarous* truth; . . . I. vi. 12. 2
At sight whereof his *barbarous* heart was fired, . . . VI. xi. 4. 1

Barbican. Within the *Barbican* a Porter sate, . . . II. ix. 25. 1

Barbs. with golden sell And goodly gorgeous *barbes,* . . . II. ii. 11. 7

Bard. *See* **Barred.**
that Ascraean *bard,* whose fame now rings . . . *Gn.* 149
that blinde *bard* did him immortall make . . . *Ti.* 430

Bards. *Bardes,* that . . . Can tune their timely voices . . . I. v. 3. 6
Bards tell of many wemen valorous, . . . III. iii. 54. 4
With wanton *Bardes,* and Rymers impudent, . . . III. xii. 5. 5

Bare. *See* **Bore, Threadbare.**
he *bare* The tree of peace, . . . *Bel.*[1] vii. 10
wine of hooredome in a cup she *bare.* . . . *Rev.* ii. 8
what might arise of the *bare* sheepe, . . . *S.C.* May 107
left both *bare* and barrein now at erst; . . . *S.C.* D. 105
Cockel for corne, and chaffe for barley, *bare:* . . . *S.C.* D. 124
vertues *bare* regard advaunced bee, . . . *Hub.* 638
Ne did he leave the mountaines *bare* unseene, . . . *Mui.* 155
path . . . that beaten seemd most *bare,* . . . I. i. 11. 3

Bare—*Continued.*
His feete all *bare*, his beard all hoarie gray, . . . I. i. 29. 3
on his backe a heavy load he *bare* . . . I. iii. 16. 7
All *bare* through peoples feet which thether traveiled. . . . I. iv. 2. 9
in his hand his Portesse still he *bare*, . . . I. iv. 19. 1
in his hand a burning hart he *bare*, . . . I. iv. 25. 3
Me, silly maid, away with him he *bare*, . . . I. iv. 47. 7
That in his armour *bare* a croslet red? . . . I. vi. 36. 6
From top to toe no place appeared *bare*, . . . I. vii. 29. 6
youth, . . . His speare of heben wood behind him *bare*, . . . I. vii. 37. 2
His *bare* thin cheekes for want of better bits, . . . I. viii. 41. 3
Her necke and brests were ever open *bare*, . . . I. x. 30. 7
bare wretched wights he dayly clad, . . . I. x. 39. 6
was their manner then but *bare* and playne; . . . I. xii. 14. 7
Unto an aged woman, poore and *bare*, . . . II. v. 17. 3
in their metal *bare* The antique shapes of kings . . . II. vii. 5. 8
Her snowy brest was *bare* . . . II. xii. 78. 1
in his fall so well him selfe he *bare*, . . . III. i. 6. 8
in late yeares so faire a blossome *bare*, . . . III. iv. 3. 7
they robbed *bare* Of bounty, and of beautie, . . . III. vi. 4. 8
how them she *bare* . . . III. vi. 5. 3
all naked *bare* displayd. . . . III. vi. 7. 4
the burning hart which on his brest He *bare*, . . . III. viii. 45. 5
boy . . . He snatcht from Ida hill, and with him *bare*: . . . III. xi. 34. 5
either *bare* The other downe . . . IV. i. 41. 7
Shew'd all his bodie *bare* unto the cruell dent. . . . IV. vi. 15. 9
of great mother Venus *bare* the name, . . . IV. x. 5. 4
All which the Oceans daughter to him *bare*, . . . IV. xi. 48. 4
mans age . . . the first blossome of faire vertue *bare*; . . . V. Pr. 1. 4
Whose scalp is *bare*, that bondage doth bewray, . . . V. ii. 6. 7
nought else but *bare* life doth remaine; . . . V. x. 21. 7
eke to th' earth his burden with him *bare*; . . . V. xi. 9. 2
all his teeth wide *bare* One might have seene . . . V. xi. 9. 7
His side all *bare* and naked overtooke, . . . V. xi. 13. 8
in his wide great mouth away her *bare* . . . VI. iii. 24. 4
the *bare* ground with hoarie mosse bestrowed . . . VI. iv. 14. 4
His shield, his helmet, and his curats *bare*; . . . VI. v. 8. 7
'He lyes' (said he) 'upon the cold *bare* ground, . . . VI. vii. 16. 6
Some whet their knives, and strip their elboes *bare*: . . . VI. viii. 39. 6
Gathered together and them homeward *bare*: . . . VI. ix. 15. 5
Arrived in the Isle, though *bare* and blunt, . . . VI. xi. 9. 5
Do seize upon some beast whose flesh is *bare*, . . . VI. xi. 48. 2
When thy great mother Venus first thee *bare*, . . . *H.L.* 52
the gentle streame, the which them *bare*, . . . *Proth.* 47
Bared. shortly balde and *bared* she became. . . . *Van.* vii. 12
His *bared* boughes were beaten with stormes, . . . *S.C.* F. 112
sitting so with *bared* scalpe, . . . *S.C.* Jul. 221
The Turtle on the *bared* braunch . . . *S.C.* N. 138
All comfortlesse upon the *bared* bow, . . . *T.M.* 245
bared all his head unto the bone; . . . II. vi. 31. 8
Her *bared* bosome she doth broad display; . . . II. xii. 74. 8
His face was covered, and his head was *bar'd*, . . . V. iv. 22. 5
the Culver, on the *bared* bough, . . . *Am.* lxxxviii. 1
Barehead. That *bare-head* knight . . . Would faine have fled, . I. ix. 34. 7
Bargains. a Farmer, that would sell *Bargaines* of woods, . . . *Hub.* 872
Barge. A Ladie on rough waves row'd in a sommer *barge*. . . . VI. ii. 44. 9
Bargemen. backward yode, as *Bargemen* wont to fare . . . VII. vii. 35. 7
Bark. *See* **Fisher-bark.**
if that Envie *barke* at thee, . . . *To his Booke* 5
He has a Dogge to byte or to *barke*; . . . *S.C.* S. 181
at midnight he would *barke* and ball, . . . *S.C.* S. 190
mouthes doo bay And *barke* out flames, . . . *Gn.* 346
Through their hard *barke* his silver sound receav'd. . . . *Gn.* 456
There eke my feeble *barke* a while may stay, . . . I. xii. 1. 8
to the wished haven bring thy weary *barke!*' . . . II. i. 32. 9
The little *barke* unto the shore to draw, . . . II. vi. 4. 3
the flitt *barke*, obaying to her mind, . . . II. vi. 20. 3
In Phaedrias flitt *barck* over that perlous shard. . . . II. vi. 38. 9
envy base to *barke* at sleeping fame. . . . II. viii. 13. 7
he eftsoones gan launch his *barke* forthright. . . . II. xi. 4. 4
Wherein my feeble *barke* is tossed long . . . III. iv. 8. 2
a dogge . . . That durst not *barke*; . . . III. ix. 14. 8
the dogs did *barke* and howle About the house, . . . IV. v. 41. 6
after them did *barke*, and still backbite, . . . IV. viii. 36. 3
Her weary *barke* at last uppon mine Isle did rest. . . . V. iv. 11. 9
At him began aloud to *barke* and bay . . . V. xii. 41. 2
in this shore To rest my *barcke*, . . . VI. ix. 31. 4
my silly *barke* was tossed sore: . . . *Am.* lxiii. 4
her brest, lyke a rich laden *barke*, . . . *Am.* lxxxi. 5
Barked. he bayd and loudly *barkt* at mee, . . . VI. i. 9. 5
Some were of dogs, that *barked* day and night; . . . VI. xii. 27. 3
Barking. balefull *barking* bringes in hast Pyne, . . . *S.C.* Jul. 23
that curre, *barking* with bitter sownd, . . . VI. v. 19. 5
Barking and biting all that him doe bate, . . . VI. xii. 40. 5
Barks. As when two *Barkes*, . . . contrary courses sew, . . . IV. ix. 26. 7
Barley. Cockel for corne, and chaffe for *barley*, . . . *S.C.* D. 124
Barnaby. With *Barnaby* the bright, . . . *Epith.* 266
Barow. *See* **Barrow.**
Barraine. *See* **Barren.**
Barred. with his body *bard* the way atwixt them twaine. . . . I. viii. 13. 9
All *bard* with golden bendes, . . . II. iii. 27. 4
All *bard* with double bends, . . . II. vii. 30. 3
They found the gates fast *barred* long ere night, . . . II. ix. 10. 8
foolish garde, . . . kept th' yron dore fast *bard*, . . . III. xi. 31. 6
flame, . . . passage *bard* to all that thither came, . . . III. xii. 43. 4
He lent against a tree, that backeward onset *bard*. . . . VI. v. 18. 9
Barren. 'Thou *barrein* ground, whome winters wrath hath wasted, . . . *S.C.* Ja. 19
left both bare and *barrein* now at erst; . . . *S.C.* D. 105
Let th' earth be *barren*, . . . *D.* 334

Barren—*Continued.*
back returnedst to this *barrein* soyle, . . . *Col.* 656
Receive, dear Lord, in worth, the fruit of *barren* field. . . . *Ded. Son.* v. 14
With thornes and *barren* brakes environd round, . . . IV. i. 20. 5
The *barren* ground was full of wicked weedes, . . . IV. i. 25. 2
Nought leaving but their *barren* ashes without seede. . . . VII. vii. 24. 9
Which in the *barraine* cold he doth inspyre. . . . *H.L.* 98
Vouchsafe to shed into my *barren* spright . . . *H.H.L.* 45
Barrow. the goodly *Barow* which doth hoord Great heapes of salmons . . . IV. xi. 43. 5
Barry. lyes a litle space From the swift *Barry*, . . . III. iii. 8. 5
Bars. neither yron *barres*, nor brasen locke, . . . IV. xi. 3. 3
Bartas. gins *Bartas* hie to rayse His heavenly Muse, . . . *Ro.* Env. 11
Basan. bigge Bulles of *Basan* brace hem about, . . . *S.C.* S. 124
Basciante. *Basciante* did him selfe most courteous shew; . . . III. i. 45. 5
Bascimano. Gan choose his Dame with *Bascimano* (*Basciomani) gay, . . . III. i. 56. 8
Base. *See* **Bass.**
shining Christall, which from top to *base* . . . *Bel.* ii. 6
Upon foure corners of the *base* . . . *Bel.* iii. 9
Loath this *base* world, . . . *Pet.²* vii. 12
how ever *base* thou bee, . . . *Ro.* xxxii. 12
The *base* kinred of so simple swaine. . . . *S.C.* May 271
In rymes, in ridles, and in bydding *base*; . . . *S.C.* O. 5
Abandon, then, the *base* and viler clowne; . . . *S.C.* O. 37
Base is the style, and matter meane withall. . . . *Hub.* 44
Let us all servile *base* subjection scorne; . . . *Hub.* 134
such vile vassals, borne to *base* vocation, . . . *Hub.* 156
though his vesture were but meane and *bace*, . . . *Hub.* 229
following that trade so *base* and vile; . . . *Hub.* 366
to weare garments *base* of wollen twist, . . . *Hub.* 460
farre unfit it is, that person *bace* . . . *Hub.* 464
loath such *base* condition, . . . *Hub.* 719
as people *base* And simple men, . . . *Hub.* 833
borowe *base*, and some good Ladies gifts: . . . *Hub.* 852
dwell in dust inglorious and *bace*, . . . *Hub.* 981
to be learned it a *base* thing deeme: . . . *T.M.* 87
Through their bad dooings, or *base* slothfulnesse, . . . *T.M.* 99
Blind Error, scornefull Follie, and *base* Spight, . . . *T.M.* 317
the *base* vulgar, that with hands uncleane . . . *T.M.* 567
with *base* thoughts are into blindnesse led, . . . *T.M.* 592
I, *base* shepheard, bold and blind, . . . *Col.* 348
Such loftie flight *base* shepheard seemeth not, . . . *Col.* 618
As *base*, or blunt, unmeet for melodie. . . . *Col.* 710
their desire is *base*, and doth not merit The name of love, . . *Col.* 891
Not then to her that scorned thing so *base*, . . . *Col.* 935
to let thy name be writt In this *base* Poeme, . . . *Ded. Son.* ii. 5
spirit, . . . Might long perhaps have lien in silence *bace*, . *Ded. Son.* xiii. 5
with remembraunce of your gracious name, . . . adorne these verses *base*. . . . *Ded. Son.* xvi. 5
By that same hole an entraunce darke and *bace*, . . . I. v. 31. 4
her *base* Elfin brood there for thee left: . . . I. x. 65. 8
My ragged rimes are all too rude and *bace* . . . I. xii. 23. 4
yield his sence to bee too blunt and *bace*, . . . II. Pr. 4. 4
Had vertue pourd into their waters *bace*, . . . II. i. 6. 8
fowle revenging rage, and *base* contentious jarre. . . . II. ii. 30. 9
did deeme Such entertainment *base*, . . . II. ii. 35. 2
all, that els this worlds enclosure *base* Hath great . . . II. ii. 41. 3
Streight at his foot in *base* humilitee, . . . II. iii. 8. 8
quenched *bace* desyre. . . . II. iii. 23. 9
to be easd of that *base* burden still did erne. . . . II. iii. 46. 9
it was a groome of *base* degree, . . . II. iv. 24. 3
Disguised like that groome of *base* degree, . . . II. iv. 27. 8
To them that list these *base* regardes I lend; . . . II. vii. 33. 5
Others through friendes; others for *base* regard, . . . II. vii. 47. 4
love In heavenly spirits to these creatures *bace*, . . . II. viii. 1. 2
envy *base* to barke at sleeping fame. . . . II. viii. 13. 7
Distempred through misrule and passions *bace*; . . . II. ix. 1. 6
twixt them both a quadrate was the *base*, . . . II. ix. 22. 6
Seagulles hoars and *bace*, . . . II. xii. 8. 4
as the one stird up affections *bace*, . . . III. i. 46. 3
doth *base* affections move In brutish mindes, . . . III. iii. 1. 5
disguising both in straunge And *base* atyre, . . . III. iii. 7. 2
Shee, that *base* Braggadochio did affray, . . . III. v. 27. 7
'But, foolish boy, what bootes thy service *bace* . . . III. v. 47. 1
his *base* thought with terrour and with aw So inly smot, . . III. vii. 13. 5
conceiv'd affection *bace*, And cast to love her . . . III. vii. 15. 7
'Thy offers *base* I greatly loth, . . . III. x. 29. 6
Trompart *bace* Had it purloyned . . . III. x. 54. 3
boldly bad him *bace*, . . . III. xi. 5. 5
both were bent t' avenge his usage *base*, . . . IV. iv. 4. 7
in *base* mind nor friendship dwels nor enmity. . . . IV. iv. 11. 9
Now *base* and contemptible did appeare, . . . IV. v. 14. 2
so *base* and vilde To be unjustly blamd, . . . IV. viii. 28. 8
this Dwarfe, her dearling *base*, . . . IV. viii. 54. 5
frame in earth, and forme of substance *base*, . . . IV. x. 21. 7
cropt the branches of the sient *base*, . . . V. i. 1. 8
In the *base* blood of such a rascall crew; . . . V. ii. 52. 5
'Thou losell *base*, That hast with borrowed plumes . . . V. iii. 20. 6
armes dishonour with *base* villanie, . . . V. iii. 38. 7
That he of womens hands so *base* a death should dy. . . . V. iv. 22. 9
put to that *base* service of her band, . . . V. iv. 32. 7
they were borne to *base* humilitie, . . . V. v. 25. 8
proudest harts *base* love hath blynded.' . . . V. v. 40. 9
Which had her Lord in her *base* prison pent, . . . V. vi. 18. 8
So ran they all, as they had bene at *bace*, . . . V. viii. 5. 4
downe descend unto the *base*: . . . V. ix. 16. 7
hearing pleas of people meane and *base*: . . . V. ix. 36. 5
blotted with condition vile and *base*, . . . V. ix. 38. 5
Yet glad at last to make most *base* submission, . . . V. x. 27. 4

Base—*Continued.*
Borne of the brooding of Echidna *base,* . . . V. xi. 23. 5
he loathd leasing and *base* flattery, . . . VI. i. 3. 8
him to beare she thought it thing too *base* . . . VI. ii. 47. 5
reed Me then to be full *base* . . . VI. iii. 31. 8
Did scorne the challenge of so *base* a thrall; . . . VI. iii. 36. 4
Gan him entreat even with submission *base,* . . . VI. iii. 38. 5
howsoever *base* and meane it were, . . . VI. iv. 15. 1
running streight upon that villaine *base,* . . . VI. vi. 22. 3
By such discourteous deeds discovering his *base* kind. . . . VI. vii. 1. 9
him bewayling with affection *base,* . . . VI. vii. 18. 3
Though of meane parentage and kindred *base,* . . . VI. vii. 28. 4
To follow sheepe and shepheards *base* attire: . . . VI. ix. 24. 4
being bred under *base* shepheards wings, . . . VI. ix. 35. 4
The gentle heart scornes *base* disparagement. . . . VI. x. 37. 5
Base thing I can no more endure to view: . . . *Am.* iii. 6
is close implide, Scorn of *basc* things, . . . *Am.* v. 6
Shoot out his darts to *base* affections wound; . . . *Am.* viii. 6
seemes to scorne *Base* thing, . . . *Am.* xiii. 10
she should scorne *Base* things, . . . *Am.* lxi. 12
The which the *base* affections doe obay, . . . *Epith.* 196
lust, Whose *base* affect through cowardly distrust . . . *H.L.* 180
base affections, which your eares would bland . . . *H.B.* 171
From this *base* world unto thy heavens hight, . . . *H.H.L.* 2
Whose root from earths *base* groundworke shold begin. . . . *H.H.L.* 105
Therefore of clay, *base,* vile, and next to nought, . . . *H.H.L.* 106
in what rags, and in how *base* aray, . . . *H.H.L.* 228
loves, with which the world doth . . . stirre up affections *base,* *H.H.L.* 263
this *base* world, subject to fleshly eye, . . . *H.H.B.* 23
may Be seene of all his creatures vile and *base,* . . . *H.H.B.* 116

Base-begot. Say, thou wert *base-begot* with blame; . . . *To his Booke* 14

Base-born. Scorning the boldnes of such *base-borne* men, . . . *T.M.* 219
The *base-borne* brood of blindnes cannot gesse, . . . *T.M.* 392
Admir'd of *base-borne* men from farre away: . . . *Ti.* 424
To be so scorned of a *base-borne* thrall, . . . V. v. 47. 4
baseborne mynds such lamps regard the lesse, . . . *H.L.* 173

Basely. (so *basely* was he borne) . . . *Hub.* 808
Whose service high so *basely* they ensew, . . . *Col.* 767
a war-monger to be *basely* nempt; . . . III. x. 29. 5
to adorne With so brave badges one so *basely* borne: . . . VI. vi. 36. 5

Base-minded. *Base minded* they that want intelligence; . . . *T.M.* 88

Baseness. squallid Fortune, into *basenes* flong, . . . *T.M.* 543
So great her pride that she such *basenesse* much abhord. . . . V. v. 27. 9
that one in *basenesse* set Doth noble courage shew . . . VI. iii. 1. 8
even the Prince his *basenesse* did despize; . . . VI. vi. 32. 4
He for such *basenesse* shamefully him shent, . . . VI. vi. 33. 2
by her from *basenesse* raysed; . . . *Am.* iii. 4
Nor unto Glasse; such *basenesse* mought offend her. . . . *Am.* ix. 12
it all sordid *basenesse* doth expell, . . . *H.L.* 191
And all that pompe . . . Seemes to them *basenesse,* . . . *H.H.B.* 279

Basenet. *See* **Basinet.**

Baser. Ne brest of *baser* birth doth thee embrace, . . . *S.C.* O. 82
Exceeding all this *baser* worldes good: . . . *Ti.* 620
give leave a while To *baser* wit . . . *Ded.Son.*xii.10
The royall virgin . . . rising forth out of her *baser* bowre, I. ii. 7. 6
Ne thought of honour ever did assay His *baser* brest, . . . II. iii. 4. 4
drowne his *baser* mind, . . . III. iv. 56. 6
The *baser* wit, . . . It stirreth up to sensuall desire, . . . III. v. 1. 4
With golden foyle doth finely over-spread Some *baser* metall, . IV. v. 15. 3
Made cruell havocke of the *baser* crew, . . . V. xi. 59. 6
Even so the *baser* mind it selfe displayes . . . VI. vii. 1. 3
Such love, not lyke to lusts of *baser* kynd, . . . *Am.* vi. 3
that high look, . . . bow to a *baser* make, . . . *Am.* x. 11
let *baser* things devize To dy in dust, . . . *Am.* lxxv. 9

Bases. the *bases* were of richest golde, . . . *Bel.*[1] iv. 2
bases were of richest metalls warke, . . . *Bel.*[2] iv. 2
Instead of Curiets and *bases* fit for fight. . . . V. v. 20. 9
to course about their *bases* light; . . . VI. x. 8. 4

Basest. meane regard, and *basest* fortunes scorne, . . . *Hub.* 60
makes it servaunt to her *basest* part, . . . II. i. 57. 6
The love and service of the *basest* crew? . . . III. v. 47. 7
the boldnesse of thy *basest* thrall, . . . V. Pr. 11. 6

Bashan. *See* **Basan.**

Bashed. *bashed* not For Guyons lookes, . . . II. iv. 37. 8

Bashful. The *bashfull* blood her snowy cheekes did dye, . . . II. ix. 41. 4
peepe foorth with *bashfull* modestee, . . . II. xii. 74. 5
Whereto her *bashful* shamefastnesse ywrought A great increase V. iii. 23. 3
His face with *bashfull* blood did flame, . . . *Epig.* iii. 5

Bashfulness. did his head for *bashfulnesse* abase, . . . VI. viii. 5. 5

Basil. Sound Savorie, and *Bazil* hartie-hale, . . . *Mui.* 198

Basilisk. the *Basiliske,* of serpents seede, . . . IV. viii. 39. 7

Basin. in a silver *basin* layd, . . . III. xii. 21. 2

Basinet. He sent to her his *basenet* as a faithfull band. . . . VI. i. 31. 9

Basin-wide. stare . . . with big lookes *basen wide,* . . . *Hub.* 670

Basket. he left behind In the *basket* . . . *S.C.* May 289
his *basket* did latch: . . . *S.C.* May 291
a little wicker *basket,* Made of fine twigs, . . . *Proth.* 24

Baskets. 'To make . . . *Baskets* of bulrushes, . . . *S.C.* D. 80
they all out of their *baskets* drew . . . *Proth.* 73

Bass. In his big *base* them fitly answered; . . . II. xii. 33. 2
the *base* murmure of the waters fall; . . . II. xii. 71. 6
Certein sad words with hollow voice and *bace,* . . . III. ii. 50. 5

Bass'. taught to beare A *Bases* part . . . *T.M.* 28

Bastard. To banish cowardize and *bastard* feare: . . . I. vi. 24. 2
Thought in his *bastard* armes her to embrace. . . . II. iii. 42. 6

Basted. *Basted* with bends of gold on every side, . . . V. v. 3. 2

Bat. upleaning on his *batt,* . . . *Gn.* 154
In stead of them a handsome *bat* he held, . . . *Hub.* 217
on his shoulders high his *bat* to beare, . . . *Hub.* 238
The lether-winged *Batt,* dayes enimy; . . . II. xii. 36. 6

Bate. *See* **Bait, Baited, Bit.**
civile *bate* Made me the spoile and bootie . . . *Bel.*[1] viii. 9
They looken bigge as Bulls that bene *bate,* . . . *S.C.* S. 44
inly *bate* Deep in his flesh, . . . II. v. 7. 8
to *bayt* His tyred armes for toylesome wearinesse, . . . II. xii. 29. 7
Bate somewhat of that Majestie and awe . . . V. ix. 35. 7

Bated. *See* **Baited.**

Bath. *See* **Bathe.**
th' English *Bath,* and eke the German Spau; . . . I. xi. 30. 7
Might not be purgd with water nor with *bath;* . . . II. ii. 4. 2
in his costly *Bath* causd to bee site. . . . III. xii. 46. *or.* 4
as als' of wondrous *Bath,* . . . IV. xi. 31. 8
in bloody *bath* . . . her cruell hands embrew. . . . *Am.* xxxi. 11

Bathe. in this blessed brooke Doe *bathe* your brest, . . . *S.C.* Ap. 38
Wherein the Nymphes doe *bathe;* . . . *S.C.* Jul. 80
his thristy blade To *bathe* in blood . . . I. v. 15. 3
they gan . . . *bathe* in pleasaunce of the joyous shade, . . . I. vii. 4. 2
Some wrestle, some do run, some *bathe* in christall flood. . . . I. xii. 7. 9
usd to *bath* themselves in that deceiptfull shade, . . . II. xii. 30. 9
bathe him in a fountaine by some covert glade: . . . III. i. 35. 9
with ambrosiall kisses *bathe* his eyes; . . . III. i. 36. 4
Shee ofte did *bathe,* and ofte againe did dry; . . . III. ii. 34. 7
To *bath* their hands in bloud of dearest freend, . . . IV. vi. 17. 8
To *bath* in joy and amorous desire, . . . IV. x. 38. 7
bathe in fountaines that do freshly flowe . . . VII. vi. 39. 4
In her sweet streames Diana used oft . . . To *bathe* . . . VII. vi. 42. 3
he might her Lady see When she her selfe did *bathe,* . . . VII. vi. 43. 9
So much delight to *bathe* her limbes she tooke: . . . VII. vi. 54. 4
now would *bathe* his limbes . . . VII. vii. 29. 9
my fraile fancy . . . Doth *bath* in blisse, . . . *Am.* lxxii. 10

Bathed. She *bathed* oft with teares, and dried oft: . . . *As.* 164
Bathed in wanton blis and wicked joy. . . . I. i. 47. 6
Till we be *bathed* in a living well: . . . I. ii. 43. 4
Some *bathed* kisses, and did soft embrew . . . II. v. 33. 5
those which therein *bathed* mote offend. . . . II. xii. 63. 4
kisses bathe his eyes; And whilst he *bath'd* . . . III. i. 36. 5
She *bath'd* her brest the boyling heat t' allay; . . . III. vi. 6. 7
She *bath'd* with roses red and violets blew, . . . III. vi. 6. 8
bath'd in bloud and sweat together ment; . . . V. v. 12. 5
Where still he *bathed* lay in his owne bloody gore. . . . VI. vii. 8. 9
doffing her array, She *bath'd* her lovely limbes, . . . VII. vi. 45. 9
bath'd in the sacred brooke Of Helicon, . . . *Am.* i. 9
then she *bath'd* him in a dainty well, . . . *Epig.* iv. 47
To be so *bath'd* in Venus blis? . . . *Epig.* iv. 50
In th' Ocean billowes he hath *bathed* fayre, . . . *Proth.* 165

Bathes. *See* **Baths.**
bathes him selfe in courtly blis, . . . II. iii. 40. 2

Bathing. Ran *bathing* all the creakie shore . . . *Bel.*[2] ix. 7
Now in the same *bathing* his tender feete; . . . *Mui.* 182
Bathing her selfe in origane and thyme: . . . I. ii. 40. 7
therein *bathing* seemed to contend . . . II. xii. 63. 7
Being through former *bathing* mollifide, . . . III. vi. 7. 6
With *bathing* in the Acidalian brooke. . . . *Epith.* 310
Bathing thy wings in her ambrosiall kisse, . . . *H.L.* 25

Baths. These wals, these arcks, these *baths,* . . . *Ro.* xxvii. 4
Behold the boyling *bathes* at Cairbadon, . . . II. x. 26. 2

Baton. with his yron *batton* which he bore . . . VI. vii. 46. 3

Batt. *See* **Bat.**

Battailant. did beare (as *batteilant*) A gilden towre, . . . *Van.* viii. 3

Battail(e), Battaill, Battail(l)es, Battayle. *See* **Battle, Battle's, Battles.**

Battailous. him selfe prepayre In sunbright armes, and *battailous* array; . . . I. v. 2. 8
Glistring in armes and *battailous* aray, . . . II. vii. 37. 2
match his brother proud in *battailous* aray. . . . II. viii. 22. 9
strong siege and *battailous* assault, . . . II. xi. 9. 2
hungry whelpes, his *battailous* bold brood, . . . III. iii. 47. 4
With which he wont to stirre up *battailous* alarmes. . . . V. v. 21. 9
her cause in *battailous* array Against him justifie, . . . V. xi. 40. 3
in *battailous* array Wayting his foe, . . . V. xii. 12. 7
well approv'd in *batteilous* affray, . . . VI. i. 2. 8
in *batteilous* array I may beare armes, . . . VI. ii. 33. 5
warres darraine Against the heaven in order *battailous,* . . . VI. vii. 41. 7

Batteil(l), Batteilant, Batteilles, Batteilous, *etc.* *See* **Battailant, Battailous, Battle, Battle's, Battles.**

Battered. impresse Deepe dinted furrowes in the *battred* mayle: I. v. 6. 8
him to dust thought to have *battred* quight, . . . I. vii. 14. 3
fowly *battered* his comely corse, . . . II. v. 23. 5
They *battred* day and night, and entraunce did awate. . . . II. xi. 6. 9
bowd his *battred* visour to his brest: . . . III. vii. 42. 5
His *battred* ballances in peeces lay, . . . V. ii. 50. 7
they his shield in peeces *battred* have, . . . V. xi. 46. 2
That bloudie scutchin, being *battered* sore, . . . V. xi. 54. 4
brusht and *battred* them without remorse, . . . V. xii. 7. 4

Batteree. *See* **Battery.**

Batteries. All those against that fort did bend their *batteries.* II. xi. 10. 9

Battering. Which *battring* downe, it on the church doth glance, IV. vi. 14. 4

Battery. when he saw his . . . subtile engines bett from *batteree;* . . . I. vi. 5. 2
fort . . . will at last be wonne with *battrie* long, . . . I. ix. 11. 3
cruell *battry* bend Gainst fort of Reason, . . . II. iv. 34. 7
towre, Whom foe with double *battry* doth assaile, . . . II. viii. 35. 8
they dayly made most dreadfull *battery.* . . . II. xi. 7. 9
that fourth band which cruell *battry* bent . . . II. xi. 12. 1
Rather for pleasure then for *battery* or fight. . . . II. xii. 43. 9
with huge strokes and cruell *battery* . . . III. vii. 32. 3
no wals so strong, But that continuall *battery* will rive, . . . III. x. 10. 2
As three great Culverings for *battrie* bent, . . . V. x. 34. 6
And lay incessant *battery* to her heart; . . . *Am.* xiv. 10
Ne your incessant *battry* more to beare: . . . *Am.* lvii. 4

Battill, Battilment. *See* **Battle, Battlement.**
Battle. bad him *battaile* even to his jawes: . . . *Van.* x. 8
thwarting his huge shield, Them *battell* bad, . . . *Gn.* 515
To prove his puissance in *battell* brave . . . I. i. 3. 7
So both to *batteill* fierce arraunged arre, . . . I. ii. 36. 5
prepare Himselfe to *batteill* with his couched speare. . . . I. iii. 34. 4
they gan . . . Redoubted *battaile* ready to darrayne, . . . I. iv. 40. 2
A shrilling trompett . . . unto *battaill* bad them selves addresse: I. v. 6. 2
End of the doubtfull *battaile* deemed tho . . . I. v. 11. 7
two knights, . . . arraung'd in *batteill* new, . . . I. vi. 38. 4
ofte refreshed, *battell* oft renue. . . . I. vi. 44. 3
lefte the doubtfull *battell* hastily, . . . I. vi. 46. 4
Did to him pace sad *battaile* to darrayne, . . . I. vii. 11. 5
Whom when the Prince, to *batteill* new addrest . . . I. viii. 22. 1
Is this the *battaile* which thou vauntst to fight . . . I. ix. 52. 8
all knights on earth, that *batteill* undertake.' . . . I. xi. 2. 9
shoke his scales to *battaile* ready drest, . . . I. xi. 15. 7
boystrous *battaile* make, each other to avenge. . . . I. xi. 21. 9
new-borne knight to *battell* new did rise. . . . I. xi. 34. 9
did himselfe to *battaile* ready dight; . . . I. xi. 52. 3
him in hardy *battayle* overcame, . . . I. xii. 20. 4
prickt with courage kene, did cruell *battell* breath. . . . II. i. 27. 9
unto *battell* sterne themselves prepar'd. . . . II. ii. 19. 9
Thenceforth in *battaile* never sword to beare, . . . II. iii. 17. 8
soone thyselfe prepaire To *batteile,* . . . II. vi. 28. 6
Withhold your bloody handes from *battaill* fierce; . . . II. vi. 33. 3
Not this rude kynd of *battaill,* . . . II. vi. 34. 2
Sith late with him I *batteill* vaine would boste; . . . II. vi. 50. 6
threaten *batteill* to the Faery knight; . . . II. vii. 42. 4
Who likewise gan himselfe to *batteill* dight, . . . II. vii. 42. 5
unto *batteil* doe your selves addresse; . . . II. viii. 18. 2
gan themselves prepare to *batteill* greedily. . . . II. viii. 18. 9
So ready dight fierce *battaile* to assay, . . . II. viii. 22. 8
when this breathlesse woxe, that *batteil* gan renew. . . . II. viii. 47. 9
he an end of *batteill* and of life did make. . . . II. x. 16. 9
Encountred him in *batteill* well ordaind, . . . II. x. 18. 4
Raisd warre, and him in *batteill* overthrew. . . . II. x. 33. 6
An army brought, and with him *batteile* fought, . . . II. x. 51. 2
There she with them a cruell *batteill* tryde, . . . II. x. 55. 1
shortly was by Coyll in *batteill* slaine: . . . II. x. 58. 5
in *batteill* vanquished Those spoylefull Picts, . . . II. x. 63. 1
to him brought, fresh *batteill* to renew; . . . II. xi. 28. 3
of the *battell* balefull end had made, . . . II. xi. 29. 7
gan him selfe to second *battaill* bend, . . . II. xi. 35. 5
all knights that ever *batteill* tryde, . . . II. xii. 32. 5
did darrayne Fiers *battaill* against one . . . III. i. 20. 9
Both slaine in *battaile* upon Layburne playne, . . . III. iii. 37. 4
usd the same in *batteill* aye to beare; . . . III. iii. 60. 3
unto *battaill* did her selfe prepayre. . . . III. iv. 14. 3
he must do *battail* with the Sea-nymphes sonne. . . . III. iv. 20. 9
to forbeare The bloody *batteill* . . . III. iv. 24. 8
gan the *battaile* freshly to begin; . . . III. v. 22. 5
to the *batteill* doth her selfe prepare: . . . III. vii. 39. 6
she list not the *batteill* to abide, . . . III. vii. 44. 3
bide him *batteill* without further treat. . . . III. viii. 16. 5
the which made *Batteill* against the Gods, . . . III. xi. 22. 9
Signe of nigh *battaill,* or got victory: . . . III. xii. 1. 6
The hurts whereof me now from *battell* stay, . . . IV. i. 40. 4
Yet would not let their *battell* so be broken, . . . IV. ii. 21. 4
battell strong to wage Gainst all those knights, . . . IV. ii. 28. 7
battell made the dreddest daungerous . . . IV. ii. 32. 3
Upon which ground this same great *battell* grew, . . . IV. ii. 54. 6
battell twixt three brethren with Cambell for Canacee: . . . IV. iii. Arg. 1
Rusht fiercely forth the *battell* to renew, . . . IV. iii. 14. 6
cruell *battell* twixt themselves doe make, . . . IV. iii. 16. 6
Thus did the *battell* varie to and fro, . . . IV. iii. 28. 1
As if but then the *battell* had begonne: . . . IV. iii. 36. 2
Desirous both to have the *battell* donne; . . . IV. iii. 36. 5
Whom formerly he had in *battell* wonne, . . . IV. iv. 8. 7
for her sake refus'd to enterprize The *battell,* . . . IV. iv. 11. 5
had in many a *battell* oft bene tride, . . . IV. iv. 17. 8
none against them *battell* durst maintaine: . . . IV. iv. 25. 5
Unable he new *battell* to darraine, . . . IV. iv. 26. 7
As if but now the *battell* wexed warme. . . . IV. iv. 35. 5
by him in *battell* wonne long sens: . . . IV. v. 23. 7
readie were new *battell* to darraine. . . . IV. v. 24. 6
Whilest thus in *battell* they embusied were, . . . IV. vii. 29. 1
Ne thenceforth ever strike in *battell* stroke, . . . IV. vii. 39. 3
foure of them the *battell* best beseemed, . . . IV. ix. 20. 4
As if but then the *battell* had begonne; . . . IV. ix. 27. 2
would them faine from *battell* to surceasse, . . . IV. ix. 32. 8
To rip up wrong that *battell* once hath tried; . . . IV. ix. 37. 3
Expert in *battell* and in deedes of armes; . . . V. ii. 5. 4
dreadfull *battaile* twixt them do darraine: . . . V. ii. 15. 5
So sharpe a *battell,* that so many did dismay. . . . V. iii. 21. 9
To warne her foe to *battell* soone be prest: . . . V. vii. 27. 2
Was to the *battell* whilome ready dight. . . . V. vii. 27. 6
After that them in *battell* he had wonne: . . . V. x. 30. 6
aside had set The use of armes, and *battell* quite forgone: . . . V. xi. 37. 4
courage chill Kindling afresh, gan *battell* to renew, . . . VI. i. 35. 8
loth t' assay The proofe of *battell* now . . . VI. iii. 41. 4
him selfe to *battell* he did frame; . . . VI. vi. 25. 8
sleepe, they sayd, would make her *battill* better: . . . VI. viii. 38. 3
The spoiles of Princes hang'd which were in *battel* won. . . . VI. viii. 42. 9
had endured many a dreadfull stoure In bloudy *battell* . . . VI. xii. 3. 8
cruell warriour, doth herselfe addresse To *battell,* . . . *Am.* xi. 4
passions doe awake To *battaile,* . . . *Am.* xliv. 12
Battlement. Beaten with stones downe from the *battilment,* V. ii. 20. 6
Unto the *battilment* to be upbrought, . . . V. ii. 23. 5
Battlements. from the *battlements* she ready seem'd to fall. VI. i. 34. 9
Battle-order. They rose in armes, and all in *battell* order stood. . . . V. ii. 51. 9
Battle's. to tell . . . this *battels* end, will need another place. I. vi. 48. 9
whence she might behold that *battailles* proof, . . . I. xi. 5. 3
He gan to faint toward the *battels* end, . . . IV. iii. 32. 7
with dint of sword And *battailes* doubtfull proofe . . . V. iv. 6. 2
That *battells* utmost triall to adventer. . . . V. v. 5. 5
Battles. Of dreadfull *battailes* of renowmed Knights; . . . *Hub.* 767
All those great *battels,* which thou boasts to win . . . I. ix. 43. 3
bitter *battailes* all are fought? . . . I. x. 62. 8
many bloody *battailes* fought in face, . . . I. x. 65. 3
have beheld the *battailes* which it wan.' . . . II. iii. 16. 9
write the *battailes* of his great godhed: . . . II. iii. 24. 4
many *battailes* fought and many fraies . . . II. iii. 38. 5
He fought great *batteils* with his salvage fone; . . . II. x. 10. 3
with great honour many *batteills* try; . . . III. iii. 31. 4
Where be the *batteilles,* where the shield and speare, . . . III. iv. 1. 4
cruell *battailes,* which he whilome fought . . . III. xi. 29. 6
sundry *battels,* which she hath atchieved . . . V. iv. 33. 6
Fought many *battels* without wound or losse; . . . V. xi. 53. 7
And in three *battailes* did so deadly daunt, . . . VI. iv. 29. 8
in all *battels* bore away the baies: . . . VI. vi. 4. 5
Batton. *See* **Baton.**
Battred, Battrie, Battring, Battry. *See* **Battered, Battering,** *etc.*
Baude. *See* **Bawd.**
Baudricke, Bauldricke. *See* **Baldric.**
Bawd. serving her . . . was, as it were, her *baude* . . . IV. i. 31. 3
Bawl. at midnight he would barke and *ball,* . . . *S.C.* S. 190
Bay. mouthes doo *bay* And barke out flames, . . . *Gn.* 345
there *bay* Manie great bandogs . . . *Gn.* 539
The wakefull dogs did never cease to *bay,* . . . I. v. 30. 2
it was a still And calmy *bay,* . . . II. xii. 30. 3
having at a *bay* The salvage beast . . . III. i. 22. 1
at the length unto a *bay* he brought her, . . . IV. vi. 41. 3
he her brought Unto his *bay,* . . . IV. viii. 48. 5
At him began aloud to barke and *bay* . . . V. xii. 41. 2
Into this *bay* of perill and disgrace? . . . VI. i. 12. 2
Like a wylde Bull, that, being at a *bay,* . . . VI. v. 19. 1
Like as a Mastiffe having at a *bay* A salvage Bull, . . . VI. vii. 47. 1
making many a borde and many a *bay,* . . . VI. xii. 1. 6
the *bay,* which I unto her gave, . . . *Am.* xxix. 3
The *bay* . . . is of the victours borne, . . . *Am.* xxix. 5
Bay-branches. Bene they not *Bay braunches* which they doe beare, . . . *S.C.* Ap. 104
Bayed. Spite bites the dead, that living never *baid.* . . . *Ti.* 215
he *bayd* and loudly barkt at mee, . . . VI. i. 9. 5
Bay-leaves. *Bay leaves* betweene, And primroses greene, . . . *S.C.* Ap. 61
Bays. that were wont greene *bayes* to weare, . . . *S.C.* N. 146
match that Muse when it with *bayes* is crowned, . . . *Col.* 414
And crownes their ashes with immortall *baies.* . . . *Ded. Son.* iv. 12
crownd with lasting *baies* of hevenlie blis . . . *Ded. Son.* xv. 4
bayes His sweatie forehead in the breathing wynd, . . . I. vii. 3. 1
their proud girlonds of tryumphant *bayes* . . . III. xi. 52. 7
To win a willow bough, whilest other weares the *bayes.* . . . IV. i. 47. 9
Crowned with girlonds of immortall *baies;* . . . V. xi. 34. 6
in all battels bore away the *baies:* . . . VI. vi. 4. 5
decke her head with glorious *bayes,* . . . *Am.* xxix. 13
Bazil. *See* **Basil.**
Be (*partial list*). *See* **Albe, Been, Be it, How be, If so be, Shall be, So be, Will be.**
he shall *be* their God, . . . *Rev.* iv. 6
calme seem'd the sea to *bee,* . . . *Pet.* ii. 4
Much richer then that vessell seem'd to *bee,* . . . *Bel.*[2] xiii. 1
these seven hils, which *be* nowe Tombes . . . *Ro.* iv. 7
Rome onely might to Rome compared *bee,* . . . *Ro.* vi. 9
Pallaces, which maystred *bee* Of time, . . . *Ro.* xviii. 3
how ever base thou *bee,* . . . *Ro.* xxxii. 12
made all other Foules his thralls to *bee:* . . . *Van.* iv. 4
forget not what you *be:* . . . *Van.* xii. 12
I deeme thy braine emperished *bee* . . . *S.C.* F. 53
I wene thou *bee* assot; . . . *S.C.* Mar. 25
Let *be,* as may *be,* . . . That is to come, let *be* forecast; . . . *S.C.* Mar. 58, 59
Els had he sore *be* daunted. . . . *S.C.* Mar. 114
'Of fayre Elisa *be* your silver song, . . . *S.C.* Ap. 46
playen while their flockes *be* unfedde: . . . *S.C.* May 44
Had lever my foe then my freend he *be;* . . . *S.C.* May 167
Flye to my love, where ever that she *bee,* . . . *S.C.* Jun. 99
I weene thou *be* affrayd . . . *S.C.* Jul. 71
(thanked *be* God . . . *S.C.* Jul. 169
Colin Clout, I wene, *be* his selfe boye, . . . *S.C.* S. 176
blessed *be* the day, . . . *Hub.* 589
Though nought at all but ruines now I *bee,* . . . *Ti.* 39
'Ah far *be* it . . . fro me, . . . *Col.* 464
though there she *be;* . . . *Col.* 525
amongst them *bee* Full many persons . . . *Col.* 751
ye, my fellow shepheards, . . . for ever witnesse *bee,* . . . *Col.* 949
shew what ye *bee;* . . . I. i. 19. 2
he should have cloven *bee.* . . . I. v. 12. 9
if thou *be,* as thou art pourtrahed . . . I. viii. 33. 7
So few there *bee,* That chose the narrow path, . . . I. x. 10. 3
'let *be* thy deepe advise: . . . II. iii. 16. 1
What ever *bee* the cause, it sure beseemes you ill.' . . . II. ix. 37. 9
Yet had the bodie not dismembred *bee,* . . . IV. iii. 21. 7
Ne let hob Goblins . . . Fray us with things that *be* not: . . . *Epith.* 344
That wondrous Paterne, wheresoere it *bee,* . . . *H.B.* 36
were goodly to *bee* seene . . . *Proth.* 168
Beacon. like a goodly *beacon* high addrest, . . . *Col.* 562
Beacons. two broad *Beacons,* sett in open fieldes, . . . I. xi. 14. 3
Two goodly *Beacons,* set in watches stead, . . . II. ix. 46. 3
eies, Like two great *Beacons,* glared bright and wyde, . . . VI. vii. 42. 2

Bead-men. *See* **Beadsmen.**
Bead-roll. On Fames eternall *beadroll* worthie to be fyled. . . IV. ii. 32. 9
Beads. Bidding his *beades* all day for his trespas, . . . I. i. 30. 7
that old woman . . . did pray Upon her *beads*, . . . I. iii. 13. 7
for feare her *beads* she did forgett: . . . I. iii. 14. 5
All night she spent in bidding of her *bedes*, . . . I. x. 3. 8
all this while was busy at her *beades;* . . . I. x. 8. 3
Beadsmen. seven *Bead-men* . . . Did spend their daies in doing godly thing. . . . I. x. 36. 3
Beak. Himselfe smote with his *beake*, as in disdaine, . . . *Pet.* v. 10
Beaks. Owles, with *beckes* uncomely bent; . . . II. xi. 8. 3
Beam. *See* **Shiny-beam, Sunbeam, Wagon-beam.**
All as the Sunnye *beame* so bright, . . . *S.C.* Au. 81
from *beam* to *beame* he fled . . . *Hub.* 1373
being lightned with his beawties *beme*, . . . *T.M.* 585
The *beame* of beautie sparkled from above, . . . *Col.* 468
From fiery wheeles of his faire chariot Hurled his *beame* . . . I. ii. 29. 5
the stiffe *beame* quaked as affrayd, . . . I. xi. 20. 5
The blazing brightnesse of her beauties *beame*, . . . I. xii. 23. 1
ear that wished day his *beame* disclosd, . . . II. iv. 22. 1
her broad beauties *beam* great brightnes threw . . . II. vii. 45. 2
All were the *beame* in bignes like a mast, . . . III. vii. 40. 6
when he saw that blazing beauties *beame*, . . . III. viii. 22. 5
shoot forth his *beame*. . . . III. xi. 41. 5
Whose beauties *beame* eftsoones did shine so bright, . . . IV. v. 10. 8
right sate in the middest of the *beame* alone. . . . V. ii. 48. 9
Gins to abate the brightnesse of his *beme*, . . . V. ix. 35. 3
The *beame* of light, whom mortal eyes admyre; . . . *Am.* lxi. 10
His golden *beame* upon the hils doth spred, . . . *Epith.* 20
Beauties glorious *beame*. . . . *H.L.* 116
faire immortall *beame* Hath darted fyre . . . *H.B.* 23
that faire *beame* which therein is empight. . . . *H.B.* 49
flowing from the *beame* Of thy bright starre, . . . *H.B.* 55
Beam-like. at him his *beam-like* speare he aimed, . . . IV. iv. 24. 1
Beams. *See* **Shiny beams.**
cleare as Christall gainst the Sunnie *beames*, . . . *Bel.* xii. 2
On everie side a thousand shining *beames:* . . . *Bel.*² xi. 10
when he sawe how broade her *beames* did spredde, . . . *S.C.* Ap. 75
When shee the *beames* of her beauty displayes, . . . *S.C.* Ap. 84
golde, which underlayes The summer *beames*, . . . *Gn.* 100
Hyperion, throwing foorth his *beames* full hott, . . . *Gn.* 156
did his *beames* abroad dispred, . . . *Mui.* 52
Shot her sharp pointed *beames* through purest aire. . . . *As.* 58
As Sunny *beames* in fairest somers day, . . . *As.* 158
Forth darting *beames* of beautie from her eyes: . . . *As.* 190
goodly *beames* though they be overdight . . . *Col.* 493
Faire Galathea with bright shining *beames*, . . . *Col.* 518
Her lookes were like *beames* of the morning Sun, . . . *Col.* 604
Darting her *beames* into each feeble mynd: . . . *Col.* 874
Shed thy faire *beames* into my feeble eyne, . . . I. Pr. 4. 5
While flashing *beames* do daze his feeble eyen, . . . I. iv. 9. 6
Under your *beames* I will me safely shrowd . . . I. iv. 48. 3
Phoebus . . . hurld his glistring *beams* through gloomy ayre. . I. v. 2. 5
As when a cloud his *beames* doth over-lay; . . . I. vii. 34. 7
amazd At flashing *beames* of that sunshiny shield, . . . I. viii. 20. 2
Like sunny *beames* threw from her Christall face . . . I. x. 12. 7
could not endure those *beames* bright, . . . II. Pr. 5. 4
As morning Sunne her *beames* dispredden cleare, . . . II. ii. 40. 8
the morrow fayre with purple *beames* . . . II. iii. 1. 1
darted fyrie *beames* out of the same, . . . II. iii. 23. 3
as the Sunny *beames* do glaunce and glide . . . II. v. 2. 4
The sunny *beames* which on the billowes bett, . . . II. xii. 63. 3
Moystened their fierie *beames*, with which she thrild . . . II. xii. 78. 7
the wonder of her *beames* bright, . . . III. Pr. 4. 8
doth farre outcast His hearie *beames*, . . . III. i. 16. 6
the bright glister of their *beames* cleare . . . III. i. 32. 8
Breakes forth her silver *beames*, . . . III. i. 43. 4
Their *beames* shall ofte breake forth, . . . III. iii. 44. 9
Speed thee to spred abroad thy *beames* bright, . . . III. iv. 60. 4
When the bright sunne his *beams* thereon doth beat: . . . III. v. 49. 6
whose bright shining *beames* Adorne the world . . . III. v. 53. 1
Phoebus with faire *beames* did her adorne, . . . III. vi. 2. 8
When Titan faire his *beames* did display, . . . III. vi. 6. 5
nether Phoebus *beams* could through them throng, . . . III. vi. 44. 8
sith the Sunne now ginnes to slake his *beames* . . . III. viii. 51. 3
like sunny *beames*, . . . shewe their golden gleames, . . . III. ix. 20. 6
from his fearefull eyes two fierie *beames*, . . . IV. viii. 39. 1
Cambridge or Oxford, Englands goodly *beames*. . . . IV. xi. 35. 6
Both darting forth faire *beames* to each mans eye, . . . V. iii. 19. 3
Whose skirts were bordred with bright sunny *beames*, . . . V. ix. 28. 6
is ought so bright And beautifull as glories *beames* appeare, . V. xi. 62. 8
as Titans *beames* forth brust Through the thicke clouds . . . VI. iii. 13. 5
joyous day . . . in sunny *beames* bedight, . . . VI. iii. 45. 2
The *beames* whereof did kindle lovely fire . . . VI. vii. 28. 8
Through the bright heaven doth her *beams* display, . . . VI. x. 13. 7
With starrie *beames* about her shining bright, . . . VI. xi. 13. 5
To sparke out litle *beames*, . . . VI. xi. 21. 9
In which faire *beames* of beauty did appeare . . . VII. vi. 31. 2
round about such *beames* of splendor threw, . . . VII. vii. 6. 7
The goodly Sun encompast all with *beames* bright. . . . VII. vii. 44. 9
your bright *beams* . . . May kindle living fire . . . *Am.* vii. 11
your bright *beams* doth not the blinded guest . . . *Am.* viii. 5
by which your fayre *beames* darkned be. . . . *Am.* xlv. 14
now shew theyr goodly *beams* . . . *Epith.* 94
beames with such disparagements Be dimd, . . . *H.B.* 164
Through mutuall receipt of *beames* bright, . . . *H.B.* 235
For he his *beames* doth still to them extend, . . . *H.H.L.* 72
Whose glorious *beames* all fleshly sense doth daze . . . *H.H.L.* 278
show Some litle *beames* to mortall eyes below . . . *H.H.B.* 12

Beams—*Continued.*
The Suns bright *beames* when he on us doth shyne, . . . *H.H.B.* 121
From whence proceed her *beames* so pure and bright . . . *H.H.B.* 160
That with his *beames* enlumineth the darke And dampish aire, *H.H.B.* 164
Through heavenly vertue which her *beames* doe breed. . . . *H.H.B.* 175
From whose pure *beams* al perfect beauty springs, . . . *H.H.B.* 296
Hot Titans *beames*, which then did glyster fayre; . . . *Proth.* 4
Beams'. feeles the warmth of sunny *beames* reflection, . . . IV. xii. 34. 7
Bear. *See* **Bare.**
seven heads, ten crounes, ten hornes did *beare*, . . . *Rev.* i. 2
Feete of a *beare*, a Lions throte she had. . . . *Rev.* i. 5
Ten hornes also the stately beast did *beare*. . . . *Rev.* ii. 5
To *beare* the frame, foure great Lyons . . . *Bel.* iii. 10
The top thereof a pot did seeme to *beare*, . . . *Bel.*² iii. 5
doth *beare* aboord The ploughmans hope . . . *Ro.* xiv. 3
the foule, that serves to *beare* the lightning, . . . *Ro.* xvii. 13
At last, not able to *beare* so great weight, . . . *Ro.* xx. 12
forkhed sting that death in it did *beare*, . . . *Van.* vi. 4
on his backe did *beare* . . . A gilden towre, . . . *Van.* viii. 3
The blossome which my braunch of youth did *beare* . . . *S.C.* Ja. 39
if thou can *beare* . . . Winters wrathful cheare; . . . *S.C.* F. 25
her lot To *beare* such an one. . . . *S.C.* Ap. 94
Bene they not Bay braunches which they doe *beare*, . . . *S.C.* Ap. 104
To helpen the Ladyes their Maybush *beare!*) . . . *S.C.* May 34
Three thinges to *beare* bene very burdenous, . . . *S.C.* May 132
all burdens, that a man can *beare*, . . . *S.C.* May 140
a fooles talke to *beare* and to heare. . . . *S.C.* May 141
beare of the sharpe showres; . . . *S.C.* May 157
Beare witnesse all of thys so wicked deede: . . . *S.C.* Jun. 108
Whom Ida hyll dyd *beare*, . . . *S.C.* Jul. 146
beare witnesse of my woe, . . . *S.C.* Au. 151
Eche thing imparted is more eath to *beare:* . . . *S.C.* S. 17
bearen the cragge so stiffe and so state, . . . *S.C.* S. 45
As they han brewed, so let hem *beare* blame. . . . *S.C.* S. 101
the white *beare* to the stake did bring. . . . *S.C.* O. 48
for her girlond Olive braunches *beare*, . . . *S.C.* N. 144
if that Hobbinol right judgement *bare*, . . . *S.C.* D. 45
neither sword nor dagger he did *beare;* . . . *Hub.* 215
on his shoulders high his bat to *beare*, . . . *Hub.* 238
All jolly Prelates, worthie rule to *beare*, . . . *Hub.* 423
Ne is the paines so great, but *beare* ye may, . . . *Hub.* 446
Newes may perhaps some good unweeting *beare*.' . . . *Hub.* 606
Who now in Court doth *beare* the greatest sway, . . . *Hub.* 616
the nigh aymed ring away to *beare*. . . . *Hub.* 742
oft unsweare, a Diademe to *beare?* . . . *Hub.* 1058
the King did favour to them *beare;* . . . *Hub.* 1076
So much as they were able well to *beare*, . . . *Hub.* 1157
taught to *beare* A Bases part . . . *T.M.* 27
Fortunes freakes, is wisely taught to *beare:* . . . *T.M.* 130
Deare unto all that true affection *beare:* . . . *Ti.* 243
The Harpe well knowne beside the Northern *Beare*. . . . *Ti.* 616
The Arke did *beare* with him above the skie, . . . *Ti.* 668
Her sonne to Psyche secrete love did *beare*, . . . *Mui.* 131
that flie them in her wings doth *beare*. . . . *Mui.* 144
on his backe Her through the sea did *beare;* . . . *Mui.* 279
Griefe findes some ease by him that like does *beare*. . . . *D.* 67
unto his loved lasse, . . . him dolefully did *beare*. . . . *As.* 148
to the shiny Mulla he did *beare*, . . . *Col.* 93
yet doth *beare*, and ever will, . . . *Col.* 94
without harme us farre away did *beare*, . . . *Col.* 225
that frame, which us did *beare;* . . . *Col.* 287
for the love which thou doest *beare* . . . *Ded. Son.* iii. 10
the knight whose semblaunt he did *beare*, . . . I. ii. 12. 1
He set her on her steede, and forward forth did *beare*. . . . I. ii. 45. 9
he . . . saw the Red-crosse which the knight did *beare*, . . . I. iii. 34. 2
Through shield and body eke he should him *beare:* . . . I. iii. 35. 5
from his sadle quite he did him *beare*. . . . I. iii. 35. 7
he . . . in his hand did *beare* a bouzing can, . . . I. iv. 22. 6
rugged heare, . . . Was like the person selfe whom he did *beare:* . . . I. iv. 24. 4
Goe say, his foe thy shield with his doth *beare*.' . . . I. v. 13. 4
His trembling hand . . . Upon the Lyon and the rugged *Beare;* I. vi. 24. 4
he would . . . ryde their backes, not made to *beare;* . . . I. vi. 24. 7
The Lyon whelpes she saw how he did *beare*, . . . I. vi. 27. 8
lesser pangs can *beare* who hath endur'd the chief. . . . I. vi. 37. 9
Who hath endur'd the whole can *beare* ech part. . . . I. vii. 25. 5
Can speake his prowesse that did earst you *beare*, . . . I. vii. 48. 4
It booted nought to thinke such thunderbolts to *beare*. . . . I. viii. 7. 9
What mortall wight could ever *beare* so monstrous blow? . . I. viii. 18. 9
'Whose feeble thighes, . . . him scarse to light could *beare;* I. viii. 40. 8
The things, that grievous were to doe, or *beare*, . . . I. viii. 44. 2
like infirmity like chaunce may *beare;* . . . I. ix. 30. 8
mountaines . . . She would commaund themselves to *beare* away, I. x. 20. 7
all with patience wisely she did *beare*, . . . I. x. 28. 8
To *beare* so great a weight: . . . I. xi. 18. 6
Snatcht up both horse and man, to *beare* them quite away. I. xi. 18. 9
Vere the maine shete, and *beare* up with the land, . . . I. xii. 1. 3
As chained *beare* whom cruell dogs doe bait, . . . I. xii. 35. 7
Goodly comportaunce each to other *beare*, . . . II. i. 29. 3
he honour still away did *beare*, . . . II. i. 35. 3
to the Palmer gave to *beare;* . . . II. ii. 11. 2
As when a *Beare* and Tygre, being met . . . II. ii. 22. 5
Doth *beare* the fayrest flowre in honourable seed. . . . II. iii. 10. 9
Thenceforth in battaile never sword to *beare*, . . . II. iii. 17. 8
What great despight doth fortune to thee *beare*, . . . II. iv. 25. 7
such hideous puissaunce on foot to *beare;* . . . II. v. 3. 9
Would oftentimes emongst them *beare* a part, . . . II. vi. 25. 2
beare the rigour of his bold mesprise; . . . II. vii. 39. 8
nothing seemd mote *beare* so monstrous might: . . . II. viii. 38. 2

Bear—*Continued.*
So did Prince Arthur *beare* himselfe in fight, ... II. viii. 48. 8
Beare ye the picture of that Ladies head? . . . . II. ix. 2. 8
Whose faire retraitt I in my shield doe *beare;* . . . . . . II. ix. 4. 2
Others to *beare* the same away did mynd; . . . . II. ix. 31. 8
Them closely into Armorick did *beare:* . . . . II. x. 64. 5
every one did bow and arrowes *beare.* . . . . II. xi. 8. 7
So fast as his good Courser could him *beare;* . . . . . . II. xi. 25. 8
a *Beare,* whom angry curres have touzd, ... II. xi. 33. 3
It booted not to thinke that throw to *beare,* . . . . . . II. xi. 36. 4
beare him farre from hope of succour usuall. . . . . . . II. xi. 45. 9
All monsters to subdew to him that did it *beare.* . . . . . II. xii. 40. 9
the downy heare Did . . . silken blossoms *beare.* . . . . . II. xii. 79. 9
Ne armes to *beare* against the others syde: . . . . III. i. 12. 6
downe the next did *beare.* . . . . III. i. 28. 9
wemen wont in warres to *beare* most sway, ... III. ii. 2. 8
nine monethes did *beare* . . . Her tender babe, ... III. ii. 11. 6
The wisard could no lenger *beare* her bord, ... III. iii. 19. 1
Long time ye both in armes shall *beare* great sway, ... III. iii. 28. 5
the kingdom he from them should *beare.* . . . . III. iii. 45. 9
usd the same in batteill aye to *beare;* . . . . III. iii. 60. 3
did *beare* This warlike sonne unto an earthly peare, ... III. iv. 19. 4
They easely unto her charett *beare:* . . . . III. iv. 42. 2
the boughes doe laughing blossoms *beare,* . . . . III. vi. 42. 3
From peril free he away her did *beare;* . . . . III. vii. 24. 8
in foote doth *beare* A trembling Culver, ... III. vii. 39. 1
I will away her *beare.'* . . . . III. viii. 12. 9
Besought them humbly him to *beare* withall, ... III. ix. 18. 5
The which she meant away with her to *beare;* . . . . III. x. 12. 5
that Guest did *beare* her forcibly, ... III. x. 13. 8
al good knights, that armes doe *bear* this day, ... III. x. 27. 8
I pardon yield, and with thy rudenes *beare;* . . . . III. x. 31. 3
He ran as fast as both his feet could *beare,* . . . . III. x. 53. 2
like as a *Beare,* . . . . III. x. 53. 4
he the powre of chaste hands might not *beare,* . . . . . . III. xi. 6. 3
Ne in that stownd wist how her selfe to *beare;* . . . . . . III. xi. 22. 2
both in flowres doe live, and love thee *beare,* . . . . . . III. xi. 37. 4
Whom Jove . . . chose his cup to *beare;* . . . . III. xii. 7. 4
in his hand a windy fan did *beare,* . . . . III. xii. 8. 8
in face And outward shew faire semblance they did *beare;* . . . IV. i. 17. 6
a gloomie cloud, . . . doth *beare* An hideous storme, ... IV. i. 45. 5
too long I *beare* The open wrongs . . . . IV. ii. 13. 1
Did *beare* them both to fell avenges end, ... IV. ii. 15. 2
gan therefore close spight to him to *beare;* . . . . IV. ii. 26. 5
mightie strokes . . . seemed death in them to *beare;* . . . . IV. iii. 7. 7
horse and man to ground he quite did *beare,* . . . . IV. iv. 20. 8
Satyrane that day was judg'd to *beare* the bell. . . . . . . IV. iv. 25. 9
The which this famous Britomart did *beare;* . . . . IV. iv. 46. 5
wivehood true, to all that did it *beare;* . . . . IV. v. 3. 2
pearelesse she was thought that did it *beare.* . . . . IV. v. 6. 5
she downe did *beare* The Salvage Knight . . . . IV. v. 8. 4
she should surely *beare* the bell away; . . . . IV. v. 13. 6
some celestiall shape that flesh did *beare:* . . . . IV. v. 14. 7
With which he all that met him downe did *beare.* . . . . . IV. vi. 6. 5
from him his fairest love did *beare.* . . . . IV. vi. 7. 3
ne unto whom I more true love did *beare:* . . . . IV. vi. 35. 9
of mortall stroke the stound doth *beare,* . . . . IV. vi. 37. 5
now he her away with him did *beare* . . . . IV. vii. 24. 7
he his hand so carefully did *beare,* . . . . IV. vii. 27. 5
bootlesse thing it was to think such blowes to *beare.* . . . . IV. vii. 28. 9
with her dolefull accent *beare* with him a part. . . . . . . IV. viii. 3. 9
on his warlike beast them both did *beare,* . . . . IV. viii. 22. 8
The burden of the deadly brunt did *beare* . . . . IV. viii. 42. 2
seemed nought the souse thereof could *beare,* . . . . IV. viii. 44. 5
zeale Which I to him as to my soule did *beare,* . . . . . . IV. viii. 55. 3
To guide the beast that did his maister *beare,* . . . . . . IV. ix. 5. 4
with him did *beare* Faire Amoret, ... IV. ix. 17. 6
did those two them selves so bravely *beare,* . . . . IV. ix. 30. 6
as they him downe would *beare;* . . . . IV. ix. 33. 3
that huge River, which doth *beare* his name . . . . IV. xi. 21. 8
with him *beare* where none of her might know: . . . . IV. xii. 15. 2
He wist not how her thence away to *bere,* . . . . IV. xii. 15. 8
though his limbs could not his bodie *beare,* . . . . IV. xii. 35. 3
on his steed her set to *beare* her out of sight. . . . . . . V. i. 17. 9
Beare for his penaunce that same Ladies head, ... V. i. 26. 8
He chose with shame to *beare* that Ladies head: . . . . . . V. i. 27. 8
with it *beare* the burden of defame, ... V. i. 28. 8
To *beare* that Ladies head before his breast, ... V. i. 29. 4
He tooke it up, and thence with him did *beare,* . . . . . . V. i. 29. 8
ne *beare* him selfe upright; . . . . V. ii. 17. 8
He could no longer *beare,* but forth issewed, ... V. iii. 20. 4
'That shield, which thou doest *beare,* . . . . V. iii. 21. 1
this the arme the which that shield did *beare,* . . . . . . V. iii. 22. 2
As when a *Beare* hath seiz'd her cruell clawes . . . . . . V. iv. 40. 6
beare with you both wine and juncates fit, ... V. iv. 49. 8
like a greedie *Beare* unto her pray, ... V. v. 9. 7
Beare off the burden of her raging yre: . . . . V. v. 16. 4
well to *beare* The storme of fortunes frowne . . . . V. v. 38. 2
I will a while with his first folly *beare,* . . . . V. v. 48. 8
To *beare* unto her love the message of her mind. . . . . . . V. vi. 7. 9
through the aire doth *beare;* . . . . V. vi. 40. 5
afterwards a sonne to him shalt *beare,* . . . . V. vii. 23. 7
'This token *beare* Unto the man . . . . V. vii. 32. 4
his wingfooted coursers him did *beare* So fast away . . . . . V. viii. 33. 4
Fast did they fly as them their feete could *beare* . . . . . V. viii. 39. 1
Did *beare* the pendants through their nimblesse bold: . . . . V. ix. 29. 3
made it *beare* the yoke of Inquisition, ... V. x. 27. 2
th' Adamantine shield which he did *beare* . . . . V. xi. 10. 7
in his hand an huge Polaxe did *beare,* . . . . V. xii. 14. 7
to *beare* themselves aright To all of each degree . . . . . . VI. ii. 1. 3

Bear—*Continued.*
to launch the salvage hart . . . of many a *Beare,* . . . . . . VI. ii. 6. 8
enforst to *beare* though to my paine, ... VI. ii. 12. 5
a slender dart, Fellow of this I *beare,* . . . . VI. ii. 12. 7
I yet glad to *beare* the packe . . . . VI. ii. 21. 7
zeale Which to thy noble personage I *beare,* . . . . VI. ii. 26. 6
Of him that did the kingly Scepter *beare,* . . . . VI. ii. 29. 4
I may *beare* armes, ... VI. ii. 33. 6
the courteous care which he did *beare* . . . . VI. ii. 46. 8
him to *beare* she thought it thing too base. . . . . VI. ii. 47. 5
To *beare* this burden on your dainty backe; . . . . VI. ii. 47. 8
My selfe will *beare* a part, ... VI. ii. 47. 9
And twixt them both with parted paines did *beare,* . . . . . VI. ii. 48. 5
by outragious force away did *beare:* . . . . VI. iii. 18. 7
If I would *beare* behinde a burden of such scorne. . . . . . VI. iii. 31. 9
Or *beare* her on thy backe with pleasing payne, ... VI. iii. 32. 4
whylest an Infant from a *Beare* He saves, ... VI. iv. Arg.
from his mothers wombe, which him did *beare,* . . . . VI. iv. 4. 8
A cruell *Beare,* the which an infant bore . . . . VI. iv. 17. 8
the wearie *Beare* Ere long he overtooke . . . . VI. iv. 20. 1
seemed nothing might *Beare* off their blowes . . . . VI. v. 18. 5
Above a launces length him forth did *beare,* . . . . VI. vii. 11. 3
could no lenger *beare* so great abuse . . . . VI. vii. 45. 4
Till they him force the buxome yoke to *beare:* . . . . VI. viii. 12. 4
that leg, which did his body *beare,* . . . . VI. viii. 16. 4
wherefore doe you *beare* This bottle . . . . VI. viii. 23. 6
of the pray each one a part doth *beare.* . . . . VI. viii. 41. 5
Above all other lasses *beare* the bell; . . . . VI. x. 26. 4
fared like a furious wyld *Beare,* . . . . VI. xi. 25. 8
th' empire sought from them to *beare.* . . . . VII. vi. 1. 9
therein to *beare* Nights burning lamp, ... VII. vi. 12. 2
(Such sway doth beauty even in Heaven *beare*) . . . . VII. vi. 31. 4
Of all that *beare* the British Islands name, ... VII. vi. 38. 3
Yet he (poore soule!) with patience all did *beare;* . . . . . VII. vi. 49. 6
new bloosmes did *beare,* . . . . VII. vii. 28. 3
in his hand a javelin he did *beare,* . . . . VII. vii. 28. 6
him did *beare* With crooked crawling steps . . . . VII. vii. 35. 5
Day did *beare* upon his scepters hight The goodly Sun . . . . VII. vii. 44. 8
raign and *bear* the greatest sway; . . . . VII. vii. 47. 4
reare My Trophee, and from all the triumph *beare?* . . . . . VII. vii. 56. 5
it is the badge that I doe *beare,* . . . . *Am.* xxviii. 3
Ne your incessant battry more to *beare:* . . . . *Am.* lvii. 4
To *beare* the message of her gentle spright. . . . . *Am.* lxxxi. 12
The false reports that flying tales doe *beare,* . . . . . . *H.L.* 261
Dost *beare* unto thy blisse, ... *H.L.* 279
That heavenly riches which in you ye *beare,* . . . . *H.B.* 185
in thy brest his blessed image *beare.* . . . . *H.H.L.* 259

Beard. Long was his *beard,* . . . . *Bel.*[1] vii. 3
With side-long *beard,* . . . . *Bel.*[2] ix. 3
gan his newe-budded *beard* to stroke. . . . . *S.C.* May 214
from my *beard* the fat away have swept; . . . . *Hub.* 78
beard all overgrowne, ... *D.* 44
With hoary head and deawy dropping *beard,* . . . . *Col.* 250
His feete all bare, his *beard* all hoarie gray, ... I. i. 29. 3
An old old man, with *beard* as white as snow, ... I. viii. 30. 2
fire, that flashing in his *beard* Him all amazd, ... I. xi. 26. 4
bitt his tawny *beard* to shew his raging yre. . . . . II. iv. 15. 9
His head and *beard* with sout were ill bedight, ... II. vii. 3. 7
sprinckled frost upon his deawy *beard:* . . . . III. viii. 30. 4
the cold ysickles from his rough *beard* . . . . III. viii. 35. 3
through likenesse of his gotish *beard,* . . . . III. x. 47. 6
his hore *beard* Was fowly dight, ... III. x. 52. 4
With rugged *beard,* and hoarie shagged heare, ... IV. v. 34. 8
With head all hoary, and his *beard* all gray, ... IV. xi. 25. 8
First he his *beard* did shave, ... V. iii. 37. 5
strongly flew With all her body at his head and *beard,* . . . V. xi. 30. 7
that knights *berd,* for toll which they for passage pay.' . . . VI. i. 13. 9
Wilt give thy *beard,* though it but little bee? . . . . . . VI. i. 19. 8
with unjust detraction him did *beard,* . . . . VI. v. 12. 7
Whose silver lockes bedeckt his *beard* and hed, ... VI. ix. 13. 7
by his goatish *beard* some did him haile: . . . . VII. vi. 49. 5
on his hoary *beard* his breath did freese, ... VII. vii. 31. 3

Bearded. *See* **Shaggy-bearded.**
next to him rode lustfull Lechery Upon a *bearded* Gote, . . . I. iv. 24. 2

Beards. the fat from their *beards* doen lick: . . . . *S.C.* S. 123
With *beards* of Knights and locks of Ladies lynd: . . . . . VI. i. 15. 5

Beare. *See* **Bier.**

Bearest. what ever man *bearst* worldlie sway, ... *Ti.* 208
that royall mace Which now thou *bear'st,* . . . . II. x. 4. 4

Beareth. *beareth* fruit of honour and all chast desyre. . . . III. v. 52. 9

Bearing. *See* **Harness-bearing.**
Bearing close envie to these riches rare, ... *Bel.*[2] xiii. 6
Bearing the fire with which heaven doth us fray, ... *Ro.* xvii. 2
Bearing a trusse of tryfles . . . . *S.C.* May 239
Best knowne by *bearing* up great Cynthiaes traine: . . . . . *Col.* 509
wearied with *bearing* of her bag . . . . I. i. 6. 3
bearing with him treasure in close store, ... III. x. 19. 3
Bearing that precious relicke in an arke Of gold, ... IV. iv. 15. 2
in his armes her *bearing* Ran, ... IV. vii. 8. 6
Bearing a litle Dwarfe before his steed, ... IV. viii. 38. 3
Bearing the shield which I had conquerd late, ... IV. x. 14. 2
Bearing his sixe deformed heads on hye, ... IV. xi. 32. 2
bearing in his targe A Ladie . . . . VI. ii. 44. 8
Into the wood was *bearing* her apace. . . . . VI. iii. 25. 2
The trustie damzell *bearing* it abrode . . . . VI. xii. 7. 1
the badge which I doe beare, Ye, *bearing* it, ... *Am.* xxviii. 4

Bear's. *See* **She bear's.**
What of the Persian *Beares* outragiousnesse, ... *Ti.* 66
The other like a *beares* uneven paw, ... I. viii. 48. 8
ragged weed Made of *Beares* skin, ... III. xii. 11. 2

Bears. The kingly Bird, that *beares* Joves thunder-clap, . . . *Van.* iv. 1
Seest howe brag yond Bullocke *beares,* . . . *S.C.* F. 71
Chloris . . . Of Olive braunches *beares* a Coronall: . . . *S.C.* Ap. 123
beares on his shoulders the heavens height. . . . *S.C.* May 143
many a fayre sight Of *Beres* and Tygres, . . . *S.C.* Au. 28
That balefull sorrow he no longer *beares* . . . *Gn.* 644
I saw two *Beares,* as white as anie milke, . . . *Ti.* 561
these *Beares* lay sleeping sound, . . . *Ti.* 570
Beares in his wings so manie a changefull token. . . . *Mui.* 101
all harts that hornes the highest *beares;* . . . *Col.* 714
Unlesse that some gay Mistresse badge he *beares:* . . . *Col.* 780
He . . . *Beares* her away upon his courser light: . . . I. iii. 43. 8
Whose shield he *beares* renverst, the more to heap disdayn. . I. iv. 41. 9
'he *beares* a charmed shield, . . . I. iv. 50. 5
with her *beares* the fowle welfavoured witch. . . . I. v. 28. 2
beares an equall eie? . . . I. ix. 47. 2
The godly Matrone . . . him *beares* Forth from her presence, . I. x. 35. 1
So boldly he him *beares,* . . . II. ii. 25. 1
Them on her bulwarke *beares,* . . . II. viii. 35. 9
Beares, Lyons, and Buls, which romed them arownd. . . . III. i. 14. 9
Beares he himselfe with portly majestee, . . . III. iii. 32. 4
the house that *beares* the stile Of roiall majesty . . . III. iii. 48. 7
Beares in his boasted fan, . . . III. xi. 47. 8
in his shield he *beares* . . . the heads of many broken speares; IV. i. 48. 8
With *Beares* and Tygers taking heavie part, . . . IV. vii. 2. 7
hunting then the Libbards and the *Beares* . . . IV. vii. 23. 7
other food then that wilde forrest *beares,* . . . IV. vii. 41. 5
could have perst the hearts of Tigres and of *Beares,* . . . IV. viii. 4. 9
other Isle, that greater bredth now *beares.* . . . V. iv. 7. 9
was not borne Of *Beares* and Tygres, . . . V. v. 40. 6
Beares, that groynd continually; . . . VI. xii. 27. 5
in his hand a broad deepe boawle he *beares,* . . . VII. vii. 41. 8
In all things else she *beares* the greatest sway: . . . VII. viii. 1. 5
That boldned innocence *beares* in hir eies; . . . *Am.* v. 10
His faith, his fortune, in his breast he *beares.* . . . *H.L.* 224

Beast. I saw an ugly *beast* come from the sea, . . . *Rev.* i. 1
then came from the sea a savage *beast,* . . . *Rev.* i. 11
make all wights adore The *beast,* . . . *Rev.* i. 14
a Woman sitting on a *beast* . . . *Rev.* ii. 1
Ten hornes also the stately *beast* did beare. . . . *Rev.* ii. 5
Then did I see the *beast* and Kings . . . *Rev.* iii. 11
this fierce hatefull *beast* and all hir traine . . . *Rev.* iii. 13
a strange *beast* with seven heads . . . *Bel.*[2] viii. 5
pincht the haunches of that (this[1]) gentle *beast,* . . . *Pet.* i. 9
forst this hideous *beast* to open wide . . . *Van.* iii. 9
it was a perilous *beast* above all, . . . *S.C.* S. 214
So wilde a *beast* so tame ytaught to bee, . . . *Hub.* 625
Without a gowned *beast* him fast beside, . . . *Hub.* 749
'Arise, (said Mercurie) thou sluggish *beast,* . . . *Hub.* 1327
the royall *Beast* forbore beleeving, . . . *Hub.* 1365
What difference twixt man and *beast* is left, . . . *T.M.* 487
where is that same great seven-headded *beast,* . . . *Ti.* 71
Like *beast* whose breath but in his nostrels is, . . . *Ti.* 356
An hairie hide of some wilde *beast,* . . . *Mui.* 66
ne fear'd the wildest *beast,* . . . *D.* 135
to a *beast* his noble hart embase, . . . *D.* 180
No *beast* so salvage but he could it kill; . . . *As.* 83
A cruell *beast* of most accursed brood . . . *As.* 116
with so much speede As her slowe *beast* could make; . . . I. ii. 8. 2
From her unhastie *beast* she did alight; . . . I. iii. 4. 2
'The Lyon, Lord of everie *beast* in field,' . . . I. iii. 7. 1
The kingly *beast* upon her gazing stood: . . . I. iii. 8. 4
that disdainfull *beast,* Encountring fierce, . . . I. iii. 19. 6
Her servile *beast* yet would not leave her so, . . . I. iii. 44. 6
too weake and feeble was the forse Of salvage *beast* . . . I. iii. 42. 2
most like a brutish *beast,* He spued up his gorge, . . . I. iv. 21. 8
Who had more joy to . . . chase the salvage *beast* . . . I. vi. 21. 8
everie *beast* for feare of him did fly, and quake. . . . I. vi. 24. 9
there abode, whylst any *beast* of name Walkt . . . I. vi. 29. 3
A monstrous *beast* ybredd in filthy fen he chose, . . . I. vii. 16. 8
Upon this dreadfull *Beast* with sevenfold head . . . I. vii. 18. 8
Arthure . . . wounds the *beast,* . . . I. viii. Arg.
Duessa came, High mounted on her many headed *beast,* . . I. viii. 6. 2
she hastily did draw Her dreadfull *beast;* . . . I. viii. 12. 4
Enforst her purple *beast* with all her might, . . . I. viii. 13. 3
So downe he fell before the cruell *beast,* . . . I. viii. 15. 1
He . . . to the *beast* gan turne his enterprise, . . . I. viii. 15. 7
the fruitfull-headed *beast,* . . . Became stark blind, . . . I. viii. 20. 1
the dreadful *Beast* drew nigh to hand, . . . I. xi. 8. 1
The wrathfull *beast* about him turned light, . . . I. xi. 16. 7
Exceeding rage enflam'd the furious *Beast,* . . . I. xi. 17. 5
The *beast,* impatient of his smarting wound . . . I. xi. 25. 6
The hell-bred *beast* threw forth unto the skies, . . . I. xi. 40. 3
the ever damned *Beast* Durst not approch, . . . I. xi. 49. 1
thereby dead that balefull *Beast* did deeme, . . . I. xii. 2. 7
Rejoycing at the fall of that great *beast,* . . . I. xii. 4. 8
In case he could that monstrous *beast* destroy, . . . I. xii. 41. 7
Such wounded *beast* as that I did not see, . . . II. iii. 33. 5
In mind to marke the *beast.* . . . II. iii. 34. 6
The truncked *beast* fast bleeding did him fowly dight. . . . II. v. 4. 9
To wreake it selfe on *beast* all innocent, . . . II. v. 5. 4
that furious *beast* His precious horne . . . Strikes in the stocke, II. v. 10. 6
Ne man nor *beast* may rest, . . . II. ix. 16. 6
His *Beast* he felly prickt on either syde, . . . II. xi. 24. 3
turning quicke aside His light-foot *beast,* . . . II. xi. 25. 6
To be a *beast,* and lacke intelligence!' . . . II. xii. 87. 5
having at a bag The salvage *beast* . . . III. i. 22. 2
To hunt the salvage *beast* in forrest wyde, . . . III. i. 37. 4
lov'd a Bul, and learnd a *beast* to bee. . . . III. ii. 41. 6

Beast—*Continued.*
the wilde *beast* shall dy in starved den. . . . III. iii. 34. 9
alighted from her light-foot *beast,* . . . III. iv. 7. 1
through swiftnesse of his speedie *beast,* . . . III. v. 14. 2
as shee pursewd the chace Of some wilde *beast,* . . . III. v. 28. 2
Well hoped shee the *beast* engor'd had beene, . . . III. v. 28. 7
deemd the *beast* had bene depriv'd Of life, . . . III. v. 37. 4
escaped from a ravenous *beast,* . . . III. vii. 1. 2
An hideous *beast* of horrible aspect, . . . III. vii. 22. 2
he lightly lept Upon the *beast,* . . . III. vii. 33. 7
with it bownd the *beast,* that lowd did rore . . . III. vii. 36. 3
Thus as he led the *Beast* along the way, . . . III. vii. 37. 1
He lefte his captive *Beast* at liberty, . . . III. vii. 38. 2
Where late he left the *Beast* he overcame, . . . III. vii. 61. 6
the *Beast,* which by her wicked art Late foorth she sent, . III. viii. 2. 5
a monstrous *beast* The Palfrey whereon she did travell slew, . III. viii. 49. 2
every bird and *beast* awarned made To shrowd themselves, . . III. x. 46. 8
man and *beast* with powre imperious Subdeweth . . . III. xii. 22. 4
The *beast* astonisht stands in middest of his smart. . . . IV. i. 49. 9
His neather lip was not like man nor *beast,* . . . IV. vii. 6. 1
on his warlike *beast* them both did beare, . . . IV. viii. 22. 8
Upon his usuall *beast* it firmely bound, . . . IV. ix. 4. 8
To guide the *beast* that did his maister beare, . . . IV. ix. 5. 4
The tast of bloud of some engored *beast,* . . . IV. ix. 31. 6
Bound like a *beast* appointed to the stall: . . . V. i. 22. 6
Uppon the carkasse of some *beast* too weake, . . . V. iv. 40. 7
To heare the piteous *beast* pleading her plaintiffe cause. . . . V. iv. 40. 9
Warn'd man and *beast* in quiet rest be shrowded, . . . V. iv. 45. 3
Earely calling forth both man and *beast* . . . V. v. 1. 3
putting spurres unto her fiery *beast,* . . . V. vi. 39. 2
she to hunt the *beast* first tooke in hond; . . . V. vii. 30. 8
doth wreake her wrath On man and *beast* . . . V. viii. 49. 5
An huge great *Beast* it was, . . . V. xi. 23. 1
Both man and *beast* doe fly, and succour doe inquyre. . . . V. xi. 58. 9
A monster, which the Blatant *Beast* men call, . . . V. xii. 37. 7
the Blatant *Beast,* by them set on, . . . V. xii. 41. 1
'The Blattant *Beast* . . . I doe pursew, . . . VI. i. 7. 1
'What is that Blattant *Beast?*' . . . VI. i. 7. 6
'I such a *Beast* did see, . . . VI. i. 9. 2
'That surely is that *Beast*' . . . VI. i. 10. 1
Calidore . . . Pursues the Blatant *Beast:* . . . VI. iii. Arg.
The Blatant *Beast* forth rushing unaware . . . VI. iii. 24. 2
The *Beast,* . . . was bearing her apace . . . VI. iii. 25. 1
ne ever of wyld *beast* Did taste the bloud, . . . VI. iv. 14. 8
the *beast* enrag'd to loose his pray Upon him turned, . . . VI. iv. 20. 5
The Blatant *Beast* the fittest meanes they found . . . VI. v. 14. 8
They sent that Blatant *Beast* to be a baite . . . VI. v. 15. 3
no one *beast* in forrest, wylde or tame, . . . VI. v. 15. 7
their late woundes, the which the Blatant *Beast* Had given them, . . . VI. v. 39. 8
Such were the wounds the which that Blatant *Beast* Made . VI. vi. 2. 1
that same *beast* was bred of hellish strene, . . . VI. vi. 9. 7
This hellish Dog, that hight the Blatant *Beast;* . . . VI. vi. 12. 2
the biting of that harmefull *Beast* Was throughly heal'd. . . VI. vi. 15. 5
the *beast* doth rage and loudly rore; . . . VI. vii. 47. 6
sith I left him last Sewing the Blatant *Beast;* . . . VI. ix. 2. 3
If such a *beast* they saw, . . . VI. ix. 5. 9
They answer'd him that no such *beast* they saw, . . . VI. ix. 6. 1
Who now does follow the foule Blatant *Beast,* . . . VI. x. 1. 1
When he the *beast* saw ready now to rend . . . VI. x. 35. 7
Do seize upon some *beast* whose flesh is bare, . . . VI. xi. 48. 2
Calidore doth the Blatant *Beast* Subdew, . . . VI. xii. Arg.
To his atchievement of the Blatant *Beast:* . . . VI. xii. 2. 7
That monstrous *Beast* by finall force to quell, . . . VI. xii. 22. 7
yet that foule *Beast* . . . the more did tosse and teare, . . . VI. xii. 24. 6
Full cruelly the *Beast* did rage and rore . . . VI. xii. 31. 1
Such was the fury of this hellish *Beast,* . . . VI. xii. 32. 6
when the *Beast* saw he mote nought availe By force, . . . VI. xii. 33. 1
Yet greatly did the *Beast* repine . . . VI. xii. 36. 1
To see him leade that *Beast* in bondage strong; . . . VI. xii. 37. 5
much admyr'd the *Beast,* but more admyr'd the Knight. . . . VI. xii. 37. 9
some *beast* of strange and forraine race . . . VII. vi. 28. 7
some wicked *beast* unware That breakes into her Dayr' house, VII. vi. 48. 3
the *beast* that whylome did forray The Nemaean forrest, . . . VII. vii. 36. 5
And reigneth over every *beast* in field, . . . *Am.* xx. 6
every *beast* that to his den was fled, . . . *Am.* xl. 10
doth find A feeble *beast,* doth felly him oppresse. . . . *Am.* lvi. 4
that tree, and that same *beast,* am I, . . . *Am.* lvi. 13
Strange thing, me seemd, to see a *beast* so wyld, . . . *Am.* lxvii. 13
he was wakened with the noyse And saw the *beast* so small; . *Epig.* iv. 6

Beastlihead. I be relieved by your *beastlyhead.* . . . *S.C.* May 265

Beastlike. 'Daunger without discretion to attempt Inglorious, [*and] *beastlike* is: . . . III. xi. 23. 2

Beastliness. their owne mother loathd their *beastlinesse,* . . II. x. 9. 3

Beastly. All for her shepheards bene *beastly* and blont. . . . *S.C.* S. 109
With brutishnesse and *beastlie* filth hath stained. . . . *T.M.* 270
So as he rag'd emongst that *beastly* rout, . . . *As.* 115
her *beastly* bodie raizd With doubled forces . . . I. i. 18. 3
from her most *beastly* companie I gan refraine, . . . I. ii. 41. 5
More mild in *beastly* kind then that her *beastly* foe. . . . I. iii. 44. 9
With *beastly* sin thought her to have defilde, . . . I. vi. 3. 4
burnt his *beastly* hart t' efforce her chastitye. . . . I. vi. 4. 9
A Satyre . . . made her person thrall unto his *beastly* kind. . . I. vi. 22. 9
He loudly brayd with *beastly* yelling sownd, . . . I. viii. 11. 3
With *beastly* brutish rage gan him assay, . . . II. iv. 6. 7
hideous Giaunts, and halfe *beastly* men, . . . II. x. 7. 2
'See the mind of *beastly* man, . . . II. xii. 87. 1
Breathing out *beastly* lust her to defyle: . . . III. i. 17. 3
brutish lust, that was so *beastly* tind. . . . III. vii. 15. 9

Beastly—*Continued.*
Beastly he threwe her downe, ... III. viii. 26. 8
In *beastly* use, all that I ever finde: . . . . III. xi. 4. 4
Thereof by force to take their *beastly* pleasure: . . . . VI. viii. 43. 6

Beast's. To save the innocent from the *beastes* pawes, ... *S.C.* Au. 33
Hath tracted forth some salvage *beastes* trade: . . . . II. vi. 39. 5
Have by good fortune found some *beasts* fresh spoyle, ... IV. iii. 16. 2
Least that the *beasts* sharpe teeth had any wound Made . . . VI. iv. 23. 8
that *beastes* teeth, which wounded you tofore, ... VI. vi. 9. 1

Beasts. both milder *beasts* and fiercer foes . . . . *Bel.*[2] viii. 7
as the coward *beasts* use to despise . . . . *Ro.* xiv. 5
Wonts not t' enrage the hearts of equall *beasts,* . . . . *Ro.* xxiv. 2
shortly gan all other *beasts* to scorne. . . . . *Van.* viii. 8
pray of *beasts* and spoyle of living blood, ... *Van.* x. 3
Keeping your *beastes* in the budded broomes: . . . . *S.C.* F. 36
many wyld *beastes* liggen in waite . . . . *S.C.* May 217
The *beastes* in forest wayle . . . . *S.C.* N. 135
hurtful *beastes* to hont? . . . . *S.C.* D. 82
the wilde *beasts* their furie did withhold, ... *Gn.* 451
for eare-marked *beasts* abroad be bruted. . . . . *Hub.* 188
makes the scorne of other *beasts* to bee: . . . . *Hub.* 603
the wilde *beasts,* that swiftest are in chase; . . . . *Hub.* 620
so brave *beasts* she loveth best to see . . . . *Hub.* 629
seene the manners of all *beasts* on ground; . . . . *Hub.* 687
to sew the chace Of swift wilde *beasts,* . . . . *Hub.* 744
Kings of *Beasts,* and Lords of forests all . . . . *Hub.* 971
Of all the *beasts,* which in the forrests bee, ... *Hub.* 1001
that he might be seene Of the wilde *beasts* . . . . *Hub.* 1066
no wild *beasts* should do them any torte . . . . *Hub.* 1078
the proud *beasts* him readily obayd: . . . . *Hub.* 1102
all the *Beasts* him feared as they ought, ... *Hub.* 1106
a warlike equipage Of forreine *beasts,* . . . . *Hub.* 1119
unto him all monstrous *beasts* resorted . . . . *Hub.* 1122
all wylde *beasts* made vassals of his pleasures, ... *Hub.* 1129
the wilde *beasts* whom armes did glorifie, ... *Hub.* 1184
troubled kingdome of wilde *beasts* beheld, ... *Hub.* 1231
the forrest, where wilde *beasts* doo breed, ... *Hub.* 1248
spoyles, by salvage *beasts* committed? . . . . *Hub.* 1253
the herds Of ravenous wilde *beasts,* . . . . *Hub.* 1285
Each place defilde with blood of guiltles *beasts,* . . . . *Hub.* 1307
the *beasts* therein Fled fast away . . . . *Hub.* 1347
all the *beasts* he caus'd assembled bee, ... *Hub.* 1377
like brute *beasts* doo lie in loathsome den . . . . *T.M.* 531
Two fairer *beasts* might not elswhere be found, ... *Ti.* 566
Wylde *beasts* and forrests after him to lead, ... *Ti.* 608
That did all other *Beasts* in beawtie staine. . . . . *D.* 112
of the race that all wild *beastes* do feare, ... *D.* 123
with your carkasses wild *beasts* be glutted. . . . . *D.* 350
where salvage *beasts* do most abound, ... *As.* 82
Thousand wyld *beasts* with deep mouthes . . . . *Col.* 202
other men and *beasts* and birds doth feed: . . . . *Col.* 297
this was drawne of six unequall *beasts,* . . . . I. iv. 18. 1
Like carkases of *beastes* in butchers stall. . . . . I. v. 49. 2
He nousled up . . . Emongst wild *beastes* and woods, ... I. vi. 23. 9
would him advise The angry *beastes* not rashly to despise, . . I. vi. 25. 5
Wyld *beastes* in yron yokes he would compell; . . . . I. vi. 26. 2
face he made all *beastes* to feare, ... I. x. 42. 7
wherewith she queld The salvage *beastes* . . . . II. iii. 29. 4
The wood is fit for *beasts,* . . . . II. iii. 39. 9
Of fowles and *beastes* he made the piteous prayes, ... II. v. 26. 7
more wretched were the cace Of men then *beasts.* . . . . II. viii. 1. 5
wild like *beastes* lurking in loathsome den, ... II. x. 7. 4
A man, of many parts from *beasts* deryv'd, ... II. x. 70. 6
an hideous bellowing Of many *beasts,* . . . . II. xii. 39. 2
Untill they came in vew of those wilde *beasts,* . . . . II. xii. 39. 6
those unruly *beasts* to hold without; . . . . II. xii. 43. 3
those wild-*beasts* that rag'd with furie mad; . . . . II. xii. 84. 5
what meant those *beastes* which there did ly? . . . . II. xii. 84. 9
'These seeming *beasts* are men indeed, ... II. xii. 85. 1
streight of *beastes* they comely men became; . . . . II. xii. 86. 2
to refraine From chase of greater *beastes,* . . . . III. i. 37. 7
all wilde *beastes* do rest, ... III. ii. 32. 2
of wilde *beastes* if she had chased beene; . . . . III. iv. 51. 4
Your glory sett to chace the salvage *beasts,* . . . . III. vi. 22. 2
Some made for *beasts,* some made for birds to weare; . . . . III. vi. 35. 6
Nor wicked *beastes* their tender buds did crop, ... III. vi. 43. 5
Thereto so swifte that it all *beasts* did pas: . . . . III. vii. 22. 6
suffred *beastes* her body to deflowre, ... III. vii. 49. 7
Least salvage *beastes* her person have despoyld: . . . . III. x. 39. 8
In power of herbes, and tunes of *beasts* and burds; . . . . IV. ii. 35. 6
brute *beasts,* forst to refraine fro meat, ... IV. iv. 47. 3
on ravin and on rape Of men and *beasts;* . . . . IV. vii. 5. 8
Of *beasts,* or of the earth, I have not red, ... IV. vii. 7. 8
doe the salvage *beasts* begin to play . . . . IV. x. 46. 1
Peace universall rayn'd mongst men and *beasts,* . . . . V. Pr. 9. 6
to make experience Upon wyld *beasts,* . . . . V. i. 7. 8
even wilde *beasts* did feare his awfull sight, ... V. i. 8. 4
shortly did all other *beasts* subdew. . . . . V. vii. 16. 7
Their bodies to his *beastes* for provender did spred,) . . . . V. viii. 28. 9
mongst wyld *beasts,* and salvage woods, to dwell; . . . . V. ix. 1. 5
none but *beasts* may be of her despoyled; . . . . V. ix. 2. 5
For *beasts* and foules to feede upon for their repast. . . . . V. ix. 19. 9
bands of nature, that wilde *beastes* restraine, ... V. xii. 1. 5
Ne scarse wyld *beasts* durst come, ... VI. iv. 13. 9
Mongst salvage *beasts* both rudely borne and bred, ... VI. v. 2. 3
Amongst wilde *beastes* in desert forrests bred, ... VI. v. 29. 7
their *beasts* there in the budded broomes Beside them fed, . . VI. ix. 5. 4
Ne mote wylde *beastes* . . . Thereto approch; . . . . VI. x. 7. 4
for chace of *beasts* with hound or boawe, ... VII. vi. 39. 2
'As for her tenants, that is, man and *beasts,* . . . . VII. vii. 19. 1

Beasts—*Continued.*
The *beasts* we daily see massacred dy . . . . VII. vii. 19. 2
all other *beastes* of bloody race . . . . *Am.* xxxi. 5
his spotted hyde Doth please all *beasts,* . . . . *Am.* liii. 2
Love wounded my Loves hart, But Diane *beasts* with Cupids dart *Epig.* ii. 8

Beat. *See* **Bet, Sea-beat, Storm-beat.**
So *beate* his old boughes my tender side, ... *S.C.* F. 175
beate upon the solitarie Brere; . . . . *S.C.* F. 227
the Sunnbeame so sore doth us *beate,* . . . . *S.C.* Au. 47
I *beate* the bush, the byrds to them doe flye: . . . . *S.C.* O. 17
with their spredding armes Do *beat* their buds, ... *T.M.* 78
with brave plumes doth *beate* the azure skie, ... *Ti.* 423
Did rend his haire, and *beat* his blubbred face, ... *D.* 551
they gan to . . . *beat* their brests, and naked flesh to teare: . I. iii. 22. 5
Both stricken stryke, and beaten both doe *beat,* . . . . I. v. 7. 7
whenas him list the ayre to *beat,* . . . . I. xi. 10. 6
The rolling billowes *beate* the ragged shore, ... I. xi. 21. 3
the villein sore did *beate* . . . his manly face; . . . . II. iv. 9. 1
Why doe thy cruel billowes *beat* so strong, ... III. iv. 8. 4
When the bright sunne his beams thereon doth *beat:* . . . . III. v. 49. 6
The roring billowes *beat* his bowre so boystrously. . . . . III. x. 58. 9
Did *beat* and bounse his head and brest ful sore: . . . . III. xi. 27. 6
with wide winges to *beat* the buxome ayre: . . . . III. xi. 34. 2
So dreadfully he did the andvile *beat,* . . . . IV. v. 37. 5
beat his breast unworthy of such blame, ... IV. viii. 4. 7
either *beat* him in, or drive him out. . . . . IV. x. 19. 5
with their boughes the gentle plants did *beat:* . . . . V. i. 1. 5
Else he doth hold him backe or *beat* away. . . . . V. ii. 6. 5
with their might *beat* downe licentious lust, ... V. iv. 2. 4
Did *beat* uppon the gates to enter in; . . . . V. iv. 37. 2
With his great yron sledge doth strongly on it *beat.* . . . . V. v. 7. 9
Doth *beat* upon the gentle bird in vaine, ... V. v. 15. 6
the Goddesse with her rod him backe did *beat.* . . . . V. vii. 15. 9
he the bush did *beat,* . . . . V. ix. 17. 4
soone as he their outrage backe doth *beat,* . . . . V. xi. 45. 8
lends unto it leave the emptie ayre to *beat.* . . . . V. xii. 18. 9
does *beat* her brest and forhead knockes. . . . . V. xii. 38. 9
menaced me from the field to *beat,* . . . . VI. i. 40. 5
beat her breast, and piteously her selfe torment. . . . . VI. v. 4. 9
doe him sharpe assay On every side, and *beat* about him round; VI. v. 19. 4
he did repell And *beat* them back, ... VI. vi. 23. 9
did the more her *beate* and bruse: . . . . VI. vii. 40. 5
such a Lady so to *beate* and bruse; . . . . VI. vii. 45. 5
Traceth his ground, and round about doth *beat,* . . . . VI. vii. 47. 4
The more they him misust, and cruelly did *beat.* . . . . VI. viii. 3. 9
See, how they doe that Squire *beat* and revile! . . . . VI. viii. 6. 6
he his face, his head, his brest did *beat,* . . . . VI. xi. 33. 4
The wingd-foot God so fast his plumes did *beat,* . . . . VII. vi. 17. 1
for my faults ye will me gently *beat.* . . . . *Am.* xxiv. 14
with his heavy sledge he can it *beat,* . . . . *Am.* xxxii. 3
Doe *beat* on th' andvile of her stubberne wit . . . . *Am.* xxxii. 8

Beaten. *See* **Sea-beaten, Storm-beaten, Weatherbeaten.**
he all wallowed in the weedes downe *beaten,* . . . . *Van.* ii. 8
The kene cold blowes through my *beaten* hyde, ... *S.C.* F. 3
His bared boughes were *beaten* with stormes, ... *S.C.* F. 112
With painfull torments to be sorely *beaten.* . . . . *Gn.* 352
his shooes *beaten* out with traveling. . . . . *Hub.* 214
path . . . that *beaten* seemd most bare, ... I. i. 11. 3
That path he kept which *beaten* was most plaine. . . . . I. i. 28. 3
the *beaten* marinere, That long hath wandred . . . . I. iii. 31. 1
He leaves the welkin way most *beaten* playne, ... I. iv. 9. 7
Both stricken stryke, and *beaten* both doe beat, ... I. v. 7. 7
Through which a *beaten* broad high way did trace, ... II. vii. 21. 3
a broad gate all built of *beaten* gold: . . . . II. vii. 40. 2
Through griesly shadowes by a *beaten* path, ... II. vii. 51. 3
led him to the Castle by the *beaten* way. . . . . II. xi. 48. 9
Her garments all were wrought of *beaten* gold, ... III. i. 15. 6
beaten were and chased all about. . . . . IV. iv. 43. 4
Beaten with stones downe from the battilment, ... V. ii. 20. 6
hath bene *beaten* late With stormes of fortune . . . . VI. ix. 31. 4

Beateth. strongly *beateth* downe The malice of her foes, . . . V. viii. 17. 5

Beathed. *beath'd* in fire for steele to be in sted. . . . . IV. vi. 7. 6

Beating. *beating* downe these walls with furious mood . . . *Ro.* xi. 11
Beating the withered leafe from the tree, ... *S.C.* S. 51
The soothe of byrdes by *beating* of their winges, ... *S.C.* D. 87
th' hayling darts of heaven *beating* hard. . . . . *Mui.* 80
Did alwaies sore, *beating* his yron wings; . . . . II. vii. 23. 2
feeling by his pulses *beating* rife . . . . III. v. 31. 3
beating downe what ever nigh him came, ... IV. iv. 41. 7
sound Of many yron hammers *beating* ranke, ... IV. v. 33. 7
billowes *beating* from the maine: . . . . IV. xii. 5. 9
by often *beating* Doe pearce the rockes, ... IV. xii. 7. 1
amidst the billowes *beating* of her, ... V. iv. 10. 6
She thus oft times was *beating* off and on, ... V. v. 43. 2
Now *beating* his hard head upon a stone, ... VI. v. 4. 5
beating at his gates full earnestly, ... VII. vi. 15. 3

Beats. forth she *beates* the dusty path: . . . . III. iv. 12. 8
Beates downe both leaves and buds without regard, ... III. vi. 39. 8
storme, . . . *Beats* on it strongly, it to ruinate. . . . . *Am.* lvi. 8

Beauperes. From his *Beauperes,* and from bright heavens vew, III. i. 35. 7

Beauteous. brave Courtier, in whose *beauteous* thought . . . *Hub.* 717
others tell that it so *beautious* was, ... VII. vii. 6. 6
A *beauteous* soule, with faire conditions thewed, ... *H.B.* 137
the soule is faire and *beauteous* still, ... *H.B.* 159
shadow yet shynes in your *beauteous* face. . . . . *H.B.* 168

Beauties. Of both their *beauties* to make paragone . . . . V. iii. 24. 3
in all that world of *beauties* rare, ... VI. x. 4. 6
those heavenly *beauties* be enfyred As things divine, ... *H.L.* 169
Though all their *beauties* joynd together were; . . . . *H.H.B.* 103
their *beauties* bright, That shone as heavens light, ... *Proth.* 51

Beauties'. To sharpe my sence with sundry *beauties* vew, . . *Ded.Son.*xvii.7
with like *beauties* parts be inly deckt; . . . *H.B.* 193
Beautified. Which with their presence fayre the place much *beautifide.* . . . I. iv. 7. 9
goodly *beautifide* With all the ornaments . . . II. xii. 50. 4
With such an one was Thamis *beautifide;* . . . IV. xi. 28. 7
Beautifies. All that is perfect, which th' heaven *beautefies;* . *Ro.* xix. 1
Beautiful. is ought so bright And *beautifull* as glories beames appeare, . . . V. xi. 62. 8
in *beautyfull* array Above all other lasses . . . VI. x. 26. 3
beautifull of face As any of the Goddesses . . . VII. vi. 28. 4
Were no lesse faire and *beautifull* then shee; . . . VII. vi. 40. 8
most *beautifull* and brave Their fleshly bowre, . . . *H.B.* 122
Into his face most *beautifull* and fayre, . . . *H.H.L.* 111
Whose utmost parts so *beautifull* I fynd; . . . *H.H.B.* 108
For all thats good is *beautifull* and faire. . . . *H.H.B.* 133
Beautifullest. Helpe to addorne my *beautifullest* bride: . . . *Epith.* 105
Beautify. *beautefie* the shinie firmament, . . . *Hub.* 1269
with Comick sock to *beautifie* The painted Theaters, . . . *T.M.* 176
did her beautie much more *beautifie.* . . . *D.* 217
So made by art to *beautify* the rest, . . . II. xii. 55. 2
Each did the others worke more *beautify;* . . . II. xii. 59. 6
Wherewith dame Nature doth her *beautify,* . . . III. vi. 30. 2
with rare light his bote did *beautifye,* . . . III. viii. 22. 6
Wherewith the Craftsman wonts it *beautify,* . . . III. xii. 20. 3
rivers . . . Which doe the earth enrich and *beautifie:* . . . IV. xi. 20. 2
Clare and Harwitch both doth *beautify:* . . . IV. xi. 33. 5
beautifie this sacred hymne of thyne: . . . *H.B.* 21
Beauty. Cruell death vanquishing so noble *beautie,* . . . *Pet.* i. 13
Her match in *beautie* was not anie one. . . . *Van.* vii. 5
Both borrowed pride, and native *beautie* stained. . . . *Van.* viii. 12
dirks the *beauty* of my blossomes rownd: . . . *S.C.* F. 134
When shee the beames of her *beauty* displayes, . . . *S.C.* Ap. 84
Never dempt more right of *beautye,* . . . *S.C.* Au. 137
Ne pictures *beautie,* nor the glauncing rayes . . . *Gn.* 101
Narcisse, that, in a well Seeing his *beautie,* . . . *Gn.* 680
The *beautie* of the world hath lately wasted, . . . *T.M.* 248
With *beawtie* kindled, and with pleasure fed, . . . *T.M.* 364
the Mother of delight, And Queene of *beautie,* . . . *T.M.* 398
hir *beautie* was wonte to feede mine eyes: . . . *U.V.* 14
'To tell the *beawtie* of my buildings fayre, . . . *Ti.* 85
once that *beautie* did beholde, . . . *Ti.* 531
had lost their *beautie* faire. . . . *D.* 28
That did all other Beasts in *beawtie* staine. . . . *D.* 112
did her *beautie* much more beautifie. . . . *D.* 217
Be it riches, *beautie,* or honors pride, . . . *D.* 500
Forth darting beames of *beautie* from her eyes: . . . *As.* 190
The beame of *beautie* sparkled from above, . . . *Col.* 468
Whose *beautie* shyneth as the morning cleare, . . . *Col.* 506
with sparks of hevenlie *beautie* fired. . . . *Col.* 563
beautie is the bayt which . . . Doth man allure . . . *Col.* 871
Beautie, the burning lamp of heavens light, . . . *Col.* 873
thou now full deeply hast divynd Of Love and *beautie;* . . . *Col.* 897
And native *beauty* deck with heavenlie grace: . . . *Ded.Son.*xv.12
of *beautie* soveraigne Queene, Fayre Venus, . . . I. i. 48. 1
'Whose forged *beauty* he did take . . . to have exceeded . . . I. ii. 36. 1
'Whose borrowed *beautie* now appeareth plaine . . . I. ii. 39. 2
beautie brought t' unworthie wretchednesse . . . I. iii. 1. 3
how can *beautie* maister the most strong, . . . I. iii. 6. 4
her bright blazing *beautie* did assay To dim the brightnesse . I. iv. 8. 7
He all his Peeres in *beauty* did surpas, . . . I. v. 37. 3
Then gan her *beautie* shyne as brightest skye, . . . I. vi. 4. 8
All stand astonied at her *beautie* bright, . . . I. vi. 9. 8
They, in . . . wonder of her *beautie* soverayne, . . . I. vi. 12. 6
That flowre of fayth and *beautie* excellent. . . . I. vi. 15. 5
Of wondrous *beauty,* and of bounty rare, . . . I. x. 30. 2
Wherewith her heavenly *beautie* she did hide, . . . I. xii. 22. 4
marre the blossom of your *beauty* bright: . . . II. i. 14. 4
Sith her Prince Arthur of . . . borrowd *beauty* spoyld. . . . II. i. 22. 7
For feare . . . her *beauty* to disgrace? . . . II. iii. 25. 9
with her wondrous *beauty* ravisht quight, . . . II. iii. 42. 4
Thus lowly to abase thy *beautie* bright, . . . II. iv. 25. 8
One boastes her *beautie,* . . . II. v. 33. 7
His frayle eye with spoyle of *beauty* feedes: . . . II. v. 34. 3
man, Of wondrous *beauty* and of freshest yeares, . . . II. viii. 5. 21
yf the *beauty* of her mind ye knew, . . . II. ix. 3. 5
your faire *beautie* doe with sadnes spill? . . . II. ix. 37. 6
Doth florish in all *beautie* excellent; . . . II. xi. 2. 7
Beautie and Money, they that Bulwarke sorely rent. . . . II. xi. 9. 9
depriv'd Of their proud *beautie,* . . . II. xii. 31. 4
picturing the parts of *beauty* daynt, . . . III. Pr. 2. 7
Whose soveraine *beautie* hath no living pere; . . . III. i. 26. 3
When first her tender hart was with his *beautie* smit. . . . III. i. 34. 9
a woman of great bountihed, And of rare *beautie,* . . . III. i. 41. 6
Such was the *beautie* and the shining ray, . . . III. i. 43. 8
So shamelesse *beauty* soone becomes a loathly sight. . . . III. i. 48. 9
Defaste the *beautie* of the shyning skye, . . . III. ii. 28. 2
that sweete fit that doth true *beautie* love, . . . III. iii. 1. 7
in chace of *beauty* excellent Shee lefte, . . . III. iv. 45. 5
ne lettest see The *beautie* of his worke? . . . III. iv. 56. 4
The goodly ornaments of *beautie* bright; . . . III. v. 8. 6
The whiles her matchlesse *beautie* him dismayd. . . . III. v. 43. 7
Fayre ympes of *beautie,* . . . III. v. 53. 1
shall embellish more your *beautie* bright, . . . III. v. 53. 7
both encreast her *beautie* excellent: . . . III. v. 55. 8
Of bounty, and of *beautie,* and all vertues rare. . . . III. vi. 4. 9
glorious Features of *beautie,* and all shapes select, . . . III. vi. 12. 4
that faire flowre of *beautie* fades away, . . . III. vi. 38. 8
Of grace and *beautie* noble Paragone, . . . III. vi. 52. 2

Beauty—*Continued.*
T' adore thing so divine as *beauty* were but right. . . . III. vii. 11. 9
That *beautie* durst presume to violate, . . . III. viii. 36. 2
beauty doth her bounty far surpasse; . . . III. ix. 4. 5
With wonder of her *beauty* fed their hongry vew. . . . III. ix. 23. 9
'Fayre Helene, flowre of *beautie* excellent, . . . III. ix. 35. 1
a lovely Boy Of . . . *beautie* without peare, . . . III. xii. 7. 2
Wherewith the worlds faire *beautie* she hath blent: . . . III. xii. 29. 5
under maske of *beautie* and good grace . . . IV. i. 17. 7
To sell her borrowed *beautie* to abuse: . . . IV. i. 31. 4
The snowy Florimell, whose *beautie* bright Made him seeme happie . . . IV. ii. 4. 7
After each *beautie* that appeard in sight, . . . IV. ii. 5. 3
with her *beautie,* bountie did compare, . . . IV. iii. 39. 8
The prize of her which did in *beautie* most excell. . . . IV. iv. 5. 9
Whose *beautie* each of them thought excellent, . . . IV. iv. 6. 3
To be the prize of *beautie* and of might; . . . IV. iv. 16. 2
The prize of *beautie* still hath joyned beene; . . . IV. v. 1. 3
passing *beautie* did eftsoones reveale, . . . IV. v. 10. 4
with her forged *beautie* did seduce The hearts . . . IV. v. 11. 3
to the Queene of *beautie* close did call, . . . IV. v. 26. 4
beautie, which was made to represent . . . IV. viii. 32. 1
of strength and *beautie* his desire Was spoyle to make, . . IV. viii. 48. 6
were her vertue like her *beautie* bright, . . . IV. viii. 49. 6
eke the famous prize of *beauty* from them wonne. . . . IV. ix. 28. 9
The Queene of *beautie,* and of love the mother, . . . IV. x. 29. 6
it in shape and *beautie* did excell All other Idoles . . . IV. x. 40. 1
Queene of *beautie* and of grace, . . . IV. x. 44. 1
That glorious spoyle of *beautie* with me lead, . . . IV. x. 58. 3
Admyr'd her *beautie* much, . . . IV. xii. 33. 4
ruth of *beautie* will it mollifie. . . . V. v. 13. 6
Yet did appeare rare *beautie* in her face, . . . V. ix. 38. 4
To blot your *beautie,* that unblemisht is, . . . V. xi. 62. 3
beautie is more glorious bright and clere, . . . VI. vii. 29. 7
Did boast her *beautie* had such soveraine might, . . . VI. vii. 31. 6
when first the flowre Of *beauty* gan to bud, . . . VI. viii. 20. 2
Such was the *beauty* of this goodly band . . . VI. x. 14. 1
Seem'd all the rest in *beauty* to excell, . . . VI. x. 14. 4
Divine resemblaunce, *beauty* soveraine rare, . . . VI. x. 27. 4
did but lament . . . And waste her goodly *beauty,* . . . VI. x. 44. 5
In which faire beames of *beauty* did appeare . . . VII. vi. 31. 2
(Such sway doth *beauty* even in Heaven beare) . . . VII. vi. 31. 4
wondrous *beauty* fit to kindle love; . . . VII. vii. 45. 3
The soverayne *beauty* which I doo admyre, . . . *Am.* iii. 1
In chast desires, on heavenly *beauty* bound . . . *Am.* viii. 8
so fayre *beauty* was so fowly shamed. . . . *Am.* xli. 14
mercy doth with *beautie* best agree, . . . *Am.* liii. 13
So oft as I her *beauty* doe behold, . . . *Am.* lv. 1
The glorious image of the Makers *beautie,* . . . *Am.* lxi. 1
stormes, which now his *beauty* blend, Shall turne to caulmes, *Am.* lxii. 11
when that soverayne *beauty* it doth spy, . . . *Am.* lxxii. 5
On the sweet spoyle of *beautie* they did pray; . . . *Am.* lxxvi. 8
That is true *beautie:* . . . *Am.* lxxix. 9
from whom al true And perfect *beauty* did at first proceed: . *Am.* lxxix. 12
many have err'd in this *beauty.'* . . . *Epig.* iii. 8
Her *beauty* to disgrace. . . . *Epith.* 120
The inward *beauty* of her lively spright, . . . *Epith.* 186
Fayre childe of *beauty!* . . . *Epith.* 288
Venice . . . next to them in *beauty* draweth neare, . . . *Com. Son.* iv.11
Lewkenors stile that hath her *beautie* told. . . . *Com. Son.* iv.14
in the conquests of your *beautie* bost, . . . *H.L.* 37
That same is *Beautie,* borne of heavenly race. . . . *H.L.* 112
with the brightnesse of her *beautie* cleare, . . . *H.B.* 11
great Goddesse! Queene of *Beauty,* . . . *H.B.* 15
perfect *Beautie,* which all men adore; . . . *H.B.* 40
beautie is nought else but mixture made Of colours . . . *H.B.* 65
Beautie is not, . . . An outward shew . . . *H.B.* 90
A comely corpse, with *beautie* faire endewed, . . . *H.B.* 135
goodly *beautie,* albe heavenly borne, . . . *H.B.* 149
to make your *beautie* more appeare, . . . *H.B.* 183
all, that like the *beautie* which they see, . . . *H.B.* 208
An heavenly *beautie* to his fancies will; . . . *H.B.* 222
To decke thy *beautie* with their dainties store, . . . *H.B.* 262
conquering *beautie* doth captive My trembling hart . . . *H.B.* 275
shew what wondrous powre your *beauty* hath, . . . *H.B.* 286
though not in powre so great, Yet full of *beautie,* . . . *H.H.L.* 54
images . . . Whose wondrous *beauty,* breathing sweet delights *H.H.B.* 4
beames . . . Of that immortall *beautie,* there with thee, . . *H.H.B.* 13
Th' eternall fountaine of that heavenly *beauty.* . . . *H.H.B.* 21
And all with admirable *beautie* deckt. . . . *H.H.B.* 35
his perfect end Of purest *beautie* . . . *H.H.B.* 47
That to their *beautie* may compared bee, . . . *H.H.B.* 58
to bethinke how great that *beautie* is, . . . *H.H.B.* 107
Which he hath made in *beauty* excellent, . . . *H.H.B.* 129
His goodnesse, which his *beautie* doth declare; . . . *H.H.B.* 132
For she . . . Angels eke, in *beautie* doth excell, . . . *H.H.B.* 206
Could once come neare this *beauty* soverayne. . . . *H.H.B.* 217
Whose *beautie* filles the heavens with her light, . . . *H.H.B.* 228
From whose pure beams al perfect *beauty* springs, . . . *H.H.B.* 296
Beauty's. The shepheard of Ida that judged *beauties* Queene. . *S.C.* Au. 138
As vertues braunch and *beauties* budde, . . . *S.C.* N. 88
For *beauties* prayse and pleasaunce had no peere; . . . *S.C.* N. 94
blazon foorth an earthlie *beauties* praise . . . *T.M.* 369
being lightned with her *beawties* beme, . . . *T.M.* 585
with their *beauties* amorous reflexion, . . . *Col.* 546
to draw the semblant treu Of *beauties* Queene, . . . *Ded. Son.* xvii. 6
to compare Whether in *beauties* glorie did exceede: . . . I. ii. 37. 4
a dull blast, that . . . Dimmed her former *beauties* shining ray, I. ii. 38. 7
boastes in *beauties* chaine not to be bownd, . . . I. ix. 11. 7

Beauty's—*Continued.*
The blazing brightnesse of her *beauties* beame, . . . I. xii. 23. 1
Inflamed was to follow *beauties* pray, . . . II. ii. 7. 7
her broad *beauties* beam great brightnes threw . . . II. vii. 45. 2
Would not so lightly follow *beauties* chace, . . . III. i. 19. 2
quite devourd her *beauties* scornefull grace. . . . III. vii. 23. 5
when he saw that blazing *beauties* beame, . . . III. viii. 22. 5
Where *beauties* prize shold win that pretious spoyle: . . . IV. iv. 48. 8
The controverse of *beauties* soveraine grace; . . . IV. v. 2. 3
the Paragon to see Of *beauties* praise, . . . IV. v. 9. 9
Whose *beauties* beame eftsoones did shine so bright, . . . IV. v. 10. 8
For Chian folke to pourtraict *beauties* Queene, . . . IV. v. 12. 7
whose *beauties* wonderment She lesse esteem'd . . . IV. v. 20. 8
obedience To doe to so divine a *beauties* excellence. . . . IV. vi. 21. 9
left that Tourneyment for *beauties* prise, . . . IV. vii. 3. 2
purchased this peerelesse *beauties* spoile, . . . IV. x. 3. 3
Shyning with *beauties* light and heavenly vertues grace. . . . IV. x. 52. 9
The semblant of this false by his faire *beauties* Queene. . . . V. iii. 19. 9
Nought under heaven so strongly doth allure . . . As *beauties*
lovely baite, . . . V. viii. 1. 3
Adornd with goodly gifts of *beauties* grace, . . . VI. viii. 2. 2
the traine of *beauties* Queene, . . . VI. x. 17. 5
appeare t' adorne her *beauties* grace? . . . *Am.* xxi. 4
When I behold that *beauties* wonderment, . . . *Am.* xxiv. 1
so goodly giftes of *beauties* grace! . . . *Am.* xxxi. 2
that same glorious *beauties* ydle boast . . . *Am.* xli. 9
my loves conquest, peerelesse *beauties* prise, . . . *Am.* lxix. 7
doe still adorne her *beauties* pride, . . . *Epith.* 104
Adornd with *beautyes* grace and vertues store? . . . *Epith.* 170
Beauties glorious beame. . . . *H.L.* 116
nathemore is that faire *beauties* blame, . . . *H.B.* 155
Disloiall lust faire *beauties* foulest blame, . . . *H.B.* 170
O great *Beauties* Queene, . . . *H.B.* 267
Compar'd to that celestiall *beauties* blaze, . . . *H.H.L.* 277
with false *beauties* flattring bait misled, . . . *H.H.B.* 290
Beaver. his dreadfull hideous hedd, Close couched on the *bever,* I. vii. 31. 6
to his brest his *bever* bent. . . . II. v. 6. 9
Pierst through his *bever* quite into his brow, . . . IV. iii. 11. 8
The glauncing sparkles through her *bever* glared, . . . V. vi. 38. 7
Full on his *bever* did him strike so sore, . . . VI. vii. 8. 6
Beavers. Crocodiles, Dragons, *Beavers,* and Centaures: . . . *Hub.* 1124
doen upreare Their *bevers* bright . . . II. i. 29. 2
they their *bevers* up did reare, . . . IV. vi. 25. 8
Beawtie. *See* **Beauty.**
Became. shortly balde and bared she *became.* . . . *Van.* vii. 12
like a handsome swaine it him *became.* . . . *Hub.* 242
juggle finely, that *became* him well. . . . *Hub.* 700
became their thrall, . . . *Ti.* 114
shee *became* so meeke and milde of cheare, . . . *D.* 125
what of him *became* I cannot weene. . . . *D.* 567
the fruitfull-headed beast, . . . *Became* stark blind, . . . I. viii. 20. 3
His name was Zele, that him right well *became:* . . . I. x. 6. 6
enterteynd them both, as best *became,* . . . I. x. 11. 7
Shortly therein so perfect he *became,* . . . I. x. 45. 6
as seemes thee best *became.'* . . . I. x. 66. 9
purveyaunce meet Of all, that royall Princes court *became;* I. xii. 13. 6
bowed low, that her right well *became,* . . . I. xii. 24. 3
as knight of so much worth *became,* . . . II. ii. 14. 2
In goodly garments that her well *became,* . . . II. ii. 14. 7
nothing well they her *became;* . . . II. vi. 6. 6
nought againe Him answered, as courtesie *became;* . . . II. viii. 23. 3
Did dewty to their Lady, as *became;* . . . II. ix. 28. 7
her *became,* as polisht yvory . . . II. ix. 41. 5
streight of beastes they comely men *became;* . . . II. xii. 86. 2
She shortly like a pyned ghost *became* . . . III. ii. 52. 5
till he *became* A mighty man at armes, . . . III. iv. 20. 4
To tell what tydings of fayre Florimell *became.* . . . III. vii. 61. 9
such vaine uses that him best *became:* . . . III. viii. 14. 5
hond Where ill *became* him rashly would have thrust; . . . III. viii. 25. 7
fairely them saluted, as *became,* . . . III. ix. 26. 8
deeds of armes which unto them *became,* . . . III. ix. 32. 4
With extreme fury he *became* quite mad, . . . III. x. 54. 5
for her sake a cowheard vile *became* . . . III. xi. 39. 3
attended duly on her, As well *became* a knight, . . . IV. i. 8. 9
what of them *became* themselves did scarsly weete. . . . IV. i. 41. 9
as best it her *became,* . . . IV. v. 16. 4
Companion she *became,* and so continued long. . . . IV. viii. 5. 9
the which *became* A God of seas . . . IV. xi. 13. 4
him before there went, as best *became,* . . . IV. xi. 24. 4
yet her well *became,* . . . IV. xi. 45. 3
what of it *became* none understood: . . . V. iii. 26. 6
full blyth the Lady streight *became,* . . . VI. i. 32. 1
this his Ladie (that him ill *became*) . . . VI. ii. 10. 2
through feare what of his childe *became.* . . . VI. iii. 17. 9
Whom Calepine saluting (as *became*) . . . VI. iii. 31. 1
That it *became* a famous knight well knowne, . . . VI. iv. 38. 8
now corrupt and curelesse they *became:* . . . VI. vi. 2. 5
Wayting what tydings of her folke *became.* . . . VI. vi. 30. 3
Revyling him, that them most vile *became,* . . . *H.H.L.* 152
Because (*partial list*).
Both for *because* your griefe doth great appeare, . . . *Hub.* 73
And eke *because* my selfe am touched neare: . . . *Hub.* 74
because you shall not us misdeeme, . . . *Hub.* 375
Because I nothing noble have to sing. . . . *T.M.* 108
Because that mourning matter I have none. . . . *T.M.* 168
dead, *because* him dead thou dost adore . . . *Ti.* 249
halfe in doubt, *because* of his disguize, . . . *D.* 57
I hate the heaven, *because* it doth withhold . . . *D.* 400
I hate the earth, *because* it is the mold . . . *D.* 402
I hate the fire, *because* to nought it flyes; . . . *D.* 404

Because—*Continued.*
I hate the Ayre, *because* sighes of it be; . . . *D.* 405
I hate the Sea, *because* it teares supplyes. . . . *D.* 406
I hate the day, *because* it lendeth light . . . *D.* 407
Because they breed sad balefulnesse . . . *D.* 410
I hate all times, *because* all times doo flye . . . *D.* 411
The one, *because* as I they wretched are; . . . *D.* 422
The other, for *because* I doo not finde . . . *D.* 423
life I hate, *because* it will not last; . . . *D.* 425
death I hate, *because* it life doth marre; . . . *D.* 426
the world, . . . I hate, *Because* it changeth . . . *D.* 429
So hight *because* of this deceitfull traine, . . . *Col.* 118
th' one (said shee) *Bycause* he wonne; . . . II. v. 19. 5
Because of traveill long, . . . III. i. 2. 2
Because I could not give her many a Jane.' . . . III. vii. 58. 4
Because she knew, she said, I would disclose Her counsell, . . . III. vii. 58. 8
Because to yield him love she doth deny, . . . III. xi. 17. 3
Because his sinfull lust she would not serve, . . . IV. i. 4. 2
Because to man so mercifull he was, . . . IV. i. 30. 3
Because of one that wrought him fowle despight.' . . . VI. iii. 40. 5
Is it *because* your eyes have powre to kill? . . . *Am.* xlix. 2
It lov'd it selfe, *because* it selfe was faire; . . . *H.H.L.* 29
Beck. (His black eye-brow, whose doomefull dreaded *beck* VII. vi. 22. 2
Beckes. *See* **Beaks.**
Beckoned. she signes did make, And *beckned* him, . . . II. iv. 13. 3
to him *beckned* to approch more neare, . . . II. xii. 68. 8
Beckoning. to the vulgare *beckning* with his hand, . . . III. xii. 4. 3
Become. Now to *become* nought els but heaped sands? . . . *Ro.* xv. 14
Thus is this Ape *become* a shepheard swaine, . . . *Hub.* 303
what had of long *Become* of him; . . . *Hub.* 1326
Bee now *become* most wretched wightes on ground. . . . *T.M.* 312
call to count what is of them *become:* . . . *Ti.* 58
Where now he is *become* an heavenly signe, . . . *Ti.* 601
As to *become* unmyndfull of his owne. . . . *As.* 112
valiant knight *become* a caytive thrall, . . . I. vii. 19. 3
As might *become* a Squyre so great persons to greet. . . . I. x. 7. 9
The deare Charissa, where is she *become?* . . . I. x. 16. 2
What is *become* of great Acrates sonne? . . . II. v. 35. 6
Where is the Antique glory now *become,* . . . III. iv. 1. 1
to see what was *become* Of all those persons . . . III. xii. 30. 2
did her ill *become,* . . . III. xii. 30. 7
As fresh and fragrant as the floure-deluce She was *become,* . . . IV. i. 31. 8
So mortall was their malice, and so sore *Become,* . . . IV. ii. 18. 9
now *become* to live a Ladies thrall, . . . IV. vi. 28. 8
What is of her *become,* or whether reft, . . . IV. vi. 35. 2
What shall of me, unhappy maid, *become?* . . . IV. vii. 11. 3
He louted lowly, as did him *becum,* . . . IV. vii. 44. 7
all one at last *become.* . . . IV. xi. 43. 9
the golden age, . . . It's now at earst *become* a stonie one; . . . V. Pr. 2. 2
Ne would for ought obay, as did *become,* . . . V. i. 29. 3
his faith had plight Her vassall to *become,* . . . V. v. 23. 9
Made him *become* most faithless and unsound: . . . V. xii. 2. 4
Doth best *become* and greatest grace doth gaine: . . . VI. ii. 2. 8
Of whom what was *becomen* no man knew. . . . VI. vii. 34. 3
For mans deare sake he did a man *become.* . . . *H.H.L.* 147
Becomes. *Becomes* more fierce and fervent in his gate; . . . *D.* 195
Becomes more fell, and all . . . Treads down . . . II. xi. 33. 5
So shamelesse beauty soone *becomes* a loathly sight. . . . III. i. 48. 9
ill *becomes* you, . . . To scorne the joy . . . III. vi. 22. 5
whenas forme and feature it does ketch, *Becomes* a body, . . . III. vi. 37. 4
Looke ever lovely, as *becomes* you best; . . . *Am.* vii. 10
Becometh. 'Ah! deare Sir Guyon, well *becommeth* you, . . . II. i. 28. 3
Becoming. And courteous withall, *becomming* her degree. . . . VI. iii. 20. 9
Bed. *See* **Bade, Bid, Child-bed.**
Maias bowre, That newe is upryst from *bedde:* . . . *S.C.* Mar. 18
bedde, or bowre, both which I fill with cryes, . . . *S.C.* Au. 167
There mayst thou ligge in a vetchy *bed,* . . . *S.C.* S. 256
The bush my *bedde,* the bramble was my bowre, . . . *S.C.* D. 65
lying reastlesse in heavy *bedde,* . . . *U.V.* 4
If in *Bed,* tell hir, that my eyes can take no reste: . . . *U.V.* 7
Looking aside I saw a stately *Bed,* . . . *Ti.* 631
suddeinly both *bed* and all was gone, . . . *Ti.* 643
From *bed* to *bed,* from one to other border, . . . *Mui.* 170
My *bed* the ground that hardest I may finde; . . . *D.* 377
there Tethys his wet *bed* Doth ever wash, . . . I. i. 39. 6
she . . . seemde unto his *bed* to bring Her, . . . I. i. 48. 2
Those twoo he tooke, and in a secrete *bed,* . . . I. ii. 3. 7
Retourning to his *bed* in torment great, . . . I. ii. 6. 1
Weary of aged Tithones saffron *bed,* . . . I. ii. 7. 2
Home is he brought, and layd in sumptuous *bed,* . . . I. v. 17. 1
most heavenly melody About the *bed* . . . I. v. 17. 7
a Groome, that forth him ledd . . . and laid in easie *bedd* . . . I. x. 17. 8
deck with dainty flowres their brydall *bed,* . . . I. x. 42. 3
the deawy *bed* Of aged Tithone . . . I. xi. 51. 2
Like roses in a *bed* of lillies shed, . . . II. iii. 22. 6
On a sweet *bed* of lillies softly laid, . . . II. v. 32. 3
In sumptuous *bed* shee made him to be layd; . . . II. xi. 49. 8
earst was sought to deck both *bed* and bowre . . . II. xii. 75. 4
Upon a *bed* of Roses she was layd, . . . II. xii. 77. 1
sumptuous *bed* That glistred all with gold . . . III. i. 41. 2
Lightly arose out of her wearie *bed,* . . . III. i. 59. 6
to her *bed* approching, . . . III. i. 60. 5
She lightly lept out of her filed *bedd,* . . . III. i. 62. 2
oft out of her *bed* she did astart, . . . III. ii. 29. 6
downe againe her in her warme *bed* dight: . . . III. ii. 30. 5
her downe she layd In her warme *bed* . . . III. ii. 47. 3
she did lye All night in old Tithonus frozen *bed,* . . . III. iii. 20. 6
Where you him lately lefte, in Mars his *bed:* . . . III. vi. 24. 3
every sort is in a sondry *bed* Sett by it selfe, . . . III. vi. 35. 3
their maister, who in *bed* was layd, . . . III. ix. 10. 5

Bed—*Continued.*
she receivd againe to *bed* and bord, . . . III. x. 51. 5
to her *bed,* which she was wont forbeare, . . . IV. i. 15. 8
He seemed brought to *bed* in Paradise, . . . IV. ii. 9. 8
Before that day her wooed to his *bed,* . . . IV. xi. 8. 6
to his *bed* was brought, . . . IV. xii. 20. 8
Let him lodge hard, and lie in strawen *bed,* . . . V. v. 50. 5
she threw Her selfe uppon her *bed,* and did lament: . . . V. vi. 13. 7
the *bed,* where she should lie, . . . V. vi. 27. 6
But faire Priscilla . . . Would to no *bed,* . . . VI. iii. 10. 2
the bare ground . . . Must be their *bed;* . . . VI. iv. 14. 5
Vowing that never he in *bed* againe . . . VI. iv. 40. 6
For feare of wetting them before their *bed.* . . . VI. ix. 13. 5
To thrust faire Phoebe from her silver *bed,* . . . VII. vi. 21. 3
Unto whose *bed* false Bregog whylome stole, . . . VII. vi. 40. 4
her he would receive unto his *bed:* . . . VII. vi. 53. 6
lyke a Strawberry *bed;* . . . *Am.* lxiv. 9
The Rosy Morne long since left Tithones *bed,* . . . *Epith.* 75
in her *bed* her lay; . . . *Epith.* 301
Shall fly and flutter round about your *bed,* . . . *Epith.* 359
The bridale bowre and geniall *bed* remaine, . . . *Epith.* 399
let your *bed* with pleasures chast abound, . . . *Proth.* 103
Bedded. All bent to mirth before the bride was *bedded,* . . . IV. i. 3. 5
Bedding. (Whylome for ventrous Knights the *bedding* best) IV. v. 39. 4
Bedecked. conquerours *bedecked* with his greene (leaves[1]), . . *Bel.* v. 3
an almond tree . . . With blossoms brave *bedecked* daintily; I. vii. 32. 7
A little Gondelay, *bedecked* trim . . . II. vi. 2. 7
bedeckt Uppon the bosse with stones that shined wide, . . . V. v. 3. 6
Whose silver lockes *bedeckt* his beard and hed, . . . VI. ix. 13. 7
With many deare delights *bedecked* fyne. . . . *Am.* lxxi. 12
Bedes. *See* **Beads.**
Bedewed. *See* **Salt-bedewed.**
So oft *bedeawed* with our learned layes, . . . *T.M.* 272
The same with bitter teares they all *bedewed.* . . . *As.* 204
salt teares *bedeawd* the hearers cheaks. . . . I. xii. 16. 9
with kisses light . . . his lips *bedewd,* . . . II. xii. 73. 6
Bedeaw'd with teares there left it in the place: . . . VI. xii. 8. 4
Bedford. Brave Impe of *Bedford!* grow apace in bountie, . . . *Ti.* 272
Bedide. *See* **Bedyed.**
Bedight. were he not with love so ill *bedight,* . . . *S.C.* O. 89
Lord of himselfe, with palme *bedight,* . . . *Gn.* 113
the morning starre . . . with flaming lockes *bedight,* . . . I. xii. 21. 6
'Fayre Lady, through fowle sorrow ill *bedight,* . . . II. i. 14. 2
Furor, oh! Furor hath me thus *bedight:* . . . II. vi. 50. 2
His head and beard with sout were ill *bedight,* . . . II. vii. 3. 7
All in a canvas thin he was *bedight,* . . . II. xi. 22. 6
all the ground, with pretious deaw *bedight,* . . . III. vi. 43. 8
like salvage weed With woody mosse *bedight,* . . . IV. iv. 39. 5
with Justice hath *bedight.* . . . V. Pr. 10. 5
so ill *bedight* With bleeding wounds, . . . VI. iii. 4. 1
joyous day . . . in sunny beames *bedight,* . . . VI. iii. 45. 2
Well as she could she got, and did *bedight;* . . . VI. v. 7. 6
To see him so *bedight* with bloodie gore, . . . VI. vii. 14. 4
Beds. dreame . . . With bowres, and *beds,* and ladies deare delight: . . . I. i. 55. 7
rownd about it many *beds* were dight, . . . III. i. 39. 2
From her sweete bowres, and *beds* with pleasures fraught? . . III. vi. 20. 4
In *beds,* in bowres, in banckets, and in feasts: . . . III. vi. 22. 4
other *beds* the Priests there used none, . . . V. vii. 9. 1
lie like Gods in yvorie *beds* arayd, . . . *H.L.* 285
Beducked. deepe him selfe *beducked* in the same, . . . II. vi. 42. 3
Bedyed. Bryton fieldes with Sarazin blood *bedyde,* . . . I. xi. 7. 3
streames of blood his armour all *bedide.* . . . IV. iv. 24. 7
Bee. *See* **Honey-bee.**
Th' other in hers an hony-laden *Bee.* . . . III. xii. 18. 8
Your selfe unto the *Bee* ye doe compare; . . . *Am.* lxxi. 2
peace shall see Betweene the Spyder and the gentle *Bee.* . . *Am.* lxxi. 14
A gentle *Bee* . . . About him flew . . . *Epig.* iv. 3
The *Bee* him stung . . . *Epig.* iv. 26
Beech. The warlike *Beech;* . . . I. i. 9. 7
Been (*partial list*).
his flock, that had *bene* long ypent: . . . *S.C.* Ja. 4
thy gyfts *bene* vayne; . . . *S.C.* Ja. 59
thy yeares greene, as now *bene* myne, . . . *S.C.* F. 59
it had *bene* an auncient tree, . . . *S.C.* F. 207
Mought her necke *bene* joynted . . . *S.C.* Mar. 53
bene thine eyes attempred to the yeare, . . . *S.C.* Ap. 5
if hys ditties *bene* so trimly dight, . . . *S.C.* Ap. 29
Bene they not Bay braunches . . . *S.C.* Ap. 104
How falles it, then, we no merrier *bene,* . . . *S.C.* May 3
Withouten dreade of Wolves to *bene* ytost: . . . *S.C.* Jun. 12
We *bene* of fleshe, . . . *S.C.* S. 238
how *bene* thy verses meint . . . *S.C.* N. 203
In Court . . . all fashions *beene;* . . . *Hub.* 674
none of these, how ever sweete they *beene,* . . . *Mui.* 157
asses *been* not all whose eares exceed, . . . *Col.* 713
Through judgement of the gods to *been* ywroken, . . . *Col.* 921
in diverse doubt they *been.* . . . I. i. 10. 9
'Right well . . . ye have advised *bin,*' . . . I. i. 33. 4
Dead long ygoe, I wote, thou haddest *bin,* . . . I. ii. 18. 3
So *been* they parted both, with harts on edge . . . I. iv. 43. 3
had he *beene* where earst his armes were lent, . . . I. vi. 42. 7
The pitteous pray of his fiers cruelty have *bin.* . . . I. vii. 45. 9
nought they *beene* For all his washing cleaner. . . . II. ii. 3. 5
seeme to have *ben* seard . . . II. vii. 3. 8
'Certes, Sir knight, ye *bene* too much to blame, . . . II. viii. 13. 2
why *beene* ye thus dismayd, . . . II. ix. 37. 5
By which the mightiest things efforced *bin:* . . . II. xii. 43. 7
now together on their way they *bin,* . . . V. i. 13. 6
forged showes, as fitter *beene* For courting fooles . . . VI. v. 38. 7

Been—*Continued.*
in mynd to *bene* ywroken Of all the vile demeane . . . VI. vi. 18. 3
Had it *bene* death, yet . . . *H.L.* 243
all this world, the which thy vassals *beene,* . . . *H.B.* 269
As each had *bene* a Bryde; . . . *Proth.* 23
Bees. winde, much like the sowne Of swarming *Bees,* . . . I. i. 41. 5
Like many swarmes of *Bees* assembled round, . . . II. ix. 51. 4
like a sort of *Bees* in clusters swarmed: . . . V. iv. 36. 7
Bees-alluring. Faire Marigoldes, and *Bees-alluring* Thime . . *Mui.* 191
Beetle. Bent hollow *beetle* browes, . . . II. ix. 52. 6
Beetle-stock. to be a *beetle-stock* Of thy great Masters will, . *Hub.* 507
Befall. *See* **Befelled.**
All in a sunneshine day, as did *befall,* . . . *S.C.* Ja. 3
Mischiefe mought to that mischaunce *befall,* . . . *S.C.* Au. 13
if such fortune doo to us *befall,* . . . *Hub.* 617
To see what end of fight should him *befall* . . . I. viii. 2. 9
life eke everlasting did *befall:* . . . I. xi. 46. 6
Then to thy lucklesse parents did *befall.* . . . II. i. 37. 5
well may thee *befall,* . . . II. iii. 37. 6
Least by her presence daunger mote *befall;* . . . II. iii. 44. 2
use thy fortune as it doth *befall;* . . . II. viii. 52. 2
To seeke adventures which mote him *befall,* . . . III. iv. 4. 7
to see what new successe Mote him *befall* . . . III. xi. 20. 3
Of which he dealt large almes, as did *befall:* . . . IV. iv. 32. 4
That she unto their portion might *befall.* . . . IV. v. 26. 5
Unto some resting place, which mote *befall,* . . . IV. vi. 39. 4
An hard adventure, which did then *befall,* . . . V. i. 3. 4
Departed on his way, as did *befall,* . . . V. iv. 20. 8
He purposd to proceed, what so *befall,* . . . V. vii. 43. 8
To whether should the victory *befall,* . . . V. xi. 15. 8
Of all things, to dissemble, fouly may *befall!'* . . . V. xi. 56. 9
although good Fortune me *befall,* . . . VI. i. 6. 6
for feare Of . . . ought that might *befall:* . . . VI. ii. 35. 4
as did by chaunce *befall,* . . . VI. vi. 19. 1
Which should *befall* to Calidores immortall name. . . . VI. ix. 1. 9
Befallen. *See* **Befelled.**
perils sad Which in his travell him *befallen* had, . . . I. xii. 15. 5
'Not one, nor other,' . . . 'Hath him *befalne;* . . . II. viii. 24. 7
adventures, which had . . . to him *befallen* late. . . . VI. iii. 22. 6
Like as is now *befalne* to this faire Mayd, . . . VI. xi. 2. 1
Befalls. To feede abroad where pasture best *befalls.* . . . *Gn.* 72
The which by course *befals* me here to tell: . . . IV. iv. 2. 5
Befell. 'It there *befell,* as I the fields did range . . . *D.* 106
The passed fortunes, which to thee *befell* . . . *Col.* 33
as *befell* Twixt him and thee, . . . *Col.* 176
Nymph . . . Was out of Dianes favor, as it then *befell.* . . . I. vii. 4. 9
Whereon she leaned ever, as *befell;* . . . I. x. 14. 7
It fortuned, (as fayre it then *befell*) . . . I. xi. 29. 1
late *befell* Me for to meet, . . . II. i. 30. 3
occasion straunge, Which to her Nymph *befell.* . . . II. ii. 7. 2
let them still be bloody, as *befell,* . . . II. ii. 10. 4
By other accident, that earst *befell,* . . . II. ii. 11. 8
So forth he far'd, as now *befell,* on foot . . . II. iii. 3. 1
entertained them right fairely, as *befell.* . . . II. ix. 17. 9
fayrest fortune to the Prince *befell,* . . . III. iv. 47. 6
What end unto that fearefull Damozell . . . *befell:* . . . III. vi. 54. 4
As it *befell,* that she could flie no more, . . . III. vii. 25. 5
Least worse on sea then us on land *befell.'* . . . III. viii. 24. 5
the strife, which late *befell* Betwixt us both unknowne.' . . . III. ix. 51. 8
That each to other made, as oft *befell:* . . . IV. i. 5. 3
It so *befell* one evening, that they came Unto a Castell, . . . IV. i. 9. 1
the drunken fray, The which amongst the Lapithees *befell;* . IV. i. 23. 2
Misdoubted lost through mischiefe that *befell.* . . . IV. ii. 23. 7
It lately so *befell,* . . . IV. ii. 25. 6
love each other deare, what ever them *befell.* . . . IV. ii. 53. 9
It often fals, (as here it earst *befell*) . . . IV. iv. 1. 1
Twixt Cambell and Sir Triamond *befell,* . . . IV. iv. 2. 2
they told, as then *befell,* Of that great turney . . . IV. iv. 5. 6
It so *befell,* as oft it fals in chace, . . . IV. vii. 24. 1
how their harmes *befell?* . . . IV. viii. 21. 3
as to him *befell,* . . . IV. ix. 41. 6
their dueful service, as to them *befell.* . . . IV. xi. 44. 9
Yet were they all in order, as *befell,* . . . IV. xii. 3. 4
shew the wounds which unto thee *befell;* . . . V. iii. 21. 7
as by fortune then *befell,* . . . V. iii. 29. 3
that piteous storie, which *befell* About that wofull couple . . V. iii. 31. 1
Amongst the rest, which in that space *befell,* . . . V. x. 6. 1
Being then new made widow (as *befell*) . . . V. x. 11. 7
Whereof *befell* what now is in your sight.' . . . VI. ii. 23. 4
'and right, Me seemes, that him *befell* . . . VI. ii. 23. 6
There him *befell,* unlooked for before, . . . VI. iv. 17. 6
by what meanes that shame to her *befell,* . . . VI. vi. 17. 1
Found her by fortune, which to him *befell,* . . . VI. ix. 14. 5
rest himselfe till supper time *befell;* . . . VI. ix. 17. 4
what straunge fortunes unto him *befell,* . . . VI. ix. 46. 7
what *befell* her in that theevish wonne, . . . VI. x. 44. 8
It so *befell,* (as Fortune had ordayned) . . . VI. xi. 3. 3
befell This fatall chaunce, this dolefull accident, . . . VI. xi. 31. 1
He went forth on his quest, and did that him *befell.* . . . VI. xii. 13. 9
Befelled. *See* **Befallen.**
To weet what sudden tidings was *befeld:* . . . IV. iii. 50. 3
Befit. Which so to doe may thee right well *befit,* . . . *Ded. Son.* iii. 5
Before (*partial list*).
a ghost appeare *before* mine eyes . . . *Bel.*[1] i. 5
Excelling all that ever went *before.* . . . *Ro.* Env. 10
ought may happen, that hath bene *beforne* . . . *S.C.* May 104
layen her faults the world *beforne,* . . . *S.C.* May 160
The flattring fruite is fallen to grownd *before.* . . . *S.C.* D. 106
minde that ill use doth *before* deprave, . . . *Gn.* 91
blood Which she . . . had shed *before;* . . . *Gn.* 174

Before—*Continued.*
Acornes were our foode, *before* That Ceres seede . . . *Gn.* 206
For looking back, being forbid *before:* . . . *Gn.* 435
The faults which life hath trespassed *before.* . . . *Gn.* 448
having well *before* approoved The feends . . . *Gn.* 465
Whilome (said she) *before* the world was civill, . . . *Hub.* 45
to lay the meate *before:* . . . *Hub.* 435
That *before* God we may appeare more gay, . . . *Hub.* 462
never seene In Court *before,* . . . *Hub.* 674
(as they heard *before*) . . . *Mui.* 126
Whose like *before* mine eye had seldome seene, . . . *D.* 114
My pipe, *before* that aemuled of many, . . . *Col.* 73
Before he die, alreadie dead with feare, . . . *Col.* 205
I *before* had tryde, . . . *Col.* 673
long *before* the world he was ybore, . . . *Col.* 839
soone to lose, *before* he once would lin; . . . I. i. 24. 5
He strowd an *Ave-Mary* after and *before.* . . . I. i. 35. 9
Before that angry heavens list to lowre, . . . I. ii. 22. 4
'To have *before* bewitched all mens sight: . . . I. ii. 39. 3
A damzell spyde, slow footing her *before,* . . . I. iii. 10. 8
Face of fayre Lady she *before* did vew, . . . I. iii. 11. 8
his eies he fixt *before.* . . . I. iii. 30. 8
him *before,* I saw . . . The bold Sansfoy . . . I. v. 23. 1
the vele that hong her face *before:* . . . I. vi. 4. 7
With heaped strokes more hugely then *before;* . . . I. vi. 45. 4
Whose fall did never foe *before* behold: . . . I. vii. 51. 6
Him to avenge *before* his blood were cold, . . . I. ix. 37. 5
nought but death *before* his eies . . . I. ix. 50. 2
sate wayting ever them *before,* . . . I. x. 36. 8
Present *before* the majesty divine, . . . I. x. 51. 8
cloudes *before* him fledd . . . I. xi. 10. 8
before his flightes end: . . . I. xi. 19. 4
before that cursed Dragon got That happy land, . . . I. xi. 29. 6
fall *before* his enimy. . . . I. xi. 33. 9
Whom far *before* did march a goodly band . . . I. xii. 5. 6
as is *before* exprest, . . . I. xii. 15. 8
He was affyaunced long time *before,* . . . I. xii. 27. 2
Singing *before* th' eternall majesty, . . . I. xii. 39. 4
Before, behind, and round about him laies; . . . II. ii. 25. 8
falling them *beforne,* Besought them . . . II. ii. 27. 4
Before, they fastned were under her knee . . . II. iii. 27. 6
the land that lay them faire *before,* . . . II. vi. 11. 8
had never mett *before* So puissant foe, . . . II. vi. 30. 1
As eie of man did never see *before,* . . . II. vii. 31. 5
That living eye *before* did never see. . . . II. vii. 38. 2
far *before* a light-foote Page . . . II. viii. 10. 4
greater fury then *before* was fownd; . . . II. ix. 15. 2
The one *before,* by which all in did pas, . . . II. ix. 23. 2
Early, *before* the Morne with cremosin ray . . . II. xi. 3. 1
fled asonder, and him fell *before;* . . . II. xi. 19. 3
reysd him up much stronger then *before,* . . . II. xi. 45. 5
here *before* a perlous passage lyes, . . . II. xii. 17. 8
brought to grownd that never wast *before;* . . . III. i. 7. 7
faire *before* the gate a spatious playne, . . . III. i. 20. 6
Dare not adventure on the stubborne pray, Ne byte *before,* . . . III. i. 22. 4
As did this knight, *before* ye hither came.' . . . III. i. 27. 5
Which two did yield *before* she did them smight. . . . III. i. 29. 6
him in everie part *before* her fashioned. . . . III. ii. 16. 9
Yet him in everie part *before* she knew, . . . III. ii. 17. 1
before that day His joyous face did to the world revele, . . . III. ii. 48. 1
A litle whyle *Before* that Merlin dyde, . . . III. iii. 10. 2
Then ever him *before,* or after, living wight: . . . III. iii. 11. 9
In the last field *before* Menevia, . . . III. iii. 55. 3
ryding on forray Few dayes *before,* . . . III. iii. 58. 5
But hurt his hart, the which *before* was sound, . . . III. v. 42. 4
Such as the Angels weare *before* Gods tribunall! . . . III. v. 53. 9
had not her thereof *before* aviz'd, . . . III. vi. 19. 4
before the sunny rayes He us'd to slug, . . . III. vii. 12. 7
A little bote lay hoving her *before,* . . . III. vii. 27. 4
She bore *before* her lap a dolefull Squire, . . . III. vii. 37. 6
The inward smoke, that did *before* but steeme, . . . III. viii. 26. 4
Satyrane his chaunce Was her *before,* . . . III. ix. 27. 2
Before that angry Gods . . . Upon thee heapt . . . III. ix. 33. 4
long *before* the ten yeares siege of Troy, . . . III. ix. 36. 2
by him cald Paros, which *before* Hight Nausa: . . . III. ix. 37. 1
To quench the flames which she had tyn'd *before,* . . . III. x. 13. 3
seemd more grievous then it was *before.* . . . III. x. 18. 5
'She wonneth in the forrest there *before.*' . . . III. x. 38. 3
Early, *before* the heavens fairest light . . . III. x. 52. 6
who behind him was, Ne scarsely who *before:* . . . III. x. 53. 4
Holding a lattis still *before* his face, . . . III. xii. 15. 8
her *before* the vile Enchaunter sate, . . . III. xii. 31. 1
hope, which she *before* Conceived had, . . . III. xii. 44. 7
All bent to mirth *before* the bride was bedded, . . . IV. i. 3. 5
make his praise *before* his owne preferd: . . . IV. iv. 36. 8
He held the Lady forth *before* him right, . . . IV. vii. 26. 3
There she alighting fell *before* her feet, . . . IV. viii. 9. 5
Bearing a litle Dwarfe *before* his steed, . . . IV. viii. 38. 3
celestiall sound Of dainty musicke . . . *Before* the spouse: . . . IV. xi. 23. 3
And her *before* there paced Pages twaine, . . . IV. xi. 47. 7
Which never she *before* disclosd to none, . . . IV. xii. 5. 4
mourn'd to see her losse *before* her eyne, . . . IV. xii. 21. 7
on her knee *before* him falling lowe, . . . IV. xii. 29. 5
Liftes up his head that did *before* decline, . . . IV. xii. 34. 8
gins to spread his leafe *before* the faire sunshine. . . . IV. xii. 34. 9
All th' East, *before* untam'd, did over-ronne, . . . V. i. 2. 2
It was not long *before* he overtooke Sir Sanglier, . . . V. i. 20. 6
He wilfull lost that he *before* attayned: . . . V. v. 17. 8
put *before* his lap a napron . . . V. v. 20. 8
As if *before* she had not counted trew: . . . V. vi. 5. 5

Before—*Continued.*
It was not long *before* she heard the sound . . . V. vi. 28. 6
Whose like *before* she never saw nor red; . . . V. vii. 5. 7
Who, long *before* awoke, . . . Was to the battell . . . V. vii. 27. 3
as he had beene *Before* directed by his Lord; . . . V. viii. 29. 8
Then brought he forth . . . her face *before,* . . . V. ix. 48. 8
did wound his enemy Behinde, beside, *before,* . . . V. xi. 6. 9
A rout of people they *before* them kend, . . . V. xi. 43. 7
To leave the love that ye *before* embraced, . . . V. xi. 63. 4
the dismall day Appointed her Irenas death *before,* . . . V. xii. 11. 2
the huge stroke, which he *before* intended, . . . V. xii. 21. 1
Atchiev'd so hard a quest, as few *before;* . . . VI. i. 5. 8
when he saw his foe *before* in vew, . . . VI. i. 35. 6
Prevented him *before* his stroke could light, . . . VI. i. 38. 7
Before his feet her selfe she did project; . . . VI. i. 45. 5
slaine The day *before* . . . VI. iii. 17. 3
There him befell, unlooked for *before,* . . . VI. iv. 17. 6
Which at the first, *before* it had infected, . . . VI. vi. 8. 3
th' other, not so swift as she *before,* . . . VI. vii. 9. 8
What meaneth this which here I see *before?* . . . VI. vii. 14. 7
Her stubborne hart, which love *before* disdayned, . . . VI. vii. 36. 7
in two yeares *before,* . . . She had destroyed two and twenty . . . VI. vii. 38. 6
Were bound about and voyded from *before;* . . . VI. vii. 43. 8
before Having subdew'd yet did to life restore;) . . . VI. viii. 4. 4
else abide the death that hard *before* you stands.' . . . VI. viii. 7. 9
Whose like *before* his eye had never seene; . . . VI. x. 17. 2
Whom they *before* in diverse spoyles had caught; . . . VI. xi. 11. 3
leave to take *before* his friends doe dye. . . . VI. xi. 18. 9
'That ever I did live . . . and was not dead *before,* . . . VI. xi. 29. 3
Before I saw faire Pastorella dye.' . . . VI. xi. 29. 4
So forth they goe together (God *before*) . . . VI. xi. 36. 1
all those flockes, which they *before* Had reft from Meliboe . . . VI. xi. 51. 6
she, whose sides *before* with secret wound . . . empierced were, . . . VI. xii. 4. 7
closing it againe like as *before,* . . . VI. xii. 8. 3
more scath he wrought . . . then he had done *before;* . . . VI. xii. 39. 2
him bring *before* his presence prest. . . . VII. vi. 16. 9
come *before* him Jove . . . VII. vi. 17. 9
Before they could new counsels re-allie, . . . VII. vi. 23. 4
For to betray my Right *before* I have it tride. . . . VII. vi. 34. 9
Before great Natures presence . . . VII. vi. 36. 3
On her whose sight *before* so much he sought. . . . VII. vi. 47. 6
at the time that was *before* agreed, . . . VII. vii. 3. 1
Which through the flood *before* did softly slyde . . . VII. vii. 43. 4
doe myne humbled hart *before* her poure; . . . *Am.* xx. 2
lothe the things which they did like *before,* . . . *Am.* xxxv. 11
doe me not *before* my time to dy. . . . *Am.* xlii. 14
did ye see So fayre a creature in your towne *before;* . . . *Epith.* 168
She commeth in, *before* th' Almighties view; . . . *Epith.* 211
The which *before* had lyen confused ever. . . . *H.L.* 77
Whatever ill *before* he did aby: . . . *H.L.* 242
Before this worlds great frame . . . found any being-place, . . . *H.H.L.* 22
With him he raignd, *before* all time prescribed, . . . *H.H.L.* 36
In which he stood *before* his haplesse fate. . . . *H.H.L.* 140
Meeke Lambe of God, *before* all worlds behight, . . . *H.H.L.* 173
pure glorie present still *Before* thy face, . . . *H.H.L.* 285

Beforn(e). *See* **Before.**

Beg. *Beg* amongst those that beggers doo defie.' . . . *Hub.* 192
manie *beg* which are thereof ashamed. . . . *Hub.* 352
beg the sute the which the other ment. . . . *Hub.* 882
Go *beg* with us, and be companions still, . . . *T.M.* 407

Began. *See* **Begon, Gan.**
My spirit . . . *Began* to enter into meditation . . . *Van.* i. 3
her garland so much honoured *Began* to die, . . . *Van.* vii. 10
His Vellet head *began* to shoote out, . . . *S.C.* May 185
thy oaten pype *began* to sound, . . . *S.C.* Jun. 58
Began to comfort me in chearfull wise, . . . *Hub.* 19
the Ape . . . thus *began* t' advise. . . . *Hub.* 113
began T' enquire of custome, . . . *Hub.* 244
they *began* to threat the neighbour sky; . . . *Hub.* 1174
Began her grievous plaint as doth ensew. . . . *T.M.* 114, 174, 234, 300
Began her piteous plaint, as doth ensew. . . . *T.M.* 360
Began her grievous plaint, as doth ensew. . . . *T.M.* 420
Began her plaint, as doth herein ensew. . . . *T.M.* 480
Began her mournfull plaint, as doth ensew. . . . *T.M.* 540
began to kindle fast, . . . *Mui.* 34
with good speed *began* to take his flight. . . . *Mui.* 147
sprights *began* to faint, . . . *D.* 542
Soone as his oaten pipe *began* to shrill, . . . *As.* 44
Clorinda . . . *began* this dolefull lay. . . . *As.* 214
began his mournfull tourne: . . . *As.* Interl. 221
Jove himselfe his powre *began* to dread, . . . *Col.* 809
Through him the cold *began* to covet heat, . . . *Col.* 847
She . . . th' unacquainted light *began* to feare, . . . I. v. 21. 4
his rash syre *began* to rend His heare, . . . I. v. 39. 4
when fayling breath *began* to faint, . . . II. ii. 8. 1
Since errant armes to sew he first *began:* . . . II. ii. 17. 5
them *began* With goodly meanes to pacifie, . . . II. ii. 21. 8
Then she *began* a treaty to procure, . . . II. ii. 32. 6
began these words aloud to sownd. . . . II. ii. 39. 9
Got from great Atlas daughters, hence *began,* . . . II. vii. 54. 6
Since he this hardy enterprize *began:* . . . II. vii. 65. 7
Whose tender bud to blossome new *began,* . . . II. viii. 5. 3
he *began* to doubt his dazeled sight, . . . II. xi. 40. 2
he *began* to faint, and life decay: . . . II. xi. 48. 6
excellence Of his creation, when he life *began,* . . . II. xii. 87. 3
snatching his bright sword *began* to close With her . . . III. i. 9. 3
then she thus *began.* . . . III. iii. 16. 1
The bud of youth to blossome faire *began,* . . . III. v. 29. 8
When so the froward skye *began* to lowre; . . . III. v. 51. 7

Began—*Continued.*
Then Paridell *began* to chaunge his theme, ... III. ix. 10. 8
he thus *began* amaine: . . . . IV. i. 52. 5
Her cause of comming she to tell *began*. . . . . IV. ii. 49. 5
She then *began* them humbly to intreate . . . . IV. ii. 51. 1
evermore, when he *began* to winke, ... IV. v. 41. 3
day out of the Ocean mayne *Began* to peepe . . . . IV. v. 45. 4
The Prince halfe rapt *began* on her to dote; . . . . IV. ix. 6. 7
Began to doubt, when she them saw embrace, ... IV. ix. 10. 5
Began to faint, and feele their corage cold. . . . . IV. x. 18. 5
the wicked seede of vice *Began* to spring; . . . . V. i. 1. 4
their hearts *began* to faile, ... V. ii. 24. 7
When they thus ended had, the Knight *began:* . . . . V. iv. 16. 1
Came forth into the rout, and them t' array *began*. . . . . V. iv. 36. 9
The Trumpets sounded, and the field *began;* . . . . V. v. 6. 1
With bitter strokes it both *began* and ended. . . . . V. v. 6. 2
to her turning thus *began* againe: . . . . V. v. 30. 6
There she *began* to make her monefull plaint . . . . V. vi. 12. 1
soone as he *began* to lay about . . . . V. vi. 30. 1
Began the streight conditions to propound, ... V. xii. 28. 2
Then Zele *began* to urge her punishment, ... V. ix. 49. 7
When one in armes she saw, *began* to fly; . . . . V. x. 19. 6
With his huge flaile *began* to lay about; . . . . V. xi. 47. 7
He drawing neare *began* to greete them faire, ... V. xi. 48. 2
Those knights *began* afresh them to assayle, ... V. xi. 59. 2
At him *began* aloud to barke and bay . . . . V. xii. 41. 2
Began to quake and tremble with dismay; . . . . V. xii. 41. 5
There then *began* a fearefull cruell fray . . . . VI. i. 36. 1
wherefore Betwixt you two *began* this strife . . . . VI. ii. 8. 9
Phoebus . . . Unto his Inne *began* to draw apace; . . . . . VI. iii. 29. 2
even his ruder hart *began* to rew, ... VI. iv. 3. 5
Then thus *began* the lamentable Dame: . . . . VI. iv. 29. 1
began to assay T' amend what was amisse, ... VI. v. 10. 8
To these sicke twaine, that now *began* to droupe: . . . . . VI. v. 32. 3
She starting up *began* to shrieke aloud; . . . . VI. vi. 31. 2
Began to tremble every limbe and vaine; . . . . VI. vii. 22. 2
began Him to invite unto his simple home; . . . . VI. ix. 16. 3
He thus *began:* . . . . VI. xi. 30. 2
Began to mitigate his swelling sourse, ... VI. xi. 34. 3
Began some smacke of comfort new to tast, ... VI. xi. 45. 3
How she at first her selfe *began* to reare . . . . VII. vi. 1. 8
He thus againe in milder wise *began:* . . . . VII. vi. 31. 6
his planet cleare *Began* in me to move, ... *Am.* lx. 6

Beget. the great God Pan . . . dyd himselfe *beget?* . . . . *S.C.* Jul. 52
like himselfe desire for to *beget:* . . . . *Col.* 864
Of whom he did great Constantine *begett,* . . . . II. x. 60. 1
doth *beget* True love and faithfull friendship, ... IV. vi. 46. 8
they did then *beget* This hellish Dog, ... VI. vi. 12. 1
next he did *beget* . . . Angels bright, ... *H.H.L.* 54

Begets. *Begets* and eke conceives, ne needeth other none. . . . IV. x. 41. 9

Beggar's. *Beggers* life is best; . . . . *Hub.* 180

Beggars. Free men some *beggers* call, but they be free, . . . *Hub.* 161
they which call them so more *beggers* bee; . . . . *Hub.* 162
Beg amongst those that *beggers* doo defie.' . . . . *Hub.* 192

Beggary. But few returned, having scaped hard, With balefull
beggery, ... I. iv. 3. 4

Begging. Oft-times to *begging* are content to fall. . . . . . *Hub.* 182
now is thought a civile *begging* sect. . . . . *Hub.* 198
their *begging* now them failed quyte, ... *Hub.* 347
Much like to *begging,* but much better named, ... *Hub.* 351

Begin. *See* **Begon, Gin.**
The blossomes of lust to bud did *beginne,* . . . . *S.C.* May 187
Begin, thou eldest Sister of the crew, ... *T.M.* 53
'More eath . . . How to *begin,* then know how to have donne. *Col.* 591
with new day new worke at once *begin:* . . . . I. i. 33. 2
Like to an holy Monck, the service to *begin*. . . . . I. iv. 18. 9
recovering hart, he does *begin* To rubb her temples, ... I. vii. 21. 4
Begin, and end the bitter balefull stound; . . . . I. vii. 25. 8
Each goodly thing is hardest to *begin;* . . . . I. x. 6. 1
wretched we, . . . Must now anew *begin* . . . . II. i. 32. 7
did *begin* To plaine of wronges, ... II. iii. 13. 4
Must first *begin,* and well her amenage: . . . . II. iv. 11. 2
to rayse our house to honour did *begin*. . . . . II. iv. 36. 9
they fiercely then *begin* to showre; . . . . II. viii. 48. 5
Begin then, O my dearest sacred Dame! . . . . III. iii. 4. 1
Begin, O Clio! and recount from hence . . . . III. iii. 4. 6
The hard *beginne* that meetes thee in the dore, ... III. iii. 21. 8
'For so must all things excellent *begin;* . . . . III. iii. 22. 1
death with darknesse doth *begin*. . . . . III. iv. 59. 9
gan the battaile freshly to *begin;* . . . . III. v. 22. 5
Ere that we to efforce it doe *begin:* . . . . III. ix. 9. 4
discord harder is to end then to *begin*. . . . . IV. i. 20. 9
panting breath *begin* to fayle, ... IV. vi. 16. 2
then his bloudy banket should *beginne*. . . . . IV. vii. 20. 9
beasts *begin* to play Their pleasant friskes, ... IV. x. 46. 1
till time they should *begin* the fight. . . . . V. v. 4. 9
There then a piteous slaughter did *begin;* . . . . V. vii. 35. 5
now I *begin* To tread an endlesse trace, ... VI. i. 6. 1
You calme the storme that passion did *begin,* . . . . *Am.* viii. 11
I must *begin* and never bring to end: . . . . *Am.* xxiii. 10
This joyous day, deare Lord, with joy *begin;* . . . . *Am.* lxviii. 5
Begin his witlesse note apace to clatter. . . . . *Am.* lxxxiv. 4
after stormes, when clouds *begin* to cleare, ... *H.L.* 276
Whose root from earths base groundworke shold *begin*. . . . *H.H.L.* 105
Beginne from first, where he encradled was . . . . *H.H.L.* 225

Beginner. in my woes *beginner* it to end: . . . . II. iv. 31. 4

Beginners. The first *beginners* of my endles care: . . . . . *D.* 301

Beginneth. *See* **Ginneth.**
The carefull cold *beginneth* for to creep, ... I. vii. 39. 4
He first her hands *beginneth* to unbind, ... VI. viii. 50. 5

Beginning. the Ape, *beginning* well to wey This hard adventure, *Hub.* 112
In their *beginning* they are weake and wan, ... II. iv. 34. 3
Though straunge *beginning* had, ... III. ii. 42. 2
Great matter growing of *beginning* small, ... IV. ii. 54. 7
Thereby to make their loves *beginning* their lives end. . . . IV. vi. 17. 9
For her *beginning* a more fearefull fray, ... V. viii. 10. 6
gave *beginning* to her woe and wretchednesse. . . . . V. x. 11. 9
Beginning then below, with th' easie vew . . . . *H.H.B.* 22

Beginnings. favour my *beginnings* graciously; . . . . *Gn.* 38
'Well hoped I, and faire *beginnings* had, ... I. vii. 49. 1

Begins. *See* **Gins.**
Winters wrath *beginnes* to quell, ... *S.C.* Mar. 8
How bragly it *beginnes* to budde, ... *S.C.* Mar. 14
when with Wine the braine *begins* to sweate, ... *S.C.* O. 107
beginnes To shew in Heaven his brightnes orient; . . . . . . *Ti.* 388
Soone as thy dreadfull trompe *begins* to sownd, ... I. xi. 6. 6
now my teme *begins* to faint and fayle, ... III. xii. 47. *or.* 3
Towards the westerne brim *begins* to draw, ... V. ix. 35. 2
Alreadie seemes that fortunes headlong wheele *Begins* to turne, V. x. 20. 8
The new *begins* his compast course anew: . . . . *Am.* lxii. 2
Beginnes his owne, and my old fault renewes. . . . . *H.H.L.* 21

Begon. *See* **Began, Begun, Woebegone.**
And yet, alas! but now my spring *begonne,* . . . . *S.C.* Ja. 29
then againe *begonne;* 'My weaker yeares, ... I. i. 52. 4
well *begonne,* end all so well, I pray! . . . . I. viii. 28. 4
All ends that was *begonne:* . . . . I. ix. 42. 3
Affyaunce made, my happinesse *begonne,* . . . . II. iv. 21. 4
fresh *begon* That castle to assaile . . . . II. xi. 5. 3
In playner wise to tell her grievaunce she *begonne*. . . . . III. i. 52. 9
Which to prove, I this voyage have *begonne*. . . . . III. ii. 8. 5
'Things ofte impossible' (quoth she) 'seeme, ere *begonne*. . III. ii. 36. 9
love, that is in gentle brest *begonne,* . . . . III. ii. 51. 7
begonne By false illusion of a guilefull Spright . . . . . III. iii. 13. 3
they both *begonne* To make exceeding mone, ... III. vii. 19. 8
was as far at last, as when I first *begon*. . . . . III. vii. 59. 9
that other knight *begonne* To wex exceeding wroth, ... III. viii. 17. 7
begonne His stolen steed to thunder furiously, ... III. x. 33. 5
As if but then the battell had *begonne:* . . . . IV. iii. 36. 2
he last ended, having first *begonne*. . . . . IV. v. 7. 5
As if but then the battell had *begonne;* . . . . IV. ix. 27. 2
That harder may be ended, then *begonne:* . . . . IV. x. 3. 4
with so strong attempt I had *begonne*. . . . . IV. x. 53. 5
There Justice first her princely rule *begonne*. . . . . . . V. i. 2. 5
what ensu'd shall in next Canto be *begonne*. . . . . VI. ii. 48. 9
As fiercely yet as when he first *begonne,* . . . . VI. iv. 2. 7
in sort as he at first *begonne,* . . . . VI. x. 32. 4
Will in another Canto better be *begonne*. . . . . VI. x. 44. 9
when I thinke to end that I *begonne,* . . . . *Am.* xxiii. 9

Begored. ten thousand monsters . . . gaping griesly, all *begor'd.* IV. xi. 3. 9

Begot. *See* **Base-begot.**
Which Pan, the shepheards God, of her *begot:* . . . . *S.C.* Ap. 51
proud that ever he *begot* Such a Bellibone; . . . . *S.C.* Ap. 91
begot amisse By yawning Sloth . . . . *T.M.* 262
Which wast *begot* in Daemogorgons hall, ... I. v. 22. 5
how they were *begott,* . . . . II. x. 8. 1
There he this knight of her *begot,* . . . . III. iv. 20. 1
'Night . . . wast *begot* in heaven, ... III. iv. 55. 3
wondrously they were *begot* and bred . . . . III. vi. 6. 1
her of his owne mother Earth Whylome *begot,* . . . . III. vii. 47. 9
'Anchyses sonne, *begott* of Venus fayre,' . . . . III. ix. 41. 1
Which that great Gyant Blomius *begot* . . . . IV. xi. 42. 2
by him *begot* in loves delight . . . . V. ix. 31. 5
'Of Cerberus whilome he was *begot* . . . . VI. i. 8. 1
bred of hellish strene, . . . *Begot* of foule Echidna, . . . VI. vi. 9. 9
By him *begot* of faire Eurynome, ... VI. x. 22. 2
were *begot,* In Joves sweet paradice of Day and Night; . . . *Epith.* 98
When he *begot* the great Tirynthian groome: . . . . *Epith.* 329
with thy selfe did lie And *begot* Majesty. . . . . *Epith.* 331
Begot of Plentie and of Penurie, ... *H.L.* 53
and of it selfe *begot,* . . . his eldest sonne . . . . *H.H.L.* 30
begot of any earthly Seede, ... *Proth.* 65

Begotten. By him *begotten* of fowle infamy; . . . . *T.M.* 316
A Satyres sonne . . . there *begotten* of a Lady myld, ... I. vi. 21. 3
Begotten by her kingly Paramoure, ... II. x. 19. 2
Five sonnes he left, *begotten* of one wife, ... II. x. 44. 1
wondrously *begotten,* and begonne . . . . III. iii. 13. 3
Begotten by two fathers of one mother, ... IV. x. 32. 4
Orthrus *begotten* by great Typhaon And foule Echidna . . . . V. x. 10. 7
there should to him a sonne Be gotten, not *begotten;* . . . . VI. iv. 32. 7
ye *begotten* were And borne here in this world; . . . . . . VII. vii. 53. 8

Beguile. layen baytes to *beguile* her brother; . . . . *S.C.* S. 39
he us'd oft to *beguile* Poore suters, ... *Hub.* 877
doth *beguile* Their greedie mouthes of the expected spoyle; . *Hub.* 1285
Led with delight, they thus *beguile* the way, ... I. i. 10. 1
sweet musicke . . . Him to *beguile* of griefe . . . . I. v. 17. 8
Those guestes, beguyled, did *beguyle* their eyes Of kindly
sleepe . . . . II. ii. 46. 6
So goodly did *beguile* the Guyler of his pray. . . . . II. vii. 64. 9
Illusion that did *beguile* his sense, ... II. xi. 39. 6
to *beguyle* A simple maide, ... III. ii. 12. 7
thought so to *beguile* her grievous smart; . . . . III. iv. 6. 2
Hellenors both eyes did eke *beguyle,* . . . . III. x. 5. 4
fedd on fodder to *beguile* her sight. . . . . III. xi. 42. 4
her griefe with errour to *beguyle,* . . . . V. vi. 5. 3
Gan forth to lay his bayte her to *beguyle,* . . . . V. ix. 12. 8
The better to *beguile* whom she so fond did finde. . . . . . V. xi. 23. 9
The birds to catch, or fishes to *beguyle;* . . . . VI. ix. 23. 6
Is but a bayt such wretches to *beguile,* . . . . *Am.* xli. 10
dying, doe themselves of payne *beguyle*. . . . . *Am.* xlvii. 12
faine my griefe with chaunges to *beguile,* . . . . *Am.* lxxxvi. 10

Beguiled. *See* **Late-beguiled.**
He stole away, and weetingly *beguyld*. . . . . *As.* 22
The maker selfe, . . . Was nigh *beguiled* with so goodly sight. . I. i. 45. 7
seemd she to appease Her mournefull plaintes, *beguiled* of her art, ... I. i. 54. 7
The knight was wroth to see his stroke *beguyld*, ... I. xi. 25. 1
My liefest Lord she thus *beguiled* had; . . . . II. i. 52. 5
Those guestes, *beguyled*, did beguyle their eyes . . . . . II. ii. 46. 6
Suffers her selfe through sleepe *beguild* to bee, ... II. viii. 6. 8
And his slow eies *beguiled* of their sight, ... II. viii. 9. 2
Beguyld thus with delight of novelties, ... II. x. 77. 1
was with the love thereof *beguyld;* . . . . III. ii. 44. 8
faire Amoret, . . . Being thereof *beguyld*, ... III. xii. 44. 9
Being likewise *beguiled* in her thought, ... IV. viii. 56. 3
of their private loves *beguyled*, ... IV. ix. 36. 5
Conceived close in her *beguiled* hart, ... V. vi. 43. 8
Even so Clarinda her owne Dame *beguyld*, ... V. v. 53. 5
By her *beguyled* and confounded quight: . . . . V. ix. 40. 5
doubting to be wronged or *beguyled*, ... VI. vii. 33. 7
panting hounds *beguiled* of their pray: . . . . *Am.* lxvii. 4
So goodly wonne, with her owne will *beguyled*. . . . . . . *Am.* lxvii. 14
Begun. *See* **Begon.**
her course *begun* with brave intent. . . . . *Ro.* xxi. 8
everie thing that is *begun* with reason . . . . *Hub.* 126
returne from whence he first *begun*, ... *Hub.* 306
To end thy glorie which he hath *begun:* . . . . *Col.* 409
Finish the storie which thou hast *begunne*.' . . . . *Col.* 589
the fleecie cattell have *begun* . . . to make their feast. . . . *Col.* 606
In love were either ended or *begunne:* . . . . IV. Pr. 3. 5
he now *begunne* To challenge her anew, ... IV. iv. 8. 5
Even in the dore him meeting, she *begun:* . . . . V. vi. 9. 1
With shew of morning mylde he hath *begun*, ... *Am.* lxii. 3
Behalf. purchase honour in his friends *behalve*, ... IV. iv. 27. 3
In the *behalfe* of wronged weake did fight: . . . . V. viii. 30. 8
in thine owne *behalfe* maist partiall seeme: . . . . . . VII. vi. 35. 3
Behappen. Which unto any knight *behappen* may, ... V. xi. 52. 4
Behave. thereto did himselfe right well *behave* Her to obay, . V. v. 23. 7
ye better shall your selfe *behave* . . . . VI. i. 42. 7
Towards all womenkind them kindly to *behave*. . . . . . . VI. ii. 14. 9
Behaved. This gentle knight himselfe so well *behaved*, ... V. vi. 2. 2
Behaves. his mynd *Behaves* with cares, ... II. iii. 40. 7
Behavior. his *behaviour* altogether was *Alla Turchesca*, . . . *Hub.* 676
in his . . . *behaveour* hee Did labour lively . . . . I. x. 6. 7
Her light *behaviour* and loose dalliaunce . . . . II. vi. 8. 1
they grew Greatly confused in *behaveoure*. . . . . III. iii. 50.7
Gainst natures law and good *behaveoure;* . . . . III. vii. 49. 2
With daily shew of courteous kind *behaviour*, ... V. v. 35. 7
Beheast, -s. *See* **Behest, -s.**
Beheld. Then I *beholde* the faire Dodonian tree, ... *Bel.*[1] v. 1
when suddaine I *beholde*, ... *Bel.*[2] vii. 9
*When I *beheld* this tickle trustles state . . . . *Pet.*[2] vii. 1
I, which this sight *beheld*, was much dismayed . . . . . . *Van.* vii. 13
that great warre, which Trojanes oft *beholde?* . . . . *Gn.* 498
oft *beheld* the warlike Greekish forces, ... *Gn.* 499
Which when the Priest *beheld*, he vew'd it nere, ... *Hub.* 379
troubled kingdome of wilde beasts *beholde*, ... *Hub.* 1231
since these two eyes *beheld* A mightie Prince, ... *Ti.* 183
I *beheld* where stood A Knight . . . . *Ti.* 645
The gods, which all things see, this same *beheld*, ... *As.* 181
His eies . . . stared sterne on all that him *beheld;* . . . . . I. iv. 36. 6
when the knight *beheld*, his mightie shild . . . . I. viii. 6. 6
Virgin which *beheld* from farre, . . . The whole atchievement I. viii. 26. 1
Which when the knights *beheld* amazd they were, ... I. viii. 49. 1
with this unlucky eye I late *beheld;* . . . . I. ix. 26. 8
when the carle *beheld*, and saw his guest . . . . I. ix. 54. 2
when that fairest Una she *beheld*, ... I. x. 8. 6
so dismayd when that his foe *beheld*, ... I. xi. 28. 6
his deare Lady, that *beheld* it all, ... I. xi. 55. 3
she *beheld* those maydens meriment . . . . I. xii. 8. 1
Speake they which have *beheld* the battailes which it wan.' . II. iii. 16. 9
when her goodly visage he *beheld*, ... II. iii. 37. 1
fayre Phaedria, that *beheld* That deadly daunger, ... II. vi. 32. 1
Infinite moe tormented in like paine He there *beheld*, ... II. vii. 63. 2
great workmans skill Whenas those knightes *beheld* . . . . . II. ix. 33. 2
Whom when the knights *beheld*, ... II. ix. 36. 4
Had not his gentle Squire *beheld* his paine, ... II. xi. 29. 8
Ne ever land *beheld*, ne living wight, ... II. xii. 2. 2
trembled as them passing they *beheld:* . . . . II. xii. 40. 7
Which when those knights *beheld*, ... III. i. 40. 7
Late dayes ensample, which these eyes *beheld:* . . . . . . III. iii. 55. 2
Which when the Prince *beheld*, a lothfull sight, ... III. iv. 52. 4
when shee better him *beheld* . . . . III. v. 30. 7
whenas he *beheld* the heavenly Mayd, ... III. v. 43. 4
soone as she *beheld* that suddein stound, ... III. vii. 7. 4
Which whenas Satyrane *beheld*, ... III. vii. 38. 1
Which whenas they *beheld*, they smitten were . . . . III. ix. 23. 1
Which they far off *beheld* from Trojan toures, ... III. ix. 35. 5
Whom when as Britomart *beheld* . . . . III. xi. 4. 5
Such when those Knights and Ladies all about *Beheld* her, . . IV. i. 14. 2
Whom when as Paridel more plaine *beheld*, ... IV. i. 34. 2
Which when his other companie *beheld*, ... IV. i. 37. 1
Which when as Blandamour *beheld*, ... IV. i. 44. 1
Which when as Blandamour . . . *Beheld*, ... IV. ii. 5. 4
when at last she had *beheld* her fill, ... IV. ii. 49. 3
Whom when on ground his brother next *beheld*, ... IV. iii. 14. 1
They which that piteous spectacle *beheld* Were much amaz'd . IV. iii. 21. 1
Which when as all the lookers-on *beheld*, ... IV. iii. 35. 1
All which when gentle Canacee *beheld*, ... IV. iii. 50. 1
All which when Blandamour from end to end *Beheld*, ... IV. iv. 45. 6
Which when they all *beheld* they chaft, ... IV. v. 27. 1

Beheld—*Continued.*
having long *beheld*, at last enquired The cause . . . . . . IV. v. 38. 3
when as Scudamour, who now abrayd, *Beheld*, ... IV. vi. 24. 2
Beheld the lovely face of Artegall . . . . IV. vi. 26. 2
ever when his visage she *beheld*, ... IV. vi. 27. 3
drawing nigh, ere he her well *beheld*, ... IV. vii. 36. 7
Whom when the Prince *beheld*, ... IV. viii. 20. 1
Which when that Squire *beheld*, he woxe full glad . . . . . IV. viii. 46. 1
soone as faire Aemylia *beheld* . . . . IV. ix. 9. 1
all the while *beheld* their wrathfull moode, ... IV. ix. 22. 3
Whom when the Briton Prince afarre *beheld* . . . . IV. ix. 32. 1
beheld with gazefull eye, ... IV. x. 28. 2
soone as I *beheld*, ... IV. x. 53. 1
emblazond she *beheld*, ... IV. x. 55. 4
soone as he *beheld* that angels face . . . . IV. xii. 34. 1
There they *beheld* a mighty Gyant . . . . V. ii. 30. 1
Which when as Marinell *beheld* likewise, ... V. iii. 18. 1
Which when as all that present were *beheld*, ... V. iii. 26. 1
Whom soone as he *beheld* he knew, ... V. iv. 25. 9
Whom when as Artegall in that distresse By chaunce *beheld*, . V. iv. 41. 2
whom when Britomart Had long *beheld*, ... V. vi. 7. 7
To have *beheld* a spectacle so bad; . . . . V. vii. 38. 5
Which when his Ladie from the castles hight *Beheld*, ... V. viii. 45. 5
sternely him *beheld* with grim and ghastly looke. . . . . . V. xi. 12. 9
when as she first *beheld* The armed Prince . . . . V. xi. 26. 1
all the people which *beheld* that day Gan shout aloud, . . . V. xi. 34. 1
Whom when those knights so froward and forlore *Beheld*, . . V. xi. 61. 9
With dreadfull looke he Artegall *beheld*, ... V. xii. 16. 2
Which haynous sight when Calidore *beheld*, ... VI. i. 18. 1
The sad Briana which all this *beheld;* . . . . VI. i. 44. 6
When he *beheld* the streames of purple blood . . . . VI. iv. 12. 2
Which when that Squire *beheld*, he to them stept . . . . . VI. v. 25. 6
Which when the Salvage . . . *Beheld*, ... VI. vi. 22. 2
Whose cruell handling when that Squire *beheld*, ... VI. vii. 45. 1
Which she *beheld* with lamentable eye, ... VI. viii. 3. 2
whenas Enias *Beheld* two such, ... VI. viii. 5. 8
Which when the Prince *beheld*, there standing by, ... VI. viii. 12. 6
when he *beheld* That huge great foole oppressing th' other . VI. viii. 28. 1
There I *beheld* such vainenesse as I never thought. . . . . . VI. ix. 24. 9
With lustfull eyes *beheld* that lovely guest, ... VI. xi. 3. 7
There she *beheld* . . . Her father . . . . VI. xi. 23. 1
when the hardy Titanesse *beheld* The goodly building . . . . VII. vi. 10. 1
when the haughty Titanesse *beheld*, ... VII. vi. 25. 1
Unseene of any, yet of all *beheld;* . . . . VII. vii. 13. 4
Behest. To fall before her feete at her *beheast*, ... *Ti.* 73
without *beheast* So carefull was for them, ... *D.* 137
straight obay his soveraine *beheast;* . . . . *D.* 270
Where I will live or die at her *beheast*, ... *Col.* 254
salvage nation . . . learnes her wise *beheast*. . . . . I. vi. Arg.
his *beheast* they feared as a tyrans law. . . . . I. vi. 26. 9
With forced fury following his *behest*, ... I. ix. 7. 5
me had warnd old Timons wise *behest*, ... I. ix. 9. 5
Gan him instruct in everie good *behest*, ... I. x. 33. 3
in every good *behest*, . . . Shee him instructed . . . . . . I. x. 45. 3
The waves, obedient to theyr *beheast*, ... III. iv. 31. 8
the swift bird obayd not her *behest*, ... IV. viii. 10. 7
So litle did they hearken to her sweet *beheast*. . . . . . . IV. ix. 31. 9
sternly gan repine at his *beheast;* . . . . V. i. 29. 2
Next gan Religion gainst her to impute High Gods *beheast*, . V. ix. 44. 6
To him assynd her high *beheast* to doo, ... V. xii. 3. 7
in atchievement of her high *behest* I should no creature joyne . . . . VI. ii. 37. 7
obaying natures first *beheast*. . . . . VI. iv. 14. 9
Did gladly hearken to his grave *beheast*, ... VI. vi. 15. 2
Unmyndfull of his vow, and high *beheast* . . . . VI. x. 1. 3
made unfit to serve his lawlesse mindes *behest*. . . . . . . VI. xi. 7. 9
when all the earth she thus had brought To her *behest*, . . . VII. vi. 7. 2
Sith I needs must follow thy *behest*, ... VII. vii. 2. 1
duly well observed his *beheast;* . . . . *H.L.* 93
Through observation of her high *beheast*, ... *H.H.B.* 202
Behests. slaine to serve the Apes *beheasts:* . . . . *Hub.* 1308
sage Counsellours . . . Taught to obay their bestiall *beheasts*, I. iv. 18. 3
To her faire presence and discrete *behests*. . . . . II. ii. 32. 5
We both are bownd to follow heavens *beheasts*, ... III. vi. 22. 7
Liagore much praisd for wise *behests;* . . . . IV. xi. 51. 4
Justice . . . did divide her dred *beheasts:* . . . . V. Pr. 9. 9
Restraines those sterne *behests* and cruell doomes of his. . . V. vii. 22. 9
dy As thralls and vassals unto mens *beheasts;* . . . . VII. vii. 19. 3
Thou must him love, and his *beheasts* embrace; . . . . . . *H.H.L.* 261
Behight. They bene all Ladyes of the lake *behight*, ... *S.C.* Ap. 120
I, a waylfull widdowe *behight*, ... *S.C.* May 201
It fortuned (as heavens had *behight*) . . . . *Mui.* 241
the keies are to thy hand *behight* . . . . I. x. 50. 7
Didst thou *behight* me borne of English blood, ... I. x. 64. 6
the journey which he had *behight:* . . . . II. iii. 1. 7
streight *behight* To seeke Occasion, ... II. iv. 43. 5
At last, him turning to his charge *behight*, ... II. viii. 9. 5
The Ferriman, as Alma had *behight*, ... II. xi. 4. 2
he *behight* Those gates to be unbar'd, ... II. xi. 17. 3
That Geauntesse Argante is *behight*, ... III. vii. 47. 2
A Knight much better then thy selfe *behight*, ... IV. i. 44. 4
lowly to her lowting thus *behight:* . . . . IV. ii. 23. 3
whilst all the lookers-on Him dead *behight*, ... IV. iii. 31. 2
The second was to Triamond *behight*, ... IV. v. 7. 6
Till Britomart him fairely thus *behight:* . . . . IV. vi. 38. 5
for his paines a whistle him *behight*, ... IV. xi. 6. 8
Whom . . . he knew, and thus *behight:* 'Sir Turpine! haplesse man, ... V. iv. 25. 9
fild with heavenly fury, thus he her *behight*. . . . . V. vii. 20. 9
behight Unto that Damzell in her Ladies right, ... V. ix. 3. 4

Behight—*Continued.*
Yet for the time this answere he to him *behight*. . . . . . . VI. ii. 36. 9
So with her marched forth, as she did him *behight*. . . . . . VI. ii. 39. 9
him, that is *behight* Father of Gods and men . . . . VII. vi. 35. 4
thanks to him, that it deserves, *behight;* *Com.Son.*ii.12
Meeke Lambe of God, before all worlds *behight,* . . . . *H.H.L.* 173

Behind (*partial list*).
a bell, which he left *behind* . . . . *S.C.* May 288
Her like shee has not left *behinde* . . . . *S.C.* N. 40
leave this lamentable plaint *behinde:* . . . . *Gn.* 635
all the rest must needs be left *behinde:* . . . . *Ti.* 586
Leaving *behind* them nought but griefe . . . . *D.* 398
set His sevenfold teme *behind* the stedfast starre . . . . . . I. ii. 1. 2
fast she fled, ne ever lookt *behynd,* . . . . I. iii. 12. 1
Duess' had forst him leave *behind;* . . . . I. vi. 2. 2
left *behinde* alone, ... I. vi. 33. 3
and eke *behind* His scrip did hang, ... I. vi. 35. 8
leaving all *behind* her fled away: . . . . I. viii. 25. 6
she growing had *behind* A foxes taile, ... I. viii. 48. 3
As if his feare still followed him *behynd:* . . . . I. ix. 21. 6
sin, Not purg'd nor heald, *behind* remained still, ... I. x. 25. 3
all the land *behind* him farre, ... I. xi. 11. 6
Behynd his backe, unweeting, where he stood, ... I. xi. 29. 2
Before, *behind,* and round about him laies; . . . . II. ii. 25. 8
low *behinde* her backe were scattered: . . . . II. iii. 30. 5
bide alone *behinde;* . . . . II. iii. 32. 4
him *behynd* a wicked Hag did stalke, ... II. iv. 4. 1
all *behinde* was bald, ... II. iv. 4. 7
His sandy lockes, long hanging downe *behind,* . . . . II. v. 14. 4
Having his warlike weapons cast *behynd,* . . . . II. v. 28. 7
Guyon was loath to leave his guide *behind,* . . . . II. vi. 20. 1
from *behind* it forth there lept . . . . II. vii. 26. 6
dreadfull feend, which did *behinde* him wayt, ... II. vii. 64. 4
casting wronges and all revenge *behind,* . . . . II. viii. 51. 3
Ne ought, I weene, are ye therein *behynd,* . . . . II. ix. 38. 8
therefore was removed far *behind,* . . . . II. ix. 55. 2
Least that his Lord they should *behinde* invade; . . . . II. xi. 31. 5
Whiles the dredd daunger does *behind* remaine. . . . . II. xii. 21. 4
th' other by his bote *behind* did stay. . . . . II. xii. 38. 6
Nigh a speares length *behind* his crouper fell; . . . . III. i. 6. 7
her faire yellow locks *behind* her flew, ... III. i. 16. 3
faire Britomart . . . did stay *behynd,* . . . . III. i. 19. 3
Ne bubling rowndell they *behinde* them sent. . . . . III. iv. 33. 7
his good Squire late lefte *behinde,* . . . . III. v. 12. 4
as if her former dred Were hard *behind,* . . . . III. vii. 2. 6
loth to leave his liefest pelfe *behinde;* . . . . III. x. 15. 6
in his eare him rownded close *behinde:* . . . . III. x. 30. 4
Here for to stay in safetie *behynd:* . . . . III. x. 41. 6
Did all the way him follow hard *behynd;* . . . . III. x. 55. 6
Whom when as Britomart beheld *behinde* . . . . III. xi. 4. 5
Behinde him was Reproch, Repentaunce, Shame; . . . . III. xii. 24. 1
Reproch the first, Shame next, Repent *behinde:* . . . . III. xii. 24. 2
More for the love which he had left *behynd,* . . . . IV. i. 37. 8
'Sir knight, why ride ye dumpish thus *behind,* . . . . IV. ii. 5. 7
each not farre *behinde* him had his make, ... IV. ii. 30. 5
staffe asunder brake, And left the head *behinde:* . . . . IV. iii. 10. 7
The other halfe, *behind* yet sticking fast, ... IV. iii. 12. 3
And left *behind* her in her secret bowre . . . . IV. v. 5. 4
behind her crest So sorely he her strooke, ... IV. vi. 13. 2
That quite it chynd his backe *behind* the sell, ... IV. vi. 13. 8
To Scudamour, whom she had left *behind:* . . . . IV. vi. 46. 5
When suddenly *behind* her backe she heard . . . . IV. vii. 4. 3
hard *behind* his backe his foe was prest, ... IV. viii. 41. 6
on th' other sate Delay, *Behinde* the gate . . . . IV. x. 13. 2
both *behind* upheld her spredding traine; . . . . IV. xi. 47. 4
stone; Such as *behind* their backs . . . Were throwne . . . . V. Pr. 2. 6
Ne was Sir Artegall *behinde:* so both Together ran . . . . . V. ii. 12. 3
they have him enclosed so *behind,* . . . . V. iii. 9. 4
The other stayd *behind* to gard the pray: . . . . V. iii. 11. 7
that same wretched man, . . . They left *behind* them, ... V. iv. 25. 2
that gibbet, which is there *behind,* . . . . V. iv. 32. 3
the Prince pursew'd him close *behind.* . . . . V. viii. 42. 1
wound his enemy *Behinde,* beside, before, ... V. xi. 6. 9
To hide the horrour which did lurke *behinde,* . . . . V. xi. 23. 8
as he past afore . . . Bit him *behind,* . . . . V. xii. 39. 9
He rather should have taken up *behind;* . . . . VI. ii. 11. 5
Unto the place where me he left *behind:* . . . . VI. ii. 21. 3
To take him up *behinde* upon his steed; . . . . VI. iii. 31. 5
would beare *behinde* a burden of such scorne. . . . . VI. iii. 31. 9
refuge was still *Behind* his Ladies back; . . . . VI. iii. 49. 6
Who her, . . . With th' Hermit leaves *behynd.* . . . . VI. v. Arg.
armes which Calepine whyleare Had left *behind* . . . . VI. v. 8. 5
creeping still *behinde,* doth him incomber, ... VI. v. 19. 6
Creeping *behinde* him . . . . VI. v. 20. 5
forced there to leave them both *behynd* . . . . VI. v. 41. 3
Feeling some curre *behinde* his heeles to bite, ... VI. vi. 27. 6
him following *behynd,* Him often scourg'd, ... VI. vii. 49. 4
in this bag, which I *behinde* me don, ... VI. viii. 24. 4
And yet his feare did follow him *behynd:* . . . . VI. xi. 27. 6
Ne durst abide *behind,* for dread of worse effort. . . . . . . VI. xi. 42. 9
Behind the bushes, where she did her hyde, ... VI. xii. 8. 6
in some snare or gin set close *behind,* . . . . VII. vi. 48. 6
Behinde his back a sithe, ... VII. vii. 36. 8
When once the Crab *behind* his back he sees. . . . . *Epith.* 269

Behold. loe (quod he) *beholde* . . . . *Bel.*[1] i. 9
the birde that dares *beholde* the Sunne, ... *Bel.*[1] vi. 1
beholde the bright abode Of God and men. . . . . *Rev.* iv. 5
crying lowd, Loe! now *beholde* . . . . *Bel.*[2] i. 9
Whiles thus I did *behold,* . . . . *Bel.*[2] ii. 12
When I *behold* this tickle trustles state . . . . *Pet.*[2] vii. 1

Behold—*Continued.*
Beholde what wreake, what ruine, and what wast, ... *Ro.* iii. 5
The Romane triumphs glorie to *behold,* . . . . *Ro.* xiv. 12
When ye sometimes *behold* the ruin'd pride . . . . *Ro.* xv. 12
astonisht dost *behold* The antique pride . . . . *Ro.* xxvii. 1
An hideous Dragon, dreadfull to *behold,* . . . . *Van.* vi. 1
Art made a myrrhour to *behold* my plight: . . . . *S.C.* Ja. 20
How mought we, Diggon, hem *be-hold?* . . . . *S.C.* S. 229
about him gan *beholde* What God or Fortune . . . . *Gn.* 300
that passers by Might it *behold,* . . . . *Gn.* 662
chieflie joyes on foote them to *beholde,* . . . . *Hub.* 623
Which when he did with lothfull eyes *beholde,* . . . . *Hub.* 1314
Heare, and *behold* the miserable state Of us, ... *T.M.* 59
Behold the fowle reproach and open shame, ... *T.M.* 61
Through knowledge we *behold* the worlds creation, ... *T.M.* 499
There we *behold* the heavens great Hierarchie, ... *T.M.* 507
Thence I *behold* the miserie of men, ... *T.M.* 529
least he my Loove happely chaunce to *beholde.* . . . . *Tetrasticon* 4
I did *behold* A Woman sitting, ... *Ti.* 8
Deignd to *behold* me and their gifts bestowe, ... *Ti.* 81
Let them *behold* the piteous fall of mee, ... *Ti.* 461
Let him *behold* the horror of my fall, ... *Ti.* 466
did the same from farre *beholde,* . . . . *Ti.* 493
once that beautie did *beholde,* . . . . *Ti.* 531
Behold (said it) and by ensample see, ... *Ti.* 582
So soone as Clarion he did *beholde,* . . . . *Mui.* 355
shall never more *behold* Faire thing on earth, ... *D.* 491
travailers, which it from far *behold.* . . . . *Col.* 115
and longs death to *behold,* . . . . *Col.* 204
Behold! an huge great vessell to us came, ... *Col.* 213
Did never mortall eye *behold* such heavenly grace. . . . . . . I. iii. 4. 9
Her from her Palfrey pluckt, her visage to *behold.* . . . . . I. iii. 40. 9
It was a goodly heape for to *behould,* . . . . I. iv. 5. 1
Ah heavens! that doe this hideous act *behold,* . . . . I. vi. 5. 6
The wooddy nymphes, . . . Her to *behold* do thither runne . I. vi. 18. 2
did stay In secret shadow all this to *behold;* . . . . I. vi. 48. 3
His living like saw never living eye, Ne durst *behold:* . . . . I. vii. 8. 8
instruments . . . That doe this deadly spectacle *behold,* . . . I. vii. 22. 2
Whose fall did never foe before *behold:* . . . . I. vii. 51. 6
Behold what ye this day have done for mee, ... I. viii. 27. 8
very uncouth sight was to *behold,* . . . . I. viii. 31. 1
That greatest Princes presence might *behold.* . . . . I. viii. 35. 4
Such as she was their eies might her *behold,* . . . . I. viii. 46. 6
The authour of this fact we here *behold,* . . . . I. ix. 37. 7
that all this doth *behold* From highest heven, ... I. ix. 47. 1
horrour made to all that did *behold;* . . . . I. x. 13. 5
When him his dearest Una did *behold* Disdeining life, ... I. x. 22. 7
babes . . . Playing their sportes, that joyd her to *behold;* . I. x. 31. 2
As Eagles eie that can *behold* the Sunne. . . . . I. x. 47. 6
The fairest peece that eie *beholden* can, ... I. x. 59. 3
High heven *behold* the tedious toyle . . . . I. xi. 1. 9
From whence she might *behold* that battailles proof, ... I. xi. 5. 3
Behold! I see the haven nigh at hand . . . . I. xii. 1. 1
when his daughter deare he does *behold,* . . . . I. xii. 12. 8
when his eie did her *behold,* . . . . I. xii. 40. 8
In this fayre mirrhour maist *behold* thy face, ... II. Pr. 4. 7
feeble eyes your glory may *behold,* . . . . II. Pr. 5. 3
when the good Sir Guyon did *behold,* . . . . II. i. 42. 1
hevens just with equall brow Vouchsafed to *behold* us . . . II. i. 50. 4
Behold the ymage of mortalitie, ... II. i. 57. 2
to *behold* the water worke and play . . . . II. vi. 7. 8
'*Behold,* O man! that toilesome paines doest take, ... II. vi. 15. 1
none could *behold* The hew thereof; . . . . II. vii. 29. 3
'*Behold,* thou Faeries sonne, with mortall eye, ... II. vii. 38. 1
goodly was their glory to *behold;* . . . . II. vii. 54. 2
Which to *behold* he clomb up to the bancke, ... II. vii. 57. 1
In which the damned soules he did *behold,* . . . . II. vii. 63. 5
Behold this heavy sight, thou reverend Sire! . . . . II. viii. 7. 6
Behold, who list, both one and other in this place. . . . . . II. ix. 1. 9
The sonnes of men amazd their sternnesse to *behold.* . . . . II. x. 7. 9
Behold the boyling bathes at Cairbadon, ... II. x. 26. 2
'*Behold* th' ensamples in our sights . . . . II. xii. 9. 2
seem'd to fly for feare them to *behold.* . . . . II. xii. 25. 5
they *behold* arownd A large and spacious plaine, ... II. xii. 50. 1
to slacke his pace Them to *behold,* . . . . II. xii. 68. 5
Need but *behold* the pourtraict of her hart; . . . . III. Pr. 1. 8
scarse them leasure gave her passing to *behold.* . . . . III. i. 15. 9
By straunge occasion she did him *behold,* . . . . III. ii. 18. 1
'*Behold* the man! and tell me, Britomart, ... III. iii. 32. 1
A fayrer wight did never Sunne *behold;* . . . . III. v. 5. 5
'*Behold,* Sir, how your pitifull complaint . . . . III. ix. 40. 1
the howre that first he did them lett The same *behold,* . . . III. x. 34. 9
Wondrous delight it was there to *behould* . . . . III. xi. 34. 6
beware how thou those dartes *behold.*) . . . . III. xi. 48. 5
she did *behold* How . . . was likewise writ, *Be bolde,* . . . . III. xi. 54. 1
Of chearefull looke and lovely to *behold:* . . . . III. xii. 13. 2
his proud spoile . . . he might *behold* in perfect kinde; . . . III. xii. 22. 8
from shore *behold* the dreadfull sight . . . . IV. ii. 16. 7
thronging thicke her to *behold,* . . . . IV. iii. 41. 2
both shield and she whom I *behold* . . . . IV. x. 4. 8
An hideous Giant, dreadfull to *behold,* . . . . IV. x. 16. 6
soone as they his countenance did *behold,* . . . . IV. x. 18. 4
Unwilling to *behold* that lovely band. . . . . IV. x. 33. 5
behold! with happy eye I spyde . . . . IV. x. 48. 6
nayld on high that all might them *behold.* . . . . V. ii. 26. 9
All that *behold* so strange prodigious sight, ... V. iii. 19. 5
dare even deathes most dreadfull face *behold?* . . . . V. v. 31. 4
Whose goodly building when she did *behould,* . . . . V. vii. 5. 3
joyed to *behold* Her selfe adorn'd with gems . . . . V. vii. 13. 8
Ventailes reare each other to *behold.* . . . . V. viii. 12. 5

Behold—*Continued.*
Where they a stately pallace did *behold* . . . . V. ix. 21. 4
there no Monster did *behold*. . . . . V. xi. 21. 9
Whom when they thus distressed did *behold*, ... V. xi. 47. 1
At last some fisher-barke doth neare *behold*, ... VI. iv. 1. 4
Whom when as he thus combred did *behold*, ... VI. iv. 22. 1
daily doe *behold* The glorie of the great . . . . VI. ix. 28. 1
Whom whylest she did with watrie eyne *behold*, ... VI. xii. 7. 6
In covert shade, where none *behold* her may; . . . . . . VII. vi. 42. 5
'Therein the changes infinite *beholde*, ... VII. vii. 23. 1
When ye *behold* that Angels blessed looke, ... *Am.* i. 11
Well is he borne, that may *behold* you ever. . . . . . . *Am.* viii. 14
that which fairest is, but few *behold*, ... *Am.* xv. 13
When I *behold* that beauties wonderment, ... *Am.* xxiv. 1
Still to *behold* the object of their paine, ... *Am.* xxxv. 2
in my selfe, my inward selfe, . . . *behold* your semblant trew. . . . . *Am.* xlv. 4
So oft as I her beauty doe *behold*, ... *Am.* lv. 1
let my thoughts *behold* her selfe in mee. . . . . *Am.* lxxviii. 14
Onely *behold* her rare perfection, ... *Am.* lxxxiii. 13
Behold your faces as the christall bright, ... *Epith.* 64
abashed to *behold* So many gazers . . . . *Epith.* 159
Behold, whiles she before the altar stands, ... *Epith.* 223
Behold how goodly my faire love does ly, ... *Epith.* 305
Behold them both in their right visnomy . . . . *Com. Son.* ii. 5
not so fayre her buildinges to *behold* As Lewkenors stile . *Com.Son.*iv.13
To make al things such as we now *behold*, ... *H.B.* 30
where-ever that thou doest *behold* A comely corpse, ... *H.B.* 134
they *behold* A thousand Graces . . . . *H.B.* 253
(Not this round heaven, which we from hence *behold*, . . . *H.H.L.* 58
Where they *behold* the glorie of his light, ... *H.H.L.* 69
In whom He might His mightie selfe *behould*; . . . . . . *H.H.L.* 117
That thou his soveraine bountie mayst *behold*, ... *H.H.L.* 223
I faine to tell the things that I *behold*, ... *H.H.B.* 6
Whence they doe still *behold* the glorious face . . . . . *H.H.B.* 80
Him to *behold*, is on his workes to looke, ... *H.H.B.* 128
Angels, which her goodly face *behold* . . . . *H.H.B.* 232
whom God . . . lets his owne Beloved to *behold*; . . . . . *H.H.B.* 241
Beholder. At every rash *beholder* passing by. . . . . *Am.* xvi. 8
Beholder's. Bereave of sence each rash *beholders* sight. . . . *Col.* 547
could have dazd the rash *beholders* sight, ... I. x. 12. 8
bereav'd the rash *beholders* sight: . . . . II. iii. 23. 5
with their brightnesse daz'd the straunge *beholders* eye. . . V. ix. 21. 9
to burne at first *beholders* sight. . . . . *H.B.* 210
Beholdeth. *Beholdeth* free from fleshes frayle infection. . . *H.B.* 217
Beholding. Far of *beholding* Ephialtes tide, ... *Gn.* 375
in Court full oft *Beholding* them, ... *Mui.* 106
I, *beholding* it, with deepe dismay . . . . *D.* 186
They all, *beholding* worldly wights in place, ... I. v. 36. 1
men, *beholding* so great excellence . . . . II. ii. 41. 6
all which passen by, *Beholding* it from farre, ... III. ix. 45. 9
beholding earnestly The goodly ordinaunce . . . . III. xi. 53. 1
Beholding how the thrids of life they span: . . . . IV. ii. 49. 2
Artegall, *beholding* his mischaunce, ... IV. vi. 11. 1
her *beholding* with attentive eye, ... IV. viii. 10. 1
He her *beholding* at her feet downe fell, ... IV. viii. 13. 1
That faire Poeana, them *beholding* both, ... IV. ix. 9. 6
beholding all the way The goodly workes, ... IV. x. 15. 4
Beholding all that womanish weake fight; . . . . V. iv. 25. 8
And when he long had him *beholding* stood, ... VI. ii. 24. 8
Stood on the further bancke *beholding* him; . . . . VI. iii. 34. 2
The fearfull swayne *beholding* death so nie, ... VI. vii. 12. 1
Dayly *beholding* the faire Pastorell, ... VI. ix. 34. 3
Beholding all, yet of them unespyde. . . . . VI. x. 11. 5
Whom she *beholding*, now all desolate, ... VI. x. 34. 8
Beholding me, that all the pageants play, ... *Am.* liv. 3
she, *beholding* me with constant eye, ... *Am.* liv. 9
she, *beholding* me with mylder looke, Sought not to fly, . . *Am.* lxvii. 9
beholding the Idaea playne, ... *Am.* lxxxvii. 9
Which he *beholding* still with constant sight, ... *H.L.* 195
Beholds. When she *beholds* from her celestiall throne . . . *D.* 380
she *beholds*, with high aspiring thought, ... *Col.* 612
Diana in fresh sommers day *Beholdes* her nymphes . . . . . I. xii. 7. 8
High heven *beholdes* sad lovers nightly theeveryes. . . . . III. xi. 45. 9
Behoof. framed speaches fit for his *behoofe*, ... IV. vii. 37. 7
Behote. better mought they have *behote* him Hate. . . . . . *S.C.* D. 54
Ne living wight would have him life *behott*: . . . . I. xi. 38. 4
so sore that none him life *behote*. . . . . IV. iv. 40. 9
Behove. little wote what doth thereto *behove*. . . . . . . *T.M.* 396
grieve my ghost, that ill mote him *behove*, ... *D.* 265
In all that seemly shepheard might *behove*. . . . . *As.* 10
That loves and honours thee, as doth *behove*. . . . . . . *Ded. Son.* iii. 14
Of falsehood or of slouth, when most it may *behove*. . . . III. viii. 27. 9
Whom having wedded, as did him *behove*, ... IV. i. 2. 8
I may her seeke, as doth *behove*.' . . . . IV. vi. 34. 9
well accept, as well it did *behove*, ... IV. viii. 60. 3
Ne lend an eare to ought that might *behove*. . . . . IV. ix. 31. 4
beare themselves aright . . . as doth *behove*? . . . . . . VI. ii. 1. 4
as it mote a faithfull friend *behove*, ... VI. iii. 15. 7
Saying and doing all that mote *behove*; . . . . VI. xi. 5. 7
all the postes adorne as doth *behove*, ... *Epith.* 206
what can us lesse then that *behove*? . . . . *H.H.L.* 178
Behoved. Observ'd th' appointed way, as her *behooved*, . . . *Gn.* 467
Cordeill said she lov'd him as *behoov'd*: . . . . II. x. 28. 5
honourd him with all that her *behoved*. . . . . V. x. 39. 5
Him well *behoved* so; . . . . VI. v. 20. 1
Behoves. him *behooves* to vew in compasse round . . . . . *Ro.* xxvi. 5
it *behoves*, ere that into the race We enter, ... *Hub.* 122
It most *behoves* the honorable race . . . . *T.M.* 79
learnd themselves *behoves* to bee, ... *T.M.* 83

Behoves—*Continued.*
fained cheare, as for the time *behoves*, ... II. ii. 34. 3
Wherefore it now *behoves* us to advise What way is best . . VII. vi. 21. 6
It you *behoves* to love, ... *H.B.* 184
Behoveth. me *behoveth* rather to upbrayd, ... II. i. 28. 4
'Here now *behoveth* us well to avyse, ... II. xii. 17. 6
Being (*partial list of participle*).
Being one day at my window all alone, ... *Pet.* i. 1
all things which beneath the Moone have *being* . . . . . *Ro.* ix. 10
all things turne to their first *being*. . . . . *Ro.* xviii. 14
being downe, is trodde in the durt . . . . *S.C.* F. 235
No *being* for those that truely mene; . . . . *S.C.* S. 33
Eurydice . . . *being* forbid before: . . . . *Gn.* 435
live in good estate, . . . *Being* some honest Curate, . . . *Hub.* 429
being driven hence, I thether fly. . . . . *T.M.* 528
beeing nimbler joynted than the rest, ... *Mui.* 121
By his there *being* might not be bewraid, ... *Mui.* 399
'Name have I none (quoth she) nor anie *being*, ... *Ti.* 34
Of former *being* in this mortall hous, ... *Ti.* 354
being former foes, they wexed friends, ... *Col.* 851
Being in deed old Archimage, did stay . . . . I. vi. 48. 2
being on his way, approched neare . . . . II. viii. 3. 5
fetch their *being* from the sacred mould Of her immortall womb, ... III. iv. 11. 8
All things from thence doe their first *being* fetch, ... III. vi. 37. 1
gave him *being*, commune to them twayne: . . . . III. xii. 9. 4
inly *being* more then seeming sad: . . . . III. xii. 16. 4
this young man . . . *being* moov'd with pittie . . . . . . VI. ii. 23. 2
yet past a boy, And *being* now high time . . . . VI. ii. 32. 9
Being unarm'd and set in secret shade. . . . . VI. iii. 8. 5
Being unhable else alone to ride, ... VI. iii. 46. 3
All *beeing* with so bold attempt amazed, ... VII. vi. 13. 8
The rest which doe the world in *being* hold; . . . . VII. vii. 27. 3
Sommer, *being* dight In a thin silken cassock . . . . . . VII. vii. 29. 1
The sixt was August, *being* rich arrayd . . . . VII. vii. 37. 1
Time, who doth them all disseise Of *being*: . . . . VII. vii. 48. 4
the rule of all, all *being* rul'd by you.' . . . . VII. vii. 56. 9
yet, *being* rightly wayd, ... VII. vii. 58. 3
by their change their *being* do dilate, ... VII. vii. 58. 5
being caught, may craftily enfold . . . . *Am.* xxxvii. 7
Fondnesse it were for any, *being* free, ... *Am.* xxxvii. 13
Whome, *being* caught, she kills . . . . *Am.* xlvii. 7
The first my *being* to me gave by kind, ... *Am.* lxxiv. 5
Their *being* have, and dayly are increast . . . . *H.L.* 96
Who first to us our life and *being* gave, ... *H.H.L.* 191
Being-place. Before this worlds great frame, . . . found any *being-place*, ... *H.H.L.* 23
Be it. *Be it* by fortune, or by course of kinde, ... *Ro.* ix. 3
Be it where the yerely starre doth scortch . . . . *Ro.* xxvi. 7
in ought . . . repose assurance, *Be it* riches, ... *D.* 500
Bel-accoil. her salewd with seemely *bel-accoyle*, ... IV. vi. 25. 4
Belaid. jacket . . . Of Lincolne greene, *belayd* with silver lace; VI. ii. 5. 7
Belamour. Therein to shrowd her sumptuous *Belamoure*; . . . II. vi. 16. 7
her *Belamour*, the partner of his sheet: . . . . III. x. 22. 9
Whereof was Lord the good Sir *Bellamoure*; . . . . VI. xii. 3. 4
with secret wound Of love to *Bellamoure* empierced were, . . VI. xii. 4. 8
Bellamour againe so well her pleased . . . . VI. xii. 5. 1
Sir *Bellamour* . . . so with his keepers wrought, ... VI. xii. 6. 1
long continu'd Claribell a thrall, And *Bellamour* in bands; . VI. xii. 10. 2
For *Bellamour* knew Calidore right well, ... VI. xii. 11. 2
With thanks to *Bellamour* and Claribell, ... VI. xii. 13. 8
Belamours. snowy browes, like budded *Bellamoures*; . . . . *Am.* lxiv. 7
Belamy. fayre Critias, his dearest *Belamy*! . . . . II. vii. 52. 9
Belay. those small forts which ye were wont *belay*: . . . . *Am.* xiv. 6
Belch. Doth *belch* out flames, and rockes in peeces broke, . . I. xi. 44. 6
Belcheth. *belcheth* forth his superfluity, ... II. xii. 3. 8
Beldam. '*Beldame*, your words doe worke me litle ease; . . . III. ii. 43. 1
'*Beldame*, by that ye tell . . . . III. iii. 17. 4
'*Beldame*, be not wroth With silly Virgin, ... III. vii. 8. 6
welcom'd of that honest syre And of his aged *Beldame* . . . VI. ix. 17. 2
Belgard. Unto the Castle of *Belgard* her brought, ... VI. xii. 3. 3
Belgards. Working *belgardes* and amorous retrate; . . . . . II. iii. 25. 3
In speaking many false *belgardes* at her let fly. . . . . . III. ix. 52. 9
Ten thousand sweet *belgards*, ... *H.B.* 256
Belge. takes the enterprize For *Belgee* (**Belge*) for to fight: . V. x. Arg.
Her name was *Belgae*; . . . . V. x. 7. 1
came to this, where *Belge* then did dwell . . . . V. x. 11. 5
restore *Belge* unto her right. . . . . V. xi. Arg.
As by sad *Belge* seemes; . . . . V. xi. 1. 7
How that the Lady *Belge* now had found A Champion, . . . V. xi. 2. 2
Belge, with her sonnes, prostrated low . . . . V. xi. 16. 1
Belge selfe was therewith stonied sore, ... V. xi. 30. 3
went forth his gladnesse to partake With *Belge*, ... V. xi. 32. 8
There he with *Belgae* (**Belge*) did awhile remaine . . . . V. xi. 35. 1
Full loath to *Belgae* and to all the rest; . . . . V. xi. 35. 6
for like cause faire *Belge* did oppresse, ... V. xii. 2. 6
Belge's. Gerioneos Seneschall He slayes in *Belges* right. . . V. x. Arg.
Belgic. Whose warlike prowesse . . . Hath fild sad *Belgicke* . *Ded. Son.* xiv.10
Stretch her white rod over the *Belgicke* shore, ... III. iii. 49. 7
Belied. He wept, and wayld, and false laments *belyde*, . . . III. x. 7. 7
Belief. Full easy was for her to have *beliefe*, ... III. i. 54. 1
Believe. *beleeve* that anie thing could please Fell Cerberus, . . *Gn.* 439
Were but lost labour, that few would *beleeve*, ... *Ti.* 90
more foule . . . Then womans shape man would *beleeve* to bee. I. ii. 41. 4
Least thou of her *believe* too lightly blame, ... I. iv. 1. 5
Soone shalt thou see, and then *beleeve* for troth, ... II. viii. 22. 3
Did easely *beleeve* her strong extremitye. . . . . III. i. 53. 9
Thou that hast never lov'd canst not *beleeve* . . . . *H.L.* 257
beleeve me there is more then so, ... *H.B.* 85
Believed. I to much *beleeved* my shepherd peeres,) . . . . . *S.C.* D. 39

Believed—*Continued.*
of Giaunts, hard to be *beleeved;* . . . *Hub.* 31
all things to excuse, Though nought *belev'd,* . . . III. ix. 18. 9
made her famous, more then is *believed;* . . . V. iv. 33. 8
too well *believ'd* that which tofore Jealous suspect as true untruely drad: . . . V. vii. 38. 6
The knights *beleev'd* that all he sayd was trew; . . . VI. vii. 5. 1
Believing. the royall Beast forbore *beleeving,* . . . *Hub.* 1365
Belinus. Brennus and *Belinus,* kinges of Britany. . . . II. x. 40. 9
Belinus'. Gurgiunt, great *Belinus* (**Bellinus*) sonne, . . . II. x. 41. 1
Belive. All for he did his devoyr *belive!* . . . *S.C.* S. 227
downe to Plutoes house are come *bilive:* . . . I. v. 32. 3
Unto Old Timon he me brought *bylive;* . . . I. ix. 4. 1
saide then th' enchaunter *blive,* . . . II. iii. 18. 1
to those brethren sayd; 'Rise, rise *bylive,* . . . II. viii. 18. 1
The Prince and Guyon equally *bylive* Her selfe pursewd, . . . III. i. 18. 6
Forthwith themselves . . . they gan arme *bylive,* . . . III. v. 16. 2
will be made The vassall of the victors will *bylive:* . . . III. x. 10. 7
With dreadfull force he flies at her *bylive,* . . . V. iv. 42. 6
Bell. *See* **Larum-bell.**
a *bell,* which he left behind . . . *S.C.* May 288
With price whereof they buy a golden *bell,* . . . *Col.* 725
When one so oft a night did ring his matins *bell.* . . . III. x. 48. 9
Satyrane that day was judg'd to beare the *bell.* . . . IV. iv. 25. 9
she should surely beare the *bell* away; . . . IV. v. 13. 6
First rings his silver *Bell* t' each sleepy wight, . . . V. vi. 27. 3
Above all other lasses beare the *bell;* . . . VI. x. 26. 4
Bellamour. *See* **Belamour.**
Bellay. *Bellay,* first garland of free Poesie . . . *Ro.* Env. 1
Bellibone. proud that ever he begot Such a *Bellibone;* . . . *S.C.* Ap. 92
I saw the bouncing *Bellibone,* . . . *S.C.* Au. 61
Bellies. when my Gates shall han their *bellies* layd, . . . *S.C.* O. 119
Their *bellies* swolne he saw with fulnesse burst, . . . I. i. 26. 5
Bellisont. The second had to name Sir *Bellisont,* . . . V. iii. 5. 3
Bellman. the native *Belman* of the night, . . . V. vi. 27. 1
Bellodant. for the sake of *Bellodant* the bold, . . . V. iv. 30. 2
Bellona. With queint *Bellona* in her equipage! . . . *S.C.* O. 114
Like as *Bellona* . . . Hath loosd her helmet . . . III. ix. 22. 1
thought . . . *Bellona* in that warlike wise To them appear'd, . . . IV. i. 14. 6
drad *Bellona,* that doth sound on hie Warres . . . VII. vi. 3. 7
Bellona, whose great glory thou doost spight, . . . VII. vi. 32. 5
Bellowing. sownd, Which through the wood loud *bellowing* did rebownd, . . . I. vii. 7. 5
Bulles, . . . fill the fieldes with troublous *bellowing:* . . . I. viii. 11. 8
Breathing out wrath, and *bellowing* disdaine, . . . II. viii. 42. 6
an hideous *bellowing* Of many beasts, . . . II. xii. 39. 1
Bellows. blow the *bellowes* to his swelling vanity. . . . II. iii. 9. 9
One with great *bellowes* gathered filling ayre, . . . II. vii. 36. 1
An huge great payre of *bellowes,* . . . II. ix. 30. 4
eke the breathfull *bellowes* blew amaine, . . . IV. v. 38. 7
Sighes the *bellows* weare. . . . IV. v. 38. 9
threats his horns, and *bellowes* like the thonder: . . . VI. v. 19. 8
Bellows'. The *bellowes* noyse disturb'd his quiet rest, . . . IV. v. 41. 4
Bells. an Elephant, Adorn'd with *bells* and bosses . . . *Van.* viii. 2
bells, and babes, and glasses, in hys packe: . . . *S.C.* May 240
With *bells* and bosses that full lowdly rung, . . . *Hub.* 583
Whose bridle rung with golden *bels* and bosses brave. . . . I. ii. 13. 9
having filcht her *bells,* her up he cast . . . III. x. 35. 7
Like *belles* in greatnesse orderly succeed, . . . IV. v. 36. 8
freed From *bels* and jesses which did let her flight, . . . VI. iv. 19. 8
Ring ye the *bels,* ye yong men of the towne, . . . *Epith.* 261
Ring ye the *bels,* to make it weare away, . . . *Epith.* 274
Bell-wether. drive to follow after their *Belwether.'* . . . *Hub.* 296
Belly. leaning on (against[1]) the *belly* of a pot, . . . *Bel.* ix. 5
Upon her *bellie* th' antique Palatine, . . . *Ro.* iv. 10
With his great *bellie* spreds the dimmed world, . . . *Ro.* xx. 6
His *belly* was upblowne with luxury, . . . I. iv. 21. 3
hee . . . both from backe and *belly* still did spare, . . . I. iv. 28. 4
with timely fruit her *belly* sweld, And bore a boy . . . I. vi. 23. 3
Wondred to see her *belly* so upblone, . . . III. vi. 9. 8
Her tender sides; her *bellie* white and clere, . . . VI. viii. 42. 4
hunger . . . Had by the *belly* oft him pinched . . . VII. vii. 30. 5
Belly-ful. Poure not by cups, but by the *belly full,* . . . *Epith.* 251
Belong. *See* **Long.**
uppon all those Knights that did to her *belong.* . . . V. viii. 24. 9
Belonged. areed That unto him the horse *belong'd,* . . . V. iii. 35. 2
Belongs. To you th' inheritance *belonges* by right . . . I. iv. 48. 5
Beloved. *See* **Best-beloved, Dear-beloved.**
belov'd full faine Of her owne brother river, . . . *Col.* 116
Belov'd of high and low with faithfull harts. . . . *Col.* 531
Faire Florimell *belov'd* of many a knight, . . . III. v. 8. 8
To visite her *beloved* Paramoure, . . . IV. v. 5. 2
stolne away from her *beloved* mate, . . . IV. vi. 47. 7
of my lifes deare love *beloved* be: . . . IV. xii. 10. 3
Of both *beloved* well, but litle frended, . . . V. v. 57. 7
With her two sonnes, right deare of her *beloved,* . . . V. x. 39. 7
Calidore, *beloved* over-all, . . . VI. i. 2. 2
a faire Damzell, my *beloved* deare, . . . VI. i. 16. 2
Unworthy she to be *belov'd* so dere, . . . VI. vii. 29. 5
I was *belov'd* of many a gentle Knight, . . . VI. viii. 20. 5
Of her *beloved* Fanchin did obtaine, . . . VII. vi. 53. 5
Go to the bowre of my *beloved* love, . . . *Epith.* 23
know ech other here *belov'd* to bee. . . . *H.B.* 203
For love doth love the thing *belov'd* to see, . . . *H.H.L.* 118
whom God . . . lets his owne *Beloved* to behold; . . . *H.H.B.* 241
Below (*partial list*). He blusht to see another Sunne *belowe,* . . . *S.C.* Ap. 77
My seely sheepe like well *belowe,* . . . *S.C.* Jul. 105
The Lilly fresh, and Violet *belowe;* . . . *Gn.* 667
not with kissed hand *belowe* the knee, . . . *Hub.* 730
greatest god *below* the skye, . . . II. vii. 8. 2

Below—*Continued.*
which the sea *below* Had . . . devoured deepe, . . . III. iv. 22. 5
thrust downe to hell *below,* . . . III. iv. 55. 4
that young Squyre him reared from *below;* . . . III. ix. 16. 8
raised from *below* Out of the dwellings of the damned sprights, . . . IV. i. 19. 7
To enter in, or issue forth *below;* . . . IV. xii. 15. 4
entreat that iron man *below* To cease his outrage, . . . V. ii. 22. 5
She heard a wondrous noise *below* the hall: . . . V. vi. 27. 5
An hideous tempest seemed from *below* To rise . . . V. vii. 14. 2
if that any were on earth *belowe* That did . . . her molest, . . . VII. vi. 16. 5
Since thou hast seene her dreadfull power *belowe,* . . . VII. vi. 32. 6
Or from high hilles or from the dales *belowe,* . . . VII. vi. 39. 5
Whether those same on high, or these *belowe;* . . . VII. vii. 20. 2
show Some litle beames to mortall eyes *below* . . . *H.H.B.* 12
Beginning then *below,* with th' easie vew . . . *H.H.B.* 22
Belphoebe. to entertaine His fayre *Belphoebe,* . . . *Ti.* 525
Braggadocchio, . . . is of fayre *Belphoebe* fowle forlorne. . . . II. iii. Arg.
Or in *Belphoebe* fashioned to bee; . . . III. Pr. 5. 8
Belphebe findes him almost dead, . . . III. v. Arg.
Belphoebe was her name, as faire as Phoebus sunne. . . . III. v. 27. 9
As did *Belphoebe,* in the bloody place, . . . III. v. 37. 3
Which seeing fayre *Belphoebe* gan to feare, . . . III. v. 49. 1
this faire virgin, this *Belphebe* fayre; . . . III. v. 54. 2
birth of fayre *Belphoebe* and Of Amorett . . . III. vi. Arg.
to this faire *Belphoebe* in her berth . . . III. vi. 2. 1
She bore *Belphoebe;* . . . III. vi. 4. 4
of her selfe, her name *Belphoebe* red: . . . III. vi. 28. 5
Amoret rapt by greedie lust *Belphebe* saves from dread: . . . IV. vii. Arg.
Belphebe with her peares, The woody Nimphs, . . . IV. vii. 23. 5
Belphebe, raunging in that forrest wide, . . . IV. vii. 29. 2
mov'd *Belphebe* her no lesse to hate, . . . IV. vii. 34. 6
Which was by him *Belphebe* rightly rad. . . . IV. vii. 46. 5
who was that *Belphebe* he ne wist; . . . IV. vii. 46. 6
faire *Belphebe* had With one sterne looke so daunted, . . . IV. viii. 2. 2
all the bounty which *Belphebe* threw On him, . . . IV. viii. 6. 4
she came where wonned his *Belphebe* faire. . . . IV. viii. 8. 9
After that Timias had againe recured the favour of *Belphebe* . . . VI. v. 12. 2
Belt. Embost with buegle about the *belt:* . . . *S.C.* F. 66
by his *belt* his booke he hanging had: . . . I. i. 29. 4
girded with a *belt* of twisted brake: . . . II. xi. 22. 7
That glorious *belt* did in it selfe containe, . . . IV. v. 2. 8
brought with her from thence that goodly *belt* away. . . . IV. v. 5. 9
That goodly *belt* was Cestus hight by name, . . . IV. v. 6. 1
golden *belt* by doome of all Graunted to her, . . . IV. v. 16. 1
snatching from her hand halfe angrily The *belt* . . . IV. v. 19. 9
Artegall that golden *belt* uptooke, . . . V. iii. 27. 1
About their middles that faire *belt* to knit; . . . V. iii. 28. 2
With an embrodered *belt* of mickell pride; . . . V. v. 3. 5
by his side Under his *belt* he bore a sickle . . . VII. vii. 36. 9
Belts. Ygyrt with *belts* of glitterand gold, . . . *S.C.* Jul. 177
Belus. Great *Belus,* Phoeax, and Agenor best; . . . IV. xi. 15. 7
Beme. *See* **Beam.**
Bemoan. now these scorned fields *bemone* her fall, . . . *Ro.* xii. 13
care that any should *bemone* My hard mishap, . . . *D.* 75
will my case *bemone,* And pitie me . . . *D.* 382
each the other gan . . . privately *bemone.* . . . IV. i. 16. 4
to her selfe her sorrow did *bemone:* . . . IV. xii. 5. 5
He could no more but her great misery *bemone.* . . . IV. xii. 12. 9
Crying in vaine to her him to *bemone;* . . . VI. vi. 30. 5
to men, whose fall she did *bemone,* . . . VII. vi. 11. 5
Bemoaned. To be *bemoned* with compassion kinde, . . . *Ti.* 160
Bemoaning. still *bemoning* her unworthy paine. . . . IV. xii. 17. 5
Benches. The seates and *benches* shone as yvorie, . . . *Bel.* xii. 9
Bend. *See* **Bended.**
a fresh *bend* Of lovely Nymphs. . . . *S.C.* May 32
To this his minde and senses he doth *bend,* . . . *Gn.* 138
against the others bodie *bend* His cursed steele, . . . *Gn.* 412
daylie doth her changefull counsels *bend* . . . *D.* 153
Ne ever would to any byway *bend,* . . . I. i. 28. 4
Thether Duessa badd him *bend* his pace, . . . I. iv. 3. 7
pilgrimage To yonder same Hierusalem doe *bend,* . . . I. x. 61. 4
the haven . . . To which I meane my wearie course to *bend;* . . . I. xii. 1. 2
Thereto his subtile engins he does *bend,* . . . II. i. 3. 5
When I at her my murdrous blade did *bend,* . . . II. iv. 31. 7
cruell battry *bend* Gainst fort of Reason, . . . II. iv. 34. 7
Ne ever will it breake, ne ever *bend:* . . . II. viii. 21. 5
All those against that fort did *bend* their batteries. . . . II. xi. 10. 9
gan him selfe to second battaill *bend,* . . . II. xi. 35. 5
though she did *bend* Her earnest minde, . . . III. xi. 54. 8
deadly points at eithers breast to *bend,* . . . IV. ii. 14. 8
spies him toward *bend* His dreadfull souse, . . . IV. iii. 19. 5
Till evening that the Sunne gan downward *bend.* . . . IV. iv. 43. 6
myselfe did *bend* Him to recomfort . . . IV. viii. 57. 3
He should his flale to final execution *bend.* . . . V. viii. 29. 9
I, . . . *bend* my carelesse wit To salvage chace, . . . VI. ii. 9. 4
both at once with equall spight Did *bend* their speares, . . . VI. vii. 7. 5
But *bend* your force against your enemyes: . . . *Am.* xlix. 8
So doe I hope her stubborne hart to *bend,* . . . *Am.* li. 11
Bended. in his hand a *bended* bow was seene, . . . II. xi. 21. 1
Bender's. The Eugh, obedient to the *benders* will; . . . I. i. 9. 4
Bending. *Bending* her horned browes, did put her back; . . . VII. vi. 12. 6
Bending their force contrary to their face; . . . VII. vii. 35. 8
Bends. *bends* what ever power his aged yeares Him lent, . . . *Gn.* 646
Which to expresse he *bends* his gentle wit: . . . I. ii. 30. 5
All bard with golden *bendes,* . . . II. iii. 27. 4
All bard with double *bends,* . . . II. vii. 30. 3
Basted with *bends* of gold on every side, . . . V. v. 3. 2
to his will she *bends;* . . . V. x. 24. 8
Then to the rest his wrathfull hand he *bends;* . . . VI. viii. 49. 5
Nether to one her selfe nor other *bends.* . . . *Am.* lix. 12

Beneath. all things which *beneath* the Moone have being . . . *Ro.* ix. 10
levin, That seeldome falles *bynethe*. . . . *S.C.* Jul. 92
All pav'd *beneath* with Jaspar shining bright, . . . II. xii. 62. 8
placed high above Or low *beneath*, . . . VI. ii. 1. 6
(not pleasd in mortall things *Beneath* the Moone to raigne) . VII. vi. Arg.
all the world *beneath* for terror quooke, . . . VII. vi. 30. 8
faulcon . . . That flags awhile her fluttering wings *beneath*, . *H.H.B.* 27
Benefice. How to a *Benefice* he might aspire? . . . *Hub.* 482
These lookes (nought saying) doo a *benefice* seeke, . . . *Hub.* 500
So maist thou chaunce mock out a *Benefice*, . . . *Hub.* 509
T' accept a *Benefice* in peeces riven. . . . *Hub.* 540
they a *Benefice* twixt them obtained; . . . *Hub.* 555
Benefices. He crammed them with crumbs of *Benefices*, . . . *Hub.* 1153
Beneficial. How to obtaine a *Beneficiall*. . . . *Hub.* 486
Benefit. either for some gainfull *benefit*, . . . *Hub.* 639
In hope by him great *benefite* to gaine, . . . V. ii. 33. 4
Benempt. he That is so oft *bynempt?* . . . *S.C.* Jul. 214
Kidde or Cosset, which I thee *bynempt*. . . . *S.C.* N. 46
Bynempt a sacred vow, which none should ay releace. . . . II. i. 60. 9
Benevolence. The Courtier needes must recompenced bee With
a *Benevolence*, . . . *Hub.* 517
with sweet love and sure *benevolence*, . . . V. v. 33. 4
Benign. unto all his creatures so *benigne*, . . . IV. i. 30. 4
Of her faire light and bounty most *benigne*, . . . VII. vi. 11. 8
Benombd. *See* **Benumbed.**
Bent. *See* **Bow-bent.**
Had all the world in armes against her *bent*, . . . *Ro.* xxi. 6
His hornes bene as broade as Rainebowe *bent*, . . . *S.C.* F. 73
To nought more, Thenot, my mind is *bent* . . . *S.C.* F. 94
to the roote *bent* his sturdy stroake, . . . *S.C.* F. 201
I *bent* my bolt against the bush, . . . *S.C.* Mar. 70
silver bowe, . . . Which lightly he *bent* at me: . . . *S.C.* Mar. 84
For naught caren that bene so lewdly *bent*. . . . *S.C.* Ap. 157
All for they nould be buxome and *bent*. . . . *S.C.* S. 149
ybent to song and musicks mirth, . . . *S.C.* D. 40
frogs . . . their jarring voyces *bent*, . . . *Gn.* 230
inconstant fortune, *bent* to ill, . . . *Gn.* 247
fervent eyes to his destruction *bent*. . . . *Gn.* 296
stifly *bent* his vowed life to spill . . . *Gn.* 603
'that thou are *bent* To die alone, . . . *D.* 78
Yet I her fram'd, and wan so to my *bent*, . . . *D.* 124
Which way his course the wanton Bregog *bent*; . . . *Col.* 135
Thereto our ship her course directly *bent*, . . . *Col.* 268
there is sad Alcyon *bent* to mourne, . . . *Col.* 384
To menage of most grave affaires is *bent*, . . . *Ded. Son.* ix. 2
to the ground his eyes were lowly *bent*, . . . I. i. 29. 6
bent his speare, and spurd his horse with yron heele. . . . I. iii. 34. 9
O! who does know the *bent* of womens fantasy? . . . I. iv. 24. 9
Their backward *bent* knees teach her humbly to obay. . . . I. vi. 11. 9
bent his enimy to quell, . . . I. vi. 43. 3
To wreake the guilt of mortall sins is *bent*, . . . I. viii. 9. 2
dearely sure her love was to me *bent*, . . . I. ix. 14. 3
ever up to heven, . . . Her stedfast eyes were *bent*, . . . I. x. 14. 9
With folded hands, and knees full lowly *bent*, . . . I. xi. 32. 6
Themselves to ground with gracious humblesse *bent*, . . . I. xii. 8. 3
On the long voiage whereto she is *bent*: . . . I. xii. 42. 8
sword Against her snowy brest he fiercely *bent*, . . . II. i. 11. 7
hid her visage, and her head downe *bent*, . . . II. i. 15. 7
For Gods deare love be not so wilfull *bent*, . . . II. i. 16. 2
cursed steele against that badge I *bent*, . . . II. i. 27. 5
with *bent* lowring browes, . . . II. ii. 35. 7
her Javelin bright Against him *bent*, . . . II. iii. 42. 8
to his brest his bever *bent*. . . . II. v. 6. 9
bent to wreake on him The wrath . . . II. vi. 2. 2
full *bent* To prove extremities of bloody fight, . . . II. vi. 36. 1
bent his hastie course towardes the ydle flood. . . . II. vi. 41. 9
to a stedfast starre his course hath *bent*, . . . II. vii. 1. 2
Both fiercely *bent* to have him disaraid; . . . II. viii. 17. 3
his balefull speare he fiercely *bent* . . . II. viii. 32. 1
Bent hollow beetle browes, . . . II. ix. 52. 6
gainst the Romanes *bent* their proper powre; . . . II. x. 57. 6
Owles, with beckes uncomely *bent*; . . . II. xi. 8. 3
Their wicked engins they against it *bent*; . . . II. xi. 9. 6
that fourth band which cruell battry *bent* . . . II. xi. 12. 1
his mischievous bow full readie *bent*, . . . II. xi. 24. 4
bent his dreadful speare against the others head. . . . III. i. 5. 9
she saw him *bent* to cruell play, . . . III. i. 37. 3
faire Malecasta *bent* Her crafty engins . . . III. i. 57. 4
though my love be not so lewdly *bent* . . . III. ii. 43. 2
So beene they three three sondry wayes *ybent*; . . . III. iv. 47. 5
more *bent* to eke my smartes . . . III. vii. 55. 7
His bloody speare eftesoones he boldly *bent* . . . III. viii. 12. 5
As if he were on some adventure *bent*, . . . III. viii. 44. 8
The Boaster at him sternely *bent* his browe, . . . III. x. 24. 1
Gainst whom he alwayes *bent* a brasen shield, . . . III. xii. 12. 8
All *bent* to mirth before the bride was bedded, . . . IV. i. 3. 5
as *bent* to charge them new: . . . IV. i. 38. 6
seeing both *bent* to so bloudy games, . . . IV. ii. 20. 4
Yet one, of many, was so strongly *bent* By Priamond, . . . IV. iii. 8. 1
both were *bent* t' avenge his usage base, . . . IV. iv. 4. 7
A mightie speare eftsoones at him he *bent*; . . . IV. iv. 28. 6
he to fell reveng was fully *bent*: . . . IV. v. 30. 9
Bent to revenge on blamelesse Britomart The crime . . . IV. v. 31. 1
Full busily unto his worke *ybent*; . . . IV. v. 34. 2
he was full *bent* to some mischievous deede. . . . IV. vi. 2. 9
went Forth on his way to which he was *ybent*; . . . IV. vi. 44. 5
With bow in hand and arrowes ready *bent*, . . . IV. vii. 29. 6
'Then have they all themselves against me *bent*: . . . IV. viii. 16. 4
I, that was not *bent* to former love . . . IV. viii. 60. 1
Him selfe he *bent* their furies to abate, . . . IV. ix. 34. 6

Bent—*Continued.*
th' other backeward *bent*, . . . IV. x. 12. 4
In hope thereby her to his *bent* to draw: . . . IV. xi. 2. 6
bent against them selves their cruell hands; . . . V. iv. 5. 7
fully *bent* her That battells utmost triall to adventer. . . . V. v. 5. 4
right fully *bent* To fierce avengement . . . V. vi. 18. 6
rather *bent* To peace then needlesse trouble to constraine, . . V. vi. 19. 6
Unto the land of Amazons, as she was *bent*. . . . V. vii. 24. 9
ever as she rode her eye was backeward *bent*. . . . V. viii. 4. 9
So both together, ylike felly *bent*, Like fiercely met. . . . V. viii. 7. 5
For zeale of Justice, was against her *bent*: . . . V. ix. 49. 5
Hastily *bent* that enterprise to heare, . . . V. x. 15. 4
As three great Culverings for battrie *bent*, . . . V. x. 34. 6
Gainst whom my selfe I long in vaine have *bent* . . . V. xi. 51. 3
Upon our way to which we weren *bent*, . . . VI. ii. 16. 2
As *bent* to some malicious enterprise, . . . VI. iii. 48. 3
face to face against him *bent*: . . . VI. v. 20. 8
Bull . . . busie *bent* To fight with many foes . . . VI. vi. 27. 4
was *bent* her to abuse; . . . VI. vii. 40. 7
smote him on the knee that never yet was *bent*. . . . VI. viii. 15. 9
It never yet was *bent*, ne *bent* it now, . . . VI. viii. 16. 1
On which his hungry eye was alwayes *bent*; . . . VI. ix. 26. 7
sturdy March, with brows full sternly *bent* . . . VII. vii. 32. 3
Bents. No more then for the stroke of strawes or *bents*: . . . VI. iv. 4. 7
Benumbed. hath the Crampe thy joynts *benomd* . . . *S.C.* Au. 4
A stonie coldnesse hath *benumbd* the sence . . . *T.M.* 253
sences all were straight *benumbd* and starke. . . . I. i. 44. 5
with the frosen cold *Benumbd* so inly, . . . III. viii. 34. 8
His powrelesse arme, *benumbd* with secret feare, . . . IV. vi. 21. 3
Benumbs. deadly pallied hew *Benumbes* her cheekes: . . . VI. viii. 40. 7
Bequeath. Did equally *bequeath* his lands in fee, . . . V. iv. 7. 4
Bequeathed. Forgoe that royal maides *bequeathed* care, . . . I. x. 63. 7
As she *bequeathd* in her last testament; . . . II. ii. 10. 6
The which the Faery Queene had long afore *Bequeath'd* to
him, . . . VI. xii. 12. 5
Bequeathing. 'Them therefore as *bequeathing* to the winde, . *Gn.* 633
Bequest. Amoret, whom Fortune by *bequest* Had left . . . IV. ix. 17. 7
Which in his last *bequest* he to us spake, . . . *H.H.L.* 207
Beraft. *See* **Bereft.**
Bere. *See* **Bier.**
Bereave. Seemeth thou dost their soule of sence *bereave*; . . *S.C.* O. 27
Bereave of sence each rash beholders sight. . . . *Col.* 547
Her swollen hart her speech seemd to *bereave*, . . . I. i. 52. 3
thou didst these goods *bereave* From rightfull owner . . . II. vii. 19. 3
vengeaunce utterly the guilt *bereave*: . . . II. viii. 29. 5
she might his wretched life *bereave*. . . . V. v. 37. 5
no new loves impression ever could *Bereave* it thence: . . . V. vi. 2. 9
Thus to *bereave* thy loves deare sight from thee: . . . VI. x. 29. 5
it doth *bereave* Their soule of sense, . . . *H.H.B.* 257
Bereaved. the shrill woods, which were of sense *bereav'd*, . . *Gn.* 455
had the use of his right arme *bereaved*. . . . *Hub.* 208
all my senses were *bereaved* quight, . . . *Ti.* 577
all my senses were *bereaved* quight: . . . I. ii. 42. 5
Ne ought he car'd whom he . . . *bereav'd* of right: . . . II. ii. 18. 8
bereav'd the rash beholders sight: . . . II. iii. 23. 5
To war on those which him had of his realme *bereav'd*. . . . II. x. 31. 9
made more haste the life to have *bereav'd*; . . . III. v. 28. 8
They were through wonder nigh of sence *berev'd*, . . . III. vi. 27. 5
Right sorrowfully mourning her *bereaved* cares. . . . IV. xii. 17. 9
gan inquire how was that steed *bereaved*, . . . V. iii. 30. 8
Thinking to have her griefe by death *bereaved*: . . . V. v. 10. 4
all she sought was mens good name to have *bereaved*. . . . V. xii. 33. 9
Berecynthian. Such as the *Berecynthian* Goddesse bright, . . *Ro.* vi. 1
Bereft. of their tailes are utterlie *bereft*. . . . *Hub.* 1384
he that is of reasons skill *bereft*, . . . *T.M.* 139
th' ornaments of wisdome are *bereft?* . . . *T.M.* 489
Bereft of both by Fates unjust decreeing. . . . *Ti.* 35
So all my senses from me are *bereft*. . . . *D.* 420
all his sences seemd *berefte* attone: . . . II. i. 42. 4
thousand women of their love *beraft*, . . . IV. ii. 10. 5
She ran in hast his life to have *bereft*; . . . IV. vii. 32. 2
each one of sence *bereft* Fled fast into the towne, . . . V. vii. 34. 8
Hath you thus long away from me *bereft?* . . . VI. v. 23. 8
In yron chaines of liberty *bereft*, . . . VI. viii. 1. 4
That so rich frute should be from us *bereft*; . . . VI. ix. 1. 7
thence all goodnesse he *bereft*, . . . VI. xii. 23. 5
Beres. *See* **Bears.**
Berobbed. That of your selfe ye thus *berobbed* arre, . . . I. viii. 42. 8
an enraged cow That is *berobbed* of her youngling dere, . . . V. viii. 46. 2
Berries. scarlot *berries* in Sommer time? . . . *S.C.* F. 168
A fruitfull Olyve tree, with *berries* spredd, . . . *Mui.* 326
Berth. *See* **Birth.**
Bescattered. Unto her waste, with flowres *bescattered*, . . . IV. xi. 46. 2
Bescratched. was *bescracht* and both his feet nigh lame. . . III. v. 3. 9
Beseech. 'I thee *beseche* . . . Hearken awhile, . . . *S.C.* D. 13
Mote I *beseech* to succour his sad plight, . . . II. viii. 25. 7
those Knights he humbly did *beseech* To stay their hands, . . IV. ii. 21. 1
Beseeching. *Beseeching* him with prayer and with praise, . . I. v. 41. 6
Beseek. By all that unto them was deare, did them *beseeke*. . IV. iii. 47. 9
lodging did for her *beseeke*. . . . VI. iii. 37. 9
Beseem. Well mought it *beseme* any harvest Queene. . . . *S.C.* Au. 36
howe ill did him *beseme* . . . II. vi. 27. 4
Mote Princes place *be seeme* so deckt to bee. . . . III. i. 33. 4
As meetest may *beseeme* a noble mayd: . . . III. v. 5. 3
Take here your owne, that doth you best *beseeme*, . . . V. i. 28. 7
Ne better doth *beseeme* brave chevalry, . . . V. ii. 1. 2
right well Did her *beseeme*: . . . VI. x. 14. 6
Beseemed. His reverend heares . . . The knight much honord,
as *beseemed* well; . . . I. viii. 32. 2
Was clad in blew, that her *beseemed* well; . . . I. x. 14. 2

Beseemed—*Continued.*
faire them quites, as him *beseemed* best, . . . I. x. 15. 8
beseemed it To be the shield of some redoubted knight; . . . II. iv. 38. 5
They did obeysaunce, as *beseemed* right, . . . II. ix. 26. 7
as *beseemed* best, Her entertaynd: . . . III. i. 55. 5
him saluting as *beseemed* best, . . . III. viii. 45. 7
Which . . . he wore, as him *beseemed* well. . . . IV. ii. 25. 9
somewhat redder then *beseem'd* aright, . . . IV. vi. 19. 8
foure of them the battell best *beseemed*, . . . IV. ix. 20. 4
they received were . . . as them *beseemed* best; . . . V. vi. 22. 7
Beseemeth. So well his golden Circlet him *beseemeth*. . . . *Hub.* 627
They to him hearken, as *beseemeth* meete, . . . II. xii. 14. 1
Call me the Squyre of Dames; that me *beseemeth* well. . . . III. vii. 51. 9
well *beseemeth* that in Princes hall . . . VI. i. 1. 3
Beseeming. him salute with well *beseeming* glee; . . . I. x. 15. 7
to a courage great It is no lesse *beseeming* . . . V. v. 38. 2
With stayed steps and grave *beseeming* grace: . . . VI. v. 36. 5
Beseeming well the bower of anie Queene, . . . *Proth.* 170
Beseems. well *beseemes* all knights of noble name, . . . I. x. 59. 4
That ill *beseemes* thee, such as I thee see, . . . II. v. 17. 6
What ever bee the cause, it sure *beseemes* you ill.' . . . II. ix. 37. 9
Him ill *beseemes* anothers fault to name, . . . II. ix. 38. 4
It ill *beseemes* a knight of gentle sort, . . . III. ii. 12. 6
ill *beseemes* it to upbrayd A dolefull heart . . . III. vi. 21. 7
'Her well *beseemes* that Quest,' . . . III. vii. 53. 1
in vertue that *beseemes* her well . . . VI. x. 26. 5
So well it her *beseemes*, . . . *Epith.* 152
Beseen. *See* **Gay-beseen, Well-beseen.**
As tokens of her thankefull mind *beseene*, . . . V. x. 17. 3
Of costly Ivory full rich *beseene*, . . . V. x. 28. 3
Deckt with greene boughes and flowers gay *beseene*: . . . VI. v. 38. 5
such joyance hath thee well *beseene*. . . . VII. vii. 11. 9
That goodly Idoll, now so gay *beseene*, . . . *Am.* xxvii. 5
Beset. *See* **Ill-beset.**
Of that strong stownd which him so sore *beset*. . . . *D.* 560
him *beset* With strokes of mortall steele . . . II. ii. 22. 2
there so hard *besett*: . . . III. i. 8. 5
sore *beset* on every side arownd, . . . III. i. 21. 2
Beside (*partial list*). *See* **Therebeside.**
Beside the fruitfull shore of muddie Nile, . . . *Van.* iii. 1
thou art *beside* thy wit, . . . *S.C.* May 306
Beside a learned well. . . . *S.C.* Jul. 48
Besyde, . . . There is a hyllye place, . . . *S.C.* Jun. 57
The gentle shepheard satte *beside* a springe, . . . *S.C.* D. 1
you *beside* the honourable band . . . *Gn.* 479
'Neighbour Ape, and my Gossip eke *beside*, . . . *Hub.* 53
Beside, we may have lying by our sides . . . *Hub.* 475
Without a gowned beast him fast *beside*, . . . *Hub.* 749
His Crowne and Scepter lying him *beside*, . . . *Hub.* 953
a thousand deathes, and shame *beside?*' . . . *Hub.* 976
Beside the silver Springs of Helicone, . . . *T.M.* 5
Some few *beside* . . . *T.M.* 583
beside the shore Of silver streaming Thamesis . . . *Ti.* 1
The Harpe well knowne *beside* the Northern Beare. . . . *Ti.* 616
He, sitting me *beside* . . . *Col.* 68
At sea, *beside* a thousand moe at land: . . . *Col.* 261
Ladie rode him faire *beside*, . . . I. i. 4. 1
wayting her *besyde*; . . . I. iii. 26. 2
him *beside* rides fierce revenging Wrath, . . . I. iv. 33. 1
them *besyde*, Forth ryding . . . I. v. 53. 6
there *beside* . . . was built An Altare, . . . I. viii. 36. 1
There grew a goodly tree him faire *beside*, . . . I. xi. 46. 1
early foe awaiting him *beside* . . . I. xi. 52. 4
He left his steed without, and speare *besyde*, . . . II. iii. 3. 8
fast *beside* there trickled softly downe . . . II. v. 30. 1
her sweete selfe . . . She sett *beside*, . . . II. vi. 14. 6
fast *beside* him sat tumultuous Strife: . . . II. vii. 21. 6
him *beside* an aged Squire there rode, . . . III. i. 4. 3
whome hee lately brake *Beside* Cayr Verolame . . . III. iii. 52. 8
Beside those armes there stood a mightie speare, . . . III. iii. 60. 1
Her bow and gilden quiver lying him *beside*. . . . III. v. 34. 9
Beside the same a dainty place there lay, . . . III. v. 40. 1
Sitting *beside* a fountaine in a rew; . . . III. vi. 17. 4
Satyrane his chaunce Was her before, and Paridell *beside*; . . . III. ix. 27. 2
cast himselfe on ground her fast *besyde*: . . . III. x. 7. 5
him *beside* marcht amorous Desyre, . . . III. xii. 9. 1
Together with this Hag *beside* her set, . . . IV. iv. 9. 6
And fast *beside* a little brooke did pas . . . IV. v. 33. 3
Sitting in shade *beside* his grazing steede; . . . IV. vi. 2. 6
Upon a day as she him sate *beside*, . . . IV. viii. 6. 1
those two other, which *beside* them stoode, . . . IV. ix. 22. 1
An headlesse Ladie lying him *beside* . . . V. i. 14. 3
With golden hands and silver feete *beside*, . . . V. ii. 10. 2
But Artegall was better breath'd *beside*, . . . V. ii. 17. 5
Like the true saint *beside* the image set, . . . V. iii. 24. 2
them *beside* two seemely damzells stood, . . . V. iv. 4. 6
wound his enemy Behinde, *beside*, before, . . . V. xi. 6. 9
And them *beside* a Ladie faire he saw . . . VI. ii. 4. 1
beside him sate . . . His wofull Ladie, . . . VI. ii. 41. 1
on his steede her did sustaine . . . soft footing her *beside*; . . . VI. iii. 28. 6
Sitting *beside* his Ladie there at ease, . . . VI. vi. 40. 2
is slaine; and him *beside* His aged wife, . . . VI. xi. 18. 4
'Yet mauger Jove, and all his gods *beside*, . . . VII. vii. 17. 1
Yet many wondrous things there are *beside*: . . . *Am.* xvii. 8
Besides. their holie things to say, . . . *besides* their Anthemes *Hub.* 451
Besides, he could doo manie other poynts, . . . *Hub.* 696
Besides, he usde another slipprie slight, . . . *Hub.* 859
Besides all this, . . . *Hub.* 877
Besides the infinite extortions, . . . *Hub.* 1311
Besides, in hunting such felicitie, . . . he found, . . . *As.* 79

Besides—*Continued.*
And then, *besides*, those little streames . . . *Col.* 141
Besides her peerlesse skill . . . *Col.* 188
Besides an hundred Nymphs . . . *Col.* 256
Besides most goodly rivers there appeare, . . . *Col.* 300
Besides yet many mo . . . *Col.* 576
Besides the endlesse routes . . . I. v. 51. 1
Besides them both, . . . The dead corse . . . II. i. 41. 1
Besides he feard her wrath, . . . II. iii. 43. 4
Besides subjected France and Germany, . . . II. x. 40. 6
them unwares *besides* the Severne did enclose. . . . II. x. 54. 9
Besides all hope, . . . III. v. 30. 4
Besides, her golden girdle, which did fall . . . III. vii. 31. 8
Besides, . . . I found her golden girdle . . . III. viii. 49. 7
Besides the huge massacres, which he wrought . . . III. xi. 29. 8
Besides her modest countenance he saw . . . IV. vi. 33. 4
Besides ten thousand monsters . . . IV. xi. 3. 8
besides, three thousand more there were . . . IV. xi. 52. 6
Besides the rest dismayd, . . . V. v. 19. 7
Besides, a thousand more of such as sings Hymns . . . V. ix. 29. 4
Besides the double strength which in them was: . . . V. xi. 6. 3
Besides, unto themselves they gotten had A monster, . . . V. xii. 37. 6
Besides the great dishonour and defame, . . . VI. ix. 1. 8
Besides, for recompence hereof I shall You well reward, . . . VI. ix. 32. 5
Besides a thousand more . . . VI. x. 21. 7
Besides, through sicknesse now so wan and weake, . . . VI. xi. 12. 7
Besides the losse of so much loos . . . VI. xii. 12. 8
Besides, her countenaunce and her likely hew, . . . VI. xii. 18. 7
now no place *besides* unsought had left, . . . VI. xii. 23. 7
Besides, her face and countenance . . . We changed see . . . VII. vii. 50. 6
Besides, that power and vertue which ye spake, . . . VII. vii. 54. 4
'*Besides*, the sundry motions of your Spheares, . . . VII. vii. 55. 1
Besiege. The enimies of Temperaunce *Besiege* her dwelling place: II. xi. Arg.
doe that sence *besiege* with light illusions. . . . II. xi. 11. 9
Besieged. He has them now fowr years *besiegd* to make them thrall. . . . I. vii. 44. 9
The house of Temperance, . . . *Besiegd* of many foes, . . . II. ix. Arg.
Seven yeares this wize they us *besieged* have, . . . II. ix. 12. 8
Besit. *Which so to doe may thee right well *besit*, . . . *Ded. Son.* iii. 5
Besits. 'Me ill *besits*, . . . II. vii. 10. 1
Besitting. that which is for Ladies most *besitting*, . . . IV. ii. 19. 1
Besmear. With wicked herbes and oyntments did *besmeare* My body . . . I. ii. 42. 3
Besmeared. *Besmeard* with pretious Balme, . . . I. xi. 50. 5
Besmeard with smoke that nigh his eye-sight blent; . . . IV. v. 34. 7
Besought. That shepheard I *besought* to me to tell, . . . *Col.* 229
Of that old woman tidings he *besought*, . . . I. iii. 24. 8
Who, all in rage, his Sea-god syre *besought* . . . I. v. 38. 1
Una faire *besought* That straunger knight his name . . . tell; . I. ix. 2. 6
fayrely eke *besought* Himselfe to chearish, . . . I. x. 29. 4
Una her *besought*, . . . to schoole her knight, . . . I. x. 32. 5
Her deare *besought* to let her die a mayd. . . . II. ii. 8. 5
Besought them . . . Their deadly cruell discord to forbeare, . II. ii. 27. 5
She them *besought*, during their quiet treague, . . . II. ii. 33. 3
She Guyon deare *besought* of curtesie To tell . . . II. ii. 39. 4
him *besought*, . . . to counsell me the best: . . . II. iv. 23. 6
Besought that Damzell suffer him depart, . . . II. vi. 36. 8
great Mammon fayrely he *besought* . . . II. vii. 65. 8
Archimage *besought*, him that afford Which . . . II. viii. 19. 3
They her *besought* of favour speciall . . . II. ix. 20. 7
them *besought* To thinke . . . II. x. 77. 6
besought The Prince of grace to let him ronne that turne. . III. i. 5. 1
her *besought*, well as they might, . . . III. i. 30. 7
there with many gentle termes her faire *besought*. . . . III. viii. 35. 9
Another knight, . . . late entrance deare *besought*: . . . III. ix. 12. 4
Besought them humbly him to beare withall, . . . III. ix. 18. 5
besought Them go to rest. . . . III. ix. 53. 8
Besought him his great corage to appease, . . . III. x. 30. 8
her *besought* To graunt her boone, . . . IV. ii. 50. 1
pardon her *besought* his errour frayle, . . . IV. vi. 22. 6
Then her *besought*, as she to her was deare, . . . IV. vi. 25. 6
She deare *besought* the Prince of remedie; . . . IV. viii. 64. 7
Besought her to graunt ease unto my smart, . . . IV. x. 48. 4
'She often prayd, and often me *besought*, . . . IV. x. 57. 1
Whom she *besought* to find some remedie, . . . IV. xi. 6. 7
she came, and him *besought*, . . . IV. xii. 24. 6
She her *besought* of gratious redresse. . . . V. i. 4. 4
rather of his hand *besought* to die. . . . V. i. 18. 4
him faire *besought*; . . . V. ii. 22. 6
her *besought* to take it well in gree, . . . V. vi. 21. 7
Ne doffe her armes, though he her much *besought*: . . . V. vi. 23. 5
earnestly *besought* to wend that day With her, . . . V. ix. 3. 8
To make abode that night he greatly was *besought*. . . . VI. iii. 2. 9
He him by all the bands of love *besought*, . . . VI. iii. 15. 6
he *besought* him downe by him to sit, . . . VI. iii. 22. 3
Whom Calepine . . . *Besought* of courtesie, . . . VI. iii. 31. 2
often him *besought*, and prayd, and vowd, . . . VI. vi. 31. 7
to tell him courteously *besought*, . . . VI. ix. 5. 8
him *besought* himselfe to disattyre, . . . VI. ix. 17. 3
Bespake. What ever that good old man *bespake*. . . . *S.C.* F. 97
I him *bespake* againe; . . . *D.* 173
Calling to me (ay me!) this wise *bespake*; . . . *D.* 262
him thus atweene *bespake*: . . . *Col.* 81
him Thestylis *bespake*; . . . *Col.* 156
So having said, Aglaura him *bespake*: . . . *Col.* 584
doubting much his sence, he thus *bespake*: . . . I. ii. 32. 4
he her comforted, and faire *bespake*: . . . I. vii. 52. 2
with sweet joyous cheare him thus *bespake*: . . . I. viii. 26. 6
Him yett againe, . . . *bespake* The gentle knight; . . . I. ix. 24. 6
in her modest maner thus *bespake*: . . . I. xi. 1. 6

Bespake—*Continued.*
them approching, thus the knight *bespake;* . . . II. i. 8. 6
Till her that Squyre *bespake:* . . . II. i. 16. 1
thus fayre *bespake;* . . . II. ii. 5. 2
him spying thus *bespake:* . . . II. iii. 32. 6
him thus *bespake* their soveraine Lord and syre; . . . II. vii. 37. 9
roughly him *bespake:* . . . II. vii. 63. 6
That sire he fowl *bespake:* . . . II. viii. 12. 2
Till Alma him *bespake:* . . . II. ix. 43. 6
them the wary Boteman thus *bespake:* . . . II. xii. 17. 5
at last she thus *bespake.* . . . III. ii. 42. 9
at length him thus *bespake:* . . . III. iii. 43. 4
Conceiv'd a bold devise, and thus *bespake:* . . . III. iii. 52. 2
The knight, approching, sternely her *bespake:* . . . III. iv. 14. 4
gazing each on other nought *bespake.* . . . III. vi. 27. 6
trembling yet through feare the Squire *bespake:* . . . III. vii. 47. 1
Forthy he thus to Paridel *bespake:* . . . IV. i. 40. 1
Sir Blandamour, . . . thus fiercely him *bespake:* . . . IV. ii. 25. 2
charging him afresh thus felly him *bespake.* . . . IV. iii. 10. 9
Yet nigh approching he them fowle *bespake,* . . . IV. iv. 4. 1
Him (*he) thus *bespake:* 'Certes, Sir Artegall, . . . IV. vi. 28. 6
Her thus *bespake:* 'But, Sir, without offence . . . IV. vi. 34. 5
being mov'd with ruth she thus *bespake:* . . . IV. viii. 14. 6
sighing inly deepe, her thus *bespake:* . . . IV. viii. 16. 3
Then good Sir Claribell him thus *bespake:* . . . IV. ix. 40. 1
Where that same Damzell lowdly him *bespake,* . . . V. iv. 50. 8
To her *bespake:* 'Sir Knight, it seemes to me . . . V. vii. 18. 6
Him thus *bespake:* . . . V. xi. 16. 4
Whom Calidore . . . At length *bespake;* . . . VI. ii. 7. 2
Which when as he perceiv'd he thus *bespake:* . . . VI. ii. 47. 6
Him thus *bespake:* . . . VI. v. 23. 5
with reprochfull words him thus *bespake* on hight. . . . VI. vi. 24. 9
did thrust it farre away, And thus *bespake:* . . . VI. ix. 33. 3
Until that Jove himselfe her selfe *bespake:* . . . VII. vi. 25. 6
having pauz'd awhile, Jove thus *bespake:* . . . VII. vi. 29. 1

Bespoke. he nought could say, Till him the childe *bespoke;* II. viii. 7. 3
turning to those brethren, thus *bespoke:* . . . II. viii. 27. 1
faire *bespoke* with words, . . . VI. xi. 35. 9

Bespotted. tayle, . . . *Bespotted* as with shieldes of red and blacke, . . . I. xi. 11. 5

Bespread. all the floore was . . . *Bespredd* with costly scarlott I. xii. 13. 8
Faire Helenore with girlonds all *bespredd,* . . . III. x. 44. 5

Besprent. now morne with teares *besprint;* . . . *S.C.* N. 111
My head *besprent* with hoary frost I fynd, . . . *S.C.* D. 135

Besprinkled. armour all with blood *besprincled* was; . . . II. i. 41. 3
besprinckled was throughout With golden aygulets, . . . II. iii. 26. 6
Hogh, *besprincled* with the gore Of mighty Goemot, . . . II. x. 10. 7
otherwhiles, with gold *besprinkeled,* . . . II. xii. 45. 8
besprinckled all the grassy greene: . . . III. v. 28. 5
were with sweet Ambrosia all *besprinckled* light. . . . III. vi. 18. 9
Betwixt his bloodie jawes, *besprinckled* all with gore. . . . VI. iv. 17. 9

Besprint. *See* **Besprent.**

Best. Since of all workmen helde in reckning *best;* . . . *Ro.* xxvii. 7
nor for his *best,* Open the dore . . . *S.C.* May 225
I hold it *best* for us home to hye. . . . *S.C.* May 317
in fields where falls hem *best.* . . . *S.C.* Jun. 76
Shepheards they weren of the *best,* . . . *S.C.* Jul. 121
Whilom thou was peregall to the *best,* . . . *S.C.* Au. 8
Little lacketh Perigot of the *best,* . . . *S.C.* Au. 126
Badde is the *best;* . . . *S.C.* S. 105
Mought needes decay, when it is at *best.* . . . *S.C.* S. 241
the worthy whome shee loveth *best,* . . . *S.C.* O. 47
thy due meede that thou deservest *best,* . . . *Gn.* 60
feede abroad where pasture *best* befalls. . . . *Gn.* 72
Where breathe on them the whistling wind mote *best;* . . . *Gn.* 236
Abides in highest place above the *best,* . . . *Gn.* 614
What course ye weene is *best* for us to take, . . . *Hub.* 115
Beggers life is *best;* . . . *Hub.* 180
they, that thinke themselves the *best* of all, . . . *Hub.* 181
We may seeke favour of the *best* of all?' . . . *Hub.* 618
brave beasts she loveth *best* to see . . . *Hub.* 629
the *best* speaches with ill meaning spill, . . . *Hub.* 716
thereof gathers for himselfe the *best.* . . . *Hub.* 726
the *best* helpe, which chiefly him sustain'd, . . . *Hub.* 853
Twixt *best* and worst, when both alike are dedd; . . . *T.M.* 448
gathered more store . . . than the others *best;* . . . *Mui.* 123
lavish Nature, in her *best* attire, . . . *Mui.* 163
Then gan I him to comfort all my *best,* . . . *D.* 190
do not spare the *best* or fayrest, . . . *D.* 202
In one thing onely fayling of the *best,* . . . *As.* 11
meanes deviz'd to shew his sorrow *best.* . . . *As.* 208
As everie one in order lov'd him *best,* . . . *As.* Interl. 224
(*best* knowen by that name) . . . *Col.* 1
Best knowne by bearing up . . . *Col.* 509
best of all that honourable crew, . . . *Col.* 517
I deeme it *best* to hold eternally . . . *Col.* 581
best can handle his deceitfull wit . . . *Col.* 693
which doe byte their hasty supper *best;* . . . I. i. 23. 4
Untroubled night . . . gives counsell *best.'* . . . I. i. 33. 3
The noblest mind the *best* contentment has. . . . I. i. 35. 4
her, whome she loved *best.* . . . I. ii. 8. 9
seemde *best* the person to put on Of that good knight, . . . I. ii. 11. 1
How with that pensive Maid he *best* might thence arise. . . . I. vi. 32. 9
Best musicke breeds delight in loathing eare; . . . I. viii. 44. 4
'knowes *best* the termes established; . . . I. ix. 41. 7
enterteynd them both, as *best* became, . . . I. x. 11. 7
Who faire them quites, as him beseemed *best,* . . . I. x. 15. 8
The first of them, that eldest was and *best,* . . . I. x. 37. 1
as seemes thee *best* became.' . . . I. x. 66. 9
retire A little backeward for his *best* defence, . . . I. xi. 45. 3

Best—*Continued.*
bids thee be advized for the *best,* . . . I. xii. 26. 5
best shall bee to them that lived *best;* . . . II. i. 59. 4
the *best* and noblest knight alive Prince Arthur is, . . . II. iii. 18. 3
There maist thou *best* be seene, and *best* maist see: . . . II. iii. 39. 8
to counsell me the *best:* . . . II. iv. 23. 7
laid forth for ensample of the *best:* . . . II. vi. 12. 5
thing that likte him *best,* . . . II. vii. 27. 3
The next could of thinges present *best* advize; . . . II. ix. 49. 2
called Cornwaile, yet so called *best;* . . . II. x. 12. 5
As for her Syre and king her seemed *best;* . . . II. x. 31. 7
should matched have the *best:* . . . II. x. 43. 6
each might *best* offend his proper part, . . . II. xi. 6. 3
A place pickt out by choyce of *best* alyve, . . . II. xii. 42. 3
as beseemed *best,* Her entertaynd: . . . III. i. 55. 5
To order them as *best* to thee doth seeme, . . . III. iii. 2. 3
by what means his love might *best* be wrought: . . . III. iii. 6. 6
did the *best* His grievous hurt to guarish, . . . III. v. 41. 5
Perforce her carried where ever he thought *best.* . . . III. vii. 2. 9
which way were *best* Him selfe to fashion . . . III. viii. 8. 5
such vaine uses that him *best* became: . . . III. viii. 14. 5
entertained her the *best* he might, . . . III. viii. 38. 2
she a mortall creature loved *best:* . . . III. viii. 39. 7
him saluting as beseemed *best,* . . . III. viii. 45. 7
So huge a scope at first him seemed *best,* . . . III. ix. 46. 5
With purpose how they might it *best* betray; . . . III. x. 34. 7
I thinke *best* Here for to stay . . . III. x. 41. 5
'Then is it *best,'* (said he) . . . III. x. 42. 1
Whom of all living wightes she loved *best.* . . . III. xii. 41. 2
Such as the maker selfe could *best* by art devize. . . . IV. iii. 38. 9
that loveth *best,* And *best* is lov'd . . . IV. Pr. 4. 6, 7
Like as it seemed *best* to every one; . . . IV. iv. 14. 8
yeeld the prize To Triamond and Cambell as the *best.* . . . IV. iv. 36. 4
That can her *best* defend from villenie; . . . IV. v. 1. 7
Satyrane the first day *best* had donne: . . . IV. v. 7. 4
all the rest which had the *best* afore, . . . IV. v. 8. 6
For last is deemed *best.* . . . IV. v. 8. 8
as *best* it her became, . . . IV. v. 16. 4
the judges did arret her Unto the second *best* . . . IV. v. 21. 5
(Whylome for ventrous Knights the bedding *best*) . . . IV. v. 39. 4
Its *best* to hope the *best,* though of the worst affrayd.' . . . IV. vi. 37. 9
how *best* he mote darrayne That enterprize . . . IV. ix. 4. 4
foure of them the battell *best* beseemed, . . . IV. ix. 20. 4
That which of them was *best* mote not be deemed. . . . IV. ix. 20. 5
purchase me some place amongst the *best.* . . . IV. x. 4. 5
unto her obayed all the *best.* . . . IV. x. 49. 4
wade in doubt what *best* were to be donne; . . . IV. x. 53. 2
it fitteth *best* For Cupids man . . . IV. x. 54. 6
Great Belus, Phoeax, and Agenor *best;* . . . IV. xi. 15. 7
Nereus, th' eldest and the *best,* . . . IV. xi. 18. 5
as *best* became, . . . IV. xi. 24. 4
were wont have *best* insight, . . . V. Pr. 8. 2
old Saturne, that was wont be *best.* . . . V. Pr. 8. 9
to her he seem'd *best* skild in righteous lore. . . . V. i. 4. 9
Take here your owne, that doth you *best* beseeme, . . . V. i. 28. 7
Marinell that day deserved *best.* . . . V. iii. 7. 8
best to him to whom the *best* should fall. . . . V. iii. 14. 4
Sixe of thy fellowes of the *best* array, . . . V. iv. 49. 7
as *best* was seeming for a Knight, . . . V. v. 1. 8
th' Amazon, as *best* it likt her selfe to dight. . . . V. v. 1. 9
From time to time, when thou it *best* shalt see, . . . V. v. 34. 4
Yet to awayt fit time she weened *best,* . . . V. v. 44. 8
in an other Canto will be *best* contayned. . . . V. v. 57. 9
every place thought *best,* . . . V. vi. 7. 2
they received were . . . as them beseemed *best;* . . . V. vi. 22. 7
As sundry chaunge her seemed *best* to ease. . . . V. vi. 26. 4
I am adjur'd *best* counsell to impart . . . V. vii. 19. 8
(as seemed *best*) . . . V. vii. 26. 1
thought it *best* With that his wife in friendly wise to deale, . . . V. viii. 21. 1
thinking *best* by counterfet disguise . . . V. viii. 25. 1
Gan to advize what *best* were to be done. . . . V. ix. 8. 5
her recomforted the *best* he might, . . . V. xi. 17. 2
To please the *best,* and th' evill to embase; . . . VI. i. 3. 7
By all the meanes she mote it *best* explaine: . . . VI. i. 46. 5
Doth *best* become and greatest grace doth gaine: . . . VI. ii. 2. 8
'The widow Queene . . . Thought *best* away me to remove . . . VI. ii. 29. 7
like as she *best* could understand, . . . VI. ii. 44. 5
and thinke what reliefe Were *best* devise . . . VI. ii. 46. 4
to him their cause they *best* esteemed Whole to commit, . . . VI. iii. 13. 3
But his *best* succour and refuge was still . . . VI. iii. 49. 5
He stayed not t' advize which way were *best* . . . VI. iv. 5. 1
that wyld man did apply His *best* endevour . . . VI. iv. 16. 2
To weet which way were *best* to entertaine . . . VI. iv. 24. 4
as he them *best* could frame, . . . VI. v. 4. 3
sought by all the meanes that he could *best* . . . VI. v. 6. 3
his backe for *best* safegard He lent against a tree, . . . VI. v. 18. 8
Howbe that carefull Hermite did his *best,* . . . VI. vi. 2. 6
'The *best'* (sayd he) 'that I can you advize, . . . VI. vi. 14. 1
The which for him she could imagine *best:* . . . VI. vi. 41. 5
To doe some thing that seemed to him *best;* . . . VI. vii. 19. 7
The *best* advizement was, of bad, to let her Sleepe . . . VI. viii. 38. 1
diversely dispose As each thought *best* . . . VI. viii. 39. 3
Sith they know *best* what is the *best* for them; . . . VI. ix. 29. 3
not that which men covet most is *best,* . . . VI. ix. 29. 6
thought it *best* To chaunge the manner of his loftie looke; . . . VI. ix. 36. 1
He would commend his guift, and make the *best;* . . . VI. ix. 40. 5
thought it *best,* . . . to pretend Some shew of favour, . . . VI. xi. 6. 5
in charge of one, the *best* Of many worst, . . . VI. xi. 24. 2
how they mote *best* assay. . . . VI. xi. 36. 9
Sir Calidore him arm'd as he thought *best,* . . . VI. xi. 42. 4

Best—*Continued.*
Of which the *best* he did his love betake; VI. xi. 51. 5
What way is *best* to drive her to retire, VII. vi. 21. 7
Areed, ye sonnes of God, as *best* ye can devise.' VII. vi. 21. 9
gan now advise What course were *best* to take VII. vi. 22. 9
For triall of their Titles and *best* Rights: VII. vi. 36. 4
(Beeing of old the *best* and fairest Hill VII. vi. 37. 6
Oft to resort there-to, when seem'd them *best*, VII. vi. 38. 5
Then thinkes what punishment were *best* assign'd, VII. vi. 48. 8
Looke ever lovely, as becomes you *best;* *Am.* vii. 10
The heavens know *best* what is the *best* for me. *Am.* xlvi. 6
Fit medicines for my bodies *best* reliefe. *Am.* l. 4
mercy doth with beautie *best* agree, *Am.* liii. 13
in theyr Maker ye them *best* may see. *Am.* liii. 14
sith so heaven ye lykened are the *best,* *Am.* lv. 13
he most happy, who such one loves *best.* *Am.* lix. 14
Clad all in white, that seemes a virgin *best.* *Epith.* 151
For they can doo it *best:* *Epith.* 258
so hard handling those which *best* thee serve, *H.L.* 163
please her *best,* and grace unto him gaine; *H.L.* 222
He may embosomd bee and loved *best;* *H.L.* 249
yet not *best,* but to be lov'd alone; *H.L.* 250
their *best* service lend *Proth.* 124
Bestad(e). *See* **Bested.**
Bestain. all her silken garments did with blood *bestaine.* IV. vii. 27. 9
Best-beloved. With th' Elfin Knight, her Ladies *best beloved:* V. v. 35. 6
Bestead. *See* **Bested.**
Besteaded. *See* **Bested.**
the Ladie, ill of friends *bestedded,* IV. i. 3. 7
Bested. *See* **Ill-bested.**
What the foule evill hath thee so *bestadde?* *S.C.* Au. 7
both attonce on both sides him *bestad,* III. v. 22. 8
who so straungely had him seene *bestadd,* III. x. 54. 7
sore *bestedde* With heapes of strokes, IV. iii. 25. 3
From whom he now so sorely was *bestad,* IV. vii. 46. 4
then being sore *bestad.* IV. xii. 33. 9
doth lie In wretched bondage, wofully *bestad.'* V. vi. 10. 7
she was right sore *bestad,* V. vi. 17. 5
Uppon an hard adventure sore *bestad,* VI. i. 4. 2
he, that hath your Knight so ill *bestad,* VI. ii. 45. 5
With which he had those two so ill *bestad:* VI. vi. 18. 5
Bestial. sage Counsellours . . . Taught to obay their *bestiall* beheasts, I. iv. 18. 3
none so *bestiall* Nor salvage hart, III. vii. 9. 5
Shame most ill-favourd, *bestiall,* and blinde: III. xii. 24. 5
She in my stead supplide his *bestiall* desire.' IV. vii. 19. 9
made the baite of *bestiall* delight: IV. viii. 32. 4
Bestir. Lord! how he gan for to *bestirre* him tho, *Mui.* 252
Bestow. Deignd to behold me and their gifts *bestowe,* *Ti.* 81
did *bestow* Upon the daughter of this woman blind, I. iii. 18. 2
All is but lost, that living we *bestow,* I. x. 41. 6
on me she deigned to *bestowe* Order of Maydenhead, II. ii. 42. 3
he did *bestow* Both guestes and meate, II. ix. 28. 3
to their sire their carcasses left to *bestow.* V. vi. 40. 9
their huge strokes full daungerously *bestow,* V. xii. 17. 3
skill it is such duties timely to *bestow.* VI. ii. 1. 9
'These three on men all gracious gifts *bestow,* VI. x. 23. 1
To bandie Crownes, and Kingdoms to *bestowe:* VII. vi. 32. 8
Bestowed. were those goodly favours *Bestowd* on thee, *Col.* 586
meed, Which she on me *bestowd,* *Col.* 593
certes seemes *bestowed* not amis: III. ii. 42. 4
that great favour Which I on her *bestowed,* V. iv. 12. 6
bestowed on me The portion of that good V. iv. 12. 6
on those Priests *bestowed* rich reward; V. vii. 24. 3
Bestows. God his gifts there plenteously *bestowes,* *Col.* 326
Bestrewed. *bestrowed* all with rich aray Of pearles III. iv. 18. 4
the bare ground with hoarie mosse *bestrowed* VI. iv. 14. 4
Bestride. made him stoupe, till he did him *bestride:* IV. xii. 13. 7
Bestrode. whiles he his backe *bestrad.* V. ii. 13. 9
Bestrowed. *See* **Bestrewed.**
Bet. what I the *bett* for-thy? *S.C.* O. 15
Bett back the furie of the Trojan fyre. *Gn.* 496
long the dore with rage and threats he *bett,* I. iii. 19. 1
when he saw his . . . subtile engines *bett* from batteree; I. vi. 5. 2
Long tost with stormes, and *bet* with bitter wind, I. vii. 28. 7
on his shield like yron sledges *bet:* II. ii. 22. 4
Whom sore he *bett,* and gor'd with many a wownd, II. iv. 3. 8
Yet still he *bet* the water, II. vi. 42. 9
The sunny beames which on the billowes *bett,* II. xii. 63. 3
thousand Fancies *bett* his ydle brayne III. iv. 54. 4
So long he held him, and him *bett* so long, III. vii. 35. 2
Him *bett* so sore, that life and sence did much dismay. III. viii. 31. 9
with their axes both so sorely *bet,* IV. iii. 15. 3
he shall have the Hag that is *ybet,* IV. iv. 9. 8
The better had, and *bet* the others backe; IV. ix. 25. 2
Yet still he *bet* and bounst uppon the dore, V. ii. 21. 6
he ere long the former fiftie *bet,* V. iii. 11. 8
with his club *bet* backe his brondyron bright VI. viii. 10. 4
bet abacke, threatning in vaine to bite, VI. xii. 29. 4
Betake. ere that anie way I doo *betake,* *Hub.* 69
here ly downe, and to thy rest *betake,* I. ix. 44. 2
to his handes that writt he did *betake,* I. xii. 25. 8
did her selfe *betake* Unto her boat again, II. vi. 18. 5
Unto the mighty streame him to *betake,* II. x. 16. 8
Them to *betake* unto their kindly rest: III. i. 58. 2
to their tryed swords them selves *betake;* IV. iv. 29. 2
None other way will I this day *betake,* V. ii. 10. 6
to his handy swimming him *betake.* V. ii. 16. 3
Forst . . . to *betake* him selfe to fearefull flight; VI. iii. 25. 8
Unto his heeles himselfe he did *betake,* VI. vi. 29. 2

Betake—*Continued.*
Of which the best he did his love *betake;* VI. xi. 51. 5
Betakes. to her yron wagon she *betakes,* I. v. 28. 1
Beteem. *Beteeme* to you this sword, you to defend, II. viii. 19. 6
Bethink. Her to *bethinke* of that mote to her selfe pertaine. III. ii. 22. 9
He gan *bethinke* him in what perilous plight VI. vi. 37. 4
When I *bethinke* me on that speech VII. viii. 1. 1
to *bethinke* how great that beautie is, *H.H.B.* 107
Bethinking. better him *bethinking* of the right, IV. ix. 6. 8
Whereof she now *bethinking,* gan t' advize VI. iii. 8. 6
Bethinks. old Sylvanus selfe *bethinkes* not what To thinke I. vi. 16. 3
Bethought. At last she her *bethought* III. vi. 16. 3
againe he him *bethought* to live, III. x. 7. 6
he *bethought* How to prevent the perill IV. ii. 37. 7
sitting downe, her selfe awhile *bethought* VI. viii. 32. 7
would have *bethought* On Phrygian Paris by Plexippus brooke, VI. ix. 36. 6
he *bethought* To leave his love, VI. xii. 13. 2
Bethrall. For she it is, that did my Lord *bethrall,* I. viii. 28. 6
Betid. *See* **Betided.**
some new mishap Had him *betidde,* II. i. 26. 9
What great misfortune hath *betidd* this knight? II. viii. 24. 2
deadly daunger, which to him *betidd;* III. v. 13. 2
There unto him *betid* a disaventrous case. IV. xii. 4. 9
What evil hap to Marinell *betid,* V. iii. 10. 6
That had to any happily *betid,* V. xii. 32. 2
Betide. *See* **Betid, Betided.**
not but well mought him *betight:* *S.C.* S. 173
By straunge adventure as it did *betyde,* I. vi. 21. 2
To weete of newes that did abroad *betide,* I. vi. 34. 5
as if some new mishap, Had him *betide,* II. i. 26. 9
Through many hard assayes which did *betide;* II. i. 35. 2
for feare of worse that may *betide,* II. iii. 46. 1
Least worse *betide* thee by some later chaunce. II. iv. 36. 5
Pyrochles, O Pyrochles! what is thee *betyde?'* II. vi. 43. 9
Dreadfull of daunger that mote him *betyde,* III. i. 37. 5
till thou tidings learne what her *betide,* III. v. 11. 7
For doubt of daunger which mote him *betide;* III. v. 12. 6
least ought did ill *betide* To that faire Maide, III. vii. 31. 4
There found she her (as then it did *betide*) IV. viii. 9. 1
tydings what did unto him *betide,* IV. viii. 18. 6
To whom they told all that did them *betide,* IV. viii. 21. 4
all That did betwixt him and that Squire *betide:* V. i. 23. 4
Which she would sure performe, *betide* her wele or wo. V. vi. 23. 9
when fit occasion did *betyde,* V. xi. 6. 4
To weet what issue would thereof *betyde:* VI. iii. 47. 2
what so else were unto him *betyde;* VI. v. 3. 8
Least unto me *betide* a greater ill; VI. viii. 30. 4
did him *betide* A great adventure, VI. viii. 30. 8
What did *betide* to the faire Pastorell VI. xii. 14. 3
Betided. As if some evill were to her *betight?* *S.C.* N. 174
a strange adventure, that *betided* *Hub.* 37
The rest of thine adventures, that *betyded.'* *Col.* 329
Betight. *See* **Betide, Betided.**
Betimes. Beware therefore, ye groomes, I read *betimes,* *Col.* 925
Whiles they are weake, *betimes* with them contend; II. iv. 34. 5
all this cursed plot . . . discovered was *betymes,* V. ix. 42. 4
Betoken. they doe nought but right or wrong *betoken;* V. ii. 47. 5
Betokening. *Betokening* peace and plenty to ensew. *Am.* lxii. 4
Betook. Her power to Peters successor *betooke;* *Ro.* xviii. 12
ere that unto armes I me *betooke,* *Hub.* 291
other bywaies he himselfe *betooke,* I. vii. 50. 3
he him selfe *betooke* another way, III. i. 2. 7
Dame Phoebe to a Nymphe her babe *betooke* III. vi. 28. 3
to her feet *betooke* her doubtfull sickernesse. III. vii. 25. 9
Unto her sword and shield her soone *betooke;* IV. vi. 14. 8
from the water to the land *betooke* his flight. V. ii. 17. 9
And Calidore *betooke* him to depart, VI. ii. 36. 2
Himselfe unto his weapon he *betooke,* VI. vii. 24. 6
she *betooke* her selfe to rest: VI. viii. 34. 5
Betray. fish, which they with baits usde to *betraie,* *Ti.* 152
How he might anie in his trap *betray.* *Mui.* 248
Ne suffred lust his safety to *betray.* II. vii. 64. 8
With purpose how they might it best *betray;* III. x. 34. 7
eke the knight attonce she did *betray;* V. v. 52. 7
will ye *betray* My life now too, V. vi. 25. 2
Least any should *betray* his Lady treacherously. V. vi. 26. 9
Him to *betray* unto a straunger swaine: VI. vii. 22. 5
False Fortune did her safety *betray* VI. viii. 34. 8
For to *betray* my Right before I have it tride. VII. vi. 34. 9
Betrayed. Preserved from being to his foes *betrayde;* *Van.* xi. 11
fortune false *betraide* me to thy powre, I. ii. 22. 5
her knight, . . . subtily *betrayd* Through that late vision I. iii. 3. 5
With Elfin sword most shamefully *betrade?* I. v. 22. 8
by subtile sleights she him *betraid* Unto his foe, I. vii. 51. 1
breach of love and loialty *betrayd.* I. xii. 31. 5
to my foe *betrayd* when least I feared ill.' I. xii. 32. 9
Betrayd his countrey unto forreine spoyle. II. x. 48. 8
She weened well that then she was *betraide:* IV. ix. 7. 5
with guyle My heart at first *betrayd,* V. vi. 25. 2
they were all *betrayd* And murdred cruelly VI. vii. 34. 8
entrapt of love, which him *betrayd,* VI. x. 1. 7
betrayd To tell what time he might her Lady see VII. vi. 43. 7
Him thither brought, and her to him *betraid?* VII. vi. 51. 6
He taken was, *betrayd,* and false accused; *H.H.L.* 240
Betraying. *Betraying* him into the traines of hys foe. *S.C.* May 200
Betrothed. *See* **Late-betrothed.**
'He, . . . *Betrothed* me unto the onely haire I. ii. 23. 2
Fayre Una to the Redcrosse Knight *Betrouthed* is I. xii. Arg.
Bett. *See* **Bet.**
Better. *See* **Bet.**

Better—*Continued.*
when time serves may bring things *better* forth. . . . *Van.* i. 14
(no *better* doe him call,) . . . *S.C.* Ja. 1
(But now I trowe can *better* good,) . . . *S.C.* Mar. 56
I cannot compare *Better* then to the Apes . . . *S.C.* May 96
Better is then the lowly playne, . . . *S.C.* Jul. 7
his hap . . . shall be *better* in time. . . . *S.C.* Jul. 230
Were not *better* to shunne the scortching heate? . . . *S.C.* Au. 48
In hope of *better* that was uncouth! . . . *S.C.* S. 60
seeldome chaunge the *better* brought: . . . *S.C.* S. 69
better leave of with a little losse, . . . *S.C.* S. 134
Better it were a little to feyne, . . . *S.C.* S. 137
they had be *better* come at their cal; . . . *S.C.* S. 146
the prayse is *better* then the price, . . . *S.C.* O. 19
Tom Piper makes us *better* melodie. . . . *S.C.* O. 78
better learne of hem that learned bee, . . . *S.C.* N. 29
better dayes death hath shut up in woe? . . . *S.C.* N. 74
better mought they have behote him Hate. . . . *S.C.* D. 54
Who to entrappe the fish . . . Was *better,* seene, . . . *S.C.* D. 82
never pype of reede did *better* sounde. . . . *S.C.* D. 142
The *better* please, the worse despise; . . . *S.C.* Env. 12
Two fellowes might no where be *better* fitted. . . . *Hub.* 50
meane for *better* winde about to throwe. . . . *Hub.* 80
two is *better* than one head.' . . . *Hub.* 82
this might *better* be the world of gold; . . . *Hub.* 152
like to begging, but much *better* named, . . . *Hub.* 351
since their souldiers pas no *better* spedd, . . . *Hub.* 357
Ne make one title worse, ne make one *better:* . . . *Hub.* 384
A garment *better* than of wooll or heare. . . . *Hub.* 474
Whereas thou maist compound a *better* penie, . . . *Hub.* 523
Better a short tale than a bad long shriving: . . . *Hub.* 543
may *better* thrive than thousands . . . *Hub.* 642
To loose good dayes, that might be *better* . . . *Hub.* 897
with him far'd some *better* chaunce to fynde. . . . *Hub.* 942
better farre it were to hide their names, . . . *T.M.* 101
who can *better* sing . . . *Ti.* 316, 323
they heare thine, and thine doo *better* praise. . . . *Ti.* 336
worthie of a *better* place was she: . . . *D.* 366
in affliction wast my *better* age: . . . *D.* 374
With *better* fortune than did me succeed, . . . *D.* 521
till he were *better* eased . . . *D.* 559
her much *better* to preferre, . . . *Col.* 121
better shepheards be not under skie, . . . *Col.* 377
Nor *better* hable, . . . *Col.* 378
'the perill of this place I *better* wot then you: . . . I. i. 13. 2
Better new friend then an old foe is said.' . . . I. ii. 27. 4
That to strange knight no *better* countenance allowd. . . . I. iv. 15. 9
The *better* part now of the lingring day . . . I. vi. 34. 1
Were it not *better* I that Lady had . . . I. vi. 47. 3
Such helplesse harmes yts *better* hidden keep, . . . I. vii. 39. 7
Where he his *better* dayes hath wasted all: . . . I. viii. 28. 8
His bare thin cheekes for want of *better* bits, . . . I. viii. 41. 3
Is it not *better* to doe willinglie, . . . I. ix. 47. 7
Who *better* can the way to heaven aread . . . I. x. 51. 4
Death *better* were; death did he oft desire, . . . I. xi. 28. 4
let that man with *better* sence advize, . . . II. Pr. 2. 1
Long maist thou live, and *better* thrive withall . . . II. i. 37. 4
I him recured to a *better* will, . . . II. i. 54. 7
were not *better* fayre it to accord . . . II. ii. 30. 2
which *better* to approve, He promised to bring me . . . II. iv. 24. 6
better first I thought To wreake my wrath on him . . . II. iv. 30. 4
death were *better* then such agony . . . II. iv. 33. 3
Ne thou for *better* hope, if thou his presence stay.' . . . II. iv. 40. 9
she *better* can abstaine: . . . II. vi. 1. 7
Better safe port then be in seas distrest.' . . . II. vi. 23. 8
better reason will aswage The rash revengers heat. . . . II. viii. 26. 6
recompenst them with a *better* scorse: . . . II. ix. 55. 8
unto *better* fortune doth her selfe prepayre. . . . II. xi. 36. 9
him avizing *better,* . . . II. xii. 28. 4
better were to dy. . . . III. i. 25. 4
chaunged her weary side the *better* ease to take. . . . III. i. 61. 9
'perhaps ye should it *better* find: . . . III. ii. 13. 5
better fortune thine, and *better* howre, . . . III. ii. 45. 5
Farre *better* I it deeme to die with speed . . . III. iv. 38. 3
when shee *better* him beheld . . . III. v. 30. 7
His readie wound with *better* salves new drest: . . . III. v. 41. 4
Paridell kept *better* watch then hee, . . . III. x. 4. 1
as he *better* did their shape avize, . . . III. x. 21. 2
Was never *better* time to shew thy smart . . . III. x. 26. 3
In *better* quarell then defence of right, . . . III. x. 28. 4
He did the *better* counterfeite aright: . . . III. x. 47. 7
now made *better* speed t' escape his feared foe. . . . III. xi. 5. 9
them apply To *better* boot; . . . III. xi. 19. 6
faire Alcmena *better* match did make, . . . III. xi. 33. 6
better were in vertues discipled, . . . IV. Pr. 1. 8
that she may the *better* deigne to heare, . . . IV. Pr. 5. 1
for to hide her fained sex the *better* . . . IV. i. 7. 3
The other no whit *better* was then shee, . . . IV. i. 18. 6
A Knight much *better* then thy selfe behight, . . . IV. i. 44. 4
God send you *better* gaine!' . . . IV. ii. 6. 5
To draw them longer out, and *better* twine, . . . IV. ii. 51. 2
Now this the *better* had, now had his fo; . . . IV. iii. 28. 3
For evill deedes may *better* then bad words be bore. . . . IV. iv. 4. 9
with no *better* fortune then the rest: . . . IV. iv. 21. 2
still the Knights of Maidenhead the *better* wonne; . . . IV. iv. 38. 9
with no *better* fortune then the rest afore. . . . IV. iv. 45. 9
Unto the second best that lov'd her *better;* . . . IV. v. 21. 5
Ne *better* had he, ne for *better* cared: . . . IV. v. 35. 2
Where *better* seem'd he mote himselfe repose; . . . IV. v. 40. 4
Whose fire were *better* turn'd to other flame; . . . IV. vi. 32. 3

Better—*Continued.*
Shew'd change of *better* cheare: . . . IV. vi. 38. 3
then *better* doe advise: . . . IV. viii. 15. 6
Bad them not looke for *better* entertayne; . . . IV. viii. 27. 4
I with *better* reason him aviz'd, . . . IV. viii. 58. 1
better him bethinking of the right, . . . IV. ix. 6. 8
To *better* termes of myldnesse did entreat . . . IV. ix. 14. 2
Till he had made of her some *better* priefe; . . . IV. ix. 15. 5
sometimes Paridell and Blandamour The *better* had, . . . IV. ix. 25. 2
Let them record them that are *better* skild, . . . IV. xi. 17. 5
Thame was stronger, and of *better* stay; . . . IV. xi. 25. 6
In *better* case, . . . V. Pr. 7. 3
Ne *better* doth beseeme brave chevalry, . . . V. ii. 1. 2
Uncertaine whether had the *better* side; . . . V. ii. 17. 2
Artegall was *better* breath'd beside, . . . V. ii. 17. 5
change his shield with him, to be the *better* hid. . . . V. iii. 10. 9
What *better* dowre can to a dame be hight? . . . V. iv. 9. 5
Both goodly portions, but of both the *better* she. . . . V. iv. 12. 9
showre of arrowes, which them staid, And *better* bad advise, . . . V. iv. 38. 5
'Which that thou mayst the *better* bring to pas, . . . V. v. 34. 1
thus thy *better* dayes are drowned In sad despaire, . . . V. v. 36. 4
art mov'd to wish me *better,* . . . V. v. 37. 8
Yet doe I not of *better* times despeyre; . . . V. v. 38. 7
'Unworthy sure' (quoth he) 'of *better* day, . . . V. v. 39. 5
They mote the *better* tend to their devotion. . . . V. vii. 9. 9
better skild in Tilt and Turnament, . . . V. viii. 7. 7
better to reforme then to cut off the ill. . . . V. x. 2. 9
The *better* to confirme her fearelesse confidence. . . . V. x. 12. 9
He did him selfe encourage and take *better* cheare. . . . V. xi. 2. 9
The *better* to beguile whom she so fond did finde. . . . V. xi. 23. 9
The other nothing *better* was then shee, . . . V. xii. 33. 1
To him that hath it *better* justifyde, . . . VI. i. 18. 8
some *better* Knight Then thou, . . . VI. i. 25. 6
To prove if *better* foote then horsebacke would ensew. . . . VI. i. 35. 9
ye *better* shall your selfe behave . . . VI. i. 42. 7
To lend him day his *better* right to trie, . . . VI. ii. 19. 4
And for their *better* comfort to them nigher drew. . . . VI. ii. 41. 9
he him found much *better* then he was; . . . VI. iii. 14. 5
Through that same perillous foord with *better* heede, . . . VI. iii. 31. 4
th' other, ayming *better,* did him smite Full in the shield . . . VI. vii. 8. 1
entyrely prayd T' advize him *better* . . . VI. vii. 22. 4
to entreat The one or th' other *better* her to use; . . . VI. vii. 40. 2
sleepe, they sayd, would make her battill *better:* . . . VI. viii. 38. 3
yet *better* so To lodge then in the salvage fields to rome. . . . VI. ix. 16. 6
No *better* doe I weare, no *better* doe I feed. . . . VI. ix. 20. 9
may perhaps you *better* much withall, . . . VI. ix. 32. 7
Will in another Canto *better* be begonne. . . . VI. x. 44. 9
With *better* tearmes she did him entertaine, . . . VI. xi. 7. 2
Nor *better* cheare to shew in misery, . . . VI. xi. 8. 7
better were with them to have bene dead, . . . VI. xi. 32. 6
with *better* reason cast How he might save her life, . . . VI. xi. 34. 4
they for *better* hyre did shortly looke: . . . VI. xi. 40. 8
Mongst which he found a sword of *better* say, . . . VI. xi. 47. 5
Therefore do you, my rimes, keep *better* measure, . . . VI. xii. 41. 8
that to all may *better* yet appeare, . . . VII. vi. 1. 6
better able it to guide alone; . . . VII. vi. 11. 4
to quit her with a *better;* . . . VII. vi. 44. 2
better were attonce to let me die, . . . *Am.* xxv. 5
pryde depraves each other *better* part, . . . *Am.* xxxi. 3
the *better* may . . . her cruell hands embrew. . . . *Am.* xxxi. 11
Well worthy thou to have found *better* hyre, . . . *Am.* xlviii. 5
for *better* be allured, Ne feard with worse . . . *Am.* lix. 3
chuse the *better* of them both . . . *Com. Son.* ii. 11
mayest them make it *better* to deserve, . . . *H.L.* 166

Bettered. Of rustick muse full hardly to be *betterd.* . . . *D.* 231

Between (*partial list*). Bay leaves *betweene,* And primroses *S.C.* Ap. 61
betweene the Cuppe And golden Diademe: . . . *S.C.* Jul. 19
strife *betweene* them . . . *Mui.* 309
kind speeches they *betweene* them spend, . . . I. x. 15. 3
difference *Betweene* the vulgar and the noble seed, . . . II. iv. 1. 3
That seven fold shield . . . He cast *between* . . . II. viii. 32. 6
reconcilement was *betweene* them knitt, . . . III. i. 12. 1
aye *betweene* the cups she did prepare . . . III. i. 51. 7
union shall be made *Betweene* the nations . . . III. iii. 49. 2
smote downe all that was *betweene,* . . . IV. iv. 34. 2
creepe *betweene* his legs, . . . IV. x. 19. 3
mailes *betweene,* and laced close afore; . . . V. v. 3. 3
the Prince hard preased in *betweene,* . . . V. x. 37. 6
A privy token which *betweene* them past, . . . VI. i. 29. 3
peace shall see *Betweene* the Spyder and the gentle Bee . . . *Am.* lxxi. 14
still throw *betweene* Some graces to be seene; . . . *Epith.* 106
Betweene the toylefull Oxe and humble Asse, . . . *H.H.L.* 227

Betwixt (*partial list*). His tayle he clapt *betwixt* his legs twayne, . . . *S.C.* May 280
Betwixt the forrest wide and starrie sky: . . . *Gn.* 34
that betided *Betwixt* the Foxe and th' Ape . . . *Hub.* 38
Betwixt two mightie ones of great estate, . . . *Mui.* 3
Betwixt the centred earth and azure skies, . . . *Mui.* 19
Of the late love the which *betwixt* us past, . . . *D.* 289
The marriage to accomplish vowd *betwixt* you twayn. . . . I. xii. 19. 9
By breaking of the band *betwixt* us twaine; . . . I. xii. 34. 4
a pleasant dale that lowly lay *Betwixt* two hils, . . . II. i. 24. 4
by that same sacred band *Betwixt* us both, . . . II. iv. 23. 7
Betwixt them both was but a litle stride, . . . II. vii. 24. 8
Hel-gate them both *betwext.* . . . II. vii. 25. 9
Betwixt the lowest earth and hevens hight, . . . III. ii. 19. 3
Betwixt two shady mountaynes doth arize: . . . III. ii. 24. 7
Betwixt her feeble armes her quickly keight, . . . III. ii. 30. 4
The soveraine weede *betwixt* two marbles plaine . . . III. v. 33. 1
Her up *betwixt* his rugged hands he reard, . . . III. viii. 35. 1

Betwixt—*Continued.*
which late befell *Betwixt* us both unknowne.' III. ix. 51. 9
Should equally be shard *betwixt* us tway. IV. ii. 13. 5
in a privy place, *betwixt* us hight, IV. vii. 17. 7
had not . . . *Betwixt* him and his hurt bene IV. viii. 43. 7
And him embracing fast *betwixt* them held, IV. ix. 9. 3
Betwixt the Medway and the Thames agreed. IV. xi. 8. 4
the limit *betwixt* Logris land And Albany: IV. xi. 36. 6
Artegall dealeth right *betwixt* Two brethren V. iv. Arg.
this is things compacte *betwixt* you two, V. vi. 16. 7
cruell fray *Betwixt* them two VI. i. 36. 2
wherefore *Betwixt* you two began this strife VI. ii. 8. 9
an infant bore *Betwixt* his bloodie jawes, VI. iv. 17. 9
Then tooke he up *betwixt* his armes twaine VI. iv. 23. 1
whatever chaunce were blowne *Betwixt* them to divide, VI. vii. 3. 9

Bever, -s. *See* **Beaver, -s.**

Bevy. whither rennes this *bevie* of Ladies bright, *S.C.* Ap. 118
A lovely *bevy* of faire Ladies sate, II. ix. 34. 2
A *bevie* of fayre damzels close did lye, IV. x. 48. 8
A *bevie* of faire Virgins clad in white, V. ix. 31. 2

Bewail. if thou wilt *bewayle* my wofull tene, *S.C.* N. 41
Whom all the Muses did *bewaile* long space, *T.M.* 17
who will *bewaile* my heavy chaunce? *U.V.* 19
rocke . . . That lay in waite her wrack for to *bewaile,* I. vi. 1. 3
each did other much *bewaile* and mone, IV. vii. 20. 2

Bewaileth. me no man *bewaileth,* but in game, *Ti.* 162

Bewailing. him *bewayling* with affection base, VI. vii. 18. 3

Beware. wit to *beware,* *S.C.* May 181
Beware therefore, ye groomes, I read betimes, *Col.* 925
Therefore I read *beware.'* I. i. 13. 8
Beware of fraud, *beware* of ficklenesse, I. iv. 1. 3
ofte of secret ill bids us *beware:* II. xii. 47. 7
beware how thou those dartes behold.) III. xi. 48. 5
Well warned to *beware* with whom he dar'd to dallie. IV. i. 36. 9
warned him of womens love *beware,* IV. xii. 27. 2

Bewitch. the soyle that so doth thee *bewitch:* *S.C.* Jun. 18
Ne let vaine words *bewitch* thy manly hart, I. ix. 53. 2
in vain sheows, that wont yong knights *bewitch,* III. vii. 29. 6

Bewitched. I wote ne, Hobbin, how I was *bewitcht* *S.C.* S. 74
Hath so wise men *bewitcht,* *Ti.* 457
"Fye, fye! . . . 'To have before *bewitched* all mens sight: I. ii. 39. 3

Bewray. Which now their dusty reliques do *bewray;* *Ro.* xv. 4
The previe marks I would *bewray,* *S.C.* Mar. 35
of my woe cannot *bewray* least part) *S.C.* Au. 176
did the bankets of the Gods *bewray,* *Gn.* 386
Commaunding them their cause of strife *bewray;* *Hub.* 1096
Clad all in black, that mourning did *bewray,* *D.* 40
With drery shriekes did also her *bewray;* I. v. 30. 7
To tempt the cause it selfe for to *bewray,* I. vii. 38. 8
chaunge of hew great passion did *bewray;* I. ix. 16. 2
treasons could *bewray,* and foes convince: III. ii. 21. 8
that none might them *bewray,* III. iii. 7. 2
Disguiz'd in thousand shapes, that none might him *bewray.*) III. vi. 11. 9
did to her *bewray* A litle valley III. vii. 4. 7
Till triall doe more certeine truth *bewray.'* III. viii. 50. 5
the treasure which he did *bewray,* III. x. 34. 5
that nights ensample did *bewray* III. x. 48. 7
he gan *bewray* Some argument III. xii. 4. 5
His chaunge of cheere that anguish did *bewray,* IV. i. 50. 7
Whose scalp is bare, that bondage doth *bewray,* V. ii. 6. 7
all things secrete wisely could *bewray,* V. ii. 25. 4
ere one could it *bewray.* V. iii. 25. 9
that mote his shame *bewray;* V. v. 21. 7
all that treason there intended did *bewray.* V. vi. 30. 9
did to them *bewray* A straunge adventure, V. ix. 4. 4
'That shall I unto you' (quoth he) *'bewray,* V. xi. 52. 7
Would not *bewray* the state in which she stood. VI. viii. 51. 5
Mote not *bewray* the secret of her lode, VI. xii. 7. 3
So did their ghastly gaze *bewray* their hidden feares. VII. vi. 28. 9

Bewrayed. Had not a Goose the treachery *bewrayde;* *Van.* xi. 8
By his there being might not be *bewraid,* *Mui.* 399
all that might . . . entyse she unto him *bewrayd;* II. xii. 66. 8
To cloke the cause that hath it selfe *bewrayd?* III. iii. 19. 4
In him *bewraid* great grudge and maltalent: III. iv. 61. 8
Phoebus Lamp *Bewrayed* had the world with early light, III. x. 1. 2
soone as they with wrathfull eie *bewraide,* IV. ix. 28. 4
to the gloomy world itselfe *bewray'd:* IV. x. 52. 7
every where *Bewrayd* it selfe, IV. xi. 45. 8
Bewrayd the signes of feature excellent; V. v. 12. 7
a man by nothing is so well *bewrayd* As by his manners; VI. iii. 1. 3
Or loth to let her sorrowes be *bewrayd:* VI. iv. 27. 4
'twas Molanna which her so *bewraid.* VII. vi. 51. 8

Bewrayedst. That thou *bewray'dst* his mothers wantonnesse, III. xi. 36. 4

Bewraying. *Bewraying* him that did of late destroy His eldest brother; I. iv. 39. 3

Bewrays. Merlin *bewrayes* to Britomart The state of Arthegall; III. iii. Arg.
Like as the gentle hart it selfe *bewrayes* VI. vii. 1. 1

Beyond. I *beyond* all these am carried *Gn.* 419
traversing . . . *Beyond* the compasse of his pointed path, *T.M.* 10
left *beyond* that Ydle lake, II. vii. 2. 2
Lo! where *beyond* he lyeth languishing, III. i. 38. 1
beyond the Africk Ismael Or th' Indian Peru III. iii. 6. 7
Him so transfixed she before her bore *Beyond* his croupe, III. iv. 16. 7
carried her *beyond* all jeopardy; III. vii. 3. 4
overbore *beyond* his crouper IV. iv. 40. 7
in my way, a little here *beyond,* V. ii. 4. 5
Yet is that Highest farre *beyond* all telling, *H.H.B.* 101

Biblis. Nor so did *Biblis* spend her pining hart; III. ii. 41. 2

Bickerment. Did stay a while their greedy *bickerment,* V. iv. 6. 8

Bid. Diggon Davie! I *bidde* her god day; *S.C.* S. 1

Bid—*Continued.*
'Tho gan my lovely Spring *bid* me farewel, *S.C.* D. 55
Bid strange mischance his quietnes to spill. *Gn.* 248
Whose part once past all men *bid* take away: *Hub.* 932
Bid me, O! *bid* me quicklie come to thee, *Ti.* 307
When fairer faces were *bid* standen by: I. iv. 24. 8
Nor leave his stand untill his Captaine *bed.'* I. ix. 41. 5
The knight and Una . . . *bid* her joy I. x. 32. 2
bid them sleepe in everlasting peace. II. i. 60. 6
Bid thee to them thy fruitlesse labors yield, II. vi. 16. 3
Ne gave him leave to *bid* that aged sire Adieu; II. vi. 20. 5
bid them strike the marke which he had eyde; II. xi. 21. 7
Yet list them *bid* their businesse to unfold, III. iii. 15. 3
bid his faithlesse chickens overronne The fruitfull plaines, III. iii. 46. 7
bid His mighty waters to them buxome bee: III. iv. 32. 5
No need to *bid* her fast away to flie: III. vii. 24. 2
bide him batteill without further treat. III. viii. 16. 5
pacing fairely forth did *bid* all haile, IV. iii. 46. 5
bid him eate: henceforth he oft shall hungry sit.' V. iv. 49. 9
like one unto a banquet *bid,* V. xii. 32. 7
Was wont his howres and holy things to *bed;* VI. v. 35. 7
Sternely did *bid* him quickely thence avaunt, VI. vi. 21. 2
Boldly she *bid* the Goddesse downe descend, VII. vi. 11. 1
To *bid* her leave faire Cynthias silver bower; VII. vi. 18. 7
Bid her therefore her selfe soone ready make, *Am.* lxx. 9
Bid her awake; for Hymen is awake, *Epith.* 25
Bid her awake therefore, *Epith.* 30

Biddest. *See* **Bidst.**

Biddeth. Whose secret filth good manners *biddeth* not be told. I. viii. 46. 9

Bidding. In rymes, in ridles, and in *bydding* base; *S.C.* O. 5
Bidding his beades all day for his trespas, I. i. 30. 7
Bidding the dwarfe . . . to bring away The Sarazins shield, I. ii. 20. 6
ruefull plaints, me *bidding* guiltlesse blood to spare?' I. ii. 32. 9
All night she spent in *bidding* of her bedes, I. x. 3. 8
bidding bold defyaunce to his foeman neare. I. xi. 15. 9
He stayd not for more *bidding,* II. iii. 19. 1
Bidding his winged vessell fairely forward fly: II. vii. 1. 9
Bidding them nigher draw unto the shore, II. xii. 15. 2
bidding her sit downe, to rest III. vii. 10. 4
Bidding her feare no more her foeman vilde, III. viii. 34. 3
Bidding them fight for honour of their love, IV. ii. 19. 6
Yet for no *bidding* . . . Would he restrayned be VI. vi. 18. 8
Bidding him turne againe, false traytour knight, VI. vii. 7. 2
She at his *bidding* meekely did arise, VI. ix. 15. 1
New yeare, . . . *bidding* th' old Adieu, *Am.* iv. 3

Bide. *See* **Bid.**
What hell it is in suing long to *bide:* *Hub.* 896
Love and Lordship *bide* no paragone. *Hub.* 1026
blustring breath of Heaven, that none can *bide,* I. iii. 31. 5
he durst not *byde,* I. vi. 8. 8
she would no lenger *byde,* I. vii. 2. 4
brought thee up in ploughmans state to *byde,* I. x. 66. 5
her vertues in her water *byde,* II. ii. 9. 6
fly away, or *bide* alone behinde; II. iii. 32. 4
Or *bide* the chaunce at thine owne jeopardee.' II. iv. 39. 5
By every fournace many feendes did *byde,* II. vii. 35. 6
who nill *bide* the burden of distresse, III. xi. 14. 8
Could *bide* the force of that enchaunted speare, IV. iv. 46. 4
He by his former combate would not *bide,* IV. vii. 29. 7
bide the horror of his wreakfull hand, V. i. 8. 8
To *bide* that judgement ye shall us afford.' V. iv. 16. 5
He will not *bide* the daunger of such dread, V. xii. 18. 7
in the covert of the wood did *byde,* VI. x. 11. 4
at her perill *bide* the wrathfull Thunders wrack. VII. vi. 12. 9
Sought not to fly, but fearelesse still did *bide;* *Am.* lxvii. 10
There whylome wont the Templer Knights to *byde,* *Proth.* 135

Bideth. That substaunce is eterne, and *bideth* so; III. vi. 37. 6

Biding. where him she *byding* fond II. vi. 19. 5
The moniments whereof there *byding* beene, IV. i. 24. 8

Bids. *bids* make readie Maias bowre, *S.C.* Mar. 17
bids him clayme with rigorous rage hys right: *S.C.* D. 130
Tell Rosalind, her Colin *bids* her adieu.' *S.C.* D. 156
Remembraunce . . . *Bids* me, most noble Lady, to adore *Ded. Son.* xv. 8
Sweet slombring deaw, the which to sleep them *biddes.* I. i. 36. 4
He *bids* thee . . . send for his intent A fit false dreame, I. i. 43. 8
thus perforce he *bids* me do, or die. I. i. 51. 6
bids thee be advized for the best, I. xii. 26. 5
So *bids* thee well to fare, Thy neither friend nor foe, I. xii. 28. 9
bids them nought availe. II. viii. 35. 9
ofte of secret ill *bids* us beware: II. xii. 47. 7
scornes thy ydle scoffe, and *bids* thee be defyde.' VI. i. 27. 9
he taking oddes, streight *bids* him dight Himselfe VI. ii. 18. 4
Bids all old thoughts to die in dumpish spright: *Am.* iv. 4
when I pleade, she *bids* me play my part; *Am.* xviii. 9
My cruell fayre streight *bids* me wend my way: *Am.* xlvi. 2

Bidst. redoubled crime with vengeaunce new Thou *biddest* me to eeke? I. v. 42. 8
since thou *bidst,* thy pleasure shalbe donne. I. x. 52. 1

Bier. Yet saw I on the *beare* when it was brought; *S.C.* N. 161
he at last laid forth on balefull *beare.* *T.M.* 162
I saw him die . . . and brought foorth on *beare;* *Ti.* 191
him dolefully did beare. The dolefulst *beare* that ever *As.* 149
Nor wayld of friends, nor layd on groning *beare,* I. v. 23. 4
The ruefull Strich, still waiting on the *bere;* II. xii. 36. 7
He was surprisd, and buried under *beare,* III. iii. 11. 2
strowe with flowres the lamentable *beare.* III. iv. 42. 5
his shield, . . . like to an hollow *beare;* VI. ii. 48. 2
With bleeding wounds, brought home upon a *beare* VI. iii. 4. 2

Big. An hideous bodie big and strong *Bel.* ix. 2
The bodie *bigge,* and mightely pight, *S.C.* F. 106

Big—*Continued.*
They looken *bigge* as Bulls that bene bate, *S.C.* S. 44
bigge Bulles of Basan brace hem about, *S.C.* S. 124
thy Ball is a bold *bigge* curre, *S.C.* S. 164
with *big* words, and with a stately pace, *Hub.* 646
stare . . . with *big* lookes basen wide, *Hub.* 670
with *big* thundring voice revyld him lowd: II. iii. 7. 3
In his *big* base them fitly answered; II. xii. 33. 2
Whose *big* embodied braunches shall not lin III. iii. 22. 3
Big looking like a doughty Doucepere, III. x. 31. 1
his *bigge* hart loth'd so uncomely vew: V. v. 22. 5
Bigger. if thee please in *bigger* notes to sing, *S.C.* O. 46
speak to thee In *bigger* notes, *Gn.* 11
In *bigger* tunes to sound your living prayse. *Ded.Son.*xiii.14
victory in *bigger* notes to sing VII. vii. 1. 7
Biggin. A *Biggen* he had got about his brayne, *S.C.* May 241
Bight. *See* **Bite.**
Bigness. Thy wast *bignes* but combers the grownd, *S.C.* F. 133
All were the beame in *bignes* like a mast, III. vii. 40. 6
Bilbo. Not *Bilbo* steele, nor brasse from Corinth fet, *Mui.* 77
Bilive. *See* **Belive.**
Bill. *See* **Forest-bill.**
The warie foule his *bill* doth backward wring; VI. vii. 9. 4
from his purpled *bill* As from a limbeck VII. vii. 31. 4
Billiards. With dice, with cards, with *balliards* farre unfit *Hub.* 803
Billows. river swift, whose fomy *billowes* *Bel.*[2] viii. 1
Eftsoones of thousand *billowes* shouldred narre, *Ro.* xvi. 3
with good speed the fomie *billowes* scowre: *Gn.* 564
The *billowes* striving to the heavens to reach, *Gn.* 575
Tost on salt *billowes,* round about doth stray. *Gn.* 592
in the bosome of the *billowes* breed. *Col.* 243
the river Dee . . . His tombling *billowes* rolls with gentle rore; I. ix. 4. 8
blood-red *billowes,* like a walled front, I. x. 53. 3
The rolling *billowes* beate the ragged shore, I. xi. 21. 3
steepe His fierie face in *billowes* of the west, I. xi. 31. 2
Meetes two contrarie *billowes* II. ii. 24. 4
Through the dull *billowes* thicke as troubled mire, II. vi. 20. 7
Yet still he bet the water, and the *billowes* dasht. II. vi. 42. 9
the salt brine out of the *billowes* sprong. II. xii. 10. 5
the *billowes* rore Outragiously, II. xii. 22. 1
Ye might have seene the frothy *billowes* fry II. xii. 45. 1
The sunny beames which on the *billowes* bett, II. xii. 63. 3
thy cruel *billowes* beat so strong, III. iv. 8. 4
Eftsoones the roaring *billowes* still abid, III. iv. 32. 7
her bowre Is built of hollow *billowes* heaped hye, III. iv. 43. 2
The roring *billowes* in their proud disdaine, III. viii. 37. 3
all men feare to tempt his *billowes* strong, III. ix. 45. 5
The roring *billowes* beat his bowre so boystrously. III. x. 58. 9
therewith fierce did stryke The raging *billowes,* III. xi. 40. 6
As when two *billowes* . . . Do meete together, IV. i. 42. 1
The powre to rule the *billowes,* IV. xi. 12. 9
billowes beating from the maine: IV. xii. 5. 9
amidst the *billowes* beating of her, V. iv. 10. 6
prove thy manhood on the *billowes* vayne.' VI. iii. 32. 5
bad his *billowes* spare To wet their silken feathers, *Proth.* 48
In th' Ocean *billowes* he hath bathed fayre, *Proth.* 165
Bills. With *bils* and glayves making a dreadfull luster, V. xi. 58. 5
Bind. *Binde* your fillets faste, *S.C.* Ap. 133
in the wine a solemne oth they *bynd* I. v. 4. 8
His cruell wounds . . . They *binden* up I. v. 29. 7
in which his needments he did *bind.* I. vi. 35. 9
those two knights, fast friendship for to *bynd,* I. ix. 18. 6
the pennes, that did his pineons *bynd,* I. xi. 10. 4
My conscience cleare with guilty bands would *bynd?* I. xii. 30. 5
fast to *bind* their league, II. ii. 33. 1
Guyon does Furor *bind* in chaines, II. iv. Arg.
With hundred yron chaines he did him *bind,* II. iv. 15. 1
the faith which she to me did *bynd;* II. iv. 22. 8
To *bind* their dooers to receive their meed? II. viii. 56. 3
That man to hard conditions to *bind,* III. ii. 13. 7
She with her scarf did *bind* the wound III. v. 33. 9
with thy charmes the sharpest sight doest *binde,* III. x. 4. 5
to her service *bind* each living creature, IV. ii. 44. 4
Therewith to *bind* lascivious desire, IV. v. 4. 7
did *bind* About the turtles necke, IV. viii. 7. 2
the gentle hart should most assured *bind.* IV. ix. 1. 9
there in chaynes her cruelly did *bind,* IV. xi. 2. 5
now they doe with captive bands him *bind;* V. iii. 9. 7
With which wise Nature did them strongly *bynd* V. v. 25. 3
Chiefely by him whose life her law doth *bynd,* V. v. 41. 7
by the holy vow which me doth *bind,* V. vii. 19. 7
'Nathlesse,' (quoth he) 'if need doe not you *bynd,* VI. iv. 28. 6
Led in a rope which both his hands did *bynd;* VI. vii. 49. 2
fast with cords do *bynde,* VI. viii. 12. 3
friendly offices that *bynde,* VI. x. 23. 5
doth the Blatant Beast Subdew, and *bynd* in bands. VI. xii. Arg.
Let her, yf please her, *bynd* with adamant chayne: *Am.* xlii. 10
Bynd up the locks the which hang scatterd light, *Epith.* 62
Eternally *bind* thou this lovely band, *Epith.* 396
Bindeth. vertue is the band that *bindeth* harts most sure. IV. ii. 29. 9
Binding. *See* **Heart-binding.**
did far away espye *Binding* her sister, II. xi. 28. 9
bynding up her locks and weeds, V. x. 24. 9
Bynding himselfe most firmely to obay, VI. i. 44. 2
Binds. dread of God, that devils *bindes,* V. xii. 1. 3
Birch. The *Birch* for shaftes; I. i. 9. 5
Birchen. swarme Of flyes upon a *birchen* bough doth cluster, V. xi. 58. 2
Bird. the *birde* that dares beholde the Sunne, *Bel.*[1] vi. 1
A *Bird* all white, well feathered *Bel.* xi. 5

Bird—*Continued.*
the *Bird* that can the sun endure, *Bel.*[2] vii. 1
Strange *bird* (*birde*[1]) he was, *Pet.* v. 3
So long as Joves great *Bird* did make his flight, *Ro.* xvii. 1
I saw a little *Bird* cal'd Tedula, *Van.* iii. 7
The kingly *Bird,* that beares Joves thunder-clap, *Van.* iv. 1
the Nightingale . . . That blessed *byrd,* *S.C.* Au. 184
Junoes *Bird* in her ey-spotted traine *Mui.* 95
No braunch whereon a fine *bird* did not sitt; II. vi. 13. 2
No *bird* but did her shrill notes sweetely sing; II. vi. 13. 3
she, more sweete then any *bird* on bough, II. vi. 25. 1
Upon her fist the *bird,* which shonneth vew, II. ix. 40. 7
Joves harnesse-bearing *Bird* from hye II. xi. 43. 1
The *bird* that knowes not the false fowlers call, III. i. 54. 8
each Paramor his leman knowes, Each *bird* his mate; III. vi. 41. 8
As glad of that small rest as *Bird* of tempest gon. III. vii. 10. 9
every *bird* and beast awarned made To shrowd themselves, III. x. 46. 8
the proud *Bird,* ruffing his fethers wyde III. xi. 32. 6
this gentle *bird* to him did use to repaire IV. viii. 5. 1
the *bird,* when she did find Her selfe so deckt, IV. viii. 7. 5
that sweet *bird* departing flew forthright, IV. viii. 8. 7
the swift *bird* obayd not her behest, IV. viii. 10. 7
Doth beat upon the gentle *bird* in vaine, V. v. 15. 6
The *bird* that warned Peter of his fall, V. vi. 27. 2
till that at last Into a *bird* it chaung'd, V. ix. 17. 5
In which he liv'd alone, like carelesse *bird* in cage. VI. vi. 4. 9
Caught like the *bird* which gazing still on others stands. VI. ix. 11. 9
each *bird* that sits on spray, *Am.* xl. 9
The gentle *birde* feeles no captivity *Am.* lxv. 7
Lyke as a *byrd* . . . to it doth make his flight: *Am.* lxxiii. 5
Birds. *birdes* from aire descending *Rev.* iii. 9
store of *birds* (*birdes*[1]) therein yshrowded were, *Pet.* iii. 5
Wherein the *byrds* were wont to build their bowre, *S.C.* Ja. 32
For *birds* in bushes tooting, *S.C.* Mar. 66
where *Byrds* of every kynde . . . tunes attemper *S.C.* Jun. 7
Whose Echo . . . taught the *byrds,* *S.C.* Jun. 53
Ye carelesse *byrds* are privie to my cryes, *S.C.* Au. 153
Helpe me, ye banefull *byrds,* *S.C.* Au. 173
I beate the bush, the *byrds* to them doe flye: *S.C.* O. 17
where the chaunting *birds* luld me asleepe, *S.C.* D. 71
The soothe of *byrdes* by beating of their winges, *S.C.* D. 87
the small *Birds,* in their wide boughs embowring, *Gn.* 225
'Let *birds* be silent on the naked spray, *D.* 330
all their *birds* with silence to complaine: *Col.* 24
other men and beasts and *birds* doth feed: *Col.* 297
all as glad as *birdes* of joyous Pryme, I. vi. 13. 5
chearefull *birds* of sundry kynd I. vii. 3. 4
the mery *birdes* of every sorte II. v. 31. 6
Trees, braunches, *birds,* and songs, were framed fitt II. vi. 13. 5
all the quire of *birds* did sweetly sing, II. vi. 24. 8
Cormoyraunts, with *birds* of ravenous race, II. xii. 8. 5
all the nation of unfortunate And fatall *birds* II. xii. 36. 2
Birdes, voices, instruments, windes, waters, II. xii. 70. 9
The joyous *birdes,* shrouded in chearefull shade II. xii. 71. 1
gan all the quire of *birdes* II. xii. 76. 1
sweet *birdes* thereto applide Their daintie layes III. i. 40. 3
the *birds* song many a lovely lay III. v. 40. 3
Some made for beasts, some made for *birds* to weare; III. vi. 35. 6
The whiles the joyous *birdes* make their pastyme III. vi. 42. 7
young *birds,* which he had taught to sing, III. vii. 17. 3
In power of herbes, and tunes of beasts and *burds;* IV. ii. 35. 6
the merry *birds,* thy prety pages, IV. x. 45. 6
Charmes to the *birds* full many a pleasant lay, V. ix. 13. 2
The *birds* to catch, or fishes to beguyle; VI. ix. 23. 6
Spredding pavilions for the *birds* to bowre, VI. x. 6. 6
a thousand *birds* had built their bowres VII. vii. 28. 4
the quyre of *Byrds* resounded, Their anthemes *Am.* xix. 5
Hark! how the cheerefull *birds* do chaunt *Epith.* 78
Two fairer *Birds* I yet did never see; *Proth.* 39
All which upon those goodly *Birds* they threw *Proth.* 76
'Ye gentle *Birdes!* the worlds faire ornament, *Proth.* 91
those joyous *Birdes* did passe along, *Proth.* 114
Birds'. Joying to heare the *birdes* sweete harmony, I. i. 8. 2
hearken to the *birds* love-learned song, *Epith.* 88
Birth. fight against the Gods of heavenly *berth,* *Ro.* xii. 3
Ne brest of baser *birth* doth thee embrace, *S.C.* O. 82
the Muse so wrought me from my *byrth,* *S.C.* D. 38
like as at the ingate of their *berth* *Ti.* 47
you, my liefe, yborn of hevenly *berth.* I. iii. 28. 9
Most vertuous virgin, borne of hevenly *berth,* I. x. 9. 3
by her stately portance borne of heavenly *birth.* II. iii. 21. 9
birth of fayre Belphoebe and Of Amorett III. vi. Arg.
in her *berth* The hevens so favorable were III. vi. 2. 1
Her *berth* was of the wombe of Morning dew, III. vi. 3. 1
being but halfe twin of that *berth:* III. vii. 47. 9
at that *berth* another Babe she bore; III. vii. 48. 1
there made gods, though borne of mortall *berth,* IV. iii. 44. 3
Then came Nobilitie of *birth,* V. ix. 45. 7
His Saviour's *birth* his mind so much did glad. VII. vii. 41. 4
Birthright. Titan . . . Saturnes elder brother by *birth-right,* VII. vi. 27. 2
Bisaltis. Ne ought but deare *Bisaltis* ay could make him glad. III. xi. 41. 9
Bishop. Both that the *Bishop* may admit of thee, *Hub.* 533
Bishopric. cast a figure for a *Bishoprick;* *Hub.* 511
Scarse can a *Bishoprick* forpas them by, *Hub.* 519
Bit. *See* **Bate, Cannon-bit.**
leade me forth on Fancies *bitte* to playe: *S.C.* D. 64
This with full *bit* doth catch the utmost top *Gn.* 83
The *bit* of balefull steele and bitter stownd, *Mui.* 62
Defended from foule Envies poisnous *bit.* *Ded. Son.* iii. 4
His angry steede did chide his foming *bitt,* I. i. 1. 6

Bit—*Continued.*	
thrise three times did fast from any *bitt;*	I. iii. 14. 4
The yron rowels into frothy fome he *bitt.*	I. vii. 37. 9
smott, and *bitt,* and kickt, and scratcht, and rent,	II. iv. 6. 8
bitt his tawny beard to shew his raging yre.	II. iv. 15. 9
arriving forcibly On his broad shield, *bitt* not,	II. v. 4. 4
pierced to the skin, but *bit* no more;	II. viii. 44. 8
bit his lip for felonous despight,	IV. x. 33. 8
tameth stubborne youth With iron *bit,*	IV. xii. 13. 4
It *bit* the earth for very fell despight,	V. ii. 18. 6
th' one hand seizing on his golden *bit,*	V. iii. 29. 6
by the shoulder him so sore he *bit,*	V. iii. 33. 8
glauncing on her shoulder-plate it *bit* Unto the bone,	V. vii. 33. 2
with furious *bit* Snatching at every thing	V. viii. 49. 3
Abasht at his rebuke, that *bit* her neare,	V. xi. 64. 2
Bit him behind, that long the marke was to be read.	V. xii. 39. 9
he with his tooth impure Him heedlesse *bit,*	VI. v. 16. 9
Thereat frown'd Coridon, and his lip closely *bit.*	VI. ix. 41. 9
bit them with his banefull teeth of injury.	VI. xi. 28. 9
He grind, hee *bit,* he scratcht, he venim threw,	VI. xii. 31. 8
every *bit* which thenceforth I did eat,	*Am.* xxxix. 14
Bitch. at his feete a *bitch* Wolfe did give sucke	*Bel.*[1] vii. 9
at his feete a *bitch* wolfe suck did yeeld	*Bel.*[2] ix. 9
As a mad *bytch,* when as the franticke fit	V. viii. 49. 1
Bite. *See* **Bate.**	
He has a Dogge to *byte* or to barke;	*S.C.* S. 181
the right gentle minde woulde *bite* his lip,	*Hub.* 711
which doe *byte* their hasty supper best;	I. i. 23. 4
The cruell steele . . . doth *bight* In tender flesh,	I. v. 9. 3
His harder hyde would nether perce nor *bight,*	I. xi. 16. 4
The fish that once was caught new bait wil hardly *byte.*	II. i. 4. 9
suffred not his blowes to *byte* him nere,	II. ii. 23. 3
teach the cursed steele to *bight* In his owne flesh,	II. vi. 32. 8
gnawing Gealosy . . . his bitter lips did *bight;*	II. vii. 22. 5
glauncing downe would not his owner *byte;*	II. viii. 38. 4
Dare not adventure on the stubborne pray, Ne *byte* before,	III. i. 22. 4
had no powre in his soft flesh to *bite.*	III. v. 19. 5
with gnashing teeth did *bite* The bitter earth,	III. v. 22. 1
doth felly *bite* and teare The stone	IV. viii. 36. 5
feeling him thus *bite* upon the bayt,	V. v. 42. 6
bite, and cruelly torment.'	VI. i. 8. 9
none of them in his soft flesh did *bite;*	VI. v. 18. 7
where they *bite* it booteth not to weene . . . It ever to amend:	VI. vi. 9. 4
Feeling some curre behinde his heeles to *bite,*	VI. vi. 27. 6
The tempred steele did not into his braynepan *byte.*	VI. vi. 30. 9
To see her sore lament and *bite* her tender lip.	VI. vii. 44. 9
Gan him to hale, and teare, and scratch, and *bite;*	VI. viii. 28. 7
he would loure And *byte* his lip,	VI. ix. 39. 3
snatch, and *byte,* and rend, and tug, and teare;	VI. xi. 17. 6
bet abacke, threatning in vaine to *bite,*	VI. xii. 29. 4
Her lips lyke cherryes charming men to *byte,*	*Epith.* 174
Bites. yet spite *bites* neare.	*Hub.* 424
Spite *bites* the dead, that living never baid.	*Ti.* 215
Biting. The *byting* frost nipt his stalke dead,	*S.C.* F. 231
His *biting* sword, and his devouring speare,	I. vii. 48. 2
Embost with bale, and bitter *byting* griefe,	I. ix. 29. 2
When he these bitter *byting* wordes had red,	I. xii. 29. 1
Where *byting* deepe so deadly it imprest,	IV. vi. 13. 7
byting th' earth for very deaths disdaine;	V. xi. 14. 7
byting deepe therein did sticke so fast	V. xii. 21. 8
the *biting* of that harmefull Beast Was throughly heal'd.	VI. vi. 15. 5
Barking and *biting* all that him doe bate,	VI. xii. 40. 5
Bits. lavish cups and thriftie *bitts* of meate,	*S.C.* O. 105
steedes . . . on their rusty *bits* did champ	I. v. 20. 9
His bare thin cheekes for want of better *bits,*	I. viii. 41. 3
brought to nought by little *bits?*	IV. ii. 33. 9
Bitter. nothing doth endure, But *bitter* griefe	*Pet.* vi. 12
Heaven envious, and *bitter* stepdame Nature!	*Ro.* ix. 2
where colde Boreas blowes his *bitter* stormes.	*Ro.* xxvi. 8
These *bitter* blasts never ginne tasswage?	*S.C.* F. 2
That shall alegge this *bitter* blast,	*S.C.* Mar. 5
One *bitter* blast blewe all away.	*S.C.* N. 119
Now bringen *bitter* Eldre braunches seare;	*S.C.* N. 147
Winter is come that blowes the *bitter* blaste,	*S.C.* D. 143
Into this *bitter* bale I am outcast,	*Gn.* 330
With *bitter* woundes her owne deere babes to slay,	*Gn.* 399
With *bitter* torture, and impatient paines,	*Gn.* 628
Oxeye still greene, and *bitter* Patience;	*Gn.* 678
raged sore In *bitter* words,	*Hub.* 1089
Against the *bitter* throwes of dolours darts:	*T.M.* 134
far more *bitter* storme than winters stowre	*T.M.* 247
those *bitter* stounds Of raging love	*T.M.* 373
a brackish flood Of *bitter* teares,	*T.M.* 416
The bit of balefull steele and *bitter* stownd,	*Mui.* 62
Notes sad enough t' expresse this *bitter* throw:	*Mui.* 414
whose brackish *bitter* well, I wasted have,	*D.* 250
Feede ye hencefoorth on *bitter* Astrofell,	*D.* 346
When she beholds . . . My *bitter* penance,	*D.* 382
The same with *bitter* teares they all bedewed.	*As.* 204
The Mirrhe sweete-bleeding in the *bitter* wound;	I. i. 9. 6
And *bitter* anguish of his guilty sight,	I. ii. 6. 2
'That keepes thy body from the *bitter* fitt!	I. ii. 18. 2
plaines, Where Boreas doth blow full *bitter* bleake,	I. ii. 33. 7
she . . . does steepe Her tender brest in *bitter* teares all night;	I. iii. 15. 8
that harlott . . . That causd her shed so many a *bitter* teare;	I. iii. 25. 4
many mischiefes follow cruell Wrath: . . . *Bitter* despight,	I. iv. 35. 4
nourish bloody vengeaunce in his *bitter* mind.	I. iv. 38. 9
I saw with *bitter* eyes The bold Sansfoy shrinck	I. v. 23. 1
They pas the *bitter* waves of Acheron,	I. v. 33. 1
he al enrag'd these *bitter* speaches said.	I. vi. 46. 9
Bitter—*Continued.*	
Begin, and end the *bitter* balefull stound;	I. vii. 25. 8
Long tost with stormes, and bet with *bitter* wind,	I. vii. 28. 7
Soone as I thinke upon my *bitter* bale.	I. vii. 39. 6
ghosts . . . Have felt the *bitter* dint of his avenging blade.	I. vii. 47. 9
Embost with bale, and *bitter* byting griefe,	I. ix. 29. 2
That makes frayle flesh to feare the *bitter* wave,	I. ix. 40. 5
bitter Penaunce, with an yron whip,	I. x. 27. 1
have mind of that last *bitter* throw;	I. x. 41. 8
The *bitter* doome of death and balefull mone	I. x. 53. 8
bitter battailes all are fought?	I. x. 62. 8
bitter sence of his deepe rooted ill,	I. xi. 22. 8
When he these *bitter* byting wordes had red,	I. xii. 29. 1
many *bitter* throbs did throw,	II. i. 47. 3
The *bitter* pangs that doth your heart infest.	II. i. 48. 5
wordes with *bitter* teares did steepe:	II. ii. 1. 9
Sad be the sights, and *bitter* fruites of warre,	II. ii. 30. 6
the Hag, with many a *bitter* threat,	II. iv. 9. 3
Her *bitter* rayling and foule revilement,	II. iv. 12. 5
Streight gan he him revyle, and *bitter* rate,	II. vi. 39. 3
'lett be thy *bitter* scorne,	II. vii. 18. 1
gnawing Gealosy . . . his *bitter* lips did bight;	II. vii. 22. 5
A song of bale and *bitter* sorrow sings,	II. vii. 23. 7
trees of *bitter* Gall, and Heben sad;	II. vii. 52. 2
dipped in the *bitter* wave Of hellish Styx,	II. viii. 20. 8
He cast between to ward the *bitter* stownd:	II. viii. 32. 6
exercise most *bitter* tyranny	II. xi. 1. 7
was not so hardy to abide That *bitter* stownd,	II. xi. 25. 5
commen to his reskew, ere his *bitter* bane.	II. xi. 29. 9
full many a *bitter* stownd I have endurd,	III. i. 24. 8
First did it shew the *bitter* balefull stowre,	III. i. 34. 7
with hart-thrilling throbs and *bitter* stowre,	III. ii. 5. 3
Whose root and stalke so *bitter* yet did taste,	III. ii. 17. 6
tyrannizeth in the *bitter* smarts	III. ii. 23. 3
through many a *bitter* stowre:	III. iii. 3. 5
full of *bitter* griefe and pensife thought,	III. iv. 31. 5
Thou art the roote and nourse of *bitter* cares,	III. iv. 57. 2
So them with *bitter* words he stird to bloodie yre.	III. v. 15. 9
with gnashing teeth did bite The *bitter* earth,	III. v. 22. 2
with bold words and *bitter* threat	III. viii. 16. 2
Gan blowen up a *bitter* stormy blast,	III. ix. 11. 5
did his hart with *bitter* thoughts engore,	III. x. 45. 4
festred up with *bitter* milke of tine,	III. xi. 1. 4
Untroubled of vile feare or *bitter* fell.	III. xi. 2. 5
forth breaking into *bitter* plaintes	III. xi. 9. 1
Each other of loves *bitter* fruit despoile.	III. xii. 47. *or.* 2
The deare compassion of whose *bitter* fit	IV. i. 1. 6
Seven moneths he so her kept in *bitter* smart,	IV. i. 4. 1
All carelesse of his taunt and *bitter* rayle;	IV. i. 43. 2
gan this *bitter* answere to him make:	IV. ii. 14. 2
bitter gall away to chace,	IV. iii. 43. 3
Covered with cloudie storme and *bitter* showre,	IV. v. 32. 2
adding anguish to the *bitter* wound	IV. vii. 1. 7
bitter thoughts, which deepe therein infixed lay.	IV. viii. 1. 9
breathed forth with blast of *bitter* wind;	IV. viii. 26. 5
All which he did from *bitter* bondage free,	IV. ix. 8. 6
that same *bitter* corsive,	IV. ix. 14. 4
With many *bitter* teares shed from his blubbred eyne.	V. i. 13. 9
With *bitter* taunts and termes of vile disgrace.	V. iv. 23. 4
With *bitter* strokes it both began and ended.	V. v. 6. 2
into *bitter* termes forth brust,	V. viii. 22. 4
Miscalling me by many a *bitter* name,	V. viii. 22. 8
bitter curses, horrible to tell;	V. xi. 28. 3
With *bitter* rage and fell contention,	V. xii. 41. 3
among most *bitter* wordes they spake,	V. xii. 42. 1
with *bitter* wracke To wreake on me the guilt	VI. ii. 21. 5
To wype his wounds, and ease their *bitter* payning.	VI. ii. 41. 5
bring us bale and *bitter* sorrowings,	VI. iii. 5. 5
all the night for *bitter* anguish weepe,	VI. iii. 10. 4
the *bitter* stoure Of his sore vengeaunce,	VI. iii. 48. 4
that curre, barking with *bitter* sownd,	VI. v. 19. 5
The *bitter* anguish of their sharpe disease	VI. v. 32. 5
Not sparing him with *bitter* words to taunt,	VI. vi. 21. 7
with *bitter* mockes and mowes	VI. vii. 49. 6
life Which Shepheards lead, without debate or *bitter* strife.	VI. ix. 18. 9
Blew up a *bitter* storme of foule adversity.	VI. x. 38. 9
With *bitter* termes of shamefull infamy;	VI. xii. 33. 4
Streight *bitter* stormes, and balefull countenance	VII. vii. 23. 5
when I feele the *bitter* balefull smart,	*Am.* xxiv. 5
Sweet is the Nut, but *bitter* is his pill;	*Am.* xxvi. 6
In *bitter* hyve to grope for honny:	*Epig.* i. 4
Faine would I seeke to ease my *bitter* smart	*H.L.* 5
With *bitter* wounds through hands, through feet, and syde!	*H.H.L.* 245
Bitter-breathing. *bitter-breathing* windes with harmfull blast,	*Ti.* 405
Bitterly. Duessa wept full *bitterly.*	I. v. 17. 9
eke blaspheming heaven *bitterly,*	II. vii. 60. 8
the Palmer gan full *bitterly* Her to rebuke	II. xii. 16. 5
ever hasty Night he blamed *bitterlie.*	III. iv. 54. 9
To be unjustly blamd, and *bitterly* revilde.	IV. viii. 28. 9
Gan both envy, and *bitterly* to ban;	IV. ix. 9. 7
with sharpe words did *bitterly* upbrayd:	VI. vi. 33. 3
Bittern. as a *Bittur* in the Eagles clawe,	II. viii. 50. 2
Bitterness. Strife and debate, bloodshed and *bitternesse,*	II. vii. 12. 7
few drops of *bitternesse,*	III. x. 25. 9
oft with *bitternesse* It forth would breake,	IV. viii. 24. 4
gan t' augment her *bitternesse* much more;	VI. i. 32. 2
Bittur. *See* **Bittern.**	
Bize. *See* **Byze.**	
Black. *See* **Coal-black, Tomb-black.**	
with *black* horror did the ayre appall:	*Bel.*[2] viii. 4

Black—*Continued.*
the one was *blacke* (*black*[1]), the other white: . . . *Pet.* i. 7
jawes, that with *blacke* venime swell. . . . *Van.* iii. 12
Her mantle *black* through heaven gan overhaile: . . . *S.C.* Ja. 75
night-ravenes lodge, more *black* then pitche, . . . *S.C.* Jun. 23
To quite it from the *blacke* bowre of sorrowe. . . . *S.C.* S. 97
The blew in *black*, . . . is tinct; . . . *S.C.* N. 107
the *blacke* Holme that loves the watrie vale; . . . *Gn.* 215
To the *black* shadowes of the Stygian shore, . . . *Gn.* 383
blacke Laestrigones, a people stout: . . . *Gn.* 538
Black stormes and fogs are blowen up from farre, . . . *Gn.* 572
Borne in the bosome of the *black* Abysse, . . . *T.M.* 260
overgrowen with *blacke* oblivions rust. . . . *Ti.* 98
Clad all in *black*, that mourning did bewray, . . . *D.* 40
over all a *blacke* stole shee did throw: . . . I. i. 4. 5
A floud of poyson horrible and *blacke*, . . . I. i. 20. 2
Deformed monsters, fowle, and *blacke* as inke, . . . I. i. 22. 7
An aged Sire, in long *blacke* weedes yclad, . . . I. i. 29. 2
He bad awake *blacke* Plutoes griesly Dame; . . . I. i. 37. 4
sad Night over him her mantle *black* doth spred. . . . I. i. 39. 9
a *black* stole, most like to seeme for Una fit. . . . I. i. 45. 9
Under *blacke* stole hyding her bayted hooke; . . . I. i. 49. 6
mourning altars . . . The *black* infernall Furies doen aslake: I. iii. 36. 8
sluggish Idlenesse, . . . Arayd in habit *blacke*, . . . I. iv. 18. 8
Who rough, and *blacke*, and filthy, did appeare, . . . I. iv. 24. 5
Doest thou sit wayling by *blacke* Stygian lake, . . . I. v. 10. 6
Night, . . . in a foule *blacke* pitchy mantle clad, . . . I. v. 20. 3
two *blacke* as pitch, And two were browne, . . . I. v. 28. 4
Bespotted as with shieldes of red and *blacke*, . . . I. xi. 11. 5
A gushing river of *blacke* gory blood, . . . I. xi. 22. 4
A comely Palmer, clad in *black* attyre, . . . II. i. 7. 2
gan his voyage make With his *blacke* Palmer, . . . II. i. 34. 4
that *blacke* Palmer, his most trusty guide, . . . II. iv. 2. 4
the *Blacke* Palmer suffred still to stond, . . . II. vi. 19. 7
fowle smoke and clouds more *black* then Jett. . . . II. vii. 28. 9
More fitt emongst *black* fiendes then men to have his place. . . II. vii. 41. 9
direfull deadly *black*, both leafe and bloom, . . . II. vii. 51. 8
Dead sleeping Poppy, and *black* Hellebore; . . . II. vii. 52. 3
a *blacke* flood, which flow'd about it round. . . . II. vii. 56. 7
under the *blacke* vele of guilty Night, . . . III. i. 59. 7
Thy dwelling is in Herebus *black* hous, . . . III. iv. 55. 6
(*Black* Herebus, thy husband, is the foe Of all the Gods,) . . III. iv. 55. 7
'Under thy mantle *black* there hidden lye . . . III. iv. 58. 1
white seemes fayrer macht with *blacke* attone; . . . III. ix. 2. 4
By strong enchauntments and *blacke* Magicke leare, . . . III. xi. 16. 7
Full *blacke* and griesly did his face appeare, . . . IV. v. 34. 6
Within his mouth a *blacke* spot doth appeare, . . . V. iii. 32. 8
Enwallow'd in his owne *blacke* bloudy gore, . . . V. xi. 14. 6
Breathing out clouds of sulphure fowle and *blacke*, . . . V. xi. 32. 2
with *black* dishonor And foule defame . . . VI. vi. 25. 4
his locks, as *blacke* as pitchy night, . . . VI. vii. 43. 7
His brode *black* wings had . . . dispred, . . . VI. viii. 44. 5
Drawne of two steeds, th' one *black*, the other white, . . . VII. vi. 9. 2
(His *black* eye-brow, whose doomefull dreaded beck . . . VII. vi. 22. 2
Th' one on a Palfrey *blacke*, the other white; . . . VII. vii. 44. 3
covered her uncomely face With a *blacke* veile, . . . VII. vii. 44. 5
And al her faults in thy *black* booke enroll: . . . *Am.* x. 12
Black-browed. His mother was the *blacke-browd* Cymoent, . . III. iv. 19. 3
Black-lidded. he vewes, with his *black-lidded* eye, . . . *Hub.* 1228
Blacksmith. some *blacksmith* dwelt in that desert ground. . . IV. v. 33. 9
His name was Care; a *blacksmith* by his trade, . . . IV. v. 35. 6
Blackwater. of the English man Is cal'de *Blacke-water*, . . . IV. xi. 41. 6
Bladder. that monstrous mas . . . like an emptie *blader* was. . I. viii. 24. 9
Bladders. like *bladders* blowen up with wynd, . . . *Col.* 717
Her dried dugs, lyke *bladders* lacking wind, Hong downe, . . . I. viii. 47. 6
Blade. Nor the deep wounds of victours raging *blade*, . . . *Ro.* xiii. 2
Now with his sharp bore-spear, now with his *blade*. . . . *As.* 108
with his trenchand *blade* her boldly kept . . . I. i. 17. 3
his thristy *blade* To bathe in blood . . . I. v. 15. 2
Semiramis, whose sides transfixt With sonnes own *blade* . . I. v. 50. 4
scarsely could he weeld his bootlesse single *blade*. . . . I. vii. 11. 9
Thereby his mortall *blade* full comely hong In yvory sheath, . I. vii. 30. 6
ghosts . . . Have felt the bitter dint of his avenging *blade*. . I. vii. 47. 9
with *blade* all burning bright He smott off his left arme, . . I. viii. 10. 5
high advauncing his blood-thirstie *blade*, . . . I. viii. 16. 1
His sparkling *blade* about his head he blest, . . . I. viii. 22. 3
fercely tooke his trenchand *blade* in hand, . . . I. xi. 24. 1
High brandishing his bright deaw-burning *blade*, . . . I. xi. 35. 6
Inflam'd with wrath, his raging *blade* he hefte, . . . I. xi. 39. 6
shyning *blade* unsheathd, . . . II. ii. 21. 6
rusheth forth Betweene them both by conduct of his *blade*. . II. ii. 25. 2
When I at her my murdrous *blade* did bend, . . . II. iv. 31. 7
With his bright *blade* did smite at him . . . II. v. 4. 2
soone his dreadfull *blade* about he cast, . . . II. v. 12. 3
where hath he hong up his mortall *blade*, . . . II. v. 35. 7
Guyons angry *blade* so fiers did play . . . II. vi. 31. 5
hurling up his harmefull *blade* on hy, . . . II. viii. 33. 5
He stroke so hugely with his borrowd *blade*, . . . II. viii. 45. 2
them perforce withheld with threatned *blade*, . . . II. xi. 31. 4
brave retourning, with his brandisht *blade* . . . II. xi. 37. 1
His speares default to mend with cruell *blade*; . . . III. i. 10. 3
Threatning the point of her avenging *blaed*; . . . III. i. 63. 8
a rusty *blade* In th' other was; . . . III. xii. 11. 5
fiercely forth her mortall *blade* she drew, . . . III. xii. 33. 8
snatching forth his direfull deadly *blade* . . . IV. vi. 12. 2
garnisht all with gold upon the *blade* . . . V. i. 10. 3
How ever gay their blossome or their *blade* Doe flourish now, V. ii. 40. 4
with his trenchant *blade* . . . he shared quite away, . . . V. v. 9. 1
swearing faith to either on his *blade*, . . . V. viii. 14. 7
Upon the Image with his naked *blade* . . . he strooke; . . . V. xi. 22. 1

Blade—*Continued.*
laying hand upon his wrathfull *blade* . . . VI. v. 26. 6
fiercely drawing forth his *blade*, . . . VI. xi. 15. 7
Blades. Your *blades* in your owne bowels you embrew'd? . . *Ro.* xxiv. 8
wretched boy, they slew with guiltie *blades*; . . . *Gn.* 403
burning *blades* about their heades doe blesse, . . . I. v. 6. 4
To see their *blades* so greedily imbrew, . . . I. vi. 38. 7
the knights with their bright burning *blades* . . . II. ix. 15. 6
Their wrathfull *blades* downe fell out of their hand, . . . IV. iii. 48. 4
cruell *blades*, yet steeming with whot bloud, . . . IV. ix. 29. 4
Bladud. Whose footsteps *Bladud* following, . . . II. x. 25. 6
Which *Bladud* made by Magick art of yore, . . . III. iii. 60. 2
Blame. No *blame* to thee, whosoever dost abide By Nyle, . . . *Ro.* xxxi. 3
Say, thou wert base-begot with *blame*; . . . *To his Booke* 14
who my song doth prayse or *blame*, . . . *S.C.* Jun. 73
Thus holy hylles to *blame*, . . . *S.C.* Jul. 38
As they han brewed, so let hem beare *blame*. . . . *S.C.* S. 101
who such sports and sweet delights doth *blame*, . . . *Gn.* 7
caytives, which had bred him *blame*. . . . *Hub.* 1318
be aveng'd on those that breed thy *blame*.' . . . *Hub.* 1332
good men *blame*, and losels magnify. . . . *T.M.* 324
Untill he quite him of this guiltie *blame*. . . . *Ti.* 230
Laies of sweet love, without rebuke or *blame*, . . . *Col.* 3
by breeding him some blot of *blame*, . . . *Col.* 697
the *blame* Which thou imputest, is too generall, . . . *Col.* 731
'*Blame* is . . . more blamelesse generall, . . . *Col.* 749
Though *blame* do light on those that faultie bee; . . . *Col.* 756
who with *blame* can justly her upbrayd . . . *Col.* 913
How rashly *blame* of Rosalind ye raise.' . . . *Col.* 926
to my selfe the *blame* that lookt so hie: . . . *Col.* 936
Ne may I, without blot of endlesse *blame*, . . . *Ded. Son.* xvi. 1
with *blame* . . . asked him, for what he came. . . . I. i. 43. 4
glauncing downe his shield from *blame* him fairly blest. . . I. ii. 18. 9
Least thou of her believe too lightly *blame*, . . . I. iv. 1. 5
holy righteousnesse, without rebuke or *blame*. . . . I. x. 45. 9
often *blame* the too importune fate . . . I. xii. 16. 5
fairely quit him of th' imputed *blame*; . . . II. i. 20. 2
withouten *blame* or blot, . . . II. iii. 22. 3
First her restraine from her reprochfull *blame* . . . II. iv. 11. 3
he to her, withouten blott or *blame*; . . . II. iv. 20. 6
'Certes, Sir knight, ye bene too much to *blame*, . . . II. viii. 13. 2
Ne *blame* your honor with so shamefull vaunt . . . II. viii. 16. 3
Resolv'd to put away that loathly *blame*, . . . II. viii. 44. 4
knew them how to order without *blame*, . . . II. ix. 28. 5
'How is it that this mood in me ye *blame*, . . . II. ix. 38. 2
did away that *blame* . . . II. x. 23. 4
United all his powres to purge him selfe from *blame*. . . II. xi. 31. 9
he gan to feare His toward perill, and untoward *blame*, . . III. i. 9. 7
laid the *blame*, not to his carriage, . . . III. i. 11. 5
'Certes,' (said she) 'then beene ye sixe to *blame*, . . . III. i. 25. 1
Here have I cause in men just *blame* to find, . . . III. ii. 1. 1
t' upbrayd A gentle knight with so unknightly *blame*; . . III. ii. 9. 6
ever doe that mote deserven *blame*: . . . III. ii. 10. 3
she was pure from *blame* of sinfull blott; . . . III. ii. 23. 8
not so lewdly bent As those ye *blame*, . . . III. ii. 43. 3
least *blame* Of her miscarriage should in her be fond, . . . III. ii. 52. 7
affection faultlesse *blame* For fault of few . . . IV. Pr. 2. 4
that could deserve No spot of *blame*, . . . IV. i. 4. 8
Lest she with *blame* her honor should attaint, . . . IV. i. 5. 5
'Then tell,' (quoth Blandamour) 'and feare no *blame*: . . IV. i. 48. 5
For dread of *blame* and honours blemishment; . . . IV. ii. 36. 5
without blot or *blame* To let them passe at will, . . . IV. iv. 3. 4
for doubt of *blame* If he misdid, . . . IV. iv. 27. 7
fell away, as feeling secret *blame*. . . . IV. v. 16. 7
beat his breast unworthy of such *blame*, . . . IV. viii. 4. 7
then none may it redresse or *blame*, . . . IV. viii. 15. 1
she with *blame* would blot, and of due praise deprive. . . IV. viii. 25. 9
Gan *blame* me much for being so untrew . . . IV. viii. 56. 4
ye seemen much to *blame* . . . IV. ix. 37. 2
Ne ever for rebuke or *blame* of any balkt. . . . IV. x. 25. 9
any blemish which the worke mote *blame*; . . . IV. x. 41. 5
As if some *blame* of evill she did feare, . . . IV. x. 50. 4
that formost matrone me did *blame*, . . . IV. x. 54. 1
through his mad mothers *blame*, . . . IV. xi. 13. 5
blame me not if I have err'd in count . . . IV. xii. 2. 6
blame it is to him, that armes profest, . . . IV. xii. 8. 4
Backe to him selfe he gan returne the *blame*, . . . IV. xii. 16. 2
Let none then *blame* me, . . . V. Pr. 3. 1
die guiltie of the *blame* The which another did, . . . V. i. 15. 8
oft their lewdnes blotteth good deserts with *blame*. . . . V. iii. 38. 9
In hope ye will not turne misfortune to my *blame*. . . . V. iv. 28. 9
Left to her will by his owne wilfull *blame*, . . . V. v. 20. 2
Oft did she *blame* her selfe, and often rew, . . . V. vi. 12. 5
never did her ill, ne once deserved *blame*. . . . V. viii. 22. 9
aggravate the horror of her *blame*: . . . V. ix. 43. 4
Too much am I too (*to) *blame* for that faire Maide, . . . V. xi. 41. 2
How cleare I am from *blame* of this upbraide; . . . V. xi. 41. 7
Amongst all Knights he blotted was with *blame*, . . . V. xi. 46. 8
Least ye therefore mote happily me *blame*, . . . V. xi. 52. 8
With so foule *blame* as breach of faith once plight, . . . V. xi. 62. 4
To blot the same with *blame*, . . . V. xii. 34. 9
fowle upbrayd with faulty *blame*. . . . VI. i. 24. 9
it is no *blame* To punish those . . . VI. i. 26. 4
'Perdie great *blame*' . . . a wight unarm'd to wrong: . . . VI. ii. 8. 6
He with his speare, that was to him great *blame*, . . . VI. ii. 10. 7
I . . . gan to *blame* him for such cruelty . . . VI. ii. 11. 3
she . . . cleard that stripling of th' imputed *blame*, . . . VI. ii. 14. 2
To rayse a lyving *blame* against the dead; . . . VI. ii. 15. 7
I may not, certes, without *blame* denie, . . . VI. ii. 34. 6
gan devize How she the *blame* might salve . . . VI. iii. 8. 9

Blame—*Continued.*
and guiltlesse innocent Of *blame,* . . . VI. iii. 18. 4
Yet, as I well it meane, vouchsafe it without *blame.* . . . VI. iv. 34. 9
it was to thee reprochfull *blame* . . . VI. vi. 34. 3
I will them soone acquite, and both of *blame* assoile.' . . . VI. viii. 6. 9
Thus did the courteous Knight excuse his *blame,* . . . VI. x. 29. 8
least reprochfull *blame* With foule dishonour him mote blot . VI. xii. 12. 6
Albe they worthy *blame,* or cleare of crime: . . . VI. xii. 40. 6
let me aske you this withouten *blame;* . . . VII. vii. 53. 4
Her hardnes *blame,* which I should more commend? . . . *Am.* li. 6
T' accuse of pride, or rashly *blame* for ought. . . . *Am.* lxi. 4
hurtlesse sports, without rebuke or *blame,* . . . *H.L.* 288
nathemore is that faire beauties *blame,* . . . *H.B.* 155
Disloiall lust faire beauties foulest *blame,* . . . *H.B.* 170
Sith now that heat is quenched, quench my *blame,* . . . *H.H.L.* 18
Without all blemish or reprochfull *blame,* . . . *H.H.L.* 149
lampe . . . seems fowle, and full of sinfull *blame;* . . . *H.H.B.* 276
Blamed. Faire Rosalind of divers fowly *blamed* . . . *Col.* 908
in which she oft him *blam'd* . . . II. v. 21. 4
Did follow that ensample which he *blam'd* afore. . . . II. vi. 45. 9
ever hasty Night he *blamed* bitterlie. . . . III. iv. 54. 9
being *blam'd,* His dayes in dole doth lead. . . . IV. vii. Arg.
To be unjustly *blamd,* and bitterly revilde. . . . IV. viii. 28. 9
One while she *blam'd* her selfe; . . . V. vi. 5. 1
and *blam'd* her noble blood: . . . VI. iii. 11. 8
evermore she *blamed* Calepine, . . . VI. viii. 33. 1
Ne certes mote he greatly *blamed* be . . . VI. x. 3. 1
many causelesse caused to be *blamed.* . . . VI. xii. 38. 5
to be *blam'd* for spilling guiltlesse blood. . . . *Am.* xxxviii. 14
Blameful. embay His *blamefull* body in salt water . . . I. x. 27. 6
nothing is more *blamefull* to a knight, . . . VI. i. 41. 1
without crime Or *blamefull* blot; . . . VI. ix. 46. 4
all were they cleanest From *blamefull* blot, . . . VI. xii. 41. 4
Blameless. 'Blame is . . . more *blamelesse* generall, . . . *Col.* 749
Bent to revenge on *blamelesse* Britomart The crime . . . IV. v. 31. 1
In simple truth and *blamelesse* chastitie, . . . IV. viii. 30. 3
Blames. The soveraigne of seas he *blames* in vaine, . . . *S.C.* F. 33
telling them to blazon out their *blames.* . . . *T.M.* 102
To get small thankes, and therewith many *blames,* . . . III. vii. 61. 3
least with unworthie *blames* . . . III. ix. 1. 3
first laide on those Ladies thousand *blames,* . . . IV. ii. 20. 7
sith ye please that both our *blames* shall die, . . . V. viii. 14. 1
Artegall . . . *blames* for changing shield: . . . V. xii. Arg.
Blamest. *blamest* hem much for small encheason. . . . *S.C.* May 147
thou *blamest* me for having blent My name with guile . . . I. vi. 42. 4
Blameworthy. ought in them *blameworthie* thou doest spie.' . *Col.* 679
Blaming. *Blaming* of Fortune, which such troubles threw, . . I. vi. 31. 5
boldly *blaming* her for comming there, . . . VII. vi. 12. 7
Bland. base affections, which your eares would *bland* . . . *H.B.* 171
Blandamour. discord breedes Twixt Scudamour and *Blandamour:* . . . IV. i. Arg.
His name was *Blandamour,* that did descrie His fickle mind . IV. i. 32. 4
when as *Blandamour* approching nie . . . IV. i. 38. 7
Which when as *Blandamour* beheld, . . . IV. i. 44. 1
'Then tell,' (quoth *Blandamour*) 'and feare no blame: . . . IV. i. 48. 5
Blandamour, whenas he did espie His chaunge of cheere . . . IV. i. 50. 6
Blandamour winnes false Florimell; . . . IV. ii. Arg.
Blandamour . . . her scornd, and set at nought, . . . IV. ii. 3. 3
Which when as *Blandamour* . . . Beheld, . . . IV. ii. 5. 1
'Too boastfull *Blandamoure!* too long I beare . . . IV. ii. 13. 1
Exceeding wroth thereat was *Blandamour,* . . . IV. ii. 14. 1
you, Sir *Blandamour,* and Paridell, . . . IV. ii. 24. 2
Thereat Sir *Blandamour* . . . thus fiercely him bespake: . . . IV. ii. 25. 1
a new debate Stird up twixt *Blandamour* and Paridell, . . . IV. iv. 2. 4
Blandamour full of vainglorious spright, . . . IV. iv. 3. 6
Which *Blandamour* had riding by his side: . . . IV. iv. 7. 8
Which scornefull offer *Blandamour* gan soone despize; . . . IV. iv. 8. 9
Blandamour with those Of his . . . IV. iv. 14. 2
him against Sir *Blandamour* did ride . . . IV. iv. 19. 3
All which when *Blandamour* from end to end Beheld, . . . IV. iv. 45. 5
Blandamour, who thought he had the trew And very Florimell, IV. v. 13. 7
Blandamour thereat full greatly grudged, . . . IV. v. 22. 3
wroth with Satyran was *Blandamour;* . . . IV. v. 24. 2
wroth with *Blandamour* was Erivan; . . . IV. v. 24. 3
Love-lavish *Blandamour,* and lustfull Paridell. . . . IV. ix. 20. 9
so eke lov'd *Blandamour,* . . . IV. ix. 21. 5
sometimes Paridell and *Blandamour* The better had, . . . IV. ix. 25. 1
Blandamour, whom alwaies he envide; . . . IV. ix. 26. 4
Blandamour to Claribell relide: . . . IV. ix. 26. 5
assaid Of Claribell and *Blandamour* attone; . . . IV. ix. 30. 2
With faithlesse *Blandamour* and Paridell, . . . V. ix. 41. 3
Blandford. doth his course through *Blandford* plains direct, . IV. xi. 32. 3
Blandina. Albe his Lady, that *Blandina* hight, . . . VI. iii. 42. 6
Although *Blandina* did . . . Him otherwise perswade . . . VI. v. 33. 5
Where him *Blandina* fayrely entertayned . . . VI. vi. 41. 3
Blandishment. the Foxe, and his false *blandishment:* . . . *Hub.* 1274
trust the guile of fortunes *blandishment;* . . . *Col.* 671
With gentle *blandishment* and lovely looke, . . . I. i. 49. 8
lovely *blandishment* She to me made, . . . I. ix. 14. 1
with sweet pleasaunce, and bold *blandishment,* . . . II. ii. 1. 5
With sugred words and gentle *blandishment,* . . . III. vi. 25. 4
With faire entreatie and sweet *blandishment,* . . . IV. vi. 41. 2
Farre from all fraud or fayned *blandishment;* . . . IV. x. 26. 7
with faire *blandishment* Her chearing up, . . . VI. iv. 27. 6
Blank. Th' old woman wox half *blanck* those wordes to heare, III. iii. 17. 8
Blaspheme. *Blaspheme* his powre, or termes unworthie yield.' . *Col.* 822
his babling tongue did yet *blaspheme* . . . IV. viii. 45. 6
foule *blaspheme* that Queene for forged guyle, . . . V. ix. 25. 5
Blasphemies. *blasphemies* forth threw Against his Gods, . . . V. xi. 12. 3
Blaspheming. the vile *blaspheming* name. . . . *Rev.* i. 3
eke *blaspheming* heaven bitterly, . . . II. vii. 60. 8
Blasphemous. with *blasphemous* bannes high God in peeces tare. III. vii. 39. 9
his *blasphemous* head . . . He pitcht upon a pole . . . V. ii. 19. 3
speaches forth doth send, Even *blasphemous* words, . . . V. xi. 20. 8
fowle *blasphemous* speaches forth did cast, . . . V. xi. 28. 2
therein shut up his *blasphemous* tong, . . . VI. xii. 34. 5
Blasphemously. Swearing and banning most *blasphemously,* . V. viii. 28. 2
Blasphemy. dreadfull name of *blasphemie* . . . *Rev.* ii. 3
with reprochfull *blasphemy* defide, . . . V. ii. 20. 5
Altars fouled, and *blasphemy* spoke, . . . VI. xii. 25. 3
Blast. fell Boreas with sharpe *blast* Tossing huge tempests . *Ro.* xvi. 5
That shall alegge this bitter *blast,* . . . *S.C.* Mar. 5
make a mocke at the blustring *blast.* . . . *S.C.* S. 54
One bitter *blast* blewe all away. . . . *S.C.* N. 119
his blustring *blast* eche coste dooth scoure. . . . *S.C.* D. 132
Winter is come that blowes the bitter *blaste,* . . . *S.C.* D. 143
tost in ayre with everie windie *blast:* . . . *Gn.* 334
bitter-breathing windes with harmfull *blast,* . . . *Ti.* 405
some ungracious *blast,* out of the gate Of Aeoles raine, . . . *Mui.* 419
their greene leaves, trembling with every *blast,* . . . I. ii. 28. 5
by her hellish science raisd . . . a dull *blast,* . . . I. ii. 38. 6
once abide the terror of that *blast,* . . . I. viii. 4. 6
the fierce Northerne wind with blustring *blast* . . . II. ix. 16. 8
Loosely disperst with puff of every *blast:* . . . III. i. 16. 4
both did quite drye up and *blast;* . . . III. v. 48. 7
Nor Aeolus sharp *blast* could worke them any wrong. . . . III. vi. 44. 9
welkin . . . Gan blowen up a bitter stormy *blast,* . . . III. ix. 11. 5
with his furious *blast* Confounds both land and seas, . . . III. ix. 15. 8
driven with that stormy *blast* . . . III. xii. 27. 2
by the Northerne *blast* Quite overblowne, . . . IV. i. 45. 6
breathed forth with *blast* of bitter wind; . . . IV. viii. 26. 5
Is with the *blast* of some outragious storme Blowne downe, . . V. xi. 29. 2
Ere long enforst to breath his utmost *blast,* . . . VI. iv. 22. 7
fed with light report Of every *blaste,* . . . VI. x. 2. 9
With every *blast* that bloweth, fowle or faire: . . . VII. vii. 22. 8
Blasted. With breathed sighes is blowne away and *blasted;* *S.C.* Ja. 40
The eare that budded faire is burnt and *blasted,* . . . *S.C.* D. 99
all their blossoms *blasted;* . . . *T.M.* 250
As *blasted* bloosme through heat doth languish and decay: . IV. viii. 2. 9
their faire blossomes *blasted,* . . . V. x. 7. 6
Blasts. These bitter *blasts* never ginne tasswage? . . . *S.C.* F. 2
Blatant. A monster, which the *Blatant* Beast men call, . . . V. xii. 37. 7
the *Blatant* Beast, by them set on, . . . V. xii. 41. 1
'The *Blattant* Beast . . . I doe pursew, . . . VI. i. 7. 1
'What is that *Blattant* Beast?' . . . VI. i. 7. 6
Calidore . . . Pursues the *Blatant* Beast: . . . VI. iii. Arg.
The *Blatant* Beast forth rushing unaware . . . VI. iii. 24. 2
The *Blatant* Beast the fittest meanes they found . . . VI. v. 14. 8
They sent that *Blatant* Beast to be a baite . . . VI. v. 15. 3
woundes, the which the *Blatant* Beast Had given them, . . VI. v. 39. 8
Such were the wounds the which that *Blatant* Beast Made . VI. vi. 2. 1
This hellish Dog, that hight the *Blatant* Beast; . . . VI. vi. 12. 2
sith I left him last Sewing the *Blatant* Beast; . . . VI. ix. 2. 3
Who now does follow the foule *Blatant* Beast, . . . VI. x. 1. 1
Calidore doth the *Blatant* Beast Subdew, . . . VI. xii. Arg.
To his atchievement of the *Blatant* Beast: . . . VI. xii. 2. 7
Blattant. *See* **Blatant.**
Blaze. Greece will the olde Ephesian buildings *blaze,* . . . *Ro.* ii. 3
Helpe me to *blaze* Her worthy praise, . . . *S.C.* Ap. 43
So forth she comes; her brightnes brode doth *blaze.* . . . I. iv. 16. 6
I this man of God his godly armes may *blaze.* . . . I. xi. 7. 9
I may in trump of fame *blaze* over-all. . . . *Am.* xxix. 12
Compar'd to that celestiall beauties *blaze,* . . . *H.H.L.* 277
Blazed. *See* **Broad-blazed.**
Her *blazed* fame which all the world had fil'd, . . . *Mui.* 266
envying the Britons *blazed* fame, . . . II. x. 47. 8
'Fame *blazed* hath, that here in Faery lond . . . III. ii. 8. 1
through all Faerie lond his noble fame Now *blazed* was, . . III. iv. 21. 4
Of that great turney which was *blazed* brode, . . . IV. iv. 5. 7
The time and place was *blazed* farre and wide, . . . V. iii. 2. 5
with bold speaches which he *blazed* had, . . . V. ix. 25. 6
the starres, which round about her *blazed,* . . . VII. vi. 13. 6
Blazers. Bablers of folly, and *blazers* of cryme: . . . II. ix. 25. 6
Blazing. *See* **Bright-blazing.**
wondren at bright Argus *blazing* eye; . . . *S.C.* O. 32
Such *blazing* brightnesse through the ayer threw, . . . I. viii. 19. 4
His *blazing* eyes, like two bright shining shieldes, . . . I. xi. 14. 1
The *blazing* brightnesse of her beauties beame, . . . I. xii. 23. 1
Their *blazing* pride thou wouldest soone have blent, . . . II. iv. 26. 3
as a *blazing* starre doth farre outcast His hearie beames, . . III. i. 16. 5
when he saw that *blazing* beauties beame, . . . III. viii. 22. 5
The armed Prince with shield so *blazing* bright . . . V. xi. 26. 2
Blazon. telling them to *blazon* out their blames. . . . *T.M.* 102
blazon foorth an earthlie beauties praise . . . *T.M.* 369
To *blazon* broade emongst her learned throng: . . . I. Pr. i. 8
to *blazon* far away. . . . II. x. 3. 9
Bleak. plaines, Where Boreas doth blow full bitter *bleake,* . . I. ii. 33. 7
on a gallowes *bleak* Shall give th' enchaunter his unhappy hire. III. iii. 36. 5
Blear. To *blere* mine eyes doest thinke. . . . *S.C.* Jul. 36
Bleared. face with smoke was tand, and eies were *bleard,* . . II. vii. 3. 6
Bleating. to draw their *bleating* flocks to rest. . . . *Col.* 955
Bled. Yet bleeding lay, and yet would still have *bled,* . . . *As.* 143
his hurts, that yet still freshly *bled.* . . . I. v. 17. 3
her wound still inward freshly *bledd,* . . . III. i. 56. 3
of that cruell wound he *bled* so sore, . . . III. v. 26. 2
Bleed. she the truest shepheards hart made *bleede,* . . . *S.C.* Jun. 111
ranckling wound as yet does rifelye *bleede.* . . . *S.C.* D. 94
To stop his wound that wondrously did *bleed!* . . . *As.* 132

Bleed—*Continued.*
His poynant speare that many made to *bleed,* . . . I. vii. 19. 7
hardest heart would *bleede* to hear their piteous mone. . . . I. viii. 36. 9
many noble Greekes and Trojans made to *bleed.* . . . II. vii. 55. 9
Through losse of blood which from his wounds did *bleed,* . . . II. xi. 48. 5
sucks the blood which from my hart doth *bleed:* . . . III. ii. 37. 5
Had power to staunch al wounds that mortally did *bleed.* . . . IV. ii. 39. 9
so much her wounds did *bleede;* . . . VI. iii. 46. 4
thou madest many harts to *bleed* . . . *H.L.* 12
And let thy bowels *bleede* in every vaine, . . . *H.H.L.* 248
Bleeding. *See* **Close-bleeding, Sweet-bleeding.**
freshly *bleeding* of a grievous wounde. . . . *Rev.* i. 8
heaped spoyles of *bleeding* harts to see, . . . *Mui.* 100
wound my heart, and rend my *bleeding* chest, . . . *D.* 298
Where as the lucklesse boy yet *bleeding* lay; . . . *As.* 142
Yet *bleeding* lay, and yet would still have bled, . . . *As.* 143
They flocked all about her *bleeding* wound, . . . I. i. 25. 7
knight, . . . The *bleeding* bough did thrust into the ground, . I. ii. 44. 6
His *bleeding* hart is in the vengers hand; . . . I. iii. 20. 2
Their gory sides fresh *bleeding* fiercely frett; . . . I. vi. 44. 5
wound That launched hath my brest with *bleeding* smart. . . . I. vii. 25. 7
Wherewith enmovd, these *bleeding* words she gan to say. . . . I. vii. 38. 9
that fresh *bleeding* wound, . . . I. ix. 7. 3
The stricken Deare doth chalenge by the *bleeding* wound.' . . II. i. 12. 9
Thy litle hands embrewd in *bleeding* brest . . . II. i. 37. 8
forth her *bleeding* life does raine, . . . II. i. 38. 7
Which shee increased with her *bleeding* hart, . . . II. i. 40. 3
didst not thou see a *bleeding* Hynde, . . . II. iii. 32. 7
The truncked beast fast *bleeding* did him fowly dight. . . . II. v. 4. 9
left his headlesse body *bleeding* all the place. . . . II. viii. 52. 9
infixed faster hold Within my *bleeding* bowells, . . . III. ii. 39. 2
lay *bleding* out his hart-blood neare. . . . III. v. 32. 9
freshly *bleeding* forth her fainting spright, . . . III. xii. 20. 7
lately did dispart Her *bleeding* brest, . . . III. xii. 38. 4
Shap'd like a heart yet *bleeding* of the wound, . . . IV. viii. 6. 8
so ill bedight With *bleeding* wounds, . . . VI. iii. 4. 2
There he that knight full sorely *bleeding* found, . . . VI. iv. 9. 6
And stopt the *bleeding* straight, ere he it staunched thought. . VI. iv. 12. 9
Regardlesse of her wounds yet *bleeding* rife, . . . VI. v. 5. 2
staunch the *bleeding* of her dreary wound: . . . VI. v. 6. 5
whose yet *bleeding* hart With thousand wounds . . . *H.L.* 142
Whose *bleeding* sourse their streames yet never staunch . . *H.H.L.* 164
Blemish. No mortall *blemishe* may her blotte. . . . *S.C.* Ap. 54
cleare she dide from *blemish* criminall: . . . II. i. 37. 7
any *blemish* which the worke mote blame; . . . IV. x. 41. 5
such blot his honour *blemish* should. . . . V. vi. 2. 9
Bloud is no *blemish,* for it is no blame To punish . . . VI. i. 26. 4
'Unknightly Knight, the *blemish* of that name, . . . VI. iii. 35. 1
Firme Chastity, that spight ne *blemish* dare: . . . VI. x. 27. 5
No *blemish* she may spie. . . . *Epith.* 66
Without *blemish* or staine; . . . *Epith.* 400
Without all *blemish* or reproachfull blame, . . . *H.H.L.* 149
Blemished. all my former praise hath *blemisht* sore: . . . V. xi. 49. 4
Blemishment. For dread of blame and honours *blemishment;* IV. ii. 36. 5
voide of all *blemishment;* . . . *H.B.* 215
Blend. Regard of worldly mucke doth fowly *blend,* . . . II. vii. 10. 5
O horrible enchantment, that him so did *blend!* . . . II. xii. 80. 9
doth *blend* The shyning glory of your soveraine light; . . . III. ix. 1. 7
out of the swownd, which him did *blend,* . . . IV. iii. 35. 7
these stormes, which now his beauty *blend,* . . . *Am.* lxii. 11
Blent. Ah, foolish Boy! that is with love *yblent:* . . . *S.C.* Ap. 155
feare and yre Had *blent* so much his sense, . . . *Gn.* 311
thy throne royall with dishonour *blent:* . . . *Hub.* 1330
The eie of reason was with rage *yblent,* . . . I. ii. 5. 7
thou blamest me for having *blent* My name with guile . . . I. vi. 42. 4
reason, *blent* through passion, nought descryde; . . . II. iv. 7. 7
Their blazing pride thou wouldest soone have *blent,* . . . II. iv. 26. 3
So hast thou oft with guile thine honor *blent;* . . . II. v. 5. 7
have The faithfull light of that faire lampe *yblent,* . . . II. vii. 1. 4
their life and fame, for ever fowly *blent.* . . . II. xii. 7. 9
all thy worthie prayses being *blent* . . . III. ix. 33. 8
Wherewith the worlds faire beautie she hath *blent:* . . . III. xii. 29. 5
Besmeard with smoke that nigh his eye-sight *blent;* . . . IV. v. 34. 7
blotted out his armes with falshood *blent,* . . . V. iii. 37. 7
How to revenge that blot of honour *blent,* . . . V. vi. 13. 2
so great honour with so fowle reproch had *blent.* . . . V. vi. 18. 9
Saying that he had . . . his honour *blent,* . . . V. xii. 40. 4
Blere. *See* **Blear.**
Bless. tenne thousand sithes I *blesse* the stoure . . . *S.C.* Ja. 51
'God *blesse* thee, poore Orphane! . . . *S.C.* May 191
'Jesus *blesse* that sweete face I espye, . . . *S.C.* May 256
I *blesse* thy state, . . . *S.C.* Jun. 9
They her did praise, and my good fortune *blesse.* . . . *D.* 147
He hurles out vowes, and Neptune oft doth *blesse.* . . . I. iii. 32. 5
burning blades about their heades doe *blesse,* . . . I. v. 6. 4
were not hevenly grace that did him *blesse,* . . . I. vii. 12. 3
We met that villen, (God from him me *blesse!*) . . . I. ix. 28. 3
'Fayre Sonne, great God thy right hand *blesse,* . . . II. viii. 40. 3
Doth *blesse* her servaunts, and them high advaunce. . . . II. ix. 5. 5
So *blesse* thee God, and give thee joyance of thy dreame!' . V. vii. 23. 9
full oft for loving you I *blesse* my lot, . . . *Am.* lxxxii. 2
blesse your fortunes fayre election. . . . *Am.* lxxxiii. 14
He faines himselfe, and doth his fortune *blesse.* . . . *H.L.* 210
Blesse. *See* **Bliss.**
Blessed. in this *blessed* brooke Doe bathe your brest, . . . *S.C.* Ap. 37
Elisa . . . That *blessed* wight, The flowre of Virgins: . . . *S.C.* Ap. 47
ryse, ye *blessed* Flocks, and home apace, . . . *S.C.* Jun. 118
Feeding the *blessed* flocke of Dan, . . . *S.C.* Jul. 51
O *blessed* sheepe! O shepheard great! . . . *S.C.* Jul. 53
So hath theyr god them *blist;* . . . *S.C.* Jul. 174

Blessed—*Continued.*
the Nightingale . . . That *blessed* byrd, . . . *S.C.* Au. 184
I see thee, *blessed* soule, . . . *S.C.* N. 178
There lives shee with the *blessed* Gods in blisse, . . . *S.C.* N. 194
heavenly ranks, where *blessed* soules do rest; . . . *Gn.* 58
good men, of whom thou oft are *blest;* . . . *Gn.* 62
'Ah! sir Mule, now *blessed* be the day, . . . *Hub.* 589
Despise the brood of *blessed* Sapience. . . . *T.M.* 72
'His *blessed* spirite, full of power divine . . . *Ti.* 288
'O noble spirite! live there ever *blessed,* . . . *Ti.* 302
that *blessed* throng Of heavenlie Poets . . . *Ti.* 340
twixt their *blessed* armes it carried . . . *Ti.* 627
Eternally Him praise that hath them *blest;* . . . *D.* 286
There shall I be amongst those *blessed* ones. . . . *D.* 287
made us all so *blessed* and so blythe. . . . *Col.* 21
since I saw that Angels *blessed* eie, . . . *Col.* 40
may that *blessed* presence still enjoy, . . . *Col.* 661
glauncing downe his shield from blame him fairly *blest.* . . . I. ii. 18. 9
'His *blessed* body, spoild of lively breath, . . . I. ii. 24. 1
His sparkling blade about his head he *blest,* . . . I. viii. 22. 3
blessed sprites, . . . To God for vengeance cryde continually; I. viii. 36. 6
You to have helpt I hold my selfe yet *blest.'* . . . I. ix. 7. 7
he might see The *blessed* Angels . . . I. x. 56. 2
Where is for thee ordaind a *blessed* end: . . . I. x. 61. 5
Great God it planted in that *blessed* stedd . . . I. xi. 46. 7
well arrived are, (high God be *blest!*) . . . I. xii. 17. 8
blessed Angels he sends to and fro, . . . II. viii. 1. 8
God hath built for his owne *blessed* bowre. . . . II. ix. 47. 5
had not grace thee *blest,* thou shouldest not survive. . . . II. xi. 30. 9
To light their *blessed* lamps in Joves eternall hous. . . . III. iv. 51. 9
Dayes dearest children be the *blessed* seed . . . III. iv. 59. 5
I kisse thy *blessed* feete.' . . . III. v. 35. 9
In *blessed* Nectar and pure Pleasures well, . . . III. xi. 2. 4
raignst in blis emongst thy *blessed* Saintes, . . . III. xi. 9. 3
Prince of peace from heaven *blest.* . . . IV. Pr. 4. 9
With which it *blessed* Concord hath together tide. . . . IV. i. 30. 9
Their mother . . . had full *blessed* hap . . . IV. ii. 43. 8
blessed peace to seeke, . . . IV. iii. 47. 8
the which it fairely *blest* From foule mischance; . . . IV. vi. 13. 4
He *blest* himselfe as one sore terrifide: . . . IV. vi. 24. 7
how himselfe he *blist.* . . . IV. vii. 46. 9
Blessed the man that well can use his blis: . . . IV. x. 8. 8
Mother of *blessed* Peace and Friendship trew; . . . IV. x. 34. 2
she holds them with her *blessed* hands. . . . IV. x. 35. 7
With which high God had *blest* her happie land, . . . V. ix. 30. 4
with his club him all about so *blist,* . . . VI. viii. 13. 4
made them all accurst That God had *blest,* . . . VII. vi. 5. 8
couldst not hold thy selfe so hidden *blest,* . . . VII. vi. 46. 7
When ye behold that Angels *blessed* looke, . . . *Am.* i. 11
with the crew of *blessed* Saynts upbrought, . . . *Am.* lxi. 7
Which oft I wisht, yet never was so *blest.* . . . *Am.* lxxvi. 14
Of *blessed* Saints for to increase the count. . . . *Epith.* 423
Venus dearlings, through her bountie *blest;* . . . *H.L.* 284
O most *blessed* Spirit! pure lampe of light, . . . *H.H.L.* 43
that most *blessed* bodie, which was borne . . . *H.H.L.* 148
O *blessed* Well of Love! O Floure of Grace! . . . *H.H.L.* 169
Free that was thrall, and *blessed* that was band; . . . *H.H.L.* 184
in thy brest his *blessed* image beare. . . . *H.H.L.* 259
The house of *blessed* God, which men call Skye, . . . *H.H.B.* 52
blessed Plentie wait upon your bord; . . . *Proth.* 102
Blessedness. Would be on earth too great a *blessednesse,* . . VI. xi. 1. 4
Blesseth. *blesseth* her with his two happy hands, . . . *Epith.* 225
Blessing. she gave like *blessing* to each creture, . . . *Hub.* 146
Sometimes him *blessing* with a light eye-glance, . . . IV. ii. 9. 4
The gladfull *blessing* of posteritie, . . . VI. iv. 31. 3
Poure out your *blessing* on us plentiously, . . . *Epith.* 415
Blessings. With thousand *blessings* she is heried. . . . III. i. 43. 7
happy *blessings,* which ye have . . . upon you thrown; . . . *Am.* lxvi. 1
all thy *blessings* unto us impart. . . . *Epith.* 397
Blest. *See* **Blessed.**
Blew. *See* **Blue.**
Faire *blew* the winde into her bosome right; . . . *Van.* ix. 5
One bitter blast *blewe* all away. . . . *S.C.* N. 119
everie sound that under heaven *blew;* . . . *Hub.* 1011
The same before the Geaunts gate he *blew,* . . . I. viii. 5. 1
when myld Zephyrus emongst them *blew,* . . . II. v. 29. 8
a stormy whirlwind *blew* Throughout the house, . . . III. xii. 3. 1
sparks . . . Which still he *blew* and kindled busily, . . . III. xii. 9. 8
A trompet *blew;* they both together met . . . IV. iii. 6. 5
the trompets freshly *blew.* . . . IV. iii. 14. 9
eke the breathfull bellowes *blew* amaine, . . . IV. v. 38. 7
Triton his trompet shrill before them *blew,* . . . IV. xi. 12. 3
Blew up a bitter storme of foule adversity. . . . VI. x. 38. 9
with His onely breath them *blew* away . . . *H.H.L.* 87
Blin. Did th' other two their cruell vengeaunce *blin,* . . . III. v. 22. 7
Blind. did those earthborn brethren *blinde.* . . . *Ro.* x. 14
If the *blinde* furie, which warres breedeth oft, . . . *Ro.* xxiv. 1
doe *blinde* his gazing eye; . . . *Gn.* 100
Blinde through ambition, and with vengeance wood, . . . *Gn.* 411
(For *blind* is bold) . . . *T.M.* 266
Blind Error, scornefull Follie, and base Spight, . . . *T.M.* 317
that *blinde* bard did him immortall make . . . *Ti.* 430
I, base shepheard, bold and *blind,* . . . *Col.* 348
the *blind* God that doth me thus amate, . . . I. i. 51. 4
Truth . . . Marres *blind* Devotions mart, . . . I. iii. Arg.
I, . . . lately through her brightnes *blynd,* . . . I. iii. 1. 5
her mother *blynd* Sate in eternall night: . . . I. iii. 12. 3
bestow Upon the daughter of this woman *blind,* . . . I. iii. 18. 3
the fearfull twayne, That *blind* old woman, and her daughter I. iii. 22. 2
He would them gazing *blind,* or turne to other hew. . . . I. vii. 35. 9

Blind—*Continued.*
the fruitfull-headed beast, . . . Became stark *blind,* . . . . I. viii. 20. 3
drive me to withdraw my *blind* abused love. . . . . II. iv. 24. 9
an old old man, halfe *blind,* . . . . II. ix. 55. 5
sith both are bold and *blinde?* . . . . III. iv. 9. 9
Calles thee his goddesse, in his errour *blind,* . . . . III. iv. 56. 8
shut up fast within her prisons *blind,* . . . . III. ix. 15. 4
his *blinde* eie, that sided Paridell, ... III. ix. 27. 6
in their foolish fancy feigne thee *blinde,* . . . . III. x. 4. 4
the joy of misers *blinde.* . . . . III. x. 15. 9
Shame most ill-favourd, bestiall, and *blinde:* . . . . III. xii. 24. 5
With sting of lust that reasons eye did *blind,* . . . . IV. ii. 5. 5
So *blind* is lust false colours to descry. . . . . IV. ii. 11. 5
making *blind* love her guide. . . . . IV. v. 29. 5
Her threw into a dongeon deepe and *blind,* . . . . IV. xi. 2. 4
almost *blind* through eld, ... IV. xi. 24. 9
Your aide to guide me out of errour *blind.'* . . . . V. vii. 19. 5
it can *blynd* The wisest sight . . . . VI. Pr. 5. 6
To rule the stubborne rage of passion *blinde:* . . . . VI. vi. 5. 8
came by fortune *blynde* Whereas this Lady . . . lay. . . . . VI. viii. 36. 7
in subtile bands Of the *blynd* boy; . . . . VI. ix. 11. 7
fortune, fraught with malice, *blinde* and brute, ... VI. x. 38. 7
I starve my body, and mine eyes doe *blynd.* . . . . *Am.* lxxxvii. 14
The *blynd* boy, Venus baby, ... *Epig.* i. 2
Thou, being *blind,* letst him not see his feares, ... *H.L.* 226
it can rob both sense, and reason *blynd?* . . . . *H.B.* 77
loves, with which the world doth *blind* Weake fancies, ... *H.H.L.* 262
this darke world, whose damps the soule do *blynd,* . . . . *H.H.B.* 137
Blinded. the *blinded* god his lustfull fyre To kindle . . . . II. iii. 23. 6
That *blinded* God, which hath ye blindly smit, ... III. ii. 35. 8
Following the guydance of her *blinded* guest, ... III. iv. 6. 8
proudest harts base love hath *blynded.'* . . . . V. v. 40. 9
doth not the *blinded* guest Shoot out his darts . . . . *Am.* viii. 5
Blindfold. as a *blindfold* Bull, at randon fares, ... II. iv. 7. 8
Blyndfold he was; . . . . III. xi. 48. 1
His *blindfold* eies he bad awhile unbinde, ... III. xii. 22. 6
Blindfolded. See yee the *blindfoulded* pretie God, ... *Tetrasticon* 1
Hence farre away we will *blyndfolded* ly, ... III. x. 42. 7
Blinding. *blinding* him againe, his way he forth did take. . . . . III. xii. 23. 9
Blinding the eyes, and lumining the spright. . . . . *H.H.L.* 280
Blindly. That blinded God, which hath ye *blindly* smit, ... III. ii. 35. 8
Blindness. armd with *blindnesse* and with boldnes stout, ... *T.M.* 265
The base-borne brood of *blindnes* cannot gesse, ... *T.M.* 392
love of *blindnesse* and of ignorance, ... *T.M.* 485
with base thoughts are into *blindnesse* led, ... *T.M.* 592
Blinked. with his other *blincked* eye; . . . . III. ix. 5. 5
Bliss. thinke of heavens *blis:* . . . . *Pet.*[2] vii. 12
There lives shee with the blessed Gods in *blisse,* . . . . *S.C.* N. 194
Yet are ye both received into *blis,* . . . . *Gn.* 477
to live in *blisse* for ever. . . . . *Gn.* 624
in the bosome of all *blis* did sit, ... *T.M.* 308
want the *blis* that wisedom would them breed, ... *T.M.* 530
builde your *blis* on hope of earthly thing, ... *Ti.* 198
Where he now liveth in eternall *blis,* . . . . *Ti.* 265
Out of the bosome of the makers *blis,* . . . . *Ti.* 282
hath no hope of happinesse or *blis.* . . . . *Ti.* 357
Where mortall wreakes their *blis* may not remove; . . . . *Ti.* 397
flesh delight In earthlie *blis,* . . . . *Ti.* 528
Where drownd with him is all his earthlie *blisse.* . . . . *Ti.* 546
In state of *blis,* or stedfast happinesse? . . . . *Ti.* 569
least mishap the most *blisse* alter may? . . . . *Mui.* 220
Let now your *blisse* be turned into bale, ... *D.* 320
(In which shee joyeth in eternall *blis*) . . . . *D.* 381
My lifes sole *blisse,* . . . . *Col.* 47
Conspire in one to make contented *blisse.* . . . . *Col.* 311
through report of that lives painted *blisse,* . . . . *Col.* 685
crownd with lasting baies Of hevenlie *blis* . . . . *Ded. Son.* xv. 5
Bathed in wanton *blis* and wicked joy. . . . . I. i. 47. 6
welcome now, my light, and shining lampe of *blis!'* . . . . I. iii. 27. 9
Did love . . . above all worldly *blisse;* . . . . I. vi. 17. 7
blisse may not abide in state of mortall men. . . . . I. viii. 44. 9
he is taught . . . The way to hevenly *blesse.* . . . . I. x. Arg.
Brings them to joyous rest and endlesse *blis.* . . . . I. x. 52. 6
it hight the Bowre of *blis.* . . . . II. i. 51. 9
'Her *blis* is all in pleasure. . . . . II. i. 52. 1
happy *blis* And all delight does raigne, ... II. iii. 39. 4
bathes him selfe in courtly *blis,* . . . . II. iii. 40. 2
ydle pleasures in her Bowre of *Blisse,* . . . . II. v. 27. 3
'Loe! here the worldes *blis:* loe! here the end, ... II. vii. 32. 7
Another *blis* before mine eyes I place, ... II. vii. 33. 3
this worldes *blis,* For which ye men doe strive; . . . . II. vii. 48. 8
hope ever to aspire . . . Unto such *blisse?* . . . . II. ix. 5. 8
Guyon, . . . Doth overthrow the Bowre of *blis,* . . . . II. xii. Arg.
Whereas the Bowre of *Blisse* was situate; . . . . II. xii. 42. 2
Now are they come nigh to the Bowre of *blis,* . . . . II. xii. 69. 4
their *blisse* he turn'd to balefulnesse. . . . . II. xii. 83. 5
Joy thereof have thou and eternall *blis!'* . . . . III. ii. 42. 5
my short *blis* maligne, ... III. iv. 39. 2
To send thine Angell from her bowre of *blis* . . . . III. v. 35. 3
Should happy bee, and have immortall *blis:* . . . . III. vi. 41. 3
There now he liveth in eternall *blis,* . . . . III. vi. 48. 1
From heavens *blis* and everlasting rest: . . . . III. viii. 8. 4
From courtly *blis* and wonted happinesse, ... III. viii. 20. 8
wicked Sprightes did fall from happy *blis;* . . . . III. ix. 2. 8
raignst in *blis* emongst thy blessed Saintes, ... III. xi. 9. 3
Britomart, halfe envying their *blesse,* III.xii.46.*or.*6
crowne true lovers with immortall *blis,* . . . . IV. Pr. 2. 8
Farre from the view of gods and heavens *bliss,* . . . . IV. ii. 47. 8
Before that they in *blisse* amongst the Gods were plaste. . . . . IV. iii. 44. 9
in peace and joyous *blis* They liv'd together . . . . IV. ix. 16. 1

Bliss—*Continued.*
Blessed the man that well can use his *blis:* . . . . IV. x. 8. 8
live in lasting *blesse,* . . . . IV. x. 23. 5
I, that never tasted *blis* . . . . IV. x. 28. 1
Mother of laughter, and welspring of *blisse,* . . . . IV. x. 47. 8
Till that th' offended heavens list to lowre Upon their *blisse,* . V. x. 26. 7
one evill, which doth . . . all our *blisse* abate; . . . . VI. iv. 30. 7
To happie *blisse* he was full high uprear'd, ... VI. v. 12. 4
last forth brought The fruite of joy and *blisse,* . . . . VI. ix. 45. 9
never more delight in painted show Of such false *blisse,* . . . . VI. x. 3. 8
to thy *blisse* I made this luckelesse breach, ... VI. x. 29. 3
worthy deeme partakers of our *blisse* to bee. . . . . VII. vi. 33. 9
that Angels blessed looke, . . . my heavens *blis;* . . . . *Am.* i. 12
lordeth in licentious *blisse* Of her freewill; . . . . *Am.* x. 3
th' author of my *blisse,* . . . . *Am.* xxii. 9
As meanes of *blisse* I gladly wil embrace; . . . . *Am.* xxv. 12
All sorrowes short that gaine eternall *blisse.* . . . . *Am.* lxiii. 14
my fraile fancy . . . Doth bath in *blisse,* . . . . *Am.* lxxii. 10
here on earth to have such hevens *blisse.* . . . . *Am.* lxxii. 14
The bowre of *blisse,* the paradice of pleasure, ... *Am.* lxxvi. 3
dead my life that wants such lively *blis.* . . . . *Am.* lxxxviii. 14
To be so bath'd in Venus *blis?* . . . . *Epig.* iv. 50
Whom heaven would heape with *blis,* . . . . *Epith.* 247
Out of thy silver bowres and secret *blisse,* . . . . *H.L.* 23
In sight whereof all other *blisse* seemes vaine: . . . . *H.L.* 208
thy *blisse,* and heavens glorie. . . . . *H.L.* 279
That they might serve him in eternall *blis,* . . . . *H.H.L.* 62
Ne hath their day, ne hath their *blisse,* an end, ... *H.H.L.* 74
Out of the bosome of eternall *blisse,* . . . . *H.H.L.* 134
His truth, his love, his wisedome, and his *blis,* . . . . *H.H.B.* 110
All joy, all *blisse,* all happinesse, have place; . . . . *H.H.B.* 243
Blisses. this, That seemes in it all *blisses* to containe, ... *H.L.* 207
Blissful. One joyous howre in *blisfull* happines, ... *Hub.* 983
swimming in that sea of *blisfull* joy, ... I. xii. 41. 5
left her *blisfull* bowre of joy above: . . . . III. vi. 11. 5
Some *blisfull* houres at last must needes appeare; . . . . V. iii. 1. 4
hower Doth leade unto your lovers *blisfull* bower, ... *Proth.* 93
Blist. *See* **Blessed.**
Blistered. With *blistred* hands emongst the cinders brent, . . IV. v. 35. 3
Blithe. makes himselfe full *blythe* . . . . *Gn.* 131
made us all so blessed and so *blythe.* . . . . *Col.* 21
He rousd himselfe full *blyth,* . . . . I. xi. 4. 9
The foolish man thereat woxe wondrous *blith,* . . . . III. x. 33. 1
He woxe full *blithe,* as he had got thereby, ... IV. i. 50. 8
full *blith* eftsoones his mightie hand He heav'd, ... IV. iii. 33. 1
He wox right *blyth,* as he had got thereby, ... V. xi. 9. 6
full *blyth* the Lady streight became, ... VI. i. 32. 1
Whereof they both full glad and *blyth* did rest, ... VI. xi. 41. 8
Blive. *See* **Belive.**
Block. 'Why standst there (quoth he) thou brutish *blocke?* *S.C.* F. 127
The *blocke* oft groned under the blow, ... *S.C.* F. 215
both stand sencelesse as a *blocke,* . . . . I. ii. 16. 5
his left arme, . . . like a *block* Did fall . . . . I. viii. 10. 6
on the ground he layd him like a sencelesse *blocke.* . . . . V. i. 21. 9
Blomius. Which that great Gyant *Blomius* begot . . . . IV. xi. 42. 2
Bloncket. *See* **Blunket.**
Blont. *See* **Blunt.**
Blood. *See* **Gore-blood, Heart-blood, Jelly-blood, Life-blood.**
erst descended from the Trojan *bloud.* . . . . *Bel.*[1] v. 8
The *bloud* of Martyrs dere . . . . *Rev.* ii. 10
His precious robe I saw embrued with *bloud.* . . . . *Rev.* iii. 5
whilome from the Troyan *blood* did flow. . . . . *Bel.*[2] v. 8
embrew her teeth and clawes with lukewarm *blood* . . . . *Bel.*[2] vi. 7
the Troyan prince spilt Turnus *blood* . . . . *Bel.*[2] ix. 8
brothers *blood,* the which at first was spilt . . . . *Ro.* xxiv. 12
cram'd with guiltles *blood* and greedie pray . . . . *Van.* iii. 4
pray of beasts and spoyle of living *blood,* . . . . *Van.* x. 3
stong, that it the *blood* forth drawes, ... *Van.* x. 9
cruddles the *blood* and pricks the harte: . . . . *S.C.* F. 46
oft the *bloud* springeth from woundes wyde; . . . . *S.C.* F. 176
let out the sheepes *bloud* at his throte. . . . . *S.C.* S. 207
Faire Xanthus sprincled with Chimaeras *blood,* . . . . *Gn.* 19
When Giants *bloud* did staine Phlegraean ground. . . . . *Gn.* 40
the guiltie *blood* Which she . . . had shed before; . . . . *Gn.* 173
the two brethren borne of Cadmus *blood,* . . . . *Gn.* 409
All slaine with darts, he wallowed in their *blood.* . . . . *Gn.* 432
Simois and Xanthus *blood* outwelde; . . . . *Gn.* 502
Having the *blood* of vanquisht Hector shedd, ... *Gn.* 527
as if that he had shedd Much *blood* . . . . *Hub.* 207
late in warres have spent my deerest *blood,* . . . . *Hub.* 247
that disguised Dog lov'd *blood* to spill, ... *Hub.* 319
Each place defilde with *blood* of guiltles beasts, ... *Hub.* 1307
his pure streames with guiltles *blood* oft stained; . . . . *Ti.* 145
powre forth th' offring of his guiltles *blood:* . . . . *Ti.* 300
after greedie spoyle of *bloud* to crave: . . . . *Ti.* 565
bred was of Medusaes *blood,* . . . . *Ti.* 647
streames of *blood* foorth flowed on the gras. . . . . *Ti.* 651
all her *blood* to poysonous rancor turne: . . . . *Mui.* 344
for secret crime thy *blood* hast spilt.' . . . . *D.* 84
Which Venus *blood* did in her leaves impresse, ... *D.* 109
with fell tooth accustomed to *blood,* . . . . *As.* 118
so huge streames of *blood* thereout did flow, ... *As.* 122
With crudled *blood* and filthie gore deformed, ... *As.* 152
cole-black *blood* forth gushed from her corse. . . . . I. i. 24. 9
They . . . sucked up their dying mothers *bloud,* . . . . I. i. 25. 8
ruth . . . for her noble *blood,* and for her tender youth. . . . I. i. 50. 9
Dame . . . For whose defence he was to shed his *blood.* . . . . I. i. 55. 3
adowne his coursers side The red *bloud* trickling . . . . I. ii. 14. 9
streams of purple *bloud* new die the verdant fields. . . . . I. ii. 17. 9
out of whose rifte there came Smal drops of gory *bloud,* . . . I. ii. 30. 9

Blood—*Continued.*
His face with bashfull *blood* did flame, . . . *Epig.* iii. 5
suckes the *blood,* and drinketh up the lyfe, . . . *H.L.* 125
That is a signe to know the gentle *blood.* . . . *H.B.* 140
what can prize that thy most precious *blood?* . . . *H.H.L.* 175
Blood-desiring. Nor ruthlesse spoyle of souldiers *blood-desiring, Ro.* xiii. 3
Blooded. That ye were *blooded* in a yeelded pray. . . . *Am.* xx. 14
Blood-frozen. nathemore . . . Could his *blood frosen* hart emboldened bee, . . . I. ix. 25. 7
Blood-guiltiness. To shew how sore *bloodguiltinesse* he hat'th; II. ii. 4. 5
with *bloodguiltinesse* to heape offence, . . . II. ii. 30. 3
bloodguiltinesse or guile them blott.' . . . II. vii. 19. 5
Blood-red. *blood-red* billowes, like a walled front, . . . I. x. 53. 3
Bloodthirsty. high advauncing his *blood-thirstie* blade, . . . I. viii. 16. 1
Bloodshed. with much *bloodshed* bought full deere, . . . *Ti.* 115
many mischiefes follow cruell Wrath: Abhorred *bloodshed,* . I. iv. 35. 2
Through strife, and *blood-shed,* and avengement, . . . I. ix. 43. 4
love does give his sweet Alarmes Without *bloodshed,* . . . II. vi. 34. 8
Strife and debate, *bloodshed* and bitternesse, . . . II. vii. 12. 7
Through great *bloodshed* and many a sad assay, . . . II. x. 49. 2
Abhorred *bloodshed,* and vile felony, . . . III. iv. 58. 3
most often end in *bloudshed* and in warre. . . . IV. i. 25. 9
there with guiltie *bloudshed* charged ryfe: . . . V. ix. 48. 4
Bloody. *See* **Gore bloody.**
from his *bloodie* eyes doth sparkle fire: . . . *Van.* x. 12
them did save with *bloudy* sweat . . . *S.C.* Jul. 55
sing of *bloody* Mars, . . . *S.C.* O. 39
Fought with the *bloudie* Lapithaes at bord: . . . *Gn.* 42
No greedy riches knowes nor *bloudie* strife, . . . *Gn.* 123
all his tract with *bloudie* drops is stained . . . *Gn.* 279
bloodie eyes doo glister firie red; . . . *Gn.* 350
each with brothers *bloudie* hand was slaine. . . . *Gn.* 416
With *bloodie* night, and darke confusion; . . . *Gn.* 445
When Teucrian soyle with *bloodie* rivers swelde, . . . *Gn.* 500
Of Lovers Miseries which maketh his *bloodie* game? . . . *Tetrasticon* 2
In *bloodie* streames foorth fled . . . *Mui.* 439
No *bloodie* issues nor no leprosies, . . . *Col.* 313
After his murdrous spoyles and *bloudie* rage allayd. . . . I. Pr. 3. 9
The cruell markes of many'a *bloody* fielde; . . . I. i. 1. 4
on his brest a *bloodie* Crosse he bore, . . . I. i. 2. 1
Having all satisfide their *bloudy* thurst, . . . I. i. 26. 4
upon his coward brest A *bloody* crosse, . . . I. ii. 11. 5
With *bloudy* mouth his mother earth did kis, . . . I. ii. 19. 6
twixt them both was born the *bloudy* bold Sans loy. . . . I. ii. 25. 9
His *bloody* rage aswaged with remorse, . . . I. iii. 5. 8
on his shield *Sansloy* in *bloody* lines was dyde. . . . I. iii. 33. 9
him that slew Sansfoy with *bloody* knife: . . . I. iii. 36. 4
whilest him fortune favourd, fayre did thrive In *bloudy* field; I. iii. 37. 9
nourish *bloody* vengeaunce in his bitter mind. . . . I. iv. 38. 9
Sowen in *bloodie* field, and bought with woe: . . . I. iv. 42. 5
his shield is hangd with *bloody* hew; . . . I. v. 5. 8
quench the flame of furious despight, And *bloodie* vengeance: I. v. 14. 6
Cerberus . . . lilled forth his *bloody* flaming tong: . . . I. v. 34. 4
Of whom he meanes his *bloody* feast to make, . . . I. vi. 10. 5
In these and like delightes of *bloody* game . . . I. vi. 29. 1
Washing his *bloody* wounds, . . . I. vi. 39. 9
with their drery wounds, and *bloody* gore, . . . I. vi. 45. 5
much rejoyced in their *bloody* fray: . . . I. vi. 48. 4
bloody wordes of bold Enchaunters call; . . . I. vii. 35. 2
beast, Who on his neck his *bloody* clawes did seize, . . . I. viii. 15. 2
bodie lay, All wallowd in his owne fowle *bloody* gore, . . . I. viii. 24. 4
yet he was unfitt for *bloody* fight. . . . I. x. 2. 6
writt in stone With *bloody* letters . . . I. x. 53. 7
wash thy hands from guilt of *bloody* field: . . . I. x. 60. 8
many *bloody* battailes fought in face, . . . I. x. 65. 3
I of warres and *bloody* Mars doe sing, . . . I. xi. 7. 2
Was swoln with wrath and poyson, and with *bloody* gore; . . . I. xi. 8. 9
When Centaures blood and *bloody* verses charmd; . . . I. xi. 27. 6
'What meane these *bloody* vowes and idle threats, . . . I. xii. 30. 1
threatned death with many a *bloodie* word: . . . II. i. 11. 8
in his silver shield He bore a *bloodie* Crosse . . . II. i. 18. 9
Babes *bloody* handes may not be clensd: . . . II. ii. Arg.
His guiltie handes from *bloody* gore to cleene. . . . II. ii. 3. 4
still the litle hands were *bloody* seene: . . . II. ii. 3. 7
this babes *bloody* hand May not be clensd . . . II. ii. 10. 1
let them still be *bloody,* . . . II. ii. 10. 4
two brave knightes in *bloody* fight . . . II. ii. 21. 3
After their weary sweat and *bloody* toile, . . . II. ii. 33. 2
purvay Your selfe of sword before that *bloody* day; . . . II. iii. 15. 5
His burning eyen, whom *bloody* strakes did staine, . . . II. iv. 15. 5
A flaming fire in midst of *bloody* field, . . . II. iv. 38. 3
Drad for his derring doe and *bloody* deed; . . . II. iv. 42. 3
he is all disposd to *bloody* fight, . . . II. iv. 43. 7
Withhold your *bloody* handes from battaill fierce; . . . II. vi. 33. 3
full bent To prove extremities of *bloody* fight, . . . II. vi. 36. 2
The other brandished a *bloody* knife; . . . II. vii. 21. 8
murdrous spoiles and *bloody* pray, . . . II. viii. 6. 4
With him in *bloody* armes they rashly did debate. . . . II. viii. 11. 9
gan the *bloody* brethren both to raine; . . . II. x. 33. 1
ceased not the *bloody* fight for ought; . . . II. x. 51. 5
overcame The wicked Gobbelines in *bloody* field; . . . II. x. 73. 2
Headed with flint, and fethers *bloody* dide; . . . II. xi. 21. 4
shivering speare in *bloody* field first shooke, . . . III. i. 7. 3
tasted many a *bloody* wownd.' . . . III. i. 24. 9
Her succourd eke the Champion of the *bloody* Crosse. . . . III. i. 64. 9
Against his Saxon foes in *bloody* field to fight. . . . III. iii. 29. 9
feld Great Ulfin thrise upon the *bloody* playne; . . . III. iii. 55. 6
to forbeare The *bloody* batteill . . . III. iv. 24. 8
So them with bitter words he stird to *bloodie* yre. . . . III. v. 15. 9
As did Belphoebe, in the *bloody* place, . . . III. v. 37. 3

Bloody—*Continued.*
Forthy the *bloody* tract they followd fast, . . . III. v. 37. 6
As ever man that *bloody* field did fight; . . . III. vii. 29. 5
His *bloody* speare eftesoones he boldly bent . . . III. viii. 12. 5
Braggadochio, with his *bloody* launce, . . . III. viii. 18. 7
of his bowels made his *bloody* feast: . . . III. viii. 49. 4
a long *bloody* river through them rayld, . . . III. xi. 46. 8
Hearing him those same *bloody* lynes reherse; . . . III. xii. 36. 7
the *bloodie* feast, which sent away . . . drunken soules to hell, IV. i. 23. 3
stirre up *bloudie* frayes, . . . IV. i. 47. 8
all their armours staynd with *bloudie* gore; . . . IV. ii. 18. 6
seeing both bent to so *bloudy* games, . . . IV. ii. 20. 4
oft for her in *bloudie* armes they fought. . . . IV. ii. 37. 5
downe on the *bloudy* plaine Her selfe she threw, . . . IV. iii. 47. 4
reasons, to restraine From *blouddy* strife, . . . IV. iii. 47. 8
Far'd like a lyon in his *bloodie* game, . . . IV. iv. 41. 5
The signe whereof yet stain'd his *bloudy* lips afore. . . . IV. vii. 5. 9
then his *bloudy* banket should beginne. . . . IV. vii. 20. 9
Whose *bloudie* corse they shew'd him there beside, . . . IV. viii. 21. 7
his life ran foorth in *bloudie* streame, . . . IV. viii. 45. 8
yet he conquer'd not by *bloudie* fight, . . . IV. viii. 47. 6
greedy hold of that his *bloudy* feast: . . . IV. ix. 31. 8
A broken sword within a *bloodie* field; . . . V. i. 19. 8
by ordele, or by *blooddy* fight, . . . V. i. 25. 3
About that wofull couple . . . And their young *bloodie* babe V. iii. 31. 3
he left the *bloudy* slaughter In which he swam, . . . V. iv. 41. 2
in a cote of plate Burnisht with *bloudie* rust; . . . V. viii. 29. 2
with *bloudie* knyfe Yet dropping fresh in hand, . . . V. ix. 48. 2
Enwallow'd in his owne blacke *bloudy* gore, . . . V. xi. 14. 6
The more t' aggrate his God with such his *blouddy* guize. . . V. xi. 19. 9
That *bloudie* scutchin, being battered sore, . . . V. xi. 54. 4
The *bloudie* gore and poyson dropping lothsomely. . . . V. xii. 30. 9
lake Of *bloudy* gore congeal'd about them stood, . . . VI. i. 37. 8
Flying the fury of his *bloudy* will: . . . VI. iii. 49. 4
Betwixt his *bloudie* jawes, besprinckled all with gore. . . . VI. iv. 17. 9
He reared her up from the *bloudie* ground, . . . VI. v. 6. 2
with . . . foule defame doe decke thy *bloudy* baner? . . . VI. vi. 25. 5
Where still he bathed lay in his owne *bloody* gore. . . . VI. vii. 8. 9
To see him so bedight with *bloodie* gore, . . . VI. vii. 14. 4
Witnesse the wounds, and this wyde *bloudie* lake, . . . VI. vii. 15. 5
His *bloudy* vessels wash, and holy fire prepare. . . . VI. viii. 39. 9
When the bold Centaures made that *bloudy* fray . . . VI. x. 13. 4
had endured many a dreadfull stoure In *bloudy* battell . . . VI. xii. 3. 8
formed all about his *bloudy* jawes: . . . VI. xii. 29. 6
in *bloudy* stall Of butchers balefull hand to ground is feld, . VI. xii. 30. 7
he gan fret and fome out *bloudy* gore . . . VI. xii. 31. 3
all other beastes of *bloody* race . . . *Am.* xxxi. 5
in *bloody* bath . . . her cruell hands embrew. . . . *Am.* xxxi. 11
whylst her *bloody* hands them slay, . . . *Am.* xlvii. 9
Bloody-handed. *bloody-handed* babe . . . Did earnestly committ, II. iii. 2. 2
Bloody-mouthed. *bloody mouthed* with late cruell feast, . . . I. viii. 6. 5
Bloody red. His steed was *bloody red,* and fomed yre, . . . II. v. 2. 8
The fruitfull vine; whose liquor *blouddy red,* . . . V. vii. 11. 3
Bloom. *See* **Fir-bloom.**
direfull deadly black, both leafe and *bloom,* . . . II. vii. 51. 8
Blooms. fed, and nipt the tender *bloomes;* . . . VI. ix. 5. 5
Bloosme, -s, Bloosming. *See* **Blossom, Blossoms, Blossoming.**
Blossom. The *blossome* which my braunch of youth did beare *S.C.* Ja. 39
To thinke to ground how that faire *blossome* fell. . . . *D.* 252
The *blossome* of sweet joy and perfect love, . . . *Col.* 470
She is the *blosome* of grace and curtesie, . . . *Col.* 528
marre the *blossom* of your beauty bright: . . . II. i. 14. 4
fiers fate did crop the *blossome* of his age. . . . II. i. 41. 9
They spring, they bud, they *blossome* fresh and faire, . . . II. vi. 15. 6
Whose tender bud to *blossome* new began, . . . II. viii. 5. 3
in late yeares so faire a *blossome* bare, . . . III. iv. 3. 7
The bud of youth to *blossome* faire began, . . . III. v. 29. 8
Of all the weeds that bud and *blossome* there; . . . III. vi. 30. 8
Now in *blossome* of his freshest age. . . . III. vii. 46. 5
As blasted *bloosme* through heat doth languish and decay: . . IV. viii. 2. 9
mans age . . . the first *blossome* of faire vertue bare; . . . V. Pr. 1. 4
How ever gay their *blossome* or their blade Doe flourish now, . V. ii. 40. 4
the *bloosme* of comely courtesie; . . . VI. Pr. 4. 2
Nor spilt the *blossome* of my tender yeares . . . VI. ii. 31. 2
gan to bud, and *bloosme* delight, . . . VI. viii. 20. 2
The bud of joy, the *blossome* of the morne, . . . *Am.* lxi. 9
Blossomed. yong *blossomed* Jessemynes: . . . *Am.* lxiv. 12
Blossoming. the bushes with *bloosming* buds. . . . *S.C.* May 8
The flowre of chevalry, now *bloosming* faire, . . . *Ded. Son.* x. 2
Did seeme to bow their *bloosming* heads full lowe . . . VII. vii. 8. 8
Blossoms. *bloosmes,* wherewith your buds did flowre; . . . *S.C.* Ja. 34
It was embellisht with *blossomes* fayre, . . . *S.C.* F. 118
dirks the beauty of my *blossomes* rownd: . . . *S.C.* F. 134
With flowring *blossomes* to furnish the prime, . . . *S.C.* F. 167
The *blossomes* of lust to bud did beginne, . . . *S.C.* May 187
'My boughes with *bloosmes* that crowned were . . . *S.C.* D. 103
all their *blossoms* blasted; . . . *T.M.* 250
her braunch faire *blossomes* foorth did bring, . . . *D.* 241
an almond tree . . . With *blossoms* brave bedecked daintily; I. vii. 32. 7
flourishing fresh leaves and *blossomes* did enwrap. . . . II. iii. 30. 9
No arborett with painted *blossomes* drest . . . II. vi. 12. 7
The trees did bud, and early *blossomes* bore; . . . II. vi. 24. 7
deckt with *blossoms* dyde in white and red, . . . II. xii. 12. 5
the downy heare Did . . . silken *blossoms* beare. . . . II. xii. 79. 9
the boughes doe laughing *blossoms* beare, . . . III. vi. 42. 3
deckes his branch with *blossomes* over all, . . . IV. x. 22. 4
their faire *blossomes* blasted, . . . V. x. 7. 6
That freshly budded and new *bloosmes* did beare, . . . VII. vii. 28. 3
faire *blossomes* of youths wanton breed, . . . *H.L.* 36
Why doe not then the *blossomes* of the field, . . . *H.B.* 78

Blot. No mortall blemishe may her *blotte*. . . . . *S.C. Ap.* 54
seeke with slaunder his good name to *blot*; . . . . *Hub.* 1219
blot his brutish name Unto the world, ... *Hub.* 1240
by breeding him some *blot* of blame, ... *Col.* 697
Ne may I, without *blot* of endlesse blame, ... *Ded. Son.* xvi. 1
whether *blott* of fowle offence Might not be purgd . . . II. ii. 4. 1
withouten blame or *blot*, ... II. iii. 22. 3
'What fowle *blott* Is this to knight, ... II. iii. 43. 7
he to her, withouten *blott* or blame ; . . . . II. iv. 20. 6
with thy blood abolish so reprochfull *blott*.' . . . . . . II. iv. 45. 9
bloodguiltinesse or guile them *blott*.' . . . . II. vii. 19. 5
Thus for to *blott* the honor of the dead, ... II. viii. 13. 3
Which *blott* his sonne succeeding in his seat, ... II. x. 23. 1
Ne *blott* the bounty of all womankind, ... III. i. 49. 4
she was pure from blame of sinfull *blott* ; . . . . III. ii. 23. 8
To *blott* her honour, and her heavenly light. . . . . . . III. v. 45. 5
with fowle infamous *blot* His cruell deedes . . . did spot : . III. vi. 13. 4
though spite did oft assay To *blot* her with dishonor . . IV. i. 4. 9
all true lovers with dishonor *blotten* : . . . . IV. i. 51. 4
wisht them without *blot* or blame To let them passe . . . IV. iv. 3. 4
she with blame would *blot*, and of due praise deprive. . . IV. viii. 25. 9
the boaster, that all knights did *blot* . . . . V. iii. 16. 1
what way She mote revenge that *blot* . . . . V. iv. 47. 5
such *blot* his honour blemish should. . . . . V. vi. 2. 9
How to revenge that *blot* of honour blent, ... V. vi. 13. 2
To *blot* your beautie, that unblemisht is, ... V. xi. 62. 3
To *blot* the same with blame, ... V. xii. 34. 9
Through fowle commixture of his filthy *blot*; . . . . . . VI. i. 8. 3
blot of all that armes uppon them take, ... VI. iii. 35. 2
without crime Or blamefull *blot*; . . . . VI. ix. 46. 4
With foule dishonour him mote *blot* therefore; . . . . . VI. xii. 12. 7
all were they cleanest From blamefull *blot*, ... VI. xii. 41. 4
Loath that foule *blot*, ... *H.B.* 169
sonne . . . Eternall, pure, and voide of sinfull *blot*, . . *H.H.L.* 32
Blots. Two filthie *blots* in noble gentrie ; . . . . . . *Hub.* 734
The filthy *blottes* of sin to wash away. . . . . I. x. 27. 7
Blotted. see the salving of your *blotted* name.' . . . . II. i. 20. 7
may unwares bee *blotted* with the same : . . . . II. ix. 38. 5
blotted out his armes with falshood blent, ... V. iii. 37. 7
blotted with condition vile and base, ... V. ix. 38. 5
Amongst all Knights he *blotted* was with blame, ... V. xi. 46. 8
blotted them with infamie, ... VI. xii. 28. 8
Blotten. *See* **Blot.**
Blotteth. oft their lewdnes *blotteth* good deserts with blame. . V. iii. 38. 9
Bloud, Bloudshed, etc. *See* **Blood,** etc.
Blow. Did *blowe* new fire, ... *Ro.* xi. 7
The blocke oft groned under the *blow*, ... *S.C. F.* 215
Then *blowe* your pypes, shepheards. . . . . *S.C. Au.* 197
when they list to *blow* Their pipes aloud, ... *Col.* 378
in open plaines, Where Boreas doth *blow* full bitter bleake, . I. ii. 33. 7
lightly lept from underneath the *blow*: . . . . I. vii. 12. 6
Did grone full grievous underneath the *blow*, ... I. viii. 8. 8
What mortall wight could ever beare so monstrous *blow*? . I. viii. 18. 9
blow the fire which them to ashes brent : . . . . I. ix. 10. 6
blow the bellowes to his swelling vanity. . . . . II. iii. 9. 9
when fluttring wind does *blow* . . . . II. iii. 10. 3
Exceeding wroth was Guyon at that *blow*, ... II. v. 7. 1
Ne care, ne feare I how the wind do *blow*, ... II. vi. 10. 4
blow them quite away, and in the Ocean cast. . . . . . . II. ix. 16. 9
At last *blow* up some gentle gale of ease, ... III. iv. 10. 3
warily he did avoide the *blow*, ... III. v. 21. 6
welkin . . . Gan *blowen* up a bitter stormy blast, ... III. ix. 11. 5
Paridell sore brused with the *blow* . . . . III. ix. 16. 6
from their nosethrilles *blow* the brynie streame, ... III. xi. 41. 2
with that same *blow* To make an end of all . . . . IV. iii. 33. 2
That any little *blow* on her did light, ... IV. vii. 26. 8
thrusting boldly twixt him and the *blow*, ... IV. viii. 42. 1
weigh the winde that under heaven doth *blow* ; . . . . . V. ii. 43. 2
at the next *blow* Halfe of her shield he shared quite away, . V. v. 9. 1
from the Altar all about did *blow* The holy fire, ... V. vii. 14. 4
twixt him and the *blow* his shield did cast, ... V. xii. 21. 6
Whether more wary were to give or ward the *blow*. . . . VI. viii. 13. 9
When any winde doth under heaven *blowe* ; . . . . . . VII. vii. 20. 7
blowe his nayles to warme them if he may ; . . . . . . VII. vii. 42. 4
Blowen. *See* **Blown.**
Bloweth. *See* **Overbloweth.**
nowe the Westerne wind *bloweth* sore, ... *S.C. S.* 49
As when a windy tempest *bloweth* hye, ... II. viii. 48. 1
With every blast that *bloweth*, fowle or faire : . . . . . VII. vii. 22. 8
Blowing. *See* **High-blowing.**
Triton, *blowing* loud his wreathed horne : . . . . *Col.* 245
Which at first *blowing* take not hastie fyre ; . . . . . . *H.L.* 174
Blown. *See* **Overblown.**
With breathed sighes is *blowne* away and blasted ; . . . *S.C. Ja.* 40
Thy Ewes, that wont to have *blowen* bags, ... *S.C. F.* 81
youngth is a bubble *blown* up with breath, ... *S.C. F.* 87
All was *blowne* away of the wavering wynd. . . . . . . *S.C. D.* 126
Black stormes and fogs are *blowen* up from farre, ... *Gn.* 572
She fel away like fruit *blowne* downe with winde. . . . . *D.* 244
like bladders *blowen* up with wynd, ... *Col.* 717
through al Faery lond his famous worth was *blown*. . . . I. vi. 29. 9
everie little breath that under heaven is *blowne*. . . . . . I. vii. 32. 9
broad-blazed fame, That up to heven is *blowne*.' . . . . I. x. 11. 5
wicked discord ; whose small sparkes once *blowen* . . . . IV. ii. 1. 5
Is with the blast of some outragious storme *Blowne* downe, . V. xi. 29. 3
Being with fame through many Nations *blowen*,) . . . . VI. iv. 36. 5
whatever chaunce were *blowne* Betwixt them to divide, . . VI. vii. 3. 8
Like a vaine bubble *blowen* up with ayre : . . . . *Am.* lviii. 6

Blows. wrathfull winde, Which *blows* cold storms, ... *Bel.*² viii. 12
where colde Boreas *blowes* his bitter stormes. . . . . . . *Ro.* xxvi. 8
The kene cold *blowes* through my beaten hyde, ... *S.C. F.* 3
Winter is come that *blowes* the bitter blaste, ... *S.C. D.* 143
Winter is come, that *blowes* the balefull breath, ... *S.C. D.* 149
So soone as on them *blowes* the Northern winde, ... *D.* 396
The yron walles to ward their *blowes* are weak and fraile. . I. v. 6. 9
The Sarazin . . . heaped *blowes* like yron hammers great ; . I. v. 7. 2
they gan, . . . To thunder *blowes*, ... I. vi. 43. 2
double *blowes* about him stoutly laid, ... I. xi. 42. 4
suffred not their *blowes* to byte him nere, ... II. ii. 23. 3
He hewd, and lasht, and foynd, and thondred *blowes*, . . II. v. 9. 1
falsed oft his *blowes* t' illude him with such bayt. . . . . II. v. 9. 9
both attonce their huge *blowes* down did sway. . . . . . II. vi. 31. 2
dealt *blowes* On either side, ... II. viii. 41. 1
stoutly dealt his *blowes*, ... III. i. 21. 6
thy strong buffets and outrageous *blowes*, ... III. iv. 9. 2
To steale away that I with *blowes* have wonne, ... III. viii. 17. 2
Much was Cambello daunted with his *blowes* : . . . . . IV. iii. 26. 1
bootlesse thing it was to think such *blowes* to beare. . . . IV. vii. 28. 9
Yet still her *blowes* he bore, ... V. v. 7. 1
dealt her *blowes* unmercifully sore ; . . . . V. vii. 31. 2
Dealing his dreadfull *blowes* with large dispence, ... V. xi. 45. 4
The Tyrant thundred his thicke *blowes* so fast, ... V. xii. 17. 6
with his burdenous *blowes* him sore did overlade. . . . . V. xii. 19. 9
seemed nothing might Beare off their *blowes* . . . . . . VI. v. 18. 5
bootelesse thing him seemed to abide So mighty *blowes*, . VI. vii. 46. 9
Was much more grievous then the others *blowes* : . . . . VI. vii. 49. 8
Blubbered. Did rend his haire, and beat his *blubbred* face, . *D.* 551
With ruffled rayments, and fayre *blubbred* face, ... I. vi. 9. 3
her faire face with teares was fowly *blubbered*. . . . . . II. i. 13. 9
blubbred face with teares of her faire eyes : . . . . . . III. viii. 32. 3
With many bitter teares shed from his *blubbred* eyne. . . V. i. 13. 9
Blue. With winges of purple and *blewe* ; . . . . *S.C. Mar.* 33
The *blew* in black, . . . is tinct ; . . . . *S.C. N.* 107
In a *blew* jacket with a crosse of redd . . . . *Hub.* 205
one flowre that is both red and *blew* ; . . . . *As.* 184
It first growes red, and then to *blew* doth fade, ... *As.* 185
Her eyelids *blew*, . . . At last she up gan lift : . . . . . I. ii. 45. 4
Full of diseases was his carcas *blew*, ... I. iv. 23. 6
Her younger sister, . . . Was clad in *blew*, ... I. x. 14. 2
Enrold in duskish smoke and brimstone *blew* : . . . . . I. xi. 44. 4
all her garment *blew*, ... II. ix. 40. 5
She bath'd with roses red and violets *blew*, ... III. vi. 6. 8
Her lips were, like raw lether, pale and *blew* : . . . . . V. xii. 29. 7
Bound truelove wize, with a *blew* silke riband. . . . . . *Epith.* 44
the Violet, pallid *blew*, ... *Proth.* 30
Blunket. Our *bloncket* liveryes bene all to sadde . . . . *S.C. May* 5
Blunt. All for her shepheards bene beastly and *blont*. . . . *S.C. S.* 109
As base, or *blunt*, unmeet for melodie. . . . . *Col.* 710
All were his earthly eien both *blunt* and bad, ... I. x. 47. 3
yield his sence to bee too *blunt* and bace, ... II. Pr. 4. 4
Arrived in the Isle, though bare and *blunt*, ... VI. xi. 9. 5
Bluntly. bad her tongue that it so *bluntly* tolde. . . . . . *Hub.* 1388
Blush. My chaster Muse for shame doth *blush* to write ; . . I. viii. 48. 2
the third for shame did *blush*, ... II. ix. 35. 6
Thereat the Elfe did *blush* in privitee, ... II. ix. 44. 1
To hide the *blush* which in her visage rose . . . . V. v. 30. 2
never *blush*, Cupid, quoth I, ... *Epig.* iii. 7
But *blush* to heare her prayses sung so loud, ... *Epith.* 163
Why *blush* ye, love, to give to me your hand, ... *Epith.* 238
Blushed. He *blusht* to see another Sunne belowe, ... *S.C. Ap.* 77
Withall she laughed, and she *blusht* withall, ... II. xii. 68. 1
Thereat full inly *blushed* Britomart, ... IV. vi. 32. 8
Blushing. *See* **Fair-blushing.**
as halfe *blushing* offred him to kis, ... I. i. 49. 7
Phoebus, . . . His *blushing* face in foggy cloud implyes, . . I. vi. 6. 7
With rosy cheekes, for shame as *blushing* red : . . . . . I. xi. 51. 4
face The flashing blood with *blushing* did inflame, ... II. ix. 43. 3
blushing to her laughter gave more grace, And laughter to her
    blushing, ... II. xii. 68. 2, 3
Doth by her *blushing* tell . . . . III. iii. 20. 5
Thereat she *blushing* saide . . . . III. v. 36. 1
Sir Burbon, *blushing* halfe for shame : . . . . V. xi. 52. 6
Bluster. As when the wrathfull Boreas doth *bluster*, ... V. xi. 58. 7
Blustering. The *blustering* Boreas did encroche, ... *S.C. F.* 226
make a mocke at the *blustring* blast. . . . . *S.C. S.* 54
his *blustring* blast eche coste dooth scoure. . . . . *S.C. D.* 132
Untill the *blustring* storme is overblowne ; . . . . I. i. 10. 2
blustring breath of Heaven, that none can bide, ... I. iii. 31. 5
blustring Aeolus his boasted syre ; . . . . I. vii. 9. 2
the *blustring* brethren boldly threat To move the world ; . I. xi. 21. 7
the fierce Northerne wind with *blustring* blast . . . . . . II. ix. 16. 8
Boad, Boads. *See* **Bode, Bodes.**
Boar. He shortly met the Tygre, and the Bore, ... *Hub.* 1087
wont in charett chace the foming *bore* : . . . . I. v. 37. 2
The spotted Panther, and the tusked *Bore*, ... I. vi. 26. 3
As chauffed *Bore* his bristles doth upreare ; . . . . . . I. xi. 15. 6
Deadly engored of a great wilde *Bore* ; . . . . III. i. 38. 2
that wilde *Bore*, the which him once annoyd, ... III. vi. 48. 5
huge great teeth, like to a tusked *Bore* : . . . . IV. vii. 5. 6
Had hunted late the Libbard or the *Bore*. . . . . VII. vii. 29. 8
Board. *See* **Seaboard.**
Fought with the bloudie Lapithaes at *bord* : . . . . . . *Gn.* 42
Sitting so cheerlesse at the cheerfull *boorde*, ... *U.V.* 5
If at *Boorde*, tell hir, that my mouth can eate no meate : . *U.V.* 8
Whom thus at gaze the Palmer gan to *bord* . . . . . . II. ii. 5. 1
him the Prince with gentle court did *bord* : 'Sir knight, . . II. ix. 2. 5

Board—*Continued.*
all sitting at his *bord;* . . . . II. x. 66. 7
she in merry sort Them gan to *bord,* . . . . . II. xii. 16. 2
in open place and commune *bord* . . . . . . III. x. 6. 5
she receivd againe to bed and *bord,* . . . . . III. x. 51. 5
By faire Kilkenny and Rosseponte *boord;* . . . IV. xi. 43. 4
Who, sitting with his Lady then at *bord,* . . . . VI. iii. 42. 3
making many a *borde* and many a bay, ... VI. xii. 1. 6
blessed Plentie wait upon your *bord;* . . . . . *Proth.* 102
Boarded. with like againe he *boorded* mee, ... II. iv. 24. 1
Boars. As when two *Bores,* with rancling malice mett, . . . I. vi. 44. 4
wilde *Bores* late rouzd out of the brakes: . . . . II. xi. 10. 5
As two wild *Boares* together grapling go, ... IV. iv. 29. 8
Boar-spear. Now with his sharp *bore-spear,* now with his blade. *As.* 108
a sharpe *bore-speare* she held, ... II. iii. 29. 1
in his clownish hand a sharp *bore speare* he shooke. . . . . III. i. 17. 9
the foster with his long *bore-speare* . . . . . III. v. 20. 1
And in his left he held a sharpe *bore-speare,* . . . . VI. ii. 6. 6
Boast. Crete will *boast* the Labyrinth, ... *Ro.* ii. 8
Should *boast* himselfe of the Romane Empire, ... *Ro.* xi. 14
Well maist thou *boast,* . . . . *Ro.* xxxii. 12
Thou art a fon of thy love to *boste;* . . . . . *S.C.* F. 69
here mayst thou freely *boste.* . . . . *S.C.* Jun. 13
All Kent can rightly *boaste:* . . . . *S.C.* Jul. 44
They *boast* they han the devill at commaund, ... *S.C.* S. 94
onely *boast* of Armes and Auncestrie, ... *T.M.* 94
Mongst simple shepheards they do *boast* their skill, ... *T.M.* 329
with this mightie one in hugenes *boast;* . . . . . *Ti.* 539
Nor anie weaver, which his worke doth *boast* . . . . *Mui.* 363
in his grace did *boast* you most to be! . . . . . *As.* 130
Of which I meanest *boast* my selfe to be, ... *Col.* 538
knight was not for all his bragging *bost;* . . . . I. iii. 24. 5
boast to swallow her in greedy grave; . . . . . II. ii. 24. 6
The man was much abashed at his *boast;* . . . . . II. iii. 17. 1
Sith late with him I batteill vaine would *boste;* . . . . II. vi. 50. 6
That in advauntage would his puissaunce *bost:* . . . . II. viii. 26. 4
ye brave knights, that *boast* this Ladies love, ... III. viii. 27. 6
What boots it *boast* thy glorious descent, ... III. ix. 33. 6
the fayrest Dame That ever Greece did *boast,* . . . . III. ix. 34. 8
'the fruitlesse end Of thy vaine *boast,* . . . . . IV. i. 51. 2
O men! which *boast* your strong And valiant hearts, ... IV. xi. 22. 3
womens powre, that *boast* of mens subjection? . . . . V. iv. 26. 5
Thereat she gan to triumph with great *boast,* . . . . V. v. 10. 1
is the *boast* of that proud Ladies threat, ... VI. i. 40. 4
Did *boast* her beautie had such soveraine might, ... VI. vii. 31. 6
he his lookes despised, and his *boast* disprаized. . . . VI. viii. 26. 9
that same glorious beauties ydle *boast* . . . . . *Am.* xli. 9
in the conquests of your beautie *bost,* . . . . . *H.L.* 37
Boasted. blustring Aeolus his *boasted* syre; . . . . I. vii. 9. 2
each of Brutus *boasted* to be borne, ... II. x. 36. 7
Such as ye have him *boasted,* . . . . III. ii. 12. 7
Sometimes he *boasted* that a God he hight, ... III. viii. 39. 6
Beares in his *boasted* fan, ... III. xi. 47. 8
he *boasted,* . . . That all the world he would weigh equallie, . V. ii. 30. 4
Boaster. that *boaster* gan to quake, ... II. iii. 18. 8
Bad that same *boaster,* as he mote, on high, ... III. viii. 16. 3
The *Boaster* at him sternely bent his browe, ... III. x. 24. 1
forth the *Boaster* marching brave . . . . . . III. x. 33. 5
the *Boaster* from his loftie sell Faynd to alight, ... III. x. 38. 5
streight that *boaster* prayd, ... V. iii. 10. 8
the *boaster,* that all knights did blot . . . . . V. iii. 16. 1
to the *boaster* said; 'Thou losell base, ... V. iii. 20. 6
of those words, the which that *boaster* threw, ... V. iii. 23. 6
the proud *boaster* gan his doome upbrayd, ... V. iii. 35. 7
Talus by the backe the *boaster* hent, ... V. iii. 37. 2
Boaster's. That dreadfull sound the *bosters* hart did thrill . . III. x. 43. 5
saw that *boasters* pride and gracelesse guile, ... V. iii. 20. 3
Boasteth. 'He lives,' (quoth he) and *boasteth* of the fact, . . II. i. 12. 4
Boastful. *boastfull* men so oft abasht to heare? . . . . III. iv. 1. 7
knight he was not, but a *boastfull* swaine . . . . III. viii. 11. 6
seeing his so prowd And *boastfull* chalenge, ... IV. i. 10. 6
'Too *boastfull* Blandamoure! too long I beare . . . . IV. ii. 13. 1
boastful Braggadochio rather chose, ... IV. iv. 14. 4
with *boastfull* vaine pretense, Stept Braggadochio . . . . IV. v. 23. 5
boastfull Braggadochio to defame, ... V. iii. 29. 2
Boasting. both full liefe his *boasting* to abate: . . . . III. ix. 14. 4
bosting in their martyrdome unmeet. . . . . . . IV. x. 2. 5
Boasts. *See* **Outboasts.**
Brought foorth those signes of your presumptuous *boasts* . . . *Ro.* xv. 3
boasts his good event . . . . *Gn.* 534
'There also goodly Agamemnon *bosts,* . . . . . . *Gn.* 545
boastes in beauties chaine not to be bownd, ... I. ix. 11. 7
battels, which thou *boasts* to win Through strife, ... I. ix. 43. 3
What man is he, that *boasts* of fleshly might . . . . I. x. 1. 1
One *boastes* her beautie, ... II. v. 33. 7
Boat. *See* **Cock-boat.**
her painted *bote* streightway Turnd to the shore, ... II. vi. 4. 6
My little *boat* can safely passe this perilous bourne.' . . . . II. vi. 10. 9
did her selfe betake Unto her *boat* again, ... II. vi. 18. 6
her swift *bote* Forthwith directed to that further strand; . . II. vi. 38. 1
The Ferriman, . . . With his well-rigged *bote:* . . . . II. xi. 4. 3
running to her *boat* withouten ore, ... II. xii. 15. 7
She turnd her *bote* about, ... II. xii. 16. 9
To draw their *bote* within the utmost bound . . . . . II. xii. 20. 8
To stere the *bote* towards that dolefull Mayd, ... II. xii. 28. 2
the nimble *bote* so well her sped, ... II. xii. 38. 2
th' other by his *bote* behind did stay. . . . . . . II. xii. 38. 6
A little *bote* lay hoving her before, ... III. vii. 27. 4
being fled into the fishers *bote* . . . . III. viii. 21. 1
with rare light his *bote* did beautifye, ... III. viii. 22. 6

Boat—*Continued.*
saide his *boat* the way could wisely tell; . . . . . III. viii. 24. 7
comming to that Fishers wandring *bote,* . . . . . III. viii. 31. 1
Tossing them like a *boate* amid the mayne, ... IV. iii. 1. 6
without ship or *bote* her thence to row, ... IV. xii. 15. 7
Boatman. Said then the *Boteman,* 'Palmer, stere aright, . . . II. xii. 3. 1
them the wary *Boteman* thus bespake: . . . . . . II. xii. 17. 5
th' heedful *Boteman* strongly forth did stretch His brawnie armes, ... II. xii. 21. 1
the *Boteman* strayt Held on his course . . . . . . II. xii. 29. 5
he the *boteman* bad row easily, ... II. xii. 33. 8
Boatswain. fortune, *Boteswaine,* no assurance knowes; . . . III. iv. 9. 7
Bode. the world, in which they bootles *boad,* . . . . *Hub.* 400
At last they came whereas that Ladie *bode,* . . . . . V. xi. 60. 1
So there all day they *bode,* . . . . VI. xi. 40. 9
Bodes. Good on-set *boads* good end. . . . . VII. vi. 23. 9
Bodies. *See* **Body's.**
when their wearie limbes . . . And *bodies* were refresht . . . I. x. 18. 2
trickling blood, and gobbets raw, Of late devoured *bodies* . . I. xi. 13. 4
So both agree their *bodies* to engrave: . . . . . . II. i. 60. 1
Can call out of the *bodies* of fraile wightes; . . . . II. v. 27. 5
though they *bodies* seem, yet substaunce from them fades. . . II. ix. 15. 9
Their feet unshod, their *bodies* wrapt in rags, ... II. xi. 23. 4
the sunburnt Indians do aray Their tawney *bodies* . . . . III. xii. 8. 4
Whose *bodies* chast, when ever in his powre . . . . . IV. vii. 12. 6
Their *bodies* to his beastes for provender did spred,) . . . V. viii. 28. 9
had three *bodies* in one wast empight, ... V. x. 8. 8
Through all three *bodies* he him strooke attonce, ... V. xi. 14. 1
Made in the *bodies* of that Squire and Dame; . . . . VI. vi. 2. 2
With slaughtred *bodies* which his hand had slaine, ... VI. vi. 38. 2
till all the entry was with *bodies* mand. . . . . . VI. xi. 46. 9
Till he had strowd with *bodies* all the way; . . . . . VI. xi. 49. 5
Ne doe their *bodies* only flit and fly, ... VII. vii. 19. 7
Bodies'. Through his three *bodies* powre in one combynd; . . V. x. 9. 6
Bodragings. oft annoyd with sondry *bordragings,* . . . . II. x. 63. 4
Bodrags. No nightly *bordrags,* nor no hue and cries; . . . *Col.* 315
Body. *See* **Nobody.**
I saw hir *bodie* turned all to dust, ... *Bel.*[1] vi. 12
An hideous *bodie* (*body*[1]) big and strong . . . . . . *Bel.* ix. 2
soone her *bodie* turn'd to ashes colde. . . . . . . *Bel.*[2] vii. 12
May of the *bodie* yeeld a seeming sight, ... *Ro.* v. 6
in a vicious *bodie,* grose disease Soone growes . . . . *Ro.* xxiii. 11
All as I were through the *body* gryde: . . . . . . *S.C.* F. 4
The *bodie* bigge, and mightely pight, ... *S.C.* F. 106
this faded Oake, Whose *bodie* is sere, ... *S.C.* F. 170
To see the braunche of his *body* displaie, ... *S.C.* May 196
That some good *body* woulde once pitie mee!' . . . . . *S.C.* May 248
That did her buried *body* hould. . . . . *S.C.* N. 159
against the others *bodie* bend His cursed steele, ... *Gn.* 412
He compast Troy thrice with his *bodie* dedd. . . . . . *Gn.* 528
my weake *bodie,* set on fire with griefe, ... *Hub.* 15
when the *bodie* list to pause, ... *Hub.* 759
Though death his soule doo from his *bodie* sever; . . . . *Ti.* 257
to present His *bodie,* as a spotles sacrifise; . . . . . *Ti.* 298
His *bodie* left the spectacle of care. . . . . . . *Mui.* 440
her beastly *bodie* raizd With doubled forces . . . . . I. i. 18. 3
her huge traine All suddenly about his *body* wound, ... I. i. 18. 7
her *body,* full of filthie sin, ... I. i. 24. 7
all . . . Gathred themselves about her *body* round, ... I. i. 25. 4
he spred A seeming *body* of the subtile aire, ... I. ii. 3. 3
'Curse on that Cross,' . . . 'That keepes thy *body* . . . . . I. ii. 18. 2
'His blessed *body,* spoild of lively breath, ... I. ii. 24. 1
With wicked herbes and oyntments did besmeare My *body* . . I. ii. 42. 4
Through shield and *body* eke he should him beare: . . . . I. iii. 35. 5
fayntnes . . . like a fever fit through all his *bodie* swelt. . . I. vii. 6. 9
seven great heads out of his *body* grew, ... I. vii. 17. 7
brought not backe the balefull *body* dead: . . . . . . I. vii. 50. 5
with his *body* bard the way atwixt them twaine. . . . . I. viii. 13. 9
headlesse his unweldy *bodie* lay, ... I. viii. 24. 3
That huge great *body,* which the Gyaunt bore, ... I. viii. 24. 7
embay His blamefull *body* in salt water . . . . . . I. x. 27. 6
Each bone might through his *body* well be red . . . . . I. x. 48. 5
pyn'd his flesh to keepe his *body* low and chast. . . . . I. x. 48. 9
His *body* monstrous, horrible, and vaste; . . . . . . I. xi. 8. 7
In his bras-plated *body* to embosse, ... I. xi. 20. 3
through his armour all his *body* seard, ... I. xi. 26. 7
To save his *body* from the scorching fire, ... I. xi. 45. 4
from the head the *body* sundred quight. . . . . . . II. v. 4. 6
braunches broad dispredd and *body* great, ... II. vii. 53. 7
On this vile *body* from to wreak my wrong, ... II. viii. 28. 4
when breath the *body* first doth leave; . . . . . . II. viii. 29. 2
left his headlesse *body* bleeding all the place. . . . . II. viii. 52. 9
more faire and excellent Then is mans *body,* . . . . . II. ix. 1. 3
Weake *body* wel is chang'd for minds redoubled forse. . . . II. ix. 55. 9
in a *body* which doth freely yeeld . . . . II. xi. 2. 1
His *body* leane and meagre as a rake, ... II. xi. 22. 2
Wounds without hurt, a *body* without might, ... II. xi. 40. 5
all his *bodie* straine, ... II. xii. 21. 2
His dayes, his goods, his *bodie,* he did spend: . . . . . II. xii. 80. 8
her bright armes about her *body* dight. . . . . . . III. i. 67. 3
I, fonder, love a shade, the *body* far exyld.' . . . . . III. ii. 44. 9
No shadow but a *body* hath in powre: . . . . . . III. ii. 45. 7
That *body,* wheresoever that it light, ... III. ii. 45. 8
The slouthfull *body* . . . Doth praise thee oft, ... III. iv. 56. 5
in the sacred throne Of her chaste *bodie;* . . . . . III. vi. 5. 8
The sunbeames bright upon her *body* playd, ... III. vi. 7. 5
whenas forme and feature it does ketch, Becomes a *body,* . . III. vi. 37. 4
suffred beastes her *body* to deflowre, ... III. vii. 49. 7
The substance, whereof she the *body* made, ... III. viii. 6. 1
every member of his *body* quooke. . . . . III. x. 24. 5

Body—*Continued.*
In her tormented *bodie* to embrew: . . . III. xii. 32. 7
streightly did embrace her *body* bright, . . . III. xii. 45. *or.* 2
Her *body,* late the prison of sad paine, . . . III. xii. 45. *or.* 3
About her backe and all her *bodie* wound: . . . IV. i. 13. 5
The soule had sure out of his *bodie* rived, . . . IV. iii. 18. 3
Yet had the *bodie* not dismembred bee, . . . IV. iii. 21. 7
So did one soule out of his *bodie* flie . . . IV. iii. 30. 8
about her *body* gan it tie. . . . IV. v. 19. 9
Yet nathemore would it her *bodie* fit; . . . IV. v. 20. 1
Shew'd all his *bodie* bare unto the cruell dent. . . . IV. vi. 15. 9
with her *body,* as a buckler, . . . IV. vii. 26. 4
The more his weakened *body* so to wast, . . . IV. vii. 41. 8
To ward his *bodie* from the balefull stound, . . . IV. viii. 45. 2
namelesse there his *bodie* now doth lie; . . . IV. viii. 49. 2
all the service of the *bodie* frame, . . . IV. ix. 2. 7
love of soule doth love of *bodie* passe, . . . IV. ix. 2. 8
though his limbs could not his *bodie* beare, . . . IV. xii. 35. 3
His *bodie* was her thrall, . . . V. v. 46. 9
all his bowels in his *body* brast: . . . V. viii. 8. 6
with his mortal steel quite through the *body* strooke. . . . V. xi. 13. 9
Thereto the *body* of a dog she had, . . . V. xi. 24. 1
strongly flew With all her *body* at his head . . . V. xi. 30. 7
keepe your *body* from the daunger drad, . . . VI. i. 10. 7
Yet in his *bodie* made no wound nor bloud appeare. . . . VI. iv. 5. 9
in minde . . . And *body* have receiv'd a mortall wound, . . . VI. v. 28. 4
such as hee Did use his feeble *body* to sustaine, . . . VI. v. 39. 2
having from his craven *bodie* torne Those goodly armes, . . . VI. vi. 36. 7
Her selfe quite through the *bodie* doth engore, . . . VI. vii. 9. 6
that leg, which did his *body* beare, . . . VI. viii. 16. 4
every *body* two, and two she foure did read. . . . VI. viii. 31. 9
decke the *body* or adorne the mynde, . . . VI. x. 28. 2
Her sickenesse was not of the *body,* but the mynde. . . . VI. xi. 8. 9
Yet all are in one *body,* and as one appeare. . . . VII. vii. 25. 9
Is not the hart of all the *body* chiefe, . . . *Am.* l. 7
then my *body* shall have shortly ease: . . . *Am.* l. 11
with one salve, both hart and *body* heale. . . . *Am.* l. 14
With guifts of *body,* fortune, and of mind. . . . *Am.* lxxiv. 4
I starve my *body,* and mine eyes doe blynd. . . . *Am.* lxxxvii. 14
all her *body* like a pallace fayre, . . . *Epith.* 178
all the *bodie* to thy hest doest frame, . . . *H.L.* 44
So it the fairer *bodie* doth procure. . . . *H.B.* 129
of the soule the *bodie* forme doth take; . . . *H.B.* 132
soule is forme, and doth the *bodie* make. . . . *H.B.* 133
that most blessed *bodie,* which was borne . . . *H.H.L.* 148

Body's. Strikes at an Heron with all his *bodies* sway, . . . IV. iii. 19. 3
Of my harts wound, and of my *bodies* griefe; . . . *Am.* l. 2
Fit medicines for my *bodies* best reliefe. . . . *Am.* l. 4

Boethus'. *See* **Baetus'.**

Bogs. Onely these marishes and myrie *bogs,* . . . V. x. 23. 6

Boil. drinke of every brooke when thirst my throte doth *boyle.* . . . VI. ix. 23. 9

Boiled. The whyles the viaundes in the vessell *boyld* . . . II. ix. 30. 8
Doth burne the earth and *boyled* rivers drie, . . . IV. iv. 47. 2
her private fire, which *boyld* Her inward brest, . . . V. v. 53. 7

Boiling. from the force of Phoebus *boyling* ray, . . . *Gn.* 167
There from the *boyling* heate himselfe to hide: . . . *Gn.* 252
Through *boyling* sands of Arabie . . . I. vi. 35. 6
shade, Which shielded them against the *boyling* heat, . . . I. vii. 4. 3
burning Aetna from his *boyling* stew . . . I. xi. 44. 5
suncke so deepe into their *boyling* brests, . . . II. ii. 32. 2
Behold the *boyling* bathes at Cairbadon, . . . II. x. 26. 2
She bath'd her brest the *boyling* heat t' allay; . . . III. vi. 6. 7
Now *boyling* hot, streight friezing deadly cold; . . . VII. vii. 23. 3
hot July *boyling* like to fire, . . . VII. vii. 36. 1
I burne much more in *boyling* sweat, . . . *Am.* xxx. 7

Boisterous. His *boystrous* club, . . . He could not rearen up . . . I. viii. 10. 1
boystrous battaile make, each other to avenge. . . . I. xi. 21. 9
like as a *boystrous* winde, . . . III. ix. 15. 2
round about with *boystrous* strokes oppresse, . . . VI. vi. 26. 2

Boisterously. The roring billowes beat his bowre so *boystrously.* III. x. 58. 9

Bokes. *See* **Books.**

Bold. *See* **Over-bold.**
the *bolde* people by the Thamis brincks, . . . *Ro.* xxxi. 6
made this foolish Brere wexe so *bold,* . . . *S.C.* F. 124
So spake this *bold* brere with great disdaine: . . . *S.C.* F. 139
thy Ball is a *bold* bigge curre, . . . *S.C.* S. 164
whether God or Fortune made him *bold* . . . *Gn.* 302
Bold sure he was, and worthie spirite bore, . . . *Gn.* 437
valiant fortune made Dan Orpheus *bolde:* . . . *Gn.* 449
in avengement of their *bold* attempt, . . . *Gn.* 577
So long persisted obstinate and *bolde,* . . . *Hub.* 567
with a good *bold* face, . . . *Hub.* 645
none but such as this *bold* Ape, unblest, . . . *Hub.* 915
who is so *bold* a wretch, . . . *Hub.* 973
(For blind is *bold*) . . . *T.M.* 266
Full of brave courage and *bold* hardyhed, . . . *Mui.* 27
with . . . *bold* atchievements her did entertaine. . . . *As.* 70
Bold men, presuming life for gaine to sell, . . . *Col.* 209
how *bold* and swift the monster was, . . . *Col.* 220
I, base shepheard, *bold* and blind, . . . *Col.* 348
To make so *bold* a doome, with words unmeet, . . . *Col.* 929
A *bold* bad man, that dar'd to call . . . Gorgon, . . . I. i. 37. 7
twixt them both was born the bloudy *bold* Sans loy. . . . I. ii. 25. 9
Left in the hand of that same Paynim *bold,* . . . I. iii. 40. 6
'Ah dearest Dame,' quoth then the Paynim *bold,* . . . I. iv. 41. 1
I saw . . . The *bold* Sansfoy shrinck . . . I. v. 23. 2
The *bold* Semiramis, whose sides transfixt . . . I. v. 50. 3
hurle not flashing flames upon that Paynim *bold?* . . . I. vi. 5. 9
He led away with corage stout and *bold.* . . . I. vi. 33. 4
Bought with the blood of vanquisht Paynim *bold;* . . . I. vii. 26. 4

Bold—*Continued.*
bloody wordes of *bold* Enchaunters call; . . . I. vii. 35. 2
with constant zele and corage *bold,* . . . I. viii. 40. 4
nathemore by his *bold* hartie speach . . . I. ix. 25. 6
Sir Terwin . . . was both *bold* and free, . . . I. ix. 27. 4
in courage *bold* Him to avenge . . . I. ix. 37. 4
bidding *bold* defyaunce to his foeman neare. . . . I. xi. 15. 9
some more *bold* to measure him nigh stand, . . . I. xii. 11. 8
Witnesse . . . guilty heavens of his *bold* perjury; . . . I. xii. 27. 6
with *bold* furie armes the weakest hart: . . . II. i. 57. 8
with sweet pleasaunce, and *bold* blandishment, . . . II. ii. 1. 5
Fast by her side did sitt the *bold* Sansloy, . . . II. ii. 37. 1
Did see and grieve at his *bold* fashion; . . . II. ii. 37. 7
with *bold* grace, and comely gravity, . . . II. ii. 39. 7
all knights of worth and courage *bold* . . . II. ii. 42. 8
this liegeman gan to wexe more *bold,* . . . II. iii. 9. 2
At which *bold* word that boaster gan to quake, . . . II. iii. 18. 8
far renowmd through many *bold* emprize; . . . II. iii. 35. 4
His countenaunce was *bold,* . . . II. iv. 37. 8
For his *bold* feates and hardy confidence, . . . II. iv. 41. 3
Whom *bold* Cymochles traveiling to finde, . . . II. vi. 2. 1
beare the rigour of his *bold* mesprise; . . . II. vii. 39. 8
A sturdie villein, stryding stiffe and *bold,* . . . II. vii. 40. 4
nothing might abash the villein *bold,* . . . II. vii. 42. 8
those which Hercules, with conquest *bold* Got . . . II. vii. 54. 5
he that breathlesse seems shal corage *bold* respire. . . . II. viii. 7. 9
he which earst them combatted was Guyon *bold.* . . . II. viii. 10. 9
found him fiers and *bold.'* . . . II. viii. 13. 9
An armed knight, of *bold* and bounteous grace, . . . II. viii. 17. 5
compeld with courage *bold* To yield . . . II. viii. 41. 7
either me too *bold* ye weene, . . . II. ix. 42. 2
Of stature huge, and eke of corage *bold,* . . . II. x. 7. 8
Great Godmer threw . . . At *bold* Canutus; . . . II. x. 11. 9
many *bold* repulse and many hard Atchievement wrought, . . . II. xi. 15. 3
Transformd to fish for their *bold* surquedry; . . . II. xii. 31. 5
how more *bold* and free . . . II. xii. 74. 7
The second was Parlante, a *bold* knight; . . . III. i. 45. 3
He nought was moved at their entraunce *bold,* . . . III. iii. 15. 1
his battailous *bold* brood, . . . III. iii. 47. 4
Conceiv'd a *bold* devise, . . . III. iii. 52. 2
The *bold* Bunduca, whose victorious Exployts . . . III. iii. 54. 7
Bold Marinell of Britomart Is throwne . . . III. iv. Arg.
Homere spake Of *bold* Penthesilee, . . . III. iv. 2. 5
sith both are *bold* and blinde? . . . III. iv. 9. 9
By your good counsell, or *bold* hardiment, . . . III. v. 10. 7
bold, as ever Squyre that waited by knights side: . . . III. v. 12. 9
despight Which he had borne of his *bold* enimee: . . . III. v. 15. 4
a *bold* knight that with great hardinesse . . . III. vii. 37. 4
that *bold* knight, whom ye pursuing saw That Geauntesse, . . . III. vii. 52. 1
with *bold* words and bitter threat . . . III. viii. 16. 2
Her to recomfort, and accourage *bold,* . . . III. viii. 34. 2
that old leachour, which with *bold* assault . . . III. viii. 36. 1
through great prowesse and *bold* hardinesse, . . . III. ix. 34. 6
noble Britons sprong from Trojans *bold,* . . . III. ix. 38. 8
Subdewd with losse of many Britons *bold:* . . . III. ix. 50. 2
bold he sayd; O most redoubted Pere! . . . III. x. 26. 8
Which the *bold* Virgin seeing . . . III. xi. 13. 8
they dismounting drew their weapons *bold,* . . . III. xi. 21. 1
bold to guide the charet of the Sunne, . . . III. xi. 38. 3
Bee bold: she oft and oft it over-red, . . . III. xi. 50. 4
forward with *bold* steps into the next roome went. . . . III. xi. 50. 9
Be bolde, be bolde, and every where, *Be bold;* . . . III. xi. 54. 3
on which was writ, *Be not too bold;* . . . III. xi. 54. 8
the *bold* Britonesse was nought ydred, . . . III. xii. 2. 8
in went *Bold* Britomart, . . . III. xii. 29. 8
It was to weete the *bold* Sir Ferraugh hight, . . . IV. ii. 4. 5
So fortune friends the *bold:'* . . . IV. ii. 7. 6
Bold was the chalenge, as himselfe was *bold,* . . . IV. ii. 39. 1
Amongst those knights there were three brethren *bold,* . . . IV. ii. 41. 1
prov'd three champions *bold.* . . . IV. ii. 45. 9
'*Bold* Fay, that durst Come see the secret of the life of man, . . . IV. ii. 49. 6
Then tooke the *bold* Sir Satyrane in hand . . . IV. iv. 17. 1
Hight Bruncheval the *bold,* who fiersly forth did ride. . . . IV. iv. 17. 9
Fiercely they followd on their *bolde* emprize, . . . IV. iv. 36. 1
hold The wrathfull weapon gainst his countnance *bold:* . . . IV. vi. 27. 5
Ne ever Knight so *bold,* ne ever Dame So chast . . . IV. viii. 25. 5
in wickednesse woxe *bold,* . . . IV. viii. 31. 8
(so young mens thoughts are *bold*) . . . IV. x. 4. 6
with the terrour of his countenance *bold* . . . IV. x. 16. 8
In greater perils to be stout and *bold,* . . . IV. x. 18. 2
father of the *bold* And warlike people . . . IV. xi. 15. 8
with many a champion *bold* . . . IV. xi. 19. 5
in thoughts lesse hard and *bold,* . . . IV. xi. 22. 4
Bold Marinell with Florimell the fayre, . . . V. iv. 3. 3
for the sake of Bellodant the *bold,* . . . V. iv. 30. 2
Unknowen perill of *bold* womens pride. . . . V. iv. 38. 6
Bold Radigund with sound of trumpe on hight, . . . V. iv. 45. 4
Say on, my soverayne Ladie, and be *bold;* . . . V. v. 31. 5
'Talus, be *bold,* And tell what ever it be, . . . V. vi. 10. 1
she bad to open *bold,* That she the face . . . might see: . . . V. vii. 25. 6
So faire a creature and so wondrous *bold,* . . . V. viii. 12. 7
sending to the Souldan in despight A *bold* defyance, . . . V. viii. 27. 8
the *bold* child that perill well espying, . . . V. viii. 32. 1
Nor all the Moenades so furious were, As this *bold* woman . . . V. viii. 47. 9
To weet, a wicked villaine, *bold* and stout, . . . V. ix. 4. 6
with *bold* speaches which he blazed had, . . . V. ix. 25. 6
the *bold* title of a poet bad He on himselfe had ta'en, . . . V. ix. 25. 8
Did beare the pendants through their nimblesse *bold:* . . . V. ix. 29. 3
this *bold* Tyrant, of her widowhed Taking advantage, . . . V. x. 12. 1
He stepped forth with courage *bold* and great, . . . V. x. 15. 6

Bold—*Continued.*
with *bold* vaunts and ydle threatning, . . . V. xi. 3. 7
the *bold* Prince was forced foote to give . . . V. xi. 5. 6
Them also gan assaile with outrage *bold,* . . . V. xi. 47. 3
thy hand too *bold* it selfe embrewed In blood . . . VI. ii. 7. 3
Being oppressed by that faytour *bold,* . . . VI. iv. 1. 7
the *bold* knight no whit thereat dismayd, . . . VI. iv. 21. 1
The wife of *bold* Sir Bruin, who is Lord Of all this land, . . . VI. iv. 29. 4
gard her to defend from *bold* oppressors might. . . . VI. v. 7. 9
well they wist that Squire to be so *bold,* . . . VI. v. 15. 6
the more outrageous and *bold,* . . . VI. vi. 21. 1
the *bold* Prince defended him so well, . . . VI. vi. 23. 6
'Not that the burden of so *bold* a guest Shall chargefull be, . . . VI. ix. 32. 1
When the *bold* Centaures made that bloudy fray . . . VI. x. 13. 4
fought through fury fierce and *bold.* . . . VI. xi. 30. 9
the *bold* knight Encountring him with small resistence slew, . . . VI. xi. 43. 5
All beeing with so *bold* attempt amazed, . . . VII. vi. 13. 8
At last he bade her (with *bold* stedfastnesse) . . . VII. vi. 17. 7
changing nought his count'nance *bold,* . . . VII. vi. 19. 8
'Of that bad seed is this *bold* woman bred, . . . VII. vi. 21. 1
now with *bold* presumption doth aspire . . . VII. vi. 21. 2
What course were best to take in this hot *bold* emprize. . . . VII. vi. 22. 9
the Gods, that gave good eare To her *bold* words, . . . VII. vi. 28. 2
In this *bold* sort to Heaven claime to make, . . . VII. vi. 29. 3
bold Procrustes hire . . . Would have suffiz'd . . . VII. vi. 29. 5
Dare to renew the like *bold* enterprize, . . . VII. vi. 30. 2
Bold Alteration pleades Large Evidence: . . . VII. vii. Arg.
mens frayle eyes, which gaze too *bold,* . . . *Am.* xxxvii. 5
Base things, that to her love too *bold* aspire! . . . *Am.* lxi. 12
want of cunning made me *bold,* In bitter hyve to grope for honny: . . . *Epig.* i. 3
Ne dare lift up her countenance too *bold,* . . . *Epith.* 162
Did puffe them up with greedy *bold* ambition, . . . *H.H.L.* 79
Th' Almighty, seeing their so *bold* assay, . . . *H.H.L.* 85
Boldened. That *boldned* innocence beares in hir eies; . . . *Am.* v. 10
Bolder. My Muse . . . With *bolder* wing shall dare alofte to sty *Ded. Son.* ii. 9
Three *bolder* brethren never were yborne, . . . IV. ii. 41. 2
when my spirit doth spred her *bolder* winges, . . . *Am.* lxxii. 1
Boldest. boldlie doth amongst the *boldest* go; . . . *Hub.* 666
The most unruly and the *boldest* boy . . . II. ii. 18. 3
Boldly. Say *boldly* that these same SIX VISIONS . . . *Pet.*[1] vii. 2
boldlie doth amongst the boldest go; . . . *Hub.* 666
her *boldly* kept From turning backe, . . . I. i. 17. 3
The Sprite then gan more *boldly* him to wake, . . . I. i. 43. 1
With foule reprochfull words he *boldly* him defide. . . . I. vi. 40. 9
Then gin the blustring brethren *boldly* threat . . . I. xi. 21. 7
may I *boldly* say, . . . II. i. 19. 4
Their sharp assault right *boldly* did rebut, . . . II. ii. 23. 2
So *boldly* he him beares, . . . II. ii. 25. 1
my self I *boldly* reard. . . . II. iii. 45. 9
to Guyon first He *boldly* spake; . . . II. iv. 39. 2
Him *boldly* bad his passage there to stay, . . . III. v. 18. 7
In hand she *boldly* tooke To make another . . . III. viii. 5. 6
His bloudy speare eftesoones he *boldly* bent . . . III. viii. 12. 5
boldly bad him bace, . . . III. xi. 5. 5
He made him open chalenge, and thus *boldly* sayd; . . . IV. ii. 12. 9
To which I *boldly* came upon my feeble feete. . . . IV. vii. 17. 9
thrusting *boldly* twixt him and the blow, . . . IV. viii. 42. 1
I *boldly* thought, . . . IV. x. 4. 6
'Whom *boldly* I encountred . . . IV. x. 10. 1
He *boldly* aunswerd him, . . . V. xi. 4. 8
Declare it *boldly,* Dame, and doe not stand in dout.' . . . V. xi. 18. 9
the other . . . Yet *boldly* answer'd, . . . VI. ii. 18. 7
There he arriving *boldly* did present . . . VI. iii. 18. 1
And entraunce *boldly* unto him forbad: . . . VI. iii. 38. 3
so *boldly,* without let or shame, . . . VI. vi. 20. 3
Boldly him bad such injurie forbeare; . . . VI. xi. 15. 2
Boldly she bid the Goddesse downe descend, . . . VII. vi. 11. 1
boldly blaming her for comming there, . . . VII. vi. 12. 7
boldly preacing-on raught forth her hand . . . VII. vi. 13. 2
Shee there arriving *boldly* in did pass; . . . VII. vi. 24. 1
Him *boldly* answer'd thus to his demaund: . . . VII. vi. 26. 3
Upon a Lyon . . . He *boldly* rode, . . . VII. vii. 36. 4
there to rest themselves did *boldly* place. . . . *Am.* lxxvi. 12
in her snowy bosome *boldly* lay Their quiet heads, . . . *H.L.* 289
Boldned. *See* **Boldened.**
Boldness. Now on these ashie tombes shew *boldnesse* vaine, . . . *Ro.* xiv. 13
Scorning the *boldnes* of such base-borne men, . . . *T.M.* 219
armd with blindnesse and with *boldnes* stout, . . . *T.M.* 265
through his *boldnes* rather feare did reach; . . . I. ix. 25. 8
feared least his *boldnesse* should offend, . . . II. iii. 17. 5
The knight at his great *boldnesse* wondered; . . . II. iv. 39. 6
He from such hardy *boldnesse* was restraynd, . . . III. v. 44. 8
Pardon the *boldnesse* of thy basest thrall, . . . V. Pr. 11. 6
they that most in *boldnesse* doe excell . . . V. ix. 1. 7
Under his club with wary *boldnesse* went, . . . VI. viii. 15. 8
Bollet. *See* **Bullet.**
Bolt. *See* **Thunderbolt.**
I bent my *bolt* against the bush, . . . *S.C.* Mar. 70
Bolted. he now had *boulted* all the floure, . . . II. iv. 24. 2
Bolts. *See* **Thunderbolts.**
With bowe and *bolts* in either hand, . . . *S.C.* Mar. 65
Bon. In cyphers strange, that few could rightly read, *Bon Font;* V. ix. 26. 4
but *Bon,* that once had written bin, Was raced out, . . . V. ix. 26. 4
Bond. *See* **Bound.**
why should he that is at libertie Make himselfe *bond?* . . . *Hub.* 133
since mine he is, or free or *bond,* . . . I. xii. 28. 1
Good turnes be counted as a servile *bond* . . . II. viii. 56. 2
Are bownd with commun *bond* of frailtee, . . . III. v. 36. 8
With Canacee and Cambine linckt in lovely *bond.* . . . IV. ii. 31. 9

Bond—*Continued.*
true friendships *bond* Doth their long strife agree. . . . IV. iii. Arg.
Left in the victors powre, like vassall *bond,* . . . IV. ix. 18. 7
Enlincked fast in wedlockes loyall *bond,* . . . V. iv. 3. 2
he had brought it now in servile *bond,* . . . V. x. 27. 1
make him *bond* that bondage earst dyd fly . . . *Am.* lxv. 4
Bondage. Caried to heaven, from sinfull *bondage* losed; . . . *Ro.* xix. 12
cast to quitt them from their *bondage* quight: . . . *Van.* xi. 4
beast, From whose eternall *bondage* now they were releast. . . . I. xii. 4. 9
the partes brought into their *bondage:* . . . II. xi. 1. 8
in eternall *bondage* dye he must, . . . III. vii. 50. 7
To view the thrals which there in *bondage* lay: . . . IV. viii. 52. 3
All which he did from bitter *bondage* free, . . . IV. ix. 8. 6
Whose scalp is bare, that *bondage* doth bewray, . . . V. ii. 6. 7
find In her false hart his *bondage* to unbind, . . . V. v. 56. 5
his balefull smart In womans *bondage* . . . V. vi. 3. 4
by hard mishap doth lie In wretched *bondage,* . . . V. vi. 10. 7
hide Thy maisters shame, in harlots *bondage* tide: . . . V. vi. 11. 5
bring in *bondage* of their brutishnesse: . . . V. xi. 44. 5
them kept in *bondage* hard, . . . VI. x. 43. 5
her in *bondage* strong Detaynd, . . . VI. xi. 2. 4
To see him leade that Beast in *bondage* strong; . . . VI. xii. 37. 5
make him bond that *bondage* earst dyd fly. . . . *Am.* lxv. 4
But cast out of that *bondage* to redeeme, . . . *H.H.L.* 132
Bondmaid. th' one was ravisht of his owne *bondmaide,* . . . *Gn.* 489
Bondmen. Ye shall for ever us your *bondmen* make.' . . . *Hub.* 412
for *bondmen* there to buy, . . . VI. xi. 9. 3
Bonds. She hath the *bonds* broke of eternall night, . . . *S.C.* N. 165
passe the *bonds* of modest merimake, . . . II. vi. 21. 8
Her angrie teame breaking their *bonds* of peace . . . IV. iii. 41. 3
To breake all *bonds* of law and rules of right: . . . V. viii. 20. 5
Till Fortune would her captive *bonds* unbynde: . . . VI. xi. 8. 8
Where they for ever should in *bonds* remaine . . . *H.H.L.* 125
Bondslave. The shame of Nature, the *bondslave* of spight, . . . *Mui.* 245
vanquisht thine eternall *bondslave* make, . . . I. vii. 14. 8
the *bondslave* of defame; . . . *H.B.* 173
Bondslaves. their *bondslaves* for to buy; . . . VI. xi. 10. 2
Bonduca. 'But long ere this, *Bunduca,* Britonesse, . . . *Ti.* 106
Bunduca, that victorious conqueresse, . . . *Ti.* 108
Which seeing, stout *Bunduca* up arose, . . . II. x. 54. 6
The bold *Bunduca,* whose victorious Exployts . . . III. iii. 54. 7
Bone. *See* **Raw-bone.**
flesh, that everie *bone* doth hide. . . . *Hub.* 592
it both *bone* and muscles ryved quight. . . . *As.* 120
Each *bone* might through his body well be red . . . I. x. 48. 5
from Cerberus greedy jaw To plucke a *bone,* . . . I. xi. 41. 5
bared all his head unto the *bone;* . . . II. vi. 31. 8
through feare, as white as whales *bone:* . . . III. i. 15. 5
men . . . form'd of flesh and *bone,* . . . V. Pr. 2. 4
glauncing on her shoulder-plate it bit Unto the *bone,* . . . V. vii. 33. 3
Those he devoures, they say, both flesh and *bone.* . . . V. x. 29. 7
Being unable to digest that *bone;* . . . VI. iv. 21. 7
Bones. *See* **Cheek-bones.**
there unjoynted both her *bones:* . . . *S.C.* Mar. 52
underneath their feet, all scattered lay . . . *bones* of men . . . I. iv. 36. 9
dead mens *bones,* which round about were flong; . . . II. vii. 30. 7
through her *bones* the false instilled fire Did spred . . . III. i. 56. 4
In which old Styx her aged *bones* alway . . . doth lay. . . . IV. xi. 4. 4
His timbered *bones* all broken rudely rumbled: . . . V. ii. 50. 8
Her brothers *bones* she scattered all about; . . . V. viii. 47. 4
all his *bones* as small as sandy grayle He broke, . . . V. ix. 19. 4
all her *bones* might through her cheekes be red: . . . V. xii. 29. 6
all his *bones* in peeces nigh he brake. . . . VI. vii. 11. 5
Bonet. *See* **Bonnet.**
Bonfires. merry feasting which he made And great *bonfires,* . . . VII. vii. 41. 3
bonefiers make all day; . . . *Epith.* 275
Bonibell, Bonilasse. *See* **Bonnibel, Bonnilass.**
Bonie. *See* **Bonny.**
Bonnet. his embrodered *Bonet* sat awry: . . . III. xii. 9. 6
Bonnibel. Hey, ho, *Bonibell!* . . . *S.C.* Au. 62
Bonnilass. As the *bonilasse* passed bye, . . . *S.C.* Au. 77
Hey, ho, *bonilasse!* . . . *S.C.* Au. 78
gan a gentle *bonylasse* to speake, . . . *Col.* 172
Bonny. a *bonie* swaine, That Cuddy hight, . . . *Col.* 80
(said then that *bony* Boy) . . . *Col.* 96
Bonylasse. *See* **Bonnilass.**
Book. Goe, little *booke!* . . . *To his Booke* 1
I meane to turne the next leafe of the *booke:* . . . *Hub.* 68
by his belt his *booke* he hanging had: . . . I. i. 29. 4
A *booke,* wherein his Saveours testament Was writt . . . I. ix. 19. 7
in his eternall *booke* of fate Are written sure, . . . I. ix. 42. 4
she fast did hold A *booke,* . . . I. x. 13. 8
her sacred *Booke,* with blood ywritt. . . . I. x. 19. 1
in th' immortall *booke* of fame To be eternized, . . . I. x. 59. 5
An auncient *booke,* hight *Briton moniments,* . . . II. ix. 59. 6
Sir Guyon chaunst eke on another *booke,* . . . II. ix. 60. 1
As in that old mans *booke* they were in order told, . . . II. x. 4. 9
Guyon all this while his *booke* did read, . . . II. x. 70. 1
Unfitly furnisht with thy bag and *booke,* . . . III. x. 24. 7
Full dreadfull thinges out of that balefull *booke* He red, . . . III. xii. 36. 3
Written with teares in harts close-bleeding *book.* . . . *Am.* i. 8
And al her faults in thy black *booke* enroll: . . . *Am.* x. 12
And in the same, as in a brasen *booke,* . . . *H.H.B.* 130
Book-read. They forged another, as for Clerkes *booke-redd.* . . . *Hub.* 358
Books. *See* **Loving-books.**
Muttred of matters as their *bookes* them shewd, . . . *Hub.* 836
fill their *bookes* with discipline of vice. . . . *T.M.* 336
Her vomit full of *bookes* and papers was, . . . I. i. 20. 6
amiddes His magick *bookes,* and artes of sundrie kindes, . . . I. i. 36. 8
He cast about, and searcht his baleful *bokes* againe. . . . I. ii. 2. 9

Books—*Continued.*
old records . . . Some made in *books*, ... II. ix. 57. 8
To read those *bookes;* . . . . II. ix. 60. 9
halfe unwilling from their *bookes* them brought, ... II. x. 77. 8
As it in *bookes* hath written beene of old. . . . . III. ii. 18. 3
As it in antique *bookes* is mentioned. . . . . III. vi. 6. 3
His wicked *bookes* in hast he overthrew, ... III. xii. 32. 2
as in *bookes* is taught. . . . . VI. vi. 9. 9
stonisht are . . . and damne their lying *bookes:* . . . . VII. vii. 52. 6
Such art of eyes I never read in *bookes!* . . . . *Am.* xxi. 14
that count, which lovers *books* invent, ... *Am.* lx. 9
which those six *books* compile, ... *Am.* lxxx. 2
Boon. graunt his *boone* that most desires to dye. . . . . *D.* 357
to God he made so many an idle *boone:* . . . . III. vii. 34. 9
her besought To graunt her *boone,* . . . . IV. ii. 50. 2
meekest *boone* that they imagine mought: . . . . V. ix. 34. 5
if shee would him pleasure With this small *boone,* . . . . VII. vi. 44. 2
Doe not thy servants simple *boone* refuse; . . . . *Epith.* 124
Boord(e), Boorded. *See* **Board, Boarded.**
Boot. to seeke redresse mought little *boote;* . . . . *S.C.* S. 127
what may it *boot* To frett for anger, ... II. iii. 3. 3
them apply To better *boot;* . . . . III. xi. 19. 6
With hope of her some wishfull *boot* to have. . . . . V. ix. 10. 3
naught may *boot* to banishe them from thence; . . . . V. xi. 45. 7
It could not *boot:* needs mote she die at last. . . . . VI. xi. 32. 2
harvests riches, which he made his *boot,* . . . . VII. vii. 38. 3
Booted. It *booted* nought to thinke such thunderbolts to beare. I. viii. 7. 9
It *booted* nought to thinke to robbe him of his pray. . . . . I. xi. 41. 9
It *booted* nought Sir Guyon, ... II. v. 3. 8
Nought *booted* it the Paynim then to strive; . . . . II. viii. 50. 1
It *booted* not to thinke that throw to beare, ... II. xi. 36. 4
At last when sorrow he saw *booted* nought, ... III. x. 18. 6
to thinke to save himselfe it *booted* not. . . . . VI. ii. 19. 9
Him *booted* not to thinke them to pursew, ... VI. v. 22. 8
booted nought for prayers . . . To hope for to release . . . . VI. viii. 3. 6
Booteth. 'What *booteth* it to have been rich alive? . . . . *Ti.* 351
Him *booteth* not resist, nor succour call, ... I. iii. 20. 1
Paynim . . . From whom her *booteth* not at all to flie: . . . . I. iii. 40. 7
helplesse hap it *booteth* not to mone. . . . . I. iv. 49. 5
What *booteth* then the good and righteous deed, ... III. xi. 9. 8
it *booteth* not to weene . . . It ever to amend: . . . . VI. vi. 9. 4
what *booteth* that celestiall ray, ... *H.B.* 187
Booting. leaving watry gods, as *booting* nought, ... IV. xii. 25. 2
Bootless. Seeing the world, in which they *bootles* boad, ... *Hub.* 400
messengers of hell, . . . gan tel Their *bootelesse* paines, ... I. ii. 2. 4
with sharp shrilling shriekes doe *bootlesse* cry, ... I. v. 33. 5
when their *bootlesse* zeale she did restrayne . . . . I. vi. 19. 8
scarsely could he weeld his *bootlesse* single blade. . . . . I. vii. 11. 9
His *bootelesse* bow in feeble hand upcaught, ... III. v. 24. 6
Vaine was the watch, and *bootlesse* all the ward, ... III. xi. 31. 8
bootlesse thing it was to think such blowes to beare. . . . . IV. vii. 28. 9
when he saw it *bootelesse* to resist, ... V. i. 29. 7
with *bootlesse* paine Annoy this noble Knight, ... V. v. 15. 8
bootelesse thing him seemed to abide So mighty blowes, ... VI. vii. 46. 8
Boots. Little *bootes* all the welth and the trust, ... *S.C.* May 88
What *bootes* it then to come from glorious Forefathers, ... *T.M.* 445
what *bootes* it that I was, ... *Ti.* 41
what *bootes* it to see earthlie thing . . . . *Ti.* 554
what of gods then *boots* it to be borne, ... I. v. 23. 6
what *bootes* it to weepe . . . . II. i. 16. 5
What *bootes* it al to have, and nothing use? . . . . II. vi. 17. 6
What *bootes* it him from death to be unbownd, ... III. v. 42. 7
'But, foolish boy, what *bootes* thy service bace . . . . III. v. 47. 1
What *boots* it boast thy glorious descent, ... III. ix. 33. 6
'What *boots* it plaine that cannot be redrest, ... III. xi. 16. 1
What *boots* it then to plaine that cannot be redrest?' . . . . III. xi. 17. 9
little *bootes* against him hand to reare. . . . . VI. i. 16. 5
all *bootes* not; they hands upon her lay: . . . . VI. viii. 41. 1
Booty. me the spoile and *bootie* of the world, ... *Bel.*[1] viii. 10
to curse and ban, for lacke Of that faire *bootie,* . . . . VI. ii. 21. 5
'Where is the *bootie,* which therefore I bought, ... VI. vii. 16. 2
wandring every way To seeke for *booty,* . . . . VI. viii. 36. 7
fed on spoile and *booty,* . . . . VI. x. 39. 5
Bord. *See* **Board, Bourd.**
Border. from one to other *border,* . . . . *Mui.* 170
a faire *border* wrought of sundrie flowres, ... *Mui.* 298
from Alcluid to Panwelt did that *border* bownd. . . . . II. x. 63. 9
round about a *border* was entrayld . . . . III. xi. 46. 6
Like to a golden *border* did appeare, ... IV. vi. 20. 3
straungers to devoure, which on their *border* Were brought . VI. viii. 36. 3
Upon their neighbours which did nigh them *border,* . . . . VI. x. 39. 6
raunged farre abroad in every *border,* . . . . VII. vii. 4. 8
Bordered. Whose skirts were *bordred* with bright sunny beames, V. ix. 28. 6
round about was *bordered* with a wood . . . . VI. x. 6. 2
Bordering. mountaines *bordring* Lombardie, ... *Bel.*[2] vi. 10
Unto the Prince of Picteland, *bordering* nere; . . . . VI. xii. 4. 6
Borders. About the *borders* of our rich Coshma, ... *Col.* 522
Through both whose *borders* swiftly downe it glides, ... IV. xi. 31. 3
making nightly rode Into their neighbours *borders;* . . . . VI. viii. 35. 4
Bordragings, Bordrags. *See* **Bodragings,** *etc.*
Bore, -s. *See* **Bare, Boar, Overbore.**
the Romaine Empire bore the raine Of all the world . . . . *Van.* xi. 1
Bold sure he was, and worthie spirite *bore,* . . . . *Gn.* 437
straight to heaven him *bore,* . . . . *Ti.* 657
Therein two deadly weapons fixt he *bore,* . . . . *Mui.* 81
his mother, which him *bore* and bred, ... *Mui.* 259
Of gentlest race that ever shepheard *bore,* . . . . *As.* 2
long before the world he was *ybore,* . . . . *Col.* 839
on his brest a bloodie Crosse he *bore,* . . . . I. i. 2. 1
the dreame he *bore* In hast unto his Lord, ... I. i. 44. 8

Bore—*Continued.*
on her shoulders sad a pot of water *bore.* . . . . I. iii. 10. 9
with timely fruit her belly sweld, And *bore* a boy . . . . I. vi. 23. 4
her golden cup, Which still she *bore,* . . . . I. viii. 14. 2
body, which the Gyaunt *bore,* Was vanisht quite; . . . . I. viii. 24. 7
on his arme a bounch of keyes he *bore,* . . . . I. viii. 30. 6
in her right hand *bore* a cup of gold, ... I. x. 13. 2
Long he them *bore* above the subject plaine, ... I. xi. 19. 1
now they laurell braunches *bore* in hand, ... I. xii. 5. 8
great beene the evils which ye *bore* . . . . I. xii. 17. 2
in his silver shield He *bore* a bloodie Crosse . . . . II. i. 18. 9
Behind his backe he *bore* a brasen shield, ... II. iv. 38. 1
The trees did bud, and early blossomes *bore;* . . . . II. vi. 24. 7
Of love they ever greater glory *bore* . . . . II. vi. 35. 6
Whose squire *bore* after him an heben launce . . . . II. viii. 17. 6
her sonne, which she to Locrin *bore,* . . . . II. x. 20. 1
Upon his shield their heaped hayle he *bore,* . . . . II. xi. 19. 1
th' Earth his mother was, and first him *bore,* . . . . II. xi. 45. 2
through the Euxine seas *bore* all the flowr of Greece. . . . . II. xii. 44. 9
the Nimphe that *bore* A gyaunt babe . . . . II. xii. 52. 2
shield That *bore* a Lion passant in a golden field. . . . . III. i. 4. 9
Nathelesse it *bore* his foe not from his sell, ... III. i. 6. 4
sith warlike armes he *bore* . . . . III. i. 7. 2
Ah! gentlest knight, that ever armor *bore,* . . . . III. i. 7. 5
they still the girlond *bore* away; . . . . III. ii. 2. 4
He *bore* a crowned little Ermelin, ... III. ii. 25. 8
him perforce unto the ground it *bore.* . . . . III. iii. 60. 7
Him so transfixed she before her *bore* . . . . III. iv. 16. 6
Bove all the sonnes that were of earthly wombes *ybore.* . . . . III. iv. 21. 9
She *bore* Belphoebe; . . . . III. vi. 4. 4
she *bore* in like cace Fayre Amoretta . . . . III. vi. 4. 4
Unwares she them conceivd, unwares she *bore:* . . . . III. vi. 27. 1
She *bore* withouten paine, that she conceiv'd Withouten pleasure; . . . . III. vi. 27. 2
in his Scutchin *bore* a Satyres hedd. . . . . III. vii. 30. 6
She *bore* before her lap a dolefull Squire, ... III. vii. 37. 6
She *bore* him fast away. . . . . III. vii. 43. 6
at that berth another Babe she *bore;* . . . . III. vii. 48. 1
Florimell with him unto his bowre he *bore,* . . . . III. viii. 36. 9
With speaking lookes, that close embassage *bore,* . . . . III. ix. 28. 2
of all Asie *bore* the soveraine crowne, ... III. ix. 39. 4
greedy eares her weake hart from her *bore;* . . . . III. ix. 52. 7
bore so fayre a sayle, that none espyde His secret drift, ... III. x. 6. 3
Through open outrage he her *bore* away, ... III. x. 27. 6
in his hand a braunch of laurell *bore,* . . . . III. xii. 3. 7
that stormy blast Which . . . *bore* all away. . . . . III. xii. 27. 3
knight That *bore* great sway in armes and chivalrie, ... IV. i. 32. 2
he *bore* The God of love with wings displayed wide . . . . IV. i. 39. 2
The whiles his love away the other *bore,* . . . . IV. ii. 7. 3
bore three such, three such not to be fond! . . . . IV. ii. 41. 6
In her right hand a rod of peace shee *bore,* . . . . IV. iii. 42. 1
For evill deedes may better then bad words be *bore.* . . . . IV. iv. 4. 9
His speare he feutred, and at him it *bore,* . . . . IV. iv. 45. 8
bore The prayse of prowesse from them all away. . . . . IV. iv. 48. 3
the Knight That *bore* the Hebene speare, ... IV. v. 20. 5
secretly from thence that night her *bore* away. . . . . IV. v. 27. 9
So likewise did the hammers which they *bore,* . . . . IV. v. 36. 7
vewed The armes he *bore,* . . . . IV. vi. 3. 4
with the force, whiche in it selfe it *bore,* . . . . IV. vi. 19. 2
in his hand a tall young oake he *bore,* . . . . IV. vii. 7. 4
whence he was, or of what wombe *ybore,* . . . . IV. vii. 7. 7
through the forrest *bore* her quite away, ... IV. vii. 8. 2
Whilest he in armes her *bore,* . . . . IV. vii. 9. 2
Ne was there man so strong, but he downe *bore;* . . . . IV. viii. 48. 3
I lightly snatcht him up and with me *bore* away. . . . . IV. viii. 61. 9
all the while he by his side her *bore,* . . . . IV. ix. 19. 5
in them *bore* true lovers vowes entire: . . . . IV. x. 38. 5
the Dolphin, which him *bore* Through the Agaean seas . . . . IV. xi. 23. 6
auncient heavy burden which he *bore* . . . . IV. xi. 26. 3
Ram, which *bore* Phrixus and Helle . . . . V. Pr. 5. 6
the Bull which fayre Europa *bore:* . . . . V. Pr. 5. 9
bore upon his shield . . . A broken sword . . . . V. i. 19. 6
Ne any Knight was absent that brave courage *bore.* . . . . V. iii. 2. 9
all these knights, which that day armour *bore,* . . . . V. iii. 13. 7
his shield, Which *bore* the Sunne brode blazed . . . . V. iii. 14. 9
Both brethren, whom one wombe together *bore,* . . . . V. iv. 4. 3
To whom she *bore* most fervent love of late, ... V. iv. 30. 3
Yet still her blowes he *bore,* . . . . V. v. 7. 1
Uppon her speare she *bore* before her breast, ... V. vi. 39. 5
bore him quite out of his saddle, ... V. viii. 7. 8
By some bad spirit that it to mischiefe *bore,* . . . . V. viii. 34. 7
She forth did rome whether her rage her *bore,* . . . . V. viii. 48. 6
at his backe a great wyde net he *bore,* . . . . V. ix. 11. 6
bore Downe to the house of dole, ... V. xi. 14. 8
The same long while I *bore,* . . . . V. xi. 53. 6
So *bore* her quite away, nor well nor ill apayd. . . . . V. xi. 64. 9
The heavy Mayd, to whom none tydings *bore* . . . . V. xii. 11. 5
The Dwarfe, which *bore* that message to her knight, ... VI. i. 31. 3
Whom on his backe he *bore,* . . . . VI. iii. 2. 6
A cruell Beare, the which an infant *bore* . . . . VI. iv. 17. 8
She *bore* it thence, and ever as her owne it kept. . . . . VI. iv. 37. 9
Yet he himselfe so well and wisely *bore,* . . . . VI. v. 12. 8
in all battels *bore* away the baies: . . . . VI. vi. 4. 5
Ne ever Knight that *bore* so lofty creast, ... VI. vi. 12. 7
the cold steele . . . to the ground him *bore,* . . . . VI. vii. 8. 8
in his hand a mighty yron club he *bore.* . . . . VI. vii. 43. 9
with his yron batton which he *bore* . . . . VI. viii. 46. 3
that same day That Theseus her unto his bridale *bore,* . . . . VI. x. 13. 3
them selves so in their daunce they *bore,* . . . . VI. x. 24. 6
like to one distraught . . . towards her him *bore;* . . . . VI. xi. 45. 8

Bore—*Continued.*
his love with him *bore*. VI. xi. 51. 9
So home unto his honest wife it *bore,* VI. xii. 9. 8
The which she *bore* the whiles in prison she did dwell. VI. xii. 15. 9
Straunge bands, whose like till then he never *bore,* VI. xii. 36. 2
in his hand he *bore* A boawe and shaftes, VII. vii. 29. 6
Upon his head a wreath . . . he *bore;* VII. vii. 30. 7
Under his belt he *bore* a sickle circling wide. VII. vii. 36. 9
Boreas. fell *Boreas* with sharpe blast Tossing huge tempests *Ro.* xvi. 5
where colde *Boreas* blowes his bitter stormes. *Ro.* xxvi. 8
The blustering *Boreas* did encroche, *S.C.* F. 226
in open plaines, Where *Boreas* doth blow full bitter bleake, I. ii. 33. 7
As when the wrathfull *Boreas* doth bluster, V. xi. 58. 7
Bored. Was closed up, as it had not beene *bor'd;* III. xii. 38. 5
Born. *See* **Base-born, Bore, Borne, Earth-Born, Free-born, Hell-born, Late-born, New-born, Wood-born.**
All that's imperfect, *borne* belowe the Moone; *Ro.* xix. 2
the *borne* Souldier which Rhine running drinks: *Ro.* xxxi. 8
the two brethren *borne* of Cadmus blood, *Gn.* 409
such vile vassals, *borne* to base vocation, *Hub.* 156
(so basely was he *borne*). *Hub.* 808
Unhappie wight, *borne* to desastrous end, *Hub.* 907
borne to be a Kingly soveraigne.' *Hub.* 1032
wretched persons to misfortune *borne;* *T.M.* 154
Borne in the bosome of the black Abysse, *T.M.* 260
ignorance . . . mindes of men *borne* heavenlie doth debace. *T.M.* 498
all the rest, as *borne* of salvage brood, *T.M.* 589
Forgotten quite as they were never *borne*. *Ti.* 182
borne above the cloudes to be divin'd, *Ti.* 611
Dan Perseus, *borne* of heavenly seed, *Ti.* 648
as ye be of heavenlie off-spring *borne,* *Ti.* 684
For being *borne* an auncient Lions haire, *D.* 122
A gentle shepheard *borne* in Arcady, *As.* 1
an hundred Nymphs all heavenly *borne,* *Col.* 256
Borne without Syre or couples of one kynd; *Col.* 800
'Faire knight, *borne* under happie starre, I. i. 27. 3
that new creature, *borne* without her dew, I. i. 46. 6
Borne the sole daughter of an Emperour, I. ii. 22. 7
twixt them both was *born* the bloudy bold Sans loy. I. ii. 25. 9
At last . . . Arose the virgin, *borne* of heavenly brood, I. iii. 8. 7
you, my liefe, *yborn* of hevenly berth. I. iii. 28. 9
cole blacke steedes *yborne* of hellish brood, I. v. 20. 8
what of gods then boots it to be *borne,* I. v. 23. 6
The fall of famous children *borne* of mee, I. v. 25. 2
stood In doubt to deeme her *borne* of earthly brood: I. vi. 16. 5
A Satyres sonne, *yborne* in forrest wyld, I. vi. 21. 1
arrogant delight Of th' high descent whereof he was *yborne,* I. vii. 10. 2
Most vertuous virgin, *borne* of hevenly berth, I. x. 9. 3
both *borne* and bred In hevenly throne, I. x. 51. 5
she is hevenly *borne,* I. x. 59. 9
behight me *borne* of English blood, I. x. 64. 6
as one were *borne* that very day. I. xi. 30. 5
He was an Elfin *borne* of noble state II. i. 6. 5
'Ah! lucklesse babe, *borne* under cruell starre, II. ii. 2. 1
by her stately portance *borne* of heavenly birth. II. iii. 21. 9
Seemes to be *borne* by native influence; II. iv. 1. 5
was *borne* of noble parentage, II. iv. 19. 3
Death is for wretches *borne* under unhappy starre.' II. vi. 44. 9
borne with ill-disposed skyes, II. ix. 52. 8
All were they *borne* of her owne native slime: II. x. 9. 5
Borne of fayre Inogene of Italy; II. x. 13. 5
each of Brutus boasted to be *borne,* II. x. 36. 7
The fierce Spumador, *borne* of heavenly seed, II. xi. 19. 8
noblest *borne* of all in Britayne land; II. xi. 30. 7
newly *borne* Of th' Ocean's fruitfull froth, II. xii. 65. 3
all sixe brethren, *borne* of one parent, III. i. 44. 5
Yet is no Fary *borne,* III. iii. 26. 4
Briton babe that shal be *borne* To live in thraldome III. iii. 42. 2
whom *borne* She, of his father, Marinell did name; III. iv. 20. 1
The wretched sonne of wretched mother *borne,* III. iv. 36. 2
To beene ybredd and never *borne* to dye? III. iv. 38. 2
She, hevenly *borne* and of celestiall hew. III. v. 47. 4
all the Graces rockt her cradle being *borne*. III. vi. 2. 9
So was this virgin *borne,* so was she bred; III. vi. 3. 6
A Faerie was, *yborne* of high degree. III. vi. 4. 3
Of all things that are *borne* to live and dye, III. vi. 30. 5
Some, of *borne* brethren prov'd unnaturall; IV. i. 24. 4
she at first was *borne* of hellish brood, IV. i. 26. 7
Three bolder brethren never were *yborne,* IV. ii. 41. 2
Borne of one mother in one happie mold, IV. ii. 41. 3
Borne at one burden in one happie morne; IV. ii. 41. 4
fruitfull apples to have *borne* awhile, IV. iii. 29. 8
seemed *borne* of Angels brood, IV. iii. 39. 7
there made gods, though *borne* of mortall berth, IV. iii. 44. 3
to his powre we all are subject *borne:* IV. viii. 15. 2
her syre of whom she was *yborne*. IV. ix. 3. 9
both *borne* of heavenly seed, IV. x. 34. 3
Sixe valiant Knights of one faire Nymphe *yborne,* IV. xi. 37. 3
Terpine, *borne* to' a more unhappy howre, V. v. 18. 4
they were *borne* to base humilitie, V. v. 25. 8
was not *borne* Of Beares and Tygres, V. v. 40. 5
sacred Reverence *yborne* of heavenly strene. V. ix. 32. 9
She first was bred, and *borne* of heavenly race, V. x. 1. 8
they say that he was *borne* and bred Of Gyants race, V. x. 9. 1
Borne of the brooding of Echidna base, V. xi. 23. 5
he deem'd him *borne* of noble race: VI. ii. 5. 5
sure he weend him *borne* of noble blood, VI. ii. 24. 6
Or surely *borne* of some Heroicke sead, VI. ii. 25. 8
Then wote ye that I am a Briton *borne,* VI. ii. 27. 6
The lusty Aladine, though meaner *borne* VI. iii. 7. 6

Born—*Continued.*
reed Me then to be full base and evill *borne,* VI. iii. 31. 8
pitty craves, as he of woman was *yborne.'* VI. iii. 41. 9
Mongst salvage beasts both rudely *borne* and bred, VI. v. 2. 3
certes he was *borne* of noble blood, VI. v. 2. 7
to adorne With so brave badges one so basely *borne:* VI. vi. 36. 5
She was *borne* free, not bound to any wight, VI. vii. 30. 8
all his brethren *borne* in Britaine land; VI. xii. 39. 8
art *yborne* of heaven and heavenly Sire, VII. vii. 2. 7
Then is she mortall *borne,* how-so ye crake: VII. vii. 50. 5
Where were ye *borne?* VII. vii. 53. 5
borne here in this world; VII. vii. 53. 9
'Then are ye mortall *borne,* and thrall to me VII. vii. 54. 1
Well is he *borne,* that may behold you ever. *Am.* viii. 14
looking on the earth whence she was *borne,* *Am.* xiii. 6
of the brood of Angels hevenly *borne;* *Am.* lxi. 6
divine, and *borne* of heavenly seed; *Am.* lxxix. 10
That same is Beautie, *borne* of heavenly race. *H.L.* 112
it is heavenly *borne* and can not die, *H.B.* 104
goodly beautie, albe heavenly *borne,* *H.B.* 149
bodie, which was *borne* Without all blemish *H.H.L.* 148
did deeme Them heavenly *borne,* *Proth.* 62
Borne. *See* **Born, Long-borne, Overborne.**
these olde fragments are for paternes *borne:* *Ro.* xxvii. 8
Backe to be *borne,* though it unlawfull were *Gn.* 464
them *borne* aside Into a secret corner unespide. *Hub.* 1017
borne to heaven, for heaven a fitter pray; *D.* 164
For him so far had *borne* his light-foot steede, I. ii. 8. 3
false Duessa in her sted had *borne,* I. iv. 2. 3
powres . . . Have *borne* him hence to Plutoes balefull bowres: I. v. 14. 8
Is not short payne well *borne,* that bringes long ease, I. ix. 40. 6
Besought them by the womb which them had *born,* II. ii. 27. 5
traine . . . *borne* of two faire Damsels II. ix. 19. 5
had seven hundred yeares this scepter *borne* II. x. 36. 2
The noble Arthegall hath ever *borne* the name. III. ii. 9. 9
despight Which he had *borne* of his bold enimee: III. v. 15. 4
way through which his wings Had *borne* him, III. vi. 12. 7
Unwares had *borne* two babes, III. vi. 26. 9
hath him *borne* a chyld, III. vi. 50. 7
As if the wind him on his winges had *borne;* III. x. 55. 2
Let then this plaint unto his eares be *borne,* IV. xii. 8. 3
crusht the Crab, and quite him *borne* V. Pr. 6. 3
So he my love away with him hath *borne,* V. i. 18. 8
armes had *borne,* but little good could finde, V. vi. 32. 4
goodly building . . . *Borne* uppon stately pillours, V. vii. 5. 4
under his fierce horses feet have *borne,* V. viii. 31. 8
ere that it she backe again had *borne,* V. xi. 29. 7
And *borne* great sway in armes amongst his peares; VI. iii. 3. 3
The bay . . . is of the victours *borne,* *Am.* xxix. 5
Borrel. I am but rude and *borrell,* *S.C.* Jul. 95
Borrow. now nill be quitt with baile nor *borrowe*. *S.C.* May 131
Nay, say I thereto, by my deare *borrowe,* *S.C.* May 150
lette me thy tale *borrowe* *S.C.* May 308
that great Pan bought with deare *borrow,* *S.C.* S. 96
borowe base, and some good Ladies gifts: *Hub.* 852
Doth *borrow* grace, the fancie to aggrate; *T.M.* 406
Whence all that lives does *borrow* life and light, II. x. 2. 2
borrow matter whereof they are made; III. vi. 37. 2
Borrowed. Both *borrowed* pride, and native beautie stained. *Van.* viii. 12
'Whose *borrowed* beautie now appeareth plaine I. ii. 39. 2
with extorted powre, and *borrow'd* strength, I. vii. 18. 3
such the sight . . . when her *borrowed* light Is laid away, I. viii. 49. 5
Sith her Prince Arthur of . . . *borrowd* beauty spoyld. II. i. 22. 7
He stroke so hugely with his *borrowd* blade, II. viii. 45. 2
three Moones with *borrowd* brothers light III. iii. 16. 2
her bright browes were deckt with *borrowed* haire; III. xii. 14. 7
To sell her *borrowed* beautie to abuse: IV. i. 31. 4
His *borrowed* waters forst to redisbourse, IV. iii. 27. 7
with *borrowed* plumes thy selfe endewed, V. iii. 20. 7
all that Venus in her selfe doth vaunt Is *borrowed* of them. VI. x. 15. 6
Shall doffe her fleshes *borrowd* fayre attyre, *Am.* xxvii. 6
Bosom. beating downe these walls . . . Into her mothers *bosome,* *Ro.* xi. 12
Doth plonge himselfe in Tethys *bosome* faire; *Ro.* xx. 4
Faire blew the winde into her *bosome* right; *Van.* ix. 5
Borne in the *bosome* of the black Abysse, *T.M.* 260
in the *bosome* of all blis did sit, *T.M.* 308
th' Almighties *bosome,* where he nests; *T.M.* 389
Sate in the *bosome* of his Soveraine, *Ti.* 188
Out of the *bosome* of the makers blis, *Ti.* 282
in the *bosome* of the billowes breed. *Col.* 243
bred above in Venus *bosome* deare: *Col.* 840
in the *bosome* of the billowes breed. *Col.* 243
fast gan flye Into great Tethys *bosome,* II. xii. 26. 9
Her bared *bosome* she doth broad display; II. xii. 74. 8
Out of their hollow *bosome* forth to throw III. iv. 22. 4
in her *bosome* she compriz'd Well as she might, III. vi. 19. 7
in her *bosome* she thee long had nurst, III. xi. 1. 3
into her faire *bosome* made his grapes decline. III. xi. 43. 9
Great *heapes* of salmons in his deepe *bosome:* IV. xi. 43. 6
was shed Into her pregnant *bosome,* V. vii. 11. 2
whilest in Morpheus *bosome* safe she lay, VI. viii. 34. 6
Rent up her brest, and *bosome* open layd, VI. xii. 19. 4
Out of her fruitfull *bosome* made to growe Most dainty trees, VII. vii. 8. 6
goodly *bosome,* lyke a Strawberry bed; *Am.* lxiv. 9
him take, and in your *bosome* bright Gently encage, *Am.* lxxiii. 9
Him lodging in your *bosome* to have lent. *Am.* lxxiii. 14
Fayre *bosome!* fraught with vertues richest tresure, *Am.* lxxvi. 1
in her snowy *bosome* boldly lay Their quiet heads, *H.L.* 289
Out of the *bosome* of eternall blisse, *H.H.L.* 134
There in his *bosome* Sapience doth sit, *H.H.B.* 183

Boss. bedeckt Uppon the *bosse* with stones that shined wide, . . . V. v. 3. 7
His deare Redeemers badge upon the *bosse:* . . . V. xi. 53. 5
Bosses. an Elephant, Adorn'd with bells and *bosses* . . . *Van.* viii. 2
With bells and *bosses* that full lowdly rung, . . . *Hub.* 583
Whose bridle rung with golden bels and *bosses* brave. . . . I. ii. 13. 9
Bost(e), Boster, *etc.* *See* **Boast, Boaster,** *etc.*
Both (*partial list*).
Sudden *both* Palme and Olive fell away, . . . *Bel.*[2] ix. 13
I saw *both* ship and mariners each one, . . . *Bel.*[2] xiii. 12
both her feete . . . *Ro.* iv. 13
The firie sunnes *both* one and other hous: . . . *Ro.* x. 8
there unjoynted *both* her bones: . . . *S.C.* Mar. 52
what account *both* these will make; . . . *S.C.* May 51
keepe *both* our flockes from straying. . . . *S.C.* May 173
bedde, or bowre, *both* which I fill with cryes, . . . *S.C.* Au. 167
they *both* doe mortall foes remaine, . . . *Gn.* 415
Both seeming now full glad . . . *Gn.* 483
both of them . . . Renown'd . . . *Gn.* 486
For *both* were craftie . . . *Hub.* 49
Both their habiliments unto them tooke, . . . *Hub.* 110
Such will we fashion *both* our selves to bee, . . . *Hub.* 167
The pasport ended, *both* they forward went; . . . *Hub.* 203
twixt them *both* they not a lambkin left, . . . *Hub.* 321
who, striken *both* with feare, . . . *Hub.* 1068
his Crowne and scepter *both* he wanted, . . . *Hub.* 1339
both eares pared of their hight; . . . *Hub.* 1382
when *both* alike are dedd; . . . *T.M.* 448
So thou *both* here and there immortall art, . . . *Ti.* 342
now *both* woods and fields and floods revive, . . . *Col.* 29
So piped we, until we *both* were weary.' . . . *Col.* 79
Both male and female through commixture joynd: . . . *Col.* 802
Lost *both* his eyes . . . *Col.* 922
Come, *both;* and with you bring triumphant Mart, . . . I. Pr. 3. 7
Them *both* together laid to joy in vaine delight. . . . I. ii. 3. 9
so *both* away do fly. . . . I. ii. 6. 9
Soone meete they *both, both* fell and furious, . . . I. ii. 15. 4
So stood these twaine, . . . *Both* staring fierce, . . . I. ii. 16. 8
twixt them *both* was born the bloudy bold Sans loy. . . . I. ii. 25. 9
Both which fraile men doe oftentimes mistake, . . . I. ii. 32. 7
Both seemde to win, and *both* seemde won to bee, . . . I. ii. 37. 6
Shee found them *both* in darksome corner pent; . . . I. iii. 13. 5
when they *both* had wept and wayld their fill, . . . I. iii. 22. 6
hee . . . *both* from backe and belly still did spare, . . . I. iv. 28. 4
So been they parted *both,* with harts on edge . . . I. iv. 43. 3
Feasting and courting *both* in bowre and hall; . . . I. iv. 43. 6
'what oddes can ever bee, Where *both* doe fight alike, . . . I. iv. 50. 4
The warlike feates of *both* those knights to see. . . . I. v. 5. 5
Both stricken stryke, and beaten *both* doe beat, . . . I. v. 7. 7
With hideous horror *both* together smight, . . . I. v. 8. 6
Great pains, and greater praise, *both* never to be donne.' . . . I. v. 43. 9
The Antelope, and Wolfe *both* fiers and fell; . . . I. vi. 26. 5
see that knight *both* living and eke ded.' . . . I. vi. 36. 9
Both breathing vengeaunce, *both* of wrathfull hew. . . . I. vi. 38. 5
Therewith they gan, *both* furious and fell, To thunder blowes, I. vi. 43. 1
with their force they perst *both* plate and maile, . . . I. vi. 43. 4
Both hongred after death; *both* chose to win, or die. . . . I. vi. 43. 9
Til breathlesse *both* themselves aside retire, . . . I. vi. 44. 6
They *both,* deformed, scarsely could bee known. . . . I. vi. 45. 6
Both loftie towres and highest trees hath rent, . . . I. viii. 9. 7
left hand . . . is through rage more strong then *both* were erst; I. viii. 18. 3
Both feet and face one way are wont to lead. . . . I. viii. 31. 6
all the good is Gods, *both* power and eke will. . . . I. x. 1. 9
court they see, *Both* plaine and pleasaunt . . . I. x. 6. 3
The auncient Dame . . . enterteynd them *both,* . . . I. x. 11. 7
A booke, that was *both* signd and seald with blood; . . . I. x. 13. 8
of youre toyle . . . Ye *both* forwearied be: . . . I. x. 17. 4
They bene ymett, *both* ready to affrap, . . . II. i. 26. 6
So beene they *both* at one, . . . II. i. 29. 1
So courteous conge *both* did give and take, . . . II. i. 34. 1
Besides them *both,* upon the soiled gras . . . II. i. 41. 1
Betwixt them *both* can measure out a meane; . . . II. i. 58. 2
Thrise happy man, who fares them *both* atweene! . . . II. i. 58. 5
both alike, when death hath *both* suppresst, . . . II. i. 59. 5
So *both* agree their bodies to engrave: . . . II. i. 60. 1
both against the middest meant to worken woe. . . . II. ii. 13. 9
Both knightes and ladies forth right angry far'd, . . . II. ii. 19. 8
both with greedy forse Attonce upon him ran, . . . II. ii. 22. 1
scorning *both* their spights, does make wide way, . . . II. ii. 24. 7
Does ride on *both* their backs, . . . II. ii. 24. 9
rusheth forth Betweene them *both* . . . II. ii. 25. 2
both their champions bad Pursew the end . . . II. ii. 28. 2
stablish terms betwixt *both* their requests, . . . II. ii. 32. 7
their natures bad appeard in *both;* . . . II. ii. 34. 5
both did at their second sister grutch . . . II. ii. 34. 6
Betwixt them *both* the faire Medina sate . . . II. ii. 38. 1
both his foen with equall foyle to daunt. . . . II. iii. 13. 3
dead through great affright They *both* nigh were, . . . II. iii. 19. 8
Both fled attonce, . . . II. iii. 19. 9
both doe strive their fearefulnesse to faine. . . . II. iii. 20. 6
both her hands fast bound unto a stake, . . . II. iv. 13. 5
both his hands fast bound behind his backe, . . . II. iv. 14. 8
both his feet in fetters to an yron racke. . . . II. iv. 14. 9
by that same sacred band Betwixt us *both,* . . . II. iv. 23. 7
I meant to purge *both* with a third mischiefe, . . . II. iv. 31. 3
Whose bounty more then might, yet *both,* he wondered. . . . II. v. 14. 9
Both what she was, and what that usage ment, . . . II. vi. 9. 3
both did gnash their teeth, and *both* did threten life. . . . II. vii. 21. 9
Here Sleep, ther Richesse, and Hel-gate them *both* betwext. . II. vii. 25. 9
both his handes, most filthy feculent, . . . II. vii. 61. 4
though they *both* stood stiffe; yet could not *both* withstond. . II. viii. 41. 9

Both—*Continued.*
they *both* yfere Forth passed on their way . . . II. ix. 2. 3
They *both* attone Did dewty to their Lady, . . . II. ix. 28. 6
so *both* divided were. . . . III. xi. 6. 9
The cause of *both,* of *both* their minds depends, . . . IV. iv. 1. 4
So did the Ladies *both,* . . . V. i. 17. 4
(*Both* two her paramours, *both* by her hyred, . . . V. ix. 41. 4
Did set uppon us flying *both* for feare; . . . VI. i. 16. 4
leave them *both* behynd In that good Hermits charge; . . . VI. v. 41. 3
Of that good Hermite *both* they tooke their leave, . . . VI. vi. 15. 8
armed *both* agreeably, And *both* combynd, . . . to divide, . VI. vii. 3. 7, 8
else *both* you, and she, Will *both* together . . . *Am.* xlvi. 11, 12
see The ods twixt *both,* of *both* them deem aright, . . . *Com. Son.* ii. 10
Doe *both* expresse the faces first impression. . . . *H.B.* 182
Bottle. wherefore doe you beare This *bottle* . . . VI. viii. 23. 7
'Here in this *bottle* . . . I put the tears of my contrition, . VI. viii. 24. 1
Yet is the *bottle* leake, and bag so torne, . . . VI. viii. 24. 6
Bottom. Shaking the hill even from the *bottome* deepe, . . . *Bel.*[1] ii. 13
The *bottome* yellow like the shining land, . . . *Bel.*[1] x. 3
The *bottome* yeallow, like the golden grayle . . . *Bel.*[2] xii. 3
Shee sight from *bottome* of her wounded brest; . . . II. i. 47. 2
Ne ought mote ever sinck downe to the *bottom* there. . . . II. vi. 46. 9
through the waves one might the *bottom* see, . . . II. xii. 62. 7
Lay hidden in the *bottome* of the pot. . . . III. ii. 26. 5
Deepe in the *bottome* of the sea . . . III. iv. 43. 1
His bowre is in the *bottom* of the maine, . . . III. viii. 37. 1
Downe in the *bottome* of the deepe Abysse, . . . IV. ii. 47. 6
thousand vowes from *bottome* of his hart, . . . IV. vi. 43. 4
Deepe in the *bottome* of an huge great rocke . . . IV. xi. 3. 1
doth their *bottome* tread; . . . IV. xi. 14. 8
it shakes the *bottome* of the bulke, . . . V. xi. 29. 3
foot of man might sound the *bottome* plaine, . . . V. xii. 5. 3
Bouget. *See* **Budget.**
Bough. *See* **Laurel-bough.**
From *bough* to *bough* he lepped light, . . . *S.C.* Mar. 92
All comfortlesse upon the bared *bow,* . . . *T.M.* 245
to frame A girlond . . . He pluckt a *bough;* . . . I. ii. 30. 8
knight, . . . The bleeding *bough* did thrust into the ground, . I. ii. 44. 6
she, more sweete then any bird on *bough,* . . . II. vi. 25. 1
having hong upon a *bough* on high Her bow . . . III. vi. 18. 1
To win a willow *bough,* . . . IV. i. 47. 9
as a swarme Of flyes upon a birchen *bough* doth cluster, . . . V. xi. 58. 2
Sweet is the Junipere, but sharpe his *bough;* . . . *Am.* xxvi. 2
the Culver, on the bared *bough,* . . . *Am.* lxxxviii. 1
Boughs. *See* **Laurel-boughs.**
The honour of these noble *boughs* (*bowes*[1]) . . . *Bel.* v. 11
I see your teares that from your *boughes* doe raine, . . . *S.C.* Ja. 35
As on your *boughes* the ysicles depend. . . . *S.C.* Ja. 42
His bared *boughes* were beaten with stormes, . . . *S.C.* F. 112
So beate his old *boughes* my tender side, . . . *S.C.* F. 175
balefull *boughes* of Cypres doen advaunce; . . . *S.C.* N. 145
'My *boughes* with bloosmes that crowned were . . . *S.C.* D. 103
Others the utmost *boughs* of trees doe crop, . . . *Gn.* 81
whose *boughes* she doth enfold . . . *Gn.* 220
Birds, in their wide *boughs* embowring, . . . *Gn.* 225
with greene *boughes* decking a gloomy glade, . . . I. vii. 4. 4
With *boughes* and arbours woven cunningly, . . . II. vi. 2. 8
Cover'd with *boughes* and shrubs from heavens light, . . . II. vii. 3. 2
being goodly dight With *bowes* and braunches, . . . II. xii. 53. 8
the weake *boughes,* with so rich load opprest . . . II. xii. 55. 5
the *boughes* doe laughing blossoms beare, . . . III. vi. 42. 3
Whose shady *boughes* sharp steele did never lop, . . . III. vi. 43. 4
with their *boughes* the gentle plants did beat: . . . V. i. 1. 5
Where he with *boughes* hath built his shady stand, . . . V. viii. 35. 8
Deckt with greene *boughes* and flowers gay beseene: . . . VI. v. 38. 5
Bought. shepheard great! That *bought* his flocke so deare, . . *S.C.* Jul. 54
Whose love he *bought* to deare; . . . *S.C.* Jul. 148
though my bale with death I *bought,* . . . *S.C.* Au. 105
that great Pan *bought* with deare borrow, . . . *S.C.* S. 96
(a lesson derely *bought*) . . . *S.C.* N. 156
Adieu, my deare, whose love I *bought* so deare; . . . *S.C.* D. 152
all be brethren ylike dearly *bought:* . . . *Hub.* 142
with much bloodshed *bought* full deere, . . . *Ti.* 115
O short pleasure, *bought* with lasting paine! . . . *Ti.* 526
so deare his love he *bought.'* . . . *Col.* 155
O, too deare love, love *bought* with death too deare!' . . . I. ii. 31. 7
Sowen in bloodie field, and *bought* with woe: . . . I. iv. 42. 5
loves . . . *Bought* with the blood of vanquisht Paynim bold; I. vii. 26. 4
Ladies love to leave, so dearely *bought?* . . . I. x. 62. 6
So deare thee, babe, I *bought;* . . . II. i. 53. 8
I cast to pay that I so dearely *bought.* . . . II. iv. 30. 7
deare wisedom *bought* too late! . . . III. iv. 37. 9
'for which is *bought* Endlesse renowm, . . . III. xi. 19. 8
Whens dearely she with death *bought* her desire. . . . III. xi. 33. 5
Scudamour her *bought* In perilous fight . . . IV. i. 2. 1
That she might win some time, though dearly *bought,* . . . V. ii. 23. 7
'Where is the bootie, which therefore I *bought,* . . . VI. vii. 16. 2
though long time dearely *bought.* . . . VI. ix. 45. 9
Him first to love that us so dearely *bought,* . . . *H.H.L.* 188
Boughts. wrapt his scalie *boughts* with fell despight, . . . *Gn.* 255
taile . . . in knots and many *boughtes* upwound, . . . I. i. 15. 3
Whose wreathed *boughtes* when ever he unfoldes, . . . I. xi. 11. 3
Bounce. Did beat and *bounse* his head and brest ful sore: . . . III. xi. 27. 6
They snuf, they snort, they *bounce,* they rage, . . . V. ii. 15. 6
Bounced. Yet still he bet and *bounst* upon the dore, . . . V. ii. 21. 6
Bouncing. I saw the *bouncing* Bellibone, . . . *S.C.* Au. 61
Bound. *See* **Bounden.**
Their armes . . . *bounde* at their backes. . . . *Bel.*[1] xi. 10
With armes *bound* at their backs . . . *Bel.*[2] xv. 10
bound in sheaves, and layd in comely rowes, . . . *Ro.* xxx. 7

Bound—*Continued.*
Why should we be *bound* to such miseree? . . . *S.C.* S. 239
Fast *bound* with serpents that him oft invades; . . . *Gn.* 374
Before his noble heart he firmely *bound,* . . . *Mui.* 58
brought away fast *bound* with silver chaine. . . . *D.* 119
To thee are all true lovers greatly *bound.* . . . *Col.* 899
I now doe live, *bound* yours by vassalage; . . . *Ded. Son.* vii. 5
Upon a great adventure he was *bond,* . . . I. i. 3. 1
a loose Leman to vile service *bound:* . . . I. i. 48. 6
I . . . hold me to you *bound:* . . . I. i. 54. 3
Yet live perforce in balefull darkenesse *bound?* . . . I. viii. 38. 5
boastes in beauties chaine not to be *bownd,* . . . I. ix. 11. 7
the way that does to heaven *bownd!'* . . . I. x. 67. 4
Attacht that faytor false, and *bound* him strait; . . . I. xii. 35. 5
bound him hand and foote with yron chains; . . . I. xii. 36. 2
bownd by them to live in lives despight; . . . II. i. 36. 4
In chaines of lust and lewde desyres *ybownd,* . . . II. i. 54. 3
His sunbroad shield about his wrest he *bond,* . . . II. ii. 21. 5
whither now on new adventure *bownd:* . . . II. ii. 39. 6
many-folded shield he *bound* about his wrest. . . . II. iii. 1. 9
both her handes fast *bound* unto a stake, . . . II. iv. 13. 5
both his hands fast *bound* behind his backe, . . . II. iv. 14. 8
whom your victorious might Hath now fast *bound,* . . . II. iv. 32. 4
whither with such hasty flight Art thou now *bownd?* . . . II. iv. 43. 3
'Then loe! wher *bound* she sits, . . . II. iv. 44. 8
His owne woes author, who so *bound* it findes, . . . II. v. 1. 8
where he them *bound* did see, . . . II. v. 18. 8
without the utmost *bound* Of this great gardin, . . . II. vii. 56. 4
Guyons shield about his wrest he *bond:* . . . II. viii. 22. 7
But to be ever *bound*'— . . . II. viii. 55. 9
knightes by oath *bound* to withstond Oppressours powre . . . II. viii. 56. 4
from Alcluid to Panwelt did that border *bownd.* . . . II. x. 63. 9
within the utmost *bound* Of his wide Labyrinth, . . . II. xii. 20. 8
formerly were *bownd* Up in one knott, . . . II. xii. 67. 2
both them strongly *bound* In captive bandes, . . . II. xii. 82. 4
round about the Pots mouth *bound* the thread; . . . III. ii. 50. 3
Them *bownd* till his retourne their labour not to slake. . . . III. iii. 10. 9
the stubborne feendes he to his service *bownd.* . . . III. iii. 14. 9
firmely *bound* with faithfull band, . . . III. iii. 27. 6
A friendly league . . . She with him *bound,* . . . III. iv. 4. 5
Are *bownd* with commun bond of frailtee, . . . III. v. 36. 8
We both are *bownd* to follow heavens beheasts, . . . III. vi. 22. 7
with it *bownd* the beast, that lowd did rore . . . III. vii. 36. 3
with a teeme of scaly Phocas *bownd* . . . III. viii. 30. 8
that is the *bownd* Toward the land; . . . III. ix. 46. 3
two rivers *bownd* the rest. . . . III. ix. 46. 4
al good knights, . . . Are *bownd* for to revenge, . . . III. x. 27. 9
the Lady, which by him stood *bound.* . . . III. xii. 34. 3
He *bound* that pitteous Lady prisoner, . . . III. xii. 41. 7
Himselfe she *bound,* more worthy to be so, . . . III. xii. 41. 8
by the tailes together firmely *bound,* . . . IV. iii. 42. 4
mighty spirites *bound* with mightier band, . . . IV. iii. 48. 7
bound Upon an hard adventure yet in quest, . . . IV. vi. 42. 2
of the perils whereto he was *bound,* . . . IV. vi. 45. 3
Kings and Keasars to thy service *bound;* . . . IV. vii. 1. 4
if so be they were not *bound,* . . . IV. vii. 33. 7
with a litle golden chaine about it *bound.* . . . IV. viii. 6. 9
eke his cave in which they both were *bond:* . . . IV. viii. 21. 8
Upon his usuall beast it firmely *bound,* . . . IV. ix. 4. 8
bound them with inviolable bands; . . . IV. x. 35. 4
The dongeon was, in which her *bound* he left, . . . IV. xi. 3. 2
Bound like a beast appointed to the stall: . . . V. i. 22. 6
To doe her service so as I am *bond:* . . . V. ii. 4. 4
every one doe know their certaine *bound,* . . . V. ii. 36. 2
Ne loose that he hath *bound* with stedfast band. . . . V. ii. 42. 4
Fast *bound* on every side with iron bands, . . . V. iv. 5. 2
ever to my lore be *bound;* . . . V. iv. 49. 3
There *bound* t' obay that Amazons proud law, . . . V. v. 22. 3
as *bound* to me he may continue still: . . . V. v. 32. 9
'*Bound* unto me but not with such hard bands . . . V. v. 33. 1
I to your selfe should rest for ever *bound,* . . . V. v. 42. 4
She quickly caught her sword, and shield about her *bound.* . . . V. vi. 28. 9
To serve her so as she the rest had *bound:* . . . V. vii. 28. 4
With a strong yron chaine and coller *bound,* . . . V. ix. 33. 6
Gave leave unto his ghost from thraldome *bound* . . . V. x. 33. 5
whose everlasting praise They all were *bound* . . . to raise. . . V. xi. 34. 9
by that Tyrant is in wretched thraldome *bound:* . . . V. xi. 38. 9
whom all the bands Which may a Knight assure had surely *bound,* . . . V. xii. 2. 2
Both hand and foote unto a tree was *bound;* . . . VI. i. 11. 4
Me . . . Till his returne unto this tree he *bond;* . . . VI. i. 16. 8
Her selfe acknowledg'd *bound* for that accord, . . . VI. i. 45. 8
her selfe *bound* to him for evermore; . . . VI. i. 46. 8
But I am *bound* by vow, . . . VI. ii. 37. 5
From him to whom she was for ever *bound:* . . . VI. ii. 43. 7
She was borne free, not *bound* to any wight, . . . VI. vii. 30. 8
Were *bound* about and voyded from before; . . . VI. vii. 43. 8
the Carle upon him layd, And *bound* him fast: . . . VI. vii. 48. 7
Him to have *bound* and thrald without delay; . . . VI. viii. 11. 7
all this while stood there beside them *bound,* . . . VI. viii. 27. 2
So leave we her in wretched thraldome *bound,* . . . VI. xi. 24. 8
This daughter thought in wedlocke to have *bound* . . . VI. xii. 4. 5
Against his will fast *bound* in yron chaine, . . . VI. xii. 35. 3
In chast desires, on heavenly beauty *bound.* . . . *Am.* viii. 8
league . . . that loyal love hath *bound:* . . . *Am.* lxv. 10
of lillyes and of roses, *Bound* truelove wize, . . . *Epith.* 44
that mightie *bound* which doth embrace The rolling Spheres, . . . *H.H.L.* 25
And *bound* therto with an eternall band, . . . *H.H.L.* 187
Untill they come to their first Movers *bound,* . . . *H.H.B.* 72
two Garlands *bound* Of freshest Flowres . . . *Proth.* 83

Bounded. With loftie flight above the earth he *bounded,* . . . *Ti.* 599
th' Aire . . . firmely *bounded* On everie side, . . . *H.H.B.* 38
Not *bounded,* not corrupt, as these same bee, . . . *H.H.B.* 66
Bounden. I *bownden* am streight after this emprize, . . . I. xii. 18. 4
Fast *bounden* hand and foote with cords of wire, . . . III. vii. 37. 8
both whose hands Were *bounden* fast, . . . III. xii. 30. 7
That I her *bounden* thrall by her may live, . . . *H.B.* 278
Bounding. often *bounding* on the brused gras, . . . I. xi. 15. 3
Bounds. Nor *bounds* nor banks his headlong ruine may sustayne. II. xi. 18. 9
looser thoughts to lawfull *bounds* withdraw; . . . IV. vi. 33. 7
Dare not henceforth, above the *bounds* of dewtie, . . . *Am.* lxi. 3
Bounse, Bounst. *See* **Bounce,** *etc.*
Bounteous. Ladie, in whose *bounteous* brest All heavenly grace . . . *Pet.*[2] vii. 9
who so else his *bounteous* minde did trie, . . . *Ti.* 233
Their *bounteous* deeds and noble favours shrynd, . . . *Col.* 582
Ne wanted ought to shew her *bounteous* or wise. . . . I. x. 11. 9
to the mighty victor yields a *bounteous* feast. . . . II. v. 10. 9
Did breath out *bounteous* smels, . . . II. v. 29. 9
how brave she decks her *bounteous* boure, . . . II. vi. 16. 5
thy *bounteous* baytes and pleasing charmes, . . . II. vii. 10. 3
An armed knight, of bold and *bounteous* grace, . . . II. viii. 17. 5
to her guestes doth *bounteous* banket dight, . . . II. xi. 2. 8
Thereto so *bounteous* and so debonayre, . . . III. i. 26. 4
love does alwaies bring forth *bounteous* deeds, . . . III. i. 49. 8
Should ever enter in his *bounteous* thought, . . . III. ii. 10. 2
In gentle Ladies breste and *bounteous* race Of woman kind . . . III. v. 52. 7
more *bounteous* creature never far'd On foot . . . III. xi. 10. 3
magnanimity Dwells in thy *bounteous* brest! . . . III. xi. 19. 3
bounteous Trent, that in him selfe enseames . . . IV. xi. 35. 8
your *bounteous* proffer Be farre fro me, . . . VI. ix. 33. 3
Bounteously. Feeding upon their pleasures *bounteouslie,* . . . *Mui.* 151
Bountiest. The *bountiest* virgin and most debonaire . . . III. v. 8. 2
Bountiful. The next to her is *bountifull* Charillis: . . . *Col.* 542
Bountihead. such soveraine glory and great *bountyhed?* . . . II. x. 2. 9
On firme foundation of true *bountyhed:* . . . II. xii. 1. 5
She seemd a woman of great *bountihed,* . . . III. i. 41. 5
Emongst his young ones shall divide with *bountyhed.* . . . III. iii. 47. 9
In all chaste vertue and true *bounti-hed,* . . . III. vi. 3. 8
Bounty. not so common was his *bountie* shared: . . . *Hub.* 1194
with rich *bountie,* and deare cherishment, . . . *T.M.* 573
Brave Impe of Bedford! grow apace in *bountie,* . . . *Ti.* 272
In whom all *bountie* and all vertuous love Appeared . . . *Ti.* 283
robd her race of *bountie* quight. . . . *D.* 221
grace was great, and *bounty* most rewardfull. . . . *Col.* 187
She is the well of *bountie* and brave mynd, . . . *Col.* 496
Be witnesse of her *bountie* here alive, . . . *Col.* 646
That doest their *bountie* still so much commend. . . . *Col.* 902
All goodly *bountie* and true honour sits. . . . *Ded. Son.* v. 12
Noble Lord, . . . Through whose large *bountie,* . . . *Ded. Son.* vii. 3
Of wondrous beauty, and of *bounty* rare, . . . I. x. 30. 2
One that to *bountie* never cast his mynd, . . . II. iii. 4. 2
Her yvorie forhead, full of *bountie* brave, . . . II. iii. 24. 1
Whose *bounty* more then might, yet both, he wondered. . . . II. v. 14. 9
The guifts of soveraine *bounty* did embrace: . . . II. vii. 16. 4
full of princely *bounty* and great mind, . . . II. viii. 51. 1
That is, her *bounty,* and imperiall powre, . . . II. ix. 3. 6
with her *bounty* and glad countenaunce Doth blesse . . . II. ix. 5. 4
Her *bountie* she abated, and his cheare empayrd. . . . II. x. 30. 9
Ne blott the *bounty* of all womankind, . . . III. i. 49. 4
his large *bountie* rightly doth areed: . . . III. iv. 59. 4
Her soveraine *bountie* and celestiall hew, . . . III. v. 44. 5
Of *bounty,* and of beautie, and all vertues rare. . . . III. vi. 4. 9
beauty doth her *bounty* far surpasse; . . . III. ix. 4. 5
all *bountie* naturall And treasures of true love . . . IV. Pr. 4. 3
with her beautie, *bountie* did compare, . . . IV. iii. 39. 8
all the *bounty* which Belphebe threw On him, . . . IV. viii. 6. 4
Dew'd with her drops of *bountie* Soveraine, . . . IV. viii. 33. 5
For her great *bounty* knowen over all . . . V. viii. 17. 3
heavenly seedes of *bounty* soveraine, . . . VI. Pr. 3. 7
Of her faire light and *bounty* most benigne, . . . VII. vi. 11. 8
him enricht with *bounty* of the soyle: . . . VII. vii. 38. 4
Venus dearlings, through her *bountie* blest; . . . *H.L.* 284
That thou his soveraine *bountie* mayst behold, . . . *H.H.L.* 223
Bountyhed. *See* **Bountihead.**
Bounty's. To loose both her and *bounties* ornament. . . . *D.* 224
Bourbon. 'My name is *Burbon* hight, . . . V. xi. 49. 1
Sir *Burbon,* blushing halfe for shame: . . . V. xi. 52. 6
'Yet let me you of courtesie request' (Said *Burbon*) . . . V. xi. 57. 2
Burbon, streight dismounting from his steed, . . . V. xi. 61. 1
Which *Burbon* seeing her againe assayd; . . . V. xi. 64. 6
Artegall doth Sir *Burbon* aide, . . . V. xii. Arg.
Witnesse may *Burbon* be; . . . V. xii. 2. 1
Bourd. The wisard could no lenger beare her *bord,* . . . III. iii. 19. 1
turning all to game And pleasaunt *bord,* . . . IV. iv. 13. 2
Boure, -s. *See* **Bower, -s.**
Bourn. My little boat can safely passe this perilous *bourne.'* . . . II. vi. 10. 9
Bourne. *See* **Born.**
Bousing-can. he . . . in his hand did beare a *bouzing can,* . . . I. iv. 22. 6
Bout. *See* **About.**
Deepe busied *bout* worke of wondrous end, . . . III. iii. 14. 7
Whilest thus they busied were *bout* Florimell, . . . V. iii. 29. 1
Bout which whilest he was busied thus hard, . . . VI. v. 11. 1
Bouzing-can. *See* **Bousing-can.**
Bove. *See* **Above.**
brave heroick thought *Bove* womens weaknes, . . . *Ti.* 110
T' endow her sonne . . . *Bove* all the sonnes . . . III. iv. 21. 9
Bove all her sexe that ever yet was seene. . . . IV. Pr. 4. 5
Satyrane, *bove* all the other crew, . . . IV. iv. 37. 4
name then would I raise *Bove* all the gods, . . . *H.L.* 304

Bow, -s. *See* **Bough, -s, Saddle-bow.**
bowe your eares unto my dolefull dittie: . . . *S.C.* Ja. 16
With *bowe* and bolts in either hand, . . . *S.C.* Mar. 65
silver *bowe,* which was but slacke, . . . *S.C.* Mar. 83
bowe and shafts as then none had, . . . *S.C.* Mar. 113
his stiffe armes to stretch with Eughen *bowe,* . . . *Hub.* 747
stouping, like an arrowe from a *bowe,* . . . *Hub.* 1262
so manie sundrie colours arre In Iris *bowe;* . . . *Mui.* 93
The one his *bowe* and shafts, . . . *Mui.* 292
Then got he *bow* and shafts of gold and lead, . . . *Col.* 807
Lay now thy deadly Heben *bowe* apart, . . . I. Pr. 3. 5
Diana he her takes to be, But misseth *bow* and shaftes, . . . I. vi. 16. 9
Love! lay down thy *bow,* the whiles I may respyre. . . . I. ix. 8. 9
So far as Ewghen *bow* a shaft may send, . . . I. xi. 19. 2
she the woodes with *bow* and shaftes did raunge, . . . II. ii. 7. 3
at her backe a *bow* and quiver gay, . . . II. iii. 29. 2
Wandreth alone with *bow* and arrowes keene, . . . II. iii. 31. 4
having laid his cruell *bow* away . . . II. viii. 6. 2
His cruel *bow,* wherewith he thousands hath dismayd. . . . II. ix. 34. 9
every one did *bow* and arrowes beare . . . II. xi. 8. 7
in his hand a bended *bow* was seene, . . . II. xi. 21. 1
his mischievous *bow* full readie bent, . . . II. xi. 24. 4
his hands Discharged of his *bow* and deadly quar'le, . . . II. xi. 33. 8
boughes, . . . Did *bow* adowne as overburdened. . . . II. xii. 55. 6
Drew out a deadly *bow* and arrow keene, . . . III. i. 65. 2
His bootelesse *bow* in feeble hand upcaught, . . . III. v. 24. 6
Her *bow* and gilden quiver lying him beside. . . . III. v. 34. 9
Her *bow* and painted quiver, . . . III. vi. 18. 2
to the ground him meekely made to *bowe,* . . . III. x. 24. 3
When her discolourd *bow* she spreds through hevens hight. . . . III. xi. 47. 9
A mortall *bow* and arrowes keene did hold, . . . III. xi. 48. 2
Did to that image *bowe* their humble knee, . . . III. xi. 49. 4
Like shaft out of a *bow* preventing speed: . . . IV. i. 41. 3
with the force it backward forced him to *bow.* . . . IV. iii. 11. 9
With *bow* in hand and arrowes ready bent, . . . IV. vii. 29. 6
in her *bow* she ready shewed The arrow . . . IV. vii. 30. 3
with his killing *bow* And cruell shafts, . . . IV. x. 55. 3
Her goodly *bow,* which paints the liquid ayre, . . . V. iii. 25. 3
seem'd a marble pillour it could *bow;* . . . VI. viii. 16. 3
for chace of beasts with hound or *boawe,* . . . VII. vi. 39. 2
Did seeme to *bow* their bloosming heads full lowe . . . VII. vii. 8. 8
in his hand he bore A *boawe* and shaftes, . . . VII. vii. 29. 7
that high look, . . . *bow* to a baser make, . . . *Am.* x. 11
Bow-bent. the Bull hath with his *bow-bent* horne . . . V. Pr. 6. 1
Bowed. *bowed* low, that her right well became, . . . I. xii. 24. 3
Meekely shee *bowed* downe, . . . III. v. 31. 1
bowd his battred visour to his brest: . . . III. vii. 42. 5
to his saddle-bow thereby He *bowed* low, . . . IV. viii. 43. 5
seem'd to stoupe afore With *bowed* backe, . . . IV. xi. 26. 2
her *bowd* Upon her knee, intreating him for grace, . . . VI. vi. 31. 5
Bowels. Your blades in your owne *bowels* you embrew'd? . . . *Ro.* xxiv. 8
Made him to swell, that nigh his *bowells* brust, . . . *Van.* vi. 10
have in mine owne *bowels* made my grave, . . . *Ti.* 26
bowels so with ranckling poyson swelde, . . . *Mui.* 255
he saw . . . *bowels* gushing forth: . . . I. i. 26. 6
Morpheus house . . . Amid the *bowels* of the earth . . . I. i. 39. 4
Oke, which he had torne Out of his mothers *bowelles,* . . . I. vii. 10. 8
within my secret *bowelles* bee. . . . II. vi. 49. 9
first opened The *bowels* of wide Fraunce, . . . II. x. 23. 7
infixed faster hold Within my bleeding *bowells,* . . . III. ii. 39. 2
in thy troubled *bowels* raignes and rageth ryfe. . . . III. iv. 8. 9
Closely the wicked flame his *bowels* brent, . . . III. vii. 16. 1
of his *bowels* made his bloody feast: . . . III. viii. 49. 4
the wyde wound, which . . . riven *bowels* gor'd, . . . III. xii. 38. 4
all his *bowels* in his body brast: . . . V. viii. 8. 6
did his *bowels* disentrayle, . . . V. ix. 19. 5
Stryving in vaine that nigh his *bowels* brast, . . . VI. iv. 22. 2
And let thy *bowels* bleede in every vaine, . . . *H.H.L.* 248
Bower. Wherein the byrds were wont to build their *bowre* . . . *S.C.* Ja. 32
bids make readie Maias *bowre,* . . . *S.C.* Mar. 17
of St. Brigets *bowre,* . . . Kent can rightly boaste: . . . *S.C.* Jul. 43
tell thee more, And of our Ladyes *bowre;* . . . *S.C.* Jul. 74
bedde, or *bowre,* both which I fill with cryes, . . . *S.C.* Au. 167
To quite it from the blacke *bowre* of sorrowe. . . . *S.C.* S. 97
did fetch his dame From Plutoes balefull *bowre* . . . *S.C.* O. 29
The bush my bedde, the bramble was my *bowre,* . . . *S.C.* D. 65
perfect pleasure buildes her joyous *bowre,* . . . *Gn.* 135
A pleasant *bowre* with all delight abounding . . . *Gn.* 187
the darksome *bowre* Of Herebus . . . *Gn.* 313
pallid Yvie, building his owne *bowre;* . . . *Gn.* 675
Into her silver *bowre* the Sunne received; . . . *Hub.* 4
in Venus silver *bowre* were bred, . . . *T.M.* 362
For the Shriche-owle to build her balefull *bowre:* . . . *Ti.* 130
All happinesse in Hebes silver *bowre,* . . . *Ti.* 384
Merily masking both in *bowre* and hall. . . . *As.* 28
purchace highest rowmes in *bowre* and hall: . . . *Col.* 726
In whose high thoughts Pleasure hath built her *bowre,* . . . *Ded. Son.* viii. 6
The royall virgin . . . rising forth out of her baser *bowre,* . . . I. ii. 7. 6
Feasting and courting both in *bowre* and hall; . . . I. iv. 43. 6
came rushing forth from inner *bowre,* . . . I. viii. 5. 6
nor wight was seene in *bowre* or hall. . . . I. viii. 29. 9
Through every rowme he sought, and everie *bowr,* . . . I. viii. 37. 1
The faulty soules . . . brought to his heavenly *bowre.* . . . I. x. 40. 9
it hight the *Bowre of blis.* . . . II. i. 51. 9
She led him up into a goodly *bowre,* . . . II. ii. 15. 1
in a darkesome inner *bowre* Her oft to meete: . . . II. iv. 24. 5
ydle pleasures in her *Bowre* of Blisse, . . . II. v. 27. 3
how brave she decks her bounteous *boure,* . . . II. vi. 16. 5
God hath built for his owne blessed *bowre.* . . . II. ix. 47. 5
Guyon, . . . Doth overthrow the *Bowre* of blis, . . . II. xii. Arg.

Bower—*Continued.*
Whereas the *Bowre* of Blisse was situate; . . . II. xii. 42. 2
forth from virgin *bowre* she comes in th' early morne. . . . II. xii. 50. 9
Now are they come nigh to the *Bowre* of blis, . . . II. xii. 69. 4
earst was sought to deck both bed and *bowre* . . . II. xii. 75. 4
be led in courteous wize Into a *bowre,* . . . III. i. 42. 4
Her fearfull feete towards the *bowre* she mov'd, . . . III. i. 60. 2
Yet she might all men vew out of her *bowre?* . . . III. ii. 20. 5
th' aged Nourse, her calling to her *bowre,* . . . III. ii. 49. 4
Most famous fruites of matrimoniall *bowre,* . . . III. iii. 3. 7
To enter into that same balefull *Bowre,* . . . III. iii. 8. 8
Banisht from princely *bowre* to wastefull wood! . . . III. iii. 42. 6
her *bowre* Is built of hollow billowes . . . III. iv. 43. 1
To send thine Angell from her *bowre* of blis . . . III. v. 35. 3
left her blisfull *bowre* of joy above: . . . III. vi. 11. 5
devoure Her native flesh and staine her brothers *bowre,* . . . III. vii. 49. 5
Florimell with him unto his *bowre* he bore. . . . III. viii. 36. 9
His *bowre* is in the bottom of the maine, . . . III. viii. 37. 1
in close *bowre* her mewes from all mens sight, . . . III. ix. 5. 8
They beene ybrought into a comely *bowre,* . . . III. ix. 19. 1
The roring billowes beat his *bowre* so boystrously. . . . III. x. 58. 9
left behind her in her secret *bowre* . . . IV. v. 5. 4
forced them to seeke some covert *bowre,* . . . IV. v. 32. 5
dayly feasting both in *bowre* and hall, . . . IV. vi. 39. 7
To come forthwith unto his Ladies *bowre:* . . . IV. viii. 59. 3
in her delitious *boure* The faire Poeana . . . IV. ix. 6. 1
recoure His Leman from the Stygian Princes *boure:* . . . IV. x. 58. 5
Being returned to his mothers *bowre,* . . . IV. xii. 19. 1
Then Britomart unto a *bowre* was brought, . . . V. vi. 23. 2
She forth yssew'd out of her loathed *bowre,* . . . V. vi. 35. 3
lay Under the Idols feete in fearelesse *bowre,* . . . V. vii. 15. 2
The warlike Amazon out of her *bowre* did peepe. . . . V. vii. 26. 9
Thenceforth she streight into a *bowre* him brought, . . . V. vii. 41. 1
Fit for Adicia there to build her wicked *bowre.* . . . V. ix. 1. 9
it in silver *bowre* does hidden ly . . . VI. Pr. 3. 3
though it on a lowly stalke doe *bowre,* . . . VI. Pr. 4. 3
When Calidore . . . Unto his *bowre* was brought, . . . VI. iii. 9. 8
this your cabin both my *bowre* and hall: . . . VI. ix. 32. 4
Spredding pavilions for the birds to *bowre,* . . . VI. x. 6. 6
To bid her leave faire Cynthia's silver *bower;* . . . VII. vi. 18. 7
brought forth with pompous showes Out of her *bowre,* . . . VII. vi. 41. 5
that long hath slept in cheerlesse *bower,* . . . *Am.* iv. 6
spotlesse Pleasure builds her sacred *bowre.* . . . *Am.* lxv. 14
in her winters *bowre* not well awake; . . . *Am.* lxx. 6
The *bowre* of blisse, the paradice of pleasure, . . . *Am.* lxxvi. 3
her *bowre* with her late presence deckt; . . . *Am.* lxxviii. 6
nor in field nor *bowre* I her can fynd; . . . *Am.* lxxviii. 7
Yet field and *bowre* are full of her aspect: . . . *Am.* lxxviii. 8
Goe visit her in her chast *bowre* of rest . . . *Am.* lxxxiii. 7
Go to the *bowre* of my beloved love, . . . *Epith.* 23
To honors seat and chastities sweet *bowre.* . . . *Epith.* 180
The bridale *bowre* and geniall bed remaine, . . . *Epith.* 399
Their fleshly *bowre,* most fit for their delight, . . . *H.B.* 123
Within the closet of her chastest *bowre,* . . . *H.H.B.* 249
Doth leade unto your lovers blisfull *bower,* . . . *Proth.* 93
Beseeming well the *bower* of anie Queene, . . . *Proth.* 170
Bowers. Forsake your watry *bowres,* . . . *S.C.* Ap. 39
our chast *bowers,* in which all vertue rained, . . . *T.M.* 269
A goodly worke, full fit for kingly *bowres;* . . . *Mui.* 300
who shall dight your *bowres,* sith she is dead . . . *D.* 318
dreame . . . With *bowres,* and beds, and ladies deare delight: . . . I. i. 55. 7
galleries . . . Full of faire windowes and delightful *bowres:* . . . I. iv. 4. 8
powres . . . Have borne him hence to Plutoes balefull *bowres:* . . . I. v. 14. 8
Fell from high Princes courtes, or Ladies *bowres,* . . . I. v. 51. 6
mighty brawned *bowrs* Were wont to rive steele plates, . . . I. viii. 41. 6
a whyle I read you rest, and to your *bowres* recoyle.' . . . I. x. 17. 5
The woods, the nymphes, my *bowres,* my midwives, weare: . . . II. i. 53. 7
How oft do they their silver *bowers* leave, . . . II. viii. 2. 1
When ever they their heavenly *bowres* forlore; . . . II. xii. 52. 7
all those pleasaunt *bowres,* and Pallace brave, . . . II. xii. 83. 1
Unto their *bowres* to guyden every guest. . . . III. i. 58. 4
From her sweete *bowres,* and beds with pleasures fraught? . . . III. vi. 20. 4
In beds, in *bowres,* in banckets, and in feasts: . . . III. vi. 22. 4
all unto their *bowres* were brought. . . . III. ix. 53. 9
Their girlonds rent, their *bowres* despoyled all; . . . IV. i. 24. 7
Delightfull *bowres,* to solace lovers trew; . . . IV. x. 24. 7
breake forth out of his lusty *bowres,* . . . IV. x. 45. 4
In which the fearefull ewftes do build their *bowres,* . . . V. x. 23. 7
Princes *bowres* adorne with painted imagery. . . . VII. vii. 10. 9
a thousand birds had built their *bowres* . . . VII. vii. 28. 4
to decke their lovers *bowres.* . . . *Am.* lxiv. 4
To deck the bridale *bowers.* . . . *Epith.* 47
Now bring the Bryde into the brydall *boures.* . . . *Epith.* 299
Out of thy silver *bowres* and secret blisse, . . . *H.L.* 23
first descent Out of their heavenly *bowres,* . . . *H.B.* 202
gemmes Fit to decke maydens *bowres,* . . . *Proth.* 15
studious Lawyers have their *bowers,* . . . *Proth.* 134
Bowing. gently to them *bowing* in his gate, . . . *Hub.* 1084
bowing downe her aged backe, she kist The wicked witch, . . . I. v. 27. 1
to the Prince, *bowing* with reverence dew . . . II. viii. 55. 3
bowing low before her Majestie, . . . V. ix. 34. 3
Bowl. With patience to forbeare the offred *bowle?* . . . *S.C.* May 139
A mighty Mazer *bowle* of wine was sett, . . . II. xii. 49. 3
overthrew his *bowle* disdainfully, . . . II. xii. 49. 8
in his hand a broad deepe *boawle* he beares, . . . VII. vii. 41. 8
Her brest like to a *bowle* of creame uncrudded, . . . *Epith.* 175
Bownd. *See* **Bound.**
Bows. everie one with meekenesse to her *bowes.* . . . II. iii. 25. 5
a border . . . Of broken *bowes* and arrowes shivered short; . . . III. xi. 46. 7
broke their *bowes,* and did their shooting marre, . . . V. iv. 44. 4

Box. *Box,* yet mindfull of his olde offence; *Gn.* 676
to give largely to the *boxe* refused. *Hub.* 1224
Prince Arthur gave a *boxe* of Diamond sure, I. ix. 19. 1
Boxes. Wont to robbe . . . poore mens *boxes* of their due reliefe, I. iii. 17. 3
Boy. A shepeheards *boye* . . . Led forth his flock, *S.C.* Ja. 1
the pensife *boy;* halfe in despight, Arose, *S.C.* Ja. 76
Colin thou kenst, the Southerne shepheardes *boye;* *S.C.* Ap. 21
Ah, foolish *Boy!* that is with love yblent: *S.C.* Ap. 155
Cuddie, fresh Cuddie, the liefest *boye,* *S.C.* Au. 195
Colin Clout, I wene, be his selfe *boye,* *S.C.* S. 176
wretched *boy,* they slew with guiltie blades; *Gn.* 403
Wake, shepheards *boy,* at length awake for shame! *Ti.* 231
Ah! wretched *boy,* the shape of dreryhead, *As.* 133
Where as the lucklesse *boy* yet bleeding lay; *As.* 142
The shepheards *boy* (best knowen by that name) *Col.* 1
(said then that bony *Boy*) *Col.* 96
told her father by a shepheards *boy,* *Col.* 147
Nought hast thou, foolish *boy,* seene in thy daies.' *Col.* 303
pensive *boy,* pursue that brave conceipt *Col.* 388
that false winged *boy* Her chaste hart had subdewd I. i. 47. 8
which the lovely *boy* Did love as life, I. vi. 17. 6
with timely fruit her belly sweld, And bore a *boy* I. vi. 23. 4
find some other play-fellowes, mine own sweet *boy.'* I. vi. 28. 9
prouder vaunt that proud avenging *boy* Did soone pluck downe, I. ix. 12. 3
The most unruly and the boldest *boy* II. ii. 18. 3
A litle *boy* did on him still attend To reach, II. ix. 58. 4
That *boy* them sought and unto him did lend: II. ix. 58. 7
with what sleights and sweet allurements she Entyst the *Boy,* III. i. 35. 2
that same wretched *boy* Was of him selfe the ydle Paramoure, III. ii. 45. 1
they saw that goodly *boy* with blood Defowled, III. v. 38. 1
'But, foolish *boy,* what bootes thy service bace III. v. 47. 1
'Goe, Dame; goe, seeke your *boy,* III. vi. 24. 2
reape sweet pleasure of the wanton *boy:* III. vi. 46. 3
the winged *boy,* Sporting him selfe in safe felicity: III. vi. 49. 3
On faire Oenone got a lovely *boy,* III. ix. 36. 4
behinde The fearefull *boy* so greedily poursew, III. xi. 4. 6
On which the winged *boy* in colours cleare Depeincted was, III. xi. 7. 7
the Trojane *boy* so fayre He snatcht from Ida hill, III. xi. 34. 4
The winged *boy* did thrust into his throne, III. xi. 35. 6
the sad distresse In which that *boy* thee plonged, III. xi. 36. 3
Fansy, like a lovely *Boy* Of rare aspect, III. xii. 7. 1
with that lovely *boy,* Was hunting IV. vii. 23. 6
Like as it fell to this unhappy *boy,* IV. viii. 2. 1
turning backe unto that gentle *boy,* VI. ii. 24. 1
yet past a *boy,* And being now high time VI. ii. 32. 8
these words burst forth: 'Ah, sory *boy!* VI. iii. 4. 6
The hardy *boy* . . . Upon him set, VI. v. 16. 1
in subtile bands Of the blynd *boy;* VI. ix. 11. 7
Life was like a faire young lusty *boy,* VII. vii. 46. 6
The blynd *boy,* Venus baby, *Epig.* i. 2
the cruell *boy* . . . Would needs the fly pursue; *Epig.* iv. 21
The wanton *boy* was shortly wel recured *Epig.* iv. 51
that imperious *boy* Doth therwith tip his . . . darts, *H.L.* 120
Boyne. The pleasant *Boyne,* the fishy fruitfull Ban, IV. xi. 41. 4
Boy's. like the *boyes* blood therein shed, II. xii. 45. 6
Boys. Theyr *boyes* can looke to those. *S.C.* Jul. 196
'Now leave, ye shepheards *boyes,* your merry glee; *S.C.* D. 139
Mingled emongst loose Ladies and lascivious *boyes.* II. v. 28. 9
with curious ymageree . . . and shapes of naked *boyes,* II. xii. 60. 6
Many faire Ladies and lascivious *boyes,* II. xii. 72. 8
Confusd with womens cries and shouts of *boyes,* IV. iii. 37. 8
shapes seem'd not like to terrestriall *boyes,* IV. x. 42. 4
Yet was admired much of fooles, women, and *boys.* V. ii. 30. 9
'Ah! my sweet *boyes,'* (Sayd she) V. x. 20. 3
ye fresh *boyes,* that tend upon her groome, *Epith.* 112
The whyles the *boyes* run up and downe the street, *Epith.* 137
Boystrous. *See* **Boisterous.**
Brace. bigge Bulles of Basan *brace* hem about, *S.C.* S. 124
Braced. *See* **Iron-braced.**
Bracidas. 'Now, *Bracidas,* let this likewise be showne; V. iv. 18. 2
so the threasure yours is, *Bracidas,* by right.' V. iv. 19. 9
Bracidas and Lucy were right glad, V. iv. 20. 3
Brackish. His *brackish* waves be meynt. *S.C.* Jul. 84
forst to overflow with *brackish* teares, *T.M.* 29
she powred foorth a *brackish* flood Of bitter teares, *T.M.* 415
whose *brackish* bitter well, I wasted have, *D.* 250
ever sprinckle *brackish* teares among, *D.* 530
through the *brackish* waves their passage sheare; III. iv. 42. 7
his hoarie hed Dropped with *brackish* deaw: III. xi. 40. 4
Brag. Seest howe *brag* yond Bullocke beares, *S.C.* F. 71
Braggadochio. Vaine *Braggadocchio,* . . . is made the scorne Of knighthood II. iii. Arg.
Trompart, fitt man for *Braggadochio,* II. iii. 10. 1
Braggadocchio saide; 'Once I did sweare, II. iii. 17. 6
In which vaine *Braggadocchio* was mewd, II. iii. 34. 3
I,' (said *Braggadocchio*) 'thought no lesse, II. iii. 44. 8
afford Which he had brought for *Braggadochio* vaine. II. viii. 19. 4
Shee, that base *Braggadochio* did affray, III. v. 27. 7
Proud *Braggadocchio,* that in vaunting vaine III. viii. 11. 8
Proud man himselfe then *Braggadochio* deem'd, III. viii. 13. 6
(said *Braggadochio*) 'needes thou wilt Thy daies abridge III. viii. 18. 1
Braggadochio, with his bloody launce, III. viii. 18. 7
it was scornefull *Braggadochio,* III. x. 23. 1
from *Braggadocchio* whilome reft The snowy Florimell, IV. ii. 4. 6
Which Ferrau late from *Braggadochio* wonne: IV. iv. 8. 2
Braggadochio said, he never thought . . . His person to emperill IV. iv. 10. 4
Braggadochio rather chose, For glorie vaine, IV. iv. 14. 4
Braggadocchio seeing had no will To hasten IV. iv. 20. 1

Braggadochio—*Continued.*
Stept *Braggadochio* forth, and as his thrall Her claym'd, IV. v. 23. 6
At last to *Braggadochio* selfe alone She came IV. v. 26. 8
By *Braggadochio* lately was redeemed; IV. ix. 20. 7
Braggadochio is uncas'd In all the Ladies sights. V. iii. Arg.
With *Braggadochio,* whom he lately met V. iii. 10. 3
To *Braggadochio* did his shield restore, V. iii. 13. 2
Came *Braggadochio,* and did shew his shield, V. iii. 14. 8
Braggadochio selfe with dreriment So daunted was V. iii. 26. 7
boastfull *Braggadochio* to defame, V. iii. 29. 2
Braggadochio would not let him pas, V. iii. 30. 3
Braggadochio's. Don *Braggadochios* name resounded thrise: V. iii. 15. 4
Bragging. Hard by his side grewe a *bragging* Brere, *S.C.* F. 115
knight was not for all his *bragging* bost; I. iii. 24. 5
Bragly. How *bragly* it beginnes to budde, *S.C.* Mar. 14
Braid. *See* **Breded.**
Braies. *See* **Brays.**
Brain. I deeme thy *braine* emperished bee *S.C.* F. 53
A Biggen he had got about his *brayne,* *S.C.* May 241
therewith bruzd his *brayne;* *S.C.* Jul. 226
when with Wine the *braine* begins to sweate, *S.C.* O. 107
Whose wordes recording in my troubled *braine,* *Ti.* 481
As one . . . whose dryer *braine* Is tost with troubled sights I. i. 42. 7
That troublous dreame gan freshly tosse his *braine* I. i. 55. 6
foule evill, . . . rotts the marrow, and consumes the *braine.* I. iv. 26. 8
th' aboundance of an ydle *braine* Will judged be, II. Pr. 1. 3
cruell passage made Quite through his *brayne.* II. viii. 45. 6
thousand Fancies bett his ydle *brayne* III. iv. 54. 4
thousands like which flowed in his *braine,* III. x. 8. 7
It would have cleft his *braine* downe to his brest. IV. iii. 34. 7
feare His ydle *braine* gan busily molest, IV. v. 43. 7
it empierced to the very *braine,* V. vii. 33. 8
To breake his sleepe, and waste his ydle *braine:* *H.L.* 256
sullein care . . . did afflict my *brayne,* *Proth.* 9
Brained. with his club me threatned to have *brayned,* IV. x. 36. 5
Brain-pan. The tempred steele did not into his *braynepan* byte. VI. vi. 30. 9
Brains. Counted but toyes to busie ydle *braines;* *Col.* 704
it will stonn thy feeble *braines;* III. iii. 9. 5
Brake. *See* **Broke.**
Till Thestylis at last their silence *brake,* *Col.* 651
At last his solemn silence thus he *brake,* I. xii. 29. 5
twixt the perles and rubins softly *brake* A silver sound, II. iii. 24. 8
girded with a belt of twisted *brake:* II. xi. 22. 7
Ne hedge ne ditch his readie passage *brake;* II. xi. 26. 5
Yet when his love was false he with a peaze it *brake.* III. ii. 20. 9
whome hee lately *brake* . . . in victorious fight, III. iii. 52. 7
at the last they *brake* His slomber, IV. i. 43. 8
the staffe asunder *brake,* And left the head behinde: IV. iii. 10. 6
the which his quiet slomber *brake:* IV. v. 44. 7
eftsoones he *brake,* His sodaine silence IV. viii. 16. 1
old despight . . . forth newly *brake* Gainst Blandamour, IV. ix. 26. 3
thus *brake* forth, IV. x. 43. 9
for joy he *brake* His bands, V. iii. 34. 7
They hew'd their helmes, and plates asunder *brake,* VI. i. 37. 4
all his bones in peeces nigh he *brake.* VI. vii. 11. 5
with one fall his necke he almost *brake;* VI. ix. 44. 3
Ne shee the lawes of Nature onely *brake,* VII. vi. 6. 1
At length she . . . The silence *brake,* VII. vii. 57. 9
Brakes. Was nought but *brakes* and brambles *S.C.* D. 102
wilde Bores late rouzd out of the *brakes:* II. xi. 10. 5
With thornes and barren *brakes* environd round, IV. i. 20. 5
through thicke woods and *brakes* and briers him drew, VI. v. 17. 3
Bramble. The bush my bedde, the *bramble* was my bowre, *S.C.* D. 65
Bramble-bush. The *Bramble bush,* where Byrds of every kynde *S.C.* Jun. 7
Bramble-leaves. with sharpe teeth the *bramble leaves* doth lop, *Gn.* 85
Brambles. Was nought but brakes and *brambles* *S.C.* D. 102
Brame. through long languour and hart-burning *brame,* III. ii. 52. 4
Branch. *See* **Laurel-branch, Poplar-branch.**
The blossome which my *braunch* of youth did beare *S.C.* Ja. 39
Als my budding *braunch* thou wouldest cropp; *S.C.* F. 58
To see the *braunche* of his body displaie, *S.C.* May 196
As vertues *braunch* and beauties budde, *S.C.* N. 88
The *braunch* once dead, the budde . . . must quaile; *S.C.* N. 91
The Turtle on the bared *braunch* *S.C.* N. 138
then he pearcheth on some *braunch* thereby, *Mui.* 183
her *braunch* faire blossomes foorth did bring, *D.* 241
She is the *braunch* of true nobilitie, *Col.* 530
the chastest flowre that aye did spring On earthly *braunch,* I. i. 48. 5
'Fayre *braunch* of noblesse, flowre of chevalrie, I. viii. 26. 7
As budding *braunch* rent from the native tree, II. ii. 2. 6
No *braunch* whereon a fine bird did not sitt; II. vi. 13. 2
The noble *braunch* from th' antique stocke was torne II. x. 36. 4
in his hand a *braunch* of laurell bore, III. xii. 3. 7
deckes his *branch* with blossomes over all, IV. x. 22. 4
the Firbloome, but his *braunche* (**braunches*) is (**om.*) rough; *Am.* xxvi. 4
Faire *branch* of Honor, *Proth.* 150
Branched. *Braunched* with gold and perle II. ix. 19. 4
Seem'd like a grove faire *braunched* over-hed: VI. v. 35. 4
Branches. *See* **Bay-branches, Elder-branches, Laurel-branches, Olive-branches.**
heavenly *branches* did I see arise *Pet.* iii. 1
His honor decayed, his *braunches* sere. *S.C.* F. 114
Whose bodie is sere, whose *braunches* broke, *S.C.* F. 170
his cancker-wormes light Upon my *braunches,* *S.C.* F. 180
the high Palme trees, with *braunches* faire, *Gn.* 190
load the *braunches* of the fruitfull vine; *Col.* 601
thinking of those *braunches* greene to frame A girlond I. ii. 30. 6
with greene *braunches* strowing all the ground, I. vi. 13. 8
The mossy *braunches* of an Oke halfe ded. I. x. 48. 4

Branches—*Continued.*
No tree whose *braunches* did not bravely spring; . . . . . . II. vi. 13. 1
Trees, *braunches,* birds, and songs, were framed fitt . . . . II. vi. 13. 5
braunches broad dispredd and body great, ... II. vii. 53. 7
his broad *braunches,* laden with rich fee, ... II. vii. 56. 3
being goodly dight With bowes and *braunches,* . . . . II. xii. 53. 8
Whose big embodied *braunches* shall not lin . . . . III. iii. 22. 3
Well worthie stock, from which the *branches* sprong . . . . III. iv. 3. 6
knitting their rancke *braunches,* . . . . III. vi. 44. 4
far abroad his mightie *braunches* threw . . . . III. ix. 47. 8
Like three faire *branches* budding farre and wide, ... IV. ii. 43. 5
with their *braunches* spred all Britany, ... IV. xi. 26. 6
cropt the *branches* of the sient base, ... V. i. 1. 8
two more of his armes did fall away, Like fruitlesse *braunches,* V. xi. 11. 8
in their lower *braunches* sung aloud; . . . . VI. x. 6. 7
*sweet is the firbloome, but his *braunches* rough. . . . . . *Am.* xxvi. 4
Brancheth. *brancheth* forth in brave nobilitie, ... VI. Pr. 4. 4
Branching. mucky filth his *braunching* armes annoyes, . . . II. vii. 15. 8
Brand. *See* **Firebrand, Levin-brand, Lightning-brand.**
he perced . . . With thrilling point of deadly yron *brand,* . . I. iii. 42. 7
in his hand a burning *brond* he hath, ... I. iv. 33. 3
grace . . . doth quench the *brond* of hellish smart, ... I. ix. 53. 7
Her hellish *brond* hath kindled with despight, ... II. ii. 29. 3
He hath a sword that flames like burning *brond.* . . . . . . II. iii. 18. 5
quench the *brond* of his conceived yre: . . . . II. vi. 27. 6
Kindled through his infernall *brond* of spight, ... II. vi. 50. 5
I can carve with this inchaunted *brond* . . . . II. viii. 22. 4
the third brunt of this my fatall *brond:* . . . . II. viii. 37. 8
To yield wide way to his hart-thrilling *brond;* . . . . II. viii. 41. 8
did his yron *brond* so fast applie, ... IV. iii. 25. 7
stroke the Pagan with his steely *brand* . . . . IV. viii. 43. 3
When so he list in wrath lift up his steely *brand,* . . . . . . V. i. 8. 9
Which steely *brand,* to make him dreaded more, ... V. i. 9. 1
fenst himselfe about with many a flaming *brand.* . . . . . . V. viii. 35. 9
Whose long rest rusted the bright steely *brand;* . . . . . . V. ix. 30. 7
with his raging *brond* divide Their thickest troups, ... VI. xi. 48. 8
Brandiron. with his *brondiron* round about him layd; . . . . IV. iv. 32. 3
with his club bet backe his *brondyron* bright . . . . VI. viii. 10. 4
Brandirons. Shame burning *brond-yrons* in her hand did hold: III. xii. 24. 8
Brandished. With *brandisht* tongue the emptie aire did gride, *Gn.* 254
The other *brandished* a bloody knife; . . . . II. vii. 21. 8
most gent, That ever *brandished* bright steele on hye! . . . . II. xi. 17. 6
brave retourning, with his *brandisht* blade . . . . II. xi. 37. 1
Brandisheth. a burning brond . . . The which he *brandisheth*
about his hed: . . . . I. iv. 33. 4
Brandishing. High *brandishing* his bright deaw-burning blade, I. xi. 35. 6
Brands. beast; . . . threatned all his heades like flaming
brandes. . . . . I. viii. 12. 6
Another did the dying *bronds* repayre . . . . II. vii. 36. 3
bounded On everie side, with pyles of flaming *brands,* . . . . *H.H.B.* 39
Bransles. *Bransles,* Ballads, virelayes, and verses vaine; . . . III. x. 8. 5
Brasen. *See* **Brazen.**
Brass. shields of *brasse* that shone like burnisht golde, . . . *Van.* vi. 3
stoute as steede of *brasse.* . . . . *S.C.* Jul. 156
Not Bilbo steele, nor *brasse* from Corinth fet, ... *Mui.* 77
An yron brest, and back of scaly *bras,* . . . . I. vii. 17. 8
shield . . . Not made of steele, nor of enduring *bras,* . . . . I. vii. 33. 3
captives to redeeme with price of *bras* . . . . I. x. 40. 3
all armd in shyning *bras.* . . . . II. ii. 17. 9
not of wood, nor of enduring *bras,* . . . . II. ix. 23. 4
upon the glassy See A bridge of *bras,* . . . . II. x. 73. 9
everlasting moniments of *brasse,* . . . . III. ix. 50. 8
Whose raging rigour neither steele nor *bras* Could stay, . . . IV. vi. 15. 5
perfect gold surmounts the meanest *brasse.* . . . . IV. ix. 2. 9
neither pretious stone, nor durefull *brasse,* . . . . IV. x. 39. 4
hundred mouthes, and voice of *brasse* I had, ... IV. xi. 9. 7
to thinke gold that is *bras;* . . . . VI. Pr. 5. 7
More firme and durable then steele or *brasse,* . . . . *H.H.B.* 153
Brass-paved. when she does ride . . . through heavens *bras-paved* way, ... I. iv. 17. 7
Brass-plated. In his *bras-plated* body to embosse, ... I. xi. 20. 3
Brass-scaly. Does overspred his long *bras-scaly* back, ... I. xi. 11. 2
Brast. *See* **Burst, Outbrast.**
dreadfull Furies, which their chaines have *brast,* . . . . . . I. v. 31. 8
with that percing noise flew open quite, or *brast.* . . . . . . I. viii. 4. 9
Als flew his steed as he his bandes had *brast,* . . . . I. ix. 21. 7
glauncing on the tempred metall, *brast* In thousand shivers, . III. vii. 40. 8
Therewith asunder in the midst it *brast,* . . . . IV. iii. 12. 1
with the straint his wesand nigh he *brast.* . . . . V. ii. 14. 5
all his bowels in his body *brast:* . . . . V. viii. 8. 6
Did quake to heare, and nigh asunder *brast:* . . . . V. xi. 28. 5
all they cleft or *brast.* . . . . V. xii. 17. 9
As if his lungs and lites were nigh asunder *brast.* . . . . . . VI. iii. 26. 9
Stryving in vaine that nigh his bowels *brast,* . . . . VI. iv. 22. 2
all her hart-strings *brast,* . . . . VI. xi. 22. 8
Shouting as they the heavens would have *brast;* . . . . VII. vi. 52. 7
Braught. *See* **Brought.**
Brave. this *brave* monument with flash did rend. . . . . . . *Bel.*[2] iii. 14
Which that *brave* races greatnes did attest, ... *Bel.*[2] v. 7
her *brave* writings, which her famous merite . . . . *Ro.* v. 12
As that *brave* sonne of Aeson, ... *Ro.* x. 1
So this *brave* Towne, that in her youthlie daies . . . . *Ro.* x. 5
Did *brave* about the corpes of Hector colde; . . . . *Ro.* xiv. 10
these *brave* Pallaces, which maystred bee Of time, ... *Ro.* xviii. 3
that same *brave* Citie, Which . . . Sustein'd the shocke of common enmitie . . . . *Ro.* xxi. 2
her course begun with *brave* intent. . . . . *Ro.* xxi. 8
that *brave* honour of the Latine name, ... *Ro.* xxii. 1
the *brave* warlicke brood of Alemaine, ... *Ro.* xxxi. 7
France . . . though fruitfull of *brave* wits, ... *Ro.* Env. 2

Brave—*Continued.*
semblants outward *brave!* . . . . *Gn.* 93
The great Argoan ships *brave* ornament, ... *Gn.* 210
brave Knights, and their renowned Squires; . . . . *Hub.* 29
so *brave* beasts she loveth best to see . . . . *Hub.* 629
the *brave* Courtier, in whose beauteous thought . . . . *Hub.* 717
Desire of honor or *brave* thought of armes . . . . *Hub.* 825
thought of honor, nor *brave* gest, ... *Hub.* 978
who would ever care to doo *brave* deed, ... *T.M.* 451
Large streetes, *brave* houses, sacred sepulchers, ... *Ti.* 94
lifting up her *brave* heroick thought . . . . *Ti.* 109
Brave Impe of Bedford! grow apace in bountie, ... *Ti.* 272
with *brave* plumes doth beate the azure skie, ... *Ti.* 423
So *brave* a Trompe, thy noble acts to sound! . . . . *Ti.* 434
Ne of so *brave* a building ought remained, ... *Ti.* 559
purchas Through *brave* atcheivements from his enemies; . . . *Ti.* 655
Full of *brave* courage and bold hardyhed, ... *Mui.* 27
with *brave* deeds to her sole service vowed, ... *As.* 69
pursue that *brave* conceipt In thy sweete Eglantine . . . . . *Col.* 388
In whose *brave* mynd, as in a golden cofer, ... *Col.* 488
She is the well of bountie and *brave* mynd, ... *Col.* 496
Ne any there doth *brave* or valiant seeme, ... *Col.* 779
But where thy selfe hast thy *brave* mansione: . . . . *Ded. Son.* v. 8
And ye, *brave* Lord, whose goodly personage . . . . *Ded. Son.* vi. 1
Yet *brave* ensample of long passed daies, ... *Ded. Son.* x. 9
That their *brave* deeds she might immortalize . . . . *Ded. Son.* xiv. 3
through immortall merit Of his *brave* vertues, ... *Ded. Son.* xv. 4
Then that *brave* court doth to mine eie present, ... *Ded.Son.*xvii.11
To prove his puissance in battell *brave* . . . . I. i. 3. 7
The Champion . . . dismounted from his courser *brave,* . . . . I. i. 11. 8
Whose bridle rung with golden bels and bosses *brave.* . . . . I. ii. 13. 9
most *brave* embellished With royall robes . . . . I. iv. 8. 3
Athwart his brest a bauldrick *brave* he ware, ... I. vii. 29. 8
an almond tree . . . With blossoms *brave* bedecked daintily; . I. vii. 32. 7
brave poursuitt of chevalrous emprize, ... I. ix. 1. 4
writt with golden letters rich and *brave:* . . . . I. ix. 19. 8
both sweet and *brave* They might appeare, ... I. x. 42. 4
she saw where he upstarted *brave* . . . . I. xi. 34. 1
The *brave* adventures of this faery knight, ... II. Pr. 5. 7
two *brave* knightes in bloody fight . . . . II. ii. 21. 3
Brave be her warres, and honorable deeds, ... II. ii. 31. 5
that *brave* steed there finding ready dight, ... II. iii. 4. 8
Her yvorie forhead, full of bountie *brave,* . . . . II. iii. 24. 1
my corage *brave* Dismay with feare, ... II. iii. 45. 3
In *brave* poursuitt of honorable deed, ... II. iv. 1. 1
how *brave* she decks her bounteous boure, ... II. vi. 16. 5
I in armes, and in atchievements *brave,* . . . . II. vii. 33. 6
of his victories *Brave* moniments remaine, ... II. x. 21. 9
brave ensample, both of martiall And civil rule, ... II. x. 74. 8
brave retourning, with his brandisht blade . . . . II. xi. 37. 1
this *brave* knight, that for this vertue fightes, ... II. xii. 1. 6
his *brave* shield, full of old moniments, ... II. xii. 80. 3
all those pleasaunt bowres, and Pallace *brave,* . . . . II. xii. 83. 1
the *brave* Mayd would not disarmed bee, ... III. i. 42. 7
Of their *brave* gestes and prowesse martiall: . . . . III. ii. 1. 6
Brave Captaines, and most mighty warriours, ... III. iii. 23. 3
comming forth shall spred his banner *brave* . . . . III. iii. 30. 3
Shall of him selfe a *brave* ensample shew, ... III. iii. 45. 2
with *brave* bauldrick garnished. . . . . III. iii. 59. 9
Where be the *brave* atchievements doen by some? . . . . . . III. iv. 1. 3
in *brave* sprite it kindles goodly fire, ... III. v. 1. 8
the *brave* youthly Champions to assay . . . . III. vii. 41. 6
ye *brave* knights, that boast this Ladies love, ... III. viii. 27. 6
All the *brave* knightes that doen in armes excell . . . . . . III. viii. 46. 7
The heavie losse of their *brave* Paramours, ... III. ix. 35. 4
forth the Boaster marching *brave* . . . . III. x. 33. 5
To giust with that *brave* straunger knight a cast, ... III. x. 35. 4
Then they march forward *brave.* . . . . III. x. 42. 9
the *brave* Mayd would not for courtesy . . . him abrade, . . . III. xi. 8. 3
the *brave* Maid, which al this while was plast . . . . III. xii. 27. 4
brave exploits which great Heroes wonne, ... IV. Pr. 3. 4
In *brave* aray and goodly amenance, ... IV. iii. 5. 5
'*Brave* Knights and Ladies, certes, ye doe wrong . . . . . . IV. iv. 12. 2
Manie a *brave* knight and manie a daintie dame, ... IV. iv. 13. 8
with that *brave* Britonesse Had left . . . . IV. vii. 3. 1
this same *brave* emprize for me did rest, ... IV. x. 4. 7
Brave thoughts and noble deedes did evermore aspire. . . . . IV. x. 26. 9
Ne better doth beseeme *brave* chevalry, ... V. ii. 1. 2
Ne any Knight was absent that *brave* courage bore. . . . . . V. iii. 2. 9
goodly gan to greet his *brave* emprise, ... V. iii. 15. 7
From all *brave* knights be banisht with defame; . . . . V. iii. 38. 8
All the *brave* Knights that hold of Maidenhead, ... V. iv. 29. 6
he round about him saw Many *brave* Knights, ... V. v. 22. 2
A sordid office for a mind so *brave:* . . . . V. v. 23. 4
his owne *brave* mind Subjected hath to my unequall might. . . V. v. 32. 2
her good Knights, of which so *brave* a band Serves her . . . . V. viii. 18. 6
the *brave* Prince for honour and for right, . . . did fight: . . V. viii. 30. 6
The noble Briton Prince with his *brave* Peare; . . . . V. x. 15. 2
sent redresse thereof by this *brave* Briton Knight. . . . . . . V. xi. 1. 9
brancheth forth in *brave* nobilitie, ... VI. Pr. 4. 4
this proud gyant should with *brave* emprize Quite overthrow; VI. iv. 33. 4
More *brave* and noble knights have raysed beene . . . . VI. iv. 36. 3
thought that those *brave* imps were sowen Here by the Gods, . VI. iv. 36. 7
With those *brave* armours lying on the ground, ... VI. v. 25. 4
Was greatly growne in love of that *brave* pere,) . . . . VI. vi. 41. 8
through prowesse and their *brave* emprize . . . . VI. vi. 35. 7
to adorne With so *brave* badges . . . . VI. vi. 36. 5
What *brave* exploit, what perill hardly wrought . . . . *H.L.* 220
most beautifull and *brave* Their fleshly bowre, ... *H.B.* 122
some *brave* muse may sing . . . . *Proth.* 159

Bravely. head, full *bravely* with a morion hidd (armed[1]), *Bel.* xv. 5
A goodly ship with banners *bravely* dight, *Van.* ix. 2
A goodly building *bravely* garnished; I. iv. 2. 6
her streight legs most *bravely* were embayld II. iii. 27. 2
No tree whose braunches did not *bravely* spring; II. vi. 13. 1
bravely furnished as ship might bee, II. xii. 19. 3
did those two them selves so *bravely* beare, IV. ix. 30. 6
bravely mounted to his most mishap: IV. x. 9. 7
Braver. No *braver* Poeme can be under Sun. *Col.* 411
Ne *braver* proofe in any of thy powre III. iii. 3. 2
no *braver* president this day Remaines on earth, V. iv. 2. 6
Bravery. all the *braverie* that eye may see, *Hub.* 608
oft maintain'd his masters *braverie.* *Hub.* 858
to him avaunting in great *bravery,* II. iii. 6. 3
with how great vaunt of *braverie* He them abused V. iii. 39. 7
Bravest. miserie doth *bravest* mindes abate, *Hub.* 256
shortly must repent that now so vainely *bravest.'* V. vii. 32. 9
Brawned. mighty *brawned* bowrs Were wont to rive steele plates, I. viii. 41. 6
Brawny. strongly forth did stretch His *brawnie* armes, II. xii. 21. 2
brawney armes had lost their knowen might, IV. xii. 20. 4
Bray. Therewith enrag'd she loudly gan to *bray,* I. i. 17. 5
they gan loudly *bray,* With hollow houling, I. iii. 23. 1
Her shrill outcryes and shrieks so loud did *bray,* I. vi. 7. 5
shrill trompets lowd did *bray,* III. xii. 6. 6
shrilling trompets loudly gan to *bray,* IV. iv. 48. 5
The Tyrant selfe came forth with yelling *bray,* IV. viii. 62. 2
The Lyons rore; the Tygres loudly *bray;* IV. x. 46. 3
which she doth *bray* Out of her poysnous entrails V. xi. 20. 9
With that aloude she gan to *bray* and yell, V. xi. 28. 1
So dreadfully his hundred tongues did *bray:* V. xii. 41. 7
Brayed. He loudly *brayd* with beastly yelling sownd, I. viii. 11. 3
He lowdly *brayd,* that like was never heard; I. xi. 26. 2
He *brayd* aloud for very fell despight; V. xi. 8. 2
Thereat he *brayed* loud, and yelled dreadfully. V. xii. 20. 9
Brays. *Braies* out her latest breath, and up her eies doth seele. II. i. 38. 9
Brazen. A *brasen* voice that may with shrilling cryes *T.M.* 117
brasen Pillours never to be fired, *Ti.* 410
Upon a *brazen* pillour standing hie, *Ti.* 660
fast embard in mighty *brasen* wall, I. vii. 44. 8
'Lo! yonder is' . . . 'The *brasen* towre, I. xi. 3. 2
over all with *brasen* scales was armd, I. xi. 9. 1
He badd to open wyde his *brasen* gate, I. xii. 3. 6
Behind his backe he bore a *brasen* shield, II. iv. 38. 1
brasen Caudrons thou shalt rombling heare, III. iii. 9. 3
A *brasen* wall in compas to compyle III. iii. 10. 3
Untill that *brasen* wall they up doe reare; III. iii. 11. 7
Nor *brasen* walls, nor many wakefull spyes, III. ix. 7. 5
through the roofe of her strong *brasen* towre III. xi. 31. 3
Gainst whom he alwayes bent a *brasen* shield, III. xii. 12. 8
That *brasen* dore flew open, III. xii. 29. 7
Upon a *brasen* pillour, by the which she stands. III. xii. 30. 9
that great *brasen* pillour broke in peeces small. III. xii. 37. 9
seem'd his shrikes would rend the *brasen* skie: IV. viii. 38. 5
eke an hundred *brasen* caudrons bright, IV. x. 38. 6
neither yron barres, nor *brasen* locke, IV. xi. 3. 3
That Romaine Monarch built a *brasen* wall, IV. xi. 36. 2
As if they would have rent the *brasen* skies. VI. viii. 40. 4
Fayth doth fearlesse dwell in *brasen* towre, *Am.* lxv. 13
th' Earth, . . . engirt with *brasen* bands; *H.H.B.* 37
And in the same, as in a *brasen* booke, *H.H.B.* 130
Of Gods high praise, that filles the *brasen* sky; *H.H.B.* 263
Breach. some old sorowe that made a newe *breache:* *S.C.* May 210
No reach, no *breach,* that might him profit bring, *Hub.* 1141
breach of lawes to privie ferme did let: *Hub.* 1160
the *breach* Which love and fortune in her heart had wrought; I. vii. 42. 3
Each dore he opened without any *breach,* I. viii. 34. 8
forst, at last he made through silence suddein *breach.* I. ix. 25. 9
in his conscience made a secrete *breach,* I. ix. 48. 3
breach of love and loialty betrayd. I. xii. 31. 5
with faire semblaunt sought to hyde the *breach,* II. ix. 39. 3
Ne was there outward *breach,* nor grudge in hart, II. x. 14. 7
so untimely *breach* . . . halfe seemed to offend; II. x. 68. 6
th' utmost sandy *breach* they shortly fetch, II. xii. 21. 3
with daintie *breach* Of her fine fingers, II. xii. 56. 4
vile ungentlenesse, or hospitages *breach.* III. x. 6. 9
let not my rudenes be no *breach* Unto your patience, III. x. 25. 3
Threatning into his life to make a *breach,* III. xi. 12. 7
Did find it fit withouten *breach* or let. IV. v. 19. 5
With *breach* of faith and loyaltie unsound, IV. vi. 28. 4
so sore a *breach* That sudden newes had made IV. vi. 38. 3
For *breach* of faith to her, V. vi. 12. 9
Seeking by every way to make some *breach;* V. viii. 37. 2
lastly Justice charged her with *breach* of lawes. V. ix. 44. 9
With so foule blame as *breach* of faith once plight, V. xi. 62. 4
the stroke That . . . had made so strong a *breach* VI. ii. 13. 3
with so unknightly *breach* Of armes, VI. ii. 42. 4
to thy blisse I made this luckelesse *breach,* VI. x. 29. 3
well agree withouten *breach* or jar. *Epith.* 132
Breaches. The *breaches* of her singults did supply. *T.M.* 232
the ragged *breaches* hong Embost with massy gold II. vii. 28. 3
Provoked them the *breaches* to assay, II. xi. 14. 7
Supplide her sobbing *breaches* with sad complement. III. iv. 35. 9
of like former *breaches* Made in their friendship, IV. ii. 12. 4
In my sweet peace such *breaches* to have bred! *Am.* lxxxv. 12
Bread. *See* **Bred.**
Theyr sheepe han crustes, and they the *bread;* *S.C.* Jul. 187
The *bread* of life powr'd downe from heavenly place. *Hub.* 438
My *bread* shall be the anguish of my mind, *D.* 375
who with gratious *bread* the hungry feeds, I. iv. 32. 3
Bread—*Continued.*
make them cheese and *bredd;* III. x. 36. 8
doe also serve To her for *bread,* IV. i. 26. 2
bread and water or like feeble thing, V. iv. 31. 8
ere he tasted *bread* He would her succour, VI. i. 31. 4
Breaded. *See* **Breded.**
Breadth. To be the measure of her *bredth* and length: *Ro.* viii. 4
to measure Her length, her *breadth,* her deepnes, *Ro.* xxvi. 4
other Isle, that greater *bredth* now beares. V. iv. 7. 9
Break. Against a Rocke to *breake* with dreadfull poyse: *Ro.* xvi. 4
anie fortunes wreakes Could *breake* her course *Ro.* xxi. 8
Let *breake* your sounder sleepe, *S.C.* Au. 191
the shepheard would *breake* his sleepe, *S.C.* S. 193
Breake we our pypes, that shrild *S.C.* N. 71
all their learned instruments did *breake:* *T.M.* 599
'The sevenfold yron gates . . . To *breake,* *Ti.* 375
in their wrath *breake* off the vitall bands, *D.* 18
could great Cynthiaes sore displeasure *breake,* *Col.* 174
When as death these vitall bands shall *breake,* *Col.* 630
He . . . would not all his silence *breake.* I. i. 42. 9
who can . . . *breake* the chayne of strong necessitee, I. v. 25. 5
gan to *breake* the bands of their captivitee. II. v. 18. 9
least Force or Fraud should unaware *Breake* in, II. vii. 25. 4
Ne ever will it *breake,* ne ever bend: II. viii. 21. 5
within his flesh Did *breake* the launce, II. viii. 36. 7
It might *breake* out and set the whole on fyre, II. ix. 30. 2
his purposes to *breake,* III. iii. 36. 4
Their beames shall ofte *breake* forth, III. iii. 44. 9
breake forth into bright burning flame, III. iii. 48. 6
none might thorough *breake,* nor overstride. III. vi. 31. 4
breake the vow that to faire Columbell I plighted have, III. vii. 51. 6
doe *breake* by force Into an heard, IV. iv. 35. 6
oft with bitternesse It forth would *breake,* IV. viii. 24. 5
In case his burning lust should *breake* into excesse. IV. ix. 18. 9
see The spring *breake* forth out of his lusty bowres, IV. x. 45. 4
rather chose his challenge off to *breake,* V. i. 24. 3
it would lose or *breake,* V. iii. 28. 9
his contempt, that did her judg'ment *breake.* V. iv. 40. 5
To *breake* all bonds of law and rules of right: V. viii. 20. 5
Whom he did all to peeces *breake,* V. xi. 33. 8
streight commaundement . . . Which none durst *breake,* V. xii. 10. 5
they that *breake* bands of civilitie, VI. i. 26. 6
'loth were I . . . yet *breake* it should againe, VI. ii. 7. 7
Gan *breake* to him the fortunes of his love, VI. iii. 15. 2
His heart . . . forth at last did *breake* in speaches sharpe VI. iii. 34. 9
at the last *breake* forth in his owne proper kynd. VI. v. 1. 9
the strong course of their displeasure *breake,* VI. v. 30. 7
his lives threed to *breake.* VI. xi. 34. 9
Breake forth at length out of the inner part, *Am.* ii. 5
if I silent be, my hart will *breake,* *Am.* xliii. 3
Out of my prison I will *breake* anew; *Am.* lxxx. 6
Let not one sparke of filthy lustfull fyre *Breake* out, *Am.* lxxxiii. 2
Breake gentle sleepe with misconceived dout. *Epith.* 337
To *breake* his sleepe, and waste his ydle braine: *H.L.* 256
Breaking. *See* **Heart-breaking.**
breaking foorth at last, thus dearnelie plained: *D.* 196
By *breaking* of the band betwixt us twaine; I. xii. 34. 4
breaking off the end for want of breath, II. i. 56. 2
with her brest *breaking* the fomy wave, II. ii. 24. 8
on the rocke the waves *breaking* aloft II. xii. 33. 3
forth *breaking* into bitter plaintes III. xi. 9. 1
breaking quite his garlond ever greene, III. xi. 37. 8
Her angrie teame *breaking* their bonds of peace IV. iii. 41. 3
They *breaking* forth with rude unruliment IV. ix. 23. 5
breaking forth dare tempt the deepest flood IV. x. 46. 5
Which *breaking* open with indignant ire, V. vii. 37. 4
breaking forth out at a posterne dore, V. viii. 48. 8
Which *breaking* off he toward them did pace VI. v. 36. 4
For *breaking* of their daunce, VI. x. 11. 3
breaking forth in laughter, VII. vi. 46. 5
Thence *breaking* forth, did . . . throng. *Am.* xii. 8
Breaking his prison, forth to you doth fly. *Am.* lxxiii. 4
Breaks. open *breakes* the dore in furious wize, I. iii. 19. 5
At last *breakes* forth with furious unrest, II. xi. 32. 5
Breakes forth her silver beames, III. i. 43. 4
Whence foorth it *breakes* in sighes and anguish ryfe, III. ii. 32. 8
Then forth it *breakes,* III. ix. 15. 8
At length *breakes* downe in raine, IV. ix. 33. 6
Breakes forth, and makes his way more violent; VI. i. 21. 5
Like as a flowre, . . . At length *breakes* forth, VI. ii. 35. 9
breakes into her Dayr' house, VII. vi. 48. 4
Breane. The morish Cole, and the soft sliding *Breane,* IV. xi. 29. 6
Breares. *See* **Briers.**
Breast. castles under her *brest* did coure, *Bel.*[2] viii. 6
Ladie, in whose bounteous *brest* All heavenly grace *Pet.*[2] vii. 9
I gan in my engrieved *brest* To scorne *Van.* xii. 5
in this blessed brooke Doe bathe your *brest,* *S.C.* Ap. 38
Ne *brest* of baser birth doth thee embrace, *S.C.* O. 82
with pure *brest* from carefull sorrow free, *Gn.* 107
His glittering *breast* he lifteth up on hie, *Gn.* 258
The canker worme of everie gentle *brest;* *Hub.* 736
into whose *brest* Never crept thought of honor, *Hub.* 977
She armes the *brest* with constant patience *T.M.* 133
felt my heart nigh riven in my *brest* *Ti.* 30
did enrich that noble *breast* of his *Ti.* 285
inlie greeving in my groning *brest,* *Ti.* 484
With fruitfull hope his aged *breast* he fed *Mui.* 25
whose empierced *brest* Sharpe sorrowe did . . . rive. *D.* 6
The stormie passion of his troubled *brest,* *D.* 192
let compassion creepe Into his *brest,* *D.* 249

Breast—*Continued.*
yet are deepe engraven in my *brest,* . . . *D.* 296
her faire *brest,* the threasury of joy, . . . *As.* 161
sole possession in so chaste a *brest!* . . . *Col.* 555
celestiall rage Of Love . . . is breath'd into thy *brest,* . . . *Col.* 824
To you, right noble Lord, whose carefull *brest* . . . *Ded. Son.* ix. 1
on his *breast* a bloodie Crosse he bore, . . . I. i. 2. 1
knockt his *brest,* as one that did repent. . . . I. i. 29. 9
sore grieved in her gentle *brest,* . . . I. ii. 8. 8
upon his coward *brest* A bloody crosse, . . . I. ii. 11. 4
when corage hott The fire of love, . . . kindled in my *brest,* . . . I. ii. 35. 3
she . . . does steepe Her tender *brest* in bitter teares all night; I. iii. 15. 8
seizing cruell clawes on trembling *brest,* . . . I. iii. 19. 8
they gan to . . . beat their *brests,* and naked flesh to teare: . . I. iii. 22. 5
life forsooke his stubborne *brest.* . . . I. iii. 42. 9
since my *brest* was launcht with lovely dart . . . I. iv. 46. 5
An yron *brest,* and back of scaly bras, . . . I. vii. 17. 8
lively breath her sad *brest* did forsake; . . . I. vii. 20. 8
wound That launched hath my *brest* with bleeding smart. . . I. vii. 25. 7
Athwart his *brest* a bauldrick brave he ware, . . . I. vii. 29. 8
head . . . Had riven many a *brest* with pikehead square: . . . I. vii. 37. 4
life nigh crusht out of his panting *brest:* . . . I. viii. 15. 3
soone as breath out of his *brest* did pas, . . . I. viii. 24. 6
wound . . . doth rancle in my riven *brest,* . . . I. ix. 7. 4
To kindle love in every living *brest:* . . . I. ix. 9. 4
Ne fleshly *brest* can armed be so sownd, . . . I. ix. 11. 2
consuming thought To put away out of his carefull *brest.* . . . I. x. 29. 6
O! gently come into my feeble *brest;* . . . I. xi. 6. 1
Forelifting up a-loft his speckled *brest,* . . . I. xi. 15. 2
never felt his imperceable *brest* So wondrous force . . . I. xi. 17. 7
advaunce his broad discoloured *brest* Above his wonted pitch, . I. xi. 31. 7
remaynd Some lingring life within his hollow *brest,* . . . I. xii. 10. 4
his sharpe sword Against her snowy *brest* . . . II. i. 11. 7
Thy litle hands embrewd in bleeding *brest* . . . II. i. 37. 8
In whose white alabaster *brest* did stick . . . II. i. 39. 5
Shee sight from bottome of her wounded *brest;* . . . II. i. 47. 2
with her *brest* breaking the fomy wave, . . . II. ii. 24. 8
with her tresses torne And naked *brest,* . . . II. ii. 27. 3
His puissant armes about his noble *brest,* . . . II. iii. 1. 8
Ne thought of honour ever did assay His baser *brest,* . . . II. iii. 4. 4
forelay Athwart her snowy *brest,* . . . II. iii. 29. 6
Which his sad speach infixed in my *brest,* . . . II. iv. 23. 2
to his *brest* it selfe intended right: . . . II. iv. 46. 4
to his *brest* his bever bent. . . . II. v. 6. 9
on his *brest* his victor foote he thrust: . . . II. v. 12. 6
Gan sucke this vitall ayre into his *brest,* . . . II. vii. 66. 6
speare he fiercely bent Against the Pagans *brest,* . . . II. viii. 32. 2
downe to his manly *brest* Have cleft his head . . . II. viii. 33. 8
An open passage through his riven *brest,* . . . II. xi. 37. 4
crusht his carcas so against his *brest,* . . . II. xi. 42. 2
His stubborne *brest* gan secret pleasaunce to embrace. . . . II. xii. 65. 9
Her snowy *brest* was bare . . . II. xii. 78. 1
it is shrined in my Soveraines *brest,* . . . III. Pr. 1. 5
fairest knight alive, when armed was her *brest.* . . . III. ii. 4. 9
rive with thousand throbs thy thrilled *brest:* . . . III. ii. 32. 5
love hath gryde My feeble *brest* of late, . . . III. ii. 37. 9
Her alablaster *brest* she soft did kis, . . . III. ii. 42. 7
love, that is in gentle *brest* begonne, . . . III. ii. 51. 7
housed is within her hollow *brest,* . . . III. iii. 18. 7
Strooke her full on the *brest,* . . . III. iv. 15. 8
did vexe his noble *brest,* . . . III. iv. 54. 3
Ever to creepe into his noble *brest;* . . . III. v. 2. 4
Long while he strove in his corageous *brest* . . . III. v. 44. 1
In gentle Ladies *brest* and bounteous race Of woman kind . . III. v. 52. 7
She bath'd her *brest* the boyling heat t' allay; . . . III. vi. 6. 7
He knockt his *brest* with desperate intent, . . . III. vii. 20. 3
bowd his battred visour to his *brest:* . . . III. vii. 42. 5
would have algates riv'd The hart out of his *brest:* . . . III. viii. 3. 6
thrise his *brest* he stroke, . . . III. viii. 22. 3
Dropped adowne upon her yvory *brest:* . . . III. viii. 35. 4
So firmely she had sealed up her *brest.* . . . III. viii. 39. 5
the burning hart which on his *brest* He bare, . . . III. viii. 45. 4
Whilest deadly torments doe her chast *brest* rend, . . . III. xi. 11. 3
powre of hand, nor skill of learned *brest,* . . . III. xi. 16. 3
Love to conceive in her disdainfull *brest;* . . . III. xi. 17. 6
magnanimity Dwells in thy bounteous *brest!* . . . III. xi. 19. 3
Did beat and bounse his head and *brest* ful sore: . . . III. xi. 27. 6
brushing his faire *brest,* . . . III. xi. 32. 7
privy love his *brest* empierced had, . . . III. xi. 41. 8
Her *brest* all naked, as nett yvory . . . III. xii. 20. 1
litle drops empurpled her faire *brest.* . . . III. xii. 33. 5
lately did dispart Her bleeding *brest,* . . . III. xii. 38. 4
deadly points at eithers *breast* to bend, . . . IV. ii. 14. 8
It would have cleft his braine downe to his *brest.* . . . IV. iii. 34. 7
In whose chast *brest* all bountie naturall . . . IV. Pr. 4. 3
Ne suffred sleepe to settle in his *brest.* . . . IV. v. 41. 5
This feeble *brest* endured hath, . . . IV. vii. 14. 4
all his hairy *brest* with gory bloud was fild. . . . IV. vii. 31. 9
beat his *breast* unworthy of such blame, . . . IV. viii. 4. 7
about her purple *brest* That precious juell, . . . IV. viii. 10. 2
Of his old love conceav'd in secret *brest,* . . . IV. ix. 17. 4
inward grudge fild his heroicke *brest:* . . . IV. ix. 32. 4
To beare that Ladies head before his *breast,* . . . V. i. 29. 4
whereas they *brest* to *brest* Should meete, . . . V. ii. 12. 5
Out of his *breast* the very heart have rended: . . . V. v. 6. 5
Which long concealing in her covert *brest,* . . . V. v. 27. 1
Within the closet of her covert *brest,* . . . V. v. 44. 6
her private fire, which boyld Her inward *brest,* . . . V. v. 53. 8
Uppon her speare she bore before her *breast,* . . . V. vi. 39. 5
in unquiet *brest* Did closely harbour such a jealous guest) . V. vii. 27. 4

Breast—*Continued.*
she, whose Princely *brest* was touched nere With piteous ruth . V. ix. 50. 1
does beat her *brest* and forhead knockes. . . . V. xii. 38. 9
all her garments from her snowy *brest,* . . . VI. i. 17. 7
And flame forth honour in thy noble *brest;* . . . VI. ii. 37. 4
Full on the *breast* him strooke, . . . VI. iv. 5. 7
beat her *breast,* and piteously her selfe torment. . . . VI. v. 4. 9
her *breast,* new launcht with murdrous knife, . . . VI. v. 5. 4
well disburdened her engrieved *brest,* . . . VI. viii. 34. 2
Her yvorie neck; her alablaster *brest;* . . . VI. viii. 42. 1
with a naked knife Readie to launch her *brest,* . . . VI. viii. 48. 9
each hath his fortune in his *brest.* . . . VI. ix. 29. 9
Ne him could find to fancie in her *brest:* . . . VI. ix. 40. 7
with lovely dart Dinting his *brest* . . . VI. x. 31. 8
he no word could speake, but smit his *brest,* . . . VI. xi. 28. 5
he his face, his head, his *brest* did beat, . . . VI. xi. 33. 4
Upon the litle *brest,* like christall bright, . . . VI. xii. 7. 7
having her snowy *brest* As yet not laced, . . . VI. xii. 15. 2
on her *brest* I . . . did view The litle purple rose . . . VI. xii. 18. 4
Rent up her *brest,* and bosome open layd, . . . VI. xii. 19. 4
that which she hath fylde In her owne *breast,* . . . VI. xii. 21. 4
made his hart to tickle in his *brest,* . . . VII. vi. 46. 2
in my feeble *brest* Kindle fresh sparks . . . VII. vii. 2. 3
to kindle new desire In gentle *brest,* . . . *Am.* vi. 10
May kindle living fire within my *brest.* . . . *Am.* vii. 12
if in your hardned *brest* ye hide . . . *Am.* xxv. 9
your gentle *brest* inspire With sweet infusion, . . . *Am.* xxviii. 6
in your *brest* his leafe and love embrace. . . . *Am.* xxviii. 14
lend you me another living *brest.* . . . *Am.* xxxiii. 14
Her *brest,* lyke Lillyes, . . . *Am.* lxiv. 11
Her *brest* that table was, so richly spredd; . . . *Am.* lxxvii. 13
her *brest,* lyke a rich laden barke, . . . *Am.* lxxxi. 5
pure affections bred in spotlesse *brest,* . . . *Am.* lxxxiii. 5
Her *brest* like to a bowle of creame uncrudded, . . . *Epith.* 175
my feeble *breast* inspire With gentle furie, . . . *H.L.* 27
Thou hast enfrosen her disdainefull *brest,* . . . *H.L.* 146
His faith, his fortune, in his *breast* he beares, . . . *H.L.* 224
in her inmost *brest* He may embosomd bee . . . *H.L.* 248
my feeble *breast,* too full of thee? . . . *H.B.* 3
in thy *brest* his blessed image beare. . . . *H.H.L.* 259
that shall thy feeble *brest* Inflame with love, . . . *H.H.L.* 269
Vouchsafe . . . To shed into my *breast* some sparkling light . *H.H.B.* 10

Breast-plate. His *breastplate* first, that was of substance pure, *Mui.* 57

Breasts. pierce immortall *breasts* with mortall smarts? . . . *T.M.* 48
From thence infused into mortall *brests.* . . . *T.M.* 390
Her necke and *brests* were ever open bare, . . . I. x. 30. 7
suncke so deepe into their boyling *brests,* . . . II. ii. 32. 2
'If ever love of Lady did empierce Your yron *brestes,* . . . II. vi. 33. 2
burnest mightily In living *brests,* . . . III. iii. 1. 2
which he did earst revive In their sterne *brests,* . . . III. v. 16. 5
her lanck loynes ungirt, and *brests* unbraste, . . . III. vi. 18. 4
their soules they would attonce have rent Out of their *brests,* . IV. ii. 18. 3
Psamathe for her brode snowy *brests;* . . . IV. xi. 51. 5
their soules they wold have ryven quight Out of their *breasts* . V. x. 32. 5
rends her golden locks, and snowy *brests* embrew. . . . VI. viii. 40. 9

Breath. *See* **Breathe.**
with enflamed *breath* . . . hot rage instil'd. . . . *Ro.* xi. 7
youngth is a bubble blown up with *breath,* . . . *S.C.* F. 87
She stoppeth the *breath* of her youngling. . . . *S.C.* May 100
With dogges of noysome *breath,* . . . *S.C.* Jul. 22
Winter is come, that blowes the balefull *breath,* . . . *S.C.* D. 149
Corrupted had th' ayre with his noysome *breath,* . . . *Hub.* 7
a race, T' enlarge his *breath,* . . . *Hub.* 745
(large *breath* in armes most needfull) . . . *Hub.* 745
flesh, a bubble-glas of *breath,* . . . *Ti.* 50
whilest the fates afoord me vitall *breath,* . . . *Ti.* 309
into me that sacred *breath* inspire, . . . *Ti.* 314
Like beast whose *breath* but in his nostrels is, . . . *Ti.* 356
doo in darknesse not abridge my *breath,* . . . *D.* 445
suckt the wasting *breath* Out of his lips . . . *As.* 165
'His blessed body, spoild of lively *breath,* . . . I. ii. 24. 1
blustring *breath* of Heaven, that none can bide, . . . I. iii. 31. 5
every *breath* of heaven shaked itt: . . . I. iv. 5. 7
stayd, To gather *breath* in many miseryes. . . . I. vi. 19. 4
with his *breath* . . . Her hollow womb did secretly inspyre, . . I. vii. 9. 3
th' only *breath* him daunts, who hath escapt the stroke. . . I. vii. 13. 9
lively *breath* her sad brest did forsake; . . . I. vii. 20. 8
everie little *breath* that under heaven is blowne. . . . I. vii. 32. 9
soone as *breath* out of his brest did pas, . . . I. viii. 24. 6
Her sowre *breath* abhominably smeld. . . . I. viii. 47. 5
A wyde way made to let forth living *breath:* . . . I. ix. 30. 3
let him dye, that loatheth living *breath,* . . . I. ix. 38. 8
Braies out her latest *breath,* and up her eies doth seele. . . II. i. 38. 9
In these sad wordes she spent her utmost *breath:* . . . II. i. 49. 4
breaking off the end for want of *breath,* . . . II. i. 56. 2
when fayling *breath* began to faint, . . . II. ii. 8. 1
*Sometimes she laught, that nigh her *breth* was gone, . . . II. vi. 3. 4
when *breath* the body first doth leave; . . . II. viii. 29. 2
payre of bellowes . . . cooling *breath* inspyre, . . . II. ix. 30. 5
through poyson stopped was his *breath;* . . . II. x. 67. 8
from thy hand Did commun *breath* and nouriture receave. . II. x. 69. 6
th' ydle *breath* all utterly exprest. . . . II. xi. 42. 4
If any puffe of *breath* or signe of sence shee fond. . . . III. i. 60. 9
Panting for *breath,* and almost out of hart, . . . III. v. 4. 1
So long as *breath* and hable puissaunce . . . III. vii. 3. 1
whilest his *breath* did strength to him supply, . . . III. vii. 24. 7
His money, which he lov'd as living *breath;* . . . III. x. 2. 8
finding that the *breath* gan him to fayle, . . . IV. i. 43. 5
for want of *breath* gan to abate, . . . IV. iii. 26. 6
panting *breath* begin to fayle, . . . IV. vi. 16. 2

Breath—*Continued.*
But noysome *breath*, and poysnous spirit sent . . . . IV. viii. 26. 3
for lacke Of *breath*, ... IV. ix. 25. 8
So long as in his steedes the flaming *breath* did last. . . . V. viii. 33. 9
that made his grone And gaspe for *breath*, ... VI. iv. 21. 6
wanting *breath* him downe to ground he cast; . . . . VI. iv. 22. 5
onely *breath*, sith that I did forgive.' . . . . VI. vi. 36. 6
the cold steele . . . did devowre His vitall *breath*, ... VI. vii. 8. 8
on his hoary beard his *breath* did freese, ... VII. vii. 31. 3
Yet is he nought but parting of the *breath*; . . . . VII. vii. 46. 3
gather to myselfe new *breath* awhile. . . . . *Am.* lxxx. 4
with His onely *breath* them blew away . . . . *H.H.L.* 87
Breathe. now did *breathe* corrupted smel. . . . . *Bel.*[1] viii. 14
Where *breathe* on them the whistling wind mote best; . . . *Gn.* 236
I walkt abroade to *breath* the freshing ayre . . . . *D.* 26
fainting, each themselves to *breathen* lett, ... I. vi. 44. 2
none can *breath*, nor see, nor heare at will, ... I. vii. 13. 7
downe he fell, and forth his life did *breath*, ... I. xi. 54. 1
prickt with courage kene, did cruell battell *breath*. . . . II. i. 27. 9
shee gan to *breath* out living aire. . . . . II. i. 43. 9
Did *breath* out bounteous smels, ... II. v. 29. 9
It lettes not scarse this Prince to *breath* at all, ... III. v. 2. 8
to stay to rest, or *breath* at large, ... III. vii. 23. 3
Yet scarcely once to *breath* would they relent, ... IV. ii. 18. 7
Shall *breath* it selfe awhile after so long a went. . . . . IV. v. 46. 9
To see his foe *breath* out his spright in vaine: . . . . IV. viii. 46. 2
Of all this day on ground that *breathen* living spright! . . . VI. i. 4. 9
Ne once to *breath* awhile their angers tempest ceast. . . . . VI. i. 36. 9
he nould let him *breath*, nor gather spright, ... VI. iii. 26. 7
Ere long enforst to *breath* his utmost blast, ... VI. iv. 22. 7
Till she her selfe for stronger flight can *breath*. . . . . *H.H.B.* 28
Breathed. *See* **Outbreathed.**
With *breathed* sighes is blowne away and blasted; . . . . *S.C.* Ja. 40
'Most gentle spirite, *breathed* from above . . . . *Ti.* 281
celestiall rage Of Love . . . is *breath'd* into thy brest, . . . *Col.* 824
Then backe to fight againe, new *breathed* and entire. . . . . I. vi. 44. 9
when these knights had *breathed* once, ... I. vi. 45. 1
breathed ever forth a filthie banefull smell. . . . . I. viii. 39. 9
These words she *breathed* forth from riven chest: . . . . II. i. 47. 5
Unworthie of the commune *breathed* ayre, ... II. iii. 7. 5
That *breathed* strife and troublous enmitie. . . . . II. viii. 10. 5
tombling downe on ground, *Breathed* out his ghost, ... II. viii. 45. 7
still it *breathed* forth sweet spirit and holesom smell: . . . II. xii. 51. 9
wide nosethrils burnd With *breathed* flames, ... III. ix. 22. 4
breathed forth with blast of bitter wind; . . . . IV. viii. 26. 5
Artegall was better *breath'd* beside, ... V. ii. 17. 5
when the Shepheard *breathed* had awhyle, ... VI. xi. 30. 1
He *breath'd* his sword, and rested him till day; . . . . VI. xi. 47. 2
modest thoughts *breathd* from weltempred sprites, ... *Am.* lxxxiii. 6
He man did make, and *breathd* a living spright . . . . *H.H.L.* 110
Breathes. *breathes* out wrath and hainous crueltee: . . . . II. iv. 43. 8
man that *breathes* a more immortall mynd, ... *H.L.* 103
Breathest. Which thou there *breathest* perfect and entire. . . *Ti.* 315
Breatheth. 'What man henceforth that *breatheth* vitall ayre . . *D.* 197
none that *breatheth* living aire does know . . . . II. Pr. 1. 6
Breathful. Fresh Costmarie, and *breathfull* Camomill, ... *Mui.* 195
eke the *breathfull* bellowes blew amaine, ... IV. v. 38. 7
Breathing. *See* **Bitter-breathing, Sweet-breathing.**
breathing furie from his inward gall . . . . *Bel.*[2] xiv. 11
with gentle murmure of the *breathing* ayre, ... *Gn.* 186
Ye gentle Spirits, *breathing* from above, ... *T.M.* 361
raisd . . . a dull blast, that *breathing* on her face . . . . I. ii. 38. 6
With pleasaunce of the *breathing* fields yfed, ... I. iv. 38. 2
Both *breathing* vengeaunce, both of wrathfull hew. . . . . I. vi. 38. 5
bayes His sweatie forehead in the *breathing* wynd, ... I. vii. 3. 2
I, *breathing* yre, Sore chauffed at my stay . . . . II. iv. 32. 6
Breathing out wrath, and bellowing disdaine, ... II. viii. 42. 6
The dales for shade, the hilles for *breathing* space, ... II. xii. 58. 6
Breathing out beastly lust her to defyle: . . . . III. i. 17. 3
After her heat the *breathing* cold to taste: . . . . III. vi. 18. 5
The other *breathing* now another spright, ... IV. iii. 35. 8
Breathing out clouds of sulphure fowle and blacke, ... V. xi. 32. 2
images . . . Whose wondrous beauty, *breathing* sweet delights . *H.H.B.* 4
Breathless. he fled All *breathles*, ... *Hub.* 1374
in the ende he *breathlesse* did remaine, ... *Mui.* 430
Til *breathlesse* both themselves aside retire, ... I. vi. 44. 6
wondred at his *breathlesse* hasty mood: . . . . I. xii. 25. 3
He soone approched, panting, *breathlesse*, ... II. iv. 37. 6
all *breathlesse*, weary, faint, Him spying, ... II. v. 11. 2
He seemed *breathlesse*, hartlesse, faint, and wan; . . . . II. vi. 41. 5
he that *breathlesse* seems shal corage bold respire. . . . . II. viii. 7. 9
when this *breathlesse* woxe, that batteil gan renew. . . . . II. viii. 47. 9
nigh he *breathlesse* grew, ... III. i. 21. 3
Like as a *Deare*, . . . now nigh *breathlesse*. III.xii.44.*or.*9
Whiles with long fight on foot he *breathlesse* was, ... IV. vi. 15. 2
Bred. *See* **Home-bred, Hell-bred.**
The seedes, of which all things at first were *bred*, ... *Ro.* xxii. 13
there *bred* A litle wicked worme, ... *Van.* vii. 6
such sight hath *bred* my bane. . . . . *S.C.* Ja. 53
So nowe fayre Rosalind hath *bredde* hys smart, ... *S.C.* Ap. 27
which love within his heart had *bredd*, ... *S.C.* Jun. 86
The memory of hys misdeede that *bred* her woe. . . . . *S.C.* Au. 186
frogs, *bred* in the slimie scowring . . . . *Gn.* 229
ever as they *bred*, They slue them, ... *Hub.* 317
forreine beasts, not in the forest *bred*, ... *Hub.* 1119
monstrous beasts . . . *Bred* of two kindes, ... *Hub.* 1123
caytives, which had *bred* him blame. . . . . *Hub.* 1318
Where being *bredd*, he light and heaven does hate; . . . . *T.M.* 190
in Venus silver bowre were *bred*, ... *T.M.* 362
to have been nobly *bredd*? . . . . *T.M.* 446

Bred—*Continued.*
bred was of Medusaes blood, ... *Ti.* 647
all those flowres, . . . that *bred* her spight, ... *Mui.* 141
his mother, which him bore and *bred*, ... *Mui.* 259
'No age hath *bred* . . . more vertue in a wight; . . . . *D.* 218
bred above in Venus bosome deare: . . . . *Col.* 840
Of the wilde fruit which salvage soyl hath *bred*; . . . . *Ded. Son.* v. 2
Of her there *bred* A thousand yong ones, ... I. i. 15. 4
all three *bred* Of one bad sire, ... I. ii. 25. 7
A monstrous beast *ybredd* in filthy fen He chose, ... I. vii. 16. 8
Helmet . . . Both glorious brightnesse and great terrour *bredd*: I. vii. 31. 2
Dragon, . . . *Bred* in the loathly lakes of Tartary, ... I. vii. 44. 3
That to have heard great horror would have *bred*; . . . . I. viii. 17. 2
both borne and *bred* In hevenly throne, ... I. x. 51. 5
That sight thereof *bredd* cold congealed feare; . . . . I. xi. 13. 5
in dead parents balefull ashes *bred*, ... II. ii. 2. 2
so her smart was much more grievous *bredd*, ... III. iv. 6. 3
of immortall seed To beene *ybredd* . . . . III. iv. 38. 2
So was this virgin borne, so was she *bred*; . . . . III. vi. 3. 6
wondrously they were begot and *bred* . . . . III. vi. 6. 1
Infinite shapes of creatures there are *bred*, ... III. vi. 35. 1
false rumors . . . *Bred* in assemblies of the vulgar sort, . . . IV. i. 28. 4
Your high displesure, through misdeeming *bred*: . . . . IV. viii. 17. 3
Of an huge Geauntesse whylome was *bred*, ... IV. viii. 47. 2
Venus of the fomy sea was *bred*, ... IV. xii. 2. 2
being *bred* Of mortall sire, ... IV. xii. 4. 1
Such as behind their backs (so backward *bred*) . . . . V. Pr. 2. 6
that *bread* Great ruth through her misfortunes tragicke stowre; V. ix. 45. 7
Sith in th' Almighties everlasting seat She first was *bred*, . . V. x. 1. 8
they say that he was borne and *bred* Of Gyants race, ... V. x. 9. 1
'It is a Monster *bred* of hellishe race,' . . . . VI. i. 7. 7
Out of the countrie wherein I was *bred*, ... VI. ii. 30. 3
Mongst salvage beasts both rudely borne and *bred*, ... VI. v. 2. 3
Amongst wilde beastes in desert forrests *bred*, ... VI. v. 29. 7
that same beast was *bred* of hellish strene, ... VI. vi. 9. 7
being *bred* under base shepheards wings, ... VI. ix. 35. 4
had *bred* his restlesse paine; . . . . VI. x. 31. 8
Of that bad seed is this bold woman *bred*, ... VII. vi. 21. 1
the faire Shure, in which are thousand Salmons *bred*. . . . VII. vi. 54. 9
This great Grandmother of all creatures *bred*, ... VII. vii. 13. 1
all that from her springs, and is *ybredde*, ... VII. vii. 18. 1
all that are of others *bredd* doth slay; . . . . VII. vii. 24. 7
she was *bred* and nurst On Cynthus hill, ... VII. vii. 50. 3
Unquiet thought! whom at the first I *bred* . . . . *Am.* ii. 1
pure affections *bred* in spotlesse brest, ... *Am.* lxxxiii. 5
In my sweet peace such breaches to have *bred*! . . . . *Am.* lxxxv. 12
Through the sharpe sorrowes which thou hast me *bred*, . . . *H.L.* 16
were they *bred* of Somers-heat, ... *Proth.* 67
Breded. she roundly did uptye In *breaded* tramels, ... II. ii. 15. 8
trebly *breaded* in a threefold lace, ... III. ii. 50. 2
Breech. graffed to the ground is my *breche*: . . . . *S.C.* F. 242
underneath, his *breech* was all to-torne and jagged. . . . . V. ix. 10. 9
Breeches. His *breeches* were made after the new cut, ... *Hub.* 211
Breed. Such stormy stoures doo *breede* my balefull smart, . . . *S.C.* Ja. 27
Ah, God! that love should *breede* both joy and payne! . . . *S.C.* Ja. 54
Such follie great sorow to Niobe did *breede*: . . . . *S.C.* Ap. 87
Ere the breme Winter *breede* you greater griefe. . . . . *S.C.* D. 148
ne of Greeke, that *breede* Doubts mongst Divines, ... *Hub.* 386
the thing that doth thy sorrow *breed*: . . . . *Hub.* 596
the forrest, where wilde beasts doo *breed*, ... *Hub.* 1248
be aveng'd on those that *breed* thy blame.' . . . . *Hub.* 1332
want the blis that wisedom would them *breed*, ... *T.M.* 530
even their heavie song would *breede* delight; . . . . *D.* 13
Because they *breed* sad balefulnesse in mee; . . . . *D.* 410
with your piteous layes have learnd to *breed* Compassion . . . *As.* Pr. 3
like her that did him *breed*, ... *As.* 16
ragged ruines *breed* great ruth and pittie . . . . *Col.* 114
in the bosome of the billowes *breed*. . . . . *Col.* 243
wherin there *breed* Ten thousand kindes of creatures, ... I. i. 21. 6
More old then Jove, whom thou at first didst *breede*, ... I. v. 22. 3
many heades . . . Did *breed* him endlesse labor to subdew. . . I. vii. 17. 5
earthly sight can nought but sorrow *breed*, ... I. vii. 23. 6
Ne car'd to hoord for those whom he did *breede*: . . . . I. x. 38. 5
(all flesh doth frayltie *breed*) . . . . II. i. 52. 6
Her faultie Handmayd, which that bale did *breede*, ... II. iv. 29. 8
the Monster filth did *breede*: . . . . II. iv. 35. 5
Doe *breede* repentaunce late, and lasting infamy.' . . . . II. v. 13. 9
cause of death betweene two doughtie knights do *breed*! . . . II. vi. 33. 9
Such as Laomedon of Phoebus race did *breed*. . . . . II. xi. 19. 9
all that els does horror *breed*, ... II. xii. 37. 1
Mote *breede* him scath unwares; . . . . III. i. 37. 8
but more annoiaunce *breed*: . . . . III. ii. 37. 2
in her doth such torment *breed*.' . . . . III. iii. 18. 9
he her first did *breed* . . . . III. iv. 59. 7
in his cold complexion doe *breed* A filthy blood, ... III. x. 59. 3
Your vertue selfe her owne reward shall *breed*, ... III. xii. 39. 5
Cambell . . . Perceiv'd would *breede* great mischiefe, . . . IV. ii. 37. 7
th' onely remnant of that royall *breed*, ... IV. viii. 33. 8
poysnous bale did *breede* To all that on him lookt . . . . IV. viii. 39. 4
my last bale to *breed*.' . . . . V. v. 29. 9
Is wont to cut off all that doubt may *breed*, ... VI. ii. 29. 6
gentle bloud will gentle manners *breed*; . . . . VI. iii. 2. 2
now her wounds corruption gan to *breed*: . . . . VI. v. 31. 5
With flaming sword in hand his terror more to *breed*. . . . VI. vii. 11. 9
on him which did this mischiefe *breed*, ... VI. vii. 13. 7
cattell for to *breed*, ... VI. viii. 35. 6
The fields my food, my flocke my rayment *breed*; . . . . VI. ix. 20. 8
to us all exceeding feare did *breed*, ... VII. vi. 20. 4
that same would spill The Wood-gods *breed*, ... VII. vi. 50. 4
Ne any living creatures doth he *breed*, ... VII. vii. 24. 6

Briers. Scattred with bushy thornes and ragged *breares,* . . . I. x. 35. 3
sharp thornes and *breres* the way forstall, . . . III. i. 46. 7
With *briers* and bushes all to-rent and scratcht; . . . IV. vii. 8. 3
through thicke wood and brakes and *briers* him drew, . . . VI. v. 17. 3
Through hils and dales, through bushes and through *breres,* . VI. viii. 32. 1
Brigadore. called *Brigadore,* (so was he hight,) . . . V. iii. 34. 3
Brigandine, -s. *See* **Brigantine, -s.**
Brigands. A lawlesse people, *Brigants* hight of yore, . . . VI. x. 39. 3
Now made the spoile of theeves and *Brigants* bad, . . . VI. x. 40. 7
Hither those *Brigants* brought their present pray, . . . VI. x. 43. 1
Such was the conflict of those cruell *Brigants* there. . . . VI. xi. 17. 9
Albe with all their might those *Brigants* her did keepe. . . . VI. xi. 23. 9
how those *Brigants* vyle . . . Spoyld all our cots, . . . VI. xi. 30. 3
all the *Brigants* flocking in great store . . . VI. xi. 46. 3
Brigands'. raught Faire Pastorella from those *Brigants* powre, VI. xii. 3. 2
Brigantine. Like as a warlike *Brigandine,* . . . *Mui.* 84
Brigantines. As when two warlike *Brigandines* at sea, . . . IV. ii. 16. 1
Briget's. *See* **Bridget's.**
Bright. *See* **Fiery-bright, Sun-bright, Sunny-bright.**
beholde the *bright* abode Of God and men. . . . *Rev.* iv. 5
the seeling *bright* Did shine . . . *Bel.*[2] ii. 9
a sharped spyre of Diamond *bright,* . . . *Bel.*[2] iii. 1
Upon an hill a *bright* flame . . . *Bel.*[2] xi. 1
golden grayle That *bright* Pactolus washeth . . . *Bel.*[2] xii. 4
The skie . . . did show full *bright* and faire: . . . *Pet.* ii. 5
Such as the Berecynthian Goddesse *bright,* . . . *Ro.* vi. 1
whither rennes this bevie of Ladies *bright,* . . . *S.C.* Ap. 118
the *bright* Sunne gynneth to dismount; . . . *S.C.* May 315
when Phoebe shineth *bright:* . . . *S.C.* Jun. 31
All as the Sunnye beame so *bright,* . . . *S.C.* Au. 81
the *bright* starre Seemeth ay greater . . . *S.C.* S. 76
wondren at *bright* Argus blazing eye; . . . *S.C.* O. 32
his *bright* eyes, glauncing full dreadfullie, . . . *Gn.* 262
With their *bright* firebronds me to terrifie. . . . *Gn.* 424
That her *bright* glorie else hath much defamed. . . . *Col.* 910
O Goddesse heavenly *bright!* . . . I. Pr. 4. 1
Her angels face . . . shyned *bright,* . . . I. iii. 4. 7
Of her, that was the Lady of that Pallace *bright.* . . . I. iv. 6. 9
a rich throne, as *bright* as sunny day; . . . I. iv. 8. 2
Now his *bright* armes assaying, . . . *Hub.* 741
thine owne sister, peerles Ladie *bright,* . . . *Ti.* 317
Lastly his shinie wings as silver *bright,* . . . *Mui.* 89
ne heaven doth shine so *bright,* . . . *Mui.* 93
Then gan the Goddesse *bright* Her selfe . . . to dight. . . . *Mui.* 303
my fair Starre (that shinde on me so *bright*) . . . *D.* 480
Her yellow locks that shone so *bright* and long, . . . *As.* 157
Her worlds *bright* sun, her heavens fairest light, . . . *Col.* 41
in remembrance of that glorious *bright,* . . . *Col.* 46
Yet through that darksome vale do glister *bright;* . . . *Col.* 495
in her hand she held a mirrhour *bright,* . . . I. iv. 10. 6
the armes, that earst so *bright* did show, . . . I. v. 9. 5
all the ayre it fills, and flyes to heaven *bright.* . . . I. v. 16. 9
All stand astonied at her beautie *bright,* . . . I. vi. 9. 8
From flaming mouth *bright* sparckles fiery redd, . . . I. vii. 31. 7
Gloriane, great Queene of glory *bright,* . . . I. vii. 46. 6
with blade all burning *bright* . . . I. viii. 10. 5
he has redd his end In that *bright* shield, . . . I. viii. 21. 5
that fire-mouthed Dragon, horrible and *bright?* . . . I. ix. 52. 9
that glistreth *bright* With burning starres . . . I. x. 50. 5
that *bright* towre, all built of christall clene, . . . I. x. 58. 5
this *bright* Angels towre quite dims that towre of glas.' . . . I. x. 58. 9
as the clashing of an Armor *bright,* . . . I. xi. 9. 8
High brandishing his *bright* deaw-burning blade, . . . I. xi. 35. 6
high her burning torch set up in heaven *bright.* . . . I. xi. 49. 9
The weapon *bright* . . . Ran through his mouth . . . I. xi. 53. 5
As *bright* as doth the morning starre appeare . . . I. xii. 21. 5
should not be quenched . . ., but burnen ever *bright.* . . . I. xii. 37. 9
could not endure those beames *bright,* . . . II. Pr. 5. 4
marre the blossom of your beauty *bright:* . . . II. i. 14. 4
doen upreare Their bevers *bright* . . . II. i. 29. 2
all in *bright* armour clad, . . . II. i. 45. 4
Had slayne Sir Mordant and his Lady *bright:* . . . II. iii. 13. 8
hevenly pourtraict of *bright* Angels hew, . . . II. iii. 22. 2
So passing persant, and so wondrous *bright,* . . . II. iii. 23. 4
golden aygulets, that glistred *bright* Like twinckling starres; II. iii. 26. 7
her Javelin *bright* Against him bent, . . . II. iii. 42. 7
Thus lowly to abase thy beautie *bright,* . . . II. iv. 25. 8
One in *bright* armes embatteiled full strong, . . . II. v. 2. 3
as the Sunny beames . . . so shined *bright,* . . . II. v. 2. 5
With his *bright* blade did smite at him . . . II. v. 4. 2
in Stygian lake, ay burning *bright,* Had kindled: . . . II. v. 22. 7
With wrathfull fire his corage kindled *bright,* . . . II. vi. 30. 7
his whott fyre burnes in mine entralles *bright,* . . . II. vi. 50. 4
Faire shields, gay steedes, *bright* armes be my delight; . . . II. vii. 10. 8
hundred fournaces all burning *bright:* . . . II. vii. 35. 5
Their fruit were golden apples glistring *bright,* . . . II. vii. 54. 1
their *bright* Squadrons round about us plant; . . . II. viii. 2. 7
Two Paynim knights al armd as *bright* as skie, . . . II. viii. 10. 2
why should a dead dog be deckt in armour *bright?'* . . . II. viii. 15. 9
made thee soldier of that Princesse *bright,* . . . II. ix. 5. 3
Alma she called was; a virgin *bright,* . . . II. ix. 18. 1
all armed *bright* In glistring steele, . . . II. ix. 26. 2
set in silver sockets *bright,* . . . II. ix. 46. 6
to him gave for wife his daughter *bright,* . . . II. x. 59. 4
Alma, like a virgin Queene most *bright,* . . . II. xi. 2. 6
The windowes of *bright* heaven opened had, . . . II. xi. 3. 2
Sir Guyon, in *bright* armour clad, . . . II. xi. 3. 5
most gent, That ever brandished *bright* steele on hye! . . . II. xi. 17. 6
his *bright* shield that nought him now avayld; . . . II. xi. 41. 8

Bright—*Continued.*
when appeared the third Morrow *bright* . . . II. xii. 2. 4
Bright Scolopendraes arm'd with silver scales; . . . II. xii. 23. 8
All pav'd beneath with Jaspar shining *bright,* . . . II. xii. 62. 8
starry light . . . does seeme more *bright.* . . . II. xii. 78. 9
the wonder of her beames *bright,* . . . III. Pr. 4. 8
snatching his *bright* sword began to close With her . . . III. i. 9. 3
the *bright* glister of their beames cleare . . . III. i. 32. 8
From his Beauperes, and from *bright* heavens vew, . . . III. i. 35. 7
her *bright* hed Discovers to the world discomfited: . . . III. i. 43. 4
her *bright* armes about her body dight. . . . III. i. 67. 3
a flake Of lightning through *bright* heven fulmined: . . . III. ii. 5. 8
Through whose *bright* ventayle, . . . III. ii. 24. 3
a sore evill, which this virgin *bright* Tormenteth . . . III. iii. 16. 4
now all Britany doth burne in armes *bright.* . . . III. iii. 52. 9
one, all in armour *bright,* . . . III. iv. 12. 2
griesly shadowes covered heaven *bright,* . . . III. iv. 52. 2
Speed thee to spred abroad thy beames *bright,* . . . III. iv. 60. 4
Dwarfe, aread what is that Lady *bright* . . . III. v. 7. 7
The goodly ornaments of beautie *bright;* . . . III. v. 8. 6
that Lady *bright,* Besides all hope, . . . III. v. 30. 3
When the *bright* sunne his beams theron doth beat: . . . III. v. 49. 6
shall embellish more your beautie *bright,* . . . III. v. 53. 7
The sunbeames *bright* upon her body playd, . . . III. vi. 7. 5
Her golden lockes, that late in tresses *bright* Embreaded were . III. vi. 18. 6
The one of yron, the other of *bright* gold, . . . III. vi. 31. 3
one, which hath gaz'd On the *bright* Sunne unwares, . . . III. vii. 13. 7
Then drew he his *bright* sword, . . . III. ix. 16. 9
He did resemble to his lady *bright;* . . . III. x. 21. 8
in thy colours *bright* Wast there enwoven, . . . III. xi. 36. 1
to win Deucalions daughter *bright,* . . . III. xi. 42. 5
the proud Pavone . . . or Iris *bright,* . . . III. xi. 47. 8
*discolourd bow she spreds through heaven *bright.* . . . III. xi. 47. 9
her *bright* browes were deckt with borrowed haire; . . . III. xii. 14. 7
Without adorne of gold or silver *bright,* . . . III. xii. 20. 2
streightly did embrace her body *bright,* . . . III. xii. 45. *or.* 2
The snowy Florimell, whose beautie *bright* . . . IV. ii. 4. 7
Where is my part then of this Ladie *bright,* . . . IV. ii. 13. 6
a Ladie, passing faire And *bright,* . . . IV. iii. 39. 7
One in *bright* armes, with ready speare in rest, . . . IV. iv. 6. 6
were like faire and *bright,* . . . IV. iv. 10. 8
Hewing and slashing shields and helmets *bright,* . . . IV. iv. 41. 6
Whose beauties beame eftsoones did shine so *bright,* . . . IV. v. 10. 8
The heavenly pourtraict of *bright* Angels hew. . . . IV. v. 13. 4
all afore that seemed fayre and *bright,* . . . IV. v. 14. 1
Where hardly eye mote see *bright* heavens face . . . IV. vii. 38. 7
The great Creatours owne resemblance *bright,* . . . IV. viii. 32. 2
when he saw the Prince in armour *bright,* . . . IV. viii. 40. 6
were her vertue like her beautie *bright,* . . . IV. viii. 49. 6
Ne helmets *bright* ne hawberks strong did spare, . . . IV. ix. 27. 3
eke an hundred brasen caudrons *bright,* . . . IV. x. 38. 6
With *bright* Chrysaor in his cruell hand, . . . V. ii. 18. 2
that same other Damzell, Lucy *bright,* . . . V. iv. 9. 2
flakes of fire, *bright* as the sunny ray, . . . V. v. 8. 3
Like coles that through a silver Censer sparkle *bright.* . . . V. vi. 38. 9
Whereof there was great store, and armors *bright,* . . . V. vii. 41. 4
shone as *bright* as doth the heaven sheene: . . . V. viii. 29. 5
the firie-mouthed steedes, which drew The Sunnes *bright* wayne V. viii. 40. 2
seeing all in armour *bright* as day, . . . V. ix. 24. 2
Upon a throne of gold full *bright* and sheene, . . . V. ix. 27. 5
Whose skirts were bordred with *bright* sunny beames, . . . V. ix. 28. 6
Whose long rest rusted the *bright* steely brand; . . . V. ix. 30. 7
As the *bright* sunne, . . . Gins to abate the brightnesse . . . V. ix. 35. 1
sunne to shine more *bright* then it was wont, . . . V. x. 20. 8
gan hew So hideously uppon his armour *bright,* . . . V. xi. 5. 4
his *bright* shield display. . . . V. xi. 21. 5
The armed Prince with shield so blazing *bright* . . . V. xi. 26. 2
is ought so *bright* And beautifull as glories beames appeare, . V. xi. 62. 7
that *bright* sword, the sword of Justice lent, . . . V. xii. 40. 5
with the faire sight Of the *bright* mettall . . . VI. ii. 39. 4
beautie is more glorious *bright* and clere, . . . VI. vii. 29. 7
eies, Like two great Beacons, glared *bright* and wyde, . . . VI. vii. 42. 2
with his club bet backe his brondyron *bright* . . . VI. viii. 10. 4
Then he was tride unto his Lady *bright;* . . . VI. viii. 33. 7
doffing his *bright* armes . . . VI. ix. 36. 3
Through the *bright* heaven doth her beams display, . . . VI. x. 13. 7
With starrie beames about her shining *bright,* . . . VI. xi. 13. 5
twixt the twinckling of her eye-lids *bright* . . . VI. xi. 21. 8
Upon the litle brest, like christall *bright,* . . . VI. xii. 7. 7
The goodly building of her Palace *bright,* . . . VII. vi. 10. 2
the Moones *bright* wagon still did stand, . . . VII. vi. 13. 7
Have wonne the Empire of the Heavens *bright;* . . . VII. vi. 33. 7
sister unto Mulla faire and *bright,* . . . VII. vi. 40. 3
Her garment was so *bright* and wondrous sheene, . . . VII. vii. 7. 3
The goodly Sun encompast all with beames *bright.* . . . VII. vii. 44. 9
Now hornd, now round, now *bright,* . . . VII. vii. 50. 8
your *bright* beams . . . May kindle living fire . . . *Am.* vii. 11
Thrugh your *bright* beams doth not the blinded guest . . . *Am.* viii. 5
star, that wont with her *bright* ray Me to direct, . . . *Am.* xxxiv. 5
him take, and in your bosome *bright* Gently encage, . . . *Am.* lxxiii. 9
With his *bright* Tead that flames with many a flake, . . . *Epith.* 27
Behold your faces as the christall *bright,* . . . *Epith.* 64
More *bright* then Hesperus his head doth rere. . . . *Epith.* 95
Her goodly eyes lyke Saphyres shining *bright,* . . . *Epith.* 171
With Barnaby the *bright,* . . . *Epith.* 266
the *bright* evening-star with golden creast Appeare . . . *Epith.* 286
whose is that faire face that shines so *bright?* . . . *Epith.* 373
a thousand torches flaming *bright* Doe burne, . . . *Epith.* 410
The Sunne more *bright* and glorious doth appeare; . . . *H.L.* 277

Bright—*Continued.*
flowing from the beame Of thy *bright* starre, . . . H.B. 56
That golden wyre, those sparckling stars so *bright*, . . . H.B. 97
your *bright* glorie darkned quight; . . . H.B. 165
Through mutuall receipt of beames *bright*, . . . H.B. 235
An infinite increase of Angels *bright*, . . . H.H.L. 55
thy *bright* radiant eyes shall plainely see . . . H.H.L. 283
On that *bright* shynie round still moving Masse, . . . H.H.B. 51
heavens, . . . Unmoving, uncorrupt, and spotlesse *bright*, . . . H.H.B. 68
Yet farre more faire be those *bright* Cherubins, . . . H.H.B. 92
Yet fairer then they both, and much more *bright*, . . . H.H.B. 96
His glorious face! which glistereth else so *bright*, . . . H.H.B. 118
The Suns *bright* beames when he on us doth shyne, . . . H.H.B. 121
On that *bright* Sunne of Glorie fixe thine eyes, . . . H.H.B. 139
From whence proceed her beames so pure and *bright* . . . H.H.B. 160
Is many thousand times more *bright*, more cleare, . . . H.H.B. 170
their beauties *bright*, That shone as heavens light, . . . Proth. 51
Which decke the Bauldricke of the Heavens *bright*; . . . Proth. 174

Bright-blazing. her *bright blazing* beautie did assay To dim the brightnesse . . . I. iv. 8. 7
Light, farre exceeding that *bright blazing* sparke . . . H.H.B. 162

Bright-burning. the knights with their *bright burning* blades . . . II. ix. 15. 6
breake forth into *bright burning* flame, . . . III. iii. 48. 6

Bright-burnished. Through the greene gras his long *bright burnisht* back declares. . . . III. xi. 28. 9

Bright-embroidered. Him by the *bright embrodered* hed-stall tooke; . . . V. iii. 33. 7

Brighter. gemmes and jewels . . . that *brighter* then the starres appeare, . . . H.H.B. 188

Brightest. night had all displayd Her coleblacke curtein over *brightest* skye; . . . I. iv. 44. 2
dreaded Night in *brightest* day hath place, . . . I. v. 24. 4
Then gan her beautie shyne as *brightest* skye, . . . I. vi. 4. 8
armour . . . Like glauncing light of Phoebus *brightest* ray; . . . I. vii. 29. 5
Panthea, seemd the *brightest* thing that was; . . . I. x. 58. 6
The *brightest* Angell, even the Child of Light, . . . H.H.L. 83

Bright-glistering. all their tops *bright glistering* with gold, . . . V. ix. 21. 7

Brightness. Hir *brightnesse* greater was than can be founde, . . . Rev. iv. 8
joying in the *brightnes* of your day, . . . Ro. xv. 2
Let him . . . His *brightnesse* compare With hers, . . . S.C. Ap. 80
of that *brightnes* now appeares no shade, . . . Ti. 124
To shew in Heaven his *brightnes* orient; . . . Ti. 389
I, . . . lately through her *brightnes* blynd, . . . I. iii. 1. 5
purest skye with *brightnesse* they dismaid: . . . I. iv. 4. 5
To dim the *brightnesse* of her glorious throne, . . . I. iv. 8. 8
So forth she comes; her *brightnes* brode doth blaze. . . . I. iv. 16. 6
never did such *brightnes* there appeare; . . . I. v. 21. 5
haughtie Helmet, . . . Both glorious *brightnesse* and great terrour bredd: . . . I. vii. 31. 2
The light . . . Such blazing *brightnesse* through the ayer threw, I. viii. 19. 4
dazed were his eyne Through passing *brightnes*, . . . I. x. 67. 7
The blazing *brightnesse* of her beauties beame, . . . I. xii. 23. 1
with their *brightnesse* made that darknes light, . . . II. vii. 42. 2
beam great *brightnes* threw Through the dim shade, . . . II. vii. 45. 2
with too much *brightnes* daz'd, . . . III. vii. 13. 8
dim the *brightnesse* of the welkin rownd, . . . III. x. 46. 7
The whiles the passing *brightnes* her fraile sences dazd. . . . III. xi. 49. 9
with their *brightnesse* daz'd the straunge beholders eye. . . . V. ix. 21. 9
Gins to abate the *brightnesse* of his beme, . . . V. ix. 35. 3
with her *brightnesse* doth inflame . . . VI. Pr. 6. 6
being now with her huge *brightnesse* dazed, . . . Am. iii. 5
with such *brightnesse* whylest I fill my mind, . . . Am. lxxxvii. 13
with the *brightnesse* of her beautie cleare, . . . H.B. 11
adde more *brightnesse* to your goodly hew, . . . H.B. 178
stars . . . Whereof each other doth in *brightnesse* passe, . . . H.H.B. 54
His throne is . . . hid in his owne *brightnesse* . . . H.H.B. 178
And make her native *brightnes* seem more cleare. . . . H.H.B. 189

Bright-shining. Our lovely Lasses, or *bright shining* Brides: . . . Hub. 476
Faire Galathea with *bright shining* beames, . . . Col. 518
His blazing eyes, like two *bright shining* shieldes, . . . I. xi. 14. 1
whose *bright shining* beames Adorne the world . . . III. v. 53. 1
The heavens *bright-shining* baudricke to enchace; . . . V. i. 11. 7
To whose *bright shining* palace straight she came, . . . VII. vi. 8. 3
the light of your *bright shyning* starre. . . . H.B. 175

Brim. by whose utmost *brim* Wayting to passe, . . . II. vi. 2. 4
to the *brim* with Coltwood did it fill, . . . III. ii. 49. 8
upon the *brim* Of the Rich Strond, . . . III. iv. 34. 1
Upon the *brim* of his brode-plated shield, . . . IV. iii. 34. 6
was with Nepenthe to the *brim* upfild. . . . IV. iii. 42. 9
Towards the westerne *brim* begins to draw, . . . V. ix. 35. 2
when as Calepine came to the *brim*, . . . VI. iii. 34. 5
Till to the *brim* I have it full defrayd: . . . VI. viii. 24. 3
A good full pecke within the utmost *brim*, . . . VI. xii. 26. 6

Brimstone. fire and *brimstone*, which for ever shall remaine. . . . I. ix. 49. 9
Enrold in duskish smoke and *brimstone* blew: . . . I. xi. 44. 4
their entrailles, full of quick *Brimston*, . . . II. x. 26. 4

Brine. the salt *brine* out of the billowes sprong. . . . II. xii. 10. 5
His dewy lockes did drop with *brine* apace . . . IV. xi. 11. 3

Bring. Caligulaes Must still *bring* forth to rule . . . Bel.[1] viii. 15
Which eare the frutefull graine doth shortly *bring*; . . . Ro. xxx. 4
That when time serves may *bring* things better forth. . . . Van. i. 14
asked who thee forth did *bring*, . . . To his Booke 8
'*Bring* hether the Pincke and purple Cullambine, . . . S.C. Ap. 136
Bring Coronations, and Sops in wine, . . . S.C. Ap. 138
home they *bringen* in a royall throne, . . . S.C. May 29
of hys keepe A sacrifice to *bring*, . . . S.C. Jul. 134
the white beare to the stake did *bring*. . . . S.C. O. 48
Now *bringen* bitter Eldre braunches seare; . . . S.C. N. 147
season more secure Shall *bring* forth fruit, . . . Gn. 10
No reach, no breach, that might him profit *bring*, . . . Hub. 1141

Bring—*Continued.*
when he ought would *bring* to pas, . . . Hub. 1167
out of her happie womb did *bring* The sacred brood . . . Ti. 278
thence the soules to *bring* awaie . . . Ti. 375
Sith time doth greatest things to ruine *bring?* . . . Ti. 556
bring to her so precious a pray. . . . Mui. 112
morning faire may *bring* fowle evening late, . . . Mui. 219
bring to hand that yet had never beene; . . . D. 116
her braunch faire blossomes foorth did *bring*, . . . D. 241
th' earth be barren, and *bring* foorth no flowres, . . . D. 334
cease henceforth things kindly forth to *bring*, . . . D. 339
his mother Him forth did *bring*, . . . As. 14
with you *bring* triumphant Mart, . . . I. Pr. 3. 7
she . . . seemde unto his bed to *bring* Her, . . . I. i. 48. 2
Bidding the dwarfe . . . to *bring* away The Sarazins shield, . . . I. ii. 20. 6
her kindly skil To *bring* forth fruit, . . . I. iii. 28. 8
They *bring* them wines of Greece and Araby, . . . I. v. 4. 5
So towards old Sylvanus they her *bring*; . . . I. vi. 14. 5
In hope to *bring* her to her last decay. . . . I. vi. 48. 7
O! welcome thou, that doest of death *bring* tydings trew.' . . . I. viii. 38. 9
time in her just term the truth to light should *bring*.' . . . I. ix. 5. 9
Ne *bring* him forth in face of dreadfull fight, . . . I. ix. 20. 7
She cast to *bring* him where he chearen might, . . . I. x. 2. 8
unto an holy Hospitall . . . she did him *bring*; . . . I. x. 36. 2
might I happily Unto you *bring*, . . . I. xi. 3. 9
to the world does *bring* long-wished light: . . . I. xii. 21. 8
to the wished haven *bring* thy weary barke!' . . . II. i. 32. 9
He promised to *bring* me at that howre, . . . II. iv. 24. 7
such agony As griefe and fury unto me did *bring*; . . . II. iv. 33. 4
planted there did *bring* forth fruit of gold; . . . II. vii. 54. 7
To *bring* the sowle into captivity? . . . II. xi. 1. 4
she from farre did thither *bring*: . . . II. xii. 72. 4
love does alwaies *bring* forth bounteous deeds, . . . III. i. 49. 8
to *bring* to perfect end: . . . III. iii. 10. 5
to *bring* his will to pas: . . . III. iii. 24. 5
To this his native soyle thou backe shalt *bring*, . . . III. iii. 27. 7
He shall his dayes with peace *bring* to his earthly In. . . . III. iii. 30. 9
skil, which practize small Wil *bring*, . . . III. iii. 53. 9
bring my ship, ere it be rent, . . . III. iv. 10. 4
To *bring* her sonne unto his last decay. . . . III. iv. 28. 5
To *bring* to passe his mischievous intent, . . . III. iv. 45. 2
bring with him his long expected light? . . . III. iv. 60. 2
Oft from the forrest wildings he did *bring*, . . . III. vii. 17. 1
To *bringe* her backe againe, or worke her finall bale. . . . III. vii. 21. 9
should *bring* their names And pledges, . . . III. vii. 54. 8
their lately bruzed parts to *bring* in plight. . . . III. ix. 19. 9
One may his journey *bring* too soone to evill end.' . . . III. x. 40. 9
seedes of evill wordes . . . *Bring* foorth an infinite increase, . . . IV. i. 25. 7
sought to *bring* all things unto decay; . . . IV. i. 29. 4
great riches, . . . She in short space did often *bring* to nought, IV. i. 29. 6
Unto his last confusion to *bring*, . . . IV. i. 30. 7
all knights with them their Ladies are to *bring*: . . . IV. ii. 26. 9
These three so noble babes to *bring* forth at one clap. . . . IV. ii. 43. 9
forth to *bring* those thrals which there he held. . . . IV. ix. 8. 3
To *bring* forth stormes, or fast them to upbinde, . . . IV. xi. 52. 4
To *bring* it to her husband new ordained, . . . V. iv. 13. 7
'Which that thou mayst the better *bring* to pas, . . . V. v. 34. 1
then *bring* me newes Of his demeane; . . . V. v. 51. 1
forth did *bring* a Lion of great might, . . . V. vii. 16. 6
bring in bondage of their brutishnesse: . . . V. xi. 44. 5
from your selfe I doe this vertue *bring*, . . . VI. Pr. 7. 2
bring us bale and bitter sorrowings, . . . VI. iii. 5. 5
To *bring* him to the place where he would faine, . . . VI. iv. 24. 5
it forth doth *bring* Sorrow, and anguish, . . . VI. vi. 8. 5
the first, whose force her first doth *bring*, . . . VI. vii. 9. 5
Unlesse to me thou hether *bring* with speed The wretch . . . VI. vii. 13. 4
being gone, none can them *bring* in place, . . . VI. x. 20. 4
Yet none of them could ever *bring* him into band. . . . VI. xii. 39. 9
bring into a mighty Peres displeasure, . . . VI. xii. 41. 6
him *bring* before his presence prest. . . . VII. vi. 16. 9
Me from these woods and pleasing forrests *bring*, . . . VII. vii. 1. 2
Bring therefore all the forces . . . Am. xiv. 9
I must begin and never *bring* to end: . . . Am. xxiii. 10
hard t' atchieve and *bring* to end. . . . Am. li. 8
having harrowd hell, didst *bring* away Captivity . . . Am. lxviii. 3
Bring with you all the Nymphes that you can heare . . . Epith. 37
bring in hand Another gay girland, . . . Epith. 41
let them eeke *bring* store of other flowers, . . . Epith. 46
Bring her up to th' high altar, . . . Epith. 215
bring home the bride againe; . . . Epith. 242
Bring home the triumph of our victory: . . . Epith. 243
Bring home with you the glory of her gaine . . . Epith. 244
With joyance *bring* her and with jollity. . . . Epith. 245
Now *bring* the Bryde into the brydall boures. . . . Epith. 299
Till they *bring* forth the fruitfull progeny; . . . Epith. 403

Bringeth. *bringeth* forth the fruite of sommers pryde; . . . S.C. D. 74
from them redeemes, And *bringeth* backe againe. . . . VI. xi. Arg.

Bringing. *bringing* them to their appointed place, . . . V. viii. 27. 1
bringing light into the heavens fayre, . . . V. x. 16. 7
the morning, *bringing* earely light . . . VI. v. 40. 2
forth her *bringing* to the joyous light, . . . VI. xi. 50. 4

Brings. balefull barking *bringes* in hast Pyne, . . . S.C. Jul. 23
knewe we, fooles, what it us *bringes* until, . . . S.C. N. 185
The joyous Spring out of the ground *brings* forth, . . . Gn. 683
Brings to reproach and common infamie! . . . Hub. 222
Brings downe the stowtest hearts to lowest state; . . . Hub. 255
He daylie eekes, and *brings* to excellence. . . . Hub. 792
Faire virgin . . . *Brings* Arthure to the fight: . . . I. viii. Arg.
'O! who is that, which *bringes* me happy choyce Of death, . . . I. viii. 38. 3
Is not short payne well borne, that *bringes* long ease, . . . I. ix. 40. 6

Brings—*Continued.*
Her faithfull knight faire Una *brings* To house of Holinesse; . I. x. Arg.
Brings them to joyous rest and endlesse blis. . . . . I. x. 52. 6
after to his Pallace he them *bringes,* . . . . I. xii. 13. 1
The sea unto him voluntary *brings;* . . . . III. iv. 23. 7
the man that of him tydings to her *brings.* . . . . III. vi. 12. 9
She with her *bringes* into a secret Ile, ... III. vii. 50. 6
brings forth glorious flowres of fame, ... IV. Pr. 2. 7
passing joy, which so great marvaile *brings,* . . . . IV. iii. 49. 8
to his daughter *brings,* that dwels thereby; . . . . V. ii. 9. 2
Talus *brings* newes to Britomart . . . . V. vi. Arg.
Calidore *brings* Priscilla home; . . . . VI. iii. Arg.
Is this the hope . . . Thou *brings?* . . . . VI. iii. 4. 8
Which th' earth *brings* forth; . . . . VII. vii. 33. 8
humbled harts *brings* captive unto thee, ... *Am.* x. 7
which loathing *brings* Of this vile world . . . . *H.H.B.* 298
Brink. 'There next the utmost *brinck* doth he abide, ... *Gn.* 385
the fruit which grew upon the *brincke;* . . . . II. vii. 58. 5
his head he gan a litle reare Above the *brincke* . . . . . . V. ii. 18. 4
From th' utmost *brinke* of the Americke shore . . . . V. x. 3. 6
Brinks. the bolde people by the Thamis *brincks,* . . . . . . *Ro.* xxxi. 6
Briny. from their nosethrilles blow the *brynie* streame, . . III. xi. 41. 2
Bristles. At them he gan to reare his *bristles* strong, . . . I. v. 34. 5
As chauffed Bore his *bristles* doth upreare; . . . . I. xi. 15. 6
Bristol. *Bristow* faire, which on his waves he builded hath. IV. xi. 31. 9
Britain. *See* **Britany.**
*High reard their royall throne in *Britane* land, ... I. x. 65. 4
hold of him, as subject to *Britayne.* . . . . II. x. 41. 9
noblest borne of all in *Britayne* land; . . . . II. xi. 30. 7
Whom straunge adventure did from *Britayne* sett . . . . . . III. i. 8. 7
is by name The greater *Brytayne,* . . . . III. ii. 7. 9
Sith him whylome in *Britayne* she did vew, ... III. ii. 17. 3
warlike people which the *Britaine* Islands hold: . . . . . . IV. xi. 15. 9
all his brethren borne in *Britaine* land; . . . . VI. xii. 39. 8
Britain's. that Citie, which the garland wore Of *Britaines* pride, ... *Ti.* 37
High reard their royall throne in *Britans* land, ... I. x. 65. 4
Britany. *See* **Britain.**
In *Britannie* was none to match with mee, ... *Ti.* 100
Locrine left chiefe Lord of *Britany.* . . . . II. x. 13. 7
The gratious Numa of great *Britany;* . . . . II. x. 39. 6
Brennus and Belinus, kinges of *Britany.* . . . . II. x. 40. 9
comprovincial In auncient times unto great *Britainee,* . . . . III. iii. 32. 7
now all *Britany* doth burne in armes bright. . . . . III. iii. 52. 9
with their braunches spred all *Britany,* . . . . IV. xi. 26. 6
British. three hundred Lords he slew Of *British* blood, . . . II. x. 66. 7
in queint disguise Of *British* armes doest maske thy royall blood, ... V. vii. 21. 2
Of all that beare the *British* Islands name, ... VII. vi. 38. 3
Britomart. Guyon encountreth *Britomart:* . . . . III. i. Arg.
Even the famous *Britomart* it was, ... III. i. 8. 6
The whiles faire *Britomart* . . . did stay behynd, ... III. i. 19. 1
When *Britomart* him saw, she ran apace . . . . III. i. 22. 7
'Perdy,' (said *Britomart*) 'the choise is hard; . . . . III. i. 27. 6
With which fayre *Britomart* gave light unto the day. . . . . III. i. 43. 9
to faire *Britomart* they all but shadowes beene. . . . . III. i. 45. 9
Britomart dissembled it with ignoraunce. . . . . III. i. 50. 9
Britomart would not such guilfull message know. . . . . . . III. i. 51. 9
The Lady did faire *Britomart* entreat . . . . III. i. 52. 3
The noble *Britomartis* her arayd, ... III. i. 67. 2
Redcrosse knight to *Britomart* Describeth Artegall: . . . . . III. ii. Arg.
faire *Britomart,* whose prayse I wryte; . . . . III. ii. 3. 2
Such secrete ease felt gentle *Britomart,* . . . . III. ii. 15. 7
One day it fortuned fayre *Britomart* . . . . III. ii. 22. 1
bewrayes to *Britomart* The state of Arthegall; . . . . III. iii. Arg.
fayre *Britomartis,* thus arayd, ... III. iii. 19. 5
'It was not, *Britomart,* thy wandring eye . . . . III. iii. 24. 1
ordaynd to bee The spouse of *Britomart,* . . . . III. iii. 26. 2
'Behold the man! and tell me, *Britomart,* . . . . III. iii. 32. 1
'Ah! read,' (quoth *Britomart*) 'how is she hight?' . . . . . III. iii. 56. 1
old Glauce thither led Faire *Britomart,* . . . . III. iii. 59. 7
The Redcrosse Knight diverst, but forth rode *Britomart.* . . . III. iii. 62. 9
Bold Marinell of *Britomart* Is throwne . . . . III. iv. Arg.
Cannot with noble *Britomart* compare, ... III. iv. 3. 2
Britomart kept on her former course, ... III. iv. 5. 1
fayre *Britomart,* having disclo'ste Her clowdy care . . . . . III. iv. 13. 7
Paridell giusts with *Britomart:* . . . . III. ix. Arg.
looking still askaunce Gainst *Britomart,* . . . . III. ix. 27. 4
the noble *Britomart* heard tell . . . . III. ix. 38. 1
there,' (said *Britomart*) 'afresh appeared The glory . . . . . III. ix. 44. 1
Faire *Britomart* and that same Faery knight Uprose, ... III. x. 1. 5
his late fight With *Britomart* . . . . III. x. 1. 8
Britomart chaceth Ollyphant; . . . . III. xi. Arg.
of faire *Britomart* ensample take, ... III. xi. 2. 8
Whom when as *Britomart* beheld . . . . III. xi. 4. 5
Britomart the flowre of chastity; . . . . III. xi. 6. 2
Fayre *Britomart* so long him followed, ... III. xi. 7. 1
Greatly thereat was *Britomart* dismayd, ... III. xi. 22. 1
That wondrous sight faire *Britomart* amazd, ... III. xi. 49. 6
Britomart redeemes faire Amoret . . . . III. xii. Arg.
in went Bold *Britomart,* . . . . III. xii. 29. 8
Before faire *Britomart* she fell prostrate, ... III. xii. 39. 1
Britomart, uprearing her from grownd, ... III. xii. 40. 1
Britomart, halfe envying their blesse, ... III. xii. 46. *or.* 6
Fayre *Britomart* saves Amoret: . . . . IV. i. Arg.
Untill such time as noble *Britomart* Released her, ... IV. i. 4. 3
Yet *Britomart* attended duly on her, ... IV. i. 8. 8
From farre espide the famous *Britomart,* . . . . IV. i. 33. 2
'Discourteous, disloyall *Britomart,* . . . . IV. i. 53. 1
evermore sought *Britomart* to cleare: . . . . IV. i. 54. 6

Britomart—*Continued.*
Britomart winnes the prize from all, ... IV. iv. Arg.
The which this famous *Britomart* did beare; . . . . IV. iv. 46. 5
So did the warlike *Britomart* restore The prize . . . . IV. iv. 48. 1
To *Britomart* was given by good right; . . . . IV. v. 8. 3
Britomart would not thereto assent, ... IV. v. 20. 6
of *Britomart* it here doth neede . . . to tell, ... IV. v. 28. 7
Bent to revenge on blamelesse *Britomart* The crime . . . . . IV. v. 31. 1
Scudamour and Arthegall Doe fight with *Britomart:* . . . . . IV. vi. Arg.
He wist right well that it was *Britomart,* . . . . IV. vi. 7. 2
So both to wreake their wrathes on *Britomart* agreed. . . . . IV. vi. 8. 9
Britomart with sharpe avizefull eye . . . . IV. vi. 26. 1
Thereat full inly blushed *Britomart,* . . . . IV. vi. 32. 8
To whom thus *Britomart:* . . . . IV. vi. 35. 1
Till *Britomart* him fairely thus behight: . . . . IV. vi. 38. 5
made way Unto the love of noble *Britomart,* . . . . IV. vi. 40. 2
Where sorie *Britomart* had lost her late; . . . . IV. vi. 47. 2
so and so to noble *Britomart:* . . . . IV. vii. 2. 2
heavie sleepe the eye-lids did surprise Of *Britomart,* . . . . IV. vii. 3. 8
Britomart heard not the shrilling sound, ... IV. vii. 4. 8
Britomart fightes with many Knights; . . . . IV. ix. Arg.
Britomart and gentle Scudamour; . . . . IV. ix. 22. 2
did *Britomart* assay To speake to them, ... IV. ix. 31. 1
To weet faire *Britomart,* . . . . IV. ix. 36. 2
Britomart did him importune hard . . . . IV. ix. 41. 2
that cruell stroke Which *Britomart* him gave, ... IV. xi. 5. 9
Talus brings newes to *Britomart* . . . . V. vi. Arg.
his owne love, the noble *Britomart,* . . . . V. vi. 3. 1
Then *Britomart* unto a bowre was brought, ... V. vi. 23. 2
There all that night remained *Britomart,* . . . . V. vi. 24. 5
(that which to *Britomart* Unknowen was) . . . . V. vi. 31. 6
Britomart comes to Isis Church, ... V. vii. Arg.
Unto whose temple when as *Britomart* Arrived, ... V. vii. 3. 6
whom when *Britomart* Had long beheld, ... V. vii. 7. 6
In which stout *Britomart* her selfe did rest, ... V. vii. 26. 3
Which *Britomart* withstood with courage stout, ... V. vii. 31. 3
Full sad and sorrowfull was *Britomart* . . . . V. vii. 44. 1
left his love, . . . Faire *Britomart* in languor and unrest, . . V. viii. 3. 5
Britomart's. Through heavy stroke of *Britomartis* hond. . . III. iv. 29. 4
of the hardie *Britomarts* successe: . . . . III. xii. 43. *or.* 5
Awayted there for *Britomarts* returne, ... III. xii. 45. 2
Strange were the words in *Britomartis* eare, ... V. vi. 38. 1
Briton. Tanaquill, Whom that most noble *Briton* Prince Sought . . . . I. Pr. 2. 6
Bryton fieldes with Sarazin blood bedyde, ... I. xi. 7. 3
The *Briton* Prince recov'ring his stolne sword, ... II. ix. 2. 2
'Thrise happy man,' (said then the *Briton* knight) . . . . . II. ix. 5. 1
An auncient booke, hight *Briton moniments,* . . . . II. ix. 59. 6
A chronicle of *Briton* kings, ... II. x. Arg.
oft the *Briton* kings against them strongly swayd. . . . . . II. x. 49. 9
the *Briton* Prince him rouzd Out of his holde, ... II. xi. 33. 1
The famous *Briton* Prince and Faery knight, ... III. i. 1. 1
To aske this *Briton* Maid, what uncouth wind . . . . III. ii. 4. 5
everlasting woe, Be to the *Briton* babe . . . . III. iii. 42. 2
So shall the *Briton* blood their crowne agayn reclame. . . . III. iii. 48. 9
Through fine abusion of that *Briton* mayd; . . . . IV. i. 7. 2
Upon all which the *Briton* Prince made seasure, ... IV. ix. 12. 5
Scudamour and that same *Briton* maide . . . . IV. ix. 28. 2
Whom when the *Briton* Prince afarre beheld . . . . IV. ix. 32. 1
The *Briton* Prince him readie did awayte, ... V. viii. 29. 3
The *Briton* Prince was sore empassionate, ... V. ix. 46. 2
The noble *Briton* Prince with his brave Peare; . . . . V. x. 15. 2
sent redresse thereof by this brave *Briton* Knight. . . . . . V. xi. 1. 9
Then wote ye that I am a *Briton* borne, ... VI. ii. 27. 6
What fortune to the *Briton* Prince did lite, ... VI. vi. 17. 5
Britoness. 'But long ere this, Bunduca, *Britonnesse,* . . . . *Ti.* 106
when the *Britonesse* saw all the rest Avoided . . . . III. i. 58. 5
the bold *Britonesse* was nought ydred, ... III. xii. 2. 8
The warlike *Britonesse* her soone addrest, ... IV. i. 36. 1
the most redoubted *Britonesse* . . . . IV. v. 13. 1
with that brave *Britonesse* Had left that Turneyment . . . . IV. vii. 3. 1
The which that *Britonesse* had to them donne . . . . IV. ix. 28. 6
the wrothfull *Britonesse* Stayd not . . . . V. vii. 34. 1
Britons. The land which warlike *Britons* now possesse, . . . II. x. 5. 1
taking armes the *Britons* to her drew; . . . . II. x. 54. 7
of the *Britons* first crownd Soveraine. . . . . II. x. 58. 7
The weary *Britons,* whose war-hable youth . . . . II. x. 62. 1
The feeble *Britons,* broken with long warre, ... III. iii. 23. 6
'Whiles thus thy *Britons* doe in languour pine, ... III. iii. 35. 1
the *Britons,* late dismayd and weake, ... III. iii. 36. 7
the raine Of *Britons* eke with him attonce shall dye; . . . . III. iii. 40. 2
displace The *Britons* for their sinnes dew punishment . . . . III. iii. 41. 8
in this thraldome *Britons* shall abide; . . . . III. iii. 44. 2
the crowne, which they from *Britons* wonne . . . . III. iii. 46. 2
A band of *Britons,* ryding on forray . . . . III. iii. 58. 4
noble *Britons* sprong from Trojans bold, ... III. ix. 38. 8
Subdewd with losse of many *Britons* bold: . . . . III. ix. 50. 2
this to you, O *Britons!* most pertaines, ... IV. xi. 22. 6
Which mote the feebled *Britons* strongly flancke . . . . . . IV. xi. 36. 3
Dee, which *Britons* long ygone Did call divine, ... IV. xi. 39. 3
Britons'. no moniment Of Brutus, nor of *Britons* glorie auncient. II. x. 36. 9
envying the *Britons* blazed fame, ... II. x. 47. 8
to assist the *Britons* fone. . . . . III. iii. 33. 9
the full time . . . of *Britons* regiment: . . . . III. iii. 40. 6
Brize. *See* **Breeze.**
Broach. To stirre up strife and troublous contecke *broch:* . . III. i. 64. 5
Broad. *See* **Sun-broad.**
His hornes bene as *broade* as Rainebowe bent, ... *S.C.* F. 73
when he sawe how *broade* her beames did spredde, ... *S.C.* Ap. 75
his *broad* forhead like two hornes divide, ... *Gn.* 22

Broad—*Continued.*
about his shoulders *broad* he threw An hairie hide . . . . . *Mui.* 65
To blazon *broade* emongst her learned throng: . . . . . I. Pr. 1. 8
Did spred so *broad,* that heavens light did hide, ... I. i. 7. 5
when *broad* day the world discovered has, ... I. iii. 21. 1
towards it a *broad* high way that led, ... I. iv. 2. 8
her brightnes *brode* doth blaze. . . . . . I. iv. 16. 6
Whom *broad* awake she findes, ... I. iv. 45. 1
muddy shore of *broad* seven-mouthed Nile, ... I. v. 18. 2
All keepe the *broad* high way, ... I. x. 10. 5
two *broad* Beacons, sett in open fieldes, ... I. xi. 14. 3
he, cutting way With his *broad* sayles, ... I. xi. 18. 7
his left wing, then *broad* displayd: . . . . . I. xi. 20. 7
advaunce his *broad* discoloured brest Above his wonted pitch, I. xi. 31. 7
The Northerne winde his wings did *broad* display . . . . . II. iii. 19. 3
Like a *broad* table did it selfe dispred, ... II. iii. 24. 2
arriving forcibly On his *broad* shield, bitt not, ... II. v. 4. 4
Through which a beaten *broad* high way did trace, ... II. vii. 21. 3
a *broad* gate all built of beaten gold: . . . . . II. vii. 40. 2
her *broad* beauties beam great brightnes threw . . . . . II. vii. 45. 2
braunches *broad* dispredd and body great, ... II. vii. 53. 7
his *broad* braunches, laden with rich fee, ... II. vii. 56. 3
Full large he was of limbe, and shoulders *brode,* . . . . . II. xi. 20. 7
the *brode* shadow of an hoarie hill; . . . . . II. xii. 30. 4
did *broad* dilate Their clasping armes . . . . . II. xii. 53. 8
Her bared bosome she doth *broad* display; . . . . . II. xii. 74. 8
Whiles on his *broad* rownd backe they softly slid, ... III. iv. 32. 2
their *brode* flaggy finnes no fome did reare, ... III. iv. 33. 6
an Island spatious and *brode,* . . . . . III. ix. 49. 2
made a long *broad* dyke, ... III. xi. 40. 7
at his backe a *brode* Capuccio had, ... III. xii. 10. 3
With scutchins gilt and banners *broad* displayd; . . . . . IV. iii. 5. 6
Of that great turney which was blazed *brode,* . . . . . IV. iv. 5. 7
Ne hostes of men with banners *brode* dispred, ... IV. viii. 47. 7
Psamathe for her *brode* snowy brests; . . . . . IV. xi. 51. 5
To weather his *brode* sailes, ... V. iv. 42. 3
and *brode* displayes his smyling hew. . . . . . VI. ii. 35. 9
Covered with mossie shrubs, which spredding *brode* . . . . . VI. iv. 13. 6
His *brode* black wings had . . . dispred, ... VI. viii. 44. 5
in his hand a *broad* deepe boawle he beares, ... VII. vii. 41. 8
Thrugh the *broad* world doth spred . . . . . *Am.* xl. 8
Spread thy *broad* wing over my love and me, ... *Epith.* 319
on Themmes *brode* aged backe . . . . . *Proth.* 133
Broad-blazed. Ledd with thy prayses, and *broad-blazed* fame, I. x. 11. 4
bore the Sunne *brode blazed* in a golden field. . . . . . V. iii. 14. 9
Broad-outstretched. His *broad outstretched* hornes, his hayrie thies, ... *Mui.* 335
Broad-plated. Upon the brim of his *brode-plated* shield, . . . IV. iii. 34. 6
Broad-spreading. *broad spreading* like an aged tree, ... *Ti.* 452
her *brode-spreading* wings did wyde unfold; . . . . . V. ix. 28. 5
Broadwater. Allo hight, *Broad-water* called farre; . . . . . *Col.* 123
Brocage. *See* **Brokage.**
Broch. *See* **Broach.**
Brockwell. Shall backe repulse the valiaunt *Brockwell* twise, III. iii. 35. 5
Brode. *See* **Broad.**
Broil. Both falling out doe stirre up strifefull *broyle,* . . . . . IV. iii. 16. 5
Brokage. filthie *brocage,* and unseemly shifts, ... *Hub.* 851
Broke. *See* **Brake, Broken.**
So *broke* his oaten pype, and downe dyd lye. . . . . . *S.C.* Ja. 72
Whose bodie is sere, whose braunches *broke,* . . . . . *S.C.* F. 170
hast thy selfe his slomber *broke,* . . . . . *S.C.* Mar. 29
is thy Bagpype *broke,* that soundes so sweete? . . . . . *S.C.* Ap. 3
Hys pleasaunt Pipe . . . He wylfully hath *broke,* . . . . . *S.C.* Ap. 15
her solein silence she *broke,* . . . . . *S.C.* May 213
She weend the shell-fishe to have *broke,* . . . . . *S.C.* Jul. 225
She hath the bonds *broke* of eternall night, ... *S.C.* N. 165
Their wraths at length *broke* into open warre. . . . . . *Mui.* 8
Alexis *broke* his tale asunder, ... *Col.* 352
he snatcht the wood, And quite a sunder *broke*. . . . . . I. xi. 22. 3
Doth belch out flames, and rocks in peeces *broke,* . . . . . I. xi. 44. 6
She *broke* his wanton darts, and quenched bace desyre. . . . II. iii. 23. 9
That *broke* the violence of his intent, ... II. v. 6. 6
The Prince now stood, having his weapon *broke;* . . . . . II. viii. 39. 6
Those Champions *broke* on them, ... II. ix. 14. 6
Broke their rude troupes, and orders did confownd, ... II. ix. 15. 7
Perforce their studies *broke,* . . . . . II. x. 77. 6
broke his caytive bands; . . . . . II. xi. 33. 2
On whose sharp cliftes the ribs of vessels *broke;* . . . . . II. xii. 7. 3
broke his staffe with which he charmed semblants sly. . . . II. xii. 49. 9
Guyon *broke* downe with rigour pittilesse; . . . . . II. xii. 83. 2
he had *broke* his band, And was returnd . . . . . III. vii. 61. 7
Broke into open fire and rage extreme; . . . . . III. viii. 26. 5
Their swerds and speres were *broke,* . . . . . III. xi. 52. 6
that great brasen pillour *broke* in peeces small. . . . . . III. xii. 37. 9
Marshals of the field *Broke* up the listes, ... IV. iii. 35. 4
broke The puissance of his intended stroke: . . . . . IV. vii. 26. 4
all he *broke* And threw away, ... IV. vii. 39. 1
all his ribs he quite in peeces *broke,* . . . . . V. iii. 33. 4
broke his sword in twaine, ... V. iii. 37. 9
broke their bowes, and did their shooting marre, ... V. iv. 44. 4
broke his sword, for feare of further harmes, ... V. v. 21. 8
his owne waight his necke asunder *broke,* . . . . . V. viii. 8. 3
strongly either strooke And *broke* their speares; . . . . . V. viii. 9. 7
all his bones as small as sandy grayle He *broke,* . . . . . V. ix. 19. 5
wroke His wrath on him that first occasion *broke;* . . . . . VI. ii. 13. 5
Out of their ambush *broke,* and gan him to invade. . . . . . VI. v. 17. 9
broke his bag-pipe quight, ... VI. x. 18. 5
From thence into the sacred Church he *broke,* . . . . . VI. xii. 25. 1
he *broke* his yron chaine, ... VI. xii. 38. 8
The Damzell *broke* his misintended dart. . . . . . *Am.* xvi. 12

Broken. *See* **Broke.**
With sodaine falling *broken* all to dust. . . . . . *Bel.*[1] iv. 14
Untill he came unto the *broken* tree, ... *Pet.* v. 5
his hose *broken* high above the heeling, ... *Hub.* 213
with the weight their backs nigh *broken* were: . . . . . *Hub.* 1158
In her right hand a *broken* rod she held, ... *Ti.* 13
this *broken* verse, *Broken* with sighes, ... *Ti.* 678, 679
those little streames so *broken* . . . . . *Col.* 141
holding idely The *broken* reliques of their former cruelty. . . I. ii. 16. 9
Like the old ruines of a *broken* towre, ... I. ii. 20. 2
thou *broken* hast The law of armes . . . . . II. viii. 31. 6
Throwing away her *broken* chaines and bands, ... II. xi. 47. 4
all in peeces it was *broken* fond, ... II. xii. 57. 4
The feeble Britons, *broken* with long warre, ... III. iii. 23. 6
*Tyde with her *broken* girdle, ... III. viii. 2. 7
Her heart nigh *broken* was with weary toyle, ... III. viii. 32. 4
broken bowes and arrowes shivered short; . . . . . III. xi. 46. 7
on a *broken* reed he still did stay His feeble steps, ... III. xii. 10. 8
There were rent robes and *broken* scepters plast; . . . . . IV. i. 21. 4
Witnesse their *broken* bandes there to be seene, ... IV. i. 24. 6
the heads of many *broken* speares; . . . . . IV. i. 48. 9
Yet would not their battell so be *broken,* . . . . . IV. ii. 21. 4
A *broken* sword within a bloodie field; . . . . . V. i. 19. 8
almost would his balances have *broken;* . . . . . V. ii. 47. 2
His timbered bones all *broken* rudely rumbled: . . . . . V. ii. 50. 8
Was lately *broken* by some fortune ill; . . . . . V. v. 15. 4
broken with some fearefull dreames affright, ... V. vi. 14. 2
Though nothing whole, but all to-brusd and *broken,* . . . . . V. viii. 44. 2
Dealing just judgements, that mote not be *broken* . . . . . V. ix. 24. 8
'loth were I to have *broken* The law of armes: . . . . . VI. ii. 7. 6
unable to support So huge a burden on such *broken* geare, . VI. viii. 16. 7
His dearest joynt he sure had *broken* quight. . . . . . VI. ix. 44. 5
Into their cloysters now he *broken* had, ... VI. xii. 24. 1
Fearing least Chaos *broken* had his chaine, ... VII. vi. 14. 6
fruitlesse worke is *broken* with least wynd. . . . . . *Am.* xxiii. 14
Broker. Then would he be a *Broker,* . . . . . *Hub.* 869
Brokest. Seeking to kisse her, *brok'st* the Gods decree, ... *Gn.* 471
Brond, -s, Brondiron, -s. *See* **Brand, -s, Brandiron, -s.**
Brontes. Farre passing *Bronteus* or Pyracmon great, ... IV. v. 37. 2
Great *Brontes;* and Astraeus, ... IV. xi. 13. 7
Bronteus. *See* **Brontes.**
Brood. that Nation, th' earths new Giant *brood,* . . . . . *Ro.* xi. 9
the brave warlicke *brood* of Alemaine, ... *Ro.* xxxi. 7
mount Parnasse, the Muses *brood,* . . . . . *Gn.* 21
the bad daughter of old Cadmus *brood,* . . . . . *Gn.* 171
The golden *brood* of great Apolloes wit, ... *T.M.* 2
Despise the *brood* of blessed Sapience. . . . . . *T.M.* 72
He now hath placed his accursed *brood,* . . . . . *T.M.* 315
The base-borne *brood* of blindnes cannot gesse, ... *T.M.* 392
all the rest, as borne of salvage *brood,* . . . . . *T.M.* 589
The sacred *brood* of learning and all honour; . . . . . *Ti.* 279
the puissant *brood* Of golden girt Alcmena, ... *Ti.* 379
the goodlie criew Of white Strimonian *brood* . . . . . *Ti.* 593
A cruell beast of most accursed *brood* . . . . . *As.* 116
all the *brood* of Greece so highly praised, ... *Col.* 413
Her scattered *brood,* . . . Gathred themselves about her body I. i. 25. 1
At last . . . Arose the virgin, borne of heavenly *brood,* . . . . I. iii. 8. 7
Th' eternall *brood* of glorie excellent: . . . . . I. v. 1. 4
cole blacke steedes yborne of hellish *brood,* . . . . . I. v. 20. 8
all the hellish *brood* Of feends infernall . . . . . I. v. 32. 7
In doubt to deeme her borne of earthly *brood:* . . . . . I. vi. 16. 5
bid her joy of that her happy *brood;* . . . . . I. x. 32. 2
to thee is unknowne the cradle of thy *brood*. . . . . . I. x. 64. 9
her base Elfin *brood* there for thee left: . . . . . I. x. 65. 8
in the hollow earth have their eternall *brood*. . . . . . II. vii. 8. 9
The martiall *brood* accustomed to fight: . . . . . III. i. 13. 5
those same antique Peres, the hevens *brood,* . . . . . III. iii. 22. 8
hungry whelpes, his battailous bold *brood,* . . . . . III. iii. 47. 4
not as other wemens commune *brood* . . . . . III. vi. 5. 6
her deare *brood,* her deare delight: . . . . . III. vi. 40. 4
an huge nation of the Geaunts *broode* . . . . . III. ix. 49. 8
she at first was borne of hellish *brood,* . . . . . IV. i. 26. 7
seemed borne of Angels *brood,* . . . . . IV. iii. 39. 7
Phorcys, the father of that fatall *brood,* . . . . . IV. xi. 13. 1
No lesse then do her elder sisters *broode*. . . . . . IV. xi. 26. 7
thy linage, and thy Lordly *brood,* . . . . . V. vii. 21. 7
Had left her now but five of all that *brood:* . . . . . V. x. 8. 2
In which thou lurkest lyke to vipers *brood;* . . . . . *Am.* ii. 6
For . . . she is, divinely wrought, And of the *brood* of Angels *Am.* lxi. 6
His second *brood,* though not in powre so great, ... *H.H.L.* 53
like the native *brood* of Eagles kynd, ... *H.H.B.* 138
Ran all in haste to see that silver *brood,* . . . . . *Proth.* 56
Brood's. gan abhorre her *broods* unkindly crime, ... II. x. 9. 4
Brooding. Borne of the *brooding* of Echidna base, ... V. xi. 23. 5
Brook. in this blessed *brooke* Doe bathe your brest, ... *S.C.* Ap. 37
Her owne like image in a christall *brooke*. . . . . . *Gn.* 88
many a Nymph both of the wood and *brooke,* . . . . . *As.* 43
his faire Leman flying through a *brooke* She overhent, . . . II. x. 18. 8
well did *brooke* Her noble deeds, ... III. iv. 44. 8
Whether she would them love, or in her liking *brooke*. . . . IV. ii. 40. 9
fast beside a little *brooke* did pas . . . . . IV. v. 33. 3
burning all to ashes powr'd it downe the *brooke*. . . . . . V. ii. 27. 9
Flowne at a flush of Ducks foreby the *brooke,* . . . . . V. ii. 54. 2
Through slipperie footing fell into the *brooke,* . . . . . V. v. 43. 3
With which he seldome fished at the *brooke,* . . . . . V. ix. 11. 7
Ne could he *brooke* the coldnesse of the stony masse. . . . . VI. iv. 21. 9
all the water which doth ronne In the next *brooke,* . . . . . VI. iv. 32. 9
drinke of every *brooke* when thirst my throte doth boyle. . . . VI. ix. 23. 9
On Phrygian Paris by Plexippus *brooke,* . . . . . VI. ix. 36. 7
In haste forth started from the guilty *brooke;* . . . . . VII. vi. 47. 2

Brook—*Continued.*
Thence-forth abandond her delicious *brooke,* . . . . VII. vi. 54. 2
bath'd in the sacred *brooke* Of Helicon, ... *Am.* i. 9
nothing else they *brooke,* . . . . *Am.* xxxv. 10
Thinking to quench her thirst at the next *brooke:* . . . . *Am.* lxvii. 8
With bathing in the Acidalian *brooke.* . . . . *Epith.* 310
Brooks. Soft rombling *brookes,* that gentle slomber drew ; . IV. x. 24. 4
As that in rivers swim, or *brookes* doe wade ; . . . . . . IV. xi. 9. 5
the Nymphes from all the *brooks* thereby . . . . VII. vii. 10. 6
Broom-flower. Sweet is the *Broome-flowre,* . . . . . . *Am.* xxvi. 7
Brooms. Keeping your beastes in the budded *broomes:* . . . . *S.C.* F. 36
there in the budded *broomes* Beside them fed, ... VI. ix. 5. 4
Brother. *See* **Brethren.**
with his elder *brother* Themis . . . . *S.C.* Jul. 83
This had a *brother* . . . . *S.C.* Jul. 161
Colin Clout rafte me of his *brother,* . . . . *S.C.* Au. 40
make like account of his *brother.* . . . . *S.C.* Au. 43
layen baytes to beguile her *brother;* . . . . *S.C.* S. 39
Say, my faire *brother* now, ... *Hub.* 93
'Now surely *brother* (said the Foxe anon) . . . . *Hub.* 124
'I cannot, my lief *brother,* like but well . . . . *Hub.* 177
my owne deare *brother,* . . . . *Hub.* 1003
Nath'les (my *brother*) . . . . *Hub.* 1047
So hee his sonnes both Syre and *brother* hight. . . . . *T.M.* 264
'He dyde, and after him his *brother* dyde, ... *Ti.* 239
His *brother* Prince, his *brother* noble Peere, ... *Ti.* 240
With his yong *brother* Sport, ... *Mui.* 290
most resembling . . . Her *brother* deare, ... *As.* 214
Her owne *brother* river, Bregog hight, ... *Col.* 117
Bewraying him that did of late destroy His eldest *brother;* . I. iv. 39. 4
'Pyrochles is his name, . . . The *brother* of Cymochles, ... II. iv. 41. 5
to tell his funerall Unto his *brother,* . . . . II. v. 25. 9
his *brother* burns in furious fyre. . . . . II. vi. Arg.
'Good or bad,' gan his *brother* fiers reply, ... II. viii. 15. 1
th' other *brother* gan his helme unlace, ... II. viii. 17. 2
match his *brother* proud in battailous aray. . . . . II. viii. 22. 9
Which when his *brother* saw, fraught with great griefe . . . II. viii. 33. 1
his *brother* saw the red blood rayle . . . . II. viii. 37. 3
fierce Cundah gan shortly to envy His *brother* Morgan, ... II. x. 33. 3
Stird Porrex up to put his *brother* downe ; . . . . II. x. 35. 3
faire Elferon, The eldest *brother,* . . . . II. x. 75. 7
brother unto Cador, Cornish king ; . . . . III. iii. 27. 2
Whose *brother* Oswin, daunted with like dread, ... III. iii. 39. 5
did drive Their *brother* to reproch . . . . III. v. 16. 6
the third *brother* him did sore assay, ... III. v. 21. 3
the *brother* deare Of that Argante . . . . III. xi. 3. 6
Whom when on ground his *brother* next beheld, ... IV. iii. 14. 1
evill plight, in which her dearest *brother* Now stood, ... IV. iii. 40. 7
First to her *brother,* whom she loved deare, ... IV. iii. 46. 6
Hate was the elder, Love the younger *brother;* . . . . IV. x. 32. 7
The whilest their eldest *brother* was away, ... IV. x. 42. 6
Cupid their eldest *brother;* . . . . IV. x. 42. 7
my younger *brother,* Amidas, ... V. iv. 9. 1
to my *brother* did ellope streight way, ... V. iv. 9. 8
My *brother* here declared hath to you: . . . . V. iv. 15. 3
his *brother* . . . tooke the roiall high degree, ... VI. ii. 28. 6
Titan . . . Was Saturnes elder *brother* . . . . VII. vi. 27. 2
knittest each to each, as *brother* unto *brother.* . . . . . . VII. vii. 14. 9
Brother's. *brothers* blood, the which at first was spilt . . . . *Ro.* xxiv. 12
the Poplar happely should rew Her *brothers* strokes, ... *Gn.* 220
each with *brothers* bloudie hand was slaine. . . . . *Gn.* 416
brothers death to wreak, Sansjoy doth chaleng . . . . I. iv. Arg.
That *brothers* hand shall dearely well requight, ... I. iv. 42. 6
th' inheritance . . . Of *brothers* prayse, ... I. iv. 48. 6
his *brothers* shield, which hong thereby: . . . . I. v. 10. 3
Arvirage his *brothers* place supplyde . . . . II. x. 51. 6
three Moones with borrowd *brothers* light . . . . III. iii. 16. 2
devoure Her native flesh and staine her *brothers* bowre, . . . III. vii. 49. 5
As in reversion of his *brothers* right ; . . . . IV. iii. 14. 7
throwne it up unto my *brothers* share: . . . . V. iv. 8. 4
Your *brothers* land the which the sea hath layd Unto your part, V. iv. 17. 3
Your *brothers* threasure, which from him is strayd, ... V. iv. 18. 3
Her *brothers* bones she scattered all about ; . . . . V. viii. 47. 4
Brought. Proud that so manie Gods she *brought* to light ; . *Ro.* vi. 3
Brought foorth those signes of your presumptuous boasts . . *Ro.* xv. 3
All that which Athens ever *brought* forth wise ; . . . . . . *Ro.* xxix. 9
All that which Afrike ever *brought* forth strange ; . . . . . *Ro.* xxix. 10
first garland of free Poesie That France *brought* forth, . . . *Ro.* Env. 2
brought forth in her last declining season, ... *Van.* i. 7
broughten this Oake to this miserye ; . . . . *S.C.* F. 212
I *brought* him up without the Dambe: . . . . *S.C.* Au. 39
seeldome chaunge the better *brought:* . . . . *S.C.* S. 69
mightie manhode *brought* a bedde of ease, ... *S.C.* O. 68
Yet saw I on the beare when it was *brought;* . . . . *S.C.* N. 161
from Indian seas *brought* far away ; . . . . *Gn.* 106
His worke he shortly to good purpose *brought,* . . . . *Gn.* 655
whom wicked fate Hath *brought* to Court, ... *Hub.* 893
shortly *brought* to hopelesse wretchednesse. . . . . *Hub.* 934
were all those plaints unto him *brought* . . . . *Hub.* 1252
forth with shame unto his judgement *brought.* . . . . *Hub.* 1376
ye three Twins, to light by Venus *brought,* . . . . *T.M.* 403
Her mightie hoast against my bulwarkes *brought,* . . . . . . *Ti.* 107
I saw him die, . . . and *brought* foorth on beare ; . . . . . *Ti.* 191
Worthie of heaven it selfe, which *brought* it forth. . . . . . *Ti.* 287
when most in perill it was *brought,* . . . . *Ti.* 624
untill it forth have *brought* Her long borne Infant, ... *D.* 31
harken well till it to ende bee *brought,* . . . . *D.* 97
brought away fast bound with silver chaine. . . . . *D.* 119
brought him presents, flowers if it were prime, ... *As.* 47
pure and spotlesse Cupid forth she *brought,* . . . . *Col.* 803

Brought—*Continued.*
being knit, they *brought* forth other kynds . . . . *Col.* 853
and *brought* forth chearfull day: . . . . *Col.* 856
At length it *brought* them to a hollowe cave . . . . I. i. 11. 6
The which at last out of the wood them *brought.* . . . . . . I. i. 28. 6
when that ydle dreame was to him *brought,* . . . . I. i. 46. 1
Who soone him *brought* into a secret part, ... I. ii. 5. 3
faire Hesperus . . . *brought* forth dawning light ; . . . . . . I. ii. 6. 7
The dwarfe him *brought* his steed ; . . . . I. ii. 6. 9
That many errant knights hath *broght* to wretchednesse. . . . I. ii. 34. 9
Then *brought* she me into this desert waste, ... I. ii. 42. 6
beautie *brought* t' unworthie wretchednesse . . . . I. iii. 1. 3
wished tydinges none of him unto her *brought.* . . . . I. iii. 3. 9
all . . . Unto this house he *brought,* . . . . I. iii. 18. 2
he to her *brought* part of his stolen things. . . . . I. iii. 18. 9
hard mishap . . . hath thee . . . *brought* to taste mine yre? . I. iii. 39. 3
So goodly *brought* them to the lowest stayre . . . . I. iv. 13. 5
whom he . . . slew, and *brought* to shamefull grave: . . . . . I. iv. 47. 6
forth have *brought* Th' eternall brood of glorie excellent: . . I. v. 1. 3
She is *ybrought* unto a paled greene, ... I. v. 5. 3
Heralds . . . to him *brought* the shield, ... I. v. 15. 9
Home is he *brought,* and layd in sumptuous bed, ... I. v. 17. 1
they . . . *brought* the heavy corse with easy pace . . . . . . I. v. 31. 2
From surging gulf two Monsters streight were *brought,* . . . I. v. 38. 3
Them *brought* to Aesculape, that by his art . . . . I. v. 39. 8
To Aesculapius *brought* the wounded knight: . . . . I. v. 41. 3
she . . . *Brought* forth this monstrous masse of earthly slyme, I. vii. 9. 8
Him to his castle *brought* with hastie forse, ... I. vii. 15. 8
The everburning lamps from thence it *braught,* . . . . I. vii. 18. 4
the Faery Queene it *brought* To Faerie lond, ... I. vii. 36. 8
'Faire Sir, I hope good hap hath *brought* You . . . . I. vii. 42. 5
brought not backe the balefull body dead: . . . . I. vii. 50. 5
To see his loved Squyre into such thraldom *brought:* . . . . I. viii. 15. 9
Squyre her . . . So *brought* unto his Lord as his deserved pray. I. viii. 25. 9
'Unto Old Timon he me *brought* bylive ; . . . . I. ix. 4. 1
what adventure . . . Hath *brought* you hither into Faery land, ... I. ix. 6. 4
wound . . . Me hither *brought* by wayes yet never found, . . . I. ix. 7. 6
brought unto him swords, ropes, poison, fire, ... I. ix. 50. 6
What grace hath thee now hither *brought* this way? . . . . . I. x. 9. 8
Whom, thus recover'd . . . they to Una *brought;* . . . . . . I. x. 29. 2
Charissa, late in child-bed *brought,* . . . . I. x. 29. 7
To her fayre Una *brought* this unacquainted guest. . . . . . I. x. 29. 9
The faulty soules . . . *brought* to his heavenly bowre. . . . . I. x. 40. 9
'Thence she thee *brought* into this Faery lond, ... I. x. 66. 1
brought thee up in ploughmans state to byde, ... I. x. 66. 5
a manchild forth I *brought* . . . . II. i. 53. 6
with one sword seven knightes I *brought* to end, ... II. iii. 17. 7
What hard mishap him *brought* to such distresse, ... II. iv. 16. 8
She *brought* to mischiefe through Occasion, ... II. iv. 17. 8
with him *brought* Pryene, ... II. iv. 28. 2
'let that message to thy Lord be *brought.*' . . . . II. iv. 44. 9
Now *brought* to him a flaming fyer brond, ... II. v. 22. 6
They bene *ybrought;* . . . . II. v. 38. 1
brought Unto the other side of that wide strond . . . . . . II. vi. 19. 1
shee soone to hond Her ferry *brought,* . . . . II. vi. 19. 5
Tho him she *brought* abord, ... II. vi. 38. 1
At last him to a litle dore he *brought,* . . . . II. vii. 24. 5
shortly *brought* Unto another rowme, ... II. vii. 35. 1
He *brought* him, through a darksom narrow strayt, ... II. vii. 40. 1
He *brought* him in. The rowme was large. . . . . II. vii. 43. 3
to guyde him backe, as he him *brought.* . . . . II. vii. 65. 9
backe againe him *brought* to living light. . . . . II. vii. 66. 4
to that shady delve him *brought* at last, ... II. viii. 4. 6
afford Which he had *brought* for Braggadochio vaine. . . . . II. viii. 19. 4
seven fold shield, which he from Guyon *brought,* . . . . . . II. viii. 32. 5
brought them up into her castle hall ; . . . . II. ix. 20. 2
Jett or Marble far from Ireland *brought;* . . . . II. ix. 24. 3
Thence she them *brought* into a stately Hall, ... II. ix. 27. 1
by a conduit pipe it thence were *brought:* . . . . II. ix. 32. 4
Was close convaid, and to the backgate *brought,* . . . . . . II. ix. 32. 7
soone into a goodly Parlour *brought,* . . . . II. ix. 33. 6
Up to a stately Turret she them *brought,* . . . . II. ix. 44. 8
brought them to the second rowme, ... II. ix. 53. 2
By sea to have bene from the Celticke maynland *brought.* . . . II. x. 5. 9
They *brought* forth Geaunts, ... II. x. 8. 8
he *brought* them to these salvage parts, ... II. x. 25. 8
shortly *brought* to civile governaunce, ... II. x. 38. 8
wholesome Statutes to her husband *brought.* . . . . II. x. 42. 6
An army *brought,* and with him batteile fought, ... II. x. 51. 2
brought with him the holy grayle, ... II. x. 53. 8
Hengist eke soon *brought* to shamefull death. . . . . II. x. 67. 6
halfe unwilling from their bookes them *brought,* . . . . . . II. x. 77. 8
the partes *brought* into their bondage: . . . . II. xi. 1. 8
to him *brought,* fresh batteill to renew ; . . . . II. xi. 28. 3
all his labor *brought* to happy end ; . . . . II. xi. 35. 2
had from hoggish forme him *brought* to naturall. . . . . . . II. xii. 86. 9
brought to grownd that never wast before ; . . . . III. i. 7. 7
Eftsoones them *brought* unto their Ladies sight, ... III. i. 31. 8
Thence they were *brought* to that great Ladies vew, ... III. i. 41. 1
what uncouth wind *Brought* her into those partes, ... III. ii. 4. 6
Thou have it lastly *brought* unto her Excellence. . . . . . . III. iii. 4. 9
Hath hither *brought* for succour to appele ; . . . . III. iii. 19. 8
shee bad her charett to be *brought;* . . . . III. iv. 31. 2
great grace or fortune thither *brought* Comfort . . . . III. v. 27. 3
Shee fownd, and *brought* it to her patient deare, ... III. v. 32. 8
Thither they *brought* that wounded Squyre, ... III. v. 41. 1
her that from deathes dore Me *brought?* . . . . III. v. 46. 3
many plaintes to her were *brought,* . . . . III. vi. 15. 3
what cause her *brought* Into that wildernesse . . . . III. vi. 20. 2

Brought—*Continued.*
Shee *brought* her to her joyous Paradize, . . . III. vi. 29. 1
Hither great Venus *brought* this infant fayre, . . . III. vi. 51. 1
She *brought* her forth into the worldes vew, . . . III. vi. 52. 3
what devill had her thither *brought*, . . . III. vii. 8. 2
by adventure *brought* Unto your dwelling, . . . III. vii. 8. 7
brought she was now to so hard constraint, . . . III. vii. 10. 7
the squirrell wild He *brought* to her in bands, . . . III. vii. 17. 7
Till her he had attaind and *brought* in place, . . . III. vii. 23. 4
many hath to foule confusion *brought*. . . . III. vii. 48. 4
Ere they into the lightsom world were *brought*, . . . III. vii. 48. 7
meant unto her prison to have *brought*, . . . III. vii. 51. 3
I with me *brought*, and did to her present: . . . III. vii. 55. 6
brutishly *brought* up, that nev'r did fashions see.' . . . III. vii. 57. 9
then she forth her *brought* Unto her sonne . . . III. viii. 9. 6
brought through points of many perilous swords: . . . III. viii. 17. 3
What hard misfortune *brought* me to this same; . . . III. viii. 23. 8
Removing her, into his charet *brought*, . . . III. viii. 35. 8
Thither he *brought* the sory Florimell, . . . III. viii. 38. 1
Another knight, whom tempest thither *brought*, . . . III. ix. 12. 2
They beene *ybrought* into a comely bowre, . . . III. ix. 19. 1
towres of Ilion . . . *Brought* unto balefull ruine, . . . III. ix. 34. 4
all unto their bowres were *brought*. . . . III. ix. 53. 9
what furie furst *Brought* thee from balefull house of Proserpine, . . . III. xi. 1. 2
mighty kings and kesars into thraldome *brought*. . . . III. xi. 29. 9
with force her *brought* From twentie Knights . . . IV. i. 2. 3
eke the Ladie selfe he *brought* away, . . . IV. i. 2. 7
Brought in that mask of love which late was showen; . . . IV. i. 3. 6
He seemed *brought* to bed in Paradise, . . . IV. ii. 9. 8
brought to nought by little bits? . . . IV. ii. 33. 9
That she might see her childrens thrids forth *brought*, . . . IV. ii. 50. 3
So Florimell with Ate forth was *brought*, . . . IV. iv. 10. 2
Whereof when newes to Triamond was *brought* . . . IV. iv. 33. 1
brought with her from thence that goodly belt away. . . . IV. v. 5. 9
Cambello *brought* into their view His faire Cambina, . . . IV. v. 10. 1
By view of all the fairest to him *brought*, . . . IV. v. 12. 8
Which being *brought*, about her middle small They thought to gird, . . . IV. v. 16. 3
brought forth speeches myld when she would have missayd. . . . IV. vi. 27. 9
'Ye gentle Knights, whom fortune here hath *brought* . . . IV. vi. 30. 2
at the length unto a bay he *brought* her, . . . IV. vi. 41. 3
Since I was *brought* into this dolefull den; . . . IV. vii. 13. 3
unhappy houre me thither *brought*, . . . IV. vii. 18. 1
Me hether *brought* with him as swift as wind, . . . IV. vii. 18. 7
Thence she them *brought* toward the place . . . IV. vii. 35. 1
what evill guide Them thether *brought*, . . . IV. viii. 21. 3
he her *brought* Unto his bay, . . . IV. viii. 48. 4
Him wretched thrall unto his dongeon *brought*, . . . IV. viii. 51. 8
'Then was I taken and before her *brought*, . . . IV. viii. 56. 1
Should wilfully be into thraldome *brought*, . . . IV. viii. 58. 7
have perforce him hether *brought* away.' . . . IV. viii. 62. 5
forth were *brought* to him above a score . . . IV. ix. 8. 4
being *brought* in daunger to relent too late. . . . IV. ix. 34. 9
when Paris *brought* his famous prise, . . . IV. xi. 19. 3
with him *brought* a present joyfully . . . IV. xi. 33. 7
she in time forth *brought* These three faire sons, . . . IV. xi. 42. 7
to his bed was *brought*, . . . IV. xii. 20. 8
thence Apollo, King of Leaches, *brought*. . . . IV. xii. 25. 4
So thence him farre she *brought* Into a cave . . . V. i. 6. 6
Is with the tide unto another *brought*: . . . V. ii. 39. 8
by him *brought* againe to Faerie land, . . . V. iii. 2. 3
So backe he *brought* Sir Marinell againe; . . . V. iii. 12. 1
Then forth he *brought* his snowy Florimele, . . . V. iii. 17. 1
So forth the noble Ladie was *ybrought*, . . . V. iii. 23. 1
in this coffer which she with her *brought* . . . V. iv. 13. 1
what cause *brought* that man to decay, . . . V. iv. 23. 6
him restoring . . . So *brought* unto his Lord, . . . V. iv. 25. 7
to this shame am *brought*, . . . V. iv. 27. 6
So being clad she *brought* him from the field, . . . V. v. 21. 1
sad tydings . . . Talus to her *brought*; . . . V. vi. 3. 4
Brought in untimely houre, ere it was sought: . . . V. vi. 3. 5
Then Britomart unto a bowre was *brought*, . . . V. vi. 23. 2
many *brought* to shame by treason treacherous. . . . V. vi. 32. 9
Thence forth unto the Idoll they her *brought*; . . . V. vii. 6. 1
forth she *brought* The fruitfull vine; . . . V. vii. 11. 2
She for a present to their Goddesse *brought*. . . . V. vii. 24. 5
Whereof when newes to Radigund was *brought*, . . . V. vii. 25. 1
Thenceforth she streight into a bowre him *brought*, . . . V. vii. 41. 1
brought that Damzell as his purchast pray; . . . V. viii. 26. 8
Commaunded straight his armour to be *brought*; . . . V. viii. 28. 3
He up did take, and with him *brought* away, . . . V. viii. 44. 3
misween'd for her owne Knight, That *brought* her backe: . . . V. viii. 46. 7
brought the pillage home, whence none could get it out. . . . V. ix. 4. 9
Eftsoones *brought* forth the villaine, . . . V. ix. 10. 2
So he it *brought* with him unto the knights, . . . V. ix. 18. 1
Those two strange nights were to her presence *brought*; . . . V. ix. 34. 2
Then was there *brought*, as prisoner to the barre, . . . V. ix. 38. 1
Was *brought* to her sad doome, . . . V. ix. 42. 9
many other crimes of foule defame Against her *brought*, . . . V. ix. 43. 3
reasons *brought* that no man could refute: . . . V. ix. 44. 4
He *brought* forth that old hag of hellish hew, . . . V. ix. 47. 3
The cursed Ate, *brought* her face to face, . . . V. ix. 47. 4
Then *brought* he forth . . . Abhorred Murder, . . . V. ix. 48. 1
Then *brought* he forth Sedition, . . . V. ix. 48. 5
Then *brought* he forth Incontinence of lyfe, . . . V. ix. 48. 7
brought that land to his subjection, . . . V. x. 9. 5
he had *brought* it now in servile bond, . . . V. x. 27. 1
Whereof when newes was to that Tyrant *brought*, . . . V. xi. 2. 1
Then in he *brought* her, . . . V. xi. 33. 5

Brought—*Continued.*
Surprized was, and to Grantorto *brought*, . . . V. xi. 39. 8
She forth was *brought* in sorrowfull dismay . . . V. xii. 12. 4
'Unhappy Squire! what hard mishap thee *brought* . . . VI. i. 12. 1
The Dwarfe . . . *Brought* aunswere backe, . . . VI. i. 31. 4
the boast of that proud Ladies threat . . . *brought* to this? . . . VI. i. 40. 6
till he him *brought* Unto the Castle . . . VI. iii. 2. 6
With bleeding wounds, *brought* home upon a beare . . . VI. iii. 4. 2
to what case her name should now be *brought*: . . . VI. iii. 6. 9
When Calidore . . . Unto his bowre was *brought*, . . . VI. iii. 9. 8
had weetingly Now *brought* her selfe, . . . VI. iii. 11. 8
till to her fathers house he had her *brought*. . . . VI. iii. 15. 9
Which answer . . . *brought* To Calepine, . . . VI. iii. 43. 3
in another Canto shall to end be *brought*. . . . VI. iii. 51. 9
A certaine herbe from thence unto him *brought*, . . . VI. iv. 12. 6
Thether he *brought* these unacquainted guests, . . . VI. iv. 14. 1
when that infant unto him she *brought*, . . . VI. iv. 38. 5
brought them also ease, . . . VI. v. 40. 3
If yet he were alive, or to destruction *brought*. . . . VI. vi. 37. 9
Thence he him *brought* away, . . . VI. vi. 39. 7
shortly *brought* Unto the barre . . . VI. vii. 36. 1
Ere she againe to Calepine was *brought*: . . . VI. vii. 50. 7
on their border Were *brought* by errour . . . VI. viii. 36. 4
If such a beast they saw, which he had thether *brought*. . . . VI. ix. 5. 9
brought home and noursed well As his owne chyld; . . . VI. ix. 14. 7
What time the golden apple was unto him *brought*. . . . VI. ix. 36. 9
when Coridon unto her *brought* . . . litle sparrowes . . . VI. ix. 40. 1
last forth *brought* The fruite of joy and blisse, . . . VI. ix. 45. 8
Have for more honor *brought* her to this place, . . . VI. x. 26. 8
at the last unto his will he *brought* her; . . . VI. x. 38. 3
Hither those Brigants *brought* their present pray, . . . VI. x. 43. 1
when faire Pastorell Into this place was *brought*, . . . VI. x. 43. 7
Were *brought* unto their Captaine, . . . VI. xi. 9. 8
Then forth the good old Meliboe was *brought*, . . . VI. xi. 11. 1
Unto their hellish dens those theeves them *brought*; . . . VI. xi. 41. 2
Like lyfull heat to nummed senses *brought*, . . . VI. xi. 45. 4
Unto the Castle of Belgard her *brought*, . . . VI. xii. 3. 3
in dew time a mayden child forth *brought*: . . . VI. xii. 6. 5
Till time that Calidore *brought* Pastorella thether. . . . VI. xii. 10. 9
sought Throughout the world, and to destruction *brought*. . . . VI. xii. 13. 5
Brought forth with him the dreadfull dog of hell, . . . VI. xii. 35. 2
brought Into like bands, ne maystred any more: . . . VI. xii. 39. 3
when all the earth she thus had *brought* To her behest, . . . VII. vi. 7. 1
brought againe on them eternall night; . . . VII. vi. 14. 7
He from his Jove such message to her *brought*, . . . VII. vi. 18. 6
brought forth with pompous showes Out of her bowre, . . . VII. vi. 41. 4
then into the open light they forth him *brought*. . . . VII. vi. 47. 9
Him thither *brought*, and her to him betraid? . . . VII. vi. 51. 6
Sweet fruit of pleasure, *brought* from Paradice . . . *Am.* lxxvii. 11
The Latmian shepherd once unto thee *brought*, . . . *Epith.* 380
Lo! one, whom later age hath *brought* to light, . . . *Com. Son.* iii. 9

Broughten. *See* **Brought.**

Brouze, -s. *See* **Browse, -s.**

Brow. I match with that sweet smile and chearfull *brow*, . . . *D.* 306
delay The rugged *brow* of carefull Policy, . . . *Ded. Son.* i. 12
hevens just with equall *brow* Vouchsafed . . . II. i. 50. 3
The Boaster at him sternely bent his *browe*, . . . III. x. 24. 1
Pierst through his bever quite into his *brow*, . . . IV. iii. 11. 8
with his *brow* . . . Made signe to them . . . VII. vi. 22. 1

Browed. *See* **Black-browed.**

Brown. *See* **Rusty-brown.**
helmes unbruzed wexen dayly *browne*. . . . *S.C.* O. 42
two blacke as pitch, And two were *browne*, . . . I. v. 28. 5
now round, now bright, now *browne* and gray; . . . VII. vii. 50. 8

Brows. Comes the breme Winter with chamfred *browes*, . . . *S.C.* F. 43
With hollow *browes* and greisly countenaunce, . . . *T.M.* 185
with bent lowring *browes*, . . . II. ii. 35. 7
Under the shadow of her even *browes*, . . . II. iii. 25. 2
Bent hollow beetle *browes*, . . . II. ix. 52. 6
her bright *browes* were deckt with borrowed haire; . . . III. xii. 14. 7
Bending her horned *browes*, did put her back; . . . VII. vi. 12. 6
sturdy March, with *brows* full sternly bent . . . VII. vii. 32. 3
his *browes* with sweat did reek and steem, . . . VII. vii. 40. 4
snowy *browes*, like budded Bellamoures; . . . *Am.* lxiv. 7

Browse. To *brouze*, or play, or what shee thought good: . . . *S.C.* May 179
brouze the woodbine twigges . . . *Gn.* 82

Browses. The whiles their Gotes upon the *brouzes* fedd, . . . III. x. 45. 8

Bruin. bold Sir *Bruin*, who is Lord Of all this land, . . . VI. iv. 29. 4
The good Sir *Bruin* growing farre in yeares, . . . VI. iv. 33. 6

Bruise. *bruze* with clownish fistes his manly face; . . . II. iv. 9. 2
Least they their finnes should *bruze*, . . . III. iv. 34. 5
Shee pownded small, and did in peeces *bruze*; . . . III. v. 33. 2
T' abate all spasme, and soke the swelling *bruze*; . . . III. v. 33. 7
rather did the more her beate and *bruse*: . . . VI. vii. 40. 5
such a Lady so to beate and *bruse*; . . . VI. vii. 45. 5

Bruised. *See* **Lately-bruised, To-bruised.**
being downe, is . . . *brouzed* and sorely hurt. . . . *S.C.* F. 236
therewith *bruzd* his brayne; . . . *S.C.* Jul. 226
often bounding on the *brused* gras, . . . I. xi. 15. 3
Sore *bruzed* with the fall he slow uprose, . . . II. v. 5. 1
Paridell sore *brused* with the blow . . . III. ix. 16. 6
their lately *bruzed* parts to bring in plight. . . . III. ix. 19. 9
of that Carle she sorely *bruz'd* had beene, . . . IV. vii. 35. 8
How scourgd, how crownd, how buffeted, how *brused*; . . . *H.H.L.* 243

Bruises. through the *bruses* of his former fight, . . . IV. i. 39. 8
all his wounds, and all his *bruses* guarisht; . . . IV. iii. 29. 5

Bruiseth. rod . . . With which he *bruseth* all his foes to dust, . . . *H.H.B.* 156

Bruising. with his hand him rashly *bruzing* slewe . . . *Gn.* 290
Of every place that was with *bruzing* harmd, . . . II. vi. 51. 4

Bruited. for eare-marked beasts abroad be *bruted*. . . . *Hub.* 188

Bruncheval. Hight *Bruncheval* the bold, who fiersly forth did ride. . . . IV. iv. 17. 9
Brunchildis. warreyd on *Brunchild* In Henault, . . . II. x. 21. 7
did sad *Brunchildis* see The greene shield dyde . . . II. x. 24. 6
Brunell. The third was *Brunell,* famous in his dayes; . . . V. iii. 5. 5
Brunt. the third *brunt* of this my fatall brond: . . . II. viii. 37. 8
The burden of the deadly *brunt* did beare . . . IV. viii. 42. 2
when as overblowen was that *brunt,* . . . V. xi. 59. 1
being readie met . . . at the instant *brunt,* . . . VI. xi. 9. 7
Too feeble I t' abide the *brunt* so strong, . . . *Am.* xii. 9
Bruse, -d, -s. *See* **Bruise,** *etc.*
Brush. passing by, did *brush* With his long tayle, . . . I. xi. 16. 8
With his stiffe oares did *brush* the sea so strong, . . . II. xii. 10. 2
All suddenly out of the thickest *brush,* . . . III. i. 15. 1
With his long taile the bryzes *brush* away. . . . VI. i. 24. 5
Brushed. *brusht* and battred them without remorse, . . . V. xii. 7. 4
Brusheth. their tender wings He *brusheth* oft, . . . I. i. 23. 9
Brushing. the proud Bird, . . . *brushing* his faire brest, . . . III. xi. 32. 7
Brust, -ing. *See* **Burst, -ing.**
Brute. *See* **Brutus.**
like *brute* beasts doo lie in loathsome den . . . *T.M.* 531
brute beasts, forst to refraine fro meat, . . . IV. iv. 47. 3
fortune, fraught with malice, blinde and *brute,* . . . VI. x. 38. 7
Bruted. *See* **Bruited.**
Bruteness. with thy *brutenesse* shendst thy comely age, . . . II. viii. 12. 3
Brutish. 'Why standst there (quoth he) thou *brutish* blocke? *S.C.* F. 127
blot his *brutish* name Unto the world, . . . *Hub.* 1240
ugly Barbarisme, And *brutish* Ignorance, . . . *T.M.* 188
the *brutish* nation to enwrap: . . . *As.* 98
With *brutish* barbarisme is overspredd: . . . *Ded. Son.* v. 4
most like a *brutish* beast, He spued up his gorge, . . . I. iv. 21. 8
A Satyre . . . kindling coles of lust in *brutish* eye, . . . I. vi. 22. 7
With beastly *brutish* rage gan him assay, . . . II. iv. 6. 7
How *brutish* is it not to understand . . . II. x. 69. 7
beastes, whose *brutish* pryde Mote breede him scath . . . III. i. 37. 7
doth base affections move In *brutish* mindes, . . . III. iii. 1. 6
for thy bad And *brutish* shape . . . III. iv. 55. 4
cast to love her in his *brutish* mind: . . . III. vii. 15. 8
brutish lust, that was so beastly tind. . . . III. vii. 15. 9
powring forth their bloud in *brutishe* wize, . . . V. x. 28. 8
In such a salvage wight, of *brutish* kynd, . . . VI. v. 29. 6
Brutishly. *brutishly* brought up, that nev'r did fashions see.' III. vii. 57. 9
Brutishness. With *brutishnesse* and beastlie filth hath stained. *T.M.* 270
close appeard in that rude *brutishnesse,* . . . IV. vii. 45. 5
bring in bondage of their *brutishnesse:* . . . V. xi. 44. 5
Brutus. Briton kings, From *Brute* to Uthers rayne; . . . II. x. Arg.
Brutus, anciently deriv'd From roiall stocke . . . II. x. 9. 6
Brute this Realme unto his rule subdewd, . . . II. x. 13. 1
The second *Brute,* the second both in name . . . II. x. 23. 2
each of *Brutus* boasted to be borne, . . . II. x. 36. 7
no moniment Of *Brutus,* nor of Britons glorie auncient. . . . II. x. 36. 9
'The Trojan *Brute* did first that citie fownd, . . . III. ix. 46. 1
that same *Brute,* whom much he did advaunce . . . III. ix. 48. 1
Brutus'. Here ended *Brutus* sacred progeny, . . . II. x. 36. 1
such as claymd themselves *Brutes* rightfull hayres, . . . II. x. 37. 5
Brutus warlicke sonne, Locrinus, . . . IV. xi. 38. 1
Bruzd, Bruzing, Bruze. *See* **Bruise, -d,** *etc.*
Bryzes. *See* **Breezes.**
Bubble. youngth is a *bubble* blown up with breath, . . . *S.C.* F. 87
Like a vaine *bubble* blowen up with ayre: . . . *Am.* lviii. 6
Bubble-glass. flesh, a *bubble-glas* of breath, . . . *Ti.* 50
Bubbles. the light *bubles* daunced all along, . . . II. xii. 10. 4
by the dauncing *bubbles* did divine, . . . II. ix. 30. 6
Bubbling. *bubbling* wave did ever freshly well, . . . I. vii. 4. 6
Beside a *bubling* fountaine low she lay, . . . II. i. 40. 2
Ne *bubling* rowndell they behinde them sent. . . . III. iv. 33. 7
Buck. *See* **Roebuck.**
(For he was swift as any *Bucke* in chace) . . . VI. iv. 8. 3
Buckle. gan him streight to *buckle* to the fight, . . . V. xii. 16. 8
Buckled. soone him *buckled* to the field. . . . I. vi. 41. 9
buckled with a golden tong. . . . I. vii. 30. 9
Therewith the Gyant *buckled* him to fight, . . . I. viii. 7. 1
Ere he were throughly *buckled* to his geare, . . . V. xi. 10. 2
Buckler. with her body, as a *buckler,* . . . IV. vii. 26. 4
Buckling. *buckling* him eftsoones unto the fight, . . . V. xi. 57. 8
buckling soone him selfe, gan fiercely fly . . . VI. viii. 12. 8
Bucks. *See* **Roebucks.**
Bud. How bragly it beginnes to *budde,* . . . *S.C.* Mar. 14
The blossomes of lust to *bud* did beginne, . . . *S.C.* May 187
As vertues braunch and beauties *budde,* . . . *S.C.* N. 88
the *budde* eke needes must quaile; . . . *S.C.* N. 91
the woodbine twigges that freshly *bud;* . . . *Gn.* 82
'He, noble *bud,* his Grandsires livelie hayre, . . . *Ti.* 267
you, fresh *budd* of vertue springing fast, . . . I. viii. 27. 1
there it might be fownd To *bud* out faire, . . . II. vi. 12. 9
They spring, they *bud,* they blossome fresh and faire, . . . II. vi. 15. 6
The trees did *bud,* and early blossomes bore; . . . II. vi. 24. 7
Whose tender *bud* to blossome new began, . . . II. viii. 5. 3
Of mortall life the leafe, the *bud,* the flowre; . . . II. xii. 75. 2
The *bud* of youth to blossome faire began, . . . III. v. 29. 8
Of all the weeds that *bud* and blossome there; . . . III. vi. 30. 8
any *bud* thereof doth scarse remaine, . . . IV. viii. 33. 2
whose silken leaves small Long shut up in the *bud* . . . VI. ii. 35. 8
when first the flowre Of beauty gan to *bud,* . . . VI. viii. 20. 2
did all winter as in sommer *bud,* . . . VI. x. 6. 5
The *bud* of joy, the blossome of the morne, . . . *Am.* lxi. 9
Budded. *See* **New-budded, Newly-budded.**
Keeping your beastes in the *budded* broomes: . . . *S.C.* F. 36
The eare that *budded* faire is burnt . . . *S.C.* D. 99
there in the *budded* broomes Beside them fed, . . . VI. ix. 5. 4

Budded—*Continued.*
To crop his thousand heads, the which still new Forth *budded,* VI. xii. 32. 5
flowres That freshly *budded* . . . VII. vii. 28. 3
like *budded* Bellamoures; . . . *Am.* lxiv. 7
Her paps lyke lyllies *budded,* . . . *Epith.* 176
Budding. seven heads, *budding* monstrous crimes anew, . . . *Bel.*[2] x. 12
Als my *budding* braunch thou wouldest cropp; . . . *S.C.* F. 58
with the *budding* rod Did rule the Jewes, . . . *Hub.* 439
many heades, out *budding* ever new, . . . I. vii. 17. 4
As *budding* braunch rent from the native tree, . . . II. ii. 2. 6
Like three faire branches *budding* farre and wide, . . . IV. ii. 43. 5
Budget. out of his *bouget* forth he drew . . . treasure, . . . III. x. 29. 1
Buds. bloosmes, wherewith your *buds* did flowre; . . . *S.C.* Ja. 34
My timely *buds* with wayling all are wasted; . . . *S.C.* Ja. 38
the bushes with bloosming *buds.* . . . *S.C.* May 8
With Hawthorne *buds,* and swete Eglantine, . . . *S.C.* May 13
any *buddes* of Poesie, . . . *S.C.* O. 73
paint with pallid greene her *buds* of gold. . . . *Gn.* 222
with their spredding armes Do beat their *buds,* . . . *T.M.* 78
those fresh *buds,* which wont so faire to flowre, . . . *T.M.* 249
Their tender *buds* or leaves to violate; . . . II. xii. 51. 4
Beates downe both leaves and *buds* without regard, . . . III. vi. 39. 8
Nor wicked beastes their tender *buds* did crop, . . . III. vi. 43. 5
wanton as a Kid whose horne new *buds:* . . . VII. vii. 33. 2
all the fairest flowres and freshest *buds* . . . VII. vii. 33. 7
lips, like rosy *buds* in May, . . . *H.B.* 258
Buegle. *See* **Bugle.**
Buff. The Sarazin, sore daunted with the *buffe,* . . . I. ii. 17. 1
so extremely did the *buffe* him quell, . . . I. xi. 24. 7
Nathelesse so sore a *buff* to him it lent, . . . II. v. 6. 8
Buffeted. How scourgd, how crownd, how *buffeted,* how brused; *H.H.L.* 243
Buffets. thy strong *buffets* and outrageous blowes, . . . III. iv. 9. 2
Buffs. with redoubled *buffes* them backe did put: . . . II. ii. 23. 4
Bug. As ghastly *bug,* does greatly them affeare: . . . II. iii. 20. 5
Bugle. Embost with *buegle* about the belt: . . . *S.C.* F. 66
Then tooke that Squire an horne of *bugle* small, . . . I. viii. 3. 5
Bugs. Be but as *bugs* to fearen babes withall, . . . II. xii. 25. 8
Build. *See* **Ybuilded.**
To *builde,* with levell of my loftie style, . . . *Ro.* xxv. 13
Wherein the byrds were wont to *build* their bowre, . . . *S.C.* Ja. 32
For the Shriche-owle to *build* her balefull bowre: . . . *Ti.* 130
builde your blis on hope of earthly thing, . . . *Ti.* 198
all of Christall did Panthea *build:* . . . II. x. 73. 4
In his free thought to *build* her sluggish nest, . . . III. v. 2. 2
Resolv'd to *build* his balefull mansion . . . III. x. 58. 2
Fit for Adicia there to *build* her wicked bowre. . . . V. ix. 1. 9
In which the fearefull ewftes do *build* their bowres, . . . V. x. 23. 7
I greater am in bloud (whereon I *build*) . . . VII. vi. 26. 8
Will *builde* an altar to appease her yre; . . . *Am.* xxii. 10
Builded. *See* **Built.**
Nigh to a castle *builded* strong and hye: . . . I. viii. 2. 2
wals and towres were *builded* high and strong . . . I. x. 55. 4
Bristow faire, which on his waves he *builded* hath. . . . IV. xi. 31. 9
Builder. The *builder* Oake, sole king of forrests all; . . . I. i. 8. 8
Buildest. *buildest* strong warke upon a weake ground: . . . *S.C.* May 145
Building. Threwe downe this *building* to the lowest stone. . . *Bel.*[1] ii. 14
pallid Yvie, *building* his owne bowre; . . . *Gn.* 675
Ne of so brave a *building* ought remained, . . . *Ti.* 559
till at last they see A goodly *building* bravely garnished; . . . I. iv. 2. 6
Which in that stately *building* wont to dwell: . . . I. viii. 32. 4
What stately *building* durst so high extend . . . I. x. 56. 7
To view the *building* of that uncouth place, . . . IV. xii. 4. 6
Whose goodly *building* when she did behould, . . . V. vii. 5. 3
The goodly *building* of her Palace bright, . . . VII. vi. 10. 2
Buildings. Greece will the olde Ephesian *buildings* blaze, . . *Ro.* ii. 3
Renewes herselfe with *buildings* rich and gay; . . . *Ro.* xxvii. 11
'To tell the beawtie of my *buildings* fayre, . . . *Ti.* 85
Their banket houses burne; their *buildings* race; . . . II. xii. 83. 8
Her stately towres and *buildings* sunny sheene, . . . V. x. 25. 5
antique Babel . . . Upreard her *buildinges* to the threatned skie: *Com. Son.* iv. 2
not so fayre her *buildinges* to behold As Lewkenors stile . . . *Com. Son.* iv. 13
Builds. perfect pleasure *buildes* her joyous bowre, . . . *Gn.* 135
buildes so stronglie on so frayle a soyle, . . . *Ti.* 513
spotlesse Pleasure *builds* her sacred bowre. . . . *Am.* lxv. 14
Built. *See* **Builded.**
on sand was *built* the goodly frame: . . . *Bel.*[2] xiv. 4
these old Romane works, *built* with your hands, . . . *Ro.* xv. 13
where the Eagle *built* his towring nest, . . . *Van.* iv. 6
huge Colosses *built* with costlie paine, . . . *Ti.* 409
Was (O great pitie!) *built* of brickle clay, . . . *Ti.* 499
Built all of richest stone that might bee found, . . . *Ti.* 506
Had lately *built* his hatefull mansion; . . . *Mui.* 246
In whose high thoughts Pleasure hath *built* her bowre, . . . *Ded. Son.* viii. 6
A stately Pallace *built* of squared bricke, . . . I. iv. 4. 1
The house of endlesse paine is *built* thereby, . . . I. v. 33. 7
there beside of marble stone was *built* An Altare, . . . I. viii. 36. 1
The new Hierusalem, that God has *built* . . . I. x. 57. 2
that bright towre, all *built* of christall clene, . . . I. x. 58. 5
Built on a rocke adjoyning to the seas: . . . II. ii. 12. 7
a broad gate all *built* of beaten gold: . . . II. vii. 40. 2
Not *built* of bricke, ne yet of stone and lime, . . . II. ix. 21. 4
king Nine whilome *built* Babell towre. . . . II. ix. 21. 6
It was a vaut *ybuilt* for great dispence, . . . II. ix. 29. 1
that, which antique Cadmus whylome *built* In Thebes, . . . II. ix. 45. 6
towre That God hath *built* for his owne blessed bowre. . . . II. ix. 47. 5
built Cairleill, and *built* Cairleon strong. . . . II. x. 25. 3
built that gate which of his name is hight, . . . II. x. 46. 6
He of his name Coylchester *built* of stone and lime. . . . II. x. 58. 9
He *built* by art upon the glassy See . . . II. x. 73. 8
her bowre Is *built* of hollow billowes heaped hye, . . . III. iv. 43. 2

Built—*Continued.*
A little cottage, *built* of stickes and reedes . . . . III. vii. 6. 2
built Nausicle by the Pontick shore; . . . . III. ix. 37. 3
Troynovant was *built* of old Troyes ashes cold. . . . . III. ix. 38. 9
There was an Altar *built* of pretious stone . . . . III. xi. 47. 2
Much more then that which was in Paphos *built,* . . . . . . IV. x. 5. 6
It was a bridge *ybuilt* in goodly wize . . . . IV. x. 6. 6
That Romaine Monarch *built* a brasen wall, ... IV. xi. 36. 2
Where he with boughes hath *built* his shady stand, ... V. viii. 35. 8
before this Castle greene *Built* a faire Chappell, ... V. x. 28. 2
a thousand birds had *built* their bowres . . . . VII. vii. 28. 4
Her temple fayre is *built* within my mind, ... *Am.* xxii. 5
His throne is *built* upon Eternity, ... *H.H.B.* 152
Bulk. it shakes the bottome of the *bulke,* . . . . V. xi. 29. 3
Bull. I saw a *Bull* as white as driven snowe, ... *Van.* ii. 2
how Jove did abuse Europa like a *Bull,* . . . . *Mui.* 278
it true Sea, and true *Bull,* ye would weene. . . . . *Mui.* 280
Before the *Bull* she pictur'd winged Love, ... *Mui.* 289
as a blindfold *Bull,* at randon fares, ... II. iv. 7. 8
salvage *Bull,* whom two fierce mastives bayt, ... II. viii. 42. 1
lov'd a *Bul,* and learnd a beast to bee. . . . . III. ii. 41. 6
like a *Bull,* Europa to withdraw: . . . . III. xi. 30. 6
the *Bull* which fayre Europa bore: . . . . V. Pr. 5. 9
And eke the *Bull* hath with his bow-bent horne . . . . V. Pr. 6. 1
Like a wylde *Bull,* that, being at a bay, ... VI. v. 19. 1
Like a fierce *Bull,* that being busie bent . . . . VI. vi. 27. 4
having at a bay A salvage *Bull,* . . . . VI. vii. 47. 2
Upon a *Bull* he rode, ... VII. vii. 33. 3
Bullet. Engin, . . . ramd with *bollet* rownd, ordaind to kill, . I. vii. 13. 4
Bullion. all of purest *bullion* framed were, ... III. i. 32. 6
Bullock. Seest howe brag yond *Bullocke* beares, ... *S.C.* F. 71
Like as a *bullocke,* that in bloudy stall . . . . VI. xii. 30. 7
Bulls. They looken bigge as *Bulls* that bene bate, ... *S.C.* S. 44
bigge *Bulles* of Basan brace hem about, ... *S.C.* S. 124
wyld roring *Buls* he would him make To tame, ... I. vi. 24. 6
when in Cymbrian plaine An heard of *Bulles,* . . . complaine, . I. viii. 11. 6
Beares, Lyons, and *Buls,* which romed them arownd. . . . . III. i. 14. 9
As two fierce *Buls,* that strive the rule to get . . . . IV. iv. 18. 3
The raging *Buls* rebellow through the wood, ... IV. x. 46. 4
Bulrushes. 'To make . . . Baskets of *bulrushes,* . . . . *S.C.* D. 80
Bulwark. the Squire . . . did like a *bulwarke* stand. . . . . . . I. viii. 12. 9
Them on her *bulwarke* beares, ... II. viii. 35. 9
unto each a *Bulwarke* did arrett, ... II. xi. 7. 3
against the *bulwarke* of the Sight . . . . II. xi. 9. 1
Beautie and Money, they that *Bulwarke* sorely rent. . . . . . II. xi. 9. 9
The second *Bulwarke* was the Hearing sence, ... II. xi. 10. 1
the fourth *Bulwarke,* that is the Taste, ... II. xi. 12. 2
Against that same fift *bulwarke* they continued fight. . . . . II. xi. 13. 9
like a *bulwarke* firmely did abyde, ... V. x. 35. 4
Bulwarks. Her mightie hoast against my *bulwarkes* brought, . *Ti.* 107
Against the five great *Bulwarkes* of that pyle, ... II. xi. 7. 2
hideous Ordinaunce Upon the *Bulwarkes* cruelly did play, . . II. xi. 14. 4
Bunch. on his craven crest A *bounch* of heares . . . . I. ii. 11. 6
A *bounch* of heares discolourd diversly, ... I. vii. 32. 2
on his arme a *bounch* of keyes he bore, ... I. viii. 30. 6
he . . . key found not at all Emongst that *bounch* . . . . . I. viii. 37. 5
lyke to a *bounch* of Cullambynes; . . . . *Am.* lxiv. 10
Bunches. vine, Whose *bounches* hanging downe seemd to entice II. xii. 54. 3
Knotted with blood in *bounches* rudely ran; . . . . III. v. 29. 6
Bunduca. *See* **Bonduca.**
Burbon. *See* **Bourbon.**
Burden. Findes greater *burthen* of his miserie. . . . . *T.M.* 306
the huge *burden* of my cares unlade. . . . . *D.* 489
sway The *burdeine* of this kingdom mightily, ... *Ded. Son.* i. 10
The *burdein* of this kingdomes governement, ... *Ded. Son.* ix. 4
Against the day of wrath to *burden* thee? . . . . I. ix. 46. 5
my wombe her *burdein* would forbeare, ... II. i. 53. 4
His double *burden* did him sore disease. . . . . II. ii. 12. 4
to be easd of that base *burden* still did erne. . . . . II. iii. 46. 9
As if that age badd him that *burden* spare, ... III. i. 4. 5
Till thy wombes *burden* thee from them do call, ... III. iii. 28. 6
Till that unweeldy *burden* she had reard, ... III. vi. 10. 4
She threw away her *burden* angrily; . . . . III. vii. 44. 2
opprest With *burdein* of great treasure, ... III. x. 41. 5
who nill bide the *burden* of distresse, ... III. xi. 14. 8
heavy eyes with natures *burdein* deare, ... III. xi. 55. 7
Borne at one *burden* in one happie morne; . . . . IV. ii. 41. 4
The *burden* of the deadly brunt did beare . . . . IV. viii. 42. 2
auncient heavy *burden* which he bore . . . . IV. xi. 26. 3
with it beare the *burden* of defame, ... V. i. 28. 8
As rated Spaniell takes his *burden* up for feare. . . . . . . V. i. 29. 9
forst the *burden* of their prize to stay. . . . . V. iii. 11. 4
Beare off the *burden* of her raging yre: . . . . V. v. 16. 4
He threw his *burden* downe, and fast away did fly. . . . . . V. ix. 14. 9
eke to th' earth his *burden* with him bare; . . . . V. xi. 9. 2
The heavy *burden* of whose dreadfull might . . . . VI. i. 22. 1
To beare this *burden* on your dainty backe; . . . . VI. ii. 47. 8
would beare behinde a *burden* of such scorne. . . . . VI. iii. 31. 9
heavy armes . . . Whose *burden* mote empeach his needfull speed, ... VI. iv. 19. 2
Rather then once his *burden* to sustaine: . . . . VI. vii. 46. 7
unable to support So huge a *burden* . . . . VI. viii. 16. 7
'Not that the *burden* of so bold a guest Shall chargefull be, . . VI. ix. 32. 1
clogd with *burden* of mortality; . . . . *Am.* lxxii. 4
Burdened. *See* **Overburdened.**
heaped snowe *burdned* him so sore, ... *S.C.* F. 233
Burdenous. Three things to beare bene very *burdenous,* . . . *S.C.* May 132
to kepe is a *burdenous* smart: . . . . *S.C.* S. 16
Her soule unbodied of the *burdenous* corpse. . . . . *S.C.* N. 166
with his *burdenous* blowes him sore did overlade. . . . . . V. xii. 19. 9
Burdens. all *burdens,* that a man can beare, ... *S.C.* May 140
Burganet. *See* **Burgonet.**
Burgeon. hasting Prime did make them *burgein* round. . . . VII. vii. 43. 8
Burgonet. Upon his head his glistering *Burganet,* . . . . . . *Mui.* 73
it empierst the Pagans *burganet;* . . . . II. viii. 45. 3
from his head his heavy *burganet* did light. . . . . III. v. 31. 9
Burial. after death and *buriall* done, ... I. x. 43. 1
Religious reverence doth *buriall* teene; . . . . II. i. 59. 6
Buried. lyeth *buryed* long in Winters bale; . . . . *S.C.* N. 84
That did her *buried* body hould. . . . . *S.C.* N. 159
the light of simple veritie *Buried* in ruines, ... *Ti.* 172
His boystrous club, so *buried* in the grownd, ... I. viii. 10. 1
great good . . . Should . . . *buried* be in thankles thought. . . I. ix. 2. 9
in oblivion ever *buried* is; . . . . II. iii. 40. 4
As one in wilfull bale for ever *buried.* . . . . III. ii. 31. 9
He was surprisd, and *buried* under beare, ... III. iii. 11. 2
For ever dye, and ever *buried* bee . . . . III. vi. 47. 2
'Troy, that . . . in thine ashes *buried* low dost lie, ... III. ix. 33. 2
buried in the ground from jeopardy, ... III. x. 42. 4
both are fallen, . . . And *buried* now in their own ashes ly; . *Com. Son.* iv. 7
Burly. *See* **Hurly-burly.**
Burn. thinking yet on her I *burne* and quake; . . . . *Pet.* vi. 2
once assai'd to *burne* this world so wide. . . . . *Gn.* 376
the ships which they did seeke to *burne.* . . . . *Gn.* 512
Where Phlegeton with quenchles flames doth *burne;* . . . . . *Gn.* 622
Yet did she inly fret and felly *burne,* . . . . *Mui.* 343
inflames the skyen With fire not made to *burne,* . . . . . . I. iv. 9. 9
The forlorne mayd did with loves longing *burne,* . . . . . . I. vi. 22. 1
Did *burne* with wrath, and sparkled living fyre: . . . . I. xi. 14. 2
should not be quenched . . . , but *burnen* ever bright. . . . . I. xii. 37. 9
Gan *burne* in filthy lust; . . . . II. iii. 42. 5
Burnt I doe burne. . . . . II. iv. 38. 5
'I *burne,* I *burne,* I *burne!*' then lowd he cryde, ... II. vi. 44. 1
'O! how I *burne* with implacable fyre; . . . . II. vi. 44. 2
Their banket houses *burne;* their buildings race; . . . . . . II. xii. 83. 8
whose fiery feete did *burne* The verdant gras . . . . III. i. 5. 5
the greene grasse that groweth they shall *bren,* . . . . . . III. iii. 34. 8
now all Britany doth *burne* in armes bright. . . . . III. iii. 52. 9
all too long I *burne* with envy sore . . . . III. iv. 2. 3
To *burn* the same with unquenchable fire, ... III. ix. 17. 7
Misdeeming sure that her those flames did *burne;* . . . . . . III. xii. 45. 5
this doth hatred make in love to *brenne,* . . . . IV. iii. 45. 7
Doth *burne* the earth and boyled rivers drie, ... IV. iv. 47. 2
He gan to *burne* in rage, ... V. xi. 2. 6
She gan to *burne* in her ambitious spright, ... VII. vi. 10. 5
when it once doth *burne,* it doth divide . . . . *Am.* vi. 7
I *burne* much more in boyling sweat, ... *Am.* xxx. 7
What then remaines but I to ashes *burne,* . . . . *Am.* xxxii. 13
Not water; for her love doth *burne* like fyre: . . . . *Am.* lv. 6
a thousand torches flaming bright Doe *burne,* . . . . *Epith.* 411
streight to *burne* at first beholders sight. . . . . *H.B.* 210
Burned. *See* **Burnt.**
So whot she *burned* in that lustfull fyre; . . . . III. vii. 49. 8
wide nosethrils *burnd* With breathed flames, ... III. ix. 22. 3
when he marked how his money *burnd,* . . . . III. x. 15. 3
Like lightening flash that hath the gazer *burned,* . . . . . . V. viii. 38. 1
he streightway with haughtie choler *burned,* . . . . VI. ii. 12. 3
Burnest. Most sacred fyre, that *burnest* mightily . . . . III. iii. 1. 1
Burning. *See* **Bright-burning, Dew-burning, Ever-burning, Fair-burning, Heart-burning, Hot-burning, Lamp-burning.**
'Ne feard the *burning* waves of Phlegeton, ... *Gn.* 441
A *burning* Teade about his head did move, ... *Mui.* 293
Beautie, the *burning* lamp of heavens light, ... *Col.* 873
the flashing fier flies, . . . out of their *burning* shields; . . . I. ii. 17. 8
in his hand a *burning* hart he bare, ... I. iv. 25. 3
in his hand a *burning* brond he hath, ... I. iv. 33. 3
burning all with rage, He to him lept, ... I. iv. 39. 4
burning blades about their heades doe blesse, ... I. v. 6. 4
with blade all *burning* bright . . . . I. viii. 10. 5
burning starres and everliving fire, ... I. x. 50. 6
As *burning* Aetna from his boyling stew . . . . I. xi. 44. 5
high her *burning* torch set up in heaven bright. . . . . . . I. xi. 49. 9
Witnesse the *burning* Altars, which he swore, ... I. xii. 27. 5
He hath a sword that flames like *burning* brond. . . . . . . II. iii. 18. 5
His *burning* eyen, whom bloody strakes did staine, ... II. iv. 15. 5
in Stygian lake, ay *burning* bright, Had kindled: . . . . . . II. v. 22. 7
Burning in flames, yet no flames can I see, ... II. vi. 45. 3
hundred fournaces all *burning* bright: . . . . II. vii. 35. 5
a mightie fornace, *burning* whott, ... II. ix. 29. 6
burning both with fervent fire . . . . II. ix. 60. 6
having quencht her *burning* fier-brands, ... II. xi. 47. 5
With *burning* charet wheeles it nigh to smite; . . . . III. vii. 41. 7
two *burning* lampes she set . . . . III. viii. 7. 1
Ne ought your *burning* fury mote abate; . . . . III. viii. 28. 7
the *burning* hart which on his brest He bare, ... III. viii. 45. 4
the *burning* torment which he felt; . . . . III. xi. 27. 3
There was he painted full of *burning* dartes, ... III. xi. 44. 8
Shame *burning* brond-yrons in her hand did hold: . . . . . . III. xii. 24. 8
yron tongs did take Out of the *burning* cinders, ... IV. v. 44. 3
In case his *burning* lust should breake into excesse, ... IV. ix. 18. 9
all *burning* with a fresh desire . . . . IV. ix. 29. 1
burning all to ashes powr'd it downe the brooke. . . . . . . V. ii. 27. 9
inly *burning* To be avenged . . . . V. vi. 31. 1
Her *burning* tongue with rage inflamed hath, ... V. viii. 49. 2
Burning with inward rancour and despight, ... VI. v. 18. 2
therein to beare Nights *burning* lamp, ... VII. vi. 12. 3
eft his *burning* levin-brond in hand he tooke. . . . . VII. vi. 30. 9
Burning in flames of pure and chast desyre: . . . . *Am.* xxii. 12
For feare of *burning* her sunshyny face, ... *Epith.* 119

Burning—*Continued.*
To quench the flame which they in *burning* fynd; . . . . . . *H.L.* 102
lampe doth yet remaine Fresh *burning* . . . . . . *H.L.* 132
Adornd with thousand lamps of *burning* light, ... *H.H.L.* 59
and set thee all on fire With *burning* zeale, ... *H.H.L.* 271
And those eternall *burning* Seraphins, ... *H.H.B.* 94
Burnished. *See* **Bright-burnished.**
shields of brasse that shone like *burnisht* golde, ... *Van.* vi. 3
The one faire fram'd of *burnisht* Yvory, ... I. i. 40. 2
hilts were *burnisht* gold, and handle strong Of mother perle; I. vii. 30. 8
some were of *burnisht* gold, ... II. xii. 55. 1
in a cote of plate *Burnisht* with bloudie rust; . . . . . . V. viii. 29. 2
Burns. my heart yet *burnes* in paine. . . . . . . *Pet.*[1] v. 12
yet my heart *burnes* in exceeding paine . . . . . . *Pet.*[2] v. 12
for which intent He inly *burns*, ... *Gn.* 275
his brother *burns* in furious fyre. . . . . . . II. vi. Arg.
his whott fyre *burnes* in mine entralles bright, ... II. vi. 50. 4
Burnt. *See* **Brent.**
Burnt up his yong ones, and himselfe distrest; . . . . . . *Van.* iv. 8
The eare that budded faire is *burnt* . . . . . . *S.C.* D. 99
my sommer *burnt* up quite; . . . . . . *S.C.* D. 128
the East . . . *Burnt* th' Attick towres, ... *Gn.* 44
he *burnt* with gealous fire; . . . . . . I. ii. 5. 6
When nigh he drew . . . He *burnt* in fire; . . . . . . I. iii. 34. 3
burnt his beastly hart t' efforce her chastitye. . . . . . . I. vi. 4. 9
The God himselfe, . . . *burnt* in his intent; . . . . . . I. vi. 15. 7
With firie zeale he *burnt* in courage bold . . . . . . I. ix. 37. 4
Whom fyrie steele now *burnt*, that erst him armd; . . . . . . I. xi. 27. 8
Burnt I doe burne. . . . . . . II. iv. 38. 5
The driest wood is soonest *burnt* to dust. . . . . . . III. viii. 25. 5
ever when he *burnt* in lustfull fire, ... IV. vii. 19. 8
My children and my people, *burnt* in flame . . . . . . V. xi. 19. 7
eke many a one *Burnt* in her love, ... VI. ix. 10. 3
inly *burnt* with flames most raging whot, ... VI. xi. 4. 2
Burst. *See* **Brast.**
wrathfull winde . . . *burst* out of Scithian mew, ... *Bel.*[2] viii. 12
Made him to swell, that nigh his bowells *brust.* . . . . . . *Van.* vi. 10
nigh with griefe thereof my heart was *brust.* . . . . . . *Ti.* 518
Least that his toyle should of their troups be *brust.* . . . . . . *As.* 106
Their bellies swolne he saw with fulnesse *burst*, ... I. i. 26. 5
into termes of open outrage *brust*, ... III. i. 48. 2
kindled heat that soone in flame forth *brust:* . . . . . . III. viii. 25. 4
eke thy childrens thrids to be asunder *burst!*' . . . . . . IV. ii. 49. 9
when his speare was *brust*, his sword he drew, ... IV. iv. 41. 3
as if her hart Would quite have *burst* . . . . . . IV. xii. 11. 9
into bitter termes forth *brust*, ... V. viii. 22. 4
her entrailes . . . the which, once being *brust*, ... V. xi. 31. 4
no lesse Then all the rest *burst* out to all outragiousnesse. . . . V. xii. 2. 9
it to ripenesse grew and forth to honour *burst.* . . . . . . VI. Pr. 3. 9
He *burst* into these wordes, ... VI. ii. 24. 9
so dolefull dreare, That he these words *burst* forth: . . . . . . VI. iii. 4. 6
Titans beames forth *brust* Through the thicke clouds . . . . VI. iii. 13. 5
all their statutes *burst:* . . . . . . VII. vi. 5. 4
Bursting. *brusting* forth in laughter, ... III. iii. 19. 2
Bursting forth teares like springs out of a banke), ... V. i. 15. 2
bursting forth in teares, ... V. x. 20. 3
Then *bursting* forth in teares, ... VI. viii. 19. 1
Bush. *See* **Bramble-bush, Holly-bush, May-bush.**
Where in a *bush* he did him hide, ... *S.C.* Mar. 32
I bent my bolt against the *bush*, ... *S.C.* Mar. 70
I beate the *bush*, the byrds to them doe flye: . . . . . . *S.C.* O. 17
The *bush* my bedde, the bramble was my bowre, ... *S.C.* D. 65
On everie *bush*, and everie hollow rocke, ... *Gn.* 235
crept into a *bush*, ... II. iii. 21. 3
Unto the *bush* her eye did suddein glaunce, ... II. iii. 34. 2
in the *bush* he lay, ... II. iii. 43. 5
both over banck and *bush*, ... III. i. 17. 5
He in a *bush* did hyde his fearefull hedd. . . . . . . III. x. 44. 2
out of the *bush* . . . he crept full light, ... III. x. 47. 1
Ne banck nor *bush* could stay him, ... III. x. 55. 3
Then to a *bush* himselfe he did transforme; . . . . . . V. ix. 17. 3
he the *bush* did beat, ... V. ix. 17. 4
layd her underneath a *bush* to sleepe, ... VI. iii. 44. 6
Enclos'd the *bush* about, and there him tooke, ... VII. vi. 47. 4
Within a *bush* his dreadfull head doth hide, ... *Am.* liii. 3
Bushes. in his small *bushes* used to shrowde . . . . . . *S.C.* F. 122
For birds in *bushes* tooting, ... *S.C.* Mar. 66
the *bushes* with bloosming buds. . . . . . . *S.C.* May 8
doth shrowde Emong the *bushes* rancke? . . . . . . *S.C.* Jul. 4
With briers and *bushes* all to-rent and scratcht; . . . . . . IV. vii. 8. 3
hid themselves in holes and *bushes* from his vew. . . . . . . V. ii. 53. 9
Through hils and dales, through *bushes* and through breres, . VI. viii. 32. 1
drew a litle space Behind the *bushes*, ... VI. xii. 8. 6
Bushes'. Lay sleeping soundly in the *bushes* shade, ... VI. xi. 38. 4
Bushy. All in the shadowe of a *bushye* brere, ... *S.C.* D. 2
the *bushie* shrubs which growe thereby. . . . . . . *Gn.* 80
Scattred with *bushy* thornes and ragged breares, ... I. x. 35. 3
the *bushy* Teade a groome did light, ... I. xii. 37. 6
Busied. He is with greater matter *busied* Than a Lambe, . . . *Hub.* 1215
Deepe *busied* bout worke of wondrous end, ... III. iii. 14. 7
Whilest thus they *busied* were bout Florimell, ... V. iii. 29. 1
Bout which whilest he was *busied* thus hard, ... VI. v. 11. 1
Busily. thereupon did raise full *busily* . . . . . . *Gn.* 659
seeking all the forrest *busily*, ... *Hub.* 1319
she her selfe thus *busily* did frame . . . . . . II. ii. 16. 1
Shee softly felt, and rubbed *busily*, ... III. ii. 34. 4
he him selfe so *busily* addrest, ... III. viii. 35. 5
sparks . . . Which still he blew and kindled *busily*, ... III. xii. 9. 8
Full *busily* unto his worke ybent; . . . . . . IV. v. 34. 2
feare His ydle braine gan *busily* molest, ... IV. v. 43. 7

Busily—*Continued.*
full *busily* About their holy things . . . . . . V. vii. 17. 7
Then all their helpes they *busily* applyde . . . . . . VI. xi. 22. 3
Business. let us turne to our first *businesse.* . . . . . . *Gn.* 64
he would learne their *busines* secretly, ... *Hub.* 879
sternely bad him other *businesse* plie . . . . . . I. vi. 46. 7
Ne other worldly *busines* did apply: . . . . . . I. x. 46. 7
They did about their *businesse* sweat, and sorely toyld. . . . II. ix. 30. 9
Th' uneven nomber for this *busines* is most fitt.' . . . . . . III. ii. 50. 9
Yet list them bid their *businesse* to unfold, ... III. iii. 15. 3
Whom she thought fittest for that *businesse;* . . . . . . V. iv. 48. 2
Busiran(e). *See* **Busyrane.**
Buskets. To gather May *bus-kets* and smelling brere: . . . . *S.C.* May 10
Buskin. teache her tread aloft in *buskin* fine, ... *S.C.* O. 113
The Stage with Tragick *buskin* to adorne, ... *T.M.* 152
Buskins. Diana he her takes to be, But misseth . . . *buskins* I. vi. 16. 9
embayld In gilden *buskins* of costly Cordwayne, ... II. iii. 27. 3
had unlaste Her silver *buskins* . . . . . . III. vi. 18. 3
on her legs she painted *buskins* wore, ... V. v. 3. 1
Buskins he wore of costliest cordwayne, ... VI. ii. 6. 1
Buss. every Satyre first did give a *busse* To Hellenore; . . . . III. x. 46. 3
Busses. every Satyre first did give a busse . . . so *busses* did abound. . . . . . . III. x. 46. 4
Bustling. I heard a busie *bustling.* . . . . . . *S.C.* Mar. 69
Busy. I heard a *busie* bustling. . . . . . . *S.C.* Mar. 69
finde nought to *busie* me: . . . . . . *T.M.* 166
takes survey, with curious *busie* eye, ... *Mui.* 171
Counted but toyes to *busie* ydle braines; . . . . . . *Col.* 704
paynd himselfe with *busie* care to reare Her out of carelesse swowne. . . . . . . I. ii. 45. 3
chase the salvage beast with *busie* payne, ... I. vi. 21. 8
thrise he her reviv'd with *busie* paine. . . . . . . I. vii. 24. 4
all this while was *busy* at her beades; . . . . . . I. x. 8. 3
wants she health, or *busie* is elswhere?' . . . . . . I. x. 16. 3
every feend his *busie* paines applyde . . . . . . II. vii. 35. 8
backe againe turning his *busie* hond, ... II. viii. 41. 6
she had cause to *busie* them withall; . . . . . . II. xii. 15. 3
displayd The clothes about her round with *busy* ayd; . . . . III. ii. 47. 5
She cast to comfort him with *busie* paine . . . . . . III. v. 31. 5
Busie (as seem'd) about some wicked gin: . . . . . . III. vii. 7. 3
chaunst Malbecco *busie* be elsewhere, ... III. x. 12. 2
all men *busie* to suppresse the flame, ... III. x. 16. 2
as she backward cast her *busie* eye . . . . . . III. xi. 50. 1
With *busie* care they strove him to awake, ... IV. i. 43. 6
day and night employ'd his *busie* paine . . . . . . V. xii. 26. 3
So well he did his *busie* paines apply, ... VI. iii. 28. 1
Of this wyld man, whom they full *busie* found . . . . . . VI. v. 25. 2
Bull . . . *busie* bent To fight with many foes . . . . . . VI. vi. 27. 4
After he gotten had with *busie* paine Some of their weapons . VI. vi. 38. 7
with full *busie* care His bloudy vessels wash, ... VI. viii. 39. 8
Like as an huswife, that with *busie* care . . . . . . VII. vi. 48. 1
Them well disposed by his *busie* paine, ... VII. vii. 4. 7
Busying. *busying* his quicke eies her face to view, ... I. ii. 26. 6
Busyrane. Assayes the house of *Busyrane*, ... III. xi. Arg.
Why then is *Busirane* with wicked hand Suffred, ... III. xi. 10. 7
that same vile Enchauntour *Busyran*, ... IV. i. 3. 1
But (*partial list*).
nought in this worlde *but* griefe endures. . . . . . . *Bel.*[1] iii. 12
that which *but* the picture is of thee. . . . . . . *Ro.* v. 4
But by her selfe, her equall match could see. . . . . . . *Ro.* vi. 8
Were first enclosures *but* of salvage soyle; . . . . . . *Ro.* xviii. 2
This Citie, which was first *but* shepheards shade, ... *Ro.* xx. 9
hath left *but* feeble holde, ... *Ro.* xxviii. 4
left of it *but* these olde markes . . . . . . *Ro.* xxx. 11
alas! *but* now my spring begonne, ... *S.C.* Ja. 29
Thy wast bignes *but* combers the grownd, ... *S.C.* F. 133
And, *but* your goodnes the same recure, ... *S.C.* F. 154
Nought aske I, *but* onely to hold my right; . . . . . . *S.C.* F. 186
Let none come there *but* that Virgins bene, ... *S.C.* Ap. 129
It was not long, . . . *But* the false Foxe came . . . . . . *S.C.* May 236
Yet not so previlie *but* the Foxe him spyed; . . . . . . *S.C.* May 253
little lack of dead, *But* I be relieved . . . . . . *S.C.* May 265
thous *but* a laesie loord, ... *S.C.* Jul. 33
Sike a song never heardest thou *but* Colin sing. . . . . . . *S.C.* Au. 50
you cannot wel ken, *But* it be by his pryde, ... *S.C.* S. 43
That waketh and if *but* a leafe sturre. . . . . . . *S.C.* S. 183
But knewe we, . . . Dye would we . . . . . . *S.C.* N. 185
I cannot . . . like *but* well The purpose . . . . . . *Hub.* 177
But that we are as honest as we seeme, ... *Hub.* 376
Why should ye doubt, then, *but* that ye likewise . . . . . . *Hub.* 425
Ne is the paines so great, *but* beare ye may, ... *Hub.* 446
Got him small gaines, *but* shameles flatterie, ... *Hub.* 850
But that with thunder bolts he had him slaine, ... *Hub.* 1236
all Apes *but* halfe their eares have left, ... *Hub.* 1383
There now is *but* an heap of lyme and sand, ... *Ti.* 129
'All is *but* fained, ... *Ti.* 204
Like beast whose breath *but* in his nostrels is, ... *Ti.* 356
'What hart so stony hard *but* that would weepe, ... *D.* 246
What Timon *but* would let compassion creepe . . . . . . *D.* 248
they be all *but* vaine, ... *D.* 395
Her, and *but* her, of love he worthie deemed; . . . . . . *As.* 65
Full litle faileth *but* thou shalt be dead, ... *As.* 135
nor any forth can set *But* he . . . . . . *As.* 172
but who the Godhead can define. . . . . . . *Col.* 347
but that the glooming skies Warnd them . . . . . . *Col.* 954
words that could not chose *but* please: . . . . . . I. i. 54. 8
Ne ever wist *but* that she was the same; . . . . . . I. ii. 40. 3
nothing faire *but* her on earth . . . . . . I. vi. 18. 9
all he taught . . . was *but* To banish cowardize . . . . . . I. vi. 24. 1
nought *but* sorrow . . . . . . I. vii. 23. 6

But—*Continued.*
'No faith so fast . . . *but* flesh does paire.' I. vii. 41. 8
never wight that heard . . . *But* trembling feare did feel I. viii. 4. 2
so firme and fast, *But* with that percing noise flew I. viii. 4. 9
can armed be so sownd, *But* will at last be wonne I. ix. 11. 3
garment, nought *but* many ragged clouts, I. ix. 36. 1
What justice can *but* judge against thee I. ix. 37. 8
luxurious pompe is swollen up *but* late. I. xii. 14. 9
I did *but* as I ought. II. i. 33. 5
Was never man, . . . *But* sometimes had II. v. 15. 4
No bird *but* did her shrill notes II. vi. 13. 3
Ne wote I *but* thou didst these goods bereave II. vii. 19. 3
wight Like ever saw, *but* they from hence were sold; II. vii. 54. 4
Full litle wanted *but* he had him slaine, II. xi. 29. 6
him that loves *but* one: III. i. 25. 6
they all *but* shadowes beene. III. i. 45. 9
That *but* the fruit more sweetnes did contayne, III. ii. 17. 7
Sad Amaranthus, made a flowre *but* late, III. vi. 45. 6
And, *but* God turne the same to good III. viii. 50. 2
never . . . Is suffred here to enter, *but* he seeme Such III. ix. 6. 4
No flowre in field, . . . *But* there was planted, IV. x. 22. 5
Else would the waters overflow . . . *But* that she holds IV. x. 35. 7
Rich Oranochy, though *but* knowen late; IV. xi. 21. 7
He could no more *but* her great misery bemone. IV. xii. 12. 9
for no cause, *but* as I shall you shew. V. i. 16. 5
a Bridge . . . Which is *but* narrow, *but* exceeding long; V. ii. 7. 7
But like a little Mount V. iv. 7. 7
doubting least his hold was *but* unsound V. v. 42. 7
For houres, *but* dayes; for weekes . . . She told *but* moneths, V. vi. 5. 6, 7
Ne wight *but* onely Talus with him went, V. viii. 3. 8
see not perfect things *but* in a glas: VI. Pr. 5. 5
Yet were her words *but* wynd, and all her teares *but* water. VI. vi. 42. 9
Yet not so freely, *but* that nathelesse VI. vii. 37. 5
with paine Saved him selfe *but* that he there him slew; VI. viii. 9. 4
Yet sav'd not so, *but* that the bloud it drew, VI. viii. 9. 5
any other twaine . . . *But* those whom heaven *H.B.* 206
As he would speake, *but* that he lackt a tong, *Proth.* 116
Butcher's. Like carkases of beastes in *butchers* stall. I. v. 49. 2
Of *butchers* balefull hand to ground is feld, VI. xii. 30. 8
But for. *But for* the ladde . . . Nowe loves a lasse *S.C.* Ap. 10
But, for she had a motherly care *S.C.* May 180
But, for the Sunnbeame so sore doth us beate, *S.C.* Au. 47
But for her father . . . Did warily still watch *Col.* 132
But for he was unhable them to fett, A little boy II. ix. 58. 3
But for she saw him bent to cruell play, III. i. 37. 3
But for he was halfe mortall, IV. xii. 4. 1
But for so much as to my lot here lights, V. iii. 3. 7
But if. Good is no good, *but if* it be spend; *S.C.* May 71
she shalbe mine, *But if* thou can her obteine. *S.C.* Au. 112
they nill listen . . . *But-if* he call hem *S.C.* S. 143
That *but if* she did lend her short reliefe III. i. 53. 5
but if remedee Thou her afford, III. iii. 16. 8
but if she Mercie would him give, that he mote algates dye, III. x. 7. 8
But-if the heavens helpe to redresse her wrong, IV. vii. 23. 3
But-if few plants, preserv'd through heavenly ayd, IV. viii. 33. 3
no meanes . . . *But if* that Dwarfe I could IV. viii. 61. 8
'*But if* in his owne powre occasion lay, V. v. 39. 2
Butt. with theyr hornes *butten* the more stoute; *S.C.* S. 125
Butted. the heard, Who *butted* him with hornes on every syde, III. x. 52. 3
the Bull hath . . . So hardly *butted* those two twinnes of Jove, V. Pr. 6. 2
Butt-end. Pounching me with the *butt end* of his speare, VI. ii. 22. 6
Butter. *Butter* enough, honye, milke, and whay, *S.C.* May 115
Butterfly. She turn'd into a winged *Butterflie,* *Mui.* 138
when he spide the joyous *Butterflie* *Mui.* 249
Emongst these leaves she made a *Butterflie,* *Mui.* 329
Buttevant. doth run downe right To *Buttevant,* *Col.* 111
Buxom. All for they nould be *buxome* and bent. *S.C.* S. 149
so tame . . . And *buxome* to his bands, *Hub.* 626
therewith scourge the *buxome* aire so sore, I. xi. 37. 6
Of them that to him *buxome* are and prone: III. ii. 23. 4
bid His mighty waters to them *buxome* bee: III. iv. 32. 6
with wide winges to beat the *buxome* ayre: III. xi. 34. 2
Till they him force the *buxome* yoke to beare: VI. viii. 12. 4
Buy. So you may *buye* golde to deere. *S.C.* Au. 108
they will *buy* his sheepe out of the cote, *S.C.* S. 40
To *buy* his Masters frivolous good will, *Hub.* 889
Justice he solde injustice for to *buy,* *Hub.* 1147
With price whereof they *buy* a golden bell, *Col.* 725
With price of silver shall his kingdome *buy;* III. iii. 39. 6

Buy—*Continued.*
He had small lust to *buy* his love so deare, IV. i. 34. 6
for bondmen there to *buy,* VI. xi. 9. 3
their bondslaves for to *buy;* VI. xi. 10. 2
Ne ought would *buy,* VI. xi. 14. 4
all lyke deare didst *buy,* *Am.* lxviii. 11
Buyeth. Ne frankincens he from Panchaea *buyth:* *Gn.* 133
Buzzed. flyes Which *buzzed* all about, II. ix. 51. 2
By (*partial list*). *See* **Comers-by, Passers-by, Whereby.**
calling me then *by* my propre name, *Bel.*[1] i. 7
Nay, say I thereto, *by* my deare borrowe, *S.C.* May 150
be ruld *by* mee, *S.C.* May 221
As the bonilasse passed *bye,* *S.C.* Au. 77
rayes Of precious stones, whence no good commeth *by;* *Gn.* 102
passing *by* with rolling wreathed pace, *Gn.* 253
this Curdog, *by* my coste, . . . will serve *Hub.* 294
Scarse can a Bishoprick forpas them *by,* *Hub.* 519
'Now sure, and *by* my hallidome, *Hub.* 545
Upon his tiptoes, stalketh stately *by,* *Hub.* 664
when he ought not pleasing would put *by* *Hub.* 1169
as a speedie post that passeth *by.* *D.* 413
When passing *by* ye read these wofull layes, *D.* 536
fairer faces were bid standen *by:* I. iv. 24. 8
He ghest his nature *by* his countenance I. viii. 34. 4
will I abyde *By* you, I. ix. 32. 7
'Who travailes *by* the wearie wandring way, I. ix. 39. 1
By this Charissa, . . . Was woxen strong, I. x. 29. 7
glauncing *by,* foorth passed I. xi. 16. 5
him so rudely, passing *by,* did brush I. xi. 16. 8
her two other sisters, standing *by,* II. ii. 28. 1
'here comes, and is hard *by,* A knight II. iv. 40. 5
lightly shunned it; and, passing *by,* II. v. 4. 1
Guyon standing *by* their uncouth strife does see. II. v. 20. 9
Atin *by* no way She would admit, II. vi. 4. 8
By this she had him lulled II. vi. 18. 1
who, passing *by,* forth ledd her guestes II. ix. 28. 8
they needes must passen *by,* II. xii. 14. 4
as he passed *by,* II. xii. 32. 1
So did he eke Sir Guyon passing *by;* II. xii. 49. 6
The trembling groves, the christall running *by,* II. xii. 58. 7
sett her *by* to watch, and sett her *by* to weepe. III. ii. 47. 9
Her to encounter ere she passed *by;* III. vii. 38. 4
when Proteus she did see her *by.* (*thereby) III. viii. 33. 9
manie *by* in place That present were to testifie the case.' IV. i. 49. 4
they avoyded were, and vainely *by* did slyde. IV. iii. 7. 9
each of them his Ladie had him *by,* IV. iv. 6. 2
knowne *by* fame, and *by* an Hebene speare, IV. vi. 6. 4
lovers heaven must passe *by* sorrowes hell.' IV. vi. 32. 7
The armed knights stopping his passage *by,* V. ix. 14. 8
twelve of them he did *by* times devoure, V. x. 8. 3
'Now sure and *by* my life, V. xi. 41. 1
By his owne sword, and *by* the crosse thereon, VI. i. 43. 6
when he saw his faire Priscilla *by* VI. iii. 11. 4
Seeing the ugly Monster passing *by,* VI. v. 16. 2
that same Knight and Salvage standing *by,* VI. vi. 23. 2
being carried with his force forthright Glaunst swiftly *by;* VI. vii. 7. 8
the other, which was passed *by,* VI. vii. 10. 1
glauncing *by* deceiv'd him of that he desynd. VI. vii. 10. 9
lightly slipping *by,* Unwares defrauded his intended destiny: VI. viii. 8. 8
Which when the Prince beheld, there standing *by,* VI. viii. 12. 6
snar at all that ever passed *by:* VI. xii. 27. 7
Far passing those which Hercules came *by,* *Am.* lxxvii. 7
By and by. Their troublous strife they stinted *by and by,* *Hub.* 1092
each one *by and by* Departed to his home *Hub.* 1108
The noble knight alighted *by and by* From loftie steed, I. viii. 2. 7
yields *by and by,* I. x. 1. 4
by and by It cut away upon the yielding wave, II. vi. 5. 5
So *by and by* Through that thick covert he him led, II. vii. 20. 5
He *by and by* His feeble feet directed II. viii. 4. 4
did *by and by* out find IV. xii. 25. 6
by and by The loft was raysd againe, V. vi. 27. 8
he bad me *by and by* For to alight: VI. ii. 17. 5
he *by and by* . . . a Capias Should issue forth VI. vii. 35. 3
by-and-by Bade Order call them all VII. vii. 27. 8
Bye. *She death shall *by.* V. xi. 40. 6
Bylive, Bynempt, Bynethe. *See* **Belive,** *etc.*
By-way. Ne ever would to any *byway* bend, I. i. 28. 4
By-ways. other *bywaies* he himselfe betooke, I. vii. 50. 3
Byze. Which mear'd her rule with Africa, and *Byze,* *Ro.* xxii. 2

C

Cabin. in secret *cabin* there he held Her captive I. vi. 23. 1
Of grace do me unto his *cabin* guyde.' I. ix. 32. 4
there he his *cabin* made. IV. vii. 38. 9
Having espide this *Cabin* far away, IV. vii. 42. 5
this your *cabin* both my bowre and hall: VI. ix. 32. 4
Cabinet. Hearken awhile, from thy greene *cabinet,* *S.C.* D. 17
To turne aside unto my *Cabinet,* *D.* 558
Cabinets. their gardins did deface; . . . their *Cabinets* suppresse; II. xii. 83. 7
Cabins. lurke emongst your Nimphes . . . Or keepe their *cabins:* III. vi. 23. 3
Cadmus. that, which antique *Cadmus* whylome built In Thebes, I. ix. 45. 6
Cadmus'. the bad daughter of old *Cadmus* brood, *Gn.* 171
the two brethren borne of *Cadmus* blood, *Gn.* 409
Cador. brother unto *Cador,* Cornish king; III. iii. 27. 2
Caduceus. He tooke *Caduceus,* his snakie wand, *Hub.* 1292
Of which *Caduceus* whilome was made, II. xii. 41. 2
Caduceus, the rod of Mercury, II. xii. 41. 3
Cadwallader. the good *Cadwallader* . . . be hable it to remedy, III. iii. 40. 3
Cadwallader, not yielding to his ills, III. iii. 41. 3

Cadwallin. *Cadwallin* . . . all those wrongs shall wreake; III. iii. 36. 1
'Whereat *Cadwallin* wroth shall forth issew, III. iii. 39. 1
with guifts his Lord *Cadwallin* pacify. III. iii. 39. 9
'Then shall *Cadwallin* die; III. iii. 40. 1
Cadwan. *Cadwan,* pittying his peoples ill, III. iii. 35. 8
Caecily. great Gurgustus, then faire *Caecily,* II. x. 34. 3
Caelia. Dame *Caelia* men did her call, I. x. 4. 1
Then said the aged *Caelia,* 'Deare dame, I. x. 17. 1
came to *Caelia* to declare her smart; I. x. 23. 1
leave they take of *Caelia* I. x. 68. 9
Caelian. *Caelian* on the right; *Ro.* iv. 13
Caer. *See* **Cair.**
Caesar. High *Caesar,* great Pompey, and fiers Antonius. I. v. 49. 9
warlike *Caesar,* tempted with the name II. x. 47. 6
by him *Caesar* got the victory, II. x. 49. 1
Caesar's. So Maro oft did *Caesars* cares allay. *Ded. Son.* i. 8
Caesars. Those antique *Caesars,* sleeping long in darke, *Ro.* xxv. 3
Caesura. Without full point, or other *Cesure* right; II. x. 68. 3

Cage. Fearing least from her *cage* the wearie soule would flit. . III. xi. 12. 9
Small was his house, and like a little *cage*, ... VI. v. 38. 3
In which he liv'd alone, like carelesse bird in *cage*. . . . . . VI. vi. 4. 9
feeles no captivity Within her *cage*; . . . . *Am.* lxv. 8
Cages. 'To make fine *cages* for the Nightingale, ... *S.C.* D. 79
Chirpe loud to thee out of their leavy *cages*, ... IV. x. 45. 8
Caicus. Mightie Chrysaor; and *Caicus* strong; . . . . IV. xi. 14. 3
Cair. Beside *Cayr* Verolame in victorious fight, ... III. iii. 52. 8
Cairbadon. Behold the boyling bathes at *Cairbadon*, ... II. x. 26. 2
Cairleill. built *Cairleill*, and built Cairleon strong. . . . . II. x. 25. 3
Carileon. built Cairleill, and built *Cairleon* strong. . . . . . II. x. 25. 3
Cair-Merdin. is now by chaunge Of name *Cayr-Merdin* cald, . III. iii. 7. 4
A brasen wall in compas to compyle About *Cairmardin*, . . III. iii. 10. 4
Caitiff. cause a *caytive* corage to aspire; . . . . *S.C.* O. 95
'Goe, *caytive* Elfe, him quickly overtake, ... I. v. 11. 1
caytive wretched thralls, that wayled night and day: . . . . I. v. 45. 9
valiant knight become a *caytive* thrall, ... I. vii. 19. 3
Whom great Orgoglio . . . Had made his *caytive* thrall: . . . I. viii. 32. 8
yeeldes his *caytive* neck to victours most despight. . . . . . I. ix. 11. 9
'Vile *Caytive*, vassall of dread and despayre, ... II. iii. 7. 4
Forth creeping on his *caitive* hands and thies; . . . . II. iii. 35. 7
the *caytive* spoile Of that same outcast carcas, ... II. viii. 12. 4
'*Caytive*, curse on thy cruell hond, ... II. viii. 37. 6
Vile *caitive* wretches, ragged, rude, deformd, ... II. ix. 13. 4
broke his *caytive* bands; . . . . II. xi. 33. 2
His *caytive* thought durst not so high aspire: . . . . III. vii. 16. 5
all the passions . . . vex his *caytive* spright. . . . . III. x. 17. 9
Why then is Amoret in *caytive* band, ... III. xi. 10. 2
'This dismall day hath thee a *caytive* made, ... IV. vii. 12. 1
Where this same cursed *caytive* did appeare . . . . IV. vii. 24. 4
when as the *caytive* carle Should issue forth, ... V. ix. 9. 1
'Art thou the *caytive* that defyest me? . . . . VI. i. 19. 6
sav'd from being to that *caytive* thrall. . . . . VI. iv. 15. 4
Whereof thou, *caytive*, so unworthie art, ... VI. vi. 33. 6
That cursed *caytive*, my strong enemy, ... VI. vii. 16. 3
'Abide, ye *caytive* treachetours untrew, ... VI. viii. 7. 4
At last the *caytive*, after long discourse, ... VI. viii. 14. 6
Caitiff's. out of *caytives* handes Himselfe he frees . . . . . . II. i. 1. 7
that *caytives* thrall, the thrall of wretchednesse. . . . . . . II. iv. 16. 9
Caitiffs. worke the avengement . . . On those two *caytives*, . . *Hub.* 1318
in that uprore Ye with those *caytives* saw, ... V. xi. 49. 6
Cakes. the shepherds entertayne With *cakes* and cracknells, . *S.C.* N. 96
Calamint. the flowre Of Camphora, and *Calamint*, and Dill; . III. ii. 49. 6
Calamities. th' only comfort in *calamities*. . . . . *T.M.* 132
'Those two be those two great *calamities*, ... *Ti.* 442
Of lovers sad *calamities* of old . . . . IV. i. 1. 1
Full many great *calamities* and rare . . . . IV. vii. 14. 3
Calamity. Yf chaunce him fall into *calamitie*, ... *T.M.* 305
Than question made of his *calamitie*, ... *D.* 90
As if she did some great *calamitie* deplore. . . . . V. ix. 8. 9
At whose *calamity*, . . . He laughed, ... VI. iii. 34. 3
much lamented his *calamity*, ... VI. viii. 3. 4
Calcineth. every thing consumes, and *calcineth* by art. . . . III. v. 48. 9
Caldron. *See* **Cauldron.**
Calendar. I have made a *Calender* for every yeare, ... *S.C.* Env. 1
Goe, lyttle *Calender!* . . . . *S.C.* Env. 7
Calepine. whilest *Calepine* By Turpine is oppressed. . . . . . VI. iii. Arg.
Sir *Calepine* (so hight) Came to the place . . . . VI. iii. 27. 1
Whom *Calepine* saluting (as became) . . . . VI. iii. 31. 1
Sir *Calepine* her thanckt; . . . . VI. iii. 33. 1
when as *Calepine* came to the brim, ... VI. iii. 34. 5
So much the more was *Calepine* offended, ... VI. iii. 36. 6
Which answer . . . brought To *Calepine*, ... VI. iii. 43. 4
Then *Calepine*, . . . forth on his journey goth. . . . . VI. iii. 45. 6
Calepine. . . . From Turpine reskewed is; . . . . VI. iv. Arg.
Chasing the gentle *Calepine* around, ... VI. iv. 2. 8
when as *Calepine* was woxen strong, ... VI. iv. 17. 1
did meane for helpe to call To *Calepine*, ... VI. iv. 18. 4
Whom when as *Calepine* saw so dismayd, ... VI. iv. 27. 5
Right glad was *Calepine* to be so rid . . . . VI. iv. 38. 1
But *Calepine*, now being left alone . . . . VI. iv. 39. 1
long time he lacked had The good Sir *Calepine*, ... VI. v. 3. 2
Those warlike armes which *Calepine* whyleare Had left behind VI. v. 8. 4
Sir *Calepine* himselfe away had hidden it. . . . . VI. v. 8. 9
I was erewhile the love of *Calepine*; . . . . VI. v. 28. 6
Wrought to Sir *Calepine* so foule despight; . . . . VI. vi. 17. 7
Ere she againe to *Calepine* was brought: . . . . VI. vii. 50. 7
Serena, found of Salvages, By *Calepine* is freed. . . . . . . VI. viii. Arg.
evermore she blamed *Calepine*, ... VI. viii. 33. 1
The good Sir *Calepine*, her owne true Knight, ... VI. viii. 33. 2
to this grove Sir *Calepine*, . . . fortune hether drove, ... VI. viii. 46. 7
Calf. an Hynde, whose *calfe* is falne unwares . . . . IV. xii. 17. 6
Calidore. if Sir *Calidore* could it presage, ... III. viii. 28. 8
Calidore saves from Maleffort A Damzell . . . . VI. i. Arg.
Calidore, beloved over-all, ... VI. i. 2. 2
Calidore thus first: 'Haile, noblest Knight . . . . VI. i. 4. 8
happy man,' (sayd then Sir *Calidore*) . . . . VI. i. 5. 6
'That surely is that Beast' (saide *Calidore*) . . . . VI. i. 10. 1
Sir *Calidore* thence travelled not long, ... VI. i. 11. 1
'A shamefull use . . . Sayd *Calidore*, ... VI. i. 14. 2
Which haynous sight when *Calidore* beheld, ... VI. i. 18. 1
Calidore, that was well skild in fight, ... VI. i. 20. 5
Such was the fury of Sir *Calidore*: . . . . VI. i. 21. 6
Whom *Calidore* perceiving fast to flie, ... VI. i. 22. 6
Calidore did follow him so fast, ... VI. i. 23. 3
whilest *Calidore* Did enter in, ... VI. i. 23. 8
Calidore uprose againe full light, ... VI. i. 34. 1
Calidore did with her there abyde . . . . VI. i. 30. 2
Ne ought dismayed was Sir *Calidore*, ... VI. i. 32. 4
Calidore, that was more quicke of sight . . . . VI. i. 38. 5

Calidore—*Continued.*
Sir *Calidore* upcheard, and to her teld . . . . VI. i. 44. 8
unto Sir *Calidore* She freely gave that Castle . . . . VI. i. 46. 6
Calidore himselfe would not retaine . . . . VI. i. 47. 1
Calidore sees young Tristram slay . . . . VI. ii. Arg.
That well in courteous *Calidore* appeares; . . . . VI. ii. 3. 1
Whom *Calidore* . . . At length bespake; . . . . VI. ii. 7. 1
'Perdie great blame' (then said Sir *Calidore*) . . . . VI. ii. 8. 6
Much did Sir *Calidore* admyre his speach . . . . VI. ii. 13. 1
Sayd then Sir *Calidore*; 'Neither will I Him charge . . . . . VI. ii. 14. 3
(then said Sir *Calidore*) 'and right, Me seemes, that him befell VI. ii. 23. 5
when well Sir *Calidore* had heard, ... VI. ii. 34. 1
And *Calidore* betooke him to depart, ... VI. ii. 36. 2
Whereat Sir *Calidore* did much delight, ... VI. ii. 36. 6
And *Calidore* forth passed to his former payne. . . . . VI. ii. 38. 9
And turne we backe to good Sir *Calidore*; . . . . VI. ii. 40. 2
Which sorie sight when *Calidore* did vew . . . . VI. ii. 41. 6
When *Calidore* this ruefull storie had Well understood, . . . VI. ii. 44. 1
Then gan Sir *Calidore* to ghesse streightway, ... VI. ii. 45. 1
Calidore brings Priscilla home; . . . . VI. iii. Arg.
As well may be in *Calidore* descryde, ... VI. iii. 2. 3
Whom *Calidore* thus carried on his chine; . . . . VI. iii. 3. 8
That to Sir *Calidore* was easie geare; . . . . VI. iii. 6. 5
But *Calidore* with all good courtesie . . . . VI. iii. 9. 1
When *Calidore* in seemly good array . . . . VI. iii. 9. 7
the onely helpe . . . Seem'd to be *Calidore*: . . . . VI. iii. 12. 9
Calidore rising up as fresh as day . . . . VI. iii. 13. 8
That *Calidore* it dearly deepe did move: . . . . VI. iii. 15. 4
Sir *Calidore* his faith thereto did plight . . . . VI. iii. 16. 1
thousand thankes to *Calidore* . . . Did yeeld: . . . . VI. iii. 19. 3
Sir *Calidore* approaching nye, ... VI. iii. 21. 1
Calidore, Who was more light of foote . . . . VI. iii. 25. 3
For he durst not abide with *Calidore* to fight. . . . . VI. iii. 25. 9
Calidore hostes with Meliboe, ... VI. ix. Arg.
Great travell hath the gentle *Calidore* . . . endured, ... VI. ix. 2. 1
To whom Sir *Calidore* yet sweating comes, ... VI. ix. 5. 7
Her whyles Sir *Calidore* there vewed well, ... VI. ix. 11. 1
Now seeing *Calidore* left all alone, ... VI. ix. 16. 2
in each mans self' (said *Calidore*) 'It is . . . . VI. ix. 31. 1
So there that night Sir *Calidore* did dwell, ... VI. ix. 34. 1
Calidore perceiving, thought it best To chaunge . . . . VI. ix. 36. 1
when he came in companie Where *Calidore* was present, . . . VI. ix. 39. 2
Calidore should lead the ring, ... VI. ix. 41. 7
Calidore, of courteous inclination, ... VI. ix. 42. 1
Did chalenge *Calidore* to wrestling game; . . . . VI. ix. 43. 6
Calidore he greatly did mistake, ... VI. ix. 44. 1
Given to *Calidore* as his due right; . . . . VI. ix. 44. 7
Thus *Calidore* continu'd there long time . . . . VI. ix. 46. 1
Calidore sees the Graces daunce . . . . VI. x. Arg.
Whilest *Calidore* does follow that faire Mayd, ... VI. x. 1. 2
Like to one sight which *Calidore* did vew? . . . . VI. x. 4. 2
Much wondred *Calidore* at this straunge sight, ... VI. x. 17. 1
Calidore, though no lesse sory wight . . . . VI. x. 18. 7
'Right sory I,' (saide then Sir *Calidore*) . . . . VI. x. 20. 6
Sayd *Calidore*: 'Now sure it yrketh mee, ... VI. x. 29. 2
But *Calidore* soone comming to her ayde, ... VI. x. 35. 6
Calidore did not despise him quight, ... VI. x. 37. 6
one day, when *Calidore* Was hunting in the woods, ... VI. x. 39. 1
Her *Calidore* from them redeemes, ... VI. xi. Arg.
turne we backe to *Calidore* where we him found. . . . . . . VI. xi. 24. 9
'Die? out alas!' then *Calidore* did cry, ... VI. xi. 29. 5
When *Calidore* these ruefull newes had raught, ... VI. xi. 33. 1
Yet *Calidore* so well him wrought with meed, ... VI. xi. 35. 8
Calidore Had, underneath, him armed privily. . . . . VI. xi. 36. 3
Calidore recomforting his griefe, ... VI. xi. 38. 1
chiefly *Calidore*, whom griefe had most possest. . . . . VI. xi. 41. 9
Sir *Calidore* him arm'd as he thought best, ... VI. xi. 42. 4
Calidore with huge resistlesse might The dores assayled, . . . VI. xi. 43. 2
when as *Calidore* was comen in, ... VI. xi. 44. 1
Ne lesse in hart rejoyced *Calidore*, ... VI. xi. 45. 6
Calidore in th' entry close did stand, ... VI. xi. 46. 6
Calidore doth the Blatant Beast Subdew, ... VI. xii. Arg.
Sir *Calidore* . . . Unto the Castle of Belgard her brought, . . VI. xii. 3. 1
Till time that *Calidore* brought Pastorella thether. . . . . . VI. xii. 10. 9
For Bellamour knew *Calidore* right well, ... VI. xii. 11. 2
Tho gan Sir *Calidore* him to advize Of his first quest, ... VI. xii. 12. 1
let us tell Of *Calidore*; . . . . VI. xii. 22. 6
seeing *Calidore*, away he flew, ... VI. xii. 25. 7
Calidore, thereof no whit afrayd, ... VI. xii. 29. 1
Whilest *Calidore* him under him downe threw: . . . . VI. xii. 32. 7
The proved powre of noble *Calidore*, ... VI. xii. 36. 7
by the maystring might Of doughty *Calidore*, ... VI. xii. 38. 2
long time after *Calidore*, ... VI. xii. 39. 5
Calidore's. Which should befall to *Calidores* immortall name. VI. ix. 1. 9
Caligulas. So many Neroes and *Caligulaes* . . . . *Bel.* x. 13
Call. *See* **Caul.**
for your antique furie here doo *call*, ... *Ro.* i. 12
that which Rome men *call*. . . . . *Ro.* iii. 4
you up to *call* To honours seat, ... *Van.* xii. 11
A shepeheards boye, (no better doe him *call*,) . . . . *S.C.* Ja. 1
lowdly she gan to *call* Her Kidde; . . . . *S.C.* May 296
But-if he *call* hem at theyr good choyce; . . . . *S.C.* S. 143
they had be better come at their *cal*; . . . . *S.C.* S. 146
he had eft learned a curres *call*,) . . . . *S.C.* S. 191
had he cond the shepherds *call*, ... *S.C.* S. 215
she would *cal* him often heame, ... *S.C.* N. 98
Night . . . her teemed steedes gan *call*, ... *Gn.* 314
No Muses aide me needes heretoo to *call*; . . . . *Hub.* 43
Free men some beggers *call*, ... *Hub.* 161
they which *call* them so more beggers bee; . . . . *Hub.* 162

Call—*Continued.*
I read that we our counsells *call*, . . . *Hub.* 189
Nor anie one doth care to *call* us in, . . . *T.M.* 343
none vouchsafes to answere to our *call;* . . . *T.M.* 352
call to count what is of them become: . . . *Ti.* 58
his owne end unto remembrance *call;* . . . *Ti.* 467
her play-fellowes aide to *call,* . . . *Mui.* 282
stayed not, till I againe did *call:* . . . *D.* 60
To carelesse heavens I doo daylie *call;* . . . *D.* 354
cruell Death doth scorne to come at *call,* . . . *D.* 356
I to minde will *call* How my fair Starre . . . *D.* 479
From this day forth do *call* it Astrophel: . . . *As.* 196
call it forth, O *call* him forth to thee, . . . *Col.* 408
my lambs, when for their dams they *call,* . . . *Col.* 638
lambs, . . . Ile teach to *call* for Cynthia by name. . . . *Col.* 639
none them in doth *call.'* . . . *Col.* 730
Then do they cry and *call* to love apace, . . . *Col.* 879
A . . . man, that dar'd to *call* by name Great Gorgon, . . . I. i. 37. 7
His Lady, . . . Did yield her comely person to be at my *call.* . I. ii. 36. 9
approching she to her gan *call,* . . . I. iii. 11. 1
ready entraunce was not at his *call;* . . . I. iii. 16. 6
Him booteth not resist, nor succour *call,* . . . I. iii. 20. 1
proud Lucifera men did her *call,* . . . I. iv. 12. 1
The roiall Dame, . . . for her coche doth *call:* . . . I. iv. 16. 2
Aurora . . . Out of the East the dawning day doth *call.* . . . I. iv. 16. 5
Which doen, the Chamberlain, Slowth, did to rest them *call.* . I. iv. 43. 9
lowd to him gan *call* The false Duessa, . . . I. v. 11. 8
him as onely God to *call* upon; . . . I. v. 47. 3
bloody wordes of bold Enchaunters *call;* . . . I. vii. 35. 2
To warde the same, nor answere commers *call.* . . . I. viii. 3. 4
Unto the Gyaunt lowdly she gan *call;* . . . I. viii. 20. 8
O heare, how piteous he to you for ayd does *call!'* . . . I. viii. 28. 9
Then gan he lowdly through the house to *call;* . . . I. viii. 29. 6
Through which he sent his voyce, and lowd did *call* . . . I. viii. 37. 7
Thy life shutt up for death so oft did *call;* . . . I. ix. 45. 6
Dame Caelia men did her *call,* . . . I. x. 4. 1
An auncient matrone she to her does *call,* . . . I. x. 34. 2
To *call* in commers-by that needy were . . . I. x. 36. 9
Such, men do Chaungelings *call,* . . . I. x. 65. 9
did it *call* The tree of life, . . . I. xi. 46. 8
mery wynd and weather *call* her thence away. . . . I. xii. 1. 9
to his Lord and Lady lowd gan *call,* . . . I. xii. 2. 8
Witnes, ye heavens, whom she in vaine to help did *call.* . . . II. i. 10. 9
he hoped faire To *call* backe life . . . II. i. 43. 7
bad me *call* Lucina to me neare. . . . II. i. 53. 5
doe for mercy *call.* . . . II. iii. 8. 4
whom Cymochles men did *call.* . . . II. v. 25. 9
Can *call* out of the bodies of fraile wightes; . . . II. v. 27. 5
Him needed not long *call;* . . . II. vi. 19. 4
Ne wind and weather at his pleasure *call:* . . . II. vi. 23. 3
'God of the world and worldlings I me *call,* . . . II. vii. 8. 1
did disdayne . . . who so did him *call:* . . . II. vii. 41. 2
Thereby more lovers unto her to *call:* . . . II. vii. 45. 6
in despight of life for death doe *call.'* . . . II. viii. 52. 4
lowd unto the knights did *call,* . . . II. ix. 11. 7
part, Which of himselfe Albania he did *call;* . . . II. x. 14. 3
of her name now Severne men do *call:* . . . II. x. 19. 8
all that now America men *call:* . . . II. x. 72. 6
they Glorian *call* that glorious flowre: . . . II. x. 76. 8
loud to them can *call,* . . . II. xii. 15. 1
They in that place him Genius did *call:* . . . II. xii. 47. 1
good Agdistes *call;* . . . II. xii. 48. 2
Now soft, now loud, unto the wind did *call;* . . . II. xii. 71. 8
The bird that knowes not the false fowlers *call,* . . . III. i. 54. 8
The worde gone out she backe againe would *call,* . . . III. ii. 9. 1
thence pourd into men, which men *call* Love! . . . III. iii. 1. 4
could *call* out of the sky Both Sunne and Moone, . . . III. iii. 12. 1
Till thy wombes burden thee from them do *call,* . . . III. iii. 28. 6
call Their sondry kings to do their homage severall. . . . III. iii. 32. 8
'Fayre Angela' (quoth she) 'men do her *call,* . . . III. iii. 56. 2
themselves of her name *Angles call.* . . . III. iii. 56. 7
Alowd to her he oftentimes did *call,* . . . III. iv. 48. 6
to his first poursuit him forward still doth *call.* . . . III. v. 2. 9
Angell, or Goddesse doe I *call* thee right? . . . III. v. 35. 5
him the Father of all formes they *call:* . . . III. vi. 47. 8
Call me the Squyre of Dames; . . . III. vii. 51. 9
To *call* them all in order to her ayde, . . . III. viii. 4. 6
hearing them to *call* For fire in earnest, . . . III. ix. 18. 2
slacke attendaunce unto straungers *call.* . . . III. ix. 18. 7
to him did cry And *call* alowd for helpe, . . . III. x. 13. 7
The wretched man hearing her *call* for ayd, . . . III. x. 14. 1
call to count the things that then were donne, . . . IV. Pr. 3. 2
Yet he to them so earnestly did *call,* . . . IV. ii. 21. 6
Whereto her selfe he did to witnesse *call;* . . . IV. v. 23. 8
to the Queene of beautie close did *call,* . . . IV. v. 26. 4
as if one him suddenly did *call:* . . . IV. v. 42. 7
call ye me the Salvage Knight, . . . IV. vi. 4. 9
She gan eftsoones it to her mind to *call* . . . IV. vi. 26. 4
Her name men Sclaunder *call.* . . . IV. viii. 24. 9
I persever'd still to knocke and *call,* . . . IV. x. 11. 6
thee their mother *call* to coole their kindly rages. . . . IV. x. 45. 9
fish . . . the which they Ruffins *call.* . . . IV. xi. 33. 9
yet thereof Gualsever they doe *call:* . . . IV. xi. 36. 5
Dee, which Britons long ygone Did *call* divine, . . . IV. xi. 39. 4
Of which the auncient Lincolne men doe *call:* . . . IV. xi. 39. 8
Whom of their sire Nereides men *call,* . . . IV. xi. 48. 3
For that which all men then did vertue *call,* . . . V. Pr. 4. 1
Into redoubted perill forth did *call;* . . . V. i. 3. 5
To *call* to count, or weigh his workes anew, . . . V. ii. 42. 6
Then for that stranger knight they loud did *call,* . . . V. iii. 14. 5

Call—*Continued.*
he bad them Florimell forth *call.* . . . V. iii. 22. 9
To follow his old quest, the which him forth did *call.* . . . V. iv. 20. 9
'Her name' (quoth he) 'they Radigund doe *call,* . . . V. iv. 31. 3
she did *call* Her nearest handmayd, . . . V. v. 29. 1
with guilefull *call* Did cast for to allure . . . V. v. 52. 8
should their mindes up to devotion *call,* . . . V. vi. 27. 4
Upon his first adventure which him forth did *call.* . . . V. vii. 43. 9
'Her name Mercilla most men use to *call* . . . V. viii. 17. 1
Therefore by name Malengin they him *call,* . . . V. ix. 5. 8
to their Queene for judgement loudly *call,* . . . V. ix. 49. 8
unto gratious great Mercilla *call* For ayde . . . V. x. 14. 3
willing them forth to *call* Into the field . . . V. x. 31. 4
On his first quest, the which him forth did *call,* . . . V. xi. 36. 3
A monster, which the Blatant Beast men *call,* . . . V. xii. 37. 7
Of Court, it seemes, men Courtesie doe *call,* . . . VI. i. 1. 1
you into such perils presently doth *call?'* . . . VI. i. 6. 9
So he him dubbed, and his Squire did *call.* . . . VI. ii. 35. 5
him to no revenge he forth could *call,* . . . VI. iii. 36. 7
did meane for helpe to *call* To Calepine, . . . VI. iv. 18. 3
to revile, and rate, and recreant *call,* . . . VI. vii. 26. 8
Whom they by name there Portamore did *call;* . . . VI. vii. 35. 8
Fortune aunswerd not unto his *call;* . . . VI. viii. 10. 1
which skill men *call* Civility. . . . VI. x. 23. 9
To *call* the soule backe to her home againe; . . . VI. xi. 22. 4
gan aloud for Pastorell to *call,* . . . VI. xi. 44. 2
ere he new helpe could *call,* . . . VI. xii. 30. 5
Gan *call* to him aloud with all their might . . . VII. vi. 15. 4
their minds (which they immortall *call*) . . . VII. vii. 19. 8
these, that Gods themselves do *call,* . . . VII. vii. 26. 2
to thy presence *call* The rest . . . VII. vii. 27. 2
Bade Order *call* them all before her Majesty. . . . VII. vii. 27. 9
sweetly sung to *call* forth Paramours) . . . VII. vii. 28. 5
none can *call* againe the passed time. . . . *Am.* lxx. 14
Men *call* you fayre, and you doe credit it, . . . *Am.* lxxix. 1
if thou be indeede, as men thee *call,* . . . *H.L.* 155
In praise of that mad fit which fooles *call* love, . . . *H.H.L.* 9
The house of blessed God, which men *call* Skye, . . . *H.H.B.* 52
Called. I saw a little Bird *cal'd* Tedula, . . . *Van.* iii. 7
A little fish, that men *called* Remora, . . . *Van.* ix. 10
called Lowder, with a hollow throte, . . . *S.C.* S. 217
Love they him *called* . . . *S.C.* D. 53
Nor ought *cald* mine or thine: . . . *Hub.* 149
he Mercurie unto him *cal'd,* . . . *Hub.* 1246
I heard a voyce, which loudly to me *called,* . . . *Ti.* 580
I heard a voyce that *called* farre away, . . . *Ti.* 638
oft she *cald* to him, . . . *As.* 167
That hearbe of some Starlight is *cald* by name, . . . *As.* 193
Allo hight, Broad-water *called* farre; . . . *Col.* 123
forth he *cald* . . . Legions of Sprights, . . . I. i. 38. 1
Who, whiles he livde, was *called* proud Sans foy, . . . I. ii. 25. 6
false Duessa . . . *Called* Fidess', and so supposd to be, . . . I. iv. 2. 4
a Porter . . . *Cald* Malvenu, who entrance none denide: . . . I. iv. 6. 4
Then *called* she a Groome, . . . I. x. 17. 6
thou *Saint George* shalt *called* bee, . . . I. x. 61. 8
His trusty sword he *cald* to his last aid, . . . I. xi. 42. 2
forth he *called* that his daughter fayre, . . . I. xii. 21. 1
The noyse thereof *cald* forth that straunger knight, . . . II. ii. 21. 1
He might . . . Be *called* Ruddymane; . . . II. iii. 2. 8
Still *cald* upon to kill him in the place. . . . II. iv. 9. 4
called for his armes, for he would algates fight: . . . II. v. 37. 9
He lowdly *cald* to such as were abord . . . II. vi. 4. 2
lowdly *cald;* 'Help, helpe! O Archimage! . . . II. vi. 48. 2
cald; 'Pyrochles! what is this I see? . . . II. vi. 49. 1
Disdayne he *called* was, and did disdayne To be so *cald,* . . . II. vii. 41. 1, 2
a voyce that *called* lowd and cleare, . . . II. viii. 3. 7
To weet who *called* so importunely: . . . II. viii. 4. 2
Alma she *called* was; a virgin bright, . . . II. ix. 18. 1
The maister Cooke was *cald* Concoction; . . . II. ix. 31. 1
called Cornwaile, yet so *called* best; . . . II. x. 12. 5
The which he *cald* Canutium, . . . II. x. 12. 8
He *cald* his daughters, . . . II. x. 27. 8
two sonnes, whose eldest, *called* Lud, . . . II. x. 46. 1
That man so made he *called* Elfe, . . . II. x. 71. 1
It *called* was the quicksand of Unthriftyhed. . . . II. xii. 18. 9
called was the Whirlepoole of decay; . . . II. xii. 20. 2
lowd to them for succour *called* evermore. . . . II. xii. 27. 9
is now by chaunge Of name Cayr-Merdin *cald,* . . . III. iii. 7. 4
Shall Hevenfield be *cald* to all posterity. . . . III. iii. 38. 9
Great father he of generation Is rightly *cald,* . . . III. vi. 9. 2
Her Amoretta *cald,* to comfort her dismayd. . . . III. vi. 28. 9
called is by her lost lovers name, . . . III. vi. 29. 8
out of her hidden cave she *cald* An hideous beast . . . III. vii. 22. 1
It forth she *cald,* and gave it streight in charge . . . III. vii. 23. 1
'That was by him *cald* Paros, . . . III. ix. 37. 1
Cald by strong charmes out of eternall night, . . . III. xii. 19. 5
Dernly unto her *called* to abstaine . . . III. xii. 34. 4
At last she came . . . And to him *cald;* . . . III. xii. 43. *or.* 8
The Seneschall was *cal'd* to deeme the right: . . . IV. i. 12. 1
I *cal'd* her loud, I sought her farre and neare, . . . IV. vi. 36. 8
He *cald* to him aloud his case to rew, . . . IV. viii. 40. 7
Corflambo was he *cald* aright, . . . IV. viii. 49. 1
The Dwarfe *cald* at the doore of Amyas . . . IV. viii. 59. 2
she *cald* to him for aide; . . . IV. ix. 7. 2
I *cald,* but no man answred to my clame: . . . IV. x. 11. 5
To whom I *cald* aloud, halfe angry therewithall. . . . IV. x. 11. 9
of the English man Is *cal'de* Blacke-water, . . . IV. xi. 41. 6
One *cald* the Theise, the other *cald* the Crane, . . . IV. xi. 47. 2
vertue . . . Is now *cald* vice; . . . V. Pr. 4. 2
True love despiseth shame, when life is *cald* in dread. . . . V. i. 27. 9

Called—*Continued.*
called Brigadore, (so was he hight,) . . . V. iii. 34. 3
A goodly citty . . . of her owne name, she *called* Radegone. . V. iv. 35. 9
She *called* forth to her a trusty mayd, . . . V. iv. 48. 1
Then they that Damzell *called* to them nie, . . . V. viii. 16. 1
his name was *called* Zele. . . . V. ix. 39. 4
Called aloud unto the watchfull ward . . . V. x. 31. 3
Till he an Herauld *cald,* and to him spake, . . . V. xii. 8. 5
He through occasion *called* was away . . . V. xii. 27. 2
him *called* to his aide: . . . VI. i. 11. 6
a Seneschall assynd, *Cald* Maleffort, . . . VI. i. 15. 8
a Dwarfe she *cald* to her in hast, . . . VI. i. 29. 1
forth he *cald* from sorrowfull dismay . . . VI. i. 44. 5
And *called* oft with prayers loud and shrill, . . . VI. iii. 49. 7
From a great Gyant, *called* Cormoraunt, . . . VI. iv. 29. 6
The first of them by name was *cald* Despetto, . . . VI. v. 13. 6
Causde me be *called* to accompt therefore; . . . VI. viii. 22. 2
streight the slaves should forth be *called,* . . . VI. xi. 10. 8
For which it loudly *cald,* and pittifully cryde. . . . VI. xii. 8. 9
damned ghosts, *cald* up with mighty spels, . . . *Epith.* 347
eeke for comfort often *called* art . . . *Epith.* 394
Calleth. Flora now *calleth* forth eche flower, . . . *S.C.* Mar. 16
Calling. *calling* me then by my propre name, . . . *Bel.*[1] i. 7
Which, *calling* me by name, . . . *Bel.*[2] i. 7
he will come, without *calling,* . . . *S.C.* May 153
Calling in vaine for rest, and can have none. . . . *Gn.* 392
Calling on Itis, Itis! evermore, . . . *Gn.* 402
I (to her *calling*) askt what her so vexed. . . . *Ti.* 21
Calling to me (ay me!) this wise bespake; . . . *D.* 262
calling forth straight way A diverse Dreame . . . I. i. 44. 1
to Diana *calling* lowd for ayde, . . . II. ii. 8. 4
Calling thy help in vaine . . . II. v. 36. 9
The knight him *calling* asked who he was? . . . II. vii. 62. 1
th' aged Nourse, her *calling* to her bowre, . . . III. ii. 49. 4
Malbecco, . . . to them *calling* from the castle wall, . . . III. ix. 18. 4
often to him *calling* to take surer hould. . . . III. xi. 34. 9
Calling men to their daily exercize: . . . III. xii. 28. 7
Him *calling* theefe, them whores; . . . IV. viii. 35. 4
earely *calling* forth both man and beast . . . V. v. 1. 3
calling her apart, Gan to demaund of her some tydings good, . V. v. 45. 1
Calling him great Osyris, . . . V. vii. 2. 5
and *calling* oft for ayde; . . . VI. iii. 24. 6
each to other *calling* . . . VI. xi. 20. 4
calling forth out of sad Winters night . . . *Am.* iv. 5
Calliope. 'I see *Calliope* speede her to the place, . . . *S.C.* Ap. 100
I sawe *Calliope* wyth Muses moe, . . . *S.C.* Jun. 57
faire *Calliope* did lose Her loved Twinnes, . . . *T.M.* 13
Meane-while, O Clio! lend *Calliope* thy quill. . . . VII. vi. 37. 9
Calls. *calls* foorth men unto their toylsome trade, . . . *D.* 485
And to him *cals;* 'Rise, rise! . . . I. ii. 4. 6
his restlesse spright, . . . *calles* to you above . . . I. iv. 48. 8
The Elfe him *calls* alowd, But answer none receives; . . . I. v. 13. 8
calles to mind his pourtraiture alive, . . . I. vi. 17. 3
A man of hell that *calls* himselfe Despayre: . . . I. ix. 28. 5
Calles thee his goddesse, in his errour blind, . . . III. iv. 56. 8
He to them *calles* and speakes, yet nought avayles; . . . V. viii. 39. 7
he streight *Cals* for his armes, . . . V. x. 31. 7
Calm. Milde was the winde, *calme* seem'd the sea . . . *Pet.* ii. 4
the gentle warbling wynde, So *calme,* so coole, . . . *S.C.* Jun. 5
With gentle *calme* the world had quieted, . . . *Mui.* 50
their greene leaves, . . . Made a *calme* shadowe . . . I. ii. 28. 6
to allay, and *calme* her storming paine, . . . I. vii. 38. 5
calme the tempest of his passion wood: . . . II. iv. 11. 8
in the *calme* of pleasaunt womankind. . . . II. vi. 8. 9
calme the sea of their tempestuous spight. . . . II. vi. 36. 4
To *calme* the tempest of his troubled thought: . . . IV. ii. 3. 2
naught the same may *calme* ne mitigate, . . . IV. viii. 1. 5
mollifie, and *calme* her raging heat: . . . IV. ix. 14. 7
They doe his anger *calme,* and cruell vengeance stay. . . . V. ix. 31. 9
Saturne oft doth . . . *calme* his crabbed lookes. . . . VII. vii. 52. 8
You *calme* the storme that passion did begin, . . . *Am.* viii. 11
let the night be *calme,* and quietsome, . . . *Epith.* 326
Calme was the day, . . . *Proth.* 1
Calmed. With pittie *calmd* downe fell his angry mood. . . . I. iii. 8. 5
He . . . *calmd* his wrath with goodly temperance. . . . I. viii. 34. 5
He smote the sea, which *calmed* was with speed, . . . II. xii. 26. 7
soone as *calmed* was the christall ayre, . . . III. v. 51. 8
when *calmed* was her furious heat, . . . V. v. 47. 8
having somewhat *calm'd* his wrathfull heat . . . VI. i. 40. 2
Calms. Eurypulus, that *calmes* the waters wroth; . . . IV. xi. 14. 4
all these stormes, . . . Shall turne to *caulmes,* . . . *Am.* lxii. 12
Calmy. it was a still And *calmy* bay, . . . II. xii. 30. 3
Cambden. *See* **Camden.**
Cambell. Couragious *Cambell,* and stout Triamond, . . . IV. ii. 31. 8
Cambell, that was stout and wise, . . . IV. ii. 37. 6
battell twixt three brethren with *Cambell* for Canacee: . . . IV. iii. Arg.
For Canacee with *Cambell* for to fight. . . . IV. iii. 3. 2
Then entred *Cambell* first into the list, . . . IV. iii. 5. 1
Whom so dismayd when *Cambell* had espide, . . . IV. iii. 10. 1
Out of his headpeece *Cambell* fiercely reft, . . . IV. iii. 12. 4
Which faire adventure when *Cambello* spide, . . . IV. iii. 20. 1
Against *Cambello* fiercely him addrest; . . . IV. iii. 22. 8
Much was *Cambello* daunted with his blowes: . . . IV. iii. 26. 1
Cambell still more strong and greater grew, . . . IV. iii. 29. 1
Which *Cambell* seeing come . . . IV. iii. 33. 4
First to her brother, . . . And next to *Cambell,* . . . IV. iii. 46. 8
Cambel tooke Cambina to his fere, . . . IV. iii. 52. 6
Twixt *Cambell* and Sir Triamond befell, . . . IV. iv. 2. 2
Cambell thus did shut up all in jest: . . . IV. iv. 12. 1
Which *Cambell* seeing, though he could not salve, . . . IV. iv. 27. 1

Cambell—*Continued.*
Which vauntage *Cambell* did pursue so fast, . . . IV. iv. 30. 5
Lightly *Cambello* leapt downe from his steed . . . IV. iv. 31. 1
Cambello it away before had got. . . . IV. iv. 33. 5
he came where he had *Cambell* seene . . . IV. iv. 34. 4
did yeeld the prize To Triamond and *Cambell* . . . IV. iv. 36. 4
But Triamond to *Cambell* it relest, . . . IV. iv. 36. 5
Cambell it to Triamond transferd, . . . IV. iv. 36. 6
Which *Cambell* seeing much the same envyde, . . . IV. iv. 44. 7
Cambell victour was in all mens sight, . . . IV. v. 7. 8
Cambello brought into their view His faire Cambina, . . . IV. v. 10. 1
Cambell's. *Cambelloes* sister was fayre Canacee, . . . IV. ii. 35. 1
Ne lesse approved was *Cambelloes* might, . . . IV. iii. 7. 3
Through *Cambels* shoulder it unwarely went, . . . IV. iii. 8. 3
Cambels fate that fortune did prevent; . . . IV. iii. 18. 5
falling heavie on *Cambelloes* crest, . . . IV. iii. 34. 2
Cambelloes armes therefore he on him threw, . . . IV. iv. 33. 6
Camber. *Camber* did possesse the Westerne quart, . . . II. x. 14. 4
Cambina. With Canacee and *Cambine* linckt in lovely bond. . IV. ii. 31. 9
Cambina with true friendships bond Doth their long strife agree. . . . IV. iii. Arg.
wise *Cambina,* taking by her side Faire Canacee, . . . IV. iii. 51. 6
Cambel tooke *Cambina* to his fere, . . . IV. iii. 52. 6
faire *Cambina* with perswasions myld . . . IV. iv. 5. 1
Cambello brought into their view His faire *Cambina,* . . . IV. v. 10. 2
Cambria. wedded . . . thother to the king of *Cambria.* . . . II. x. 29. 2
that of *Cambry* king confirmed late, . . . II. x. 38. 5
Cambridge. Thence doth by Huntingdon and *Cambridge* flit, . IV. xi. 34. 6
My mother *Cambridge,* whom as with a Crowne He doth adorne, IV. xi. 34. 7
Cambridge or Oxford, Englands goodly beames. . . . IV. xi. 35. 6
Cambry. *See* **Cambria.**
Camden. '*Cambden!* the nourice of antiquitie, . . . *Ti.* 169
Cambden! . . . thy just labours ever shall endure. . . . *Ti.* 174
Came. then *came* from the sea a savage beast, . . . *Rev.* i. 11
Untill he *came* unto the broken tree, . . . *Pet.* v. 5
mounting up againe from whence he *came,* . . . *Ro.* xx. 5
That *came* to passe, . . . *Ro.* xxiii. 13
gently tooke that ungently *came;* . . . *S.C.* F. 22
the false Foxe *came* to the dore anone: . . . *S.C.* May 236
in *came* The false Foxe, . . . *S.C.* May 278
they *came* where thou thy skill didst showe, . . . *S.C.* Jun. 62
the brethren were That *came* from Canaan: . . . *S.C.* Jul. 142
when at even he *came* to the flocke, . . . *S.C.* S. 204
oft in the night *came* to the shepe-cote, . . . *S.C.* S. 216
Came the bad daughter of old Cadmus brood, . . . *Gn.* 171
there *came* to visite mee Some friends, . . . *Hub.* 17
'From royall Court I lately *came* (said he) . . . *Hub.* 607
what he toucht *came* not to light againe; . . . *Hub.* 702
simple men, which never *came* in place Of worlds affaires, . . *Hub.* 834
Of all the which there *came* a secret fee, . . . *Hub.* 875
whenas they *came* they fell at words, . . . *Hub.* 1019
the Sheepe . . . *Came* to the Court, . . . *Hub.* 1208
till that he *came* with steep descent Unto the place . . . *Hub.* 1260
unto the Pallace nigh he *came.* . . . *Hub.* 1265
He would no more endure, but *came* his way, . . . *Hub.* 1315
At last he *came* unto his mansion, . . . *Hub.* 1349
to the Lion *came,* full lowly creeping, . . . *Hub.* 1361
thether *came* to heare their musick sweet, . . . *T.M.* 32
Soone after this a Giaunt *came* in place, . . . *Ti.* 533
Came downe to prove the truth, . . . *Mui.* 267
Toward those parts *came* flying carelesslie, . . . *Mui.* 391
There *came* unto my minde a troublous thought, . . . *D.* 29
Into a forest wide and waste he *came,* . . . *As.* 93
By fate or fortune *came* unto the place, . . . *As.* 141
when I asked from what place he *came,* . . . *Col.* 64
he *came* far from the main-sea deepe, . . . *Col.* 67
to the sea we *came;* . . . *Col.* 196
Behold! an huge great vessell to us *came,* . . . *Col.* 213
Untill that we to Cynthiaes presence *came:* . . . *Col.* 332
by descent from Royall lynage *came* . . . I. i. 5. 3
Halfe furious unto his foe he *came,* . . . I. i. 24. 3
Halfe angrie asked him, for what he *came.* . . . I. i. 43. 5
messengers of hell, . . . *Came* to their wicked maister, . . . I. ii. 2. 3
of whose most innocent death When tidings *came* to mee, . . I. ii. 24. 4
they *came* at last Where grew two goodly trees, . . . I. ii. 28. 2
out of whose rifte there *came* Smal drops of gory bloud, . . . I. ii. 30. 8
home she *came,* whereas her mother blynd Sate . . . I. iii. 12. 3
the fearfull twayne . . . *Came* forth; . . . I. iii. 22. 3
Ere long he *came* where Una traveild slow, . . . I. iii. 26. 1
with faire fearefull humblesse towards him shee *came:* . . . I. iii. 26. 9
proud Paynim forward *came* so ferce . . . I. iii. 35. 1
With gaping jawes full greedy at him *came,* . . . I. iii. 41. 4
Soon as the Elfin knight in presence *came,* . . . I. iv. 13. 1
Returne from whence ye *came,* and rest a while, . . . I. iv. 51. 3
Phoebus . . . *Came* dauncing forth, . . . I. v. 2. 4
I to thee *came,* Duessa I, . . . I. v. 26. 8
when she *came,* she found the Faery knight Departed thence; I. v. 45. 3
came to shamefull end. . . . I. v. 53. 6
a noble warlike knight . . . to that forrest *came* . . . I. vi. 20. 2
His loving mother *came* . . . to see her little sonne; . . . I. vi. 27. 1
now he thither *came* for like intent; . . . I. vi. 30. 5
soone he *came,* as he the place had ghest, . . . I. vi. 40. 4
monstrous enimy With sturdie steps *came* stalking in his sight, I. vii. 8. 3
So willingly she *came* into his armes, . . . I. vii. 15. 3
untill they *came* Nigh to a castle . . . I. viii. 2. 1
In hast *came* rushing forth from inner bowre, . . . I. viii. 5. 6
after him the proud Duessa *came,* . . . I. viii. 6. 1
Her dreadfull beast; . . . *Came* ramping forth . . . I. viii. 12. 5
the Gyaunt . . . *Came* hurtling in full fiers, . . . I. viii. 17. 9
The roiall Virgin . . . *Came* running fast . . . I. viii. 26. 4

Came—*Continued.*
with creeping crooked pace forth *came* An old old man, . . . I. viii. 30. 1
At last he *came* unto an yron doore, . . . I. viii. 37. 3
'Thither the great magicien Merlin *came,* . . . I. ix. 5. 1
gladly did them guide, till to the Hall they *came.* . . . I. x. 6. 9
'Thy selfe to see, . . . (quoth she) 'I hither *came;* . . . I. x. 11. 2
two most goodly virgins *came* in place, . . . I. x. 12. 2
labors long, through which ye hither *came,* . . . I. x. 17. 3
came to Caelia to declare her smart; . . . I. x. 23. 1
lodging unto all that *came* and went; . . . I. x. 37. 5
So *came* to Una, who him joyd to see; . . . I. x. 68. 6
Forth *came* that auncient Lord, and aged Queene, . . . I. xii. 5. 1
Unto that doughtie Conquerour they *came,* . . . I. xii. 6. 1
The comely virgins *came,* with girlands dight, . . . I. xii. 6. 6
they *came* where that faire virgin stood: . . . I. xii. 7. 6
when to her they *came,* . . . I. xii. 8. 2
they *came* where that dead Dragon lay, . . . I. xii. 9. 6
So fairely dight when she in presence *came,* . . . I. xii. 24. 1
Came running in, much like a man dismayd, . . . I. xii. 24. 8
with king Oberon he *came* to Faery land. . . . II. i. 6. 9
they *came* at last Into a pleasant dale . . . II. i. 24. 2
his aged Guide in presence *came;* . . . II. i. 31. 3
Lucina *came;* a manchild forth I brought . . . II. i. 53. 6
at last they to a Castle *came,* . . . II. ii. 12. 6
Newes hereof to her other sisters *came,* . . . II. ii. 16. 3
when Guyon *came* to part their fight, . . . II. ii. 23. 8
their faire loves, *Came* with them eke, . . . II. ii. 34. 2
To tell from whence he *came* through jeopardy, . . . II. ii. 39. 5
Sith earst into this forrest wild I *came.* . . . II. iii. 33. 6
One day unto me *came* in friendly mood, . . . II. iv. 22. 4
he *came* unto th' appointed place, . . . II. iv. 28. 1
When he in presence *came,* . . . II. iv. 39. 1
Came to a river, by whose utmost brim . . . II. vi. 2. 4
The varlett saw, when to the flood he *came,* . . . II. vi. 42. 1
By fortune *came,* ledd with the troublous sowne: . . . II. vi. 47. 7
At last he *came* unto a gloomy glade, . . . II. vii. 3. 1
At length they *came* into a larger space, . . . II. vii. 21. 1
they *came* unto an yron dore, . . . II. vii. 31. 2
Some scumd the drosse that from the metall *came;* . . . II. vii. 36. 7
They never creature saw that *cam* that way: . . . II. vii. 37. 5
that straunger knight in presence *came,* . . . II. viii. 23. 1
when they *came* in sight, . . . II. ix. 10. 6
report . . . *Came* to the Ladies eare . . . II. ix. 17. 6
Both guestes and meate, when ever in they *came,* . . . II. ix. 28. 4
Soone as the gracious Alma *came* in place, . . . II. ix. 36. 1
warlike Caesar . . . hither *came.* . . . II. x. 47. 9
Hither *came* Joseph of Arimathy, . . . II. x. 53. 7
those forreyners which *came* from farre, . . . II. x. 65. 5
Until he *came* unto a standing lake; . . . II. xi. 46. 6
Came rushing, in the fomy waves enrold, . . . II. xii. 25. 4
Untill they *came* in view of those wilde beasts, . . . II. xii. 39. 6
all Which thither *came;* . . . II. xii. 46. 3
he *came* unto another gate; . . . II. xii. 53. 6
The way they *came,* the same retourn'd they right, . . . II. xii. 84. 3
fiercely forward *came* withouten dread, . . . III. i. 5. 8
stoutly forward *came:* . . . III. i. 9. 4
At length they *came* into a forest wyde, . . . III. i. 14. 5
as nigh out of the wood she *came,* . . . III. i. 20. 1
As did this knight, before ye hither *came.'* . . . III. i. 27. 5
Where when confusedly they *came,* . . . III. i. 63. 4
For such intent into these partes I *came,* . . . III. ii. 7. 6
whence, to none inferior, ye *came,* . . . III. iii. 54. 3
till that to Faery lond They *came,* . . . III. iii. 62. 2
Tydings hereof *came* to his mothers eare: . . . III. iv. 19. 2
At last they *came* unto a double way; . . . III. iv. 46. 6
Chace her away, from whence she *came,* to hell: . . . III. iv. 60. 6
he asked, whence he lately *came,* . . . III. v. 3. 6
Tho to his brethren *came,* for they were three . . . III. v. 15. 5
The gentle Squyre *came* ryding that same way, . . . III. v. 18. 2
Shortly she *came* whereas that wofull Squire, . . . III. v. 29. 1
Shortly unto the wastefull woods she *came,* . . . III. vi. 17. 1
To Faery court she *came;* . . . III. vi. 52. 7
at length she *came* To an hilles side, . . . III. vii. 4. 6
came at last in weary wretched plight . . . III. vii. 5. 7
slew him cruelly ere any reskew *came.* . . . III. vii. 28. 9
seeming sory that she ever *came* Into his powre, . . . III. viii. 14. 7
Fiercely that straunger forward *came:* . . . III. viii. 16. 1
rudely askte her, how she thither *came?* . . . III. viii. 23. 6
Another knight, . . . *Came* to that Castle, . . . III. ix. 12. 3
to that shed . . . He *came,* . . . III. ix. 13. 4
Ne would they eate till she in presence *came.* . . . III. ix. 26. 6
Shee *came* in presence with right comely grace, . . . III. ix. 26. 7
sayling thence to th' isle of Paros *came.* . . . III. ix. 36. 9
Gave them safe conduct, till to end they *came.* . . . III. x. 16. 7
Paridell *came* pricking fast Upon the plaine; . . . III. x. 35. 2
let him passe as lightly as he *came:* . . . III. x. 39. 2
The jolly Satyres . . . *Came* dauncing forth, . . . III. x. 44. 4
till he *came* unto the place . . . III. x. 54. 1
he *came* unto a rocky hill . . . III. x. 56. 3
she at last *came* to a fountaine sheare, . . . III. xi. 7. 2
stoutly *came* unto the Castle gate, . . . III. xi. 21. 2
the winged God him selfe *Came* riding . . . III. xii. 22. 2
At last she *came* unto the place, . . . III. xii. 43. *or.* 1
passage bard to all that thither *came,* . . . III. xii. 43. 4
one evening, that they *came* Unto a Castell, . . . IV. i. 9. 1
seemd their ends out shortly *came.* . . . IV. ii. 50. 9
the doughty chalenger *came* forth, . . . IV. iii. 6. 1
came forth in hast to take his part, . . . IV. iii. 40. 8
where so he *came* in place, . . . IV. iv. 4. 4
where so they rode or *came,* . . . IV. iv. 13. 3

Came—*Continued.*
Unto the place of turneyment they *came;* . . . IV. iv. 13. 6
Then first of all forth *came* Sir Satyrane, . . . IV. iv. 15. 1
he *came* where he had Cambell seene . . . IV. iv. 34. 4
day *came,* when all those knightes againe Assembled were . . . IV. iv. 37. 1
Seven Knights, one after other as they *came:* . . . IV. iv. 41. 2
beating downe what ever nigh him *came,* . . . IV. iv. 41. 7
Much wondred all men what or whence he *came,* . . . IV. iv. 42. 1
overthrew what ever *came* her neare, . . . IV. iv. 46. 7
each one thought as to their fancies *came.* . . . IV. v. 17. 2
looke to whom she voluntarie *came,* . . . IV. v. 25. 7
to Braggadochio selfe alone She *came* of her accord, . . . IV. v. 26. 9
unto her his congee *came* to take; . . . IV. vi. 42. 6
till he *came* to th' end of all his way, . . . IV. vii. 8. 7
To which I boldly *came* upon my feeble feete. . . . IV. vii. 17. 9
Came to the cave; and rolling thence the stone, . . . IV. vii. 20. 4
came rudely rushing in, . . . IV. vii. 20. 6
when he *came* in sight, He durst not nigh approch, . . . IV. vii. 37. 3
His owne deare Lord Prince Arthure *came* that way, . . . IV. vii. 42. 2
she *came* where wonned his Belphebe faire. . . . IV. viii. 8. 9
A Squire *came* gallopping, as he would flie, . . . IV. viii. 38. 2
Him overtooke before he *came* in vew: . . . IV. viii. 40. 5
Came to that Squire, yet trembling every vaine; . . . IV. viii. 41. 3
before the harme *came* neare: . . . IV. viii. 42. 4
With which he killed all that *came* within his might. . . . IV. viii. 47. 9
Gyants daughter *came* upon a day Unto the prison, . . . IV. viii. 52. 1
when tydings *came* unto mine eare, . . . IV. viii. 55. 1
Insteed of whom forth *came* I, Placidas, . . . IV. viii. 59. 4
The Tyrant selfe *came* forth with yelling bray, . . . IV. viii. 62. 2
In presence *came,* desirous t' understand Tydings . . . IV. viii. 62. 8
that Squire of low degree *Came* forth . . . IV. ix. 8. 9
they *came* whereas a troupe of Knights They saw . . . IV. ix. 20. 1
to the place of perill shortly *came:* . . . IV. x. 5. 2
to the Bridges utter gate I *came;* . . . IV. x. 11. 2
'Into the inmost Temple thus I *came,* . . . IV. x. 37. 1
In order as they *came* could I recount them well. . . . IV. xi. 9. 9
First *came* great Neptune, . . . IV. xi. 11. 1
after them the royall issue *came,* . . . IV. xi. 12. 6
Next *came* the aged Ocean and his Dame . . . IV. xi. 18. 1
all the rest of those two parents *came,* . . . IV. xi. 18. 3
after him the famous rivers *came,* . . . IV. xi. 20. 1
Soone after whom the lovely Bridegroome *came,* . . . IV. xi. 24. 2
Then *came* his neighbour floods . . . IV. xi. 30. 1
there *came* Stoure with terrible aspect, . . . IV. xi. 32. 1
Then *came* the Rother, . . . IV. xi. 33. 1
the plenteous Ouse *came* far from land, . . . IV. xi. 34. 1
Next these *came* Tyne, . . . IV. xi. 36. 1
Then *came* those sixe sad brethren, . . . IV. xi. 37. 1
These after *came* the stony shallow Lone, . . . IV. xi. 39. 1
Then *came* the Bride, the lovely Medua *came,* . . . IV. xi. 45. 1
Who thither with her *came,* . . . IV. xii. 3. 8
backe he *came* unto her patient; . . . IV. xii. 23. 7
Unto himselfe she *came,* and him besought, . . . IV. xii. 24. 6
Apollo *came;* . . . IV. xii. 25. 5
the which by fortune *came* Upon your seas, . . . IV. xii. 31. 3
it would pierce or cleave, where so it *came,* . . . V. i. 10. 7
There *came* this knight, . . . V. i. 16. 8
When to the place they *came,* . . . V. i. 23. 1
Unto the place he *came* within a while, . . . V. ii. 11. 1
A villaine to them *came* with scull all raw, . . . V. ii. 11. 5
them against *came* all that list to giust, . . . V. iii. 6. 1
into the field they *came,* . . . V. iii. 7. 2
The third day *came,* that should due tryall lend . . . V. iii. 8. 1
Sir Artegall into the Tilt-yard *came,* . . . V. iii. 10. 2
Came to the open hall to listen . . . V. iii. 13. 8
thether also *came* in open sight Fayre Florimell, . . . V. iii. 14. 1
that stranger knight . . . Who *came* not forth; . . . V. iii. 14. 7
for Sir Artegall *Came* Braggadochio, . . . V. iii. 14. 8
then to him *came* fayrest Florimell, . . . V. iii. 15. 6
Forth from the thickest preasse of people *came,* . . . V. iii. 29. 4
their Queene . . . *Came* forth into the rout, . . . V. iv. 36. 9
So forth she *came* out of the citty gate . . . V. v. 4. 1
Then forth *came* Artegall out of his tent, . . . V. v. 5. 1
Soone after eke *came* she, . . . V. v. 5. 3
She to a window *came* that opened West, . . . V. vi. 7. 4
there *came* unto her chamber dore Two Knights . . . V. vi. 29. 1
Till to the perillous Bridge she *came;* . . . V. vi. 38. 3
till she *came* without relent Unto the land of Amazons, . . . V. vii. 24. 8
Stayd not till she *came* to her selfe againe, . . . V. vii. 34. 2
all that ever *came* within his reach . . . V. vii. 35. 6
the noble Conqueresse Her selfe *came* in, . . . V. vii. 36. 2
when as to her owne Love she *came,* . . . V. vii. 38. 1
So forth he *came,* all in a cote of plate . . . V. viii. 29. 1
when as ny He *came* unto his cave, . . . V. ix. 14. 7
not for those she now in question *came,* . . . V. ix. 40. 6
came Many grave persons that against her pled. . . . V. ix. 43. 5
First there *came* Pittie with full tender hart, . . . V. ix. 45. 3
then *came* Daunger, threatning hidden dread . . . V. ix. 45. 5
Then *came* Nobilitie of birth, . . . V. ix. 45. 7
There *came* two Springals of full tender yeares, . . . V. x. 6. 2
came to this, where Belge then did dwell . . . V. x. 11. 5
well she wist this knight *came* succour to supply. . . . V. x. 19. 9
They *came* unto a Citie farre up land, . . . V. x. 25. 1
To whom when tydings thereof *came,* . . . V. x. 31. 6
till that he *came* at last Unto the Castle . . . V. xi. 3. 3
opening streight the Sparre, forth to him *came,* . . . V. xi. 4. 2
So to the Church he *came,* . . . V. xi. 21. 6
To many a one which *came* unto her schoole, . . . V. xi. 25. 8
in ray *Came* dauncing forth, . . . V. xi. 34. 4
deeme it doen of will, that through inforcement *came.* . . . V. xi. 52. 9

Came—*Continued.*
At last they *came* whereas that Ladie bode, . . . V. xi. 60. 1
when they *came* to the sea coast . . . V. xii. 4. 1
By this *came* tydings to the Tyrants eare, . . . V. xii. 6. 4
not for such slaughters sake He thether *came,* . . . V. xii. 8. 8
Who *came* at length with proud presumpteous gate . . . V. xii. 14. 1
passing forth into the hall he *came,* . . . VI. i. 24. 6
ere he *came* . . . that youth had kild That armed knight, . . VI. ii. 4. 6
Came to the place whereas ye heard afore . . . VI. ii. 40. 4
Till to that Ladies fathers house he *came;* . . . VI. iii. 17. 8
Came to the place where he his Lady found . . . VI. iii. 27. 2
when as Calepine *came* to the brim, . . . VI. iii. 34. 5
By this the other *came* in place likewise, . . . VI. iii. 48. 1
wyld man . . . *Came* to her creeping . . . VI. iv. 11. 2
How ever by hard hap he hether *came,* . . . VI. v. 2. 8
All arm'd to point *came* ryding thetherward; . . . VI. v. 11. 3
at length unto a woody glade He *came,* . . . VI. v. 17. 7
towards night they *came* unto a plaine, . . . VI. v. 34. 7
now lie In piteous languor since ye hither *came,* . . . VI. vi. 6. 7
Ne stayd, till that he *came* into the hall; . . . VI. vi. 19. 3
Ere long to him a homely groome there *came,* . . . VI. vi. 20. 1
Came forth in hast; . . . VI. vi. 24. 5
So did his forty yeomen, which there with him *came.* . . . VI. vi. 25. 9
At last he up into the chamber *came* . . . VI. vi. 30. 1
Ere long they *came,* . . . VI. vii. 17. 7
the foole, which did that end awayte, *Came* running in; . . VI. viii. 11. 2
came by fortune blynde Whereas this Lady . . . lay. . . . VI. viii. 36. 7
Then *came* to them a good old aged syre, . . . VI. ix. 13. 6
home *came* the fayrest Pastorell, . . . VI. ix. 17. 5
when he *came* in companie Where Calidore was present, . . . VI. ix. 39. 1
When to the Cave they *came,* they found it fast; . . . VI. xi. 43. 1
Still slew the formost that *came* first to hand . . . VI. xi. 46. 8
all that nere him *came* did hew and slay, . . . VI. xi. 49. 4
to his love sometimes he *came* in place; . . . VI. xii. 6. 3
Came to the place; . . . VI. xii. 9. 4
At all that *came* within his ravenings; . . . VI. xii. 28. 4
To whose bright shining palace straight she *came,* . . . VII. vi. 8. 3
soone he *came* where-as the Titanesse Was striving . . . VII. vi. 17. 2
thither also *came* all other creatures, . . . VII. vii. 4. 1
Before her *came* dame Mutability; . . . VII. vii. 13. 6
Then *came* the jolly Sommer, . . . VII. vii. 29. 1
Then *came* the Autumne all in yellow clad, . . . VII. vii. 30. 1
Lastly, *came* Winter cloathed all in frize, . . . VII. vii. 31. 1
after them the Monthes all riding *came.* . . . VII. vii. 32. 2
Next *came* fresh Aprill, full of lustyhed, . . . VII. vii. 33. 1
Then *came* faire May, . . . VII. vii. 34. 1
after her *came* jolly June, . . . VII. vii. 35. 1
Then *came* hot July boyling like to fire, . . . VII. vii. 36. 1
Then *came* October full of merry glee; . . . VII. vii. 39. 1
after him *came* next the chill December: . . . VII. vii. 41. 1
Then *came* old January, . . . VII. vii. 42. 1
lastly *came* cold February, . . . VII. vii. 43. 1
after these there *came* the Day and Night, . . . VII. vii. 44. 1
Then *came* the Howres, . . . VII. vii. 45. 1
after all *came* Life, and lastly Death; . . . VII. vii. 46. 1
There *came* to me a leach, . . . *Am.* l. 3
But *came* the waves, and washed it away: . . . *Am.* lxxv. 2
But *came* the tyde, and made my paynes his pray. . . . *Am.* lxxv. 4
apples . . . Far passing those which Hercules *came* by, . . . *Am.* lxxvii. 7
little Cupid humbly *came,* . . . *Epig.* iii. 2
Unto his mother straight he weeping *came,* . . . *Epig.* iv. 31
When him the silly Shepheards *came* to see, . . . *H.H.L.* 230
As they *came* floating on the Christal Flood; . . . *Proth.* 57
they all to mery London *came,* . . . *Proth.* 127
There when they *came,* . . . *Proth.* 132

Camel. with the simple *Camell* raged sore . . . *Hub.* 1088
greedy Avarice by him did ride, Uppon a *Camell* . . . I. iv. 27. 2

Cameleon. *See* **Chameleon.**

Camest. whence thou *camst,* flye backe to heaven . . . *S.C.* O. 84
To Faery court thou *cam'st* to seek for fame, . . . I. x. 66. 8
Till thou *cam'st* hither to augment our mone: . . . IV. vii. 13. 8

Camilla. how *Camill'* hath slaine The huge Orsilochus, . . . III. iv. 2. 8

Camillus. here the antique fame of stout *Camill* Doth ever live; *Gn.* 601

Camis. in a silken *Camus* lilly whight, . . . II. iii. 26. 4
All in a *Camis* light of purple silke . . . V. v. 2. 1

Camlet. wav'd upon, like water *Chamelot,* . . . IV. xi. 45. 6

Camomile. Fresh Costmarie, and breathfull *Camomill,* . . . *Mui.* 195

Camphor. Rew, and Savine, and the flowre Of *Camphora,* . . . III. ii. 49. 6

Camus. *See* **Camis.**

Can (*partial list*). *See* **Bousing-can, Cannot, Couth, Gan.**
Hir brightnesse greater was than *can* be founde, . . . *Rev.* iv. 8
Seemeth thy flocke thy counsell *can,* . . . *S.C.* F. 77
(But now I trowe *can* better good,) . . . *S.C.* Mar. 56
who *can* counsell a thristie soule, . . . *S.C.* May 138
the Pedler *can* chat, . . . *S.C.* May 284
well he meanes, but little *can* say. . . . *S.C.* May 312
lightfoote Nymphes, *can* chace the lingring Night . . . *S.C.* Jun. 26
taught me homely, as I *can,* to make; . . . *S.C.* Jun. 82
The Woodes *can* witnesse many a wofull stowre. . . . *S.C.* D. 66
Calling in vaine for rest, and *can* have none. . . . *Gn.* 392
now the Pylote *can* no loadstarre see, . . . *Gn.* 573
they must feed themselves, doo what we *can.* . . . *Hub.* 434
Though they of sorrowe heavilie *can* sing; . . . *D.* 12
Not that these few lines *can* in them comprise . . . *Ded.Son.*xvi.6
Much *can* they praise the trees . . . I. i. 8. 5
Tho *can* she weepe, to stirre up gentle ruth . . . I. i. 50. 8
this good knight, soone as he them *can* spie, . . . I. ii. 29. 1
His dronken corse he scarse upholden *can:* . . . I. iv. 22. 8
(O who *can* then refrayn?) . . . I. iv. 41. 8
With gentle wordes, he *can* her fayrely greet, . . . I. iv. 46. 1

Can—*Continued.*
'what oddes *can* ever bee, Where both doe fight alike, . . . I. iv. 50. 3
none *can* wound the man that does them wield.' . . . I. iv. 50. 7
How *can* ye vengeance just so long withhold, . . . I. vi. 5. 8
What witt of mortal wight *Can* now devise . . . I. vi. 6. 9
Where none appeares *can* make her selfe a way, . . . I. vi. 7. 2
lesser pangs *can* beare who hath endur'd the chief. . . . I. vi. 37. 9
What justice *can* but judge against thee right . . . I. ix. 37. 8
who *can* quickly ryse . . . I. xi. 23. 7
From loathed soil he *can* him lightly reare, . . . I. xi. 39. 3
I present was, and *can* it witnesse well, . . . II. i. 19. 6
to pacifie, well as he *can.* . . . II. ii. 21. 9
Thou litle wotest what this right-hand *can:* . . . II. iii. 16. 8
Ne *can* the man that moulds in ydle cell . . . attaine: . . II. iii. 41. 3
them espying, loud to them *can* call, . . . II. xii. 15. 1
In shame of knighthood, as I largely *can* report. . . . III. ii. 12. 9
nought that wanteth rest *can* long aby: . . . III. vii. 3. 5
can and dare Redresse the wrong . . . III. x. 28. 1
He *can* let drive at him . . . And with his axe him smote . IV. iii. 20. 4
They up againe them selves *can* lightly reare, . . . IV. iv. 29. 1
th' other thus *can* say: 'Ah, gentle Scudamour! . . . IV. vi. 3. 6
her enhaunced hand she downe *can* soft withdraw. . . . IV. vi. 26. 9
The Fayrie, . . . *Can* yeeld great thankes . . . V. v. 55. 5
So *can* they both them selves full eath perswade . . . V. viii. 14. 4
his axe he raught . . . And *can* let drive . . . V. xi. 10. 3
as they past together on their way, He *can* devize . . . VI. iii. 16. 8

Canaan. the brethren were That came from *Canaan:* . . . *S.C.* Jul. 142

Canace. With *Canacee* and Cambine linckt in lovely bond. . IV. ii. 31. 9
Cambelloes sister was fayre *Canacee,* . . . IV. ii. 35. 1
In love of *Canacee* they joyned all: . . . IV. ii. 54. 5
battell twixt three brethren with Cambell for *Canacee:* . . . IV. iii. Arg.
For *Canacee* with Cambell for to fight. . . . IV. iii. 3. 2
Fayre *Canacee* upon a stately stage Was set, . . . IV. iii. 4. 6
Canacee gan wayle her dearest frend. . . . IV. iii. 35. 5
All which when gentle *Canacee* beheld, . . . IV. iii. 50. 1
Faire *Canacee,* as fresh as morning rose, . . . IV. iii. 51. 7
Triamond had *Canacee* to wife, . . . IV. iii. 52. 4
The face of his deare *Canacee* unheale; . . . IV. v. 10. 7
But Triamond lov'd *Canacee,* and other none. . . . IV. v. 21. 9

Cancelled. Hast sumd in one, and *cancelled* for aye: . . . *Epith.* 318

Candida. Ne thee lesse worthie, curteous *Candida,* . . . *Col.* 574

Candle-light. But now weake age had dimd his *candle-light:* . VI. iii. 3. 4
Ne lightned was with window, . . . But with continuall *candle-light,* . . . VI. x. 42. 8
but hardly seene by *candle-light,* . . . VI. xi. 13. 2
the *candle-light* Out quenched leaves no skill . . . VI. xi. 16. 8

Candles. lighting *candles* new, gan search anone, . . . VI. xi. 20. 8

Canker. all worm-eaten and full of *canker* holes. . . . II. ix. 57. 9

Cankered. 'Cause have I none . . . of *cancred* will . . . *Col.* 680
did chaw Between his *cankred* teeth a venemous tode, . . . I. iv. 30. 3
That conning Architect of *cancred* guyle, . . . II. i. 1. 1
'Therein a *cancred* crabbed Carle does dwell, . . . III. ix. 3. 5
with *cancred* malice lind, . . . IV. viii. 26. 4
not of *cancred* will . . . I have forbore this duetie to fulfill; V. v. 41. 1
His father Dolon had . . . shewd his *cankred* hate. . . . V. vi. 33. 9
Agreeing in bad will and *cancred* kynd; . . . V. xii. 33. 2
In *cancred* malice and revengefull spight: . . . VI. vii. 1. 4
His *cancred* foes, his fights, his toyle, his strife, . . . *H.H.L.* 234

Cankering. people should With *cancring* laisure not be overworne: . . . *Ro.* xxiii. 4

Cankerworm. The *canker worme* of everie gentle brest; . . . *Hub.* 736
O cursed Eld! the *cankerworme* of writs, . . . IV. ii. 33. 6
That *cancker-worme,* that monster, Gelosie, . . . *H.L.* 267

Cankerworms. oft he lets his *canker-wormes* light . . . *S.C.* F. 179

Cannon-bit. His stubborne steed with curbed *canon bitt,* . . I. vii. 37. 6

Cannot (*partial list*).
So great riches as like *cannot* be found! . . . *Pet.* ii. 14
cleanly cover that *cannot* be cured: . . . *S.C.* S. 138
worse than that I have I *cannot* meete. . . . *Hub.* 89
brood of blindnes *cannot* gesse, . . . *T.M.* 392
what of him became I *cannot* weene. . . . *D.* 567
death their hearts *cannot* divide, . . . *As.* 179
I *cannot* thinke according to her worth: . . . *Col.* 627
Most wretched he, that is and *cannot* tell.' . . . *Col.* 659
names I *cannot* readily now ghesse: . . . *Col.* 740
ease of paine which *cannot* be recured. . . . *Col.* 946
In vaine he seekes that having *cannot* hold. . . . I. vi. 33. 7
what I *cannot* quite requite with usuree. . . . I. viii. 27. 9
I *can not* read aright: . . . III. iii. 16. 7
'In vaine he feares that which he *cannot* shonne; . . . III. ix. 7. 1
Cannot employ your most victorious speare . . . III. x. 28. 3
a crew, As like *can not* be seene . . . *Cannot* find . . . IV. v. 18. 4, 5
The wonder that my wit *cannot* endite. . . . *Am.* iii. 14

Canopy. She is . . . placed under stately *canapee,* . . . I. v. 5. 4

Canst (*partial list*).
yet *canst* not when thou should; . . . *S.C.* Ja. 70
Why fearest thou, that *canst* not hope . . . I. v. 43. 3
thou *canst* not see, . . . III. x. 4. 3
thou . . . Ne *canst* her ayde, ne *canst* her foe dismay; . . . III. xi. 11. 7

Canticle. Shall for another *canticle* be spared: . . . IV. v. 46. 7

Cantium. *Cantium,* which Kent we comenly inquyre. . . . II. x. 12. 9

Canto. will reserve it for a *Canto* new. . . . IV. ii. 54. 9
sith they cannot in this *Canto* well Comprised be, . . . IV. ix. 41. 8
So ended he his tale, where I this *Canto* end. . . . IV. x. 58. 9
Unto an other *Canto* I will overpas. . . . IV. xi. 53. 9
in an other *Canto* will be best contayned. . . . V. v. 57. 9
That for another *Canto* will more fitly fall. . . . V. vii. 45. 9
what ensu'd shall in next *Canto* be begonne. . . . VI. ii. 48. 9
in another *Canto* shall to end be brought. . . . VI. iii. 51. 9
Will in another *Canto* better be begonne. . . . VI. x. 44. 9

Canute. *See* **Canutus.**
Canutium. The which he cald *Canutium,* for his hyre; . . . II. x. 12. 8
Canutus. Great Godmer threw . . . At bold *Canutus;* . . . II. x. 11. 9
Canute had his portion from the rest, . . . II. x. 12. 7
Canvas. like mayne-yardes with flying *canvas* lynd; . . . I. xi. 10. 5
winged *canvas* with the wind to fly: . . . II. vi. 5. 4
All in a *canvas* thin he was bedight, . . . II. xi. 22. 6
Cap. Upon his head an old Scotch *cap* he wore, . . . *Hub.* 209
on his head a steele *cap* he did weare . . . V. xii. 14. 5
Cape. Thus was the ape . . . put into Malbeccoes *cape.* . . . III. ix. 31. 9
Caphareus. Some on the rocks of *Caphareus* are throwne; . . . *Gn.* 586
Capias. a *Capias* Should issue forth . . . VI. vii. 35. 4
Capitayn, -s. *See* **Captain, -s.**
Capitol. Possest nigh of the *Capitol* through slight, . . . *Van.* xi. 7
Capon's. did nigh affray That *Capons* corage: . . . III. viii. 15. 6
Caprifoil. Eglantine and *Caprifole* emong, . . . III. vi. 44. 6
Captain. That flocks grand *Captaine* and most trustie guide . *Gn.* 268
Nor leave his stand untill his *Captaine* bed.' . . . I. ix. 41. 5
evermore their cruell *Captaine* Sought . . . II. ix. 15. 3
Them in twelve troupes their *Captein* did dispart, . . . II. xi. 6. 1
their wicked *Capitayn* Provoked them . . . II. xi. 14. 6
When as their *Capteine* heard, . . . II. xi. 20. 2
he which was their *Capitaine* profest, . . . VI. xi. 3. 4
Were brought unto their *Captaine,* . . . VI. xi. 9. 8
This their request the *Captaine* much appalled, . . . VI. xi. 10. 6
the *Captaine* in full angry wize Made answere, . . . VI. xi. 12. 1
then the *Captaine,* fraught with more displeasure, . . . VI. xi. 14. 7
Was by the *Captaine* all this while defended, . . . VI. xi. 19. 2
Their *Captaine* there they cruelly found kild, . . . VI. xi. 21. 1
Their *Captaine* long withstood, and did her death forstall. . . VI. xi. 31. 9
Captain's. he streight went to the *Captaines* nest: . . . VI. xi. 42. 7
Endure their *Captains* flaming head to see? . . . *H.H.B.* 60
Captains. By reason that the *Captaines* on her syde, . . . II. x. 55. 3
their *Capitayns,* which hight Hengist and Horsus, . . . II. x. 65. 1
Brave *Captaines,* and most mighty warriours, . . . III. iii. 23. 3
mightie Conquerours and *Captaines* strong, . . . III. xi. 52. 3
the two knights themselves their *captains* did subdew. . . . V. xi. 59. 9
Captivance. reskewed from *captivaunce* Of his strong foe, . . III. vii. 45. 7
The whole discourse of his *captivance* sad, . . . V. vi. 17. 2
Captive. The whiles the *captive* heard his nets did rend. . . *As.* 125
there he held Her *captive* to his sensuall desyre, . . . I. vi. 23. 2
The Redcrosse knight is *captive* made . . . I. vii. Arg.
That he my *captive* langour should redeeme: . . . I. vii. 49. 2
till I have acquitt your *captive* knight, . . . I. vii. 52. 6
that weake *captive* wight now wexed strong, . . . I. ix. 2. 3
To thinke of those her *captive* Parents deare, . . . I. xi. 1. 2
thyselfe my *captive* yield for ay. . . . II. iii. 7. 8
to her *captive* sonne yield his first libertee. . . . II. v. 17. 9
both them strongly bound In *captive* bandes, . . . II. xii. 82. 5
some for wrath to see their *captive* Dame: . . . II. xii. 86. 5
Late king, now *captive;* late lord, now forlorne; . . . III. iii. 42. 4
He lefte his *captive* Beast at liberty, . . . III. vii. 38. 2
captive with her led to wretchednesse and wo. . . . III. xii. 41. 9
They have him taken *captive,* though it grieve him sore. . . IV. iv. 32. 9
Like *captive* thral two other Knights atweene: . . . IV. iv. 34. 5
setst thy kingdome in the *captive* harts Of Kings . . . IV. vii. 1. 3
she him still detaines in *captive* hold, . . . IV. viii. 53. 7
Her *captive* lovers friend, young Placidas, . . . IV. viii. 63. 2
Before the ryder, as he *captive* were, . . . IV. ix. 5. 2
He her unwares attacht, and *captive* held by might. . . . IV. ix. 6. 9
the *captive* Squire she lov'd so deare, . . . IV. ix. 10. 6
that *captive* Lady faire, The faire Poeana, . . . IV. ix. 13. 1
now they doe with *captive* bands him bind; . . . V. iii. 9. 7
Gan cast a secret liking to this *captive* straunge. . . . V. v. 26. 9
in the streightnesse of that *captive* state . . . V. vi. 2. 1
In which her wretched love was *captive* layd: . . . V. vii. 37. 3
long in *captive* shade Had shrowded bene, . . . V. vii. 43. 1
To *captive* men, and make them all the world reject. . . . V. viii. 2. 9
He like a dog was led in *captive* case, . . . VI. viii. 5. 4
Then turning backe unto that *captive* thrall, . . . VI. viii. 27. 1
all his people *captive* led away; . . . VI. x. 40. 3
carried *captive* by those theeves away; . . . VI. x. 41. 2
Till Fortune would her *captive* bonds unbynde: . . . VI. xi. 8. 8
So led this Knight his *captyve* with like conquest wonne. . . . VI. xii. 35. 9
Rejoyced much to see his *captive* plight, . . . VI. xii. 37. 8
humbled harts brings *captive* unto thee, . . . *Am.* x. 7
Accoumpts my self her *captive* quite forlorne. . . . *Am.* xxix. 4
bring away Captivity thence *captive,* . . . *Am.* lxviii. 4
conquering beautie doth *captive* My trembling hart . . . *H.B.* 275
Captived. The faire Ixione *captiv'd* from Troy; . . . *Gn.* 490
'My weaker yeares, *Captiv'd* to fortune . . . I. i. 52. 5
sithens fortunes guile, . . . hath now *captived* you, Returne . I. iv. 51. 2
Wherein *captiv'd,* of life or death he stood in doubt. . . . I. vii. 26. 9
long *captived* soules from weary thraldome free. . . . II. i. 36. 9
when as Guyon Furor had *captivd,* . . . II. iv. 16. 1
thee to endlesse bale *captived* lead. . . . II. v. 16. 6
Captiv'd eternally in yron mewes . . . II. v. 27. 8
Frayle men are oft *captiv'd* to covetise; . . . II. vii. 15. 2
Rather then fly, or be *captiv'd,* . . . II. x. 55. 9
the *captiv'd* Acrasia he sent, . . . III. i. 2. 1
Faire Ladies, that to love *captived* arre, . . . III. i. 49. 1
To succor wretched wights whom we *captived* see.' . . . III. v. 36. 9
To be *captived* in endlesse duraunce Of sorrow . . . III. v. 42. 8
whilome *captived* in their dayes To cruell love, . . . III. xi. 52. 4
Nations *captived,* and huge armies slaine: . . . IV. i. 21. 8
Where she, *captived* long, great woes did prove; . . . IV. vi. 34. 8
brought Unto his bay, and *captived* her thought: . . . IV. viii. 48. 5
She lenger yet is like *captiv'd* to bee; . . . IV. xi. 1. 8
In which *captiv'd* she many moneths did mourne, . . . V. iii. 1. 8
him *captived* hath in haplesse woe.' . . . V. vi. 11. 3

Captived—*Continued.*
mote appall An hardie courage, like *captived* thrall . . . V. ix. 33. 5
thee *captyved* in this shamefull place?' . . . VI. i. 12. 4
when he up did looke And saw him selfe *captiv'd,* . . . VI. vii. 48. 8
To be *captiv'd* and handled as he list, . . . VI. viii. 13. 2
yield for pledge my poore *captyved* hart; . . . *Am.* xlii. 8
In whose streight bands ye now *captived* are . . . *Am.* lxxi. 7
Being my self *captyved* here in care, . . . *Am.* lxxiii. 1
Perforce subdude my poore *captived* hart, . . . *H.L.* 2
Captives. *captives* to redeeme with price of bras . . . I. x. 40. 3
that those same *captives* there Mote . . . Be sold, . . . VI. xi. 10. 3
first of all their *captives* they doe kill, . . . VI. xi. 18. 1
all the *captives,* which they here had hent, . . . VI. xi. 31. 4
Lyke *captives* trembling at the victors sight. . . . *Am.* i. 4
Captiving. Who, me *captiving* streight . . . *Am.* xii. 11
Captivity. The hidden cause of their *captivitie;* . . . I. v. 46. 3
hold sad life in long *captivitee;* . . . II. i. 48. 3
gan to breake the bands of their *captivitee.* . . . II. v. 18. 9
To bring the sowle into *captivity?* . . . II. xi. 1. 4
tell the course of his *captivitie,* . . . IV. viii. 64. 2
The whiles his Pastorell is led Into *captivity.* . . . VI. x. Arg.
feeles no *captivity* Within her cage; . . . *Am.* lxv. 7
having harrowd hell, didst bring away *Captivity* . . . *Am.* lxviii. 4
Capuccio. at his backe a brode *Capuccio* had, . . . III. xii. 10. 3
Car. Phoebus fiery *carre* In hast was climbing . . . I. ii. 1. 7
lights the world forth from his firie *carre.* . . . *H.B.* 112
Carados. *Carados* her hand withheld From rash revenge, . . . III. iii. 55. 7
Yet *Carados* himselfe from her escapt with payne.' . . . III. iii. 55. 9
Carausius. gan *Carausius* tirannize anew, . . . II. x. 57. 5
Carcass. in my carrion *carcas* abounds.' . . . *S.C.* May 258
Full of diseases was his *carcas* blew, . . . I. iv. 23. 6
nought he car'd his *carcas* long unfed; . . . I. x. 48. 7
awaiting shortly to obtayn Thy *carcas* . . . II. vi. 28. 9
carcas deepe was drent Within the river, . . . II. vii. 61. 2
the caytive spoile Of that same outcast *carcas,* . . . II. viii. 12. 5
with fowle cowardize his *carcas* shame, . . . II. viii. 13. 4
for his (*this) *carkas* pardon I entreat, . . . II. viii. 27. 8
make his *carkas* as the outcast dong? . . . II. viii. 28. 5
Yet lives his memorie, though *carcas* sleepe in rest. . . . II. x. 43. 9
through his *carcas* one might playnly see. . . . II. xi. 38. 3
crusht his *carcas* so against his brest, . . . II. xi. 42. 2
Downe on the ground his *carkas* groveling fell: . . . III. v. 23. 7
The *carcas* with the streame was carried downe, . . . III. v. 25. 6
Upon that milke-white Palfreyes *carcas* fedd, . . . III. vii. 30. 8
dint of steele his *carcas* could not quell; . . . III. vii. 35. 8
she put a Spright to rule the *carcas* dead: . . . III. viii. 7. 9
him assayling sore his *carkas* teare, . . . III. x. 53. 7
Uppon the *carkasse* of some beast too weake, . . . V. iv. 40. 7
His *carkasse,* tumbling on the threshold, . . . V. x. 36. 8
The *carkasse* tumbling downe within the dore . . . VI. i. 23. 6
Streight to the *carkasse* of that Knight he went, . . . VI. iii. 17. 1
ymet About some *carcase* by the common way, . . . VI. xi. 17. 2
Carcasses. with wide wounds their *carcases* doth rend; . . . *Gn.* 414
with your *carkasses* wild beasts be glutted. . . . *D.* 350
Like *carkases* of beastes in butchers stall. . . . I. v. 49. 2
A Donghill of dead *carcases* he spyde; . . . I. v. 53. 8
grave, That still for carrion *carcases* doth crave: . . . I. ix. 33. 5
carcases were scattred on the greene, . . . I. ix. 34. 5
carkases . . . Of fowles and beastes he made the piteous prayes, II. v. 26. 6
their vile *carcases* now left unburied. . . . II. vii. 30. 9
carcases on ground were horribly prostrate. . . . II. viii. 54. 9
stuck with *carkases* exanimate . . . II. xii. 7. 5
fieldes . . . strowne With *carcases* of noble warrioures . . . III. ix. 35. 7
to their sire their *carcasses* left to bestow. . . . V. vi. 40. 9
the heapes which he did make Of slaughtred *carkasses,* . . . V. vii. 36. 5
feedes on all the *carkasses* that die In sacrifize . . . V. xi. 20. 3
covered with confused preasse Of *carcases,* . . . VI. xi. 20. 2
when they mov'd the *carcases* aside, . . . VI. xi. 22. 1
Through the dead *carcases* he made his way, . . . VI. xi. 47. 4
Card. Upon his *card* and compas firmes his eye, . . . II. vii. 1. 6
Withouten compasse or withouten *card,* . . . III. ii. 7. 7
went at will withouten *card* or sayle, . . . III. viii. 31. 2
To spin, to *card,* to sew, to wash, to wring; . . . V. iv. 31. 6
Carde. *See* **Cared.**
Carding. Spinning and *carding* all in comely rew, . . . V. v. 22. 4
Cards. With dice, with *cards,* with balliards farre unfit, . . . *Hub.* 803
nether spinnes nor *cards,* ne cares nor fretts, . . . II. vi. 16. 8
Care. May seeme he lovd, or els some *care* he tooke; . . . *S.C.* Ja. 9
Thy maysters mind is overcome with *care:* . . . *S.C.* Ja. 46
ever my flocke was my chiefe *care,* . . . *S.C.* F. 23
Thomalin, have no *care* for-thy; . . . *S.C.* Mar. 37
on him was all my *care* and joye, . . . *S.C.* Ap. 23
For naught *caren* that bene so lewdly bent. . . . *S.C.* Ap. 157
caren as little as they What fallen the flocke, . . . *S.C.* May 48
With them it sits to *care* for their heire, . . . *S.C.* May 77
to the Apes folish *care,* . . . *S.C.* May 96
a motherly *care* Of her young sonne, . . . *S.C.* May 180
the great *care* I have of thy health . . . *S.C.* May 215
What neede hem *caren* for their flocks, . . . *S.C.* Jul. 195
they casten too much of worlds *care,* . . . *S.C.* S. 114
Nought easeth the *care* that doth me forhaile; . . . *S.C.* S. 243
Ne wont with crabbed *care* the Muses dwell: . . . *S.C.* O. 101
Nought reaped but a weedye crop of *care;* . . . *S.C.* D. 122
the causer of my *care,* . . . *Gn.* Ded. 2
Pales To whome the honest *care* of husbandrie . . . *Gn.* 29
Have *care* for to pursue his footing light . . . *Gn.* 31
This all his *care,* this all his whole indevour, . . . *Gn.* 137
Through whose not costly *care* each shepheard sings . . . *Gn.* 147
Devoid of *care,* and feare of all falshedd; . . . *Gn.* 246
Alceste lives inviolate, Free from all *care,* . . . *Gn.* 426

Care—*Continued.*
more for thrift did *care* than for gay clothing: . . . *Hub.* 231
Or *care* to overlooke, or trust to gather, . . . *Hub.* 279
they without *care* or feare Cruelly fell upon their flock . . . *Hub.* 334
All his *care* was, his service well to saine, . . . *Hub.* 392
he will *care* for all the rest to shift, . . . *Hub.* 532
All his *care* was himselfe how to advaunce, . . . *Hub.* 845
No *care* of justice, nor no rule of reason, . . . *Hub.* 1131
care of thrift, and husbandry, . . . *Hub.* 1170
Let God, . . . if please, *care* for the manie, . . . *Hub.* 1195
I for my selfe must *care* before else anie. . . . *Hub.* 1196
The *care* of Kings and power of Empires stand, . . . *Hub.* 1226
vertuous deeds . . . they *care* not to atchive. . . . *T.M.* 96
Nor anie one doth *care* to call us in, . . . *T.M.* 343
none doth *care* to comfort us at all; . . . *T.M.* 350
Ne doo they *care* to have the auncestrie . . . *T.M.* 439
care that late posteritie Should know their names, . . . *T.M.* 441
Who would ever *care* to doo brave deed, . . . *T.M.* 451
the *care* of Kesars and of Kings. . . . *T.M.* 570
Care now his idle bagpipe up to raise, . . . *Ti.* 226
His bodie left the spectacle of *care*. . . . *Mui.* 440
care that any should bemone My hard mishap, . . . *D.* 75
no worlds sad *care* nor wasting woe . . . *D.* 283
The first beginners of my endles *care:* . . . *D.* 301
life drawes *care*, and care continuall woe; . . . *D.* 450
he for none of them did *care* a whit, . . . *As.* 49
His *care* was all how he them all might kill, . . . *As.* 109
Where cold and *care* and penury do dwell, . . . *Col.* 657
Seemed in heart some hidden *care* she had, . . . I. i. 4. 8
dogges . . . Watching to banish *Care* their enimy, . . . I. i. 40. 5
paynd himselfe with busie *care* to reare Her out of carelesse swowne. . . . I. ii. 45. 3
of devotion he had little *care*, . . . I. iv. 19. 3
thorough daily *care* To get, and nightly feare to lose . . . I. iv. 28. 7
hop'd to reape the crop of all my *care*, . . . I. iv. 47. 2
not a pin Does *care* for looke of living creatures eye. . . . I. v. 4. 4
Her love is firme, her *care* continuall, . . . I. viii. 1. 5
loe! that wicked woman . . . The roote of all your *care* . . . I. viii. 45. 5
what need him *care* for more? . . . I. x. 38. 8
whose *care* Was guests to welcome, . . . I. x. 44. 2
Forgoe that royal maides bequeathed *care*, . . . I. x. 63. 7
'His be that *care*, whom most it doth concerne,' . . . II. iv. 43. 1
care of vow'd revenge and cruell fight, . . . II. vi. 8. 4
Ne *care*, ne feare I how the wind do blow, . . . II. vi. 10. 4
Yet no man for them taketh paines or *care*, . . . II. vi. 15. 8
to her mother Nature all her *care* she letts. . . . II. vi. 16. 9
of no worldly thing he *care* did take: . . . II. vi. 18. 2
Ne of his safetie seemed *care* he kept; . . . II. vi. 42. 5
Before the dore sat selfe-consuming *Care*, . . . II. vii. 25. 1
And is there *care* in heaven? . . . II. viii. 1. 1
The *care* thereof my selfe unto the end, . . . II. viii. 8. 4
All naked without shame or *care* of cold, . . . II. x. 7. 6
With constancy and *care*, gainst daunger and dismay. . . . II. xii. 38. 9
powre, to whom the *care* Of life, . . . perteines . . . II. xii. 47. 2
great *care* she tooke, and greater feare, . . . III. iii. 5. 6
disclo'ste Her clowdy *care* into a wrathfull stowre, . . . III. iv. 13. 8
unto Psyche with great trust and *care* Committed her, . . . III. vi. 51. 3
Have *care*, I pray, to guide the cock-bote well, . . . III. viii. 24. 4
told his *secret* care . . . III. ix. 28. 3
care of credite, or of husband old, . . . III. x. 11. 4
doth with curelesse *care* consume the hart, . . . III. x. 59. 6
Unquiet *Care*, and fond Unthriftyhead; . . . III. xii. 25. 4
With busie *care* they strove him to awake, . . . IV. i. 43. 6
Amoret, companion of her *care:* . . . IV. v. 30. 5
His name was *Care;* a blacksmith by his trade, . . . IV. v. 35. 6
having left that restlesse house of *Care*, . . . IV. vi. 2. 1
she went to seeke faire Amoret, Her second *care*, . . . IV. vi. 46. 7
Ne *care* he had, ne pittie of the pray, . . . IV. vii. 8. 4
Him to recomfort in his greatest *care*, . . . IV. viii. 5. 4
his deare companion of his *care*. . . . IV. viii. 8. 6
manly limbs endur'd with litle *care* . . . IV. viii. 27. 8
So was his toyle the more, the more that was his *care*. . . . IV. viii. 37. 9
Then either *care* of parents could refraine, . . . IV. ix. 3. 4
still with *care* was moved. . . . IV. x. 1. 9
if any Gods at all Have *care* of right, . . . IV. xii. 9. 2
understood the cause of all her *care* . . . IV. xii. 12. 2
For love of Nymphes she thought she need not *care*, . . . IV. xii. 27. 4
The *care* whereof, and hope of his successe, . . . V. vii. 44. 6
That false Duessa, which had wrought great *care* . . . V. ix. 40. 3
had to name The Kingdomes *Care*, . . . V. ix. 43. 8
Importune *care* of their owne publicke cause; . . . V. ix. 44. 8
Unto his way, which now was all his *care* and count. . . . V. x. 16. 9
leaving Artegall to his owne *care*, . . . V. x. 17. 4
from her balefull minde all *care* he banished. . . . V. x. 39. 9
watch advauntage how to worke his *care*, . . . V. xi. 13. 4
unfit For . . . worke of greater *care*, . . . VI. ii. 9. 3
She thankt him . . . for the courteous *care* . . . VI. ii. 46. 8
did with plenteous teares His *care* . . . compassionate, . . . VI. iii. 12. 2
gan . . . with equall *care* to cast . . . VI. iii. 12. 6
Who with the horrour of her haplesse *care* . . . VI. iii. 24. 7
He wore no armour, ne for none did *care*, . . . VI. vii. 43. 1
with full busie *care* His bloudy vessels wash, . . . VI. viii. 39. 8
inward shame . . . through *care* of womanhood, . . . VI. viii. 51. 2
Did *care* a whit, ne any liking lend: . . . VI. ix. 10. 8
each his sundrie sheepe with severall *care* Gathered together, . . . VI. ix. 15. 4
growes dayly more Without my *care*, . . . VI. ix. 21. 6
left in heavy *care* Through daily mourning . . . VI. xii. 14. 4
Like as an huswife, that with busie *care* . . . VII. vi. 48. 1
Whom if ye please, I *care* for other none! . . . *Am.* i. 14
Being my self captyved here in *care*, . . . *Am.* lxxiii. 1

Care—*Continued.*
they seeke onely, without further *care*, . . . *H.L.* 101
His *care*, his joy, his hope, is all on this, . . . *H.L.* 206
sullein *care*, . . . did afflict my brayne, . . . *Proth.* 5

Cared. Ne *car'd* with them his daintie lips to sweeten: . . . *Van.* ii. 9
what *car'd* he for God, or godlinesse? . . . *Hub.* 844
As for the rascall Commons least he *cared*, . . . *Hub.* 1193
Not honored nor *cared* for of anie, . . . *T.M.* 225
they living *cared* not to cherishe No gentle wits, . . . *Ti.* 362
Nought *carde* I then for worldly change or chaunce, . . . *D.* 103
For one alone he *cared*, for one he sigh't, . . . *As.* 53
neither *car'd* for wynd, nor haile, nor raine, . . . *Col.* 221
He . . . *cared* not for God or man a point. . . . I. ii. 12. 9
Ne *car'd* for blood in his avengement: . . . I. iv. 34. 5
no man *car'd* to answere to his crye: . . . I. viii. 29. 7
Ne *car'd* to hoord for those whom he did breede: . . . I. x. 38. 5
nought he *car'd* his carcas long unfed; . . . I. x. 48. 7
Ne ought he *car'd* whom he endamaged . . . II. ii. 18. 7
Ne *car'd* he greatly for her presence vayne, . . . II. iii. 43. 6
ne *car'd* for his saufgard, . . . II. v. 8. 8
Ne *cared* she her course for to apply; . . . II. vi. 5. 7
The Conquerour nought *cared* him to slay; . . . II. viii. 51. 2
ne *car'd* to hyde Their dainty partes . . . II. xii. 63. 8
Ne for them ne for honour *cared* hee, . . . II. xii. 80. 5
ne *car'd* to spill Her garments gay . . . III. viii. 26. 8
cared not to spare that should be shortly spent. . . . IV. iii. 6. 9
Ne either *car'd* to ward, or perill shonne, . . . IV. iii. 36. 4
Ne either *cared* life to save or spill, . . . IV. iii. 36. 6
nought he *car'd* for friend or enemy, . . . IV. iv. 11. 8
he nought *car'd* for all that they could say, . . . IV. v. 27. 6
Ne better had he, ne for better *cared:* . . . IV. v. 35. 2
Thenceforth he *car'd* no more which way he strooke, . . . V. xi. 12. 6
Ne *cared* as a coward so to be condemned. . . . VI. iii. 36. 9
He *cared* not for dint of sword nor speere, . . . VI. iv. 4. 6
What *cared* she who sighed for her sore, . . . VI. vii. 30. 5
For other worldly wealth they *cared* nought. . . . VI. ix. 5. 6
cared more for Colins carolings . . . VI. ix. 35. 7
Ne *cared* she her wound in teares to steepe, . . . VI. xi. 23. 8

Career. To stop his wearie *cariere* suddenly: . . . *Ro.* xvi. 8

Careful. The *carefull* travailes of the painefull day: . . . *Bel.*[1] i. 4
The *carefull* thoughts of mortall miseries; . . . *Bel.*[2] i. 4
'A thousand sithes I curse that *carefull* hower . . . *S.C.* Ja. 49
hanging heads did seeme his *carefull* case to weepe. . . . *S.C.* Ja. 78
Your *carefull* heards with cold bene annoied: . . . *S.C.* F. 48
carefull thoughts in her heart did creepe) . . . *S.C.* May 190
keepe your corpse from the *carefull* stounds . . . *S.C.* May 257
my *carefull* case to frame: . . . *S.C.* Jun. 78
O, *carefull* Colin! I lament thy case; . . . *S.C.* Jun. 113
The hollow Echo of my *carefull* cryes: . . . *S.C.* Au. 160
O *carefull* verse! . . . *S.C.* N. 62, 72, 82, 92, 102, 112, 122, 132, 142, 152, 162
The rurall song of *carefull* Colinet. . . . *S.C.* D. 18
'The *carefull* cold hath nypt my rugged rynde, . . . *S.C.* D. 133
with pure brest from *carefull* sorrow free, . . . *Gn.* 107
So wander we all *carefull* comfortlesse, . . . *T.M.* 349
So *carefull* was for them, and for my good, . . . *D.* 138
her old sire more *carefull* of her good, . . . *Col.* 120
carefull pipe may make the hearer rew: . . . *Col.* 397
mourning stole of *carefull* wydowhead, . . . *Col.* 494
delay The rugged brow of *carefull* Policy, . . . *Ded. Son.* i. 12
To you, right noble Lord, whose *carefull* brest . . . *Ded. Son.* ix. 1
His heavie head, devoide of *careful* carke; . . . I. i. 44. 4
Whose case whenas the *careful* Dwarfe had tould, . . . I. v. 52. 1
The pitteous mayden, *carefull*, comfortlesse, . . . I. vi. 6. 1
So fast he carried her with *carefull* paine, . . . I. vi. 33. 8
cruell fates the *carefull* threds unfould, . . . I. vii. 22. 5
in constant *carefull* mind, She fedd her wound . . . I. vii. 28. 5
The *carefull* cold beginneth for to creep, . . . I. vii. 39. 4
That when the *carefull* knight gan well avise, . . . I. viii. 15. 5
From that day forth I cast in *carefull* mynd, . . . I. ix. 15. 6
sent with *carefull* diligence, To fetch a Leach, . . . I. x. 23. 6
consuming thought To put away out of his *carefull* brest. . . . I. x. 29. 6
the *carefull* charge of him she gave, . . . I. x. 34. 6
As *carefull* Nourse her child from falling oft does reare. . . . I. x. 35. 9
The gentle knight her soone with *carefull* paine Uplifted . . . II. i. 46. 1
Yet no man to them can his *carefull* paines compare. . . . II. vi. 15. 9
The *carefull* servaunt stryving with his raging Lord. . . . II. vi. 47. 9
A *carefull* man, and full of comely guyse. . . . II. ix. 31. 2
The noble Elfe and *carefull* Palmer . . . II. xii. 81. 1
carefull thoughts did quite assoile. . . . III. i. 58. 9
taught the *carefull* Mariner to play, . . . III. viii. 20. 3
then that *carefull* Fay Departed thence . . . IV. ii. 53. 1
Those be unquiet thoughts that *carefull* minds invade. . . . IV. v. 35. 9
There he continued in this *carefull* plight, . . . IV. vii. 41. 1
did so well employ his *carefull* paine, . . . IV. xi. 7. 2
piteously complaind her *carefull* grieffe, . . . IV. xii. 5. 3
By that same *carefull* Squire did then abide, . . . V. i. 23. 2
She chaw'd the cud of lover's *carefull* plight; . . . V. v. 27. 2
Which long he usd with *carefull* diligence, . . . V. x. 12. 8
by them long with *carefull* labour nurst, . . . VI. Pr. 3. 8
with *carefull* hand . . . To wype his wounds, . . . VI. ii. 41. 4
her did sustaine With *carefull* hands, . . . VI. iii. 28. 6
day and night did vexe her *carefull* thought, . . . VI. v. 6. 8
weary now with *carefull* keeping ward, . . . VI. v. 21. 2
Howbe that *carefull* Hermite did his best, . . . VI. vi. 2. 6
Till then I wander *carefull*, comfortlesse, . . . *Am.* xxxiv. 13
with *carefull* heed The silver scaly trouts doe tend . . . *Epith.* 56
drinketh up the lyfe, Of *carefull* wretches . . . *H.L.* 126

Carefully. doen so *carefully* theyr flocks tend. . . . . *S.C.* S. 179
In th' hearts of men to rule them *carefully,* . . . . *T.M.* 314
Full *carefully* he kept them day and night, ... *As.* 5
he gave . . . That scarlot whore to keepen *carefully;* . . . . I. viii. 29. 2
the old-woman *carefully* displayd The clothes . . . . III. ii. 47. 4
as her Squyre attend her *carefully.* . . . . III. iii. 61. 5
no lesse *carefully* her tendered Then her owne daughter . . . III. vi. 51. 6
To counsell her, so *carefully* dismayd, ... III. viii. 4. 8
he his hand so *carefully* did beare, ... IV. vii. 27. 5
Like to a Spaniell wayting *carefully* . . . . V. vi. 26. 8
then most *carefully* . . . did him selfe apply. . . . . VI. iii. 19. 8
he did her attend most *carefully,* . . . . VI. v. 9. 6
Carefulness. ne them keepe with *carefulnesse.* . . . . III. xi. 53. 9
Careless. Then is your *carelesse* corage accoied, ... *S.C.* F. 47
youth and course of *carelesse* yeeres, ... *S.C.* Jun. 33
Ye *carelesse* byrds are privie to my cryes, ... *S.C.* Au. 153
his *carelesse* time This Shepheard drives, ... *Gn.* 153
His dearest life did trust to *careles* sleep; . . . . *Gn.* 243
Thy *careles* limbs in loose sleep dost display. . . . . *Gn.* 336
careles hear'st my intollerable cares. . . . . *Gn.* 632
when all shrowded were In *careles* sleep, ... *Hub.* 334
Playing alone *carelesse* on hir heavenlie Virginals. . . . . . *U.V.* 6
as one *carelesse* of suspition, ... *Com. Son.* i. 5
his Colin, *carelesse* Colin Cloute, ... *Ti.* 225
For to entrap the *careles* Clarion, ... *Mui.* 375
His *carelesse* locks uncombed and unshorne, ... *D.* 43
drown'd in *carelesse* quiet deepe; . . . . *D.* 136
closde her eyes with *carelesse* quietnesse; . . . . *D.* 257
To *carelesse* heavens I doo daylie call; . . . . *D.* 354
do feed Your *carelesse* flocks on hils . . . . *D.* 520
carelesse Quiet lyes Wrapt in eternall silence . . . . I. i. 41. 8
you in *carelesse* sleepe are drowned quight.' . . . . I. i. 53. 4
Paynd himselfe . . . to reare Her out of *carelesse* swowne. . . . I. ii. 45. 4
when all men *carelesse* slept, ... I. iii. 17. 6
Both *carelesse* of his health, and of his fame; . . . . I. vii. 7. 3
if that *carelesse* hevens,' (quoth she) 'despise . . . . II. i. 36. 1
As *carelesse* of his woe, or innocent . . . . II. ii. 1. 7
For to allure fraile mind to *carelesse* ease: . . . . II. vi. 13. 6
Carelesse the man soone woxe, ... II. vi. 13. 7
Like as the sacred Oxe that *carelesse* stands, ... III. iv. 17. 1
in lewd slouth to wast his *carelesse* day; . . . . III. v. 1. 7
all *carelesse* of her needes; . . . . III. vii. 6. 5
Downe to her foot with *carelesse* modestee. . . . . III. ix. 21. 6
Reproch despightfull, *carelesse,* and unkinde; . . . . III. xii. 24. 4
All *carelesse* of his taunt and bitter rayle; . . . . IV. i. 43. 2
As she sate *carelesse* by a cristall flood . . . . IV. ii. 45. 4
Carelesse of perill in their fiers affret, ... IV. iii. 6. 7
by their many wounds and *carelesse* harmes, ... IV. iv. 38. 3
I, . . . bend my *carelesse* wit To salvage chace, ... VI. ii. 9. 4
In which he liv'd alone, like *carelesse* bird in cage. . . . . VI. vi. 4. 9
the whyles the Prince did rest In *carelesse* couch, ... VI. vi. 44. 2
sitting *carelesse* on the scorners stoole, ... VI. viii. 21. 7
All *carelesse* how my life for her decayes: . . . . *Am.* xxxviii. 10
she, all *carelesse* of his griefe . . . . *Am.* xlviii. 9
Goe to my love, where she is *carelesse* layd, ... *Am.* lxx. 5
forgets the cruell *carelesse* elfe His mothers heast to prove. . . *Epig.* iv. 57
greedy pleasure, *carelesse* of your toyes, ... *Epith.* 365
Carelessly. her yeolow locks . . . *carelesle* downe trailing, . . . *Ti.* 11
came flying *carelesslie,* Where hidden was . . . . *Mui.* 391
There he him found all *carelesly* displaid, ... II. v. 32. 1
suffred her so *carelesly* disguiz'd Be overtaken. . . . . . . III. vi. 19. 5
with the tide drove forward *carelesly;* . . . . III. viii. 21. 4
Uncomb'd, uncurl'd, and *carelesly* unshed; . . . . IV. vii. 40. 6
And *carelesly* into the river goth, ... VI. iii. 33. 3
Carelessness. Sweete slumbring deaw in *carelesnesse* did steepe, *Gn.* 323
with reproch of *carelesnes* unkynd Upbrayd, ... I. vii. 3. 7
Caren. *See* **Care.**
Care's. Scudamour, comming to *Cares* House, ... IV. v. Arg.
Cares. whiles that my daylie *cares* did sleepe, ... *Van.* i. 1
Ne *cares* he if the fleece, which him arayes, ... *Gn.* 97
sad *cares* that rich mens hearts devowre. . . . . *Gn.* 136
careles hear'st my intollerable *cares.* . . . . *Gn.* 632
wondrous *cares* . . . full sore opprest; . . . . *Gn.* 642
To fret thy soule with crosses and with *cares;* . . . . *Hub.* 903
leave me here distressed With mortall *cares* . . . . *Ti.* 305
'Nought *cares* at all . . . . *D.* 87
carest for one that for himselfe *cares* nought, ... *D.* 93
cares finde quiet! . . . . *D.* 447
the huge burden of my *cares* unlade. . . . . *D.* 489
So Maro oft did Caesars *cares* allay. . . . . *Ded. Son.* i. 8
From worldly *cares* himselfe he did esloyne, ... I. iv. 20. 1
Forgetfull of his owne that mindes an others *cares.* . . . . . I. v. 18. 9
doubly is distrest twixt joy and *cares* . . . . I. vi. 1. 7
By tryall of his former harmes and *cares,* . . . . II. i. 4. 7
his mynd Behaves with *cares,* . . . . II. iii. 40. 7
whom he hurts nought *cares.* . . . . II. iv. 7. 9
nether spinnes nor cards, ne *cares* nor fretts, ... II. vi. 16. 8
Which with sad *cares* empeach our native joyes. . . . . II. vii. 15. 6
To taken counsell of their common *cares;* . . . . II. x. 37. 7
mortall men their weary *cares* Do lay away, ... III. ii. 32. 1
Thou art the roote and nourse of bitter *cares,* . . . . III. iv. 57. 2
Ne *cares* what men say of him, ... III. ix. 3. 7
whereby all *cares* forepast Are washt away . . . . IV. iii. 44. 6
all the *cares* and evill which they meet . . . . IV. x. 2. 2
count my *cares* when none is nigh to heare, ... IV. xii. 6. 2
Cares not what evils hap to wretched wight; . . . . IV. xii. 6. 8
Right sorrowfully mourning her bereaved *cares.* . . . . IV. xii. 17. 9
will my *cares* unfolde, in hope to find Your aide . . . . . . V. vii. 19. 4
store of *cares* doth follow riches store. . . . . VI. ix. 21. 4
Me no such *cares* nor combrous thoughts offend, ... VI. ix. 22. 6

Cares—*Continued.*
Wrapped in wretched *cares* and hearts unrest, ... VI. xi. 3. 2
all my *cares,* which cruell Love collected, ... *Epith.* 317
That maketh them all worldly *cares* forget, ... *H.H.B.* 265
Cares'. Fit matter for his *cares* increase would finde, ... *D.* 3
Carest. *carest* for one that for himselfe cares nought, ... *D.* 93
Careticus. 'All which his sonne *Careticus* awhile Shall well defend, ... III. iii. 33. 1
Carians'. Mausolus worke will be the *Carians* glorie; . . . . *Ro.* ii. 7
Cariere. *See* **Career.**
Caring. Nor *caring* how . . . She her gay painted plumes disorderid: . . . . II. iii. 36. 3
Not *caring* his long labours to deface; . . . . III. xii. 32. 3
spake reprochfully, not *caring* where nor when. . . . . VI. xii. 27. 9
Cark. the wight whose absence is our *carke;* . . . . *S.C.* N. 66
His heavie head, devoide of careful *carke;* . . . . I. i. 44. 4
Carl. when the *carle* beheld, and saw his guest . . . . I. ix. 54. 2
that fiers *Carle* commaunding to forbeare, ... II. vii. 43. 2
For her defence against that *Carle* to fight, ... II. xi. 16. 7
Soone as the *Carle* from far the Prince espyde . . . . II. xi. 24. 1
Now had the *Carle* Alighted from his Tigre, ... II. xi. 33. 6
He to the *Carle* him selfe agayn addrest, ... II. xi. 37. 2
the *Carle* as fast Gan heap huge strokes on him, ... II. xi. 43. 8
wrong'd by *Carle,* by Proteus sav'd, ... III. viii. Arg.
'Therein a cancred crabbed *Carle* does dwell, ... III. ix. 3. 5
evermore the *Carle* of courtesie accusd. . . . . III. ix. 12. 9
that uncurteous *Carle,* their commune foe, ... III. ix. 17. 8
the wicked *carle,* the maister Smith, ... IV. v. 44. 1
Of this accursed *Carle* of hellish kind, ... IV. vii. 18. 4
hardly could he come the *carle* to touch, ... IV. vii. 27. 3
of that *Carle* she sorely bruz'd had beene, ... IV. vii. 35. 8
that selfe arrow which the *Carle* had kild; . . . . IV. vii. 36. 5
Of that same wicked *Carle,* . . . . IV. viii. 21. 6
streight leapt the *Carle* unblest, ... V. ii. 12. 7
To wreake your wrath on such a *carle* as hee: . . . . V. iii. 36. 8
neither will one foot, till we that *carle* have hent.' . . . . V. ix. 7. 9
when as the caytive *carle* Should issue forth, ... V. ix. 9. 1
A cruell *carle,* the which all strangers slew, ... V. x. 10. 3
They saw that *Carle* from farre, ... VI. i. 17. 5
Whenas the *Carle* no longer could sustaine, ... VI. i. 22. 2
Looking at that same *Carle* . . . . VI. iii. 34. 7
Led by a *Carle* and foole which by her side did passe. . . . . VI. vii. 27. 9
So did the Squire, the whiles the *Carle* did fret . . . . . . VI. vii. 47. 7
Till heavy hand the *Carle* upon him layd, ... VI. vii. 48. 6
the *Carle* with paine Saved him selfe . . . . VI. viii. 9. 3
gan fiercely fly Upon that *Carle* . . . . VI. viii. 12. 9
Slay not that *Carle,* though worthy to be slaine, ... VI. viii. 17. 7
Carleil. *See* **Cairleill.**
Carl's. end of that *Carles* dayes and his owne paynes did make. II. xi. 46. 9
Carls. for these *Carles* to carry much more comely were?' . . . VI. viii. 23. 9
at variaunce fell With those two *Carles,* . . . . VI. viii. 31. 4
Carnal. With stinges of *carnall* lust, ... II. xi. 13. 7
Carnation. her pure yvory Into a cleare *Carnation* suddeine dyde; . . . . III. iii. 20. 3
Carnations. Bring *Coronations,* and Sops in wine, ... *S.C.* Ap. 138
Carol. Tho wouldest thou learne to *caroll* of Love, ... *S.C.* F. 61
carroll (*carrol) lowde, and leade the Myllers rownde, . . . *S.C.* O. 52
to my pype to *caroll* and to daunce. . . . . *D.* 105
For he could pipe, and daunce, and *caroll* sweet, ... *As.* 31
Or *carol* made to praise thy loved lasse.' . . . . *Col.* 87
to *caroll,* as they sate Keeping their sheepe, ... VI. x. 33. 5
carroll of Loves praise. . . . . *Epith.* 79
thereunto doe daunce and *carrol* sweet, ... *Epith.* 135
The whiles the maydens doe theyr *carroll* sing, ... *Epith.* 259
And *caroll* Hymnes of love both day and night. . . . . *H.H.L.* 70
Caroled. His maistresse praises sweetly *caroled:* . . . . III. vii. 17. 4
Fit song of Angels *caroled* to bee! . . . . III. viii. 43. 1
Caroling. told that gardins pleasures in their *caroling.* . . . . II. vi. 24. 9
Ay *caroling* of love and jollity, ... III. i. 40. 5
Playing on pipes and *caroling* apace, ... VI. ix. 5. 3
caroling her name both day and night, ... VI. ix. 9. 8
Carolings. cared more for Colins *carolings* . . . . VI. ix. 35. 7
And heare such heavenly notes and *carolings,* . . . . *H.H.B.* 262
Carols. sings Hymns to high God, and *carols* heavenly things, . V. ix. 29. 5
Came dauncing forth, and joyous *carrols* song: . . . . V. xi. 34. 4
Carpers. Such as no *carpers* may contrayre reveale; . . . . . *Hub.* 494
Carriage. Through Venus grace, and vertues *cariage.* . . . . *Gn.* 488
Through due deserts and comely *carriage,* . . . . *Hub.* 777
His *carriage* was full comely and upright; . . . . II. i. 6. 1
With sober grace and goodly *carriage:* . . . . II. ii. 38. 2
laid the blame, not to his *carriage,* . . . . III. i. 11. 5
And saw his *carriage* past that perill well, ... VI. iii. 34. 6
comely *carriage* of her count'nance trim, ... VI. ix. 9. 4
gracious gifts bestow, . . . As comely *carriage,* . . . . . . VI. x. 23. 4
His humble *carriage,* his unfaulty wayes, ... *H.H.L.* 233
Carried. *Caried* to heaven, from sinfull bondage losed; . . . *Ro.* xix. 12
'I *carried* am into waste wildernesse, ... *Gn.* 369
I beyond all these am *carried* faine, ... *Gn.* 419
Carried in clowdes of all-concealing night. . . . . *Hub.* 340
be *carried* with the common winde . . . . *Hub.* 722
twixt their blessed armes it *carried* . . . . *Ti.* 627
his unstaid desire Him wholly *caried,* . . . . *Mui.* 162
forth *caried* Into the cursed cobweb, ... *Mui.* 422
so true-seeming grace It *carried,* . . . . I. v. 27. 5
So fast he *carried* her with carefull paine, ... I. vi. 33. 8
Upon his shoulders *carried* him perforse . . . . II. xi. 46. 4
Carried her forward with her first intent: . . . . III. iv. 50. 5
Carried away with wings of speedy feare.' . . . . III. v. 6. 6
The carcas with the streame was *carried* downe, ... III. v. 25. 6
with them *carried* to be fostered. . . . . III. vi. 28. 2

Carried—*Continued.*
Perforce her *carried* where ever he thought best. III. vii. 2. 9
carried her beyond all jeopardy; III. vii. 3. 4
What wonder then, if she were likewise *carried?* III. x. 9. 9
Caried with fervent zeale: IV. iv. 34. 3
this *caried* with the tide, That with the wind, IV. ix. 26. 7
His corps was *carried* downe along the Lee, V. ii. 19. 1
being *carried* farre from forraine lands. V. iv. 5. 5
Yet fled she fast . . . *Carried* with wings of feare, V. viii. 4. 7
An hart not *carried* with too curious eyes, VI. ii. 16. 8
Thence they him *carried* to a Castle neare, VI. ii. 48. 7
Whom Calidore thus *carried* on his chine; VI. iii. 3. 8
being *carried* with his force forthright VI. vii. 7. 7
carried captive by those theeves away; VI. x. 41. 2
Spoyld all our cots, and *caried* us from hence; VI. xi. 30. 5
Carries. *carries* thee so swifte and light.' II. iv. 43. 4
carries into smoake with rage and horror great. II. xi. 32. 9
As *carries* them into an extasy, *H.H.B.* 261
Carriest. *cariest* him to that which he hath eyde, *H.L.* 227
Carrion. a fowling net, Which he for *carrion* Crowes had set *S.C.* Mar. 110
in my *carrion* carcas abounds.' *S.C.* May 258
grave, That still for *carrion* carcases doth crave: I. ix. 33. 5
Why should not that dead *carrion* satisfye The guilt II. viii. 28. 6
having scruzd out of his *carrion* corse The lothfull life, II. xi. 46. 2
In loathly wise like to a *carrion* corse, III. vii. 43. 5
Having his *carrion* corse quite sencelesse left IV. vii. 32. 4
it approve upon his *carrion* corse. V. iii. 30. 5
an hungry hound That hunting after game hath *carrion* found, V. viii. 36. 5
There they him left a *carrion* outcast V. ix. 19. 8
Unto some *carrion* offered to his sight; VI. viii. 28. 5
Carry. semblance she did *carrie* under feigned hew. I. i. 46. 9
to her watry chamber swiftly *carry* him. III. iv. 42. 9
Timely to joy and *carrie* comely cheare: V. v. 38. 5
they fled As fast as feete could *carry* them away; V. x. 36. 2
carry colours faire that feeble eies misdeeme. VI. Pr. 4. 9
for these Carles to *carry* much more comely were?' VI. viii. 23. 9
exchange Their dwelling places, as the streames them *carrie:* VII. vii. 21. 6
Whose ymage yet I *carry* fresh in mynd. *Am.* lxxviii. 4
whither, Love! wilt thou now *carrie* mee? *H.B.* 1
Which *carrie* privie message to the spright, *H.B.* 236
And *carrie* all the rest with him around; *H.H.B.* 74
Carrying. *Carrying* compassion to their lovely foe; *H.B.* 243
Cart. On every side of his embatteld *cart,* V. viii. 34. 3
Carthage. *Carthage* towres from spoile should be forborne, *Ro.* xxiii. 2
To whom the ruin'd walls of *Carthage* vow'd, *Gn.* 615
Carve. they will *carven* the shepheards throte. *S.C.* S. 41
I can *carve* with this inchaunted brond II. viii. 22. 4
Through cruell knife that her deare heart did *kerve:* IV. i. 4. 5
Carved. yvory sheath, *ycarv'd* with curious slights, I. vii. 30. 7
An Altare, *carv'd* with cunning ymagery, I. viii. 36. 2
Carven. *See* **Carve.**
Carver. The *carver* Holme; I. i. 9. 9
Case. In *case* thy greatnes he can gesse in harte, *Ro.* v. 3
hanging heads did seeme his carefull *case* to weepe. *S.C.* Ja. 78
my carefull *case* to frame: *S.C.* Jun. 78
O, carefull Colin! I lament thy *case;* *S.C.* Jun. 113
my *case* I thus complaine *Gn. Ded.* 3
sorie my sad *case* to see, *Hub.* 18
plaine his *case* with words unkinde. *Hub.* 52
Thus therefore I advize upon the *case,* *Hub.* 129
Its an hard *case,* when men of good deserving *Hub.* 369
In *case* thou ever there wilt hope to thrive, *Hub.* 632
In *case* his paines were recompenst with reason. *Hub.* 887
In *case* the good . . . they would wisely take. *Hub.* 962
Came to the Court, her *case* there to complaine; *Hub.* 1208
To whom shall I my evill *case* complaine, *T.M.* 421
shame and sorrow and accursed *case* *T.M.* 519
A dolefull *case* desires a dolefull song, *T.M.* 541
in my *case* their owne ensample see. *Ti.* 462
Hath made fit mate thy wretched *case* to heare, *D.* 65
I will to thee this heavie *case* relate: *D.* 96
Therefore more plaine areade this doubtfull *case.'* *D.* 182
will my *case* bemone, And pitie me *D.* 382
Help me to wayle my miserable *case,* *D.* 510
I sore griev'd to see his wretched *case.* *D.* 553
Let him be moov'd to pity such a *case.* *As.* Pr. 18
'More eath . . . it is in such a *case* *Col.* 590
And for your owne high merit in like *cace:* *Ded. Son.* xi. 7
Which ever after in most wretched *case,* . . . by the hedges lay. I. iv. 3. 5
To wayle his wofull *case* she would not stay, I. v. 19. 8
Whose *case* whenas the careful Dwarfe had tould, I. v. 52. 1
to tell her lamentable *cace,* I. vi. 48. 8
wondrous faith . . . Was firmest fixt in myne extremest *case.* I. ix. 17. 5
'Then shall I you recount a ruefull *cace,'* I. ix. 26. 6
'These, that have it attaynd, were in like *cace,* I. x. 62. 3
he could not endure so cruell *cace,* I. xi. 26. 8
In *case* he could that monstrous beast destroy, I. xii. 41. 7
'Deare Lady! how shall I declare thy *cace,* II. i. 9. 6
Sore chauffed at my stay in such a *cace,* II. iv. 32. 7
Like Angels life was then mens happy *cace;* II. vii. 16. 5
more wretched were the *cace* Of men then beasts. II. viii. 1. 4
by your powre protect his feeble *cace?* II. viii. 25. 8
Guyon mervayld at her uncouth *cace;* II. ix. 43. 5
As every one seem'd meetest in that *cace.* II. xi. 6. 5
never was she in so evill *cace,* II. xi. 16. 3
whose unhappy *cace* . . . them driven hath II. xii. 8. 7
as if his *case* she rewd. II. xii. 73. 9
In *case* he have no Lady nor no love, III. i. 26. 8
dare thou not, I charge, in any *cace* To enter III. iii. 8. 7
where long in wretched *cace* He liv'd, III. iii. 41. 4

Case—*Continued.*
How him in deadly *case* theyr Lady fownd, III. v. 38. 4
she bore in like *cace* Fayre Amoretta III. vi. 4. 4
attaine My Ladies love in such a desperate *case,* III. vii. 60. 7
succor send to her distressed *cace;* III. viii. 29. 4
humid evening ill for sicke folkes *cace;* III. ix. 26. 4
Was never wretched man in such a wofull *cace.* III. x. 14. 9
Vouchsafe with mild regard a wretches *cace* to heare.' III. x. 26. 9
That present were to testifie the *case.'* IV. i. 49. 5
in *case* it had arrived Where it was ment, IV. iii. 18. 1
Whilst thus the *case* in doubtfull ballance hong, IV. iii. 37. 1
To deeme this doutfull *case,* for which they all contended. IV. v. 6. 9
at which so suddain *case* He wondred much. IV. vi. 3. 5
all the gods did mone her miserable *case.* IV. vii. 30. 9
Full of sad anguish and in heavy *case:* IV. vii. 38. 4
She knew him not, but pittied much his *case,* IV. viii. 12. 8
wondred much at his so selcouth *case;* IV. viii. 14. 2
The evill *case* in which those Ladies lay; IV. viii. 20. 2
He cald to him aloud his *case* to rew, IV. viii. 40. 7
An hard mishap and disaventrous *case* IV. viii. 51. 3
diversly conferred of their *case,* IV. ix. 10. 2
In *case* his burning lust should breake into excesse. IV. ix. 18. 9
There unto him betid a disaventrous *case.* IV. xii. 4. 9
So feelingly her *case* she did complaine, IV. xii. 5. 6
She gan afresh thus to renew her wretched *case.* IV. xii. 8. 9
In better *case,* V. Pr. 7. 3
the more Rejoyced at his miserable *case,* V. iv. 23. 2
That ever in this wretched *case* ye were? V. iv. 26. 3
With which in *case* thou canst him not invade, V. v. 49. 7
In *case* she might finde favour in his eye, V. v. 55. 2
if she would free him from that *case,* V. v. 55. 8
With fayned colours shading a true *case;* V. vii. 2. 7
The tryall of a great and weightie *case,* V. ix. 36. 7
privie was and partie in the *case:* V. ix. 47. 5
Sith ye thus farre have tendred my poore *case,* V. xi. 18. 3
Hard is the *case* the which ye doe complaine; V. xi. 55. 2
Such was Irenas countenance, such her *case,* V. xii. 13. 7
'My haplesse *case* Is not occasiond through my misdesert, VI. i. 12. 5
His mightie hart their mournefull *case* can rew, VI. ii. 41. 4
That was a straunger to her wretched *case;* VI. ii. 47. 4
Too greatly grieve at any his unlucky *case.'* VI. iii. 5. 9
thinking to what *case* her name should now be brought. VI. iii. 6. 9
whilest he was in this distressed *case,* VI. iii. 30. 5
the Knight, now in so needy *case,* VI. iii. 38. 4
when he had devized of her *case,* VI. iv. 34. 3
To seeke some comfort in that sorie *case.* VI. v. 7. 4
was fall'n into this feeble *case* Through many wounds, VI. vi. 20. 7
with the ruth of her so wicked *case,* VI. vi. 31. 8
Much did the Craven seeme to mone his *case,* VI. vii. 18. 1
plainely gan to him declare the *case* VI. vii. 21. 2
Throughout the world in this uncomely *case,* VI. vii. 38. 2
Ensample take of Mirabellaes *case,* VI. viii. 2. 7
He like a dog was led in captive *case,* VI. viii. 5. 4
inward shame of her uncomely *case* She did conceive, VI. viii. 51. 1
Yet could not remedie her wretched *case;* VI. xii. 8. 2
'Ne is the water in more constant *case,* VII. vii. 20. 1
Expecting th' end of this so doubtfull *case,* VII. vii. 57. 5
Whose want too well now feeles my freendles *case;* *Proth.* 140
Cases. made most ugly *cases.* V. xii. 28. 9
as is by law ordayned In *cases* like; VI. vii. 36. 6
Caspian. Who swelling sayles in *Caspian* sea doth crosse, II. vii. 14. 3
(As wonts the Tartar by the *Caspian* lake, II. xi. 26. 7
Cassibalane. *Cassibalane,* their Eme, II. x. 47. 1
Cassiopeia's. Aldeboran . . . Above the shinie *Cassiopeias* chaire, I. iii. 16. 2
Cassock. th' Ape a *cassocke* sidelong hanging downe; *Hub.* 354
a thin silken *cassock* coloured greene, VII. vii. 29. 2
Cast. *See* **Counter-cast, Outcast, Overcast.**
cast to quitt them from their bondage quight: *Van.* xi. 4
he *cast* him to scold And snebbe the good Oake, *S.C.* F. 125
oft his hoarie locks downe doth *cast,* *S.C.* F. 181
To this the Oake *cast* him to replie *S.C.* F. 189
I *cast* to goe a shooting. *S.C.* Mar. 63
he *cast* me downe hys pack, *S.C.* May 245
I *cast* to have lorne this grounde: *S.C.* S. 57
I *cast* for to compare Whether . . . did exceede: I. ii. 37. 3
they *casten* too much of worlds care, *S.C.* S. 114
let us *cast* with what delight to chace, *S.C.* O. 2
cast hem out as rotten and unsoote. *S.C.* D. 118
The loser Lasse I *cast* to please no more; *S.C.* D. 119
by their huge Navy *cast,* *Gn.* 47
Into the same mishap I now am *cast,* *Gn.* 363
They *cast* in course to waste the wearie howres. *Hub.* 27
Or *cast* a figure for a Bishoprick; *Hub.* 511
he by meanes might *cast* them to prevent, *Hub.* 881
he *cast* to leave The Court, *Hub.* 935
cast to seeke the Lion where he may, *Hub.* 1316
to the other side To *cast* mine eye, *Ti.* 588
After his guize did *cast* abroad to fare: *Mui.* 55
gan to *cast* how I her compasse might, *D.* 115
He gan to *cast* great lyking to my lore, *Col.* 180
humor . . . on them *cast* Sweet slombring deaw, I. i. 36. 3
ever-drizling raine . . . did *cast* him in a swowne. I. i. 41. 5
over it *Cast* a black stole, I. i. 45. 9
He *cast* about, and searcht his baleful bokes againe. I. ii. 2. 9
I *cast* for to compare Whether . . . did exceede: I. ii. 37. 3
What not by right she *cast* to win by guile; I. ii. 38. 3
that dredd Lyons looke her *cast* in deadly hew. I. iii. 11. 9
Into new woes unweeting I was *cast* I. iv. 47. 3
to *cast* his eye . . . Upon his brothers shield, I. v. 10. 1

Cast—*Continued.*
Of all attonce he *cast* avengd to be, . . . I. v. 12. 6
besought Some cursed vengeaunce on his sonne to *cast*. . . . I. v. 38. 2
first he *cast* by treatie, . . . Her to persuade . . . I. vi. 3. 6
cast her coulours . . . To seeme like truth, . . . I. vii. 1. 4
ryder from her loftie sted Would have *cast* downe, . . . I. viii. 17. 6
Her golden cup she *cast* unto the ground, . . . I. viii. 25. 2
From that day forth I *cast* in carefull mynd, . . . I. ix. 15. 6
as he fledd his eye was backward *cast,* . . . I. ix. 21. 5
She *cast* to bring him where he chearen might, . . . I. x. 2. 8
With lookes full lowly *cast,* . . . I. x. 5. 6
To Una back he *cast* him to retyre, . . . I. x. 68. 2
He *cast* to suffer him no more respire, . . . I. xi. 28. 7
Monster, having *kest* His wearie foe into that living well, . . . I. xi. 31. 5
He *cast* at once him to avenge for all; . . . I. xi. 40. 6
That I may *cast* to compas your reliefe, . . . II. i. 48. 8
cast to seek him forth through danger . . . II. i. 52. 9
One that to bountie never *cast* his mynd, . . . II. iii. 4. 2
to court he *cast* t' advaunce his first degree. . . . II. iii. 5. 9
he *cast* for to uphold His ydle humour . . . II. iii. 9. 7
Then him to ground he *cast,* . . . II. iv. 14. 7
I *cast* to pay that I so dearely bought. . . . II. iv. 30. 7
soone his dreadfull blade about he *cast,* . . . II. v. 12. 3
He *cast* him downe to ground, . . . II. v. 23. 3
Having his warlike weapons *cast* behynd, . . . II. v. 28. 7
He *cast* between to ward the bitter stownd: . . . II. viii. 32. 6
(Who Guyons shield *cast* ever him before, . . . II. viii. 43. 2
through his nimble sleight did under him down *cast*. . . . II. viii. 49. 9
Did not once move, nor upward *cast* his eye, . . . II. viii. 50. 6
blow them quite away, and in the Ocean *cast*. . . . II. ix. 16. 9
Over the which was *cast* a wandring vine, . . . II. ix. 24. 4
Unto the grownd she *cast* her modest eye, . . . II. ix. 41. 2
he espying *cast* her to restraine . . . II. xi. 28. 4
adowne he *kest* The lumpish corse . . . II. xi. 42. 5
Adowne he *kest* it with so puissant wrest, . . . II. xi. 42. 7
Gan heap huge strokes on him, as ere he down was *cast*. . . . II. xi. 43. 9
Therefore to grownd he would him *cast* no more, . . . II. xi. 45. 7
Hedlong her selfe did *cast* into that lake; . . . II. xi. 47. 6
The cup to ground did violently *cast,* . . . II. xii. 57. 3
Old Glauce *cast* to cure this Ladies griefe; . . . III. iii. 5. 2
cast t' avenge him of that fowle despight . . . III. v. 15. 3
She *cast* to comfort him with busie paine. . . . III. v. 31. 5
Forthy she thither *cast* her course t' apply, . . . III. vi. 16. 8
she to none of them her love did *cast,* . . . III. vi. 53. 1
Ne ever *cast* his mind to covet prayse, . . . III. vii. 12. 5
cast to love her in his brutish mind: . . . III. vii. 15. 8
she *cast* In secret wize herselfe thence to withdraw, . . . III. vii. 18. 2
he *cast* Her to encounter ere she passed by; . . . III. vii. 38. 3
He *cast* to punish for his hainous fault: . . . III. viii. 36. 3
cast him up upon the shore; . . . III. viii. 36. 8
With harder meanes he *cast* her to subdew, . . . III. viii. 40. 7
I found her golden girdle *cast* astray, . . . III. viii. 49. 8
cast himselfe on ground her fast besyde: . . . III. x. 7. 5
when againe he backeward *cast* his eye, . . . III. x. 14. 4
Ten thousand wayes he *cast* in his confused thought. . . . III. x. 18. 9
To giust with that brave straunger knight a *cast,* . . . III. x. 35. 4
her up he *cast* To the wide world, . . . III. x. 35. 7
as she backward *cast* her busie eye . . . III. xi. 50. 1
there sleights and art She *cast* to use, . . . III. xii. 28. 2
rownd about Shee *cast* her eies . . . III. xii. 30. 2
Cast how to salve, that both the custome showne Were kept, . . . IV. i. 11. 7
having *cast* him in a foolish trance, . . . IV. ii. 9. 7
cast t' avenge his friends indignity. . . . IV. iv. 28. 5
To stumble, that his rider nigh he *cast;* . . . IV. iv. 30. 4
cast t' avenge the shame doen to his freend: . . . IV. iv. 45. 2
He gan to *cast* how to appease the same, . . . IV. v. 25. 2
To whom she did her liking lightly *cast,* . . . IV. viii. 52. 6
Cast into sundry shapes by wondrous skill, . . . IV. x. 15. 6
Then did he *cast* to steale her thence away, . . . IV. xii. 15. 1
Not so to leave her, nor away to *cast,* . . . V. i. 18. 3
Did *cast* about by sleight the truth thereout to straine; . . . V. i. 24. 9
Either the other from his steede to *cast;* . . . V. ii. 14. 7
Over the Castle wall adowne her *cast,* . . . V. ii. 27. 3
with their troupes did far asunder *cast;* . . . V. iv. 43. 8
Gan *cast* a secret liking to this captive straunge. . . . V. v. 26. 9
Therefore I *cast* how I may him unbind, . . . V. v. 32. 7
gan thenceforth to *cast* affection, . . . V. v. 43. 7
with guilefull call Did *cast* for to allure . . . V. v. 52. 9
She gan to *cast* in her misdoubtfull mynde A thousand feares, V. vi. 3. 8
did *cast* How to revenge that blot of honour blent, . . . V. vi. 13. 1
The other over side the Bridge she *cast* Into the river, . . . V. vi. 39. 8
ever round about he *cast* his looke: . . . V. ix. 11. 5
he then stones at it so long did *cast,* . . . V. ix. 17. 7
fowle blasphemous speaches forth did *cast,* . . . V. xi. 28. 2
cast his shield about to be in readie plight. . . . V. xii. 16. 9
twixt him and the blow his shield did *cast,* . . . V. xii. 21. 6
at him still did she scold, And stones did *cast;* . . . V. xii. 43. 7
him upon the ground he groveling *cast;* . . . VI. i. 39. 4
one stroke or twaine; Which I, . . . *cast* to requite; . . . VI. ii. 12. 6
gan . . . with equall care to *cast* How to save . . . VI. iii. 12. 6
He *cast* to keepe him selfe so safely as he may. . . . VI. iii. 47. 9
left that couple nere their utmost *cast:* . . . VI. iv. 9. 5
Upon a day he *cast* abrode to wend, . . . VI. iv. 17. 2
wanting breath him downe to ground he *cast;* . . . VI. iv. 22. 5
she *cast* to leave the place, . . . VI. v. 7. 2
sad dispaire away did *cast*. . . . VI. v. 21. 9
She on her way *cast* forward to proceede, . . . VI. v. 31. 2
when a *cast* of Faulcons make their flight . . . VI. vii. 9. 1
The end whereof Ile keepe untill another *cast*. . . . VI. viii. 51. 9
In that same quest which fortune on him *cast,* . . . VI. ix. 2. 7

Cast—*Continued.*
That worldly chaunces doe amongst them *cast,* . . . VI. xi. 1. 3
with better reason *cast* How he might save her life, . . . VI. xi. 34. 4
That litle Infant had, which forth she *kest,* . . . VI. xii. 15. 7
she gan to *cast* In her conceiptfull mynd . . . VI. xii. 16. 1
th' Images, for all their goodly hew, Did *cast* to ground, . . . VI. xii. 25. 5
Did *cast* his shield atweene; . . . VI. xii. 30. 2
She gan to *cast* in her ambitious thought . . . VII. vi. 7. 3
she *cast* by force and tortious might Her to displace, . . . VII. vi. 10. 7
straight gan *cast* their counsell grave and wise. . . . VII. vi. 22. 6
To Joves high Palace straight *cast* to ascend, . . . VII. vi. 23. 8
They gan to *cast* what penaunce him to give. . . . VII. vi. 50. 2
all his garments he had *cast* away. . . . VII. vii. 36. 2
love of things so vaine to *cast* away; . . . VII. viii. 1. 7
this worlds great Workmaister did *cast* To make al things . . . *H.B.* 29
That they gan *cast* their state how to increase . . . *H.H.L.* 80
Cast to supply the same, and to enstall . . . *H.H.L.* 103
But *cast* out of that bondage to redeeme, . . . *H.H.L.* 132
Castalia. *See* **Castalion.**
the sweete waves of sounding *Castaly* . . . *Gn.* 23
thou, our Syre, that raignst in *Castalie* . . . *T.M.* 57
dipt in deaw of *Castalie:* . . . *Ti.* 431
like showers of *Castaly,* . . . *D.* 228
Castalion. *See* **Castalia.**
speaking streames of pure *Castalion,* . . . *T.M.* 273
Castaly. *See* **Castalia.**
Casten. *See* **Cast.**
Castilian. those huge castles of *Castilian* King, . . . *Ded. Son.* vi. 7
Casting. *See* **Forecasting.**
Casting mine eyes farre off, . . . *Bel.*[2] xiii. 3
casting downe his towres, . . . *Van.* viii. 11
suddenly *casting* aside his vew, . . . *Gn.* 294
casting up a sdeinfull eie at me, . . . *D.* 549
casting up a deadly looke, . . . II. i. 47. 1
casting wronges and all revenge behind, . . . II. viii. 51. 3
casting from her that enchaunted launce, . . . IV. vi. 14. 7
casting secret flakes of lustfull fire . . . IV. viii. 48. 8
Castle. Him to his *castle* brought with hastie forse, . . . I. vii. 15. 8
Themselves . . . He forst to *castle* strong to take their flight; I. vii. 44. 7
untill they came Nigh to a *castle* . . . I. viii. 2. 2
all the *castle* quaked from the grownd, . . . I. viii. 5. 2
as a *Castle,* . . . Is undermined from the lowest ground, . . . I. viii. 23. 1
he himselfe . . . Into the *Castle* entred forcibly, . . . I. viii. 29. 4
Una faire, Did in that *castle* afterwards abide, . . . I. viii. 50. 7
to spoyle the *Castle* of his health?' . . . I. ix. 31. 2
at last they to a *Castle* came, . . . II. ii. 12. 6
Whenas they spide a goodly *castle,* . . . II. ix. 10. 3
with long siege us in the *castle* hould. . . . II. ix. 12. 7
Of that faire *Castle* to affoord them vew: . . . II. ix. 20. 8
That *castle* to assaile on every side, . . . II. xi. 5. 4
Against that *Castle* restlesse siege did lay, . . . II. xi. 14. 2
led him to the *Castle* by the beaten way. . . . II. xi. 48. 9
A stately *Castle* far away she spyde, . . . III. i. 20. 2
That *Castle* was most goodly edifyde, . . . III. i. 20. 4
stately port of *Castle* Joyeous, . . . III. i. 31. 2
(For so that *Castle* hight by commun name) . . . III. i. 31. 3
the great *Castle* smite so sore withall, . . . III. iii. 49. 8
to yonder *castle* turne your gate.' . . . III. viii. 51. 9
Forth marched to a *Castle* them before; . . . III. viii. 52. 2
entertaynd, as seemed meet, Into that *Castle,* . . . III. ix. 3. 4
Came to that *Castle,* . . . III. ix. 12. 3
one evening, that they came Unto a *Castell,* . . . IV. i. 9. 2
to his *castle* they approched neare; . . . IV. ix. 5. 5
gan they ransacke that same *Castle* strong, . . . IV. ix. 12. 1
a *castle* faire and strong . . . IV. x. 7. 2
'Before that *Castle* was an open plaine, . . . IV. x. 8. 1
all the *castle* ringed with the clap. . . . IV. x. 9. 5
drownes Lady Munera, Does race her *castle* quight. . . . V. ii. Arg.
It will be at the *Castle* of the Strond; . . . V. ii. 4. 2
unto the *Castle* he did wend, . . . V. ii. 20. 1
lastly all that *Castle* quite he raced, . . . V. ii. 28. 1
Departed from the *Castle* of the Strond . . . V. iv. 3. 5
in her necke a *Castle* huge had made, . . . V. x. 25. 8
That *Castle* was the strength of all that state, . . . V. x. 26. 1
Both goodly *Castle,* and both goodly Towne, . . . V. x. 26. 5
before this *Castle* greene Built a faire Chappell, . . . V. x. 28. 1
thence unto the *castle* marched right, . . . V. x. 33. 8
all the rest which in that *Castle* were, . . . V. x. 38. 1
Thenceforth into that *Castle* he her led . . . V. x. 39. 6
till that he came at last Unto the *Castle* . . . V. xi. 3. 4
Which when the Lady from the *Castle* saw, . . . V. xi. 15. 1
there stands a *castle* strong, . . . VI. i. 13. 2
'The Lady, which doth owne This *Castle,* . . . VI. i. 14. 6
Which to provide she hath this *Castle* dight, . . . VI. i. 15. 6
streight he tooke his flight Toward the *Castle,* . . . VI. i. 22. 4
the rest the which the *Castle* kept . . . VI. i. 24. 1
So all returning to the *Castle* glad, . . . VI. i. 46. 1
She freely gave that *Castle* for his paine, . . . VI. i. 46. 7
Thence they him carried to a *Castle* neare, . . . VI. ii. 48. 7
till he him brought Unto the *Castle* . . . VI. iii. 2. 7
the Knight, the which that *Castle* ought, . . . VI. iii. 2. 8
with his Lady to the *Castle* rid, . . . VI. iii. 37. 3
doth thus strongly ward the *Castle* of the Ford?' . . . VI. iii. 39. 9
Unto the *Castle* of Belgard her brought, . . . VI. xii. 3. 3
Castle-gate. Unto the *castle gate* they come againe, . . . II. ix. 17. 2
Seven of the same against the *Castle gate* . . . II. xi. 6. 6
to the *Castle gate* approcht in quiet wise. . . . III. ix. 9. 9
stoutly came unto the *Castle gate,* . . . III. xi. 21. 2
Eftsoones his Page drew to the *Castle gate,* . . . V. ii. 21. 1
He sternely marcht before the *Castle gate,* . . . V. xi. 3. 6

Castle-green. *See* **Castle, Green.**
Castle-hall. brought them up into her *castle hall;* . . . II. ix. 20. 2
Castle's. To vew her *Castles* other wondrous frame: . . . II. ix. 44. 7
th' assieged *Castles* ward . . . II. xi. 15. 1
Against that *Castles* Lord they gan conspire, . . . III. ix. 17. 4
to maintaine that *castels* ancient rights. . . . IV. x. 7. 9
Which when his Ladie from the *castles* hight Beheld, . . . V. viii. 45. 4
Castles. townes and *castles* under her brest did coure, . . . *Bel.*[2] viii. 6
their olde *Castles* to the ground to fall, . . . *Hub.* 1179
huge *castles* . . . ye did before you chace; . . . *Ded. Son.* vi. 7
Castles surprizd, great cities sackt and brent: . . . II. vii. 13. 8
Great cities ransackt, and strong *castles* rast; . . . IV. i. 21. 7
In which were many towres and *castels* set, . . . IV. xi. 27. 8
Gaynst such strong *castles* needeth greater might . . . *Am.* xiv. 5
Castle-wall. Forth ryding underneath the *castell wall,* . . . I. v. 53. 7
He marched forth towardes that *castle wall,* . . . I. viii. 3. 2
the watchman on the *castle-wall;* . . . I. xii. 2. 6
wind his horne under the *castle wall,* . . . II. ix. 11. 4
she them led up to the *Castle wall,* . . . II. ix. 21. 1
Within this *castle wall* a Lady fayre, . . . III. i. 26. 2
to them calling from the *castle wall,* . . . III. ix. 18. 4
the Lady forth appeared Uppon the *Castle wall;* . . . V. ii. 22. 2
powred forth over the *Castle wall,* . . . V. ii. 23. 6
Over the *Castle wall* adowne her cast, . . . V. ii. 27. 3
ryding streight under the *Castle wall,* . . . V. x. 31. 2
There where she stood uppon the *Castle wall,* . . . VI. i. 34. 6
Castory. fayre vermilion or pure *Castory.* . . . II. ix. 41. 7
Casts. Who ever *casts* to compasse weightye prise, . . . *S.C.* O. 103
he *casts* to sew the chace . . . *Hub.* 743
He *casts* his glutton sense to satisfie, . . . *Mui.* 179
castes up a mount of clay. . . . I. viii. 9. 9
a Snake, . . . *Casts* off his ragged skin . . . IV. iii. 23. 9
forth he *casts* in his unquiet thought, . . . *H.L.* 218
Catastrophes. Full of sad sights and sore *Catastrophees;* . . . *T.M.* 158
Catch. *See* **Catched.**
when the Kidde stooped downe to *catch,* . . . *S.C.* May 290
This Wolvish sheepe woulde *catchen* his pray, . . . *S.C.* S. 197
This with full bit doth *catch* the utmost top . . . *Gn.* 83
lefte the doubtfull battell hastily, To *catch* her, . . . I. vi. 46. 5
To *ketch* him at a vauntage in his snares. . . . II. i. 4. 5
To *catchen* hold of that long chaine, . . . II. vii. 46. 6
if I *catch* him in this company, . . . III. vi. 24. 6
whenas forme and feature it does *ketch,* . . . III. vi. 37. 3
He may them *catch* unable to gainestrive, . . . IV. vii. 12. 7
Fit to *catch* hold of all that he could weld, . . . V. ix. 11. 3
The birds to *catch,* or fishes to beguyle; . . . VI. ix. 23. 6
Disperseth them to *catch* his choysest pray; . . . VI. xi. 49. 2
lurke In close awayt, to *catch* her unaware: . . . *Am.* lxxi. 4
Catched. *See* **Caught.**
A shepeheard, when Mnemosyne he *catcht;* . . . III. xi. 35. 3
Catching. *catching* hastie holde Of a yong alder . . . *Gn.* 298
suddeine *catching* hold, did her dismay . . . I. iii. 12. 5
by her cleanly garment *catching* hold, Her from her Palfrey pluckt, . . . I. iii. 40. 8
catching up in hast his three-square shield . . . I. vi. 41. 8
catching hold of her ungratious tonge . . . II. iv. 12. 8
catching hold him strongly stayd From drowning. . . . II. vi. 46. 3
catching hold of him, as downe he lent, . . . II. xi. 29. 1
on him *catching* hold gan loud to crie . . . V. i. 18. 2
catching hold of this Sea-beaten chest, . . . V. iv. 11. 6
catching her fast by her ragged weed . . . V. xi. 61. 3
catching up in hand a ragged stone . . . VI. iv. 21. 2
catching up his arms, streight to the noise forth past. . . . VI. viii. 47. 9
Whom *catching* greedily, for great desire Rent up her brest, . . . VI. xii. 19. 3
catching hold on thine owne wicked hed, . . . *Am.* lxxxv. 10
Cats. some of *cats,* that wrawling still did cry; . . . VI. xii. 27. 4
Cattell. *See* **Cattle.**
Cattle. is trodde in the durt Of *cattell,* . . . *S.C.* F. 236
Cattell to keep, or grounds to oversee; . . . *Hub.* 283
Or corne, or *cattle,* or such other ware, . . . *Hub.* 873
the fleecie *cattell* have begun . . . to make their feast. . . . *Col.* 606
for her sake her *cattell* fedd awhile, . . . III. xi. 39. 2
cattell for to breed, . . . VI. viii. 35. 6
Caudron, -s. *See* **Caldron, -s.**
Caught. *See* **Catched, Overcaught.**
A stinging serpent by the heele her *caught:* . . . *Pet.* vi. 8
How he him *caught* upon a day, . . . *S.C.* Mar. 107
by the hyde the Wolfe Lowder *caught;* . . . *S.C.* S. 223
him at last the Lyon spide, and *caught,* . . . *Hub.* 1375
Out of the swelling streame it lightly *caught,* . . . *Ti.* 626
I her *caught* disporting on the greene, . . . *D.* 118
The fish that once was *caught* new bait wil hardly byte. . . . II. i. 4. 9
Woe never wants where every cause is *caught;* . . . II. iv. 44. 6
up he *caught* him twixt his puissant hands, . . . II. xi. 46. 1
Betwixt her feeble armes her quickly *keight,* . . . III. ii. 30. 4
Rather then of the tyrant to be *caught:* . . . III. vii. 26. 8
She *caught* in hand an huge great yron mace, . . . III. vii. 40. 1
'Me, seely wretch, she so at vauntage *caught,* . . . III. vii. 51. 1
him unawares there *caught;* . . . IV. viii. 51. 6
Delay . . . *Caught* hold on me, . . . IV. x. 14. 6
there was *caught* to her confusion: . . . V. v. 43. 4
She quickly *caught* her sword, . . . V. vi. 28. 9
in his hand his thresher ready keight. . . . V. vi. 29. 7
Out of her fist the wicked weapon *caught:* . . . V. viii. 48. 4
The Blatant Beast . . . *Caught* her . . . VI. iii. 24. 3
Caught like the bird which gazing still on others stands. . . . VI. ix. 11. 9
Whom they before in diverse spoyles had *caught;* . . . VI. xi. 11. 3
Entrapped him, and *caught* into her traine; . . . VII. vi. 48. 7
being *caught,* may craftily enfold . . . *Am.* xxxvii. 7
Whome, being *caught,* she kills with cruell pryde, . . . *Am.* xlvii. 7

Caught—*Continued.*
your selfe were *caught* in cunning snare . . . *Am.* lxxi. 5
in his hand . . . Him *caught* for to subdue. . . . *Epig.* iv. 24
Caul. when they had despoyld her tire and *call,* . . . I. viii. 46. 5
Cauldron. There placed was a *caudron* wide and tall . . . II. ix. 29. 5
So long as any thing it in the *caudron* gott. . . . II. ix. 29. 9
About the *Caudron* many Cookes accoyld . . . II. ix. 30. 6
Cauldrons. brasen *Caudrons* thou shalt rombling heare, . . . III. iii. 9. 3
eke an hundred brasen *caudrons* bright, . . . IV. x. 38. 6
Caulmes. *See* **Calms.**
Cause. Thou onely *cause,* O Civill furie! art, . . . *Ro.* xxxi. 9
such *cause* hath she none) . . . *S.C.* May 98
lengd to know the *cause* of his complaint: . . . *S.C.* May 250
Asked the *cause* of his great distresse, . . . *S.C.* May 260
Sike question ripeth up *cause* of newe woe, . . . *S.C.* S. 13
cause a caytive corage to aspire; . . . *S.C.* O. 95
Such *cause* of mourning never hadst afore; . . . *S.C.* N. 54
ne *cause* of speaking mooved; . . . *Gn.* 469
Cause of my death and just complaint to tell: . . . *Gn.* 629
The Foxe, that first this *cause* of griefe did finde, . . . *Hub.* 51
Commaunding them their *cause* of strife bewray; . . . *Hub.* 1096
there was *cause,* els doo it he would not: . . . *Hub.* 1220
his false counsellor, the *cause* of all, . . . *Hub.* 1243
Might be the *cause* of so impatient plight? . . . *T.M.* 44
Untill my *cause* of sorrow be redrest. . . . *T.M.* 228
please his fancie, nor him *cause* t' abide: . . . *Mui.* 158
The *cause* why he this Flie so maliced . . . *Mui.* 257
given like *cause* with thee to waile . . . *D.* 66
To tell the *cause* which thee theretoo constrained, . . . *D.* 81
in watch did spend, If *cause* requir'd, . . . *D.* 130
their *cause* of meriment, . . . *Col.* 30
how that shepheard strange thy *cause* advanced.' . . . *Col.* 357
'*Cause* have I none . . . *Col.* 680
That doest their *cause* so mightily defend: . . . *Col.* 900
who can tell what *cause* had that faire Mayd . . . *Col.* 911
procure your needlesse smart Where *cause* is none; . . . I. i. 54. 5
For present *cause* was none of dread her to dismay. . . . I. ii. 20. 9
Good *cause* of mine excuse, . . . I. iii. 29. 6
they, . . . Making obeysaunce, did the *cause* declare, . . . I. iv. 13. 7
wept, that *cause* of weeping none he had; . . . I. iv. 30. 8
as a sacred pledge His *cause* in combat . . . to try: . . . I. iv. 43. 2
Cause of my new griefe, *cause* of my new joy; . . . I. iv. 45. 5
the shield, the *cause* of enmitie. . . . I. v. 15. 9
the old *cause* of my continued paine . . . I. v. 42. 3
Good *cause* he had to hasten thence away; . . . I. v. 45. 6
The hidden *cause* of their captivitie; . . . I. v. 46. 3
commeth out To weet the *cause,* . . . I. vi. 14. 7
The *cause* was this: . . . I. vii. 5. 1
To tempt the *cause* it selfe for to bewray, . . . I. vii. 38. 8
This is my *cause* of griefe, . . . I. vii. 51. 9
'Certes, Madame, ye have great *cause* of plaint; . . . I. vii. 52. 3
stoutest heart, I weene, could *cause* to quake: . . . I. vii. 52. 4
to read aright The course of heavenly *cause,* . . . I. ix. 6. 7
Me hither sent for *cause* to me unghest; . . . I. ix. 7. 2
The secrete *cause* of his perplexitie: . . . I. ix. 25. 5
gives not rather *cause* it to forsake? . . . I. ix. 44. 5
the *cause* and root of all his ill, . . . I. x. 25. 1
'What end . . . should *cause* us take such paine, . . . I. x. 50. 1
Who did her *cause* into thy hand committ, . . . I. x. 63. 8
Abett that virgins *cause* disconsolate, . . . I. x. 64. 2
truth is strong her rightfull *cause* to plead, . . . I. xii. 28. 7
tell the *cause* of your conceived payne; . . . II. i. 14. 6
Great *cause,* I weene, you guided, . . . II. i. 29. 9
Reserve her *cause* to her eternall doome; . . . II. i. 58. 8
cause not well conceived ye mistake: . . . II. ii. 5. 5
more to mighty hands then rightfull *cause* doth trust. . . . II. ii. 29. 9
were there rightfull *cause* of difference, . . . II. ii. 30. 1
cause one foot to flye, . . . II. iii. 45. 4
Which was the *cause,* . . . II. iii. 45. 6
Ne ever thing could *cause* us disagree. . . . II. iv. 19. 7
when the *cause* of that outrageous deede Demaunded, . . . II. iv. 29. 6
Great *cause,* that carries thee so swifte and light.' . . . II. iv. 43. 4
'that does seeke Occasion to wrath, and *cause* of strife: . . . II. iv. 44. 2
Woe never wants where every *cause* is caught; . . . II. iv. 44. 6
Of courtesie to mee the *cause* aread . . . II. v. 16. 8
That to her might move *cause* of meriment: . . . II. vi. 3. 6
cause of death betweene two doughtie knights do breed! . . . II. vi. 33. 9
To covet more then I have *cause* to use? . . . II. vii. 39. 4
lowd and wyde be hard When *cause* requyrd, . . . II. ix. 25. 8
What ever bee the *cause,* it sure beseemes you ill.' . . . II. ix. 37. 9
in haste he yode The *cause* to weet, . . . II. xi. 20. 3
she had *cause* to busie them withall; . . . II. xii. 15. 3
The *cause* of their dissention and outrageous yre. . . . III. i. 23. 9
prove his *cause.*' . . . III. i. 28. 6
Here have I *cause* in men just blame to find, . . . III. ii. 1. 1
Defending Ladies *cause* and Orphans right, . . . III. ii. 14. 6
The *cause,* some say, is this: . . . III. iii. 10. 1
either fatall end, Or other mightie *cause,* . . . III. iii. 15. 9
Doth course of naturall *cause* farre exceed, . . . III. iii. 18. 6
To cloke the *cause* that hath it selfe bewrayd? . . . III. iii. 19. 4
what *cause* her brought Into that wildernesse . . . III. vi. 20. 2
did ye see Just *cause* of dread, . . . III. viii. 48. 6
that young Squyre Gan them informe the *cause,* . . . III. viii. 52. 7
The *cause* why Satyrane and Paridell Mote not be entertaynd, . . . III. ix. 3. 2
the *cause* why never any knight Is suffred here to enter, . . . III. ix. 6. 3
Gan *causen* why she could not come in place; . . . III. ix. 26. 2
countries *cause,* and commune foes disdayne. . . . III. ix. 40. 4
hast thou, Lord, of good mens *cause* no heed? . . . III. xi. 9. 6
your *cause* is nothing lesse Then is your sorrow certes, . . . III. xi. 18. 3
The golden Apple, *cause* of all their wrong, . . . IV. i. 22. 5

Cause—*Continued.*
justifie my *cause* on yonder knight.' . . . IV. i. 40. 6
rather die then Ladies *cause* release: . . . IV. ii. 19. 7
Drew nigh, to weete the *cause* of their debate: . . . IV. ii. 20. 6
First he desir'd their *cause* of strife to see: . . . IV. ii. 22. 1
That doth ill *cause* or evill end enure; . . . IV. ii. 29. 8
Her *cause* of comming she to tell began. . . . IV. ii. 49. 5
The *cause* of both, of both their minds depends, . . . IV. iv. 1. 4
at last enquired The *cause* and end thereof, . . . IV. v. 38. 4
'Great *cause* of sorrow certes, Sir, ye have; . . . IV. vi. 38. 6
The *cause* of that his sorrowfull constraint; . . . IV. vii. 45. 3
made her understand His sorrowes *cause,* . . . IV. viii. 12. 4
With forged *cause* them falsely to defame; . . . IV. viii. 25. 7
he gan enquire his *cause* of dread: . . . IV. viii. 41. 4
cause of feare, sure, had she none . . . IV. ix. 19. 1
Cause of their discord and so fell debate . . . IV. ix. 24. 1
the *cause* of their so cruell heat . . . IV. ix. 35. 8
some ill whose *cause* did not appeare. . . . IV. x. 12. 9
'The *cause* why she was covered with a vele . . . IV. x. 41. 1
As every one had *cause* of good or ill. . . . IV. x. 43. 6
understood the *cause* of all her care . . . IV. xii. 12. 2
The secret *cause* and nature of his teene; . . . IV. xii. 21. 4
And for what *cause;* . . . IV. xii. 30. 7
would some rightfull *cause* pretend, . . . IV. xii. 30. 9
To sit in his own seate, his *cause* to end, . . . V. Pr. 10. 8
for no *cause,* but as I shall you shew. . . . V. i. 16. 5
if ye please that I your *cause* decide, . . . V. i. 25. 5
t' inquire The *cause* of their array, . . . V. ii. 52. 9
Till he had questioned the *cause* of their dissent. . . . V. iv. 6. 9
To weete the *cause* of their assemblaunce wide: . . . V. iv. 21. 5
Did aske what *cause* brought that man to decay, . . . V. iv. 23. 6
'The *cause,* they say, of this her cruell hate . . . V. iv. 30. 1
To heare the piteous beast pleading her plaintiffe *cause.* . . . V. iv. 40. 9
she gan unfold The *cause* of her conceived maladie, . . . V. v. 31. 8
gan enquire . . . The certaine *cause* of Artegals detaine, . . . V. vi. 15. 7
To lodge with him that night, unles good *cause* empeach. . . V. vi. 21. 9
for what *cause* so great mischievous smart Was ment . . . V. vi. 31. 8
For his departure, her new *cause* of griefe: . . . V. vii. 44. 2
either others *cause* to maintaine mutually. . . . V. viii. 14. 9
for what *cause* they chased so that Mayd? . . . V. viii. 15. 4
for what *cause* pursu'd of them attone. . . . V. viii. 16. 5
To th' hearing of that former *cause* in hand . . . V. ix. 37. 2
Importune care of their owne publicke *cause;* . . . V. ix. 44. 8
Yet at the last she will her owne *cause* right: . . . V. xi. 1. 6
her *cause* in battailous array Against him justifie, . . . V. xi. 40. 3
as they approcht the *cause* to know, . . . V. xi. 44. 1
for like *cause* faire Belge did oppresse, . . . V. xii. 2. 6
to trie the right Of fayre Irenaes *cause* . . . V. xii. 8. 9
Sir Artegall did *cause* his tent There to be pitched . . . V. xii. 10. 1
by what meanes . . . And for what *cause?* . . . VI. i. 14. 4
To weet the *cause* of so uncomely fray, . . . VI. ii. 4. 4
What *cause* could make him so dishonourable . . . VI. ii. 15. 3
refused To take me up . . . for no just *cause* accused, . . . VI. ii. 22. 4
And him . . . mortally did wound, Withouten *cause,* . . . VI. ii. 43. 6
to him their *cause* they best esteemed Whole to commit, . . . VI. iii. 13. 3
To give faire colour to that Ladies *cause* in sight. . . . VI. iii. 16. 9
The *cause* of all this evill, who was slaine . . . VI. iii. 17. 2
for what *cause,* declare; so mote ye not repent.' . . . VI. iv. 27. 9
this my *cause* of griefe to you appeares; . . . VI. iv. 33. 8
'If that the *cause* of this your languishment . . . VI. iv. 35. 1
the *cause,* whence evill doth arize, . . . VI. vi. 14. 3
That mucky masse, the *cause* of mens decay, . . . VI. ix. 33. 5
Sith they that were the *cause* of all were gone: . . . VI. xi. 20. 6
for hyre She should it *cause* be fostred . . . VI. xii. 6. 9
to knowe The *cause* of this so strange astonishment, . . . VII. vi. 16. 3
Strong thrugh your *cause,* but by your vertue weak. . . . *Am.* viii. 12
teach to speak, and my just *cause* to plead; . . . *Am.* xliii. 10
Remove the *cause* by which your fayre beames darkned be. . *Am.* xlv. 14
ere she could thy *cause* wel understand, . . . *Am.* xlviii. 3
plead thy maisters *cause,* unjustly payned. . . . *Am.* xlviii. 8

Caused. *Caused* of wrong and cruell constraint, . . . *S.C.* F. 152
my plaints, *causd* of discurtesee, . . . *S.C.* Jun. 97
all the beasts he *caus'd* assembled bee, . . . *Hub.* 1377
flocks and shepheards *caused* to rejoyce. . . . *D.* 315
that harlott . . . That *causd* her shed so many a bitter teare; I. iii. 25. 4
Eftesoones shee *causd* him up to be convayd, . . . II. xi. 49. 6
She *caused* them be led in courteous wize . . . III. i. 42. 3
King Ryence *caused* to be hanged hy . . . III. iii. 59. 2
in his costly Bath *caused* to bee site. . . . III. xii. 46. *or.* 4
caus'd to be proclaim'd each where A solemne feast, . . . IV. ii. 26. 7
pacifie the strife, which *causd* so deadly smart. . . . IV. iii. 40. 9
She *caused* him to make experience Upon wyld beasts, . . . V. i. 7. 7
causde great sackes . . . to be upbrought, . . . V. ii. 23. 4
Causd all her people to surcease from fight; . . . V. iv. 45. 5
Causd his pavilion to be richly pight . . . V. iv. 46. 4
Terpine . . . She *caused* to be attacht, . . . V. v. 18. 6
caused him to be disarmed quight . . . V. v. 20. 3
she *causd* his warlike armes Be hang'd on high, . . . V. v. 21. 6
She *caused* her Pavilion be pight; . . . V. vii. 26. 2
caused streight a Trumpet loud to shrill . . . V. vii. 27. 1
causd him those uncomely weedes undight; . . . V. vii. 41. 2
He *caused* them be hung in all mens sight, . . . V. viii. 45. 2
Whom she had *causd* be kept as prisonere . . . V. viii. 46. 5
Then *caused* he the gates be opened wyde; . . . V. viii. 51. 1
There him he *causd* to kneele, . . . VI. ii. 35. 1
Causde me be called to accompt therefore; . . . VI. viii. 22. 2
many causelesse *caused* to be blamed. . . . VI. xii. 38. 5
They would have *caused* much confusion and disorder. . . . VII. vii. 4. 9

Causeless. *Causelesse* complained, . . . *S.C.* F. 148
they shrowd themselves from *causeles* feare; . . . II. iii. 20. 2

Causeless—*Continued.*
'Deare sonne, thy *causelesse* ruth represse, . . . II. v. 24. 5
To chaunge love *causelesse* is reproch to warlike knight.' . . II. vii. 50. 9
To thinke how *causelesse,* of her owne accord, . . . III. viii. 1. 3
causelesse crimes continually to frame, . . . IV. viii. 25. 2
through pittie of his *causelesse* smart. . . . V. v. 43. 9
many *causelesse* caused to be blamed. . . . VI. xii. 38. 5

Causen. *See* **Cause.**

Causer. you (great Lord) the *causer* of my care, . . . *Gn.* Ded. 2
To follow her that was the *causer* of their ill. . . . I. iii. 22. 9

Causers. their great sinnes, the *causers* of their paine, . . . *Ro.* xix. 13

Cause's. this doubtfull *causes* right . . . V. i. 25. 1
More in his *causes* truth he trusted then in might. . . . V. viii. 30. 9
But by their trueth and by the *causes* right: . . . V. xi. 17. 5

Causes. those secret *causes* to display; . . . *T.M.* 50
Shall I accuse . . . mightie *causes* wrought in heaven above, . I. i. 51. 3
their rightfull *causes* downe to tread; . . . I. x. 43. 7
thousand *causes* wrought. . . . II. v. 19. 9
guyde the heavenly *causes* to their constant terme. . . . III. iii. 25. 9
were for other *causes* firme and sound; . . . III. vii. 60. 3
Welds kingdomes *causes* and affaires of state, . . . IV. Pr. 1. 2
Thou doest not know the *causes,* nor their courses dew. . . V. ii. 42. 9
To messengers that come for *causes* just: . . . V. viii. 22. 2

Causeth. With that he *causeth* sleep to seize the eyes, . . . *Hub.* 1295
She *causeth* them be hang'd up out of hand; . . . V. iv. 32. 4

Cave. I saw a Wolfe under a rockie *cave* . . . *Bel.*[2] vi. 1
the *cave* where Phoebe layed The shepheard . . . *S.C.* Jul. 63
Lying together in a mightie *cave,* . . . *Ti.* 562
The *Cave,* in which these Beares lay sleeping sound, . . . *Ti.* 570
the *cave* in which he lurking dwelt, . . . *Mui.* 358
Or some deepe *cave,* or solitarie shade; . . . *D.* 487
a hollowe *cave* Amid the thickest woods. . . . I. i. 11. 6
Me, . . . ever since hath kept in darksom *cave,* . . . I. iv. 47. 8
would have backe retyred to her *cave,* . . . I. v. 21. 6
a *Cave* ywrought by wondrous art, . . . I. v. 36. 5
His dwelling has, low in an hollow *cave,* . . . I. ix. 33. 2
That darkesome *cave* they enter, . . . I. ix. 35. 1
in secret *cave* . . . her selfe hath hid, . . . II. iii. 36. 1
Lyke an huge *cave* hewne out of rocky clifte, . . . II. vii. 28. 2
fire, the which in hollow *cave* Hath long bene underkept . II. xi. 32. 1
It is an hideous hollow *cave* . . . III. iii. 8. 3
in drowsie *cave* Hath long time slept, . . . III. iii. 30. 1
in a rocky *cave,* . . . Long time she fostred up, . . . III. iv. 20. 3
a strong rocky *Cave,* . . . Hewen underneath that Mount, . III. vi. 48. 8
out of her hidden *cave* she cald An hideous beast . . . III. vii. 22. 1
Therein is eaten out an hollow *cave,* . . . III. viii. 37. 5
at the last he found a *cave* with entrance small. . . . III. x. 57. 9
Unto his *cave* farre from all peoples hearing, . . . IV. vii. 8. 8
Came to the *cave;* and rolling thence the stone, . . . IV. vii. 20. 4
eke his *cave* in which they both were bond: . . . IV. viii. 21. 8
him farre she brought Into a *cave* from companie exilde, . V. i. 6. 7
The cry whereof entring the hollow *cave* . . . V. ix. 10. 1
when as ny He came unto his *cave,* . . . V. ix. 14. 7
When to the *Cave* they came, they found it fast; . . . VI. xi. 43. 1
in great store Unto the *cave* gan preasse, . . . VI. xi. 46. 4

Caved. the mouldred earth had *cav'd* the banke; . . . IV. v. 33. 2

Caves. darkesome *caves* in pleasaunt vallies pight, . . . *Gn.* 117
fild her hidden *caves* with stormie yre, . . . I. vii. 9. 5
Shee, . . . lurkt in rocks and *caves,* long unespide. . . . I. viii. 50. 5
Lurking in rockes and *caves* far under ground, . . . II. i. 22. 3
Out of the rockes and *caves* adjoyning nye; . . . II. ix. 13. 3
in th' earthes hollow *caves* hath long ben hid . . . III. ix. 15. 3
appointed have her place Mongst rocks and *caves,* . . . VI. vi. 11. 4
their way was made Through hollow *caves,* . . . VI. x. 42. 2
did themselves convay Into their *caves,* . . . VI. xi. 49. 8

Cayr, Cayr-Merdin. *See* **Cair,** *etc.*

Caytive, -s. *See* **Caitiff, -'s, -s.**

Cease. *Cease* not to sound these olde antiquities; . . . *Ro.* xxxii. 10
Ne wote I how to *cease* it. . . . *S.C.* Mar. 102
Tho gan the streames of flowing wittes to *cease,* . . . *S.C.* O. 71
Cease now, my Muse, now *cease* thy sorrowes sourse; . . . *S.C.* N. 171
Ceasse now, my song, . . . *S.C.* N. 201
'*Cease,* foolish man! . . . To seeke . . . *D.* 71
cease henceforth things kindly forth to bring, . . . *D.* 339
Cease, Shepheard! *cease,* and end thy undersong.' . . . *D.* 539
The wakefull dogs did never *cease* to bay, . . . I. v. 30. 2
Soone as the terme of those six yeares shall *cease,* . . . I. xii. 19. 7
taught the land from wearie wars to *cease:* . . . II. x. 25. 5
till Genuissa gent Persuaded him to *ceasse,* . . . II. x. 52. 9
'What is there ells but *cease* these fruitlesse paines, . . . III. xi. 24. 1
Now *cease* your worke, and . . . play: . . . III. xii. 47. *or.* 8
Now *cease* your work; to morrow is an holy day. . . . III. xii. 47. *or.* 9
trumpets sound to *cease* did them compell: . . . IV. iv. 25. 8
ne did he *ceasse,* Till that he came where he had Cambell seene IV. iv. 34. 3
naturall affection soone doth *cesse,* . . . IV. ix. 2. 1
entreat that iron man below To *cease* his outrage, . . . V. ii. 22. 6
make him *cease* for ought. . . . V. ii. 22. 9
'*Cease,* thou bad newes-man! . . . V. vi. 11. 4
ne ever howre did *cease* Till he redeemed had that Lady thrall: V. vii. 45. 7
Them guyded through the throng, that did their clamors *ceasse.* V. ix. 23. 9
your victorious arme will not yet *cease,* . . . V. xi. 18. 5
Nor *cease* her sorrow and impatient stound, . . . VI. v. 6. 7
when as he was dead, the fray gan *ceasse;* . . . VI. xi. 20. 3
Ceasse to molest the Moone to walke at large, . . . VII. vi. 17. 8
'Will never mortall thoughts *ceasse* to aspire . . . VII. vi. 29. 2
'Then *ceasse* thy idle claime, thou foolish gerle; . . . VII. vi. 34. 1
'*Ceasse,* Saturnes sonne, to seeke by proffers vaine . . . VII. vi. 34. 7
'*Cease* therefore, daughter, further to aspire, . . . VII. vii. 59. 1
Ceasse then, till she vouchsafe . . . *Am.* xxxiii. 13
shall their ruthlesse torment never *cease;* . . . *Am.* xxxvi. 2

Cease—*Continued.*
Ceasse then, myne eyes, to seeke her selfe to see; . . . *Am.* lxxviii. 13
Now *ceasse,* ye damsels, your delights fore-past; . . . *Epith.* 296
let the mayds and yongmen *cease* to sing; . . . *Epith.* 332
Till which we *cease* our hopefull hap to sing; . . . *Epith.* 388
we *cease* your further prayse to sing; . . . *Epith.* 407
cease till then our tymely joyes to sing: . . . *Epith.* 425
Cease then, my tongue! and lend unto my mynd . . . *H.H.B.* 106
ceasse to gaze on matter of thy grief: . . . *H.H.B.* 294
Ceased. when lust of meat and drinke was *ceast,* . . . II. ii. 39. 3
Now after all was *ceast,* . . . II. vi. 36. 7
day and night it brent, ne *ceased* not, . . . II. ix. 29. 8
ceased not the bloody fight for ought; . . . II. x. 51. 5
He *ceast;* and then gan all the quire of birdes . . . II. xii. 76. 1
Her dolour soone she *ceast,* . . . III. iv. 12. 4
Ne *ceased* not, till him oppressed hard The heavie plague . . . III. v. 14. 8
when it *ceast,* . . . trompets lowd did bray, . . . III. xii. 6. 6
when they *ceast,* it gan againe to play, . . . III. xii. 6. 8
When as their sharpe contention he had *ceased,* . . . V. iv. 20. 7
They *ceast* their clamors upon them to gaze; . . . V. ix. 24. 1
Ne *ceassed* not, till all their scattred crew Into the sea he drove . . . V. xi. 65. 3
Ne once to breath awhile their angers tempest *ceast.* . . . VI. i. 36. 9
Yet *ceast* he not for all that cruell wound, . . . VI. iii. 51. 1
in short space their malady was *ceast,* . . . VI. vi. 15. 4
Yet *ceast* he not to sew, . . . VI. xi. 5. 5
So having said, he *ceast;* . . . VII. vi. 22. 1
Ceaseless. For which I thus doe mourne, and poure forth *ceaselesse* teares.' . . . VI. iv. 33. 9
Ceasest. *ceassest* not thy weary soles to lead; . . . I. x. 9. 7
Cedar. High on a hill a goodly *Cedar* grewe, . . . *Van.* vii. 1
the *Cedar* proud and tall; . . . I. i. 8. 6
From lowest Juniper to *Ceder* tall, . . . IV. x. 22. 2
Cedar-tree. incense of precious *Cedar* (*Ceder*[1]) *tree,* . . . *Bel.* xi. 3
Ceiled. *sield* With moniments of many Knights decay, . . . V. v. 21. 3
Ceiling. the *sielyng* eke Did shine . . . *Bel.*[1] ii. 9
the *seeling* bright Did shine . . . *Bel.*[2] ii. 9
Celaeno. sad *Celeno,* sitting on a clifte, . . . II. vii. 23. 6
Celebrate. To *celebrate* the solemne bridall cheare . . . VII. vii. 12. 4
Celestial. The sectaries of my *celestiall* skill, . . . *T.M.* 73
The precious store of this *celestiall* riches? . . . *T.M.* 146
Such high conceipt of that *celestiall* fire, . . . *T.M.* 391
Can no whit savour this *celestiall* food, . . . *T.M.* 591
influence of all *celestiall* grace, . . . *Ti.* 289
'In purenesse and in all *celestiall* grace, . . . *D.* 211
Saints and Angels in *celestiall* thrones . . . *D.* 285
When she beholds from her *celestiall* throne . . . *D.* 380
some *celestiall* rage Of Love . . . is breath'd into thy brest, . . . *Col.* 823
things *celestiall* which ye never saw. . . . *Col.* 930
that great house of Gods *caelestiall,* . . . I. v. 22. 4
through *celestiall* doome thrown out of dore, . . . I. v. 47. 4
she him taught *celestiall* discipline. . . . I. x. 18. 8
Did wonder much at her *celestial* sight: . . . I. xii. 23. 8
So glorious mirrhour of *celestiall* grace, . . . II. iii. 25. 6
shee is some powre *celestiall?* . . . II. iii. 44. 4
Not that *celestiall* powre, . . . II. xii. 47. 2
Her soveraine bountie and *celestiall* hew, . . . III. v. 44. 5
She, hevenly borne and of *celestiall* hew. . . . III. v. 47. 4
The heritage of all *celestiall* grace; . . . III. vi. 4. 7
such as that *celestiall* Psalmist was, . . . IV. ii. 2. 1
some *celestiall* shape that flesh did beare: . . . IV. v. 14. 7
worship her as some *celestiall* vision. . . . IV. vi. 24. 9
a most *celestiall* sound Of dainty musicke, . . . IV. xi. 23. 1
touch *celestiall* seats with earthly mire? . . . VII. vi. 29. 4
ravisht with delight Of his *celestiall* song, . . . VII. vii. 12. 9
At wondrous sight of so *celestiall* hew. . . . *Am.* iii. 8
The fayre Idea of your *celestiall* hew . . . remaines . . . *Am.* xlv. 7
Had ye once seene these her *celestial* threasures, . . . *Epith.* 200
The flaming light of that *celestiall* fyre . . . *H.L.* 186
through infusion of *celestiall* powre, . . . *H.B.* 50
lampe, from whose *celestiall* ray That light proceedes, . . . *H.B.* 99
That goodly beautie, . . . and that *celestiall* hew, . . . *H.B.* 150
what booteth that *celestiall* ray, . . . *H.B.* 187
Love is a *celestiall* harmonie . . . *H.B.* 197
Some little drop of thy *celestiall* dew, . . . *H.H.L.* 46
Compar'd to that *celestiall* beauties blaze, . . . *H.H.L.* 277
With sweete enragement of *celestiall* love, . . . *H.H.L.* 286
Transported with *celestiall* desyre Of those faire formes, . . . *H.H.B.* 18
For in the view of her *celestiall* face . . . *H.H.B.* 242
Celia. *See* **Caelia.**
Cell. Doth rather choose to sit in idle *Cell,* . . . *T.M.* 221
Silly old man, that lives in hidden *cell,* . . . I. i. 30. 6
the man that moulds in ydle *cell* . . . II. iii. 41. 3
to her chamber went like solitary *cell.* . . . V. vi. 11. 9
taking them apart into his *cell,* . . . VI. vi. 6. 1
poure that vertue from our heavenly *cell* . . . VII. vii. 48. 7
Cells. searched all their *cels* and secrets neare: . . . VI. xii. 24. 4
Celtic. By sea to have bene from the *Celticke* maynland brought, . . . II. x. 5. 9
Celtic. By sea to have bene from the *Celticke* maynland brought, II. x. 5. 9
Cemitare. *See* **Scimiter.**
Censer. from a golden *Censer* forth doth rise, . . . *Col.* 609
Like coles that through a silver *Censer* sparkle bright. . . . V. vi. 38. 9
Censors. these Stoicke *censours* cannot well deny . . . IV. Pr. 3. 9
Censure. And wipe their faults out of your *censure* grave. . . . *Ded. Son.* ix. 14
Centaur. Then like a *Centaure;* then like to a storme . . . III. viii. 41. 3
to a *Centaure* did him selfe transmove. . . . III. xi. 43. 5
it a dreadfull *Centaure* was in sight, . . . VII. vii. 40. 8
Centaur's. When *Centaures* blood and bloody verses charmd; . . . I. xi. 27. 6
Centaurs. th' halfe-horsy people, *Centaures* hight, . . . *Gn.* 41
Crocodiles, Dragons, Beavers, and *Centaures,* . . . *Hub.* 1124
Infernall Hags, *Centaurs,* feendes, Hippodames, . . . II. ix. 50. 8
When the bold *Centaures* made that bloudy fray . . . VI. x. 13. 4
Centaurs'. sent away So many *Centaures* drunken soules to hell, IV. i. 23. 4
Centonell. *See* **Sentinel.**
Centre. lose The worlds foundations from his *centre* fixt: . . . III. xii. 2. 4
The earth was in the middle *centre* pight, . . . V. ii. 35. 5
From rudely pressing to the middle *center;* . . . V. v. 5. 7
Centred. Betwixt the *centred* earth and azure skies, . . . *Mui.* 19
Cephise. *See* **Cephissus.**
Cephissus. Ne can *Cephise,* nor Hebrus, match this well: . . . I. xi. 30. 8
Cephissus'. fonder then *Cephisus* foolish chyld, . . . III. ii. 44. 6
Cerberus. *Cerberus,* whose many mouthes doo bay . . . *Gn.* 345
beleeve that anie thing could please Fell *Cerberus,* . . . *Gn.* 440
dreadfull *Cerberus* His three deformed heads did lay along, . . . I. v. 34. 1
Cerberus, when Orpheus did recoure His Leman . . . IV. x. 58. 4
'Of *Cerberus* whilome he was begot . . . VI. i. 8. 1
Cerberus'. from *Cerberus* greedy jaw To plucke a bone, . . . I. xi. 41. 4
Ceremonies. With other divelish *ceremonies* met: . . . VI. viii. 45. 7
The sacred *ceremonies* there partake, . . . *Epith.* 216
Ceres. fruitfull *Ceres* and Lyaeus fatt . . . III. i. 51. 3
Ceres'. before That *Ceres* seede of mortall men were knowne, . *Gn.* 207
Certain. shall we tie our selves for *certaine* yeares . . . *Hub.* 120
not to anie *certaine* trade or place, . . . *Hub.* 130
never standeth in one *certaine* state, . . . *D.* 430
the *certeine* perill he stood in, . . . I. i. 24. 2
For hoped love to winne me *certaine* hate? . . . I. i. 51. 5
the *certein* Sire, From which I sprong, . . . I. ix. 3. 3
Are written sure, and have their *certein* date. . . . I. ix. 42. 5
By *certein* signes . . . He may it fynd; . . . II. Pr. 4. 2
not firme land, nor any *certein* wonne, . . . II. xii. 11. 4
Ne made for shipping any *certeine* port, . . . II. xii. 13. 3
them awayted there a *certaine* space, . . . III. i. 19. 4
he ne wonneth in one *certeine* stead, . . . III. ii. 14. 3
Certein sad words with hollow voice and bace, . . . III. ii. 50. 5
sheweth at the least Her *certeine* losse, . . . III. viii. 49. 6
Till triall doe more *certeine* truth bewray.' . . . III. viii. 50. 5
By chance he *certaine* miniments forth drew, . . . IV. viii. 6. 2
every one doe know their *certaine* bound, . . . V. ii. 36. 2
For *certaine* losse of so great expectation: . . . V. ii. 51. 5
gan enquire . . . The *certaine* cause of Artegals detaine, . . . V. vi. 15. 7
There she continu'd for a *certaine* space, . . . V. vii. 45. 1
leveld all against one *certaine* place, . . . V. x. 34. 7
By *certaine* signes he plainly him descryde . . . VI. iii. 47. 4
A *certaine* herbe from thence unto him brought, . . . VI. iv. 12. 6
Gan mutter close a *certaine* secret charme, . . . VI. viii. 45. 6
Ne ought was feared of his *certaine* harmes: . . . VI. viii. 47. 4
certaine of the theeves there by them left, . . . VI. xi. 37. 4
That he by them might *certaine* tydings weene . . . VI. xi. 39. 3
Directs her course unto one *certaine* cost, . . . VI. xii. 1. 2
'Most *certaine* markes' (sayd she) 'do me it teach; . . . VI. xii. 18. 3
She found at last, by very *certaine* signes . . . VI. xii. 20. 3
Ne have the watry foules a *certaine* grange . . . VII. vii. 21. 7
Know this for *certaine,* . . . *H.B.* 136
Certainly. *certeinly* to mee areed, . . . II. iii. 14. 8
thought *certainely* To have supplyde the first, . . . VI. viii. 9. 8
Certainty. dismayd With needlesse dread, till *certaintie* ye heare; . . . IV. vi. 37. 7
Certes. *'Certes* . . . I meane me to disguize . . . *Hub.* 83
Ne, *certes,* may I take it well in part, . . . *Hub.* 1217
'Certes, Alcyon, painfull is thy plight, . . . *D.* 174
Certes, Madame, ye have great cause of plaint; . . . I. vii. 52. 3
'Certes,' (sayd he) 'hence shall I never rest, . . . I. ix. 32. 1
False traytour *certes,'* . . . II. i. 17. 6
'Certes, . . . I wote not how he hight, . . . II. i. 18. 5
'Certes,' . . . 'well mote I shame to tell . . . II. i. 30. 1
Ne *certes,* Sir, strive you it to withstand, . . . II. ii. 10. 3
'Certes, . . . (said he) 'that shall I soone, . . . II. iii. 15. 1
'Certes' (sayd he) 'I n' ill thine offred grace, . . . II. vii. 33. 1
'Certes, Sir knight, ye bene too much to blame, . . . II. viii. 13. 2
'Certes,' (then said the Prince) . . . II. ix. 7. 1
certes it great pitty was to see . . . II. xii. 79. 3
'Certes,' (said she) 'then beene ye sixe to blame, . . . III. i. 25. 1
Certes ye misavised beene . . . III. ii. 9. 5
certes seemes bestowed not amis: . . . III. ii. 42. 4
Certes I should be loth thee to molest; . . . III. iii. 18. 4
Ne *certes,* daughter, that same warlike wize, . . . III. iii. 53. 5
'Now *certes,* swaine,' (saide he) 'such one, I weene, . . . III. v. 6. 1
'Certes was but a common Courtisane; . . . III. vii. 58. 2
your cause is nothing lesse Then is your sorrow *certes,* . . . III. xi. 18. 4
Certes, me seemes, bene not advised well; . . . IV. ii. 24. 5
Ne *certes* can that friendship long endure, . . . IV. ii. 29. 6
'Brave Knights and Ladies, *certes,* ye doe wrong . . . IV. iv. 12. 2
certes his right name was otherwize, . . . IV. iv. 42. 7
Ne *certes* wonder, for no powre of man Could bide . . . IV. iv. 46. 3
'Certes,' (sayd he) 'ye mote as now excuse Me . . . IV. vi. 4. 6
Certes some hellish furie or some feend . . . IV. vi. 17. 6
Him thus bespake: *'Certes,* Sir Artegall, . . . IV. vi. 28. 6
'Certes, Sir Knight, What is of her become, . . . IV. vi. 35. 1
'Great cause of sorrow *certes,* Sir, ye have; . . . IV. vi. 38. 6
certes was with milke of Wolves and Tygres fed. . . . IV. vii. 7. 9
'Certes, sir Knight, ye seemen much to blame . . . IV. ix. 37. 2
'Certes, her losse ought me to sorrow most, . . . IV. ix. 38. 7
'Certes, your strife were easie to accord, . . . V. iv. 16. 2
'Certes, Clarinda, not of cancred will . . . I have forbore . . . V. v. 41. 1
'Certes,' (sayd she) 'sith ye so well have spide . . . V. vii. 19. 1
'Certes me needeth more To crave the same; . . . V. viii. 13. 7
'Certes I wote not well,' . . . V. viii. 15. 5

Certes—*Continued.*
'*Certes,* Sir knight, Hard is the case . . . . V. xi. 55. 1
'*Certes*' (said he) 'loth were I to have broken . . . . VI. ii. 7. 6
'*Certes,* Sir Knight' (sayd she) 'full loth I were . . . . . . VI. ii. 15. 6
Well may I, *certes,* such an one thee read, ... VI. ii. 25. 6
I may not, *certes,* without blame denie, ... VI. ii. 34. 6
his life . . . was *certes* in great jeopardy, ... VI. iii. 51. 5
'And, *certes,* it hath oftentimes bene seene, ... VI. iv. 36. 1
certes he was borne of noble blood, ... VI. v. 2. 7
'*Certes,*' (sayd then the Prince) 'the God is just, ... VI. viii. 23. 1
certes I your happinesse envie, ... VI. ix. 19. 8
Ne *certes* mote he greatly blamed be . . . . VI. x. 3. 1
Yet was she *certes* but a countrey lasse; . . . . VI. x. 25. 8
Yet *certes* by her face and physnomy, ... VII. vii. 5. 5
Certes small glory doest thou winne hereby, ... *H.L.* 153
Cerule. *caerule* streame, rombling in Pible stone, ... *Gn.* 163
Cesse. *See* **Cease.**
Cestus. That goodly belt was *Cestus* hight by name, ... IV. v. 6. 1
Cesure. *See* **Caesura.**
Chace. *See* **Chase.**
Chafe. To rubb her temples, and to *chaufe* her chin, ... I. vii. 21. 5
She gan afresh to *chafe,* and grieve in every vaine. . . . . IV. xii. 27. 9
With cruell *chaufe* their courages they whet, ... V. ii. 15. 3
gan to *chaufe* and sweat, ... V. xi. 12. 7
After long search and *chauff* he turned backe . . . . VI. ii. 21. 2
in his *chauffe* he digs the trampled ground, ... VI. v. 19. 7
Chafed. After the *chafed* Lyons cruell bayting, ... *Hub.* 6
chafte at that indignitie right sore: . . . . *Hub.* 1338
his hot ryder spurd his *chauffed* side: . . . . I. iii. 33. 6
he perced through his *chaufed* chest . . . . I. iii. 42. 6
steed . . . *chauft* that any on his backe should sitt: . . . . . I. vii. 37. 8
As *chauffed* Bore his bristles doth upreare; . . . . I. xi. 15. 6
seeming sorely *chauffed* at his band, ... I. xii. 35. 6
chaufd and fom'd with corage fiers and sterne, ... II. iii. 46. 8
Sore *chauffed* at my stay in such a cace, ... II. iv. 32. 7
they *chaft,* and rag'd, And woxe nigh mad . . . . IV. v. 27. 1
yet he did labour long, And swat, and *chauf'd,* . . . . V. ii. 46. 8
A while she walkt, and *chauft;* . . . . V. vi. 13. 6
He *chauft,* he griev'd, he fretted, and he sight, ... VI. xi. 25. 7
chauffed inly, seeing now no more His liberty was left . . . VI. xii. 36. 4
from which, as he had *chauffed* been, The sweat did drop; . . VII. vii. 29. 5
Chaff. Cockel for corne, and *chaffe* for barley, ... *S.C.* D. 124
Soone as the *chaffe* should in the fan be fynd, ... *S.C.* D. 125
Like scattred *chaffe* the which the wind away doth fan. . . . V. xi. 47. 9
Chaffer. Ne *chaffar* words, prowd corage to provoke, ... II. v. 3. 2
Chaffered. bene they *chaffred,* or at mischiefe dead? . . . . . *S.C.* S. 10
He *chaffred* Chayres in which Churchmen were set, ... *Hub.* 1159
Chafing. *Chaufing* and foming choler each against his fo. . . . IV. iv. 29. 9
Chain. Enchaste with *chaine* and circulet of golde. . . . . . *Hub.* 624
his late *chayne* his Liege unmeete esteemeth; . . . . *Hub.* 628
brought away fast bound with silver *chaine.* . . . . *D.* 119
wights Have knit themselves in Venus shameful *chaine:* . . . I. ii. 4. 8
who can . . . breake the *chayne* of strong necessitee, ... I. v. 25. 5
O goodly golden *chayne,* wherewith yfere The vertues linked are I. ix. 1. 1
boastes in beauties *chaine* not to be bownd, ... I. ix. 11. 7
Pyrochles . . . Furors *chayne* untyes, ... II. v. Arg.
She held a great gold *chaine* ylincked well, ... II. vii. 46. 2
To catchen hold of that long *chaine,* . . . . II. vii. 46. 6
with that golden *chaine* of concord tyde. . . . . III. i. 12. 8
that mightie *chaine,* . . . adowne gan fall, ... III. xii. 37. 7
With that great *chaine,* . . . Himselfe she bound, ... III. xii. 41. 6
that of Amorets hart-binding *chaine,* . . . . IV. i. 1. 4
that great golden *chaine* quite to divide, ... IV. i. 30. 8
linckt with me in the same *chaine* attone? . . . . IV. vii. 14. 7
with a litle golden *chaine* about it bound. . . . . IV. viii. 6. 9
in sad thraldomes *chayne;* . . . . IV. xi. 1. 5
With a strong yron *chaine* and coller bound, ... V. ix. 33. 6
thereunto a great long *chaine* he tight, ... VI. xii. 34. 8
Against his will fast bound in yron *chaine,* . . . . VI. xii. 35. 3
he broke his yron *chaine,* . . . . VI. xii. 38. 8
Fearing least Chaos broken had his *chaine,* . . . . VII. vi. 14. 6
Let her, yf please her, bynd with adamant *chayne:* . . . . . *Am.* xlii. 10
My trembling hart in her eternall *chaine,* . . . . *H.B.* 276
Chained. As *chained* beare whom cruell dogs doe bait, ... I. xii. 35. 7
The which I found sure lockt and *chained* fast. . . . . IV. x. 11. 3
Chains. Girt with long snakes, and thousand yron *chaynes,* . . *Gn.* 626
dreadfull Furies, which their *chaines* have brast, ... I. v. 31. 8
Aesculapius . . . Emprisond was in *chaines* remedilesse; . . I. v. 36. 8
Infernall furies with their *chaines* untyde. . . . . I. ix. 24. 5
bound him hand and foote with yron *chains;* . . . . I. xii. 36. 2
In *chaines* of lust and lewde desyres ybownd, ... II. i. 54. 3
Guyon does Furor bind in *chaines,* . . . . II. iv. Arg.
With hundred yron *chaines* he did him bind, ... II. iv. 15. 1
thralled her in *chaines* with strong effort, ... II. v. 17. 4
Throwing away her broken *chaines* and bands, ... II. xi. 47. 4
her in *chaines* of adamant he tyde; . . . . II. xii. 82. 6
such ghastly noyse of yron *chaines* . . . . III. iii. 9. 2
Faire Amorett must dwell in wicked *chaines,* . . . . III. xi. 24. 3
All deckt with crownes, and *chaynes,* and girlands gay, . . . IV. x. 37. 6
there in *chaynes* her cruelly did bind, ... IV. xi. 2. 5
Cold yron *chaines* with which let him be tide; . . . . V. v. 50. 8
In yron *chaines* of liberty bereft, ... VI. viii. 1. 4
Together linkt with Adamantine *chaines;* . . . . *H.L.* 89
Chair. on he upon triumphing *chaire,* . . . . *Bel.*[1] iv. 7
in triumphant *chayre* was set on hie, ... *Bel.*[2] iv. 7
Angels waighting on th' Almighties *chayre.* . . . . *T.M.* 510
Aldeboran . . . Above the shinie Cassiopeias *chaire,* . . . . . I. iii. 16. 2
strove to match, . . . Great Junoes golden *chayre;* . . . . . I. iv. 17. 5
The foule Duessa, next unto the *chaire* Of proud Lucifer,' . . I. iv. 37. 5

Chair—*Continued.*
she sitting in an yvory *chayre.* . . . . I. x. 31. 9
Amidst them all he in a *chaire* was sett, ... II. ix. 58. 1
In hast she from her lofty *chaire* descended, ... IV. iii. 50. 2
did set in sumptuous *chaire* To feast . . . . IV. ix. 13. 3
To pluck her downe perforce from off her *chaire;* . . . . . VII. vi. 13. 3
Chairs. He chaffred *Chayres* in which Churchmen were set, . . *Hub.* 1159
Chalk. weening hys whyte head was *chalke,* . . . . *S.C.* Jul. 223
Chalky. The *chaulky* Kenet, and the Thetis gray, ... IV. xi. 29. 5
Challenge. So meane Harpes worke may *chalenge* for her meed? . *Ro.* xxxii. 4
Sith nought on earth can *chalenge* long endurance? . . . . . *Van.* xi. 14
chalenge to our selves our portions dew . . . . *Hub.* 137
The Goddesse selfe to *chalenge* to the field, ... *Mui.* 270
Minerva did the *chalenge* not refuse, ... *Mui.* 273
Sansjoy Doth *chaleng* him to fight. . . . . I. iv. Arg.
'as sure as hound The stricken Deare doth *chalenge* . . . . . II. i. 12. 9
Not to debate the *chalenge* of your right, ... II. viii. 27. 7
That *challenge* did too peremptory seeme, ... III. viii. 16. 6
seeing his so prowd And boastfull *chalenge,* . . . . IV. i. 10. 6
That did her win and free from *chalenge* set: . . . . IV. i. 12. 4
Will *chalenge* yond same other for my fee.' . . . . IV. i. 35. 8
He made him open *chalenge,* . . . . IV. ii. 12. 9
Against all those that *chalenge* it to gard . . . . IV. ii. 27. 7
Bold was the *chalenge,* as himselfe was bold, ... IV. ii. 39. 1
These three that hardie *chalenge* tooke in hand, ... IV. iii. 3. 1
Assembled were in field the *chalenge* to define. . . . . . . IV. iii. 3. 9
All arm'd to point, his *chalenge* to abet: . . . . IV. iii. 6. 2
he now begunne To *challenge* her anew, ... IV. iv. 8. 6
Her to demaund and *chalenge* as their rights, ... IV. v. 23. 3
To whom each one his *chalenge* should disclame, ... IV. v. 25. 5
she that wrongfull *challenge* soone assoyled, ... IV. ix. 36. 7
rather chose his *challenge* off to breake, ... V. i. 24. 3
To *chalenge* all in right of Florimell, ... V. iii. 4. 8
Where falling downe his *challenge* he releast: . . . . V. vi. 39. 7
Both *challenge* it with equall greedinesse: . . . . V. vii. 30. 3
I defie thee; and here *challenge* make, ... VI. iii. 35. 4
Did scorne the *challenge* of so base a thrall; . . . . VI. iii. 36. 4
But both his *challenge* and him selfe contemned, ... VI. iii. 36. 8
no one beast in forrest, . . . but he it *challenge* would, . . . VI. v. 15. 8
Did *chalenge* Calidore to wrestling game; . . . . VI. ix. 43. 6
chalenge th' heritage of this our skie; . . . . VII. vi. 30. 3
May *challenge* ought in Heavens interesse; . . . . VII. vi. 33. 3
challenge to themselves the whole worlds raign, ... VII. vii. 15. 3
she will the conquest *challeng* needs, ... *Am.* xxix. 9
Challenged. From everie worke he *chalenged* essoyne, ... I. iv. 20. 3
his redeemer *chalengd* for his foe, ... II. v. 20. 3
strongly *challenged* The crowne . . . . II. x. 67. 3
That *chaleng'd* ought in Florimell, ... IV. ii. 28. 9
he *chalenged* the thiefe to fight: . . . . V. iii. 31. 6
Challenger. the doughty *chalenger* came forth, ... IV. iii. 6. 1
Challengers. gan the part of *Chalengers* anew To range the field, IV. iv. 25. 3
that late weaker band of *chalengers* relieved. . . . . IV. iv. 46. 9
Challenges. Till then your *challenges* ye may prolong; . . . . IV. iv. 12. 7
Challengeth. The signe by which he *chalengeth* the place; . . *Mui.* 317
Challenging. *chalenging* the Virgin as his dew, ... IV. iii. 14. 8
Chamber. sacred lamp in secret *chamber* hide, ... I. xii. 37. 7
His *chamber* was dispainted all within . . . . II. ix. 50. 1
all the *chamber* filled was with flyes . . . . II. ix. 51. 1
That *chamber* seemed ruinous and old, ... II. ix. 55. 1
His *chamber* all was hangd about with rolls . . . . II. ix. 57. 6
through a *Chamber* long and spacious, ... III. i. 31. 7
the sumptuous aray Of that great *chamber* . . . . III. i. 32. 2
So was that *chamber* clad in goodly wize: . . . . III. i. 39. 1
to the troubled *chamber* all in armes did throng. . . . . . . III. i. 62. 9
to her watry *chamber* swiftly carry him. . . . . III. iv. 42. 9
The maske of Cupid, and th' enchanted *Chamber* . . . . . . III. xii. Arg.
marcht . . . About the *chamber* by the Damozell; . . . . . . III. xii. 26. 7
Into a long large *chamber,* which was sield With moniments . V. v. 21. 3
to her *chamber* went like solitary cell. . . . . V. vi. 11. 9
comming with close intent Towards her *chamber;* . . . . . . V. vi. 28. 8
At last he up into the *chamber* came . . . . VI. vi. 30. 1
up convayd Into the *chamber,* where that Dame . . . . . . VI. vi. 39. 8
Lyke Phoebe, from her *chamber* of the East, ... *Epith.* 149
Chamber-door. there came unto her *chamber dore* Two Knights V. vi. 29. 1
at her *chamber dore* awayt, ... *Epith.* 52
Chamber-floor. they appeare . . . Like a Brydes *Chamber flore.* *Proth.* 82
Chamberlain. Which doen, the *Chamberlain,* Slowth, did to rest them call. I. iv. 43. 9
Chamber's. gazing on that *Chambers* ornament, ... III. xii. 29. 2
Chameleon. As ever could *Cameleon* colours new; . . . . . . IV. i. 18. 4
Chamelot. *See* **Camlet.**
Chamfered. Comes the breme Winter with *chamfred* browes, . *S.C.* F. 43
Champ. on their rusty bits did *champ* as they were wood. . . I. v. 20. 9
foming tarre, their bridles they would *champ,* . . . . I. v. 28. 8
Champaign. all the *champain* (*champion) o're he soared light; *Mui.* 149
The richest *champain* (*champian) that may else be rid; . . VII. vi. 54. 8
Champian. The same is now nought but a *champian* wide, . . *Ro.* xxxi. 1
*And all the *champion* he soared light, ... *Mui.* 149
In the wide *champian* of the Ocean plaine, ... V. ii. 15. 2
And by good fortune the plaine *champion* wonne: . . . . . . VI. iv. 26. 3
*doth over-looke The richest *champian* . . . . VII. vi. 54. 8
Champion. *See* **Champian.**
The *Champion* stout Eftsoones dismounted . . . . I. i. 11. 7
when she saw her *champion* fall . . . . I. ii. 20. 1
To seeke her strayed *Champion* if she might attayne. . . . . I. iii. 8. 9
that wilde *champion* wayting her besyde; . . . . I. iii. 26. 2
heard abroad of that her *champion* trew, ... I. vi. 36. 5
At her so pitteous cry was much amoov'd Her *champion* stout I. viii. 21. 2
Which when that *Champion* heard, . . . his hart was thrilled I. viii. 39. 1

Champion—*Continued.*
that great *Champion* of the antique world, ... I. xi. 27. 1
where that *champion* stout . . . did remaine, ... I. xii. 12. 3
now this Ladies *Champion,* . . . . II. ii. 18. 9
Her succourd eke the *Champion* of the bloody Crosse. . . . . III. i. 64. 9
with many a *champion* bold . . . . IV. xi. 19. 5
The *Champion* of true Justice, Artegall: . . . . V. i. 3. 2
Him entertayn'd and did her *champion* chose; . . . . V. x. 12. 7
A *Champion,* that had with his *Champion* fought, ... V. xi. 2. 3
if that no *champion* doe appeare, ... V. xi. 40. 2
how long space Hath he her lent a *Champion* to provide?' . V. xi. 42. 2
Championess. the *Championesse* now entred has The utmost rowme, ... III. xi. 27. 7
laid the noble *Championesse* strong hond Upon th' enchaunter III. xii. 41. 3
The *Championesse* . . . Was glad to yeeld . . . . V. vi. 22. 1
So did the *Championesse* those two there strow, ... V. vi. 40. 8
The *Championesse* them greeting, as she could, ... V. vii. 5. 1
Champion's. with that same Faery *champions* page, ... I. iv. 39. 2
eke her *champions* glorie sounded overall. . . . . V. xii. 24. 9
Champions. both their *champions* bad Pursew the end . . . . II. ii. 28. 2
Those *Champions* broke on them, ... II. ix. 14. 6
Malecastaes *champions* are defaced. . . . . III. i. Arg.
those sixe knights, that ladies *Champions* . . . . III. i. 63. 1
Those two great *champions* did attonce pursew . . . . III. iv. 46. 2
the brave youthly *Champions* to assay . . . . III. vii. 41. 6
babes, that prov'd three *champions* bold. . . . . IV. ii. 45. 9
These warlike *Champions,* all in armour shine, ... IV. iii. 3. 8
Thereat the *Champions* both stood still a space, ... IV. iii. 38. 1
Those warlike *champions* both together chose . . . . IV. iii. 51. 4
So these two *champions* to the ground were feld, ... IV. iv. 18. 6
Chance. (O grievous *chance!*) . . . . *Bel.*[2] xi. 12
if that fortune *chaunce* you up to call . . . . *Van.* xii. 11
Whereby by *chaunce* I him knewe. . . . . *S.C.* Mar. 36
My sheepe for that may *chaunce* to swerve, ... *S.C.* Mar. 44
if he *chaunce* come . . . . *S.C.* May 223
sike happy cheere is turnd to heavie *chaunce,* . . . . *S.C.* N. 103
Shall *chaunce,* through power of some divining spright, . . . *Gn. Ded.* 6
So maist thou *chaunce* mock out a Benefice, ... *Hub.* 509
with him far'd some better *chaunce* to fynde. . . . . *Hub.* 942
their owne happie *chaunce* Them freely offred, ... *Hub.* 962
What did of late *chaunce* happen to the Lyon stearne, ... *Hub.* 1250
Yf *chaunce* him fall into calamitie, ... *T.M.* 305
who will bewaile my heavy *chaunce?* . . . . *U.V.* 19
least he my Loove happely *chaunce* to beholde. . . . . . . *Tetrasticon,* 4
Nought carde I then for worldly change or *chaunce,* . . . . *D.* 103
true Lovers! whom desastrous *chaunce* Hath farre exiled . . . *D.* 505
thither led by *chaunce,* . . . . *Col.* 63
Much seemed he to mone her haplesse *chaunce,* . . . . I. iii. 25. 6
'Yt was my *chaunce* (my *chaunce* was faire and good) . . . I. vii. 47. 1
his shield, that covered was, Did loose his vele by *chaunce,* I. viii. 19. 2
like infirmity like *chaunce* may beare; . . . . I. ix. 30. 8
That feared *chaunce* from her to turne away: . . . . I. xi. 32. 5
It chaunst, (eternall God that *chaunce* did guide) . . . . . I. xi. 45. 6
Great cause, I weene, you guided, or some uncouth *chaunce.'* . II. i. 29. 9
'Fayre sonne, God give you happy *chaunce,* . . . . II. i. 31. 7
direfull *chaunce,* armd with avenging fate, ... II. i. 44. 6
to stay the mortall *chaunce,* . . . . II. iii. 34. 7
Least worse betide thee by some later *chaunce.* . . . . . . II. iv. 36. 5
Or bide the *chaunce* at thine owne jeopardee.' . . . . II. iv. 39. 5
to him that mindes his *chaunce* t' abye?' . . . . II. iv. 40. 4
One cursed creature he by *chaunce* espide, ... II. vii. 57. 8
The Prince by *chaunce* did on a Lady light, ... II. ix. 36. 6
Into this land by *chaunce* have driven bene; . . . . II. x. 8. 5
who can shun the *chance* that dest'ny doth ordaine? . . . . III. i. 37. 9
If *chaunce* I him encounter paravaunt; . . . . III. ii. 16. 4
Did *chaunce* to still into her weary spright, ... III. ii. 29. 2
he by *chaunce* did wander that same way, ... III. iv. 19. 8
Whose *chaunce* it was, that soone he did repent, ... III. iv. 47. 7
gan to make Exceeding mone, and curst that cruell *chaunce* . III. vii. 45. 4
Whom I in countrey cottage fownd by *chaunce:* . . . . III. vii. 59. 2
There them by *chaunce* encountred on the way . . . . III. viii. 15. 2
May meete againe, and each take happy *chaunce.'* . . . . . III. viii. 18. 4
Satyrane his *chaunce* Was her before, ... III. ix. 27. 1
Rather let try extremities of *chaunce,* . . . . III. xi. 24. 8
Much was he grieved with that gracelesse *chaunce;* . . . . . IV. iii. 8. 5
Now falne into their fellowship by *chance:* . . . . IV. iv. 7. 4
by *chaunce* doth fall Into the hunters toile, ... IV. iv. 32. 5
By *chance* he certaine miniments forth drew, ... IV. viii. 6. 2
By fortune in that place did *chance* to light: . . . . IV. ix. 28. 3
as he to and fro by *chaunce* did trace, ... IV. xii. 4. 8
All change is perillous, and all *chaunce* unsound. . . . . . V. ii. 36. 7
I by *chaunce* then wandring on the shore . . . . V. iv. 12. 1
Whom when as Artegall in that distresse By *chaunce* beheld, . V. iv. 41. 2
by *chaunce* hath spide A Goshauke, ... V. iv. 42. 3
to upbrayd that *chaunce* which him misfell, ... V. v. 10. 2
Having by *chaunce* espide advantage neare, ... V. vii. 32. 2
by *chaunce* he met uppon a day With Artegall, ... VI. i. 4. 3
by *chaunce* a comely Squire he found, ... VI. i. 11. 2
Subject to fortunes *chance,* still chaunging new: . . . . . . VI. i. 41. 8
Having by *chaunce* a close advantage vew'd, ... VI. iii. 50. 4
a wondrous *chaunce* his reskue wrought, ... VI. iii. 51. 6
by some deadly *chaunce* be done to pine . . . . VI. v. 28. 8
as did by *chaunce* befall, ... VI. vi. 19. 1
whatever *chaunce* were blowne Betwixt them to divide, . . . VI. vii. 3. 8
by *chaunce* more then by choyce, ... VI. viii. 46. 7
This fatall *chaunce,* this dolefull accident, ... VI. xi. 31. 2
this young Mayd, whom *chance* to her presents, ... VI. xii. 20. 5
to her creatures every minute *chaunce;* . . . . VII. vii. 23. 2
if . . . Thou *chance* to come, fall lowly at her feet; . . . . *Am.* ii. 10
when he by *chance* doth find A feeble beast, ... *Am.* lvi. 3

Chance—*Continued.*
Devouring tyme and changeful *chance* have prayd, ... *Am.* lviii. 7
Ne feard with worse to any *chaunce* to start; . . . . *Am.* lix. 4
ye waving *chance* to marke; . . . . *Am.* lxxxi. 2
by *chaunce,* against the course of kynd, ... *H.B.* 143
For feare, lest if he *chaunce* to looke on thee, ... *H.H.B.* 146
Chanced. Casting mine eyes farre off, I *chaunst* to see . . . *Bel.*[2] xiii. 3
Which th' husbandman behind him *chanst* to scater. . . . . *Ro.* xxx. 14
Yt *chaunced* after upon a day, ... *S.C.* F. 143
I *chaunst* to fall asleepe with sorowe . . . . *S.C.* Mar. 47
chaunst to stomble at the threshold flore: . . . . *S.C.* May 230
what my selfe knowe *Chaunced* to Roffynn . . . . *S.C.* S. 171
they *chaunst* to meet upon the way . . . . *Hub.* 227
chaunst with a formall Priest to meete, ... *Hub.* 361
At last they *chaunst* to meete upon the way . . . . *Hub.* 581
It *chaunced* me on day beside the shore . . . . *Ti.* 1
lincked *chaunst* with thee to bee, ... *Ti.* 248
As if to me had *chanst* some evill tourne! . . . . *D.* 266
such mishap, as *chaunst* to me, ... *D.* 516
a straunge shepheard *chaunst* to find me out, ... *Col.* 60
His Lady, seeing all that *chaunst* from farre, ... I. i. 27. 1
they *chaunst* to meet upon the way An aged Sire, ... I. i. 29. 1
him *chaunst* to meete . . . A faithlesse Sarazin, ... I. ii. 12. 5
it *chaunced* this proud Sarazin To meete me wandring; . . . I. ii. 25. 1
Me *chaunced* of a knight encountred bee, ... I. ii. 35. 7
I *chaunst* to see her in her proper hew, ... I. ii. 40. 6
the Paynim *chaunst* to cast his eye, ... I. v. 10. 1
she *chaunst* their stubborne mouths to twitch; . . . . I. v. 28. 7
A Satyre *chaunst* her wandring for to finde; . . . . I. vi. 22. 6
His loving mother . . . *chaunst* unwares to meet him . . . . I. vi. 27. 3
'I *chaunst* this day, This fatall day . . . . I. vi. 38. 1
she *chaunced* by good hap to meet . . . . I. vii. 29. 1
him *chaunced* false Duessa meete, ... I. vii. 50. 6
'I lately *chaunst* (Would I had never *chaunst!*) . . . . . I. ix. 27. 1
It *chaunst,* (eternall God that chaunce did guide) . . . . . I. xi. 45. 6
would, O! would it so had *chaunst,* . . . . II. i. 10. 1
what bootes it to weepe . . . When ill is *chaunst,* . . . . . II. i. 16. 6
as *chaunst* them by a forest side To passe, ... II. i. 35. 5
Dan Faunus *chaunst* to meet her by the way, ... II. ii. 7. 5
by the way he *chaunced* to espy One . . . . II. iii. 6. 1
oft himselfe he *chaunst* to hurt unwares, ... II. iv. 7. 6
There *chaunced* to the Princes hand to rize . . . . II. ix. 59. 5
Sir Guyon *chaunst* eke on another booke, ... II. ix. 60. 1
it *chaunst* a knight To passe that way, ... III. vii. 29. 2
A knight that way there *chaunced* to repaire; . . . . III. viii. 11. 5
chaunst Malbecco busie be elsewhere, ... III. x. 12. 2
chaunced on a craggy cliff to light, ... III. x. 57. 7
they *chaunced* to espie Two other knights, ... IV. i. 38. 4
they *chaunst* to overtake Two knights . . . . IV. ii. 30. 2
It *chaunst* Sir Satyrane his steed . . . To stumble, ... IV. iv. 30. 2
Upon his heavie eye-lids *chaunst* to fall, ... IV. v. 42. 2
it *chaunst* That . . . So sorely he her strooke, ... IV. vi. 13. 1
The wicked stroke upon her helmet *chaunst,* . . . . IV. vi. 19. 1
Glauce, seeing all that *chaunced* there, ... IV. vi. 25. 1
if it *chaunst,* (as needs it must in fight) . . . . IV. vii. 26. 6
there *chaunst* a turtle Dove To come . . . . IV. viii. 3. 2
He *chaunst* to come where those two Ladies . . . . IV. viii. 19. 2
An hard mishap and disaventrous case Him *chaunst:* . . . . IV. viii. 51. 4
she *chaunced* there to see This lovely swaine, ... IV. viii. 52. 4
Him for to aide, if aide he *chaunst* to neede, ... V. i. 13. 2
He *chaunst* to meet a Dwarfe in hasty course, ... V. ii. 2. 2
He *chaunst* to come whereas two comely Squires, ... V. iv. 4. 2
She *chaunst* unwares to light upon this coffer, ... V. iv. 10. 8
He *chaunst* to come, where happily he spide A rout . . . . V. iv. 21. 2
all the ill which *chaunst* to me of late, ... V. iv. 28. 7
She *chaunst* to meete, toward the even-tide, A Knight . . . V. vi. 19. 3
he *chaunst* far off to heed A Damzell, ... V. viii. 4. 1
had he *chaunced* not his shield to reare, ... V. xi. 10. 4
At length it *chaunst* that both . . . . VI. i. 38. 1
I *chaunst* to meete this knight, who there lyes slaine, . . . VI. ii. 9. 8
I will the truth discover as it *chaunst* whylere. . . . . . VI. ii. 15. 9
We *chaunst* to come foreby a covert glade . . . . VI. ii. 16. 3
He *chaunst* to come whereas a jolly Knight . . . . VI. iii. 20. 2
He *chaunst* to spie a faire and stately place, ... VI. iii. 29. 7
He *chaunst* far off an armed Knight to spy . . . . VI. iii. 46. 6
Well then him *chaunst* his heavy armes to want, ... VI. iv. 19. 1
It *chaunst* some furniture about her steed To be disordred . VI. v. 10. 2
He *chaunst* to spy a sort of shepheard groomes, ... VI. ix. 5. 2
He *chaunst* to come . . . Unto a place . . . . VI. x. 5. 3
if any grace *chaunst* to arize To him, ... VI. x. 33. 8
There *chaunst* to them a dangerous accident: . . . . VI. x. 34. 3
It *chaunst* a sort of merchants . . . Arrived in this Isle, . . VI. xi. 9. 2
He *chaunst* one comming towards him to spy, ... VI. xi. 27. 2
They *chaunst,* upon an hill . . . shepheards to espy; . . . . VI. xi. 36. 6
Chaunst to espy upon her yvory chest The rosie marke, . . . VI. xii. 15. 5
nothing knew Of all that *chaunced* heere, ... VII. vi. 14. 2
Mongst whom some beast . . . Unwares is *chaunc't,* . . . . . VII. vi. 28. 8
She *chaunst* to come where Cupid lay, ... *Epig.* ii. 2
A Flocke of Nymphes I *chaunced* to espy, ... *Proth.* 20
Chanceful. In this adventures *chauncefull* jeopardie: . . . . *Hub.* 98
Chancel. robd the *Chancell,* and the deskes downe threw, . . VI. xii. 25. 2
Chances. Such *chaunces* oft exceed all humaine thought! . . VI. iii. 51. 8
That worldly *chaunces* doe amongst them cast, ... VI. xi. 1. 3
Change. *See* **Counterchange.**
O grevous *chaunge!* . . . . *Bel.*[1] ix. 12
In hundred formes to *change* his fearefull hew; . . . . . . *Bel.*[2] viii. 10
O mervelous great *change!* . . . . *Ro.* xxix. 12
With sight of such as *chaunge* my restlesse woe. . . . . . . *S.C.* Au. 172
To cheerefull songs can *chaunge* my cherelesse cryes. . . . . *S.C.* Au. 182
seeldome *chaunge* the better brought: . . . . *S.C.* S. 69

Change—*Continued.*
Neede feare no *chaunge* of frowning fate; . . . *S.C.* S. 71
Nor *chaunge* of labour may intreated bee; . . . *Gn.* 418
Continuallie subject unto *chaunge*. . . . *Hub.* 92
Abroad, where *change* is, good may gotten bee.' . . . *Hub.* 101
they unto their fortunes *change* to tosse: . . . *Hub.* 342
they their occupation meant to *change*, . . . *Hub.* 355
Of kingdomes *change*, of divers gouvernment, . . . *Hub.* 766
th' intent of Counsells, and the *change* Of states, . . . *Hub.* 786
Now *change* the tenor of your joyous layes, . . . *T.M.* 367
Now *change* your praises into piteous cries, . . . *T.M.* 371
All things doo *change* that under heaven abide, . . . *Ti.* 206
Ne feareth *change* of time, . . . *Ti.* 465
His choicefull sense with every *change* doth flit: . . . *Mui.* 159
varietie And *change* of sweetnesse, (for all *change* is sweete) . *Mui.* 178
Nought carde I then for worldly *change* or chaunce, . . . *D.* 103
before the *chaunge* Which Venus blood . . . *D.* 108
By *chaunge* of turnes, each making other mery; . . . *Col.* 77
For trumpets sterne to *chaunge* mine Oaten reeds, . . . I. Pr. 1. 4
With *chaunge* of chear the . . . maid Let fal her eien, . . . I. ii. 27. 5
'We may not *chaunge*,' (quoth he,) 'this evill plight, . . . I. ii. 43. 3
beware of ficklenesse, In . . . *chaunge* of thy deare-loved Dame ; I. iv. 1. 4
compassion mov'd . . . and *change* in that great mothers face : I. v. 24. 7
Which, . . . quakes in every lim With *chaunge* of feare . . . I. vi. 10. 9
chaunge of hew great passion did bewray; . . . I. ix. 16. 2
she no whitt did *chaunge* her constant mood: . . . I. x. 13. 6
Confest how Philemon her wrought to *chaunge* her weede. . . II. iv. 29. 9
Therefore, I thee exhort To *chaunge* thy will, . . . II. v. 17. 8
Can *chaunge* my cheare, or make me ever mourne: . . . II. vi. 10. 8
Avise thee well, and *chaunge* thy wilfull mood, . . . II. vii. 38. 8
To *chaunge* love causelesse is reproch to warlike knight.' . . II. vii. 50. 9
chaunge of colour did perforce unfold, . . . II. ix. 39. 4
To *chaunge* my liefe, and love another Dame; . . . III. i. 24. 3
Ne list me *chaunge;* . . . III. i. 24. 7
is now by *chaunge* Of name Cayr-Merdin cald, . . . III. iii. 7. 3
That suddein *chaunge* she straunge adventure thought. . . . III. vi. 20. 5
To *chaunge* her hew, and sondry formes to don, . . . III. vi. 38. 4
feed her fancy with delightfull *chaunge:* . . . III. vii. 50. 3
late mischaunce had her compeld to *chaunge* The land for sea, III. viii. 20. 4
losse of chastitie, or *chaunge* of love: . . . III. viii. 42. 2
his hew Gan greatly *chaunge* . . . III. viii. 48. 2
Then Paridell began to *chaunge* his theme, . . . III. ix. 10. 8
Inconstant *Chaunge* and false Disloyalty; . . . III. xii. 25. 6
sight of such a *chaunge* her much dismayd . . . III. xii. 42. 5
fresh . . . She was become, by *chaunge* of her estate, . . . IV. i. 31. 8
His *chaunge* of cheere that anguish did bewray, . . . IV. i. 50. 7
Not all the gods can *chaunge*, . . . IV. ii. 51. 9
For that had might to *change* the hearts of men . . . IV. iii. 45. 5
Fro love to hate, a *change* of evill choise: . . . IV. iii. 45. 6
Made her to *change* her hew, and hidden love t' appeare. . . IV. iii. 46. 9
Wonder it is that sudden *change* to see: . . . IV. iii. 49. 2
When all men saw this sudden *change* of things, . . . IV. iii. 49. 6
Shew'd *change* of better cheare: . . . IV. vi. 38. 3
Ne ought mote make him *change* his wonted tenor, . . . IV. vii. 47. 3
Fearelesse of fortunes *chaunge* or envies dread, . . . IV. viii. 18. 3
admyrde her *change*, and spake her praise. . . . IV. ix. 16. 9
change his liking, and new Lemans prove; . . . IV. ix. 21. 6
gan they *change* their sides, . . . IV. ix. 26. 1
If wind and tide doe *change*, their courses *change* anew. . . IV. ix. 26. 9
Would *change* with me, but I did it denye, . . . V. i. 17. 3
Yet for no pitty would he *change* the course Of Justice, . . . V. ii. 26. 1
mongst them al no *change* hath yet beene found; . . . V. ii. 36. 4
All *change* is perillous, and all chaunce unsound. . . . V. ii. 36. 7
To *change* his shield with him, to be the better hid. . . . V. iii. 10. 9
For any death to *chaunge* life, though most bad: . . . V. iv. 11. 5
having chosen, now he might not *chaunge*. . . . V. v. 26. 6
Therewith she gan at first to *change* her mood, . . . V. v. 45. 4
By *change* of place seeking to ease her paine; . . . V. vi. 15. 5
As sundry *chaunge* her seemed best to ease. . . . V. vi. 26. 4
even she her selfe much wondered At such a *chaunge*, . . . V. vii. 13. 8
by the *change* of her uncheerefull looke, . . . V. vii. 18. 1
by your *change* of cheare is easie for to see.' . . . V. vii. 18. 9
Could ought on earth so wondrous *change* have wrought, . . V. vii. 40. 6
the *change* of aire and place Would *change* her paine, . . . V. vii. 45. 3, 4
change of love for any worlds delight! . . . V. xi. 62. 5
Nether of envy nor of *chaunge* afeard: . . . VI. v. 12. 5
or *chaunge* to you at all; . . . VI. ix. 32. 2
To *change* the manner of his loftie looke; . . . VI. ix. 36. 2
Proud *Change* (not pleasd in mortall things . . . to raigne) VII. vi. Arg.
Of *Change*, the which all mortall things doth sway, . . . VII. vi. 1. 2
made him *change* his gray attire to greene: . . . VII. vii. 11. 8
So turne they still about, and *change* in restlesse wise. . . VII. vii. 18. 9
men themselves do *change* continually, . . . VII. vii. 19. 4
Still *change* and vary thoughts, as new occasions fall. . . VII. vii. 19. 9
Still tost and turned with continuall *change*, . . . VII. vii. 21. 2
To thousand sorts of *Change* we subject see: . . . VII. vii. 25. 3
Whether . . . *Change* doth not raign . . . VII. vii. 47. 4
Times do *change* and move continually: . . . VII. vii. 47. 6
though he lesse appeare To *change* his hew, . . . VII. vii. 51. 2
your owne natures *change;* . . . VII. vii. 54. 6
by their *change* their being do dilate, . . . VII. vii. 58. 5
over them *Change* doth not rule and raigne, But they raigne
over *Change*, . . . VII. vii. 58. 8, 9
none no more *change* shal see.' . . . VII. vii. 59. 5
that same time when no more *Change* shall be, . . . VII. viii. 2. 2
all that moveth doth in *Change* delight: . . . VII. viii. 2. 6
So let us, which this *chaunge* of weather vew, . . . *Am.* lxii. 5
Chaunge eke our mynds, and former lives amend; . . . *Am.* lxii. 6
chaunge old yeares annoy to new delight. . . . *Am.* lxii. 14
eyther *change* thy cruelty, Or give like leave unto the fly.' . . *Epig.* iv. 19

Changeable. Whatever thing lacketh *chaungeable* rest, . . . *S.C.* S. 240
Changed. So now his frend is *chaunged* for a frenne. . . . *S.C.* Ap. 28
His *chaunged* powres at first them selves not felt; . . . I. vii. 6. 6
three Moones have *changed* thrice their hew, . . . I. viii. 38. 6
do Chaungelings call, so *chaung'd* by Faeries theft. . . . I. x. 65. 9
He *chaungd* his mynd from one to other ill; . . . II. i. 5. 4
when they had markt the *chaunged* skyes, . . . II. ii. 46. 8
too oft she *chaung'd* her native hew. . . . II. ix. 40. 4
Weake body wel is *chang'd* for minds redoubled forse. . . II. ix. 55. 9
chaunged her weary side the better ease to take. . . . III. i. 61. 9
Chaunged thy lively cheare, and living made thee dead? . . III. ii. 30. 9
All suddeinly abasht shee *chaunged* hew, . . . III. v. 30. 5
chaunged is, and often altred to and froe. . . . III. vi. 37. 9
The substaunce is not *chaungd* nor altered, . . . III. vi. 38. 1
Transformed oft, and *chaunged* diverslie; . . . III. vi. 47. 7
chaung'd from one to other feare: . . . III. viii. 33. 2
into a golden showre Him selfe he *chaung'd*, . . . III. xi. 31. 2
false Duessa . . . now had *chang'd* her former wonted hew; . IV. i. 18. 2
chaung'd at pleasure for those impes of thine! . . . IV. ii. 51. 7
Ne *chaunged* was into a starre in sky; . . . IV. iii. 13. 5
friends profest are *chaungd* to foemen fell: . . . IV. iv. 1. 3
all things else in time are *chaunged* quight: . . . V. Pr. 4. 5
His Lyons skin *chaungd* to a pall of gold, . . . V. v. 24. 7
She *chang'd* that threatfull mood, . . . V. v. 47. 9
till that at last Into a bird it *chaung'd*, . . . V. ix. 17. 5
chang'd from hand to hand, . . . V. xi. 7. 7
So wondrously now *chaung'd* from that she was afore. . . . VI. i. 46. 9
pitty her sad plight, so *chang'd* from pleasaunt hew. . . . VI. xi. 2. 9
she the face of earthly things so *changed*, . . . VII. vi. 5. 1
having *chang'd* his cheare, . . . VII. vi. 31. 5
Yet is she *chang'd* in part, and eeke in generall: . . . VII. vii. 17. 9
Unlike in forme, and *chang'd* by strange disguise: . . . VII. vii. 18. 8
Which every howre is *chang'd* and altred cleane . . . VII. vii. 22. 7
Yet are they *chang'd* . . . Into themselves, . . . VII. vii. 25. 4
all things . . . Are *chaung'd* of Time, . . . VII. vii. 48. 3
moves them all, and makes them *changed* be? . . . VII. vii. 48. 8
likewise *chang'd* and subject unto mee? . . . VII. vii. 49. 9
her face and countenance every day We *changed* see . . . VII. vii. 50. 7
Mars . . . is *changed* most; . . . VII. vii. 52. 1
Is checkt and *changed* from his nature trew, . . . VII. vii. 54. 8
all things stedfastnesse do hate And *changed* be; . . . VII. vii. 58. 3
They are not *changed* from their first estate; . . . VII. vii. 58. 4
time shall come that all shall *changed* bee, . . . VII. vii. 59. 4
Nor to the Moone; for they are *changed* never; . . . *Am.* ix. 6
Changeful. The *chaungfull* turning of mens slipperie state, . . *Gn.* 554
Beares in his wings so manie a *changefull* token. . . . *Mui.* 101
daylie doth her *changefull* counsels bend . . . *D.* 153
sent into the *chaungefull* world agayne, . . . III. vi. 33. 7
'as *changefull* as the Moone' men use to say. . . . VII. vii. 50. 9
Devouring tyme and *changeful* chance . . . *Am.* lviii. 7
Changelings. Such, men do *Chaungelings* call, so chaung'd by
Faeries theft. . . . I. x. 65. 9
Change's. affrayd of every *chaunges* dread. . . . VI. ix. 27. 9
Changes. 'The divelish hag by *chaunges* of my cheare Per-
ceiv'd my thought; . . . I. ii. 42. 1
'Therein the *changes* infinite beholde, . . . VII. vii. 23. 1
flashing lights that thousand *changes* make. . . . VII. vii. 23. 9
doth many *changes* take, . . . VII. vii. 54. 5
faine my griefe with *chaunges* to beguile, . . . *Am.* lxxxvi. 10
Changeth. Because it *changeth* ever too and fro, . . . *D.* 429
Changing. by *changing* fate for fate. . . . *Gn.* 427
Oft *chaunging* sides, and oft new place electing, . . . IV. v. 40. 3
every place seem'd painefull, and ech *changing* vaine. . . . IV. v. 40. 9
changing all that forme of common-weale . . . V. vii. 42. 4
Artegall . . . blames for *changing* shield: . . . V. xii. Arg.
Subject to fortunes chance, still *chaunging* new: . . . VI. i. 41. 8
changing nought his count'nance bold, . . . VII. vi. 19. 8
Channel. to slide In silver *channell*, . . . *Ti.* 135
flood Through every *channell* running one might see; . . . II. xii. 60. 4
(That on each side her silver *channell* crowne) . . . VII. vi. 41. 8
Channels. in *chanels* cleare To romble gently downe . . . *T.M.* 25
Chant. Free libertie to *chaunt* our charmes at will, . . . *T.M.* 244
They cherelie *chaunt*, and rymes at randon fling, . . . *T.M.* 321
birds . . . Doe *chaunt* sweet musick . . . I. vii. 3. 5
some one did *chaunt* this lovely lay: . . . II. xii. 74. 1
how the cheerefull birds do *chaunt* theyr laies . . . *Epith.* 78
Chanted. *Chaunted* their sundrie tunes with sweete consent; . *Gn.* 226
Chaunted alowd their cheerefull harmonee, . . . II. v. 31. 7
Chanticleer. chearefull *Chaunticlere* with his note shrill . . I. ii. 1. 6
Chanting. *Chaunting* in shade their sundrie melodie, . . . *Pet.* iii. 6
where the *chaunting* birds luld me asleepe, . . . *S.C.* D. 71
on shrill reedes *chaunting* his rustick rime, . . . *Gn.* 155
Chaos. destinie this huge *Chaos* turmoyling, . . . *Ro.* xix. 9
An huge eternall *Chaos*, which supplyes The substaunces . . III. vi. 36. 8
Demogorgon, . . . The hideous *Chaos* keepes, . . . IV. ii. 47. 9
As if instead thereof they *Chaos* would restore. . . . IV. ix. 23. 9
Fearing least *Chaos* broken had his chaine, . . . VII. vi. 14. 6
Chaos'. Shall in great *Chaos* wombe againe be hid. . . . *Ro.* xxii. 14
great Earth, great *Chaos* child; . . . VII. vi. 26. 6
Out of great *Chaos* ugly prison crept, . . . *H.L.* 58
Chapel. a litle wyde There was an holy *chappell* edifyde, . . I. i. 34. 5
On top whereof a sacred *chappell* was, . . . I. x. 46. 3
before this Castle greene Built a faire *Chappell*, . . . V. x. 28. 2
nigh thereto a little *Chappell* stoode, . . . VI. v. 35. 1
Chapelet, -s. *See* **Chaplet,** *etc.*
Chaplain. would not let me be her *Chappellane*, . . . III. vii. 58. 7
Chaplet. A *chapelet* on her head she wore, . . . *S.C.* Au. 69
Hey, ho, *chapelet!* . . . *S.C.* Au. 70
A *Chapelet* of sundry flowers she wore, . . . IV. xi. 46. 6

Chaplets. The coloured *chaplets* wrought with a chiefe, . . . *S.C.* N. 115
Gay *chapelets* of flowers and gyrlonds trim. . . . *As.* 42
Chapters. The *chapters* Alablaster, . . . *Bel.* iv. 3
Character. Whose *character* . . . so firmely was engraved, . . V. vi. 2. 6
Characters. writing straunge *characters* in the grownd, . . . III. iii. 14. 8
Figuring straunge *characters* of his art: . . . III. xii. 31. 2
With living blood he those *characters* wrate, . . . III. xii. 31. 3
Chare. lapped up her silken leaves most *chayre,* . . . III. v. 51. 6
Charet. In her swifte *charret* with high turrets crownde, . . . *Ro.* vi. 2
his golden *Charet* glistering light; . . . *Gn.* 67
traversing the *charret* of the Sunne . . . *T.M.* 9
Before the dore her yron *charet* stood, . . . I. v. 20. 6
So lay him in her *charett,* . . . I. v. 29. 9
Their mournefull *charett,* fild with rusty blood, . . . I. v. 32. 2
wont in *charett* chace the foming bore: . . . I. v. 37. 2
steedes aghast Both *charett* swifte and huntsman overcast: . . I. v. 38. 5
Una her did marke Clymbe to her *charet,* . . . I. xi. 51. 7
did them drive before His whirling *charet* . . . II. xii. 22. 4
shee bad her *charett* to be brought; . . . III. iv. 31. 2
Drew the smooth *charett* of sad Cymoent: . . . III. iv. 33. 2
They easely unto her *charett* beare: . . . III. iv. 42. 2
His *charett* swifte in hast he thither steard, . . . III. viii. 30. 7
Removing her, into his *charet* brought, . . . III. viii. 35. 8
tyde behind his *charet,* to aggrate The virgin . . . III. viii. 36. 5
bold to guide the *charet* of the Sunne, . . . III. xi. 38. 3
That his swift *charet* might have passage wyde . . . III. xi. 40. 8
One in a *charet* of straunge furniment . . . IV. iii. 38. 4
The *charet* decked was in wondrous wize . . . IV. iii. 38. 6
In her great iron *charet* wonts to ride, . . . IV. xi. 28. 2
Mounted in Phoebus *charet* fierie bright, . . . V. iii. 19. 2
mounting straight upon a *charret* hye, . . . V. viii. 28. 4
If he too rashly to his *charet* drew, . . . V. viii. 32. 2
Oft drew the Prince unto his *charret* nigh, . . . V. viii. 33. 1
they did draw The yron *charet,* . . . V. viii. 41. 6
Charets. Bad eke attonce their *charetts* to be sought: . . . III. iv. 31. 4
their *charets* they forlore, . . . III. iv. 34. 2
Charet-wheels. With burning *charet wheeles* it nigh to smite; III. vii. 41. 7
His *charret wheeles* about him whirled round, . . . V. viii. 36. 2
Charge. Those faytours little regarden their *charge,* . . . *S.C.* May 39
take his *charge* of kyne? . . . *Hub.* 286
lent to him the *charge* Of all his flocke, . . . *Hub.* 299
the *charge* is wondrous great, . . . *Hub.* 431
The Nimph, which of that water course has *charge,* . . . *Col.* 109
the shepheard which hath *charge* in chief, . . . *Col.* 244
Have in the Ocean *charge* to me assignd; . . . *Col.* 253
The ledden of straunge languages in *charge:* . . . *Col.* 744
charge of them was to a Porter hight, . . . I. iv. 6. 3
he gave in *charge* unto his Squyre, That scarlot whore . . . I. viii. 29. 1
he had *charge* my discipline to frame, . . . I. ix. 5. 3
the carefull *charge* of him she gave, . . . I. x. 34. 6
Of all the house had *charge* and governement, . . . I. x. 37. 2
The fift had *charge* sick persons to attend, . . . I. x. 41. 1
The sixt had *charge* of them now being dead, . . . I. x. 42. 1
The seventh . . . Had *charge* the tender Orphans . . . I. x. 43. 2
The *charge* thereof unto a covetous Spright Commaunded was, II. vii. 32. 1
'The *charge,* which God doth unto me arrett, . . . II. viii. 8. 1
At last, him turning to his *charge* behight, . . . II. viii. 9. 5
both attonce him *charge* on either syde . . . II. viii. 35. 1
when againe They gave fresh *charge,* . . . II. ix. 14. 3
They all that *charge* did fervently apply . . . II. xi. 7. 6
perteines in *charge* particulare, . . . II. xii. 47. 4
dare thou not, I *charge,* in any cace To enter . . . III. iii. 8. 7
gave it streight in *charge* . . . III. vii. 23. 1
As her Creatresse had in *charge* to her ordain'd, . . . III. viii. 10. 9
hath the *charge* of Neptunes mighty heard; . . . III. viii. 30. 2
as bent to *charge* them new: . . . IV. i. 38. 6
her Dwarfe, which had me in his *charge,* . . . IV. viii. 61. 2
Unto whose trust the *charge* thereof was lent: . . . IV. x. 12. 2
Which hath in *charge* the ingate of the yeare: . . . IV. x. 12. 6
have the sea in *charge* to them assinde, . . . IV. xi. 52. 2
his mothers former *charge* Gainst womens love, . . . IV. xii. 14. 5
The *charge* of Justice given was in trust, . . . V. iv. 2. 2
'Neither will I Him *charge* with guilt, . . . VI. ii. 14. 4
For his sicke *charge* some harbour there to seeke; . . . VI. iii. 37. 6
his young *charge* whereof he skilled nought, . . . VI. iv. 38. 2
In that good Hermits *charge;* . . . VI. v. 41. 4
They left her so, in *charge* of one, . . . VI. xi. 24. 2
laying feare aside to doe his *charge,* . . . VII. vi. 17. 6
the *charge* to them foreshewed By mighty Jove; . . . VII. vii. 45. 5
ne ever did their *charge* forsake. . . . VII. vii. 45. 9
sith of wemens labours thou hast *charge,* . . . *Epith.* 383
Charged. We are but *charg'd* to lay the meate before: . . . *Hub.* 435
himselfe was *charged* heavily Of hardy Nennius, . . . II. x. 49. 3
charg'd his spere At him that first appeared . . . IV. iv. 40. 1
charg'd his powrefull speare At Artegall, . . . IV. iv. 44. 1
Foure *charged* two, and two surcharged one; . . . IV. ix. 30. 5
lastly Justice *charged* her with breach of lawes. . . . V. ix. 44. 9
there with guiltie bloudshed *charged* ryfe: . . . V. ix. 48. 4
fiercely *charged* them with all his force: . . . V. xii. 7. 2
And him unarm'd, . . . *Charg'd* with his speare, . . . VI. ii. 43. 5
charged him so fierce and furiously, . . . VI. v. 16. 5
Chargeful. 'Not that the burden of so bold a guest Shall *chargefull* be, . . . VI. ix. 32. 2
Charges. tend our *charges* with obeisaunce meeke. . . . III. vi. 22. 8
Charging. *charging* him afresh thus felly him bespake. . . . IV. iii. 10. 9
fiercely *charging* him with all his might, . . . VI. iii. 25. 6
Charillis. Phyllis, *Charillis,* and sweet Amaryllis. . . . *Col.* 540
The next to her is bountifull *Charillis:* . . . *Col.* 542
sweet *Charillis* is the Paragone Of peerlesse price, . . . *Col.* 548
Chariot. From fiery wheeles of his faire *chariot* Hurled his beame . . . I. ii. 29. 4
Charissa. faire *Charissa* to a lovely fere Was lincked, . . . I. x. 4. 8
The deare *Charissa,* where is she become? . . . I. x. 16. 2
By this *Charissa,* . . . Was woxen strong, . . . I. x. 29. 7
Albe *Charissa* were their chiefest founderesse. . . . I. x. 44. 9
Charity. Ah, deare Lord! and sweete Saint *Charitee!* . . . *S.C.* May 247
godly worke of Almes and *charitee,* . . . I. x. 45. 4
welcomde more for feare then *charitee;* . . . III. ix. 19. 4
Charlemagne. *Charlemaine* amongst the Starris seaven. . . . *T.M.* 462
Charm. Here we our slender pypes may safely *charme.* . . . *S.C.* O. 118
Had not that *charme* from thee forwarned itt: . . . I. ii. 18. 4
By subtilty, nor slight, nor might, nor mighty *charme.* . . . I. xi. 36. 9
The *charme* fulfild, dead suddeinly he downe did sincke. . . II. i. 55. 9
the *charme* and veneme which they dronck, . . . II. ii. 4. 6
Does *charme* her lovers, . . . II. v. 27. 4
The art of mightie words that men can *charme;* . . . V. v. 49. 6
well could *charme* his tongue, . . . V. ix. 39. 3
Gan mutter close a certaine secret *charme,* . . . VI. viii. 45. 6
O mighty *charm!* which makes men love theyr bane, . . . *Am.* xlvii. 13
Charmed. he forward gan advaunce . . . his *charmed* launce. I. iii. 25. 9
'he beares a *charmed* shield, . . . I. iv. 50. 5
'*Charmd* or enchaunted,' . . . 'I no whitt reck; . . . I. iv. 50. 8
the Paynim lay, . . . Coverd with *charmed* cloud . . . I. v. 29. 4
God you never let his *charmed* speaches heare!' . . . I. ix. 30. 9
As he were *charmed* with inchaunted rimes; . . . I. ix. 48. 8
when Centaures blood and bloody verses *charmd;* . . . I. xi. 27. 6
With cup thus *charmd* him parting she deceivd; . . . II. i. 55. 3
with a love lay she thus him sweetly *charmd.* . . . II. vi. 14. 9
evermore with mightie spels them *charmd;* . . . II. vi. 51. 7
broke his staffe with which he *charmed* semblants sly. . . . II. xii. 49. 9
where they lately had *Charm'd* those wild-beasts . . . II. xii. 84. 5
doth the *charmed* Snake in slomber lay. . . . III. ii. 15. 6
Glauncing unwares in *charmed* looking glas, . . . III. iii. 24. 2
Charming. *Charming* his oaten pipe unto his peres, . . . *Col.* 5
The *charming* smiles, that rob sence . . . *Am.* xvii. 10
Her lips lyke cherryes *charming* men to byte, . . . *Epith.* 174
Charms. Through fatall *charmes* transformd to such an one; . *Gn.* 205
by *charmes* Atcheived the golden Fleece . . . *Ro.* x. 1
with his wicked *charmes* And strong conceipts . . . *Hub.* 826
Free libertie to chaunt our *charmes* at will, . . . *T.M.* 244
To heare the *charmes* of his enchanting skill; . . . *As.* 46
mighty *charmes* to trouble sleepy minds. . . . I. i. 36. 9
all this while, with *charmes* and hidden artes, . . . I. i. 45. 1
besmeare My body all, through *charmes* and magicke might, I. ii. 42. 4
In *charmes* and magick to have wondrous might, . . . I. iii. 38. 8
If either salves, or oyles, or herbes, or *charmes,* . . . I. v. 41. 7
after *charmes* and some enchauntments said, . . . I. viii. 14. 6
thy bounteous baytes and pleasing *charmes,* . . . II. vii. 10. 3
weenest words or *charms* may force withstond: . . . II. viii. 22. 2
His mighty staffe, that could all *charmes* defeat. . . . II. xii. 40. 3
Her mighty *charmes,* her furious loving fitt; . . . II. xii. 44. 5
No ydle *charmes* so lightly may remove: . . . III. ii. 51. 8
Nor herbes, nor *charmes,* nor counsel, . . . III. iii. 5. 4
With herbs, with *charms,* with counsel, and with teares; . . III. vii. 21. 2
tears, nor *charms,* nor herbs, nor counsell, . . . III. vii. 21. 3
His maker with her *charmes* had framed him so well. . . . III. vii. 35. 9
with thy *charmes* the sharpest sight doest binde, . . . III. x. 4. 5
redeemes faire Amoret through *charmes* decayd. . . . III. xii. Arg.
Cald by strong *charmes* out of eternall night, . . . III. xii. 19. 5
when *charmes* had closed it afore. . . . III. xii. 27. 9
Nether of ydle showes, nor of false *charmes* aghast. . . . III. xii. 29. 9
A thousand *charmes* he formerly did prove, . . . III. xii. 31. 8
thousand *charmes* could not her stedfast hart remove. . . . III. xii. 31. 9
his *charmes* back to reverse. . . . III. xii. 36. 2
more emboldned by the wicked *charmes,* . . . V. ii. 5. 5
powr of *charms,* which she against him wrought, . . . V. ii. 22. 8
Charmes to the birds full many a pleasant lay, . . . V. ix. 13. 2
did with *charmes* or Magick her molest, . . . VII. vi. 16. 6
mischivous witches with theyr *charmes,* . . . *Epith.* 342
Charon. spoyld of *Charon* too and fro am tost. . . . *Gn.* 339
Charret. *See* **Charet.**
Charybdis. deep *Charybdis* gulphing in and out: . . . *Gn.* 542
Chase. Two eager dogs did her pursue in *chace,* . . . *Pet.* i. 6
twincling starres the daylight hence *chase.* . . . *S.C.* Ap. 161
lightfoote Nymphes, can *chace* the lingring Night . . . *S.C.* Jun. 26
not good Dogges hem needeth to *chace,* . . . *S.C.* S. 166
let us cast with what delight to *chace,* . . . *S.C.* O. 2
the Wolves, that *chase* the wandring sheepe, . . . *S.C.* N. 136
joyed oft to *chace* the trembling Pricket, . . . *S.C.* D. 27
the wilde beasts, that swiftest are in *chase;* . . . *Hub.* 620
to sew the *chace* Of swift wilde beasts, . . . *Hub.* 743
No *chace* so hard, but he therein had skill. . . . *As.* 84
A sort of shepheards, sewing of the *chace,* . . . *As.* 139
Like flying doves ye did before you *chace;* . . . *Ded. Son.* vi. 9
Did *chace* away sweet sleepe from sluggish eye, . . . I. iv. 44. 4
wont in charett *chace* the foming bore: . . . I. v. 37. 2
chase the salvage beast with busie payne, . . . I. vi. 21. 8
Phoebe fayre . . . was following the *chace,* . . . I. vii. 5. 2
to *chace* the cheareleasse darke; . . . I. xi. 51. 8
*Inflamed was to follow beauties *chace,* . . . II. ii. 7. 7
when the flying Libbard she did *chace,* . . . II. iii. 28. 8
Through woods and plaines so long I did her *chace,* . . . II. iv. 32. 2
in the *chace* was slaine of them that fled, . . . II. x. 57. 3
Whenas the Russian him in fight does *chace*) . . . II. xi. 26. 8
Would not so lightly follow beauties *chace,* . . . III. i. 19. 2
The salvage beast embost in wearie *chace,* . . . III. i. 22. 2
to refraine From *chase* of greater beastes, . . . III. i. 37. 7
in *chace* of beauty excellent Shee lefte, . . . III. iv. 45. 5

Chase—*Continued.*
chace away this too long lingring night; . . . III. iv. 60. 5
Chace her away, from whence she came, to hell: . . . III. iv. 60. 6
as shee pursewd the *chace* Of some wilde beast, . . . III. v. 28. 1
the former *chace* Had undertaken after her, . . . III. v. 37. 1
After late *chace* of their embrewed game, . . . III. vi. 17. 3
Your glory sett to *chace* the salvage beasts, . . . III. vi. 22. 2
with like fiercenesse did ensew the *chace*. . . . III. xi. 5. 2
As a dismayed Deare in *chace* embost, . . . III. xii. 17. 8
thirstinesse, Which he in *chace* endured hath, . . . III. xii. 44. *or.* 9
From her high spirit *chase* imperious feare, . . . IV. Pr. 5. 3
in *chace* The Parthian strikes a stag with shivering dart, . . . IV. i. 49. 7
bitter gall away to *chace*, . . . IV. iii. 43. 3
any of the Thracian Nimphes in salvage *chase*. . . . IV. vii. 22. 9
as oft it fals in *chace*, . . . IV. vii. 24. 1
toile which she had tride In salvage *chase*, . . . IV. viii. 9. 4
gan from their eye-lids *chace* The drowzie humour . . . IV. viii. 34. 3
His cheared heart eftsoones away gan *chace* Sad death, . . . IV. xii. 34. 3
They being chased that did others *chase*. . . . V. viii. 5. 5
So cruelly did him pursew and *chace*, . . . V. viii. 36. 6
following his *chace* in dewy morne, . . . V. viii. 43. 2
he was swift in *chace*. . . . V. ix. 16. 2
through the world incessantly doe *chase*, . . . VI. i. 7. 2
unto his hand in *chase* did happen neare. . . . VI. ii. 6. 9
I, . . . bend my carelesse wit To salvage *chace*, . . . VI. ii. 9. 5
Latonaes sonne After his *chace* on woodie Cynthus . . . VI. ii. 25. 5
my most delight . . . To hunt the salvage *chace*, . . . VI. ii. 31. 7
more light of foote and swift in *chace*, . . . VI. iii. 25. 4
like a wilde goate round about did *chace* . . . VI. iii. 49. 3
at length, after long weary *chace*, . . . VI. iii. 50. 3
(For he was swift as any Bucke in *chace*) . . . VI. iv. 8. 3
no one beast in forrest, . . . Met him in *chase* . . . VI. v. 15. 8
nigh tyrd with former *chace*, . . . VI. v. 21. 1
Still looking after him that did him *chace*, . . . VI. vi. 29. 8
cruelty and hardnesse from you *chace*, . . . VI. viii. 2. 4
There on a day, as he pursew'd the *chace*, . . . VI. ix. 5. 1
them thence didst *chace*, . . . VI. x. 20. 2
for *chace* of beasts with hound or boawe, . . . VII. vi. 39. 2
(After her sweaty *chace* and toylesome play) . . . VII. vi. 42. 2
those Woods, and all that goodly *Chase* . . . VII. vi. 55. 7
back again doth *chace* Their looser lookes . . . *Am.* xxi. 7
fly no more, fayre Love, from Phebus *chace*, . . . *Am.* xxviii. 13
with theyr terrour al the rest may *chace*, . . . *Am.* xxxi. 7
Like as a huntsman after weary *chace* . . . *Am.* lxvii. 1
I all weary had the *chace* forsooke, . . . *Am.* lxvii. 6
with your steele darts doo *chace* from comming neer; . . . *Epith.* 70

Chased. *chaced* her that fast from him did fly; . . . II. ii. 7. 8
chaste so fiercely after fearefull flight, . . . II. x. 16. 5
both as swift on foot as *chased* Stags; . . . II. xi. 23. 5
Fayre Florimell is *chaced*. . . . III. i. Arg.
of wilde beastes if she had *chased* beene; . . . III. iv. 51. 4
Him he *chaced* long Through the thicke woods . . . III. v. 13. 6
who that was which *chaced* her along the lands. . . . III. vii. 46. 9
with . . . hatefull outrage long him *chaced* thus; . . . III. xi. 3. 5
beaten were and *chased* all about. . . . IV. iv. 43. 4
Then did he take that *chaced* Squire, . . . IV. ix. 5. 1
deckt with smyles that all sad humors *chaced*, . . . IV. x. 50. 8
overthrew, And *chaced* quite out of the field, . . . V. iii. 12. 6
her full fiercely *chast* In hope to have her overhent at last: . V. viii. 4. 4
They being *chased* that did others chase. . . . V. viii. 5. 5
for what cause they *chased* so that Mayd? . . . V. viii. 15. 4
like wyld Goates them *chaced* all about, . . . V. viii. 50. 7
chaced them both over hill and dale. . . . V. xi. 59. 7
whence he them *chast* away, . . . V. xii. 5. 8
He him pursu'd and *chaced* through the plaine, . . . VI. i. 22. 7
But *chaste* him still for all his Ladies cry; . . . VI. iii. 51. 2
He followed fast, and *chaced* him so nie, . . . VI. ix. 4. 6
Through which the Monckes he *chaced* here and there, . . . VI. xii. 24. 2
chast With all their hounds . . . VII. vi. 52. 2

Chaseth. Britomart *chaceth* Ollyphant; . . . III. xi. Arg.
Corflambo *chaseth* Placidas, And is by Arthure slaine. . . . IV. viii. Arg.

Chasing. his *chacing* steedes aghast Both charett swifte and huntsman overcast: . . . I. v. 38. 4
Chasing, and laying on them heavy lode, . . . IV. iv. 23. 7
Now cuffing close, now *chacing* to and fro, . . . IV. iv. 29. 6
Of a rude rout him *chasing* to and fro, . . . V. xi. 44. 3
Chasing the gentle Calepine around, . . . VI. iv. 2. 8
nor be delayd From *chacing* him, . . . VI. x. 1. 6

Chast. *See* **Chased, Chaste.**

Chaste. *See* **Chased.**
'There *chast* Alceste lives inviolate, . . . *Gn.* 425
allure *Chast* Ladies eares to fantasies impure. . . . *Hub.* 820
our *chast* bowers, in which all vertue rained, . . . *T.M.* 269
followed her make like turtle *chaste*, . . . *As.* 178
sole possession in so *chaste* a brest! . . . *Col.* 555
thy *chaste* life and vertue I esteeme: . . . *Col.* 573
with *chaste* heart to honor him alway: . . . *Col.* 888
that false winged boy Her *chaste* hart had subdewd . . . I. i. 47. 9
The Lyon . . . a strong gard Of her *chast* person, . . . I. iii. 9. 3
his members *chast* Scattered on every mountaine . . . I. v. 38. 7
The eldest two, most sober, *chast*, and wise, . . . I. x. 4. 5
chaste in worke and will: . . . I. x. 30. 6
pyn'd his flesh to keepe his body low and *chast*. . . . I. x. 48. 9
As a *chaste* Virgin that had wronged beene: . . . II. i. 21. 5
it is *chaste* and pure as purest snow, . . . II. ii. 9. 7
be for all *chaste* Dames an endlesse moniment.' . . . II. ii. 10. 9
Through goodly temperaunce and affection *chaste*; . . . III. i. 12. 2
chaste desires doe nourish in your mind, . . . III. i. 49. 2
the *chaste* damzell . . . Did easely beleeve . . . III. i. 53. 7

Chaste—*Continued.*
beareth fruit of honour and all *chast* desyre. . . . III. v. 52. 9
In all *chaste* vertue and true bounti-hed, . . . III. vi. 3. 8
in the sacred throne Of her *chaste* bodie; . . . III. vi. 5. 8
Lodestarre of all *chaste* affection . . . III. vi. 52. 5
she, that is so *chaste* a wight.' . . . III. vii. 52. 9
did abide for ever *chaste* and sownd.' . . . III. vii. 56. 7
Seeking to match the *chaste* with th' unchaste Ladies traine.' . III. vii. 60. 9
he the powre of *chaste* hands might not beare, . . . III. xi. 6. 3
Whilest deadly torments doe her *chast* brest rend, . . . III. xi. 11. 3
In whose *chast* brest all bountie naturall . . . IV. Pr. 4. 3
wondrous *chast* of life, yet lov'd of Knights and Lords. . . . IV. ii. 35. 9
That girdle gave the vertue of *chast* love, . . . IV. v. 3. 1
Whose bodies *chast*, when ever in his powre . . . IV. vii. 12. 6
ne ever Dame So *chast* and loyall liv'd, . . . IV. viii. 25. 6
on *chast* vertue grounded their desire, . . . IV. x. 26. 6
Speedy Hippothoe, and *chaste* Actea, . . . IV. xi. 50. 1
That had despisde so *chast* and faire a dame, . . . IV. xii. 16. 7
Unlesse that she were continent and *chast*, . . . V. iii. 28. 8
Did the most *chast* Penelope possesse . . . V. vii. 39. 2
dints the parts entire With *chast* affects . . . *Am.* vi. 12
In *chast* desires, on heavenly beauty bound. . . . *Am.* viii. 8
Burning in flames of pure and *chast* desyre: . . . *Am.* xxii. 12
Goe visit her in her *chast* bowre of rest . . . *Am.* lxxxiii. 7
the *chast* wombe informe with timely seed, . . . *Epith.* 386
So many millions of *chaste* pleasures play. . . . *H.B.* 259
let your bed with pleasures *chast* abound, . . . *Proth.* 103

Chaster. My *chaster* Muse for shame doth blush to write; . . . I. viii. 48. 2

Chastest. the *chastest* flowre that aye did spring . . . I. i. 48. 4
Within the closest of her *chastest* bowre, . . . *H.H.B.* 249

Chastise. Threatning to *chastize* me, . . . VI. ii. 11. 9

Chastised. Would her have *chastiz'd* with his yron flaile, . . . V. xii. 43. 3

Chastity. We be not tyde to wilfull *chastitie*, . . . *Hub.* 477
faire flower of *chastitie*, . . . *Ti.* 251
Adorn'd with wisedome and with *chastitie*, . . . *D.* 215
The floure of vertue and pure *chastitie*, . . . *Col.* 469
her . . . That was the flowre of faith and *chastity*: . . . I. iii. 23. 5
burnt his beastly hart t' efforce her *chastitye*. . . . I. vi. 4. 9
And win rich spoile of ransackt *chastitee*. . . . I. vi. 5. 5
Of *chastity* and honour virginall: . . . II. i. 10. 8
Shee is the flowre of grace and *chastity* . . . II. ix. 4. 3
It falls me here to write of *Chastity*, . . . III. Pr. 1. 1
In th' one her rule; in th' other her rare *chastitee*. . . . III. Pr. 5. 9
for pure *chastitee* and vertue rare, . . . III. iv. 3. 4
In stedfast *chastitie* and vertue rare, . . . III. v. 8. 5
Of *chastity* and vertue virginall, . . . III. v. 53. 6
in perfect love and spotlesse fame Of *chastitie*, . . . III. v. 54. 4
In so great prayse of stedfast *chastity* . . . III. v. 55. 1
all the gifts of grace and *chastitee* . . . III. vi. 2. 5
chastitee Had lodging in so meane a maintenaunce; . . . III. vii. 59. 3
chastity did for it selfe embrace, . . . III. vii. 60. 2
soveraine favor towards *chastity*, . . . III. viii. 29. 3
losse of *chastitie*, or chaunge of love: . . . III. viii. 42. 2
t' advance thy goodly *chastitee* . . . III. viii. 43. 3
Britomart the flowre of *chastity*; . . . III. xi. 6. 2
In simple truth and blamelesse *chastitie*, . . . IV. viii. 30. 3
They tied were to stedfast *chastity* . . . V. vii. 9. 7
Firme *Chastity*, that spight ne blemish dare: . . . VI. x. 27. 5
Adorn'd with honour, love, and *chastity*! . . . *Am.* lxix. 8
There dwels sweet love, and constant *chastity*, . . . *Epith.* 191

Chastity's. To honors seat and *chastities* sweet bowre. . . . *Epith.* 180

Chat. After his chere the Pedler can *chat*, . . . *S.C.* May 284
to holden *chat* With seely shepherds swayne, . . . *S.C.* Jul. 29
Thus *chatten* the people in theyr steads, . . . *S.C.* S. 120

Chatten. *See* **Chat.**

Chattering. The trembling ghosts . . . *Chattring* their iron teeth, I. v. 32. 6
Chattering his teeth for cold . . . VII. vii. 31. 2

Chaucer. Dan *Chaucer*, well of English undefyled, . . . IV. ii. 32. 8

Chaufe, Chauff(e). *See* **Chafe.**

Chaufing. *See* **Chafing.**

Chaw. *See* **Jaw.**
chaw the tender prickles in her Cud; . . . *Gn.* 86
malicious Envy . . . still did *chaw* . . . a venemous tode, . . I. iv. 30. 2
all the poison ran about his *chaw*; . . . I. iv. 30. 4

Chawed. The whiles his flock their *chawed* cuds do eate. . . . *Gn.* 144
inwardly he *chawed* his owne maw At neighbours welth, . . . I. iv. 30. 5
Long thus he *chawd* the cud of inward griefe, . . . III. x. 18. 1
She *chaw'd* the cud of lover's carefull plight; . . . V. v. 27. 2
though she hungrily Earst *chawed* thereon, . . . V. xii. 39. 6

Chawing. *chawing* vengeaunce all the way I went, . . . II. iv. 29. 2
Chawing the cud of griefe and inward paine, . . . V. vi. 19. 2

Chayre. *See* **Chare.**

Cheap. To keepe their flockes for litle hyre and *chepe*, . . . VI. xi. 40. 7

Check. even the highest Powers of heaven to *check*) . . . VII. vi. 22. 4

Checked. by the *checked* wave they did descry It plaine, . . . II. xii. 18. 7
being *checkt* he did abstaine streightway, . . . VI. viii. 29. 4
Is *checkt* and changed from his nature trew, . . . VII. vii. 54. 8

Checklaton. *See* **Ciclaton.**

Checkmate. Love they him called that gave me *checkmate*, . . . *S.C.* D. 53

Cheek. so stremes the trickling teares Adowne thy *cheeke*, . . . *S.C.* Ap. 8
In either *cheeke* depeincten lively chere: . . . *S.C.* Ap. 69
did purely shyne Upon her snowy *cheeke*; . . . III. vii. 9. 4
Privily moystening his horrid *cheeke*: . . . III. xi. 44. 7
Approching nigh unto him, *cheeke* by *cheeke*, . . . V. ii. 49. 7
Decking her *cheeke* with a vermilion rose; . . . V. xii. 30. 4

Cheek-bones. His *cheeke-bones* raw, and eie-pits hollow grew, IV. xii. 20. 3

Cheeks. outraging her *cheekes* and golden haire, . . . *Bel.*[2] x. 3
with pallid *cheekes* The Romane triumphs glorie to beholde, . *Ro.* xiv. 11
those pallid *cheekes* and ashy hew, . . . *D.* 302

Cheeks—*Continued.*
His *cheekes* wext pale, . . . *D.* 542
From her red *cheeks* the roses rent away; . . . *As.* 160
His bare thin *cheekes* for want of better bits, . . . I. viii. 41. 3
His raw-bone *cheekes* . . . Were shronke into his jawes, . . . I. ix. 35. 8
With rosy *cheekes,* for shame as blushing red: . . . I. xi. 51. 4
salt teares bedeawd the hearers *cheaks.* . . . I. xii. 16. 9
rosy red Did paint his chearefull *cheekes,* . . . II. i. 41. 5
in her *cheekes* the vermeill red did shew . . . II. iii. 22. 5
cheekes with teares, and sydes with blood, did all abownd. . . II. iv. 3. 9
The bashfull blood her snowy *cheekes* did dye, . . . II. ix. 41. 4
With hollow eyes and rawbone *cheekes* forspent, . . . IV. v. 34. 4
in her *cheekes* made roses oft appeare: . . . IV. x. 50. 5
all her bones might through her *cheekes* be red: . . . V. xii. 29. 6
deadly pallied hew Benumbes her *cheekes:* . . . VI. viii. 40. 7
ruddy *cheekes,* lyke unto Roses red . . . *Am.* lxiv. 6
when the rose in her red *cheekes* appeares; . . . *Am.* lxxxi. 3
hew . . . With which the *cheekes* are sprinckled, . . . *H.B.* 93
Her *cheekes* lyke apples which the sun hath rudded, . . . *Epith.* 173
How the red roses flush up in her *cheekes,* . . . *Epith.* 226

Cheer. beare Cherefully the Winters wrathful *cheare;* . . . *S.C.* F. 26
In either cheeke depeincten lively *chere:* . . . *S.C.* Ap. 69
With singing, and shouting, and jolly *chere:* . . . *S.C.* May 21
After his *chere* the Pedler can chat, . . . *S.C.* May 284
The chippes, and they the *chere:* . . . *S.C.* Jul. 188
Hey, ho, heavie *cheere!* . . . *S.C.* Au. 106
With cakes and cracknells, and such country *chere:* . . . *S.C.* N. 96
sike happy *cheere* is turnd to heavie chaunce, . . . *S.C.* N. 103
now morne with heavy *cheare,* . . . *S.C.* N. 151
shee became so meeke and milde of *cheare,* . . . *D.* 125
of his *cheere* did seeme too solemne sad; . . . I. i. 2. 8
With chaunge of *chear* the . . . maid Let fal her eien, . . . I. ii. 27. 5
hag by chaunges of my *cheare* Perceiv'd my thought; . . . I. ii. 42. 1
with trembling *cheare* Her up he tooke, . . . I. ii. 45. 6
his Lady did so well him *cheare,* . . . I. iii. 34. 7
be of *cheare,* and comfort to you take; . . . I. vii. 52. 5
with sweet joyous *cheare* him thus bespake: . . . I. viii. 26. 6
She cast to bring him where he *chearen* might, . . . I. x. 2. 8
With hartie wordes her knight she gan to *cheare,* . . . I. xi. 1. 5
Whose sight my feeble soule doth greatly *cheare:* . . . I. xi. 3. 5
forth proceeding with sad sober *cheare,* . . . I. xii. 21. 4
fained *cheare,* as for the time behoves, . . . II. ii. 34. 3
One thought her *cheare* too litle, . . . II. ii. 34. 9
Can chaunge my *cheare,* or make me ever mourne: . . . II. vi. 10. 8
Her selfe to cherish, and her guest to *cheare.* . . . II. vi. 21. 4
seemeth by your troubled *cheare,* . . . II. ix. 42. 1
Her bountie she abated, and his *cheare* empayrd. . . . II. x. 30. 9
Chaunged thy lively *cheare,* and living made thee dead? . . . III. ii. 30. 9
faynd to *cheare* his lady in dismay, . . . III. viii. 15. 7
That chearful word his weak heart much did *cheare,* . . . III. x. 26. 6
Downe hanging his dull head with heavy *chere,* . . . III. xii. 16. 3
The morrowe next appeard with joyous *cheare,* . . . III. xii. 28. 6
His chaunge of *cheere* that anguish did bewray, . . . IV. i. 50. 7
whose sad ruefull *cheare* Made her to change her hew, . . . IV. iii. 46. 8
Thence to depart with glee and gladsome *chere.* . . . IV. iii. 51. 3
Shew'd change of better *cheare:* . . . IV. vi. 38. 3
to rue the others heavy *cheare;* . . . IV. vii. 34. 7
al the world shews joyous *cheare.* . . . IV. x. 44. 9
when her bridale *cheare* Should be solemniz'd; . . . V. ii. 3. 7
Timely to joy and carrie comely *cheare:* . . . V. v. 38. 5
For he, their host, them goodly well did *cheare,* . . . V. vi. 22. 8
by your change of *cheare* is easie for to see.' . . . V. vii. 18. 9
Souldan, with presumpteous *cheare* And countenance sublime . V. viii. 30. 3
with goodly *chere* Them entertayn'd, . . . V. x. 5. 3
her gan *cheare* with what she there had vewed, . . . V. x. 38. 8
He did him selfe encourage and take better *cheare.* . . . V. xi. 2. 9
She gan rejoyce and shew triumphant *chere,* . . . V. xi. 33. 2
hanging down her head with heavie *cheare,* . . . V. xi. 64. 4
it did her dead hart *cheare,* . . . V. xii. 12. 8
then would she make Great *cheare,* . . . V. xii. 32. 7
Temper his griefe, and turned it to *cheare,* . . . VI. iii. 6. 2
To *cheare* his guests whom he had stayd that night, . . . VI. iii. 6. 3
afterwards to *cheare* with speaches kind; . . . VI. viii. 50. 7
Nor better *cheare* to shew in misery, . . . VI. xi. 8. 7
With gladfull speaches and with lovely *cheare;* . . . VI. xi. 50. 3
with sterne count'naunce and disdainfull *cheare,* . . . VII. vi. 12. 5
having chang'd his *cheare,* . . . VII. vi. 31. 5
To celebrate the solemne bridall *cheare* . . . VII. vii. 12. 4
Mark when she smiles with amiable *cheare,* . . . *Am.* xl. 1
cheare you your heavy spright, . . . *Am.* lxii. 13

Cheered. when he saw him slaine himselfe he *cheard.* . . . *Gn.* 312
That *cheard* his friendes, and did his foes amate: . . . II. i. 6. 4
cheared well with wine and spiceree: . . . III. i. 42. 5
much *cheard* the feeble spright Of the sicke virgin, . . . III. ii. 47. 1
downe to rest Her selfe she set, and comfortably *cheard:* . . . III. vi. 10. 7
She much was *cheard* to heare him mentiond, . . . III. xii. 41. 1
His *cheared* heart eftsoones away gan chace Sad death, . . . IV. xii. 34. 3
But that faire Lady would be *cheard* for nought, . . . VI. iii. 6. 6
And, having *cheared* her, thus said: . . . VI. iv. 34. 6
So my storme-beaten hart likewise is *cheared* . . . *Am.* xl. 13

Cheerful. the foule that shunnes the *cherefull* light . . . *Bel.*[1] vi. 13
Frame to thy songe their *chereful* cheriping, . . . *S.C.* Jun. 55
To *cheerefull* songs can chaunge my cherelesse cryes. . . . *S.C.* Au. 182
From *cheerefull* lookes great mirth and gladsome glee. . . . *Gn.* 184
The Marigolde, and *cherefull* Rosemarie; . . . *Gn.* 668
Began to comfort me in *chearfull* wise, . . . *Hub.* 19
Receyved them with *chearefull* entertayne. . . . *Hub.* 1085
Sitting so cheerlesse at the *cheerfull* boorde, . . . *U.V.* 5
With pleasures choyce to feed his *cheerefull* sprights: . . . *Ti.* 522
she started up with *cherefull* sight, . . . *Ti.* 642

Cheerful—*Continued.*
Embathed Balme, and *chearfull* Galingale, . . . *Mui.* 194
I match with that sweet smile and *chearfull* brow, . . . *D.* 306
drery horror dim the *chearfull* light, . . . *D.* 328
brought forth *chearfull* day: . . . *Col.* 856
He, . . . Remounted up as light as *chearefull* Larke; . . . I. i. 44. 7
cheareful Chaunticlere with his note shrill . . . I. ii. 1. 6
My *chearefull* day is turnd to chearelesse night, . . . I. iii. 27. 7
His *chearfull* whistle merily doth sound, . . . I. iii. 31. 8
That Phoebus *chearefull* face durst never vew, . . . I. v. 20. 2
chearefull birds of sundry kynd . . . I. vii. 3. 4
chereful blood in fayntnes chill did melt, . . . I. vii. 6. 8
His *chearefull* words reviv'd her chearelesse spright, . . . I. vii. 52. 8
Since I the heavens *chearefull* face did vew, . . . I. viii. 38. 8
drave Far from that haunt all other *chearefull* fowle, . . . I. ix. 33. 8
Not all so *chearefull* seemed she . . . I. x. 14. 3
entertaynes with friendly *chearefull* mood. . . . I. x. 32. 4
she beheld those maydens meriment With *chearefull* vew; . . I. xii. 8. 2
rosy red Did paint his *chearefull* cheekes, . . . II. i. 41. 5
Chaunted alowd their *chearefull* harmonee, . . . II. v. 31. 7
vew of *cherefull* day Did never . . . it selfe display, . . . II. vii. 29. 4
heavens *chearefull* face enveloped, . . . II. xii. 34. 7
The joyous birdes, shrouded in *chearefull* shade . . . II. xii. 71. 1
Her *chearefull* words much cheard the feeble spright . . . III. ii. 47. 1
chearfull looks as earst did shew. . . . III. iii. 50. 9
Which *chearefull* signe did send unto her sight . . . III. vii. 5. 4
That *chearful* word his weak heart much did cheare, . . . III. x. 26. 6
Of *chearefull* looke and lovely to behold: . . . III. xii. 13. 2
She *chearfull,* fresh, and full of joyaunce glad, . . . III. xii. 18. 4
hardly of her *chearefull* speech Did comfort take, . . . IV. vi. 38. 1
his wonted *chearefull* hew Gan fade, . . . IV. xii. 20. 1
chearefull signes he shewed outwardly. . . . IV. xii. 35. 5
A *chearefull* countenance on them let fall, . . . V. ix. 34. 8
With such his *chearefull* speaches he doth wield Her mind . . V. x. 24. 7
to the world display His *chearefull* face, . . . V. xii. 11. 4
rather did more *chearefull* seeme therefore: . . . VI. i. 32. 5
The Ladie, . . . Gan reare her eyes as to the *chearefull* light, . VI. ii. 42. 8
to see that *chearefull* sight. . . . VI. iii. 45. 5
Had never joyance felt nor *chearefull* thought, . . . VI. xi. 45. 2
looking up with *chearefull* view, . . . VII. vii. 57. 8
Fed on the fulnesse of that *chearefull* glaunce, . . . *Am.* xxxix. 12
Hark! how the *cheerefull* birds do chaunt . . . *Epith.* 78
chearefull grace and amiable sight; . . . *H.B.* 131

Cheerfully. beare *Cherefully* the Winters wrathful cheare; . . *S.C.* F. 26
All which together song full *chearefully* . . . III. xii. 5. 6
How *chearefully* thou lookest from above, . . . *Epith.* 291

Cheerfulness. her against sweet *Cherefulnesse* was placed, . . IV. x. 50. 6

Cheering. great Dame Natures handmaide *chearing* every kind. III. iv. 56. 9
with faire blandishment Her *chearing* up, . . . VI. iv. 27. 7

Cheerless. To cheerefull songs can chaunge my *cherelesse* cryes. *S.C.* Au. 182
All comfortlesse doth hide her *chearlesse* head . . . *T.M.* 239
Sitting so *cheerlesse* at the cheerfull boorde, . . . *U.V.* 5
My chearefull day is turnd to *chearelesse* night, . . . I. iii. 27. 7
His chearefull words reviv'd her *chearelesse* spright, . . . I. vii. 52. 8
The *chearelesse* man, whom sorrow did dismay, . . . I. viii. 43. 7
to chace the *chearelesse* darke; . . . I. xi. 51. 8
whenas *chearelesse* Night ycovered had Fayre heaven . . . III. xii. 1. 1
(welcommed with cold And *chearelesse* hunger) . . . IV. viii. 28. 2
that long hath slept in *cheerlesse* bower, . . . *Am.* iv. 6

Cheerly. They *cherelie* chaunt, . . . *T.M.* 321

Cheers. *chears* my dulled spright. . . . VI. Pr. 1. 9

Cheese. make them *cheese* and bredd; . . . III. x. 36. 8

Cherish. Eke *cherish* his child, . . . *S.C.* May 86
cared not to *cherishe* No gentle wits, . . . *Ti.* 362
to *cherish* him with diets daint, . . . I. x. 2. 7
Una . . . besought Himselfe to *chearish,* . . . I. x. 29. 5
Her selfe to *cherish,* and her guest to cheare. . . . II. vi. 21. 4
To *cherish* her with all things choice and rare; . . . VI. xii. 14. 7
Which if she graunt, then live, and my love *cherish:* . . . *Am.* ii. 13
that, which shall you make immortall, *cherish.* . . . *Am.* xxvii. 14

Cherished. Still when as he enfeebled was, him *cherisht,* . . IV. iii. 29. 4
Where all that night them selves they *cherished,* . . . V. x. 39. 8

Cherishment. with rich bountie, and deare *cherishment,* . . . *T.M.* 573

Cherries. Queene-apples, and red *Cherries* from the tree, . . VII. vi. 43. 6
Her lips lyke *cherryes* charming men to byte, . . . *Epith.* 174

Cherry. me in mirth do *cherry!* . . . VI. x. 22. 9

Cherubim. Yet farre more faire be those bright *Cherubins,* . . *H.H.B.* 92

Cherwell. The Churne and *Charwell,* two small streames, . . IV. xi. 25. 3

Chest. wound my heart, and rend my bleeding *chest,* . . . *D.* 298
he perced through his chaufed *chest* . . . I. iii. 42. 6
When corage first does creepe in manly *chest,* . . . I. ix. 9. 2
These words she breathed forth from riven *chest:* . . . II. i. 47. 5
When the hart blood should gush out of his *chest,* . . . II. xi. 37. 7
Sorrow is heaped in thy hollow *chest,* . . . III. ii. 32. 7
Unwares it strooke into her snowie *chest,* . . . III. xii. 33. 4
catching hold of this Sea-beaten *chest,* . . . V. iv. 11. 6
Chaunst to espy upon her yvory *chest* The rosie marke, . . VI. xii. 15. 5

Chester. Dee, . . . that doth by *Chester* tend; . . . IV. xi. 39. 4

Chests. huge great yron *chests,* and coffers strong, . . . II. vii. 30. 2

Chevalrous, -ry. *See* **Chivalrous,** *etc.*

Chevisance. The pretie Pawnce, And the *Chevisaunce,* . . . *S.C.* Ap. 143
They maken many a wrong *chevisaunce,* . . . *S.C.* May 92
'Fortune, the foe of famous *chevisaunce,* . . . II. ix. 8. 1
reft from him so faire a *chevisaunce,* . . . III. vii. 45. 5
shameful . . . t' abandon noble *chevisaunce* . . . III. xi. 24. 6

Chew, *etc.* *See* **Chaw,** *etc.*

Chian. The *Chian* Peincter, when he was requirde . . . *Ded. Son.* xvii. 1
For *Chian* folke to pourtraict beauties Queene, . . . IV. v. 12. 7

Chicken. courd it tenderly, As *chicken* newly hatcht, . . . II. viii. 9. 9

Chickens. bid his faithlesse *chickens* overronne . . . III. iii. 46. 7

Chide. His angry steede did *chide* his foming bitt, ... I. i. 1. 6
him doth *chyde* as false and fraudulent, ... IV. xii. 23. 2
gan first to scold And *chyde* at him . . . . . IV. xii. 26. 4
Chief. herein I tooke (toke herein[1]) my *chiefe* delight, ... *Pet.* iv. 9
ever my flocke was my *chiefe* care, ... *S.C.* F. 23
They never stroven to be *chiefe,* . . . . . *S.C.* Jul. 167
nowe is in his *chiefe* sovereigntee, ... *S.C.* S. 50
The coloured chaplets wrought with a *chiefe,* . . . . . *S.C.* N. 115
Man is not like an Ape In his *chiefe* parts, ... *Hub.* 1043
The Realmes *chiefe* strength and girlond of the crowne. . . . *Hub.* 1185
That wont to be the worlds *chiefe* ornament, ... *T.M.* 74
It is my *chiefe* profession to compyle; . . . . . *T.M.* 432
They thinke to be *chiefe* praise of Poetry; . . . . . *T.M.* 555
the shepheard which hath charge in *chief,* . . . . . *Col.* 244
courts *chief* garlond with all vertues dight, ... *Col.* 499
Unmindfull of *chiefe* parts of manlinesse; . . . . . *Col.* 764
O holy virgin! *chiefe* of nyne, ... I. Pr. 2. 1
lesser pangs can beare who hath endur'd the *chief.* . . . . . I. vi. 37. 9
the richesse of all heavenly grace In *chiefe* degree . . . . . II. ii. 41. 2
Locrine left *chiefe* Lord of Britany. . . . . . II. x. 13. 7
the *chiefe* dominion By strength was wielded . . . . . II. x. 39. 7
their *chiefe* and th' authour of that strife: . . . . . II. xi. 16. 8
chiefe And choicest med'cine for sick harts reliefe: . . . . . III. iii. 5. 4
caused to be hanged hy In his *chiefe* Church, ... III. iii. 59. 3
of her name and nation be *chiefe,* . . . . . III. iv. 11. 7
Whose *chiefe* desire is love and friendly aid . . . to nourish . . IV. i. 46. 3
Thereto he offred for to make him *chiefe* . . . . . IV. ix. 15. 7
his honor, which she tendred *chiefe,* . . . . . V. vii. 44. 4
In evils counsell is the comfort *chiefe;* . . . . . VI. iv. 34. 7
those three in the midst doe *chiefe* on her attend. . . . . VI. x. 21. 9
had the *chiefe* commaund of all the rest, ... VI. xi. 3. 5
Is not the hart of all the body *chiefe,* . . . . . *Am.* l. 7
Chiefdom. take that *chiefedome* which ye doe abuse. . . . . VI. viii. 1. 9
Chiefest. Chloris, that is the *chiefest* Nymph of all, ... *S.C.* Ap. 122
whilome wast the worldes *chiefst* riches, ... *Ti.* 675
great Cynthia her in *chiefest* grace Doth hold, ... *Col.* 500
The first and *chiefest* of the seven, ... I. x. 44. 2
Albe Charissa were their *chiefest* founderesse. . . . . . I. x. 44. 9
three the *chiefest* and of greatest powre, ... II. ix. 47. 7
His *chiefest* letts and authors of his harmes, ... II. xi. 31. 3
Which alwaies of his paines he made the *chiefest* meed. . . . III. iv. 4. 9
from my *chiefest* foe me to release, ... V. xi. 18. 4
some other of the *chiefest* theeves . . . . . VI. xi. 15. 1
This day the sunne is in his *chiefest* hight, ... *Epith.* 265
Chiefly. *chieflie* joyes on foote them to beholde, ... *Hub.* 623
wise desire, That *chieflie* doth each noble minde adorne, . . *Hub.* 831
the best helpe, which *chiefly* him sustain'd, ... *Hub.* 853
'Of such . . . I *chiefly* doe inquere, ... I. i. 31. 5
But *chiefly* skill to ride seemes a science . . . . . II. iv. 1. 7
chiefely Paridell his hart did grate . . . . . III. ix. 14. 5
In which her kingdomes throne is *chiefly* resiant. . . . . IV. xi. 28. 9
chiefly of the fairest Florimell, ... V. ii. 2. 8
Chiefely by him whose life her law doth bynd, ... V. v. 41. 7
chiefly by that yron page he ghest, ... V. vi. 34. 3
chiefly Talus with his yron flayle, ... V. xi. 59. 4
chiefly Calidore, whom griefe had most possest. . . . . VI. xi. 41. 9
chiefely Mercury, that next doth raigne, ... VII. vi. 14. 8
Chieftain. forst their *chiefetain,* for his safeties sake, . . . II. x. 16. 6
(Their *Chiefetain* Humber named was aright,) . . . . . II. x. 16. 7
Child. *See* **Chilled, Foster-child, Maiden-child, Man-child.**
As *child* whose parent is unkent, ... To his Booke 2
Palinodie, thou art a worldes *childe:* . . . . . *S.C.* May 73
Eke cherish his *child,* . . . . . *S.C.* May 86
O come, (thou sacred *childe*) come sliding soft, ... *Gn.* 37
thou, (dread sacred *child*) . . . . . *Gn.* 54
Hyperions fierie *childe* Ascending . . . . . *Mui.* 51
Exceeding shone, like Phoebus fayrest *childe,* . . . . . I. iv. 9. 1
childe ne kinsman living had he none To leave them to; . . I. iv. 28. 6
hart that . . . is with *childe* of glorious great intent, ... I. v. 1. 2
O welcome, *child!* whom I have longd to see, ... I. v. 27. 8
For ransome leaving him the late-borne *childe;* . . . . . I. vi. 23. 6
As carefull Nourse her *child* from falling oft does reare. . . . I. x. 35. 9
her foolehardy *chyld* Did come too neare, ... I. xii. 11. 1
Me then he left enwombed of this *childe,* . . . . . II. i. 50. 8
This luckles *childe,* whom thus ye see with blood defild. . . . II. i. 50. 9
the *childe* Uptaking, to the Palmer gave to beare; . . . . . II. ii. 11. 1
he nought could say, Till him the *childe* bespoke; . . . . . II. viii. 7. 3
fonder then Cephisus foolish *chyld,* . . . . . III. ii. 44. 6
hath him borne a *chyld,* . . . . . III. vi. 50. 7
The royall *child* with readie quicke foresight . . . . . IV. viii. 44. 8
minde did travell as with *chylde* . . . . . IV. ix. 17. 3
Upon a day she found this gentle *childe* . . . . . V. i. 6. 2
to receive In her owne mouth the food ment for her *chyld,* . . V. v. 53. 2
Like as a wayward *childe,* . . . . . V. vi. 14. 1
the bold *child* that perill well espying, ... V. viii. 32. 1
seizd not, where it was hight, Uppon the *childe,* . . . . . V. xi. 8. 8
Nought fear'd the *childe* his lookes, ... V. xi. 13. 1
aread, Thou gentle *chyld,* wherefore . . . . . VI. ii. 8. 8
Threatning to chastize me, as doth t'a *chyld* pertaine. . . . VI. ii. 11. 9
'Faire *chyld,* the high desire . . . which in you doth aspire, . VI. ii. 34. 4
Chyld Tristram prayd that he with him might goe . . . . . VI. ii. 36. 3
through feare what of his *childe* became. . . . . . VI. iii. 17. 9
That from his sides some noble *chyld* should rize, ... VI. iv. 33. 2
The noble *childe,* preventing his desire, ... VI. viii. 15. 7
brought home and noursed well As his owne *chyld;* . . . . . VI. ix. 14. 8
how the heavens had her graste To save her *chylde,* . . . . VI. xii. 16. 9
Who ever is the mother of one *chylde,* . . . . . VI. xii. 21. 1
great Earth, great Chaos *child;* . . . . . VII. vi. 26. 6
thee, faire Titans *child,* I rather weene, ... VII. vi. 32. 1
yet a *chyld,* renewing still thy yeares, ... *H.L.* 55
Child—*Continued.*
Fayre *childe* of beauty! . . . . . *Epith.* 288
The brightest Angell, even the *Child* of Light, ... *H.H.L.* 83
Childbed. Charissa, late in *child-bed* brought, ... I. x. 29. 7
Childed. A little mayde, the which ye *chylded* tho; . . . . . VI. xii. 17. 7
Childhood. With which she from her *childhood* had bene fed; . IV. i. 26. 6
Childish. lull in rugged armes withouten *childish* feare. . . . I. vi. 27. 9
Their wanton sportes and *childish* mirth did play, ... I. xii. 7. 2
shewst th' ensample of thy *childishe* might, ... II. iv. 45. 4
Amongst his peres playing his *childish* sport; . . . . . V. i. 6. 3
Children. *See* **Foster-children.**
the *children* of the earth Heapt hils on hils . . . . . *Ro.* xii. 1
in gathering Into her lap the *children* of the spring. . . . . *Mui.* 128
who shall not great Nightes *children* scorne, ... I. v. 23. 8
Night . . . can the *children* of fayre light deface.' . . . . . I. v. 24. 5
The fall of famous *children* borne of mee, ... I. v. 25. 2
a Lyonesse . . . did lowd requere Her *children* . . . . . I. vi. 27. 7
them before the fry of *children* yong . . . . . I. xii. 7. 1
The *children* of one syre by mothers three; . . . . . II. ii. 13. 2
fooles, lovers, *children,* Dames. . . . . . II. ix. 50. 9
So many *children* he did multiply: . . . . . II. x. 22. 4
her sisters *children,* woxen strong, ... II. x. 32. 6
Dayes dearest *children* be the blessed seed . . . . . III. iv. 59. 5
Ungratious *children* of one gracelesse syre, ... III. v. 15. 6
Foolhardy as th' Earthes *children,* . . . . . III. xi. 22. 8
whose *children* werne All three as one; . . . . . IV. ii. 41. 7
in seeking for her *children* three Long life, ... IV. iii. 2. 2
slaine her *children* ruefully, alas! . . . . . V. x. 6. 9
Giving her dearest *children* one by one Unto a dreadfull Monster . . . . . V. x. 13. 6
Ere all her *children* he from her had reft: . . . . . V. x. 14. 5
all her other *children* . . . Had hid themselves, ... V. x. 19. 3
My *children* and my people, burnt in flame . . . . . V. xi. 19. 7
Be lacke of *children* to supply your place, ... VI. iv. 35. 2
Children's. th' earth under her *childrens* weight did grone, . . *Ro.* xii. 7
eke thy *childrens* thrids to be asunder burst!' . . . . . IV. ii. 49. 9
That she might see her *childrens* thrids forth brought, ... IV. ii. 50. 3
Latonaes *childrens* wrath that all her issue wasted. . . . . . V. x. 7. 9
With their great deedes, and fild their *childrens* eares? . . . *Com. Son.* iii. 4
Chill. This *chill,* that cold; this crooked, that wrye; . . . . *S.C.* F. 28
sadde winters wrathe, and season *chill,* . . . . . *S.C.* N. 33
The Ape, that earst did nought but *chill* and quake, ... *Hub.* 993
cheareful blood in fayntness *chill* did melt, ... I. vii. 6. 8
The yron man, . . . did inly *chill* and quake, ... V. vi. 9. 6
courage *chill* Kindling afresh, gan battell to renew, ... VI. i. 35. 7
Chattering his teeth for cold that did him *chill;* . . . . . VII. vii. 31. 2
after him came next the *chill* December: . . . . . VII. vii. 41. 1
Chilled. his hart was inly *child* With great amazement, . . . VI. ii. 4. 8
Chimera. fell *Chimaera,* in her darkesome den, ... VI. i. 8. 2
Chimera's. Faire Xanthus sprincled with *Chimaeras* blood, . . *Gn.* 19
Chimney. And one great *chimney,* . . . . . II. ix. 29. 3
Chimneys. Fewe *chymneis* reeking you shall espye: . . . . . *S.C.* S. 117
Chin. spring forth ranckly under his *chinne.* . . . . . *S.C.* May 188
There thristy Tantalus hong by the *chin;* . . . . . I. v. 35. 5
To rubb her temples, and to chaufe her *chin,* . . . . . I. vii. 21. 5
Deepe was he drenched to the upmost *chin,* . . . . . II. vii. 58. 1
to the *chin* he clefte his head in twaine. . . . . . III. v. 23. 6
cleft his head asunder to his *chin.* . . . . . VI. i. 23. 5
Chine. Whom Calidore thus carried on his *chine;* . . . . . VI. iii. 3. 8
Chined. it *chynd* his backe behind the sell, ... IV. vi. 13. 8
Chink. he peeped out through a *chinck,* . . . . . *S.C.* May 252
Chips. Theyr sheepe han . . . The *chippes,* . . . . . *S.C.* Jul. 188
Chiron. The seed of Saturne and faire Nais, *Chiron* hight. . . VII. vii. 40. 9
Chirp. *Chirpe* loud to thee out of their leavy cages, ... IV. x. 45. 8
Chirped. shrill grashoppers *chirped* them around; . . . . . *Gn.* 231
Chirruping. Frame to thy songe their chereful *cheriping,* . . . *S.C.* Jun. 55
Chivalrous. brave poursuitt of *chevalrous* emprize, ... I. ix. 1. 4
did apply Their mindes to prayse and *chevalrous* desyre: . . . II. x. 22. 6
Her lovers shape and *chevalrous* aray: . . . . . III. iv. 5. 5
Chivalry. the president Of Noblesse and of *chevalree:* . . . To his Booke 4
some of love, and some of *chevalrie;* . . . . . *S.C.* F. 99
To all that armes professe and *chevalry.* . . . . . *Ded. Son.* iv. 4
The flowre of *chevalry,* . . . Doth promise fruite . . . . . *Ded. Son.* x. 2
when corage hott The . . . joy of *chevalree,* First kindled . . I. ii. 35. 2
him destroy, That was the flowre of . . . *chevalrye;* . . . . . I. iv. 45. 8
Greatly advauncing his gay *chevalree:* . . . . . I. v. 16. 5
'Fayre braunch of noblesse, flowre of *chevalrie,* . . . . . I. viii. 26. 7
By dew desert of noble *chevalree,* . . . . . I. xii. 20. 8
The scorne of knighthood and trew *chevalrye,* . . . . . II. iii. 10. 5
He had not trayned bene in *chevalree.* . . . . . . II. iii. 46. 5
To whom no share in armes and *chevalree* They doe impart, . . III. ii. 1. 4
they mervaild at her *chevalree* And noble prowesse, ... III. ix. 24. 5
bore great sway in armes and *chivalrie,* . . . . . IV. i. 32. 2
Ne more renowmed for their *chevalrie,* . . . . . IV. iii. 2. 8
with the praise of armes and *chevalrie* . . . . . IV. v. 1. 2
Ne better doth beseeme brave *chevalry,* . . . . . V. ii. 1. 2
To deedes of armes and proofe of *chevalrie* . . . . . V. iii. 4. 3
what prescribed were by lawes of *chevalrie.* . . . . . V. vii. 28. 9
none more noble then is *chevalrie*) . . . . . VI. ii. 34. 8
Whether ye list him traine in *chevalry,* . . . . . VI. iv. 35. 8
flower of *Chevalrie!* . . . . . *Proth.* 150
Chloris. *Chloris,* that is the chiefest Nymph of all, ... *S.C.* Ap. 122
Chockt. *See* **Choked.**
Choice. if *choice* were to me, ... *S.C.* May 166
he call hem at theyr good *choyce;* . . . . . *S.C.* S. 143
When *choise* I had to choose my wandring waye, ... *S.C.* D. 62
Renown'd in *choyce* of happie marriage . . . . . *Gn.* 487
He made small *choyce;* . . . . . *Hub.* 849
the *choice* Of all that ever did in rimes rejoice, ... *Ti.* 333
With pleasures *choyce* to feed his cheerefull sprights: . . . . *Ti.* 522

Choice—*Continued.*
beware of ficklenesse, In *choice*, . . . of thy deare-loved Dame; . . . I. iv. 1. 4
'O! who is that, which bringes me happy *choyce* Of death, . I. viii. 38. 3
A place pickt out by *choyce* of best alyve, . . . II. xii. 42. 3
'Perdy,' (said Britomart) 'the *choise* is hard; . . . III. i. 27. 6
Fro love to hate, a change of evill *choise:* . . . IV. iii. 45. 6
Yet at her *choice* they all did greatly muse. . . . IV. v. 21. 3
Unto my *choise* by no meanes would assent, . . . IV. vii. 16. 3
of their loves *choise* they might freedom clame, . . . IV. ix. 37. 7
by chaunce more then by *choyce,* . . . VI. viii. 46. 7
To cherish her with all things *choice* and rare; . . . VI. xii. 14. 7
Therefore in *choice* of love he doth desyre . . . *H.L.* 110
in your *choice* of Loves, . . . *H.B.* 190
Choiceful. His *choicefull* sense with every change doth flit: . . *Mui.* 159
Choicely. *choycely* picked out from all the rest, . . . II. vi. 12. 4
Choicest. *choicest* witt Cannot your glorious pourtraict figure playne, . . . III. Pr. 3. 6
choicest med'cine for sick harts reliefe: . . . III. iii. 5. 5
Disperseth them to catch his *choysest* pray; . . . VI. xi. 49. 2
Choir. all the *quire* of birds did sweetly sing, . . . II. vi. 24. 8
gan all the *quire* of birdes . . . II. xii. 76. 1
Of all which there was doing in that *quire:* . . . VI. viii. 48. 4
the *quyre* of Byrds resounded, Their anthemes . . . *Am.* xix. 5
th' unpleasant *Quyre* of Frogs still croking . . . *Epith.* 349
Choke. Redounding teares did *choke* th' end of her plaint, . . I. iii. 8. 1
Sthenoboea . . . her selfe did *choke* With wilfull chord . . . I. v. 50. 5
all the ayre doth *choke,* That none can breath, . . . I. viii. 13. 6
al the land with stench and heven with horror *choke.* . . . I. xi. 44. 9
Both horse and man nigh able for to *choke;* . . . II. v. 3. 5
A flaming fire, . . . did all entraunce *choke,* . . . III. xi. 21. 8
Did *choke* the entraunce with a lumpe of sin, . . . VI. i. 23. 7
Choked. welnigh *choked* with the deadly stinke, . . . I. i. 22. 2
flame, Which *chokt* the porch of that enchaunted gate . . III. xii. 43. 3
Dart, nigh *chockt* with sands of tinny mines. . . . IV. xi. 31. 5
him nigh *choked* with the deadly stinke. . . . V. xi. 31. 8
he nigh *choked* was, Being unable to digest that bone; . . VI. iv. 21. 6
strained him so streightly that he *chokt* him neare. . . . VI. xii. 33. 9
choked be with overflowing gall. . . . *Am.* xliii. 4
Choking. *Choking* the remnant of his plaintife speach, . . III. xi. 12. 4
Make us to wish theyr *choking.* . . . *Epith.* 350
Choler. when *choler* is inflamed with rage, . . . *S.C.* May 136
The man straightway his *choler* up did move, . . . *Hub.* 364
Trembling through hasty rage when *choler* in him sweld. . I. iv. 33. 9
grieved mindes, which *choler* did englut, . . . II. ii. 23. 5
Chaufing and foming *choler* each against his fo. . . . IV. iv. 29. 9
As fayning *choler* which was turn'd to cold: . . . IV. vi. 27. 2
rather in them kindled *choler* new: . . . V. ii. 13. 4
Guyon did his *choler* pacify, . . . V. iii. 36. 5
softly royne, when salvage *choler* gan redound. . . . V. ix. 33. 9
he streightway with haughtie *choler* burned, . . . VI. ii. 12. 3
Choose. Thenot, to that I *choose* thou doest me tempt; . . *S.C.* N. 49
choise I had to *choose* my wandring waye, . . . *S.C.* D. 62
the yong lustie gallants he did *chose* To follow, . . . *Hub.* 797
wish him to *chuse* His Master, . . . *Hub.* 884
I *chose* before a life of wretchednes. . . . *Hub.* 984
Doth rather *choose* to sit in idle Cell, . . . *T.M.* 221
None would *choose* goodnes of his owne freewill. . . . *T.M.* 456
Whose merits they to glorifie do *chose.* . . . *Ti.* 371
chuse What storie she will for her tapet take. . . . *Mui.* 275
Thrise happie she, whom he to praise did *chose.* . . . *As.* 36
made me in that desart *chose* to dwell. . . . *Col.* 91
fed with words that could not *chose* but please: . . . I. i. 54. 8
prowest knight, That ever Ladie to her love did *chose,* . . . I. v. 14. 3
bad him *choose* what death he would desire; . . . I. ix. 50. 8
So few there bee, That *chose* the narrow path, . . . I. x. 10. 4
yeares More rype us reason lent to *chose* our Peares, . . . II. iv. 18. 5
Refuse such fruitlesse toile, and present pleasures *chuse.'* . . II. vi. 17. 9
choose my flitting houres to spend, . . . II. vii. 33. 7
no'te he *chuse* But beare the rigour . . . II. vii. 39. 7
him streight did *choose* Their king, . . . II. x. 37. 8
either Gloriana let her *chuse,* . . . III. Pr. 5. 7
Gan *choose* his Dame with *Bascimano* gay, . . . III. i. 56. 8
Their fit disports with faire delight doe *chose,* . . . III. ii. 31. 4
'The second was an holy Nunne to *chose,* . . . III. vii. 58. 6
They by consent should *chose* the stoutest three . . . IV. ii. 38. 7
Him entertayn'd and did her champion *chose;* . . . V. x. 12. 7
Unto your selfe I freely leave to *chose,* . . . VI. viii. 29. 8
Some with their eyes the daintest morsels *chose;* . . . VI. viii. 39. 4
They for their Judge did Pastorella *chose;* . . . VI. ix. 43. 3
ne wist what way to *chose:* . . . VII. vi. 24. 5
Chose rather to be praysed for dooing good, . . . *Am.* xxxviii. 13
Let the world *chose* to envy or to wonder. . . . *Am.* lxxxiv. 14
Who could not *chose* but laugh at his fond game, . . . *Epig.* iv. 33
To *chose* the longest day in all the yeare, . . . *Epith.* 271
chuse the better of them both . . . *Com. Son.* ii. 11
Choosed. *See* **Chosen.**
skill them rightly to have *chusd,* . . . II. ii. 5. 8
Chooseth. he *chooseth* with vile difference To be a beast, . . II. xii. 87. 4
choseth vertue for his dearest Dame, . . . III. iii. 1. 8
Choosing. *choosing* out few words most horrible, . . . I. i. 37. 1
Which *choosing* for that evenings hospitale, . . . II. ix. 10. 5
choosing solitarie to abide . . . III. vii. 6. 6
Chopped. eke her feete . . . *Chopt* off, . . . V. ii. 26. 9
he to peeces would have *chopt* it quight, . . . V. xi. 5. 5
Chord. *See* **Cord.**
to the trembling *chord* Can tune their timely voices . . . I. v. 3. 6
Sthenoboea . . . her selfe did choke With wilfull *chord* . . . I. v. 50. 6
Choristers. The *Choristers* the joyous Antheme sing, . . . *Epith.* 221
Chorl. *See* **Churl.**

Chose. *See* **Choose.**
chose with scornfull shame Him to avenge, . . . *Hub.* 1239
chose that guiltie hands of enemies . . . *Ti.* 299
rather *chose* back to my sheep to tourne, . . . *Col.* 672
The Lyon *chose* his mate, . . . *Col.* 865
Chose for his love the fairest in his sight. . . . *Col.* 869
Of those he *chose* out two, the falsest twoo, . . . I. i. 38. 6
chose in Faery court, of meere goodwil, . . . I. iii. 28. 5
Upon a slouthfull Asse he *chose* to ryde, . . . I. iv. 18. 7
both *chose* to win, or die. . . . I. vi. 43. 9
A monstrous beast ybredd in filthy fen He *chose,* . . . I. vii. 16. 9
He *chose* an halter from among the rest, . . . I. ix. 54. 4
chose for love to fight. . . . II. ii. 18. 9
'Disleall Knight, whose coward corage *chose* . . . II. v. 5. 3
each a damzell *chose.* . . . II. ix. 36. 5
rather *chose* to dye for sorow great, . . . III. v. 49. 8
chose emongst the jolly Satyres still to wonne. . . . III. x. 51. 9
Whom Jove did love and *chose* his cup to beare; . . . III. xii. 7. 4
both together *chose* Homeward to march, . . . IV. iii. 51. 4
Braggadochio rather *chose,* For glorie vaine, . . . IV. iv. 14. 4
chose out a gloomy glade, Where hardly eye mote see . . . IV. vii. 38. 6
for his love he *chose.* . . . IV. xii. 26. 9
Chose Artegall to right her to restore; . . . V. i. 4. 8
rather *chose* his challenge off to breake, . . . V. i. 24. 3
rather guilty *chose* himselfe to yield: . . . V. i. 24. 5
He *chose* with shame to beare that Ladies head: . . . V. i. 27. 8
I rather *chose* to die in lives despight, . . . V. iv. 32. 8
She *chose* this Arlo; . . . VII. vi. 39. 6
Chosen. *See* **Choosed.**
Chosen to be her dearest Paramoure. . . . *Ti.* 385
weighing the . . . shrunken synewes of her *chosen* knight, . . I. ix. 20. 5
Why shouldst thou then despeire, that *chosen* art? . . . I. ix. 53. 5
For those to dwell in that are *chosen* his, . . . I. x. 57. 3
His *chosen* people, purg'd from sinful guilt . . . I. x. 57. 4
It was a *chosen* plott of fertile land, . . . II. vi. 12. 1
by the people *chosen* in their sted, . . . II. x. 47. 2
having *chosen,* now he might not chaunge. . . . V. v. 26. 6
Christ. That same hath Jesus *Christ* now to him raught, . . *Hub.* 441
Christall, -ine. *See* **Crystal, -line.**
Christendom. Nor in all Kent, nor in *Christendome;* . . . *S.C.* S. 153
Christianity. Lucius, That first received *Christianity,* . . . II. x. 53. 4
Christians'. An Altare, . . . On which trew *Christians* blood was often spilt, . . . I. viii. 36. 3
Christmas. gather nuttes to make me *Christmas* game, . . *S.C.* D. 26
Christ's. The sacred pledge of *Christes* Evangely. . . . II. x. 53. 5
Chronicle. A *chronicle* of Briton kings, . . . II. x. Arg.
Chroniclers. many *Chroniclers,* that can record Old loves, . . I. v. 3. 8
Chrysaor. Mightie *Chrysaor;* and Caicus strong; . . . IV. xi. 14. 3
steely brand, . . . *Chrysaor* it was hight; . . . V. i. 9. 7
Chrysaor, that all other swords excelled, . . . V. i. 9. 8
With bright *Chrysaor* in his cruell hand, . . . V. ii. 18. 2
He stroke him with *Chrysaor* on the hed, . . . V. xii. 23. 2
Chrysogone. Her mother was the faire *Chrysogonee,* . . . III. vi. 4. 1
faire *Chrysogone* Conceiv'd these infants, . . . III. vi. 5. 2
So sprong these twinnes in womb of *Chrysogone;* . . . III. vi. 9. 6
whereas lay Faire *Crysogone* in slombry traunce . . . III. vi. 26. 7
The yonger daughter of *Chrysogonee,* . . . III. vi. 51. 2
Church. *See* **Kirk.**
Unto his *Church* for to present a wight, . . . *Hub.* 526
tooke their ready way Unto the *Church,* . . . III. ii. 48. 4
holy *Church* with faithlesse handes deface, . . . III. iii. 34. 2
caused to be hanged by In his chiefe *Church,* . . . III. iii. 59. 3
it on the *church* doth glance, . . . IV. vi. 14. 4
sacrilege me seem'd the *Church* to rob, . . . IV. x. 53. 3
Britomart comes to Isis *Church,* . . . V. vii. Arg.
in this *Church* hereby There stands an Idole . . . V. xi. 19. 1
So to the *Church* he came, . . . V. xi. 21. 6
From thence into the sacred *Church* he broke, . . . VI. xii. 25. 1
Churches. Wont to robbe *churches* of their ornaments, . . . I. iii. 17. 2
Churchmen. chaffred Chayres in which *Churchmen* were set, . *Hub.* 1159
Church's. growes lifes fruite unto the *Churches* good. . . . *Rev.* iv. 14
The *Churches* part, and Ploughmans portion, . . . II. x. 39. 4
Churl. the *Chorle* . . . conceiv'd affection bace, . . . III. vii. 15. 6
seeing with that *Chorle* so faire a wight, . . . III. viii. 12. 1
The fearefull *Chorle* durst not gainesay nor dooe, . . . III. viii. 13. 1
a rude *churle,* whom often he accused . . . VI. iii. 33. 5
Churn. The *Churne* and Charwell, two small streames, . . . IV. xi. 25. 3
Chuse. *See* **Choose.**
Chymneis. *See* **Chimneys.**
Chynd. *See* **Chined.**
Ciclaton. quilted richly rare Upon *checklaton,* . . . VI. vii. 43. 4
Cicones. 'Againe the dreadfull *Cycones* him dismay, . . . *Gn.* 537
Cicuta. Mortall Samnitis, and *Cicuta* bad, . . . II. vii. 52. 5
Cilician. Saffron, sought for in *Cilician* soyle; . . . *Gn.* 671
Cimmerian. Waste wildernes, amongst *Cymerian* shades, . . . *Gn.* 370
Cimmerians'. Darknesse more than *Cymerians* daylie night: . *T.M.* 256
Cinders. spirites, whose ashie *cinders* lie Under deep ruines, . *Ro.* i. 1
With blistred hands emongst the *cinders* brent, . . . IV. v. 35. 3
yron tongs did take Out of the burning *cinders,* . . . IV. v. 44. 3
Cinnamon. My *Sinamon* smell too much annoieth: . . . *S.C.* F. 136
Ciphered. Ease, on his robe in golden letters *cyphered.* . . . III. xii. 4. 9
Ciphers. In which there written was, with *cyphres* old, . . . III. ii. 25. 5
May learned be by *cyphers,* or by Magicke might. . . . III. ii. 45. 9
In *cyphers* strange, that few could rightly read, . . . V. ix. 26. 3
Circle. Nine was the *circle* sett in heavens place: . . . II. ix. 22. 8
Thence to the *Circle* of the Moone she clambe, . . . VII. vi. 8. 1
Downe to the *Circle* of the Moone, . . . VII. vi. 16. 2
Circled. Whose *circled* waters rapt with whirling sway, . . II. xii. 20. 5
in great heapes them *circled* all about, . . . V. v. 5. 8
Circle's. In which her *circles* voyage is fulfild, . . . *Am.* lx. 3

Circles. Whose sides with dapled *circles* weren dight; . . . . II. i. 18. 7
Circlet. Enchaste with chaine and *circulet* of golde . . . . *Hub.* 624
So well his golden *Circlet* him beseemeth. . . . . *Hub.* 627
like the *circlet* of a Turtle true, ... *Col.* 340
Her faire lockes in rich *circlet* be enrold, ... III. v. 5. 4
Circling. Under his belt he bore a sickle *circling* wide. . . . VII. vii. 36. 9
Circular. The frame thereof seemd partly *circulare,* . . . . II. ix. 22. 1
Circulet. *See* **Circlet.**
Circumstance. well considering of the *circumstaunce,* . . . . *Hub.* 174
Circumvent. So did Decetto eke him *circumvent;* . . . . . . VI. v. 20. 6
Citadel. So farre from court and royall *Citadell,* . . . . . III. vi. 1. 5
Cited. holde A Visitation, and them *cyted* thether: . . . . . *Hub.* 569
Cities. mongst all *Cities* florished much more. . . . . . . *Ro.* xxviii. 14
Castles surprizd, great *cities* sackt and brent: . . . . II. vii. 13. 8
all thy *Citties* they shall sacke and race, ... III. iii. 34. 7
She then the *Cities* sought from gate to gate, ... III. vi. 14. 1
Towres, *citties,* kingdomes, ye would ruinate . . . . III. viii. 28. 5
Cannot two fairer *Cities* find this day, ... III. ix. 51. 4
Great *cities* ransackt, and strong castles rast; . . . . IV. i. 21. 7
Out of the pleasant soyle and *cities* glad, ... V. x. 18. 5
My *cities* sackt, and their sky-threating towres Raced . . . . V. x. 23. 4
Him first from court he to the *citties* coursed, ... VI. ix. 3. 6
from the *citties* to the townes him prest, ... VI. ix. 3. 7
City. The holy *Citie* of the Lorde, from hye . . . . *Rev.* iv. 3
Square was this *Citie,* . . . . *Rev.* iv. 9
I saw a *Citie* like unto that same, ... *Bel.*[2] xiv. 2
The weake foundations of this *citie* faire. . . . . *Bel.*[2] xiv. 14
Such was this *Citie* in her good daies fownd: . . . . *Ro.* vi. 4
This *Citie,* more than that great Phrygian mother . . . . . . *Ro.* vi. 5
This *Citie,* which was first but shepheards shade, ... *Ro.* xx. 9
that same brave *Citie,* Which . . . Sustein'd the shocke . . . *Ro.* xxi. 2
The which this auncient *Citie* whilome made! . . . . *Ro.* xxv. 4
Was wont this auncient *Citie* to adorne, ... *Ro.* xxix. 7
th' auncient Genius of that *Citie* brent: . . . . *Ti.* 19
that *Citie,* which the garland wore Of Britaines pride, ... *Ti.* 36
Clayming that sea-coast *Citie* as his right. . . . . *Mui.* 314
It giveth name unto that auncient *Cittie,* . . . . *Col.* 112
A little path . . . to a goodly *Citty* led his vew, ... I. x. 55. 3
The *Citty* of the greate king hight it well, ... I. x. 55. 8
with great joy into that *Citty* wend, ... I. x. 56. 4
Now are they Saints all in that *Citty* sam, ... I. x. 57. 8
The fairest *citty* was that might be seene; . . . . I. x. 58. 4
this great *Citty* that does far surpas, ... I. x. 58. 8
By whose advise old Priams *cittie* fell, ... II. ix. 48. 6
Trojan warres and Priams *citie* sackt, ... III. ix. 38. 2
'The Trojan Brute did first that *citie* fownd, ... III. ix. 46. 1
that faire *City,* wherein make abode So many learned impes, . IV. xi. 26. 4
By many a *city* and by many a towne . . . . IV. xi. 34. 2
A goodly *citty* and a mighty one, ... V. iv. 35. 8
the watchman . . . all the *city* warned . . . . V. iv. 36. 2
magistrates of all that *city* made, ... V. vii. 43. 3
They came unto a *Citie* farre up land, ... V. x. 25. 1
that same *citie,* so now ruinate, ... V. x. 26. 3
City-gate. Before the *city gate,* in open sight; . . . . . . V. iv. 46. 5
So forth she came out of the *citty gate* . . . . V. v. 4. 1
City's. one would weene that one sole *Cities* strength . . . *Ro.* viii. 2
such this *Cities* honour was of yore, ... *Ro.* xxviii. 13
He was not in the *cities* wofull fyre Consum'd, ... III. ix. 40. 8
gathering them unto her *citties* gate, ... V. iv. 45. 6
there stood gazing from the *Citties* wall . . . . V. xi. 15. 6
Civil. *civile* bate Made me the spoile and bootie . . . . . . *Bel.*[1] viii. 9
civill warres me made The whole worlds spoile, ... *Bel.*[2] x. 9
Through idlenes would turne to *civill* rage, ... *Ro.* xxiii. 7
Thou onely cause, O *Civill* furie! art, ... *Ro.* xxxi. 9
before the world was *civill,* . . . . *Hub.* 45
now is thought a *civile* begging sect. . . . . *Hub.* 198
Whom they in *civill* manner first did greete, ... *Hub.* 362
for wise and *civill* governaunce. . . . . *Hub.* 782
Mecaenas . . . to all that *civil* artes professe, ... *Ded.Son.*xiii.10
shortly brought to *civile* governaunce, ... II. x. 38. 8
making vantage of their *civile* jarre, ... II. x. 65. 4
brave ensample, both of martiall And *civil* rule, ... II. x. 74. 9
Till universall peace compound all *civill* jarre. . . . . . . III. iii. 23. 9
civile armes to exercise no more: . . . . III. iii. 49. 5
far expell All *civile* usage and gentility, ... III. vi. 1. 8
Was the disturber of all *civill* life, ... III. vi. 14. 8
of *civill* uses lore, ... V. Pr. 3. 2
mutining to stirre up *civill* faction . . . . V. ii. 51. 4
roote of *civill* conversation: . . . . VI. i. 1. 6
this continuall, cruell, *civill* warre, ... *Am.* xliv. 5
Civility. had them traynd in all *civilitee,* . . . . III. i. 44. 6
spreds it selfe through all *civilitie;* . . . . VI. Pr. 4. 5
they that breake bands of *civilitie,* . . . . VI. i. 26. 6
which skill men call *Civility.* . . . . VI. x. 23. 9
Clad. *Clad* like a Nimph, that wings of silver weares, ... *Bel.*[2] iv. 6
clad with reliques of some Trophees olde, ... *Ro.* xxviii. 2
Yclad in Scarlot, like a mayden Queene, ... *S.C.* Ap. 57
when all is *ycladd* With pleasaunce: . . . . *S.C.* May 6
They bene *yclad* in purple and pall, ... *S.C.* Jul. 173
Ycladde in clothing of seely sheepe, ... *S.C.* S. 188
Mecaenas is *yclad* in claye, ... *S.C.* O. 61
they bene all *yclad* in clay; . . . . *S.C.* N. 118
The Ape *clad* Souldierlike, ... *Hub.* 204
he was *clad* in strange accoustrements, ... *Hub.* 672
Clad all in black, that mourning did bewray, ... *D.* 40
Ycladd in mightie armes and silver shielde, ... I. i. 1. 2
loftie trees, *yclad* with sommers pride, ... I. i. 7. 4
An aged Sire, in long blacke weedes *yclad,* . . . . I. i. 29. 2
Her all in white he *clad,* . . . . I. i. 45. 8
Then up he rose, and *clad* him hastily: . . . . I. ii. 6. 8

Clad—*Continued.*
In mighty armes he was *yclad* anon, ... I. ii. 11. 3
A goodly Lady *clad* in scarlot red, ... I. ii. 13. 2
In greene vine leaves he was right fitly *clad,* . . . . I. iv. 22. 1
an errant knight in armes *ycled,* . . . they new arrived find: . I. iv. 38. 4
Night, . . . In a foule blacke pitchy mantle *clad,* . . . . . . I. v. 20. 3
frowning forheades, with rough hornes *yclad,* . . . . I. vi. 11. 5
him . . . Who earst in flowres of freshest youth was *clad.* . . . I. viii. 42. 4
a gentle Squyre, . . . *clad* in comely sad attyre; . . . . . . I. x. 7. 3
Her younger sister, . . . Was *clad* in blew, ... I. x. 14. 2
bare wretched wights he dayly *clad,* . . . . I. x. 39. 6
A comely Palmer, *clad* in black attyre, ... II. i. 7. 2
all in bright armour *clad,* . . . . II. i. 45. 4
A goodly Ladie *clad* in hunters weed, ... II. iii. 21. 7
was *yclad* . . . All in a silken Camus . . . . II. iii. 26. 3
richly *cladd* in robes of royaltye, ... II. vii. 44. 7
yclad in red Downe to the ground, ... II. ix. 27. 5
Sir Guyon, in bright armour *clad,* . . . . II. xi. 3. 5
Clad in fayre weedes but fowle disordered, ... II. xii. 55. 8
So was that chamber *clad* in goodly wize: . . . . III. i. 39. 1
'Royally *clad*' (quoth he) 'in cloth of gold, ... III. v. 5. 2
then of him are *clad* with other hew, ... III. vi. 33. 6
al *yclad* in garments light . . . . III. x. 21. 6
Yclad in costly garments fit for tragicke Stage. . . . . . . III. xii. 3. 9
Doubt, who was *yclad* In a discolour'd cote . . . . III. xii. 10. 2
Griefe all in sable sorrowfully *clad,* . . . . III. xii. 16. 2
Clad in a vesture of unknowen geare . . . . IV. xi. 45. 2
Both *clad* in colours like, and like array, ... IV. xi. 47. 8
So being *clad* she brought him from the field, ... V. v. 21. 1
All *clad* in linnen robes with silver hemd; . . . . V. vii. 4. 4
when as she him anew had *clad,* . . . . V. vii. 41. 8
Him *clad* in th' armour of a Pagan knight, ... V. viii. 26. 2
A bevie of faire Virgins *clad* in white, ... V. ix. 31. 2
A Lions clawes, with powre and rigour *clad,* . . . . V. xi. 24. 3
faire she was, and richly *clad* In roiall robes, ... V. xi. 60. 6
All in a woodmans jacket he was *clad* . . . . VI. ii. 5. 6
What manner wight he was, and how *yclad,* . . . . VI. ii. 44. 3
of stature large, *Clad* all in gilden armes, ... VI. ii. 44. 7
To *clad* his corpse with meete habiliments, ... VI. iv. 4. 5
a faire Mayden *clad* in mourning weed, ... VI. vi. 16. 7
Yclad in home-made greene that her owne hands had dyde. . VI. ix. 7. 9
though it were a cottage *clad* with lome, ... VI. ix. 16. 5
So being *clad* unto the fields he went . . . . VI. ix. 37. 1
Like the faire Morning *clad* in misty fog . . . . VI. xi. 3. 9
Both *clad* in shepheards weeds agreeably, ... VI. xi. 36. 2
though full many a day He saw her *clad,* . . . . VII. vi. 42. 8
Him in Deares skin to *clad;* . . . . VII. vi. 50. 8
Then came the Autumne all in yellow *clad,* . . . . VII. vii. 30. 1
Clad all in white, that seemes a virgin best. . . . . *Epith.* 151
Clad like a Queene in royall robes, ... *H.H.B.* 185
Claim. bids him *clayme* with rigorous rage hys right: . . . . *S.C.* D. 130
as their due by Nature doo it *clame.* . . . . *Hub.* 166
I *claime* my selfe more fit Than you to rule; . . . . *Hub.* 1038
where ye *claime* your selfe for outward shape . . . . *Hub.* 1041
The sacred Muses have made alwaies *clame* . . . . *Ded. Son.* iv. 1
sith ye this Lady *clame,* . . . . IV. iv. 9. 1
of their loves choise they might freedom *clame,* . . . . . . IV. ix. 37. 7
no man answred to my *clame:* . . . . IV. x. 11. 5
the Sea-gods, which to themselves doe *clame* The powre . . . IV. xi. 12. 8
from the heritage, which she did *clame,* . . . . V. i. 3. 8
And both the living Lady *claime* your right, ... V. i. 26. 2
His owne good steed, which he had stolne, to *clame;* . . . . V. iii. 29. 5
By what right doe you *claime* to be your owne?' . . . . . . V. iv. 18. 5
but rather doe quite *clame:* . . . for you he spake it, ... VI. ii. 14. 4
In this bold sort to Heaven *claime* to make, ... VII. vi. 29. 3
'Then ceasse thy idle *claime,* thou foolish gerle; . . . . . . VII. vi. 34. 1
These gods do *claime* the worlds whole soverainty, ... VII. vii. 16. 2
do *claime* the rule and soverainty; . . . . VII. vii. 26. 3
King of all the rest, as ye doe *clame,* . . . . VII. vii. 53. 2
Claimed. thundring Jove, . . . she *claymed* for her syre, . . . I. iv. 11. 6
such as *claymd* themselves Brutes rightfull hayres, ... II. x. 37. 5
She *claim'd* that to her selfe, as Ladies det, ... IV. i. 12. 7
as his thrall Her *claym'd,* . . . . IV. v. 23. 7
like to this be *clamed.* . . . . IV. x. 30. 9
a waift . . . he *claym'd* as propertie: . . . . IV. xii. 31. 4
Claiming. *Clayming* that sea-coast Citie as his right. . . . *Mui.* 314
Clamb. *See* **Climbed, Clomb.**
Thence to the Circle of the Moone she *clambe,* . . . . . . VII. vi. 8. 1
Clambering. *clambring* through the hollow cliffes on hy . . . *Gn.* 79
Emongst the rest the *clambring* Yvie grew, ... *Gn.* 217
Clame, -d. *See* **Claim,** *etc.*
Clamor. To weeten what that sudden *clamour* ment: . . . . IV. iii. 38. 2
Clamors. Them guyded through the throng, that did their *clamors* ceasse. V. ix. 23. 9
They ceast their *clamors* upon them to gaze; . . . . V. ix. 24. 1
through great confusione Of cryes and *clamors* . . . . VI. xi. 32. 4
Clap. *See* **Thunder-clap.**
seing hir striken fall with *clap* of thunder, ... *Bel.*[1] xi. 13
downe she stricken fell with *clap* of thunder, ... *Bel.*[2] xv. 13
As the great *clap* of thunder which doth ryve . . . . *Gn.* 519
As Hellene, . . . Did *clap* her hands, ... III. x. 12. 9
These three so noble babes to bring forth at one *clap.* . . . IV. ii. 43. 9
all the castle ringed with the *clap.* . . . . IV. x. 9. 5
Clapped. His tayle he *clapt* betwixt his legs . . . . *S.C.* May 280
clapt his yron wings as victor he did dwell. . . . . I. xi. 31. 9
a stormy whirlwind . . . *clapped* every dore, ... III. xii. 3. 2
clapt on hye his coulourd winges twaine, ... III. xii. 23. 7
Clapping. Shouting, and *clapping* all their hands on hight, . I. v. 16. 8
Claps. *See* **Thunder-claps.**
Clare. *Clare* and Harwitch both doth beautify: . . . . IV. xi. 33. 5

Claribel. faire *Claribell* with all her art,	II. iv. 26. 5
sterne Druon, and lewd *Claribell,*	IV. ix. 20. 8
Claribell enraged rife With fervent flames,	IV. ix. 21. 3
Blandamour to *Claribell* relide:	IV. ix. 26. 5
assaid Of *Claribell* and Blandamour attone;	IV. ix. 30. 2
Then good Sir *Claribell* him thus bespake:	IV. ix. 40. 1
Her name was *Claribell;*	VI. xii. 4. 1
Thus long continu'd *Claribell* a thrall,	VI. xii. 10. 1
Claribell Ne lesse did tender the faire Pastorell,	VI. xii. 11. 4
he bethought To leave his love . . . With *Claribell;*	VI. xii. 13. 4
With thanks to Bellamour and *Claribell,*	VI. xii. 13. 8
The daughter of her Lady *Claribell,*	VI. xii. 15. 8
Claribell's. Pryene, rich arayd, In *Claribellaes* clothes.	II. iv. 28. 3
Clarin. Her name was *Clarin,*	V. iv. 48. 3
'Clarin,' (said she) 'thou seest yond Fayry Knight,	V. v. 32. 1
Ne ever did deceiptfull *Clarin* find	V. v. 56. 4
Clarinda. *'Clarinda,* whom of all I trust alive,	V. v. 29. 3
Goe now, *Clarinda;*	V. v. 34. 6
'Certes, *Clarinda,* not of cancred will . . . I have forbore	V. v. 41. 1
'What now is left, *Clarinda?*	V. v. 48. 1
Even so *Clarinda* her owne Dame beguyld,	V. v. 53. 5
Clarin's. He is . . . wrought by *Clarins* wile.	V. v. Arg.
Clarion. now I will my golden *Clarion* rend,	*T.M.* 463
sad *Clarion* did at last decline	*Mui.* 14
Clarion, the eldest sonne and haire Of Muscaroll;	*Mui.* 22
Yong *Clarion,* with vauntfull lustie-head,	*Mui.* 54
Thus the fresh *Clarion,* being readie dight,	*Mui.* 145
O *Clarion,* though fairest thou Of all thy kinde,	*Mui.* 233
where yong *Clarion* Was wont to solace him,	*Mui.* 242
So soone as *Clarion* he did beholde,	*Mui.* 355
For to entrap the careles *Clarion,*	*Mui.* 375
The luckles *Clarion,* whether cruell Fate	*Mui.* 417
Clarions. With shaumes, and trompets, and with *Clarions* sweet;	I. xii. 13. 2
shril trompets and loud *clarions* sweetly playd	IV. iii. 5. 9
Clarke, -s. *See* **Clerk,** *etc.*	
Clash. they . . . *clash* their shields, and shake their swerds	I. iv. 40. 3
Clashing. as the *clashing* of an Armor bright,	I. xi. 9. 8
glittering he did spy Or *clashing* heard,	III. xii. 12. 5
Clasping. dilate Their *clasping* armes in wanton wreathings	II. xii. 53. 9
clasping twixt his armes, her up did reare	V. xi. 64. 7
Clatter. I see thou doest but *clatter,*	*S.C.* Jul. 207
Begin his witlesse note apace to *clatter.*	*Am.* lxxxiv. 4
Claudius. Good *Claudius,* that next was Emperour,	II. x. 51. 1
Clave. *See* **Cleaved, Cleft, Clove.**	
their crooked keeles the surges *clave.*	*Gn.* 568
Claw. by myne eie the Crow his *clawe* dooth wright:	*S.C.* D. 136
one of them was like an Eagles *claw,*	I. viii. 48. 6
from his cruell *claw* To reave	I. xi. 41. 5
as a Bittur in the Eagles *clawe,*	II. viii. 50. 2
Claws. T' embrew her teeth and *clawes*	*Bel.*[2] vi. 7
Or armed be with *clawes,* or scalie creasts,	*Ro.* xxiv. 4
all his glory in his cruell *clawes.*	*Van.* x. 6
her unruly Page With his rude *clawes* the wicket open rent,	I. iii. 13. 2
seizing cruell *clawes* on trembling brest,	I. iii. 19. 8
did weene the same Have reft away with his sharp . . . *clawes:*	I. iii. 41. 6
From Lyons *clawes* to pluck the gryped pray.	I. vi. 7. 4
beast, Who on his neck his bloody *clawes* did seize,	I. viii. 15. 2
The sharpnesse of his cruel rending *clawes:*	I. xi. 12. 2
with his cruell *clawes* he snatcht the wood,	I. xi. 22. 2
nayles like *clawes* appeard.	II. vii. 3. 9
He over him did hold his cruell *clawes,*	II. vii. 27. 6
some had *clawes* to teare:	II. xi. 8. 5
Whose *clawes* were newly dipt in cruddy blood,	III. iii. 47. 5
Whence he with crooked *clawes* so long did crall,	III. x. 57. 8
seiz'd her cruell *clawes* Uppon the carkasse	V. iv. 40. 6
first the Tygre *clawes* thereon did lay,	V. vii. 30. 4
A Lions *clawes,* with powre and rigour clad,	V. xi. 24. 3
Her Lions *clawes* he from her feete away did wipe.	V. xi. 27. 9
with long nayles over-raught, Like puttocks *clawes;*	V. xii. 30. 3
threatning his sharpe *clawes,* now wanting powre to traine.	VI. iv. 22. 9
with fell *clawes* full of fierce gourmandize,	VI. x. 34. 5
As if he would have rent him with his cruell *clawes:*	VI. xii. 29. 9
Clay. Mecaenas is yclad in *claye,*	*S.C.* O. 61
they bene all yclad in *clay;*	*S.C.* N. 118
built of brickle *clay,*	*Ti.* 499
the good knight, . . . with fresh *clay* did close the wooden wound:	I. ii. 44. 8
So deepely dinted in the driven *clay,*	I. viii. 8. 5
castes up a mount of *clay.*	I. viii. 9. 9
The images of God in earthly *clay;*	I. x. 39. 7
A lesson too too hard for living *clay*	III. iv. 26. 3
Are wont to cleave unto the lowly *clay,*	III. v. 1. 5
'Thou clod of vilest *clay,*	III. x. 31. 2
nor shining gold, nor mouldring *clay* it was;	IV. x. 39. 5
that same lumpe of *clay,*	V. x. 37. 2
fall away . . . even to corrupted *clay:*	*H.B.* 96
Therefore of *clay,* base, vile, and next to nought,	*H.H.L.* 106
Cle. The *Cle,* the Were, the Grant, the Sture, the Rowne.	IV. xi. 34. 5
Clean. all their teares he shall wipe *cleane* away.	*Rev.* iv. 7
devoure The spring . . . and all *cleane* out of sight.	*Pet.* iv. 11
with *cleane* minde, and heart sincere,	*Gn.* 122
His yron-headed spade tho making *cleene,*	*Gn.* 653
And their disloiall powre defaced *clene,*	*Ded. Son.* xi. 11
All *cleane* dismayd to see so uncouth sight,	I. i. 50. 1
all of Diamond perfect pure and *cleene*	I. vii. 33. 5
His rawbone armes, . . . Were *clene* consum'd;	I. viii. 41. 8
the river Dee, as silver *cleene,*	I. ix. 4. 7
that bright towre, all built of christall *clene,*	I. x. 58. 5
Clean—*Continued.*	
guilt of sinfull crimes *cleane* wash away;	I. xi. 30. 2
he . . . His shackles emptie lefte, himselfe escaped *cleene.*	II. i. 1. 9
Laid first his filthie hands on virgin *cleene,*	II. i. 10. 4
the *cleane* waves with purple gore did ray:	II. i. 40. 4
Her sisters, . . . Strive her to banish *cleane.*	II. ii. Arg.
His guiltie handes from bloody gore to *cleene.*	II. ii. 3. 4
filth wipe *cleane* away:	II. iv. 35. 8
one old Nymph, hight Panope, to keepe it *cleane.*	III. viii. 37. 9
her skin all snowy *cleene.*	III. xii. 20. 9
vanisht utterly and *cleane* subverst	III. xii. 42. 3
Seaven women by him slaine, and eaten *clene:*	IV. vii. 13. 5
in whose waters *cleane* Ten thousand fishes play	IV. xi. 29. 8
in the sight of all men *cleane* disgraced,	V. iii. 39. 3
Sate goodly Temperance in garments *clene,*	V. ix. 32. 8
from her partie eftsoones was drawen *cleene:*	V. ix. 49. 3
defaced *cleene* Her stately towres	V. x. 25. 4
yet inly neate and *clene,*	VI. v. 38. 4
cleane were gone, which way he never knew;	VI. x. 18. 3
Which every howre is chang'd and altred *cleane*	VII. vii. 22. 7
cleane without his usuall spheere to fare;	VII. vii. 52. 4
in your glasse of cristall *clene,*	*Am.* xlv. 1
with thy deare blood *clene* washt	*Am.* lxviii. 7
Cleaner. nought they beene For all his washing *cleaner.*	II. ii. 3. 6
nothing *cleaner* were for such intent,	II. vii. 61. 7
Cleanest. all were they *cleanest* From blamefull blot,	VI. xii. 41. 3
Cleanly. *cleanly* cover that cannot be cured:	*S.C.* S. 138
coosinage and *cleanly* knaverie,	*Hub.* 857
he thousands *cleanly* coosined:	*Hub.* 862
his fine handling, and his *cleanly* play,	*Hub.* 1015
by her *cleanly* garment catching hold,	I. iii. 40. 8
Right *cleanly* clad in comely sad attyre;	I. x. 7. 3
Cleanse. And *clense* the guilt of that infected cryme	*H.H.L.* 167
Cleansed. Babes bloody handes may not be *clensd:*	II. ii. Arg.
this babes bloody hand May not be *clensd*	II. ii. 10. 2
Clear. lively streame, more *cleere* than Christall	*Rev.* iv. 12
As *cleare* (*clere*[1]) as Christall	*Bel.* xii. 2
His face, more *cleare* then Christall glasse,	*S.C.* Jul. 159
As *cleare* as the christall glasse;	*S.C.* Au. 80
the cloudes wexen *cleare.*	*S.C.* S. 18
if I ever sonet song so *cleare,*	*S.C.* D. 15
in chanels *cleare* To romble gently downe	*T.M.* 25
unto Allo, or to Mulla *cleare:*	*Col.* 302
beautie shyneth as the morning *cleare,*	*Col.* 506
gold and jewels shining *cleare,*	I. v. 21. 2
the streame, as *cleare* as christall glas:	I. vii. 6. 3
she wist his cryme could els be never *cleare.*	I. x. 28. 9
My conscience *cleare* with guilty bands would bynd?	I. xii. 30. 5
cleare she dide from blemish criminall:	II. i. 37. 7
As morning Sunne her beames dispredden *cleare,*	II. ii. 40. 8
Gan *cleare* the deawy ayre	II. iii. 1. 4
a horne that shrilled *cleare*	II. iii. 20. 7
Cleare as the skye,	II. iii. 22. 3
a voyce that called lowd and *cleare,*	II. viii. 3. 7
with her light the earth enlumines *cleare:*	II. ix. 4. 7
at last the weather gan to *cleare,*	II. xii. 37. 5
Few drops, more *cleare* then Nectar,	II. xii. 78. 4
Whose face did seeme as *cleare* as Christall stone,	III. i. 15. 4
the bright glister of their beames *cleare*	III. i. 32. 8
her pure yvory Into a *cleare* Carnation suddeine dyde;	III. iii. 20. 3
the *cleare* ayre engroste,	III. iv. 13. 2
Whom such whenas Malbecco spyed *clere,*	III. x. 23. 4
On which the winged boy in colours *cleare* Depeincted was,	III. xi. 7. 7
yet doth not passe so *cleare,*	IV. i. 45. 7
evermore sought Britomart to *cleare:*	IV. i. 54. 6
Amongst the lesser starres in evening *cleare.*	IV. v. 14. 4
To frame such subtile wire, so shinie *cleare;*	IV. vi. 20. 6
eyes, like twinkling stars in evening *cleare,*	IV. x. 50. 7
all mankinde do nourish with their waters *clere.*	IV. xi. 52. 9
The sunne at length his joyous face doth *cleare:*	V. iii. 1. 2
in the sunshine of her countenance *cleare*	V. v. 38. 4
prove her *cleare* Of all those crimes	V. xi. 40. 4
How *cleare* I am from blame of this upbraide;	V. xi. 41. 7
when that Knight from perill *cleare* was freed,	V. xi. 48. 1
Whose goodly light then Phoebus lampe doth shine more *cleare?*	V. xi. 62. 9
it me concernes my selfe to *clere,*	VI. ii. 15. 8
his own thought he knew most *cleare* from wite:	VI. iii. 16. 6
beautie is more glorious bright and *clere,*	VI. vii. 29. 7
Her tender sides; her bellie white and *clere,*	VI. viii. 42. 4
Albe they worthy blame, or *cleare* of crime:	VI. xii. 40. 6
did sing the spousall hymne full *cleere,*	VII. vii. 12. 7
lovely light to *cleare* my cloudy grief,	*Am.* xxxiv. 12
his planet *cleare* Began in me to move,	*Am.* lx. 5
stormes, . . . Shall turne to caulmes, and tymely *cleare* away.	*Am.* lxii. 12
after stormes, when clouds begin to *cleare,*	*H.L.* 276
with the brightnesse of her beautie *cleare,*	*H.B.* 11
so still more *cleare* And faire it growes,	*H.H.B.* 45
Is many thousand times more bright, more *cleare,*	*H.H.B.* 170
And make her native brightnes seem more *cleare.*	*H.H.B.* 189
Cleared. Albe her guiltlesse conscience her *cleard,*	III. vi. 10. 2
th' ayre was milde and *cleared* was the skie,	III. viii. 21. 5
she . . . *cleard* that stripling of th' imputed blame,	VI. ii. 14. 2
sunshine, when cloudy looks are *cleared.*	*Am.* xl. 14
Clear'd from grosse mists of fraile infirmities.	*H.H.B.* 140
Clearer. *Clearer* then cristall, would therein appere.	*Am.* xlv. 12
Clearest. *my former writs, all were they *clearest* From blamefull blot,	VI. xii. 41. 3
Ne ought I see, though in the *clearest* day,	*Am.* lxxxvii. 5

Cleareth. And clowdie Welkin *cleareth*. *S.C.* Mar. 12
Cleave. That Romane Eagle seene to *cleave* asunder, *Ro.* xvii. 10
O, how the rurall routes to thee doe *cleave!* *S.C.* O. 26
cleave The flitting skyes, like flying Pursuivant, II. viii. 2. 3
all his seede the curse doth often *cleave,* II. viii. 29. 4
Uplifting high . . . to *cleave* his head. II. viii. 30. 7
Are wont to *cleave* unto the lowly clay III. v. 1. 5
no substance . . . But it would pierce or *cleave,* V. i. 10. 7
Cleaved. *See* **Clave, Cleft, Clove.**
with . . . wings he *cleav'd* The liquid clowdes, *Hub.* 1258
Cleaves. as the thonder *cleaves* the cloudes, *S.C.* Au. 85
So *cleaves* thy soule asonder: *S.C.* Au. 88
with her pineons *cleaves* the liquid firmament. III. iv. 49. 9
Cleaving. *cleaving* the hard steele, did deepe invade II. viii. 45. 4
Cleft. *See* **Clave, Cleaved, Clove.**
So hugely stroke, that it . . . *cleft* his head. I. ii. 19. 5
his bloody wounds, that through the steele were *cleft.'* I. vi. 39. 9
his huge taile he quite a sonder *clefte;* I. xi. 39. 8
with which she *clefte* The slouthfull wave II. vi. 18. 6
Have *cleft* his head in twaine, II. viii. 33. 9
to the chin he *clefte* his head in twaine. III. v. 23. 6
His weasand-pipe it through his gorget *cleft.* IV. iii. 12. 7
It would have *cleft* his braine downe to his brest. IV. iii. 34. 7
It would have *cleft* him to the girding place; IV. viii. 43. 8
As they the cliffe in peeces would have *cleft;* IV. xi. 3. 7
She with one stroke both head and helmet *cleft.* V. vii. 34. 6
all they *cleft* or brast. V. xii. 17. 9
cleft his head asunder to his chin. VI. i. 23. 5
the which my coulter hath not *cleft;* VI. ix. 1. 4
Clefts. through the *clifts* the vermeil bloud out sponne, IV. ix. 27. 4
Clemence. To shew that *clemence* oft, . . . Restraines V. vii. 22. 8
Clemencies. worthie paterns of her *clemencies;* V. x. 5. 7
Clemency. *See* **Clemence.**
Use them but well, with gracious *clemencye,* *Hub.* 1080
his avenging wrath to *clemency* incline. I. x. 51. 9
such is the might Of courteous *clemency* II. vi. 36. 6
The sacred pledge of peace and *clemencie,* V. ix. 30. 3
Cleopatra. High minded *Cleopatra* . . . her selfe did stoutly kill; I. v. 50. 7
Cleopatra's. neglect The worlds whole rule for *Cleopatras* sight. V. viii. 2. 7
Cleopolis. Whose kingdomes seat *Cleopolis* is red; I. vii. 46. 7
great *Cleopolis* . . . The fairest citty was I. x. 58. 2
Cleopolis, . . . The fairest peece that eie beholden can; I. x. 59. 2
Cannot two fairer Cities find this day Except *Cleopolis:* III. ix. 51. 5
Cleopolis'. Elfinan, who laid *Cleopolis* foundation first of all: II. x. 72. 8
Clepe. I saw the fish (if fish I may it *cleepe*) *Van.* v. 2
Cleped. Cittie, Which Kilnemullah *cleped* is of old; *Col.* 113
cleeped him his liege, II. iii. 8. 9
cleped was Port Esquiline, II. ix. 32. 8
he Anamnestes *cleped* is; II. ix. 58. 8
of them *cleeped* was the Lady of Delight. III. i. 31. 9
is *ycleped* Florimell the fayre, III. v. 8. 7
The other *cleped* Cruelty by name: III. xii. 19. 3
'Concord she *cleeped* was in common reed, IV. x. 34. 1
old Gall, that now is *cleeped* France, IV. xi. 16. 4
Sir Sanglier, (so *cleeped* was that Knight) V. i. 20. 7
Therefore it rightly *cleeped* was mount Acidale. VI. x. 8. 9
Clergy. to the *Clergy* now was come at last; VI. xii. 23. 3
Clerk. *See* **Kitchen-clerk.**
th' Ape his Parish *Clarke* procur'd to bee. *Hub.* 557
Clerks. They forg'd another, as for *Clerkes* booke-redd. *Hub.* 358
'It seemes . . . right well that ye be *Clerks,* *Hub.* 415
they, that are great *Clerkes,* have nearer wayes, *Hub.* 537
Clerks they to loathly idlenes entice, *T.M.* 335
Some *Clarkes* doe doubt in their devicefull art V. x. 1. 1
sundry wayes and fashions as *clerkes* faine, VII. vii. 55. 2
Clew. untwisting his deceiptfull *clew,* II. i. 8. 3
Clews. alwaies in her hand two *clewes* of silke she twynd. III. xii. 14. 9
Cliff. tree, High growing on the top of rocky *clift,* I. viii. 22. 6
His dwelling . . . underneath a craggy *clift* ypight, I. ix. 33. 3
clift, Whose false foundacion waves have washt away, I. xi. 54. 5
sad Celeno, sitting on a *clifte,* II. vii. 23. 6
Lyke an huge cave hewne out of rocky *clifte,* II. vii. 28. 2
craggie *clift* Depending from on high, II. xii. 4. 2
still sat wayting on that wastfull *clift* II. xii. 8. 6
chaunced on a craggy *cliff* (*clift?*) to light, III. x. 57. 7
As they the *cliffe* in peeces would have cleft; IV. xi. 3. 7
Under the hanging of an hideous *clieffe* IV. xii. 5. 1
downe the *cliffe* the wretched Gyant tumbled; V. ii. 50. 6
Cliffs. clambring through the hollow *cliffes* on hy *Gn.* 79
Some on th' Euboick *Cliffs* in pieces rent; *Gn.* 587
His goodly corps, on ragged *cliffs* yrent, I. v. 38. 6
carcases were . . . throwne about the *cliffs.* I. ix. 34. 6
On whose sharp *cliftes* the ribs of vessels broke; II. xii. 7. 3
gainst the craggy *clifts* did loudly rore, III. iv. 7. 5
dauncing on the craggy *cliffes* at will; V. ix. 15. 5
Clift, -s. *See* **Cliff, -s, Clefts.**
Climb. God shield, man, that I should *clime,* *S.C.* Jul. 9
affrayd To *clime* this hilles height. *S.C.* Jul. 72
Alsoone may shepheard *clymbe* to skye *S.C.* Jul. 101
sith thys hyll Thou hast such doubt to *climbe.* *S.C.* Jul. 232
love does teach him *climbe* so hie, *S.C.* O. 91
Into the highest top of heaven gan *clime,* *Gn.* 157
Still wayting to preferment up to *clime,* *Hub.* 76
thou to a tree mayst *clyme,* *Hub.* 990
So forth she comes, and to her coche does *clyme,* I. iv. 17. 1
Una her did marke *Clymbe* to her charet, I. xi. 51. 7
To *climbe* aloft, and others to excell: II. vii. 46. 7
so high as foe might not it *clime,* II. ix. 21. 2
Then all the rest into their coches *clim,* III. iv. 42. 6

Climb—*Continued.*
the heavy trees they *clyme,* III. vi. 42. 5
and thinke how she to heaven may *clime;* *Am.* xiii. 10
All ready to her silver coche to *clyme;* *Epith.* 76
Climbed. *See* **Clamb, Clomb.**
She *climbed* up to heaven in the smoke. *Bel.*[1] ix. 8
Climbers. Great *clymbers* fall unsoft. *S.C.* Jul. 12
Climbing. Phoebus fiery carre . . . was *climbing* up the Easterne hill, I. ii. 1. 8
Climbs. Unto the type of kingdomes title *clymes!* V. ix. 42. 7
Clim(e). *See* **Climb.**
Climene. the sonne of *Climene,* he did repent; III. xi. 38. 2
Clink. creeping close behind the Wickets *clink,* *S.C.* May 251
Clio. Begin, O *Clio!* and recount from hence III. iii. 4. 6
Meane-while, O *Clio!* lend Calliope thy quill. VII. vi. 37. 9
Clip. Ile *clip* his wanton wings, that he no more shall flye.' VI. iv. 24. 9
Clipped. Lightly he *clipt* her twixt his armes twaine, III. xii. 45. *or.* 1
Clipping. fast her *clipping* twixt his armes twayne, III. viii. 10. 1
Cloak. His colowred crime with craft to *cloke.* *S.C.* F. 162
The *cloke* was care of thrift, and husbandry, *Hub.* 1170
still he strove to *cloke* his inward bale, I. ix. 16. 3
To *cloke* her guile with sorrow and sad teene; II. i. 21. 7
for helps to *cloke* her crime withall. II. vii. 45. 9
To *cloke* the cause that hath it selfe bewrayd? III. iii. 19. 4
So courage lent a *cloke* to cowardise. V. iii. 15. 5
Now glooming sadly, so to *cloke* her matter; VI. vi. 42. 8
To *cloke* the mischiefe which he inly ment, VI. vii. 4. 2
Cloaked. Abusing manie through their *cloaked* guile, *Hub.* 344
The false Duessa, *cloked* with Fidessaes name. I. vii. 1. 9
this false footman, *clokt* with simplenesse, I. xii. 34. 6
Cloath, -ed, -s. *See* **Clothe, -d, -s.**
Clod. covering with a *clod* their closed eye, II. i. 60. 4
'Thou *clod* of vilest clay, I pardon yield, III. x. 31. 2
Clods. to us wretched earthly *clods* . . . lend desired light; *Epith.* 411
Clogged. her up he cast . . . He nould be *clogd.* III. x. 35. 9
clogd with burden of mortality; *Am.* lxxii. 4
Cloisters. Into their *cloysters* now he broken had, VI. xii. 24. 1
Clomb. *See* **Clamb, Climbed.**
to what end they *clomb* that tedious hight? I. x. 49. 9
to behold he *clomb* up to the bancke, II. vii. 57. 1
Tho to their ready Steedes they *clombe* full light, III. iii. 61. 6
She to her wagon *clombe; clombe* all the rest, III. iv. 31. 6
clombe unto his steed. III. iv. 61. 6
Unto his lofty steede he *clombe* anone, IV. v. 46. 1
Clonmel. making way By sweet *Clonmell,* IV. xi. 43. 2
Clorinda. first his sister that *Clorinda* hight, *As.* 211
Close. Bearing *close* envie to these riches rare, *Bel.* xiii. 6
peeping *close* into the thicke, *S.C.* Mar. 73
we *close* shrowded in thys shade alone. *S.C.* Ap. 32
creeping *close* behind the Wickets clink, *S.C.* May 251
till my last sleepe Doe *close* mine eyes: *S.C.* Au. 171
sorrow *close* shrouded in hart, *S.C.* S. 15
Drawne into danger through *close* ambushment; *Gn.* 532
With whom he *close* confers *Hub.* 763
all the skill Of *close* conveyance, *Hub.* 856
Scarse anie left to *close* his eylids neare; *Ti.* 194
love did beare, And long it *close* conceal'd, *Mui.* 132
thousand perills lie in *close* awaite *Mui.* 221
Himselfe he *close* upgathered . . . Into his den, *Mui.* 397
when life parts vouchsafe to *close* mine eye. *D.* 511
none is nigh, thine eylids up to *close,* *As.* 137
creeping *close* into his secrecie; *Col.* 698
knight, . . . with fresh clay did *close* the wooden wound: I. ii. 44. 8
in *close* hart shutting up her payne, I. iii. 8. 6
close in night conceald. I. v. 29. 9
his dreadfull hideous hedd *Close* couched on the bever, I. vii. 31. 5
creeping *close,* as Snake in hidden weedes, I. ix. 28. 8
Close creeping twixt the marow and the skin: I. x. 25. 5
did glyde *Close* under his left wing, I. xi. 20. 7
coming *close* to Trompart II. iii. 12. 1
How they within their fouldings *close* enwrapped bee: II. iii. 27. 9
Whereby *close* fire into his heart does creepe: II. v. 34. 7
Some by *close* shouldring; some by flatteree; II. vii. 47. 3
Doubly disparted, it did locke and *close,* II. ix. 23. 6
when it opened, no man might it *close,* II. ix. 23. 8
close convaid, and to the backgate brought, II. ix. 32. 7
Close rownd about her tuckt with many a plight: II. ix. 40. 6
keepes in coverts *close* from living wight, II. ix. 40. 8
in the secret of your hart *close* lyes, II. ix. 42. 4
Through many covert groves and thickets *close,* II. xii. 76. 6
snatching his bright sword began to *close* With her III. i. 9. 3
false instilled fire Did spred it selfe, and venime *close* inspire. III. i. 56. 5
bent Her crafty engins to her *close* intent. III. i. 57. 5
feeling one *close* couched by her side, III. i. 62. 1
Where they in secret counsell *close* conspird, III. iii. 51. 5
Litle shee weend that love he *close* conceald. III. v. 49. 4
in *close* bowre her mewes from all mens sight, III. ix. 5. 8
sent *close* messages of love to her at will. III. ix. 27. 9
With speaking lookes, that *close* embassage bore, III. ix. 28. 2
By such *close* signes they secret way did make III. ix. 31. 5
Cupid selfe, it seeing, *close* did smyle III. x. 5. 7
bearing with him treasure in *close* store, III. x. 19. 3
hoved *close* under a forest side, III. x. 20. 8
in his eare him rownded *close* behinde: III. x. 30. 4
close creeping as he might, III. x. 44. 1
creeping *close* amongst the hives III. x. 53. 5
Hath in a dungeon deepe her *close* embard, III. xi. 16. 8
Woven with gold and silke, so *close* and nere III. xi. 28. 3
Twixt both his hands few sparks he *close* did strayne, III. xii. 9. 7
gan therefore *close* spight to him to beare; IV. ii. 26. 5

Close—*Continued.*
in *close* disguise Of fayned love, . . . IV. ii. 30. 1
aventred With doubled force *close* underneath his shield, . . . IV. iii. 9. 2
With point of steele that *close* his hartbloud spild, . . . IV. iii. 22. 5
through the seame, which did his hauberk *close,* . . . IV. iii. 30. 3
reaching forth his sweard *Close* underneath his shield, . . . IV. iii. 33. 7
allur'd with *close* delight, . . . IV. iv. 16. 4
Now cuffing *close,* now chacing to and fro, . . . IV. iv. 29. 6
to the Queene of beautie *close* did call, . . . IV. v. 26. 4
When gentle sleepe his heavie eyes would *close;* . . . IV. v. 40. 2
Artegall *close* smyling joy'd in secret hart. . . . IV. vi. 32. 9
she heard some one *close* by her side . . . IV. vii. 10. 1
close appeard in that rude brutishnesse, . . . IV. vii. 45. 5
close venim doth convay Into the lookers hart, . . . IV. viii. 39. 8
Delay in *close* awaite . . . IV. x. 14. 5
A bevie of fayre damzels *close* did lye, . . . IV. x. 48. 8
He saw no way but *close* with him in hast; . . . V. ii. 14. 2
Keeping there *close* with him . . . his false Ladie, . . . V. iii. 13. 4
Artegall . . . Stood in the preasse *close* covered, . . . V. iii. 20. 2
painted buskins . . . laced *close* afore; . . . V. v. 3. 3
Conceived *close* in her beguiled hart, . . . V. v. 43. 8
Her selfe there *close* afflicted long in vaine, . . . V. vi. 15. 2
He should his purpose misse, which *close* he ment: . . . V. vi. 24. 3
Of armed men comming with *close* intent . . . V. vi. 28. 7
with sweete rest her heavy eyes did *close,* . . . V. vii. 12. 3
did *close* implie The course of all her fortune . . . V. vii. 12. 8
Yet still the Prince pursew'd him *close* behind. . . . V. viii. 42. 1
from *close* friends, that dar'd not to appeare, . . . V. xii. 10. 8
maintayne That Tyrants part with *close* or open ayde, . . . V. xii. 25. 6
couching *close* his speare and all his powre, . . . VI. iii. 48. 2
Having by chaunce a *close* advantage vew'd, . . . VI. iii. 50. 4
all about did *close* the compasse of his eye. . . . VI. iv. 24. 9
scattering Contagious poyson *close* through every vaine, . . . VI. vi. 8. 8
joyning *close* huge lode at him did lay; . . . VI. vi. 28. 8
He watcht in *close* awayt with weapons prest, . . . VI. vi. 44. 3
Gan mutter *close* a certaine secret charme, . . . VI. viii. 45. 6
joyed long in *close* felicity, . . . VI. x. 38. 6
Unto their dwelling did them *close* convay. . . . VI. x. 41. 5
Calidore in th' entry *close* did stand, . . . VI. xi. 46. 6
Where all the Gods she found in counsell *close,* . . . VII. vi. 24. 2
him placed where he *close* might view . . . VII. vi. 45. 2
in some snare or gin set *close* behind, Entrapped him, . . . VII. vi. 48. 6
Which of her Nymphes, or other *close* consort, . . . VII. vi. 51. 5
in those lofty lookes is *close* implide, . . . *Am.* v. 5
In the *close* covert of her guilefull eyen, . . . *Am.* xii. 7
A *close* intent at last to shew me grace; . . . *Am.* xxv. 10
the Spyder, that doth lurke In *close* awayt, . . . *Am.* lxxi. 4
one of hers did *close* convay . . . *Epig.* ii. 5
mercie seate, *Close* covered with the Lambes integrity . . . *H.H.B.* 149
Close-bleeding. Written with teares in harts *close-bleeding* book. *Am.* i. 8
Closed. *closde* her eyes with carelesse quietnesse; . . . *D.* 257
Wherein were *closd* few drops of liquor pure, . . . I. ix. 19. 3
covering with a clod their *closed* eye, . . . II. i. 60. 4
they *closd* the earth agayne. . . . II. i. 61. 9
open to their friendes, and *closed* to their foes. . . . II. ix. 23. 9
That the dim eies . . . I mote have *closed,* . . . III. iv. 39. 5
fast *closed* in some hollow greave, . . . III. x. 42. 3
when charmes had *closed* it afore. . . . III. xii. 27. 9
closd up, as it had not beene bor'd; . . . III. xii. 38. 5
streight he *closd* the gate: . . . IV. x. 14. 4
The Lists were *closed* fast, . . . V. v. 5. 6
He with him *closd,* and, laying mightie hold Upon his throte, VI. iv. 22. 3
Closely. The subtill vermin, creeping *closely* neare, . . . *Van.* vi. 7
the next morrowes meed they *closely* ment, . . . *Hub.* 331
not so *closely* hide His craftie feates, . . . *Hub.* 919
closely as he might, he cast to leave The Court, . . . *Hub.* 935
the false Foxe . . . Fled *closely* forth, . . . *Hub.* 1360
lurking *closely,* in awayte now lay, . . . *Mui.* 247
Full *closely* creeping by the hinder side, . . . *Mui.* 403
streames . . . He under ground so *closely* did convay, . . . *Col.* 142
Where that false couple were full *closely* ment . . . I. ii. 5. 4
resemblaunce of Deceipt, I wist, Did *closely* lurke; . . . I. v. 27. 4
His wandring perill *closely* did lament, . . . I. vi. 32. 2
His warlike shield all *closely* cover'd was, . . . I. vii. 33. 1
closely did awayt Avauntage, . . . II. v. 9. 6
Them *closely* into Armorick did beare: . . . II. x. 64. 5
In strong entrenchments he did *closely* place, . . . II. xi. 6. 7
with teares which *closely* she did weepe. . . . III. ii. 28. 9
Was taken with her love, and by her *closely* lay. . . . III. iv. 19. 9
Mongst whom might be that he did *closely* lye, . . . III. vi. 16. 6
Closely the wicked flame his bowels brent, . . . III. vii. 16. 1
closely as she might, . . . III. vii. 18. 6
ever *closely* eide Sir Satyrane, . . . III. ix. 27. 4
So *closely* yet, that none but she it vewd, . . . III. x. 9. 4
He *closely* nearer crept the truth to weet: . . . III. x. 22. 6
So *closely* as he could he to them crept, . . . III. x. 49. 1
twixt her eielids *closely* spyde . . . III. xi. 32. 8
Did *closely* with a cruell one consent . . . IV. viii. 16. 7
Which all that while I *closely* had conceld; . . . IV. x. 55. 2
closely rankled under th' orifis: . . . IV. xii. 22. 7
Did *closely* harbour such a jealous guest) . . . V. vii. 27. 5
They in awayt would *closely* him ensnarle, . . . V. ix. 9. 3
Appear'd like Aspis sting that *closely* kils, . . . V. xii. 36. 4
his Ladie, . . . *closely* hid her selfe . . . VI. ii. 20. 4
The more he laughes, and does her *closely* quip, . . . VI. vii. 44. 8
closely tempted with their craftie spyes; . . . VI. viii. 43. 4
Thereat frown'd Coridon, and his lip *closely* bit. . . . VI. ix. 41. 9
all his paines did *closely* emulate; . . . VI. x. 33. 4
in his mind had *closely* made A further purpose, . . . VI. xi. 38. 7
closely did her wed, but knowne to few: . . . VI. xii. 5. 4

Closely—*Continued.*
One of those archers *closely* I did spy, . . . *Am.* xvi. 9
his mother *closely* smiling . . . *Epig.* iv. 11
Closes. The little Dazie, that at evening *closes,* . . . *Proth.* 31
Closet. In the deare *closett* of her painefull syde . . . III. ii. 11. 7
Into her fathers *closet* to repayre; . . . III. ii. 22. 2
She to his *closet* went, where all his wealth Lay hid; . . . III. x. 12. 3
Within the *closet* of her covert brest, . . . V. v. 44. 6
Deepe, in the *closet* of my parts entyre, . . . *Am.* lxxxiv. 9
Within the *closet* of her chastest bowre, . . . *H.H.B.* 249
Closing. it the Posterne did from *closing* stay: . . . V. x. 37. 5
closing it againe like as before, . . . VI. xii. 8. 3
Closure. in *closure* of a thankfull mynd, . . . *Col.* 580
Untill the *closure* of the Evening: . . . III. iii. 27. 5
Cloth. *See* **Clothe.**
Adorned all with costly *cloth* of gold, . . . *Ti.* 632
High above all a *cloth* of State was spred, . . . I. iv. 8. 1
in that *cloth* was wrought as if it lively grew. . . . III. i. 38. 9
'Royally clad' (quoth he) 'in *cloth* of gold, . . . III. v. 5. 2
All over her a *cloth* of state was spred, . . . V. ix. 28. 1
Not of rich tissew, nor of *cloth* of gold, . . . V. ix. 28. 2
Seemed those litle Angels did uphold The *cloth* of state, . . . V. ix. 29. 2
Clothd. *See* **Clothed.**
Clothe. Colours meete to *clothe* a mayden Queene? . . . *S.C.* F. 132
Where thickest grasse did *cloath* the open hills. . . . *Gn.* 74
To *cloath* her selfe in colours fresh and new, . . . *Gn.* 684
when flowres doo *clothe* the fruitful ground, . . . *Mui.* 114
of warlike armes despoile, And *cloth* in womens weedes: . . . V. iv. 31. 4
Clothed. now are *clothd* with mosse and hoary frost, . . . *S.C.* Ja. 33
Clothed with cold, and hoary wyth frost, . . . *S.C.* F. 79
the Ape anon Himselfe had *cloathed* like a Gentleman, . . . *Hub.* 660
He *cloathed* them with all colours, save white, . . . *Hub.* 1155
In a greene gowne he *clothed* was full faire, . . . I. iv. 25. 1
All in a kirtle of discolourd say He *clothed* was, . . . I. iv. 31. 2
feeble nature *cloth'd* with fleshly tyre. . . . II. i. 57. 3
the Moone, *cloathed* with clowdy night, . . . II. vii. 29. 8
Clothed with leaves, that none the wood mote see, . . . II. vii. 53. 8
flowing low and thick her *cloth'd* arownd, . . . II. xii. 67. 4
round about the walls *yclothed* were With goodly arras . . . III. xi. 28. 1
Daunger, *cloth'd* in ragged weed . . . III. xii. 11. 1
clothed all in garments made of line, . . . V. vii. 6. 4
Lastly, came Winter *cloathed* all in frize, . . . VII. vii. 31. 1
Clothes. *See* **Grave-clothes.**
with vile *cloaths* approach Gods majestie, . . . *Hub.* 465
other *clothes* he could not weare for heate; . . . I. iv. 22. 2
clothes meet to keepe keene cold away, . . . I. x. 39. 4
if that no spare *clothes* to give he had, . . . I. x. 39. 8
Pryene, rich arayd, In Claribellaes *clothes.* . . . II. iv. 28. 3
With costly *clothes* of Arras and of Toure; . . . III. i. 34. 2
displayd The *clothes* about her round . . . III. ii. 47. 5
he *clothes* with sinfull mire, . . . III. vi. 32. 7
That her gay *clothes* did in discolour die. . . . V. i. 14. 5
fearing death, and next to death the lacke Of *clothes* . . . VI. viii. 50. 4
Clotheth. this earthly myne Which *clotheth* it thereafter . . . *H.B.* 47
Clothing. with sheepes *clothing* doen hem disguise. . . . *S.C.* S. 157
Ycladde in *clothing* of seely sheepe, . . . *S.C.* S. 188
more for thrift did care than for gay *clothing:* . . . *Hub.* 231
Clotho. Sad *Clotho* held the rocke, . . . IV. ii. 48. 5
Which *Clotho* graunting shewed her the same. . . . IV. ii. 50. 6
Love . . . by *Clotho* being waked: . . . *H.L.* 63
Cloths. *See* **Clothes.**
Clotted. *See* **Clouted.**
Clouch, -es. *See* **Clutch, -es.**
Cloud. Into a *clowde* of dust sperst in the aire . . . *Bel.*[2] xiv. 13
a darke *clowde* (*cloude*[1]) shrouded her . . . *Pet.* vi. 7
No otherwise than raynie *cloud,* . . . *Ro.* xx. 1
On which the *clowde* of ghastly night did sit, . . . *D.* 305
A *cloud* of cumbrous gnattes doe him molest, . . . I. i. 23. 5
on those . . . dazed eyes . . . The *cloude* of death did sit. . . . I. iii. 39. 8
since faire Sunne hath sperst that lowring *clowd,* . . . I. iv. 48. 1
a darkesome *clowd* Upon him fell: . . . I. v. 13. 6
Covering your foe with *cloud* of deadly night, . . . I. v. 14. 7
knight . . . Lay cover'd with inchaunted *cloud* . . . I. v. 19. 6
the Paynim lay, . . . Coverd with charmed *cloud* . . . I. v. 29. 4
Phoebus, . . . His blushing face in foggy *cloud* implyes, . . . I. vi. 6. 7
Through smouldry *cloud* of duskish stincking smoke; . . . I. vii. 13. 8
As when a *cloud* his beames doth over-lay; . . . I. vii. 34. 7
A *cloud* of smoothering smoke, and sulphure seare, . . . I. xi. 13. 7
round about a *cloud* of dust did fly, . . . II. iv. 37. 4
as a *cloud* doth seeme to dim the skies; . . . II. ix. 16. 5
it doth, as *cloud* from sea, aryse. . . . II. ix. 42. 5
Is in a noyous *cloud* enveloped, . . . III. i. 43. 2
Covered with secret *cloud* of silent night, . . . III. iii. 61. 8
There a sad *cloud* of sleepe her overkest, . . . III. vi. 10. 8
in a *cloud* their light did long time stay, . . . III. ix. 20. 7
ycovered had Fayre heaven with an universall *clowd,* . . . III. xii. 1. 2
Like as a gloomie *cloud,* . . . the skie doth overcast . . . IV. i. 45. 5
A watry *cloud* doth overcast the skie, . . . IV. iv. 47. 7
To *cloud* my daies in dolefull misery, . . . IV. viii. 16. 8
in a watry *cloud* displayed wide Her goodly bow, . . . V. iii. 25. 2
though this *cloud* have now me overcast, . . . V. v. 38. 6
like a *cloud,* as likest may be told, . . . V. ix. 28. 4
with a *cloud* of night him covering, . . . V. xi. 14. 8
envies *cloud* still dimmeth vertues ray. . . . V. xii. 27. 7
With *cloud* of death upon her eyes displayd; . . . VI. xi. 21. 5
Yet did the *cloud* make . . . Seeme much more lovely . . . VI. xi. 21. 6
cloud of pryde, which oft doth dark Her goodly light, . . . *Am.* lxxxi. 7
like stars that dimmed were With darksome *cloud,* . . . *Epith.* 94
Clouded. *See* **Heavy-clouded.**
yclowded With fearefull shadowes of deformed night, . . . V. iv. 45. 1

Clouds. pierce the *cloudes,* and with hir wings — *Bel.*[1] vi. 7
with a larger flight To pierce the *cloudes,* — *Bel.*[2] vii. 6
sperst these *cloudes;* — *Bel.*[2] viii. 13
as the thonder cleaves the *cloudes,* — *S.C.* Au. 85
the *cloudes* wexen cleare. — *S.C.* S. 18
cloudes han all overcast. — *S.C.* D. 138
clap of thunder . . . *cloudes* asunder dryve. — *Gn.* 520
Carried in *clowdes* of all-concealing night. — *Hub.* 340
The liquid *clowdes,* and lucid firmament; — *Hub.* 1259
borne above the *cloudes* to be divin'd, — *Ti.* 611
he dared to stie Up to the *clowdes,* — *Mui.* 43
The day with *cloudes* was suddeine overcast, — I. i. 6. 5
Through riven *cloudes* and molten firmament; — I. viii. 9. 5
The *cloudes* before him fledd for terror great, — I. xi. 10. 8
Enwrapt in coleblacke *clowds* and filthy smoke, — I. xi. 44. 8
That vanisht into smoke and *cloudes* swift; — I. xi. 54. 2
drery death . . . made darke *clouds* appeare: — II. i. 45. 3
fowle smoke and *clouds* more black then Jett. — II. vii. 28. 9
cloudes of deadly night . . . his heavy eylids cover'd have, — II. viii. 24. 7
The *clowdes,* as thinges affrayd, before him flye; — II. viii. 48. 3
Like to thicke *clouds* that threat a stormy showre, — III. iv. 43. 3
a ship, whose Lodestar suddeinly Covered with *cloudes* — III. iv. 53. 4
water of the ford, Or of the *clouds,* — III. vi. 34. 8
The soring *clouds* into sad showres ymolt; — III. xi. 25. 8
rould in *clouds* to heaven did aspire, — IV. x. 38. 4
thee the winds, the *clouds* doe feare, — IV. x. 44. 6
Breathing out *clouds* of sulphure fowle and blacke, — V. xi. 32. 2
Through the thicke *clouds* in which they steeped lay — VI. iii. 13. 6
Like a sweet Angell twixt two *clouds* uphild; — VI. xi. 21. 3
the *clouds* are also tost and roll'd, — VII. vii. 20. 8
I, whose star, . . . with *cloudes* is over-cast, — *Am.* xxxiv. 6
after stormes, when *clouds* begin to cleare, — *H.L.* 276

Cloudy. And *clowdie* Welkin cleareth. — *S.C.* Mar. 12
In *clowdie* teares my case I thus complaine — *Gn. Ded.* 3
cloudy tempests have The faithfull light . . . yblent, — II. vii. 1. 3
the Moone, cloathed with *clowdy* night, — II. vii. 29. 8
More hidden are then Sunne in *cloudy* vele; — III. iii. 19. 6
disclo'ste Her *clowdy* care into a wrathfull stowre, — III. iv. 13. 8
Covered with *cloudie* storme and bitter showre, — IV. v. 32. 2
lovely light to cleare my *cloudy* grief, — *Am.* xxxiv. 12
that sunshine, when *cloudy* looks are cleared. — *Am.* xl. 14

Clout. laughes the songs that Colin *Clout* doth make. — *S.C.* Ja. 66
His hinder heele was wrapt in a *clout,* — *S.C.* May 243
Colin *Clout* rafte me of his brother, — *S.C.* Au. 40
Colin *Clout,* I wene, be his selfe boye, — *S.C.* S. 176
Colin *Cloute* she would not once disdayne; — *S.C.* N. 101
unwise and witlesse Colin *Cloute,* — *S.C.* D. 91
his Colin, carelesse Colin *Cloute,* — *Ti.* 225
'Ah far be it (quoth Colin *Clout*) fro me, — *Col.* 464
they all agree That Colin *Clout* should pipe, — VI. ix. 41. 6
That jolly shepheard . . . was Poore Colin *Clout,* — VI. x. 16. 4
(who knowes not Colin *Clout?*) — VI. x. 16. 4

Clouted. Ewe, Whose *clouted* legge her hurt doth shewe, — *S.C.* Mar. 50
give him curds and *clouted* Creame. — *S.C.* N. 99

Clouts. His garment, nought but many ragged *clouts,* — I. ix. 36. 1

Clove. *See* **Clave, Cleaved, Cleft.**
there *clove* unto her keele A little fish, — *Van.* ix. 9
into diverse doubt his wavering wonder *clove.* — II. ii. 3. 9
quite it *clove* his plumed crest in tway, — II. vi. 31. 7

Cloven. Had he not stouped so, he should have *cloven* bee. — I. v. 12. 9
He had him surely *cloven* quite in twaine: — V. xi. 10. 6

Clown. The homely shepheard, nor the ruder *clowne;* — *Pet.* iv. 4
Abandon, then, the base and viler *clowne;* — *S.C.* O. 37
boldly bent Against the silly *clowne,* — III. viii. 12. 6
Such homely what as serves the simple *clowne,* — VI. ix. 7. 4
ne mote the ruder *clowne,* Thereto approch; — VI. x. 7. 4
seem'd to be some sorie simple *clowne,* — VI. xi. 27. 3

Clownish. a barbarous troupe of *clownish* fone — *Bel.*[2] v. 10
His *clownish* gifts and curtsies I disdaine, — *S.C.* Ja. 57
with his *clownish* hands their tender wings He brusheth — I. i. 23. 8
bruze with *clownish* fistes his manly face; — II. iv. 9. 2
in his *clownish* hand a sharp bore speare he shooke. — III. i. 17. 9

Cloyed. with his cruell tuske him deadly *cloyd:* — III. vi. 48. 4
'With sight whereof soone *cloyd,* — VI. ix. 25. 1

Club. lifting up his dreadfull *club* on hight, — I. viii. 7. 3
His boystrous *club,* . . . He could not rearen up — I. viii. 10. 1
whiles he strove his combred *clubbe* to quight — I. viii. 10. 4
his hideous *club* aloft he dites, — I. viii. 18. 4
In his right hand an yron *club* he held, — II. vii. 40. 6
His harmefull *club* he gan to hurtle hye, — II. vii. 42. 3
with his craggy *club* in his right hand — IV. vii. 25. 6
with his *club* me threatned to have brayned, — IV. x. 36. 5
monstrous tyrants with his *club* subdewed: — V. i. 2. 8
The *club* of Justice dread with kingly powre endewed. — V. i. 2. 9
his huge *club,* which had subdew'd of old So many monsters — V. v. 24. 5
after that his monstrous father fell Under Alcides *club,* — V. x. 11. 3
in his hand a mighty yron *club* he bore. — VI. vii. 43. 9
with his yron *club* to ground him strooke; — VI. vii. 48. 4
when she saw him fall Under that villaines *club,* — VI. vii. 50. 2
with his yron *club* preparing way, — VI. viii. 8. 2
with his *club* bet backe his brondyron bright — VI. viii. 10. 4
with his *club* him all about so blist, — VI. viii. 13. 4
Under his *club* with wary boldnesse went, — VI. viii. 15. 8

Clubs. Some with unweldy *clubs,* some with long speares, — II. ix. 13. 6

Cluster. *cluster* thicke unto his leasings vaine, — V. ii. 33. 2
as a swarme Of flyes upon a birchen bough doth *cluster,* — V. xi. 58. 2

Clustering. in the aire their *clustring* army flies, — II. ix. 16. 4

Clusters. Her deeds were like great *clusters* of ripe grapes, — *Col.* 600
like a sort of Bees in *clusters* swarmed: — V. iv. 36. 7

Clutch. Ever to come into his *clouch* againe, — III. x. 20. 2

Clutches. in the compasse of his *clouches* tooke; — V. ix. 11. 4

Cnidus. Or it in *Gnidus* bee, I wote not well; — III. vi. 29. 5

Coach. The roiall Dame, . . . for her *coche* doth call: — I. iv. 16. 2
So forth she comes, and to her *coche* does clyme, — I. iv. 17. 1
Eftsoones out of her *Coch* she gan availe, — IV. iii. 46. 4
Unto her *Coch* remounting, home did ride, — IV. iii. 51. 8
All ready to her silver *coche* to clyme; — *Epith.* 76

Coaches. Then all the rest into their *coches* clim, — III. iv. 42. 6

Coal. (whote *cole* on her tongue!) — *S.C.* S. 112
Then first the *cole* of kindly heat appeares — I. ix. 9. 3
as a *cole* to kindle fleshly flame, — III. i. 50. 2

Coal-black. *cole-black* blood forth gushed from her corse. — I. i. 24. 9
darkesome night had all displayd Her *coleblacke* curtein — I. iv. 44. 2
cole blacke steedes yborne of hellish brood, — I. v. 20. 8
Enwrapt in *coleblacke* clowds and filthy smoke, — I. xi. 44. 8
His *cole-blacke* hands did seeme to have ben seard — II. vii. 3. 8
A streame of *coleblacke* bloud thence gusht amaine, — IV. vii. 27. 8

Coals. his enemie Had kindled such *coles* of displeasure, — *S.C.* F. 191
kindle *coales* of conteck and yre, — *S.C.* S. 86
A Satyre . . . kindling *coles* of lust in brutish eye, — I. vi. 22. 7
love fresh *coles* unto her fire did lay; — I. vii. 27. 5
Coles of contention and whot vengeaunce tind. — II. viii. 11. 5
kindling *coles* of cruell enmity, — II. x. 33. 5
Did privily put *coles* unto his secret fire. — IV. ii. 11. 9
Like *coles* that through a silver Censer sparkle bright. — V. vi. 38. 9
In my true love did stirre up *coles* of yre; — *Am.* lxxxv. 8

Coast. *See* **Sea-coast.**
I chaunst to see Upon the Latine *Coast* — *Bel.*[2] xiii. 4
from the Northerne *coast* a storme arose, — *Bel.*[2] xiv. 10
angry Gods pursue from *coste* to *coste,* — *S.C.* Jun. 15
That wardes the Westerne *coste?* — *S.C.* Jul. 42
his blustring blast eche *coste* dooth scoure. — *S.C.* D. 132
this Curdog, by my *coste,* . . . will serve — *Hub.* 294
from the one he could to th' other *coast* Stretch — *Ti.* 540
Through the wide compas of the ayrie *coast;* — *Mui.* 38
Where towards me a sory wight did *cost,* — *D.* 39
to the Easterne *coast* of heaven makes speedy way: — I. v. 19. 9
From every *coast* that heaven walks about — I. vii. 45. 3
contend With either of those knightes on even *coast,* — II. iii. 17. 3
Under what *coast* of heaven the man did dwell, — III. iii. 6. 5
The watry Southwinde, from the seabord *coste* Upblowing, — III. iv. 13. 4
Once thinke to match three such on equall *cost,* — IV. iii. 24. 8
First from one *coast,* — IV. ix. 33. 7
From every *coast* and countrie under sunne: — V. iii. 6. 2
Towards which *coast* her love his way addrest: — V. vi. 7. 5
in one day they with the *coast* did fall; — V. xii. 4. 6
At length espyes at hand the happie *cost,* — VI. xi. 44. 8
Directs her course unto one certaine *cost,* — VI. xii. 1. 2
Bade her attonce from heavens *coast* to pack, — VII. vi. 12. 8
Thieves should rob and spoile that *Coast* around: — VII. vi. 55. 6

Coasted. So towardes them they *coasted,* — V. ii. 29. 8

Coasts. In forrein *costes* men sayd was plentye; — *S.C.* S. 28
were wount To skim those *coastes* — VI. xi. 9. 3

Coat. tooke out the Woolfe in his counterfect *cote,* — *S.C.* S. 206
Ne . . . would he sometimes scorne A Pandares *coate* — *Hub.* 808
thred-bare *cote,* and cobled shoes, hee ware; — I. iv. 28. 2
His owne *cote* he would cut, — I. x. 39. 9
cote of steele, so couched neare That nought mote perce; — I. xi. 9. 2
His yron *cote,* all overgrowne with rust, — II. vii. 4. 1
a discolour'd *cote* of straunge disguyse, — III. xii. 10. 2
So forth he came, all in a *cote* of plate — V. viii. 29. 1
All armed in a *cote* of yron plate — V. xii. 14. 3

Coat-armour. In whose *cote-armour* richly are displayd — *Am.* lxx. 2

Coated. *See* **Iron-coated.**

Cobbled. thred-bare cote, and *cobled* shoes, hee ware; — I. iv. 28. 2

Cobweb. like a *cobweb* weaving slenderly, — *Gn.* 3
forth caried Into the cursed *cobweb,* — *Mui.* 423

Coch(e), -s. *See* **Coach, -s.**

Cock. As *cocke* on his dunghill crowing cranck. — *S.C.* S. 46
now the crowing *Cocke,* and now the Owle — IV. v. 41. 8

Cockatrices. kill with looks as *Cockatrices* doo: — *Am.* xlix. 10

Cock-boat. to guide the *cock-bote* well, — III. viii. 24. 4

Cocked. under the *cocked* hay. — *S.C.* N. 12

Cockle. *Cockel* for corne, and chaffe for barley, — *S.C.* D. 124

Cocytus. Gorgon, . . . At which *Cocytus* quakes, — I. i. 37. 9
That is the river of *Cocytus* deepe, — II. vii. 56. 8
by the grim floud of *Cocytus* slow, — III. iv. 55. 5

Coffer. A curious *Coffer* made of Heben wood, — *Ti.* 618
In whose brave mynd, as in a golden *cofer,* — *Col.* 488
there before them stood a *Coffer* strong — V. iv. 5. 1
She chaunst unwares to light upon this *coffer,* — V. iv. 10. 8
in this *coffer* which she with her brought — V. iv. 13. 1

Coffers. Two iron *coffers* hong on either side, — I. iv. 27. 3
huge great yron chests, and *coffers* strong, — II. vii. 30. 2
therewith fill The *coffers* of her wicked threasury, — V. ii. 9. 4

Cognizance. Eftsoones of him had perfect *cognizaunce,* — II. i. 31. 5

Coil(l)us. *See* **Coyll.**

Coin. in his lap an heap of *coine* he told; — I. iv. 27. 5
in his lap a masse of *coyne* he told, — II. vii. 4. 7
Gan *coyne* streight lawes to curb their liberty: — III. ii. 2. 6

Coined. Her deeds were forged, and her words false *coynd,* — III. xii. 14. 8

Colchester. He of his name *Coylchester* built of stone and lime. — II. x. 58. 9

Colchic. on *Colchicke* strand Her brothers bones she scattered — V. viii. 47. 3

Colchid. Atcheived the golden Fleece in *Colchid* land, — *Ro.* x. 2
With them that cruell *Colchid* mother dwells, — *Gn.* 397

Cold. *See* **Stony-cold.**
her bodie turn'd to ashes *colde.* — *Bel.*[2] vii. 12
wrathfull winde, Which blows *cold* storms, — *Bel.*[2] viii. 12
Into the Gothicke *colde* hot rage instil'd. — *Ro.* xi. 8
Did brave about the corpes of Hector *colde;* — *Ro.* xiv. 10

Cold—*Continued.*
where *colde* Boreas blowes his bitter stormes. . . . *Ro.* xxvi. 8
My life-bloud friesing with unkindly *cold;* . . . *S.C.* Ja. 26
The kene *cold* blowes through my beaten hyde, . . . *S.C.* F. 3
Yet never complained of *cold* nor heate, . . . *S.C.* F. 19
This chill, that *cold;* this crooked, that wrye; . . . *S.C.* F. 28
Tho gynne you, fond flyes! the *cold* to scorne, . . . *S.C.* F. 39
Your carefull heards with *cold* bene annoied: . . . *S.C.* F. 48
Clothed with *cold,* and hoary wyth frost, . . . *S.C.* F. 79
The rather Lambes bene starved with *cold,* . . . *S.C.* F. 83
with great *cold* he had gotte the gout. . . . *S.C.* May 244
All the *cold* season to wach and waite; . . . *S.C.* S. 237
'The carefull *cold* hath nypt my rugged rynde, . . . *S.C.* D. 133
Colde Lettuce, and refreshing Rosmarine. . . . *Mui.* 200
on the *cold* deare earth himselfe did throw; . . . *As.* 124
Where *cold* and care and penury do dwell, . . . *Col.* 657
Through him the *cold* began to covet heat, . . . *Col.* 847
though a tree I seme, yet *cold* and heat me paines.' . . . I. ii. 33. 9
full of . . . *cold* affray, Gan shut the dore. . . . I. iii. 12. 7
faith . . . The creeping deadly *cold* away did shake: . . . I. v. 12. 4
suddein *cold* did ronne through every vaine, . . . I. vi. 37. 2
crudled *cold* his corage gan assayle, . . . I. vii. 6. 7
let the stony dart of sencelesse *cold* Perce to my hart, . . . I. vii. 22. 7
The carefull *cold* beginneth for to creep, . . . I. vii. 39. 4
Him to avenge before his blood were *cold,* . . . I. ix. 37. 5
cold that makes the hart to quake, . . . I. ix. 44. 7
The crudled *cold* ran to her well of life, . . . I. ix. 52. 2
clothes meet to keepe keene *cold* away, . . . I. x. 39. 4
Himselfe refreshing with the liquid *cold,* . . . II. i. 24. 8
his fresh blood did frieze with fearefull *cold,* . . . II. i. 42. 3
if the stony *cold* Have not all seized . . . II. i. 46. 5
Yet *colde* through feare . . . II. ii. 9. 3
Nor sea of licour *cold,* nor lake of myre: . . . II. vi. 44. 4
Cold Coloquintida, and Tetra mad; . . . II. vii. 52. 4
the *cold* liquor which he waded in; . . . II. vii. 58. 3
Vile is the vengeaunce on the ashes *cold,* . . . II. viii. 13. 6
Now seeming flaming whott, now stony *cold:* . . . II. ix. 39. 5
All naked without shame or care of *cold,* . . . II. x. 7. 6
as *cold* and drery as a snake, . . . II. xi. 22. 4
Nor scorching heat, nor *cold* intemperate, . . . II. xii. 51. 5
shewd him many sights that corage *cold* could reare. . . . II. xii. 68. 9
To doe the frosen *cold* away to fly; . . . III. ii. 34. 5
The *cold* earth was his couch, . . . III. iv. 53. 9
did bind the wound from *cold* to keepe. . . . III. v. 33. 9
After her heat the breathing *cold* to taste: . . . III. vi. 18. 5
her faint hart was with the frosen *cold* Benumbd . . . III. viii. 34. 7
the *cold* ysickles from his rough beard . . . III. viii. 35. 3
Troynovant was built of old Troyes ashes *cold.* . . . III. ix. 38. 9
overthrowne and laide on th' earth full *cold,* . . . III. ix. 50. 5
in his *cold* complexion doe breed A filthy blood, . . . III. x. 59. 3
There on the *cold* earth him now thrown she found, . . . III. xii. 43. *or.*6
As fayning choler which was turn'd to *cold:* . . . IV. vi. 27. 2
(welcommed with *cold* And chearelesse hunger) . . . IV. viii. 28. 1
Her graunted love, but with affection *cold,* . . . IV. viii. 53. 5
feele their corage *cold.* . . . IV. x. 18. 5
Cold yron chaines with which let him be tide; . . . V. v. 50. 8
bake their sides upon the *cold* hard stone, . . . V. vii. 9. 3
These eyes him saw upon the *cold* earth sprad, . . . VI. ii. 45. 7
to sleepe, Cover'd with *cold,* and wrapt in wretchednesse; . . . VI. iii. 44. 7
giveth comfort to her courage *cold:* . . . VI. iv. 1. 5
On the *cold* ground maugre himselfe he threw . . . VI. iv. 40. 3
the *cold* steele, through piercing, did devowre His vitall breath, VI. vii. 8. 7
gainst the *cold* hard earth so sore him strake, . . . VI. vii. 11. 4
'He lyes' (said he) 'upon the *cold* bare ground, . . . VI. vii. 16. 6
Now boyling hot, streight friezing deadly *cold;* . . . VII. vii. 23. 3
Chattering his teeth for *cold* that did him chill; . . . VII. vii. 31. 2
he was faint with *cold,* and weak with eld, . . . VII. vii. 31. 8
through merry feasting . . . did not the *cold* remember; . . . VII. vii. 41. 3
wrapped well . . . to keep the *cold* away; . . . VII. vii. 42. 2
lastly came *cold* February, . . . VII. vii. 43. 1
her *cold* so great Is not dissolv'd . . . *Am.* xxx. 2
delayd by her hart-frosen *cold;* . . . *Am.* xxx. 6
yse, which is congeald with sencelesse *cold,* . . . *Am.* xxx. 11
Which in the barraine *cold* he doth inspyre. . . . *H.L.* 98
Cold-congealed. That sight thereof bredd *cold congealed* feare; I. xi. 13. 5
Coldness. A stonie *coldnesse* hath benumbd the sence . . . *T.M.* 253
Ne could he brooke the *coldnesse* of the stony masse. . . . VI. iv. 21. 9
Cole. The morish *Cole,* and the soft sliding Breane, . . . IV. xi. 29. 6
Coles. *See* **Coals.**
Coleworts. Fat *Colworts,* and comforting Perseline, . . . *Mui.* 199
Colin. *Colin* them gives to Rosalind againe. . . . *S.C.* Ja. 60
laughes the songs that *Colin* Clout doth make. . . . *S.C.* Ja. 66
Colin thou kenst, the Southerne shepheardes boye; . . . *S.C.* Ap. 21
Lo! *Collin,* here the place . . . *S.C.* Jun. 1
Colin, to heare thy rymes . . . *S.C.* Jun. 49
O, carefull *Colin!* I lament thy case; . . . *S.C.* Jun. 113
Colin Clout rafte me of his brother, . . . *S.C.* Au. 40
never heardest thou but *Colin* sing. . . . *S.C.* Au. 50
a doolefull verse Of Rosalend . . . That *Colin* made? . . . *S.C.* Au. 142
O *Colin, Colin!* the shepheards joye, . . . *S.C.* Au. 193
Colin Clout, I wene, be his selfe boye, . . . *S.C.* S. 176
(Ah, for *Colin,* he whilome my ioye!) . . . *S.C.* S. 177
Colin fittes such famous flight to scanne; . . . *S.C.* O. 88
Colin, my deare, when shall it please thee sing, . . . *S.C.* N. 1
Should *Colin* make judge of my fooleree: . . . *S.C.* N. 28
The songs that *Colin* made you in her praise, . . . *S.C.* N. 78
Colin Cloute she would not once disdayne; . . . *S.C.* N. 101
Up, *Colin* up! ynough thou morned hast; . . . *S.C.* N. 207
The gentle shepheard . . . That *Colin* hight, . . . *S.C.* D. 3
The wiser Muses after *Colin* ranne. . . . *S.C.* D. 48

Colin—*Continued.*
unwise and witlesse *Colin* Cloute, . . . *S.C.* D. 91
Tell Rosalind, her *Colin* bids her adieu.' . . . *S.C.* D. 156
his *Colin,* carelesse *Colin* Cloute, . . . *Ti.* 225
her own Shepheard, *Colin,* her owne Shepherd, . . . *D.* 229
'*Colin,* my liefe, my life, . . . *Col.* 16
I would request thee, *Colin,* for my sake, . . . *Col.* 83
Who all that *Colin* makes do covet faine.' . . . *Col.* 99
Worthie of *Colin* selfe, that did it make. . . . *Col.* 158
But tell on further, *Colin,* as befell . . . *Col.* 176
(then quoth *Colin*) . . . *Col.* 292
Colin, thy selfe thou mak'st us more to wonder, . . . *Col.* 354
nay (said *Colin*) . . . *Col.* 376
'Ah far be it (quoth *Colin* Clout) fro me, . . . *Col.* 464
'*Colin,* well worthie were those goodly favours . . . *Col.* 585
'*Colin,* (said Cuddy then) . . . *Col.* 616
bountie . . . Which she to *Colin* her poore shepheard shewed.' *Col.* 647
'Why *Colin,* since thou foundst such grace . . . *Col.* 652
'Happie indeed (said *Colin*) I him hold, . . . *Col.* 660
'Ah! *Colin,* (then said Hobbinol) . . . *Col.* 731
(said *Colin*) passeth reasons reach, . . . *Col.* 837
'*Colin,* thou now full deeply hast divynd . . . *Col.* 896
'Ah! shepheards, (then said *Colin*) . . . *Col.* 927
they all agree That *Colin* Clout should pipe, . . . VI. ix. 41. 6
That jolly shepheard . . . was Poore *Colin* Clout, . . . VI. x. 16. 4
(who knowes not *Colin* Clout?) . . . VI. x. 16. 4
That Shepheard *Colin* dearely did condole, . . . VII. vi. 40. 5
Colinet. The rurall song of carefull *Colinet.* . . . *S.C.* D. 18
Colin's. was thilk same song of *Colins* owne making? . . . *S.C.* Ap. 154
thou shalt ycrouned be In *Colins* stede, . . . *S.C.* Au. 146
cared more for *Colins* carolings . . . VI. ix. 35. 7
the Graces daunce To *Colins* melody; . . . VI. x. Arg.
Collar. He would have slipt the *coller* handsomly, . . . *Hub.* 269
on his *collar* laying puissaunt hand, . . . III. vii. 43. 1
Uppon his iron *coller* griped fast, . . . V. ii. 14. 4
With a strong yron chaine and *coller* bound, . . . V. ix. 33. 6
his left hand upon his *collar* layd. . . . VI. vii. 25. 6
Collected. all my cares, which cruell Love *collected,* . . . *Epith.* 317
Colled. Shee streightly straynd, and *colled* tenderly; . . . III. ii. 34. 2
Collusion. the Foxe, maister of *collusion:* . . . *S.C.* May 219
Colony. enstall A new unknowen *Colony* therein, . . . *H.H.L.* 104
Coloquintida. Cold *Coloquintida,* and Tetra mad; . . . II. vii. 52. 4
Color. a Woman . . . of Orenge *colour* hew: . . . *Rev.* ii. 2
under *colour* of shepeheards, . . . *S.C.* May 126
I am a poore sheepe, albe my *coloure* donne, . . . *S.C.* May 266
we may *coulor* it with some pretext . . . *Hub.* 988
under *colour* of the confidence . . . *Hub.* 1164
could not *colour* yet so well the troth, . . . II. ii. 34. 4
chaunge of *colour* did perforce unfold, . . . II. xi. 39. 4
What *colour* were their waters that same day, . . . II. x. 24. 3
Colour thy name with foule reproaches rust! . . . IV. i. 53. 7
a steele-cap he did weare Of *colour* rustie-browne, . . . V. xii. 14. 6
To give faire *colour* to that Ladies cause . . . VI. iii. 16. 9
he *colour* might Both his estate and love from skill . . . VI. x. 37. 8
Colorable. 'Glauce, what needes this *colourable* word . . . III. iii. 19. 3
Colored. *See* **Divers-colored.**
His *colowred* crime with craft to cloke. . . . *S.C.* F. 162
craft, *coloured* with simplicitie: . . . *S.C.* May 303
The *coloured* chaplets wrought with a chiefe, . . . *S.C.* N. 115
like the *coloured* Rainbowe arched wide: . . . *Ti.* 550
Shakt his long locks *colourd* like copper-wyre, . . . II. iv. 15. 8
the rich metall was so *coloured,* . . . II. xii. 61. 3
I in *colourd* showes may shadow itt, . . . III. Pr. 3. 8
Her mantle, *colour'd* like the starry skyes, . . . III. i. 36. 2
clapt on hye his *coulourd* winges twaine, . . . III. xii. 23. 7
with *colourd* ribbands drest: . . . IV. viii. 10. 4
the blame might salve with *coloured* disguize. . . . VI. iii. 8. 9
a thin silken cassock *coloured* greene, . . . VII. vii. 29. 2
Colors. To peinct their girlonds with his *colowres;* . . . *S.C.* F. 121
Colours meete to clothe a mayden Queene? . . . *S.C.* F. 132
Theyr sondry *colours* tourne. . . . *S.C.* N. 129
With sundrie *colours* paints the sprinckled lay: . . . *Gn.* 110
To cloath her selfe in *colours* fresh and new, . . . *Gn.* 684
He cloathed them with all *colours,* save white, . . . *Hub.* 1155
so gay were dyde In *colours* divers, . . . *T.M.* 238
Painted with thousand *colours,* . . . *Mui.* 90
Not halfe so manie sundrie *colours* . . . *Mui.* 92
So many goodly *colours* doth containe. . . . *Mui.* 96
His glorious *colours,* and his glistering eies. . . . *Mui.* 336
In which all *colours* of the rainbow bee; . . . *Col.* 341
cast her *coulours* . . . To seeme like truth, . . . I. vii. 1. 4
On which was drawen faire, in *colours* fit, . . . II. iv. 38. 2
breath out bounteous smels, and painted *colors* shew. . . . II. v. 29. 9
dispainted all within With sondry *colours,* . . . II. ix. 50. 2
wanting *colours* fayre To paint it forth, . . . II. x. 28. 6
in living *colours,* and right hew, . . . III. Pr. 4. 1
with fresh *colours* decke the wanton Pryme, . . . III. vi. 42. 4
thousand spots of *colours* queint elect, . . . III. vii. 22. 5
by the *colours* in his crest, That Paridell it was. . . . III. viii. 45. 5
On which the winged boy in *colours* cleare Depeincted was, . III. xi. 7. 7
in thy *colours* bright Wast there enwoven, . . . III. xi. 36. 1
winges it had with sondry *colours* dight, . . . III. xi. 47. 6
More sondry *colours* then the proud Pavone Beares . . . III. xi. 47. 7
As ever could Cameleon *colours* new; . . . IV. i. 18. 4
So could she forge all *colours,* save the trew. . . . IV. i. 18. 5
So blind is lust false *colours* to descry. . . . IV. ii. 11. 5
a riband new, In which his Ladies *colours* were, . . . IV. viii. 7. 2
Both clad in *colours* like, . . . IV. xi. 47. 8
Dismayd so with the stroke that he no *colours* knew. . . . V. iv. 39. 9
With fayned *colours* shading a true case; . . . V. vii. 2. 7

Come—*Continued.*
now I *come* into my course againe, VI. xii. 2. 6
to the Clergy now was *come* at last; VII. xii. 23. 3
come before high Jove her dooings to discharge. VII. vi. 17. 9
Till to the Plaine she *come,* whose Valleyes she doth drowne. VII. vi. 41. 9
time shall *come* that all shall changed bee, VII. vii. 59. 4
if . . . Thou chance to *come,* fall lowly at her feet; *Am.* ii. 10
For lusty Spring . . . Is ready to *come* forth, *Am.* iv. 10
But Angels *come* to lead fraile mindes to rest *Am.* viii. 7
She chaunst to *come* where Cupid lay, *Epig.* ii. 2
For lo! the wished day is *come* at last, *Epith.* 31
when you *come* whereas my love doth lie, *Epith.* 65
Come now, ye damzels, daughters of delight, *Epith.* 96
first *come* ye fayre houres, *Epith.* 98
Now is my love all ready forth to *come:* *Epith.* 110
When so ye *come* into those holy places, *Epith.* 213
lende me leave to *come* unto my love? *Epith.* 279
The night is *come,* now soon her disaray, *Epith.* 300
Come, then, O *come,* thou mightie God of Love, *H.L.* 22
Come softly, and my feeble breast inspire *H.L.* 27
To *come* at length unto the wished scope *H.L.* 296
Untill they *come* to their first Movers bound, *H.H.B.* 72
Could once *come* neare this beauty soverayne. *H.H.B.* 217
two Swannes . . . *Come* softly swimming *Proth.* 38
Comedy. mask in myrth lyke to a *Comedy:* *Am.* liv. 6
Comeliness. augment her price through praise of *comlinesse.* VI. xi. 11. 9
Comely. bound in sheaves, and layd in *comely* rowes, *Ro.* xxx. 7
walkes upright with *comely* stedfast pace, *Hub.* 728
Through due deserts and *comely* carriage, *Hub.* 777
excelling far each other, In *comely* shape, *As.* 16
His Lady, . . . Did yield her *comely* person to be at my call. I. ii. 36. 9
Thereby his mortall blade full *comely* hong I. vii. 30. 6
entertaines with *comely* courteous glee; I. x. 6. 5
a gentle Squyre, . . . clad in *comely* sad attyre; I. x. 7. 3
With goodly grace and *comely* personage, I. x. 30. 3
The *comely* virgins came, with girlands dight, I. xii. 6. 6
Of *comely* services, or courtly trayne? I. xii. 14. 4
His carriage was full *comely* and upright; II. i. 6. 1
A *comely* Palmer, clad in black attyre, II. i. 7. 2
A sober sad and *comely* courteous Dame; II. ii. 14. 5
She led him up . . . And *comely* courted II. ii. 15. 2
Unworthy of faire Ladies *comely* governaunce. II. ii. 35. 9
with bold grace, and *comely* gravity, II. ii. 39. 7
fowly battered his *comely* corse, II. v. 23. 5
with thy brutenesse shendst thy *comely* age, II. viii. 12. 3
With *comely* compasse and compacture strong, II. ix. 24. 8
At th' upper end there sate . . . a *comely* personage, II. ix. 27. 6
A carefull man, and full of *comely* guyse. II. ix. 31. 2
A *comely* personage of stature tall, II. xii. 46. 4
Under that Porch a *comely* dame did rest II. xii. 55. 7
streight of beastes they *comely* men became; II. xii. 86. 2
they were entertaynd with courteous And *comely* glee III. i. 31. 5
Without regard of grace or *comely* amenaunce. III. i. 41. 9
A jolly person, and of *comely* vew; III. i. 45. 2
A *comely* knight, all arm'd in complete wize, III. ii. 24. 2
Sett by it selfe, and ranckt in *comely* rew; III. vi. 35. 4
a *comely* personage And lovely face, III. vii. 46. 2
They beene ybrought into a *comely* bowre, III. ix. 19. 1
Shee came in presence with right *comely* grace, III. ix. 26. 7
With *comely* haveour and count'nance sage, III. xii. 3. 8
with her feeble feete did move a *comely* pace. III. xii. 19. 9
The which he never wont to combe, or *comely* sheare. IV. v. 34. 9
her against sate *comely* Curtesie, IV. x. 51. 3
sad Asopus, *comely* with his hoarie head. IV. xi. 14. 9
Adorn'd with honor and all *comely* grace: V. iii. 23. 2
two *comely* Squires, Both brethren, V. iv. 4. 2
Spinning and carding all in *comely* rew, V. v. 22. 4
Timely to joy and carrie *comely* cheare: V. v. 38. 5
gan gently her salute . . . in the most *comely* wize; V. vi. 20. 2
with long locks *comely* kemd, V. vii. 4. 5
the bloosme of *comely* courtesie; VI. Pr. 4. 2
comely guize withall And gracious speach, VI. i. 2. 5
by chaunce a *comely* Squire he found, VI. i. 11. 2
forth together rode, a *comely* couplement. VI. v. 24. 9
A faire young Mayden, full of *comely* glee; VI. vi. 10. 7
for these Carles to carry much more *comely* were?' VI. viii. 23. 9
comely carriage of her count'nance trim, VI. ix. 9. 4
gracious gifts bestow, . . . As *comely* carriage, VI. x. 23. 4
to recomfort him all *comely* meanes did frame. VI. x. 29. 9
nor her golden haire Into their *comely* tresses dewly drest, VI. xii. 15. 4
Unspotted fayth, and *comely* womanhood, *Epith.* 192
He fashiond them as *comely* as he could, *H.B.* 33
comely composition Of parts well measurd, *H.B.* 69
A *comely* corps, with beautie faire endewed, *H.B.* 135
Comen. *See* **Come.**
Comenly. *See* **Commonly.**
Comer's. To warde the same, nor answere *commers* call. I. viii. 3. 4
Comers-by. To call in *commers-by* that needy were I. x. 36. 9
Comes. *See* **Overcomes.**
Comes the breme Winter with chamfred browes, *S.C.* F. 43
the Sprite . . . unto Morpheus *comes,* I. i. 40. 8
He . . . to the virgin *comes;* I. iii. 40. 1
So forth she *comes;* her brightnes brode doth blaze. I. iv. 16. 6
So forth she *comes,* and to her coche does clyme, I. iv. 17. 1
Uprose Duessa . . . And to the Paynims lodging *comes* I. iv. 44. 9
forth he *comes* into the commune hall; I. v. 3. 1
Soone after *comes* the cruell Sarazin, I. v. 4. 1
At last forth *comes* that far renowmed Queene: I. v. 5. 1
comes unto the place where th' Hethen knight . . . Lay I. v. 19. 4
loe! he *comes,* he *comes* fast after mee.' I. ix. 25. 2

Comes—*Continued.*
help never *comes* too late.' II. i. 44. 9
'From thence it *comes,* that this babes II. ii. 10. 1
'here *comes,* and is hard by, A knight II. iv. 40. 5
Shee *comes* unsought, and shonned followes eke. II. iv. 44. 3
yonder *comes* the prowest knight alive, II. viii. 18. 3
Now *comes* to point of that same perilous sted, II. xii. 1. 7
forth from virgin bowre she *comes* in th' early morne. II. xii. 50. 9
soone *comes* age that will her pride deflowre; II. xii. 75. 7
soone as maistery *comes* III. i. 25. 8
their forren foe that *commes* from farre, III. iii. 23. 8
He *comes* not here; we scorne his foolish joy, III. vi. 24. 4
Like as the tide, that *comes* fro th' Ocean mayne, IV. iii. 27. 1
Sweete is the love that *comes* alone with willingnesse. IV. v. 25. 9
He *comes* to Proteus hall, IV. xi. Arg.
Who all that *comes* doth take, V. ii. 9. 3
So *comes* it now to Florimell by tourne, V. iii. 1. 6
Britomart *comes* to Isis Church, V. vii. Arg.
Till that, as *comes* by course, I doe recite VI. vi. 17. 4
To whom Sir Calidore yet sweating *comes,* VI. ix. 5. 7
How *comes* it then *Am.* xxx. 2
how *comes* it that my exceeding heat *Am.* xxx. 5
Comes forth afresh out of their late dismay, *Am.* xl. 11
Loe! where she *comes* along with portly pace, *Epith.* 148
Thereof it *comes* that these faire soules, *H.B.* 120
Comest. Now *comest* thou to rob my house unmand, VI. i. 25. 4
Comet. A *commett* stird up that unkindly heate, *S.C.* D. 59
Cometh. after Winter *commeth* timely death. *S.C.* D. 150
whence no good *commeth* by; *Gn.* 102
He *commeth* on, and all things in his way *Gn.* 271
Sildome but some good *commeth* ere the end.' *Hub.* 172
The day is spent; and *commeth* drowsie night, I. iii. 15. 1
Who, with the noyse awaked, *commeth* out I. vi. 14. 6
throw his ragged rift On whoso *cometh* nigh; II. xii. 4. 6
So fitly now here *commeth* next in place, IV. v. 2. 1
On man and beast that *commeth* in her path. V. viii. 49. 5
The which, as *commeth* now by course, I will declare. VI. x. 4. 9
That *commeth* in to you. *Epith.* 209
She *commeth* in, before th' Almighties view; *Epith.* 211
Comfort. So as I can I wil thee *comfort;* *S.C.* S. 255
Began to *comfort* me in chearfull wise, *Hub.* 19
th' only *comfort* in calamities. *T.M.* 132
none doth care to *comfort* us at all; *T.M.* 350
It is the onelie *comfort* which they have, *T.M.* 494
comfort can I, wretched creature, have? *Ti.* 23
to *comfort* wakefull Lovers, *Ti.* 132
Yet it is *comfort* in great languishment, *Ti.* 159
Ne other *comfort* in this world can be, *Ti.* 584
Then gan I him to *comfort* all my best, *D.* 190
What frayes ye, that were wont to *comfort* me affrayd?' I. i. 52. 9
all . . . shew a semblance glad To *comfort* her; I. vi. 11. 8
Yet outwardly some little *comfort* shewes. I. vii. 21. 3
My last left *comfort* is my woes to weepe and waile.' I. vii. 39. 9
be of cheare, and *comfort* to you take; I. vii. 52. 5
feeling wondrous *comfort* in her weaker eld: I. x. 8. 9
wise Speranza gave him *comfort* sweet, I. x. 22. 1
to . . . *comfort* those in point of death which lay; I. x. 41. 2
them most needeth *comfort* in the end, I. x. 41. 3
offred hope of *comfort* did despise: II. i. 15. 3
What *comfort* can I, wofull wretch, conceave? II. i. 17. 2
fayre Lady, *comfort* to you make, II. i. 18. 1
He gan to *comfort,* and his woundes to dresse. II. iv. 16. 6
Yet in himselfe some *comfort* he did find, II. v. 14. 7
Voide of all succour and needfull *comfort;* II. v. 17. 5
quickned the dull spright with musicall *comfort.* II. v. 31. 9
evermore himselfe with *comfort* feedes II. vii. 2. 4
To *comfort* him in his infirmity. II. xi. 49. 5
lend her short reliefe And doe her *comfort,* III. i. 53. 6
conceiving hope of *comfort* glad, III. iii. 51. 3
meeke wordes to stay and *comfort* her withall. III. iv. 48. 9
'Dwarfe, *comfort* to thee take, III. v. 11. 6
of *comfort* him thou shalt deprive, III. v. 26. 8
Comfort to him that comfortlesse now lay. III. v. 27. 4
She cast to *comfort* him with busie paine. III. v. 31. 5
To *comfort* me in my distressed plight. III. v. 35. 4
Her Amoretta cald, to *comfort* her dismayd. III. vi. 28. 9
The *comfort* of her age and weary dayes, III. vii. 12. 2
Without all hope of *comfort* or reliefe; III. viii. 1. 6
Great *comfort* of her presence he conceiv'd, III. viii. 23. 3
'Therefore, faire Sir, doe *comfort* to you take, III. xi. 15. 1
faire Lady, *comfort* to you take, III. xii. 40. 6
His dearest love, the *comfort* of his dayes, III. xii. 44. *or.* 2
heavy heart with *comfort* doth rejoyce. IV. iii. 45. 8
great *comfort* in her sad misfare Was Amoret, IV. v. 30. 4
hardly of her chearefull speech Did *comfort* take, IV. vi. 38. 2
comfort take; for, by this heavens light, I vow IV. vi. 38. 7
Withouten *comfort* and withouten guide, IV. vii. 2. 8
Striving to *comfort* him all that they can, IV. ix. 9. 4
Give her great *comfort* and some harts content. V. v. 35. 3
To all that shall require my *comfort* in their smart.' V. vii. 19. 9
Gave unto her great *comfort* and reliefe; V. vii. 44. 7
through *comfort* of this noble knight.' V. x. 20. 9
she take *comfort* which God now did send: V. x. 22. 8
Such secret *comfort* and such heavenly pleasures, VI. Pr. 2. 1
And for their better *comfort* to them nigher drew. VI. ii. 41. 9
bitter sorrowings, Instead of *comfort* VI. iii. 5. 6
Yet had no meanes to *comfort,* VI. iii. 43. 9
giveth *comfort* to her courage cold: VI. iv. 1. 5
In evils counsell is the *comfort* chiefe; VI. iv. 34. 7
To seeke some *comfort* in that sorie case. VI. v. 7. 4

Comfort—*Continued.*
Finde harbour fit to *comfort* her great neede; VI. v. 31. 4
may her feeble leaves with *comfort* glade— VI. x. 44. 7
Began some smacke of *comfort* new to tast, VI. xi. 45. 3
Since I have lackt the *comfort* of that light, *Am.* lxxxvii. 1
Ne joy of ought . . . Can *comfort* me, *Am.* lxxxviii. 10
That may our *comfort* breed: *Epith.* 387
eeke for *comfort* often called art *Epith.* 394
Their joy, their *comfort*, their desire, their gaine, *H.H.B.* 271
Comfortable. Whom having laid in *comfortable* couch, III. i. 64. 2
Comfortably. downe to rest Her selfe she set, and *comfortably* cheard: III. vi. 10. 7
Comforted. *comforted* with curteous kind reliefe: I. vi. 37. 6
he her *comforted*, and faire bespake: I. vii. 52. 2
th' other forst him staye, and *comforted* in feare. I. ix. 34. 9
Her wisely *comforted* all that she might, I. x. 23. 4
Therewith much *comforted* she gan unfold The cause V. v. 31. 7
Comforting. Fat Colworts, and *comforting* Perseline, *Mui.* 199
Comfortless. To eate thy heart through *comfortlesse* dispaires; *Hub.* 904
All *comfortlesse* doth hide her chearlesse head *T.M.* 239
All *comfortlesse* upon the bared bow, *T.M.* 245
So wander we all carefull *comfortlesse*, *T.M.* 349
Deepe, darke, uneasy, doleful, *comfortlesse*. I. v. 36. 6
The pitteous mayden, carefull, *comfortlesse*, I. vi. 6. 1
'From whom retourning sad and *comfortlesse*, I. ix. 28. 1
comfortlesse through tyranny or might: III. ii. 14. 8
Comfort to him that *comfortlesse* now lay. III. v. 27. 4
Till then I wander carefull, *comfortlesse*, *Am.* xxxiv. 13
a tree alone all *comfortlesse*, *Am.* lvi. 7
Comic. with *Comick* sock to beautefie The painted Theaters, *T.M.* 176
all that els the *Comick* Stage . . . graced, *T.M.* 199
Coming. Typhoeus sister *comming* neare; *Bel.*[2] xv. 4
First *comming* to the world with weeping eye, *T.M.* 159
The dawning day forth *comming* from the East. *As.* 34
comming where the knight in slomber lay, I. i. 47. 2
Night . . . She findes forth *comming* from her darksome mew, I. v. 20. 4
comming to that sowle-diseased knight, I. x. 24. 1
comming down to ground, does free it selfe I. xi. 19. 9
coming to this well, he stoupt to drincke: II. i. 55. 8
coming close to Trompart II. iii. 12. 1
rowze as *comming* late from rest. II. iii. 35. 9
It booted nought Sir Guyon, *comming* neare, II. v. 3. 8
the villein, *comming* to their ayd, II. xi. 29. 4
cumming to his Squyre that kept his steed, II. xi. 48. 2
of their *comming* well he wist afore; III. iii. 15. 2
comming forth shall spred his banner brave III. iii. 30. 3
comming to the place, III. iv. 34. 7
He, *comming* home at undertime, III. vii. 13. 1
He *comming* present, where the Monster vilde III. vii. 30. 7
comming to that Fishers wandring bote, III. viii. 31. 1
comming nigh, eftsoones he gan to gesse, III. viii. 45. 3
comming him before low louted on the lay. III. x. 23. 9
Her cause of *comming* she to tell began. IV. ii. 49. 5
comming home, in warlike fresh aray Them found IV. ii. 53. 3
Scudamour, *comming* to Cares House, IV. v. Arg.
Whom when the watch . . . Saw *comming* home, IV. ix. 5. 7
comming to her sonne, IV. xii. 26. 3
Which lawlesse multitude him *comming* too V. ii. 52. 1
Which when as Radigund there *comming* heard, V. iv. 37. 6
comming to this knight, she purpose fayned, V. v. 54. 1
at last she spide One *comming* towards her V. vi. 8. 2
He *comming* neare gan gently her salute V. vi. 20. 1
the sound Of armed men *comming* V. vi. 28. 7
comming down to seeke them where they wond, V. vi. 35. 6
comming full before his horses vew, V. viii. 37. 8
comming present there, She at her ran V. viii. 46. 7
She *comming* forth . . . was greatly queld, V. xi. 26. 1
comming to the place, and finding there Sir Artegall, V. xii. 12. 6
Then th' other *comming* neare gan him revile, V. xii. 40. 1
The *comming* of that so much threatned Knight; VI. i. 30. 3
comming forth yet full of late affray VI. i. 44. 7
comming to the rivers side, he found VI. iii. 30. 1
And, *comming* likewise to the wounded knight, VI. iv. 12. 1
the Salvage, *comming* now in place, VI. vi. 22. 1
To whom false Turpine *comming* courteously, VI. vii. 4. 1
this way *comming* from feastfull glee VI. x. 22. 4
Calidore soone *comming* to her ayde, VI. x. 35. 6
He chaunst one *comming* towards him to spy, VI. xi. 27. 2
boldly blaming her for *comming* there, VII. vi. 12. 7
Who now is *comming* forth with girland crouned. *Am.* xix. 4
Comming to kisse her lyps, *Am.* lxiv. 1
with your steele darts doo chace from *comming* neer; *Epith.* 70
T' awayt the *comming* of your joyous make, *Epith.* 87
Prepare your selves; for he is *comming* strayt. *Epith.* 113
Command. They boast they han the devill at *commaund*, *S.C.* S. 94
She would *commaund* the hasty Sunne to stay, I. x. 20. 2
huge mountaines . . . She would *commaund* themselves to beare away, I. x. 20. 7
his wings did broad display At his *commaund*, II. iii. 19. 4
Who fares on sea may not *commaund* his way, II. vi. 23. 2
At thy *commaund* lo! all these mountaines bee: II. vii. 9. 2
his heaped waves he did *commaund* III. iv. 22. 3
Badd her *commaund* my life to save or spill. III. vii. 54. 2
To th' insolent *commaund* of womens will; V. vi. 1. 4
The which did her *commaund* without needing perswade. V. x. 25. 9
had the chiefe *commaund* of all the rest, VI. xi. 3. 5
halfe confused with his great *commaund*, VII. vi. 26. 1
Commanded. that great Queene, . . . *Commaunded* them their fury to refraine; I. iv. 40. 7
The charge thereof unto a covetous Spright *Commaunded* was, II. vii. 32. 2

Commanded—*Continued.*
Thence she *commaunded* me to prison new; IV. viii. 56. 7
full of scorne to be *commaunded* so, V. i. 21. 2
Commaunded them their daily workes renew, V. v. 1. 4
Commaunded straight his armour to be brought; V. viii. 28. 3
Commaunded him from slaughter to recoyle, V. xi. 65. 7
since that loving Lord *Commaunded* us to love them *H.H.L.* 205
Commanding. *Commaunding* them their cause of strife bewray; *Hub.* 1096
that fiers Carle *commaunding* to forbeare, II. vii. 43. 2
Commaunding Proteus straight t' enlarge the mayd, IV. xii. 32. 3
commaunding peace, Them guyded through the throng, V. ix. 23. 8
Commandment. they neglected his *commaundement*. *Hub.* 566
To have in her *commandement* at hand.' *Col.* 263
wretched woman, . . . made thrall to your *commandement*, I. ii. 22. 3
From her fayre eyes he tooke *commandement*, I. iii. 9. 8
So greatly his *commandement* they feare, III. iii. 11. 5
To the long raynes at her *commaundement*: III. iv. 33. 4
Her teme at her *commaundement* quiet stands, III. iv. 42. 3
Her *commaundment* he could not withstand, IV. x. 33. 7
he had given streight *commaundement* V. xii. 10. 3
streight he held his hand at his *commaundement*. VI. vi. 40. 9
by *commaund'ment* of Diana, VII. vi. 53. 3
Commandments. kept so well his wise *commaundements*, VI. vi. 15. 3
Commen, Commers, *etc.* *See* **Come, Comer's,** *etc.*
Commence. 'Where shall I then *commence* This wofull tale? VI. xi. 30. 2
Commend. worthie to *commend* For prize of value, *T.M.* 465
That doest their bountie still so much *commend*. *Col.* 902
The mightie martiall handes doe most *commend*: II. vi. 35. 5
his deare safety, I to thee *commend*; II. viii. 8. 2
did it *commend* Unto these Sprights III. iii. 10. 4
so fitte tide Him to *commend* to her, III. ix. 32. 9
which *commend* he will Unto the vulgar for good gold IV. v. 15. 3
Lindus that his pikes doth most *commend*, IV. xi. 39. 7
her glorie to *commend*, V. ix. 32. 7
Unto his soveraine Queene her suite for to *commend*. V. xi. 37. 9
every action doth them much *commend*, VI. ii. 2. 3
Gan highly to *commend* the happie life VI. ix. 18. 8
He would *commend* his guift, VI. ix. 40. 5
Could not maligne him, but *commend* him needs; VI. ix. 45. 4
Her hardnes blame, which I should more *commend*? *Am.* li. 6
Commend to you by loves abused name, *H.B.* 172
may it more to mortall eyes *commend*, *H.B.* 263
How wondrously would he her face *commend*, *H.H.B.* 222
Commended. Right noble Nymphs, and high to be *commended*: *Col.* 577
Was favoured and to her grace *commended*. VI. ix. 46. 6
Comment. wheresoever they *comment* the same, VII. vii. 53. 7
Commissaries. To Deanes, to Archdeacons, to *Commissaries*, *Hub.* 421
Commission. And sit in Gods owne seat without *commission*; *H.H.L.* 82
Commit. dare not yet *committ* Her single person I. vi. 12. 1
Who did her cause into thy hand *committ*, I. x. 63. 8
unto her truth Did earnestly *committ*, II. iii. 2. 3
Ne him *committ* to grave terrestriall, II. xi. 45. 8
safe *committ* to her soft fethered nest, III. i. 58. 7
T' avenge that shame they did on him *commit*, V. iv. 39. 4
she did at last *commit* All to his hands, V. x. 13. 1
their cause they best esteemed Whole to *commit*, VI. iii. 13. 4
Committed. spoyles, by salvage beasts *committed*? *Hub.* 1253
till thou have to my trustie eare *Committed* *D.* 70
That had almost *committed* crime abhord, II. i. 27. 3
wronges, which had *committed* bin By Guyon, II. iii. 13. 5
unto Psyche with great trust and care *Committed* her, III. vi. 51. 4
oft *committed* fowle Idolatree. III. xi. 49. 5
Defil'd the pledge *committed* to thy trust? IV. i. 53. 5
keyes of every prison dore By her *committed* be, IV. viii. 54. 7
In flesh at first the guilt *committed* was, *H.H.L.* 141
Commixtion. 'Of that *commixtion* they did then beget This hellish Dog, VI. vi. 12. 1
Commixture. Both male and female through *commixture* joynd: *Col.* 802
Through fowle *commixture* of his filthy blot; VI. i. 8. 3
Commodity. for their most *commodity* Be sold, VI. xi. 10. 4
Common. I say not, as the *common* voyce doth say, *Ro.* ix. 9
Sustein'd the shocke of *common* enmitie; *Ro.* xxi. 4
things exceeding reach of *common* reason; *Van.* i. 4
Whatever thing seems small in *common* eyes. *Van.* v. 14
Must not the world wend in his *commun* course, *S.C.* F. 11
Dight gaudy Girlonds was my *common* (*comen) trade, *S.C.* Jun. 45
To be partaker of their *common* woe; *Hub.* 14
Brings to reproach and *common* infamie! *Hub.* 222
that which *common* is, and knowne to all, *Hub.* 613
common Courtiers love to gybe and fleare *Hub.* 714
the *common* winde Of Courts inconstant mutabilitie, *Hub.* 722
In taking on himselfe, in *common* sight, *Hub.* 860
For to encrease the *common* treasures store; *Hub.* 1171
not so *common* was his bountie shared: *Hub.* 1194
No *common* things may please a wavering wit. *Mui.* 160
Gods with *common* mockerie Might laugh at them, *Mui.* 372
And the dim vele, with which from *commune* vew *Ded. Son.* ix. 10
forth he comes into the *commune* hall; I. v. 3. 1
well acquainted with that *commune* plight, I. x. 23. 2
the *common* In of rest; II. i. 59. 2
Unworthie of the *commune* breathed ayre, II. iii. 7. 5
from tender dug of *commune* nourse II. iv. 18. 3
'It was my fortune, *commune* to that age, II. iv. 19. 1
To taken counsell of their *common* cares; II. x. 37. 7
from thy hand Did *commun* breath and nouriture receave. II. x. 69. 6
(For so that Castle hight by *commun* name) III. i. 31. 3
not as other wemens *commune* brood III. vi. 5. 6
nor with *commune* food, As other wemens babes, III. vi. 5. 8
To *commun* accidents stil open layd, III. v. 36. 7
Are bownd with *commun* bond of frailtee, III. v. 36. 8

Common—*Continued.*
'Certes was but a *common* Courtisane; . . . III. vii. 58. 2
ought evermore To errant knights be *commune:* . . . III. viii. 52. 5
that uncurteous Carle, their *commune* foe, . . . III. ix. 17. 8
countries cause, and *commune* foes disdayne. . . . III. ix. 40. 4
in open place and *commune* bord . . . III. x. 6. 5
with *commune* speach He courted her; . . . III. x. 6. 6
the whole worlds *commune* remedy.' . . . III. x. 26. 5
every one as *commune* good her handeled. . . . III. x. 36. 9
By any ridling skill, or *commune* wit. . . . III. xi. 54. 5
gave him being, *commune* to them twayne: . . . III. xii. 9. 4
it prodigious seemes in *common* peoples sight. . . . IV. i. 13. 9
on their *common* harmes together did devise. . . . IV. vi. 10. 9
Ne signe of sence did shew, ne *common* wit, . . . IV. vii. 44. 3
as *common* words are ment, . . . IV. viii. 26. 1
gainst *common* sence, . . . IV. x. 2. 4
Low looking dales, disloignd from *common* gaze; . . . IV. x. 24. 6
'Concord she cleeped was in *common* reed, . . . IV. x. 34. 1
seemed strange to *common* vew, . . . IV. xi. 27. 7
I doe not forme them to the *common* line . . . V. Pr. 3. 3
when he understood by *common* fame . . . V. iii. 10. 5
thether also came . . . into the *common* hall, . . . V. iii. 14. 2
termes to entertaine of *common* guize, . . . V. vi. 20. 4
of sundry things did *commen:* . . . V. ix. 4. 3
It often fals, in course of *common* life, . . . V. xi. 1. 1
she used often to resort To *common* haunts, . . . V. xii. 34. 7
soothly it was sayd by *common* fame, . . . VI. v. 37. 1
To make a *common* feast, and feed with gurmandize. . . . VI. viii. 38. 9
mote not be prophan'd of *common* eyes, . . . VI. viii. 43. 2
by *common* voice esteemed The father . . . VI. ix. 14. 1
ymet About some carcase by the *common* way, . . . VI. xi. 17. 2
Commoned. So long as Guyon with her *commoned,* . . . II. ix. 41. 1
Commonly. As *commonly* as frend does with his frend. . . . I. x. 56. 5
Cantium, which Kent we *comenly* inquyre. . . . II. x. 12. 9
Commonplace. well discourst Upon this *Commonplace,* . . . *Hub.* 542
Commons. As for the rascall *Commons* least he cared, . . . *Hub.* 1193
by consent of *Commons* and of Peares, . . . II. x. 62. 8
Lordings curbe that *commons* over-aw, . . . V. ii. 38. 8
Commons'. Then gan the Peoples cry and *Commons* sute . . . V. ix. 44. 7
Common weal. Therewith containes his heavenly *Common-weale:* V. vii. 1. 8
changing all that forme of *common-weale* . . . V. vii. 42. 4
Both to her selfe and to her *common-weale,* . . . V. viii. 21. 4
She was about affaires of *common-wele,* . . . V. ix. 36. 3
How to reforme that ragged *common-weale:* . . . V. xii. 26. 4
Common weals. lawes of men, that *common-weales* containe, . . . V. xii. 1. 4
Commonwealths. though time doth *Commonwealths* devowre, . *Ro.* viii. 11
Of *commen-wealthes,* of states, of pollicy, . . . II. ix. 53. 6
Commun(e). *See* **Common.**
Communed. Whiles thus they *communed,* . . . IV. vi. 9. 1
Compact. this is things *compacte* betwixt you two, . . . V. vi. 16. 7
Compacted. All which *compacted* made a goodly Diapase. . . II. ix. 22. 9
Perforce disparted their *compacted* gyre, . . . III. i. 23. 6
Compacture. with comely compasse and *compacture* strong, . . II. ix. 24. 8
Companies. to resort To common haunts, and *companies* frequent, . . . V. xii. 34. 7
Companing. *companing* with feends and filthy Sprights . . . II. x. 8. 6
Companion. wise Curius, *companion* Of noble vertues, . . . *Gn.* 609
reft fro me my sweete *companion,* . . . *D.* 159
Hee had a faire *companion* of his way, . . . I. ii. 13. 1
Of her leawd parts to make *companion:* . . . II. ii. 37. 5
her owne daughter Pleasure, to whom shee Made her *companion,* . . . III. vi. 51. 8
Amoret, *companion* of her care: . . . IV. v. 30. 5
Companion she became, and so continued long. . . . IV. viii. 5. 9
his deare *companion* of his care. . . . IV. viii. 8. 6
Companions. Such were for him no fit *companions,* . . . *Hub.* 795
The sweete *companions* of the Muses late, . . . *T.M.* 404
Go beg with us, and be *companions* still, . . . *T.M.* 407
With two *companions* of like qualitie, . . . IV. i. 32. 7
With these two lewd *companions,* and no more, . . . VI. viii. 22. 7
Company. dauncing all in *companie,* . . . *Gn.* 27
To face, to forge, to scoffe, to *companie,* . . . *Hub.* 506
from her most beastly *companie* I gan refraine, . . . I. ii. 41. 5
Such one was Idlenesse, first of this *company.* . . . I. iv. 20. 9
the great felicitee Of proud Lucifera, and his owne *companee.* . I. iv. 31. 9
whenas Morpheus had . . . Arrested all that courtly *company,* I. iv. 44. 7
The forlorne mayd . . . could not lacke her lovers *company;* I. vi. 22. 2
Thenceforth he kept her goodly *company,* . . . I. vi. 31. 8
With a fayre knight to keepen *companee,* . . . I. ix. 27. 2
From highest heven in gladsome *companee,* . . . I. x. 56. 3
Her joyous presence, and sweet *company,* . . . I. xii. 41. 1
present Unto her vew, and *company* unsought; . . . III. i. 44. 3
Sweete love such lewdnes bands from his faire *companee.* . . III. ii. 41. 9
To search the secret haunts of Dianes *company.* . . . III. vi. 16. 9
if I catch him in this *company,* . . . III. vi. 24. 6
to enjoy Her deare Adonis joyous *company,* . . . III. vi. 46. 2
With many of the Gods in *company* . . . III. vi. 49. 2
Florimell It was with whom in *company* he yode, . . . III. viii. 19. 7
ne keepe her *company,* . . . III. ix. 5. 7
the sight And *company* at meat, . . . III. ix. 25. 9
After whom marcht a jolly *company,* . . . III. xii. 5. 8
did survay his goodly *company;* . . . III. xii. 23. 3
Which when his other *companie* beheld, . . . IV. i. 37. 1
made good semblance to his *companie,* . . . IV. i. 38. 2
That offer pleased all the *company:* . . . IV. iv. 10. 1
So loth she was his *companie* for to forsake. . . . IV. vi. 45. 9
Him to recomfort with my *companie,* . . . IV. viii. 57. 4
him farre she brought Into a cave from *companie* exilde, . . . V. i. 6. 7
having in *companie* This lucklesse Ladie . . . V. i. 16. 8

Company—*Continued.*
Glad from his *companie* to be so sondred; . . . V. v. 19. 4
There did Typhaon with her *company;* . . . VI. vi. 11. 7
She wander should in *companie* of those, . . . VI. vii. 37. 8
her *companie* to gaine, . . . VI. ix. 34. 7
when he came in *companie* Where Calidore was present, . . . VI. ix. 39. 1
neither could to *company* of th' other creepe. . . . VI. xii. 5. 9
Compare. ship to which none other might *compare:* . . . *Bel.*[2] xiii. 8
her princely grace, Can you well *compare?* . . . *S.C.* Ap. 67
Let him . . . His brightnesse *compare* With hers, . . . *S.C.* Ap. 80
Sike mens follie I cannot *compare* . . . *S.C.* May 95
in derring-doe *compare* With shepheards swayne . . . *S.C.* D. 43
Not that great Idoll might with this *compaire,* . . . *Ti.* 495
to *compare* with her in curious skill Of workes . . . *Mui.* 271
With this so curious networke to *compare.* . . . *Mui.* 368
With those sweet sugred speaches doo *compare,* . . . *D.* 299
Such greatnes I cannot *compare* to ought: . . . *Col.* 335
I cast for to *compare* Whether . . . did exceede: . . . I. ii. 37. 3
from backe and belly still did spare, . . . richesse to *compare:* I. iv. 28. 5
thinkes . . . Pholoe fowle, when her to this he doth *compaire.* I. vi. 15. 9
when her curteous deeds he did *compare,* . . . I. vi. 31. 3
a woman . . . That was on earth not easie to *compare;* . . . I. x. 30. 4
art, stryving to *compayre* With nature, . . . II. v. 29. 1
Yet no man to them can his carefull paines *compare.* . . . II. vi. 15. 9
Lives ought that to her linage may *compaire;* . . . II. x. 2. 3
if ought with Eden mote *compayre.* . . . II. xii. 52. 9
never any mote with her *compayre:* . . . III. i. 26. 5
Cannot with noble Britomart *compare,* . . . III. iv. 3. 2
Lives none this day that may with her *compare* . . . III. v. 8. 4
none living may *compayre:* . . . III. v. 54. 4
with her beautie, bountie did *compare,* . . . IV. iii. 39. 8
present time The image of the antique world *compare,* . . . V. Pr. 1. 2
then together doe them both *compare;* . . . V. ii. 48. 5
To which what can *compare?*) . . . VI. x. 4. 8
Ne ought . . . can it *compare:* . . . VI. x. 4. 8
all her peres cannot with her *compare,* . . . VI. x. 27. 7
my fraile wit cannot devize to what It to *compare,* . . . VII. vii. 7. 5
to what I might *compare* Those powrefull eies, . . . *Am.* ix. 1
therewith doe her cruelty *compare,* . . . *Am.* lv. 2
Your selfe unto the Bee ye doe *compare;* . . . *Am.* lxxi. 2
Compared. Rome onely might to Rome *compared* bee, . . . *Ro.* vi. 9
(*compar'd* to all the rest Of each degree) . . . *Hub.* 179
My wealth, *compar'd* to thine owne miserie, . . . *Hub.* 598
With my great forces might *compared* bee: . . . *Ti.* 103
might be *compar'd* to it. . . . *Ti.* 511
So darke are earthly thinges *compard* to things divine. . . . I. x. 67. 9
next to death is Sleepe to be *compard;* . . . II. vii. 25. 7
compar'd to these by many parts: . . . II. ix. 48. 3
Compared to the creatures in the seas entrall. . . . II. xii. 25. 9
Compar'd to her that shone as Phebes light . . . IV. v. 14. 3
That to their beautie may *compared* bee, . . . *H.H.B.* 58
Compared to his least resplendent sparke? . . . *H.H.B.* 126
Ne can on earth *compared* be to ought. . . . *H.H.B.* 210
Compar'd to that celestiall beauties blaze, . . . *H.H.L.* 277
Comparing. times *comparing* with their accidents, . . . VI. xii. 20. 2
Compass. Your toombs devoted *compasse* over-all, . . . *Ro.* i. 10
cloud . . . Eftsoones in *compas* arch't, . . . *Ro.* xx. 3
Him behooves to vew in *compasse* round . . . *Ro.* xxvi. 5
his trees of state in *compasse* rownd: . . . *S.C.* F. 146
casten to *compasse* many wrong emprise: . . . *S.C.* S. 83
Who ever casts to *compasse* weightye prise, . . . *S.C.* O. 103
squaring it in *compasse* well beseene, . . . *Gn.* 651
to *compas* anie sute not hard, . . . *Hub.* 886
Beyond the *compasse* of his pointed path, . . . *T.M.* 10
Above the *compasse* of the arched skie; . . . *T.M.* 370
Through the wide *compas* of the ayrie coast; . . . *Mui.* 38
Mars sleeping with his wife to *compasse* in, . . . *Mui.* 371
gan to cast how I her *compasse* might, . . . *D.* 115
As the wide *compasse* of the firmament . . . *Ded. Son.* ix. 5
Made a calme shadowe far in *compasse* round: . . . I. ii. 28. 6
A thing without the *compas* of my witt; . . . I. ix. 3. 2
That I may cast to *compas* your reliefe, . . . II. i. 48. 8
Upon his card and *compas* firmes his eye, . . . II. vii. 1. 6
with comely *compasse* and compacture strong, . . . II. ix. 24. 8
Withouten *compasse* or withouten card, . . . III. ii. 7. 7
To *compas* thy desire, and find that loved knight.' . . . III. ii. 46. 9
A brasen wall in *compas* to compyle . . . III. iii. 10. 3
To be the *compasse* of his kingdomes seat: . . . III. ix. 46. 6
to *compasse* Philliras hard love, . . . III. xi. 43. 7
in *compasse* round About her backe . . . IV. i. 13. 4
Within the *compasse* of that Islands space; . . . IV. x. 21. 2
in small *compasse* hild? . . . IV. xi. 17. 4
alwaies doe their powre within just *compasse* pen. . . . V. ii. 19. 9
That we may *compasse* this our enterprize? . . . V. v. 48. 2
Of all that on this earthly *compasse* wonnes; . . . V. vi. 33. 3
in the *compasse* of his clouches tooke; . . . V. ix. 11. 4
all about did close the *compasse* of his eye. . . . VI. iv. 24. 9
like a girlond did in *compasse* stemme: . . . VI. x. 12. 5
ne hath her *compasse* lost: . . . VI. xii. 1. 7
No way he found to *compasse* his desire, . . . VII. vi. 43. 1
That in his mightie *compasse* doth comprize, . . . *H.H.B.* 73
Compassed. the *compast* course of the universe . . . is ronne, *Ro.* xxii. 9
kingdomes, *compassed* With rustie horrour . . . *Gn.* 442
He *compast* Troy thrice with his bodie dedd. . . . *Gn.* 528
Although the *compast* world were sought around. . . . *Ti.* 567
all the storie She *compast* with a wreathe . . . *Mui.* 328
having overrun The *compast* skie, . . . *D.* 25
was with dread and horror *compassed* arownd. . . . II. vii. 20. 9
this great gardin, *compast* with a mound; . . . II. vii. 56. 5

Compassed—*Continued.*
Like highest heaven *compassed* around, . . . II. ix. 45. 2
like a girlond *compassed* the hight; . . . III. vi. 43. 6
Might [*be] by the witch or by (*that) her sonne *compast*. . III. vii. 18. 5
ere the yeare his course had *compassid*, . . . III. vii. 55. 3
So sore he sowst him on the *compast* creast, . . . IV. iv. 30. 7
The new begins his *compast* course anew: . . . *Am.* lxii. 2
Compassing. Both heaven and earth in roundnesse *compassing;* *Ro.* iv. 4
Compassion. all her Sisters, with *compassion* like, . . . *T.M.* 231
For pitties sake *compassion* our paine, . . . *T.M.* 346
all her sisters, with *compassion* like, . . . *T.M.* 477
To be bemoned with *compassion* kinde, . . . *Ti.* 160
let *compassion* creepe Into his brest, . . . *D.* 248
heavenly spirits have *compassion* On mortall men, . . . *D.* 384
to breed *Compassion* in a countrey lasses hart . . . *As.* Pr. 4
Nought . . . That moves more deare *compassion* of mind. . I. iii. 1. 2
Her hart gan melt in great *compassion;* . . . I. iii. 6. 8
Her feeling speaches some *compassion* mov'd . . . I. v. 24. 6
They, in *compassion* of her tender youth, . . . I. vi. 12. 5
may *compassion* of their evilles move? . . . II. viii. 1. 3
For great *compassion* of their sorow, . . . III. iv. 32. 5
With womanish *compassion* of her plaint, . . . III. vii. 10. 2
My heart doth melt with meere *compassion,* . . . III. viii. 1. 2
Deepe indignation and *compassion* frayle . . . III. viii. 31. 4
not empierst with deepe *compassiowne,* . . . III. ix. 39. 7
The deare *compassion* of whose bitter fit . . . IV. i. 1. 6
With deare *compassion* deeply did emmove, . . . IV. viii. 3. 7
The peoples great *compassion* unto her allure. . . . V. ix. 38. 9
inly touched with *compassion* deare, . . . VI. iii. 4. 4
feele *compassion* of his evill plight, . . . VI. iv. 3. 6
His deepe *compassion* of her dolefull stound, . . . VI. iv. 11. 4
Without *compassion* of her cruell smarts: . . . VI. v. 33. 4
Was touched with *compassion* entire, . . . VI. viii. 3. 3
in dongeon deepe Without *compassion* cruelly he threw; . . . VI. xii. 5. 7
Carrying *compassion* to their lovely foe; . . . *H.B.* 243
Compassionate. did . . . His care more then her owne *compassionate,* . . . VI. iii. 12. 2
Compel. their cruell Judge *compell* With bitter torture, . . . *Gn.* 627
who can love *compell?* . . . *Col.* 914
king of Babylon, That would *compell* all nations . . . I. v. 47. 2
Wyld beastes in yron yokes he would *compell;* . . . I. vi. 26. 2
he did *compell* . . . with him to matchen equall fight: . . . II. v. 4. 7
many foes, whom straunger knightes to flight *compell.* . . . II. ix. Arg.
the large leape which Debon did *compell* Coulin to make, . . II. x. 11. 2
trumpets sound to cease did them *compell:* . . . IV. iv. 25. 8
to alight on foote her algates did *compell:* . . . IV. vi. 13. 9
He thought her to *compell* by crueltie and awe. . . . IV. xi. 2. 9
Do you by duresse him *compell* thereto, . . . IV. xii. 10. 5
did her *compell* To perils great; . . . V. iii. 27. 6
with threat Doth them *compell* to worke, . . . V. iv. 31. 5
did *compell* To stay their cruell hands . . . VI. xi. 20. 4
roring horribly, did him *compell* To see the hatefull sunne, . VI. xii. 35. 4
still *compell* To keepe his course? . . . VII. vii. 48. 5
compell To keepe them selves within their sundrie raines, . *H.L.* 87
Compelled. she had this Knight from far *compeld.* . . . I. i. 5. 9
At last he was *compeld* to cry perforse, . . . II. v. 23. 7
compeld with courage bold To yield . . . II. viii. 41. 7
soone *compeld* to hearken unto peace. . . . III. i. 23. 7
Ne may love be *compeld* by maistery; . . . III. i. 25. 7
late mischaunce had her *compeld* to chaunge The land for sea, III. viii. 20. 4
this faire many were *compeld* at last . . . III. ix. 11. 7
He was *compeld* to seeke some refuge neare, . . . III. ix. 13. 2
him *compeld* To open unto him the prison dore, . . . IV. ix. 8. 1
shortly them *compelled* to retrate, . . . IV. ix. 34. 8
Thereto *compelled* through hart-murdring paine; . . . V. v. 30. 8
Not by strong hand *compelled* thereunto, . . . V. vi. 16. 4
All this accord to which he Crudor had *compeld.* . . . VI. i. 44. 9
Compelled were themselves awhile to rest, . . . VI. iv. 15. 6
Compeld him soone the spoyle adowne to lay. . . . VI. iv. 20. 4
Compelling. *Compelling* them which way he list, . . . *Col.* 251
Compelling her, wher she would not, . . . VI. vii. 44. 3
Compels. to his law *compels* all creatures to obay. . . . IV. x. 42. 9
Compile. That which no hands can evermore *compyle.* . . . *Ro.* xxv. 14
It is my chiefe profession to *compyle;* . . . *T.M.* 432
Thy gracious Soverains praises to *compile,* . . . *Ded. Son.* xii. 6
his prayses to *compyle,* . . . III. ii. 12. 5
A brasen wall in compas to *compyle* . . . III. iii. 10. 3
So great perfections did in her *compile,* . . . III. vi. 1. 3
with lewd poems which he did *compyle;* . . . V. ix. 25. 7
which those six books *compile,* . . . *Am.* lxxx. 2
Compiled. As in the smoky forge it was *compilde,* . . . III. vii. 30. 5
As that renowmed Poet them *compyled* With warlike numbers IV. ii. 32. 6
a lamentable lay, So sensibly *compyld,* . . . IV. viii. 4. 4
when the Prince had perfectly *compylde,* . . . IV. ix. 17. 1
Compyld by me, which thy poore liegeman am! . . . *H.B.* 273
Complain. makes me much and ever to *complaine;* . . . *Pet.* iii. 13
those that did thy Rosalind *complayne,* . . . *S.C.* N. 44
my case I thus *complaine* Unto yourselfe, . . . *Gn.* Ded. 3
they all eternally *complaine* Of others wrong, . . . *Gn.* 407
To whom may I more trustely *complaine* . . . *Hub.* 55
The honest man, that heard him thus *complaine,* . . . *Hub.* 259
Came to the Court, her case there to *complaine,* . . . *Hub.* 1208
he heard each one *complaine* Of foule abuses . . . *Hub.* 1275
Therefore we mourne and pittilesse *complaine,* . . . *T.M.* 353
To whom shall I my evill case *complaine,* . . . *T.M.* 421
for my selfe *complaine,* . . . *T.M.* 533
at all *complaine* My good to heare, . . . *D.* 279
all their birds with silence to *complaine:* . . . *Col.* 24
Daphnaida Upon her neeces death I did *complaine:* . . . *Col.* 511

Complain—*Continued.*
Bulles, . . . Doe for the milky mothers want *complaine,* . . . I. viii. 11. 7
to that mighty Princesse did *complaine* . . . II. ii. 43. 2
having not *complaine,* and having it upbrayd?' . . . II. vi. 14. 9
Yet many Ladies fayre did oft *complaine,* . . . III. iv. 26. 7
His Faery Queene, for whom he did *complaine,* . . . III. iv. 54. 7
gan *complaine* The want of his good Squire . . . III. v. 12. 3
She sweetly heard *complaine,* . . . III. vi. 15. 8
The wofull husbandman doth lowd *complaine* . . . III. vii. 34. 7
Ne lesse thereat did Paridell *complaine,* . . . IV. v. 22. 6
So feelingly her case she did *complaine,* . . . IV. xii. 5. 6
some pit, where she him heares *complaine,* . . . IV. xii. 17. 7
Nor unto any meaner to *complaine;* . . . IV. xii. 29. 3
Hard is the case the which ye doe *complaine;* . . . V. xi. 55. 2
Whom pitying to heare so sore *complaine,* . . . VI. iv. 23. 3
that proud And shamefull Knight of whom she did *complaine.* VI. v. 34. 4
ne did of want *complaine,* . . . VI. v. 39. 4
Gan to *complaine* of great discourtesie, . . . VI. vii. 4. 3
often did of love, and oft of lucke *complaine.* . . . VI. viii. 32. 9
having small yet doe I not *complaine* Of want, . . . VI. ix. 20. 3
oft *complaine* Of Pastorell to all the shepheards . . . VI. xi. 38. 7
Ne wight he found to whom he might *complaine,* . . . VI. xi. 26. 1
I doo *complaine,* Against your eies, . . . *Am.* xii. 13
having, pine; and, having not, *complaine.* . . . *Am.* xxxv. 4
Complained. Yet never *complained* of cold nor heate, . . . *S.C.* F. 19
Causelesse *complained,* and lowdly cryed . . . *S.C.* F. 148
to the Ordinarie of them *complain'd,* . . . *Hub.* 562
Thus as they them *complayned* too and fro, . . . *Hub.* 949
It was *complaind* that thou hadst done great tort . . . II. v. 17. 2
she sighed deepe, and after thus *complaynd.* . . . III. iv. 7. 9
unto them *complayned* how that he Had used beene . . . V. v. 15. 7
in blood Accomplished, that many deare *complaind:* . . . III. ix. 42. 7
Paridell *complaynd,* . . . That ryde he could not, . . . III. x. 1. 7
piteously *complaind* her carefull grieffe, . . . IV. xii. 5. 3
the which that mayd *complained* To have bene done . . . V. viii. 24. 2
And oft *complayn'd* of fate, and fortune oft defyde. . . . VI. iv. 26. 9
he to her *complayned* The piteous passion . . . *Am.* xlviii. 11
he weeping came, And of his griefe *complayned:* . . . *Epig.* iv. 32
Complainest. Lewdly *complainest* thou, laesie ladde, . . . *S.C.* F. 9
Complaining. To whome *complayning* his unhappy stound, . *Hub.* 940
Ladies and Lordes she everywhere mote heare *Complayning,* . III. vi. 13. 7
Complayning of her cruell Paramoure, . . . IV. ix. 6. 3
Great sorts of lovers piteously *complayning,* . . . IV. x. 43. 2
To whom *complayning* her afflicted plight, . . . V. i. 4. 3
In vaine *complayning* to be so abused; . . . VI. ii. 22. 7
His wofull Ladie, piteously *complayning* . . . VI. ii. 41. 2
Complayning out on me that would not on them rew. . . . VI. viii. 20. 9
Complains. thou art he whom my poore ghost *complaines* . *Gn.* 630
when she *complaines,* The more he laughes, . . . VI. vii. 44. 7
Complaint. lengd to know the cause of his *complaint:* . . . *S.C.* May 250
May by this Gnatts *complaint* be easily knowen. . . . *Gn.* Ded. 14
Cause of my death and just *complaint* to tell: . . . *Gn.* 629
Renewing her *complaint* with passion strong, . . . *Ti.* 479
your pitifull *complaint* Hath fownd another partner . . . III. ix. 40. 1
All which *complaint* when Marinell had heard, . . . IV. xii. 12. 1
Complaints. the *complaints* thereof could not be tolde. . . *Hub.* 1313
In funerall *complaints* and waylfull tyne, . . . *Mui.* 12
womanish *complaints* she did represse, . . . V. vii. 44. 8
pittifull *complaints* which there she made, . . . VI. x. 44. 2
Now lay those sorrowfull *complaints* aside; . . . *Epith.* 12
Love doest laugh and scorne At their *complaints,* . . . *H.L.* 135
Complement. *See* **Compliment.**
For a full *complement* of all their ill, . . . *Hub.* 338
Supplide her sobbing breaches with sad *complement.* . . . III. iv. 35. 9
So all did make in her a perfect *complement.* . . . III. v. 55. 9
Of natures skill the onely *complement;* . . . *Am.* xxiv. 3
Complete. A comely knight, all arm'd in *complete* wize, . . . III. ii. 24. 2
Complexion. Of swarth *complexion,* and of crabbed hew, . . II. ix. 52. 4
through impression Of the sunbeames in moyst *complexion,* III. vi. 8. 5
Meet for her temper and *complexion:* . . . III. vi. 38. 5
in his cold *complexion* doe breed A filthy blood, . . . III. x. 59. 3
Complexions. Through goodly mixture of *complexions* dew; II. iii. 22. 4
pure *complexions,* that shall quickly fade . . . *H.B.* 67
Compliment. his fine feates and Courtly *complement;* . . . *Hub.* 692
as a *complement* for courting vaine. . . . *Col.* 790
Compliments. Without vaine art or curious *complements;* . . *T.M.* 542
all the *complements* of curtesie: . . . VI. x. 23. 6
Complines. Their penie Masses, and their *Complynes* meete, . *Hub.* 452
Complishing. kept from *complishing* the faith which I did owe. V. xi. 41. 9
Complot. The purpose of the *complot* which ye tell; . . . *Hub.* 178
They did this *complot* twixt them selves devise: . . . V. viii. 25. 3
Comportance. Goodly *comportaunce* each to other beare, . . II. i. 29. 3
Compose. layes of love he also could *compose:* . . . *As.* 35
soone she did her countenance *compose,* . . . V. v. 30. 5
The Priest him selfe a garland doth *compose* . . . VI. viii. 39. 7
Composed. likely harts *composd* of starres concent, . . . *H.B.* 198
Composition. made a *composition* With their next neighbor . *Hub.* 571
life enjoy for any *composition:* . . . V. x. 27. 5
Withouten dowre or *composition;* . . . VI. i. 43. 8
comely *composition* Of parts well measurd, . . . *H.B.* 69
Compound. Whereas thou maist *compound* a better penie, . . *Hub.* 523
eftsoones he did *compownd;* . . . II. vii. 17. 7
Till universall peace *compound* all civill jarre. . . . III. iii. 23. 9
with whom they did *compound* To passe them over . . . V. xii. 4. 3
They did their counsels now in one *compound:* . . . VI. v. 14. 6
Comprehend. No thought of earthly wight Can *comprehend,* . *H.H.L.* 41
Comprehended. nought but gall and venim *comprehended,* . IV. i. 27. 4
Comprise. naming Rome, ye land and sea *comprize:* . . . *Ro.* xxvi. 12
Not that these few lines can in them *comprise* . . . *Ded. Son.* xvi. 6

Comprise—*Continued.*
the same could one of these *comprize*. . . . . II. ix. 49. 5
What meaning mote those uncouth words *comprize*, ... VI. viii. 18. 4
That in his mightie compasse doth *comprize*, ... *H.H.B.* 73
Comprised. in her bosome she *compriz'd* Well as she might, . . III. vi. 19. 7
sith they cannot in this Canto well *Comprised* be, ... IV. ix. 41. 9
Comprize, -zd. *See* **Comprise, -d.**
Comprovincial. Islands, *comprovinciall* In auncient times unto great Britainee, ... III. iii. 32. 6
Comptroll. *See* **Control.**
Compulsion. Of strong *compulsion* and streight violence, . . . V. v. 33. 2
Con. Of Muses, Hobbinol, I *conne* no skill, ... *S.C.* Jun. 66
they that *con* of Muses skill . . . . *S.C.* Jul. 45
they *con* to heaven the high-way, ... *S.C.* S. 90
Yet, as I *conne*, my conning I will strayne. . . . . *S.C.* N. 52
Much more there is unkend then thou doest *kon*, ... *Col.* 294
Conan. Griffyth *Conan* also shall upreare His dreaded head, . III. iii. 45. 6
Conceal. where I did long *conceale* My selfe, ... IV. viii. 55. 4
From peoples knowledge labour'd to *concele*: . . . . IV. x. 41. 3
what so Envie good or bad did fynd She did *conceale*, ... V. xii. 33. 5
(Unlesse thou in these woods thy selfe *conceale* . . . . . VI. ii. 26. 2
Did inly grudge, yet did it well *conceale*; . . . . VII. vi. 35. 8
Concealed. love did beare, And long it close *conceal'd*, ... *Mui.* 132
Oft times to plaine your loves *concealed* smart; . . . . . . *As.* Pr. 2
So lay him in her charett, close in night *conceald*. . . . . . I. v. 29. 9
Litle shee weend that love he close *conceald*. . . . . III. v. 49. 4
to her reveald . . . but from all men *conceald*: . . . . . . III. viii. 6. 5
Which all that while I closely had *conceld*; . . . . IV. x. 55. 2
that which he most *concealed*, ... IV. xii. 22. 8
Conceald through covert night. . . . . *Epith.* 363
Concealing. *See* **All-concealing.**
double griefs afflict *concealing* harts, ... I. ii. 34. 5
Which long *concealing* in her covert brest, ... V. v. 27. 1
Conceit. Such high *conceipt* of that celestiall fire, ... *T.M.* 391
pursue that brave *conceipt* In thy sweete Eglantine . . . . . *Col.* 388
To steale a snatch of amorous *conceipt*, ... II. v. 34. 6
Which vaine *conceipt* now nourishing no more, ... V. vii. 38. 8
wouldest needs thine owne *conceit* areed! . . . . VII. vi. 46. 8
wonders doe they reede To their *conceipt*, ... *H.B.* 247
Conceited. *See* **High-conceited.**
Conceitful. she gan to cast In her *conceiptfull* mynd . . . . VI. xii. 16. 2
Conceits. with his wicked charmes And strong *conceipts* . . *Hub.* 827
Conceive. What comfort can I, wofull wretch, *conceave?* . . . II. i. 17. 2
Conceive such soveraine glory and great bountyhed? . . . . . II. x. 2. 9
Doe life *conceive* and quickned are by kynd: . . . . III. vi. 8. 6
Love to *conceive* in her disdainfull brest; . . . . III. xi. 17. 6
He gan in mind *conceive* a fit reliefe . . . . VI. iv. 34. 4
he cannot expresse his simple minde, Ne yours *conceive*, . . . VI. v. 30. 4
inward shame of her uncomely case She did *conceive*, ... VI. viii. 51. 2
Is long ere it *conceive* the kindling fyre; . . . . *Am.* vi. 6
Such subtile craft my Damzell doth *conceave*, ... *Am.* xxiii. 5
Wil soon *conceive*, and learne to construe well. . . . . . . *Am.* xliii. 14
Whereof such wondrous pleasures they *conceave*, ... *H.H.B.* 256
Conceived. *See* **Deep-Conceived, Old-conceived.**
The which *conceiv'd* in her revengefull minde . . . . *Gn.* 398
Like as he had *conceiv'd* it in his thought. . . . . *Gn.* 656
Fled back to heaven, whence she was first *conceived*, ... *Hub.* 3
Which she *conceived* hath through meditation . . . . *D.* 33
ever by her lookes *conceived* her intent. . . . . I. iii. 9. 9
fild her hidden caves with stormie yre, That she *conceiv'd*; . . I. vii. 9. 6
tell the cause of your *conceived* payne; . . . . II. i. 14. 6
cause not well *conceived* ye mistake: . . . . II. ii. 5. 5
colde through feare and old *conceived* dreads; . . . . II. ii. 9. 3
of him selfe great hope and help *conceiv'd*, ... II. iii. 5. 2
quench the brond of his *conceived* yre: . . . . II. vi. 27. 6
Her fickle hart *conceived* hasty fyre, ... III. i. 47. 6
Conceiv'd a bold devise, and thus bespake: . . . . III. iii. 52. 2
faire Chrysogone *Conceiv'd* these infants, ... III. vi. 5. 3
Unwares she them *conceivd*, unwares she bore: . . . . III. vi. 27. 1
bore withouten paine, that she *conceiv'd* Withouten pleasure; III. vi. 27. 2
conceiv'd affection bace, And cast to love her . . . . . . III. vii. 15. 7
apply His nimble feet to her *conceived* feare, ... III. vii. 24. 6
Great comfort of her presence he *conceiv'd*, ... III. viii. 23. 3
soone they life *conceiv'd*, and forth . . . did fly. . . . . . III. xii. 9. 9
hope, which she before *Conceived* had, ... III. xii. 44. 8
confidence . . . *Conceived* by a ring which she him sent, . . . IV. ii. 39. 7
Of his old love *conceav'd* in secret brest, ... IV. ix. 17. 4
She inly yet *conceived* great disgrace: . . . . V. iii. 23. 7
Through dolorous despaire which she *conceyved*, ... V. iv. 10. 2
she gan unfold The cause of her *conceived* maladie, ... V. v. 31. 8
Conceived close in her beguiled hart, ... V. v. 43. 8
For very fell despight which she *conceived*, ... V. v. 47. 3
Scarse so *conceived* in her jealous thought, ... V. vi. 3. 2
what ever evill she *conceived*, ... V. xii. 33. 6
soone allayd that Knights *conceiv'd* displeasure, ... VI. iii. 22. 2
many gealous thoughts *conceiv'd* in vaine, ... VI. ix. 38. 4
Conceives. Begets and eke *conceives*, ne needeth other none. . IV. x. 41. 9
Conceiveth. that divelish yron Engin . . . *Conceiveth* fyre, . . I. vii. 13. 5
Conceiving. *conceiving* hope of comfort glad, ... III. iii. 51. 3
Whereof *conceiving* shame and foule disgrace, ... III. vi. 10. 1
Whereof *conceiving*, she in time forth brought . . . sons, . . IV. xi. 42. 7
The trustie Mayd, *conceiving* her intent, ... V. v. 35. 1
conceiving then great feare Of my fraile safetie, ... VI. ii. 29. 2
Concele, -ld. *See* **Conceal, -ed.**
Concent. A lay of loves delight with sweet *concent*: . . . . . III. xii. 5. 7
likely harts composd of starres *concent*, ... *H.B.* 198
Concented. Such Musicke is wise words, with time *concented*, . IV. ii. 2. 5
Conception. her *conception* of the joyous Prime; . . . . . . III. vi. 3. 2
So straunge ensample of *conception*; . . . . III. vi. 8. 2
Concern. 'His be that care, whom most it doth *concerne*,' . . . II. iv. 43. 1
Concerning. wondrous things *concerning* our welfare, ... II. xii. 47. 5
first, *concerning* her that is the first, ... VII. vii. 50. 1
Concerns. ye then, whom onely it *concernes*, ... *T.M.* 49
it me *concernes* my selfe to clere, ... VI. ii. 15. 8
Concluded. Which might *concluded* be by mutuall consent. . . V. iii. 21. 9
Conclusions. My Song thus now in thy *Conclusions*, ... *Pet.*[1] vii. 1
Concoction. The maister Cooke was cald *Concoction*; . . . . II. ix. 31. 1
Concord. So conteck soone by *concord* mought be ended. . . . *S.C.* May 163
what *concord* han light and darke sam? . . . . *S.C.* May 168
lovely *concord*, and most sacred peace, ... II. ii. 31. 1
with that golden chaine of *concord* tyde. . . . . III. i. 12. 8
How she might overthrow the things that *Concord* wrought. . IV. i. 29. 9
With which it blessed *Concord* hath together tide. . . . . . IV. i. 30. 9
'*Concord* she cleeped was in common reed, ... IV. x. 34. 1
Concrew. He let to grow and griesly to *concrew*, ... IV. vii. 40. 5
Cond. *See* **Conned.**
Condemn. I him *condemne*, and deeme his paine, ... IV. xii. 11. 3
Condemned. Theseus *condemned* to endlesse slouth by law; . . I. v. 35. 8
They were . . . *Condemned* to that Dongeon mercilesse, . . . I. v. 46. 8
nought that falles . . . but is *condemned* to be drent, ... II. xii. 6. 9
By wicked doome *condemn'd* a wretched death to die. . . . . IV. xii. 29. 9
She him *condemn'd* as trustlesse and untrew; . . . . V. vi. 5. 2
Ne cared as a coward so to be *condemned*. . . . . VI. iii. 36. 9
Ye shall *condemned* be of many a one. . . . . *Am.* xxxvi. 14
Condescend. Thereto they both did franckly *condiscend*, . . . V. i. 25. 8
Condign. Her selfe of all that rule she deemed most *condigne*. VII. vi. 11. 9
Condition. happie then Was the *condition* of mortall men. . . *Hub.* 150
Content with little in *condition* sicker. . . . . *Hub.* 430
a composition . . . for light *condition*, ... *Hub.* 572
loath such base *condition*, ... *Hub.* 719
Upon *condition*, that ye ruled bee In all affaires, ... *Hub.* 1051
The sharpe dislikes of each *condition*: . . . . *Com. Son.* i. 4
Whose bad *condition* yet it doth retaine, ... IV. xi. 38. 8
In which *condition* I right now did stand: . . . . V. iv. 32. 5
blotted with *condition* vile and base, ... V. ix. 38. 5
orders new Imposd on it with many a hard *condition*, ... V. x. 27. 7
to release his former foule *condition*. . . . . VI. i. 43. 9
As graunt me live in like *condition*; . . . . VI. ix. 28. 7
Above the fortune of their first *condition*, ... *H.H.L.* 81
Conditioned. every substaunce is *conditioned* To chaunge her hew, III. vi. 38. 3
Conditions. Such would descrie his lewd *conditions*; . . . . *Hub.* 796
With like *conditions* to their kindes applyde: . . . . I. iv. 18. 4
to her just *conditions* of faire peace to heare. . . . . II. ii. 27. 9
All shap't according their *conditions*: . . . . II. xi. 11. 6
That man to hard *conditions* to bind, ... III. ii. 13. 7
far unlike *conditions* has; . . . . III. ix. 4. 7
in *conditions* to be loath'd no lesse; . . . . IV. viii. 24. 2
O vaine judgement, and *conditions* vaine, ... IV. xii. 11. 1
these *conditions* doe to him propound: . . . . V. iv. 49. 1
Scorning her offers and *conditions* vaine; . . . . V. v. 46. 2
Began the streight *conditions* to propound. . . . . V. vii. 28. 2
For his faire usage and *conditions* sound, ... VI. i. 3. 3
With these *conditions* which I will propound: . . . . VI. i. 42. 6
A beauteous soule, with faire *conditions* thewed, ... *H.B.* 137
Condole. That Shepheard Colin dearely did *condole*, ... VII. vi. 40. 5
Conduct. *See* **Safe-conduct.**
Under whose *conduct* most victorious, ... *Gn.* 548
rusheth forth Betweene them both by *conduct* of his blade. . . II. ii. 25. 2
conduct me well In these strange waies . . . . VI. Pr. 2. 7
Withouten guide her to *conduct* aright, ... VI. v. 7. 8
To wend with him, and be his *conduct* trew . . . . VI. xi. 35. 3
By *conduct* of some star, doth make her way; . . . . *Am.* xxxiv. 2
Conducted. So he them streight *conducted* to his Lord; . . . V. iv. 51. 1
they her forth *conducted*, ... VI. v. 31. 3
Conducting. *See* **Safe-conducting.**
Conduit-pipe. by a *conduit pipe* it thence were brought: . . . II. ix. 32. 4
Conference. through wise speaches and grave *conference* . . *Hub.* 791
Conferred. diversely *conferred* of their case, ... IV. ix. 10. 2
Confers. With whom he close *confers* with wise discourse, . . *Hub.* 763
Confess. As one that would *confesse*, yet faine would it denie. V. v. 31. 9
Shall find by tryall, and *confesse* it then, ... *H.B.* 89
Confessed. *Confest* how Philemon her wrought to chaunge . . II. iv. 29. 9
Who, being askt, accordingly *confessed* all. . . . . IV. v. 23. 9
to her *confessed* short That 'twas Molanna . . . . VII. vi. 51. 7
Confidence. In God alone do stay my *confidence*. . . . . . . *Bel.*[1] i. 14
In God alone my *confidence* do stay. . . . . *Bel.*[2] i. 14
under colour of the *confidence* . . . . *Hub.* 1164
For his bold featés and hardy *confidence*, ... II. iv. 41. 3
vertues might and values *confidence*: . . . . III. xi. 14. 7
Most *confidence* and hope of happie speed, ... IV. ii. 39. 6
I was emboldned with more *confidence*; . . . . IV. x. 56. 5
counsels him, through *confidence* of might, ... V. viii. 20. 4
The better to confirme her fearelesse *confidence*. . . . . . . V. x. 12. 9
thinkes through *confidence* of might, . . . To wrong the weaker, VI. ii. 23. 7
'Speake, thou fraile woman, speake with *confidence*; . . . . . VII. vi. 25. 7
Confident. kept her place with courage *confident*, ... V. vi. 28. 4
Confines. devides The Cornish and the Devonish *confines*; . . . IV. xi. 31. 2
Confirm. to *confirme*, and fast to bind their league, ... II. ii. 33. 1
Yet ought mens good endevours them *confirme*, ... III. iii. 25. 8
The better to *confirme* her fearelesse confidence. . . . . . . V. x. 12. 9
Confirmed. auncient truth *confirm'd* with credence old. . . . *Col.* 103
that of Cambry king *confirmed* late, ... II. x. 38. 5
settled he his kingdome, and *confirmd* his right: . . . . . . II. x. 60. 9
peace being *confirm'd* amongst them all, ... IV. vi. 39. 2
Jove *confirm'd* in his imperiall see. . . . . VII. vii. 59. 7
Conflict. The lucklesse *conflict* with the Gyaunt stout, ... I. vii. 26. 8
combrous *conflict* which they did sustaine, ... II. ix. 17. 5
This cruell *conflict* raised thereabout, ... IV. ix. 24. 8
Such was the *conflict* of those cruell Brigants there. . . . . VI. xi. 17. 9
'In that same *conflict* (woe is me!) befell This fatall chaunce, VI. xi. 31. 1

Conforming. *conforming* it unto the light, H.B. 218
Confound. *See* **Confounded.**
as halfe with shame *confound* S.C. Jun. 64
Sith ignorance our kingdome did *confound,* T.M. 311
was . . . in her owne skill *confound,* Mui. 262
whose glorious vew Their frayle amazed senses did *confound:* I. iv. 7. 3
one that with his prowesse may . . . thy foes *confownd.* I. ix. 16. 8
did quite *confound* His feeble sence, I. x. 67. 7
Do arme your self against that day, them to *confownd'* II. iii. 15. 9
realmes and rulers thou doest both *confound,* II. vii. 13. 2
Broke their rude troupes, and orders did *confownd,* II. ix. 15. 7
which Alexander did *confound;* II. ix. 45. 7
doth *confownd* Them comfortlesse III. ii. 14. 7
all the world *confound* with cruelty; III. x. 33. 8
sweetnesse . . . The feeble sences wholy did *confound,* III. xii. 6. 4
Wherewith the hellish fiends he doth *confound:* IV. iii. 42. 7
curse his God that did him so *confound:* IV. viii. 45. 7
all the world *confound* with wide uprore, IV. ix. 23. 8
Through these his slights he many doth *confound:* V. ix. 6. 1
eke him selfe did threaten to *confound;* V. xi. 2. 5
right and wrong most cruelly *confound:* V. xii. 2. 7
To worke his utter shame, and throughly him *confound.* VI. v. 14. 9
fruitfull issue . . . Which may your foes *confound,* Proth. 105
Confounded. *See* **Confound.**
those two Sarazins *confounded* late, II. viii. 54. 8
Much was the man *confounded* in his mind, V. iv. 27. 1
By her beguyled and *confounded* quight: V. ix. 40. 5
So all *confounded* and disordered there: VI. xii. 25. 6
Thou turne to nought, and quite *confounded* be. H.H.B. 147
Confounds. with his furious blast *Confounds* both land and seas, III. ix. 15. 9
Confused. to my selfe, for whose *confusde* decay D. 353
He them encountred, a *confused* rout, II. x. 16. 1
suddeine horrour and *confused* cry II. xi. 20. 1
this great Universe seemd one *confused* mas. II. xii. 34. 9
As smoke and sulphure mingled with *confused* stryfe. III. ii. 32. 9
they grew Greatly *confused* in behaveoure. III. iii. 50. 7
Ten thousand wayes he cast in his *confused* thought. III. x. 18. 9
after them a rude *confused* rout Of persons flockt, III. xii. 25. 1
Confusd with wemens cries and shouts of boyes, IV. iii. 37. 8
His foe *confused* through his sodaine fall, V. ii. 8. 7
she star'd A while about her with *confused* eye; V. v. 13. 8
As one adaw'd, and halfe *confused* stood; V. v. 45. 5
She was *confused* in her troublous thought; V. vii. 25. 3
Flocking together in *confusde* array; V. xi. 43. 8
a soft murmure and *confused* sound Of senselesse words, VI. iv. 11. 7
with the peoples voyce *Confused,* VI. viii. 46. 6
All on *confused* heapes themselves assay, VI. xi. 17. 5
covered with *confused* preasse Of carcases, VI. xi. 20. 1
halfe *confused* with his great commaund, VII. vi. 26. 1
to amaze weak mens *confused* skil, Am. xvii. 2
Crying aloud with strong *confused* noyce, Epith. 138
The which before had lyen *confused* ever. H.L. 77
Confusedly. Where when *confusedly* they came, III. i. 63. 4
Confusion. he has voued thy last *confusion.* S.C. May 220
With bloodie night, and darke *confusion;* Gn. 445
turning all unto the Apes *confusion,* Hub. 1364
they see not the way of their *confusion.* Ti. 458
renownd For tongues *confusion* in Holie Writ, Ti. 510
The foe of faire things, th' author of *confusion,* Mui. 244
Least thy foolhardize worke thy sad *confusion.'* II. iv. 42. 9
many hath to foule *confusion* brought, III. vii. 48. 4
Unto his last *confusion* to bring, IV. i. 30. 7
out throwen Into this world to worke *confusion,* IV. ii. 1. 3
thorough rude *confusion* of the rout, IV. iii. 41. 6
there was caught to her *confusion:* V. v. 43. 4
I onely scapt through great *confusione* VI. xi. 32. 3
They would have caused much *confusion* and disorder. VII. vii. 4. 9
Threatning their owne *confusion* and decay: H.L. 82
Congealed. *See* **Cold-congealed.**
His cruell wounds, with cruddy bloud *congeald,* I. v. 29. 6
with dry drops *congealed* in her eye, II. i. 49. 3
The Christall humor stood *congealed* rownd; III. v. 29. 4
Yet still he wasted, as the snow *congeald* III. v. 49. 5
purest snow in massy mould *congeald,* III. viii. 6. 2
in his *congealed* flesh III. viii. 25. 1
Congealed litle drops which doe the morne adore. IV. xi. 46. 9
lake Of bloudy gore *congeal'd* about them stood, VI. i. 37. 8
yse, which is *congeald* with sencelesse cold, Am. xxx. 11
Congee. Where taking *Conge,* each one by and by Departed Hub. 1108
So courteous *conge* both did give and take, II. i. 34. 1
taking *Conge* of that virgin pure, II. iii. 2. 1
taking courteous *conge,* II. xi. 17. 3
They courteous *conge* tooke, and forth together yode. III. i. 1. 9
Conge tooke withall; III. iv. 4. 5
unto her his *congee* came to take; IV. vi. 42. 6
Congregate. With all the Gods about him *congregate:* VII. vi. 19. 5
Conjectured. For not to grow of nought he it *conjectured.* II. iv. 39. 9
Conjoined. Where singled forces faile, *conjoynd* may gaine. VI. v. 14. 7
Conjure. Unlesse thou canst one *conjure* by device, Hub. 510
them *conjure* t' avenge this shamefull injury. I. xii. 27. 9
her *conjure* . . . to traine his tender youth, II. iii. 2. 3
them *conjure,* upon eternall paine, To counsell her, III. viii. 4. 7
When those gainst states and kingdomes do *conjure,* V. x. 26. 8
Conjured. them *conjur'd* by some well knowen token, IV. ii. 21. 7
Conned. Which I *cond* of Tityrus in my youth, S.C. F. 92
had well *ycond* his lere, S.C. May 262
had he *cond* the shepherds call, S.C. S. 215
(for well that skill he *cond;*) Col. 74
They all were fled for feare; but whether, nether *kond.* V. vi. 35. 9
Conning. *See* **Cunning.**
Conquer. Doest *conquer* greatest conquerors on ground, IV. vii. 1. 2
though sweet love to *conquer* glorious bee, IV. x. 3. 8
Conquered. *conquer'd,* dare the Conquerour disdaine. Ro. xiv. 14
Harten against her selfe her *conquer'd* spoile, Ro. xxii. 6
by force I *conquered* were Of hardie Saxons, Ti. 113
The which my soule first *conquerd* and possest, D. 300
Though *conquered* now he lye on lowly land; I. iii. 37. 7
seemd himselfe as *conquered* to yield. I. viii. 20. 5
That he in ods of armes was *conquered:* II. v. 14. 6
hong their *conquerd* armes . . . On gallow trees, II. v. 26. 8
After the Paynim brethren *conquer'd* were, II. ix. 2. 1
Goemot, whome in stout fray Corineus *conquered,* II. x. 10. 9
taught her first how to be *conquered;* II. x. 23. 8
this sweet Island never *conquered,* II. x. 47. 7
the spoile of the countrey *conquered* III. iii. 47. 8
having *conquered* The maistring raines out of her weary wrest, III. vii. 2. 7
as *conquered* To be her thrall, III. vii. 17. 7
From slaughter of the Giaunts *conquered;* III. ix. 22. 2
Albion had *conquered* first by warlike feat.' III. ix. 46. 9
Hath *conquered* you anew in second fight: IV. vi. 31. 3
whylome they have *conquerd* sea and land, IV. vi. 31. 4
yet he *conquer'd* not by bloudie fight, IV. viii. 47. 6
Bearing the shield which I had *conquerd* late, IV. x. 14. 2
Unto the Castle which they *conquerd* had: V. xi. 3. 4
this land, late *conquer'd* by his sword VI. iv. 29. 5
Conqueress. Bunduca, that victorious *conqueresse,* Ti. 108
the noble *Conqueresse* Her selfe came in, V. vii. 36. 1
Conquering. he bare . . . in left the *conquering* Palme, Bel.[1] vii. 11
conquering beautie doth captive My trembling hart H.B. 275
Conqueror. conquer'd, dare the *Conquerour* disdaine. Ro. xiv. 14
made the Easterne *Conquerour* to crie, Ti. 432
The Sarazins shield, signe of the *conqueroure.* I. ii. 20. 7
Unto that doughtie *Conquerour* they came, I. xii. 6. 1
The *Conquerour* nought cared him to slay; II. viii. 51. 2
now alone he *conquerour* remaines: II. xi. 48. 1
Conquerors. *conquerours* (*Conquerors*[1]) bedecked Bel. v. 3
The Laurell, meed of mightie *Conquerours* I. i. 9. 1
mighty kings and *conquerours* in warre, II. x. 4. 5
girlond of the mighty *Conquerours,* III. ix. 35. 2
victorious prayes Of mightie *Conquerours* III. xi. 52. 3
Doest conquer greatest *conquerors* on ground, IV. vii. 1. 2
the heyre of ancient kings And mightie *Conquerors,* V. ix. 29. 8
Conquest. so oft thee, (Rome) their *conquest* made; Ro. xiii. 4
with *conquest* of their might and maine, Ti. 62
When the Naemean *Conquest* he did win. Mui. 72
This simple trophe of her great *conquest.'*— Col. 951
The *conquest* yours; I yours; I. v. 14. 9
greater *conquest* of hard love he gaynes, I. vi. 3. 8
the suitt of earthly *conquest* shonne, I. x. 60. 7
atchievde so great a *conquest* by his might. I. xi. 55. 9
those which Hercules, with *conquest* bold Got II. vii. 54. 5
of this lands first *conquest* did devize, II. ix. 59. 7
His goodly *conquest* of the golden fleece, II. xii. 44. 6
through *conquest* of your wondrous might, III. v. 53. 4
As if the *conquest* his he surely wist. IV. iii. 5. 3
Scudamour doth his *conquest* tell Of vertuous Amoret: IV. x. Arg.
quaile in *conquest* of that land of gold. IV. xi. 22. 5
all the West with equall *conquest* wonne, V. i. 2. 7
No fayrer *conquest* then that with goodwill is gayned. V. v. 17. 9
Till I the *conquest* of my will recover.' V. v. 51. 5
his late *conquest* which he gotten had: VI. i. 4. 5
rather seem'd the *conquest* of his might, VI. v. 9. 4
was the *conquest* of the gentlest Knight VI. x. 40. 8
he himselfe which did that *conquest* make: VI. xi. 12. 5
So led this Knight his captyve with like *conquest* wonne. VI. xii. 35. 9
we by *conquest* . . . Have wonne the Empire VII. vi. 33. 5
she will the *conquest* challeng needs, Am. xxix. 9
memory Of my loves *conquest,* Am. lxix. 7
What puissant *conquest,* what adventurous paine, H.L. 221
Advance the banner of thy *conquest* hie, H.B. 268
Conquest's. With his faire paragon, his *conquests* part, IV. i. 33. 4
Conquests. Was never man, who most *conquestes* atchiev'd, II. v. 15. 3
That hath so many haughty *conquests* wonne? II. v. 35. 8
In meed of these great *conquests* by them gott, II. x. 12. 1
shall their *conquests* through all lands extend, III. iii. 23. 4
all the *conquests* which them high did reare, III. iv. 1. 5
in all His famous *conquests* highly magnifide: III. vii. 31. 7
thy victorious *conquests* to areed, H.L. 11
in the *conquests* of your beautie bost, H.L. 37
Conscience. in his *conscience* made a secrete breach, I. ix. 48. 3
trembling horror did his *conscience* daunt, I. ix. 49. 3
that disease of grieved *conscience,* I. x. 23. 8
Una . . . joyous of his cured *conscience,* I. x. 29. 3
My *conscience* cleare with guilty bands would bynd? I. xii. 30. 5
Albe her guiltlesse *conscience* her cleard, III. vi. 10. 2
According to the line of *conscience,* V. i. 7. 4
with *conscience* Of his ill newes, V. vi. 9. 5
Consent. Chaunted their sundrie tunes with sweete *consent;* Gn. 226
The fields, the floods, the heavens, with one *consent,* I. ix. 12. 8
They soone *consent:* II. ii. 33. 6
with Guyon knitt in one *consent,* II. iii. 11. 8
Accord of friendes, *consent* of Parents sought, II. iv. 21. 3
by *consent* of Commons and of Peares, II. x. 62. 8
all her sister Nymphes with one *consent* III. iv. 35. 8
They by *consent* should chose the stoutest three IV. ii. 38. 7
they all with one *consent* . . . Agreed to travell, IV. iv. 6. 1
with one *consent* did yeeld the prize To Triamond IV. iv. 36. 3
she yeelded her *consent* To be his love, IV. vi. 41. 7
consent To cloud my daies in dolefull misery, IV. viii. 16. 7

Consent—*Continued.*
lodging there without her owne *consent:* IV. viii. 28. 5
with him to wend, gainst all her friends *consent.* IV. viii. 50. 9
ne would for ought *Consent* IV. viii. 58. 6
thereto did with readie will *consent,* IV. viii. 64. 8
lovers lincked in true harts *consent,* IV. x. 26. 4
he thereto would by no meanes *consent,* V. i. 30. 6
Which might concluded be by mutuall *consent.* V. viii. 21. 9
they all gave one *consent* VI. viii. 38. 4
Were by them slaine by generall *consent:* VI. xi. 31. 5
They all *consent* that ye begotten were VII. vii. 53. 8
So goodly all agree, with sweet *consent,* *Epith.* 83
Consented. to my foe hath guilefully *consented:* V. xi. 50. 8
Consider. 'I well *consider* all that ye have said, VII. vii. 58. 1
Considering. well *considering* of the circumstaunce, *Hub.* 174
Consisted. *Consisted* much in that adventures priefe: V. vii. 44. 5
Consort. To him assembled with one full *consort,* I. xii. 4. 7
made emongst them selves a sweete *consort,* II. v. 31. 8
On thother side in one *consort* there sate II. vii. 22. 1
Some song in sweet *consort;* II. ix. 35. 2
wonder was to heare their trim *consort.* III. i. 40. 6
The Lyon there did with the Lambe *consort,* IV. viii. 31. 1
Coridon durst not with him *consort,* VI. xi. 42. 8
With whom the woody Gods did oft *consort,* VII. vi. 39. 8
Which of her Nymphes, or other close *consort,* VII. vi. 51. 5
Consorted. *See* **Well-consorted.**
Memprise, . . . being *consorted* with Manild, II. x. 21. 4
there *consorted* in one harmonee; II. xii. 70. 8
Consorts. to beare A Bases part amongst their *consorts* oft, *T.M.* 28
Conspire. all the heavenly powres *Conspire* in one to wreake *Gn.* 579
Conspire in one to make contented blisse. *Col.* 311
conspyre With fire and sword the region to invade: I. xi. 14. 5
Against that Castles Lord they gan *conspire,* III. ix. 17. 4
Fortune did not with his will *conspire;* VI. viii. 15. 5
al powers *conspire,* That . . . naught else be counted *Am.* viii. 3
Yet heresy nor treason didst *conspire,* *Am.* xlviii. 7
conspire In my sweet peace such breaches to have bred! *Am.* lxxxv. 11
to *conspyre* Each against other *H.L.* 80
Conspired. Where they in secret counsell close *conspird,* III. iii. 51. 5
had her counsels false *conspyred* V. ix. 41. 2
Conspiring. Starres *conspiring* wretched men t' afflict, *T.M.* 482
So both *conspiring* gan to intimate VI. iii. 12. 4
conspiring all together plaine, VI. v. 14. 5
Constancy. With *constancy* and care, gainst daunger II. xii. 38. 9
Constant. *constant* Curtius, Who, stifly bent *Gn.* 602
She armes the brest with *constant* patience *T.M.* 133
he . . . Her *constant* hart did tempt with diverse guile: I. vi. 4. 3
in *constant* carefull mind, She fedd her wound I. vii. 28. 5
with *constant* zele and corage bold, I. viii. 40. 4
Ne divelish thoughts dismay thy *constant* spright: I. ix. 53. 3
she no whitt did chaunge her *constant* mood: I. x. 13. 6
all that might his *constant* hart Withdraw II. vi. 25. 5
constant keepe the way in which ye stand; II. ix. 8. 6
In *constant* peace their kingdomes did contayne. II. x. 34. 4
The *constant* payre heard all that he did say, II. xii. 76. 4
constant mind Would not so lightly follow beauties chace, III. i. 19. 1
guyde the heavenly causes to their *constant* terme. III. iii. 25. 9
Her *constant* mind could move IV. xi. 2. 8
with *constant* firme intent For zeale of Justice, V. ix. 49. 4
Her *constant* mynd could not a whit remove, VI. xi. 5. 2
'Ne is the water in more *constant* case, VII. vii. 20. 1
you, Dan Jove, that only *constant* are, VII. vii. 53. 1
she, beholding me with *constant* eye, *Am.* liv. 9
her too *constant* stiffenesse doth constrayn. *Am.* lxxxiii. 12
There dwels sweet love, and *constant* chastity, *Epith.* 191
Which he beholding still with *constant* sight, *H.L.* 195
Constantine. Of whom he did great *Constantine* begett, II. x. 60. 1
They crownd the second *Constantine* with joyous teares. II. x. 62. 9
the sonnes of *Constantine,* which fled, II. x. 67. 1
Constantius. *Constantius,* a man of mickle might, II. x. 59. 2
from the head Of his coosen *Constantius,* III. iii. 29. 5
Constitution. And so doe make contrarie *constitution* V. Pr. 4. 8
Constrain. so small so mightie can *constraine?* *Van.* iii. 14
The evill plight that doth me sore *constraine,* *Hub.* 56
everie wight to shrowd it did *constrain;* I. i. 6. 8
soone to loose her wicked bands did her *constraine.* I. i. 19. 9
them *constraine* in equall teme to draw. I. vi. 26. 6
such as want of harbour did *constraine:* I. x. 37. 8
did him at last *constraine* To let them downe I. xi. 19. 3
ravenous hunger did thereto *constraine:* I. xi. 37. 4
nor stroks mote him *constraine* To loose, I. xi. 43. 2
fraile affection did *constraine* His stout courage to stoupe, II. i. 42. 8
hundred knots, that did him sore *constraine;* II. iv. 15. 2
my lucklesse lott doth me *constrayne* Hereto perforce. III. Pr. 3. 4
her for to awake he did the more *constraine.* III. x. 49. 9
by torture he would her *constraine* III. xi. 17. 5
two villeins . . . Her forward still with torture did *constraine,* III. xii. 21. 8
My softened heart so sorely doth *constraine,* IV. i. 1. 7
love of fairest Ladie could *constraine;* IV. ix. 3. 5
Feare of her safety did her not *constraine;* IV. ix. 18. 1
Proteus to *constraine;* IV. xii. 14. 8
he for nought could him thereto *constraine;* V. iii. 31. 7
Even so did Radigund . . . sorely him *constraine.* V. v. 15. 9
rather bent To peace then needlesse trouble to *constraine,* V. vi. 19. 7
That it to such a streight mote you *constraine*) V. xi. 55. 4
When as necessitie doth it *constraine.'* V. xi. 56. 5
if need *constraine,* His hope of refuge used to remaine: VI. i. 22. 4
Whom he likewise right sorely did *constraine,* VI. vi. 38. 5
he did him *constraine* To give him ground, VI. vii. 46. 5

Constrain—*Continued.*
her too constant stiffenesse doth *constrayn.* *Am.* lxxxiii. 12
Constrained. *constrain'd* that trade to overgive, I driven am *Hub.* 249
th' evill will Of all their Parishners they had *constraind;* *Hub.* 561
the cause which thee theretoo *constrained,* *D.* 81
he is perforce *constraynd* To throw his ryder; I. xi. 23. 6
The God, though loth, yet was *constraynd* t' obay; II. vii. 66. 1
As if some pensive thought *constraind* her gentle spright. II. ix. 36. 9
him vanquisht she to fly *constraind:* II. x. 18. 5
The same to love he strongly was *constraynd;* III. v. 44. 6
he with old Latinus was *constraind* To contract wedlock, III. ix. 42. 4
constrayned To utter forth the anguish of his hart: *Am.* xlviii. 9
Constraining. through Loves *constrayning* Tormented sore, IV. x. 43. 7
her sad selfe . . . *constrayning,* To wype his wounds, VI. ii. 41. 4
Constrains. greater conquest of hard love he gaynes, . . . then he that it *constraines.* I. vi. 3. 9
When too huge toile and labour them *constraines,* III. iii. 9. 7
Constraint. Caused of wrong and cruell *constraint,* *S.C.* F. 152
Well heard Kiddie al this sore *constraint,* *S.C.* May 249
Whether rejoyce or weepe for great *constrainte.* *S.C.* N. 205
With tender ruth to see her sore *constraint;* *Ti.* 31
His Lady, sad to see his sore *constraint,* I. i. 19. 1
she saide, . . . deare *constraint,* Lets me not sleepe, I. i. 53. 1
sad to see her sorrowfull *constraint,* I. iii. 8. 3
when her face is staynd with magicke arts *constraint.* I. vii. 34. 9
sinews woxen weake and raw, Through . . . hard *constraint,* I. x. 2. 4
Whom late I left in languorous *constraynt?* II. i. 9. 7
to weepe for sore *constraint;* II. ii. 8. 3
through great *constraint* He made him stoup II. v. 11. 5
brought she was now to so hard *constraint,* III. vii. 10. 7
nothing may impresse so deare *constraint* III. ix. 40. 3
The cause of that his sorrowfull *constraint;* IV. vii. 45. 3
Till strong *constraint* did her thereto enforce: V. x. 4. 6
true love doth tye Without *constraynt,* *Am.* lxv. 6
Construe. yet could not *construe* it By any ridling skill, III. xi. 54. 4
Wil soon conceive, and learne to *construe* well. *Am.* xliii. 14
Consume. all that doth *consume* our pleasures soone; *Ro.* xix. 4
'Harrow! the flames which me *consume,'* II. vi. 49. 8
with plagues and murrins pestilent *Consume,* III. iii. 40. 9
Doth it *consume* and into nothing goe, III. vi. 37. 8
saw the wicked fire so furiously *Consume* his hart, III. x. 14. 6
did *consume* his gall with anguish sore: III. x. 18. 2
doth with curelesse care *consume* the hart, III. x. 59. 6
Nor to the Fire; for they *consume* not ever; *Am.* ix. 8
Consume thee quite, that didst with guile conspire *Am.* lxxxv. 11
Consumed. With sodain fall to dust *consumed* quight. *Bel.*^{2} iv. 14
Eftsoones *consum'd* to fall downe feebily, *Ro.* xvi. 11
these mountaines, now *consum'd* to pouder; *Ro.* xvii. 12
The Dorick flames *consum'd* the Iliack posts. *Gn.* 549
the Oetaean wood Had him *consum'd,* *Ti.* 382
nigh *consumed* is the lingring day. I. iv. 3. 9
Consumed had their goods and thriftlesse howres, I. v. 51. 8
Such earthly mettals soon *consumed* beene, I. vii. 33. 4
His rawbone armes, . . . Were clene *consum'd;* I. viii. 41. 8
After lost credit and *consumed* thrift, II. xii. 8. 8
In one sad night *consumd* and throwen downe: III. ix. 39. 5
He was not in the cities wofull fyre *Consum'd,* III. ix. 40. 9
all his substance was *consum'd* to nought, III. x. 57. 3
quenched quite like a *consumed* torch, III. xii. 42. 8
Through wilfull penury *consumed* quight, IV. vii. 41. 3
th' Aire . . . Never *consum'd,* nor quencht with mortall hands; *H.H.B.* 40
Consumes. That rotts the marrow, and *consumes* the braine. I. iv. 26. 8
every thing *consumes,* and calcineth by art. III. v. 48. 9
Consuming. *See* **Life-consuming, Self-consuming.**
spends his wit in loves *consuming* smart: *Col.* 429
consuming thought To put away I. x. 29. 5
with loves *consuming* rage, III. vii. 46. 4
That he might taste the sweet *consuming* woe, III. xi. 45. 4
In wilfull languor and *consuming* smart, III. xii. 16. 8
evermore encreased her *consuming* paine. III. xii. 21. 9
Consuming Riotise, and guilty Dread III. xii. 25. 7
nourisheth her owne *consuming* smart? IV. vi. 1. 4
makes himself his owne *consuming* pray: VII. vii. 24. 5
Time shall soon cut down with his *consuming* sickle. VII. viii. 1. 9
drinketh up the lyfe . . . with *consuming* griefe. *H.L.* 126
After long sorrow and *consuming* smart. *H.B.* 28
Kindled the flame of His *consuming* yre, *H.H.L.* 86
Contagion. scarce the skin the strong *contagion* helde. *Mui.* 256
through the great *contagion* direful deadly stonck. II. ii. 4. 9
nought The fell *contagion* may thereof restraine, V. vii. 11. 8
In which a puddle of *contagion* was, V. xi. 32. 3
Contagious. scattering *Contagious* poyson close through every vaine, VI. vi. 8. 8
Contain. The map of all the wide world doth *containe.* *Ro.* xxvi. 14
So many goodly colours doth *containe.* *Mui.* 96
narrow leaves cannot in them *contayne* The large discourse I. xii. 14. 5
No song but did *containe* a lovely ditt. II. vi. 13. 4
In constant peace their kingdomes did *contayne.* II. x. 34. 4
the fruit more sweetnes did *contayne,* III. ii. 17. 7
seemd the Ocean could not *containe* them there. III. vi. 35. 9
in strong bancks his violence *containe,* (D.) III. vii. 34. 2
But fast goodwill, . . . May her perhaps *containe,* III. ix. 7. 9
Ne in small meares *containe* his glory great, III. ix. 46. 8
That glorious belt did in it selfe *containe,* IV. v. 2. 8
could not *containe* it still, IV. x. 43. 8
all that did within them all *containe,* V. ii. 31. 6
Al which the heavens *containe,* V. ii. 35. 9
Ne feed on ought the which doth bloud *containe,* V. vii. 10. 2
Ne within reasons rule her madding mood *containe.* V. vii. 11. 9

Contain—*Continued.*
As to abandon that which doth *containe* Your honours stile, . . . V. xi. 55. 5
lawes of men, that common-weales *containe,* . . . V. xii. 1. 4
From that they most affect, and in due termes *containe.* . . . VI. vi. 7. 9
seemed to *containe* A full good pecke . . . VI. xii. 26. 5
He could him not *containe* in silent rest; . . . VII. vi. 46. 4
Arlo scarsly could them all *containe,* . . . VII. vii. 4. 4
my love doth in her selfe *containe* All . . . riches . . . *Am.* xv. 5
this, That seemes in it all blisses to *containe,* . . . *H.L.* 207
doe *containe* All mortall Princes and imperiall States; . . . *H.H.B.* 87
And all the creatures which they both *containe;* . . . *H.H.B.* 198
Contained. What under this great Temple is *containde,* . . . *Bel.*[1] i. 10
Whatever thing was in the world *contaynd,* . . . III. ii. 19. 2
the heaven is in his course *contained.* . . . IV. x. 35. 1
in this so narrow verse *Contayned* . . . IV. xi. 17. 4
In whose right hands great power is *contayned,* . . . V. ii. 19. 7
Great threasure sithence we did finde *contained,* . . . V. iv. 13. 2
in an other Canto will be best *contayned.* . . . V. v. 57. 9
What wondrous vertue is *contaynd* in you, . . . *Am.* vii. 2
things that are *contained* Within this goodly cope, . . . *H.L.* 94
all that in this mortall frame *Contained* is, . . . *H.L.* 114
worlds great frame, in which al things Are now *containd,* . . . *H.H.L.* 23
Contains. Whatso the heaven in his wide vawte *containes,* . . . *Hub.* 1229
Therewith *containes* his heavenly Common-weale: . . . V. vii. 1. 8
spheare of Cupid fourty yeares *containes:* . . . *Am.* lx. 10
Conteck. So *conteck* soone by concord mought be ended. . . . *S.C.* May 163
kindle coales of *conteck* and yre, . . . *S.C.* S. 86
To stirre up strife, and troublous *contecke* broch: . . . III. i. 64. 5
Contemned. *See* **Contempt.**
both his challenge and him selfe *contemned,* . . . VI. iii. 36. 8
Contemplation. In *contemplation* of things heavenlie wrought: *T.M.* 526
From everie worke he chalenged essoyne, For *contemplation* sake: . . . I. iv. 20. 4
His name was hevenly *Contemplation;* . . . I. x. 46. 8
In *contemplation* of divinitee: . . . III. ix. 24. 4
The *contemplation* of whose heavenly hew, . . . *Am.* lxxx. 11
Through *contemplation* of my purest part, . . . *Am.* lxxxvii. 10
Through *contemplation* of those goodly sights, . . . *H.H.B.* 2
To *contemplation* of th' immortall sky; . . . *H.H.B.* 25
Mount up aloft through heavenly *contemplation,* . . . *H.H.B.* 136
Contempt. Let not my small demaund be so *contempt.* . . . *S.C.* N. 48
to wreake their rash *contempt,* . . . *Gn.* 579
scornfull Follie with *Contempt* is crept, . . . *T.M.* 212
his *contempt,* that did her judg'ment breake. . . . V. iv. 40. 5
Contemptible. Now base and *contemptible* did appeare, . . . IV. v. 14. 2
Contend. Whilst each does for the Soveraignty *contend,* . . . *Gn.* 410
th' one with fire and weapons did *contend* . . . *Gn.* 521
His foes . . . with whom he should *contend.* . . . I. i. 26. 9
sorrowfull assay . . . greater grew the more she did *contend,* . I. vii. 27. 3
hagard hauke, presuming to *contend* With hardy fowle . . . I. xi. 19. 5
whoso would *contend* With either of those knightes . . . II. iii. 17. 2
Whiles they are weake, betimes with them *contend;* . . . II. iv. 34. 5
That joyes for crownes and kingdomes to *contend:* . . . II. vii. 10. 7
Out of his swowne arose, fresh to *contend,* . . . II. xi. 35. 4
seemed to *contend* And wrestle wantonly, . . . II. xii. 63. 7
long while did *contend;* . . . V. xi. 27. 7
Contended. When she with her for excellence *contended,* . . . *Mui.* 263
both the parts did speake, and both *contended;* . . . IV. i. 27. 7
this doutfull case, for which they all *contended.* . . . IV. v. 6. 9
Contending. Arte, with her *contending,* doth aspire . . . *Mui.* 165
contending to excell The reach of men, . . . II. x. 26. 8
Content. not *content* with loyall obeysaunce, . . . *S.C.* May 120
Content who lives with tryed state . . . *S.C.* S. 70
content us in thys humble shade, . . . *S.C.* O. 116
Content with any food that God doth send; . . . *Gn.* 140
Oft-times to begging are *content* to fall. . . . *Hub.* 182
The Husbandman was meanly well *content* . . . *Hub.* 297
Content with little in condition sicker. . . . *Hub.* 430
was *content* to attempt that enterprise, . . . *Hub.* 995
I with reason meete will rest *content,* . . . *Hub.* 1049
The knight was well *content;* . . . I. i. 33. 8
Not all *content,* yet seemd she to appease Her . . . plaintes, I. i. 54. 6
the . . . mayd Did her *content* to please their feeble eyes, . . . I. vi. 19. 2
In full *content* he there did long enjoy; . . . I. xii. 41. 2
not *content* so fowly to devoure Her native flesh . . . III. vii. 49. 4
cruell Cupid, not herewith *content,* . . . III. xi. 38. 7
Content to heare him speake, . . . IV. ii. 21. 9
to his speeches was *content* To lend an eare, . . . IV. vi. 41. 4
spotlesse pleasures and sweet loves *content.* . . . IV. x. 26. 2
Give her great comfort and some harts *content.* . . . V. v. 35. 3
Yet not *content,* . . . Would thumpe her forward . . . VI. ii. 10. 5
that mote *content* An hart . . . VI. ii. 16. 7
Some place of succour to *content* his mynd, . . . VI. iv. 26. 5
doe my selfe with that I have *content;* . . . VI. ix. 20. 5
his speach, that wrought him great *content,* . . . VI. ix. 26. 5
With which the Knight him selfe did much *content,* . . . VI. x. 30. 3
Fit to keepe sheepe, unfit for loves *content:* . . . VI. x. 37. 4
thee *content* thus to be rul'd by mee, . . . VII. vii. 59. 2
To worke ech others joy and true *content,* . . . *H.B.* 200
the cruell boy, not so *content,* Would needs the fly pursue; . *Epig.* iv. 21
Joy may you have, and gentle hearts *content* . . . *Proth.* 94
Contented. *Contented* I: then, will I singe his laye . . . *S.C.* Ap. 33
leave the sweetnes of *contented* home, . . . *Hub.* 947
not *contented* us themselves to scorne, . . . *T.M.* 65
Conspire in one to make *contented* blisse. . . . *Col.* 311
Departed thence with full *contented* mynd; . . . IV. ii. 53. 2
Would not so rest *contented* with his right; . . . V. i. 17. 6
doth litle crave *contented* to abyde. . . . VI. ix. 17. 9
that might *contented* live. . . . VI. ix. 22. 5
fittest is, that all *contented* rest With that they hold: . . . VI. ix. 29. 8

Contented—*Continued.*
Fortune, not with all this wrong *Contented,* . . . VI. xi. 2. 6
He nathemore can so *contented* rest, . . . *H.L.* 246
Contention. Both fierce and furious in *contention* Encountred, *Gn.* 517
Their fell *contention* still increased more, . . . II. v. 22. 1
Whom all that folke with such *contention* . . . II. vii. 48. 5
Coles of *contention* and whot vengeaunce tind. . . . II. viii. 11. 5
threw, in fierce *contention,* At bold Canutus; . . . II. x. 11. 8
When as their sharpe *contention* he had ceased, . . . V. iv. 20. 7
With bitter rage and fell *contention,* . . . V. xii. 41. 3
Did strive to match with strong *contention,* . . . VI. x. 33. 3
Contentious. fowle revenging rage, and base *contentious* jarre. II. ii. 30. 9
Some troublous uprore or *contentious* fray, . . . II. iv. 3. 3
not for malice and *contentious* crymes, . . . III. i. 13. 3
breedes Tumultuous trouble, and *contentious* jarre, . . . IV. i. 25. 8
stirs up anguish and *contentious* rage: . . . IV. iii. 43. 4
Of warres delight and worlds *contentious* toyle, . . . VI. v. 37. 6
Contentment. all things needfull for *contentment* meeke, . . . *Hub.* 911
I feede on sweet *contentment* of my thought, . . . *T.M.* 524
feed on sweet *contentment* of that sight: . . . *Col.* 43
The noblest mind the best *contentment* has. . . . I. i. 35. 4
Gave wondrous great *contentment* to the knight, . . . II. vi. 8. 2
With no *contentment* can themselves suffize; . . . *Am.* xxxv. 3
Her harts desire with most *contentment* please. . . . *Am.* lxxii. 12
pleasures they conceave, And sweete *contentment,* . . . *H.H.B.* 257
All happie joy and full *contentment* fynd. . . . *H.H.B.* 287
Contents. were too long their infinite *contents* Here to record, II. x. 74. 5
Continence. A harder lesson to learne *Continence* . . . II. vi. 1. 1
They tied were to stedfast chastity And *continence* of life, . . V. vii. 9. 8
Continent. in the seas, That raignest also in the *Continent,* . III. iv. 10. 2
Shee threw her selfe downe on the *Continent,* . . . III. iv. 30. 5
th' head fell backeward on the *Continent;* . . . III. v. 25. 7
Unlesse that she were *continent* and chast, . . . V. iii. 28. 8
Continual. Returneth by *continuall* successe, . . . *Gn.* 30
Whereas *continuall* shade is to be seene, . . . *Gn.* 118
Of Natures workes, of heavens *continuall* course, . . . *Hub.* 764
life drawes care, and care *continuall* woe; . . . *D.* 450
wrought so well with his *continuall* paine; . . . *Col.* 124
Her love is firme, her care *continuall,* . . . I. viii. 1. 5
with *continual* watch did warely keepe. . . . I. xii. 36. 3
his peace is but *continual* jarre: . . . II. ii. 26. 8
through *continuall* practise and usage . . . II. ix. 54. 4
wearie wax of his *continuall* stay. . . . II. x. 30. 5
There those five sisters had *continuall* trade, . . . II. xii. 30. 8
The world in his *continuall* course to keepe, . . . III. iv. 56. 2
There is *continuall* Spring, and harvest there *Continuall,* . . III. vi. 42. 1, 2
keepe *continuall* spy Upon her . . . III. ix. 5. 4
no wals so strong, But that *continuall* battery will rive, . . . III. x. 10. 2
continuall feare Of that rocks fall, . . . III. x. 58. 3
Out of her thraldome and *continuall* feare: . . . III. xi. 16. 5
did lay *Continuall* siege unto her gentle hart; . . . IV. vi. 40. 4
the watch, that kept *continuall* ward, . . . IV. ix. 5. 6
with waves *continuall* Doe eate the earth, . . . V. ii. 39. 4
Ne lightned was with window, . . . But with *continuall* candle-light, . . . VI. x. 42. 8
kept them with *continuall* watch and ward; . . . VI. x. 43. 2
Still tost and turned with *continuall* change, . . . VII. vii. 21. 2
To be acquit fro my *continual* smart; . . . *Am.* xlii. 6
this *continuall,* cruell, civill warre, . . . *Am.* xliv. 5
Continually. *Continuallie* subject unto chaunge. . . . *Hub.* 92
The which in Court *continually* hooved, . . . *Col.* 666
A shaking fever raignd *continually.* . . . I. iv. 20. 8
hungry wolves *continually* did howle . . . I. v. 30. 8
Gehons golden waves doe wash *continually:* . . . I. vii. 43. 9
To God for vengeance cryde *continually;* . . . I. viii. 36. 7
In those sad waves, . . . Plonged *continually* . . . II. vii. 57. 4
bellowes, which did styre *Continually,* . . . II. ix. 30. 5
gave light, and flamd *continually;* . . . II. ix. 46. 4
Infinit streames *continually* did well . . . II. xii. 62. 1
causelesse crimes *continually* to frame, . . . IV. viii. 25. 2
watcht *continually,* Lying without her dore . . . V. vi. 26. 6
Beares, that groynd *continually;* . . . VI. xi. 27. 5
men themselves do change *continually,* . . . VII. vii. 19. 4
Times do change and move *continually:* . . . VII. vii. 47. 6
continually About the sacred Altare doe remaine, . . . *Epith.* 229
Continuance. Ne rust of age hating *continuance,* . . . *Ro.* xiii. 6
all this glee had no *continuaunce:* . . . *S.C.* F. 224
through long *continuance* of his course, . . . the world . . . V. Pr. 1. 6
some small *continuance* He there did make, . . . VI. iii. 19. 7
The firmest flint doth in *continuance* weare: . . . *Am.* xviii. 4
Continue. to *continue* their wont countenaunce: . . . *S.C.* May 80
It shall *contineewe* till the worlds dissolution, . . . *S.C.* Env. 4
daunger well he wist long to *continue* there. . . . IV. xii. 15. 9
as bound to me he may *continue* still: . . . V. v. 32. 9
His kingdome would *continue* but a while. . . . VI. viii. 23. 5
at more ease *continue* there his thrall: . . . VI. xi. 6. 8
Continued. the old cause of my *continued* paine . . . I. v. 42. 3
In which we long time . . . *contynewd* as was fitt; . . . II. iv. 18. 8
Against that same fift bulwarke they *continued* fight. . . . II. xi. 13. 9
all that night her course *contineewed,* . . . III. vii. 2. 2
Long while they then *continued* in that wize, . . . IV. iii. 36. 1
So he *continued* all that day throughout, . . . IV. iv. 43. 5
There he *continued* in this carefull plight, . . . IV. vii. 41. 1
Companion she became, and so *continued* long. . . . IV. viii. 5. 9
continu'd there a while To rest him selfe, . . . IV. ix. 12. 6
they long while *continued* in fight; . . . IV. ix. 28. 1
still *continu'd* his assault the more, . . . V. ii. 24. 1
there all day *contineew'd* cruell fight, . . . V. iii. 7. 3
Thus there long while *continu'd* Artegall, . . . V. v. 26. 1
There she *continu'd* for a certaine space, . . . V. vii. 45. 1

Continued—*Continued.*
like hound full greedy . . . *Continu'd* still his course, ... V. viii. 7. 3
those knights *continu'd* there . . . . V. x. 5. 1
Thus Calidore *continu'd* there long time . . . . VI. ix. 46. 1
Thus long *continu'd* Claribell a thrall, ... VI. xii. 10. 1
Contract. To *contract* wedlock, . . . Wedlocke *contract* in blood, . III. ix. 42. 5, 6
Contrair. Such as no carpers may *contrayre* reveale ; . . . . *Hub.* 494
Made no resistance, ne could her *contraire,* . . . . VII. vi. 7. 8
That is *contrayr* to Mutabilitie ; . . . . VII. viii. 2. 5
Contrariwise. Yet rather counseld him *contrarywize,* . . . . VI. vii. 22. 6
this coy Damzell thought *contrariwize,* . . . . VI. vii. 30. 1
Contrary. some that weene the *contrarie* in thought, ... *Ro.* ix. 13
Meetes two *contrarie* billowes . . . . II. ii. 24. 4
quite *contrary* to her sisters kynd ; . . . . II. ii. 36. 3
contrary to the worke which ye intend : . . . . II. viii. 19. 9
his *contrary* object most deface, ... II. xi. 6. 4
this same was to that quite *contrary,* . . . . II. xii. 48. 3
All ignorant of her *contrary* sex, ... III. i. 47. 2
Of filthy lust, *contrary* unto kinde ; . . . . III. ii. 40. 4
She turned her *contrary* to the Sunne ; . . . . III. ii. 51. 2
Thrise she her turnd *contrary,* and returnd All *contrary ;* . . III. ii. 51. 3, 4
With squinted eyes *contrarie* wayes intended, ... IV. i. 27. 2
The other backe retired and *contrarie* trode. . . . . IV. i. 28. 9
Forcibly driven by *contrarie* tydes, ... IV. i. 42. 2
Flowes up the Shenan with *contrarie* forse, ... IV. iii. 27. 2
whosoever *contrarie* doth prove, ... IV. v. 3. 3
From one to other so quite *contrary :* . . . . IV. vi. 33. 3
There was I found, *contrary* to my thought, ... IV. vii. 18. 3
two Barkes, . . . *contrary* courses sew, ... IV. ix. 26. 8
of *contrarie* natures each to other : . . . . IV. x. 32. 5
And so doe make *contrarie* constitution . . . . V. Pr. 4. 8
for her, on the *contrarie* part, Rose many advocates . . . . . V. ix. 45. 1
But evermore *contrary* hath bene tryde, ... VI. iii. 2. 1
the wyld man, *contrarie* to her feare, ... VI. iv. 11. 1
they find, *contrarie* to their thought, That Pastorell yet liv'd ; VI. xi. 41. 5
Bending their force *contrary* to their face ; . . . . VII. vii. 35. 8
with *contrary* forces to conspyre Each against other . . . . *H.L.* 80
tempering . . . Their *contrary* dislikes with loved meanes, . . *H.L.* 86
Contrayr(e). *See* **Contrair.**
Contrition. 'Here in this bottle . . . I put the tears of my *contrition,* . . . . VI. viii. 24. 2
Contrive. Three ages, such as mortall men *contrive,* . . . . . II. ix. 48. 5
other none such passion can *contrive* . . . . VI. xii. 21. 5
Control. she doth *comptroll* All this worlds pride, ... *Am.* x. 10
Controverse. The *controverse* of beauties soveraine grace ; . . IV. v. 2. 3
Controversies. Ne medled with their *controversies* vaine ; . . *Hub.* 391
Convaid, Convayd. *See* **Conveyed.**
Convenable. with his word his worke is *convenable.* . . . . . *S.C.* S. 175
Convenient. it were *convenient* To tell the cause . . . . . . *D.* 80
time and place *convenient* to areed, ... V. xii. 9. 3
I . . . as was *convenient,* Have trayned bene . . . . VI. ii. 31. 3
For to avenge in time *convenient,* . . . . VI. vii. 4. 7
so soone as they *convenient* may, ... V. x. 43. 3
Conveniently. all thinges did *conveniently* purvay. . . . . . . III. iii. 58. 2
Shall more *conveniently* in other place be ended. . . . . . . VI. ix. 46. 9
Convent. every parts inholders to *convent,* . . . . VII. vii. 17. 4
Conversation. roote of civill *conversation :* . . . . VI. i. 1. 6
Conversest. *Conversest,* and doost heare their heavenlie layes, *Ti.* 335
Conversing. thus *conversing* with this noble Knight ; . . . . IV. viii. 29. 5
Convert. into plaints *convert* your joyous playes, ... *D.* 321
to strive Into their names the title to *convart,* . . . . . . III. ix. 43. 4
her proud mind *convert* To meeke obeysance . . . . V. v. 28. 7
Her selfe eftsoones she gan *convert* againe : . . . . V. ix. 37. 3
Those engins can the proudest love *convert :* . . . . *Am.* xiv. 12
Converting. Her former sorrow into suddein wrath . . . *Converting,* . . . . III. iv. 12. 8
Convey. streames . . . He under ground so closely did *convay,* *Col.* 142
her to Faery court safe to *convay ;* . . . . III. i. 2. 4
close venim doth *convay* Into the lookers hart, ... IV. viii. 39. 8
if that Dwarfe I could with me *convay,* . . . . IV. viii. 61. 8
as his purchast prize with him *convay* . . . . V. viii. 25. 7
And how ye may him hence, . . . *Convay* to be recur'd.' . . . VI. ii. 46. 6
How thence she might *convay* him to some place ; . . . . . VI. ii. 47. 2
from the Goat her kidde, how to *convay :* . . . . VI. ix. 23. 4
Unto their dwelling did them close *convay.* . . . . VI. x. 41. 5
did themselves *convay* Into their caves, ... VI. xi. 49. 7
one of hers did close *convay* Into the others stead : . . . . . *Epig.* ii. 5
Conveyance. all the skill Of close *conveyance,* . . . . *Hub.* 856
Conveyed. 'His blessed body, . . . Was afterward, . . . *convaid,* I. ii. 24. 2
He is *convaide ;* but how, or where, here fits not tell. . . . . II. ii. 11. 9
Was close *convaid,* and to the backgate brought, ... II. ix. 32. 7
Eftesoones she causd him up to be *convayd,* . . . . II. xi. 49. 6
Themselves they forth *convaid,* and passed forward right. . . III. iii. 61. 9
They did him set theron, and forth with them *convayd.* . . . III. v. 38. 9
Venus hers thence far away *convayd,* . . . . III. vi. 28. 6
all the keyes *convayd* Unto their maister, ... III. ix. 10. 4
Conveyed quite away to living wight unknowen. . . . . IV. i. 3. 9
on his way they had him forth *convayd :* . . . . IV. i. 37. 5
she was thence *convayd,* And stolne away . . . . IV. vi. 47. 6
the weake in state, To be *convayed* in, ... V. iv. 45. 9
them *convayd* out at a Posterne dore. . . . . V. x. 38. 4
him . . . up *convayd* Into the chamber, ... VI. vi. 39. 7
whether by force, or sleight, . . . they were away *convayd ?* . VI. vii. 34. 6
Convince. treasons could bewray, and foes *convince :* . . . . III. ii. 21. 8
Conway. *Conway,* which out of his streame doth send . . . . IV. xi. 39. 5
Cook. The maister *Cooke* was cald Concoction ; . . . . II. ix. 31. 1
Cooks. About the Caudron many *Cookes* accoyld . . . . II. ix. 30. 6
Cool. the gentle warbling wynde, So calme, so *coole,* . . . . *S.C.* Jun. 5
In some *coole* shadow from the scorching heat, ... *Gn.* 143
Coole Violets, and Orpine growing still, ... *Mui.* 193

Cool—*Continued.*
For the *coole* shade him thither hastly got : . . . . I. ii. 29. 2
The valley did with *coole* shade overcast : . . . . II. i. 24. 5
To rest thy weary person in the shadow *coole ?'* . . . . . . II. vii. 63. 9
a Deare, that greedily embayes In the *cool* soile, ... III. xii. 44. *or.* 8
mother call to *coole* their kindly rages. . . . . IV. x. 45. 9
Cooled. Enaunter his rage mought *cooled* bee ; . . . . *S.C.* F. 200
So hasty heat soone *cooled* to subdew : . . . . II. viii. 47. 8
Ne ought the water *cooled* their whot bloud, ... V. ii. 13. 3
Cooling. *Cooling* againe his former kindled heate, ... *Ro.* xi. 5
Hee feedes upon the *cooling* shade, ... I. vii. 3. 1
payre of bellowes . . . *cooling* breath inspyre. . . . . II. ix. 30. 5
Cools. my corage *cooles* ere it be warme : . . . . *S.C.* O. 115
Cooly. amongst the *cooly* shade Of the greene alders . . . . *Col.* 58
Coop. sonne-bright honour pend in shamefull *coupe.* . . . . . *S.C.* O. 72
Coosen. *See* **Cousin.**
Coosin, -age, -ed. *See* **Cozen, Cozenage,** *etc.*
Cope. Will *cope* with thee in reasonable wise ; . . . . *Hub.* 527
things that are contained Within this goodly *cope,* . . . . . *H.L.* 95
Copemate. the Foxe, his *copesmate* he had found, ... *Hub.* 939
Copesmate. *See* **Copemate.**
Coportion. My selfe will beare a part, *coportion* of your packe.' VI. ii. 47. 9
Copper-wire. Shakt his long locks colourd like *copper-wyre,* . II. iv. 15. 8
Coradin. advaunce Mine auncestry from famous *Coradin,* . . . II. iv. 36. 8
Corbe. *See* **Courbe.**
Corbes. With curious *Corbes* and pendants graven faire, . . . IV. x. 6. 7
Corceca. Abessa, daughter of *Corceca* slow, ... I. iii. 18. 4
Cord. *See* **Chord.**
with an hempen *cord* He like a dog was led . . . . VI. viii. 5. 3
Cordeill. *See* **Cordelia.**
Cordelia. *Cordeill* said she lov'd him as behoov'd : . . . . . . II. x. 28. 5
the wise *Cordelia* Was sent to Aggannip of Celtica. . . . . . II. x. 29. 4
He to *Cordelia* him selfe addrest, ... II. x. 31. 5
Cordial. that sweet *Cordiall,* which can restore A love-sick hart, III. v. 50. 6
Cordials. costly *Cordialles* she did apply, ... III. v. 50. 4
with some *cordialls,* seeke first to appease The inward languor *Am.* l. 9
such sweet *cordialls* passe Physitions art. . . . . *Am.* l. 12
her lookes, which like to *Cordials* bee ; . . . . *H.B.* 250
Cords. With fine small *cords* about it stretched wide, ... *Mui.* 359
Fast bounden hand and foote with *cords* of wire, ... III. vii. 37. 8
fast with *cords* do bynde, ... VI. viii. 12. 3
Cordwain. embayld In gilden buskins of costly *Cordwayne,* . . II. iii. 27. 3
Buskins he wore of costliest *cordwayne,* . . . . VI. ii. 6. 1
Corflambo. *Corflambo* chaseth Placidas, And is by Arthure slaine. IV. viii. Arg.
Corflambo was he cald aright, ... IV. viii. 49. 1
Coridon. *See* **Corydon.**
Corineus. Goemot, whome in stout fray *Corineus* conquered, . II. x. 10. 9
Corineus had that Province utmost west . . . . II. x. 12. 2
The noble daughter of *Corineus* . . . . II. x. 18. 1
the great Goemagot of strong *Corineus,* . . . . III. ix. 50. 4
Corinth. Corinth skil'd in curious workes to grave ; . . . . . *Ro.* xxix. 4
Not Bilbo steele, nor brasse from *Corinth* fet, ... *Mui.* 77
Cork. Encloseth *Corke* with his devided flood ; . . . . IV. xi. 44. 4
Cormorant. From a great Gyant, called *Cormoraunt,* . . . . . VI. iv. 29. 6
Cormorants. *Cormoyraunts,* with birds of ravenous race, . . . II. xii. 8. 5
Corn. crowing in pypes made of greene *corne,* . . . . *S.C.* F. 40
The *corne* is theyrs, let other thresh, ... *S.C.* Jul. 191
Cockel for *corne,* and chaffe for barley, ... *S.C.* D. 124
Or *corne,* or cattle, or such other ware, ... *Hub.* 873
There fruitfull *corne,* faire trees, fresh herbage is, ... *Col.* 298
With ears of *corne* of every sort, ... VII. vii. 30. 7
the which was cround With eares of *corne,* . . . . VII. vii. 37. 5
Corner. them borne aside Into a secret *corner* unespide. . . . *Hub.* 1018
Fled here and there, and everie *corner* sought, ... *Hub.* 1357
Shee found them both in darksome *corner* pent ; . . . . . . I. iii. 13. 5
in another *corner* wide were strowne . . . . I. v. 49. 3
Me leading, in a secret *corner* layd, ... II. iv. 27. 5
in coward *corner* ly. . . . . III. ix. 14. 9
Corners. Upon foure *corners* of the base . . . . *Bel.* iii. 9
but, in darke *corners* mewd, ... *Hub.* 835
Thou in dull *corners* doest thy selfe inclose ; . . . . III. ii. 31. 5
hid them selves in *corners* here and there ; . . . . V. ii. 24. 8
Corner-stone. reckned him the kingdomes *corner stone.* . . . *Hub.* 1166
Cornewale. *See* **Cornwall.**
Corn-fed. later ages pride, like *corn-fed* steed, ... II. vii. 16. 6
Cornish. brother unto Cador, *Cornish* king ; . . . . III. iii. 27. 2
devides The *Cornish* and the Devonish confines ; . . . . . . IV. xi. 31. 2
Cornwall. called *Cornwaile,* yet so called best ; . . . . II. x. 12. 5
king Meliogras which did rayne In *Cornewale,* . . . . VI. ii. 28. 3
Coronal. That bene the honor of your *Coronall :* . . . . *S.C.* F. 178
Chloris . . . Of Olive braunches beares a *Coronall :* . . . . . *S.C.* Ap. 123
crowne your heades with heavenly *coronall,* . . . . III. v. 53. 8
by his side his Queene with *coronall,* . . . . IV. xi. 11. 5
Crowne ye God Bacchus with a *coronall,* . . . . *Epith.* 255
Coronations. *See* **Carnations.**
Coronet. Upon her head a Cremosin *coronet,* . . . . *S.C.* Ap. 59
on his head like to a *Coronet* He wore, ... IV. xi. 27. 6
Coronis. So lovedst thou the faire *Coronis* deare ; . . . . . . III. xi. 37. 2
Corpes. *See* **Corpse.**
Corpse. A worthie tombe for such a worthie *corps.* . . . . . *Bel.*[1] iii. 11
The *corpes* of Rome in ashes is entombed, ... *Ro.* v. 9
Did brave about the *corpes* of Hector colde ; . . . . *Ro.* xiv. 10
keepe your *corpse* from the carefull stounds . . . . *S.C.* May 257
Her soule unbodied of the burdenous *corpse.* . . . . *S.C.* N. 166
a gulph . . . with his owne *corps* did fill, ... *Gn.* 605
Upon his fleshly *corpse* to make invasion : . . . . *Hub.* 1090
senseles, like the *corpse* deceast, ... *Hub.* 1328
ward his gentle *corpes* from cruell wound ; . . . . *Mui.* 60
her fine *corpes* to a bag of venim grewe. . . . . *Mui.* 352
Forth-with her ghost out of her *corps* did flit, ... *As.* 177

Corpse—*Continued.*
His goodly *corps,* . . . Was quite dismembred, ... I. v. 38. 6
To spoyle her dainty *corps,* so faire and sheene . . . . II. i. 10. 5
this dead *corpse* . . . the good Sir Mortdant was: . . . . . . II. i. 49. 7
His *corps* was carried downe along the Lee, ... V. ii. 19. 1
To clad his *corpse* with meete habiliments, ... VI. iv. 4. 5
A comely *corpse,* with beautie faire endewed, ... *H.B.* 135
Corrosives. he meant his *corrosives* to apply, ... I. x. 25. 8
Corrupt. lawlesse lustes, *corrupt* envyes, ... II. xi. 8. 8
She ment him to *corrupt* with goodly meede; . . . . V. ii. 23. 3
now *corrupt* and curelesse they became: . . . . VI. vi. 2. 5
to *corrupt* Molanna, this her maid, ... VII. vi. 43. 2
corrupt, and wrested unto will: . . . . *H.B.* 158
Not bounded, not *corrupt,* as these same bee, ... *H.H.B.* 66
Corrupted. Of Sulphure now did breathe *corrupted* smel. . . . *Bel.*[1] ix. 14
They soone myght be *corrupted,* . . . . *S.C.* Jul. 110
Corrupted had th' ayre with his noysome breath, ... *Hub.* 7
all *corrupted* through the rust of time . . . . *T.M.* 433
when your mawes are with those weeds *corrupted,* . . . . . . *D.* 348
soone in him was lefte no one *corrupted* jott. . . . . I. x. 26. 9
Corrupted by Paulinus, from her swerv'd: . . . . II. x. 55. 4
Full many wounds in his *corrupted* flesh . . . . III. vii. 32. 6
present dayes, which are *corrupted* sore, ... V. Pr. 3. 4
fall away . . . even to *corrupted* clay: . . . . *H.B.* 96
Corruptful. with *corruptfull* brybes is to untruth mis-trayned.' V. xi. 54. 9
Corruptible. Ne dare looke up with *corruptible* eye . . . . . *H.H.B.* 144
Corrupting. The Galles were, by *corrupting* of a mayde, . . . *Van.* xi. 6
Corruption. Inward *corruption* and infected sin, ... I. x. 25. 2
Fleshly *corruption,* nor mortall payne. . . . . III. vi. 33. 4
now her wounds *corruption* gan to breed: . . . . VI. v. 31. 5
permanent and free From frayle *corruption,* . . . . *Am.* lxxix. 8
things immortall no *corruption* take. . . . . *H.B.* 161
Corrupts. *Corrupts* the stomacke with gall vitious, ... III. x. 59. 7
Corse. It's like a *corse* drawne forth out of the tombe . . . . *Ro.* v. 7
Againe on foote to reare her pouldred *corse.* . . . . *Ro.* xxvii. 14
The faded flowres her *corse* embrave. . . . . *S.C.* N. 109
cole-black blood forth gushed from her *corse.* . . . . I. i. 24. 9
Then forth I went his woefull *corse* to find, ... I. ii. 24. 6
To have attonce devourd her tender *corse;* . . . . I. iii. 5. 6
his *corse* left on the strand. . . . . I. iii. 20. 5
he was strong, and of so mightie *corse,* . . . . I. iii. 42. 3
His dronken *corse* he scarse upholden can: . . . . I. iv. 22. 8
they . . . brought the heavy *corse* with easy pace . . . . . . I. v. 31. 2
For that Hippolytus rent *corse* he did redresse. . . . . I. v. 36. 9
up he tooke the slombred sencelesse *corse,* . . . . I. vii. 15. 6
thighes, unable to uphold His pined *corse,* . . . . I. viii. 40. 8
A dreary *corse,* whose life away did pas, ... I. ix. 36. 5
In ashes and sackcloth he did array His daintie *corse,* . . . . . I. x. 26. 2
ne might his *corse* bee harmd . . . . I. xi. 9. 3
The sencelesse *corse* appointed for the grave: . . . . I. xi. 48. 8
*To spoile her daintie *corse* so faire and sheene, ... II. i. 10. 5
The dead *corse* of an armed knight was spred, ... II. i. 41. 2
fowly battered his comely *corse,* . . . . II. v. 23. 5
Keeping that slombred *corse* to him assind: . . . . II. viii. 11. 7
at his feet . . . an armed *corse* did lye, ... II. viii. 23. 8
all decrepit in his feeble *corse,* . . . . II. ix. 55. 6
his dead *corse* should fall upon the flore; . . . . II. xi. 37. 8
his dead *corse* upon the flore fell nathemore. . . . . II. xi. 37. 9
adowne he kest The lumpish *corse* . . . . II. xi. 42. 6
having scruzd out of his carrion *corse* The lothfull life, . . . II. xi. 46. 2
Whiles they the *corse* into her wagon reare, ... III. iv. 42. 4
In loathly wise like to a carrion *corse,* . . . . III. vii. 43. 5
each awhile lay like a sencelesse *corse.* . . . . III. ix. 16. 5
finding no fit seat, the lifelesse *corse* it left. . . . . IV. iii. 21. 9
Having his carrion *corse* quite sencelesse left . . . . IV. vii. 32. 4
Whose bloudie *corse* they shew'd him there beside, ... IV. viii. 21. 7
like a lifelesse *corse* immoveable he stood. . . . . V. iii. 26. 9
it approve upon his carrion *corse.* . . . . V. iii. 30. 5
yeelding the last honour to her wretched *corse.* . . . . V. x. 4. 9
Both through his haberjeon and eke his *corse;* . . . . V. x. 33. 3
on the ground he left full many a *corse;* . . . . V. xii. 7. 5
To be aveng'd on him and to devoure his *corse.* . . . . VI. iv. 20. 9
At sight of his most sacred heavenly *corse,* . . . . *H.H.L.* 249
Corses. wide Sigaean shores were spred with *corses,* . . . . . *Gn.* 501
many *corses* . . . Of murdred men, ... I. v. 53. 2
In seemely sort their *corses* to engrave, ... I. x. 42. 2
They lay therein their *corses* tenderly, ... II. i. 60. 5
rive Out of their wretched *corses,* . . . . IV. ix. 22. 9
Corsive. *corsive,* which did eat Her tender heart . . . . . . IV. ix. 14. 4
Corybantes'. by unjust . . . meanes, through *Corybantes* slight, VII. vi. 27. 4
Corydon. is the sea (quoth *Coridon*) so fearfull?' . . . . . . *Col.* 200
there is *Corydon* though meanly waged, ... *Col.* 382
Coridon envies him, ... VI. ix. Arg.
the shepheard *Coridon* For her did languish, ... VI. ix. 10. 5
Coridon most helpe did give. . . . . VI. ix. 15. 9
Coridon, who her likewise Long time had lov'd, ... VI. ix. 38. 1
when *Coridon* unto her brought . . . litle sparrowes . . . . . VI. ix. 40. 1
Thereat frown'd *Coridon,* and his lip closely bit. . . . . VI. ix. 41. 9
Tooke *Coridon* and set him in his place, ... VI. ix. 42. 2
Coridon could daunce, and trimly trace: . . . . VI. ix. 42. 4
Then *Coridon* woxe frollicke, that earst seemed dead. . . . . . VI. ix. 42. 9
Coridon forth stepping openly Did chalenge Calidore . . . . . VI. ix. 43. 5
Gave it to *Coridon,* and said he wonne it well. . . . . VI. ix. 44. 9
the shepheard *Coridon* . . . Did strive to match . . . . VI. x. 33. 1
Which *Coridon* first hearing ran in hast To reskue her; . . . VI. x. 35. 1
Coridon for cowherdize reject, ... VI. x. 37. 3
With them also was taken *Coridon,* . . . . VI. x. 41. 1
Coridon with many other moe, ... VI. xi. 11. 2
Coridon, escaping craftily, ... VI. xi. 18. 6
Coridon it was, the silly shepherds hynd. . . . . VI. xi. 27. 9

Corydon—*Continued.*
Tho *Coridon* he prayd . . . To wend with him, ... VI. xi. 35. 1
Right well knew *Coridon* his owne late sheepe, ... VI. xi. 37. 6
Whom *Coridon* him counseld to invade . . . . VI. xi. 38. 5
right so as *Coridon* had taught: . . . . VI. xi. 41. 7
Coridon durst not with him consort, ... VI. xi. 42. 8
He did them all to *Coridon* restore: . . . . VI. xi. 51. 8
Corydon's. did it put on *Coridons* instead: . . . . VI. ix. 42. 8
Corylas. say on further (then said *Corylas*) . . . . *Col.* 328
is Love then (said *Corylas*) once knowne . . . . *Col.* 771
Coshma. About the borders of our rich *Coshma,* . . . . . . *Col.* 522
Cosset. I shall thee give yond *Cosset* . . . . *S.C.* N. 42
Much greater gyfts . . . Then Kidde or *Cosset,* . . . . *S.C.* N. 46
Thyne be the *cossette,* . . . . *S.C.* N. 206
Cost. what they spent in *cost,* . . . . *S.C.* May 69
loose thy labour and thy fruitles *cost.* . . . . *Hub.* 636
The roiall riches and exceeding *cost* . . . . III. i. 32. 4
that me right dearely *cost;* . . . . IV. i. 35. 2
I, without your perill or your *cost,* Will chalenge . . . . . . IV. i. 35. 7
Yet did the workmanship farre passe the *cost:* . . . . IV. iv. 15. 8
Hath me much sorrow and much travell *cost:* . . . . IV. ix. 38. 4
framed With endlesse *cost* . . . . IV. x. 30. 7
for sparing litle *cost* or paines, ... IV. xi. 22. 8
Then life were least, that us so litle *cost.* . . . . *H.H.L.* 182
Cost(e), -s. *See* **Coast, -s.**
Costliest. Buskins he wore of *costliest* cordwayne, ... VI. ii. 6. 1
Costly. the *costly* rate Of riotise, ... *Gn.* 92
Through whose not *costly* care each shepheard sings . . . . . *Gn.* 147
costly trappings that to ground downe hung. . . . . *Hub.* 584
With courtizans, and *costly* riotize, ... *Hub.* 805
huge Colosses built with costlie *paine,* . . . . *Ti.* 409
made of golde and *costlie* yvorie, ... *Ti.* 605
Adorned all with *costly* cloth of gold, ... *Ti.* 632
costly Oricalche from strange Phoenice, ... *Mui.* 78
which was on every side With . . . *costly* arras dight. . . . . I. iv. 6. 6
Bespredd with *costly* scarlott of great name, ... I. xii. 13. 8
embayld In gilden buskins of *costly* Cordwayne, ... II. iii. 27. 3
With balme, and wine, and *costly* spicery, ... II. xi. 49. 4
With *costly* clothes of Arras and of Toure; . . . . III. i. 34. 2
costly Cordialles she did apply, ... III. v. 50. 4
Decked with many a *costly* ornament, ... III. viii. 12. 2
Yclad in *costly* garments fit for tragicke Stage. . . . . III. xii. 3. 9
in his *costly* Bath causd to bee site. . . . . III. xii. 46. *or.* 4
whose goodly pride And *costly* frame . . . . IV. x. 16. 3
an altar of some *costly* masse, ... IV. x. 39. 2
an Altar framed Of *costly* Ivory . . . . V. x. 28. 3
eke that Idoll deem'd so *costly* dere, ... V. xi. 33. 7
Costmary. The purple Hyacinthe, and fresh *Costmarie;* . . . *Gn.* 670
Fresh *Costmarie,* and breathfull Camomill, ... *Mui.* 195
Cot. Which in her *cott* she daily practized? . . . . II. vi. 9. 4
Cotage. *See* **Cottage.**
Cote. *See* **Coat, Sheep-cote.**
The first of all his *cote,* . . . . *S.C.* Jul. 162
they will buy his sheepe out of the *cote,* . . . . *S.C.* S. 40
they holden shame of theyr *cote:* . . . . *S.C.* S. 111
Cotes. learnd of lighter timber *cotes* to frame, ... *S.C.* D. 77
Cots. to the litle *cots,* where shepherds lie . . . . VI. ix. 4. 8
Spoyld all our *cots,* and caried us from hence; . . . . VI. xi. 30. 5
Cottage. if to my *cotage* thou wilt resort, ... *S.C.* S. 254
in their *cotage* small that night she rest her may. . . . . . . I. iii. 14. 9
A little *cottage,* built of stickes and reedes . . . . III. vii. 6. 2
Whom I in countrey *cottage* fownd by chaunce: . . . . III. vii. 59. 2
They spide a little *cottage,* . . . . IV. v. 32. 9
A little *cotage* farre away they spide, ... IV. viii. 23. 2
though it were a *cottage* clad with lome, ... VI. ix. 16. 5
saw his shepheards *cottage* spoyled quight, ... VI. xi. 25. 2
Cottages. were shepheards *cottages* somewhile. . . . . *Ro.* xviii. 4
in the rurall *cottages* inquir'd; . . . . III. vi. 15. 2
Couch. That might for anie Princes *couche* be red, ... *Ti.* 633
The knight of the Redcrosse, . . . Gan fairely *couch* his speare, I. ii. 15. 3
The verdant gras my *couch* did goodly dight, ... I. ix. 13. 3
The knight gan fayrely *couch* his steady speare, ... I. xi. 16. 1
Uprose from drowsie *couch,* . . . . II. iii. 1. 6
seemd to *couch* under his shield threesquare, ... III. i. 4. 4
Whom having laid in comfortable *couch,* . . . . III. i. 64. 2
often steepe Her dainty *couch* with teares . . . . III. ii. 28. 9
There they him laide in easy *couch* well dight, ... III. iv. 43. 6
The cold earth was his *couch,* . . . . III. iv. 53. 9
In easie *couch* his feeble limbes to rest. . . . . III. v. 41. 2
the whyles the Prince did rest In carelesse *couch,* . . . . . . VI. vi. 44. 2
Couchant. His crest was covered with a *couchant* Hownd, . . . III. ii. 25. 1
Couched. in this golden vessel *couched* weare The ashes . . . *Bel.* iii. 7
prepare Himselfe to batteill with his *couched* speare. . . . . . I. iii. 34. 4
his dreadfull hideous hedd, Close *couched* on the bever, ... I. vii. 31. 6
cote of steele, so *couched* neare That nought mote perce; . . . I. xi. 9. 2
feeling one close *couched* by her side, ... III. i. 62. 1
His mighty speare he *couched* warily, ... III. vii. 38. 7
Their steel-hed speares they strongly *coucht,* . . . . III. ix. 16. 1
coucht his speare, and ran at him amaine. . . . . VI. i. 33. 4
Couches. The warlike youthes, on dayntie *couches* layd, . . . I. iv. 44. 3
Rashly out of their rouzed *couches* sprong, ... III. i. 62. 8
Couching. fayrly *couching* his steeleheaded speare, ... II. v. 3. 6
couching close his speare and all his powre, ... VI. iii. 48. 2
Could (*partial list*).
Or that . . . I *could,* with pencill fine, Fashion . . . . *Ro.* xxv. 9
could beleeve that anie thing *could* please Fell Cerberus, . . . *Gn.* 439
as if they *could* him understand; . . . . *Gn.* 454
if one *could,* it were but a schoole trick. . . . . *Hub.* 512
but yet *could* never win The Fort, ... I. ii. 25. 3
with that suddein horror *could* no member move. . . . . I. ii. 31. 9

Could—*Continued.*
'Her neather partes . . . I *could* not see; I. ii. 41. 2
all the hinder partes, that few *could* spie, Were ruinous and old, I. iv. 5. 8
Scarse *could* he once uphold his heavie hedd, I. iv. 19. 5
other clothes he *could* not weare for heate; I. iv. 22. 2
he . . . well *could* daunce, and sing with ruefulnesse; I. iv. 25. 7
gout tormented him . . . That well he *could* not touch, I. iv. 29. 8
cryme in her *could* never creature find; I. vi. 2. 5
The forlorne mayd . . . *could* not lacke her lovers company; I. vi. 22. 2
Ne in this new acquaintaunce *could* delight; I. vi. 32. 3
Una, . . . *Could* not for sorrow follow him so fast; I. vi. 40. 3
floods of blood *could* not them satisfie: I. vi. 43. 8
They both, deformed, scarsely *could* bee known. I. vi. 45. 6
speare it never percen *could,* I. vii. 33. 8
he that never would *Could* never: I. vii. 41. 4
His boystrous club, . . . He *could* not rearen up I. viii. 10. 2
What mortall wight *could* ever beare so monstrous blow? I. viii. 18. 9
she *could* not endure that dolefull stound I. viii. 25. 5
he *could* not them use, I. viii. 30. 9
Who answerd him full soft, *he could not tell.* I. viii. 32. 5
no where *could* he find that wofull thrall: I. viii. 37. 2
his foot *could* find no flore, I. viii. 39. 7
nor filthy bands, Nor noyous smell, his purpose *could* withhold, I. viii. 40. 8
Whose feeble thighes, . . . him scarse to light *could* beare; I. viii. 40. 8
Could not endure th' unwonted sunne to view; I. viii. 41. 2
empty sides . . . *Could* make a stony hart his hap to rew; I. viii. 41. 5
With all the court'sies that she *could* devyse, I. x. 11. 8
sunny beames . . . *could* have dazd the rash beholders sight, I. x. 12. 8
That none *could* reade except she did them teach, I. x. 19. 2
documents . . . That weaker witt of man *could* never reach; I. x. 19. 5
great hostes of men she *could* dismay; I. x. 20. 4
well *could* cure the same: I. x. 23. 9
Could hardly him intreat to tell his grief: I. x. 24. 2
she wist his cryme *could* els be never cleare. I. x. 28. 9
could not colour yet so well the troth, II. ii. 34. 4
No solace *could* her Paramour intreat Her once to show, II. ii. 35. 5
Hardly *could* he endure his hardiment, II. ii. 37. 8
A song . . . That hart of flint asonder *could* have rifte; II. vii. 23. 8
We would, and would againe, if that we *could;* II. ix. 12. 5
them greeting, as she *could,* Was thence V. vii. 5. 1
flie with all the speed he *could* To Crudor; VI. i. 29. 4
Some goodly person, . . . That *could* his good to all; VI. v. 36. 8
love so much *could.* VI. ix. 37. 9
mould He fashiond them as comely as he *could,* *H.B.* 33

Couldst (*partial list*).
what *couldst* thou more, III. xi. 19. 3
How *couldst* thou weene, . . . To hide thy state V. vii. 21. 4
couldst not hold thy selfe so hidden blest, VII. vi. 46. 7

Coulin. the large leape which Debon did compell *Coulin* to make, II. x. 11. 3
Coulin of Debon old, Were overthrowne III. ix. 50. 4

Coulter. *See* **Colter.**

Council. Where they in secret *counsell* close conspird, III. iii. 51. 5
Where all the Gods she found in *counsell* close, VII. vi. 24. 2
all the Gods in *councell* did agree *Am.* xxiv. 9

Counsel. Seemeth thy flocke thy *counsell* can, *S.C.* F. 77
who can *counsell* a thristie soule, *S.C.* May 138
Of ayde or *counsell* in my decaye. *S.C.* S. 247
to me, my trustie friend, aread Thy *councell:* *Hub.* 82
Through the Priests holesome *counsell* lately tought, *Hub.* 553
Eftsones by *counsell* of the Foxe alone, *Hub.* 1112
with milde *counsaile* strove to mitigate *D.* 191
So you, great Lord, that with your *counsell* sway *Ded. Son.* i. 9
Untroubled night, . . . gives *counsell* best.' I. i. 33. 3
he was . . . Not meet to be of *counsell* to a king, I. iv. 23. 3
counsell mitigates the greatest smart: I. vii. 40. 8
With goodly *counsell* and advisement right; I. x. 23. 5
to her gossibs gan in *counsell* say; I. xii. 11. 4
goodly *counsell,* that for wounded hart Is meetest med'cine, II. i. 44. 2
with pitthy words, and *counsell* sad, II. ii. 28. 5
to *counsell* me the best: II. iv. 23. 7
Abandon this forestalled place . . . I *counsell* thee: II. iv. 39. 4
Helpe with thy hand, or with thy *counsell* sage: II. vi. 48. 4
Weake handes, but *counsell* is most strong in age.' II. vi. 48. 5
in demeanure sober, and in *counsell* sage. II. ix. 27. 9
To take *counsell* of their common cares; II. x. 37. 7
counsell sage in steed thereof to him applyde. II. xii. 82. 9
counsel, that is chiefe And choicest med'cine III. iii. 5. 4
I deeme that *counsel* aye most fit, III. iii. 52. 3
By your good *counsell,* or bold hardiment, III. v. 10. 7
With herbs, with charms, with *counsel,* and with teares; III. vii. 21. 2
tears, nor charms, nor herbs, nor *counsell,* III. vii. 21. 3
I would disclose Her *counsell,* III. vii. 58. 9
To *counsell* her, so carefully dismayd, III. viii. 4. 8
That *counsell* pleased well: III. viii. 52. 1
That *counsell* pleasd: III. ix. 9. 8
Their *counsell* crav'd in daunger imminent. III. x. 41. 3
That *counsell* pleased not Malbeccoes mynd, III. x. 41. 8
hearken to his lore, and all his *counsell* hyde. III. x. 50. 9
Of the bad issue of his *counsell* vaine, IV. ii. 6. 2
her friends with *counsell* sage Dissuaded her IV. viii. 50. 4
I am adjur'd best *counsell* to impart V. vii. 19. 8
taxing *counsell* of a wise man red, VI. ii. 30. 1
In evils *counsel* is the comfort chiefe; VI. iv. 34. 7
Which with sage *counsell* . . . He could enforme, VI. vi. 3. 7
Give salves to every sore, but *counsell* to the minde. VI. vi. 5. 9
sith we need good *counsell,'* VI. vi. 13. 8
'Aread, good Sire, some *counsell* that may us sustaine.' VI. vi. 13. 9
Whether by open force, or *counsell* wise: VII. vi. 21. 8
straight gan cast their *counsell* grave and wise. VII. vi. 22. 6

Counsell. *See* **Council, Counsel.**

Counselled. The Foxe then *counsel'd* th' Ape for to require *Hub.* 325
Be therefore *counselled* herein by me, *Hub.* 985
ruled bee In all affaires, and *counselled* by mee; *Hub.* 1052
The which to leave, thenceforth he *counseld* mee, *Col.* 184
counseld him abstaine from perilous fight; II. vii. 42. 7
counselled faire Alma how to governe well. II. ix. 48. 9
Let all that live hereby be *counselled* II. xii. 9. 8
counseld well him forward thence did draw. II. xii. 69. 3
When so he *counseld* with his sprights encompast round. III. iii. 7. 9
counseld with her Nourse III. iii. 57. 7
him *counseld* to forbeare The bloody batteill III. iv. 24. 7
The Ladie *counseld* him the place to shonne, V. x. 30. 8
Yet rather *counseld* him contrarywize, VI. vii. 22. 6
Whom Coridon him *counseld* to invade VI. xi. 38. 5

Counsellor. his false *counsellor,* the cause of all, *Hub.* 1243

Counsellors. On which her six sage *Counsellours* did ryde, I. iv. 18. 2

Counsel's. Whose *counsels* depth thou canst not understand; V. ii. 42. 7

Counsels. I read that we our *counsells* call, *Hub.* 189
To marke th' intent of *Counsells,* *Hub.* 786
To ayme their *counsels* to the fairest scope, *Hub.* 960
daylie doth her changefull *counsels* bend *D.* 153
Those prudent heads, that with theire *counsels* wise *Ded. Son.* i. 1
six wisards . . . with their *counsels* bad, her kingdome did uphold. I. iv. 12. 9
all her witt in secret *counsels* spent, I. vi. 32. 5
Bad *counsels,* prayses, and false flatteries: II. xi. 10. 8
So readie rype to ill ill wemens *counsels* bee! III. x. 11. 9
As if they secret *counsels* did partake; IV. ii. 30. 4
counsels him, through confidence of might, V. viii. 20. 4
had her *counsels* false conspyred V. ix. 41. 2
They did their *counsels* now in one compound: VI. v. 14. 6
Before they could new *counsels* re-allie, VII. vi. 23. 4

Count. eft, when ye *count* you freed from feare, *S.C.* F. 42
he no *count* made of Nobilitie, *Hub.* 1183
call to *count* what is of them become: *Ti.* 58
Whom England high in *count* of honour held, *Ti.* 185
count of wisedome more than of thy Countie. *Ti.* 273
call to *count* the things that then were donne, IV. Pr. 3. 2
That were too long a worke to *count* them all; IV. i. 24. 2
I *count* as naught, and tread downe under feet, IV. x. 2. 7
Were cowards knowne, and litle *count* did hold, IV. x. 18. 7
'No tree, that is of *count,* IV. x. 22. 1
To tell the sands, or *count* the starres on hye, IV. xi. 53. 2
To *count* the seas abundant progeny, IV. xii. 1. 2
if I have err'd in *count* Of Gods, IV. xii. 2. 6
count my cares when none is nigh to heare, IV. xii. 6. 2
To call to *count,* or weigh his workes anew, V. ii. 42. 6
She fayn'd to *count* the time againe anew, V. vi. 5. 4
Unto his way, which now was all his care and *count.* V. x. 16. 9
by that *count,* which lovers books invent, *Am.* lx. 9
Of blessed Saints for to increase the *count.* *Epith.* 423
creatures which by name Thou canst not *count,* *H.H.B.* 33

Counted. dead is now, as living, *counted* deare, *Ti.* 242
Counted but toyes to busie ydle braines; *Col.* 704
Good turnes be *counted* as a servile bond II. viii. 56. 2
in his crown he *counted* her no hayre, II. x. 28. 8
so much as doth need must needs be *counted* here. III. vi. 30. 9
That thing of course he *counted* love to entertaine. III. ix. 29. 9
As if before she had not *counted* trew: V. vi. 5. 5
counted but a recreant Knight with endles shame. V. xi. 46. 9
seeke to please; that now is *counted* wise mens threasure. VI. xii. 41. 9
That to the world naught else be *counted* deare; *Am.* viii. 4

Countenance. The faithfull man with flaming *countenaunce,* *Rev.* iii. 2
to continue their wont *countenaunce:* *S.C.* May 80
all their craft is in their *countenaunce,* *S.C.* S. 168
With greislie *countenaunce* and visage grim, *Gn.* 326
Supports his credite and his *countenaunce.* *Hub.* 668
to uphold his courtly *countenaunce* *Hub.* 846
that he his *countenaunce* might bee. *Hub.* 876
ne could upholde His *countenance* *Hub.* 928
with their noble *countenaunce* to grace *T.M.* 81
With hollow browes and greisly *countenaunce,* *T.M.* 185
Under the shadow of thy *countenaunce* *Ti.* 268
by the semblant of his *countenaunce* *D.* 51
arts of schoole have there small *countenance,* *Col.* 703
vouchsafe thy noble *countenaunce* *Ded. Son.* ii. 13
by thy *countenaunce* doth crave to bee Defended *Ded. Son.* iii. 3
Shee turning backe, with ruefull *countenaunce,* Cride, 'Mercy, I. ii. 21. 1
Faire Una framed words and *count'naunce* fitt; I. iii. 14. 7
That to strange knight no better *countenance* allowd. I. iv. 15. 9
read her sorrow in her *count'nance* sad; I. vi. 11. 4
They, . . . fawne on her with *count'nance* fayne. I. vi. 12. 9
With staring *countenance* sterne, as one astownd, I. viii. 5. 7
He ghest his nature by his *countenance,* I. viii. 34. 4
With *countenance* demure, and modest grace, I. x. 12. 4
that infernall Monster, . . . with *countenance* fell, I. xi. 31. 8
with utt'rance grave, and *count'nance* sad, I. xii. 15. 7
With sober *countenance* thus to him sayd: I. xii. 33. 3
His *countenance* demure and temperate; II. i. 6. 2
with faire *countenance* and flattring style II. i. 8. 5
to these Ladies love did *countenaunce,* II. ii. 16. 8
She scould, and frownd with froward *countenaunce;* II. ii. 35. 8
threatned death with dreadfull *countenaunce,* II. iii. 14. 2
His *countenaunce* was bold, II. iv. 37. 8
with grim looke And *count'naunce* sterne, II. v. 14. 2
Crying with pitteous voyce, and *count'nance* wan, II. vi. 32. 4
Elfe, That darest view my direfull *countenaunce,* II. vii. 7. 7
with her bounty and glad *countenaunce* Doth blesse II. ix. 5. 4
told her meaning in her *countenaunce;* III. i. 50. 8

Countenance—*Continued.*
with faire *countenaunce,* as beseemed best, Her entertaynd: III. i. 55. 5
From her faire eyes and gratious *countenaunce.* III. v. 42. 6
All which she of him tooke with *countenance* meeke and mild. III. vii. 17. 9
in her *countenaunce* Dwelt simple truth III. vii. 59. 5
with gentle *countenaunce,* retain'd Enough III. viii. 10. 6
With comely haveour and *count'nance* sage, III. xii. 3. 8
Shewing his nature in his *countenaunce:* III. xii. 15. 5
hanging downe his heavy *countenaunce;* III. xii. 18. 3
Yet could she not but curteous *countenance* to her make. IV. i. 5. 9
With golden words and goodly *countenance,* IV. ii. 9. 2
with *countenance* sterne All full of wrath, IV. ii. 25. 1
With stately steps and fearelesse *countenance,* IV. iii. 5. 2
Whereat they shewed curteous *countenaunce.* IV. iv. 7. 5
hold The wrathfull weapon gainst his *countnance* bold: IV. vi. 27. 5
her modest *countenance* he saw So goodly grave, IV. vi. 33. 4
Ne ever laught, ne once shew'd *countenance* glad, IV. viii. 2. 7
gladsome *countenaunce* nor pleasaunt glee; IV. ix. 13. 5
with the terrour of his *countenance* bold IV. x. 16. 8
soone as they his *countenance* did behold, IV. x. 18. 4
graver *countenance* then all the rest; IV. x. 49. 2
with sterne *countenance* and indignant pride V. i. 23. 5
with fell intent And *countenaunce* fierce, V. v. 5. 4
soone she did her *countenance* compose, V. v. 30. 5
in the sunshine of her *countenance* cleare V. v. 38. 4
Souldan, with presumpteous cheare And *countenance* sublime V. viii. 30. 4
A chearefull *countenance* on them let fall, V. ix. 34. 8
A Ladie of great *countenance* and place, V. ix. 38. 2
with dull *countenance* and with dolefull spright V. xii. 12. 3
Such was Irenas *countenance,* such her case, V. xii. 13. 7
His face was ugly and his *countenance* sterne, V. xii. 15. 6
Was with his ghastly *count'nance* nothing queld; V. xii. 16. 7
with sterne *count'naunce* thus unto him spake: VI. i. 19. 5
through support of *count'nance* proud . . . To wrong the weaker, VI. ii. 23. 8
Looking at that same Carle with *count'nance* grim, VI. iii. 34. 7
comely carriage of her *count'nance* trim, VI. ix. 9. 4
her *countenaunce* and her likely hew, VI. xii. 18. 7
with sterne *count'naunce* and disdainfull cheare, VII. vi. 12. 5
changing nought his *count'nance* bold, VII. vi. 19. 8
As well for horror of their *count'naunce* ill, VII. vii. 3. 7
bitter stormes, and balefull *countenance* VII. vii. 23. 5
her face and *countenance* every day We changed see VII. vii. 50. 6
her faire *countenance,* like a goodly banner, *Am.* v. 11
that same lofty *countenance* seemes to scorne *Am.* xiii. 9
with sterne *countenance,* *Am.* xxi. 7
A dreadfull *countenaunce* she given hath; *Am.* xxxi. 6
Ne dare lift up her *countenance* too bold, *Epith.* 162
glancing through the eyes with *countenance* coy *H.L.* 122

Counter. With kindly *counter* under Mimick shade, *T.M.* 207
Is met of many a *counter* winde and tyde, VI. xii. 1. 3

Counter-cast. He can devize this *counter-cast* of slight, VI. iii. 16. 8

Counterchange. Could not arise the *counterchaunge* to scorse, III. ix. 16. 7

Counterfect. *See* **Counterfeit.**

Counterfeisance. his man Reynold, with fine *counterfesaunce,* *Hub.* 667
Fine *Counterfesaunce,* and unhurtfull Sport, *T.M.* 197
when her borrowed light Is laid away, and *counterfesaunce* knowne.' I. viii. 49. 6
he in *counterfesaunce* did excell, III. viii. 8. 8
This goodly *counterfesaunce* he did frame: IV. iv. 27. 4

Counterfeit. tooke out the Woolfe in his *counterfect* cote, *S.C.* S. 206
the *counterfet* should shame The thing it selfe: III. viii. 5. 5
He did the better *counterfeite* aright: III. x. 47. 7
disguized Her worke, and *counterfet* her selfe so nere, IV. ix. 11. 4
by *counterfet* disguise To their deseigne to make the easier way, V. viii. 25. 1
Did *counterfeit* kind pittie where was none: VI. vii. 18. 4

Counterfeited. wrought by art and *counterfetted* shew, II. vii. 45. 5

Counterfeits. when these *counterfeits* were thus uncased V. iii. 39. 1

Counterpoint. No *counterpoint* of cunning policie, *Hub.* 1140

Counterpoise. If ought he had the same to *counterpoys;* V. ii. 30. 6
counterpeise the same with so much wrong.' V. ii. 46. 2

Counterstroke. He met him with a *counterstroke* so swift, V. xi. 7. 8

Countervail. those lovers, with sweet *countervayle,* III. xii. 47. *or.* 1
For nought against their wils might *countervaile:* VII. vi. 49. 7

Countervailed. him with equall valew *countervayld:* II. vi. 29. 4

Counting. *Counting* it fairer then it is indeede, *H.B.* 230

Countless. thereof she *countlesse* summes did reare, III. x. 12. 4

Countries. In tho *countryes,* whereas I have bene, *S.C.* S. 32
spred his glory through all *countryes* wide. II. i. 35. 4
overflowd all *countries* far away, II. x. 15. 4
Whose *countries* he redus'd to quiet state, II. x. 38. 7
Full many *Countreyes* they did overronne, III. i. 3. 4
Through *countreyes* waste, and eke well edifyde, III. i. 14. 2
read the salvage *cuntreis* thorough which they pace. IV. xi. 40. 9
In three great rivers ran, and many *countreis* scowrd. IV. xi. 42. 9

Country. No such *countrye* as there to remaine; *S.C.* S. 35
With cakes and cracknells, and such *country* chere: *S.C.* N. 96
where the *countrey* Nymphs are rife, *Gn.* 146
Dooing my *Countrey* service as I might, *Hub.* 61
passing through the *Countrey* in disguize, *Hub.* 575
in *countrey* and in towne, *Ti.* 263
all the *countrey* wide he did possesse, *Mui.* 150
to breed Compassion in a *countrey* lasses hart *As.* Pr. 4
joyd that *country* shepheard ought could fynd *Col.* 366
all this *countrie,* farre and neare.' I. i. 31. 4
Their kingdome spoild, and *countrey* wasted quight: I. vii. 44. 5
Betrayd his *countrey* unto forreine spoyle. II. x. 48. 8
'Deare *countrey!* O! how dearely deare II. x. 69. 3
You and your *countrey* both I wish welfare, III. ii. 10. 8

Country—*Continued.*
Strongly to ayde his *countrey* III. iii. 27. 8
the spoile of the *countrey* conquered III. iii. 47. 8
in the *countrey* she abroad him sought, III. vi. 15. 1
all the *countrey* seemes to be a Maine, III. vii. 34. 5
over all the *countrie* she did raunge III. vii. 50. 1
Whom I in *countrey* cottage fownd by chaunce: III. vii. 59. 2
I greet you well Your *countrey* kin; III. ix. 51. 7
purchast all the *countrey* lying ny V. ii. 9. 7
From every coast and *countrie* under sunne: V. iii. 6. 2
To hinder thee . . . from thy *countrey* deare: V. vii. 23. 4
robbed all the *countrie* there about, V. ix. 4. 8
I my *countrie* have forlorne, VI. ii. 27. 8
to send me quight Out of the *countrie* VI. ii. 30. 3
from the townes into the *countrie* forsed, VI. ix. 3. 8
from the *country* back to private farmes he scorsed. VI. ix. 3. 9
Yet was she certes but a *countrey* lasse; VI. x. 25. 8
all other *countrey* lasses farre did passe: VI. x. 25. 9
Thy *country* may be freed *Proth.* 156

Country's. his vowed life to spill For *Countreyes* health, *Gn.* 604
So life exchanging for his *countries* good. *Ti.* 301
Yet not unworthie of the *countries* store. *As.* 52
Their *countreys* auncestry to understond, II. ix. 60. 7
naturall desire of *countryes* state, II. x. 77. 2
countries cause, and commune foes disdayne. III. ix. 40. 4
mindfull still of your first *countries* sight, *H.B.* 166

Counts. dewly adayes *counts* mine. *S.C.* Mar. 42
sole aspect he *counts* felicitye. *H.L.* 217

County. count of wisedome more than of thy *Countie.* *Ti.* 273

Coupe. *See* **Coop.**

Couple. Then gan this craftie *couple* to devize, *Hub.* 655
this faire *couple* eke to shroud themselves were fain. I. i. 6. 9
Where that false *couple* were full closely ment I. ii. 5. 4
The loving *couple* neede no reskew feare, III. x. 16. 3
he far away espide A *couple,* III. x. 20. 7
About that wofull *couple* which were slaine, V. iii. 31. 2
left that *couple* nere their utmost cast: VI. iv. 9. 5

Couplement. Allide with bands of mutuall *couplement;* IV. iii. 52. 3
forth together rode, a comely *couplement.* VI. v. 24. 9
gentle hearts content Of your loves *couplement;* *Proth.* 95

Couples. Borne without Syre or *couples* of one kynd; *Col.* 800
Venus selfe doth soly *couples* seeme, *Col.* 801
Thus marched these six *couples* forth in faire degree. III. xii. 18. 9
The knights in *couples* marcht with ladies linckt attone. IV. iv. 14. 9

Courage. did her *courage* to the heavens advaunce. *Ro.* vi. 14
with stout *courage* arm'd against mischaunce, *Ro.* xxi. 3
He well foresaw how that the Romane *courage,* *Ro.* xxiii. 5
Then is your carelesse *corage* accoied, *S.C.* F. 47
Thy flocks father his *corage* hath lost. *S.C.* F. 80
My *courage* earnd it to awake, *S.C.* Mar. 77
cause a caytive *corage* to aspire; *S.C.* O. 95
my *corage* cooles ere it be warme: *S.C.* O. 115
To learned wits givest *courage* worthily, *Gn.* 36
Now gan some *courage* unto him to take, *Hub.* 994
Full of brave *courage* and bold hardyhed, *Mui.* 27
skill, matcht with such *courage* as he had, *As.* 85
Whose warlike prowesse and manly *courage,* *Ded. Son.* xiv. 8
Whose *corage* when the feend perceived to shrinke, I. i. 22. 4
repining *courage* yields No foote to foe: I. ii. 17. 6
when *corage* hott The fire of love, . . . First kindled I. ii. 35. 1
lust did now inflame His *corage* more, I. iii. 41. 8
passion did . . . torment The flaming *corage* I. v. 1. 6
spices . . . To kindle heat of *corage* privily; I. v. 4. 7
The dreadlesse *courage* of this Elfin knight, I. vi. 1. 8
sturdie *courage* tame with dreadfull aw, I. vi. 26. 8
courage haught Desyrd of forreine foemen to be knowne, I. vi. 29. 5
He led away with *corage* stout and bold. I. vi. 33. 4
crudled cold his *corage* gan assayle, I. vii. 6. 7
at him fiersly flew, with *corage* fild, I. viii. 6. 8
Therewith his sturdie *corage* soon was quayd, I. viii. 14. 8
with constant zele and *corage* bold, I. viii. 40. 4
When *corage* first does creepe in manly chest, I. ix. 9. 2
in *courage* bold Him to avenge I. ix. 37. 4
prickt with *courage,* and thy forces pryde, I. x. 66. 7
The sparke of noble *corage* now awake, I. xi. 2. 6
nought their kindled *corage* may aswage: I. xi. 6. 5
his froth-fomy steed, whose *courage* stout I. xi. 23. 3
Ne yet hath any knight his *courage* crackt.' II. i. 12. 5
prickt with *courage* kene, did cruell battell breath. II. i. 27. 9
fraile affection did constraine His stout *courage* to stoupe, II. i. 42. 9
when him high *corage* did emmove, II. i. 50. 5
Sterne melancholy did his *courage* pas, II. ii. 17. 8
all knights of worth and *courage* bold II. ii. 42. 8
her great words did appall My feeble *corage,* II. iii. 44. 6
my *corage* brave Dismay with feare, II. iii. 45. 3
chaufd and fom'd with *corage* fiers and sterne, II. iii. 46. 8
enrage Her frantick sonne, and kindles his *corage;* II. iv. 11. 5
prowd *corage* to provoke, II. v. 3. 2
'Disleall Knight, whose coward *corage* chose II. v. 5. 3
kindling new his *corage* seeming queint, II. v. 11. 4
With wrathfull fire his *corage* kindled bright, II. vi. 30. 7
he that breathlesse seems shal *corage* bold respire. II. viii. 7. 9
False Archimage provokte their *corage* prowd, II. viii. 11. 3
Ne was there ever noble *corage* seene, II. viii. 26. 3
Glad was the knight, and with fresh *courage* fraught, II. viii. 40. 5
compeld with *courage* bold To yield II. viii. 41. 7
Ne thenceforth life ne *corage* did appeare; II. viii. 46. 3
Of stature huge, and eke of *corage* bold, II. x. 7. 8
corage fierce that all men did affray, II. x. 15. 2
with *courage* stout He them defeated II. x. 16. 3

Courage—*Continued.*
gathering force and *corage* valorous, II. x. 18. 3
with fresh *corage* on the victor servd: II. x. 55. 7
when she your *courage* hath inclind II. xii. 29. 1
shewd him many sights that *corage* cold could reare. II. xii. 68. 9
So is his angry *corage* fayrly pacifyde. III. i. 11. 9
With stedfast *corage* and stout hardiment: III. i. 19. 8
The noble *corage* never weeneth ought III. ii. 10. 4
the old sparkes renew Of native *corage,* III. iii. 45. 8
it ought your *corage* much inflame III. iii. 54. 1
equall *corage* to thee take.' III. iii. 56. 9
generous stout *courage* did inspyre, III. iii. 57. 4
her great *courage* would not let her weepe, III. iv. 11. 3
Love and despight attonce her *courage* kindled hath. III. iv. 12. 9
Yet he her followd still with *corage* keene III. iv. 51. 5
His coward *courage* gan emboldned bee, III. v. 15. 2
native *corage* unto him supply, III. vii. 3. 2
could the stoutest *corage* have appald; III. vii. 22. 3
fear gave her wings, and need her *corage* taught. III. vii. 26. 9
did nigh affray That Capons *corage:* III. viii. 15. 6
in his old *corage* new delight To gin awake, III. viii. 23. 4
thinking for to make her stubborne *corage* quayle. III. viii. 40. 9
Besought him his great *corage* to appease, III. x. 30. 8
Nought therewith daunted was her *courage* prowd, III. xii. 1. 7
still with stedfast eye and *courage* stout III. xii. 37. 5
haughtie *courage* soften, IV. Pr. 5. 8
courage full of haughtie hardiment, IV. ii. 39. 2
Their days mote be abridged through their *corage* stout. IV. ii. 46. 9
paine, that did the more enhaunce His haughtie *courage* IV. iii. 8. 8
with stout *courage* turnd upon them all, IV. iv. 32. 2
What yron *courage* ever could endure IV. vi. 17. 1
Therewith her wrathfull *courage* gan appall, IV. vi. 26. 7
now his *courage* being throughly fired, IV. ix. 35. 1
feele their *corage* cold. IV. x. 18. 5
mighty *courage* mollifide, IV. xii. 13. 2
Ne any Knight was absent that brave *courage* bore. V. iii. 2. 9
So *courage* lent a cloke to cowardise. V. iii. 15. 5
though powre faild, her *courage* did accrew; V. v. 7. 4
to a *courage* great It is no lesse beseeming V. v. 38. 1
That may pull downe the *courage* of his pride; V. v. 50. 6
kept her place with *courage* confident, V. vi. 28. 4
fild with *courage* and with joyous glee, V. vii. 25. 4
Which Britomart withstood with *courage* stout, V. vii. 31. 3
Could so great *courage* stouped have to ought? V. vii. 40. 8
much renound For noble *courage* V. viii. 36. 8
All which he did assault with *courage* stout, V. viii. 50. 5
mote appall An hardie *courage,* V. ix. 33. 5
for great ruth his *courage* gan relent: V. ix. 46. 6
He stepped forth with *courage* bold and great, V. x. 15. 6
gan with *courage* fierce addresse him to the fight. V. x. 31. 9
he gan her with *courage* fierce assay, V. xi. 26. 6
nought was terrifide, but greater *courage* tooke. V. xi. 28. 9
courage chill Kindling afresh, gan battell to renew, VI. i. 35. 7
That mote thy kindled *courage* set on fire, VI. ii. 37. 3
Doth noble *courage* shew with curteous manners met. VI. iii. 1. 9
Or had no *courage,* or else had no gall. VI. iii. 36. 5
giveth comfort to her *courage* cold: VI. iv. 1. 5
laying yet afresh, with *courage* stout, Upon the rest VI. vi. 38. 3
wheres no *courage,* theres no ruth nor mone. VI. vii. 18. 5
Threatning to yoke them two and tame their *corage* stout. VI. viii. 11. 9
entertayning them with *courage* stout, VI. xi. 46. 7
threatens all with *corage* stout. *Epig.* iv. 10

Courageous. Redoubted Lord, in whose *corageous* mind *Ded. Son.* x. 1
nathemore would that *corageous* swayne To her yeeld passage I. viii. 13. 6
underneath him his *courageous* steed, II. xi. 19. 6
Long while he strove in his *corageous* brest III. v. 44. 1
Couragious Cambell, and stout Triamond, IV. ii. 31. 8

Courages. Eftsoones their stubborne *corages* were queld, II. xii. 40. 4
With cruell chaufe their *courages* they whet, V. ii. 15. 3

Courbe. So on thy *corbe* shoulder it leanes amisse. *S.C.* F. 56

Course. *See* **Water-course.**
all which did against his *course* oppose, *Bel.*[2] xiv. 12
Be it by fortune, or by *course* of kinde, *Ro.* ix. 3
her *course* begun with brave intent. *Ro.* xxi. 8
the compast *course* of the universe . . . is ronne, *Ro.* xxii. 9
stopt her *course,* and held her by the heele, *Van.* ix. 11
Must not the world wend in his commun *course,* *S.C.* F. 11
youth and *course* of carelesse yeeres, *S.C.* Jun. 33
can undoe Dame Natures kindly *course;* *S.C.* N. 124
delay Thy nightly *course,* to heare his melodie? *Gn.* 460
They cast in *course* to waste the wearie howres. *Hub.* 27
What *course* ye weene is best for us to take, *Hub.* 115
ere the yeare have halfe his *course* out-run, *Hub.* 305
some good *course* that we might undertake; *Hub.* 411
in their speedie *course* and nimble flight *Hub.* 621
Of Natures workes, of heavens continuall *course,* *Hub.* 764
There now no rivers *course* is to be seene, *Ti.* 139
She fell away against all *course* of kinde. *D.* 242
should it not thy readie *course* restraine, *Col.* 82
Which way his *course* the wanton Bregog bent; *Col.* 135
Thereto our ship her *course* directly bent, *Col.* 268
'to what *course* thou please thy selfe advance: *Col.* 425
to read aright The *course* of heavenly cause, I. ix. 6. 7
Would not a while her forward *course* pursew, I. ix. 20. 6
Sunne to stay, Or backward turne his *course* I. x. 20. 3
To which I meane my wearie *course* to bend; I. xii. 1. 2
To weete what *course* he takes, II. i. 4. 4
when him ronning in full *course* he spyes, II. v. 10. 5
Ne cared she her *course* for to apply; II. vi. 5. 7
bent his hasty *course* towardes the ydle flood. II. vi. 41. 9

Course—*Continued.*
nimbly ran her wonted *course* II. vi. 20. 6
to a stedfast starre his *course* hath bent, II. vii. 1. 2
Whereby her *course* is stopt and passage staid: II. ix. 8. 4
taking his full *course* Until he came II. xi. 46. 5
stere aright, And keepe an even *course;* II. xii. 3. 2
old Syre, thy *course* doe thereunto apply.' II. xii. 10. 9
Quit from that danger forth their *course* they kept; II. xii. 27. 1
Held on his *course* with stayed stedfastnesse, II. xii. 29. 6
The land to which their *course* they leveled; II. xii. 34. 4
every river eke his *course* forbeares, III. ii. 32. 3
From *course* of nature and of modestee? III. ii. 41. 8
Doth *course* of naturall cause farre exceed, III. iii. 18. 6
the streight *course* of hevenly destiny, III. iii. 24. 3
Britomart kept on her former *course,* III. iv. 5. 1
From love in *course* of nature to refraine. III. iv. 26. 4
ne her right *course* for ought forsooke. III. iv. 44. 9
The world in his continuall *course* to keepe, III. iv. 56. 2
his *cours* they did restraine. III. v. 39. 9
Forthy she thither cast her *course* t' apply, III. vi. 16. 8
decay By *course* of kinde and by occasion; III. vi. 38. 7
all that night her *course* continewed, III. vii. 2. 2
ere the yeare his *course* had compassid, III. vii. 55. 3
That thing of *course* he counted love to entertaine. III. ix. 29. 9
backe agayne To turne your *course,* III. ix. 40. 6
by fatall *course* they driven were III. ix. 49. 1
Aread what *course* of you is safest dempt, III. xi. 23. 3
towards them did ply With speedie *course,* IV. i. 38. 6
Drives backe the current of his kindly *course,* IV. iii. 27. 4
The which by *course* befals me here to tell: IV. iv. 2. 5
toward them his *course* seem'd to apply: IV. iv. 6. 7
Which th' other seeing gan his *course* relent, IV. iv. 7. 1
his speare he gan abase And voide his *course:* IV. vi. 3. 5
in this Ladie wrought Against the *course* of kind, IV. vi. 30. 5
tell the *course* of his captivitie, IV. viii. 64. 2
The *course* of loose affection to forstall, IV. ix. 19. 3
the heaven is in his *course* contained. IV. x. 35. 1
doth his *course* through Blandford plains direct, IV. xi. 32. 3
through long continuance of his *course,* . . . the world V. Pr. 1. 6
his creatures from their *course* astray, V. Pr. 6. 8
ne keepes his *course* more right, V. Pr. 7. 3
He chaunst to meet a Dwarfe in hasty *course,* V. ii. 2. 2
Yet for no pitty would he change the *course* Of Justice, V. ii. 26. 1
Till we may be assur'd they shall their *course* retaine.' V. ii. 36. 9
To whom his *course* he hastily applide, V. iv. 21. 4
The *course* of all her fortune and posteritie. V. vii. 12. 9
hound full greedy of his pray, . . . Continu'd still his *course,* V. viii. 7. 3
It often fals, in *course* of common life, V. xi. 1. 1
Kept on his *course* as he did it direct, V. xii. 21. 2
of necessity His *course* of Justice he was forst to stay, V. xii. 27. 4
yet he for nought would swerve From his right *course,* V. xii. 43. 8
long restrayned of his ready *course,* VI. i. 21. 3
And moved speach to him of things of *course,* VI. iii. 14. 6
the strong *course* of their displeasure breake, VI. v. 30. 7
Till that, as comes by *course,* I doe recite VI. vi. 17. 4
seemed nought the *course* thereof could stay, VI. viii. 8. 5
first it falleth me by *course* to tell Of faire Serena; VI. viii. 31. 1
A monstrous cruelty gainst *course* of kynde! VI. viii. 36. 5
Then gan they to devize what *course* to take; VI. viii. 37. 6
The which, as commeth now by *course,* I will declare. VI. x. 4. 9
to *course* about their bases light; VI. x. 8. 4
after griefe awhile had had his *course,* VI. xi. 34. 1
Directs her *course* unto one certaine cost, VI. xii. 1. 2
Whose *course* is often stayd, yet never is astray. VI. xii. 1. 9
Though out of *course,* yet hath not bene missayd, VI. xii. 2. 3
now I come into my *course* againe, VI. xii. 2. 6
why she did her wonted *course* forslowe; VII. vi. 16. 4
gan now advise What *course* were best to take VII. vi. 22. 9
still compell To keepe his *course?* VII. vii. 48. 6
he his *course* doth alter every yeare, VII. vii. 51. 3
it can alter all the *course* of kynd. *Am.* xxx. 14
Out of her *course* doth wander far astray! *Am.* xxxiv. 4
part The raging waves, and keepes her *course* *Am.* lix. 6
in *course* of heavenly spheares are skild, *Am.* lx. 1
The new begins his compast *course* anew: *Am.* lxii. 2
by chaunce, against the *course* of kynd, *H.B.* 143

Coursed. as they *courst,* and turneyd here and theare, IV. iv. 30. 1
as they *coursed* here and there, IV. vi. 13. 1
Them sorely vext, and *courst,* and overran, V. iv. 44. 3
There he him *courst* a-fresh, V. ix. 16. 8
Him first from court he to the citties *coursed,* VI. ix. 3. 6

Courser. The Champion . . . dismounted from his *courser* I. i. 11. 8
he sate upon his *courser* free, I. ii. 11. 8
One . . . Full strongly armd, and on a *courser* free I. iii. 33. 3
He . . . Beares her away upon his *courser* light: I. iii. 43. 8
Raunging the forest wide on *courser* free, I. ix. 12. 7
He smote his *courser* in the trembling flanck, II. iii. 6. 5
On goodly *courser* thondring with his feet, II. iii. 11. 4
well that valiaunt *courser* did discerne; II. iii. 46. 6
So proudly pricketh on his *courser* strong, II. v. 38. 8
So fast as his good *Courser* could him beare; II. xi. 25. 8
to her *Courser* mounting light: III. iv. 12. 5
his warlike *courser,* which was strayd III. v. 38. 6
Fast flying, on a *Courser* dapled gray, III. vii. 37. 3
An armed knight upon a *courser* strong, III. viii. 15. 3
if thee list to see thy *Courser* ronne, III. viii. 17. 4
Upon his *Courser* sett the lovely lode, III. viii. 19. 4
having from his *courser* her downe throwne, V. i. 17. 7
the *courser* whereuppon he rad Could swim V. ii. 13. 8

Courser's. adowne his *coursers* side The red bloud trickling I. ii. 14. 8

Coursers. from their sweaty *Coursers* did avale, II. ix. 10. 7
his wingfooted *coursers* him did beare So fast away V. viii. 33. 4
Courses. *See* **Water-courses.**
Let streaming floods their hastie *courses* stay, *D.* 332
till the horned moone three *courses* did expire. IV. vi. 43. 9
two Barkes, . . . contrary *courses* sew, IV. ix. 26. 8
their *courses* change anew. IV. ix. 26. 9
And search the *courses* of the rowling spheares, V. Pr. 5. 2
Al which the heavens containe, and in their *courses* guide. V. ii. 35. 9
Thou doest not know the causes, nor their *courses* dew. V. ii. 42. 9
Like as the workeman had their *courses* taught; V. v. 2. 5
their well-knowen *courses* they forwent; V. viii. 40. 6
Court. if thee list unto the *Court* to throng, *Hub.* 502
without reward Livings in *Court* be gotten, *Hub.* 514
'From royall *Court* I lately came (said he) *Hub.* 607
now in *Court* doth beare the greatest sway, *Hub.* 616
if fortune thee in *Court* to live, *Hub.* 631
How for the *Court* themselves they might aguize; *Hub.* 656
to the *Court* in seemly sort they come; *Hub.* 662
devises, never seene In *Court* before, *Hub.* 674
The which in *Court* him served to good stead; *Hub.* 697
Poore suters, that in *Court* did haunt some while; *Hub.* 878
being one of great regard In *Court*, *Hub.* 886
whom wicked fate Hath brought to *Court*, *Hub.* 893
will to *Court* for shadowes vaine to seeke, *Hub.* 912
Out of the *Court* for ever banished. *Hub.* 924
he cast to leave The *Court*, *Hub.* 936
dreadles bad them come to *Corte*, *Hub.* 1077
to appeare The morrow next at *Court*, it to defend; *Hub.* 1099
the Sheepe . . . Came to the *Court*, *Hub.* 1208
Thus dight, into the *Court* he tooke his way, *Hub.* 1300
sway in *Court* with pride and rashnes rude; *T.M.* 328
Find entertainment or in *Court* or Schoole; *T.M.* 410
in *Court* full oft Beholding them, *Mui.* 105
The which in *Court* continually hooved, *Col.* 666
As ever else in Princes *Court* thou vewest. *Col.* 738
is Love then . . . once knowne In *Court*, *Col.* 772
as Exuls out of his *court* be thrust.' *Col.* 894
Then that brave *court* doth to mine eie present, *Ded.Son.*xvii.11
in Faery *court*, . . . Where noblest knights I. iii. 28. 5
In living Princes *court* none ever knew Such endlesse richesse, I. iv. 7. 4
in that *court* whylome her well they knew: I. iv. 15. 5
goodly *court* he made still to his Dame, I. vii. 7. 1
With lovely *court* he gan her entertaine; I. vii. 38. 2
Forthwith to *court* of Gloriane I sped, I. vii. 46. 5
entred in, a spatious *court* they see, I. x. 6. 2
To Faery *court* thou cam'st to seek for fame, I. x. 66. 8
purveyaunce meet Of all, that royall Princes *court* became; I. xii. 13. 6
Sith him in Faery *court* he late avizd; II. i. 31. 6
to show, ne *court*, nor dalliaunce; II. ii. 35. 6
in *court* gay portaunce he perceiv'd, II. iii. 5. 7
to *court* he cast t' advaunce his first degree. II. iii. 5. 9
To serve at *court* in view of vaunting eye; II. iii. 10. 2
doest not it for joyous *court* exchaunge, II. iii. 39. 3
the *court* is fitt for thee.' II. iii. 39. 9
'In Princes *court*'—The rest she would have sayd, II. iii. 42. 1
Did *court* the handmayd of my Lady deare, II. iv. 25. 2
him the Prince with gentle *court* did bord: II. ix. 2. 5
the Palmer him forth drew From Faery *court*. II. ix. 9. 8
gentle *court* and gracious delight Shee to them made, II. ix. 20. 3
they gan dispose Themselves to *court*, II. ix. 36. 5
with *court* and goodly game II. ix. 44. 4
her to Faery *court* safe to convay; III. i. 2. 4
I lately did depart From Faery *court*, III. v. 4. 4
fowre since Florimell the *Court* forwent, III. v. 10. 2
So farre from *court* and royall Citadell, III. vi. 1. 5
First she him sought in *Court*, III. vi. 13. 1
To Faery *court* she came; III. vi. 52. 7
now in Faery *court* all men do tell, III. viii. 46. 2
has no skill of *Court* nor courtesie, III. ix. 3. 6
Therefore he her did *court*, IV. ii. 8. 6
greatest Princes *court* would welcome fayne; IV. viii. 27. 2
In Princess *Court* doe hap to sprout againe, IV. viii. 33. 4
out of *court* him scourged openly. V. iii. 38. 5
with him convay Unto the Souldans *court*, V. viii. 25. 8
When first to Faery *court* he saw her wend, V. xi. 37. 8
He through occasion called was away To Faerie *Court*, V. xii. 27. 3
still the way did hold To Faerie *Court*; V. xii. 43. 9
doe adorne your *Court* where courtesies excell. VI. Pr. 7. 9
Of *Court*, it seemes, men Courtesie doe call, VI. i. 1. 1
Right so in Faery *court* it did redound, VI. i. 1. 7
ne was there Lady found In Faery *court*, VI. i. 3. 2
on a day, when Cupid kept his *court*, VI. vii. 32. 6
Him first from *court* he to the citties coursed, VI. ix. 3. 6
leaving home, to roiall *court* I sought, VI. ix. 24. 6
in it She used most to keepe her royall *court*, VI. x. 9. 7
long fruitlesse stay in Princes *Court*, *Proth.* 7
Courted. With fawning wordes he *courted* her a while; I. vi. 4. 1
comely *courted* with meet modestie; II. ii. 15. 2
Courted of many a jolly Paramoure, II. ix. 34. 3
with commune speach He *courted* her; III. x. 6. 7
Courteins. *See* **Curtains.**
Courteous. excelling all the crewe In *curteous* usage *Mui.* 120
Ne thee lesse worthie, *curteous* Candida, *Col.* 574
faire him quited, as that *courteous* was; I. i. 30. 2
when her *curteous* deeds he did compare, I. vi. 31. 3
comforted with *curteous* kind reliefe; I. vi. 37. 6
Thereat the *courteous* knight displeased was, I. viii. 33. 3
'Ah! *courteous* Knight,' (quoth she) I. ix. 7. 8
entertaines with comely *courteous* glee; I. x. 6. 5

Courteous—*Continued.*
So *courteous* conge both did give and take, II. i. 34. 1
A sober sad and comely *courteous* Dame; II. ii. 14. 5
The knight was *courteous*, II. vi. 21. 5
As to despise so *curteous* seeming part II. vi. 26. 4
such is the might Of *courteous* clemency II. vi. 36. 6
Of kindnesse and of *courteous* aggrace; II. viii. 56. 8
the Prince in *courteous* maner sayd; II. ix. 37. 4
taking *courteous* conge, II. xi. 17. 3
They *courteous* conge tooke, and forth together yode. III. i. 1. 9
they were entertaynd with *courteous* And comely glee III. i. 31. 4
be led in *courteous* wize Into a bowre, III. i. 42. 3
they all seemed *courteous* and gent, III. i. 44. 4
Basciante did him selfe most *courteous* shew; III. i. 45. 5
mote I weet of you, right *courteous* knight, Tydings III. ii. 8. 6
'How ever, Sir, ye fyle Your *courteous* tongue III. ii. 12. 5
Wise, warlike, personable, *courteous*, and kind. III. iv. 5. 9
singled from the crew Of *courteous* knights, III. iv. 45. 4
she was so *courteous* and kynde, III. v. 55. 2
through her so kind And *courteise* use, III. vii. 15. 7
shewd her selfe in all a gentle *courteous* Dame. III. ix. 26. 9
Courteous to all and seeming debonaire, III. xii. 14. 4
Yet could she not but *curteous* countenance to her make. IV. i. 5. 9
She, that no lesse was *courteous* then stout, IV. i. 11. 6
Whereat they shewed *curteous* countenaunce. IV. iv. 7. 5
With daily shew of *courteous* kind behaviour, V. v. 35. 7
gan gently her salute With *curteous* words, V. vi. 20. 2
Where *curteous* Knights and Ladies most did won VI. i. 1. 8
none more *courteous* Knight Then Calidore, VI. i. 2. 1
Thy *courteous* lore, that doest my love deride, VI. i. 27. 8
That well in *courteous* Calidore appeares; VI. ii. 3. 1
sith ye so *courteous* seemed late, VI. ii. 27. 4
'Glad would I surely be, thou *courteous* Squire, VI. ii. 37. 1
So taking *courteous* leave they parted twayne, VI. ii. 38. 8
The Ladie, hearing his so *courteous* speach, VI. ii. 42. 7
She thankt him . . . for the *courteous* care VI. ii. 46. 8
Doth noble courage shew with *curteous* manners met. VI. iii. 1. 9
By late ensample of that *courteous* deed VI. iii. 2. 4
Yet was he *courteous* still to every wight, VI. iii. 3. 5
to them he seemed, A *courteous* Knight VI. iii. 13. 2
And *courteous* withall, becomming her degree. VI. iii. 20. 9
Such was the state of this most *courteous* knight VI. iv. 1. 6
By all the *courteous* meanes he could invent; VI. v. 32. 6
The Squire, for that he *courteous* was indeed, VI. vi. 16. 4
With all the *courteous* glee and goodly feast VI. vi. 41. 4
(That was that *courteous* Knight, VI. viii. 4. 4
Did litle whit regard his *courteous* guize, VI. ix. 35. 6
Calidore, of *courteous* inclination, VI. ix. 42. 1
Thus did the *courteous* Knight excuse his blame, VI. x. 29. 8
Courteously. the bold Virgin . . . spake thus *courtesly*:— III. xi. 13. 9
To whome false Turpine comming *courteously*, VI. vii. 4. 1
to tell him *courteously* besought, VI. ix. 5. 8
Courtesan. 'Certes was but a common *Courtisane*; III. vii. 58. 2
Courtesans. With *courtizans*, and costly riotize, *Hub.* 805
Courtesies. His clownish gifts and *curtsies* I disdaine, *S.C.* Ja. 57
With all the *court'sies* that she could devyse, I. x. 11. 8
them requites with *court'sies* seeming meet, I. x. 32. 3
entertaine themselves with *court'sies* meet. II. i. 29. 4
fast goodwill, with gentle *courtesyes*, III. ix. 7. 7
entertaining her with *curt'sies* meet, IV. iii. 50. 8
Them fairely entertayned with *curt'sies* meete, V. iv. 51. 5
Both doing and receiving *curtesies* V. x. 5. 2
doe adorne your Court where *courtesies* excell. VI. Pr. 7. 9
And unto him did shew all lovely *courtesyes*. VI. ii. 16. 9
fitter beene For courting fooles that *curtesies* would faine, VI. v. 38. 8
With all kind *courtesies* he could invent; VI. ix. 34. 6
Courtesy. unto everie one doo *curtesie* meeke: *Hub.* 499
unto all doth yeeld due *curtesie*; *Hub.* 729
She is the blosome of grace and *curtesie*, *Col.* 528
Masked with faire dissembling *curtesie*, *Col.* 700
each one himselfe did payne . . . faire *courtesie* to shew, I. iv. 15. 4
them receives a gentle Squyre, Of . . . rare *courtesee*, I. x. 7. 2
them encounters with like *courtesee*: I. x. 15. 2
Your *court'sie* takes on you anothers dew offence.' II. i. 28. 9
She Guyon deare besought of *curtesie* To tell II. ii. 39. 4
Of *courtesie* to mee the cause aread II. v. 16. 8
nought againe Him answered, as *courtesie* became; II. viii. 23. 3
'Sir knight, mote I of you this *court'sy* read, II. ix. 2. 6
he his ydle *curtesie* defide, II. xii. 49. 7
The great schoolmaistresse of all *courtesy*: III. vi. 1. 6
The which thy proffred *curtesie* denayd? III. vii. 57. 7
has no skill of Court nor *courtesie*, III. ix. 3. 6
evermore the Carle of *courtesie* accusd. III. ix. 12. 9
Then they Malbecco prayd of *courtesy*, III. ix. 25. 7
the brave Mayd would not for *courtesy* . . . him abrade, III. xi. 8. 3
Nor more ennobled for their *courtesie*, IV. iii. 2. 6
her against sate comely *Curtesie*, IV. x. 51. 3
Can yeeld great thankes for such her *curtesie*; V. v. 55. 5
That *curt'sie* with like kindnesse to repay, V. xi. 11. 5
'Yet let me you of *courtesie* request' V. xi. 57. 1
the bloosme of comely *courtesie*; VI. Pr. 4. 2
in the triall of true *curtesie*, VI. Pr. 5. 1
The goodly praise of Princely *curtesie*, VI. Pr. 6. 3
Of Court, it seemes, men *Courtesie* doe call, VI. i. 1. 1
Both noble armes and gentle *curtesie*. VI. i. 26. 8
doe instead thereof mild *curt'sie* showe VI. i. 27. 3
court'sie doth as well as armes professe, VI. i. 41. 2
his exceeding *courtesie*, that pearst Her stubborne hart VI. i. 45. 3
What vertue is so fitting for a knight . . . As *Curtesie*; VI. ii. 1. 3
with all good *courtesie* Fain'd her to frolicke, VI. iii. 9. 1

Courtesy—*Continued.*
his kyndly *courtesie* to prove, VI. iii. 15. 5
That he gainst *courtesie* so fowly did default. VI. iii. 21. 9
Whom Calepine . . . Besought of *courtesie,* VI. iii. 31. 2
host, That should to me such *curtesie* afford, VI. iii. 39. 6
That *curtesie* and manhood ever disagree. VI. iii. 40. 9
Or *curtesie* with rudenesse to requite: VI. iii. 41. 5
And offred him, his *courtesie* to requite, VI. iv. 39. 7
How each to entertaine with *curt'sie* well beseene. VI. v. 36. 9
as he that did excell In *courtesie* VI. ix. 18. 4
he, that did in *courtesie* excell, VI. ix. 44. 8
courtesie amongst the rudest breeds Good will VI. ix. 45. 5
all the complements of *curtesie:* VI. x. 23. 6
with such *courtesie* doth grace, VI. x. 27. 6
To shew the *courtesie* by him profest VI. xii. 2. 4
Courtier. The *Courtier* needes must recompenced bee *Hub.* 516
the brave *Courtier,* in whose beauteous thought *Hub.* 717
Such is the rightfull *Courtier* in his kinde, *Hub.* 793
Courtier's. No art of schoole, but *Courtiers* schoolery. *Col.* 702
Courtiers. *Courtiers,* as the tide, doo rise and fall.' *Hub.* 614
good *Courtiers* may ye bee!' *Hub.* 653
gan the *Courtiers* gaze on everie side, *Hub.* 669
common *Courtiers* love to gybe and fleare *Hub.* 714
Courting. thereto doth his *Courting* most applie: *Hub.* 784
when the *courting* masker louteth lowe, *Ti.* 202
as a complement for *courting* vaine. *Col.* 790
With . . . *courting* dalliaunce, She intertainde her lover I. ii. 14. 1
That night they pas . . . Feasting and *courting* I. iv. 43. 6
no *courting* nicetee, But simple, trew, I. x. 7. 7
forged showes, as fitter beene For *courting* fooles VI. v. 38. 8
Courtisane, -izans. *See* **Courtesan, -s.**
Courtly. his fine feates and *Courtly* complement; *Hub.* 692
when this *Courtly* Gentleman with toyle Himselfe hath wearied, *Hub.* 753
to uphold his *courtly* countenaunce *Hub.* 846
Wherewith that *courtly* garlond most ye grace *Ded. Son.* xvi. 4
Some frounce their curled heare in *courtly* guise; I. iv. 14. 7
whenas Morpheus had . . . Arrested all that *courtly* company, I. iv. 44. 7
Of comely services, or *courtly* trayne? I. xii. 14. 4
bathes him selfe in *courtly* blis, II. iii. 40. 2
With whom he ment to make his sport and *courtly* play. III. i. 56. 9
vain sheows . . . And *courtly* services, III. vii. 29. 7
From *courtly* blis and wonted happinesse, III. viii. 20. 8
courtly favour, VI. x. 2. 8
Court's. the common winde Of *Courts* inconstant mutabilitie, *Hub.* 723
courts chief garlond with all vertues dight, *Col.* 499
Courts. Fell from high Princes *courtes,* or Ladies bowres, I. v. 51. 6
picturals Of Magistrates, of *courts,* of tribunals, II. ix. 53. 5
in Princes *courts* to worke great scath and hindrance: V. ix. 22. 9
Cousin. ye my *cousin* Wolfe so fowly thwart, *Hub* 1218
coosen unto king Ambrosius; III. iii. 13. 8
from the head Of his *coosen* Constantius, III. iii. 29. 5
Both *coosen* passions of distroubled spright, III. iv. 12. 7
Couth. Well *couth* he tune his pipe *S.C.* Ja. 10
the Oake cast him to replie Well as he *couth;* *S.C.* F. 190
Well *couth* he wayle his Woes, *S.C.* Jun. 85
Such favour *couth* he fynd, *S.C.* Jul. 138
So well she *couth* the shepherds entertayne *S.C.* N. 95
He daily dyde, yet never throughly dyen *couth.* II. vii. 58. 9
Covenant. The *covenant* was, that every spoyle or pray Should equally be shard IV. ii. 13. 4
Cover. cleanly *cover* that cannot be cured: *S.C.* S. 138
With cryme doe not it *cover,* but disclose the same.' I. xii. 30. 9
The more that she it sought to *cover* and to hyde. V. v. 53. 9
clothes to *cover* what they ought by kind, VI. viii. 50. 4
though the night did *cover* her disgrace, VI. viii. 51. 3
Covered. wall; . . . *cover'd* all with griesly shadowes, *Bel.*[2] viii. 3
Tartar *covered* With bloodie night, *Gn.* 444
his Moother with a Veale hath *coovered* his Face? *Tetrasticon* 3
Covered with darkenes and misdeeming night, I. ii. 3. 8
A foggy mist had *covered* all the land; I. iv. 36. 7
knight . . . Lay *cover'd* with inchaunted cloud I. v. 19. 6
the Paynim lay, *Coverd* with charmed cloud I. v. 29. 4
His warlike shield all closely *cover'd* was, I. vii. 33. 1
his shield, that *covered* was, Did loose his vele I. viii. 19. 1
all was *covered* with darknesse dire: I. xi. 40. 4
cover'd heaven with hideous dreriment, II. vii. 1. 5
Cover'd with boughes and shrubs from heavens light, II. vii. 3. 2
He much rejoyst, and *courd* it tenderly, II. viii. 9. 8
bore after him an heben launce And *coverd* shield. II. viii. 17. 7
cloudes of deadly night . . . his heavy eylids *cover'd* have, II. viii. 24. 8
The one upon his *covered* shield did fall, II. viii. 38. 3
Cover'd with lids deviz'd of substance sly, II. ix. 46. 7
That quicksand nigh with water *covered;* II. xii. 18. 6
both awhile would *covered* remaine, II. xii. 64. 4
Her with a scarlott mantle *covered* III. i. 59. 8
His crest was *covered* with a couchant Hownd, III. ii. 25. 1
Covered with secret cloud of silent night, III. iii. 61. 8
griesly shadowes *covered* heaven bright, III. iv. 52. 2
a ship, whose Lodestar suddeinly *Covered* with cloudes III. iv. 53. 4
All *coverd* with thick woodes that quite it overcame. III. vii. 4. 9
whenas chearelesse Night *ycovered* had Fayre heaven III. xii. 1. 1
evening Her *covered* with her sable vestiment, III. xii. 29. 4
His faire Cambina, *covered* with a veale; IV. v. 10. 2
Covered with cloudie storme and bitter showre, IV. v. 32. 2
mossy trees, which *covered* all with shade IV. vii. 38. 8
covered with a slender veile afore; IV. x. 40. 7
'The cause why she was *covered* with a vele IV. x. 41. 1
Whose yvorie shoulders weren *covered* all, IV. xi. 11. 7
Covered from peoples gazement with a vele: V. iii. 17. 3
Artegall . . . Stood in the preasse close *covered,* V. iii. 20. 2
Covered—*Continued.*
His face was *covered,* and his head was bar'd, V. iv. 22. 5
to sleepe, *Cover'd* with cold, and wrapt in wretchednesse; VI. iii. 44. 7
a hollow glade *Covered* with mossie shrubs, VI. iv. 13. 6
Island . . . *Covered* with shrubby woods, VI. x. 41. 7
shade From view of living wight and *covered* over; VI. x. 42. 4
covered with confused preasse Of carcases, VI. xi. 20. 1
With a Deeres-skin they *covered,* VII. vi. 52. 2
Night had *covered* her uncomely face VII. vii. 44. 4
mercie seate . . . Close *covered* with the Lambes integrity *H.H.B.* 149
Covering. *Covering* your foe with cloud of deadly night, I. v. 14. 7
with greene mosse *cov'ring* her nakednesse II. i. 22. 4
covering with a clod their closed eye, II. i. 60. 4
The shield it drove, and did the *covering* reare: IV. viii. 42. 7
The which she *covering* with her purple pall V. ix. 50. 8
with a cloud of night him *covering,* V. xi. 14. 8
with her garment *covering* him from sight, VI. vi. 31. 3
Coverings. Through their thin *covering* appearing fayre, *Gn.* 286
Coverlets. With silken courtens and gold *coverletts,* II. vi. 16. 6
odourd sheetes, and Arras *coverlets.* *Epith.* 304
Covert. Enforst to seeke some *covert* nigh at hand, I. i. 7. 1
The which O! pardon me thus to enfold In *covert* vele, II. Pr. 5. 2
Through that thick *covert* he him led, II. vii. 20. 6
Through many *covert* groves and thickets close, II. xii. 76. 6
bathe him in a fountaine by some *covert* glade: III. i. 35. 9
Within that wood there was a *covert* glade, III. v. 17. 1
till they arrived were In that same shady *covert* III. vi. 26. 6
in the thickest *covert* of that shade III. vi. 44. 1
forced them to seeke some *covert* bowre, IV. v. 32. 5
Thrust to an Hynd within some *covert* glade, IV. vi. 12. 4
Sitting in *covert* shade of arbors sweet, IV. viii. 9. 2
Amongst the flags and *covert* round about. V. ii. 54. 6
Which long concealing in her *covert* brest, V. v. 27. 1
Within the closet of her *covert* brest, V. v. 44. 6
Cannot come neare him in the *covert* wood, V. viii. 35. 7
We chaunst to come foreby a *covert* glade VI. ii. 16. 3
his Ladie, . . . Into the *covert* did her selfe withdraw, VI. ii. 20. 3
when she fled into that *covert* greave, VI. ii. 43. 8
In *covert* shade him selfe did safely rest, VI. iii. 20. 3
whose *covert* stopt his further sight: VI. v. 17. 7
The *covert* was so thicke that did no passage shew. VI. v. 22. 9
in the *covert* of the wood did byde, VI. x. 24. 5
Simple and true, from *covert* malice free; VI. x. 24. 5
in the *covert* of the night, VI. x. 41. 3
her dainty limbes to lay In *covert* shade, VII. vi. 42. 5
In the close *covert* of her guilefull eyen, *Am.* xii. 7
Conceald through *covert* night. *Epith.* 363
Covertly. Lay lurking *covertly* him to surprise; *Mui.* 386
Coverts. keepes in *coverts* close from living wight, II. ix. 40. 8
Through many woods and shady *coverts* flowes, VII. vi. 41. 7
Coverture. Where hast thou *coverture?* *S.C.* Jul. 26
throughly arm'd against such *coverture,* *Hub.* 683
Covet. Shall hap to heare, or *covet* them to read: *As.* Pr. 14
'Hobbin, thou temptest me to that I *covet:* *Col.* 37
Who all that Colin makes do *covet* faine.' *Col.* 99
I do *covet* most the same to heare, *Col.* 161
As men use most to *covet* forreine thing.' *Col.* 162
Through him the cold began to *covet* heat, *Col.* 847
That *covett* in th' immortall booke of fame To be eternized, I. x. 59. 5
'Which, for my part, I *covet* to performe I. xii. 20. 1
To them that *covet* such eye-glutting gaine II. vii. 9. 8
To *covet* more then I have cause to use? II. vii. 39. 4
Did *covet,* as they passed by that way, II. xii. 20. 7
Thy selfe thou *covet* to see pictured, III. Pr. 4. 2
Ne ever cast his mind to *covet* prayse, III. vii. 12. 5
not that which men *covet* most is best, VI. ix. 29. 6
if ye algates *covet* to assay This simple sort of life VI. ix. 33. 7
To *covet* fetters, though they golden bee! *Am.* xxxvii. 14
Coveted. That maketh it be *coveted* the more: *Am.* xxvi. 10
Coveting. *coveting,* with his high tops extent, *Gn.* 212
gaped still as *coveting* to drinke II. vii. 58. 2
Covetise. they bene false, and full of *covetise,* *S.C.* S. 82
Tickled with glorie and rash *covetise:* *Hub.* 996
Gluttonie, malice, pride, and *covetize,* *Hub.* 1309
through pride or *covetize,* *Ti.* 363
Whose need had end, but no end *covetise;* I. iv. 29. 3
he gnasht his teeth . . . with griple *Covetyse;* I. iv. 31. 7
mortgaging their lives to *Covetise,* I. v. 46. 4
Outrageous wrong, and hellish *covetize,* II. vii. 12. 8
Frayle men are oft captiv'd to *covetise;* II. vii. 15. 2
their devouring *covetize* restraynd; III. iv. 7. 8
greedy *covetize* Still to behold the object *Am.* xxxv. 1
Covetous. rend the greedie mindes of *covetous* men, *Gn.* 95
the Foxe guilefull, and most *covetous;* *Hub.* 1022
feede his eye And *covetous* desire II. vii. 4. 9
If ever *covetous* hand, or lustfull eye, II. vii. 27. 2
The charge thereof unto a *covetous* Spright II. vii. 32. 1
From other *covetous* feends it to defend, II. vii. 32. 4
corrupt envyes, And *covetous* aspects, II. xi. 8. 9
lurking from the vew of *covetous* guest, II. xii. 55. 4
Covets. From that which feeble nature *covets* faine: II. vi. 1. 5
Cow. Streight downe she ranne, like an enraged *cow* V. viii. 46. 1
Coward. as the *coward* beasts use to despise *Ro.* xiv. 5
upon his *coward* brest A bloody crosse, I. ii. 11. 4
To hide his *coward* head II. iii. 21. 4
He was dismayed in his *coward* minde, II. iii. 32. 2
'Disleall Knight, whose *coward* corage chose II. v. 5. 3
What *coward* hand shall doe thee next to dye, II. vi. 39. 8
crownd his *coward* crest with knightly stile; II. viii. 12. 7
His *coward* courage gan emboldned bee, III. v. 15. 2

Coward—*Continued.*
in *coward* corner ly, . . . III. ix. 14. 9
Flying from place to place with *cowheard* shame; . . . V. viii. 50. 8
Nor undertake the same for *cowheard* feare, . . . V. x. 15. 5
'*Cowherd!*' (quoth she) . . . VI. i. 28. 5
Ne cared as a *coward* so to be condemned. . . . VI. iii. 36. 9
that craven *cowherd* Knight Was at his backe . . . VI. vi. 26. 6
'Vile *cowheard* dogge! now doe I much repent, . . . VI. vi. 33. 4
by this thy *cowheard* feare: . . . VI. vi. 34. 2
The *coward* Turpine, whereof now I treat; . . . VI. vii. 2. 2
the *cowheard*, deaded with affright, . . . VI. vii. 25. 7
Through *cowherd* feare he fled away . . . VI. x. 35. 3
Cowardice. bad him put all *cowardize* away: . . . *Hub.* 958
To banish *cowardize* and bastard feare: . . . I. vi. 24. 2
with fowle *cowardize* his carcas shame, . . . II. viii. 13. 4
As scorning his unmanly *cowardize:* . . . IV. iv. 11. 2
So courage lent a cloke to *cowardise.* . . . V. iii. 15. 5
cowardize doth still in villany delight. . . . VI. vi. 26. 9
To shew such faintnesse and foule *cowardize* . . . VI. vi. 35. 2
Yet durst he not for very *cowardize* Effect the same, . . . VI. vi. 44. 6
Coridon for *cowherdize* reject, . . . VI. x. 37. 3
Cowardly. from the fielde most *cowardly* doth fly! . . . I. x. 1. 5
cowardly distrust Of his weake wings . . . *H.L.* 180
Cowardry. shake off this vile harted *cowardree.* . . . *Hub.* 986
Cowards. (despeyre makes *cowards* stout,) . . . *As.* 117
From fearefull *cowards* entrance to forstall . . . IV. x. 17. 3
in hard assaies Were *cowards* knowne, . . . IV. x. 18. 7
Cower. townes and castles under her brest did *coure,* . . . *Bel.*^{2} viii. 6
Cowhe(a)rd. *See* **Coward.**
Cowherd. for her sake a *cowheard* vile became . . . III. xi. 39. 3
The servant of Admetus, *cowheard* vile, . . . III. xi. 39. 4
Kept by a *cowheard,* high Eurytion, . . . V. x. 10. 2
Cowslips. *Cowslips,* and Kingcups, and loved Lillies: . . . *S.C.* Ap. 141
Coy. Their match in glorie, mightie, fierce, and *coy;* . . . *Gn.* 494
he feining seemely merth, And shee *coy* lookes: . . . I. ii. 27. 9
Still solemne sad, or still disdainfull *coy;* . . . II. vi. 37. 5
Another seemed envious or *coy,* . . . II. ix. 35. 7
everie looke was *coy* and wondrous quaint, . . . IV. i. 5. 7
coy lookes tempring with loose dalliance; . . . IV. ii. 9. 5
sense of man so *coy* and curious nice, . . . IV. x. 22. 6
Seeing his face so lovely sterne and *coy,* . . . VI. ii. 24. 3
this *coy* Damzell thought contrariwize, . . . VI. vii. 30. 1
glancing through the eyes with countenance *coy* . . . *H.L.* 122
Coylchester. *See* **Colchester.**
Coyll. Then *Coyll;* and after him good Lucius, . . . II. x. 53. 3
shortly was by *Coyll* in batteill slaine: . . . II. x. 58. 5
With whome king *Coyll* made an agreement, . . . II. x. 59. 3
Coyly. *Coyly* rebutted his embracement light; . . . III. viii. 10. 5
Cozen. Thereby to *coosin* men not well aware: . . . *Hub.* 874
Cozenage. *coosinage* and cleanly knaverie, . . . *Hub.* 857
Cozened. With which he thousands cleanly *coosined:* . . . *Hub.* 862
Crab. That they have crusht the *Crab,* . . . V. Pr. 6. 3
Upon a *Crab* he rode, . . . VII. vii. 35. 5
When once the *Crab* behind his back he sees. . . . *Epith.* 269
Crabbed. Ne wont with *crabbed* care the Muses dwell: . . . *S.C.* O. 101
Of swarth complexion, and of *crabbed* hew, . . . II. ix. 52. 4
'Therein a cancred *crabbed* Carle does dwell, . . . III. ix. 3. 5
Saturne oft doth . . . calme his *crabbed* lookes. . . . VII. vii. 52. 8
Crack. did uncomely speaches *crake.* . . . V. iii. 16. 7
makes her ribs to *cracke* as they were torne; . . . V. xi. 29. 4
Then is she mortall borne, how-so ye *crake:* . . . VII. vii. 50. 5
Cracked. Ne yet hath any knight his courage *crackt.*' . . . II. i. 12. 5
my feeble vessell, crazd and *crackt* . . . III. iv. 9. 1
It *crackt* throughout, (yet did no bloud appeare,) . . . VI. viii. 16. 5
his leg . . . Was *crackt* in twaine, . . . VI. viii. 25. 8
Cracknels. His kiddes, his *cracknelles,* and his early fruit. . . *S.C.* Ja. 58
the shepherds entertayne With cakes and *cracknells,* . . . *S.C.* N. 96
Cracks. Leasinges, backbytinges, and vain-glorious *crakes,* . . II. xi. 10. 7
Cradle. How in his *cradle* first he fostred was; . . . *T.M.* 500
The *cradle* of her owne creation, . . . *Col.* 613
to thee is unknowne the *cradle* of thy brood. . . . I. x. 64. 9
Whyles yet in infant *cradle* he did crall; . . . III. iii. 26. 7
all the Graces rockt her *cradle* being borne. . . . III. vi. 2. 9
Even from the *cradle* of his infancie, . . . V. i. 5. 2
The wondrous *cradle* of thine infancie, . . . *H.L.* 51
Craesie. *See* **Crazy.**
Craft. *See* **Leechcraft.**
His colowred crime with *craft* to cloke. . . . *S.C.* F. 162
craft, coloured with simplicitie: . . . *S.C.* May 303
all their *craft* is in their countenaunce, . . . *S.C.* S. 168
when through *craft* he her out ran. . . . II. vii. 54. 9
had learned skill in leaches *craft,* . . . III. iv. 41. 3
perfectly practiz'd in womans *craft,* . . . IV. ii. 10. 2
Thereto the villaine used *craft* in fight; . . . IV. vii. 26. 1
he right well in Leaches *craft* was seene; . . . VI. vi. 3. 1
Such subtile *craft* my Damzell doth conceave, . . . *Am.* xxiii. 5
Craftily. which the Lemnian God framde *craftily,* . . . *Mui.* 370
himselfe had *craftily* devisd To be her Squire, . . . II. i. 21. 8
Coridon, escaping *craftily,* . . . VI. xi. 18. 6
craftily enfold Theyr weaker harts, . . . *Am.* xxxvii. 7
Craftiness. my slie wyles and subtil *craftinesse,* . . . *Hub.* 1045
Craft's. So cunningly she wrought her *crafts* assay, . . . V. v. 52. 5
Craftsman. not with skill of *craftsman* polished: . . . *Gn.* 130
yvory Which cunning *Craftesman* hand hath overlayd . . . II. ix. 41. 6
Wherewith the *Craftsman* wonts it beautify, . . . III. xii. 20. 3
Craftsman's. No worke it seem'd of earthly *craftsmans* wit, . *Bel.*^{2} iv. 9
*Which cunning *Craftesmans* hand hath overlayd . . . II. ix. 41. 6
A greater *craftesmans* hand thereto doth neede, . . . *Am.* xvii. 13
Craftsmen. Not such as *Craftes-men* by their idle skill . . . VII. vii. 8. 3

Crafty. if foxes bene so *crafty* as so, . . . *S.C.* May 312
both were *craftie* and unhappie witted; . . . *Hub.* 49
craftie Reynold was a Priest ordained, . . . *Hub.* 556
Then gan this *craftie* couple to devize, . . . *Hub.* 655
this Foxe could not so closely hide His *craftie* feates, . . . *Hub.* 920
Strongly encorag'd by the *crafty* Foxe; . . . *Hub.* 1104
wearie traveiler . . . Doth meete a cruell *craftie* Crocodile, . . I. v. 18. 4
so wise . . . As to discry the *crafty* cunning traine, . . . I. vii. 1. 2
Her *crafty* head was altogether bald, . . . I. viii. 47. 1
she suborned hath This *crafty* messenger . . . I. xii. 34. 2
Still as he went he *craftie* stales did lay, . . . II. i. 4. 1
where him that *crafty* Squyre Supposd to be. . . . II. i. 13. 3
Therefore this *craftie* engine he did frame, . . . II. i. 23. 7
the treachour did remove His *craftie* engin, . . . II. iv. 27. 4
with her two *crafty* spyes She secretly would search . . . III. i. 36. 5
Still did he rove at her with *crafty* glaunce . . . III. i. 50. 6
bent Her *crafty* engins to her close intent. . . . III. i. 57. 5
That stratageme had oftentimes assayd This *crafty* Paramoure, III. x. 10. 9
'Ah! but,' (said *crafty* Trompart) 'weete ye well, . . . III. x. 40. 2
he so *crafty* was to forge and face, . . . V. ix. 5. 4
closely tempted with their *craftie* spyes; . . . VI. viii. 43. 4
Crag. bearen the *cragge* so stiffe and so state, . . . *S.C.* S. 45
Craggy. 'How often have I scaled the *craggie* Oke, . . . *S.C.* D. 31
His dwelling . . . underneath a *craggy* clift ypight, . . . I. ix. 33. 3
craggie clift Depending from on high, . . . II. xii. 4. 2
gainst the *craggy* clifts did loudly rore, . . . III. iv. 7. 5
chaunced on a *craggy* cliff to light, . . . III. x. 57. 7
with his *craggy* club in his right hand . . . IV. vii. 25. 6
dauncing on the *craggy* cliffes at will; . . . V. ix. 15. 5
Crags. Like wailefull widdowes hangen their *crags;* . . . *S.C.* F. 82
Crake, -s. *See* **Crack, -s.**
Crall, -ing. *See* **Crawl, -ing.**
Crammed. *cram'd* with guiltles blood and greedie pray . . . *Van.* iii. 4
He *crammed* them with crumbs of Benefices, . . . *Hub.* 1153
Cramp. hath the *Crampe* thy joynts benomd . . . *S.C.* Au. 4
Crane. like a *Crane* his necke was long and fyne . . . I. iv. 21. 5
the other cald the *Crane,* . . . IV. xi. 47. 2
stalking stately, like a *Crane,* . . . VI. vii. 42. 5
Crank. Cocke on his dunghill crowing *cranck.* . . . *S.C.* S. 46
Cranks. So many turning *cranks* these have, . . . VII. vii. 52. 9
Craples. With ugly *craples* crawling in their way, . . . V. viii. 40. 4
Crased. *See* **Crazed.**
Cratch. In simple *cratch,* wrapt in a wad of hay, . . . *H.H.L.* 226
Crave. In wanton dalliance the teate to *crave,* . . . *Bel.*^{2} vi. 3
Crave pardon for my hardyhedde. . . . *To his Booke* 12
after greedie spoyle of bloud to *crave:* . . . *Ti.* 565
by thy countenaunce doth *crave* to bee Defended . . . *Ded. Son.* iii. 3
her grace . . . Which of all earthly thinges he most did *crave:* I. i. 3. 5
'Yet, O thou dreaded Dame! I *crave* Abyde, . . . I. v. 21. 8
grave, That still for carrion carcases doth *crave:* . . . I. ix. 33. 5
happy ease, which thou doest want and *crave,* . . . I. ix. 40. 2
I ought *crave* pardon, till I there have beene.' . . . I. xii. 18. 9
The thing, that thou didst *crave* so earnestly, . . . II. vii. 38. 3
crave but rowme to rest while tempest overblo'th.' . . . III. vii. 8. 9
'Sir Salvage knight, Let me this *crave,* . . . IV. vi. 9. 7
I humbly *crave* your Majestie It to replevie, . . . IV. xii. 31. 7
'Certes me needeth more To *crave* the same; . . . V. viii. 13. 8
since ye mercie now doe need to *crave,* . . . VI. i. 42. 4
good Sir, . . . Let me this *crave,* . . . VI. ii. 33. 3
if he needes will fight, *crave* leave till morne, . . . VI. iii. 41. 6
doth litle *crave* contented to abyde. . . . VI. ix. 17. 9
Craved. therefore *crav'd* to come unto the King, . . . *Hub.* 1211
Whereof he *crav'd* redresse. . . . II. ii. 43. 5
entraunce *crav'd* which was denied erst. . . . II. ix. 17. 3
Crav'd leave of Alma and that aged sire . . . II. ix. 60. 8
Their counsell *crav'd* in daunger imminent. . . . III. x. 41. 3
With which those Amazons his love still *craved,* . . . V. vi. 2. 4
pardon *crav'd* for his so rash default, . . . VI. iii. 21. 8
Craven. on his *craven* crest A bounch of heares . . . I. ii. 11. 5
There he this most discourteous *craven* found, . . . VI. iv. 2. 6
evermore that *craven* cowherd Knight Was at his backe . . . VI. vi. 26. 6
having from his *craven* bodie torne Those goodly armes, . . . VI. vi. 36. 7
Much did the *Craven* seeme to mone his case, . . . VI. vii. 18. 1
Craves. Muse . . . *craves* protection of her feeblenesse: . . . *Ded.Son.*xiii.12
misery *craves* rather mercy then repriefe. . . . III. viii. 1. 9
an errant Knight, That house-rome *craves;* . . . VI. iii. 41. 3
That pitty *craves,* as he of woman was yborne.' . . . VI. iii. 41. 9
Craveth. when nature *craveth* sleepe, . . . *S.C.* Au. 177
Craving. *Craving* your goodlihead to aswage . . . *S.C.* F. 184
Craving of you, . . . To doe none ill, . . . I. ii. 26. 3
Then *craving* sucke, and then the sucke refusing: . . . V. vi. 14. 8
Crawl. swarming all about his legs did *crall,* . . . I. i. 22. 8
Whyles yet in infant cradle he did *crall;* . . . III. iii. 26. 7
Whence he with crooked clawes so long did *crall,* . . . III. x. 57. 8
Crawled. he *crauld* out of his nest, . . . II. iii. 35. 6
Crawling. Ten thousand snakes *cralling* about his hed . . . *Gn.* 348
crooked *crawling* shankes, of marrowe empted; . . . *Mui.* 350
With ugly craples *crawling* in their way, . . . V. viii. 40. 4
With crooked *crawling* steps an uncouth pase, . . . VII. vii. 35. 6
Crazed. my feeble vessell, *crazd* and crackt . . . III. iv. 9. 1
Her *crased* helth, her late recourse to rest, . . . III. ix. 26. 3
Crazy. be their pipes untunable and *craesie,* . . . *Col.* 374
Creakie. *See* **Creeky.**
Cream. give him curds and clouted *Creame.* . . . *S.C.* N. 99
the white fomy *creame* Did shine with silver, . . . III. xi. 41. 4
Her brest like to a bowle of *creame* uncrudded, . . . *Epith.* 175
Creaming-pans. there doth draine Her *creaming pannes,* . . VII. vi. 48. 5
Creast, -ed, -s. *See* **Crest,** *etc.*
Create. why did they then *create* The world so fayre, . . . *D.* 204
Did not he all *create* To die againe? . . . I. ix. 42. 2

Create—*Continued.*
Do not I kings *create,* . . . II. vii. 11. 6
how first Prometheus did *create* A man, . . . II. x. 70. 5
she, whom Nature did so faire *create* . . . IV. ix. 16. 5
Created. All things, as they *created* were, doe grow, . . . III. vi. 34. 3
As it at first *created* was of yore: . . . III. vi. 36. 5
since the day that they *created* beene, . . . IV. v. 12. 4
they all *created* were . . . by their Makers might; . . . V. ii. 35. 1
Their dainty parts, which nature had *created* So faire . . . V. vii. 29. 6
To Nenna first, that first this worke *created,* . . . *Com. Son.* ii. 13
Creates. The Witch *creates* a snowy Lady . . . III. viii. Arg.
Creation. Through knowledge we behold the worlds *creation,* *T.M.* 499
The cradle of her owne *creation,* . . . *Col.* 613
Like as himselfe was fairest by *creation:* . . . *Col.* 870
most hevenly faire . . . She by *creation* was, . . . II. vii. 45. 8
so soone forgot the excellence Of his *creation,* . . . II. xii. 87. 3
all her whole *creation* did her shew Pure . . . III. vi. 3. 3
his faire sister for *creation* Ministreth matter fit, . . . VII. vi. 9. 3
Creator. in despight of his *Creatour* . . . *Ti.* 537
The grace of his *Creator* doth despise, . . . IV. viii. 15. 8
Creator's. 'The antique world . . . Fownd no defect in his *Creators* grace; . . . II. vii. 16. 2
The great *Creatours* owne resemblance bright, . . . IV. viii. 32. 2
Creatress. As her *Creatresse* had in charge to her ordain'd. . III. viii. 10. 9
Creature. ye doo weld th' affaires of earthlie *creature;* . . . *Ro.* ix. 4
a Brize, a scorned little *creature,* . . . *Van.* ii. 10
she gave like blessing to each *creture,* . . . *Hub.* 146
Man, the Lord of everie *creature,* . . . *Hub.* 1030
Most miserable *creature* under sky . . . *T.M.* 127
comfort can I, wretched *creature,* have? . . . *Ti.* 23
What more felicitie can fall to *creature* . . . *Mui.* 209
This cursed *creature,* mindfull of that olde Enfested grudge, . *Mui.* 353
such a cursed *creature* lives so long a space.' . . . I. i. 31. 9
that new *creature,* borne without her dew, . . . I. i. 46. 6
so . . . hot That living *creature* mote it not abide; . . . I. ii. 29. 6
every *creature* shrowded is in sleepe. . . . I. iii. 15. 2
by his side rode loathsome Gluttony, Deformed *creature,* . . . I. iv. 21. 2
creature never past, That backe retourned . . . I. v. 31. 6
cryme in her could never *creature* find; . . . I. vi. 2. 5
living *creature* none he did espye. . . . I. viii. 29. 5
More ugly shape yet never living *creature* saw. . . . I. viii. 48. 9
So fayre a *creature* yet saw never sunny day. . . . I. ix. 13. 9
ne word to *creature* spake. . . . I. xii. 29. 4
wist no *creature* whence that hevenly sweet Proceeded, . . . I. xii. 39. 6
They never *creature* saw that cam that way: . . . II. vii. 37. 5
One cursed *creature* he by chaunce espide, . . . II. vii. 57. 8
A goodly *creature,* whom he deemd in mynd . . . II. x. 71. 5
maketh every *creature* glad, . . . II. xi. 3. 4
tract of living *creature* none they fownd, . . . III. i. 14. 8
If ay more goodly *creature* thou didst see? . . . III. iii. 32. 2
The fayrest *creature* that he ever saw . . . III. vii. 13. 2
No living *creature* could his cruelty asswage. . . . III. viii. 28. 9
she a mortall *creature* loved best: . . . III. viii. 39. 7
living *creature* it would terrify To looke adowne, . . . III. x. 56. 5
more bounteous *creature* never far'd On foot . . . III. xi. 10. 3
Whereas no living *creature* he mistooke, . . . III. xi. 13. 4
living *creature* none she saw appeare. . . . III. xi. 55. 2
to her service bind each living *creature,* . . . IV. ii. 44. 4
weend no mortall *creature* she should bee, . . . IV. v. 14. 6
which no *creature* may Long time resist, . . . IV. v. 43. 3
To worke such outrage on so faire a *creature;* . . . IV. vi. 17. 2
This ugly *creature* in his armes her snatcht, . . . IV. vii. 8. 1
Ne *creature* saw, but hearkned now and then . . . IV. vii. 33. 3
A foule and lothsome *creature,* did appeare, . . . IV. vii. 34. 4
A foule and loathly *creature* sure in sight, . . . IV. viii. 24. 1
never two so like did living *creature* see. . . . IV. viii. 55. 9
Full weake and crooked *creature* seemed shee, . . . IV. xi. 24. 8
So faire a *creature* and so wondrous bold, . . . V. viii. 12. 7
So ugly *creature,* she was nigh dismayd, . . . V. ix. 12. 2
I should no *creature* joyne unto mine ayde: . . . VI. ii. 37. 8
seldome yet did living *creature* see . . . VI. iii. 40. 8
Where foot of living *creature* never trode, . . . VI. iv. 13. 8
Who can aread what *creature* mote she bee, . . . VI. x. 25. 3
Whether a *creature,* or a goddesse graced With heavenly gifts VI. x. 25. 4
That could not any *creature* well descry; . . . VII. vii. 5. 7
did ye see So fayre a *creature* in your towne before; . . . *Epith.* 168
Seeing him lie like *creature* long accurst . . . *H.H.L.* 129
Creature's. a pin Does care for looke of living *creatures* eye. . I. v. 4. 4
being ment of mortall *creatures* sead, . . . IV. xii. 27. 3
Creatures. though ye be the fairest of Gods *creatures,* . . . *Pet.*[2] vii. 13
'Ah, my soveraigne! Lord of *creatures* all, . . . *S.C.* F. 163
Such grace did God unto his *creatures* give. . . . *Hub.* 402
all the heavens on lower *creatures* smilde, . . . *Mui.* 53
th' armies of their *creatures* all and some . . . *Mui.* 229
all things else that living *creatures* need. . . . *Col.* 299
rules the *creatures* by his powrfull saw: . . . *Col.* 884
Rashly to wyten *creatures* so divine; . . . *Col.* 916
Ten thousand kindes of *creatures,* partly male And partly femall, I. i. 21. 7
of punishment The cursed *creatures* doe eternally torment . . I. v. 33. 9
Deformed *creatures,* horrible in sight; . . . II. vii. 35. 7
made him scorne all *creatures* great and small, . . . II. vii. 41. 7
'Most cursed of all *creatures* under skye, . . . II. vii. 59. 4
love In heavenly spirits to these *creatures* bace, . . . II. viii. 1. 2
highest God that loves his *creatures* so, . . . II. viii. 1. 6
Deformed *creatures,* in straunge difference, . . . II. xi. 10. 3
Compared to the *creatures* in the seas entrall. . . . II. xii. 25. 9
T' afflict the *creatures* which therein did dwell; . . . II. xii. 51. 6
*Yet tract of living *creatures* none they found, . . . III. i. 14. 8
Infinite shapes of *creatures* men doe fynd . . . III. vi. 8. 8
Infinite shapes of *creatures* there are bred, . . . III. vi. 35. 1

Creatures—*Continued.*
unto all his *creatures* so benigne, . . . IV. i. 30. 4
none did ever see More happie *creatures* . . . IV. iii. 2. 5
to his law compels all *creatures* to obay. . . . IV. x. 42. 9
The fertile Nile, which *creatures* new doth frame; . . . IV. xi. 20. 3
she all living *creatures* did excell; . . . IV. xii. 33. 5
his *creatures* from their course astray, . . . V. Pr. 6. 8
All *creatures* must obey the voice of the Most Hie. . . . V. ii. 40. 9
The earth to all her *creatures* lodging lends.' . . . V. x. 24. 6
two old ill favour'd Hags he met . . . Two griesly *creatures:* . V. xii. 28. 6
eke all other *creatures* her bad dooings rewed. . . . VII. vi. 4. 9
thither also came all other *creatures,* . . . VII. vii. 4. 1
This great Grandmother of all *creatures* bred, . . . VII. vii. 13. 1
Which any of thy *creatures* do to other . . . VII. vii. 14. 6
We daily see new *creatures* to arize, . . . VII. vii. 18. 6
all *creatures* to maintaine In state of life? . . . VII. vii. 22. 4
to her *creatures* every minute chaunce; . . . VII. vii. 23. 2
Ne any living *creatures* doth he breed, . . . VII. vii. 24. 6
how all *creatures* laught when her they spide . . . VII. vii. 34. 7
in all thy *creatures* more or lesse . . . VII. vii. 47. 3
all *creatures,* looking in her face, . . . VII. vii. 57. 4
therein reed The endlesse kinds of *creatures* . . . *H.H.B.* 32
may Be seene of all his *creatures* vile and base, . . . *H.H.B.* 116
lower *creatures* all Subjected to her powre imperiall. . . . *H.H.B.* 195
And all the *creatures* which they both containe; . . . *H.H.B.* 198
Creatures'. His owne faire mother, for all *creatures* sake, . . . *H.L.* 72
Credence. auncient truth confirm'd with *credence* old. . . . *Col.* 103
Ne let it seeme that *credence* this exceedes: . . . I. vii. 36. 1
him too light of *credence* did mislead, . . . VI. vii. 20. 7
Credit. Supports his *credite* and his countenaunce. . . . *Hub.* 668
Thus did the Ape at first him *credit* gaine, . . . *Hub.* 689
With whom his *credite* he did often leave . . . *Hub.* 864
giving hastie *credit* to th' accuser, . . . *Mui.* 135
His *credit* now in doubtfull ballaunce hong: . . . II. i. 3. 8
After lost *credit* and consumed thrift, . . . II. xii. 8. 8
they more fond that *credit* to thee give! . . . III. iv. 37. 2
His glory did repose, and *credit* did maintaine, . . . III. viii. 11. 9
care of *credite,* or of husband old, . . . III. x. 11. 4
Men call you fayre, and you doe *credit* it, . . . *Am.* lxxix. 1
Creeky. flowing all along the *creekie* shoare . . . *Bel.*[1] vii. 7
bathing all the *creakie* shore aflot, . . . *Bel.*[2] ix. 7
Creep. carefull thoughts in her heart did *creepe*) . . . *S.C.* May 190
of sike pastoures howe done the flocks *creepe?* . . . *S.C.* S. 140
ever *creepe* into the shepheards den. . . . *Gn.* 96
He will not *creepe,* nor crouche with fained face, . . . *Hub.* 727
brave thought of armes Did ever *creepe,* . . . *Hub.* 826
And I *creepe* under ground, . . . *Hub.* 991
They crying *creep* out of their mothers woomb . . . *Ti.* 48
let compassion *creepe* Into his brest, . . . *D.* 248
The carefull cold beginneth for to *creep,* . . . I. vii. 39. 4
When corage first does *creepe* in manly chest, . . . I. ix. 9. 2
Whereby close fire into his heart does *creepe:* . . . II. v. 34. 7
Through which the damned ghosts doen often *creepe* . . . II. xii. 6. 5
Low his lascivious armes adown did *creepe,* . . . II. xii. 61. 6
ungentlenesse Ever to *creepe* into his noble brest; . . . III. v. 2. 4
creepe betweene his legs, . . . IV. x. 19. 3
neither could to company of th' other *creepe.* . . . VI. xii. 5. 9
Creepeth. The drouping night thus *creepeth* on them fast; . . I. i. 36. 1
Creeping. The subtill vermin, *creeping* closely neare, . . . *Van.* vi. 7
Into his nosthrils *creeping,* so him pained, . . . *Van.* viii. 10
creeping close behind the Wickets clink, . . . *S.C.* May 251
to the Lion came, full lowly *creeping,* . . . *Hub.* 1361
Full closely *creeping* by the hinder side, . . . *Mui.* 403
By *creeping* close into his secrecie; . . . *Col.* 698
creeping sought way in the weedy gras: . . . I. i. 20. 8
faith . . . The *creeping* deadly cold away did shake: . . . I. v. 12. 4
with *creeping* crooked pace forth came An old old man, . . . I. viii. 30. 1
Those *creeping* flames by reason to subdew, . . . I. ix. 9. 6
creeping close, as Snake in hidden weedes, . . . I. ix. 28. 8
Close *creeping* twixt the marow and the skin: . . . I. x. 25. 5
Forth *creeping* on his caitive hands and thies; . . . II. iii. 35. 7
Whiles *creeping* slomber made him to forget . . . II. v. 30. 8
In which they *creeping* did at last display . . . II. xii. 76. 7
a litle *creeping* sleepe Surprisd her sence: . . . III. ii. 47. 6
close *creeping* as he might, . . . III. x. 44. 1
creeping close amongst the hives . . . III. x. 53. 5
Came to her *creeping* like a fawning hound, . . . VI. iv. 11. 2
creeping still behinde, doth him incomber, . . . VI. v. 19. 6
Creeping behinde him still to have destroyde; . . . VI. v. 20. 5
Creeps. Into the same he *creepes,* . . . III. x. 58. 1
Creepes forth of dores, whilst darknes him doth hide, . . . VI. xi. 18. 7
Cremosin, Cremsin. *See* **Crimson.**
Crept. There *crept* in Wolves, . . . *S.C.* May 127
Crept under mosse as greene as any goord, . . . *Gn.* 164
into whose brest Never *crept* thought of honor, . . . *Hub.* 978
now *crept,* now backward drew, . . . *Hub.* 1012
ycrept of late Out of dredd darknes . . . *T.M.* 188
scornfull Follie with Contempt is *crept,* . . . *T.M.* 212
the whiles the Foxe is *crept* Into the hole, . . . *Ti.* 216
everie living wight *Crept* forth like wormes . . . *Col.* 860
Into her mouth they *crept,* . . . I. i. 15. 9
he by conning sleights in at the window *crept.* . . . I. iii. 17. 9
crept into a bush, . . . II. iii. 21. 3
He closely nearer *crept* the truth to weet: . . . III. x. 22. 6
Upon his handes and feete he *crept* full light, . . . III. x. 47. 2
So closely as he could he to them *crept,* . . . III. x. 49. 1
he emongst the rest *crept* forth in sory plight. . . . III. x. 52. 9
Crept in by stouping low, . . . IV. x. 18. 9
Mongst which *crept* litle Angels through the glittering gleames. V. ix. 28. 9
Out of great Chaos ugly prison *crept,* . . . *H.L.* 58

Crest. With purple wings, and *crest* of golden hewe; . . . *Pet.* v. 2
His *creste* above, spotted with purple die, . . . *Gn.* 260
on his craven *crest* A bounch of heares . . . I. ii. 11. 5
upon his *crest* With rigor so outrageous he smitt, . . . I. ii. 18. 6
upon his *crest* he stroke him so, . . . I. v. 11. 5
all the *crest* a Dragon did enfold . . . I. vii. 31. 3
Upon the top of all his loftie *crest,* . . . I. vii. 32. 1
every head was crowned on his *creast,* . . . I. viii. 6. 4
Eftsoones he gan advance his haughty *crest,* . . . I. xi. 15. 5
Upon his *crest* the hardned yron fell, . . . I. xi. 24. 4
his more hardned *crest* was armd so well, . . . I. xi. 24. 5
Ne reard above the earth his flaming *creast,* . . . I. xii. 2. 3
his lofty *crest* Did fiercely shake, . . . II. iii. 35. 8
he smote his haughty *crest* so hye, . . . II. v. 12. 4
quite it clove his plumed *crest* in tway, . . . II. vi. 31. 7
in the lake his loftie *crest* was stept, . . . II. vi. 42. 4
crownd his coward *crest* with knightly stile; . . . II. viii. 12. 7
Smote him so hugely on his haughtie *crest,* . . . II. viii. 33. 6
His *crest* was covered with a couchant Hownd, . . . III. ii. 25. 1
the fether in her lofty *crest,* . . . III. ii. 27. 1
Badd her old Squyre unlace her lofty *creast:* . . . III. iv. 7. 3
made him low incline his lofty *crest,* . . . III. vii. 42. 4
by the colours in his *crest,* That Paridell it was. . . . III. viii. 45. 5
whenas vailed was her lofty *crest,* . . . III. ix. 20. 3
falling heavie on Cambelloes *crest,* . . . IV. iii. 34. 2
So sore he sowst him on the compast *creast,* . . . IV. iv. 30. 7
behind her *crest* So sorely he her strooke, . . . IV. vi. 13. 2
that warriouresse with haughty *crest* Did forth issue . . . V. vii. 27. 7
Ne ever Knight that bore so lofty *creast,* . . . VI. vi. 12. 7
the bright evening-star with golden *creast* Appeare . . . *Epith.* 286
Crested. Upon his *crested* scalp so sore did smite, . . . I. xi. 35. 7
the shining skie . . . Is *creasted* all with lines of firie light, . . . IV. i. 13. 8
Crest-front. Whereas his temples did his *creast-front* tyre; . . . *Gn.* 308
Crests. armed be with clawes, or scalie *creasts,* . . . *Ro.* xxiv. 4
lowly did abase their lofty *crests* . . . II. ii. 32. 4
rearing fercely their upstaring *crests,* . . . II. xii. 39. 8
high advaunced *crests* downe meekely feld; . . . II. xii. 40. 5
ill becomes you, with your lofty *creasts,* . . . III. vi. 22. 5
Crete. *Crete* will boast the Labyrinth, . . . *Ro.* ii. 8
Some say in *Crete* by name, . . . VII. vii. 53. 5
Creusa. Yt seemd thenchaunted flame which did *Creusa* wed. . . . II. xii. 45. 9
Crevice. Where one stood peeping through a *crevis* small, . . . IV. x. 11. 8
Crew. often crost with the priestes *crewe,* . . . *S.C.* F. 209
Equall in honour to the former *crue,* . . . *Gn.* 594
As that same Apish *crue* is wont to doo: . . . *Hub.* 731
wonts to decke the Gods immortall *crew* . . . *Hub.* 1268
Begin, thou eldest Sister of the *crew,* . . . *T.M.* 53
the goodlie *criew* Of white Strimonian brood . . . *Ti.* 592
excelling all the *crewe* In curteous usage . . . *Mui.* 119
best of all that honourable *crew,* . . . *Col.* 517
With Cynthia and all her noble *crew;* . . . *Col.* 653
the other *crew* Of shepheards daughters . . . *Col.* 931
gave more honourable prize . . . then did the Martiall *crew,* . . . *Ded. Son.* xiv. 2
A fairer *crew* yet no where could I see . . . *Ded.Son.*xvii.10
a noble *crew* Of Lords and Ladies stood on every side, . . . I. iv. 7. 7
Right glad with him to have increast their *crew;* . . . I. iv. 15. 2
Such one was Gluttony, the second of that *crew.* . . . I. iv. 23. 9
Have thither come the noble Martial *crew* . . . I. vii. 45. 4
that faire *crew* of knights, . . . I. viii. 50. 6
A noble *crew* about them waited rownd . . . I. xii. 5. 4
Another Damsell of that gentle *crew,* . . . II. ix. 40. 2
with a *crew* Of hungry whelpes, . . . III. iii. 47. 3
singled from the *crew* Of courteous knights, . . . III. iv. 45. 3
The love and service of the basest *crew?* . . . III. v. 47. 7
Whereas she found the Goddesse with her *crew,* . . . III. vi. 17. 2
some Goddesse, or of Dianes *crew,* . . . III. vii. 11. 7
this gallant with his goodly *crew* . . . IV. i. 33. 1
Unmindfull both of that discordfull *crew,* . . . IV. ii. 30. 8
There this faire *crewe* arriving did divide . . . IV. iv. 14. 1
Appear'd in place, with all his noble *crew:* . . . IV. iv. 26. 3
There he in troupe found all that warlike *crew,* . . . IV. iv. 33. 8
Satyrane, bove all the other *crew,* . . . IV. iv. 37. 4
so faire a *crew,* As like can not be seene . . . IV. v. 18. 3
This gentle *crew* gan from their eye-lids chace . . . IV. viii. 34. 3
this gentle *crew* Is now so well accorded . . . IV. ix. 40. 4
These marched farre afore the other *crew:* . . . IV. xi. 12. 1
The eares and hearts of all that goodly *crew,* . . . IV. xi. 23. 5
Full many people gathered in a *crew;* . . . V. ii. 29. 5
In the base blood of such a rascall *crew;* . . . V. ii. 52. 5
then this warlike *crew* Together met . . . V. iii. 8. 2
To set afresh on all the other *crew:* . . . V. iii. 12. 4
Made cruell havocke of the baser *crew,* . . . V. xi. 59. 6
all their scattred *crew* Into the sea he drove . . . V. xi. 65. 3
Then found he many missing of his *crew,* . . . VI. vii. 34. 1
ever, as the *crew* About her daunst, . . . VI. x. 14. 6
Where was his Pastorell? where all the other *crew?* . . . VI. xi. 28. 9
all the heavenly *crew* Of happy wights, . . . VII. vi. 14. 3
ungracious *crew* which faines demurest grace. . . . VII. vii. 35. 9
with the *crew* of blessed Saynts upbrought, . . . *Am.* lxi. 7
To wayt on Love amongst his lovely *crew;* . . . *Am.* lxx. 10
Shewing us mercie (miserable *crew!*) . . . *H.H.L.* 214
Cried. He *cride* to me, and loe (quod he) . . . *Bel.*[1] i. 9
One *cride* aloude. . . . *Rev.* i. 9
With thondring voice *cride* out aloude, . . . *Rev.* ii. 13
Then *cried* a shining Angell . . . *Rev.* iii. 8
lowdly *cryed* Unto his lord, . . . *S.C.* F. 148
He *cryed* out, to make his undersong; . . . *Col.* 169
His Lady, . . . *Cride* out, 'Now, now, . . . I. i. 19. 2
Shee turning backe, . . . *Cride,* 'Mercy, mercy, Sir, . . . I. ii. 21. 2
'Then *cride* she out, "Fye, fye! deformed wight, . . . I. ii. 39. 1

Cried—*Continued.*
Una *cride,* 'O! hold that heavie hand, . . . I. iii. 37. 2
Then *cryde* the Dwarfe, 'Lo! yonder is the same, . . . I. viii. 2. 3
blessed sprites, . . . To God for vengeance *cryde* continually; . . . I. viii. 36. 7
with the uncouth smart the Monster lowdly *cryde.* . . . I. xi. 20. 9
He *cryde,* as raging seas are wont to rore . . . I. xi. 21. 1
'Lo! yonder he,' *cryde* Archimage alowd, . . . II. i. 25. 1
cryde, 'Mercie, Sir Knight! and mercie, Lord, . . . II. i. 27. 1
a ruefull voice, that dearnly *cride* . . . II. i. 35. 7
Then loud he *cryde;* . . . II. iii. 8. 2
when the Palmer saw, he loudly *cryde,* . . . II. iv. 10. 1
With that he *cryde;* 'Mercy! . . . II. v. 12. 7
Fiercely approching to him lowdly *cryde,* . . . II. v. 35. 3
'Harrow now out, and well away!' he *cryde,* . . . II. vi. 43. 6
'I burne, I burne, I burne!' then lowd he *cryde,* . . . II. vi. 44. 1
'These flames, these flames,' (he *cryde*) 'doe me torment.' . . . II. vi. 49. 5
full of anger fiersly to him *cryde;* . . . II. viii. 31. 5
Cryde out; 'Deare countrey! . . . II. x. 69. 3
harmefull fowles about them fluttering *cride,* . . . II. xii. 35. 7
cride to heven, from humane helpe exild. . . . III. viii. 27. 5
when to him she *cryde,* to her he turnd, . . . III. x. 15. 1
the Nymphes eke Hylas *cryde.* . . . III. xii. 7. 9
'Fy, fy! false knight,' (then false Duessa *cryde*) . . . IV. i. 51. 6
for helpe aloud in earnest *cride:* . . . V. ix. 12. 3
They both arose, and at him loudly *cryde,* . . . V. xii. 38. 4
loude to him he *cryde:* . . . VI. i. 18. 6
Cryde out; 'Ah mercie, Sir! . . . VI. i. 39. 8
who to him *cryde,* And called oft . . . VI. iii. 49. 6
woman kynd, Which to her selfe lamenting loudly *cryde,* . . . VI. iv. 26. 8
aloude the faire Serena *cryde* Unto the Knight, . . . VI. v. 27. 1
Then one of them aloud unto him *cryde,* . . . VI. vii. 7. 1
Cryde out aloud for mercie, . . . VI. vii. 12. 2
Cryde mercie, to abate the extremitie of law. . . . VI. vii. 36. 9
Which when the Lady saw, she *cryde* amaine; . . . VI. viii. 17. 4
For which it loudly cald, and pittifully *cryde.* . . . VI. xii. 8. 9
alasse, he *cryde,* and wel-away! . . . *Epig.* iv. 27
Cries. *See* **Outcries.**
Ye carelesse byrds are privie to my *cryes,* . . . *S.C.* Au. 153
The hollow Echo of my carefull *cryes:* . . . *S.C.* Au. 160
bedde, or bowre, both which I fill with *cryes,* . . . *S.C.* Au. 167
my deadly *cryes* 'Most ruthfully to tune: . . . *S.C.* Au. 174
as my *cryes* . . . Increase, . . . *S.C.* Au. 175
To cheerefull songs can chaunge my cherelesse *cryes.* . . . *S.C.* Au. 182
the sound Of these my nightly *cryes* . . . *S.C.* Au. 189
Did now rebound with nought but rufull *cries,* . . . *T.M.* 23
with shrilling *cryes* Pierce the dull heavens . . . *T.M.* 117
lowd shrieks and drerie dolefull *cries.* . . . *T.M.* 172
Now change your praises into piteous *cries,* . . . *T.M.* 371
Did throw forth shrieks and *cries* . . . *T.M.* 538
where shall I finde lamentable *cryes,* . . . *Mui.* 411
No nightly bordrags, nor no hue and *cries;* . . . *Col.* 315
No . . . peoples troublous *cryes,* . . . Might there be heard; . . . I. i. 41. 6
Does throw out thrilling shriekes, and shrieking *cryes,* . . . I. vi. 6. 2
Hart cannot thinke what outrage and what *cries,* . . . I. xi. 40. 1
with their piteous *cryes,* and yelling shrightes, . . . II. vii. 57. 5
Confusd with womens *cries* and shouts of boyes, . . . IV. iii. 37. 8
with piteous sound Of his shrill *cries* . . . VI. i. 11. 6
Then out aloud she *cries,* . . . VI. viii. 40. 7
through great confusione Of *cryes* and clamors . . . VI. xi. 32. 4
Let no lamenting *cryes* . . . Be heard . . . *Epith.* 334
Crime. His colowred *crime* with craft to cloke. . . . *S.C.* F. 162
pretext . . . that may excuse the *cryme:* . . . *Hub.* 989
through unnoble sloth, or sinfull *crime,* . . . *T.M.* 435
Of her pretended *crime,* though *crime* none were: . . . *Mui.* 143
for secret *crime* thy blood hast spilt.' . . . *D.* 84
When Witches wont do penance for their *crime,*) . . . I. ii. 40. 5
redoubled *crime* with vengeaunce new Thou biddest me to . . . I. v. 42. 7
cryme in her could never creature find; . . . I. vi. 2. 5
she . . . walketh forth without suspect of *crime.* . . . I. vi. 13. 4
masse of earthly slyme, . . . fild with sinfull *cryme.* . . . I. vii. 9. 9
she wist his *cryme* could els be never cleare. . . . I. x. 28. 9
The tree of life, the *crime* of our first fathers fall. . . . I. xi. 46. 9
With *cryme* doe not it cover, but disclose the same.' . . . I. xii. 30. 9
That had almost committed *crime* abhord, . . . II. i. 27. 3
overcome Of anguish, rather then of *crime,* . . . II. i. 58. 7
mortal vengeaunce joyne to *crime* abhord? . . . II. ii. 30. 4
'Thus heaping *crime* on *crime,* . . . II. iv. 31. 1
helps to cloke her *crime* withall. . . . II. vii. 45. 9
thou art partaker of his *cryme:* . . . II. viii. 30. 3
Bablers of folly, and blazers of *cryme:* . . . II. ix. 25. 6
gan abhorre her broods unkindly *crime,* . . . II. x. 9. 4
To purge away the guilt of sinfull *crime.* . . . II. x. 50. 4
Whilest loving thou mayst loved be with equall *crime.* . . . II. xii. 75. 9
lets me not hyde My *crime,* (if *crime* it be) . . . III. ii. 37. 7
Pure and unspotted from all loathly *crime* . . . III. vi. 3. 4
The *crime* which cursed Ate kindled earst, . . . IV. v. 31. 2
with no *crime* defilde, . . . V. i. 6. 4
heaped shame to shame, And *crime* to *crime,* . . . VI. vi. 34. 2
He gan to him object his haynous *crime,* . . . VI. vii. 26. 7
now your *crime* with cruelty pursew! . . . VI. viii. 7. 7
without *crime* Or blamefull blot; . . . VI. ix. 46. 3
Albe they worthy blame, or cleare of *crime:* . . . VI. xii. 40. 6
out of their decay and mortall *crime,* . . . VII. vii. 18. 5
And clense the guilt of that infected *cryme* . . . *H.H.L.* 167
Crimes. seven springing heds of monstrous *crimes,* . . . *Bel.*[1] viii. 13
seven heads, budding monstrous *crimes* anew, . . . *Bel.*[2] x. 12
them of *crimes* and heresies accus'd, . . . *Hub.* 564
All these through fained *crimes* he thrust adowne, . . . *Hub.* 1186
The ugly vew of his deformed *crimes;* . . . I. ix. 48. 6
guilt of sinfull *crimes* cleane wash away; . . . I. xi. 30. 2

Crimes—*Continued.*
not for malice and contentious *crymes,* . . . III. i. 13. 3
causelesse *crimes* continually to frame, . . . IV. viii. 25. 2
False *crimes* and facts, such as they never ment, . . . IV. viii. 35. 6
lay on heaven the guilt of their owne *crimes.* . . . V. iv. 28. 3
Of many haynous *crymes* by her enured; . . . V. ix. 39. 6
th' actours won the meede meet for their *crymes.* . . . V. ix. 42. 5
many other *crimes* of foule defame Against her brought, . . . V. ix. 43. 2
prove her cleare Of all those *crimes* . . . V. xi. 40. 5
could reveale All hidden *crimes,* . . . V. xii. 26. 6
Of all those *crymes* she there indited was: . . . VI. vii. 35. 2
Criminal. pillage . . . got abroad by purchas *criminall.* . . . I. iii. 16. 9
cleare she dide from blemish *criminall:* . . . II. i. 37. 7
cut off by practise *criminall* Of secrete foes, . . . III. iii. 28. 8
Crimson. Upon her head a *Cremosin* coronet, . . . *S.C.* Ap. 59
before the Morne with *cremosin* ray . . . II. xi. 3. 1
Like *crimsin* dyde in grayne: . . . *Epith.* 228
Crimson-red. Dyed in Lilly white and *Cremsin redde,* . . . *S.C.* F. 130
Crisped. Her yellow lockes, *crisped* like golden wyre, . . . II. iii. 30. 1
Critias. fayre *Critias,* his dearest Belamy! . . . II. vii. 52. 9
to his *Critias,* . . . Of love full manie lessons did apply, . . . IV. Pr. 3. 7
Critic. doest note with *critique* pen . . . *Com. Son.* i. 3
Croaking. Yeeld me an hostry mongst the *croking* frogs, . . . V. x. 23. 8
th' unpleasant Quyre of Frogs still *croking* . . . *Epith.* 349
Crock. *See* **Honey-crock.**
Crocodile. In monstrous length, a mightie *Crocodile,* . . . *Van.* iii. 3
wearie traveiler . . . Doth meete a cruell craftie *Crocodile,* . . . I. v. 18. 4
at her feete a *Crocodile* was rold, . . . V. vii. 6. 8
One foote was set uppon the *Crocodile,* . . . V. vii. 7. 1
the *Crocodile,* which sleeping lay Under the Idols feete . . . V. vii. 15. 1
that same *Crocodile* doth represent The righteous Knight . . . V. vii. 22. 3
that same *Crocodile* Osyris is, . . . V. vii. 22. 6
Crocodiles. *Crocodiles,* Dragons, Beavers, and Centaures: . . . *Hub.* 1124
Croesus. There also was king *Croesus,* . . . I. v. 47. 6
Croked. *See* **Crooked.**
Crook. In hope her to attaine by hooke or *crooke,* . . . III. i. 17. 6
The which her sire had scrapt by hooke and *crooke,* . . . V. ii. 27. 8
forthwith led Unto the *crooke,* . . . V. v. 18. 7
Crooked. to rule this *croked* shore. . . . *Bel.*[1] viii. 15
Out of these *crooked* shores . . . *Bel.*[2] x. 14
This chill, that cold; this *crooked,* that wrye; . . . *S.C.* F. 28
their *crooked* keeles the surges clave. . . . *Gn.* 568
crooked crawling shankes, of marrowe empted; . . . *Mui.* 350
with creeping *crooked* pace forth came An old old man, . . . I. viii. 30. 1
thrise three tymes had fild her *crooked* hornes, . . . II. i. 53. 3
With her two *crooked* handes she signes did make, . . . II. iv. 13. 2
with her *crooked* keele the land she strooke: . . . II. xii. 38. 3
Whence he with *crooked* clawes so long did crall, . . . III. x. 57. 8
like withered tree . . . She old and *crooked* were, . . . IV. i. 31. 6
old and *crooked* and not good for ought. . . . IV. ii. 3. 5
By which few *crooked* sallowes grew in ranke: . . . IV. v. 33. 5
Full weake and *crooked* creature seemed shee, . . . IV. xi. 24. 8
With *crooked* crawling steps an uncouth pase, . . . VII. vii. 35. 6
Crooks. So many turning cranks these have, so many *crookes.* . VII. vii. 52. 9
Crop. Als my budding braunch thou wouldest *cropp;* . . . *S.C.* F. 58
Nought reaped but a weedye *crop* of care; . . . *S.C.* D. 122
Others the utmost boughs of trees doe *crop,* . . . *Gn.* 81
hop'd to reape the *crop* of all my care, . . . I. iv. 47. 2
fiers fate did *crop* the blossome of his age. . . . II. i. 41. 9
Nor wicked beastes their tender buds did *crop,* . . . III. vi. 43. 5
labourd long in vaine To *crop* his thousand heads, . . . VI. xii. 32. 4
Cropped. *cropt* the branches of the sient base, . . . V. i. 1. 8
at one stroke *cropt* off her head with scorne, . . . V. i. 18. 6
Hath pruned from the native tree, and *cropped* quight. . . . V. xi. 11. 9
with fine Fingers *cropt* full feateously . . . *Proth.* 27
Croslet. *See* **Crosslet.**
Cross. *See* **Red Cross.**
with a *crosse* of redd And manie slits, . . . *Hub.* 205
I, poore swaine, of many, greatest *crosse!* . . . *Col.* 18
on his brest a bloodie *Crosse* he bore, . . . I. i. 2. 1
upon his coward brest A bloody *crosse,* . . . I. ii. 11. 5
'Curse on that *Cross,*' (quoth then the Sarazin,) . . . I. ii. 18. 1
fast towards him do *crosse.* . . . I. vi. 34. 9
in his silver shield He bore a bloodie *Crosse* . . . II. i. 18. 9
that deare *Crosse* uppon your shield devizd, . . . II. i. 31. 8
Who swelling sayles in Caspian sea doth *crosse,* . . . II. vii. 14. 3
Her succourd eke the Champion of the bloody *Crosse.* . . . III. i. 64. 9
greater *crosse* To see frends grave, . . . III. iv. 38. 8
hast to *crosse* him by the nearest way, . . . IV. vii. 25. 2
Whose sight to her is greatest *crosse* may fall, . . . V. xii. 31. 4
By his owne sword, and by the *crosse* thereon, . . . VI. i. 43. 6
Cross-cuts. *Cros-cuts* the liver with internall smart, . . . III. x. 59. 8
Crossed. often *crost* with the priestes crewe, . . . *S.C.* F. 209
Jaakob staffe in hand devoutlie *crost,* . . . *D.* 41
Through vainly *crossed* shield he quite did perce; . . . I. iii. 35. 3
The Redcrosse knight toward him *crossed* fast, . . . I. ix. 23. 1
some light displeasure which him *crost,* . . . III. vi. 11. 3
crost the nearest way, by which he cast Her to encounter . . . III. vii. 38. 3
The hot-spurre youth so scorning to be *crost,* . . . IV. i. 35. 5
With greedie force And furie to be *crossed* in his way, . . . VI. iv. 20. 7
For fell despight to be so sorely *crost;* . . . VI. iv. 40. 4
With which her winged speed is let and *crost,* . . . VI. xii. 1. 4
Crosses. To fret thy soule with *crosses* and with cares; . . . *Hub.* 903
Al holding *crosses* in their hands on hye, . . . III. iii. 38. 6
Crosslet. That in his armour bare a *croslet* red? . . . I. vi. 36. 6
Crost. *See* **Crossed.**
Crouch. To *crouche,* to please, to be a beetle-stock . . . *Hub.* 507
He will not creepe, nor *crouche* with fained face, . . . *Hub.* 727
To fawne, to *crowche,* to waite, to ride, to ronne, . . . *Hub.* 905

Crouching. Kissing his hands, and *crouching* to the ground; . VI. iv. 11. 5
Croud. *See* **Crowd.**
Croun, -d. *See* **Crown, -ed.**
Croup. Him so transfixed she before her bore Beyond his *croupe,* . . . III. iv. 16. 7
Crouper. *See* **Crupper.**
Crow. *See* **Overcrow.**
by myne eie the *Crow* his clawe dooth wright: . . . *S.C.* D. 136
Crowd. the stout Faery mongst the middest *crowd* Thought . . . I. iv. 15. 6
The pipe, the tabor, and the trembling *Croud,* . . . *Epith.* 131
Crowed. *See* **Overcrowed.**
Crowing. *crowing* in pypes made of greene corne, . . . *S.C.* F. 40
As cocke on his dunghill *crowing* cranck. . . . *S.C.* S. 46
now the *crowing* Cocke, and now the Owle . . . IV. v. 41. 8
Crown. To *crowne* her golden locks: . . . *S.C.* Jun. 46
those that weld the awful *crowne,* . . . *S.C.* O. 40
His *Crowne* and Scepter lying him beside, . . . *Hub.* 953
May we his *Crowne* and Mace take from the ground, . . . *Hub.* 968
ye shall have both *crowne* and government, . . . *Hub.* 1050
upon his head The *Crowne,* . . . *Hub.* 1062
Realmes chiefe strength and girlond of the *crowne.* . . . *Hub.* 1185
when his *Crowne* and scepter both he wanted, . . . *Hub.* 1339
Have purchast him in heaven an happie *crowne,* . . . *Ti.* 264
I would her lyken to a *crowne* of lillies, . . . *Col.* 337
He gave her . . . triple *crowne* set on her head full hye, . . . I. vii. 16. 4
Prince Arthure, *crowne* of Martiall band?' . . . I. ix. 6. 5
his victorious handes did earst restore To native *crowne* . . . II. i. 2. 7
Whose hoary locks great gravitie did *crowne,* . . . II. vi. 47. 5
throw the *crowne* Sometimes to him . . . II. vii. 11. 6
In her owne hand the *crowne* she kept in store, . . . II. x. 20. 3
in his *crown* he counted her no hayre, . . . II. x. 28. 8
Their aged Syre, thus eased of his *crowne,* . . . II. x. 29. 6
to his *crowne* she him restord againe; . . . II. x. 32. 1
O! the greedy thirst of royall *crowne,* . . . II. x. 35. 1
he first wore *crowne* of gold for dignity. . . . II. x. 39. 9
Next whom Morindus did the *crowne* sustayne; . . . II. x. 43. 3
Even thrise eleven descents the *crowne* retaynd, . . . II. x. 45. 8
Both in his armes and *crowne,* . . . II. x. 51. 7
their uncle Vortigere Usurpt the *crowne* . . . II. x. 64. 3
The *crowne* which Vortiger did long detayne: . . . II. x. 67. 4
Did high advaunce the *crowne* of Faery: . . . II. x. 75. 5
To *crowne* his golden lockes with honour dew; . . . III. i. 35. 5
Shall take the *crowne* that was his fathers right, . . . III. iii. 29. 6
crowne himselfe in th' others stead: . . . III. iii. 29. 7
crowne with martiredome his sacred head: . . . III. iii. 39. 4
peaceably Enjoy the *crowne,* . . . III. iii. 46. 2
from the Daniske Tyrants head shall rend Th' usurped *crowne,* III. iii. 47. 7
So shall the Briton blood their *crowne* agayn reclame. . . . III. iii. 48. 9
Decline her head, and touch her crouper with her *crown.* . . . III. iv. 15. 9
every one did teare her girlond from her *crowne.* . . . III. iv. 30. 9
mischief fel upon the meaners *crowne.* . . . III. v. 25. 8
crowne your heades with heavenly coronall, . . . III. v. 53. 8
crowne of heavenly prayse with Saintes above, . . . III. viii. 42. 7
of all Asie bore the soveraine *crowne,* . . . III. ix. 39. 4
crowne true lovers with immortall blis, . . . IV. Pr. 2. 8
love, That is the *crowne* of knighthood, . . . IV. vi. 31. 7
steale away the *crowne* of their good name: . . . IV. viii. 25. 4
hard unto his *crowne* The shield it drove, . . . IV. viii. 42. 6
on her head a *crowne* She wore, . . . IV. x. 31. 6
as with a *Crowne* He doth adorne, . . . IV. xi. 34. 7
kept the *crowne* in which she should succeed: . . . V. i. 13. 5
Uppon her head she wore a *Crowne* of gold; . . . V. vii. 6. 6
Moone-like Mitre to a *Crowne* of gold; . . . V. vii. 13. 6
the just heritage Of thy sires *Crowne,* . . . V. vii. 23. 4
soveraine grace, with which her royall *crowne* She doth support, . . . V. viii. 17. 4
Seekes to subvert her *Crowne* and dignity, . . . V. viii. 18. 4
how for to depryve Mercilla of her *crowne,* . . . V. ix. 41. 7
Had bene the keye of all that kingdomes *crowne;* . . . V. x. 26. 4
When her that Tyrant did of *Crowne* deprive; . . . V. xi. 38. 4
And lost the *crowne* . . . VI. ii. 27. 9
did weare a *crowne* Of sundry flowres . . . VI. ix. 7. 7
Then was the oaken *crowne* by Pastorell Given to Calidore . . . VI. ix. 44. 6
In the woods shade which did the waters *crowne,* . . . VI. x. 7. 7
the *crowne,* which Ariadne wore . . . VI. x. 13. 1
woods . . . (That on each side her silver channell *crowne*) . . . VII. vi. 41. 8
Crowne ye God Bacchus with a coronall, . . . *Epith.* 255
Hymen also *crowne* with wreathes of vine; . . . *Epith.* 256
her they *crowne* their Goddesse and their Queene, . . . *H.L.* 292
on her head a *crowne* of purest gold Is set, . . . *H.H.B.* 190
gemmes Fit to . . . *crowne* their Paramours . . . *Proth.* 16
Crowned. In her swifte charret with high turrets *crownde,* . . . *Ro.* vi. 2
Crowned as king: . . . *S.C.* May 30
thou shalt *ycrouned* be In Colins stede, . . . *S.C.* Au. 145
My boughes with bloosmes that *crowned* were . . . *S.C.* D. 103
Like virgin Queenes, with laurell garlands *cround* . . . *T.M.* 309
with rosie garland *crownd!* . . . *D.* 312
match that Muse when it with bayes is *crowned,* . . . *Col.* 414
sung by them with flowry gyrlonds *crownd.* . . . *Col.* 643
crownd with lasting baies Of hevenlie blis; . . . *Ded. Son.* xv. 4
freshest Flora her with Yvie girlond *crownd.* . . . I. i. 48. 9
That made her selfe a Queene, and *crownd* to be; . . . I. iv. 12. 2
Do worship her as Queene with olive girlond *cround.* . . . I. vi. 13. 9
every head was *crowned* on his creast, . . . I. viii. 6. 4
she . . . *crowned* mitre rudely threw asyde: . . . I. viii. 25. 3
hill, . . . For ever with a flowring girlond *crownd:* . . . I. x. 54. 5
crowned her twixt earnest and twixt game: . . . I. xii. 8. 7
with laurell girlond *cround.* . . . II. iii. 38. 9
The *crowned* often slaine, the slayer *cround;* . . . II. vii. 13. 5

Crowned—*Continued.*
crownd his coward crest with knightly stile; II. viii. 12. 7
crowned with a garland of sweete Rosiere. II. ix. 19. 9
of the Britons first *crownd* Soveraine. II. x. 58. 7
They *crownd* the second Constantine with joyous teares. II. x. 62. 9
He bore a *crowned* little Ermelin, III. ii. 25. 8
With gilden hornes and flowry girlonds *crownd,* III. iv. 17. 2
both were with one olive garland *crownd,* IV. iii. 42. 5
that was Arion *crownd;* IV. xi. 23. 3
The pleasaunt Bandon *crownd* with many a wood; IV. xi. 44. 2
Might else have with felicitie bene *crowned:* V. v. 36. 7
with Diademe hath ever *crowned* beene.' V. ix. 20. 9
Crowned with girlonds of immortall baies; VI. xi. 34. 6
Crownd with a rosie girlond VI. x. 14. 5
the which was *cround* With eares of corne, VII. vii. 37. 4
is comming forth with girland *crouned.* *Am.* xix. 4
having all your heads with girlands *crownd,* *Epith.* 13
being *crowned* with a girland greene, *Epith.* 157
Whom he therefore with equall honour *crownd.* *H.H.L.* 35
How scourgd, how *crownd,* how buffeted, how brused; *H.H.L.* 243
Their snowie Foreheads therewithall they *crownd,* *Proth.* 86
Crowns. seven heads, ten *crownes,* ten hornes did beare, *Rev.* i. 2
His head did shine with *crounes* set therupon. *Rev.* iii. 3
And *crownes* their ashes with immortall baies. *Ded. Son.* iv. 12
a Persian mitre . . . with *crowns* and owches garnished, I. ii. 13. 5
Nereus *crownes* with cups; his mates him pledg around. I. iii. 31. 9
That joyes for *crownes* and kingdomes to contend: II. vii. 10. 7
crownes and kingdomes to thee multiply. II. vii. 11. 5
crownes, and Diademes, and titles vaine, II. vii. 43. 8
All deckt with *crownes,* and chaynes, and girlands gay, IV. x. 37. 6
To bandie *Crownes,* and Kingdoms to bestowe: VII. vi. 32. 8
Crows. a fowling net, Which he for carrion *Crowes* had set *S.C.* Mar. 110
Crucified. And lastly, how twixt robbers *crucifyde,* *H.H.L.* 244
Cruddles, Cruddy, Crudled. *See* **Curdles,** *etc.*
Crudor. Calidore . . . Doth vanquish *Crudor;* VI. i. Arg.
'His name is *Crudor;* VI. i. 15. 1
flie with all the speed he could To *Crudor;* VI. i. 29. 5
All this accord to which he *Crudor* had compeld. VI. i. 44. 9
Cruel. The *cruell* Leopard she resembled much: *Rev.* i. 4
in their *cruell* race They pincht the haunches *Pet.* i. 8
Cruell death vanquishing so noble beautie, *Pet.* i. 13
Ye *cruell* starres, and eke ye Gods unkinde, *Ro.* ix. 1
Emongst themselves with *cruell* furie striving, *Ro.* x. 11
each to other working *cruell* wrongs, *Ro.* xxiv. 7
all his glory in his *cruell* clawes. *Van.* x. 6
Caused of wrong and *cruell* constraint, *S.C.* F. 152
whom *cruell* fate And angry Gods pursue *S.C.* Jun. 14
Agaynst his *cruell* scortching heate, *S.C.* Jul. 25
Ne runs in perill of foes *cruell* knife, *Gn.* 125
Cruell Agave, flying vengeance sore *Gn.* 172
hastning his *cruell* fate. *Gn.* 328
lockes uncombed *cruell* adders be. *Gn.* 344
With them that *cruell* Colchid mother dwells, *Gn.* 397
approoved The feends to be too *cruell* and severe, *Gn.* 466
cruell Orpheus, thou much crueller, *Gn.* 470
the *cruell* fiends of hell, *Gn.* 625
their *cruell* Judge compell With bitter torture, *Gn.* 627
After the chafed Lyons *cruell* bayting, *Hub.* 6
With fowle reproach, and *cruell* banishment? *T.M.* 426
he saw my *cruell* foes me pained, *Ti.* 144
times decay, and envies *cruell* tort, *Ti.* 167
ward his gentle corpes from *cruell* wound; *Mui.* 60
Whose *cruell* fate is woven even now *Mui.* 235
cruell Fate . . . him misled, *Mui.* 417
A *cruell* Satyre with his murdrous dart, *D.* 156
No nurse, but Stepdame, *cruell,* mercilesse. *D.* 342
cruell Death doth scorne to come at call, *D.* 356
pardon that unto the *cruell* skies, *As.* 113
A *cruell* beast of most accursed brood *As.* 116
being to that swaine too *cruell* hard, *Col.* 909
Faire Venus sonne, that with thy *cruell* dart I. Pr. 3. 2
The *cruell* markes of many' a bloody fielde; I. i. 1. 4
Seemd in their song to scorne the *cruell* sky. I. i. 8. 4
Shall I accuse the hidden *cruell* fate, I. i. 51. 2
with *cruell* spies Does seeke to perce; I. ii. 17. 5
Hurled his beame so scorching *cruell* hot, I. ii. 29. 5
whose nature weake A *cruell* witch, . . . Hath thus transformd, I. ii. 33. 5
How does he find in *cruell* hart to hate Her, I. iii. 7. 7
of his *cruell* rage Nigh dead with feare, I. iii. 13. 3
seizing *cruell* clawes on trembling brest, I. iii. 19. 8
Cruell revenge, which he in hart did hyde; I. iii. 33. 8
His *cruel* facts he often would repent; I. iv. 34. 7
Full many mischiefes follow *cruell* Wrath: I. iv. 35. 1
Soone after comes the *cruell* Sarazin, I. v. 4. 1
The *cruell* steele . . . doth bight In tender flesh, I. v. 9. 3
wearie traveiler . . . Doth meete a *cruell* craftie Crocodile, I. v. 18. 4
His *cruell* wounds, with cruddy bloud congeald, I. v. 29. 6
His *cruell* step-dame . . . Her wicked daies . . . did end, I. v. 39. 1
The Pardale swift, and the Tigre *cruell,* I. vi. 26. 4
After his sportes and *cruell* pastime donne; I. vi. 27. 4
That *cruell* word her tender hart so thrild, I. vi. 37. 1
Where foming wrath their *cruell* tuskes they whett, I. vi. 44. 7
increasing more Their puissant force, and *cruell* rage I. vi. 45. 3
cruell fates the carefull threds unfould, I. vii. 22. 5
their *cruell* cursed enemy . . . Their kingdome spoild, I. vii. 44. 1
proofe he since hath made . . . in many a *cruell* fight; I. vii. 47. 7
bloody mouthed with late *cruell* feast, I. viii. 6. 5
So downe he fell before the *cruell* beast, I. viii. 15. 1
With *cruell* malice and strong tyranny: I. viii. 36. 5
The sharpnesse of his *cruel* rending clawes: I. xi. 12. 2

Cruel—*Continued.*
with his *cruell* clawes he snatcht the wood, I. xi. 22. 2
he could not endure so *cruell* cace, I. xi. 26. 8
The *cruell* wound enraged him so sore, I. xi. 37. 1
from his *cruell* claw To reave I. xi. 41. 5
So tossed was in fortunes *cruell* freakes: I. xii. 16. 8
As chained beare whom *cruell* dogs doe bait, I. xii. 35. 7
prickt with courage kene, did *cruell* battell breath. II. i. 27. 9
whose sides with *cruell* steele Through launched, II. i. 38. 6
did stick A *cruell* knife II. i. 39. 6
a lovely babe did play His *cruell* sport, II. i. 40. 6
the *cruell* steel He lightly snatcht, II. i. 43. 1
cursed hand, hath plaid this *cruell* part, II. i. 44. 7
Accusing fortune, and too *cruell* fate, II. i. 56. 8
'Ah! lucklesse babe, borne under *cruell* starre, II. ii. 2. 1
cruell combat joynd in middle space: II. ii. 20. 3
being met In *cruell* fight II. ii. 22. 6
Their deadly *cruell* discord to forbeare, II. ii. 27. 8
downe they lett their *cruell* weapons fall, II. ii. 32. 3
Furor, cursed *cruel* wight, II. iv. 10. 6
with which *cruell* intent, II. iv. 31. 6
with my heat kindled his *cruell* fyre; II. iv. 32. 8
cruell battry bend Gainst fort of Reason, II. iv. 34. 7
Full oft approvd in many a *cruell* warre; II. iv. 41. 4
stirre him up to strife and *cruell* fight. II. iv. 42. 7
like a *cruell* tygre far'd. II. v. 8. 9
yeilded passage to his *cruell* knife. II. v. 9. 4
Eftsoones his *cruel* hand Sir Guyon stayd, II. v. 13. 1
With *cruell* purpose bent to wreake on him II. vi. 2. 2
care of vow'd revenge and *cruell* fight, II. vi. 8. 4
how can Your *cruell* eyes endure so pitteous sight, II. vi. 32. 6
Such *cruell* game my scarmoges disarmes. II. vi. 34. 5
'Debatefull strife, and *cruell* enmity, II. vi. 35. 1
Delighting all in armes and *cruell* warre, II. vi. 37. 6
'That cursed man, that *cruel* feend of hell, II. vi. 50. 1
On thother side . . . there sate *Cruell* Revenge, II. vii. 22. 2
He over him did hold his *cruell* clawes, II. vii. 27. 6
when his *cruell* foes he queld. II. vii. 40. 9
Plonged continually of *cruell* Sprightes, II. vii. 57. 4
having laid his *cruell* bow away II. viii. 6. 2
his *cruell* foes, that stand here-by, II. viii. 25. 1
Had reard him selfe againe to *cruel* fight II. viii. 34. 7
thy *cruell* hond, That twise hath spedd; II. viii. 37. 6
cruell passage made Quite through his brayne. II. viii. 45. 5
evermore their *cruell* Capitaine Sought II. ix. 15. 3
His *cruel* bow, wherewith he thousands hath dismayd. II. ix. 34. 9
young Hectors blood by *cruell* Greekes was spilt. II. ix. 45. 9
kindling coles of *cruell* enmity, II. x. 33. 5
with most *cruell* hand him murdred pittilesse. II. x. 35. 9
with wrath outrageous And *cruell* rancour II. x. 43. 5
There she with them a *cruell* batteill tryde, II. x. 55. 1
What warre so *cruel,* or what siege so sore, II. xi. 1. 1
To see a *cruell* fight doen by the prince this day. II. xi. 4. 9
covetous aspects, all *cruell* enimyes. II. xi. 8. 9
that fourth band which *cruell* battry bent II. xi. 12. 1
All deadly daungerous, all *cruell* keene, II. xi. 21. 3
at him a *cruell* shaft he sent: II. xi. 24. 5
His speares default to mend with *cruell* blade; III. i. 10. 3
Vyle rancor to avoid and *cruel* surquedry. III. i. 13. 9
Fiers battaill against one with *cruell* might and mayne. III. i. 20. 9
she saw him bent to *cruell* play, III. i. 37. 3
Hath me subjected to loves *cruell* law: III. ii. 38. 5
Ne slake the fury of her *cruell* flame, III. ii. 52. 2
cruell Feendes should thee unwares devowre: III. iii. 8. 9
The worlds reproch; the *cruell* victors scorne; III. iii. 42. 5
thy *cruel* billowes beat so strong, III. iv. 8. 4
thy *cruell* wrath and spightfull wrong III. iv. 8. 7
their malice they did whet With *cruell* threats III. v. 17. 9
A *cruell* shaft, headed with deadly ill, III. v. 20. 4
Did th' other two their *cruell* vengeaunce blin, III. v. 22. 7
of that *cruell* wound he bled so sore, III. v. 26. 2
of his lucklesse lott and *cruell* love thus playnd: III. v. 44. 9
His *cruell* deedes and wicked wyles did spot: III. vi. 13. 5
with his *cruell* tuske him deadly cloyd: III. vi. 48. 4
His feeble hart wide launched with loves *cruel* wownd. III. vi. 52. 9
with huge strokes and *cruell* battery III. vii. 32. 3
Which when his *cruell* enimy espyde, III. vii. 42. 8
curst that *cruell* chaunce III. vii. 45. 4
that *cruell* Queene avengeresse, III. viii. 20. 6
afterwardes affray with *cruell* threat, III. ix. 9. 3
angry Gods and *cruell* skie III. ix. 33. 4
With zelous envy of Greekes *cruell* fact III. ix. 38. 5
he with *cruell* warre was entertaind III. ix. 42. 2
Soone as the *cruell* flames yslaked were, III. x. 17. 1
wreake your sorrow on your *cruell* foe; III. xi. 15. 5
That *cruell* element, which all things feare, III. xi. 22. 4
cruell Mulciber would not obay His threatfull pride, III. xi. 26. 5
cruell battailes, which he whilome fought III. xi. 29. 6
cruell Cupid, not herewith content, III. xi. 38. 7
Ne did he spare (so *cruell* was the Elfe) III. xi. 45. 1
in his *cruell* fist A mortall bow III. xi. 48. 1
whilome captived in their dayes To *cruell* love, III. xi. 52. 5
rather stird to *cruell* enmity, III. xii. 1. 8
(The worke of *cruell* hand) III. xii. 20. 8
he much rejoyced in his *cruell* minde. III. xii. 22. 9
Seeming transfixed with a *cruell* dart; III. xii. 31. 5
The *cruell* steele, which thrild her dying hart, III. xii. 38. 1
Through *cruell* knife that her deare heart did kerve: IV. i. 4. 5
With murdrous weapons arm'd to *cruell* fight, IV. ii. 16. 2
Have rays'd this *cruell* warre and outrage fell, IV. ii. 24. 4

Cruel—*Continued.*
That *cruell* Atropos eftsoones undid, . . . IV. ii. 48. 7
cruell battell twixt themselves doe make, . . . IV. iii. 16. 6
Now made forget their former *cruell* mood, . . . IV. iii. 39. 4
when she saw that *cruell* war so ended, . . . IV. iii. 50. 4
he amongst them *cruell* havocke makes, . . . IV. iv. 34. 6
Shew'd all his bodie bare unto the *cruell* dent. . . . IV. vi. 15. 9
Ah, *cruell* hand! and thrise more *cruell* hart, . . . IV. vi. 16. 8
cruell sword out of his fingers slacke Fell downe . . . IV. vi. 21. 5
with thy *cruell* darts Doest conquer . . . IV. vii. 1. 1
the relickes of his feast And *cruell* spoyle, . . . IV. vii. 6. 4
Latonaes daughter, *cruell* kynde, . . . IV. vii. 30. 5
With fell despight her *cruell* arrowes tynde . . . IV. vii. 30. 7
wrath of *cruell* wight on thee ywrake, . . . IV. viii. 14. 8
theirs that have so *cruell* thee forlorne! . . . IV. viii. 15. 4
Did closely with a *cruell* one consent . . . IV. viii. 16. 7
his *cruell* foe that him pursewd in sight. . . . IV. viii. 40. 9
Complayning of her *cruell* Paramoure, . . . IV. ix. 6. 3
This *cruell* conflict raised thereabout, . . . IV. ix. 24. 8
on his foes did worke full *cruell* wracke: . . . IV. ix. 25. 4
Faint friends when they fall out most *cruell* fomen bee. . . . IV. ix. 27. 9
cruell blades, yet steeming with whot bloud, . . . IV. ix. 29. 4
they for nought their *cruell* hands would stay, . . . IV. ix. 31. 3
the cause of their so *cruell* heat . . . IV. ix. 35. 8
with his killing bow And *cruell* shafts, . . . IV. x. 55. 4
that *cruell* stroke Which Britomart him gave, . . . IV. xi. 5. 8
his foe, A *cruell* Tyrant, . . . IV. xii. 29. 8
As withered weed through *cruell* winters tine, . . . IV. xii. 34. 6
Against that *cruell* Tyrant, which opprest The faire Irena . . . V. i. 13. 3
A cursed *cruell* Sarazin doth wonne, . . . V. ii. 4. 6
With *cruell* chaufe their courages they whet, . . . V. ii. 15. 3
With bright Chrysaor in his *cruell* hand, . . . V. ii. 18. 2
whom *cruell* tempest drives Upon a rocke . . . V. ii. 50. 1
being freed from Proteus *cruell* band . . . V. iii. 2. 1
there all day continew'd *cruell* fight, . . . V. iii. 7. 3
this the sword which wrought those *cruell* stounds, . . . V. iii. 22. 1
bent against them selves their *cruell* hands; . . . V. iv. 5. 7
To joyne the combate with *cruell* intent, . . . V. iv. 6. 6
suffred *cruell* shipwracke by the way: . . . V. iv. 13. 8
Meaning on him their *cruell* hands to lay, . . . V. iv. 23. 8
'The cause, they say, of this her *cruell* hate . . . V. iv. 30. 1
So *cruell* doale amongst her maides divide . . . V. iv. 39. 3
seiz'd her *cruell* clawes Uppon the carkasse . . . V. iv. 40. 6
No hand so *cruell,* nor no hart so hard, . . . V. v. 13. 5
cruell heavens have heapt an heavy fate; . . . V. v. 36. 3
Which when the *cruell* Amazon perceived, . . . V. v. 47. 1
Restraines those sterne behests and *cruell* doomes of his. . . . V. vii. 22. 9
Nath'lesse that stroke so *cruell* passage found, . . . V. vii. 33. 1
Crying to them their *cruell* hands to stay, . . . V. viii. 10. 8
'To all which *cruell* tyranny, they say, He is provokt, . . . V. viii. 20. 1
drawne of *cruell* steedes which he had fed With flesh of men, V. viii. 28. 6
Did stay her *cruell* hand ere she her raught; . . . V. viii. 48. 2
after that he had foyled The *cruell* Souldan, . . . V. ix. 2. 8
They doe his anger calme, and *cruell* vengeance stay. . . . V. ix. 31. 9
A *cruell* carle, the which all strangers slew, . . . V. x. 10. 3
For ayde against that *cruell* Tyrants theft, . . . V. x. 14. 4
cruell enemies increased more, . . . V. xi. 54. 2
Made *cruell* havocke of the baser crew, . . . V. xi. 59. 6
Artegall, seeing his *cruell* deed, . . . V. xi. 65. 6
Which *cruell* outrage when as Artegall Did well avize, . . . V. xii. 18. 1
high did reare His *cruell* hand to smite him mortally, . . . V. xii. 20. 3
What *cruell* hand thy wretched thraldome wrought, . . . VI. i. 12. 3
There then began a fearefull *cruell* fray . . . VI. i. 36. 1
Their *cruell* strokes and terrible affright; . . . VI. i. 36. 7
what *cruell* hand hath thus arayd This knight . . . VI. ii. 42. 3
Yet ceast he not for all that *cruell* wound, . . . VI. iii. 51. 1
And saved from his *cruell* villany. . . . VI. iii. 51. 7
Seeing his sharpe assault and *cruell* stoure, . . . VI. iv. 3. 3
A *cruell* Beare, the which an infant bore . . . VI. iv. 17. 8
Gnashing his *cruell* teeth at him in vaine, . . . VI. iv. 22. 8
to these happie fortunes *cruell* fate . . . VI. iv. 30. 5
Without compassion of her *cruell* smarts: . . . VI. v. 33. 4
Cruell Typhoon, whose tempestuous rage . . . VI. vi. 11. 8
With all the evill termes and *cruell* meane . . . VI. vii. 39. 5
Whose *cruell* handling when that Squire beheld, . . . VI. vii. 45. 1
Bull, whose *cruell* hornes doe threat Desperate daunger, . . . VI. vii. 47. 2
his *cruell* hand to stay, . . . VI. viii. 29. 2
out of his *cruell* hands; . . . VI. ix. 11. 8
Such was the conflict of those *cruell* Brigants there. . . . VI. xi. 17. 9
To stay their *cruell* hands from slaughter fell, . . . VI. xi. 20. 5
with unkind disdaine And *cruell* rigour . . . VI. xi. 24. 4
With *cruell* rage and dreadfull violence, . . . VI. xi. 30. 4
Oft cursing th' heavens, that so *cruell* were To her, . . . VI. xi. 33. 6
As if he would have rent him with his *cruell* clawes: . . . VI. xii. 29. 9
doth play Her *cruell* sports to many mens decay? . . . VII. vi. 1. 5
with their death his *cruell* life dooth feed; . . . VII. vii. 24. 8
She, *cruell* warriour, doth herselfe addresse . . . *Am.* xi. 3
Have ever since me kept in *cruell* bands . . . *Am.* xii. 12
But she, more *cruell,* and more salvage wylde, . . . *Am.* xx. 9
in bloody bath . . . her *cruell* hands embrew. . . . *Am.* xxxi. 12
through tempests *cruel* wracke, . . . *Am.* xxxviii. 1
To be so *cruell* to an humbled foe? . . . *Am.* xli. 2
this continuall, *cruell,* civill warre, . . . *Am.* xliv. 5
My *cruell* fayre streight bids me wend my way: . . . *Am.* xlvi. 2
Whome, . . . she kills with *cruell* pryde, . . . *Am.* xlvii. 7
they take pleasure in her *cruell* play, . . . *Am.* xlvii. 11
whom too *cruell* hand Did make the matter . . . *Am.* xlviii. 1
Fayre *cruell!* why are ye so fierce and *cruell?* . . . *Am.* xlix. 1
Right so my *cruell* fayre with me doth play; . . . *Am.* liii. 5
which her made attonce so *cruell* faire, . . . *Am.* lv. 4

Cruel—*Continued.*
Fayre ye be sure, but *cruell* and unkind, . . . *Am.* lvi. 1
to make these *cruel* stoures. . . . *Am.* lvii. 10
Ye *cruell* one! what glory can be got, . . . *Am.* lvii. 11
the *cruell* boy . . . Would needs the fly pursue; . . . *Epig.* iv. 21
forgets the *cruell* carelesse elfe His mothers heast to prove. . . *Epig.* iv. 57
all my cares, which *cruell* Love collected, . . . *Epith.* 317
by thy *cruell* darts to thee subdewed. . . . *H.L.* 14
The *cruell* worker of your kindly smarts, . . . *H.L.* 32
Making their *cruell* rage thy scornefull game, . . . *H.L.* 47
He freely gave to be both rent and torne Of *cruell* hands, . . *H.H.L.* 151
Crueler. cruell Orpheus, thou much *crueller,* . . . *Gn.* 470
Cruelly. *Cruelly* fell upon their flock in folde, . . . *Hub.* 335
slaine her Lambe most *cruellie,* . . . *Hub.* 1210
My dearest Lord . . . *cruelly* was slaine; . . . I. ii. 23. 9
blood, which *cruelly* was spilt On cursed tree, . . . I. x. 57. 5
Her golden lockes most *cruelly* she rent, . . . II. i. 15. 4
so *cruelly* have swayd Against that knight! . . . II. viii. 46. 7
Yet sith his fate so *cruelly* did fall, . . . II. viii. 52. 7
conquered, and *cruelly* did slay. . . . II. x. 10. 9
Of that third troupe was *cruelly* assayd; . . . II. xi. 11. 2
Cruelly they assayed that fift Fort, . . . II. xi. 13. 5
hideous Ordinaunce Upon the Bulwarkes *cruelly* did play, . . II. xi. 14. 4
eke himselfe her *cruelly* exyld: . . . III. vi. 50. 5
slew him *cruelly* ere any reskew came. . . . III. vii. 28. 9
My Lady and my love so *cruelly* to pen! . . . III. xi. 10. 9
'My Lady and my love is *cruelly* pend . . . III. xi. 11. 1
erst all entrers wont so *cruelly* to scorch. . . . III. xii. 42. 9
in his side The mortall point most *cruelly* empight; . . . IV. iii. 10. 4
So *cruelly* these Knights strove for that Ladies sake. . . . IV. iii. 16. 9
afterwardes themselves doth *cruelly* devoure. . . . IV. vii. 12. 9
there in chaynes her *cruelly* did bind, . . . IV. xi. 2. 5
All whom a Scythian king . . . Slew *cruelly,* . . . IV. xi. 37. 9
So *cruelly* did him pursew and chace, . . . V. viii. 36. 6
right and wrong most *cruelly* confound: . . . V. xii. 2. 7
cruelly does wound whom so she wils: . . . V. xii. 36. 5
bite, and *cruelly* torment.' . . . VI. i. 8. 9
With full intent him *cruelly* to kill, . . . VI. iii. 49. 2
murdred *cruelly* by a rebellious Mayd. . . . VI. vii. 34. 9
The more they him misust, and *cruelly* did beat. . . . VI. viii. 3. 9
Their Captaine there they *cruelly* found kild, . . . VI. xi. 21. 1
in dongeon deepe Without compassion *cruelly* he threw; . . . VI. xii. 5. 7
Full *cruelly* the Beast did rage and rore . . . VI. xii. 31. 1
The love which me so *cruelly* tormenteth, . . . *Am.* xlii. 1
thou art disposed *cruelly,* . . . *Epig.* iv. 17
Cruel-minded. his *cruell minded* hart Empierced was . . . V. v. 13. 1
Three mightie ones, and *cruell minded* eeke, . . . VI. v. 13. 3
Cruelness. gan renew her former *cruelnesse:* . . . V. v. 14. 4
the reproch of pride and *cruelnesse.* . . . VI. i. 41. 4
But taketh glory in her *cruelnesse.* . . . *Am.* xx. 12
Cruelties. Let them feele the utmost of your *crueltyes;* . . . *Am.* xlix. 9
Cruelty. *crueltie,* the signe of currish kinde, . . . *Hub.* 1134
Against the seas encroching *crueltie.* . . . *Col.* 275
holding idely The broken reliques of their former *cruelty.* . . I. ii. 16. 9
joyd to make proofe of her *cruelty* . . . I. vi. 31. 6
they . . . The pitteous pray of his fiers *cruelty* have bin. . . . I. vii. 45. 9
Drew . . . A handsom stripling with great *crueltee,* . . . II. iv. 3. 7
breathes out wrath and hainous *crueltee:* . . . II. iv. 43. 8
y scuith gogh, signe of sad *crueltee.* . . . II. x. 24. 9
with fell *cruelty* In their avenge . . . III. iii. 46. 8
felt the *cruelty* Of his sharpe dartes . . . III. vi. 14. 4
with spoiles and *cruelty* Ransackt the world, . . . III. vi. 49. 5
with great *cruelty* Rored and raged . . . III. vii. 33. 7
refuge from the Monsters *cruelty,* . . . III. viii. 21. 2
No living creature could his *cruelty* asswage. . . . III. viii. 28. 9
The hevens such *crueltie* abhore.' . . . III. viii. 48. 9
all the world confound with *cruelty;* . . . III. x. 33. 8
How suffrest thou such shamefull *cruelty* . . . III. xi. 9. 4
The other cleped *Cruelty* by name: . . . III. xii. 19. 3
They did much more their *cruelty* encrease; . . . IV. ii. 19. 5
she it all did mar with *cruelty* and pride. . . . IV. ix. 14. 9
He thought her to compell by *crueltie* and awe. . . . IV. xi. 2. 9
Yet still her *crueltie* increased more, . . . V. v. 7. 3
Such is the *crueltie* of womenkynd, . . . V. v. 25. 1
Their hardned hearts, enur'd to bloud and *cruelty.* . . . V. viii. 1. 9
Tygres scath In *crueltie* and outrage she did pas, . . . V. viii. 49. 8
now his *cruelty* so sore she drad, . . . V. x. 18. 7
for more horror and more *crueltie,* . . . V. x. 29. 1
Had stayned with reprochfull *crueltie* In guiltlesse blood . . V. xii. 40. 6
I . . . gan to blame him for such *cruelty* . . . VI. ii. 11. 3
if men you of *cruelty* accuse, . . . VI. viii. 1. 8
cruelty and hardnesse from you chace, . . . VI. viii. 2. 4
they gan augment Their *cruelty,* . . . VI. viii. 4. 7
now your crime with *cruelty* pursew! . . . VI. viii. 7. 7
A monstrous *cruelty* gainst course of kynde! . . . VI. viii. 36. 5
to torment me thus with *cruelty,* . . . *Am.* xxv. 7
Such *cruelty* she would have soone abhord . . . *Am.* xxxi. 14
their *cruelty* doth still increace, . . . *Am.* xxxvi. 7
Onely let her abstaine from *cruelty.* . . . *Am.* xlii. 13
through your *cruelty,* With sorrow dimmed . . . it were, . . *Am.* xlv. 9
therewith doe her *cruelty* compare, . . . *Am.* lv. 2
change thy *cruelty,* Or give like leave unto the fly.' . . . *Epig.* iv. 19
againe enured His former *cruelty.* . . . *Epig.* iv. 54
Crumbs. He crammed them with *crumbs* of Benefices, . . . *Hub.* 1153
Crumenal. Is nowe fast stalled in her *crumenall.* . . . *S.C.* S. 119
Crupper. Nigh a speares length behind his *crouper* fell; . . . III. i. 6. 7
touch her *crouper* with her crown. . . . III. iv. 15. 9
overbore beyond his *crouper* quight; . . . IV. iv. 40. 7
Crushed. life nigh *crusht* out of his panting brest: . . . I. viii. 15. 3
crusht his carcas so against his brest, . . . II. xi. 42. 2
That they have *crusht* the Crab, . . . V. Pr. 6. 3

Crusts. Theyr sheepe han *crustes,* . . . . *S.C.* Jul. 187

Cry. *See* **Outcry.**

rout of Faunes With hideous *cry* assembled . . . . *Bel.*[1] x. 12

Soone as my younglings *cryen* for the dam . . . . *S.C.* Ap. 95

(then gan he *crye*) . . . . *S.C.* May 255

he heavily departed With piteous *crie,* . . . . *Gn.* 640

unto them the Foxe alowd did *cry,* . . . . *Hub.* 1070

'But whie (unhappie wight!) doo I thus *crie,* . . . . *Ti.* 176

made the Easterne Conquerour to *crie,* . . . . *Ti.* 432

heavens refuse to heare a wretches *cry;* . . . . *D.* 355

Horrible, hideous, roaring with hoarse *crie.*' . . . . *Col.* 199

Then do they *cry* and call to love apace, ... *Col.* 879

With hollow houling, and lamenting *cry;* . . . . I. iii. 23. 2

cry, and curse, and raile, and rend her heare, ... I. iii. 25. 2

ghosts . . . with sharp shrilling shriekes doe bootlesse *cry,* . . I. v. 33. 5

Duessa loud to him gan *crye,* . . . . I. vii. 14. 4

At her so pitteous *cry* was much amoov'd Her champion . . . I. viii. 21. 1

no man car'd to answere to his *crye:* . . . . I. viii. 29. 7

Ay wont to laugh when them I heard to *cry,* . . . . I. ix. 10. 5

like a Lyon he would *cry* and rore, ... I. x. 28. 2

At last he was compeld to *cry* perforse, ... II. v. 23. 7

Then gan the cursed wretch alowd to *cry,* . . . . II. vii. 60. 6

all the fields resounded with the ruefull *cry.* . . . . II. viii. 3. 9

His feeble feet directed to the *cry;* . . . . II. viii. 4. 5

with outragious *cry* A thousand villeins rownd about them . II. ix. 13. 1

They reard a most outrageous dreadfull yelling *cry:* . . . . . II. xi. 17. 9

suddeine horrour and confused *cry* . . . . II. xi. 20. 1

th' one of them with dreadfull yelling *crye,* . . . . II. xi. 47. 3

they heard a ruefull *cry* . . . . II. xii. 27. 2

ill it were to hearken to her *cry,* . . . . II. xii. 28. 6

with earnest *cry* Badd those same six forbeare . . . . . . III. i. 22. 8

to her *cry* they list not lenden eare, ... III. i. 23. 1

streight embraced she to him did *cry* . . . . III. x. 13. 6

he stampt, he lowd did *cry,* . . . . III. x. 17. 7

all the way full loud for aide did *crie,* . . . . IV. viii. 38. 4

with his *cry* The Tyrant selfe came forth . . . . IV. viii. 62. 1

Then gan she loudly *cry,* and weepe, and waile, ... IV. ix. 7. 6

on him catching hold gan loud to *crie* . . . . V. i. 18. 2

The *cry* whereof entring the hollow cave . . . . V. ix. 10. 1

Then gan the Peoples *cry* and Commons sute . . . . V. ix. 44. 7

Then gan she *cry* much louder then afore, ... V. xi. 30. 1

looking up unto the *cry* to lest, ... VI. i. 17. 4

he for dread of death gan loude to *crie* . . . . VI. i. 22. 8

But chaste him still for all his Ladies *cry;* . . . . VI. iii. 51. 2

Gan *cry* aloud with horrible affright, ... VI. iv. 8. 8

As if his *cry* did meane for helpe to call . . . . VI. iv. 18. 3

by the *cry* he follow'd, and pursewed fast. . . . . VI. iv. 18. 9

had not the Ladies *cry* Procur'd the Prince . . . . VI. viii. 29. 1

Gan *cry* to them aloud to helpe her . . . . VI. x. 34. 9

'Die? out alas!' then Calidore did *cry,* . . . . VI. xi. 29. 5

The hue and *cry* was raysed all about; . . . . VI. xi. 46. 2

Led with the infants *cry* that loud did weepe, ... VI. xii. 9. 3

cats, that wrawling still did *cry;* . . . . VI. xii. 27. 4

when I laugh, she mocks; and, when I *cry,* She laughes, . . . *Am.* liv. 11

when he saw me stung and *cry,* He tooke his wings . . . . . *Epig.* i. 5

Crying. *crying* lowd, Loe! now beholde . . . . *Bel.*[2] i. 9

They *crying* creep out of their mothers woomb, ... *Ti.* 48

my voyce is spent with *crying;* . . . . *D.* 414

a piteous yelling voice was heard, *Crying,* . . . . I. ii. 31. 2

crying, 'Mercy!' loud, ... II. iii. 6. 9

Trompart forth stept . . . Out *crying:* . . . . II. iii. 34. 8

Crying; 'Let be that Lady debonaire, ... II. vi. 28. 4

Crying with pitteous voyce, ... II. vi. 32. 4

Led with that wofull Ladies piteous *crying,* . . . . IV. vii. 25. 3

Her selfe then tooke he . . . In vaine loud *crying,* . . . . . V. ii. 27. 2

Crying to them their cruell hands to stay, ... V. viii. 10. 8

Crying to them in vaine that nould his *crying* heare. . . . . V. viii. 41. 9

Crying for helpe aloud: . . . . V. ix. 14. 6

Crying in vaine for helpe, when helpe was past: . . . . . . V. ix. 19. 6

Crying, and holding up her wretched hands . . . . V. xi. 44. 8

a ruefull shrieke Of one loud *crying,* . . . . VI. i. 17. 2

Crying aloud (*in vaine) to shew her sad misfare . . . . . VI. iii. 24. 5

his lovely litle spoile *Crying* for food . . . . VI. iv. 25. 8

Crying in vaine to her him to bemone; . . . . VI. vi. 30. 5

Wringing her hands, and ruefully loud *crying?* . . . . VI. xi. 23. 7

Crying aloud with strong confused noyce, ... *Epith.* 138

Crysogone. *See* **Chrysogone.**

Crystal. *Christall* frises, ... *Bel.*[1] iv. 3

lively streame, more cleere than *Christall* is, ... *Rev.* iv. 12

shining *Christall,* which from top to base . . . . *Bel.* ii. 6

As cleare as *Christall* . . . . *Bel.* xii. 2

the fryses *christall,* . . . . *Bel.*[2] iv. 3

to kisse their *christall* faces, ... *S.C.* Jun. 30

Her owne like image in a *christall* brooke. . . . . *Gn.* 88

fresh springing wells, as *christall* neate, ... *Gn.* 119

looke into the *Christall* firmament: . . . . *T.M.* 506

where the *christall* Thamis wont to slide . . . . *Ti.* 134

To mount aloft unto the *Cristall* skie, ... *Mui.* 44

parching drougth drie up the *christall* wells; . . . . *D.* 333

Both *christall* wells and shadie groves forsooke, ... *As.* 45

Thereby a *christall* streame did gently play, ... I. i. 34. 8

Fidelia . . . Like sunny beames threw from her *Christall* face I. x. 12. 7

that bright towre, all built of *christall* clene, ... I. x. 58. 5

Some wrestle, some do run, some bathe in *christall* flood. . . . I. xii. 7. 9

all of *Christall* did Panthea build: . . . . II. x. 73. 4

The trembling groves, the *christall* running by, ... II. xii. 58. 7

drops of *Christall* seemd for wantones to weep. . . . . . . II. xii. 61. 9

through the *christall* waves appeared plaine: . . . . II. xii. 64. 7

Crystal—*Continued.*

The *Christall* humor stood congealed rownd; . . . . III. v. 29. 4

soone as calmed was the *christall* ayre, ... III. v. 51. 8

adowne out of her *christall* eyne . . . . III. vii. 9. 1

As she sate carelesse by a *cristall* flood . . . . IV. ii. 45. 4

Laomedia like the *christall* sheene; . . . . IV. xi. 51. 3

Upon the litle brest, like *christall* bright, ... VI. xii. 7. 7

up-held With thousand *Crystall* pillors . . . . VII. vi. 10. 4

Nor unto *Cristall;* for nought may them sever; . . . . *Am.* ix. 11

in your glasse of *cristall* clene, ... *Am.* xlv. 1

Clearer then *cristall,* would therein appere. . . . . *Am.* xlv. 12

Behold your faces as the *christall* bright, ... *Epith.* 64

And, last, that mightie shining *christall* wall, ... *H.H.B.* 41

floating on the *Christal* Flood; . . . . *Proth.* 57

Crystal-glass. His face, more cleare then *Christall glasse,* . . *S.C.* Jul. 159

As cleare as the *christall glasse;* . . . . *S.C.* Au. 80

the streame, as cleare as *christall glas:* . . . . I. vii. 6. 3

like to *christall glasse,* . . . . IV. x. 39. 7

the waves, glittering like *Christall glas.* . . . . IV. xi. 27. 3

Crystal-stone. face did seeme as cleare as *Christall stone,* . . III. i. 15. 4

Crystalline. their yellow heare *Christalline* humor dropped . . II. xii. 65. 6

Cteatus. The rich *Cteatus;* and Eurytus long; . . . . IV. xi. 14. 1

Cubits. frame, An hundred *cubits* (*cubites*[1]) high . . . . . *Bel.* ii. 2

Cubits'. depth exceeded not three *cubits* hight, ... II. xii. 62. 6

Cubs. He fed his *cubs* with fat of all the soyle, ... *Hub.* 1151

Cuckold. Whom she hath vow'd to dub a fayre *Cucquold.* . . . III. x. 11. 5

Cuckoo. The merry *Cuckow,* messenger of Spring, ... *Am.* xix. 1

unlesse she turne to thee Ere *Cuckow* end . . . . *Am.* xix. 14

So does the *Cuckow,* when the Mavis sings, ... *Am.* lxxxiv. 3

Cud. chaw the tender prickles in her *Cud;* . . . . *Gn.* 86

Long thus he chawd the *cud* of inward griefe, ... III. x. 18. 1

She chaw'd the *cud* of lover's carefull plight; . . . . V. v. 27. 2

Chawing the *cud* of griefe and inward paine, ... V. vi. 19. 2

Cuddy. *Cuddie,* I wote thou kenst little good, ... *S.C.* F. 85

Sike a judge as *Cuddie* were for a king. . . . . *S.C.* Au. 52

Now say it, *Cuddie,* as thou art a ladde: . . . . *S.C.* Au. 143

Cuddie, fresh *Cuddie,* the liefest boye, ... *S.C.* Au. 195

Cuddie, for shame! hold up thy heavye head, ... *S.C.* O. 1

What good thereof to *Cuddie* can arise? . . . . *S.C.* O. 18

Cuddie, the prayse is better then the price, ... *S.C.* O. 19

Cuddie shall have a Kidde to store his farme. . . . . *S.C.* O. 120

a bonie swaine, That *Cuddy* hight, ... *Col.* 81

(then *Cuddy* sayd) . . . . *Col.* 290

'Ah! *Cuddy* (then quoth Colin) . . . . *Col.* 292

'Colin, (said *Cuddy* then) . . . . *Col.* 616

some celestiall rage Of love (quoth *Cuddy*) . . . . *Col.* 824

Cuddy's. So mought our *Cuddies* name to heaven sownde. . . *S.C.* O. 54

Cuds. The whiles his flock their chawed *cuds* do eate. . . . . *Gn.* 144

Cuff. Who well it wards, and quyteth *cuff* with *cuff:* . . . . . I. ii. 17. 3

Cuffing. Now *cuffing* close, now chacing to and fro, ... IV. iv. 29. 6

Cuirass. Instead of *Curiets* and bases fit for fight. . . . . . V. v. 20. 9

Stayd not, till through his *curat* it did glyde, ... V. viii. 34. 8

His shield, his helmet, and his *curats* bare; . . . . VI. v. 8. 7

Cullambine, -bynes. *See* **Columbine, -s.**

Culver. More light then *Culver* in the Faulcons fist. . . . . . II. vii. 34. 6

in foote doth beare A trembling *Culver,* . . . . III. vii. 39. 2

the *Culver,* on the bared bough, Sits mourning . . . . *Am.* lxxxviii. 1

Culverins. As three great *Culverings* for battrie bent, ... V. x. 34. 6

Culvers. Like wofull *Culvers,* doo sit wayling now, ... *T.M.* 246

Cumbered. whiles he strove his *combred* clubbe to quight . . . I. viii. 10. 4

whiles he *combred* was therewith so sore, ... V. xii. 22. 8

Whom when as he thus *combred* did behold, ... VI. iv. 22. 1

Cumbers. Thy wast bignes but *combers* the grownd, ... *S.C.* F. 133

Cumbrous. With mortall cares and *cumbrous* worlds anoy! . . . *Ti.* 305

A cloud of *cumbrous* gnattes doe him molest, ... I. i. 23. 5

combrous conflict which they did sustaine, ... II. ix. 17. 5

streight his *combrous* armes aside did lay . . . . VI. v. 10. 6

Me no such cares nor *combrous* thoughts offend, ... VI. ix. 22. 6

Cumin. *Cummin* good for eyes, ... *Mui.* 188

Cumming. *See* **Coming.**

Cundah. fierce *Cundah* gan shortly to envy . . . . II. x. 33. 2

Cunedag, Cunedagius. *See* **Cundah.**

Cunning. Yet, as I conne, my *conning* I will strayne. . . . . *S.C.* N. 52

Made me by arte more *cunning* in the same. . . . . *S.C.* D. 42

all the *cunning* meanes he could devise: . . . . *Hub.* 847

No counterpoint of *cunning* policie, ... *Hub.* 1140

his *cunning* theeveries He wonts to worke, ... *Hub.* 1287

judge of Natures *cunning* operation, ... *T.M.* 501

Might in their divers *cunning* ever dare . . . . *Mui.* 367

Of each a part I stole by *cunning* thefte: . . . . *Ded.Son.* xvii.13

he by *conning* sleights in at the window crept. . . . . I. iii. 17. 9

His *cunning* hand gan to his wounds to lay, ... I. v. 44. 2

to discry the crafty *cunning* traine, ... I. vii. 1. 2

An Altare, carv'd with *cunning* ymagery, ... I. viii. 36. 2

hopelesse, hartlesse, gan the *cunning* thiefe Perswade us dye, I. ix. 29. 7

That *conning* Architect of cancred guyle, ... II. i. 1. 1

With *cunning* traynes him to entrap unwares, ... II. i. 4. 2

In *cunning* sleightes and practick knavery. . . . . II. iii. 9. 6

by Natures *cunning* hand Bene choycely picked out . . . . . . II. vi. 12. 3

Arachne high did lifte Her *cunning* web, ... II. vii. 28. 8

yvory Which *cunning* Craftesman hand hath overlayd . . . . . II. ix. 41. 6

As well in curious instruments as *cunning* laies. . . . . . . II. x. 59. 9

defects From her most *cunning* hand escaped bee; . . . . . . II. xii. 23. 4

with *cunning* hand was pourtrahed The love of Venus . . . . III. i. 34. 3

Framed in goldsmithes forge and *cunning* hand: . . . . IV. vi. 20. 4

goldsmithes *cunning* could not understand . . . . IV. vi. 20. 5

to his *cunning* feat The stubborne mettall seeketh to subdew, . V. v. 7. 6

So well as could with *cunning* hand be wrought, ... V. vii. 6. 3

your selfe were caught in *cunning* snare . . . . *Am.* lxxi. 5

want of *cunning* made me bold, ... *Epig.* i. 3

Cunningly. At that good knight so *cunningly* didst rove, . . I. Pr. 3. 3
bricke, Which *cunningly* was without morter laid, ... I. iv. 4. 2
Were ruinous and old, but painted *cunningly*. . . . . . . I. iv. 5. 9
Bardes, that . . . Can tune their timely voices *cunningly*; . I. v. 3. 7
With boughes and arbours woven *cunningly*, ... II. vi. 2. 8
Of that same wood it fram'd was *cunningly*, ... II. xii. 41. 1
(so *cunningly* the rude And scorned partes were mingled . . II. xii. 59. 1
that same net so *cunningly* was wound, ... II. xii. 82. 2
So *cunningly* enwoven were, ... IV. xi. 27. 4
So *cunningly* she wrought her crafts assay, ... V. v. 52. 5
in her person *cunningly* did shade . . . . V. vii. 3. 3
with sly skill so *cunningly* them dresses, ... *Am.* xxxvii. 3
Cup. wine of hooredome in a *cup* she bare. . . . . *Rev.* ii. 8
betweene the *Cuppe* And golden Diademe: . . . . *S.C.* Jul. 19
such a *cup* hast thou ever sene? . . . . *S.C.* Au. 35
his *cup* embost with Imagery . . . . *Gn.* 103
Then tooke the angrie witch her golden *cup*, ... I. viii. 14. 1
Her golden *cup* she cast unto the ground, ... I. viii. 25. 2
in her right hand bore a *cup* of gold, ... I. x. 13. 2
With *cup* thus charmd him parting she deceivd; . . . . . . II. i. 55. 3
In her left hand a *Cup* of gold she held, ... II. xii. 56. 1
Whose sappy liquor . . . Into her *cup* she scruzd . . . . . II. xii. 56. 4
The *cup* to ground did violently cast, ... II. xii. 57. 3
The guilty *cup* she fained to mistake, ... III. ix. 31. 2
Whom Jove . . . chose his *cup* to beare; . . . . III. xii. 7. 4
in her other hand a *cup* she hild, ... IV. iii. 42. 8
Her golden *cup* to them for drinke she raught, ... IV. iii. 48. 8
That I mote drinke the *cup* whereof she dranke, ... V. i. 15. 7
Cupid. *Cupide* . . . Did lend her secret aide, ... *Mui.* 126
Cupid selfe of them ashamed is, ... *Col.* 768
pure and spotlesse *Cupid* forth she brought, ... *Col.* 803
Hast *Cupid* selfe depainted in his kynd, ... *Col.* 898
Like as *Cupido* on Idaean hill, ... II. viii. 6. 1
litle *Cupid* playd His wanton sportes, ... II. ix. 34. 6
Cupid still emongest them kindled lustfull fyres. . . . . . III. i. 39. 9
she her dearest sonne *Cupido* sought, ... III. vi. 20. 7
Pleasure, the daughter of *Cupid* and Psyche late. . . . . . III. vi. 50. 9
Cupid selfe, it seeing, close did smyle . . . . III. x. 5. 7
cruell *Cupid*, not herewith content, ... III. xi. 38. 7
The maske of *Cupid*, and th' enchanted Chamber . . . . . . III. xii. Arg.
Cupid their eldest brother; . . . . IV. x. 42. 7
Cupid, with his killing bow . . . . IV. x. 55. 3
on a day, when *Cupid* kept his court, ... VI. vii. 32. 6
Which when as *Cupid* heard, he wexed wroth; . . . . VI. vii. 33. 6
All which when *Cupid* heard, ... VI. vii. 35. 3
Cupid selfe about her fluttred all in greene. . . . . VII. vii. 34. 9
Such as they faine Dan *Cupid* to have beene, ... VII. vii. 46. 7
spheare of *Cupid* fourty yeares containes: . . . . *Am.* lx. 10
She chaunst to come where *Cupid* lay, ... *Epig.* ii. 2
to my Dame How little *Cupid* humbly came, ... *Epig.* iii. 2
never blush, *Cupid*, quoth I, ... *Epig.* iii. 7
Cupid's. freed is from *Cupids* yoke by fate, ... *Col.* 566
Cupids wanton snare As hell she hated; . . . . I. x. 30. 5
Mars is *Cupidoes* frend, ... II. vi. 35. 7
had not yet felt *Cupides* wanton rage; . . . . II. ix. 18. 2
all *Cupids* warres they did repeate, ... III. xi. 29. 5
To shew Dan *Cupids* powre and great effort: . . . . III. xi. 46. 5
quenched is with *Cupids* greater flame: . . . . IV. ix. 2. 2
Cupids man with Venus mayd to hold, ... IV. x. 54. 7
wondred much at *Cupids* judg'ment wise, ... VI. viii. 25. 2
Love wounded my Loves hart, But Diane beasts with *Cupids* dart. *Epig.* ii. 8
Cups. Let powre in lavish *cups* and thriftie bitts . . . . . . *S.C.* O. 105
Nereus crownes with *cups*; his mates him pledg around. . . . I. iii. 31. 9
aye the *cups* their bancks did overflow; . . . . III. i. 51. 6
betweene the *cups* she did prepare Way to her love, ... III. i. 51. 7
Poure not by *cups*, but by the belly full, ... *Epith.* 251
Cur. thy Ball is a bold bigge *curre*, ... *S.C.* S. 164
Never had shepheard so kene a *kurre*, ... *S.C.* S. 182
As Shepheardes *curre*, that in darke evenings shade . . . . II. vi. 39. 4
Like as a *curre* doth felly bite and teare . . . . IV. viii. 36. 5
that *curre*, barking with bitter sownd, ... VI. v. 19. 5
Feeling some *curre* behinde his heeles to bite, ... VI. vi. 27. 6
Curate. Being some honest *Curate*, or some Vicker . . . . . *Hub.* 429
Curat(s). *See* **Cuirass.**
Curb. As stubborne steed, that is with *curb* restrained, ... *D.* 194
As much disdayning to the *curbe* to yield: . . . . I. i. 1. 7
Gan coyne streight lawes to *curb* their liberty: . . . . . . III. ii. 2. 6
Lordings *curbe* that commons over-aw, ... V. ii. 38. 8
Curbed. His stubborne steed with *curbed* canon bitt, ... I. vii. 37. 6
that proud avenging boy . . . *curbd* my libertee. . . . . . . I. ix. 12. 4
Curdled. With *crudled* blood and filthie gore deformed, . . . *As.* 152
crudled cold his corage gan assayle, ... I. vii. 6. 7
through every vaine The *crudled* cold ran . . . . I. ix. 52. 2
Curdles. *cruddles* the blood and pricks the harte: . . . . . . *S.C.* F. 46
Cur dog. this *Curdog*, by my coste, (Meaning the Foxe) . . . *Hub.* 294
Is bayted of a mastiffe and a hound And a *curre-dog*, ... VI. v. 19. 3
Curds. give him *curds* and clouted Creame. . . . . *S.C.* N. 99
Curdy. His cruell wounds, with *cruddy* bloud congeald, . . . I. v. 29. 6
Whose clawes were newly dipt in *cruddy* blood, ... III. iii. 47. 5
in gore And *cruddy* blood enwallowed . . . . III. iv. 34. 8
Cure. kydst not ene to *cure* thy sore hart-roote, ... *S.C.* D. 93
Duessa . . . for His *cure* to hell does goe. . . . . I. v. Arg.
let stay Aveugles sonne there in the leaches *cure*; . . . . . . I. v. 44. 6
a Leach, . . . could *cure* the same: . . . . I. x. 23. 9
Old Glauce cast to *cure* this Ladies griefe; . . . . III. iii. 5. 2
To *cure* her sonne, as he his faith had lent, ... IV. xii. 23. 4
From your owne will to *cure* your maladie. . . . . VI. vi. 7. 3
Who can him *cure* that will be cur'd of none? . . . . VI. vi. 7. 4
Cured. cleanly cover that cannot be *cured*: . . . . *S.C.* S. 138
Una . . . joyous of his *cured* conscience, ... I. x. 29. 3

Cured—*Continued.*
Ne can be *cured* of that cruell stroke . . . . IV. xi. 5. 8
his old hurt, which was not throughly *cured*. . . . . IV. xii. 23. 6
Who can him cure that will be *cur'd* of none? . . . . VI. vi. 7. 4
Cureless. Love is a *curelesse* sorrowe. . . . . *S.C.* Au. 104
doth with *curelesse* care consume the hart, ... III. x. 59. 6
now corrupt and *curelesse* they became: . . . . VI. vi. 2. 5
Cures. *Cures* all their sorrowes with one sweete aspect. . . . *H.B.* 245
Curiets. *See* **Cuirass.**
Curious. Corinth skil'd in *curious* workes to grave; . . . . . *Ro.* xxix. 4
Without vaine art or *curious* complements; . . . . *T.M.* 542
A *curious* Coffer made of Heben wood, ... *Ti.* 618
takes survey, with *curious* busie eye, ... *Mui.* 171
in *curious* skill Of workes with loome, ... *Mui.* 271
With this so *curious* networke to compare. . . . . *Mui.* 368
stand astonisht at his *curious* skill, ... *Col.* 8
yvory sheath, ycarv'd with *curious* slights, ... I. vii. 30. 7
apply Her *curious* skill the warbling notes to play, ... I. xii. 38. 7
entayld With *curious* antickes, ... II. iii. 27. 5
A worke of rich entayle and *curious* mould, ... II. vii. 4. 5
As well in *curious* instruments as cunning laies. . . . . . II. x. 59. 9
Most goodly it with *curious* ymageree Was overwrought, . . II. xii. 60. 5
to shifte their *curious* request, ... III. ix. 26. 1
With *curious* Corbes and pendants graven faire, ... IV. x. 6. 7
sense of man so coy and *curious* nice, ... IV. x. 22. 6
An hart not carried with too *curious* eyes, ... VI. ii. 16. 8
Painter . . . Which pictured Venus with so *curious* quill, . . *H.H.B.* 212
Curiously. glistering Burganet, . . . *curiously* engraven, . . *Mui.* 75
A gorgeous girdle, *curiously* embost . . . . IV. iv. 15. 6
basket, Made of fine twigs, entrayled *curiously*, ... *Proth.* 25
Curious-nice. *See* **Curious, Nice.**
Curius. wise *Curius*, companion Of noble vertues, ... *Gn.* 609
Curled. Some frounce their *curled* heare in courtly guise; . . I. iv. 14. 7
Curled with thousand adders venemous, ... I. v. 34. 3
curld uncombed heares Upstaring stiffe, ... I. ix. 22. 2
His snowy front, *curled* with golden heares, ... II. viii. 5. 5
With golden wyre to weave her *curled* head; . . . . III. viii. 7. 6
long *curld* locks that downe his shoulders shagged; . . . . . V. ix. 10. 6
Current. to prove whether his powre would pas As *currant*, . . *Hub.* 1095
divydes The doubtfull *current* into divers wayes. . . . . . IV. i. 42. 6
Drives backe the *current* of his kindly course, ... IV. iii. 27. 4
Currish. crueltie, the signe of *currish* kinde, ... *Hub.* 1134
more enfierced through his *currish* play, ... II. iv. 8. 6
Ne from his *currish* will a whit reclame. . . . . VI. iii. 43. 2
Curry. to *curry* favour With th' Elfin Knight, ... V. v. 35. 5
Cur's. he had eft learned a *curres* call,) . . . . *S.C.* S. 191
Curs. a Beare, whom angry *curres* have touzd, ... II. xi. 33. 3
Like dastard *Curres* . . . . III. i. 22. 1
As it had bene two shepheards *curres* . . . . V. xii. 38. 5
Curse. 'A thousand sithes I *curse* that carefull hower . . . . *S.C.* Ja. 49
I *curse* the stounde . . . . *S.C.* S. 56
Mischiefe light on him, and Gods great *curse!* . . . . *S.C.* S. 212
That *curse* God send unto mine enemie! . . . . *Hub.* 914
'*Curse* on that Cross,' (quoth then the Sarazin,) . . . . . . I. ii. 18. 1
cry, and *curse*, and raile, and rend her heare, ... I. iii. 25. 2
all his seede the *curse* doth often cleave, ... II. viii. 29. 4
'Caytive, *curse* on thy cruell hond, ... II. viii. 37. 6
full of rage he gan to *curse* and sweare, ... IV. viii. 44. 2
blaspheme And *curse* his God . . . . IV. viii. 45. 7
There gan he me to *curse* . . . . VI. ii. 21. 4
we all are subject to that *curse*, ... VII. vi. 6. 8
There-on an heavy haplesse *curse* did lay; . . . . VII. vi. 55. 3
Cursed. blood Which she with *cursed* hands had shed before; . *Gn.* 174
go, *cursed* damosells, Whose bridale torches . . . . *Gn.* 393
against the others bodie bend His *cursed* steele, ... *Gn.* 413
who will record my *cursed* end? . . . . *U.V.* 20
This *cursed* creature, mindfull of that olde Enfested grudge, *Mui.* 353
forth caried Into the *cursed* cobweb, ... *Mui.* 423
hurling her hideous taile About her *cursed* head; . . . . . . I. i. 16. 3
fruitfull *cursed* spawne of serpents small, ... I. i. 22. 6
such a *cursed* creature lives so long a space.' . . . . I. i. 31. 9
He . . . *cursed* heven; . . . . I. i. 37. 5
A cruell witch, her *cursed* will to wreake, ... I. ii. 33. 5
He knocked fast, and often *curst*, and sware, ... I. iii. 16. 5
ten thousand sorts of punishment The *cursed* creatures . . . torment. . . . . I. v. 33. 9
besought Some *cursed* vengeaunce on his sonne to cast. . . . I. v. 38. 2
Antiochus, the which advaunst His *cursed* hand gainst God, . I. v. 47. 9
'Arise, thou *cursed* Miscreaunt, ... I. vi. 41. 1
their cruell *cursed* enemy . . . Their kingdome spoild, ... I. vii. 44. 1
That *cursed* wight, from whom I scapt whyleare, ... I. ix. 28. 4
That *cursed* man, low sitting on the ground, ... I. ix. 35. 2
Out of his hand she snatcht the *cursed* knife, ... I. ix. 52. 4
Arise, sir Knight, arise, and leave this cursed *place*.' . . . I. ix. 53. 9
blood, which cruelly was spilt On *cursed* tree, ... I. x. 57. 6
Till from her *cursed* foe thou have her freely quitt.' . . . . I. x. 63. 9
before that *cursed* Dragon got That happy land, ... I. xi. 29. 6
cursed steele against that badge I bent, ... II. i. 27. 5
cursed hand, hath plaid this cruell part, ... II. i. 44. 7
The *cursed* land where many wend amis, ... II. i. 51. 8
what *cursed* evil Spright, Or fell Erinnys, ... II. ii. 29. 1
Furor, *cursed* cruel wight, ... II. iv. 10. 6
teach the *cursed* steele to bight In his owne flesh, ... II. vi. 32. 8
'What dismall day hath lent this *cursed* light, ... II. vi. 43. 7
'That *cursed* man, that cruel feend of hell, ... II. vi. 50. 1
gan a *cursed* hand the quiet wombe . . . to wound, ... II. vii. 17. 1
well could weld That *cursed* weapon, ... II. vii. 40. 9
One *cursed* creature he by chaunce espide, ... II. vii. 57. 8
'Most *cursed* of all creatures under skye, ... II. vii. 59. 4
Then gan the *cursed* wretch alowd to cry, ... II. vii. 60. 6

Cursed—*Continued.*
His *cursed* life out of her lodge have rent; . . . . II. viii. 32. 3
'By Mahoune, *cursed* thiefe, ... II. viii. 33. 3
may Thy *cursed* hand so cruelly have swayd . . . . II. viii. 46. 7
yielding succour to that *cursed* Swaine, ... II. xi. 28. 5
One of Malegers *cursed* darts did take, ... II. xi. 47. 8
seemes some *cursed* witches deed, ... III. iii. 18. 8
Cursed the hand that did so deadly smight . . . . III. iv. 44. 4
cursed night that reft from him so goodly scope. . . . . III. iv. 52. 9
gan to make Exceeding mone, and *curst* that cruell chaunce III. vii. 45. 4
His *cursed* hand withheld, ... III. xii. 32. 9
gan streight to over-looke Those *cursed* leaves, ... III. xii. 36. 2
Where she in darknes wastes her *cursed* daies and nights. . IV. i. 19. 9
those same *cursed* seedes doe also serve To her for bread, . IV. i. 26. 1
both . . . with many a *cursed* oth Sweare she is yours, . . . IV. i. 47. 7
O *cursed* Eld! the cankerworme of writs, ... IV. ii. 33. 6
With *cursed* knife cutting the twist in twaine. . . . . IV. ii. 48. 8
The crime which *cursed* Ate kindled earst, ... IV. v. 31. 2
cursed usage and ungodly trade . . . . IV. vii. 12. 3
Where this same *cursed* caytive did appeare . . . . IV. vii. 24. 4
A *cursed* cruell Sarazin doth wonne, ... V. ii. 4. 6
curst the hand which did that vengeance on him dight. . . V. ii. 18. 9
with many a *cursed* threat, ... V. v. 47. 6
Like as the *cursed* son of Theseus, ... V. viii. 43. 1
all this *cursed* plot . . . discovered was betymes, ... V. ix. 42. 3
that old hag of hellish hew, The *cursed* Ate, ... V. ix. 47. 4
that *cursed* Idole, farre proclamed, ... V. x. 28. 4
Under that *cursed* Idols altar-stone . . . . V. x. 29. 2
curst, and band, and blasphemies forth threw . . . . V. xi. 12. 3
In sacrifize unto that *cursed* feend; . . . . V. xi. 20. 4
the *cursed* felon high did reare His cruell hand . . . . . . V. xii. 20. 2
with th' one of which she scratcht Her *cursed* head, ... V. xii. 30. 4
her *cursed* tongue, full sharpe and short, ... V. xii. 36. 3
The *cursed* Serpent . . . was not all so dead . . . . V. xii. 39. 5
their owne *cursed* tongs did straine. . . . . V. xii. 41. 9
That *cursed* caytive, my strong enemy, ... VI. vii. 16. 3
with *cursed* hands uncleane Whipping her horse, ... VI. vii. 39. 7
since th' Earths *cursed* seed Sought to assaile . . . . VII. vi. 20. 2
this off-scum of that *cursed* fry . . . . VII. vi. 30. 1
is there one more *cursed* then they all, ... *H.L.* 266
Curses. none of all those *curses* overtooke The warlike Maide, III. iv. 44. 6
With *curses* vaine in his avengefull ire; . . . . IV. viii. 40. 3
vile *curses* and reprochfull shame . . . . IV. xii. 16. 4
bitter *curses,* horrible to tell; . . . . V. xi. 28. 3
Cursing. ghosts . . . *Cursing* high Jove, ... I. v. 33. 6
Cursing his Gods, and him selfe damning deepe: . . . . . . II. viii. 37. 2
Cursing his hand that had that visage mard: . . . . V. v. 13. 4
Oft *cursing* th' heavens, that so cruell were To her, ... VI. xi. 33. 6
Curst. *See* **Cursed.**
Curtain. night had all displayd Her coleblacke *curtein* . . . . I. iv. 44. 2
day . . . Nights humid *curtaine* from the heavens withdrew, . V. v. 1. 2
Curtains. With silkin *curtens* and gold coverletts, ... II. vi. 16. 6
silken *courteins* over her display, ... *Epith.* 303
Curtaxe. With *curtaxe* used Diamond to smite, ... IV. ii. 42. 7
speare and *curtaxe* both usd Priamond in field. . . . . IV. ii. 42. 9
Curtius. constant *Curtius,* Who, stifly bent . . . . *Gn.* 602
Curtsie, -s. *See* **Courtesy, Courtesies.**
Custody. The third had of their wardrobe *custody,* . . . . . . I. x. 39. 1
Custom. Of *custome* for to survewe his grownd, ... *S.C.* F. 145
T' enquire of *custome,* what and whence they were? . . . . *Hub.* 245
Sate (as his *custome* was) upon a day, ... *Col.* 4
The *custome* of that place was such, ... IV. i. 9. 7
that both the *custome* showne Were kept, ... IV. i. 11. 7
As whylome was the *custome* ancient . . . . IV. vi. 44. 7
According to the *custome* of their law: . . . . V. ii. 11. 7
doth observe a *custome* lewd and ill, ... VI. i. 13. 3
it was to thee reprochfull blame To erect this wicked *custome,* VI. vi. 34. 4
Custometh. on a Bridge he *custometh* to fight, ... V. ii. 7. 6
Customs. wicked *customes* of that Bridge refourmed; . . . . . V. ii. 28. 8
breake bands of civilitie, And wicked *customes* make, ... VI. i. 26. 7
Cut. As halfe unwilling to *cutte* the graine; . . . . *S.C.* F. 204
cutte of hys dayes with untimely woe, ... *S.C.* May 199
To *cut* the ships from turning home againe To Argos; . . . *Gn.* 522
His breeches were made after the new *cut,* . . . . *Hub.* 211
th' Apes long taile . . . he quight *Cut* off, ... *Hub.* 1382
They have *cut* downe, and all their pleasaunce mard, ... *T.M.* 281
In liquid waves to *cut* their fomie waie, ... *Ti.* 149
His owne cote he would *cut,* . . . . I. x. 39. 9
he *cutt* a lock of all their heare, ... II. i. 61. 2
Gan with new rage their shieldes to hew and *cut;* . . . . . . II. ii. 23. 7
It *cut* away upon the yielding wave, ... II. vi. 5. 6
fixed at his backe to *cut* his ayery wayes. . . . . II. viii. 5. 9
this sad realme, *cut* into sondry shayres . . . . II. x. 37. 4
Too rathe *cut* off by practise criminall . . . . III. iii. 28. 8
her way does *cut* amaine, ... III. ix. 49. 5
He wilfully did *cut* and shape anew; . . . . IV. vii. 40. 2
When as he saw she should be *cut* in twaine, ... V. i. 27. 4
better to reforme then to *cut* off the ill. . . . . V. x. 2. 9
Whose gealous dread . . . Is wont to *cut* off all . . . . VI. ii. 29. 6
the necke thereof did *cut* in twaine, ... VI. iii. 17. 5
Time shall soon *cut* down with his consuming sickle. . . . . VII. viii. 1. 9
Either with nimble wings to *cut* the skies, ... *H.H.L.* 66
Cuts. *See* **Cross-cuts.**
Cutting. *See* **Air-cutting.**
he, *cutting* way With his broad sayles, ... I. xi. 18. 6
With cursed knife *cutting* the twist in twaine. . . . . IV. ii. 48. 8
cutting off through hasty accidents, ... *Epith.* 429
Cybele. Old *Cybele,* arayd with pompous pride, ... IV. xi. 28. 4
Cybele's. *Cybeles* franticke rites have made them mad: . . . I. vi. 15. 3
Cycilly. *See* **Caecily.**
Cyclops. Then doo the Aetnean *Cyclops* him affray, ... *Gn.* 541

Cymbeline. *See* **Kimbeline.**
Cymbrian. when in *Cymbrian* plaine An heard of Bulles, . . . complaine, ... I. viii. 11. 5
Cymerian. *See* **Cimmerian.**
Cymo. *Cymo,* Eupompe, and Themiste just; . . . . IV. xi. 51. 6
Cymochles. 'Pyrochles . . . The brother of *Cymochles,* . . . II. iv. 41. 5
Atin to *Cymochles* for ayd flyes. . . . . II. v. Arg.
whom *Cymochles* men did call. . . . . II. v. 25. 9
There Atin fownd *Cymochles* sojourning, ... II. v. 28. 1
'*Cymochles;* oh! no, but Cymochles shade, ... II. v. 35. 4
Guyon . . . Fights with *Cymochles,* . . . . II. vi. Arg.
Whom bold *Cymochles* traveiling to finde, ... II. vi. 2. 1
when far off *Cymochles* heard and saw, ... II. vi. 4. 1
Cymochles of her questioned Both what she was, ... II. vi. 9. 2
Cymochles, that had never mett before So puissant foe, . . II. vi. 30. 1
Cymochles with that wanton mayd . . . . II. vi. 40. 8
Then sayd *Cymochles:* 'Palmer, thou doest dote, ... II. viii. 14. 1
To whom *Cymochles* said; 'For what art thou, ... II. viii. 28. 1
speare he thrust . . . At proud *Cymochles,* . . . . II. viii. 36. 4
with his troncheon he so rudely stroke *Cymochles* twise, . . II. viii. 39. 9
Eft to *Cymochles* twise so many fold; . . . . II. viii. 41. 5
when *Cymochles* saw the fowle reproch, ... II. viii. 44. 1
Cymochles'. 'Cymochles; oh! no, but *Cymochles* shade, . . . II. v. 35. 4
by this *Cymochles* howre was spent, ... II. vi. 27. 1
Cymochles sword on Guyons shield yglaunst, ... II. vi. 31. 3
Cymodoce. *Cymodoce,* and stout Autonoe, ... IV. xi. 50. 6
the mother was Of luckless Marinell, *Cymodoce;* . . . . . IV. xi. 53. 7
Amongst the rest was faire *Cymodoce,* . . . . IV. xii. 3. 6
Cymoent. His mother was the blacke-browd *Cymoent,* . . . . III. iv. 19. 3
Drew the smooth charett of sad *Cymoent:* . . . . III. iv. 33. 2
Cymothoe. Lightfoote *Cymothoe,* and sweete Melite, ... IV. xi. 49. 4
Cynthia. 'Shewe thyselfe, *Cynthia,* with thy silver rayes, . . . *S.C.* Ap. 82
Of *Cynthia* the Ladie of the Sea, ... *Col.* 166
wend with him, his *Cynthia* to see; . . . . *Col.* 186
a great shepheardesse, that *Cynthia* hight, ... *Col.* 234
surges hie, On which faire *Cynthia* her heards doth feed: . . *Col.* 241
the shepheards which my *Cynthia* serve At sea, ... *Col.* 260
land and sea my *Cynthia* doth deserve . . . . *Col.* 262
the fields In which dame *Cynthia* her landheards fed; . . . *Col.* 277
In faithfull service of faire *Cynthia:* . . . . *Col.* 381
were he knowne to *Cynthia* as he ought, ... *Col.* 402
do their *Cynthia* immortall make: . . . . *Col.* 453
favour thee, and honour *Cynthia:* . . . . *Col.* 458
great *Cynthia* her in chiefest grace Doth hold, ... *Col.* 500
Worthie next after *Cynthia* to tread, ... *Col.* 514
She there then waited upon *Cynthia,* . . . . *Col.* 520
Besides yet many mo that *Cynthia* serve, ... *Col.* 576
lambs . . . Ile teach to call for *Cynthia* by name. . . . . . *Col.* 639
With *Cynthia* and all her noble crew; . . . . *Col.* 653
those that do to *Cynthia* expound . . . . *Col.* 743
Cynthia doth in sciences abound, ... *Col.* 745
Cynthia . . . doth steepe In silver deaw his ever-drouping hed, I. i. 39. 7
silver *Cynthia* wexed pale and faynt, ... I. vii. 34. 8
'Now had fayre *Cynthia* . . . measured . . . . II. i. 53. 1
His *Cynthia,* his heavens fayrest light? . . . . III. Pr. 4. 6
Ne let his fayrest *Cynthia* refuse . . . . III. Pr. 5. 5
As when fayre *Cynthia,* in darkesome night, ... III. i. 43. 1
Where *Cynthia* raignes in everlasting glory, ... VII. vi. 8. 2
Where *Cynthia* did sit, that never still did stand. . . . . . VII. vi. 8. 9
Was striving with faire *Cynthia* for her seat; . . . . VII. vi. 17. 3
none of all there-in more pleasure found Then *Cynthia,* . . . VII. vi. 38. 7
Cynthia; whom so much ye make Joves dearest darling, . . VII. vii. 50. 2
Is it not *Cinthia,* she that never sleepes, ... *Epith.* 374
Cynthia doth shend The lesser starres. . . . . *Proth.* 121
Cynthia's. as Dame *Cynthias* silver raye, ... *S.C.* Au. 89
could great *Cynthiaes* sore displeasure breake, ... *Col.* 174
To wash faire *Cynthiaes* sheep, when they be shorne, . . . *Col.* 258
put us all ashore on *Cynthias* land. . . . . *Col.* 289
Untill that we to *Cynthiaes* presence came: . . . . *Col.* 332
'By wondring at thy *Cynthiaes* praise, ... *Col.* 353
Best knowne by bearing up great *Cynthiaes* traine: . . . . *Col.* 509
great *Cynthiaes* goodnesse, and high grace, ... *Col.* 588
Let thy faire *Cinthias* praises be thus rudely showne . . . *Ded.Son.*viii.14
To bid her leave faire *Cynthias* silver bower; . . . . VII. vi. 18. 7
him esteemed nought, No more then *Cynthia's* selfe; . . . . VII. vi. 18. 9
Cynthia's selfe, more angry then the rest, ... VII. vi. 51. 1
Cynthus. Of swift Eurotas, or on *Cynthus* greene, ... II. iii. 31. 2
Latonaes sonne After his chace on woodie *Cynthus* . . . . . VI. ii. 25. 5
she was bred and nurst On *Cynthus* hill, ... VII. vii. 50. 4
Cyparesse. *See* **Cypress.**
Cyparissa. ginneth to revive His ancient love, and dearest *Cyparisse;* . . . . I. vi. 17. 2
Cypress. balefull boughes of *Cypres* doen advaunce; . . . . . *S.C.* N. 145
the sweete *Cypresse,* signe of deadly bale. . . . . *Gn.* 216
Vouchsafe to deck the same with *Cyparesse;* . . . . *D.* 529
the *Cypresse* funerall; . . . . I. i. 8. 9
governing . . . aged limbs on *cypresse* stadle stout, ... I. vi. 14. 8
with sad *Cypresse* seemely it embrace; . . . . II. i. 60. 3
There mournfull *Cypresse* grew in greatest store, ... II. vii. 52. 1
Sweet is the *Cypresse,* but his rynd is tough; . . . . *Am.* xxvi. 5
Cyprian. the *Cyprian* goddesse, newly borne . . . . II. xii. 65. 3
ye three handmayds of the *Cyprian* Queene, ... *Epith.* 103
thy soveraine might, O *Cyprian* Queene! . . . . *H.B.* 55
Cyprus. That which was in Paphos built, Or that in *Cyprus,* . IV. x. 5. 7
Cyrus'. Ooraxes, feared for great *Cyrus* fate, ... IV. xi. 21. 5
Cytherea. Faire *Cytheree,* the Mother of delight, ... *T.M.* 397
The Archer God, the sonne of *Cytheree,* . . . . *Mui.* 98
Goodly she gan faire *Cytherea* greet, ... III. vi. 20. 1
All those, O *Cytherea!* . . . . *H.B.* 260
Cytheron. Whether in Paphos, or *Cytheron* hill, ... III. vi. 29. 4
her owne *Cytheron* . . . She in regard hereof refusde . . . . VI. x. 9. 6

D

Daedal. His *daedale* hand would faile and greatly faynt, . . . III. Pr. 2. 4
doth the *daedale* earth throw forth to thee . . . IV. x. 45. 1
Daemogorgon's. *See* **Demogorgon's.**
Daffadowndillies. Strowe me the ground with *Daffadowndillies*, *S.C.* Ap. 140
Daffodillies. Thy sommer prowde, with *Daffadillies* dight; . . . *S.C.* Ja. 22
With Damaske roses and *Daffadillies* set: . . . *S.C.* Ap. 60
With Roses dight and Goolds and *Daffadillies;* . . . *Col.* 339
Gathering sweete *daffadillyes*, to have made Gay girlonds . . . III. iv. 29. 8
her in *daffadillies* sleeping made . . . III. xi. 32. 4
Dagger. neither sword nor *dagger* he did beare; . . . *Hub.* 215
on his *dagger* still his hand he held, . . . I. iv. 33. 8
He to him raught a *dagger* sharpe and keene, . . . I. ix. 51. 2
Daily. Neroes and Caligulaes . . . must *dayly* rayse?' . . . *Bel.*² x. 14
whiles that my *daylie* cares did sleepe, . . . *Van.* i. 1
Albee my love he seeke with *dayly* suit; . . . *S.C.* Ja. 56
Which I your poore Vassall *dayly* endure; . . . *S.C.* F. 153
Now she is a stone, And makes *dayly* mone, . . . *S.C.* Ap. 89
The fame whereof doth *dayly* greater growe. . . . *S.C.* Jun. 92
To renne hys *daily* race, . . . *S.C.* Jul. 60
helmes unbruzed wexen *daily* browne. . . . *S.C.* O. 42
Dye would we *dayly*, . . . *S.C.* N. 186
How manie honest men see ye arize *Daylie* . . . *Hub.* 420
daylie more augment . . . *Hub.* 691
he *daylie* doth devise: . . . *Hub.* 738
He *daylie* eekes, and brings to excellence. . . . *Hub.* 792
Darknesse more than Cymerians *daylie* night: . . . *T.M.* 256
I *dayly* starve, . . . *U.V.* 17
I doo *dailie* see things highest placed, . . . *Ti.* 180
perills lie in close awaite About us *daylie*, . . . *Mui.* 222
dayly dooth my weaker wit possesse, . . . *D.* 30
Daylie resort to me from farre and neare, . . . *D.* 143
daylie doth her changefull counsels bend . . . *D.* 153
To carelesse heavens I doo *daylie* call; . . . *D.* 354
She . . . Will send for me; for which I *daylie* long; . . . *D.* 390
'So doo I live, so doo I *daylie* die, . . . *D.* 435
Which *daily* more and more he did augment, . . . *As.* 19
To her my thoughts I *daily* dedicate, . . . *Col.* 472
A thousand yong ones, which she *dayly* fed, . . . I. i. 15. 5
Through woods and wastnes wide him *daily* sought; . . . I. iii. 3. 8
To many knights did *daily* worke disgrace; . . . I. iii. 29. 4
a dry dropsie . . . by misdiet *daily* greater grew. . . . I. iv. 23. 8
daily care To get, and nightly feare to lose his owne, . . . I. iv. 28. 7
the thing, which *daily* yet I rew, . . . I. v. 42. 2
to make him *daily* fall, . . . I. viii. 1. 2
further from it *daily* wanderest: . . . I. ix. 40. 3
bare wretched wights he *dayly* clad, . . . I. x. 39. 6
Here hauntes that feend, and does his *dayly* spoyle; . . . I. xi. 2. 3
Titan rose to runne his *daily* race; . . . I. xi. 33. 2
All were she *daily* with himselfe in place, . . . I. xii. 23. 7
death him did awaite in *daily* wretchednesse. . . . I. xii. 33. 9
daily . . . Regions are discovered, . . . II. Pr. 2. 3
Still did they strive and *daily* disagree; . . . II. ii. 13. 7
daily warre against his foeman moves, . . . II. ii. 19. 3
Which in her cott she *daily* practized? . . . II. vi. 9. 4
dying *dayly*, *dayly* yet revive. . . . II. vi. 45. 4
He *daily* dyde, yet never throughly dyen couth. . . . II. vii. 58. 9
Some *daily* seene and knowen by their names, . . . II. ix. 50. 6
Romanes *daily* did the weake subdew: . . . II. x. 54. 5
daily spectacle of sad decay: . . . II. x. 62. 5
they *dayly* made most dreadfull battery. . . . II. xi. 7. 9
th' ulcer groweth *daily* more and more; . . . III. ii. 39. 5
his bad deedes, which *daily* he increast, . . . III. v. 14. 7
Daily she dressed him, . . . III. v. 41. 5
Whiles *dayly* playsters to his wownd she layd, . . . III. v. 43. 5
Daily they grow, and *daily* forth are sent . . . III. vi. 36. 1
Dayly he tempted her with this or that, . . . III. viii. 39. 1
continuall battery will rive, Or *daily* siege, . . . III. x. 10. 3
Calling men to their *daily* exercize: . . . III. xii. 28. 7
dayly more offensive unto each degree. . . . IV. i. 18. 9
all dissention which doth *dayly* grow . . . IV. i. 19. 2
Yet he to her did *dayly* service more, . . . IV. ii. 11. 1
dayly more deceived was thereby; . . . IV. ii. 11. 2
his *dayly* feare His ydle braine gan busily molest, . . . IV. v. 43. 6
dayly feasting both in bowre and hall, . . . IV. vi. 39. 7
heaping stormes of trouble on them *daily* more? . . . IV. vii. 1. 9
dayly yet thou doest the same repayre; . . . IV. x. 47. 2
In which I *daily* dying am too long: . . . IV. xii. 9. 5
Ne *dayly* food did take, ne nightly sleepe, . . . IV. xii. 19. 8
once amisse growes *daily* wourse and wourse: . . . V. Pr. 1. 9
dayly he his wrongs encreaseth more; . . . V. ii. 6. 1
th' earth it selfe how *daily* its increast . . . V. ii. 37. 6
things subject to thy *daily* vew . . . V. ii. 42. 8
Comaunded them their *daily* workes renew, . . . V. v. 1. 4
With *daily* shew of courteous kind behaviour, . . . V. v. 35. 7
So *daily* he faire semblant did her shew, . . . V. v. 56. 1
She *daily* told her love he did defye; . . . V. v. 56. 8
did attend Uppon the rites and *daily* sacrifize, . . . V. vii. 4. 3
Approving *daily* to their noble eyes . . . V. x. 5. 5
He offred up for *daily* sacrifize My children . . . V. xi. 19. 6
I long in vaine have bent . . . and *daily* meanes assay; . . . V. xi. 51. 4
Nymphs . . . Which *daily* may to thy sweete lookes repayre, . VI. ii. 25. 3
His best endevour and his *daily* paine . . . VI. iv. 16. 2
having long time, as his *daily* weed, . . . VI. iv. 19. 4
he dare not returne for all his *daily* vaunt. . . . VI. iv. 29. 9
that foule feend, who *dayly* doth attend . . . VI. iv. 31. 8

Daily—*Continued.*
The litle that I have growes *dayly* more . . . VI. ix. 21. 5
my flockes father *daily* doth amend it. . . . VI. ix. 21. 8
in the Princes gardin *daily* wrought: . . . VI. ix. 24. 8
daily doe behold The glorie of the great . . . VI. ix. 28. 1
your meane food shall be my *daily* feast, . . . VI. ix. 32. 3
Dayly beholding the faire Pastorell, . . . VI. ix. 34. 3
He *daily* did apply him selfe to donne All dewfull service, . . VI. x. 32. 5
daily more her favour to augment; . . . VI. x. 37. 2
With humble service, and with *daily* sute, . . . VI. x. 38. 2
darkenesse dred and *daily* night did hover . . . VI. x. 42. 5
With *dayly* service and attendance dew, . . . VI. xii. 5. 2
Through *daily* mourning and nightly misfare: . . . VI. xii. 14. 5
all this world is woxen *daily* worse. . . . VII. vi. 6. 6
We *daily* see new creatures to arize, . . . VII. vii. 18. 6
The beasts we *daily* see massacred dy . . . VII. vii. 19. 2
Which they did *daily* watch, and nightly wake . . . VII. vii. 45. 8
Dayly when I do seeke and sew for peace, . . . *Am.* xi. 1
dayly more augment my miseryes? . . . *Am.* xxxvi. 8
For that your selfe ye *dayly* such doe see: . . . *Am.* lxxix. 2
From whence declining *daily* by degrees, . . . *Epith.* 267
dayly are increast . . . *H.L.* 96
Those unto all he *daily* doth display, . . . *H.H.B.* 113
Daint. to cherish him with diets *daint*, . . . I. x. 2. 7
picturing the parts of beauty *daynt*, . . . III. Pr. 2. 7
to tell The diverse usage, and demeanure *daint*, . . . IV. i. 5. 2
Daintest. that may *dayntest* fantasy aggrate, . . . II. xii. 42. 7
Some with their eyes the *daintest* morsels chose; . . . VI. viii. 39. 4
Dainties. doth despise the *dainties* of the towne. . . . VI. ix. 7. 5
Deckt all with *dainties* of her seasons pryde, . . . VII. vii. 34. 2
Dainties'. To decke thy beautie with their *dainties* store, . . . *H.B.* 262
Daintiest. Full of sweete flowres and *daintiest* delights, . . . *Ti.* 520
*Or that may *dayntiest* fantasie aggrate, . . . II. xii. 42. 7
Daintily. With blossoms brave bedecked *daintily;* . . . I. vii. 32. 7
deckt with flowers and herbars *daintily:* . . . II. ix. 46. 2
With diverse flowres he *daintily* was deckt, . . . II. xii. 49. 1
Dainty. Ne car'd with them his *daintie* lips to sweeten: . . . *Van.* ii. 9
Cedar . . . That farre abroad her *daintie* odours threwe; . . . *Van.* vii. 3
'Ye *dayntye* Nymphs, that in this blessed brooke . . . *S.C.* Ap. 37
now ye *daintie* Damsells may depart . . . *S.C.* Ap. 147
The grassye ground with *daintye* Daysies dight, . . . *S.C.* Jun. 6
With troublous noyse did dull their *daintie* eares. . . . *T.M.* 30
deckt with *daintie* flowres, . . . *Ti.* 634
up she tooke Her *daintie* feete, . . . *Mui.* 284
Of gentle wit and *daintie* sweet device, . . . *As.* Interl. 218
And *dainty* love learnd sweetly to endite. . . . *Ded. Son.* viii. 7
Whose grosse defaults thy *daintie* pen may file, . . . *Ded. Son.* xii. 11
so *dainty*, they say, maketh derth. . . . I. ii. 27. 9
thinking . . . to frame A girlond for her *dainty* forehead fit, . I. ii. 30. 7
on the grasse her *dainty* limbs did lay . . . I. iii. 4. 3
The warlike youthes, on *dayntie* couches layd, . . . I. iv. 44. 3
daintie spices fetch from furthest Ynd, . . . I. v. 4. 6
store they fownd of al that *dainty* was and rare. . . . I. viii. 50. 9
a royall Mayd Her *daintie* limbes . . . down did lay: . . . I. ix. 13. 8
In ashes and sackcloth he did array His *daintie* corse, . . . I. x. 26. 2
deck with *dainty* flowres their brydall bed, . . . I. x. 42. 3
ne once adowne would lay Her *dainty* limbs . . . I. xi. 32. 8
streame of Balme, most soveraine And *dainty* deare, . . . I. xi. 48. 3
What needes of *dainty* dishes to devize . . . I. xii. 14. 3
To spoyle her *dainty* corps, so faire and sheene . . . II. i. 10. 5
stray about her *daintie* eares. . . . II. ii. 15. 9
Their minds to pleasure, and their mouths to *dainty* fare. . . II. ii. 33. 9
did divide Her *daintie* paps; . . . II. iii. 29. 7
In *daintie* delices, and lavish joyes, . . . II. v. 28. 6
daintie odours round about them threw: . . . II. v. 29. 6
does yield to vew Her *dainty* limbes . . . II. v. 33. 8
No *daintie* flowre or herbe that growes on grownd, . . . II. vi. 12. 6
A *daintie* damsell dressing of her heare, . . . II. xii. 14. 8
with *daintie* breach Of her fine fingers, . . . II. xii. 56. 4
the most *daintie* Paradise on ground . . . II. xii. 58. 1
ne car'd to hyde Their *dainty* partes . . . II. xii. 63. 9
all that mote delight a *daintie* eare, . . . II. xii. 70. 2
She secretly would search each *daintie* lim, . . . III. i. 36. 6
Him to a *dainty* flowre she did transmew, . . . III. i. 38. 8
Their *daintie* layes and dulcet melody, . . . III. i. 40. 4
Nought wanted there that *dainty* was and rare, . . . III. i. 51. 5
every *daintie* limbe with horrour shake; . . . III. ii. 5. 5
often steepe Her *dainty* couch with teares . . . III. ii. 28. 9
Beside the same a *dainty* place there lay, . . . III. v. 40. 1
That *daintie* Rose, the daughter of her Morne, . . . III. v. 51. 1
From off their *dainty* limbs the dusty sweat . . . III. vi. 17. 6
Threw forth most *dainty* odours and most sweet delight. . . . III. vi. 43. 9
From scorching heat her *daintie* limbes to shade; . . . III. xi. 32. 5
that same *daintie* lad, which was so deare . . . III. xii. 7. 5
Manie a brave knight and manie a *daintie* dame, . . . IV. iv. 13. 8
To be embaulm'd, and sweat out *dainty* dew, . . . IV. vii. 40. 4
No flowre in field, that *daintie* odour throwes, . . . IV. x. 22. 3
a most celestiall sound Of *dainty* musicke, . . . IV. xi. 23. 2
ne spared not Their *dainty* parts, . . . V. vii. 29. 6
Thereon distill and deaw her *daintie* face, . . . V. xii. 13. 4
To beare this burden on your *dainty* backe; . . . VI. ii. 47. 8
did with his smarting toole Oft whip her *dainty* selfe, . . . VI. vii. 39. 9
of her *dainty* flesh they did devize To make a common feast, . VI. viii. 38. 8
Those *daintie* parts, the dearlings of delight, . . . VI. viii. 43. 1
other *daintie* thing for her addrest, . . . VI. ix. 40. 4

Dainty—*Continued.*
Tell me, what mote these *dainty* Damzels be, ... VI. x. 19. 6
To make it seeme more deare and *dainty*, ... VI. xi. 1. 9
on the soft And downy grasse her *dainty* limbes to lay . . . VII. vi. 42. 4
made to growe Most *dainty* trees, ... VII. vii. 8. 7
wont to please Some *dainty* eares, ... *Am.* xxxviii. 6
store Of all that deare and *daynty* is . . . . *Am.* lxiii. 8
flowres, That *dainty* odours from them threw . . . . *Am.* lxiv. 3
bath'd him in a *dainty* well, ... *Epig.* iv. 47
to the sense most *daintie* odours yield, ... *H.B.* 80
meades adornd with *daintie* gemmes . . . . *Proth.* 14
Dairy. Thinks of her *Dairy* to make wondrous gaine, ... VII. vi. 48. 2
Dairy-house. breakes into her *Dayr' house*, ... VII. vi. 48. 4
Dais. *See* **Dess.**
Daisies. The grassye ground with daintye *Daysies* dight, . . . *S.C.* Jun. 6
Sweet Marjoram, and *Daysies* decking prime: . . . . *Mui.* 192
Daisy. The little *Dazie*, that at evening closes, ... *Proth.* 31
Dale. Tripping over the *dale* alone, ... *S.C.* Au. 63
with the same fill every hill and *dale*. . . . . *D.* 322
the Northside of Armulla *dale*) . . . . *Col.* 105
His fattie waves . . . overflow each plaine and lowly *dale*: . . I. i. 21. 4
A litle lowly Hermitage . . . Downe in a *dale*, ... I. i. 34. 2
every hil and *dale*, . . . Did search, ... I. ii. 8. 7
High over hills, and lowe adowne the *dale*, ... I. vii. 28. 8
they came at last Into a pleasant *dale* . . . . II. i. 24. 3
Still he him guided over *dale* and hill, ... II. i. 34. 5
Into a shady *dale* she soft him led, ... II. vi. 14. 3
castle, plaste Foreby a river in a pleasaunt *dale*; . . . . II. ix. 10. 4
Nor hedge, nor ditch, nor hill, nor *dale* she staies, ... IV. vii. 22. 1
chaced them both over hill and *dale*. . . . . V. xi. 59. 7
Downe in a *dale* forby a rivers syde . . . . VI. iii. 29. 6
Dales. to the *dales* resort, where shepheards ritch, ... *S.C.* Jun. 21
on hylls, or *dales*, or other where, ... *S.C.* Jun. 107
In humble *dales* is footing fast, ... *S.C.* Jul. 13
stremis Adowne the *dales* of Kent, ... *S.C.* Jul. 82
leades in lowly *dales*, ... *S.C.* Jul. 102
Through hils and *dales* he speedy way did make, ... II. xi. 26. 4
The *dales* for shade, the hilles for breathing space, ... II. xii. 58. 6
High over hilles and over *dales* he fledd, ... III. x. 55. 1
Low looking *dales*, disloignd from common gaze; . . . . IV. x. 24. 6
The hils doe not the lowly *dales* disdaine, ... V. ii. 41. 3
The *dales* doe not the lofty hils envy. . . . . V. ii. 41. 4
High over hilles, and lowly over *dales*, ... V. viii. 39. 2
Through hils and *dales*, through bushes and through breres, . VI. viii. 32. 1
through *dales*, through forests, and through plaines, ... VI. ix. 2. 6
in hils, in woods, in *dales*, ... VI. x. 3. 6
Or from high hilles or from the *dales* belowe, ... VII. vi. 39. 5
through the flowry *Dales* she tumbling downe . . . . VII. vi. 41. 6
all the woods and *dales* . . . Did ring againe, ... VII. vi. 52. 8
Dalliance. In wanton *dalliance* the teate to crave, ... *Bel.*[2] vi. 3
Marring my joyous gentle *dalliaunce*. . . . . *T.M.* 186
With . . . courting *dalliaunce*, She intertainde her lover . . . I. ii. 14. 1
Where he with his Duessa *dalliaunce* fownd, ... I. viii. 5. 5
to show, ne court, nor *dalliaunce*; . . . . II. ii. 35. 6
Her light behaviour and loose *dalliaunce* . . . . II. vi. 8. 1
Her *dalliaunce* he despis'd, ... II. vi. 21. 9
Now faining *dalliaunce* and wanton sport, ... II. xii. 16. 3
To whom he made great *dalliance* and delight: . . . . IV. ii. 4. 4
coy lookes tempring with loose *dalliance*; . . . . IV. ii. 9. 5
Dally. To *dally* thus with death is no fit toy: . . . . I. vi. 28. 8
Well warned to beware with whom he dar'd to *dallie*. . . . IV. i. 36. 9
Dam. *See* **Mill-dam.**
folowing th' example of hir *damme*: . . . . *Bel.*[1] vi. 4
Soone as my younglings cryen for the *dam* . . . . *S.C.* Ap. 95
Tho went the pensife *Damme* out of dore, ... *S.C.* May 229
Home when the doubtfull *Damme* had her hyde, ... *S.C.* May 294
I brought him up without the *Dambe*: . . . . *S.C.* Au. 39
Their *dam* upstart out of her den effraide, ... I. i. 16. 1
To see th' unkindly Impes, . . . Devoure their *dam*; . . . . I. i. 26. 3
More dear unto their God then younglings to their *dam*.' . . . I. x. 57. 9
Damage. For all the *damage* which he had him doen afore. . . III. v. 18. 9
to wreake the *dammage* by thee donne. . . . . IV. i. 44. 6
To doe most *dammage* where as most they ment: . . . . V. xii. 17. 4
Lying in waite how him he *damadge* might; . . . . VI. i. 20. 7
Damask. With *Damaske* roses and Daffadillies set: . . . . *S.C.* Ap. 60
In dieper, in *damaske*, or in lyne, ... *Mui.* 364
Damb(e). *See* **Dam, Mill-dam.**
Dame. *See* **Stepdame.**
The huge Leviathan, *dame* Natures wonder, ... *Van.* v. 6
Let *dame* Elisa thanke you for her song: . . . . *S.C.* Ap. 150
The Gate her *dame*, that had good reason, ... *S.C.* May 177
as *Dame* Cynthias silver raye, ... *S.C.* Au. 89
To deck her *Dame*, and enrich her heyre, ... *S.C.* S. 115
All as the shepheard that did fetch his *dame* . . . . *S.C.* O. 28
can undoe *Dame* Natures kindly course; . . . . *S.C.* N. 124
surcease, good *Dame*, and hence depart.' . . . . *Hub.* 1221
unto thee most deare, O dearest *Dame!* . . . . *Ti.* 244
they be daughters of *Dame* Memorie . . . . *Ti.* 368
dame Venus, on a day In spring, ... *Mui.* 113
Such as *Dame* Pallas . . . Could not accuse. . . . . *Mui.* 301
the fields In which *dame* Cynthia her landheards fed; . . . *Col.* 277
He bad awake blacke Plutoes griesly *Dame*; . . . . I. i. 37. 4
subdewd to learne *Dame* Pleasures toy. . . . . I. i. 47. 9
Dame,' (quoth he,) 'what hath ye thus dismayd? . . . . I. i. 52. 8
'Deare *dame*, I rew, That . . . such griefe unto you grew. . . I. i. 53. 8
Much griev'd to thinke that gentle *Dame* so light, ... I. i. 55. 2
'Mercy, mercy, Sir, vouchsafe to show On silly *Dame*, . . . I. ii. 21. 3
'Deare *dame*, your suddein overthrow Much rueth me; . . . . I. ii. 21. 7
'Thensforth I tooke Duessa for my *Dame*, ... I. ii. 40. 1
Dame Una, weary *Dame*, and entrance did requere: . . . . I. iii. 12. 9

Dame—*Continued.*
He thereto meeting said, 'My dearest *Dame*, ... I. iii. 28. 1
his soveraine *Dame* So rudely handled by her foe he saw, . . . I. iii. 41. 2
beware of ficklenesse, In choice, . . . of thy deare-loved *Dame*; I. iv. 1. 4
Suddein upriseth from her stately place The roiall *Dame*, . . I. iv. 16. 2
'Ah dearest *Dame*,' quoth then the Paynim bold, ... I. iv. 41. 1
'Faire *Dame*, be nought dismaid For sorrowes past; . . . . I. iv. 49. 1
'Why, *dame*,' (quoth he) 'what oddes can ever bee, ... I. iv. 50. 3
'Yet, O thou dreaded *Dame!* I crave Abyde, ... I. v. 21. 8
up, dreary *Dame*, of darknes Queene! . . . . I. v. 24. 1
'Ah *Dame*,' (quoth he) 'thou temptest me in vaine, ... I. v. 42. 1
Duessa . . . Returnd to stately pallace of *Dame* Pryde: . . . . I. v. 45. 2
Sometimes *dame* Venus selfe he seemes to see; . . . . I. vi. 16. 6
The fearefull *Dame* all quaked at the sight, ... I. vi. 28. 1
make proofe of her cruelty On gentle *Dame*, ... I. vi. 31. 7
Deare *dame*,' (quoth he) 'well may I rew . . . . I. vi. 36. 7
'Ah! dearest *dame*,' . . . 'how might I see . . . . I. vi. 39. 3
that false *Dame*, The false Duessa, ... I. vii. 1. 8
goodly court he made still to his *Dame*, ... I. vii. 7. 1
'Dear *Dame*, (quoth he) 'you sleeping sparkes awake, ... I. ix. 8. 1
Dame Caelia men did her call, ... I. x. 4. 1
them to his *Dame* he leades, That aged *Dame*, ... I. x. 8. 1, 2
The auncient *Dame* Him goodly greeted . . . . I. x. 11. 5
'Deare *dame*, And you, good Sir, ... I. x. 17. 1
had he not that *Dame* respected more, ... I. x. 49. 4
doen their service to that soveraigne *Dame*, ... I. x. 59. 7
O thou sacred Muse! most learned *Dame*, ... I. xi. 5. 6
Should have mine onely daughter to his *Dame*, ... I. xii. 20. 5
wrapped be in loves of former *Dame*, ... I. xii. 30. 8
Fidessa hight the falsest *Dame* on grownd, ... I. xii. 32. 3
far be it,' (said he) 'Deare *dame*, fro mee, ... II. i. 48. 1
from their sourse indewd By great *Dame* Nature, ... II. ii. 6. 2
A sober sad and comely courteous *Dame*; . . . . II. ii. 14. 5
made love unto the eldest *Dame*, ... II. ii. 17. 1
would abuse so gentle *Dame!* . . . . II. iv. 20. 9
in honour of his dearest *Dame*. . . . . II. v. 26. 9
His dearest *Dame* is that Enchaunteresse, ... II. v. 27. 1
'Ah, *Dame!* perdy ye have not doen me right, ... II. vi. 22. 7
Themselves did solace each one with his *Dame*, ... II. ix. 44. 5
wide Fraunce, a forlorne *Dame*, ... II. x. 23. 7
had to wife *Dame* Mertia the fayre, ... II. x. 42. 3
Such as *Dame* Nature selfe mote feare to see, ... II. xii. 23. 2
Under that Porch a comely *dame* did rest . . . . II. xii. 55. 7
some for wrath to see their captive *Dame*: . . . . II. xii. 86. 5
Most goodly meede, the fairest *Dame* alive: . . . . III. i. 18. 8
To chaunge my liefe, and love another *Dame*; . . . . III. i. 24. 3
That she is fairer then our fairest *Dame*; . . . . III. i. 27. 4
'Mongst thousands good one wanton *Dame* to find: . . . . III. i. 49. 5
Nought so of love this looser *Dame* did skill, ... III. i. 50. 1
Gan choose his *Dame* with *Bascimano* gay, ... III. i. 56. 8
the *Dame*, halfe dedd Through suddein feare . . . . III. i. 62. 4
that old *Dame* said many an idle verse, ... III. ii. 48. 8
choseth vertue for his dearest *Dame*, ... III. iii. 1. 8
Begin then, O my dearest sacred *Dame!* . . . . III. iii. 4. 1
great *Dame* Natures handmaide chearing every kind. . . . . III. iv. 56. 9
Of my deare *Dame* is loved dearely well: . . . . III. v. 9. 2
'Goe, *Dame*; goe, seeke your boy, ... III. vi. 24. 2
Dame Phoebe to a Nymphe her babe betooke . . . . III. vi. 28. 3
Wherewith *dame* Nature doth her beautify, ... III. vi. 30. 2
tell the idle tidings to his *Dame*: . . . . III. vii. 28. 6
was returnd againe unto his *Dame*, ... III. vii. 61. 8
To make another like the former *Dame*, ... III. viii. 5. 7
He gan make gentle purpose to his *Dame* . . . . III. viii. 14. 2
In th' heart of every honourable *Dame*, ... III. viii. 43. 5
shewd her selfe in all a gentle courteous *Dame*. . . . . III. ix. 26. 9
Purpose was moved by that gentle *Dame* . . . . III. ix. 32. 2
the fayrest *Dame* That ever Greece did boast, ... III. ix. 34. 7
Upon his lips hong faire *Dame* Hellenore . . . . III. ix. 52. 2
This second Helene, fayre *Dame* Hellenore, ... III. x. 13. 1
was he loth to loose his loved *Dame*, ... III. x. 15. 5
I enjoyd the gentlest *Dame* alive; . . . . III. x. 27. 2
let us goe to seeke my dearest *Dame*, ... III. x. 39. 5
love a Shephards daughter for his dearest *Dame*. . . . . III. xi. 38. 9
He loved Isse for his dearest *Dame*, ... III. xi. 39. 1
there marcht a most faire *Dame*, ... III. xii. 19. 1
that same dolorous Faire *Dame* he might behold . . . . III. xii. 22. 8
thou this *Dame* do presently Restore unto her health . . . III. xii. 35. 5
'Gentle *Dame*, reward enough I weene, ... III. xii. 40. 2
many a knight, and many a lovely *Dame*, Was then assembled IV. i. 9. 3
'Take then to you this *Dame* of mine,' . . . . IV. i. 35. 6
The aged *Dame*, him seeing so enraged, ... IV. i. 54. 1
'Fond *dame*, that deem'st of things divine As of humane, . . IV. ii. 51. 5
rather stird by his discordfull *Dame*, ... IV. iv. 3. 7
Manie a brave knight and manie a daintie *dame*, ... IV. iv. 13. 8
Dame Venus girdle, by her steemed deare . . . . IV. v. 3. 7
Graunted to her, as to the fayrest *Dame*. . . . . IV. v. 16. 2
forgoe so light For that strange *Dame*, ... IV. v. 20. 8
First in the midst to set that fayrest *Dame*, ... IV. v. 25. 4
that old aged *Dame*, his faithfull Squire, ... IV. v. 39. 6
That peerelesse paterne of *Dame* Natures pride . . . . IV. vi. 24. 5
faire Ladie knight, my dearest *Dame*, ... IV. vi. 32. 1
ne ever *Dame* So chast and loyall liv'd, ... IV. viii. 25. 5
the Dwarfe did me reveale, And told his *Dame* . . . . IV. viii. 55. 6
Not to despise that *dame* which lov'd him liefe, ... IV. ix. 15. 4
The warlike *Dame* was on her part assaid . . . . IV. ix. 30. 1
therein sate an amiable *Dame*, ... IV. x. 31. 3
'Nathlesse that *Dame* so well them tempred both, ... IV. x. 33. 1
The nourslling of *Dame* Memorie his deare, ... IV. xi. 10. 2
the aged Ocean and his *Dame* Old Tethys, ... IV. xi. 18. 1
Dame Venus sonne, ... IV. xii. 13. 3

Dame—*Continued.*
That had despisde so chast and faire a *dame,* IV. xii. 16. 7
That was to succour a distressed *Dame* V. i. 3. 6
He askt who had that *Dame* so fouly dight, V. i. 14. 8
eke their *dame* halfe dead did hide her self for feare. V. ii. 24. 9
met Upon the way with that his snowy *Dame:* V. iii. 10. 4
What better dowre can to a *dame* be hight? V. iv. 9. 5
Even so Clarinda her owne *Dame* beguyld, V. v. 53. 5
him she told her *Dame* his freedome did denye. V. v. 56. 9
to her *Dame* him still she discommended, V. v. 57. 4
backe returning where his *Dame* did lie, V. vi. 30. 7
this proude *Dame,* disdayning all accord, V. viii. 22. 3
By that proud *dame* which her so much disdained, V. viii. 24. 4
all that wrong unto that wofull *Dame* So long had done, V. xi. 4. 5
Declare it boldly, *Dame,* and doe not stand in dout.' V. xi. 18. 9
will ye, fond *Dame,* attempted bee Unto a strangers love, V. xi. 63. 1
that discourteous *Dame* with scornfull pryde VI. i. 30. 4
great helpe *dame* Nature selfe doth lend; VI. ii. 2. 1
Through thicke and thin, unfit for any *Dame:* VI. ii. 10. 4
For what he spake, for you he spake it, *Dame;* VI. ii. 14. 5
he said: 'Ye dolefull *Dame,* VI. ii. 42. 2
'*Dame,* be no longer sad; VI. ii. 45. 4
For safe conducting of his sickely *Dame* VI. iii. 31. 3
For pitty of his *Dame* whom she saw so diseased. VI. iii. 32. 9
for pitty of his dearest *Dame,* VI. iii. 43. 7
'What be you, wofull *Dame,* which thus lament, VI. iv. 27. 8
A wofull *dame* ye have me termed well; VI. iv. 28. 3
Then thus began the lamentable *Dame:* VI. iv. 29. 1
'Faire *Dame,* In evils counsell is the comfort chiefe; VI. iv. 34. 6
Albe that *Dame,* by all the meanes she might, VI. iv. 39. 5
By gentle usage of that wretched *Dame:* VI. v. 2. 6
backe returning to that sorie *Dame,* VI. v. 4. 1
To draw him from his deare beloved *dame* VI. v. 15. 4
The wretchedest *Dame* that lives this day on ground; VI. v. 28. 2
that Squire and *Dame* So faint and feeble were, VI. v. 40. 6
The Hermite heales both Squire and *dame* VI. vi. Arg.
Made in the bodies of that Squire and *Dame;* VI. vi. 2. 2
'Faire daughter *Dame,* And you, faire Sonne, VI. vi. 6. 5
his *Dame,* him seeing in such guize, VI. vi. 32. 5
where that *Dame* remayned With her unworthy knight, VI. vi. 39. 8
Then forth issewed (great goddesse) great *dame* Nature VII. vii. 5. 1
the solemne bridall cheare Twixt Peleus and *Dame* Thetis VII. vii. 12. 5
Before her came *dame* Mutability; VII. vii. 13. 6
to my *Dame* . . . Cupid humbly came, *Epig.* iii. 1
Ne once move ruth in that rebellious *Dame,* *H.L.* 151

Dames. Forgive it me, faire *Dames,* sith lesse ye have not lefte, *Ded.Son.*xvii.14
'Whose forged beauty . . . All other *Dames* . . . exceeded farre: I. ii. 36. 2
the direfull *dames* doe drive Their mournefull charett, I. v. 32. 1
be for all chaste *Dames* an endlesse moniment.' II. ii. 10. 9
fooles, lovers, children, *Dames.* II. ix. 50. 9
Satyrane saves the Squyre of *Dames* III. vii. Arg.
Call me the Squyre of *Dames;* III. vii. 51. 9
above all *Dames* is deemd, And above many knightes III. vii. 52. 4
read, thou Squyre of *Dames,* what vow is this, III. vii. 53. 2
I might doe service unto gentle *Dames,* III. vii. 54. 6
Till I so many other *Dames* had fownd, III. vii. 56. 4
'Perdy' (sayd Satyrane) 'thou Squyre of *Dames,* III. vii. 61. 1
having ended with that Squyre of *Dames* III. viii. 44. 1
(said then the Squyre of *Dames*) III. viii. 51. 1
Redoubted knights, and honorable *Dames,* III. ix. 1. 1
From whom the Squyre of *Dames* was reft whylere; III. xi. 3. 8
Was from those *Dames* so farre and so unfitting, IV. ii. 19. 3
a Squire, even he the Squire of *Dames,* IV. ii. 20. 2
Which when that scornefull Squire of *Dames* did vew, IV. v. 18. 1
Plenty of pearles to decke his *dames* withall; IV. xi. 39. 6
faire *Dames!* the worlds deare ornaments *H.B.* 162

Damn. To *damne* to death, or dole perpetuall, *Hub.* 1244
To *damne* him selfe by every evil name, IV. xii. 16. 5
stonisht are . . . and *damne* their lying bookes: VII. vii. 52. 6

Damned. *See* **Ever-damned, Fore-damned.**
thereby mad'st her ever *damn'd* to be. *Gn.* 472
With which the *damned* ghosts he governeth, *Hub.* 1293
As one aghast with feends or *damned* sprights, I. ii. 4. 5
'What voice of *damned* Ghost from Limbo lake, I. ii. 32. 5
'Nor *damned* Ghost, . . . to thee these words doth speake; I. ii. 33. 1
damned sprights sent forth to make ill men aghast. I. v. 31. 9
Phlegeton, Whereas the *damned* ghosts in torments fry, I. v. 33. 4
'Thou *damned* wight, The authour of this fact I. ix. 37. 6
The *damned* ghosts that doe in torments waile, I. ix. 49. 7
Whom when the *damned* feend so fresh did spy, I. xi. 35. 1
damned ghoste In flaming Phlegeton II. vi. 50. 8
many *damned* wightes In those sad waves, II. vii. 57. 2
In which the *damned* soules he did behold, II. vii. 63. 5
Through which the *damned* ghosts doen often creepe II. xii. 6. 5
There let her with the *damned* spirits dwell, III. iv. 60. 8
Out of the dwellings of the *damned* sprights, IV. i. 19. 8
justly *damned* by the doome Of his owne mouth, V. v. 17. 3
to perpetuall paine Had *damn'd* her sonnes V. vii. 10. 8
There let her with the *damned* spirits dwell, III. iv. 60. 8
doome a-rights Against Duessa, *damned* by them all; V. x. 4. 4
her he deemes already but a *damned* ghoste.' V. xi. 42. 9
damned to endure this direfull smart, VI. viii. 19. 8
swarmes of *damned* soules to hell he sends: VI. viii. 49. 7
Where with such *damned* fiends she should in darknesse dwell. VI. x. 43. 9
damned ghosts which dwell For aye in darkenesse, VI. xii. 35. 7
damned ghosts, cald up with mighty spels, *Epith.* 347
to provoke the yre Of *damned* fiends, *H.L.* 235
can restore a *damned* wight from death. *H.B.* 287
To deepest hell, and lake of *damned* fyre, *H.H.L.* 89

Damnified. As if late fight had nought him *damnifyde,* I. xi. 52. 7
To see my Lord so deadly *damnifyde?* II. vi. 43. 8

Damning. the Evill *damning* evermore to dy: *Com. Son.* i. 12
Cursing his Gods, and him selfe *damning* deepe: II. viii. 37. 2
Damning all Wrong and tortious Injurie, VII. vii. 14. 5

Damon. *Damon* and Pythias, whom death could not sever: IV. x. 27. 6

Damosell, Damozell. *See* **Damsel.**

Damp. the shady *damp* Out of the goodly heven amoved quight, III. x. 1. 3
misty *dampe* of misconceyving night, III. x. 47. 5
Sith shady *dampe* had dimd the heavens reach, V. vi. 21. 8
the day with *dampe* was overcast, V. vii. 8. 6
Bad doe away the *dampe* of drouzie sleepe, V. vii. 26. 8
Having disperst the nights unchearefull *dampe,* *Epith.* 21

Dampish. All suddeinly dim wox the *dampish* ayre, III. iv. 52. 1
The drowzie humour of the *dampish* night, IV. viii. 34. 4
enlumineth the darke And *dampish* aire, *H.H.B.* 165

Damps. this darke world, whose *damps* the soule do blynd, *H.H.B.* 137

Dams. my lambs, when for their *dams* they call, *Col.* 638

Damsel. that *Damzell* . . . She turn'd into a winged Butterflie, *Mui.* 137
the presumptuous *Damzell* rashly dar'd *Mui.* 269
Not anie *damzell,* which her vaunteth most *Mui.* 361
she has A *damzel* spyde, slow footing her before, I. iii. 10. 8
The doubtfull *Damzell* dare not yet committ I. vi. 12. 1
when he saw the *Damsell* passe away, I. vi. 48. 5
Or ever gentle *Damzell* so abuse: II. i. 19. 3
did enterpris Th' adventure of the Errant *damozell;* II. i. 19. 8
the wanton *Damsell* found New merth II. vi. 6. 1
Ne staied for his *Damsell* to inquire, II. vi. 27. 8
Besought that *Damzell* suffer him depart, II. vi. 36. 8
to that *Damsell* thankes gave for reward. II. vi. 38. 6
each a *damzell* chose. II. ix. 36. 5
Another *Damsell* of that gentle crew, II. ix. 40. 2
'Fayre *Damzell,* seemeth by your troubled cheare, II. ix. 42. 1
A daintie *damsell* dressing of her heare, II. xii. 14. 8
of a single *damzell* thou wert mett III. i. 8. 4
she th' Errant *Damzell* hight; III. i. 24. 7
Forthy, faire Sir, yours be the *Damozell,* III. i. 30. 3
the chaste *damzell* . . . Did easely beleeve III. i. 53. 7
Therefore, faire *Damzell,* be ye well aware, III. ii. 10. 6
The *Damzell* well did vew his Personage III. ii. 26. 1
The *Damzell* pauzd; and then thus fearfully: III. ii. 35. 1
the faire *Damzel* from the holy herse III. ii. 48. 6
the sicke *Damosell* . . . vewed her straunge lovers shade, III. iii. 6. 2
More neede of leach-crafte hath your *Damozell,* III. iii. 17. 5
The *Damzell* was full deepe empassioned III. iii. 43. 1
into the mynd Of the yong *Damzell* sunke, III. iii. 57. 2
did attonce pursew The fearefull *damzell* III. iv. 46. 3
that way in which that *Damozell* Was fledd afore, III. iv. 47. 8
the shame he did To that faire *Damzell:* III. v. 13. 6
Ye wonder how this noble *Damozell* III. vi. 1. 2
What end unto that fearefull *Damozell* . . . befell: III. vi. 54. 2
The *Damzell* there arriving entred in; III. vii. 7. 1
the *Damzell,* full of doubtfull thought, III. vii. 8. 5
Whom when the fearefull *Damzell* nigh espide, III. vii. 24. 1
'The third a *Damzell* was of low degree, III. vii. 59. 1
This gentle *Damzell,* whom I write upon, III. viii. 1. 4
The warlike *Damzell* was empassiond sore, III. xi. 18. 2
About the chamber by the (*with that) *Damozell;* III. xii. 26. 7
the stout *Damzell,* to him leaping light, III. xii. 32. 8
Every of which was to a *damzell* hight; IV. x. 38. 8
Th' enchaunted *Damzell* vanisht into nought: V. iii. 24. 6
that same other *Damzell,* Lucy bright, V. iv. 9. 2
this same other *Damzell* V. iv. 13. 4
'Goe, *damzell,* quickly, doe thy selfe addresse V. iv. 48. 4
The *Damzell* streight obayd, V. iv. 50. 1
Where that same *Damzell* lowdly him bespake, V. iv. 50. 8
'Faire *Damzell,* that with ruth . . . Of my mishaps V. v. 37. 7
he chaunst far off to heed A *Damzell,* V. viii. 4. 2
the *Damzell,* who those deadly ends Of both her foes had seene, V. viii. 10. 4
lo! the *Damzell* selfe, whence all did grow, V. viii. 15. 8
Then they that *Damzell* called to them nie, V. viii. 16. 1
So said this *Damzell,* that hight Samient; V. viii. 23. 7
that *Damzell,* the sad Samient, V. viii. 25. 6
taking with him . . . That *Damzell,* V. viii. 26. 4
brought that *Damzell* as his purchast pray; V. viii. 26. 8
did of him requere That *Damsell* whom he held V. viii. 27. 9
when she saw that *Damzell* there. V. viii. 47. 9
behight Unto that *Damzell* in her Ladies right, V. ix. 3. 5
that *Damzell* did to them bewray A straunge adventure, V. ix. 4. 4
Which when the *Damzell* neare at hand did spy, V. ix. 8. 3
The *Damzell* straight went, as she was directed, V. ix. 9. 6
Him when the *damzell* saw fast by her side, V. ix. 12. 1
There they alighting by that *Damzell* were Directed in, V. ix. 22. 1
saves from Maleffort A *Damzell* used vylde: VI. i. Arg.
a faire *Damzell,* my beloved deare, VI. i. 16. 2
to his *damzell,* as their rightfull meed VI. i. 47. 5
this coy *Damzell* thought contrariwize, VI. vii. 30. 1
The *damzell* was attacht, and shortly brought Unto the barre VI. vii. 36. 1
The *Damzell* wakes; VI. viii. 40. 1
The *Damzell* was before the altar set, VI. viii. 45. 2
he there besyde Saw a faire *damzell,* VI. ix. 7. 7
aged syre, . . . That wild the *damzell* rise; VI. ix. 13. 9
was placed Another *Damzell,* VI. x. 12. 7
The trustie *damzell* bearing it abrode VI. xii. 7. 1
Untill the *Damzell* gan to wex more sound and strong. VI. xii. 11. 9
The *Damzell* broke his misintended dart. *Am.* xvi. 12
Such subtile craft my *Damzell* doth conceave, *Am.* xxiii. 5
the stubborne *damzell* doth deprave *Am.* xxix. 1

Damsel's. meant them to the *damzels* fantazy. VI. ix. 12. 9

Damsels. now ye daintie *Damsells* may depart	*S.C.* Ap. 147
go, cursed *damosells,* Whose bridale torches	*Gn.* 393
her faire *damzels,* flocking her arownd,	*Mui.* 116
faire *Damsels!* Shepheards dere delights,	*D.* 526
Amidst a flock of *Damzelles* fresh and gay,	II. v. 32. 4
traine . . . borne of two faire *Damsels*	II. ix. 19. 5
Two naked *Damzelles* he therein espyde,	II. xii. 63. 6
all was full of *Damzels* and of Squyres,	III. i. 39. 6
her *Damzells,* which the former chace Had undertaken	III. v. 37. 1
She made those *Damzels* search;	III. v. 38. 8
woxe halfe wroth against her *damzels* slacke,	III. vi. 19. 3
forth her *damzells* sent Through all the woods,	III. vi. 25. 7
Ladies, knights, and *Damsels* gent,	III. xi. 46. 1
all the Priests were *damzels* in soft linnen dight	IV. x. 38. 9
A bevie of fayre *damzels* close did lye,	IV. x. 48. 8
All goodly *damzels,* deckt with long greene haire,	IV. xi. 48. 2
them beside two seemely *damzells* stood,	V. iv. 4. 6
those *Damzells* did forestall Their furious encounter,	V. iv. 5. 8
she came . . . Guarded with many *Damzels*	V. v. 4. 3
all the *damzels* of that towne	V. xi. 34. 3
Tell me, what mote these dainty *Damzels* be,	VI. x. 19. 6
Are Venus *Damzels,* all within her fee,	VI. x. 21. 4
flowres . . . For *damzels* fit	*Am.* lxiv. 4
Come now, ye *damzels,* daughters of delight,	*Epith.* 96
the *Damzels* doe delite When they their tymbrels smyte,	*Epith.* 133
Now ceasse, ye *damsels,* your delights fore-past;	*Epith.* 296
Now it is night, ye *damsels* may be gon,	*Epith.* 311
Damsons. When *Damsines* I gether,	*S.C.* Ap. 152
Dan. Feeding the blessed flocke of *Dan,*	*S.C.* Jul. 51
did *Dan* Orpheus represse The streames of Hebrus	*Gn.* 180
valiant fortune made *Dan* Orpheus bolde;	*Gn.* 449
Dan Orpheus was seene Wylde beasts . . . to lead,	*Ti.* 607
Dan Perseus, borne of heavenly seed,	*Ti.* 648
Dan Faunus chaunst to meet her by the way,	II. ii. 7. 5
all his windes *Dan* Aeolus did keepe	III. viii. 21. 6
To shew *Dan* Cupids powre and great effort:	III. xi. 46. 5
Dan Chaucer, well of English undefyled,	IV. ii. 32. 8
For which *Dan* Phebus selfe cannot a salve provide	IV. vi. 1. 9
Dan Aeolus, in great displeasure	IV. ix. 23. 1
bade *Dan* Phoebus scribe her Appellation seale	VII. vi. 35. 9
old *Dan* Geffrey . . . durst not with it mel,	VII. vii. 9. 3
The same wherewith *Dan* Jove . . . was nourisht	VII. vii. 41. 6
Such as they faine *Dan* Cupid to have beene,	VII. vii. 46. 7
you, *Dan* Jove, that only constant are,	VII. vii. 53. 1
Danae. faire *Danae* to vew;	III. xi. 31. 2
Dance. she did seeme to *daunce,* as in delight,	*Van.* ix. 7
pray him leaden our *daunce*	*S.C.* Mar. 24
They *dauncen* deffly, and singen soote,	*S.C.* Ap. 111
a fourth Grace, to make the *daunce* even?	*S.C.* Ap. 113
they *dauncen,* eche one with his mayd.	*S.C.* May 24
Made my heart after the pype to *daunce:*	*S.C.* May 26
Pan . . . Will pype and *daunce*	*S.C.* Jun. 31
now I have learnd a newe *daunce;*	*S.C.* Au. 11
where death doth leade the *daunce,*	*S.C.* N. 105
wont with her to sing and *daunce,*	*S.C.* N. 143
he could play, and *daunce,* and vaute, and spring,	*Hub.* 693
flockes to leap and *daunce,*	*Ti.* 326
wont full merrilie to pipe and *daunce,*	*D.* 55
to my pype to caroll and to *daunce*	*D.* 105
For he could pipe, and *daunce,* and caroll sweet,	*As.* 31
he . . . well could *daunce,* and sing with ruefulnesse;	I. iv. 25. 7
heares . . . Did shake, and seemd to *daunce* for jollity,	I. vii. 32. 4
Some fell to *daunce,* some fel to hazardry,	III. i. 57. 1
They fell to *daunce:*	VI. ix. 41. 5
he should lead the *daunce,* as was his fashion;	VI. ix. 42. 3
Coridon could *daunce,* and trimly trace:	VI. ix. 42. 4
Calidore sees the Graces *daunce* To Colins melody;	VI. x. Arg.
to *daunce,* when they to *daunce* would faine,	VI. x. 8. 3
For breaking of their *daunce,*	VI. x. 11. 3
Three other Ladies did both *daunce* and sing,	VI. x. 12. 3
daunce there day and night:	VI. x. 15. 3
them selves so in their *daunce* they bore,	VI. x. 24. 6
faire sun-shine, that makes all skip and *daunce;*	VII. vii. 23. 4
thereunto doe *daunce* and carrol sweet,	*Epith.* 135
let the Graces *daunce* unto the rest,	*Epith.* 257
daunce about them, and about them sing,	*Epith.* 276
Danced. proud Antiochus . . . on his altares *daunst*	I. v. 47. 9
the light bubles *daunced* all along,	II. xii. 10. 4
She, . . . full glade, *Daunst* lively,	III. x. 44. 9
All day they *daunced* with great lusty-hedd,	III. x. 45. 6
All they without were raunged in a ring, And *daunced*	VI. x. 12. 2
ever, as the crew About her *daunst,*	VI. x. 14. 7
He pypt apace, whilest they him *daunst* about.	VI. x. 16. 5
leapt and *daunc't* as they had ravisht beene!	VII. vii. 34. 8
Dancing. With pyping and *dauncing* did passe the rest	*S.C.* Au. 10
dauncing all in companie, Adorne that God:	*Gn.* 27
With many Fairies oft were *dauncing* seene	*Gn.* 179
The Shepheards daughters *dauncing* in a rownd!	*D.* 310
Dauncing upon the waters back to lond,	*Col.* 214
Amongst the shepheards daughters *dancing* rownd,	*Col.* 641
the Graces seemed all to sing, . . . *dauncing* all around;	I. i. 48. 8
Phoebus . . . Came *dauncing* forth, shaking his deawie hayre,	I. v. 2. 4
Faunes . . . were *dauncing* in a rownd,	I. vi. 7. 8
Thence lead her forth, about her *dauncing* round,	I. vi. 13. 6
all *dauncing* on a row, The comely virgins came,	I. xii. 6. 5
Dauncing and reveling both day and night,	III. i. 39. 7
by the *dauncing* bubbles did divine,	III. ix. 30. 6
The jolly Satyres . . . Came *dauncing* forth,	III. x. 44. 4
still he far'd as *dauncing* in delight,	III. xii. 8. 7
dauncing on the craggy cliffes at will;	V. ix. 15. 5
Dancing—*Continued.*	
in ray Came *dauncing* forth,	V. xi. 34. 4
There he a troupe of Ladies *dauncing* found	VI. x. 10. 7
All raunged in a ring and *dauncing* in delight	VI. x. 11. 9
Dandled. Then those which have bene *dandled* in the lap:	VI. iv. 36. 6
Danger. unawares doe into *daunger* fall	*Van.* xii. 8
him to much rebuke and *Daunger* drove,	*S.C.* Jun. 69
No *daunger* there the shepheard can astert;	*S.C.* N. 187
I of doubted *daunger* had no feare:	*S.C.* D. 22
Drawne into *danger* through close ambushment;	*Gn.* 532
we shall ronne Into great *daunger,*	*Hub.* 184
Unweeting of the *danger* hee is in,	*T.M.* 491
faulty men, which *daunger* to thee threat:	*Com. Son.* i. 8
As he that did all *daunger* quite despise,	*Mui.* 390
of *daunger* nought ydrad,	*As.* 87
As if it scornd the *daunger* of the same;	*Col.* 215
withouten dread or *daunger:*	*Col.* 317
ne ward the *daunger* of the wound;	*Col.* 876
The *danger* hid, the place unknowne and wilde,	I. i. 12. 3
if of *daunger,* . . . ye desire to heare,	I. i. 31. 1
For *danger* great, . . . I saw before mine eyes,	I. ii. 41. 8
'no *daunger* now is nye.'	I. ix. 26. 5
eke be safe from *daunger* far descryde	I. xi. 5. 4
or hidden *danger* did entrap;	II. i. 26. 9
through *danger* and great dreed	II. i. 52. 9
Seeing at last her selfe from *daunger* rid,	II. iii. 36. 5
Least by her presence *daunger* mote befall;	II. iii. 44. 2
Seeking for *daunger* and adventures vaine?	II. vi. 17. 5
fayre Phaedria, that beheld That deadly *daunger,*	II. vi. 32. 2
(So Love the dread of *daunger* doth despise)	II. vi. 46. 2
In *daunger* rather to be drent then brent?'	II. vi. 49. 7
Ne darkenesse him, ne *daunger* might dismay	II. vii. 26. 4
Firme is thy faith, whom *daunger* never fro me drew,	II. viii. 53. 9
most deadly *daunger* and distressed plight	II. xii. 11. 9
Whiles the dredd *daunger* does behind remaine	II. xii. 21. 4
Quit from that *danger* forth their course they kept;	II. xii. 27. 1
Worse is the *daunger* hidden then descride,	II. xii. 35. 5
constancy and care, gainst *daunger* and dismay	II. xii. 38. 9
Dreadfull of *daunger* that mote him betyde,	III. i. 37. 5
Of hurt unwist most *daunger* doth redound;	III. ii. 26. 6
nor *daunger* from thy dew reliefe Shall me debarre:	III. ii. 33. 8
For dread of *daunger* which it might portend;	III. iii. 14. 4
Shamefull deceipt, and *daunger* imminent,	III. iv. 58. 4
For doubt of *daunger* which mote him betide;	III. v. 12. 6
deadly *daunger,* which to him betidd;	III. v. 13. 2
shortly he from *daunger* was releast,	III. v. 14. 4
Him selfe from deadly *daunger* to defend:	III. vii. 32. 5
Her selfe not saved yet from *daunger* dredd	III. viii. 33. 1
Their counsell crav'd in *daunger* imminent	III. x. 41. 3
daunger vaine it were to have assayd That cruell element,	III. xi. 22. 3
'*Daunger* without discretion to attempt Inglorious,	III. xi. 23. 1
for feare Of secret *daunger,*	III. xi. 55. 6
With him went *Daunger,* cloth'd in ragged weed	III. xii. 11. 1
evermore on *Daunger* fixt his eye,	III. xii. 12. 7
he was forst from *daunger* of the throwes Backe to retire,	IV. iii. 26. 3
Him selfe to save, and *daunger* to defend,	IV. iii. 32. 4
feare and *danger* of that dismall wight	IV. vii. 33. 9
her great *daunger* did him much dismay	IV. viii. 20. 5
being brought in *daunger* to relent too late,	IV. ix. 34. 9
'His name was *Daunger,*	IV. x. 17. 1
'No lesse did *Daunger* threaten me with dread,	IV. x. 58. 1
daunger well he wist long to continue there	IV. xii. 15. 9
It's late in death of *daunger* to advize,	IV. xii. 28. 6
every one his *daunger* did eschew:	V. iii. 8. 7
Which to her in that *daunger* hope of life did offer	V. iv. 10. 9
From the dread *daunger* of his weapon keene,	V. v. 8. 7
thenceforth unto *daunger* opened way	V. v. 9. 4
deadly *daunger* seem'd in all mens sight To tempt such steps,	V. ix. 15. 6
then came *Daunger,* threatning hidden dread	V. ix. 45. 5
Wayting what end would be of that same *daunger* drad	V. xi. 32. 9
He will not bide the *daunger* of such dread,	V. xii. 18. 7
keepe your body from the *daunger* drad,	VI. i. 10. 7
seeing in what *daunger* he was plast,	VI. i. 39. 7
My knight hers . . . to *daunger* drove,	VI. ii. 20. 5
no need Of dreaded *daunger* might his doubtfull humor feed	VI. ii. 29. 9
To succour her from *daunger* of dismay,	VI. ii. 38. 4
him selfe he thought from *daunger* free,	VI. iii. 20. 6
Whom now in deadly *daunger* he did see,	VI. iii. 43. 8
Unwares into the *daunger* of defame;	VI. v. 15. 5
seeing one in so great *daunger* set	VI. v. 22. 2
Whom when the Salvage saw from *daunger* free,	VI. vi. 40. 1
Devizing of his love more then of *daunger* drad	VI. vii. 6. 9
Bull, whose cruell hornes doe threat Desperate *daunger,*	VI. vii. 47. 3
Ne would endure the *daunger* of their might,	VI. viii. 14. 4
seeing nought Which doubt of *daunger* to her offer mought,	VI. viii. 32. 5
For dread of *daunger* not to be redrest,	VI. ix. 3. 4
wicked feend . . . *daunger* to them draw;	VI. ix. 6. 3
Ne durst abide the *daunger* of the end;	VI. x. 35. 4
As if he did from some late *daunger* fly,	VI. xi. 27. 5
by all meanes the *daunger* knowne did shonne:	VI. xi. 35. 7
none his *daunger* daring to abide	VI. xi. 49. 6
warne to shun the *daunger* of theyr wrath	*Am.* xxxi. 8
He dreads no *danger,* nor misfortune feares,	*H.L.* 223
Dangered. The evil stownd that *daungerd* her estate,	I. viii. 12. 2
Dangerous. Now was the Prince in *daungerous* distresse,	II. viii. 34. 1
All deadly *daungerous,* all cruell keene,	II. xi. 21. 3
A *daungerous* and detestable place,	II. xii. 8. 2
He lowrd on her with *daungerous* eyeglaunce,	III. xii. 15. 4
battell made the dreddest *daungerous* That ever shrilling trumpet did resound;	IV. ii. 32. 3

Dangerous—*Continued.*
gan shun his dreadfull sight, . . . in *daungerous* affright. . . . IV. iv. 41. 9
The end whereof and *daungerous* event . . . IV. v. 46. 6
dangerous successe depended yet in doubt: . . . IV. ix. 24. 9
That is both swift and *dangerous* deepe withall; . . . V. ii. 8. 2
she saw The *daungerous* state in which she stood, . . . V. ii. 22. 3
how Fortune would resolve that *daungerous* dout. . . . V. v. 5. 9
They saw a Knight in *daungerous* distresse . . . V. xi. 44. 2
In saving him from *daungerous* despaire . . . V. xi. 48. 4
'forborne Your owne good shield in *daungerous* dismay? . . . V. xi. 52. 2
Which he endured had through *daungerous* debate: . . . VI. iii. 22. 9
seas, Which tosse the rest in *daungerous* disease; . . . VI. ix. 19. 5
There chaunst to them a *dangerous* accident: . . . VI. x. 34. 3
In dread of death, and *daungerous* dismay, . . . *Am.* lxiii. 3
Dangerously. their huge strokes full *daungerously* bestow, . . V. xii. 17. 3
dangerously did round about enclose: . . . VI. v. 20. 3
Danger's. their flocks, devoyd of *dangers* feare, . . . *Col.* 54
slack her threatfull hand for *daungers* dout; . . . III. xii. 37. 4
Fro *dangers* dread his doubtfull life to save; . . . V. xi. 46. 4
Without suspect of ill or *daungers* hidden dred. . . . VI. iii. 23. 9
Yet would not neare approch in *daungers* eye, . . . VI. vii. 3. 2
mote empaire my peace with *daungers* dread; . . . VI. ix. 33. 6
Affrayd of every *dangers* least dismay. . . . *Am.* lxxxvii. 4
Dangers. In sea of deadly *daungers* was distrest: . . . I. xii. 17. 6
Mongst thousand *dangers*, and ten thousand Magick mights. . II. xii. 1. 9
Where *daungers* dwelt, and perils most did wonne, . . . III. i. 3. 2
in that wastefull wildernesse . . . many *dangers* dwell; . . . III. x. 40. 4
by searching *daungers* new, . . . Their days mote be abridged . IV. ii. 46. 7
From *daungers* dread to ward his naked side, . . . IV. iii. 20. 3
able was all *daungers* to withstond: . . . IV. ix. 18. 4
all those *daungers* unto them declar'd; . . . IV. ix. 41. 7
The doubts, the *daungers*, the delayes, the woes, . . . *H.L.* 262
Daniel. rouze thy feathers quickly, *Daniell*, . . . *Col.* 424
Danish. from the *Daniske* Tyrants head shall rend Th' usurped crowne, . . . III. iii. 47. 6
much like unto a *Danisk* hood, . . . IV. x. 31. 7
Danius. then Kimarus; and then *Danius:* . . . II. x. 43. 2
Daphnaida. she to whom *Daphnaida* Upon her neeces death I did complaine: . . . *Col.* 510
Daphne. '*Daphne* thou knewest, quoth he, . . . *D.* 183
my *Daphne* they have tane away; . . . *D.* 365
My *Daphne* hence departing bad me so; . . . *D.* 454
Fayre *Daphne* Phoebus hart with love did gore; . . . II. xii. 52. 5
Fled fearfull *Daphne* on th' Aegaean strond, . . . III. vii. 26. 4
he thrild thee . . . To love faire *Daphne*, . . . III. xi. 36. 7
More swift then Myrrh' or *Daphne* in her race, . . . IV. vii. 22. 8
Proud *Daphne*, scorning Phoebus lovely fyre, . . . *Am.* xxviii. 9
Daphne's. Lamenting lowde my *Daphnes* Elegie, . . . *D.* 509
rue my *Daphnes* wrong, And mourne for me . . . *D.* 537
for *Daphnes* death doth tourn Sweet layes . . . *Col.* 386
Dapled. *See* **Dappled.**
Dapper. The *dapper* ditties, that I wont devise . . . *S.C.* O. 13
Dappled. a Courser *dapled* gray, . . . III. vii. 37. 3
Whose sides with *dapled* circles weren dight; . . . II. i. 18. 7
Dare. conquer'd, *dare* the Conquerour disdaine. . . . *Ro.* xiv. 14
Let him, if he *dare*, His brightnesse compare . . . *S.C.* Ap. 79
Wherefore with myne thou *dare* thy musick matche? . . . *S.C.* Au. 2
if in rymes with me thou *dare* strive, . . . *S.C.* Au. 21
by my soule, I *dare* undersaye . . . *S.C.* S. 91
Dare not to match thy pype with Tityrus his style. . . . *S.C.* Env. 9
should *dare* To come unto his haunt; . . . *Gn.* 273
No lesse, I *dare* saie, than the prowdest wight; . . . *Hub.* 62
dare his hardy hand to those outstretch, . . . *Hub.* 974
dare their follies forth so rashlie throwe, . . . *T.M.* 220
Ne ever *dare* their dunghill thoughts aspire . . . *T.M.* 393
oft would *dare* to tempt the troublous winde. . . . *Mui.* 48
Might in their divers cunning ever *dare* . . . *Mui.* 367
Bold men . . . *Dare* tempt that gulf . . . *Col.* 210
dare with evil deed or leasing vaine Blaspheme . . . *Col.* 821
My Muse . . . With bolder wing shall *dare* alofte to sty, . . . *Ded. Son.* ii. 9
Ne *dare* to weepe, nor seeme to understand . . . I. iii. 20. 7
victory they *dare* not wish to either side. . . . I. v. 9. 9
'thou temptest me . . . To *dare* the thing, . . . I. v. 42. 2
The doubtfull Damzell *dare* not yet committ . . . I. vi. 12. 1
How *dare* I thinke such glory to attaine?' . . . I. x. 62. 2
So hard a workemanship adventure *darre*, . . . III. Pr. 2. 8
Dare not adventure on the stubborne pray, . . . III. i. 22. 3
Dare not for dread his hardy hand expose, . . . III. i. 46. 8
dare thou not, I charge, in any cace To enter . . . III. iii. 8. 7
hand should *dare* for to engore Her noble blood? . . . III. viii. 48. 8
Both first and second Troy shall *dare* to equalize. . . . III. ix. 44. 9
can and *dare* Redresse the wrong . . . III. x. 28. 1
feare Of that rocks fall, . . . he *dare* never sleepe, . . . III. x. 58. 6
the man . . . That *dare* fro me thinke Florimell to take!' . . . IV. ii. 25. 4
Ne *dare* I like; but, through infusion sweete Of thine owne spirit . . . IV. ii. 34. 6
All which who so *dare* thinke for to enchace, . . . IV. v. 12. 1
breaking forth *dare* tempt the deepest flood . . . IV. x. 46. 5
thy basest thrall, That *dare* discourse . . . V. Pr. 11. 7
with his souce, which none enduren *dare*, . . . V. iv. 42. 7
none . . . did *darre* Him to assault, . . . V. iv. 44. 5
dare even deathes most dreadfull face behold? . . . V. v. 31. 4
the man, that say or doe so *dare*, . . . V. vi. 1. 6
none should *dare* him once to entertaine; . . . V. xii. 10. 4
Unlesse thou *dare*, for thy deare Ladies sake . . . VI. iii. 35. 7
he *dare* not returne for all his daily vaunt. . . . VI. iv. 29. 9
ne ever knighthood *dare* Hence to professe; . . . VI. vi. 36. 3
what it *dare* not doe by open might, . . . VI. vii. 1. 7
To *dare* not to pollute so sacred threasure . . . VI. viii. 43. 8
Firme Chastity, that spight ne blemish *dare:* . . . VI. x. 27. 5

Dare—*Continued.*
'How could the death *dare* ever her to quell? . . . VI. xi. 29. 6
Dare to renew the like bold enterprize, . . . VII. vi. 30. 2
loosely they ne *dare* to looke upon her. . . . *Am.* v. 8
find I nought on earth, to which I *dare* . . . *Am.* ix. 3
let no thought of joy, . . . *Dare* to approch, . . . *Am.* lii. 10
Dare not henceforth, . . . T' accuse of pride, . . . *Am.* lxi. 3
heavenly formes ought rather worshipt be, Then *dare* be lov'd . *Am.* lxi. 14
pride *dare* not approch, . . . *Am.* lxv. 9
Ne *dare* lift up her countenance too bold, . . . *Epith.* 162
dare not to heaven fly, . . . *H.L.* 181
no higher *dare* aspyre, . . . *H.L.* 184
Ne *dare* looke up with corruptible eye . . . *H.H.B.* 144
How then *dare* I, the novice of his Art, . . . *H.H.B.* 225
Dared. Never shall be sayde that Perigot was *dared*. . . . *S.C.* Au. 24
he *dared* to stie Up to the clowdes, . . . *Mui.* 42
dar'd The Goddesse selfe to chalenge . . . *Mui.* 269
A . . . man, that *dar'd* to call by name Great Gorgon, . . . I. i. 37. 7
to weet what suddein stowre . . . *dar'd* his dreaded powre. . I. viii. 5. 9
never knight, that *dared* warlike deed, . . . I. ix. 45. 3
dared not his victor to withstand, . . . III. vii. 36. 5
Well warned to beware with whom he *dar'd* to dallie. . . . IV. i. 36. 9
Ne any *dar'd* their perill to partake . . . IV. iv. 29. 5
dared of all sinnes the secrets to unfold. . . . IV. viii. 31. 9
from close friends, that *dar'd* not to appeare, . . . V. xii. 10. 8
Like *darred* Larke, not daring up to looke . . . VII. vi. 47. 5
Had they not *dar'd* their Lord to disobay. . . . *H.H.L.* 77
Darent. the still *Darent*, in whose waters cleane . . . IV. xi. 29. 8
Dares. the birde that *dares* beholde the Sunne, . . . *Bel.*[1] vi. 1
Dares to pollute her hidden mysterie; . . . *T.M.* 568
in doubt ne *dares* To joy at his foolhappie oversight: . . . I. vi. 1. 5
With which he *dares* our offers thus despize: . . . V. v. 48. 5
Ne any *dares* with him for it debate. . . . VI. iv. 30. 4
Darest. Elfe, That *darest* view my direfull countenaunce, . II. vii. 7. 7
Daring. *Daring* the foe that cannot him defend: . . . *Ro.* xiv. 8
not *daring* to expresse my paine, . . . *Gn.* Ded. 1
daring not too rashly mount on hight, . . . *Col.* 421
daring tempt the Queene of heaven to sin; . . . I. v. 35. 2
not one of all them *daring*. . . . IV. x. 56. 9
none his daunger *daring* to abide . . . VI. xi. 49. 6
Like darred Larke, not *daring* up to looke . . . VII. vi. 47. 5
Orpheus, *daring* to provoke the yre . . . *H.L.* 234
Dark. Above the wast a *darke* clowde shrouded her, . . . *Pet.* vi. 7
Those antique Caesars, sleeping long in *darke*, . . . *Ro.* xxv. 3
what concord han light and *darke* sam? . . . *S.C.* May 168
now at earst the *dirke* night doth hast. . . . *S.C.* S. 6
speake not so *dirke;* . . . *S.C.* S. 102
The sonne of all the world is dimme and *darke:* . . . *S.C.* N. 67
With bloodie night, and *darke* confusion; . . . *Gn.* 445
but, in *darke* corners mewd, Muttred of matters . . . *Hub.* 835
darke night fast approched, . . . *D.* 557
calling forth . . . A diverse Dreame out of his prison *darke*, I. i. 44. 2
her *darke* griesly looke them much dismay: . . . I. v. 30. 5
By that same hole an entraunce, *darke* and bace, . . . I. v. 31. 4
Deepe, *darke*, uneasy, dolefull, comfortlesse. . . . I. v. 36. 6
a deepe descent, as *darke* as hell, . . . I. viii. 39. 8
His dwelling . . . *Darke*, dolefull, dreary, like a greedy grave, . I. ix. 33. 4
Wherein *darke* things were writt, hard to be understood. . . . I. x. 13. 9
So *darke* are earthly thinges compard to things divine. . . . I. x. 67. 9
into his *darke* abysse all ravin fell. . . . I. xi. 12. 9
to chace the chearelesse *darke;* . . . I. xi. 51. 8
drery death . . . made *darke* clouds appeare: . . . II. i. 45. 3
Does waste his dayes in *darke* obscuritee, . . . II. iii. 40. 3
As Shepheardes curre, that in *darke* eveninges shade . . . II. vi. 39. 4
that *darke* dreadfull hole of Tartare steepe . . . II. xii. 6. 4
Darke was the Evening, fit for lovers stealth, . . . III. x. 12. 1
Which drawing softly forth out of the *darke*, . . . IV. iv. 15. 4
Where ever in the *darke* he could them spie, . . . V. vi. 30. 5
glyding through the ayre lights all the heavens *darke*. . . . VI. vii. 7. 9
Though faire all night, yet is she *darke* all day: . . . VII. vii. 51. 6
Dark is the world, where your light shined never; . . . *Am.* viii. 13
eies, which lighten my *dark* spright; . . . *Am.* ix. 2
cloud of pryde, which oft doth *dark* Her goodly light, . . . *Am.* lxxxi. 7
Dark is my day, whyles her fayre light I mis, . . . *Am.* lxxxviii. 13
in the secret *darke*, that none reproves, . . . *Epith.* 360
In sight of whom both Sun and Moone are *darke*, . . . *H.H.B.* 125
this *darke* world, whose damps the soule do blynd, . . . *H.H.B.* 137
That with his beames enlumineth the *darke* And dampish aire, *H.H.B.* 164
Darkened. *darkned* was the welkin all about, . . . *Pet.* iii. 10
glistring glosse, *darkned* with filthy dust, . . . II. vii. 4. 3
though *darkned* be her light. . . . V. v. 12. 9
Mean-while the lower World . . . was *darkned* quite; . . . VII. vi. 14. 2
fills the *darkned* world with terror and dismay. . . . VII. vii. 51. 9
by which your fayre beames *darkned* be. . . . *Am.* xlv. 14
your bright glorie *darkned* quight; . . . *H.B.* 165
Darkest. May reach from hence to depth of *darkest* hell, . . . *Ro.* i. 6
Darkness. The hatefull *darknes* now had put to flight; . . . *Gn.* 69
made them dwell in *darknes* of disgrace; . . . *Hub.* 1187
The sonnes of *darknes* and of ignoraunce, . . . *T.M.* 68
Shall die in *darknesse*, and lie hid in slime: . . . *T.M.* 106
dredd *darknes* of the deepe Abysme, . . . *T.M.* 189
dimd with *darknesse* their intelligence, . . . *T.M.* 255
Darknesse more than Cymerians daylie night: . . . *T.M.* 256
To dwell in *darknesse* without sovenance? . . . *T.M.* 486
hell, and *darkenesse*, and the grislie grave, . . . *T.M.* 496
in loathsome den Of ghostly *darkenes*, . . . *T.M.* 532
With fearfull fiends, that in deep *darknes* dwell. . . . *Ti.* 126
shall in rustie *darknes* ever lie, . . . *Ti.* 349
Out of dread *darkenesse* to eternall day, . . . *Ti.* 376
let the dreadfull Queene Of *Darkenes* deepe come . . . *D.* 20

Darkness—*Continued.*
I hate the *darkenesse* and the drery night, . . . *D.* 409
doo in *darknesse* not abridge my breath, . . . *D.* 445
to give them light Which dwell in *darknes,* . . . *D.* 479
gan heaven out of *darknesse* dread For to appeare, . . . *Col.* 855
light through *darknesse* for to wade.' . . . I. i. 12. 9
Ay wont in desert *darknes* to remaine, . . . I. i. 16. 8
Great Gorgon, prince of *darknes* and dead night; . . . I. i. 37. 8
he cald out of deepe *darknes* dredd . . . I. i. 38. 1
Covered with *darkenes* and misdeeming night, . . . I. ii. 3. 8
the *darknes* him does shrowd. . . . I. v. 13. 9
up, dreary Dame, of *darknes* Queene! . . . I. v. 24. 1
arose away The mother of dredd *darknesse,* . . . I. v. 44. 5
darknesse he in deepest dongeon drove, . . . I. vii. 23. 3
Yet live perforce in balefull *darkenesse* bound? . . . I. viii. 38. 5
nether *darkenesse* fowle, nor filthy bands, . . . I. viii. 40. 1
all was covered with *darknesse* dire: . . . I. xi. 40. 4
Lamenting Sorrow did in *darknes* lye, . . . II. vii. 22. 8
Ne *darkenesse* him, ne daunger might dismay. . . . II. vii. 26. 4
hid in *darkenes,* that none could behold . . . II. vii. 29. 3
with their brightnesse made that *darknes* light, . . . II. vii. 42. 2
How to direct theyr way in *darkenes* wide, . . . II. xii. 35. 2
The world in *darkenes* dwels; . . . III. iv. 13. 3
Which *darknesse* shall subdue and heaven win: . . . III. iv. 59. 6
death with *darknesse* doth begin. . . . III. iv. 59. 9
That hast from *darkenes* me returnd to light, . . . III. v. 35. 7
In hatefull *darknes* and in deepe horrore, . . . III. vi. 36. 7
with the Prince of *Darkenes* fell somewhyle . . . III. viii. 8. 3
both full loth in *darkenesse* to debate; . . . III. ix. 14. 2
to build his balefull mansion In drery *darkenes* . . . III. x. 58. 3
pend In dolefull *darkenes* from the vew of day, . . . III. xi. 11. 2
shadowes gan . . . wrap in *darkenes* dreare; . . . III. xi. 55. 4
every wight dismayd with *darkenes* sad . . . III. xii. 1. 3
Where she in *darknes* wastes her cursed daies and nights. . . IV. i. 19. 9
it all the skie doth overcast With *darknes* dred, . . . IV. i. 45. 9
Demogorgon, in dull *darknesse* pent . . . IV. ii. 47. 7
darknesse and dread horrour where she dwelt, . . . IV. vii. 9. 7
The heavens abhorre, and into *darkenesse* drive; . . . IV. vii. 12. 4
To sinfull men with *darknes* overdight, . . . IV. viii. 34. 2
darkenesse dredd that never viewed day, . . . IV. xi. 4. 2
Now seeking *darkenesse,* and now seeking light, . . . V. vi. 14. 7
No more shall now the *darkenesse* of the night Defend thee . . V. vi. 37. 6
An hideous monster doth in *darknesse* lie, . . . V. x. 29. 3
Titans beames . . . lay All night in *darkenesse,* . . . VI. iii. 13. 7
Twixt *darkenesse* dread and hope of living light, . . . VI. iii. 45. 4
In fearefull *darkenesse,* furthest from the skie . . . VI. vi. 11. 2
darkenesse dred and daily night did hover . . . VI. x. 42. 5
Where with such damned fiends she should in *darknesse* dwell. VI. x. 43. 9
in dreadfull *darknesse* layd Amongst those theeves, . . . VI. xi. 2. 3
Creepes forth of dores, whilst *darknes* him doth hide, . . . VI. xi. 18. 7
Seeme much more lovely in that *darknesse* layd, . . . VI. xi. 21. 7
In dreadfull *darknesse* dreadfully aghast; . . . VI. xi. 32. 5
damned ghosts which dwell For aye in *darkenesse,* . . . VI. xii. 35. 8
sleep and *darknesse* round about did trace: . . . VII. vii. 44. 7
wander now, in *darknesse* and dismay, . . . *Am.* xxxiv. 7
your light . . . in my *darknesse,* greater doth appeare, . . . *Am.* lxvi. 12
I wander as in *darkenesse* of the night, . . . *Am.* lxxxvii. 3
In dreadfull *darknesse* lend desired light; . . . *Epith.* 412
in deepe *darknesse* kept, . . . *H.L.* 60
If it in *darknesse* be enshrined ever, . . . *H.B.* 188
That *darknesse* there appeareth never none; . . . *H.H.L.* 73
Where they in *darknesse* and dread horror dwell, . . . *H.H.L.* 90

Darks. *dirks* the beauty of my blossomes rownd: . . . *S.C.* F. 134
And *darkes* the earth with shadow of her sight? . . . *H.H.B.* 229

Darksome. the *darksome* river Of Styx, . . . *Ro.* xv. 5
darkesome caves in pleasaunt vallies pight, . . . *Gn.* 117
the *darksome* bowre Of Herebus . . . *Gn.* 313
round about me heapt in *darksome* glades; . . . *Gn.* 372
I will withdraw me to some *darksome* place, . . . *D.* 486
Yet through that *darksome* vale do glister bright; . . . *Col.* 495
forth unto the *darksom* hole he went, . . . I. i. 14. 3
Shee found them both in *darksome* corner pent; . . . I. iii. 13. 5
darkesome night had all displayd Her coleblacke curtein . . . I. iv. 44. 1
Me, . . . ever since hath kept in *darksom* cave, . . . I. iv. 47. 8
a *darkesome* clowd Upon him fell: . . . I. v. 13. 6
Night . . . She findes forth comming from her *darksome* mew, I. v. 20. 4
I scarse in *darksome* place Could it discerne, . . . I. v. 27. 5
beast . . . which he had kept long time in *darksom* den. . . . I. vii. 16. 9
now in *darkesome* dungeon, wretched thrall, . . . I. vii. 51. 7
That *darkesome* cave they enter, . . . I. ix. 35. 1
he laid him privily Downe in a *darksome* lowly place . . . I. x. 25. 7
deepe emperst his *darksom* hollow maw, . . . I. xi. 53. 8
in a *darkesome* inner bowre Her oft to meete: . . . II. iv. 24. 5
I not descerned in that *darkesome* shade, . . . II. iv. 28. 4
Captiv'd eternally in yron mewes And *darksom* dens, . . . II. v. 27. 9
A *darkesome* way, which no man could descry, . . . II. vii. 20. 7
through a *darksom* narrow strayt, . . . II. vii. 40. 1
this *darksom* neather world her light Doth dim . . . II. vii. 49. 3
in *darkesome* night, Is in a noyous cloud enveloped, . . . III. i. 43. 1
darksom night he eke could turne to day: . . . III. iii. 12. 4
rashly through thy *darksom* dore Unwares have prest; . . . III. iii. 15. 7
It is a *darkesome* delve farre under ground, . . . IV. i. 20. 4
nought but *darkesome* drerinesse she found, . . . IV. vii. 33. 2
fell Chimaera, in her *darkesome* den, . . . VI. i. 8. 2
long in *darksome* Stygian den upbrought, . . . VI. vi. 9. 8
In doubtfull shadow of the *darkesome* night . . . VI. xi. 13. 4
when as towards *darksome* night it drew, . . . VI. xi. 41. 1
like stars that dimmed were With *darksome* cloud, . . . *Epith.* 94

Darling. Like as the *dearling* of the Summers pryde, . . . *T.M.* 235
Faire Marian, the Muses onely *darling:* . . . *Col.* 505

Darling—*Continued.*
'Ah Satyrane, my *dearling* and my joy, . . . I. vi. 28. 6
dred infant, Venus *dearling* dove, . . . IV. Pr. 5. 2
this Dwarfe, her *dearling* base, . . . IV. viii. 54. 5
whom so much ye make Joves dearest *darling,* . . . VII. vii. 50. 3
you, faire Venus *dearling,* . . . *H.B.* 281
The soveraine *dearling* of the Deity, . . . *H.H.B.* 184

Darlings. Her loved Twinnes, the *dearlings* of her joy, . . . *T.M.* 14
Those daintie parts, the *dearlings* of delight, . . . VI. viii. 43. 1
Hercules and Hebe, and the rest Of Venus *dearlings,* . . . *H.L.* 284

Darraine, Darrayne. *See* **Deraign.**

Darred. *See* **Dared.**

Dart. *dart* abroad the thunder bolts of warre, . . . *Ro.* xi. 10
Drerily shooting his stormy *darte,* . . . *S.C.* F. 45
Him Love hath wounded with a deadly *darte:* . . . *S.C.* Ap. 22
through the glaunce Of envies *dart,* . . . *Gn.* 558
A cruell Satyre with his murdrous *dart,* . . . *D.* 156
it may empierse With dolours *dart* . . . *As.* Pr. 10
Faire Venus sonne, that with thy cruell *dart* . . . I. Pr. 3. 2
since my brest was launcht with lovely *dart* . . . I. iv. 46. 5
slew with glauncing *dart* amisse A gentle Hynd, . . . I. vi. 17. 5
let the stony *dart* of senceless cold Perce to my hart, . . . I. vii. 22. 7
thrilling sorrow throwne his utmost *dart:* . . . I. vii. 25. 2
almightie Jove, . . . Hurles forth his thundring *dart* . . . I. viii. 9. 3
Their God . . . Shott many a *dart* . . . I. ix. 10. 8
the *dart* of sinfull guilt the soule dismayes. . . . I. x. 21. 9
pricking him with his sharp-pointed *dart,* . . . II. v. 36. 1
With that he stifly shooke his steelhead *dart:* . . . II. vi. 40. 1
at him a quiv'ring *dart* he threw, . . . III. v. 19. 1
Through an unwary *dart,* which did rebownd . . . III. v. 42. 5
Shee sent at him one fyrie *dart,* . . . III. ix. 28. 8
doth transfixe the soule with deathes eternall *dart.* . . . III. x. 59. 9
felt the point of his hart-percing *dart,* . . . III. xi. 30. 2
Forthy he thrild thee with a leaden *dart* . . . III. xi. 36. 6
inward wounds of dolours *dart.* . . . III. xii. 16. 9
Quite through transfixed with a deadly *dart,* . . . III. xii. 21. 3
Seeming transfixed with a cruell *dart;* . . . III. xii. 31. 5
The Parthian strikes a stag with shivering *dart,* . . . IV. i. 49. 8
being whylome launcht with lovely *dart,* . . . IV. vi. 40. 5
*Great God of love, that with thy cruell *dart* . . . IV. vii. 1. 1
Dart, nigh chockt with sands of tinny mines. . . . IV. xi. 31. 5
wyder made the wound of th' hidden *dart.* . . . V. v. 28. 5
She wounded was with her deceipts owne *dart,* . . . V. v. 43. 6
threw A shivering *dart* with so impetuous force, . . . V. viii. 32. 6
Againe the Pagan threw another *dart,* . . . V. viii. 34. 1
In his right hand he held a trembling *dart,* . . . VI. ii. 6. 4
with a slender *dart,* . . . Strooke him, . . . VI. ii. 12. 6
with lovely *dart* Dinting his brest . . . VI. x. 31. 7
both lyfe and death forth from you *dart,* . . . *Am.* vii. 3
The Damzell broke his misintended *dart.* . . . *Am.* xvi. 12
death out of theyr shiny beames doe *dart;* . . . *Am.* xxiv. 7
all the gods he threats with thundring *dart:* . . . *Am.* xxxix. 4
Love wounded my Loves hart, But Diane beasts with Cupids *dart.* *Epig.* ii. 8
he wounded hath my selfe With his sharpe *dart* of love: . . . *Epig.* iv. 56
dart at them their litle fierie launces; . . . *H.B.* 241
Dolours of death into his soule did *dart,* . . . *H.H.L.* 159
Which from their faces *dart* out fierie light; . . . *H.H.B.* 95

Darted. *darted* fyrie beames out of the same, . . . II. iii. 23. 3
darted forth delights the which her goodly graced. . . . IV. x. 50. 9
darted fyre into my feeble ghost, . . . *H.B.* 24
sparke Which *darted* is from Titans flaming head, . . . *H.H.B.* 163

Darting. Forth *darting* beames of beautie from her eyes: . . . *As.* 190
Darting her beames into each feeble mynd: . . . *Col.* 874
Both *darting* forth faire beames to each mans eye, . . . V. iii. 19. 3
loves . . . *Darting* their deadly arrowes, . . . *Am.* xvi. 7

Darts. *See* **Thunder-darts.**
All slaine with *darts,* lie wallowed in their blood. . . . *Gn.* 432
Against the bitter throwes of dolours *darts:* . . . *T.M.* 134
th' hayling *darts* of heaven beating hard. . . . *Mui.* 80
griefe, Which love had launched with his deadly *darts,* . . . I. ix. 29. 3
She broke his wanton *darts,* . . . II. iii. 23. 9
quiver gay, Stuft with steele-headed *dartes,* . . . II. iii. 29. 3
in his hand two *dartes,* . . . II. iv. 38. 7
With that one of his thrillant *darts* he threw, . . . II. iv. 46. 1
Armed with *dartes* of sensuall Delight, . . . II. xi. 13. 6
One of Malegers cursed *darts* did take, . . . II. xi. 47. 8
secret *darts* did throw; . . . III. i. 51. 8
thy dredd *dartes* in none doe triumph more, . . . III. iii. 3. 1
his sharpe *dartes* and whot artilleree: . . . III. vi. 14. 5
laying his sad *dartes* Asyde, . . . III. vi. 49. 8
There was he painted full of burning *dartes,* . . . III. xi. 44. 8
beware how thou those *dartes* behold.) . . . III. xi. 48. 5
the *darts* which his right hand did straine . . . III. xii. 23. 5
with thy cruell *darts* Doest conquer . . . IV. vii. 1. 1
Though *darts* from shore and stones they at him threw; . . . V. xii. 5. 5
His wanton wings and *darts* of deadly power. . . . *Am.* iv. 8
Shoot out his *darts* to base affections wound; . . . *Am.* viii. 6
With your steele *darts* doo chace from comming neer; . . . *Epith.* 70
by thy cruell *darts* to thee subdewed. . . . *H.L.* 14
The piercing points of his avengefull *darts;* . . . *H.L.* 30
therwith tip his sharp empoisned *darts,* . . . *H.L.* 121
Thence to the soule *darts* amorous desyre, . . . *H.B.* 60

Dashed. O, how art thou *dasht!* . . . *S.C.* Ap. 85
Yet still he bet the water, and the billowes *dasht.* . . . II. vi. 42. 9
Bacchus fruit . . . He on the table *dasht,* . . . III. ix. 30. 4
As fast as water-sprinkles gainst a rocke are *dasht.* . . . IV. iii. 25. 9

Dashing. feare The *dashing* of the waves, . . . *Mui.* 283
billowes . . . *dashing* on all sides, . . . IV. i. 42. 4

Dastard. Like *dastard* Curres . . . III. i. 22. 1
The *dastard,* that did heare him selfe defyde, . . . VI. iii. 36. 1

Dastards. as at Troy most *dastards* of the Greekes . . . . Ro. xiv. 9
Date. from their first untill their utmost *date,* . . . . Ti. 45
Are written sure, and have their certein *date.* . . . . I. ix. 42. 5
good lucke prolonged hath thy *date,* . . . . I. ix. 45. 7
Thus fowle to hasten your untimely *date?* . . . . II. i. 44. 8
did his life her fatall *date* expyre, ... II. viii. 24. 3
feeble age Nigh to his utmost *date* . . . . II. x. 27. 7
Till they outraigned had their utmost *date,* . . . . II. x. 45. 2
To whom sweet Poets verse hath given endlesse *date.* . . . . III. vi. 45. 9
right willing to prolong his *date:* . . . . III. xii. 35. 9
know the measure of their utmost *date* . . . . IV. ii. 50. 4
To draw their dayes unto the utmost *date,* . . . . IV. iii. 1. 2
the same *date* . . . repayd on his owne pate: . . . . IV. xi. 38. 2
the utmost *date* assynde For his returne . . . . V. vi. 3. 6
his passed *date* Bids all old thoughts to die . . . . Am. iv. 3
Daughter. woes the Widdowes *daughter* of the glenne; . . . . S.C. Ap. 26
shee is Syrinx *daughter* without spotte, ... S.C. Ap. 50
Dido! the greate shepehearde his *daughter* sheene. . . . . S.C. N. 38
the bad *daughter* of old Cadmus brood, ... Gn. 171
Great Nereus his *daughter* and his joy. . . . . Gn. 492
faire Eurydice, her *daughter* deere, ... D. 464
He had a *daughter* fresh as floure of May, ... Col. 106
Mulla, the *daughter* of old Mole, ... Col. 108
he that river for his *daughter* wonne: . . . . Col. 125
the *daughter* of a king, Now a loose Leman . . . . I. i. 48. 5
Borne the sole *daughter* of an Emperour, ... I. ii. 22. 7
she . . . Though true as touch, though *daughter* of a king, ... I. iii. 2. 5
bestow Upon the *daughter* of this woman blind, ... I. iii. 18. 3
Abessa, *daughter* of Corceca slow, ... I. iii. 18. 4
That blind old woman, and her *daughter* dear, ... I. iii. 22. 2
Of griesly Pluto she the *daughter* was, ... I. iv. 11. 1
'Deare *daughter,* rightly may I rew The fall . . . . I. v. 25. 1
Duessa I, the *daughter* of Deceipt and Shame.' . . . . I. v. 26. 9
Fayre Thyamis, the *daughter* of Labryde, ... I. vi. 21. 4
Am th' onely *daughter* of a King and Queene, ... I. vii. 43. 3
when his *daughter* deare he does behold, ... I. xii. 12. 8
your *daughter* can ye well advize, ... I. xii. 18. 5
mine onely *daughter* to his Dame, ... I. xii. 20. 5
Both *daughter* and eke kingdome lo! I yield to thee.' . . . . I. xii. 20. 9
forth he called that his *daughter* fayre, ... I. xii. 21. 1
The fairest Un', his onely *daughter* deare, ... I. xii. 21. 2
His onely *daughter* and his only hayre; . . . . I. xii. 21. 3
The wofull *daughter* and forsaken heyre . . . . I. xii. 26. 3
thy *daughter* linck, in holy band Of wedlocke, ... I. xii. 26. 6
to the knight his *daughter* deare he tyde . . . . I. xii. 36. 8
That goodly one . . . my *daughter* is: . . . . II. vii. 48. 6
The noble *daughter* of Corineus . . . . II. x. 18. 1
eke her *daughter* deare, ... II. x. 19. 1
His *daughter* gan despise his drouping day, ... II. x. 30. 4
to his *daughter* Regan he repayrd, ... II. x. 30. 6
to him allide His *daughter* Genuiss' in marriage: . . . . II. x. 52. 4
to him gave for wife his *daughter* bright, ... II. x. 59. 4
his *daughter* deare He gave in wedlocke . . . . II. x. 61. 1
Being his onely *daughter* and his hayre; . . . . III. ii. 22. 4
'Ah! my deare *daughter,* ah! my dearest dread, ... III. ii. 30. 6
'O *daughter* deare!' (said she) 'despeire no whit; . . . . III. ii. 35. 6
'*Daughter,*' (said she) 'what need ye be dismayd? . . . . III. ii. 40. 1
'Come *daughter,* come; come, spit upon my face; . . . . III. ii. 50. 7
Daughter of Phoebus and of Memorye, ... III. iii. 4. 2
Matilda, *daughter* to Pubidius, ... III. iii. 13. 6
'*Daughter,* I deeme that counsel aye most fit, ... III. iii. 52. 3
Ne certes, *daughter,* that same warlike wize, ... III. iii. 53. 5
blacke-browd Cymoent, The *daughter* of great Nereus, ... III. iv. 19. 4
Truth is his *daughter;* . . . . III. iv. 59. 7
the Mayd And *daughter* of a woody Nymphe, ... III. v. 36. 3
That daintie Rose, the *daughter* of her Morne, ... III. v. 51. 1
The *daughter* of Amphisa, who by race A Faerie was, ... III. vi. 4. 2
Pleasure, the *daughter* of Cupid and Psyche late. . . . . III. vi. 50. 9
The yonger *daughter* of Chrysogonee, ... III. vi. 51. 2
her owne *daughter* Pleasure, to whom shee Made her companion, III. vi. 51. 7
Argante is behight, A *daughter* of the Titans . . . . III. vii. 47. 3
love a Shephards *daughter* for his dearest Dame. . . . . III. xi. 38. 9
He loved . . . Aeolus faire *daughter,* Arne hight, ... III. xi. 42. 2
to win Deucalions *daughter* bright, ... III. xi. 42. 5
Daughter unto a Lord of high degree; . . . . IV. vii. 15. 2
Latonaes *daughter,* cruell kynde, In vengement . . . . IV. vii. 30. 5
hath he left one *daughter* . . . . IV. viii. 49. 3
'This Gyants *daughter* came upon a day . . . . IV. viii. 52. 1
All which the Oceans *daughter* to him bare, ... IV. xi. 48. 4
'*Daughter,* me seemes of double wrong ye plaine, ... IV. xii. 30. 2
With which his *daughter* doth him still support; . . . . V. ii. 5. 6
to his *daughter* brings, that dwels thereby; . . . . V. ii. 9. 2
In which the Paynims *daughter* did abide, ... V. ii. 20. 2
the *daughter* of Thaumantes faire . . . . V. iii. 25. 1
It had depriv'd her mother of a *daughter:* . . . . V. iv. 41. 7
For she was *daughter* to a noble Lord . . . . VI. iii. 7. 1
'Faire *daughter* Dame, And you, faire Sonne, ... VI. vi. 6. 5
begot of faire Eurynome, The Oceans *daughter,* . . . . VI. x. 22. 3
the *daughter* of the day . . . . VI. x. 26. 1
This *daughter* thought in wedlocke to have bound . . . . VI. xii. 4. 5
The *daughter* of her Lady Claribell, ... VI. xii. 15. 8
do surely prieve That yond same is your *daughter* sure, ... VI. xii. 18. 9
'And livest thou, my *daughter,* now againe? . . . . VI. xii. 19. 8
Is her owne *daughter,* her owne infant deare. . . . . VI. xii. 20. 6
When she so faire a *daughter* saw survive, ... VI. xii. 21. 7
a *daughter* by descent Of those old Titans . . . . VII. vi. 2. 5
th' Earths *daughter,* thogh she nought did reck Of Hermes message, ... VII. vi. 22. 7
'I am a *daughter,* by the mothers side, Of . . . great Earth, . . VII. vi. 26. 4

Daughter—*Continued.*
daughter of old Father Mole, ... VII. vi. 40. 2
'Cease therefore, *daughter,* further to aspire, ... VII. vii. 59. 1
the *daughter* of the Queene of Love, ... Am. xxxix. 1
with thy *daughter* Pleasure they doe play . . . . H.L. 287
Daughter's. Through his faire *daughters* face and flattring word. II. x. 66. 5
Out of her *daughters* hart fond fancies to reverse. . . . . III. ii. 48. 9
So thought she to undoe her *daughters* love; . . . . III. ii. 51. 6
Should of his dearest *daughters* hard misfortune heare. . . . . III. iii. 5. 9
my deare *daughters* deepe engraffed ill, ... III. iii. 18. 3
The God did graunt his *daughters* deare demaund, ... III. iv. 22. 1
Daughters. Mongst all the *daughters* of proud Libanon, ... Van. vii. 4
thereto aye wonned to repayre The shepheards *daughters* . . . . S.C. F. 120
'Ye shepheards *daughters,* that dwell on the greene, ... S.C. Ap. 127
they bene *daughters* of the hyghest Jove, ... S.C. Jun. 66
Sing now, ye shepheards *daughters,* . . . . S.C. N. 77
The Sunnes sad *daughters* waylde . . . . Gn. 198
Of us, thy *daughters,* dolefull desolate. . . . . T.M. 60
they be *daughters* of Dame Memorie . . . . Ti. 368
The Shepheards *daughters* dauncing in a rownd! . . . . D. 310
Of all the shepheards *daughters* which there bee, ... Col. 556
Amongst the shepheards *daughters* dancing rownd, ... Col. 641
the other crew Of shepheards *daughters* . . . . Col. 932
The mother of three *daughters,* well upbrought . . . . I. x. 4. 3
leave they take of Caelia and her *daughters* three. . . . . I. x. 68. 9
those which Hercules . . . Got from great Atlas *daughters,* . . II. vii. 54. 6
His learned *daughters* would to me report . . . . II. x. 3. 7
Dioclesians fifty *daughters* shene . . . . II. x. 8. 4
three faire *daughters,* which were well uptraind . . . . II. x. 27. 3
He cald his *daughters,* . . . . II. x. 27. 8
the moist *daughters* of huge Atlas . . . . III. i. 57. 8
All these the *daughters* of old Nereus were, ... IV. xi. 52. 1
All lovely *daughters* of high Jove, ... V. ix. 31. 4
Those were the Graces, *daughters* of delight, ... VI. x. 15. 1
'They are the *daughters* of sky-ruling Jove, ... VI. x. 22. 1
faire *daughters* of high Jove And timely Night; . . . . VII. vii. 45. 1
Come now, ye damzels, *daughters* of delight, ... Epith. 96
Tell me, ye merchants *daughters,* . . . . Epith. 167
For she the *daughters* of all wemens race, . . . doth excell, . H.H.B. 205
lovely *Daughters* of the Flood . . . . Proth. 21
Daunt. To *daunt* his foe by ensample of the same. . . . . Gn. 608
daunt unequall armies of his foes, ... I. vii. 34. 3
trembling horror did his conscience *daunt,* . . . . I. ix. 49. 3
did this knight twelve thousand dolours *daunt,* . . . . I. xi. 27. 7
both his foen with equall foyle to *daunt.* . . . . II. iii. 13. 3
did him deadly *daunt,* or fowle dismay; . . . . II. iv. 40. 8
the other, whom he earst did *daunt,* . . . . II. viii. 34. 6
For perdy one shall other slay, or *daunt:* . . . . III. ii. 16. 5
And in three battailes did so deadly *daunt,* . . . . VI. iv. 29. 8
Heroes, which their world did *daunt* With their great deedes, Com. Son. iii. 3
Daunted. Els had he sore be *daunted.* . . . . S.C. Mar. 114
Roaring yet lowder that all harts it *daunted,* . . . . Hub. 1368
Much *daunted* with that dint . . . . I. i. 18. 1
daunted with theyr forces hideous, Their steeds doe stagger, . I. ii. 15. 5
The Sarazin, sore *daunted* with the buffe, ... I. ii. 17. 1
So *daunted* when the Geaunt saw the knight, ... I. vii. 14. 1
daunted with like dread, ... III. iii. 39. 5
Nought therewith *daunted* was her courage prowd, ... III. xii. 1. 7
Much was Cambello *daunted* with his blowes: . . . . IV. iii. 26. 1
Much was he *daunted* with that direfull stound, ... IV. iv. 24. 8
had With one sterne looke so *daunted,* . . . . IV. viii. 2. 3
as one *daunted* with her presence dread, ... IV. viii. 13. 7
So *daunted* was in his despeyring mood, ... V. iii. 26. 8
As if he would have *daunted* him with feare; . . . . V. xii. 16. 3
He much was *daunted* with so dismall sight; . . . . VI. vii. 10. 4
As if he would have *daunted* him withall: . . . . VI. viii. 26. 4
Daunts. th' only breath him *daunts,* who hath escapt the stroke. . . . . I. vii. 13. 9
It dimmes the dazed eyen, and *daunts* the sences quight. . . . . I. viii. 21. 9
Smart *daunts* not mighty harts, ... IV. iii. 8. 9
David. Trew Jonathan and *David* trustie tryde . . . . IV. x. 27. 2
Davy. Diggon *Davie!* I bidde her god day; . . . . S.C. S. 1
Daw. himselfe will a *daw* trie; . . . . Hub. 913
Dawning. they which see the *dawning* day arize; . . . . Ro. xxii. 4
with her song doth greet The *dawning* day . . . . As. 34
where *dawning* day doth never peepe, His dwelling is; . . . . I. i. 39. 5
faire Hesperus . . . brought forth *dawning* light; . . . . I. ii. 6. 7
Aurora . . . Out of the East the *dawning* day doth call. . . . . I. iv. 16. 5
Still did he wake, and still did watch for *dawning* light. . . . . I. v. 1. 9
ere that *dawning* light Discovered had the world to heaven I. v. 52. 5
To tell that *dawning* day is drawing neare, ... I. xii. 21. 7
into the world the *dawning* day Might looke, ... II. xi. 3. 3
earely, ere the *dawning* day appear'd, ... III. vii. 19. 1
day forth *dawning* from the East . . . . V. v. 1. 1
so soone as *dawning* houre Discovered had the light . . . . V. vi. 35. 1
The morrow next, so soone as *dawning* light . . . . V. vii. 26. 7
He mote perceive a litle *dawning* sight . . . . VI. viii. 48. 3
As plaine as light discovers *dawning* day. . . . . H.B. 238
Day. *See* **Good day, Holiday, Sabbath-day, Wedding-day.**
carefull travailes of the painefull *day:* . . . . Bel.[1] i. 4
Being one *day* at my window all alone, ... Pet. i. 1
all this whole shall one *day* come to nought. . . . . Ro. ix. 14
joying in the brightnes of your *day,* . . . . Ro. xv. 2
they which see the dawning *day* arize; . . . . Ro. xxii. 4
marke how Rome, from *day* to *day,* . . . Renewes herselfe . . . Ro. xxvii. 9
One *day,* whiles that my daylie cares did sleepe, ... Van. i. 1
In summers *day,* when Phoebus fairly shone, ... Van. ii. 1
Bird . . . One *day* did scorne the simple Scarabee, ... Van. iv. 2
swanne doth sing before her dying *day,* . . . . Frag.

Day—*Continued.*

All in a sunneshine *day*, as did befall, . . . *S.C.* Ja. 3
Yt chaunced after upon a *day*, . . . *S.C.* F. 143
the *day* is nigh wasted. . . . *S.C.* F. 246
How he him caught upon a *day*, . . . *S.C.* Mar. 107
'Thy father, had he lived this *day*, . . . *S.C.* May 195
One *daye* he sat upon a hyll, . . . *S.C.* Jul. 217
the *daye* in woe, I vowed have to wayst, . . . *S.C.* Au. 179
day, that was, is wightly past, . . . *S.C.* S. 5
sleepe, as some doen, all the long *day;* . . . *S.C.* S. 233
sadde Winter welked hath the *day*, . . . *S.C.* N. 13
the shepheard, seeing *day* appeare, . . . *Gn.* 70
So soone as *day* appeard to peoples vewing, . . . *Hub.* 104
bad next *day* that all should readie be: . . . *Hub.* 329
used duly everie *day* Their service . . . to say, . . . *Hub.* 449
'Ah! sir Mule, now blessed be the *day*, . . . *Hub.* 589
Ne suffer it to house there halfe a *day*. . . . *Hub.* 828
Sitting one *day* within his turret hye, . . . *Hub.* 1227
is *day* by *day* unto us wrought . . . *T.M.* 62
It is their light, their loadstarre, and their *day;* . . . *T.M.* 495
kept from looking on the lightsome *day:* . . . *T.M.* 593
It chaunced me on *day* beside the shore . . . *Ti.* 1
Out of dread darkenesse to eternall *day*, . . . *Ti.* 376
A fairer wight saw never summers *day*. . . . *Ti.* 637
So on a Summers *day*, when season milde . . . *Mui.* 49
dame Venus, on a *day* In spring, . . . *Mui.* 113
who can him assure of happie *day*, . . . *Mui.* 218
The sea, the aire, the fire, the *day*, the night, . . . *Mui.* 228
The wretchedst man that treades this *day* on ground?' . . . *D.* 63
Would wend with me, and waite by me all *day*, . . . *D.* 128
'She is the Rose, the glorie of the *day*, . . . *D.* 232
to her ghost doo service *day* by *day*. . . . *D.* 371
'I hate the *day*, because it lendeth light . . . *D.* 407
day is turnd to night, . . . *D.* 482
soone as *day* doth shew his deawie face, . . . *D.* 484
There will I sigh, and sorrow all *day* lang, . . . *D.* 488
daie was overcast, And darke night fast approched, . . . *D.* 556
Full carefully he kept them *day* and night, . . . *As.* 5
with her song doth greet The dawning *day* . . . *As.* 34
As they the forest raunged on a *day*, . . . *As.* 140
As Sunny beames in fairest somers *day*, . . . *As.* 158
all the *day* it standeth full of deow, . . . *As.* 191
From this *day* forth do call it Astrophel: . . . *As.* 196
The gentlest shepheardesse that lives this *day*, . . . *As.* 212
Sate (as his custome was) upon a *day*, . . . *Col.* 4
Since that same *day* in nought I take delight, . . . *Col.* 44
'One *day* (quoth he) . . . *Col.* 56
The dowre agreed, the *day* assigned plaine, . . . *Col.* 126
hablest wit of most I know this *day*. . . . *Col.* 383
everie goodly meed . . . demaunds a *day;* . . . *Col.* 593
everie *day*, in which she did a deed, . . . *Col.* 594
never wist I till this present *day*, . . . *Col.* 827
brought forth chearfull *day:* . . . *Col.* 856
The *day* with cloudes was suddeine overcast, . . . I. i. 6. 5
Armory, Wherein ye have great glory wonne this *day*, . . . I. i. 27. 6
Bidding his beades all *day* for his trespas, . . . I. i. 30. 7
The Sunne, that measures heaven all *day* long, . . . I. i. 32. 8
with new *day* new worke at once begin: . . . I. i. 33. 2
now *day* is spent: . . . I. i. 33. 6
where dawning *day* doth never peepe, His dwelling is; . . . I. i. 39. 5
prickte with . . . hope to winne his Ladies hearte that *day*, . . . I. ii. 14. 7
ere my hoped *day* of spousall shone, . . . I. ii. 23. 6
One *day* in doubt I cast for to compare . . . I. ii. 37. 3
raisd . . . A foggy mist that overcast the *day*, . . . I. ii. 38. 5
Till on a *day* (that *day* is everie Prime, . . . I. ii. 40. 4
One *day*, nigh wearie of the yrkesome way, . . . I. iii. 4. 1
that old woman *day* and night did pray . . . I. iii. 13. 6
Nine hundred *Pater nosters* every *day*, . . . I. iii. 13. 8
The *day* is spent; and commeth drowsie night, . . . I. iii. 15. 1
when broad *day* the world discovered has, . . . I. iii. 21. 1
My chearefull *day* is turnd to chearelesse night, . . . I. iii. 27. 7
troupes of people traveild thetherward Both *day* and night, . . . I. iv. 3. 2
nigh consumed is the lingring *day*. . . . I. iv. 3. 9
a rich throne, as bright as sunny *day;* . . . I. iv. 8. 2
Aurora . . . Out of the East the dawning *day* doth call. . . . I. iv. 16. 5
To looken whether it were night or *day*. . . . I. iv. 19. 6
as a sacred pledge His cause . . . the next *day* to try: . . . I. iv. 43. 2
with that Pagan proud he combatt will that *day*. . . . I. v. 2. 9
Lay cover'd with inchaunted cloud all *day:* . . . I. v. 19. 6
she all *day* did hide her hated hew. . . . I. v. 20. 5
dreaded Night in brightest *day* hath place, . . . I. v. 24. 4
The sonnes of *Day* he favoureth, I see, . . . I. v. 25. 7
Coverd with charmed cloud from vew of *day*, . . . I. v. 29. 4
thundering Jove, that rules both night and *day?* . . . I. v. 42. 9
on a *day* his wary Dwarfe had spyde . . . I. v. 45. 7
caytive wretched thralls, that wayled night and *day:* . . . I. v. 45. 9
thralles . . . thither were assembled *day* by *day* . . . I. v. 51. 2
mother came upon a *day* . . . to see her little sonne; . . . I. vi. 27. 1
on a *day*, when Satyres all were gone . . . I. vi. 33. 1
The better part now of the lingring *day* . . . I. vi. 34. 1
As he had traveild many a sommers *day* . . . I. vi. 35. 5
'I chaunst this *day*, This fatall *day* . . . I. vi. 38. 1, 2
one *day*, when Phoebe fayre . . . was following the chace, . . . I. vii. 5. 1
From that *day* forth Duessa was his deare, . . . I. vii. 16. 1
'O lightsome *day!* the lampe of highest Jove, . . . I. vii. 23. 1
Was never Lady loved dearer *day* . . . I. vii. 27. 7
To see what end of fight should him befall that *day*. . . . I. viii. 2. 9
Behold what ye this *day* have done for mee, . . . I. viii. 27. 8
Have made you master of the field this *day*, . . . I. viii. 28. 2

Day—*Continued.*

my Lord . . . Whose presence I have lackt too long a *day:* . . . I. viii. 43. 2
wound, which *day* and night Whilome doth rancle . . . I. ix. 7. 3
on a *day*, prickt forth with jollitee . . . I. ix. 12. 5
So fayre a creature yet saw never sunny *day*. . . . I. ix. 13. 9
From that *day* forth I lov'd that face divyne; . . . I. ix. 15. 5
From that *day* forth I cast in carefull mynd, . . . I. ix. 15. 6
Against the *day* of wrath to burden thee? . . . I. ix. 46. 5
all the *day* in doing good and godly deedes. . . . I. x. 3. 9
it was warely watched night and *day*, . . . I. x. 5. 2
Hast wandred through the world now long a *day*, . . . I. x. 9. 6
dieted with fasting every *day*, . . . I. x. 26. 3
wont him once to disple every *day:* . . . I. x. 27. 2
If not well ended at our dying *day*. . . . I. x. 41. 7
day and night said his devotion, . . . I. x. 46. 6
as one were borne that very *day*. . . . I. xi. 30. 5
watch the noyous night, and wait for joyous *day*. . . . I. xi. 50. 9
The joyous *day* gan early to appeare; . . . I. xi. 51. 1
so soone as *day* he spyde, . . . I. xi. 52. 5
Diana in fresh sommers *day* Beholdes her nymphes . . . I. xii. 7. 7
To tell that dawning *day* is drawing neare, . . . I. xii. 21. 7
day should faile me ere I had them all declard. . . . I. xii. 31. 9
it should not be quenched *day* nor night, . . . I. xii. 37. 8
made great feast to solemnize that *day:* . . . I. xii. 38. 2
Great joy was made that *day* of young and old, . . . I. xii. 40. 1
One *day*, when him high corage did emmove, . . . II. i. 50. 5
Upon a *day*, As she the woodes . . . did raunge, . . . II. ii. 7. 2
heroick worth He shewd that *day*, . . . II. ii. 25. 4
That may this *day* in all the world be found. . . . II. ii. 42. 5
The *day* that first doth lead the yeare around, . . . II. ii. 42. 7
'There this old Palmer shewd himselfe that *day*, . . . II. ii. 43. 1
Why livest thou, dead dog, a lenger *day*, . . . II. iii. 7. 6
From that *day* forth he cast for to uphold . . . II. iii. 9. 7
purvay Your selfe of sword before that bloody *day;* . . . II. iii. 15. 5
Do arme your self against that *day*, . . . II. iii. 15. 9
The *day* that first of Priame she was seene, . . . II. iii. 31. 7
day and night her dores to all stand open wide. . . . II. iii. 41. 9
that *day* too farre did seeme. . . . II. iv. 21. 6
ear that wished *day* his beame disclosd, . . . II. iv. 22. 1
One *day* unto me came in friendly mood, . . . II. iv. 22. 4
One *day* . . . He woo'd her thus: . . . II. iv. 25. 5
For he has vowd to beene avengd that *day* . . . II. v. 38. 5
(That *day* it selfe him seemed all too long) . . . II. v. 38. 6
'What dismall *day* hath lent this cursed light, . . . II. vi. 43. 7
Day and night keeping wary watch and ward, . . . II. vii. 25. 2
An ugly feend, more fowle then dismall *day*, . . . II. vii. 26. 7
vew of cherefull *day* Did never . . . it selfe display, . . . II. vii. 29. 4
warily awaited *day* and night, . . . II. vii. 32. 3
till that *day* They never creature saw . . . II. vii. 37. 5
After so wicked deede why liv'st thou lenger *day?* . . . II. viii. 46. 9
'Paynim, this is thy dismall *day;* . . . II. viii. 51. 5
by whose most gratious ayd I live this *day*, . . . II. viii. 55. 6
Day and night duely keeping watch and ward; . . . II. ix. 25. 2
day and night it brent, . . . II. ix. 29. 8
But later *day*, Finding in it fit ports . . . II. x. 6. 7
can witnes yet unto this *day* . . . II. x. 10. 6
What colour were their waters that same *day*, . . . II. x. 24. 3
How oft that *day* did sad Brunchildis see . . . II. x. 24. 6
his daughter gan despise his drouping *day*, . . . II. x. 30. 4
lost his sword, yet to be seene this *day*. . . . II. x. 49. 5
long before that *day* . . . II. x. 53. 6
into the world the dawning *day* Might looke, . . . II. xi. 3. 3
To see a cruell fight doen by the prince this *day*. . . . II. xi. 4. 9
They battred *day* and night, and entraunce did awate. . . . II. xi. 6. 9
Ne once did yield it respitt *day* nor night; . . . II. xi. 9. 3
day and night . . . they continued fight. . . . II. xi. 13. 8
had not bene removed many a *day;* . . . II. xi. 35. 8
afterwards did rule the night and *day:* . . . II. xii. 13. 7
In springing flowre the image of thy *day*. . . . II. xii. 74. 3
So passeth, in the passing of a *day*, . . . II. xii. 75. 1
Dauncing and reveling both *day* and night, . . . III. i. 39. 7
With which fayre Britomart gave light unto the *day*. . . . III. i. 43. 9
T' abridg their journey long, and lingring *day;* . . . III. ii. 4. 3
One *day* it fortuned fayre Britomart, . . . III. ii. 22. 1
all the *day*, when as thine equall peares . . . III. ii. 31. 3
one *day*, as me misfortune led, . . . III. ii. 38. 6
day His joyous face did to the world revele, . . . III. ii. 48. 1
In a deepe delve, farre from the vew of *day*, . . . III. iii. 7. 7
there doe toyle and traveile *day* and night, . . . III. iii. 11. 6
darksom night he eke could turne to *day:* . . . III. iii. 12. 4
to this *day* . . . The feends do quake . . . III. iii. 12. 8
Ne other to himselfe is knowne this *day*, . . . III. iii. 26. 8
where the *day* out of the sea doth spring, . . . III. iii. 27. 4
'Great ayd . . . shall give in that sad *day;* . . . III. iii. 28. 2
on a *day* Finding the Nymph asleepe . . . III. iv. 19. 6
she inquir'd One *day* of Proteus . . . III. iv. 25. 2
she gave him warning every *day* . . . III. iv. 26. 1
day discovers all dishonest wayes, . . . III. iv. 59. 1
Our life is *day*, but death with darknesse doth begin. . . . III. iv. 59. 9
'O! when will *day* then turne to me againe, . . . III. iv. 60. 1
yield her rowme to *day* that can it governe well.' . . . III. iv. 60. 9
in lewd slouth to wast his carelesse *day;* . . . III. v. 1. 7
I have many a *day* Served a gentle Lady . . . III. v. 4. 4
Lives none this *day* that may with her compare . . . III. v. 8. 4
on a *day*, as shee pursewd the chace . . . III. v. 28. 1
It was upon a Sommers shinie *day*. . . . III. vi. 6. 4
two babes, as faire as springing *day*. . . . III. vi. 26. 9
attend About him *day* and night, . . . III. vi. 32. 4
all the *day* before the sunny rayes . . . III. vii. 12. 7

Day—*Continued.*
ere the dawning *day* appear'd, . . . III. vii. 19. 1
never learned he such service till that *day*. . . . III. vii. 36. 9
on a *day*, as he disposed was To walke . . . III. viii. 11. 1
next to none after that happy *day*, . . . III. viii. 13. 7
Cannot two fairer Cities find this *day*, . . . III. ix. 51. 4
suffer her, nor night nor *day*, Out of his sight . . . III. x. 3. 7
One *day*, as hee forpassed by the plaine . . . III. x. 20. 5
al good knights, that armes doe bear this *day*, . . . III. x. 27. 8
on a *day* the Satyres her espide . . . III. x. 36. 4
All *day* they daunced with great lusty-hedd, . . . III. x. 45. 6
Nine times he heard him come aloft ere *day*, . . . III. x. 48. 5
these seven monethes *day*, . . . III. xi. 10. 8
In dolefull darkenes from the vew of *day*, . . . III. xi. 11. 2
day and night afflicts with mortall paine, . . . III. xi. 17. 2
Dying each *day* with inward wounds of dolours dart. . . . III. xii. 16. 9
that *day* for to outweare. . . . III. xii. 28. 9
All that *day* she outwore in wandering . . . III. xii. 29. 1
yokes assoyle . . . till a new *day*; . . . III. xii. 47. *or.* 6
she never joyed *day*; . . . IV. i. 2. 2
The very selfe same *day* that she was wedded, . . . IV. i. 3. 2
great riches, gathered manie a *day*, . . . IV. i. 29. 5
not in plight This *day* to wreake the dammage by thee donne. IV. i. 44. 6
The open wrongs thou doest me *day* by *day*: . . . IV. ii. 13. 2
There they, I weene, would fight untill this *day*, . . . IV. ii. 20. 1
This happie *day* I have to greete you well, . . . IV. ii. 23. 5
One *day*, when all that troupe of warlike wooers . . . IV. ii. 38. 1
There on a *day* a noble youthly knight, . . . IV. ii. 45. 1
The *day* was set, that all might understand, . . . IV. iii. 3. 3
That *day*, the dreddest *day* that living wight Did ever see . . IV. iii. 3. 5
To view and deeme the deedes of armes that *day*: . . . IV. iii. 4. 4
upon th' appointed *day* . . . they came; . . . IV. iv. 13. 5
Which doughty Triamond had wrought that *day* . . . IV. iv. 22. 5
Satyrane that *day* was judg'd to beare the bell. . . . IV. iv. 25. 9
So that the doome was to another *day* differd. . . . IV. iv. 36. 9
day came, when all those knightes againe Assembled were . . IV. iv. 37. 1
Full many deedes that *day* were shewed plaine: . . . IV. iv. 37. 3
The doughtiest knight that liv'd that *day*, . . . IV. iv. 42. 9
So he continued all that *day* throughout, . . . IV. iv. 43. 5
in sommers *day*, when raging heat Doth burne the earth . . . IV. iv. 47. 1
restore The prize to knights of Maydenhead that *day*, . . . IV. iv. 48. 2
The same one *day* . . . she from her middle loosd, . . . IV. v. 5. 1
Satyrane the first *day* best had donne: . . . IV. v. 7. 4
since the *day* that they created beene, . . . IV. v. 12. 4
hath this *day* so many so unmanly shent.' . . . IV. v. 18. 9
The more it gauld and griev'd him night and *day*, . . . IV. v. 31. 8
neither *day* nor night from working spared, . . . IV. v. 35. 7
in Lipari doe *day* and night Frame thunderbolts . . . IV. v. 37. 3
The things, that *day* most minds, at night doe most appeare. . IV. v. 43. 9
day out of the Ocean mayne Began to peepe . . . IV. v. 45. 3
The next *day*, as he on his way did ride, . . . IV. vi. 2. 2
almost had against you trespassed this *day*.' . . . IV. vi. 3. 9
'This other *day*' (sayd he) 'a stranger knight . . . IV. vi. 5. 6
When ever he this way shall passe by *day* or night.' . . . IV. vi. 5. 9
'Till on a *day*, as through a desert wyld We travelled, . . . IV. vi. 36. 1
all she did was but to weare out *day*. . . . IV. vi. 45. 5
many a knight had sought so many a *day*. . . . IV. vii. 8. 5
'This dismall *day* hath thee a caytive made, . . . IV. vii. 12. 1
on a *day*, unweeting unto wight, . . . IV. vii. 17. 5
yet untouched till this present *day*, . . . IV. vii. 18. 8
on a *day*, by fortune as it fell, . . . IV. vii. 42. 1
alwaies wept and wailed night and *day*, . . . IV. viii. 2. 8
Till on a *day*, as in his wonted wise . . . IV. viii. 3. 1
every *day*, for guerdon of her song, . . . IV. viii. 5. 6
Upon a *day* as she him sate beside, . . . IV. viii. 6. 1
Till on a *day*, as through that wood he rode, . . . IV. viii. 19. 1
soone as *day* discovered heavens face . . . IV. viii. 34. 1
Gyants daughter came upon a *day* Unto the prison, . . . IV. viii. 52. 1
From *day* to *day* she woo'd and prayd him fast, . . . IV. viii. 52. 8
So on a *day*, as by the flowrie marge . . . IV. viii. 61. 5
From that *day* forth in peace . . . IV. ix. 16. 1
the *day* that first with deadly wound My heart was launcht, . IV. x. 1. 7
time to steale, the threasure of mans *day*, . . . IV. x. 14. 8
day and night did watch and duely ward . . . IV. x. 17. 2
my love was lodged *day* and night, . . . IV. x. 29. 4
darkenesse dredd that never viewed *day*, . . . IV. xi. 4. 2
Ne ever from the *day* the night descride, . . . IV. xi. 4. 8
Before that *day* her wooed to his bed, . . . IV. xi. 8. 6
They all on him this *day* attended well, . . . IV. xi. 30. 3
joy likewise this solemne *day* to see? . . . IV. xi. 40. 5
One *day*, as she to shunne the season whot . . . IV. xi. 42. 4
All which that *day* in order seemly good . . . IV. xi. 44. 7
Her silver feet, faire washt against this *day*: . . . IV. xi. 47. 6
In which his wretched love lay *day* and night . . . IV. xii. 19. 4
weeping *day* and night did him attend, . . . IV. xii. 21. 6
Upon a *day* she found this gentle childe . . . V. i. 6. 2
in that same *day* when Jove those Gyants quelled: . . . V. i. 9. 9
'That ever I this dismall *day* did see! . . . V. i. 15. 3
This *day* as I in solace sate hereby . . . V. i. 16. 6
for a twelve moneths *day* . . . V. i. 26. 7
None other way will I this *day* betake, . . . V. ii. 10. 6
By which as they did travell on a *day*, . . . V. ii. 29. 3
To tell the glorie of the feast that *day*, . . . V. iii. 3. 1
Full many deeds of armes that *day* were donne, . . . V. iii. 6. 5
all that *day* the greatest prayse redounded To Marinell, . . . V. iii. 6. 8
The second *day*, so soone as morrow light Appear'd . . . V. iii. 7. 1
there all *day* continew'd cruell fight, . . . V. iii. 7. 3
Marinell that *day* deserved best. . . . V. iii. 7. 8
The third *day* came, that should due tryall lend . . . V. iii. 8. 1
all these knights, which that *day* armour bore, . . . V. iii. 13. 7

Day—*Continued.*
To whom that *day* they should the girlond yield, . . . V. iii. 14. 6
Approv'd that *day* that she all others did excell. . . . V. iii. 15. 9
what he did that *day*, he did it not For her, . . . V. iii. 16. 3
What strokes, what dreadfull stoure, it stird this *day*; . . . V. iii. 21. 6
never word from that *day* forth he spoke. . . . V. iii. 33. 5
no braver president this *day* Remaines on earth, . . . V. iv. 2. 6
By what good right doe you withhold this *day*?' . . . V. iv. 17. 5
what other deadly dismall *day* Is falne on you . . . V. iv. 26. 6
made the scorne of Knighthod this same *day*: . . . V. iv. 27. 7
Weary of toile and travell of that *day*, . . . V. iv. 46. 3
For the rebuke which she sustain'd that *day*, . . . V. iv. 47. 2
As she had seene that *day*, . . . V. iv. 47. 9
day forth dawning from the East . . . V. v. 1. 1
In which he had bene trayned many a *day*, . . . V. v. 21. 2
it tormented her both *day* and night: . . . V. v. 27. 5
one *day* she thus him proved. . . . V. v. 35. 9
'Unworthy sure' (quoth he) 'of better *day*, . . . V. v. 39. 5
One *day* her Ladie, calling her apart, . . . V. v. 45. 1
One *day* when as she long had sought for ease . . . V. vi. 7. 1
I wote when ye did watch both night and *day* . . . V. vi. 25. 5
the *day* with dampe was overcast, . . . V. vii. 8. 6
Untill she spide the lampe of lightsome *day* . . . V. vii. 17. 3
Ne *day* nor night did ever idly rest; . . . V. viii. 3. 7
Which he unto her people does each *day*; . . . V. viii. 19. 2
stird up *day* and night . . . V. viii. 20. 2
Justice that *day* of wrong her selfe had wroken; . . . V. viii. 44. 7
the Prince, as victour of that *day*, . . . V. viii. 51. 2
earnestly besought to wend that *day* With her, . . . V. ix. 3. 8
Stood open wyde to all men *day* and night; . . . V. ix. 22. 4
seeing all in armour bright as *day*, . . . V. ix. 24. 2
Upon Joves judgement-seat wayt *day* and night; . . . V. ix. 31. 7
till this *day* mongst many living are, . . . V. x. 5. 8
Ne *day* nor night did sleepe t' attend them on, . . . V. x. 10. 4
all his armours readie dight that *day*, . . . V. x. 16. 3
That same is it which fought for you this *day*. . . . V. xi. 17. 6
all the people which beheld that *day* Gan shout aloud, . . . V. xi. 34. 1
ne ever *day* did rest. . . . V. xi. 35. 9
now he hath to her prefixt a *day*, . . . V. xi. 40. 1
He *day* and night doth ward both farre and wide, . . . V. xi. 42. 7
from the *day* that he thus did it leave, . . . V. xi. 46. 7
in one *day* they with the coast did fall; . . . V. xii. 4. 6
ne gave him longer *day*: . . . V. xii. 9. 8
the dismall *day* Appointed for Irenas death . . . V. xii. 11. 1
Most squalid garments, fit for such a *day*; . . . V. xii. 12. 2
There wayting for the Tyrant till it was farre *day*. . . . V. xii. 13. 9
day and night employ'd his busie paine . . . V. xii. 26. 3
by chaunce he met uppon a *day* With Artegall, . . . VI. i. 4. 3
Of all this *day* on ground that breathen living spright! . . . VI. i. 4. 9
this same *day*, as I that way did come . . . VI. i. 16. 1
a Steare, in heat of sommers *day*, . . . VI. i. 24. 4
this *day* I was enraunging it, . . . VI. ii. 9. 7
'This *day*, . . . We chaunst to come . . . VI. ii. 16. 1
He him requested, . . . To lend him *day* . . . VI. ii. 19. 4
since the *day* that armes I first did reare, . . . VI. ii. 26. 8
fortune hath this *day* Given to me the spoile . . . VI. ii. 33. 7
when *day* gan to uplooke, . . . VI. iii. 11. 1
Calidore rising up as fresh as *day* . . . VI. iii. 13. 8
who was slaine The *day* before . . . VI. iii. 17. 3
Where he arriving with the fall of *day* . . . VI. iii. 37. 7
When *day* is spent, and rest us needeth most, . . . VI. iii. 39. 2
so soone as joyous *day* Did shew it selfe . . . VI. iii. 45. 1
Upon a *day* he cast abrode to wend, . . . VI. iv. 17. 2
So all that *day* in wandring vainely he did spend. . . . VI. iv. 25. 9
day and night vexe her carefull thought, . . . VI. v. 6. 8
faithfully did serve both *day* and night . . . VI. v. 9. 7
Upon a *day*, as on their way they went, . . . VI. v. 10. 1
Upon a *day*, as they the time did waite, . . . VI. v. 15. 1
The wretchedst Dame that lives this *day* on ground; . . . VI. v. 28. 2
every *day* them duely drest. . . . VI. vi. 2. 9
One *day*, as he was searching of their wounds, . . . VI. vi. 5. 1
Now smyling smoothly, like to sommers *day*, . . . VI. vi. 42. 7
neither *day* nor weeke He would surceasse, . . . VI. vii. 13. 8
on a *day*, when Cupid kept his court, . . . VI. vii. 32. 6
day, that doth discover bad and good, . . . VI. viii. 51. 7
day nor night he suffred him to rest, . . . VI. ix. 3. 2
There on a *day*, as he pursew'd the chace, . . . VI. ix. 5. 1
caroling her name both *day* and night, . . . VI. ix. 9. 8
untill the flying *day* Was farre forth spent, . . . VI. ix. 12. 5
the *day* did now expyre. . . . VI. ix. 13. 9
For so great kindnesse as he found that *day* . . . VI. ix. 18. 5
all the *day* to what I list I doe attend. . . . VI. ix. 22. 9
every *day*, her companie to gaine, . . . VI. ix. 34. 7
With the faire Pastorella every *day*, . . . VI. ix. 37. 2
One *day*, when as the shepheard swaynes together Were met, . VI. ix. 41. 1
One *day*, as he did raunge the fields abroad, . . . VI. x. 5. 1
that same *day* That Theseus her unto his bridale bore, . . . VI. x. 13. 2
daunce there *day* and night: . . . VI. x. 15. 3
the daughter of the *day* . . . VI. x. 26. 1
One *day*, as they all three together went . . . VI. x. 34. 1
From that *day* forth she gan him to affect, . . . VI. x. 37. 1
one *day*, when Calidore Was hunting in the woods, . . . VI. x. 39. 1
day and night she nought did but lament . . . VI. x. 44. 3
One *day*, as he did all his prisoners vew, . . . VI. xi. 3. 6
From that *day* forth he kyndnesse to her showed, . . . VI. xi. 4. 6
Ne *day* nor night he suffred her to rest, . . . VI. xi. 5. 8
her all night did watch, and all the *day* molest. . . . VI. xi. 5. 9
'That ever I did live this *day* to see, This dismall *day*, . . . VI. xi. 29. 2, 3
gently waking them gave them the time of *day*. . . . VI. xi. 38. 9
So there all *day* they bode, . . . VI. xi. 40. 9

Day—*Continued.*

He breath'd his sword, and rested him till *day;* . . . VI. xi. 47. 2
in whottest sommers *day,* . . . VI. xi. 48. 1
Appointed to attend her dewly *day* and night. . . . VI. xii. 14. 9
Some were of dogs, that barked *day* and night; . . . VI. xii. 27. 3
duly her attended *day* and night; . . . VII. vi. 9. 4
though full many a *day* He saw her clad, . . . VII. vi. 42. 7
as her manner was on sunny *day,* . . . VII. vi. 45. 6
Doth to this *day* with Wolves and Thieves abound: . . . VII. vi. 55. 8
this same *day* when she on Arlo sat, . . . VII. vii. 7. 2
since the *day* That all the gods whylome assembled were . . . VII. vii. 12. 1
every *day* We see his parts, . . . VII. vii. 24. 2
holding all the *day* An hatchet . . . VII. vii. 42. 5
after these there came the *Day* and Night, . . . VII. vii. 44. 1
Day did beare upon his scepters hight The goodly Sun . . . VII. vii. 44. 8
her face . . . every *day* We changed see . . . VII. vii. 50. 6
though faire all night, yet is she darke all *day:* . . . VII. vii. 51. 6
One *day* I sought . . . To make a truce, . . . *Am.* xii. 1
One *day* as I unwarily did gaze . . . *Am.* xvi. 1
on so holy *day,* . . . *Am.* xxii. 3
my thoughts doo *day* and night attend, . . . *Am.* xxii. 7
the worke that she all *day* did make, . . . *Am.* xxiii. 3
The laurel-leafe, which you this *day* doe weare, . . . *Am.* xxviii. 1
the fayre sunshine in somers *day;* . . . *Am.* xl. 6
Lord of lyfe! that, on this *day,* Didst make thy triumph . . . *Am.* lxviii. 1
This joyous *day,* . . . with joy begin; . . . *Am.* lxviii. 5
One *day* I wrote her name upon the strand; . . . *Am.* lxxv. 1
when as *day* the heaven doth adorne, . . . *Am.* lxxxvi. 5
I wish that night the noyous *day* would end: . . . *Am.* lxxxvi. 6
I wish that *day* would shortly reascend. . . . *Am.* lxxxvi. 8
Ne ought I see, though in the clearest *day,* . . . *Am.* lxxxvii. 5
Dark is my *day,* whyles her fayre light I mis, . . . *Am.* lxxxviii. 13
As Diane hunted on a *day,* . . . *Epig.* ii. 1
Upon a *day,* as Love lay sweetly slumbring . . . *Epig.* iv. 1
For lo! the wished *day* is come at last, . . . *Epith.* 31
In Joves sweet paradice of *Day* and Night; . . . *Epith.* 99
Fit for so joyfull *day:* . . . *Epith.* 115
The joyfulst *day* that ever sunne did see. . . . *Epith.* 116
let this *day,* let this one *day,* be myne; . . . *Epith.* 125
Never had man more joyfull *day* then this, . . . *Epith.* 246
Make feast therefore now all this live-long *day;* . . . *Epith.* 248
This *day* for ever to me holy is. . . . *Epith.* 249
leave your wonted labors for this *day:* . . . *Epith.* 262
This *day* is holy; . . . *Epith.* 263
This *day* the sunne is in his chiefest hight, . . . *Epith.* 265
To chose the longest *day* in all the yeare, . . . *Epith.* 271
Yet never *day* so long, but late would passe. . . . *Epith.* 273
bonefiers make all *day;* . . . *Epith.* 275
when will this long weary *day* have end, . . . *Epith.* 278
Enough it is that all the *day* was youres: . . . *Epith.* 297
now *day* is doen, and night is nighing fast, . . . *Epith.* 298
For it will soone be *day:* . . . *Epith.* 369
As plaine as light discovers dawning *day.* . . . *H.B.* 238
And caroll Hymnes of love both *day* and night. . . . *H.H.L.* 70
Both *day,* and night, is unto them all one; . . . *H.H.L.* 71
Ne hath their *day,* ne hath their blisse, an end, . . . *H.H.L.* 74
But those two most, which, ruling night and *day,* . . . *H.H.B.* 55
Calme was the *day,* . . . *Proth.* 1
Against the Brydale *day,* . . . *Proth.* 17, 35
Against their Brydale *day,* . . . *Proth.* 53
So fresh they seem'd as *day,* . . . *Proth.* 70
Even as their Brydale *day,* . . . *Proth.* 71
this Lay, Prepar'd against that *Day,* . . . *Proth.* 88
Against their Brydale *day,* . . . *Proth.* 89
Upon your Brydale *day,* . . . *Proth.* 107
their brydale *daye* should not be long; . . . *Proth.* 111
Against the bridale *daye,* . . . *Proth.* 143
Upon the Brydale *day,* . . . *Proth.* 161
Against their Brydale *day,* . . . *Proth.* 179

Daylight. twincling starres the *daylight* hence chase. . . . *S.C.* Ap. 161
all the Kirke pillours eare *day light,* . . . *S.C.* May 12
while it was *daye-light,* . . . *S.C.* S. 3
the drouping *day-light* gan to fade, . . . I. xi. 49. 5
darknesse, which *day-light* doth shonne: . . . VI. xii. 35. 8

Dayr'house. *See* **Dairy-house.**

Day's. *See* **Midday's.**

After his *dayes* long labour drew to rest, . . . *D.* 23
untill *Dayes* enemy Did him appease; . . . I. v. 34. 6
This *daies* ensample hath this lesson deare Deepe written . . . I. viii. 44. 7
for memory of that *dayes* ruth, . . . II. iii. 2. 7
henceforth by this *daies* ensample trow, . . . II. v. 13. 7
The lether-winged Batt, *dayes* enimy; . . . II. xii. 36. 6
through long watch, and late *daies* wearie toile, . . . III. i. 58. 8
by ensample of the last *dayes* losse, . . . III. i. 64. 6
Late *dayes* ensample, which these eyes beheld: . . . III. iii. 55. 2
Dayes dearest children be the blessed seed . . . III. iv. 59. 5
The third *dayes* prize unto that straunger Knight, . . . IV. v. 8. 1
this *dayes* honour sav'd to Marinell: . . . V. iii. 21. 2
daies faire shinie-beame, yclowded . . . V. iv. 45. 1
That he mote fresher be against the next *daies* fight. . . . V. iv. 51. 9
mindefull to pursew The last *daies* purpose . . . V. v. 1. 6
Yet being forst to abide the *daies* returning, . . . V. vi. 31. 3
After that long *daies* toile and weary plight: . . . V. vii. 12. 4
discourse Of former *daies* mishap, . . . VI. iii. 14. 9
forth he passed thorough that *daies* paine, . . . VI. iii. 17. 7
So goodly all agree . . . To this *dayes* merriment. . . . *Epith.* 84
That long *daies* labour doest at last defray, . . . *Epith.* 316

Days. *See* **Adays, Holidays, Now-a-days.**

right worthie sure . . . of immortall *dayes,* . . . *Bel.*[2] xiv. 7
Such was this Citie in her good *daies* fownd: . . . *Ro.* vi. 4

Days—*Continued.*

in her youthlie *daies* An Hydra was . . . *Ro.* x. 5
All the mishap the which our *daies* outweares, . . . *Ro.* xix. 5
can to other give eternall *dayes:* . . . *Ro.* Env. 8
Thy *dayes* therefore are endles, . . . *Ro.* Env. 9
Phyllis is myne for many *dayes.* . . . *S.C.* F. 64
cutte of hys *dayes* with untimely woe, . . . *S.C.* May 199
I more delight then larke in Sommer *dayes:* . . . *S.C.* Jun. 51
As shee was wont in youngth and sommer *dayes;* . . . *S.C.* N. 20
better *dayes* death hath shut up in woe? . . . *S.C.* N. 74
fond men doe all their *dayes* turmoyle. . . . *Gn.* 152
her husbands *daies* She did prolong . . . *Gn.* 426
by the wayling shores to waste my *dayes,* . . . *Gn.* 621
To doo you faithfull service all my *dayes.* . . . *Hub.* 253
in his Princes service spends his *dayes,* . . . *Hub.* 773
To loose good *dayes,* that might be better spent; . . . *Hub.* 897
all his *dayes,* like dolorous Trophees, . . . *T.M.* 160
draw the *dayes* of men forth in extent; . . . *Ti.* 18
As if his *daies* for ever should remaine? . . . *Ti.* 54
By heavens doome doo ende my earthlie *daies:* . . . *Ti.* 312
O, happie were those *dayes,* thrice happie were! . . . *Ti.* 329
in their *daies* most famouslie did florish; . . . *Ti.* 359
ye, faire Ladie, th' honour of your *daies,* . . . *Ti.* 680
'"Our *daies* are full of dolor and disease, . . . *D.* 274
why seeke I to prolong My wearie *daies* . . . *D.* 440
mourne for me that languish out my *dayes.* . . . *D.* 538
Far passing all the pastors of his *daies,* . . . *As.* 9
To her he vowd the service of his *daies,* . . . *As.* 61
Nought hast thou, foolish boy, seene in thy *daies.'* . . . *Col.* 303
Vassall to one, whom all my *dayes* I serve; . . . *Col.* 467
former *dayes* Had in rude fields bene altogether spent, . . . *Col.* 668
they their *dayes* to ydlenesse divide, . . . *Col.* 761
Yet brave ensample of long passed *daies,* . . . *Ded. Son.* x. 9
that most Heroicke spirit, . . . the glory of our *daies,* . . . *Ded. Son.* xv. 2
that wicked wight his *dayes* doth weare; . . . I. i. 31. 7
in loves and lusty-hed His wanton *daies* . . . led, . . . I. ii. 3. 5
Banisht from living wights, our wearie *daies* we waste.' . . . I. ii. 42. 9
Still drownd in sleepe, and most of his *daies* dedd: . . . I. iv. 19. 4
Her wicked *daies* with wretched knife did end, . . . I. v. 39. 2
He would at her request prolong her nephews *daies.* . . . I. v. 41. 9
Where he his better *dayes* hath wasted all: . . . I. viii. 28. 8
all my *daies* he traind mee up in vertuous lore. . . . I. ix. 4. 9
draw thy *dayes* forth to their last degree? . . . I. ix. 46. 2
he desirde to end his wretched *dayes:* . . . I. x. 21. 8
Did spend their *daies* in doing godly thing. . . . I. x. 36. 5
mighty man of God . . . Dwelt forty *daies* . . . I. x. 53. 6
with that old Dragon fights Two *days* incessantly: . . . I. xi. Arg.
end their *daies* with irrenowmed shame. . . . II. i. 23. 4
Therein I have spent all my youthly *daies,* . . . II. iii. 38. 4
Does waste his *dayes* in darke obscuritee, . . . II. iii. 40. 3
he in his *dayes* Had doen to death, . . . II. v. 26. 4
that in . . . honours suit my vowed *daies* do spend, . . . II. vii. 10. 2
three *dayes* of men were full outwrought, . . . II. vii. 65. 6
An happy man in his first *dayes* he was, . . . II. x. 22. 1
till his *dayes,* . . . II. x. 39. 7
The which was dew in his dead fathers *daies.* . . . II. x. 41. 5
The justest man and trewest in his *daies,* . . . II. x. 42. 2
joyd his *dayes* in great tranquillity. . . . II. x. 53. 2
most famous hight . . . of all in her *daies,* . . . II. x. 59. 8
With which the world did in those *dayes* abound: . . . II. x. 63. 6
end of that Carles *dayes* and his owne paynes did make. . . . II. xi. 46. 9
Two *dayes* now in that sea he sayled has, . . . II. xii. 2. 1
spent their looser *daies* in leud delightes, . . . II. xii. 9. 5
His *dayes,* his goods, his bodie, he did spend: . . . II. xii. 80. 8
Her wretched *dayes* in dolour she mote waste, . . . III. ii. 17. 8
Till death make one end of my *daies* and miseree!' . . . III. ii. 39. 9
He shall his *dayes* with peace bring to his earthly In. . . . III. iii. 30. 9
ryding on forray Few *dayes* before, . . . III. iii. 58. 5
'But if the heavens did his *dayes* envie, . . . III. iv. 39. 1
Halfe of thy *dayes* doest lead in horrour hideous. . . . III. iv. 55. 9
'Five *daies* there be since he (they say) was slaine, . . . III. v. 10. 1
The comfort of her age and weary *dayes,* . . . III. vii. 12. 2
all my *dayes* am like to waste in vaine, . . . III. vii. 60. 8
Thy *daies* abridge through proofe of puissaunce, . . . III. viii. 18. 2
all his *dayes* he drownes in privitie, . . . III. ix. 3. 8
In dolefull thraldome all his *dayes* to dwell? . . . III. ix. 8. 3
my *dayes* to spend In seewing deeds of armes, . . . III. ix. 37. 8
As if his *dayes* were come to their last reach: . . . III. xi. 12. 5
spare thy happy *daies,* . . . III. xi. 19. 5
whilome captived in their *dayes* To cruell love, . . . III. xi. 52. 4
His dearest love, the comfort of his *dayes,* . . . III. xii. 44. *or.* 2
What time the *dayes* with scorching heat abound, . . . IV. i. 13. 7
Where she in darknes wastes her cursed *daies* and nights. . . . IV. i. 19. 9
That was the learnedst Ladie in her *dayes,* . . . IV. ii. 35. 2
in privie place Did spend her *dayes,* . . . IV. ii. 44. 9
Their *days* mote be abridged through their corage stout. . . . IV. ii. 46. 9
desirous th' end of all their *dayes* To know, . . . IV. ii. 47. 1
Most wretched men, whose *dayes* depend on thrids so vaine! . . . IV. ii. 48. 9
So did they surely during all their *dayes,* . . . IV. ii. 54. 1
To draw their *dayes* unto the utmost date, . . . IV. iii. 1. 2
theire *daies* they spent In perfect love, . . . IV. iii. 52. 1
since their *dayes* such lovers were not found elswhere. . . . IV. iii. 52. 9
His *dayes* in dole doth lead. . . . IV. vii. Arg.
'Now twenty *daies* . . . have past through heven sheene, . . . IV. vii. 13. 1
wast his wretched *daies* in wofull plight; . . . IV. vii. 39. 8
Spending his *daies* in dolour and despaire, . . . IV. vii. 43. 2
daies in wilfull woe are worne, . . . IV. viii. 15. 7
To cloud my *daies* in dolefull misery, . . . IV. viii. 16. 8
That she mote match the fairest of her *daies,* . . . IV. ix. 16. 6
I wast my life, and doe my *daies* devowre . . . IV. ix. 39. 5

Days—*Continued.*
let me die and end my *daies* attone, . . . IV. xii. 9. 8
the common line Of present *dayes*, . . . V. Pr. 3. 4
Within three *daies*,' (quoth he) . . . V. ii. 4. 1
The third was Brunell, famous in his *dayes;* . . . V. iii. 5. 5
Spending their joyous *dayes* and gladfull nights, . . . V. iii. 40. 2
thus thy better *dayes* are drowned In sad despaire, . . . V. v. 36. 4
though she still have worne Her *dayes* in warre, . . . V. v. 40. 5
his abridged *dayes* in dolour wast, . . . V. v. 46. 6
For houres, but *dayes;* for weekes . . . She told but moneths, V. vi. 5. 6
his *daies* there to deplore. . . . V. xi. 14. 9
'Ten *daies*,' (quoth he) 'he graunted hath of grace, . . . V. xi. 42. 3
if I live till those ten *daies* have end, . . . V. xi. 43. 2
Doe spend my *dayes* and bend my carelesse wit . . . VI. ii. 9. 4
my *daies* I have not lewdly spent, . . . VI. ii. 31. 1
through the long experience of his *dayes*, . . . VI. vi. 3. 2
As any one that lived in his *daies*, . . . VI. vi. 4. 2
her good *dayes* in dolorous disgrace: . . . VI. vii. 38. 4
thy joyous *dayes* Here leadest in this goodly merry-make, . . VI. x. 19. 2
sung of thee in all his *dayes*, . . . VI. x. 28. 5
all that I in many *dayes* doo weave, . . . *Am.* xxiii. 7
al my *dayes* in pining langour spend, . . . *Am.* xxxvi. 3
short her wayes, . . . or else short my *dayes*. . . . *Am.* lx. 14
Many long weary *dayes* I have outworne; . . . *Am.* lxxxvi. 2
The *daies* they waste, the nights they grieve . . . *H.L.* 129
Through which he past his miserable *dayes*, . . . *H.H.L.* 236
those wits, the wonders of their *dayes*, . . . *H.H.B.* 218

Daysman. what art thou, That mak'st thy selfe his *dayesman*, II. viii. 28. 2

Day-spring. He wooed her till *day-spring* he espyde, . . . III. x. 52. 1

Daze. While flashing beames do *daze* his feeble eyen, . . . I. iv. 9. 6
shewd by outward signes that dread her sence did *daze*. . . III. vii. 7. 9
False Labyrinthes, fond runners eyes to *daze;* . . . IV. x. 24. 8
The glaunce whereof their dimmed eies would *daze*, . . . VI. x. 4. 3
his garments so did *daze* their eyes. . . . VII. vii. 7. 9
Whose glorious beames all fleshly sense doth *daze* . . . *H.H.L.* 278

Dazed. with that dint her sence was *dazd;* . . . I. i. 18. 1
on those guilefull *dazed* eyes . . . The cloude of death did sit. I. iii. 39. 7
beast, . . . Became stark blind, and all his sences *dazd*, . . . I. viii. 20. 3
It dimmes the *dazed* eyen, . . . I. viii. 21. 9
sunny beames . . . could have *dazd* the rash beholders sight, . . I. x. 12. 8
dazed were his eyne Through passing brightnes, . . . I. x. 67. 6
with too much brightnes *daz'd*, . . . III. vii. 13. 8
Assotted had his sence, or *dazed* was his eye. . . . III. viii. 22. 9
The whiles the passing brightnes her fraile sences *dazd*. . . III. xi. 49. 9
daz'd the eyes of all as with exceeding light. . . . IV. v. 10. 9
with their brightnesse *daz'd* the straunge beholders eye. . . V. ix. 21. 9
being now with her huge brightnesse *dazed*, . . . *Am.* iii. 5

Dazie. *See* **Daisy.**

Dazzled. eyes . . . would bee *dazled* with exceeding light. . . II. Pr. 5. 5
he began to doubt his *dazeled* sight, . . . II. xi. 40. 2

Dead. *See* **Never-dead, Stone-dead.**
He that hath seene a great Oke drie and *dead*, . . . *Ro.* xxviii. 1
Rome, . . . *dead*, is now the worlds sole moniment. . . . *Ro.* xxix. 14
give a second life to *dead* decayes! . . . *Ro.* Env. 6
dead himselfe he wisheth for despight. . . . *Van.* x. 13
The byting frost nipt his stalke *dead*, . . . *S.C.* F. 231
when they bene *dead*, . . . *S.C.* May 67
little lack of *dead*, . . . *S.C.* May 264
The God of shepheards, Tityrus, is *dead*, . . . *S.C.* Jun. 81
Nowe *dead* he is, . . . *S.C.* Jun. 89
the saynets Which han be *dead* of yore. . . . *S.C.* Jul. 116
bene they chaffred, or at mischiefe *dead?* . . . *S.C.* S. 10
thou in sleepe art *dead*. . . . *S.C.* O. 6
great Augustus long ygoe is *dead*, . . . *S.C.* O. 62
deade is Dido, *dead*, alas! and drent; . . . *S.C.* N. 37
dead shee is, that myrth thee made of yore. . . . *S.C.* N. 57
Dido, my deare, alas! is *dead*, . . . *S.C.* N. 58
Dead, and lyeth wrapt in lead. . . . *S.C.* N. 59
The braunch once *dead*, the budde . . . must quaile; . . . *S.C.* N. 91
Dido nis *dead*, but into heaven hent. . . . *S.C.* N. 169
He compast Troy thrice with his bodie *dedd*. . . . *Gn.* 528
all within were *dead* and hartles left; . . . *Hub.* 1355
for feare now almost *ded;* . . . *Hub.* 1374
Our pleasant Willy, ah! is *dead* of late: . . . *T.M.* 208
when both alike are *dedd;* . . . *T.M.* 448
'He now is *dead*, and all is with him *dead*, . . . *Ti.* 211
evill men, now *dead*, his deeds upbraid: . . . *Ti.* 214
Spite bites the *dead*, that living never baid. . . . *Ti.* 215
'He now is *dead*, and all his glorie gone, . . . *Ti.* 218
dead is now, as living, counted deare, . . . *Ti.* 242
being *dead*, is happie now much more; . . . *Ti.* 247
dead, because him *dead* thou dost adore . . . *Ti.* 249
sleepes in dust, *dead* and inglorious, . . . *Ti.* 355
To sing his living praises being *dead*, . . . *Ti.* 437
Nor alive nor *dead* be of the Muse adorned! . . . *Ti.* 455
But was th' Harpe of Philisides now *dead*. . . . *Ti.* 609
Least that the world thee *dead* accuse of guilt, . . . *D.* 82
'She now is *dead;*' ne more endured to say, . . . *D.* 184
who shall dight your bowres, sith she is *dead* . . . *D.* 318
when ye heare that I am *dead* or slaine, . . . *D.* 523
Made not to please the living but the *dead*. . . . *As.* Pr. 16
Full litle faileth but thou shalt be *dead*, . . . *As.* 135
all *dead* in dole did lie: . . . *Col.* 22
That us, late *dead*, has made againe alive: . . . *Col.* 31
alreadie *dead* with feare, . . . *Col.* 205
after Astrofell is *dead* and gone: . . . *Col.* 449
verse of noblest shepheard lately *dead* . . . *Col.* 534
eke to make the *dead* againe alive. . . . *Col.* 599
long while after I am *dead* and rotten, . . . *Col.* 640
dead, as living, ever him ador'd: . . . I. i. 2. 4

Dead—*Continued.*
Great Gorgon, prince of darknes and *dead* night; . . . I. i. 37. 8
Dead long ygoe, I wote, thou haddest bin, . . . I. ii. 18. 3
There lies he now with foule dishonor *dead*, . . . I. ii. 25. 5
turning to his Lady, *dead* with feare her fownd. . . . I. ii. 44. 9
Her seeming *dead* he fownd with feigned feare, . . . I. ii. 45. 1
of his cruell rage Nigh *dead* with feare, . . . I. iii. 13. 4
Still drownd in sleepe, and most of his daies *dedd:* . . . I. iv. 19. 4
As ashes pale of hew, and seeming *ded;* . . . I. iv. 33. 7
underneath their feet, all scattered lay *Dead* sculls . . . I. iv. 36. 9
Dead is Sansfoy, his vitall paines are past, . . . I. iv. 49. 6
I . . . with Sansfoyes *dead* dowry you endew.' . . . I. iv. 51. 5
Such wondrous science . . . that could the *dead* revive, . . . I. v. 40. 2
A Donghill of *dead* carcases he spyde; . . . I. v. 53. 8
see that knight both living and eke *ded*.' . . . I. vi. 36. 9
dead was his hart within, . . . I. vii. 21. 2
resolving him to find Alive or *dead;* . . . I. vii. 28. 3
brought not backe the balefull body *dead:* . . . I. vii. 50. 5
This was the . . . foster father of the Gyaunt *dead;* . . . I. viii. 31. 8
halfe *dead* with dying feare; . . . I. ix. 30. 6
The sixt had charge of them now being *dead*, . . . I. x. 42. 1
even *dead* we honour should. . . . I. x. 42. 8
God, me graunt, I *dead* be not defould! . . . I. x. 42. 9
the tender Orphans of the *dead* . . . I. x. 43. 2
The mossy braunches of an Oke halfe *ded*. . . . I. x. 48. 4
Dead was it sure, as sure as death in deed, . . . I. xi. 12. 3
unto life the *dead* it could restore, . . . I. xi. 30. 1
to the earth him drove, as stricken *dead;* . . . I. xi. 38. 3
thereby *dead* that balefull Beast did deeme, . . . I. xii. 2. 7
dead now was their foe, which them forrayed late. . . . I. xii. 3. 9
they came where that *dead* Dragon lay, . . . I. xii. 9. 6
Halfe *dead* through feare, . . . I. xii. 11. 3
Or false or trew, or living or else *dead*, . . . I. xii. 28. 2
to thy mother *dead* attest That cleare she dide . . . II. i. 37. 6
lay, halfe *dead*, halfe quick; . . . II. i. 39. 4
The *dead* corse of an armed knight was spred, . . . II. i. 41. 2
rosy red Did paint his chearefull cheekes, yett being *ded;* . . II. i. 41. 5
this *dead* corpse . . . the good Sir Mortdant was: . . . II. i. 49. 7
dead suddeinly he downe did sincke. . . . II. i. 55. 9
The *dead* knights sword out of his sheath he drew, . . . II. i. 61. 1
in *dead* parents balefull ashes bred, . . . II. ii. 2. 2
Why livest thou, *dead* dog, . . . II. iii. 7. 6
dead through great affright . . . II. iii. 19. 7
Hable to heale the sicke, and to revive the *ded*. . . . II. iii. 22. 9
Him deeming *dead*, as then he seemd in sight, . . . II. v. 25. 7
dead mens bones, which round about were flong; . . . II. vii. 30. 7
Fitt to adorne the *dead*, . . . II. vii. 51. 9
Dead sleeping Poppy, and black Hellebore; . . . II. vii. 52. 3
Thus for to blott the honor of the *dead*, . . . II. viii. 13. 3
Bad therefore I him deeme that thus lies *dead* on field.' . . II. viii. 14. 9
why should a *dead* dog be deckt in armour bright?' . . . II. viii. 15. 9
To spoile the *dead* of weed Is sacrilege, . . . II. viii. 16. 4
In whose *dead* face he redd great magnanimity. . . . II. viii. 23. 9
Why should not that *dead* carrion satisfye The guilt . . . II. viii. 28. 6
doth against the *dead* his hand upheave, . . . II. viii. 29. 7
by Termagaunt thou shalt be *dead*.' . . . II. viii. 30. 4
Full lively is the semblaunt, though the substance *dead*.' . . II. ix. 2. 9
'if in that picture *dead* Such life ye read, . . . II. ix. 3. 1
The faire Sabrina, almost *dead* with feare, . . . II. x. 19. 3
His sonne Rivall' his *dead* rowme did supply; . . . II. x. 34. 1
The which was dew in his *dead* fathers daies. . . . II. x. 41. 5
an Helmet light, Made of a *dead* mans skull, . . . II. xi. 22. 9
his *dead* corse should fall upon the flore; . . . II. xi. 37. 8
his *dead* corse upon the flore fell nathemore. . . . II. xi. 37. 9
when he felt him *dead*, . . . II. xi. 42. 5
the Dame, halfe *dedd* Through suddein feare . . . III. i. 62. 4
Me lever were with point of foemans speare be *dead*. . . . III. ii. 6. 9
Chaunged thy lively cheare, and living made thee *dead?* . . III. ii. 30. 9
full shortly I her *dead* shall see.' . . . III. iii. 16. 9
'With thee yet shall he leave . . . his ymage *dead*, . . . III. iii. 29. 2
Beene they all *dead*, and laide in dolefull herse, . . . III. iv. 1. 8
If they be *dead*, then woe is me therefore; . . . III. iv. 2. 1
dead the grave selfe to engrosse. . . . III. iv. 38. 9
Belphebe findes him almost *dead*, . . . III. v. Arg.
Till him alive or *dead* she did invent. . . . III. v. 10. 4
They three be *dead* with shame, . . . III. v. 25. 9
That Ladies all may follow her ensample *dead*. . . . III. v. 54. 9
sith her *dedd* He surely dempt, . . . III. viii. 3. 6
she put a Spright to rule the carcas *dead;* . . . III. viii. 7. 9
dead through feare Fell streight to ground . . . III. viii. 12. 6
turne his steede about, or sure he should be *dedd*. . . . III. viii. 17. 9
offrest sacrifice unto the *dead:* . . . III. viii. 47. 4
dead, I surely doubt, thou maist aread . . . III. viii. 47. 5
downe tombled *dedd* From top of Hemus . . . III. ix. 22. 5
shortly doen be *dedd*.' . . . III. x. 32. 9
He fainted, and was almost *dead* with feare, . . . III. x. 37. 7
fell to ground half *dedd*. . . . III. x. 43. 9
Sorrow seeming *dead;* . . . III. xii. 25. 5
to ground He fell halfe *dead:* . . . III. xii. 34. 2
In wilfull anguish and *dead* heavinesse, . . . III. xii. 43. *or.* 7
The aged Dame . . . Was *dead* with feare; . . . IV. i. 54. 2
being *dead* in vaine yet many strive: . . . IV. ii. 34. 5
downe he fell as *dead* in all mens sight; . . . IV. iii. 30. 5
Yet *dead* he was not, yet he sure did die, . . . IV. iii. 30. 6
whilst all the lookers-on Him *dead* behight, . . . IV. iii. 31. 2
both at once fell *dead* upon the field, . . . IV. iii. 34. 8
wholly *dead* Himselfe he wisht have beene, . . . IV. iv. 22. 8
I vow you *dead* or living not to leave, . . . IV. vi. 38. 8
she, deare Ladie, all the way was *dead*, . . . IV. vii. 9. 1
Emong the living, or emong the *dead?* . . . IV. vii. 11. 2

Dead—*Continued.*
almost *dead* and desperate Through her late hurts, . . . IV. viii. 19. 7
Then did her glorious flowre wex *dead* and wan, . . . IV. viii. 32. 8
'ye both the *dead* deny, And both the living Lady claime . . . V. i. 26. 1
Let both the *dead* and living equally Devided be . . . V. i. 26. 3
To witnesse to the world that she by him is *dead*.' . . . V. i. 26. 9
to him selfe be shared *dead;* . . . V. i. 27. 6
beare the burden of defame, Your owne *dead* Ladies head, . . . V. i. 28. 9
eke their dame halfe *dead* did hide her self for feare. . . . V. ii. 24. 9
some hath put to shame, and many done be *dead*. . . . V. iv. 29. 9
dead long since in dolorous distresse, . . . V. vii. 39. 4
his necke asunder broke, And left there *dead*. . . . V. viii. 8. 4
whom ye may see There *dead* on ground. . . . V. viii. 11. 7
when they saw their foes *dead* out of doubt, . . . V. viii. 12. 3
As that I did mistake the living for the *ded*. . . . V. viii. 13. 9
Like one of those two Knights which *dead* there lay; . . . V. viii. 25. 5
ere they were halfe *ded* . . . V. viii. 28. 8
earst was *dead,* restor'd to life againe, . . . V. xi. 16. 6
it did her *dead* hart cheare, . . . V. xii. 12. 8
was not all so *dead* . . . V. xii. 39. 6
alive or *dead* Her foe deliver up . . . VI. i. 31. 5
She deem'd him sure to have bene *dead* on ground; . . . VI. i. 34. 7
To rayse a lyving blame against the *dead;* . . . VI. ii. 15. 7
fortune hath . . . Given to me the spoile of this *dead* knight, . VI. ii. 33. 8
Tristram, then despoyling that *dead* knight . . . VI. ii. 39. 1
Upon the steed of her owne late *dead* knight; . . . VI. ii. 39. 8
He, her not finding, both them thus nigh *dead* did leave. . . . VI. ii. 43. 9
Where I had surely long ere this bene *dead,* . . . VI. v. 29. 2
with the *dead* He saw the ground all strow'd, . . . VI. vi. 24. 5
still did lie as *dead,* and quake, and quiver, . . . VI. vi. 32. 3
th' one is *dead,* and th' other soone shall die, . . . VI. vii. 13. 3
He weened well that he in deed was *dead,* . . . VI. vii. 20. 2
many there were missing; which were *ded,* . . . VI. vii. 33. 3
though she were with wearinesse nigh *dead,* . . . VI. vii. 40. 8
Being alreadie *dead* with fearefull fright: . . . VI. viii. 45. 3
Then Coridon woxe frollicke, that earst seemed *dead*. . . . VI. ix. 42. 9
when as he was *dead,* the fray gan cease; . . . VI. xi. 20. 3
was not *dead* before, . . . VI. xi. 29. 3
better were with them to have bene *dead,* . . . VI. xi. 32. 6
if that *dead,* how he her death might wreake, . . . VI. xi. 34. 6
all the rest Were *dead,* . . . VI. xi. 41. 7
In *dead* of night, when all the theeves did rest, . . . VI. xi. 42. 2
faire Pastorell through great affright Was almost *dead,* . . . VI. xi. 43. 8
Through the *dead* carcases he made his way, . . . VI. xi. 47. 4
long had lyen *dead,* . . . VI. xi. 50. 9
art thou yet alive, whom *dead* I long did faine?' . . . VI. xii. 19. 9
having thought long *dead* she fyndes alive, . . . VI. xii. 21. 2
being *dead,* To turne againe unto their earthly slime: . . . VII. vii. 18. 3
mote enlarge her living prayses, *dead*. . . . *Am.* xxxiii. 4
dead my life that wants such lively blis. . . . *Am.* lxxxviii. 14
Dead-doing. hold your *dead-doing* hand,' . . . II. iii. 8. 1
Which hold my life in their *dead-doing* might, . . . *Am.* i. 2
Deaded. all joy and jolly meriment Is also *deaded,* . . . *T.M.* 210
lively spirits *deaded* quight: . . . IV. xii. 20. 2
the cowheard, *deaded* with affright, . . . VI. vii. 25. 7
His hart quite *deaded* was with anguish great, . . . VI. xi. 33. 2
Deadliest. was to him on earth the *deadliest* despight. . . . VI. vii. 20. 9
Dead-living. How to take life from that *dead-living* swayne, . II. xi. 44. 7
Deadly. With *deadly* force so in their cruell race . . . *Pet.* i. 8
Him Love hath wounded with a *deadly* darte: . . . *S.C.* Ap. 22
that wrought so *deadly* spight. . . . *S.C.* Jun. 101
my *deadly* cryes 'Most ruthfully to tune: . . . *S.C.* Au. 174
did sing of warres and *deadly* drede, . . . *S.C.* O. 59
all we dwell in *deadly* night. . . . *S.C.* N. 69
death, and dreaded sisters *deadly* spight, . . . *S.C.* N. 163
No *deadly* fight of warlick fleete doth feare; . . . *Gn.* 124
the sweete Cypresse, signe of *deadly* bale. . . . *Gn.* 216
Lightned with *deadly* lamps on everie post? . . . *Gn.* 341
Even from the doore of death and *deadlie* dreed! . . . *Gn.* 355
judgement seates, whose Judge is *deadlie* dred, . . . *Gn.* 446
threatned death, and thousand *deadly* dolours, . . . *Hub.* 1341
I sing of *deadly* dolorous debate, . . . *Mui.* 1
Therein two *deadly* weapons fixt he bore, . . . *Mui.* 81
Gave her the fatall wound of *deadlie* smart, . . . *D.* 158
All were my self, through griefe, in *deadly* drearing. . . . *D.* 189
deadly accents, which like swords Did wound my heart, . . . *D.* 297
those hollow eyes and *deadly* view, . . . *D.* 304
'To live I finde it *deadly* dolorous, . . . *D.* 449
So *deadly* was the dint and deep the wound, . . . *As.* 121
Lay now thy *deadly* Heben bowe apart, . . . I. Pr. 3. 5
light she hated as the *deadly* bale, . . . I. i. 16. 7
welnigh choked with the *deadly* stinke, . . . I. i. 22. 2
falling to the ground, Groning full *deadly,* . . . I. i. 25. 3
when all drownd in *deadly* sleepe he findes, . . . I. i. 36. 6
ever to have toucht her I did *deadly* rew. . . . I. ii. 40. 9
with pale and *deadly* hew, At last she up gan lift: . . . I. ii. 45. 5
that dredd Lyons looke her cast in *deadly* hew. . . . I. iii. 11. 9
all in *deadly* sleepe did drowned lye . . . I. iii. 16. 3
Loth . . . To taste th' untryed dint of *deadly* steele: . . . I. iii. 34. 6
he perced . . . With thrilling point of *deadly* yron brand, . . I. iii. 42. 7
each to *deadly* shame would drive his foe: . . . I. v. 9. 2
faith . . . The creeping *deadly* cold away did shake: . . . I. v. 12. 4
Covering your foe with cloud of *deadly* night, . . . I. v. 14. 7
griesly Night, with visage *deadly* sad, . . . I. v. 20. 1
the stout Sansjoy doth sleepe in *deadly* shade. . . . I. v. 22. 9
he was wary of that *deadly* stowre, . . . I. vii. 12. 5
saw the signes that *deadly* tydinges spake, . . . I. vii. 20. 6
instruments . . . That doe this *deadly* spectacle behold, . . . I. vii. 22. 2
eyes . . . seeled up with death shall have their *deadly* meed.' . I. vii. 23. 9
Thrise did she sinke adowne in *deadly* swownd, . . . I. vii. 24. 3

Deadly—*Continued.*
deadly dint of steele endanger may. . . . I. vii. 29. 7
Mine onely foe, mine onely *deadly* dread; . . . I. vii. 50. 7
Hurles forth his thundring dart with *deadly* food . . . I. viii. 9. 3
Dismayed with so desperate *deadly* wound, . . . I. viii. 11. 1
griefe, Which love had launched with his *deadly* darts, . . . I. ix. 29. 3
lever had I die then see his *deadly* face.' . . . I. ix. 32. 9
his hollow eyne Lookt *deadly* dull, . . . I. ix. 35. 7
Both *deadly* sharp, that sharpest steele exceeden farre. . . . I. xi. 11. 9
found no place his *deadly* point to rest. . . . I. xi. 17. 4
The *deadly* dint his dulled sences all dismaid. . . . I. xi. 35. 9
deadly wounds could heale, . . . I. xi. 48. 7
he was *deadly* made, . . . I. xi. 49. 2
the last *deadly* smoke aloft did steeme, . . . I. xii. 2. 4
In sea of *deadly* daungers was distrest: . . . I. xii. 17. 6
He could escape fowle death or *deadly* pains? . . . I. xii. 36. 5
object of his spight And *deadly* food he makes: . . . II. i. 3. 2
a *deadly* shrieke she forth did throw . . . II. i. 38. 1
Pitifull spectacle of *deadly* smart, . . . II. i. 40. 1
he did her *deadly* wounds repaire, . . . II. i. 43. 8
As one out of a *deadly* dreame affright, . . . II. i. 45. 6
casting up a *deadly* looke, . . . II. i. 47. 1
through the great contagion direful *deadly* stonck. . . . II. ii. 4. 9
Each other does envy with *deadly* hate, . . . II. ii. 19. 2
in bloody fight With *deadly* rancour . . . II. ii. 21. 4
Their *deadly* cruell discord to forbeare, . . . II. ii. 27. 8
many whelmd in *deadly* paine; . . . II. ii. 43. 4
towards gan a *deadly* shafte advaunce, . . . II. iii. 34. 5
withhold this *deadly* howre. . . . II. iii. 34. 9
Those *deadly* tooles which in her hand she held, . . . II. iii. 37. 3
drew his *deadly* weapon to maintaine his part. . . . II. iv. 9. 9
Of *deadly* drugs I gave him drinke anon, . . . II. iv. 30. 8
two dartes, exceeding flit And *deadly* sharp, . . . II. iv. 38. 8
did him *deadly* daunt, or fowle dismay; . . . II. iv. 40. 8
Deadly dismayd with horror of that dint . . . II. v. 8. 1
fayre Phaedria, that beheld That *deadly* daunger, . . . II. vi. 32. 2
to stay your *deadly* stryfe a space.' . . . II. vi. 33. 5
doolefull sorrow heape with *deadly* harmes: . . . II. vi. 34. 4
To see my Lord so *deadly* damnifyde? . . . II. vi. 43. 8
His *deadly* woundes within my liver swell, . . . II. vi. 50. 3
direfull *deadly* black, both leafe and bloom, . . . II. vii. 51. 8
those sad waves, which direfull *deadly* stancke, . . . II. vii. 57. 3
All which he did to do him *deadly* fall . . . II. vii. 64. 1
all his sences were with *deadly* fit opprest. . . . II. vii. 66. 9
deadly fitt thy pupill doth dismay. . . . II. viii. 7. 5
with sorrowfull demayne And *deadly* hew, . . . II. viii. 23. 8
cloudes of *deadly* night . . . his heavy eylids cover'd have, . II. viii. 24. 7
wisely watch to ward that *deadly* stowre; . . . II. viii. 35. 4
oft the Paynim sav'd from *deadly* stowre: . . . II. viii. 43. 6
All *deadly* daungerous, all cruell keene, . . . II. xi. 21. 3
his hands Discharged of his bow and *deadly* quar'le, . . . II. xi. 33. 8
most *deadly* daunger and distressed plight. . . . II. xii. 11. 9
soone as they approcht with *deadly* threat, . . . II. xii. 40. 1
Deadly engored of a great wilde Bore; . . . III. i. 38. 2
Was drowned in the depth of *deadly* sleepe; . . . III. i. 59. 3
Drew out a *deadly* bow and arrow keene, . . . III. i. 65. 2
Whiles thus he lay in *deadly* stonishment, . . . III. iv. 19. 1
This was that woman, this that *deadly* wownd, . . . III. iv. 28. 1
shee up out of her *deadly* fitt Arose, . . . III. iv. 31. 1
The lucklesse Marinell lying in *deadly* swownd, . . . III. iv. 34. 9
so *deadly* smight Her dearest sonne, . . . III. iv. 44. 4
So deepe the *deadly* feare of that foule swaine . . . III. iv. 49. 2
deadly daunger, which to him betidd; . . . III. v. 13. 2
A cruell shaft, headed with *deadly* ill, . . . III. v. 20. 4
from his steed he fell in *deadly* swowne: . . . III. v. 26. 3
lay in *deadly* swownd; . . . III. v. 29. 2
How him in *deadly* case theyr Lady fownd, . . . III. v. 38. 4
with his cruell tuske him *deadly* cloyd: . . . III. vi. 48. 4
with fell looke and hollow *deadly* gaze . . . III. vii. 7. 6
Him selfe from *deadly* daunger to defend: . . . III. vii. 32. 5
He from that *deadly* throw made no defence, . . . III. ix. 29. 1
deadly dent The blood hath of so many thousands shedd, . . III. x. 32. 5
Whilest *deadly* torments doe her chast brest rend, . . . III. xi. 11. 3
Quite through transfixed with a *deadly* dart, . . . III. xii. 21. 3
When her from *deadly* thraldome he redeemed, . . . IV. i. 8. 4
Through mischievous debate and *deadly* feood, . . . IV. i. 26. 4
deadly points at eithers breast to bend, . . . IV. ii. 14. 8
did not seeke t' appease their *deadly* hate, . . . IV. ii. 20. 8
stroke, . . . (so *deadly* it was ment) . . . IV. iii. 18. 2
it fell, and *deadly* slept. . . . IV. iii. 20. 9
Him selfe to save from that so *deadly* throw; . . . IV. iii. 33. 5
pacifie the strife, which causd so *deadly* smart. . . . IV. iii. 40. 9
deadly foes so faithfully affrended, . . . IV. iii. 50. 5
So dreadfull were his strokes, so *deadly* was his hond. . . . IV. iv. 23. 9
snatching forth his direfull *deadly* blade . . . IV. vi. 12. 2
Where byting deepe so *deadly* it imprest, . . . IV. vi. 13. 7
His hart was thrild with point of *deadly* feare, . . . IV. vi. 37. 2
The arrow to his *deadly* marke desynde. . . . IV. vii. 30. 4
The burden of the *deadly* brunt did beare . . . IV. viii. 42. 2
with *deadly* wound My heart was launcht, . . . IV. x. 1. 7
He ment the thiefe there *deadly* to have smit: . . . V. iii. 29. 8
what other *deadly* dismall day Is falne on you . . . V. iv. 26. 6
He to her lept with *deadly* dreadfull looke, . . . V. v. 11. 7
Into the river, where he drunke his *deadly* last. . . . V. vi. 39. 9
those *deadly* ends Of both her foes had seene, . . . V. viii. 10. 4
with most fell despight and *deadly* hate . . . V. viii. 18. 3
Working to all that love her *deadly* woe, . . . V. viii. 20. 8
deadly daunger seem'd in all mens sight To tempt such steps, V. ix. 15. 6
Wrapt in great dolours and in *deadly* feares . . . V. x. 6. 7
There did the Prince him leave in *deadly* swound, . . . V. x. 33. 7

Deadly—*Continued.*
powred forth his wretched life in *deadly* dreare. . . . . . . V. x. 35. 9
Full *deadly* wounds where so it is empight; . . . . V. xi. 24. 6
suffred *deadly* doole: . . . . V. xi. 25. 6
him nigh choked with the *deadly* stinke. . . . . . . V. xi. 31. 8
new life to her lent in midst of *deadly* feare. . . . . . . V. xii. 12. 9
to ward the *deadly* feare; . . . . V. xii. 14. 4
did against him weld His *deadly* weapon . . . . V. xii. 16. 5
Right in the flanke him strooke with *deadly* dreare, ... V. xii. 20. 5
the *deadly* swound, in which full deepe . . . . VI. iii. 10. 7
Like one that out of *deadly* dreame awooke: . . . . VI. iii. 11. 3
In dolorous dismay and *deadly* plight, ... VI. iii. 27. 3
Whom now in *deadly* daunger he did see, ... VI. iii. 43. 8
God . . . had them freed from that *deadly* feare, ... VI. iv. 15. 3
And in three battailes did so *deadly* daunt, ... VI. iv. 29. 8
by some *deadly* chaunce be done to pine . . . . VI. v. 28. 8
Kept and delivered me from *deadly* dread. . . . . . . VI. v. 29. 5
Whom when the Prince so *deadly* saw dismayd, ... VI. vi. 33. 1
That other swayne, like ashes *deadly* pale, ... VI. vii. 17. 8
deadly pallied hew Benumbes her cheekes: . . . . VI. viii. 40. 6
Her wretched life shut up in *deadly* shade, ... VI. x. 44. 4
Now boyling hot, straight friezing *deadly* cold; . . . . VII. vii. 23. 3
His wanton wings and darts of *deadly* power. . . . . . . *Am.* iv. 8
Darting their *deadly* arrowes, fyry bright, ... *Am.* xvi. 7
the night Raven, that still *deadly* yels; . . . . *Epith.* 346
That He for him might pay sinnes *deadly* hyre, ... *H.H.L.* 138
Dead-seeming. To wreake your wrath on this *dead seeming* knight, ... II. viii. 27. 4
Dead-sleeping. *Dead sleeping* Poppy, and black Hellebore; . . II. vii. 52. 3
Deal. *See* **Somedeal.**
sixe months greater a great *deele;* . . . . *Ro.* xviii. 8
Here is a great *deale* of good matter Lost . . . . *S.C.* Jul. 205
Too good for him had bene a great *deale* worse; . . . . . . *S.C.* S. 213
doth true justice *deale* To his inferiour Gods, ... V. vii. 1. 6
did true Justice *deale,* . . . . V. vii. 42. 7
With that his wife in friendly wise to *deale,* . . . . V. viii. 21. 2
His studie was true Justice how to *deale,* . . . . V. xii. 26. 2
ye have much adoe to *deale* withall.' . . . . VI. i. 10. 8
Right to all dost *deale* indifferently, ... VII. vii. 14. 4
Dealed. *See* **Dealt.**
What time king Ryence raign'd and *dealed* right, ... III. ii. 18. 5
Dealeth. All is his justly that all freely *dealth.* . . . . IV. i. 6. 5
both to good and bad he *dealeth* right, ... V. Pr. 10. 4
Artegall *dealeth* right betwixt Two brethren . . . . V. iv. Arg.
Dealing. unto them was *dealing* righteous doome: . . . . . V. ix. 23. 5
Dealing just judgements, that mote not be broken . . . . V. ix. 24. 8
Dealing with Justice with indifferent grace, ... V. ix. 36. 4
Dealing his dreadfull blowes with large dispence, ... V. xi. 45. 4
and to his *dealing* just. . . . . VI. iii. 13. 4
Dealt. *See* **Dealed.**
dealt blowes On either side, ... II. viii. 41. 1
stoutly *dealt* his blowes, ... III. i. 21. 6
Of which he *dealt* large almes, as did befall: . . . . IV. iv. 32. 4
dealt her blowes unmercifully sore; . . . . V. vii. 31. 2
candle-light, which *delt* A doubtfull sense of things, ... VI. x. 42. 8
Deans. To *Deanes,* to Archdeacons, to Commissaries, ... *Hub.* 421
Dear. The bloud of Martyrs *dere* . . . . *Rev.* ii. 10
With inward ruth and *deare* affection, ... *Van.* xii. 3
ladde, whome long I lovd so *deare,* . . . . *S.C.* Ap. 10
Nay, say I thereto, by my *deare* borrowe, ... *S.C.* May 150
Ah, *deare* Lord! and sweete Saint Charitee! . . . . *S.C.* May 247
nought he deemed *deare* for the jewell: . . . . *S.C.* May 277
her sonne had sette to *deere* a prise . . . . *S.C.* May 299
loved her most *dere.* . . . . *S.C.* Jun. 112
shepheard great! That bought his flocke so *deare,* . . . . . . *S.C.* Jul. 54
Whose love he bought to *deare;* . . . . *S.C.* Jul. 148
you may buye golde to *deere.* . . . . *S.C.* Au. 108
that great Pan bought with *deare* borrow, ... *S.C.* S. 96
Colin, my *deare,* when shall it please thee sing, ... *S.C.* N. 1
Dido, my *deare,* alas! is dead, ... *S.C.* N. 58
shee deemed nothing too *deere* for thee. . . . . *S.C.* N. 117
Adieu, my *deare,* whose love I bought so *deare;* . . . . . *S.C.* D. 152
thy life more *deare* and precious Was than mine owne, . . . *Gn.* 331
With bitter woundes her owne *deere* babes to slay, ... *Gn.* 399
'Ah! my *deare* Gossip, ... *Hub.* 71
'Right well, *deere* Gossip, ye advized have, ... *Hub.* 193
askt an almes for Gods *deare* love. . . . . *Hub.* 363
my owne *deare* brother, ... *Hub.* 1003
with rich bountie, and *deare* cherishment, ... *T.M.* 573
did the losse of some *deer* love lament, ... *Ti.* 16
I with much bloodshed bought full *deere,* . . . . *Ti.* 115
late him loved *deare:* . . . . *Ti.* 193
dead is now, as living, counted *deare,* . . . . *Ti.* 242
Deare unto all that true affection beare: . . . . *Ti.* 243
unto thee most *deare,* O dearest Dame! . . . . *Ti.* 244
thy lost *deare* love deplore. . . . . *Ti.* 250
Sorrowing tempered with *deare* delight, ... *Ti.* 319
Thus, *deare!* adieu, whom I expect ere long."— . . . . *D.* 292
faire Eurydice, her daughter *deere,* . . . . *D.* 464
faire Damsels! Shepheards *dere* delights, ... *D.* 526
His lifes desire, and his *deare* loves delight. . . . . . . *As.* 54
on the cold *deare* earth himselfe did throw; . . . . *As.* 124
To whom alive was nought so *deare* as hee: . . . . *As.* 128
with . . . her *deare* favours dearly well adorned; . . . . . *As.* 154
The shepheards all which loved him full *deare,* . . . . . . *As.* 200
sure full *deare* of all he loved was, ... *As.* 201
most resembling . . . Her brother *deare,* . . . . *As.* 214
Whom Astrophel full *deare* did entertaine, ... *As.* Interl. 219
so *deare* his love he bought.' . . . . *Col.* 155
Ne lesse praise-worthie is her sister *deare,* . . . . *Col.* 504

Dear—*Continued.*
it embracing *deare* without disdaine, ... *Col.* 554
All full of love, and love, and love my *deare,* . . . . *Col.* 777
bred above in Venus bosome *deare:* . . . . *Col.* 840
chose . . . the Turtle Dove Her *deare,* . . . . *Col.* 866
For having loved ever one most *deare:* . . . . *Col.* 904
They unto thee, and thou to them, most *deare:* . . . . . . *Ded. Son.* iii. 12
Deare as thou art unto thy selfe, ... *Ded. Son.* iii. 13
Receive, *dear* Lord, in worth, the fruit of barren field. . . . *Ded. Son.* v. 14
The which vouchsafe, *dear* Lord, your favorable doome. . . . *Ded. Son.* vii.14
Thy soveraine Goddesses most *deare* delight, ... *Ded. Son.* viii. 2
The *deare* remembrance of his dying Lord, ... I. i. 2. 2
their Parent *deare* They saw so rudely falling . . . . I. i. 25. 1
'Ah! my *dear* sonne,' (quoth he) . . . . I. i. 30. 5
'Your owne *deare* sake forst me . . . to leave My fathers . . . I. i. 52. 1
she saide, . . . *deare* constraint, Lets me not sleepe, ... I. i. 53. 1
'*Deare* dame, I rew, That . . . such griefe unto you grew. . . I. i. 53. 8
all so *deare* as life is to my hart, I deeme your love, ... I. i. 54. 2
dreame . . . With bowres, and beds, and ladies *deare* delight: I. i. 55. 7
'*Deare* dame, your suddein overthrow Much rueth me; . . . I. ii. 21. 7
that happened . . . to this wretched Lady, my *deare* love; . . I. ii. 31. 6
O, too *deare* love, love bought with death too *deare!'* . . . I. ii. 31. 7
Nought . . . That moves more *deare* compassion of mind, . . I. iii. 1. 2
the late losse of her *deare* loved knight, ... I. iii. 15. 6
That blind old woman, and her daughter *dear,* . . . . . . I. iii. 22. 2
ought . . . That should as death unto my *deare* heart light: I. iii. 27. 5
Deare Sir, what ever that thou be in place: . . . . I. iii. 37. 3
he of Ladies oft was loved *deare,* . . . . I. iv. 24. 7
'Ah *deare* Sansjoy, next dearest to Sansfoy, ... I. iv. 45. 4
my brest was launcht with lovely dart Of *deare* Sansfoy, . . . I. iv. 46. 6
Thyselfe thy message do to german *deare;* . . . . I. v. 13. 2
Why suffredst thou thy Nephewes *deare* to fall, ... I. v. 22. 7
bold Sansfoy . . . to me too dearely *deare.* . . . . I. v. 23. 5
'*Deare* daughter, rightly may I rew The fall . . . . I. v. 25. 1
sad, that Una, his *deare* dreed, Her truth had staynd . . . . I. vi. 2. 3
a Lyonesse . . . did lowd requere Her children *deare,* . . . . I. vi. 27. 7
her *deare* heart with anguish did torment, ... I. vi. 32. 4
Deare dame,' (quoth he) 'well may I rew . . . . I. vi. 36. 7
From that day forth Duessa was his *deare,* . . . . I. vii. 16. 1
For whose *deare* sake so many troubles her did tosse. . . . I. vii. 27. 9
'Ah Lady *deare,'* quoth then the gentle knight, ... I. vii. 40. 1
parents *deare* . . . Did spred their rule . . . . I. vii. 43. 4
Parents *deare* from tyrants powre deliver might. . . . . . I. vii. 46. 9
the record . . . of my dolefull disaventurous *deare.* . . . . . I. vii. 48. 7
Faire virgin, to redeeme her *deare,* . . . . I. viii. Arg.
Therefore, *deare* Sir, your mightie powres assay.' . . . . . I. viii. 2. 6
That when his *deare* Duessa heard, ... I. viii. 12. 1
with percing point Of pitty *deare* his hart was thrilled sore; I. viii. 39. 2
This daies ensample hath this lesson *deare* Deepe written . . I. viii. 44. 7
'*Dear* Dame,' (quoth he) 'you sleeping sparkes awake, . . . I. ix. 8. 1
and badd me love her *deare;* . . . . I. ix. 14. 2
'For Gods *deare* love, Sir knight, doe me not stay; . . . . . I. ix. 25. 1
Now praysd, hereafter *deare* thou shalt repent; . . . . . . I. ix. 43. 5
by him had many pledges *dere.* . . . . I. x. 4. 9
your sister *deare,* The *deare* Charissa, ... I. x. 16. 1, 2
'*Deare* dame, And you, good Sir, ... I. x. 17. 1
His owne *deare* Una, ... I. x. 28. 4
that *deare* Lord who oft thereon was fownd, ... I. x. 54. 4
More *dear* unto their God then younglings to their dam.' . . I. x. 57. 9
To thinke of those her captive Parents *deare,* . . . . . . I. xi. 1. 2
'*Deare* knight, as *deare* as ever knight was *deare,* . . . . . I. xi. 1. 7
my parents *deare* . . . emprisond be; . . . . I. xi. 3. 2
more mindfull of his honour *deare* . . . . I. xi. 39. 1
streame of Balme, most soveraine And dainty *deare,* . . . . I. xi. 48. 3
the second fall Of her *deare* knight, ... I. xi. 50. 2
his *deare* Lady, that beheld it all, ... I. xi. 55. 3
when his daughter *deare* he does behold, ... I. xii. 12. 8
'*Deare* Sonne, great beene the evils which ye bore . . . . . I. xii. 17. 2
The fairest Un', his onely daughter *deare,* . . . . I. xii. 21. 2
her own *deare* loved knight . . . Did wonder much . . . . . I. xii. 23. 6
to the knight his daughter *deare* he tyde . . . . I. xii. 36. 8
His *deare* delights were hable to annoy: . . . . I. xii. 41. 4
'*Deare* Lady! how shall I declare thy cace, ... II. i. 9. 6
For Gods *deare* love be not so wilfull bent, ... II. i. 16. 2
'Ah! *deare* Sir Guyon, well becommeth you, ... II. i. 28. 3
that *deare* Crosse uppon your shield devizd, ... II. i. 31. 8
deare Lady, which the ymage art Of ruefull pitty . . . . . II. i. 44. 4
Speake, O *dear* Lady, speake! help never comes too late.' . . II. i. 44. 9
far be it,' (said he) '*Deare* dame, fro mee, ... II. i. 48. 1
My Lord, my love, my *deare* Lord, my *deare* love! . . . . . II. i. 50. 2
So *deare* thee, babe, I bought; . . . . II. i. 53. 8
nought too *dear* I deemd, while so my *deare* I sought. . . . II. i. 53. 9
Her *deare* besought to let her die a mayd. . . . . . . II. ii. 8. 5
by the loves which were to them most *deare,* . . . . II. ii. 27. 6
Be, therefore, O my *deare* Lords! pacifide, ... II. ii. 31. 8
She Guyon *deare* besought of curtesie To tell . . . . II. ii. 39. 4
O *deare* Lord! hold your dead-doing hand,' . . . . II. iii. 8. 1
Did court the handmayd of my Lady *deare,* . . . . II. iv. 25. 2
I may more delight in thy embracement *deare.* . . . . . . II. iv. 26. 9
'*Deare* sonne, thy causelesse ruth represse, ... II. v. 24. 5
Made dronke with drugs of *deare* voluptuous receipt. . . . . II. v. 34. 9
On him, that did Pyrochles *deare* dismay: . . . . II. v. 38. 7
should he but his owne *deare* Lord there see, ... II. vi. 43. 3
His owne *deare* Lord Pyrochles in sad plight, ... II. vi. 43. 4
every pillour decked was full *deare* With crownes, ... II. vii. 43. 7
'That goodly one, . . . my *deare,* my daughter is: . . . . . II. vii. 48. 6
'The charge . . . Of his *deare* safety, ... II. viii. 8. 2
His life for dew revenge should *deare* abye? . . . . II. viii. 28. 8
his *deare* hart the picture gan adore; . . . . II. viii. 43. 5
'*Deare* sir, whom . . . I long have lackt, ... II. viii. 53. 7

Dear—*Continued.*
My liefe, my liege, my Soveraine, my *deare,* . . . II. ix. 4. 5
eke her daughter *deare,* . . . II. x. 19. 1
his daughter *deare* He gave in wedlocke . . . II. x. 61. 1
'*Deare* countrey! O! how dearely *deare* . . . II. x. 69. 3
Which now him turnd to disadvantage *deare;* . . . II. xi. 34. 1
good Sir Guyon *deare* besought The Prince of grace . . . III. i. 5. 1
For whose *deare* sake full many a bitter stownd . . . III. i. 24. 8
In the *deare* closett of her painefull syde . . . III. ii. 11. 7
'Ah! my *deare* daughter, ah! my dearest dread, . . . III. ii. 30. 6
by this most sacred head Of my *deare* foster childe, . . . III. ii. 33. 6
with kisses *deare* Shee ofte did bathe, . . . III. ii. 34. 6
'O daughter *deare!*' (said she) 'despeire no whit; . . . III. ii. 35. 6
my *Deare,* (welfare thy heart, my *deare!*) . . . III. ii. 42. 1
her father *deare* Should . . . hard misfortune heare . . . III. iii. 5. 8
my *deare* daughters deepe engraffed ill, . . . III. iii. 18. 3
Proud of his dying honor and *deare* bandes, . . . III. iv. 17. 3
The God did graunt his daughters *deare* demaund, . . . III. iv. 22. 1
all that els was pretious and *deare,* . . . III. iv. 23. 6
Tryde often to the scath of many *Deare,* . . . III. iv. 24. 2
Her *deare* sonnes destiny to her to tell, . . . III. iv. 25. 4
Which when his mother *deare* did understond, . . . III. iv. 29. 5
Shee made so piteous mone and *deare* wayment, . . . III. iv. 35. 6
'*Deare* image of my selfe, (she sayd) . . . III. iv. 36. 1
so deepe wound through these *deare* members drive . . . III. iv. 37. 4
deare wisedom bought too late! . . . III. iv. 37. 9
the dim eies of my *deare* Marinell . . . III. iv. 39. 4
Of my *deare* Dame is loved dearely well: . . . III. v. 9. 2
brought it to her patient *deare,* . . . III. v. 32. 8
'Mercy, *deare* Lord!' (said he) . . . III. v. 35. 1
More *deare* then life she tendered, . . . III. v. 51. 2
her *deare* brood, her *deare* delight: . . . III. vi. 40. 4
to enjoy Her *deare* Adonis joyous company, . . . III. vi. 46. 2
wandring for to seeke her lover *deare,* . . . III. vi. 54. 6
Her lover *deare,* her dearest Marinell, . . . III. vi. 54. 7
'this Lady is my *deare;* . . . III. viii. 12. 8
late entrance *deare* besought: . . . III. ix. 12. 4
madest many Ladies *deare* lament . . . III. ix. 35. 3
nothing may impresse so *deare* constraint . . . III. ix. 40. 3
in blood Accomplished, that many *deare* complaind: . . . III. ix. 42. 7
Sir Paridell, all were he *deare;* . . . III. x. 37. 2
the brother *deare* Of that Argante . . . III. xi. 3. 6
redeeme my *deare* Out of her thraldome . . . III. xi. 16. 4
So lovedst thou the faire Coronis *deare;* . . . III. xi. 37. 2
for his owne *deare* sonne, . . . III. xi. 38. 1
Ne ought but *deare* Bisaltis ay could make him glad . . . III. xi. 41. 9
He loved eke Iphimedia *deare,* . . . III. xi. 42. 1
Ne did he spare . . . His owne *deare* mother, . . . III. xi. 45. 2
heavy eyes with natures burdein *deare,* . . . III. xi. 55. 7
lad . . . so *deare* To great Alcides, . . . III. xii. 7. 5
to see her own *deare* knight, . . . III. xii. 44. 8
the sweet lodge of love and *deare* delight: . . . III. xii. 45. *or.* 4
her *deare* nourslings losse no lesse did mourne, . . . III. xii. 45. 7
magnifying lovers *deare* debate; . . . IV. Pr. 1. 5
The *deare* compassion of whose bitter fit . . . IV. i. 1. 6
Through cruell knife that her *deare* heart did kerve: . . . IV. i. 4. 5
Some, of *deare* lovers foes perpetuall: . . . IV. i. 24. 5
He had small lust to buy his love so *deare,* . . . IV. i. 34. 6
Yet thou, false Squire, his fault shalt *deare* aby, . . . IV. i. 53. 8
Full many knights, that loved her like *deare,* . . . IV. ii. 26. 2
those two Ladies their two lovers *deare;* . . . IV. ii. 31. 7
robd the world of threasure endlesse *deare,* . . . IV. ii. 33. 4
love each other *deare,* what ever them befell . . . IV. ii. 53. 9
First to her brother, whom she loved *deare,* . . . IV. iii. 46. 6
By all that unto them was *deare,* . . . IV. iii. 47. 9
Dame Venus girdle, by her steemed *deare* . . . IV. v. 3. 7
as her life by her esteemed *deare* . . . IV. v. 6. 2
The face of his *deare* Canacee unheale; . . . IV. v. 10. 7
The which ere long full *deare* he shall abie: . . . IV. vi. 8. 5
Then her besought, as she to her was *deare,* . . . IV. vi. 25. 6
Ne ever was there wight to me more *deare* . . . IV. vi. 35. 8
she, *deare* Ladie, all the way was dead, . . . IV. vii. 9. 1
griefe, that her *deare* hart nigh swelt, . . . IV. vii. 9. 4
A leman fit for such a lover *deare:* . . . IV. vii. 34. 5
His owne *deare* Lord Prince Arthure came that way, . . . IV. vii. 42. 2
albeit his owne *dear* Squire he were, . . . IV. vii. 43. 5
With *deare* compassion deeply did emmove, . . . IV. viii. 3. 7
his *deare* companion of his care . . . IV. viii. 8. 6
all mindlesse of his owne *deare* Lord . . . IV. viii. 18. 4
lov'd me *deare,* as dearest thing alive . . . IV. viii. 56. 6
her *deare* hart full deepely made to rew, . . . IV. viii. 64. 3
She *deare* besought the Prince of remedie; . . . IV. viii. 64. 7
The *deare* affection unto kindred sweet, . . . IV. ix. 1. 5
when she perceived Her owne *deare* sire, . . . IV. ix. 7. 2
the captive Squire she lov'd so *deare,* . . . IV. ix. 10. 6
For losse of his *deare* love by Neptune hent, . . . IV. ix. 23. 2
such gaine was gotten *deare* . . . IV. ix. 30. 9
great Hercules and Hyllus *deare* . . . IV. x. 27. 1
forst to seeke my lifes *deare* patronnesse: . . . IV. xi. 28. 8
The nourslng of Dame Memorie his *deare,* . . . IV. xi. 10. 2
of my lifes *deare* love beloved be: . . . IV. xii. 10. 3
For his *deare* sake, . . . IV. xii. 19. 5
that same Squire, to whom she was more *dere,* . . . V. i. 27. 3
for his owne *deare* Ladies sake, . . . V. iii. 16. 4
With all *deare* delices and rare delights, . . . V. iii. 40. 4
gave them gifts and things of *deare* delight . . . V. iv. 51. 6
'Ah! my *deare* dread,' (said then the faithfull Mayd) . . . V. v. 31. 1
on their mother Earths *deare* lap did lie, . . . V. vii. 9. 2
To hinder thee . . . from thy countrey *deare:* . . . V. vii. 23. 4
Unto the man whom thou doest love so *deare;* . . . V. vii. 32. 5

Dear—*Continued.*
'Ah, my *deare* Lord! what sight is this?' . . . V. vii. 40. 1
an enraged cow That is berobbed of her youngling *dere,* . . . V. viii. 46. 2
her owne *deare* flesh did teare: . . . V. viii. 47. 6
'Nathlesse,' (said he) '*deare* Ladie, with me goe; . . . V. x. 24. 1
downe he fell uppon his mother *deare,* . . . V. x. 35. 8
With her two sonnes, right *deare* of her beloved, . . . V. x. 39. 7
Deare Lady, deedes ought not be scand . . . V. xi. 17. 3
eke that Idoll deem'd so costly *dere,* . . . V. xi. 33. 7
in which he did endosse His *deare* Redeemers badge . . . V. xi. 53. 5
Is ought on earth so pretious or *deare* As prayse and honour? . V. xi. 62. 6
For faire Irena, whom they loved *deare:* . . . V. xii. 10. 6
him did *deare* embrace . . . VI. i. 3. 2
She long time hath *deare* lov'd a doughty Knight, . . . VI. i. 14. 8
a faire Damzell, my beloved *deare,* . . . VI. i. 16. 2
perhaps he mote it *deare* aby.' . . . VI. i. 28. 4
him adoring as her lives *deare* Lord, . . . VI. i. 45. 6
For *deare* affection and unfayned zeale . . . VI. ii. 26. 5
She thankt him *deare* . . . VI. ii. 46. 6
inly touched with compassion *deare,* . . . VI. iii. 4. 4
And *deare* affection of so dolefull dreare, . . . VI. iii. 4. 5
But sigh'd and sorrow'd for her lover *deare,* . . . VI. iii. 6. 7
present The fearefull Lady to her father *deare,* . . . VI. iii. 18. 2
Unlesse thou dare, for thy *deare* Ladies sake . . . VI. iii. 35. 7
His *dear* affect with silence did restraine, . . . VI. v. 24. 4
quickely thence avaunt, Or *deare* aby; . . . VI. vi. 21. 3
his *deare* Ladie shent: . . . VI. vii. 4. 5
for his sake his *deare* life had forgone; . . . VI. vii. 18. 2
Unworthy she to be belov'd so *dere,* . . . VI. vii. 29. 5
first they spoile her of her jewels *deare,* . . . VI. viii. 41. 2
For her did languish, and his *deare* life spend; . . . VI. ix. 10. 6
have learn'd to love more *deare* This lowly quiet life . . . VI. ix. 25. 8
she did love a stranger swayne then him more *dere* . . . VI. ix. 38. 9
Thus to bereave thy loves *deare* sight from thee: . . . VI. x. 29. 5
ready now to rend His loves *deare* spoile, . . . VI. x. 35. 8
To make it seeme more *deare* and dainty, . . . VI. xi. 1. 9
To make the prises of the rest more *deare* . . . VI. xi. 15. 5
backe returning to his dearest *deare,* . . . VI. xi. 50. 1
had endured many a dreadfull stoure . . . for a Ladie *deare,* VI. xii. 3. 8
Is her owne daughter, her owne infant *deare* . . . VI. xii. 20. 6
all that she so *deare* did way, . . . VII. vi. 55. 1
Rudely thou wrongest my *deare* harts desire, . . . *Am.* v. 1
naught else be counted *deare;* . . . *Am.* viii. 4
that most sacred Empresse, my *dear* dred, . . . *Am.* xxxiii. 2
From presence of my dearest *deare* exylde, . . . *Am.* lii. 7
store Of all that *deare* and daynty is . . . *Am.* lxiii. 8
This joyous day, *deare* Lord, with joy begin; . . . *Am.* lxviii. 5
with thy *deare* blood clene washt . . . *Am.* lxviii. 7
all lyke *deare* didst buy, . . . *Am.* lxviii. 11
caught in cunning snare Of a *deare* foe, . . . *Am.* lxxi. 6
With many *deare* delights bedecked fyne . . . *Am.* lxxi. 12
The well of *deare* delight . . . *Epig.* iv. 48
Ah! my *deere* love, why doe ye sleepe thus long, . . . *Epith.* 85
Ay me! *deere* Lord! . . . *H.L.* 294
in honour of thy Mother *deare,* . . . *H.B.* 9
faire Dames! the worlds *deare* ornaments . . . *H.B.* 162
in *deare* loves delight . . . *H.B.* 233
faire Venus dearling, my *deare* dread! . . . *H.B.* 281
For mans *deare* sake he did a man become . . . *H.H.L.* 147
pierst the piteous hart Of that *deare* Lord . . . *H.H.L.* 157
What . . . thought can think the depth of so *deare* wound? . . . *H.H.L.* 163
Even he himselfe, in his *deare* sacrament, . . . *H.H.L.* 195
Learne him to love that loved thee so *deare,* . . . *H.H.L.* 258
ravisht with devouring great desire Of his *deare* selfe, . . . *H.H.L.* 269

Dear-beloved. To draw him from his *deare beloved* dame . . . VI. v. 15. 4

Deare, -s. *See* **Deer, Deer's.**

Dearer. Was never Lady loved *dearer* day . . . I. vii. 27. 7
her honor, *dearer* then her life, . . . IV. i. 6. 6
Much *dearer* be the things which come through hard distresse. IV. x. 28. 9
Dearer is love then life, and fame then gold; . . . V. xi. 63. 8
dearer then them both your faith once plighted hold.' . . . V. xi. 63. 9
His life he steemed *dearer* then his frend: . . . VI. x. 35. 5

Dearest. His *dearest* life did trust to careles sleep; . . . *Gn.* 243
late in warres have spent my *deerest* blood, . . . *Hub.* 247
unto thee most deare, O *dearest* Dame! . . . *Ti.* 244
Chosen to be her *dearest* Paramoure . . . *Ti.* 385
The presence of your *dearest* loves delight, . . . *D.* 513
all heedlesse of his *dearest* hale, . . . *As.* 103
unto . . . His *dearest* love, him dolefully did beare . . . *As.* 148
The dolefulst beare . . . Was Astrophel, but *dearest* unto mee! *As.* 150
lov'd this shepheard *dearest* in degree, . . . *Col.* 14
The which to heare vouchsafe, O *dearest* dread, . . . I. Pr. 4. 9
My *dearest* Lord fell from high honors staire . . . I. ii. 23. 7
He thereto meeting said, 'My *dearest* Dame, . . . I. iii. 28. 1
'Ah *dearest* Dame,' quoth then the Paynim bold, . . . I. iv. 41. 1
His *dearest* love, . . . Is there possessed of the traytour vile; I. iv. 42. 2
'Ah deare Sansjoy, next *dearest* to Sansfoy, . . . I. iv. 45. 4
ginneth to revive His ancient love, and *dearest* Cyparisse; . . I. vi. 17. 2
'Ah! *dearest* Lord,' (quoth she) 'how might that bee, . . . I. vi. 39. 1
'Ah! *dearest* dame,' . . . 'how might I see . . . I. vi. 39. 3
she it is, that did my Lord bethrall, My *dearest* Lord, . . . I. viii. 28. 7
'Ah *dearest* Lord! what evill starre On you hath frownd, . . . I. viii. 42. 6
When him his *dearest* Una did behold . . . I. x. 22. 7
Ah, *dearest* God, me graunt, . . . I. x. 42. 9
'Ah *dearest* Lord!' said then that doughty knight, . . . I. xii. 18. 1
in honour of his *dearest* Dame . . . II. iv. 26. 9
His *dearest* Dame is that Enchaunteresse, . . . II. v. 27. 1
fayre Critias, his *dearest* Belamy! . . . II. vii. 52. 9
his *dearest* life For her defence . . . II. xi. 16. 6
'Ah! my deare daughter, ah! my *dearest* dread, . . . III. ii. 30. 6

Dearest—*Continued.*
choseth vertue for his *dearest* Dame, III. iii. 1. 8
Begin then, O my *dearest* sacred Dame! III. iii. 4. 1
Should of his *dearest* daughters hard misfortune heare. III. iii. 5. 9
Her *dearest* sonne, her *dearest* harts delight: III. iv. 44. 5
Dayes *dearest* children be the blessed seed III. iv. 59. 5
'Ah, *dearest* God!' (quoth he) 'that is great woe, III. v. 6. 7
she her *dearest* sonne Cupido sought, III. vi. 20. 7
Phoebus paramoure And *dearest* love; III. vi. 45. 4
for his *dearest* sake endured sore Sore trouble III. vi. 53. 5
Her lover deare, her *dearest* Marinell, III. vi. 54. 7
the *dearest* to his dounghill minde, III. x. 15. 8
let us goe to seeke my *dearest* Dame, III. x. 39. 5
love a Shephards daughter for his *dearest* Dame. III. xi. 38. 9
He loved Isse for his *dearest* Dame, III. xi. 39. 1
His *dearest* love, the comfort of his dayes, III. xii. 44. *or.* 2
making way unto his *dearest* life, IV. iii. 12. 6
Canacee gan wayle her *dearest* frend. IV. iii. 35. 5
evill plight, in which her *dearest* brother Now stood, IV. iii. 40. 7
workst such wrecke on her to whom thou *dearest* art! IV. vi. 16. 9
To bath their hands in bloud of *dearest* freend, IV. vi. 17. 8
faire Ladie knight, my *dearest* Dame, IV. vi. 32. 1
Her *dearest* love full loth so shortly to forsake. IV. vi. 42. 9
likewise late had lost her *dearest* love, IV. viii. 3. 4
'Ne any but your selfe, O *dearest* dred, IV. viii. 17. 1
lov'd me deare, as *dearest* thing alive. IV. viii. 56. 6
When he in place his *dearest* love did spy; IV. xii. 35. 2
Giving her *dearest* children one by one Unto a dreadfull Monster V. x. 13. 6
Though I this *dearest* life for her doe spend.' V. xi. 43. 4
for pitty of his *dearest* Dame, VI. iii. 43. 7
His *dearest* joynt he sure had broken quight. VI. ix. 44. 5
backe returning to his *dearest* deare, VI. xi. 50. 1
whom so much ye make Joves *dearest* darling, VII. vii. 50. 3
Amongst thy *deerest* relicks to be kept. *Am.* xxii. 14
From presence of my *dearest* deare exylde, *Am.* lii. 7
Unmindfull of that *dearest* Lord of thyne; *H.H.L.* 221

Dearling, -s. *See* **Darling, -s.**

Dear-loved. the late losse of her *deare loved* knight, I. iii. 15. 6
beware of ficklenesse, In choice, . . . of thy *deare-loved* Dame; I. iv. 1. 4
her own *deare loved* knight . . . Did wonder much I. xii. 23. 6

Dearly. (a lesson *derely* bought) *S.C.* N. 156
Yet all be brethren ylike *dearly* bought: *Hub.* 142
I, it seeing, *dearelie* did lament. *Ti.* 504
with . . . her deare favours *dearly* well adorned; *As.* 154
That brothers hand shall *dearely* well requight, I. iv. 42. 6
That whylome was to me too *dearely* deare. I. v. 23. 5
A gentle youth, his *dearely* loved Squire, I. vii. 37. 1
For *dearely* sure her love was to me bent, I. ix. 14. 3
Una . . . Him *dearely* kist, I. x. 29. 4
Ladies love to leave, so *dearely* bought? I. x. 62. 6
that hoarie king, . . . Her *dearely* doth imbrace, I. xii. 12. 9
he *dearely* shall abyde, II. i. 20. 3
But vaine; for ye shall *dearely* do him rew, II. i. 25. 5
thou maist love, and *dearly* loved be, II. iii. 39. 6
after soone I *dearely* did lament; II. iv. 29. 5
I cast to pay that I so *dearely* bought. II. iv. 30. 7
Which to avenge on him they *dearly* vowd, II. viii. 11. 1
That direfull stroke thou *dearely* shalt aby:' II. viii. 33. 4
sacked Rome too *dearely* did assay, II. x. 40. 3
O! how *dearely* deare II. x. 69. 3
with sharpe speare the rest made *dearly* knowne. III. iv. 15. 6
Her Sea-god syre she *dearely* did perswade III. iv. 21. 7
Of my deare Dame is loved *dearely* well: III. v. 9. 2
he *dearly* shall abye: III. vi. 24. 8
her he *dearely* loved, III. vii. 31. 6
ere long shall *dearely* it repent; III. x. 32. 7
Whens *dearely* she with death bought her desire. III. xi. 33. 5
that me right *dearely* cost; IV. i. 35. 2
These three did love each other *dearely* well, IV. ii. 43. 1
made them *dearely* lov'd of each degree; IV. iii. 2. 7
My Sire, who me too *dearely* well did love, IV. vii. 16. 2
Nathlesse his pride full *dearely* he did pryse; IV. xi. 5. 5
That she might win some time, though *dearly* bought, V. ii. 23. 7
To have him slaine, or *dearely* doen aby; V. iii. 36. 4
That Calidore it *dearly* deepe did move: VI. iii. 15. 4
life so *dearely* did redeeme.' VI. vii. 15. 9
When his foote slipt, (that slip he *dearely* rewd) VI. vii. 48. 3
though long time *dearely* bought. VI. ix. 45. 9
who so hardie hand on her doth lay, It *dearely* shall aby, VI. xi. 15. 9
These eyes saw die, and *dearely* did lament; VI. xi. 31. 7
That Shepheard Colin *dearely* did condole, VII. vi. 40. 5
things hard gotten men more *dearely* deeme. *H.L.* 168
Him first to love that us so *dearely* bought, *H.H.L.* 188

Dearnelie, Dearnly. *See* **Dernly.**

Dearth. so dainty, they say, maketh *derth.* I. ii. 27. 9
The earth shall sooner . . . make eternal *derth,* I. iii. 28. 8

Death. Cruell *death* vanquishing so noble beautie, *Pet.* i. 13
death shall spoyle your goodly features. *Pet.*[2] vii. 14
forkhed sting that *death* in it did beare, *Van.* vi. 4
feeles the deepe delight that is in *death,* *Frag.*
Whose witt is weakenesse, whose wage is *death,* *S.C.* F. 88
Death on hym such outrage showe?) *S.C.* Jun. 90
Pyne, plagues, and dreery *death.* *S.C.* Jul. 24
though my bale with *death* I bought, *S.C.* Au. 105
my *death* shall weepe, *S.C.* Au. 119
whose shrieking sound Ys signe of dreery *death,* *S.C.* Au. 174
better dayes *death* hath shut up in woe? *S.S.* N. 74
where *death* doth leade the daunce, *S.C.* N. 105
that dreerie *Death* should strike so mortall stroke, *S.C.* N. 123

Death—*Continued.*
Laments the wound that *death* did launch. *S.C.* N. 139
maugre *death,* and dreaded sisters deadly spight, *S.C.* N. 163
We deeme of *Death* as doome of ill desert; *S.C.* N. 184
after Winter dreerie *death* does hast. *S.C.* D. 144
after Winter commeth timely *death.* *S.C.* D. 150
Warnd him awake, from *death* himselfe to keep. *Gn.* 288
Even from the doore of *death* and deadlie dreed! *Gn.* 355
Tydings of *death* and massacre unkinde: *Gn.* 396
A judge, that after *death* doth punish sore *Gn.* 447
him to *death* unfaithfull Paris sent; *Gn.* 530
death on everie side to them appeares *Gn.* 583
Cause of my *death* and just complaint to tell: *Gn.* 629
that Gnats *death,* which deeply was imprest, *Gn.* 645
powr'd on th' earth plague, pestilence, and *death.* *Hub.* 8
Where nought but dread and *death* do seeme in show? *Hub.* 966
If he awake, yet is not *death* the next, *Hub.* 987
To damne to *death,* or dole perpetuall, *Hub.* 1244
threatned *death,* and thousand deadly dolours, *Hub.* 1341
streightway of *death* afeard, *Hub.* 1360
Life, and *Death,* is in thy doomefull writing! *Com. Son.* i. 13
reare a trophee for devouring *death,* *Ti.* 52
after *death* all friendship doth decaie: *Ti.* 207
Though *death* his soule doo from his bodie sever; *Ti.* 257
untill that timelie *death* . . . doo ende my earthlie daies: *Ti.* 311
after *death* no token doth survive *Ti.* 353
bands of impacable fate, And power of *death,* *Ti.* 396
sung the prophecie Of his owne *death* *Ti.* 595
his life from yron *death* assure, *Mui.* 59
The engines which in them sad *death* doo hyde: *Mui.* 86
Deem the occasion of his *death* to bee; *D.* 88
The whiles soft *death* away her spirit hent, *D.* 258
In which sad *Death* his pourtraicture had writ, *D.* 303
cruell *Death* doth scorne to come at call, *D.* 356
Els surely *death* should be no punishment, *D.* 362
death I hate, because it life doth marre; *D.* 426
doo not dye then in despight of *death;* *D.* 443
As if that *death* he in the face had seene, *D.* 565
With dolours dart for *death* of Astrophel. *As.* Pr. 10
His palled face, impictured with *death,* *As.* 163
To prove that *death* their hearts cannot divide, *As.* 179
and longs *death* to behold, *Col.* 204
for Daphnes *death* doth tourn Sweet layes *Col.* 386
Daphnaida Upon her neeces *death* I did complaine: *Col.* 511
when as *death* these vitall bands shall breake, *Col.* 630
Making her *death* their life, I. i. 25. 9
You, . . . destinie Hath made judge of my life or *death* I. i. 51. 9
of whose most innocent *death* When tidings came to mee, I. ii. 24. 3
O, too deare love, love bought with *death* too deare!' I. ii. 31. 7
yielded pryde and proud submission, Still dreading *death,* I. iii. 6. 7
ought . . . That should as *death* unto my deare heart light: I. iii. 27. 5
eke my night of *death* the shadow is; I. iii. 27. 8
on those . . . dazed eyes . . . The cloude of *death* did sit. I. iii. 39. 8
with *death* opprest He ror'd aloud, I. iii. 42. 8
brothers *death* to wreak, Sansjoy Doth chaleng I. iv. Arg.
death it was, when any good he saw; I. iv. 30. 7
'Ah me! that is a double *death,'* I. iv. 51. 6
The messenger of *death,* the ghastly owle, I. v. 30. 6
In *death* avowing th' innocence of her sonne. I. v. 39. 3
charmes, A fordonne wight from dore of *death* mote raise, I. v. 41. 8
scornd of God and man, a shamefull *death* he dide. I. v. 48. 9
death ensewd if any him descryde. I. v. 52. 9
Which, quitt from *death,* yet quakes in every lim I. vi. 10. 8
To dally thus with *death* is no fit toy: I. vi. 28. 8
wonne from *death,* she bad him tellen plaine I. vi. 37. 7
Both hongred after *death;* I. vi. 43. 9
eyes . . . seeled up with *death* shall have their deadly meed.' I. vii. 23. 9
If *death* it be, it is not the first wound I. vii. 25. 6
captiv'd, of life or *death* he stood in doubt. I. vii. 26. 9
rather *death* desire then such despight. I. vii. 49. 6
Death and despeyre did many thereof sup, I. viii. 14. 3
'O! who is that, which bringes me happy choyce Of *death,* I. viii. 38. 4
O! welcome thou, that doest of *death* bring tydings trew.' I. viii. 38. 9
A ruefull spectacle of *death* and ghastly drere. I. viii. 40. 9
is the point of *death* now turnd fro mee, I. ix. 26. 3
'With which sad instrument of hasty *death,* I. ix. 30. 1
None els to *death* this man despayring drive I. ix. 38. 5
his owne guiltie mind, deserving *death.* I. ix. 38. 6
death after life, does greatly please.' I. ix. 40. 9
shunne the *death* ordaynd by destinie? I. ix. 42. 8
When houre of *death* is come, I. ix. 42. 9
'Thou, wretched man, of *death* hast greatest need, I. ix. 45. 1
Thy life shutt up for *death* so oft did call; I. ix. 45. 6
death then would the like mishaps forestall, I. ix. 45. 8
Death is the end of woes: I. ix. 47. 9
nought but *death* before his eies he saw, I. ix. 50. 2
bad him choose what *death* he would desire; I. ix. 50. 8
death was dew to him that had provokt Gods ire. I. ix. 50. 9
death he could not worke himselfe thereby; I. ix. 54. 6
those in point of *death* which lay; I. x. 41. 2
sin, and hell, and *death,* doe most dismay I. x. 41. 4
after *death* and buriall done, I. x. 43. 1
The bitter doome of *death* and balefull mone I. x. 53. 8
Dead was it sure, as sure as *death* in deed, I. xi. 12. 3
Death better were; *death* did he oft desire, I. xi. 28. 4
death will never come when needes require. I. xi. 28. 5
Into that same he fell, which did from *death* him save. I. xi. 48. 9
death him did awaite in daily wretchednesse. I. xii. 33. 9
Who then would thinke . . . He could escape fowle *death* I. xii. 36. 5
none but *death* for ever can divide; I. xii. 37. 2

Death—*Continued.*
threatned *death* with many a bloodie word: . . . . II. i. 11. 8
Death were too litle paine for such a fowle despight. . . . . II. i. 17. 9
The sacred badge of my Redeemers *death,* . . . . II. i. 27. 6
Yet can they not warne *death* from wretched wight. . . . . . II. i. 36. 5
Come, then; come soone; come sweetest *death,* to me, ... II. i. 36. 6
where that sad pourtraict Of *death* and dolour lay, ... II. i. 39. 4
On which the drery *death* did sitt . . . . II. i. 45. 2
As heven accusing guilty of her *death,* . . . . II. i. 49. 2
give *death* to him that *death* does give, ... II. i. 55. 4
ended all her woe in quiet *death.* . . . . II. i. 56. 4
'*death* is an equall doome . . . . II. i. 59. 1
after *death* the tryall is to come, ... II. i. 59. 3
when *death* hath both supprest, ... II. i. 59. 5
For all so great shame after *death* I weene, ... II. i. 59. 8
taught T' avenge his Parents *death* . . . . II. iii. 2. 9
doest not unto *death* thyselfe prepayre? . . . . II. iii. 7. 7
threatned *death* with dreadfull countenaunce, ... II. iii. 14. 2
death were better then such agony . . . . II. iv. 33. 3
Had doen to *death,* subdewde in equall frayes . . . . II. v. 26. 5
cause of *death* betweene two doughtie knights do breed! . . . II. vi. 33. 9
whither dost thou flye The shame and *death,* . . . . II. vi. 39. 7
Nothing but *death* can doe me to respyre.' . . . . II. vi. 44. 5
After pursewing *death* . . . . II. vi. 44. 7
Death is for wretches borne under unhappy starre.' . . . . . II. vi. 44. 9
O Atin! helpe to me last *death* to give.' . . . . II. vi. 45. 5
Of *death* and dolor telling sad tidings; . . . . II. vii. 23. 5
next to *death* is Sleepe to be compard; . . . . II. vii. 25. 7
dread of *death* and dolor doe away; . . . . II. viii. 7. 7
what doth his bad *death* now satisfy . . . . II. viii. 15. 3
dreadfull *Death* behynd thy backe doth stond.' . . . . II. viii. 37. 9
waytes for *death* with dread and trembling aw; . . . . II. viii. 50. 4
in despight of life for *death* doe call.' . . . . II. viii. 52. 4
All threatning *death,* all in straunge manner armd; . . . . . II. ix. 13. 5
in bands, where he till *death* remaind; . . . . II. x. 18. 7
he dyde, made ripe for *death* by eld, ... II. x. 32. 2
Whose *death* t' avenge, his mother mercilesse, ... II. x. 35. 6
Till by his *death* he it recovered: . . . . II. x. 44. 8
Shee triumphed on *death,* in enemies despight. . . . . II. x. 56. 9
Hengist eke soon brought to shamefull *death.* . . . . II. x. 67. 6
they to direfull *death* their groning ghosts did send. . . . . II. xi. 15. 9
shunne Rocke of Reproch, and it as *death* to dred!' . . . . . II. xii. 9. 9
The dreadfull Fish that hath deserv'd the name Of *Death,* . . II. xii. 24. 2
For *death* sate on the point of that enchaunted speare: . . . III. i. 9. 9
it importunes *death* and dolefull dreryhedd. . . . . III. i. 16. 9
That *death* me liefer were then such despight, ... III. i. 24. 4
yield the pray of love to lothsome *death* at last. . . . . . III. ii. 17. 9
death nor daunger from thy dew reliefe Shall me debarre: . . III. ii. 33. 8
it must doubled bee with *death* of twaine? . . . . III. ii. 35. 4
nought for me but *death* there doth remaine.' . . . . III. ii. 35. 5
Till *death* make one end of my daies and miseree!' . . . . . III. ii. 39. 9
needs love or *death* must bee thy lott, ... III. ii. 46. 7
nought but *death* her dolour mote depart. . . . . III. iv. 6. 5
Ne doest by others *death* ensample take, ... III. iv. 14. 7
So life is losse, and *death* felicity: . . . . III. iv. 38. 7
Sad life worse then glad *death;* . . . . III. iv. 38. 8
Sister of heavie *death,* and nourse of woe, ... III. iv. 55. 2
The dreary image of sad *death* appeares: . . . . III. iv. 57. 7
death with darknesse doth begin. . . . . III. iv. 59. 9
threatned *death* for his outrageous wrong. . . . . III. v. 13. 9
What bootes it him from *death* to be unbownd, ... III. v. 42. 7
Fayre *death* it is, to shonne more shame, to dy: . . . . . . III. v. 45. 8
shund dishonor which as *death* she feard: . . . . III. vi. 10. 5
She you from *death,* you me from dread, redeemd; . . . . . . III. vii. 52. 7
To doe fowle *death* to die, ... III. ix. 17. 9
Two things he feared, but the third was *death;* . . . . . . III. x. 2. 6
yet did his *death* forgive. . . . . III. x. 7. 9
had from *death* to life him newly wonne. . . . . III. x. 33. 4
he of *death* afeard. . . . . III. x. 52. 5
death and life attonce unto him gives, ... III. x. 60. 3
renowm, that, more then *death,* is to be sought.' . . . . . III. xi. 19. 9
Whens dearely she with *death* bought her desire. . . . . . . III. xi. 33. 5
Yet was thy love her *death,* and her *death* was thy smart. . III. xi. 36. 9
Vile Poverty; and, lastly, *Death* with infamy. . . . . III. xii. 25. 9
death, or if that ought doe *death* exceed; . . . . III. xii. 35. 3
He, glad of life, that lookt for *death* but late, ... III. xii. 35. 8
mightie strokes . . . seemed *death* in them to beare; . . . . IV. iii. 7. 7
gan shun his dreadfull sight, No lesse then *death* . . . . . IV. iv. 41. 9
seemed nought but *death* mote be her destinie. . . . . IV. vi. 18. 9
Shall *death* be th' end, or ought else worse, ... IV. vii. 11. 4
Death is to him, that wretched life doth lead, ... IV. vii. 11. 7
Then *death* it selfe more dread and desperate; . . . . IV. viii. 1. 4
unto *death* had doen him unredrest, ... IV. viii. 41. 8
Damon and Pythias, whom *death* could not sever: . . . . IV. x. 27. 6
By timely *death* shall winne her wished rest, ... IV. xii. 8. 2
if ye deeme me *death* . . . . IV. xii. 9. 6
It's late in *death* of daunger to advize, ... IV. xii. 28. 6
By wicked doome condemn'd a wretched *death* to die. . . . . . IV. xii. 29. 9
death t' adward I ween'd did appertaine . . . . IV. xii. 30. 4
away gan chace Sad *death,* . . . . IV. xii. 34. 4
dismayd with dreadfull sight Of *death,* . . . . V. ii. 54. 4
as the *death* he hated such despight, ... V. iii. 31. 8
doth from *death* reprive. . . . . V. iv. Arg.
Thinking to have her griefe by *death* bereaved: . . . . V. iv. 10. 4
Twixt life and *death* long to and fro she weaved, ... V. iv. 10. 7
When as the paine of *death* she tasted had, ... V. iv. 11. 2
For any *death* to chaunge life, though most bad: . . . . . . V. iv. 11. 5
From dreadfull mouth of *death,* . . . . V. iv. 12. 3
That he of womens hands so base a *death* should dy. . . . . . V. iv. 22. 9
horrour of fowle *death* for Knight unfit, ... V. iv. 25. 4

Death—*Continued.*
pangs of *death* her spirit overtooke. . . . . V. v. 11. 5
might have had of life or *death* election: . . . . V. v. 26. 5
many hath with dread of *death* dismayd, ... V. v. 31. 3
To thinke how this long *death* thou mightest disinherit.' . . . V. v. 36. 9
Like fruitles seede, of which untimely *death* should grow. . . V. vii. 31. 9
tryumph in their blood whom she to *death* did dryve. . . . . V. ix. 41. 9
she of *death* was guiltie found by right, ... V. ix. 50. 4
Is liker lingring *death* then loathed life to bee.' . . . . . V. x. 21. 9
Whom she did put to *death,* deceived like a foole. . . . . . V. xi. 25. 9
She *death* shall sure aby.' . . . . V. xi. 40. 6
Gainst which the pallid *death* findes no defence; . . . . . . V. xi. 45. 5
the dismall day Appointed for Irenas *death* . . . . V. xii. 11. 2
seemed nought could him from *death* protect; . . . . V. xii. 21. 4
he for dread of *death* gan loude to crie . . . . VI. i. 22. 8
all this while did dwell In dread of *death,* . . . . VI. i. 43. 2
After whose *death* his brother, . . . tooke the roiall . . . . VI. ii. 28. 6
Twixt life and *death,* not knowing what was donne. . . . . . VI. ii. 48. 6
As if her vitall powers were at strife With stronger *death,* . VI. v. 5. 8
every joynt for dread of *death* did quake, ... VI. vi. 29. 7
The fearfull swayne beholding *death* so nie, ... VI. vii. 12. 1
That other swayne . . . Lay in the lap of *death,* . . . . . VI. vii. 17. 9
Or else abide the *death* that hard before you stands.' . . . VI. viii. 7. 9
Ne list the Knight . . . Whose doome was *death;* . . . . . . VI. viii. 8. 8
My life will by his *death* have lamentable end. . . . . . . VI. viii. 17. 9
to the dore of *death* for sorrow drew, ... VI. viii. 20. 8
The rest, that scape his sword and *death* eschew, ... VI. viii. 49. 8
fearing *death,* and next to *death* the lacke Of clothes . . VI. viii. 50. 3
A thousand times him thankt that had her *death* prevented. . VI. x. 36. 9
It dearely shall aby, and *death* for handsell pay. . . . . . VI. xi. 15. 9
making way for *death* at large to walke; . . . . VI. xi. 16. 5
With cloud of *death* upon her eyes displayd; . . . . VI. xi. 21. 5
Renew'd her *death* by timely *death* denying. . . . . VI. xi. 23. 5
'How could the *death* dare ever her to quell? . . . . VI. xi. 29. 6
Their Captaine long withstood, and did her *death* forstall. . VI. xi. 31. 9
death it selfe unto himselfe did threat; . . . . VI. xi. 33. 5
if that dead, how he her *death* might wreake, ... VI. xi. 34. 6
long for *death* had sought. . . . . VI. xi. 45. 5
their heads from *death* to hide, ... VI. xi. 49. 8
death for life exchanged foolishlie: . . . . VII. vi. 6. 4
death, instead of life, have sucked from our Nurse! . . . . VII. vi. 6. 9
with their *death* his cruell life dooth feed; . . . . VII. vii. 24. 8
lastly *Death; Death* with most grim and griesly visage . . . VII. vii. 46. 1, 2
chast affects that naught but *death* can sever; . . . . . . *Am.* vi. 12
both lyfe and *death* forth from you dart, ... *Am.* vii. 3
since that lyfe is more then *death* desyred, ... *Am.* vii. 9
Such *death* the sad ensample of your might. . . . . *Am.* vii. 14
death out of theyr shiny beames doe dart; . . . . *Am.* xxiv. 7
in the shade of *death* it selfe shall shroud, ... *Am.* xxvii. 3
his *death,* which some perhaps will mone, ... *Am.* xxxvi. 13
Allur'd a Dolphin him from *death* to ease. . . . . *Am.* xxxviii. 4
In dread of *death,* and daungerous dismay, ... *Am.* lxiii. 3
make thy triumph over *death* and sin; . . . . *Am.* lxviii. 2
whenas *death* shall all the world subdew, ... *Am.* lxxv. 13
Which *death,* or love, or fortunes wreck did rayse, ... *Epith.* 8
Had it bene *death,* yet would he die againe, ... *H.L.* 243
nought but *death* can stint his dolours smart? . . . . *H.B.* 74
can restore a damned wight from *death.* . . . . *H.B.* 287
Fell . . . Into the mouth of *death,* . . . . *H.H.L.* 123
Dolours of *death* into his soule did dart, ... *H.H.L.* 159
Us wretches from the second *death* did save; . . . . *H.H.L.* 193

Death's. sing of sorrowe and *deathes* dreeriment; . . . . . . *S.C.* N. 36
hast thy *deathes* wound? . . . . *S.C.* D. 95
The Shepheard hath thy *deaths* record engraved. . . . . *Gn.* 688
His life was nigh unto *deaths* dore yplaste; . . . . I. iv. 28. 1
Whom these sad eyes saw nigh unto *deaths* dore, ... I. viii. 27. 2
The man that . . . lay at *deathes* dore. . . . . I. x. 27. 9
The ill-faste Owle, *deaths* dreadfull messengere; . . . . . . I. xii. 36. 4
her that from *deathes* dore Me brought? . . . . III. v. 46. 2
doth transfixe the soule with *deathes* eternall dart. . . . . III. x. 59. 9
Had *Deathes* owne ymage figurd in her face, ... III. xii. 19. 6
every houre they knocke at *deathes* gate? . . . . IV. iii. 1. 7
Well knowing her to be his *deaths* sole instrument. . . . . . IV. vii. 29. 9
From *deathes* dore at which he lately lay, ... V. iv. 35. 2
dare even *deathes* most dreadfull face behold? . . . . V. v. 31. 4
byting th' earth for very *deaths* disdaine; . . . . V. xi. 14. 7
Looking each houre into *deathes* mouth to fall, ... VI. xi. 44. 7

Deaths. a thousand *deathes,* and shame beside?' . . . . *Hub.* 976
thousand *deathes* me lever were to dye . . . . III. vii. 51. 5
thousand *deathes* deviseth in her vengefull mind. . . . . . . VII. vi. 48. 9

Deaths'. Me liefer were ten thousand *deathes* priefe . . . . . II. iv. 28. 8

Deaw, Deaw(e)d, *etc. See* **Dew, Dewed,** *etc.*

Debace, -d. *See* **Debase, -d.**

Debar. nor daunger from thy dew reliefe Shall me *debarre:* . . III. ii. 33. 9

Debarred. from her presence faultlesse him *debard.* . . . . . *Col.* 167
Utterers of secrets he from thence *debard,* . . . . II. ix. 25. 5
so them still *debar'd.* . . . . III. ii. 21. 5
None was *debard,* but all had leave that lust. . . . . V. iii. 6. 3
at the sight of these those were awhile *debard.* . . . . . . V. ix. 36. 9

Debars. want *debarres* myne eyes from sleepe. . . . . *S.C.* Au. 162

Debase. ignorance . . . mindes of men borne heavenlie doth *debace.* . . . . *T.M.* 498

Debased. all that humble is, and meane *debaced,* . . . . . . *Van.* i. 6
honour with indignitie *debased!* . . . . V. xi. 63. 7

Debate. I sing of deadly dolorous *debate,* . . . . *Mui.* 1
She made the storie of the olde *debate* . . . . *Mui.* 305
Well could he tourney, and in lists *debate,* . . . . II. i. 6. 7
Strife and *debate,* bloodshed and bitternesse, ... II. vii. 12. 7
With him in bloody armes they rashly did *debate.* . . . . . . II. viii. 11. 9
Not to *debate* the chalenge of your right, ... II. viii. 27. 7

Debate—*Continued.*
gan he to discourse the whole *debate*, . . . II. viii. 54. 6
Who after long *debate*, . . . II. x. 58. 6
With double sences, and with false *debate*, . . . III. iv. 28. 8
both full loth in darkenesse to *debate;* . . . III. ix. 14. 2
magnifying lovers deare *debate;* . . . IV. Pr. 1. 5
mother of *debate* And all dissention . . . IV. i. 19. 1
Through mischievous *debate* and deadly feood, . . . IV. i. 26. 4
Drew nigh, to weete the cause of their *debate:* . . . IV. ii. 20. 6
now a new *debate* Stird up . . . IV. iv. 2. 3
They liv'd together long without *debate;* . . . IV. ix. 16. 2
Cause of their discord and so fell *debate* . . . IV. ix. 24. 1
him maystred still in all *debate*. . . . IV. x. 32. 9
Which he endured had through daungerous *debate:* . . . VI. iii. 22. 9
Ne any dares with him for it *debate*. . . . VI. iv. 30. 4
Himselfe addrest unto this new *debate*, . . . VI. viii. 13. 3
life Which Shepheards lead, without *debate* or bitter strife. . VI. ix. 18. 9
Debateful. '*Debatefull* strife, and cruell enmity, . . . II. vi. 35. 1
Debatement. He with Pyrochles sharp *debatement* made: . . II. vi. 39. 2
Debating. on both sides was then *debating* hard; . . . V. ix. 36. 8
Thus whylest they were *debating* diverslie, . . . VI. vii. 23. 7
Debon. the large leape which *Debon* did compell Coulin to make, . . . II. x. 11. 2
Goemagot of strong Corineus, and Coulin of *Debon* old, . . . III. ix. 50. 4
Debonair. Was never Prince so meeke and *debonaire*, . . . I. ii. 23. 5
Crying; 'Let be that Lady *debonaire*, . . . II. vi. 28. 4
Thereto so bounteous and so *debonayre*, . . . III. i. 26. 4
The bountiest virgin and most *debonaire* . . . III. v. 8. 2
Courteous to all and seeming *debonaire*, . . . III. xii. 14. 4
Most sacred wight, most *debonayre* and free, . . . V. ix. 20. 7
Debon's. *Debons* shayre was that is Devonshyre: . . . II. x. 12. 6
Deborah. how stout *Debora* strake Proud Sisera, . . . III. iv. 2. 7
Debt. In gage for his gay Masters hopelesse *dett:* . . . *Hub.* 865
nor reave Out of your endlesse *debt*, . . . *Ded. Son.* vii. 7
as Ladies *det*, He as a Knight might justly be admitted; . . IV. i. 12. 7
to forbeare doth not forgive the *det*.' . . . IV. iii. 11. 5
And pay the price, all were his *debt* extreeme. . . . *H.H.L.* 133
Debtor. For such your kind regard I can but rest your *detter*. V. v. 37. 9
he vow'd to be her *debter* For many moe good turnes . . . VII. vi. 44. 7
Debtors. all women are thy *debtors* found, . . . *Col.* 901
Decay. onely God surmounts all times *decay*, . . . *Bel.*^{2} i. 13
faire greene Lawrell branch did quite *decay*. . . . *Bel.*^{2} ix. 14
Are temporall, and subject to *decay:* . . . *Ro.* ix. 11
For nought mought they quitten him from *decay*, . . . *S.C.* F. 213
With your ayd to fore-stall my neere *decay*.' . . . *S.C.* May 273
Mought needes *decay*, when it is at best. . . . *S.C.* S. 241
Of ayde or counsell in my *decaye*. . . . *S.C.* S. 247
waylde the rash *decay* Of Phaeton, . . . *Gn.* 198
safe delivered from sad *decay*, . . . *Gn.* 335
Doth as a vapour vanish, and *decaie*. . . . *Ti.* 56
to lament My long *decay*, . . . *Ti.* 157
times *decay*, and envies cruell tort, . . . *Ti.* 167
after death all friendship doth *decaie:* . . . *Ti.* 207
thoughts of men do as themselves *decay;* . . . *Ti.* 401
Above the reach of ruinous *decay*, . . . *Ti.* 422
to worke our *decay;* . . . *Mui.* 222
to my selfe, for whose confusde *decay* . . . *D.* 353
danger great, if not assurd *decay*, I saw before mine eyes, . . I. ii. 41. 8
Through wicked pride and wasted welthes *decay*. . . . I. v. 51. 4
In hope to bring her to her last *decay*. . . . I. vi. 48. 7
O foolish men! why hast ye to your own *decay?* . . . I. x. 10. 9
long *decay* Renew, as one were borne that very day. . . . I. xi. 30. 4
give you eke good helpe to their *decay*. . . . II. iii. 15. 2
So shall wrath, gealosy, griefe, love, die and *decay*.' . . . II. iv. 35. 9
overgrowne with dust and old *decay*, . . . II. vii. 29. 2
Eternall God thee save from such *decay!* . . . II. vii. 34. 7
More glory thought to give life then *decay*, . . . II. viii. 51. 4
save your selves from neare *decay;* . . . II. ix. 12. 3
Threatning unheedy wrecke and rash *decay*, . . . II. x. 6. 5
since it greatly did *decay*. . . . II. x. 53. 9
daily spectacle of sad *decay:* . . . II. x. 62. 5
now it gan to threaten neare *decay:* . . . II. xi. 14. 5
To shonne the engin of his meant *decay;* . . . II. xi. 36. 3
th' utmost yssew of his owne *decay*. . . . II. xi. 41. 5
he began to faint, and life *decay:* . . . II. xi. 48. 6
called was the Whirlepoole of *decay;* . . . II. xii. 20. 2
Ne more doth florish after first *decay*, . . . II. xii. 75. 3
Made them recoile, and fly from dredd *decay*, . . . III. i. 21. 8
envious Men, fearing their rules *decay*, . . . III. ii. 2. 5
To bring her sonne unto his last *decay*. . . . III. iv. 28. 5
formes are variable, and *decay* . . . III. vi. 38. 6
All things *decay* in time, and to their end doe draw. . . . III. vi. 40. 9
is the spectacle of ruinous *decay*. . . . III. vii. 41. 9
Her certeine losse, if not her sure *decay:* . . . III. viii. 49. 6
sought to bring all things unto *decay;* . . . IV. i. 29. 4
As blasted bloosme through heat doth languish and *decay:* . IV. viii. 2. 9
Amoret, so neare unto *decay*, . . . IV. viii. 20. 4
That his *decay* should happen by a mayd. . . . IV. xii. 28. 5
Till they arrive at their last ruinous *decay*. . . . V. Pr. 6. 9
So did this Ladies goodly forme *decay*, . . . V. iii. 25. 8
Of rude oblivion and long times *decay*, . . . V. iv. 2. 8
tract of time, that all things doth *decay*, . . . V. iv. 8. 1
when Philtra saw my lands *decay* . . . V. iv. 9. 6
what cause brought that man to *decay*, . . . V. iv. 23. 6
to lead your selfe unto your owne *decay?*' . . . V. iv. 26. 9
sield With moniments of many Knights *decay*, . . . V. v. 21. 4
drew The Sunnes bright wayne to Phaetons *decay*, . . . V. viii. 40. 2
when in wrath he threats the worlds *decay*, . . . V. ix. 31. 8
glad of spoyle and ruinous *decay*, . . . V. ix. 47. 6
Out of her poysnous entrails fraught with dire *decay*.' . . . V. xi. 20. 9

Decay—*Continued.*
For to receive the doome of her *decay:* . . . V. xii. 12. 5
when I gin to feele *decay* of might, . . . VI. Pr. 1. 8
her vitall powers were at strife . . . and feared their *decay:* . VI. v. 5. 8
to allure such fondlings . . . unto their owne *decay:* . . . VI. vi. 42. 4
Unto a straunge mischaunce that menac'd her *decay*. . . . VI. viii. 34. 9
downe themselves doe drive To sad *decay*, . . . VI. ix. 22. 5
That mucky masse, the cause of mens *decay*, . . . VI. ix. 33. 5
doth play Her cruell sports to many mens *decay?* . . . VII. vi. 1. 5
Yet see we soone *decay;* . . . VII. vii. 18. 3
out of their *decay* and mortall crime, . . . VII. vii. 18. 5
To lose their heat and shortly to *decay;* . . . VII. vii. 24. 4
thy *decay* thou seekst by thy desire; . . . VII. vii. 59. 3
weake harts doth . . . tempte to theyr *decay;* . . . *Am.* xlvii. 6
She doth allure me to mine owne *decay*, . . . *Am.* liii. 7
I my selfe shall lyke to this *decay*, . . . *Am.* lxxv. 7
Threatning their owne confusion and *decay:* . . . *H.L.* 82
The whyles thou doest triumph in their *decay;* . . . *H.L.* 137
that same goodly hew . . . shal *decay*, . . . *H.B.* 93
Shall never be extinguisht nor *decay;* . . . *H.B.* 101
Ne ever should their happinesse *decay*, . . . *H.H.L.* 76
Decayed. *See* **Late-decayed.**
Repayring her *decayed* fashion, . . . *Ro.* xxvii. 10
To see so goodly thing so soone *decayed*. . . . *Van.* vii. 14
His honor *decayed*, his braunches sere. . . . *S.C.* F. 114
shortly the foundation *decaid*, . . . *Ti.* 500
all his vitall powres *Decayd*, . . . I. viii. 41. 9
weighing the *decayed* plight . . . of her chosen knight, . . I. ix. 20. 4
so often as his life *decayd*, . . . II. xi. 45. 3
their *decayed* kingdomes shall amend: . . . III. iii. 23. 5
his hart woxe sore, and health *decayd:* . . . III. v. 43. 2
her sonne whose senses were *decayd*. . . . III. viii. 4. 9
redeemes faire Amoret through charmes *decayd*. . . . III. xii. Arg.
all their glory quite *decayd;* . . . III. xii. 42. 4
now it is so utterly *decayd*, . . . IV. viii. 33. 1
now their forces greatly were *decayd*, . . . IV. ix. 34. 1
lives although *decay'd*, yet loves *decayed* never. . . . IV. x. 27. 9
as he still *decayd* so he encreased more. . . . VI. i. 21. 9
The sight of whom, though now *decayd* and mard, . . . VI. xi. 13. 1
Her lovely light was dimmed and *decayd* . . . VI. xi. 21. 4
the Templer Knights to byde, Till they *decayed* through pride: . . . *Proth.* 136
Decays. give a second life to dead *decayes!* . . . *Ro.* Env. 6
when the life *decayes* and forme does fade, . . . III. vi. 37. 7
wrought their owne *decayes*. . . . III. xi. 52. 5
All carelesse how my life for her *decayes* (**decayse*): . . . *Am.* xxxviii. 10
Decease. the whilest you mourne for his *decease*, . . . *Ti.* 237
Since whose *decease*, learning lies unregarded, . . . *Ti.* 440
After her Noble husbands late *decesse;* . . . V. x. 11. 8
Deceased. liest senseles, like the corpse *deceast*, . . . *Hub.* 1328
Deceit. Through fleshes frailtie, and *deceipt* of sin. . . . *T.M.* 492
Duessa I, the daughter of *Deceipt* and Shame.' . . . I. v. 26. 9
The false resemblaunce of *Deceipt* . . . Did closely lurke; . . I. v. 27. 3
deceipt doth maske in visour faire, . . . I. vii. 1. 3
So he them deceives, deceivd in his *deceipt*, . . . II. v. 34. 8
Shamefull *deceipt*, and daunger imminent, . . . III. iv. 58. 4
By treacherous *deceipt* did me deprive: . . . III. x. 27. 5
litle knew Of such *deceipt*, . . . III. xi. 31. 6
So did *deceipt* the selfe-deceiver fayle. . . . V. ix. 19. 7
Deceitful. *deceitfull* meaning is double eyed. . . . *S.C.* May 254
that his *deceitfull* traine . . . might not be bewraid, . . . *Mui.* 398
So hight because of this *deceitfull* traine . . . *Col.* 118
handle his *deceitfull* wit In subtil shifts, . . . *Col.* 693
No . . . *deceiptfull* traine, Might once abide . . . I. viii. 4. 5
untwisting his *deceiptfull* clew, . . . II. i. 8. 3
through treason and *deceiptfull* gin, . . . II. iii. 13. 7
well perceived his *deceiptfull* sleight, . . . II. vii. 64. 7
usd to bath themselves in that *deceiptfull* shade. . . . II. xii. 30. 9
his *deceiptfull* eyes did never lin To looke . . . III. viii. 24. 8
Ne ever did *deceiptfull* Clarin find . . . V. v. 56. 4
Hast after vaine *deceiptfull* shadowes sought, . . . *H.H.B.* 291
Deceit's. She wounded was with her *deceipts* owne dart, . . . V. v. 43. 6
Deceits. they did employ . . . several *deceipts*, but all in vaine; VI. v. 14. 2
Deceive. how to *deceave* With talke, . . . *Hub.* 23
Now like a Merchant, Merchants to *deceave*, . . . *Hub.* 863
Him to *deceive*, for all his watchfull ward, . . . *Col.* 136
the man, that ever would *deceave* A gentle Lady, . . . II. i. 17. 7
all he did was to *deceive* good knights, . . . II. i. 23. 1
sure yt would *deceive* thy labor and thy might.' . . . II. viii. 21. 9
who can *deceive* his destiny, . . . III. iv. 27. 1
deceive Fraile Ladies hart with loves consuming rage, . . . III. vii. 46. 3
Two eies him needeth, . . . Who lovers will *deceive*. . . . III. ix. 31. 8
Him selfe he did of his new love *deceave;* . . . IV. i. 36. 5
Vaine is the art that seekes it selfe for to *deceive*. . . . IV. vi. 40. 9
doeth *deceive* The infant, . . . V. v. 53. 3
Me to *deceive* of faith unto me plight, . . . V. vi. 16. 8
could *deceive* one looking in his face: . . . V. ix. 5. 7
Deviz'd a Web her wooers to *deceave;* . . . *Am.* xxiii. 2
Deceived. empty sides *deceived* of their dew, . . . I. viii. 41. 4
With cup thus charmd him parting she *deceivd;* . . . II. i. 55. 3
with selfe-loved personage *deceiv'd*, . . . II. iii. 5. 4
So he them deceives, *deceivd* in his deceipt, . . . II. v. 34. 8
when he stroke most strong the dint *deceiv'd*, . . . II. viii. 49. 3
her expectation greatly was *deceav'd*. . . . III. v. 28. 9
of his forward hope *deceived* quight; . . . III. vii. 28. 2
the Thebane Semelee, *Deceivd* of gealous Juno, . . . III. xi. 33. 2
dayly more *deceived* was thereby; . . . IV. ii. 11. 2
Deceived through great likenesse of their face: . . . IV. ix. 10. 7
Whether by might extort, or else by slight *deceaved?* . . . V. iii. 30. 9
see how much her purpose was *deceaved!* . . . V. iv. 10. 5

Deceived—*Continued.*
And drawing backe *deceived* their intent: V. iv. 24. 2
Least by such slight he were unwares *deceived;* V. xi. 7. 3
Whom she did put to death, *deceived* like a foole. V. xi. 25. 9
As if she doubted to have bene *deceived,* VI. iv. 27. 3
glauncing by *deceiv'd* him of that he desynd. VI. vii. 10. 9
Deceiver. *See* **Self-deceiver.**
Deceives. So he them *deceives,* deceivd in his deceipt, II. v. 34. 8
December. after him came next the chill *December:* VII. vii. 41. 1
Decent. corses . . . lay Without remorse or *decent* funerall; I. v. 53. 4
Decesse. *See* **Decease.**
Decetto. The second, not so strong but wise, *Decetto;* VI. v. 13. 8
So did *Decetto* eke him circumvent; VI. v. 20. 6
Decide. if ye please that I your cause *decide,* V. i. 25. 5
That which he doth with righteous doome *decide,* V. iv. 1. 4
Decii. Here Fabii and *Decii* doo dwell, *Gn.* 599
Deck. To *deck* her Dame, and enrich her heyre, *S.C.* S. 115
The gaudie girlonds *deck* her grave, *S.C.* N. 108
wonts to *decke* the Gods immortall crew *Hub.* 1268
to *decke* thy sable Herse. *Ti.* 679
Vouchsafe to *deck* the same with Cyparesse; *D.* 529
As fittest flowres to *deck* his mournfull hearse. *As.* Interl. 228
And native beauty *deck* with hevenlie grace: *Ded. Son.* xv. 12
ye grace And *deck* the world, *Ded. Son.* xvi. 5
to . . . *deck* with dainty flowres their brydall bed, I. x. 42. 3
all the people *decke* with girlands greene, II. iii. 28. 3
decke the world with their rich pompous showes; II. vi. 15. 7
Fitt to . . . *deck* the drery toombe. II. vii. 51. 9
To *decke* his herce, and trap his tomb-blacke steed.' II. viii. 16. 7
To *decke* my song withall, II. x. 3. 8
like a pompous bride Did *decke* her, II. xii. 50. 8
earst was sought to *deck* both bed and bowre II. xii. 75. 4
with fresh colours *decke* the wanton Pryme, III. vi. 42. 4
decke his pleasant streame. IV. xi. 29. 9
Plenty of pearles to *decke* his dames withall; IV. xi. 39. 6
with black dishonor And foule defame doe *decke* thy bloudy baner? VI. vi. 25. 5
decke the body or adorne the mynde, VI. x. 23. 2
as a girlond seemes to *deck* the locks VII. vi. 41. 3
Did *deck* himselfe in freshest faire attire; VII. vii. 11. 2
with divers-colord flowre To *decke* hir selfe, *Am.* iv. 12
decke her head with glorious bayes, *Am.* xxix. 13
fit to *decke* their lovers bowres. *Am.* lxiv. 4
To *deck* the bridale bowers. *Epith.* 47
To helpe to *decke* her, and to help to sing, *Epith.* 72
all the pillours *deck* with girlands trim, *Epith.* 207
decke with floures thy altars well beseene. *H.L.* 293
To *decke* thy beautie with their dainties store, *H.B.* 262
daintie gemmes Fit to *decke* maydens bowres, *Proth.* 15
vermeil Roses, To *decke* their Bridegromes posies *Proth.* 34
Which *decke* the Bauldricke of the Heavens bright; *Proth.* 173
Decked. Elisa, *decked* as thou art In royall aray; *S.C.* Ap. 145
Well *decked* in a frocke of gray; *S.C.* Au. 65
The Mule all *deckt* in goodly rich aray, *Hub.* 582
Delight, and Laughter, *deckt* in seemly sort. *T.M.* 198
deckt with daintie flowres, *Ti.* 634
deckt . . . With manie garlands *Ti.* 652
deckt himselfe with fethers youthly gay, I. xi. 34. 5
Her nathelesse Th' enchaunter . . . *deckt* with due habiliments. II. i. 22. 9
shewd them naked, *deckt* with many ornaments. II. v. 32. 9
every pillour *decked* was . . . With crownes, II. vii. 43. 7
two sharpe winged sheares, *Decked* with diverse plumes, II. viii. 5. 8
why should a dead dog be *deckt* in armour bright?' II. viii. 15. 9
deckt with flowers and herbars daintily: II. ix. 46. 2
deckt with blossoms dyde in white and red, II. xii. 12. 5
With diverse flowres he daintily was *deckt,* II. xii. 49. 1
Mote Princes place be seeme so *deckt* to bee. III. i. 33. 4
deckt the azure field with her fayre pouldred skin. III. ii. 25. 9
the faire flowres that *decked* him afore: III. iv. 17. 8
with thousand starres was *decked* fayre: III. iv. 52. 3
With which high God his workmanship hath *deckt;* III. vi. 12. 5
Him shaped thus she *deckt* in garments gay, III. viii. 9. 1
Decked with many a costly ornament, III. viii. 12. 2
her bright browes were *deckt* with borrowed haire; III. xii. 14. 7
The charet *decked* was in wondrous wize IV. iii. 38. 6
when she did find Her selfe so *deckt,* IV. viii. 7. 6
All *deckt* with crownes, and chaynes, and girlands gay, IV. x. 37. 6
deckt with smyles that all sad humors chaced, IV. x. 50. 8
deckt with pearles which th' Indian seas for her prepaire. IV. xi. 11. 9
All *decked* in a robe of watchet hew, IV. xi. 27. 2
the Rother, *decked* all with woods IV. xi. 33. 1
All goodly damzels, *deckt* with long greene haire, IV. xi. 48. 2
Fresh Alimeda *deckt* with girlond greene; IV. xi. 51. 1
deckt with Mitre on her hed V. vii. 13. 2
being all with Yvy overspred *Deckt* all the roofe, VI. v. 35. 3
Deckt with greene boughes and flowers gay beseene: VI. v. 38. 5
deckt with wondrous giftes of natures grace, VI. vii. 28. 5
deckt it all with flowres which they nigh hand obtayned. VI. viii. 44. 9
All fairely *deckt* with heavens goodly storie; VII. vi. 8. 4
Deckt all with dainties of her seasons pryde, VII. vii. 34. 2
Deckt all with flowres, and wings of gold VII. vii. 46. 9
her bowre with her late presence *deckt;* *Am.* lxxviii. 6
With which my love should duly have been *dect,* *Epith.* 428
with like beauties parts be inly *deckt;* *H.B.* 193
And all with admirable beautie *deckt.* *H.H.B.* 35
Decking. hundred pillers . . . *decking* the front, *Bel.*[1] ii. 3
Sweet Marjoram, and Daysies *decking* prime: *Mui.* 192
with greene boughes *decking* a gloomy glade, I. vii. 4. 4
Decking her cheeke with a vermilion rose; V. v. 30. 4
Decks. *Decks* all the forrest with embellishment; *Gn.* 214
That *decks* and armes your shield with faire defence: II. i. 28. 8
how brave she *decks* her bounteous boure, II. vi. 16. 5
decks the girlonds of her Paramoures, III. vi. 30. 3
deckes his branch with blossomes over all, IV. x. 22. 4
Declare. 'That shall I eke (quoth he) to you *declare:* *Col.* 163
they, . . . Making obeysaunce, did the cause *declare,* I. iv. 13. 7
Then gan she to *declare* the whole discourse V. vii. 20. 1
came to Caelia to *declare* her smart; I. x. 23. 1
'Deare Lady! how shall I *declare* thy cace, II. i. 9. 6
'Dreadlesse,' (said he) 'that shall I soone *declare.* II. v. 17. 1
all her goodly deedes doe well *declare.* III. iv. 3. 5
It were a goodly storie to *declare* III. vi. 5. 1
to *declare* the mournfull Tragedyes III. xi. 45. 6
dreadfull tidings which thou doest *declare,'* IV. vii. 14. 1
doe it *declare* unto me trew.' V. i. 16. 2
Declare at once: and hath he lost or wun?' V. vi. 9. 3
Then gan she to *declare* the whole discourse V. vii. 20. 1
them to their posterities doe still *declare.* V. x. 5. 9
Declare it boldly, Dame, and doe not stand in dout.' V. xi. 18. 9
'That shall I, sooth,' . . . to you *declare.* VI. ii. 9. 1
for what cause, *declare;* so mote ye not repent.' VI. iv. 27. 9
plainely gan to him *declare* the case VI. vii. 21. 2
The which, as commeth now by course, I will *declare.* VI. x. 4. 9
to *declare* What did betide to the faire Pastorell VI. xii. 14. 2
who alive can perfectly *declare* *H.L.* 50
His goodnesse, which his beautie doth *declare;* *H.H.B.* 132
Declared. day should faile me ere I had them all *declard.* I. xii. 31. 9
His wondrous worth *declared* in all mens view, IV. iv. 37. 5
All which was thus to him *declared* by that Squire. IV. viii. 46. 9
all those daungers unto them *declar'd:* IV. ix. 41. 7
My brother here *declared* hath to you: V. iv. 15. 3
to his Lord *Declar'd* the message VI. iii. 42. 2
as shall *declared* be elsewhere. VI. v. 41. 9
Declares. Through the greene gras his long bright burnisht back *declares.* III. xi. 28. 9
Decline. did at last *decline* To lowest wretchednes: *Mui.* 14
Phoebus gan *decline* in haste His weary wagon II. ix. 10. 1
Decline her head, and touch her crouper with her crown. III. ix. 15. 9
into her faire bosome made his grapes *decline.* III. xi. 43. 9
Liftes up his head that did before *decline,* IV. xii. 34. 8
Declined. though somewhat they *declind;* II. ix. 55. 4
He is *declyned* from that marke of theirs Nigh thirtie minutes V. Pr. 7. 7
Declines. meeting Plim, to Plimmouth thence *declines:* IV. xi. 31. 4
Declining. brought forth in her last *declining* season, *Van.* i. 7
From whence *declining* daily by degrees, *Epith.* 267
Decorum. Without regard, or due *Decorum* kept; *T.M.* 214
Decree. So did the Gods by heavenly doome *decree,* *Ro.* vi. 11
Seeking to kisse her, brok'st the Gods *decree,* *Gn.* 471
whether through the Gods *decree,* *Gn.* 569
I will pay Penance to her, according their *decree,* *D.* 370
Amongst them all this end he did *decree;* IV. ii. 38. 5
what the Fates do once *decree,* Not all the gods can chaunge, IV. ii. 51. 8
Unweeting of the Fates divine *decree* IV. iii. 21. 4
Till fortune did perforce it so *decree:* IV. viii. 58. 8
if that life ye unto me *decree,* IV. xii. 10. 1
to *decree* And judge, whether with truth or falshood V. ii. 47. 8
by heavens high *decree,* V. viii. 44. 6
by eternall doome of Fates *decree,* VII. vi. 33. 6
And slew the Just by most unjust *decree.* *H.H.L.* 154
Decreed. his realme he equally *decreed* To have divided. II. x. 27. 5
th' heavens have *decreed* to displace The Britons III. iii. 41. 7
Yet mote he not withstand what was *decreede,* IV. v. 9. 4
thought t' appeale from that which was *decreed* IV. v. 22. 7
to that avenge by you *decreed* IV. vi. 8. 6
Unto the Castle where they had *decreed:* VI. iii. 2. 7
Fayre Mirabellaes punishment For Loves disdaine *decreed.* VI. vii. Arg.
(according as they had *decreed*) VII. vi. 52. 1
Decreeing. Bereft of both by Fates unjust *decreeing.* *Ti.* 35
Decrepit. all *decrepit* in his feeble corse, II. ix. 55. 6
Decretals. Of lawes, of judgementes, and of *decretals,* II. ix. 53. 7
Decrewed. renewed His strength still more, but she still more *decrewed.* IV. vi. 18. 5
Dect. *See* **Decked.**
Dedicate. To her my thoughts I daily *dedicate,* *Col.* 472
Dedicated. *dedicated* is t' Olympick Jove, II. v. 31. 3
Deducted. in his *deducted* spright Some sparks remaining *H.L.* 106
Dee. the river *Dee* . . . His tombling billowes rolls with gentle rore; I. ix. 4. 7
passing *Dee,* with hardy enterprise III. iii. 35. 4
Dee, which Britons long ygone Did call divine, IV. xi. 39. 3
Deed. *See* **Indeed.**
Beare witnesse all of thys so wicked *deede:* *S.C.* Jun. 108
him to heare, or matter of his *deede.* *S.C.* Au. 148
Where the reward of my so piteous *deed?* *Gn.* 357
I would be readie, both in *deed* and word, *Hub.* 252
he that dreadfull *deed* Forbore, *Hub.* 1238
who would ever care to doo brave *deed,* *T.M.* 451
everie day, in which she did a *deed,* *Col.* 594
with evil *deed* or leasing vaine Blaspheme *Col.* 821
Right faithfull true he was in *deede* and word, I. i. 2. 7
she . . . nor in word nor *deede* ill meriting, I. iii. 2. 7
'Is not his *deed,* what ever thing is donne I. ix. 42. 1
never knight, that dared warlike *deed,* I. ix. 45. 3
In word and *deede* that shewd great modestee, I. x. 7. 4
without desert of gentle *deed* And noble worth, II. iii. 10. 6
wreake on them their hainous hatefull *deed.'* II. iii. 14. 9
In brave poursuitt of honorable *deed,* II. iv. 1. 1
when the cause of that outrageous *deede* Demaunded, II. iv. 29. 6
Drad for his derring doe and bloody *deed;* II. iv. 42. 3

Deed—*Continued.*
That am the authour of this hainous *deed,* II. vi. 33. 8
most hevenly faire in *deed* and vew II. vii. 45. 7
'For knighthoods love doe not so fowle a *deed,* II. viii. 16. 2
After so wicked *deede* why liv'st thou lenger day?' II. viii. 46. 9
seemes some cursed witches *deed,* III. iii. 18. 8
win him worship through his warlike *deed,* III. iv. 4. 8
ment To her no evill thought nor evill *deed;* III. iv. 50. 3
Thy life she saved by her gratious *deed;* III. v. 45. 3
most sweet hymnes of this thy famous *deed* III. viii. 42. 8
loosenesse of her love and loathly *deed,* III. x. 50. 4
What booteth then the good and righteous *deed,* III. xi. 9. 8
Yield you in lieu of this your gracious *deed?* III. xii. 39. 4
through her gentle *deed* Was . . . restor'd, IV. i. 15. 1
inly thought of that despightfull *deede* IV. v. 9. 5
he was full bent to some mischievous *deede* IV. vi. 2. 9
Ne more sincere in word and *deed* profest; IV. xi. 18. 7
To be avenged for so fowle a *deede,* V. vi. 31. 2
yeeld great thankes for their so goodly *deed,* V. xi. 48. 3
forced me to so infamous *deed,* V. xi. 57. 4
Artegall, seeing his cruell *deed,* V. xi. 65. 6
Nor land nor fee for hyre of his good *deede,* VI. i. 47. 2
Whose every *deed* . . . Was like enchantment, VI. ii. 3. 2
that courteous *deed* Done to that wounded Knight VI. iii. 2. 4
They should accomplish both a knightly *deed,* VI. vii. 4. 8
hath doen to thee this wrongfull *deed,* VI. vii. 5. 8
The wretch that hyr'd you to this wicked *deed.'* VI. vii. 13. 5
was the tyme ordayned For such a dismall *deed,* VI. viii. 44. 7
of her selfe in very *deede* so deemed; VI. ix. 14. 3
Hath wrought this wicked *deed:* VI. xi. 29. 9
how we then defeated all their *deed,* VII. vi. 20. 5
Ensampled it by his most righteous *deede,* *H.H.L.* 213

Deeds. scorned bene *dedes* of fond foolerie. *S.C.* May 62
doubting nought their *deeds,* *Hub.* 328
practising the proofe of warlike *deedes,* *Hub.* 740
What furie, or what feend with felon *deeds* *T.M.* 45
vertuous *deeds* . . . they care not to atchive. *T.M.* 95
Have both desire of worthie *deeds* forlorne, *T.M.* 437
evill men, now dead, his *deeds* upbraid: *Ti.* 214
Whose great good *deeds,* in countrey and in towne, *Ti.* 263
'For *deeds* doe die, how ever noblie donne, *Ti.* 400
with vertuous *deeds* assay To mount to heaven, *Ti.* 425
In spight of envie that his *deeds* would spot: *Ti.* 439
with brave *deeds* to her sole service vowed, *As.* 69
both in *deeds* and words he nourtred was, *As.* 71
Their bounteous *deeds* and noble favours shrynd, *Col.* 582
Her *deeds* were like great clusters of ripe grapes, *Col.* 600
with lewd speeches, and licentious *deeds,* *Col.* 787
brave Lord, whose goodly personage And noble *deeds,* *Ded. Son.* vi. 2
for your . . . noble *deeds,* have your deserved place *Ded. Son.* xi. 2
That their brave *deeds* she might immortalize *Ded. Son.* xiv. 3
to . . . sing of Knights and Ladies gentle *deeds;* I. Pr. 1. 5
He hated all good workes and vertuous *deeds,* I. iv. 32. 1
when her curteous *deeds* he did compare, I. vi. 31. 3
knowne . . . To have done much more admirable *deedes.* I. vii. 36. 3
Inquireth of our states, and of our knightly *deedes.* I. ix. 28. 9
all the day in doing good and godly *deedes.* I. x. 3. 9
deeds of armes must I at last be faine . . . to leave, I. x. 62. 5
not so good of *deedes* as great of name, II. ii. 17. 3
Brave be her warres, and honorable *deeds,* II. ii. 31. 5
My Soveraine, Whose glory is in gracious *deeds,* II. ii. 43. 6
fowle *deedes,* too hideous to bee told, II. ii. 44. 7
Through *deeds* of armes and prowesse martiall. II. iii. 37. 8
his own vertues and praise-worthie *deedes.* II. vii. 2. 5
noble *deeds* above the Northern starre II. x. 4. 7
salved both their infamies With noble *deedes,* II. x. 21. 7
dim'd his valorous And mightie *deedes,* II. x. 43. 6
maintaynd With mightie *deedes* their sondry governments; II. x. 74. 4
From seeking praise and *deeds* of armes abrode, III. i. 1. 8
love does alwaies bring forth bounteous *deeds,* III. i. 49. 8
Does all their *deedes* deface, and dims their glories all. III. ii. 1. 9
'All my delight on *deedes* of armes is sett, III. ii. 7. 1
Whence spring all noble *deedes* and never dying fame: III. iii. 1. 9
all her goodly *deeds* doe well declare. III. iv. 3. 5
well did brooke Her noble *deeds,* III. iv. 44. 9
the dew reward Of his bad *deedes,* III. v. 14. 7
His cruell *deedes* and wicked wyles did spot: III. vi. 13. 5
reproches rife Of his mischievous *deedes,* III. vi. 14. 7
her divelish *deedes* And hellish arts III. vii. 6. 7
in martiall law And *deedes* of armes III. vii. 52. 4
deedes of armes had ever in despaire, III. viii. 11. 7
they thy vertuous *deedes* may imitate, III. viii. 43. 6
deeds of armes which unto them became, III. ix. 32. 4
my dayes to spend In seewing *deeds* of armes, III. ix. 37. 9
To prove some *deeds* of armes upon an equall pere?' III. x. 24. 9
Her *deeds* were forged, III. xii. 14. 8
Scudamour and Blandamour: Their fight and warlike *deedes.* IV. i. Arg.
Was then assembled *deeds* of armes to see: IV. i. 9. 4
The seedes of evill wordes and factious *deedes;* IV. i. 25. 5
She modest was in all her *deedes* and words, IV. ii. 35. 8
To view and deeme the *deedes* of armes that day: IV. iii. 4. 4
For evill *deedes* may better then bad words be bore. IV. iv. 4. 9
gan to treate of *deeds* of armes abrode, IV. iv. 5. 4
their *deedes* of armes to shew. IV. iv. 37. 2
Full many *deedes* that day were shewed plaine: IV. iv. 37. 3
she wondrous *deeds* of arms atchieved, IV. iv. 46. 6
Brave thoughts and noble *deedes* did evermore aspire. IV. x. 26. 9
did in noble *deedes* of armes excell, IV. xi. 37. 4
Their greatest glory for their rightfull *deedes,* V. ii. 1. 6
Expert in battell and in *deedes* of armes; V. ii. 5. 4

Deeds—*Continued.*
Her name is Munera, agreeing with her *deedes.* V. ii. 9. 9
To *deedes* of armes and proofe of chevalrie V. iii. 4. 3
Full many *deeds* of armes that day were donne, V. iii. 6. 5
There Marinell great *deeds* of armes did shew, V. iii. 8. 4
Through hard adventures *deedes* of armes to try, V. iv. 29. 2
all obedience both to words and *deeds* They quite forgot, V. viii. 41. 3
deedes ought not be scand By th' authors manhood, V. xi. 17. 3
To loose the badge that should his *deedes* display.' V. xi. 52. 5
The gentle mind by gentle *deeds* is knowne: VI. iii. 1. 2
to make avoure Of the lewd words and *deedes* VI. iii. 48. 6
(As their victorious *deedes* have often showen, VI. iv. 36. 4
And did right noble *deedes;* the which els where are showne. VI. iv. 38. 9
In doing gentle *deedes* with franke delight, VI. vii. 1. 2
By such discourteous *deeds* discovering his base kind. VI. vii. 1. 9
the gentle knight himselfe abeare . . . in all his *deeds,* VI. ix. 45. 2
To sing the glory of their famous *deedes.* *Am.* xxix. 8
great *deeds* and valarous emprize. *Am.* lxix. 4
Heroes, which the world did daunt With their great *deedes,* *Com. Son.* iii. 4

Deele. *See* **Deal.**

Deem. You *deemen* the Spring is come attonce; *S.C.* F. 38
I *deeme* thy braine emperished bee *S.C.* F. 53
Of Heaven to *demen* so; *S.C.* Jul. 94
Fayth of my soule, I *deeme* ech have gayned: *S.C.* Au. 131
We *deeme* of Death as doome of ill desert; *S.C.* N. 184
to be learned it a base thing *deeme:* *T.M.* 87
Did surely *deeme* the victorie his due: *Mui.* 319
Deem the occasion of his death to bee; *D.* 88
her wisdome, none Can *deeme,* but who *Col.* 347
thy true love and loyaltie I *deeme.* *Col.* 575
I *deeme* it best *Col.* 581
him the greatest of the Gods we *deeme,* *Col.* 799
Thus ought all lovers of their lord to *deeme,* *Col.* 887
all so deare as life is to my hart, I *deeme* your love, I. i. 54. 3
In doubt to *deeme* her borne of earthly brood: I. vi. 16. 5
thereby dead that balefull Beast did *deeme,* I. xii. 2. 7
did *deeme* Such entertainment base, II. ii. 35. 1
my falser friend did no less joyous *deeme.* II. iv. 21. 9
'Varlet, this place most dew to me I *deeme,* II. iv. 40. 1
Ne *deeme* thy force by fortunes doome unjust, II. v. 12. 8
deeme them roote of all disquietnesse; II. vii. 12. 2
Ne canst of prowesse ne of knighthood *deeme,* II. viii. 14. 2
Bad therefore I him *deeme* II. viii. 14. 9
deeme him bourne with ill-disposed skyes, II. ix. 52. 8
surely *deeme* it to bee yvie trew: II. xii. 61. 5
Well did Antiquity a God thee *deeme,* III. iii. 2. 1
I *deeme* that counsel aye most fit, III. iii. 52. 3
Farre better I it *deeme* to die with speed III. iv. 38. 3
so disloyally *Deeme* of her high desert, III. v. 45. 7
doubted her to *deeme* an earthly wight, III. vii. 11. 6
'Extremely mad the man I surely *deeme,* III. ix. 6. 7
golden pray, . . . loath as doung, ne *deeme* my dew reward: III. x. 31. 6
The Seneschall was cal'd to *deeme* the right: IV. i. 12. 1
In doubt to whom she victorie should *deeme,* IV. ii. 17. 5
To view and *deeme* the deedes of armes that day: IV. iii. 4. 4
To *deeme* this doutfull case, for which they all contended. IV. v. 6. 9
when your pleasure is to *deeme* aright, IV. viii. 17. 4
Hard is the doubt, and difficult to *deeme,* IV. ix. 1. 1
if one did rightly *deeme;* IV. x. 39. 8
if ye *deeme* me death IV. xii. 9. 6
I him condemne, and *deeme* his paine, IV. xii. 11. 3
deeme unworthy or of love or life, IV. xii. 16. 6
thine I *deeme* The living Lady, V. i. 28. 2
'Of things unseene how canst thou *deeme* aright,' V. ii. 39. 1
vaine it is to *deeme* of things aright, V. iv. 1. 6
'Your right is good,' (sayd he) 'and so I *deeme,* V. iv. 17. 8
'Your right is good,' (sayd he) 'and so I *deeme,* V. iv. 18. 8
Some men, I wote, will *deeme* in Artegall Great weaknesse, V. vi. 1. 1
deeme it doen of will, that through inforcement came. V. xi. 52. 9
Him they did *deeme,* . . . A courteous Knight VI. iii. 13. 1
My due reward, the which right well I *deeme* I yearned have, VI. vii. 15. 8
worthy *deeme* partakers of our blisse to bee. VII. vi. 33. 9
thee, O Jove! no equall Judge I *deeme* VII. vi. 35. 1
heaven and earth I both alike do *deeme,* VII. vii. 15. 6
Whereon he rode not easie was to *deeme;* VII. vii. 40. 7
The world that cannot *deeme* of worthy things *Am.* lxxxiv. 1
But not to *deeme* of her desert aspyre. *Am.* lxxxiv. 8
see The ods twixt both, of both them *deem* aright, *Com. Son.* ii. 10
things hard gotten men more dearely *deeme.* *H.L.* 168
did *deeme* Them heavenly borne, *Proth.* 61

Deemed. *See* **Dempt, Well-deemed.**
nought he *deemed* deare for the jewell: *S.C.* May 277
shee *deemed* nothing too deere for thee. *S.C.* N. 117
Tho *deemed* I my spring would ever laste. *S.C.* D. 30
His wisdome he above their learning *deemed.* *Hub.* 1192
Her, and but her, of love he worthie *deemed;* *As.* 65
Albe of love I alwayes humbly *deemed,* *Col.* 828
Saint George himselfe ye would have *deemed* him to be. I. ii. 11. 9
End of the doubtfull battaile *deemed* tho The lookers on; I. v. 11. 7
nought too dear I *deemd,* II. i. 53. 9
Her many *deemd* to have beene of the Fayes, II. x. 42. 7
deemd in mynd To be no earthly wight, II. x. 71. 5
shee inly *deemd* Her love too light, III. i. 55. 6
deemd the beast had bene depriv'd Of life, III. v. 37. 4
above all Dames is *deemd,* And above many knightes III. vii. 52. 4
Proud man himselfe then Braggadochio *deem'd,* III. viii. 13. 6
Made her not yeeld so much as due she *deemed.* IV. i. 8. 7
Nathlesse proud man himselfe the other *deemed,* IV. ii. 8. 1
With diverse fortune doubtfull to be *deemed:* IV. iii. 28. 2
For last is *deemed* best. IV. v. 8. 8

Deemed—*Continued.*
That which of them was best mote not be *deemed*. . . . IV. ix. 20. 5
So was she guiltie *deemed* of them all. . . . V. ix. 49. 6
eke that Idoll *deem'd* so costly dere, . . . V. xi. 33. 7
She *deem'd* him sure to have bene dead on ground; . . . VI. i. 34. 7
he *deem'd* him borne of noble race: . . . VI. ii. 5. 5
her worthy *deemed* To be a Princes Paragone esteemed, . . . VI. ix. 11. 4
of her selfe in very deede so *deemed;* . . . VI. ix. 14. 3
Her selfe of all that rule she *deemed* most condigne. . . . VII. vi. 11. 9
Deemest. *deem'st* of things divine As of humane, . . . IV. ii. 51. 5
Deemeth. not by that which is, the world now *deemeth,* . . . *Hub.* 649
Deeming. Him *deeming* dead, as then he seemd in sight, . . . II. v. 25. 7
thereby *deeming* sure the thing as donne, . . . III. viii. 3. 3
Deeming them doughtie, as they did appeare, . . . IV. ii. 31. 2
In all the skill of *deeming* wrong and right, . . . V. i. 8. 2
Deems. her he *deemes* already but a damned ghoste.' . . . V. xi. 42. 9
Deene. *See* Din.
Deep. Out of *deepe* vaute threw forth a thousand rayes . . . *Bel.*[1] ii. 7
Shaking the hill even from the bottome *deepe,* . . . *Bel.*[1] ii. 13
Under *deep* ruines, with huge walls oppress, . . . *Ro.* i. 2
let those *deep* Abysses open rive, . . . *Ro.* i. 7
her head, earth'd in her foundations *deep,* . . . *Ro.* viii. 13
Nor the *deep* wounds of victours raging blade, . . . *Ro.* xiii. 2
to enter into meditation *deepe* . . . *Van.* i. 3
sweepe The fomie waves out of the dreadfull *deep,* . . . *Van.* v. 5
feeles the *deepe* delight that is in death, . . . *Frag.*
Pampred in pleasures *deepe:* . . . *S.C.* Jul. 198
in my face *deepe* furrowes eld hath pight: . . . *S.C.* D. 134
His little needle there infixing *deep,* . . . *Gn.* 287
Okes, *deep* grounded in the earthly molde, . . . *Gn.* 453
deep Charybdis gulphing in and out: . . . *Gn.* 542
Of such *deep* learning little had he neede, . . . *Hub.* 385
Much good *deep* learning one thereout may reed; . . . *Hub.* 484
the Foxe, *deep* groning in his sprite, . . . *Hub.* 588
Therefore I mourne with *deep* harts sorrowing, . . . *T.M.* 107
lie drowned in *deep* wretchednes, . . . *T.M.* 149
dredd darknes of the *deepe* Abysme, . . . *T.M.* 189
with *deepe* Oracles their verses fill: . . . *T.M.* 562
With fearfull fiends, that in *deep* darknes dwell. . . . *Ti.* 126
to thee sings with *deep* harts sorrowing, . . . *Ti.* 318
all astonished with *deepe* dismay, . . . *Ti.* 473
downe hee fell into the *deepe* Abisse, . . . *Ti.* 545
a wilde wildernes of waters *deepe:* . . . *Mui.* 287
let the dreadfull Queene Of Darkenes *deepe* come . . . *D.* 20
He sighed soft, and inly *deepe* did grone, . . . *D.* 48
'One, whome like wofulnesse, impressed *deepe* . . . *D.* 64
harts *deep* sorrow hates both life and light. . . . *D.* 91
drown'd in carelesse quiet *deepe;* . . . *D.* 136
with *deepe* dismay Was much appald, . . . *D.* 186
yet are *deepe* engraven in my brest, . . . *D.* 296
Or some *deepe* cave, or solitarie shade; . . . *D.* 487
So deadly was the dint and *deep* the wound, . . . *As.* 121
he came far from the main-sea *deepe,* . . . *Col.* 67
beasts with *deep* mouthes gaping direfull . . . *Col.* 202
seeme, by this thy *deep* insight, . . . *Col.* 831
deep waters which her drownd alway: . . . *Col.* 858
Wherein old dints of *deepe* woundes did remaine, . . . I. i. 1. 3
he cald out of *deepe* darknes dredd . . . I. i. 38. 1
through the world of waters wide and *deepe,* . . . I. i. 39. 2
Morpheus . . . drowned *deepe* In drowsie fit . . . I. i. 40. 8
al that in the wide *deepe* wandring arre; . . . I. ii. 1. 5
And wast his inward gall with *deepe* despight, . . . I. ii. 6. 4
groning *deep;* . . . I. ii. 33. 1
it is empassioned so *deepe,* . . . I. iii. 2. 1
greeved ghost for vengeance *deep* do grone: . . . I. iv. 49. 7
hewen helmets (*helmets hewen) *deepe* shew marks of eithers might. . . . I. v. 7. 9
yawning gulfe of *deepe* Avernus hole. . . . I. v. 31. 3
Deepe, darke, uneasy, dolefull, comfortlesse. . . . I. v. 36. 6
in a dungeon *deepe* huge nombers lay . . . I. v. 45. 8
her coulours, died *deepe* in graine, . . . I. vii. 1. 4
he . . . in a Dongeon *deepe* him threw without remorse. . . . I. vii. 15. 9
hart, so plungd in sea of sorrowes *deep,* . . . I. vii. 39. 2
So *deepe* did settle in her gracious thought, . . . I. vii. 42. 2
three yardes *deepe* a furrow up did throw. . . . I. viii. 8. 6
she it is, that did my Lord . . . *deepe* in dongeon lay, . . . I. viii. 28. 7
his foot could find no flore, But all a *deepe* descent, . . . I. viii. 39. 8
sad dull eies, *deepe* sunck in hollow pits, . . . I. viii. 41. 1
Deepe written in my heart with yron pen, . . . I. viii. 44. 8
through fatal *deepe* foresight, . . . I. ix. 7. 1
Witnes the dungeon *deepe,* wherein . . . I. ix. 45. 5
his faint steedes watred in Ocean *deepe,* . . . I. xi. 31. 3
as in a dreame of *deepe* delight, . . . I. xi. 50. 4
The weapon . . . *deepe* emperst his darksom hollow maw, . . . I. xi. 53. 8
they him layd full low in dungeon *deepe,* . . . I. xii. 36. 1
after gave a grone so *deepe* and low . . . II. i. 38. 3
into a *deepe* sanguine dide the grassy grownd. . . . II. i. 39. 9
his mighty ghost gan *deepe* to grone, . . . II. i. 42. 5
ruth emperced *deepe* In that knightes hart, . . . II. ii. 1. 8
suncke so *deepe* into their boyling brests, . . . II. ii. 32. 2
in Ocean *deep* . . . His flaming head did hasten for to steep, . II. ii. 46. 1
'let be thy *deepe* advise: . . . II. iii. 16. 1
inly bate *Deepe* in his flesh, . . . II. v. 7. 9
His wandring thought in *deepe* desire does steepe, . . . II. v. 34. 2
Thus in still waves of *deepe* delight to wade, . . . II. v. 35. 2
him to ferry over that *deepe* ford. . . . II. vi. 4. 4
despiteously entayld *Deepe* in their flesh, . . . II. vi. 29. 8
deepe him selfe beducked in the same, . . . II. vi. 42. 3
Where drenched *deepe* he fownd . . . The carefull servaunt . II. vi. 47. 8
deep descended through the hollow grownd, . . . II. vii. 20. 8

Deep—*Continued.*
That is the river of Cocytus *deepe,* . . . II. vii. 56. 8
drenched lay full *deepe* under the Garden side. . . . II. vii. 57. 9
Deepe was he drenched to the upmost chin, . . . II. vii. 58. 1
groning *deepe,* thus answerd him againe; . . . II. vii. 59. 3
wretch, whose carcas *deepe* was drent . . . II. vii. 61. 2
word so *deepe* did in their harts impresse, . . . II. viii. 18. 7
all his sences drowned in *deep* sencelesse wave: . . . II. viii. 24. 9
Cursing his Gods, and him selfe damning *deepe:* . . . II. viii. 37. 2
did *deepe* invade Into his head, . . . II. viii. 45. 4
deepe engorgeth all this worldes pray; . . . II. xii. 3. 5
sucking the seas into his entralles *deepe,* . . . II. xii. 6. 2
nought that falles into this direfull *deepe* . . . II. xii. 6. 7
Some *deepe* empurpled as the Hyacine, . . . II. xii. 54. 7
swimming *deepe* in sensuall desyres; . . . III. i. 39. 8
Into the Ocean *deepe* to drive their weary drove. . . . III. i. 57. 9
the world in silence *deepe* Yshrowded was, . . . III. i. 59. 1
yet was the wound not *deepe,* . . . III. i. 65. 6
By his *deepe* science and hell-dreaded might, . . . III. ii. 18. 7
sad sighes and sorrowes *deepe* Kept watch . . . III. ii. 28. 6
Through *deepe* impression of thy secret might, . . . III. iii. 2. 7
In a *deepe* delve, farre from the vew of day, . . . III. iii. 7. 7
From under that *deepe* Rock most horribly rebowndes. . . . III. iii. 9. 9
Deepe busied bout worke of wondrous end, . . . III. iii. 14. 7
enrooted *deepe* must be that Tree, . . . III. iii. 22. 2
The Damzell was full *deepe* empassioned . . . III. iii. 43. 1
so *deepe* into the mynd Of the yong Damzell sunke, . . . III. iii. 57. 1
the *deepe* wound more *deep* engord her hart, . . . III. iv. 6. 4
Thereat she sighed *deepe,* . . . III. iv. 7. 9
sighing softly sore, and inly *deepe,* . . . III. iv. 11. 1
Ythrild with *deepe* disdaine of his proud threat, . . . III. iv. 15. 1
Had in his greedy gulfe devoured *deepe,* . . . III. iv. 22. 6
so *deepe* wound through these deare members drive. . . . III. iv. 37. 4
Deepe in the bottome of the sea . . . III. iv. 43. 1
So *deepe* the deadly feare of that foule swaine . . . III. iv. 49. 2
oft from Stygian *deepe* Calles thee his goddesse, . . . III. iv. 56. 7
labour'd long in that *deepe* ford . . . III. v. 19. 9
after having searcht the intuse *deepe,* . . . III. v. 33. 8
groning inly *deepe,* . . . III. v. 34. 2
In hatefull darknes and in *deepe* horrore, . . . III. vi. 36. 7
Deepe indignation and compassion frayle . . . III. viii. 31. 4
Downe in a Dongeon *deepe* he let her fall, . . . III. viii. 41. 8
not empierst with *deepe* compassiowne, . . . III. ix. 39. 7
Into huge waves of griefe . . . Full *deepe* emplonged was, . III. x. 17. 5
awfull terror *deepe* into him strooke, . . . III. x. 24. 4
Hath in a dungeon *deepe* her close embard, . . . III. xi. 16. 8
the frayle soule in *deepe* delight nigh drownd: . . . III. xii. 6. 5
Entrenched *deep* with knyfe accursed keene, . . . III. xii. 20. 6
Albe the wound were nothing *deepe* imprest, . . . III. xii. 33. 7
Th' Enchaunter selfe, . . . *deepe* engrieved was. . . . III. xii. 43. 9
Downe in the bottome of the *deepe* Abysse, . . . IV. ii. 47. 6
Where byting *deepe* so deadly it imprest, . . . IV. vi. 13. 7
like a wide *deepe* poke, . . . IV. vii. 6. 2
deepe disdaine and great indignity, . . . IV. vii. 36. 3
bitter thoughts, which *deepe* therein infixed lay. . . . IV. viii. 1. 9
sighing inly *deepe,* her thus bespake: . . . IV. viii. 16. 3
Scudamour, then sighing *deepe,* . . . IV. ix. 38. 6
inly groning *deepe* and sighing oft, . . . IV. x. 48. 3
Her threw into a dongeon *deepe* and blind, . . . IV. xi. 2. 4
Deepe in the bottome of an huge great rocke . . . IV. xi. 3. 1
Deepe Indus, and Maeander intricate, . . . IV. xi. 21. 2
the Liffar *deep,* . . . IV. xi. 41. 6
Great heapes of salmons in his *deepe* bosome; . . . IV. xi. 43. 6
The thought whereof empierst his hart so *deepe.* . . . IV. xii. 19. 6
That is both swift and dangerous *deepe* withall; . . . V. ii. 8. 2
'This griefes *deepe* wound I would to thee disclose, . . . V. v. 30. 7
with *deepe* sighes and singults few. . . . V. vi. 13. 9
Restlesse, recomfortlesse, with heart *deepe* grieved, . . . V. vi. 24. 6
Her heart gan grudge for very *deepe* despight . . . V. vii. 37. 8
how *deepe* no man can tell, . . . V. ix. 6. 4
with hollow eyes *deepe* pent, . . . V. ix. 10. 5
Then up arose a person of *deepe* reach, . . . V. ix. 39. 1
byting *deepe* therein did sticke so fast . . . V. xii. 21. 8
to make them pierce and wound more *deepe,* . . . V. xii. 42. 6
vertues seat is *deepe* within the mynd, . . . VI. Pr. 5. 8
pearst Her stubborne hart with inward *deepe* effect, . . . VI. i. 45. 4
the deadly swound, in which full *deepe* . . . VI. iii. 10. 7
That Calidore it dearly *deepe* did move: . . . VI. iii. 15. 4
His *deepe* compassion of her dolefull stound, . . . VI. iv. 11. 4
There she long groveling and *deepe* groning lay, . . . VI. v. 5. 6
he sighed *deepe* for inward tyne: . . . VI. v. 24. 1
deepe emboweld in the earth entyre: . . . VI. viii. 15. 4
Full many a one for me *deepe* groand and sight, . . . VI. viii. 20. 7
His poysnous point *deepe* fixed in his hart . . . VI. x. 31. 2
to forray the land, or scoure the *deepe.* . . . VI. xi. 40. 5
them in dongeon *deepe* . . . cruelly he threw; . . . VI. xii. 5. 6
through the river him have drive And ducked *deepe;* . . . VII. vi. 50. 6
in his hand a broad *deepe* boawle he beares, . . . VII. vii. 41. 8
Deepe is the wound, that dints the parts . . . *Am.* vi. 11
her *deep* wit, that true harts thought can spel, . . . *Am.* xliii. 13
In *deep* discovery of the mynds disease; . . . *Am.* l. 6
diving *deepe* through amorous insight, . . . *Am.* lxxvi. 7
Deepe, in the closet of my parts entyre, . . . *Am.* lxxxiv. 9
in *deepe* darknesse kept, . . . *H.L.* 60
In that *deepe* horror of despeyred hell, . . . *H.H.L.* 130
loves *deepe* wound, that pierst the piteous hart . . . *H.H.L.* 156
Deep-conceived. gentle knight! whose *deep conceived* griefe . III. xi. 14. 1
Deep-devouring. his *deepe devouring* jawes Wyde gaped, . . . I. xi. 12. 7
Deep-digged. *deep digd* vawtes; . . . *Gn.* 444
Deep-dinted. they do impresse *Deepe dinted* furrowes . . . I. v. 6. 8

Deep-engraffed. my deare daughters *deepe engraffed* ill, . . . III. iii. 18. 3
Deep-engulfed. Like an huge Aetn' of *deepe engulfed* gryefe, . III. ii. 32. 6
Deeper. ay *deeper* and *deeper* sinck. . . . *S.C.* S. 133
Scorns th' one and th' other in his *deeper* skill. . . . *Ti.* 448
Yet if their *deeper* sence be inly wayd, . . . *Ded. Son.* ix. 9
deeper dint therein it would not make; . . . I. xi. 24. 6
her guilefull bayt She will embosome *deeper* in your mind, . II. xii. 29. 3
Deepest. all that in the *deepest* earth remaines, . . . *Hub.* 1230
that divelish yron Engin, wrought In *deepest* Hell, . . . I. vii. 13. 2
darknesse he in *deepest* dongeon drove, . . . I. vii. 23. 3
tempt the *deepest* flood To come . . . IV. x. 46. 5
I will thrust downe into the *deepest* maine, . . . V. ii. 38. 4
Whose image printing in his *deepest* wit, . . . *H.L.* 197
To *deepest* hell, and lake of damned fyre, . . . *H.H.L.* 89
Deep-groaning. his *deepe-groning* spright In bloodie streames foorth fled . . . *Mui.* 438
Deeply. Long having *deeply* gron'd these Visions sad, . . . *Bel.*^{2} xiv. 1
that Gnats death, which *deeply* was imprest, . . . *Gn.* 645
Deeply doo your sad words my wits awhape, . . . *Hub.* 72
deepelie muzing at her doubtfull speach, . . . *Ti.* 485
my soule it *deepely* doth empassion. . . . *D.* 35
full *deeply* hast divynd Of Love and beautie; . . . *Col.* 896
So *deepely* dinted in the driven clay, . . . I. viii. 8. 5
deepely did it thrill: . . . III. v. 20. 7
With deare compassion *deeply* did emmove, . . . IV. viii. 3. 7
her deare hart full *deepely* made to rew, . . . IV. viii. 64. 3
whilest her earthly parts . . . did *deeply* drowned lie, . . . V. vii. 12. 6
He *deepely* sigh'd, and groaned inwardly, . . . VI. iii. 11. 5
Deepness. Her length, her breadth, her *deepnes*, or her hight; *Ro.* xxvi. 4
Deep-rooted. bitter sence of his *deepe rooted* ill, . . . I. xi. 22. 8
Seeking to drive away *deepe-rooted* dreede . . . V. x. 22. 4
Deeps. tosse the *deepes*, and teare the firmament, . . . IV. ix. 23. 7
Deep-wounded. A virgin widow, whose *deepe wounded* mind . I. ii. 24. 8
his *deepe wounded* hart in two did rive; . . . II. vi. 45. 7
Deer. Like hartlesse *deare*, dismayd with thunders sound. . . *Col.* 9
forth they ran, like two amazed *deare*, . . . I. iii. 22. 7
'as sure as hound The stricken *Deare* doth chalenge . . . II. i. 12. 9
As a dismayed *Deare* in chace embost, . . . III. xii. 17. 8
a *Deare*, that greedily embayes In the cool soile, . . . III. xii. 44. *or.* 7
like mazed *deare* dismayfully they flew. . . . V. viii. 38. 9
Like as a Lion mongst an heard of *dere*, . . . VI. xi. 49. 1
fled more fast Then any *Deere*, . . . VII. vi. 52. 5
The gentle *deare* returnd the selfe-same way, . . . *Am.* lxvii. 7
*eke ye lightfoot mayds which keepe the *deere*, . . . *Epith.* 67
Deer's. Him in *Deares* skin to clad; . . . VII. vi. 50. 8
With a *Deeres*-skin they covered, . . . VII. vi. 52. 2
Deface. Why do vaine men mean things so much *deface*, . . *Van.* xi. 12
with sharp quips joy'd others to *deface*, . . . *Hub.* 707
doth all fairest things on earth *deface*, . . . *T.M.* 434
Ne with his feete their silken leaves *deface*, . . . *Mui.* 175
that proud people, . . . didst first *deface*: . . . *Ded. Son.* vi. 11
knight he now shall never more *deface*: . . . I. iii. 29. 5
Night . . . can the children of fayre light *deface*.' . . . I. v. 24. 5
grace, . . . that accurst hand-writing doth *deface*. . . . I. ix. 53. 8
That it should not *deface* all others lesser light? . . . II. iv. 25. 9
with his pride all others powre *deface*: . . . II. vii. 41. 8
First prayse of knighthood is fowle outrage to *deface*.' . . . II. viii. 25. 9
Prince Arthure them repelles, and fowle Maleger doth *deface*. . II. xi. Arg.
his contrary object most *deface*, . . . II. xi. 6. 4
to see Him his nobility so fowle *deface*: . . . II. xii. 79. 4
Their groves he feld; their gardins did *deface*; . . . II. xii. 83. 6
Does all their deedes *deface*, and dims their glories all. . . . III. ii. 1. 9
holy Church with faithlesse handes *deface*, . . . III. iii. 34. 2
doest all thinges *deface*, . . . III. iv. 56. 3
Not caring his long labours to *deface*; . . . III. xii. 32. 3
with lewd termes their lovers to *deface*. . . . IV. iv. 4. 5
Before misfortune did his hew *deface*; . . . IV. viii. 14. 5
that fowle rudenesse which did her *deface*; . . . IV. ix. 14. 3
with strong hand their fruitful rancknes did *deface*. . . . V. i. 1. 9
others worth with leasings doest *deface*, . . . V. viii. 20. 8
all her other honour did obscure, And titles of nobilitie *deface*: V. ix. 38. 7
those shames, that erst ye spake me to *deface*.' . . . VI. i. 28. 9
all your other praises will *deface*, . . . VI. viii. 2. 5
Should harbour'd be and all those Woods *deface*, . . . VII. vi. 55. 5
all those pretious ornaments *deface*. . . . *Am.* xxxi. 4
Defaced. Where-with my fresh flowretts bene *defast*: . . . *S.C.* F. 182
are wholly now *defaced*; . . . *T.M.* 202
hath our fayre light *defaced*; . . . *T.M.* 266
thy Kingdome is *defaced* quight, . . . *T.M.* 399
all my antique moniments *defaced*? . . . *Ti.* 179
And their disloiall powre *defaced* clene, . . . *Ded. Son.* xi. 11
all his power was utterly *defaste*, . . . II. iv. 14. 3
feele the law the which thou hast *defast*.' . . . II. viii. 31. 9
Malecastaes champions are *defaced*. . . . III. i. Arg.
To let not others honour be *defaste* . . . III. i. 12. 4
Defaste the beautie of the shyning skye, . . . III. ii. 28. 2
shall their name for ever be *defaste*, . . . III. iii. 43. 8
knighthood fowle *defaced* by a faithlesse knight. . . . III. ix. 1. 9
Altars defyld, and holy things *defast*; . . . IV. i. 21. 5
Time . . . That famous moniment hath quite *defaste*, . . . IV. ii. 33. 3
with lewd loves . . . Had it *defaste*, . . . IV. ix. 16. 8
all the hewen stones thereof *defaced*, . . . V. ii. 28. 3
defaced cleene Her stately towres . . . V. x. 25. 4
Them fouly rent, and shamefully *defaced* had. . . . V. xi. 60. 9
let your fame with falshood be *defaced*? . . . V. xi. 63. 5
all his joyes *defaced*! . . . *H.L.* 272
Defame. hong their conquerd armes, for more *defame*, . . . II. v. 26. 8
Then must he her foregoe with fowle *defame*, . . . III. i. 27. 2
as thing deviz'd her to *defame*. . . . IV. v. 17. 5
With forged cause them falsely to *defame*; . . . IV. viii. 25. 7

Defame—*Continued.*
eke the love of Ladies foule *defame*; . . . IV. ix. 37. 5
with it beare the burden of *defame*, . . . V. i. 28. 8
boastfull Braggadochio to *defame*, . . . V. iii. 29. 2
From all brave knights be banisht with *defame*; . . . V. iii. 38. 8
many other crimes of foule *defame* Against her brought, . . . V. ix. 43. 2
defame Both noble armes and gentle curtesie. . . . VI. i. 26. 7
Unwares into the daunger of *defame*; . . . VI. v. 15. 5
to infest The noblest wights with notable *defame*: . . . VI. vi. 12. 6
with black dishonor And foule *defame* . . . VI. vi. 25. 5
Besides the great dishonour and *defame*, . . . VI. ix. 1. 8
the bondslave of *defame*; . . . *H.B.* 173
Defamed. Be with the worke of losels wit *defamed*, . . . *Hub.* 813
That her bright glorie else hath much *defamed*. . . . *Col.* 910
With his vile tongue, which many had *defamed*, . . . VI. xii. 38. 4
Defames. The which himselfe then Ladies more *defames*, . . III. viii. 44. 3
Defaming. For never more *defaming* gentle Knight, . . . VI. xii. 34. 6
Defast(e). *See* **Defaced.**
Default. His speares *default* to mend with cruell blade; . . . III. i. 10. 3
Which by *default* I have not yet defraide: . . . V. xi. 41. 5
pardon crav'd for his so rash *default*, . . . VI. iii. 21. 8
That he gainst courtesie so fowly did *default*. . . . VI. iii. 21. 9
Defaults. Whose grosse *defaults* thy daintie pen may file, . . *Ded.Son.*xii.11
Defeasance. After his foes *defeasaunce* did remaine, . . . I. xii. 12. 4
Defeat. The Patrone . . . Foule Errour doth *defeate*: . . . I. i. Arg.
after Archimagoes fowle *defeat*, . . . I. vi. 3. 1
Doth overthrow the Bowre of blis, And Acrasy *defeat*. . . . II. xii. Arg.
His mighty staffe, that could all charmes *defeat*. . . . II. xii. 40. 3
Shall stoutly him *defeat*, and thousand Saxons kill. . . . III. iii. 35. 9
Shall him *defeate* withouten blood imbrewd: . . . III. iii. 38. 7
He Turpine doth *defeate*, . . . VI. vi. Arg.
Defeated. he them *defeated* evermore, . . . II. x. 10. 4
He them *defeated* in victorious fight, . . . II. x. 16. 4
being all *defeated*, save a few, . . . II. x. 55. 8
I them both with equall hap *defeated*. . . . IV. x. 10. 4
Defeated had the other faytour quight, . . . V. viii. 8. 5
how we then *defeated* all their deed, . . . VII. vi. 20. 5
Defeature. mischiefe framd for their first loves *defeature*, . . IV. vi. 17. 7
Defect. The antique world . . . Fownd no *defect* in his Creators grace; . . . II. vii. 16. 2
Defects. *defects* From her most cunning hand escaped bee; . II. xii. 23. 3
Defence. *See* **Defense.**
Defend. Daring the foe that cannot him *defend*: . . . *Ro.* xiv. 8
th' other strove for to *defend* The force of Vulcane . . . *Gn.* 523
appeare . . . at Court, it to *defend*; . . . *Hub.* 1099
That doest their cause so mightily *defend*: . . . *Col.* 900
I send This present . . . it to *defend*. . . . *Ded. Son.* iv. 14
that by land and seas Have vowd you to *defend*. . . . I. iii. 29. 9
He hath no powre to hurt, nor to *defend*, . . . I. viii. 21. 7
one that with his prowesse may *Defend* thine honour, . . . I. ix. 16. 8
him to *defend* thereby. . . . I. xi. 42. 9
Should neede of all his armes him to *defend*, . . . II. iii. 17. 4
From other covetous feends it to *defend*, . . . II. vii. 32. 4
defend Against his foe and mine: . . . II. viii. 8. 5
Beteeme to you this sword, you to *defend*, . . . II. viii. 19. 6
The stroke thereof from entraunce may *defend*; . . . II. viii. 21. 2
Ne shield *defend* the thunder of his throwes: . . . II. viii. 41. 3
those two brethren Gyauntes did *defend* The walles . . . II. xi. 15. 6
thence to *defend* The sunny beames . . . II. xii. 63. 2
mightily *defend* Against their forren foe . . . III. iii. 23. 7
Shall well *defend*, and Saxons powre suppresse; . . . III. iii. 33. 2
Him selfe from deadly daunger to *defend*: . . . III. vii. 32. 5
This hand her wonne, this hand shall her *defend*.' . . . IV. ii. 14. 6
from his force seemes nought may it *defend*; . . . IV. iii. 19. 4
Him selfe to save, and daunger to *defend*, . . . IV. iii. 32. 4
That can her best *defend* from villenie; . . . IV. v. 1. 7
evermore my shield did me *defend* . . . IV. x. 58. 6
to *defend* the feeble in their right, . . . V. ii. 1. 3
Guarded of many which did her *defend*: . . . V. ii. 20. 3
I will it *defend* whilest ever that I may.' . . . V. iv. 14. 9
No more shall now the darkenesse of the night *Defend* thee . V. vi. 37. 7
O ye Heavens, *defend!* and turne away From her . . . V. viii. 19. 5
Her to *defend* against all forrein foes . . . V. x. 12. 4
An hideous monster that doth it *defend*, . . . V. xi. 20. 2
he was not presently in plight Her to *defend*, . . . VI. ii. 19. 2
without sword his person to *defend*: . . . VI. iv. 17. 5
So that for want of heires it to *defend*, . . . VI. iv. 31. 6
gard her to *defend* from bold oppressors might. . . . VI. v. 7. 9
Defended. by thy countenaunce doth crave to bee *Defended* . *Ded. Son.* iii. 4
From that first flaw him selfe right well *defended*. . . . V. v. 6. 7
she saw no meanes to be *defended*, . . . VI. iv. 10. 5
the bold Prince *defended* him so well, . . . VI. vi. 23. 6
Was by the Captaine all this while *defended*, . . . VI. xi. 19. 2
Defending. *Defending* Ladies cause and Orphans right, . . . III. ii. 14. 6
Defends. *Defends* him selfe, and saves his gotten pray: . . . IV. vii. 25. 7
Defense. nor God nor man can fynd *Defence*, . . . *Col.* 876
Dame . . . For whose *defence* he was to shed his blood. . . . I. i. 55. 3
I in *defence* of mine did likewise stand, . . . I. ii. 36. 3
did dread in their *defence*; . . . I. x. 43. 6
retire A little backeward for his best *defence*, . . . I. xi. 45. 3
That decks and armes your shield with faire *defence*: . . . II. i. 28. 8
fayre *defence* and goodly menaging Of armes . . . II. iv. 8. 3
for his Realmes *defence*, . . . II. x. 15. 8
his dearest life For her *defence* . . . II. xi. 16. 7
He from that deadly throw made no *defence*, . . . III. ix. 29. 1
In better quarrell then *defence* of right, . . . III. x. 28. 4
the Squire, in her *defence*, her sore astound. . . . IV. viii. 19. 9
for *defence* thereof . . . There reared was a castle . . . IV. x. 7. 1
'He is' (said he) 'a man of great *defence*, . . . V. ii. 5. 3
She wore for her *defence* a mayled habergeon. . . . V. v. 2. 9

Defense—*Continued.*
did waite Uppon her person for her sure *defence,* . . . V. v. 4. 4
Doth in *defence* thereof full stoutly stond: . . . V. vii. 30. 6
now needing strong *defence,* . . . V. x. 12. 6
Gainst which the pallid death findes no *defence;* . . . V. xi. 45. 5
All armed in a cote of yron plate Of great *defence* . . . V. xii. 14. 4
for thine owne *defence,* on foote alight . . . VI. iii. 35. 8
was sav'd with strong *defence;* . . . VI. xi. 30. 7
Defer. I will *deferre* the end untill another tide. . . . IV. vii. 47. 9
Deferred. So that the doome was to another day *differd.* . . . IV. iv. 36. 9
Defetto. The third, nor strong nor wise, but spightfullest, *Defetto.* . . . VI. v. 13. 9
most of all *Defetto* him annoyde, . . . VI. v. 20. 4
Deffly. *See* **Deftly.**
Defiance. bad *defiance* to his enemie. . . . *Van.* vi. 6
bidding bold *defyaunce* to his foeman neare. . . . I. xi. 15. 9
too weake To aunswere his *defiaunce* in the field, . . . V. i. 24. 2
sending to the Souldan in despight A bold *defyance,* . . . V. viii. 27. 8
Three times, as in *defiance,* there he strooke; . . . V. xi. 22. 2
'To take *defiaunce* at a Ladies word . . . VI. i. 28. 1
Spreds in *defiaunce* of all enemies. . . . *Am.* v. 12
Defied. I saw a wasp, that fiercely him *defide,* . . . *Van.* x. 7
With railing tearmes *defied* the Jewish hoast, . . . *Ti.* 538
With foule reprochfull words he boldly him *defide.* . . . I. vi. 40. 9
streight *defyde* Both Guyon and Pyrochles; . . . II. v. 19. 3
he his ydle curtesie *defide,* . . . II. xii. 49. 7
so *defyde* them each, and so *defyde* them both. . . . III. ix. 13. 9
when he was *defyde,* . . . III. ix. 14. 9
Be thou, . . . Loathed of ladies all, and of all knights *defyde!'* IV. i. 51. 9
sith first I was *defyde,* . . . IV. vi. 9. 7
his accuser thereuppon *defide;* . . . V. i. 23. 7
with reprochfull blasphemy *defide,* . . . V. ii. 20. 5
turne thee soone to him of whom thou art *defyde.'* . . . VI. i. 18. 9
scornes thy ydle scoffe, and bids thee be *defyde.'* . . . VI. i. 27. 9
The dastard, that did heare him selfe *defyde,* . . . VI. iii. 36. 1
And oft complayn'd of fate, and fortune oft *defyde.* . . . VI. iv. 26. 9
Bidding him turne againe, . . . for he him *defyde.* . . . VI. vii. 7. 3
Defies. A prowd rebellious Unicorn *defyes,* . . . II. v. 10. 2
Defiest. 'Art thou the caytive that *defyest* me? . . . VI. i. 19. 6
Defile. Breathing out beastly lust her to *defyle:* . . . III. i. 17. 3
in all shamefull sort him selfe with her *defile.* . . . III. vii. 50. 9
Defiled. mought needes be *defilde;* . . . *S.C.* May 74
Each place *defilde* with blood of guiltles beasts, . . . *Hub.* 1307
Her filthie parbreake all the place *defiled* has. . . . I. i. 20. 9
With beastly sin thought her to have *defilde,* . . . I. vi. 3. 4
all the floore . . . *Defiled* was, . . . I. viii. 35. 8
in al abuse thou hast thy selfe *defild?* . . . I. ix. 46. 9
with innocent blood *Defyld* those sacred waves, . . . I. xi. 29. 8
This luckles childe, whom thus ye see with blood *defild.* . . . II. i. 50. 9
his sad fathers armes with blood *defilde,* . . . II. ii. 11. 3
when she is nigh *defild* Of filthy wretch? . . . III. viii. 27. 7
Altars *defyld,* and holy things defast; . . . IV. i. 21. 5
Defil'd the pledge committed to thy trust? . . . IV. i. 53. 5
defiled with foule villanie The sacred pledge . . . IV. vi. 8. 2
Whom seeing fit, and with no crime *defilde,* . . . V. i. 6. 4
Where none may be with her lewd parts *defyled,* . . . V. ix. 2. 4
to be with guiltlesse bloud *defylde,* . . . *Am.* xx. 11
Define. who the Godhead can *define.* . . . *Col.* 347
of his nature rightly to *define,* . . . *Col.* 836
Assembled were in field the chalenge to *define.* . . . IV. iii. 3. 9
this same vertue that doth right *define:* . . . V. vii. 1. 3
Since I him lately lost, uneath is to *define.* . . . VI. v. 28. 9
Defined. not in outward shows, but inward thoughts *defynd.* VI. Pr. 5. 9
Deflower. soone comes age that will her pride *deflowre;* . . . II. xii. 75. 7
suffred beastes her body to *deflowre,* . . . III. vii. 49. 7
He with his shamefull lust doth first *deflowre,* . . . IV. vii. 12. 8
for feare it to *deflore,* . . . *H.B.* 39
Deflowered. This Gyant found her and by force *deflowr'd;* . . . IV. xi. 42. 6
Deform. he did *deforme* Both borrowed pride, . . . *Van.* viii. 11
She likewise did *deforme,* like him to bee. . . . *As.* 156
who-so kild that monster most *deforme,* . . . I. xii. 20. 3
greedy Rosmarines with visages *deforme.* . . . II. xii. 24. 9
gentle sprite *deforme* with rude rusticity. . . . III. vi. 1. 9
soyle, which did *deforme* their lively hew; . . . III. vi. 17. 7
Straunge horrour to *deforme* his griesly shade: . . . III. xii. 11. 4
Deformed. *Deformd* with filth and fowle iniquitie; . . . *T.M.* 122
With crudled blood and filthie gore *deformed,* . . . *As.* 152
Deformed monsters, fowle, and blacke as inke, . . . I. i. 22. 7
'Then cride she out, "Fye, fye! *deformed* wight, . . . I. ii. 39. 1
by his side rode loathsome Gluttony, *Deformed* creature, . . . I. iv. 21. 2
dreadfull Cerberus His three *deformed* heads did lay along, . . . I. v. 34. 2
They both, *deformed,* scarsely could bee known. . . . I. vi. 45. 6
Stroke one of those *deformed* heades so sore, . . . I. viii. 16. 2
they . . . wondred at so fowle *deformed* wight. . . . I. viii. 49. 2
Dismayd with that *deformed* dismall sight, . . . I. ix. 30. 5
The ugly vew of his *deformed* crimes; . . . I. ix. 48. 6
him in blood and durt *deformed* quight. . . . II. v. 22. 4
Deformed creatures, horrible in sight; . . . II. vii. 35. 7
Vile caitive wretches, ragged, rude, *deformd,* . . . II. ix. 13. 4
Deformed creatures, in straunge difference, . . . II. xi. 10. 3
so *deformd* is luxury, . . . II. xi. 12. 6
more *deformed* Monsters thousand fold, . . . II. xii. 25. 2
that wofull Squire, With blood *deformed,* . . . III. v. 29. 2
he, through privy griefe . . . Is woxen so *deform'd* . . . III. x. 60. 8
With matchlesse eares *deformed* and distort, . . . IV. i. 28. 2
With heary glib *deform'd* and meiger face, . . . IV. viii. 12. 6
Much more *deformed* fearefull, ugly were, . . . IV. x. 20. 4
Bearing his sixe *deformed* heads on hye, . . . IV. xi. 32. 2
all his face *deform'd* with infamie, . . . V. iii. 38. 4
yclowded With fearefull shadowes of *deformed* night, . . . V. iv. 45. 2

Deformed—*Continued.*
Whom like disguize no lesse *deformed* had, . . . V. vii. 38. 2
A dreadfull feend with fowle *deformed* looke, . . . V. xi. 22. 5
Then downe to ground fell that *deformed* Masse, . . . V. xi. 32. 1
With sorrow dimmed and *deform'd* . . . *Am.* xlv. 10
mynd Dwels in *deformed* tabernacle drownd, . . . *H.B.* 142
deform'd with some foule imperfection. . . . *H.B.* 147
Deformity. her light Doth dim with horror and *deformity;* . . . II. vii. 49. 4
All dreadfull pourtraicts of *deformitee:* . . . II. xii. 23. 5
Much like in foulnesse and *deformity* Unto that Monster, . . . V. xi. 25. 1
wrapt In sad misfortunes foule *deformity* . . . VI. v. 1. 3
Defouled. God, me graunt, I dead be not *defould!* . . . I. x. 42. 9
they saw that goodly boy with blood *Defowled,* . . . III. v. 38. 2
Defrauded. Unwares *defrauded* his intended destiny: . . . VI. viii. 8. 9
Defray. Can Night *defray* The wrath of thundring Jove, . . . I. v. 42. 8
nought but dire revenge his anger mote *defray.* . . . IV. v. 31. 9
That long daies labour doest at last *defray,* . . . *Epith.* 316
Defrayed. Arthur all that reckoning *defrayd:* . . . II. x. 49. 8
Which by default I have not yet *defraide:* . . . V. xi. 41. 5
Till to the brim I have it full *defrayd:* . . . VI. viii. 24. 3
Deftly. dauncen *deffly,* and singen soote, . . . *S.C.* Ap. 111
Defy. Beg amongst those that beggers doo *defie.'* . . . *Hub.* 192
As if the highest God *defy* he would: . . . II. vii. 40. 5
'Foole!' . . . 'I thy gift *defye,* . . . II. viii. 52. 1
a proud Amazon did late *defy* All the brave Knights . . . V. iv. 29. 5
She daily told her love he did *defye;* . . . V. v. 56. 8
I *defie* thee; and here challenge make, . . . VI. iii. 35. 4
Degendered. ere long will be *degendered.* . . . V. Pr. 2. 9
Degendering. *Degendering* to hate, fell from above . . . *H.H.L.* 94
Degenerate. doth *degenerate* the noble race, . . . *T.M.* 436
Degree. So grew the Romane Empire by *degree,* . . . *Ro.* xxx. 9
Learne by their losse to love the low *degree;* . . . *Van.* xii. 10
like in eche *degree* The flocke . . . *S.C.* Jul. 131
To love the lowe *degree*) ; . . . *S.C.* Jul. 220
(compar'd to all the rest Of each *degree*) . . . *Hub.* 180
Ye a great master are in your *degree:* . . . *Hub.* 546
sdeign'd the low *degree;* . . . *Hub.* 679
to raise Himselfe to high *degree,* . . . *Hub.* 775
lov'd this shepheard dearest in *degree,* . . . *Col.* 14
For high desert, advaunst to that *degree.* . . . *Col.* 527
th' youngest is the highest in *degree.* . . . *Col.* 543
Great troupes of people . . . of each *degree* and place; . . . I. iv. 3. 2
pourtrahed With natures pen, in ages grave *degree,* . . . I. viii. 33. 8
In fowle reproch of knighthoodes fayre *degree,* . . . I. ix. 22. 6
him againe lov'd in the least *degree;* . . . I. ix. 27. 7
draw thy dayes forth to their last *degree?* . . . I. ix. 46. 2
knew his good to all of each *degree,* . . . I. x. 7. 5
from the first unto the last *degree,* . . . I. x. 45. 7
the richesse of all heavenly grace In chiefe *degree* . . . II. ii. 41. 2
to court he cast t' advaunce his first *degree.* . . . II. iii. 5. 9
he despisd to tread in dew *degree,* . . . II. iii. 46. 7
To love a Lady fayre of great *degree,* . . . II. iv. 19. 2
it was a groome of base *degree,* . . . II. iv. 24. 3
Disguised like that groome of base *degree,* . . . II. iv. 27. 8
Some thought to raise themselves to high *degree* . . . II. vii. 47. 1
unto all that live in high *degree,* . . . II. vii. 60. 3
Exceeding much the state of meane *degree,* . . . III. i. 33. 7
A Faerie was, yborne of high *degree.* . . . III. vi. 4. 3
'The third a Damzell was of low *degree,* . . . III. vii. 59. 1
Thus marched these six couples forth in faire *degree.* . . . III. xii. 18. 9
dayly more offensive unto each *degree.* . . . IV. i. 18. 9
courtesie, That made them dearely lov'd of each *degree;* . . . IV. iii. 2. 7
had done outrage in so high *degree:* . . . IV. vi. 22. 7
Daughter unto a Lord of high *degree;* . . . IV. vii. 15. 2
Yet was he but a Squire of low *degree;* . . . IV. vii. 15. 7
for his meane *degree* might not aspire . . . IV. viii. 50. 3
This lovely swaine, the Squire of low *degree;* . . . IV. viii. 52. 5
her Squire of low *degree* Did secretly . . . IV. viii. 55. 6
The Squire of low *degree,* releast, Aemylia takes to wife: . . . IV. ix. Arg.
that Squire of low *degree* Came forth . . . IV. ix. 8. 8
sooth is said, and tride in each *degree,* . . . IV. ix. 27. 8
Might match with this by many a *degree:* . . . IV. x. 30. 5
I them all according their *degree* Cannot recount, . . . IV. xi. 40. 7
is the Virgin, sixt in her *degree,* . . . V. i. 11. 8
like a little Mount of small *degree,* . . . V. iv. 7. 7
guyded by *degree* Unto the presence of that gratious Queene; . . . V. ix. 27. 1
beare themselves aright To all of each *degree* . . . VI. ii. 1. 4
Upon him tooke the roiall high *degree,* . . . VI. ii. 28. 8
Of what *degree* and what race he is growne: . . . VI. iii. 1. 5
And courteous withall, becomming her *degree.* . . . VI. iii. 20. 9
from the high *degree* of happy state Fell . . . VI. viii. 2. 8
From pitch of higher place unto this low *degree.'* . . . VI. ix. 28. 9
differing in honour and *degree:* . . . VI. x. 21. 5
how to each *degree* and kynde We should our selves demeane, VI. x. 23. 7
Excelling much the meane of her *degree;* . . . VI. x. 27. 3
rageth sore in each *degree* and state, . . . VI. xii. 40. 2
Then dare be lov'd by men of meane *degree.* . . . *Am.* lxi. 14
Shall lift you up unto an high *degree.* . . . *Am.* lxxxii. 14
Garnisht with heavenly guifts of high *degree,* . . . *Epith.* 187
striving . . . To be advanced highest in *degree.* . . . *Com. Son.* ii. 8
Next to Himselfe in glorious *degree,* . . . *H.H.L.* 93
How much lesse those, much higher in *degree,* . . . *H.H.B.* 61
Degrees. Uprising by *degrees,* grewe to such height, . . . *Ro.* xx. 10
by dew *degrees,* and long protense, . . . III. iii. 4. 8
by *degrees* they all were disagreed; . . . IV. v. 36. 6
According their *degrees* disposed well. . . . IV. xii. 3. 5
Made signe to them in their *degrees* to speake, . . . VII. vi. 22. 5
From whence declining daily by *degrees,* . . . *Epith.* 267
And as these heavens still by *degrees* arize, . . . *H.H.B.* 71
So those likewise doe by *degrees* redound, . . . *H.H.B.* 75

Deheubarth. In *Deheubarth,* that now South-wales is hight, . . . III. ii. 18. 4
Deify. With which ye use your loves to *deifie,* . . . *T.M.* 368
mortall men have powre to *deifie:* . . . *T.M.* 460
her with heavenly hymnes doth *deifie,* . . . *D.* 230
thou doest so enforce to *deifie:* . . . *Col.* 481
Deign. so be thou *deigne* to heare Rude ditties, . . . *S.C.* D. 13
if me thou *deigne* to serve and sew, . . . II. vii. 9. 1
that she may the better *deigne* to heare, . . . IV. Pr. 5. 1
Those lamping eyes will *deigne* sometimes to look, . . . *Am.* i. 6
They *deigne* to see, and seeing it still dye. . . . *H.L.* 133
Deigne to let fall one drop of dew reliefe, . . . *H.B.* 284
Deigned. my Lute, whom Phoebus *deignd* to give, . . . *Ro.* xxxii. 9
Deignd to behold me and their gifts bestowe, . . . *Ti.* 81
deign'd with her the paragon to make: . . . *Mui.* 274
on me she *deigned* to bestowe Order of Maydenhead, . . . II. ii. 42. 3
since ye *deignd* so goodly to relent . . . *Am.* lxxxii. 9
Deigns. Shee *deignes* not my good will, . . . *S.C.* Ja. 63
deignes to pitie a perplexed hart; . . . *T.M.* 424
heven thee *deignes* to hold in living state, . . . II. i. 37. 3
Deity. that . . . Greeke, That for his love refused *deitye.* . . . I. iii. 21. 6
All that is by the working of thy *Deitee.* . . . III. x. 4. 9
Ne dare looke . . . On the dred face of that great *Deity,* . . . *H.H.B.* 145
The soveraine dearling of the *Deity,* . . . *H.H.B.* 184
Delay. *delay* Thy nightly course, to heare his melodie? . . . *Gn.* 459
times *delay* new hope of helpe still breeds. . . . *Hub.* 327
With like delightes . . . *delay* The rugged brow . . . *Ded. Son.* i. 11
after labors long and sad *delay,* . . . I. x. 52. 5
sparks, seed, drops, and filth, do thus *delay;* . . . II. iv. 35. 6
to *delay* the heat, least by mischaunce . . . II. ix. 30. 1
Till Diamond, disdeigning long *delay* . . . IV. iii. 17. 6
the time for to *delay,* . . . IV. vi. 45. 2
Till time the tempest doe thereof *delay* . . . IV. viii. 1. 6
She drew her far, and led with slow *delay.* . . . IV. viii. 11. 7
'On th' one side he, on th' other sate *Delay,* . . . IV. x. 13. 1
Delay in close awaite Caught hold on me, . . . IV. x. 14. 5
Some of their losse, some of their loves *delay,* . . . IV. x. 43. 3
That ye will make me Squire without *delay,* . . . VI. ii. 33. 4
The which discourse as now I must *delay,* . . . VI. vii. 50. 8
Him to have bound and thrald without *delay;* . . . VI. viii. 11. 7
discoursing diversely . . . to worke *delay;* . . . VI. ix. 12. 7
otherwhyles, their dying to *delay,* . . . *H.L.* 138
lightly did *delay* Hot Titans beames, . . . *Proth.* 3
Delayed. The hasty heat of his avowd revenge *delayd.* . . . II. vi. 40. 9
I am els *delaid* With hard adventure . . . II. ix. 8. 7
Those dreadfull flames she also found *delayd* . . . III. xii. 42. 7
nor be *delayd* From chacing him, . . . VI. x. 1. 5
all that hetherto hath long *delayd* This gentle knight . . . VI. xii. 2. 1
delayd by her hart-frosen cold; . . . *Am.* xxx. 6
Delays. wearied his life with dull *delayes.* . . . III. xii. 44. *or.* 4
The doubts, the daungers, the *delayes,* the woes, . . . *H.L.* 262
Delectable. grassy greene of *delectable* hew; . . . II. xii. 12. 3
Delian. plac'd in thy sacred wood (O *Delian* Goddesse!) . . . *Gn.* 170
Delice. *See* **Fleur-de-lis.**
Delices. In daintie *delices,* and lavish joyes, . . . II. v. 28. 6
Abounding all with *delices* most rare, . . . IV. x. 6. 2
With all deare *delices* and rare delights, . . . V. iii. 40. 4
Delicious. Now made of Maa, the Nymph *delitious.* . . . *Col.* 523
mournefull meed of joyes *delicious!* . . . II. xii. 85. 7
that same *delitious* Poet . . . III. Pr. 5. 1
a most *delitious* harmony . . . was sweetly heard . . . III. xii. 6. 1
in her *delitious* boure The faire Poeana . . . IV. ix. 6. 1
Thence-forth abandond her *delicious* brooke, . . . VII. vi. 54. 2
Delight. *See* **Self-delight.**
The bloud of Martyrs dere were hir *delite.* . . . *Rev.* ii. 10
faire as mote the greatest god *delite;* . . . *Pet.* i. 5
herein I tooke (toke herein[1]) my chiefe *delight,* . . . *Pet.* iv. 9
she did seeme to daunce, as in *delight,* . . . *Van.* ix. 7
feeles the deepe *delight* that is in death, . . . *Frag.*
Tho shall we sporten in *delight,* . . . *S.C.* Mar. 19
thou lackest somedele their *delight.* . . . *S.C.* May 56
Of my old age have this one *delight,* . . . *S.C.* May 202
what wants me here to worke *delyte?* . . . *S.C.* Jun. 3
musick for their more *delight:* . . . *S.C.* Jun. 29
I more *delight* then larke in Sommer dayes: . . . *S.C.* Jun. 51
forsayd From places of *delight,* . . . *S.C.* Jul. 70
Ne in good nor goodnes taken *delight,* . . . *S.C.* S. 85
let us cast with what *delight* to chace, . . . *S.C.* O. 2
The dapper ditties . . . *Delighten* much; . . . *S.C.* O. 15
Delight is layd abedde; . . . *S.C.* D. 137
With pype of fennie reedes doth him *delight.* . . . *Gn.* 112
There his milk-dropping Goats be his *delight,* . . . *Gn.* 115
A pleasant bowre with all *delight* abounding . . . *Gn.* 187
the *delight* thereof me much releeved. . . . *Hub.* 32
The Lyon now doth take the most *delight;* . . . *Hub.* 622
with sweete *delight* Of Musicks skill . . . *Hub.* 755
Sweete Ladie Muses, Ladies of *delight,* . . . *Hub.* 761
all that els was wont to worke *delight* . . . *T.M.* 37
Delight, and Laughter, deckt in seemly sort. . . . *T.M.* 198
in the lap of soft *delight* Beene long time luld, . . . *T.M.* 301
Faire Cytheree, the Mother of *delight,* . . . *T.M.* 397
Have now quite lost their naturall *delight,* . . . *T.M.* 552
what *delight* (quoth she) in earthlie thing, . . . *Ti.* 22
Sorrowing tempered with deare *delight,* . . . *Ti.* 319
flesh *delight* In earthlie blis, . . . *Ti.* 527
To come to her, and seeke her loves *delight.* . . . *Ti.* 641
to enjoy *delight* with libertie, . . . *Mui.* 210
in this wretched life dooth take *delight,* . . . *D.* 9
even their heavie song would breede *delight;* . . . *D.* 13
may allure the senses to *delight,* . . . *D.* 324

Delight—*Continued.*
ne feed on false *delight* . . . *D.* 492
The presence of your dearest loves *delight,* . . . *D.* 513
His lifes desire, and his deare loves *delight.* . . . *As.* 54
Since that same day in nought I take *delight,* . . . *Col.* 44
allured with my pipes *delight,* . . . *Col.* 61
wrought to win *delight.* . . . *Col.* 119
she thenceforth therein gan take *delight;* . . . *Col.* 361
In loves soft laies and looser thoughts *delight.* . . . *Col.* 423
Faire spreading forth her leaves with fresh *delight,* . . . *Col.* 545
bayt which with *delight* Doth man allure . . . *Col.* 871
Thy soveraine Goddesses most deare *delight,* . . . *Ded. Son.* viii. 2
Led with *delight,* they thus beguile the way, . . . I. i. 10. 1
dreame . . . With bowres, and beds, and ladies deare *delight:* . . . I. i. 55. 7
Them both together laid to joy in vaine *delight.* . . . I. ii. 3. 9
in her selfe-lov'd semblance took *delight;* . . . I. iv. 10. 8
in vaine glorious frayes he litle did *delight.* . . . I. vi. 20. 9
Ne in this new acquaintaunce could *delight;* . . . I. vi. 32. 3
chaunt sweet musick to *delight* his mynd. . . . I. vii. 3. 5
arrogant *delight* Of th' high descent whereof he was yborne, . . . I. vii. 10. 1
'What worlds *delight,* or joy of living speach, . . . I. vii. 39. 1
The chearelesse man, . . . Had no *delight* to treaten of his griefe; . . . I. viii. 43. 8
Them to renew, I wote, breeds no *delight,* . . . I. viii. 44. 3
Best musicke breeds *delight* in loathing eare: . . . I. viii. 44. 4
Was never hart so ravisht with *delight,* . . . I. ix. 14. 6
take *delight* With many rather for to goe astray, . . . I. x. 10. 5
take *delight* To see sad pageaunts . . . II. i. 36. 2
'Her blis is all in pleasure, and *delight,* . . . II. i. 52. 1
as in a dreame of deepe *delight,* . . . I. xi. 50. 4
poured out in pleasure and *delight:* . . . II. ii. 36. 5
with *delight* of that he wisely spake . . . II. ii. 46. 5
happy blis And all *delight* does raigne, . . . II. iii. 39. 5
fild with *delight* Of her sweete words . . . II. iii. 42. 2
I may more *delight* in thy embracement deare. . . . II. iv. 26. 9
all in blood and spoile is his *delight.* . . . II. iv. 42. 4
Thus in still waves of deepe *delight* to wade, . . . II. v. 35. 2
As her fantasticke wit did most *delight:* . . . II. vi. 7. 2
With one sweete drop of sensuall *delight.* . . . II. vi. 8. 7
said and did all that mote him *delight,* . . . II. vi. 22. 2
of her joy And vaine *delight* . . . II. vi. 37. 3
Faire shields, gay steedes, bright armes be my *delight;* . . . II. vii. 10. 8
gentle court and gracious *delight* Shee to them made, . . . II. ix. 20. 3
with rare *delight* And gazing wonder . . . II. ix. 33. 2
At last, quite ravisht with *delight* . . . II. x. 69. 1
Beguyld thus with *delight* of novelties, . . . II. x. 77. 1
Attempred goodly well for health and for *delight.* . . . II. xi. 2. 9
Armed with dartes of sensuall *Delight,* . . . II. xi. 13. 6
suffred no *delight* To sincke into his sence, . . . II. xii. 53. 2
all that mote *delight* a daintie eare, . . . II. xii. 70. 2
greedily depasturing *delight;* . . . II. xii. 73. 4
her faire eyes, sweet smyling in *delight,* . . . II. xii. 78. 6
My sences lulled are in slomber of *delight.* . . . III. Pr. 4. 9
of them cleeped was the Lady of *Delight.* . . . III. i. 31. 9
Some for untimely ease, some for *delight,* . . . III. i. 39. 4
poured forth in sensuall *delight,* . . . III. i. 48. 6
'All my *delight* on deedes of armes is sett, . . . III. ii. 7. 1
Their fit disports with faire *delight* doe chose, . . . III. ii. 31. 4
Her dearest sonne, her dearest harts *delight:* . . . III. iv. 44. 5
In other none, but him, she sets *delight;* . . . III. v. 9. 3
All her *delight* is set on Marinell, . . . III. v. 9. 4
greatest Princes liking it mote well *delight.* . . . III. v. 40. 9
So my *delight* is all in joyfulnesse, . . . III. vi. 22. 3
her deare brood, her deare *delight:* . . . III. vi. 40. 4
Threw forth most dainty odours and most sweet *delight.* . . . III. vi. 43. 9
all were her whole *delight* In mischiefe, . . . III. vii. 9. 8
in vain sheows . . . tooke no *delight;* . . . III. vii. 29. 7
Enough to hold a foole in vaine *delight.* . . . III. viii. 10. 7
in his old corage new *delight* To gin awake, . . . III. viii. 23. 4
To winne her liking unto his *delight:* . . . III. viii. 38. 5
Depriv'd of kindly joy and naturall *delight* . . . III. ix. 5. 9
they tooke *delight* In their first error, . . . III. ix. 23. 7
to doe them more *delight.* . . . III. ix. 25. 9
The jolly Satyres, full of fresh *delight,* . . . III. x. 44. 3
Wondrous *delight* it was . . . III. xi. 34. 6
A lay of loves *delight* with sweet concent: . . . III. xii. 5. 7
the frayle soule in deepe *delight* nigh drownd: . . . III. xii. 6. 5
still he far'd as dauncing in *delight,* . . . III. xii. 8. 7
the sweet lodge of love and deare *delight:* . . . III. xii. 45. *or.* 4
none . . . to them tydings tell that mote their harts *delight.* . . . IV. i. 16. 9
his wanton hart Was tickled with *delight,* . . . IV. i. 33. 6
Love is free, and led with selfe *delight,* . . . IV. i. 46. 8
To whom he made great dalliance and *delight:* . . . IV. ii. 4. 4
More wise they weend to make of love *delight* Then life to hazard . . . IV. ii. 40. 5
Priamond on foote had more *delight;* . . . IV. ii. 42. 5
(for small *delight* They had . . . IV. iii. 47. 1
The eyes of all, allur'd with close *delight,* . . . IV. iv. 16. 4
laugh aloud, and gather great *delight.* . . . IV. vii. 26. 9
made the baite of bestiall *delight:* . . . IV. viii. 32. 4
she given is to vaine *delight,* . . . IV. viii. 49. 8
walke about her gardens of *delight,* . . . IV. viii. 54. 3
with the sweetnesse of her rare *delight* . . . IV. ix. 6. 6
Druons *delight* was all in single life, . . . IV. ix. 21. 1
She is the nourse of pleasure and *delight,* . . . IV. x. 35. 8
of a fishes shell was wrought with rare *delight.* . . . IV. xi. 6. 9
Erato that doth in love *delite,* . . . IV. xi. 49. 7
greedy seas doe in the spoile of life *delight.* . . . IV. xii. 6. 9
of no worldly thing he tooke *delight;* . . . IV. xii. 19. 7

Delight—*Continued.*
Her vertue was the dowre that did *delight*. . . . . V. iv. 9. 4
gave them gifts and things of deare *delight*. . . . . V. iv. 51. 6
Amongst loose Ladies lapped in *delight*: . . . . . V. vi. 6. 8
with soft *delight* Of sencelesse sleepe . . . . . V. vii. 12. 5
Well solast in that Souldans late *delight*, ... V. ix. 3. 2
by him begot in loves *delight* . . . . . V. ix. 31. 5
change of love for any worlds *delight*! . . . . . V. xi. 62. 5
nigh ravisht with rare thoughts *delight*, ... VI. Pr. 1. 6
more meete . . . for loves *delight*, ... VI. ii. 18. 2
my most *delight* hath alwaies been To hunt . . . . . VI. ii. 31. 6
Whereat Sir Calidore did much *delight*, ... VI. ii. 36. 6
Joying together in unblam'd *delight*; . . . . . VI. ii. 43. 3
To solace with his Lady in *delight*: . . . . . VI. iii. 20. 4
troubled had their quiet loves *delight*: . . . . . VI. iii. 21. 5
divers flowres distinct with rare *delight*, ... VI. iii. 23. 5
Him seem'd his feet did fly and in their speed *delight*. . . . . VI. iv. 19. 9
Of warres *delight* and worlds contentious toyle, ... VI. v. 37. 6
Subdue desire, and bridle loose *delight*; . . . . . VI. vi. 14. 6
cowardize doth still in villany *delight*. . . . . VI. vi. 26. 9
In doing gentle deedes with franke *delight*, ... VI. vii. 1. 2
so would ever live, and love her owne *delight*. . . . . VI. vii. 30. 9
gan to bud, and bloosme *delight*, ... VI. viii. 20. 2
For love in soft *delight* thereon to rest; . . . . . VI. viii. 42. 3
Those daintie parts, the dearlings of *delight*, ... VI. viii. 43. 1
Would never more *delight* in painted show Of such false blisse, VI. x. 3. 7
by natures skill Devized to worke *delight* . . . . . VI. x. 5. 7
to serve to all *delight*, ... VI. x. 8. 2
All raunged in a ring and dauncing in *delight*. . . . . VI. x. 11. 9
Those were the Graces, daughters of *delight*, ... VI. x. 15. 1
with *delight* his greedy fancy fed . . . . . VI. x. 30. 4
what through wonder, and what through *delight*. . . . . VI. xi. 13. 7
In much *delight*, and many joyes among, ... VI. xii. 11. 8
So much *delight* to bathe her limbes she tooke: . . . . . VII. vi. 54. 4
might *delight* the smell, or please the view, ... VII. vii. 10. 5
all the gods were ravisht with *delight* . . . . . VII. vii. 12. 8
waves, through which he waded for his loves *delight*. . . . . VII. vii. 33. 9
In planting eeke he took no small *delight*. . . . . VII. vii. 40. 6
all that moveth doth in Change *delight*: . . . . . VII. viii. 2. 6
Doth seeme to promise hope of new *delight*: . . . . . *Am.* iv. 2
Through sweet illusion of her lookes *delight*; . . . . . *Am.* xvi. 4
take *delight* t' encrease a wretches woe; . . . . . *Am.* xli. 7
Ne ought for fayrer weathers false *delight*. . . . . *Am.* lix. 8
chaunge old yeares annoy to new *delight*. . . . . *Am.* lxii. 14
a rest; Whose least *delight* sufficeth . . . . . *Am.* lxiii. 11
my fraile fancy, fed with full *delight*, ... *Am.* lxxii. 9
he there may learne, with rare *delight*, ... *Am.* lxxiii. 11
The neast of love, the lodging of *delight*, ... *Am.* lxxvi. 2
In her unspotted pleasauns to *delight*. . . . . *Am.* lxxxviii. 12
The well of deare *delight*. . . . . *Epig.* iv. 48
Pay to her usury of long *delight*: . . . . . *Epith.* 33
Come now, ye damzels, daughters of *delight*, ... *Epith.* 96
sing the thing that mote thy mind *delight*, ... *Epith.* 123
the Damzels doe *delite* When they their tymbrels smyte, . . . *Epith.* 133
To filch away sweet snatches of *delight*, ... *Epith.* 362
the sweet pleasures of theyr loves *delight* . . . . . *Epith.* 401
Fayre Venice, flower of the last worlds *delight*; . . . . . *Com. Son.* iv. 10
in their roring taking great *delight*; . . . . . *H.L.* 48
Turning all loves *delight* to miserie, ... *H.L.* 269
all *delight* and joyous happie rest, ... *H.L.* 281
Mother of love, and of all worlds *delight*, ... *H.B.* 16
The duller earth it quickneth with *delight*, ... *H.B.* 51
Their fleshly bowre, most fit for their *delight*, ... *H.B.* 123
doth the world with her *delight* adorne, ... *H.B.* 151
in deare loves *delight* . . . . . *H.B.* 233
A thousand Graces masking in *delight*; . . . . . *H.B.* 254
That in no earthly thing thou shalt *delight*, ... *H.H.L.* 272
The hearts of men, which . . . feed on vaine *delight*, ... *H.H.B.* 17
bereave Their soule of sense, through infinite *delight*, ... *H.H.B.* 258
That in nought else on earth they can *delight*, ... *H.H.B.* 283
two faire Brides, their Loves *delight*; . . . . . *Proth.* 176

Delightful. There was no pleasure nor *delightfull* play, . . . *As.* 29
goodly galleries . . . Full of faire windowes and *delightful* bowres: . . . . . I. iv. 4. 8
made *delightfull* musick all the way, ... I. xii. 7. 5
out of his *delightfull* dreame The man awoke, ... II. v. 37. 1
with *delightfull* sport To loose her warlike limbs . . . . . III. i. 52. 4
All that in this *delightfull* Gardin growes . . . . . III. vi. 41. 2
feed her fancy with *delightfull* chaunge: . . . . . III. vii. 50. 3
The onely pleasant and *delightfull* place . . . . . IV. x. 21. 4
Delightfull bowres, to solace lovers trew; . . . . . IV. x. 24. 7
ought to heare that mote *delightfull* bee: . . . . . V. vi. 21. 2
In this *delightfull* land of Faery, ... VI. Pr. 1. 2
So downe he sate, and with *delightfull* pleasure . . . . . VI. iii. 22. 7
Layes of sweete love and youthes *delightfull* heat: . . . . . VI. ix. 4. 4
Full of *delightfull* health and lively joy, ... VII. vii. 46. 8

Delighting. *Delighting* all in armes and cruell warre, ... II. vi. 37. 6

Delights. To other *delights* they would encline: . . . . . *S.C.* F. 60
Shepheards *delights* he dooth them all forsweare; . . . . . *S.C.* Ap. 13
In such *delights* did joy . . . . . *S.C.* Jun. 35
draweth newe *delightes* with hoary heares. . . . . *S.C.* Jun. 40
loatheth sike *delightes* as thou doest prayse: . . . . . *S.C.* N. 18
'Adieu, *delightes*, that lulled me asleepe; . . . . . *S.C.* D. 151
who such sports and sweet *delights* doth blame, ... *Gn.* 7
Delights (with Phoebus friendly leave) . . . . . *Gn.* 52
In such *delights* whilst thus his carelesse time . . . . . *Gn.* 153
Delights of life, and ornaments of light! . . . . . *Hub.* 762
To such *delights* the noble wits he led . . . . . *Hub.* 821
fruitles follies and unsound *delights*. . . . . *Hub.* 823
Where be the sweete *delights* of learnings treasure . . . . . *T.M.* 175

Delights—*Continued.*
gentle mindes with lewd *delights* distaine; . . . . . *T.M.* 334
Full of sweete flowres and daintiest *delights*, ... *Ti.* 520
Nor the ranke grassie fennes *delights* untride. . . . . *Mui.* 156
T' excell the naturall with made *delights*; . . . . . *Mui.* 166
faire Damsels! Shepheards dere *delights*, ... *D.* 526
With like *delightes* . . . delay The rugged brow . . . . . *Ded. Son.* i. 11
dwel . . . gentle Nymphes, *delights* of learned wits; . . . . *Ded. Son.* v. 10
To sing his sweet *delights* in lowlie laies; . . . . . *Ded. Son.* xv. 7
In these and like *delightes* of bloody game . . . . . I. vi. 29. 1
His deare *delights* were hable to annoy: . . . . . I. xii. 41. 4
To slug in slouth and sensuall *delights*, ... II. i. 23. 3
with vaine *delightes*, And ydle pleasures . . . . . II. v. 27. 2
strove with most *delights* Him to aggrate, ... II. v. 33. 1
his eyes and sences fed With false *delights*, ... II. vi. 14. 2
drowne in dissolute *delights* apart, ... II. vi. 25. 7
Diverse *delights* they fownd them selves to please; . . . . . II. ix. 35. 1
Foolish *delights*, and fond abusions, ... II. xi. 11. 8
Where Pleasure dwelles in sensuall *delights*, ... II. xii. 1. 8
spent their looser daies in leud *delightes*, ... II. xii. 9. 5
all that might . . . entyse To her *delights* . . . . . II. xii. 66. 8
'The donghill kinde *Delightes* in filth . . . . . II. xii. 87. 7
with amorous *delights* And pleasing toyes . . . . . III. x. 8. 1
darted forth *delights* the which her goodly graced. . . . . IV. x. 50. 9
The royall banquets, and the rare *delights*, ... V. iii. 3. 5
With all deare delices and rare *delights*, ... V. iii. 40. 4
Mongst these sterne stounds to mingle soft *delights*; . . . . VII. vi. 37. 4
she, . . . *Delights* not in my merth, nor rues my smart: . . . *Am.* liv. 10
With many deare *delights* bedecked fyne. . . . . *Am.* lxxi. 12
Accompanyde with angelick *delightes*. . . . . *Am.* lxxxiii. 8
Now ceasse, ye damsels, your *delights* fore-past; . . . . . *Epith.* 296
images . . . Whose wondrous beauty, breathing sweet *delights* *H.H.B.* 4

Deliver. Parents deare from tyrants powre *deliver* might. . . I. vii. 46. 9
Till he these wordes to him *deliver* might: . . . . . I. ix. 23. 6
I will, . . . *Deliver* her fro thence, ... III. xi. 18. 9
Deliver hence out of this dungeon strong, ... IV. xii. 9. 4
bad *Deliver* him his owne, ... V. xi. 3. 8
alive or dead Her foe *deliver* up into her hand: . . . . . VI. i. 31. 6
Deliver from the doome of my desart, ... VI. viii. 19. 6

Deliverance. sorie bee For my *deliverance*, ... *D.* 279
For whose *deliverance* she this Prince doth thither guyd. . . . I. viii. 1. 9
Then meanes I gan devise for his *deliveraunce*. . . . . II. i. 54. 9
meane of your *deliverance* have beene. . . . . III. xii. 40. 5
his large paines in her *deliveraunce* . . . . . VI. iii. 19. 4

Delivered. safe *delivered* from sad decay, ... *Gn.* 335
delivered unto me By Romane Victors, ... *Ti.* 37
calling . . . A diverse Dreame . . . *Delivered* it to him, . . . I. i. 44. 3
streight *deliver'd* to a Fary knight, ... I. ix. 3. 8
As she to me *delivered* all that night; . . . . . I. ix. 14. 8
Delivered up the Lord of life to dye, ... II. vii. 62. 6
As it *delivered* was from hond to hond: . . . . . II. ix. 60. 5
Of her fayre twins was there *delivered*, ... II. xii. 13. 6
But unto her *delivered* Florimell: . . . . . IV. xii. 33. 2
Till he to her *delivered* had his shield, ... V. v. 16. 8
Kept and *delivered* me from deadly dread. . . . . VI. v. 29. 5
the former token Which faire Serene to him *delivered* had, . . VI. vi. 18. 2
Till that he him *delivered* to his punishment. . . . . VI. vii. 21. 9
Delivered hath into your hands by gift, ... VI. viii. 1. 5
Which she . . . *Delivered* to her handmayd, ... VI. xii. 6. 8

Delivers. Guyon . . . *Delivers* Phaon, ... II. iv. Arg.

Dell. Fell headlong into a *dell*, ... *S.C.* Mar. 51
all the moore twixt Elversham and *Dell*, ... II. x. 24. 4

Delos. 'As th' Isle of *Delos* whylome, ... II. xii. 13. 1

Delt. *See* **Dealt.**

Deluce. *See* **Fleur-de-lis.**

Delude. A fit false dreame, that can *delude* the sleepers sent.' . I. i. 43. 9
whether dreames *delude*, or true it were, ... I. ix. 14. 5

Deluded. all in rage to see his skilfull might *Deluded* so, . . . I. ii. 2. 6
halfe in rage to be *deluded* thus, ... II. xi. 38. 5
long *deluded* With idle hopes . . . . . VI. ix. 25. 1
With which his eyes mote have *deluded* beene. . . . . VI. x. 17. 7

Deluding. no *deluding* dreames, nor dreadfull sights, ... *Epith.* 338

Delve. Guyon findes Mamon in a *delve* . . . . . II. vii. Arg.
to that shady *delve* him brought at last, ... II. viii. 4. 6
In a deepe *delve*, farre from the vew of day, ... III. iii. 7. 7
It is a darksome *delve* farre under ground, ... IV. i. 20. 4

Demand. Let not my small *demaund* be so contempt. . . . . *S.C.* N. 48
Aread in graver wise what I *demaund* of thee.' . . . . . I. viii. 33. 9
to *demaund* of his renowmed guest: . . . . . I. xii. 15. 6
thy *demaund*, O Lady! doth revive Fresh memory . . . . . II. ii. 40. 1
The God did graunt his daughters deare *demaund*, ... III. iv. 22. 1
Her to *demaund* and chalenge as their rights, ... IV. v. 23. 3
He gently gan him to *demaund* of all . . . . . V. i. 23. 3
Gan to *demaund* of her some tydings good, ... V. v. 45. 2
many things *demaund*, to which she answer'd light. . . . . V. vi. 20. 9
he gan of her *demand*, What manner wight he was, ... VI. ii. 44. 2
did not his *demaund* approve, ... VI. iii. 42. 4
to *demand* What and from whence she was, ... VI. v. 27. 6
Yet could he not their just *demaund* deny, ... VI. xi. 10. 7
Him boldly answer'd thus to his *demaund*: . . . . . VII. vi. 26. 3
Of all the which *demand* in generall, ... VII. vii. 27. 5

Demanded. the cause of that outrageous deede *Demaunded*, . II. iv. 29. 7

Demands. The vaunted verse a vacant head *demaundes*, . . . *S.C.* O. 100
everie goodly meed . . . *demaunds* a day; . . . . . *Col.* 593
Demaunds a yeare it duly to display. . . . . *Col.* 595
for no *demaunds* he staide, ... VI. i. 11. 8
Ne ought *demaunds* but that we loving bee, ... *H.H.L.* 185

Demayne. *See* **Demean.**

Demean. with sorrowfull *demayne* And deadly hew, ... II. viii. 23. 7
right fayre and modest of *demayne*, ... II. ix. 40. 3

Demean—*Continued.*
then bring me newes Of his *demeane:* V. v. 51. 2
ywroken Of all the vile *demeane* and usage bad, VI. vi. 18. 4
The whiles that mighty man did her *demeane* VI. vii. 39. 4
how to each degree and kynde We should our selves *demeane,* VI. x. 23. 8
Demeaned. To quite them ill, that me *demeand* so well: *Col.* 681
Demeanor. With gentle usage and *demeanure* myld: *As.* 20
them receives a gentle Squyre, Of myld *demeanure* I. x. 7. 2
in *demeanure* sober, and in counsell sage. II. ix. 27. 9
loath'd the loose *demeanure* of that wanton sort. III. i. 40. 9
All his *demeasnure* from his sight did hide: III. ix. 27. 7
to tell The diverse usage, and *demeanure* daint, IV. i. 5. 2
when he long had marked his *demeanor,* IV. vii. 47. 1
her sad semblant and *demeanure* wyse: IV. x. 49. 6
markt her rare *demeanure,* VI. ix. 11. 2
Demeanure, Demeasnure. *See* **Demeanor.**
Demigods. *demigods* they be and first did spring From heaven, *Col.* 917
Demiss. like a most *demisse* And abject thrall, *H.H.L.* 136
Demogorgon. Where *Demogorgon* . . . The hideous Chaos keepes, IV. ii. 47. 7
Demogorgon's. Which wast begot in *Daemogorgons* hall, I. v. 22. 5
Demon. the Romaine *Daemon* Doth yet himselfe . . . enforce, *Ro.* xxvii. 12
Demonstration. by *demonstration* me to teach, *Ti.* 488
Demophoon. tree, in which *Demophoon* . . . Eternall hurte left *Gn.* 201
Dempt. *See* **Deemed.**
Never *dempt* more right of beautye, *S.C.* Au. 137
I *dempt* there much to have eeked my store, *S.C.* S. 30
partiall Paris *dempt* it Venus dew, II. vii. 55. 7
sith her dedd He surely *dempt,* III. viii. 3. 7
Aread what course of you is safest *dempt,* III. xi. 23. 3
Demure. With countenance *demure,* and modest grace, I. x. 12. 4
His countenance *demure* and temperate; II. i. 6. 2
Demurest. ungracious crew which faines *demurest* grace. VII. vii. 35. 9
Den. Safe in his dreadles *den* him thought to hide: *Van.* x. 4
ever creepe into the shepheards *den.* *Gn.* 96
Ah, wretched world! the *den* of wickednesse, *T.M.* 121
in loathsome *den* Of ghostly darkenes, *T.M.* 531
close upgathered more and more Into his *den,* *Mui.* 398
rushing with fierce might Out of his *den,* *Mui.* 435
Errours *den,* A monster vile, I. i. 13. 6
Her huge long taile her *den* all overspred, I. i. 15. 2
Their dam upstart out of her *den* effraide, I. i. 16. 1
beast . . . which he had kept long time in darksom *den.* I. vii. 16. 9
albe his drowsy *den* were next; II. vii. 25. 6
wild like beastes lurking in loathsome *den,* II. x. 7. 4
the wilde beast shall dy in starved *den.* III. iii. 34. 9
in secret *den* My Lady and my love so cruelly to pen! III. xi. 10. 8
Since I was brought into this dolefull *den;* IV. vii. 13. 3
ere unto his hellish *den* he raught, IV. vii. 31. 2
forth she past into his dreadfull *den,* IV. vii. 33. 1
There let her ever keepe her damned *den,* V. ix. 2. 3
Where she might sit nigh to the *den* alone, V. ix. 8. 7
Ere to his *den* he backward could recoyle, V. ix. 9. 4
fell Chimaera, in her darkesome *den,* VI. i. 8. 2
long in darksome Stygian *den* upbrought, VI. vi. 9. 8
every beast that to his *den* was fled, *Am.* xl. 10
Denay, -d. *See* **Deny, Denied.**
Denial. made this faire *denyall:* IV. ii. 6. 3
whom one *deniall* Excludes from fairest hope IV. x. 17. 8
it ought be rendred her without *deniall.'* V. iv. 15. 9
Denied. a Porter . . . Cald Malvenu, who entrance none *denide:* I. iv. 6. 4
That wanton Mayd of passage had *denide,* II. viii. 3. 3
entraunce crav'd which was *denied* erst. II. ix. 17. 3
The which thy proffred curtesie *denayd?* III. vii. 57. 7
love forbid him, that is life *denayd;* IV. xii. 28. 7
he entrance sought, but was *denide,* V. ii. 20. 4
let what ever he desires be him *denide.* V. v. 50. 9
Denies. *Denies* them quite for servitors of his.' *Col.* 770
Denmark. He Easterland subdewd, and *Denmarke* (*Danmark) wonne, II. x. 41. 3
Dens. Captiv'd eternally in yron mewes And darksom *dens,* II. v. 27. 9
Whylest thus she in these hellish *dens* remayned, VI. xi. 3. 1
Unto their hellish *dens* those theeves them brought; VI. xi. 41. 2
into those theevish *dens* he went, VI. xi. 51. 1
ransacke all their *dennes* from most to least, VI. xii. 24. 8
Dent. deadly *dent* The blood hath of so many thousands shedd, III. x. 32. 5
Shew'd all his bodie bare unto the cruell *dent.* IV. vi. 15. 9
Deny. (For manie did, which doo it now *denie,*) *Ti.* 235
All for she Scudamore will not *denay.* III. xi. 11. 5
to yield him love she doth *deny,* III. xi. 17. 3
these Stoicke censours cannot well *deny* IV. Pr. 3. 9
Would change with me, but I did it *denye,* V. i. 17. 3
'ye both the dead *deny,* And both the living Lady claime V. i. 26. 1
that his foe should him the field *denie,*) V. iii. 32. 4
As one that would confesse, yet faine would it *denie.* V. v. 31. 9
her Dame his freedome did *denye.* V. v. 56. 9
when as she could nought *deny,* VI. ii. 14. 1
I may not, certes, without blame *denie,* VI. ii. 34. 6
Yet could he not their just demaund *deny,* VI. xi. 10. 7
with great rage he stoutly doth *denay;* VI. xi. 15. 6
that to be My heritage Jove's selfe cannot *denie,* VII. vii. 16. 7
who can *deny* But to be subject still VII. vii. 47. 8
Great wrong I doe, I can it not *deny,* *Am.* xxxiii. 1
Denying. I die, nought to the world *denying,* *Col.* 950
Renew'd her death by timely death *denying.* VI. xi. 23. 5
Deow. *See* **Dew.**
Depainted. *See* **Depeinct, -ed.**
Hast Cupid selfe *depainted* in his kynd, *Col.* 898
That on his shield *depainted* he did see: II. v. 11. 8
Depart. now ye daintie Damsells may *depart* *S.C.* Ap. 147

Depart—*Continued.*
life out of his members did *depart:* *Gn.* 293
I now *depart,* returning to thee never, *Gn.* 634
surcease, good Dame, and hence *depart.'* *Hub.* 1221
' "I . . . must needes *depart* from thee, *D.* 269
to your rest *depart.'* I. i. 54. 5
Doth license him *depart* at sound of morning droome.' I. ix. 41. 9
when the carle . . . saw his guest Would safe *depart,* I. ix. 54. 3
Depart to woods untoucht, and leave so proud disdayne.' II. iii. 43. 9
Let us soone hence *depart.'* II. iii. 46. 2
ever her desired to *depart.* II. vi. 26. 7
Besought that Damzell suffer him *depart,* II. vi. 36. 8
quart, Which Severne now from Logris doth *depart:* II. x. 14. 5
let us hence *depart* whilest wether serves and winde.' II. xii. 87. 9
depart From course of nature III. ii. 41. 7
nought but death her dolour mote *depart.* III. iv. 6. 5
I lately did *depart* From Faery court, III. v. 4. 3
that lewd lover did the most lament For her *depart,* III. vii. 20. 2
His sonne Iulus did from thence *depart* III. ix. 43. 5
Forthy from that same rowme not to *depart* Till morrow III. xii. 28. 3
Thence to *depart* for further aide t' enquire: III. xii. 45. 8
Thence to *depart* with glee and gladsome chere. IV. iii. 51. 3
doth fall in love, And soone from her *depart.* IV. vi. Arg.
Fit time for him thence to *depart* it found, IV. vi. 42. 4
wonne her will to suffer him *depart;* IV. vi. 43. 2
He seeing her *depart* arose up light, IV. vii. 37. 1
Yet taking leave of her he did *depart.* V. vi. 24. 4
Did enter in, ne would that night *depart;* V. vii. 3. 8
never doth from doome of right *depart,* V. x. 2. 7
To weet the cause . . . And to *depart* them, VI. ii. 4. 5
through the wound his spirit shortly did *depart.'* VI. ii. 12. 9
And Calidore betooke him to *depart,* VI. ii. 36. 2
Whom when her Host saw readie to *depart,* VI. v. 8. 1
with him eke the salvage, . . . Would needes *depart;* VI. v. 41. 9
So oft as homeward I from her *depart,* *Am.* lii. 1
Ne ought for tempest doth from it *depart,* *Am.* lix. 7
Departed. he heavily *departed* With piteous crie, *Gn.* 639
Departed to his home in dreadfull awe, *Hub.* 1109
she found the Faery knight *Departed* thence; I. v. 45. 4
the Redcrosse knight he understands To beene *departed* II. i. 1. 5
Departed thence with full contented mynd; IV. ii. 53. 2
departed thence with speed, And follow'd them, IV. v. 28. 2
Soone as they thence *departed* were afore, IV. viii. 35. 1
Departed straight to Proteus therewithall; IV. xii. 32. 7
'him soone to overtake That hence so long *departed,* V. i. 19. 4
Departed from the Castle of the Strond V. iv. 3. 5
Artegall . . . *Departed* on his way, V. iv. 20. 8
So she *departed* full of griefe and sdaine, V. v. 51. 6
so would have *departed* on their way; V. ix. 3. 6
till that her syre *Departed* life, VI. xii. 10. 3
Departing. My Daphne hence *departing* bad me so; *D.* 454
The feeble soule *departing* hence away. I. x. 41. 5
Great thankes . . . He thens *departing* gave for his paynes hyre I. x. 68. 5
From the *departing* land it launched light, II. xii. 15. 8
that sweet bird *departing* flew forthright, IV. viii. 8. 7
Departs. with them all *departes* to tell his great distresse. I. vii. 19. 9
Departure. For her *departure,* had no word to say; *Ti.* 474
Since whose *departure,* day is turnd to night, *D.* 482
desirous was Of his *departure* thence; II. vi. 37. 2
when of his *departure* she despayrd, II. x. 30. 8
offended That his *departure* thence should be so short, IV. xii. 18. 4
For his *departure,* her new cause of griefe: V. vii. 44. 2
Depasturing. Or greedily *depasturing* delight; II. xii. 73. 4
Depeinct. In either cheeke *depeincten* lively chere: *S.C.* Ap. 69
Depeincted. *See* **Depainted.**
On which the winged boy in colours cleare *Depeincted* was, III. xi. 7. 8
Depend. As on your boughes the ysicles *depend.* *S.C.* Ja. 42
Most wretched men, whose dayes *depend* on thrids so vaine! IV. ii. 48. 9
more on him doth then him selfe *depend:* VI. viii. 17. 8
They all are Graces which on her *depend,* VI. x. 21. 6
About him wait, and on his will *depend,* *H.H.L.* 65
Depended. such, as he *depended* most upon; *Hub.* 818
dangerous successe *depended* yet in doubt: IV. ix. 24. 9
Dependent. sleeves *dependaunt* Albanese-wyse: III. xii. 10. 4
Depending. craggie clift *Depending* from on high, II. xii. 4. 3
Twixt feare and hope *depending* doubtfully! *Am.* xxv. 4
Depends. The cause of both, of both their minds *depends,* IV. iv. 1. 4
Deplore. thy lost deare love *deplore.* *Ti.* 250
left me here his losse for to *deplore.* *Ti.* 658
my fortune to *deplore;* *D.* 475
Seemed some great misfortune to *deplore,* II. xii. 27. 8
my hard fortune to *deplore,* And languish, III. ii. 39. 7
His hard mishap in dolor to *deplore,* IV. vii. 39. 7
Unto the wyld wood ranne, her dolours to *deplore.* V. viii. 48. 9
As if she did some great calamitie *deplore.* V. ix. 8. 9
his daies there to *deplore.* V. xi. 14. 9
Let them that list their lucklesse lot *deplore,* VI. vii. 30. 7
Deposed. nought him griev'd to beene from rule *deposed* downe. II. x. 29. 9
Deposed was from princedome soverayne, II. x. 44. 5
Deprave. With minde that ill use doth before *deprave,* *Gn.* 91
How to *deprave* and slaunderously upbrayd, V. xii. 34. 3
doth *deprave* My simple meaning *Am.* xxix. 1
every one doth seeke but to *deprave* it. *H.B.* 154
Depraves. pryde *depraves* each other better part, *Am.* xxxi. 3
Depravest. 'Lewdly thou my love *depravest,* V. vii. 32. 8
Deprive. therefore, of life him not *deprive.'* I. iii. 37. 9
Of endlesse life he might him not *deprive,* I. v. 40. 4
men of happinesse *deprive.* III. iv. 57. 9
of comfort him thou shalt *deprive,* III. v. 26. 8
By treacherous deceipt did me *deprive:* III. x. 27. 5

Deprive—*Continued.*
each of life sought others to *deprive*, ... IV. i. 23. 8
with blame would blot, and of due praise *deprive*. . . . . IV. viii. 25. 9
Out of their wretched corses, and their lives *deprive*. . . . . IV. ix. 22. 9
all, in his revenge, of spirite would *deprive*. . . . . V. vii. 36. 9
how for to *depryve* Mercilla of her crowne, ... V. ix. 41. 6
When her that Tyrant did of Crowne *deprive;* . . . . . V. xi. 38. 4
Whom though high Jove of kingdome did *deprive*, ... VII. vi. 2. 8
to *deprive* Remembrance of all paines . . . . . *Am.* lxiii. 11
Deprived. *Depriv'd* of sense and ordinarie reason, ... *Hub.* 11
men *depriv'd* of sense and minde. . . . . *T.M.* 156
of all happines hath us *deprived*. . . . . *Mui.* 416
Did fall to ground, *depriv'd* of native might: . . . . . I. viii. 10. 7
Whom that mad man of life nigh late *deprivd*, ... II. iv. 16. 3
depriv'd Of native strength . . . . . II. ix. 57. 4
them of their unjust possession *depriv'd*. . . . . II. x. 9. 9
he was by Jove *depryv'd* Of life . . . . . II. x. 70. 8
were *depriv'd* Of their proud beautie, ... II. xii. 31. 3
deemd the beast had bene *depriv'd* Of life, ... III. v. 37. 4
as one nigh of her wits *depriv'd*, ... III. vii. 14. 5
Wherewith she many had of life *depriv'd;* . . . . . III. vii. 40. 2
himselfe he thought *depriv'd* Quite of all hope . . . . . III. viii. 3. 7
Depriv'd of kindly joy and naturall delight . . . . . III. ix. 5. 9
In whom he liv'd anew, of former life *deprived*. . . . . IV. iii. 13. 9
like one that hopelesse was *depryv'd* . . . . . V. iv. 35. 1
It had *depriv'd* her mother of a daughter: . . . . . V. iv. 41. 7
Whereof that Tyrant had her now *deprived*, ... V. x. 18. 3
Depth. May reach from hence to *depth* of darkest hell, ... *Ro.* i. 6
depth exceeded not three cubits hight, ... II. xii. 62. 6
Was drowned in *depth* of deadly sleepe; . . . . . III. i. 59. 3
Thinking to hide the *depth* by troubling of the flood. . . . . IV. vi. 29. 9
Alebius, that know'th The waters *depth*, ... IV. xi. 14. 8
all the *depth* of rightfull doome was taught . . . . . V. i. 5. 3
durst the *depth* of any water sownd. . . . . V. ii. 16. 7
Whose counsels *depth* thou canst not understand; . . . . . V. ii. 42. 7
A dreadfull *depth;* how deepe no man can tell, ... V. ix. 6. 4
Now drowned in the *depth* of sleepe all fearelesse lay. . . . . VI. viii. 36. 9
What . . . thought can think the *depth* of so deare wound? . *H.H.L.* 163
Deraign. they gan . . . Redoubted battaile ready to *darrayne*, I. iv. 40. 2
Did to him pace sad battaile to *darrayne*, ... I. vii. 11. 5
to *darraine* A triple warre with triple enmitee, ... II. ii. 26. 2
six knights, that did *darrayne* Fiers battaill against one . . . III. i. 20. 8
Unable he new battell to *darraine*, ... IV. iv. 26. 7
readie were new battell to *darraine*. . . . . IV. v. 24. 6
how best he mote *darrayne* That enterprize . . . . . IV. ix. 4. 4
And dreadfull battaile twixt them do *darraine:* . . . . . V. ii. 15. 5
In which they two the combat might *darraine*. . . . . V. xii. 9. 4
those old Gyants, which did warres *darraine* . . . . . VI. vii. 41. 6
Der-doing. in *der-doing* armes . . . my vowed daies do spend, II. vii. 10. 1
Deride. vertue to advaunce, and vice *deride*, ... *Hub.* 812
all men him uncased gan *deride*, ... *Hub.* 930
makes wrong doers justice to *deride*, ... V. iv. 1. 7
Thy courteous lore, that doest my love *deride*, ... VI. i. 27. 8
Did laugh at her that many did *deride*, ... VI. vii. 32. 4
Derive. Whose lignage from this Lady I *derive* along. . . . . III. iv. 3. 9
'From him my linage I *derive* aright, ... III. ix. 36. 1
from great Neptune do *derive* their parentage. . . . . IV. xi. 17. 9
That she might it unto her selfe *deryve*, ... V. ix. 41. 8
Derived. her dew loves *deryv'd* to that vile witches shayre. . I. iii. 2. 9
Honour and dignitie from her alone *Derived* are, ... II. vii. 48. 8
old records from auncient times *derivd*, ... II. ix. 57. 7
though from earth it be *derived* right . . . . . II. x. 2. 4
From this renowmed Prince *derived* arre, ... II. x. 4. 2
Brutus, anciently *deriv'd* From roiall stocke . . . . . II. x. 9. 6
A man, of many parts from beasts *deryv'd*, ... II. x. 70. 6
What mister wight that was, and whence *deriv'd*, ... III. vii. 14. 2
branches . . . from one roote *deriv'd* their vitall sap: . . . . . IV. ii. 43. 6
through traduction was eftsoones *derived*, ... IV. iii. 13. 6
the band Of noble minds *derived* from above, ... IV. vi. 31. 8
Return'd to heaven, whence she *deriv'd* her race; . . . . . V. i. 11. 4
Up to the skies, whence first *deriv'd* it was, ... V. x. 3. 4
being *derived* at furst From heavenly seedes . . . . . VI. Pr. 3. 6
From my great Grandsire Titan unto mee *Deriv'd* . . . . . VII. vii. 16. 9
Of Helicon, whence she *derived* is; . . . . . *Am.* i. 10
From mothers womb *deriv'd* by dew descent: . . . . . *Am.* lxxiv. 6
Deriv'd from that fayre Spirit, ... *Am.* lxxix. 11
titles vaine, *Derived* farre from famous Auncestrie: . . . . . *Com. Son.* ii. 4
the soule, the which *derived* was, ... *H.B.* 106
Together with that third from them *derived*, ... *H.H.L.* 38
Derives. Whence all the world *derives* the glorious Features of beautie, ... III. vi. 12. 3
Dernly. breaking foorth at last, thus *dearnelie* plained: . . . *D.* 196
a ruefull voice, that *dearnly* cride . . . . . II. i. 35. 7
whylome full *dernly* tryde. . . . . III. i. 14. 4
Dernly unto her called to abstaine . . . . . III. xii. 34. 4
Derth. *See* **Dearth.**
Derring do. who in *derring-doe* were dreade, ... *S.C.* O. 65
in *derring-doe* compare With shepheards swayne . . . . . *S.C.* D. 43
Drad for his *derring doe* and bloody deed; . . . . . II. iv. 42. 3
Renowmed much in armes and *derring-doe;* . . . . . VI. v. 37. 4
Derring doers. All mightie men and dreadfull *derring-dooers*, IV. ii. 38. 3
Desart, -s. *See* **Desert, -s.**
Descant. the Mavis *descant* playes: . . . . . *Epith.* 81
Descend. a tempest from the heaven *descend*, ... *Bel.*[2] iii. 13
from mine eyes the drizling teares *descend*, ... *S.C.* Ja. 41
see The blessed Angels to and fro *descend* . . . . . I. x. 56. 2
'Renowmed kings . . . shall from thee *descend;* . . . . . III. iii. 23. 2
From whence *descend* all hopelesse remedies: . . . . . III. v. 34. 5
From whom I Paridell by kin *descend:* . . . . . III. ix. 37. 6
downe *descend* unto the base: . . . . . V. ix. 16. 7

Descend—*Continued.*
Sir Artegall with that old knight Did forth *descend*, ... V. xii. 6. 2
Boldly she bid the Goddesse downe *descend*, ... VII. vi. 11. 1
Descended. erst *descended* from the Trojan bloud. . . . . *Bel.*[1] v. 8
descended Downe from the mountaines . . . . . *Bel.*[2] vi. 9
Descended all from Rome by linage due; . . . . . *Gn.* 596
deep *descended* through the hollow grownd, ... II. vii. 20. 8
mace . . . *descended* farre From mighty kings . . . . . II. x. 4. 4
In hast she from her lofty chaire *descended*, ... IV. iii. 50. 2
Into the Martian field adowne *descended* . . . . . IV. v. 6. 8
His soule *descended* downe into the Stygian reame. . . . . IV. viii. 45. 9
with such monstrous poise adowne *descended*, ... V. xii. 21. 3
he was *descended* of the hous Of those old Gyants, ... VI. vii. 41. 5
The which *descended* with such dreadfull sway, ... VI. viii. 8. 4
downe to them *descended* in that earthy vew. . . . . VI. ix. 8. 9
He downe *descended*, . . . in fleshes fraile attyre, ... *H.H.L.* 136
this noble Lord . . . *Descended* to the Rivers open vewing, . . *Proth.* 166
Descendeth. *Descendeth* garnisht as a loved spouse. . . . . *Rev.* iv. 4
Descending. An Angell then *descending* downe from Heaven, . *Rev.* ii. 12
birdes from aire *descending* downe on earth . . . . . *Rev.* iii. 9
Two Angels, downe *descending* with swift flight, ... *Ti.* 625
From heaven *descending* to appease their strife, ... *Ti.* 667
down *descending*, he along would flie . . . . . *Mui.* 46
forth *descending* to that perlous porch . . . . . III. xii. 42. 6
descending backe in haste he sought If yet he were alive, . . VI. vi. 37. 8
Descends. an entraunce . . . *Descends* to hell: . . . . . I. v. 31. 6
even as his right hand adowne *descends*, ... VI. viii. 49. 2
Descent. farre abroad through each *descent;* . . . . . *Gn.* 77
till that he came with steep *descent* . . . . . *Hub.* 1260
For honor of your name and high *descent*. . . . . *Ded. Son.* x. 14
by *descent* from Royall lynage came . . . . . I. i. 5. 3
arrogant delight Of th' high *descent* whereof he was yborne, I. vii. 10. 2
his foot could find no flore, But all a deepe *descent*, ... I. viii. 39. 8
Ne that approcheth nigh the wyde *descent*, ... II. xii. 6. 8
What boots it boast thy glorious *descent*, ... III. ix. 33. 6
of them sprung by lineall *descent:* . . . . . IV. xi. 12. 7
a daughter by *descent* Of those old Titans . . . . . VII. vi. 2. 5
unto mee Deriv'd by dew *descent;* . . . . . VII. vii. 16. 9
From mothers womb deriv'd by dew *descent:* . . . . . *Am.* lxxiv. 6
first *descent* Out of their heavenly bowres. . . . . *H.B.* 201
Descents. Even thrise eleven *descents* the crowne retaynd, . . II. x. 45. 8
all their Ofspring, in their dew *descents;* . . . . . II. x. 74. 2
Thou doest effect in destined *descents*, ... III. iii. 2. 6
Describe. earthly tong Cannot *describe*, ... I. x. 55. 6
Long were it to *describe* the goodly frame, ... III. i. 31. 1
Described. *Described* by that famous Tuscane penne: . . . . . IV. iii. 45. 4
Great Venus Temple is *describ'd;* . . . . . IV. x. Arg.
She then . . . Him thus *describ'd;* . . . . . VI. ii. 44. 6
By many signes which she *described* had, ... VI. ii. 45. 2
Had in his *Plaint of kinde describ'd* it well: . . . . . VII. vii. 9. 7
Describeth. Redcrosse knight to Britomart *Describeth* Artegall: . III. ii. Arg.
Descried. Lest he should be *descried* by his trayne. . . . . *S.C.* May 281
they gan to be *descryed* Of everie one, ... *Hub.* 345
they were *descride* At length . . . . . *Hub.* 920
through the gard, which never him *descride*, ... *Hub.* 1301
not so secret, but it was *descride*, ... *Col.* 146
at length we land far off *descryde;* . . . . . *Col.* 265
those wretches which I there *descryde*.' . . . . . *Col.* 675
death ensewd if any him *descryde*. . . . . I. v. 52. 9
sober lookes her wisedome well *descryde:* . . . . . I. x. 34. 3
he from far *descryde* Those glistring armes . . . . . I. xi. 4. 7
be safe from daunger far *descryde*. . . . . I. xi. 5. 4
he *descryde* and shonned still his slight: . . . . . II. i. 4. 8
reason, blent through passion, nought *descryde;* . . . . . II. iv. 7. 7
Worse is the daunger hidden then *descride*. . . . . II. xii. 35. 5
The doubtfull Mayd, seeing her selfe *descryde*, ... III. iii. 20. 1
she, having him *descryde*, Her selfe to fight addrest, . . . III. vii. 38. 8
To save his life, ne let him be *descryde*, ... III. x. 50. 8
th' one of them he perfectly *descride* To be Sir Scudamour, . . IV. i. 39. 1
Sent forth their Squire to have them both *descride*, ... IV. iv. 2. 8
In quyent disguise, full hard to be *descride:* . . . . . IV. iv. 39. 3
soone as them approaching he *descride*, ... IV. vi. 2. 7
they plaine *descryde* To be the same . . . . . IV. vi. 9. 4
he plaine *descride* That peerelesse paterne . . . . . IV. vi. 24. 4
Him seeking evermore, yet no where him *descride*. . . . . IV. viii. 18. 9
Ne ever from the day the night *descride*, ... IV. xi. 4. 8
he plainely then *descride* To be a troupe of women, ... V. iv. 21. 7
by the watchman were *Descried* streight; . . . . . V. iv. 36. 2
ere him she plaine *descride*, ... V. vi. 8. 3
A tall young man, . . . as well he him *descryde*, ... VI. ii. 3. 8
As well may be in Calidore *descryde*, ... VI. iii. 2. 3
By certaine signes he plainly him *descryde* . . . . . VI. iii. 47. 4
kept aloofe for dread to be *descryde*, ... VI. vii. 3. 3
For dread of them unwares to be *descryde*, ... VI. x. 11. 2
Descrive. How shall frayle pen *descrive* her heavenly face, . II. iii. 25. 8
this mothers joy *descrive;* . . . . . VI. xii. 21. 4
Descry. *See* **Scried.**
Such would *descrie* his lewd conditions; . . . . . *Hub.* 796
so wise . . . As to *discry* the crafty cunning traine, ... I. vii. 1. 2
all so soyld that none could him *descry:* . . . . . II. iv. 37. 7
A darkesome way, which no man could *descry*, ... II. vii. 20. 7
'Lo! I the land *descry;* . . . . . II. xii. 10. 8
by the checked wave they did *descry* It plaine, ... II. xii. 18. 7
shortly gan *descry* The land . . . . . II. xii. 34. 3
when her wayes he could no more *descry*, ... III. iv. 53. 1
she did *descry* A little smoke, ... III. vii. 5. 1
Expecting . . . when some foe she might *descry*. . . . . III. xi. 1. 9
did *descrie* His fickle mind . . . . . IV. i. 32. 4
So blind is lust false colours to *descry*. . . . . IV. ii. 11. 5
She through his late disguizement could him not *descrie!* . IV. v. 29. 9

Descry—*Continued.*
these, which I *descry,* . . . IV. xi. 53. 4
further right by tokens to *descrie,* . . . V. iii. 32. 5
who he was uneath was to *descry;* . . . V. iv. 22. 6
To weete if shipping readie he mote there *descry.* . . . V. xii. 3. 9
one might *descry* The bloudie gore . . . V. xii. 30. 8
He could no path nor tract of foot *descry,* . . . VI. iv. 24. 6
O what an easie thing is to *descry* The gentle bloud, . . . VI. v. 1. 1
In lieu whereof he would to him *descrie* Great treason . . . VI. vii. 12. 3
that none Mote them *descry,* . . . VI. x. 41. 4
That could not any creature well *descry;* . . . VII. vii. 5. 7
Most goodly temperature ye may *descry;* . . . *Am.* xiii. 4
I doe at length *descry* the happy shore, . . . *Am.* lxiii. 5

Desert. We deeme of Death as doome of ill *desert;* . . . *S.C.* N. 184
everie where through excellent *desart.* . . . *Ti.* 343
When ye doo heare me in that *desert* place . . . *D.* 508
Wearie your selves in wandring *desert* wayes, . . . *D.* 534
made me in that *desart* chose to dwell. . . . *Col.* 91
For high *desert,* advaunst to that degree. . . . *Col.* 527
Ay wont in *desert* darknes to remaine, . . . I. i. 16. 8
Then brought she me into this *desert* waste, . . . I. ii. 42. 6
By dew *desert* of noble chevalree, . . . I. xii. 20. 8
without *desert* of gentle deed And noble worth, . . . II. iii. 10. 6
T' adorne thy forme according thy *desart,* . . . II. iv. 26. 2
nought but *desert* wildernesse shewed all around. . . . II. vii. 2. 9
That here in *desert* hast thine habitaunce, . . . II. vii. 7. 2
dye with honour and *desert* of fame; . . . II. viii. 44. 5
fog over-spred With his dull vapour all that *desert* . . . II. xi. 34. 6
to all high *desert* and honour doth aspire. . . . III. v. 1. 9
so disloyally Deeme of her high *desert,* . . . III. v. 45. 7
She grew familiare in that *desert* place. . . . III. vii. 15. 5
To leave that *desert* mansion, . . . III. vii. 18. 2
Lesse she thee lov'd then was thy just *desart,* . . . III. xi. 36. 8
for your *desart* Good lucke presents you with yond lovely mayd, . . . IV. i. 33. 7
What vengeance due can equall thy *desart,* . . . IV. i. 53. 3
seemed some blacksmith dwelt in that *desert* ground. . . . IV. v. 33. 9
as through a *desert* wyld We travelled, . . . IV. vi. 36. 1
Backe to that *desert* forrest they retyred, . . . IV. vi. 47. 1
The Gate of Good *Desert,* . . . IV. x. 16. 2
The meede of his *desert* for that despight, . . . VI. ii. 45. 8
though he were still in this *desert* wood, . . . VI. v. 2. 2
Amongst wilde beastes in *desert* forrests bred, . . . VI. v. 29. 7
Deliver from the doome of my *desart,* . . . VI. viii. 19. 6
thee, O Jove! no equall Judge I deeme Of my *desert,* . . . VII. vi. 35. 2
But not to deeme of her *desert* aspyre. . . . *Am.* lxxxiv. 8

Deserts. Through due *deserts* and comely carriage, . . . *Hub.* 777
none of all their due *deserts* resoundest.' . . . *Col.* 463
she . . . In wildernesse and wastfull *deserts* strayd, . . . I. iii. 3. 4
Long she thus traveiled through *deserts* wyde, . . . I. iii. 10. 1
not regard dew right and just *desarts?* . . . II. ii. 29. 7
Thre hundred pledges for my good *desartes,* . . . III. vii. 55. 4
In salvage forrests and in *deserts* wide . . . IV. vii. 2. 6
oft their lewdnes blotteth good *deserts* with blame. . . . V. iii. 38. 9
of malice, without her *desarts,* . . . VI. v. 33. 7
In these wylde *deserts* where she now abode, . . . VI. viii. 35. 1
by right *deserts,* t' attaine, Unto the type of true Nobility; . *Com. Son.* ii. 1

Deserve. doth *deserve* to have small faults remitted, . . . *Gn.* 474
Good garments for their service should *deserve;* . . . *Hub.* 468
should not *deserve* to weare A garment better . . . *Hub.* 473
land and sea my Cynthia doth *deserve* . . . *Col.* 262
I of gentle Mayds should ill *deserve!* . . . *Col.* 465
if I all should praise as they *deserve,* . . . *Col.* 578
Ne did it then *deserve* a name to have, . . . II. x. 6. 1
ever doe that mote *deserven* blame: . . . III. ii. 10. 3
Thy life she gave, thy life she doth *deserve;* . . . III. v. 46. 8
Did aske me, how I could her love *deserve,* . . . III. vii. 53. 8
that could *deserve* No spot of blame, . . . IV. i. 4. 7
she most fit his service doth *deserve,* . . . IV. v. 1. 8
readie to *deserve* what grace I found.' . . . V. v. 42. 5
He wold, by all good means he might, *deserve* such grace. . . V. v. 55. 9
To punish those that doe *deserve* the same; . . . VI. i. 26. 5
praise likewise *deserve* good thewes . . . VI. ii. 2. 9
mayest them make it better to *deserve,* . . . *H.L.* 166

Deserved. *See* **Well-deserved.**
'What have I, wretch, *deserv'd,* . . . *Gn.* 329
If none should yeeld him his *deserved* meed, . . . *T.M.* 453
for your worthinesse . . . have your *deserved* place . . . *Ded. Son.* xi. 2
So brought unto his Lord as his *deserved* pray. . . . I. viii. 25. 9
Not with so good successe as shee *deserv'd;* . . . II. x. 55. 2
The dreadful Fish that hath *deserv'd* the name Of Death, . . II. xii. 24. 1
Right well *deserved,* as his duefull meed, Her love, . . . IV. i. 6. 3
Deserved for their perils recompense. . . . IV. v. 23. 4
For his deare sake, that ill *deserv'd* that plight: . . . IV. xii. 19. 5
place *deserved* with the Gods on hy. . . . V. ii. 1. 7
Marinell that day *deserved* best. . . . V. iii. 7. 8
never did her ill, ne once *deserved* blame. . . . V. viii. 22. 9
speake so ill of him that well *deserved,* . . . V. xii. 43. 2
never so *deserved* to endite. . . . VI. xii. 41. 7
Doing him die that never it *deserved,* . . . *H.H.L.* 160

Deserver. *See* **Not-deserver.**

Deserves. As shee *deserves* that wrought so deadly spight. . . *S.C.* Jun. 101
Who but thy selfe *deserves* sike Poetes prayse? . . . *S.C.* N. 23
Deserves to taste his follies fruit, repented payne.' . . . II. v. 24. 9
'Another Grace she well *deserves* to be, . . . VI. x. 27. 1
thanks to him, that it *deserves,* behight; . . . *Com. Son.* ii. 12

Deservest. thy due meede that thou *deservest* best, . . . *Gn.* 60

Deserving. men of good *deserving* . . . *Hub.* 369
Deserving never here to be forgot, . . . *Ti.* 438
his owne guiltie mind, *deserving* death. . . . I. ix. 38. 6

Design. seemd some perilous tumult to *desine,* . . . IV. iii. 37. 7
To their *deseigne* to make the easier way, . . . V. viii. 25. 2

Designed. The arrow to his deadly marke *desynde.* . . . IV. vii. 30. 4
glauncing by deceiv'd him of that he *desynd.* . . . VI. vii. 10. 9
letters . . . With which that happy name was first *desynd,* . *Am.* lxxiv. 2

Designing. By outward shew her inward sence *desining:* . . V. vii. 8. 3

Designment. *Gainst which the second troupe *dessignment* makes; . . . II. xi. 10. 2

Designs. trayterous *desynes* Gainst loiall Princes, . . . V. ix. 42. 2

Desine, Desining. *See* **Design,** *etc.*

Desire. *See* **Praise-desire.**
With vayne *desire* and hope to be enricht; . . . *S.C.* S. 75
Respite till morrow t' answere his *desire;* . . . *Hub.* 326
all the happinesse that heart *desire,* . . . *Hub.* 609
like *desire* and praise of noble fame, . . . *Hub.* 769
Desire of honor or brave thought of armes . . . *Hub.* 825
kindle wise *desire,* . . . *Hub.* 830
Have both *desire* of worthie deeds forlorne, . . . *T.M.* 437
loath this drosse of sinfull worlds *desire!* . . . *Ti.* 686
to subject his *desire* To loathsome sloth, . . . *Mui.* 35
To the gay gardins his unstaid *desire* Him wholly caried, . . *Mui.* 161
Why then should I *desire* here to remaine! . . . *D.* 277
His lifes *desire,* and his deare loves delight. . . . *As.* 54
prick him foorth with proud *desire* of praise . . . *As.* 86
like himselfe *desire* for to beget: . . . *Col.* 864
their *desire* is base, and doth not merit The name of love, . . *Col.* 891
To like *desire* of honor may ye raise, . . . *Ded. Son.* x. 11
if of . . . homebredd evil ye *desire* to heare, . . . I. i. 31. 2
if ought higher were than that, did it *desyre.* . . . I. iv. 11. 9
there he held Her captive to his sensuall *desyre,* . . . I. vi. 23. 2
rather death *desire* then such despight. . . . I. vii. 49. 6
he himselfe with greedie great *desyre* Into the Castle entred . I. viii. 29. 3
I will revele what ye so much *desire.* . . . I. ix. 8. 8
With fresh *desire* his voyage to pursew; . . . I. ix. 18. 4
O! never, Sir, *desire* to try his guilefull traine.' . . . I. ix. 31. 9
desire To draw thy dayes forth . . . I. ix. 46. 1
bad him choose what death he would *desire;* . . . I. ix. 50. 8
To shew it to this knight, according his *desire.'* . . . I. x. 50. 9
gan him *desyre* Of her adventure myndfull for to bee. . . . I. x. 68. 7
Death better were; death did he oft *desire,* . . . I. xi. 28. 4
henceforth *desyre* To see faire heavens face, . . . II. i. 17. 3
to melt in pleasures whott *desyre,* . . . II. i. 58. 3
broke his wanton darts, and quenched bace *desyre.* . . . II. iii. 23. 9
His wandring thought in deepe *desire* does steepe, . . . II. v. 34. 2
Guyon is of immodest Merth Led into loose *desyre;* . . . II. vi. Arg.
forth launched quickly as she did *desire,* . . . II. vi. 20. 4
Might not revive *desire* of knightly exercize. . . . II. vi. 25. 9
fairly tempring, fond *desire* subdewd, . . . II. vi. 26. 6
feede his eye And covetous *desire* . . . II. vii. 4. 9
the matter of his huge *desire* And pompous pride . . . II. vii. 17. 6
That was Ambition, rash *desire* to sty, . . . II. vii. 46. 8
wrathfull hand wrought not her owne *desire?* . . . II. viii. 15. 5
infinite *desire* into your spirite poure. . . . II. ix. 3. 9
losse of thousand lives, to die at her *desire.'* . . . II. ix. 5. 9
My whole *desire* hath beene . . . To serve that Queene . . . II. ix. 7. 3
gently answered, They entraunce did *desire.* . . . II. ix. 11. 9
Through great *desire* of glory and of fame; . . . II. ix. 38. 7
gladly graunted their *desire.* . . . II. ix. 60. 9
did apply Their mindes to prayse and chevalrous *desyre:* . . II. x. 22. 6
naturall *desire* of countryes state, . . . II. x. 77. 2
shortly brent into extreme *desyre,* . . . III. i. 47. 8
in each gentle hart *desire* of honor breeds. . . . III. i. 49. 9
Such love is hate, and such *desire* is shame. . . . III. i. 50. 5
all attonce discovered her *desire* . . . III. i. 53. 1
Till she mote winne fit time for her *desire;* . . . III. i. 56. 2
Can have no ende nor hope of my *desire,* . . . III. ii. 44. 2
To compas thy *desire,* and find that loved knight.' . . . III. ii. 46. 9
great *desire* Of warlike armes . . . III. iii. 57. 2
It stirreth up to sensuall *desire,* . . . III. v. 1. 6
desire No service but thy safety and ayd; . . . III. v. 36. 3
beareth fruit of honour and all chast *desyre.* . . . III. v. 52. 9
All that to come into the world *desire:* . . . III. vi. 32. 2
ye first *desire* to learne What end . . . III. vi. 54. 1
unto her to utter his *desire;* . . . III. vii. 16. 4
Whom she did meane to make the thrall of her *desire.* . . . III. vii. 37. 9
all that might not slake her sensuall *desyre:* . . . III. vii. 49. 9
dore Was shut to all which lodging did *desyre:* . . . III. viii. 52. 8
Shewing *desire* her inward flame to slake. . . . III. ix. 31. 4
I would to heare *desyre* What to Aeneas fell; . . . III. ix. 40. 6
The God of his *desire,* the joy of misers blinde. . . . III. x. 15. 9
With greedy will and envious *desire,* . . . III. xi. 26. 3
Whens dearely she with death bought her *desire.* . . . III. xi. 33. 5
him beside marcht amorous *Desyre,* . . . III. xii. 9. 1
Whose chiefe *desire* is love and friendly aid . . . to nourish . IV. i. 46. 3
Ate soone discovering his *desire,* . . . IV. ii. 11. 6
O! why doe wretched men so much *desire* . . . IV. iii. 1. 1
Therewith to bind lascivious *desire,* . . . IV. v. 4. 7
That needed much her weake age to *desire,* . . . IV. v. 39. 8
his felonous intent Returning disappointed his *desire,* . . . IV. vi. 11. 7
No longer space thereto he did *desire,* . . . IV. vi. 43. 8
She in my stead supplide his bestiall *desire.'* . . . IV. vii. 19. 9
he greatly did *desire* To know what Virgin . . . IV. viii. 22. 1
of strength and beautie his *desire* Was spoyle to make, . . . IV. viii. 48. 6
her new love, the hope of her *desire.* . . . IV. ix. 13. 9
all burning with a fresh *desire* . . . IV. ix. 29. 1
whose great *desire* He glad to satisfie, . . . IV. ix. 41. 3
since ye so *desire,* . . . IV. x. 3. 5
on chast vertue grounded their *desire,* . . . IV. x. 26. 6
frankely there their loves *desire* possesse; . . . IV. x. 28. 6
To bath in joy and amorous *desire,* . . . IV. x. 38. 7

Desire—*Continued.*
where thou doest draw them with *desire*. . . . . IV. x. 46. 6
to enquire What thing so many nations met did there *desire*. . V. ii. 29. 9
he Talus to them sent . . . truce for to *desire*. . . . . V. ii. 52. 9
he gently did *desyre* To stay her stroks, ... V. v. 16. 5
For great *desire* that Monster to assay, ... V. xi. 21. 2
Unto her ran with greedie great *desyre*, ... V. xi. 61. 2
impotent *desire* of men to raine! . . . . V. xii. 1. 2
desire him that he would Vouchsafe . . . . VI. i. 29. 5
the high *desire* . . . which in you doth aspire, ... VI. ii. 34. 4
'My liefe, my lifes *desire*, ... VI. v. 23. 5
Subdue *desire*, and bridle loose delight; . . . . VI. vi. 14. 6
The noble childe, preventing his *desire*, ... VI. viii. 15. 7
He staide his hand according her *desire*, ... VI. viii. 18. 1
Ne could with seeing satisfie his great *desire*. . . . . . . VI. viii. 27. 9
When pride of youth forth pricked my *desire*, ... VI. ix. 24. 2
to insinuate his harts *desire*, ... VI. ix. 27. 2
for great *desire* Rent up her brest, ... VI. xii. 19. 3
If that her might were match to her *desire*. . . . . VII. vi. 21. 5
No way he found to compasse his *desire*, ... VII. vi. 43. 1
learned minds inflameth with *desire* Of heavenly things: . . . VII. vii. 2. 5
Had in him kindled youthfull fresh *desire*, ... VII. vii. 11. 7
thy decay thou seekst by thy *desire*; . . . . VII. vii. 59. 3
Rudely thou wrongest my deare harts *desire*, ... *Am.* v. 1
new *desire* . . . that shall endure for ever: . . . . *Am.* vi. 9
Burning in flames of pure and chast *desyre*: . . . . *Am.* xxii. 12
Th' importune suit of my *desire* to shonne: . . . . *Am.* xxiii. 6
dissolv'd through my so hot *desyre*, ... *Am.* xxx. 3
Not fyre: for she doth friese with faint *desire*. . . . . . . *Am.* lv. 8
Her harts *desire* with most contentment please. . . . . *Am.* lxxii. 12
Ne one light glance of sensuall *desyre* . . . . *Am.* lxxxiii. 3
with *desyre* Lifted aloft, ... *H.L.* 67
Therefore in choice of love he doth *desyre* . . . . *H.L.* 110
Such fancies feele no love, but loose *desyre*. . . . . *H.L.* 175
fyre Which kindleth love in generous *desyre*, ... *H.L.* 187
nought may quench his infinite *desyre*, ... *H.L.* 202
the wished scope Of my *desire*, ... *H.L.* 297
Thou in me kindlest much more great *desyre*, ... *H.B.* 5
Thence to the soule darts amorous *desyre*, ... *H.B.* 60
ye that wont with greedy vaine *desire* . . . . *H.H.L.* 15
ravisht with devouring great *desire* Of his deare selfe, . . . *H.H.L.* 268
Thenceforth all worlds *desire* will in thee dye, ... *H.H.L.* 274
Transported with celestiall *desyre* Of those faire formes, . . . *H.H.B.* 18
Their joy, their comfort, their *desire*, their gaine, ... *H.H.B.* 271
pompe to which proud minds aspyre . . . and so much *desyre*, *H.H.B.* 278
Desired. Shrines made of the mettall most *desired*, ... *Ti.* 411
' "I goe, and long *desired* have to goe, ... *D.* 281
I him *desirde* . . . To turne aside unto my Cabinet, ... *D.* 556
it *desir'd* at timely houres to heare, ... *Col.* 362
desird Of all the fairest Maides to have the vew. *Ded.Son.*xvii.3
courage haught *Desyrd* of forreine foemen to be knowne, . . I. vi. 29. 6
he *desirde* to end his wretched dayes: . . . . I. x. 21. 8
To hinder soule from her *desired* rest, ... II. i. 48. 2
ever her *desired* to depart. . . . . II. vi. 26. 7
his disciples both *desyrd* to bee; . . . . II. ix. 54. 8
refte from men the worldes *desired* vew, ... III. ii. 28. 3
to possesse the purpose they *desird*: . . . . III. iii. 51. 7
So from the wearie spirit thou doest drive *Desired* rest, . . . III. iv. 57. 9
she *desyrd* th' abridgement of her fate, ... III. viii. 2. 3
soft knocking entrance he *desyrd*. . . . . III. ix. 10. 1
seeing still the more *desir'd* to see, ... III. ix. 24. 2
With sober words, that sufferance *desired*, ... IV. i. 54. 4
First he *desir'd* their cause of strife to see: . . . . IV. ii. 22. 1
instantly *desired* T' asswage his wrath, ... IV. ix. 35. 3
When good was onely for it selfe *desyred*, ... V. Pr. 3. 6
many Lords have her to wife *desired*, ... V. ii. 10. 3
'The wretched mayd, that earst *desir'd* to die, ... V. iv. 11. 1
Talus *desir'd* that he might have prepared The way . . . . . V. vi. 38. 4
greatly it *desir'd* of her to learne, ... V. ix. 7. 3
Nigh to the place which ye *desir'd* to see: . . . . V. ix. 20. 5
Him oft *desired* home with her to wend, ... VI. iv. 39. 6
for pleasure might *Desired* be, ... VI. x. 8. 6
her alone he for his part *desired* . . . . VI. xi. 4. 3
since that lyfe is more then death *desyred*, ... *Am.* vii. 9
a byrd, that in ones hand doth spy *Desired* food, ... *Am.* lxxiii. 6
In dreadful darknesse lend *desired* light; . . . . *Epith.* 412
Desires. My sad *desires*, rest therefore moderate; . . . . . . *Ro.* vii. 12
Impatient of pleasures faint *desires*, ... *Ro.* xxiii. 6
A dolefull case *desires* a dolefull song, ... *T.M.* 541
Rather *desires* to be forgotten quight, ... *D.* 89
graunt his boone that most *desires* to dye. . . . . *D.* 357
Hobbin *desires*, thou maist it not forsake;— . . . . *Col.* 50
Duessa . . . Inveigled him to follow her *desires* unmeete. . . I. vii. 50. 9
In chaines of lust and lewde *desyres* ybownd, ... II. i. 54. 3
swimming deepe in sensuall *desyres*; . . . . III. i. 39. 8
So th' other did mens rash *desires* apall, ... III. i. 46. 4
chaste *desires* do nourish in your mind, ... III. i. 49. 2
therewith their keene *desires* were whett. . . . . III. x. 34. 9
stirred up with different *desires*, ... V. iv. 4. 4
let what ever he *desires* be him denide. . . . . V. v. 50. 9
In chast *desires*, on heavenly beauty bound. . . . . *Am.* viii. 8
Desiring. *See* **Blood-desiring.**
Disdeining life, *desiring* leave to dye, ... I. x. 22. 8
with revenge *desyring* soone to dye, ... II. viii. 47. 2
Desiring of his Amoret to heare . . . . IV. vi. 34. 3
Desirous. She no lesse glad then he *desirous* was . . . . . . II. vi. 37. 1
The rest hidd underneath him more *desirous* made. . . . . . . II. xii. 66. 9
desirous th' end of all their dayes To know, ... IV. ii. 47. 1
Desirous both to have the battell donne; . . . . IV. iii. 36. 5
desirous t' understand Tydings . . . . IV. viii. 62. 8

Desirous—*Continued.*
'Being *desirous* . . . deedes of armes to try, ... V. iv. 29. 1
desirous rather to rest mute, ... V. vi. 20. 3
desirous of the offred meed: . . . . VI. vi. 5. 6
Desks. robd the Chancell, and the *deskes* downe threw, . . . VI. xii. 25. 2
Desolate. Of us, thy daughters, dolefull *desolate*. . . . . . . *T.M.* 60
The Lyon would not leave her *desolate*, ... I. iii. 9. 1
The wyld woodgods . . . find the virgin, doolfull, *desolate*, . . I. vi. 9. 2
'Thenceforth me *desolate* he quite forsooke, ... I. vii. 50. 1
To aide a virgin *desolate*, foredonne; . . . . I. x. 60. 4
Island . . . was all *desolate*, ... II. x. 5. 8
'But since this Ladie is all *desolate*, ... VI. ii. 38. 1
Whom she beholding, now all *desolate*, ... VI. x. 34. 8
here to see all *desolate* and wast, ... VI. xi. 32. 7
a ship, of succour *desolate*, Doth suffer wreck . . . . *Am.* lvi. 11
wandring here and there all *desolate*, ... *Am.* lxxxviii. 7
Desolation. saw his sudden *desolation*, ... V. ii. 51. 2
Despair. now unto *despaire* I gin to growe, ... *Hub.* 79
(*despeyre* makes cowards stout,) . . . . *As.* 117
she . . . Is from her knight divorced in *despayre*, ... I. iii. 2. 8
If then it find not helpe, and breeds *despaire*.' . . . . I. vii. 41. 6
'*Despaire* breeds not' . . . 'where faith is staid.' . . . . . I. vii. 41. 7
Death and *despeyre* did many thereof sup, ... I. viii. 14. 3
Sir Trevisan flies from *Despeyre*, ... I. ix. Arg.
A man of hell that calls himselfe *Despayre*: . . . . I. ix. 28. 5
To drive him to *despaire*, and quite to quaile, ... I. ix. 49. 5
Why shouldst thou then *despeire*, that chosen art? . . . . . . I. ix. 53. 5
vassall of dread and *despayre*, ... II. iii. 7. 4
'O daughter deare!' (said she) '*despeire* no whit; . . . . . . III. ii. 35. 6
despeyre she from her flong. . . . . III. iv. 41. 9
sorrow and *despeyre* without aleggeaunce! . . . . III. v. 42. 9
deedes of armes had ever in *despaire*, ... III. viii. 11. 7
His expectation to *despaire* did turne, ... III. xii. 45. 4
Spending his daies in dolour and *despaire*, ... IV. vii. 43. 2
all dismayd through mercilesse *despaire* . . . . IV. viii. 51. 7
Else should afflicted wights oftimes *despeire*: . . . . V. iii. 1. 5
Through dolorous *despaire* which she conceyved, ... V. iv. 10. 2
This squalid weede, the patterne of *dispaire*, ... V. iv. 34. 6
thus thy better dayes are drowned In sad *despaire*, ... V. v. 36. 5
Yet doe I not of better times *despeyre*; . . . . V. v. 38. 7
They . . . drive his wife Adicia to *despaire*. . . . . V. viii. Arg.
In saving him from daungerous *despaire* . . . . V. xi. 48. 4
he through lives *despeire* Untimely dyde, ... VI. ii. 28. 3
sad *dispaire* away did cast. . . . . VI. v. 21. 9
Despaired. when of his departure she *despayrd*, ... II. x. 30. 8
High God, whose goodnesse he *despaired* quight, ... V. ii. 18. 8
In that deepe horror of *despeyred* hell, ... *H.H.L.* 130
Despairful. them driven hath to this *despairefull* drift. . . . II. xii. 8. 9
Despairing. None els to death this man *despayring* drive . . . I. ix. 38. 5
So daunted was in his *despeyring* mood, ... V. ii. 26. 8
Despairs. To eate thy heart through comfortlesse *dispaires*; . *Hub.* 904
Despeire, Despeyre, -d, *etc.* *See* **Despair, Despaired,** *etc.*
Desperate. Am like for *desperate* doole to dye, ... *S.C.* F. 155
It was a *desperate* shot. *S.C.* Au. 100
Dismayed with so *desperate* deadly wound, ... I. viii. 11. 1
all *desperate*, as loathing light, ... II. viii. 47. 1
His sinfull sowle with *desperate* disdaine . . . . III. v. 23. 8
He knockt his brest with *desperate* intent, ... III. vii. 20. 3
in *desperate* distresse, ... III. vii. 25. 8
attaine My Ladies love in such a *desperate* case, ... III. vii. 60. 7
All *desperate* of his fore-damned spright, ... III. x. 56. 8
Twixt dolour and despight halfe *desperate*, ... III. xii. 43. *or.* 3
Ne *desperate* of glorious victorie; . . . . IV. iii. 25. 2
Then death it selfe more dread and *desperate*; . . . . IV. viii. 1. 4
almost dead and *desperate* Through her late hurts, ... IV. viii. 19. 7
Bull, whose cruell hornes doe threat *Desperate* daunger, . . . VI. vii. 47. 3
Despetto. The first of them by name was cald *Despetto*, . . . VI. v. 13. 6
stout *Despetto* in his greater pryde Did front him, ... VI. v. 20. 7
Despight, -ful. *See* **Despite, -ful.**
Despise. the foule, that doth the light *dispise*, ... *Bel.*[2] vii. 13
despise The noble Lion after his lives end, ... *Ro.* xiv. 5
Hereby I learned have not to *despise* . . . . *Van.* v. 13
The better please, the worse *despise*; . . . . *S.C.* Env. 12
he through pride and fatnes gan *despise* Their meanesse; . . *Hub.* 586
Despise the brood of blessed Sapience. . . . . *T.M.* 72
despize The precious store of this celestiall riches? . . . . . *T.M.* 145
we silly Maides, whom they *dispize* . . . . *T.M.* 339
How ever yet they mee *despise* and spight, ... *T.M.* 523
As he that did all daunger quite *despise*, ... *Mui.* 390
would him advise The angry beastes not rashly to *despise*, . . I. vi. 25. 5
none did others safety *despize*, ... I. ix. 1. 5
offred hope of comfort did *despise*: . . . . II. i. 15. 3
if that carelesse hevens,' (quoth she) '*despise* . . . . II. i. 36. 1
As to *despise* so curteous seeming part . . . . II. vi. 26. 4
(So Love the dread of daunger doth *despise*) . . . . II. vi. 46. 2
That noble heart as great dishonour doth *despize*. . . . . . . II. vii. 12. 9
Such superfluities they would *despise*, ... II. vii. 15. 5
His daughter gan *despise* his drouping day, ... II. x. 30. 4
threatning to devoure all that his powre *despise*. . . . . II. xii. 21. 9
Acrasia . . . will slip away, and all our drift *despise*. . . . II. xii. 69. 9
great rebuke it is love to *despise*, ... III. i. 55. 3
Strokes, wounds, wards, weapons, all they did *despise*, . . . IV. iii. 36. 3
Which scornefull offer Blandamour gan soone *despize*; . . . . IV. iv. 8. 9
in your minde wont to *despise* them all.' . . . . IV. vi. 28. 9
The grace of his Creator doth *despise*, ... IV. viii. 15. 8
Not to *despise* that dame which lov'd him liefe, ... IV. ix. 15. 4
(ah! who would her *despyse*?) . . . . IV. xi. 5. 2
With which he dares our offers thus *despize*: . . . . V. v. 48. 5
rather then she kindnesse would *despize*, ... V. vi. 20. 5
The salvage nation doth all dread *despize*, ... VI. iv. 6. 6

Despise—*Continued.*
now ginnes to *despize* The good Sir Bruin . . . VI. iv. 33. 5
even the Prince his basenesse did *despize;* . . . VI. vi. 32. 4
the more she did all love *despize,* . . . VI. vii. 30. 3
wreake him selfe on them that him *despise.* . . . VI. viii. 25. 4
doth *despise* the dainties of the towne. . . . VI. ix. 7. 5
His layes, his loves, his lookes, she did them all *despize.* . . . VI. ix. 35. 9
Calidore did not *despise* him quight, . . . VI. x. 37. 6
him, whose life, though ye *despyse,* . . . *Am.* xxxvi. 11
him that doeth thy lovely heasts *despize,* . . . *H.L.* 160
Despised. Are now *despizd,* and made a laughing game. . . . *T.M.* 204
To see that vertue should *dispised* bee . . . *Ti.* 450
wander up and downe *despys'd* of all; . . . *Col.* 728
he *despisd* to tread in dew degree, . . . II. iii. 46. 7
Her dalliaunce he *despis'd,* . . . II. vi. 21. 9
As one that loathed life, and yet *despysd* to dye. . . . II. viii. 50. 9
them *despised* all; for all was in her powre. . . . III. iv. 18. 9
she both offers and the offerer *Despysde,* . . . III. viii. 38. 9
take to his new love, and leave her old *despysd.* . . . III. x. 8. 9
His sorrowes cause, to be of her *despis'd:* . . . IV. viii. 12. 4
eke that age *despysed* nicenesse vaine, . . . IV. viii. 27. 5
Despisd and troden downe of all that over-ran. . . . IV. viii. 32. 9
Marinell, Who her *despysd* . . . IV. xi. 5. 2
That had *despisde* so chast and faire a dame, . . . IV. xii. 16. 7
he his lookes *despised,* and his boast dispraized. . . . VI. viii. 26. 9
Despiseth. True love *despiseth* shame, . . . V. i. 27. 9
she them all *despiseth* for great pride.' . . . V. ii. 10. 4
Despite. *See* **Self-despite.**
In great *despight* (*despite*[1]) he dide, . . . *Pet.* v. 11
dead himselfe he wisheth for *despight.* . . . *Van.* x. 13
the pensife boy, halfe in *despight,* Arose, . . . *S.C.* Ja. 76
the East with tyranous *despight* . . . *Gn.* 43
wrapt his scalie boughts with fell *despight,* . . . *Gn.* 255
backbite Anies good name for envie or *despite:* . . . *Hub.* 720
Hath stirred up so mischievous *despight?* . . . *T.M.* 46
in *despight* of his Creatour . . . *Ti.* 537
Stir'd up through wrathfull Nemesis *despight,* . . . *Mui.* 2
'Why doo I longer live in lifes *despight,* . . . *D.* 442
doo not dye then in *despight* of death; . . . *D.* 443
wondrous wroth, for that so foule *despight,* . . . *Col.* 148
He is repayd with scorne and foule *despite,* . . . *Col.* 905
He thought have slaine her in his fierce *despight;* . . . I. i. 50. 3
And wast his inward gall with deepe *despight,* . . . I. ii. 6. 4
many mischiefes follow cruell Wrath: . . . Bitter *despight,* I. iv. 35. 4
No knight, but treachour full of false *despight* . . . I. iv. 41. 5
quench the flame of furious *despight,* . . . I. v. 14. 5
rather death desire then such *despight.* . . . I. vii. 49. 6
'To doe her die,' (quoth Una) 'were *despight,* . . . I. viii. 45. 7
yeeldes his caytive neck to victours most *despight.* . . . I. ix. 11. 9
To be avenged of so great *despight;* . . . I. xi. 17. 6
The beast, impatient . . . of so fierce and forcible *despight,* I. xi. 25. 7
For griefe thereof and divelish *despight,* . . . I. xi. 44. 1
if he live that hath you doen *despight;* . . . II. i. 14. 7
Death were too litle paine for such a fowle *despight.* . . . II. i. 17. 9
bownd by them to live in lives *despight;* . . . II. i. 36. 4
herselfe, in great *despight,* She groveling threw to ground, . . II. i. 45. 8
Her hellish brond hath kindled with *despight,* . . . II. ii. 29. 3
till he avenged bee Of that *despight,* . . . II. iii. 12. 8
mote him honour win to wreak so foule *despight.* . . . II. iii. 13. 9
In fowle reproch, and termes of vile *despight,* . . . II. iv. 5. 2
Occasion; the roote of all wrath and *despight.* . . . II. iv. 10. 9
more for ranck *despight* then for great paine, . . . II. iv. 15. 7
What great *despight* doth fortune to thee beare, . . . II. iv. 25. 7
fraught with fowle *despight,* . . . II. iv. 29. 1
that vengeable *despight* To punish: . . . II. iv. 30. 3
In poyson and in blood of malice and *despight.* . . . II. iv. 38. 9
The sonnes of old Acrates and *Despight;* . . . II. iv. 41. 6
Headed with yre and vengeable *despight.* . . . II. iv. 46. 2
weetlesse eke of lately wrought *despight,* . . . II. v. 36. 5
He then uprose, inflamd with fell *despight,* . . . II. v. 37. 8
with envious *despight* His prowd presumed force increased . . II. vi. 30. 2
Ready to drowne him selfe for fell *despight:* . . . II. vi. 43. 5
Cruell Revenge, and rancorous *Despight,* . . . II. vii. 22. 2
allay the storme of your *despight,* . . . II. viii. 27. 5
His honour staines with rancour and *despight,* . . . II. viii. 29. 8
in *despight* of life for death doe call.' . . . II. viii. 52. 4
every loup fast lockt, as fearing foes *despight.* . . . II. ix. 10. 9
Shee triumphed on death, in enemies *despight.* . . . II. x. 56. 9
yet the vanquished had no *despight.* . . . III. i. 13. 7
That death me liefer were then such *despight,* . . . III. i. 24. 4
with felonous *despight* And fell intent, . . . III. i. 65. 3
Love and *despight* attonce her courage kindled hath. . . . III. iv. 12. 9
thy voyage rashly make . . . in my *despight,* . . . III. iv. 14. 6
She, she it is, that hath me done *despight:* . . . III. iv. 60. 7
cast t' avenge him of that fowle *despight* . . . III. v. 15. 3
Vile rancour their rude harts had fild with such *despight.* . . III. v. 16. 9
With so fell force, and villeinous *despite,* . . . III. v. 19. 2
with villeinous *despight* To blott her honour, . . . III. v. 45. 4
Yet no'te she find redresse for such *despight:* . . . III. vi. 40. 7
to avenge his divelish *despight,* . . . III. vii. 28. 7
For great *despight* of that unwonted band, . . . III. vii. 36. 4
The quarry throwes to ground with fell *despight,* . . . III. vii. 39. 5
The rest she fyr'd, for sport, or for *despight;* . . . III. x. 12. 6
drowned nye Twixt inward doole and felonous *despight:* . . . III. x. 17. 6
Griefe, and *despight,* and gealosy, and scorne, . . . III. x. 55. 5
'This is' . . . 'the dolorous *despight,* . . . III. xi. 23. 5
for *despight* That thou bewray'dst his mothers wantonnesse, . III. xi. 36. 3
th' one *Despight,* The other . . . Cruelty . . . III. xii. 19. 2
he thought, for villeinous *despight,* . . . III. xii. 32. 6
Twixt dolour and *despight* halfe desperate, . . . III. xii. 43. *or.* 3

Despite—*Continued.*
He now unable was to wreake his old *despight.* . . . IV. i. 39. 9
for passing great *despight,* Staid not to answer; . . . IV. i. 52. 1
Whose Lord hath done my love this foule *despight?* . . . IV. i. 52. 8
with termes of foule *despight,* . . . IV. ii. 3. 3
They stemme ech other with so fell *despight,* . . . IV. ii. 16. 4
with which *despight* He all enrag'd . . . IV. iii. 10. 7
rather stir'd to vengeance and *despight,* . . . IV. iii. 14. 4
in revengement of his owne *despight;* . . . IV. iv. 35. 3
woxe nigh mad for very harts *despight,* . . . IV. v. 27. 2
On whom I waite to wreake that foule *despight,* . . . IV. vi. 5. 8
swell in every inner part For fell *despight,* . . . IV. vi. 7. 5
With fell *despight* her cruell arrowes tynde . . . IV. vii. 30. 7
on him selfe to wreake his follies owne *despight.* . . . IV. vii. 39. 9
she was stuft with rancour and *despight* . . . IV. viii. 24. 3
all full of fell *despight,* . . . IV. ix. 20. 3
old *despight* which now forth newly brake . . . IV. ix. 26. 3
hatred, murther, treason, and *despight,* . . . IV. x. 20. 6
bit his lip for felonous *despight,* . . . IV. x. 33. 8
most free from fowle *despight,* . . . IV. xi. 18. 8
shall in *despight* Beare for his penaunce . . . V. i. 26. 7
It bit the earth for very fell *despight,* . . . V. ii. 18. 6
as the death he hated such *despight,* . . . V. iii. 31. 8
I rather chose to die in lives *despight,* . . . V. iv. 32. 8
never had she suffred such *despight:* . . . V. iv. 43. 4
shun the dred *despight* Of her fierce wrath, . . . V. v. 16. 1
Yet he it tooke in his owne selfes *despight,* . . . V. v. 23. 6
For very fell *despight* which she conceived, . . . V. v. 47. 3
kicks, and squals, and shriekes for fell *despight;* . . . V. vi. 14. 5
for *despight* The glauncing sparkles through her bever glared, V. vi. 38. 6
proud Radigund, with fell *despight,* . . . V. vii. 32. 1
Her heart gan grudge for very deepe *despight* . . . V. vii. 37. 8
with most fell *despight* and deadly hate . . . V. viii. 18. 3
sending to the Souldan in *despight* A bold defyance, . . . V. viii. 27. 7
All flaming with revenge and furious *despight.* . . . V. viii. 46. 9
To keepe out guyle, and malice, and *despight,* . . . V. ix. 22. 7
ryven quight Out of their breasts with furious *despight:* . . . V. x. 32. 5
yeeld to his *despight;* . . . V. xi. 5. 7
He brayd aloud for very fell *despight;* . . . V. xi. 8. 2
Made kill her selfe for very hearts *despight* . . . V. xi. 25. 4
forst her turne againe in her *despight* To save her selfe, . . . V. xi. 26. 7
proud *despight* of his selfe-pleasing mynd, . . . VI. i. 15. 2
executes her wicked will with worse *despight.* . . . VI. i. 15. 9
oft recuile to shunne his sharpe *despight:* . . . VI. i. 20. 4
both inflam'd with furious *despight;* . . . VI. i. 36. 5
I may avenge him of so foule *despight.'* . . . VI. ii. 42. 6
The meede of his desert for that *despight,* . . . VI. ii. 45. 8
in *despight* to be so fowle abused . . . VI. iii. 33. 4
for more *despight,* He laught, . . . VI. iii. 34. 3
one that wrought him fowle *despight.'* . . . VI. iii. 40. 5
greedy to avenge that vile *despight,* . . . VI. iii. 45. 7
him avenge of that so villenous *despight.* . . . VI. iv. 3. 9
For fell *despight* to be so sorely crost; . . . VI. iv. 40. 4
Three mightie enemies did him most *despight,* . . . VI. v. 13. 2
Burning with inward rancour and *despight,* . . . VI. v. 18. 2
Tell me what worlds *despight,* or heavens yre, . . . VI. v. 23. 7
Wrought to Sir Calepine so foule *despight;* . . . VI. vi. 17. 7
He woxe nigh mad with wrath and fell *despight,* . . . VI. vi. 24. 8
His rancorous *despight* did not releasse, . . . VI. vi. 43. 8
To this attempt to wreake his hid *despight,* . . . VI. vii. 12. 8
was to him on earth the deadliest *despight.* . . . VI. vii. 20. 9
foule Infamie and fell *Despight* Gave evidence, . . . VI. vii. 34. 7
Yond Lady and her Squire with foule *despight* Abusde, . . . VI. viii. 6. 3
for fell *despight* Of that displeasure, . . . VI. x. 18. 4
for very fell *despight,* . . . VI. xi. 25. 5
made him almost mad for fell *despight:* . . . VI. xii. 31. 7
he drew him forth, even in his own *despight.* . . . VI. xii. 34. 9
Hope to escape his venemous *despite,* . . . VI. xii. 41. 2
Upon the fruitfull earth, which doth us yet *despite.* . . . VII. vi. 20. 9
Then doe I more augment my foes *despight;* . . . *Am.* xliv. 10
Despiteful. when she heard, as in *despightfull* wise . . . II. i. 15. 1
Reproch *despightfull,* carelesse, and unkinde; . . . III. xii. 24. 4
inly thought of that *despightfull* deede . . . IV. v. 9. 5
with *despightfull* shame Revyling him, . . . *H.H.L.* 151
Despitefully. To heare him threaten so *despightfully,* . . . III. ix. 14. 6
at him throwes it most *despightfully:* . . . V. xii. 39. 4
Despiteous. *See* **Dispiteous.**
to Jewes *despiteous* Delivered up the Lord . . . II. vii. 62. 5
In your avengement and *despiteous* rage, . . . III. viii. 28. 6
Against her rode, full of *despiteous* ire, . . . IV. vi. 11. 4
despiteous dreare And heavie sway, . . . IV. viii. 42. 5
had wounded sore . . . in his *despiteous* pryde: . . . VI. ii. 40. 6
Despiteously. *despiteously* entayld Deepe in their flesh, . . . II. vi. 29. 7
From thence he threw him selfe *despiteously,* . . . III. x. 56. 7
He saw his life powrd forth *despiteously;* . . . VI. iii. 51. 4
Despites. Would for it selfe redresse, and punish such *despights.* VI. viii. 18. 9
How with most scornefull taunts, and fell *despights,* . . . *H.H.L.* 241
Despoil. a Groome, . . . gan *despoile* Of puissant armes, . . . I. x. 17. 7
she gan her selfe *despoile,* . . . III. i. 58. 6
He wist not how him to *despoile* of life, . . . III. vii. 33. 1
Each other of loves bitter fruit *despoile.* . . . III. xii. 47. *or.* 2
she doth them of warlike armes *despoile,* . . . V. iv. 31. 3
thou dost of arms *despoile,* . . . VI. vi. 34. 6
lastly to *despoyle* of knightly bannerall. . . . VI. vii. 26. 9
Despoiled. The goodly fields . . . quite *despoyled* hath, . . . *T.M.* 238
when they had *despoyld* her tire and call, . . . I. viii. 46. 5
Sir Guyon, . . . is by Acrates sonnes *despoyld;* . . . II. viii. Arg.
of his armes *despoyled* easily . . . II. xi. 49. 7
Least salvage beastes her person have *despoyld:* . . . III. x. 39. 8
Of her dew honour was *despoyled* quight; . . . III. xii. 20. 4

Despoiled—*Continued.*
Their girlonds rent, their bowres *despoyled* all; . . . . IV. i. 24. 7
of their publicke praise had them *despoyled,* . . . . IV. ix. 36. 4
none but beasts may be of her *despoyled;* . . . . V. ix. 2. 5
by some other violence *despoyled:* . . . . VI. vii. 33. 5
Despoyled of those joyes and jolly-head, ... VI. xi. 32. 8
Despoyld of warlike armes and knowen shield. . . . . *Am.* lii. 4
Despoiling. Tristram, then *despoyling* that dead knight . . . . VI. ii. 39. 1
Where he him found *despoyling* all . . . . VI. xii. 23. 9
Dess. Ne ever once did looke up from her *desse,* . . . . IV. x. 50. 3
Destined. Thou doest effect in *destined* descents, ... III. iii. 2. 6
Destinies. whiles equal *destinies* Did ronne about, ... I. vii. 43. 4
'thy *destinies* withstand My wrathfull will, ... II. iii. 8. 3
Destiny. makes me wayle so hard a *destenie* (*destinie*[1]) . . . . *Pet.* i. 14
destinie this huge Chaos turmoyling, ... *Ro.* xix. 9
Was this (ye Romanes) your hard *destinie,* . . . . *Ro.* xxiv. 9
Doo weave the direfull threds of *destinie,* . . . . *D.* 17
You, whom my hard avenging *destinie* Hath made judge . . . . I. i. 51. 8
who can turne the stream of *destinee,* . . . . I. v. 25. 4
shunne the death ordaynd by *destinie?* . . . . I. ix. 42. 8
this grace I have Me given by eternall *destiny,* . . . . II. iii. 45. 2
courd it tenderly . . . from dreaded *destiny,* . . . . II. viii. 9. 9
The hellish Harpyes, prophets of sad *destiny.* . . . . II. xii. 36. 9
who can shun the chance that *dest'ny* doth ordaine? . . . . III. i. 37. 9
the streight course of hevenly *destiny,* . . . . III. iii. 24. 3
doe by all dew meanes thy *destiny* fulfill.' . . . . III. iii. 24. 9
Penda, fearefull of like *desteny,* . . . . III. iii. 37. 8
the full time, prefixt by *destiny,* . . . . III. iii. 40. 5
Her deare sonnes *destiny* to her to tell, ... III. iv. 25. 4
who can deceive his *destiny,* . . . . III. iv. 27. 1
Ne can thy irrevocable *desteny* bee wefte. . . . . III. iv. 36. 9
Upon thee heapt a direfull *destinie;* . . . . III. ix. 33. 5
unto them what *destinie* was assynd, . . . she did not tell; . . . . IV. ii. 53. 5
Like as his mother prayd the *Destinie,* . . . . IV. iii. 13. 7
seemed nought but death mote be her *destinie.* . . . . IV. vi. 18. 9
'Ay me,' (quoth she) 'what wicked *destinie!* . . . . V. vi. 10. 8
Unwares defrauded his intended *destiny:* . . . . VI. viii. 8. 9
what *destiny* . . . Hath wrought this wicked deed: . . . . VI. xi. 29. 7
Destitute. All *destitute* of helpe doth headlong fall; . . . . V. ii. 8. 4
Destroy. The fatall Sisters, did for spight *destroy,* . . . . *T.M.* 16
No ravenous wolves the good mans hope *destroy* . . . . *Col.* 318
Bewraying him that did of late *destroy* His eldest brother; . . . . I. iv. 39. 3
greevd to thinke how foe did him *destroy,* . . . . I. iv. 45. 7
In case he could that monstrous beast *destroy,* . . . . I. xii. 41. 7
Queene Of Amazons whom Pyrrhus did *destroy,* . . . . II. iii. 31. 6
after Greekes did Priams realme *destroy,* . . . . III. ix. 36. 7
finally *destroy* Proud Priams towne. . . . . IV. xi. 19. 6
by force could him *destroy,* . . . . VI. v. 14. 3
Whom ye doe wreck, doe ruine, and *destroy.* . . . . *Am.* lvi. 14
Destroyed. Spying the tree *destroid* (*destroyde*[1]), ... *Pet.* v. 9
That Monster can be maistred or *destroyd:* . . . . II. iv. 10. 3
It she reduced, but himselfe *destroyed* quight. . . . . III. v. 41. 9
whom he had earst *destroyd* She weend, ... III. viii. 2. 8
Good Knights and Ladies true and many else *destroyd.* . . . . VI. i. 7. 9
Creeping behinde him still to have *destroyde;* . . . . VI. v. 20. 5
She had *destroyed* two and twenty more. . . . . VI. vii. 38. 8
them *destroyed* quite; . . . . VII. vi. 20. 6
Destruction. fervent eyes to his *destruction* bent. . . . . *Gn.* 296
shun'd *destruction* doth *destruction* render: . . . . *Gn.* 364
let *destruction* be the punishment, ... *Gn.* 367
If yet he were alive, or to *destruction* brought. . . . . VI. vi. 37. 9
sought Throughout the world, and to *destruction* brought. . . . . VI. xii. 13. 5
Desynd(e), Desynes. *See* **Designed,** *etc.*
Det(t), -er. *See* **Debt, -or.**
Detain. The crowne which Vortiger did long *detayne:* . . . . II. x. 67. 4
gan enquire . . . The certaine cause of Artegals *detaine,* . . . . V. vi. 15. 7
Detained. there *detained* bee For looking back, ... *Gn.* 434
she by force is still fro me *detayned,* . . . . V. xi. 54. 8
her in bondage strong *Detaynd,* . . . . VI. xi. 2. 5
Detains. she him still *detaines* in captive hold, ... IV. viii. 53. 7
Deteast. *See* **Detest.**
Detect. Reveale to me, and all the meanes *detect,* . . . . *Mui.* 13
his tract she mote *detect:* . . . . III. vi. 12. 7
Like never yet did living eie *detect;* . . . . III. vii. 22. 7
Abhorred Murder, who, . . . did her *detect,* . . . . V. ix. 48. 3
Detected. For feare she should of lightnesse be *detected:* . . . . IV. xii. 35. 8
Determined. *determined* to seeke Their fortunes farre abroad, ... *Hub.* 47
Detest. the fires scorn'd furie to *detest;* . . . . *Gn.* 612
lothefull idlenes he doth *detest,* . . . . *Hub.* 735
He spued up his gorge, that all did him *deteast.* . . . . I. iv. 21. 9
al that life preserved did *detest;* . . . . I. xi. 49. 3
all his fained kindnes did *detest,* . . . . III. viii. 39. 4
Detestable. That *detestable* sight him much amazde, ... I. i. 26. 1
A daungerous and *detestable* place, ... II. xii. 8. 2
Detests. she that vertue loves and vice *detests,* . . . . IV. xi. 51. 7
Detraction. Her name was hight *Detraction,* . . . . V. xii. 35. 5
with unjust *detraction* him did beard, ... VI. v. 12. 7
Deucalion. stone; Such as . . . Were throwne by Pyrrha and *Deucalione:* . . . . V. Pr. 2. 7
Deucalion's. to win *Deucalions* daughter bright, ... III. xi. 42. 5
Device. Shepheards *devise* she hateth as the snake, ... *S.C.* Ja. 65
to heare novells of his *devise;* . . . . *S.C.* F. 95
Say . . . if this *device* Doth like you, ... *Hub.* 93
shall we varie our *device* at will, ... *Hub.* 118
Unlesse thou canst one conjure by *device,* . . . . *Hub.* 510
Burganet . . . wrought by wonderous *device* . . . . *Mui.* 74
With excellent *device* and wondrous slight, ... *Mui.* 330
Of gentle wit and daintie sweet *device,* . . . . *As.* Interl. 218
The same by my *device* I undertake . . . . II. iii. 18. 6
So fashioned a Porch with rare *device.* . . . . II. xii. 54. 1

Device—*Continued.*
A worke of rare *device* and wondrous wit. . . . . III. i. 34. 6
Conceiv'd a bold *devise,* and thus bespake: . . . . III. iii. 52. 2
read to me, by what *devise* or wit . . . . IV. vii. 19. 3
Nor hart could wish for any queint *device,* . . . . IV. x. 22. 8
could be fram'd by workmans rare *device;* . . . . V. ix. 27. 8
kindle fyre by wonderfull *devyse!* . . . . *Am.* xxx. 12
Deviceful. the *devicefull* matter of my song; . . . . *T.M.* 386
The goodly service, the *devicefull* sights, ... V. iii. 3. 2
Some Clarkes doe doubt in their *devicefull* art . . . . V. x. 1. 1
Devices. Fashion'd with queint *devises,* . . . . *Hub.* 673
Devices, dreames, opinions unsound, ... II. ix. 51. 7
Devil. They boast they han the *devill* at commaund, ... *S.C.* S. 94
what *devill* had her thither brought, ... III. vii. 8. 2
The one a feend, the other an incarnate *devill.* . . . . IV. ii. 3. 9
Devilish. he praisd his *divelish* arts, ... I. i. 9. 4
'The *divelish* hag . . . Perceiv'd my thought; . . . . I. ii. 42. 1
that *divelish* yron Engin, wrought In deepest Hell, ... I. vii. 13. 1
Ne *divelish* thoughts dismay thy constant spright: . . . . I. ix. 53. 3
For griefe thereof and *divelish* despight, ... I. xi. 44. 1
hellish feend raysd up through *divelish* science. . . . . II. xi. 39. 9
her *divelish* deedes And hellish arts . . . . III. vii. 6. 7
by her *divelish* arts thought to prevaile . . . . III. vii. 21. 8
to avenge his *divelish* despight, ... III. vii. 28. 7
With other *divelish* ceremonies met: . . . . V. viii. 45. 7
Devil's. shepeheardes for the *Devils* stedde, ... *S.C.* May 43
Devils. dread of God, that *devils* bindes, ... V. xii. 1. 3
Devise. *See* **Device.**
All that which Aegypt whilome did *devise,* . . . . *Ro.* xxix. 1
(as I can well *devise*) . . . . *S.C.* May 174
The dapper ditties, that I wont *devise* . . . . *S.C.* O. 13
meanes of gladsome solace to *devise:* . . . . *Hub.* 20
I will *devise* A pasport for us both . . . . *Hub.* 195
as you can *devise,* . . . . *Hub.* 488
Then gan this craftie couple to *devize,* . . . . *Hub.* 655
he daylie doth *devise:* . . . . *Hub.* 738
all the cunning meanes he could *devise:* . . . . *Hub.* 847
I Did first *devise* the plot by pollicie; . . . . *Hub.* 1036
devise Unto his heavenlie maker to present His bodie, ... *Ti.* 296
Such as on earth man could not more *devize,* . . . . *Ti.* 521
his gins . . . Drest in good order as he could *devise.* . . . . *Mui.* 388
to *devise* Notes sad enough . . . . *Mui.* 413
The wily lover did *devise* this slight: . . . . *Col.* 137
finest sleights *devise,* . . . . *Col.* 694
of love, and of his sacred lere, . . . otherwise *devise,* . . . . *Col.* 784
doth need a golden quill . . . them rightly to *devise;* . . . . *Ded. Son.* xvi. 11
Her Lordes and Ladies all this while *devise* Themselves . . . . I. iv. 14. 5
What witt of mortal wight Can now *devise* . . . . I. vi. 6. 9
glad to gain such favour, gan *devise,* . . . . I. vi. 32. 8
friendly each did others praise *devize,* . . . . I. ix. 1. 7
With all the court'sies that she could *devyse,* . . . . I. x. 11. 8
Thus as they gan of sondrie thinges *devise,* . . . . I. x. 12. 1
What needes of dainty dishes to *devize,* . . . . I. xii. 14. 3
Let us *devize* of ease and everlasting rest.' . . . . I. xii. 17. 9
'Of ease or rest I may not yet *devize;* . . . . I. xii. 18. 2
Then meanes I gan *devise* for his deliveraunce. . . . . II. i. 54. 9
Yet others she more urgent did *devise;* . . . . II. v. 21. 8
Matter of merth enough . . . She could *devise;* . . . . II. vi. 3. 8
other whiles vaine toyes she would *devize,* . . . . II. vi. 7. 1
did of joy and jollity *devize,* . . . . II. vi. 21. 3
set them forth, as well he could *devise.* . . . . II. ix. 31. 5
if ought else that I mote not *devyse,* . . . . II. ix. 42. 7
of this lands first conquest did *devize,* . . . . II. ix. 59. 7
each gan diversely *devize.* . . . . III. i. 33. 9
to *devize* Their goodly entertainement . . . . III. i. 42. 1
Now this, now that, twixt them they did *devize,* . . . . III. iii. 51. 8
So faire a place as Nature can *devize:* . . . . III. vi. 29. 3
She gan for me *devise* a grievous punishment; . . . . III. vii. 55. 9
she did *devyse* With golden wyre . . . . III. viii. 7. 5
why doe wee *devise* of others ill, ... III. ix. 8. 6
He gan *devise* how her he reskew mought: . . . . III. x. 18. 8
one was armed, . . . Whom to be Paridell he did *devize;* . . . . III. x. 21. 5
So diversely each one did sundrie doubts *devise.* . . . . IV. i. 14. 9
all things did *devise,* and all things doe, ... IV. ii. 8. 8
Such as the maker selfe could best by art *devize.* . . . . IV. iii. 38. 9
on their common harmes together did *devise.* . . . . IV. vi. 10. 9
Both through a forest ryding did *devise* T' alight, ... IV. vii. 3. 5
To come where he his dolors did *devise,* . . . . IV. viii. 3. 3
as list them to *devise;* . . . . IV. ix. 35. 7
Now gan he in his grieved minde *devise,* . . . . IV. xii. 14. 1
rather gan in troubled mind *devize* . . . . IV. xii. 28. 8
Ne wist he what to thinke, or to *devise;* . . . . V. iii. 18. 3
Devize how to enlarge him out of hould. . . . . V. v. 55. 3
Then gan the other further to *devize* Of things abrode, ... V. vi. 20. 7
What doe ye then *devise* Of more revenge? . . . . V. viii. 11. 7
They did this complot twixt them selves *devise:* . . . . V. viii. 25. 3
gan eftsoones *devize* to be aveng'd for it. . . . . V. viii. 45. 9
The Prince staid not his aunswere to *devize,* . . . . V. xi. 4. 1
With all the tortures that he could *devize,* . . . . V. xi. 19. 8
so goodly as ye can *devize,* . . . . VI. i. 5. 7
and thinke what reliefe Were best *devise* . . . . VI. ii. 46. 4
Yet could she not *devise* . . . How thence she might convay him VI. ii. 47. 1
gan *devize* How she the blame might salve . . . . VI. iii. 8. 8
He can *devize* this counter-cast of slight, ... VI. iii. 16. 8
He gan *devize* to be aveng'd anew . . . . VI. vii. 2. 6
To joyne with him and vengeance to *devize,* . . . . VI. vii. 22. 8
Then gan they to *devize* what course to take; . . . . VI. viii. 37. 6
of her dainty flesh they did *devize* To make a common feast, VI. viii. 38. 8
some of them gan mongst themselves *devize* . . . . VI. viii. 43. 5
fooles therefore They are which fortunes doe by vowes *devize,* VI. ix. 30. 8

Devise—*Continued.*
Then all that he could doe, or ever *devize:* . . . VI. ix. 35. 8
Areed, ye sonnes of God, as best ye can *devise.'* . . . VII. vi. 21. 9
my fraile wit cannot *devize* to what It to compare, . . . VII. vii. 7. 4
For though he colours could *devize* at will, . . . *Am.* xvii. 5
What trophee then shall I most fit *devize,* . . . *Am.* lxix. 5
let baser things *devize* To dy in dust, . . . *Am.* lxxv. 9
Devised. meanes *deviz'd* to shew his sorrow best. . . . *As.* 208
He then *devisde* himselfe how to disguise; . . . I. ii. 10. 1
himselfe had craftily *devisd* To be her Squire, . . . II. i. 21. 8
that deare Crosse uppon your shield *devizd,* . . . II. i. 31. 8
devisd redresse for such annoyes: . . . II. ii. 43. 8
Cover'd with lids *deviz'd* of substance sly, . . . II. ix. 46. 7
Ne can *devized* be of mortall wit; . . . II. ix. 50. 5
Pleasures porter was *devizd* to bee, . . . II. xii. 48. 8
The great Magitien Merlin had *deviz'd,* . . . III. ii. 18. 6
It fortuned, as they *devised* had: . . . III. v. 18. 1
She there *deviz'd* a wondrous worke to frame, . . . III. viii. 5. 2
Oft purposes, oft riddles, he *devysd,* . . . III. x. 8. 6
time and place, which shortly shee *Devized* hath, . . . III. x. 11. 7
Devized by the Gods, for to asswage Harts grief, . . . IV. iii. 43. 2
as thing *deviz'd* her to defame. . . . IV. v. 17. 5
to accord them all this meanes *deviz'd:* . . . IV. v. 25. 3
And eft againe *deviz'd* some what to say, . . . IV. vi. 45. 7
there a piteous ditty new *deviz'd,* . . . IV. viii. 12. 2
As each one had his furnitures *deviz'd.* . . . V. iii. 4. 5
Now she *deviz'd* . . . to seeke her errant Knight; . . . V. vi. 6. 5
full many treasons vile His father Dolon had *deviz'd* . . . V. vi. 33. 8
as they had *deviz'd,* . . . V. viii. 26. 1
Which warlike uses had *deviz'd* of yore: . . . V. viii. 34. 5
when he had *devized* of her case, . . . VI. iv. 34. 3
as they *devised* had, . . . VI. v. 16. 1
by natures skill *Devized* to worke delight . . . VI. x. 5. 7
Deviz'd all goodly meanes from her to drive The sad . . . VI. xi. 50. 6
That, some do say, was so by skill *devized,* . . . VII. vii. 6. 1
Their anthemes sweet, *devized* of loves prayse, . . . *Am.* xix. 6
Deviz'd a Web her wooers to deceave; . . . *Am.* xxiii. 2
Deviseth. thousand deathes *deviseth* in her vengefull mind. . . VII. vi. 48. 9
Devising. *Devizing* how that doughtie turnament . . . he atchieven might: . . . I. v. 1. 7
Thereof *devising* shortly to be wroke, . . . II. vi. 30. 8
in this distressed case, *Devising* what to doe, . . . VI. iii. 30. 6
Devizing of his love more then of daunger drad. . . . VI. vii. 6. 9
Devoid. *Devoid* of care, and feare of all falshedd; . . . *Gn.* 246
Sweete Love *devoyd* of villanie or ill, . . . *T.M.* 387
their flocks, *devoyd* of dangers feare, . . . *Col.* 54
His heavie head, *devoide* of careful carke; . . . I. i. 44. 4
the Paynim lay, *Devoid* of outward sence . . . I. v. 29. 3
'When I awoke, and found her place *devoyd,* . . . I. ix. 15. 1
devoyd of dreed, Upon him lightly leaping . . . II. viii. 49. 4
Had she not beene *devoide* of mortall slime, . . . III. iv. 35. 3
In perfect love, *devoide* of hatefull strife, . . . IV. xi. 52. 2
Their quiet heads, *devoyd* of guilty shame, . . . *H.L.* 290
Devoir. All for he did his *devoyr* belive! . . . *S.C.* S. 227
Devon. Which to avenge Sir *Devon* him did dight, . . . IV. iv. 21. 1
Devonish. devides The Cornish and the *Devonish* confines; . . IV. xi. 31. 2
Devonshire. Debons shayre was that is *Devonshyre:* . . . II. x. 12. 6
Devoted. Your toombs *devoted* compasse over-all, . . . *Ro.* i. 10
Devotion. *devotion* Taught him the fires scorn'd furie to detest; *Gn.* 611
It is enough to doo our small *devotion,* . . . *Hub.* 457
of *devotion* he had little care, . . . I. iv. 19. 3
day and night said his *devotion,* . . . I. x. 46. 6
With great *devotion,* and with little zele: . . . III. ii. 48. 5
turning feare to faint *devotion,* . . . IV. vi. 24. 8
should their mindes up to *devotion* call, . . . V. vi. 27. 4
They mote the better tend to their *devotion.* . . . V. vii. 9. 9
From his *devotion* streight he troubled was; . . . VI. v. 36. 3
Men to *devotion* ought to be inclynd: . . . *Am.* xxii. 2
Devotion's. Truth . . . Marres blind *Devotions* mart, . . . I. iii. Arg.
Devour. with equall ravine to *devoure.* . . . *Bel.*[2] viii. 8
the gaping earth *devoure* The spring, the place, . . . *Pet.* iv. 10
The pray of time, which all things doth *devowre!* . . . *Ro.* iii. 8
though time doth Commonwealths *devowre,* . . . *Ro.* viii. 11
sad cares that rich mens hearts *devowre.* . . . *Gn.* 136
left his whelps their kingdomes to *devoure?* . . . *Ti.* 70
To see th' unkindly Impes, . . . *Devoure* their dam; . . . I. i. 26. 3
how great wonder would your thoughts *devoure,* . . . II. ix. 3. 8
threatning to *devoure* all that his powre despise. . . . II. xii. 21. 9
Ran towards to *devoure* those unexpected guests. . . . II. xii. 39. 9
cruell Feendes should thee unwares *devowre:* . . . III. iii. 8. 9
so fowly to *devoure* Her native flesh . . . III. vii. 49. 4
met, As if that each ment other to *devoure;* . . . IV. iii. 15. 2
afterwardes themselves doth cruelly *devoure.* . . . IV. vii. 12. 9
I wast my life, and doe my daies *devowre* . . . IV. ix. 39. 5
fire *devoure* the ayre, and hell them quight, . . . IV. x. 35. 6
did streight *devoure* Both flames and tempest: . . . V. vii. 15. 5
Where still the stronger doth the weake *devoure,* . . . V. ix. 1. 6
twelve of them he did by times *devoure,* . . . V. x. 8. 3
Unto a dreadfull Monster to *devoure,* . . . V. x. 13. 7
As if that he attonce would me *devoure:* . . . VI. i. 9. 6
ran at him, as he would *devoure* His life . . . VI. iii. 48. 7
To be aveng'd on him and to *devoure* his corse. . . . VI. iv. 20. 9
the cold steele . . . did *devowre* His vitall breath, . . . VI. vii. 8. 7
straungers to *devoure,* which on their border Were brought . VI. viii. 36. 3
Was readie oft his owne heart to *devoure,* . . . VI. ix. 39. 4
the Lyon . . . disdeigneth to *devoure* The silly lambe . . . *Am.* xx. 7
the wylde wolves, which seeke them to *devoure,* . . . *Epith.* 69
Devoured. *See* **Late-devoured.**
the spring, that late *devoured* was. . . . *Pet.* v. 6
often *devoured* their owne sheepe, . . . *S.C.* May 128

Devoured—*Continued.*
He would have *devoured* both hidder and shidder. . . . *S.C.* S. 211
Devour'd of Time, in time to nought doo passe. . . . *Ti.* 420
To have attonce *devourd* her tender corse; . . . I. iii. 5. 6
early foe awaiting him beside To have *devourd,* . . . I. xi. 52. 5
Had in his greedy gulfe *devoured* deepe, . . . III. iv. 22. 6
quite *devourd* her beauties scornefull grace. . . . III. vii. 23. 5
sith workes of heavenly wits Are quite *devourd,* . . . IV. ii. 33. 9
Was of his hounds *devour'd* in Hunters hew. . . . VII. vi. 45. 5
Devouring. *See* **Deep-devouring, Life-devouring, Wide-devouring.**
reare a trophee for *devouring* death, . . . *Ti.* 52
The griesly gates of his *devouring* hell, . . . *Van.* iii. 10
Dragon . . . With murdrous ravine, and *devouring* might, . . I. vii. 44. 4
His biting sword, and his *devouring* speare, . . . I. vii. 48. 2
owre, not purifide Of Mulcibers *devouring* element; . . . II. vii. 5. 4
whiles they fly that Gulfes *devouring* jawes, . . . II. xii. 4. 8
their *devouring* covetize restraynd; . . . III. iv. 7. 8
this *devouring* Sea, that naught doth spare, . . . V. iv. 8. 2
For dread of their *devouring* enemie, . . . V. iv. 44. 8
The which whyleare she was so greedily *Devouring,* . . . V. xii. 39. 3
Devouring tyme and changeful chance . . . *Am.* lviii. 7
ravisht with *devouring* great desire Of his deare selfe, . . . *H.H.L.* 268
Devours. al good things with venemous tooth *devowres,* . . . *Mui.* 302
Yt now *devoures* with flames and scorching heat, . . . II. xi. 32. 8
Those he *devoures,* they say, both flesh and bone. . . . V. x. 29. 7
Devout. Yet of the *devout* people is ador'd, . . . *Ro.* xxviii. 10
Devoutly. Jaakob staffe in hand *devoutlie* crost, . . . *D.* 41
pray Upon her beads, *devoutly* penitent: . . . I. iii. 13. 7
for his safetie gan *devoutly* pray, . . . I. xi. 50. 8
gan *devoutly* sweare; . . . II. i. 61. 4
Dew. *See* **Due, Honey-dew.**
sudden dropping of a silver *dew* . . . *Bel.*[2] xi. 11
often halowed with holy-water *dewe:* . . . *S.C.* F. 210
The kindelye *dewe* drops from the higher tree, . . . *S.C.* N. 31
Theyr rootes bene dryed up for lacke of *dewe,* . . . *S.C.* D. 111
Sweete slumbring *deaw* in carelesnesse did steepe, . . . *Gn.* 323
dipt in *deaw* of Castalie: . . . *Ti.* 431
the *deaw* which yet on them does lie, . . . *Mui.* 181
all the day it standeth full of *deow,* . . . *As.* 191
silver *deaw* upon the roses pearling. . . . *Col.* 507
Sweet slombring *deaw,* the which to sleep them biddes. . . . I. i. 36. 4
Cynthia . . . doth steepe In silver *deaw* his ever-drouping hed, I. i. 39. 8
that holy water *dew* Wherein he fell, . . . I. xi. 36. 2
morning *deaw* upon their leaves doth light; . . . I. xii. 6. 8
themselves dipping in the silver *dew* . . . II. xii. 61. 7
nets, which oft we woven see Of scorched *deaw,* . . . II. xii. 77. 9
Her berth was of the wombe of Morning *dew,* . . . III. vi. 3. 1
Some of them washing with the liquid *dew* . . . III. vi. 17. 5
all the ground, with pretious *deaw* bedight, . . . III. vi. 43. 8
gan the humid vapour shed the grownd With perly *deaw,* . . III. x. 46. 6
his hoarie hed Dropped with brackish *deaw:* . . . III. xi. 40. 4
An holy-water sprinckle, dipt in *deowe,* . . . III. xii. 13. 6
With pearly *dew* sprinkling the morning grasse: . . . IV. v. 45. 5
To be embaulm'd, and sweat out dainty *dew,* . . . IV. vii. 40. 4
With few drops thereof did softly *dew,* Her wounds, . . . IV. viii. 20. 8
Thereon distill and *deaw* her daintie face, . . . V. xii. 13. 4
Some *deaw* of grace into my withered hart, . . . *H.B.* 27
Some little drop of thy celestiall *dew,* . . . *H.H.L.* 46
Dew-burning. High brandishing his bright *deaw-burning* blade, I. xi. 35. 6
Dewed. *See* **Nectar-dewed.**
dewed with teares they han be ever among. . . . *S.C.* D. 112
As it had *deawed* bene with timely raine: . . . I. xi. 48. 5
Their welheads spring, and are with moisture *deawd;* . . . II. ii. 6. 3
Deawd with ambrosiall kisses, . . . IV. Pr. 5. 6
Deawed with silver drops through sweating sore, . . . IV. vi. 19. 7
Dew'd with her drops of bountie Soveraine, . . . IV. viii. 33. 5
Deawed with silver drops that trickled downe alway. . . . IV. xi. 25. 9
Dewlap. His *dewelap* as lythe as lasse of Kent: . . . *S.C.* F. 74
Dewy. for the *deawie* night now doth nye, . . . *S.C.* May 316
soone as day doth shew his *deawie* face, . . . *D.* 484
Morning . . . Had spred her purple robe through *deawy* aire, I. ii. 7. 3
Phoebus . . . Came dauncing forth, shaking his *deawie* hayre, I. v. 2. 4
Out of the sea faire Titans *deawy* face, . . . I. xi. 33. 4
the *deawy* bed Of aged Tithone . . . I. xi. 51. 2
Gan cleare the *deawy* ayre . . . II. iii. 1. 4
His *deawy* face out of the sea doth reare; . . . II. xii. 65. 2
her faire *deawy* eies . . . Shee ofte did bathe, . . . III. ii. 34. 6
her faire *deawy* lockes yrent; . . . III. iv. 30. 2
ere the morrow did upreare His *deawy* head . . . III. iv. 61. 4
His watry eies drizling like *deawy* rayne, . . . III. v. 34. 3
sprinckled frost upon his *deawy* beard: . . . III. viii. 30. 4
In *deawy* vapours of the westerne mayne, . . . III. viii. 51. 4
From her faire eyes wiping the *deawy* wet . . . IV. vii. 35. 5
His *dewy* lockes did drop with brine apace . . . IV. xi. 11. 3
the *deawy* humour shed Did tricle downe . . . IV. xi. 46. 7
following his chace in *dewy* morne, . . . V. viii. 43. 2
Like to the Evening starre adorn'd with *deawy* ray. . . . VI. vii. 19. 9
Her *deawy* humour gan on th' earth to shed, . . . VI. ix. 13. 2
The *deawy* leaves among! . . . *Epith.* 89
Dewy-dropping. With hoary head and *deawy dropping* beard, *Col.* 250
Dha. Howell *Dha* shall goodly well indew . . . III. iii. 45. 4
Diadem. betweene the Cuppe And golden *Diademe:* . . . *S.C.* Jul. 20
to steale the *Diademe* away . . . *Hub.* 1034
oft unsweare, a *Diademe* to beare? . . . *Hub.* 1058
The sacred *Diademe* in peeces rent, . . . II. vii. 13. 6
on him tooke the roiall *Diademe,* . . . II. x. 47. 3
Under his *Diademe* imperiall: . . . IV. xi. 11. 4
a *Diademe* embattild wide With hundred turrets, . . . IV. xi. 28. 5
with *Diademe* hath ever crowned beene.' . . . V. ix. 20. 9

Diadems. crownes, and *Diademes,* and titles vaine, ... II. vii. 43. 8
Dial. on the top a *Diall* told the timely howres. . . . . . . I. iv. 4. 9
Diamond. hundred pillers . . . of fine *Diamant* . . . . *Bel.*[1] ii. 3
a sharped spyre of *Diamond* (*diamant*[1]) . . . . *Bel.* iii. 1
pillours . . . All wrought with *Diamond* . . . . *Bel.*[2] ii. 4
As rock of *Diamond* stedfast evermore. . . . . I. vi. 4. 5
all of *Diamond* perfect pure and cleene . . . . I. vii. 33. 5
The second *Dyamond,* the youngest Triamond. . . . . . . IV. ii. 41. 9
Prince Arthur gave a boxe of *Diamond* sure, ... I. ix. 19. 1
Strong *Diamond,* but not so stout a knight; . . . . IV. ii. 42. 2
horse and foote knew *Diamond* to wield: . . . . IV. ii. 42. 6
With curtaxe used *Diamond* to smite, ... IV. ii. 42. 7
Till *Diamond,* disdeigning long delay . . . Resolv'd to end it . IV. iii. 17. 6
seem'd a rocke of *Diamond* it could rive . . . . IV. v. 37. 8
like a *Diamond* of rich regard, ... VI. xi. 13. 3
Nor to the *Diamond;* for they are more tender; . . . . . *Am.* ix. 10
the hard *diamond,* which them both doth passe. . . . . . *H.H.B.* 154
Diana. Sometimes *Diana* he her takes to be, ... I. vi. 16. 8
Diana in fresh sommers day Beholdes her nymphes . . . . I. xii. 7. 7
to *Diana* calling lowd for ayde, ... II. ii. 8. 4
Diana by the sandy shore Of swift Eurotas, ... II. iii. 31. 1
Thereat *Diana* gan to smile, ... III. vi. 21. 1
Not that same famous Temple of *Diane,* . . . . IV. x. 30. 1
for his sake *Diana* did lament, ... V. viii. 43. 6
In her sweet streames *Diana* used oft . . . To bathe . . . . VII. vi. 42. 1
Diana, with her Nymphes about her, ... VII. vi. 45. 7
So did *Diana* and her maydens all Use silly Faunus, ... VII. vi. 49. 1
by commaund'ment of *Diana,* . . . . VII. vi. 53. 3
Diana, full of indignation, ... VII. vi. 54. 1
As *Diane* hunted on a day, ... *Epig.* ii. 1
Love wounded my Loves hart, But *Diane* beasts with Cupids dart. . . . . *Epig.* ii. 8
Diana's. By *Dianes* meanes, who was Hippolyts frend, ... I. v. 39. 7
Nymph . . . Was out of *Dianes* favor, as it then befell. . . . . I. vii. 4. 9
To search the secret haunts of *Dianes* company. . . . . . . III. vi. 16. 9
some Goddesse, or of *Dianes* crew, ... III. vii. 11. 7
how Arlo, through *Dianaes* spights, . . . Was made the most unpleasant . . . . VII. vi. 37. 5
by *Dianaes* doom unjust Slew great Orion; . . . . VII. vii. 39. 7
Diapase. make a tunefull *Diapase* of pleasures, ... *T.M.* 549
All which compacted made a goodly *Diapase.* . . . . II. ix. 22. 9
Diaper. In *dieper,* in damaske, or in lyne, ... *Mui.* 364
Diapered. *diapred* lyke the discolored mead. . . . . *Epith.* 51
Dice. With *dice,* with cards, with balliards farre unfit . . . . *Hub.* 803
Just *Dice,* wise Eunomie, myld Eirene; . . . . V. ix. 32. 6
Did (*partial list of auxiliary*).
eager dogs *did* her pursue . . . . *Pet.* i. 6
downe *dyd* lye, ... *S.C.* Ja. 72
Will doe as *did* the Foxe by the Kidde. . . . . *S.C.* May 171
With pyping and dauncing *did* (*didst) passe the rest. . . . *S.C.* Au. 10
All for he *did* his devoyr belive! . . . . *S.C.* S. 227
a wicked maladie . . . that manie *did* to die, ... *Hub.* 10
little thrift for him he *did* it too: . . . . *Hub.* 240
What *did* they then, but made a composition . . . . *Hub.* 571
Thinking that their disgracing *did* him grace: . . . . *Hub.* 708
What else then *did* he by progression, ... *Hub.* 842
on his backe the skin he *did,* . . . . *Hub.* 1062
did he good to none, to manie ill, ... *Hub.* 1197
everie day, in which she *did* a deed, ... *Col.* 594
he shortly *did,* and Una left to mourne. . . . . I. xii. 41. 9
all he *did* was to deceive good knights, ... II. i. 23. 1
almost it *did* haynous violence . . . . II. i. 28. 6
all I *did,* I *did* but as I ought. . . . . II. i. 33. 5
ere they *did* their utmost obsequy, ... II. i. 60. 7
said and *did* all that mote him delight, ... II. vi. 22. 2
So *did* she all that might his constant hart Withdraw . . . . II. vi. 25. 5
wars and spoiles, the which he *did* of yore.' . . . . II. vi. 35. 9
All which he *did* to do him deadly fall . . . . II. vii. 64. 1
They both attone, *Did* dewty to their Lady, ... II. ix. 28. 7
The knightes there entring *did* him reverence dew, ... II. ix. 59. 1
did away that blame . . . . II. x. 23. 4
As *did* this knight, before ye hither came.' . . . . III. i. 27. 5
nought she *did* but wayle, ... III. ii. 28. 8
ever what she *did* was streight undonne. . . . . III. ii. 51. 5
Such happinesse *did,* maulgre, to me spight, ... III. v. 7. 5
To bene avenged of the shame he *did* . . . . III. v. 13. 5
did the best His grievous hurt to guarish, ... III. v. 41. 5
'So well I to faire Ladies service *did,* . . . . III. vii. 55. 1
It pleased; so he *did.* . . . . III. x. 42. 9
both *did* and sayd Full many things . . . . IV. i. 7. 4
attended duly on her, . . . and *did* to her all honor. . . . . IV. i. 8. 9
So much they *did,* that at the last they brake His slomber, . IV. i. 43. 8
Yet he to her *did* dayly service more, ... IV. ii. 11. 1
So *did* they surely during all their dayes, ... IV. ii. 54. 1
all she *did* was but to weare out day. . . . . IV. vi. 45. 5
saw that all he said and *did* was vaine, ... IV. vii. 47. 2
more then ever *did* Cambridge or Oxford, ... IV. xi. 35. 5
never wight so evill *did* or thought, ... IV. xii. 30. 8
die guiltie of the blame The which another *did,* . . . . . . V. i. 15. 9
So *did* the Ladies both, as may be knowne: . . . . V. i. 17. 4
so *did* the fire the aire; . . . . V. ii. 32. 4
He *did* so first, and then the false he layd . . . . V. ii. 45. 6
So *did* he; and then plaine it did appeare, ... V. ii. 48. 7
what he *did* that day, he *did* it not For her, ... V. iii. 16. 3
ne ought he sayd, Ne ought he *did,* . . . . V. iii. 18. 6
with faire words, but words *did* little good, ... V. iv. 4. 8
what he *did,* and in what state he stood, ... V. vi. 15. 8
never *did* her ill, ne once deserved blame. . . . . V. viii. 22. 9
for th' evill which he *did* therein, ... V. ix. 26. 7
Did to her myld obeysance, as they ought, ... V. ix. 34. 4

Did—*Continued.*
if she heard of ill that any *did,* . . . . V. xii. 32. 5
he fouly *did* to die. . . . . V. xii. 40. 9
So off he *did* his shield, ... VI. ii. 48. 1
And what he *did,* he *did* himselfe to save: . . . . VI. ii. 14. 6
nought weighing what he sayd or *did,* . . . . VI. iii. 37. 1
Whiles he him selfe all night *did* nought but weepe, ... VI. iii. 44. 8
When ought he *did,* that did their lyking gaine. . . . . . . VI. iv. 16. 5
Ne she lesse glad; for she so wisely *did,* . . . . VI. iv. 38. 3
And *did* right noble deedes; the which els where are showne. VI. iv. 38. 9
Howbe that carefull Hermite *did* his best, ... VI. vi. 2. 6
So *did* his forty yoemen, which there with him came. . . . . VI. vi. 25. 9
So *did* the Squire, the whiles the Carle did fret . . . . . . VI. vii. 47. 7
What ever thing he *did* her to aggrate, ... VI. x. 33. 2
day and night she nought *did* but lament . . . . VI. x. 44. 3
He went forth on his quest, and *did* that him befell. . . . . VI. xii. 13. 9
Yet *did* that auncient matrone all she might, ... VI. xii. 14. 6
So Orpheus *did* for his owne bride! . . . . *Epith.* 16
Dide. *See* **Died, Dyed.**
Dido. deade is *Dido,* dead, alas! and drent; . . . . *S.C.* N. 37
Dido! the greate shepehearde his daughter sheene. . . . . . *S.C.* N. 38
Dido, my deare, alas! is dead, ... *S.C.* N. 58
Dido nis dead, but into heaven hent. . . . . *S.C.* N. 169
'*Dido* is gone afore; . . . . *S.C.* N. 193
Didst (*partial list*).
Didst arme thy hand . . . . *Ro.* xxxi. 11
with Love thou *diddest* fight: . . . . *S.C.* Mar. 104
*With pyping and dauncing, *didst* passe the rest. . . . . . *S.C.* Au. 10
never *didst* thou heare more haplesse fate. . . . . *D.* 98
So whylome *didst* thou to faire Florimell, ... IV. vii. 2. 1
Which *didst* that service unto Florimell. . . . . V. iii. 21. 4
Or shew the sweat with which thou *diddest* sway . . . . . . V. iii. 21. 8
Die. *See* **Dye.**
which shall never *die* Through your faire verses, ... *Ro.* i. 3
her garland so much honoured Began to *die,* . . . . *Van.* vii. 10
Am like for desperate doole to *dye,* . . . . *S.C.* F. 155
if for gracelesse greefe I *dye,* . . . . *S.C.* Au. 113
Nowe is time to *dye:* . . . . *S.C.* N. 81
Dye would we dayly, ... *S.C.* N. 186
manie did to *die,* . . . . *Hub.* 10
Shall *die* in darknesse, and lie hid in slime: . . . . *T.M.* 106
die forgot from whence at first they sprong, ... *T.M.* 443
Nowe doe I alwayes *dye,* . . . . *U.V.* 18
if I *dye,* who will saye: *this was Immerito?* . . . . *U.V.* 21
the Evill damning evermore to *dy:* . . . . *Com. Son.* i. 12
'I saw him *die,* I saw him *die,* . . . . *Ti.* 190
I saw him *die,* and no man left to mone . . . . *Ti.* 192
For, when thou diest, all shall with thee *die.* . . . . *Ti.* 210
by thee thy Lord shall never *die.* . . . . *Ti.* 252
'Thy Lord shall never *die,* . . . . *Ti.* 253
'Ne shall his sister, ne thy father *die,* . . . . *Ti.* 260
'Ne may I let thy husbands sister *die,* . . . . *Ti.* 274
Die in obscure oblivion, ... *Ti.* 346
them immortall make, which els would *die* . . . . *Ti.* 377
'For deedes doe *die,* how ever noblie donne. . . . . *Ti.* 400
Could save the sonne of Thetis from to *die;* . . . . *Ti.* 429
Feeling the fit that him forwarnd to *die,* . . . . *Ti.* 598
I for dole was almost like to *die.* . . . . *Ti.* 672
seeke alone to weepe, and *dye* alone.' . . . . *D.* 77
To *die* alone, unpitied, unplained; . . . . *D.* 79
ere thou *die,* it were convenient . . . . *D.* 80
For age to *dye* is right, but youth is wrong; . . . . *D.* 243
'Yet fell she not as one enforst to *dye,* . . . . *D.* 253
graunt his boone that most desires to *dye.* . . . . *D.* 357
pitie me that living thus doo *die;* . . . . *D.* 383
dying lives, and living still does *dye.* . . . . *D.* 434
'So doo I live, so doo I daylie *die,* . . . . *D.* 435
doo not *dye* then in despight of death; . . . . *D.* 443
uneath To leave this life, or dolorous to *dye?* . . . . *D.* 448
to *dye* must needes be joyeous, ... *D.* 451
As one disposed wilfullie to *die,* . . . . *D.* 552
longs death to behold, Before he *die,* . . . . *Col.* 205
Where I will live or *die* at her beheast, ... *Col.* 254
graunt them grace that otherwise would *die.* . . . . *Col.* 882
for ever witnesse bee, That hers I *die,* . . . . *Col.* 950
thus perforce he bids me do, or *die.* . . . . I. i. 51. 6
Die is my dew; yet rew my wretched state, ... I. i. 51. 7
Let me not *die* in languor and long teares.' . . . . I. i. 52. 7
such is the *dye* of warre. . . . . I. ii. 36. 7
When such I see, . . . all for pitty I could *dy.* . . . . I. iii. 1. 9
they should live in wo, and *dye* in wretchednesse. . . . . . I. v. 46. 9
both chose to win, or *die.* . . . . I. vi. 43. 9
Hold for my sake, and doe him not to *dye,* . . . . I. vii. 14. 7
holy Martyres often doen to *dye* With cruell malice . . . . . I. viii. 36. 4
Now in your powre, to let her live, or *die.'* . . . . I. viii. 45. 6
'To doe her *die,'* (quoth Una) 'were despight, ... I. viii. 45. 7
Least so great good . . . Should *die* unknown, ... I. ix. 2. 9
him that would have forced me to *dye?* . . . . I. ix. 26. 2
Perswade us *dye,* to stint all further strife: . . . . I. ix. 29. 8
lever had I *die* then see his deadly face.' . . . . I. ix. 32. 9
he should *dye* who merites not to live? . . . . I. ix. 38. 4
let him *dye,* that loatheth living breath, ... I. ix. 38. 8
let him *die* at ease, that liveth here uneath? . . . . I. ix. 38. 9
Did not he all create To *die* againe? . . . . I. ix. 42. 3
Let every sinner *die;* Die shall all flesh? . . . . I. ix. 47. 5, 6
die soone, O faeries sonne!' . . . . I. ix. 47. 9
not doe him *die,* Till he should *die* his last, ... I. ix. 54. 8, 9
Disdeining life, desiring leave to *dye,* . . . . I. x. 22. 8
That tree through one mans fault hath doen us all to *dy.* . . I. xi. 47. 9
die with you in sorrow, ... II. i. 48. 9

Die—*Continued.*
As selfe to *dyen* bad, unburied bad to beene.' . . . . II. i. 59. 9
Her deare besought to let her *die* a mayd. . . . . II. ii. 8. 5
Dy, or thyselfe my captive yield for ay. . . . . II. iii. 7. 8
'Betwixt them both they have me doen to *dye,* . . . . II. iv. 33. 1
So shall wrath, gealosy, griefe, love, *die* and decay.' . . . . . II. iv. 35. 9
he cryde; 'Mercy! doe me not *dye,* . . . . II. v. 12. 7
th' equall *die* of warre he well did know: . . . . II. v. 13. 4
Will *die* for thrist, and water doth refuse? . . . . II. vi. 17. 8
What coward hand shall doe thee next to *dye,* . . . . II. vi. 39. 8
Threatning with greedy gripe to doe him *dye,* . . . . II. vii. 27. 7
th' unjust Atheniens made to *dy* Wise Socrates; . . . . . . II. vii. 52. 6
He daily dyde, yet never throughly *dyen* couth. . . . . . . II. vii. 58. 9
Lo! here I now for want of food doe *dye:* . . . . II. vii. 59. 7
As author of unjustice, there to let him *dye.* . . . . II. vii. 60. 9
Delivered up the Lord of life to *dye,* . . . . II. vii. 62. 6
To proove he lived il that did thus fowly *dye.* . . . . II. viii. 12. 9
thousand Sar'zins fowly donne to *dye.'* . . . . II. viii. 18. 6
The trespass still doth live, albee the person *dye.'* . . . . . II. viii. 28. 9
dye with honour and desert of fame; . . . . II. viii. 44. 5
with revenge desyring soone to *dye,* . . . . II. viii. 47. 2
As one that loathed life, and yet despysd to *dye.* . . . . . . II. viii. 50. 9
say, that I not overcome doe *dye,* . . . . II. viii. 52. 3
losse of thousand lives, to *die* at her desire.' . . . . II. ix. 5. 9
The eldest brother, did untimely *dy;* . . . . II. x. 75. 7
could not *die,* yet seemd a mortall wight, ... II. xi. 40. 7
The whistler shrill, that whoso heares doth *dy;* . . . . II. xii. 36. 8
Dye rather would he then endure that same. . . . . III. i. 9. 5
better were to *dy.* . . . . III. i. 25. 4
she mote algates *dye:* . . . . III. i. 53. 6
Is not enough that I alone doe *dye,* . . . . III. ii. 35. 3
feed on shadowes whiles I *die* for food, ... III. ii. 44. 3
even the wilde beast shall *dy* in starved den. . . . . III. iii. 34. 9
Shall tread adowne, and doe him fowly *dye;* . . . . III. iii. 39. 8
'Then shall Cadwallin *die;* . . . . III. iii. 40. 1
with him attonce shall *dye;* . . . . III. iii. 40. 2
maugre thee will passe or *dy.'* . . . . III. iv. 15. 4
they for love of him would algates *dy:* . . . . III. iv. 26. 8
Dy, who so list for him, he was loves enimy. . . . . III. iv. 26. 9
they that *dye* doe nether love nor hate: . . . . III. iv. 37. 6
To beene ybredd and never borne to *dye?* . . . . III. iv. 38. 2
Farre better I it deeme to *die* with speed . . . . III. iv. 38. 3
Thus much afford me, ere that he did *die,* . . . . III. iv. 39. 3
Dye rather, *dye,* then so disloyally . . . . III. v. 45. 6
Fayre death it is, to shonne more shame, to *dy:* . . . . . . III. v. 45. 8
Dye rather, *dy,* then ever love disloyally. . . . . III. v. 45. 9
Dye rather, *dye,* and dying doe her serve; . . . . III. v. 46. 6
Dye rather, *dye,* then ever from her service swerve. . . . . . III. v. 46. 9
dye meekly for her sake: . . . . III. v. 47. 8
Dye rather, *dye,* then ever so faire love forsake!' . . . . . . III. v. 47. 9
rather chose to *dye* for sorow great, ... III. v. 49. 8
Of all things that are borne to live and *dye,* . . . . III. vi. 30. 5
For ever *dye,* and ever buried bee . . . . III. vi. 47. 2
She flyes; he faines to *dy.* . . . . III. vii. Arg.
it she shund no lesse then dread to *die;* . . . . III. vii. 24. 4
muchell blood did spend, Yet might not doe him *die:* . . . . . III. vii. 32. 8
in eternall bondage *dye* he must, ... III. vii. 50. 7
thousand deathes me lever were to *dye* . . . . III. vii. 51. 5
Dy, if thou it gainesay: . . . . III. viii. 12. 9
Dye had she rather in tormenting griefe . . . . III. viii. 42. 3
rather had he *dy* Then . . . in coward corner ly. . . . . . . III. ix. 14. 8
To doe fowle death to *die,* . . . . III. ix. 17. 9
Mercie . . . give, That he mote algates *dye,* . . . . III. x. 7. 9
meant to ravish her, that rather had to *dy.* . . . . III. x. 13. 9
Yet can he never *dye,* but dying lives, ... III. x. 60. 1
Deliver her fro thence, or with her for you *dy.* . . . . III. xi. 18. 9
let me *die* that ought: . . . . III. xi. 19. 6
More is more losse; one is enough to *dy.'* . . . . III. xi. 19. 7
Scudamore here *die* with sorrowing.' . . . . III. xi. 24. 4
to abstaine From doing him to *dy.* . . . . III. xii. 34. 5
Be sure that nought may save thee from to *dy* . . . . III. xii. 35. 4
This doe, and live, els *dye* undoubtedly.' . . . . III. xii. 35. 7
Die had she lever with Enchanters knife . . . . IV. i. 6. 8
rather *die* then Ladies cause release: . . . . IV. ii. 19. 7
Yet dead he was not, yet he sure did *die,* . . . . IV. iii. 30. 6
bad him rise, or surely he should *die.* . . . . IV. vi. 23. 6
die or live, for nought he would upstand, ... IV. vi. 23. 7
lives a loathed life, and wishing cannot *die.* . . . . IV. vii. 11. 9
make me loath this life, still longing for to *die.* . . . . . IV. viii. 16. 9
Greeks and Trojans which therein did *die;* . . . . IV. xi. 20. 7
To let her *die* whom he might have redrest.' . . . . IV. xii. 8. 5
let me *die* and end my daies attone, ... IV. xii. 9. 8
By wicked doome condemn'd a wretched death to *die.* . . . . IV. xii. 29. 9
Proteus, that hath ordayn'd my sonne to *die;* . . . . IV. xii. 31. 2
die guiltie of the blame The which another did, ... V. i. 15. 8
rather of his hand besought to *die.* . . . . V. i. 18. 4
when they *die* They turne to that whereof they first were made? V. ii. 40. 6
'They live, they *die,* like as he doth ordaine, ... V. ii. 41. 1
'The wretched mayd, that earst desir'd to *die,* . . . . V. iv. 11. 1
That he of womens hands so base a death should *dy.* . . . . . V. iv. 22. 9
that same wretched man, ordayned to *die,* . . . . V. iv. 25. 1
I rather chose to *die* in lives despight, ... V. iv. 32. 8
Die rather would he in penurious paine, ... V. v. 46. 5
To fight with him, and goodly *die* her last. . . . . V. vi. 13. 3
sith ye please that both our blames shall *die,* . . . . V. viii. 14. 1
feedes on all the carkasses that *die* In sacrifize . . . . . . V. xi. 20. 3
Dye, rather then doe ought that mote dishonour yield.' . . . . V. xi. 55. 9
he fouly did to *die.* . . . . V. xii. 40. 9
th' one is dead, and th' other soone shall *die,* . . . . VI. vii. 13. 3
at the last through dreary dolour *die:* . . . . VI. vii. 31. 4

Die—*Continued.*
let them love that list, or live or *die,* . . . . VI. viii. 21. 1
Me list not *die* for any lovers doole; . . . . VI. viii. 21. 2
He would with whipping him have done to *dye:* . . . . . . VI. viii. 29. 3
Ne stayeth leave to take before his friends doe *dye.* . . . . . VI. xi. 18. 9
Before I saw faire Pastorella *dye.'* . . . . VI. xi. 29. 4
'*Die?* out alas!' then Calidore did cry, ... VI. xi. 29. 5
These eyes saw *die,* and dearely did lament; . . . . VI. xi. 31. 7
needs mote she *die* at last. . . . . VI. xi. 32. 2
Then to *die* with her, ... VI. xi. 34. 9
all living wights have learn'd to *die,* . . . . VII. vi. 6. 5
The beasts we daily see massacred *dy* . . . . VII. vii. 19. 2
If not, *die* soone; and I with thee will perish. . . . . . . *Am.* ii. 14
Bids all old thoughts to *die* in dumpish spright: . . . . . . *Am.* iv. 4
Then doe I *die,* as one with lightning fyred. . . . . *Am.* vii. 8
To force me live, and will not let me *dy.* . . . . *Am.* xi. 12
fall downe and *dy* before her; . . . . *Am.* xiv. 13
better were attonce to let me *die,* . . . . *Am.* xxv. 5
doe me not before my time to *dy.* . . . . *Am.* xlii. 14
like a stupid stock in silence *die!* . . . . *Am.* xliii. 8
thinck they *dy* with pleasure, live with payne. . . . . *Am.* xlvii. 14
for whom thou diddest *dye,* . . . . *Am.* lxviii. 6
let baser things devize to *dy* in dust, ... *Am.* lxxv. 10
They deigne to see, and seeing it still *dye.* . . . . *H.L.* 133
To let her live thus free, and me to *dy.* . . . . *H.L.* 154
Had it bene death, yet would he *die* againe, ... *H.L.* 243
it is heavenly borne and can not *die,* . . . . *H.B.* 104
Doing him *die* that never it deserved, ... *H.H.L.* 160
Thenceforth all worlds desire will in thee *dye,* . . . . *H.H.L.* 274

Died. *See* **Dyed.**
faire greene Laurel witherd up and *dide.* . . . . *Bel.*[1] vii. 14
Fell to the ground, and there untimely *dide.* . . . . *Pet.* i. 12
foorthwith in great despight he *dide.* . . . . *Pet.* v. 11
'He *dyde,* and after him his brother *dyde,* . . . . *Ti.* 239
Ne *dyde* with dread and grudging discontent, ... *D.* 254
sad Alcyon *dyde* in lifes disdaine. . . . . *D.* 525
Which gives them life, that els would soone have *dide,* . . . . *Ded. Son.* iv. 11
scornd of God and man, a shamefull death he *dide.* . . . . . I. v. 48. 9
The messenger of so unhappie newes Would faine have *dyde:* . I. vii. 21. 2
when he *dyde,* the Faery Queene it brought To Faerie lond, . I. vii. 36. 8
Els should this Redcrosse knight in bands have *dyde,* . . . . I. viii. 1. 8
cleare she *dide* from blemish criminall: . . . . II. i. 37. 7
to ayd her ere she *dyde.* . . . . II. iii. 3. 9
him restor'd to helth that would have algates *dyde.* . . . . . II. vi. 51. 9
He daily *dyde,* yet never throughly *dyen* couth. . . . . . . II. vii. 58. 9
'What doe I recke, sith that he *dide* entire? . . . . II. viii. 15. 2
he *dyde,* made ripe for death by eld, ... II. x. 32. 2
Donwallo *dyde,* (for what may live for ay?) . . . . II. x. 40. 1
He *dide,* and him succeeded Marius, ... II. x. 53. 1
This good king shortly without issew *dide,* . . . . II. x. 54. 1
A litle whyle Before that Merlin *dyde,* . . . . III. iii. 10. 2
he swownd, he perdy *dyde,* . . . . III. x. 7. 4
when as he *dyde,* He wailed womanlike . . . . III. xii. 7. 6
he through lives despeire Untimely *dyde,* . . . . VI. ii. 28. 4

Dies. when th' one *dies,* th' other then beginnes . . . . . . *Ti.* 388
'the evill donne *Dyes* not, ... II. viii. 29. 2
Who *dyes,* the utmost dolor doth abye; . . . . III. iv. 38. 5
dyes like ill grounded seeds. . . . . IV. iv. 1. 9

Diest. Why *dyest* thou stil, ... *S.C.* D. 96
For, when thou *diest,* all shall with thee die. . . . . *Ti.* 210

Diet. Scarce this right hand the mouth with *diet* feedeth, . . . *Hub.* 274
with streight *diet* tame his stubborne malady. . . . . I. x. 25. 9
He Steward was, hight *Diet;* . . . . II. ix. 27. 8
'Some of his *diet* doe from him withdraw, ... V. v. 50. 1
his scarse *diet* somewhat was amended, ... V. v. 57. 2
Meat fit for such a monsters monsterous *dyeat:* . . . . V. xii. 31. 9
I . . . all her pray and all her *diet* know. . . . . VI. ii. 32. 4
Use scanted *diet,* and forbeare your fill; . . . . VI. vi. 14. 7

Dieted. *dieted* with fasting every day, ... I. x. 26. 3

Diets. to cherish him with *diets* daint, ... I. x. 2. 7

Differd. *See* **Deferred.**

Difference. To scorne all *difference* of great and small, ... *Van.* xii. 6
That there might be no *difference* nor strife, ... *Hub.* 148
breede Doubts mongst Divines, and *difference* of texts, . . . *Hub.* 387
What *difference* twixt man and beast is left, ... *T.M.* 487
were there rightfull cause of *difference,* . . . . II. ii. 30. 1
great *difference* Betweene the vulgar and the noble seed, . . . II. iv. 1. 2
Deformed creatures, in straunge *difference,* . . . . II. xi. 10. 3
The waters fall with *difference* discreet, ... II. xii. 71. 7
he chooseth with vile *difference* To be a beast, ... II. xii. 87. 4
leaves no skill nor *difference* of wight. . . . . VI. xi. 16. 9

Different. Where other powers farre *different* I see, ... *Gn.* 420
Of forreine lands, of people *different,* . . . . *Hub.* 765
Betweene the nations *different* afore, ... III. iii. 49. 2
stirred up with *different* desires, ... V. iv. 4. 4
With like fierce minds, but meanings *different;* . . . . . . V. viii. 30. 2
So *different* from that which earst ye seem'd in sight?' . . . . VI. vii. 14. 9

Differing. *diff'ring* both in willes agreed in fine: . . . . . . II. xii. 59. 7
differing in honour and degree: . . . . VI. x. 21. 5

Difficult. Hard is the doubt, and *difficult* to deeme, ... IV. ix. 1. 1

Diffuse. they to each such fortune doe *diffuse,* . . . . VI. ix. 29. 4

Diffused. Being *diffused* through the senceless tronck, ... II. ii. 4. 8
From whose sterne presence they *diffused* ran, ... V. xi. 47. 8

Dig. To *dig* up sods out of the flowrie grasse, ... *Gn.* 654
the hid treasures . . . With Sacriledge to *dig.* . . . . II. vii. 17. 4

Digest. Yet could it not so thoroughly *digest,* . . . . V. v. 27. 3
Being unable to *digest* that bone; . . . . VI. iv. 21. 7

Digestion. The kitchin clerke, that hight *Digestion,* . . . . . II. ix. 31. 3

Digged. *See* **Deep-digged.**
how mount Athos . . . Was *digged* downe, ... *Gn.* 46

Diggon. *Diggon* Davie! I bidde her god day; . . . . *S.C.* S. 1
Or *Diggon* her is, or I missaye. . . . . *S.C.* S. 2
Diggon, areede who has thee so dight? . . . . *S.C.* S. 7
Diggon, I am so stiffe and so stanck, ... *S.C.* S. 47
Now say on, *Diggon,* what ever thou hast. . . . . *S.C.* S. 55
Diggon, I praye thee, speake not so dirke; . . . . . . *S.C.* S. 102
Diggon, I see thou speakest to plaine; . . . . *S.C.* S. 136
Fye on thee, *Diggon,* . . . . *S.C.* S. 150
Say it out, *Diggon,* whatever it hight, ... *S.C.* S. 172
Marry, *Diggon,* what should him affraye . . . . *S.C.* S. 208
How mought we, *Diggon,* hem be-hold? . . . . *S.C.* S. 229
Ah, *Diggon!* thilke same rule were too straight, ... *S.C.* S. 236
Diggon, I lament The haplesse mischiefe . . . . *S.C.* S. 248
Diggon should soone find favour and ease: . . . . *S.C.* S. 253
Diggon on fewe such freends did ever lite. . . . . . . *S.C.* S. 259

Dight. *See* **Overdight.**
The floore of Jasp and Emeraude was *dight.* . . . . *Bel.*[2] ii. 11
A goodly ship with banners bravely *dight,* . . . . *Van.* ix. 2
Thy sommer prowde, with Daffadillies *dight;* . . . . . . *S.C.* Ja. 22
if hys ditties bene so trimly *dight,* . . . . *S.C.* Ap. 29
home they hasten the postes to *dight,* . . . . *S.C.* May 11
The grassye ground with daintye Daysies *dight,* . . . . . *S.C.* Jun. 6
Dight gaudy Girlonds was my common trade, ... *S.C.* Jun. 45
areede who has thee so *dight?* . . . . *S.C.* S. 7
Where bene the nosegayes that she *dight* for thee? . . . . *S.C.* N. 114
To spil the flowres that should her girlond *dight?* . . . . *S.C.* D. 114
groves, with green leaves *dight.* . . . . *Gn.* 32
bad the Ape him *dight* To play his part, ... *Hub.* 233
when he was all *dight,* . . . . *Hub.* 1064
on his head his dreadfull hat he *dight,* . . . . *Hub.* 1279
Thus *dight,* into the Court he tooke his way, ... *Hub.* 1300
her awaking bad her quickly *dight,* . . . . *Ti.* 639
his shinie wings . . . he did about him *dight:* . . . . . . *Mui.* 91
Thus the fresh Clarion, being readie *dight,* . . . . . . *Mui.* 145
Her selfe likewise unto her worke to *dight.* . . . . . . *Mui.* 304
The silken downe with which his backe is *dight,* . . . . . *Mui.* 334
who shall *dight* your bowres, sith she is dead . . . . . . *D.* 318
well I wot my rymes bene rudely *dight.* . . . . *As.* Pr. 12
they promised to *dight* for him Gay chapelets . . . . . . *As.* 41
wont to be with flowers and gyrlonds *dight,* . . . . . . *As.* 153
Gan *dight* themselves t' expresse their inward woe, ... *As.* Interl. 225
With Roses *dight* and Goolds and Daffadillies; . . . . . . *Col.* 339
All were my notes but rude and roughly *dight,* . . . . . . *Col.* 363
courts chief garlond with all vertues *dight,* . . . . . . *Col.* 499
which was on every side With . . . costly arras *dight.* . . . . I. iv. 6. 6
others trimly *dight* Their gay attyre; . . . . I. iv. 14. 8
ere he could his armour on him *dight,* . . . . I. vii. 8. 1
A foxes taile, with dong all fowly *dight;* . . . . I. viii. 48. 4
The verdant gras my couch did goodly *dight,* . . . . . . I. ix. 13. 3
His aery plumes doth rouze, full rudely *dight;* . . . . . . I. xi. 9. 6
did himselfe to battaile ready *dight;* . . . . I. xi. 52. 3
The comely virgins came, with girlands *dight,* . . . . . . I. xii. 6. 6
Oft had he seene her faire, but never so faire *dight.* . . . . I. xii. 23. 9
So fairely *dight* when she in presence came, ... I. xii. 24. 1
Most false Duessa, royall richly *dight,* . . . . I. xii. 32. 4
steede . . . Whose sides with dapled circles weren *dight;* . . II. i. 18. 7
that brave steed there finding ready *dight,* . . . . II. iii. 4. 8
whose heads were *dight* In poyson . . . . II. iv. 38. 8
The truncked beast fast bleeding did him fowly *dight.* . . . II. v. 4. 9
gan him *dight* to succour his distresse, ... II. v. 24. 2
he quickly does him *dight,* . . . . II. v. 38. 1
fresh flowrets *dight* About her necke, ... II. vi. 7. 4
Who likewise gan himselfe to batteill *dight,* . . . . . . II. vii. 42. 5
'What herce or steed' . . . 'should he have *dight,* . . . . . II. viii. 16. 8
So ready *dight* fierce battaile to assay, ... II. viii. 22. 8
ready *dight* with drapets festivall, ... II. ix. 27. 3
with royall arras richly *dight,* . . . . II. ix. 33. 7
as yet ashamd how rude Pan did her *dight.* . . . . II. ix. 40. 9
to her guestes doth bounteous banket *dight,* . . . . . . II. xi. 2. 8
Eftsoones himselfe in glitterand armes he *dight,* . . . . . II. xi. 17. 1
being goodly *dight* With bowes and braunches, ... II. xii. 53. 7
As faint through heat, or *dight* to pleasant sin; . . . . . II. xii. 77. 2
rownd about it many beds were *dight,* . . . . III. i. 39. 2
Supper was shortly *dight,* . . . . III. i. 51. 1
her bright armes about her body *dight,* . . . . III. i. 67. 3
downe againe her in her warme bed *dight:* . . . . III. ii. 30. 5
Another harnesse . . . About her selfe she *dight,* . . . . . III. iii. 61. 3
on her *dight* Her Helmet, ... III. iv. 12. 4
There they him laide in easy couch well *dight,* . . . . . III. iv. 43. 6
was al within most richly *dight,* . . . . III. v. 40. 8
With this fayre flowre your goodly girlonds *dight,* . . . . III. v. 53. 5
her loose lockes to *dight* in order dew . . . . III. vii. 11. 2
Girlonds of flowres . . . He fine would *dight;* . . . . . . III. vii. 17. 6
In his proud furnitures she freshly *dight,* . . . . III. vii. 18. 8
Supper was *dight;* . . . . III. ix. 25. 6
his hore beard Was fowly *dight,* . . . . III. x. 52. 5
winges it had with sondry colours *dight,* . . . . III. xi. 47. 6
paynted plumes in goodly order *dight,* . . . . III. xii. 8. 2
They both uprose and to their waies them *dight:* . . . . . IV. i. 16. 6
Casts off his ragged skin and freshly doth him *dight.* . . . IV. iii. 23. 9
Which to avenge Sir Devon him did *dight,* . . . . IV. iv. 21. 1
The shield and armes . . . he on himselfe did *dight,* . . . . IV. iv. 27. 8
her selfe she lightly gan To *dight,* . . . . IV. vi. 10. 5
Till I thereto had all things ready *dight.* . . . . IV. vii. 17. 4
Gan *dight* him selfe unto his wonted sinne; . . . . IV. vii. 20. 8
did themselves unto their journey *dight.* . . . . IV. viii. 34. 5
walkes and alleyes *dight* With divers trees . . . . IV. x. 25. 1
all the Priests were damzels in soft linnen *dight.* . . . . IV. x. 38. 9
to this feast with Neptunes seed was *dight.* . . . . IV. xi. 16. 9

Dight—*Continued.*
He askt who had that Dame so fouly *dight,* . . . . V. i. 14. 8
curst the hand which did that vengeance on him *dight.* . . . V. ii. 18. 9
a troupe of women, warlike *dight,* . . . . V. iv. 21. 8
nimbly did him *dight* to guide the way . . . . V. iv. 35. 5
She fiercely towards him her selfe gan *dight,* . . . . . . V. iv. 43. 2
Artegall him selfe to rest did *dight,* . . . . V. iv. 51. 8
th' Amazon, as best it likt her selfe to *dight.* . . . . . . V. v. 1. 9
she made him to be *dight* In womans weedes, ... V. v. 20. 6
streight her selfe did *dight,* and armor don, ... V. vi. 17. 8
A raskall rout, with weapons rudely *dight;* . . . . V. vi. 29. 4
Was to the battell whilome ready *dight.* . . . . V. vii. 27. 6
Kept himselfe still in his straunge armour *dight:* . . . . . V. viii. 27. 5
all his armours readie *dight* that day, ... V. x. 16. 3
richly clad In roiall robes, and many jewels *dight;* . . . . V. xi. 60. 7
on her selfe did *dight* Most squalid garments, ... V. xii. 12. 1
Which to provide she hath this Castle *dight,* . . . . . . VI. i. 15. 6
having soone his armes about him *dight,* . . . . VI. i. 32. 6
he taking oddes, streight bids him *dight* Himselfe . . . . VI. ii. 18. 4
after having them upon him *dight,* . . . . VI. ii. 39. 6
That she her selfe had to the journey *dight,* . . . . . . VI. iii. 16. 3
the place, the which was *dight* with divers flowres . . . . VI. iii. 23. 4
About the sad Serena things to *dight,* . . . . VI. v. 25. 3
having all things well about her *dight,* . . . . VI. v. 31. 1
gan them selves to *dight* Unto their journey; . . . . . . VI. v. 40. 5
in a Jacket, quilted richly rare . . . he was straungely *dight;* VI. vii. 43. 4
supper readie *dight* they to it fell . . . . VI. ix. 17. 7
Was *dight* with flowers that voluntary grew . . . . VII. vii. 10. 2
lusty Spring, all *dight* in leaves of flowres . . . . VII. vii. 28. 2
Sommer, being *dight* In a thin silken cassock . . . . . . VII. vii. 29. 1
garlonds goodly *dight* Of all the fairest flowres . . . . . VII. vii. 33. 6
dight His wanton wings and darts . . . . *Am.* iv. 7
The gate with pearles and rubyes richly *dight;* . . . . . *Am.* lxxxi. 10
Bid her awake therefore, and soone her *dight,* . . . . . . *Epith.* 30
whylest she doth her *dight,* . . . . *Epith.* 34
Helpe quickly her to *dight:* . . . . *Epith.* 97
it more fairely *dight* With chearefull grace . . . . *H.B.* 130

Dighting. when this Maiden faire Was *dighting* her, ... VI. xii. 15. 2

Dights. his hideous club aloft he *dites,* . . . . I. viii. 18. 4
With his faire mother he him *dights* to play, ... II. viii. 6. 5

Dignify. of their grace us *dignifie:* . . . . *Col.* 818

Dignities. Them entertayn'd, fit for their *dignities,* . . . . V. x. 5. 4

Dignity. as if he aspyr'd To *dignitie,* . . . . *Hub.* 679
Then was shee held in soveraigne *dignitie,* . . . . *T.M.* 563
set in highest seat of *dignitee,* . . . . II. iv. 19. 4
every linck thereof a step of *dignity.* . . . . II. vii. 46. 9
Honour and *dignitie* from her alone Derived are, ... II. vii. 48. 7
incontinent Doth loose his *dignity* and native grace: . . . . II. ix. 1. 8
he first wore crowne of gold for *dignity.* . . . . II. x. 39. 9
For their high merits and great *dignitie,* . . . . IV. iii. 44. 4
To overthrow my state and *dignitie.* . . . . IV. vii. 15. 5
Seekes to subvert her Crowne and *dignity,* . . . . V. viii. 18. 4
you to reward with greater *dignitie.'* . . . . VI. ii. 34. 9
She was a Ladie of great *dignitie,* . . . . VI. vii. 28. 1
striving both for termes of *dignitie,* . . . . *Com. Son.* ii. 7

Digs. in his chauffe he *digs* the trampled ground, ... VI. v. 19. 7

Dike. The raging billowes, . . . made a long broad *dyke,* . . . III. xi. 40. 7

Dilate. that wofull theame For to *dilate* at large, ... II. v. 37. 4
braunches, which did broad *dilate* Their clasping armes . . . II. xii. 53. 8
Of diverse thinges discourses to *dilate,* . . . . III. iii. 62. 4
he gan at large to her *dilate* The whole discourse . . . . . V. vi. 17. 1
Tho gan that shepheard thus for to *dilate:* . . . . VI. x. 21. 1
by their change their being do *dilate,* . . . . VII. vii. 58. 5
your light doth more itselfe *dilate,* . . . . *Am.* lxvi. 11

Diligence. sent with carefull *diligence,* To fetch a Leach, . . I. x. 23. 6
Which long he usd with carefull *diligence,* . . . . V. x. 12. 8

Diligent. he wayted *diligent,* With humble service . . . . . I. iii. 9. 6
With onely Talus wayting *diligent,* . . . . V. xi. 36. 7
kept her sheepe with *diligent* attent, ... VI. ix. 37. 3
by *diligent* inquest Provided him a sword . . . . VI. xi. 42. 5

Dill. Veyne-healing Verven, and hed-purging *Dill,* . . . . . *Mui.* 197
the flowre Of Camphora, and Calamint, and *Dill;* . . . . . III. ii. 49. 6

Dim. The sonne of all the world is *dimme* and darke: . . . . *S.C.* N. 67
drery horror *dim* the chearfull light, ... *D.* 328
And the *dim* vele . . . aside be layd, ... *Ded. Son.* ix. 10
To *dim* the brightnesse of her glorious throne, ... I. iv. 8. 8
her *dim* eie-lids she up gan reare, ... II. i. 45. 1
Which, mingled all with sweate, did *dim* his eye. . . . . . II. iv. 37. 5
beam great brightnes threw Through the *dim* shade, ... II. vii. 45. 3
her light Doth *dim* with horror and deformity; . . . . . . II. vii. 49. 4
as a cloud doth seeme to *dim* the skies; . . . . II. ix. 16. 5
Thrise shined faire, and thrise seemd *dim* and wan, ... III. iii. 16. 3
the *dim* eies of my deare Marinell . . . . III. iv. 39. 4
All suddeinly *dim* wox the dampish ayre, ... III. iv. 52. 1
dim the brightnesse of the welkin rownd, ... III. x. 46. 7
all the rest like lesser lamps did *dim:* . . . . VI. ix. 9. 5
T' illuminate my *dim* and dulled eyne, ... *H.B.* 20

Dimd. *See* **Dimmed.**

Diminish. Th' one to *diminish,* th' other for to eeke; . . . . V. ii. 49. 4

Dimmed. With his great bellie spreds the *dimmed* world, . . . *Ro.* xx. 6
dimd with darknesse their intelligence, ... *T.M.* 255
mine eyes are *dimd* with teares; . . . . *D.* 417
blast, that . . . *Dimmed* her former beauties shining ray, . . I. ii. 38. 7
Her eyelids blew, And *dimmed* sight, . . . she up gan lift: . . I. ii. 45. 5
Huge flames that *dimmed* all the hevens light, ... I. xi. 44. 3
dim'd his valorous And mightie deedes, ... II. x. 43. 5
Sith shady dampe had *dimd* the heavens reach, ... V. vi. 21. 8
seemed to outshine the *dimmed* skye, ... V. ix. 21. 8
But now weake age had *dimd* his candle-light: . . . . . . VI. iii. 3. 4

Dimmed—*Continued.*
The glaunce whereof their *dimmed* eies would daze, . . . VI. x. 4. 3
quite are *dimmed* when she is in place: . . . VI. x. 27. 8
Her lovely light was *dimmed* and decayd . . . VI. xi. 21. 4
make even that *dimmed* light Seeme much more lovely . . . VI. xi. 21. 6
Whenas a storme hath *dimd* her trusty guyde, . . . *Am.* xxxiv. 3
With sorrow *dimmed* and deform'd . . . *Am.* xlv. 10
like stars that *dimmed* were With darksome cloud, . . . *Epith.* 93
beames with such disparagements Be *dimd,* . . . *H.B.* 164
Dimmeth. envies cloud still *dimmeth* vertues ray. . . . V. xii. 27. 7
Dims. It *dimmes* the dazed eyen, . . . I. viii. 21. 9
this bright Angels towre quite *dims* that towre of glas.' . . . I. x. 58. 9
Does all their deedes deface, and *dims* their glories all. . . . III. ii. 1. 9
the drosse which *dims* the light . . . *H.B.* 48
Din. Fled fast away from that so dreadfull *din.* . . . *Hub.* 1348
all the rest her dolefull *din* augmented . . . *T.M.* 357
When that tumultuous rage and fearfull *deene* . . . *Ded. Son.* xi. 9
All full of people making troublous *din* . . . V. ix. 23. 3
Dine. Were shronke into his jawes, as he did never *dyne.* . . . I. ix. 35. 9
nought was given them to sup or *dyne,* . . . V. v. 22. 8
Dint. backe was arm'd against the *dint* of speare . . . *Van.* vi. 2
Such pleasaunce now displast by dolors *dint:* . . . *S.C.* N. 104
So deadly was the *dint* and deep the wound, . . . *As.* 121
with that *dint* her sence was dazd; . . . I. i. 18. 1
Loth . . . To taste th' untryed *dint* of deadly steele: . . . I. iii. 34. 6
deadly *dint* of steele endanger may. . . . I. vii. 29. 7
Ne *dint* of direfull sword divide the substance would. . . . I. vii. 33. 9
ghosts . . . Have felt the bitter *dint* of his avenging blade. . . . I. vii. 47. 9
With *dint* of swerd, nor push of pointed speare: . . . I. xi. 9. 4
deeper *dint* therein it would not make; . . . I. xi. 24. 6
The deadly *dint* his dulled sences all dismaid. . . . I. xi. 35. 9
They gan abstaine from *dint* of direfull stroke, . . . II. ii. 28. 8
Deadly dismayd with horror of that *dint* . . . II. v. 8. 1
no enchauntment from his *dint* might save; . . . II. viii. 20. 6
It seizd in his right side, and there the *dint* did stay. . . . II. viii. 38. 9
when he stroke most strong the *dint* deceiv'd, . . . II. viii. 49. 3
by *dint* of sword approve, That she is fairer . . . III. i. 27. 3
dint of steele his carcas could not quell; . . . III. vii. 35. 8
every *dint* the ghost would rive . . . IV. ix. 22. 8
Ne any armour could his *dint* out-ward; . . . V. i. 10. 8
with *dint* of sword . . . their rights to try, . . . V. iv. 6. 1
He cared not for *dint* of sword nor speere, . . . VI. iv. 4. 6
Inflicts with *dint* of sword, . . . VI. vi. 1. 2
Dinted. *See* **Deep-dinted.**
So deepely *dinted* in the driven clay, . . . I. viii. 8. 5
Dinting. with lovely dart *Dinting* his brest . . . VI. x. 31. 8
Dints. Wherein old *dints* of deepe woundes did remaine, . . . I. i. 1. 3
that *dints* the parts entire With chast affects . . . *Am.* vi. 11
Dioclesian's. *Dioclesians* fifty daughters shene . . . II. x. 8. 4
Dipped. not to have been *dipt* in Lethe lake, . . . *Ti.* 428
dipt in deaw of Castalie: . . . *Ti.* 431
dipped in the bitter wave Of hellish Styx, . . . II. viii. 20. 8
Whose clawes were newly *dipt* in cruddy blood, . . . III. iii. 47. 5
An holy-water sprinckle, *dipt* in deowe, . . . III. xii. 13. 6
Dipping. themselves *dipping* in the silver dew . . . II. xii. 61. 7
Dire. all was covered with darknesse *dire:* . . . I. xi. 40. 4
nought but *dire* revenge his anger mote defray. . . . IV. v. 31. 9
Out of her poysnous entrails fraught with *dire* decay.' . . . V. xi. 20. 9
Direct. wontst the tragick stage for to *direct,* . . . *Mui.* 11
I hope . . . your wisedome will *direct* my thought, . . . I. vii. 42. 7
Those could he well *direct* and streight as line, . . . II. xi. 21. 6
How to *direct* theyr way in darkenes wide, . . . II. xii. 35. 2
all their actions to *direct* aright: . . . III. iii. 2. 4
Or succour her, or me *direct* the way, . . . III. v. 10. 8
none That to their willes could them *direct* aright, . . . IV. i. 16. 8
her footing to *direct* aright, . . . IV. xi. 25. 4
doth his course through Blandford plains *direct,* . . . IV. xi. 32. 3
sent to him a Page that mote *direct* his way. . . . V. viii. 26. 9
Kept on his course as he did it *direct,* . . . V. xii. 21. 2
star, that wont with her bright ray Me to *direct,* . . . *Am.* xxxiv. 6
when myne eyes I thereunto *direct,* . . . *Am.* lxxviii. 9
Directed. Forthwith *directed* to that further strand; . . . II. vi. 38. 2
His feeble feet *directed* to the cry; . . . II. viii. 4. 5
as Merlin them *directed* late: . . . III. iii. 62. 2
as he had beene Before *directed* by his Lord; . . . V. viii. 29. 8
The Damzell straight went, as she was *directed,* . . . V. ix. 9. 6
There they alighting by that Damzell were *Directed* in, . . . V. ix. 22. 2
directed Unto a litle grove not farre asyde, . . . VI. viii. 44. 1
Directing. her swords point *directing* forward right . . . III. xi. 25. 3
Direction. falne on you by heavens hard *direction* . . . V. iv. 26. 7
T' obay a womans tyrannous *direction,* . . . V. v. 26. 4
good *direction* how to enter in, . . . VI. i. 6. 3
will not yield unto her formes *direction,* . . . *H.B.* 146
Directly. Thereto our ship her course *directly* bent, . . . *Col.* 268
to the gate *directly* did incline . . . II. ix. 24. 7
To which her steps *directly* she did frame. . . . III. i. 20. 3
directly fly Unto her rest in Plutoes griesly land; . . . IV. iii. 13. 2
I would you guyde *directly* to the place.' . . . V. ix. 7. 7
ne did the other stay, But after went *directly* . . . VI. iii. 37. 5
Directs. *Directs* her course unto one certaine cost, . . . VI. xii. 1. 2
Direful. Doo weave the *direfull* threds of destinie, . . . *D.* 17
he endured not the *direfull* stound, . . . *As.* 123
beasts with deep mouthes gaping *direfull* . . . *Col.* 202
the *direfull* dames doe drive Their mournefull charett, . . . I. v. 32. 1
Ne dint of *direfull* sword divide the substance would. . . . I. vii. 33. 9
whenas the *direfull* feend She saw not stirre, . . . I. xi. 55. 5
direfull chaunce, armd with avenging fate, . . . II. i. 44. 6
through the great contagion *direful* deadly stonck. . . . II. ii. 4. 9
They gan abstaine from dint of *direfull* stroke, . . . II. ii. 28. 8
Direfull impatience, and hart-murdring love: . . . II. v. 16. 4

Direful—*Continued.*
Elfe, That darest view my *direfull* countenaunce, . . . II. vii. 7. 7
direfull deadly black, both leafe and bloom, . . . II. vii. 51. 8
those sad waves, which *direfull* deadly stancke, . . . II. vii. 57. 3
That *direfull* stroke thou dearely shalt aby:' . . . II. viii. 33. 4
they to *direfull* death their groning ghosts did send. . . . II. xi. 15. 9
nought that falles into this *direfull* deepe . . . II. xii. 6. 7
Their *direfull* rancour rather did encreasse; . . . III. i. 23. 4
Upon thee heapt a *direfull* destinie; . . . III. ix. 33. 5
A *direfull* stench of smoke and sulphure mixt Ensewd, . . . III. xii. 2. 5
The *direfull* distaffe standing in the mid, . . . IV. ii. 48. 2
Yet still that *direfull* stroke kept on his way, . . . IV. iii. 34. 1
Much was he daunted with that *direfull* stound, . . . IV. iv. 24. 8
snatching forth his *direfull* deadly blade . . . IV. vi. 12. 2
Radigund . . . from her *direfull* doome acquit, . . . V. iv. 39. 2
'Echidna is a Monster *direfull* dred, . . . VI. vi. 10. 1
damned to endure this *direful* smart, . . . VI. viii. 19. 8
other *dyrefull* hap from heaven or hell . . . VI. xi. 29. 8
Dirges. Their *Diriges,* their Trentals, and their shrifts, . . . *Hub.* 453
Diriges. *See* **Dirges.**
Dirke, Dirks. *See* **Dark, -s.**
Dirt. is trodde in the *durt* Of cattell, . . . *S.C.* F. 235
him in blood and *durt* deformed quight. . . . II. v. 22. 4
Drew him through *durt* and myre . . . II. v. 23. 4
Distaynd with *durt* and blood, . . . III. viii. 49. 9
trode downe in the *durt,* . . . III. x. 52. 4
he did all to peeces breake, and foyle In filthy *durt,* . . . V. xi. 33. 9
fell to ground, like to a lumpe of *durt;* . . . VI. viii. 16. 8
Seeme *durt* and drosse in thy pure-sighted eye, . . . *H.H.L.* 276
Dirty. as she lay upon the *durtie* ground, . . . I. i. 15. 1
ryder . . . Would have cast downe, and trodd in *durty* myre, I. viii. 17. 6
downe he tumbled on the *durtie* field, . . . I. viii. 20. 4
with *durty* blood distaynd, . . . I. xi. 23. 8
soyld with *durtie* gore, . . . II. vi. 41. 7
there her drowned in the *durty* mud; . . . V. ii. 27. 4
Her hands were foule and *durtie,* . . . V. xii. 30. 1
His dunghill thoughts . . . themselves enure To *dirtie* drosse, . *H.L.* 184
And doest thy mynd in *durty* pleasures moyle, . . . *H.H.L.* 220
Disable. Them to *disable* from revenge adventuring. . . . V. iv. 31. 9
Disabled. And him *dishabled* quyte. . . . II. v. 21. 6
Disaccord. but she did *disaccord,* Ne could her liking . . . VI. iii. 7. 3
Disadvance. enterprised praise for dread to *disavaunce.'* . . . III. xi. 24. 9
forced him his shield to *disadvaunce.* . . . IV. iii. 8. 4
vaunted speare eftsoones to *disadvaunce,* . . . IV. iv. 7. 2
Disadvantage. fort . . . unawares at *disavantage* fownd. . . . I. ix. 11. 4
Which now him turnd to *disavantage* deare; . . . II. xi. 34. 1
Disadventure. through great *disaventure,* or mesprize, . . . II. xii. 19. 4
to and fro at *disaventure* strayd; . . . III. iv. 53. 2
Disadventures. never knight . . . More luckless *dissaventures* did amate: . . . I. ix. 45. 4
And all his *disadventures* to unfold, . . . VI. iii. 15. 3
Disadventurous. *disadventrous,* and quite fortunelesse; . . . *Hub.* 100
the record . . . of my dolefull *disaventurous* deare. . . . I. vii. 48. 7
Doth soonest fall in *disaventrous* fight, . . . I. ix. 11. 8
An hard mishap and *disaventrous* case . . . IV. viii. 51. 3
There unto him betid a *disaventrous* case. . . . IV. xii. 4. 9
As she had seene that day, a *disaventerous* sight. . . . V. iv. 47. 9
losse of fame in *disaventrous* field: . . . V. xi. 55. 8
Disagree. Seemed the heavens with the earth did *disagree,* . . *Ti.* 664
Still did they strive and daily *disagree;* . . . II. ii. 13. 7
Ne ever thing could cause us *disagree.* . . . II. iv. 19. 7
To stirre up strife, and garre them *disagree:* . . . II. v. 19. 7
in bad maner they did *disagree,* . . . V. xii. 33. 3
That curtesie and manhood ever *disagree.* . . . VI. iii. 40. 9
Disagreed. For which th' Idaean Ladies *disagreed,* . . . II. vii. 55. 6
by degrees they all were *disagreed;* . . . IV. v. 36. 6
Disappointed. felonous intent Returning *disappointed* his desire, IV. vi. 11. 7
Disaraid, Disaray, -d. *See* **Disarray,** *etc.*
Disarm. all his left side it did quite *disarme;* . . . II. v. 7. 7
Would him *disarme* and treaten shamefully; . . . II. viii. 25. 3
of his weapons did himselfe *disarme.* . . . II. xi. 34. 5
did faire Britomart entreat Her to *disarme,* . . . III. i. 52. 4
weening to have arm'd him, she did quite *disarme.* . . . III. iv. 27. 9
Offred his service to *disarme* the Knight; . . . V. viii. 27. 2
Disarmed. *Disarmed* all of yron-coted Plate; . . . I. vii. 2. 8
Disarmd, disgraste, and inwardly dismayde; . . . I. vii. 11. 6
him *disarmed,* dissolute, dismaid, Unwares surprised, . . . I. vii. 51. 3
laying his head *disarmd* In her loose lap, . . . II. vi. 14. 6
him attonce *disarm'd;* . . . II. vi. 51. 2
disarmed for to be, . . . III. i. 42. 4
The Redcrosse Knight was soon *disarmed* there; . . . III. i. 42. 6
the brave Mayd would not *disarmed* bee, . . . III. i. 42. 7
Now were *disarmd,* and did them selves present . . . III. i. 44. 2
They him *disarmd;* and, spredding on the grownd . . . III. iv. 40. 4
Having her thus *disarmed* of her shield, . . . V. v. 11. 1
caused him to be *disarmed* quight . . . V. v. 20. 3
So, as I then *disarmed* did remaine, . . . *Am.* xii. 5
Disarms. Such cruell game my scarmoges *disarmes.* . . . II. vi. 34. 5
Disarray. In ragged robes and filthy *disaray;* . . . II. iv. 4. 2
did loosely *disaray* Her upper partes . . . II. v. 32. 7
Was for like need enforst to *disaray:* . . . III. ix. 20. 2
Who overtaking him did *disaray,* . . . V. iii. 38. 3
The night is come, now soon her *disaray.* . . . *Epith.* 300
Disarrayed. of their leaves they were *disarayde:* . . . *S.C.* F. 105
Whome having softly *disaraid* of armes, . . . I. v. 41. 4
So, as she bad, that witch they *disaraid,* . . . I. viii. 46. 1
Both fiercely bent to have him *disaraid;* . . . II. viii. 17. 3
was arayd, or rather *disarayd,* . . . II. xii. 77. 3
Disastrous. Unhappie wight, borne to *desastrous* end, . . . *Hub.* 907
true Lovers! whom *desastrous* chaunce Hath farre exiled . . *D.* 505

Disattire. him besought himselfe to *disattyre,* . . . VI. ix. 17. 3
Disavantage. *See* **Disadvantage.**
Disavaunce. *See* **Disadvance.**
Disaventerous, Disaventrous, *etc.* *See* **Disadventurous.**
Disaventure, -s. *See* **Disadventure, -s.**
Disavow. The name of knighthood he did *disavow;* . . . VI. v. 37. 7
Disboweled. halfe *disbowel'd* lies above the ground, . . . *Ro.* xxviii. 5
Disburdened. that gay payre . . . *Disburdned* her. . . . II. vi. 11. 7
well *disburdened* her engrieved brest, . . . VI. viii. 34. 2
Discarded. he that helpe from her against her will *discarded.* . . . V. v. 8. 9
Discern. heedy shepheards to *discerne* their face; . . . *S.C.* S. 167
I scarse in darksome place Could it *discerne,* . . . I. v. 27. 6
well that valiaunt courser did *discerne;* . . . II. iii. 46. 6
well mote I *discerne* Great cause, . . . II. iv. 43. 3
no man can *Discerne* the hew thereof. . . . II. vi. 41. 8
none could him *discerne;* . . . IV. iv. 27. 9
grief unknowne, which he could not *discerne:* . . . IV. xii. 24. 2
whether man or monster one could scarse *discerne.* . . . V. xii. 15. 9
Discerned. Living to get, and not to be *discern'd.* . . . *Hub.* 536
Her proper face I not *discerned* . . . II. iv. 28. 4
she uneath *discerned* whether whether weare. . . . IV. ix. 10. 9
Discharge. The weary sowle from thence it would *discharge;* II. v. 6. 7
To Proteus selfe to sue for her *discharge:* . . . IV. xii. 14. 4
come before high Jove her dooings to *discharge.* . . . VII. vi. 17. 9
Discharged. his hands *Discharged* of his bow and deadly quar'le, . . . II. xi. 33. 8
Dischord. *See* **Discord.**
Discided. as her tongue so was her hart *discided,* . . . IV. i. 27. 8
Discipled. better were in vertues *discipled,* . . . IV. Pr. 1. 8
Disciples. his *disciples* both desyrd to bee; . . . II. ix. 54. 8
Discipline. Great thankes I yeeld you for your *discipline,* . . . *Hub.* 547
fill their bookes with *discipline* of vice. . . . *T.M.* 336
The precepts of my heavenlie *discipline;* . . . *T.M.* 518
learnd her *discipline* of faith and verity. . . . I. vi. 31. 9
he had charge my *discipline* to frame, . . . I. ix. 5. 3
she him taught celestiall *discipline,* . . . I. x. 18. 8
them to warlike *discipline* did trayne, . . . IV. viii. 27. 7
them with maystring *discipline* doth tame, . . . IV. ix. 2. 4
if in *discipline* Of vertue . . . V. Pr. 3. 1
all the *discipline* of justice there him taught. . . . V. i. 6. 9
needes wise read and *discipline,* . . . VI. vi. 13. 3
Disciplined. rather needed to be *disciplinde* . . . VI. vi. 5. 6
Disclaim. He left his wife; money did love *disclame:* . . . III. x. 15. 4
To whom each one his chalenge should *disclame,* . . . IV. v. 25. 5
Disclame. *See* **Disclaim.**
Disclose. to whom he might *disclose* His witlesse pleasance, . *Hub.* 798
The same to wight he never wont *disclose,* . . . I. vii. 34. 1
her perswaded to *disclose* the breach . . . I. vii. 42. 3
With cryme doe not it cover, but *disclose* the same.' . . . I. xii. 30. 9
I would *disclose* Her counsell, . . . III. vii. 58. 8
to *disclose* Which of the Nymphes . . . IV. xii. 26. 6
'This griefes deepe wound I would to thee *disclose,* . . . V. v. 30. 7
Yet durst she not *disclose* her fancies wound, . . . V. v. 44. 1
Doe it *disclose* to ease your grieved spright: . . . VI. iv. 28. 7
Disclosed. her sacred Booke, . . . She unto him *disclosed* . . . I. x. 19. 3
ear that wished day his beame *disclosd,* . . . II. iv. 22. 1
having *disclo'ste* Her clowdy care . . . III. iv. 13. 7
it as oft was from about her wast *disclos'd:* . . . IV. v. 16. 9
never she before *disclosd* to none, . . . IV. xii. 5. 4
Disclosing. he *disclosing* read thus, as the paper spake: . . . I. xii. 25. 9
Discolor. That her gay clothes did in *discolour* die. . . . V. i. 14. 5
Discolored. A bounch of heares *discolourd* diversly. . . . I. ii. 11. 6
All in a kirtle of *discolourd* say He clothed was, . . . I. iv. 31. 1
A bounch of heares *discolourd* diversly, . . . I. vii. 32. 2
advaunce his broad *discoloured* brest Above his wonted pitch, . I. xi. 31. 7
descry It plaine, and by the sea *discoloured:* . . . II. xii. 18. 8
garments light *Discolourd* like to womanish disguise, . . . III. x. 21. 7
Like a *discolourd* Snake, . . . III. xi. 28. 8
When her *discolourd* bow she spreds through hevens hight. . III. xi. 47. 9
a *discolour'd* cote of straunge disguyse, . . . III. xii. 10. 2
diapred lyke the *discolored* mead. . . . *Epith.* 51
Discomfit. his proud foes *discomfit* in victorious field. . . . III. iii. 31. 9
Discomfited. her bright hed Discovers to the world *discomfited:* III. i. 43. 5
Discomfort. Full of *discomfort* and disquiet plight, . . . IV. viii. 8. 4
Discommended. to her Dame him still she *discommended,* . . . V. v. 57. 4
Disconsolate. naked left and *disconsolate,* . . . *S.C.* F. 230
Abett that virgins cause *disconsolate,* . . . I. x. 64. 2
I alone, now left *disconsolate,* . . . *Am.* lxxxviii. 5
Discontent. To wast long nights in pensive *discontent;* . . . *Hub.* 898
Ne dyde with dread and grudging *discontent,* . . . *D.* 254
evermore did seeme As *discontent* . . . II. ii. 35. 4
halfe *discontent,* mote nathelesse Himselfe appease, . . . II. vi. 24. 1
Paridell, though partly *discontent* With his late fall . . . III. ix. 25. 1
That stryfull hag with gealous *discontent* Had fild, . . . IV. v. 30. 8
rayle at them with grudgefull *discontent,* . . . IV. viii. 28. 4
right *discontent* In minde he grew, . . . V. vi. 24. 1
Through *discontent* of my long fruitlesse stay . . . *Proth.* 6
Discontentment. signes of grudge and *discontentment* vaine. II. viii. 23. 5
Discord. shall backe reverse To their first *discord,* . . . *Ro.* xxii. 12
So hard the *discord* was to be agreede. . . . I. ii. 37. 7
themselves at *discord* fell, . . . II. ii. 20. 2
Their deadly cruell *discord* to forbeare, . . . II. ii. 27. 8
this misseeming *discord* meekely lay aside.' . . . II. iii. 31. 9
braunch from th' antique stocke was torne Through *discord,* . II. x. 36. 5
So *dischord* ofte in Musick makes the sweeter lay:— . . . III. ii. 15. 9
Duessa *discord* breedes Twixt Scudamour and Blandamour: . IV. i. Arg.
discord harder is to end then to begin. . . . IV. i. 20. 9
All which the sad effects of *discord* sung: . . . IV. i. 21. 3
the dreadfull *discord,* which did drive . . . to outrage fell; . IV. i. 23. 6

Discord—*Continued.*
Firebrand of hell . . . Is wicked *discord;* . . . IV. ii. 1. 5
never *discord* did amongst them fall, . . . IV. ii. 54. 2
new *discord* to maintaine. . . . IV. v. 22. 9
soone as she them saw to *discord* set, . . . IV. v. 29. 1
Cause of their *discord* and so fell debate . . . IV. ix. 24. 1
So was their *discord* by this doome appeased, . . . V. iv. 20. 5
pride dare not approch, nor *discord* spill The league . . . *Am.* lxv. 9
Discordant. It is no love, but a *discordant* warre, . . . *H.B.* 195
Discordful. Unmindfull both of that *discordfull* crew, . . . IV. ii. 30. 8
rather stird by his *discordfull* Dame, . . . IV. iv. 3. 7
Discounselled. With temperate advice *discounselled,* . . . II. xii. 34. 2
By such good meanes he him *discounselled* . . . III. i. 11. 1
Discountenance. with reprochfull scorne *discountenaunce,* . . . *T.M.* 340
Discouraged. She was no whit thereby *discouraged* . . . III. xi. 50. 7
Discoure. *See* **Discover.**
Discourse. he close confers with wise *discourse,* . . . *Hub.* 763
So Mother Hubberd her *discourse* did end, . . . *Hub.* 1385
by *discourse* them to indignifie.' . . . *Col.* 583
With faire *discourse* the evening so they pas; . . . I. i. 35. 5
Then gan the Dwarfe the whole *discourse* declare; . . . I. vii. 26. 1
goodly gan *discourse* of many a noble gest. . . . I. x. 15. 9
The large *discourse* of roiall Princes state. . . . I. xii. 14. 6
gan he to *discourse* the whole debate, . . . II. viii. 54. 6
Grew pensive through that amarous *discourse,* . . . III. iv. 5. 3
A long *discourse* of his adventures vayne, . . . III. viii. 44. 2
Every *discourse,* and every argument, . . . III. ix. 53. 7
of their evils as they did *discourse,* . . . IV. vii. 20. 1
thy basest thrall, That dare *discourse* . . . V. Pr. 11. 7
Till he of tidings mote with him *discourse.* . . . V. ii. 2. 4
he gan at large to her dilate The whole *discourse* . . . V. vi. 17. 2
Then gan she to declare the whole *discourse* . . . V. vii. 20. 1
he namely did to him *discourse* Of former daies mishap, . . . VI. iii. 14. 8
The which *discourse* as now I must delay, . . . VI. vii. 50. 8
At last the caytive, after long *discourse,* . . . VI. viii. 14. 6
Discoursed. have I not well *discourst* Upon this Commonplace, *Hub.* 541
Discourst his voyage long, according his request. . . . I. xi. 15. 9
discoursed diversly Of straunge affaires, . . . III. ix. 53. 1
whilest they *discoursed* both together, . . . VI. iii. 23. 1
Discourses. Diverse *discourses* in their way they spent; . . . II. vi. 9. 1
Of diverse thinges *discourses* to dilate, . . . III. iii. 62. 4
In such *discourses* they together spent Long time, . . . VI. x. 30. 1
Discoursing. *Discoursing* of her dreadful late distresse, . . . I. iii. 32. 7
So diversly *discoursing* of their loves, . . . I. ix. 18. 1
discoursing diversly Of sundry things as fell, . . . VI. ix. 12. 6
Discourteise. *See* **Discourteous.**
Discourteous. in *discourteise* wise Scorne the faire offer . . . III. i. 55. 1
'*Discourteous,* disloyall Britomart, . . . IV. i. 53. 1
that *discourteous* Dame with scornfull pryde . . . VI. i. 30. 4
slay A proud *discourteous* knight: . . . VI. ii. Arg.
that *discourteous* knight, (Whom Tristram slew) . . . VI. ii. 43. 1
did free from feare Of a *discourteous* Knight, . . . VI. iii. 18. 6
that same *discourteous* Knight . . . laught, and mockt . . . VI. iii. 34. 1
There he this most *discourteous* craven found, . . . VI. iv. 2. 6
By such *discourteous* deeds discovering his base kind. . . . VI. vii. 1. 9
That well appears in this *discourteous* knight, . . . VI. vii. 2. 1
Discourtesies. The foule *discourt'sies* and unknightly parts, . VI. v. 33. 2
Discourtesy. my plaints, causd of *discurtesee,* . . . *S.C.* Jun. 97
fowle *discourtesie,* unfit for Knight, . . . VI. iii. 33. 6
Gan to complaine of great *discourtesie,* . . . VI. vii. 4. 3
Discover. gan to him *discover* all his harmes, . . . I. v. 41. 5
Whome if ye please for to *discover* plaine, . . . I. xii. 34. 7
if please you it *discure,* . . . II. ix. 42. 8
that none might her *discoure,* . . . III. ii. 20. 4
secretly he saw, yet note *discoure:* . . . III. iii. 50. 4
whenso her face She list *discover,* . . . IV. ii. 44. 7
all the artes, that subtill wits *discover,* . . . IV. iii. 40. 2
the truth *discover* plaine, . . . IV. xii. 30. 7
They do to thee in this same dreame *discover;* . . . V. vii. 22. 2
I will the truth *discover* . . . VI. ii. 15. 9
Her weed she then withdrawing did him *discover;* . . . VI. vi. 32. 1
day, that doth *discover* bad and good, . . . VI. viii. 51. 7
Through hollow caves, that no man mote *discover* . . . VI. x. 42. 2
Her to *discover* for some secret hire: . . . VII. vi. 43. 3
Discovered. the high hils Titan *discovered,* . . . I. ii. 7. 4
when broad day the world *discovered* has, . . . I. iii. 21. 1
ere that dawning light *Discovered* had the world to heaven . I. v. 52. 6
from the world that her *discovered* wide, Fled . . . I. viii. 50. 2
through hardy enterprize Many great Regions are *discovered,* II. Pr. 2. 4
That plaine *discovered* her incontinence; . . . III. i. 48. 3
all attonce *discovered* her desire . . . III. i. 53. 1
Therein *discovered* was, ne ought mote pas, . . . III. ii. 19. 6
passing by, his name *discovered,* . . . III. xii. 4. 8
which eftsoones *discovered,* to it drew The eyes of all, . . . IV. iv. 16. 3
Whose face, *discovered,* plainely did expresse . . . IV. v. 13. 3
soone as day *discovered* heavens face . . . IV. viii. 34. 1
Whom when *discovered* they had throughly eide, . . . V. iii. 17. 4
when as he *discovered* had her face, . . . V. v. 12. 1
so soone as dawning houre *Discovered* had the light . . . V. vi. 35. 2
For doubt to be *discovered* by his sight, . . . V. viii. 27. 4
all this cursed plot . . . *discovered* was betymes, . . . V. ix. 42. 4
Discovering. Ate soone *discovering* his desire, . . . IV. ii. 11. 6
excuse Me from *discovering* you my name aright, . . . IV. vi. 4. 7
Then Artegall, himselfe *discovering* plaine, . . . V. viii. 50. 1
by *discovering* my estate, Harme may arise . . . VI. ii. 27. 2
By such discourteous deeds *discovering* his base kind. . . . VI. vii. 1. 9
Discovers. her bright hed *Discovers* to the world discomfited: . III. i. 43. 5
day *discovers* all dishonest wayes, . . . III. iv. 59. 1
As plaine as light *discovers* dawning day. . . . *H.B.* 238

Discovery. Without *discoverie* of my thoughts pretence, . . . V. v. 33. 7
In deep *discovery* of the mynds disease; . . . *Am.* l. 6
Discreet. Mishaps are maistred by advice *discrete,* . . . I. vii. 40. 7
To her faire presence and *discrete* behests. . . . II. ii. 32. 5
The waters fall with difference *discreet,* . . . II. xii. 71. 7
Discretion. 'Daunger without *discretion* to attempt Inglorious, III. xi. 23. 1
have you lost your selfe and your *discretion,* . . . V. iv. 26. 2
without *discretion* He at him ran . . . V. viii. 9. 2
Discure. *See* **Discover.**
Discurtesee. *See* **Discourtesy.**
Discuss. of good passed newly to *discus,* . . . *Col.* 38
Discussed. all regard of shame she had *discust,* . . . III. i. 48. 7
Disdain. the roote in hie *disdaine* Sende forth . . . *Bel.*[1] v. 13
in great (hie[1]) *disdaine* . . . send forth . . . *Bel.* v. 13
Himselfe smote with his beake, as in *disdaine,* . . . *Pet.* v. 10
conquer'd, dare the Conquerour *disdaine.* . . . *Ro.* xiv. 14
greatest things the least *disdaine,* . . . *Van.* iii. 13
The nations gan their soveraigntie *disdaine,* . . . *Van.* xi. 3
His clownish gifts and curtsies I *disdaine,* . . . *S.C.* Ja. 57
So spake this bold brere with great *disdaine:* . . . *S.C.* F. 139
disdayne The base kinred of so simple swaine. . . . *S.C.* May 270
Colin Cloute she would not once *disdayne;* . . . *S.C.* N. 101
for *disdaine* of sinfull worlds upbraide . . . *Hub.* 2
for my Sisters eake whom they *disdaine.* . . . *T.M.* 534
disdaine to subject his desire To loathsome sloth, . . . *Mui.* 35
My wearie daies in dolor and *disdaine!* . . . *D.* 440
sad Alcyon dyde in lifes *disdaine.* . . . *D.* 525
it embracing deare without *disdaine,* . . . *Col.* 554
Most lothsom, filthie, foule, and full of vile *disdaine.* . . . I. i. 14. 9
His gall did grate for . . . high *disdaine;* . . . I. i. 19. 6
steede, Pricked with . . . fiery fierce *disdaine,* . . . I. ii. 8. 4
Her loathly visage viewing with *disdaine,* . . . I. ii. 39. 5
her fiers servant, full of kingly aw And high *disdaine,* . . . I. iii. 41. 2
Looking to heaven, for earth she did *disdayne,* . . . I. iv. 10. 2
Whose shield he beares renverst, the more to heap *disdayn.* . . . I. iv. 41. 9
Inflamd with scornefull wrath and high *disdaine,* . . . I. viii. 7. 2
Duessa, full of . . . fiers *disdaine* to be affronted so, . . . I. viii. 13. 2
As Lion, grudging in his great *disdaine,* . . . II. i. 42. 6
leave so proud *disdayne.'* . . . II. iii. 43. 9
to grind His grated teeth for great *disdeigne,* . . . II. v. 14. 3
without dread or *disdayn* She sett beside, . . . II. vi. 14. 5
In great *disdaine* he answerd: . . . II. vii. 7. 6
Disdayne he called was, and did *disdayne* To be so cald, . . . II. vii. 41. 1
with sterne lookes, and stomachous *disdaine,* . . . II. viii. 23. 4
Breathing out wrath, and bellowing *disdaine,* . . . II. viii. 42. 6
For vile *disdaine* and rancour, which did gnaw . . . II. viii. 50. 7
prickt with proud *disdaine* . . . II. x. 33. 3
Archigald, who for his proud *disdayne* Deposed . . . II. x. 44. 4
With murmurous *disdayne* doth inly rave, . . . II. xi. 32. 3
Stoupes at a flying heron with proud *disdayne,* . . . II. xi. 43. 2
the great sea, puft up with proud *disdaine,* . . . II. xii. 21. 7
I swell with great *disdaine.* . . . III. iv. 2. 9
Ythrild with deepe *disdaine* of his proud threat, . . . III. iv. 15. 1
In stead thereof sad sorow and *disdaine* . . . III. iv. 54. 2
as halfe in great *disdaine,* . . . III. iv. 61. 5
His sinfull sowle with desperate *disdaine* . . . III. v. 23. 8
The roring billowes in their proud *disdaine,* . . . III. viii. 37. 3
countries cause, and commune foes *disdayne.* . . . III. ix. 40. 4
He looked round about with sterne *disdayne,* . . . III. xii. 23. 2
as in *disdaine* Against that Knight, . . . IV. ii. 6. 7
may not *disdaine* that womans hand Hath conquered you . . . IV. vi. 31. 2
deepe *disdaine* and great indignity, . . . IV. vii. 36. 3
this trustie squire with proud *disdaine* . . . IV. ix. 3. 7
The hils doe not the lowly dales *disdaine,* . . . V. ii. 41. 3
With proud *disdaine* did scornefull answere make, . . . V. iii. 16. 2
through stout *disdaine* of manly mind . . . V. iv. 32. 1
For high *disdaine* of such indignity, . . . V. vii. 28. 6
Therewith all fraught with fury and *disdaine,* . . . V. xi. 8. 1
byting th' earth for very deaths *disdaine;* . . . V. xi. 14. 7
From view of men, and wicked worlds *disdaine;* . . . VI. Pr. 3. 4
through high *disdaine* And proud despight . . . VI. i. 15. 1
I doe much *disdaine* Thy courteous lore, . . . VI. i. 27. 7
Did well endure her womanish *disdaine,* . . . VI. i. 30. 8
Wherewith he wroth, and full of proud *disdaine,* . . . VI. ii. 11. 6
Fayre Mirabellaes punishment For Loves *disdaine* decreed. . . VI. vii. Arg.
This was *Disdaine,* who led that Ladies horse . . . VI. vii. 44. 1
Prince Arthure overcomes *Disdaine;* . . . VI. viii. Arg.
He in his necke had set his foote with fell *disdaine.* . . . VI. viii. 10. 9
With these two lewd companions, . . . *Disdaine* and Scorne, . VI. viii. 22. 8
Then suffred he *Disdaine* up to arise, . . . VI. viii. 25. 5
hight, that seem'd th' earth to *disdaine;* . . . VI. x. 6. 3
with unkind *disdaine* And cruell rigour . . . VI. xi. 24. 3
Disdayne to yield unto the first assay. . . . *Am.* xiv. 8
drery sad *disdayne* Of all worlds gladnesse, . . . *Am.* lii. 11
Their lives they loath, and heavens light *disdaine;* . . . *H.L.* 130
Disdained. th' Elfin knight, . . . *Disdaind* to loose the meed I. iv. 39. 8
that reprochfull fall right fowly he *disdaynd;* . . . I. xi. 23. 9
Guyon much *disdeigned* so loathly sight. . . . II. v. 23. 6
Would not endure to bee so vile *disdaind,* . . . II. x. 18. 2
in their raging surquedry *disdaynd* . . . III. iv. 7. 6
none *disdained* low to him to lout: . . . IV. xi. 30. 5
Sangliere *disdained* much his doome, . . . V. i. 29. 1
him revil'd, and rated, and *disdayned,* . . . V. iii. 35. 8
By that proud dame which her so much *disdained,* . . . V. viii. 24. 4
trampled downe in dust his thoughts *disdained* scorne. . . . V. viii. 31. 9
Her stubborne hart, which love before *disdayned,* . . . VI. vii. 36. 7
I *disdain'd* . . . To follow sheepe . . . VI. ix. 24. 3
Disdaineth. Lyon . . . *disdeigneth* to devoure The silly lambe . *Am.* xx. 7
Disdainful. Thought all things lesse than his *disdainful* pride. *Van.* iii. 6

Disdainful—*Continued.*
He lookt aside as in *disdainefull* wise, . . . *D.* 59
Her . . . love with foule *disdainefull* spight He would not shend; . . . I. i. 53. 7
that *disdainfull* beast, Encountring fierce, . . . I. iii. 19. 6
With . . . *disdaineful* spight Her vildly entertaines; . . . I. iii. 43. 6
She thancked them in her *disdainefull* wise; . . . I. iv. 14. 2
From dreaded storme of his *disdainfull* spight: . . . I. iv. 48. 4
(So love does loath *disdainefull* nicitee) . . . II. ii. 3. 3
Still solemne sad, or still *disdainfull* coy; . . . II. vi. 37. 5
halfe in *disdaineful* wise, . . . II. ix. 38. 1
the *disdainfull* sowle he thence dispatcht, . . . II. xi. 42. 3
Full of *disdainfull* wrath he fierce uprose . . . III. i. 9. 1
upbrayd A dolefull heart with so *disdainfull* pride: . . . III. vi. 21. 8
Love to conceive in her *disdainfull* brest; . . . III. xi. 17. 6
not of cancred will, . . . nor obstinate *disdainefull* mind, . . . V. v. 41. 2
backstarting with *disdainefull* yre . . . V. xi. 61. 5
fume in his *disdainefull* mynd the more, . . . VI. vii. 47. 8
with sterne count'naunce and *disdainfull* cheare, . . . VII. vi. 12. 5
deprave My simple meaning with *disdaynfull* scorne; . . . *Am.* xxix. 2
Thou hast enfrosen her *disdainefull* brest, . . . *H.L.* 146
Disdainfully. overthrew his bowle *disdainfully,* . . . II. xi. 49. 8
downe againe himselfe *disdainfully* Abjecting, . . . III. xi. 13. 6
Disdaining. As much *disdayning* to the curbe to yield: . . . I. i. 1. 7
Disdeining life, desiring leave to dye, . . . I. x. 22. 8
Disdeigning to bee held so long in fight. . . . II. vi. 30. 4
much *disdeigning* to be so misdempt, . . . III. x. 29. 4
Till Diamond, *disdeigning* long delay . . . IV. iii. 17. 6
In royall heart *disdaining* to be thrall. . . . IV. iv. 32. 7
much *disdaining* unto him to lout, . . . IV. x. 19. 2
Some of their pride, some paragons *disdayning,* . . . IV. x. 43. 4
this proude Dame, *disdayning* all accord, . . . V. viii. 22. 3
I no lesse *disdayning,* backe returned His . . . taunts . . . VI. ii. 12. 1
Disdains. Much he *disdaines* that anie one should dare . . . *Gn.* 273
he *disdaines* himselfe t' embase theretoo. . . . *Hub.* 732
plaine attire such glorious gallantry *Disdaines* . . . *Col.* 730
Disdeign, -ing, *etc.* *See* **Disdain,** *etc.*
Disease. grose *disease* Soone growes through humours superfluitie. . . . *Ro.* xxiii. 11
Why done we them *disease?* . . . *S.C.* Jul. 124
' "Our daies are full of dolor and *disease,* . . . *D.* 274
Who had enough, yett wished ever more; A vile *disease:* . . . I. iv. 29. 6
that *disease* of grieved conscience, . . . I. x. 23. 8
His double burden did him sore *disease.* . . . II. ii. 12. 4
Whom raging windes . . . doe diversly *disease,* . . . II. ii. 24. 3
fell to vaine voluptuous *disease:* . . . II. x. 17. 5
labour'd long in that deepe ford with vaine *disease.* . . . III. v. 19. 9
Dissembling his *disease* and evill plight; . . . IV. i. 38. 3
Nought could she read the roote of his *disease,* . . . IV. xii. 22. 1
soone as he had sought Through his *disease,* . . . IV. xii. 25. 6
Lying without her dore in great *disease:* . . . V. vi. 26. 7
The bitter anguish of their sharpe *disease* . . . VI. v. 32. 5
So all that night they past in great *disease,* . . . VI. v. 40. 1
seas, Which tosse the rest in daungerous *disease;* . . . VI. ix. 19. 5
In deep discovery of the mynds *disease;* . . . *Am.* l. 6
Diseased. *See* **Soul-diseased.**
So by the small the great is oft *diseased.* . . . *Van.* ii. 14
All were my spirite heavie and *diseased,* . . . *Hub.* 40
The griefe thereof him wondrous sore *diseasd,* . . . I. xi. 38. 8
'Squyre, sore have ye beene *diseasd,* . . . II. iv. 33. 8
For pitty of his Dame whom she saw so *diseased.* . . . VI. iii. 32. 9
Diseases. Full of *diseases* was his carcas blew, . . . I. iv. 23. 6
Disentrail. As if he thought her soule to *disentrayle.* . . . IV. vi. 16. 7
did his bowels *disentrayle,* . . . V. ix. 19. 5
Disentrailed. the *disentrayled* blood Adowne their sides . . . stremed, . . . IV. iii. 28. 6
Disfigured. Her swollen eyes were much *disfigured,* . . . II. i. 13. 8
gins her feathers fowle *disfigured* Prowdly to prune, . . . II. iii. 36. 7
Disgrace. See that your rudenesse doe not you *disgrace:* . . . *S.C.* Ap. 132
made them dwell in darknes of *disgrace;* . . . *Hub.* 1187
To thrust downe other into foule *disgrace,* . . . *Col.* 691
To wish you backe returne with foule *disgrace,* . . . I. i. 13. 3
to all knighthood it is foule *disgrace,* . . . I. i. 31. 8
a dull blast, that . . . with foule ugly forme did her *disgrace;* I. ii. 38. 8
a felon strong To many knights did daily worke *disgrace;* I. iii. 29. 4
having scaped hard, With balefull beggery, or foule *disgrace;* I. iv. 3. 4
fly away for feare of fowle *disgrace:* . . . I. vi. 18. 7
The goddesse wroth gan fowly her *disgrace,* . . . I. vii. 5. 5
For feare . . . her beauty to *disgrace?* . . . II. iii. 25. 9
The knight, yet wrothfull for his late *disgrace,* . . . II. xi. 34. 6
Whereof conceiving shame and foule *disgrace,* . . . III. vi. 10. 1
for feare of shame and fowle *disgrace.* . . . III. vii. 60. 5
In vengement of her mothers great *disgrace,* . . . IV. vii. 30. 6
what heavens hard *disgrace,* Or wrath of cruell wight . . . IV. viii. 14. 7
When they are all restor'd thou shalt rest in *disgrace.* . . . V. iii. 20. 9
She inly yet conceived great *disgrace:* . . . V. iii. 23. 7
With bitter taunts and termes of vile *disgrace.* . . . V. iv. 23. 4
Did her appeach; and, to her more *disgrace,* . . . V. ix. 47. 7
'What foule *disgrace* is this To so faire Ladie, . . . V. xi. 62. 1
Into this bay of perill and *disgrace?* . . . VI. i. 12. 2
to *disgrace* With all those shames, . . . VI. i. 28. 8
let it not you seeme *disgrace* To beare this burden . . . VI. ii. 47. 7
Were vanquished, and put to foule *disgrace;* . . . VI. vii. 21. 5
her good dayes in dolorous *disgrace:* . . . VI. vii. 38. 4
though the night did cover her *disgrace,* . . . VI. viii. 51. 3
Her beauty to *disgrace.* . . . *Epith.* 120
Disgraced. Griefe of good mindes, to see goodnesse *disgraced!* *Van.* i. 8
Disarmd, *disgraste,* and inwardly dismayde; . . . I. vii. 11. 6
it would lose or breake, that many had *disgrast.* . . . V. iii. 28. 9

Disgraced—*Continued.*
in the sight of all men cleane *disgraced,* . . . V. iii. 39. 3
He was revyld, *disgrast,* and foule abused; . . . *H.H.L.* 242
Disgraces. their *disgraces* Did much the more augment, . . . V. xii. 28. 8
Disgracing. Thinking that their *disgracing* did him grace: . . . *Hub.* 708
Disgracing them, him selfe thereby to grace, . . . IV. iv. 4. 2
Disgrast(e). *See* **Disgraced.**
Disguise. Then was the Germane Raven in *disguise* . . . *Ro.* xvii. 9
with sheepes clothing doen hem *disguise*. . . . *S.C.* S. 157
I meane me to *disguize* In some straunge habit, . . . *Hub.* 83
passing through the Countrey in *disguize,* . . . *Hub.* 575
standing by the gates in strange *disguize,* . . . *Hub.* 1271
the faire Scene with rudenes foule *disguize*. . . . *T.M.* 192
halfe in doubt, because of his *disguize,* . . . *D.* 57
He then devisde himselfe how to *disguise;* . . . I. ii. 10. 1
diverse plots did frame to maske in strange *disguise*. . . . III. iii. 51. 9
Let us in feigned armes our selves *disguize,* . . . III. iii. 53. 2
Least he like one of them him selfe *disguize,* . . . III. vi. 23. 4
Discolourd like to womanish *disguise,* . . . III. x. 21. 7
here did rove In straunge *disguyze,* . . . III. xi. 30. 4
a discolour'd cote of straunge *disguise,* . . . III. xii. 10. 2
it was a maske of strange *disguise:* . . . IV. i. 14. 8
in close *disguise* Of fayned love, . . . IV. ii. 30. 1
In quyent *disguise,* full hard to be descride: . . . IV. iv. 39. 3
Most answerable to his wyld *disguize* . . . IV. iv. 42. 5
in queint *disguise* Of British armes doest maske thy royall blood, . . . V. vii. 21. 1
Whom like *disguize* no lesse deformed had, . . . V. vii. 38. 2
by counterfet *disguise* To their deseigne to make the easier way, . . . V. viii. 25. 1
the blame might salve with coloured *disguize*. . . . VI. iii. 8. 9
their glorious Lord in strange *disguise* Transfigur'd . . . VII. vii. 7. 8
Unlike in forme, and chang'd by strange *disguise:* . . . VII. vii. 18. 8
Disguised. that *disguised* Dog lov'd blood to spill, . . . *Hub.* 319
So had false Archimago her *disguysd,* . . . II. i. 21. 6
Disguised like that groome of base degree, . . . II. iv. 27. 8
the king was by a Treachetour *Disguised* slaine, . . . II. x. 51. 4
into these fearefull shapes *disguiz'd* . . . II. xii. 26. 3
what inquest Made her dissemble her *disguised* kind? . . . III. ii. 4. 7
Disguiz'd in thousand shapes, that none might him bewray.) . . . III. vi. 11. 9
suffred her so carelesly *disguiz'd* Be overtaken. . . . III. vi. 19. 5
His garment was *disguysed* very vayne, . . . III. xii. 9. 5
All which *disguized* marcht in masking wise . . . III. xii. 26. 6
Whom when she saw in wretched weedes *disguiz'd,* . . . IV. viii. 12. 5
our like persons, eath to be *disguiz'd,* . . . IV. viii. 58. 3
nature had so well *disguized* Her worke, . . . IV. ix. 11. 3
through that *disguized* hood, To hide thy state . . . V. vii. 21. 4
Of men *disguiz'd* in womanishe attire, . . . V. vii. 37. 7
Disguisement. in so straunge *disguizement* there did maske, . . . III. vii. 14. 3
She through his late *disguizement* could him not descrie! . . . IV. v. 29. 9
Disguising. them selves *disguising* both in straunge And base atyre, . . . III. iii. 7. 1
Disguysing diversly my troubled wits. . . . *Am.* liv. 4
Dish. in a silver *dish* did ly Twoo golden apples . . . *Am.* lxxvii. 5
Dishabled. *See* **Disabled.**
Disheartened. her olde Nourse was nought *dishartened,* . . . III. iii. 20. 8
Dishes. What needes of dainty *dishes* to devize, . . . I. xii. 14. 3
Disheveled. With garments rent, and heare *discheveled,* . . . II. i. 13. 6
Dishonest. day discovers all *dishonest* wayes, . . . III. iv. 59. 1
Dishonesty. her accusing of *dishonesty,* . . . I. iii. 23. 4
Dishonor. thy throne royall with *dishonour* blent: . . . *Hub* 1330
There lies he now with foule *dishonor* dead, . . . I. ii. 25. 5
That noble heart as great *dishonour* doth despize. . . . II. vii. 12. 9
Late foule *dishonour* and reprochfull spight, . . . III. ii. 8. 8
shund *dishonor* which as death she feard: . . . III. vi. 10. 5
though spite did oft assay To blot her with *dishonor* . . . IV. i. 4. 9
dread of shame and doubt of fowle *dishonor* . . . IV. i. 8. 6
all true lovers with *dishonor* blotten: . . . IV. i. 51. 4
Shame and *dishonour* hath unto me donne, . . . IV. vi. 5. 7
forst him backe with fowle *dishonor* to retreat. . . . IV. vii. 37. 9
'Sir knight, it would *dishonour* bee . . . V. iii. 36. 6
armes *dishonour* with base villanie, . . . V. iii. 38. 7
Dye, rather then doe ought that mote *dishonour* yield.' . . . V. xi. 55. 9
The which shal nought to you but foule *dishonor* yearne. . . . VI. i. 40. 9
with black *dishonor* And foule defame . . . VI. vi. 25. 4
Besides the great *dishonour* and defame, . . . VI. ix. 1. 8
With foule *dishonour* him mote blot therefore; . . . VI. xii. 12. 7
and sdeigne of foule *dishonor:* . . . *Am.* v. 6
Dishonorable. with *dishonorable* termes her to entreat. . . . III. v. 49. 9
What cause could make him so *dishonourable* . . . VI. ii. 15. 3
Dishonored. He fownd him selfe *dishonored* so sore. . . . III. i. 7. 4
To be by them *dishonoured* and shent: . . . V. viii. 23. 4
Disinherit. how this long death thou mightest *disinherit.'* . . . V. v. 36. 9
Disleal. '*Disleall* Knight, whose coward corage chose . . . II. v. 5. 3
Dislike. Ne do your selfe *dislike* a whit the more; . . . IV. i. 46. 7
Without disquiet or *dislike* of ether, . . . VI. xii. 10. 8
no jot Of loves *dislike* or pride was to be found, . . . *H.H.L.* 34
hath vertue to remove All Loves *dislike,* . . . *Proth.* 99
Disliked. *See* **Self-disliked.**
Dislikeful. *Dislikefull* paine so sad a taske to take, . . . IV. ix. 40. 3
Dislikes. The sharpe *dislikes* of each condition: . . . *Com. Son.* i. 4
of all old *dislikes* they made faire weather; . . . IV. ii. 29. 3
tempering . . . Their contrary *dislikes* with loved meanes, . . . *H.L.* 86
Disliking. *disliking* of their evill And hard estate, . . . *Hub.* 46
great *dislyking* to my lucklesse lot, . . . *Col.* 181
Dislodge. to *dislodge* the Raven of her nest? . . . *S.C.* D. 32
love for to *dislodge* out of his nest: . . . III. v. 44. 3
them *dislodge,* all were they liefe or loth; . . . III. ix. 13. 8
Would streight *dislodge* the wretched wearie life. . . . VI. v. 5. 5
I hunt the Fox, . . . and him *dislodge* away; . . . VI. ix. 23. 2
Dislodged. finding life not yet *dislodged* quight, . . . II. viii. 9. 7
Disloined. Low looking dales, *disloignd* from common gaze; . . . IV. x. 24. 6
Disloyal. not merit The name of love, but of *disloyall* lust: . . . *Col.* 892
And their *disloiall* powre defaced clene, . . . *Ded. Son.* xi. 11
Disloyall Treason, and hart-burning Hate; . . . II. vii. 22. 3
Such was the end that to *disloyall* love did fall. . . . II. x. 19. 9
'Discourteous, *disloyall* Britomart, . . . IV. i. 53. 1
made him dreame those two *disloyall* were: . . . IV. v. 43. 8
Disloiall lust faire beauties foulest blame, . . . *H.B.* 170
Disloyally. *disloyally* Deeme of her high desert, . . . III. v. 45. 6
Dye rather, dy, then ever love *disloyally*. . . . III. v. 45. 9
Disloyalty. By his *disloyalty* lamented sore, . . . *Gn.* 202
if to love *disloyalty* it bee, . . . III. v. 46. 1
Inconstant Chaunge, and false *Disloyalty;* . . . III. xii. 25. 6
to *disloyalty* she will not be allured. . . . IV. x. 2. 9
Ne ever shewed signe of foule *disloyalty*. . . . VI. v. 9. 9
Dismaid(e). *See* **Dismayed.**
Dismailed. Their mightie strokes their haberjeons *dismayld,* . . . II. vi. 29. 5
Dismal. Was turned now to *dismall* heavinesse, . . . *T.M.* 41
with staggring pace and *dismall* lookes dismay, . . . *D.* 564
Dismayd with that deformed *dismall* sight, . . . I. ix. 30. 5
'What *dismall* day hath lent this cursed light, . . . II. vi. 43. 7
An ugly feend, more fowle then *dismall* day, . . . II. vii. 26. 7
'Paynim, this is thy *dismall* day; . . . II. viii. 51. 5
'This *dismall* day hath thee a caytive made, . . . IV. vii. 12. 1
feare and danger of that *dismall* wight. . . . IV. vii. 33. 9
'That ever I this *dismall* day did see! . . . V. i. 15. 3
what other deadly *dismall* day Is falne on you . . . V. iv. 26. 6
the *dismall* day Appointed for Irenas death . . . V. xii. 11. 1
He much was daunted with so *dismall* sight; . . . VI. vii. 10. 4
was the tyme ordayned For such a *dismall* deed, . . . VI. viii. 44. 7
'That ever I did live this day to see, This *dismall* day, . . . VI. xi. 29. 3
Dismay. 'Againe the dreadfull Cycones him *dismay,* . . . *Gn.* 537
Therefore herewith doo not your selfe *dismay;* . . . *Hub.* 445
all astonished with deepe *dismay,* . . . *Ti.* 473
with deepe *dismay* Was much appald, . . . *D.* 186
With staggring pace and dismall lookes *dismay,* . . . *D.* 564
Threatning her angrie sting, him to *dismay;* . . . I. i. 17. 7
For present cause was none of dread her to *dismay*. . . . I. ii. 20. 9
suddeine catching hold, did her *dismay* . . . I. iii. 12. 5
her darke griesly looke them much *dismay:* . . . I. v. 30. 5
whenas monsters huge he would *dismay,* . . . I. vii. 34. 2
The chearelesse man, whom sorrow did *dismay,* . . . I. viii. 43. 7
Ne divelish thoughts *dismay* thy constant spright: . . . I. ix. 53. 3
great hostes of men she could *dismay;* . . . I. x. 20. 4
sin, and hell, and death, doe most *dismay* . . . I. x. 41. 4
rolling downe great Neptune doth *dismay:* . . . I. xi. 54. 8
The sight with ydle feare did them *dismay,* . . . I. xii. 9. 8
The hartlesse Hynd and Robucke to *dismay,* . . . II. ii. 7. 4
Dismay with feare, or cause one foot to flye, . . . II. iii. 45. 4
did him deadly daunt, or fowle *dismay;* . . . II. iv. 40. 8
that stroke of living arme Should him *dismay,* . . . II. v. 7. 3
On him, that did Pyrochles deare *dismay:* . . . II. v. 38. 7
Ne darkenesse him, ne daunger might *dismay*. . . . II. vii. 26. 4
ugly shapes did nigh the man *dismay,* . . . II. vii. 37. 7
deadly fitt thy pupill doth *dismay*. . . . II. viii. 7. 5
Whome Romane warres . . . could no whit *dismay;* . . . II. x. 62. 7
Yet would he not for all his great *dismay* . . . II. xi. 41. 2
constancy and care, gainst daunger and *dismay*. . . . II. xii. 38. 9
Huge hostes of men he could alone *dismay,* . . . III. iii. 12. 5
let no whit thee *dismay* The hard beginne . . . III. iii. 21. 7
A virgin straunge and stout him should *dismay* or kill. . . . III. iv. 25. 9
That Proteus prophecide should him *dismay;* . . . III. iv. 28. 2
faynd to cheare his lady in *dismay,* . . . III. viii. 15. 7
Him bett so sore, that life and sence did much *dismay* . . . III. viii. 31. 9
With upstart haire and staring eyes *dismay,* . . . III. x. 54. 8
Ne canst her ayde, ne canst her foe *dismay;* . . . III. xi. 11. 7
Yet fairely well he did them all *dismay,* . . . IV. i. 2. 5
She . . . their possessours often did *dismay:* . . . IV. i. 29. 7
'do not *dismay* Your selfe for this; . . . IV. i. 40. 7
Ne word had he to speake for great *dismay,* . . . IV. i. 50. 2
had so great *dismay* so well amended: . . . IV. iii. 50. 7
The sight of whom once seene did all the rest *dismay*. . . . IV. v. 13. 9
her great daunger did him much *dismay*. . . . IV. vii. 20. 5
doubtfull through *dismay,* In presence came, . . . IV. viii. 62. 7
without *dismay* or dread; . . . IV. xi. 14. 6
drives Upon a rocke with horrible *dismay,* . . . V. ii. 50. 2
Yet nought they could him hurt, ne ought *dismay:* . . . V. ii. 53. 4
So sharpe a battell, that so many did *dismay*. . . . V. iii. 21. 9
Partly with shame, and partly with *dismay,* . . . V. iv. 27. 2
Seem'd to awake in horrible *dismay,* . . . V. vii. 15. 3
So did the sight thereof their sense *dismay,* . . . V. viii. 38. 2
There he her found in sorrow and *dismay,* . . . V. x. 19. 1
'forborne Your owne good shield in daungerous *dismay?* . . . V. xi. 52. 2
She forth was brought in sorrowfull *dismay* . . . V. xii. 12. 4
Began to quake and tremble with *dismay;* . . . V. xii. 41. 5
hearts *dismay* and inward dolour queld, . . . VI. i. 18. 3
of the Lady selfe in sad *dismay* He was ymett, . . . VI. i. 24. 7
forth he cald from sorrowfull *dismay* . . . VI. i. 44. 5
To succour her from daunger of *dismay,* . . . VI. ii. 38. 4
In dolorous *dismay* and deadly plight, . . . VI. iii. 27. 3
Serena full of dolorous *dismay,* . . . VI. iii. 45. 3
his fierce steed that mote him much *dismay:* . . . VI. iv. 6. 5
With the fierce Lapithes which did them *dismay,* . . . VI. x. 13. 5
full of fresh *dismay,* . . . VI. xi. 28. 3
fills the darkned world with terror and *dismay*. . . . VII. vii. 51. 9
Playnts, prayers, vowes, ruth, sorrow, and *dismay;* . . . *Am.* xiv. 11
with one looke, she doth my life *dismay;* . . . *Am.* xxi. 10
wander now, in darknesse and *dismay,* . . . *Am.* xxxiv. 7
Comes forth afresh out of their late *dismay,* . . . *Am.* xl. 11

Dismay—*Continued.*
In dread of death, and daungerous *dismay,* . . . *Am.* lxiii. 3
Affrayd of every dangers least *dismay.* . . . *Am.* lxxxvii. 4
Dismayed. I, which this sight beheld, was much *dismayed* . . . *Van.* vii. 13
All suddenly *dismaid,* and hartles quight, . . . *Gn.* 297
would have fled with terror all *dismayde.* . . . *Hub.* 956
My spirits now *dismayd* with sorrow dull . . . *T.M.* 291
her silence, signe of one *dismaid,* . . . *Mui.* 341
Like hartlesse deare, *dismayd* with thunders sound. . . . *Col.* 9
cleane *dismayd* to see so uncouth sight, . . . I. i. 50. 1
Dame,' (quoth he,) 'what hath ye thus *dismayd?* . . . I. i. 52. 8
Her faithfull gard remov'd, her hope *dismaid,* . . . I. iii. 43. 3
purest skye with brightnesse they *dismaid:* . . . I. iv. 4. 5
'Faire Dame, be nought *dismaid* For sorrowes past; . . . I. iv. 49. 1
it made His mortall mace, wherewith his foemen he *dismayde.* I. vii. 10. 9
Disarmd, disgraste, and inwardly *dismayde;* . . . I. vii. 11. 6
The groning ghosts of many one *dismaide* . . . I. vii. 47. 8
him disarmed, dissolute, *dismaid,* Unwares surprised, . . . I. vii. 51. 3
The Gyaunt selfe, *dismaied* with that sownd, . . . I. viii. 5. 4
Dismayed with so desperate deadly wound, . . . I. viii. 11. 1
all his sences were with suddein dread *dismayd.* . . . I. viii. 14. 9
dismaid with uncouth dread: . . . I. ix. 22. 3
To weet what mister wight was so *dismayd.* . . . I. ix. 23. 2
Dismayd with that deformed dismall sight, . . . I. ix. 30. 5
The sight whereof so throughly him *dismaid,* . . . I. ix. 50. 1
so *dismayd* when that his foe beheld, . . . I. xi. 28. 6
The deadly dint his dulled sences all *dismaid.* . . . I. xi. 35. 9
He woxe *dismaid,* and gan his fate to feare: . . . I. xi. 52. 8
Came running in, much like a man *dismayd,* . . . I. xii. 24. 8
'My Lord, my king, be nought hereat *dismayd,* . . . I. xii. 31. 2
Great pitty is to see you thus *dismayd,* . . . II. i. 14. 3
quite *dismayd* With stony feare . . . II. ii. 8. 7
two so mighty warriours he *dismade.* . . . II. ii. 25. 5
He was *dismayed* in his coward minde, . . . II. iii. 32. 2
her sweete words that all his sence *dismayd,* . . . II. iii. 42. 3
Deadly *dismayd* with horror of that dint . . . II. v. 8. 1
maistring might on enimy *dismayd;* . . . II. v. 13. 3
though himselfe were at the sight *dismayd,* . . . II. vii. 6. 8
stony feare . . . all his sence *dismayd,* . . . II. viii. 46. 2
faire Sir, be not herewith *dismaid,* . . . II. ix. 8. 5
His cruel bow, wherewith he thousands hath *dismayd.* . . . II. ix. 34. 9
why beene ye thus *dismayd,* . . . II. ix. 37. 5
some like to Apes, *dismayd,* . . . II. xi. 11. 4
much *dismayed* with that dreadful sight, . . . II. xi. 16. 2
huge Sea monsters, such as living sence *dismayd:* . . . II. xii. 22. 9
Thereat they greatly were *dismayd,* . . . II. xii. 35. 1
nigh he breathlesse grew, yet nought *dismaid,* . . . III. i. 21. 3
The fourth was by that other knight *dismayd,* . . . III. i. 29. 3
with so troublous terror they were all *dismayd.* . . . III. i. 63. 9
with her dreadfull strokes were all *dismayd:* . . . III. i. 66. 4
'what need ye be *dismayd?* . . . III. ii. 40. 1
the Britons, late *dismayd* and weake, . . . III. iii. 36. 7
other ghastly spectacle *dismayd,* . . . III. iii. 50. 3
His uncouth shield and straunge armes her *dismayd,* . . . III. iv. 51. 1
her Pilott hath *dismayd;* . . . III. iv. 53. 4
The whiles her matchlesse beautie him *dismayd.* . . . III. v. 43. 7
Her Amoretta cald, to comfort her *dismayd.* . . . III. vi. 28. 9
dismayd At that same last extremity . . . III. vii. 25. 1
To counsell her, so carefully *dismayd,* . . . III. viii. 4. 8
He was *dismayd;* and thrise his brest he stroke, . . . III. viii. 22. 3
Paridell . . . seemd *dismaid* to bee; . . . III. viii. 48. 2
In his disquiet mind was much *dismayd:* . . . III. x. 14. 3
Greatly thereat was Britomart *dismayd,* . . . III. xi. 22. 1
every wight *dismayd* with darkenes sad . . . III. xii. 1. 3
As a *dismayed* Deare in chace embost, . . . III. xii. 17. 8
all that did not her *dismaied* make, . . . III. xii. 37. 3
sight of such a chaunge her much *dismayd* . . . III. xii. 42. 5
he shewd him selfe to be *dismayd* . . . IV. i. 37. 7
by slight And foule advantage this good Knight *dismayd,* . . . IV. i. 44. 3
Whom so *dismayd* when Cambell had espide, . . . IV. iii. 10. 1
As one that seemed doubtfull or *dismayd.* . . . IV. iv. 20. 4
looking round about, like one *dismaid,* . . . IV. iv. 22. 3
He with their multitude was nought *dismayd,* . . . IV. iv. 32. 1
By his sole manhood and atchievement stout *Dismay'd,* . . . IV. iv. 43. 3
ghesse the man to be *dismayd* with gealous dread. . . . IV. v. 45. 9
Yet she no whit *dismayd* her steed forsooke, . . . IV. vi. 14. 6
He was therewith right wondrously *dismayd;* . . . IV. vi. 24. 3
'Faire Sir, be nought *dismayd* With needlesse dread, . . . IV. vi. 37. 6
Which sodaine accident him much *dismaid,* . . . IV. viii. 7. 8
all *dismayd* through mercilesse despaire . . . IV. viii. 51. 7
nought *dismayd,* them stoutly well withstood; . . . IV. ix. 29. 7
'By her I entring half *dismayed* was; . . . IV. x. 36. 1
dismayd with dreadfull sight Of death, . . . V. ii. 54. 3
He was therewith exceedingly *dismayd,* . . . V. iii. 18. 2
Dismayd so with the stroke that he no colours knew. . . . V. iv. 39. 9
Besides the rest *dismayd,* . . . V. v. 19. 7
many hath with dread of death *dismayd,* . . . V. v. 31. 3
With sight whereof she was *dismayd* right sore, . . . V. vi. 28. 1
doubtfully *dismayd* through that so uncouth sight. . . . V. vii. 16. 9
Or ill apayd or much *dismayd* ye be; . . . V. vii. 18. 8
She was *dismayd,* or faynted through affright, . . . V. viii. 45. 7
she was nigh *dismayd,* . . . V. ix. 12. 2
She could it sternely draw, that all the world *dismayde.* . . . V. ix. 30. 9
much *dismayd* with that dismayfull sight, . . . V. xi. 26. 4
Her halfe *dismayd* they found in doubtfull plight, . . . V. xi. 60. 4
Ne ought *dismayed* was Sir Calidore, . . . VI. i. 32. 4
Whereat the other starting up *dismayd,* . . . VI. ii. 18. 6
like men *dismayde,* Ran after fast . . . VI. iii. 24. 8
the bold knight no whit thereat *dismay'd,* . . . VI. iv. 21. 1
Whom when as Calepine saw so *dismayd,* . . . VI. iv. 27. 5

Dismayed—*Continued.*
leaving there this Ladie all *dismayd,* . . . VI. v. 3. 5
Whom when the Prince so deadly saw *dismayd,* . . . VI. vi. 33. 1
he was *dismayd,* Ne powre had to withstand, . . . VI. vii. 48. 8
being halfe *dismayd,* . . . VI. xii. 16. 7
Mongst wretched men (*dismaide* with her affright) . . . VII. vi. 32. 7
Be nought *dismayd* that her unmoved mind . . . *Am.* vi. 1
Retourne agayne, my forces late *dismayd,* . . . *Am.* xiv. 1
Dismayful. much dismayd with that *dismayfull* sight, . . . V. xi. 26. 4
Dismayfully. like mazed deare *dismayfully* they flew. . . . V. viii. 38. 9
Dismays. the dart of sinfull guilt the soule *dismayes.* . . . I. x. 21. 9
horse and man he equally *dismaies,* . . . V. ii. 8. 8
Dismembered. him . . . *dismembred* hath: . . . I. iii. 20. 4
His goodly corps, . . . Was quite *dismembred,* . . . I. v. 38. 7
Yet had the bodie not *dismembred* bee, It would have lived, IV. iii. 21. 7
Dismissed. Then was that whole assembly quite *dismist,* . . . VII. vii. 59. 8
Dismount. the bright Sunne gynneth to *dismount;* . . . *S.C.* May 315
Dismounted. The Champion stout Eftsoones *dismounted* . . . I. i. 11. 8
him *dismounted* low he did compell . . . II. v. 4. 7
him *dismounted* on the plaine . . . did far away espye . . . II. xi. 28. 7
Let not thee grieve *dismounted* to have beene, . . . III. i. 7. 6
all of them likewise *dismounted* were; . . . IV. iv. 46. 2
Dismounting. *Dismounting* lightly from his loftie steed, . . . I. iii. 36. 1
dismounting straict From his tall steed, . . . II. i. 39. 1
from his loftie steed *dismounting* low . . . III. iv. 53. 6
they *dismounting* drew their weapons bold, . . . III. xi. 21. 1
from my lofty steede *dismounting* low . . . IV. x. 15. 3
low *dismounting* from his loftie steede . . . V. x. 22. 2
streight *dismounting* from his steed, . . . V. xi. 61. 1
soft *dismounting,* like a weary lode, . . . VI. vi. 19. 4
Dismounting light, his shield about him threw, . . . VI. viii. 7. 2
Disobey. his lore do *disobay.* . . . *Col.* 890
durst he not his mother *disobay,* . . . IV. xii. 18. 6
Had not they dar'd their Lord to *disobay.* . . . *H.H.L.* 77
Disobeyed. 'Faire Sir, be not displeasd if *disobayd:* . . . II. xii. 28. 5
Not one was left that durst her once have *disobayd.* . . . V. xii. 25. 9
But she his precept proudly *disobayes,* . . . *Am.* xix. 11
Disorder. none of them he rudely doth *disorder,* . . . *Mui.* 174
with other much *disorder.* . . . VI. x. 39. 9
They would have caused much confusion and *disorder.* . . . VII. vii. 4. 9
Disordered. barbarous villaines in *disordred* heape, . . . *Bel.*[1] v. 10
Disordred hong about his shoulders round, . . . I. ix. 35. 5
She her gay painted plumes *disorderid;* . . . II. iii. 36. 4
Clad in fayre weedes but fowle *disordered,* . . . II. xii. 55. 8
To be *disordred* by some accident, . . . VI. v. 10. 3
So all confounded and *disordered* there: . . . VI. xii. 25. 6
Disorderly. One might have seene enraung'd *disorderly,* . . . V. xi. 9. 8
Dispace. Thus wise long time he did himselfe *dispace* . . . *Gn.* 265
Dispacing. In this faire plot *dispacing* too and fro, . . . *Mui.* 250
Dispainted. *dispainted* all within With sondry colours, . . . II. ix. 50. 1
Disparage. Dissuaded her from such a *disparage:* . . . IV. viii. 50. 5
Disparaged. Nought is thy worth *disparaged* thereby; . . . *Ded. Son.* ii. 6
fraile pen, with feare *disparaged,* . . . I. x. 2. 8
Disparagement. great *disparagment* makes to his former might.' II. viii. 29. 9
thought that match a fowle *disparagement:* . . . III. viii. 12. 4
for his meannesse and *disparagement,* . . . IV. vii. 16. 1
The gentle heart scornes base *disparagement.* . . . VI. x. 37. 5
one *disparagement* they to you gave, . . . *Am.* lxvi. 3
Disparagements. beames with such *disparagements* Be dimd, *H.B.* 164
Dispart. Them in twelve troupes their Captein did *dispart,* . . II. xi. 6. 1
Themselves they did *dispart,* . . . III. iv. 46. 8
lately did *dispart* Her bleeding brest, . . . III. xii. 38. 3
doe *dispart* the hart with powre extreme, . . . IV. ix. 1. 3
Both linckt together never to *dispart;* . . . IV. x. 51. 7
cryde Unto the Knight, them to *dispart* in twaine; . . . VI. v. 27. 2
Disparted. On either side *disparted* with his rod, . . . I. x. 53. 4
quite *disparted* all the linked frame, . . . II. viii. 44. 7
Doubly *disparted,* it did locke and close, . . . II. ix. 23. 6
Perforce *disparted* their compacted gyre, . . . III. i. 23. 6
So they *disparted* were, and all men went to rest. . . . V. iii. 7. 9
they *disparted* them, maugre their might, . . . V. iv. 43. 7
Dispatched. the disdainfull sowle he thence *dispatcht,* . . . II. xi. 42. 3
of the deadly swound . . . she at the length *dispacht* him, . . VI. iii. 10. 8
Dispense. one loving howre For many yeares of sorrow can
dispence; . . . I. iii. 30. 3
It was a vaut ybuilt for great *dispence,* . . . II. ix. 29. 1
poured forth with plentifull *dispence,* . . . II. xii. 42. 8
When so it needs with rigour to *dispence:* . . . V. i. 7. 5
Dealing his dreadfull blowes with large *dispence,* . . . V. xi. 45. 4
Dispensed. such fond favours sparingly *dispenst:* . . . IV. ii. 9. 3
Disperse. all his manly powres it did *disperse,* . . . I. ix. 48. 7
doth *disperse* the vapour lo'ste, . . . III. iv. 13. 5
So did that Squire his foes *disperse* and drive asonder. . . . VI. v. 19. 9
Dispersed. Of this faire fire the faire *dispersed* rayes . . . *Bel.*[1] ix. 9
Her power, *disperst* through all the world did vade; . . . *Ro.* xx. 13
The force, which wont in two to be *disperst,* . . . he now
unites, . . . I. viii. 18. 1
Disperst the shadowes of the misty night, . . . II. iii. 1. 2
when they had that troublous rout *disperst,* . . . II. ix. 17. 1
Infinite shapes of thinges *dispersed* thin; . . . II. ix. 50. 3
with his sword *disperst* the raskall flockes, . . . II. xi. 19. 2
Loosely *disperst* with puff of every blast: . . . III. i. 16. 4
Was all *disperst* out of the firmament, . . . III. i. 67. 8
To seeke their loves *dispersed* diversly, . . . IV. ix. 19. 8
Dispersed all their troupe incontinent, . . . V. iv. 24. 7
like a sort of sheepe *dispersed* farre . . . V. iv. 44. 7
Having *disperst* the nights unchearefull dampe, . . . *Epith.* 21
Disperseth. *Disperseth* them to catch his choysest pray; . . VI. xi. 49. 2
Dispiteous. *See* **Despiteous.**
Spurring so hote with rage *dispiteous,* . . . I. ii. 15. 2

Dispiteous—*Continued.*
leaving there in that *dispiteous* plight, . . . V. viii. 8. 7
With so fell fury and *dispiteous* forse, . . . VI. i. 33. 6
Through her *dispiteous* pride, . . . VI. vii. 38. 7
Displace. That vainly threatned kingdomes to *displace,* . . . *Ded. Son.* vi. 8
displace The Britons for their sinnes dew punishment . . . III. iii. 41. 7
doth *displace* The soring clouds . . . III. xi. 25. 7
he did it soone *displace,* . . . VI. ix. 42. 7
'That my ill fortune did them hence *displace;* . . . VI. x. 20. 7
she cast by force and tortious might Her to *displace,* . . . VII. vi. 10. 8
mild pleasance, which doth pride *displace,* . . . *Am.* xxi. 5
All other loves, . . . Thou must renounce and utterly *displace,* *H.H.L.* 264
Displaced. Such pleasaunce now *displast* by dolors dint: . . . *S.C.* N. 104
Displaid(e). *See* **Displayed.**
Display. To see the braunche of his body *displaie,* . . . *S.C.* May 196
There may thy Muse *display* her fluttryng wing, . . . *S.C.* O. 43
*soone as spring his mantle doth *displaye,* . . . *S.C.* N. 85
Sommer season sped him to *display* . . . *S.C.* D. 56
On the soft grasse his limbs doth oft *display,* . . . *Gn.* 108
Thy careles limbs in loose sleep dost *display.* . . . *Gn.* 336
those secret causes to *display;* . . . *T.M.* 50
Demaunds a yeare it duly to *display.* . . . *Col.* 595
In ampler wise it selfe will forth *display.* . . . *Ded.Son.*xvi.14
Faire feeling words he wisely gan *display,* . . . I. vii. 38. 6
hide the smoke that did his fire *display,* . . . I. ix. 16. 4
His flaggy winges, when forth he did *display,* . . . I. xi. 10. 1
The Northerne winde his wings did broad *display* . . . II. iii. 19. 3
by it his wearie limbes *display,* . . . II. v. 30. 7
vew of cherefull day Did never . . . it selfe *display,* . . . II. vii. 29. 5
His glory did enhaunce, and pompous pryde *display.* . . . II. vii. 44. 9
he gan *display* His painted nimble wings, . . . II. viii. 8. 8
did themselves through all the North *display:* . . . II. x. 15. 7
her powre she did *display* . . . II. x. 20. 5
Her bared bosome she doth broad *display;* . . . II. xii. 74. 8
did at last *display* That wanton Lady . . . II. xii. 76. 7
cannot *display* The roiall riches and exceeding cost . . . III. i. 32. 3
then his spirite thus gan foorth *display:* . . . III. iii. 21. 5
the Redcrosse knight did earst *display* Her lovers shape . . . III. iv. 5. 4
When Titan faire his beames did *display,* . . . III. vi. 6. 5
Her golden locks, . . . did them selves adowne *display* . . . III. ix. 20. 5
Till Blandamour . . . did her *display,* . . . IV. v. 13. 8
all the engins of her wit *display;* . . . V. v. 52. 2
The plot of all her practise did *display,* . . . V. ix. 47. 8
his bright shield *display.* . . . V. xi. 21. 5
To loose the badge that should his deedes *display.'* . . . V. xi. 52. 5
So soone as it did to the world *display* His chearefull face, . . . V. xii. 11. 3
far his fame *display.* . . . VI. i. 2. 9
Another while I baytes and nets *display* . . . VI. ix. 23. 5
to whom ye ill *display* That mucky masse, . . . VI. ix. 33. 4
Through the bright heaven doth her beams *display,* . . . VI. x. 13. 7
They loosely did theyr wanton winges *display,* . . . *Am.* lxxvi. 11
when so she doth *display* The gate . . . *Am.* lxxxi. 9
silken courteins over her *display,* . . . *Epith.* 303
your likenesse doth *display;* . . . *H.B.* 180
to their eyes that inmost faire *display,* . . . *H.B.* 237
Those unto all he daily doth *display,* . . . *H.H.B.* 113
Displayed. th' auncient Plot of Rome, *displayed* plaine, . . . *Ro.* xxvi. 13
With armes full strong and largely *displayd,* . . . *S.C.* F. 104
soone as spring his mantle hath *displayde,* . . . *S.C.* N. 85
sleep oppressed him *Displaid* on ground, . . . *Gn.* 240
ugly monster . . . Halfe like a serpent horribly *displaide,* . . . I. i. 14. 7
taile . . . whose folds *displaid* Were stretcht now forth . . . I. i. 16. 3
golden foile all over them *displaid,* . . . I. iv. 4. 4
darkesome night had all *displayd* Her coleblacke curtein . . . I. iv. 44. 1
griefe' . . . 'does greater grow *displaid,'* . . . I. vii. 41. 5
ornaments that richly were *displaid;* . . . I. viii. 46. 3
pillow was my helmett fayre *displayd;* . . . I. ix. 13. 4
with his waving wings *displayed* wyde, . . . I. xi. 18. 1
his left wing, then broad *displayd:* . . . I. xi. 20. 7
There he him found all carelesly *displaid,* . . . II. v. 32. 1
heavenly grace so plenteously *displayd!* . . . II. x. 50. 6
her two lilly paps aloft *displayd,* . . . II. xii. 66. 6
displayd The clothes about her round . . . III. ii. 47. 4
all naked bare *displayd.* . . . III. vi. 7. 4
now it plaine *display'd:* . . . III. x. 10. 9
maske of Cupid, and th' enchanted Chamber are *displayd;* . . . III. xii. Arg.
The God of love with wings *displayed* wide . . . IV. i. 39. 3
With scutchins gilt and banners broad *displayd;* . . . IV. iii. 5. 6
her nimble wings *displaid,* And flew away . . . IV. viii. 7. 6
Hath in a watry cloud *displayed* wide Her goodly bow, . . . V. iii. 25. 2
that losell, plainely now *displayd,* . . . V. iii. 35. 5
Loosely *displayd* upon the grassie ground, . . . VI. vii. 18. 8
Tho when as all her plaints she had *displayd,* . . . VI. viii. 34. 1
when thy glory shall be farre *displayd* To future age, . . . VI. x. 28. 8
With cloud of death upon her eyes *displayd;* . . . VI. xi. 21. 5
In which that rose she plainely saw *displayd:* . . . VI. xii. 19. 5
In whose cote-armour richly are *displayd* . . . *Am.* lxx. 2
With rose and lillies over them *displayd.* . . . *H.L.* 286
Displays. When shee the beames of her beauty *displayes,* . . . *S.C.* Ap. 84
That fame in tromp of gold eternally *displayes.* . . . III. iii. 3. 9
The prayses of high God he faire *displayes,* . . . III. iv. 59. 3
and brode *displayes* his smyling hew. . . . VI. ii. 35. 9
Even so the baser mind it selfe *displayes* . . . VI. vii. 1. 3
Disple. bitter Penaunce, . . . Was wont him once to *disple* every day: . . . I. x. 27. 2
Displeasance. him to *displeasaunce* moov'd, . . . II. x. 28. 7
Without *displeasance* for to prove his spere. . . . IV. vi. 4. 3
Displease. ought have done, that ye *displeasen* might, . . . I. iii. 27. 4
That stroke the hardy Squire did sore *displease,* . . . III. v. 19. 6
pardon simple man that rash him *displease.* . . . III. x. 30. 9

Displease—*Continued.*
She would her selfe *displease;* . . . V. vi. 20. 6
should it not *displease* thee it to tell, . . . VI. ii. 26. 1
lately sought his Lord for to *displease:* . . . VI. vi. 40. 4
Displeased. Thereat the courteous knight *displeased* was, . . . I. viii. 33. 3
'that thee so sore *displeased* hath? . . . II. v. 18. 2
'Faire Sir,' (quoth she) 'be not *displeasd* at all, . . . II. vi. 23. 1
Mammon was much *displeasd,* . . . II. vii. 39. 7
'Faire Sir, be not *displeasd* if disobayd: . . . II. xii. 28. 5
Whom whenas Venus saw so sore *displeasd,* . . . III. vi. 25. 1
wondrous sore Thereat *displeasd* they were, . . . III. viii. 52. 6
Sorely thereat he was *displeased,* . . . III. ix. 12. 7
he woxe therewith *displeased* sore, . . . IV. iv. 45. 6
her therewith full sore *displeasd* he found, . . . IV. vi. 42. 7
in her mind *displeased.* . . . IV. vi. 44. 3
Both Amidas and Philtra were *displeased;* . . . V. iv. 20. 2
his Lady much *displeased* Did him reprove, . . . VI. iii. 32. 6
Displeasing. gnasht his yron tuskes at that *displeasing* sight. . IV. x. 33. 9
Displeasure. Least thou the price of my *displeasure* prove.' . . *S.C.* F. 138
his enemie Had kindled such coles of *displeasure,* . . . *S.C.* F. 191
Tityus, mindefull yet Of thy *displeasure,* O Latona . . . *Gn.* 378
Displeasure too implacable was it, . . . *Gn.* 379
could great Cynthiaes sore *displeasure* breake, . . . *Col.* 174
upon eternall paine Of high *displeasure* that ensewen might, . I. iv. 40. 6
Whom Princes late *displeasure* left in bands, . . . II. i. 1. 2
nought regarding her *displeasure,* . . . II. xii. 57. 9
some light *displeasure* which him crost, . . . III. vi. 11. 3
After them went *Displeasure* and Pleasaunce, . . . III. xii. 18. 1
In great *displeasure* that he could not get her. . . . IV. v. 21. 7
displeasure of the mighty is Then death it selfe more dread . IV. viii. 1. 3
Her gentle Squire through her *displeasure* did pertake. . . . IV. viii. 9. 9
to wreake on worthlesse wight Your high *displesure,* . . . IV. viii. 17. 3
Dan Aeolus, in great *displeasure* . . . IV. ix. 23. 1
lay aside this griefe, . . . For that *displeasure,* . . . VI. ii. 46. 3
soone allayd that Knights conceiv'd *displeasure,* . . . VI. iii. 22. 2
the strong course of their *displeasure* breake, . . . VI. v. 30. 7
In great *displeasure* wild a Capias Should issue forth . . . VI. vi. 35. 4
for fell despight Of that *displeasure,* . . . VI. x. 18. 5
then the Captaine, fraught with more *displeasure,* . . . VI. xi. 14. 7
bring into a mighty Peres *displeasure,* . . . VI. xii. 41. 6
Displeasure's. For dread of her *displeasures* utmost proofe: . IV. vii. 37. 5
Displeasures. forepast *displeasures* to repeale. . . . V. viii. 21. 5
Disport. With faire *disport,* . . . She intertainde her lover . . . I. ii. 14. 1
Full of *disport,* still laughing, loosely light, . . . II. ii. 36. 2
They sdeigned such lascivious *disport,* . . . III. i. 40. 8
Her to *disport* and idle time to pas . . . III. viii. 11. 3
Disporting. I her caught *disporting* on the greene, . . . *D.* 118
Disports. She list not heare, but her *disports* poursewd, . . . II. vi. 26. 8
Their fit *disports* with faire delight doe chose, . . . III. ii. 31. 4
gives ye so good ayd To your *disports:* . . . III. vi. 21. 5
Dispose. Then must thou thee *dispose* another way: . . . *Hub.* 504
Who then can save what they *dispose* to spill? . . . *Mui.* 232
they gan *dispose* Themselves to court, . . . II. ix. 36. 4
Whose sleepie head she in her lap did soft *dispose.* . . . II. xii. 76. 9
The rest themselves in troupes did else *dispose,* . . . IV. iv. 14. 7
wheresoever he did himselfe *dispose,* . . . IV. v. 40. 7
He may *dispose* by his imperiall might, . . . V. iv. 19. 6
sith your fortunes thus *dispose,* . . . VI. viii. 29. 6
diversely *dispose* As each thought best . . . VI. viii. 39. 2
when as they did *dispose* To practise games . . . VI. ix. 43. 1
when she did *dispose* Her selfe to pleasaunce, . . . VI. x. 9. 1
in his soveraine throne gan straight *dispose* Himselfe, . . . VII. vi. 24. 7
Disposed. *See* **Ill-disposed.**
well *dispos'd* him some reliefe to showe, . . . *Hub.* 261
As one *disposed* wilfullie to die, . . . *D.* 552
he is all *disposd* to bloody fight, . . . II. iv. 43. 7
Words, well *dispost,* Have secrete powre . . . II. viii. 26. 7
Gently attempred, and *disposd* so well, . . . II. xii. 51. 8
onely three they were *disposd* so well; . . . III. vii. 57. 3
as he *disposed* was To walke the woodes . . . III. viii. 11. 1
A womans will, which is *disposd* to go astray. . . . III. ix. 6. 9
To moderate stiffe mindes *disposd* to strive: . . . IV. ii. 2. 6
at th' one side sixe judges were *dispos'd,* . . . IV. iii. 4. 3
disposd To visite her beloved Paramoure, . . . IV. v. 5. 1
So diversly these foure *disposed* were to love. . . . IV. ix. 21. 9
According their degrees *disposed* well. . . . IV. xii. 3. 5
To be by her *disposed* diversly To Gods and men, . . . VII. vi. 3. 5
Them well *disposed* by his busie paine, . . . VII. vii. 4. 7
thou art *disposed* cruelly, . . . *Epig.* iv. 17
Disposition. hath a zealous *disposition* To God, . . . *Hub.* 491
parts well measurd, with meet *disposition!* . . . *H.B.* 70
Dispossess. him of heavens Empire sought to *dispossesse?* . VII. vii. 1. 9
Dispossessed. cleft his head in twaine, and life thence *dispossest.* . . . II. viii. 33. 9
Disprad. *See* **Dispread.**
Dispraise. Praise who so list, yet I will him *dispraise,* . . . *Ti.* 229
Dispraised. such, as signes of ill luck, bene *dispraised;*) . . . *S.C.* May 232
he his lookes despised, and his boast *dispraized.* . . . VI. viii. 26. 9
Dispread. looslie on the grassie greene *dispredd,* . . . *Gn.* 242
did his beames abroad *dispred,* . . . *Mui.* 52
each where thou hast *dispredd* thy fame, . . . *Ded.Son.*xiv.13
fayre Pecocks, . . . full of Argus eyes their tayles *dispredden* wide. . . . I. iv. 17. 9
As morning Sunne her beames *dispredden* cleare, . . . II. ii. 40. 8
Like a broad table did it selfe *dispred,* . . . II. iii. 24. 2
They waved like a penon wyde *dispred,* . . . II. iii. 30. 4
did an Arber greene *dispred,* . . . II. v. 29. 2
braunches broad *dispredd* and body great, . . . II. vii. 53. 7
Wherein were many tables fayre *dispred,* . . . II. ix. 27. 2
the grownd *dispred* With grassy greene . . . II. xii. 12. 2

Dispread—*Continued.*
a blazing starre doth . . . flaming lockes *dispredd,* III. i. 16. 6
She did it fayre *dispred* and let to florish fayre. III. v. 51. 9
Thus finely did he his false nets *dispred,* III. x. 9. 6
over all his shoulders did *dispred,* IV. vii. 40. 8
Ne hostes of men with banners brode *dispred,* IV. viii. 47. 7
all *dispred* With shining gold, V. vii. 5. 4
To throw amongst the good which others had *disprad.* V. xii. 36. 9
had through the heavens wyde By this *dispred,* VI. viii. 44. 6
Dispreads. *Dispreds* the glorie of her leaves gay; V. xii. 13. 6
Dispred(d), Dispredden, Dispreds. *See* **Dispread, -s.**
Disprofess. His armes, which he had vowed to *disprofesse,* III. xi. 20. 4
Disproved. now his wisedome is *disprooved* quite; *Ti.* 446
Dispurveyance. through *dispurvayaunce* long And lacke of reskewes, III. x. 10. 3
Disquiet. In his *disquiet* mind was much dismayd: III. x. 14. 3
In such *disquiet* and hart-fretting payne IV. v. 45. 1
Full of discomfort and *disquiet* plight, IV. viii. 8. 4
Without *disquiet* or dislike of ether, VI. xii. 10. 8
Nor any dread *disquiet* once annoy *Epith.* 324
Disquieted. Till the prowde Romanes him *disquieted,* II. x. 47. 5
Disquietness. deeme them roote of all *disquietnesse;* II. vii. 12. 2
Without affliction or *disquietnesse* VI. xi. 1. 2
Disrobe. The holy Saints of their rich vestiments He did *disrobe,* I. iii. 17. 6
Disrobed. in hast, *disroabed* as he was, *Hub.* 1343
when they had the witch *disrobed* quight, I. viii. 49. 7
Disseise. Time, who doth them all *disseise* Of being: VII. vii. 48. 3
Disseised. He so *disseized* of his gryping grosse, I. xi. 20. 1
Dissemblance. *Dissemblaunce* and Suspect Marcht in one rancke, III. xii. 14. 1
as *Dissemblaunce* laught on him, III. xii. 15. 3
without guile Or false *dissemblaunce* VI. x. 24. 4
Dissemble. what inquest Made her *dissemble* her disguised kind? III. ii. 4. 7
Right plaine appeard, though she it would *dissemble,* IV. vi. 29. 7
fairely did *dissemble* her sad thoughts unrest. V. v. 44. 9
Of all things, to *dissemble,* fouly may befall!' V. xi. 56. 9
Dissembled. he inly quooke; But it *dissembled,* *Hub.* 1061
for my part, I vow, *dissembled* not a whitt. II. iv. 18. 9
she the same *Dissembled* faire, II. ix. 44. 3
Britomart *dissembled* it with ignoraunce. III. i. 50. 9
she to him *dissembled* womanish guyle, III. iii. 17. 3
He it *dissembled* well, and light seemd to esteeme III. viii. 16. 9
they *dissembled* what they did not see, III. ix. 19. 5
Dissembling. Masked with faire *dissembling* curtesie, *Col.* 700
Dissembling his disease and evill plight; IV. i. 38. 3
Dissension. The cause of their *dissention* and outrageous yre. II. i. 23. 9
mother of debate And all *dissention* IV. i. 19. 2
Dissent. who does *dissent* from this my read, V. i. 26. 6
Till he had questioned the cause of their *dissent.* V. iv. 6. 9
Dissention. *See* **Dissension.**
Disshivered. *Disshivered* speares, and shields ytorne in twaine; IV. i. 21. 6
Dissolute. him disarmed, *dissolute,* dismaid, Unwares surprised, I. vii. 51. 3
rownd about him *dissolute* did play II. v. 32. 5
drowne in *dissolute* delights apart, II. vi. 25. 7
With termes of love and lewdnesse *dissolute;* III. viii. 14. 3
Dissolution. It shall continewe till the worlds *dissolution,* *S.C.* Env. 4
toward his *dissolution.* V. Pr. 4. 9
Dissolved. Till it *dissolved* be from earthly band. II. xi. 30. 5
The mist of griefe *dissolv'd* did into vengeance powre. III. iv. 13. 9
dissolv'd through my so hot desyre, *Am.* xxx. 3
Dissolving. *dissolving* his moist frame, *Ro.* xx. 7
Dissuade. thee did hence *dissuade.'* *Col.* 177
'Let bee therefore my vengeaunce to *disswade,* III. ii. 13. 1
gan first *disswade* From such foule outrage, IV. ix. 34. 3
for nought may feare *disswade,* VI. xi. 38. 2
Dissuaded. *disswaded* them from needlesse feare, *Hub.* 1075
Dissuaded her from such a disparage: IV. viii. 50. 5
Distaff. The direfull *distaffe* standing in the mid, IV. ii. 48. 2
in his hand a *distaffe* to him gave, V. v. 23. 2
apply His mightie hands the *distaffe* vile to hold V. v. 24. 4
A *distaffe* in her other hand she had, V. xii. 36. 6
Distain. gentle mindes with lewd delights *distaine;* *T.M.* 334
Distained. if my temples were *distaind* with wine, *S.C.* O. 110
with durty blood *distaynd,* I. xi. 23. 8
distaind her honorable blood, II. iv. 22. 7
Distaynd with durt and blood, III. viii. 49. 9
Distains. *Distaines* the pillours and the holy grownd, III. iv. 17. 7
Distempered. *Distempred* through misrule and passions bace; II. ix. 1. 6
Distent. *distent* Into great Ingowes and to wedges square; II. vii. 5. 5
Disthronised. Peridure and Vigent him *disthronized.* II. x. 44. 9
Distil. soone as few drops of raine Thereon *distill* V. xii. 13. 4
As from a limbeck did adown *distill.* VII. vii. 31. 5
Distilled. Few drops, more cleare then Nectar, forth *distild,* II. xii. 78. 4
Distinct. With divers flowres *distinct* with rare delight, VI. iii. 23. 5
Distinguished. *Distinguished* with manie a twinckling starre; *Mui.* 94
Distort. With matchlesse eares deformed and *distort,* IV. i. 28. 2
Her face was ugly, and her mouth *distort,* V. xii. 36. 1
Distrain. he knew Some secret sorrow did her heart *distraine;* I. vii. 38. 4
neither guile nor force might it *distraine.* II. xii. 82. 3
Distraught. *Distraught* twixt feare and pitie; *Ti.* 579
'What franticke fit, (quoth he) 'hath thus *distraught* Thee, I. ix. 38. 1
Thus whilest their minds were doubtfully *distraught,* IV. iii. 48. 6
thrild His greedy throte, therewith in two *distraught,* IV. vii. 31. 7
Such an huge stroke, that it of sence *distraught* her; V. iv. 41. 5
Trayled with ribbands diversly *distraught,* V. v. 2. 4
like one enfelon'd or *distraught,* V. viii. 48. 5
all his wits with doole were nigh *distraught,* VI. xi. 33. 3
like to one *distraught* And robd of reason, VI. xi. 45. 7

Distraughted. Which in my weake *distraughted* mynd I see; *H.H.B.* 14
Distress. Asked the cause of his great *distresse,* *S.C.* May 260
there huge Othos sits in sad *distresse,* *Gn.* 373
he driven was to great *distresse,* *Hub.* 933
yeeld us some reliefe in this *distresse;* *T.M.* 347
In pitie of my undeserv'd *distresse,* *D.* 531
no . . . wight May ever passe, but thorough great *distresse.'* I. i. 32. 3
Discoursing of her dreadful late *distresse,* I. iii. 32. 7
cryes, The last vaine helpe of wemens great *distresse,* I. vi. 6. 3
with them all departes to tell his great *distresse.* I. vii. 19. 9
throw This gentle knight into so great *distresse,* I. xii. 33. 8
What hard mishap him brought to such *distresse,* II. iv. 16. 8
gan him dight to succour his *distresse,* II. v. 24. 2
hath to Paynim knights wrought gret *distresse,* II. viii. 18. 5
Now was the Prince in daungerous *distresse,* II. viii. 34. 1
Whom when the Palmer saw in such *distresse,* II. viii. 40. 1
In such *distresse* and doubtfull jeopardy III. i. 22. 6
in desperate *distresse,* And to her feet betooke her III. vii. 25. 8
Lying athwart her horse in great *distresse,* III. vii. 37. 7
Driven to great *distresse* by fortune straunge, III. viii. 20. 2
In such *distresse* and sad perplexity III. viii. 33. 8
A silly Pilgrim driven to *distresse,* III. x. 25. 6
who nill bide the burden of *distresse,* III. xi. 14. 8
the sad *distresse* In which that boy thee plonged, III. xi. 36. 2
She left Sir Scudamour in great *distresse,* III. xii. 43. *or.* 2
all his joy, he said, in that *distresse* IV. viii. 57. 6
the things which come through hard *distresse.* IV. x. 28. 9
Whom when as Artegall in that *distresse* By chaunce beheld, V. iv. 41. 1
Who yeester day drove us to such *distresse:* V. iv. 48. 7
in revenge both of her loves *distresse* V. vii. 34. 3
dead long since in dolorous *distresse,* V. vii. 39. 4
They saw a Knight in daungerous *distresse* V. xi. 44. 2
oft I driven am to great *distresse,* V. xi. 51. 8
having freed Irena from *distresse,* V. xii. 27. 8
So downe he tooke his Lady in *distresse,* VI. iii. 44. 5
in such *distresse* He wist not to which side him to addresse: VI. vi. 26. 4
Distressed. Burnt up his yong ones, and himselfe *distrest;* *Van.* iv. 8
To see so great things by so small *distrest.* *Van.* xii. 4
leave me here *distressed* With mortall cares *Ti.* 304
doubly is *distrest* . . . The dreadlesse corage I. vi. 1. 7
Una greatly with those newes *distrest.* I. vii. Arg.
In this *distressed* doubtfull agony, I. x. 22. 6
In sea of deadly daungers was *distrest:* I. xii. 17. 6
Better safe port then be in seas *distrest.'* II. vi. 23. 8
most deadly daunger and *distressed* plight. II. xii. 11. 9
To comfort me in my *distressed* plight. III. v. 35. 4
succor send to her *distressed* cace; III. viii. 29. 4
He was therewith *distressed* diversely, III. x. 14. 7
Britomart chaceth Ollyphant; Findes Scudamour *distrest:* III. xi. Arg.
th' enchaunter which had her *distrest* So sore, III. xii. 41. 4
That was to succour a *distressed* Dame V. i. 3. 6
After long tossing in the seas *distrest,* V. iv. 11. 8
by wracke that wretches hath *distrest,* V. iv. 19. 5
Whom when they thus *distressed* did behold, V. xi. 47. 1
Ran after fast to reskue the *distressed* mayde. VI. iii. 24. 9
whilest he was in this *distressed* case, VI. iii. 30. 5
Whom when the Salvage saw so sore *distrest,* VI. v. 6. 1
Distribute. His owne cote he would cut, and it *distribute* glad. I. x. 39. 9
Distroubled. Both coosen passions of *distroubled* spright, III. iv. 12. 7
Distrust. cowardly *distrust* Of his weake wings *H.L.* 180
Distrustful. The vaine surmizes, the *distrustfull* showes, *H.L.* 260
Disturbance. He should without *disturbance* her possesse: IV. v. 25. 8
Disturbed. The bellowes noyse *disturb'd* his quiet rest, IV. v. 41. 4
all the sea, *disturbed* with their traine, V. ii. 15. 7
Disturber. Was the *disturber* of all civill life, III. vi. 14. 8
Dit. *See* **Ditty.**
No song but did containe a lovely *ditt.* II. vi. 13. 4
Ditch. To hedge, to *ditch,* to thrash, to thetch, to mowe? *Hub.* 264
Ne hedge ne *ditch* his readie passage brake; II. xi. 26. 5
Nor hedge, nor *ditch,* nor hill, nor dale she staies, IV. vii. 22. 1
Dites. *See* **Dights.**
Ditt. *See* **Dit.**
Ditties. if hys *ditties* bene so trimly dight, *S.C.* Ap. 29
The dapper *ditties,* that I wont devise *S.C.* O. 13
Rude *ditties,* tund to shepheards Oaten reede, *S.C.* D. 14
Ditty. *See* **Dit.**
bowe your eares unto my dolefull *dittie:* *S.C.* Ja. 16
What *dittie* did that other shepheard sing: *Col.* 160
fit to frame an everlasting *dittie,* *Col.* 385
Too high a *ditty* for my simple song. I. x. 55. 7
(O too high *ditty* for my simple rime!) II. x. 50. 7
there a piteous *ditty* new deviz'd, IV. viii. 12. 2
Divelish. *See* **Devilish.**
Divers. *See* **Diverse.**
Of kingdomes change, of *divers* gouvernment, *Hub.* 766
so gay were dyde In colours *divers,* *T.M.* 238
Might in their *divers* cunning ever dare *Mui.* 367
Faire Rosalind of *divers* fowly blamed *Col.* 908
Therein were *divers* rowmes; and *divers* stages; II. ix. 47. 6
divydes The doubtfull current into *divers* wayes. IV. i. 42. 6
As diverse wits affected *divers* beene. IV. v. 11. 5
divers trees enrang'd in even rankes; IV. x. 25. 2
With *divers* fortune fit for such a game, V. iii. 7. 4
the place, the which was dight With *divers* flowres VI. iii. 23. 5
Divers-colored. with *divers-colord* flowre To decke hir selfe, *Am.* iv. 11
Diverse. *See* **Divers.**
which of them to take in *diverse* doubt they been. I. i. 10. 9
calling forth . . . A *diverse* Dreame out of his prison darke, I. i. 44. 2
he . . . Her constant hart did tempt with *diverse* guile: I. vi. 4. 3
into *diverse* doubt his wavering wonder clove. II. ii. 3. 9

Diverse—*Continued.*
stryfull mind and *diverse* qualitee . . . II. ii. 13. 5
vowd to so *diverse* loves, . . . II. ii. 19. 1
Diverse discourses in their way they spent; . . . II. vi. 9. 1
two sharpe winged sheares, Decked with *diverse* plumes, . . . II. viii. 5. 8
Diverse delights they fownd them selves to please; . . . II. ix. 35. 1
With *diverse* flowres he daintily was deckt, . . . II. xii. 49. 1
Their *diverse* notes t' attune unto his lay, . . . II. xii. 76. 2
As *diverse* witts to *diverse* things apply; . . . III. i. 57. 3
diverse plots did frame to maske in strange disguise. . . . III. iii. 51. 9
Of *diverse* thinges discourses to dilate, . . . III. iii. 62. 4
Wonder it is to see in *diverse* mindes . . . III. v. 1. 1
to tell The *diverse* usage, and demeanure daint, . . . IV. i. 5. 2
With *diverse* fortune doubtfull to be deemed: . . . IV. iii. 28. 2
As *diverse* wits affected divers beene. . . . IV. v. 11. 5
He knew the *diverse* went of mortall wayes, . . . VI. vi. 3. 5
Whom they before in *diverse* spoyles had caught; . . . VI. xi. 11. 3
Diversed. The Redcrosse Knight *diverst,* but forth rode Britomart. . . . III. iii. 62. 9
Diversely. *See* **Diversly.**
each gan *diversely* devize. . . . III. i. 33. 9
He was therewith distressed *diversely,* . . . III. x. 14. 7
They searched *diversely,* so both divided were. . . . III. xi. 6. 9
So *diversely* each one did sundrie doubts devise. . . . IV. i. 14. 9
diversely dispose As each thought best . . . VI. viii. 39. 2
Divers-feathered. little winged loves, Like *divers-fethered* doves, *Epith.* 358
Diversity. From whence arise *diversitie* of sects, . . . *Hub.* 388
all agreed, through sweete *diversity,* . . . II. xii. 59. 8
Diversly. *See* **Diversely.**
as ye see huge flames spred *diverslie,* . . . *Ro.* xvi. 9
through his entrailes spredding *diversly,* . . . *Van.* vi. 9
to be In this or that praysd *diversly* apart, . . . *Col.* 569
A bounch of heares discolourd *diversly.* . . . I. ii. 11. 6
bounch of heares discolourd *diversly,* . . . I. vii. 32. 2
diversly discoursing of their loves, . . . I. ix. 18. 1
So *diversly* them selves in vaine they fray; . . . I. xii. 11. 7
Whom raging windes, . . . doe *diversly* disease, . . . II. ii. 24. 3
gan to bord, and purpose *diversly;* . . . II. xii. 16. 2
How *diversly* love doth his pageaunts play, . . . III. v. 1. 2
Transformed oft, and chaunged *diverslie;* . . . III. vi. 47. 7
discoursed *diversly* Of straunge affaires, . . . III. ix. 53. 1
diversly conferred of their case, . . . IV. ix. 10. 2
To seeke their loves dispersed *diversly,* . . . IV. ix. 19. 8
So *diversly* these foure disposed were to love. . . . IV. ix. 21. 9
Trayled with ribbands *diversly* distraught, . . . V. v. 2. 4
Thus whylest they were debating *diverslie,* . . . VI. vii. 23. 7
discoursing *diversly* Of sundry things as fell, . . . VI. ix. 12. 6
To be by her disposed *diversly* To Gods and men, . . . VII. vi. 3. 5
Disguysing *diversly* my troubled wits. . . . *Am.* liv. 4
Divide. his broad forhead like two hornes *divide,* . . . *Gn.* 22
As the great Ocean doth himselfe *divide.* . . . *Gn.* 160
Let us our fathers heritage *divide,* . . . *Hub.* 136
the rich fee, which Poets wont *divide,* . . . *T.M.* 471
To prove that death their hearts cannot *divide,* . . . *As.* 179
they their dayes to ydlenesse *divide,* . . . *Col.* 761
most heavenly melody . . . sweet musicke did *divide,* . . . I. v. 17. 7
Ne dint of direfull sword *divide* the substance would. . . . I. vii. 33. 9
with strong flight did forcibly *divyde* The yielding ayre, . . . I. xi. 18. 3
none but death for ever can *divide;* . . . I. xii. 37. 2
dying whylome did *divide* this fort . . . II. ii. 13. 3
Whom they in equall pray hope to *divide,* . . . II. ii. 22. 8
did *divide* Her daintie paps; . . . II. iii. 29. 6
did the house of Richesse from hell-mouth *divide.* . . . II. vii. 24. 9
did her selfe in sondry parts *divide,* . . . II. x. 54. 3
Musicke did *divide* Her looser notes with Lydian harmony; . . . III. i. 40. 1
Emongst his young ones shall *divide* . . . III. iii. 47. 9
did it selfe *divide* with equall space, . . . III. xi. 25. 5
that great golden chaine quite to *divide,* . . . IV. i. 30. 8
Which did her powre into three parts *divyde;* . . . IV. ii. 43. 4
like that roote that doth her life *divide,* . . . IV. ii. 43. 7
did *divide* Them selves asunder: . . . IV. iv. 14. 1
Her tender hart in peeces would *divide:* . . . IV. vii. 10. 3
daies, by which the sonnes of men *Divide* their works, . . . IV. vii. 13. 2
To whom he did *divide* part of his purchast spoile. . . . IV. ix. 12. 9
thought it all one night that did no houres *divide.* . . . IV. xi. 4. 9
Justice . . . did *divide* her dred beheasts: . . . V. Pr. 9. 9
True Justice unto people to *divide,* . . . V. iv. 1. 2
So cruell doale amongst her maides *divide* . . . V. iv. 39. 3
to them stepping did them soone *divide,* . . . VI. v. 27. 3
whatever chaunce were blowne Betwixt them to *divide,* . . . VI. vii. 3. 9
A great adventure, which did him from them *devide.* . . . VI. viii. 30. 9
with his raging brond *divide* Their thickest troups, . . . VI. xi. 48. 8
as she them list *divide;* . . . VII. vi. 3. 6
As if ye please it into parts *divide,* . . . VII. vii. 17. 3
doth burne, it doth *divide* Great heat, . . . *Am.* vi. 7
Divided. the rayne Twixt them *divided* into even twaine, . . . *Hub.* 1024
Archimago, when his guests He saw *divided* . . . I. ii. 9. 2
his realme he equally decreed To have *divided.* . . . II. x. 27. 6
They searched diversely, so both *divided* were. . . . III. xi. 6. 9
Her lying tongue was in two parts *divided,* . . . IV. i. 27. 6
Divided them, how ever loth to rest; . . . IV. ix. 32. 7
Encloseth Corke with his *devided* flood; . . . IV. xi. 44. 4
Devided be betwixt you here in sight, . . . V. i. 26. 4
earth uptake And all the sea, *divided* each from either: . . . V. ii. 31. 2
Divides. *divydes* The doubtfull current into divers wayes. . . . IV. i. 42. 5
devides The Cornish and the Devonish confines; . . . IV. xi. 31. 1
Dividing. The which *dividing* with importune sway, . . . II. viii. 38. 8
Divine. By paterne of great Virgils spirit *divine!* . . . *Ro.* xxv. 11
To make the mountaines touch the starres *divine,* . . . *Gn.* 213

Divine—*Continued.*
Through the *divine* infusion of their skill, . . . *T.M.* 38
Thoughts halfe *devine,* full of the fire of love, . . . *T.M.* 363
they that scorne the schoole of arts *divine,* . . . *T.M.* 520
Divine Elisa, sacred Emperesse! . . . *T.M.* 579
'His blessed spirite, full of power *divine* . . . *Ti.* 288
to judge of things *divine:* . . . *Col.* 345
needs his priest t' expresse his powre *divine.* . . . *Col.* 838
Rashly to wyten creatures so *divine;* . . . *Col.* 916
of *divine* regard and heavenly hew, . . . *Col.* 933
Mirrour of grace and Majestie *divine,* . . . I. Pr. 4. 2
From that day forth I lov'd that face *divyne;* . . . I. ix. 15. 5
heare the wisedom of her wordes *divine.* . . . I. x. 18. 6
Present before the majesty *divine,* . . . I. x. 51. 8
So darke are earthly thinges compard to things *divine.* . . . I. x. 67. 9
They all perfumde with frankincense *divine,* . . . I. xii. 38. 3
O worke *divine!* . . . II. ix. 22. 2
old Assaracus, and Inachus *divine.* . . . II. ix. 56. 9
voyces made To th' instruments *divine* respondence meet; . . . II. xii. 71. 4
The fatall purpose of *divine* foresight . . . III. iii. 2. 5
whether yt *divine* Tobacco were, Or Panachaea, . . . III. v. 32. 6
T' adore thing so *divine* as beauty were but right. . . . III. vii. 11. 9
by the dauncing bubbles did *divine,* . . . III. ix. 30. 6
turnest love *divine* To joylesse dread, . . . III. xi. 1. 5
In his *divine* resemblance wondrous lyke: . . . III. xi. 40. 2
deem'st of things *divine* As of humane, . . . IV. ii. 51. 5
Unweeting of the Fates *divine* decree . . . IV. iii. 21. 4
obedience To doe to so *divine* a beauties excellence. . . . IV. vi. 21. 9
The which right well her workes *divine* did shew: . . . IV. x. 34. 5
Divine Scamander, purpled yet with blood . . . IV. xi. 20. 6
Dee, which Britons long ygone Did call *divine,* . . . IV. xi. 39. 4
Adorn'd with all *divine* perfection, . . . IV. xii. 34. 2
dare discourse of so *divine* a read . . . V. Pr. 11. 7
Nought is on earth more sacred or *divine,* . . . V. vii. 1. 1
To shew that she had powre in things *divine:* . . . V. vii. 6. 7
by his *divine* permission, . . . V. ix. 32. 1
drawne forth from her by *divine* extreate: . . . V. x. 1. 4
To offer sacrifice *divine* thereon; . . . VI. viii. 42. 6
Divine resemblaunce, beauty soveraine rare, . . . VI. x. 27. 4
Babblers unworthy been of so *divine* a meed. . . . VII. vi. 46. 9
assembled were On Haemus hill in their *divine* array, . . . VII. vii. 12. 3
shew Thing so *divine* to vew of earthly eye, . . . *Am.* xlv. 6
Great shame it is, thing so *divine* in view, . . . *Am.* liii. 9
that doth argue you To be *divine,* . . . *Am.* lxxix. 10
nought more *divine* doth seeme, . . . *H.L.* 114
those heavenly beauties be enfyred As things *divine,* . . . *H.L.* 170
Or more or lesse, by influence *divine,* . . . *H.B.* 44
face Of the *Divine* Eternall Majestie; . . . *H.H.B.* 81
The glory of that Majestie *Divine,* . . . *H.H.B.* 124
More excellent, more glorious, more *divine,* . . . *H.H.B.* 171
Presume to picture so *divine* a wight, . . . *H.H.B.* 226
Divined. borne above the cloudes to be *divin'd,* . . . *Ti.* 611
Living on earth like Angell new *divinde,* . . . *D.* 214
thou now full deeply hast *divynd* Of Love and beautie; . . . *Col.* 896
Divinely. His snowy front, . . . *Divinely* shone; . . . II. viii. 5. 7
she her selfe likewise *divinely* grew; . . . IV. x. 34. 4
Faire Amphitrite, most *divinely* faire, . . . IV. xi. 11. 6
For being, as she is, *divinely* wrought, . . . *Am.* lxi. 5
Divines. Doubts mongst *Divines,* and difference of texts, . . . *Hub.* 387
mocke *Divines* and their profession. . . . *Hub.* 841
Divinest. Be fild with praises of *divinest* wits, . . . *T.M.* 581
skill That whilome in *divinest* wits did rayne, . . . III. Pr. 3. 2
Diving. *diving* deepe through amorous insight, . . . *Am.* lxxvi. 7
Divining. through power of some *divining* spright, . . . *Gn.* Ded. 6
Divinities. The goodly Maide, ful of *divinities* . . . III. v. 34. 7
Divinity. In contemplation of *divinitee:* . . . III. ix. 24. 4
Division. this lands . . . old *division* into Regiments, . . . II. ix. 59. 8
Divorced. she . . . Is from her knight *divorced* in despayre, . . . I. iii. 2. 8
Divorces. the strong *divorces* Of that great warre, . . . *Gn.* 497
Do (*partial list of auxiliary*). *See* **Derring do.**
In God alone *do* stay my confidence. . . . *Bel.*[1] i. 14
sights, that *doo* her peace molest. . . . *Pet.*[2] vii. 8
what ever nature, arte, And heaven could *doo,* . . . *Ro.* v. 2
Doo ye not feele your torments . . . *Ro.* xv. 11
if that time *doo* let thy glorie live, . . . *Ro.* xxxii. 11
doe into daunger fall. . . . *Van.* xii. 8
(no better *doe* him call,) . . . *S.C.* Ja. 1
shake, As *doen* high Towers . . . *S.C.* F. 6
Nymphs, that . . . *Doe* bathe your brest, . . . *S.C.* Ap. 38
Will *doe* as did the Foxe by the Kidde. . . . *S.C.* May 171
So be your goodlihead *doe* not disdayne . . . *S.C.* May 270
(As garments *doen,* which wexen old above,) . . . *S.C.* Jun. 39
That als we mought *doe* soe. . . . *S.C.* Jul. 120
Why *done* we them disease? . . . *S.C.* Jul. 124
As Lordes *done* other where; . . . *S.C.* Jul. 186
That shall I *doe,* . . . *S.C.* Au. 23
sleepe, as some *doen,* all the long day; . . . *S.C.* S. 233
What shall I *doe?* . . . *S.C.* S. 244
If nor in Princes pallace thou *doe* sitt, . . . *S.C.* O. 80
seeing kindly sleep refuse to *doe* His office, . . . *Hub.* 21
As if good service he were fit to *doo;* . . . *Hub.* 239
To *doo* you faithfull service all my dayes. . . . *Hub.* 253
To *doo* their kindly services as needeth. . . . *Hub.* 273
they must feed themselves, *doo* what we can. . . . *Hub.* 434
we need to *doo* no more. . . . *Hub.* 436
It is enough to *doo* our small devotion, . . . *Hub.* 457
unto everie one *doo* curtesie meeke: . . . *Hub.* 499
he could *doo* manie other poynts, . . . *Hub.* 696
As that same Apish crue is wont to *doo:* . . . *Hub.* 731

Do—*Continued.*
had not power to *doo* him good or ill. . . . . . *Hub.* 890
be rul'd to *doo* as I doo teach' . . . . . . *Hub.* 992
ye be fine and nimble it to *doo;* . . . . . . *Hub.* 1000
no wild beasts should *do* them any torte . . . . . . *Hub.* 1078
there was cause, els *doo* it he would not: . . . . . . *Hub.* 1220
Arise, and *doo* thyself redeeme . . . . . . *Hub.* 1331
all her sisters, seeing her *doo* soe, ... *T.M.* 297
rime at riot, and *doo* rage in love; . . . . . . *T.M.* 395
who would ever care to *doo* brave deed, ... *T.M.* 451
as he was wont to *doo* For her . . . . . . *As.* 39
do not thy selfe that wrong, ... *Col.* 406
Which so to *doe* may thee right well befit, ... *Ded. Son.* iii. 5
he gave . . . The other . . . other worke to *doo.* . . . . . . I. i. 38. 9
thus perforce he bids me *do,* or die. . . . . . . I. i. 51. 6
To *doe* none ill, if please ye not *doe* well.' . . . . . . I. ii. 26. 4
When Witches wont *do* penance for their crime,) . . . . . . I. ii. 40. 5
Thyselfe thy message *do* to german deare; . . . . . . I. v. 13. 2
To *do* their service to Sylvanus old, ... I. vi. 33. 2
Hold for my sake, and *doe* him not to dye, ... I. vii. 14. 7
'The things, that grievous were to *doe,* or beare, ... I. viii. 44. 2
'To *doe* her die,' (quoth Una) 'were despight, ... I. viii. 45. 7
will ryde Against my liking backe to *doe* you grace: . . . . . . I. ix. 32. 6
Is it not better to *doe* willinglie . . . . . . I. ix. 47. 7
feends that *doe* them endlesse paine . . . . . . I. ix. 49. 8
it could not *doe* him die, ... I. ix. 54. 8
Of love, and righteousnes, and well to *donne;* . . . . . . I. x. 33. 4
doen their service to that soveraigne Dame, ... I. x. 59. 7
He shall you *doe* dew recompence agayne, ... II. i. 14. 8
How that same knight should *doe* so fowle amis, ... II. i. 19. 2
To be her Squire, and *do* her service well aguisd. . . . . . . II. i. 21. 9
But vaine; for ye shall dearely *do* him rew, ... II. i. 25. 5
dew vengeaunce *doe* forbeare, ... II. i. 61. 7
That speare is him enough to *doen* a thousand grone.' . . . . . . II. iii. 12. 9
mote I wisely you advise to *doon,* . . . . . . II. iii. 15. 3
but *doe* purvay Your selfe of sword . . . . . . II. iii. 15. 4
doe unwilling worship to the Saint, ... II. v. 11. 7
'Mercy! *doe* me not dye, ... II. v. 12. 7
*To stirre up strife, and *do* them disagree: . . . . . . II. v. 19. 7
to *do* him laugh, ... II. vi. 7. 6
which *doe* men in bale to sterve, ... II. vi. 34. 3
What coward hand shall *doe* thee next to dye, ... II. vi. 39. 8
Nothing but death can *doe* me to respyre.' . . . . . . II. vi. 44. 5
Threatning with greedy gripe to *doe* him dye, ... II. vii. 27. 7
All which he did to *do* him deadly fall . . . . . . II. vii. 64. 1
dread of death and dolor *doe* away; . . . . . . II. viii. 7. 7
'For knighthoods love *doe* not so fowle a deed, ... II. viii. 16. 2
Therewith to *doen* his foes eternall smart. . . . . . . II. viii. 20. 4
to *doen* outrage to a sleeping ghost; . . . . . . II. viii. 26. 2
His single speare could *doe* him small redresse . . . . . . II. viii. 34. 3
Ne what to say, ne what to *doe* at all: . . . . . . II. xi. 39. 4
could *doe* harme, yet could not harmed bee, ... II. xi. 40. 6
(God *doe* us well acquight!) . . . . . . II. xii. 3. 3
Who can it *doe* more lively, or more trew, ... III. Pr. 4. 3
Shall *doe* unto her service, ... III. i. 26. 9
Ne to your Lady will I service *done,* . . . . . . III. i. 28. 4
lend her short reliefe And *doe* her comfort, ... III. i. 53. 6
ever *doe* that mote deserven blame: . . . . . . III. ii. 10. 3
(as maydens use to *done*) . . . . . . III. ii. 23. 5
Therefore away *doe* dread; . . . . . . III. ii. 33. 7
To *doe* the frosen cold away to fly; . . . . . . III. ii. 34. 5
Can *doe*' (said she) 'that which cannot be donne.' . . . . . . III. ii. 36. 8
call Their sondry kings to *do* their homage severall. . . . . . . III. iii. 32. 9
Shall tread adowne, and *doe* him fowly dye; . . . . . . III. iii. 39. 8
How can they other *doe,* . . . . . . III. iv. 9. 9
he must *do* battail with the Sea-nymphes sonne. . . . . . . III. iv. 20. 9
To *doen* his Nephew in all riches flow; . . . . . . III. iv. 22. 2
To *doe* away vaine doubt and needlesse dreed: . . . . . . III. iv. 48. 7
Do one or other good, I you most humbly pray. . . . . . . III. v. 10. 9
What service may I *doe* unto thee meete, ... III. v. 35. 6
Ah God! what other could he *do* at least, ... III. v. 43. 8
What can I lesse *doe* then her love therefore, ... III. v. 46. 4
To *doe* him ease, or *doe* him remedy. . . . . . . III. v. 50. 2
A laesy loord, for nothing good to *donne,* . . . . . . III. vii. 12. 3
muchell blood did spend, Yet might not *doe* him die: . . . . . . III. vii. 32. 8
The fearefull Chorle durst not gainesay nor *dooe,* . . . . . . III. viii. 13. 1
Forcyng to *doe* that did him fowle misseeme. . . . . . . III. viii. 26. 7
with feare, nor favour, nor with all He els could *doe,* . . . III. viii. 41. 7
To *doe* fowle death to die, ... III. ix. 17. 9
have the sight . . . to *doe* them more delight. . . . . . . III. ix. 25. 9
stood aloofe, unweeting what to *doe;* . . . . . . III. x. 22. 3
durst he not against it *doe* or say, ... III. x. 45. 3
faire Sir, *doe* comfort to you take, ... III. xi. 15. 1
Till so she *doe,* she must in doole remaine, ... III. xi. 17. 7
This *doe,* and live, els dye undoubtedly.' . . . . . . III. xii. 35. 7
all things did devise, and all things *dooe,* . . . . . . IV. ii. 8. 8
As all men *do,* that lose the living spright. . . . . . . IV. iii. 30. 7
ye *doe* wrong To stirre up strife, ... IV. iv. 12. 2
all in vaine: for what might one *do* more? . . . . . . IV. iv. 32. 8
For ought that Glauce could or *doe* or say. . . . . . . IV. v. 31. 6
obedience To *doe* to so divine a beauties excellence. . . . . . . IV. vi. 21. 9
wisht it were in her to *doe* him any grace. . . . . . . IV. viii. 12. 9
For ought that ever she could *doe* or say; . . . . . . IV. x. 15. 2
nought That ever she to me could say or *doe,* . . . . . . IV. x. 57. 4
teaching others to *doe* right. . . . . . . IV. xi. 18. 9
To *doe* their dueful service, ... IV. xi. 44. 9
let mee live as lovers ought to *do,* . . . . . . IV. xii. 10. 2
doe what ever thing he did intend: . . . . . . V. i. 12. 5
To *doe* her service so as I am bond: . . . . . . V. ii. 4. 4
what he list *doe,* he may. . . . . . . V. ii. 41. 9

Do—*Continued.*
He much was troubled, ne wist what to *doo:* . . . . . . V. ii. 52. 3
to *doe* all the ill Which she could *doe* . . . . . . V. iv. 30. 8, 9
To *doe* the message which I shall expresse. . . . . . . V. iv. 48. 5
What ever he shall like to *doe* or say. . . . . . . V. iv. 49. 5
Nought could he *do* . . . . . . V. v. 16. 1
To *doe* those workes to them appointed dew; . . . . . . V. v. 22. 7
'Say and *do* all that may thereto prevaile; . . . . . . V. v. 49. 1
the man, that say or *doe* so dare, ... V. vi. 1. 6
Bad *doe* away the dampe of drouzie sleepe, ... V. vii. 26. 8
making all her Knights and people to *do* so. . . . . . . V. viii. 20. 9
Nought feared they what he could *doe* or say, ... V. viii. 38. 7
whylome wont to *doe* so many quake, ... V. ix. 35. 8
To *doe* whatever he thought good or fit: . . . . . . V. x. 13. 3
to *doe* unto his Idole most untrew. . . . . . . V. x. 27. 9
Dye, rather then *doe* ought that mote dishonour yield.' . . . V. xi. 55. 9
To him assynd her high beheast to *doo,* . . . . . . V. xii. 3. 7
To *doe* most dammage where as most they ment: . . . . . . V. xii. 17. 4
So stoutest knights *doen* oftentimes in field. . . . . . . V. xii. 19. 5
for all that ever he could *doe,* . . . . . . V. xii. 22. 4
pay thee with thy right; And if none *do,* . . . . . . VI. i. 25. 9
'If I *doe* so,' . . . . . . VI. i. 28. 7
he wild her *doe* away all dread; . . . . . . VI. i. 31. 7
Ye may *doe* well, . . . To succour her . . . . . . VI. ii. 38. 3
in this distressed case, Devising what to *doe,* . . . . . . VI. iii. 30. 6
let thy Lady likewise *doe* the same, ... VI. iii. 32. 3
who nought could *do* but shun The perill . . . . . . VI. iii. 48. 8
eke could *doe* as well as say the same; . . . . . . VI. vi. 6. 4
his two knights *Doe* gaine their treasons meed: . . . . . . VI. vii. Arg.
what it dare not *doe* by open might, ... VI. vii. 1. 7
To *doe* some thing that seemed to him best; . . . . . . VI. vii. 19. 7
What could the Gods *doe* more, but *doe* it more aright? . . VI. vii. 31. 9
wont *doe* suit and service to his might, ... VI. vii. 34. 2
for nought that he could say or *doe,* . . . . . . VI. viii. 50. 8
well could *doe* and say, ... VI. ix. 18. 4
Then all that he could *doe,* or ever devize: . . . . . . VI. ix. 35. 8
He daily did apply him selfe to *donne* All dewfull service, . VI. x. 32. 5
all that ever he could *doe* or say . . . . . . VI. xi. 5. 1
With which none had to *doe,* ne ought partake, ... VI. xi. 12. 4
doe feare away, and tell.' . . . . . . VI. xi. 29. 9
'But what could he gainst all them *doe* alone? . . . . . . VI. xi. 32. 1
laying feare aside to *doe* his charge, ... VII. vi. 17. 6
if Jove should *do* still what he can. . . . . . . VII. vi. 31. 9
Which any of thy creatures *do* to other . . . . . . VII. vii. 14. 6
Great wrong I *doe,* . . . . . . *Am.* xxxiii. 1
doe me not before my time to dy. . . . . . . *Am.* xlii. 14
kill with looks as Cockatrices *doo:* . . . . . . *Am.* xlix. 10
For they can *doo* it best: . . . . . . *Epith.* 258
what ye *do,* albe it good or ill. . . . . . . *Epith.* 367
any service I might *do* to thee, ... *H.L.* 6
Why then *do* I this honor unto thee, ... *H.L.* 148
What he may *do,* her favour to obtaine; . . . . . . *H.L.* 219
idle hopes, which still *doe* fly away, ... *Proth.* 8

Doale. *See* **Dole.**
Docks. The fierce Spumador, trode them downe like *docks;* . . II. xi. 19. 7
Doctrine. missay Both of their *doctrine,* and of theyr faye. . *S.C.* S. 107
Documents. heavenly *documents* thereout did preach, ... I. x. 19. 4
Dodonian. the faire **Dodonian** tree . . . . . . *Bel.* v. 1
Doe. the fawne I practise from the *Doe,* . . . . . . VI. ix. 23. 3
Doen. *See* **Do, Done.**
Doer. to the shamefull *doer* it afford. . . . . . . VI. i. 26. 3
Doer's. deedes ought not be scand By . . . the *doers* might, . . V. xi. 17. 4
Doers. *See* **Derring doers, Wrong-doers.**
To bind their *dooers* to receive their meed? . . . . . . II. viii. 56. 3
Does (*partial list of auxiliary*).
such end, perdie, *does* all hem remayne, ... *S.C.* May 304
'Who life *dooes* loath, ... *D.* 85
As commonly as frend *does* with his frend. . . . . . . I. x. 56. 5
Which he unto her people *does* each day; . . . . . . V. viii. 19. 2
So *does* the Cuckow, when the Mavis sings, ... *Am.* lxxxiv. 3
Doest. *See* **Dost.**
Doff. nould she *d'off* her weary armes, ... III. xi. 55. 5
Ne *doffe* her armes, though he her much besought: . . . . V. vi. 23. 5
Shall *doffe* her fleshes borrowd fayre attyre, ... *Am.* xxvii. 6
Doffed. having *doft* for heate his dreadfull hide: . . . . . . *Hub.* 954
that Ambrosiall hew . . . He *doft,* . . . . . . *Hub.* 1270
when them the gorgeous Flie had *doft,* . . . . . . *Mui.* 109
Ne ever *dofte* her armes, ... III. iv. 5. 2
Shee also *dofte* her heavy haberjeon, ... III. ix. 21. 1
her glistring helmet she unlaced; Which *doft,* . . . . . . IV. i. 13. 2
doft his helmet, and undid his mayle: . . . . . . IV. i. 43. 7
Doffing. *doffing* his bright armes himselfe addrest In shepheards weed; . . . . . . VI. ix. 36. 3
doffing her array, She bath'd her lovely limbes, ... VII. vi. 45. 8
Doft. *See* **Doffed.**
Dog. *See* **Cur-dog.**
*hunts he fast, with *Dogge* of noysome breath, ... *S.C.* Jul. 22
So lost the *Dogge* the flesh in his mouth. . . . . . . *S.C.* S. 61
He has a *Dogge* to byte or to barke; . . . . . . *S.C.* S. 181
(for so his *dog* hote) . . . . . . *S.C.* S. 194
The *dog* his maisters voice did it wene, ... *S.C.* S. 219
the hot Syrian *Dog* on him awayting, ... *Hub.* 5
And the false Foxe his *dog* . . . . . . *Hub.* 304
that disguised *Dog* lov'd blood to spill, ... *Hub.* 319
Why livest thou, dead *dog,* . . . . . . II. iii. 7. 6
why should a dead *dog* be deckt in armour bright?' . . . . . . II. viii. 15. 9
As if he did a *dogge* in kenell rate . . . . . . III. ix. 14. 7
Me like a *dog* she out of dores did thrust, ... V. viii. 22. 7
With his two-headed *dogge* that Orthrus hight; . . . . . . V. x. 10. 6
Thereto the body of a *dog* she had, ... V. xi. 24. 1

Dog—*Continued.*
This hellish *Dog*, that hight the Blatant Beast; . . . VI. vi. 12. 2
'Vile cowheard *dogge!* now doe I much repent, . . . VI. vi. 33. 4
He like a *dog* was led in captive case, . . . VI. viii. 5. 4
Brought forth with him the dreadfull *dog* of hell, . . . VI. xii. 35. 2
like a fearefull *dog* him followed through the land. . . . VI. xii. 36. 9
Dogs. Two eager *dogs* did her pursue in chace, . . . *Pet.* i. 6
With *dogges* of noysome breath, . . . *S.C.* Jul. 22
not good *Dogges* hem needeth to chace, . . . *S.C.* S. 166
wakeful *dogges* before them farre doe lye, . . . I. i. 40. 4
The wakefull *dogs* did never cease to bay, . . . I. v. 30. 2
As chained beare whom cruell *dogs* doe bait, . . . I. xii. 35. 7
Like two mad *dogs* they ran about the lands, . . . II. xi. 47. 2
a Beare, . . . the wakefull *dogs* espy, . . . III. x. 53. 6
all the night the *dogs* did barke and howle . . . IV. v. 41. 6
harbour here in safety from those ravenous *dogs*.' . . . V. x. 23. 9
Like as a sort of hungry *dogs*, . . . VI. xi. 17. 1
Some were of *dogs*, that barked day and night; . . . VI. xii. 27. 3
Doing. *See* **Dead-doing, Der-doing, Well-doing.**
Dooing my Countrey service as I might, . . . *Hub.* 61
Due praise, that is the spur of *dooing* well? . . . *T.M.* 454
wonted feare of *doing* ought amis, . . . I. i. 49. 2
all the day in *doing* good and godly deedes. . . . I. x. 3. 9
Did spend their daies in *doing* godly thing. . . . I. x. 36. 5
Ay *doing* thinges that to his fame redownd, . . . III. ii. 14. 5
to abstaine From *doing* him to dy. . . . III. xii. 34. 5
Doing him selfe, and teaching others to doe right. . . . IV. xi. 18. 9
as she was *doing* sacrifize To Isis, . . . V. vii. 13. 1
Both *doing* and receiving curtesies . . . V. x. 5. 2
Can keepe from outrage and from *doing* wrong, . . . V. xii. 1. 6
To thrust him out of dore *doing* his worst assay. . . . VI. vi. 21. 9
In *doing* gentle deedes with franke delight, . . . VI. vii. 1. 2
Of all which there was *doing* in that quire: . . . VI. viii. 48. 4
Saying and *doing* all that mote behove; . . . VI. xi. 5. 7
unto lovely Lady *doing* wrong; . . . VI. xii. 34. 7
Chose rather to be praysd for *dooing* good, . . . *Am.* xxxviii. 13
Doing away the drosse which dims the light . . . *H.B.* 48
Doing him die that never it deserved, . . . *H.H.L.* 160
Offending none, and *doing* good to all, . . . *H.H.L.* 237
Doings. Through their bad *dooings*, or base slothfulnesse, . . . *T.M.* 99
He there did stand That would his *doings* justifie . . . V. xi. 4. 9
all other creatures her bad *dooings* rewed. . . . VII. vi. 4. 9
come before high Jove her *dooings* to discharge. . . . VII. vi. 17. 9
his *doings* to relate Unto his Lord; . . . VII. vi. 19. 2
Dole. Am like for desperate *doole* to dye, . . . *S.C.* F. 155
all that may augment My *doole*, draw neare! . . . *S.C.* Au. 165
How dolefully his *doole* thou didst rehearse! . . . *S.C.* Au. 196
'Againe great *dole* on either partie grewe, . . . *Gn.* 529
To damme to death, or *dole* perpetuall, . . . *Hub.* 1244
I for *dole* was almost like to die. . . . *Ti.* 672
all dead in *dole* did lie: . . . *Col.* 22
full many had with haplesse *doole* Beene suncke, . . . II. xii. 20. 3
drowned nye Twixt inward *doole* and felonous despight: . . . III. x. 17. 6
Till so she doe, she must in *doole* remaine, . . . III. xi. 17. 7
His dayes in *dole* doth lead. . . . IV. vii. Arg.
as in his wonted wise His *doole* he made, . . . IV. viii. 3. 2
So cruell *doale* amongst her maides divide . . . V. iv. 39. 3
bore Downe to the house of *dole*, . . . V. xi. 14. 9
suffred deadly *doole*: . . . V. xi. 25. 6
much augment her *doole*. . . . VI. vii. 39. 9
Me list not die for any lovers *doole*; . . . VI. viii. 21. 2
all his wits with *doole* were nigh distraught, . . . VI. xi. 33. 3
Him, wretch, in *doole* would let no lenger dwell, . . . *H.H.L.* 131
Doleful. bowe your eares unto my *dolefull* dittie: . . . *S.C.* Ja. 16
to heare a *doolefull* verse Of Rosalend . . . *S.C.* Au. 140
bene thy verses meint With *doleful* (**doolful*) pleasaunce, . . . *S.C.* N. 204
Can rightfully aread so *dolefull* lay. . . . *T.M.* 52
Of us, thy daughters, *dolefull* desolate. . . . *T.M.* 60
lowd shrieks and drerie *dolefull* cries. . . . *T.M.* 172
all the rest her *dolefull* din augmented . . . *T.M.* 357
A *dolefull* case desires a *dolefull* song, . . . *T.M.* 541
mourne my fall with *dolefull* dreriment. . . . *Ti.* 158
no man left to mone His *dolefull* fate, . . . *Ti.* 193
With *dolefull* shrikes shee vanished away, . . . *Ti.* 471
sung the prophecie . . . in *dolefull* Elegie. . . . *Ti.* 595
grisly Ghosts, to heare the *dolefull* teene. . . . *D.* 21
th' ayre be filled with noyse of *dolefull* knells, . . . *D.* 335
place my *dolefull* plaint your plaints emong. . . . *As.* Pr. 6
Clorinda . . . began this *dolefull* lay. . . . *As.* 214
expresse their inward woe, With *dolefull* layes . . . *As.* Interl. 226
Deepe, darke, uneasy, *dolefull*, comfortlesse. . . . I. v. 36. 6
The wyld woodgods, . . . find the virgin, *doolfull*, desolate, . . . I. vi. 9. 2
Hath thee incenst to hast thy *dolefull* fate? . . . I. vi. 47. 2
'Ye dreary instruments of *dolefull* sight, . . . I. vii. 22. 1
the record . . . of my *dolefull* disaventurous deare . . . I. vii. 48. 7
she could not endure that *dolefull* stound . . . I. viii. 25. 5
His dwelling . . . Darke, *dolefull*, dreary, like a greedy grave, . . . I. ix. 33. 4
That bare-head knight, for dread and *dolefull* teene, . . . I. ix. 34. 7
With percing shriekes and many a *dolefull* lay; . . . II. i. 35. 8
frye in hartlesse griefe and *dolefull* tene: . . . II. i. 58. 4
'Tell on, fayre Sir, . . . that *dolefull* tale, . . . II. ii. 45. 1
doolefull sorrow heape with deadly harmes: . . . II. vi. 34. 4
Whose *dolefull* moniments who list to rew, . . . II. x. 66. 8
To stere the bote towards that *dolefull* Mayd, . . . II. xii. 28. 2
The hoars Night-raven, trump of *dolefull* drere; . . . II. xii. 36. 5
it importunes death and *dolefull* dreryhedd. . . . III. i. 16. 9
doth plonge in *dolefull* plight, . . . III. iii. 16. 5
Beene they all dead, and laide in *dolefull* herse, . . . III. iv. 1. 8
ill beseemes it to upbrayd A *dolefull* heart . . . III. vi. 21. 8
She bore before her lap a *dolefull* Squire, . . . III. vii. 37. 6

Doleful—*Continued.*
In *dolefull* thraldome all his dayes to dwell? . . . III. ix. 8. 3
joyed at that *dolefull* sight. . . . III. x. 12. 9
In *dolefull* darkenes from the vew of day, . . . III. xi. 11. 2
She, *dolefull* Lady, like a dreary Spright . . . III. xii. 19. 4
Since I was brought into this *dolefull* den; . . . IV. vii. 13. 3
with her *dolefull* accent beare with him a part. . . . IV. viii. 3. 9
To cloud my daies in *dolefull* misery, . . . IV. viii. 16. 8
not, as women wont, in *dolefull* fit She was dismayd, . . . V. viii. 45. 6
With dull countenance and with *doleful* spright . . . V. xii. 12. 3
he said: 'Ye *dolefull* Dame, . . . VI. ii. 42. 2
deare affection of so *dolefull* dreare, . . . VI. iii. 4. 5
His deepe compassion of her *dolefull* stound, . . . VI. iv. 11. 4
for to tell the *dolefull* dreriment . . . VI. x. 44. 1
This fatall chaunce, this *dolefull* accident, . . . VI. xi. 31. 2
to lament Your *dolefull* dreriment: . . . *Epith.* 11
Let no lamenting cryes, nor *dolefull* teares, Be heard . . . *Epith.* 334
Dolefulest. dolefully did beare. The *dolefulst* beare that ever *As.* 149
Dolefully. How *dolefully* his doole thou didst rehearse! . . . *S.C.* Au. 196
him *dolefully* did beare. . . . *As.* 148
Dolon. She goes to seeke him, *Dolon* meetes, . . . V. vi. Arg.
The goodman of this house was *Dolon* hight; . . . V. vi. 32. 1
full many treasons vile His father *Dolon* had deviz'd . . . V. vi. 33. 8
Dolon's. efte in *Dolons* subtile surprysall. . . . *Gn.* 536
Dolor. Is also deaded, and in *dolour* drent. . . . *T.M.* 210
' "Our daies are full of *dolor* and disease, . . . *D.* 274
My wearie daies in *dolor* and disdaine! . . . *D.* 440
where that sad pourtraict Of death and *dolour* lay, . . . II. i. 39. 4
Of death and *dolor* telling sad tidings; . . . II. vii. 23. 5
dread of death and *dolor* doe away; . . . II. viii. 7. 7
Her wretched dayes in *dolour* she mote waste, . . . III. ii. 17. 8
nought but death her *dolour* mote depart. . . . III. iv. 6. 5
Her *dolour* soone she ceast, . . . III. iv. 12. 4
Who dyes, the utmost *dolor* doth abye; . . . III. iv. 38. 5
shortly she his *dolour* hath redrest, . . . III. v. 41. 7
Sought by all meanes his *dolor* to prolong, . . . III. vii. 35. 7
Twixt *dolour* and despight halfe desperate, . . . III. xii. 43. *or.* 3
His hard mishap in *dolor* to deplore, . . . IV. vii. 39. 7
Spending his daies in *dolour* and despaire, . . . IV. vii. 43. 2
his abridged dayes in *dolour* wast, . . . V. v. 46. 6
hearts dismay and inward *dolour* queld, . . . VI. i. 18. 3
at the last through dreary *dolour* die: . . . VI. vii. 31. 4
Dolorous. the Greekes themselves, more *dolorous*, . . . *Gn.* 550
all his dayes, like *dolorous* Trophees, . . . *T.M.* 160
I sing of deadly *dolorous* debate, . . . *Mui.* 1
uneath To leave this life, or *dolorous* to dye? . . . *D.* 448
'To live I finde it deadly *dolorous*, . . . *D.* 449
Had with dew rites and *dolorous* lament . . . II. ii. 1. 2
The greene shield dyde in *dolorous* vermell? . . . II. x. 24. 7
'This is' . . . 'the *dolorous* despight, . . . III. xi. 23. 5
that same *dolorous* Faire Dame . . . III. xii. 22. 7
Through *dolorous* despaire which she conceyved, . . . V. iv. 10. 2
dead long since in *dolorous* distresse, . . . V. vii. 39. 4
his Lady found In *dolorous* dismay . . . VI. iii. 27. 3
Serena full of *dolorous* dismay, . . . VI. iii. 45. 3
Such were this Ladies pangs and *dolorous* assay. . . . VI. v. 5. 9
her good dayes in *dolorous* disgrace: . . . V. vii. 38. 4
Dolor's. Such pleasaunce now displast by *dolors* dint: . . . *S.C.* N. 104
Against the bitter throwes of *dolours* darts: . . . *T.M.* 134
it may empierse With *dolours* dart . . . *As.* Pr. 10
inward wounds of *dolours* dart. . . . III. xii. 16. 9
nought but death can stint his *dolours* smart? . . . *H.B.* 74
Dolors. threatned death, and thousand deadly *dolours*, . . . *Hub.* 1341
voyce These pitteous plaintes and *dolours* did resound: . . . I. viii. 38. 2
many soules in *dolours* had fordonne: . . . I. x. 33. 7
did this knight twelve thousand *dolours* daunt, . . . I. xi. 27. 7
To come where he his *dolors* did devise, . . . IV. viii. 3. 3
Unto the wyld wood ranne, her *dolours* to deplore. . . . V. viii. 48. 9
Wrapt in great *dolours* and in deadly feares . . . V. x. 6. 7
Dolours of death into his soule did dart, . . . *H.H.L.* 159
Dolphin. chose . . . the *Dolphin* his owne Dolphinet; . . . *Col.* 866
He turnd him selfe into a *Dolphin* fayre; . . . III. xi. 42. 6
the *Dolphin*, which him bore . . . IV. xi. 23. 6
As when a *Dolphin* and a Sele are met . . . V. ii. 15. 1
Allur'd a *Dolphin* him from death to ease. . . . *Am.* xxxviii. 4
move the *Dolphin* from her stubborn will, . . . *Am.* xxxviii. 8
Dolphinet. chose . . . the Dolphin his owne *Dolphinet*; . . . *Col.* 866
Dolphins. A teme of *Dolphins* raunged in aray . . . III. iv. 33. 1
Dome. *See* Doom.
Dominations. And heavenly *Dominations* are set, . . . *H.H.B.* 90
Dominion. the chiefe *dominion* By strength was wielded . . . II. x. 39. 7
(O hideous hunger of *dominion!*) . . . II. x. 47. 9
Doubly supplide, in spousall and *dominion*. . . . II. x. 75. 9
In this small plot of your *dominion*, . . . VI. ix. 28. 4
Rule and *dominion* to her selfe to gaine; . . . VII. vi. 4. 2
Don. Advent'rous knighthood on her selfe to *don*; . . . III. iii. 57. 6
To chaunge her hew, and sondry formes to *don*, . . . III. vi. 38. 4
she could *d'on* so manie shapes in sight, . . . IV. i. 18. 3
Don Braggadochios name resounded thrise: . . . V. iii. 15. 4
streight her selfe did dight, and armor *don*, . . . V. vi. 17. 8
in this bag, which I behinde me *don*, . . . VI. viii. 24. 4
Done. *See* Do.
And yet, alas! yt is already *done*. . . . *S.C.* Ja. 30
answerd his mother, all should be *done*. . . . *S.C.* May 228
Wailing the wrong which he had *done* of late, . . . *Gn.* 327
things lightly *done* amis . . . *Gn.* 475
When that was *done*, he might attend his playes: . . . *Hub.* 394
nothing there is *done* without a fee: . . . *Hub.* 515
Which *done*, he bad the Lyon . . . *Hub.* 1254
Done through the Foxes great oppressions, . . . *Hub.* 1312

Done—*Continued.*
'For deeds doe die, how ever noblie *donne*, ... *Ti.* 400
It almost drowned was, and *done* to nought, ... *Ti.* 622
For she it is that hath me *done* this wrong, ... *D.* 341
The place appointed where it should be *doone*. . . . . . . *Col.* 127
know how to have *donne*. . . . . *Col.* 591
Which hardly *doen*, at length she gan them pray, ... I. iii. 14. 8
ought have *done*, that ye displeasen might, ... I. iii. 27. 4
Which *doen* away, He left him lying so, ... I. iii. 39. 8
Which *doen*, the Chamberlain, Slowth, did to rest them call. I. iv. 43. 9
warres for Ladies *doen* by many a Lord. . . . . I. v. 3. 9
His cruell step-dame, seeing what was *donne*, ... I. v. 39. 1
Great pains, and greater praise, both never to be *donne*.' . I. v. 43. 9
After his sportes and cruell pastime *donne*; . . . . I. vi. 27. 4
The thing that might not be, and yet was *donne*?' . . . . . I. vi. 39. 4
knowne . . . To have *done* much more admirable deedes. . . . I. vii. 36. 3
Behold what ye this day have *done* for mee, ... I. viii. 27. 8
holy Martyres often *doen* to dye With cruell malice . . . . . I. viii. 36. 4
what ever thing is *donne* In heaven and earth? . . . . I. ix. 42. 1
What then must needs be *donne*, ... I. ix. 47. 6
Which *doen*, she up arose with seemely grace, ... I. x. 8. 4
after death and buriall *done*, ... I. x. 43. 1
since thou bidst, thy pleasure shalbe *donne*. . . . . I. x. 52. 1
'That *done*, he leads him to the highest Mount, ... I. x. 53. 1
one mans fault hath *done* us all to dy. . . . . I. xi. 47. 9
since that band ye cannot . . . *doen* undo, ... I. xii. 19. 6
if he live that hath you *doen* despight, ... II. i. 14. 7
Of late most hard atchiev'ment by you *donne*, ... II. i. 32. 2
innocent Of that was *doen*; . . . . II. ii. 1. 8
There wanted nought but few rites to be *donne*, ... II. iv. 21. 5
'Betwixt them both they have me *doen* to dye, ... II. iv. 33. 1
thou hadst *done* great tort Unto an aged woman, ... II. v. 17. 2
Had *doen* to death, subdewde in equall frayes . . . . II. v. 26. 5
Is all his force forlorne, and all his glory *donne*? . . . . . II. v. 35. 9
perdy ye have not *doen* me right, ... II. vi. 22. 7
Which *doen*, he balmes and herbes thereto applyde, ... II. vi. 51. 6
Had he so *doen*, he had him snatcht away, ... II. vii. 34. 5
thousand Sar'zins fowly *donne* to dye.' . . . . II. viii. 18. 6
'the evill *donne* Dyes not, ... II. viii. 29. 1
'Traytour, what hast thou *doen*? . . . . II. viii. 46. 6
Suffise that I have *done* my dew in place.' . . . . II. viii. 56. 6
they weened fowle reproch Was to them *doen*, ... II. ix. 11. 2
Hengist, seeming sad for that was *donne*, ... II. x. 66. 3
To see a cruell fight *doen* by the prince this day. . . . . . II. xi. 4. 9
one that hath unto me *donne* Late foule dishonour . . . . . III. ii. 8. 7
oft hath wonders *donne*.' . . . . III. ii. 36. 6
Can doe' (said she) 'that which cannot be *donne*.' . . . . . III. ii. 36. 8
Nor so fowle outrage *doen* by living men; . . . . III. iii. 34. 6
Where be the brave atchievements *doen* by some? . . . . . . III. iv. 1. 3
great adventures by him *donne*: . . . . III. iv. 20. 6
She, she it is, that hath me *done* despight: . . . . III. iv. 60. 7
For all the damage which he had him *doen* afore. . . . . . . III. v. 18. 9
both how and what Her sonne had to them *doen*; . . . . . . III. vi. 15. 9
wrong Which he supposed *donne* to Florimell, ... III. vii. 35. 6
thereby deeming sure the thing as *donne*, ... III. viii. 3. 3
shortly *doen* be dedd.' . . . . III. x. 32. 9
As if the word so spoken were halfe *donne*, ... III. x. 33. 2
As if no trespas ever had beene *donne*: . . . . III. x. 51. 6
Which *doen*, he backe retyred soft away, ... III. xii. 4. 7
as I have *done* of late, ... IV. Pr. 1. 4
call to count the things that then were *donne*, ... IV. Pr. 3. 2
Which *done*, she passed forth, ... IV. i. 36. 7
my selfe will for you fight, As ye have *done* for me: . . . . IV. i. 40. 9
to wreake the dammage by thee *donne*. . . . . IV. i. 44. 6
Whose Lord hath *done* my love this foule despight? . . . . . IV. i. 52. 8
Which *doen*, the doughty chalenger came forth, ... IV. iii. 6. 1
Desirous both to have the battell *donne*; . . . . IV. iii. 36. 5
Yee shall her winne, as I have *done*, in fight: . . . . IV. iv. 9. 4
though he could not salve, Ne *done* undoe, ... IV. iv. 27. 2
cast t' avenge the shame *doen* to his freend: . . . . IV. iv. 45. 2
Satyrane the first day best had *donne*: . . . . IV. v. 7. 4
she her selfe did thinke it *doen* for spight, ... IV. v. 17. 3
have ye it for some occasion *donne*? . . . . IV. vi. 5. 4
Shame and dishonour hath unto me *donne*, ... IV. vi. 5. 7
Hath *doen* to noble knights, that many makes him dread: . . IV. vi. 7. 9
had *done* outrage in so high degree: . . . . IV. vi. 22. 7
I have so *done*, as she to me hath showne; . . . . IV. vii. 19. 7
Hath *done* this wrong, to wreake on worthlesse wight . . . . IV. viii. 17. 2
Ne ever thing so well was *doen* alive, ... IV. viii. 25. 8
unto death had *doen* him unredrest, ... IV. viii. 41. 8
so great outrage *donne*: . . . . IV. ix. 27. 7
The which that Britonesse had to them *donne* . . . . IV. ix. 28. 6
your will be *donne*. . . . . IV. x. 3. 5
wade in doubt what best were to be *donne*; . . . . IV. x. 53. 2
that I have *doen* such wrong, ... IV. xi. 1. 3
Which the proud Humber unto them had *donne*, ... IV. xi. 38. 3
If I should graunt that I have *doen* the same, ... V. i. 15. 6
That *done*, unto the Castle he did wend, ... V. ii. 20. 1
Which *done*, unto his former journey he retourned: . . . . . V. ii. 28. 9
'What ever thing is *done* by him is *donne*, ... V. ii. 42. 1
Full many deeds of armes that day were *donne*, ... V. iii. 6. 5
To have him slaine, or dearely *doen* aby: . . . . V. iii. 36. 4
some hath put to shame, and many *done* be dead. . . . . . . V. iv. 29. 9
Tho gan she tell her all that she had *donne*, ... V. v. 45. 8
'When thou hast all this *doen*, then bring me newes . . . . . V. v. 51. 1
To have bene *done* against her Lady Queene . . . . V. viii. 24. 3
Gan to advize what best were to be *done*. . . . . V. ix. 8. 5
all that wrong unto that wofull Dame So long had *done*, . . . V. xi. 4. 6
she had him *done* to rew. . . . . V. xi. 30. 9
deeme it *doen* of will, that through inforcement came. . . . V. xi. 52. 9

Done—*Continued.*
grudge at all That ever she sees *doen* prays-worthily; . . . . V. xii. 31. 3
whatsoever good by any sayd Or *doen* she heard, ... V. xii. 34. 2
After his chace on woodie Cynthus *donne*; . . . . VI. ii. 25. 5
Twixt life and death, not knowing what was *donne*. . . . . VI. ii. 48. 6
that courteous deed *Done* to that wounded Knight . . . . . VI. iii. 2. 5
the lewd . . . deedes which he had *done*: . . . . VI. iii. 48. 6
To understand what there was to be *donne*: . . . . VI. iv. 2. 5
well perceiving what was *done*, ... VI. v. 4. 7
by some deadly chaunce be *done* to pine . . . . VI. v. 28. 8
great discourtesie . . . Had *doen* to him, ... VI. vii. 4. 5
hath *doen* to thee this wrongfull deed, ... VI. vii. 5. 8
He would with whipping him have *done* to dye; . . . . VI. viii. 29. 3
Which *doen*, he gan aloft t' advance his arme, ... VI. viii. 45. 8
to see what should be *donne*; . . . . VI. xi. 35. 4
nought having dout Of that was *doen*, ... VI. xi. 46. 5
This *doen*, into those theevish dens he went, ... VI. xi. 51. 1
tell To griesly Pluto what on earth was *donne*, ... VI. xii. 35. 6
more scath he wrought . . . then he had *done* before; . . . . VI. xii. 39. 2
Can tell things *doen* in heaven so long ygone, ... VII. vii. 2. 8
Had she not so *doon*, sure I had bene slayne; . . . . *Am.* xvi. 13
Which *done*, doe at her chamber dore awayt, ... *Epith.* 52
Now al is *done*: bring home the bride againe; . . . . *Epith.* 242
Now day is *doen*, and night is nighing fast, ... *Epith.* 298
So hast thou often *done* . . . . *H.L.* 141
Dongeon. *See* **Dungeon.**
Donne. *See* **Done, Dun.**
Donwallo. *Donwallo* dyde, (for what may live for ay?) . . . II. x. 40. 1
Dony. For this was *Dony*, Florimels owne Dwarfe, ... V. ii. 3. 1
Dooe, Dooers. *See* **Do, Doers.**
Doole, Dool(e)ful. *See* **Dole, Doleful.**
Doom. So did the Gods by heavenly *doome* decree, ... *Ro.* vi. 11
Till it by fatall *doome* adowne did fall. . . . . *Ro.* xvi. 14
Perigot is well pleased with the *doome*: . . . . *S.C.* Au. 135
We deeme of Death as *doome* of ill desert; . . . . *S.C.* N. 184
Through *doome* of that their cruell Judge compell . . . . . *Gn.* 627
To heare their *doome*, and sad ensample see. . . . . *Hub.* 1378
whom thou, great Jove, by *doome* unjust . . . . *T.M.* 69
By heavens *doome* doo ende my earthlie daies: . . . . *Ti.* 312
in their secret *doome* Ordained have, ... *Mui.* 225
To make so bold a *doome*, ... *Col.* 929
The which vouchsafe, dear Lord, your favorable *doome*. . . . *Ded.Son.*vii.14
through celestiall *doome* thrown out of dore, ... I. v. 47. 4
foolish man, so rash a *doome* to give? . . . . I. ix. 38. 2
'Who life did limit by almightie *doome*,' . . . . I. ix. 41. 6
The bitter *doome* of death and balefull mone . . . . I. x. 53. 8
'despise The *doome* of just revenge, ... II. i. 36. 2
Reserve her cause to her eternall *doome*; . . . . II. i. 58. 8
'death is an equall *doome* . . . . II. i. 59. 1
Ne deeme thy force by fortunes *doome* unjust, ... II. v. 12. 8
by unrighteous And wicked *doome*, ... II. vii. 62. 5
By Phoebus *doome* the wisest thought alive, ... II. ix. 48. 2
it usurped by unrighteous *doome*: . . . . II. x. 60. 5
So that the *doome* was to another day differd. . . . . IV. iv. 36. 9
by *doome* of all Graunted to her, ... IV. v. 16. 1
The which did seeme, unto my simple *doome*, ... IV. x. 21. 3
By equall *dome* repayd on his owne pate: . . . . IV. xi. 38. 4
if he should through pride your *doome* undo, ... IV. xii. 10. 4
By wicked *doome* condemn'd a wretched death to die. . . . . IV. xii. 29. 9
to thy people righteous *doome* aread, ... V. Pr. 11. 4
all the depth of rightfull *doome* was taught . . . . V. i. 5. 3
Alwayes to execute her stedfast *doome*, ... V. i. 12. 3
to his *doome* with listfull eares did both attend. . . . . . . V. i. 25. 9
Well pleased with that *doome* was Sangliere, ... V. i. 27. 1
Sangliere disdained much his *doome*, ... V. i. 29. 1
in the mind the *doome* of right must bee: . . . . V. ii. 47. 6
the proud boaster gan his *doome* upbrayd, ... V. iii. 35. 7
That which he doth with righteous *doome* decide, ... V. iv. 1. 4
for assurance to my *doome* to stand, ... V. iv. 16. 6
So was their discord by this *doome* appeased, ... V. iv. 20. 5
Radigund . . . from her direfull *doome* acquit, ... V. iv. 39. 2
justly damned by the *doome* Of his owne mouth, ... V. v. 17. 3
eke of powre her owne *doome* to undo, ... V. v. 41. 8
But his owne *doome*, that none can now undoo.' . . . . V. vi. 16. 5
unto them was dealing righteous *doome*: . . . . V. ix. 23. 5
Was brought to her sad *doome*, ... V. ix. 42. 9
never doth from *doome* of right depart, ... V. x. 2. 7
When they had seene and heard her *doome* . . . . V. x. 4. 3
though her *dome* she doe prolong, ... V. xi. 1. 5
For to receive the *doome* of her decay: . . . . V. xii. 12. 5
In execution of her lawlesse *doome* . . . . VI. i. 16. 3
did the rigour of his *doome* represse; . . . . VI. vii. 37. 4
Ne list the Knight . . . Whose *doome* was death; . . . . VI. viii. 8. 8
Deliver from the *doome* of my desart, ... VI. viii. 19. 6
by eternal *doome* of Fates decree, ... VII. vi. 33. 6
Nature soone Her righteous *Doome* areads. . . . . VII. vii. Arg.
by Dianaes *doom* unjust Slew great Orion; . . . . VII. vii. 39. 7
gave her *doome* in speeches few. . . . . VII. vii. 57. 9
His grace, his *doome*, his mercy, and his might, ... *H.H.B.* 111
Doomful. Life, and Death, is in thy *doomefull* writing! . . . *Com. Son.* i. 13
(His black eye-brow, whose *doomefull* dreaded beck . . . . . VII. vi. 22. 2
Dooms. Restraines those sterne behests and cruell *doomes* . . V. vii. 22. 9
Doon(e). *See* **Done.**
Door. *See* **Chamber-door, Prison-door.**
Open the *dore* at his request.' . . . . *S.C.* May 226
Tho went the pensife Damme out of *dore*, ... *S.C.* May 229
Kiddie the *dore* sperred after her fast. . . . . *S.C.* May 234
the false Foxe came to the *dore* anone: . . . . *S.C.* May 236
at the *dore* he cast me downe hys pack, ... *S.C.* May 245
Tho opened he the *dore*, ... *S.C.* May 278

Door—*Continued.*
the *dore* to make fast, . . . *S.C.* May 292
see the *dore* stand open wyde. . . . *S.C.* May 295
he opened the *dore*, . . . *S.C.* S. 220
Even from the *doore* of death and deadlie dreed! . . . *Gn.* 355
shouldred is, or out of *doore* quite shit, . . . *Col.* 709
backe returning by the Yvorie *dore*, . . . I. i. 44. 6
full of ghastly fright . . . Gan shut the *dore*. . . . I. iii. 12. 8
One knocked at the *dore*, and in would fare: . . . I. iii. 16. 4
long the *dore* with rage and threats he bett, . . . I. iii. 19. 1
open breakes the *dore* in furious wize, . . . I. iii. 19. 5
His life was nigh unto deaths *dore* yplaste; . . . I. iv. 28. 1
Before the *dore* her yron charet stood, . . . I. v. 20. 6
charmes, A fordonne wight from *dore* of death mote raise, . . I. v. 41. 8
through celestiall doome thrown out of *dore*, . . . I. v. 47. 4
every *dore* of freewill open flew. . . . I. viii. 5. 3
Whom these sad eyes saw nigh unto deaths *dore*, . . . I. viii. 27. 2
Those were the keyes of every inner *dore*; . . . I. viii. 30. 8
Each *dore* he opened without any breach, . . . I. viii. 34. 8
At last he came unto an yron *doore*, . . . I. viii. 37. 3
Which shaking off, he rent that yron *dore* . . . I. viii. 39. 5
Arrived there, the *dore* they find fast lockt, . . . I. x. 5. 1
The man that . . . lay at deathes *dore*. . . . I. x. 27. 9
At last him to a litle *dore* he brought, . . . II. vii. 24. 5
Before the *dore* sat selfe-consuming Care, . . . II. vii. 25. 1
the *dore* To him did open . . . II. vii. 26. 1
the *dore* streight way Did shutt, . . . II. vii. 26. 5
they came unto an yron *dore*, . . . II. vii. 31. 2
dore forthright To him did open, . . . II. vii. 35. 2
through thy darksom *dore* Unwares have prest; . . . III. iii. 15. 7
The hard beginne that meetes thee in the *dore*, . . . III. iii. 21. 8
her that from deathes *dore* Me brought? . . . III. v. 46. 2
why that same *dore* Was shut to all . . . III. viii. 52. 7
past the foremost *dore*; . . . III. xi. 27. 8
kept th' yron *dore* fast bard, . . . III. xi. 31. 6
Over the *dore* thus written she did spye, . . . III. xi. 50. 3
over that same *dore* was likewise writ, . . . III. xi. 54. 2
she spyde . . . Another yron *dore*, on which was writ, . . . III. xi. 54. 7
a stormy whirlwind . . . clapped every *dore*, . . . III. xii. 3. 2
the *dore* streightway Fast locked, . . . III. xii. 27. 1
went unto the *dore* To enter in, . . . III. xii. 27. 6
That brasen *dore* flew open, . . . III. xii. 29. 7
Should either winne him one, or lye without the *dore*. . . . IV. i. 9. 9
in the very *dore* him overcaught, . . . IV. vii. 31. 5
The Dwarfe cald at the *doore* of Amyas . . . IV. viii. 59. 2
Proteus house they fild even to the *dore*; . . . IV. xii. 3. 3
Yet still he bet and bounst uppon the *dore*, . . . V. ii. 21. 6
at the length he was yrent the *dore*, . . . V. ii. 24. 3
From deathes *dore* at which he lately lay, . . . V. iv. 35. 2
Even in the *dore* him meeting, . . . V. vi. 9. 1
now seeing night at *dore*, . . . V. vi. 22. 1
Lying without her *dore* in great disease: . . . V. vi. 26. 7
Whiles Talus watched at the *dore* all night. . . . V. vii. 26. 4
on a tree before the Tyrants *dore* . . . V. viii. 45. 1
breaking forth out at a posterne *dore*, . . . V. viii. 48. 8
them convayd out at a Posterne *dore*. . . . V. x. 38. 4
The carkasse tumbling downe within the *dore* . . . VI. i. 23. 6
To thrust him out of *dore* doing his worst assay. . . . VI. vi. 21. 9
to the *dore* of death for sorrow drew, . . . VI. viii. 20. 8
ye lightfoot mayds, which keepe the *dore*, . . . *Epith.* 67

Doors. her *dores* to all stand open wide. . . . II. iii. 41. 9
all the *dores* to rattle round about: . . . III. xii. 37. 2
Me like a dog she out of *dores* did thrust, . . . V. viii. 22. 7
Creepes forth of *dores*, whilst darknes him doth hide, . . . VI. xi. 18. 7
with huge resistlesse might The *dores* assayled, . . . VI. xi. 43. 3

Doost. *See* **Dost.**

Doric. hundred pillers . . . all in *Dorike* wise. . . . *Bel.*[1] ii. 4
wrought with Diamond after *Dorick* wize: . . . *Bel.*[2] ii. 4
After th' Ionicke, Atticke, *Doricke* guise; . . . *Ro.* xxix. 3
The *Dorick* flames consum'd the Iliack posts. . . . *Gn.* 549
stately pillours fram'd after the *Doricke* guize. . . . IV. x. 6. 9

Doris. the Oceans daughter . . . The gray-eyde *Doris*; . . . IV. xi. 48. 5
snowy neckd *Doris*, and milkewhite Galathaea: . . . IV. xi. 49. 9

Dortours. them pursu'd into their *dortours* sad, . . . VI. xii. 24. 3

Dost (*partial list of auxiliary*).
Thou that at Rome astonisht *dost* behold . . . *Ro.* xxvii. 1
doost heare their heavenlie layes, . . . *Ti.* 335
when thou *doest* me wrong?' . . . *Col.* 171
Well worthy *doest* thy service for her grace, . . . I. x. 60. 3
what *doest* thou here Unfitly furnisht . . . III. x. 24. 6
The open wrongs thou *doest* me day by day: . . . IV. ii. 13. 2
So *doest* thou now to her of whom I tell, . . . IV. vii. 2. 3
Bellona, whose great glory thou *doost* spight, . . . VII. vi. 32. 5
Love, that . . . *Doest* tyrannize . . . *H.L.* 4

Dotard. *'Dotard,'* (said he) 'let be thy deepe advise: . . . II. iii. 16. 1
That sire he fowl bespake: Thou *dotard* vile, . . . II. viii. 12. 2
we suffer this same *dotard* old . . . III. ix. 8. 7

Dote. 'Palmer, thou doest *dote*, . . . II. viii. 14. 1
The Prince halfe rapt began on her to *dote*; . . . IV. ix. 6. 7

Doted. sencelesse speach, and *doted* ignorance, . . . I. viii. 34. 2

Doth (*partial list of auxiliary*).
the time when rest . . . *Doth* drowne . . . *Bel.*[1] i. 3
He . . . his tressed locks *dooth* teare. . . . *S.C.* Ap. 12
mortall mindes *doth* inwardly infect . . . *T.M.* 484
Love *dothe* appall the weake stomacke: . . . *U.V.* 11
trussing me, as Eagle *doth* his pray, . . . IV. vii. 18. 6
that *doth* to travellers such harmes?' . . . V. ii. 5. 2
doth from death reprive. . . . V. iv. Arg.
him that *doeth* thy lovely heasts despize, . . . *H.L.* 160

Doto. Light *Doto*, wanton Glauce, and Galene glad: . . . IV. xi. 48. 9

Double. The *double* front of a triumphall Arke: . . . *Bel.* iv. 4
My selfe will have a *double* eye, . . . *S.C.* Mar. 38
dubble losse by her hath on them light, . . . *D.* 223
By *dubble* usurie doth twise renew it. . . . *Col.* 39
double gates he findeth locked fast, . . . I. i. 40. 1
his guests He saw divided into *double* parts, . . . I. ii. 9. 2
double griefs afflict concealing harts, . . . I. ii. 34. 5
'Ah me! that is a *double* death,' . . . I. iv. 51. 6
She, more amazd, in *double* dread doth dwell; . . . I. vi. 10. 1
double quite for that he on them spent; . . . I. x. 37. 7
double blowes about him stoutly laid, . . . I. xi. 42. 4
the weake minde with *double* woe torment?' . . . II. i. 16. 7
His *double* burden did him sore disease. . . . II. ii. 12. 4
So *double* was his paines, so *double* be his praise. . . . II. ii. 25. 9
gazers sence with *double* pleasure fed, . . . II. iii. 22. 8
All bard with *double* bends, . . . II. vii. 30. 3
towre, Whom foe with *double* battry doth assaile, . . . II. viii. 35. 8
With *double* sences, and with false debate, . . . III. iv. 28. 8
At last they came unto a *double* way; . . . III. iv. 46. 6
double gates it had which opened wide, . . . III. vi. 31. 5
Old Genius, the which a *double* nature has. . . . III. vi. 31. 9
Als as she *double* spake, so heard she *double*, . . . IV. i. 28. 1
Againe he drove at him with *double* might, . . . IV. iii. 10. 2
him fild With *double* life and griefe; . . . IV. iii. 22. 3
He sends the sea his owne with *double* gaine, . . . IV. iii. 27. 8
Doubt, that had a *double* face, . . . IV. x. 12. 3
ye *double* noursery Of Arts! . . . IV. xi. 26. 8
To see an helplesse evill *double* griefe doth lend. . . . IV. xii. 21. 9
me seemes of *double* wrong ye plaine, . . . IV. xii. 30. 2
them repaide againe with *double* more. . . . V. vii. 31. 4
Through his three *double* hands thrise multiplyde, . . . V. xi. 6. 2
Besides the *double* strength which in them was: . . . V. xi. 6. 3
he was rapt with *double* ravishment, . . . VI. ix. 26. 4
Long languishing in *double* malady . . . *Am.* l. 1

Doubled. Seeing the *doubled* shadowes low to fall, . . . *Gn.* 318
her beastly bodie raizd With *doubled* forces . . . I. i. 18. 4
The knight . . . *doubled* strokes, like dreaded thunders threat; I. v. 7. 5
all the woods with *doubled* Eccho ring; . . . I. vi. 14. 2
it must *doubled* bee with death of twaine? . . . III. ii. 35. 4
aventred With *doubled* force close underneath his shield, . . . IV. iii. 9. 2

Double-eyed. deceitfull meaning is *double eyed*. . . . *S.C.* May 254

Double-folded. His *double folded* necke she reard upright, . . III. v. 31. 6

Doubleth. to the ground it *doubleth* him full low: . . . I. viii. 18. 8
Doubleth her hast for feare to bee for-hent, . . . III. iv. 49. 8

Doubling. *doubling* all his powres redoubled every stroke. . . II. vi. 30. 9

Doubly. *doubly* faire wox both in mynd and face. . . . *As.* 18
doubly lov'd of ladies, unlike faire, . . . I. ii. 37. 1
doubly is distrest twixt joy and cares . . . I. vi. 1. 7
Doubly disparted, it did locke and close, . . . II. ix. 23. 6
Whose emptie place the mightie Oberon *Doubly* supplide, . . II. x. 75. 9
doubly overcommen, her ador'd. . . . IV. i. 15. 4
never thoght one thing, but *doubly* stil was guided. . . . IV. i. 27. 9
doubly him did grieve when so himselfe he found. . . . IV. iv. 26. 9
being *doubly* smitten likewise *doubly* smit. . . . IV. ix. 29. 9

Doubt. sith thys hyll Thou hast such *doubt* to climbe. . . . *S.C.* Jul. 232
halfe in *doubt* he opened the dore, . . . *S.C.* S. 220
As pausing in great *doubt*, awhile he staid, . . . *Hub.* 175
I this *doubt* will save; . . . *Hub.* 194
They were in *doubt*, and flatly set abord. . . . *Hub.* 324
Why should ye *doubt*, then, but that ye . . . *Hub.* 425
doo not *doubt* but duly to encline My wits thereto. . . . *Hub.* 548
Ne do I *doubt* but that ye well can fashion . . . *Hub.* 651
Then wandreth he in error and in *doubt*, . . . *T.M.* 490
Whether she were one of that Rivers Nymphes, . . . I *doubt*; *Ti.* 17
halfe in *doubt*, because of his disguize, . . . *D.* 57
whilest I was thus without dread or *dout*, . . . *D.* 155
makes them *doubt* their wits be not their owne: . . . I. i. 10. 7
which of them to take in diverse *doubt* they been. . . . I. i. 10. 9
One day in *doubt* I cast for to compare . . . I. ii. 37. 3
in *doubt* ne dares To joy at his foolhappie oversight: . . . I. vi. 1. 5
stood In *doubt* to deeme her borne of earthly brood: . . . I. vi. 16. 5
captiv'd, of life or death he stood in *doubt*. . . . I. vii. 26. 9
she had great *doubt* of his safety, . . . I. xi. 33. 8
into diverse *doubt* his wavering wonder clove. . . . II. ii. 3. 9
he began to *doubt* his dazeled sight, . . . II. xi. 40. 2
of their first intent gan make new *dout*, . . . III. iii. 14. 3
To doe away vaine *doubt* and needlesse dreed: . . . III. iv. 48. 7
For *doubt* of daunger which mote him betide; . . . III. v. 12. 6
Nor *doubt* himselfe; and who he was her told: . . . III. viii. 34. 4
I surely *doubt*, thou maist aread . . . III. viii. 47. 5
cause of dread, that makes ye *doubt* so sore? . . . III. viii. 48. 6
Such as no *doubt* of him he neede misdeeme.' . . . III. ix. 6. 5
of her safety in great *doubt* I ame, . . . III. x. 39. 7
least *doubt* of us ye have, . . . III. x. 42. 6
Matter of *doubt* and dread suspitious, . . . III. x. 59. 5
Next after him went *Doubt*, . . . III. xii. 10. 1
slack her threatfull hand for daungers *dout*: . . . III. xii. 37. 4
dread of shame and *doubt* of fowle dishonor . . . IV. i. 8. 6
hard t' accord two things so far in *dout*. . . . IV. i. 11. 9
every one gan grow in secret *dout* Of this and that, . . . IV. i. 14. 3
why should I *doubt* to tell the same?' . . . IV. i. 48. 4
In *doubt* to whom she victorie should deeme, . . . IV. ii. 17. 5
she gan to *dout* Their safetie; . . . IV. ii. 46. 6
some, that would seeme wise, their wonder turnd to *dout*. . . IV. iii. 41. 9
for *doubt* of blame If he misdid, . . . IV. iv. 27. 7
Hard is the *doubt*, and difficult to deeme, . . . IV. ix. 1. 1
Began to *doubt*, when she them saw embrace, . . . IV. ix. 10. 5
dangerous successe depended yet in *doubt*: . . . IV. ix. 24. 9
His name was *Doubt*, that had a double face, . . . IV. x. 12. 3

Doubt—*Continued.*
wade in *doubt* what best were to be donne; . . . IV. x. 53. 2
shaking off all *doubt* and shamefast feare . . . IV. x. 53. 6
how Fortune would resolve that daungerous *dout*. . . . V. v. 5. 9
gan to *doubt* least she him sought t' appeach Of treason, . . V. v. 37. 3
for *doubt* of being sdayned, . . . V. v. 44. 2
to ease her selfe of *dout*. . . . V. vi. 6. 4
Yet stirred not at all for *doubt* of more, . . . V. vi. 28. 3
when they saw their foes dead out of *doubt*, . . . V. viii. 12. 3
For *doubt* to be discovered by his sight, . . . V. viii. 27. 4
Some Clarkes doe *doubt* in their devicefull art . . . V. x. 1. 1
Declare it boldly, Dame, and doe not stand in *dout*.' . . . V. xi. 18. 9
as well approv'd in many a *doubt*, . . . V. xi. 47. 5
Yet *doubt* thou not, but that some better Knight . . . VI. i. 25. 6
Is wont to cut off all that *doubt* may breed, . . . VI. ii. 29. 6
withouten *doubt* or dreed; . . . VI. v. 10. 7
seeing nought Which *doubt* of daunger to her offer mought, . VI. viii. 32. 5
nought having *dout* Of that was doen, . . . VI. xi. 46. 4
he did assoyle . . . where it in *doubt* did stand, . . . VII. vii. 38. 8
The *doubt* which ye misdeeme, fayre love, is vaine, . . . *Am.* lxv. 1
Breake gentle sleepe with misconceived *dout*. . . . *Epith.* 337
Doubted. *doubted* Knights, whose woundlesse armour rusts, . *S.C.* O. 41
I of *doubted* daunger had no feare: . . . *S.C.* D. 22
doubted whether his late enimy It were, . . . I. xi. 35. 3
doubted whether he himselfe should shew, . . . II. iii. 32. 3
He *doubted* least it were some magicall Illusion . . . II. xi. 39. 5
doubted her to deeme an earthly wight, . . . III. vii. 11. 6
As if she *doubted* to have bene deceived, . . . VI. iv. 27. 3
He *doubted* much what mote their meaning bee; . . . VI. vii. 24. 2
Doubtful. Home when the *doubtfull* Damme had her hyde, . *S.C.* May 294
deepelie muzing at her *doubtfull* speach, . . . *Ti.* 485
Therefore more plaine areade this *doubtfull* case.' . . . *D.* 182
doubtfull words made that redoubted knight Suspect her truth: I. i. 53. 5
voice . . . Sends to my *doubtful* eares these speaches rare, . . I. ii. 32. 8
seeing . . . The *doubtfull* ballaunce equally to sway, . . . I. ii. 38. 2
End of the *doubtfull* battaile deemed tho . . . I. v. 11. 7
The *doubtfull* Damzell dare not yet committ . . . I. vi. 12. 1
lefte the *doubtfull* battell hastily, . . . I. vi. 46. 4
The whole atchievement of this *doubtfull* warre, . . . I. viii. 26. 3
In this distressed *doubtfull* agony, . . . I. x. 22. 6
With *doubtfull* eyes fast fixed on his guest: . . . I. xii. 29. 6
His credit now in *doubtfull* ballaunce hong; . . . II. i. 3. 8
him perforce restraynd, and to him *doubtfull* sayd: . . . II. vii. 6. 9
In such distresse and *doubtfull* jeopardy . . . III. i. 22. 6
The *doubtfull* Mayd, seeing her selfe descryde, . . . III. ii. 20. 1
doubtfull which to take, her to reskew, . . . III. iv. 46. 7
the Damzell, full of *doubtfull* thought, . . . III. vii. 8. 5
to her feet betooke her *doubtfull* sickernesse. . . . III. vii. 25. 9
Full of sad feare and *doubtfull* agony . . . III. vii. 32. 1
Full many things so *doubtfull* to be wayd, . . . IV. i. 7. 5
divydes The *doubtfull* current into divers wayes. . . . IV. i. 42. 6
doubtfull fortune wavering to and fro, . . . IV. iii. 17. 7
With diverse fortune *doubtfull* to be deemed: . . . IV. iii. 28. 2
Whilst thus the case in *doubtfull* ballance hong, . . . IV. iii. 37. 1
As one that seemed *doubtfull* or dismayd. . . . IV. iv. 20. 4
To deeme this *doutfull* case, for which they all contended. IV. v. 6. 9
twixt *doubtfull* feare And feeble hope hung . . . IV. vi. 34. 1
doubtfull through dismay, . . . IV. viii. 62. 7
all voide of *doubtfull* feare, . . . IV. ix. 5. 7
this *doubtfull* causes right . . . V. i. 25. 1
Then very *doubtfull* was the warres event, . . . V. ii. 17. 1
with dint of sword And battailes *doubtfull* proofe . . . V. iv. 6. 2
dread of shame my *doubtfull* lips doth still restraine.' . . . V. v. 30. 9
Fro dangers dread his *doubtfull* life to save; . . . V. xi. 46. 4
Her halfe dismayd they found in *doubtfull* plight, . . . V. xi. 60. 4
He staggered to and fro in *doubtfull* sted. . . . V. xii. 23. 4
no need Of dreaded daunger might his *doubtfull* humor feed. VI. ii. 29. 9
loth t' assay . . . now in *doubtfull* night, . . . VI. iii. 41. 4
candle-light, which delt A *doubtfull* sense of things, . . . VI. x. 42. 9
In *doubtfull* shadow of the darkesome night . . . VI. xi. 13. 4
Expecting th' end of this so *doubtfull* case, . . . VII. vii. 57. 5
Doubtfully. their minds were *doubtfully* distraught, . . . IV. iii. 48. 6
doubtfully dismayd through that so uncouth sight. . . . V. vii. 16. 9
So *doubtfully*, that hardly one could know . . . VI. viii. 13. 8
Twixt feare and hope depending *doubtfully!* . . . *Am.* xxv. 4
Doubting. The goodman granted, *doubting* nought their deeds, *Hub.* 328
doubting much his sence, he thus bespake: . . . I. ii. 32. 4
Yet *doubting* least his hold was but unsound . . . V. v. 42. 7
Doubting sad end of principle unsound: . . . V. xi. 2. 7
doubting to be wronged or beguyled, . . . VI. vii. 33. 7
Doubting least Typhon were againe uprear'd, . . . VII. vi. 15. 8
Doubtless. For, *doubtlesse*, death ensewd if any him descryde. I. v. 52. 9
Doubts. breede *Doubts* mongst Divines, and difference of texts, *Hub.* 387
the place unknowne and wilde, Breedes dreadfull *doubts*. . . I. i. 12. 4
So diversely each one did sundrie *doubts* devise. . . . IV. i. 14. 9
The *doubts*, the daungers, the delayes, the woes, . . . *H.L.* 262
Doughtiest. The *doughtiest* knight that liv'd that day, . . . IV. iv. 42. 9
Doughty. Devizing how that *doughtie* turnament . . . he atchieven might: . . . I. v. 1. 7
doughty knights, whom Faery land did raise, . . . I. vii. 46. 3
freshly up arose the *doughty* knight, . . . I. xi. 52. 1
Unto that *doughtie* Conquerour they came, . . . I. xii. 6. 1
'Ah dearest Lord!' said then that *doughty* knight, . . . I. xii. 18. 1
To let him weet his *doughtie* valiaunce, . . . II. iii. 14. 5
Full many *doughtie* knightes he . . . Had doen to death, . . . II. v. 26. 4
cause of death betweene two *doughtie* knights do breed! . . II. vi. 33. 9
Thereto he was a *doughty* dreaded knight, . . . III. iv. 24. 1
Big looking like a *doughty* Doucepere, . . . III. x. 31. 1
Deeming them *doughtie*, as they did appeare, . . . IV. ii. 31. 2

Doughty—*Continued.*
the *doughty* chalenger came forth, . . . IV. iii. 6. 1
they were *doughtie* knights of dreaded name, . . . IV. iv. 3. 2
Which *doughty* Triamond had wrought that day . . . IV. iv. 22. 5
many *doughty* warriours, often tride . . . IV. x. 18. 1
She long time hath deare lov'd a *doughty* Knight, . . . VI. i. 14. 8
In hope he sure would prove a *doughtie* knight: . . . VI. ii. 36. 8
he had bene a *doughty* Knight, . . . VI. vi. 4. 1
by the maystring might Of *doughty* Calidore, . . . VI. xii. 38. 2
Douglas. after him Sir *Douglas* him addrest, . . . IV. iv. 21. 4
Doune. The *Doune* and eke the Frith, . . . IV. xi. 47. 9
Doung, -hill. *See* **Dung,** *etc.*
Doure. *See* **Dower.**
Douzepere. Big looking like a doughty *Doucepere*, . . . III. x. 31. 1
Dove. *See* **Turtle-dove.**
prune his plumes like ruffed *Dove*. . . . *T.M.* 402
light fluttering . . . as each had been a *Dove;* . . . *Mui.* 291
Like as a fearefull *Dove*, . . . III. iv. 49. 4
Was from her fled as flit as ayery *Dove*, . . . III. vi. 11. 4
dred infant, Venus dearling *dove*, . . . IV. Pr. 5. 2
the *Dove* Would flit a litle forward, . . . IV. viii. 11. 1
eke the *Dove* sate by the Faulcons side; . . . IV. viii. 31. 2
Seek with my playnts to match that mournful *dove*. . . . *Am.* lxxxviii. 8
Doves. *See* **Turtle-doves.**
Like flying *doves* ye did before you chace; . . . *Ded. Son.* vi. 9
made to fly like *doves* whom the Eagle doth affray. . . . V. xii. 5. 9
Fly like a flocke of *doves* before a Faulcons vew. . . . VI. viii. 49. 9
little winged loves, Like divers-fethered *doves*, . . . *Epith.* 358
Dower. The *dowre* agreed, the day assigned plaine, . . . *Col.* 126
without *dowre* the wise Cordelia Was sent . . . II. x. 29. 4
With whom a goodly *doure* I should have got, . . . V. iv. 8. 8
To whom but little *dowre* allotted was: . . . V. iv. 9. 3
Her vertue was the *dowre* that did delight. . . . V. iv. 9. 4
What better *dowre* can to a dame be hight? . . . V. iv. 9. 5
Withouten *dowre* or composition; . . . VI. i. 43. 8
th' hearts of men, as your eternall *dowre*, . . . VI. viii. 1. 3
Nature me endu'd with plenteous *dowre* Of all her gifts, . . VI. viii. 20. 3
Th' eternall portion of her precious *dowre*, . . . *H.H.B.* 250
Down (*partial list of adv. and prep.*). *See* **Thistle-down, Upside down.**
Threw *downe* this building. . . . *Bel.*[1] ii. 14
stroke *downe* this noble monument. . . . *Bel.*[1] iii. 14
descending *downe* from Heaven, . . . *Rev.* ii. 12
All flaming *downe* she on the plaine was felde, . . . *Bel.* vii. 11
Threw *down* the seats, . . . *Bel.* xii. 14
soft sliding *downe* From heavens hight . . . *Bel.*[2] i. 1
honour of these noble boughs *down* threw: . . . *Bel.*[2] v. 11
descended *Downe* from the mountaines . . . *Bel.*[2] vi. 10
and locks *down* hanging . . . *Bel.*[2] ix. 3
by a rivers bancke that swift *downe* slidd, . . . *Bel.*[2] xv. 7
Then *downe* she stricken fell . . . *Bel.*[2] xv. 13
water, mildly rumbling *downe*, . . . *Pet.* iv. 2
Mow'd *downe* themselves with slaughter . . . *Ro.* x. 12
downe to ground did fall, . . . *Ro.* xii. 6
to fall *downe* feebily, . . . *Ro.* xvi. 11
in the weedes *downe* beaten, . . . *Van.* ii. 8
casting *downe* his towres, . . . *Van.* viii. 11
and *downe* dyd lye. . . . *S.C.* Ja. 72
as the lowring Wether lookes *downe*, . . . *S.C.* F. 29
his hoarie locks *downe* doth cast, . . . *S.C.* F. 181
downe to the earth he fell . . . *S.C.* F. 218
The watrie wette weighed *downe* his head, . . . *S.C.* F. 232
being *downe*, is trodde in the durt . . . *S.C.* F. 235
wandring up and *downe* the land, . . . *S.C.* Mar. 64
cast me *downe* hys pack, And layd him *downe*, . . . *S.C.* May 245, 246
Come *downe*, and learne . . . *S.C.* Jul. 31
An Eagle . . . A shell-fish *downe* let flye: . . . *S.C.* Jul. 224
sitte thee *downe*, . . . *S.C.* Au. 49
Sitte we *downe* here . . . *S.C.* S. 52
the sweete waves . . . doth slide *downe* easily. . . . *Gn.* 24
how mount Athos . . . Was digged *downe*, . . . *Gn.* 46
weighing *down* his drouping drowsie hedd, . . . *Gn.* 244
loftie type of honour . . . is *downe* in dust prostrate, . . . *Gn.* 558
downe on them to fall . . . *Gn.* 580
Brings *downe* the stowtest hearts . . . *Hub.* 255
a cassocke sidelong hanging *downe;* . . . *Hub.* 354
powr'd *downe* from heavenly place. . . . *Hub.* 438
that to ground *downe* hung. . . . *Hub.* 584
driven *downe* to hell, . . . *Hub.* 1237
romble gently *downe* with murmur soft, . . . *T.M.* 26
arbors sweet . . . They have cut *downe*, . . . *T.M.* 281
About her shoulders careleslie *downe* trailing, . . . *Ti.* 11
With her owne weight *down* pressed . . . *Ti.* 76
In silver channell, *downe* along the Lee, . . . *Ti.* 135
Then *downe* it fell, . . . *Ti.* 502
That *downe* hee fell . . . *Ti.* 545
all the rest *downe* shortlie fell, . . . *Ti.* 558
Two Angels, *downe* descending . . . *Ti.* 625
Whence, *down* descending, . . . *Mui.* 46
Came *downe* to prove the truth, . . . *Mui.* 267
The silken *downe* with which his backe is dight, . . . *Mui.* 334
Downe to the earth . . . *D.* 46
like fruit blowne *downe* . . . *D.* 244
downe doth lye, So lay she *downe*, . . . *D.* 255, 256
doth run *downe* right To Buttevant, . . . *Col.* 110
did roll *downe* from his hill . . . *Col.* 149
waies leading *down* to hell. . . . *Col.* 211
To thrust *downe* other into foule disgrace, . . . *Col.* 691
wander up and *downe* . . . *Col.* 728

Down—*Continued.*
And th' heavie *downe* to peize; . . . *Col.* 849
A litle lowly Hermitage . . . *Downe* in a dale, . . . I. i. 34. 2
streame from high rock tumbling *downe,* . . . I. i. 41. 2
downe did lay His heavie head, . . . I. i. 44. 3
tumbling *downe* alive, . . . I. ii. 19. 5
downe fell his angry mood. . . . I. iii. 8. 5
her pitcher *downe* she threw, . . . I. iii. 11. 6
Sad Una *downe* her laies . . . I. iii. 15. 3
He, tombling rudely *downe,* . . . I. iii. 35. 8
fast trickled *downe* the sweat. . . . I. iv. 22. 4
that streames of blood *down* flow; . . . I. v. 9. 4
bowing *downe* her aged backe, . . . I. v. 27. 1
downe to Plutoes house . . . I. v. 32. 3
downe his taile he hong, . . . I. v. 34. 7
unto hell did thrust him *downe* . . . I. v. 40. 5
With dying fitt, that *downe* she fell . . . I. vi. 37. 4
lying *downe* upon the sandie graile, . . . I. vii. 6. 2
downe againe she fell unto the ground, . . . I. vii. 24. 1
His monstrous scalpe *downe* to his teeth it tore, . . . I. viii. 16. 4
He *downe* let fall his arme, . . . I. viii. 19. 7
downe he tumbled on the durtie field, . . . I. viii. 20. 4
downe he tombled; . . . I. viii. 22. 5
a Castle . . . At last *downe* falles; . . . I. viii. 23. 5
Her dried dugs . . . Hong *downe,* . . . I. viii. 47. 7
Did soone pluck *downe,* and curbd my libertee. . . . I. ix. 12. 4
downe to sleepe me layd, . . . I. ix. 13. 2
Her daintie limbes full softly *down* did lay: . . . I. ix. 13. 8
Downe in a darksome lowly place . . . I. x. 25. 7
their rightfull causes *downe* to tredd; . . . I. x. 43. 7
lett *downe* that haughtie string, . . . I. xi. 7. 7
So *downe* he fell, . . . I. xi. 54. 1,3,5,9
her head *downe* bent, . . . II. i. 15. 7
dead suddeinly he *downe* did sincke. . . . II. i. 55. 9
inclyning on his knee *Downe* to that well, . . . II. ii. 3. 2
downe they lett their cruell weapons fall, . . . II. ii. 32. 3
Downe fell to ground, . . . II. iii. 21. 3
being *downe* the villein sore did beate . . . II. iv. 9. 1
lockes, long hanging *downe* behind, . . . II. v. 14. 4
trickled softly *downe* A gentle streame, . . . II. v. 30. 1
their huge blowes *down* did sway. . . . II. vi. 31. 2
downe them poured through an hole . . . II. vii. 6. 4
did strive his fellow *downe* to throw. . . . II. vii. 47. 9
downe to his manly brest Have cleft his head . . . II. viii. 33. 8
to overthrowe and *downe* him tred: . . . II. viii. 49. 7
did under him *down* cast. . . . II. viii. 49. 9
from her shoulder to her heele *downe* raught; . . . II. ix. 19. 2
yclad in red *Downe* to the ground, . . . II. ix. 27. 6
Held *downe* her head, . . . II. ix. 43. 2
to beene from rule deposed *downe.* . . . II. x. 29. 9
Stird Porrex up to put his brother *downe;* . . . II. x. 35. 3
as *downe* he lent, . . . II. xi. 29. 1
long bene underkept and *down* supprest, . . . II. xi. 32. 2
he *down* was cast. . . . II. xi. 43. 9
threatneth *downe* to throw his ragged rift . . . II. xii. 4. 5
high advaunced crests *downe* meekely feld; . . . II. xii. 40. 5
then *downe* againe Her plong, . . . II. xii. 64. 2
oft inclining *downe,* . . . II. xii. 73. 5
bowres, and Pallace brave, Guyon broke *downe* . . . II. xii. 83. 2
downe him smot . . . and *downe* the next did beare. . . . III. i. 28. 8, 9
downe againe her in her warme bed dight: . . . III. ii. 30. 5
her *downe* she layd . . . to sleepe, . . . III. ii. 47. 2
Shee . . . The dronken lamp *down* in the oyl did steepe, . . . III. ii. 47. 8
tread *downe* the victors surquedry. . . . III. iii. 46. 9
that same Armory *Downe* taking, . . . III. iii. 59. 8
made her *downe* Decline her head, . . . III. iv. 15. 8
Downe himselfe he layd . . . III. iv. 53. 7
thrust *downe* to hell below, . . . III. iv. 55. 4
Downe on the ground his carkas groveling fell: . . . III. v. 23. 7
their glory to the ground *downe* flings, . . . III. vi. 39. 5
Beates *downe* both leaves and buds without regard, . . . III. vi. 39. 8
Downe in her lap she hid her face, . . . III. viii. 32. 9
Downe in a Dongeon deepe . . . III. viii. 41. 8
Transfixed with her speare *downe* tombled dedd . . . III. ix. 22. 5
consumd and throwen *downe.* . . . III. ix. 39. 5
downe againe himselfe disdainfully Abjecting, . . . III. xi. 13. 6
feare least *down* he fallen should, . . . III. xi. 34. 8
Downe hanging his dull head with heavy chere, . . . III. xii. 16. 3
unto her heeles *downe* traced, . . . IV. i. 13. 3
Downe in the bottome of the deepe Abysse, . . . IV. ii. 47. 6
downe he fell as dead . . . IV. iii. 30. 5
cleft his braine *downe* to his brest. . . . IV. iii. 34. 7
downe . . . Her selfe she threw, . . . IV. iii. 47. 4
blades *downe* fell out of their hand, . . . IV. iii. 48. 4
him likewise he quickly *downe* did smight, . . . IV. iv. 21. 3
smote *downe* all that was betweene, . . . IV. iv. 34. 2
Him at the first encounter *downe* he smote, . . . IV. iv. 40. 6
beating *downe* what ever nigh him came, . . . IV. iv. 41. 7
he all that met him *downe* did beare. . . . IV. vi. 6. 5
having me, . . . *downe* feld, . . . IV. vi. 6. 8
fell humbly *downe* upon his knee, . . . IV. vi. 22. 2
her enhaunced hand she *downe* can soft withdraw. . . . IV. vi. 26. 9
downe hanging low, . . . IV. vii. 6. 2
downe both sides . . . did glow, And raught *downe* . . . IV. vii. 6. 7, 8
she felt Her selfe *downe* soust, . . . IV. vii. 9. 3
Despisd and troden *downe* . . . IV. viii. 32. 9
descended *downe* into the Stygian reame. . . . IV. viii. 45. 9
Whether shall weigh the balance *downe;* . . . IV. ix. 1. 4
He, running *downe,* . . . IV. ix. 5. 8
breakes *downe* in raine, and haile . . . IV. ix. 33. 6

Down—*Continued.*
taking *downe* the shield . . . IV. x. 10. 9
drops that trickled *downe* alway. . . . IV. xi. 25. 9
swiftly *downe* it glides, . . . IV. xi. 31. 3
Into his waters as he passeth *downe,* . . . IV. xi. 34. 4
the Nene *downe* softly slid; . . . IV. xi. 35. 7
the Liffy rolling *downe* the lea, . . . IV. xi. 41. 1
Did tricle *downe* her haire, . . . IV. xi. 46. 8
having from his courser her *downe* throwne, . . . V. i. 17. 7
a trap was letten *downe* to fall . . . V. ii. 12. 6
was carried *downe* along the Lee, . . . V. ii. 19. 1
Beaten with stones *downe* from the battilment, . . . V. ii. 20. 6
He pulleth *downe,* he setteth up . . . V. ii. 41. 7
the wrongs could not a litle right *downe* way. . . . V. ii. 46. 9
beat *downe* licentious lust, . . . V. iv. 2. 4
let each lay *downe* his sword; . . . V. iv. 16. 7
it raught *Downe* to her lowest heele; . . . V. v. 2. 8
ne ever lookt aside, But still right *downe;* . . . V. vi. 18. 5
strongly beateth *downe* The malice . . . V. viii. 17. 5
trampled *downe* in dust . . . V. viii. 31. 9
it goeth *downe* to hell: . . . V. ix. 6. 5
locks that *downe* his shoulders shagged; . . . V. ix. 10. 6
pour'd *down* on men by influence of grace. . . . V. x. 1. 9
that state by strength was pulled *downe;* . . . V. x. 26. 2
Downe streight to ground fell . . . V. xi. 9. 1
Downe to the house of dole, his daies there to deplore. . . . V. xi. 14. 9
hanging *down* her head . . . V. xi. 64. 4
tumbling *downe* within the dore . . . VI. i. 23. 6
He with strong hand *downe* from his steed me throw'th . . . VI. ii. 17. 8
So *downe* he sate, . . . VI. iii. 22. 7
stouping *downe* . . . Uprear'd her from the ground . . . VI. iii. 27. 7
Downe in a dale forby a rivers syde . . . VI. iii. 29. 6
So *downe* he tooke his Lady . . . VI. iii. 44. 5
wanting breath him *downe* to ground he cast; . . . VI. iv. 22. 5
So up and *downe* he wandred many a mile . . . VI. iv. 25. 4
made him *downe* unto the earth encline; . . . VI. v. 26. 4
That *downe* he kept him . . . VI. viii. 11. 4
They *downe* him hold, . . . VI. viii. 12. 3
trodden *downe* of Scorne, . . . VI. viii. 24. 8
Downe on his golden feete he often gazed, . . . VI. viii. 26. 6
downe him plucking, . . . VI. viii. 28. 6
that the bloud *downe* followeth. . . . VI. viii. 28. 9
Were *downe* to them descended . . . VI. ix. 8. 9
downe themselves doe drive To sad decay, . . . VI. ix. 22. 4
His silver waves did softly tumble *downe,* . . . VI. x. 7. 2
fell *down* with him in drerie swound. . . . VI. xi. 19. 9
as there he romed up and *downe,* . . . VI. xi. 27. 1
and the deskes *downe* threw, . . . VI. xii. 25. 2
And, being *downe,* . . . VI. xii. 30. 5
on him threw, and fast *downe* held: . . . VI. xii. 30. 6
Is forcibly kept *downe,* . . . VI. xii. 30. 9
Calidore him under him *downe* threw; . . . VI. xii. 32. 7
Boldly she bid the Goddesse *downe* descend, . . . VII. vi. 11. 1
Downe to the Circle of the Moone, . . . VII. vi. 16. 2
downe to hell . . . VII. vi. 16. 7
to hellish dungeons *downe* hast feld. . . . VII. vi. 27. 8
In garment all of gold *downe* to the ground; . . . VII. vii. 37. 2
So was the Titanesse put *downe* and whist, . . . VII. vii. 59. 6
Time shall soon cut *down* . . . VII. viii. 1. 9
Treading *downe* earth as lothsome . . . *Am.* xiii. 11
fall *downe* and dy before her; . . . *Am.* xiv. 13
And tread my life *downe* in the lowly floure. . . . *Am.* xx. 4
It *down* is weighd . . . *Am.* lxxii. 3
The whyles the boyes run up and *downe* the street, . . . *Epith.* 137
This day is holy; doe ye write it *downe,* . . . *Epith.* 263
Downe from the top of purest heavens hight . . . *H.B.* 109
He *downe* descended, . . . in fleshes fraile attyre, . . . *H.H.L.* 136
softly swimming *downe* along the Lee; . . . *Proth.* 38
downe along by pleasant Tempes shore, . . . *Proth.* 79
Down-rolling. doo thou haunt the soft *downe-rolling* river, . *Gn.* 636
Downs. by your flocks on Kentish *downes* abyde, . . . *S.C.* N. 63
My little flocke on westerne *downes* to keepe, . . . *D.* 100
lie, On hills and *downes,* . . . *Col.* 317
Downward. Till evening that the Sunne gan *downward* bend. . . IV. iv. 43. 6
and *downeward* layd upon the ground, . . . VI. ii. 48. 1
Ne could it upward come, nor *downward* passe, . . . VI. iv. 21. 8
Downy. the *downy* heare Did now but freshly spring, . . . II. xii. 79. 8
on the soft And *downy* grasse her dainty limbes to lay . . . VII. vi. 42. 4
Dowries. all the *dowries* of a noble mind, . . . *D.* 216
Dowry. I . . . with Sansfoyes dead *dowry* you endew.' . . . I. iv. 51. 5
Together with her selfe in *dowry* free; . . . V. iv. 12. 8
Being the *dowry* of his wife well knowne, . . . V. iv. 18. 4
Drad. *See* **Dread.**
Draft. *See* **Draught.**
Dragged. *drag'd* him through the waves in scornfull state, . . . III. viii. 36. 7
Dragon. The mightie *Dragon* gave to hir his power. . . . *Rev.* i. 6
What one is like . . . This honoured *Dragon,* . . . *Rev.* i. 10
An hideous *Dragon,* dreadfull to behold, . . . *Van.* vi. 1
Upon his foe, a *Dragon* horrible and stearne. . . . I. i. 3. 9
Now like a foxe, now like a *dragon* fell; . . . I. ii. 10. 6
A dreadfull *Dragon* with an hideous trayne; . . . I. iv. 10. 5
a Gryfon . . . A *Dragon* fiers encountreth . . . I. v. 8. 3
all the crest a *Dragon* did enfold With greedie pawes, . . . I. vii. 31. 3
An huge great *Dragon* horrible in sight, . . . I. vii. 44. 2
that fire-mouthed *Dragon,* horrible and bright? . . . I. ix. 52. 9
The knight with that old *Dragon* fights . . . I. xi. Arg.
Eftsoones that dreadful *Dragon* they espyde, . . . I. xi. 4. 4
before that cursed *Dragon* got That happy land, . . . I. xi. 29. 6
that dredd *Dragon* all did overthrow. . . . I. xi. 47. 5
they came where that dead *Dragon* lay, . . . I. xii. 9. 6

Dragon—*Continued.*
A wounded *Dragon* under him did ly, . . . III. xi. 48. 6
A monstrous *Dragon,* full of fearefull uglinesse. . . . VI. vi. 10. 9
And the great *Dragon* strongly doth represse, . . . *H.H.B.* 157
Dragonets. nest Of many *Dragonettes,* his fruitfull seede: . . I. xii. 10. 6
Dragon's. a savage beast, With *Dragons* speche, . . . *Rev.* i. 12
engendred men of armes Of *Dragons* teeth, . . . *Ro.* x. 4
To tell how he had seene the *Dragons* fatall fall. . . . I. xii. 2. 9
A *Dragons* taile, whose sting . . . Full deadly wounds . . . V. xi. 24. 5
Dragons. Crocodiles, *Dragons,* Beavers, and Centaures: . . . *Hub.* 1124
Dragons, and Minotaures, and feendes of hell, . . . III. x. 40. 5
Drain. there doth *draine* Her creaming pannes, . . . VII. vi. 48. 4
Dram. A *dram* of sweete is worth a pound of sowre. . . . I. iii. 30. 4
For every *dram* of hony therein found . . . IV. x. 1. 4
not a *dram* was missing of their right: . . . V. ii. 35. 4
Drank. *See* **Dronk.**
That I mote drinke the cup whereof she *dranke,* . . . V. i. 15. 7
Drapets. ready dight with *drapets* festivall, . . . II. ix. 27. 3
Draught. by that *draught* Did drive the Romanes . . . II. x. 51. 7
in her lap did shed her idle *draught,* . . . III. ix. 31. 3
by his false allurements wylie *draft* . . . IV. ii. 10. 4
ech drunk an harty *draught;* . . . IV. iii. 48. 9
She sent an arrow forth with mighty *draught,* . . . IV. vii. 31. 4
Drave. *See* **Drive, Drived, Drove.**
drave them to a foord, . . . *Gn.* 162
he his heard back from that water foord *Drave,* . . . *Gn.* 167
From highest staire to lowest step me *drave,* . . . *Ti.* 25
drave Far from that haunt all other chearefull fowle, . . . I. ix. 33. 7
us *drave* To this attempt to wreake his hid despight, . . . VI. vii. 12. 7
Draw. all that may augment My doole, *draw* neare! . . . *S.C.* Au. 165
woulden *drawe* with hem many moe. . . . *S.C.* S. 99
and *draw* in Both wares and money, . . . *Hub.* 869
let none other ever *drawe* Your minde from me, . . . *Hub.* 1053
three fatall Impes Which *draw* the dayes of men forth . . . *Ti.* 18
Through secret sence which thereto doth them *draw.* . . . *Col.* 886
How great a guilt upon your heads ye *draw,* . . . *Col.* 928
to *draw* their bleating flocks to rest. . . . *Col.* 955
to *draw* the semblant trew Of beauties Queene, . . . *Ded. Son.* xvii. 5
fifty sisters water in leke vessels *draw.* . . . I. v. 35. 9
them constraine in equall teme to *draw.* . . . I. vi. 26. 6
she hastily did *draw* Her dreadfull beast; . . . I. viii. 12. 3
desire To *draw* thy dayes forth . . . I. ix. 46. 2
all that might him to perdition *draw;* . . . I. ix. 50. 7
Thrise he assayd it from his foote to *draw,* . . . I. xi. 41. 7
thrise in vaine to *draw* it did assay; . . . I. xi. 41. 8
his life blood forth with all did *draw.* . . . I. xi. 53. 9
draw them from pursuit of praise and fame . . . II. i. 23. 2
from the right way seeke to *draw* him wide, . . . II. iv. 2. 7
The little barke unto the shore to *draw,* . . . II. vi. 4. 3
preaced to *draw* nere To th' upper part, . . . II. vii. 44. 3
Bidding them nigher *draw* unto the shore, . . . II. xii. 15. 2
To *draw* their bote within the utmost bound . . . II. xii. 20. 8
draw from on this journey to proceed.' . . . II. xii. 26. 5
counseld well him forward thence did *draw.* . . . II. xii. 69. 3
then some hope I might unto me *draw;* . . . III. ii. 38. 2
All things decay in time, and to their end doe *draw.* . . . III. vi. 40. 9
Which foure great Hippodames did *draw* in temewise tyde. . III. xi. 40. 9
That no man forth might *draw,* . . . III. xi. 48. 9
To *draw* them longer out, . . . IV. ii. 51. 2
desire To *draw* their dayes unto the utmost date, . . . IV. iii. 1. 2
Ne thinke th' affection of her hart to *draw* . . . IV. vi. 33. 2
Unto that purposd place I did me *draw,* . . . IV. x. 29. 3
where thou doest *draw* them with desire. . . . IV. x. 46. 6
In hope thereby her to his bent to *draw:* . . . IV. xi. 2. 6
When as they to the passage gan to *draw,* . . . V. ii. 11. 4
all the wealth of rich men to the poore will *draw.*' . . . V. ii. 38. 9
they did *draw* The yron charet, . . . V. viii. 41. 5
She could it sternely *draw,* that all the world dismayde. . . . V. ix. 30. 9
Towards the westerne brim begins to *draw,* . . . V. ix. 35. 2
She towards him in hast her selfe did *draw* . . . V. xi. 15. 3
To whom himselfe he hastily did *draw* . . . VI. ii. 4. 3
knowing that her Knight now neare did *draw,* . . . VI. iii. 26. 3
Phoebus . . . Unto his Inne began to *draw* apace; . . . VI. iii. 29. 2
To *draw* him from his deare beloved dame . . . VI. v. 15. 4
See, how they doe the Lady hale and *draw!* . . . VI. viii. 6. 7
wicked feend . . . daunger to them *draw;* . . . VI. ix. 6. 3
Nor *draw* unto the lure of his lewd lay, . . . VI. xi. 5. 3
Yet durst he not *draw* backe, . . . VI. xii. 36. 6
That all this world . . . May *draw* to thee, . . . *H.B.* 270
through the Skie *draw* Venus silver Teeme; . . . *Proth.* 63
Draweth. let us homeward, for night *draweth* on, . . . *S.C.* Ap. 160
draweth newe delightes with hoary heares. . . . *S.C.* Jun. 40
when as drouping Titan *draweth* neere . . . *D.* 468
'Now, . . . *draweth* toward night, . . . I. i. 32. 4
Venice, . . . next to them in beauty *draweth* neare, . . . *Com. Son.* iv. 11
Drawing. *Drawing* in teemes along the starrie skie; . . . *Gn.* 458
They, *drawing* nigh, . . . present That flowre of fayth . . . I. vi. 15. 4
drawing nigh him, said; 'Ah! misborn Elfe, . . . I. vi. 42. 1
To tell that dawning day is *drawing* neare, . . . I. xii. 21. 7
Drawing to him the eies of all arownd, . . . II. ii. 39. 8
the steele . . . Which *drawing* backe, . . . II. xi. 37. 6
drawing both their swords, . . . on other flew, . . . IV. ii. 17. 7
with unwearied fingers *drawing* out The lines of life, . . . IV. ii. 48. 3
Which *drawing* softly forth out of the darke, . . . IV. iv. 15. 4
drawing nigh, when as he plaine descride . . . IV. vi. 24. 4
drawing nigh, ere he her well beheld, . . . IV. vii. 36. 7
drawing him out of the open hall . . . V. iii. 37. 3
And *drawing* backe deceived their intent: . . . V. iv. 24. 2
when she reckned them, still *drawing* neare, . . . V. vi. 5. 8
He *drawing* neare began to greete them faire, . . . V. xi. 48. 2

Drawing—*Continued.*
now time *drawing* ny . . . V. xii. 3. 6
drawing thence his speach another way, . . . VI. ix. 18. 7
fiercely *drawing* forth his blade, . . . VI. xi. 15. 7
Drawing out of the object of their eyes . . . *H.B.* 213
Drawn. It's like a corse *drawne* forth out of the tombe . . . *Ro.* v. 7
Drawne into danger through close ambushment; . . . *Gn.* 532
Drawne into armes . . . Through prowd ambition . . . *Mui.* 4
love will not be *drawne,* but must be ledde; . . . *Col.* 129
Be ever *drawne* together into one . . . *Col.* 845
Drawne of fayre Pecocks, that excell in pride, . . . I. iv. 17. 8
this was *drawne* of six unequall beasts, . . . I. iv. 18. 1
a brasen shield, On which was *drawen* faire, . . . II. iv. 38. 2
they have ofte *drawne* many a wandring wight . . . II. xii. 11. 8
The rest, of other fishes *drawen* weare, . . . III. iv. 33. 8
drawne upon the waves that fomed him arownd. . . . III. viii. 30. 9
At that wide orifice her trembling hart Was *drawne* forth, . . III. xii. 21. 2
Drawne it was . . . Of two grim lyons, . . . IV. iii. 39. 1
Drawne with the powre of an heart-robbing eye, . . . V. viii. 1. 6
arm'd dreadfully And *drawne* of cruell steedes . . . V. viii. 28. 6
from her partie eftsoones was *drawen* cleene: . . . V. ix. 49. 3
drawne forth from her by divine extreate: . . . V. x. 1. 4
have her *drawne* to all this troublous strife, . . . V. xi. 41. 3
A salvage man, . . . *Drawne* with that Ladies loud and piteous shright, . . . VI. iv. 2. 3
Would not for ought be *drawne* to former drede, . . . VI. xi. 35. 6
Drawne of two steeds, th' one black, the other white, . . . VII. vi. 9. 2
Drawne of two fishes, . . . VII. vii. 43. 3
I joy to see how, in your *drawen* work, . . . *Am.* lxxi. 1
Drawne with sweet pleasures bayt, . . . *Am.* lxxxii. 7
Draws. stong, that it the blood forth *drawes,* . . . *Van.* x. 9
my yeare *drawes* to his latter terme, . . . *S.C.* D. 127
life *drawes* care, and care continuall woe; . . . *D.* 450
forth his swerd he *drawes.* . . . I. iii. 41. 9
what within his reach he ever *drawes.* . . . I. xi. 12. 5
nigh it *drawes* All passengers, . . . II. xii. 4. 6
Her smile me *drawes;* . . . *Am.* xxi. 12
Dread. Withouten *dreade* of Wolves to bene ytost: . . . *S.C.* Jun. 12
did sing of warres and deadly *drede,* . . . *S.C.* O. 59
who in derring-doe were *dreade,* . . . *S.C.* O. 65
Withouten *dreade* of Wolves to bene espyed. . . . *S.C.* D. 24
thou, most *dread* (Octavius), . . . *Gn.* 35
thou, (*dread* sacred child) . . . *Gn.* 54
Even from the doore of death and deadlie *dreed!* . . . *Gn.* 355
judgement seates, whose Judge is deadlie *dred,* . . . *Gn.* 446
Where nought but *dread* and death do seeme in show? . . . *Hub.* 966
dredd darknes of the deepe Abysme, . . . *T.M.* 189
Of ghostly darkenes, and of gastlie *dreed;* . . . *T.M.* 532
His hope is faild, and come to passe his *dread,* . . . *Ti.* 213
Out of *dread* darkenesse to eternall day, . . . *Ti.* 376
with her weapon *dredd* She smote the ground, . . . *Mui.* 324
whilest I was thus without *dread* or dout, . . . *D.* 155
Ne dyde with *dread* and grudging discontent, . . . *D.* 254
withouten *dread* or daunger: . . . *Col.* 317
O dreaded *Dread,* do not thy selfe that wrong, . . . *Col.* 406
she doth *new* bands adventure *dread;*— . . . *Col.* 567
Ah! my *dread* Lord, that doest liege hearts possesse, . . . *Col.* 793
that God, that is so greatly *dred;* . . . *Col.* 798
Jove himselfe his powre began to *dread,* . . . *Col.* 809
gan heaven out of darknesse *dread* For to appeare, . . . *Col.* 855
The which to heare vouchsafe, O dearest *dread,* . . . I. Pr. 4. 9
nothing did he *dread,* but ever was *ydrad.* . . . I. i. 2. 9
therein shrouded from the tempest *dred,* . . . I. i. 8. 3
he cald out of deepe darknes *dredd* . . . I. i. 38. 1
For present cause was none of *dread* her to dismay. . . . I. ii. 20. 9
The Fort, that Ladies hold in soveraign *dread.* . . . I. ii. 25. 4
that *dredd* Lyons looke her cast in deadly hew. . . . I. iii. 11. 9
needlesse *dread* for to remove away, . . . I. iii. 14. 6
for *dread* hee durst not show Him selfe too nigh at hand, . . I. iii. 26. 3
With *dread* whereof his chacing steedes aghast . . . I. v. 38. 4
arose away The mother of *dredd* darknesse, . . . I. v. 44. 5
more sad, that Una, his deare *dreed,* Her truth had staynd . . I. vi. 2. 3
She, more amazd, in double *dread* doth dwell; . . . I. vi. 10. 1
oft, for *dread* of hurt, would him advise . . . I. vi. 25. 4
The ground eke groned under him for *dreed:* . . . I. vii. 8. 6
He sett the false Duessa, for more aw and *dread.* . . . I. vii. 18. 9
Mine onely foe, mine onely deadly *dread;* . . . I. vii. 50. 7
all his sences were with suddein *dread* dismayd. . . . I. viii. 14. 9
dismaid with uncouth *dread:* . . . I. ix. 22. 3
That bare-head knight, for *dread* and dolefull teene, . . . I. ix. 34. 7
redeeme . . . From tyrans rage and ever-dying *dread,* . . . I. x. 9. 5
whether *dread* did dwell Or anguish in her hart, . . . I. x. 14. 4
Ne ought the powre of mighty men did *dread* . . . I. x. 43. 5
For *dread* of that huge feend . . . I. xi. 3. 3
with *dread* of shame sore terrifide. . . . I. xi. 45. 9
that *dredd* Dragon all did overthrow. . . . I. xi. 47. 5
Durst not approch for *dread* which she misdeemd; . . . I. xi. 55. 4
She weakely started, yet she nothing *drad:* . . . II. i. 45. 7
through danger and great *dreed.* . . . II. i. 52. 9
vassall of *dread* and despayre, . . . II. iii. 7. 4
To hide his coward head from dying *dreed:* . . . II. iii. 21. 4
with *dredd* Majestie and awfull yre, . . . II. iii. 23. 8
For *dread* of soring hauke her selfe hath hid, . . . II. iii. 36. 2
Drad for his derring doe and bloody deed; . . . II. iv. 42. 3
That thee against me drew with so impetuous *dread.* . . . II. v. 16. 9
without *dread* or disdayn She sett beside, . . . II. vi. 14. 5
(So Love the *dread* of daunger doth despise) . . . II. vi. 46. 2
First got with guile, and then preserv'd with *dread,* . . . II. vii. 12. 3
with *dread* and horror compassed arownd. . . . II. vii. 20. 9
dread of death and dolor doe away; . . . II. viii. 7. 7

Dread—*Continued.*
devoyd of *dreed,* Upon him lighty leaping . . . . II. viii. 49. 4
waytes for death with *dread* and trembling aw; . . . . II. viii. 50. 4
Was never king more . . . *dredd* of Romanes, ... II. x. 52. 2
For *dread* of whom, and for those Picts annoyes, ... II. x. 64. 6
shunne Rocke of Reproch, and it as death to *dred!'* . . . . II. xii. 9. 9
Whiles the *dredd* daunger does behind remaine. . . . . II. xii. 21. 4
By that same wicked witch, to worke us *dreed,* . . . . II. xii. 26. 4
O *dredd* Soverayne! . . . . III. Pr. 3. 5
fiercely forward came withouten *dread,* . . . . III. i. 5. 8
Made them recoile, and fly from *dredd* decay, ... III. i. 21. 8
Dare not for *dread* his hardy hand expose, ... III. i. 46. 8
Ah! my deare daughter, ah! my dearest *dread,* . . . . III. ii. 30. 6
Therefore away doe *dread;* . . . . III. ii. 33. 7
thy *dredd* dartes in none doe triumph more, ... III. iii. 3. 1
For *dread* of daunger which it might portend; . . . . III. iii. 14. 4
without *dread* Shall take the crowne . . . . III. iii. 29. 5
daunted with like *dread,* . . . . III. iii. 39. 5
To doe away vaine doubt and needlesse *dreed:* . . . . III. iv. 48. 7
With no lesse hast, and eke with no lesse *dreed,* . . . . III. iv. 50. 1
whose sad annoy The Gods doe *dread,* . . . . III. vi. 24. 8
as if her former *dred* Were hard behind, ... III. vii. 2. 5
shewd by outward signes that *dread* her sence did daze. . . . III. vii. 7. 9
it she shund no lesse then *dread* to die; . . . . III. vii. 24. 4
From *dread* of her revenging fathers hond; . . . . III. vii. 26. 2
She you from death, you me from *dread,* redeemd; . . . . III. vii. 52. 7
Her selfe not saved yet from daunger *dredd* . . . . III. viii. 33. 1
'Thy labour all is lost, I greatly *dread,* . . . . III. viii. 47. 2
did ye see Just cause of *dread,* . . . . III. viii. 48. 6
That Ladies safetie is sore to be *dradd.* . . . . III. viii. 50. 3
With showre and hayle so horrible and *dred,* . . . . III. ix. 11. 6
Empoisned was with privy lust and gealous *dredd.* . . . . III. ix. 28. 9
durst not for *dread* approchen nie, ... III. x. 22. 2
She was astonisht with exceeding *dreed,* . . . . III. x. 50. 5
Matter of doubt and *dread* suspitious, ... III. x. 59. 5
turnest love divine To joylesse *dread,* . . . . III. xi. 1. 6
alwayes did their *dread* encounter fly: . . . . III. xi. 6. 4
enterprised praise for *dread* to disavaunce.' . . . . III. xi. 24. 9
As if no sorrow she ne felt ne *drad;* . . . . III. xii. 18. 5
guilty *Dread* Of heavenly vengeaunce; . . . . III. xii. 25. 7
when he had long in *drede* Awayted . . . . III. xii. 45. 1
dred infant, Venus dearling dove, ... IV. Pr. 5. 2
dread of shame and doubt of fowle dishonor . . . . IV. i. 8. 6
it all the skie doth overcast With darknes *dred,* . . . . IV. i. 45. 9
For *dread* of blame and honours blemishment; . . . . IV. ii. 36. 5
dread thereof and his redoubted might Did . . . appall, ... IV. ii. 40. 2
From daungers *dread* to ward his naked side, ... IV. iii. 20. 3
To let them passe at will, for *dread* of shame. . . . . IV. iv. 3. 5
ghesse the man to be dismayd with gealous *dread.* . . . . IV. v. 45. 9
that many makes him *dread:* . . . . IV. vi. 7. 9
'Faire Sir, be nought dismayd With needlesse *dread,* . . . . IV. vi. 37. 7
Amoret rapt by greedie lust Belphebe saves from *dread:* . . . . IV. vii. Arg.
she waked out of *dread* Streight into griefe, ... IV. vii. 9. 3
darknesse and *dread* horrour where she dwelt, ... IV. vii. 9. 7
'whose *dread* Untride is lesse . . . . IV. vii. 11. 5
For *dread* of her displeasures utmost proofe: . . . . IV. vii. 37. 5
Then death it selfe more *dread* and desperate; . . . . IV. viii. 1. 4
Withouten *dread* of perill to repaire . . . . IV. viii. 5. 2
as one daunted with her presence *dread,* . . . . IV. viii. 13. 7
'Ne any but your selfe, O dearest *dred,* . . . . IV. viii. 17. 1
Fearelesse of fortunes chaunge or envies *dread,* . . . . IV. viii. 18. 3
he gan enquire his cause of *dread:* . . . . IV. viii. 41. 4
'No lesse did Daunger threaten me with *dread,* . . . . IV. x. 58. 1
darkenesse *dredd* that never viewed day. . . . . IV. xi. 4. 2
without dismay or *dread;* . . . . IV. xi. 14. 6
Justice . . . did divide her *dred* beheasts: . . . . V. Pr. 9. 9
Dread Soverayne Goddesse, that doest highest sit . . . . V. Pr. 11. 1
filles with awful *dread,* . . . . V. Pr. 11. 5
The club of Justice *dread* with kingly powre endewed. . . . . V. i. 2. 9
True love despiseth shame, when life is cald in *dread.* . . . . V. i. 27. 9
for *dread* of being drownd, ... V. ii. 16. 2
For *dread* of their devouring enemie, ... V. iv. 44. 8
To keepe a nightly watch for *dread* of treachery. . . . . V. iv. 46. 9
From the *dread* daunger of his weapon keene, ... V. v. 8. 7
shun the *dred* despight Of her fierce wrath, ... V. v. 16. 1
dread of shame my doubtfull lips doth still restraine.' . . . . V. v. 30. 9
'Ah! my deare *dread,'* (said then the faithfull Mayd) . . . . V. v. 31. 1
'Can *dread* of ought your dreadlesse hart withhold, ... V. v. 31. 2
many hath with *dread* of death dismayd, ... V. v. 31. 3
lay upon him, for his greater *dread,* Cold yron chaines . . . . V. v. 50. 7
Whereat her heart was fild with hope and *drede,* . . . . V. vi. 8. 7
Jealous suspect as true untruely *drad:* . . . . V. vii. 38. 7
Which she against the *dred* Mercilla oft did frame. . . . . V. ix. 40. 9
then came Daunger, threatning hidden *dread* . . . . V. ix. 45. 5
He that whylome in Spain so sore was *dred* . . . . V. x. 9. 3
now his cruelty so sore she *drad,* . . . . V. x. 18. 7
Seeking to drive away deepe-rooted *dreede* . . . . V. x. 22. 4
with huge terrour, to be more *ydrad,* . . . . V. xi. 3. 5
Wayting what end would be of that same daunger *drad.* . . . V. xi. 32. 9
Fro dangers *dread* his doubtfull life to save; . . . . V. xi. 46. 4
dread of God, that devils bindes, ... V. xii. 1. 3
He will not bide the daunger of such *dread,* . . . . V. xii. 18. 7
A dreadfull feend, of gods and men *ydrad,* . . . . V. xii. 37. 8
as he past afore withouten *dread,* . . . . V. xii. 39. 8
keepe your body from the daunger *drad,* . . . . VI. i. 10. 7
he for *dread* of death gan loude to crie . . . . VI. i. 22. 8
for *dread* of shame, forgoe This evill manner . . . . VI. i. 27. 1
he wild her doe away all *dread;* . . . . VI. i. 31. 7
all this while did dwell In *dread* of death, ... VI. i. 43. 2
Whose gealous *dread* induring not a peare . . . . VI. ii. 29. 5

Dread—*Continued.*
by vow, which I profest To my *dread* Soveraine, ... VI. ii. 37. 6
Without suspect of ill or daungers hidden *dred.* . . . . VI. iii. 23. 9
forst him gape and gaspe, with *dread* aghast, ... VI. iii. 26. 8
Twixt darkenesse *dread* . . . . VI. iii. 45. 4
The salvage nation doth all *dread* despize, ... VI. iv. 6. 6
withouten doubt or *dreed;* . . . . VI. v. 10. 7
Kept and delivered me from deadly *dread.* . . . . VI. v. 29. 5
'Echidna is a Monster direfull *dred,* . . . . VI. vi. 10. 1
The Lady, for that she was much in *dred,* . . . . VI. vi. 16. 2
every joynt for *dread* of death did quake, ... VI. vi. 29. 7
kept aloofe for *dread* to be descryde, ... VI. vii. 3. 3
Devizing of his love more then of daunger *drad.* . . . . VI. vii. 6. 9
Prince Arthure . . . Quites Mirabell from *dreed:* . . . . VI. viii. Arg.
So fresh the image of her former *dread,* . . . . VI. viii. 31. 6
For *dread* of daunger not to be redrest, ... VI. ix. 3. 4
affrayd of every chaunges *dread.* . . . . VI. ix. 27. 9
mote empaire my peace with daungers *dread;* . . . . VI. ix. 33. 6
For *dread* of them unwares to be descryde, ... VI. x. 11. 2
darkenesse *dred* and daily night did hover . . . . VI. x. 42. 5
Would not for ought be drawne to former *drede,* . . . . VI. xi. 35. 6
Ne durst abide behind, for *dread* of worse effort. . . . . VI. xi. 42. 9
(for *dread* least if her syre Should know thereof . . . . VI. xii. 6. 6
drad Bellona, that doth sound on hie Warres . . . . VII. vi. 3. 7
voyd of speech in that *drad* audience, ... VII. vi. 25. 5
so sore him *dread* aghast. . . . . VII. vi. 52. 5
that most sacred Empresse, my dear *dred,* . . . . *Am.* xxxiii. 2
In *dread* of death, and daungerous dismay, ... *Am.* lxiii. 3
Without constraynt, or *dread* of any ill: . . . . *Am.* lxv. 6
guydest lovers through the nights sad *dread,* . . . . *Epith.* 290
Nor any *dread* disquiet once annoy . . . . *Epith.* 324
Till then, *dread* Lord! vouchsafe . . . . *H.L.* 306
faire Venus dearling, my deare *dread!* . . . . *H.B.* 281
on his owne *dread* presence to attend, ... *H.H.L.* 68
Where they in darknesse and *dread* horror dwell, ... *H.H.L.* 90
Ne dare looke . . . On the *dred* face of that great Deity, . . *H.H.B.* 145

Dreaded. *See* **Hell-dreaded, Ydreaded.**
maugre death, and *dreaded* sisters deadly spight, ... *S.C.* N. 163
most art *dreaded* for thy thunder darts; . . . . *T.M.* 56
O *dreaded* Dread, do not thy selfe that wrong, ... *Col.* 406
thou, most *dreaded* impe of highest Jove, ... I. Pr. 3. 1
the *dreaded* name Of Hecate: . . . . I. i. 43. 2
Without regard of armes and *dreaded* fight: . . . . I. ii. 3. 6
I will me safely shrowd From *dreaded* storme . . . . I. iv. 48. 4
doubled strokes, like *dreaded* thunders threat; . . . . I. v. 7. 5
'Yet, O thou *dreaded* Dame! I crave Abyde, ... I. v. 21. 8
dreaded Night in brightest day hath place, ... I. v. 24. 4
for to make her *dreaded* more of men, ... I. vii. 16. 6
to weet what suddein stowre . . . dar'd his *dreaded* powre. . I. viii. 5. 9
my *dreaded* name to raise Above the Moone, ... II. iii. 38. 7
Joves *dreaded* thunder light Does scorch not halfe so sore, II. vi. 50. 7
courd it tenderly . . . from *dreaded* destiny. . . . . II. viii. 9. 9
auncestryes Of my most *dreaded* Soveraigne I recount, . . . II. x. 1. 8
his mighty puissaunce And *dreaded* name . . . . III. iii. 28. 2
shall upreare His *dreaded* head, ... III. iii. 45. 7
dreaded more then all The other Saxons, ... III. iii. 56. 5
Thereto he was a doughty *dreaded* knight, ... III. iv. 24. 1
chevalrie That made them *dreaded* much of all men . . . . IV. iii. 2. 9
they were doughtie knights of *dreaded* name, ... IV. iv. 3. 2
'His name was Daunger, *dreaded* over-all, ... IV. x. 17. 1
to make him *dreaded* more, ... V. i. 9. 1
they that most in boldnesse doe excell Are *dredded* most, . V. ix. 1. 8
So sitting high in *dreaded* soverayntie, ... V. ix. 34. 1
set a Seneschall of *dreaded* might, ... V. x. 30. 2
pardon me, most *dreaded* Soveraine, ... VI. Pr. 7. 1
no need Of *dreaded* daunger might his doubtfull humor feed. VI. ii. 29. 9
durst her *dreaded* reskue enterprize, ... VI. viii. 18. 7
(His black eye-brow, whose doomefull *dreaded* beck . . . VII. vi. 22. 2

Dreadest. battell made the *dreddest* daungerous . . . . IV. ii. 32. 3
the *dreddest* day that living wight Did ever see . . . . IV. iii. 3. 5

Dreadful. I was with so *dreadfull* sight afrayde, ... *Bel.*[1] xi. 11
This *dreadfull* shape was vanished to nought. . . . . *Bel.*[2] viii. 14
assaile this ship with *dreadfull* threat, ... *Bel.*[2] xiii. 7
dreadfull name of blasphemie . . . . *Rev.* ii. 3
Against a Rocke to breake with *dreadfull* poyse: . . . . *Ro.* xvi. 4
sweepe The fomie waves out of the *dreadfull* deep, ... *Van.* v. 5
An hideous Dragon, *dreadfull* to behold, ... *Van.* vi. 1
not these leaves do sing that *dreadfull* stound, ... *Gn.* 39
Through their Syres *dreadfull* jurisdiction, ... *Gn.* 484
'Againe the *dreadfull* Cycones him dismay, ... *Gn.* 537
skies and seas doo make most *dreadfull* warre; . . . . *Gn.* 574
He lately slue his *dreadfull* foe in fight. . . . . *Gn.* 648
Of *dreadfull* battailes of renowmed Knights; . . . . *Hub.* 767
having doft for heate his *dreadfull* hide: . . . . *Hub.* 954
Departed to his home in *dreadfull* awe, ... *Hub.* 1109
he that *dreadfull* deed Forbore, ... *Hub.* 1238
on his head his *dreadfull* hat he dight, ... *Hub.* 1279
Fled fast away from that so *dreadfull* din. . . . . *Hub.* 1348
Was turned now to *dreadfull* uglinesse. . . . . *T.M.* 42
Full sad and *dreadfull* is that ships event; . . . . *T.M.* 143
The *dreadfull* accents of their outcries shrill. . . . . *T.M.* 286
spredding all his backe, with *dreadfull* view . . . . *Mui.* 69
let the *dreadfull* Queene Of Darkenes deepe come . . . . *D.* 19
shady woods resound with *dreadfull* yells; . . . . *D.* 331
as ghastly *dreadfull,* as it seemes, ... *Col.* 208
the place unknowne and wilde, Breedes *dreadfull* doubts. . . . I. i. 12. 4
At last whenas the *dreadfull* passion Was overpast, ... I. ii. 32. 1
Discoursing of her *dreadfull* late distresse, ... I. iii. 32. 7
underneath her scornefull feete was layne A *dreadfull* Dragon I. iv. 10. 5
dreadfull Furies, which their chaines have brast, ... I. v. 31. 8

Dreadful—*Continued.*

dreadfull Cerberus His three deformed heads did lay along, . . . I. v. 34. 1
The *dreadfull* spectacle of that sad house of Pryde. . . . . . I. v. 53. 9
sturdie courage tame with *dreadfull* aw, . . . I. vi. 26. 8
For love of me leave off this *dreadfull* play; . . . I. vi. 28. 7
at the last he heard a *dreadfull* sownd, . . . I. vii. 7. 4
he gan . . . towardes him with *dreadfull* fury praunce; . . . I. vii. 11. 3
this *dreadfull* Beast with sevenfold head . . . I. vii. 18. 8
his *dreadfull* hideous hedd, Close couched on the bever, . . . I. vii. 31. 5
Which have endured many a *dreadfull* stowre, . . . I. vii. 48. 3
lifting up his *dreadfull* club on hight, . . . I. viii. 7. 3
she hastily did draw Her *dreadfull* beast; . . . I. viii. 12. 4
the Prince, . . . threatning high his *dreadfull* stroke, . . . I. viii. 22. 2
all the floore . . . Defiled was, that *dreadfull* was to vew, . . . I. viii. 35. 8
Ne bring him forth in face of *dreadfull* fight, . . . I. ix. 20. 7
Eftsoones that *dreadful* Dragon they espyde, . . . I. xi. 4. 4
Soone as thy *dreadfull* trompe begins to sownd, . . . I. xi. 6. 6
the *dreadful* Beast drew nigh to hand, . . . I. xi. 8. 1
Those glaring lampes were sett that made a *dreadfull* shade. I. xi. 14. 9
With *dreadfull* poyse is from the mayneland rift, . . . I. xi. 54. 7
To weet what *dreadfull* thing was there in hond; . . . II. ii. 21. 2
threatned death with *dreadfull* countenaunce, . . . II. iii. 14. 2
soone his *dreadfull* blade about he cast, . . . II. v. 12. 3
'Fly, O Pyrochles! fly the *dreadfull* warre . . . II. v. 16. 1
That *dreadfull* feend, which did behinde him wayt, . . . II. vii. 64. 4
dreadfull Death behynd thy backe doth stond.' . . . II. viii. 37. 9
with his *dreadfull* hornes them drives afore, . . . II. viii. 42. 4
such *dreadful* wights As far exceeded men . . . II. x. 8. 8
having overcome The Romane legion in *dreadfull* fight. . . . II. x. 60. 8
they dayly made most *dreadfull* battery. . . . II. xi. 7. 9
the fift troupe . . . is *dreadfull* to report; . . . II. xi. 13. 2
these twelve troupes with *dreadfull* puissaunce . . . II. xi. 14. 1
much dismayed with that *dreadful* sight, . . . II. xi. 16. 2
They reard a most outrageous *dreadfull* yelling cry: . . . II. xi. 17. 9
th' one of them with *dreadfull* yelling crye, . . . II. xi. 47. 3
Depending from on high, *dreadfull* to sight, . . . II. xii. 4. 3
that darke *dreadfull* hole of Tartare steepe . . . II. xii. 6. 4
All *dreadfull* pourtraicts of deformitee: . . . II. xii. 23. 5
The *dreadful* Fish that hath deserv'd the name Of Death, . . . II. xii. 24. 1
like him lookes in *dreadfull* hew; . . . II. xii. 24. 2
dreadfull noise and hollow rombling rore . . . II. xii. 25. 3
all that here on earth we *dreadfull* hold, . . . II. xii. 25. 7
all that *dreadfull* Armie fast gan flye . . . II. xii. 26. 8
The ill-faste Owle, deaths *dreadfull* messengere; . . . II. xii. 36. 4
bent his *dreadful* speare against the others head. . . . III. i. 5. 9
Dreadfull of daunger that mote him betyde, . . . III. i. 37. 5
with her *dreadfull* strokes were all dismayd: . . . III. i. 66. 4
with fantastick sight Of *dreadfull* things, . . . III. ii. 29. 5
go to see that *dreadfull* place. . . . III. iii. 8. 2
the *dreadfull* Mage there fownd Deepe busied . . . III. iii. 14. 6
Then shall he issew forth with *dreadfull* might . . . III. iii. 29. 8
The *dreadful* speare and shield to exercize: . . . III. iii. 53. 4
thou sendest troublous feares And *dreadfull* visions, . . . III. iv. 57. 6
Her *dreadfull* weapon she to him addrest, . . . III. vii. 42. 2
To *dreadfull* shapes he did him selfe transforme; . . . III. viii. 41. 1
That *dreadfull* sound the bosters hart did thrill . . . III. x. 43. 5
many *dreadfull* feends hath pointed to her gard. . . . III. xi. 16. 9
with griesly hate And *dreadfull* horror . . . III. xi. 21. 8
With *dreadfull* thunder and lightning atwixt, . . . III. xii. 2. 2
Beares skin, that him more *dreadfull* made; . . . III. xii. 11. 2
his owne face was *dreadfull*, . . . III. xii. 11. 3
With ghastly looks and *dreadfull* drerihed; . . . III. xii. 17. 3
Full *dreadfull* thinges out of that balefull booke He red, . . . III. xii. 36. 3
Those *dreadfull* flames she also found delayd . . . III. xii. 42. 7
that fained *dreadfull* flame, . . . III. xii. 43. 2
the *dreadfull* discord, which did drive . . . to outrage fell; IV. i. 23. 6
from shore behold the *dreadfull* sight . . . IV. ii. 16. 7
All mightie men and *dreadfull* derring-dooers, . . . IV. ii. 38. 3
Farre under ground . . . their *dreadfull* dwelling is. . . . IV. ii. 47. 9
met With *dreadfull* force and furious intent, . . . IV. iii. 6. 6
The *dreadfull* stroke, in case it had arrived . . . IV. iii. 18. 1
spies him toward bend His *dreadfull* souse, . . . IV. iii. 19. 6
So *dreadfull* were his strokes, so deadly was his hond. . . . IV. iv. 23. 9
With that he drives at them with *dreadfull* might, . . . IV. iv. 35. 1
every one gan shun his *dreadfull* sight, . . . IV. iv. 41. 8
dreadfull seem'd to every living wight, . . . IV. v. 32. 3
With *dreadfull* force falles on some steeple hie; . . . IV. vi. 14. 3
dreadfull tidings which thou doest declare,' . . . IV. vii. 14. 1
With *dreadfull* strokes let drive at him so sore, . . . IV. vii. 28. 3
forth she past into his *dreadfull* den, . . . IV. vii. 33. 1
With *dreadfull* weapon aymed at his head, . . . IV. viii. 41. 7
would have maz'd a man his *dreadfull* face to vew: . . . IV. viii. 38. 9
So *dreadfull* strokes each did at other drive, . . . IV. ix. 22. 6
An hideous Giant, *dreadfull* to behold, . . . IV. x. 16. 6
the storme of every *dreadfull* stoure: . . . IV. x. 58. 7
no *dreadfull* trompets sound; . . . V. Pr. 9. 5
durst withstand His *dreadfull* heast, . . . V. i. 8. 7
And *dreadfull* battaile twixt them do darraine: . . . V. ii. 15. 5
dismayd with *dreadfull* sight Of death, . . . V. ii. 54. 3
So terribly his *dreadfull* strokes did thonder, . . . V. iii. 8. 8
What strokes, what *dreadfull* stoure, it stird this day; . . . V. iii. 21. 6
From *dreadfull* mouth of death, . . . V. iv. 12. 3
With *dreadfull* force he flies at her bylive, . . . V. iv. 42. 6
He to her lept with deadly *dreadfull* looke, . . . V. v. 11. 7
dare even deathes most *dreadfull* face behold? . . . V. v. 31. 4
at which *dreadfull* stound She quickly caught her sword, . . . V. vi. 28. 8
Like one adawed with some *dreadfull* spright: . . . V. vii. 20. 8
Let drive at him with all her *dreadfull* might, . . . V. vii. 32. 3
Which *dreadfull* sight when all her warlike traine . . . saw, . . . V. vii. 34. 7
Where is that *dreadfull* manly looke? . . . V. vii. 40. 3

Dreadful—*Continued.*

The *dreadfull* sight did them so sore affray, . . . V. viii. 40. 5
with *dreadfull* fate Had utterly subverted his unrighteous state. . . . V. ix. 2. 8
A *dreadfull* depth; how deepe no man can tell, . . . V. ix. 6. 4
Full *dreadfull* wight he was as ever went Upon the earth, . . . V. ix. 10. 4
Through the sad terror of so *dreadfull* fate, . . . V. ix. 46. 4
Of horrible aspect and *dreadfull* mood, . . . V. x. 8. 7
Unto a *dreadfull* Monster to devoure, . . . V. x. 13. 7
Whose *dreadfull* shape was never seene of none . . . V. x. 29. 4
A *dreadfull* feend with fowle deformed looke, . . . V. xi. 22. 5
Dealing his *dreadfull* blowes with large dispence, . . . V. xi. 45. 4
With bils and glayves making a *dreadfull* luster, . . . V. xi. 58. 5
With *dreadfull* looke he Artegall beheld, . . . V. xii. 16. 2
With *dreadfull* terror and with fell intent; . . . V. xii. 17. 2
A *dreadfull* feend, of gods and men ydrad, . . . V. xii. 37. 8
The heavy burden of whose *dreadfull* might . . . VI. i. 22. 1
Like as a ship with *dreadfull* storme long tost, . . . VI. iv. 1. 1
for her so *dreadfull* face, . . . VI. vi. 11. 1
With *dreadfull* force they all did him assaile, . . . VI. vi. 26. 1
when he once his *dreadfull* strokes had tasted, . . . VI. vi. 28. 1
His lookes were *dreadfull*, and his fiery eies, . . . VI. vii. 42. 1
The which descended with such *dreadfull* sway, . . . VI. viii. 8. 4
His *dreadfull* hand he heaved up aloft, . . . VI. viii. 15. 1
with his *dreadfull* instrument of yre . . . VI. viii. 15. 2
in *dreadfull* darknesse layd Amongst those theeves, . . . VI. xi. 2. 3
In thousand *dreadful* shapes doth mongst them stalke, . . . VI. xi. 16. 7
With cruell rage and *dreadfull* violence, . . . VI. xi. 30. 4
In *dreadfull* darknesse dreadfully aghast; . . . VI. xi. 32. 5
there gan a *dreadfull* fight. . . . VI. xi. 47. 9
had endured many a *dreadfull* stoure . . . VI. xii. 3. 7
Brought forth with him the *dreadfull* dog of hell, . . . VI. xii. 35. 2
Since thou hast seene her *dreadfull* power belowe, . . . VII. vi. 32. 6
dreadfull thunder-claps (that make them quake) . . . VII. vii. 23. 8
Upon a *dreadfull* Scorpion he did ride, . . . VII. vii. 39. 6
it a *dreadfull* Centaure was in sight, . . . VII. vii. 40. 8
A *dreadfull* countenaunce she given hath; . . . *Am.* xxxi. 6
The *dreadfull* tempest of her wrath appease, . . . *Am.* xxxviii. 7
when a *dreadfull* storme away is flit, . . . *Am.* xl. 7
Within a bush his *dreadfull* head doth hide, . . . *Am.* liii. 3
no deluding dreames, nor *dreadfull* sights, . . . *Epith.* 338
In *dreadful* darknesse lend desired light; . . . *Epith.* 412
Whose *dreadfull* name . . . did thunder, . . . *Proth.* 147

Dreadfully. bright eyes, glauncing full *dreadfullie*, . . . *Gn.* 262
He oftentimes me *dreadfullie* doth threaten . . . *Gn.* 351
So *dreadfully* he towardes him did pas, . . . I. xi. 15. 1
a rocky hill Over the sea suspended *dreadfully*, . . . III. x. 56. 4
the darts . . . Full *dreadfully* he shooke, . . . III. xii. 23. 6
Dreadfully dropping from her dying hart, . . . III. xii. 31. 4
So *dreadfully* he did the andvile beat, . . . IV. v. 37. 5
lashing *dreadfully* at every part, . . . IV. vi. 16. 6
Full *dreadfully* empurpled all with bloud; . . . IV. vii. 6. 6
(With yron wheeles and hookes arm'd *dreadfully*, . . . V. viii. 28. 5
The whilest at him so *dreadfully* he drive, . . . V. xi. 5. 8
can let drive at him so *dreadfullie*, . . . V. xi. 10. 3
Thereat he brayed loud, and yelled *dreadfully*. . . . V. xii. 20. 9
So *dreadfully* his hundred tongues did bray: . . . V. xii. 41. 7
Like troubled ghost, did *dreadfully* appeare, . . . VI. vi. 32. 8
Let drive at him so *dreadfully* amaine, . . . VI. vii. 46. 4
In dreadfull darknesse *dreadfully* aghast; . . . VI. xi. 32. 5

Dreading. yielded . . . proud submission, Still *dreading* death, I. iii. 6. 7
As no whit *dreading* any living wight; . . . VI. vii. 43. 2

Dreadless. Safe in his *dreadles* den him thought to hide: . . . *Van.* x. 4
dreadles bad them come to Corte, . . . *Hub.* 1077
The *dreadlesse* corage of this Elfin knight, . . . I. vi. 1. 8
'*Dreadlesse*,' (said he) 'that shall I soone declare. . . . II. v. 17. 1
Whom he assayld with *dreadlesse* hardiment, . . . V. iii. 11. 3
Unlesse it be perform'd with *dreadlesse* might; . . . V. iv. 1. 8
'Can dread of ought your *dreadlesse* hart withhold, . . . V. v. 31. 2

Dreads. colde through feare and old conceived *dreads*; . . . II. ii. 9. 3
He *dreads* no danger, nor misfortune feares, . . . *H.L.* 223

Dream. we here siten as drownd in a *dreme*. . . . *S.C.* May 16
layed The shepheard long to *dreame*. . . . *S.C.* Jul. 64
As one then in a *dreame*, . . . He mumbled soft, . . . I. i. 42. 7
A fit false *dreame*, that can delude the sleepers sent.' . . . I. i. 43. 9
calling forth . . . A diverse *Dreame* out of his prison darke, . I. i. 44. 2
the *dreame* he bore In hast unto his Lord, . . . I. i. 44. 8
when that ydle *dreame* was to him brought, . . . I. i. 46. 1
made him *dreame* of loves and lustfull play, . . . I. i. 47. 4
That troublous *dreame* gan freshly tosse his braine . . . I. i. 55. 6
That feigning *dreame*, and that faire-forged Spright, . . . I. ii. 2. 2
Out of his swowning *dreame* he gan awake; . . . I. v. 12. 2
as in a *dreame* of deepe delight, . . . I. xi. 50. 4
As one out of a deadly *dreame* affright, . . . II. i. 45. 6
out of his delightfull *dreame* The man awoke, . . . II. v. 37. 1
he awoke out of his ydle *dreme*; . . . II. vi. 27. 2
slumbring fast In senceles *dreame*; . . . II. viii. 4. 9
his *dreame* that did him long entraunce, . . . III. vii. 45. 2
thought he yet did *dreame* Not well awakte; . . . III. viii. 22. 7
none him durst awake out of his *dreme*; . . . III. ix. 10. 6
one out of a *dreame* not waked well . . . III. x. 49. 7
hong adowne his head as he did *dreame*; . . . III. xi. 41. 7
upstarted . . . As men awaked rashly out of *dreme*, . . . IV. ii. 17. 2
As one that had out of a *dreame* bene reard, . . . IV. iii. 31. 4
made him *dreame* those two disloyall were: . . . IV. v. 43. 8
Like one that from his *dreame* is waked suddenlye. . . . V. v. 13. 9
They do to thee in this same *dreame* discover; . . . V. vii. 22. 2
So blesse thee God, and give thee joyance of thy *dreame*!' V. vii. 23. 9
Like one that out of deadly *dreame* awooke: . . . VI. iii. 11. 3
Was it a *dreame*, or did I see it playne; . . . *Am.* lxxvii. 1

Dream's. broken with some fearefull *dreames* affright, V. vi. 14. 2
Dreams. after troublous sights And *dreames*, I. ii. 4. 3
whether *dreames* delude, or true it were, I. ix. 14. 5
Devices, *dreames*, opinions unsound, II. ix. 51. 7
with *dreames*, and with fantastick sight III. ii. 29. 4
My love is now awake out of her *dreames*, *Epith.* 92
no deluding *dreames*, nor dreadfull sights, *Epith.* 338
Drear. A ruefull spectacle of death and ghastly *drere* I. viii. 40. 9
others like Gryphons *dreare;* II. xi. 8. 4
The hoars Night-raven, trump of dolefull *drere;* II. xii. 36. 5
wrap in darkenes *dreare;* III. xi. 55. 4
despiteous *dreare* And heavie sway, IV. viii. 42. 5
powred forth his wretched life in deadly *dreare.* V. x. 35. 9
Right in the flanke him strooke with deadly *dreare,* V. xii. 20. 5
Both to her love and to her selfe in that sad *dreare.* VI. ii. 46. 9
deare affection of so dolefull *dreare,* VI. iii. 4. 5
Drearihead. She grew to hideous shape of *dryrihed,* *Mui.* 347
Ah! wretched boy, the shape of *dreryhead,* *As.* 133
it importunes death and dolefull *dreryhedd.* III. i. 16. 9
Through suddein feare and ghastly *drerihedd,* III. i. 62. 5
with sad *drearyhead* Chaunged thy lively cheare, III. ii. 30. 8
With ghastly looks and dreadfull *drerihed;* III. xii. 17. 3
Drearily. *Drerily* shooting his stormy darte, *S.C.* F. 45
Dreariment. sing of sorrowe and deathes *dreeriment,* *S.C.* N. 36
mourne my fall with dolefull *dreriment.* *Ti.* 158
Full of sad feare and ghastly *dreriment,* I. ii. 44. 4
Enrold in flames, and smouldring *dreriment,* I. viii. 9. 4
in her sad *dreriment,* But praying still I. xi. 32. 8
scratcht her face with ghastly *dreriment;* II. i. 15. 5
She fled away with ghastly *dreriment,* II. iv. 31. 8
shaking off his drowsy *dreriment,* II. vi. 27. 3
cover'd heaven with hideous *dreriment,* II. vii. 1. 5
gamesom merth to grievous *dreriment:* III. iv. 30. 4
Fowle horror, and eke hellish *dreriment:* III. iv. 58. 5
fled away with ghastly *dreriment,* IV. vii. 29. 8
Braggadochio selfe with *dreriment* So daunted was V. iii. 26. 7
for to tell the dolefull *dreriment* VI. x. 44. 1
to lament Your dolefull *dreriment:* *Epith.* 11
Dreariness. empeach His foltring toung with pangs of *dreri-nesse,* III. xi. 12. 3
nought but darkesome *drerinesse* she found, IV. vii. 33. 2
Drearing. All were my self, through griefe, in deadly *drearing.* *D.* 189
Dreary. Whose drops in *drery* ysicles remaine. *S.C.* Ja. 36
Pyne, plagues, and *dreery* death, *S.C.* Jul. 24
Whose shrieking sound Ys signe of *dreery* death, *S.C.* Au. 174
that *dreerie* Death should strike so mortall stroke, *S.C.* N. 123
after Winter *dreerie* death does hast. *S.C.* D. 144
lowd shrieks and *drerie* dolefull cries. *T.M.* 172
shrieks and cries and *dreery* yells. *T.M.* 538
the *drerie* stownd is now arrived, *Mui.* 415
drery horror dim the chearfull light, *D.* 328
I hate the darknesse and the *drery* night, *D.* 409
up, *dreary* Dame, of darknes Queene! I. v. 24. 1
the ghastly owle, With *drery* shriekes I. v. 30. 7
with their *drery* wounds, and bloody gore, I. vi. 45. 5
returning from the *drery* Night, I. vii. 2. 1
'Ye *dreary* instruments of dolefull sight, I. vii. 22. 1
an hollow, *dreary,* murmuring voyce I. viii. 38. 1
His dwelling . . . Darke, dolefull, *dreary,* like a greedy grave, I. ix. 33. 4
A *dreary* corse, whose life away did pas, I. ix. 36. 5
On which the *drery* death did sitt II. i. 45. 2
Fitt to . . . deck the *drery* toombe. II. vii. 51. 9
as cold and *drery* as a snake, II. xi. 22. 4
The *dreary* image of sad death appeares: III. iv. 57. 7
to build his balefull mansion In *drery* darkenes III. x. 58. 3
like a *dreary* Spright III. xii. 19. 4
Which *drery* sight the gentle Squire espying IV. vii. 25. 1
when Briana saw that *drery* stound, VI. i. 34. 5
He also gan uplooke with *drery* eye, VI. iii. 11. 2
stouping downe to her in *drery* swound VI. iii. 27. 7
staunch the bleeding of her *dreary* wound: VI. v. 6. 5
hath me driven to this *drery* stound. VI. v. 28. 5
at the last through *dreary* dolour die: VI. viii. 31. 4
fell down with him in *drerie* swound. VI. xi. 19. 9
in his armes the *dreary* dying mayd, VI. xi. 21. 2
With *drearie* drouping eyne lookt up like one aghast. VI. xi. 22. 9
drery sad disdayne Of all worlds gladnesse, *Am.* lii. 11
Let none of these theyr *drery* accents sing; *Epith.* 351
Dred(e), Dredd. *See* **Dread.**
Dreed. *See* **Dread.**
Dreere, Dreeriment. *See* **Dreary, Dreariment.**
Drench. With holy water they doen hem all *drench.* *S.C.* S. 89
To *drench* himselfe in moorish slime did trace, *Gn.* 251
Drenched. *See* **Drent.**
hath so often with his overflowing Thee *drenched.* *Ro.* xiii. 12
the well, wherein he *drenched* lay: I. xi. 34. 2
Where *drenched* deepe he fownd . . . The carefull servaunt II. vi. 47. 8
drenched lay full deepe under the Garden side II. vii. 57. 9
Deepe was he *drenched* to the upmost chin, II. vii. 58. 1
river, where he late Had *drenched* them, IV. xi. 38. 6
swound, in which full deepe He *drenched* was, VI. iii. 10. 8
Drent. *See* **Drenched.**
deade is Dido, dead, alas! and *drent;* *S.C.* N. 37
'Some in the greedie flouds are sunke and *drent;* *Gn.* 585
Is also deaded, and in dolour *drent.* *T.M.* 210
In daunger rather to be *drent* then brent?' II. vi. 49. 7
carcas deepe was *drent* Within the river, II. vi. 61. 2
nought that falles . . . but is condemned to be *drent.* II. xii. 6. 9
To see her Lord, that was reported *drent* V. vii. 39. 3

Drere, Drerie, Drerihed(d), etc. *See* **Drear, Dreary, Dreari-head,** *etc.*
Dress. He gan to comfort, and his woundes to *dresse,* II. iv. 16. 6
their Lady *dresse* his wownd, III. v. 38. 2
His armes, . . . She gathered up and did about him *dresse,* III. xi. 20. 5
her wel-pointed wepons did about her *dresse.* III. xi. 55. 9
In seeking . . . For herbes to *dresse* their wounds; VI. iv. 16. 4
Dressed. my rymes bene rough, and rudely *drest;* *S.C.* Jun. 77
his gins, . . . *Drest* in good order as he could devise. *Mui.* 388
With sprincled pearle and gold full richly *drest,* I. vii. 32. 3
thousand times he so him selfe had *drest,* I. ix. 54. 7
shoke his scales to battaile ready *drest,* I. xi. 15. 7
No arborett with painted blossomes *drest* II. vi. 12. 7
Faire Lady she him seemd, like Lady *drest.* III. ii. 4. 8
Hast *drest* my sinfull wounds? III. v. 35. 9
His readie wound with better salves new *drest:* III. v. 41. 4
Daily she *dressed* him, III. v. 41. 5
like a Faerie knight him selfe he *drest,* III. viii. 40. 1
with colourd ribbands *drest:* IV. viii. 10. 4
ill your goddesse services are *drest* By virgins, IV. x. 54. 8
Such were these Hags, and so unhandsome *drest:* V. xii. 38. 1
every day them duely *drest.* VI. vi. 2. 9
her infestred wound . . . by any to be *drest.* VI. xi. 24. 7
nor her golden haire Into their comely tresses dewly *drest,* VI. xii. 15. 4
She *drest* his wound, *Epig.* iv. 45
Dresses. with sly skill so cunningly them *dresses,* *Am.* xxxvii. 3
Dressing. al the while his wounds were *dressing* by him stayd, II. xi. 49. 9
A daintie damsell *dressing* of her heare, II. xii. 14. 8
Drest. *See* **Dressed.**
Drevill. *See* **Drivel.**
Drew. They drewe abacke, *S.C.* Jun. 63
drew the wicked Shepheard to his will. *Hub.* 320
now crept, now backward *drew,* *Hub.* 1012
After his dayes long labour *drew* to rest, *D.* 23
to the pray when as he *drew* more ny, I. iii. 5. 7
nigh he *drew* unto this gentle payre, I. iii. 34. 1
Whenas this knight nigh to the Lady *drew,* I. vii. 38. 1
Nigh as he *drew,* they might perceive his head I. ix. 22. 1
wrath . . . That *drew* on men Gods hatred I. x. 33. 6
the dreadful Beast *drew* nigh to hand, I. xi. 8. 1
She nigher *drew,* and saw that joyous end: I. xi. 55. 7
drew her on the ground; II. i. 11. 6
The dead knights sword out of his sheath he *drew,* II. i. 61. 1
Drew them in partes, and each made others foe: II. ii. 13. 6
Whereto he *drew* in hast II. iv. 3. 4
Drew by the heare along upon the grownd II. iv. 3. 6
drew his deadly weapon to maintaine his part. II. iv. 9. 9
With that he *drew* his flaming sword, II. v. 6. 1
That thee against me *drew* with so impetuous dread. II. v. 16. 9
Drew him through durt and myre II. v. 23. 4
So him away he *drew* II. v. 25. 1
his sword forth *drew,* II. vi. 29. 3
Atin *drew* nigh to weet what it mote bee, II. vi. 43. 1
Firme is thy faith, whom daunger never fro me *drew.* II. viii. 53. 9
the Palmer him forth *drew* From Faery court. II. ix. 9. 7
Arraught the rule, and from their father *drew;* II. x. 34. 8
taking armes the Britons to her *drew;* II. x. 54. 7
Still as the greedy knight nigh to him *drew;* II. xi. 27. 2
when Guyon saw, he *drew* him neare, II. xii. 65. 7
Elfe and carefull Palmer *drew* So nigh them, II. xii. 81. 1
Drew out a deadly bow and arrow keene, III. i. 65. 2
Drew the smooth charett of sad Cymoent: III. iv. 33. 2
ever as he nigher to her *drew,* III. iv. 48. 3
Then *drew* he his bright sword, III. ix. 16. 9
as he nigher *drew,* he easily Might scerne III. x. 22. 7
forth he *drew* Great store of treasure, III. x. 29. 1
they dismounting *drew* their weapons bold, III. xi. 21. 1
drew her selfe aside in sickernesse, III. xi. 55. 8
A murdrous knife out of his pocket *drew,* III. xii. 32. 5
fiercely forth her mortall blade she *drew,* III. xii. 33. 8
to her bed . . . Now freely *drew,* IV. i. 15. 9
the lovely paire *drew* nigh to hond: IV. i. 34. 1
thrise he *drew* it backe; so did at last forbeare. IV. i. 54. 9
a Squire, . . . *Drew* nigh, to weete the cause of their debate: IV. ii. 20. 6
to it *drew* The eyes of all, IV. iv. 16. 3
when his speare was brust, his sword he *drew,* IV. iv. 41. 3
to them *drew* nere, And her salewd IV. vi. 25. 3
drew thereto, making her eare her guide: IV. vii. 29. 4
He to it *drew,* to weet who there did wonne; IV. vii. 42. 6
By chance he certaine miniments forth *drew,* IV. viii. 6. 2
stay Till she *drew* neare, and then againe remove; IV. viii. 11. 3
into that forrest wide She *drew* her far, IV. viii. 11. 7
Eftsoones that pretious liquour forth he *drew,* IV. viii. 20. 6
To which they *drew* ere night upon them fell; IV. viii. 23. 3
Soft rombling brookes, that gentle slomber *drew;* IV. x. 24. 4
unto him *drew* The eares and hearts of all IV. xi. 23. 4
his sword he *drew* all wrathfully, V. i. 18. 5
Eftsoones his Page *drew* to the Castle gate, V. ii. 21. 1
Thence he her *drew* By the faire lockes, V. ii. 25. 6
Till that at length nigh to the sea they *drew;* V. ii. 29. 2
In sdeignfull wize he *drew* unto him neare, V. ii. 33. 8
with th' other *drew* his sword; V. iii. 29. 7
He nigh them *drew* to stay th' avengers forse, V. iii. 30. 7
the purple bloud forth *drew.* V. v. 9. 9
drew him on with hope fit leasure to awayt. V. v. 42. 9
as she nigh unto them *drew,* V. vi. 37. 2
he so neare her *drew* V. vii. 16. 4
They *drew* their swords, V. viii. 10. 2
touched with intire affection nigh him *drew;* V. viii. 12. 9

Drew—*Continued.*
If he too rashly to his charet *drew*, V. viii. 32. 2
Oft *drew* the Prince unto his charret nigh, V. viii. 33. 1
At last from his victorious shield he *drew* The vaile, V. viii. 37. 6
the firie-mouthed steedes, which *drew* The Sunnes bright wayne V. viii. 40. 1
Talus soone him overtooke, and backward *drew*. V. ix. 18. 9
as he nigher *drew*, three knights he spyde, V. x. 34. 1
They *drew* unto his aide; V. xi. 47. 2
when as nigh unto the shore they *drew* V. xii. 5. 2
So sounded the retraite, and *drew* his folke away. V. xii. 9. 9
he therewith the knight *drew* all about: V. xii. 22. 3
And for their better comfort to them nigher *drew*. VI. ii. 41. 9
arriving with the fall of day *Drew* to the gate, VI. iii. 37. 8
he stayd, till that he nearer *drew*, VI. iii. 47. 1
from his steed him nigh he *drew* againe: VI. iv. 7. 5
He to her *drew*, and with faire blandishment VI. iv. 27. 6
through thicke woods and brakes and briers him *drew*, VI. v. 17. 3
Whereof exceeding glad he to him *drew*, VI. v. 23. 3
Yet say'd not so, but that the bloud it *drew*, VI. viii. 9. 5
to the dore of death for sorrow *drew*, VI. viii. 20. 8
So forth he *drew* much gold, and toward him it drive. VI. ix. 32. 9
He nigher *drew* to weete what mote it be: VI. x. 10. 6
seeing him to mourne, *Drew* neare, VI. x. 18. 9
Him hardly forward *drew*, VI. xi. 38. 3
when as towards darksome night it *drew*, VI. xi. 41. 1
drew a little space Behind the bushes, VI. xii. 8. 5
he *drew* him forth, even in his own despight. VI. xii. 34. 9
drew To this sweet spring; VII. vi. 45. 7
Thence forth they *drew* him by the hornes, VII. vi. 47. 7
Drew millions more against their God to fight *H.H.L.* 84
they all out of their baskets *drew* *Proth.* 73

Dried. Spying the tree destroid, the water *dride*. *Pet.* v. 9
flouds do gaspe, for *dryed* is theyr sourse, *S.C.* N. 126
Theyr rootes bene *dryed* up *S.C.* D. 111
throat through thirst to nought nigh being *dride* *Gn.* 387
A sea of teares that never may be *dryde*, *T.M.* 116
She bathed oft with teares, and *dried* oft: *As.* 164
soild with dust of the long *dried* way; I. vi. 35. 2
Her *dried* dugs, lyke bladders lacking wind, Hong downe, I. viii. 47. 6
As withered leaves drop from their *dryed* stockes, II. xi. 19. 4
skin all withered like a *dryed* rooke; II. xi. 22. 3
Th' one faire and fresh, the other old and *dride*. III. vi. 31. 7
The durefull Oake, whose sap is not yet *dride*, *Am.* vi. 5

Driest. The *driest* wood is soonest burnt to dust. III. viii. 25. 5

Drift. in woods and forrests, Th' end of his *drift*, I. ii. 9. 4
The mightie trunck, . . . fall with fearefull *drift*. I. viii. 22. 9
of all his *drifte* the aymed end: II. i. 3. 4
them driven hath to this despairefull *drift*. II. xii. 8. 9
Acrasia, . . . will slip away, and all our *drift* despise. II. xii. 69. 9
none espyde His secret *drift*, III. x. 6. 4
Whose hidden *drift* he could not well perceive; V. v. 37. 2

Drifts. favour not The wicked *driftes* of trayterous desynes V. ix. 42. 2

Drink. Did in his *drinke* shed poyson privilie; *Van.* vi. 8
My *drink* the teares which fro mine eyes do raine, *D.* 376
Whose mind in meat and *drinke* was drowned so, I. iv. 23. 4
all that *drinke* thereof do faint and feeble grow. I. vii. 5. 9
His office was the . . . thristy give to *drinke*; I. x. 38. 3
coming to this well, he stoupt to *drincke*: II. i. 55. 8
when lust of meat and *drinke* was ceast, II. ii. 39. 3
Of deadly drugs I gave him *drinke* anon, II. iv. 30. 8
gaped still as coveting to *drinke* Of the cold liquor II. vii. 58. 2
Of grace I pray thee, give to eat and *drinke* to mee!' II. vii. 59. 9
Thereof she usd to give to *drinke* to each, II. xii. 56. 7
That she may sucke their life, and *drinke* their blood, IV. i. 26. 5
Nepenthe is a *drinck* of soverayne grace, IV. iii. 43. 1
Are by the Gods to *drinck* thereof assynd; IV. iii. 43. 8
such as *drinck*, eternall happinesse do fynd. IV. iii. 43. 9
Are wont . . . To *drincke* hereof, IV. iii. 44. 6
Her golden cup to them for *drinke* she raught, IV. iii. 48. 8
Ne other *drinke* there did he ever tast IV. vii. 41. 6
That I mote *drinke* the cup whereof she dranke, V. i. 15. 7
Ne *drinke* of wine; for wine, they say, is blood, V. vii. 10. 3
which should *drinke* And dry up all the water VI. iv. 32. 7
Offred him *drinke* to quench his thirstie heat, VI. ix. 6. 8
drinke of every brooke when thirst my throte doth boyle. VI. ix. 23. 9

Drinketh. suckes the blood, and *drinketh* up the lyfe, *H.L.* 125

Drinking. Though eating hipps, and *drinking* watry fome. *Hub.* 948

Drink-quickening. Dull Poppie, and *drink-quickning* Setuale, *Mui.* 196

Drinks. the borne Souldier which Rhine running *drinks*: *Ro.* xxxi. 8
There *drincks* she Nectar with Ambrosia mixt, *S.C.* N. 195
meates and *drinkes* of every kinde I. xii. 15. 1
when of meats and *drinks* they had their fill, III. ix. 32. 1
with full satietie Of meates and *drinkes* V. iii. 4. 2
he freely *drinks* an health to all his peeres. VII. vii. 41. 9

Drive. *See* **Thunder-drive.**
If too great winde against the port him *drive*, *Ro.* xxi. 13
His little Goats gan *drive* out of their stalls, *Gn.* 71
clap of thunder . . . cloudes asunder *dryve*. *Gn.* 520
drive to follow after their Belwether.' *Hub.* 296
he would it *drive* away, *Hub.* 827
Proteus eke with him does *drive* his heard *Col.* 248
melody, To *drive* away the dull melancholy; I. v. 3. 5
each to deadly shame would *drive* his foe: I. v. 9. 2
the direfull dames doe *drive* Their mournefull charett, I. v. 32. 1
None els to death this man despayring *drive* I. ix. 38. 5
To *drive* him to despaire, and quite to quaile, I. ix. 49. 5
The streame thereof would *drive* a water-mill: I. xi. 22. 6
To *drive* away the dull Melancholy; I. xii. 38. 8
So parted we, and on our journey *drive*; II. i. 55. 7

Drive—*Continued.*
drive me to withdraw my blind abused love. II. iv. 24. 9
Nor timely tides did *drive* out of their sluggish sourse. II. vi. 20. 9
Did *drive* the Romanes to the weaker syde, II. x. 51. 8
thee fierce Fortune did so nearely *drive*, II. xi. 30. 8
mightily doth *drive* The hollow vessell II. xii. 5. 5
after them did *drive* with all her power and might. II. xii. 15. 9
did them *drive* before His whirling charet II. xii. 22. 3
Into the Ocean deepe to *drive* their weary drove. III. i. 57. 9
so deepe wound through these deare members *drive*. III. iv. 37. 4
So from the wearie spirit thou doest *drive* Desired rest, III. iv. 57. 8
did *drive* Their brother to reproch III. v. 16. 5
saw his drover *drive* along the streame, III. viii. 22. 2
th' inland folke, which sought him backe to *drive*, III. ix. 42. 3
daily siege, . . . will to parley *drive*; III. x. 10. 4
with fowle force unto his will did *drive*; III. x. 27. 7
did *drive* The noble Argonauts to outrage fell; IV. i. 23. 6
Them reconcyld againe, and to their homes did *drive*. IV. ii. 2. 9
He can let *drive* at him with all his power, IV. iii. 20. 4
seem'd to dust he shortly would it *drive*: IV. v. 37. 6
The heavens abhorre, and into darkenesse *drive*; IV. vii. 12. 4
With dreadfull strokes let *drive* at him so sore, IV. vii. 28. 3
suffred that same Dwarfe me to her dongeon *drive*. IV. viii. 56. 9
So dreadfull strokes each did at other *drive*, IV. ix. 22. 6
Against those two let *drive*, IV. ix. 29. 5
either beat him in, or *drive* him out. IV. x. 19. 5
Her from the quarrey he away doth *drive*, V. iv. 42. 8
They seeing that let *drive* at him streightway, V. vi. 29. 8
Let *drive* at her with all her dreadfull might, V. vii. 32. 3
They . . . *drive* his wife Adicia to despaire. V. viii. Arg.
he with his yron flayle Gan *drive* at him V. ix. 19. 3
tryumph in their blood whom she to death did *dryve*. V. ix. 41. 9
Seeking to *drive* away deepe-rooted dreede V. x. 22. 4
The whilest at him so dreadfully he *drive*, V. xi. 5. 8
can let *drive* at him so dreadfullie, V. xi. 10. 3
What new occasion doth thee hither *drive*, V. xi. 38. 5
He gan at him let *drive* more fiercely then afore. V. xii. 22. 9
gan to *drive* at him more hard. VI. i. 20. 9
whose swelling sourse Shall *drive* a Mill, VI. i. 21. 2
To *drive* you so on foot, VI. ii. 15. 4
So did that Squire his foes disperse and *drive* asonder. VI. v. 19. 9
Let *drive* at him with so malitious mynd, VI. vii. 10. 6
Let *drive* at him so dreadfully amaine, VI. vii. 46. 4
for to *drive* The painefull plough, VI. viii. 35. 5
To helpe faire Pastorella home to *drive* Her fleecie flocke; VI. ix. 15. 8
through ambition downe themselves doe *drive* VI. ix. 22. 4
So forth he drew much gold, and toward him it *drive*. VI. ix. 32. 9
Watching to *drive* the ravenous Wolfe away, VI. ix. 37. 4
from her to *drive* The sad remembrance VI. xi. 50. 6
What way is best to *drive* her to retire, VII. vi. 21. 7
Others would through the river him have *drive* VII. vi. 50. 5

Drived. *See* **Drave, Drive, Drove.**
Ne her out of the stedfast sadle *driv'd*; III. vii. 40. 7

Drivel. that false witch, and that foule aged *drevill*; IV. ii. 3. 8

Driven. *See* **Drive.**
I saw a Bull as white as *driven* snowe, *Van.* ii. 2
Driven for neede to come home agayne. *S.C.* S. 67
I *driven* am to seeke some meanes to live: *Hub.* 250
driven be perforce to sterving, *Hub.* 370
are *driven* T' accept a Benefice *Hub.* 539
he *driven* was to great distresse, *Hub.* 933
had him slaine, And *driven* downe to hell, *Hub.* 1237
being *driven* hence, I thether fly. *T.M.* 528
Driven with streames of wretchednesse and woe, *D.* 433
So deepely dinted in the *driven* clay, I. viii. 8. 5
Some others were new *driven*, and distent Into great Ingowes II. vii. 5. 5
Into this land by chaunce have *driven* bene; II. x. 8. 5
Driven by fatall error here arriv'd, II. x. 9. 8
them *driven* hath to this despairefull drift. II. xii. 8. 9
Driven to great distresse by fortune straunge, III. viii. 20. 2
by fatall course they *driven* were Into an Island III. ix. 49. 1
A silly Pilgrim *driven* to distresse, III. x. 25. 6
driven with that stormy blast III. xii. 27. 2
billowes . . . Forcibly *driven* by contrarie tydes, IV. i. 42. 2
oft I *driven* am to great distresse, V. xi. 51. 8
hath me *driven* to this drery stound. VI. v. 28. 5
He *driven* was to ground in selfe despight; VI. viii. 10. 7

Drives. shining land, That golden Pactol *drives* *Bel.*[1] x. 4
his carelesse time This Shepheard *drives*, *Gn.* 154
with his dreadfull hornes them *drives* afore, II. viii. 42. 4
with his staffe, that *drives* his heard astray, III. viii. 31. 8
the tide, . . . *Drives* backe the current of his kindly course, IV. iii. 27. 4
With that he *drives* at them with dreadfull might, IV. iv. 35. 1
whom cruell tempest *drives* Upon a rocke V. ii. 50. 1
her frowne me *drives* away. *Am.* xxi. 12
that cloud of pryde . . . with smiles she *drives* away. *Am.* lxxxi. 8

Driving. Along the fomy waves *driving* his finny drove, III. viii. 29. 9
Towards them *driving*, like a storme out sent. IV. iii. 38. 5
to him *driving* strongly downe the tide V. ii. 14. 3

Drizzling. *See* **Ever-drizzling.**
from mine eyes the *drizling* teares descend, *S.C.* Ja. 41
drizling teares did shed for pure affection. I. iii. 6. 9
His watry eies *drizling* like deawy rayne, III. v. 34. 3
And *drizling* drops, that often doe redound, *Am.* xviii. 3

Droil. Drudge in the world, and for their living *droyle*, *Hub.* 157

Dromedary. Ryding upon a *Dromedare* on hie, IV. viii. 38. 7

Dronk. *See* **Drank, Drunk.**
the thirsty land *Dronke* up his life; I. iii. 20. 5
dronke with blood, yet thristed after life: I. vi. 38. 8
this gentle knight . . . *Dronke* of the streame, I. vii. 6. 3

Dronk—*Continued.*
the charme and veneme which they *dronck,* (*druncke) . . . II. ii. 4. 6
Made *dronke* (*drunke) with drugs of deare voluptuous receipt. II. v. 34. 9
dronke with blood of men slaine by his might, . . . III. vii. 47. 7
when *droncke* with drowsinesse he woke, . . . III. viii. 22. 1
the Geaunts broode . . . *dronck* mens vitall blood. . . . III. ix. 49. 9
Droop. To these sicke twaine, that now began to *droupe:* . . . VI. v. 32. 3
Drooping. *See* **Ever-drooping.**
weighing down his *drouping* drowsie hedd, . . . *Gn.* 244
when as *drouping* Titan draweth neere . . . *D.* 468
The *drouping* night thus creepeth on them fast; . . . I. i. 36. 1
the *drouping* day-light gan to fade, . . . I. xi. 49. 5
His daughter gan despise his *drouping* day, . . . II. x. 30. 4
Till *drouping* Phoebus gan to hyde his golden hedd. . . . III. x. 45. 9
the *drouping* night, Covered with cloudie storme . . . IV. v. 32. 1
With drearie *drouping* eyne lookt up like one aghast. . . . VI. xi. 22. 9
to the light lift up theyr *drouping* hed. . . . *Am.* xl. 12
Drop. molten starres doe *drop* like weeping eyes; . . . I. vi. 6. 5
Nor *drop* of blood in all his face appeares, . . . I. ix. 22. 4
if any *drop* Of living blood . . . II. i. 43. 4
With one sweete *drop* of sensuall delight. . . . II. vi. 8. 7
As withered leaves *drop* from their dryed stockes, . . . II. xi. 19. 4
Ne *drop* of blood appeared shed to bee, . . . II. xi. 38. 1
any *drop* of slombring rest . . . III. ii. 29. 1
from their fruitfull sydes sweet gum did *drop,* . . . III. vi. 43. 7
Yet from the wound no *drop* of bloud there fell, . . . IV. iii. 8. 6
did not from him let One *drop* of bloud to fall, . . . IV. iii. 24. 3
His dewy lockes did *drop* with brine apace . . . IV. xi. 11. 3
not a *drop* can slide: . . . V. ii. 35. 8
from which . . . The sweat did *drop;* . . . VII. vii. 29. 6
no one *drop* of pitie there doth rest. . . . *H.L.* 147
One *drop* of grace at length will to me give, . . . *H.B.* 277
Deigne to let fall one *drop* of dew reliefe, . . . *H.B.* 284
Some little *drop* of thy celestiall dew, . . . *H.H.L.* 46
Dropped. their yellow heare Christalline humor *dropped* downe II. xii. 65. 6
Dropped adowne upon her yvory brest: . . . III. viii. 35. 4
his hoarie hed *Dropped* with brackish deaw: . . . III. xi. 40. 4
Dropping. *See* **Dewy-dropping, Milk-dropping, Silver-dropping.**
sodain *dropping* of a golden shoure . . . *Bel.*[1] ix. 11
sudden *dropping* of a silver dew . . . *Bel.*[2] xi. 11
my heart-blood *dropping* weares, . . . *D.* 251
His subtile tong like *dropping* honny mealt'h Into the heart, I. ix. 31. 5
Sweete wordes like *dropping* honny she did shed; . . . II. iii. 24. 7
sweet wordes, *dropping* like honny dew; . . . II. v. 33. 4
Dreadfully *dropping* from her dying hart, . . . III. xii. 31. 4
with bloudie knyfe Yet *dropping* fresh in hand, . . . V. ix. 48. 3
Yet *dropping* fresh out of the Indian fount, . . . V. x. 16. 6
The bloudie gore and poyson *dropping* lothsomely. . . . V. xii. 30. 9
Yet cannot I, with many a *dropping* teare . . . *Am.* xviii. 5
Drops. Whose *drops* in drery ysicles remaine. . . . *S.C.* Ja. 36
if on me some little *drops* would flowe . . . *S.C.* Jun. 93
The kindelye dewe *drops* from the higher tree, . . . *S.C.* N. 31
all his tract with bloudie *drops* is stained . . . *Gn.* 279
out of whose rifte there came Smal *drops* of gory bloud, . . . I. ii. 30. 9
Wherein were closd few *drops* of liquor pure, . . . I. ix. 19. 3
drops of blood thence like a well did play: . . . I. x. 27. 4
with dry *drops* congealed in her eye, . . . II. i. 49. 3
The flood of *drops,* the Monster filth did breede: . . . II. iv. 35. 5
sparks, seed, *drops,* and filth, do thus delay; . . . II. iv. 35. 6
The *drops* dry up, . . . II. iv. 35. 8
drops of Christall seemd for wantones to weep. . . . II. xii. 61. 9
Few *drops,* more cleare then Nectar, . . . II. xii. 78. 4
drops of purple blood thereout did weepe, . . . III. i. 65. 8
many *drops* of milk and blood through it did spill. . . . III. ii. 49. 9
tears . . . in his eies, few *drops* of bitternesse. . . . III. x. 25. 9
litle *drops* empurpled her faire brest. . . . III. xii. 33. 5
with *drops* of melting love, . . . Sprinckle her heart, . . . IV. Pr. 5. 5
Deawed with silver *drops* through sweating sore, . . . IV. vi. 19. 7
with few *drops* thereof did softly dew, Her wounds, . . . IV. viii. 20. 8
Dew'd with her *drops* of bountie Soveraine, . . . IV. viii. 33. 5
Deawed with silver *drops* that trickled downe alway. . . . IV. xi. 25. 9
Congealed litle *drops* which doe the morne adore. . . . IV. xi. 46. 9
Few perling *drops* from her faire lampes of light; . . . V. ix. 50. 7
soone as few *drops* of raine Thereon distill . . . V. xii. 13. 3
the dull *drops,* that . . . did adown distill. . . . VII. vii. 31. 4
And drizling *drops,* that often doe redound, . . . *Am.* xviii. 3
Dropsy. a dry *dropsie* through his flesh did flow, . . . I. iv. 23. 7
Dross. loath this *drosse* of sinfull worlds desire! . . . *Ti.* 686
Some scumd the *drosse* that from the metall came; . . . II. vii. 36. 7
all worlds glorie is but *drosse* uncleane, . . . *Am.* xxvii. 2
His dunghill thoughts . . . themselves enure To dirtie *drosse,* . *H.L.* 184
the *drosse* which dims the light . . . *H.B.* 48
Seeme durt and *drosse* in thy pure-sighted eye, . . . *H.H.L.* 276
Seemes to them basenesse, and all riches *drosse,* . . . *H.H.B.* 279
Drossy. hinders heavenly thoughts with *drossy* slime. . . . *Am.* xiii. 12
Drought. parching *drougth* drie up the christall wells; . . . *D.* 333
he sterv'd with hunger, and with *drouth,* . . . II. vii. 58. 8
with untimely *drought* nigh withered was, . . . V. xii. 13. 2
Drove. *See* **Drave, Drive, Drived.**
drove the Nymphes away (to flight[1]). . . . *Bel.* xii. 14
drove in Joves owne lap his egs to lay; . . . *Van.* iv. 10
Arose, and homeward *drove* his sonned sheepe, . . . *S.C.* Ja. 77
him to much rebuke and Daunger *drove,* . . . *S.C.* Jun. 69
blast . . . perforce him *drove* on hed, . . . *Mui.* 420
darknesse he in deepest dongeon *drove,* . . . I. vii. 23. 3
to the earth him *drove,* as stricken dead; . . . I. xi. 38. 3
him into great amaz'ment *drove,* . . . II. ii. 3. 8
did assayle, And *drove* them to recoile; . . . II. ix. 14. 2
Guyon *drove* so furious and fell, . . . III. i. 6. 2
Into the Ocean deepe to drive their weary *drove.* . . . III. i. 57. 9

Drove—*Continued.*
drove at him with all his might and mayne . . . III. v. 21. 4
with the tide *drove* forward carelesly; . . . III. viii. 21. 4
Along the fomy waves driving his finny *drove.* . . . III. viii. 29. 9
They rudely *drove* to ground both man and horse, . . . III. ix. 16. 4
Againe he *drove* at him with double might, . . . IV. iii. 10. 2
hard unto his crowne The shield it *drove,* . . . IV. viii. 42. 7
Who yeester day *drove* us to such distresse: . . . V. iv. 48. 7
all their scattred crew Into the sea he *drove* . . . V. xi. 65. 4
My knight hers . . . to daunger *drove,* . . . VI. ii. 20. 5
And *drove* away the stound . . . VI. iii. 10. 9
The selfe same evening fortune hether *drove,* . . . VI. viii. 46. 8
drove away their flocks; . . . VI. x. 39. 9
So *drove* them all away, and his love with him bore. . . . VI. xi. 51. 9
Drover. saw his *drover* drive along the streame, . . . III. viii. 22. 2
Drowes. Sad *Trowis,* that once his people over-ran, . . . IV. xi. 41. 7
Drown. *drowne* in the forgetfulnesse of slepe, . . . *Bel.*[1] i. 3
In the forgetfulnes of sleepe doth *drowne* . . . *Bel.*[2] i. 3
drowne in dissolute delights apart, . . . II. vi. 25. 7
Ready to *drowne* him selfe for fell despight: . . . II. vi. 43. 5
strove in vaine, the one him selfe to *drowne,* . . . II. vi. 47. 2
drowne his baser mind, . . . III. iv. 56. 6
in the sea to *drowne* herselfe she fond, . . . III. vii. 26. 7
drowne all Holland with his excrement, . . . IV. xi. 35. 3
ne filth mote therein *drowne:* . . . VI. x. 7. 5
Till to the Plaine she come, whose Valleyes she doth *drowne.* VII. vi. 41. 9
Drowned. see lost and *drown'd* (*drownde*[1]), So great riches . . . *Pet.* ii. 13
all that treasure, *drowned* in the maine: . . . *Bel.*[2] xiii. 13
we here sitten as *drownd* in a dreme. . . . *S.C.* May 16
In th' Hellespont being nigh *drowned* all. . . . *Gn.* 552
lie *drowned* in deep wretchednes, . . . *T.M.* 149
Where *drownd* with him is all his earthlie blisse. . . . *Ti.* 546
It almost *drowned* was, . . . *Ti.* 622
All were I *drown'd* in carelesse quiet deepe; . . . *D.* 136
drownded lie in pleasures wastefull well, . . . *Col.* 762
deep waters which her *drownd* alway: . . . *Col.* 858
when all *drownd* in deadly sleepe he findes, . . . I. i. 36. 6
Morpheus . . . *drowned* deepe In drowsie fit he findes: . . . I. i. 40. 8
you in carelesse sleepe are *drowned* quight.' . . . I. i. 53. 4
drownd in sleepie night, . . . did besmeare My body . . . I. ii. 42. 2
all in deadly sleepe did *drowned* lye . . . I. iii. 16. 3
Still *drownd* in sleepe, and most of his daies dedd: . . . I. iv. 19. 4
Whose mind in meat and drinke was *drowned* so, . . . I. iv. 23. 4
blood . . . *drowned* all the land whereon he stood; . . . I. xi. 22. 5
Calling thy help in vaine that here in joyes art *dround.*' . . . II. v. 36. 9
all her wordes she *drownd* with laughter vaine, . . . II. vi. 6. 7
all his sences *drowned* in deep sencelesse wave: . . . II. viii. 24. 9
then to have them *dround.* . . . II. xii. 20. 9
Was *drowned* in the depth of deadly sleepe; . . . III. i. 59. 3
Full deepe emplonged was, and *drowned* nye . . . III. x. 17. 5
the frayle soule in deepe delight nigh *drownd:* . . . III. xii. 6. 5
in the river *drowned* quight. . . . IV. xi. 37. 9
he *drowned* him againe, . . . IV. xi. 38. 6
for dread of being *drownd,* . . . V. ii. 16. 2
there her *drowned* in the durty mud; . . . V. ii. 27. 4
in the sea him *dround.* . . . V. ii. 49. 9
thus thy better dayes are *drowned* In sad despaire, . . . V. v. 36. 4
whilest her earthly parts . . . did deeply *drowned* lie, . . . V. vii. 12. 6
Now *drowned* in the depth of sleepe all fearelesse lay. . . . VI. viii. 36. 9
mynd Dwels in deformed tabernacle *drownd,* . . . *H.B.* 142
Drowning. him strongly stayd From *drowning.* . . . II. vi. 46. 4
both from *drowning* for to save, . . . II. vi. 47. 3
them of *drowning* made affeard. . . . II. xii. 2. 9
Drowns. all his dayes he *drownes* in privitie, . . . III. ix. 3. 8
Artegall . . . *drownes* Lady Munera, . . . V. ii. Arg.
either both them *drownes,* or trayterously slaies. . . . V. ii. 8. 9
Drowsihead. The royall virgin shooke off *drousy-hed;* . . . I. ii. 7. 5
Drowsiness. when dronck with *drowsinesse* he woke, . . . III. viii. 22. 1
Drowsy. weighing down his drouping *drowsie* hedd, . . . *Gn.* 244
Morpheus . . . drowned deepe In *drowsie* fit he findes: . . . I. i. 40. 8
The day is spent; and commeth *drowsie* night, . . . I. iii. 15. 1
Uprose from *drowsie* couch, . . . II. iii. 1. 6
shaking off his *drowsy* dreriment, . . . II. vi. 27. 3
albe his *drowsy* den were next; . . . II. vii. 25. 6
in *drowsie* cave Hath long time slept, . . . III. iii. 30. 1
The *drowzie* humour of the dampish night, . . . IV. viii. 34. 4
Bad doe away the dampe of *drouzy* sleepe, . . . V. vii. 26. 8
Drudge. *Drudge* in the world, and for their living droyle, . . *Hub.* 157
Drugs. Purged from *drugs* of fowle intemperaunce: . . . II. i. 54. 8
Of deadly *drugs* I gave him drinke anon, . . . II. iv. 30. 8
Made dronke with *drugs* of deare voluptuous receipt. . . . II. v. 34. 9
Drum. Doth license him depart at sound of morning *droome.*' I. ix. 41. 9
Drunk. such as *drunke* her life the which them nurst! . . . I. i. 26. 7
*all that *drunke* thereof, did faint and feeble grow. . . . I. vii. 5. 9
*the charme and venim, which they *druncke,* . . . II. ii. 4. 6
*Made *drunke* with drugs of deare voluptuous receipt. . . . II. v. 34. 9
The which Rinaldo *drunck* in happie howre, . . . IV. iii. 45. 3
ech *drunk* an harty draught; . . . IV. iii. 48. 9
Into the river, where he *drunke* his deadly last. . . . V. vi. 39. 9
Drunken. His *dronken* corse he scarse upholden can: . . . I. iv. 22. 8
delight, Wherewith she makes her lovers *dronken* mad; . . . II. i. 52. 2
The *dronken* lamp down in the oyl did steepe, . . . III. ii. 47. 8
there the relicks of the *drunken* fray, . . . IV. i. 23. 1
sent away So many Centaures *drunken* soules to hell, . . . IV. i. 23. 4
That they may sweat, and *drunken* be withall. . . . *Epith.* 254
Druon. sterne *Druon,* and lewd Claribell, . . . IV. ix. 20. 8
Paridell and *Druon* fiercely laid At Scudamour, . . . IV. ix. 30. 3
Druon's. *Druons* delight was all in single life, . . . IV. ix. 21. 1
Paridell did take to *Druons* side, . . . IV. ix. 26. 2
Dry. He that hath seene a great Oke *drie* and dead, . . . *Ro.* xxviii. 1

Dry—*Continued.*
'All so my lustfull leafe is *drye* and sere, . . . *S.C.* Ja. 37
his moyst wings to *dry*. . . . *Mui.* 184
parching drougth *drie* up the christall wells; . . . *D.* 333
the Poplar never *dry;* . . . I. i. 8. 7
scorching Sunne does *dry* my secret vaines; . . . I. ii. 33. 8
a *dry* dropsie through his flesh did flow, . . . I. iv. 23. 7
with *dry* drops congealed in her eye, . . . II. i. 49. 3
The drops *dry* up, . . . II. iv. 35. 8
Shee ofte did bathe, and ofte againe did *dry;* . . . III. ii. 34. 7
The Land to sea, and sea to maineland *dry,* . . . III. iii. 12. 3
both did quite *drye* up and blast; . . . III. v. 48. 7
moysten their roots *dry;* . . . III. vi. 34. 8
the *drie* withered stocke it gan refresh, . . . III. viii. 25. 3
To *dry* them selves by Vulcanes flaming light, . . . III. ix. 19. 8
Doth burne the earth and boyled rivers *drie,* . . . IV. iv. 47. 2
till nought thereof be *drie,* . . . IV. ix. 33. 7
washeth Winborne meades in season *drye*. . . . IV. xi. 32. 4
usd to fish for fooles on the *dry* shore, . . . V. ix. 11. 8
And *dry* up all the water which doth ronne . . . VI. iv. 32. 8
a lewd foole her leading thorough *dry* and wet. . . . VI. vi. 16. 9
Dryads. Woodgods, and Satyres, and swift *Dryades,* . . . *Gn.* 178
Dryer. whose *dryer* braine Is tost with troubled sights . . . I. i. 42. 7
Dry-foot. his army *dry-foot* through them yod, . . . I. x. 53. 5
did on *dry-foot* pas Into old Gall, . . . IV. xi. 16. 3
Drying. The whiles his nets were *drying* on the sand. . . . III. vii. 27. 6
Dryope. His owne fayre *Dryope* now he thinkes not faire, . . . I. vi. 15. 8
Dryrihed. *See* **Drearihead.**
Dry-shod. *Dry-shod* to passe she parts the flouds in tway; . . . I. x. 20. 5
Dub. Whom she hath vow'd to *dub* a fayre Cucquold. . . . III. x. 11. 5
Du Bartas. *See* **Bartas.**
Dubbed. 'True is that I at first was *dubbed* knight . . . V. xi. 53. 1
So he him *dubbed,* . . . VI. ii. 35. 5
Ducked. th' one her selfe low *ducked* in the flood, . . . II. xii. 66. 3
through the river him have drive And *ducked* deepe; . . . VII. vi. 50. 6
Ducks. Flowne at a flush of *Ducks* foreby the brooke, . . . V. ii. 54. 2
Due. as in season *due* the husband mowes . . . *Ro.* xxx. 5
thy *due* meede that thou deservest best, . . . *Gn.* 60
punishment is *due* to the offender. . . . *Gn.* 366
Descended all from Rome by linage *due;* . . . *Gn.* 596
hope thereof to finde *due* remedie? . . . *Hub.* 57
chalenge to our selves our portions *dew* . . . *Hub.* 137
as their *due* by Nature doo it clame. . . . *Hub.* 166
unto all doth yeeld *due* curtesie; . . . *Hub.* 729
Through *due* deserts and comely carriage, . . . *Hub.* 777
with homage *due* Themselves to humble . . . *Hub.* 1082
Without regard, or *due* Decorum kept; . . . *T.M.* 214
know their names, or speak their praises *dew,* . . . *T.M.* 442
Due praise, that is the spur of dooing well? . . . *T.M.* 454
thereby wanting *due* intelligence, . . . *T.M.* 556
due reward For her prais-worthie workmanship . . . *Mui.* 267
Did surely deeme the victorie his *due:* . . . *Mui.* 319
none of all their *due* deserts resoundest.' . . . *Col.* 463
she might . . . sound their praises *dew?* . . . *Ded. Son.* xiv. 4
that new creature, borne without her *dew,* . . . I. i. 46. 6
Die is my *dew;* yet rew my wretched state, . . . I. i. 51. 7
her *dew* loves deryv'd to that vile witches shayre. . . . I. iii. 2. 9
Wont to robbe . . . poore mens boxes of their *due* reliefe, . . . I. iii. 17. 3
due recompence Of all her passed paines: . . . I. iii. 30. 1
Both those the lawrell girlonds to the victor *dew*. . . . I. v. 5. 9
thrust from heaven *dew,* . . . I. v. 42. 5
trebling the *dew* time In which the wombes of wemen . . . I. vii. 9. 6
empty sides deceived of their *dew,* . . . I. viii. 41. 4
their powres . . . With *dew* repast they had recured well, . . . I. ix. 2. 2
He pluckt from us all hope of *dew* relief, . . . I. ix. 29. 5
Is then unjust to each his *dew* to give? . . . I. ix. 38. 7
death was *dew* to him that had provokt Gods ire. . . . I. ix. 50. 9
bodies were refresht with *dew* repast, . . . I. x. 18. 2
By *dew* desert of noble chevalree, . . . I. xii. 20. 8
He shall you doe *dew* recompence agayne, . . . II. i. 14. 8
Her nathelesse Th' enchaunter . . . deckt with *dew* habiliments. . . . II. i. 22. 9
To fly the vengeaunce for his outrage *dew:* . . . II. i. 25. 4
Your court'sie takes on you anothers *dew* offence.' . . . II. i. 28. 9
play His cruell sport, in stead of sorrow *dew;* . . . II. i. 40. 6
To lett a weary wretch from her *dew* rest, . . . II. i. 47. 7
Robs reason of her *dew* regalitie, . . . II. i. 57. 5
If I, or thou, *dew* vengeaunce doe forbeare, . . . II. i. 61. 7
Had with *dew* rites and dolorous lament . . . II. ii. 1. 2
not regard *dew* right and just desarts? . . . II. ii. 29. 7
they would strive *dew* reason to exceed, . . . II. ii. 38. 6
for feare of *dew* vengeaunce Doe lurke, . . . II. iii. 14. 7
Through goodly mixture of complexions *dew;* . . . II. iii. 22. 4
That unto thee *dew* worship I may rightly frame.' . . . II. iii. 33. 9
he despisd to tread in *dew* degree, . . . II. iii. 46. 7
'Varlet, this place most *dew* to me I deeme, . . . II. iv. 40. 1
ever as he went *dew* watch upon him kept. . . . II. vii. 26. 9
partiall Paris dempt it Venus *dew,* . . . II. vii. 55. 7
dew praise or *dew* reproch them yield; . . . II. viii. 14. 8
His life for *dew* revenge should deare abye? . . . II. viii. 28. 8
to the Prince, bowing with reverence *dew* . . . II. viii. 55. 3
Suffise that I have done my *dew* in place.' . . . II. viii. 56. 6
when they rested had a season *dew,* . . . II. ix. 20. 6
in good order, and with *dew* regard; . . . II. ix. 25. 4
The knightes there entring did him reverence *dew,* . . . II. ix. 59. 1
all mens harts in *dew* obedience held; . . . II. x. 32. 5
The which was *dew* in his dead fathers daies. . . . II. x. 41. 5
raynd By *dew* successe, . . . II. x. 45. 7
Till aged Hely by *dew* heritage it gaynd. . . . II. x. 45. 9
all their Ofspring, in their *dew* descents; . . . II. x. 74. 2

Due—*Continued.*
To enter in and reape the *dew* reward. . . . III. i. 30. 8
To crowne his golden lockes with honour *dew;* . . . III. i. 35. 5
nor daunger from thy *dew* reliefe Shall me debarre: . . . III. ii. 33. 8
by *dew* degrees, and long protense, . . . III. iii. 4. 8
doe by all *dew* meanes thy destiny fulfill.' . . . III. iii. 24. 9
for their sinnes *dew* punishment . . . III. iii. 41. 8
of the time doth *dew* advauntage take. . . . III. iii. 52. 4
findeth *dew* effect or soone or late; . . . III. iv. 27. 5
the *dew* reward Of his bad deedes, . . . III. v. 14. 6
With reason *dew* the passion to subdew, . . . III. v. 44. 2
Sith I her *dew* reward cannot restore? . . . III. v. 46. 5
Till to her *dew* perfection she were ripened. . . . III. vi. 3. 9
her loose lockes to dight in order *dew* . . . III. vii. 11. 2
I woo'd her with *due* observaunce, . . . III. vii. 59. 7
To heape on him *dew* vengeaunce for his hire. . . . III. ix. 17. 5
With vigilant regard and *dew* attent, . . . III. ix. 52. 3
ne deeme my *dew* reward: . . . III. x. 31. 6
Of her *dew* honour was despoyled quight: . . . III. xii. 20. 4
To give him the reward for such vile outrage *dew*. . . . III. xii. 33. 9
Made her not yeeld so much as *due* she deemed. . . . IV. i. 8. 7
when to ripenesse *due* they growen arre, . . . IV. i. 25. 6
What vengeance *due* can equall thy desart, . . . IV. i. 53. 3
Yet was it in *due* triall but a wandring weft. . . . IV. ii. 4. 9
steale from thee the meede of thy *due* merit, . . . IV. ii. 34. 3
chalenging the Virgin as his *dew,* . . . IV. iii. 14. 8
yeeld the fayrest her *due* fee. . . . IV. v. 9. 9
as her *dew* right, It yielded was . . . IV. v. 20. 2
of *due* praise deprive. . . . IV. viii. 25. 9
Ye will recount to us in order *dew* . . . IV. ix. 40. 7
Faire lawnds, to take the sunne in season *dew;* . . . IV. x. 24. 2
In equall ballance with *due* recompence, . . . V. i. 7. 2
Thou doest not know the causes, nor their courses *dew*. . . . V. ii. 42. 9
due tryall lend Of all the rest; . . . V. iii. 8. 1
Whereof to make *due* tryall, . . . V. iii. 33. 1
Them selves thereto preparde in order *dew;* . . . V. v. 1. 7
To doe those workes to them appointed *dew;* . . . V. v. 22. 7
the honour that is *dew* To God, . . . V. x. 27. 8
her adored with *due* humblenesse . . . V. xii. 24. 7
Forget his patience, and yeeld vengeaunce *dew* . . . V. xii. 42. 4
To pay each with his owne is right and *dew;* . . . VI. i. 42. 3
With all *due* thankes and dutifull respect, . . . VI. i. 45. 7
unrighteous ire . . . had given him his owne *due* hire? . . . VI. ii. 13. 9
From that they most affect, and in *due* termes containe. . . . VI. vi. 7. 9
Therefore now yeeld . . . My *due* reward, . . . VI. vii. 15. 8
sude and sought with all the service *dew:* . . . VI. viii. 20. 6
Ne rested he himselfe, but natures *dew,* . . . VI. ix. 3. 3
did pype and sing her prayses *dew,* . . . VI. ix. 8. 6
Of forreine helpes to lifes *due* nourishment: . . . VI. ix. 20. 7
Given to Calidore as his *due* right; . . . VI. ix. 44. 7
Scarse yeelding her *due* food or timely rest, . . . VI. xi. 24. 5
With dayly service and attendance *dew,* . . . VI. xii. 5. 2
in *dew* time a mayden child forth brought: . . . VI. xii. 6. 5
for his hire to so foole-hardy *dew,* . . . VII. vi. 45. 4
Of which the greatest part is *due* to me, . . . VII. vii. 15. 4
that is onely *dew* unto thy might . . . VII. vii. 16. 3
unto mee Deriv'd by *dew* descent; . . . VII. vii. 16. 9
their *dew* places found. . . . VII. vii. 43. 9
unto me addoom that is my *dew;* . . . VII. vii. 56. 8
my toung would speak her praises *dew,* . . . *Am.* iii. 9
Shall be by him amearst with penance *dew*. . . . *Am.* lxx. 12
From mothers womb deriv'd by *dew* descent: . . . *Am.* lxxiv. 6
With strong endevour and attention *dew*. . . . *Am.* lxxx. 8
Dew to thy selfe, that it for me prepard! . . . *Am.* lxxxv. 14
For to receyve this Saynt with honour *dew,* . . . *Epith.* 208
Ye would not stay your *dew* time to expect, . . . *Epith.* 430
with *dew* fealtie Adore the powre . . . *H.B.* 270
Deigne to let fall one drop of *dew* reliefe, . . . *H.B.* 284
Into the mouth of death, to sinners *dew,* . . . *H.H.L.* 123
From thence to mount aloft, by order *dew,* . . . *H.H.B.* 24
Dueful. Right well deserved, as his *duefull* meed, . . . IV. i. 6. 3
To doe their *dueful* service, as to them befell. . . . IV. xi. 44. 9
He daily did apply him selfe to donne All *dewfull* service, . . . VI. x. 32. 6
Of my desert, or of my *dewfull* Right; . . . VII. vi. 35. 2
Duessa. 'The author . . . of all my smarts, Is one *Duessa,* . . . I. ii. 34. 8
Lyke a faire Lady, but did fowle *Duessa* hyde. . . . I. ii. 35. 9
ever false *Duessa* seemde as faire as shee. . . . I. ii. 37. 9
'Thensforth I tooke *Duessa* for my Dame, . . . I. ii. 40. 1
false *Duessa,* . . . Heard how in vaine Fradubio did lament, . . . I. ii. 44. 1
To sinfull hous of Pryde *Duessa* Guydes . . . I. iv. Arg.
false *Duessa* in her sted had borne, . . . I. iv. 2. 3
Thether *Duessa* badd him bend his pace, . . . I. iv. 3. 7
false *Duessa* seeming Lady fayre, . . . I. iv. 13. 2
to *Duess'* each one himselfe did payne All kindnesse . . . I. iv. 15. 3
Emongst the rest rode . . . The foule *Duessa,* . . . I. iv. 37. 5
Uprose *Duessa* from her resting place, . . . I. iv. 44. 8
his . . . foe; Whom false *Duessa* saves, . . . I. v. Arg.
in all mens open vew *Duessa* placed is, . . . I. v. 5. 7
lowd to him gan call The false *Duessa,* . . . I. v. 11. 9
In haste *Duessa* from her place arose, . . . I. v. 14. 1
Duessa wept full bitterly. . . . I. v. 17. 9
So wept *Duessa* untill eventyde, . . . I. v. 19. 1
when she saw *Duessa,* sunny bright, . . . I. v. 21. 1
She stayd; and foorth *Duessa* gan proceede: . . . I. v. 22. 1
'I, that do seeme not I, *Duessa* ame,' . . . I. v. 26. 6
Duessa I, the daughter of Deceipt and Shame.' . . . I. v. 26. 9
The false *Duessa* . . . Returnd to stately pallace . . . I. v. 45. 1
speed The fayre *Duess'* had forst him leave behind; . . . I. vi. 2. 2
The false *Duessa,* cloked with Fidessaes name. . . . I. vii. 1. 9
Duessa loud to him gan crye, . . . I. vii. 14. 4

Duessa—*Continued.*	
From that day forth *Duessa* was his deare,	I. vii. 16. 1
Upon this dreadfull Beast . . . He sett the false *Duessa,*	I. vii. 18. 9
him chaunced false *Duessa* meete,	I. vii. 50. 6
Arthure . . . strips *Duessa* quight.	I. viii. Arg.
Where he with his *Duessa* dalliaunce fownd,	I. viii. 5. 5
after him the proud *Duessa* came,	I. viii. 6. 1
That when his deare *Duessa* heard,	I. viii. 12. 1
The proud *Duessa,* full of wrathful spight,	I. viii. 13. 1
Whose grievous fall when false *Duessa* spyde,	I. viii. 25. 1
such the sight Of fowle *Duessa,*	I. viii. 49. 5
sold thy selfe to serve *Duessa* vild,	I. ix. 46. 8
false *Duessa,* . . . Her false sleightes doe imploy.	I. xii. Arg.
Most false *Duessa,* royall richly dight,	I. xii. 32. 4
under simple shew, and semblant plaine, Lurkt false *Duessa*	II. i. 21. 4
Duessa discord breedes Twixt Scudamour and Blandamour:	IV. i. Arg.
The one of them the false *Duessa* hight,	IV. i. 18. 1
Her false *Duessa,* . . . raised from below	IV. i. 19. 5
Such was that hag which with *Duessa* roade;	IV. i. 31. 1
Faithlesse *Duessa,* and false Paridell,	IV. i. 32. 8
'Ah gentle knight!' then false *Duessa* sayd,	IV. i. 46. 1
So false *Duessa;* but vile Ate thus:	IV. i. 47. 1
'Fy, fy! false knight,' (then false *Duessa* cryde)	IV. i. 51. 6
did Paridell produce His false *Duessa,*	IV. v. 11. 2
through lewd upbraide Of Ate and *Duessa,*	IV. ix. 24. 6
First gan he tell how this . . . *Duessa* hight;	V. ix. 40. 2
That false *Duessa,* which had wrought great care	V. ix. 40. 3
false *Duessa,* now untitled Queene,	V. ix. 42. 8
her doome a-rights Against *Duessa,* damned by them all;	V. x. 4. 4
Duessa's. I the . . . roote of *Duessaes* race.	I. v. 27. 7
Duessaes traines and Malecastaes champions are defaced.	III. i. Arg.
Duest. driven downe to hell, his *dewest* meed:	*Hub.* 1237
Dug. from tender *dug* of commune nourse	II. iv. 18. 3
Dugs. yong ones, . . . Sucking upon her poisnous *dugs;*	I. i. 15. 6
Her dried *dugs,* lyke bladders lacking wind, Hong downe,	I. viii. 47. 6
Duke. the Troyan *Duke* with Turnus fought.	*Bel.*[1] vii. 8
Dulcet. Their daintie layes and *dulcet* melody,	III. i. 40. 4
Dull. With troublous noyse did *dull* their daintie eares.	*T.M.* 30
with shrilling cryes Pierce the *dull* heavens	*T.M.* 118
My spirits now dismayd with sorrow *dull*	*T.M.* 291
Dull Poppie, and drink-quickning Setuale,	*Mui.* 196
'Yet doth not my *dull* wit well understand	*D.* 176
O, . . . sharpen my *dull* tong!	I. Pr. 2. 9
dull wearines of former fight Having yrockt asleepe	I. i. 55. 4
busying . . . his *dull* eares to heare what shee did tell;	I. ii. 26. 7
by her hellish science raisd . . . a *dull* blast,	I. ii. 38. 6
with . . . piteous plaintes, she filleth his *dull* eares,	I. iii. 44. 2
melody, To drive away the *dull* melancholy;	I. v. 3. 5
Thenceforth her waters wexed *dull* and slow,	I. vii. 5. 8
His sad *dull* eies, deepe sunck in hollow pits,	I. viii. 41. 1
his hollow eyne Lookt deadly *dull,*	I. ix. 35. 7
opened his *dull* eyes, that light mote in them shine.	I. x. 18. 9
To drive away the *dull* Melancholy;	I. xii. 38. 8
quickned the *dull* spright with musical comfort.	II. v. 31. 9
Through the *dull* billowes thicke as troubled mire,	II. vi. 20. 7
on the *dull* waves did lightly flote,	II. vi. 38. 3
he fownd in that *dull* ford The carefull servaunt	II. vi. 47. 8
fog over-spred With his *dull* vapour all that desert	II. xii. 34. 6
Thou in *dull* corners doest thy selfe inclose;	III. ii. 31. 5
Ne did she let *dull* sleepe once to relent,	III. vii. 2. 3
Lightly she leaped . . . From her *dull* horse,	III. vii. 25. 8
Downe hanging his *dull* head with heavy chere,	III. xii. 16. 3
Demogorgon, in *dull* darknesse pent	IV. ii. 47. 7
wearied his life with *dull* delayes.	III. xii. 44. *or.* 4
with *dull* countenance and with dolefull spright	V. xii. 12. 3
With her *dull* eyes did seeme to looke askew,	V. xii. 29. 2
the *dull* drops, that . . . did adown distill.	VII. vii. 31. 4
Dulled. lowd plaints have *duld* mine eares;	*D.* 415
The deadly dint his *dulled* sences all dismaid.	I. xi. 35. 9
Therewith their *dulled* sprights they edgd anew,	IV. ii. 17. 6
restore His weakned powers, and *dulled* spirits whet,	IV. iii. 24. 4
Till she had *duld* the sting which in her tongs end grew.	IV. viii. 36. 9
Looke up at last, and wake thy *dulled* spirit	V. v. 36. 8
chears my *dulled* spright.	VI. Pr. 1. 9
Titans beames . . . in darkenesse, *duld* with yron rust,	VI. iii. 13. 7
T' illuminate my dim and *dulled* eyne,	*H.B.* 20
their points rebutted backe againe Are *duld,*	*H.H.B.* 123
Duller. The *duller* earth it quickneth with delight,	*H.B.* 51
Duly. That *dewly* adayes counts mine.	*S.C.* Mar. 42
duly everie day Their service . . . to say,	*Hub.* 449
duly to encline My wits theretoo,	*Hub.* 548
Demaunds a yeare it *duly* to display.	*Col.* 595
Hermite *dewly* wont to say His holy thinges	I. i. 34. 6
they watch and *dewly* ward,	II. viii. 2. 6
Day and night *duely* keeping watch and ward;	II. ix. 25. 2
Yet Britomart attended *duly* on her,	IV. i. 8. 8
with their owne repayed *duely* weare,	IV. ix. 30. 8
day and night did watch and *duely* ward	IV. x. 17. 2
many a pretty Page Attended *duely,*	IV. xi. 29. 2
duely did attend Uppon the rites and daily sacrifize,	V. vii. 4. 2
every day them *duely* drest.	VI. vi. 2. 9
Appointed to attend her *dewly* day and night.	VI. xii. 14. 9
nor her golden haire Into their comely tresses *dewly* drest,	VI. xii. 15. 4
duly her attended day and night;	VII. vi. 9. 4
equall gave to each as Justice *duly* scann'd.	VII. vii. 38. 9
With which my love should *duly* have been dect,	*Epith.* 428
duly well observed his beheast;	*H.L.* 93
Dumarin. an earthly peare, The famous *Dumarin;*	III. iv. 19. 6
Dumb. stood still mute, as if he had beene *dum,*	IV. vii. 44. 2
Dumpish. 'Sir knight, why ride ye *dumpish* thus behind,	IV. ii. 5. 7
Bids all old thoughts to die in *dumpish* spright:	*Am.* iv. 4
Dumps. But sudden *dumps,* . . . my torment feed.	*Am.* iii. 11
Dun. I am a poore sheepe, albe my coloure *donne,*	*S.C.* May 266
Dung. had behind A foxes taile, with *dong* all fowly dight;	I. viii. 48. 4
make his carkas as the outcast *dong?*	II. viii. 28. 5
that golden pray, . . . I loath as *doung,*	III. x. 31. 6
Dungeon. in a *dungeon* deepe huge nombers lay	I. v. 45. 8
They were . . . Condemned to that *Dongeon* mercilesse,	I. v. 46. 8
thousands moe the like that did that *dongeon* fill.	I. v. 50. 9
most of all, which in that *dongeon* lay,	I. v. 51. 5
in a *Dongeon* deepe him threw without remorse.	I. vii. 15. 9
darknesse he in deepest *dongeon* drove,	I. vii. 23. 3
now in darkesome *dungeon,* wretched thrall,	I. vii. 51. 7
she it is, that did my Lord . . . deepe in *dongeon* lay,	I. viii. 28. 7
Witnes the *dungeon* (**dongeon*) deepe, wherein	I. ix. 45. 5
they him layd full low in *dungeon* deepe,	I. xii. 36. 1
Downe in a *Dongeon* deepe he let her fall,	III. viii. 41. 8
Hath in a *dungeon* deepe her close embard,	III. xi. 16. 8
Him wretched thrall unto his *dongeon* brought,	IV. viii. 51. 8
suffred that same Dwarfe me to her *dongeon* drive.	IV. viii. 56. 9
Her threw into a *dongeon* deepe and blind,	IV. xi. 2. 4
The *dongeon* was, in which her bound he left,	IV. xi. 3. 2
Deliver hence out of this *dungeon* strong,	IV. xii. 9. 4
How from that *dungeon* he might her enlarge.	IV. xii. 14. 2
them in *dongeon* deepe . . . cruelly he threw;	VI. xii. 5. 6
Dungeons. them to hellish *dungeons* downe hast feld.	VII. vi. 27. 8
Dunghill. As cocke on his *dunghill* crowing cranck.	*S.C.* S. 46
Ne ever dare their *dunghill* thoughts aspire	*T.M.* 393
A *Donghill* of dead carcases he spyde;	I. v. 53. 8
'The *donghill* kinde Delightes in filth	II. xii. 87. 6
the dearest to his *dounghill* minde,	III. x. 15. 8
Be arguments of a vile *donghill* mind,	VI. vii. 1. 6
His *dunghill* thoughts . . . themselves enure To dirtie drosse,	*H.L.* 183
Dunvallo. *See* **Donwallo.**	
Durable. More firme and *durable* then steele or brasse,	*H.H.B.* 153
Durance. and time in *durance,* shall outweare;	*S.C.* Env. 2
captived in endlesse *duraunce* Of sorrow	III. v. 42. 8
Seeing her weake and wan through *durance* long.	VI. xii. 11. 6
long ygo, Whilest ye in *durance* dwelt,	VI. xii. 17. 6
Durefull. neither pretious stone, nor *durefull* brasse,	IV. x. 39. 4
The *durefull* Oake, whose sap is not yet dride,	*Am.* vi. 5
Duress. food which in her *duresse* she had found;	IV. viii. 19. 6
Do you by *duresse* him compell thereto,	IV. xii. 10. 5
During. *During* the time of that her widowhead:	*T.M.* 240
During which time her gentle wit she plyes	I. vi. 19. 5
During which time, . . . Shee him instructed	I. x. 45. 3
during their quiet treague,	II. ii. 33. 3
during life will never be appeasd!'	II. iv. 33. 6
During which time her powre she did display	II. x. 20. 5
during their pupillage;	II. x. 64. 3
During which worke the Lady of the Lake,	III. iii. 10. 6
during eight yeares space,	III. iii. 41. 2
during this their most obscuritee;	III. iii. 44. 8
During which time the Chorle,	III. vii. 15. 6
during the whyle That he there sojourned	III. x. 5. 5
So did they surely *during* all their dayes,	IV. ii. 54. 1
During which space these sory eies have seen	IV. vii. 13. 4
all her land and lordship *during* life.	IV. ix. 15. 8
during Saturnes ancient raigne	V. Pr. 9. 1
During which time the warlike Amazon,	V. v. 26. 7
During all which, those knights continu'd	V. x. 5. 1
During which time that he did there remayne,	V. xii. 26. 1
During which time that wyld man did apply	VI. iv. 16. 1
During which time he did her entertaine	VI. ix. 34. 5
During which space that she thus sicke did lie,	VI. xi. 9. 1
What did betide . . . *During* his absence,	VI. xii. 14. 4
Durst. Ne *durst* againe his fyrye face out showe:	*S.C.* Ap. 78
I *durst* in derring-doe compare With shepheards swayne	*S.C.* D. 43
durst those lowest shadowes goe to see,	*Gn.* 438
none *durst* speake, ne none *durst* of him plaine,	*Hub.* 1199
none *durst* vewe the horror of his face,	*Ti.* 535
Durst not adventure such unknowen wayes,	*Col.* 670
of those fearfull women none *durst* rize,	I. iii. 19. 2
hee *durst* not show Him selfe too nigh at hand,	I. iii. 26. 3
visage . . . That Phoebus chearefull face *durst* never vew,	I. v. 20. 2
erthly wight that with the Night *durst* ride.	I. v. 32. 9
he *durst* not byde,	I. vi. 8. 8
His living like saw never living eye, Ne *durst* behold:	I. vii. 8. 8
faine have fled, ne *durst* approchen neare;	I. ix. 34. 8
What stately building *durst* so high extend	I. x. 56. 7
the ever damned Beast *Durst* not approch,	I. xi. 49. 2
Durst not approch for dread which she misdeemd;	I. xi. 55. 4
Ne *durst* approch him nigh to touch, or once assay.	I. xii. 9. 9
durst he nott Pursew her steps	II. iii. 43. 2
never entraunce any *durst* pretend,	II. xi. 15. 8
none of all the six before him *durst* assay.	III. i. 21. 9
None of them rashly *durst* to her approch,	III. i. 64. 7
Ne *durst* adventure rashly in to wend,	III. iii. 14. 2
none *durst* passen through that perilous glade:	III. iv. 21. 5
His caytive thought *durst* not so high aspire:	III. vii. 16. 5
Ne *durst* assay to wade the perlous seas,	III. vii. 28. 3
The fearefull Chorle *durst* not gainesay nor dooe,	III. viii. 13. 1
That beautie *durst* presume to violate,	III. viii. 36. 2
none him *durst* awake out of his dreme;	III. ix. 10. 6
a dogge . . . That *durst* not barke;	III. ix. 14. 8
durst not for dread approchen nie,	III. x. 22. 2
loth, yet *durst* he not gainesay,	III. x. 23. 8
durst he not against it doe or say,	III. x. 45. 3

Durst—*Continued.*
That none *durst* ever whilest thou wast alive, . . . IV. ii. 34. 4
none of them *durst* undertake the fight; . . . IV. ii. 40. 4
'Bold Fay, that *durst* Come see the secret of the life of man, . IV. ii. 49. 6
none against them battell *durst* maintaine: . . . IV. iv. 25. 5
none of them in field *durst* stand, . . . IV. iv. 43. 3
Yet *durst* he not make love so suddenly, . . . IV. vi. 33. 1
He *durst* not nigh approch, but kept aloofe, . . . IV. vii. 37. 4
Durst not the sternnesse of his looke abide; . . . IV. x. 18. 3
Ne ever *durst* her eyes from ground upreare, . . . IV. x. 50. 2
durst he not his mother disobay, . . . IV. xii. 18. 6
durst he not the warrant to withstand, . . . IV. xii. 33. 1
durst withstand His dreadfull heast, . . . V. i. 8. 6
durst the depth of any water sownd. . . . V. ii. 16. 7
Ne any of them *durst* come in his way, . . . V. ii. 53. 7
none Against them *durst* his head to perill shew. . . . V. iii. 12. 7
Yet *durst* she not disclose her fancies wound, . . . V. v. 44. 1
Durst not endure their sight, . . . V. viii. 36. 9
Durst not abide, but fled away for feare, . . . V. x. 38. 3
streight commaundement . . . Which none *durst* breake, . . . V. xii. 10. 5
Not one was left that *durst* her once have disobayd. . . . V. xii. 25. 9
For he *durst* not abide with Calidore to fight. . . . VI. iii. 25. 9
Ne scarse wyld beasts *durst* come, . . . VI. iv. 13. 9
durst so boldly . . . Into his Lords forbidden hall to passe? . VI. vi. 20. 3
Durst not the furie of his force abyde, . . . VI. vi. 28. 2
Yet *durst* he not for very cowardize Effect the same, . . . VI. vi. 44. 6
durst her dreaded reskue enterprize, . . . VI. viii. 18. 7
she, for nought . . . One word *durst* speake, . . . VI. viii. 50. 9
He *durst* not enter into th' open greene, . . . VI. x. 11. 1
Ne *durst* abide the daunger of the end; . . . VI. x. 35. 4
Coridon *durst* not with him consort, . . . VI. xi. 42. 8
Ne *durst* abide behind, for dread of worse effort. . . . VI. xi. 42. 9
Ne ever any *durst* till then impose; . . . VI. xii. 36. 3
Yet *durst* he not draw backe, . . . VI. xii. 36. 6
(which none yet *durst* Of Gods or men to alter . . . VII. vi. 5. 5
In his *Foules parley durst* not with it mel, . . . VII. vii. 9. 5

Duskish. smouldry cloud of *duskish* stincking smoke; . . . I. vii. 13. 8
Enrold in *duskish* smoke and brimstone blew: . . . I. xi. 44. 4

Dust. With sodaine falling broken all to *dust*. . . . *Bel.*[1] iv. 14
I saw hir bodie turned all to *dust*, . . . *Bel.*[1] vi. 12
With sodain fall to *dust* consumed quight. . . . *Bel.*[2] iv. 14
Out of her *dust* like to a worm arise. . . . *Bel.*[2] vii. 14
Into a clowde of *dust* sperst in the aire . . . *Bel.*[2] xiv. 13
In spight of time out of the *dust* doth reare, . . . *Ro.* v. 13
Lyft up thy selfe out of the lowly *dust*, . . . *S.C.* O. 38
Is faded quite, and into *dust* ygoe. . . . *S.C.* N. 76
downe in *dust* prostrate, . . . *Gn.* 558
dwell in *dust* inglorious and bace, . . . *Hub.* 981
they that dwell in lowly *dust*, . . . *T.M.* 67
out of *dust* their memories awake? . . . *T.M.* 450
All those (O pitie!) now are turnd to *dust*, . . . *Ti.* 97
sleepes in *dust*, dead and inglorious, . . . *Ti.* 355
the *dust*, to which the Oetaean wood Had him consum'd, . . . *Ti.* 381
I saw this Towre fall sodainelie to *dust*, . . . *Ti.* 517
soild with *dust* of the long dried way; . . . I. vi. 35. 2
him to *dust* thought to have battred quight, . . . I. vii. 14. 3
transmew . . . stones to *dust*, and *dust* to nought at all; . I. vii. 35. 7
round about a cloud of *dust* did fly, . . . II. iv. 37. 4
The smouldring *dust* did rownd about him smoke, . . . II. v. 3. 4
thus low me laid in *dust*.' . . . II. v. 12. 9
His sandy lockes, . . . Knotted in blood and *dust*, . . . II. v. 14. 5
glistring glosse, darkned with filthy *dust*, . . . II. vii. 4. 3
him that low in *dust* doth ly, . . . II. vii. 11. 7
overgrowne with *dust* and old decay, . . . II. vii. 29. 2
The driest wood is soonest burnt to *dust*. . . . III. viii. 25. 5
Troy againe out of her *dust* was reard . . . III. ix. 44. 3
I tread in *dust* thee and thy money both, . . . III. x. 29. 8
Troden in *dust* with fury insolent, . . . III. xi. 52. 8
For hast did over-runne, in *dust* enrould: . . . IV. iii. 41. 5
seem'd to *dust* he shortly would it drive: . . . IV. v. 37. 6
they into *dust* shall vade. . . . V. ii. 40. 5
trampled downe in *dust* his thoughts disdained scorne. . . . V. viii. 31. 9
By whom my spirit out of *dust* was raysed: . . . *Am.* lxxiv. 10
let baser things devize To dy in *dust*, . . . *Am.* lxxv. 10
Lifting himselfe out of the lowly *dust* . . . *H.L.* 177
Shall turne to *dust*, and loose their goodly light. . . . *H.B.* 98
rod . . . With which he bruseth all his foes to *dust*, . . . *H.H.B.* 156

Dusty. Which now their *dusty* reliques do bewray; . . . *Ro.* xv. 4
forth she beates the *dusty* path: . . . III. iv. 12. 8
From off their dainty limbs the *dusty* sweat . . . III. vi. 17. 6
Lightly upstarted from the *dustie* ground, . . . III. vii. 7. 5
Sate downe upon the *dusty* ground anon; . . . III. vii. 10. 8

Duties. with last *duties* of this broken verse, . . . *Ti.* 678
He lives that shall him pay his *dewties* last, . . . I. iv. 49. 8
skill it is such *duties* timely to bestow. . . . VI. ii. 1. 9

Dutiful. He did her service *dewtifull*, . . . III. x. 9. 2
With all due thankes and *dutifull* respect, . . . VI. i. 45. 7

Duty. Those for Gods sake his *dewty* was to entertaine. . . . I. x. 37. 9
Did *dewty* to their Lady, as became; . . . II. ix. 28. 7
Endite I would as *dewtie* doth excyte; . . . III. ii. 3. 5
I have forbore this *duetie* to fulfill; . . . V. v. 41. 3
Dare not henceforth, above the bounds of *dewtie*, . . . *Am.* lxi. 3
whose soverayne grace and kindly *dewty* . . . *H.B.* 17
And learne to love, with zealous humble *dewty*, . . . *H.H.B.* 20

Dwarf. Behind her farre away a *Dwarfe* did lag, . . . I. i. 6. 1
to the *Dwarfe* a while his needlesse spere he gave. . . . I. i. 11. 9
'Fly, fly!' (quoth then The fearefull *Dwarfe*) . . . I. i. 13. 9
The *dwarfe* him brought his steed; . . . I. ii. 6. 9
Lookt for her knight, . . . And for her *dwarfe*, . . . I. ii. 7. 8
Bidding the *dwarfe* . . . to bring away The Sarazins shield, . I. ii. 20. 6
his wary *Dwarfe* had spyde . . . I. v. 45. 7

Dwarf—*Continued.*
Whose case whenas the careful *Dwarfe* had tould, . . . I. v. 52. 1
The wofull *Dwarfe*, which saw his maisters fall . . . I. vii. 19. 1
when her eyes she on the *Dwarfe* had set, . . . I. vii. 20. 5
Then gan the *Dwarfe* the whole discourse declare; . . . I. vii. 26. 1
the *Dwarfe* the way to her assynd; . . . I. vii. 28. 4
forth they went, the *Dwarfe* them guiding ever right. . . . I. vii. 52. 9
Then cryde the *Dwarfe*, 'Lo! yonder is the same, . . . I. viii. 2. 3
He met a *Dwarfe* that seemed terrifyde . . . III. v. 3. 3
The *Dwarfe* him answerd; . . . III. v. 4. 2
Dwarfe, aread what is that Lady bright . . . III. v. 7. 7
'*Dwarfe*, comfort to thee take, . . . III. v. 11. 6
So with the *Dwarfe* he back retourn'd againe, . . . III. v. 12. 1
Bearing a litle *Dwarfe* before his steed, . . . IV. viii. 38. 3
both Squire and *dwarfe* did tomble downe . . . IV. viii. 42. 8
that same *dwarfe* right sorie seem'd and sad, . . . IV. viii. 46. 3
Which keeper is this *Dwarfe*, . . . IV. viii. 54. 5
till that the *Dwarfe* did me reveale, . . . IV. viii. 55. 5
suffred that same *Dwarfe* me to her dongeon drive. . . . IV. viii. 56. 9
The *Dwarfe* cald at the doore of Amyas . . . IV. viii. 59. 2
her *Dwarfe*, which had me in his charge, . . . IV. viii. 61. 2
if that *Dwarfe* I could with me convay, . . . IV. viii. 61. 8
his *Dwarfe*, though with unwilling ayd, . . . IV. ix. 5. 3
tooke he that same *Dwarfe*, . . . IV. ix. 8. 1
He chaunst to meet a *Dwarfe* in hasty course, . . . V. ii. 2. 2
Loth was the *Dwarfe*, yet did he stay perforse, . . . V. ii. 2. 5
For this was Dony, Florimels owne *Dwarfe*, . . . V. ii. 3. 1
a *Dwarfe* she cald to her in hast, . . . VI. i. 29. 1
The *Dwarfe* his way did hast, . . . VI. i. 30. 1
The *Dwarfe*, which bore that message to her knight, . . . VI. i. 31. 3

Dwell. you Virgins, that on Parnasse *dwell*, . . . *S.C.* Ap. 41
'Ye shepheards daughters, that *dwell* on the greene, . . . *S.C.* Ap. 127
systers nyne, which *dwell* on Parnasse hight, . . . *S.C.* Jun. 28
they *dwell* (As goteheards wont) upon a hill, . . . *S.C.* Jul. 46
Here will I *dwell* apart . . . *S.C.* Au. 169
Ne wont with crabbed care the Muses *dwell*: . . . *S.C.* O. 101
wets the little plants that lowly *dwell*. . . . *S.C.* N. 32
all we *dwell* in deadly night. . . . *S.C.* N. 69
love then in the Lyons house did *dwell*) . . . *S.C.* D. 57
Here Fabii and Decii doo *dwell*, . . . *Gn.* 599
dwell in dust inglorious and bace, . . . *Hub.* 981
made them *dwell* in darknes of disgrace; . . . *Hub.* 1187
they that *dwell* in lowly dust, . . . *T.M.* 67
To *dwell* in darkenesse without sovenance? . . . *T.M.* 486
With fearfull fiends, that in deep darknes *dwell*. . . . *Ti.* 126
to give them light Which *dwell* in darknes, . . . *D.* 479
made me in that desart chose to *dwell*. . . . *Col.* 91
world . . . In which I saw no living people *dwell*. . . . *Col.* 231
Where cold and care and penury do *dwell*, . . . *Col.* 657
There, in deede, *dwel* faire Graces many one, . . . *Ded. Son.* v. 9
daunger, which hereby doth *dwell*, . . . I. i. 31. 1
friendlesse, unfortunate, Now miserable I, Fidessa, *dwell*, . I. ii. 26. 2
He in great passion al this while did dwell, . . . I. ii. 26. 5
'Are you in this misformed hous to *dwell?*' . . . I. ii. 43. 2
thundring Jove, that high in heaven doth *dwell* . . . I. iv. 11. 5
he no lenger would There *dwell* . . . I. v. 52. 4
She, more amazd, in double dread doth *dwell*; . . . I. vi. 10. 1
The sacred Nymph, which therein wont to *dwell*, . . . I. vii. 4. 8
people . . . Which in that stately building wont to *dwell*: . I. viii. 32. 4
Them list no lenger there at leasure *dwell*, . . . I. ix. 2. 4
whether dread did *dwell* Or anguish in her hart, . . . I. x. 14. 4
Wherein eternall peace and happinesse doth *dwell*. . . . I. x. 55. 9
For those to *dwell* in that are chosen his, . . . I. x. 57. 3
In which that fairest Faery Queene doth *dwell*, . . . I. x. 58. 3
the place where all our perilles *dwell*; . . . I. xi. 2. 2
clapt his yron wings as victor he did *dwell*. . . . I. xi. 31. 9
it may *dwell* In her sonnes flesh, . . . II. ii. 10. 7
The house was raysd, and all that in did *dwell*. . . . II. ii. 20. 7
in waves, in warres, she wonts to *dwell*, . . . II. iii. 41. 1
in which Doth sober Alma *dwell*, . . . II. ix. Arg.
Came to the Ladies eare which there did *dwell*, . . . II. ix. 17. 6
These three in these three rowmes did sondry *dwell*, . . . II. ix. 48. 8
T' afflict the creatures which therein did *dwell*; . . . II. xii. 51. 6
Nor guidaunce of herselfe in her did *dwell*: . . . III. ii. 49. 3
Under what coast of heaven the man did *dwell*, . . . III. iii. 6. 5
In which the Gods doe *dwell* eternally; . . . III. iv. 43. 5
There let her with the damned spirits *dwell*, . . . III. iv. 60. 8
knowledge of those woods where he did *dwell*, . . . III. v. 14. 3
Sith that in salvage forests she did *dwell*, . . . III. vi. 1. 4
Wher most she wonnes when she on earth does *dwell*; . . . III. vi. 29. 2
In which a witch did *dwell*, . . . III. vii. 6. 4
'Therein a cancred crabbed Carle does *dwell*, . . . III. ix. 3. 5
In dolefull thraldome all his dayes to *dwell?* . . . III. ix. 8. 3
the fresh Swayne would not his leasure *dwell*, . . . III. x. 38. 7
in that wastefull wildernesse . . . many dangers *dwell*; . . . III. x. 40. 4
it was he which by her side did *dwell*; . . . III. x. 49. 5
in his stead let Love for ever *dwell*; . . . III. xi. 2. 2
Faire Amorett must *dwell* in wicked chaines, . . . III. xi. 24. 3
As if but one soule in them all did *dwell*, . . . IV. ii. 43. 3
in the midst thereof did horror *dwell*, . . . IV. xi. 4. 1
his neighbour floods which nigh him *dwell*, . . . IV. xi. 30. 1
wonned there where now Yorke people *dwell*; . . . IV. xi. 37. 5
Astraea here mongst earthly men did *dwell*, . . . V. i. 5. 8
mongst wyld beasts, and salvage woods, to *dwell*; . . . V. ix. 1. 5
the rocke, in which he wonts to *dwell*, . . . V. ix. 6. 2
from forrein land where they did *dwell*, . . . V. x. 6. 3
came to this, where Belge then did *dwell* . . . V. x. 11. 5
Ye sacred imps, that on Parnasso *dwell*, . . . VI. Pr. 2. 2
Faire Lords and Ladies which about you *dwell*, . . . VI. Pr. 7. 8
all this while did *dwell* In dread of death, . . . VI. i. 43. 1
For love amongst the woodie Gods to *dwell*) . . . VI. ii. 26. 3

Dwell—*Continued.*
here doe *dwell* at ease, . . . VI. ix. 19. 2
So there that night Sir Calidore did *dwell,* . . . VI. ix. 34. 1
of all the rest which there did *dwell,* . . . VI. ix. 46. 5
the Graces, that here wont to *dwell,* . . . VI. x. 26. 7
with such damned fiends she should in darknesse *dwell.* . . . VI. x. 43. 9
There they a while together thus did *dwell* . . . VI. xii. 11. 7
the whiles in prison she did *dwell.* . . . VI. xii. 15. 9
damned ghosts which *dwell* For aye in darkenesse, . . . VI. xii. 35. 7
The pure well head of Poesie did *dwell*) . . . VII. vii. 9. 4
all things else that under heaven *dwell* . . . VII. vii. 48. 2
Fayth doth fearlesse *dwell* in brasen towre, . . . *Am.* lxv. 13
forme, which now doth *dwell* In his high thought, . . . *H.L.* 193
Where they in darknesse and dread horror *dwell,* . . . *H.H.L.* 90
Him, wretch, in doole would let no lenger *dwell,* . . . *H.H.L.* 131
foule which in his flood did *dwell* . . . *Proth.* 119
that great Lord, which therein wont to *dwell,* . . . *Proth.* 139
Dwelled. The hylls where *dwelled* holy saints . . . *S.C.* Jul. 113
Where they for ever incorrupted *dweld:* . . . II. ix. 56. 7
Dwellers. *See* **In-dwellers.**
Dwelleth. *dwelleth* here Within this castle wall a Lady fayre, . III. i. 26. 1
Dwelling. 'in wastfull wildernesse His *dwelling* is, . . . I. i. 32. 2
where dawning day doth never peepe, His *dwelling* is; . . . I. i. 39. 6
His *dwelling* is low in a valley greene, . . . I. ix. 4. 5
they come where that same wicked wight His *dwelling* has, I. ix. 33. 2
Within a wandring Island . . . her *dwelling* is. . . . II. i. 51. 6
For there their *dwelling* was. . . . II. iii. 24. 6
Thy *dwelling* is in Herebus black hous, . . . III. iv. 55. 6
Where was their *dwelling,* in a pleasant glade . . . III. v. 39. 2
by adventure brought Unto your *dwelling,* . . . III. vii. 8. 8
Hard by the gates of hell her *dwelling* is; . . . IV. i. 20. 1
Farre under ground . . . their dreadfull *dwelling* is. . . . IV. ii. 47. 9
to guide the way Unto the *dwelling* of that Amazone: . . . V. iv. 35. 6
little wide by West, His *dwelling* was, . . . V. vi. 22. 5
her *dwelling* Was neare to Envie, . . . V. xii. 35. 5
the image of her former dread, Yet *dwelling* in her eye, . . . VI. viii. 31. 7
wisht that with that shepheard he mote *dwelling* share. . . . VI. x. 30. 9
The *dwelling* of these shepheards did invade, . . . VI. x. 39. 7
Unto their *dwelling* did them close convay. . . . VI. x. 41. 5
Their *dwelling* in a little Island was, . . . VI. x. 41. 6
Dwelling-place. To weet if *dwelling place* were nigh at hand; I. iii. 11. 2
The enimies of Temperaunce Besiege her *dwelling place:* . . II. xi. Arg.
eke the fastnesse of his *dwelling place,* . . . V. ix. 5. 2
To understand that villeins *dwelling place,* . . . V. ix. 7. 2
Dwelling-places. evermore exchange Their *dwelling places,* . . VII. vii. 21. 6
Dwellings. hath our *dwellings* raced . . . *T.M.* 268
Out of the *dwellings* of the damned sprights, . . . IV. i. 19. 8
Dwells. With them that cruell Colchid mother *dwells,* . . . *Gn.* 397
Where Pleasure *dwelles* in sensuall delights, . . . II. xii. 1. 8
The world in darknes *dwels;* . . . III. iv. 13. 3
There *dwels* he ever, miserable swaine, . . . III. x. 60. 5
magnanimity *Dwels* in thy bounteous brest! . . . III. xi. 19. 3
in base mind nor friendship *dwels* nor enmity. . . . IV. iv. 11. 9
to his daughter brings, that *dwels* thereby; . . . V. ii. 9. 2
There *dwels* sweet love, and constant chastity, . . . *Epith.* 191
mynd *Dwels* in deformed tabernacle drownd, . . . *H.B.* 142
Dwelt. in a siege seaven yeres about me *dwelt.* . . . *Ti.* 105
the cave in which he lurking *dwelt,* . . . *Mui.* 358
On top whereof ay *dwelt* the ghastly Owle, . . . I. ix. 33. 6
mighty man of God . . . *Dwelt* forty daies . . . I. x. 53. 6
Therein three sisters *dwelt* . . . II. ii. 13. 1
there *dwelt* three honorable sages, . . . II. ix. 47. 8
far in land a salvage nation *dwelt* . . . II. x. 7. 1
the sted Whereas those Mermayds *dwelt:* . . . II. xii. 30. 2
Where daungers *dwelt,* and perils most did wonne, . . . III. i. 3. 2
in her countenaunce *Dwelt* simple truth . . . III. vii. 59. 6
like two senceles stocks in long embracement *dwelt.* . . . III. xii. 45. *or.* 9
that same soule which therein *dwelt* . . . IV. iii. 22. 1
seemed some blacksmith *dwelt* in that desert ground. . . . IV. v. 33. 9
darknesse and dread horrour where she *dwelt,* . . . IV. vii. 9. 7
Within the land where *dwelt* that Ladie sad; . . . V. x. 18. 2
a noble Lord Which *dwelt* thereby, . . . VI. iii. 7. 2
this fresh young Knight who *dwelt* her ny, . . . VI. iii. 7. 5
in her soveraine lyking he *dwelt* evermore . . . VI. v. 12. 9
There *dwelt* a salvage nation, . . . VI. viii. 35. 2
Through all the inner parts, wherein they *dwelt;* . . . VI. x. 42. 6
long ygo, Whilest ye in durance *dwelt,* . . . VI. xii. 17. 6

Dye. *See* **Die.**
Be not twice steeped in Assyrian *dye;* . . . *Gn.* 98
His creste above, spotted with purple *die,* . . . *Gn.* 260
The Rose engrained in pure scarlet *die;* . . . *Gn.* 666
streams of purple bloud new *die* the verdant fields. . . . I. ii. 17. 9
The bashfull blood her snowy cheekes did *dye,* . . . II. ix. 41. 4
did staine, And the gray Ocean into purple *dy:* . . . II. x. 48. 4
That her gay clothes did in discolour *die.* . . . V. i. 14. 5
all his armour did with purple *dye:* . . . V. xii. 20. 8
Dyeat. *See* **Diet.**
Dyed. *Dyed* in Lilly white and Cremsin redde, . . . *S.C.* F. 130
fields, that earst so gay were *dyde* In colours . . . *T.M.* 237
'All is but fained, and with oaker *dide,* . . . *Ti.* 204
on his shield *Sansloy* in bloody lines was *dyde.* . . . I. iii. 33. 9
armes . . . Into a pure vermillion now are *dyde.* . . . I. v. 9. 6
her coulours, *died* deepe in graine, . . . I. vii. 1. 4
As they in pure vermilion had been *dide,* . . . I. xi. 46. 3
into a deepe sanguine *dide* the grassy grownd. . . . II. i. 39. 9
Ne lets her waves with any filth be *dyde;* . . . II. ii. 9. 8
The greene shield *dyde* in dolorous vermell? . . . II. x. 24. 7
Headed with flint, and fethers bloody *dide;* . . . II. xi. 21. 4
deckt with blossoms *dyde* in white and red, . . . II. xii. 12. 5
her pure yvory Into a cleare Carnation suddeine *dyde;* . . . III. iii. 20. 3
dyde in sanguine red her skin . . . III. xii. 20. 9
though she were most faire, and goodly *dyde,* . . . IV. ix. 14. 8
That all his garments and the grasse in vermeill *dyde.* . . . VI. ii. 40. 9
he saw the way all *dyde* With streames of bloud; . . . VI. vii. 17. 5
Yclad in home-made greene that her owne hands had *dyde.* . . VI. ix. 7. 9
Like crimsin *dyde* in grayne: . . . *Epith.* 228
Dyes. *streames of purple bloud new *dies* the verdant fields. . I. ii. 17. 9
Dying. *See* **Ever-dying, Never-dying.**
swanne doth sing before her *dying* day, . . . *Frag.*
His worthie praise, and vertues *dying* never, . . . *Ti.* 256
dooth multiplye My *dying* paines, . . . *D.* 74
I hate to tast, for food withholds my *dying;* . . . *D.* 416
dying lives, and living still does dye. . . . *D.* 434
heare the languors of my too long *dying,* . . . *Col.* 948
The deare remembrance of his *dying* Lord, . . . I. i. 2. 2
They . . . sucked up their *dying* mothers bloud, . . . I. i. 25. 8
I his shield have quit from *dying* foe.' . . . I. v. 11. 4
all her sences fild With *dying* fitt, . . . I. vi. 37. 4
me . . . that here lye *dying* every stound, . . . I. viii. 38. 4
halfe dead with *dying* feare . . . I. ix. 30. 6
If not well ended at our *dying* day. . . . I. x. 41. 7
trouble *dying* soules tranquilitee; . . . II. i. 47. 8
dying whylome did divide this fort . . . II. ii. 13. 3
He lately heard that *dying* Lady grone, . . . II. iii. 3. 7
To hide his coward head from *dying* dreed: . . . II. iii. 21. 4
dying dayly, dayly yet revive. . . . II. vi. 45. 4
Another did the *dying* bronds repayre . . . II. vii. 36. 3
dying left none heire them to withstand, . . . II. x. 61. 8
Three sonnes he *dying* left, . . . II. x. 64. 1
He *dying* left the fairest Tanaquill, . . . II. x. 76. 4
huge hills Of *dying* people, . . . III. iii. 41. 2
Proud of his *dying* honor and deare bandes, . . . III. iv. 17. 3
Dye rather, dye, and *dying* doe her serve; . . . III. v. 46. 6
Dying her serve, and living her adore; . . . III. v. 46. 7
The which he *dying* lefte next in remaine . . . III. ix. 37. 4
Yet can he never dye, but *dying* lives, . . . III. x. 60. 1
Dying each day with inward wounds of dolours dart. . . . III. xii. 16. 9
Dreadfully dropping from her *dying* hart, . . . III. xii. 31. 4
The cruell steele, which thrild her *dying* hart, . . . III. xii. 38. 1
In which I daily *dying* am too long: . . . IV. xii. 9. 5
By all that *dying* to it turned be? . . . V. ii. 37. 7
By all that *dying* into it doe fade; . . . V. ii. 40. 2
Of carcases, which *dying* on her fell. . . . VI. xi. 20. 2
in his armes the dreary *dying* mayd, . . . VI. xi. 21. 2
having saved her from *dying,* . . . VI. xi. 23. 4
reade the sorrowes of my *dying* spright, . . . *Am.* i. 7
So *dying* live, and living do adore her. . . . *Am.* xiv. 14
How long shall this lyke *dying* lyfe endure, . . . *Am.* xxv. 1
And, *dying,* doe themselves of payne beguyle. . . . *Am.* xlvii. 12
The piteous passion of his *dying* smart. . . . *Am.* xlviii. 12
otherwhyles, their *dying* to delay, . . . *H.L.* 138
And in her ashes shrowd my *dying* shame; . . . *H.H.L.* 19
Dynamene. White hand Eunica, proud *Dynamene,* . . . IV. xi. 49. 1
Dynevor. Emongst the woody hilles of *Dynevowre:* . . . III. iii. 8. 6

E

Each (*partial list*).
Eche gate was of an orient perfect pearle, . . . *Rev.* iv. 10
I saw both ship and mariners *each* one, . . . *Bel.*[2] xiii. 12
each thing at last we see . . . *Pet.* v. 7
each to other working cruell wrongs, . . . *Ro.* xxiv. 7
*ye daintie Damsells may depart *echeone* her way, . . . *S.C.* Ap. 148
may depart *Eche* one her way. . . . *S.C.* Ap. 148
they daunceu, *eche* one with his mayd. . . . *S.C.* May 24
That shepheardes so witen *ech* others life, . . . *S.C.* May 159
done *eache* of hem scorne. . . . *S.C.* May 161
like in *eche* degree The flocke . . . *S.C.* Jul. 131
I deeme *ech* have gayned: . . . *S.C.* Au. 131
Then listneth *ech* unto my heavy laye, . . . *S.C.* Au. 149
Eche thing imparted is more eath to beare: . . . *S.C.* S. 17
his blustring blast *eche* coste dooth scoure. . . . *S.C.* D. 132
farre abroad through *each* descent, . . . *Gn.* 77
each shepheard sings As merrie notes . . . *Gn.* 147
each does for the Soveraignty contend, . . . *Gn.* 410
Each doth against the others bodie bend . . . *Gn.* 412

Each—*Continued.*
Sith *each* with brothers bloudie hand was slaine. . . . *Gn.* 416
(compar'd to all the rest Of *each* degree) . . . *Hub.* 180
each thing fained ought more warie bee. . . . *Hub.* 495
each one by and by Departed . . . *Hub.* 1108
he heard *each* one complaine . . . *Hub.* 1275
an ey-witnes of *each* thing to bee. . . . *Hub.* 1278
Each place abounding . . . *Each* place defilde . . . *Hub.* 1305, 1307
The foes of learning and *each* gentle thought; . . . *T.M.* 64
As with *each* storme does fall away, . . . *Ti.* 514
pastures on the pleasures of *each* place. . . . *Mui.* 176
each doth chuse . . . *Mui.* 275
as *each* had been a Dove; . . . *Mui.* 291
Each of the Gods, . . . *Mui.* 310
A sclender swaine, excelling far *each* other, . . . *As.* 15
each making other mery; . . . *Col.* 77
and *each* an end of singing made . . . *Col.* 179
prais'd and rais'd above *each* other starre. . . . *Col.* 535
Moves me of *each,* . . . to tell . . . *Col.* 683

Each—*Continued.*
Where *each* one seeks with malice, . . . *Col.* 690
each mans worth is measured . . . *Col.* 711
gan by litle learne to love *each* other: . . . *Col.* 852
they gan *each* one his like to love, . . . *Col.* 863
yrkes *each* gentle heart . . . *Col.* 906
And loath *each* lowly thing . . . *Col.* 938
And steale from *each* some part of ornament. . . . *Ded. Son.* xvii. 8
Of *each* a part I stole by cunning thefte: . . . *Ded.Son.*xvii.13
each one (**each*one) Of sundrie shapes, yet all ill-favored: . I. i. 15. 6
wont to say His holy thinges *each* morne and eventyde: . . I. i. 34. 7
her dwarfe, that wont to wait *each* howre: . . . I. ii. 7. 8
and *ech* to other yealdeth land. . . . I. ii. 15. 9
Each others equall puissaunce envies, . . . I. ii. 17. 4
Faire seemely pleasaunce *each* to other makes, . . . I. ii. 30. 1
Great troupes of people . . . of *each* degree and place; . . . I. iv. 3. 2
each others greater pride does spight. . . . I. iv. 14. 9
each one himselfe did payne All kindnesse . . . to shew, . . . I. iv. 15. 3
people, . . . Doe ride *each* other upon her to gaze: . . . I. iv. 16. 8
To be aveng'd *each* on his enimy. . . . I. iv. 43. 4
With greedy force *each* other doth assayle, . . . I. v. 6. 6
each to deadly shame would drive his foe: . . . I. v. 9. 2
yet *each* to *each* unlich, . . . I. v. 28. 5
they gan, . . . fiersly to assaile *Each* other, . . . I. vi. 43. 3
fainting, *each* themselves to breathen lett, . . . I. vi. 44. 2
friendly *each* did others praise devize, . . . I. ix. 1. 7
love establish *each* to other trew, . . . I. ix. 18. 7
Is then unjust to *each* his dew to give? . . . I. ix. 38. 7
Each goodly thing is hardest to begin; . . . I. x. 6. 1
knew his good to all of *each* degree, . . . I. x. 7. 5
greatly joy *each* other for to see: . . . I. x. 15. 4
Each bone might through his body well be red . . . I. x. 48. 5
boystrous battaile make, *each* other to avenge. . . . I. xi. 21. 9
each one felt secretly Himselfe thereby refte of his sences . I. xii. 39. 7
doen upreare Their bevers bright *each* other for to greet; . II. i. 29. 2
Goodly comportaunce *each* to other beare, . . . II. i. 29. 3
feedes *each* living plant with liquid sap, . . . II. ii. 6. 4
each made others foe: . . . II. ii. 13. 6
Accourting *each* her frend with lavish fest: . . . II. ii. 16. 5
to his mistresse *each* himselfe strove to advaunce. . . . II. ii. 16. 9
Each other does envy with deadly hate, . . . II. ii. 19. 2
then *each* to rest him hyes. . . . II. ii. 46. 9
each bad other flye: . . . II. iii. 19. 8
Each trembling leafe and whistling wind they heare, . . . II. iii. 20. 4
Each strove to please, . . . II. iv. 19. 9
naked made *each* others manly spalles; . . . II. vi. 29. 6
each one sought his Lady to aggrate: . . . II. ix. 34. 5
and *each* a damzell chose. . . . II. ix. 36. 5
Themselves did solace *each* one with his Dame, . . . II. ix. 44. 5
each his portion peaceably enjoyd, . . . II. x. 14. 6
each his paynes to others profit still employd. . . . II. x. 14. 9
each of Brutus boasted to be borne, . . . II. x. 36. 7
Where *each* might best offend . . . II. xi. 6. 3
unto *each* a Bulwarke did arrett, . . . II. xi. 7. 3
each thing by which the eyes may fault: . . . II. xi. 9. 7
each doth in him selfe it well perceive to bee. . . . II. xii. 47. 9
she usd to give to drinke to *each*, . . . II. xii. 56. 7
striving *each* th' other to undermine, *Each* did the others worke II. xii. 59. 5, 6
each the other from to rise restraine; . . . II. xii. 64. 5
and *each* gan diversely devize. . . . III. i. 33. 9
in *each* gentle hart desire of honor breeds. . . . III. i. 49. 9
for *each* of other worthy are.' . . . III. ii. 10. 9
like a Gyaunt in *each* manly part . . . III. iii. 32. 3
each to other, well affectionate, . . . III. iii. 62. 7
thy moyst mountaines *each* on others throng, . . . III. iv. 8. 5
they did dispart, *each* to assay . . . III. iv. 46. 8
sheweth *each* thing as it is in deed: . . . III. iv. 59. 2
each did other more augment, . . . III. v. 55. 6
gazing *each* on other . . . III. vi. 27. 6
each one a babe uptooke, . . . III. vi. 28. 1
each Paramor his leman knowes, *Each* bird his mate; . . . III. vi. 41. 7, 8
and *each* at other wondered. . . . III. vii. 14. 9
And so defyde them *each*, . . . III. ix. 13. 9
Each gan undight Their garments wett, . . . III. ix. 19. 6
each on other, . . . Stood gazing, . . . III. ix. 23. 3
And of *each* one he mett . . . III. x. 19. 9
each did strive the other to outgoe: . . . III. xi. 5. 6
Long were to tell *each* other lovely fitt; . . . III. xi. 39. 6
All three to *each* unlike, . . . III. xii. 24. 9
That *each* to other made, . . . IV. i. 5. 3
each one did sundrie doubts devise. . . . IV. i. 14. 9
ech of them had ryding by his side . . . IV. i. 17. 3
dayly more offensive unto *each* degree. . . . IV. i. 18. 9
each of life sought others to deprive, . . . IV. i. 23. 8
Forgetfull *each* to have bene ever others frend. . . . IV. ii. 14. 9
Each other horse and man to ground did send; . . . IV. ii. 15. 7
stemme *ech* other with so fell despight, . . . IV. ii. 16. 4
each on other flew, . . . IV. ii. 17. 8
each other did assayle, . . . IV. ii. 18. 1
did love *each* other dearely well, . . . IV. ii. 43. 1
'the terme of *each* mans life . . . IV. ii. 52. 1
love *each* other . . . IV. ii. 53. 9
dearely lov'd of *each* degree; . . . IV. iii. 2. 7
ech drunk an harty draught; . . . IV. iii. 48. 9
each other kissed glad, . . . IV. iii. 49. 3
Each labouring t' advance the others gest, . . . IV. iv. 36. 7
each of other gan inquire his name. . . . IV. iv. 42. 3
the which *each* other did outgoe. . . . IV. v. 11. 9
each one thought as to their fancies came. . . . IV. v. 17. 2
Each one profest to be her paramoure, . . . IV. v. 24. 7

Each—*Continued.*
each one his chalenge should disclame, . . . IV. v. 25. 5
when she long had lookt upon *each* one, . . . IV. v. 26. 6
how *each* one did succeede, . . . IV. v. 28. 5
every place seem'd painefull, and *ech* changing vaine. . . . IV. v. 40. 9
sooth is said, and tride in *each* degree, . . . IV. ix. 27. 8
of contrarie natures *each* to other: . . . IV. x. 32. 5
love . . . that leads *each* living kind. . . . IV. xii. 25. 9
each of either take his share aright: . . . V. i. 26. 5
divided *each* from either: . . . V. ii. 31. 2
of *each* equall share, . . . V. ii. 48. 4
And *each* one had his right. . . . V. iv. 20. 6
it mote be like in *each* respect. . . . V. v. 3. 9
Each hour did seeme a moneth, . . . V. vi. 5. 9
Which he unto her people does *each* day; . . . V. viii. 19. 2
whenas *each* of other had a sight, . . . VI. i. 4. 6
tryde all waies how *each* mote entrance make . . . VI. i. 37. 2
To pay *each* with his owne is right . . . VI. i. 42. 3
beare themselves aright To all of *each* degree . . . V. ii. 1. 4
gan to intimate *Each* others griefe . . . VI. iii. 12. 5
did they *each* other entertaine . . . VI. v. 34. 5
ne *ech* would other leave: . . . VI. vi. 15. 9
As he is wont at *each* Saint Valentide, . . . VI. vii. 32. 7
of the pray *each* one apart doth beare. . . . VI. viii. 41. 5
each his sundrie sheepe . . . Gathered together, . . . VI. ix. 15. 4
they to *each* such fortune doe diffuse, . . . VI. ix. 29. 4
each hath his fortune in his brest. . . . VI. ix. 29. 9
each unto himselfe his life may fortunize.' . . . VI. ix. 30. 9
They teach us how to *each* degree . . . VI. x. 23. 7
rageth sore in *each* degree and state, . . . VI. xii. 40. 2
knittest *each* to *each*, as brother unto brother. . . . VII. vii. 14. 9
equall gave to *each* as Justice duly scann'd. . . . VII. vii. 38. 9
each of you, That vertue have or this . . . VII. vii. 54. 6
pryde depraves *each* other better part, . . . *Am.* xxxi. 3
Seekes . . . to salve *each* others wound: . . . *Am.* lxv. 12
to conspyre *Each* against other . . . *H.L.* 81
To worke *ech* others joy and true content, . . . *H.B.* 200
know *ech* other here belov'd to bee. . . . *H.B.* 203
stars . . . Whereof *each* other doth in brightnesse passe, . . . *H.H.B.* 54
These thus in faire *each* other farre excelling, . . . *H.H.B.* 99
each one had a little wicker basket, . . . *Proth.* 24

Each where. The skie *eachwhere* did show full bright . . . *Pet.* ii. 5
and shot *each where* . . . glistering light; . . . *Gn.* 66
Tisiphone *each where* doth shake and shiver . . . *Gn.* 342
That rang'd *each where* without suspition. . . . *Mui.* 376
in the ground *each where* will it engrosse, . . . *Col.* 634
each where thou hast dispredd thy fame, . . . *Ded.Son.*xiv.13
Through famous Poets verse *each where* renownd. . . . I. x. 54. 7
walkte *each where* for feare of hid mischaunce, . . . III. xii. 15. 7
proclaim'd *each where* A solemne feast, . . . IV. ii. 26. 7
seeke *each where*, where last I sawe her face, . . . *Am.* lxxviii. 3

Eager. Two *eager* (*egre*[1]) dogs did her pursue . . . *Pet.* i. 6
eger greedinesse through every member thrild. . . . I. viii. 6. 9
Gan towards them to pricke with *eger* speede, . . . IV. vi. 2. 8
as doth an *eger* hound Thrust to an Hynd . . . IV. vi. 12. 3
an *eager* mastiffe once doth prove The tast of bloud . . . IV. ix. 31. 5
with more *eager* felnesse him pursew'd; . . . VI. iii. 50. 2
when his foe he still so *eager* saw, . . . VI. vi. 29. 1

Eagerness. to her ran with hasty *egernesse*, . . . III. xii. 44. *or.* 6

Eagle. That Romane *Eagle* seene to cleave asunder, . . . *Ro.* xvii. 10
thence th' Imperiall *Eagle* rooting tooke, . . . *Ro.* xviii. 10
where the *Eagle* built his towring nest, . . . *Van.* iv. 6
An *Eagle* sored hye, . . . *S.C.* Jul. 222
as an *Eagle*, seeing pray appeare, . . . I. xi. 9. 5
As *Eagle*, fresh out of the ocean wave, . . . I. xi. 34. 3
hart-strings of an *Aegle* ryv'd. . . . II. x. 70. 9
having spide on hight An *Eagle* . . . III. vii. 39. 3
trussing me, as *Eagle* doth his pray, . . . IV. vii. 18. 6
Like to an *Eagle*, in his kingly pride . . . V. iv. 42. 1
made to fly like doves whom the *Eagle* doth affray. . . . V. xii. 5. 9
like fresh *Eagle*, make his hardie flight . . . *H.L.* 69

Eagle's. one of them was like an *Eagles* claw, . . . I. viii. 48. 6
As *Eagles* eie that can behold the Sunne. . . . I. x. 47. 6
as a Bittur in the *Eagles* clawe, . . . II. viii. 50. 2
Twise was he seene in soaring *Eagles* shape, . . . III. xi. 34. 1
And *Eagles* wings, for scope and speedinesse, . . . V. xi. 24. 7
like the native brood of *Eagles* kynd, . . . *H.H.B.* 138

Eagles. Apes, Lyons, *Aegles*, Owles, . . . II. ix. 50. 9

Ear. from a stalke into an *eare* forth-growes, . . . *Ro.* xxx. 3
Which *eare* the frutefull graine doth shortly bring; . . . *Ro.* xxx. 4
to yield the timely *eare*, . . . *S.C.* O. 58
The *eare* that budded faire is burnt . . . *S.C.* D. 99
though the vulgar yeeld an open *eare*, . . . *Hub.* 713
his *eare* he lent To everie sound . . . *Hub.* 1010
to my trustie *eare* Committed . . . *D.* 69
to mine oaten pipe enclin'd her *eare*, . . . *Col.* 360
That may thy tunefull *eare* unseason quite? . . . *Ded. Son.* viii. 4
Best musicke breeds delight in loathing *eare*; . . . I. viii. 44. 4
with patient *eare* The brave adventures . . . to heare; . . . II. Pr. 5. 6
The Palmer lent his *eare* unto the noyce, . . . II. viii. 4. 1
report . . . Came to the Ladies *eare* . . . II. ix. 17. 6
all that mote delight a daintie *eare*, . . . II. xii. 70. 2
all that pleasing is to living *eare* . . . II. xii. 70. 7
to her cry they list not lenden *eare*, . . . III. i. 23. 1
lent her wary *eare* to understand . . . III. i. 60. 8
standing high aloft low lay thine *eare*, . . . III. iii. 9. 1
Tydings hereof came to his mothers *eare*: . . . III. iv. 19. 2
Peece, that unto parley *eare* will give, . . . III. x. 10. 5
in his *eare* him rownded close behinde: . . . III. x. 30. 4
He whispered in her *eare*, . . . III. x. 49. 4

Ear—*Continued.*
sow vaine sorrow in a fruitlesse *eare,* . . . III. xi. 16. 2
Ne let his speeches come unto their *eare.* . . . IV. v. 38. 6
To lend an *eare,* and softly to relent. . . . IV. vi. 41. 5
drew thereto, making her *eare* her guide: . . . IV. vii. 29. 4
them seeing past the reach of *eare,* . . . IV. viii. 36. 7
when tydings came unto mine *eare,* . . . IV. viii. 55. 1
Ne lend an *eare* to ought that might behove. . . . IV. ix. 31. 4
heaven, that unto all lends equall *eare,* . . . IV. xii. 6. 5
The *eare* must be the ballance, . . . V. ii. 47. 8
Strange were the words in Britomartis *eare,* . . . V. vi. 38. 1
By this came tydings to the Tyrants *eare,* . . . V. xii. 6. 4
all that pleasant is to *eare* or eye, . . . VI. *Pr.* 1. 5
with greedy *eare* Hong still upon his melting mouth attent; . VI. ix. 26. 1
the Gods, that gave good *eare* To her bold words, . . . VII. vi. 28. 1
Earl. Thy father, that good *Earle* of rare renowne, . . . *Ti.* 261
Early. His kiddes, his cracknelles, and his *early* fruit. . . . *S.C.* Ja. 58
wander may thy flocke, *early* or late, . . . *S.C.* Jun. 11
oppress With *early* frosts, . . . *D.* 28
Where *earely* waite him many a gazing eye, . . . I. v. 3. 2
earely rose; and, ere that dawning light . . . I. v. 52. 5
made him pray both *earely* and eke late: . . . I. x. 26. 5
The morrow next gan *earely* to appeare, . . . I. xi. 33. 1
earely, ere the morrow . . . I. xi. 33. 3
The joyous day gan *early* to appeare; . . . I. xi. 51. 1
Whose *early* foe awaiting him beside . . . I. xi. 52. 4
The trees did bud, and *early* blossomes bore; . . . II. vi. 24. 7
Early and late it rong, . . . II. ix. 25. 9
Early, before the Morne . . . II. xi. 3. 1
forth from virgin bowre she comes in th' *early* morne. . . . II. xii. 50. 9
So *earely* . . . They tooke their steeds, . . . III. i. 67. 7
Earely, the morrow next, . . . III. ii. 48. 1
earely, ere the morrow did upreare His deawy head . . . III. iv. 61. 3
earely, ere the dawning day appear'd, . . . III. vii. 19. 1
Bewrayed had the world with *early* light, . . . III. x. 1. 2
Early, before the heavens fairest light . . . III. x. 52. 6
early in the morrow next, he went . . . IV. vi. 44. 4
earely calling forth both man and beast . . . V. v. 1. 3
Earely, so soone as Titans beames forth brust . . . VI. iii. 13. 5
the morning, bringing *earely* light . . . VI. v. 40. 2
The morrow next the Prince did *early* rize, . . . VI. vi. 44. 8
twixt her paps, (like *early* fruit in May, . . . *Am.* lxxvi. 9
Early . . . Doe ye awake; . . . *Epith.* 19
Ear-marked. for *eare-marked* beasts abroad be bruted. . . . *Hub.* 188
Earn. His heart did *earne* against his hated foe, . . . *Mui.* 254
his hart did *earne* To prove his puissance . . . I. i. 3. 6
when in rage he for revenge did *earne.* . . . I. vi. 25. 9
to be easd of that base burden still did *erne.* . . . II. iii. 46. 9
my heart did inly *earne,* . . . IV. x. 9. 1
gan her heart to faint, and quake, and *earne,* . . . IV. xii. 24. 4
compell to worke, to *earne* their meat, . . . V. iv. 31. 5
what their hands could *earne* by twisting linnen twyne. . . . V. v. 22. 9
gan *earne* To understand that villeins dwelling place, . . . V. ix. 7. 1
his heart gan *earne* For great desire . . . V. xi. 21. 1
The which shal nought to you but foule dishonor *yearne.* . . . VI. i. 40. 9
Earned. My courage *earnd* it to awake, . . . *S.C.* Mar. 77
Una *earnd* her traveill to renew. . . . I. ix. 18. 5
his faint hart much *earned* at the sight: . . . III. x. 21. 9
'Now sure ye well have *earn'd* your meed; . . . VI. vii. 13. 2
My due reward, the which right well I deeme I *yearned* have, . VI. vii. 15. 9
Earnest. A shaft in *earnest* snatched, . . . *S.C.* Mar. 96
crowned her twixt *earnest* and twixt game: . . . I. xii. 8. 7
So can he turne his *earnest* unto game, . . . II. i. 31. 1
did her *earnest* end in jest. . . . II. vi. 23. 9
somewhat gan relent his *earnest* pace; . . . II. xii. 65. 8
with *earnest* cry Badd those same six forbeare . . . III. i. 22. 8
with *earnest* mone, . . . late entrance deare besought: . . . III. ix. 12. 3
hearing them to call For fire in *earnest,* . . . III. ix. 18. 3
late he fled from his too *earnest* foe: . . . III. x. 23. 3
though she did bend Her *earnest* minde, . . . III. xi. 54. 9
gotten by her slight And *earnest* search, . . . V. i. 9. 3
How *earnest* suit she earst for him had made . . . V. v. 54. 2
for helpe aloud in *earnest* cride: . . . V. ix. 12. 3
He gan his *earnest* fervour to augment, . . . V. ix. 46. 8
earnest tooke To keepe their flockes . . . VI. xi. 40. 6
'Twixt *earnest* and twixt game: . . . *Epig.* iv. 12
Earnestly. Doth urge her fellow Furies *earnestlie* . . . *Gn.* 423
unto her truth Did *earnestly* committ, . . . II. iii. 2. 3
The thing, that thou didst crave so *earnestly,* . . . II. vii. 38. 3
beholding *earnestly* The goodly ordinaunce . . . III. xi. 53. 1
Yet he to them so *earnestly* did call, . . . IV. ii. 21. 6
her of pardon prayd more *earnestlie,* . . . IV. vi. 23. 8
oft of them did *earnestly* inquire, . . . IV. viii. 22. 3
earnestly besought to wend that day With her, . . . V. ix. 3. 8
earnestly entreated, that they might Finde favour . . . VI. iii. 42. 8
beating at his gates full *earnestly,* . . . VII. vi. 15. 3
Ears. Up to his *eares* the verdant grasse did growe, . . . *Van.* ii. 5
bowe your *eares* unto my dolefull dittie: . . . *S.C.* Ja. 16
yond Bullocke beares . . . his pricked *eares?* . . . *S.C.* F. 72
allure Chast Ladies *eares* to fantasies impure. . . . *Hub.* 820
both *eares* pared of their hight; . . . *Hub.* 1382
all Apes but halfe their *eares* have left, . . . *Hub.* 1383
With troublous noyse did dull their daintie *eares.* . . . *T.M.* 30
with pleasure The listners eyes and *eares* with melodie; . . . *T.M.* 178
They feede the *eares* of fooles with flattery, . . . *T.M.* 323
pierce his frosen *eares?* . . . *D.* 249
lowd plaints have duld mine *eares;* . . . *D.* 415
with greedie listfull *eares,* . . . *Col.* 7
With hungrie *eares* to heare his harmonie: . . . *Col.* 53
The staie whereof shall nought these *eares* annoy, . . . *Col.* 98

Ears—*Continued.*
measured by his weed, As . . . asses by their *eares:* . . . *Col.* 712
asses been not all whose *eares* exceed, . . . *Col.* 713
Unlesse he swim in love up to the *eares.* . . . *Col.* 782
busying . . . his dull *eares* to heare what shee did tell; . . . I. ii. 26. 7
'What voice . . . Sends to my doubtful *eares* these speaches . I. ii. 32. 8
with . . . piteous plaintes, she filleth his dull *eares,* . . . I. iii. 44. 2
with her gealous termes his open *eares* abusd: . . . I. v. 37. 9
Her golden locks . . . were loosely shed About her *eares,* . . . I. xi. 51. 6
stray about her daintie *eares.* . . . II. ii. 15. 9
they encombred all mens *eares* and eyes; . . . II. ix. 51. 3
greedy *eares* her weake hart from her bore; . . . III. ix. 52. 7
With matchlesse *eares* deformed and distort, . . . IV. i. 28. 2
as her *eares,* so eke her feet were odde, . . . IV. i. 28. 6
downe both sides two wide long *eares* did glow, . . . IV. vii. 6. 7
More great then th' *eares* of Elephants by Indus flood. . . . IV. vii. 6. 9
passing through the *eares* would pierce the hart, . . . IV. viii. 26. 6
all mens *eares* possest, . . . IV. x. 4. 2
The *eares* and hearts of all that goodly crew, . . . IV. xi. 23. 5
Let then this plaint unto his *eares* be borne, . . . IV. xii. 8. 3
to his doome with listfull *eares* did both attend. . . . V. i. 25. 9
with rude flaring lockes About her *eares,* . . . V. xii. 38. 9
enchantment, that through both the *eares* (*eyes) . . . did
steale the hart . . . VI. ii. 3. 3
Calepine, whose *eares* those shrieches shrill, . . . VI. iv. 18. 4
Your eies, your *eares,* your tongue, your talk restraine . . . VI. vi. 7. 8
enrold With *ears* of corne of every sort, . . . VII. vii. 30. 7
the which was cround With *eares* of corne, . . . VII. vii. 37. 5
wont to please Some dainty *eares,* . . . Am. xxxviii. 6
daunt With their great deedes, and fild their childrens *eares?* *Com. Son.* iii. 4
base affections, which your *eares* would bland . . . *H.B.* 171
Earst. *See* **Erst.**
Earth. *See* **Mother earth.**
Ere it be long within the *earth* to rest. . . . *Pet.*[1] vii. 4
birdes from aire descending downe on *earth* . . . *Rev.* iii. 9
I saw new *Earth,* new Heaven, . . . *Rev.* iv. 1
the gaping *earth* devoure The spring, the place . . . *Pet.* iv. 10
Alas, on (in[1]) *earth* so nothing doth endure, . . . *Pet.* vi. 11
Both heaven and *earth* in roundnesse compassing; . . . *Ro.* iv. 4
The lowest *earth* join'd to the heaven hie; . . . *Ro.* viii. 8
Out of the *earth* engendred men of armes . . . *Ro.* x. 3
the children of the *earth* Heapt hils on hils . . . *Ro.* xii. 1
th' *earth* under her childrens weight did grone, . . . *Ro.* xii. 7
His wings which wont the *earth* to overspredd, . . . *Ro.* xvii. 6
The *earth* . . . forth sent That antique horror, . . . *Ro.* xvii. 7
The least of thousands which on *earth* abide, . . . *Van.* iii. 8
Sith nought on *earth* can chalenge long endurance? . . . *Van.* xi. 14
downe to the *earth* he fell forthwith. . . . *S.C.* F. 218
Thearth shronke under him, . . . *S.C.* F. 220
lyves on *earth,* and loved her most dere . . . *S.C.* Jun. 112
never thing on *earth* so pleaseth me . . . *S.C.* Au. 147
The *earth* now lacks her wonted light, . . . *S.C.* N. 68
thing on *earth* that is of most availe, . . . *S.C.* N. 87
nys on *earth* assuraunce to be sought; . . . *S.C.* N. 157
While here on *earth* she did abyde. . . . *S.C.* N. 199
An heape of *earth* he hoorded up on hie, . . . *Gn.* 657
He planted there, and reard a mount of *earth,* . . . *Gn.* 685
powr'd on th' *earth* plague, pestilence, and death. . . . *Hub.* 8
all that in the deepest *earth* remaines, . . . *Hub.* 1230
earth, that all thing breeds, . . . *T.M.* 43
naught on *earth* her griefe might pacifie; . . . *T.M.* 356
doth all fairest things on *earth* deface, . . . *T.M.* 434
Hath powrd on *earth* this noyous pestilence, . . . *T.M.* 483
loathing *earth,* I looke up to the sky, . . . *T.M.* 527
all that lives on face of sinfull *earth!* . . . *Ti.* 44
made one meare of th' *earth* and of their raine? . . . *Ti.* 63
no footing now on *earth* appeares? . . . *Ti.* 65
Loathing this sinfull *earth* and earthlie slime, . . . *Ti.* 290
Such as on *earth* man could not more devize, . . . *Ti.* 521
The Cave . . . Was but *earth,* . . . *Ti.* 571
With loftie flight above the *earth* he bounded, . . . *Ti.* 599
Seemed the heavens with the *earth* did disagree, . . . *Ti.* 664
the *earth* did grieve exceedingly, . . . *Ti.* 671
Betwixt the centred *earth* and azure skies, . . . *Mui.* 19
To raine in th' aire from th' *earth* to highest skie, . . . *Mui.* 212
what on *earth* can long abide in state, . . . *Mui.* 217
Downe to the *earth* his heavie eyes were throwne, . . . *D.* 46
Living on *earth* like Angell new divinde, . . . *D.* 214
nought on *earth* may lessen or appease; . . . *D.* 276
Let th' *earth* be barren, . . . *D.* 334
I hate the *earth,* because it is the mold . . . *D.* 402
no sweet on *earth* is left; . . . *D.* 418
shall never more behold Faire thing on *earth,* . . . *D.* 492
on the cold deare *earth* himselfe did throw; . . . *As.* 124
if I her like ought on *earth* might read, . . . *Col.* 336
Next gan the *earth* to shew her naked head, . . . *Col.* 857
Whylom the pillours of th' *earth* did sustaine, . . . *Ded. Son.* i. 2
Morpheus house . . . Amid the bowels of the *earth* . . . I. i. 39. 4
Let fal her eien, as shamefast, to the *earth,* . . . I. ii. 27. 6
Where noblest knights were to be found on *earth.* . . . I. iii. 28. 6
The *earth* shall sooner leave her kindly skil . . . I. iii. 28. 7
Looking to heaven, for *earth* she did disdayne, . . . I. iv. 10. 2
henceforth nothing faire but her on *earth* they find. . . . I. vi. 18. 9
trample th' *earth,* the whiles they may respire, . . . I. vi. 44. 8
Arriv'd wher they in *erth* their fruitles blood had sown. . . . I. vi. 45. 9
all the *earth* for terror seemd to shake, . . . I. vii. 7. 6
The greatest *Earth* his uncouth mother was, . . . I. vii. 9. 1
The sad *earth,* . . . Did grone full grievous . . . I. viii. 8. 7
shooting in the *earth,* castes up a mount of clay. . . . I. viii. 9. 9
his combred clubbe to quight Out of the *earth,* . . . I. viii. 10. 5

Earth—*Continued.*
Gyaunts fall, that seemd to shake The stedfast globe of *earth*, . I. viii. 23. 9
Old Timon . . . is the wisest now on *earth* I weene: . . . . I. ix. 4. 4
what ever thing is donne In heaven and *earth?* . . . . . . I. ix. 42. 2
her embracing, said; 'O happy *earth*, ... I. x. 9. 1
a woman . . . That was on *earth* not easie to compare; . . . I. x. 30. 4
come, thou man of *earth*, and see the way, ... I. x. 52. 2
Above all knights on *earth*, ... I. xi. 2. 9
with their horror heven and *earth* did ring; . . . . I. xi. 7. 5
they the *earth* would shoulder from her seat; . . . . I. xi. 21. 4
can quickly ryse From off the *earth*, ... I. xi. 23. 8
to the *earth* him drove, as stricken dead; . . . . I. xi. 38. 3
the face of *earth* and wayes of living wight, ... I. xi. 49. 8
th' *earth* him underneath Did grone, ... I. xi. 54. 3
Ne reard above the *earth* his flaming creast, ... I. xii. 2. 3
the *earth*, great mother of us all, ... II. i. 10. 6
medling with their blood and *earth* . . . . II. i. 61. 3
they closd the *earth* agayne. . . . . II. i. 61. 9
over all the *earth* it may be seene, ... II. ii. 40. 7
that which noblest knight on *earth* doth weare.' . . . . . . II. iii. 17. 9
From off the *earth* to take his aerie flight. . . . . II. iii. 19. 5
downe them poured . . . Into the hollow *earth*, ... II. vii. 6. 5
in the hollow *earth* have their eternall brood. . . . . . . II. vii. 8. 9
whiles they on *earth* did rayne. . . . . II. vii. 43. 9
Not such as *earth* out of her fruitfull woomb . . . . II. vii. 51. 6
On *earth* like never grew, ... II. vii. 54. 3
no living wight Below the *earth* . . . . II. vii. 66. 3
with her light the *earth* enlumines cleare: . . . . II. ix. 4. 7
Soone it must turne to *earth;* . . . . II. ix. 21. 9
though from *earth* it be derived right . . . . II. x. 2. 4
freshly to arize From th' *earth*, ... II. xi. 44. 9
th' *Earth* his mother was, ... II. xi. 45. 2
all that here on *earth* we dreadfull hold, ... II. xii. 25. 7
richest substance that on *earth* might bee, ... II. xii. 60. 2
Nothing on *earth* mote alwaies happy beene: . . . . III. i. 10. 7
Where now on *earth*, or how, he may be fownd; . . . . III. ii. 14. 2
Betwixt the lowest *earth* and hevens hight, ... III. ii. 19. 3
through the *earth* have spredd their living prayse, ... III. iii. 3. 8
quite from off the *earth* their memory be raste?' . . . . . . III. iii. 43. 9
the fast *earth* affronted them so sore, ... III. iv. 7. 7
Now lyest thou a lumpe of *earth* forlorne; . . . . III. iv. 36. 7
The cold *earth* was his couch, ... III. iv. 53. 9
with gnashing teeth did bite The bitter *earth*, ... III. v. 22. 2
Looking with myld aspect upon the *earth* . . . . III. vi. 2. 3
Wher most she wonnes when she on *earth* does dwell; . . . III. vi. 29. 2
Whose like on *earth* was never framed yit; . . . . III. viii. 5. 3
overthrowne and laide on th' *earth* full cold, ... III. ix. 50. 5
Ne he twixt heven and *earth* shall hide his hedd, ... III. x. 32. 8
th' *earth* with his faire forhead strooke: . . . . III. xi. 13. 7
Whyles thus on *earth* great Jove these pageaunts playd, . . . III. xi. 35. 5
whiles Jove to *earth* is gone.' . . . . III. xi. 35. 9
There on the cold *earth* him now thrown she found, ... III. xii. 43. *or.* 6
that most on *earth* him joyd, ... III. xii. 44. *or.* 1
Whose like alive on *earth* he weened not: . . . . IV. ii. 8. 5
Such famous men, such worthies of the *earth*, ... IV. iii. 44. 1
Doth burne the *earth* and boyled rivers drie, ... IV. iv. 47. 2
the mouldred *earth* had cav'd the banke; . . . . IV. v. 33. 2
Of beasts, or of the *earth*, I have not red, ... IV. vii. 7. 8
Ne living aide for her on *earth* appeares, ... IV. vii. 23. 2
tomble downe Unto the *earth*, ... IV. viii. 42. 9
like on *earth* no where I recken may: . . . . IV. x. 15. 7
frame in *earth*, and forme of substance base, ... IV. x. 21. 7
all other That ever were on *earth*, ... IV. x. 29. 9
doth the daedale *earth* throw forth to thee . . . . IV. x. 45. 1
Ne ought on *earth* that merry is and glad, ... IV. x. 47. 3
Ne ought on *earth* that lovely is and fayre, ... IV. x. 47. 4
rivers . . . Which doe the *earth* enrich and beautifie: . . . . IV. xi. 20. 2
Whilest here on *earth* she lived mortallie: . . . . V. i. 5. 5
It bit the *earth* for very fell despight, ... V. ii. 18. 6
He sayd that he would all the *earth* uptake . . . . V. ii. 31. 1
Like as the sea . . . Had worne the *earth;* . . . . V. ii. 32. 4
The *earth* was in the middle centre pight, ... V. ii. 35. 5
th' *earth* it selfe how daily its increast . . . . V. ii. 37. 6
with waves continuall Doe eate the *earth*, ... V. ii. 39. 5
Ne is the *earth* the lesse, or loseth ought, ... V. ii. 39. 6
'Likewise the *earth* is not augmented more . . . . V. ii. 40. 1
of the *earth* they formed were of yore: . . . . V. ii. 40. 3
what on *earth* can alwayes happie stand? . . . . V. iii. 9. 1
no braver president this day Remaines on *earth*, ... V. iv. 2. 7
doth teare Th' one from the *earth*, ... V. vi. 40. 5
Nought is on *earth* more sacred or divine, ... V. vii. 1. 1
the *earth* . . . Wroth with the Gods, ... V. vii. 10. 6
Could ought on *earth* so wondrous change have wrought, . . . V. vii. 40. 6
Full dreadfull wight he was as ever went Upon the *earth*, . . V. ix. 10. 5
That ever yet upon this *earth* was seene, ... V. ix. 20. 8
now on *earth* it selfe enlarged has . . . . V. x. 3. 5
The *earth* to all her creatures lodging lends.' . . . . V. x. 24. 6
was never seene of none That lives on *earth;* . . . . V. x. 29. 5
eke to th' *earth* his burden with him bare; . . . . V. xi. 9. 2
byting th' *earth* for very deaths disdaine; . . . . V. xi. 14. 7
Is ought on *earth* so pretious or deare As prayse and honour? . V. xi. 62. 6
by the Gods with paine Planted in *earth*, ... VI. Pr. 3. 6
most did won Of all on *earth*, ... VI. i. 1. 9
Above the *earth* upreard his flaming head, ... VI. i. 31. 2
These eyes him saw upon the cold *earth* sprad, ... VI. ii. 45. 7
made him downe unto the *earth* encline; . . . . VI. v. 26. 4
furthest from the skie And from the *earth*, ... VI. vi. 11. 3
gainst the cold hard *earth* so sore him strake, ... VI. vii. 11. 4
was to him on *earth* the deadliest despight, ... VI. vii. 20. 9
deepe emboweld in the *earth* entyre: . . . . VI. viii. 15. 4

Earth—*Continued.*
He him preventing layes on *earth* along, ... VI. viii. 49. 3
Her deawy humour gan on th' *earth* to shed, ... VI. ix. 13. 2
To passe all others on the *earth* which were: . . . . VI. x. 5. 5
hight, that seem'd th' *earth* to disdaine; . . . . VI. x. 6. 3
all the *earth* doest lighten with thy rayes, ... VI. x. 28. 2
Would be on *earth* too great a blessednesse, ... VI. xi. 1. 4
here on *earth* is no sure happinesse, ... VI. xi. 1. 7
day; . . . he spyde upon the *earth* t'encroch, ... VI. xi. 47. 3
tell To griesly Pluto what on *earth* was donne, ... VI. xii. 35. 6
That makes both heaven and *earth* to tremble at her pride. . VII. vi. 3. 9
first, on *earth* she sought it to obtaine; . . . . VII. vi. 4. 5
now, when all the *earth* she thus had brought To her behest, . VII. vi. 7. 1
if that any were on *earth* belowe That did . . . her molest, . VII. vi. 16. 5
did alite Upon the fruitfull *earth*, ... VII. vi. 20. 9
great *Earth*, great Chaos child; . . . . VII. vi. 26. 6
th' *Earth* herselfe, of her owne motion, ... VII. vii. 8. 5
all the *earth* far underneath her feete . . . . VII. vii. 10. 1
heaven and *earth* I both alike do deeme, ... VII. vii. 15. 6
Sith heaven and *earth* are both alike to thee, ... VII. vii. 15. 7
the *Earth* (great mother of us all) . . . . VII. vii. 17. 6
Ayre to Water sheere, And Water into *Earth;* . . . . VII. vii. 25. 7
Water fights With Fire, and Ayre with *Earth*, ... VII. vii. 25. 8
Ops, of the *earth;* . . . . VII. vii. 26. 6
ripened fruits the which the *earth* had yold. . . . . VII. vii. 30. 9
Which on the *earth* he strowed as he went, ... VII. vii. 32. 8
Which th' *earth* brings forth; . . . . VII. vii. 33. 8
Liv'd here on *earth*, and plenty made abound; . . . . VII. vii. 37. 7
warnes the *Earth* . . . To decke hir selfe, ... *Am.* iv. 11
Yet find I nought on *earth*, ... *Am.* ix. 3
looking on the *earth* whence she was borne, ... *Am.* xiii. 6
Whatso is fayrest shall to *earth* returne. . . . . *Am.* xiii. 8
Treading downe *earth* as lothsome . . . . *Am.* xiii. 11
Not *earth*, for her high thoghts more heavenly are: . . . . . *Am.* lv. 5
on *earth* nought hath enduraunce. . . . . *Am.* lviii. 12
Could not on *earth* have found one fit for mate, ... *Am.* lxvi. 6
All sorts of flowers, the which on *earth* do spring, ... *Am.* lxx. 3
here on *earth* to have such hevens blisse. . . . . *Am.* lxxii. 14
suffrest neyther gods in sky, Nor men in *earth*, to rest: . . *Epig.* iv. 16
from the *earth*, which they may long possesse . . . . *Epith.* 418
They both are fallen, that all the *earth* did feare, ... *Com. Son.* iv. 6
The *earth*, the ayre, the water, and the fyre, ... *H.L.* 78
Ayre hated *earth*, and water hated fyre, ... *H.L.* 83
seemes on *earth* most heavenly to embrace, ... *H.L.* 111
like a moldwarpe in the *earth* doth ly. . . . . *H.L.* 182
the native might Of heavie *earth*, ... *H.L.* 189
As thing on *earth* so heavenly . . . . *H.L.* 214
Nothing on *earth* seemes fayre to fleshly sight, ... *H.B.* 18
Whether in *earth* layd up in secret store, ... *H.B.* 37
The duller *earth* it quickneth with delight, ... *H.B.* 51
Then rouze thy selfe, O *Earth!* out of thy soyle, ... *H.H.L.* 218
First, th' *Earth*, on adamantine pillers founded . . . . . . *H.H.B.* 36
as every thing . . . further is from *earth*, ... *H.H.B.* 45
Both heaven and *earth* obey unto her will, ... *H.H.B.* 197
Ne can on *earth* compared be to ought. . . . . *H.H.B.* 210
And darkes the *earth* with shadow of her sight? . . . . . . *H.H.B.* 229
Of all on *earth* whom God so much doth grace, ... *H.H.B.* 240
Ne ought on *earth* can want unto the wight . . . . *H.H.B.* 244
That in nought else on *earth* they can delight, ... *H.H.B.* 283
each Flower and weede The *earth* did fresh aray; . . . . . *Proth.* 69
Earth-born. did those *earthborn* brethren blinde. . . . . . *Ro.* x. 14
Earthed. her head, *earth'd* in her foundations deep, ... *Ro.* viii. 13
Earthen. All which she in a *earthen* Pot did poure, ... III. ii. 49. 7
Earthly. No worke it seem'd of *earthly* craftsmans wit, . . . *Bel.*[2] iv. 9
Your glorie, fairest of all *earthly* thing! . . . . *Ro.* i. 14
That other *earthlie* power should not resemble Her . . . . *Ro.* vi. 12
ye doo weld th' affaires of *earthlie* creature; . . . . *Ro.* ix. 4
earthly vapours gathered in the ayre, ... *Ro.* xx. 2
My spirit shaking off her *earthly* prison, ... *Van.* i. 2
'O trustlesse state of *earthly* things, ... *S.C.* N. 153
what might be in *earthlie* mould, ... *S.C.* N. 158
th' Okes, deep grounded in the *earthly* molde, ... *Gn.* 453
blazon foorth an *earthlie* beauties praise . . . . *T.M.* 369
what delight (quoth she) in *earthlie* thing, ... *Ti.* 22
builde your blis on hope of *earthly* thing, ... *Ti.* 198
Loathing this sinfull earth and *earthlie* slime, ... *Ti.* 290
By heavens doome doo ende my *earthlie* daies: . . . . *Ti.* 312
'In vaine doo *earthly* Princes, ... *Ti.* 407
All such vaine moniments of *earthlie* masse, ... *Ti.* 419
flesh delight In *earthlie* blis, ... *Ti.* 528
Where drownd with him is all his *earthlie* blisse. . . . . . *Ti.* 546
what bootes it to see *earthlie* thing . . . . *Ti.* 554
Her now I seek throughout this *earthlie* soyle, ... *D.* 167
their judgments share Mongst *earthlie* wightes, ... *D.* 200
Ne feeling have in any *earthly* pleasure, ... *Col.* 45
by paragone Of *earthly* things, to judge of things divine: . . *Col.* 345
her grace . . . Which of all *earthly* thinges he most did crave: . I. i. 3. 5
the chastest flowre that aye did spring On *earthly* braunch, . I. i. 48. 5
erthly wight that with the Night durst ride. . . . . I. v. 32. 9
stood In doubt to deeme her borne of *earthly* brood: . . . . I. vi. 16. 5
What man so wise, what *earthly* witt so ware, ... I. vii. 1. 1
she . . . Brought forth this monstrous masse of *earthly* slyme, I. vii. 9. 8
Why doe ye . . . liking find to gaze on *earthly* mould, . . . I. vii. 22. 4
earthly sight can nought but sorrow breed, ... I. vii. 23. 6
Such *earthly* mettals soon consumed beene, ... I. vii. 33. 4
Nothing is sure that growes on *earthly* grownd; . . . . . . I. ix. 11. 5
wondrous faith, exceeding *earthly* race, ... I. ix. 17. 4
The images of God in *earthly* clay; . . . . I. x. 39. 1
All were his *earthly* eien both blunt and bad, ... I. x. 47. 3
earthly tong Cannot describe, ... I. x. 55. 5

Earthly—*Continued.*
Cleopolis, for *earthly* frame, The fairest peece . . . I. x. 59. 2
the suitt of *earthly* conquest shonne, . . . I. x. 60. 7
So darke are *earthly* thinges compard to things divine. . . I. x. 67. 9
Too false and strong for *earthly* skill or might, . . . I. xii. 32. 7
what ever hevenly powre, Or *earthly* wight thou be, . . . II. iii. 34. 9
earthly thing may not my corage brave Dismay . . . II. iii. 45. 3
when an *earthly* wight they present saw . . . II. vii. 37. 1
never *earthly* Prince in such aray His glory did enhaunce, . . II. vii. 44. 8
I, that am fraile flesh and *earthly* wight, . . . II. vii. 50. 3
no'te avoyded be by *earthly* skill or powre. . . . II. viii. 43. 9
grace of *earthly* Prince so soveraine, . . . II. ix. 6. 2
no *earthly* thing is sure. . . . II. ix. 21. 9
lifted high above this *earthly* masse, . . . II. ix. 45. 3
all *earthly* Princes she doth far surmount. . . . II. x. 1. 9
deemd in mynd To be no *earthly* wight, . . . II. x. 71. 6
Till it dissolved be from *earthly* band. . . . II. xi. 30. 5
He shall his dayes with peace bring to his *earthly* In. . . . III. iii. 30. 9
did beare This warlike sonne unto an *earthly* peare, . . . III. iv. 19. 5
Bove all the sonnes that were of *earthly* wombes ybore. . . . III. iv. 21. 9
Good both for *erthly* med'cine and for hevenly food. . . . III. iv. 40. 9
As it an *earthly* Paradize had beene: . . . III. v. 40. 5
did in stocke of *earthly* flesh enrace, . . . III. v. 52. 5
doubted her to deeme an *earthly* wight, . . . III. vii. 11. 6
No word they spake, nor *earthly* thing they felt, . . . III. xii. 45. *or.* 8
it could overreach the wisest *earthly* wight. . . . IV. ii. 10. 9
Began to peepe above this *earthly* masse, . . . IV. v. 45. 4
as the soule doth rule the *earthly* masse, . . . IV. ix. 2. 6
seem'd unlike unto his *earthly* home: . . . IV. xii. 4. 7
And men . . . at first were framed Of *earthly* mould, . . . V. Pr. 2. 4
Astraea here mongst *earthly* men did dwell, . . . V. i. 5. 8
Of all that on this *earthly* compasse wonnes; . . . V. vi. 33. 3
whilest her *earthly* parts . . . did deeply drowned lie, . . . V. vii. 12. 5
herein doest all *earthly* Princes pas? . . . V. x. 3. 2
So tickle is the state of *earthly* things, . . . VI. iii. 5. 2
downe to them descended in that *earthly* vew. . . . VI. ix. 8. 9
she the face of *earthly* things so changed, . . . VII. vi. 5. 1
touch celestiall seates with *earthly* mire? . . . VII. vi. 29. 4
both heavenly Powers and *earthly* wights, . . . VII. vi. 36. 2
To turne againe unto their *earthly* slime: . . . VII. vii. 18. 4
shew Thing so divine to vew of *earthly* eye, . . . *Am.* xlv. 6
It down is weighd with thoght of *earthly* things, . . . *Am.* lxxii. 3
to us wretched *earthly* clods . . . lend desired light; . . . *Epith.* 411
Ne can his feeble *earthly* eyes endure . . . *H.L.* 185
Thereof as every *earthly* thing partakes . . . *H.B.* 43
the grosse matter of this *earthly* myne . . . *H.B.* 46
Farre above feeble reach of *earthly* sight, . . . *H.H.L.* 5
no thought of *earthly* wight Can comprehend, . . . *H.H.L.* 40
That in no *earthly* thing thou shalt delight, . . . *H.H.L.* 272
From whom all *earthly* governance is fet. . . . *H.H.B.* 91
Or idle thought of *earthly* things, remaine; . . . *H.H.B.* 268
begot of any *earthly* Seede, . . . *Proth.* 65

Earth-pot. Upon an huge great *Earth-pot* steane he stood, . . VII. vii. 42. 8

Earthquake. A sodein *earthquake* loe, . . . *Bel.*[1] ii. 12
An *earthquake* shooke the hill . . . *Bel.*[2] ii. 13
As doen high Towers in an *earthquake*: . . . *S.C.* F. 6
earth, . . . did like an *erthquake* show. . . . I. viii. 8. 9
As it an *Earth-quake* were: . . . III. ii. 42. 9
With dreadfull thunder . . . And an *earthquake*, . . . III. xii. 2. 3

Earth's. *See* **Mother earth's.**
Her that did match the whole *earths* puissaunce, . . . *Ro.* vi. 13
that Nation, th' *earths* new Giant brood, . . . *Ro.* xi. 9
The great *earthes* wombe they open to the sky, . . . II. i. 60. 2
ere the grosse *Earthes* gryesy shade Was all disperst . . . III. i. 67. 7
in th' *earthes* hollow caves hath long ben hid . . . III. ix. 15. 3
th' *Earthes* gloomy shade Did dim the brightnesse . . . III. x. 46. 6
Foolhardy as th' *Earthes* children, . . . III. xi. 22. 8
since th' *Earthes* cursed seed Sought to assaile . . . VII. vi. 20. 2
th' *Earths* daughter, thogh she nought did reck Of Hermes message, . . . VII. vi. 22. 7
What idle errand hast thou *earths* mansion to forsake?' . . . VII. vi. 25. 9
Whose root from *earths* base groundworke shold begin. . . . *H.H.L.* 105
all *earthes* glorie, on which men do gaze, . . . *H.H.L.* 275

Ease. in a people given all to *ease*, . . . *Ro.* xxiii. 9
unlucky Muse, that wontst to *ease* My musing mynd, . . . *S.C.* Ja. 69
But little *ease* of thy lewd tale I tasted: . . . *S.C.* F. 245
here liven at *ease* and leasure? . . . *S.C.* May 66
Diggon should soone find favour and *ease*: . . . *S.C.* S. 253
mightie manhode brought a bedde of *ease*, . . . *S.C.* O. 68
herbs, both which can hurt and *ease*, . . . *S.C.* D. 88
lying all at *ease* from guile or spight, . . . *Gn.* 111
His sense to seeke for *ease* turnes every way: . . . *Gn.* 388
make our *ease* our treasure. . . . *Hub.* 160
having overlookt their pas at *ease*, . . . *Hub.* 396
bad him stay at *ease* till further preeving. . . . *Hub.* 1366
houres in *ease* to wast, . . . *Mui.* 36
Griefe findes some *ease* by him that like does beare. . . . *D.* 67
ease of paine which cannot be recured. . . . *Col.* 946
slyding softly forth, she turnd as to her *ease*. . . . I. i. 54. 9
let him die at *ease*, that liveth here uneath? . . . I. ix. 38. 9
happy *ease*, which thou doest want and crave, . . . I. ix. 40. 2
Is not short payne well borne, that bringes long *ease*, . . . I. ix. 40. 6
Ease after warre, death after life, . . . I. ix. 40. 9
to *ease* he him recured brief, . . . I. x. 24. 7
tydings glad . . . to *ease* you of your misery!' . . . I. xi. 3. 9
Let us devize of *ease* and everlasting rest.' . . . I. xii. 17. 9
'Of *ease* or rest I may not yet devize; . . . I. xii. 18. 2
feele some secret *ease*. . . . II. i. 16. 9
So long they traveiled with litle *ease*, . . . II. ii. 12. 5
Where *ease* abownds yt's eath to doe amis: . . . II. iii. 40. 5

Ease—*Continued.*
For to allure fraile mind to carelesse *ease*: . . . II. vi. 13. 6
some ydly satt at *ease*; . . . II. ix. 35. 3
To *ease* you of that ill, . . . II. ix. 42. 9
insolent wox through unwonted *ease*, . . . II. x. 17. 2
That he might know and *ease* her sorrow sad; . . . II. xii. 28. 3
Some for untimely *ease*, some for delight, . . . III. i. 39. 4
chaunged her weary side the better *ease* to take. . . . III. i. 61. 9
Such secrete *ease* felt gentle Britomart, . . . III. ii. 15. 7
Yet wist she was not well at *ease* perdy; . . . III. ii. 27. 8
to *ease* thy griefe And win thy will: . . . III. ii. 33. 6
'Beldame, your words doe worke me litle *ease*; . . . III. ii. 43. 1
At last blow up some gentle gale of *ease*, . . . III. iv. 10. 3
To doe him *ease*, or doe him remedy. . . . III. v. 50. 2
Perhaps this hand may helpe to *ease* your woe, . . . III. xi. 15. 4
Ease, on his robe in golden letters cyphered. . . . III. xii. 4. 9
He by no meanes could wished *ease* obtaine: . . . IV. v. 40. 8
found no *ease* of griefe nor hope of grace, . . . IV. vii. 38. 2
Ne ought mote *ease* or mitigate his paine, . . . IV. vii. 47. 4
That much did *ease* his mourning and misfare: . . . IV. viii. 5. 5
Besought her to graunt *ease* unto my smart, . . . IV. x. 48. 4
nought, She saw, could *ease* his rankling maladie, . . . IV. xi. 6. 4
to *ease* her selfe of dout. . . . V. vi. 6. 4
she long had sought for *ease* In every place, . . . V. vi. 7. 1
By change of place seeking to *ease* her paine; . . . V. vi. 15. 5
As sundry chaunge her seemed best to *ease*. . . . V. vi. 26. 4
Would change her paine, and sorrow somewhat *ease*, . . . V. vii. 45. 4
He lightly reft his head to *ease* him of his paine. . . . V. xii. 23. 9
Spake, as was meet, for *ease* of my regret: . . . VI. ii. 23. 3
To wype his wounds, and *ease* their bitter payning. . . . VI. ii. 41. 5
Doe it disclose to *ease* your grieved spright: . . . VI. iv. 28. 7
never . . . His limbes would rest, ne lig in *ease* embost, . . . VI. iv. 40. 7
To seeke some place the which mote yeeld some *ease* . . . VI. v. 32. 2
brought them also *ease*, . . . VI. v. 40. 3
Sitting beside his Ladie there at *ease*, . . . VI. vi. 40. 2
here doe dwell at *ease*, . . . VI. ix. 19. 2
at more *ease* continue there his thrall: . . . VI. xi. 6. 8
seeke some succour both to *ease* my smart, . . . *Am.* ii. 7
Allur'd a Dolphin him from death to *ease*. . . . *Am.* xxxviii. 4
then my body shall have shortly *ease*: . . . *Am.* l. 11
There my fraile fancy . . . mantleth most at *ease*; . . . *Am.* lxxii. 10
Faine would I seeke to *ease* my bitter smart . . . *H.L.* 5
Walkt forth to *ease* my payne . . . *Proth.* 10

Eased. his heart was greatly *eased*. . . . *Hub.* 710
till he were better *eased* Of that strong stownd . . . *D.* 559
to be *easd* of that base burden still did erne. . . . II. iii. 46. 9
all your hurts may soone through temperance be *easd*.' . . . II. iv. 33. 9
Their aged Syre, thus *eased* of his crowne, . . . II. x. 29. 6
Hart that is inly hurt is greatly *eased* With hope . . . III. ii. 15. 3
She much was *eased* in her troublous thought, . . . V. vii. 24. 2
would on her owne Palfrey him have *eased*, . . . VI. iii. 32. 8

Easement. Yet found no *easement* in her troubled wits, . . . V. vi. 15. 3
Glad of that *easement*, though it were but small; . . . VI. iv. 15. 7

Easeth. this long tale Nought *easeth* the care . . . *S.C.* S. 243

Easier. To their deseigne to make the *easier* way, . . . V. viii. 25. 2

Easily. Ambition is engendred *easily*; . . . *Ro.* xxiii. 10
by this Gnatts complaint be *easily* knowen. . . . *Gn. Ded.* 14
With liquid foote doth slide downe *easily*. . . . *Gn.* 24
The Queene of hell to move as *easily*, . . . *Gn.* 462
Ne new ones could he *easily* provide, . . . *Hub.* 929
can more *easily* be thought then said.' . . . I. vii. 41. 2
Ye well may hope, and *easely* attaine? . . . II. ix. 6. 4
of his armes despoiled *easily* . . . II. xi. 49. 7
he the boteman bad row *easily*, . . . II. xii. 33. 8
Did *easely* beleeve her strong extremitye, . . . III. i. 53. 9
Into his hidden nett full *easely* doth fall. . . . III. i. 54. 9
They *easely* unto her charett beare: . . . III. iv. 42. 2
as he nigher drew, he *easily* Might scerne . . . III. x. 22. 7
up his head he reared *easily*, . . . III. xi. 15. 8
That by his gate might *easily* appeare; . . . III. xii. 8. 6
none the same may *easily* out-win: . . . IV. i. 20. 6
That by her monstrous shape might *easily* be red. . . . IV. i. 26. 9
so would hope him *easily* to foyle. . . . V. ix. 9. 5
To which he *easily* did them perswade. . . . VI. iv. 13. 4

East. stretch her selfe at large from *East* to West; . . . *S.C.* O. 44
the *East* with tyranous despight . . . *Gn.* 43
overran the *East* with greedie powre, . . . *Ti.* 69
The dawning day forth comming from the *East*. . . . *As.* 34
Forth looking through the windowes of the *East*, . . . *Col.* 605
had . . . Their scepters stretcht from *East* to Westerne shore, . I. i. 5. 5
Aurora . . . Out of the *East* the dawning day doth call. . . . I. iv. 16. 5
Phoebus in the glooming *East* . . . I. xii. 2. 1
doth the morning starre appeare Out of the *East*, . . . I. xii. 21. 6
Lookt foorth, as Phoebus face out of the *east* . . . III. ii. 24. 6
The wealth of th' *East*, and pompe of Persian kings: . . . III. iv. 23. 4
reeled to and fro from *east* to west. . . . III. vii. 42. 7
who from *East* to West will endlong seeke, . . . III. ix. 51. 3
light Out of the ruddy *East* was fully reard, . . . III. x. 52. 7
As like can not be seene from *East* to West, . . . IV. v. 18. 4
All th' *East*, before untam'd, did over-ronne, . . . V. i. 2. 2
weigh the light that in the *East* doth rise; . . . V. ii. 43. 3
day forth dawning from the *East* . . . V. v. 1. 1
Lyke Phoebe, from her chamber of the *East*, . . . *Epith.* 149
Appeare out of the *East*. . . . *Epith.* 287
antique Babel, Empresse of the *East*, . . . *Com. Son.* iv. 1

Easterland. He *Easterland* subdewd, and Denmarke wonne, . . II. x. 41. 3

Easterlings. Those spoylefull Picts, and swarming *Easterlings*, II. x. 63. 2

Eastern. made the *Easterne* Conquerour to crie, . . . *Ti.* 432
Phoebus fiery carre . . . was climbing up the *Easterne* hill, . I. ii. 1. 8
to the *Easterne* coast of heaven makes speedy way: . . . I. v. 19. 9

Eastern—*Continued.*
Titan, playing on the *eastern* streames, II. iii. 1. 3
The *Easterne* Saxons from the Southerne ny, IV. xi. 33. 4
Easy. An *easie* running verse with tender feete. *Gn.* 53
An *easie* life, and fit high God to please. *Hub.* 395
fairly paced forth with *easie* paine, *Hub.* 1264
they . . . brought the heavy corse with *easy* pace I. v. 31. 2
Three miles it might be *easy* heard arownd, I. viii. 4. 3
a Groome, that forth him ledd . . . and laid in *easie* bedd. I. x. 17. 8
a woman . . . That was on earth not *easie* to compare; I. x. 30. 4
easy was t' inveigle weaker sight: I. xii. 32. 5
cannot so *easy* mis. II. iii. 40. 7
easy is the way and passage plaine II. iii. 41. 7
So *easie* was to quench his flamed minde II. vi. 8. 6
So *easie* is t' appease the stormy winde Of malice II. vi. 8. 8
The sea is wide, and *easy* for to stray; II. vi. 23. 4
easie to be thought II. ix. 33. 9
they overran all parts with *easy* hand. II. x. 61. 9
Full *easy* was for her to have beliefe, III. i. 54. 1
with *easy* shifte . . . quilt she lightly up did lifte, III. i. 61. 1
'Ne soothlich is it *easie* for to read III. ii. 14. 1
There they him laide in *easy* couch well dight, III. iv. 43. 6
In *easie* couch his feeble limbes to rest. III. v. 41. 2
So may he long him selfe full *easie* hide; III. vi. 23. 6
the winged boy . . . full *easie* to be knowne, And he thereby, III. xi. 7. 8
More *easie* issew now then entrance late III. xii. 43. 1
But not so *easie* will I her forsake; IV. ii. 14. 5
was *easie* to be showen. IV. iv. 38. 5
With *easie* steps so soft as foot could stryde, IV. viii. 37. 2
By which it's *easie* him to know againe, V. i. 19. 7
'Certes, your strife were *easie* to accord, V. iv. 16. 2
by your change of cheare is *easie* for to see.' V. vii. 18. 9
found No *easie* meanes according to his mind: V. viii. 42. 3
That to Sir Calidore was *easie* geare; VI. iii. 6. 5
O what an *easie* thing is to descry The gentle bloud, VI. v. 1. 1
Mote *easie* be supprest with little thing; VI. vi. 8. 4
To some hid end to make more *easie* way, VI. vi. 42. 2
Whereon he rode not *easie* was to deeme; VII. vii. 40. 7
easie things, that may be got at will, *Am.* xxvi. 11
with th' *easie* vew Of this base world, *H.H.B.* 22
Eat. Should warre upon the kings, and *eate* their flesh. *Rev.* iii. 10
The whiles his flock their chawed cuds do *eate*. *Gn.* 144
Eate they that list, *Hub.* 436
To *eate* thy heart through comfortlesse dispaires; *Hub.* 904
tell hir, that my mouth can *eate* no meate: *U.V.* 8
That which I *eate* did I joy, and that which I greedily gorged, *Ex Tempore* 1
the hungry t' *eat*, *Col.* 849
He . . . did his stout heart *eat*, I. ii. 6. 3
a courser . . . the sharpe yron did for anger *eat*, I. iii. 33. 5
as he rode he somewhat still did *eat*, I. iv. 22. 5
rend his flesh, and his owne synewes *eat*. I. x. 28. 3
he would *eat* His neighbour element in his revenge: I. xi. 21. 5
whoso did *eat*, eftsoones did know Both good and ill, I. xi. 47. 7
ne ought would *eat*, II. ii. 35. 2
Of grace I pray thee, give to *eat* and drinke to mee!' II. vii. 59. 9
Ne would they *eate* till she in presence came. III. ix. 26. 6
of us three to morrow he will sure *eate* one.' IV. vii. 13. 9
corsive, which did *eat* Her tender heart IV. ix. 14. 4
with waves continuall Doe *eate* the earth, V. ii. 39. 5
Ne doth she give them other thing to *eat* V. iv. 31. 7
bid him *eate*: henceforth he oft shall hungry sit.' V. iv. 49. 9
He gan to threaten her likewise to *eat*, V. vii. 15. 8
vexeth so that makes her *eat* her gall; V. xii. 31. 5
when she wanteth other thing to *eat*, V. xii. 31. 6
To *eate* the fleshe of men whom they mote fynde, VI. viii. 36. 2
then her *eate* attonce, or many meales to make. VI. viii. 37. 9
if he hungry were, him offred eke to *eat*. VI. ix. 6. 9
every bit which thenceforth I did *eat*. *Am.* xxxix. 14
Eaten. *See* **Worm-eaten.**
the gay floures did offer to be *eaten*; *Van.* ii. 6
Therein is *eaten* out an hollow cave, III. viii. 37. 5
Seaven women by him slaine, and *eaten* clene: IV. vii. 13. 5
As if that long she had not *eaten* ought; V. xii. 30. 7
Eath. thence the passage *ethe*; *S.C.* Jul. 90
Eche thing imparted is more *eath* to beare: *S.C.* S. 17
From the right way full *eath* may wander *Hub.* 404
by his like visnomie *Eathe* to be knowen; *Mui.* 311
'More *eath* (quoth he) it is in such a case *Col.* 590
Where ease abownds yt's *eath* to doe amis: II. iii. 40. 5
It's *eath* his ydle fury to aswage, II. iv. 11. 7
More *eath* to number with how many eyes III. xi. 45. 8
More *eath* was new impression to receive; IV. vi. 40. 6
our like persons, *eath* to be disguiz'd, IV. viii. 58. 3
more *eath* it were for mortall wight IV. xi. 53. 1
much more *eath* to tell the starres on hy, IV. xii. 1. 5
them selves full *eath* perswade To faire accordaunce, V. viii. 14. 4
Eating. Though *eating* hipps, and drinking watry fome. *Hub.* 948
Eats. *eates* the hart and feedes upon the gall, *H.L.* 268
Ebb. every River still doth *ebbe* and flowe; VII. vii. 20. 4
Ebon. Made all of *Heben* and white Yvorie; *Pet.* ii. 2
A curious Coffer made of *Heben* wood, *Ti.* 618
Lay now thy deadly *Heben* bowe apart, I. Pr. 3. 5
youth . . . His speare of *heben* wood behind him bare, I. vii. 37. 2
trees of bitter Gall, and *Heben* sad; II. vii. 52. 2
bore after him an *heben* launce And coverd shield. II. viii. 17. 6
Whom all men term'd Knight of the *Hebene* speare, IV. v. 8. 2
the Knight That bore the *Hebene* speare, IV. v. 20. 5
knowne by fame, and by an *Hebene* speare, IV. vi. 6. 4
Ebranck. *Ebranck* salved both their infamies II. x. 21. 6
Ecastor. The fourth *Ecastor*, of exceeding might; V. iii. 5. 6
Echidna. Orthrus begotten by great Typhaon And foule *Echidna* V. x. 10. 8
Borne of the brooding of *Echidna* base, V. xi. 23. 5
bred of hellish strene, . . . Begot of foule *Echidna*, VI. vi. 9. 9
'*Echidna* is a Monster direfull dred, VI. vi. 10. 1
Echo. *See* **Re-echo.**
Whose *Echo* made the neyghbour groves to ring, *S.C.* Jun. 52
The hollow *Echo* of my carefull cryes: *S.C.* Au. 160
All which the ayrie *Echo* did resound, *Gn.* 232
feeble *Eccho* now laments *T.M.* 285
Her name to *eccho* unto heaven hie. *Col.* 483
all the woods with doubled *Eccho* ring; I. vi. 14. 2
through the woods their *Eccho* did rebound. VI. x. 10. 5
The woods shall to me answer, and my *Eccho* ring. *Epith.* 18
That all the woods may answer, and your *eccho* ring. *Epith.* 36
The woods shall to you answer, and your *Eccho* ring. *Epith.* 55
That all the woods may answer, and your *eccho* ring. *Epith.* 73
all the woods them answer, and theyr *eccho* ring. *Epith.* 91
The whiles the woods shal answer, and your *eccho* ring. *Epith.* 109
all the woods shal answer, and theyr *eccho* ring. *Epith.* 128
al the woods them answer, and theyr *eccho* ring. *Epith.* 147
That all the woods may answer, and your *eccho* ring. *Epith.* 166
To which the woods did answer, and your *eccho* ring? *Epith.* 184
al the woods should answer, and your *echo* ring. *Epith.* 203
That al the woods may answere, and their *eccho* ring. *Epith.* 222
That all the woods may answere, and your *eccho* ring. *Epith.* 241
To which the woods shall answer, and theyr *eccho* ring. *Epith.* 260
That all the woods may answer, and your *eccho* ring. *Epith.* 277
all the woods them answer, and their *echo* ring! *Epith.* 295
The woods no more shall answere, nor your *echo* ring. *Epith.* 314
Ne let the woods them answer nor theyr *eccho* ring. *Epith.* 333, 352
Ne will the woods now answer, nor your *Eccho* ring. *Epith.* 371
Ne let the woods us answere, nor our *Eccho* ring. *Epith.* 389
Ne any woods shall answer, nor your *Eccho* ring. *Epith.* 408
The woods no more us answer, nor our *eccho* ring! *Epith.* 426
gentle *Eccho* . . . Their accents did resound. *Proth.* 112
Echoed. *See* **Re-echoed.**
her plaint, Which softly *ecchoed* from the neighbour wood; I. iii. 8. 2
the *ecchoed* report Of their new joy, I. xii. 4. 2
Throughout the wood that *ecchoed* againe, II. iii. 20. 8
Echoes. Were wont redoubled *Echoes* to rebound, *T.M.* 22
Ecchoes three aunswer'd it selfe againe: I. viii. 4. 4
The woods did nought but *ecchoes* vaine rebound; VI. xi. 26. 6
all the woods theyr *ecchoes* back rebounded, *Am.* xix. 7
Eclipsed. Yet is he oft *eclipsed* by the way, VII. vii. 51. 8
Ecstasy. some *extasye* Assotted had his sence, III. viii. 22. 8
To set upon them in that *extasie*, VII. vi. 23. 5
As carries them into an *extasy*, *H.H.B.* 261
Ecstatic. suddein fitt, and halfe *extatick* stoure, III. iii. 50. 5
Eden. most mighty king of *Eden* fayre, I. xii. 26. 1
To beene departed out of *Eden* landes, II. i. 1. 5
Eden selfe, if ought with *Eden* mote compayre. II. xii. 52. 9
Eden, though but small, IV. xi. 36. 7
Edge. The Axes *edge* did oft turne againe, *S.C.* F. 203
bene not thy teeth on *edge*, *S.C.* May 35
with harts on *edge* To be aveng'd I. iv. 43. 3
sharper *edge* did feele, I. xi. 36. 3
Edged. Therewith their dulled sprights they *edgd* anew, IV. ii. 17. 6
Edges. weld his naked sword, and try the *edges* keene, IV. vii. 45. 9
Edified. A little mount, of greene turffs *edifide*; *Gn.* 660
that great Arche, which Trajan *edifide*, *Ti.* 551
a litle wyde There was an holy chappell *edifyde*, I. i. 34. 5
Through countreyes waste, and eke well *edifyde*, III. i. 14. 2
That Castle was most goodly *edifyde*, III. i. 20. 4
Edmund. Such one King *Edmond*, but was rent for gaine. *Ti.* 418
Edwin. On his sonne *Edwin* all those wrongs shall wreake; III. iii. 36. 2
Till both the sonnes of *Edwin* he have slayne, III. iii. 37. 2
Effect. The roote whereof and tragicall *effect*, Vouchsafe, *Mui.* 9
Give over to *effect* his first intent, II. xi. 41. 3
Thou doest *effect* in destined descents, III. iii. 2. 6
How to *effect* so hard an enterprize, III. iii. 51. 6
findeth dew *effect* or soone or late; III. iv. 27. 5
she feared The sad *effect* of her neare overthrowe; V. ii. 22. 4
thereon seizing tooke no great *effect*; V. xii. 21. 7
pearst Her stubborne hart with inward deepe *effect*, VI. i. 45. 4
when the cause . . . Removed is, th' *effect* surceaseth still. VI. vi. 14. 4
Yet durst he not for very cowardize *Effect* the same, VI. vi. 44. 7
Encline thy will t' *effect* our wishfull vow, *Epith.* 385
seeing her faire eyes so sharpe *effect*, *H.B.* 244
Effects. All which the sad *effects* of discord sung: IV. i. 21. 3
Effierced. with fell woodnes he *effierced* was, III. xi. 27. 4
Efforce. burnt his beastly hart t' *efforce* her chastitye. I. vi. 4. 9
Them to *efforce* by violence or wrong: II. vii. 30. 4
Yet list the same *efforce* with faind gainesay; III. ii. 15. 8
Ere that we to *efforce* it doe begin: III. ix. 9. 4
It vaine she thought with rigorous uprore For to *efforce*, III. xii. 27. 9
He gan t' *efforce* the evidence anew, V. ix. 47. 1
Efforced. Againe he heard a more *efforced* voyce, II. viii. 4. 3
the mightiest things *efforced* bin: II. xii. 43. 7
To have *efforst* the love of that faire lasse, III. xii. 43. 8
Effort. thralled her in chaines with strong *effort*, II. v. 17. 4
strong *effort* Of feeling pleasures, II. xi. 13. 7
To loose her warlike limbs and strong *effort*; III. i. 52. 5
To shew Dan Cupids powre and great *effort*: III. xi. 46. 5
he stil them holds, and keepes with strong *effort*. V. ii. 5. 9
Ne durst abide behind, for dread of worse *effort*. VI. xi. 42. 9
Effrayed. Their dam upstart out of her den *effraide*, I. i. 16. 1
Eft. But *eft* . . . Comes the breme Winter *S.C.* F. 42
he had *eft* learned a curres call,) *S.C.* S. 191
eft did sing of warres *S.C.* O. 59

Eft—*Continued.*
efte in Dolons subtile surprysall. . . . . *Gn.* 536
Eft looking back would faine have runne away; . . . . . I. ix. 25. 3
Eft through the thicke they heard one rudely rush, ... II. iii. 21. 1
eft, . . . Our selves in league of vowed love wee knitt: . . . . . II. iv. 18. 4
Eft to Cymochles twise so many fold; . . . . . II. viii. 41. 5
Eft fierce retourning, ... II. xi. 36. 6
It would have lived, and revived *eft;* . . . . . IV. iii. 21. 8
eft them turned both againe to fight: . . . . . IV. iii. 47. 3
eft aventring his steele-headed launce, ... IV. vi. 11. 3
And *eft* againe deviz'd some what to say, ... IV. vi. 45. 7
eft gan into tender teares to melt. . . . . . IV. vii. 9. 5
The Lady to alight did *eft* require, ... V. i. 21. 3
which he unbuckling *eft* Presented to the fayrest Florimell, . V. iii. 27. 7
Yet seem'd the soyle both fayre and frutefull *eft,* . . . . . VI. ix. 1. 5
eft his burning levin-brond in hand he tooke. . . . . . VII. vi. 30. 9
eft him placed where he close might view . . . . . VII. vi. 45. 2
When she in fleshly seede is *eft* enraced, ... *H.B.* 114

Efts. In which the fearefull *ewftes* do build their bowres, . . . V. x. 23. 7

Eftsoons. *Eftsoones* of thousand billowes shouldred narre, . . . *Ro.* xvi. 3
Eftsoones having his wide wings spent in wast, ... *Ro.* xvi. 7
Eftsoones consum'd to fall downe feebily, ... *Ro.* xvi. 11
Eftsoones their rule of yearely Presidents . . . . . *Ro.* xviii. 7
Eftsoones in compas arch't, ... *Ro.* xx. 3
eftsones Winter gan to approche; . . . . . *S.C.* F. 225
Eftsoones more fierce in visage, ... *Gn.* 269
Eftsoones he gins to fashion . . . . . *Gn.* 650
Eftsoones the Ape himselfe gan up to reare, ... *Hub.* 237
of the Priest *eftsoones* gan to enquire, ... *Hub.* 481
Eftsones by counsell of the Foxe . . . . . *Hub.* 1112
Eftsoones such store of teares shee forth did powre, ... *T.M.* 595
Eftsoones that Damzell . . . She turn'd into a . . . . . *Mui.* 137
Eftsoones her white streight legs were altered . . . . . *Mui.* 349
Eftsoones . . . Full greedily into the heard he thrust, . . . *As.* 103
The Champion stout *Eftsoones* dismounted . . . . . I. i. 11. 8
Eftsoones he tooke that miscreated faire, ... I. ii. 3. 1
the sleeping spark . . . gan *eftsoones* revive; . . . . . I. ii. 19. 2
Eftsoones I thought her such as she me told, ... I. ii. 39. 6
gan *eftsoones* prepare Himselfe to batteill . . . . . I. iii. 34. 3
Eft soones he perced through his chaufed chest . . . . . I. iii. 42. 6
Eftsoones his manly forces gan to fayle, ... I. vii. 6. 4
eftsoones he gan apply relief . . . . . I. x. 24. 4
Eftsoones unto an holy Hospitall, ... I. x. 36. 1
Eftsoones that dreadful Dragon they espyde, ... I. xi. 4. 4
Eftsoones he gan advance his haughty crest, ... I. xi. 15. 5
whoso did eat, *eftsoones* did know . . . . . I. xi. 47. 7
Eftsoones the Gard, . . . Attacht that faytor false, ... I. xii. 35. 4
Eftsoones untwisting his deceiptfull clew, ... II. i. 8. 3
Eftsoone she said; . . . . . II. i. 17. 1
Eftsoones of him had perfect cognizaunce, ... II. i. 31. 5
Eftsoones devisd redresse . . . . . II. ii. 43. 8
Eftsoones to court he cast t' advaunce his first degree. . . . II. iii. 5. 9
Eftsoones this liegeman gan to wexe more bold, ... II. iii. 9. 2
Eftsoones supposed him a person meet . . . . . II. iii. 11. 5
Eftsoone there stepped foorth A goodly Ladie . . . . . II. iii. 21. 6
'*Eftsoones* he came unto th' appointed place, ... II. iv. 28. 1
Eftsoones he fled away, and might no where be seene. . . . II. iv. 46. 9
Eftsoones his cruel hand Sir Guyon stayd, ... II. v. 13. 1
Eftsoones her shallow ship away did slide, ... II. vi. 5. 1
Eftsoones he gan to rage, and inly frett, ... II. vi. 28. 3
the matter . . . *eftsoones* he did compownd; . . . . . II. vii. 17. 7
eftsoones he gan display His . . . wings, ... II. viii. 8. 8
both *eftsoones* upstarted furiously, ... II. viii. 18. 8
Eftsoones forth looked . . . The watch, ... II. ix. 11. 6
eftsoones arrived here three hoyes Of Saxons, ... II. x. 64. 8
he *eftsoones* gan launch his barke forthright. . . . . . II. xi. 4. 4
Eftsoones himselfe in glitterand armes he dight, ... II. xi. 17. 1
Eftesoones shee causd him up to be convayd, ... II. xi. 49. 6
Eftsoones they saw an hideous hoast . . . . . II. xii. 22. 8
Eftesoones their stubborne corages were queld, ... II. xii. 40. 4
Eftsoones they heard a most melodious sound, ... II. xii. 70. 1
Eftsoones them brought unto their Ladies sight, ... III. i. 31. 8
Eftsoones shee grew to great impatience, ... III. i. 48. 1
Eftesoones long waxen torches weren light . . . . . III. i. 58. 3
Eftsoones there was presented to her eye A comely knight, . III. ii. 24. 1
Eftsoones, her goodly shield addressing fayre, ... III. iv. 14. 1
Eftsoones his heaped waves he did commaund . . . . . III. iv. 22. 3
Eftesoones both flowres and girlonds far away Shee flong, . . III. iv. 30. 1
Eftesoones the roaring billowes still abid, ... III. iv. 32. 7
Eftsoones his warlike courser . . . She made those Damzels
search; . . . . . III. v. 38. 6
Eftsoones her steps she thereunto applyd, ... III. vii. 5. 6
Eftesoones out of her hidden cave she cald . . . . . III. vii. 22. 1
Eftsoones she badd me, ... III. vii. 54. 3
His bloody speare *eftesoones* he boldly bent . . . . . III. viii. 12. 5
comming nigh, *eftsoones* he gan to gesse, ... III. viii. 45. 3
the flame; the which *eftesoones* gave place, ... III. xi. 25. 4
Forst him *eftsoones* to follow other game, ... III. xi. 38. 8
eftsoones his wanton hart Was tickled with delight, ... IV. i. 33. 5
eftsoones it prickt his wanton mind With sting of lust . . . IV. ii. 5. 4
That cruell Atropos *eftsoones* undid, ... IV. ii. 48. 7
Eftsoones his life may passe into the next: . . . . . IV. ii. 52. 6
through traduction was *eftsoones* derived, ... IV. iii. 13. 6
eftsoones his mightie hand He heav'd on high, ... IV. iii. 33. 1
Eftsoones out of her Coch she gan availe, ... IV. iii. 46. 4
vaunted speare *eftsoones* to disadvaunce, ... IV. iv. 7. 2
which *eftsoones* discovered, to it drew The eyes of all, . . . IV. iv. 16. 3
Eftsoones he gan to gather up around His weapons . . . . . IV. iv. 23. 1
A mightie speare *eftsoones* at him he bent; . . . . . IV. iv. 28. 6
passing beautie did *eftsoones* reveale, ... IV. v. 10. 4

Eftsoons—*Continued.*
Whose beauties beame *eftsoones* did shine so bright, ... IV. v. 10. 8
when they thought it fast, *eftsoones* it was untide. . . . . . IV. v. 17. 9
Eftsoones one of those villeins him did rap . . . . . IV. v. 42. 3
She gan *eftsoones* it to her mind to call . . . . . IV. vi. 26. 4
Eftsoones she flew unto his fearelesse hand, ... IV. viii. 12. 1
eftsoones he brake, His sodaine silence . . . . . IV. viii. 16. 1
Eftsoones that pretious liquour forth he drew, ... IV. viii. 20. 6
Eftsoones the Prince tooke downe those Ladies twaine . . . IV. viii. 41. 1
Eftsoones the others did the field recoure, ... IV. ix. 25. 3
Eftsoones all burning with a fresh desire . . . . . IV. ix. 29. 1
Eftsoones him selfe he to their aide addrest, ... IV. ix. 32. 5
Eftsoones outsprung two more of equall mould; . . . . . IV. x. 10. 3
Eftsoones, advauncing that enchaunted shield, ... IV. x. 19. 6
His cheared heart *eftsoones* away gan chace Sad death, . . . IV. xii. 34. 3
Eftsoones him selfe he from his hold unbownd, ... V. ii. 16. 4
Eftsoones his Page drew to the Castle gate, ... V. ii. 21. 1
Eftsoones he stood as still as any stake, ... V. iii. 34. 5
Eftsoones the people all to harnesse ran, ... V. iv. 36. 6
Eftsoones that warriouresse . . . Did forth issue . . . . . V. vii. 27. 7
Eftsoones they gan their wrothfull hands to hold, ... V. viii. 12. 4
gan *eftsoones* devize to be aveng'd for it. . . . . . V. viii. 45. 9
Eftsoones brought forth the villaine, ... V. ix. 10. 2
Her selfe *eftsoones* she gan convert againe: . . . . . V. ix. 37. 3
from her partie *eftsoones* was drawen cleene: . . . . . V. ix. 49. 3
Eftsoones forth pricked proudly in his might, ... V. x. 31. 8
Eftsoones againe his axe he raught on hie, ... V. xi. 10. 1
buckling him *eftsoones* unto the fight, ... V. xi. 57. 8
Eftsoones he loosd that Squire, ... VI. i. 18. 2
Those warlike armes . . . he gan *eftsoones* prepare, ... VI. v. 8. 5
Eftsoones he spide a Knight approching nye; . . . . . VI. v. 22. 1
eftsoones he all enraged grew, ... VI. vi. 22. 2
Eftsoones they pricked forth with forward pryde, ... VI. vii. 6. 5
Eftsoones the Prince to him full nimbly stept, ... VI. viii. 17. 1
Eftsoones he saw one with a naked knife . . . . . VI. viii. 48. 8
Eftsoones she cast . . . Her to displace, ... VII. vi. 10. 7
Eftsoones the sonne of Maia forth he sent . . . . . VII. vi. 16. 1
Eftsoones she thus resolv'd; . . . . . VII. vi. 23. 1
Eftsoones the time and place appointed were, ... VII. vi. 36. 1
Eftsoones he wypes quite out of memory . . . . . *H.L.* 241
Eftsoones the Nymphes, . . . Ran all in haste . . . . . *Proth.* 55

Eger. *See* **Eager.**

Eggs. drove in Joves owne lap his *egs* to lay; . . . . . *Van.* iv. 10
Forst with the filth his *egs* to fling away: . . . . . *Van.* iv. 12

Eglantine. With Hawthorne buds, and swete *Eglantine,* . . . *S.C.* May 13
In thy sweete *Eglantine* of Meriflure; . . . . . *Col.* 389
the fragrant *Eglantine* did spred His prickling armes, ... II. v. 29. 4
Eglantine and Caprifole emong, ... III. vi. 44. 6
Sweet is the *Eglantine,* but pricketh nere; . . . . . *Am.* xxvi. 3
woodbynd flowers and fragrant *Eglantine;* . . . . . *Am.* lxxi. 10

Egre. *See* **Eager.**

Egypt. All that which *Aegypt* whilome did devise, ... *Ro.* xxix. 1

Egyptian. father Nilus gins to swell . . . above the *Aegyptian*
vale . . . . . I. i. 21. 2
of thing like to that *Aegyptian* slime, ... II. ix. 21. 5
Wherein th' *Aegyptian* Phao long did lurke . . . . . III. ii. 20. 3
Aegyptian wisards old, Which in Star-read . . . have best
insight, ... V. Pr. 8. 1
Of th' old *Aegyptian* Kings that whylome were, ... V. vii. 2. 6

Eide. *See* **Eyed.**

Eien. *See* **Eyes.**

Eight. being *eight* lugs of grownd, ... II. x. 11. 3
during *eight* yeares space, ... III. iii. 41. 2

Eione. Neso, and *Eione* well in age, ... IV. xi. 50. 7

Eirene. Just Dice, wise Eunomie, myld *Eirene;* . . . . . V. ix. 32. 6

Either. With bowe and bolts in *either* hand, ... *S.C.* Mar. 65
In *either* cheeke depeincten lively chere: . . . . . *S.C.* Ap. 69
For *eyther* the shepeheards bene ydle and still, ... *S.C.* S. 80
shed his whirling flames on *either* side, ... *Gn.* 159
great dole on *either* partie grewe, ... *Gn.* 529
here the praise of *either* Scipion Abides . . . . . *Gn.* 613
Must *either* driven be perforce to sterving, ... *Hub.* 370
But *either* for some gainfull benefit, ... *Hub.* 639
either (algates) would be Lords alone; . . . . . *Hub.* 1025
if that wrong on *eyther* side there were, ... *Hub.* 1097
About whose flowrie bankes on *either* side . . . . . *Ti.* 136
Strongly outlaunced towards *either* side, ... *Mui.* 82
Either by slaundring his well-deemed name, ... *Col.* 695
For *either* they be puffed up with pride, ... *Col.* 759
Their horned fronts so fierce on *either* side Doe meete, . . . I. ii. 16. 3
Two iron coffers hong on *either* side, ... I. iv. 27. 3
if that *either* to that shield had right, ... I. iv. 40. 8
victory they dare not wish to *either* side. . . . . . I. v. 9. 9
If *either* salves, or oyles, or herbes, or charmes, ... I. v. 41. 7
On *either* side disparted with his rod, ... I. x. 53. 4
in *either* jaw Three ranckes of yron teeth . . . . . I. xi. 13. 1
Either for grievous shame, or for great teene, ... II. i. 15. 8
her on *either* side doe sore assay, ... II. ii. 24. 5
contend With *either* of those knightes . . . . . II. iii. 17. 3
He, *either* envying my toward good, Or . . . . . II. iv. 22. 2
both attonce him charge on *either* syde . . . . . II. viii. 35. 1
dealt blowes On *either* side, ... II. viii. 41. 2
Matchable *either* to Semiramis, ... II. x. 56. 2
no earthly wight, but *either* Spright, Or Angell, ... II. x. 71. 6
His Beast he felly prickt on *either* syde, ... II. xi. 24. 3
either Gloriana let her chuse, ... III. Pr. 5. 7
for *cither* fatall end, Or other mightie cause, ... III. iii. 15. 8
girt in with two walls on *either* side; . . . . . III. vi. 31. 2
Either for want of handsome time and place, ... III. vii. 60. 4
with a shaft was shot through *either* eye, ... III. xi. 48. 8

Either—*Continued.*
Matchable *ether* to that ympe of Troy, . . . III. xii. 7. 3
In love were *either* ended or begunne: . . . IV. Pr. 3. 5
Should *either* winne him one, . . . IV. i. 9. 9
either bare The other downe . . . IV. i. 41. 7
Full many mightie strokes on *either* side Were sent, . . . IV. iii. 7. 6
either sdeignes with other to partake: . . . IV. iii. 16. 8
Ne *either* car'd to ward, or perill shonne, . . . IV. iii. 36. 4
Ne *either* cared life to save or spill, . . . IV. iii. 36. 6
either doth on other much relie. . . . IV. v. 1. 5
Then *either* care of parents could refraine, . . . IV. ix. 3. 4
Either through gifts, or guile, or such like waies, . . . IV. x. 18. 8
either beat him in, or drive him out. . . . IV. x. 19. 5
On *either* side of her two young men stood, . . . IV. x. 32. 1
Therefore on *either* side she was sustained . . . IV. xi. 25. 1
ill perhaps mote fall to *either* side; . . . V. i. 25. 4
each of *either* take his share aright: . . . V. i. 26. 5
Either the other from his steede to cast; . . . V. ii. 14. 7
earth uptake And all the sea, divided each from *either*: . . . V. ii. 31. 2
Ne *either* sought the others strokes to shun, . . . V. vii. 29. 3
strongly *either* strooke And broke their speares; . . . V. viii. 9. 6
Either embracing other lovingly, . . . V. viii. 14. 6
swearing faith to *either* on his blade, . . . V. viii. 14. 7
either others cause to maintaine mutually. . . . V. viii. 14. 9
He *either* spoiles, . . . Or to his part allures, . . . V. viii. 18. 8
Eyther for th' evill which he did therein, . . . V. ix. 26. 7
As *either* might for wealth have gotten bene, . . . V. ix. 27. 7
heare the matter throughly scand On *either* part, . . . V. ix. 37. 8
Past through his shield and pierst through *either* syde; . . . V. x. 35. 7
Either for fame, or else for exercize, . . . VI. vi. 35. 5
Without disquiet or dislike of *ether*, . . . VI. xii. 10. 8
on *eyther* side Supported her . . . VII. vii. 34. 5
more salvage wylde, Then *either* Lyon or . . . *Am.* xx. 10
eyther change thy cruelty, Or give like leave . . . *Epig.* iv. 19
Either by chaunce, against the course of kynd, . . . *H.B.* 143
Either with nimble wings to cut the skies, . . . *H.H.L.* 66

Either's. So parted they, as *eithers* way them led. . . . *Hub.* 551
hewen helmets deepe shew marks of *eithers* might. . . . I. v. 7. 9
deadly points at *eithers* breast to bend, . . . IV. ii. 14. 8

Eke (*partial list of adv.*).
an hundred pillers *eke* about, . . . *Bel.*[1] ii. 2
the sielyng *eke* Did shine . . . *Bel.*[1] ii. 9
And *eke* tenne thousand sithes . . . *S.C.* Ja. 51
I have a syre, A stepdame *eke*, . . . *S.C.* Mar. 41
To be wise, and *eke* to love, . . . *S.C.* Mar. Emb. 1
And *eke* you Virgins, . . . *S.C.* Ap. 41
God, that gave . . . *Eke* cherish his child, . . . *S.C.* May 86
My fancye *eke* from former follies move . . . *S.C.* Jun. 37
They han the fleece, and *eke* the flesh, . . . *S.C.* Jul. 189
The glory *eke* much greater then the gayne: . . . *S.C.* O. 20
the budde *eke* needes must quaile; . . . *S.C.* N. 91
and my Gossip *eke* beside, . . . *Hub.* 53
There must thou fashion *eke* a godly zeale, . . . *Hub.* 493
Yet manie *eke* of them . . . are driven . . . *Hub.* 539
and *eke* of private men . . . *Hub.* 787
and *eke* scorne The Sectaries thereof, . . . *Hub.* 832
And for my Sisters *eake* . . . *T.M.* 534
That goodly Ladie, sith she *eke* did spring . . . *Ti.* 275
will till then my painfull penance *eeke*. . . . *D.* 391
and *eke* my love from me; . . . *D.* 401
But read now *eke*, . . . *Col.* 159
'That shall I *eke* . . . to you declare: . . . *Col.* 163
And Proteus *eke* with him does drive . . . *Col.* 248
There *eke* is Palin . . . *Col.* 392
after him uprose *eke* all the rest: . . . *Col.* 953
And with them *eke*, O Goddesse . . . I. Pr. 4. 1
And *eke* the Graces . . . I. i. 48. 7
Up Una rose, up rose the lyon *eke*; . . . I. iii. 21. 2
Through shield and body *eke* . . . I. iii. 35. 5
And *eke* unhable once to stirre or go; . . . I. iv. 23. 2
and *eke* in foote and hand . . . I. iv. 29. 6
And *eke* the verse of famous Poets witt . . . I. iv. 32. 6
to you *eke* longes his love. . . . I. iv. 48. 6
And *eke* enchaunted armes, . . . I. iv. 50. 6
redoubled crime with vengeaunce new Thou biddest me to *eeke*? . . . I. v. 42. 8
both living and *eke* ded.' . . . I. vi. 36. 9
The ground *eke* groned under him . . . I. vii. 8. 6
haplesse, and *eke* hopelesse, . . . I. vii. 11. 4
Of wondrous worth, and *eke* of wondrous mights, . . . I. vii. 30. 2
So thought I *eke* of him, . . . I. vii. 49. 9
Your fortune maister *eke* with governing, . . . I. viii. 28. 3
both power and *eke* will. . . . I. x. 1. 9
made him pray both earely and *eke* late: . . . I. x. 26. 5
fayrely *eke* besought Himselfe to chearish, . . . I. x. 29. 4
both gratious and *eke* liberall: . . . I. x. 34. 5
th' English Bath, and *eke* the German Spau; . . . I. xi. 30. 7
For happy life . . . And life *eke* everlasting . . . I. xi. 46. 6
Another like faire tree *eke* grew thereby, . . . I. xi. 47. 6
Both daughter and *eke* kingdome lo! I yield . . . I. xii. 20. 9
two froward sisters . . . Came with them *eke*, . . . II. ii. 34. 2
Love . . . makes *eke* one will; . . . II. iv. 19. 8
and shonned followes *eke*. . . . II. iv. 44. 3
Deadly dismayd . . . and grieved *eke* . . . II. v. 8. 2
And weetlesse *eke* of lately wrought despight, . . . II. v. 36. 5
Him followed *eke* Sir Guyon . . . II. vii. 26. 3
Here *eke* that famous golden Apple grew, . . . II. vii. 55. 4
and solemne *eke* in sight, . . . II. ix. 36. 8
Sir Guyon chaunst *eke* on another booke, . . . II. ix. 60. 1
and *eke* of corage bold, . . . II. x. 7. 8

Eke—*Continued.*
She *eke* . . . Did life with usury to him restore, . . . II. xi. 45. 3
So did he *eke* Sir Guyon . . . II. xii. 49. 6
countreyes waste, and *eke* well edifyde, . . . III. i. 14. 2
men that prayse gin *eke* t' envy. . . . III. ii. 2. 9
what needeth thee to *eke* my payne? . . . III. ii. 35. 2
no lesse hast, and *eke* with no lesse dreed, . . . III. iv. 50. 1
horror, and *eke* hellish dreriment: . . . III. iv. 58. 5
Spare, gentle sister, with reproch my paine to *eeke*; . . . III. vi. 22. 9
her selfe *eke* with her went . . . III. vi. 26. 3
more bent to *eke* my smartes . . . III. vii. 55. 7
his worke is *eke* Faire Lincolne, . . . III. ix. 51. 1
And Hellenors both eyes did *eke* beguyle, . . . III. x. 5. 4
He loved *eke* Iphimedia deare, . . . III. xi. 42. 1
oft for Venus, and how often *eek* For . . . III. xi. 44. 4
Nymphes *eke* Hylas cryde. . . . III. xii. 7. 9
And *eke* the love of Ladies foule defame; . . . IV. ix. 37. 5
Begets and *eke* conceives, . . . IV. x. 41. 9
the rest were *eke* her equall peares, . . . IV. x. 49. 3
Th' one to diminish, th' other for to *eeke*; . . . V. ii. 49. 4
eke came she, . . . V. v. 5. 3
both Knights envide, and Ladies *eke* did spight. . . . V. vi. 6. 9
There *eke* he placed a strong garrisone, . . . V. x. 30. 1
Both through his haberjeon and *eke* his corse; . . . V. x. 33. 3
they *eke* him greeted all. . . . V. xi. 15. 9
if that any ill she heard of any, She would it *eeke*, . . . V. xii. 35. 2
Three mightie ones, and cruell minded *eeke*, . . . VI. v. 13. 3
eke thy selfe, . . . And *eke* all knights hast shamed . . . VI. vi. 33. 8, 9
where is *eke* your friend . . . VI. vii. 16. 5
And *eeke* that angry foole . . . VI. vii. 39. 6
terrible by nature, And *eeke* . . . huge and hideous, . . . VI. vii. 41. 2
soft and tender *eeke* in mynde . . . VI. viii. 2. 3
And *eeke* this wallet . . . VI. viii. 23. 8
if he hungry were, him offred *eke* to eat. . . . VI. ix. 6. 9
And *eeke* them selves . . . they bore, . . . VI. x. 24. 6
and *eke* from whence they were: . . . VI. xi. 39. 6
So did he *eeke* long after this remaine, . . . VI. xii. 38. 6
Not men onely . . . But *eke* all other creatures . . . VII. vi. 4. 9
lawes of Nature . . . But *eke* of Justice, . . . VII. vi. 6. 2
chang'd in part, and *eeke* in generall: . . . VII. vii. 17. 9
But *eeke* their minds . . . VII. vii. 19. 8
And *eek* my name bee wyped out . . . *Am.* lxxv. 8
let them *eeke* bring store of other flowers, . . . *Epith.* 46
And *eeke* for comfort often called art . . . *Epith.* 394
herein *eke* thy glory seemeth more, . . . *H.L.* 162
An honourable Hymne I *eke* should frame, . . . *H.B.* 10

Eked. I dempt there much to have *eeked* my store, . . . *S.C.* S. 30
how their lives were *eekt*, she did not tell; . . . IV. ii. 53. 6

Ekes. He daylie *eekes*, and brings to excellence. . . . *Hub.* 792

Eking. such *eeking* hath made my hart sore. . . . *S.C.* S. 31

Elbow. upleaning on her *elbow* weake, . . . III. ii. 42. 6
leaning on his *elbowe*, these few words lett fly. . . . III. xi. 15. 9

Elbows. Some whet their knives, and strip their *elboes* bare: VI. viii. 39. 6

Eld. Through rusty *elde*, that hath rotted thee: . . . *S.C.* F. 54
to wrong holy *eld* did forbeare; . . . *S.C.* F. 206
thend of this Ambitious brere, For scorning *Eld*— . . . *S.C.* F. 238
in my face deepe furrowes *eld* hath pight: . . . *S.C.* D. 134
he leaned, as one farre in *elde*. . . . *Hub.* 218
as in hate of honorable *eld*, . . . I. viii. 47. 2
feeling wondrous comfort in her weaker *eld*: . . . I. x. 8. 9
that weake *eld* hath left thee nothing wise; . . . II. iii. 16. 3
Ne suffred them to perish through long *eld*, . . . II. ix. 56. 4
made ripe for death by *eld*, . . . II. x. 32. 2
O cursed *Eld!* the cankerworme of writs, . . . IV. ii. 33. 6
almost blind through *eld*, . . . IV. xi. 24. 9
Great Nature, ever young, yet full of *eld*; . . . VII. vii. 13. 2
From youth to *eld*, from wealth to poverty, . . . VII. vii. 19. 5
he was faint with cold, and weak with *eld*, . . . VII. vii. 31. 8

Elder. we tway bene men of *elder* witt. . . . *S.C.* May 18
with his *elder* brother Themis . . . *S.C.* Jul. 83
as the springe gives place to *elder* time, . . . *S.C.* D. 73
Ne Troynovant, though *elder* sister shee, . . . *Ti.* 102
So Ennius the *elder* Africane, . . . *Ded. Son.* i. 7
Hate was the *elder*, Love the younger brother; . . . IV. x. 32. 7
stronger in his state Then th' *elder*, . . . IV. x. 32. 9
No lesse then do her *elder* sisters broode. . . . IV. xi. 26. 7
To whom the *elder* did this aunswere frame: . . . V. iv. 7. 1
Then turning to the *elder* thus he sayd: . . . V. iv. 18. 1
The one of them, that *elder* did appeare, . . . V. xii. 29. 1
Titan . . . Was Saturnes *elder* brother . . . VII. vi. 27. 2
The younger thrust the *elder* from his right: . . . VII. vi. 27. 5
elder then thine owne nativitie, . . . *H.L.* 54

Elder-branches. Now bringen bitter *Eldre braunches* seare; . *S.C.* N. 147

Elder's. Yet was that other swayne this *elders* syre, . . . III. xii. 9. 3

Eldest. Begin, thou *eldest* Sister of the crew, . . . *T.M.* 53
Clarion, the *eldest* sonne and haire Of Muscaroll; . . . *Mui.* 22
Phyllis, the faire, is *eldest* of the three: . . . *Col.* 541
proud Sans foy, The *eldest* of three brethren; . . . I. ii. 25. 7
Bewraying him that did of late destroy His *eldest* brother; . I. iv. 39. 4
The *eldest* two, most sober, chast, and wise, . . . I. x. 4. 5
the *eldest*, that Fidelia hight, . . . I. x. 12. 6
The first of them, that *eldest* was and best, . . . I. x. 37. 1
The *eldest* did against the youngest goe, . . . II. ii. 13. 8
made love unto the *eldest* Dame, . . . II. ii. 17. 1
Elissa (so the *eldest* hight) . . . II. ii. 35. 1
The *eldest*, Gonorill, gan to protest . . . II. x. 28. 1
two sonnes, whose *eldest*, called Lud, . . . II. x. 46. 1
The first and *eldest*, which that scepter swayd, . . . II. x. 72. 4
faire Elferon, The *eldest* brother, . . . II. x. 75. 7
the *eldest* of the three, . . . IV. ii. 52. 4

Eldest—*Continued.*
The whilest their *eldest* brother was away, IV. x. 42. 6
Cupid their *eldest* brother; IV. x. 42. 7
Nereus, th' *eldest* and the best, IV. xi. 18. 5
The *eldest* of the which was slaine erewhile By Artegall, V. vi. 33. 4
these two, her *eldest* sonnes, she sent V. x. 14. 6
yet the *eldest* of the heavenly Peares? *H.L.* 56
begot, Like to it selfe his *eldest* sonne and heire, *H.H.L.* 31
Elect. thousand spots of colours queint *elect,* III. vii. 22. 5
Electing. Oft chaunging sides, and oft new place *electing,* IV. v. 40. 3
Election. might have had of life or death *election:* V. v. 26. 5
blesse your fortunes fayre *election.* *Am.* lxxxiii. 14
Elegies. Eulogies turne into *Elegies.* *T.M.* 372
Elegy. sung the prophecie . . . in dolefull *Elegie.* *Ti.* 595
Lamenting lowde my Daphnes *Elegie,* *D.* 509
Element. proudly thrust into *Thelement,* *S.C.* F. 116
trampling the fine *element* would fiercely ramp. I. v. 28. 9
Her flitting parts, and *element* unsound, I. xi. 18. 5
he would eat His neighbour *element* in his revenge: I. xi. 21. 6
owre, not purifide Of Mulcibers devouring *element;* II. vii. 5. 4
Makes the huge *element,* . . . To move III. ix. 15. 5
That cruell *element,* which all things feare, III. xi. 22. 4
another *Element* inquire Whereof she mote be made, *Am.* lv. 9
Elements. The bands of th' *elements* shall backe reverse *Ro.* xxii. 11
Elephant. Soone after this I saw an *Elephant,* *Van.* viii. 1
Elephants. More great then th' eares of *Elephants* by Indus IV. vii. 6. 9
Elevate. none . . . Himselfe therefore to heaven should *elevate;* *Gn.* 556
Eleven. Even thrise *eleven* descents the crowne retaynd, II. x. 45. 8
Elf. *Thelf* was so wanton and so wood, *S.C.* Mar. 55
To heare thee sing, a simple silly *Elfe?* *Col.* 371
Which when the valiant *Elfe* perceiv'd, I. i. 17. 1
Returne . . . Till morrow next that I the *Elfe* subdew, I. iv. 51. 4
Which when the wakeful *Elfe* perceiv'd, I. v. 2. 6
'Goe, caytive *Elfe,* him quickly overtake, I. v. 11. 1
The *Elfe* him calls alowd, I. v. 13. 8
drawing nigh him, said: 'Ah! misborn *Elfe,* I. vi. 42. 1
Th' *Elfe,* therewith astownd, Upstarted I. vii. 7. 7
'Hardy *Elfe,* . . . I read thee rash II. vii. 7. 6
'Vaine glorious *Elfe,*' (saide he) II. vii. 11. 1
The warlike *Elfe* much wondred at this tree, II. vii. 56. 1
Thereat the *Elfe* did blush in privitee, II. ix. 44. 1
That man so made he called *Elfe,* II. x. 71. 1
The noble *Elfe* and carefull Palmer II. xii. 81. 1
he by an *Elfe* was gotten of a Fay: III. iii. 26. 9
(so cruell was the *Elfe*) III. xi. 45. 1
Taught to obay the menage of that *Elfe* III. xii. 22. 3
Who was to weet a wretched wearish *elfe,* IV. v. 34. 3
I with that *Elfe* did play, IV. viii. 61. 6
'Thou foolishe *Elfe,*' (said then the Gyant wroth) V. ii. 37. 1
so let his Idols serve the *Elfe!* V. viii. 19. 9
Pastorella, wofull wretched *Elfe,* VI. xi. 19. 1
forgets the cruell carelesse *elfe* His mothers heast to prove. *Epig.* iv. 57
Elfant. *Elfant* was of most renowmed fame, II. x. 73. 3
Elfar. *Elfar,* who two brethren gyauntes kild, II. x. 73. 5
Elferon. faire *Elferon,* The eldest brother, II. x. 75. 6
Elficleos. After all these *Elficleos* did rayne, II. x. 75. 1
The wise *Elficleos,* in great Majestie, II. x. 75. 2
Elfiline. *Elfiline* enclosd it with a golden wall. II. x. 72. 9
Elfin. Unto that *Elfin* knight he bad him fly, I. i. 46. 2
'But how long time,' said then the *Elfin* knight, I. ii. 43. 1
Soone as the *Elfin* knight in presence came, I. iv. 13. 1
th' *Elfin* knight, . . . Disdaind to loose the meed I. iv. 39. 7
Him litle answerd th' angry *Elfin* knight; I. iv. 42. 8
He lives that . . . guiltie *Elfin* blood shall sacrifice in hast.' I. iv. 49. 9
With *Elfin* sword most shamefully betrade? I. v. 22. 8
The dreadlesse corage of this *Elfin* knight, I. vi. 1. 8
There when the *Elfin* knight arrived was, I. x. 44. 1
her base *Elfin* brood there for thee left: I. x. 65. 8
To serve againe his soveraine *Elfin* Queene, II. i. 1. 6
He was an *Elfin* borne of noble state II. i. 6. 5
'Me list not' (said the *Elfin* knight) II. vii. 19. 1
th' *Elfin* knight with wonder all the way II. vii. 24. 3
And rolls of *Elfin* Emperours, II. x. Arg.
the first author of all *Elfin* kynd; II. x. 71. 2
The first and eldest . . . Was *Elfin;* II. x. 72. 5
high accompt through out all *Elfin* land, III. v. 4. 6
the *Elfin* Knight, Weary of toile . . . Causd his pavilion V. iv. 46. 2
to curry favour With th' *Elfin* Knight, V. v. 35. 6
th' *Elfin* swayne, that oft had seene like sight, V. xii. 16. 6
Unto this place when as the *Elfin* Knight Approcht, VI. x. 10. 1
The *Elfin* Knight . . . into a Monastere did light, VI. xii. 23. 6
Elfinan. *Elfinan,* who laid Cleopolis foundation first of all: II. x. 72. 7
Elfinell. His sonne was *Elfinell,* II. x. 73. 1
Elfinor. *Elfinor,* who was in magick skild; II. x. 73. 7
Elfin's. How ever now accompted *Elfins* sonne, I. x. 60. 2
Eliidurus. pitteous *Elidure* put in his sted; II. x. 44. 6
Elisa, -es. *See* **Eliza, -'s.**
Eliseis. His *Eliseis* would be redde anew. *Col.* 403
Elissa. *Elissa* . . . did deeme Such entertainment base, II. ii. 35. 1
Eliza. Of fayre *Elisa,* Queene of shepheardes all, *S.C.* Ap. 34
'Of fayre *Elisa* be your silver song, *S.C.* Ap. 46
braunches . . . All for *Elisa* in her hand to weare? *S.C.* Ap. 105
'Now ryse up, *Elisa,* *S.C.* Ap. 145
Let dame *Elisa* thanke you for her song: *S.C.* Ap. 150
Whither thou list in fayre *Elisa* rest, *S.C.* O. 45
All were *Elisa* one of thilke same ring; *S.C.* O. 53
Divine *Elisa,* sacred Emperesse! *T.M.* 579
'Ne let *Elisa,* royall Shepheardesse, . . . envy, *D.* 225
Elizabeths. Ye three *Elizabeths!* for ever live, *Am.* lxxiv. 13
Eliza's. great *Elisaes* glorious name may ring *Proth.* 157
Elm. The vine-propp *Elme;* I. i. 8. 7
Eloin. From worldly cares himselfe he did *esloyne,* I. iv. 20. 1
Elope. to my brother did *ellope* streight way, V. iv. 9. 8
Eloquence. with great wisedome and grave *eloquence* I. xii. 24. 5
Else (*partial list*).
And what *els* in the world *Ro.* ii. 11
May seeme he lovd, or *els* some care he tooke; *S.C.* Ja. 9
Els had he sore be daunted. *S.C.* Mar. 114
so coole, as no where *else* I fynde: *S.C.* Jun. 5
Or to what labour *els* he was prepar'd, *Hub.* 265
But little *els* . . . could thereof skill; *Hub.* 381
must thy selfe apply; *Els* as a thistle-downe *Hub.* 634
'How *els* (said he) but with a good bold face, *Hub.* 645
And all that *els* pertaines to reveling, *Hub.* 694
Or *els* by wrestling to wex strong *Hub.* 746
warlike amenaunce, Or *else* for . . . governaunce. *Hub.* 782
What *else* then did he by progression, *Hub.* 842
For we may colour it . . . *Else* we may flye; *Hub.* 990
I for my selfe must care before *els* anie. *Hub.* 1196
all that *els* did come were sure to faile. *Hub.* 1203
there was cause, *els* doo it he would not: *Hub.* 1220
all that *els* he met. *Hub.* 1371
all that *els* was wont to worke delight *T.M.* 37
all that *els* seemd faire and fresh in sight, *T.M.* 39
all that *els* the Comick Stage . . . graced, *T.M.* 199
or *else* Sitting so cheerlesse . . . or *else* Playing *U.V.* 4, 5
which no man *els* doth mone, *Ti.* 157
who so *els* did goodnes by him gaine, And who so *els* his bounteous minde did trie, *Ti.* 232, 233
immortall make, which *els* would die *Ti.* 377
I in watch did spend, . . . or *els* in sleepe, *D.* 130
Els surely death should be no punishment, *D.* 362
Small needments *else* need shepheard to prepare. *Col.* 195
all things *else* that living creatures need. *Col.* 299
who *else* vouchsafed thee of grace?' *Col.* 484
all their vaunted vanitie, Nought *else* but smoke, *Col.* 720
As ever *else* in Princes Court thou vewest. *Col.* 738
For how should *else* things so far from attone, *Col.* 843
That her bright glorie *else* hath much defamed. *Col.* 910
Which gives them life, that *els* would soone have dide, *Ded. Son.* iv. 11
Strangle her, *els* she sure will strangle thee.' I. i. 19. 4
none *else* from hence may us unbynd.' I. ii. 43. 9
if that any *else* did Jove excell; I. iv. 11. 7
whether right he went, or *else* astray. I. iv. 19. 9
Or *else* goe them avenge, I. v. 24. 3
thy famous might In medicine, that *els* hath to thee wonne I. v. 43. 8
all things *els* the which his art did teach: I. v. 44. 3
maintain Thy guilty wrong, or *els* thee guilty yield.' I. vi. 41. 6
Els should this Redcrosse knight in bands have dyde, I. viii. 1. 8
helpe! or *els* we perish I. viii. 20. 9
None *els* . . . But his owne guiltie mind, I. ix. 38. 5
Els had his sinnes, so great I. x. 22. 4
his cryme could *els* be never cleare. I. x. 28. 9
Els never could the force of fleshly arme, I. xi. 36. 6
Or false or trew, or living or *else* dead, I. xii. 28. 2
Which *ells* could not endure those beames bright, II. Pr. 5. 4
Els, be ye sure, he dearely shall abyde, II. i. 20. 3
all, that *els* this worlds enclosure bace Hath II. ii. 41. 3
Els never should thy judgement be so frayle II. iii. 16. 4
Yet was there not with her *else* any one, II. vi. 3. 5
There is: *else* much more wretched II. viii. 1. 4
ought that *els* your honour might maintaine; II. viii. 19. 7
Els mote it needes . . . Have cleft II. viii. 33. 8
were it not that I am *els* delaid II. ix. 8. 7
nor serviceable *elles* for ought, II. ix. 32. 2
if ought *else* that I mote not devyse, II. ix. 42. 7
Ne suffred them to perish . . . As all things *els* II. ix. 56. 5
all that *els* does horror breed, II. xii. 37. 1
whom we must surprise, *Els* she will slip away, II. xii. 69. 9
For nothing *else* might keepe her safe II. xii. 82. 7
what steed, what stedd, And what so *else* III. ii. 16. 7
these, and all that *els* had puissaunce, III. iv. 3. 1
'For *els* my feeble vessell . . . Cannot endure, III. iv. 9. 1
all that *els* was pretious and deare, III. iv. 23. 6
Lifteth it up that *els* would lowly fall: III. v. 2. 6
Now God thee keepe, . . . *Els* shall thy loving Lord III. v. 26. 7
seeke *els* without hazard of thy hedd.' III. viii. 17. 6
nor with all He *els* could doe, III. viii. 41. 7
perdie, *elles* how mote it ever bee, III. viii. 48. 7
May her perhaps containe, that *else* would algates fleet.' III. ix. 7. 9
'What is there *ells* but cease these fruitlesse paines, III. xi. 24. 1
else her paine Should be remedilesse; III. xii. 34. 5
This doe, and live, *els* dye undoubtedly.' III. xii. 35. 7
her, that *else* was like to sterve IV. i. 4. 4
Else how could one of equall might IV. iii. 24. 6
The rest themselves in troupes did *else* dispose, IV. iv. 14. 7
The prize . . . Which *else* was like to have bene lost, IV. iv. 48. 3
how each one did succeede, Shall *else* be told IV. v. 28. 6
Shall death be th' end, or ought *else* worse, aread?' IV. vii. 11. 4
Full many did affray, that *else* faine enter would. IV. x. 16. 9
all that *else* I saw, IV. x. 29. 1
all, that *else* through all the world is named IV. x. 30. 8
Else would the waters overflow the lands, IV. x. 35. 5
all things *else,* that nourish vitall blood, IV. x. 46. 7
Whose like none *else* could shew, IV. xi. 33. 9
all things *else* V. Pr. 4. 5
makes his passage-penny pay: *Else* he doth hold V. ii. 6. 5
Else should afflicted wights oftimes despeire: V. iii. 1. 5
Whether by rage of waves . . . Or *else* by wracke V. iv. 19. 5

Else—*Continued.*
merit Might *else* have . . . bene crowned: . . . . V. v. 36. 7
else he sure had left not one alive, ... V. vii. 36. 8
Nor of ought *else* that may be richest red, ... V. ix. 28. 3
nought *else* but bare life doth remaine; . . . . V. x. 21. 7
Else should he thrise have needed . . . . V. xi. 14. 3
'What is there *else*' (sayd he) 'left . . . . V. xi. 18. 8
where what him fell shall *else* be told. . . . . V. xii. 43. 9
Till I him overtake, or *else* subdew: . . . . VI. i. 7. 3
Good Knights and Ladies true, and many *else* destroyd. . . . VI. i. 7. 9
whatsoever *else* he would requere. . . . . VI. i. 43. 4
bids him . . . to yeeld his Love, or *else* to fight: . . . . VI. ii. 18. 5
Or had no courage, or *else* had no gall. . . . . VI. iii. 36. 5
Being unhable *else* alone to ride, ... VI. iii. 46. 3
shun The perill . . . or *else* be over-run. . . . . VI. iii. 48. 9
Both horse and armes and what so *else* to lend, ... VI. iv. 39. 8
Or what so *else* were unto him betyde: . . . . VI. v. 3. 8
Or *else* remained in most wretched state, ... VI. v. 29. 3
Either for fame, or *else* for exercize, ... VI. vi. 35. 5
For *else* his feare could not be satisfyde. . . . . VI. vii. 17. 4
relent: *Else* had he surely there bene slaine, ... VI. vii. 45. 9
The richest champain that may *else* be rid; . . . . VII. vi. 54. 8
those three sacred Saints, though *else* most wise, Yet . . . . VII. vii. 7. 6
all things *else* that under heaven dwell . . . . VII. vii. 48. 2
In all things *else* she beares the greatest sway: . . . . VII. viii. 1. 5
naught *else* be counted deare; . . . . *Am.* viii. 4
nothing *else* they brooke, ... *Am.* xxxv. 10
Aswage your storms; or *else* both you, and she, ... *Am.* xlvi. 11
or *else* short my dayes. . . . . *Am.* lx. 14
By any service . . . Or ought that *else* . . . . *H.L.* 7
That men the more admyre . . . For *else* what booteth . . . *H.B.* 187
That are unable *else* to see his face, ... *H.H.B.* 117
His glorious face! which glistereth *else* so bright, ... *H.H.B.* 118
That in nought *else* on earth they can delight, ... *H.H.B.* 283
Elsewhere. of more private persons seeke *elswhere*, ... *Hub.* 522
might not *elswhere* be found, ... *Ti.* 566
Me seemd I had his person seene *elsewhere*, ... *D.* 52
that *elsewhere* I ever yet did see, ... *Col.* 558
Such . . . shapes *elswher* may no man reed. . . . . I. i. 21. 9
wants she health, or busie is *elswhere?*' . . . . I. x. 16. 3
had passage found *elsewhere;* . . . . II. viii. 3. 4
might not . . . be heard *elsewhere:* . . . . II. xii. 70. 4
helpe may have *elsewhere*, ... III. iii. 17. 6
As was in all the lond of Faery, or *else wheare*. . . . . III. iv. 23. 9
As ye may *elswhere* reade that ruefull history. . . . . III. vi. 53. 9
chaunst Malbecco busie be *elsewhere*, ... III. x. 12. 2
since their dayes such lovers were not found *elswhere*. . . . IV. iii. 52. 9
And did right noble deedes; the which *els where* are showne. . VI. iv. 38. 9
as shall declared be *elsewhere*. . . . . VI. v. 41. 9
Whilest his faire Pastorella was *elsewhere*, ... VI. x. 5. 2
now sought hyre *elswhere*. . . . . VI. xi. 39. 9
Eversham. all the moore twixt *Eversham* and Dell, ... II. x. 24.4
Elves. Th' ofspring of *Elves* and Faeryes there he fond, . . . II. ix. 60. 4
ne sib at all To *Elfes*, ... III. iii. 26. 5
Elvish. Nor *elvish* ghosts, nor gastly owles doe flee. . . . . *S.C.* Jun. 24
Elysian. Walke in *Elisian* fieldes so free. . . . . *S.C.* N. 179
must passe over to th' *Elisian* plaine: . . . . *Gn.* 421
now in *Elisian* fields so free, ... *Ti.* 332
the happie soules, which doe possesse Th' *Elysian* fields . . . IV. x. 23. 5
Emathian. sowing in th' *Aemathian* fields thy spight, . . . *Ro.* xxxi. 10
Embailed. her streight legs most bravely were *embayld* . . . II. iii. 27. 2
Embalm. wash his woundes wide, And softly gan *embalme* . . I. v. 17. 5
Embalmed. wont with ointment sweet To be *embaulm'd*, . . . IV. vii. 40. 4
She drest his wound, and it *embaulmed* wel With salve . . . *Epig.* iv. 45
Embarred. My tender sides in this rough rynd *embard;* . . . I. ii. 31. 3
fast *embard* in mighty brasen wall, ... I. vii. 44. 8
Hath in a dungeon deepe her close *embard*, ... III. xi. 16. 8
Embase. no time should so low *embase* their hight, ... *Ro.* viii. 12
he disdaines himselfe t' *embase* theretoo. . . . . *Hub.* 732
Should to a beast his noble hart *embase*, ... *D.* 180
vouchsafed to *embace* Her goodly port, ... III. vii. 15. 2
To please the best, and th' evill to *embase;* . . . . VI. i. 3. 7
the Prince, him fayning to *embase*, ... VI. vi. 20. 5
this worlds worthlesse glory to *embase*, ... *Am.* xvii. 3
Embased. Of friend or foe, who ever it *embaste;* . . . . III. i. 12. 5
Their ofspring hath *embaste*, ... III. ix. 33. 9
That are so much by so meane love *embased*. . . . . *Am.* lxxxii. 4
Embaseth. to the ground her eie-lids low *embaseth*, ... *Am.* xiii. 3
Embassade. when her words *embassade* forth she sends, . . . *H.B.* 251
Embassage. With speaking lookes, that close *embassage* bore, III. ix. 28. 2
Embassy. (After returne of Hermes *Embassie*) . . . . VII. vi. 23. 2
Embaste. *See* **Embased.**
Embathed. *Embathed* Balme, and chearfull Galingale, ... *Mui.* 194
Embattled. One in bright armes *embatteiled* full strong, . . . II. v. 2. 3
a Diademe *embattild* wide With hundred turrets, ... IV. xi. 28. 5
On every side of his *embatteld* cart, ... V. viii. 34. 3
Embay. In the warme Sunne he doth himselfe *embay*, ... *Mui.* 206
Repentance used to *embay* His blamefull body in salt water . I. x. 27. 5
in her streaming blood he did *embay* His litle hands, ... II. i. 40. 7
others did them selves *embay* in liquid joyes. . . . . II. xii. 60. 9
that doth his golden wings *embay* In blessed Nectar . . . . III. xi. 2. 3
Embayed. *See* **Wide-embayed.**
every sence the humour sweet *embayd*, ... I. ix. 13. 5
His hart with great affection was *embayd*, ... II. viii. 55. 2
where they *embayd* With so sweet sence . . . . III. vi. 7. 7
in her blood yet steeming fresh *embayd:* . . . . III. xii. 21. 4
Embays. a Deare, that greedily *embayes* In the cool soile, . III. xii. 44. *or.* 7
Embellish. *Embellish* the sweete Violet. . . . . *S.C.* Ap. 63
your face; Which with your vertues ye *embellish* more, . . . *Ded. Son.* xv. 11
shall *embellish* more your beautie bright, ... III. v. 53. 7

Embellished. It was *embellisht* with blossomes fayre, ... *S.C.* F. 118
most brave *embellished* With royall robes and gorgeous array, I. iv. 8. 3
Embellishment. Decks all the forrest with *embellishment;* . . *Gn.* 214
Embers. all the *embers* strow Uppon the ground; . . . . V. vii. 14. 5
Emblazoned. *emblazond* she beheld, ... IV. x. 55. 4
Embodied. Whose big *embodied* braunches shall not lin . . . III. iii. 22. 3
To be *embodied* here, ... *H.B.* 110
Emboiled. Faynt, wearie, sore, *emboyled*, grieved, brent, . . . I. xi. 28. 1
Emboiling. *See* **Hot-emboiling.**
The knight *emboyling* in his haughtie hart . . . . II. iv. 9. 6
Emboldened. Could his blood frosen hart *emboldened* bee, . . I. ix. 25. 7
His coward courage gan *emboldned* bee, ... III. v. 15. 2
I was *emboldned* with more confidence; . . . . IV. x. 56. 5
more *emboldned* by the wicked charmes, ... V. ii. 5. 5
Embosom. glad t' *embosome* his affection vile, ... II. iv. 25. 3
her guilefull bayt She will *embosome* deeper in your mind, . II. xii. 29. 3
Embosomed. He may *embosomd* bee and loved best; . . . . *H.L.* 249
Emboss. assayd In his bras-plated body to *embosse*, ... I. xi. 20. 3
Ne in so glorious spoile themselves *embosse:* . . . . III. i. 64. 8
Embossed. *Embost* with buegle about the belt: . . . . *S.C.* F. 66
his cup *embost* with Imagery . . . . *Gn.* 103
Nor anie skil'd in workmanship *embost*, ... *Mui.* 365
A knight her mett in mighty armes *embost*, ... I. iii. 24. 4
when he . . . felt our feeble harts *Embost* with bale, ... I. ix. 29. 2
the ragged breaches hong *Embost* with massy gold . . . . II. vii. 28. 4
The salvage beast *embost* in wearie chace, ... III. i. 22. 2
with great perles and pretious stones *embost;* . . . . III. i. 32. 7
As a dismayed Deare in chace *embost*, ... III. xii. 17. 8
A gorgeous girdle, curiously *embost* . . . . IV. iv. 15. 6
all *embost* with Lyons and with Flourdelice. . . . . V. ix. 27. 9
never . . . His limbes would rest, ne lig in ease *embost*, . . . VI. iv. 40. 7
Embowed. With gilden hornes *embowed* like the Moone, . . . *Van.* ii. 3
a boxe . . . *Embowd* with gold and gorgeous ornament, . . . I. ix. 19. 2
Embowelled. having him *embowelled* To fill his hellish gorge, III. vii. 29. 1
have . . deepe *emboweld* in the earth entyre: . . . . VI. viii. 15. 4
Embowering. Birds, in their wide boughs *embowring*, ... *Gn.* 225
Embrace. Ne brest of baser birth doth thee *embrace*, ... *S.C.* O. 82
doo *embrace* The precepts of my heavenlie discipline; . . . . *T.M.* 517
Too soone for all that did his love *embrace*, ... *Ti.* 292
T' *embrace* the service of sweete Poetry, ... *Ded. Son.* iv. 7
evermore *embrace* My faithfull service, ... I. iii. 29. 7
Her dearely doth *imbrace*, and kisseth manifold. . . . . I. xii. 12. 9
His warlike armes about him gan *embrace*, ... II. i. 26. 2
Thought in his bastard armes her to *embrace*. . . . . II. iii. 42. 6
The guifts of soveraine bounty did *embrace:* . . . . II. vii. 16. 4
all his workes with mercy doth *embrace*, ... II. viii. 1. 7
that which ye so much *embrace?* . . . . II. ix. 43. 7
His stubborne brest gan secret pleasaunce to *embrace*. . . . II. xii. 65. 9
chastity did for it selfe *embrace*, ... III. vii. 60. 2
So much high God doth innocence *embrace*. . . . . III. viii. 29. 5
streightly did *embrace* her body bright, ... III. xii. 45. *or.* 2
I saw him kisse; I saw him her *embrace;* . . . . IV. i. 49. 2
him with streight *embras* Enfolding, ... IV. viii. 63. 4
when she them saw *embrace*, ... IV. ix. 10. 5
him did deare *embrace* . . . . VI. i. 3. 2
Instead of comfort which we should *embrace:* . . . . VI. iii. 5. 6
Being now soft and fit them to *embrace;* . . . . VI. iv. 35. 7
him did oft *embrace*, and oft admire, ... VI. viii. 27. 8
Each gan his fellow solace and *embrace* . . . . VI. viii. 37. 4
As meanes of blisse I gladly wil *embrace;* . . . . *Am.* xxv. 12
in your brest his leafe and love *embrace*. . . . . *Am.* xxviii. 14
The more I love and doe *embrace* my bane. . . . . *Am.* xlii. 4
seemes on earth most heavenly to *embrace*, ... *H.L.* 111
that mightie bound which doth *embrace* The rolling Spheres, *H.H.L.* 25
Thou must him love, and his beheasts *embrace*. . . . . *H.H.L.* 261
Embraced. Picturing that which I in minde *embraced*, ... *Van.* i. 11
In his strong armes he stifly him *embraste*, ... II. iv. 14. 1
streight *embraced* she to him did cry . . . . III. x. 13. 6
Embraced of a Satyre rough and rude, ... III. x. 48. 3
The Ladies both on horse, together fast *embraced*. . . . . IV. viii. 34. 9
oft *imbrast*, as if that I were hee, ... IV. viii. 59. 8
Would have *embraced* her with hart entyre; . . . . V. xi. 61. 4
To leave the love that ye before *embraced*, ... V. xi. 63. 4
A thousand times *embrast*, and kist a thousand more. . . . VI. xi. 45. 9
A thousand times she her *embraced* nere, ... VI. xii. 20. 8
Embracement. wanton lust and leud *enbracement:* . . . . I. ii. 5. 5
I may more delight in thy *embracement* deare. . . . . II. iv. 26. 9
Coyly rebutted his *embracement* light; . . . . III. viii. 10. 5
like two senceles stocks in long *embracement* dwelt. . . . III. xii. 45. *or.* 9
Embracing. with her hard hold, and straight *embracing*, . . *S.C.* May 99
it *embracing* deare without disdaine, ... *Col.* 554
her *embracing*, said; 'O happy earth, ... I. x. 9. 1
Archt over head with an *embracing* vine, ... II. xii. 54. 2
him *embracing* fast betwixt them held, ... IV. ix. 9. 3
Either *embracing* other lovingly, ... V. viii. 14. 6
him *embracing* twixt his armes entire, ... VI. v. 23. 4
her *embracing* twixt her armes twaine, ... VI. xii. 19. 6
it *embracing* in his mind entyre, ... *H.B.* 223
Embraided. late in tresses bright *Embreaded* were . . . . III. vi. 18. 7
Embras, -te. *See* **Embrace, -d.**
Embrave. All that which Greece their temples to *embrave* . . *Ro.* xxix. 2
The faded flowres her corse *embrave*. . . . . *S.C.* N. 109
with sad Cypresse seemely it *embrave;* . . . . II. i. 60. 3
Embrew, -ed. *See* **Imbrue, -d.**
Embroidered. *See* **Bright-embroidered.**
Th' *embroder'd* quilt she lightly up did lifte, ... III. i. 61. 3
his *embrodered* Bonet sat awry: . . . . III. xii. 9. 6
With an *embrodered* belt of mickell pride; . . . . V. v. 3. 5
Embrued. *See* **Imbrued.**
Embusied. Whilest thus in battell they *embusied* were, ... IV. vii. 29. 1

Eme. Cassibalane, their *Eme,* II. x. 47. 1
Emerald. The floor was Jaspis, and of *Emeraude.* *Bel.*[1] ii. 11
The floore of Jasp and *Emeraude* was dight. *Bel.*[2] ii. 11
Emeralds. faire *Emeraudes,* not yet well ripened. II. xii. 54. 9
Emilia. *See* **Aemilia.**
Emiline. Renowmed Martia; and redoubted *Emmilen.* III. iii. 54. 9
'The widow Queene my mother, . . . Faire *Emiline,* VI. ii. 29. 2
Emmarble. Thou doest *emmarble* the proud hart of her *H.L.* 139
Emmeline. *See* **Emiline.**
Emmove, -d. *See* **Inmove, -d.**
Emong, Emongst. *See* **Among, Amongst.**
Empale, Empanel, *etc.* *See* **Impale, Impaneled,** *etc.*
Empeopled. what unknowen nation there *empeopled* were? I. x. 56. 9
Emperished. I deeme thy braine *emperished* bee *S.C.* F. 53
Least his fraile senses were *emperisht* quight, III. vii. 20. 8
Ne felt his blood to wast, ne powres *emperisht,* IV. iii. 29. 2
Emperor. The ashes of a mightie *Emperour:* *Bel.* iii. 8
Borne the sole daughter of an *Emperour,* I. ii. 22. 7
that great *Emperour* of all the West; I. xii. 26. 4
Good Claudius, that next was *Emperour,* II. x. 51. 1
the *Emperour* to him allide His daughter Genuiss' II. x. 52. 3
tooke on him the robe of *Emperoure:* II. x. 57. 8
Who afterward was *Emperour* of Rome, II. x. 60. 2
Emperors. And rolls of Elfin *Emperours,* II. x. Arg.
'Renowmed kings, and sacred *Emperours,* III. iii. 23. 1
Emperst. *See* **Empierced.**
Empierce. whose softened hearts it may *empierse* *As.* Pr. 9
can *empierce* a Princes mightie hart. *Col.* 431
'If ever love of Lady did *empierce* Your yron brestes, II. vi. 33. 1
Ne mortall steele *emperce* his miscreated mould. II. vii. 42. 9
Empierced. *empierced* brest Sharpe sorrowe did . . . rive. *D.* 6
deepe *emperst* his darksom hollow maw, I. xi. 53. 8
ruth *emperced* deepe In that knightes hart, II. ii. 1. 8
it *empierst* the Pagans burganet; II. viii. 45. 3
through the linked mayles *empierced* quite, III. v. 19. 4
hart, . . . Is not *empierst* with deepe compassiowne, III. ix. 39. 7
For privy love his brest *empierced* had, III. xi. 41. 8
The thought whereof *empierst* his hart so deepe, IV. xii. 19. 6
his cruell minded hart *Empierced* was V. v. 13. 2
it *empierced* to the very braine, V. vii. 33. 8
Whose sensefull words *empierst* his hart so neare, VI. ix. 26. 3
with secret wound Of love to Bellamoure *empierced* were, VI. xii. 4. 8
Empight. ere it *empight* In the meant marke, II. iv. 46. 5
Exceeding griefe that wound in him *empight,* III. v. 20. 8
in his side The mortall point most cruelly *empight;* IV. iii. 10. 4
had three bodies in one wast *empight,* V. x. 8. 8
Into the Princes shield where it *empight,* V. x. 32. 7
Full deadly wounds where so it is *empight;* V. xi. 24. 6
therein were a thousand tongs *empight* VI. xii. 27. 1
that faire beame which therein is *empight.* *H.B.* 49
Empire. Nought from the Romane *Empire* might be quight; *Ro.* viii. 10
Should boast himselfe of the Romane *Empire,* *Ro.* xi. 14
So grew the Roman *Empire* by degree, *Ro.* xxx. 9
the Romaine *Empire* bore the raine Of all the world *Van.* xi. 1
he rul'd not the *Empire,* as he ought? *Hub.* 1251
doo possesse the *Empire* of the aire, *Mui.* 18
therein have their mighty *empire* raysd, II. x. 5. 2
spred his *empire* to the utmost shore, II. x. 10. 2
soone by meanes thereof the *Empire* wan, II. x. 61. 4
Whose *empire* lenger here then ever any stood?' III. iii. 42. 9
fought . . . to make his *empire* great; III. xi. 29. 7
Soring through his wide *Empire* of the aire V. iv. 42. 2
th' *empire* sought from them to beare. VII. vi. 1. 9
T' attempt the *empire* of the heavens hight, VII. vi. 7. 4
To thrust . . . eke our selves from heavens high *Empire,* VII. vi. 21. 4
Have wonne the *Empire* of the Heavens bright; VII. vi. 33. 7
him of heavens *Empire* sought to dispossesse? VII. vii. 1. 9
As King and Queene, the heavens *Empire* sway; *H.H.B.* 56
Empires. The care of Kings and power of *Empires* stand, *Hub.* 1226
Emplonged. *See* **Implunged.**
Employ. In whatso please *employ* his personage, *Hub.* 778
false Duessa, . . . Her false sleightes doe *imploy.* I. xii. Arg.
Cannot *employ* your most victorious speare III. x. 28. 3
T' *employ* her puissaunce to his reskew, III. xi. 4. 8
did so well *employ* his carefull paine, IV. xi. 7. 2
now high time these strong joynts to *imploy.* VI. ii. 32. 9
Oftimes their sundry powres they did *employ,* VI. v. 14. 1
wings of gold fit to *employ.* VII. vii. 46. 9
Employed. each his paynes to others profit still *employd.* II. x. 14. 9
Great shame to lose so long *employed* paines, V. v. 48. 3
day and night *employ'd* his busie paine V. xii. 26. 3
Employs. Me, all unfitt for so great purpose, she *employes.* II. ii. 43. 9
Saxons, whom he for his safety *imployes.* II. x. 64. 9
Empoisoned. that the wicked steele *empoysned* were: III. v. 49. 3
with his *empoysned* shot Their wofull harts he wounded had III. vi. 13. 7
Empoisned was with privy lust and gealous dredd. III. ix. 28. 9
therwith tip his sharp *empoisned* darts, *H.L.* 121
Empress. Divine Elisa, sacred *Emperesse!* *T.M.* 579
of the whole world as thou wast the *Empresse,* *Ti.* 83
High in the favour of that *Empresse,* *Ded. Son.* xi. 3
That soveraine Queene, that mightie *Emperesse,* V. i. 4. 5
that most sacred *Empresse,* my dear dred, *Am.* xxxiii. 2
antique Babel, *Empresse* of the East, *Com. Son.* iv. 1
Emprise. casten to compasse many wrong *emprise:* *S.C.* S. 83
brave poursuitt of chevalrous *emprize,* I. ix. 1. 4
I bownden am streight after this *emprize,* I. xii. 18. 4
far renowmd through many bold *emprize;* II. iii. 35. 4
Sir Guyon left his first *emprise,* II. iv. 12. 1
give me leave to follow mine *emprise.'* II. vii. 39. 6
t' atchieve an hard *emprize;* III. iii. 53. 7

Emprise—*Continued.*
both fitt for hard *emprize:* III. xii. 28. 2
Fiercely they followd on their bolde *emprize,* IV. iv. 36. 1
this same brave *emprize* for me did rest, IV. x. 4. 7
goodly gan to greet his brave *emprise,* V. iii. 15. 7
to knights of great *emprise* V. iv. 2. 1
So to pursue a perillous *emprize,* V. vii. 21. 3
Then to his first *emprize* his mind he lent, V. xi. 35. 5
His whole exploite and valorous *emprize,* VI. i. 5. 4
this proud gyant should with brave *emprize* Quite overthrow VI. iv. 33. 4
through prowesse and their brave *emprize* VI. vi. 35. 7
What course were best to take in this hot bold *emprize.* VII. vi. 22. 9
great deeds and valorous *emprize.* *Am.* lxix. 4
Emprisoned. *See* **Imprisoned.**
Emptied. crooked crawling shankes, of marrowe *empted;* *Mui.* 350
Emptiness. Like a swift Otter, fell through *emptinesse,* III. iii. 33. 7
wastefull *emptinesse* And solemne silence III. xi. 53. 6
Empty. With brandisht tongue the *emptie* aire did gride, *Gn.* 254
loose like an *emptie* gut; *Hub.* 212
Or guilefull spright wandring in *empty* aire, I. ii. 32. 6
masse of earthly slyme, Puft up with *emptie* wynd, I. vii. 9. 9
scourging th' *emptie* ayre with his long trayne, I. viii. 17. 3
that monstrous mas, . . . like an *emptie* blader was. I. viii. 24. 9
empty sides . . . Could make a stony hart his hap to rew; I. viii. 41. 4
His shackles *emptie* lefte, himselfe escaped cleene. II. i. 1. 9
The Palmer seeing his lefte *empty* place, II. viii. 9. 1
Whose *emptie* place the mightie Oberon Doubly supplide, II. x. 75. 8
rushing forth into the *emptie* field, IV. iii. 22. 7
th' *emptie* girdle which about her wast was wrought. V. iii. 24. 9
Standing with *emptie* hands all weaponlesse, V. v. 14. 2
Each rowme she sought, but them all *empty* fond. V. vi. 35. 8
lends unto it leave the *emptie* ayre to beat. V. xii. 18. 9
The playnes all waste and *emptie* did appeare; VI. xi. 26. 7
bearing it abrode Into the *emptie* fields, VI. xii. 7. 2
a waste and *emptie* place In His wyde Pallace, *H.H.L.* 101
doe fly away, Like *empty* shaddowes, *Proth.* 9
Empurpled. Some deepe *empurpled* as the Hyacine, II. xii. 54. 7
sides *empurpled* were with smyling red; III. vii. 17. 2
litle drops *empurpled* her faire brest. III. xii. 33. 5
Full dreadfully *empurpled* all with bloud; IV. vii. 6. 6
Emulate. all his paines did closely *emulate;* VI. x. 33. 4
Emuled. before that *aemuled* of many, *Col.* 73
Emuling. *aemuling* my pipe, he tooke in hond *Col.* 72
Enabled. So long as age *enabled* him thereto, VI. v. 37. 2
I should *enabled* be thy actes to sing. *H.L.* 21
Enamored. so *enamoured* of her young one, *S.C.* May 97
He was so *enamored* with the newell, *S.C.* May 276
Shee greatly gan *enamoured* to wex III. i. 47. 4
Enaunter. *Enaunter* his rage mought cooled bee; *S.C.* F. 200
Enaunter their heritage doe impaire. *S.C.* May 78
Enaunter they mought be inly knowe. *S.C.* S. 161
Enbracement. *See* **Embracement.**
Encage. him take, and in your bosome bright Gently *encage,* *Am.* lxxiii. 10
Enceladus. proud *Encelade,* whose wide nosethrils burnd III. ix. 22. 3
Enchace, -d. *See* **Enchase, -d.**
Enchant. him the poysoned garment did *enchaunt,* I. xi. 27. 5
Enchanted. he forward gan advaunce His fair *enchaunted* steed, I. iii. 25. 9
'he beares . . . *enchaunted* armes, that none can perce; I. iv. 50. 6
'Charmd or *enchaunted,*' . . . 'I no whitt reck; I. iv. 50. 8
knight . . . Lay cover'd with *inchaunted* cloud I. v. 19. 6
As he were charmed with *inchaunted* rimes; I. ix. 48. 8
I can carve with this *inchaunted* brond II. viii. 22. 4
Yt seemd *thenchaunted* flame which did Creusa wed. II. xii. 45. 9
That speare *enchaunted* was which layd thee on the greene. III. i. 7. 9
For death sate on the point of that *enchaunted* speare: III. i. 9. 9
The maske of Cupid, and th' *enchanted* Chamber III. xii. Arg.
chokt the porch of that *enchaunted* gate III. xii. 43. 3
Could bide the force of that *enchaunted* speare, IV. iv. 46. 4
casting from her that *enchaunted* launce, IV. vi. 14. 7
in that *enchaunted* glasse she saw; IV. vi. 26. 6
advauncing that *enchaunted* shield, IV. x. 19. 6
Th' *enchaunted* Damzell vanisht into nought: V. iii. 24. 6
Nymphes, or Faeries, or *enchaunted* show, VI. x. 17. 6
Enchanter. *Enchaunter* parts The Redcrosse Knight from Truth: I. ii. Arg.
that late vision which th' *Enchaunter* wrought, I. iii. 3. 6
th' *enchaunter* joyous seemde no lesse Then the glad marchant, I. iii. 32. 2
Th' *enchaunter* vaine his errour should not rew: I. vi. 42. 8
an *Enchaunter* bad His sence abusd, I. vii. 49. 3
th' *Enchaunter* would not spare his payne, II. i. 5. 1
Her nathelesse Th' *enchaunter* . . . Did thus revest, II. i. 22. 8
Th' *enchaunter* greatly joyed in the vaunt, II. iii. 13. 1
saide then th' *enchaunter* blive, II. iii. 18. 1
kend him . . . Th' *enchaunter* by his armes and amenaunce, II. viii. 17. 8
'So would I,' (said th' *enchaunter*) II. viii. 19. 5
Therewith th' *Enchaunter* softly gan to smyle III. iii. 17. 1
Shall give th' *enchaunter* his unhappy hire. III. iii. 36. 6
her before the vile *Enchaunter* sate, III. xii. 31. 1
th' *enchaunter* which had her distrest So sore, III. xii. 41. 4
Th' *Enchaunter* selfe, which all that fraud did frame III. xii. 43. 7
that same vile *Enchauntour* Busyran, IV. i. 3. 1
Enchanter's. bloody wordes of bold *Enchaunters* call; I. vii. 35. 2
Die had she lever with *Enchanters* knife IV. i. 6. 8
from that time I from *enchaunters* theft Her freed, IV. vi. 35. 4
Enchanting. *See* **Soul-enchanting.**
To heare the charmes of his *enchanting* skill; *As.* 46
Enchantment. No false *enchauntment* . . . Might once abide I. viii. 4. 5
no *enchauntment* from his dint might save; II. viii. 20. 6
O horrible *enchantment,* that him so did blend! II. xii. 80. 9
Some thought that some *enchantment* faygned it; IV. i. 14. 5
Whose every deed and word, . . . Was like *enchantment,* VI. ii. 3. 3

Enchantments. after charmes and some *enchauntments* said, I. viii. 14. 6
By strong *enchauntments* and blacke Magicke leare, III. xi. 16. 7
So mighty be th' *enchauntments* which the same do stay. III. xi. 23. 9
Enchantress. Acrasia, a false *enchaunteresse*, II. i. 51. 3
when the vile *Enchaunteresse* perceiv'd, II. i. 55. 1
His dearest Dame is that *Enchaunteresse*, II. v. 27. 1
The faire *Enchauntresse*, so unwares opprest, II. xii. 81. 8
men indeed, Whom this *Enchauntresse* hath transformed II. xii. 85. 2
Enchase. hundred steps of Afrike golds *enchase:* *Bel.*² ii. 8
Her heavenly lineaments for to *enchace*, I. xii. 23. 5
All which who so dare thinke for to *enchace*, IV. v. 12. 1
The heavens bright-shining baudricke to *enchace;* V. i. 11. 7
Did all their speares attonce on him *enchace*. V. x. 34. 5
spotlesse spirit in which ye may *enchace* Whatever formes VI. iv. 35. 5
Enchased. Wherein is *enchased* many a fayre sight *S.C.* Au. 27
Enchaste with chaine and circulet of golde. *Hub.* 624
vine, *Enchaced* with a wanton yvie twine; II. ix. 24. 5
With golden letters goodly well *enchaced;* IV. x. 8. 7
Amidst a ring most richly well *enchaced*, VI. x. 12. 8
enchased Your glorious name in golden moniment. *Am.* lxxxii. 7
Encheason. blamest hem much for small *encheason*. *S.C.* May 147
For such *encheason*, if you goe nye, *S.C.* S. 116
'well mote I shame to tell The fond *encheason* II. i. 30. 2
Encheer. mote *encheare* his friends, and foes mote terrifie. VII. vi. 24. 9
Encline, -d. *See* **Incline, -d.**
Enclose. with his raskall routs t' *enclose* them rownd, II. ix. 15. 4
them unwares besides the Severne did *enclose*. II. x. 54. 9
Thou in dull corners doest thy selfe *inclose;* III. ii. 31. 5
Whiles all her Nymphes did like a girlond her *enclose*. III. vi. 19. 9
in strong bancks his violence *enclose*, III. vii. 34. 2
dangerously did round about *enclose:* VI. v. 20. 3
Enclosed. In which all good and evill was *enclosed*, *Ro.* xix. 10
Enclosde therein for endles memorie Of him, *Ti.* 662
enclosd in wooden wals . . . our wearie daies we waste.' I. ii. 42. 8
Elfiline *enclosd* it with a golden wall. II. x. 72. 9
Goodly it was *enclosed* rownd about, II. xii. 43. 1
In whose *enclosed* shadow there was pight A faire Pavilion, III. v. 40. 6
While in their mothers wombe *enclosd* they were, III. vii. 48. 6
The field with listes was all about *enclos'd*, IV. iii. 4. 1
An hundred knights had him *enclosed* round, IV. iv. 31. 6
Full oft about her wast she it *enclos'd*, IV. v. 16. 8
they have him *enclosed* so behind, V. iii. 9. 4
Enclos'd the bush about, and there him tooke, VII. vi. 47. 4
Encloseth. *Encloseth* Corke with his devided flood; IV. xi. 44. 4
Enclosing. *Enclosing* you in thrice three wards for ever, *Ro.* xv. 7
Enclosing it with banks on everie side, *Gn.* 658
Enclosure. all, that els this worlds *enclosure* bace Hath great II. ii. 41. 3
Enclosures. Were first *enclosures* but of salvage soyle; *Ro.* xviii. 2
Enclouded. The heavens on everie side *enclowded* bee: *Gn.* 571
Encomber, Encombrance, Encombred. *See* **Encumber,** *etc.*
Encompass. his three foes Sought to *encompasse* him VI. v. 20. 2
Encompassed. he counseld with his sprights *encompast* round. III. iii. 7. 9
it *encompast* round as with a golden fret. IV. xi. 27. 9
Encompassed the throne on which she sate,— V. ix. 29. 6
The goodly Sun *encompast* all with beames bright. VII. vii. 44. 9
wall, Wherewith he hath *encompassed* this All. *H.H.B.* 42
His throne is all *encompassed* around, *H.H.B.* 177
Encounter. Him thought at first *encounter* to have slaine. I. viii. 7. 5
fresh *encounter* towardes him addrest; I. xi. 17. 2
in his first *encounter*, I. xi. 53. 1
Unhable their *encounter* to sustaine; II. ix. 14. 4
If chaunce I him *encounter* paravaunt; III. ii. 16. 4
he cast Her to *encounter* ere she passed by; III. vii. 38. 4
this sad *encounter* shonne, And seeke els III. viii. 17. 5
alwayes did their dread *encounter* fly: III. xi. 6. 4
Him at the first *encounter* downe he smote, IV. iv. 40. 6
They two enough t' *encounter* an whole Regiment. V. i. 30. 9
those Damzells did forestall Their furious *encounter*, V. iv. 5. 9
She at the first *encounter* on him ran V. v. 6. 3
They both *encounter* in the middle plaine, V. x. 32. 1
Encountered. Both fierce and furious in contention *Encountred*, *Gn.* 518
the two first whome he *encountred* *Hub.* 1067
Me chaunced of a knight *encountred* bee, I. ii. 35. 7
That never yet *encountred* enemy II. iv. 40. 7
He them *encountred*, a confused rout, II. x. 16. 1
Encountred him in batteill well ordaind, II. x. 18. 4
There them by chaunce *encountred* on the way III. viii. 15. 2
They were *encountred* of a lustie Knight IV. ii. 4. 2
'Whom boldly I *encountred* IV. x. 10. 1
Meant them to have *encountred* ere they left the shore: V. xii. 6. 9
Encountereth. a Gryfon . . . A Dragon fiers *encountreth* I. v. 8. 3
Guyon *encountreth* Britomart: III. i. Arg.
Encountering. shiver Her flaming fire-brond, *encountring* me, *Gn.* 343
There grim Persephone, *encountring* mee, *Gn.* 422
that disdainfull beast, *Encountring* fierce, I. iii. 19. 7
Encountring fiers with single sword in hand; I. viii. 12. 8
Encountring him with small resistence slew, VI. xi. 43. 6
Encounters. for knightly giusts and fierce *encounters* fitt. I. i. 1. 9
them *encounters* with like courtesee; I. x. 15. 2
Encourage. He did him selfe *encourage* and take better cheare. V. xi. 2. 9
Encouraged. Strongly *encorag'd* by the crafty Foxe; *Hub.* 1104
all to lawlesse lust *encouraged* II. ii. 18. 5
Encouragement. with new *encouragement* Did him assayle, IV. iii. 26. 7
otherwhile with good *encouragement* VI. v. 32. 8
Encradled. he *encradled* was In simple cratch, *H.H.L.* 225
Encrease, *etc.* *See* **Increase,** *etc.*
Encroach. The blustering Boreas did *encroche*, *S.C.* F. 226
Encroch uppon the land there under thee? V. ii. 37. 5
day; . . . he spyde upon the earth t' *encroch*, VI. xi. 47. 3
Encroached. had *encroched* upon others share; V. ii. 32. 2
Encroaching. Against the seas *encroching* crueltie. *Col.* 275
Encumber. stones, the which *encomber* might His passage, *Col.* 150
Which subtill sleight did him *encumber* much, IV. vii. 27. 1
creeping still behinde, doth him *incomber*, VI. v. 19. 6
Encumbered. him *encombred* sore, but could not hurt at all. I. i. 22. 9
when his feet *encombred* were, I. x. 35. 6
Much was the man *encombred* with his hold, I. xi. 41. 1
they *encombred* all mens eares and eyes; II. ix. 51. 3
Whose presence all their troups so much *encombred*, V. v. 19. 5
Much was he then *encombred*, VI. iv. 25. 1
Encumberment. Sleepe out her fill without *encomberment;* VI. viii. 38. 2
Encumbrance. no lesse *encombrance* she did see, VI. iv. 10. 3
From all this worlds *incombraunce* did himselfe assoyle. VI. v. 37. 9
End. *See* **Butt-end.**
if that time make *ende* of things so sure, *Ro.* vii. 13
It als will *end* the paine which I endure. *Ro.* vii. 14
To th' *end* that, having all parts in their power, *Ro.* viii. 9
To th' *end* that none . . . Should boast himselfe *Ro.* xi. 13
despise The noble Lion after his lives *end*, *Ro.* xiv. 6
To shew that all in th' *end* to nought shall fade. *Ro.* xx. 14
To th' *end* that his victorious people should *Ro.* xxiii. 3
To th' *end* that when thou wast in greatest hight, *Ro.* xxxi. 12
Now listen a while and hearken the *end*. *S.C.* F. 101
Such was *thend* of this Ambitious brere, *S.C.* F. 237
God giveth good for none other *end*. *S.C.* May 72
Such *end* had the Kidde, *S.C.* May 302
such *end*, perdie, does all hem remayne, *S.C.* May 304
At *end*, the shepheard his practise spyed, *S.C.* S. 202
there is no *end* of paine, *Gn.* 417
so to wander to the worldes *ende*, *Hub.* 87
come by readie meanes unto his *end*, *Hub.* 127
Sildome but some good commeth ere the *end*.' *Hub.* 172
that the ground-worke is, and *end* of all, *Hub.* 485
Unhappie wight, borne to desastrous *end*, *Hub.* 907
The Ape was glad to *end* the strife so light, *Hub.* 1056
So Mother Hubberd her discourse did *end*, *Hub.* 1385
who will record my cursed *end?* *U.V.* 20
By heavens doome doo *ende* my earthlie daies: *Ti.* 312
his owne *end* unto remembrance call; *Ti.* 467
see the *end* of pompe and fleshlie pride! *Ti.* 543
in the *ende* he breathlesse did remaine, *Mui.* 430
harken well till it to *ende* bee brought, *D.* 97
well did hope my joy would have no *end*, *D.* 149
Throughout the world from one to other *end*, *D.* 373
Sith all my sorrow should have *end* thereby, *D.* 446
Cease, Shepheard! cease, and *end* thy undersong.' *D.* 539
sad ensample of mans suddein *end:* *As.* 134
each an *end* of singing made *Col.* 179
fold them up, when they have made an *end*. *Col.* 259
For *end*, all good, all grace there freely growes, *Col.* 324
To *end* thy glorie which he hath begun: *Col.* 409
Furthest from *end* then, when they neerest weene, I. i. 10. 6
Till that some *end* they finde, I. i. 11. 2
well worthy *end* Of such as drunke her life I. i. 26. 6
still did follow one unto the *end*, I. i. 28. 5
in woods and forrests, Th' *end* of his drift, I. ii. 9. 4
Redounding teares did choke th' *end* of her plaint, I. iii. 8. 1
Whose need had *end*, but no *end* covetise; I. iv. 29. 3
To weet what *end* to straunger knights may fall. I. v. 3. 3
End of the doubtfull battaile deemed tho I. v. 11. 7
Her wicked daies with wretched knife did *end*, I. v. 39. 2
With like attempt to like *end* to renew. I. v. 42. 4
came to shamefull *end*. I. v. 53. 6
to tell . . . this battels *end*, will need another place. I. vi. 48. 9
Begin, and *end* the bitter balefull stound; I. vii. 25. 8
She heard with patience all unto the *end*, I. vii. 27. 1
To see what *end* of fight should him befall I. viii. 2. 9
he has redd his *end* In that bright shield, I. viii. 21. 4
well begonne, *end* all so well, I pray! I. viii. 28. 4
Death is the *end* of woes: I. ix. 47. 9
he desirde to *end* his wretched dayes: I. x. 21. 8
Mercy in the *end* his righteous soule might save. I. x. 34. 9
them most needeth comfort in the *end*, I. x. 41. 3
to what *end* they clomb that tedious hight? I. x. 49. 9
'What *end* . . . should cause us take such paine, I. x. 50. 1
end, which every living wight Should make his marke I. x. 50. 2
Where is for thee ordaind a blessed *end:* I. x. 61. 5
let them downe before his flightes *end:* I. xi. 19. 4
weening that the sad *end* of the warre; I. xi. 32. 3
She nigher drew, and saw that joyous *end:* I. xi. 55. 7
now at her journeyes *end;* I. xii. 1. 7
of all his drifte the aymed *end:* II. i. 3. 4
end their daies with irrenowmed shame, II. i. 23. 4
God guide thee, Guyon, well to *end* thy warke, II. i. 32. 8
breaking off the *end* for want of breath, II. i. 56. 2
The *end* of their sad Tragedie uptyde, II. ii. 1. 3
Thus enter we . . . with woe, and *end* with miseree!' II. ii. 2. 9
Pursew the *end* of their strong enmity, II. ii. 28. 3
of his pitteous tale he *end* did make: II. ii. 46. 4
with one sword seven knightes I brought to *end*, II. iii. 17. 7
*As ghastly bug their haire on *end* does reare: II. iii. 20. 5
in my woes beginner it to *end:* II. iv. 31. 4
soone through suff'rance growe to fearefull *end:* II. iv. 34. 4
The quivering steele his aymed *end* wel knew, II. iv. 46. 3
did her earnest *end* in jest. II. vi. 23. 9
the *end*, To which al men doe ayme, II. vii. 32. 7
Another happines, another *end*. II. vii. 33. 4
upper *end* to highest heven was knitt, II. vii. 46. 3
The care thereof my selfe unto the *end*, II. viii. 8. 4
The worth of all men by their *end* esteeme, II. viii. 14. 7

End—*Continued.*
At th' upper *end* there sate, yclad in red . . . II. ix. 27. 5
Tossing and turning them withouten *end;* . . . II. ix. 58. 2
he an *end* of batteill and of life did make. . . . II. x. 16. 9
Such was the *end* that to disloyall love did fall. . . . II. x. 19. 9
in the *end* their Syre . . . was forced to retyre. . . . II. x. 22. 8
in the *end* was left no moniment Of Brutus, . . . II. x. 36. 8
There abruptly it did *end,* . . . II. x. 68. 2
of the battell balefull *end* had made, . . . II. xi. 29. 7
all his labor brought to happy *end;* . . . II. xi. 35. 2
An huge great stone, which stood upon one *end,* . . . II. xi. 35. 7
Nigh his wits *end* then woxe th' amazed knight, . . . II. xi. 44. 1
end of that Carles dayes and his owne paynes did make. . . II. xi. 46. 9
ryv'd her trembling hart, and wicked *end* did make. . . . II. xi. 47. 9
here the *end* of all our traveill is: . . . II. xii. 69. 7
'Sad *end,*' (quoth he) 'of life intemperate, . . . II. xii. 85. 6
Till death make one *end* of my daies and miseree!' . . . III. ii. 39. 9
Short *end* of sorrowes they therby did finde; . . . III. ii. 43. 8
Can have no *ende* nor hope of my desire, . . . III. ii. 44. 2
From the worlds *end,* through many a bitter stowre: . . . III. iii. 3. 5
to bring to perfect *end:* . . . III. iii. 10. 5
Deepe busied bout worke of wondrous *end,* . . . III. iii. 14. 7
either fatall *end,* Or other mightie cause, . . . III. iii. 15. 8
'But yet the *end* is not.' . . . III. iii. 50. 1
the sad *end* of her sweet Marinell: . . . III. iv. 25. 5
The fearefull *end* of his avengement sad, . . . III. v. 24. 4
All things decay in time, and to their *end* doe draw. . . . III. vi. 40. 9
What *end* unto that fearefull Damozell . . . befell: . . . III. vi. 54. 2
at the twelve monethes *end* should bring their names . . . III. vii. 54. 8
Her will to win unto his wished *eend;* . . . III. viii. 41. 5
To whom I levell all my labours *end,* . . . III. ix. 1. 2
deeds of armes, my lives and labors *end.*' . . . III. ix. 37. 9
Gave them safe conduct, till to *end* they came. . . . III. x. 16. 7
One may his journey bring too soone to evill *end.*' . . . III. x. 40. 9
at the upper *end* of that faire rowme . . . III. xi. 47. 1
she spyde at that rowmes upper *end* . . . III. xi. 54. 6
her faire locks up stared stiffe on *end,* . . . III. xii. 36. 6
to weet what *end* would come of all. . . . III. xii. 37. 6
yokes assoyle At this same furrowes *end,* . . . III. xii. 47. *or.*6
discord harder is to *end* then to begin. . . . IV. i. 20. 9
most often *end* in bloudshed and in warre. . . . IV. i. 25. 9
'the fruitlesse *end* Of thy vaine boast, . . . IV. i. 51. 1
Did beare them both to fell avenges *end,* . . . IV. ii. 15. 2
That doth ill cause or evill *end* enure; . . . IV. ii. 29. 8
Amongst them all this *end* he did decree; . . . IV. ii. 38. 5
desirous th' *end* of all their dayes To know, . . . IV. ii. 47. 1
Yet is as nigh his *end* as he that most doth playne. . . . IV. iii. 1. 9
made an *end* of strife. . . . IV. iii. 12. 9
Diamond, . . . Resolv'd to *end* it one or other way, . . . IV. iii. 17. 8
He gan to faint toward the battels *end,* . . . IV. iii. 32. 7
To make an *end* of all that did withstand: . . . IV. iii. 33. 3
They weened sure the warre was at an *end;* . . . IV. iii. 35. 2
th' *end* of both likewise of both their ends: . . . IV. iv. 1. 5
So nought may be esteemed happie till the *end.* . . . IV. iv. 43. 9
All which when Blandamour from *end* to *end* Beheld, . . . IV. iv. 45. 5
at last enquired The cause and *end* thereof, . . . IV. v. 38. 4
The *end* whereof and daungerous event . . . IV. v. 46. 6
Thereby to make their loves beginning their lives *end.* . . . IV. vi. 17. 9
toward th' *end* Sir Arthegall renewed His strength . . . IV. vi. 18. 4
Full glad of so good *end,* . . . IV. vi. 25. 3
till he came to th' *end* of all his way, . . . IV. vii. 8. 7
Shall death be th' *end,* or ought else worse, . . . IV. vii. 11. 4
I me resolv'd the utmost *end* to prove; . . . IV. vii. 16. 7
She staid not th' utmost *end* thereof to try, . . . IV. vii. 21. 2
I will deferre the *end* untill another tide. . . . IV. vii. 47. 9
In th' *end* she her unto that place did guide, . . . IV. viii. 11. 8
the sting which in her tongs *end* grew. . . . IV. viii. 36. 9
on th' other *end* There reared was a castle . . . IV. x. 7. 1
So ended he his tale, where I this Canto *end.* . . . IV. x. 58. 9
let me die and *end* my daies attone, . . . IV. xii. 9. 8
To sit in his own seate, his cause to *end,* . . . V. Pr. 10. 8
Immoveable, resistlesse, without *end;* . . . V. i. 12. 7
Perhaps I may all further quarrell *end,* . . . V. i. 25. 6
towards th' *end* grew greater in his might, . . . V. ii. 17. 6
Together met of all to make an *end.* . . . V. iii. 8. 3
turne we here to this faire furrowes *end* . . . V. iii. 40. 6
Ne other *end* their fury would afford, . . . V. iv. 6. 3
with hard enduraunce had Heard to the *end,* . . . V. vi. 17. 5
Till to the Bridges further *end* she past; . . . V. vi. 39. 6
All which when he unto the *end* had heard, . . . V. vii. 20. 4
'The *end* whereof, and all the long event, . . . V. vii. 22. 1
All which when she unto the *end* had heard, . . . V. vii. 24. 1
end your revenge on mee.' . . . V. viii. 11. 9
to th' *end* He should his flale to final execution bend. . . . V. viii. 29. 8
Doubting sad *end* of principle unsound: . . . V. xi. 2. 7
Wayting what *end* would be of that same daunger drad. . . . V. xi. 32. 9
if I live till those ten daies have *end,* . . . V. xi. 43. 2
In th' *end,* his kyndly courtesie to prove, . . . VI. iii. 15. 5
But th' utmost *end* perforce for to aby, . . . VI. iii. 44. 3
in another Canto shall to *end* be brought. . . . VI. iii. 51. 9
An hard adventure with unhappie *end,* . . . VI. iv. 17. 7
Yet nought the nearer to his journeys *end,* . . . VI. iv. 25. 6
To leape into the same after our lives *end.* . . . VI. iv. 31. 9
wretched *end* which still attendeth on her.' . . . VI. vi. 25. 7
To some hid *end* to make more easie way, . . . VI. vi. 42. 2
the foole, which did that *end* awayte, Came running in; . . . VI. viii. 11. 1
make one *end* of him without ruth or remorse. . . . VI. viii. 14. 9
My life will by his death have lamentable *end.* . . . VI. viii. 17. 9
The *end* whereof Ile keepe untill another cast. . . . VI. viii. 51. 9
Ne durst abide the daunger of the *end;* . . . VI. x. 35. 4

End—*Continued.*
Good on-set boads good *end.* . . . VII. vi. 23. 9
Expecting th' *end* of this so doubtfull case, . . . VII. vii. 57. 5
All paine hath *end,* and every war hath peace; . . . *Am.* xi. 13
unlesse she turne to thee Ere Cuckow *end,* . . . *Am.* xix. 14
when I thinke to *end* that I begonne, . . . *Am.* xxiii. 9
I must begin and never bring to *end:* . . . *Am.* xxiii. 10
know no *end* of her owne mysery, . . . *Am.* xxv. 2
when shall these wearie woes have *end,* . . . *Am.* xxxvi. 1
so bad *end* for hereticks ordayned; . . . *Am.* xlviii. 6
hard t' achieve and bring to *end.* . . . *Am.* li. 8
I wish that night the noyous day would *end:* . . . *Am.* lxxxvi. 6
when will this long weary day have *end,* . . . *Epith.* 278
though he do not win his wish to *end,* . . . *H.L.* 211
Ne hath their day, ne hath their blisse, an *end,* . . . *H.H.L.* 74
his perfect *end* Of purest beautie . . . *H.H.B.* 46
attend On Gods owne person, without rest or *end.* . . . *H.H.B.* 98
runne softly, till I *end* my Song. . . . *Proth.* 18, 36, 54,72,90,108, 126,144,162, 180

Endamage. never more he mote *endammadge* wight . . . VI. xii. 38. 3
Endamaged. Ne ought he car'd whom he *endamaged* . . . II. ii. 18. 7
Since neither is *endamadg'd* much thereby.' . . . V. viii. 14. 3
Endanger. That deadly dint of steele *endanger* may. . . . I. vii. 29. 7
Endangerment. way he enter might without *endangerment.* . . V. ii. 20. 9
Endear. doest the more *endeere* Thy pleasures . . . *H.L.* 274
Endeavor. That all his care, this all his whole *indevour,* . . . *Gn.* 137
Him forth through infinite *endevour* to have sought. . . . III. iii. 6. 9
At least it faire *endevour* will apply.' . . . III. xi. 15. 6
through my good *endevour* . . . did helpe to save her. . . . V. iv. 12. 2
with sure promise of her good *endevour* . . . V. v. 35. 2
Like to Osyris in all just *endever:* . . . V. vii. 22. 5
that wyld man did apply His best *endevour* . . . VI. iv. 16. 2
With strong *endevour* and attention dew. . . . *Am.* lxxx. 8
Endeavored. he *endevored* with speaches milde . . . III. viii. 34. 1
Endeavoring. *Endevoring* my dreaded name to raise . . . II. iii. 38. 7
Endeavorment. Triall to make of his *endevourment;* . . . *Hub.* 298
Endeavors. By whose *endevours* they are glorifide; . . . *Ded. Son.* iv. 8
Yet ought mens good *endevours* them confirme, . . . III. iii. 25. 8
Ended. So conteck soone by concord mought be *ended.* . . . *S.C.* May 163
The pasport *ended,* both they forward went; . . . *Hub.* 203
By that he *ended* had his ghostly sermon, . . . *Hub.* 479
So *ended* shee; and then the next anew, . . . *T.M.* 113
So *ended* shee; and then the next in rew . . . *T.M.* 359, 419, 479, 539
Thus having *ended* all her piteous plaint, . . . *Ti.* 470
when all his mourning melodie He *ended* had, . . . *Ti.* 597
wrought her shame, and sorrow never *ended.* . . . *Mui.* 264
Thus when he *ended* had his heavie plaint, . . . *D.* 540
Which when she *ended* had, . . . *As.* Interl. 217
This sun would faile me ere I halfe had *ended:* . . . *Col.* 579
having *ended,* he from ground did rise, . . . *Col.* 952
Ere she had *ended* all she gan to faint: . . . I. vii. 52. 1
If not well *ended* at our dying day. . . . I. x. 41. 7
ended all her woe in quiet death. . . . II. i. 56. 4
When he thus *ended* had his sorrowing, . . . II. iv. 33. 7
Which having *ended* after him she flyeth swifte. . . . II. vii. 23. 9
Here *ended* Brutus sacred progeny, . . . II. x. 36. 1
his booke did read, Ne yet has *ended;* . . . II. x. 70. 2
having *ended* with that Squyre of Dames . . . III. viii. 44. 1
I greet you well . . . So *ended* Paridell. . . . III. ix. 51. 9
In love were either *ended* or begunne: . . . IV. Pr. 3. 5
when the next shall likewise *ended* bee, . . . IV. ii. 52. 7
when she saw that cruell war so *ended,* . . . IV. iii. 50. 4
After the proofe of prowesse *ended* well, . . . IV. v. 2. 2
now by this their feast all being *ended,* . . . IV. v. 6. 6
he last *ended,* having first begonne. . . . IV. v. 7. 5
This being *ended* thus, and all agreed, . . . IV. v. 9. 7
Which *ended,* then his bloudy banket should beginne. . . . IV. vii. 20. 9
That harder may be *ended,* then begonne: . . . IV. x. 3. 4
So *ended* he his tale, where I this Canto end. . . . IV. x. 58. 9
now by this the feast was throughly *ended,* . . . IV. xii. 18. 1
When they thus *ended* had, the Knight began: . . . V. iv. 16. 1
With bitter strokes it both began and *ended.* . . . V. v. 6. 2
where ye *ended* have, now I begin . . . VI. i. 6. 1
Shall more conveniently in other place be *ended.* . . . VI. ix. 46. 9
When thus that shepheard *ended* had his speach, . . . VI. x. 29. 1
So having *ended,* silence long ensewed; . . . VII. vii. 57. 1
High time it is this warre now *ended* were . . . *Am.* lvii. 2
So *ended* she; . . . *Proth.* 109
Endeth. Now *endeth* our roundelay.' . . . *S.C.* Au. 124
Endighting. *See* **Indicting.**
Endite. *See* **Indict, Indite.**
Endless. Should not her name and *endles* honour keep. . . . *Ro.* viii. 14
Thy dayes therefore are *endles,* . . . *Ro. Env.* 9
endles sovenaunce Emong the shepeheards swaines . . . *S.C.* N. 5
Through the worlds *endles* ages to survive. . . . *Gn.* 56
endles paines and hideous heavinesse . . . *Gn.* 371
and suffer *endles* paine. . . . *Gn.* 408
here wise Curius . . . lives in *endles* rest; . . . *Gn.* 610
Therefore I mourne, and *endlesse* sorrow make, . . . *T.M.* 473
Enclosde therein for *endles* memorie Of him, . . . *Ti.* 662
The first beginners of my *endles* care: . . . *D.* 301
tourn Sweet layes of love to *endlesse* plaints of pittie. . . . *Col.* 387
nor reave Out of your *endlesse* debt, . . . *Ded. Son.* vii. 7
Ne may I, without blot of *endlesse* blame, . . . *Ded. Son.* xvi. 1
the man so wrapt in Errours *endlesse* traine! . . . I. i. 18. 9
she did pray . . . that in *endlesse* error she might ever stray. I. iii. 23. 9
In living Princes court none ever knew Such *endlesse* richesse, I. iv. 7. 5
From wandring Stygian shores, where it doth *endlesse* move.' I. iv. 48. 9

Endless—*Continued.*
The house of *endlesse* paine is built thereby, . . . I. v. 33. 7
Theseus condemned to *endlesse* slouth by law; . . . I. v. 35. 8
Of *endlesse* life he might him not deprive, . . . I. v. 40. 4
Here *endlesse* penaunce for one fault I pay, . . . I. v. 42. 6
the *endlesse* routes of wretched thralles, . . . I. v. 51. 1
many heades . . . Did breed him *endlesse* labor to subdew. . . I. vii. 17. 5
thousand feends that doe them *endlesse* paine . . . I. ix. 49. 8
Brings them to joyous rest and *endlesse* blis. . . . I. x. 52. 6
for *endlesse* memory Of that deare Lord . . . I. x. 54. 3
A worke of labour long, and *endlesse* prayse: . . . I. xi. 7. 6
be for all chaste Dames an *endlesse* moniment.' . . . II. ii. 10. 9
thee to *endlesse* bale captived lead. . . . II. v. 16. 6
full many soules do *endlesse* wayle and weepe. . . . II. vii. 56. 9
wondred at his *endlesse* exercise: . . . II. ix. 59. 2
endlesse moniments of his great good: . . . II. x. 46. 3
with incessaunt force and *endlesse* hate . . . II. xi. 6. 8
Makes for him *endlesse* mone, . . . III. i. 38. 4
that field, for *endlesse* memory, Shall Hevenfield be cald . . . III. iii. 38. 8
for *endlesse* moniments Of his successe . . . III. iii. 59. 3
Into the balefull house of *endlesse* night, . . . III. v. 22. 3
captived in *endlesse* duraunce Of sorrow . . . III. v. 42. 8
the *endlesse* progeny Of all the weeds . . . III. vi. 30. 7
In *endlesse* rancks along enraunged were, . . . III. vi. 35. 8
To whom sweet Poets verse hath given *endlesse* date. . . . III. vi. 45. 9
be partakers of thy *endlesse* fame. . . . III. viii. 43. 7
'for which is bought *Endlesse* renowm, . . . III. xi. 19. 9
Let ugly shame and *endlesse* infamy Colour thy name . . . IV. i. 53. 6
robd the world of threasure *endlesse* deare, . . . IV. ii. 33. 4
through the *endlesse* world did wander wide, . . . IV. viii. 18. 8
seeking ever since with *endlesse* paines . . . IV. ix. 38. 3
gan their *endlesse* happinesse envye, . . . IV. x. 28. 4
framed With *endlesse* cost . . . IV. x. 30. 7
endlesse memorie that mote excell, . . . IV. xi. 9. 8
Loose so immortall glory, and so *endlesse* gaines. . . . IV. xi. 22. 9
what an *endlesse* worke have I in hand, . . . IV. xii. 1. 1
Albe they *endlesse* seeme in estimation, . . . IV. xii. 1. 6
great sackes with *endlesse* riches fraught . . . V. ii. 23. 4
Adorned all with gemmes of *endlesse* price, . . . V. ix. 27. 6
for *endlesse* horrour of his shame, . . . V. xi. 19. 5
counted but a recreant Knight with *endles* shame. . . . V. xi. 46. 9
now I begin To tread an *endlesse* trace, . . . VI. i. 6. 2
And all this land with *endlesse* losse to overflow. . . . VI. iv. 30. 9
Ne ought was tyred with his *endlesse* toyle, . . . VI. viii. 47. 3
That *endlesse* were to tell. . . . VI. xii. 23. 6
That *endlesse* pleasure shall unto me gaine! . . . *Am.* xxvi. 14
The which do *endlesse* matrimony make; . . . *Epith.* 217
for short time an *endlesse* moniment. . . . *Epith.* 433
In *endlesse* glorie and immortall might, . . . *H.H.L.* 37
Through meditation of his *endlesse* merit, . . . *H.H.L.* 255
therein reed The *endlesse* kinds of creatures . . . *H.H.B.* 32
The image of such *endlesse* perfectnesse? . . . *H.H.B.* 105
Let *endlesse* Peace your steadfast hearts accord, . . . *Proth.* 101
have thou . . . *endlesse* happinesse of thine owne name . . . *Proth.* 153

Endlong. who from East to West will *endlong* seeke, . . . III. ix. 51. 3
To seeke her *endlong* both by sea and lond. . . . III. x. 19. 5

Endore. Soft Spio, sweete *Endore*, (*Eudore) Sao sad, . . . IV. xi. 48 .8

Endoss. Her name in every tree I will *endosse*, . . . *Col.* 632
in which he did *endosse* His deare Redeemers badge . . . V. xi. 53. 4

Endow. T' *endow* her sonne with threasure and rich store . . . III. iv. 21. 8

Endowed. He . . . her *endowd* with royall majestye. . . . I. vii. 16. 5

Endowments. To tell my riches, and *endowments* rare, . . . *Ti.* 87

Endows. everie one her with a grace *endowes*, . . . II. iii. 25. 4

Ends. All *ends* that was begonne: . . . I. ix. 42. 3
therein entrayld The *ends* of all the knots, . . . II. iii. 27. 8
seemd their *ends* out shortly came. . . . IV. ii. 50. 9
th' end of both likewise of both their *ends*: . . . IV. iv. 1. 5
with th' occasion *ends*; . . . IV. iv. 1. 7
those deadly *ends* Of both her foes had seene, . . . V. viii. 10. 4

Endue. I . . . with Sansfoyes dead dowry you *endew*.' . . . I. iv. 51. 5
indew The salvage minds with skill of just and trew: . . . III. iii. 45. 4
Some fitt for reasonable sowles t' *indew*; . . . III. vi. 35. 5
every shape on him he could *endew*; . . . III. viii. 40. 2
most of all those three did her with gifts *endew*. . . . VI. x. 14. 9

Endued. some were so from their sourse *indewd* . . . II. ii. 6. 1
Whence he *indued* was with skill so merveilous. . . . III. iii. 13. 9
indewd With heavenly powre, . . . III. iii. 38. 4
Who well perceived all, and all *indewd*. . . . III. x. 9. 5
The club of Justice dread with kingly powre *endewed*. . . . V. i. 2. 9
hast with borrowed plumes thy selfe *endewed*, . . . V. iii. 20. 7
Nature me *endu'd* with plenteous dowre Of all her gifts, . . . VI. viii. 20. 3
all *endewed* With wondrous beauty . . . VII. vii. 45. 2
A comely corpse, with beautie faire *endewed*, . . . *H.B.* 135
Endewd with wisedomes riches, heavenly, rare. . . . *H.H.L.* 112

Endurance. If under heaven anie *endurance* were, . . . *Ro.* xxxii. 5
Sith nought on earth can chalenge long *endurance?* . . . *Van.* xi. 14
so his rule might lenger have *endurance*. . . . *Hub.* 1114
Be sure that they shall have no long *endurance*, . . . *D.* 501
with hard *enduraunce* had Heard to the end, . . . V. vi. 17. 4
for on earth nought hath *enduraunce*. . . . *Am.* lviii. 12

Endure. the Bird that can the sun *endure*, . . . *Bel.*[2] vii. 1
if aught under heaven might firme *endure*. . . . *Bel.*[2] xiv. 8
Alas, on (in[1]) earth so nothing doth *endure*, . . . *Pet.* vi. 11
It als will end the paine which I *endure*. . . . *Ro.* vii. 14
To frame this world that doth *endure* so long? . . . *Ro.* ix. 6
endure Upon the same to set foundation sure? . . . *Ro.* xxiv. 13
Which I your poore Vassall dayly *endure*; . . . *S.C.* F. 153
While times *enduren* of tranquillitie, . . . *S.C.* May 154
it may no painfull worke *endure*, . . . *Hub.* 275
He would no more *endure*, but came his way, . . . *Hub.* 1315

Endure—*Continued.*
yron sides that sighing may *endure*, . . . *T.M.* 119
Yet thy just labours ever shall *endure*. . . . *Ti.* 175
sdeignfull scorne *endure*; . . . *Mui.* 7
to *endure* The bit of balefull steele . . . *Mui.* 61
eye mote not the same *endure* to vew. . . . I. viii. 19. 5
she could not *endure* that dolefull stound . . . I. viii. 25. 5
eies, . . . Could not *endure* th' unwonted sunne to view; . . . I. viii. 41. 2
he could not *endure* so cruell cace, . . . I. xi. 26. 8
eyes . . . could not *endure* those beames bright, . . . II. Pr. 5. 4
as a law for ever should *endure*; . . . II. ii. 32. 8
Hardly could he *endure* his hardiment, . . . II. ii. 37. 8
he would not *endure* that wofull theame . . . II. v. 37. 3
how can Your cruell eyes *endure* so pitteous sight, . . . II. vi. 32. 6
none without the same *enduren* can: . . . II. vii. 65. 5
The faithfull steele such treason no'uld *endure*, . . . II. viii. 30. 8
So goodly workemanship should not *endure*: . . . II. ix. 21. 8
Would not *endure* to bee so vile disdaind, . . . II. x. 18. 2
Dye rather would he then *endure* that same. . . . III. i. 9. 5
Cannot *endure*, but needes it must be wrackt . . . III. iv. 9. 3
Ne certes can that friendship long *endure*, . . . IV. ii. 29. 6
How may these rimes . . . Hope to *endure*, . . . IV. ii. 33. 8
that he should not long on foote *endure*, . . . IV. iii. 32. 8
endure To worke such outrage on so faire a creature; . . . IV. vi. 17. 1
with his souce, which none *enduren* dare, . . . V. iv. 42. 7
Durst not *endure* their sight, . . . V. viii. 36. 9
No love so lasting then, that may *enduren* long. . . . V. xii. 1. 9
Ne ought could them *endure*, . . . V. xii. 17. 9
Did well *endure* her womanish disdaine, . . . VI. i. 30. 8
his great force unable to *endure*, . . . VI. v. 16. 6
To make them to *endure* the pains did them torment. . . . VI. v. 32. 9
they ne might *Endure* to travell, . . . VI. v. 40. 8
Ne would *endure* the daunger of their might, . . . VI. viii. 14. 4
damned to *endure* this direfull smart, . . . VI. viii. 19. 8
Addeem'd me to *endure* this penaunce sore; . . . VI. viii. 22. 5
never more they should *endure* the shew . . . VI. x. 4. 4
That eye of wight could not *indure* to view: . . . VII. vii. 6.5
Base thing I can no more *endure* to view: . . . *Am.* iii. 6
new desire . . . that shall *endure* for ever: . . . *Am.* vi. 10
How long shall this lyke dying lyfe *endure*, . . . *Am.* xxv. 1
Thinck ever to *endure* so taedious toyle! . . . *Am.* xxxiii. 10
can no more *endure* on them to looke. . . . *Am.* xxxv. 12
that they should *endure* through many ages, . . . *Am.* li. 3
it then more stedfast will *endure*: . . . *Am.* li. 12
Which I no lenger can *endure* to sue, . . . *Am.* lvii. 3
Ne can his feeble earthly eyes *endure* . . . *H.L.* 185
love can not *endure* a Paragone. . . . *H.L.* 251
all the paines and woes that I *endure*, . . . *H.L.* 295
Endure their Captains flaming head to see? . . . *H.H.B.* 60
That th' Angels selves can not *endure* his sight. . . . *H.H.B.* 119

Endured. *See* **Long-endured.**
Such ill, as is forced, mought nedes be *endured*. . . . *S.C.* S. 139
in his flesh *endur'd* the scorching flame, . . . *Gn.* 607
ne more *endured* to say, But fell to ground . . . *D.* 184
The which, I, wretch, *endured* have thus long. . . . *D.* 532
he *endured* not the direfull stound, . . . *As.* 123
long affliction which I have *endured*: . . . *Col.* 944
And his new Lady it *endured* not. . . . I. ii. 29. 7
how many a woefull stowre For him she late *endurd*; . . . I. iii. 30. 6
lesser pangs can beare who hath *endur'd* the chief. . . . I. vi. 37. 9
Who hath *endur'd* the whole can beare ech part. . . . I. vii. 25. 5
Which have *endured* many a dreadfull stowre, . . . I. vii. 48. 3
long enprisonment, . . . he *endured* in his late restraint, . . . I. x. 2. 5
he his paine *endur'd*, as seeming now more light. . . . I. x. 24. 9
After long wayes and perilous paines *endur'd*, . . . III. i. 1. 2
full many a bitter stownd I have *endurd*, . . . III. i. 24. 9
for his dearest sake *endured* sore Sore trouble . . . III. vi. 53. 5
no lesse griefe *endured* for your gentle sake.' . . . III. xii. 40. 9
thirstinesse, Which he in chace *endured* hath, . . . III. xii. 44. *or.*9
from the first he to the last *endured*: . . . IV. iv. 37. 6
This feeble brest *endured* hath, . . . IV. vii. 14. 4
manly limbs *endur'd* with litle care . . . IV. viii. 27. 8
they *endured* all with patience milde, . . . IV. viii. 28. 6
all that ever yet I have *endured* . . . IV. x. 2. 6
adventures . . . Which he *endured* had . . . VI. iii. 22. 9
endured for her sake Great perill of his life, . . . VI. viii. 33. 8
Great travell . . . And toyle *endured*, . . . VI. ix. 2. 2
had *endured* many a dreadfull stoure . . . VI. xii. 3. 7
tempests . . . Which hardly I *endured* . . . *Am.* lxiii. 2

Endures. nought in this worlde but griefe *endures*. . . . *Bel.*[1] iii. 12

Enduring. *See* **Long-enduring.**
The record of *enduring* memory. . . . *Ded. Son.* xi. 12
shield . . . Not made of steele, nor of *enduring* bras, . . . I. vii. 33. 3
not of wood, nor of *enduring* bras, . . . II. ix. 23. 4
Whose gealous dread *induring* not a peare . . . VI. ii. 29. 5

Endyte. *See* **Indite.**

Ene. kydst not *ene* to cure thy sore hart-roote, . . . *S.C.* D. 93

Enemies. they might Inflame the Navie of their *enemies*, . . . *Gn.* 510
the harts of all his *enemyes*; . . . *Hub.* 1296
guiltie hands of *enemies* . . . *Ti.* 299
purchas Through brave atcheivements from his *enemies*; . . . *Ti.* 655
Like two sharpe speares his *enemies* to gore: . . . *Mui.* 83
so great *enemies* as of them bee, . . . *Col.* 844
their service . . . To aide his friendes, or fray his *enimies*. . . . I. i. 38. 5
carelesse Quiet lyes . . . farre from *enimyes*. . . . I. i. 41. 9
warning give that *enimies* conspyre . . . I. xi. 14. 5
His precious horne, sought of his *enimyes*, . . . II. v. 10. 7
griefe and wrath, that be her *enemies* . . . II. vi. 1. 6
thousand *enemies* about us rave, . . . II. ix. 12. 6
made he head against his *enimies*, . . . II. x. 38. 1

Enemies—*Continued.*
Triumphed oft against her *enemis;* . . . . II. x. 56. 7
The *enimies* of Temperaunce Besiege her dwelling place: . . II. xi. Arg.
covetous aspects all cruell *enimyes.* . . . . II. xi. 8. 9
When so him list his *enimies* to fray; . . . . III. iii. 12. 7
secretly his *enemies* did slay: . . . . IV. viii. 39. 6
Ne private jarre, ne spite of *enemis,* . . . . IV. ix. 16. 3
cruell *enemies* increased more, ... V. xi. 54. 2
Three mightie *enemies* did him most despight, ... VI. v. 13. 2
Whom soone as his three *enemies* did vew, ... VI. v. 22. 6
Glauncing askew, as if his *enemies* He scorned . . . . . VI. vii. 42. 3
Spreds in defiaunce of all *enemies.* . . . . *Am.* v. 12
All fearlesse then of so false *enimies,* . . . . *Am.* xii. 3
bend your force against your *enemyes:* . . . . *Am.* xlix. 8
Enemies'. Through power of that he runnes through *enemies* swerds; . . . . *Hub.* 1283
reatch his hand into his *enemies* hoast. . . . . *Ti.* 542
So farre he past amongst his *enemies* band, ... V. iii. 9. 3
Enemy. bad defiance to his *enemie.* . . . . *Van.* vi. 6
Through felonous force of mine *enemie.'* . . . . *S.C.* F. 156
his *enemie* Had kindled such coles of displeasure, ... *S.C.* F. 190
That curse God send unto mine *enemie!* . . . . *Hub.* 914
feare he neede no force of *enemie.* . . . . *Hub.* 1126
the Wolfe, her mortall *enemie,* . . . . *Hub.* 1209
Is ignorance, the *enemy* of grace, ... *T.M.* 497
Where hidden was his hatefull *enemie.* . . . . *Mui.* 392
ye have . . . proov'd your strength on a strong *enimie,* . . . I. i. 27. 7
dogges . . . Watching to banish Care their *enimy,* . . . . . I. i. 40. 5
fretting griefe, the *enemy* of life: . . . . I. iv. 35. 5
with harts on edge To be aveng'd each on his *enimy.* . . . . I. iv. 43. 4
blade To bathe in blood of faithlesse *enimy;* . . . . . . I. v. 15. 3
untill Dayes *enemy* Did him appease; . . . . I. v. 34. 6
Plaine, faithfull, true, and *enimy* of shame, ... I. vi. 20. 7
bent his *enimy* to quell, ... I. vi. 43. 3
monstrous *enimy* With sturdie steps came stalking . . . . . I. vii. 8. 2
life recover'd had the raine, And over-wrestled his strong *enimy,* . . . . I. vii. 24. 6
their cruell cursed *enemy* . . . Their kingdome spoild, . . . I. vii. 44. 1
shame t' avenge so weake an *enimy;* . . . . I. viii. 45. 8
lovers life, As . . . vertues *enimy,* I ever scornd, ... I. ix. 10. 2
late she saw him fall before his *enimy.* . . . . I. xi. 33. 9
doubted whether his late *enimy* It were, ... I. xi. 35. 3
to all good he *enimy* was still. . . . . II. i. 5. 5
As hynd from her, so she fled from her *enimy.* . . . . . . II. ii. 7. 9
That never yet encountred *enemy* . . . . II. iv. 40. 7
shal find no greater *enimy* . . . . II. v. 1. 3
maistring might on *enimy* dismayd; . . . . II. v. 13. 3
where the *enimy* Does yield unto his foe . . . . II. vi. 34. 8
art thus fowly fledd from famous *enimy?'* . . . . II. vi. 39. 9
ruin'd wals he did reaedifye . . . gainst force of *enimy,* . . . II. x. 46. 5
The lether-winged Batt, dayes *enimy;* . . . . II. xii. 36. 6
Badd those same six forbeare that single *enimy.* . . . . . III. i. 22. 9
Dy, who so list for him, he was loves *enimy.* . . . . III. iv. 26. 9
despight Which He had borne of his bold *enimee:* . . . . . . III. v. 15. 4
The *enimy* of peace, and authour of all strife. . . . . . . III. vi. 14. 9
Great *enimy* to it, and to all the rest . . . . III. vi. 39. 1
endured sore Sore trouble of an hainous *enimy,* . . . . . . III. vi. 53. 6
Which when his cruell *enimy* espyde, ... III. vii. 42. 8
cruelty So long unwreaked of thine *enimy?* . . . . III. xi. 9. 5
nought he car'd for friend or *enemy,* . . . . IV. iv. 11. 8
Unluckie Mayd, to seeke her *enimie!* . . . . IV. v. 29. 6
For dread of their devouring *enemie,* . . . . V. iv. 44. 8
is he vanquisht by his tyrant *enemy?'* . . . . V. vi. 10. 9
to get Succour against her greedy *enimy:* . . . . V. viii. 6. 7
The wicked stroke did wound his *enemy* . . . . V. xi. 6. 8
With her unrighteous *enemy* to fight, ... V. xi. 39. 5
nimbler handed then his *enemie,* . . . . VI. i. 38. 6
Whom well he wist to be some *enemy,* . . . . VI. iii. 46. 8
No wound, which warlike hand of *enemy* Inflicts . . . . . . VI. vi. 1. 1
That cursed caytive, my strong *enemy,* . . . . VI. vii. 16. 3
All were it to his mortall *enemie,* . . . . VI. vii. 23. 4
Enemy's. mourning altars, purgd with *enimies* life, ... I. iii. 36. 7
sithens . . . *enimies* powre, hath now captived you, Returne . I. iv. 51. 2
Shee triumphed on death, in *enemies* despight. . . . . . . I. x. 56. 9
That thorough some more mighty *enemies* wrong . . . . . . VI. i. 11. 3
Enfeebled. his *enfeebled* spright Gan sucke this vitall ayre . . II. vii. 66. 5
Still when as he *enfeebled* was, him cherisht, ... IV. iii. 29. 4
Onely I feare my wits *enfeebled* late, ... *H.L.* 15
Enfeloned. like one *enfelon'd* or distraught, ... V. viii. 48. 5
Enfested. *See* **Infested.**
Enfierced. more *enfierced* through his currish play, ... II. iv. 8. 6
Enfired. those heavenly beauties be *enfyred* As things divine, . *H.L.* 169
Enflame, -d. *See* **Inflame, -d.**
Enfold. whose boughes she doth *enfold* . . . . *Gn.* 220
all the crest a Dragon did *enfold* With greedie pawes, . . . I. vii. 31. 3
how many perils doe *enfold* The righteous man, ... I. viii. 1. 1
a cup . . . In which a Serpent did himselfe *enfold,* . . . . . I. x. 13. 4
The which O! pardon me thus to *enfold* . . . . II. Pr. 5. 1
did themselves emongst the leaves *enfold,* . . . . II. xii. 55. 3
hideous tayle his lefte foot did *enfold,* . . . . III. xi. 48. 7
In which she meant him warelesse to *enfold,* . . . . V. v. 52. 3
a Crocodile . . . with her wreathed taile her middle did *enfold.* V. vii. 6. 9
craftily *enfold* Theyr weaker harts, ... *Am.* xxxvii. 7
Enfolding. him with streight embras *Enfolding,* . . . . . . IV. viii. 63. 5
Enforce. Doth yet himselfe with fatall hand *enforce,* . . . . *Ro.* xxvii. 13
Whom thou doest so *enforce* to deifie: . . . . *Col.* 481
'These six would me *enforce* by oddes of might . . . . . . III. i. 24. 2
So did these two through all the field their foes *enforce.* . . IV. iv. 35. 9
Strongly did Zele her haynous fact *enforce,* . . . . V. ix. 43. 1
Till strong constraint did her thereto *enforce:* . . . . . . V. x. 4. 6

Enforce—*Continued.*
others . . . Though they *enforce* themselves, cannot attaine; VI. ii. 2. 6
He . . . Would thumpe her forward and *inforce* to goe, . . . VI. ii. 10. 8
Enforced. him *enforst* to yeeld the victorie, ... *Van.* vi. 11
'Yet fell she not as one *enforst* to dye, ... *D.* 253
I . . . Am now *enforst,* . . . to chaunge mine Oaten reeds, . . I. Pr. 1. 3
Enforst to seeke some covert nigh at hand, ... I. i. 7. 1
Enforst her purple beast with all her might, ... I. viii. 13. 3
rage *enforst* my flight; . . . . II. iv. 32. 1
*And *Vortiger enforst* the kingdome to aband. . . . . II. x. 65. 9
straunger knight . . . Was for like need *enforst* to disaray: . III. ix. 20. 2
Enforced them their forward footing to revoke. . . . . . . III. xi. 21. 9
Love . . . Ne will *enforced* be with maisterdome or might.' . IV. i. 46. 9
soone *enforced* beene To let him loose . . . . IV. iv. 34. 7
inforced to give place Unto the passion . . . . IV. xii. 8. 6
when as foes *enforst,* or friends sought ayde, ... V. ix. 30. 8
praise likewise deserve good thewes *enforst* with paine. . . VI. ii. 2. 9
enforst to beare though to my paine, ... VI. ii. 12. 5
But more *enforst* my paine, the more my plaints to heare. . VI. ii. 22. 9
Unlesse that I were thereunto *enforst:* . . . . VI. iii. 39. 7
Ere long *enforst* to breath his utmost blast, ... VI. iv. 22. 7
backeward he *enforced* him to fall; . . . . VI. xii. 30. 4
Enforcement. doen of will, that through *inforcement* came. . . V. xi. 52. 9
Enforcing. The ydle stroke, *enforcing* furious way, ... I. viii. 8. 2
by hard meanes *enforcing* her to stay, ... I. viii. 25. 8
Enform. *See* **Inform.**
Enfouldered. With fowle *enfouldred* smoake and flashing fire, I. xi. 40. 2
Enfrozen. Thou hast *enfrosen* her disdainefull brest, . . . *H.L.* 146
Engage. life for gold *engage.* . . . . II. vii. 18. 5
Tho each to other did his faith *engage,* . . . . IV. ii. 28. 5
Engaged. his faith with her he fast *engaged,* . . . . IV. vi. 43. 3
The pledge of faith, her hand, *engaged* held . . . . IV. x. 55. 7
Engendered. Out of the earth *engendred* men of armes . . . *Ro.* x. 3
Ambition is *engendred* easily; . . . . *Ro.* xxiii. 10
Engine. that divelish yron *Engin,* wrought In deepest Hell, . I. vii. 13. 1
The fiers threeforked *engin,* . . . highest trees hath rent, . I. viii. 9. 6
Therefore this craftie *engine* he did frame, ... II. i. 23. 7
the treachour did remove His craftie *engin,* . . . . II. iv. 27. 4
To shonne the *engin* of his meant decay; . . . . II. xi. 36. 3
The wicked *engine* through false influence . . . . III. ix. 29. 3
The *Engin,* fiercely flying forth . . . . V. vi. 40. 4
Engines. The *engines* which in them sad death doo hyde: . *Mui.* 86
when he saw his . . . subtile *engines* bett from batteree; . I. vi. 5. 2
Hewen out of Adamant rocke with *engines* keene, ... I. vii. 33. 7
Castle, . . . By subtile *engins* and malitious slight Is undermined . . . . I. viii. 23. 2
Thereto his subtile *engins* he does bend, ... II. i. 3. 5
Their wicked *engins* they against it bent; . . . . II. xi. 9. 6
bent Her crafty *engins* to her close intent. . . . . III. i. 57. 5
rough Masons hand with *engines* keene . . . . III. viii. 37. 6
his false *engins* fast he plyde, ... III. x. 7. 2
all the *engins* of her wit display; . . . . V. v. 52. 2
Those *engins* can the proudest love convert: . . . . *Am.* xiv. 12
Engirt. His wast with a wreath of yvie greene *Engirt* about, . IV. vii. 7. 2
th' Earth, . . . *engirt* with brasen bands; . . . . *H.H.B.* 37
England. Whom *England* high in count of honour held, . . *Ti.* 185
Saint George of mery *England,* the signe of victoree.' . . . I. x. 61. 9
That fillest *England* with thy triumphes fame. . . . . . . *Proth.* 151
England's. Cambridge or Oxford, *Englands* goodly beames. . IV. xi. 35. 6
a noble Peer, Great *Englands* glory, ... *Proth.* 146
English. Badde is the best; (this *English* is flatt.) . . . . *S.C.* S. 105
faire ymp, sprong out from *English* race, ... I. x. 60. 1
behight me borne of *English* blood, ... I. x. 64. 6
th' *English* Bath, and eke the German Spau; . . . . I. xi. 30. 7
Dan Chaucer, well of *English* undefyled, ... IV. ii. 32. 8
water all the *English* soile throughout: . . . . IV. xi. 30. 2
many a band Of Scots and *English* both, ... IV. xi. 36. 9
balefull Oure, late staind with *English* blood, ... IV. xi. 44. 5
Englishman. of the *English man* Is cal'de Blacke-water, . . . IV. xi. 41. 5
Englut. grieved mindes, which choler did *englut,* . . . . . II. ii. 23. 5
Engore. When rancour doth with rage him once *engore,* . . . II. viii. 42. 2
hand should dare for to *engore* Her noble blood? . . . . . . III. viii. 48. 8
did his hart with bitter thoughts *engore,* . . . . III. x. 45. 4
Her selfe quite through the bodie doth *engore,* . . . . . . VI. vii. 9. 6
Engored. Deadly *engored* of a great wilde Bore; . . . . . . III. i. 38. 2
the deepe wound more deep *engord* her hart, ... III. iv. 6. 4
Well hoped shee the beast *engor'd* had beene, ... III. v. 28. 7
The tast of bloud of some *engored* beast, ... IV. ix. 31. 6
Engorged. fraught with rancour and *engorged* yre, ... I. xi. 40. 5
Engorgeth. deepe *engorgeth* all this worldes pray; . . . . . II. xii. 3. 5
Engraffed. *See* **Deep-engraffed, First-engraffed, Engraft.**
Engraft. *See* **Engraffed.**
Which that same witch had in this forme *engraft,* . . . . . IV. ii. 10. 7
Engrained. With Leaves *engrained* in lusty greene; . . . . . *S.C.* F. 131
The Rose *engrained* in pure scarlet die; . . . . *Gn.* 666
Engrasped. So both together fiers *engrasped* bee, ... II. v. 20. 8
Twixt his two mighty armes *engrasped* fast, ... II. viii. 49. 6
Engrave. *See* **Ingrave.**
In seemely sort their corses to *engrave,* . . . . I. x. 42. 2
For Love his loftie triumphes to *engrave,* . . . . II. iii. 24. 3
many wounds in his corrupted flesh He did *engrave,* . . . . III. vii. 32. 7
long while laboured it to *engrave:* . . . . III. viii. 37. 7
Engraved. *See* **Engraven.**
The shepheard hath thy deaths record *engraved.* . . . . . . *Gn.* 688
in th' Adamantine mould Of his true hart . . . was *engraved,* V. vi. 2. 7
Engraven. *See* **Engraved.**
wrought by wonderous device And curiously *engraven,* . . . *Mui.* 75
yet are deepe *engraven* in my brest, ... *D.* 296
Is in this verse *engraven* semblably, ... *Ded. Son.* vi. 13
How he the name of one *engraven* had . . . . IV. vii. 46. 2

Engraven—*Continued.*
A guilt *engraven* morion he did weare; . . . VII. vii. 28. 8
Engrieved. I gan in my *engrieved* brest To scorne . . . *Van.* xii. 5
my *engreeved* mind could find no rest, . . . II. iv. 23. 4
whose *engrieved* spright Could find no rest . . . III. i. 59. 4
she was more *engrieved,* and replide; . . . III. vi. 21. 6
Th' Enchaunter selfe, . . . deepe *engrieved* was. . . . III. xii. 43. 9
Did greatly solace his *engrieved* mind. . . . IV. viii. 7. 4
The which afflicted his *engrieved* mind; . . . IV. xii. 25. 8
sore *engriev'd* to heare, . . . V. vii. 32. 7
well disburdened her *engrieved* brest, . . . VI. viii. 34. 2
whose love his heart hath sore *engrieved.* . . . VI. x. 1. 9
Engross. in the ground each where will it *engrosse,* . . . *Col.* 634
dead the grave self to *engrosse.* . . . III. iv. 38. 9
Engrossed. *Engrost* with mud which did them fowle agrise, . II. vi. 46. 7
the cleare ayre *engroste,* . . . III. iv. 13. 2
Engulfed. *See* **Deep-engulfed.**
Engulfing. In th' huge abysse of his *engulfing* grave, . . . II. xii. 5. 8
Enhance. His glory did *enhaunce,* and pompous pryde display. II. vii. 44. 9
paine, that did the more *enhaunce* His haughtie courage . . IV. iii. 8. 7
Enhanced. Unto that Goddesse grace me first *enhanced,* . . . *Col.* 359
nought aghast, his mightie hand *enhaunst:* . . . I. i. 17. 8
Croesus, that *enhaunst* His hart too high . . . I. v. 47. 6
Both of them high attonce their handes *enhaunst,* . . . II. vi. 31. 1
her *enhaunced* hand she downe can soft withdraw. . . . IV. vi. 26. 9
Enias. They met Prince Arthure with Sir *Enias,* . . . VI. viii. 4. 3
whenas *Enias* Beheld two such, . . . VI. viii. 5. 7
Enjoined. This penaunce, which *enjoyned* is to me, . . . VI. viii. 30. 3
Enjoy. where thou dost that happines *enjoy,* . . . *Ti.* 306
to *enjoy* delight with libertie, . . . *Mui.* 210
enjoy The presence of your dearest loves delight, . . . *D.* 512
So secretly did he his love *enjoy* . . . *Col.* 145
may that blessed presence still *enjoy,* . . . *Col.* 661
'He there does now *enjoy* eternall rest . . . I. ix. 40. 1
In full content he there did long *enjoy;* . . . I. xii. 41. 2
peaceably *Enjoy* the crowne, . . . III. iii. 46. 2
to *enjoy* Her deare Adonis joyous company, . . . III. vi. 46. 1
life *enjoy* for any composition: . . . V. x. 27. 5
Enjoyed. each his portion peaceably *enjoyd,* . . . II. x. 14. 6
Enjoyd an heritage of lasting peace, . . . II. x. 25. 2
Nath'lesse the same *enjoyed* but short happy howre: . . . II. x. 57. 9
Joying his goddesse, and of her *enjoyd;* . . . III. vi. 48. 2
I *enjoyd* the gentlest Dame alive; . . . III. x. 27. 2
Enjoyment. In full *enjoyment* of felicitie, . . . *H.H.B.* 79
Enjoys. joyes *enjoyes* that mortall men doe misse. . . . *S.C.* N. 196
Where she *enjoyes* sure peace for evermore, . . . II. i. 2. 8
he *enjoyes* The wide kingdome of love . . . IV. x. 42. 7
Enlarge. a race, T' *enlarge* his breath, . . . *Hub.* 745
Doth man allure for to *enlarge* his kynd; . . . *Col.* 872
wight Were housed therewithin, whom he *enlargen* might. . I. viii. 37. 9
Great mercy, sure, for to *enlarge* a thrall, . . . II. v. 18. 3
them t' *enlarge* with long extent, . . . IV. ii. 47. 2
Finding no meanes how I might us *enlarge,* . . . IV. viii. 61. 7
How from that dungeon he might her *enlarge.* . . . IV. xii. 14. 2
Commaunding Proteus straight t' *enlarge* the mayd, . . . IV. xii. 32. 3
Devize how to *enlarge* him out of hould. . . . V. v. 55. 3
mote *enlarge* her living prayses, dead. . . . *Am.* xxxiii. 4
generation goodly dost *enlarge,* . . . *Epith.* 384
Seekes to *enlarge* his lasting progenie; . . . *H.L.* 105
loves to get Things like himselfe, and to *enlarge* his race, . . *H.H.L.* 52
Enlarged. with their spoyles *enlarg'd* his private treasures. . *Hub.* 1130
soone as Furor was *enlargd,* . . . V. ii. 19. 8
mans life For nought may lessened nor *enlarged* bee, . . . IV. ii. 52. 2
The faire Poeana, he *enlarged* free, . . . IV. ix. 13. 2
now on earth it selfe *enlarged* has . . . V. x. 3. 5
Enlargement. long *enlargement* of her painefull smart. . . . III. viii. 2. 4
Enlinked. *Enlincked* fast in wedlockes loyall bond, . . . V. iv. 3. 2
Enlocked. treasures of true love *enlocked* beene, . . . IV. Pr. 4. 4
Enlumine. lampe of light, That doth *enlumine* . . . V. Pr. 7. 2
Enlumined. your light hath once *enlumind* me, . . . *Am.* lxvi. 13
He is *enlumind* with that goodly light, . . . *H.L.* 108
Enlumines. with her light the earth *enlumines* cleare: . . . II. ix. 4. 7
Enlumineth. That with his beames *enlumineth* the darke And dampish aire. . . . *H.H.B.* 164
Enmity. Sustein'd the shocke of common *enmitie;* . . . *Ro.* xxi. 4
the shield, the cause of *enmitie.* . . . I. v. 15. 9
Against his praise to stirre up *enmitye* Of such, . . . II. i. 23. 8
to darraine A triple warre with triple *enmitee,* . . . II. ii. 26. 3
Pursew the end of their strong *enmity,* . . . II. ii. 28. 3
wanted sword to wreake his *enmitee?* . . . II. iii. 12. 4
'Debatefull strife, and cruell *enmity,* . . . II. vi. 35. 1
That breathed strife and troublous *enmitie.* . . . II. viii. 10. 5
kindling coles of cruell *enmity,* . . . II. x. 33. 5
stirring up their stormy *enmity,* . . . III. viii. 21. 7
'What monstrous *enmity* provoke we heare? . . . III. xi. 22. 7
rather stird to cruell *enmity,* . . . III. xii. 1. 8
For *enmitie,* that of no ill proceeds . . . IV. iv. 1. 6
in base mind nor friendship dwels nor *enmity.* . . . IV. iv. 11. 9
Never thenceforth to nourish *enmity,* . . . V. viii. 14. 8
To stint all strife and troublous *enmitie,* . . . V. xi. 54. 3
warres, and wreckes, and wicked *enmitie* . . . VI. ix. 19. 6
Enmoved. *See* **Inmoved.**
Ennius. So *Ennius* the elder Africane, . . . *Ded. Son.* i. 7
Ennoble. doest *ennoble* with immortall name The warlike Worthies, . . . III. iii. 4. 3
Thus to *ennoble* thy victorious name, . . . *H.L.* 149
Ennobled. Nor more *ennobled* for their courtesie, . . . IV. iii. 2. 6
Ennoblest. fame, That warlike handes *ennoblest* with immortall name; . . . I. xi. 5. 9
Enormities. Some part of those *enormities* did see, . . . *Col.* 665

Enough. Butter *enough,* honye, milke, and whay, . . . *S.C.* May 115
Enough is me to paint out my unrest, . . . *S.C.* Jun. 79
they bene hale *enough,* I trowe, . . . *S.C.* Jul. 107
ynough thou morned hast; . . . *S.C.* N. 207
One if I please, *enough* is me therefore. . . . *S.C.* D. 120
griefe *enough* it is . . . *Gn.* Ded. 11
wayes *enough* for all therein to live; . . . *Hub.* 401
Is not that name *enough* to make a living . . . *Hub.* 417
It is *enough* to doo our small devotion, . . . *Hub.* 457
mournfull tunes *enough* my griefe to show? . . . *Mui.* 412
Notes sad *enough* t' expresse this bitter throw: . . . *Mui.* 414
enough of shepheards thou hast told, . . . *Col.* 457
Enough is, that thy foe doth vanquisht stand . . . I. iii. 37. 4
Who had *enough,* yett wished ever more; . . . I. iv. 29. 5
Is not *enough,* that . . . endlesse penaunce . . . I pay, . . . I. v. 42. 5
Is not *enough* thy evill life forespent? . . . I. ix. 43. 7
Is not *enough,* that . . . Thou falsed hast thy faith . . . I. ix. 46. 6
He had *enough;* . . . I. x. 38. 8
That speare is him *enough* to doen a thousand grone.' . . . II. iii. 12. 9
Is not *enough* fowre quarters of a man, . . . II. iii. 16. 6
Matter of merth *enough,* though there were none, . . . II. vi. 3. 7
(as she could well *enough*) . . . II. vi. 25. 3
Is not *enough* that I alone doe dye, . . . III. ii. 35. 3
Enough to hold a foole in vaine delight. . . . III. viii. 10. 7
More is more losse; one is *enough* to dy.' . . . III. xi. 19. 7
thought himselfe not safe *enough* thereby, . . . III. xii. 12. 2
'Gentle Dame, reward *enough* I weene, . . . III. xii. 40. 2
They two *enough* t' encounter an whole Regiment. . . . V. i. 30. 9
It's punishment *enough* that all his shame doe see.' . . . V. iii. 36. 9
Which though I be not wise *enough* to frame, . . . VI. iv. 34. 8
Hath not *enough,* but wants in greatest store, . . . VI. ix. 30. 4
Thought not *enough* to punish him in sport, . . . VII. vi. 51. 2
Sweet is the Broome-flowre, but yet sowre *enough;* . . . *Am.* xxvi. 7
Enough it is for one man to sustaine The stormes, . . . *Am.* xlvi. 13
Enough it is (*is it) that all the day was youres: . . . *Epith.* 297
Enough is me t' admyre so heavenly thing, . . . *H.H.B.* 236
Enprisonment. *See* **Imprisonment.**
Enquire, *etc. See* **Inquire,** *etc.*
Enrace. did in stocke of earthly flesh *enrace,* . . . III. v. 52. 5
Enraced. a goddesse . . . from heven first *enraced?* . . . VI. x. 25. 5
When she in fleshly seede is eft *enraced,* . . . *H.B.* 114
Enrage. Wonts not t' *enrage* the hearts of equall beasts, . . . *Ro.* xxiv. 2
which be wont t' *enrage* the restlesse sheepe, . . . *S.C.* D. 89
hartes of great Heroes doest *enrage,* . . . I. xi. 6. 4
with which she doth *enrage* Her frantick sonne, . . . II. iv. 11. 4
Enraged. Wherewith *enrag'd* he fiercely gan upstart, . . . *Gn.* 289
Thereat *enraged,* soone he gan upstart, . . . *Hub* 1333
Therewith *enrag'd* she loudly gan to bray, . . . I. i. 17. 5
half *enraged* at her shamelesse guise, . . . I. i. 50. 2
he, *enrag'd* with rancour, nothing heares. . . . I. iii. 44. 5
'Pardon the error of *enraged* wight, . . . I. iv. 41. 2
he al *enrag'd* these bitter speaches said. . . . I. vi. 46. 9
the Gyaunt . . . all *enrag'd* with smart and frantick yre, . . I. viii. 17. 8
threw it to the ground, *enraged* rife, . . . I. ix. 52. 5
The cruell wound *enraged* him so sore, . . . I. xi. 37. 1
enraged heates, Here heaped up . . . I. xii. 30. 3
suddeinly he seemd *enragd,* . . . II. iii. 14. 1
with horrible affright And hellish fury all *enragd,* . . . II. iv. 30. 2
all *enraged* thus him loudly shent; . . . II. v. 5. 2
billowes rore Outragiously, as they *enraged* were, . . . II. xii. 22. 2
them *enraged* with fell surquedry: . . . II. xii. 39. 4
Wherewith *enrag'd* she fiercely at them flew, . . . III. i. 66. 1
Greatly he grew *enrag'd,* and furiously Hurling his sword . . III. vii. 33. 5
enrag'd, with sterne regard Her dreadfull weapon she to him addrest, . . . III. vii. 42. 1
The aged Dame, him seeing so *enraged,* . . . IV. i. 54. 1
He all *enrag'd* his shivering speare did shake, . . . IV. iii. 10. 8
Claribell *enraged* rife With fervent flames, . . . IV. ix. 21. 3
halfe *enrag'd* she grew, . . . V. v. 9. 6
Streight downe she ranne, like an *enraged* cow . . . V. viii. 46. 1
rather more *enrag'd* for those words sake; . . . VI. i. 19. 4
But he the more thereby *enraged* was, . . . VI. iii. 50. 1
With that the wyld man more *enraged* grew, . . . VI. iv. 6. 1
the beast *enrag'd* to loose his pray Upon him turned, . . . VI. iv. 20. 5
eftsoones he all *enraged* grew, . . . VI. vi. 22. 2
He ran at him *enraged,* . . . VI. x. 35. 9
halfe *enraged* at that ruefull sight; . . . VI. xi. 25. 4
Enragement. With sweete *enragement* of celestiall love, . . . *H.H.L.* 286
Enraging. Like a fell mastiffe through *enraging* heat, . . . V. xi. 12. 2
Enranged. Three linckes of yron teeth *enraunged* were, . . . I. xi. 13. 2
Beholdes her nymphes *enraung'd* in shady wood, . . . I. xii. 7. 8
two brave knightes . . . he *enraunged* fond, . . . II. ii. 21. 4
were *enraunged* ready still for fight. . . . II. ix. 26. 5
In endlesse rancks along *enraunged* were, . . . III. vi. 35. 8
In manner of a maske, *enranged* orderly. . . . III. xii. 5. 9
divers trees *enrang'd* in even rankes; . . . IV. x. 25. 2
One might have seene *enraung'd* disorderly, . . . V. xi. 9. 8
With all her Nymphes *enranged* on a rowe, . . . VII. vi. 39. 7
where those Idees on hie *Enraunged* be, . . . *H.H.B.* 83
So they, *enranged* well, . . . *Proth.* 122
Enranging. this day I was *enraunging* it, . . . VI. ii. 9. 7
Enrankled. Had so *enranckled* her malitious hart, . . . III. viii. 2. 2
Enravished. At sight thereof so much *enravisht* bee? . . . *H.L.* 119
Enregistered. To reade *enregistred* in every nooke His goodnesse, . . . *H.H.B.* 131
Enrich. To deck her Dame, and *enrich* her heyre, . . . *S.C.* S. 115
T' *enrich* the storehouse of his powerfull wit, . . . *Hub.* 790
did *enrich* that noble breast of his . . . *Ti.* 285
rivers . . . Which doe the earth *enrich* and beautifie: . . . IV. xi. 20. 2
Enriched. To leave *enriched* with that he hath spard? . . . *S.C.* May 84

Enriched—*Continued.*
With vayne desire and hope to be *enricht;* . . . *S.C.* S. 75
Enricht with spoyles of th' Ericthonian towre, . . . *Gn.* 562
if thou wilt *enriched* bee, . . . II. vii. 38. 7
him *enriched* through the overthrow . . . III. iv. 22. 7
threasure . . . which mote have *enriched* all us heare. . . . IV. ii. 33. 5
So lavishly *enricht* with Natures threasure, . . . IV. x. 23. 3
him *enricht* with bounty of the soyle: . . . VII. vii. 38. 4
Enriven. made a griesly wound in his *enriven* side. . . . V. viii. 34. 9
Enroll. to *enroll* thy memorable name In th' heart . . . III. viii. 43. 4
And al her faults in thy black booke *enroll:* . . . *Am.* x. 12
Enrolled. Hurles forth his thundring dart . . . *Enrold* in flames, I. viii. 9. 4
Enrold in duskish smoke and brimstone blew: . . . I. xi. 44. 4
enrolled is your glorious name In heavenly Regesters . . . II. i. 32. 3
In which her roiall presence is *enrold;* . . . II. ii. 44. 4
Immortall fame for ever hath *enrold;* . . . II. x. 4. 8
in the fomy waves *enrold,* . . . II. xii. 25. 4
to be in heaven *enrold.* . . . III. iv. 11. 9
Her faire lockes in rich circlet be *enrold,* . . . III. v. 5. 4
A famous history to bee *enrold* . . . III. ix. 50. 7
For hast did over-runne, in dust *enrould:* . . . IV. iii. 41. 5
Glistring like gold amongst the plights *enrold,* . . . V. ix. 28. 7
Mongst rocks and caves, where she *enrold* doth lie . . . VI. vi. 11. 4
a wreath, that was *enrold* With ears of corne . . . VII. vii. 30. 6
they would the records have *enrold* Of theyr great deeds . . . *Am.* lxix. 3
Enrooted. *enrooted* deepe must be that Tree, . . . III. iii. 22. 2
cryme Which was *enrooted* in all fleshly slyme. . . . *H.H.L.* 168
Ensample. th' *ensample* of her mothers sight: . . . *Bel.*[2] vii. 4
To daunt his foe by *ensample* of the same. . . . *Gn.* 608
A vaine *ensample* of the Persian pride; . . . *Hub.* 750
To heare their doome, and sad *ensample* see. . . . *Hub.* 1378
in my case their owne *ensample* see. . . . *Ti.* 462
Behold (said it) and by *ensample* see, . . . *Ti.* 582
Above th' *ensample* of his equall peares, . . . *Mui.* 28
sad *ensample* of mans suddein end: . . . *As.* 134
ensample, to the present age Of th' old Heroes, . . . *Ded. Son.* vi. 3
Yet brave *ensample* of long passed daies, . . . *Ded. Son.* x. 9
That doth this Redcrosse knights *ensample* plainly prove. . . . I. iv. 1. 9
made *ensample* of their mournfull sight Unto his Maister, . . . I. v. 52. 2
of his puissaunce proud *ensample* made; . . . I. viii. 16. 3
This daies *ensample* hath this lesson deare Deepe written . . . I. viii. 44. 7
'*Ensample* make of him your haplesse joy, . . . I. ix. 12. 1
rare *ensample* made, . . . II. ii. 25. 4
Ill by *ensample* good doth often gayne.' . . . II. ii. 45. 5
shewst th' *ensample* of thy childishe might, . . . II. iv. 45. 4
henceforth by this daies *ensample* trow, . . . II. v. 13. 7
laid forth for *ensample* of the best: . . . II. vi. 12. 5
How they them selves doe thine *ensample* make, . . . II. vi. 15. 3
Did follow that *ensample* which he blam'd afore. . . . II. vi. 45. 9
Ensample be of mind intemperate, . . . II. vii. 60. 4
Ensample of his wondrous faculty, . . . II. x. 26. 1
brave *ensample,* both of martiall And civil rule, . . . II. x. 74. 8
by *ensample* of the last dayes losse, . . . III. i. 64. 6
Shall of him selfe a brave *ensample* shew, . . . III. iii. 45. 2
Late dayes *ensample,* which these eyes beheld: . . . III. iii. 55. 2
her *ensample* make Unto thy selfe, . . . III. iii. 56. 8
Ne doest by others death *ensample* take, . . . III. iv. 14. 7
The warlike Maide, th' *ensample* of that might; . . . III. iv. 44. 7
To make *ensample* of his heavenly grace, . . . III. v. 52. 2
To your faire selves a faire *ensample* frame . . . III. v. 54. 1
That Ladies all may follow her *ensample* dead. . . . III. v. 54. 9
So straunge *ensample* of conception; . . . III. vi. 8. 2
To be th' *ensample* of true love alone, . . . III. vi. 52. 4
never let th' *ensample* of the bad Offend the good; . . . III. ix. 2. 1
makes *ensample* of mans wretched state, . . . III. ix. 39. 8
that nights *ensample* did bewray . . . III. x. 48. 7
of faire Britomart *ensample* take, . . . III. xi. 2. 8
made him selfe *thensample* of his follie. . . . IV. i. 36. 6
Next Hercules his like *ensample* shewed, . . . V. i. 2. 6
By like *ensample* mote for ever warned bee. . . . V. viii. 44. 9
Seeing that sad *ensample* them before, . . . V. x. 38. 2
By late *ensample* of that courteous deed . . . VI. iii. 2. 4
by the like *ensample* warned bee, . . . VI. vii. 27. 5
Ensample take of Mirabellaes case, . . . VI. viii. 2. 7
through *ensample* of thy sisters might, . . . VII. vi. 32. 4
Such death the sad *ensample* of your might. . . . *Am.* vii. 14
shew the last *ensample* of your pride; . . . *Am.* xxv. 6
now of sinne to all *ensample* bee: . . . *H.H.L.* 96
Ensampled. *Ensampled* it by his most righteous deede, . . . *H.H.L.* 213
Ensamples. Having escapt so sad *ensamples* in his sight. . . . I. vi. 1. 9
'Behold th' *ensamples* in our sights . . . II. xii. 9. 2
fetch from Faery Forreine *ensamples* . . . III. Pr. 1. 4
Enseams. in him selfe *enseames* Both thirty sorts of fish, . . . IV. xi. 35. 8
Ensew, -en, *etc. See* **Ensue,** *etc.*
Enshrined. His harts *enshrined* saint, his heavens queene, . . . *H.L.* 215
If it in darknesse be *enshrined* ever, . . . *H.B.* 188
Ensnarl. They in awayt would closely him *ensnarle,* . . . V. ix. 9. 3
Enstall, -ed. *See* **Install, -ed.**
Ensue. In whose high front was writ as doth *ensue.* . . . *Gn.* 686
let the rest in order thee *ensew.* . . . *T.M.* 54
Began her grievous plaint as doth *ensew.* . . . *T.M.* 114, 174, 234, 300, 420
Began her piteous plaint, as doth *ensew.* . . . *T.M.* 360
Began her plaint, as doth herein *ensew.* . . . *T.M.* 480
Began her mournfull plaint, as doth *ensew.* . . . *T.M.* 540
left his sonne t' *ensue* those steps of his. . . . *Ti.* 266
service high so basely they *ensew,* . . . *Col.* 767
noble Lord, the . . . Precedent of all that armes *ensue?* . . . *Ded.Son.*xiv.7
How many mischieves should *ensue* his heedlesse hast. . . . I. iv. 34. 9
upon eternall paine Of high displeasure that *ensewen* might, . . . I. iv. 40. 6

Ensue—*Continued.*
good successes which their foes *ensew:* . . . I. v. 25. 3
Th' ill to prevent, that life *ensewen* may; . . . I. ix. 44. 3
other secret vertue did *ensew;* . . . I. xi. 36. 5
next to him Jocante did *ensew;* . . . III. i. 45. 4
with like fiercenesse did *ensew* the chace, . . . III. xi. 5. 2
They loved armes, and knighthood did *ensew,* . . . IV. ii. 46. 4
musicke, which did next *ensew* Before the spouse: . . . IV. xi. 23. 2
So having sayd, the younger did *ensew:* . . . V. iv. 15. 1
Wayting what would *ensue* of that event. . . . V. vi. 28. 5
To prove if better foote then horsebacke would *ensew.* . . . VI. i. 35. 9
Did hang in long suspence what would *ensew,* . . . VII. vii. 57. 6
Betokening peace and plenty to *ensew.* . . . *Am.* lxii. 4
frayle corruption, that doth flesh *ensew.* . . . *Am.* lxxix. 8
No lesse then Angels whom he did *ensew,* . . . *H.H.L.* 121
Ensued. soone *ensued* them with heavie stowre. . . . *Gn.* 566
death *ensewd* if any him descryde. . . . I. v. 52. 9
ere her words *ensewd,* . . . II. iii. 34. 1
nature had for wantonesse *ensude* Art, . . . II. xii. 59. 3
A direfull stench of smoke and sulphure mixt *Ensewd,* . . . III. xii. 2. 6
next *ensew'd* the Paragon to see . . . IV. v. 9. 8
what *ensu'd* shall in next Canto be begonne. . . . VI. ii. 48. 9
that the blood *ensew'd* In great aboundance, . . . VI. iii. 50. 7
So having ended, silence long *ensewed;* . . . VII. vii. 57. 1
Ensues. faire Sir, whose pageant next *ensewes,* . . . II. i. 33. 6
Ensueth. Evil *ensueth* of wrong entent. . . . *S.C.* May 102
Late learnd what harme to hasty trust *ensu'th.* . . . I. vi. 12. 4
all that gentle noriture *ensu'th;* . . . II. ii. 2. 5
Ensuing. posteritie Of age *ensuing* shall you ever read? . . . *Ro.* xxxii. 2
the morrow next *ensuing,* . . . *Hub.* 103
To be a wonder to all age *ensuing,* . . . *Ti.* 552
Whom straight the Prince *ensuing* in together far'd. . . . IV. ix. 5. 9
day . . . *Ensewing,* made her knowen to him at last: . . . VI. viii. 51. 8
short her wayes, This yeare *ensuing,* . . . *Am.* lx. 14
With a great traine *ensuing.* . . . *Proth.* 167
Entail. A worke of rich *entayle* and curious mould, . . . II. vii. 4. 5
Entailed. *entayld* With curious antickes, . . . II. iii. 27. 4
despiteously *entayld* Deepe in their flesh, . . . II. vi. 29. 7
Entangle. all his gins, that him *entangle* might; . . . *Mui.* 387
She may *entangle* in that golden snare; . . . *Am.* xxxvii. 6
Entangled. *See* **Thick-entangled.**
Entangled in a fowling net, . . . *S.C.* Mar. 109
There the fond Flie, *entangled,* strugled long, . . . *Mui.* 425
Entent. *See* **Intent.**
Enter. to *enter* into meditation deepe . . . *Van.* i. 3
ere that into the race We *enter,* . . . *Hub.* 123
faintly gan into his worke to *enter,* . . . *Hub.* 1006
That none might *enter* but with issue hard: . . . *Hub.* 1116
ever *enter* in his minde; . . . *Hub.* 1133
Can griefe then *enter* into heavenly harts . . . *T.M.* 47
That darkesome cave they *enter,* . . . I. ix. 35. 1
Thus *enter* we Into this life with woe, . . . II. i. 2. 8
On which it seizing no way *enter* might, . . . II. iv. 46. 7
To *enter* in and reape the dew reward. . . . III. i. 30. 8
Should ever *enter* in his bounteous thought, . . . III. ii. 10. 2
To *enter* into that same balefull Bowre, . . . III. iii. 8. 8
never any knight Is suffred here to *enter,* . . . III. ix. 6. 4
So as he was not let to *enter* there: . . . III. ix. 13. 5
The wood they *enter,* and search . . . III. xi. 6. 8
watcht that none should *enter* nor issew: . . . III. xi. 31. 7
went unto the dore To *enter* in, . . . III. xii. 27. 7
Yet many waies to *enter* may be found, . . . IV. i. 20. 7
Full many did affray, that else faine *enter* would. . . . IV. x. 16. 9
To *enter* in, or issue forth below; . . . IV. xii. 15. 4
to invent Which way he *enter* might . . . V. ii. 20. 9
Did beat upon the gates to *enter* in; . . . V. iv. 37. 2
Made them all *enter* in before her sight; . . . V. iv. 45. 7
first the Lists did *enter:* . . . V. v. 5. 2
shee with great humility Did *enter* in, . . . V. vii. 3. 8
Pelmell with them attonce did *enter* in. . . . V. vii. 35. 4
good direction how to *enter* in, . . . VI. i. 6. 3
whilest Calidore Did *enter* in, . . . VI. i. 23. 9
He durst not *enter* into th' open greene, . . . VI. x. 11. 1
Open them wide that she may *enter* in, . . . *Epith.* 205
Enterdeal. *See* **Interdeal.**
Entered. so soone as lighter sleepe Was *entered,* . . . *Gn.* 322
so in they *entred* ar. . . . I. i. 7. 9
Into the Castle *entred* forcibly, . . . I. viii. 29. 4
Where *entred* in, his foot could find no flore, . . . I. viii. 39. 7
entred in, a spatious court they see, . . . I. x. 6. 2
being *entred* might not backe retyre; . . . II. vi. 20. 2
Soone as he *entred* was, . . . II. vii. 26. 5
their *entred* guestes to keep within, . . . II. xii. 43. 2
Thus being *entred,* they behold . . . II. xii. 50. 1
The Damzell there arriving *entred* in; . . . III. vii. 7. 1
the Championesse now *entred* has The utmost rowme, . . . III. xi. 27. 7
So soone as she was *entred,* . . . III. xii. 30. 1
Then *entred* Cambell first into the list, . . . IV. iii. 5. 1
through the mayles into his thigh it *entred,* . . . IV. iii. 9. 3
there *entered* on the other side A straunger knight, . . . IV. iv. 39. 1
Even as he ready was there to have *entred,* . . . IV. vii. 31. 3
as I *entred,* . . . IV. x. 20. 1
Who being *entred,* nought did then availe . . . V. ii. 24. 5
There *entred* in he round about him saw . . . V. v. 22. 1
She *entred* into all the partes entire: . . . V. vii. 37. 5
as they *entred* at the Scriene, . . . V. ix. 25. 1
The other which was *entred* laboured fast . . . V. x. 37. 1
the Brigants flocking . . . *entred* in a rout: . . . VI. xi. 46. 5
Whose silver gates . . . she *entred,* . . . VII. vi. 8. 7
Enterers. erst all *entrers* wont so cruelly to scorch. . . . III. xii. 42. 9

Entering. open breakes the dore . . . And *entring* is, I. iii. 19. 6
The knight and Una *entring* fayre her greet, I. x. 32. 1
The knightes there *entring* did him reverence dew, II. ix. 59. 1
First *entering,* the dreadfull Mage there fownd III. iii. 14. 6
Right as he *entring* was into the flood, III. v. 25. 3
that same soul . . . Streight *entring* into Triamond IV. iii. 22. 2
There *entring* in, they found the goodman selfe IV. v. 34. 1
Sir Scudamour there *entring* much admired IV. v. 38. 1
entring in found none therein abide, IV. viii. 23. 4
'By her I *entring* half dismayed was; IV. x. 36. 1
The cry whereof *entring* the hollow cave V. ix. 10. 1
whilest they *entring* th' one did th' other stay, V. x. 36. 5
Enterprise. was content to attempt that *enterprise,* *Hub.* 995
He . . . to the beast gan turne his *enterprise,* I. viii. 15. 7
From first to last in your late *enterprise,* I. xii. 17. 3
through hardy *enterprize* Many great Regions are discovered, II. Pr. 2. 3
did *enterpris* Th' adventure of the Errant damozell; II. i. 19. 7
Him at the threshold mett, and well did *enterprize.* II. ii. 14. 9
Withdraw from thought of warlike *enterprize,* II. vi. 25. 6
Since he this hardy *enterprize* began: II. vii. 65. 7
Equall unto this haughty *enterprise?* II. x. 1. 2
with hardy *enterprise* Shall backe repulse the valiaunt Brockwell III. iii. 35. 4
How to effect so hard an *enterprize,* III. iii. 51. 6
in all glory and great *enterprise,* III. ix. 44. 8
Before ye *enterprise* that way to wend: III. x. 40. 8
successe Mote him befall upon new *enterprise.* III. xi. 20. 3
for her sake refus'd to *enterprize* The battell, IV. iv. 11. 4
That *enterprize* for greatest glories gayne. IV. ix. 4. 5
How she that Ladies libertie might *enterprize.* IV. xii. 28. 9
That we may compasse this our *enterprize?* V. v. 48. 2
I am the wrong'd, whom ye did *enterprise* Both to redresse, V. viii. 11. 4
takes the *enterprize* For Belgee for to fight: V. x. Arg.
Hastily bent that *enterprise* to heare, V. x. 15. 4
successe Which ye have had in your late *enterprize.'* VI. i. 5. 2
As bent to some malicious *enterprise,* VI. iii. 48. 3
him force to . . . leave his *enterprize.* VI. iv. 6. 9
valiant Knights doe rashly *enterprize* VI. vi. 35. 4
passed forth to follow his first *enterprize.* VI. vi. 44. 9
durst her dreaded reskue *enterprize,* VI. viii. 18. 7
Asham'd to thinke how he that *enterprize* . . . forslacked had VI. xii. 12. 3
Dare to renew the like bold *enterprize,* VII. vi. 30. 2
Enterprised. knights . . . Have *enterpriz'd* that Monster to subdew. I. vii. 45. 2
enterprised praise for dread to disavaunce.' III. xi. 24. 9
enterpriz'd To chalenge all in right of Florimell, V. iii. 4. 7
Entertain. she couth the shepherds *entertayne* With cakes *S.C.* N. 95
Did happie winde and weather *entertaine,* *Gn.* 563
he was in sight That . . . should them *entertaine,* *Hub.* 235
no good trade of life did *entertaine,* *Hub.* 398
A thousand wayes he them could *entertaine,* *Hub.* 800
Receyved them with chearefull *entertayne.* *Hub.* 1085
with vaine toyes the vulgare *entertaine;* *T.M.* 194
Or once vouchsafeth us to *entertaine,* *T.M.* 344
to *entertaine* His fayre Belphoebe, *Ti.* 524
with . . . bold atchievements her did *entertaine.* *As.* 70
Whom Astrophel full deare did *entertaine,* *As.* Interl. 220
Goodly they all that knight doe *entertayne,* I. iv. 15. 1
The guiltlesse man with guile to *entertaine?* I. vii. 1. 7
With lovely court he gan her *entertaine;* I. vii. 38. 2
Those for Gods sake his dewty was to *entertaine.* I. x. 37. 9
Him goodly greetes, and fayre does *entertayne* I. xii. 12. 5
entertaine themselves with court'sies meet. II. i. 29. 4
to *entertaine* her new-come guest, II. ii. 16. 2
As feates of armes, and love to *entertaine:* II. iv. 1. 6
New merth her passenger to *entertaine;* II. vi. 6. 2
Proffer thy giftes, and fitter servaunts *entertaine.* II. vii. 9. 9
were your will her sold to *entertaine,* II. ix. 6. 5
the Faery knight did *entertayne* Another Damsell II. ix. 40. 1
The love of women not to *entertaine;* III. iv. 26. 2
Where she was wont her Sprightes to *entertaine,* III. viii. 4. 4
That thing of course he counted love to *entertaine.* III. ix. 29. 9
with amorous delights . . . he would her *entertaine;* III. x. 8. 2
small delight They had as then her long to *entertaine)* IV. iii. 47. 2
Bad them not looke for better *entertayne;* IV. viii. 27. 4
entertaine with her occasions sly: IV. x. 13. 4
his foes love or liking *entertaine.* V. v. 46. 7
termes to *entertaine* of common guize, V. vi. 20. 4
after all her princely *entertayne,* V. ix. 37. 1
Ne for advantage terme to *entertaine,* V. xi. 56. 4
none should dare him once to *entertaine;* V. xii. 10. 4
Most joyfully she them did *entertaine;* VI. i. 46. 2
To weet which way were best to *entertaine* VI. iv. 24. 4
As to them seemed fit time to *entertaine;* VI. v. 24. 7
This wize did they each other *entertaine* VI. v. 34. 5
How each to *entertaine* with curt'sie well beseene. VI. v. 36. 9
Therein he them full faire did *entertaine* VI. v. 38. 6
With idle hopes which them doe *entertaine,* VI. ix. 25. 2
During which time he did her *entertaine* VI. ix. 34. 5
With better tearmes she did him *entertaine,* VI. xi. 7. 2
Both whom they goodly well did *entertaine;* VI. xii. 11. 1
Prepare your selfe new love to *entertaine.* *Am.* iv. 14
To make a truce, and termes to *entertaine:* *Am.* xii. 2
With love may one another *entertayne!* *Am.* lxviii. 12
fit to *entertayne* The greatest Prince *Am.* lxxvii. 3
Entertained. She *intertainde* her lover all the way; I. ii. 14. 2
The auncient Dame . . . *enterteynd* them both, I. x. 11. 7
Shee forth issewed . . . And *entertained* them right fairely, II. ix. 17. 9
Goodly shee *entertaind* those noble knights, III. i. 20. 1
they were *entertaynd* with courteous And comely glee III. i. 31. 4
as beseemed best, Her *entertaynd:* III. i. 55. 6

Entertained—*Continued.*
Him long she so with shadowes *entertain'd,* III. viii. 10. 8
entertained her the best he might, III. viii. 38. 2
Panope her *entertaind* eke well, III. viii. 38. 3
why Satyrane and Paridell Mote not be *entertaynd,* III. ix. 3. 3
he with cruell warre was *entertaind* III. ix. 42. 2
entertaind him in so rude a wise, IV. vi. 10. 6
she in gentle wise me *entertayned,* IV. x. 36. 2
Them fairely *entertaynd* with curt'sies meete, V. iv. 51. 5
With tryumph *entertayn'd* and glorifyde, V. viii. 51. 3
with goodly chere Them *entertayn'd,* V. x. 5. 4
Him *entertayn'd* and did her champion chose; V. x. 12. 7
With her unworthy knight, who ill him *entertayned.* VI. vi. 39. 9
Where him Blandina fayrely *entertayned* VI. vi. 41. 3
Entertaining. *entertaining* her with curt'sies meet, IV. iii. 50. 8
entertayning them with courage stout, VI. xi. 46. 7
Entertainment. Find *entertainment* or in Court or Schoole; *T.M.* 410
Ne looke for *entertainement* where none was; I. i. 35. 2
His office was to give *entertainement* I. x. 37. 4
did deeme Such *entertainment* base, II. ii. 35. 2
Their goodly *entertainement* and great glee. III. i. 42. 2
Him to receive with *entertainment* meete. IV. i. 41. 6
comely carriage, *entertainement* kynde, VI. x. 23. 4
Entertains. With . . . disdaineful spight Her vildly *entertaines;* I. iii. 43. 7
entertaines with comely courteous glee; I. x. 6. 5
entertaynes with friendly chearefull mood. I. x. 32. 4
Entertake. with more myld aspect those two to *entertake.* V. ix. 35. 9
Entice. Whereto thou list their trayned willes *entice.* *S.C.* O. 24
if this device Doth like you, or may you to like *entice.'* *Hub.* 94
Clerks they to loathly idlenes *entice,* *T.M.* 335
Yet nothing could him to impatience *entise.* II. v. 21. 9
thence him forward ledd him further to *entise.* II. vii. 39. 9
travelers to him seemd to *entize:* II. xii. 46. 6
seemd to *entice* All passers by II. xii. 54. 3
all that might his melting hart *entyse* II. xii. 66. 7
frends to termes of gentle truce *entize,* III. ii. 24. 5
did fraile sense *entice.* IV. x. 22. 9
luring baytes oftimes doe heedlesse harts *entyse.* IV. x. 49. 9
all those joyes that weake mankind *entyse.* IV. xi. 5. 4
With which thou canst even Jove himselfe to love *entise.'* V. v. 34. 9
apples . . . which Atalanta did *entice;* *Am.* lxxvii. 8
Enticed. with what . . . sweet allurements she *Entyst* the Boy, III. i. 35. 2
entysd To take to his new love, III. x. 8. 8
Entyced her to him for to accord. V. xi. 50. 5
Entire. Which thou there breathest perfect and *entire.* *Ti.* 315
Then backe to fight againe, new breathed and *entire.* I. vi. 44. 9
one massy *entire* mould, Hewen out of Adamant rocke I. vii. 33. 6
(*Entire* affection hateth nicer hands) I. viii. 40. 3
Deadly dismayd . . . Pyrochles was, and grieved eke *entyre;* II. v. 8. 2
'What doe I recke, sith that he dide *entire?* II. viii. 15. 2
with *entyre* affection him receav'd, II. x. 31. 6
ransackt all her veines with passion *entyre.* III. i. 47. 9
with *entire* Affection I doe languish III. ii. 44. 4
his affection *entire* She should aread; III. vii. 16. 7
Joying his love in likenes more *entire:* III. xi. 33. 7
When first he loved her with heart *entire,* IV. v. 4. 2
there out sucking venime to her parts *entyre.* IV. viii. 23. 9
into their harts and parts *entire.* IV. viii. 48. 9
griefe *entire* For losse of her new love, IV. ix. 13. 8
in them bore true lovers vowes *entire:* IV. x. 38. 5
She entred into all the partes *entire:* V. vii. 37. 5
touched with *intire* affection nigh him drew; V. viii. 12. 9
Would have embraced her with hart *entyre;* V. xi. 61. 4
him embracing twixt his armes *entire,* VI. v. 23. 4
with *entire* affection and appearaunce plaine. VI. v. 38. 9
Was touched with compassion *entire,* VI. viii. 3. 3
deepe emboweld in the earth *entyre:* VI. viii. 15. 4
groning sore from grieved hart *entire* VI. viii. 48. 7
lived long in peace and love *entyre,* VI. xii. 10. 7
dints the parts *entire* With chast affects *Am.* vi. 11
Deepe, in the closet of my parts *entyre,* *Am.* lxxxiv. 9
it embracing in his mind *entyre,* *H.B.* 223
that deare Lord with so *entyre* affection, *H.H.L.* 157
on fire With burning zeale, through every part *entire,* *H.H.L.* 271
Entirely. gan to highest God *entirely* pray I. xi. 32. 4
you *entyrely* pray Of pardon for the strife, III. ix. 51. 7
entyrely prayd T' advize him better VI. vii. 22. 3
of her love he was *entyrely* seized, VI. xii. 5. 3
Entize. *See* **Entice.**
Entombed. The corpes of Rome in ashes is *entombed,* *Ro.* v. 9
That here in Ladies lap *entombed* art, II. v. 36. 3
be *entombed* in the raven or the kight?' II. viii. 16. 9
By which he lyes *entombed* solemnly. II. x. 46. 7
now *entombed* lies at Stoneheng by the heath. II. x. 67. 9
the place Where late his treasure he *entombed* had; III. x. 54. 2
Entrail. folds displaid Were stretcht . . . without *entraile.* I. i. 16. 4
Compared to the creatures in the seas *entrall.* II. xii. 25. 9
Entrailed. *Entrailed* with a wanton Yvie twine. *S.C.* Au. 30
therein *entrayld* The ends of all the knots, II. iii. 27. 7
His prickling armes, *entrayld* with roses red, II. v. 29. 5
With wanton yvie twine *entrayld* athwart, III. vi. 44. 5
round about a border was *entrayld* III. xi. 46. 6
Entrayled mutually in lovely lore, IV. iii. 42. 3
basket, Made of fine twigs, *entrayled* curiously, *Proth.* 25
Entrails. through his *entrailes* spredding diversly, *Van.* vi. 9
he from hellish *entrailes* did expire. I. xi. 45. 5
his whott fyre burnes in mine *entralles* bright, II. vi. 50. 4
in their *entrailles,* full of quick Brimston, II. x. 26. 4
Sucking the seas into his *entralles* deepe, II. xii. 6. 2
all my *entrailes* flow with poisnous gore, III. ii. 39. 4

Entrails—*Continued.*
all his *entrayles* wast, ... III. v. 48. 5
Asswage the fury which his *entrails* teares: . . . . III. vii. 21. 4
boyld Her inward brest, and in her *entrayles* fryde, ... V. v. 53. 8
Out of her poysnous *entrails* fraught with dire decay.' . . . V. xi. 20. 9
for her *entrailes* made an open way To issue forth; . . . V. xi. 31. 3
of her owne foule *entrayles* makes her meat; . . . . V. xii. 31. 8
all the secrets of their *entrayles* sought. . . . . VI. xi. 41. 4
Entrall, -es. *See* **Entrail, -s.**
Entrance. when he saw no *entraunce* to him graunted, . . . *Hub.* 1367
Weening their wonted *entrance* to have found . . . . I. i. 25. 5
Dame Una, weary Dame, . . . *entrance* did requere: . . . . I. iii. 12. 9
ready *entraunce* was not at his call; . . . . I. iii. 16. 6
a Porter . . . Cald Malvenu, who *entrance* none denide: . . . I. iv. 6. 4
By that same hole an *entraunce*, darke and bace, ... I. v. 31. 4
the noble Prince . . . made himselfe free *enterance*. . . . . I. viii. 34. 7
The stroke thereof from *entraunce* may defend; . . . . II. viii. 21. 2
their *entraunce* to forestall, ... II. ix. 11. 2
gently answered, They *entraunce* did desire. . . . . II. ix. 11. 9
Here may ye not have *entraunce*, ... II. ix. 12. 4
entraunce crav'd which was denied erst. . . . . II. ix. 17. 3
They battred day and night, and *entraunce* did awate. . . . II. xi. 6. 9
never *entraunce* any durst pretend, ... II. xi. 15. 8
He nought was moved at their *entraunce* bold, ... III. iii. 15. 1
his dreame that did him long *entraunce*, ... III. vii. 45. 2
they restrained were Of ready *entraunce*, ... III. viii. 52. 4
soft knocking *entrance* he desyrd. . . . . III. ix. 10. 1
late *entrance* deare besought: . . . . III. ix. 12. 4
flatly he of *entrance* was refusd. . . . . III. ix. 12. 6
entraunce late did not refuse. . . . . III. ix. 18. 9
at the last he found a cave with *entrance* small. . . . . III. x. 57. 9
A flaming fire, . . . did all *entraunce* choke, ... III. xi. 21. 8
More easie issew now then *entrance* late She found; . . . III. xii. 43. 1
He at his *entrance* charg'd his powrefull speare . . . . IV. iv. 44. 1
seeking often *entraunce* afterwards in vaine. . . . . IV. x. 13. 9
stopt the *entraunce* with his spacious stride, ... IV. x. 16. 7
From fearefull cowards *entrance* to forstall . . . . IV. x. 17. 3
Hatred would my *entrance* have restrayned, ... IV. x. 36. 4
me friended late In *entrance*, ... IV. x. 57. 9
he *entrance* sought, but was denide, ... V. ii. 20. 4
They pressed forward, *entraunce* to have made; . . . . V. iv. 38. 2
The whiles the Prince there kept the *entrance* still. . . . V. ix. 15. 2
Yet could the Seneschals no *entrance* find . . . . V. x. 32. 6
To see if *entrance* there as yet obtaine he might. . . . . V. x. 33. 9
hard preased in betweene, And *entraunce* wonne: . . . . V. x. 37. 7
Did choke the *entraunce* with a lumpe of sin, ... VI. i. 23. 7
tryde all waies how each mote *entrance* make . . . . VI. i. 37. 2
entraunce boldly unto him forbad: . . . . VI. iii. 38. 3
the theefe awaking light Unto the *entrance* ran; . . . . VI. xi. 43. 5
thou doest thy *entrance* make Unto thy heaven, ... *H.L.* 273
Entranced. like one halfe *entraunced* grew. . . . . VI. ix. 26. 9
Entrap. *entrap* in thy tender state: . . . . *S.C.* May 218
to *entrappe* the fish in winding sale . . . . *S.C.* D. 81
For to *entrap* the careles Clarion, ... *Mui.* 375
he of them great troups did soone *entrap*. . . . . *As.* 100
Hypocrisie, him to *entrappe*, ... I. i. Arg.
With cunning traynes him to *entrap* unwares, ... II. i. 4. 2
or hidden danger did *entrap;* . . . . II. i. 26. 9
to *entrap* The man most wary . . . . II. iv. 17. 4
Him to *entrap* unwares another way he wist. . . . . II. vii. 34. 9
whom he could not kill he practizd to *entrap*. . . . . III. xii. 11. 9
Awayting to *entrap* the warelesse wight . . . . IV. x. 20. 8
Dolon . . . seekes her to *entrap*. . . . . V. vi. Arg.
least his false foe did him *entrap* In traytrous traine, . . . V. vi. 4. 3
Ne yet *entrap* in treasons subtill traine. . . . . VI. v. 14. 4
to *entrap* him by false treacherie: . . . . VI. vii. 23. 5
T' *entrap* unwary fooles in their eternall bales. . . . . VI. x. 3. 9
Which sought me to *entrap* in treasons traine. . . . . *Am.* xii. 4
Let no false treason seeke us to *entrap*, ... *Epith.* 323
Entrapped. whom he with guilefull snare *Entrapped* slew, . . I. iv. 47. 6
through his traines he her *intrapped* hath, ... III. x. 11. 1
entrapt of love, which him betrayd, ... VI. x. 1. 7
Entrapped him, and caught into her traine; . . . . VII. vi. 48. 7
if ever ye *entrapped* are, ... *Am.* xxxvii. 11
Entreat. Who for the same him fowlie did *entreate;* . . . *Hub.* 922
freely doest, of what thee list, *entreat*, ... *Com. Son.* i. 9
Ne longer him *intreate* with me to staie, ... *D.* 562
we thee would *entreat*, . . . them to us to tell.' . . . . *Col.* 34
Hypocrisie, . . . doth to his home *entreate*. . . . . I. i. Arg.
woefull Lady, let me you *intrete*, ... I. vii. 40. 5
He them with speaches meet Does faire *entreat;* . . . . I. x. 7. 7
Could hardly him *intreat* to tell his grief: . . . . I. x. 24. 2
No solace could her Paramour *intreat* Her once to show, . . II. ii. 35. 5
Her selfe to shroud, and pleasures to *entreat:* . . . . II. vii. 53. 5
for his carkas pardon I *entreat*, ... II. viii. 27. 8
did faire Britomart *entreat* Her to disarme, ... III. i. 52. 3
Saxon kinges his friendship shall *intreat;* . . . . III. iii. 45. 3
I meane not thee *entreat* To passe, ... III. iv. 15. 3
with dishonorable termes her to *entreat*. . . . . III. v. 49. 9
'*entreat* The man by gentle meanes . . . . III. ix. 9. 1
all of love . . . did *entreat:* . . . . III. xi. 29. 4
She then began them humbly to *intreate* . . . . IV. ii. 51. 1
evermore, when he did grace *entreat*, ... IV. vii. 37. 6
To better termes of myldnesse did *entreat* . . . . IV. ix. 14. 2
Mote we *entreat* you, ... IV. ix. 40. 4
In those old times of which I doe *entreat*, ... V. i. 1. 2
gan *entreat* that iron man below To cease his outrage, . . V. ii. 22. 5
all those Knights . . . she fowly doth *entreate*. . . . . V. iv. 31. 2
him *entreat* for grace that had procur'd her paine. . . . . V. v. 28. 9
She chang'd that threatfull mood, and mildly gan *entreat:* . V. v. 47. 9

Entreat—*Continued.*
humbly gan that mightie Queene *entreat* . . . . V. x. 15. 8
learne Strangers no more so rudely to *entreat*, ... VI. i. 40. 7
Gan him *entreat* even with submission base, ... VI. iii. 38. 5
Ne ought it mote availe her to *entreat* . . . . VI. vii. 40. 1
For aye the more that she did them *entreat*, ... VI. viii. 3. 8
Seeking for Right, which I of thee *entreat*, ... VII. vii. 14. 3
Pardon for thee, and grace for me, *intreat:* . . . . *Am.* ii. 12
I will *intreat* . . . ye will me gently beat . . . . *Am.* xxiv. 13
harder growes the more I her *intreat!* . . . . *Am.* xxx. 4
Entreated. Nor chaunge of labour may *intreated* bee; . . . *Gn.* 418
all the twenty I likewise *entreated*, ... IV. x. 10. 5
entreated, that they might Finde favour . . . . VI. iii. 42. 8
Entreatful. With humble prayers and *intreatfull* teares; . . . V. x. 6. 5
Entreaties. Ne Ladies loves, ne sweete *entreaties*, ... II. v. 38. 3
Entreating. his hard rocky hart for no *entreating* Will yeeld, IV. xii. 7. 3
her bowd Upon her knee, *intreating* him for grace, ... VI. vi. 31. 6
Entreaty. With faire *entreatie* and sweet blandishment, . . . IV. vi. 41. 2
no *intreatie* would forgoe so glorious spoyle. . . . . IV. x. 55. 9
for no worldly meed, Nor no *entreatie*, ... IV. xi. 8. 8
wooe with fair *intreatie*, ... IV. xii. 26. 6
The more that he with meeke *intreatie* prayd . . . . V. v. 14. 8
try if thou by faire *entreatie* can Move Radigund? . . . . V. v. 40. 3
By whose *entreatie* both they overcommen Agree to goe . . . V. ix. 4. 1
fowle *entreaty* him indignifyde, ... VI. i. 30. 5
with prayers meeke And myld *entreaty* . . . . VI. iii. 37. 9
with many a dropping teare And long *intreaty*, ... *Am.* xviii. 6
Entrenched. *Entrenched* deep with knyfe accursed keene, . . . III. xii. 20. 6
Entrenchments. In strong *entrenchments* he did closely place, II. xi. 6. 7
Entry. Calidore in th' *entry* close did stand, ... VI. xi. 46. 6
till all the *entry* was with bodies mand. . . . . VI. xi. 46. 9
Entwined. Reproch sharpe stings, Repentaunce whips *en-twinde*, ... III. xii. 24. 7
Entyse, Entysd, *etc. See* **Entice,** *etc.*
Enure, -d. *See* **Inure, -d.**
Enveloped. yron cote . . . Was underneath *enveloped* with gold; II. vii. 4. 2
heavens chearefull face *enveloped*, ... II. xii. 34. 7
Is in a noyous cloud *enveloped*, ... III. i. 43. 2
was with gold and Ermines faire *enveloped*. . . . . III. i. 59. 9
on his shield *enveloped* sevenfold . . . . III. ii. 25. 7
Envenomed. *envenimd* sting . . . now gan afresh to rancle sore, VI. x. 31. 1
Envied. I (as I am) had rather be *envied*, ... *S.C.* May 57
whilste he lived was of none *envyde*, ... *Ti.* 241
Beholding them, him secretly *envide*, ... *Mui.* 106
their lasses, which my luck *envide*, ... *D.* 142
Neither envying other, nor *envied*, ... *Col.* 78
Admyr'd of all, yet *envied* of none, ... *Col.* 550
And eke from all, of whom it is *envide*, ... *Ded. Son.* iv. 9
gentle Sleepe *envyde* him any rest: . . . . III. iv. 54. 1
(let not it be *envide*.') . . . . III. vi. 23. 8
hurt far off unknowne whom ever she *envide*. . . . . III. vii. 6. 9
even Nature selfe *envide* the same, ... III. viii. 5. 4
life she him *envyde*, and long'd revenge to see: . . . . III. xi. 34. 9
Yet Paridell him *envied* therefore, ... IV. ii. 11. 3
Which Cambell seeing much the same *envyde*, ... IV. iv. 44. 7
Blandamour, whom alwaies he *envide;* . . . . IV. ix. 26. 4
both Knights *envide*, and Ladies eke did spight. . . . . V. vi. 6. 9
Nor am *envyde* of any one therefore: . . . . VI. ix. 21. 2
even he him selfe his eyes *envyde*, ... VI. x. 11. 7
Ne any left that victorie to him *envide*. . . . . VI. xi. 49. 9
(be it not *envide*) . . . . VII. vi. 26. 7
Is of the world unworthy most *envide:* . . . . *Am.* v. 4
Ne let the same of any be *envide:* . . . . *Epith.* 15
Envies. Each others equall puissaunce *envies*, ... I. ii. 17. 4
moniments remaine, which yet that land *envies*. . . . . II. x. 21. 9
lawlesse lustes, currupt *envyes*, ... II. xi. 8. 8
The foe of life, that good *envyes* to all, ... II. xii. 48. 4
Each wisheth to him selfe, and to the rest *envyes:*— . . . VI. viii. 41. 9
Coridon *envies* him, ... VI. ix. Arg.
envies lovers long prosperity, ... VI. x. 38. 8
Enviest. felicitie, Which thou *enviest*, ... *Col.* 678
Envious. Heaven *envious*, and bitter stepdame Nature! . . . *Ro.* ix. 2
Full *envious* that night so long his roome did fill: . . . . I. ii. 1. 9
envious gage Of victors glory from him snacht away: . . . I. iv. 39. 5
of no *envious* eyes he mote be spyde; . . . . I. v. 52. 8
Most *envious* man, that grieves at neighbours good; . . . . I. ix. 39. 6
Whiles nothing *envious* nature them forth throwes . . . . II. vi. 15. 4
with *envious* despight His prowd presumed force increased . II. vi. 30. 2
Those pretious hils from straungers *envious* sight, ... II. vii. 6. 3
Another seemed *envious* or coy, ... II. ix. 35. 7
envious of Uncles soveraintie, ... II. x. 48. 7
envious Men, fearing their rules decay, ... III. ii. 2. 5
With greedy will and *envious* desire, ... III. xi. 26. 3
faining to be hidd from *envious* eye; . . . . III. xi. 28. 5
far from *envious* eyes that mote him spight; . . . . VI. iii. 20. 7
Environed. With mountaines rownd about *environed*, ... III. v. 39. 3
With thornes and barren brakes *environd* round, ... IV. i. 20. 5
There he him found *environed* about With slaughtred bodies . VI. vi. 38. 1
Environ'd with a girland, . . . Of lovely lasses; . . . . VI. ix. 8. 3
Environd with tenne thousand starres around . . . . VII. vi. 9. 3
Envy. Bearing close *envie* to these riches rare, ... *Bel.*[2] xiii. 6
if that *Envie* barke at thee, ... *To his Booke* 5
so farre am I from *envie*, ... *S.C.* May 37
though *envie* it abuse: . . . . *Gn.* 6
worthie rule to beare, Who ever them *envie:* . . . . *Hub.* 424
thou canst not but *envie* My wealth, ... *Hub.* 597
backbite Anies good name for *envie* or despite: . . . . *Hub.* 720
Nor age, nor *envie*, shall them ever wast. . . . . *Ti.* 406
In spight of *envie* that his deeds would spot: . . . . *Ti.* 439
none gainsaid, nor none did him *envie*. . . . . *Mui.* 152

Envy—*Continued.*
such as *Envie* pale . . . Could not accuse. *Mui.* 301
The praises of my parted love *envy,* *D.* 226
Albe he *envie* at my rustick quill: *Col.* 393
Of fortune and of *envy* uncomptrold, *Col.* 662
fraught with *envie* that their galls do swell, *Col.* 760
next to him malicious *Envy* rode Upon a ravenous wolfe, I. iv. 30. 1
Such one vile *Envy* was, that fifte in row did sitt. I. iv. 32. 9
They *envy* her in their malitious mind, I. vi. 18. 6
their felicities The favourable heavens did not *envy.* I. vii. 43. 6
none did . . . aid *envy* to him in need that stands; I. ix. 1. 6
Ne wicked *envy,* ne vile gealosy, I. xii. 41. 3
Each other does *envy* with deadly hate, II. ii. 19. 2
unto none my graces do *envye:* II. vii. 8. 4
From whence the gods have her for *envy* thrust: II. vii. 49. 6
envy base to barke at sleeping fame. II. viii. 13. 7
such happinesse Heven doth to me *envy,* II. ix. 7. 9
fierce Cundah gan shortly to *envy* His brother Morgan, II. x. 33. 2
none does others happinesse *envye;* II. xii. 58. 4
Let later age that noble use *envy,* III. i. 13. 8
Full of great *envy* and fell gealosy III. i. 18. 2
we foolish men that prayse gin eke t' *envy.* III. ii. 2. 9
heven it selfe shall their successe *envy,* III. iii. 40. 7
all too long I burne with *envy* sore III. iv. 2. 3
'But if the heavens did his dayes *envie,* III. iv. 39. 1
with proud *envy* and indignant yre III. iv. 47. 3
that sweet Cordiall . . . she did to him *envy;* III. v. 50. 7
She did *envy* that soveraine salve in secret store. III. v. 50. 9
Ne poysnous *Envy* justly can empayre The prayse III. v. 54. 5
ne any does *envy* Their goodly meriment III. vi. 41. 8
Stygian Gods, which doe her love *envy;* III. vi. 46. 7
With zelous *envy* of Greekes cruell fact III. ix. 38. 5
His hart with secret *envie* gan to swell, IV. ii. 7. 8
much he gan his glorie to *envy,* IV. iv. 28. 4
Whereat the rest gan greatly to *envie,* IV. v. 19. 6
Gan both *envy,* and bitterly to ban; IV. ix. 9. 7
gan their endlesse happinesse *envye,* IV. x. 28. 4
nought for nicenesse nor for *envy* sparing, IV. x. 56. 6
The dales doe not the lofty hils *envy.* V. ii. 41. 4
The malice of her foes, which her *envy* V. viii. 17. 6
for that many did that shield *envie,* V. xi. 54. 1
Her name was *Envie,* knowen well thereby, V. xii. 31. 1
what so *Envie* good or bad did fynd V. xii. 33. 4
her dwelling Was neare to *Envie,* V. xii. 35. 6
A wicked hag, and *Envy* selfe excelling In mischiefe; V. xii. 35. 7
Envie first, as she that first him eyde, V. xii. 38. 7
He inly gan her lover to *envy,* VI. ii. 17. 2
Nether of *envy* nor of chaunge afeard: VI. v. 12. 5
to maligne, t' *envie,* t' use shifting slight, VI. vii. 1. 5
certes I your happinesse *envie,* VI. ix. 19. 8
'Therefore I doe not any one *envy,* VI. ix. 21. 1
t' *envie* her that in such glory raigned. VII. vi. 10. 6
Sweet thoughts! I *envy* your so happy rest, *Am.* lxxvi. 13
All that they know not *envy* or admyre; *Am.* lxxxiv. 6
Rather then *envy,* let them wonder at her, *Am.* lxxxiv. 7
Let the world chose to *envy* or to wonder. *Am.* lxxxiv. 14
do thou not *envy* My love with me to spy: *Epith.* 376
The gnawing *envie,* the hart-fretting feare, *H.L.* 259

Envying. Whose happines the heavens *envying,* *Ti.* 24
they in secret harts *envying* sore, *Mui.* 124
Neither *envying* other, nor envied, *Col.* 78
As *envying* her selfe, that too exceeding shone: I. iv. 8. 9
envying my toward good, II. iv. 22. 2
envying the Britons blazed fame, II. x. 47. 8
Britomart, halfe *envying* their blesse, III. xii. 46. *or.* 6
Envying my too great felicity, IV. viii. 16. 6
Fortune, *envying* good, hath felly frowned, V. v. 36. 2
'For th' heavens, *envying* our prosperitie, VI. iv. 31. 1

Envy's. through the glaunce Of *envies* dart, *Gn.* 558
times decay, and *envies* cruell tort, *Ti.* 167
Defended from foule *Envies* poisnous bit. *Ded. Son.* iii. 4
beautie brought t' unworthie wretchednesse Through *envies* snares, I. iii. 1. 4
Provokt with Wrath and *Envyes* false surmise, I. v. 46. 7
stop vile *envies* sting, IV. ii. 26. 6
Fearelesse of fortunes chaunge or *envies* dread, IV. viii. 18. 3
envies cloud still dimmeth vertues ray. V. xii. 27. 7

Enwallowed. in gore And cruddy blood *enwallowed* III. iv. 34. 8
Enwallow'd in his owne blacke bloudy gore, V. xi. 14. 6

Enwombed. her great spirite . . . is in the same *enwombed;* *Ro.* v. 11
Me then he left *enwombed* of this childe, II. i. 50. 8
th' eternall Lord in fleshly slime *Enwombed* was, II. x. 50. 3
They were *enwombed* in the sacred throne III. vi. 5. 7
of his game she soone *enwombed* grew, V. vii. 16. 5

Enwoven. *See* **Inwoven.**

Enwrap. subtil traines, He laid the brutish nation to *enwrap:* *As.* 98
flourishing fresh leaves and blossomes did *enwrap.* II. iii. 30. 9
With th' other he his friends ment to *enwrap;* III. xii. 11. 8
in thy sable mantle us *enwrap,* *Epith.* 321

Enwrapped. backe of that most hideous snake *Enwrapped* round, *Gn.* 306
enwrapt the nimble thyes Of his froth-fomy steed, I. xi. 23. 2
Enwrapt in coleblacke clowds and filthy smoke, I. xi. 44. 8
How they within their fouldings close *enwrapped* bee: II. iii. 27. 9
Enwrapped in fowle smoke and clouds II. vii. 28. 9

Ephesian. Greece will the olde *Ephesian* buildings blaze, *Ro.* ii. 3

Ephesus. Whose hight all *Ephesus* did oversee, IV. x. 30. 2

Ephialtes. Far of beholding *Ephialtes* tide, *Gn.* 375

Equal. Alike with *equall* ravine to devoure. *Bel.*[2] viii. 8
her *equall* match could see. *Ro.* vi. 8

Equal—*Continued.*
Wonts not t' enrage the hearts of *equall* beasts, *Ro.* xxiv. 2
the world parting by an *equall* lott, *Gn.* 158
Equall in honour to the former crue, *Gn.* 594
With *equall* plaints her sorrowe did partake. *T.M.* 298
whilst heavens with *equall* vewe Deignd to behold me *Ti.* 80
Was matchable to this in *equall* vewing. *Ti.* 553
Above th' ensample of his *equall* peares, *Mui.* 28
it in me breeds almost *equall* paine. *D.* 175
Each others *equall* puissaunce envies, I. ii. 17. 4
right and wrong ylike in *equall* ballaunce waide. I. iv. 27. 9
In *equall* lists they should the morrow next it fight. I. iv. 40. 9
So be, O Queene! you *equall* favour showe.' I. iv. 42. 7
The faithfull knight in *equall* field I. v. Arg.
them constraine in *equall* teme to draw. I. vi. 26. 6
whiles *equal* destinies Did ronne about, I. vii. 43. 4
he that high does sit, and all things see With *equall* eye, I. viii. 27. 7
beares an *equall* eie I. ix. 47. 2
They numbred even steps and *equall* pace; I. x. 12. 5
Who taught his trampling steed with *equall* steps to tread. II. i. 7. 9
He gan rencounter him in *equall* race. II. i. 26. 5
hevens just with *equall* brow Vouchsafed II. i. 50. 3
'death is an *equall* doome II. i. 59. 1
by *equall* shares in *equall* fee: II. ii. 13. 4
Whom they in *equall* pray hope to divide, II. ii. 22. 8
With *equall* measure she did moderate II. ii. 38. 3
both his foen with *equall* foyle to daunt. II. iii. 13. 3
Emongst thine *equall* peres, II. iii. 39. 4
On foot with him to matchen *equall* fight: II. v. 4. 8
th' *equall* die of warre he well did know: II. v. 13. 4
subdewde in *equall* frayes II. v. 26. 5
him with *equall* valew countervayld: II. vi. 29. 4
florish faire above his *equall* peares: II. viii. 5. 4
Equall unto this haughty enterprise? II. x. 1. 2
twixt them shayrd his realme by *equall* lottes; II. x. 29. 3
Then did he raigne alone, when he none *equall* knew. II. x. 33. 9
Whilest loving thou mayst loved be with *equall* crime. II. xii. 75. 9
thou wert mett On *equall* plaine, III. i. 8. 5
ever hope to match in *equall* fight, III. ii. 13. 8
thine *equall* peares Their fit disports . . . doe chose, III. ii. 31. 3
equall corage to thee take.' III. iii. 56. 9
She might in *equall* armes accompany, III. iii. 61. 4
none in *equall* armes him matchen might: III. iv. 24. 3
of all love taketh *equall* vew; III. v. 47. 5
fortune all in *equall* launce doth sway, III. vii. 4. 4
both in *equall* tilt May meete againe III. viii. 18. 3
To prove some deeds of armes upon an *equall* pere?' III. x. 24. 9
did it selfe divide with *equall* space, III. xi. 25. 5
What vengeance due can *equall* thy desart, IV. i. 53. 3
Sir Priamond, with *equall* worth And *equall* armes, IV. iii. 6. 3, 4
one of *equall* might with most, IV. iii. 24. 6
Once thinke to match three such on *equall* cost, IV. iii. 24. 8
Met him mid-way with *equall* hardiment, IV. iv. 28. 8
Both *equall* paines and *equall* perill shared; IV. v. 46. 5
What *equall* torment to the griefe of mind IV. vi. 1. 1
To have rencountred him in *equall* race; IV. vi. 3. 2
none *Equall* to this, where ever I have gone. IV. vii. 14. 5
Eftsoones outsprung two more of *equall* mould; IV. x. 10. 3
I them both with *equall* hap defeated. IV. x. 10. 4
all the rest were eke her *equall* peares, IV. x. 49. 3
By *equall* dome repayd on his owne pate: IV. xi. 38. 4
heaven, that unto all lends *equall* eare, IV. xii. 6. 5
all the West with *equall* conquest wonne, V. i. 2. 7
to weigh both right and wrong In *equall* ballance V. i. 7. 2
all things to an *equall* to restore, V. ii. 34. 2
two falses, of each *equall* share, V. ii. 48. 4
'For *equall* right in *equall* things doth stand; V. iv. 19. 1
try in *equall* field whether hath greater might. V. iv. 48. 9
they both like race in *equall* justice runne. V. vii. 4. 9
joyne in *equall* portion of thy realme; V. vii. 23. 6
Both challenge it with *equall* greedinesse: V. vii. 30. 3
with *equall* care to cast How to save VI. iii. 12. 6
To justifie thy fault gainst me in *equall* fight.' VI. iii. 35. 9
they both at once with *equall* spight Did bend their speares, VI. vii. 7. 4
both with *equall* might Against him ran; VI. vii. 7. 5
amongst mine *equall* peares To follow sheepe VI. ix. 24. 3
with *equall* hight Did seeme to overlooke the lowly vale; VI. x. 8. 7
Matched with *equall* years, VI. xii. 18. 8
thee, O Jove! no *equall* Judge I deeme VII. vi. 35. 1
is behight Father of Gods and men by *equall* might, VII. vi. 35. 5
In a fayre Plaine upon an *equall* Hill VII. vii. 8. 1
Sith of them all thou art the *equall* mother, VII. vii. 14. 8
equall gave to each as Justice duly scann'd. VII. vii. 38. 9
Riding together both with *equall* pase, VII. vii. 44. 2
That I may laugh at her in *equall* sort, *Am.* x. 13
pride and meeknesse, mixt by *equall* part, *Am.* xxi. 3
had the *equall* hevens so much you graced *Am.* lxxxii. 5
with *equall* insight see The ods twixt both, *Com. Son.* ii. 9
Whom he therefore with *equall* honour crownd. *H.H.L.* 35
verse With *equall* words can hope it to reherse. *H.H.L.* 42
And give me words *equall* unto my thought, *H.H.L.* 48

Equality. all things would reduce unto *equality.* V. ii. 32. 9

Equalize. if things nam'd their names doo *equalize,* *Ro.* xxvi. 10
Both first and second Troy shall dare to *equalise.* III. ix. 44. 9
as they were, them *equalize* againe. V. ii. 38. 5

Equally. seeing . . . The doubtfull ballaunce *equally* to sway, I. ii. 38. 2
she in hell and heaven had power *equally.* I. v. 34. 9
Proportiond *equally* by seven and nine: II. ix. 22. 7
his realme he *equally* decreed To have divided. II. x. 27. 5
The Prince and Guyon *equally* bylive Her selfe pursewd, III. i. 18. 6

Equally—*Continued.*
Should *equally* be shard betwixt us tway . . . IV. ii. 13. 5
Let both the dead and living *equally* Devided be . . . V. i. 26. 3
horse and man he *equally* dismaies, . . . V. ii. 8. 8
all the world he would weigh *equallie,* . . . V. ii. 30. 5
Did *equally* bequeath his lands in fee, . . . V. iv. 7. 4
That Gods and men doe *equally* adore, . . . V. vii. 1. 2
mongst them shared *equally.* . . . VI. xi. 10. 5
Equipage. With queint Bellona in her *equipage!* . . . *S.C.* O. 114
a warlike *equipage* Of forreine beasts, . . . *Hub.* 1118
The God of warre with his fiers *equipage* . . . I. xi. 6. 7
T' expresse some part of that great *equipage* . . . IV. xi. 17. 8
Equipaged. traine Of Squires and Ladies *equipaged* well, . . . II. ix. 17. 8
Equity. nor his in *equitie,* . . . IV. xii. 31. 5
equitie to measure out along . . . V. i. 7. 3
To you that are our judge of *equity,* . . . V. iii. 36. 7
That part of Justice which is *Equity,* . . . V. vii. 3. 4
Erato. *Erato* that doth in love delite, . . . IV. xi. 49. 7
Ere (*partial list*). *See* **Erelong, Ever, Whilere.**
Ere it be long . . . *Pet.*[1] vii. 4
eare day light, . . . *S.C.* May 12
Ere Roffy could for his laboure him thanck . . . *S.C.* S. 201
my corage cooles *ere* it be warme: . . . *S.C.* O. 115
rotted *ere* they were halfe mellow ripe; . . . *S.C.* D. 107
Ere the breme Winter breede you greater griefe . . . *S.C.* D. 148
ere that anie way I doo betake, . . . *Hub.* 69
ere that into the race We enter, . . . *Hub.* 122
some good commeth *ere* the end.' . . . *Hub.* 172
prevent this mischiefe *ere* it fall, . . . *Hub.* 190
ere we farther passe . . . *Hub.* 195
ere that unto armes I me betooke, . . . *Hub.* 291
For *ere* the yeare have halfe his course out-run, . . . *Hub.* 305
ere long time had passed, . . . *Hub.* 559
long *ere* this, . . . *Ti.* 106
ere his happie soule to heaven went . . . *Ti.* 295
ere thou die, . . . *D.* 80
ere that life her lodging did forsake, . . . *D.* 260
ere I goe, a pledge I leave . . . *D.* 288
ere ye be aware . . . *D.* 502
ere I halfe had ended: . . . *Col.* 579
To stay the steppe, *ere* forced to retrate . . . I. i. 13. 5
ere my hoped day of spousall shone, . . . I. ii. 23. 6
ere that dawning light Discovered had . . . I. v. 52. 5
ere he could his armour on him dight, . . . I. vii. 8. 1
ere he could out of his swowne awake, . . . I. vii. 15. 7
Ere she had ended all . . . I. vii. 52. 1
ere one be aware, . . . I. ix. 31. 7
earely, *ere* the morrow next gan reare . . . I. xi. 33. 3
But, *eare* he thus had sayd, . . . I. xii. 24. 6
Ere thou thy daughter linck, . . . I. xii. 26. 6
day should faile me *ere* I had them all declard . . . I. xii. 31. 9
to ayd her *ere* she dyde . . . II. iii. 3. 9
ear that wished day his beame disclosd, . . . II. iv. 22. 1
ere it empight In the meant marke, . . . II. iv. 46. 5
Ere on the plaine fast pricking Guyon spide One . . . II. v. 2. 2
It was not long *ere* she inflam'd him so, . . . II. v. 20. 1
long *ere* night, . . . II. ix. 10. 8
slaine, *ere* any thereof thought: . . . II. x. 51. 4
then assayle him fresh, *ere* he could shift for more . . . II. xi. 27. 9
commen to his reskew, *ere* his bitter bane . . . II. xi. 29. 9
Gan heap huge strokes on him, as *ere* he down was cast . . . II. xi. 43. 9
ere well he was aware, . . . III. i. 6. 6
downe him smot *ere* well aware he weare; . . . III. i. 28. 8
ere the grosse Earthes gryesy shade Was all disperst . . . III. i. 67. 7
it uptaking *ere* the fall, . . . III. ii. 9. 3
'Things ofte impossible' (quoth she) 'seeme, *ere* begonne.' . . . III. ii. 36. 9
The growing evill, *ere* it strength have gott, . . . III. ii. 46. 2
Ere they to former rule restor'd shal bee, . . . III. iii. 44. 6
ere two hundred yeares be full outronne, . . . III. iii. 46. 4
bring my ship, *ere* it be rent, . . . III. iv. 10. 4
Thus much afford me, *ere* that he did die, . . . III. iv. 39. 3
ere the morrow did upreare His deawy head . . . III. iv. 61. 3
earely, *ere* the dawning day appear'd, . . . III. vii. 19. 1
ere she of him were raught: . . . III. vii. 26. 6
ere any reskew came . . . III. vii. 28. 9
Her to encounter *ere* she passed by; . . . III. vii. 38. 4
Ere that we to efforce it doe begin: . . . III. ix. 9. 4
did cry . . . for helpe, *ere* helpe were past; . . . III. x. 13. 7
ere day, . . . III. x. 48. 5
forth prickt his steed . . . *ere* he him well could torne; . . . IV. ii. 6. 8
ere himselfe he could recower . . . IV. iii. 20. 2
Him weening, *ere* he nigh approcht, to have represt . . . IV. iv. 6. 9
ere him selfe he had recovered well, . . . IV. iv. 30. 6
ere his hand he reard, he overthrew Seven Knights, . . . IV. iv. 41. 1
ere night upon them fell; . . . IV. viii. 23. 3
ere that it to him approched neare, . . . IV. viii. 44. 7
ere he wist, he found . . . IV. viii. 45. 4
not long *ere* Brutus warlicke sonne, . . . IV. xi. 38. 1
joyne in one, *ere* to the sea they come; . . . IV. xi. 43. 8
ere he could him selfe recure againe, . . . V. i. 22. 1
ere thou limit what is lesse or more . . . V. ii. 34. 5
All suddenly, *ere* one can looke aside, . . . V. iii. 25. 5
ere one could it bewray . . . V. iii. 25. 9
Yet was as great and wide, *ere* many yeares, . . . V. iv. 7. 8
ere they assaid Unknowen perill . . . V. iv. 38. 5
ere she could joyne hand with him to fight, . . . V. iv. 43. 5
ere she would once retrate . . . V. iv. 45. 9
Brought in untimely houre, *ere* it was sought: . . . V. vi. 3. 5
ere him she plaine descride, . . . V. vi. 8. 3
ere they reared hand the Amazone . . . V. vii. 28. 1

Ere—*Continued.*
ere they were halfe ded . . . V. viii. 28. 8
ere his readie speare He could advance, . . . V. viii. 33. 5
Did stay her cruell hand *ere* she her raught; . . . V. viii. 48. 2
Ere to his den he backward could recoyle, . . . V. ix. 9. 4
snatching her soone up, *ere* well she knew, . . . V. ix. 14. 4
Ere proofe it tooke, . . . V. ix. 42. 4
Ere all her children he from her had reft: . . . V. x. 14. 5
Deliver him his owne, *ere* yet too late, . . . V. xi. 3. 8
ere it were espide, The wicked stroke did wound his enemy . . . V. xi. 6. 7
Ere he were throughly buckled to his geare, . . . V. xi. 10. 2
Ere that huge stroke arrived on him neare, . . . V. xi. 10. 5
ere he could his weapon backe repaire, . . . V. xi. 13. 7
ere that it she backe againe had borne, . . . V. xi. 29. 7
Meant them to have encountred *ere* they left the shore: . . . V. xii. 6. 9
ere he marched farre he with them met, . . . V. xii. 7. 1
ere they all were slaine, . . . V. xii. 9. 2
ere he coulde reforme it thoroughly, . . . V. xii. 27. 1
Ere that I in her guilefull traines was well expert . . . VI. i. 12. 9
thou wouldst fly *Ere* he doe come, . . . VI. i. 28. 6
ere he tasted bread . . . VI. i. 31. 4
Ere he had slept his fill, . . . VI. i. 35. 3
ere he could recover foote againe . . . VI. i. 39. 1
ere he came . . . that youth had kild That armed knight, . . . VI. ii. 4. 6
ere they come unto their aymed scope, . . . VI. iii. 5. 3
Ere they were well aware . . . VI. iii. 21. 2
And stopt the bleeding straight, *ere* he it staunched thought. VI. iv. 12. 9
To rescue th' infant, *ere* he did him kill: . . . VI. iv. 18. 7
ere he fled he with his tooth impure Him heedlesse bit, . . . VI. v. 16. 8
ere that litle while they ridden had, . . . VI. vii. 6. 6
Ere she againe to Calepine was brought: . . . VI. vii. 50. 7
ere he recovery could gaine, . . . VI. viii. 10. 8
ere his stroke attayned his intent, . . . VI. viii. 15. 6
Should reap the harvest *ere* it ripened were: . . . VI. ix. 38. 6
Ere he attain'd the point by him intended, . . . VI. ix. 46. 8
ere he could recou'r, he did him quell, . . . VI. x. 36. 5
ere I doe his adventures tell . . . VI. xii. 14. 1
ere he new helpe could call, . . . VI. xii. 30. 5
unlesse she turne to thee *Ere* Cuckow end, . . . *Am.* xix. 14
For *ere* this worlds still moving mightie masse . . . *H.L.* 57
ere thou doest them unto grace restore, . . . *H.L.* 164
Ere flitting Time could wag his eyas wings . . . *H.H.L.* 24
Erebus. the darksome bowre Of *Herebus* . . . *Gn.* 314
Phlegeton is sonne of *Herebus* and Night; . . . II. iv. 41. 8
Herebus sonne of Aeternitie is hight . . . II. iv. 41. 9
(Black *Herebus,* thy husband, is the foe Of all the Gods,) . . . III. iv. 55. 7
Erebus'. Thy dwelling is in *Herebus* black hous, . . . III. iv. 55. 6
Erect. There many auncient Trophees were *erect,* . . . *Bel.*[1] v. 5
The great Colosse, *erect* to Memorie; . . . *Ro.* ii. 10
reprochfull blame To *erect* this wicked custome, . . . VI. vi. 34. 4
famous warriors . . . Used Trophees to *erect* . . . *Am.* lxix. 2
Erected. an altar shortly they *erected* To slay her on . . . VI. viii. 44. 3
Erelong. th' Ape and Foxe *ere long* so well them sped, . . . *Hub.* 552
As they themselves shalbe forgot *ere long* . . . *T.M.* 444
Thus, deare! adieu, whom I expect *ere long.*" . . . *D.* 292
Ere long he came . . . I. iii. 26. 1
Ere long she fownd, . . . I. vii. 2. 6
Ere long they come where . . . I. ix. 33. 1
ere long his will to win, . . . II. iii. 13. 2
ere long the truth to let me understand . . . II. iv. 23. 9
'*Ere long* with like againe he boorded mee, . . . II. iv. 24. 1
ere long that hardy guest, . . . Should be his pray . . . II. vii. 27. 1
life *ere long* shall to her home retire, . . . II. viii. 7. 8
ere long they stronger arre . . . II. x. 65. 7
Ere long they rowed were quite out of sight, . . . II. xi. 4. 5
Ere long they heard an hideous bellowing . . . II. xii. 39. 1
ere long shall dearely it repent; . . . III. x. 32. 7
ere long they chaunced to espie Two other knights, . . . IV. i. 38. 4
The which *ere long* full deare he shall abie: . . . IV. vi. 8. 5
Ere long so weake of limbe, . . . IV. xii. 20. 6
ere long will be degendered . . . V. Pr. 2. 9
he *ere long* the former fiftie bet, . . . V. iii. 11. 8
Ere long their Queene her selfe . . . Came forth . . . V. iv. 36. 8
she therefore would him *ere long* forstall . . . V. v. 47. 7
So as *ere long* he had that knightes wound Recured well, . . . VI. iv. 16. 6
the wearie Beare *Ere long* he overtooke . . . VI. iv. 20. 2
Ere long enforst to breath his utmost blast, . . . VI. iv. 22. 7
Full like *ere long* to have escaped hard; . . . VI. v. 21. 4
Ere long to him a homely groome there came, . . . VI. vi. 20. 1
Ere long they came, . . . VI. vii. 17. 7
I hope *ere long* for to arryve: . . . *Am.* lxiii. 6
Erewhile. outcast carcas, that *erewhile* Made it selfe famous II. viii. 12. 5
Here neede you to remember, how *erewhile* . . . IV. xi. 2. 1
The which *erewhile* spake so reprochfully, . . . V. ii. 21. 4
'Sayd I not then' (quoth shee) '*erwhile* aright, . . . V. vi. 16. 6
The eldest of the which was slaine *erewhile* By Artegall, . . . V. vi. 33. 4
I was *erewhile* the love of Calepine; . . . VI. v. 28. 6
heavenly riches which she robd *erewhyle* . . . *H.B.* 119
Erichthonian. Enricht with spoyles of th' *Ericthonian* towre, . *Gn.* 562
Erigone. As he did for *Erigone* it prove) . . . III. xi. 43. 4
Erinnys. fell *Erynnis,* with hot burning tongs, . . . *Ro.* xxiv. 5
bridale torches foule *Erynnis* tynde; . . . *Gn.* 394
what cursed evil Spright, Or fell *Erinnys,* . . . II. ii. 29. 2
Erivan. wroth with Blandamour was *Erivan;* . . . IV. v. 24. 3
Ermelin. He bore a crowned little *Ermelin,* . . . III. ii. 25. 8
Ermines. Yclad in Scarlot, . . . And *ermines* white: . . . *S.C.* Ap. 58
with gold and *Ermines* faire enveloped . . . III. i. 59. 9
Errand. What idle *errand* hast thou earths mansion to forsake?' . . . VII. vi. 25. 9
Errant. *See* **Bailiff-errant.**

Errant—*Continued.*
That many *errant* knights hath brogt to wretchednesse. . . I. ii. 34. 9
an *errant* knight in armes ycled, . . . they new arrived find: I. iv. 38. 4
'Straunge thing it is an *errant* knight to see Here . . . . . I. x. 10. 1
False *erraunt* knight, infamous, ... I. xii. 27. 4
did enterpris Th' adventure of the *Errant* damozell; . . . . II. i. 19. 8
many *errant* knightes hath fowle fordonne; . . . . . II. i. 51. 4
Since *errant* armes to sew he first began: . . . . . II. ii. 17. 5
she th' *Errant* Damzell hight; . . . . . III. i. 24. 7
Great wreake to many *errant* knights of yore, ... III. vii. 48. 3
to her reveald By *errant* Sprights, ... III. viii. 6. 5
ought evermore To *errant* knights be commune: . . . . . III. viii. 52. 5
that same *errant* Knight, ... IV. ix. 36. 1
many *errant* Knights hath there fordonne; . . . . . V. ii. 4. 8
amongst the warlike rout Of *errant* Knights, ... V. vi. 6. 6
to seeke her *errant* Knight; . . . . . V. vi. 6. 6
all *errant* knights, whereso on ground; . . . . . VI. i. 42. 8
no place Of lodging fit for any *errant* Knight, ... VI. iii. 38. 8
stearne In all assaies to every *errant* Knight, ... VI. iii. 40. 4
an *errant* Knight, That house-rome craves; . . . . . VI. iii. 41. 2
To be two *errant* knights, ... VI. v. 11. 5
he was an *errant* Knight, ... VI. vi. 20. 6
his Lord of old Did hate all *errant* Knights . . . . . VI. vi. 21. 4
Gainst *errant* Knights and Ladies thou dost reare; . . . . . VI. vi. 34. 5
Slayne of that *errant* knight with whom he fought; . . . . . VI. vii. 16. 7
Erred. (if he *er'd* not,) . . . . . *Hub.* 235
if I have *err'd* in count Of Gods, ... IV. xii. 2. 6
many have *err'd* in this beauty.' . . . . . *Epig.* iii. 8
Error. monstrous *error*, flying in the ayre, ... *T.M.* 257
Blind *Error*, scornefull Follie, and base Spight, ... *T.M.* 317
Then wandreth he in *error* and in doubt, ... *T.M.* 490
through our rudenesse into *errour* led, ... *Col.* 796
Foule *Errour* doth defeate: . . . . . I. i. Arg.
she did pray . . . that in endlesse *error* she might ever stray. I. iii. 23. 9
Or thine the fault, or mine the *error* is, ... I. iii. 39. 4
'Pardon the *error* of enraged wight, ... I. iv. 41. 2
Th' enchaunter vaine his *errour* should not rew: . . . . . I. vi .42. 8
thou his *errour* shalt, I hope, now proven trew.' . . . . . I. vi. 42. 9
streight way he knew His *errour;* . . . . . II. i. 28. 2
uneath to wene That monstrous *error*, ... II. x. 8. 3
Driven by fatall *error* here arriv'd, ... II. x. 9. 8
oft of *error* did himselfe appeach: . . . . . II. xi. 40. 3
her perfections with his *error* taynt: . . . . . III. Pr. 2. 5
hold them backe that would in *error* fall: . . . . . III. i. 46. 5
Calles thee his goddesse, in his *errour* blind, ... III. iv. 56. 8
of her *errour* straunge I have great ruth . . . . . III. v. 7. 9
they tooke delight In their first *error*, ... III. ix. 23. 8
he through fatal *errour* long was led . . . . . III. ix. 41. 4
pardon her besought his *errour* frayle, ... IV. vi. 22. 6
Well weeting how their *errour* to assoyle, ... IV. vi. 25. 2
through *error* and misthought Of our like persons, ... IV. viii. 58. 2
her *error* I abusd To my friends good . . . . . IV. viii. 60. 7
whether it through skill or *errour* were. . . . . . IV. ix. 11. 7
her griefe with *errour* to beguyle, ... V. vi. 5. 3
Your aide to guide me out of *errour* blind.' . . . . . V. vii. 19. 5
whom *errour* so misled, ... V. viii. 13. 8
on their border Were brought by *errour* . . . . . VI. viii. 36. 4
Through some vaine *errour*, or inducement light, ... VII. vi. 32. 2
Error's. *Errours* den, A monster vile, ... I. i. 13. 6
the man so wrapt in *Errours* endlesse traine! . . . . . I. i. 18. 9
Errors. that which private *errours* doth pursew; . . . . . *Col.* 750
Erst. race, That *erst* descended from the Trojan bloud. . . . . . *Bel.*[1] v. 8
When *erst* of Gods and man I worshipt was? . . . . . *Bel.*[1] viii. 8
it, which *earst* so pleasant sent did yeld, ... *Bel.*[2] xi. 13
he, that *earst* seemd but to playe, ... *S.C.* Mar. 95
he that *earst* I hote. . . . . . *S.C.* Jul. 164
now at *earst* the dirke night doth hast. . . . . . *S.C.* S. 6
I have pyped *erst* so long . . . . . *S.C.* O. 7
Whereon he *earst* had taught his flocks to feede, ... *S.C.* O. 57
left both bare and barrein now at *erst;* . . . . . *S.C.* D. 105
The Ape, that *earst* did nought but chill . . . . . *Hub.* 993
Didst to the type of honour *earst* advaunce: . . . . . *T.M.* 70
The goodly fields, that *earst* so gay were dyde . . . . . *T.M.* 237
we, that *earst* were wont in sweet accord . . . . . *T.M.* 241
I, whose joy was *earst* with Spirit full . . . . . *T.M.* 289
wee that *earst* in joyance did abound, ... *T.M.* 307
'My little flocke, whom *earst* I lov'd so well, ... *D.* 344
the armes, that *earst* so bright did show, ... I. v. 9. 5
faith, that *earst* was woxen weake, ... I. v. 12. 3
he it was, that *earst* would have supprest Faire Una . . . . I. vi. 40. 7
had he beene where *earst* his armes were lent, ... I. vi. 42. 7
speake his prowesse that did *earst* you beare, ... I. vii. 48. 4
Which is through rage more strong then both were *erst;* . . . I. viii. 18. 3
Who *earst* in flowres of freshest youth was clad. . . . . . I. viii. 42. 4
I sorrowed all so much as *earst* I joyd, ... I. ix. 15. 3
That *earst* us held in love of lingring life; . . . . . I. ix. 29. 6
but *erst* lay at deathes dore. . . . . . I. x. 27. 9
that *erst* him armd; That erst him goodly armd, ... I. xi. 27. 8, 9
Shee, onely she, it is, that *earst* did throw . . . . . I. xii. 33. 7
Whom his victorious handes did *earst* restore . . . . . II. i. 2. 6
with . . . fell intent, ye did at *earst* me meet; . . . . . II. i. 29. 7
By other accident, that *earst* befell, ... II. ii. 11. 8
the Redcrosse knight he *erst* did weet . . . . . II. iii. 11. 7
The ill, which *earst* to him, he . . . ment. . . . . . II. iii. 11. 9
Whose right haunch *earst* my stedfast arrow strake? . . . . II. iii. 32. 8
Sith *earst* into this forrest wild I came. . . . . . II. iii. 33. 6
ne thinks how *erst* she did her hide. . . . . . II. iii. 36. 9
when *earst* that horne I heard, ... II. iii. 45. 6
furious fitts at *earst* quite weren quaild: . . . . . II. iv. 14. 4
Abandon this forestalled place at *erst*, ... II. iv. 39. 3
Erst—*Continued.*
What hellish fury hath at *earst* thee hent? . . . . . II. vi. 49. 2
Where Mammon *earst* did sunne his threasury; . . . . . II. viii. 4. 7
meeting *earst* with Archimago slie . . . . . II. viii. 10. 7
he which *earst* them combatted was Guyon bold. . . . . . II. viii. 10. 9
the other, whom he *earst* did daunt, ... II. viii. 34. 6
entraunce crav'd which was denied *erst*. . . . . . II. ix. 17. 3
Now one, which *earst* were many made through variaunce. II. x. 38. 9
All that did *earst* it hinder and molest, ... II. xi. 32. 7
earst was sought to deck both bed and bowre . . . . . II. xii. 75. 4
her princely gest, With which she *earst* tryumphed, ... III. ii. 27. 4
chearfull looks as *earst* did shew. . . . . . III. iii. 50. 9
the Redcrosse knight did *earst* display Her lovers shape . . . III. iv. 5. 4
Was *earst* impressed in her gentle spright. . . . . . III. iv. 49. 3
To wreake the wrath, which he did *earst* revive . . . . . III. v. 16. 4
whom he had *earst* destroyd She weend, ... III. viii. 2. 8
with furie fresh reviv'd Much more then *earst*, ... III. viii. 3. 5
with Sir Satyrane, as *earst* ye red, ... III. xi. 3. 1
despight, Which *earst* to you I playnd: . . . . . III. xi. 23. 6
those goodly rowmes, which *erst* She saw . . . . . III. xii. 42. 1
erst all entrers wont so cruelly to scorch. . . . . . III. xii. 42. 9
As fast as forward *erst* now backward to retrate. . . . . . IV. iii. 26. 9
It often fals, (as here it *earst* befell) . . . . . IV. iv. 1. 1
The crime which cursed Ate kindled *earst*, ... IV. v. 31. 2
having me, all wearie *earst*, downe feld, ... IV. vi. 6. 8
all his former parts did *earst* appere: . . . . . IV. x. 20. 5
all those same were there which *erst* I did recount. . . . . . IV. xii. 2. 9
the golden age, . . . It's now at *earst* become a stonie one; . V. Pr. 2. 2
made them stoupe that looked *earst* so hie. . . . . . V. ii. 21. 5
'The wretched mayd, that *earst* desir'd to die, ... V. iv. 11. 1
How earnest suit she *earst* for him had made . . . . . V. v. 54. 2
From whom she *earst* so fast away did flie: . . . . . V. viii. 16. 3
Of that proud Souldan whom he *earst* did slay. . . . . . V. viii. 51. 7
earst was dead, restor'd to life againe, ... V. xi. 16. 6
albe he *earst* did wyte His wavering mind, ... V. xi. 57. 6
By those which *earst* did fly away for feare, ... V. xii. 6. 5
though she hungrily *Earst* chawd thereon, ... V. xii. 39. 6
those shames, that *erst* ye spake me to deface.' . . . . . VI. i. 28. 9
Whereof she now more glad then sory *earst*, ... VI. i. 45. 1
Him much more now then *earst* he gan admire . . . . . VI. ii. 34. 2
this was he whom Tristram *earst* did slay, ... VI. ii. 45. 3
The gentle Aladine did *earst* invade, ... VI. iii. 8. 4
she at *earst* had made . . . . . VI. iii. 8. 7
'as now at *earst* When day is spent, ... VI. iii. 39. 1
shield and speare, Which *earst* he left, ... VI. iv. 13. 2
That which your selfe have *earst* ared so right? . . . . . VI. iv. 28. 2
So different from that which *earst* ye seem'd . . . . . VI. vii. 14. 9
The which I *earst* adventur'd for your sake: . . . . . VI. vii. 15. 4
Till I have sav'd so many as I *earst* did slay.' . . . . . VI. viii. 22. 9
as *earst* you heard, ... VI. viii. 31. 2
Then Coridon woxe frollicke, that *earst* seemed dead. . . . . . VI. ix. 42. 9
On which he safety hopes that *earst* feard to be lost. . . . . . VI. xi. 44. 9
all such persons as he *earst* did wrong . . . . . VI. xii. 37. 7
make him bond that bondage *earst* dyd fly. . . . . . *Am.* lxv. 4
as I *earst*, . . . So now . . . . . *H.B.* 8
all that *earst* seemd sweet seemes now offense, ... *H.H.B.* 269
all that pleased *earst* now seemes to paine; . . . . . *H.H.B.* 270
Erstwhile. That which *erstwhile* so pleasaunt scent did yelde, *Bel.*[1] ix. 13
Eryx. Fierce *Eryx:* and Alebius, ... IV. xi. 14. 7
Escape. *See* **Scape.**
'Yet shall they not *escape* so freely all, ... I. v. 26. 1
witt in secret counsels spent, How to *escape*. . . . . . I. vi. 32. 6
Who then would thinke . . . He could *escape* fowle death . I. xii. 36. 5
Out of that forest should *escape* their might: . . . . . III. v. 16. 8
one eies watch *escape:* . . . . . III. ix. 31. 6
now made better speed t' *escape* his feared foe. . . . . . III. xi. 5. 9
That nothing may *escape* her reaching might, ... V. xi. 24. 8
Hope to *escape* his venemous despite, ... VI. xii. 41. 2
Escaped. Hardly my selfe *escaped* thilke payne, ... *S.C.* S. 66
As when a ship, . . . An hidden rocke *escaped* hath unwares, I. vi. 1. 2
Having *escapt* so sad ensamples in his sight. . . . . . I. vi. 1. 9
th' only breath him daunts, who hath *escapt* the stroke. . I. vii. 13. 9
His shackles emptie lefte, himselfe *escaped* cleene. . . . . . II. i. 1. 9
Gaz'd after him, as fowle *escapt* by flight. . . . . . II. viii. 9. 4
Having off-shakt them and *escapt* their hands, ... II. xi. 33. 4
defects From her most cunning hand *escaped* bee; . . . . . II. xii. 23. 4
Yet Carados himselfe from her *escapt* with payne.' . . . . . III. iii. 55. 9
out of sight *escaped* at the least: . . . . . III. v. 14. 5
not *escaped* from the dew reward Of his bad deedes, ... III. v. 14. 6
escaped from a ravenous beast, ... III. vii. 1. 2
the same which she *escapt* whileare. . . . . . III. vii. 1. 9
the victour, through the flood *Escaped* hardly, ... III. ix. 42. 9
From Limbo lake him late *escaped* sure would say. . . . . . III. x. 54. 9
having once *escaped* perill neare, ... IV. i. 34. 8
sure they weend she was *escaped* away; . . . . . V. ii. 25. 2
Full like ere long to have *escaped* hard; . . . . . VI. v. 21. 4
Seeing the game from him *escapt* away, ... *Am.* lxvii. 2
Escaping. still from her *escaping* soft away: . . . . . IV. viii. 11. 5
Coridon, *escaping* craftily, ... VI. xi. 18. 6
Escheat. To make one great by others losse is bad *excheat*. . I. v. 25. 9
To leave to him that lady for *excheat*, ... III. viii. 16. 4
Eschew. keepe his standing, and his shaftes *eschew*, ... II. xi. 27. 7
Ziffius, whom Mariners *eschew* No lesse then rockes, ... II. xii. 24. 7
none of them foule mischiefe could *eschew*, ... III. i. 66. 3
To seeke by flight her fellowship t' *eschew*, ... IV. viii. 56. 5
every one his daunger did *eschew:* . . . . . V. iii. 8. 7
their resistlesse rigour did *eschew:* . . . . . V. vii. 32. 4
The rest, that scape his sword and death *eschew*, ... VI. viii. 49. 8
The old yeares sinnes forepast let us *eschew*, ... *Am.* lxii. 7
Eschewed. Lov'd of his freends, and of his foes *eschewd:* . . II. x. 13. 3

Eschewed—*Continued.*
having long *eschew'd* His violence in vaine; . . . VI. iii. 50. 5
they were virgins all, and love *eschewed* . . . VII. vii. 45. 4
Esloyne. *See* **Eloin.**
Especial. For his, and for your owne *especial* sake, . . . *Ded. Son.* xv. 13
Espial. at first *espiall* Of his grim face, . . . IV. x. 17. 6
Known by good markes and perfect good *espiall:* . . . V. iv. 15. 8
Espied. *See* **Aspied.**
A goodly ship . . . I *espide* . . . *Van.* ix. 3
Him when the spitefull brere had *espyed,* . . . *S.C.* F. 147
Withouten dreade of Wolves to bene *espyed.* . . . *S.C.* D. 24
for their purposes none fit *espyed.* . . . *Hub.* 226
all their sleights *espyed.* . . . *Hub.* 346
He gan to reach, but no where it *espide.* . . . *Hub.* 1336
never shew of living wight *espyde;* . . . I. iii. 10. 3
Soone as the port from far he has *espide,* . . . I. iii. 31. 7
Whom when the raging Sarazin *espyde,* . . . I. vi. 8. 6
whenas they far *espide* A weary wight . . . I. vi. 34. 2
whom when Satyrane *espide,* . . . he boldly him defide. . . I. vi. 40. 8
Whom all so soone as that proud Sarazin *Espide,* . . . I. vi. 46. 2
Eftsoones that dreadful Dragon they *espyde,* . . . I. xi. 4. 4
Before her standing she *espied* had, . . . II. i. 45. 5
One cursed creature he by chaunce *espide,* . . . II. vii. 57. 8
He lookt a litle further, and *espyde* Another wretch, . . . II. vii. 61. 1
Soone as the Carle from far the Prince *espyde* . . . II. xi. 24. 1
Two naked Damzelles he therein *espyde,* . . . II. xii. 63. 6
As hee that hath *espide* a vermeill Rose, . . . III. i. 46. 6
when she had *espyde* that mirrhour fayre, . . . III. ii. 22. 5
Having farre off *espyde* a Tassell gent, . . . III. iv. 49. 6
Whom when the fearefull Damzell nigh *espide,* . . . III. vii. 24. 1
Which when his cruell enimy *espyde,* . . . III. vii. 42. 8
Whom when as nigh approching she *espyde,* . . . III. vii. 44. 1
she plainly was *espyde* To be a woman-wight, . . . III. ix. 21. 7
none *espyde* His secret drift, . . . III. x. 6. 3
he far away *espide* A couple, . . . III. x. 20. 6
the Satyres her *espide* Straying alone . . . III. x. 36. 4
none of all the Satyres him *espyde* or heard. . . . III. x. 47. 9
He wooed her till day-spring he *espyde,* . . . III. x. 52. 1
this gallant . . . From farre *espide* the famous Britomart, . IV. i. 33. 2
Whom so dismayd when Cambell had *espide,* . . . IV. iii. 10. 1
having those two other Knights *espide* . . . IV. iv. 2. 6
Which when the noble Ferramont *espide,* . . . IV. iv. 19. 1
all unawares *espide* An armed Knight . . . IV. vi. 2. 4
Still as advantage they *espyde* thereto: . . . IV. vi. 18. 3
when that theefe approching nigh *espide* . . . IV. vii. 29. 5
Having *espide* this Cabin far away, . . . IV. vii. 42. 5
'Me when as he had privily *espide* . . . IV. x. 14. 1
they *espide* A sorie sight as ever seene with eye, . . . V. i. 14. 1
Which oddes when as Sir Artegall *espide,* . . . V. ii. 14. 1
when she *espide* Sir Terpin, . . . V. iv. 39. 1
Having by chaunce *espide* advantage neare, . . . V. vii. 32. 2
ere it were *espide,* The wicked stroke did wound his enemy . V. xi. 6. 7
when they nigh approching had *espyde* Sir Artegall, . . . V. xii. 38. 2
he nigh *espyde* An armed Knight . . . VI. iii. 30. 6
Espies. that none the same *espies;* . . . *Hub.* 1288
espies that griesly wight Approching nigh, . . . IV. vii. 22. 5
At length *espyes* at hand the happie cost, . . . VI. xi. 44. 8
Espy. One of hir heads . . . I did *espie,* . . . *Rev.* i. 7
'Jesus blesse that sweete face I *espye,* . . . *S.C.* May 256
Fewe chymneis reeking you shall *espye:* . . . *S.C.* S. 117
soone as they this mock-King did *espy,* . . . *Hub.* 1091
Which when the greisly tyrant did *espie,* . . . *Mui.* 433
I did *espie* Where towards me a sory wight did cost, . . . *D.* 38
living creature none he did *espye.* . . . I. viii. 29. 5
they gan *espy* An armed knight . . . I. ix. 21. 1
I do *espye* The watchman . . . I. xi. 3. 6
Espye a traveiler with feet surbet, . . . II. ii. 22. 7
by the way he chaunced to *espy* One . . . II. iii. 6. 1
nowhere could *espye* Tract of his foot: . . . II. iii. 19. 6
Soone as those glitterand armes he did *espye,* . . . II. vii. 42. 1
A Lyon and a Tigre doth *espye,* . . . II. ix. 14. 8
By secret wayes, that none might it *espy,* . . . II. ix. 32. 6
With his gay Squyre issewing did *espye,* . . . II. xi. 17. 8
him dismounted . . . That other Hag did far away *espye* . . II. xi. 28. 8
they sitting did *espy* A daintie damsell . . . II. xii. 14. 7
they in an Island did *espy* A seemely Maiden . . . II. xii. 27. 5
that none might them *espy,* . . . III. iii. 61. 7
when him at hand she did *espy,* . . . III. vii. 44. 7
a Beare, . . . the wakefull dogs *espy,* . . . III. x. 53. 6
they chaunced to *espie* Two other knights, . . . IV. i. 38. 4
whenas he did *espie* His chaunge of cheere . . . IV. i. 50. 6
they did *espy* One in bright armes, . . . IV. iv. 6. 5
Aemylia did *espie* Her captive lovers friend, . . . IV. viii. 63. 1
Behinde the gate that none her might *espy;* . . . IV. x. 13. 2
I by chaunce . . . Did her *espy,* . . . V. iv. 12. 2
Untill fit time and place he mote *espy,* . . . VI. vii. 3. 4
Some flockes of sheepe and shepheards to *espy;* . . . VI. xi. 36. 7
Chaunst to *espy* upon her yvory chest The rosie marke, . . . VI. xii. 15. 5
A Flocke of Nymphes I chaunced to *espy,* . . . *Proth.* 20
Espying. Which he *espying* cast her to restraine . . . II. xi. 28. 4
She, them *espying,* loud to them can call, . . . II. xii. 15. 1
The wanton Maidens, him *espying,* . . . II. xii. 66. 1
He them *espying* gan him selfe prepare, . . . III. i. 4. 7
Which drery sight the gentle Squire *espying* . . . IV. vii. 25. 1
the bold child that perill well *espying,* . . . V. viii. 32. 1
Esquiline. On her left hand the noysome *Esquiline,* . . . *Ro.* iv. 12
cleped was Port *Esquiline,* . . . II. ix. 32. 8
Essayed. her *essayd* with many a fervent fit, . . . III. i. 34. 8
Essential. How much more those *essentiall* parts of his, . . . *H.H.B.* 109
Essoin. From everie worke he chalenged *essoyne,* . . . I. iv. 20. 3
Establish. love *establish* each to other trew, . . . I. ix. 18. 7
quiet-age It doth *establish* in the troubled mynd. . . . IV. iii. 43. 6
Did her therein *establish* peaceablie, . . . V. xii. 25. 3
Established. No statute so *established* might bee, . . . *Hub.* 1161
'knowes best the termes *established;* . . . I. ix. 41. 7
ere he had *established* his throne, . . . II. x. 10. 1
Long time in peace his realme *established,* . . . II. x. 63. 3
Thenceforth it firmely was *established,* . . . II. xii. 13. 8
wrong repressed, and *establisht* right, . . . V. i. 2. 3
all which Nature had *establisht* first In good estate, . . . VII. vi. 5. 2
Establishment. setled there in sure *establishment.* . . . II. xi. 2. 5
With safe assuraunce and *establishment:* . . . V. xi. 35. 4
Estate. tell me first of thy flocks *estate.* (**astate*) . . . *S.C.* S. 24
Who so loathes not too much the poore *estate,* . . . *Gn.* 90
disliking of their evill And hard *estate,* . . . *Hub.* 47
In the meane-time to live in good *estate,* . . . *Hub.* 427
meane *estate* In safe assurance, . . . *Hub.* 909
Betwixt two mightie ones of great *estate,* . . . *Mui.* 3
in pittie of my sad *estate:* . . . I. iii. 7. 5
The evil stownd that daungerd her *estate,* . . . I. viii. 12. 2
To walke this way in Pilgrims poore *estate.* . . . I. x. 64. 4
in pompe of prowd *estate'* . . . II. iii. 40. 1
Honour, *estate,* and all this worldes good, . . . II. vii. 8. 6
so great grace and offred high *estate;* . . . II. vii. 50. 2
when her sonne to mans *estate* did wex, . . . II. x. 20. 8
of Arthegall and his *estate.* . . . III. iii. 62. 5
She learned had th' *estate* of Arthegall, . . . III. iv. 4. 2
when his meane *estate* he did revew, . . . III. v. 44. 7
fresh . . . She was become, by chaunge of her *estate,* . . . IV. i. 31. 8
gazed on their harmes, not pittying their *estate.* . . . IV. ii. 20. 9
Knowing the miserie of their *estate,* . . . IV. iii. 1. 4
Where they might tydings get of her *estate;* . . . IV. vi. 47. 4
Of whom she gan enquire of her *estate,* . . . IV. vii. 34. 8
Both in full sad and sorrowfull *estate:* . . . IV. viii. 19. 4
each *estate* quite out of order goth? . . . V. ii. 37. 3
Thus did she sit in royall rich *estate,* . . . V. ix. 33. 1
wretched ruine of so high *estate;* . . . V. ix. 46. 5
by discovering my *estate,* Harme may arise . . . VI. ii. 27. 2
How to save hole her hazarded *estate;* . . . VI. iii. 12. 7
As in his fee, with peaceable *estate,* . . . VI. iv. 30. 2
to fashion his owne lyfes *estate,* . . . VI. ix. 31. 2
he colour might Both his *estate* and love . . . VI. x. 37. 9
all which Nature had establisht first In good *estate,* . . . VII. vi. 5. 3
Was placed in his principall *Estate,* . . . VII. vi. 19. 4
They are not changed from their first *estate;* . . . VII. vii. 58. 4
Estates. Through all *estates* he found that he had past, . . . VI. xii. 23. 1
Esteem. otherwise they doo *esteeme* Of th' heavenly gift . . . *T.M.* 85
Some few beside this sacred skill *esteme,* . . . *T.M.* 583
thy chaste life and vertue I *esteeme:* . . . *Col.* 573
Ne any one himselfe doth ought *esteeme,* . . . *Col.* 781
who so else doth otherwise *esteeme,* . . . *Col.* 889
ye heavens, that all things right *esteeme,* . . . I. vii. 49. 7
Most joyous man . . . my selfe I did *esteeme,* . . . II. iv. 21. 8
The worth of all men by their end *esteeme,* . . . II. viii. 14. 7
He it dissembled well, and light seemd to *esteeme.* . . . III. viii. 16. 9
Her sharpe rebuke full litle did *esteeme;* . . . III. viii. 26. 2
much more rare and pretious to *esteeme,* . . . IV. x. 39. 6
you, Sir Knight, that love so light *esteeme,* . . . V. i. 28. 5
'What other right,' (quoth he) 'should you *esteeme,* . . . V. iv. 17. 6
'What other right,' (quoth he) 'should you *esteeme,* . . . V. iv. 18. 6
Ye will them all but fayned showes *esteeme,* . . . VI. Pr. 4. 8
Did for their soveraine goddesse her *esteeme,* . . . VI. ix. 9. 7
whose worth above all threasure They did *esteeme,* . . . VI. xi. 14. 6
gods no more then men thou doest *esteeme;* . . . VII. vii. 15. 8
having got it, may it more *esteeme;* . . . *H.L.* 167
Esteemed. *See* **Steemed.**
men of learning little he *esteemed;* . . . *Hub.* 1191
all the rest but litle he *esteemed.* . . . *As.* 66
so religiously to be *esteemed.* . . . *Col.* 830
esteemd That from like inward fire that outward smoke had steemd. . . . III. i. 55. 8
esteemd For her great worth: . . . III. vii. 52. 5
The fairest wight on ground, and most of men *esteem'd.* . . . III. viii. 13. 9
he saw him selfe *esteemd,* . . . III. viii. 41. 7
For which no service she too much *esteemed:* . . . IV. i. 8. 5
Yet victors both them selves alwayes *esteemed:* . . . IV. iii. 28. [illegible]
So nought may be *esteemed* happie till the end. . . . IV. iv. 43. 9
as her life by her *esteemed* deare. . . . IV. v. 6. 2
whose beauties wonderment She lesse *esteem'd* . . . IV. v. 20. 9
he their words as wind *esteemed* light. . . . IV. v. 27. 7
to him their cause they best *esteemed* Whole to commit, . . VI. iii. 13. 3
To be a Princes Paragone *esteemed,* . . . VI. ix. 11. 5
esteemed The father of the fayrest Pastorell, . . . VI. ix. 14. 1
Sith shee his Jove and him *esteemed* nought, . . . VII. vi. 18. 8
with selfe-same price redeemed . . . how ever of us light *esteemed.* . . . *H.H.L.* 203
Esteemeth. Ne ought the whelky pearles *esteemeth* hee, . . . *Gn.* 105
his late chayne his Liege unmeete *esteemeth;* . . . *Hub.* 628
Esthambruges. let the marsh of *Esthambruges* tell, . . . II. x. 24. 2
Estimation. Albe they endlesse seeme in *estimation,* . . . IV. xii. 1. 6
Estrange. her to *estraunge* From courtly blis . . . III. viii. 20. 7
Estranging. Him selfe *estraunging* from their joyaunce vaine, I. iv. 37. 8
Sometimes *estranging* him in sterner wise; . . . IV. ii. 9. 6
Estrild. He lov'd faire Ladie *Estrild,* leudly lov'd, . . . II. x. 17. 6
Eternal. By Magicke skill out of *eternall* night. . . . *Ro.* v. 8
can to other give *eternall* dayes: . . . *Ro.* Env. 8
She hath the bonds broke of *eternall* night, . . . *S.C.* N. 165
wont to worke *eternall* sleepe. . . . *S.C.* D. 90
Eternall hurte left unto many one: . . . *Gn.* 203
Th' *eternall* Makers majestie wee viewe, . . . *T.M.* 512

Eternal—*Continued.*
Where he now liveth in *eternall* blis, *Ti.* 265
Out of dread darkenesse to *eternall* day, *Ti.* 376
(In which shee joyeth in *eternall* blis) *D.* 381
my hearts *eternall* threasure. *Col.* 47
carelesse Quiet lyes Wrapt in *eternall* silence I. i. 41. 9
her mother blynd Sate in *eternall* night: I. iii. 12. 4
The earth shall sooner . . . make *eternal* derth, I. iii. 28. 8
upon *eternall* paine Of high displeasure that ensewen might, I. iv. 40. 5
in *eternall* woes my weaker hart Have wasted, I. iv. 46. 7
Th' *eternall* brood of glorie excellent: I. v. 1. 4
Which fast is tyde to Joves *eternall* seat? I. v. 25. 6
Eternall providence, exceeding thought, I. vi. 7. 1
vanquisht thine *eternall* bondslave make, I. vii. 14. 8
let *eternall* night so sad sight fro me hyde. I. vii. 22. 9
Th' *eternall* bale of heavie wounded harts: I. viii. 14. 5
The secret meaning of th' *eternall* might, I. ix. 6. 8
'He there does now enjoy *eternall* rest I. ix. 40. 1
times in his *eternall* booke of fate I. ix. 42. 4
Wherein *eternall* peace and happinesse doth dwell. I. x. 55. 9
(*eternall* God that chaunce did guide) I. xi. 45. 6
beast, From whose *eternall* bondage now they were releast. I. xii. 4. 9
an Angels voice Singing before th' *eternall* majesty, I. xii. 39. 4
Reserve her cause to her *eternall* doome; II. i. 58. 8
that fame may it resound In her *eternall* tromp, II. iii. 38. 9
this grace I have Me given by *eternall* destiny, II. iii. 45. 2
in the hollow earth have their *eternall* brood. II. vii. 8. 9
Eternall God thee save from such decay! II. vii. 34. 7
Therewith to doen his foes *eternall* smart. II. viii. 20. 4
there *eternall* torment found For all the sinnes II. viii. 45. 8
th' *eternall* Lord in fleshly slime Enwombed was, II. x. 50. 2
Th' *eternal* marks of treason may at Stonheng vew. II. x. 66. 9
Through ghastly horror and *eternall* shade: II. xii. 41. 5
th' *eternall* lampes . . . were halfe yspent, III. i. 57. 6
Joy thereof have thou and *eternall* blis!' III. ii. 42. 5
Emongst th' *eternall* spheres and lamping sky, III. iii. 1. 3
Led with *eternall* providence, III. iii. 24. 4
'Thenceforth *eternall* union shall be made III. iii. 49. 1
for *eternall* moniment Of thy great grace III. iv. 10. 7
through foresight of his *eternall* skill, III. iv. 25. 6
T' approve the unknowen purpose of *eternall* fate. III. iv. 28. 9
To light their blessed lamps in Joves *eternall* hous. III. iv. 51. 9
'What had th' *eternall* Maker need of thee III. iv. 56. 1
At least *eternall* meede shall you abide.' III. v. 11. 5
Eternall God, in his almightie powre, III. v. 52. 1
such as *eternall* fate Ordained hath, III. vi. 32. 6
in themselves *eternall* moisture they imply. III. vi. 34. 9
An huge *eternall* Chaos, III. vi. 36. 8
There now he liveth in *eternall* blis, III. vi. 48. 1
in *eternall* bondage dye he must, III. vii. 50. 7
them conjure, upon *eternall* paine, III. viii. 4. 7
threatned there to make her his *eternall* thrall. III. viii. 41. 9
Eternall thraldome was to her more liefe III. viii. 42. 1
doth transfixe the soule with deathes *eternall* dart. III. x. 59. 9
Cald by strong charmes out of *eternall* night, III. xii. 19. 5
On Fames *eternall* beadroll worthie to be fyled. IV. ii. 32. 9
To them ordained by *eternall* fate: IV. ii. 50. 5
such as drinck, *eternall* happinesse do fynd. IV. iii. 43. 9
hid in horrour of *eternall* night? IV. vii. 33. 6
Through thoughts aspyring to *eternall* fame: IV. ix. 2. 5
Ne with th' *eternall* Gods to bancket come; IV. xii. 4. 4
where it was kept in store In Joves *eternall* house, V. i. 9. 4
That mote remaine for an *eternall* token V. viii. 44. 4
th' hearts of men, as your *eternall* dowre, VI. viii. 1. 3
Reaping *eternall* glorie of his restlesse paines. VI. ix. 2. 9
T' entrap unwary fooles in their *eternall* bales. VI. x. 3. 9
brought againe on them *eternall* night; VII. vi. 14. 7
Sought to assaile the heavens *eternall* towers, VII. vi. 20. 3
by *eternall* doome of Fates decree, VII. vi. 33. 6
All sorrowes short that gaine *eternall* blisse. *Am.* lxiii. 14
all thensforth *eternall* peace shall see *Am.* lxxi. 13
My trembling hart in her *eternall* chaine, *H.B.* 276
That High *Eternall* Powre, which now doth move *H.H.L.* 27
sonne . . . *Eternall*, pure, and voide of sinfull blot, *H.H.L.* 32
Eternall spring of grace and wisedome trew, *H.H.L.* 44
That they might serve him in *eternall* blis, *H.H.L.* 62
But that *Eternall* Fount of love and grace, *H.H.L.* 99
Out of the bosome of *eternall* blisse, *H.H.L.* 134
Eternall King of Glorie, Lord of Might, *H.H.L.* 172
And bound therto with an *eternall* band, *H.H.L.* 187
some sparkling light Of thine *eternall* Truth, *H.H.B.* 11
Th' *eternall* fountaine of that heavenly beauty. *H.H.B.* 21
face Of the Divine *Eternall* Majestie; *H.H.B.* 81
And those *eternall* burning Seraphins, *H.H.B.* 94
For from th' *Eternall* Truth it doth proceed, *H.H.B.* 174
Th' *eternall* portion of her precious dowre, *H.H.B.* 250

Eternally. Powr'd vengeance forth on you *eternalie?* *Ro.* xxiv. 11
eternally complaine Of others wrong, *Gn.* 407
Saints and Angels . . . *Eternally* Him praise *D.* 286
to hold *eternally* Their bounteous deeds *Col.* 581
The cursed creatures doe *eternally* torment. I. v. 33. 9
Till he should die his last, that is, *eternally.* I. ix. 54. 9
Captiv'd *eternally* in yron mewes I. v. 27. 8
seeth with secret fire *eternally,* II. x. 26. 3
That fame in tromp of gold *eternally* displayes. III. iii. 3. 9
In which the Gods doe dwell *eternally;* III. iv. 43. 5
thence-forth all shall rest *eternally* VII. viii. 2. 7
Eternally bind thou this lovely band, *Epith.* 396

Eterne. That substaunce is *eterne,* and bideth so; III. vi. 37. 6
Yet is *eterne* in mutabilitie, III. vi. 47. 5

Eternity. Needes must he all *eternitie* survive, *Ro.* Env. 7
golden Trompet of *eternitie,* *T.M.* 458
Muses . . . unto men *eternitie* do give; *Ti.* 367
Jove, the father of *eternitie,* *Ti.* 369
Herebus sonne of *Aeternitie* is hight. II. iv. 41. 9
In thy great volume of *Eternitye:* III. iii. 4. 5
firmely stayd Upon the pillours of *Eternity,* VII. viii. 2. 4
this verse, vowd to *eternity,* *Am.* lxix. 9
Not for lusts sake, but for *eternitie,* *H.L.* 104
His throne is built upon *Eternity,* *H.H.B.* 152

Eternize. her *eternize* with their heavenlie writs! *T.M.* 582
My verse your vertues rare shall *eternize,* *Am.* lxxv. 11

Eternized. Love him that hath *eternized* your name. *Ded.Son.*xiv.14
covett in th' immortall booke of fame To be *eternized,* I. x. 59. 6

Ethe. *See* **Eath.**

Etheldred. Proud *Etheldred* shall from the North arise, III. iii. 35. 2

Ether. *See* **Either.**

Ethereal. Vesta, of the fire *aethereall;* VII. vii. 26. 4

Euagore. *Euagore,* and light Pontoporea, IV. xi. 50. 3

Euarne. she that vertue loves and vice detests, *Euarna,* IV. xi. 51. 8

Euboean. th' *Euboean* young man wan Swift Atalanta, II. vii. 54. 8

Euboic. Some on th' *Euboick* Cliffs in pieces rent; *Gn.* 587

Eucrate. Swift Proto, milde *Eucrate,* Thetis faire, IV. xi. 48. 7

Eudore. *See* **Endore.**

Eulimene. Lovely Pasithee, kinde *Eulimene,* IV. xi. 49. 3

Eulogies. *Eulogies* turne into Elegies. *T.M.* 372

Eumenias. token true to old *Eumenias,* V. v. 34. 3

Eumnestes. that old man *Eumnestes,* II. ix. 58. 9

Eunice. White hand *Eunica,* proud Dynamene, IV. xi. 49. 1

Eunomie. Just Dice, wise *Eunomie,* myld Eirene; V. ix. 32. 6

Euphoemus. faire *Euphoemus,* that upon them goth IV. xi. 14. 5

Euphrates. By Nyle, or Gange, or Tygre, or *Euphrate;* *Ro.* xxxi. 4
all the territories, Which Phison and *Euphrates* floweth by, I. vii. 43. 8
Great Ganges, and immortall *Euphrates,* IV. xi. 21. 1

Euphrosyne. The first of them hight mylde *Euphrosyne,* VI. x. 22. 7

Eupompe. Cymo, *Eupompe,* and Themiste just; IV. xi. 51. 6

Europa. how Jove did abuse *Europa* like a Bull, *Mui.* 278
like a Bull, *Europa* to withdraw: III. xi. 30. 6
the Bull which fayre *Europa* bore: V. Pr. 5. 9
Europa floting through th' Argolick fluds: VII. vii. 33. 4

Eurotas. by the sandy shore Of swift *Eurotas,* II. iii. 31. 2

Eurydice. sad *Eurydice* . . . no more Must turne to life, *Gn.* 433
To yeeld *Eurydice* unto her fere *Gn.* 463
Which Orpheus for *Eurydice* did make, *Ti.* 391
faire *Eurydice,* her daughter deere, *D.* 464

Eurynome. By him begot of faire *Eurynome,* VI. x. 22. 2

Eurypulus. *Eurypulus,* that calmes the waters wroth; IV. xi. 14. 4

Eurytion. Kept by a cowheard, hight *Eurytion,* V. x. 10. 2

Eurytus. The rich Cteatus; and *Eurytus* long; IV. xi. 14. 1

Euxine. through the *Euxine* seas bore all the flowr of Greece. II. xii. 44. 9
Witnesse Leander in the *Euxine* waves, *H.L.* 231

Evangely. The sacred pledge of Christes *Evangely.* II. x. 53. 5

Eve. 'It fell upon a holy *eve,* *S.C.* Au. 53
So learnd I love on a holye *eve,* *S.C.* Au. 121

Even. Shaking the hill *even* from the bottome deepe, *Bel.*[1] ii. 13
Surmount the toppes *even* of the hiest hilles, *Bel.*[1] vi. 6
mete to be assailde *Even* by an hundred *Bel.*[1] viii. 12
even at the time, when Morpheus *Bel.* xv. 1
aggreeves my hart *even* to this houre, *Pet.* iv. 12
bad him battaile *even* to his jawes: *Van.* x. 8
a fourth Grace, to make the daunce *even?* *S.C.* Ap. 113
For *even* so thy father his head upheld, *S.C.* May 205
when at *even* he came to the flocke, *S.C.* S. 204
Lowder had be slaine thilke same *even.* *S.C.* S. 225
I thee restor'd . . . *Even* from the doore of death *Gn.* 355
varie our device . . . *Even* as new occasion appeares? *Hub.* 119
At morne and *even,* besides their Anthemes sweete, *Hub.* 451
the rayne Twixt them divided into *even* twaine, *Hub.* 1024
fate is woven *even* now *Mui.* 235
Even sad Alcyon, *D.* 6
even their heavie song would breede delight; *D.* 13
Even such is all their vaunted vanitie, *Col.* 719
The prowest knight . . . *Even* stout Sansfoy, I. iv. 41. 8
Even he it was, that earst I. vi. 40. 7
They numbred *even* steps and equall pace; I. x. 12. 5
workmanship of Gods owne . . . *even* dead we honour should. I. x. 42. 8
The knight him selfe *even* trembled I. xi. 55. 1
by *even* tournes Full measured II. i. 53. 1
contend With either of those knightes on *even* coast, II. iii. 17. 3
Under the shadow of her *even* browes, II. iii. 25. 2
even heven rejoyced her sweete face to see. II. ix. 18. 9
Even thrise eleven descents the crowne retaynd, II. x. 45. 8
Even seven hundred Princes, II. x. 74. 3
stere aright, And keepe an *even* course; II. xii. 3. 2
Sir Palmer, keepe an *even* hand, II. xii. 18. 3
Even all the nation of . . . birds II. xii. 36. 1
Even the famous Britomart it was, III. i. 8. 6
even the wilde beast shall dy in starved den. III. iii. 34. 9
That *even* Nature selfe envide the same, III. viii. 5. 4
to ronne in *even* race; III. viii. 18. 6
Even immortal prayse and glory wyde, III. xii. 39. 6
That *even* th' Almightie selfe IV. i. 30. 2
even he the Squire of Dames, IV. ii. 20. 2
Even as he ready was there to have entred, IV. vii. 31. 3
divers trees enrang'd in *even* rankes; IV. x. 25. 2
Even in the lap of Womanhood IV. x. 52. 3
even to thinke thereof it inly pitties mee. IV. xi. 1. 9
Ancient Ogyges, *even* th' auncientest; IV. xi. 15. 4
even yet the Dolphin . . . Stood still IV. xi. 23. 6
Proteus house they fild *even* to the dore; IV. xii. 3. 3

Even—*Continued.*
even for griefe of minde he oft did grone, . . . IV. xii. 12. 6
upbrought *Even* from the cradle . . . V. i. 5. 2
even wilde beasts did feare his awfull sight, . . . V. i. 8. 4
Even from the sole of his foundation, . . . V. ii. 28. 2
Even so did Radigund with bootlesse paine . . . V. v. 15. 8
And dare *even* deathes . . . face behold? . . . V. v. 31. 4
thou canst *even* Jove himselfe to love entise.' . . . V. v. 34. 9
Even at the marke-white of his hart . . . V. v. 35. 8
art, *even* womens witty trade, . . . V. v. 49. 5
Even so Clarinda . . . beguyld, . . . V. v. 53. 5
Even in the dore him meeting, . . . V. vi. 9. 1
wine, they say, is blood, *Even* the bloud of Gyants, . . . V. vii. 10. 4
even she her selfe much wondered . . . V. vii. 13. 7
even to her foes her mercies multiply. . . . V. viii. 17. 9
Even foule Adulterie her face before, . . . V. ix. 48. 8
even then ruing her wilfull fall . . . V. x. 4. 7
Even seventeene goodly sonnes; . . . V. x. 7. 4
even that which thou savedst thine still to remaine?' . . . V. xi. 16. 9
speaches forth doth send, *Even* blasphemous words, . . . V. xi. 20. 8
even the Temple, wherein she was plast, . . . V. xi. 28. 4
even to the vitall parts they past, . . . V. xii. 17. 8
her dwelling Was neare to Envie, *even* her neighbour next; . V. xii. 35. 6
even that halfe-gnawen snake, . . . V. xii. 39. 3
That *even* in the Porch he him did win, . . . VI. i. 23. 4
Gan him entreat *even* with submission base, . . . VI. iii. 38. 5
even his ruder hart began to rew, . . . VI. iv. 3. 5
even the hellish fiends affrighted bee At sight thereof, . . . VI. vi. 10. 4
even the Prince his basenesse did despize; . . . VI. vi. 32. 4
Even so the baser mind it selfe displayes . . . VI. vii. 1. 3
Even for stubborne pride which her restrayned. . . . VI. vii. 36. 4
religion held *even* theeves in measure. . . . VI. viii. 43. 9
even as his right hand adowne descends, . . . VI. viii. 49. 2
even I, which daily doe behold The glorie of the great . . . VI. ix. 28. 1
even for gealousie Was readie oft his owne heart to devoure, . VI. ix. 39. 3
even they, the which his rivals were, . . . VI. ix. 45. 3
even her owne Cytheron . . . She in regard hereof refusde . VI. x. 9. 6
even he him selfe his eyes envyde, . . . VI. x. 11. 7
make *even* that dimmed light Seeme much more lovely . . . VI. xi. 21. 6
even his hart . . . he readie was to teare: . . . VI. xi. 25. 5
Even unto the lowest and the least. . . . VI. xii. 2. 5
he drew him forth, *even* in his own despight. . . . VI. xii. 34. 9
even the highest Powers of heaven to check) . . . VII. vi. 22. 4
(Such sway doth beauty *even* in Heaven beare) . . . VII. vi. 31. 4
even the gods to thee, as men to gods, do seeme. . . . VII. vii. 15. 9
daily watch, and nightly wake By *even* turnes, . . . VII. vii. 45. 9
even yee Your selves are likewise chang'd, . . . VII. vii. 49. 8
Even you, faire Cynthia; . . . VII. vii. 50. 2
even these Star-gazers stonisht are . . . VII. vii. 52. 5
even itselfe is mov'd, as wizards saine: . . . VII. vii. 55. 7
Yet, *even* whylst her bloody hands them slay, . . . *Am.* xlvii. 9
Even this verse . . . Shall be thereof immortall moniment; . *Am.* lxix. 9
Even so my hart . . . flyes backe unto your sight. . . . *Am.* lxxiii. 7
even the greatest did not greatly scorne . . . *Epith.* 4
even to the heavens . . . Doth reach . . . *Epith.* 141
even th' Angels . . . Forget their service . . . *Epith.* 229
shall fade . . . *even* to corrupted clay: . . . *H.B.* 96
The brightest Angell, *even* the Child of Light, . . . *H.H.L.* 83
Even he (*om.) himselfe, in his deare sacrament, . . . *H.H.L.* 195
Even for his sake, and for his sacred word, . . . *H.H.L.* 206
to God . . . *even* the thoughts of men, do plaine appeare; . *H.H.B.* 173
Even heavenly riches, which there hidden ly . . . *H.H.B.* 248
That kindleth love . . . *Even* the love of God; . . . *H.H.B.* 298
even the gentle streame, . . . Seem'd foule . . . *Proth.* 47
fresh . . . *Even* as their Brydale day, . . . *Proth.* 71

Evening. that same *evening*, when all shrowded were . . . *Hub.* 333
morning faire may bring fowle *evening* late, . . . *Mui.* 219
In gloomie *evening*, when the wearie Sun, . . . *D.* 22
Wend too and fro at *evening* and at morne. . . . *Col.* 247
With faire discourse the *evening* so they pas; . . . I. i. 35. 5
this *evening*, as thou art, Aray thyselfe . . . II. iv. 26. 7
faire lookes, glancing like *evening* lights; . . . II. v. 33. 3
Early and late it rong, at *evening* and at prime. . . . II. ix. 25. 9
Untill the closure of the *Evening*: . . . III. iii. 27. 5
In th' *evening* late old Glauce thither led . . . III. iii. 59. 6
All that same *evening* she in flying spent, . . . III. vii. 2. 1
humid *evening* ill for sicke folkes cace; . . . III. ix. 26. 4
so fresh at morne, and fades at *evening* late? . . . III. ix. 39. 9
Darke was the *Evening*, fit for lovers stealth, . . . III. x. 12. 1
Nor ward to waite at morne and *evening* late; . . . III. xi. 21. 4
the second *evening* Her covered . . . III. xii. 29. 3
It so befell one *evening*, that they came Unto a Castell, . . IV. i. 9. 1
By that the gloomy *evening* on them fell, . . . IV. iv. 25. 6
Till *evening* that the Sunne gan downward bend. . . . IV. iv. 43. 6
Amongst the lesser starres in *evening* cleare. . . . IV. v. 14. 4
all that *evening* . . . they together spent; . . . IV. viii. 28. 1
eyes, like twinkling stars in *evening* cleare, . . . IV. x. 50. 7
Ne ever *evening* saw, ne mornings ray, . . . IV. xi. 4. 7
mongst the rest the fight did untill *evening* last. . . . V. iv. 43. 9
Thus passing th' *evening* well, . . . V. vi. 23. 1
So they the *evening* past till time of rest; . . . VI. iii. 9. 6
towards *evening* wandering every way . . . VI. viii. 36. 6
The selfe same *evening* fortune hether drove, . . . VI. viii. 46. 8
every *evening* helping them to fold: . . . VI. ix. 37. 6
move Theyr sad protract from *evening* untill morne. . . . *Am.* lxxxvi. 4
The little Dazie, that at *evening* closes, . . . *Proth.* 31

Evening's. Shepheardes curre, that in darke *eveninges* shade . II. vi. 39. 4
Which choosing for that *evenings* hospitale, . . . II. ix. 10. 5

Evening-star. Like to the *Evening starre* adorn'd with deawy ray. VI. vii. 19. 9
Vesper, whom we the *Evening-starre* intend; . . . VII. vi. 9. 6

Evening-star—*Continued.*
the bright *evening-star* with golden creast Appeare . . . *Epith.* 286

Event. boasts his good *event* . . . *Gn.* 534
Full sad and dreadfull is that ships *event*; . . . *T.M.* 143
The end whereof and daungerous *event* . . . IV. v. 46. 6
as shall appeare by his *event*. . . . IV. viii. 64. 9
Then very doubtfull was the warres *event*, . . . V. ii. 17. 1
Wayting what would ensue of that *event*. . . . V. vi. 28. 5
'The end whereof, and all the long *event*, . . . V. vii. 22. 1

Eventide. As gentle shepheard in sweete *eventide*, . . . I. i. 23. 1
wont to say His holy thinges each morne and *eventyde*: . . . I. i. 34. 7
So wept Duessa untill *eventyde*, . . . I. v. 19. 1
As when a swarme of Gnats at *eventide* . . . II. ix. 16. 1
Thus she there wayted untill *eventyde*, . . . III. xi. 55. 1
She chaunst to meete, toward the *even-tide*, A Knight . . . V. vi. 19. 3
now the *Eventyde* His brode black wings had . . . dispred, . VI. viii. 44. 4

Events. wondring long at those so straunge *events*, . . . VI. xii. 20. 7

Ever (*partial list*). *See* **Evergreen, For ever, However, Whatever, Whatsoever, Whenever, Whensoever, Wherever, Wheresoever, Whoever, Whomever, Whosever, Whosoever.**
Which makes me much and *ever* to complaine; . . . *Pet.* iii. 13
All that which Asie *ever* had of prise, . . . *Ro.* xxix. 11
Hope ye, my verses, that posteritie . . . shall you *ever* read? . *Ro.* xxxii. 2
Ne *ever* was to Fortune foeman, . . . *S.C.* F. 21
And *ever* my flocke was my chiefe care, . . . *S.C.* F. 23
'Pan may be proud that *ever* he begot Such . . . *S.C.* Ap. 91
Syrinx rejoyce that *ever* was her lot . . . *S.C.* Ap. 93
ever since my hart did greve, . . . *S.C.* Au. 123
And *ever* at night wont to repayre . . . *S.C.* S. 186
But *ever* liggen in watch and ward, . . . *S.C.* S. 234
froward fortune doth *ever* availe: . . . *S.C.* S. 251
But who rewards him *ere* the more for-thy, . . . *S.C.* O. 33
if I *ever* sonet song so cleare, . . . *S.C.* D. 15
Tho deemed I my spring would *ever* laste. . . . *S.C.* D. 30
dewed with teares they han be *ever* among. . . . *S.C.* D. 112
No such sad cares . . . Do *ever* creepe into . . . *Gn.* 96
Ne *ever* did her ey-sight turne arere, Ne *ever* spake, . . . *Gn.* 468, 469
thereby mad'st her *ever* damn'd to be. . . . *Gn.* 472
the antique fame of stout Camill Doth *ever* live; . . . *Gn.* 602
ever as they bred, They slue them, . . . *Hub.* 317
In case thou *ever* there wilt hope to thrive, . . . *Hub.* 632
Did *ever* after scorne on foote to goe . . . *Hub.* 752
if . . . thought of armes Did *ever* creepe . . . *Hub.* 826
For none . . . Can *ever* thrive . . . *Hub.* 916
(if *ever* they would hope) . . . *Hub.* 959
ever thinke a Kingdome is your part.' . . . *Hub.* 1004
And *ever*, when he ought would bring to pas, . . . *Hub.* 1167
(for what thing can *ever* last?) . . . *Hub.* 1176
So thy renowme lives *ever* by endighting. . . . *Com. Son.* i. 14
Yet thy just labours *ever* shall endure. . . . *Ti.* 175
live there *ever* blessed, . . . *Ti.* 302
Live *ever* there, . . . *Ti.* 304
here thou livest, being *ever* song Of us, . . . *Ti.* 338
ne *ever* with regard . . . of the later age be heard, . . . *Ti.* 347
But shall in rustie darknes *ever* lie, . . . *Ti.* 349
and *ever* as he went He sighed . . . *D.* 47
it changeth *ever* too and fro, . . . *D.* 429
My wearie feete shall *ever* wandring be, . . . *D.* 457
ne will I *ever* lin, . . . *D.* 467
'And *ever* as I see the starres to fall, . . . *D.* 477
And *ever* sprinckle brackish teares among, . . . *D.* 530
and *ever* will, . . . *Col.* 94
ever and anon, . . . He cryed out, . . . *Col.* 168
And I hers *ever* onely, *ever* one: One *ever* I all vowed hers to bee, One *ever* I, . . . *Col.* 477–479
As *ever* else in Princes Court thou vewest. . . . *Col.* 738
Be *ever* drawne together . . . *Col.* 845
For having loved *ever* one most deare: . . . *Col.* 904
dead, as living, *ever* him ador'd: . . . I. i. 2. 4
nothing did he dread, but *ever* was ydrad. . . . I. i. 2. 9
And *ever* as he rode his hart did earne . . . I. i. 3. 6
lasie seemd, in being *ever* last, . . . I. i. 6. 2
Ne *ever* would to any byway bend, . . . I. i. 28. 4
there Tethys his wet bed Doth *ever* wash, . . . I. i. 39. 7
His wanton daies that *ever* loosely led, . . . I. ii. 3. 5
that shall I *ever* mone. . . . I. ii. 23. 9
And *ever* false Duessa seemde as faire as shee. . . . I. ii. 37. 9
ever to have toucht her I did deadly rew. . . . I. ii. 40. 9
ever most adord As the God of my life? . . . I. iii. 7. 8
ever by her lookes conceived her intent. . . . I. iii. 9. 9
in endlesse error she might *ever* stray. . . . I. iii. 23. 9
Ne *ever* wont in field, ne in round lists, to fight: . . . I. iii. 38. 9
if so mightie corse, As *ever* wielded speare . . . I. iii. 42. 4
ever after in most wretched case, . . . I. iv. 3. 5
Did on so weake foundation *ever* sitt: . . . I. iv. 5. 4
none *ever* knew Such endlesse richesse, . . . I. iv. 7. 4
Ne Persia selfe . . . Like *ever* saw. . . . I. iv. 7. 7
had enough, yett wished *ever* more; . . . I. iv. 29. 5
neighbours welth, that made him *ever* sad, . . . I. iv. 30. 6
all that *ever* writt. . . . I. iv. 32. 8
The prowest knight that *ever* field did fight, . . . I. iv. 41. 7
Did softly swim away, ne *ever* stamp . . . I. v. 28. 6
ne *ever* would forsake, . . . I. vi. 2. 8
ever lov'd to fight for Ladies right; . . . I. vi. 20. 8
Or *ever* hope recover her againe: . . . I. vi. 33. 6
This fatall day that shall I *ever* rew, . . . I. vi. 38. 2
Whose bubbling wave did *ever* freshly well, . . . I. vii. 4. 6
Ne *ever* would through fervent sommer fade: . . . I. vii. 4. 7
Whose many heades, out budding *ever* new, . . . I. vii. 17. 4

Ever—*Continued.*
Ne might of mortall eye be *ever* seene; . . . . I. vii. 33. 2
Had never beene, ne *ever* by his might . . . . I. vii. 47. 4
the Dwarfe them guiding *ever* right. . . . . I. vii. 52. 9
What mortall wight could *ever* beare . . . . I. viii. 18. 9
men, who *ever,* as they trace, ... I. viii. 31. 5
ne *ever* other answere made. . . . . I. viii. 32. 9
breathed *ever* forth a filthie banefull smell. . . . . . . I. viii. 39. 9
Could *ever* find to grieve the gentlest hart . . . . I. ix. 7. 9
Ne *ever* will their fervent fury slake, ... I. ix. 8. 3
'That ydle name of love . . . I *ever* scornd, ... I. ix. 10. 3
Ne living man like wordes did *ever* heare, ... I. ix. 14. 7
his balefull note, which *ever* drave Far . . . . I. ix. 33. 7
nor fruit nor leafe was *ever* seene, ... I. ix. 34. 2
What justice *ever* other judgement taught, ... I. ix. 38. 3
ever fickle fortune rageth rife; . . . . I. ix. 44. 8
thy innocent feet doe *ever* tread! . . . . I. x. 9. 2
And *ever* . . . still at hand did wayt, ... I. x. 26. 6
Her necke and brests were *ever* open bare, ... I. x. 30. 7
ever, when his feet encombred were, ... I. x. 35. 6
one sate wayting *ever* them before, ... I. x. 36. 8
as the tree does fall, so lyes it *ever* low. . . . . I. x. 41. 9
He did supply their want, and gave them *ever* free. . . . . I. x. 43. 9
deare as *ever* knight was deare, ... I. xi. 1. 7
ever ready for your foeman . . . . I. xi. 2. 5
what within his reach he *ever* drawes. . . . . I. xi. 12. 5
burnen *ever* bright. I. xii. 37. 9
ever, when his eie did her behold, ... I. xii. 40. 8
Who *ever* heard of th' Indian Peru? . . . . II. Pr. 2. 6
ever with slow pace the knight did lead, ... II. i. 7. 8
why should *ever* I henceforth desyre . . . . II. i. 17. 3
ever, like herselfe, unstayned hath beene tryde. . . . . . . II. ii. 9. 9
As *ever* of their loves they would be glad: . . . . II. ii. 28. 4
she *ever* would asswage, ... II. ii. 38. 5
in oblivion *ever* buried is; . . . . II. iii. 40. 4
wakefull watches *ever* to abide; . . . . II. iii. 41. 6
And *ever* as she went her toung did walke . . . . II. iv. 5. 1
And *ever* held his hand upon his hart; . . . . II. vi. 26. 2
ever her desired to depart. . . . . II. vi. 26. 7
And *ever* bad him stay . . . . II. vi. 26. 9
Of love they *ever* greater glory bore . . . . II. vi. 35. 6
Furious *ever* I thee knew to bee, ... II. vi. 49. 3
ever as he went . . . . II. vii. 26. 9
did never see before, Ne *ever* could . . . . II. vii. 31. 6
Ne *ever* will it breake, ne *ever* bend: . . . . II. viii. 21. 5
But *ever* at Pyrochles when he smitt, ... II. viii. 43. 1
How *ever* may Thy cursed hand so cruelly . . . . II. viii. 46. 6
How may straunge knight hope *ever* to aspire, ... II. ix. 5. 6
ever and anone with rosy red . . . . II. ix. 41. 3
Or shame that *ever* should so fowle defects . . . . II. xii. 23. 3
Ne *ever* shroncke, ne *ever* sought to bayt . . . . II. xii. 29. 7
which *ever* after they abusd to ill, ... II. xii. 31. 8
that *ever* open stood to all . . . . II. xii. 46. 2
That *ever* mixt their song . . . . II. xii. 72. 9
Of all the which they honour *ever* wonne, ... III. i. 3. 7
ever with sweet Nectar she did sprinkle him. . . . . III. i. 36. 9
ever and anone the rosy red Flasht . . . . III. ii. 5. 6
had it remayned *ever* since! . . . . III. ii. 21. 9
And *ever* what she did was streight undonne. . . . . III. ii. 51. 5
more insight Then *ever* him before, or after, ... III. iii. 11. 9
Whose empire lenger here then *ever* any stood?' . . . . . . III. iii. 42. 9
ever from fayre Ladies love did fly; . . . . III. iv. 26. 6
And *ever* as he nigher to her drew, ... III. iv. 48. 3
faithfull *ever* tride, And bold, as *ever* Squyre that waited . III. v. 12. 8, 9
Dye rather, dy, then *ever* love disloyally. . . . . III. v. 45. 9
For *ever* dye, and *ever* buried bee . . . . III. vi. 47. 2
but fled *Ever* alike, ... III. vii. 2. 5
'So liv'd they *ever* after in like sin, ... III. vii. 49. 1
deedes of armes had *ever* in despaire, ... III. viii. 11. 7
how mote it *ever* bee, That *ever* hand should dare . . . . . III. viii. 48. 7, 8
that they will *ever* rew T' have seene,' . . . . III. viii. 49. 1
ever firmely fixed did abide . . . . III. ix. 24. 3
ever closely eide Sir Satyrane, ... III. ix. 27. 4
And *ever* and anone, ... III. ix. 28. 1
(if *ever* her apart) . . . . III. x. 7. 1
with them as housewife *ever* to abide, ... III. x. 36. 7
which *ever* and anon Threates . . . . III. x. 58. 4
There dwels he *ever,* . . . . III. x. 60. 5
ever in your noble hart prepense, ... III. xi. 14. 5
But *ever* more and more upon it gazd, ... III. xi. 49. 8
Expecting *ever* when some foe she might descry. . . . . . . III. xii. 1. 9
And *ever* when his passion is allayd, ... IV. ii. 12. 6
dreddest daungerous That *ever* shrilling trumpet did . . . . IV. ii. 32. 4
It hath bene through all ages *ever* seene, ... IV. v. 1. 1
ever as they fastned it, it loos'd . . . . IV. v. 16. 6
and *ever* since withheld.' . . . . IV. vi. 6. 9
ever when he burnt in lustfull fire, ... IV. vii. 19. 8
ever when the Squire his javelin shooke, ... IV. vii. 26. 2
'Ne was he *ever* vanquished afore, But *ever* vanquisht all . IV. viii. 48. 1, 2
To whom the world this franchise *ever* yeelded, ... IV. ix. 37. 6
seeking *ever* since with endlesse paines . . . . IV. ix. 38. 3
all that *ever* yet I have endured . . . . IV. x. 2. 6
For ought that *ever* she could doe or say; . . . . IV. x. 15. 2
That *ever* troden was of footings trace: . . . . IV. x. 21. 5
Ne *ever* ought but of their true loves talkt, ... IV. x. 25. 8
nought That *ever* she to me could say . . . . IV. x. 57. 4
more then *ever* did Cambridge or Oxford, ... IV. xi. 35. 5
So *ever* loose, so *ever* happy be! . . . . IV. xii. 11. 5
'That *ever* I this dismall day did see! . . . . V. i. 15. 3
truth is one, and right is *ever* one.' . . . . V. ii. 48. 6

Ever—*Continued.*
Whom *ever* as he did the more avize, ... V. iii. 18. 8
I will it defend whilst *ever* that I may. . . . . V. iv. 14. 9
he shall . . . *ever* to my lore be bound; . . . . V. iv. 49. 3
Ne day nor night did *ever* idly rest; . . . . V. viii. 3. 7
There let her *ever* keepe her damned den, ... V. ix. 2. 3
walkt about them *ever* and anone . . . . V. x. 10. 5
And *ever,* ere he saw the stroke to land, ... V. xi. 7. 4
none *ever* saw, nor kend, That *ever* scap'd: . . . . V. xi. 20. 5, 6
she hath me *ever* since abhord, ... V. xi. 50. 7
Ay me, that *ever* guyle in wemen was invented! . . . . V. xi. 50. 9
How can he mercy *ever* hope to have? . . . . VI. i. 42. 2
none is to me unknowne that *ev'r* was seene. . . . . VI. ii. 31. 9
That curtesie and manhoode *ever* disagree. . . . . VI. iii. 40. 9
As *ever* he to Lady was affyde, To spare her Knight, ... VI. iii. 49. 8
Who, *ever* as he saw him nigh succeed, ... VI. iv. 8. 7
She bore it thence, and *ever* as her owne it kept. . . . . . VI. iv. 37. 9
And *ever* more and more . . . . VI. v. 6. 9
Ne *ever* Knight that bore so lofty creast, Ne *ever* Lady . . . VI. vi. 12. 7, 8
repent, That *ever* I this life unto thee lent, ... VI. vi. 33. 5
Ne *ever* armes ne *ever* knighthood dare . . . . VI. vi. 36. 3
And so would *ever* live, ... VI. vii. 30. 9
Had *ever* learn'd to love the lowly things, ... VI. ix. 35. 5
And *ever,* when he came in companie . . . . VI. ix. 39. 1
And *ever,* as the crew About her daunst, ... VI. x. 14. 6
if they should *ever* last . . . . VI. xi. 1. 1
'That *ever* I did live this day to see, ... VI. xi. 29. 2
Nature, *ever* young, yet full of eld; . . . . VII. vii. 13. 2
To knit the knot, that *ever* shall remaine. . . . . *Am.* vi. 14
Looke *ever* lovely, as becomes you best; . . . . *Am.* vii. 10
Well is he borne, that may behold you *ever.* . . . . *Am.* viii. 14
Nor to the Fire; for they consume not *ever;* . . . . *Am.* ix. 8
Have *ever* since kept me in cruell bands. . . . . *Am.* xii. 12
let none *ever* say, That ye were blooded . . . . *Am.* xx. 13
Thinck *ever* to endure so taedious toyle! . . . . *Am.* xxxiii. 10
if *ever* ye entrapped are, ... *Am.* xxxvii. 11
Ne . . . thing uncomely *ever* may Thereto approch . . . . . *Epith.* 198
had lyen confused *ever.* . . . . *H.L.* 77
So *ever* since they firmely have remained, ... *H.L.* 92
if they will *ever* swerve, ... *H.L.* 165
that *ever* ye that monster placed In gentle love, ... *H.L.* 271
that *ever* I might hope, ... *H.L.* 294
If it in darknesse be enshrined *ever,* . . . . *H.B.* 188
Ne *ever* should their happinesse decay, ... *H.H.L.* 76
And tell me then, what hast thou *ever* seene . . . . *H.H.B.* 57

Ever-burning. The *everburning* lamps from thence it braught, I. vii. 18. 4
ever burning wrath before him laid, ... I. ix. 50. 3
leading th' *ever-burning* lampe astray, ... V. viii. 40. 7

Ever-damned. flyes Fluttring about his *ever-damned* hedd, . . I. i. 38. 3
the *ever damned* Beast . . . . I. xi. 49. 1

Ever-drizzling. *ever-drizling* raine upon the loft, ... I. i. 41. 3

Ever-drooping. Cynthia . . . doth steepe In silver deaw his *ever-drouping* hed, ... I. i. 39. 8

Ever-dying. From tyrans rage and *ever-dying* dread, ... I. x. 9. 5
Of never-dead yet *ever-dying* paine; . . . . *H.H.L.* 126

Evergreen. moorish fennes, and marshes *ever greene.* . . . . *Ti.* 140
breaking quite his garlond *ever greene,* . . . . III. xi. 37. 8

Everlasting. Let *everlasting* lightsome glory strive, ... *Gn.* 55
fit to frame an *everlasting* dittie, ... *Col.* 385
To be the . . . Registres of *everlasting* fame, ... *Ded. Son.* iv. 3
Thy praises *everlasting* monument Is in this verse . . . . . *Ded. Son.* vi. 12
lasting baies Of . . . *everlasting* praies; . . . . *Ded. Son.* xv. 5
Lay forth out of thine *everlasting* scryne . . . . I. Pr. 2. 3
Now in the powre of *everlasting* Night? . . . . I. v. 43. 5
The Nourse of time and *everlasting* fame, ... I. xi. 5. 8
life eke *everlasting* did befall: . . . . I. xi. 46. 6
Lifting to heven her *everlasting* fame: . . . . I. xii. 8. 5
Let us devize of ease and *everlasting* rest.' . . . . I. xii. 17. 9
'Joy may you have, and *everlasting* fame, ... II. i. 32. 1
bid them sleepe in *everlasting* peace. . . . . II. i. 60. 6
With recompence of *everlasting* fame: . . . . II. x. 23. 5
'Then woe, and woe, and *everlasting* woe, ... III. iii. 42. 1
still remaines in *everlasting* store, ... III. vi. 36. 4
There now he lives in *everlasting* joy, ... III. vi. 49. 1
From heavens blis and *everlasting* rest: . . . . III. viii. 8. 4
everlasting moniments of brasse, ... III. ix. 50. 8
Where she hath now an *everlasting* place . . . . V. i. 11. 5
Sith in th' Almighties *everlasting* seat She first was bred, . . V. x. 1. 7
whose *everlasting* praise They all were bound . . . to raise. . V. xi. 34. 8
Where Cynthia raignes in *everlasting* glory, ... VII. vi. 8. 2

Ever-living. burning starres and *everliving* fire, ... I. x. 50. 6

Evermore. That which no hands can *evermore* compyle. . . . *Ro.* xxv. 14
Where wretched ghosts sit wailing *evermore.* . . . . *Gn.* 384
Calling on Itis, Itis! *evermore,* . . . . *Gn.* 402
evermore he heard each one complaine . . . . *Hub.* 1275
the Evill damning *evermore* to dy: . . . . *Com. Son.* i. 12
there thou livest, singing *evermore,* . . . . *Ti.* 337
evermore, with most varietie . . . . *Mui.* 177
evermore when I did sleepe or play, ... *D.* 132
to true loves he may us *evermore* Preferre, ... *Col.* 817
But *evermore* vouchsafe it to maintaine . . . . *Ded. Son.* xii.13
living *evermore* In the divine resemblaunce . . . . *Ded. Son.* xv. 9
and *evermore* He strowd an *Ave-Mary* after and before. . . I. i. 35. 8
evermore did weene To bee the chastest flowre . . . . I. ii. 48. 3
evermore does steepe Her tender brest in bitter teares . . . I. iii. 15. 7
evermore embrace My faithfull service, ... I. iii. 29. 7
evermore she hated, never lov'd: . . . . I. v. 24. 9
to slake the heavenly fire that raged *evermore.* . . . . . . I. v. 40. 9
As rock of Diamond stedfast *evermore.* . . . . I. vi. 4. 5
Yet *evermore* it was his maner faire, ... I. vi. 30. 1

Evermore—Continued.

evermore, in constant carefull mind,	I. vii. 28. 5
Accept therefore My simple selfe, and service evermore:	I. viii. 27. 5
It governd was, and guided evermore,	I. x. 3. 4
thankt be God, and her encrease so evermore!'	I. x. 16. 9
hearing evermore His ruefull shriekes	I. x. 28. 4
Their gates to all were open evermore,	I. x. 36. 6
That shall ye evermore renowmed make	I. xi. 2. 8
Where she enjoyes sure peace for evermore,	II. i. 2. 8
evermore did seeme As discontent	II. ii. 35. 3
evermore with mightie spels them charmd;	II. vi. 51. 7
evermore himselfe with comfort feedes	II. vii. 2. 4
Him followed eke Sir Guyon evermore,	II. vii. 26. 3
evermore him succour, and defend	II. viii. 8. 5
evermore their cruell Capitaine Sought	II. ix. 15. 3
he them defeated evermore,	II. x. 10. 4
Against the forte of reason evermore,	II. xi. 1. 3
evermore their hideous Ordinaunce	II. xi. 14. 3
evermore their wicked Capitayn Provoked them	II. xi. 14. 6
seemd to tremble evermore and quake;	II. xi. 22. 5
he looked evermore When the hart blood should gush	II. xi. 37. 6
wandreth evermore uncertain and unsure.	II. xii. 12. 9
lowd to them for succour called evermore.	II. xii. 27. 9
evermore With her soft garment wipes away the gore	III. i. 38. 4
So evermore he did increase his speed,	III. iv. 48. 4
In faithfull love, t' abide for evermore;	III. vi. 53. 4
evermore she him refused flat,	III. viii. 39. 3
ought evermore To errant knights be commune:	III. viii. 52. 4
evermore the Carle of courtesie accusd.	III. ix. 12. 9
with the like him aunswerd evermore.	III. ix. 28. 7
Fashioning worldes of fancies evermore.	III. ix. 52. 4
evermore on Daunger fixt his eye,	III. xii. 12. 7
evermore encreased her consuming paine.	III. xii. 21. 9
Whom mortally he hated evermore,	IV. i. 39. 4
friendly aid Mongst gentle Knights to nourish evermore?	IV. i. 46. 4
evermore sought Britomart to cleare:	IV. i. 54. 6
evermore, when she fit time could fynd,	IV. ii. 53. 7
Yet evermore his honour he recured,	IV. v. 37. 8
About the Andvile standing evermore.	IV. v. 36. 2
evermore, when he to sleepe did thinke,	IV. v. 41. 1
evermore, when he began to winke,	IV. v. 41. 3
evermore from villenie her kept:	IV. vi. 35. 7
evermore, when with regardfull sight She looking	IV. vii. 22. 4
fled away for evermore.	IV. vii. 36. 9
evermore, when he did grace entreat,	IV. vii. 37. 6
Him seeking evermore, yet no where him describe.	IV. viii. 18. 9
evermore he greatly did desire.	IV. viii. 22. 1
evermore their malice did augment;	IV. ix. 25. 6
evermore his eyes about him went,	IV. x. 12. 7
in the Porch did evermore abide An hideous Giant,	IV. x. 16. 5
Brave thoughts and noble deedes did evermore aspire.	IV. x. 26. 9
evermore upon the Goddesse face	IV. x. 56. 1
evermore my shield did me defend	IV. x. 58. 6
evermore some of the vertuous race Rose up,	V. i. 1. 6
as his Squire him offred evermore To serve,	V. i. 30. 3
evermore those Damzells did forestall Their furious encounter,	V. iv. 5. 8
evermore he gently did desyre To stay her stroks,	V. v. 16. 5
So praying him t' accept her service evermore.	V. v. 54. 9
evermore she did him sharpely twight.	V. vi. 12. 8
evermore Therewith containes his heavenly Common-weale:	V. vii. 1. 7
Yeeld for amends my selfe yours evermore,	V. viii. 13. 5
To be a moniment for evermore.	V. viii. 45. 3
evermore those hags them selves did paine To sharpen him,	V. xii. 41. 8
shall you most renowmed make for evermore.	VI. i. 5. 9
her selfe bound to him for evermore;	VI. i. 46. 8
evermore contrary hath bene tryde,	VI. iii. 2. 1
And evermore his lovely litle spoile Crying	VI. iv. 25. 7
in her soveraine lyking he dwelt evermore.	VI. v. 12. 9
evermore that craven cowherd Knight Was at his backe	VI. vi. 26. 6
made him evermore increase his speedie pace.	VI. vi. 29. 9
evermore she blamed Calepine,	VI. viii. 33. 1
evermore his speach he did apply To th' heards,	VI. ix. 12. 8
evermore . . . Did strive to match.	VI. x. 33. 1
Who as her owne it nurst (and named) evermore.	VI. xii. 9. 9
evermore exchange Their dwelling places,	VII. vii. 21. 5
Your goodly selfe for evermore to vew:	Am. xlv. 2
She laughes, and hardens evermore her hart.	Am. liv. 12
evermore they Hymen, Hymen sing,	Epith. 146

Ever-moving. And menageth the ever-moving sky, . . . H.H.B. 194

Ever-whirling. What man that sees the ever-whirling wheele,
Of Change, . . . VII. vi. 1. 1

Every. On everie side a thousand shining beames: . . . Bel.² xi. 10

Byrds of every kynde	S.C. Jun. 7
I have made a Calender for every yeare,	S.C. Env. 1
On everie bush, and everie hollow rocke,	Gn. 235
slumbring sleep . . . seized everie lim.	Gn. 240
His creste . . . On everie side did shine	Gn. 261
Throwing his firie eyes on everie side,	Gn. 270
now loosing everie lim,	Gn. 322
tost in th' ayre with everie windie blast:	Gn. 334
with deadly lamps on everie post?	Gn. 341
The heavens on everie side enclowded bee:	Gn. 571
death on everie side to them appeares	Gn. 583
with banks on everie side,	Gn. 658
everie streete Is full of fortunes,	Hub. 90
asked for their pas by everie squib,	Hub. 371
used duly everie day Their service . . . to say,	Hub. 449
straied . . . Through everie field	Hub. 578
round flesh, that everie bone doth hide.	Hub. 592
the Courtiers gaze on everie side,	Hub. 669

Every—Continued.

Ne after everie tattling fable flie:	Hub. 724
The canker worme of everie gentle brest;	Hub. 736
False personages fit for everie sted,	Hub. 861
Afraid of everie leafe that stir'd him by, And everie stick	Hub. 1007, 1008
his eare he lent To everie sound	Hub. 1011
the Lord of everie creature	Hub. 1030
an universall night . . . he makes on everie wight;	Hub. 1298
and everie corner sought,	Hub. 1357
everie shower will wash	Ti. 205
horror ran through everie part.	Ti. 483
His choiceful sense with every change doth flit:	Mui. 159
survey . . . Of every flowre and herbe	Mui. 172
how she in everie member shooke,	Mui. 285
Did tickle inwardly in everie vaine:	Mui. 394
fill with pleasance every wood and plaine.	D. 56
with the same fill every hill and dale.	D. 322
Nature, nurse of every living thing,	D. 337
Every field and forest far away He sought,	As. 81
everie gift, and everie goodly meed,	Col. 592
everie day, in which she did a deed,	Col. 594
Her name in every tree I will endosse,	Col. 632
everie living wight Crept forth	Col. 859
So pure . . . She was in life and every vertuous lore;	I. i. 5. 2
everie wight to shrowd it did constrain;	I. i. 6. 8
she . . . every hil and dale, . . . Did search,	I. ii. 8. 3
full large of limbe and every joint He was,	I. ii. 12. 8
their greene leaves, trembling with every blast,	I. ii. 28. 5
Till on a day (that day is everie Prime,	I. ii. 40. 4
The Lyon, Lord of everie beast in field,'	I. iii. 7. 1
Nine hundred Pater nosters every day,	I. iii. 13. 8
Thrise every weeke in ashes shee did sitt,	I. iii. 14. 2
every creature shrowded is in sleepe.	I. iii. 15. 2
every breath of heaven shaked itt:	I. iv. 5. 7
which was on every side With rich array . . . dight.	I. iv. 6. 5
a noble crew Of Lords and Ladies stood on every side,	I. iv. 7. 8
From everie worke he chalenged essoyne,	I. iv. 20. 3
So every good to bad he doth abuse;	I. iv. 32. 5
softly gan embalme on everie side:	I. v. 17. 5
on every side them stood The trembling ghosts	I. v. 32. 4
all the hellish brood . . . flockt on every side,	I. v. 32. 8
his members chast Scattered on every mountaine	I. v. 38. 8
Aesculape . . . joyned every part.	I. v. 39. 9
every tender part for feare does shake.	I. vi. 10. 2
Which, quitt from death, yet quakes in every lim	I. vi. 10. 8
everie beast for feare of him did fly, and quake.	I. vi. 24. 9
suddein cold did ronne through every vaine,	I. vi. 37. 2
so faint in every joynt and vayne,	I. vii. 11. 7
everie tender part does tosse and turne:	I. vii. 21. 6
Perce to my hart, and pas through everie side,	I. vii. 22. 8
With foltring tong, and trembling everie vaine,	I. vii. 24. 7
locks do tremble every one At everie little breath	I. vii. 32. 9
From every coast that heaven walks about	I. vii. 45. 3
trembling feare did feel in every vaine:	I. viii. 4. 2
every dore of freewill open flew.	I. viii. 5. 3
every head with fyrie tongue did flame,	I. viii. 6. 3
every head was crowned on his creast,	I. viii. 6. 4
eger greedinesse through every member thrild.	I. viii. 6. 6
Those were the keyes of every inner dore;	I. viii. 30. 8
Through every rowme he sought, and everie bowr,	I. viii. 37. 1
me . . . that here lye dying every stound,	I. viii. 38. 4
trembling horrour ran through every joynt,	I. viii. 39. 3
To kindle love in every living brest:	I. ix. 9. 4
every sence the humour sweet embayd,	I. ix. 13. 5
trembling every joynt, did inly quake.	I. ix. 24. 8
mealt'h Into the heart, and searcheth every vaine;	I. ix. 31. 6
Is not his lawe, Let every sinner die;	I. ix. 47. 5
through every vaine The crudled cold ran	I. ix. 52. 1
She unto him disclosed every whitt;	I. x. 19. 3
dieted with fasting every day,	I. x. 26. 3
wont him once to disple every day:	I. x. 27. 2
Gan him instruct in everie good behest,	I. x. 33. 3
God to us forgiveth every howre	I. x. 40. 6
in every good behest . . . Shee him instructed	I. x. 45. 3
every sinew seene, through his long fast:	I. x. 48. 6
end, which every living wight Should make his marke	I. x. 50. 2
send forth their flames far off to every shyre,	I. xi. 14. 4
meates and drinkes of every kinde.	I. xii. 15. 1
What if in every other starre unseene	II. Pr. 3. 7
feigning then in every limb to quake	II. i. 9. 3
In everie fountaine, and in everie lake,	II. ii. 5. 7
him assayle on everie side.	II. ii. 22. 9
Prowdly to prune, and sett on every side;	II. iii. 36. 8
Woe never wants where every cause is caught;	II. iv. 44. 6
fire, That seemed him to enflame on every side:	II. v. 2. 7
the mery birdes of every sorte.	II. v. 31. 6
Every of which did loosely disaray	II. v. 32. 7
every of them strove	II. v. 33. 1
redoubled every stroke.	II. vi. 30. 9
every weighty thing they did upbeare,	II. vi. 46. 8
made a priefe Of every place	II. vi. 51. 4
on every side Great heapes of gold	II. vii. 5. 1
rich metall loaded every rifte,	II. vii. 28. 5
On every side they placed were along;	II. vii. 30. 5
By every fournace many feendes did byde,	II. vii. 35. 6
every feend his busie paines applyde	II. vii. 35. 9
every pillour decked was . . . With crownes,	II. vii. 43. 7
Of every sort and nation under skye,	II. vii. 44. 2
every linck thereof a step of dignity.	II. vii. 46. 9
every loup fast lockt, as fearing foes despight.	II. ix. 10. 9

Every—*Continued.*
on *every* syde Twise sixteene warders satt, ... II. ix. 26. 1
through the world then swarmd in *every* part, ... II. x. 15. 3
health to *every* forreyne nation: . . . . . II. x. 26. 7
dawning day . . . that maketh *every* creature glad, ... II. xi. 3. 4
begon That castle to assaile on *every* side, ... II. xi. 5. 4
Islandes . . . On *every* side . . . . . II. xii. 10. 7
firmely armd for *every* hard assay, ... II. xii. 38. 8
on *every* side Strowed with pleasauns; . . . . . II. xii. 50. 2
the silver flood Through *every* channell running . . . . . II. xii. 60. 4
locks . . . disperst with puff of *every* blast: . . . . . III. i. 16. 4
sore beset on *every* side . . . . . III. i. 21. 2
every knight which doth this way repayre, ... III. i. 26. 7
cost Of *every* pillour and of *every* post, ... III. i. 32. 5
with meates of *every* sort, ... III. i. 52. 2
And *every* knight, and *every* gentle Squire, ... III. i. 56. 7
High time it seemed then for *everie* wight . . . . . III. i. 58. 1
torches . . . to guyden *every* guest. . . . . . III. i. 58. 4
every mortall wight Was drowned in . . . sleepe; . . . . . III. i. 59. 2
trembling *every* joynt, ... III. i. 60. 1
Of *every* finest fingers touch affrayd; . . . . . III. i. 61. 5
every daintie limbe with horrour shake; . . . . . III. ii. 5. 5
him in *everie* part before her fashioned . . . . . III. ii. 16. 9
him in *everie* part before she knew, ... III. ii. 17. 1
every river eke his course forbeares, ... III. ii. 32. 3
every trembling joynt and *every* vaine . . . . . III. ii. 34. 3
she gave him warning *every* day . . . . . III. iv. 26. 1
great Dame Natures handmaide chearing *every* kind. . . . . . III. iv. 56. 9
seized *every* sence with sorrow sore opprest. . . . . . III. vi. 10. 9
every Nimph full narrowly shee eide. . . . . . III. vi. 23. 9
every sort is . . . Sett by it selfe, ... III. vi. 35. 3
every substance is conditioned To chaunge her hew, ... III. vi. 38. 3
all about grew *every* sort of flowre, ... III. vi. 45. 1
every leafe, that shaketh . . . . . III. vii. 1. 4
seemd for feare to quake in *every* lim, ... III. viii. 15. 8
every shape on him he could endew; . . . . . III. viii. 40. 2
th' heart of *every* honourable Dame, ... III. viii. 43. 5
Every discourse, and *every* argument, ... III. ix. 53. 7
Thou . . . seest *every* secret of the minde; . . . . . III. x. 4. 7
yet bayted *every* word, ... III. x. 6. 7
every where he might, and *everie* while, ... III. x. 9. 1
That *every* member of his body quooke. . . . . . III. x. 24. 5
every Satyre first did give a busse . . . . . III. x. 46. 3
every bird and beast awarned made . . . . . III. x. 46. 8
Who butted him with hornes on *every* syde, ... III. x. 52. 3
Hatefull both to himselfe and *every* wight; . . . . . III. x. 60. 6
on *every* syde They trembling stood, ... III. xi. 40. 6
every wight . . . themselves did shrowd, ... III. xii. 1. 3
whirlwind . . . that clapped *every* dore, ... III. xii. 3. 2
every wood and *every* valley wyde . . . . . III. xii. 7. 8
And *every* part . . . was soone restord. . . . . . III. xii. 38. 6
whilest *every* man . . . were heedlesse . . . . . IV. i. 3. 3
everie word did tremble as she spake, And *everie* looke was coy . . . . . IV. i. 5. 6, 7
And *everie* limbe that touched her did quake; . . . . . IV. i. 5. 8
are led with *every* light report: . . . . . IV. i. 28. 5
Was so expert in *every* subtile slight, ... IV. ii. 10. 8
every spoyle or pray Should equally be shard . . . . . IV. ii. 13. 4
Well seene in *everie* science that mote bee, And *every* secret worke of natures wayes; . . . . . IV. ii. 35. 3, 4
Still watcht on *every* side, ... IV. ii. 36. 9
every houre they knocke at deathes gate? . . . . . IV. iii. 1. 7
At puffe of *every* storme doth stagger . . . . . IV. iii. 9. 9
That dreadfull seem'd to *every* living wight, ... IV. v. 32. 3
So *every* place seem'd painefull, ... IV. v. 40. 9
gan he swell in *every* inner part . . . . . IV. vi. 7. 4
lashing dreadfully at *every* part, ... IV. vi. 16. 6
Yet trembling *every* joynt through former feare; . . . . . IV. vii. 34. 2
he saw on *every* tree, ... IV. vii. 46. 1
And *every* day . . . He . . . would share; . . . . . IV. viii. 5. 6
yet trembling *every* vaine; . . . . . IV. viii. 41. 3
the keyes of *every* prison dore . . . . . IV. viii. 54. 6
every dint the ghost would rive . . . . . IV. ix. 22. 8
For *every* dram of hony therein found . . . . . IV. x. 1. 4
There worshipped of *every* living wight; . . . . . IV. x. 29. 7
Every of which was to a damzell hight; . . . . . IV. x. 38. 8
unto *every* person knew her part; . . . . . IV. x. 51. 4
the storme of *every* dreadfull stoure: . . . . . IV. x. 58. 7
To damne him selfe by *every* evil name, ... IV. xii. 16. 5
searching *every* part, ... IV. xii. 23. 8
grieve in *every* vaine. . . . . . IV. xii. 27. 9
limit what is lesse or more In *every* thing, ... V. ii. 34. 6
rudely stroke at him on *every* side; . . . . . V. ii. 53. 3
To which there did resort from *every* side . . . . . V. iii. 2. 7
From *every* coast and countrie . . . . . V. iii. 6. 2
To greet his guerdon unto *every* knight, ... V. iii. 14. 3
Fast bound on *every* side with iron bands, ... V. iv. 5. 2
And heaped strokes so fast on *every* side, ... V. iv. 38. 8
And *every* while that . . . man . . . Them sorely vext, ... V. iv. 44. 1
Basted with bends of gold on *every* side, ... V. v. 3. 2
she laid on *every* side. . . . . . V. v. 6. 9
Each hour did seeme a moneth, and *every* moneth a yeare. . . V. vi. 5. 9
had sought for ease In *every* place, and *every* place thought best, ... V. vi. 7. 2
he had with him abundant store On *every* side . . . . . V. viii. 34. 3
Seeking by *every* way . . . . . V. viii. 37. 2
He him pursewd . . . *every* place . . . . . V. ix. 16. 4
every matter worse was . . . . . V. xii. 35. 4
Ladies ayde in *every* stead and stound.' . . . . . VI. i. 42. 9
every action doth them mvch commend, ... VI. ii. 2. 3

Every—*Continued.*
Whose *every* deed . . . Was like enchantment, ... VI. ii. 3. 2
But wayt on him in *every* place and part: . . . . . VI. ii. 36. 5
Yet was he courteous still to *every* wight, ... VI. iii. 3. 5
stearne In all assaies to *every* errant Knight, ... VI. iii. 40. 4
And *every* litle limbe he searcht around, ... VI. iv. 23. 6
And *every* part that under sweath-bands lay, ... VI. iv. 23. 7
when he lookt about on *every* syde, ... VI. iv. 24. 3
doe him sharpe assay On *every* side, ... VI. v. 19. 4
Sought to encompasse him on *every* side, ... VI. v. 20. 2
and *every* day them duely drest. . . . . . VI. vi. 2. 9
Give salves to *every* sore, ... VI. vi. 5. 9
poyson close through *every* vaine, ... VI. vi. 8. 8
every joynt for dread of death did quake . . . . . VI. vi. 29. 7
the wayes to win good will Of *every* wight, ... VI. vi. 41. 7
Began to tremble *every* limbe and vaine; . . . . . VI. vii. 22. 2
did stryde At *every* step . . . . . VI. vii. 42. 6
on *every* syde He gaz'd about . . . . . VI. vii. 42. 7
shift to *every* side, ... VI. vii. 46. 6
every foote did tremble . . . . . VI. viii. 31. 8
every body two and two she foure did read. . . . . . VI. viii. 31. 9
Whooping and hallowing on *every* part, ... VI. viii. 40. 3
perfectly well shapt in *every* lim, ... VI. ix. 9. 2
My lambes doe *every* yeare increase . . . . . VI. ix. 21. 7
doe lay My limbs in *every* shade . . . And drinke of *every* brooke . . . . . VI. ix. 23. 8, 9
affrayd of *every* chaunges dread. . . . . . VI. ix. 27. 9
And *every* day . . . he with her went: . . . . . VI. ix. 34. 7
he went With the faire Pastorella *every* day, ... VI. ix. 37. 2
And *every* evening helping them to fold: . . . . . VI. ix. 37. 6
fed with light report Of *every* blaste, ... VI. x. 2. 9
do him assayle on *every* side, ... VI. xi. 48. 6
Through *every* place . . . Him follow'd . . . . . VI. xii. 22. 8
they filled *every* hill and Plaine; . . . . . VII. vii. 4. 5
raunged farre abroad in *every* border, ... VII. vii. 4. 8
And *every* parts inholders to convent, ... VII. vii. 17. 4
And *every* River still doth ebbe and flowe; . . . . . VII. vii. 20. 4
Which *every* howre is chang'd and altred cleane With *every* blast that bloweth, ... VII. vii. 22. 7,8
to her creatures *every* minute chaunce; . . . . . VII. vii. 23. 2
every day We see his parts, ... VII. vii. 24. 2
With ears of corne of *every* sort, ... VII. vii. 30. 7
her face . . . *every* day We changed see . . . . . VII. vii. 50. 6
he his course doth alter *every* yeare, ... VII. vii. 51. 3
All paine hath end, and *every* war hath peace; . . . . . *Am.* xi. 13
At *every* rash beholder passing by. . . . . . *Am.* xvi. 8
the Lyon that . . . reigneth over *every* beast . . . . . *Am.* xx. 6
every sweet with soure is tempred still, ... *Am.* xxvi. 9
A melting pleasance ran through *every* part, ... *Am.* xxxix. 7
every bit which thenceforth I did eat. . . . . . *Am.* xxxix. 14
every beast that to his den was fled, ... *Am.* xl. 10
every part remaines immortally: . . . . . *Am.* xlv. 8
To *every* planet point his sundry yeare: . . . . . *Am.* lx. 2
maketh *every* minute seeme a myle. . . . . . *Am.* lxxxvi. 12
Affrayd of *every* dangers least dismay. . . . . . *Am.* lxxxvii. 4
Doest tyrannize in *everie* weaker part: . . . . . *H.L.* 4
in *every* living wight They mixe themselves, ... *H.L.* 90
every earthly thing partakes . . . . . *H.B.* 43
in perfect limming *every* part? . . . . . *H.B.* 84
Through *every* part she doth the same impresse, ... *H.B.* 115
So *every* spirit, . . . the fairer bodie doth procure . . . . . *H.B.* 127
Him to be Lord of *every* living wight He made . . . . . *H.H.L.* 115
sharply launching *every* inner part, ... *H.H.L.* 158
And let thy bowels bleede in *every* vaine, ... *H.H.L.* 248
on fire With burning zeale, through *every* part entire, ... *H.H.L.* 271
bounded On *everie* side, with pyles of flaming brands, ... *H.H.B.* 39
To reade enregistred in *every* nooke His goodnesse, ... *H.H.B.* 131
That kindleth love in *every* godly spright . . . . . *H.H.B.* 297
Of *every* sort, which in that Meadow grew, ... *Proth.* 29

Every one. they gan to be descryed Of *everie one,* . . . . . *Hub.* 346
unto *everie one* doo curtesie meeke: . . . . . *Hub.* 499
so *everie one* was used, ... *Hub.* 1223
Walk through the world of *every one* revilde. . . . . . *T.M.* 342
Scorned of *everie one,* . . . . . *Ti.* 503
Of *everie one* he takes, and tastes . . . . . *Mui.* 203
In *every one* he vanquisht *every one,* . . . . . *As.* 77
every one did make exceeding mone, ... *As.* 205
every one did weep and waile, ... *As.* 207
locks do tremble *every one* At everie little breath . . . . . I. vii. 32. 9
everie one her with a grace endowes, ... II. iii. 25. 4
everie one with meekenesse to her bowes. . . . . . II. iii. 25. 5
every one did swincke, and *every one* did sweat. . . . . . II. vii. 36. 9
every one did strive his fellow downe to throw. . . . . . II. vii. 47. 9
at these straungers presence *every one* did hush. . . . . . II. ix. 35. 9
As *every one* seem'd meetest in that cace. . . . . . II. xi. 6. 5
every one of them had Lynces eyes; . . . . . II. xi. 8. 6
every one did bow and arrowes beare. . . . . . II. xi. 8. 7
every one did teare her girlond from her crowne. . . . . . III. iv. 30. 9
every one to ronne the swiftest stryv'd; . . . . . III. v. 37. 7
everie one did aske, did he him see? . . . . . III. vi. 14. 2
everie one her answerd, ... III. vi. 14. 3
every one threw forth reproches rife . . . . . III. vi. 14. 6
every one her likte, and *every one* her lov'd. . . . . . III. ix. 24. 9
every one his kindred and his name. . . . . . III. ix. 32. 5
every one as commune good her handeled. . . . . . III. x. 36. 9
every one gan grow in secret dout . . . . . IV. i. 14. 3
Like as it seemed best to *every one;* . . . . . IV. iv. 14. 8
every one gan shun his dreadfull sight, ... IV. iv. 41. 8
As *every one* had cause of good or ill. . . . . . IV. x. 43. 6
every one gan homeward to resort: . . . . . IV. xii. 18. 2

Every one—*Continued.*
That *every one* doe know their certaine bound, ... V. ii. 36. 2
That *every one* his daunger did eschew: . . . . V. iii. 8. 7
That by his powre oppressed *every one,* . . . . V. x. 30. 3
Why lest *everie one* with helping hands did strive, ... VI. ix. 15. 6
every one, that misseth then her make, ... *Am.* lxx. 11
every one doth seeke and sew to have it, ... *H.B.* 153
every one doth seeke but to deprave it. . . . . *H.B.* 154

Everything. *everie thing* that is begun with reason . . . . . *Hub.* 126
everie thing which they heare spoken ill, ... *Hub.* 715
all within . . . did with store of *every thing* abound, ... I. viii. 35. 3
every thing consumes, and calcineth by art. . . . . III. v. 48. 9
unto *every thing* did aunswere mum: . . . . IV. vii. 44. 5
what is lesse or more In *every thing,* . . . . V. ii. 34. 6
with furious bit Snatching at *every thing* . . . . V. viii. 49. 4
everie thing to which one is inclin'd. . . . . VI. ii. 2. 7
still as *every thing* doth upward tend, ... *H.H.B.* 44

Everyway. *See* **Every, Way.**
His sense to seeke for ease turnes *every way:* . . . . *Gn.* 388
every way did seeke into his life; . . . . II. v. 9. 2
him at first well used *every way;* . . . . II. x. 30. 7
every way, To which he turned . . . . III. i. 21. 6
searched *everie way* through which . . . . III. vi. 12. 6
warily he watcheth *every way,* . . . . III. x. 3. 4
swat, and chauf'd, and proved *every way:* . . . . V. ii. 46. 8
And *every way* did try, but all in vaine; . . . . VI. iv. 7. 2
wandering *every way* To seeke for booty, ... VI. viii. 36. 6

Everywhere. The skie gan *everie where* to overcast, ... *Pet.* iii. 9
Yougthes folke now flocken in *every where,* . . . . *S.C.* May 9
fruictfull flocks, bene *every where* to see: . . . . *S.C.* Jun. 22
Here growes Melampode *every where,* . . . . *S.C.* Jul. 85
this Shepheards flocke Lay *everie where,* . . . . *Gn.* 234
So *every where* they rule, ... *T.M.* 337
of the world admired *ev'rie where,* . . . . *Ti.* 122
everie where through excellent desart. . . . . *Ti.* 343
he shootes his arrowes *every where* . . . . *Col.* 811
Here, there, and *every where,* about her swayd . . . . III. i. 66. 5
Ladies and Lordes she *everywhere* mote heare Complayning, . III. vi. 13. 6
Throughout the wandring forest *every where;* . . . . III. vi. 26. 2
And *every where,* where with my power or skill . . . . . . III. vii. 54. 5
every where he might, and everie while, ... III. x. 9. 1
every where that . . . any meetings were; . . . . III. x. 19. 7
The wood they enter, and search *everie where;* . . . . . . III. xi. 6. 8
Yet here, and there, and *every where,* unwares . . . . . . III. xi. 28. 6
Be bolde, be bolde, and *every where, Be bold;* . . . . III. xi. 54. 3
There they her sought, and *every where* inquired . . . . . . IV. vi. 47. 3
every where Bewrayd it selfe, ... IV. xi. 45. 7
still he him did follow *every where,* . . . . V. viii. 33. 7
whiles he her pursued *every where,* . . . . VI. i. 16. 7
with a veile, that wimpled *every where,* . . . . VII. vii. 5. 8
Seeing my hart through-launced *every where* . . . . *Am.* lvii. 7

Evidence. read he could not *evidence,* nor will, ... *Hub.* 382
He gan t' efforce the *evidence* anew, ... V. ix. 47. 1
foule Infamie and fell Despight Gave *evidence,* . . . . . . VI. vii. 34. 8
Bold Alteration pleades Large *Evidence:* . . . . VII. vii. Arg.

Evident. I made plaine and *evident,* . . . . II. iv. 29. 7

Evil. In which all good and *evill* was enclosed, ... *Ro.* xix. 10
Whose knees are weake through fast and *evill* fare, ... *S.C.* Ja. 44
Evil ensueth of wrong intent. . . . . *S.C.* May 102
In *evill* houre thou hentest in hond . . . . *S.C.* Jul. 37
What the foule *evill* hath thee so bestadde? . . . . *S.C.* Au. 7
As if some *evill* were to her betight? . . . . *S.C.* N. 174
know the purporte of my *evill* plight, ... *Gn.* Ded. 8
disliking of their *evill* And hard estate, ... *Hub.* 46
The *evill* plight that doth me sore constraine, ... *Hub.* 56
th' *evill* will Of all their Parishners . . . . *Hub.* 560
evill hap Unworthy in such wretchednes doth wrap, ... *Hub.* 601
To whom shall I my *evill* case complaine, ... *T.M.* 421
the *Evill* damning evermore to dy: . . . . *Com. Son.* i. 12
evill men, now dead, his deeds upbraid: . . . . *Ti.* 214
As if to me had chanst some *evill* tourne! . . . . *D.* 266
with *evil* deed or leasing vaine Blaspheme . . . . *Col.* 821
if of . . . homebredd *evil* ye desire to heare, ... I. i. 31. 2
he slept soundly void of *evil* thought, ... I. i. 46. 3
'We may not chaunge,' (quoth he,) 'this *evill* plight, ... I. ii. 43. 3
the wayne was very *evill* ledd, ... I. iv. 19. 7
through *evill* guise, A shaking fever raignd continually. . . . I. iv. 20. 7
lewdnes fild him with reprochfull pain Of that foule *evill,* . . I. iv. 26. 7
If old Avengles sonnes so *evill* heare? . . . . I. v. 23. 7
In *evill* houre thy foes thee hither sent . . . . I. vi. 42. 2
saw The *evil* stownd that daungerd her estate, ... I. viii. 12. 2
what *evill* starre On you hath frownd, ... I. viii. 42. 6
Is not enough thy *evill* life forespent? . . . . I. ix. 43. 7
be partakers of their *evill* plight, ... I. x. 10. 7
should not be quenched . . . For feare of *evil* fates, ... I. xii. 37. 9
'Such and such *evil* God on Guyon reare, ... II. i. 61. 5
what cursed *evil* Spright, Or fell Erinnys, ... II. ii. 29. 1
Ne any *evill* meanes she did forbeare, ... II. iv. 5. 8
restraine from her reprochfull blame And *evill* meanes, ... II. iv. 11. 4
So *evill* thing to seeke unto their ayd, ... II. vii. 14. 8
evill is at hand him to offend.' . . . . II. viii. 8. 7
'the *evill* donne Dyes not, ... II. viii. 29. 1
never was she in so *evill* cace, ... II. xi. 16. 3
To loose long gotten honour with one *evill* hond. . . . . . . III. i. 10. 9
As fearing *evill* that poursewd her fast; . . . . III. i. 16. 2
Ne *evil* thing she feard, ne *evill* thing she ment. . . . . . . III. i. 19. 9
'what *evill* plight Hath thee opprest, ... III. ii. 30. 7
Then doth this wicked *evill* thee infest, ... III. ii. 32. 4
The growing *evill,* ere it strength have gott, ... III. ii. 46. 2
a sore *evill,* which this virgin bright Tormenteth . . . . . . III. iii. 16. 4

Evil—*Continued.*
this sad *evill,* which doth her infest, ... III. iii. 18. 5
seemes some cursed witches deed, Or *evill* spright, ... III. iii. 18. 9
ment To her no *evill* thought nor *evill* deed; . . . . III. iv. 50. 3
good, by paragone Of *evill,* . . . . III. ix. 2. 3
he feareth *evill* happen may; . . . . III. x. 3. 5
th' *evill* thinkes by watching to prevent: . . . . III. x. 3. 6
One may his journey bring too soone to *evill* end.' . . . . . III. x. 40. 9
The seedes of *evill* wordes and factious deedes; . . . . IV. i. 25. 5
Would afterwards afresh the sleeping *evill* reare. . . . . . . IV. i. 34. 9
Dissembling his disease and *evill* plight; . . . . IV. i. 38. 3
unwise, and warelesse of the *evill* . . . . IV. ii. 3. 6
That doth ill cause or *evill* end enure; . . . . IV. ii. 29. 8
with his axe him smote in *evill* hower, ... IV. iii. 20. 5
th' *evill* plight, in which her dearest brother Now stood, . . IV. iii. 40. 7
Fro love to hate, a change of *evill* choise: . . . . IV. iii. 45. 6
For *evill* deedes may better then bad words be bore. . . . . IV. iv. 4. 9
litle prays'd his labours *evill* speed, ... IV. v. 22. 4
right feeble through the *evill* rate Of food . . . . IV. viii. 19. 5
The *evill* case in which those Ladies lay; . . . . IV. viii. 20. 2
what *evill* guide Them thether brought, ... IV. viii. 21. 2
all the cares and *evill* which they meet . . . . IV. x. 2. 2
As if some blame of *evill* she did feare, ... IV. x. 50. 4
To damne him selfe by every *evil* name, ... IV. xii. 16. 5
To see an helplesse *evill* double griefe doth lend. . . . . . IV. xii. 21. 9
never wight so *evill* did or thought, ... IV. xii. 30. 8
Thereto he hath a groome of *evill* guize, ... V. ii. 6. 6
Sir Artegall undid the *evill* fashion, ... V. ii. 28. 7
What *evil* hap to Marinell betid, ... V. iii. 10. 6
in the rudenesse of that *evill* plight . . . . V. v. 12. 6
by his modest semblant that no *evill* ment. . . . . V. vi. 19. 9
to her that never *evill* ment in hart. . . . . V. vi. 31. 9
thorough *evill* rest of this last night, ... V. vii. 18. 7
for th' *evill* which he did therein, ... V. ix. 26. 7
he likened was to a welhed Of *evill* words, ... V. ix. 26. 9
what ever *evill* she conceived, ... V. xii. 33. 6
To please the best and th' *evill* to embase; . . . . VI. i. 3. 7
This *evill* manner which ye here maintaine, ... VI. i. 27. 2
The cause of all this *evill,* who was slaine . . . . VI. iii. 17. 2
There left on ground, though in full *evill* plight, ... VI. iii. 26. 2
reed Me then to be full base and *evill* borne, ... VI. iii. 31. 8
feele compassion of his *evill* plight, ... VI. iv. 3. 6
cruell fate Hath joyn'd one *evill,* . . . . VI. iv. 30. 6
The seede of all this *evill* first doth spring, ... VI. vi. 8. 2
the cause, whence *evill* doth arize, ... VI. vi. 14. 3
So shall you soone repaire your present *evill* plight.' . . . . VI. vi. 14. 9
Those *evill* tidings to their Lord to shew: . . . . VI. vi. 24. 3
Maintaine this *evil* use, thy foes thereby to foile. . . . . . VI. vi. 34. 9
'Perdie,' (said he) 'in *evill* houre it fell, ... VI. vii. 15. 1
in *evill* tyde . . . Lay in the lap of death, ... VI. vii. 17. 7
With all the *evill* termes and cruell meane . . . . VI. vii. 39. 5
they themselves were *evill* groomes, they sayd, ... VI. xi. 40. 3
in *evill* hower He from his Jove such message to her brought, VII. vi. 18. 5
the Pouke, nor other *evill* sprights, ... *Epith.* 341

Evil-gotten. To hoord up heapes of *evill gotten* masse, ... III. ix. 4. 2
The spoile of peoples *evil gotten* good, ... V. ii. 27. 7

Evil-matched. That *evill matched* paire they seemd to bee: . III. xii. 18. 6

Evil-ordered. marshalling the *evill-ordered* trayne, ... III. xii. 23. 4

Evil's. good growes of *evils* priefe.' . . . . I. viii. 43. 6

Evils. All these, and many *evils* moe haunt ire, ... I. iv. 35. 6
great beene the *evils* which ye bore . . . . I. xii. 17. 2
Doth not, I weene, so many *evils* meet.' . . . . II. vii. 14. 5
may compassion of their *evilles* move? . . . . II. viii. 1. 3
of their *evils* as they did discourse, ... IV. vii. 20. 1
Cares not what *evils* hap to wretched wight; . . . . IV. xii. 6. 8
Good hart in *evils* doth the *evils* much amend. . . . . . . V. x. 22. 9(*bis*)
In *evils* counsell is the comfort chiefe; . . . . VI. iv. 34. 7
th' *evils* which poore lovers greeve. . . . . *H.L.* 258

Ewe. thilke same unhappye *Ewe* . . . Fell headlong . . . . . . *S.C.* Mar. 49

Ewes. Thy *Ewes,* that wont to have blowen bags, ... *S.C.* F. 81

Ewftes. *See* **Efts.**

Exalt. soone as Titan gan his head *exault,* . . . . II. xi. 9. 4

Examine. gan *examine* him in straighter sort, ... VII. vi. 51. 4

Example. folowing th' *example* of his damme: . . . . *Bel.*[1] vi. 4
warn'd all men by their *example* to refraine. . . . . VII. vi. 29. 9

Examples. Royall *examples* of her mercies rare . . . . V. x. 5. 6
sad *examples* shewed Of her great power, ... VII. vi. 4. 6

Exanimate. stuck with carkases *exanimate* . . . . II. xii. 7. 5

Exceed. asses been not all whose eares *exceed,* . . . . *Col.* 713
to compare Whether in beauties glorie did *exceede:* . . . . . I. ii. 37. 4
his stature did *exceed* The hight of three . . . . I. vii. 8. 8
Both deadly sharp, that sharpest steele *exceeden* farre. . . . I. xi. 11. 9
sharpest steele did far *exceed* The sharpnesse of his . . . clawes: . . . . I. xi. 12. 1
they would strive dew reason to *exceed,* . . . . II. ii. 38. 6
gan *exceed* The measure of her meane . . . . II. vii. 16. 8
Is sacrilege, and doth all sinnes *exceed:* . . . . II. viii. 16. 5
volume, that doth far *excead* My leasure . . . . II. x. 70. 3
Doth course of naturall cause farre *exceed,* . . . . III. iii. 18. 6
Are still emongst them song, that far my rymes *exceed.* . . III. viii. 42. 9
in feminine And filthy lust *exceede* all womankinde, ... III. xi. 4. 2
seemes t' *exceede* the powre of patience, ... III. xi. 14. 2
if that ought doe death *exceed;* . . . . III. xii. 35. 3
he which was the last the first did farre *exceede.* . . . . . . IV. v. 36. 9
Such chaunces oft *exceed* all humaine thought! . . . . VI. iii. 51. 8
Doth she *exceede* the rest of all her race; . . . . VI. x. 26. 6
yet indeede her fairenesse doth *exceede.* . . . . *H.B.* 231
That it doth farre *exceed* all humane thought, ... *H.H.B.* 209

Exceeded. 'Whose forged beauty he did take . . . to have *exceeded* farre: . . . . I. ii. 36. 2

Exceeded—*Continued.*
in excesse *exceeded* her owne might; . . . II. ii. 36. 7
shortly gaynd that losse *exceeded* farre. . . . II. v. 15. 5
far *exceeded* men in their immeasurd mights. . . . II. x. 8. 9
His wonder far *exceeded* reasons reach, . . . II. xi. 40. 1
depth *exceeded* not three cubits hight, . . . II. xii. 62. 6
Exceedeth. my reliefe *exceedeth* living thought;) . . . *D.* 95
Exceeding. yet my heart burnes in *exceeding* paine, . . . *Pet.*[2] v. 12
things *exceeding* reach of common reason; . . . *Van.* i. 4
mount Athos through *exceeding* might Was digged downe, . . . *Gn.* 45
Therewith shee wayled with *exceeding* woe, . . . *T.M.* 295
made *exceeding* mone; . . . *T.M.* 416
To tell my sorrowes that *exceeding* bee. . . . *T.M.* 546
made *exceeding* mone, . . . *T.M.* 598
Of wondrous powre, and of *exceeding* stature, . . . *Ti.* 534
Exceeding all this baser worldes good: . . . *Ti.* 620
every one did make *exceeding* mone, . . . *As.* 205
her selfe, that too *exceeding* shone: . . . I. iv. 8. 9
Exceeding shone, like Phoebus fayrest childe, . . . I. iv. 9. 1
that great Princesse too *exceeding* prowd, . . . I. iv. 15. 8
with so' *exceeding* furie at him strake, . . . I. v. 12. 7
Eternall providence, *exceeding* thought, . . . I. vi. 7. 1
so *exceeding* was the villeins powre, . . . I. vii. 12. 7
exceeding shone, Like Hesperus . . . I. vii. 30. 3
so *exceeding* shone his glistring ray, . . . I. vii. 34. 5
Thereat he rored for *exceeding* paine, . . . I. viii. 17. 1
wondrous faith, *exceeding* earthly race, . . . I. ix. 17. 4
and too *exceding* shyne. . . . I. x. 67. 8
Exceeding rage enflam'd the furious Beast, . . . I. xi. 17. 5
loud he yelled for *exceeding* paine; . . . I. xi. 37. 2
their *exceeding* merth may not be told: . . . I. xii. 40. 3
would bee dazled with *exceeding* light. . . . II. Pr. 5. 5
now *exceeding* griefe him overcame, . . . II. i. 23. 5
in her loosenesse tooke *exceeding* joy: . . . II. ii. 37. 3
two dartes, *exceeding* flit And deadly sharp, . . . II. iv. 38. 7
Exceeding wroth was Guyon at that blow, . . . II. v. 7. 1
shewd of richesse such *exceeding* store, . . . II. vii. 31. 4
As overcome with too *exceeding* might, . . . II. vii. 66. 7
O! th' *exceeding* grace Of highest God . . . II. viii. 1. 5
two foes of so *exceeding* might, . . . II. viii. 34. 4
Nether unseemly short, nor yet *exceeding* long. . . . II. ix. 24. 9
A labor huge, *exceeding* far my might. . . . II. x. 2. 7
exceeding feare Their visages imprest . . . II. xi. 5. 8
with *exceeding* sway Threw at his foe, . . . II. xi. 36. 1
for *exceeding* feare; . . . II. xii. 22. 4
The roiall riches and *exceeding* cost . . . III. i. 32. 4
Exceeding much the state of meane degree, . . . III. i. 33. 7
Exceeding riches and all pretious things, . . . III. iv. 23. 2
Exceeding griefe that wound in him empight, . . . III. v. 20. 8
they both begonne To make *exceeding* mone, . . . III. vii. 19. 8
he gan to make *Exceeding* mone, . . . III. vii. 45. 4
With thought whereof *exceeding* mad he grew, . . . III. viii. 4. 1
that other knight begonne To wex *exceeding* wroth, . . . III. viii. 17. 8
he gan to wex *exceeding* wroth, . . . III. ix. 13. 6
She was astonisht with *exceeding* dreed, . . . III. x. 50. 5
Goodly adorned and *exceeding* faire: . . . III. xii. 14. 5
Exceeding wroth therewith the virgin grew, . . . III. xii. 33. 6
Exceeding wroth thereat was Blandamour, . . . IV. ii. 14. 1
daz'd the eyes of all as with *exceeding* light. . . . IV. v. 10. 9
Thereat *exceeding* wroth was Satyran; . . . IV. v. 24. 1
farre renowmed through *exceeding* fame, . . . IV. x. 5. 5
Witnesse th' *exceeding* fry which there are fed, . . . IV. xii. 2. 4
is but narrow, but *exceeding* long; . . . V. ii. 7. 7
The fourth Ecastor, of *exceeding* might; . . . V. iii. 5. 6
Is so *exceeding* furious and fell As wrong, . . . V. ix. 1. 2
The waies . . . Are so *exceeding* spacious and wyde, . . . VI. Pr. 1. 3
his *exceeding* courtesie, that pearst Her stubborne hart . . . VI. i. 45. 3
And makes *exceeding* mone, when he does thinke . . . VI. iv. 32. 2
for *exceeding* griefe which inly grew . . . VI. iv. 40. 1
Did wexe *exceeding* sorrowfull and sad, . . . VI. v. 3. 3
shewed semblant of *exceeding* mone . . . VI. v. 4. 2
Exceeding all the rest in powre and hight; . . . VI. v. 13. 7
Whereof *exceeding* glad he to him drew, . . . VI. v. 23. 8
Are so *exceeding* venemous and keene, . . . VI. vi. 9. 2
Exceeding much the measure of mans stature, . . . VI. vii. 41. 3
to us all *exceeding* feare did breed, . . . VII. vi. 20. 4
my *exceeding* heat Is not delayd . . . *Am.* xxx. 5
Exceeding sweet, yet voyd of sinfull vice; . . . *Am.* lxxvii. 9
others farre *exceeding* these in light, . . . *H.H.B.* 65
Light, farre *exceeding* that bright blazing sparke . . . *H.H.B.* 162
Exceedingly. A gilden towre, which shone *exceedinglie;* . . . *Van.* viii. 4
Exceedingly they troubled were in thought, . . . *Hub.* 312
the earth did grieve *exceedingly,* . . . *Ti.* 671
Whereat Excesse *exceedingly* was wroth, . . . II. xii. 57. 6
Florimell *exceedingly* did fret, . . . IV. v. 19. 7
He was therewith *exceedingly* dismayd, . . . V. iii. 18. 2
He thereat wext *exceedingly* astound, . . . VI. viii. 27. 7
It did them all *exceedingly* amate, . . . VII. vi. 19. 7
Exceeds. Ne let it seeme that credence this *exceedes;* . . . I. vii. 36. 1
Till it the pitch of highest praise *exceeds:* . . . II. ii. 31. 4
Herein the noblesse of this knight *exceedes,* . . . V. ii. 1. 8
many Princes she in wealth *exceedes,* . . . V. ii. 9. 6
her great triumph, which my skill *exceeds,* . . . *Am.* xxix. 11
Venice . . . farre *exceedes* in policie of right. . . . *Com. Son.* iv. 12
Excel. Which in her sexe doth all *excell.* . . . *S.C.* Ap. 45
Horatii that in vertue did *excell.* . . . *Gn.* 600
strive in vertue others to *excell,* . . . *T.M.* 452
In glorie, or in greatnes to *excell,* . . . *Ti.* 555
T' *excell* the naturall with made delights; . . . *Mui.* 166
She did *excell,* and seem'd of Angels race, . . . *D.* 213

Excel—*Continued.*
Such as all womankynd did far *excell;* . . . *Col.* 190
thy accent will *excell* In Tragick plaints . . . *Col.* 426
if that any else did Jove *excell;* . . . I. iv. 11. 7
Drawne of fayre Pecocks, that *excell* in pride, . . . I. iv. 17. 8
did *excell* All living wightes in might of magicke spell: . . . I. vii. 36. 4
strive your excellent selfe to *excell:* . . . I. xi. 2. 7
Both Silo this, and Jordan, did *excell,* . . . I. xi. 30. 6
who did far *excell* The other two: . . . II. ii. 14. 3
To climbe aloft, and others to *excell:* . . . II. vii. 46. 7
Did th' other far in workmanship *excell;* . . . II. ix. 23. 3
all this other worldes worke doth *excell,* . . . II. ix. 47. 3
those three monstrous stones doe most *excell,* . . . II. x. 11. 5
contending to *excell* The reach of men, . . . II. x. 26. 8
in all godly thewes . . . Did far *excell,* . . . II. x. 59. 7
All other pleasaunt places doth *excell,* . . . III. vi. 29. 7
he in counterfesaunce did *excell,* . . . III. viii. 8. 8
All the brave knightes that doen in armes *excell* . . . III. viii. 46. 7
'Fayrest of faire, that fairenesse doest *excell,* . . . IV. ii. 23. 4
In which their powre all others did *excell;* . . . IV. iii. 39. 3
The prize of her which did in beautie most *excell.* . . . IV. iv. 5. 9
to her that doth the most *excell,* . . . IV. v. 2. 4
it in shape and beautie did *excell* All other Idoles . . . IV. x. 40. 1
endlesse memorie that mote *excell,* . . . IV. xi. 9. 8
did in noble deedes of armes *excell,* . . . IV. xi. 37. 4
she all living creatures did *excell;* . . . IV. xii. 33. 5
to maintaine that she all others did *excell.* . . . V. iii. 4. 9
Approv'd that day that she all others did *excell.* . . . V. iii. 15. 9
Both her and eke all others to *excell:* . . . V. iii. 16. 6
they that most in boldnesse doe *excell* . . . V. ix. 1. 7
doe all worldly riches farre *excell,* . . . VI. Pr. 2. 4
doe adorne your Court where courtesies *excell.* . . . VI. Pr. 7. 9
So farre the meane of shepheards to *excell,* . . . VI. ix. 11. 3
as he that did *excell* In courtesie . . . VI. ix. 18. 3
he, that did in courtesie *excell,* . . . VI. ix. 44. 8
Seem'd all the rest in beauty to *excell,* . . . VI. x. 14. 4
All other lesser lights in light *excell;* . . . VI. x. 26. 2
The least of which this little pleasure should *excell.* . . . VII. vi. 44. 9
her sweet odour did them all *excell.* . . . *Am.* lxiv. 14
(Those trouts and pikes all others doo *excell;*) . . . *Epith.* 59
forme, . . . that would it selfe *excell,* . . . *H.L.* 194
doth so much *excell* All mortall sence, . . . *H.B.* 41
For she . . . Angels eke, in beautie doth *excell,* . . . *H.H.B.* 206
these twaine, that did *excell* The rest, . . . *Proth.* 120
Excelled. *Exceld* at Athens all the learned preace, . . . II. x. 25. 7
They have *exceld* in artes and pollicy, . . . III. ii. 2. 8
in the same she farre *exceld* all other: . . . IV. iii. 40. 5
Chrysaor, that all other swords *excelled,* . . . V. i. 9. 8
we nature see of art *Exceld,* . . . *H.B.* 84
Excellence. He daylie eekes, and brings to *excellence.* . . . *Hub.* 792
Admirers of her glorious *excellence;* . . . *T.M.* 584
When she with her for *excellence* contended, . . . *Mui.* 263
her great *excellence* Lifts me . . . *Col.* 620
added grace unto her *excellence:* . . . I. xii. 24. 4
men, beholding so great *excellence* . . . II. ii. 41. 6
so soone forgot the *excellence* Of his creation, . . . II. xii. 87. 2
through want of words, her *excellence* to marre. . . . III. Pr. 2. 9
Thou have it lastly brought unto her *Excellence.* . . . III. iii. 4. 9
obedience To doe to so divine a beauties *excellence.* . . . IV. vi. 21. 9
Excellencies. Still when her *excellencies* he did vew, . . . III. v. 44. 4
Excellent. hath he skill to make so *excellent,* . . . *S.C.* Ap. 19
everie where through *excellent* desart. . . . *Ti.* 343
With *excellent* device and wondrous slight, . . . *Mui.* 330
Magnificke Lord, whose vertues *excellent,* . . . *Ded. Son.* ii. 1
Th' eternall brood of glorie *excellent:* . . . I. v. 1. 4
That flowre of fayth and beautie *excellent.* . . . I. vi. 15. 5
liquor . . . Of wondrous worth, and vertue *excellent,* . . . I. ix. 19. 4
strive your *excellent* selfe to excell: . . . I. xi. 2. 7
There is no one more faire and *excellent* . . . II. ix. 1. 2
Doth florish in all beautie *excellent;* . . . II. xi. 2. 7
'For so must all things *excellent* begin; . . . III. iii. 22. 1
in chace of beauty *excellent* Shee lefte, . . . III. iv. 45. 5
both encreast her beautie *excellent:* . . . III. v. 55. 8
'Fayre Helene, flowre of beautie *excellent,* . . . III. ix. 35. 1
Whose beautie each of them thought *excellent,* . . . IV. iv. 6. 3
To see the thing, that seem'd so *excellent,* . . . V. iii. 26. 4
Bewrayd the signes of feature *excellent;* . . . V. v. 12. 7
round about her move in order *excellent.* . . . VI. x. 13. 9
never ought was *excellent* assayde Which was not hard . . . *Am.* li. 7
To speake her prayse and glory *excellent,* . . . *Am.* lxxiv. 11
Which he hath made in beauty *excellent,* . . . *H.H.B.* 129
More *excellent,* more glorious, more divine, . . . *H.H.B.* 171
Excelling. prayse *Excelling* all that ever went before. . . . *Ro.* Env. 10
excelling all the crewe In curteous usage . . . *Mui.* 119
A sclender swaine, *excelling* far each other, . . . *As.* 15
Excelling most in glorie and great light: . . . *Col.* 497
Excelling all that ever ye did see. . . . *Col.* 934
A wicked hag, and Envy selfe *excelling* In mischiefe; . . . V. xii. 35. 7
Excelling much the meane of her degree; . . . VI. x. 27. 3
These thus in faire each other farre *excelling,* . . . *H.H.B.* 99
Except. beastes in forest . . . *Except* the Wolves, . . . *S.C.* N. 136
none, *except* a God, or God him guide, May . . . *Mui.* 223
none could reade *except* she did them teach, . . . I. x. 19. 2
Cannot two fairer Cities find this day, *Except* Cleopolis: . . . III. ix. 51. 5
Excess. In riotous *excesse* doth there abound. . . . *Mui.* 168
th' antique world *excesse* and pryde did hate: . . . I. xii. 14. 8
in *excesse* exceeded her owne might; . . . II. ii. 36. 7
Whereat *Excesse* exceedingly was wroth, . . . II. xii. 57. 6
much she feard his mind would grow to some *excesse.* . . . IV. i. 7. 9
forth would breake, and gush in great *excesse,* . . . IV. viii. 24. 5

Extolled—*Continued.*
She left th' unrighteous world, and was to heaven *extold*. . . VII. vii. 37. 9
Extort. *See* **Extorted.**
Through strong expression of his powre *extort*, . . . V. ii. 5. 8
Whether by might *extort*, or else by slight deceaved? . . . V. iii. 30. 9
had bene; But now by force *extort* out of her hand . . . V. x. 25. 3
Extorted. *See* **Extort.**
with *extorted* powre, and borrow'd strength, . . . I. vii. 18. 3
Extortion. Restraining stealth and strong *extortion*, . . . II. x. 39. 5
Extortions. Besides the infinite *extortions*, . . . *Hub.* 1311
Extract. She heard that she was lineally *extract*; . . . III. ix. 38. 7
Extreat. drawne forth from her by divine *extreate*: . . . V. x. 1. 4
Extreme. Tho up he started, stird with shame *extreme*, . . . II. vi. 27. 7
of his puissaunce tryall made *extreeme*: . . . II. viii. 14. 4
shortly brent into *extreme* desyre, . . . III. i. 47. 8
seeing nigh him jeopardy *extreme*, . . . III. viii. 16. 8
For marveill of that accident *extreame*: . . . III. viii. 22. 4
Broke into open fire and rage *extreme*; . . . III. viii. 26. 5
threatned him with force and punishment *extreme*: . . . III. ix. 10. 9
With *extreme* fury he became quite mad, . . . III. x. 54. 5
with rage *extreme*, Like two mad mastiffes, . . . IV. ii. 17. 7
doe dispart the hart with powre *extreme*, . . . IV. ix. 1. 3
Lion-like shall shew his powre *extreame*. . . . V. vii. 23. 8
with such rage *extreme* Fraile men, . . . *H.L.* 117
now it wasted is with woes *extreame*, . . . *H.B.* 25
And pay the price, all were his debt *extreeme*. . . . *H.H.L.* 133
Extremely. so *extremely* did the buffe him quell, . . . I. xi. 24. 7
Extremely joyed in so happy sight, . . . III. viii. 10. 2
'*Extremely* mad the man I surely deeme, . . . III. ix. 6. 7
Extremest. wondrous faith . . . Was firmest fixt in myne *extremest* case. . . . I. ix. 17. 5
Too truely tryde in his *extremest* state. . . . II. x. 31. 3
at length, in his *extreamest* neede, . . . VI. iii. 46. 5
had he not in his *extreamest* need Bene helped . . . VI. iv. 8. 4
So pleasing is in my *extreamest* paine, . . . *Am.* xlii. 2
Extremities. The face of golden Meane: Her sisters, two *Extremities*, . . . II. ii. Arg.
moderate The strong *extremities* of their outrage. . . . II. ii. 38. 4
full bent To prove *extremities* of bloody fight, . . . II. vi. 36. 2
Rather let try *extremities* of chaunce, . . . III. xi. 24. 8
both resolv'd the last *extremities* to prove. . . . IV. ii. 19. 9
rather strove *extremities* to way, . . . V. ii. 49. 3
when ye have shewd all *extremityes*, . . . *Am.* xxxvi. 9
Extremity. fell to ground for great *extreamitie*; . . . *D.* 185
she . . . yieldes her to *extremitie* of time: . . . I. vi. 13. 2
Did easely beleeve her strong *extremitye*. . . . III. i. 53. 9
dismayd At that same last *extremity* . . . III. vii. 25. 2
prickt forth with loves *extremity* . . . III. x. 22. 4
with proofe of last *extremity*, . . . III. xi. 18. 8
since she saw the streight *extremitie*, . . . IV. xii. 28. 1
Now left alone in great *extremity*; . . . VI. vi. 16. 3
Cryde mercie, to abate the *extremitie* of law. . . . VI. vii. 36. 9
Exuls. as *Exuls* out of his court be thrust.' . . . *Col.* 894
Eyas. Ere flitting Time could wag his *eyas* wings . . . *H.H.L.* 24
Eyas-hawk. Like *Eyas hauke* up mounts unto the skies, . . . I. xi. 34. 6
Eye. *See* **Ox-eye.**
in one place all pleasures of the *eye*. . . . *Bel.*[1] x. 6
on this Lawrell fixed was mine *eie* (*eye*[1]), . . . *Pet.* iii. 8
Toward the sea turning my troubled *eye*, . . . *Van.* v. 1
My selfe will have a double *eye*, . . . *S.C.* Mar. 38
Her modest *eye*, Her Majestie, . . . *S.C.* Ap. 70
She rovde at me with glauncing *eye*, . . . *S.C.* Au. 79
Witnesse shee slewe me with her *eye*, . . . *S.C.* Au. 115
I fear me, thou have a squint *eye*: . . . *S.C.* Au. 129
wondren at bright Argus blazing *eye*; . . . *S.C.* O. 32
lofty love doth loath a lowly *eye*. . . . *S.C.* O. 96
by myne *eie* the Crow his clawe dooth wright: . . . *S.C.* D. 136
blinde his gazing *eye*; . . . *Gn.* 100
Thus wildly to wander in the worlds *eye*, . . . *Hub.* 185
other great one in the worldes *eye*, . . . *Hub.* 490
all the braverie that *eye* may see, . . . *Hub.* 608
he vewes, with his black-lidded *eye*, . . . *Hub.* 1228
First comming to the world with weeping *eye*, . . . *T.M.* 159
Ne sheddeth teares from lamentable *eie*; . . . *Ti.* 163
to the other side To cast mine *eye*, . . . *Ti.* 588
takes survey, with curious busie *eye*, . . . *Mui.* 171
To take what ever thing doth please the *eie*? . . . *Mui.* 214
Whose like before mine *eye* had seldome seene, . . . *D.* 114
when life parts vouchsafe to close mine *eye*. . . . *D.* 511
casting up a sdeinfull *eie* at me, . . . *D.* 549
(A fairer star saw never living *eie*,) . . . *As.* 57
since I saw that Angels blessed *eie*, . . . *Col.* 40
from far observ'd, with jealous *eie*, . . . *Col.* 134
A fairer Nymph yet never saw mine *eie*: . . . *Col.* 559
glorie that in simple *eie* Seeme greatest, . . . *Col.* 721
loath each lowly thing with loftie *eie*. . . . *Col.* 938
Then that brave court doth to mine *eie* present, . . . *Ded.Son.* xvii. 11
The *eie* of reason was with rage yblent, . . . I. ii. 5. 7
Her angels face, As the great *eye* of heaven, . . . I. iii. 4. 7
Did never mortall *eye* behold such heavenly grace. . . . I. iii. 4. 9
since mine *eie* your joyous sight did mis, . . . I. iii. 27. 6
Unseemely man to please faire Ladies *eye*; . . . I. iv. 24. 6
Did chace away sweet sleepe from sluggish *eye*, . . . I. iv. 44. 4
Joyous to see his ymage in mine *eye*, . . . I. iv. 45. 6
earely waite him many a gazing *eye*, . . . I. v. 3. 2
not a pin Does care for looke of living creatures *eye*. . . . I. v. 4. 4
his *eye*, His suddein *eye* flaming with wrathfull fyre, . . . I. v. 10. 1, 2
with greedy *eye* He sought all round about, . . . I. v. 15. 1
A ruefull sight as could be seene with *eie*; . . . I. v. 46. 1
to feed his fyrie lustfull *eye*, He snatcht the vele . . . I. vi. 4. 6

Eye—*Continued.*
A Satyre . . . kindling coles of lust in brutish *eye*, . . . I. vi. 22. 7
it would pitty any living *eie*. . . . I. vi. 43. 6
To catch her, newly offred to his *eie*; . . . I. vi. 46. 5
His living like saw never living *eye*, . . . I. vii. 8. 7
Duessa . . . highly honourd in his haughtie *eye*: . . . I. vii. 16. 2
Tragedy . . . these reliques sad present unto mine *eye*. . . . I. vii. 24. 9
Ne might of mortall *eye* be ever seene; . . . I. vii. 33. 2
eye mote not the same endure to vew. . . . I. viii. 19. 5
Which when the Gyaunt spyde with staring *eye*, . . . I. viii. 19. 6
he that high does sit, and all things see With equall *eye*, . . . I. viii. 27. 7
as he fledd his *eye* was backward cast, . . . I. ix. 21. 5
with this unlucky *eye* I late beheld; . . . I. ix. 26. 7
beares an equall *eie*? . . . I. ix. 47. 2
As Eagles *eie* that can behold the Sunne. . . . I. x. 47. 6
The fairest peece that *eie* beholden can; . . . I. x. 59. 3
when his *eie* did her behold, . . . I. xii. 40. 8
With living *eye* more fayre was never seene . . . II. i. 10. 7
Tounge hates to tell the rest that *eye* to see abhord.' . . . II. i. 11. 9
soone as on that knight his *eye* did glaunce, . . . II. i. 31. 4
Pitifull spectacle, as ever *eie* did vew! . . . II. i. 40. 9
with dry drops congealed in her *eye*, . . . II. i. 49. 3
covering with a clod their closed *eye*, . . . II. i. 60. 4
kindling fire at her faire-burning *eye*, . . . II. ii. 7. 6
great or glorious in mortall *eye*, . . . II. ii. 41. 4
To serve at court in view of vaunting *eye*: . . . II. iii. 10. 2
fled attonce, ne ever backe retourned *eye*; . . . II. iii. 19. 9
Unto the bush her *eye* did suddein glaunce, . . . II. iii. 34. 2
Which, mingled all with sweate, did dim his *eye*. . . . II. iv. 37. 5
His frayle *eye* with spoyle of beauty feedes: . . . II. v. 34. 3
as swift as glaunce of *eye*, A litle Gondelay, . . . II. vi. 2. 6
Upon his card and compas firmes his *eye*, . . . II. vii. 1. 6
to feede his *eye* And covetous desire . . . II. vii. 4. 8
doest hide apart From the worldes *eye*, . . . II. vii. 7. 4
It can purvay in twinckling of an *eye*; . . . II. vii. 11. 4
'yet never *eie* did vew, . . . II. vii. 19. 6
So huge a masse, and hide from heavens *eie*? . . . II. vii. 20. 2
shame his ugly face did hide from living *eye*. . . . II. vii. 22. 9
If ever covetous hand, or lustfull *eye*, . . . II. vii. 27. 2
As *eie* of man did never see before, . . . II. vii. 31. 5
'Behold, thou Faeries sonne, with mortall *eye*, . . . II. vii. 38. 1
That living *eye* before did never see. . . . II. vii. 38. 2
sith thou hast found favour in mine *eye*, . . . II. vii. 49. 7
rather fowler seemed to the *eye*; . . . II. vii. 61. 8
Did not once move, nor upward cast his *eye*, . . . II. viii. 50. 6
Unto the grownd she cast her modest *eye*, . . . II. ix. 41. 2
vew of *eye* could scarse him overtake, . . . II. xi. 26. 2
seemd so sweet and pleasaunt to the *eye*, . . . II. xii. 14. 5
It selfe doth offer to his sober *eye*, . . . II. xii. 58. 2
Still as she fledd her *eye* she backward threw, . . . III. i. 16. 1
with scornefull *eye* They sdeigned . . . III. i. 40. 7
there was presented to her *eye* A comely knight, . . . III. ii. 24. 1
'It was not, Britomart, thy wandring *eye* . . . III. iii. 24. 1
That ever living *eye*, I weene, did see. . . . III. v. 8. 3
Saw never living *eie* more heavy sight, . . . III. v. 30. 1
Like never yet did living *eie* detect; . . . III. vii. 22. 7
like a lively sanguine it seemd to the *eye*. . . . III. viii. 6. 9
Assotted had his sence, or dazed was his *eye*. . . . III. viii. 22. 9
spy Upon her with his other blincked *eye*; . . . III. ix. 5. 5
The fairest woman-wight that ever *eie* did see. . . . III. ix. 21. 9
Through gratious regard of her faire *eye*, . . . III. ix. 25. 4
his blinde *eie*, that sided Paridell, . . . III. ix. 27. 6
in his *eye* his meaning wisely redd, . . . III. ix. 28. 6
her wondring *eye* And greedy eares . . . III. ix. 52. 6
he Malbeccoes halfen *eye* did wyle; . . . III. x. 5. 2
His halfen *eye* he wiled wondrous well, . . . III. x. 5. 3
when againe he backeward cast his *eye*, . . . III. x. 14. 4
one *eye* Still ope he keepes . . . III. x. 58. 6
faining to be hidd from envious *eye*; . . . III. xi. 28. 5
with a shaft was shot through either *eye*, . . . III. xi. 48. 8
as she backward cast her busie *eye* . . . III. xi. 50. 1
evermore on Daunger fixt his *eye*, . . . III. xii. 12. 7
still with stedfast *eye* and courage stout . . . III. xii. 37. 5
many of them mov'd to *eye* her sore. . . . IV. i. 9. 6
'the thing that with this *eye* I saw, . . . IV. i. 48. 3
With sting of lust that reasons *eye* did blind, . . . IV. ii. 5. 5
His roving *eie* did on the Lady glaunce . . . IV. iv. 7. 7
Britomart with sharpe avizefull *eye* . . . IV. vi. 26. 1
Yet was he meet, unless mine *eye* did faine, . . . IV. vii. 15. 8
she saw with sodaine glauncing *eye*, . . . IV. vii. 36. 1
Where hardly *eye* mote see bright heavens face . . . IV. vii. 38. 7
His weary *eie* returnd to him againe, . . . IV. viii. 8. 3
her beholding with attentive *eye*, . . . IV. viii. 10. 1
So faire as ever yet saw living *eie*; . . . IV. viii. 49. 5
soone as they with wrathfull *eie* bewraide, . . . IV. ix. 28. 4
Should happen this with living *eye* to see, . . . IV. x. 23. 6
beheld with gazefull *eye*, . . . IV. x. 28. 2
with happy *eye* I spyde . . . IV. x. 48. 6
upon the Goddesse face Mine *eye* was fixt, . . . IV. x. 56. 2
A sorie sight as ever seene with *eye*, . . . V. i. 14. 2
'He, whether mine seem'd fayrer in his *eye*, . . . V. i. 17. 1
Both darting forth faire beames to each mans *eye*, . . . V. iii. 19. 3
It made her . . . stare with ghastly *eye*. . . . V. iv. 41. 9
she star'd A while about her with confused *eye*; . . . V. v. 13. 8
In case she might finde favour in his *eye*, . . . V. v. 55. 2
the least twinckling sleepe to start Into her *eye*, . . . V. vi. 24. 8
Discovered had the light to living *eye*, . . . V. vi. 35. 2
Drawne with the powre of an heart-robbing *eye*, . . . V. viii. 1. 6
ever as she rode her *eye* was backeward bent. . . . V. viii. 4. 9
with their brightnesse daz'd the straunge beholders *eye*. . . . V. ix. 21. 9

Eye—*Continued.*
all that pleasant is to eare or *eye,* . . . . VI. Pr. 1. 5
He also gan uplooke with drery *eye,* . . . . VI. iii. 11. 2
all about did close the compasse of his *eye.* . . . . VI. iv. 24. 9
Yet would not neare approch in daungers *eye,* . . . . . . VI. vii. 3. 2
with the onely twinckle of her *eye* . . . . VI. vii. 31. 7
Which she beheld with lamentable *eye,* . . . . VI. viii. 3. 2
The greatest shame that ever *eye* yet saw, ... VI. viii. 6. 2
the image of her former dread, Yet dwelling in her *eye,* . . VI. viii. 31. 7
On which his hungry *eye* was alwayes bent; . . . . VI. ix. 26. 7
Whose like before his *eye* had never seene; . . . . VI. x. 17. 2
much she hated sight of living *eye.* . . . . VII. vi. 42. 6
There Faunus saw that pleased much his *eye,* . . . . . . VII. vi. 46. 1
That *eye* of wight could not indure to view: . . . . VII. vii. 6. 5
judge thyselfe, by verdit of thine *eye,* . . . . VII. vii. 27. 6
When suddenly, with twincle of her *eye,* . . . . *Am.* xvi. 11
shew Thing so divine to vew of earthly *eye,* . . . . *Am.* xlv. 6
she, beholding me with constant *eye,* . . . . *Am.* liv. 9
hart, that wont on your fayre *eye* To feed his fill, ... *Am.* lxxiii. 7
some glance doth in mine *eie* remayne. . . . . *Am.* lxxxvii. 8
Fresh burning in the image of their *eye,* . . . . *H.L.* 132
Fairer then fairest, in his fayning *eye,* . . . . *H.L.* 216
He may but purchase lyking in her *eye,* . . . . *H.L.* 239
As outward it appeareth to the *eye,* . . . . *H.B.* 226
Seeme durt and drosse in thy pure-sighted *eye,* . . . . . . *H.H.L.* 276
this base world, subject to fleshly *eye,* . . . . *H.H.B.* 23
Looke thou no further, but affixe thine *eye* . . . . *H.H.B.* 50
Ne dare looke up with corruptible *eye* . . . . *H.H.B.* 144
Which they have written in their inward *ey;* . . . . *H.H.B.* 285
Eyebrow. (His black *eye-brow,* whose doomefull dreaded beck VII. vi. 22. 2
Eyebrows. Under his *eiebrowes* looking still askaunce; . . . III. xii. 15. 2
with sterne *eye-browes* stared at him oft, ... VI. viii. 26. 3
Eyed. *See* **Double-eyed, Gray-eyed, Well-eyed.**
Roffy is wise, and as Argus *eyed,*) . . . . *S.C.* S. 203
it good sport had been him to have *eyde:* . . . . *Hub.* 1013
I feard, least land we never should have *eyde:* . . . . *Col.* 267
the aymed marke which he had *eyde:* . . . . II. iv. 7. 5
bid them strike the marke which he had *eyde;* . . . . . . II. xi. 21. 7
from vew of any which them *eyd.* . . . . II. xii. 63. 9
every Nimph full narrowly shee *eide.* . . . . III. vi. 23. 9
ever closely *eide* Sir Satyrane, ... III. ix. 27. 4
Paridell, . . . thus spake, of al well *eide.* . . . . III. ix. 32. 9
missing of the marke which he had *eyde,* . . . . IV. iii. 18. 8
Whom sure he weend, that he some-wher tofore had *eide.* . . IV. iv. 7. 9
Whom when discovered they had throughly *eide,* . . . . . . V. iii. 17. 4
Envie first, as she that first him *eyde,* . . . . V. xii. 38. 7
when the Prince had once him plainely *eyde,* . . . . VI. vi. 28. 5
cariest him to that which he hath *eyde,* . . . . *H.L.* 227
Eye-glance. scornefull *eyeglaunce* at him shot. . . . . II. iv. 37. 9
He lowrd on her with daungerous *eyeglaunce,* . . . . III. xii. 15. 4
Sometimes him blessing with a light *eye-glance,* . . . . . . IV. ii. 9. 4
Eye-glances. The sweet *eye-glaunces,* that like arrowes glide; *Am.* xvii. 9
they see, through amorous *eye-glaunces,* . . . . *H.B.* 239
Eye-glutting. them that covet such *eye-glutting* gaine . . . . II. vii. 9. 8
Eyelid. on each *eyelid* sweetly doe appeare . . . . *Am.* xl. 3
Eyelid's. Whose life did lie in her least *eye-lids* fall; . . . . V. v. 47. 5
Eyelids. his *ey-lids* twinckling rare . . . . *Gn.* 284
Scarse anie left to close his *eylids* neare; . . . . *Ti.* 194
Shall ever lodge upon mine *ey-lids* more; . . . . *D.* 471
none is nigh, thine *eylids* up to close, ... *As.* 137
the sad humor loading their *eyeliddes,* . . . . I. i. 36. 2
Her *eyelids* blew, . . . At last she up gan lift: . . . . I. ii. 45. 4
her dim *eie-lids* she up gan reare, ... II. i. 45. 1
Upon her *eyelids* many Graces sate, ... II. iii. 25. 1
cloudes of deadly night . . . his heavy *eylids* cover'd have, . . II. viii. 24. 8
suffer sleepe to seaze His *eye-lids* sad, ... V. vi. 26. 6
Ne suffred slothfull sleepe her *eyelids* to oppresse. . . . . . V. vi. 34. 9
twixt the twinckling of her *eye-lids* bright . . . . VI. xi. 21. 8
to the ground her *eie-lids* low embaseth, ... *Am.* xiii. 3
within her *eye-lids* they unfold . . . . *H.B.* 255
twixt her *eielids* closely spyde . . . . III. xi. 32. 8
Upon his heavie *eye-lids* chaunst to fall, ... IV. v. 42. 2
heavie sleepe the *eye-lids* did surprise Of Britomart, ... IV. vii. 3. 7
gan from their *eye-lids* chace The drowzie humour . . . . . IV. viii. 34. 3
Eyen. *See* **Eyes.**
Eye-pits. His cheeke-bones raw, and *eie-pits* hollow grew, . . IV. xii. 20. 3
Eye's. one *eies* watch escape: . . . . III. ix. 31. 6
Eyes. Sweetely sliding into the *eyes* of men, ... *Bel.*[1] i. 2
a ghost appeare before mine *eyes* . . . . *Bel.*[1] i. 5
truely doth appeare unto our *eyes,* . . . . *Bel.*[1] xi. 2
Before mine *eyes,* of Orenge colour hew: . . . . *Rev.* ii. 2
From heavens hight into mens heavy *eyes,* . . . . *Bel.*[2] i. 2
Then did a Ghost before mine *eyes* appeare, ... *Bel.*[2] i. 5
mine *eyes* have seene so faire a sight . . . . *Bel.*[2] iv. 13
Casting mine *eyes* farre off, ... *Bel*[2]. xiii. 3
trulie doth unto our *eyes* appeare, ... *Bel.*[2] xv. 2
let mine *eyes* no more see such a sight! . . . . *Pet.*[2] v. 14
All that doth feede our spirits and our *eies,* . . . . *Ro.* xix. 3
Unto my *eyes* strange showes presented were, ... *Van.* i. 10
Whatever thing seems small in common *eyes.* . . . . *Van.* v. 14
from his bloodie *eyes* doth sparkle fire: . . . . *Van.* x. 12
from mine *eyes* the drizling teares descend, ... *S.C.* Ja. 41
bene thine *eyes* attempred to the yeare, ... *S.C.* Ap. 5
marking him with melting *eyes,* . . . . *S.C.* May 207
To blere mine *eyes* doest thinke. . . . . *S.C.* Jul. 36
debarres myne *eyes* from sleepe. . . . . *S.C.* Au. 162
till my last sleepe Doe close mine *eyes:* . . . . *S.C.* Au. 171
his bright *eyes,* glauncing full dreadfullie, ... *Gn.* 262
Throwing his firie *eyes* on everie side, ... *Gn.* 270
fervent *eyes* to his destruction bent. . . . . *Gn.* 296

Eyes—*Continued.*
bloodie *eyes* doo glister firie red; . . . . *Gn.* 350
kindly sleep . . . my feeble *eyes* forgoe, ... *Hub.* 22
mocketh th' *eyes* of all the lookers on, ... *Hub.* 1281
With that he causeth sleep to seize the *eyes,* . . . . *Hub.* 1295
Which when he did with lothfull *eyes* beholde, ... *Hub.* 1314
watrie *eyne* halfe weeping, ... *Hub.* 1362
In th' *eyes* of people they put all their praise, ... *T.M.* 93
powre into my swollen *eyes* A sea of teares . . . . *T.M.* 115
with pleasure The listners *eyes* and eares with melodie; . . *T.M.* 178
from her *eyes* a sea of teares did powre; . . . . *T.M.* 476
As if her *eyes* had beene two springing wells; . . . . *T.M.* 536
tell hir, that my *eyes* can take no reste: . . . . *U.V.* 7
hir beautie was wonte to feede mine *eyes:* . . . . *U.V.* 14
teares from her faire *eyes* forth railing: . . . . *Ti.* 12
since these two *eyes* beheld A mightie Prince, ... *Ti.* 183
Before mine *eies* strange sights presented were, ... *Ti.* 489
Could not from teares my melting *eyes* withholde. . . . . . *Ti.* 532
Cummin good for *eyes,* . . . . *Mui.* 188
His glorious colours, and his glistering *eies.* . . . . *Mui.* 336
with fast fixed *eyes* on her did stare, ... *Mui.* 340
give unto my heavie *eyes* A well of teares, ... *Mui.* 409
Downe to the earth his heavie *eyes* were throwne, ... *D.* 46
Could not abstaine mine *eyes* with teares to steepe; . . . . *D.* 171
closde her *eyes* with carelesse quietnesse; . . . . *D.* 257
those hollow *eyes* and deadly view, ... *D.* 304
My drink the teares which fro mine *eyes* do raine, ... *D.* 376
mine *eyes* are dimd with teares; . . . . *D.* 417
Ne will I rest mine *eyes* for heavinesse. . . . . *D.* 462
mine *eyes* shall never more behold Faire thing . . . . *D.* 491
from himselfe to them withdrew his *eies.* . . . . *As.* 114
Her face, the fairest face that *eye* mote see, ... *As.* 155
Forth darting beames of beautie from her *eyes:* . . . . . . *As.* 190
the teares, that from her *eyes* did flow. . . . . *As.* 192
Inflaming feeble *eyes* that her do view. . . . . *Col.* 519
Lost both his *eyes* . . . . *Col.* 922
Wherewith ye triumph over feeble *eyes,* . . . . *Ded. Son.* xvi. 8
Shed thy faire beames into my feeble *eyne,* . . . . I. Pr. 4. 5
loathly frogs and toades, which *eyes* did lacke, ... I. i. 20. 7
to the ground his *eyes* were lowly bent, ... I. ii. 29. 6
busying his quicke *eies* her face to view, ... I. ii. 26. 6
the seeming simple maid Let fal her *eien,* . . . . I. ii. 27. 6
For danger great, . . . I saw before mine *eyes,* . . . . I. ii. 41. 9
my frayle *eies* these lines with teares do steepe, ... I. iii. 2. 3
From her fayre *eyes* he tooke commandement, ... I. iii. 9. 8
his *eies* be fixt before. . . . . I. iii. 30. 8
on those . . . dazed *eyes* . . . The cloude of death did sit. . . I. iii. 39. 7
While flashing beames do daze his feeble *eyen,* . . . . . . I. iv. 9. 6
With loftie *eyes,* . . . thancked them in her disdainefull wise; I. iv. 14. 1
Her glorious glitterand light doth all mens *eies* amaze. . . . I. iv. 16. 9
fayre Pecocks, . . . full of Argus *eyes* their tayles dispredden I. iv. 17. 9
eke with fatnesse swollen were his *eyne;* . . . . I. iv. 21. 4
whally *eies* (the signe of gelosy,) . . . . I. iv. 24. 3
a kirtle of discolourd say . . . ypaynted full of *eies;* . . . . I. iv. 31. 2
His *eies* did hurle forth sparcles fiery red, ... I. iv. 33. 5
I saw with bitter *eyes* The bold Sansfoy shrinck . . . . . . I. v. 23. 1
The trembling ghosts . . . staring wide With stony *eies;* . . . I. v. 32. 7
of no envious *eyes* he mote be spyde; . . . . I. v. 52. 8
molten starres doe drop like weeping *eyes;* . . . . I. vi. 6. 5
In their rude *eyes* unworthie of so wofull plight. . . . . . . I. vi. 9. 9
mayd Did her content to please their feeble *eyes,* . . . . . I. vi. 19. 2
the sad sight which mine *eies* have red; . . . . I. vi. 36. 8
These *eies* did see that knight both living and eke ded.' . . I. vi. 36. 9
all embrewd in blood his *eyes* did shine as glas. . . . . . . I. vii. 17. 9
when her *eyes* she on the Dwarf had set, ... I. vii. 20. 5
Mine *eyes* no more on vanitie shall feed, ... I. vii. 23. 8
'The forlorne Maiden, whom your *eies* have seene . . . . . . I. vii. 43. 1
It dimmes the dazed *eyen,* . . . . I. viii. 21. 9
Whom these sad *eyes* saw nigh unto deaths dore, ... I. viii. 27. 2
His sad dull *eies,* deepe sunck in hollow pits, ... I. viii. 41. 1
Such as she was their *eies* might her behold, ... I. viii. 46. 6
From living *eies* her open shame to hide, ... I. viii. 50. 4
washed all her place with watry *eyen.* . . . . I. ix. 15. 4
staring wyde With stony *eyes* . . . . I. ix. 24. 3
his hollow *eyne* Lookt deadly dull, ... I. ix. 35. 6
nought but death before his *eies* he saw, ... I. ix. 50. 2
ever up to heven, . . . Her stedfast *eyes* were bent, ... I. x. 14. 9
opened his dull *eyes,* that light mote in them shine. . . . . I. x. 18. 9
All were his earthly *eien* both blunt and bad, ... I. x. 47. 3
dazed were his *eyne* . . . . I. x. 67. 6
His blazing *eyes,* . . . like two bright shining shieldes, . . . I. xi. 14. 1
So flam'd his *eyne* with rage and rancorous yre; . . . . . . I. xi. 14. 7
in his *eyes* did rest Yet sparckling fyre, ... I. xii. 10. 7
Another said, he saw him move his *eyes* indeed. . . . . . . I. xii. 10. 9
With doubtfull *eyes* fast fixed on his guest: . . . . I. xii. 29. 6
feeble *eyes* your glory may behold, ... II. Pr. 5. 3
Her swollen *eyes* were much disfigured, ... II. i. 13. 8
Braies out her latest breath, and up her *eies* doth seele. . . II. i. 38. 9
As from two weeping *eyes,* fresh streames do flow, ... II. ii. 9. 2
Drawing to him the *eies* of all arownd, ... II. ii. 39. 8
As with lamenting *eyes* him selfe did lately vew. . . . . . . II. ii. 45. 9
did beguyle their *eyes* Of kindly sleepe . . . . II. ii. 46. 6
In her faire *eyes* two living lamps did flame, ... II. iii. 23. 1
the hoare lockes that hong before her *eyes,* . . . . II. iv. 12. 3
His burning *eyen,* whom bloody strakes did staine, ... II. iv. 15. 5
With hart then throbbing, and with watry *eyes,* . . . . . . II. iv. 17. 1
My hart, my handes, mine *eies,* and all assayd! . . . . II. iv. 28. 7
through their lids his wanton *eies* do peepe . . . . II. v. 34. 5
Thus when shee had his *eyes* and sences fed . . . . II. vi. 14. 1
Then she with liquors strong his *eies* did steepe, ... II. vi. 18. 3

Eyes—*Continued.*
how can Your cruell *eyes* endure so pitteous sight, ... II. vi. 32. 6
eies were bleard, ... II. vii. 3. 6
with staring *eyes* fixed askaunce, ... II. vii. 7. 5
with wonder all the way Did feed his *eyes*, ... II. vii. 24. 4
Another blis before mine *eyes* I place, ... II. vii. 33. 3
Their staring *eyes* sparckling with fervent fyre . . . . . . II. vii. 37. 6
And his slow *eies* beguiled of their sight, ... II. viii. 9. 2
Staring with hollow *eies*, and stiffe upstanding heares. . . . II. ix. 13. 9
they encombred all mens eares and *eyes*; . . . . II. ix. 51. 3
sharpe staring *eyes*, That mad or foolish seemd: . . . . . . II. ix. 52. 6
every one of them had Lynces *eyes*; . . . . II. xi. 8. 6
each thing by which the *eyes* may fault: . . . . II. xi. 9. 7
th' amarous sweet spoiles to greedy *eyes* revele. . . . . . II. xii. 64. 9
He much rebukt those wandring *eyes* of his, ... II. xii. 69. 2
With her false *eyes* fast fixed in his sight, ... II. xii. 73. 2
through his humid *eyes* did sucke his spright, ... II. xii. 73. 7
bare to ready spoyle Of hungry *eies*, ... II. xii. 78. 2
her faire *eyes*, sweet smyling in delight, ... II. xii. 78. 6
with ambrosiall kisses bathe his *eyes*; . . . . III. i. 36. 4
Her wanton *eyes*, ill signes of womanhed, ... III. i. 41. 7
with crafty glaunce Of her false *eies*, ... III. i. 50. 7
her faire deawy *eies* . . . Shee ofte did bathe, ... III. ii. 34. 6
Late dayes ensample, which these *eyes* beheld: . . . . III. iii. 55. 2
the dim *eies* of my deare Marinell . . . . III. iv. 39. 4
whose faire *eyes*, like lamps of quenched fire, ... III. v. 29. 3
with melting *eies* did vew, ... III. v. 30. 4
his *eies*, His watry *eies* drizling like deawy rayne, ... III. v. 34. 2, 3
From her faire *eyes* and gratious countenaunce. . . . . III. v. 42. 6
adowne out of her christall *eyne* . . . . III. vii. 9. 1
Wiping the teares from her suffused *eyes*, ... III. vii. 10. 3
doth soone withdraw His feeble *eyne*, ... III. vii. 13. 8
Her fyrie *eyes* with furious sparkes did stare, ... III. vii. 39. 8
Instead of *eyes* two burning lampes she set . . . . III. viii. 7. 1
To stirre and roll them like to womens *eyes*: . . . . III. viii. 7. 4
his deceiptfull *eyes* did never lin To looke . . . . III. viii. 24. 8
blubbred face with teares of her faire *eyes*: . . . . III. viii. 32. 3
'These *eyes* did see that they will ever rew T' have seene,' . III. viii. 49. 1
It is not yron bandes, nor hundred *eyes*, ... III. ix. 7. 4
The wicked engine . . . Past through his *eies*, ... III. ix. 29. 4
Two *eies* him needeth, for to watch and wake, ... III. ix. 31. 7
Hellenors both *eyes* did eke beguyle, ... III. x. 5. 4
did eke beguyle, Both *eyes* and hart attonce, ... III. x. 5. 5
teares stood in his *eies*, ... III. x. 25. 9
On which their *eies* and harts were wholly sett, ... III. x. 34. 6
with pale *eyes* fast fixed on the rest, ... III. x. 41. 2
with how many *eyes* High heven beholdes . . . . III. xi. 45. 8
ne could satisfy Her greedy *eyes* . . . . III. xi. 53. 4
ne let sleepe oppresse Her heavy *eyes* . . . . III. xi. 55. 7
He lookt askew with his mistrustfull *eyes*, ... III. xii. 10. 5
His rolling *eies* did never rest in place, ... III. xii. 15. 6
His blindfold *eies* He bad awhile unbinde, ... III. xii. 22. 6
rownd about Shee cast her *eies* . . . . III. xii. 30. 2
With squinted *eyes* contrarie wayes intended, ... IV. i. 27. 2
all mens *eyes* and hearts . . . filled were with rufull tine . . IV. iii. 37. 3
that bad *eyes* might it not prophane: . . . . IV. iv. 15. 3
The *eyes* of all, allur'd with close delight, ... IV. iv. 16. 4
daz'd the *eyes* of all as with exceeding light. . . . . IV. v. 10. 9
With hollow *eyes* and rawbone cheekes forspent, ... IV. v. 34. 4
When gentle sleepe his heavie *eyes* would close; . . . . IV. v. 40. 2
these sory *eies* have seen Seaven women . . . . IV. vii. 13. 4
From her faire *eyes* wiping the deawy wet . . . . IV. vii. 35. 5
water which did well From his moist *eies*, ... IV. viii. 13. 4
from his fearefull *eyes* two fierie beames, ... IV. viii. 39. 1
From powrefull *eyes* close venim doth convay . . . . IV. viii. 39. 8
what he was whose *eyes* did flame with fire; . . . . IV. viii. 46. 8
From his false *eyes* into their harts and parts entire. . . . IV. viii. 48. 9
To see the sight perforce that both her *eyes* were loth. . . IV. ix. 9. 9
evermore his *eyes* about him went, ... IV. x. 12. 7
fond runners *eyes* to daze; . . . . IV. x. 24. 8
stedfast still her *eyes* did fixed rest, ... IV. x. 49. 7
Ne ever durst her *eyes* from ground upreare, ... IV. x. 50. 2
eyes, like twinkling stars in evening cleare, ... IV. x. 50. 7
mourn'd to see her losse before her *eyne*, ... IV. xii. 21. 7
With many bitter teares shed from his blubbred *eyne*. . . . . V. i. 13. 9
with fast fixed *eies* He gazed . . . . V. iii. 18. 6
through her *eyes* like sudden lightning flashed, ... V. v. 30. 3
her *eyes* she streight reprieved: . . . . V. vi. 24. 9
'Ye guilty *eyes*,' (sayd she) 'the which with guyle . . . . . V. vi. 25. 1
from her *eies* did flash out fiery light, ... V. vi. 38. 8
with sweete rest her heavy *eyes* did close, ... V. vii. 12. 3
with hollow *eyes* deepe pent, ... V. ix. 10. 5
To turne her *eyes* from his intent away; . . . . V. ix. 13. 7
Approving dayly to their noble *eyes* . . . . V. x. 5. 5
any yron *eyes* to see it would agrize. . . . . V. x. 28. 9
Lookt up with *eyes* full sad and hart full sore, ... V. xi. 11. 7
With her dull *eyes* did seeme to looke askew, ... V. xii. 29. 2
carry colours faire that feeble *eies* misdeeme. . . . . VI. Pr. 4. 9
Fashion'd to please the *eies* of them that pas, ... VI. Pr. 5. 4
The *eyes* of all which thereon fixed beene, ... VI. Pr. 6. 7
And in the *eyes* of men great liking find, ... VI. ii. 2. 4
enchantment, that through . . . both the *eyes* (*eares) did steale the hart . . . . VI. ii. 3. 4
An hart not carried with too curious *eyes*, ... VI. ii. 16. 8
Tristram, . . . Long fed his greedie *eyes* . . . . VI. ii. 39. 3
With heavie *eyne*, from teares uneath refrayning, ... VI. ii. 41. 7
The Ladie, . . . Gan reare her *eyes* . . . . VI. ii. 42. 8
These *eyes* him saw upon the cold earth sprad, ... VI. ii. 45. 7
far from envious *eyes* that mote him spight; . . . . VI. iii. 20. 7
From his soft *eyes* the teares he wypt away, ... VI. iv. 23. 4

Eyes—*Continued.*
shedding few soft teares from tender *eyne*, ... VI. v. 24. 3
sparkling fire out of his furious *eyne*, ... VI. v. 26. 2
Your *eies*, your eares, your tongue, your talk restraine . . . VI. vi. 7. 8
He bad his *eyes* to be unblindfold both, ... VI. vii. 33. 8
his fiery *eies*, Like two great Beacons, ... VI. vii. 42. 1
Some with their *eyes* the daintest morsels chose; . . . . . . VI. viii. 39. 4
Which when she sees with ghastly griefful *eies*, ... VI. viii. 40. 5
to their sordid *eyes* The goodly threasures of nature appeare: VI. viii. 41. 6
mote not be prophan'd of common *eyes*, ... VI. viii. 43. 2
The glaunce whereof their dimmed *eies* would daze, ... VI. x. 4. 3
even he him selfe his *eyes* envyde, ... VI. x. 11. 7
With which his *eyes* mote have deluded beene. . . . . VI. x. 17. 7
With lustfull *eyes* beheld that lovely guest, ... VI. xi. 3. 7
These marchants fixed *eyes* did so amaze, ... VI. xi. 13. 6
With cloud of death upon her *eyes* displayd; . . . . VI. xi. 21. 5
With drearie drouping *eyne* lookt up like one aghast. . . . VI. xi. 22. 9
up to heaven his *eyes* fast-streming threw: . . . . VI. xi. 28. 6
These *eyes* saw die, and dearely did lament; . . . . VI. xi. 31. 7
Whom whylest she did with watrie *eyne* behold, ... VI. xii. 7. 6
I with these *eyes* did view The litle purple rose . . . . . VI. xii. 18. 4
To see that mortall *eyes* have never seene; . . . . VII. vi. 32. 3
To hide the terror of her uncouth hew From mortall *eyes* . . VII. vii. 6. 3
his garments so did daze their *eyes*. . . . . VII. vii. 7. 9
Shall to your *eyes* appeare incontinent. . . . . VII. vii. 17. 5
with firme *eyes* affixt the ground still viewed. . . . . . . VII. vii. 57. 3
with starry light, Those lamping *eyes* will . . . look, ... *Am.* i. 6
Thretning rash *eies* which gaze on her so wide, ... *Am.* v. 7
That boldned innocence beares in hir *eies*; . . . . *Am.* v. 10
Fayre *eyes!* the myrrour of my mazed hart, ... *Am.* vii. 1
your bright beams, of my weak *eies* admyred, ... *Am.* vii. 11
No *eies* but joyes, in which al powers conspire, ... *Am.* viii. 3
Those powrefull *eies*, which lighten my dark . . . . *Am.* ix. 2
The huge massacres which her *eyes* do make; . . . . *Am.* x. 6
with her hart-thrilling *eies* To make a truce, ... *Am.* xii. 1
In the close covert of her guilefull *eyen*, ... *Am.* xii. 7
I doo complaine, Against your *eies*, ... *Am.* xii. 14
If Saphyres, loe, her *eies* be Saphyres plaine; . . . . *Am.* xv. 7
those fayre *eyes*, my loves immortall light; . . . . *Am.* xvi. 2
She to her love doth lookers *eyes* allure; . . . . *Am.* xxi. 6
her *eyes* she doth inure, ... *Am.* xxi. 9
Such art of *eyes* I never read in bookes! . . . . *Am.* xxi. 14
her fayre *eyes* unwares doe worke in mee, ... *Am.* xxiv. 6
My hungry *eyes*, through greedy covetize . . . . *Am.* xxxv. 1
lyke Narcissus vaine, Whose *eyes* him starv'd: . . . . *Am.* xxxv. 8
Yet are mine *eyes* so filled with the store . . . . *Am.* xxxv. 9
make agreement with her thrilling *eyes*; . . . . *Am.* xxxvi. 6
mens frayle *eyes*, which gaze too bold, ... *Am.* xxxvii. 5
Take heed, . . . myne *eyes*, how ye doe stare . . . . *Am.* xxxvii. 9
mine *eies*, with meek humility, ... *Am.* xliiii. 11
Love-learned letters to her *eyes* to read; . . . . *Am.* xliiii. 12
Her *eyes* looke lovely, and upon them smyle; . . . . *Am.* xlvii. 10
Is it because your *eyes* have powre to kill? . . . . *Am.* xlix. 2
To shew the powre of your imperious *eyes*; . . . . *Am.* xlix. 6
thousand arrowes, which your *eies* have shot: . . . . *Am.* lvii. 8
The beame of light, whom mortal *eyes* admyre; . . . . *Am.* lxi. 10
lovely *eyes*, lyke Pincks but newly spred; . . . . *Am.* lxiv. 8
when myne *eyes* I thereunto direct, ... *Am.* lxxviii. 9
Ceasse then, myne *eyes*, to seeke her selfe to see; . . . . . *Am.* lxxviii. 13
in her *eyes* the fyre of love does sparke. . . . . *Am.* lxxxi. 4
I starve my body, and mine *eyes* doe blynd. . . . . *Am.* lxxxvii. 14
her fayre *eyes*, like stars that dimmed were . . . . *Epith.* 93
Her modest *eyes*, abashed to behold So many gazers . . . . *Epith.* 159
Her goodly *eyes* lyke Saphyres shining bright, ... *Epith.* 171
if ye saw that which no *eyes* can see, ... *Epith.* 185
her sad *eyes*, still fastened on the ground, ... *Epith.* 234
your lovers feeble *eyes* you feed, ... *H.L.* 38
Fraile men, whose *eyes* seek heavenly things to see, ... *H.L.* 118
glancing through the *eyes* with countenance coy . . . . . . *H.L.* 122
Ne can his feeble earthly *eyes* endure . . . . *H.L.* 185
T' illuminate my dim and dulled *eyne*, ... *H.B.* 20
he before his *eyes* had plast A goodly Paterne, ... *H.B.* 31
no man may it see With sinfull *eyes*, ... *H.B.* 39
it can pierce through th' *eyes* unto the hart, ... *H.B.* 72
of loving *eyes* be vewed never? . . . . *H.B.* 189
the object of their *eyes* . . . . *H.B.* 213
lovers *eyes* more sharply sighted bee . . . . *H.B.* 232
See more then any other *eyes* can see, ... *H.B.* 234
to their *eyes* that inmost faire display, ... *H.B.* 237
may it more to mortall *eyes* commend, ... *H.B.* 263
When your faire *eyes* these fearefull lines shal read, ... *H.B.* 283
Lift up to him thy heavie clouded *eyne*, ... *H.H.L.* 222
Blinding the *eyes*, and lumining the spright. . . . . *H.H.L.* 280
thy bright radiant *eyes* shall plainely see . . . . *H.H.L.* 283
show Some litle beames to mortall *eyes* below . . . . *H.H.B.* 12
Then looke, who list thy gazefull *eyes* to feed . . . . . . *H.H.B.* 29
how can we see with feeble *eyne* . . . . *H.H.B.* 123
On that bright Sunne of Glorie fixe thine *eyes*, ... *H.H.B.* 139
sight Of all that looke thereon with *eyes* unsound; . . . . . *H.H.B.* 179
So full their *eyes* are of that glorious sight, ... *H.H.B.* 281
Their wondring *eyes* to fill; . . . . *Proth.* 59

Eyes'. With upstart haire and staring *eyes* dismay, ... III. x. 54. 8
seeing her faire *eyes* so sharpe effect . . . . *H.B.* 244

Eyesight. Ne ever did her *ey-sight* turne arere, ... *Gn.* 468
his *eye sight* him fayled long ygo; . . . . I. viii. 30. 5
Besmeard with smoke that nigh his *eye-sight* blent; . . . . . IV. v. 34. 7

Eye-spotted. Junoes Bird in her *ey-spotted* traine . . . . . . *Mui.* 95

Eye-strings. sleepe his *eie-strings* did untye, ... II. vii. 27. 4

Eyewitness. an *ey-witnes* of each thing to bee. . . . . *Hub.* 1278

Eyne. *See* **Eyes.**

F

Fabii. Here *Fabii* and Decii doo dwell, . . . *Gn.* 599
Fable. The peoples *fable,* and the spoyle of all: . . . *Ro.* vii. 8
Ne after everie tattling *fable* flie; . . . *Hub.* 724
No leasing new, nor Grandams *fable* stale, . . . *Col.* 102
Fabling. And were as faire as *fabling* wits do fayne, . . . *H.H.B.* 216
Face. A grisly forehed and Saturnelike *face.* . . . *Bel.*[1] vii. 4
The name of Mysterie writ in hir *face;* . . . *Rev.* ii. 9
'Where is . . . this whilom honoured *face?* . . . *Bel.* x. 5
Sterne *face,* and front full of Saturnlike awe . . . *Bel.*[2] ix. 4
lift her loftie *face* Against the heaven, . . . *Ro.* xii. 11
fish . . . That makes the sea before his *face* to flye, . . . *Van.* v. 3
stouping Phebus steepes his *face:* . . . *S.C.* Mar. 116
'Tell me, have ye seene her angelick *face,* . . . *S.C.* Ap. 64
Ne durst againe his fyrye *face* out showe: . . . *S.C.* Ap. 78
shee sawe in the younglings *face* . . . *S.C.* May 211
'Jesus blesse that sweete *face* I espye, . . . *S.C.* May 256
Moses . . . sawe hys makers *face,* . . . *S.C.* Jul. 158
His *face,* more cleare then Christall glasse, . . . *S.C.* Jul. 159
Glaunceth from Phoebus *face* forthright, . . . *S.C.* Au. 83
heedy shepheards to discerne their *face;* . . . *S.C.* S. 167
in my *face* deepe furrowes eld hath pight: . . . *S.C.* D. 134
To *face,* to forge, to scoffe, to companie, . . . *Hub.* 506
with a good bold *face,* . . . *Hub.* 645
He will not creepe, nor crouche with fained *face,* . . . *Hub.* 727
that faire *face,* and that Ambrosiall hew, . . . *Hub.* 1267
With fained *face,* and watrie eyne halfe weeping, . . . *Hub.* 1362
Hath mard the *face* of all that seemed fayre. . . . *T.M.* 258
Have mard the *face* of goodly Poesie, . . . *T.M.* 557
his Moother with a Veale hath coovered his *Face?* . . . *Tetrasticon* 3
all that lives on *face* of sinfull earth! . . . *Ti.* 44
none durst vewe the horror of his *face,* . . . *Ti.* 535
her faire *face* to fowle and loathsome hewe, . . . *Mui.* 351
Approaching nigh, his *face* I vewed nere, . . . *D.* 50
soone as day doth shew his deawie *face,* . . . *D.* 484
Did rend his haire, and beat his blubbred *face,* . . . *D.* 551
As if that death he in the *face* had seene, . . . *D.* 565
doubly faire wox both in mynd and *face.* . . . *As.* 18
Her *face,* the fairest *face* that eye mote see, . . . *As.* 155
His palled *face,* impictured with death, . . . *As.* 163
living evermore In the divine resemblaunce of your *face;* . . *Ded. Son.* xv. 10
there before his *face* his Ladie is, . . . I. i. 49. 5
busying his quicke eies her *face* to view, . . . I. ii. 26. 6
raisd . . . a dull blast, that breathing on her *face* . . . I. ii. 38. 6
Her angels *face,* . . . shyned bright, . . . I. iii. 4. 6
never . . . *Face* of fayre Lady she before did vew, . . . I. iii. 11. 8
Wherein her *face* she often vewed fayne, . . . I. iv. 10. 7
That Phoebus chearefull *face* durst never vew, . . . I. v. 20. 2
chaunge in that great mothers *face:* . . . I. v. 24. 7
'In that fayre *face* . . . closely lurke; . . . I. v. 27. 2
her abhorred *face,* so filthy and so fowle. . . . I. v. 30. 9
He snatcht the vele that hong her *face* before: . . . I. vi. 4. 7
Phoebus, . . . His blushing *face* in foggy cloud implyes, . . I. vi. 6. 7
With ruffled rayments, and fayre blubbred *fa e,* . . . I. vi. 9. 3
Flocke all about to see her lovely *face;* . . . I. vi. 18. 4
face all tand with scorching sunny ray, . . . I. vi. 35. 4
'O lightsome day! . . . Henceforth thy hated *face* for ever hyde, . . . I. vii. 23. 4
Phoebus golden *face* it did attaint, . . . I. vii. 34. 6
when her *face* is staynd with magicke arts constraint. . . . I. vii. 34. 9
backward still was turnd his wrincled *face:* . . . I. viii. 31. 4
Both feet and *face* one way are wont to lead. . . . I. viii. 31. 6
Since I the heavens chearefull *face* did vew. . . . I. viii. 38. 8
Such is the *face* of falshood: . . . I. viii. 49. 4
Shee, flying fast from heavens hated *face,* . . . Fled . . . I. viii. 50. 1
From that day forth I lov'd that *face* divyne; . . . I. ix. 15. 5
Ne bring him forth in *face* of dreadfull fight, . . . I. ix. 20. 7
Nor drop of blood in all his *face* appeares, . . . I. ix. 22. 4
lever had I die then see his deadly *face.'* . . . I. ix. 32. 9
His griesie lockes . . . hid his *face,* . . . I. ix. 35. 6
troubled blood through his pale *face* was seene . . . I. ix. 51. 5
Fidelia . . . Like sunny beames threw from her Christall *face* I. x. 12. 7
Whose *face* he made all beastes to feare, . . . I. x. 42. 7
In *face* of judgement he their right would plead, . . . I. x. 43. 4
many bloody battailes fought in *face,* . . . I. x. 65. 3
The scorching flame sore swinged all his *face,* . . . I. xi. 26. 6
steepe His fierie *face* in billowes of the west, . . . I. xi. 31. 2
Out of the sea faire Titans deawy *face,* . . . I. xi. 33. 4
The *face* of earth and wayes of living wight, . . . I. xi. 49. 8
To see the *face* of that victorious man, . . . I. xii. 9. 3
glorious light of her sunshyny *face,* . . . I. xii. 23. 2
In this fayre mirrhour maist behold thy *face,* . . . II. Pr. 4. 7
her faire *face* with teares was fowly blubbered. . . . II. i. 13. 9
scratcht her *face* with ghastly dreriment; . . . II. i. 15. 5
desyre To see faire heavens *face,* . . . II. i. 17. 4
The *face* of golden Meane: Her sisters, two Extremities, . . . II. ii. Arg.
in her *face* faire peace and mercy doth appeare. . . . II. ii. 40. 9
faire Phebe with her silver *face* . . . II. ii. 44. 1
Her *face* so faire as flesh it seemed not, . . . II. iii. 22. 1
How shall frayle pen descrive her heavenly *face,* . . . II. iii. 25. 8
Both feare and hope he in her *face* did finde: . . . II. iii. 32. 5
nether doth thy *face* terrestriall shew, . . . II. iii. 33. 3
eke her *face* ill-favourd, . . . II. iv. 4. 9
bruze with clownish fistes his manly *face;* . . . II. iv. 9. 2
on whom the shining Sunne Did shew his *face,* . . . II. iv. 21. 8
Her proper *face* I not descerned . . . II. iv. 28. 3

Face—*Continued.*
where Titan his *face* never shewes. . . . II. v. 27. 9
His *face* with smoke was tand, . . . II. vii. 3. 6
shame his ugly *face* did hide from living eye. . . . II. vii. 22. 9
Her *face* right wondrous faire did seeme to bee, . . . II. vii. 45. 1
Like Phoebus *face* adornd with sunny rayes, . . . II. viii. 5. 6
In whose dead *face* he redd great magnanimity. . . . II. viii. 23. 9
I joy thy *face* to vew: . . . II. viii. 53. 8
even heven rejoyced her sweete *face* to see. . . . II. ix. 18. 9
her lovely *face* The flashing blood with blushing did inflame, II. ix. 43. 2
blush in privitee, And turnd his *face* away, . . . II. ix. 44. 2
Through his faire daughters *face* and flattring word. . . . II. x. 66. 5
in his flight the villein turn'd his *face* . . . II. xi. 26. 6
shew His fearefull *face* in time of greatest storme; . . . II. xi. 24. 6
heavens chearefull *face* enveloped, . . . II. xii. 34. 7
His deawy *face* out of the sea doth reare; . . . II. xii. 65. 2
Nought but her lovely *face* she for his looking left. . . . II. xii. 67. 9
in his sparkling *face* The secrete signes of kindled lust . . . II. xii. 68. 5
in his well proportiond *face;* . . . II. xii. 79. 7
Whose *face* did seeme as cleare as Christall stone, . . . III. i. 15. 4
To get a snatch when turned is his *face.* . . . III. i. 22. 5
the rosy red Flasht through her *face,* . . . III. ii. 5. 7
His manly *face,* that did his foes agrize, . . . III. ii. 24. 4
Lookt foorth, as Phoebus *face* out of the east . . . III. ii. 24. 6
having vewed in a fountaine shere His *face,* . . . III. ii. 44. 8
His joyous *face* did to the world revele, . . . III. ii. 48. 2
Come, daughter, come; come, spit upon my *face;* . . . III. ii. 50. 7
a foggy mist hath overcast The *face* of heven, . . . III. iv. 13. 2
neither blood in *face* nor life in hart It left, . . . III. v. 48. 6
he is faire and fresh in *face* and guize . . . III. vi. 23. 7
scratcht his *face,* and with his teeth did teare . . . III. vii. 20. 4
a comely personage And lovely *face,* . . . III. vii. 46. 3
Once having turnd, no more returnd his *face,* . . . III. viii. 18. 8
To looke on her faire *face* and marke her snowy skin. . . . III. viii. 24. 9
blubbred *face* with teares of her faire eyes: . . . III. viii. 32. 3
Downe in her lap she hid her *face,* . . . III. viii. 32. 9
On her faire *face* so did he feede his fill, . . . III. ix. 27. 8
saw the wicked fire . . . scorch his Idoles *face,* . . . III. x. 14. 6
her *face* did with a Lawrell shade. . . . III. x. 44. 9
His *face* upon the grownd did groveling ly, . . . III. xi. 8. 1
upon the *face* of living land? . . . III. xi. 10. 4
Her ample shield she threw before her *face,* . . . III. xi. 25. 2
His *face* was rugged, . . . III. xi. 40. 3
his owne *face* was dreadfull, . . . III. xii. 11. 3
Holding a lattis still before his *face,* . . . III. xii. 15. 8
Had Deathes owne ymage figurd in her *face,* . . . III. xii. 19. 6
in *face* And outward shew faire semblance they did beare; IV. i. 17. 5
Her *face* most fowle and filthy was to see, . . . IV. i. 27. 1
some part Thereof did in his frouning *face* appeare: . . . IV. i. 45. 4
'Seest not the Ladie there before thy *face?'* . . . IV. ii. 22. 6
whenso her *face* She list discover, . . . IV. ii. 44. 6
The *face* of his deare Canacee unheale; . . . IV. v. 10. 7
To tell the feature of each goodly *face:* . . . IV. v. 12. 3
Whose *face,* discovered, plainely did expresse . . . IV. v. 13. 3
Full blacke and griesly did his *face* appeare, . . . IV. v. 34. 6
in his *face,* as in a looking glasse, . . . IV. v. 45. 7
He sees her *face;* doth fall in love, . . . IV. vi. Arg.
her angels *face,* unseene afore, . . . IV. vi. 19. 5
Beheld the lovely *face* of Artegall . . . IV. vi. 26. 2
Ne in his *face* or bloud or life appeard; . . . IV. vi. 37. 3
turnd her *face,* and fled away for evermore. . . . IV. vii. 36. 9
Where hardly eye mote see bright heavens *face* . . . IV. vii. 38. 7
in short time his *face* they overgrew, . . . IV. vii. 40. 7
With heary glib deform'd and meiger *face,* . . . IV. viii. 12. 6
soone as day discovered heavens *face* . . . IV. viii. 34. 1
would have maz'd a man his dreadfull *face* to vew: . . . IV. viii. 38. 9
rent his haire and scratcht his *face* for paine. . . . IV. viii. 46. 5
Deceived through great likenesse of their *face:* . . . IV. ix. 10. 7
Doubt, that had a double *face,* . . . IV. x. 12. 3
at first espiall Of his grim *face,* . . . IV. x. 17. 7
turn'd his *face* away, . . . IV. x. 33. 4
her shyning *face* Hath . . . itselfe bewray'd: . . . IV. x. 52. 6
upon the Goddesse *face* Mine eye was fixt, . . . IV. x. 56. 1
soone as he beheld that angels *face* . . . IV. xii. 34. 1
The sunne at length his joyous *face* doth cleare: . . . V. iii. 1. 2
A great increase in her faire blushing *face,* . . . V. iii. 23. 4
all his *face* deform'd with infamie, . . . V. iii. 38. 4
His *face* was covered, and his head was bar'd, . . . V. iv. 22. 5
when as he discovered had her *face,* . . . V. v. 12. 1
dare even deathes most dreadfull *face* behold? . . . V. v. 31. 4
so soone As she her *face* had wypt . . . V. v. 45. 7
she the *face* of her new foe might see: . . . V. vii. 25. 7
he saw the hindmost . . . force him turne his *face;* . . . V. viii. 5. 7
he so crafty was to forge and *face,* . . . V. ix. 5. 4
could deceive one looking in his *face:* . . . V. ix. 5. 7
Yet did appeare rare beautie in her *face,* . . . V. ix. 38. 4
The cursed Ate, brought her *face* to *face,* . . . V. ix. 47. 4
Even foule Adulterie her *face* before, . . . V. ix. 48. 8
of a Mayd she had the outward *face,* . . . V. xi. 23. 7
to the world display His chearefull *face,* . . . V. xii. 11. 4
Thereon distill and deaw her daintie *face,* . . . V. xii. 13. 4
His *face* was ugly and his countenance sterne, . . . V. xii. 15. 6
Her *face* was ugly, and her mouth distort, . . . V. xii. 36. 1
a slender slip, . . . but tall and faire of *face,* . . . VI. ii. 5. 4
Seeing his *face* so lovely sterne and coy, . . . VI. ii. 24. 3

Face—*Continued.*
some Heroicke sead, That in thy *face* appeares VI. ii. 25. 9
Did shut the gate against him in his *face,* VI. iii. 38. 2
And from his *face* the filth that did it ray; VI. iv. 23. 5
This litle babe, of sweete and lovely *face,* VI. iv. 35. 4
face to *face* against him bent: VI. v. 20. 8
her *face* and former parts professe A faire young Mayden, VI. vi. 10. 6
for her so dreadfull *face,* VI. vi. 11. 1
praise the feature of her goodly *face;* VI. vii. 28. 7
when her *face* Like the faire yvory shining they did see, VI. viii. 37. 2
soothly sure she was full fayre of *face,* VI. ix. 9. 1
he his *face,* his head, his brest did beat, VI. xi. 33. 4
she the *face* of earthly things so changed, VII. vi. 5. 1
beautifull of *face* As any of the Goddesses VII. vi. 28. 4
when he looked on her lovely *face,* VII. vi. 31. 1
certes by her *face* or physnomy, VII. vii. 5. 5
Her head and *face* was hid that mote to none appeare. VII. vii. 5. 9
her *face* did like a Lion shew, VII. vii. 6. 4
Bending their force contrary to their *face;* VII. vii. 35. 8
Night had covered her uncomely *face* VII. vii. 44. 4
her *face* and countenance every day We changed see VII. vii. 50. 6
all creatures, looking in her *face,* VII. vii. 57. 4
her faire *face* she reares up to the skie, *Am.* xiii. 2
The glorious pourtraict of that Angels *face,* *Am.* xvii. 1
tempred so the feature of her *face,* *Am.* xxi. 2
seeke each where, where last I sawe her *face,* *Am.* lxxviii. 3
His *face* with bashfull blood did flame, *Epig.* iii. 5
For feare of burning her sunshyny *face,* *Epith.* 119
Ofte peeping in her *face,* *Epith.* 232
whose is that faire *face* that shines so bright? *Epith.* 373
his goodly *face* long hidden was *H.L.* 59
face and feature doth so much excell *H.B.* 41
Light . . . which, shyning in the *face,* *H.B.* 59
shadow yet shynes in your beauteous *face.* *H.B.* 168
Into his *face* most beautifull and fayre, *H.H.L.* 111
Most lively image of thy Fathers *face,* *H.H.L.* 171
glorie present still Before thy *face,* *H.H.L.* 285
doe still behold the glorious *face* Of the Divine *H.H.B.* 80
That are unable else to see his *face,* *H.H.B.* 117
His glorious *face!* which glistereth else so bright, *H.H.B.* 118
Ne dare looke . . . On the dred *face* of that great Deity, *H.H.B.* 145
The fairenesse of her *face* no tongue can tell; *H.H.B.* 204
beautie . . . Sparkled on her from Gods owne glorious *face,* *H.H.B.* 207
How wondrously would he her *face* commend, *H.H.B.* 222
Angels, which her goodly *face* behold *H.H.B.* 232
For in the view of her celestiall *face* *H.H.B.* 242
And letteth them her lovely *face* to see, *H.H.B.* 255
Two gentle Knights of lovely *face* and feature, *Proth.* 169
Faced. *See* **Ill-faced.**
some *faste* Like loathly Toades II. xi. 12. 4
Face's. Doe both expresse the *faces* first impression. *H.B.* 182
Faces. to kisse their christall *faces,* *S.C.* Jun. 30
their faire *faces* with salt humour steep. *T.M.* 112
when painted *faces* . . . Doo fawne on you, *Ti.* 200
When fairer *faces* were bid standen by: I. iv. 24. 8
So many heavenly *faces* were not seene IV. v. 12. 5
'Under one hood to shadow *faces* twaine: V. xi. 56. 7
their *faces* Most foule and filthie were, V. xii. 28. 6
Behold your *faces* as the christall bright, *Epith.* 64
To humble your proud *faces:* *Epith.* 214
Which from their *faces* dart out fierie light; *H.H.B.* 95
Fact. The authour of this *fact* we here behold, I. ix. 37. 7
'He lives,' (quoth he) 'and boasteth of the *fact,* II. i. 12. 4
yonder he,' . . . 'That wrought the shamefull *fact* II. i. 25. 2
her from so infamous *fact* assoyld, III. viii. 32. 7
With zelous envy of Greekes cruell *fact* III. ix. 38. 5
Strongly did Zele her haynous *fact* enforce, V. ix. 43. 1
Faction. mutining to stirre up civill *faction* V. ii. 51. 4
Factions. Thenceforth this Realme was into *factions* rent, II. x. 36. 6
Factious. The seedes of evill wordes and *factious* deedes; IV. i. 25. 5
Facts. His cruel *facts* he often would repent; I. iv. 34. 7
False crimes and *facts,* such as they never ment, IV. viii. 35. 6
Faculty. Ensample of his wondrous *faculty,* II. x. 26. 1
Fade. To shew that all in th' end to nought shall *fade.* *Ro.* xx. 14
the flouret of the field doth *fade,* *S.C.* N. 83
Is turnd to smoake, that doth to nothing *fade;* *Ti.* 123
O that so faire a flower so soone should *fade,* *D.* 237
they be all but vaine, and quickly *fade;* *D.* 395
It first growes red, and then to blew doth *fade,* *As.* 185
He standes amazed how he thence should *fade:* I. v. 15. 5
wave . . . Ne ever would through fervent sommer *fade:* I. vii. 4. 7
all . . . in sight Before that shield did *fade,* and suddeine fall: I. vii. 35. 4
the drouping day-light gan to *fade,* I. xi. 49. 5
In which that manly person late did *fade.* II. v. 35. 5
a lamp, whose life does *fade* away, II. vii. 29. 7
when the life decayes and forme does *fade,* III. vi. 37. 7
fading vitall powres gan to *fade,* III. xii. 21. 7
in short space his wonted chearefull hew Gan *fade,* IV. xii. 20. 2
By all that dying into it doe *fade;* V. ii. 40. 2
fade Like to a flowre that feeles no heate of sunne, VI. x. 44. 5
Ne let theyr famous moniments to *fade?* *Am.* li. 4
All other fayre, lyke flowres, untymely *fade.* *Am.* lxxix. 14
complexions, that shall quickly *fade* And passe away, *H.B.* 67
shall *fade* and fall away To that they were, *H.B.* 95
Of that selfe mould, . . . and to the same againe shall *fade,* *H.H.L.* 199
Faded. How falls it then that this *faded* Oake, *S.C.* F. 169
Is *faded* quite, and into dust ygoe. *S.C.* N. 76
The *faded* flowres her corse embrave. *S.C.* N. 109
The *faded* lockes fall from the loftie oke, *S.C.* N. 125
Fell sodainly and *faded* under ground; *D.* 481

Faded—*Continued.*
Sith that my fairest flower is *faded* quight; *D.* 494
kisse thy lips like *faded* leaves of rose. *As.* 138
The fields with *faded* flowers did seem to mourne, *Col.* 25
he *faded* to a watry flowre: III. ii. 45. 4
His locks, like *faded* leaves fallen to grownd, III. v. 29. 5
Fades. though they bodies seem, yet substaunce from them *fades.* II. ix. 15. 9
see soone after how she *fades* and falls away. II. xii. 74. 9
that faire flowre of beautie *fades* away, III. vi. 38. 8
floures so fresh at morne, and *fades* at evening late? III. ix. 39. 9
Fading. *fading* vitall powres gan to fade, III. xii. 21. 7
flowring pride, so *fading* and so fickle, VII. viii. 1. 8
Faerie. *See* **Faery.**
Faeries. on whom did attend A fayre flocke of *Faeries,* *S.C.* May 32
frendly *Faeries,* met with many Graces, *S.C.* Jun. 25
With many *Fairies* oft were dauncing seene. *Gn.* 179
the *Faeries* and their strange attires; *Hub.* 30
The joyous Nymphes and lightfoote *Faeries* *T.M.* 31
at her parting said, She Queene of *Faeries* hight. I. ix. 14. 9
'O happy Queene of *Faeries!* I. ix. 16. 6
Th' ofspring of Elves and *Faeryes* there he fond, II. ix. 60. 4
Of whom all *Faeryes* spring, II. x. 71. 9
whylome by false *Faries* stolne away, III. iii. 26. 6
(as *Faeries* wont report) IV. v. 3. 6
Nymphes and *Faeries* by the bancks did sit VI. x. 7. 6
Nymphes, or *Faeries,* or enchaunted show, VI. x. 17. 6
Faery. were it *faerie,* feend, or snake, *S.C.* Mar. 76
To the last praises of this *Faery* Queene; *Ded. Son.* ii. 10
Both for your nearnes to that *Faerie* Queene *Ded. Son.* xi. 6
The antique rolles . . . Of *Faerie* knights, I. Pr. 2. 5
chose in *Faery* court, of meere goodwil, I. iii. 28. 5
the stout *Faery* . . . Thought all their glorie vaine I. iv. 15. 6
with that same *Faery* champions page, Bewraying him I. iv. 39. 2
torment The flaming corage of that *Faery* knight, I. v. 1. 6
Soone as the *Faerie* heard his Ladie speake, I. v. 12. 1
she found the *Faery* knight Departed thence; I. v. 45. 3
the *Faery* Queene it brought To Faerie lond, I. vii. 36. 8
streight deliver'd to a *Fary* knight, I. ix. 3. 8
In which that fairest *Faery* Queene doth dwell, I. x. 58. 3
From thence a *Faery* thee unweeting reft, I. x. 65. 6
To *Faery* court thou cam'st to seek for fame, I. x. 66. 8
Twixt that great *faery* Queene and Paynim king, I. xi. 7. 4
Backe to retourne to that great *Faery* Queene, I. xii. 18. 6
Unto his *Faery* Queene backe to retourne; I. xii. 41. 8
happy land of *Faery,* Which I so much doe vaunt, II. Pr. 1. 7
thine owne realmes in lond of *Faery,* II. Pr. 4. 8
this *faery* knight, The good Sir Guyon, II. Pr. 5. 7
'False traytour certes,' (saide the *Faerie* knight) II. i. 17. 6
Sith him in *Faery* court he late avizd; II. i. 31. 6
the *Faery* knight Besought that Damzell II. vi. 36. 7
threaten batteill to the *Faery* knight; II. vii. 42. 4
Whereon the *Faery* Queenes pourtract was writt,) II. viii. 43. 3
'Shee is the mighty Queene of *Faery,* II. ix. 4. 1
the Palmer him forth drew From *Faery* court. II. ix. 9. 8
the *Faery* knight did entertayne Another Damsell II. ix. 40. 1
Did high advaunce the crowne of *Faery:* II. x. 75. 5
'O thou fayre sonne of gentle *Faery,* II. xii. 32. 3
fetch from *Faery* Forreine ensamples III. Pr. 1. 3
The famous Briton Prince and *Faery* knight, III. i. 1. 1
her to *Faery* court safe to convay; III. i. 2. 4
Unto his *Faery* Queene he might present: III. i. 2. 6
then the *Faery* quickly raught His poynant speare, III. i. 5. 3
He wonneth in the land of *Fayeree,* III. iii. 26. 3
Yet is no *Fary* borne, III. iii. 26. 4
As was in all the lond of *Faery,* or else wheare. III. iv. 23. 9
the Prince and *Faery* gent, III. iv. 45. 4
His *Faery* Queene, for whom he did complaine, III. iv. 54. 7
that his *Faery* Queene were such as shee; III. iv. 54. 8
I lately did depart From *Faery* court, III. v. 4. 4
Amphisa, who by race A *Faerie* was, III. vi. 4. 3
To *Faery* court she came; III. vi. 52. 7
she lov'd none, but a *Faery* knight. III. viii. 39. 9
like a *Faerie* knight him selfe he drest, III. viii. 40. 1
now in *Faery* court all men doe tell, III. viii. 46. 2
that same *Faery* knight Uprose, III. x. 1. 5
Did to the *Faery* Queene her way addresse, V. i. 4. 2
Goe thou unto that stranger *Faery* Knight, V. iv. 48. 6
'thou seest yond *Fayry* Knight, V. v. 32. 1
The *Fayrie,* glad to gaine his libertie, V. v. 55. 4
When first to *Faery* court he saw her wend, V. xi. 37. 8
Appointed by that mightie *Faerie* Prince, V. xii. 3. 3
So did the *Faerie* knight himselfe abeare, V. xii. 19. 1
He through occasion called was away To *Faerie* Court, V. xii. 27. 3
still the way did hold To *Faerie* Court; V. xii. 43. 9
In this delightfull land of *Faery,* VI. Pr. 1. 2
Right so in *Faery* court it did redound, VI. i. 1. 7
ne was there Lady found In *Faery* court, VI. i. 3. 2
adviz'd to send me . . . Into the land of *Faerie,* VI. ii. 30. 5
Famous through all the land of *Faerie:* VI. vii. 28. 3
by the *Faery* Queene was on him layd, VI. x. 1. 4
The which the *Faery* Queene had long afore Bequeath'd VI. xii. 12. 4
Not finishing her Queene of *Faery,* *Am.* xxxiii. 3
Fit for the handmayd of the *Faery* Queene. *Am.* lxxx. 14
Faery-land. (That greatest Glorious Queene of *Faery lond*) I. i. 3. 3
through al *Faery lond* his famous worth was blown. I. vi. 29. 9
the Faery Queene it brought To *Faerie lond,* I. vii. 36. 8
doughty knights, whom *Faery land* did raise, I. vii. 46. 3
Hath brought you hither into *Faery land,* I. ix. 6. 4
brought into this *Faery lond,* I. x. 66. 1

Faery-land—*Continued.*
Of *faery lond* yet if he more inquyre, II. Pr. 4. 1
with king Oberon he came to *Faery land.* II. i. 6. 9
All *Faery lond* does peaceably sustene. II. ii. 40. 5
wonnes in *Faerie lond:* II. iii. 18. 4
I labour would to guide you through al *Faery land.'* II. ix. 8. 9
Antiquitee of Faery lond: II. ix. 60. 2
'Fame blazed hath, that here in *Faery lond* III. ii. 8. 1
till that to *Faery lond* They came, III. iii. 62. 1
through all *Faerie lond* his noble fame Now blazed was, III. iv. 21. 3
Whose like in *Faery lond* were seldom seene, III. iv. 51. 2
Two of the prowest Knights in *Faery lond,* IV. ii. 31. 6
by him brought againe to *Faerie land,* V. iii. 2. 3
Him through all *Faery land* he follow'd so, VI. xii. 37. 1
As I have found it registred of old In *Faery Land* VII. vi. 2. 4
so long a race as I have run Through *Faery land,* *Am.* lxxx. 2

Faery's. 'O foolish *faeries* sonne! I. vi. 47. 1
die soone, O *faeries* sonne!' I. ix. 47. 9
taking by the hand that *Faeries* sonne, I. x. 33. 2
never yet was seene of *Faeries* sonne; I. x. 52. 3
Whom all a *Faeries* sonne doen nominate?' I. x. 64. 7
do Chaungelings call, so chaung'd by *Faeries* theft. I. x. 65. 9
'Behold, thou *Faeries* sonne, with mortall eye, II. vii. 38. 1
it fell into that *Fairies* mind III. ii. 4. 4

Fail. It floureth fresh, as it should never *fayle?* *S.C.* N. 86
that thankes so much should *faile* of meed; *Gn.* 353
all that els did come were sure to *faile* *Hub.* 1203
Gan *faile,* and all the rest downe shortlie fell, *Ti.* 558
This sun would *faile* me ere I halfe had ended: *Col.* 579
His forces *faile,* ne can no lenger fight: I. i. 22. 3
when he saw his flatt'ring artes to *fayle,* I. vi. 5. 1
Eftsoones his manly forces gan to *fayle,* I. vii. 6. 4
his fraile thighes . . . Gan *faile;* I. x. 47. 9
day should *faile* me ere I had them all declard. I. xii. 31. 9
through many yeares thy wits thee *faile,* II. iii. 16. 2
If wonted force and fortune doe me not much *fayl.'* II. v. 5. 9
Awaiting passage which him late did *faile;* II. vi. 40. 7
their forces gan to *fayle,* II. ix. 14. 3
His daedale hand would *faile* and greatly faynt, III. Pr. 2. 4
when all other helpes she saw to *faile,* III. vii. 21. 6
when his force gan *faile* his pace gan wex areare. III. vii. 24. 9
Of which he now did very litle *fayle,* III. viii. 31. 7
if all *fayle,* we will by force it win, III. ix. 9. 5
now my teme begins to faint and *fayle,* III. xii. 47. *or.*3
finding that the breath gan him to *fayle,* IV. i. 43. 5
feeling life to *fayle,* it fell, IV. iii. 20. 9
as if their hearts did *faile,* IV. iii. 48. 3
It shall not *fayle* when so ye shall it need.' IV. vi. 8. 8
if I hap to *fayle,* you shall recure my right.' IV. vi. 9. 9
panting breath begin to *fayle,* IV. vi. 16. 2
their hearts began to *faile,* V. ii. 24. 7
how much it doth overflow Or *faile* thereof, V. ii. 34. 9
saw my lands decay And former livelod *fayle,* V. iv. 9. 7
So did deceipt the selfe-deceiver *fayle.* V. ix. 19. 7
if all *fayle,* yet farewell open field; V. x. 24. 5
without *faile* He jointed it, V. xi. 29. 8
Where singled forces *faile,* conjoynd may gaine. VI. v. 14. 7
His hart gan *fayle,* VI. xi. 37. 9
And, if those *fayle,* fall downe and dy *Am.* xiv. 13
words should *faile* me to relate *H.L.* 17
But feele my wits to *faile,* and tongue to fold. *H.H.B.* 7

Failed. when the object of her vertue *failed,* *Ro.* xxi. 9
when lambes *fail'd* the old sheepes lives they reft; *Hub.* 322
their begging now them *failed* quyte, *Hub.* 347
His hope is *faild,* and come to passe his dread, *Ti.* 213
his eye sight him *fayled* long ygo; I. viii. 30. 5
oft his forces *fayld,* II. iv. 14. 5
With such faire sleight him Guyon often *fayld,* II. v. 11. 1
once hath *failed* of her souse full neare, II. xi. 36. 7
never *fayld* At need till now, II. xi. 41. 6
his feeble vaines Him *faild* thereto, II. xi. 48. 4
her wits nigh *fayld,* III. viii. 34. 8
So lively and so like that living sence it *fayld.* III. xi. 46. 9
new occasion *fayld* her more to find, IV. vi. 46. 2
fayled oft through faint and feeble plight: IV. xi. 25. 5
fayld the trust which she in him had plast, IV. xii. 23. 3
had he not bene held, he nought had *fayld* of it. V. iii. 29. 9
though powre *faild,* her courage did accrew; V. v. 7. 4
For what their speares had *fayld* of their pretence: V. viii. 10. 3

Faileth. Full litle *faileth* but thou shalt be dead, *As.* 135
fayleth, trusting on his owne assurance; *Am.* lviii. 10

Failing. Nor *failing* force to former strength restore: *D.* 473
In one thing onely *fayling* of the best, *As.* 11
'At last, when *fayling* breath began to faint, II. ii. 8. 1
Which *fayling,* he gan fiercely her pursew. V. v. 7. 5

Fails. How Phoebe *fayles,* where Venus sittes, *S.C.* D. 84
Fayles of her souse, and passing by doth hurt no more. VI. vii. 9. 9

Fain. *Cf.* **Feign,** *which in Spenser sometimes is not easily distinguished in meaning from* **Fain.**
Faine would arive, but cannot for the storme, *Ro.* xxi. 12
Such an one shepeheards would make full *faine;* *S.C.* F. 67
of such falsers freendship bene *fayne.* *S.C.* May 305
I beyond all these am carried *faine,* *Gn.* 419
Who all that Colin makes do covet *faine.'* *Col.* 99
Full *faine* she lov'd, and was belov'd full *faine* *Col.* 116
this faire couple eke to shroud themselves were *fain.* I. i. 6. 9
her face she often vewed *fayne,* I. iv. 10. 7
They, . . . fawne on her with count'nance *fayne.* I. vi. 12. 9
they her Asse would worship *fayn.* I. vi. 19. 9
The messenger of so unhappie newes Would *faine* have dyde: I. vii. 21. 2

Fain—*Continued.*
Eft looking back would *faine* have runne away; I. ix. 25. 3
That bare-head knight . . . Would *faine* have fled, I. ix. 34. 8
deeds of armes must I at last be *faine* . . . to leave, I. x. 62. 5
to his force to yielden it was *faine;* I. xi. 37. 7
For such as he him thought, or *faine* would bee: II. iii. 5. 6
From that which feeble nature covets *faine:* II. vi. 1. 5
'glad and *faine* Beteeme to you this sword, II. viii. 19. 5
whoso fayre thing doest *faine* to see, II. xii. 74. 2
was she *faine* To call them all in order to her ayde, III. viii. 4. 5
ever *faine* he towards them would goe, III. x. 22. 1
fayrest floure Wouldst gather *faine,* IV. ii. 14. 4
missing it, *faine* from themselves to flie; IV. iv. 47. 5
Whereby the passion grew more fierce and *faine,* IV. vi. 33. 8
greatest Princes court would welcome *fayne;* IV. viii. 27. 2
steadie hand was *faine* his steede to guyde, IV. viii. 37. 7
would them *faine* from battell to surceasse, IV. ix. 32. 8
Gainst all that would it *faine* to force or wrong: IV. x. 7. 5
Full many did affray, that else *faine* enter would. IV. x. 16. 9
they were *fayne* to let him scape away, V. v. 19. 3
As one that would confesse, yet *faine* would it denie. V. v. 31. 9
A thousand feares, that love-sicke fancies *faine* to fynde V. vi. 3. 9
As if him selfe to solace he were *faine:* V. vi. 19. 5
full *fayne* And glad he was the slaughter so to stay; V. xii. 9. 5
Which none durst breake, though many would right *faine* V. xii. 10. 5
To show her thankefull mind and meaning *faine,* VI. i. 46. 4
The noble ympe, of such new service *fayne,* VI. ii. 38. 6
still seeming *faine* When ought he did, VI. iv. 16. 4
To bring him to the place where he would *faine,* VI. iv. 24. 5
being well suffiz'd them rested *faine.* VI. v. 39. 5
Thereof false Turpin was full glad and *faine,* VI. vii. 17. 1
when they to daunce would *faine,* VI. x. 8. 3
thou maist perhaps, if so thou *faine* VII. vi. 34. 4
faine my griefe with chaunges to beguile, *Am.* lxxxvi. 10
Faine would I seeke to ease my bitter smart *H.L.* 5
I *faine* to tell the things that I behold, *H.H.B.* 6

Faind, Faine, -d, -s, Faining. *See* **Feign,** *etc.*

Fained. That much they *faynd* to know who she mote bee; III. ix. 24. 7
fain'd to fly for feare of being thrall; V. i. 22. 8
twixt them *fained* With all their force to worke avengement V. viii. 24. 5
with all good courtesie *Fain'd* her to frolicke, VI. iii. 9. 2

Faining. As *faining* to be hidd from envious eye; III. xi. 28. 5

Fains. *faynes* to weave false tales and leasings bad, V. xii. 36. 8

Faint. Impatient of pleasures *faint* desires, *Ro.* xxiii. 6
So *faynt* they woxe, and feeble in the folde, *S.C.* Ja. 5
through inward sorrowe wexen *faint,* *Ti.* 472
sprights began to *faint,* *D.* 542
Add faith unto your force, and be not *faint;* I. i. 19. 3
of his cruell rage Nigh dead with . . . *faint* astonishment, I. iii. 13. 4
Loth was that other, and did *faint* through feare, I. iii. 34. 5
all that drinke thereof do *faint* and feeble grow. I. vii. 5. 9
so *faint* in every joynt and vayne, I. vii. 11. 7
suddeine horrour to *faint* hartes did show; I. vii. 31. 8
silver Cynthia wexed pale and *faynt,* I. vii. 34. 8
Ere she had ended all she gan to *faint:* I. vii. 52. 1
this her knight was feeble, and too *faint;* I. x. 2. 2
Faynt, wearie, sore, emboyled, grieved, brent, I. xi. 28. 1
his *faint* steedes watred in Ocean deepe, I. xi. 31. 3
faint through losse of blood, I. xi. 50. 3
seeming pale and *faynt,* II. i. 9. 4
when fayling breath began to *faint,* II. ii. 8. 1
all breathlesse, weary, *faint,* Him spying, II. v. 11. 2
He seemed breathlesse, hartlesse, *faint,* and wan; II. vi. 41. 5
a *faint* shadow of uncertein light: II. vii. 29. 6
he began to *faint,* and life decay: II. xi. 48. 6
As *faint* through heat, or dight to pleasant sin; II. xii. 77. 2
His daedale hand would faile and greatly *faynt,* III. Pr. 2. 4
faint through yrkesome wearines, III. vi. 7. 1
to rest her *faint* And wearie limbes awhile. III. vii. 10. 4
her *faint* hart was with the frosen cold Benumbd III. viii. 34. 7
ever his *faint* hart much earned at the sight: III. x. 21. 9
with vaine hope his spirits *faint* supply, III. x. 26. 7
faint Infirmity; Vile Poverty; III. xii. 25. 8
now my teme begins to *faint* and fayle, III. xii. 47. *or.*3
Amoret right fearefull was and *faint* IV. i. 5. 4
Sir Triamond at last full *faint* and feeble stood. IV. iii. 28. 9
He gan to *faint* toward the battels end, IV. iii. 32. 7
friendship, which a *faint* affection breeds IV. iv. 1. 8
turning feare to *faint* devotion, IV. vi. 24. 8
Faint friends when they fall out most cruell fomen bee. IV. ix. 27. 9
faint hearts, at first espiall IV. x. 17. 6
Began to *faint,* and feele their corage cold. IV. x. 18. 5
fayled oft through *faint* and feeble plight: IV. xi. 25. 5
gan her heart to *faint,* and quake, and earne, IV. xii. 24. 4
his *faint* foe no longer could abide His puissance, V. ii. 17. 7
their *faint* harts with senselesse horrour queld, V. iii. 26. 3
feeble spirits, that gan *faint* and reele, V. x. 20. 5
His heart gan *faint,* VI. i. 22. 3
the *faint* sprite he did revoke againe VI. iii. 28. 2
Now gan to *faint,* and further could not pas VI. v. 31. 8
that Squire and Dame So *faint* and feeble were, VI. v. 40. 7
he was *faint* with cold, and weak with eld, VII. vii. 31. 8
Not fyre: for she doth friese with *faint* desire. *Am.* lv. 8
I feare my wits . . . Should *faint,* *H.L.* 17
Ah! gentle Muse! thou art too weake and *faint* *H.H.B.* 230

Fainted. oftentimes he quakt, and *fainted* oftentimes. I. ix. 48. 9
He *fainted,* and was almost dead with feare, III. x. 37. 7
She was dismayd, or *faynted* through affright, V. viii. 45. 7

Faint-hearted. 'Fie, fie, *faint hearted* Knight! I. ix. 52. 6
Like to a weake *faint-hearted* man he fared V. vii. 20. 5

Faint-heart-fools. *faint-heart-fooles,* whom shew of perill hard
Could terrifie . . . . IV. x. 17. 4
Fainting. Tho to a hill his *faynting* flocke he ledde, ... *S.C.* Ja. 11
Fainting at last through long infirmities, ... *Ti.* 656
Ne shall with rest refresh my *fainting* sprights, ... *D.* 472
fainting, each themselves to breathen lett, ... I. vi. 44. 2
freshly bleeding forth her *fainting* spright, ... III. xii. 20. 7
Faintly. *faintly* gan into his worke to enter, ... *Hub.* 1006
fayntly fluttering, scarce his helmet raught, ... III. v. 24. 8
Faintness. cheareful blood in *fayntnes* chill did melt, ... I. vii. 6. 8
his feeble feet for *faintnesse* reeld, ... I. viii. 20. 7
To shew such *faintnesse* and foule cowardize . . . . VI. vi. 35. 2
Fair. I have seene so *faire* a thing as this, ... *Bel.*[1] iv. 13
faire greene Laurel withered up and dide. . . . . *Bel.*[1] vii. 14
Renting hir *faire* visage and golden haire, ... *Bel.*[1] viii. 4
Of this *faire* fire the *faire* dispersed rayes . . . . *Bel.*[1] ix. 9
She seemde with glorie of the scarlet *faire,* . . . . *Rev.* ii. 6
Let me no more see *faire* thing . . . . *Bel.* iv. 12
the *faire* Dodonian tree . . . . *Bel.* v. 1
So *faire* as mote the greatest god delite; . . . . *Pet.* i. 5
The skie . . . did show full bright and *faire:* . . . . *Pet.* ii. 5
so *faire* a Ladie did I spie, ... *Pet.* vi. 1
pillours fronting *faire* the same, ... *Bel.*[2] ii. 3
mine eyes have seene so *faire* a sight . . . . *Bel.*[2] iv. 13
faire greene Lawrell branch did quite decay. . . . . *Bel.*[2] ix. 14
Hard by a rivers side a virgin *faire,* . . . . *Bel.*[2] x. 1
Of this *faire* fire the scattered rayes . . . . *Bel.*[2] xi. 9
no lesse rich than *faire,* . . . . *Bel.*[2] xiv. 6
Much wondred I to see so *faire* a wall: . . . . *Bel.*[2] xiv. 9
The weake foundations of this citie *faire.* . . . . *Bel.*[2] xiv. 14
ye, *faire* Ladie, in whose bounteous brest . . . . *Pet.*[2] vii. 9
which shall never die Through your *faire* verses, ... *Ro.* i. 4
Nylus nurslings their Pyramides *faire;* . . . . *Ro.* ii. 4
Doth plonge himselfe in Tethys bosome *faire;* . . . . *Ro.* xx. 4
mowes The waving lockes of those *faire* yeallow heares, ... *Ro.* xxx. 6
Such as they were (*faire* Ladie!) take in worth, ... *Van.* i. 13
Through his *faire* hide his angrie sting did threaten, ... *Van.* ii. 11
her *faire* lockes fell from her loftie head, ... *Van.* vii. 11
Faire blew the winde into her bosome right; . . . . *Van.* ix. 5
I sawe so *fayre* a sight as shee: . . . . *S.C.* Ja. 52
It was embellisht with blossomes *fayre,* . . . . *S.C.* F. 118
why sytten we soe, . . . Upon so *fayre* a morow? . . . . *S.C.* Mar. 3
So nowe *fayre* Rosalind hath bredde hys smart, ... *S.C.* Ap. 27
Of *fayre* Elisa, Queene of shepheardes all, ... *S.C.* Ap. 34
'Of *fayre* Elisa be your silver song, ... *S.C.* Ap. 46
her angelick face, Like Phoebe *fayre?* . . . . *S.C.* Ap. 65
Shall match with the *fayre* flowre Delice. . . . . *S.C.* Ap. 144
on whom did attend A *fayre* flocke of Faeries, ... *S.C.* May 32
Wherein is enchased many a *fayre* sight . . . . *S.C.* Au. 27
Hey, ho, the *fayre* flocke! . . . . *S.C.* Au. 118
Where is the *fayre* flocke . . . . *S.C.* S. 9
when the Welkin shone *faire,* . . . . *S.C.* S. 187
Whither thou list in *fayre* Elisa rest, ... *S.C.* O. 45
Fayre fieldes and pleasaunt layes there bene; . . . . *S.C.* N. 188
The eare that budded *faire* is burnt . . . . *S.C.* D. 99
Faire Xanthus sprincled with Chimaeras blood, ... *Gn.* 19
fayre Naiades, Go too, ... *Gn.* 26
fayre Aurora, with her rosie heare, ... *Gn.* 68
that *faire* troupe of woodie Goddesses . . . . *Gn.* 182
the high Palme trees, with braunches *faire,* . . . . *Gn.* 190
Through their thin coverings appearing *fayre,* . . . . *Gn.* 286
thy displeasure, O Latona *faire!* . . . . *Gn.* 378
The *faire* Ixione captiv'd from Troy; . . . . *Gn.* 490
Say, my *faire* brother now, ... *Hub.* 93
throgh their owne *faire* handling wisely wroght, ... *Hub.* 554
read (*faire* Sir, of grace) . . . . *Hub.* 604
with *faire* exercise Of knightly feates, ... *Hub.* 737
Supplanted by fine falshood and *faire* guile; . . . . *Hub.* 788
that *faire* face, and that Ambrosiall hew, ... *Hub.* 1267
faire Calliope did lose Her loved Twinnes, ... *T.M.* 13
all that els seemd *faire* and fresh . . . . *T.M.* 39
their *faire* faces with salt humour steep. . . . . *T.M.* 112
the *faire* Scene with rudenes foule disguize. . . . . *T.M.* 192
the dearling of the Summers pryde, *Faire* Philomele, ... *T.M.* 236
those fresh buds, which wont so *faire* to flowre, ... *T.M.* 249
Hath mard the face of all that semed *fayre.* . . . . *T.M.* 258
hath our *fayre* light defaced; . . . . *T.M.* 266
Faire Ladies loves they spot with thoughts impure, ... *T.M.* 333
Faire Cytheree, the Mother of delight, ... *T.M.* 397
The Spirites and Intelligences *fayre,* . . . . *T.M.* 509
teares from her *faire* eyes forth railing: . . . . *Ti.* 12
'To tell the beawtie of my buildings *fayre,* . . . . *Ti.* 85
'High towers, *faire* temples, goodly theaters, ... *Ti.* 92
Wrought with *faire* pillours and fine imageries; . . . . *Ti.* 96
faire flower of chastitie, ... *Ti.* 251
flourish *fayre* In learned artes, ... *Ti.* 269
'So raisde they eke *faire* Ledaes warlick twinnes, ... *Ti.* 386
Placed on high upon an Altare *faire,* . . . . *Ti.* 492
to entertaine His *fayre* Belphoebe, ... *Ti.* 525
The *faire* Andromeda from perill freed: . . . . *Ti.* 649
ye, *faire* Ladie, th' honour of your daies, ... *Ti.* 680
Was none more favourable, nor more *faire,* . . . . *Mui.* 20
Full many a Ladie *faire,* in Court . . . . *Mui.* 105
so silken soft And golden *faire,* . . . . *Mui.* 108
her *faire* damzels, flocking her arownd, ... *Mui.* 116
all, that *faire* or pleasant may be found, ... *Mui.* 167
Faire Marigoldes, and Bees-alluring Thime . . . . *Mui.* 191
morning *faire* may bring fowle evening late, ... *Mui.* 219
The foe of *faire* things, th' author of confusion, ... *Mui.* 244
In this *faire* plot dispacing too and fro, ... *Mui.* 250

Fair—*Continued.*
a *faire* border wrought of sundrie flowres, ... *Mui.* 298
her *faire* face to fowle and loathsome hewe, ... *Mui.* 351
had lost their beautie *faire.* . . . . *D.* 28
a *faire* young Lionesse, White as the native Rose . . . . *D.* 107
afterwards I handled her so *fayre,* . . . . *D.* 120
why did they then create The world so *fayre,* . . . . *D.* 205
She *faire,* shee pure, most *faire,* most pure shee was, ... *D.* 208
(since *fayre* Astraea left The sinfull world) . . . . *D.* 218
O that so *faire* a flower so soone should fade, ... *D.* 237
her braunch *faire* blossomes foorth did bring, ... *D.* 241
To thinke to ground how that *faire* blossome fell. . . . . *D.* 252
faire Eurydice, her daughter deere, ... *D.* 464
my *fair* Starre (that shinde on me so bright) . . . . *D.* 480
shall never more behold *Faire* thing on earth, ... *D.* 492
faire Damsels! Shepheards dere delights, ... *D.* 526
doubly *faire* wox both in mynd and face. . . . . *As.* 18
His sports were *faire,* his joyance innocent, ... *As.* 25
Stella the *faire,* the fairest star in skie, ... *As.* 55
As *faire* as Venus or the fairest *faire,* . . . . *As.* 56
ye *fayre* Mayds, the matches of his yeares, ... *As.* 129
her *faire* brest, the threasury of joy, ... *As.* 161
surges hie, On which *faire* Cynthia her heards doth feed: . . . . *Col.* 241
To wash *faire* Cynthiaes sheep, when they be shorne, ... *Col.* 258
Faire goodly fields, ... *Col.* 278
There fruitfull corne, *faire* trees, fresh herbage is, ... *Col.* 298
like *faire* Phebes garlond shining new, ... *Col.* 342
In faithfull service of *faire* Cynthia: . . . . *Col.* 381
Faire Marian, the Muses onely darling: . . . . *Col.* 505
Faire Galathea with bright shining beames, ... *Col.* 518
Ne lesse praise-worthie *faire* Neaera is, ... *Col.* 524
Phyllis, the *faire,* is eldest of the three: . . . . *Col.* 541
Faire spreading forth her leaves with fresh delight, ... *Col.* 545
Masked with *faire* dissembling curtesie, ... *Col.* 700
Faire Rosalind of divers fowly blamed . . . . *Col.* 908
who can tell what cause had that *faire* Mayd . . . . *Col.* 911
And, in so *faire* a land as may be redd, ... *Ded. Son.* v. 5
There, in deede, dwel *faire* Graces many one, ... *Ded. Son.* v. 9
Let thy *faire* Cinthias praises be thus rudely showne. . . . . *Ded.Son.*viii. 14
The flowre of chevalry, now bloosming *faire,* . . . . *Ded. Son.* x. 2
Forgive it me, *faire* Dames, sith lesse ye have not lefte. . . . . *Ded.Son.* xvii.14
dreaded impe of highest Jove, *Faire* Venus sonne, ... I. Pr. 3. 2
Shed thy *faire* beames into my feeble eyne, ... I. Pr. 4. 5
Full jolly knight he seemd, and *faire* did sitt, ... I. i. 1. 8
A lovely Ladie rode him *faire* beside, ... I. i. 4. 1
this *faire* couple eke to shroud themselves were fain. . . . . I. i. 6. 9
Faire harbour that them seems, ... I. i. 7. 9
'*Faire* knight, borne under happie starre, ... I. i. 27. 3
He *faire* the knight saluted . . . Who *faire* him quited, ... I. i. 30. 1, 2
With *faire* discourse the evening so they pas; . . . . I. i. 35. 5
The one *faire* fram'd of burnisht Yvory, ... I. i. 40. 2
of beautie soveraigne Queene, *Fayre* Venus, ... I. i. 48. 2
Into whose stead *faire* falshood steps, ... I. ii. Arg.
Eftsoones he tooke that miscreated *faire,* . . . . I. ii. 3. 1
At last *faire* Hesperus . . . Had spent his lampe, ... I. ii. 6. 6
rosy fingred Morning *faire,* . . . Had spred her purple robe . . . . I. ii. 7. 1
Hee had a *faire* companion of his way, ... I. ii. 13. 1
With *faire* disport, . . . She intertainde her lover . . . . I. ii. 14. 1
Was never Prince so faithfull and so *faire,* . . . . I. ii. 23. 4
'*faire* lady, hart of flint would rew The undeserved woes . . . . I. ii. 26. 8
two goodly trees, that *faire* did spred . . . . I. ii. 28. 3
From fiery wheeles of his *faire* chariot Hurled his beame . . . . I. ii. 29. 4
Faire seemely pleasaunce each to other makes, ... I. ii. 30. 1
That had a like *faire* Lady by his syde; . . . . I. ii. 35. 8
Lyke a *faire* Lady, but did fowle Duessa hyde. . . . . I. ii. 35. 9
'So doubly lov'd of ladies, unlike *faire,* . . . . I. ii. 37. 1
Fraelissa was as *faire* as *faire* mote bee, ... I. ii. 37. 8
ever false Duessa seemde as *faire* as shee. . . . . I. ii. 37. 9
Then was she *fayre* alone, when none was *faire* in place. . . . . I. ii. 38. 9
she . . . *faire* as ever living wight was *fayre,* . . . . I. iii. 2. 6
From her *fayre* head her fillet she undight, ... I. iii. 4. 5
From her *fayre* eyes he tooke commandement, ... I. iii. 9. 8
never . . . Face of *fayre* Lady she before did vew, ... I. iii. 11. 8
Faire Una framed words and count'naunce fitt; . . . . I. iii. 14. 7
he forward gan advaunce His *fair* enchaunted steed, ... I. iii. 25. 9
whilest him fortune favourd, *fayre* did thrive In bloudy field; I. iii. 37. 8
after that he had *faire* Una lorne, ... I. iv. 2. 1
galleries . . . Full of *faire* windowes and delightful bowres: I. iv. 4. 8
so *faire* a mould Did on so weake foundation ever sitt: . . . . I. iv. 5. 3
Which with their presence *fayre* the place much beautifide. . . . . I. iv. 7. 9
she was wondrous *faire,* as any living wight. . . . . I. iv. 10. 9
false Duessa, seeming Lady *fayre,* . . . . I. iv. 13. 2
each one himselfe did payne . . . *faire* courtesie to shew, ... I. iv. 15. 4
As *faire* Aurora . . . the dawning day doth call. . . . . I. iv. 16. 4
Drawne of *fayre* Pecocks, that excell in pride, ... I. iv. 17. 8
Unseemely man to please *faire* Ladies eye; . . . . I. iv. 24. 6
In a greene gowne he clothed was full *faire,* . . . . I. iv. 25. 1
Such one was Avarice, the fourth of this *faire* band. . . . . I. iv. 29. 9
Emongst the rest rode that false Lady *faire,* . . . . I. iv. 37. 4
the *faire* Fidessa, loe! Is there possessed of the traytour vile; I. iv. 42. 2
since *faire* Sunne hath sperst that lowring clowd, ... I. iv. 48. 1
'*Faire* Dame, be nought dismaid For sorrowes past; . . . . I. iv. 49. 1
faire Fidessa, . . . Returne from whence ye came, ... I. iv. 51. 1
the golden Orientall gate . . . gan to open *fayre;* . . . . I. v. 2. 2
Night . . . can the children of *fayre* light deface.' . . . . I. v. 24. 5
'In that *fayre* face . . . Did closely lurke; . . . . I. v. 27. 2
Fayre Sthenoboea, that her selfe did choke . . . . I. v. 50. 5
From lawlesse lust . . . *Fayre* Una is releast: . . . . I. vi. Arg.
a ship, that flyes *fayre* under sayle, ... I. vi. 1. 1
speed The *fayre* Duess' had forst him leave behind; . . . . I. vi. 2. 2

Fair—*Continued.*

With ruffled rayments, and *fayre* blubbred face, . . . I. vi. 9. 3
His owne *fayre* Dryope now he thinkes not *faire,* . . . I. vi. 15. 8
bethinkes not what To thinke of wight so *fayre,* . . . I. vi. 16. 4
How *fayre* he was, and yet not *fayre* to this; . . . I. vi. 17. 4
faire Hamadryades, Her to behold do thither runne . . . I. vi. 18. 1
henceforth nothing *faire* but her on earth they find. . . . I. vi. 18. 9
Fayre Thyamis, the daughter of Labryde; . . . I. vi. 21. 4
Yet evermore it was his maner *faire,* . . . I. vi. 30. 1
that earst would have supprest *Faire* Una; . . . I. vi. 40. 8
Miscreaunt, That hast . . . *Faire* knighthood fowly shamed, . . . I. vi. 41. 3
deceipt doth maske in visour *faire,* . . . I. vii. 1. 3
With fowle words tempring *faire,* . . . I. vii. 3. 9
Phoebe *fayre* . . . was following the chace, . . . I. vii. 5. 1
The wanton loves of false Fidessa *fayre,* . . . I. vii. 26. 3
A goodly knight, *faire* marching by the way, . . . I. vii. 29. 2
could menage *faire* His stubborne steed . . . I. vii. 37. 5
Faire feeling words he wisely gan display, . . . I. vii. 38. 6
'*Faire* Sir, I hope good hap hath brought You . . . I. vii. 42. 5
'Yt was my chaunce (my chaunce was *faire* and good) . . . I. vii. 47. 1
'Well hoped I, and *faire* beginnings had, . . . I. vii. 49. 1
he her comforted, and *faire* bespake: . . . I. vii. 52. 2
Faire virgin, to redeeme her deare, . . . I. viii. Arg.
Did *fayre* avoide the violence him nere: . . . I. viii. 7. 8
'*Fayre* braunch of noblesse, . . . I. viii. 26. 7
the heavens, and your *faire* handeling, Have made you master I. viii. 28. 1
'*Faire* Lady,' then said that victorious knight, . . . I. viii. 44. 1
that *faire* crew of knights, and Una *faire,* . . . I. viii. 50. 6
Una *faire* besought That straunger knight his name . . . tell; I. ix. 2. 6
'*Faire* virgin,' (said the Prince,) . . . I. ix. 3. 1
pillow was my helmett *fayre* displayd; . . . I. ix. 13. 4
So *fayre* a creature yet saw never sunny day. . . . I. ix. 13. 9
In fowle reproch of knighthoodes *fayre* degree, . . . I. ix. 22. 6
With a *fayre* knight to keepen companee, . . . I. ix. 27. 2
Who first us greets, and after *fayre* areedes . . . I. ix. 28. 6
Her faithfull knight *faire* Una brings . . . I. x. Arg.
faire Charissa to a lovely fere Was lincked, . . . I. x. 4. 8
Where them does meete a francklin *faire* and free, . . . I. x. 6. 4
He them with speaches meet Does *faire* entreat; . . . I. x. 7. 7
Who *faire* them quites, as him beseemed best, . . . I. x. 15. 8
Fayre Una gan Fidelia *fayre* request, . . . I. x. 18. 3
fayre Una brought this unacquainted guest. . . . I. x. 29. 9
Adornd with gemmes and owches wondrous *fayre,* . . . I. x. 31. 6
The knight and Una entring *fayre* her greet, . . . I. x. 32. 1
'*Faire* Knight,' (quoth he) 'Hierusalem that is, . . . I. x. 57. 1
faire ymp, sprong out from English race, . . . I. x. 60. 1
High time now gan it wex for Una *fayre* . . . I. xi. 1. 1
Fayre ympe of Phoebus and his aged bryde, . . . I. xi. 5. 7
Fayre Goddesse, lay that furious fitt asyde, . . . I. xi. 7. 1
(as *fayre* it them befell) . . . I. xi. 29. 1
Out of the sea *faire* Titans deawy face, . . . I. xi. 33. 4
There grew a goodly tree him *faire* beside, . . . I. xi. 46. 1
Another like *faire* tree eke grew thereby, . . . I. xi. 47. 6
fayre Aurora from the deawy bed Of aged Tithone . . . I. xi. 51. 2
Fayre Una to the Redcrosse Knight Betrouthed is . . . I. xii. Arg.
this *fayre* virgin wearie of her way . . . I. xii. 1. 6
they came where that *faire* virgin stood: . . . I. xii. 7. 6
fayre Diana in fresh sommers day Beholdes her nymphes . . . I. xii. 7. 7
Him . . . *fayre* does entertayne . . . I. xii. 12. 5
forth he called that his daughter *fayre,* . . . I. xii. 21. 1
So *faire* and fresh that Lady shewd herselfe in sight. . . . I. xii. 21. 9
So *faire* and fresh, as freshest flowre in May; . . . I. xii. 22. 1
Oft had he seene her *faire,* but never so *faire* dight. . . . I. xii. 23. 9
most mighty king of Eden *fayre,* . . . I. xii. 26. 1
In this *fayre* mirrhour maist behold thy face, . . . II. Pr. 4. 7
Fayre marching underneath a shady hill, . . . II. i. 5. 7
with *faire* countenance and flattring style . . . II. i. 8. 5
'*Fayre* sonne of Mars, that seeke with warlike spoyle, . . . II. i. 8. 7
To spoyle her dainty corps, so *faire* and sheene . . . II. i. 10. 5
With living eye more *fayre* was never seene . . . II. i. 10. 7
her *faire* face with teares was fowly blubbered. . . . II. i. 13. 9
'*Fayre* Lady, through fowle sorrow ill bedight, . . . II. i. 14. 2
desyre To see *faire* heavens face, . . . II. i. 17. 4
fayre Lady, comfort to you make, . . . II. i. 18. 1
On that *fayre* ymage of that heavenly Mayd, . . . II. i. 28. 7
That decks and armes your shield with *faire* defence: . . . II. i. 28. 8
'*Fayre* sonne, God give you happy chaunce, . . . II. i. 31. 7
faire Sir, whose pageant next ensewes, . . . II. i. 33. 6
In this *faire* wize they traveild long yfere, . . . II. i. 35. 1
Fitt to inflame *faire* Lady with loves rage, . . . II. i. 41. 8
did the floodgate stop With his *faire* garment; . . . II. i. 43. 3
he hoped *faire* To call backe life . . . II. i. 43. 6
Fayre Sir, if ever there ye travell, . . . II. i. 51. 7
'Now had *fayre* Cynthia . . . Full measured . . . II. i. 53. 1
through wise handling and *faire* governaunce, . . . II. i. 54. 6
Which plonged had *faire* Lady in so wretched state. . . . II. i. 56. 9
thus *fayre* bespake; . . . II. ii. 5. 2
filles with flowres *fayre* Floraes painted lap: . . . II. ii. 6. 5
Fayre marching forth in honorable wize, . . . II. ii. 14. 8
faire Una late fowle outraged, . . . II. ii. 18. 2
faire her self doth save. . . . II. ii. 24. 9
The *faire* Medina, with her tresses torne . . . II. ii. 27. 2
to her just conditions of *faire* peace to heare. . . . II. ii. 27. 9
were not better *fayre* it to accord . . . II. ii. 30. 2
did abase their lofty crests To her *faire* presence . . . II. ii. 32. 5
those two froward sisters, their *faire* loves, . . . II. ii. 34. 1
Unworthy of *faire* Ladies comely governaunce. . . . II. ii. 35. 9
Betwixt them both the *faire* Medina sate . . . II. ii. 38. 1
in her face *faire* peace and mercy doth appeare. . . . II. ii. 40. 9
faire Phebe with her silver face . . . II. ii. 44. 1

Fair—*Continued.*

'Tell on, *fayre* Sir, . . . that dolefull tale, . . . II. ii. 45. 1
Braggadocchio, . . . is of *fayre* Belphoebe fowle forlorne. . . II. iii. Arg.
the morrow *fayre* with purple beames . . . II. iii. 1. 1
Through fortune of his first adventure *fayre,* . . . II. iii. 7. 2
So happy peace they made and *faire* accord. . . . II. iii. 9. 1
seeing one, that shone in armour *fayre,* . . . II. iii. 11. 3
Her face so *faire* as flesh it seemed not, . . . II. iii. 22. 1
In her *faire* eyes two living lamps did flame, . . . II. iii. 23. 1
So *faire,* and thousand thousand times more *faire,* . . . II. iii. 26. 1
full *fayre* aumayld: . . . II. iii. 27. 5
Like two *faire* marble pillours they were seene, . . . II. iii. 28. 1
fayre defence and goodly menaging . . . II. iv. 8. 3
'*Fayre* Sir' (quoth he) 'what man can shun the hap, . . . II. iv. 17. 2
To love a Lady *fayre* of great degree, . . . II. iv. 19. 2
faire Claribell with all her art, . . . II. iv. 26. 5
a brasen shield On which was drawen *faire,* . . . II. iv. 38. 2
With such *faire* sleight him Guyon often fayld, . . . II. v. 11. 1
poursewed fast The present offer of *faire* victory, . . . II. v. 12. 2
Framed of wanton Yvie, flouring *fayre,* . . . II. v. 29. 3
Some framd *faire* lookes, . . . II. v. 33. 3
therein sate a Lady fresh and *fayre,* . . . II. vi. 3. 1
Into the land that lay them *faire* before, . . . II. vi. 11. 8
there it might be fownd To bud out *faire,* . . . II. vi. 12. 9
So pleased did his wrathfull purpose *faire* appease. . . . II. vi. 13. 9
They spring, they bud, they blossome fresh and *faire,* . . . II. vi. 15. 6
'*Faire* Sir,' (quoth she) 'be not displeasd at all, . . . II. vi. 23. 1
Accompanyde with Phaedria the *faire:* . . . II. vi. 28. 2
fayre Phaedria, that beheld That deadly daunger, . . . II. vi. 32. 1
The faithfull light of that *faire* lampe . . . II. vii. 1. 4
Faire shields, gay steedes, bright armes be my delight; . . . II. vii. 10. 8
Her face right wondrous *faire* did seeme to bee, . . . II. vii. 45. 1
most hevenly *faire* in deed and vew . . . II. vii. 45. 7
fayre Philotime she rightly hight, . . . II. vii. 49. 1
fayre Critias, his dearest Belamy! . . . II. vii. 52. 9
had of her *fayre* Helen for his meed, . . . II. vii. 55. 8
tree, So *fayre* and great that shadowed all the ground, . . . II. vii. 56. 2
Beside his head there satt a *faire* young man, . . . II. viii. 5. 1
florish *faire* above his equall peares: . . . II. viii. 5. 4
With his *faire* mother he him dights to play, . . . II. viii. 6. 5
'*Fayr* Sir,' said then the Palmer suppliaunt, . . . II. viii. 16. 1
faire Sir, whose honourable sight Doth promise hope . . . II. viii. 25. 5
'*Fayre* Sonne, great God thy right hand blesse, . . . II. viii. 40. 3
'*Fayre* sonne, be no whit sad . . . II. viii. 54. 4
'*Fayre* Sir, what need Good turnes be counted . . . II. viii. 56. 1
There is no one more *faire* and excellent . . . II. ix. 1. 2
Forth passed on their way in *fayre* accord, . . . II. ix. 2. 4
'*Fayre* Sir,' (sayd he) . . . II. ix. 3. 1
Whose *faire* retraitt I in my shield doe beare; . . . II. ix. 4. 2
faire Sir, be not herewith dismaid, . . . II. ix. 8. 5
now *faire* Phoebus gan decline . . . II. ix. 10. 1
shee was *faire* as *faire* mote ever bee, . . . II. ix. 18. 6
borne of two *faire* Damsels . . . II. ix. 19. 5
Of that *faire* Castle to affoord them vew: . . . II. ix. 20. 8
all so *faire* and fensible withall; . . . II. ix. 21. 3
over it a *fayre* Portcullis hong, . . . II. ix. 24. 6
Wherein were many tables *fayre* dispred, . . . II. ix. 27. 2
backe againe *faire* Alma led them right, . . . II. ix. 33. 5
A lovely bevy of *faire* Ladies sate, . . . II. ix. 34. 2
was right *faire* and fresh as morning rose, . . . II. ix. 36. 7
your *faire* beautie doe with sadnes spill? . . . II. ix. 37. 6
'*Fayre* Sir,' said she, . . . II. ix. 38. 1
with *faire* semblaunt sought to hyde the breach, . . . II. ix. 39. 3
was right *fayre* and modest of demayne, . . . II. ix. 40. 3
fayre vermilion or pure Castory. . . . II. ix. 41. 7
'*Fayre* Damzell, seemeth by your troubled cheare, . . . II. ix. 42. 1
'Why wonder yee, *Faire* Sir, . . . II. ix. 43. 7
she the same Dissembled *faire,* . . . II. ix. 44. 3
counselled *faire* Alma how to governe well. . . . II. ix. 48. 9
wals Were painted *faire* with memorable gestes . . . II. ix. 53. 3
Ne under Sunne that shines so wide and *faire,* . . . II. x. 2. 1
Borne of *fayre* Inogene of Italy; . . . II. x. 13. 5
He lov'd *faire* Ladie Estrild, leudly lov'd, . . . II. x. 17. 6
his *faire* Leman flying through a brooke She overhent, . . . II. x. 18. 8
The *faire* Sabrina, almost dead with feare, . . . II. x. 19. 3
happy father of *faire* progeny: . . . II. x. 22. 2
three *faire* daughters, which were well uptraind . . . II. x. 27. 3
wanting colours *fayre* To paint it forth, . . . II. x. 28. 6
great Gurgustus, then *faire* Caecily, . . . II. x. 34. 3
had to wife Dame Mertia the *fayre,* . . . II. x. 42. 3
Fayre Helena, the fairest living wight; . . . II. x. 59. 5
Through his *faire* daughters face and flattring word. . . . II. x. 66. 5
faire Elferon, The eldest brother, . . . II. x. 75. 6
Fayre mote he thee, the prowest and most gent, . . . II. xi. 17. 5
fierce retourning, as a faulcon *fayre,* . . . II. xi. 36. 6
Both *faire* and fruitfull, and the ground dispred . . . II. xii. 12. 2
Of her *fayre* twins was there delivered, . . . II. xii. 13. 6
'*Faire* Sir, be not displeasd if disobayd: . . . II. xii. 28. 5
They were *faire* Ladies, . . . II. xii. 31. 1
'O thou *fayre* sonne of gentle Faery, . . . II. xii. 32. 3
the *faire* land it selfe did playnly sheow. . . . II. xii. 37. 6
fayre grassy grownd Mantled with greene, . . . II. xii. 50. 3
Fayre Daphne Phoebus hart with love did gore; . . . II. xii. 52. 5
sweet Parnasse, the haunt of Muses *fayre;* . . . II. xii. 52. 8
the *fayre* aspect Of that sweet place, . . . II. xii. 53. 1
Some like *faire* Emeraudes, . . . II. xii. 54. 9
Clad in *fayre* weedes but fowle disordered, . . . II. xii. 55. 8
so *faire* winepresse made the wine more sweet; . . . II. xii. 56. 6
that which all *faire* workes doth most aggrace, . . . II. xii. 58. 8
sweet and *faire* to see, . . . II. xii. 62. 2

Fair—*Continued.*

that *faire* Starre, the messenger of morne, . . . II. xii. 65. 1
her *faire* lockes, which formerly were bownd . . . II. xii. 67. 2
that *faire* spectacle from him was reft, . . . II. xii. 67. 6
that which reft it no lesse *faire* was fownd. . . . II. xii. 67. 7
the *faire* Witch her selfe now solacing . . . II. xii. 72. 2
Many *faire* Ladies and lascivious boyes, . . . II. xii. 72. 8
whoso *fayre* thing doest faine to see, . . . II. xii. 74. 2
her *faire* eyes, sweet smyling in delight, . . . II. xii. 78. 6
The *faire* Enchauntresse, so unwares opprest, . . . II. xii. 81. 8
Fayre Florimell is chaced: . . . III. i. Arg.
Of the *faire* Alma greatly were procur'd . . . III. i. 1. 5
They spide a knight that towards pricked *fayre;* . . . III. i. 4. 2
gan *fayre* perswade Not to provoke misfortune, . . . III. i. 10. 1
her *faire* yellow locks behind her flew, . . . III. i. 16. 3
The whiles *faire* Britomart . . . did stay behynd, . . . III. i. 19. 1
faire before the gate a spatious playne, . . . III. i. 20. 6
Within this castle wall a Lady *fayre,* . . . III. i. 26. 2
Forthy, *faire* Sir, yours be the Damozell, . . . III. i. 30. 3
glee of many gratious *Faire* Ladies, . . . III. i. 31. 6
The *fayre* Adonis, turned to a flowre; . . . III. i. 34. 5
As when *fayre* Cynthia, in darkesome night, . . . III. i. 43. 1
With which *fayre* Britomart gave light unto the day. . . . III. i. 43. 9
All were *faire* knights, and goodly well beseene; . . . III. i. 45. 8
to *faire* Britomart they all but shadowes beene. . . . III. i. 45. 9
Whom when the Lady saw so *faire* a wight, . . . III. i. 47. 1
Faire Ladies, that to love captived arre, . . . III. i. 49. 1
The Lady did *faire* Britomart entreat . . . III. i. 52. 3
to *faire* semblaunce doth light faith annexe: . . . III. i. 54. 7
Scorne the *faire* offer of good will profest; . . . III. i. 55. 2
with *faire* countenaunce, as beseemed best, Her entertaynd: . III. i. 55. 5
faire Malecasta bent Her crafty engins . . . III. i. 57. 4
Faire Malecasta, whose engrieved spright . . . III. i. 59. 4
with gold and Ermines *faire* enveloped. . . . III. i. 59. 9
faire Britomart, whose prayse I wryte; . . . III. ii. 3. 2
faire purpose gan to find, . . . III. ii. 4. 2
Faire Lady she him seemd, . . . III. ii. 4. 8
'*Faire* Sir, I let you weete, . . . III. ii. 6. 1
'*Faire* martiall Mayd, Certes ye misavised beene . . . III. ii. 9. 4
Therefore, *faire* Damzell, be ye well aware, . . . III. ii. 10. 6
if reason *faire* might you perswade . . . III. ii. 13. 3
One day it fortuned *fayre* Britomart . . . III. ii. 22. 1
when she had espyde that mirrhour *fayre,* . . . III. ii. 22. 5
thinke of that *fayre* visage written in her hart. . . . III. ii. 29. 9
Their fit disports with *faire* delight doe chose, . . . III. ii. 31. 4
her *faire* deawy eies . . . Shee ofte did bathe, . . . III. ii. 34. 6
Sweete love such lewdnes bands from his *faire* companee. . . . III. ii. 41. 9
the *faire* Damzel from the holy herse . . . III. ii. 48. 6
a *faire* Lady Nonne, that whilome hight Matilda, . . . III. iii 13. 5
Thrise shined *faire,* and thrise seemd dim and wan, . . . III. iii. 16. 3
fayre Britomartis, thus arayd, . . . III. iii. 19. 5
As *fayre* Aurora, rysing hastily, . . . III. iii. 20. 4
the third time shall *fayre* accordaunce make: . . . III. iii. 30. 7
that men them *faire* may see. . . . III. iii. 44. 9
'*Fayre* Angela' (quoth she) 'men do her call, . . . III. iii. 56. 2
No whit lesse *fayre* then terrible in fight: . . . III. iii. 56. 3
faire Infant, her ensample make Unto thy selfe, . . . III. iii. 56. 8
old Glauce thither led *Faire* Britomart, . . . III. iii. 59. 7
Faire Florimell of Arthure is Long followed, . . . III. iv. Arg.
in late yeares so *faire* a blossome bare, . . . III. iv. 3. 7
fayre Britomart, having disclo'ste Her clowdy care . . . III. iv. 13. 7
her goodly shield addressing *fayre,* . . . III. iv. 14. 1
the *faire* flowres that decked him afore: . . . III. iv. 17. 8
ever from *fayre* Ladies love did fly; . . . III. iv. 26. 6
Yet many Ladies *fayre* did oft complaine, . . . III. iv. 26. 7
from the Sun their forheads *fayr* to shade; . . . III. iv. 29. 9
her *faire* deawy lockes yrent; . . . III. iv. 30. 2
with thousand starres was decked *fayre:* . . . III. iv. 52. 3
wish that Lady *faire* mote bee His Faery Queene, . . . III. iv. 54. 6
The prayses of high God he *faire* displayes, . . . III. iv. 59. 3
Her *faire* lockes in rich circlet be enrold, . . . III. v. 5. 4
is ycleped Florimell the *fayre,* . . . III. v. 8. 7
Faire Florimell belov'd of many a knight, . . . III. v. 8. 8
Therefore, *faire* Sir, for love of knighthood gent, . . . III. v. 10. 5
the shame he did To that *faire* Damzell: . . . III. v. 13. 6
Belphoebe was her name, as *faire* as Phoebus sunne. . . . III. v. 27. 9
whose *faire* eyes, like lamps of quenched fire, . . . III. v. 29. 3
The bud of youth to blossome *faire* began, . . . III. v. 29. 8
A *faire* Pavilion, scarcely to bee seene, . . . III. v. 40. 7
his foule sore reduced to *faire* plight: . . . III. v. 41. 8
From her *faire* eyes and gratious countenaunce. . . . III. v. 42. 6
love so *fayre* a Lady that his life releast? . . . III. v. 43. 9
Fayre death it is, to shonne more shame, to dy: . . . III. v. 45. 8
Dye rather, dye, then ever so *faire* love forsake!' . . . III. v. 47. 9
Which seeing *fayre* Belphoebe gan to feare, . . . III. v. 49. 1
She did it *fayre* dispred and let to florish *fayre.* . . . III. v. 51. 9
Fayre ympes of beautie, . . . III. v. 53. 1
With this *fayre* flowre your goodly girlonds dight . . . III. v. 53. 5
To your *faire* selves a *faire* ensample frame . . . III. v. 54. 1
this *faire* virgin, this Belphebe *fayre;* . . . III. v. 54. 2
birth of *fayre* Belphoebe and Of Amorett . . . III. vi. Arg.
Well may I weene, *faire* Ladies, . . . III. vi. 1. 1
to this *faire* Belphoebe in her berth . . . III. vi. 2. 1
Phoebus with *faire* beames did her adorne, . . . III. vi. 2. 8
Her mother was the *faire* Chrysogonee, . . . III. vi. 4. 1
she bore in like cace *Fayre* Amoretta . . . III. vi. 4. 5
faire Chrysogone Conceiv'd these infants, . . . III. vi. 5. 2
When Titan *faire* his beames did display, . . . III. vi. 6. 5
his *faire* sister for creation Ministreth matter fit, . . . III. vi. 9. 3
faire Venus having lost Her little sonne, . . . III. vi. 11. 1

Fair—*Continued.*

The house of goodly formes and *faire* aspect, . . . III. vi. 12. 2
Goodly she gan *faire* Cytherea greet, . . . III. vi. 20. 1
'*Faire* sister, ill beseemes it to upbrayd A dolefull heart . . . III. vi. 21. 7
he is *faire* and fresh in face and guize . . . III. vi. 23. 7
whereas lay *Faire* Crysogone in slombry traunce . . . III. vi. 26. 7
two babes, as *faire* as springing day. . . . III. vi. 26. 9
So *faire* a place as Nature can devize: . . . III. vi. 29. 3
Th' one *faire* and fresh, the other old and dride. . . . III. vi. 31. 7
that *faire* flowre of beautie fades away, . . . III. vi. 38. 8
To see so *faire* thinges mard and spoiled quight; . . . III. vi. 40. 2
There wont *fayre* Venus often to enjoy . . . III. vi. 46. 1
with *faire* Adonis playes his wanton partes. . . . III. vi. 49. 9
his trew love *faire* Psyche with him playes, . . . III. vi. 50. 1
Fayre Psyche to him lately reconcyld, . . . III. vi. 50. 2
Hither great Venus brought this infant *fayre,* . . . III. vi. 51. 1
all *fayre* Ladies that doe live on grownd. . . . III. vi. 52. 6
So fledd *fayre* Florimell from her vaine feare, . . . III. vii. 1. 6
the *fayre* Virgin was so meeke and myld, . . . III. vii. 15. 1
Girlonds of flowres sometimes for her *faire* hed . . . III. vii. 17. 5
well they kent That their *fayre* guest was gone, . . . III. vii. 19. 8
horse Whereon *faire* Florimell was wont to ride, . . . III. vii. 31. 2
that *faire* Maide, the flowre of wemens pride; . . . III. vii. 31. 5
semblaunce of *faire* fight did make, . . . III. vii. 44. 8
reft from him so *faire* a chevisaunce. . . . III. vii. 45. 5
the vow that to *faire* Columbell I plighted have, . . . III. vii. 51. 6
a *faire* virgin that in martiall law . . . III. vii. 52. 3
'So well I to *faire* Ladies service did, . . . III. vii. 55. 1
fayre, and in her countenaunce Dwelt simple truth . . . III. vii. 59. 5
To tell what tydings of *fayre* Florimell became. . . . III. vii. 61. 9
As Florimells *fayre* heare: . . . III. viii. 7. 8
fayre resemblance above all the rest, . . . III. viii. 8. 2
To walke the woodes with that his Idole *faire,* . . . III. viii. 11. 2
seeing with that Chorle so *faire* a wight, . . . III. viii. 12. 1
To looke on her *faire* face and marke her snowy skin. . . . III. viii. 24. 9
blubbred face with teares of her *faire* eyes: . . . III. viii. 32. 3
there with many gentle termes her *faire* besought. . . . III. viii. 35. 9
offered *faire* guiftes t' allure her sight; . . . III. viii. 38. 7
They spyde a knight *fayre* pricking on the playne, . . . III. viii. 44. 7
suddein parture of *faire* Florimell . . . III. viii. 46. 5
all *faire* Ladies may for ever sory bee.' . . . III. viii. 47. 9
'*Fayre* Sir, how may I weene it trew, . . . III. viii. 48. 3
'*Faire* Sir,' (quoth he) . . . III. viii. 50. 6
Unfit *faire* Ladies service to supply; . . . III. ix. 5. 2
the *faire* welkin fowly overcast . . . III. ix. 11. 4
this *faire* many were compeld at last . . . III. ix. 11. 7
with *faire* treaty pacifide their yre. . . . III. ix. 17. 2
the *faire* feature of her limbs did hyde; . . . III. ix. 21. 2
Through gratious regard of her *faire* eye, . . . III. ix. 25. 4
On her *faire* face so did he feede his fill, . . . III. ix. 27. 8
By their *faire* handling, . . . III. ix. 31. 9
'*Fayre* Helene, flowre of beautie excellent, . . . III. ix. 35. 1
the fieldes of *faire* Scamander strowne With carcases . . . III. ix. 35. 6
On *faire* Oenone got a lovely boy, . . . III. ix. 36. 4
for *faire* ladies love and glories gaine, . . . III. ix. 37. 7
'Anchyses sonne, begott of Venus *fayre,*' . . . III. ix. 41. 1
faire it florished and long time stoud, . . . III. ix. 43. 8
his worke is eke *Faire* Lincolne, . . . III. ix. 51. 2
Upon his lips hong *faire* Dame Hellenore . . . III. ix. 52. 2
Faire Britomart and that same Faery knight Uprose, . . . III. x. 1. 5
his *faire* wife, whom honest long he kept uneath. . . . III. x. 2. 9
bore so *faire* a sayle, . . . III. x. 6. 3
Whom she hath vow'd to dub a *fayre* Cucquold. . . . III. x. 11. 5
This second Helene, *fayre* Dame Hellenore, . . . III. x. 13. 1
Night, the patronesse of love-stealth *fayre,* . . . III. x. 16. 6
all *faire* Ladies magnify your might, . . . III. x. 28. 7
Faire Helenore with girlonds all bespredd, . . . III. x. 44. 5
through the helpe of his *faire* hornes on hight, . . . III. x. 47. 4
ye, *faire* Ladies, . . . ensample take, . . . III. xi. 2. 6
of *faire* Britomart ensample take, . . . III. xi. 2. 8
Fayre Britomart so long him followed, . . . III. xi. 7. 1
For whom so *faire* a Lady feeles so sore a wound!' . . . III. xi. 11. 9
th' earth with his *faire* forhead strooke: . . . III. xi. 13. 7
'Therefore, *faire* Sir, doe comfort to you take, . . . III. xi. 15. 1
At least it *faire* endevour will apply.' . . . III. xi. 15. 6
Faire Amorett must dwell in wicked chaines, . . . III. xi. 24. 3
Many *faire* pourtraicts, and many a *faire* feate; . . . III. xi. 29. 2
like a Ram, *faire* Helle to pervart, . . . III. xi. 30. 5
faire Danae to vew; . . . III. xi. 31. 2
To win *faire* Leda to his lovely trade: . . . III. xi. 32. 2
brushing his *faire* brest, . . . III. xi. 32. 7
faire Alcmena better match did make, . . . III. xi. 33. 6
the Trojane boy so *fayre* . . . III. xi. 34. 4
faire Phoebus, in thy colours bright . . . III. xi. 36. 1
To love *faire* Daphne, . . . III. xi. 36. 7
So lovedst thou the *faire* Coronis deare; . . . III. xi. 37. 2
All which in that *faire* arras was most lively writ. . . . III. xi. 39. 9
Aeolus *faire* daughter, Arne hight, . . . III. xi. 42. 2
He turnd him selfe into a Dolphin *fayre;* . . . III. xi. 42. 6
On whom he got *faire* Pegasus that flitteth in the ayre. . . . III. xi. 42. 9
into her *faire* bosome made his grapes decline. . . . III. xi. 43. 9
at the upper end of that *faire* rowme . . . III. xi. 47. 1
That wondrous sight *faire* Britomart amazd, . . . III. xi. 49. 6
redeemes *faire* Amoret through charmes decayd. . . . III. xii. Arg.
ycovered had *Fayre* heaven with an universall clowd, . . . III. xii. 1. 2
her *fayre* lockes were woven up in gold: . . . III. xii. 13. 4
Goodly adorned and exceeding *faire:* . . . III. xii. 14. 5
Thus marched these six couples forth in *faire* degree. . . . III. xii. 18. 9
there marcht a most *faire* Dame, . . . III. xii. 19. 1
that same dolorous *Faire* Dame . . . III. xii. 22. 8

Fair—*Continued.*
Therein he them full *faire* did entertaine . . . VI. v. 38. 6
fair Serene all night could take no rest, . . . VI. v. 39. 6
'*Faire* daughter Dame, And you, *faire* Sonne, . . . VI. vi. 6. 5, 6
A *faire* young Mayden, full of comely glee; . . . VI. vi. 10. 7
a *faire* Mayden clad in mourning weed, . . . VI. vi. 16. 7
Which *faire* Serene to him delivered had, . . . VI. vi. 18. 2
thy life unto this Ladie *fayre* I given have, . . . VI. vi. 36. 1
Fayre Mirabellaes punishment For Loves disdaine decreed. . VI. vii. Arg.
Fayre Mirabella was her name, . . . VI. vii. 35. 1
the gentle Squire, with *faire* Serene, . . . VI. vii. 39. 2
The *faire* Serena . . . thought That slaine he was, . . . VI. vii. 50. 1
first it falleth me by course to tell Of *faire* Serena; . . . VI. viii. 31. 2
when her face Like the *faire* yvory shining they did see, . . VI. viii. 37. 3
Calidore . . . loves *fayre* Pastorell: . . . VI. ix. Arg.
Yet seem'd the soyle both *fayre* and frutefull eft, . . . VI. ix. 1. 5
he there besyde Saw a *faire* damzell, . . . VI. ix. 7. 7
soothly sure she was full *fayre* of face, . . . VI. ix. 9. 1
To helpe *faire* Pastorella home to drive Her fleecie flocke; . VI. ix. 15. 8
the *fayre* mayd the table ta'ne away, . . . VI. ix. 18. 2
twixt his pleasing tongue, and her *faire* hew, . . . VI. ix. 26. 8
Dayly beholding the *faire* Pastorell, . . . VI. ix. 34. 3
When he the love of *fayre* Oenone sought, . . . VI. ix. 36. 8
unto the fields he went With the *faire* Pastorella . . . VI. ix. 37. 2
As they are wont in *faire* sunshynie weather, . . . VI. ix. 41. 3
So it surely wrought With this *faire* Mayd, . . . VI. ix. 45. 7
To winne the love of the *faire* Pastorell, . . . VI. ix. 46. 2
Whilest Calidore does follow that *faire* Mayd, . . . VI. x. 1. 2
Whilest his *faire* Pastorella was elsewhere, . . . VI. x. 5. 2
that *faire* one, That in the midst was placed paravaunt, . . . VI. x. 15. 6
By him begot of *faire* Eurynome, . . . VI. x. 22. 2
Next *faire* Aglaia, last Thalia merry; . . . VI. x. 22. 8
Where his *faire* Pastorella did remaine: . . . VI. x. 32. 3
he it presented Before the feete of the *faire* Pastorell; . . . VI. x. 36. 7
Faire Pastorella, sorrowfull and sad, . . . VI. x. 40. 5
when *faire* Pastorell Into this place was brought, . . . VI. x. 43. 6
Like as is now befalne to this *faire* Mayd, . . . VI. xi. 2. 1
Faire Pastorell, of whom is now my song: . . . VI. xi. 2. 2
beheld that lovely guest, *Faire* Pastorella, . . . VI. xi. 3. 8
Like the *faire* Morning clad in misty fog . . . VI. xi. 3. 9
By his *faire* patients side . . . VI. xi. 9. 9
Gan to inquire for that *faire* shepherdesse, . . . VI. xi. 11. 6
holding fast twixt both his armes extended *Fayre* Pastorell, . VI. xi. 19. 8
Before I saw *faire* Pastorella dye.' . . . VI. xi. 29. 4
how *faire* Pastorell should have bene sold . . . VI. xi. 30. 6
faire bespoke with words, . . . VI. xi. 35. 9
faire Pastorell through great affright Was almost dead, . . . VI. xi. 43. 7
Fayre Pastorella by great hap Her parents understands. . . VI. xii. Arg.
had raught *Faire* Pastorella from those Brigants powre, . . . VI. xii. 3. 2
like a rose her silken leaves did *faire* unfold. . . . VI. xii. 7. 9
Claribell Ne lesse did tender the *faire* Pastorell, . . . VI. xii. 11. 5
taking leave of his *faire* Pastorell, . . . VI. xii. 13. 6
What did betide to the *faire* Pastorell . . . VI. xii. 14. 3
when this Maiden *faire* Was dighting her, . . . VI. xii. 15. 1
this *faire* Mayd Was that same infant, . . . VI. xii. 16. 2
When she so *faire* a daughter saw survive, . . . VI. xii. 21. 7
Acknowledg'd for his owne *faire* Pastorell. . . . VI. xii. 22. 4
all the worlds *faire* frame . . . She alter'd quite; . . . VII. vi. 5. 5
her need give lone Of her *faire* light . . . VII. vi. 11. 8
To Joves *faire* palace fixt in heavens hight; . . . VII. vi. 15. 2
Was striving with *faire* Cynthia for her seat; . . . VII. vi. 17. 3
To bid her leave *faire* Cynthia's silver bower; . . . VII. vi. 18. 7
To thrust *faire* Phoebe from her silver bed, . . . VII. vi. 21. 3
In which *faire* beames of beauty did appeare . . . VII. vi. 31. 2
thee, *faire* Titans child, I rather weene, . . . VII. vi. 32. 1
sister unto Mulla *faire* and bright, . . . VII. vi. 40. 3
Were no lesse *faire* and beautifull then shee; . . . VII. vi. 40. 8
To deck the locks Of som *faire* Bride, . . . VII. vi. 41. 4
(both combin'd) themselves in one *faire* river spred. . . . VII. vi. 53. 9
All those *faire* forrests about Arlo hid; . . . VII. vi. 54. 6
the *faire* Shure, in which are thousand Salmons bred. . . . VII. vi. 54. 9
In a *fayre* Plaine upon an equall Hill . . . VII. vii. 8. 1
Did deck himselfe in freshest *faire* attire; . . . VII. vii. 11. 2
How-ever *faire* it flourish for a time, . . . VII. vii. 18. 2
With every blast that bloweth, fowle or *faire:* . . . VII. vii. 22. 8
The *faire* doth it prolong; the fowle doth it impaire. . . . VII. vii. 22. 9
faire sun-shine, that makes all skip and daunce; . . . VII. vii. 23. 4
faire May, the fayrest mayd on ground, . . . VII. vii. 34. 1
The seed of Saturne and *faire* Nais, . . . VII. vii. 40. 9
the Howres, *faire* daughters of high Jove . . . VII. vii. 45. 1
Life was like a *faire* young lusty boy, . . . VII. vii. 46. 6
Even you, *faire* Cynthia; . . . VII. vii. 50. 2
Though *faire* all night, yet is she darke all day: . . . VII. vii. 51. 6
To decke hir selfe, and her *faire* mantle weave. . . . *Am.* iv. 12
faire flowre! in whom fresh youth doth raine, . . . *Am.* iv. 13
her *faire* countenance, like a goodly banner, . . . *Am.* v. 11
Fayre eyes! the myrrour of my mazed hart, . . . *Am.* vii. 1
More then most *faire,* full of the living fire, . . . *Am.* viii. 1
her *faire* face she reares up to the skie, . . . *Am.* xiii. 2
to leave, like one afrayd, So *fayre* a peece, . . . *Am.* xiv. 4
her *faire* hands are Silver sheene: . . . *Am.* xv. 12
unwarily did gaze On those *fayre* eyes, . . . *Am.* xvi. 2
Her temple *fayre* is built within my mind, . . . *Am.* xxii. 5
her *fayre* eyes unwares doe worke in mee, . . . *Am.* xxiv. 6
Faire Proud! now tell me, why should *faire* be proud, . . . *Am.* xxvii. 1
Shall doffe her fleshes borrowd *fayre* attyre, . . . *Am.* xxvii. 6
Faire! be no lenger proud . . . *Am.* xxvii. 13
fly no more, *fayre* Love, from Phebus chace, . . . *Am.* xxviii. 13
filled with the store Of that *faire* sight, . . . *Am.* xxxv. 10
the *fayre* sunshine in somers day; . . . *Am.* xl. 6

Fair—*Continued.*
O fayrest *fayre!* let never it be named, . . . *Am.* xli. 13
so *fayre* beauty was so fowly shamed. . . . *Am.* xli. 14
The *fayre* Idea of your celestiall hew . . . remaines . . . *Am.* xlv. 7
the cause by which your *fayre* beames darkned be. . . . *Am.* xlv. 14
My cruell *fayre* streight bids me wend my way: . . . *Am.* xlvi. 2
Fayre cruell! why are ye so fierce and cruell? . . . *Am.* xlix. 1
Right so my cruell *fayre* with me doth play; . . . *Am.* liii. 5
which her made attonce so cruell *faire,* . . . *Am.* lv. 4
Fayre ye be sure, but cruell and unkind, . . . *Am.* lvi. 1
Fayre be ye sure, but proud and pittilesse, . . . *Am.* lvi. 5
Fayre be ye sure, but hard and obstinate, . . . *Am.* lvi. 9
none so rich or wise, so strong or *fayre,* . . . *Am.* lviii. 9
Why then doe ye, proud *fayre,* misdeeme so farre, . . . *Am.* lviii. 13
let my loves *fayre* Planet short her wayes, . . . *Am.* lx. 13
Fayre soyle it seemes from far, . . . *Am.* lxiii. 7
The doubt which ye misdeeme, *fayre* love, is vaine, . . . *Am.* lxv. 1
the *fayre* tresses of your golden hayre,) . . . *Am.* lxxiii. 3
wont on your *fayre* eye To feed his fill, . . . *Am.* lxxiii. 7
Fayre bosome! fraught with vertues richest tresure, . . . *Am.* lxxvi. 1
Men call you *fayre,* and you doe credit it, . . . *Am.* lxxix. 1
the trew *fayre,* that is the gentle wit, . . . *Am.* lxxix. 3
how ever *fayre* it be, Shall turne to nought . . . *Am.* lxxix. 5
Deriv'd from that *fayre* Spirit, . . . *Am.* lxxix. 11
He onely *fayre,* and what he *fayre* hath made; . . . *Am.* lxxix. 13
All other *fayre,* lyke flowres, untymely fade. . . . *Am.* lxxix. 14
Fayre is my love, when her *fayre* golden heares . . . *Am.* lxxxi. 1
Fayre, when the rose in her red cheekes appeares; . . . *Am.* lxxxi. 3
Fayre, when her brest, lyke a rich laden barke, . . . *Am.* lxxxi. 5
Fayre, when that cloud of pryde . . . with smiles she drives away. . . . *Am.* lxxxi. 7
blesse your fortunes *fayre* election. . . . *Am.* lxxxiii. 14
Dark is my day, whyles her *fayre* light I mis, . . . *Am.* lxxxviii. 13
Another gay girland, For my *fayre* love, . . . *Epith.* 43
her *fayre* eyes, like stars that dimmed were . . . *Epith.* 93
first come ye *fayre* houres, . . . *Epith.* 98
al, that ever in this world is *fayre,* . . . *Epith.* 101
Faire Sun! shew forth thy favourable ray, . . . *Epith.* 117
did ye see So *fayre* a creature in your towne before; . . . *Epith.* 168
all her body like a pallace *fayre,* . . . *Epith.* 178
seems more *fayre,* The more they on it stare. . . . *Epith.* 232
Fayre childe of beauty! . . . *Epith.* 288
Behold how goodly my *faire* love does ly, . . . *Epith.* 305
Lyke as when Jove with *fayre* Alcmena lay, . . . *Epith.* 328
whose is that *faire* face that shines so bright? . . . *Epith.* 373
And thou, *fayre* Hebe! and thou, Hymen free! . . . *Epith.* 405
Fayre Venice, flower of the last worlds delight; . . . *Com. Son.* iv.10
not so *fayre* her buildinges to behold As Lewkenors stile . *Com. Son.* iv.13
ye, *faire* Nimphs! which oftentimes have loved . . . *H.L.* 31
ye, *faire* blossomes of youths wanton breed, . . . *H.L.* 36
His owne *faire* mother, for all creatures sake, . . . *H.L.* 72
Nothing on earth seemes *fayre* to fleshly sight, . . . *H.B.* 18
faire immortall beame Hath darted fyre . . . *H.B.* 23
now so *faire* and seemely they appeare, . . . *H.B.* 34
it more *faire* accordingly it makes, . . . *H.B.* 45
that *faire* beame which therein is empight. . . . *H.B.* 49
pleasant grace To all things *faire,* . . . *H.B.* 58
mixture made Of colours *faire,* . . . *H.B.* 66
why doe not *faire* pictures like powre shew, . . . *H.B.* 82
that *faire* lampe, from whose celestiall ray . . . *H.B.* 99
Therof it comes that these *faire* soules, . . . *H.B.* 120
A comely corpse, with beautie *faire* endewed, . . . *H.B.* 135
A beauteous soule, with *faire* conditions thewed, . . . *H.B.* 137
all that *faire* is, is by nature good; . . . *H.B.* 139
nathemore is that *faire* beauties blame, . . . *H.B.* 155
the soule is *faire* and beauteous still, . . . *H.B.* 159
faire Dames! the worlds deare ornaments . . . *H.B.* 162
Disloiall lust *faire* beauties foulest blame, . . . *H.B.* 170
Which seeing now so inly *faire* to be, . . . *H.B.* 225
to their eyes that inmost *faire* display, . . . *H.B.* 237
seeing her *faire* eyes so sharpe effect, . . . *H.B.* 244
you, *faire* Venus dearling, . . . *H.B.* 281
When your *faire* eyes these fearefull lines shal read, . . . *H.B.* 283
It lov'd it selfe, because it selfe was *faire;* . . . *H.H.L.* 29
It lov'd it selfe, . . . (For *faire* is lov'd;) . . . *H.H.L.* 30
Into his face most beautifull and *fayre,* . . . *H.H.L.* 111
love, Kindled through sight of those *faire* things above. . . *H.H.L.* 287
Transported with celestiall desyre Of those *faire* formes, . . *H.H.B.* 19
gazefull eyes to feed With sight of that is *faire,* . . . *H.H.B.* 30
so still more cleare And *faire* it growes, . . . *H.H.B.* 46
heaven then fire, appeares more pure and *fayre.* . . . *H.H.B.* 49
And rise more *faire,* till they at last arive . . . *H.H.B.* 76
at last arive To the most *faire,* whereto they all do strive. . *H.H.B.* 77
Faire is the heaven where happy soules have place, . . . *H.H.B.* 78
More *faire* is that, where those Idees on hie Enraunged be, . *H.H.B.* 82
Yet farre more *faire* be those bright Cherubins, . . . *H.H.B.* 92
These thus in *faire* each other farre excelling, . . . *H.H.B.* 99
For all thats good is beautifull and *faire.* . . . *H.H.B.* 133
And were as *faire* as fabling wits do fayne, . . . *H.H.B.* 216
that *faire* love of mightie heavens King; . . . *H.H.B.* 235
And that *faire* lampe, which useth to inflame . . . *H.H.B.* 274
beames, which then did glyster *fayre;* . . . *Proth.* 4
Soyle their *fayre* plumes with water not so *fayre,* . . . *Proth.* 50
never saw a sight so *fayre,* . . . *Proth.* 60
'Ye gentle Birdes! the worlds *faire* ornament, . . . *Proth.* 91
let *faire* Venus, . . . upon you smile, . . . *Proth.* 96
Faire branch of Honor, . . . *Proth.* 150
In th' Ocean billowes he hath bathed *fayre,* . . . *Proth.* 165
They two, . . . Received those two *faire* Brides, . . . *Proth.* 176

Fair-blushing. A great increase in her *faire blushing* face, . . V. iii. 23. 4

Fair-burning. kindling fire at her *faire-burning* eye, . . . II. ii. 7. 6

Fairer. Till *fayrer* Fortune shewe forth her head. . . . *S.C.* S. 257
Two *fairer* beasts might not elswhere be found, . . . *Ti.* 566
A *fairer* one in all the goodlie criew . . . *Ti.* 592
A *fairer* wight saw never summers day. . . . *Ti.* 637
sure those wings were *fairer* manifolde. . . . *Mui.* 104
(A *fairer* star saw never living eie,) . . . *As.* 57
None *fairer*, nor more fruitfull to be red: . . . *Col.* 279
A *fairer* Nymph yet never saw mine eie: . . . *Col.* 559
from commune vew Their *fairer* parts are hid, . . . *Ded. Son.* ix. 11
A *fairer* crew yet no where could I see . . . *Ded.Son.*xvii. 10
When *fairer* faces were bid standen by: . . . I. iv. 24. 8
Thousand times *fairer* than her mortall hew, . . . II. ix. 3. 7
Fairer and nobler liveth none this howre, . . . II. x. 76. 6
That *fairer* seemes the lesse ye see her may. . . . II. xii. 74. 6
That she is *fairer* then our fairest Dame; . . . III. i. 27. 4
A *fayrer* wight did never Sunne behold; . . . III. v. 5. 5
fayrer then her selfe, . . . III. viii. 9. 5
if ought algate Might *fayrer* be. . . . III. viii. 9. 6
white seemes *fayrer* macht with blacke attone; . . . III. ix. 2. 4
Cannot two *fairer* Cities find this day, . . . III. ix. 51. 4
Much *fayrer* then the former was that roome, . . . III. xi. 51. 1
yet this much *fairer* shined, . . . IV. x. 40. 6
'He, whether mine seem'd *fayrer* in his eye, . . . V. i. 17. 1
the *fairer* love to gaine, . . . V. i. 24. 8
No *fayrer* conquest then that with goodwill is gayned. . . . V. v. 17. 9
Amongst them all growes not a *fayrer* flowre . . . VI. Pr. 4. 1
a *fayrer* flood may no man see. . . . VII. vi. 40. 9
Fayrer then fayrest! let none ever say, . . . *Am.* xx. 13
for *fayrer* weathers false delight. . . . *Am.* lix. 8
newly fashion Unto a *fairer* forme, . . . *H.L.* 193
Fairer then fairest, in his fayning eye, . . . *H.L.* 216
So it the *fairer* bodie doth procure . . . *H.B.* 129
Counting it *fairer* then it is indeede, . . . *H.B.* 230
And so much *fairer*, and much more then these, . . . *H.H.B.* 62
As these are *fairer* then the land and seas? . . . *H.H.B.* 63
Yet *fairer* is that heaven, . . . And *fayrer* yet, . . . *H.H.B.* 85, 89
Yet *fairer* then they both, and much more bright, . . . *H.H.B.* 96
Fairer then all the rest which there appeare, . . . *H.H.B.* 102
Two *fairer* Birds I yet did never see; . . . *Proth.* 39

Fairest. though ye be the *fairest* of Gods creatures, . . . *Pet.*[2] vii. 13
Your glorie, *fairest* of all earthly thing! . . . *Ro.* i. 14
The *fayrest* May she was that ever went, . . . *S.C.* N. 39
The *fayrest* floure our gyrlond all emong . . . *S.C.* N. 75
To ayme their counsels to the *fairest* scope, . . . *Hub.* 960
doth all *fairest* things on earth deface, . . . *T.M.* 434
Of all alive did seeme the *fairest* wight. . . . *Mui.* 24
Clarion! though *fairest* thou Of all thy kinde, . . . *Mui.* 233
do not spare the best or *fayrest*, . . . *D.* 202
Sith that my *fairest* flower is faded quight; . . . *D.* 494
Full carefully he kept them . . . In *fairest* fields; . . . *As.* 6
Stella the faire, the *fairest* star in skie, . . . *As.* 55
As faire as Venus or the *fairest* faire, . . . *As.* 56
Her face, the *fairest* face that eye mote see, . . . *As.* 155
As Sunny beames in *fairest* somers day, . . . *As.* 158
her heavens *fairest* light, . . . *Col.* 41
yet there be the *fairest* under skie, . . . *Col.* 557
Chose for his love the *fairest* in his sight. . . . *Col.* 869
Like as himselfe was *fayrest* by creation: . . . *Col.* 870
one, that *fairest* Helene did revile, . . . *Col.* 920
Ne may I, . . . You, *fairest* Lady, leave out . . . *Ded. Son.* xvi. 2
desird Of all the *fairest* Maides to have the vew. . . . *Ded.Son.*xvii. 4
Faerie knights, and *fayrest* Tanaquill, . . . I. Pr. 2. 5
he her takes To be the *fairest* wight that lived yit; . . . I. ii. 30. 4
For *fairest* Unaes sake, of whom I sing, . . . I. iii. 2. 2
Exceeding shone, like Phoebus *fayrest* childe, . . . I. iv. 9. 1
Where he unwares the *fairest* Una found, . . . I. vi. 30. 6
O *fayrest* virgin! full of heavenly light, . . . I. ix. 17. 3
when that *fairest* Una she beheld, . . . I. x. 8. 6
In which that *fairest* Faery Queene doth dwell, . . . I. x. 58. 3
The *fairest* citty was that might be seene; . . . I. x. 58. 4
The *fairest* peece that eie beholden can, . . . I. x. 59. 3
The *fairest* Un', his onely daughter deare, . . . I. xii. 21. 2
thou, O *fayrest* Princesse under sky! . . . II. Pr. 4. 6
Doth beare the *fayrest* flowre in honourable seed. . . . II. iii. 10. 9
'O *fairest* under skie! . . . II. iii. 38. 1
The *fairest* wight that wonneth under skie, . . . II. vii. 49. 2
Fayre Helena, the *fairest* living wight; . . . II. x. 59. 5
He dying left the *fairest* Tanaquill, . . . II. x. 76. 4
eke the *fayrest* Alma mett him there . . . II. xi. 49. 3
of the *fayrest* late, now made the fowlest place. . . . II. xii. 83. 9
The *fayrest* vertue, far above the rest: . . . III. Pr. 1. 2
His Cynthia, his heavens *fayrest* light? . . . III. Pr. 4. 6
Ne let his *fayrest* Cynthia refuse . . . III. Pr. 5. 5
Most goodly meede, the *fairest* Dame alive: . . . III. i. 18. 8
That she is fairer then our *fairest* Dame; . . . III. i. 27. 4
fairest knight alive, when armed was her brest. . . . III. ii. 4. 9
spred Abroad thy fresh youths *fayrest* flowre, . . . III. ii. 31. 7
fayrest fortune to the Prince befell, . . . III. iv. 47. 6
she is the *fairest* wight alive, I trow.' . . . III. v. 5. 9
Affrighted had the *fairest* Florimell, . . . III. v. 23. 2
it *fayrest* Flowre doth spyre, . . . III. v. 52. 8
The *fayrest* creature that he ever saw . . . III. vii. 13. 2
The *fairest* wight on ground, and most of men esteem'd. . . . III. viii. 13. 9
fairest Florimell It was . . . III. viii. 19. 6
The *fairest* woman-wight that ever eie did see. . . . III. ix. 21. 9
the *fayrest* Dame That ever Greece did boast, . . . III. ix. 34. 7
fairest Lady knight,' . . . 'Pardon, I pray, . . . III. ix. 47. 1
before the heavens *fairest* light . . . was fully reard, . . . III. x. 52. 6
avow'd That *fairest* Amoret was his by right, . . . IV. i. 10. 3

Fairest—*Continued.*
the *fayrest* Florimell him seemed To him was fallen . . . IV. ii. 8. 3
fayrest floure Wouldst gather faine, . . . IV. ii. 14. 3
That *fayrest* Florimell was present there in place. . . . IV. ii. 22. 9
'*Fayrest* of faire, that fairenesse doest excell, . . . IV. ii. 23. 4
of them all she, that is *fayrest* found, . . . IV. ii. 27. 1
Shall to that *fairest* Ladie be prefard. . . . IV. ii. 27. 4
fairest is, and from her faith will never swerve. . . . IV. v. 1. 9
To her therefore The *fayrest* Ladie was adjudgd . . . IV. v. 8. 9
yeeld the *fayrest* her due fee. . . . IV. v. 9. 9
some that *fairest* her did weene, . . . IV. v. 11. 4
By view of all the *fairest* to him brought, . . . IV. v. 12. 8
so forged things do *fairest* shew. . . . IV. v. 15. 9
Graunted to her, as to the *fayrest* Dame. . . . IV. v. 16. 2
First in the midst to set that *fayrest* Dame, . . . IV. v. 25. 4
The *fayrest* Ladie reft, and ever since withheld.' . . . IV. vi. 6. 9
from him his *fairest* love did beare. . . . IV. vi. 7. 3
love of *fairest* Ladie could constraine; . . . IV. ix. 3. 5
That she mote match the *fairest* of her daies, . . . IV. ix. 16. 6
Excludes from *fairest* hope withouten further triall. . . . IV. x. 17. 9
Doest *fayrest* shine, and most adorne thy place; . . . IV. x. 44. 3
That same was *fayrest* Amoret in place, . . . IV. x. 52. 8
Fairest Pherusa, Phao lilly white, . . . IV. xi. 49. 5
chiefly of the *fairest* Florimell, . . . V. ii. 2. 8
then to him came *fayrest* Florimell, . . . V. iii. 15. 6
Presented to the *fayrest* Florimell, . . . V. iii. 27. 8
The *fayrest* kyne alive, but of the fiercest kynd: . . . V. x. 9. 9
The *fayrest* Pastorella her by name did hight. . . . VI. ix. 9. 9
The father of the *fayrest* Pastorell, . . . VI. ix. 14. 2
home came the *fayrest* Pastorell, . . . VI. ix. 17. 5
The *fayrest* Ladie then of all that living were: . . . VI. xii. 3. 9
(Beeing of old the best and *fairest* Hill . . . VII. vi. 37. 6
all the *fairest* flowres and freshest buds . . . VII. vii. 33. 7
faire May, the *fayrest* mayd on ground, . . . VII. vii. 34. 1
if in presence of that *fayrest* proud . . . *Am.* ii. 9
Whatso is *fayrest* shall to earth returne. . . . *Am.* xiii. 8
that which *fairest* is, . . . Her mind . . . *Am.* xv. 13
Fayrer then *fayrest!* let none ever say, . . . *Am.* xx. 13
O *fayrest* fayre! let never it be named, . . . *Am.* xli. 13
fayrest ymages Of hardest marble are of purpose made, . . . *Am.* li. 1
fayrest she, when so she doth display The gate . . . *Am.* lxxxi. 9
O *fayrest* Phoebus! father of the Muse! . . . *Epith.* 121
Hast thee, O *fayrest* Planet, to thy home, . . . *Epith.* 282
O! *fayrest* goddesse, do thou not envy . . . *Epith.* 376
Fairer then *fairest*, in his fayning eye, . . . *H.L.* 216
that *fayrest* starre Which lights the world . . . *H.B.* 111

Fair-fearful. with *faire fearefull* humblesse towards him shee came: . . . I. iii. 26. 9

Fair-filed. His practick witt and his *fayre fyled* tonge, . . . II. i. 3. 6

Fair-forged. That feigning dreame, and that *faire-forged* Spright, . . . I. ii. 2. 2

Fairies. *See* **Faeries.**

Fairly. In summers day, when Phoebus *fairly* shone, . . . *Van.* ii. 1
fairly paced forth with easie paine, . . . *Hub.* 1264
As *fairly* formd as any star in skyes; . . . *As.* 188
The knight . . . Gan *fairely* couch his speare, . . . I. ii. 15. 3
glauncing downe his shield from blame him *fairly* blest. . . . I. ii. 18. 9
skyen . . . not made to burne, but *fayrely* for to shyne. . . . I. iv. 9. 9
With gentle wordes he can her *fayrely* greet, . . . I. iv. 46. 1
The witch approching gan him *fayrely* greet, . . . I. vii. 3. 6
There *fayrely* them receives a gentle Squyre, . . . I. x. 7. 1
fayrely eke besought Himselfe to cherish, . . . I. x. 29. 4
The knight gan *fayrely* couch his steady speare, . . . I. xi. 16. 1
The which afore is *fayrly* to be kend, . . . I. xii. 1. 4
So *fairely* dight when she in presence came, . . . I. xii. 24. 1
Well may she speede, and *fairely* finish her intent! . . . I. xii. 42. 9
fairely quit him of th' imputed blame; . . . II. i. 20. 2
fairely fare on foot, how ever loth; . . . II. ii. 12. 3
Thus *fairely* shee attempered her feast, . . . II. ii. 39. 1
fayrly couching his steeleheaded speare, . . . II. v. 3. 6
fairly tempring, fond desire subdewd, . . . II. vi. 26. 6
passed *fayrely* forth. . . . II. vi. 40. 5
Bidding his winged vessell *fairely* forward fly: . . . II. vii. 1. 9
great Mammon *fayrely* he besought . . . II. vii. 65. 8
entertained them right *fairely*, as befell. . . . II. ix. 17. 9
Of hewen stone the porch was *fayrely* wrought, . . . II. ix. 24. 1
fayrely feasted as so noble knightes she ought. . . . II. x. 77. 9
goodly frame of Temperaunce *Fayrely* to rise, . . . II. xii. 1. 2
They marched *fayrly* forth, of nought ydred. . . . II. xii. 38. 7
So is his angry corage *fayrly* pacifyde. . . . III. i. 11. 9
fairely well shee thryvd, . . . III. iv. 44. 8
Shee came . . . And *fairely* them saluted, . . . III. ix. 26. 8
Yet *fairely* well he did them all dismay, . . . IV. i. 2. 5
pacing *fairely* forth did bid all haile, . . . IV. iii. 46. 5
the which it *fairely* blest From foule mischance; . . . IV. vi. 13. 4
Till Britomart him *fairely* thus behight: . . . IV. vi. 38. 5
Artegall him *fairely* gan asswage, . . . V. ii. 47. 3
Them *fairely* entertaynd with curt'sies meete, . . . V. iv. 51. 5
fairely did dissemble her sad thoughts unrest. . . . V. v. 44. 9
Where him Blandina *fayrely* entertayned . . . VI. vi. 41. 3
All *fairely* deckt with heavens goodly storie; . . . VII. vi. 8. 4
those sweete rosy leaves, so *fairely* spred . . . *H.B.* 94
more *fairely* dight With chearefull grace . . . *H.B.* 130

Fairness. sith *fairenesse* is neglected? . . . *D.* 205
'Fayrest of faire, that *fairenesse* doest excell, . . . IV. ii. 23. 4
yet indeede her *fairenesse* doth exceede. . . . *H.B.* 231
The *fairenesse* of her face no tongue can tell; . . . *H.H.B.* 204

Fair-powdered. deckt the azure field with her *fayre pouldred* skin. . . . III. ii. 25. 9

Fair-seeming. which fondly here admyre *Faire seeming* shewes, *H.H.B.* 17

Fall—*Continued.*
To weet what end to straunger knights may *fall*. . . . . . . I. v. 3. 3
twise he reeled, readie twise to *fall*: . . . . I. v. 11. 6
Why suffredst thou thy Nephewes deare to *fall*, ... I. v. 22. 7
The *fall* of famous children borne of mee, ... I. v. 25. 2
he the man that made Sansfoy to *fall*, ... I. v. 26. 3
The Antique ruins of the Romanes *fall*: . . . . I. v. 49. 4
al through that great Princesse pride did *fall*, ... I. v. 53. 5
The woodborne people *fall* before her flat, ... I. vi. 16. 1
The wofull Dwarfe, which saw his maisters *fall* . . . . . . I. vii. 19. 1
all . . . in sight Before that shield did fade, and suddeine *fall*: I. vii. 35. 4
for feare into his jawes to *fall*, ... I. vii. 44. 6
with mighty mall The monster mercilesse him made to *fall*, I. vii. 51. 5
Whose *fall* did never foe before behold: . . . . I. vii. 51. 6
perils doe enfold The righteous man, to make him daily *fall*, I. viii. 1. 2
The ydle stroke, . . . Did *fall* to ground, ... I. viii. 8. 4
like a block Did *fall* to ground, ... I. viii. 10. 7
in his *fall* his shield, . . . Did loose his vele . . . . . . I. viii. 19. 1
He downe let *fall* his arme, ... I. viii. 19. 7
Whom when his maistresse proud perceiv'd to *fall*, ... I. viii. 20. 6
The mightie trunck, . . . *fall* with fearefull drift. . . . . I. viii. 22. 9
Such was this Gyaunts *fall*, ... I. viii. 23. 8
Whose grievous *fall* when false Duessa spyde, ... I. viii. 25. 1
Doth soonest *fall* in disaventrous fight, ... I. ix. 11. 8
Into the which hereafter thou maist happen *fall*. . . . . . I. ix. 45. 9
To leade aright, that he should never *fall* . . . . I. x. 34. 7
as the tree does *fall*, so lyes it ever low. . . . . I. x. 41. 9
that reprochfull *fall* right fowly he disdaynd; . . . . . . I. xi. 23. 9
late she saw him *fall* before his enimy. . . . . I. xi. 33. 9
did fiercely *fall* Upon his sunne-bright shield, ... I. xi. 40. 8
The tree of life, the crime of our first fathers *fall*. . . . . I. xi. 46. 9
the second *fall* Of her deare knight, ... I. xi. 50. 1
The knight him selfe even trembled at his *fall*, ... I. xi. 55. 1
To tell how he had seene the Dragons fatall *fall*. . . . . . I. xii. 2. 9
Rejoycing at the *fall* of that great beast, ... I. xii. 4. 8
Hath made sad witnesse of thy fathers *fall*, ... II. i. 37. 2
Let one word *fall* that may your grief unfold, ... II. i. 46. 7
downe they lett their cruell weapons *fall*, ... II. ii. 32. 3
prostrated *fall*, And kisse my stirrup; . . . . II. iii. 8. 5
Sore bruzed with the *fall* he slow uprose, ... II. v. 5. 1
Under Sir Guyons puissaunt stroke to *fall*, ... II. v. 25. 6
most hevenly faire . . . till she did *fall*; . . . . II. vii. 45. 8
All which he did to do him deadly *fall* . . . . II. vii. 64. 1
did he *fall* by treason, or by fight? . . . . II. viii. 24. 4
The one upon his covered shield did *fall*, ... II. viii. 38. 3
Yet sith his fate so cruelly did *fall*, ... II. viii. 52. 7
with the noise it shooke as it would *fall*. . . . . II. ix. 11. 5
Such was the end that to disloyall love did *fall*. . . . . . II. x. 19. 9
his dead corse should *fall* upon the flore; . . . . II. xi. 37. 8
A second *fall* redoubling backe agayne. . . . . II. xi. 43. 5
So soone as he unto her wombe did *fall*: . . . . II. xi. 45. 6
His looser garment to the ground did *fall*, ... II. xii. 46. 7
secretly doth us procure to *fall* . . . . II. xii. 48. 5
Ne suffred storme nor frost on them to *fall*, ... II. xii. 51. 3
as did *fall*. . . . . II. xii. 68. 3
the base murmure of the waters *fall*; . . . . II. xii. 71. 6
The waters *fall* with difference discreet, ... II. xii. 71. 7
in his *fall* so well him selfe he bare, ... III. i. 6. 8
Great shame and sorrow of that *fall* he tooke; . . . . . . III. i. 7. 1
hold them backe that would in error *fall*: . . . . III. i. 46. 5
Like sparkes of fire which *fall* in sclender flex, ... III. i. 47. 7
Into his hidden nett full easely doth *fall*. . . . . III. i. 54. 9
she In love with him did *fall*. . . . . III. ii. Arg.
it uptaking ere the *fall*, ... III. ii. 9. 3
him shall make in mischiefe *fall*. . . . . III. iii. 28. 9
make him shake, and shortly learn to *fall*. . . . . III. iii. 49. 9
with mortall stroke astownd, Doth groveling *fall*, ... III. iv. 17. 6
oft let *fall* Many meeke wordes . . . . III. iv. 48. 8
Lifteth it up that els would lowly *fall*: . . . . III. v. 2. 6
It lettes not *fall*, it lettes it not to rest; . . . . III. v. 2. 7
Few trickling teares she softly forth let *fall*, ... III. vii. 9. 2
her golden girdle, which did *fall* From her in flight, . . . III. vii. 31. 8
Downe in a Dongeon deepe he let her *fall*, ... III. viii. 41. 8
wicked Sprightes did *fall* from happy blis; . . . . III. ix. 2. 8
her well-plighted frock . . . Shee low let *fall*, ... III. ix. 21. 5
discontent With his late *fall* and fowle indignity, ... III. ix. 25. 2
'O lamentable *fall* of famous towne! . . . . III. ix. 39. 2
continuall feare Of that rocks *fall*, ... III. x. 58. 4
Threates with huge ruine him to *fall* upon, ... III. x. 58. 5
Trembling through feare least down he *fallen* should, ... III. xi. 34. 8
that mightie chaine, . . . adowne gan *fall*, ... III. xii. 37. 8
answere for thy wrong as shall *fall* out in fight.' . . . . . IV. ii. 13. 9
they at last their wrothfull hands let *fall*, ... IV. ii. 21. 8
never discord did amongst them *fall*, ... IV. ii. 54. 2
did not from him let One drop of bloud to *fall*, ... IV. iii. 24. 3
by chaunce doth *fall* Into the hunters toile, ... IV. iv. 32. 5
Shall *fall* the girdle of faire Florimell: . . . . IV. v. 2. 5
Upon his heavie eye-lids chaunst to *fall*, ... IV. v. 42. 2
He sees her face; doth *fall* in love, ... IV. vi. Arg.
Saluting him gan into speach to *fall*, ... IV. vii. 43. 8
Faint friends when they *fall* out most cruell fomen bee. . . IV. ix. 27. 9
that wretched Greeke . . . Did *fall* in love: . . . . IV. x. 40. 6
For feare of perill which to him mote *fall* . . . . IV. xi. 7. 8
rules the Seas and makes them rise or *fall*; . . . . IV. xi. 11. 2
let their swelling waters low before him *fall*. . . . . . . IV. xi. 30. 9
ill perhaps mote *fall* to either side; . . . . V. i. 25. 4
Through which the rider downe doth *fall* . . . . V. ii. 7. 9
All destitute of helpe doth headlong *fall*; . . . . V. ii. 8. 4
His foe confused through his sodaine *fall*, ... V. ii. 8. 7
a trap was letten downe to *fall* . . . . V. ii. 12. 6

Fall—*Continued.*
But he was well aware, and leapt before his *fall*. . . . . . V. ii. 12. 9
Whilest he to gathering of the gold did *fall*: . . . . V. ii. 23. 8
whatsoever from one place doth *fall* . . . . V. ii. 39. 7
Weigh but one word which from thy lips doth *fall*: . . . . . V. ii. 43. 6
best to him to whom the best should *fall*. . . . . V. iii. 14. 4
by misfortune in his hand did *fall*.' . . . . V. iii. 22. 8
for it these Squires at ods did *fall*, ... V. iv. 5. 6
Whose life did lie in her least eye-lids *fall*; . . . . V. v. 47. 5
Did cast for to allure into her trap to *fall*. . . . . V. v. 52. 9
The bird that warned Peter of his *fall*, ... V. vi. 27. 2
By a false trap was let adowne to *fall* . . . . V. vi. 27. 7
if two met, the one mote needes *fall* over the lidge. . . . . V. vi. 36. 9
That for another Canto will more fitly *fall*. . . . . V. vii. 45. 9
in his *fall* misfortune him mistooke; . . . . V. viii. 8. 1
A chearefull countenance on them let *fall*, ... V. ix. 34. 8
let, instead thereof, to *fall* Few perling drops . . . . . . V. ix. 50. 6
even then ruing her wilfull *fall* . . . . V. x. 4. 7
somewhat short did *fall*, ... V. xi. 8. 8
two more of his armes did *fall* away, ... V. xi. 11. 7
made him oftentimes in field before me *fall*. . . . . V. xi. 53. 9
in one day they with the coast did *fall*; . . . . V. xii. 4. 6
He shund his strokes, where ever they did *fall*, ... V. xii. 18. 3
at her feet did *fall*, ... V. xii. 24. 6
Whose sight to her is greatest crosse may *fall*, ... V. xii. 31. 4
How they might make him into mischiefe *fall*, ... V. xii. 37. 4
from the battlements she ready seem'd to *fall*. . . . . . . VI. i. 34. 9
feeling ill Of his late *fall*, ... VI. i. 35. 5
sith now occasion fit Doth *fall*, ... VI. ii. 33. 2
They *fall* too short of our fraile reckonings, ... VI. iii. 5. 4
arriving with the *fall* of day . . . . VI. iii. 37. 7
Here they of force (as fortune now did *fall*) . . . . VI. iv. 15. 5
all this land unto his foe shall *fall*, ... VI. iv. 32. 3
when she saw him *fall* Under that villaines club, ... VI. vii. 50. 1
The villaine met him in the middle *fall*, ... VI. viii. 10. 3
As if he never had received *fall*; . . . . VI. viii. 26. 2
with one *fall* his necke he almost brake; . . . . VI. ix. 44. 3
to the waters *fall* tuning their accents fit. . . . . VI. x. 7. 9
The Theeves *fall* out for Pastorell, ... VI. xi. Arg.
They *fall* to strokes, the frute of too much talke, ... VI. xi. 16. 2
Like as a sort of hungry dogs . . . Doe *fall* together, . . . VI. xi. 17. 3
when the lot to Pastorell did *fall*, ... VI. xi. 31. 8
Looking each houre into deathes mouth to *fall*, ... VI. xi. 44. 7
backeward he enforced him to *fall*; . . . . VI. xii. 30. 4
to men, whose *fall* she did bemone, ... VII. vi. 11. 5
Typhons *fall*, or proud Ixions paine, ... VII. vi. 29. 6
Still change and vary thoughts, as new occasions *fall*. . . . VII. vii. 19. 9
times and seasons of the yeare that *fall*: . . . . VII. vii. 27. 4
To whether side should *fall* the soveraine place: . . . . . VII. vii. 57. 7
fall lowly at her feet; And, with meeke . . . . *Am.* ii. 10
fall downe and dy before her; . . . . *Am.* xiv. 13
Upon thee *fall* for thine accursed hyre . . . . *Am.* lxxxv. 6
shall fade and *fall* away To that they were, ... *H.B.* 95
Deigne to let *fall* one drop of dew reliefe, ... *H.B.* 284
emptie place . . . through those Angels *fall*, ... *H.H.L.* 102
But lowly *fall* before his mercie seate, ... *H.H.B.* 148

Fallen. *See* **Fall.**
great Babylon is *fallen*. . . . . *Rev.* ii. 14
When the rayne is *faln*, ... *S.C.* S. 18
The flattring fruite is *fallen* to grownd before, ... *S.C.* D. 106
As if againe he would have *fallen* to ground; . . . . *D.* 543
Falne into mischiefe through intemperaunce, ... II. iv. 36. 2
languish, as the leafe *faln* from the tree, ... III. ii. 39. 8
His locks, like faded leaves *fallen* to grownd, ... III. v. 29. 5
To him was *fallen* for his happie lot, ... IV. ii. 8. 4
Now *falne* into their fellowship by chance: . . . . IV. iv. 7. 4
calfe is *falne* unwares Into some pit, ... IV. xii. 17. 6
now was *falne* into new languishment . . . . IV. xii. 23. 5
Well weening that his foe was *falne* withall; . . . . V. ii. 12. 8
falne on you by heavens hard direction . . . . V. iv. 26. 7
Now when they saw it *falne*, they eke him greeted all. . . V. xi. 15. 9
Fallen into that Tyrants hand and usage bad. . . . . V. xi. 40. 9
was *fall'n* into this feeble case Through many wounds, . . VI. vi. 20. 7
had he not upon him *fallen* light, ... VI. ix. 44. 4
They both are *fallen*, that all the earth did feare, ... *Com. Son.* iv. 6

Falleth. as it *falleth*, in the gentlest harts . . . . III. ii. 23. 1
He *falleth* nigh to ground, ... IV. iii. 19. 9
falleth downe to ground like senselesse thing; . . . . . . VI. vii. 9. 7
first it *falleth* me by course to tell Of faire Serena; . . . VI. viii. 31. 1
here *falleth* fittest to unfold Her antique race . . . . . . VII. vi. 2. 1

Falling. With sodaine *falling* broken all to dust. . . . . . *Bel.*[1] iv. 14
tune hir plaint to *falling* rivers sound, ... *Bel.*[1] viii. 3
To *falling* rivers sound thus tun'd her sobs. . . . . *Bel.*[2] x. 4
their Parent deare They saw . . . *falling* to the ground, . . I. i. 25. 2
falling her before on lowly knee, ... I. v. 16. 2
her child from *falling* oft does reare. . . . . I. x. 35. 9
falling flat great humblesse he did make, ... I. xii. 25. 6
falling them beforne, Besought them . . . . II. ii. 27. 4
Both *falling* out doe stirre up strifefull broyle, ... IV. iii. 16. 5
falling heavie on Cambelloes crest, ... IV. iii. 34. 2
scarse he him upheld from *falling* in a swound. . . . . . . IV. iv. 24. 9
on her knee before him *falling* lowe, ... IV. xii. 29. 5
Where *falling* downe his challenge he releast: . . . . V. vi. 39. 7
falling on his mother earth he fed: . . . . V. xii. 23. 7
falling lowly at his feet . . . . VI. vi. 31. 5
falling downe with humble awe, ... VI. vii. 36. 8

Falls. See **Trap-falls.**
How *falls* it then that this faded Oake, ... *S.C.* F. 169
How *falles* it, then, we no merrier bene, ... *S.C.* May 3
in fields where *falls* hem best. . . . . *S.C.* Jun. 76

Falls—*Continued.*

levin, That seeldome *falles* bynethe . . . *S.C.* Jul. 92
as occasion *Falls* out, my selfe fit . . . *Hub.* 202
Truth . . . *fals* In hand of leachour . . . I. iii. Arg.
after their wofull *falles,* Through wicked pride . . . I. v. 51. 3
as a Castle . . . At last downe *falles;* . . . I. viii. 23. 5
'Unhappy *falls* that hard necessity,' . . . I. xii. 19. 1
The strong through pleasure soonest *falles,* . . . II. i. 57. 9
Hard is his hap that first *fals* in his jeopardee.' . . . II. iv. 43. 9
a large purple streame adowne their giambeux *falles.* . . . II. vi. 29. 9
The stone-dead quarrey *falls* so forciblye, . . . II. xi. 43. 3
nought that *falles* into this direfull deepe . . . II. xii. 6. 7
see soone after how she fades and *falls* away . . . II. xii. 74. 9
It *falls* me here to write of Chastity, . . . III. Pr. 1. 1
fals to ground to seeke for succor theare, . . . III. viii. 33. 5
Well *falles* it thee that I am not in plight . . . IV. i. 44. 5
It often *fals,* (as here it earst befell) . . . IV. iv. 1. 1
With dreadfull force *falles* on some steeple hie; . . . IV. vi. 14. 3
as oft it *fals* in chace, . . . IV. vii. 24. 1
(As often *falles*) of sundry things did commen: . . . V. ix. 4. 3
It often *fals,* in course of common life, . . . V. xi. 1. 1
Who ever thinkes . . . To wrong the weaker, oft *falles* . . . VI. ii. 23. 9
oft it *falles,* that . . . Knights doe rashly enterprize . . . VI. vi. 35. 3
all which I put in *fals* out anon, . . . VI. viii. 24. 7
scorneth others ayde; That soonest *fals,* . . . *Am.* lviii. 3
he, that standeth on the hyghest stayre, *Fals* lowest; . . . *Am.* lviii. 12
How *falles* it then . . . *H.L.* 158
oft it *falles* that many a gentle mynd . . . *H.B.* 141
oft it *falles,* (aye me, the more to rew!) . . . *H.B.* 148

Faln(e). *See* **Fallen.**

False. when their *false* harts bene hidde, . . . *S.C.* May 170
false Fortune such joy did him spight, . . . *S.C.* May 198
the *false* Foxe came to the dore anone: . . . *S.C.* May 236
in came The *false* Foxe, . . . *S.C.* May 279
they bene *false,* and full of covetise, . . . *S.C.* S. 82
also him that *false* Ulysses slewe, . . . *Gn.* 531
through so *false* illusion, Doth turne the name . . . *Hub.* 219
And the *false* Foxe his dog . . . *Hub.* 304
For their *false* treason and vile theeverie: . . . *Hub.* 315
False personages fit for everie sted, . . . *Hub.* 861
otherwise *false* Reynold would abuse The simple Suter, . . . *Hub.* 883
the *false* Foxe him helped to array . . . *Hub.* 1063
the *false* Foxe most kindly plaid his part; . . . *Hub.* 1137
his *false* counsellor, the cause of all, . . . *Hub.* 1243
the Foxe, and his *false* blandishment: . . . *Hub.* 1274
the *false* Foxe, when he the Lion heard, . . . *Hub.* 1359
his *false* hart, fraught with all treasons store, . . . *Mui.* 395
ne feed on *false* delight . . . *D.* 492
A fit *false* dreame, that can delude the sleepers sent.' . . . I. i. 43. 9
bad him . . . with *false* shewes abuse his fantasy, . . . I. i. 46. 4
that *false* winged boy Her chaste hart had subdewd . . . I. i. 47. 8
Eftsoones he tooke . . . that *false* other Spright, . . . I. ii. 3. 2
Come, see where your *false* Lady doth her honor staine.' . . . I. ii. 4. 9
Where that *false* couple were full closely ment . . . I. ii. 5. 4
fortune *false* betraide me to thy powre, . . . I. ii. 22. 5
'The author then,' . . . Is one Duessa, a *false* sorceresse, . . . I. ii. 34. 8
ever *false* Duessa seemde as faire as shee . . . I. ii. 37. 9
The *false* witch did my wrathfull hand withhold: . . . I. ii. 39. 8
The *false* Duessa, . . . I. ii. 44. 1
false Duessa in her sted had borne, . . . I. iv. 2. 3
false Duessa, seeming Lady fayre, . . . I. iv. 13. 2
he was *false,* and fraught with ficklenesse, . . . I. iv. 25. 5
Emongst the rest rode that *false* Lady faire, . . . I. iv. 37. 4
No knight, but treachour full of *false* despight . . . I. iv. 41. 5
Into new woes . . . cast By this *false* faytor, . . . I. iv. 47. 4
I feare the fickle freakes,' . . . 'Of fortune *false,* . . . I. iv. 50. 2
his . . . foe; Whom *false* Duessa saves, . . . I. v. Arg.
lowd to him gan call The *false* Duessa, . . . I. v. 11. 9
in *false* griefe hyding his harmefull guile, . . . I. v. 18. 5
The *false* resemblaunce of Deceipt . . . Did closely lurke; . . . I. v. 27. 3
him before His father fierce of treason *false* accusd, . . . I. v. 37. 8
The *false* Duessa . . . Returnd to stately pallace . . . I. v. 45. 1
Provokt with Wrath and Envyes *false* surmise, . . . I. v. 46. 7
that *false* Pilgrim, which that leasing told, . . . I. vi. 48. 1
that *false* Dame, The *false* Duessa, . . . I. vii. 1. 8, 9
Upon this dreadfull Beast . . . He sett the *false* Duessa, . . . I. vii. 18. 9
The wanton loves of *false* Fidessa fayre, . . . I. vii. 26. 3
him chaunced *false* Duessa meete, . . . I. vii. 50. 6
No *false* enchauntment . . . Might once abide . . . I. viii. 4. 5
Whose grievous fall when *false* Duessa spyde, . . . I. viii. 25. 1
clift, Whose *false* foundacion waves have washt away, . . . I. xi. 54. 6
false Duessa, . . . Her *false* sleightes doe imploy . . . I. xii. Arg.
False erraunt knight, infamous, . . . I. xii. 27. 4
Or *false* or trew, or living or else dead, . . . I. xii. 28. 2
this *false* woman that Fidessa hight, . . . I. xii. 32. 2
Most *false* Duessa, royall richly dight, . . . I. xii. 32. 4
Too *false* and strong for earthly skill or might, . . . I. xii. 32. 7
treasons . . . wrought by that *false* sorceresse: . . . I. xii. 33. 6
this *false* footman, clokt with simplenesse, . . . I. xii. 34. 6
the Gard . . . Attacht that faytor *false,* . . . I. xii. 35. 5
that *false* Traytour did my honour reave?' . . . II. i. 17. 5
'*False* traytour certes . . . II. i. 17. 6
under simple shew and semblant plaine Lurkt *false* Duessa . . . II. i. 21. 4
So had *false* Archimago her disguysd, . . . II. i. 21. 6
A *false* infamous faitour . . . II. i. 30. 3
Acrasia, a *false* enchaunteresse, . . . II. i. 51. 3
Till I that *false* Acrasia have wonne; . . . II. ii. 44. 6
By Guyon, and by that *false* Redcrosse knight; . . . II. iii. 13. 6
he went, and his owne *false* part playd, . . . II. iv. 27. 7
Philemon, *false* faytour Philemon, . . . II. iv. 30. 6

False—*Continued.*

his eyes and sences fed With *false* delights, . . . II. vi. 14. 2
Apple . . . emongst the gods *false* Ate threw; . . . II. vii. 55. 5
False Archimage provokte their corage prowd, . . . II. viii. 11. 3
Made it selfe famous through *false* trechery, . . . II. viii. 12. 6
'*False* traitour! miscreaunt! . . . II. viii. 31. 6
The whiles *false* Archimage and Atin fled apace . . . II. viii. 56. 9
false Acrasia, and her wicked wiles; . . . II. ix. 9. 6
Androgeus, *false* to native soyle, . . . II. x. 48. 6
Bad counsels, prayses, and *false* flatteries: . . . II. xi. 10. 8
aery spirite under *false* pretence, . . . II. xi. 39. 8
Where many Mermayds haunt making *false* melodies: . . . II. xii. 17. 9
With her *false* eyes fast fixed in his sight, . . . II. xii. 73. 2
with crafty glaunce Of her *false* eies, . . . III. i. 50. 7
The bird that knowes not the *false* fowlers call, . . . III. i. 54. 8
read where I that faytour *false* may find.' . . . III. ii. 13. 2
when his love was *false* he with a peaze it brake . . . III. ii. 20. 9
the *false* Archer, which that arrow shot . . . III. ii. 26. 7
through that *false* Ladies traine He was surprisd, . . . III. iii. 11. 1
By *false* illusion of a guilefull Spright . . . III. iii. 13. 4
whylome by *false* Faries stolne away, . . . III. iii. 26. 6
the wicked sorcery Of *false* Pellite . . . III. iii. 36. 4
With double sences, and with *false* debate, . . . III. iv. 28. 8
'Fond Proteus, father of *false* prophecis! . . . III. iv. 37. 1
Yet did *false* Archimage her still pursew, . . . III. iv. 45. 1
his *false* venim through their veines inspir'd: . . . III. vi. 15. 5
The wicked engine through *false* influence . . . III. ix. 29. 3
In speaking many *false* belgardes at her let fly . . . III. ix. 52. 9
False love! why do men say thou canst not see, . . . III. x. 4. 3
his *false* engins fast he plyde, . . . III. x. 7. 2
He wept, and wayld, and *false* laments belyde, . . . III. x. 7. 7
Thus finely did he his *false* nets dispred, . . . III. x. 9. 6
Such as *false* love doth oft upon him weare; . . . III. xi. 51. 8
deeds were forged, and her words *false* coynd, . . . III. xii. 14. 8
Inconstant Chaunge, and *false* Disloyalty; . . . III. xii. 25. 6
Nether of ydle showes, nor of *false* charmes aghast . . . III. xii. 29. 9
Through *false* allurement of that pleasing baite, . . . IV. Pr. 1. 7
Die had she lever . . . Then to be *false* in love, . . . IV. i. 6. 9
The one of them the *false* Duessa hight, . . . IV. i. 18. 1
Her *false* Duessa, . . . raised from below . . . IV. i. 19. 5
Fild with *false* rumors and seditious trouble, . . . IV. i. 28. 3
Faithlesse Duessa, and *false* Paridell, . . . IV. i. 32. 8
whether were more *false* full hard it is to tell . . . IV. i. 32. 9
'*False* faitour Scudamour, that hast by slight . . . IV. i. 44. 2
So hast thou to thy selfe *false* honour often wonne.' . . . IV. i. 44. 9
'Ah gentle knight!' then *false* Duessa sayd, . . . IV. i. 46. 1
So *false* Duessa; but vile Ate thus: . . . IV. i. 47. 1
'Fy, fy! *false* knight,' (then *false* Duessa cryde) . . . IV. i. 51. 6
'*False* traitour squire! *false* squire of falsest knight! . . . IV. i. 52. 6
Yet thou, *false* Squire, his fault shalt deare aby, . . . IV. i. 53. 8
Blandamour winnes *false* Florimell; . . . IV. ii. Arg.
Through that *false* witch, and that foule aged drevill; . . . IV. ii. 3. 8
by his *false* allurements wylie draft . . . IV. ii. 10. 4
that *false* spright . . . Was so expert . . . IV. ii. 10. 6
So blind is lust *false* colours to descry . . . IV. ii. 11. 5
did Paridell produce His *false* Duessa, . . . IV. v. 11. 2
all his gealous feare he *false* had found, . . . IV. vi. 28. 2
False crimes and facts, such as they never ment, . . . IV. viii. 35. 6
From his *false* eyes into their harts . . . IV. viii. 48. 9
false Florimel By Braggadochio lately was redeemed; . . . IV. ix. 20. 6
False Labyrinthes, fond runners eyes to daze; . . . IV. x. 24. 8
few Could weenen whether they were *false* or trew: . . . IV. xi. 27. 5
him doth chyde as *false* and fraudulent, . . . IV. xii. 23. 2
Whether old Proteus true or *false* had sayd, . . . IV. xii. 28. 4
The right or wrong, the *false* or else the trew?' . . . V. ii. 44. 6
then the *false* he layd In th' other scale; . . . V. ii. 45. 6
by no meanes the *false* will with the truth be wayd . . . V. ii. 45. 9
Keeping there close with him . . . his *false* Ladie, . . . V. iii. 13. 5
The semblant of this *false* by his faire beauties Queene . . . V. iii. 19. 9
the *false* mayden shortly turn'd againe Unto the prison, . . . V. v. 51. 8
find In her *false* hart his bondage to unbind, . . . V. v. 56. 5
least his *false* foe did him entrap . . . V. vi. 4. 3
false watches, wellaway! . . . V. vi. 25. 4
By a *false* trap was let adowne to fall . . . V. vi. 27. 7
Those two *false* brethren on that perillous Bridge, . . . V. vi. 36. 6
'Thou recreant *false* traytor, . . . V. vi. 37. 4
soone after me she sent These two *false* Knights, . . . V. viii. 23. 3
Can follow out those *false* footsteps of his, . . . V. ix. 6. 8
his *false* intent to shade, . . . V. ix. 12. 7
That *false* Duessa, which had wrought great care . . . V. ix. 40. 3
had her counsels *false* conspyred . . . V. ix. 41. 2
false Duessa, now untitled Queene, . . . V. ix. 42. 8
faynes to weave *false* tales and leasings bad, . . . V. xii. 36. 8
To her, that so *false* sclaunders at him threw . . . V. xii. 42. 5
'*False* traytor Knight!' . . . VI. i. 25. 1
Yet were her words and lookes but *false* and fayned, . . . VI. vi. 42. 1
To whom *false* Turpine comming courteously, . . . VI. vii. 4. 1
Bidding him turne againe, *false* traytour knight, . . . VI. vii. 7. 2
Thereof *false* Turpin was full glad and faine, . . . VI. vii. 17. 1
to entrap him by *false* treacherie: . . . VI. vii. 23. 5
False Fortune did her safety betray . . . VI. viii. 34. 8
never more delight in painted show Of such *false* blisse, . . . VI. x. 3. 8
without guile Or *false* dissemblaunce . . . VI. x. 24. 4
Unto whose bed *false* Bregog whylome stole, . . . VII. vi. 40. 4
All fearelesse then of so *false* enimies, . . . *Am.* xii. 3
fayrer weathers *false* delight . . . *Am.* lix. 8
Let no *false* treason seeke us to entrap, . . . *Epith.* 323
false whispers, breeding hidden feares, . . . *Epith.* 336
The *false* reports that flying tales doe beare, . . . *H.L.* 261
He taken was, betrayd, and *false* accused; . . . *H.H.L.* 240

False—*Continued.*
with *false* beauties flattring bait misled, . . . *H.H.B.* 290
Falsed. in his *falsed* fancy he her takes To be the fairest wight I. ii. 30. 3
to this Lady mild Thou *falsed* hast thy faith . . . I. ix. 46. 7
For *falsed* letters, and suborned wyle, . . . II. i. 1. 3
falsed oft his blowes t' illude him with such bayt. . . . II. v. 9. 9
His *falsed* fayth, and love too lightly flitt; . . . II. xii. 44. 7
with vaine thoughts her *falsed* fancy vex: . . . III. i. 47. 5
False-forged. *false forged* lyes, which thou didst tel, . . . *Am.* lxxxv. 7
Falsehood. Of their *falshode* more could I recount, . . . *S.C.* May 314
Devoid of care, and feare of all *falshedd;* . . . *Gn.* 246
Supplanted by fine *falshood* and faire guile; . . . *Hub.* 788
faire *falshood* . . . workes him woefull ruth. . . . I. ii. Arg.
I the mother bee Of *falshood,* . . . I. v. 27. 7
Such is the face of *falshood:* . . . I. viii. 49. 4
sore accus'd His *falshood,* . . . III. vi. 13. 4
well may she you reprove Of *falsehood* or of slouth, . . . III. viii. 27. 9
Vile treason and fowle *falshood* hidden were, . . . IV. i. 17. 8
glosse thereon doth shed To hide his *falshood,* . . . IV. v. 15. 6
With which he thresht out *falshood,* . . . V. i. 12. 9
whether with truth or *falshood* they agree. . . . V. ii. 47. 9
they with wrong or *falshood* will not fare, . . . V. ii. 48. 2
blotted out his armes with *falshood* blent, . . . V. iii. 37. 7
let your fame with *falshood* be defaced? . . . V. xi. 63. 5
Falsehood's. him to touch with *falshoods* fowle attaint, . . . V. vi. 12. 3
False-instilled. through her bones the *false instilled* fire Did spred . . . III. i. 56. 4
Falsely. holie brethren *falslie* to have praid. . . . *Ti.* 497
Sometimes he *falsely* faines himselfe to sleepe, . . . II. v. 34. 4
falsly seekst a vertuous wight to shame?' . . . IV. i. 48. 2
With forged cause them *falsely* to defame; . . . IV. viii. 25. 7
he *falsely* did revyle And foule blaspheme that Queene . . . V. ix. 25. 4
Falseness. any should of *falsenesse* her reprove, . . . III. viii. 42. 4
Falser. my *falser* friend did no less joyous deeme. . . . II. iv. 21. 9
Falser's. from the *falsers* fraude . . . to keepe. . . . *S.C.* Env. 6
Falsers'. of such *falsers* freendship bene fayne. . . . *S.C.* May 305
Falses. two *falses,* of each equall share, . . . V. ii. 48. 4
Falsest. Of those he chose out two, the *falsest* twoo, . . . I. i. 38. 6
Fidessa hight the *falsest* Dame on grownd, . . . I. xii. 32. 3
Archimago . . . The *falsest* man alive: . . . I. xii. 34. 9
'I Pilate am, the *falsest* Judge, alas! . . . II. vii. 62. 3
'False traitour squire! false squire of *falsest* knight! . . . IV. i. 52. 6
Falshedd. *See* **Falsehood.**
Faltering. With *foltring* tong, and trembling everie vaine, . . I. vii. 24. 7
foltring tongue, at last, these words seemd forth to shake; . . I. ix. 24. 9
With lips full pale and *foltring* tong opprest, . . . II. i. 47. 4
swelling throbs empeach His *foltring* toung . . . III. xi. 12. 3
Fame. With Thames inhabitants of noble *fame,* . . . *Ro.* xxii. 3
fill the world with never dying *fame!* . . . *Ro.* Env. 14
sittes not followe flying *fame,* . . . *S.C.* Jun. 75
The *fame* whereof doth dayly greater growe. . . . *S.C.* Jun. 92
fame now rings Through the wide world, . . . *Gn.* 149
th' one Aeacide did his *fame* extend; . . . *Gn.* 525
here the antique *fame* of stout Camill Doth ever live; . . . *Gn.* 601
like desire and praise of noble *fame,* . . . *Hub.* 769
His noble Spouse, and Paragon of *fame.* . . . *Ti.* 245
Fame with golden wings aloft doth flie, . . . *Ti.* 421
Her blazed *fame* which all the world had fil'd, . . . *Mui.* 266
His mistresse name, and his owne *fame* to raise. . . . *As.* 88
I found much greater then the former *fame;* . . . *Col.* 334
To let thy *fame* lie so in hidden shade: . . . *Col.* 407
To be the . . . Registres of everlasting *fame,* . . . *Ded. Son.* iv. 3
the noble Progeny, Which them succeed in *fame* . . . *Ded. Son.* iv. 6
In golden verse, worthy immortal *fame:* . . . *Ded. Son.* xii. 4
each where thou hast dispredd thy *fame,* . . . *Ded.Son.*xiv.13
Young knight . . . through long labours huntest after *fame,* I. iv. 1. 2
He had in armes abroad wonne muchell *fame,* . . . I. vi. 20. 5
Both carelesse of his health, and of his *fame;* . . . I. vii. 7. 3
Which flying *fame* throughout the world had spred, . . . I. vii. 46. 2
Ledd with thy prayses, and broad-blazed *fame,* . . . I. x. 11. 4
in th' immortall booke of *fame* To be eternized, . . . I. x. 59. 5
To Faery court thou cam'st to seek for *fame,* . . . I. x. 66. 8
The Nourse of time and everlasting *fame,* . . . I. xi. 5. 8
Lifting to heven her everlasting *fame:* . . . I. xii. 8. 5
draw them from pursuit of praise and *fame* . . . II. i. 23. 2
'Joy may you have, and everlasting *fame,* . . . II. i. 32. 1
It was an auncient worke of antique *fame,* . . . II. ii. 12. 8
that *fame* may it resound . . . II. iii. 38. 8
Which *fame* of her shrill trompet worthy reedes; . . . II. vii. 2. 7
envy base to barke at sleeping *fame.* . . . II. viii. 13. 7
dye with honour and desert of *fame;* . . . II. viii. 44. 5
Through great desire of glory and of *fame;* . . . II. ix. 38. 7
Immortall *fame* for ever hath enrold; . . . II. x. 4. 8
With recompence of everlasting *fame:* . . . II. x. 23. 5
envying the Britons blazed *fame,* . . . II. x. 47. 8
Elfant was of most renowmed *fame,* . . . II. x. 73. 3
Revivyng thought of glory and of *fame,* . . . II. xi. 31. 8
Both of their life and *fame,* . . . II. xii. 7. 9
here to seek for praise and *fame.* . . . III. ii. 7. 9
'*Fame* blazed hath, that here in Faery lond . . . III. ii. 8. 1
Ay doing thinges that to his *fame* redownd, . . . III. ii. 14. 5
Whence spring all noble deedes and never dying *fame:* . . . III. iii. 1. 9
That *fame* in tromp of gold eternally displayes. . . . III. iii. 3. 9
for terror of his *fame,* . . . III. iii. 12. 8
mickle *fame* Did get through great adventures . . . III. iv. 20. 5
through all Faerie lond his noble *fame* Now blazed was, . . III. iv. 21. 3
fame now flies, that of a forreine foe He is yslaine, . . . III. v. 9. 8
in perfect love and spotlesse *fame* Of chastitie, . . . III. v. 54. 3
The Gardin of Adonis, far renowmd by *fame.* . . . III. vi. 29. 9
be partakers of thy endlesse *fame.* . . . III. viii. 43. 7

Fame—*Continued.*
far much greater then thy *fame,* . . . III. ix. 33. 3
Sir Paris far renowmd through noble *fame;* . . . III. ix. 34. 5
Fame is my meed, and glory vertues pay: . . . III. x. 31. 7
brings forth glorious flowres of *fame,* . . . IV. Pr. 2. 7
knowne by *fame,* and by an Hebene speare, . . . IV. vi. 6. 4
Through thoughts aspyring to eternall *fame:* . . . IV. ix. 2. 5
the *fame* of this renowmed prise . . . IV. x. 4. 1
farre renowmed through exceeding *fame,* . . . IV. x. 5. 5
By whom those old Heroes wonne such *fame;* . . . IV. xi. 13. 2
Tybris, renowmed for the Romaines *fame,* . . . IV. xi. 21. 6
was of no lesse vertue then of *fame;* . . . V. i. 10. 5
all strove with perill to winne *fame;* . . . V. iii. 7. 5
when he understood by common *fame* . . . V. iii. 10. 5
after *fame* and honour for to hunt, . . . V. iv. 29. 3
With which whylome he gotten had great *fame:* . . . V. v. 20. 5
losse of *fame* in disaventrous field: . . . V. xi. 55. 8
let your *fame* with falshood be defaced? . . . V. xi. 63. 5
Dearer is love then life, and *fame* then gold; . . . V. xi. 63. 8
from low to high uplifted is your *fame.* . . . VI. Pr. 6. 9
far his *fame* display. . . . VI. i. 2. 9
hazard she at earst had made Of her good *fame;* . . . VI. iii. 8. 8
the badge of honour and of *fame,* . . . VI. iii. 35. 3
The which through *fame* should farre be magnifide, . . . VI. iv. 33. 3
Being with *fame* through many Nations blowen,) . . . VI. iv. 36. 5
soothly it was sayd by common *fame,* . . . VI. v. 37. 1
Either for *fame,* or else for exercize, . . . VI. vi. 35. 5
Besides the losse of so much loos and *fame,* . . . VI. xii. 12. 8
when Ireland florished in *fame* Of wealths . . . VII. vi. 38. 1
I may in trump of *fame* blaze over-all. . . . *Am.* xxix. 12
you shall live by *fame:* . . . *Am.* lxxv. 10
Fame in her shrill trump shal thunder, . . . *Am.* lxxxiv. 13
An house of auncient *fame:* . . . *Proth.* 131
That fillest England with thy triumphes *fame,* . . . *Proth.* 151
Fame's. On *Fames* eternall beadroll worthie to be fyled. . . . IV. ii. 32. 9
Familiar. She grew *familiare* in that desert place. . . . III. vii. 15. 5
Family. Out of his stocke and famous *familie,* . . . *Ti.* 276
The honor of the noble *familie:* . . . *Col.* 537
the whole *family,* therewith adredd, . . . III. i. 62. 7
On that vilde man and all his *family;* . . . V. vi. 35. 5
Famine. No griesly *famine,* nor no raging sweard, . . . *Col.* 314
His long endured *famine* needed more reliefe. . . . I. viii. 43. 9
spoyle, On which they weene their *famine* to asswage, . . . IV. iii. 16. 3
Famous. which her *famous* merite . . . out of the dust doth reare, . . . *Ro.* v. 12
Renowm'd for fruite of *famous* progenie, . . . *Ro.* vi. 6
Olde moniments, which of so *famous* sprights . . . *Ro.* vii. 3
Colin fittes such *famous* flight to scanne; . . . *S.C.* O. 88
famous light of all the Greekish hosts; . . . *Gn.* 547
their forefathers, *famous* over-all, . . . *Hub.* 1180
The *famous* witnesse of our wonted praise, . . . *T.M.* 274
wont the world with *famous* acts to fill; . . . *T.M.* 430
Out of his stocke and *famous* familie, . . . *Ti.* 276
Upon that *famous* Rivers further shore, . . . *Ti.* 589
Nor *famous* Ardeyn, nor fowle Arlo, is. . . . *As.* 96
of the *famous* Shure, the Nymph she is, . . . *Col.* 526
whose vertues . . . merit a most *famous* Poets witt . . . *Ded. Son.* ii. 2
make more *famous* memory Of thine Heroicke parts, . . . *Ded. Son.* ii. 11
Of th' old Heroes, whose *famous* ofspring . . . *Ded. Son.* vi. 4
In Fraunce and Ireland left a *famous* gage; . . . *Ded.Son.*xiv.11
the verse of *famous* Poets witt He does backebite, . . . I. iv. 32. 6
The fall of *famous* children borne of mee, . . . I. v. 25. 2
shew thy *famous* might In medicine, . . . I. v. 43. 7
through al Faery lond his *famous* worth was blown. . . . I. vi. 29. 9
famous harde atchievements still pursew; . . . I. vii. 45. 5
Through *famous* Poets verse each where renownd, . . . I. x. 54. 7
when thou *famous* victory hast wonne, . . . I. x. 60. 5
Whom *famous* Poetes verse so much doth vaunt, . . . I. xi. 27. 2
all this *famous* antique history . . . II. Pr. 1. 2
famous far abroad for warlike gest, . . . II. ii. 16. 7
as that *famous* Queene Of Amazons, . . . II. iii. 31. 5
advaunce Mine auncestry from *famous* Coradin, . . . II. iv. 36. 8
Famous throughout the world for warlike prayse, . . . II. v. 26. 2
The *famous* name of knighthood fowly shend; . . . II. vi. 35. 2
art thus fowly fledd from *famous* enimy?' . . . II. vi. 39. 9
Here eke that *famous* golden Apple grew, . . . II. vii. 55. 4
Made it selfe *famous* through false trechery, . . . II. viii. 12. 6
'Fortune, the foe of *famous* chevisaunce, . . . II. ix. 8. 1
memorable gestes Of *famous* Wisards, . . . II. ix. 53. 4
the *famous* auncestryes Of my most dreaded Soveraigne . . . II. x. 1. 7
three sonnes, his *famous* progeny, . . . II. x. 13. 4
Left of his life most *famous* memory, . . . II. x. 46. 2
O *famous* moniment of womens prayse! . . . II. x. 56. 1
most *famous* hight For skil in Musicke . . . II. x. 59. 7
should they be most *famous* moniments, . . . II. x. 74. 7
with rich spoyles and *famous* victorie . . . II. x. 75. 4
all the *famous* history Of Jason and Medaea . . . II. xii. 44. 3
The *famous* Briton Prince and Faery knight, . . . III. i. 1. 1
Even the *famous* Britomart it was, . . . III. i. 8. 6
Doe many *famous* knightes and Ladies wonne, . . . III. ii. 8. 2
It was a *famous* Present for a Prince, . . . III. ii. 21. 6
the *famous* Progeny, Which from them springen shall. . . . III. iii. Arg.
Most *famous* fruites of matrimoniall bowre, . . . III. iii. 3. 7
from thy wombe a *famous* Progenee Shall spring . . . III. iii. 22. 5
matter made for *famous* Poets verse, . . . III. iv. 1. 6
an earthly peare, The *famous* Dumarin; . . . III. iv. 19. 6
Too trew the *famous* Marinell it fownd, . . . III. iv. 29. 1
in all His *famous* conquests highly magnifide: . . . III. vii. 31. 7
most sweet hymmes of this thy *famous* deed . . . III. viii. 42. 8
'Most *famous* Worthy of the world, . . . III. ix. 34. 1

Famous—*Continued.*
'O lamentable fall of *famous* towne! . . . . III. ix. 39. 2
A *famous* history to bee enrold . . . . III. ix. 50. 7
From farre espide the *famous* Britomart, ... IV. i. 33. 2
when strife was growen Amongst those *famous* ympes of Greece, IV. ii. 1. 8
Time . . . That *famous* moniment hath quite defaste, ... IV. ii. 33. 3
Such *famous* men, such worthies of the earth, ... IV. iii. 44. 1
Described by that *famous* Tuscane penne: . . . . IV. iii. 45. 4
The which this *famous* Britomart did beare; . . . . IV. iv. 46. 5
The Ladies for the girdle strive Of *famous* Florimell: . . . . . IV. v. Arg.
eke the *famous* prize of beauty from them wonne. . . . . . . IV. ix. 28. 9
'Not that same *famous* Temple of Diane, ... IV. x. 30. 1
There also some most *famous* founders were . . . . IV. xi. 15. 1
when Paris brought his *famous* prise, ... IV. xi. 19. 3
after him the *famous* rivers came, ... IV. xi. 20. 1
That was to weet the *famous* Troynovant, ... IV. xi. 28. 8
no lesse *famous* then the rest they bee, ... IV. xi. 40. 2
The third was Brunell, *famous* in his dayes; . . . . V. iii. 5. 5
made her *famous*, more then is believed; . . . . V. iv. 33. 8
Famous through all the world, and honor'd far and nie. . . . V. viii. 16. 9
Well knowen by his feates, and *famous* overall. . . . . V. ix. 5. 9
More happie mother would her surely weene Then *famous* Niobe, V. x. 7. 8
That it became a *famous* knight well knowne, ... VI. iv. 38. 8
Famous through all the land of Faerie: . . . . VI. vii. 28. 3
If he for slouth forslackt so *famous* quest. . . . . VI. ix. 3. 5
To sing the glory of their *famous* deedes. . . . . *Am.* xxix. 8
Forgetfull of the *famous* golden fleece; . . . . *Am.* xliv. 3
Ne let theyr *famous* moniments to fade? . . . . *Am.* li. 4
famous warriors of anticke world . . . . *Am.* lxix. 1
Derived farre from *famous* Auncestrie: . . . . *Com. Son.* ii. 4
rapt with wonder of their *famous* praise, ... *Com. Son.* iii. 5
Famously. in their daies most *famouslie* did florish; . . . . . *Ti.* 359
Fan. Soone as the chaffe should in the *fan* be fynd, ... *S.C.* D. 125
Beares in his boasted *fan*, ... III. xi. 47. 8
in his hand a windy *fan* did beare, ... III. xii. 8. 8
Like scattred chaffe the which the wind away doth *fan*. . . . V. xi. 47. 9
Fanchin, -'s. *See* **Funsheon, -'s.**
Fancies. *See* **Fancy's.**
sike *fancies* weren foolerie, ... *S.C.* F. 211
Such fond *fantsies* shall soone be put to flight . . . . *S.C.* Au. 22
talke, that might unquiet *fancies* reave; . . . . *Hub.* 24
As one . . . whose dryer braine Is tost with . . . *fancies* weake, I. i. 42. 8
Sad, solemne, sowre, and full of *fancies* fraile, ... III. ii. 27. 5
Out of her daughters hart fond *fancies* to reverse. . . . . . III. ii. 48. 9
thousand *Fancies* bett his ydle brayne . . . . III. iv. 54. 4
Fashioning worldes of *fancies* evermore . . . . III. ix. 52. 4
with vaine poemes weeds to have their *fancies* fed. . . . . . IV. Pr. 1. 9
each one thought as to their *fancies* came. . . . . IV. v. 17. 2
A thousand feares, that love-sicke *fancies* faine to fynde. . . . V. vi. 3. 9
Many vaine *fancies* working her unrest; . . . . V. vi. 7. 7
I fynd my selfe but fed with *fancies* vayne. . . . . *Am.* lxxviii. 12
Such *fancies* feele no love, but loose desyre. . . . . *H.L.* 175
loves, with which the world doth blind Weake *fancies*, ... *H.H.L.* 263
fed On idle *fancies* of thy foolish thought, ... *H.H.B.* 289
Fancy. My *fancye* eke from former follies move . . . . . . *S.C.* Jun. 37
dapper ditties, . . . To feede youthes *fancie*, ... *S.C.* O. 14
it with pleasaunce mought thy *fancie* feede) . . . . *S.C.* D. 16
Doth borrow grace, the *fancie* to aggrate; . . . . *T.M.* 406
please his *fancie*, nor him cause t' abide: . . . . *Mui.* 158
Bregog did so well her *fancie* weld, ... *Col.* 130
in his falsed *fancy* he her takes To be the fairest wight . . . I. ii. 30. 3
with vaine thoughts her falsed *fancy* vex: . . . . III. i. 47. 5
Therewith a while she her flit *fancy* fedd, ... III. i. 56. 1
in her feigning *fancie* did pourtray Him . . . . III. iv. 5. 7
feed her *fancy* with delightfull chaunge: . . . . III. vii. 50. 3
men . . . in their foolish *fancy* feigne thee blinde, ... III. x. 4. 4
With which he fed her *fancy*, ... III. x. 8. 8
The first was *Fansy*, like a lovely Boy . . . . III. xii. 7. 1
whose *fancie* light Was alwaies flitting . . . . IV. ii. 5. 1
it his ranging *fancie* did refraine, ... IV. vi. 33. 6
Whose wandring *fancie* after lust did raunge, ... V. v. 26. 8
Ne him could find to *fancie* in her brest: . . . . VI. ix. 40. 7
with delight his greedy *fancy* fed . . . . VI. x. 30. 4
my fraile *fancy*, fed with full delight, ... *Am.* lxxii. 9
to his fayning *fansie* represent . . . . *H.L.* 254
Fancy's. leade me forth on *Fancies* bitte to playe: . . . . . *S.C.* D. 64
So stolen from their *fancies* wonderment . . . . V. iii. 26. 5
Yet durst she not disclose her *fancies* wound, ... V. v. 44. 1
His former *fancies* ruth he gan repent, ... V. ix. 49. 2
of his owne vaine *fancies* thought did frame: . . . . V. xi. 19. 4
It ravisht is with *fancies* wonderment: . . . . *Am.* iii. 12
An heavenly beautie to his *fancies* will; . . . . *H.B.* 222
Fanded. in the sea to drowne herselfe she *fond*, ... III. vii. 26. 7
Fangleness. *See* **Newfangleness.**
Fans. two such *fannes*, so silken soft . . . . *Mui.* 107
Fantasies. allure Chast Ladies eares to *fantasies* impure. . . *Hub.* 820
The fruitfull spawne of their ranke *fantasies*: . . . . *T.M.* 322
Such as in idle *fantasies* do flit; . . . . II. ix. 50. 7
All those were idle thoughtes and *fantasies*, ... II. ix. 51. 6
phantasies In wavering wemens witt, ... III. xii. 26. 3
Which as they view with lustfull *fantasyes*, ... VI. viii. 41. 8
Fantastic. As her *fantasticke* wit did most delight: . . . . II. vi. 7. 2
with *fantastick* sight Of dreadfull things, ... III. ii. 29. 4
no vision nor *fantasticke* sight, ... III. viii. 23. 2
Fantasy. *fantasie* is strong. . . . . *Hub.* 1326
made a monster of their *fantasie*. . . . . *T.M.* 558
bad him . . . with false shewes abuse his *fantasy*, ... I. i. 46. 4
O! who does know the bent of womens *fantasy*? . . . . I. iv. 24. 9
that may dayntest *fantasy* aggrate, ... II. xii. 42. 7
With thousand thoughts feeding her *fantasie*, ... V. vii. 17. 2

Fantasy—*Continued.*
meant them to the damzels *fantazy*. . . . . VI. ix. 12. 9
He thereon feeds his hungrie *fantasy*, ... *H.L.* 198
He thereon fixeth all his *fantasie*, ... *H.B.* 228
Fantsies. *See* **Fancies.**
Far. *See* **Far-forth.**
So *far* as Archer might his level see: . . . . *Bel.*[2] iii. 4
Then was the faire Dodonian tree *far* seene, ... *Bel.*[2] v. 1
odours fil'd th' ayre *farre* and nie. . . . . *Bel.*[2] xi. 4
Casting mine eyes *farre* off, ... *Bel.*[2] xiii. 3
Like as ye see the wrathfull Sea from *farre* . . . . *Ro.* xvi. 1
Cedar . . . That *farre* abroad her daintie odours threwe; . . *Van.* vii. 3
so *farre* am I from envie, ... *S.C.* May 37
To Kerke the narre, from God more *farre*, ... *S.C.* Jul. 97
renne *farre* out of frame? . . . . *S.C.* Au. 3
Seemeth ay greater when it is *farre*: . . . . *S.C.* S. 77
farre awaye, ... *S.C.* S. 196
But followe them *farre* off, ... *S.C.* Env. 11
farre abroad through each descent, ... *Gn.* 77
from Indian seas brought *far* away; . . . . *Gn.* 106
Far of beholding Ephialtes tide, ... *Gn.* 375
other powers *farre* different . . . . *Gn.* 420
from her *farre* awayes A rulesse rout . . . . *Gn.* 430
Black stormes and fogs are blowen up from *farre*, ... *Gn.* 572
Mother Hubberd, who did *farre* surpas The rest . . . . *Hub.* 34
to seeke Their fortunes *farre* abroad, ... *Hub.* 48
he leaned, as one *farre* in elde. . . . . *Hub.* 218
farre unfit it is, that person bace . . . . *Hub.* 464
fled *farre* off, where none might them surprize; . . . . *Hub.* 576
everie field and forrest *farre* and nere, ... *Hub.* 578
balliards *farre* unfit . . . . *Hub.* 803
come so *farre* to seeke for misery, ... *Hub.* 946
better *farre* it were . . . . *T.M.* 101
far more bitter storme . . . . *T.M.* 247
From my unhappie neighborhood *farre* fled, ... *Ti.* 146
Admir'd of base-borne men from *farre* away: . . . . *Ti.* 424
did the same from *farre* beholde, ... *Ti.* 493
a voyce that called *farre* away, ... *Ti.* 638
passing *farre* All Painters skill, ... *Mui.* 90
fetcht from *farre* away, ... *Mui.* 202
banisht *farre* away from hence; . . . . *D.* 10
some Pilgrim come from *farre* away. . . . . *D.* 42
Not *far* from whence Sabrinaes streame doth flow, ... *D.* 101
Daylie resort to me from *farre* and neare, ... *D.* 143
whom desastrous chaunce Hath *farre* exiled . . . . *D.* 506
Far passing all the pastors of his daies, ... *As.* 9
swaine, excelling *far* each other, ... *As.* 15
every field and forest *far* away He sought, ... *As.* 81
In forreine soyle pursued *far* away, ... *As.* 92
Hereof when tydings *far* abroad did passe, ... *As.* 199
pleasing sound yshrilled *far* about, ... *Col.* 62
he came *far* from the main-sea deepe, ... *Col.* 67
travailers, which it from *far* behold. . . . . *Col.* 115
Allo hight, Broad-water called *farre*; . . . . *Col.* 123
from *far* observ'd, with jealous eie, ... *Col.* 134
Such as all womankynd did *far* excell; . . . . *Col.* 190
without harme us *farre* away did beare, ... *Col.* 225
So *farre* that land, our mother, us did leave, ... *Col.* 226
at length we land *far* off descryde: . . . . *Col.* 265
An high headland thrust *far* into the sea, ... *Col.* 281
doth all afore him *far* surpasse; . . . . *Col.* 417
'Ah *far* be it (quoth Colin Clout) fro me, ... *Col.* 464
things so *far* from attone, ... *Col.* 843
praise her worth, though *far* my wit above. . . . . *Col.* 942
this base Poeme, for thee *far* unfitt: . . . . *Ded. Son.* ii. 5
In savadge soyle, *far* from Parnasso Mount, ... *Ded. Son.* vii. 12
a *farre* unfitter taske, ... I. Pr. i. 3
Whom to avenge she had this Knight from *far* compeld. . . . I. i. 5. 9
Behind her *farre* away a Dwarfe did lag, ... I. i. 6. 1
not *farr* away . . . . I. i. 7. 2
leading inward *farr*. . . . . I. i. 7. 8
His Lady, seeing all that chaunst from *farre*, ... I. i. 27. 1
all this countrie, *farre* and neare.' . . . . I. i. 31. 4
'*Far* hence . . . in wastfull wildernesse . . . . I. i. 32. 1
A litle . . . Hermitage . . . *Far* from resort of people . . . . . I. i. 34. 3
wakeful dogges before them *farre* doe lye, ... I. i. 40. 4
farre from enimyes. I. i. 41. 9
firme is fixt, and sendeth light from *farre* . . . . I. ii. 1. 4
her knight, who *far* away was fled, ... I. ii. 7. 7
For him so *far* had borne his light-foot steede, ... I. ii. 8. 3
The true Saint George, was wandred *far* away, ... I. ii. 12. 2
Made a calme shadowe *far* in compasse round: . . . . I. ii. 28. 6
fly *far* hence away, for feare . . . . I. ii. 31. 4
All other Dames to have exceeded *farre*: . . . . I. ii. 36. 2
Far from all peoples preace, as in exile, ... I. iii. 3. 3
In secrete shadow, *far* from all mens sight: . . . . I. iii. 4. 4
paines *far* passing that long wandring Greeke, ... I. iii. 21. 5
Far be it from your thought, and fro my wil, ... I. iii. 28. 2
Soone as the port from *far* he has espide, ... I. iii. 31. 7
ship *far* come from watrie wildernesse; . . . . I. iii. 32. 4
They had not ridden *far*, ... I. iii. 33. 1
followes her *far* off, ... I. iii. 44. 7
goodly galleries *far* over laid, ... I. iv. 4. 7
far unfitt for warlike swaine. . . . . I. iv. 37. 9
sad Aesculapius *far* apart Emprisond was . . . . I. v. 36. 7
old Ninus *far* did pas . . . . I. v. 48. 3
Faunes and Satyres *far* away . . . . I. vi. 7. 7
A seely Lamb *far* from the flock . . . . I. vi. 10. 4
Far off he wonders what them makes so glad; . . . . I. vi. 15. 1
He had . . . fild *far* landes with glorie of his might: . . . . I. vi. 20. 6

Far—*Continued.*
'And where is he thy Lord, and how *far* hence? . . . V. vi. 9. 2
Not *farre* away, but little wide by West, . . . V. vi. 22. 4
he chaunst *far* off to heed A Damzell, . . . V. viii. 4. 1
Yet fled she fast, and both them *farre* outwent, . . . V. viii. 4. 6
I Doe serve a Queene that not *far* hence doth wone, . . . V. viii. 16. 7
Famous through all the world, and honor'd *far* and nie. . . . V. viii. 16. 9
he *farre* was gone and past: . . . V. viii. 33. 6
There let her wonne, *farre* from resort of men, . . . V. ix. 2. 1
to see her Ladie thence not *farre* away. . . . V. ix. 3. 9
A straunge adventure, which not *farre* thence lay; . . . V. ix. 4. 5
wonned in a rocke not *farre* away, . . . V. ix. 4. 7
Is wondrous strong and hewen *farre* under ground, . . . V. ix. 6. 3
Those Nations *farre* thy justice doe adore; . . . V. x. 3. 8
Farre thence from forrein land where they did dwell, . . . V. x. 6. 3
They came unto a Citie *farre* up land, . . . V. x. 25. 1
that cursed Idole, *farre* proclamed, . . . V. ix. 28. 4
Sith ye thus *farre* have tendred my poore case, . . . V. xi. 18. 3
He day and night doth ward both *farre* and wide, . . . V. xi. 42. 7
farre away, amid their rakehell bands, . . . V. xi. 44. 6
ere he marched *farre* he with them met, . . . V. xii. 7. 1
There wayting for the Tyrant till it was *farre* day. . . . V. xii. 13. 9
He had not passed *farre* upon the strand, . . . V. xii. 28. 3
doe all worldly riches *farre* excell, . . . VI. Pr. 2. 4
so *farre* from that which then it was, . . . VI. Pr. 5. 2
far his fame display. . . . VI. i. 2. 9
seeing him from *farre*, . . . VI. i. 11. 5
'Not *farre* from hence, uppon yond rocky hill, . . . VI. i. 13. 1
They saw that Carle from *farre*, . . . VI. i. 17. 5
A tall young man, from thence not *farre* away, . . . VI. ii. 3. 7
far from envious eyes that mote him spight; . . . VI. iii. 20. 7
chaunst *far* off an armed Knight to spy . . . VI. iii. 46. 6
a ship . . . Now *farre* from harbour likely to be lost, . . . VI. iv. 1. 3
Farre in the forrest, by a hollow glade . . . VI. iv. 13. 5
In seeking all the woods both *farre* and nye . . . VI. iv. 16. 3
For nought but woods and forrests *farre* and nye, . . . VI. iv. 24. 8
The which through fame should *farre* be magnifide, . . . VI. iv. 33. 3
The good Sir Bruin growing *farre* in yeares, . . . VI. iv. 33. 6
The good Sir Calepine, that *farre* was strayd, . . . VI. v. 3. 2
He sought him *farre* and neare, . . . VI. v. 3. 9
Far from all neighbourhood the which annoy it may. . . . VI. v. 34. 9
'He rides' (said Turpine) 'there not *farre* afore, . . . VI. vii. 6. 1
The gentle Prince not *farre* away they spyde, . . . VI. vii. 6. 7
not *farre* away he found Whereas the Prince himselfe lay . . . VI. vii. 18. 6
was so *far* from being ought amazed, . . . VI. viii. 26. 8
Unto a litle grove not *farre* asyde, . . . VI. viii. 44. 2
They prayd high God them *farre* from them to send. . . . VI. ix. 6. 5
So *farre* the meane of shepheards to excell, . . . VI. ix. 11. 3
Although his quest were *farre* afore him gon: . . . VI. ix. 12. 3
did thrust it *farre* away, . . . VI. ix. 33. 2
your bounteous proffer Be *farre* fro me, . . . VI. ix. 33. 4
did seeme so *farre* From malicing, . . . VI. ix. 39. 6
wanton squirrels in the woods *farre* sought, . . . VI. ix. 40. 3
far from all peoples troad, . . . VI. x. 5. 3
sweete flowres that *far* did smell . . . VI. x. 14. 7
Yet she all other countrey lasses *farre* did passe: . . . VI. x. 25. 9
'So *farre*, as doth the daughter of the day . . . VI. x. 26. 1
So *farre* doth she in beautyfull array . . . VI. x. 26. 3
when thy glory shall be *farre* displayd To future age, . . . VI. x. 28. 8
upon an hill not *farre* away, . . . VI. xi. 36. 6
far straying from his peeres: . . . VII. vi. 28. 8
wealths and goodnesse, *far* above the rest . . . VII. vi. 38. 2
So *farre* past memory of man that may be knowne? . . . VII. vii. 2. 9
raunged *farre* abroad in every border, . . . VII. vii. 4. 8
Being *far* greater and more tall of stature . . . VII. vii. 5. 3
all the earth *far* underneath her feete . . . VII. vii. 10. 1
is of late *far* out of order gone. . . . VII. vii. 51. 4
he sometimes so *far* runnes out of square, . . . VII. vii. 52. 2
What needeth you to seeke so *farre* in vaine? . . . *Am.* xv. 4
riches that may *farre* be found: . . . *Am.* xv. 6
Out of her course doth wander *far* astray! . . . *Am.* xxxiv. 4
Why then doe ye, proud fayre, misdeeme so *farre*, . . . *Am.* lviii. 13
Fayre soyle it seemes from *far*, . . . *Am.* lxiii. 7
Far passing those which Hercules came by, . . . *Am.* lxxvii. 7
Their merry Musick that resounds from *far*, . . . *Epith.* 130
So *farre* from being proud. . . . *Epith.* 164
titles vaine, Derived *farre* from famous Auncestrie: . . . *Com. Son.* ii. 4
Venice . . . *farre* exceedes in policie of right. . . . *Com. Son.* iv. 12
sweeter *farre* then any Nectar is; . . . *H.L.* 26
thus *farre* happie he himselfe doth weene, . . . *H.L.* 212
Farre above feeble reach of earthly sight, . . . *H.H.L.* 5
With heavenly thoughts *farre* above humane skil, . . . *H.H.L.* 282
For *farre* above these heavens, which here we see, . . . *H.H.B.* 64
others *farre* exceeding these in light, . . . *H.H.B.* 65
their owne native light *farre* passing theirs. . . . *H.H.B.* 70
Yet *farre* more faire be those bright Cherubins, . . . *H.H.B.* 92
These thus in faire each other *farre* excelling, . . . *H.H.B.* 99
Yet is that Highest *farre* beyond all telling, . . . *H.H.B.* 101
Light, *farre* exceeding that bright blazing sparke . . . *H.H.B.* 162
That it doth *farre* exceed all humane thought, . . . *H.H.B.* 209
so *far* as Cynthia doth shend The lesser starres. . . . *Proth.* 121

Fare. Whether they *fare* on foote, or flie aloft, . . . *Ro.* xxiv. 3
Whose knees are weake through fast and evill *fare*, . . . *S.C.* Ja. 44
Winter or Sommer they mought well *fare*. . . . *S.C.* F. 24
Gathering his straying flocke, does homeward *fare*, . . . *Gn.* 319
good speed, and well to *fare*: . . . *Hub.* 550
So *fare* ye well; good Courtiers may ye bee!' . . . *Hub.* 653
After his guize did cast abroad to *fare*: . . . *Mui.* 55
He me perswaded forth with him to *fare*. . . . *Col.* 193
all the rest do most-what *fare* amis, . . . *Col.* 757

Fare—*Continued.*
At last resolving forward still to *fare*, . . . I. i. 11. 1
One knocked at the dore, and in would *fare*: . . . I. iii. 16. 4
forward *fare* as their adventures fell: . . . I. ix. 2. 5
As on the way together we did *fare*, . . . I. ix. 28. 2
streightway on that last long voiage *fare*, . . . I. x. 63. 4
So bids thee well to *fare*, Thy neither friend nor foe, . . . I. xii. 28. 9
fairely *fare* on foot, how ever loth: . . . II. ii. 12. 3
so forth with her they *fare*; . . . II. ii. 33. 6
Their minds to pleasure, and their mouths to dainty *fare*. . . . II. ii. 33. 9
Where they were served with all sumptuous *fare*, . . . III. i. 51. 2
on foot mote algates *fare* . . . III. vii. 4. 1
toward him did *fare*, . . . IV. i. 41. 2
Enur'd to hardnesse and to homely *fare*, . . . IV. viii. 27. 6
The Prince on foot, not wonted so to *fare*; . . . IV. viii. 37. 6
they much more furiously gan *fare*, . . . IV. ix. 27. 1
That none mote have accesse, nor inward *fare*, . . . IV. x. 6. 4
they with wrong or falshood will not *fare*, . . . V. ii. 48. 2
Hence *fare* on foot, till he a horse have gayned.' . . . V. iii. 35. 6
That nought the morrow next mote stay his *fare*. . . . V. x. 16. 4
Upon his voyage forth he gan to *fare* . . . V. x. 17. 5
When forward we should *fare* . . . VI. ii. 22. 2
thou hast thy steed forlorne . . . So *fare* on foote . . . VI. iii. 32. 2
He would not suffer her alone to *fare*, . . . VI. v. 8. 2
Yet was their *fare* but homely, . . . VI. v. 39. 1
Then up he made him rise, and forward *fare*, . . . VI. vii. 49. 1
streight unto her litle flocke did *fare*: . . . VI. ix. 15. 2
thence he had no will away to *fare*, . . . VI. x. 30. 8
with their little stings right felly *fare*; . . . VI. xi. 48. 4
backward yode, as Bargemen wont to *fare* . . . VII. vii. 35. 7
cleane without his usuall spheere to *fare*; . . . VII. vii. 52. 4

Fared. though mochell worse I *fared*: . . . *S.C.* Au. 23
through the world had with long travel *far'd*, . . . *Hub.* 686
with him *far'd* some better chaunce to fynde. . . . *Hub.* 942
Both knightes and ladies forth right angry *far'd*, . . . II. ii. 19. 8
So forth he *far'd*, . . . II. iii. 3. 1
like a cruell tygre *far'd*. . . . II. v. 8. 9
when late he *far'd* In Phaedrias flitt barck . . . II. vi. 38. 8
to the rivers syde they both together *far'd*: . . . II. xi. 3. 9
then in they all together *far'd*. . . . III. i. 30. 9
if ye understand Which way she *fared* hath, . . . III. v. 4. 9
So foorth they *far'd*; but he behind them stayd, . . . III. x. 2. 1
It fortuned, as they together *far'd*, . . . III. x. 35. 1
more bounteous creature never *far'd* On foot . . . III. xi. 10. 3
still he *far'd* as dauncing in delight, . . . III. xii. 8. 7
Far'd like a lyon in his bloodie game, . . . IV. iv. 41. 5
Right fit to rend the food on which he *fared*. . . . IV. v. 35. 5
forth upon his former voiage *fared*, . . . IV. v. 46. 2
Whom straight the Prince ensuing in together *far'd*. . . . IV. ix. 5. 9
To tell through what misfortune he had *far'd* . . . IV. ix. 41. 5
leaving him forth on his journey *far'd*: . . . V. i. 30. 7
with full heavy heart with them he *far'd*, . . . V. iv. 22. 7
Yet stayd she not for them, but forward *fared*, . . . V. vi. 38. 2
Like to a weake faint-hearted man he *fared* . . . V. vii. 20. 5
forth he *far'd* with all his many bad, . . . V. xi. 3. 2
So forth he *fared*, as his manner was . . . V. xi. 36. 6
fared like a furious wyld Beare, . . . VI. xi. 25. 8
fared like a feend right horrible in hew: . . . VI. xii. 31. 9
And after, when we *fared* had amisse, . . . *H.H.L.* 192

Fares. the travailer, that *fares* that way, . . . *Ti.* 6
Forth he *fares*, full of malicious mynd, . . . II. i. 2. 1
weete what course he takes, and how he *fares*, . . . II. i. 4. 4
Thrise happy man, who *fares* them both atweene! . . . II. i. 58. 5
as a blindfold Bull, at randon *fares*, . . . II. iv. 7. 8
Who *fares* on sea may not commaund his way. . . . II. vi. 23. 2
An hundred times about the pit side *fares* . . . IV. xii. 17. 8
like a Lion wood amongst them *fares*, . . . V. xi. 45. 3
Right so it *fares* with me in this long way, . . . VI. xii. 1. 8

Farewell. Now *farwell*, shepheard, . . . *S.C.* Jul. 231
'Tho gan my lovely Spring bid me *farewel*, . . . *S.C.* D. 55
eies . . . I mote have closed, and him bed *farewell*, . . . III. iv. 39. 5
farewell, my sweetest sweet! . . . III. iv. 39. 8
Farewell, my sweetest sonne, sith we no more shall meet!' . . . III. iv. 39. 9
Then, *farewell* fleshly force! . . . V. vii. 40. 9
if all fayle, yet *farewell* open field; . . . V. x. 24. 5

Far-forth. Looking *far foorth* into the Ocean wide, . . . *Van.* ix. 1
O dredd Soverayne! Thus *far-forth* pardon, . . . III. Pr. 3. 6
now the humid night was *farforth* spent, . . . III. ix. 53. 4
untill the flying day Was *farre forth* spent, . . . VI. ix. 12. 6

Far-infixed. the *far infixed* sting: . . . I. xi. 39. 4

Faring. forth *faring* on his way, . . . II. iv. 3. 1
by adventure found them *faring* so, . . . V. viii. 15. 6

Farm. Cuddie shall have a Kidde to store his *farme*. . . . *S.C.* O. 120
breach of lawes to privie *ferme* did let: . . . *Hub.* 1160
Out of her fleshly *ferme* fled to the place of paine. . . . III. v. 23. 9
an heard, farre from the husband *farme*, . . . IV. iv. 35. 7

Farmer. Then would he seeme a *Farmer*, . . . *Hub.* 871

Farms. Having great Lordships got and goodly *farmes*, . . . V. ii. 5. 7
from the country back to private *farmes* he scorsed. . . . VI. ix. 3. 9

Far-proclaimed. *See* **Far, Proclaimed.**

Far-rebounded. the *far rebownded* noyce, . . . I. vi. 8. 3

Far renowned. that *far renowmed* Queene: . . . I. v. 5. 1
O thou *far renowmed* sonne . . . I. v. 43. 6
whose warlike name Is *far renowmd* . . . II. iii. 35. 4
far renownd For the large leape . . . II. x. 11. 1
The Gardin of Adonis, *far renowmd* by fame. . . . III. vi. 29. 9
Sir Paris *far renowmd* through noble fame; . . . III. ix. 34. 5
farre renowmed through exceeding fame, . . . IV. x. 5. 5
Well knowne, and *far renowmed* heretofore, . . . V. xi. 49. 2
farre renound For his great riches . . . VI. xii. 4. 2

Far-reported. yled with *far reported* praise, . . . I. vii. 46. 1
Farther. ere we *farther* passe . . . *Hub.* 195
Fary. *See* **Faery.**
Fashion. *Fashion* the pourtraicts of these Palacis, . . . *Ro.* xxv. 10
Repayring her decayed *fashion,* . . . *Ro.* xxvii. 10
rustie horrour and fowle *fashion;* . . . *Gn.* 443
Eftsoones he gins to *fashion* forth a place; . . . *Gn.* 650
Such will we *fashion* both our selves to bee, . . . *Hub.* 167
my selfe fit for the same will *fashion.'* . . . *Hub.* 202
There must thou *fashion* eke a godly zeale, . . . *Hub.* 493
ye well can *fashion* Your selves theretoo, . . . *Hub.* 651
paint in rimes the troublous state . . . in likest *fashion,* . . . *T.M.* 382
Much like an Angell in all forme and *fashion.'* . . . *Col.* 615
How he did *fashion* his untoward pace; . . . I. viii. 31. 2
Did see and grieve at his bold *fashion;* . . . II. ii. 37. 7
th' only forme and outward *fashion;* . . . III. vi. 38. 2
Nor s'deignfull of so homely *fashion,* . . . III. vii. 10. 6
Dwelt simple truth in seemely *fashion.* . . . III. vii. 59. 6
Him selfe to *fashion* likest Florimell, . . . III. viii. 8. 6
unknowen geare And uncouth *fashion,* . . . IV. xi. 45. 3
Sir Artegall undid the evill *fashion,* . . . V. ii. 28. 7
to *fashion* his owne lyfes estate, . . . VI. ix. 31. 2
he should lead the daunce, as was his *fashion;* . . . VI. ix. 42. 3
Are wont for Princes states to *fashion;* . . . VII. vii. 8. 4
You frame my thoughts, and *fashion* me within; . . . *Am.* viii. 9
fashion to what he it list apply. . . . *Am.* xxxii. 4
newly *fashion* Unto a fairer forme, . . . *H.L.* 192
Fashioned. *fashiond* were they all in Dorike wise. . . . *Bel.*[1] ii. 4
Fashion'd with queint devises, . . . *Hub.* 673
In which trew honor yee may *fashioned* see, . . . *Ded. Son.* x. 10
some *fashioned* in the waste Like swine: . . . II. xi. 12. 5
So *fashioned* a Porch with rare device. . . . II. xii. 54. 1
Or in Belphoebe *fashioned* to bee; . . . III. Pr. 5. 8
him in everie part before her *fashioned.* . . . III. ii. 16. 9
Whose future woes so plaine he *fashioned;* . . . III. iii. 43. 3
A thousand thoughts she *fashiond* in her mind, . . . III. iv. 5. 6
Fashiond above within their inmost part, . . . III. vi. 44. 7
in those Tapets weren *fashioned* Many faire pourtraicts, . . . III. xi. 29. 1
Fashion'd to please the eies of them that pas, . . . VI. Pr. 5. 4
He *fashiond* them as comely as he could, . . . *H.B.* 33
Which He had *fashiond* in his wise foresight, . . . *H.H.L.* 109
Fashioning. *Fashioning* worldes of fancies evermore . . . III. ix. 52. 4
Fashions. yet there all *fashions* beene; . . . *Hub.* 674
brutishly brought up, that nev'r did *fashions* see.' . . . III. vii. 57. 9
sundry wayes and *fashions* as clerkes faine, . . . VII. vii. 55. 2
Thereof he *fashions* in his higher skill . . . *H.B.* 221
Fast. Whose knees are weake through *fast* and evill fare, . . . *S.C.* Ja. 44
my galage growne *fast* to my heels: . . . *S.C.* F. 244
The joyous time now nighes *fast,* . . . *S.C.* Mar. 4
Binde your fillets *faste,* . . . *S.C.* Ap. 133
Sperre the yate *fast* . . . *S.C.* May 224
Kiddie the dore sperred after her *fast.* . . . *S.C.* May 234
the dore to make *fast,* . . . *S.C.* May 292
In humble dales is footing *fast,* . . . *S.C.* Jul. 13
The rampant Lyon hunts he *fast,* . . . *S.C.* Jul. 21
how *fast* renneth the shepheard . . . *S.C.* Au. 32
The night nigheth *fast,* . . . *S.C.* Au. 198
Is nowe *fast* stalled in her crumenall. . . . *S.C.* S. 119
if thy galage once sticketh *fast,* . . . *S.C.* S. 131
to the wood would he speede him *fast.* . . . *S.C.* S. 199
Fast in theyr folds he did them locke, . . . *S.C.* S. 205
Fast by the hyde the Wolfe Lowder caught; . . . *S.C.* S. 223
nombers flowe as *fast* as spring doth ryse. . . . *S.C.* O. 108
hye we homeward *fast.* . . . *S.C.* N. 208
'I saw anothers fate approaching *fast,* . . . *Gn.* 361
Fast bound with serpents . . . *Gn.* 374
Ne are we tyde to *fast,* but when we list; . . . *Hub.* 459
Fast much, pray oft, looke lowly on the ground, . . . *Hub.* 498
Without a gowned beast him *fast* beside, . . . *Hub.* 749
At sight of him, gan *fast* away to flye; . . . *Hub.* 1069
As whome he knew to him both *fast* and true. . . . *Hub.* 1081
the Princes pallaces fell *fast* To ruine . . . *Hub.* 1175
the beasts therein Fled *fast* away . . . *Hub.* 1348
all the gates he found *fast* lockt . . . *Hub.* 1350
ginnes to shoote up *fast,* and flourish fayre . . . *Ti.* 269
lustfull yongth began to kindle *fast,* . . . *Mui.* 34
fast bound with silver chaine. . . . *D.* 119
all times doo flye So *fast* away, . . . *D.* 412
darke night *fast* approched, . . . *D.* 557
He grew up *fast* in goodnesse . . . *As.* 17
Did poure into his Lemans lap so *fast,* . . . I. i. 6. 7
The drouping night thus creepeth on them *fast;* . . . I. i. 36. 1
double gates he findeth locked *fast,* . . . I. i. 40. 1
He, prickte with pride . . . Forth spurred *fast:* . . . I. ii. 14. 8
enclosd in wooden wals full *faste,* . . . our wearie daies we waste.' . . . I. ii. 42. 8
fast fealty, Which I do owe unto all womankynd, . . . I. iii. 1. 6
Full *fast* she fled, . . . I. iii. 12. 1
thrise three times did *fast* from any bitt; . . . I. iii. 14. 4
One knocked at the dore, . . . He knocked *fast,* . . . I. iii. 16. 5
fast trickled downe the sweat. . . . I. iv. 22. 4
the chayne of strong necessitee, Which *fast* is tyde . . . I. v. 25. 6
fast away gan ryde. . . . I. vi. 8. 9
A Lyon . . . *fast* running towards him, . . . I. vi. 10. 6
turning backe gan *fast* to fly away; . . . I. vi. 28. 2
So *fast* he carried her with carefull paine, . . . I. vi. 33. 8
fast towards him do crosse. . . . I. vi. 34. 9
Could not for sorrow follow him so *fast;* . . . I. vi. 40. 3
Una, . . . *Fast* flying from that Paynims greedy pray, . . . I. vii. 20. 3
'No faith so *fast*' . . . 'but flesh does paire.' . . . I. vii. 41. 8

Fast—*Continued.*
fast embard in mighty brasen wall, . . . I. vii. 44. 8
Whose gates he fownd *fast* shutt, . . . I. viii. 3. 3
no locke so firme and *fast,* But . . . flew open . . . I. viii. 4. 8
Came running *fast* to greet his victorie, . . . I. viii. 26. 4
you, fresh budd of vertue springing *fast,* . . . I. viii. 27. 1
an yron doore, That *fast* was lockt, . . . I. viii. 37. 4
Shee, flying *fast* from heavens face, . . . I. viii. 50. 1
those two knights, *fast* friendship for to bynd, . . . I. ix. 18. 6
An armed knight towards them gallop *fast,* . . . I. ix. 21. 2
The Redcrosse knight toward him crossed *fast,* . . . I. ix. 23. 1
loe! he comes, he comes *fast* after mee.' . . . I. ix. 25. 2
Fledd *fast* away, halfe dead . . . I. ix. 30. 6
free his feet that in the myre sticke *fast?* . . . I. ix. 39. 5
the dore they find *fast* lockt, . . . I. x. 5. 1
in her other hand she *fast* did hold . . . I. x. 13. 7
She held him *fast,* and firmely did upbeare, . . . I. x. 35. 8
every sinew seene, through his long *fast:* . . . I. x. 48. 6
first thou must a season *fast* and pray, . . . I. x. 52. 7
The steely head stuck *fast* . . . I. xi. 22. 1
the knott that *fast* him tyes, . . . I. xi. 23. 4
fast trickled forth a silver flood, . . . I. xi. 29. 4
fast it stucke, ne would thereout be gott: . . . I. xi. 38. 7
grypt it *fast* withall. . . . I. xi. 40. 9
had them . . . *fast* imprisoned in sieged fort. . . . I. xii. 4. 5
fast before the king he did alight; . . . I. xii. 25. 5
chaced her that *fast* from him did fly; . . . II. ii. 7. 8
Doth nourish vertue, and *fast* friendship breeds, . . . II. ii. 31. 2
fast to bind their league, . . . II. ii. 33. 1
Fast by her side did sitt the bold Sansloy, . . . II. ii. 37. 1
Orion, flying *fast* from hissing snake, . . . II. ii. 46. 2
fast her hent By the hoare lockes . . . II. iv. 12. 2
both her handes *fast* bound . . . II. iv. 13. 5
to flye Full *fast* away, . . . II. iv. 13. 7
both his hands *fast* bound . . . II. iv. 14. 8
whom your victorious might Hath now *fast* bound, . . . II. iv. 32. 4
Whose flying feet so *fast* their way applyde, . . . II. iv. 37. 3
on the plaine *fast* pricking Guyon spide One . . . II. v. 2. 2
The truncked beast *fast* bleeding did him fowly dight. . . . II. v. 4. 9
poursewed *fast* The present offer of faire victory, . . . II. v. 12. 1
Fledd *fast* away to tell his funerall . . . II. v. 25. 8
fast beside there trickled softly downe A gentle streame, . . . II. v. 30. 1
By this she had him lulled *fast* asleepe, . . . II. vi. 18. 1
An armed knight that towardes him *fast* ran; . . . II. vi. 41. 2
fast beside him sat tumultuous Strife: . . . II. vii. 21. 6
the good Guyon he found slumbring *fast* . . . II. viii. 4. 8
brother saw the red blood rayle Adowne so *fast,* . . . II. viii. 37. 4
to th' infernall shade *Fast* flying, . . . II. viii. 45. 8
Twixt his two mighty armes engrasped *fast,* . . . II. viii. 49. 6
the gates *fast* barred . . . II. ix. 10. 8
And every loup *fast* lockt, . . . II. ix. 10. 9
'fly *fast* away, If that your lives ye love, . . . II. ix. 12. 1
Fly *fast,* and save your selves . . . II. ix. 12. 3
flying *fast* as Roebucke through the fen, . . . II. x. 7. 5
she so *fast* pursewd, that him she tooke . . . II. x. 18. 6
Her other sonne *fast* sleeping did oppresse, . . . II. x. 35. 8
fast the land behynd them fled away. . . . II. xi. 4. 6
There follow'd *fast* at hand two wicked Hags, . . . II. xi. 23. 2
fled *fast* away for feare: . . . II. xi. 25. 6
So *fast* as his good Courser could him beare; . . . II. xi. 25. 8
the Carle as *fast* Gan heap huge strokes on him, . . . II. xi. 43. 8
grounded and *fast* setteled On firme foundation . . . II. xii. 1. 4
all that dreadfull Armie *fast* gan flye . . . II. xii. 26. 8
So held them under *fast;* . . . II. xii. 81. 6
fledd so *fast* that nothing mote him hold, . . . III. i. 15. 8
As fearing evill that poursewd her *fast;* . . . III. i. 16. 2
all spurd after, *fast* as they mote fly, . . . III. i. 18. 4
never wight so *fast* in sell could sit, . . . III. iii. 60. 6
the *fast* earth affronted them so sore, . . . III. iv. 7. 7
That *fast* she from him fledd, . . . III. iv. 51. 3
whither now he traveiled so *fast?* . . . III. v. 3. 7
Fast flying through this forest from her fo, . . . III. v. 6. 2
could not stay, so *fast* she did foregoe, . . . III. v. 6. 5
make him *fast* out of the forest ronne, . . . III. v. 27. 8
Forthy the bloody tract they followd *fast,* . . . III. v. 37. 6
gan ransack *fast* His inward partes, . . . III. v. 48. 4
To whom her loving hart she linked *fast* . . . III. vi. 53. 3
fledd so *fast* from that same foster stearne . . . III. vi. 54. 3
No need to bid her *fast* away to flie: . . . III. vii. 24. 2
Not halfe so *fast* the wicked Myrrha fled . . . III. vii. 26. 1
Nor halfe so *fast* to save her maydenhed . . . III. vii. 26. 3
Fast flying, on a Courser dapled gray, . . . III. vii. 37. 3
Fast bounden hand and foote with cords of wire, . . . III. vii. 37. 8
forward gallopt *fast;* . . . III. vii. 38. 6
She bore him *fast* away. . . . III. vii. 43. 6
fast her clipping twixt his armes twayne, . . . III. viii. 10. 1
fast goodwill, with gentle courtesyes, . . . III. ix. 7. 7
before the wicket *fast* They wayted, . . . III. ix. 11. 2
his false engins *fast* he plyde, . . . III. x. 7. 2
cast himselfe on ground her *fast* besyde: . . . III. x. 7. 5
ran into her lovers armes right *fast;* . . . III. x. 13. 5
Paridell came pricking *fast* Upon the plaine; . . . III. x. 35. 2
fast closed in some hollow greave, . . . III. x. 42. 3
He ran as *fast* as both his feet could beare, . . . III. x. 53. 2
now so *fast* his feet he did apply, . . . III. xi. 6. 5
kept th' yron dore *fast* bard, . . . III. xi. 31. 6
he *fast* away did fly, . . . III. xii. 12. 5
the dore streightway *Fast* locked, . . . III. xii. 27. 2
fownd it locked *fast:* . . . III. xii. 27. 7
both whose hands Were bounden *fast,* . . . III. xii. 30. 7

Fast—*Continued.*
Where *fast* infixed, . . . the staffe asunder brake, ... IV. iii. 10. 5
The other halfe, behind yet sticking *fast*, ... IV. iii. 12. 3
Stood still awhile, and his *fast* footing kept, ... IV. iii. 20. 8
did his yron brond so *fast* applie, ... IV. iii. 25. 7
As *fast* as water-sprinkles gainst a rocke are dasht. . . . . . IV. iii. 25. 9
As *fast* as forward erst now backward to retrate. . . . . . IV. iii. 26. 9
Ne followd on so *fast*, ... IV. iii. 32. 3
Which vauntage Cambell did pursue so *fast*, ... IV. iv. 30. 5
when they thought it *fast*, eftsoones it was untide. . . . . . IV. v. 17. 9
fast beside a little brooke did pas . . . . . . IV. v. 33. 3
his faith with her he *fast* engaged, ... IV. vi. 43. 3
her pursu'd as *fast* as she did flie: . . . . . . IV. vii. 21. 7
Full *fast* she flies, and farre afore him goes, ... IV. vii. 21. 8
follow'd *fast*; but, when he came in sight, ... IV. vii. 37. 3
together *fast* embraced. . . . . . . IV. viii. 34. 9
Them follow'd *fast*, and them reviled sore, ... IV. viii. 35. 3
(so *fast* away he flew) . . . . . . IV. viii. 40. 4
she woo'd and prayd him *fast*, ... IV. viii. 52. 8
him embracing *fast* betwixt them held, ... IV. ix. 9. 3
The which I found sure lockt and chained *fast*. . . . . . . IV. x. 11. 3
a snake, whose head and tail were *fast* combyned. . . . . . . IV. x. 40. 9
flowing *fast* to Rhy; . . . . . . IV. xi. 33. 2
To bring forth stormes, or *fast* them to upbinde, ... IV. xi. 52. 4
'Which when his Ladie saw, she follow'd *fast*, ... V. i. 18. 1
Uppon his iron coller griped *fast*, ... V. ii. 14. 4
Enlincked *fast* in wedlocke's loyall bond, ... V. iv. 3. 2
Fast bound on every side with iron bands, ... V. iv. 5. 2
that rout . . . heaped strokes so *fast* on every side, ... V. iv. 38. 8
Her warlike maides about her flockt so *fast*, ... V. iv. 43. 6
The Lists were closed *fast*, ... V. v. 5. 6
Yet in my truthes assurance I rest fixed *fast*.' . . . . . . V. v. 38. 9
on the ground the other *fast* did stand; . . . . . . V. vii. 7. 2
Fled *fast* into the towne, ... V. vii. 34. 9
yet so *fast* they could not home retrate, ... V. vii. 35. 1
A Damzell, flying on a palfrey *fast* . . . . . . V. viii. 4. 2
Yet fled she *fast*, and both them farre outwent, ... V. viii. 4. 6
still from him as *fast* away did flie, ... V. viii. 6. 2
thinking to follow *fast* His other fellow Pagan . . . . . . V. viii. 8. 8
From whom she earst so *fast* away did flie: . . . . . . V. viii. 16. 3
his wingfooted courses him did beare So *fast* away . . . . . . V. viii. 33. 5
followed was of him likewise full *fast*, ... V. viii. 33. 8
made him backe agaime as *fast* to fly; . . . . . . V. viii. 36. 3
Fast did they fly as them their feete could beare . . . . . . V. viii. 39. 1
Him when the damzell saw *fast* by her side, ... V. ix. 12. 1
Ran with her *fast* away unto his mew, ... V. ix. 14. 5
He threw his burden downe, and *fast* away did fly. . . . . . . V. ix. 14. 9
he him hunted like a Foxe full *fast*: . . . . . . V. ix. 17. 2
he then tooke it up, and held *fast* in his hand. . . . . . . V. ix. 17. 9
Warning him hold it *fast* for feare of slights: . . . . . . V. ix. 18. 3
they fled As *fast* as feete could carry them away; . . . . . . V. x. 36. 2
laboured *fast* To sperre the gate; . . . . . . V. x. 37. 1
catching her *fast* by her ragged weed . . . . . . V. xi. 61. 3
the terme, approching *fast*, required speed. . . . . . . V. xi. 65. 9
The Tyrant thundred his thicke blowes so *fast*, ... V. xii. 17. 6
byting deepe therein did sticke so *fast* . . . . . . V. xii. 21. 8
Whom Calidore perceiving *fast* to flie, ... VI. i. 22. 6
Calidore did follow him so *fast*, ... VI. i. 23. 3
his foe lay *fast* in sencelesse swound; . . . . . . VI. i. 34. 2
following that faire advantage *fast*, ... VI. i. 39. 2
Ran after *fast* to reskue the distressed mayde. . . . . . . VI. iii. 24. 9
But follow'd *fast* the Monster in his flight: . . . . . . VI. iii. 26. 5
Through woods and hils he follow'd him so *fast*, ... VI. iii. 26. 6
In following of him that fled so *fast*, ... VI. iv. 9. 2
by the cry he follow'd, and pursewed *fast*. . . . . . . VI. iv. 18. 9
did gripe his gorge so *fast*, ... VI. iv. 22. 4
with his neighing *fast* Did warne his rider . . . . . . VI. v. 21. 6
They fled, and *fast* into the wood did get. . . . . . . VI. v. 22. 7
he layd about, and made them *fast* to flie. . . . . . . VI. vi. 38. 9
did him *fast* pursew. . . . . . . VI. vii. 2. 9
the Carle upon him layd, And bound him *fast*: . . . . . . VI. vii. 48. 7
fast with cords do bynde, ... VI. viii. 12. 3
in teares, which gushed *fast* Like many water streames, . . . VI. viii. 19. 1
fled *fast* away, ... VI. viii. 31. 4
he slept full *fast*; . . . . . . VI. viii. 47. 6
He followed *fast*, and chaced him so nie, ... VI. ix. 4. 6
the moystie night approching *fast* . . . . . . VI. ix. 13. 1
many feete *fast* thumping th' hollow ground, ... VI. x. 10. 4
Through cowherd feare he fled away as *fast*, ... VI. x. 35. 3
flyes away as *fast* as he can hye, ... VI. xi. 18. 8
holding *fast* twixt both his armes extended Fayre Pastorell, . VI. xi. 19. 7
to him running *fast*, ... VI. xi. 28. 1
When to the Cave they came, they found it *fast*; . . . . . . VI. xi. 43. 1
he him *fast* pursuing soone approched neare. . . . . . . VI. xii. 25. 9
Against his will *fast* bound in yron chaine, ... VI. xii. 35. 3
His shield he on him threw, and *fast* downe held: . . . . . . VI. xii. 30. 6
The wingd-foot God so *fast* his plumes did beat, ... VII. vi. 17. 1
from them fled more *fast* Then any Deere, ... VII. vi. 52. 4
This holy season, fit to *fast* and pray, ... *Am.* xxii. 1
joyous houres doe fly away too *fast*. . . . . . . *Am.* lxxxvi. 14
Now day is doen, and night is nighing *fast*, ... *Epith.* 298

Faste. *See* **Faced.**

Fasten. Thereon an yron lock did *fasten* . . . . . . II. iv. 12. 9
In hope some stroke to *fasten* on him neare, ... V. viii. 33. 2

Fastened. This goodlie bridge, one foote not *fastned* (**fastened*) well, ... *Ti.* 557
they *fastned* were under her knee . . . . . . II. iii. 27. 6
whosoever once hath *fastened* His foot thereon, ... II. xii. 12. 7
ne further *fastned* not, ... III. ii. 26. 2
Upon whose stubborne neck, . . . She *fastned* hath her foot; . III. ix. 45. 6

Fastened—*Continued.*
ever as they *fastned* it, it loos'd . . . . . . IV. v. 16. 6
Till Florimell about her *fastned* it. . . . . . . V. iii. 28. 5
this maides with whom I *fastned* hand, ... V. iv. 15. 7
least his hold was but unsound And not well *fastened*, . . . V. v. 42. 8
her sad eyes, still *fastened* on the ground, ... *Epith.* 234
in their *fastened* mynd All happie joy and full contentment fynd. . . . . . . *H.H.B.* 286

Faster. infixed *faster* hold Within my bleeding bowells, . . . III. ii. 39. 1
how she mote him *faster* tye. . . . . . . V. v. 56. 6
him selfe did *faster* hye To reskue him, ... VI. v. 22. 3

Fast-fixed. with *fast fixed* eyes on her did stare, ... *Mui.* 340
In which a rusty knife *fast fixed* stood, ... I. ix. 36. 8
fast fixed on his shield, ... I. xi. 43. 1
With doubtfull eyes *fast fixed* on his guest: . . . . . . I. xii. 29. 6
With her false eyes *fast fixed* in his sight, ... II. xii. 73. 2
with pale eyes *fast fixed* on the rest, ... III. x. 41. 2
with *fast fixed* eies He gazed . . . . . . V. iii. 18. 6
Being *fast fixed* in her wounded spright, ... V. v. 27. 4

Fast-flying. fluttring wings of thy *fast flying* Thought, . . . *U.V.* 2

Fasting. Their *fasting* flockes to keepe. . . . . . . *S.C.* Jul. 200
dieted with *fasting* every day, ... I. x. 26. 3
through long *fasting* woxen pale and wan, ... IV. vii. 43. 3

Fastness. eke the *fastnesse* of his dwelling place, ... V. ix. 5. 2
to those fennes for *fastnesse* she did fly, ... V. x. 18. 8

Fast-streaming. up to heaven his eyes *fast-streming* threw: . VI. xi. 28. 6

Fat. They han *fatte* kernes, ... *S.C.* Jul. 199
When folke bene *fat*, and riches rancke, ... *S.C.* Jul. 211
The *fatte* Oxe, that wont ligge in the stal, ... *S.C.* S. 118
the *fat* from their beards doen lick: . . . . . . *S.C.* S. 123
from my beard the *fat* away have swept; . . . . . . *Hub.* 78
He fed his cubs with *fat* of all the soyle, ... *Hub.* 1151
Fat Colworts, and comforting Perseline, ... *Mui.* 199
fed her *fatt* with feast of offerings, ... I. iii. 18. 6
Abusd her plenty and *fat* swolne encreace . . . . . . II. vii. 16. 7
fruitfull Ceres and Lyaeus *fatt* . . . . . . III. i. 51. 3
full grosse and *fat* As fed with lard, ... VII. vii. 40. 1

Fatal. Till it by *fatall* doome adowne did fall. . . . . . . *Ro.* xvi. 14
Doth yet himselfe with *fatall* hand enforce, ... *Ro.* xxvii. 13
The *fatall* sisters eke repent . . . . . . *S.C.* N. 148
Through *fatall* charmes transformd to such an one; . . . . . . *Gn.* 205
her unkindly foes, The *fatall* Sisters, ... *T.M.* 16
one of those three *fatall* Impes . . . . . . *Ti.* 17
in thy fall my *fatall* overthrowe, ... *Ti.* 79
Litle wist he his *fatall* future woe, ... *Mui.* 381
Let those three *fatall* Sisters . . . Approach hereto; . . . . *D.* 16
Gave her the *fatall* wound of deadlie smart, ... *D.* 158
This *fatall* day that shall I ever rew, ... I. vi. 38. 2
through *fatal* deepe foresight, ... I. ix. 7. 1
To tell how he had seene the Dragons *fatall* fall. . . . . . . I. xii. 2. 9
tell what *fatall* priefe Hath . . . you oppress; . . . . . . II. i. 48. 6
If ever he transgrest the *fatall* Stygian lawes. . . . . . . II. vii. 27. 9
did his life her *fatall* date expyre, ... II. viii. 24. 3
the third brunt of this my *fatall* brond: . . . . . . II. viii. 37. 8
now arrived is his *fatall* howre, ... II. viii. 43. 8
Driven by *fatall* error here arriv'd, ... II. x. 9. 8
all the nation of unfortunate And *fatall* birds . . . . . . II. xii. 36. 2
The *fatall* purpose of divine foresight . . . . . . III. ii. 2. 5
either *fatall* end, Or other mightie cause, ... III. iii. 15. 8
by *fatall* lore Hast learn'd to love, ... III. iii. 21. 6
Both joynt partakers of their *fatall* payne: . . . . . . III. iii. 37. 7
'Him shall he make his *fatall* Instrument . . . . . . III. iii. 38. 1
he through *fatall* errour long was led . . . . . . III. ix. 41. 4
by *fatall* course they driven were . . . . . . III. ix. 49. 1
Of *fatall* Thebes; of Rome that raigned long; . . . . . . IV. i. 22. 2
To the three *fatall* sisters house she went. . . . . . . IV. ii. 47. 4
when ye shred with *fatall* knife His line, ... IV. ii. 52. 3
to see their *fatall* fine, ... IV. iii. 37. 5
Phorcys, the father of that *fatall* brood, ... IV. xi. 13. 1
after him the *fatall* Welland went, ... IV. xi. 35. 1
that same former *fatall* wound of his . . . . . . IV. xii. 22. 5
lesse she feared that same *fatall* read, ... IV. xii. 27. 1
before this *fatall* teene Them overtooke . . . . . . V. x. 7. 5
the Theban Knight, The father of that *fatall* progeny, Made kill herselfe . . . . . . V. xi. 25. 3
Under her wombe his *fatall* sword he thrust, ... V. xi. 31. 2
Not satisfyde till on the *fatall* ground . . . . . . VI. iii. 51. 3
This *fatall* chaunce, this dolefull accident, ... VI. xi. 31. 2
Knowing his *fatall* hand by former feare; . . . . . . VI. xii. 25. 8

Fatally. *fatally* did vow To wreake her on that mayden messengere, ... V. viii. 46. 3

Fate. mortall men tossed by troublous *fate* . . . . . . *Pet.*[2] vii. 3
cruell *fate* And angry Gods pursue . . . . . . *S.C.* Jun. 14
Neede feare no chaunge of frowning *fate*; . . . . . . *S.C.* S. 71
hastning his cruell *fate*. . . . . . . *Gn.* 328
'I saw anothers *fate* approaching fast, ... *Gn.* 361
by changing *fate* for *fate*. . . . . . . *Gn.* 427
whom wicked *fate* Hath brought to Court, ... *Hub.* 892
no man left to mone His dolefull *fate*, ... *Ti.* 193
freed from bands of impacable *fate*, ... *Ti.* 395
for great sorrow of their sudden *fate*, ... *Ti.* 573
to sheild Achilles life from *fate* of Troyan field. . . . . . . *Mui.* 64
Whose cruell *fate* is woven even now . . . . . . *Mui.* 235
never didst thou heare more haplesse *fate*. . . . . . . *D.* 98
cruell *Fate* . . . him misled, ... *Mui.* 417
By *fate* or fortune came unto the place, ... *As.* 141
freed is from Cupids yoke by *fate*, ... *Col.* 566
Shall I accuse the hidden cruell *fate*, ... I. i. 51. 2
Hath thee incenst to hast thy dolefull *fate*? . . . . . . I. vi. 47. 2
in his eternall booke of *fate* Are written sure, ... I. ix. 42. 4

Fate—*Continued.*
He woxe dismaid, and gan his *fate* to feare: . . . I. xi. 52. 8
importune *fate* That heapd on him so many wrathfull wreakes; I. xii. 16. 5
frowning froward *fate* Hath made sad witnesse . . . II. i. 37. 1
fiers *fate* did crop the blossome of his age. . . . II. i. 41. 9
direfull chaunce, armd with avenging *fate*, . . . II. i. 44. 6
Accusing fortune, and too cruell *fate*, . . . II. i. 56. 8
My selfe well wote, and mine unequall *fate:* . . . II. vii. 50. 5
'Abide the fortune of thy present *fate;* . . . II. vii. 60. 2
Unmindfull of his wound, of his *fate* ignoraunt. . . . II. viii. 34. 9
Yet sith his *fate* so cruelly did fall, . . . II. viii. 52. 7
surrender late His life . . . unto finall *fate*. . . . II. x. 13. 9
Till he surrendered Realme and life to *fate*. . . . II. x. 45. 5
thy good fortune, having *fate* obayd, . . . III. iii. 19. 7
Ne is thy *fate*, ne is thy fortune ill, . . . III. iii. 24. 6
his last *fate* him from thee take away; . . . III. iii. 28. 7
weene by warning to avoyd his *fate?* . . . III. iv. 27. 2
T' approve the unknowen purpose of eternall *fate*. . . . III. iv. 28. 9
to accursed *fate*, The guilt I doe ascribe: . . . III. iv. 37. 8
such as eternall *fate* Ordained hath, . . . III. vi. 32. 6
Me seemes I see Amintas wretched *fate*, . . . III. vi. 45. 8
she desyrd th' abridgement of her *fate*, . . . III. viii. 2. 3
What stony hart, that heares thy haplesse *fate*, . . . III. ix. 39. 6
What fortune and his *fate* on him will lay; . . . III. x. 3. 2
happinesse: . . . that *fate* n'ould let her yet possesse. . . . III. xii. 46. *or.*9
To them ordained by eternall *fate:* . . . IV. ii. 50. 5
Cambels *fate* that fortune did prevent; . . . IV. iii. 18. 5
Which secret *fate* hath in this Ladie wrought . . . IV. vi. 30. 4
by what haplesse *fate* Or hard misfortune . . . IV. vi. 47. 5
Ooraxes, feared for great Cyrus *fate*, . . . IV. xi. 21. 5
nam'd the river of his wretched *fate* . . . IV. xi. 38. 7
who can scape what his owne *fate* hath wrought? . . . V. iv. 27. 8
To attribute their folly unto *fate*, . . . V. iv. 28. 2
cruell heavens hath heapt an heavy *fate;* . . . V. v. 36. 3
whose untimely *fate* For to avenge, . . . V. vi. 33. 6
with dreadfull *fate* Had utterly subverted his unrighteous state. V. ix. 2. 8
Through the sad terror of so dreadfull *fate*, . . . V. ix. 46. 4
thorough *fate* . . . I my countrie have forlorne, . . . VI. ii. 27. 7
And oft complayn'd of *fate*, and fortune oft defyde. . . . VI. iv. 26. 9
to these happie fortunes cruell *fate* Hath joyn'd one evill, . . VI. iv. 30. 5
With stormes of fortune and tempestuous *fate* . . . VI. ix. 31. 5
(whether wicked *fate* so framed Or fault of men,) . . . VI. xii. 38. 7
Do worke their owne perfection so by *fate:* . . . VII. vii. 58. 7
state In which he stood before his haplesse *fate*. . . . *H.H.L.* 140
Fate's. Bereft of both by *Fates* unjust decreeing. . . . *Ti.* 35
Fates. (as *fates* the same foreseeing) . . . *Ro.* xviii. 13
So soone as *Fates* their vitall thred have shorne, . . . *Ti.* 181
whilest the *fates* affoord me vitall breath, . . . *Ti.* 309
Th' importune *fates*, which vengeance on me seeke, . . . *D.* 387
'Time and suffised *fates* to former kynd Shall us restore; . I. ii. 43. 8
fates expired could renew again, . . . I. v. 40. 3
cruell *fates* the carefull threds unfould, . . . I. vii. 22. 5
should not be quenched . . . For feare of evil *fates*, . . . I. xii. 37. 9
sith *fates* can make Way for themselves . . . III. iii. 25. 4
the *fates* are firme, And may not shrinck, . . . III. iii. 25. 6
their importune *fates* all satisfide: . . . III. iii. 44. 7
(so the *fates* ordaind) . . . III. ix. 42. 5
what the *Fates* do once decree, . . . IV. ii. 51. 8
fates perverse With guilefull love . . . IV. vii. 15. 3
Fates'. Unweeting of the *Fates* divine decree . . . IV. iii. 21. 4
by eternal doome of *Fates* decree, . . . VII. vi. 33. 6
Father. *See* **Foster-father.**
Thy flocks *father* his corage hath lost. . . . *S.C.* F. 80
For once I heard my *father* say, . . . *S.C.* Mar. 106
That his *father* left by inheritaunce; . . . *S.C.* May 89
Thy *father*,' (that word she spake with payne, . . . *S.C.* May 193
'Thy *father*, had he lived this day, . . . *S.C.* May 195
so thy *father* his head upheld, . . . *S.C.* May 205
Ye may me trust as your owne ghostly *father*.' . . . *Hub.* 280
Heare, thou great *Father* of the Gods on hie, . . . *T.M.* 55
'Ne shall his sister, ne thy *father* die, . . . *Ti.* 260
Thy *father*, that good Earle of rare renowne, . . . *Ti.* 261
Jove, the *father* of eternitie, . . . *Ti.* 369
'Old *father* Mole, (Mole hight that mountain . . . *Col.* 104
her *father*, sitting still on hie, . . . *Col.* 132
told her *father* by a shepheards boy, . . . *Col.* 147
As when old *father* Nilus gins to swell . . . I. i. 21. 1
With holy *father* sits not with such thinges to mell. . . . I. i. 30. 9
with that godly *father* to his home they went. . . . I. i. 33. 9
him before His *father* fierce of treason false accusd, . . . I. v. 37. 8
'Thrise happy man,' said then the *father* grave, . . . I. x. 51. 1
But now aread, old *father*, . . . I. x. 64. 5
Whose *father* Hercules in Fraunce did quell, . . . II. x. 11. 7
happy *father* of faire progeny: . . . II. x. 22. 2
Arraught the rule, and from their *father* drew; . . . II. x. 34. 8
her *father* deare Should . . . hard misfortune heare. . . . III. iii. 5. 8
She, of his *father*, Marinell did name; . . . III. iv. 20. 2
'Fond Proteus, *father* of false prophecis! . . . III. iv. 37. 1
Great *father* he of generation Is rightly cald, . . . III. vi. 9. 1
him the *Father* of all formes they call: . . . III. vi. 47. 8
'*father*, I note read aright . . . III. viii. 23. 7
Whom . . . She, of his *Father*, Parius did name; . . . III. ix. 36. 6
loves extremity . . . the *father* of fowle gealosy, . . . III. x. 22. 5
Witnesse the *father* of Philosophie, . . . IV. Pr. 3. 6
Phorcys, the *father* of that fatall brood, . . . IV. xi. 13. 1
father of the bold And warlike people . . . IV. xi. 15. 8
full many treasons vile His *father* Dolon had deviz'd . . . V. vi. 33. 8
after that his monstrous *father* fell Under Alcides club, . . V. x. 11. 2
the Theban Knight, The *father* of that fatall progeny, Made
kill herselfe . . . V. xi. 25. 3

Father—*Continued.*
And was the *Father* of that wounded Knight, . . . VI. iii. 3. 7
present The fearefull Lady to her *father* deare, . . . VI. iii. 18. 2
The *father* of the fayrest Pastorell, . . . VI. ix. 14. 2
In which ye, *father*, here doe dwell at ease, . . . VI. ix. 19. 2
my flockes *father* daily doth amend it. . . . VI. ix. 21. 8
Give leave awhyle, good *father*, in this shore To rest my barcke, VI. ix. 31. 3
Her *father* and her friends about her lying, . . . VI. xi. 23. 2
whose *father* hight The Lord of Many Ilands, . . . VI. xii. 4. 1
Which when her *father* understood, . . . VI. xii. 5. 5
The *father* of the Gods . . . Was troubled much . . . VII. vi. 15. 6
him, that is behight *Father* of Gods and men . . . VII. vi. 35. 5
my old *father* MOLE, whom Shepheards quill Renowmed hath . VII. vi. 36. 8
daughter of old *Father* Mole, . . . VII. vi. 40. 2
O fayrest Phoebus! *father* of the Muse! . . . *Epith.* 121
Father's. To see thee succeede in thy *fathers* steade, . . . *S.C.* May 203
The old lineaments of his *fathers* grace. . . . *S.C.* May 212
Let us our *fathers* heritage divide, . . . *Hub.* 136
Unto my *fathers* sheepe I usde to looke, . . . *Hub.* 292
in his *fathers* sight . . . did seeme the fairest wight. . . . *Mui.* 23
As should be worthie of his *fathers* throne. . . . *Mui.* 32
'Your owne deare sake forst me . . . to leave My *fathers*
kingdom'— . . . I. i. 52. 2
That did presume his *fathers* fyrie wayne, . . . I. iv. 9. 2
The tree of life, the crime of our first *fathers* fall. . . . I. xi. 46. 9
Hath made sad witnesse of thy *fathers* fall, . . . II. i. 37. 2
his sad *fathers* armes with blood defilde, . . . II. ii. 11. 3
by *fathers* labour long, . . . II. x. 25. 1
In rule succeede, and eke in *fathers* praise; . . . II. x. 41. 2
The which was dew in his dead *fathers* daies. . . . II. x. 41. 5
Into her *fathers* closet to repayre; . . . III. ii. 22. 2
I in my *fathers* wondrous mirrhour saw, . . . III. ii. 38. 7
the crowne that was his *fathers* right, . . . III. iii. 29. 6
Avenge his *fathers* losse with speare and shield, . . . III. iii. 31. 8
To live in thraldome of his *fathers* foe! . . . III. iii. 42. 3
From dread of her revenging *fathers* hond; . . . III. vii. 26. 2
shewing forth signes of their *fathers* blood, . . . IV. ii. 46. 3
in her *fathers* hall . . . in that enchaunted glasse she saw; . . IV. vi. 26. 5
He had three sonnes, all three like *fathers* sonnes, . . . V. vi. 33. 1
till to her *fathers* house he had her brought. . . . VI. iii. 15. 9
Till to that Ladies *fathers* house he came; . . . VI. iii. 17. 8
Most lively image of thy *Fathers* face, . . . *H.H.L.* 171
Fathers. as holy *fathers* sayne, . . . *S.C.* Jul. 57
When holy *fathers* wont to shrieve; . . . *S.C.* Au. 55
Thy *fathers* and great Grandfathers of old, . . . II. x. 4. 6
Begotten by two *fathers* of one mother, . . . IV. x. 32. 4
(as antique *fathers* tell) . . . IV. xi. 37. 2
by the *fathers* . . . I greater am in bloud . . . VII. vi. 26. 7
Fatness. he with *fatnes* so did overflowe, . . . *Van.* ii. 7
he through pride and *fatnes* gan despise Their meanesse; . . *Hub.* 586
eke with *fatnesse* swollen were his eyne; . . . I. iv. 21. 4
Fat's. *See* **Wine-fat's.**
Fatting. he had been a *fatting* hogs of late, . . . VII. vii. 40. 3
Fatty. His *fattie* waves doe fertile slime outwell, . . . I. i. 21. 3
Faulchins. *See* **Falchions.**
Fault. Thou findest *faulte* where nys to be found, . . . *S.C.* May 144
To feele his *fault*, and not be further vext. . . . *Gn. Ded.* 12
Feareles through his own *fault* . . . *T.M.* 303
Or thine the *fault*, or mine the error is, . . . I. iii. 39. 4
Here endlesse penaunce for one *fault* I pay, . . . I. v. 42. 6
That tree through one mans *fault* hath doen us all to dy. . I. xi. 47. 9
Him ill beseemes anothers *fault* to name, . . . II. ix. 38. 4
each thing by which the eyes may *fault:* . . . II. xi. 9. 7
The cause to weet, and *fault* to remedy: . . . II. xi. 20. 3
not thy *fault*, but secret powre unseene: . . . III. i. 7. 8
Let not her *fault* your sweete affections marre, . . . III. i. 49. 3
He cast to punish for his hainous *fault:* . . . III. viii. 36. 3
Ne all are shamed by the *fault* of one: . . . III. ix. 2. 5
blame For *fault* of few that have abusd the same; . . . IV. Pr. 2. 5
Yet thou, false Squire, his *fault* shalt deare aby, . . . IV. i. 53. 8
Yet found no *fault*, but that the Hag did scold . . . IV. viii. 28. 3
through his *fault* she had Fallen into that Tyrants hand . . V. xi. 40. 8
Tooke in foule scorne that I such *fault* did find, . . . VI. ii. 11. 7
'and right, . . . that him befell by his owne *fault:* . . . VI. ii. 23. 6
Yet since it was his fortune, not his *fault*, . . . VI. iii. 21. 6
To justifie thy *fault* gainst me in equall fight.' . . . VI. iii. 35. 9
The heavens of their fortunes *fault* accuse, . . . VI. ix. 29. 2
(whether wicked fate so framed Or *fault* of men,) . . . VI. xii. 38. 8
In finding *fault* with her too portly pride: . . . *Am.* v. 2
How ever fleshes *fault* it filthy make; . . . *H.B.* 160
ye that wont . . . To reade my *fault*, . . . *H.H.L.* 16
Beginnes his owne, and my old *fault* renewes. . . . *H.H.L.* 21
Faultless. *faultlesse* fayth is turned to faithlesse fere. . . *S.C.* Jun. 110
wicked Fortune *faultles* him misled, . . . *Mui.* 418
from her presence *faultlesse* him debard. . . . *Col.* 167
affection *faultlesse* blame For fault of few . . . IV. Pr. 2. 4
Faults. layen her *faults* the world beforne, . . . *S.C.* May 160
The *faults* which life hath trespassed before. . . . *Gn.* 448
deserve to have small *faults* remitted, . . . *Gn.* 474
And wipe their *faults* out of your censure grave. . . . *Ded. Son.* ix. 14
themselves full eath perswade . . . both *faults* to shade, . . V. viii. 14. 5
And al her *faults* in thy black booke enroll: . . . *Am.* x. 12
all their *faults* with which they did offend. . . . *Am.* xxiv. 12
for my *faults* ye will me gently beat. . . . *Am.* xxiv. 14
And fly the *faults* with which we did offend. . . . *Am.* lxii. 8
Faulty. *faulty* men, which daunger to thee threat: . . . *Com. Son.* i. 8
Through blame do light on those that *faultie* bee; . . . *Col.* 756
though they *faulty* were, yet well he wayd, . . . I. x. 40. 5
The *faulty* soules . . . brought to his heavenly bowre. . . . I. x. 40. 9
if yourselfe, Sir knight, ye *faulty* fynd, . . . I. xii. 30. 7

Faulty—*Continued.*
without gealous feares Or *faultie* thoughts, ... II. iv. 18. 8
Her *faultie* Handmayd, which that bale did breede, ... II. iv. 29. 8
Our *faulty* weakenes, and your matchlesse might: . . . . . . III. i. 30. 2
faulty men use oftentimes To attribute their folly unto fate, . V. iv. 28. 1
fowle upbrayd with *faulty* blame. . . . . VI. i. 24. 9
friendships *faultie* guile For ever to assoile. . . . . *Proth.* 99
Faun. A foolish *Faune* indeed, ... VII. vi. 46. 6
Faund. *See* **Fawned.**
Fauns. a naked rout of *Faunes* With hideous cry . . . . . . *Bel.*[1] x. 11
Here han the holy *Faunes* recourse, ... *S.C.* Jul. 77
O flocks! O *Faunes!* . . . . *Gn.* 145
a ragged rout Of *Faunes* and Satyres, ... *T.M.* 268
A troupe of *Faunes* and Satyres . . . . I. vi. 7. 7
Faunus. Dan *Faunus* chaunst to meet her by the way, ... II. ii. 7. 5
Foolish god *Faunus* . . . longed foolishly To see her naked . . VII. vi. 42. 7
There *Faunus* saw that pleased much his eye, ... VII. vi. 46. 1
So did Diana and her maydens all Use silly *Faunus,* . . . . VII. vi. 49. 2
Faunus (for her paine) Of her beloved Fanchin did obtaine, . VII. vi. 53. 4
Favor. full of *favour* as kidde mought be. . . . . *S.C.* May 184
Of mercye and *favour,* then, I you pray . . . . *S.C.* May 272
Such *favour* couth he fynd, ... *S.C.* Jul. 138
Diggon should soone find *favour* and ease: . . . . *S.C.* S. 253
favour my beginnings graciously; . . . . *Gn.* 38
fortune doth you secret *favour* give.' . . . . *Hub.* 594
We may seeke *favour* of the best of all?' . . . . *Hub.* 618
after we may *favour* seeke to win?' . . . . *Hub.* 644
the King did *favour* to them beare; . . . . *Hub.* 1076
Ne fawnest for the *favour* of the great; . . . . *Com. Son.* i. 6
Whilst heaven did *favour* his felicities, ... *Mui.* 21
shepheards . . . Which *favour* thee, and honour Cynthia: . . . *Col.* 458
with none of them thou *favor* foundest, ... *Col.* 461
High in the *favour* of that Emperesse, ... *Ded. Son.* xi. 3
Who then ought more to *favour* her then you, ... *Ded. Son.* xiv. 5
So be, O Queene! you equall *favour* showe.' . . . . I. iv. 42. 7
glad to gain such *favour,* gan devise, ... I. vi. 32. 8
Nymph . . . Was out of Dianes *favor,* as it then befell. . . . I. vii. 4. 9
If lesse then that I feare, more *favour* I have found.' . . . . I. vii. 25. 9
seeme to laugh on me, and *favour* mine intent. . . . . I. ix. 12. 9
In hope to win more *favour* with his mate, ... II. ii. 19. 4
Great *favour* I thee graunt . . . . II. iii. 7. 9
sith thou hast found *favour* in mine eye, ... II. vii. 49. 7
in her *favor* high bee reckoned, ... II. ix. 6. 8
They her besought of *favour* speciall . . . . II. ix. 20. 7
found such *favour* in their loving hartes, ... III. vii. 55. 2
soveraine *favor* towards chastity, ... III. viii. 29. 3
with feare, nor *favour,* nor with all He els could doe, . . . III. viii. 41. 6
so much *favour* she to him hath hight . . . . IV. viii. 54. 1
'Thenceforth I found more *favour* at her hand, ... IV. viii. 61. 1
To laugh at me, and *favour* my pretence, ... IV. x. 56. 4
in recompence of that great *favour* . . . . V. iv. 12. 5
to curry *favour* With th' Elfin Knight, ... V. v. 35. 5
From seeking *favour* where it doth abound; . . . . V. v. 42. 2
In case she might finde *favour* in his eye, ... V. v. 55. 2
favour not The wicked driftes of trayterous desynes . . . . . V. ix. 42. 1
entreated, that they might Finde *favour* . . . . VI. iii. 42. 9
After that Timias had againe recured The *favour* of Belphebe . VI. v. 12. 2
'Let me therefore this *favour* for him finde, ... VI. v. 30. 1
Yet heavens them selves, that *favour* feeble rights, ... VI. viii. 18. 8
courtesie amongst the rudest breeds Good will and *favour.* . . VI. ix. 45. 6
shadowes vaine Of courtly *favour,* . . . . VI. x. 2. 8
daily more her *favour* to augment; . . . . VI. x. 37. 2
To graunt him *favour* or afford him love: . . . . VI. xi. 5. 4
to pretend Some shew of *favour,* . . . . VI. xi. 6. 6
Ne yielded ought for *favour* or for feare; . . . . VII. vi. 12. 4
ne *favour* seek of friends: . . . . *Am.* lix. 10
Since thou doest shew no *favour* unto mee, ... *H.L.* 150
What he may do, her *favour* to obtaine; . . . . *H.L.* 219
when he hath found *favour* to his will, ... *H.L.* 245
Favorable. *favourable* times did us afford Free libertie . . . *T.M.* 243
Was none more *favourable,* nor more faire, ... *Mui.* 20
The which vouchsafe dear Lord, your *favorable* doome. . . . *Ded. Son.* vii. 14
their felicities The *favourable* heavens did not envy, ... I. vii. 43. 6
How to advaunce with *favourable* hands, ... I. ix. 1. 8
The hevens so *favorable* were and free, ... III. vi. 2. 2
Faire Sun! shew forth thy *favourable* ray, ... *Epith.* 117
Therefore to us be *favorable* now; . . . . *Epith.* 382
Favored. *See* **Ill-favored, Well-favored.**
whilest him fortune *favourd,* fayre did thrive In bloudy field; I. iii. 37. 8
whiles good fortune *favoured* her might, ... II. x. 56. 6
Whilest Fortune *favourd* her successe in fight: . . . . V. vii. 41. 7
Was *favoured* and to her grace commended. . . . . VI. ix. 46. 6
Favoreth. The sonnes of Day he *favoureth,* I see, ... I. v. 25. 7
Favorites. Of her fond *favorites* so nam'd amis, ... II. xii. 69. 5
Favorless. happinesse Heven doth to me envy, and fortune *favourlesse.'* . . . . II. ix. 7. 9
Favor's. him receiv'd againe to former *favours* state. . . . . IV. viii. 17. 9
she knew not his *favours* likelynesse, ... V. vii. 39. 7
through that small *favours* gaine, ... VI. xi. 7. 5
Favors. Ne onelie *favours* them which it professe, ... *T.M.* 575
with . . . her deare *favours* dearly well adorned; . . . . . . *As.* 154
Their bounteous deeds and noble *favours* shrynd, ... *Col.* 582
those goodly *favours* Bestowd on thee, ... *Col.* 585
The many *favours* I with thee have fownd, ... I. x. 67. 2
she sprinckled *favours* manifold On whom she list, ... III. xii. 13. 7
such fond *favours* sparingly dispenst: . . . . IV. ii. 9. 3
For his friends sake her offred *favours* scorne, ... IV. ix. 3. 8
Fawn. To *fawne,* to crowche, to waite, to ride, to ronne, . . *Hub.* 905
Doo *fawne* on you, and your wide praises sing; . . . . *Ti.* 201
They, . . . *fawne* on her with count' nance fayne. . . . . . . I. vi. 12. 9

Fawn—*Continued.*
when her listed she could *fawne* and flatter; . . . . VI. vi. 42. 6
the *fawne* I practise from the Doe, . . . how to convay: . . . VI. ix. 23. 3
a young *fawne,* that late hath lost the hynd; . . . . *Am.* lxxviii. 2
Fawned. This fround, that *faund,* . . . . II. ix. 35. 6
Fawnest. Ne *fawnest* for the favour of the great; . . . . . . *Com. Son.* i. 6
Fawning. Her *fawning* love . . . He would not shend; . . . . I. i. 53. 7
he . . . lickt her lilly hands with *fawning* tong, ... I. iii. 6. 2
With *fawning* wordes he courted her a while; . . . . I. vi. 4. 1
yfraught with *fawning* guyle And fayre resemblance . . . . III. viii. 8. 1
all the *fawning* of the flatterer. . . . . III. viii. 38. 9
creeping like a *fawning* hound, ... VI. iv. 11. 2
Fay. missay Both of their doctrine, and of theyr *faye.* . . . . *S.C.* S. 107
mischiefes which a wicked *Fay* Had wrought, ... II. ii. 43. 3
Therefore a *Fay* he her according hight, ... II. x. 71. 8
he by an Elfe was gotten of a *Fay:* . . . . III. iii. 26. 9
Their mother was a *Fay,* . . . . IV. ii. 44. 1
'Bold *Fay,* that durst Come see the secret of the life of man, IV. ii. 49. 6
then that carefull *Fay* Departed thence . . . . IV. ii. 53. 1
Therefore this *Fay* I hold but fond and vaine, ... IV. iii. 2. 1
well instructed by the *Fay* her mother, ... IV. iii. 40. 4
neither hath religion nor *fay,* . . . . V. viii. 19. 7
Fayeree. *See* **Faery.**
Faygned. *See* **Feigned.**
Fayn(e), -d, -s. *See* **Fain,** *etc.,* **Feign,** *etc.*
Fays. Her many deemd to have beene of the *Fayes,* . . . . . II. x. 42. 7
she, as *Fayes* are wont, in privie place Did spend her dayes, . IV. ii. 44. 8
Fealty. fast *fealty,* Which I do owe unto all womankynd, . . . I. iii. 1. 6
swore him *fealty* to win or loose. . . . . II. x. 37. 9
Shall yield him selfe his liegeman, and sweare *fealty.* . . . . III. iii. 37. 9
Made them sweare *fealty* to Artegall; . . . . V. vii. 43. 6
swore to him true *fealtie* for aye. . . . . VI. i. 44. 4
with dew *fealtie* Adore the powre . . . . *H.B.* 270
Fear. heaven, that gan her force to *feare.* . . . . *Ro.* xii. 12
Gods secure *feare* not her force at all. . . . . *Ro.* xii. 14
Heaven had not *feare* of that presumptuous might, ... *Ro.* xvii. 3
eft, when ye count you freed from *feare,* . . . . *S.C.* F. 42
Semed, the sencelesse yron dyd *feare,* . . . . *S.C.* F. 205
I *feare* I have troubled your troupes to longe: . . . . *S.C.* Ap. 149
Sperre the yate fast for *feare* of fraude: . . . . *S.C.* May 224
faultlesse fayth is turned to faithlesse *fere.* . . . . *S.C.* Jun. 110
I *fear* me, thou have a squint eye: . . . . *S.C.* Au. 129
Neede *feare* no chaunge of frowning fate; . . . . *S.C.* S. 71
For *feare* of raungers and the great hunt, ... *S.C.* S. 159
I of doubted daunger had no *feare:* . . . . *S.C.* D. 22
No deadly fight of warlick fleete doth *feare;* . . . . *Gn.* 124
Devoid of care, and *feare* of all falshedd; . . . . *Gn.* 246
feare and yre Had blent so much his sense, ... *Gn.* 310
Much do I *feare* among such fiends to sit; . . . . *Gn.* 381
Much do I *feare* back to them to repayre, ... *Gn.* 382
No signe of storme, no *feare* of future paine, ... *Gn.* 565
For *feare* least we like rogues should be reputed, ... *Hub.* 187
Seemes that no foes revengement he did *feare:* . . . . *Hub.* 216
For *feare* of afterclaps, for to prevent: . . . . *Hub.* 332
they without care or *feare* Cruelly fell upon their flock . . . *Hub.* 334
To feed on hope, to pine with *feare* and sorrow; . . . . . . *Hub.* 900
striken both with *feare,* . . . . *Hub.* 1068
disswaded them from needlesse *feare,* . . . . *Hub.* 1075
feare he neede no force of enemie. . . . . *Hub.* 1126
causeth sleep to seize the eyes, And *feare* the harts . . . . *Hub.* 1296
for *feare* now almost ded; . . . . *Hub.* 1374
Are heapt with spoyles of fortune and of *feare,* . . . . *T.M.* 161
Distraught twixt *feare* and pitie; . . . . *Ti.* 579
Whereof the Goddesse gathering jealous *feare,* . . . . *Mui.* 129
feare The dashing of the waves, ... *Mui.* 282
feare of foe That hazarded his health, ... *Mui.* 377
of the race that all wild beastes do *feare,* . . . . *D.* 123
their flocks, devoyd of dangers *fecre,* . . . . *Col.* 54
'Fearful much more . . . then hart can *fear:* . . . . *Col.* 201
alreadie dead with *feare,* . . . . *Col.* 205
full of inward *feare,* . . . . *Col.* 228
all with troublous *feare* Gathred . . . about her body . . . . I. i. 25. 3
wonted *feare* of doing ought amis, ... I. i. 49. 2
of himselfe he ofte for *feare* would quake, ... I. ii. 10. 7
Still flying from his thoughts and gealous *feare:* . . . . . . I. ii. 12. 3
put *feare* apart, And tel both who ye be, ... I. ii. 21. 8
for *feare* Least to you hap that happened to me heare, . . . I. ii. 31. 4
Full of sad *feare* and ghastly dreriment, ... I. ii. 44. 4
turning to his Lady, dead with *feare* her fownd. . . . . . . I. ii. 44. 9
Her seeming dead he fownd with feigned *feare,* . . . . I. ii. 45. 1
all passed *feare,* He set her on her steede, ... I. ii. 45. 8
With suddeine *feare* her pitcher downe she threw, ... I. iii. 11. 6
quaking hands, and other signes of *feare:* . . . . I. iii. 12. 6
of his cruell rage Nigh dead with *feare,* . . . . I. iii. 13. 4
for *feare,* her beads she did forgett: . . . . I. iii. 14. 5
so forth told the story of her *feare.* . . . . I. iii. 25. 5
Loth was that other, and did faint through *feare,* . . . . . I. iii. 34. 5
had his staggering steed not shronke for *feare,* . . . . . . I. iii. 35. 4
daily care To get, and nightly *feare* to lose his owne, . . . I. iv. 28. 8
needlesse *feare* did never vantage none; . . . . I. iv. 49. 4
I *feare* the fickle freakes,' . . . 'Of fortune false, ... I. iv. 50. 1
She . . . th' unacquainted light began to *feare,* . . . . I. v. 21. 4
trembling yet through *feare* of former hate. . . . . I. vi. 9. 5
every tender part for *feare* does shake. . . . . I. vi. 10. 2
Which, . . . quakes in every lim With chaunge of *feare,* . . . I. vi. 10. 9
To comfort her; and, *feare* to put away, ... I. vi. 11. 8
twixt *feare* and hope amazd does sitt, ... I. vi. 12. 3
fly away for *feare* of fowle disgrace; . . . . I. vi. 18. 7
he taught the tender ymp . . . To banish . . . bastard *feare:* I. vi. 24. 2
everie beast for *feare* of him did fly, and quake. . . . . . . I. vi. 24. 9

Fear—*Continued.*
lull in rugged armes withouten childish *feare*. . . . I. vi. 27. 9
whom he had not taught To *feare* his force: . . . . I. vi. 29. 5
gan to turne aside For *feare*, ... I. vi. 34. 8
If lesse then that I *feare*, more favour I have found.' . . . . I. vii. 25. 9
for *feare* into his jawes to fall, ... I. vii. 44. 6
trembling *feare* did feel in every vaine: . . . . I. viii. 4. 2
earth, . . . trembling with strange *feare* . . . . I. viii. 8. 9
as it for *feare* did quake. . . . . I. viii. 23. 9
th' only good that growes of passed *feare* Is to be wise, . . . I. viii. 44. 5
his *feare* still followed him behynd: . . . . I. ix. 21. 6
adding new *Feare* to his first amazment, ... I. ix. 24. 2
through his boldnes rather *feare* did reach; . . . . I. ix. 25. 8
'*Fear* nought,' (quoth he) . . . . I. ix. 26. 5
I . . . Fledd fast away, halfe dead with dying *feare;* . . . . I. ix. 30. 6
th' other forst him staye, and comforted in *feare*. . . . . I. ix. 34. 9
That makes frayle flesh to *feare* the bitter wave, ... I. ix. 40. 5
Feare, sicknesse, age, losse, labour, sorrow, strife, ... I. ix. 44. 6
watched night and day, For *feare* of many foes; . . . . I. x. 5. 3
face he made all beastes to *feare*, ... I. x. 42. 7
That sight thereof bredd cold congealed *feare;* . . . . I. xi. 13. 5
That made the Redcrosse knight nigh quake for *feare*, ... I. xi. 15. 8
In *feare* to lose his weapon in his paw, ... I. xi. 41. 2
He woxe dismaid, and gan his fate to *feare:* . . . . I. xi. 52. 8
The sight with ydle *feare* did them dismay, ... I. xii. 9. 8
Halfe dead through *feare*, ... I. xii. 11. 3
should not be quenched . . . For *feare* of evil fates, ... I. xii. 37. 9
to quake Through inward *feare*, ... II. i. 9. 4
With stony *feare* of that rude rustick mate, ... II. ii. 8. 8
Yet colde through *feare* . . . . II. ii. 9. 3
fell flatt to ground for *feare*, ... II. iii. 6. 8
for *feare* of dew vengeaunce Doe lurke, ... II. iii. 14. 7
they shrowd themselves from causeles *feare;* . . . . II. iii. 20. 2
feare them followes still . . . . II. iii. 20. 3
For *feare* . . . her beauty to disgrace? . . . . II. iii. 25. 9
Both *feare* and hope he in her face did finde: . . . . II. iii. 32. 5
(sure I *feare* it ill) . . . . II. iii. 44. 3
Dismay with *feare*, or cause one foot to flye, ... II. iii. 45. 4
for *feare* of worse that may betide, ... II. iii. 46. 1
'*Feare* gave her winges, ... II. iv. 32. 1
For *feare* of further harme, ... II. iv. 39. 4
Ne care, ne *feare* I how the wind do blow, ... II. vi. 10. 4
trembling *Feare* still to and fro did fly, ... II. vii. 22. 6
For *feare* least Force or Fraud should unaware . . . . II. vii. 25. 3
him that walkes in *feare* and sad affright. . . . . II. vii. 29. 9
abasht he was Through *fear* and wonder . . . . II. viii. 7. 2
the stony *feare* Ran to his hart, ... II. viii. 46. 1
other ill to *feare* . . . . II. ix. 42. 3
fraile pen, with *feare* disparaged, ... II. x. 2. 8
The faire Sabrina, almost dead with *feare*, ... II. x. 19. 3
th' Infants tutors gathering to *feare*, ... II. x. 64. 4
exceeding *feare* Their visages imprest . . . . II. xi. 5. 8
fled fast away for *feare:* . . . . II. xi. 25. 6
all the seas for *feare* doe seeme away to fly. . . . . II. xii. 3. 9
for exceeding *feare;* . . . . II. xii. 22. 4
Such as Dame Nature selfe mote *feare* to see, ... II. xii. 23. 2
seem'd to fly for *feare* them to behold. . . . . II. xii. 25. 5
bugs to *fearen* babes withall, ... II. xii. 25. 8
'*Feare* nought,' then saide the Palmer . . . . II. xii. 26. 1
fild their sayles with *feare:* . . . . II. xii. 37. 2
Instead of fraying, they them selves did *feare*, ... II. xii. 40. 6
For *feare* of waking him, ... II. xii. 73. 6
Fled all away for *feare* of fowler shame. . . . . II. xii. 81. 7
For *fear*, through want of words, her excellence to marre. . . III. Pr. 2. 9
he gan to *feare* His toward perill, ... III. i. 9. 6
through *feare*, as white as whales bone: . . . . III. i. 15. 5
For *feare* least her unwares she should abrayd, ... III. i. 61. 2
Through suddein *feare* and ghastly drerihedd, ... III. i. 62. 5
striving fit to make, I *feare*, doe marre: . . . . III. ii. 3. 8
how much I *feare* least love it bee! . . . . III. ii. 33. 1
ever her importund not to *feare* . . . . III. ii. 34. 8
for *feare* least blame . . . should in her be fond, ... III. ii. 52. 7
great care she tooke, and greater *feare*, ... III. iii. 5. 7
For *feare* the cruell Feendes should thee unwares devowre: . . III. iii. 8. 9
So greatly his commandement they *feare*, ... III. iii. 11. 5
make The warlike Mertians for *feare* to quake: . . . . III. iii. 30. 5
his foes shall *feare*, ... III. iii. 45. 8
Wordes *fearen* babes. . . . . III. iv. 15. 3
feare did all invade, ... III. iv. 21. 4
The which his mother seeing gan to *feare* . . . . III. iv. 24. 4
she of womans force did *feare* no harme; . . . . III. iv. 27. 8
So deepe the deadly *feare* of that foule swaine . . . . III. iv. 49. 2
Doubleth her hast for *feare* to bee for-hent, ... III. iv. 49. 8
former *feare* of being fowly shent . . . . III. iv. 50. 4
light doe shonne for *feare* of being shent; . . . . III. iv. 58. 7
Carried away with wings of speedy *feare*.' . . . . III. v. 6. 6
fayre Belphoebe gan to *feare*, ... III. v. 49. 1
had left them languishing twixt hope and *feare*. . . . . III. vi. 13. 9
from Prince Arthure fled with wings of idle *feare*. . . . . III. vi. 54. 9
So fledd fayre Florimell from her vaine *feare*, ... III. vii. 1. 6
turning her *feare* to foolish wrath, ... III. vii. 8. 1
For *feare* of mischiefe, which she did forecast . . . . III. vii. 18. 4
Was greatly woe begon, and gan to *feare* . . . . III. vii. 20. 7
apply His nimble feet to her conceived *feare*, ... III. vii. 24. 6
fear gave her wings, and need her corage taught. . . . . III. vii. 26. 9
Full of sad *feare* and doubtfull agony . . . . III. vii. 32. 1
trembling yet through *feare* the Squire bespake: . . . . III. vii. 47. 1
for *feare* of shame and fowle disgrace. . . . . III. vii. 60. 5
dead through *feare* Fell streight to ground . . . . III. viii. 12. 6
seemd for *feare* to quake in every lim, ... III. viii. 15. 8

Fear—*Continued.*
more for *feare* of his grim sight, ... III. viii. 32. 8
chaung'd from one to other *feare:* . . . . III. viii. 33. 2
Bidding her *feare* no more her foeman vilde, ... III. viii. 34. 3
with *feare*, nor favour, nor with all He els could doe, . . . III. viii. 41. 6
Right sore I *feare*, least with unworthie blames . . . . III. ix. 1. 3
welcomde more for *feare* then charitee; . . . . III. ix. 19. 4
all men *feare* to tempt his billowes strong, ... III. ix. 45. 5
He fled for *feare* of that he had misdonne, ... III. ix. 48. 4
Fond is the *feare* that findes no remedie: . . . . III. x. 3. 3
The loving couple neede no reskew *feare*, ... III. x. 16. 3
He fainted, and was almost dead with *feare*, ... III. x. 37. 7
continuall *feare* Of that rocks fall, ... III. x. 58. 3
Untroubled of vile *feare* or bitter fell. . . . . III. xi. 2. 5
It was not Satyrane, whom he did *feare*, ... III. xi. 6. 1
Out of her thraldome and continuall *feare:* . . . . III. xi. 16. 5
That cruell element, which all things *feare*, ... III. xi. 22. 4
Trembling through *feare* least down he fallen should, ... III. xi. 34. 8
for *feare* Of secret daunger, ... III. xi. 55. 5
Next him was *Feare*, all arm'd from top to toe, ... III. xii. 12. 1
walkte each where for *feare* of hid mischaunce, ... III. xii. 15. 7
Scudamore With her . . . Squire, both full of *feare*, ... III. xii. 44. 3
From her high spirit chase imperious *feare*, ... IV. Pr. 5. 3
Thereto her *feare* was made so much the greater . . . . IV. i. 7. 1
eke fayre Amoret, now freed from *feare*, ... IV. i. 15. 6
'Then tell,' (quoth Blandamour) 'and *feare* no blame: . . . IV. i. 48. 5
The aged Dame . . . Was dead with *feare;* . . . . IV. i. 54. 2
As one in *feare* the Stygian gods t' offend, ... IV. iii. 32. 2
filled were with rufull tine And secret *feare*, ... IV. iii. 37. 5
from *feare* of treason free, ... IV. iii. 49. 4
Whether through foundring or through sodein *feare*, . . . IV. iv. 30. 3
his dayly *feare* His ydle braine gan busily molest, ... IV. v. 43. 6
His powrelesse arme, benumbd with secret *feare*, ... IV. vi. 21. 3
turning [*his] *feare* to faint devotion, ... IV. vi. 24. 8
all his gealous *feare* he false had found, ... IV. vi. 28. 2
For sudden joy and secret *feare* withall; . . . . IV. vi. 29. 3
Ne thenceforth *feare* the thing . . . . IV. vi. 30. 6
twixt doubtfull *feare* And feeble hope hung . . . . IV. vi. 34. 1
I her preserv'd from perill and from *feare*, ... IV. vi. 35. 6
His hart was thrild with point of deadly *feare*, ... IV. vi. 37. 2
The *feare* whereof seem'd much her to affray; . . . . IV. vi. 45. 4
makes her *feare* a spur to hast her flight: . . . . IV. vii. 22. 7
Pursuing that faire Lady full of *feare:* . . . . IV. vii. 24. 5
freed from *feare* and danger of that dismall wight. . . . . IV. vii. 33. 9
trembling every joynt through former *feare;* . . . . IV. vii. 34. 2
Himselfe by them on foot to succour them from *feare*. . . . IV. viii. 22. 9
all voide of doubtfull *feare*, ... IV. ix. 5. 7
Exchanged out of one into another *feare*. . . . . IV. ix. 17. 9
Feare of her safety did her not constraine; . . . . IV. ix. 18. 1
now in *feare* of shame she more did stond, ... IV. ix. 18. 5
cause of *feare*, sure, had she none . . . . IV. ix. 19. 1
As if some proved perill he did *feare*, ... IV. x. 12. 8
For *feare* of harme that might lie hidden there; . . . . IV. x. 20. 2
being free from *feare* and gealosye . . . . IV. x. 28. 5
thee the winds, the clouds doe *feare*, ... IV. x. 44. 6
As if some blame of evill she did *feare*, ... IV. x. 50. 4
shaking off all doubt and shamefast *feare* . . . . IV. x. 53. 6
for *feare* of her offence; . . . . IV. x. 56. 2
For *feare* of perill which to him mote fall . . . . IV. xi. 7. 8
For *feare* she should of lightnesse be detected: . . . . IV. xii. 35. 8
makes me *feare* in time he will us quite forsake. . . . . V. Pr. 7. 9
even wilde beasts did *feare* his awfull sight, ... V. i. 8. 4
fain'd to fly for *feare* of being thrall; . . . . V. i. 22. 8
As rated Spaniell takes his burden up for *feare*. . . . . V. i. 29. 9
The fortune of her life long time did *feare:* . . . . V. ii. 3. 4
makes all men for *feare* that passage for to shonne.' . . . . V. ii. 4. 9
filled all the house with *feare* and great uprore. . . . . V. ii. 21. 9
eke their dame halfe dead did hide her selfe for *feare*. . . . V. ii. 24. 9
thus unto him spake, without regard or *feare*. . . . . V. ii. 33. 9
broke his sword, for *feare* of further harmes, ... V. v. 21. 8
For *feare* her mistresse shold have knowledge gayned; . . . . V. v. 44. 4
secretly afflict with jealous *feare*, ... V. vi. 4. 6
for *feare* least by that art He should his purpose misse, . . . V. vi. 24. 2
They all were fled for *feare;* . . . . V. vi. 35. 9
Prince Arthure and Sir Artegall Free Samient from *feare:* . . V. viii. Arg.
Yet fled she fast, . . . Carried with wings of *feare*, ... V. viii. 4. 7
gan forward set To save her from her *feare*, ... V. viii. 6. 9
th' onely *feare* that was before their vew, ... V. viii. 38. 8
As they were follow'd of their former *feare*. . . . . V. viii. 39. 3
tost the Paynim without *feare* or awe; . . . . V. viii. 41. 7
with guilefull words her to perswade To banish *feare;* . . . . V. ix. 12. 6
Warning him hold it fast for *feare* of slights: . . . . V. ix. 18. 3
Nor undertake the same for cowheard *feare*, ... V. x. 15. 5
Durst not abide, but fled away for *feare*, ... V. x. 38. 3
He gan to burne in rage, and friese in *feare*, ... V. xi. 2. 6
By those which earst did fly away for *feare*, ... V. xii. 6. 5
new life to her lent in midst of deadly *feare*. . . . . V. xii. 12. 9
to ward the deadly *feare;* . . . . V. xii. 14. 4
As if he would have daunted him with *feare;* . . . . V. xii. 16. 3
Did set upon us flying both for *feare;* . . . . VI. i. 16. 4
Ne would he spare for pitty, nor refraine for *feare*. . . . . VI. i. 17. 9
To you I will not *feare* it to relate. . . . . VI. ii. 27. 5
conceiving then great *feare* Of my fraile safetie, ... VI. ii. 29. 2
never to be recreant for *feare* Of perill, ... VI. ii. 35. 3
Most pensive man, through *feare* what of his childe became. . VI. iii. 17. 9
did free from *feare* Of a discourteous Knight, ... VI. iii. 18. 5
and fled himselfe away for *feare*. . . . . VI. iv. 7. 9
the wyld man, contrarie to her *feare*, ... VI. iv. 11. 1
God . . . had them freed from that deadly *feare*, . . . VI. iv. 15. 3
As one that had no life him left through former *feare*. . . . VI. vi. 32. 9

Fear—*Continued.*
by this thy cowheard *feare:* . . . VI. vi. 34. 2
else his *feare* could not be satisfyde. . . . VI. vii. 17. 4
For *feare* of wetting them before their bed. . . . VI. ix. 13. 5
They, that have much, *feare* much to loose thereby, . . . VI. ix. 21. 3
Through cowherd *feare* he fled away . . . VI. x. 35. 3
scarcely yet from former *feare* exempted, . . . VI. x. 36. 8
yet his *feare* did follow him behynd: . . . VI. xi. 27. 6
doe *feare* away, and tell.' . . . VI. xi. 29. 9
whose hart through *feare* was late fordonne, . . . VI. xi. 35. 5
There did they find, that which they did not *feare,* . . . VI. xi. 37. 1
Though not his *feare,* for nought may *feare* disswade, . . . VI. xi. 38. 2
Knowing his fatall hand by former *feare;* . . . VI. xii. 25. 8
Ne yielded ought for favour or for *feare;* . . . VII. vi. 12. 4
laying *feare* aside to doe his charge, . . . VII. vi. 17. 6
to us all exceeding *feare* did breed, . . . VII. vi. 20. 4
for th' unruly fiends which they did *feare;* . . . VII. vii. 3. 8
That as some did him love, so others did him *feare.* . . . VII. vii. 28. 9
Twixt *feare* and hope depending doubtfully! . . . *Am.* xxv. 4
Such selfe-assurance need not *feare* . . . *Am.* lix. 9
fondly *feare* to loose your liberty; . . . *Am.* lxv. 2
For *feare* the stones her tender foot should wrong, . . . *Epith.* 49
For *feare* of burning her sunshyny face, . . . *Epith.* 119
From *feare* of perrill and foule horror free. . . . *Epith.* 322
They both are fallen, that all the earth did *feare,* . . . *Com. Son.* iv. 6
Onely I *feare* my wits enfeebled late, . . . *H.L.* 15
The *feare* whereof, O how doth it torment . . . *H.L.* 252
The gnawing envie, the hart-fretting *feare,* . . . *H.L.* 259
Through *feare* of loosing his felicitie. . . . *H.L.* 270
for *feare* it to deflore, . . . *H.B.* 39
Humbled with *feare* and awfull reverence, . . . *H.H.B.* 141
For *feare,* lest if he chaunce to looke on thee, . . . *H.H.B.* 146
Hercules two pillors . . . Did make to quake and *feare:* . . . *Proth.* 149

Feare. *See* **Fere.**

Feared. nought *feared* they to forgoe; . . . *S.C.* May 110
blent so much his sense, that lesse he *feard)* . . . *Gn.* 311
'Ne *feard* the burning waves of Phlegeton, . . . *Gn.* 441
all the Beasts him *feared* as they ought, . . . *Hub.* 1106
Full of the *feared* sight which late they sawe. . . . *Hub.* 1110
To hide himselfe from his owne *feared* thought. . . . *Hub.* 1358
Ne *fear'd* the Wolfe, ne *fear'd* the wildest beast, . . . *D.* 135
I *feard,* least land we never should have eyde: . . . *Col.* 267
Much *feared* I to have bene quite abhord, . . . I. iii. 27. 3
his beheast they *feared* as a tyrans law. . . . I. vi. 26. 9
That seemed from some *feared* foe to fly, . . . I. ix. 21. 3
He *feard* not once himselfe to be in need, . . . I. x. 38. 4
That *feared* chaunce from her to turne away: . . . I. xi. 32. 5
Some *feard,* and fledd; some *feard,* and well it faynd; . . . I. xii. 10. 1
to my foe betrayd when least I *feared* ill.' . . . I. xii. 32. 9
feared least his boldnesse should offend, . . . II. iii. 17. 5
he *feard* her wrath, and threatned shott, . . . II. iii. 43. 4
feard to wander in that wastefull mist, . . . II. xii. 35. 3
nought they *feard,* but past on hardily, . . . II. xii. 39. 5
Nought *feard* theyr force that fortilage to win, . . . II. xii. 43. 5
Ne evill thing she *feard,* . . . III. i. 19. 9
I *feared* love; but they that love doe live, . . . III. iv. 37. 5
she no lesse the knight *feard* then that villein rude. . . . III. iv. 50. 9
shund dishonor which as death she *feard:* . . . III. vi. 10. 5
she *feared* to be overhent Of that vile hag, . . . III. vii. 19. 5
Much *feared* he least ought did ill betide . . . III. vii. 31. 4
Two things he *feared,* but the third was death; . . . III. x. 2. 6
now made better speed t' escape his *feared* foe. . . . III. xi. 5. 9
feard each shadow moving too or froe; . . . III. xii. 12. 3
much she *feard* his mind would grow to some excesse. . . . IV. i. 7. 9
His will she *feard;* . . . IV. i. 8. 1
Feared in vaine, sith meanes, ye see, there wants theretoo. . . IV. vi. 30. 9
Ne each of other *feared* fraud or tort, . . . IV. viii. 31. 3
Ooraxes, *feared* for great Cyrus fate, . . . IV. xi. 21. 5
then he *fear'd* his mothers former charge . . . IV. xii. 14. 5
lesse she *feared* that same fatall read, . . . IV. xii. 27. 1
she *feared* The sad effect of her neare overthrowe; . . . V. ii. 22. 3
He *fear'd* least they with shame would him pursew: . . . V. ii. 52. 7
she *feared* least some hard mishap Had him misfalne . . . V. vi. 4. 1
Nought *feared* they what he could do or say, . . . V. viii. 38. 7
feared for their powre; . . . V. ix. 1. 8
Nought *fear'd* the childe his lookes, . . . V. xi. 13. 1
Yet him nought terrified that *feared* nothing ill. . . . V. xi. 22. 9
As if the onely sound thereof she *feard.* . . . V. xi. 30. 4
Her vitall powers were at strife . . . and *feared* their decay: . VI. v. 5. 8
Ne ought was *feared* of his certaine harmes; . . . VI. viii. 47. 4
On which he safety hopes that earst *feard* to be lost. . . . VI. xi. 44. 9
much he *feared* least reprochfull blame . . . VI. xii. 12. 6
his old foes that once him sorely *fear'd.* . . . VII. vi. 15. 9
He wondred much, and *feared* her no lesse: . . . VII. vi. 17. 5
for better be allured, Ne *feard* with worse . . . *Am.* lix. 4

Fearest. Ne *fearest* foolish reprehension Of faulty men, . . . *Com. Son.* i. 7
Why *fearest* thou, that canst not hope for thing; . . . I. v. 43. 3
fearest not that more thee hurten might, . . . I. v. 43. 4

Feareth. Ne *feareth* change of time, . . . *Ti.* 465
Ne *feareth* he henceforth that foe of his, . . . III. vi. 48. 3
he *feareth* evill happen may; . . . III. x. 3. 5

Fearful. *See* **Fair-fearful.**
In hundred formes to change his *fearefull* hew; . . . *Bel.*[2] viii. 10
With *fearfull* howling do all places fill; . . . *T.M.* 284
With *fearfull* fiends, that in deep darknes dwell. . . . *Ti.* 126
So did this flie outstretch his *fearefull* hornes, . . . *Mui.* 87
is the sea (quoth Coridon) so *fearfull?'* . . . *Col.* 200
'Fearful much more . . . then hart can fear: . . . *Col.* 201
When that tumultuous rage and *fearfull* deene . . . *Ded. Son.* xi. 9
'Fly, fly!' (quoth then The *fearefull* Dwarfe) . . . I. i. 13. 9

Fearful—*Continued.*
fearefull more of shame Then of the certeine perill . . . I. i. 24. 1
Whom suddenly he wakes with *fearful* frights, . . . I. ii. 4. 4
The *fearefull* shepheard, . . . Under them never sat, . . . I. ii. 28. 7
of those *fearfull* women none durst rize, . . . I. iii. 19. 2
fearefull freends weare out the wofull night, . . . I. iii. 20. 6
the *fearfull* twayne, That blind old woman, and her daughter . I. iii. 22. 1
Such *fearefull* fitt assaid her trembling hart, . . . I. vi. 11. 1
The *fearefull* Dame all quaked at the sight, . . . I. vi. 28. 1
My *feareful* flesh did tremble at their strife, . . . I. vi. 38. 6
The mightie trunck, . . . fall with *fearefull* drift. . . . I. viii. 22. 9
I, more *fearefull* or more lucky wight, . . . I. ix. 30. 4
his fresh blood did frieze with *fearefull* cold, . . . II. i. 42. 3
As *fearfull* fowle, that long . . . her selfe hath hid, . . . II. iii. 36. 1
soone through suff'rance growe to *fearefull* end: . . . II. iv. 34. 4
fly this *fearefull* stead anon, . . . II. iv. 42. 8
'Thou *fearefull* foole, Why takest not of that same fruite . . II. vii. 63. 6
chaste so fiercely after *fearefull* flight, . . . II. x. 16. 5
shew His *fearefull* face in time of greatest storme; . . . II. xii. 24. 6
into these *fearefull* shapes disguiz'd . . . II. xii. 26. 3
Her *fearfull* feete towards the bowre she mov'd, . . . III. i. 60. 2
Penda, *fearefull* of like desteny, . . . III. iii. 37. 8
When the two *fearefull* women saw, . . . III. iii. 50. 6
Threatning to swallow up my *fearefull* lyfe? . . . III. iv. 8. 6
did attonce pursew The *fearefull* damzell . . . III. iv. 46. 3
Like as a *fearefull* Dove, . . . III. iv. 49. 4
That *fearefull* Ladie fledd from him, . . . III. iv. 50. 2
The *fearefull* end of his avengement sad, . . . III. v. 24. 4
What end unto that *fearefull* Damozell . . . befell: . . . III. vi. 54. 2
Whom when the *fearefull* Damzell nigh espide, . . . III. vii. 24. 1
Fled *fearfull* Daphne on th' Aegaean strond, . . . III. vii. 26. 4
The *fearefull* Chorle durst not gainesay nor dooe, . . . III. viii. 13. 1
Like as a *fearefull* partridge, . . . III. viii. 33. 3
ran with *fearfull* speed, . . . III. ix. 18. 3
after him eke *fearefull* Trompart spedd: . . . III. x. 43. 8
He in a bush did hyde his *fearefull* hedd. . . . III. x. 44. 2
Ne stayd his flight nor *fearefull* agony, . . . III. x. 56. 2
behinde The *fearefull* boy so greedily poursew, . . . III. xi. 4. 6
the *fearefull* Ladies tender hart . . . III. xi. 30. 7
whose noyaunce fild the *fearefull* sted . . . III. xii. 2. 6
fearfull to living sight; . . . III. xii. 19. 7
Amoret right *fearefull* was and faint . . . IV. i. 5. 4
when as *fearefull* Amoret perceived, . . . IV. vii. 21. 1
from his *fearefull* eyes two fierie beames, . . . IV. viii. 39. 1
From *fearefull* cowards entrance to forstall . . . IV. x. 17. 3
Much more deformed *fearefull,* ugly were, . . . IV. x. 20. 4
yclowded With *fearefull* shadowes of deformed night, . . . V. iv. 45. 2
at her strooke with puissaunce *fearefull* fell: . . . V. v. 10. 7
broken with some *fearefull* dreames affright, . . . V. vi. 14. 2
she waked full of *fearefull* fright, . . . V. vii. 16. 8
th' other still pursu'd the *fearefull* Mayd; . . . V. viii. 6. 1
For her beginning a more *fearefull* fray, . . . V. viii. 10. 6
many *fearefull* objects to them to present. . . . V. ix. 46. 9
In which the *fearefull* ewftes do build their bowres, . . . V. x. 23. 7
Her *fearefull* speaches nought he did regard, . . . V. x. 31. 1
There then began a *fearefull* cruell fray . . . VI. i. 36. 1
present The *fearefull* Lady to her father deare, . . . VI. iii. 18. 2
And to betake him selfe to *fearefull* flight; . . . VI. iii. 25. 8
A monstrous Dragon, full of *fearefull* uglinesse. . . . VI. vi. 10. 9
In *fearefull* darkenesse, furthest from the skie . . . VI. vi. 11. 2
The *fearfull* swayne beholding death so nie, . . . VI. vii. 12. 1
Being alreadie dead with *fearefull* fright: . . . VI. viii. 45. 3
for all his *fearefull* threat, . . . VI. ix. 4. 5
like a *fearefull* dog him followed through the land. . . . VI. xii. 36. 9
When your faire eyes these *fearefull* lines shal read, . . . *H.B.* 283

Fearfully. Their fleecy flowres they *fearefully* did steepe, . . II. xii. 61. 8
The Damzell pauzd; and then thus *fearfully:* . . . III. ii. 35. 1
his right hand unarmed *fearefully* did wield. . . . III. xii. 12. 9
the Ladie *fearefully* aghast, . . . VI. iv. 9. 7

Fearfulness. both doe strive their *fearefulnesse* to faine. . . II. iii. 20. 6

Fearing. *fearing* . . . The Giants old should once againe uprise, *Ro.* iv. 5
he slumbred *fearing* not be harmd: . . . II. vi. 14. 8
every loup fast lockt, as *fearing* foes despight. . . . II. ix. 10. 9
As *fearing* evill that poursewd her fast; . . . III. i. 16. 2
envious Men, *fearing* their rules decay, . . . III. ii. 2. 5
Fearing least from her cage the wearie soule would flit. . . III. xi. 12. 9
Some *fearing* shriekt, some being harmed hould, . . . IV. iii. 41. 7
Fearing least she your loves away should woo: . . . IV. vi. 30. 8
nought feeling, ne nought *fearing.* . . . IV. vii. 8. 9
Fearing, least if she should him freely set, . . . IV. viii. 53. 8
Both strongly arm'd, as *fearing* one another; . . . IV. x. 32. 2
Some *fearing* fraud, some fraudulently fayning, . . . IV. x. 43. 5
more meete . . . for loves delight, Then *fearing* any foeman . VI. ii. 18. 3
fearing neither foe nor frend, . . . VI. iv. 17. 4
fearing death, and next to death the lacke Of clothes . . . VI. viii. 50. 3
fearing least he at length the raines would lend Unto his lust, . VI. xi. 6. 2
Fearing least Chaos broken had his chaine, . . . VII. vi. 14. 6

Fearless. As men in Summer *fearles* passe the foord . . . *Ro.* xiv. 1
Feareles through his own fault . . . *T.M.* 303
Feareles of foes and hidden jeopardie, . . . *Mui.* 251
as I the fields did range *Fearelesse* and free, . . . *D.* 107
from the ground she *fearelesse* doth arise, . . . I. vi. 13. 3
Thereby so *fearlesse* and so fell he grew, . . . I. vi. 25. 1
To whom the Palmer *fearlesse* answered: . . . II. viii. 13. 1
With stately steps and *fearelesse* countenance, . . . IV. iii. 5. 2
still the life stood *fearelesse* of her foe; . . . IV. iii. 17. 5
Where *fearelesse* I to sleepe me downe did lay: . . . IV. vi. 36. 4
Eftsoones she flew unto his *fearelesse* hand, . . . IV. viii. 12. 1
Fearlesse of fortunes chaunge or envies dread, . . . IV. viii. 18. 3
I, who stood all *fearelesse* free, . . . IV. viii. 58. 6

Fearless—*Continued.*
Unto the wall his way did *fearelesse* take, ... V. iv. 50. 6
lay Under the Idols feete in *fearelesse* bowre, ... V. vii. 15. 2
The better to confirme her *fearelesse* confidence. . . . . . . V. x. 12. 9
as if he *fearelesse* were, ... V. xii. 14. 2
Fearelesse who ought did thinke or ought did say, ... VI. iii. 16. 5
Fearelesse of foes that mote his peace molest; . . . . . . VI. vii. 19. 4
Fearelesse of ought that mote her peace molest, ... VI. viii. 34. 7
Now drowned in the depth of sleepe all *fearelesse* lay. . . . . VI. viii. 36. 9
Fearelesse of foes, and fortunes wrackfull yre . . . . VI. ix. 27. 7
Jove, all *fearlesse* forc't them to aby; . . . . VII. vi. 24. 6
All *fearelesse* then of so false enimies, ... *Am.* xii. 3
Fayth doth *fearlesse* dwell in brasen towre, ... *Am.* lxv. 13
Sought not to fly, but *fearelesse* still did bide; . . . . . . *Am.* lxvii. 10
Fears. to worke more ghastly *feares.* . . . . *Gn.* 584
my flesh is numbd with *feares:* . . . . *D.* 419
'My weaker yeares, Captiv'd to . . . frayle worldly *feares,* . . I. i. 52. 5
Ne let vaine *feares* procure your needlesse smart, ... I. i. 54. 4
ne ought he *feares* To be partaker of her wandring woe; . . . I. iii. 44. 7
to increase his *feares* . . . an hempen rope he weares, . . . I. ix. 22. 5
without gealous *feares* Or faultie thoughts, ... II. iv. 18. 7
not of nought these suddein ghastly *feares* . . . . III. ii. 31. 1
Instead of sleepe thou sendest troublous *feares* . . . . III. iv. 57. 5
to be free from hard restraynt and gealous *feares.* . . . . . . III. ix. 4. 9
'In vaine he *feares* that which he cannot shonne; . . . . . . III. ix. 7. 1
Phrixus and Helle from their stepdames *feares,* . . . . V. Pr. 5. 7
She gan to cast in her misdoubtfull mynde A thousand *feares,* . V. vi. 3. 9
stood long staring on him mongst uncertaine *feares.* . . . . . V. vii. 39. 9
Wrapt in great dolours and in deadly *feares* . . . . V. x. 6. 7
Forgetfull of her owne to minde his *feares:* . . . . VI. iii. 12. 3
she thought Her selfe now past the perill of her *feares:* . . . VI. viii. 32. 3
So did their ghastly gaze bewray their hidden *feares.* . . . . VII. vi. 28. 9
false whispers, breeding hidden *feares,* . . . . *Epith.* 336
He dreads no danger, nor misfortune *feares,* . . . . *H.L.* 223
Thou, being blind, letst him not see his *feares,* . . . . *H.L.* 226
Feast. *See* **Shearing-feast.**
summons soules unto the bridale *feast* . . . . *D.* 268
Upon the perled grasse to make their *feast.* . . . . *Col.* 607
Rest is their *feast,* and all thinges at their will: . . . . . . I. i. 35. 3
fed her fatt with *feast* of offerings, ... I. iii. 18. 6
his necke . . . With which he swallowed up excessive *feast,* . I. iv. 21. 6
Of whom he meanes his bloody *feast* to make, ... I. vi. 10. 5
bloody mouthed with late cruell *feast,* . . . . I. viii. 6. 5
Not unto such as could him *feast* againe, ... I. x. 37. 6
people, as in solemne *feast,* To him assembled . . . . I. xii. 4. 6
What needes me tell their *feast* and goodly guize, ... I. xii. 14. 1
made great *feast* to solemnize that day: . . . . I. xii. 38. 2
solemne *feast* proclaymd throughout the land, ... I. xii. 40. 2
Accourting each her frend with lavish *fest:* . . . . II. ii. 16. 5
Thus fairely shee attempered her *feast,* . . . . II. ii. 39. 1
An yearely solemne *feast* she wontes to hold, ... II. ii. 42. 6
to the mighty victor yields a bounteous *feast.* . . . . II. v. 10. 9
of his bowels made his bloody *feast:* . . . . III. viii. 49. 4
Amidst the bridale *feast,* . . . Brought in that mask of love . IV. i. 3. 3
the bloodie *feast,* which sent away . . . drunken soules to hell, IV. i. 23. 3
caus'd to be proclaim'd each where A solemne *feast,* . . . . IV. ii. 26. 8
making joyous *feast* theire daies they spent . . . . IV. iii. 52. 1
To joyous *feast* and other gentle play, ... IV. iv. 48. 7
now by this their *feast* all being ended, ... IV. v. 6. 6
the relickes of his *feast* And cruell spoyle, ... IV. vii. 6. 3
He part of his small *feast* to her would share; . . . . IV. viii. 5. 7
To *feast* and frollicke; nathemore would she . . . . IV. ix. 13. 4
greedy hold of that his bloudy *feast:* . . . . IV. ix. 31. 8
a solemne *feast* was there . . . . IV. xi. 8. 1
both agreed that this their bridale *feast* . . . . IV. xi. 9. 1
to this *feast* with Neptunes seed was dight. . . . . IV. xi. 16. 9
now by this the *feast* was throughly ended, ... IV. xii. 18. 1
To tell the glorie of the *feast* that day, ... V. iii. 3. 1
With whom great *feast* and goodly glee he fond, ... V. iv. 3. 4
seized . . . Uppon some fowle that should her *feast* prepare; . V. iv. 42. 5
Making great *feast* and joyous merriment, ... V. xi. 35. 2
goodly glee and *feast* to them she made, ... VI. i. 46. 3
the frutes of the forrest was their *feast;* . . . . VI. iv. 14. 6
With all the courteous glee and goodly *feast* . . . . VI. vi. 41. 4
To make a common *feast,* and feed with gurmandize. . . . . . VI. viii. 38. 9
your meane food shall be my daily *feast,* . . . . VI. ix. 32. 3
Make *feast* therefore now all this live-long day; . . . . *Epith.* 248
Feasted. Of which whenas they *feasted* had their fill, ... *Hub.* 337
Of whom high Jove wont whylome *feasted* bee; . . . . II. vii. 59. 6
fayrely *feasted* as so noble knightes she ought. . . . . II. x. 77. 9
Feastful. gaine a *feastfull* guerdon of their toyle, ... IV. iii. 16. 4
this way comming from *feastfull* glee . . . . VI. x. 22. 4
Feasting. That night they pas . . . *Feasting* and courting . . . I. vi. 43. 6
dayly *feasting* both in bowre and hall, ... IV. vii. 39. 7
merry *feasting* which he made And great bonfires, ... VII. vii. 41. 2
Feasts. Vaine *feastes,* and ydle superfluity: . . . . II. xi. 12. 8
In beds, in bowres, in banckets, and in *feasts:* . . . . III. vi. 22. 4
And *feasts* the Sea-gods all. . . . . IV. xi. Arg.
ador'd with solemne *feasts,* . . . . V. Pr. 9. 8
solemne *feasts* and giusts ordain'd therefore: . . . . V. iii. 2. 6
Feat. by your wondrous worth and warlike *feat* . . . . II. ix. 6. 3
Albion had conquered first by warlike *feat.'* . . . . III. ix. 46. 9
Many faire pourtraicts, and many a faire *feate;* . . . . III. xi. 29. 2
to his cunning *feat* The stubborne mettall seeketh to subdew, V. v. 7. 6
To graunt him that adventure for his former *feat.* . . . . . . V. x. 15. 9
Feather. *See* **Plume-feather.**
the *fether* in her lofty crest, ... III. ii. 27. 1
Of all whose weight he would not misse a *fether:* . . . . . . V. ii. 31. 7
Feathered. *See* **Divers - feathered, Soft - feathered, Well - feathered.**

Feathered—*Continued.*
the blindfoulded pretie God, that *feathered* Archer, ... *Tetrasticon* 1
fethered with an unlucky quill: . . . . III. v. 20. 5
Feathers. rouze thy *feathers* quickly, Daniell, ... *Col.* 424
my Muse, whose *fethers* . . . yet but flagg, ... *Ded. Son.* ii. 7
deckt himselfe with *fethers* youthly gay, ... I. xi. 34. 5
gins her *feathers* fowle disfigured Prowdly to prune, ... II. iii. 36. 7
Headed with flint, and *fethers* bloody dide; . . . . II. xi. 21. 4
the proud Bird, ruffing his *fethers* wyde . . . . III. xi. 32. 6
her long taile and *fethers* strongly shooke, ... V. xi. 22. 7
How slowly does sad Time his *feathers* move? . . . . *Epith.* 281
spare to wet their silken *feathers,* . . . . *Proth.* 49
Featously. with fine Fingers cropt full *feateously* . . . . . . *Proth.* 27
Feats. his fine *feates* and Courtly complement; . . . . *Hub.* 692
with faire exercise Of knightly *feates,* . . . . *Hub.* 738
this Foxe could not so closely hide His craftie *feates,* . . . . *Hub.* 920
all noble *feates* professe To register, ... *T.M.* 97
feates of armes did wisely understand. . . . . I. iii. 42. 5
The warlike *feates* of both those knights to see. . . . . I. v. 5. 5
Old Timon, . . . In warlike *feates* th' expertest man alive, . I. ix. 4. 3
That warlike *feats* doest highest glorifie. . . . . II. iii. 38. 3
As *feates* of armes, and love to entertaine: . . . . II. iv. 1. 6
For his bold *feates* and hardy confidence, ... II. iv. 41. 3
for his warlike *feates* renowmed is, ... III. iii. 27. 3
have full many *feats* adventurous Performd, ... III. iii. 54. 5
To heare the warlike *feates* which Homere spake . . . . III. iv. 2. 4
Traind up in *feats* of armes and knightlinesse; . . . . IV. vii. 45. 7
Well knowen by his *feates,* . . . . V. ix. 5. 9
he in slights and jugling *feates* did flow, ... V. ix. 13. 8
Feature. all his goodly *feature* . . . nought him pleased: . . . *Van.* ii. 12
To feed on flowres and weeds of glorious *feature,* . . . . . . *Mui.* 213
powred kindly heat and formall *feature,* . . . . *Col.* 862
when they had . . . all her filthy *feature* open showne, . . . I. viii. 49. 8
whenas forme and *feature* it does ketch, ... III. vi. 37. 3
the faire *feature* of her limbs did hyde; . . . . III. ix. 21. 2
Through secret understanding of their *feature.* . . . . IV. ii. 44. 5
To tell the *feature* of each goodly face: . . . . IV. v. 12. 3
The maker selfe resembling in her *feature!* . . . . IV. vi. 17. 5
Bewrayd the signes of *feature* excellent; . . . . V. v. 12. 7
praise the *feature* of her goodly face; . . . . VI. vii. 28. 7
gan her forme and *feature* to expresse, ... VI. xi. 11. 8
tempred so the *feature* of her face, ... *Am.* xxi. 2
face and *feature* doth so much excell . . . . *H.B.* 41
Two gentle Knights of lovely face and *feature,* . . . . *Proth.* 169
Features. death shall spoyle your goodly *features.* . . . . . *Pet.*[2] vii. 14
glorious *Features* of beautie, and all shapes select, ... III. vi. 12. 4
According to their sundry kinds of *features,* . . . . VII. vii. 4. 3
February. lastly came cold *February,* . . . . VII. vii. 43. 1
Feculent. *See* **Filthy-feculent.**
Fed. *See* **Corn-fed.**
raynie cloud, first *fed* With earthly vapours . . . . *Ro.* xx. 1
on her sap and vitall moysture *fed:* . . . . *Van.* vii. 8
All as his straying flocke he *fedde:* . . . . *To his Booke* 10
the while his shepe there *fedde.* . . . . *S.C.* Ja. 12
our sheepe about us safely *fedde.* . . . . *S.C.* Jun. 88
With shepheards swayne what ever *fedde* in field; . . . . . . *S.C.* D. 44
as if on fire he *fed;* . . . . *Gn.* 346
They slue them, and upon their fleshes *fed;* . . . . *Hub.* 318
By whom the flock is rightly *fed,* and taught: . . . . *Hub.* 442
their vaine humours *fed* With fruitles follies . . . . *Hub.* 822
part by land and part by water *fed;* . . . . *Hub.* 1120
He *fed* his cubs with fat of all the soyle, ... *Hub.* 1151
fed with Furies milke for sustenaunce . . . . *T.M.* 261
fed with pleasures sweet, ... *T.M.* 302
With beawtie kindled, and with pleasure *fed,* . . . . *T.M.* 364
having beene with Acorns alwaies *fed,* . . . . *T.M.* 590
With fruitfull hope his aged breast he *fed* . . . . *Mui.* 25
when he hath both plaid and *fed* his fill, ... *Mui.* 205
the fields In which dame Cynthia her landheards *fed;* . . . . *Col.* 277
A thousand yong ones, which she dayly *fed,* . . . . I. i. 15. 5
fed with words that could not chose but please: . . . . I. i. 54. 8
fed her fatt with feast of offerings, ... I. iii. 18. 6
With pleasaunce of the breathing fields *yfed,* . . . . I. iv. 38. 2
Tityus *fed* a vultur on his maw; . . . . I. v. 35. 6
She *fedd* her wound with fresh renewed bale. . . . . I. vii. 28. 6
A multitude of babes . . . still she *fed* . . . . I. x. 31. 3
happy life to all which thereon *fedd,* . . . . I. xi. 46. 5
gazers sence with double pleasure *fed,* . . . . II. iii. 22. 8
Thus when shee had his eyes and sences *fed* . . . . II. vi. 14. 1
Therewith a while she her flit fancy *fedd,* . . . . III. i. 56. 1
With such selfe-pleasing thoughts her wound she *fedd,* . . . . III. iv. 6. 1
Upon that milke-white Palfreyes carcas *fedd,* . . . . III. vii. 30. 8
all hope wherewith he long had *fedd* His foolish malady, . . III. viii. 3. 8
With wonder of her beauty *fed* their hongry vew. . . . . III. ix. 23. 9
the Geaunts broode That *fed* on living flesh. . . . . III. ix. 49. 9
With which he *fed* her fancy, ... III. x. 8. 8
The whiles their Gotes upon the brouzes *fedd,* . . . . III. x. 45. 8
for her sake her cattell *fedd* awhile, ... III. xi. 39. 2
fedd on fodder to beguile her sight. . . . . III. xi. 42. 4
with vaine poemes weeds to have their fancies *fed.* . . . . . IV. Pr. 1. 9
With which she from her childhood had bene *fed;* . . . . . IV. i. 26. 6
rape Of men and beasts; and *fed* on fleshly gore, ... IV. vii. 5. 8
certes was with milke of Wolves and Tygres *fed.* . . . . . . IV. vii. 7. 9
Witnesse th' exceeding fry which there are *fed,* . . . . IV. xii. 2. 4
He might not with immortall food be *fed,* . . . . IV. xii. 4. 3
I him find to be too proudly *fed:* . . . . V. v. 50. 2
cruell steedes which he had *fed* With flesh of men, ... V. viii. 28. 6
falling on his mother earth he *fed:* . . . . V. xii. 23. 7
On which she *fed* and gnawed hungrily, ... V. xii. 30. 6
Tristram, . . . Long *fed* his greedie eyes . . . . VI. ii. 39. 3

Fed—*Continued.*
their bad Stuard . . . Ne *fed* on flesh, VI. iv. 14. 8
brave imps . . . *fed* with heavenly sap, VI. iv. 36. 8
shepherds singing to their flockes (that *fed*) VI. ix. 4. 3
there in the budded broomes Beside them *fed,* VI. ix. 5. 5
having *fed* his fill, VI. ix. 7. 6
after he had *fed,* yet did he stay VI. ix. 12. 4
Their tender flocks, now being fully *fed,* VI. ix. 13. 4
fed with light report Of every blaste, VI. x. 2. 8
with delight his greedy fancy *fed* VI. x. 30. 4
fed on spoile and booty, VI. x. 39. 5
full grosse and fat As *fed* with lard, VII. vii. 40. 2
Unquiet thought! . . . with sighes and sorrowes *fed,* *Am.* ii. 3
Fed on the fulnesse of that chearefull glaunce, *Am.* xxxix. 12
my fraile fancy, *fed* with full delight, *Am.* lxxii. 9
the guests, which would thereon have *fedd.* *Am.* lxxvii. 14
I fynd my selfe but *fed* with fancies vayne. *Am.* lxxviii. 12
hungry soule! which long hast *fed* On idle fancies *H.H.B.* 288

Fee. Ne of land, nor *fee* in sufferaunce, *S.C.* May 106
nothing there is done without a *fee:* *Hub.* 515
Of all the which there came a secret *fee,* *Hub.* 875
the rich *fee,* which Poets wont divide, *T.M.* 471
hath so many shepheards in her *fee,* *Col.* 370
nor would for gold or *fee* Be wonne I. x. 43. 6
by equall shares in equall *fee:* II. ii. 13. 4
cleeped him his liege, to hold of him in *fee.* II. iii. 8. 9
idle offers of thy golden *fee;* II. vii. 9. 7
his broad braunches, laden with rich *fee,* II. vii. 56. 3
her knights service ought, to hold of her in *fee.* III. i. 44. 9
Will chalenge yond same other for my *fee.'* IV. i. 35. 8
yeeld the fayrest her due *fee.* IV. v. 9. 9
of Lordship with both land and *fee:* IV. ix. 13. 7
is the paine thereof much greater then the *fee.* IV. x. 3. 9
Did equally bequeath his lands in *fee,* V. iv. 7. 4
gave to them great living and large *fee:* V. vii. 43. 4
What else they have is all the Tyrants *fee;* V. x. 29. 8
Nor land nor *fee* for hyre of his good deede, VI. i. 47. 2
thousand thankes to Calidore for *fee* . . . Did yeeld: VI. iii. 19. 3
As in his *fee,* with peaceable estate, VI. iv. 30. 2
Are Venus Damzels, all within her *fee,* VI. x. 21. 4
heaven it selfe by heritage in *Fee:* VII. vii. 15. 5

Feebily. *See* **Feebly.**

Feeble. With *feeble* flight venture to mount *Bel.*[1] vi. 2
With *feeble* wings assay to mount *Bel.*[2] vii. 2
Whose foote in ground hath left but *feeble* holde, *Ro.* xxviii. 4
So faynt they woxe, and *feeble* in the folde, *S.C.* Ja. 5
'Thou *feeble* flocke, whose fleece is rough and rent, *S.C.* Ja. 43
Great freendes and *feeble* foes: *S.C.* Jul. 194
'The *feeble* flocks in field refuse their former foode, *S.C.* N. 133
kindly sleep . . . my *feeble* eyes forgoe, *Hub.* 22
scarse thy legs uphold thy *feeble* gate.' *Hub.* 600
feeble Eccho now laments *T.M.* 285
I feele my *feeble* spright Robbed of sense, *Ti.* 320
I felt such anguish wound my *feeble* heart, *Ti.* 482
feeble spirits in their force maintaine, *D.* 438
Inflaming *feeble* eyes that her do view. *Col.* 519
Darting her beames into each *feeble* mynd: *Col.* 874
In the first season of my *feeble* age, *Ded. Son.* vii. 4
Wherewith ye triumph over *feeble* eyes, *Ded. Son.* xvi. 8
Shed thy faire beames into my *feeble* eyne, I. Pr. 4. 5
All striving to infixe their *feeble* stinges, I. i. 23. 6
too weake and *feeble* was the forse Of salvage beast I. iii. 42. 1
While flashing beames do daze his *feeble* eyen, I. iv. 9. 6
mayd Did her content to please their *feeble* eyes, I. vi. 19. 2
all that drinke thereof do faint and *feeble* grow. I. vii. 5. 9
mightie strong was turnd to *feeble* frayle. I. vii. 6. 5
that fraile fountain which him *feeble* made, I. vii. 11. 8
his *feeble* feet for faintnesse reeld, I. viii. 20. 7
on a staffe his *feeble* steps did frame, I. viii. 30. 3
Whose *feeble* thighes, . . . him scarse to light could beare; I. viii. 40. 7
when he . . . felt our *feeble* harts Embost with bale, I. ix. 29. 1
'Come; come away, fraile, *feeble,* fleshly wight, I. ix. 53. 1
Una saw That this her knight was *feeble,* I. x. 2. 2
Wont on a staffe his *feeble* steps to stay I. x. 5. 7
doen thy *feeble* feet unweeting hither stray? I. x. 9. 9
The *feeble* soule departing hence away. I. x. 41. 5
did quite confound His *feeble* sence, I. x. 67. 8
Whose sight my *feeble* soule doth greatly cheare: I. xi. 3. 5
O! gently come into my *feeble* brest; I. xi. 6. 1
ayre, which nigh too *feeble* found Her flitting parts, I. xi. 18. 4
His nigh forewearied *feeble* feet did slide, I. xi. 45. 8
Did grone, as *feeble* so great load to lift; I. xi. 54. 4
There eke my *feeble* barke a while may stay, I. xii. 1. 8
Uprose with hasty joy and *feeble* speed, I. xii. 3. 1
feeble eyes your glory may behold, II. Pr. 5. 3
with a staffe his *feeble* steps did stire, II. i. 7. 4
then gan softly feel Her *feeble* pulse, II. i. 43. 4
With *feeble* hands then stretched forth on hye, II. i. 49. 1
feeble nature cloth'd with fleshly tyre. II. i. 57. 3
her great words did appall My *feeble* corage, II. iii. 44. 6
on a staffe her *feeble* steps did stay: II. iv. 4. 4
the *feeble* sprightes Can call out II. v. 27. 4
From that which *feeble* nature covets faine: II. vi. 1. 5
His *feeble* feet directed to the cry; II. viii. 4. 5
by your powre protect his *feeble* cace? II. viii. 25. 8
all decrepit in his *feeble* corse, II. ix. 55. 6
feeble age Nigh to his utmost date II. x. 27. 6
So *feeble* is mans state, II. xi. 30. 3
his *feeble* vaines Him faild thereto, II. xi. 48. 3
by self-feeling of her *feeble* sexe, III. i. 54. 2

Feeble—*Continued.*
His feeling wordes her *feeble* sence much pleased, III. ii. 15. 1
When *feeble* nature felt her selfe opprest, III. ii. 29. 3
Betwixt her *feeble* armes her quickly keight, III. ii. 30. 4
love hath gryde My *feeble* brest of late, III. ii. 37. 9
much cheard the *feeble* spright Of the sicke virgin, III. ii. 47. 1
it will stonn thy *feeble* braines; III. iii. 9. 5
The *feeble* Britons, broken with long warre, III. iii. 23. 6
Wherein my *feeble* barke is tossed long III. iv. 8. 2
my *feeble* vessell, crazd and crackt III. iv. 9. 1
So *feeble* is the powre of fleshly arme. III. iv. 27. 6
Some litle life his *feeble* sprites emong; III. iv. 41. 8
His bootelesse bow in *feeble* hand upcaught, III. v. 24. 6
In easie couch his *feeble* limbes to rest. III. v. 41. 2
His *feeble* hart wide launched with loves cruel wownd. III. vi. 52. 9
doth soone withdraw His *feeble* eyne, III. vii. 13. 8
her sonne that lay in *feeble* state; III. viii. 9. 7
whatso my *feeble* Muse can frame III. viii. 43. 2
sweetnesse . . . The *feeble* sences whidy did confound, III. xii. 6. 4
on a broken reed he still did stay His *feeble* steps, III. xii. 10. 9
with her *feeble* feete did move a comely pace. III. xii. 19. 9
Repentaunce *feeble,* sorrowfull, and lame; III. xii. 24. 3
Sir Triamond at last full faint and *feeble* stood. IV. iii. 28. 9
Her *feeble* joynts layd eke adowne to rest; IV. v. 39. 7
twixt doubtfull feare And *feeble* hope hung IV. vi. 34. 2
In *feeble* Ladies tyranning so sore, IV. vii. 1. 6
This *feeble* brest endured hath, IV. vii. 14. 4
To which I boldly came upon my *feeble* feete. IV. vii. 17. 9
right *feeble* through the evill rate Of food IV. viii. 19. 5
Passing the measure of my *feeble* powre; IV. ix. 39. 7
fayled oft through faint and *feeble* plight: IV. xi. 25. 5
feeble spirit inly felt refection: IV. xii. 34. 5
to defend the *feeble* in their right, V. ii. 1. 3
That none of them the *feeble* over-ren, V. ii. 19. 8
So *feeble* skill of perfect things the vulgar has. V. iii. 17. 9
bread and water or like *feeble* thing, V. iv. 31. 8
feeble spirits, that gan faint and reele, V. x. 20. 5
carry colours faire that *feeble* eies misdeeme. VI. Pr. 4. 9
Yet for the *feeble* Ladies sake, VI. iii. 45. 8
wend abrode, though *feeble* and forlorne, VI. v. 7. 3
such as hee Did use his *feeble* body to sustaine, VI. v. 39. 2
that Squire and Dame So faint and *feeble* were, VI. v. 40. 7
Upon the ground with *feeble* feete he trode, VI. vi. 19. 5
was fall'n into this *feeble* case Through many wounds, VI. vi. 20. 7
heavens them selves, that favour *feeble* rights, VI. viii. 18. 8
may her *feeble* leaves with comfort glade— VI. x. 44. 7
in my *feeble* brest Kindle fresh sparks VII. vii. 2. 3
With which his *feeble* steps he stayed still; VII. vii. 31. 7
Too *feeble* I t' abide the brunt so strong, *Am.* xii. 9
doth find A *feeble* beast, doth felly him oppresse. *Am.* lvi. 4
my *feeble* breast inspire With gentle furie, *H.L.* 27
your lovers *feeble* eyes you feed, *H.L.* 38
Ne can his *feeble* earthly eyes endure *H.L.* 185
my *feeble* breast, too full of thee? *H.B.* 3
darted fyre into my *feeble* ghost, *H.B.* 24
Farre above *feeble* reach of earthly sight, *H.H.L.* 5
that shall thy *feeble* brest Inflame with love, *H.H.L.* 269
how can we see with *feeble* eyne *H.H.B.* 123

Feebled. Her foundation forst, and *feebled* quight, I. viii. 23. 4
Which mote the *feebled* Britons strongly flancke IV. xi. 36. 3

Feebleness. Ne will I rest my feete for *fecblenesse,* *D.* 460
Muse . . . craves protection of her *feeblenesse:* *Ded.Son.* xiii.12
further could not pas Through *feeblenesse,* VI. v. 31. 9

Feebless. great *feeblesse,* which did oft assay Faire Amoret IV. viii. 37. 3

Feebly. Eftsoones consum'd to fall downe *feebily,* *Ro.* xvi. 11
Feebly she shriekt, but so *feebly* indeed IV. vii. 4. 7

Feed. All that doth *feede* our spirits and our eies, *Ro.* xix. 3
let him *feede,* as Nature did provide, *Van.* iii. 11
feede his flocke in fields *S.C.* Jun. 76
Shepheards, which your flocks do *feede,* *S.C.* Jun. 106
To *feede* theyr flocks at will. *S.C.* Jul. 66
Or like not of the frowie *fede,* *S.C.* Jul. 111
loved their flocks to *feede;* *S.C.* Jul. 166
The while my flocke did *feede* thereby; *S.C.* Au. 59
dapper ditties, . . . To *feede* youthes fancie, *S.C.* O. 14
Whereon he earst had taught his flocks to *feede,* *S.C.* O. 57
it with pleasaunce mought thy fancie *feede*) *S.C.* D. 16
shepheard how to *feede* his sheepe, *S.C.* Env. 5
To *feede* abroad where pasture best befalls. *Gn.* 72
they doo swinke and sweate to *feed* the other, *Hub.* 163
the charge is wondrous great, To *feed* mens soules *Hub.* 432
'To *feede* mens soules . . . is not in man; *Hub.* 433
they must *feed* themselves, doo what we can. *Hub.* 434
To *feed* on hope, to pine with feare and sorrow; *Hub.* 900
They *feede* the eares of fooles with flattery, *T.M.* 323
I *feede* on sweet contentment of my thought, *T.M.* 524
hir beautie was wonte to *feede* mine eyes: *U.V.* 14
On nectar and Ambrosia do *feede.* *Ti.* 399
With pleasures choyce to *feed* his cheerefull sprights: *Ti.* 522
To *feed* on flowres and weeds of glorious feature, *Mui.* 213
wont to *feede* with finest grasse that grew, *D.* 345
Feede ye hencefoorth on bitter Astrofell, *D.* 346
ne *feed* on false delight *D.* 492
do *feed* Your carelesse flocks on hils *D.* 519
Him forth did bring, and taught her lambs to *feed,* *As.* 14
Doth *feed* on sweet contentment of that sight: *Col.* 43
Did round about them *feed* at libertie. *Col.* 55
pastures . . . On which she useth for to *feed* her sheepe?' *Col.* 239
surges hie, On which faire Cynthia her heards doth *feed:* *Col.* 241
other men and beasts and birds doth *feed:* *Col.* 297

Feed—*Continued.*
to *feed* his fyrie lustfull eye, He snatcht the vele . . . I. vi. 4. 6
Why doe ye lenger *feed* on loathed light, . . . I. vii. 22. 3
Mine eyes no more on vanitie shall *feed,* . . . I. vii. 23. 8
His office was the hungry for to *feed,* . . . I. x. 38. 2
thousand waies invent To *feede* her foolish humour . . . II. vi. 3. 9
to *feede* his eye And covetous desire . . . II. vii. 4. 8
with wonder all the way Did *feed* his eyes, . . . II. vii. 24. 4
her lovers, which her lustes did *feed,* . . . II. xii. 85. 3
To *feed* her humor with his pleasing style, . . . III. ii. 12. 2
which on my life doth *feed,* . . . III. ii. 37. 4
feed on shadowes whiles I die for food, . . . III. ii. 44. 3
feeds on wemens flesh as others *feede* on gras. . . . III. vii. 22. 9
feed her fancy with delightfull chaunge: . . . III. vii. 50. 3
On her faire face so did he *feede* his fill, . . . III. ix. 27. 8
Ne ever is he wont on ought to *feed* But todes and frogs, . . . III. x. 59. 1
feed it selfe with selfe-consuming smart? . . . III. xi. 1. 8
gentle spright Now gan to *feede* on hope, . . . III. xii. 44. 7
To *feede* the humour of her maladie, . . . V. v. 55. 7
Ne *feed* on ought the which doth bloud containe, . . . V. vii. 10. 2
For beasts and foules to *feede* upon for their repast. . . . V. ix. 19. 9
Unto some place where they mote rest and *feede,* . . . V. x. 22. 7
no need Of dreaded daunger might his doubtfull humor *feed.* VI. ii. 29. 9
in some stable neare did set him up to *feede.* . . . VI. vi. 19. 9
on the labours of poore men to *feed,* . . . VI. viii. 35. 8
To make a common feast, and *feed* with gurmandize. . . . VI. viii. 38. 9
gave him for to *feed* . . . VI. ix. 7. 3
No better doe I weare, no better doe I *feed.* . . . VI. ix. 20. 9
Where wont the shepheards . . . *feed* an hundred flocks, . . . VI. xi. 26. 9
with their death his cruell life dooth *feed;* . . . VII. vii. 24. 8
But sudden dumps, . . . my torment *feed.* . . . *Am.* lii. 12
hart, that wont on your fayre eye To *feed* his fill, . . . *Am.* lxxiii. 8
thereon *feed* my love-affamisht hart. . . . *Am.* lxxxvii. 12
greedy pikes which use therein to *feed;* . . . *Epith.* 58
your lovers feeble eyes you *feed,* . . . *H.L.* 38
Where they doe *feede* on Nectar heavenly-wize, . . . *H.L.* 282
smiles, with which their soules they *feede,* . . . *H.B.* 248
in his deare sacrament, To *feede* our hungry soules, . . . *H.H.L.* 196
The hearts of men, which . . . *feed* on vaine delight, . . . *H.H.B.* 17
gazefull eyes to *feed* With sight of that is faire, . . . *H.H.B.* 29
that felicitie, . . . On which they *feed,* . . . *H.H.B.* 286
Feedeth. Scarce this right hand the mouth with diet *feedeth.* *Hub.* 274
Feeding. *Feeding* the blessed flocke of Dan, . . . *S.C.* Jul. 51
on the soft greene grasse *feeding* their fills, . . . *Gn.* 78
Feeding upon their pleasures bounteouslie, . . . *Mui.* 151
all their flocks from *feeding* to refraine: . . . *Col.* 26
To *feeding* of her private fire, . . . V. v. 53. 7
With thousand thoughts *feeding* her fantasie, . . . V. vii. 17. 2
feeding on the bayt of his owne bane: . . . VI. ix. 34. 4
Feeds. *feedes* him once the fuller by a graine? . . . *S.C.* O. 34
God it is that *feedes* them with his grace, . . . *Hub.* 437
What ever *feeds* in forest or in field, . . . *Col.* 820
who with gratious bread the hungry *feeds,* . . . I. iv. 32. 3
Hee *feedes* upon the cooling shade, . . . I. vii. 3. 1
feedes each living plant with liquid sap, . . . II. ii. 6. 4
His frayle eye with spoyle of beauty *feedes:* . . . II. v. 34. 3
evermore himselfe with comfort *feedes* . . . II. vii. 2. 4
feeds on wemens flesh as others feede on gras. . . . III. vii. 22. 9
inly *feeds* it selfe with thoughts unkind, . . . IV. vi. 1. 3
feedes on all the carkasses that die In sacrifize . . . V. xi. 20. 3
She *feedes* on her owne maw unnaturall, . . . V. xii. 31. 7
feeds at pleasure on the wretched pray: . . . *Am.* xlvii. 8
singes, and *feeds* her fill. . . . *Am.* lxv. 8
He thereon *feeds* his hungrie fantasy, . . . *H.L.* 198
eates the hart and *feedes* upon the gall, . . . *H.L.* 268
Feel. Doo ye not *feele* your torments to accrewe, . . . *Ro.* xv. 11
My hart-blood is wel nigh frorne, I *feele,* . . . *S.C.* F. 243
For then I little smart did *feele,* . . . *S.C.* Mar. 98
you that *feele* no woe, . . . *S.C.* Au. 187
To *feele* his fault, and not be further vext. . . . *Gn. Ded.* 12
I *feele* my feeble spright Robbed of sense, . . . *Ti.* 320
I hate to *feele,* my flesh is numbd with feares: . . . *D.* 419
I *feele* my selfe like one yrapt in spright. . . . *Col.* 623
I . . . *Feele* my hart perst with so great agony, . . . I. iii. 1. 8
hope of new good hap he gan to *feele;* . . . I. iii. 34. 8
The salvage nation *feele* her secret smart, . . . I. vi. 11. 3
more heavy plight Then that I *feele,* . . . I. vii. 25. 4
trembling feare did *feel* in every vaine: . . . I. viii. 4. 2
sharper edge did *feele,* . . . I. xi. 36. 3
feele some secret ease. . . . II. i. 16. 9
the sad pang approching shee does *feele,* . . . II. i. 38. 8
then gan softly *feel* Her feeble pulse, . . . II. i. 43. 3
feele the law the which thou hast defast.' . . . II. viii. 31. 9
she did not *feele* the wound, . . . III. ii. 26. 8
Did *feele* his pulse, . . . III. iv. 41. 7
Ne in their frosen hearts *feele* kindly flame; . . . IV. Pr. 2. 2
Began to faint, and *feele* their corage cold. . . . IV. x. 18. 5
made it seeme to *feele* her grievous paine, . . . IV. xii. 5. 8
Let him *feele* hardnesse of thy heavie arme: . . . V. v. 49. 8
'yet now I gin new life to *feele;* . . . V. x. 20. 4
when I gin to *feele* decay of might, . . . VI. Pr. 1. 8
feele compassion of his evill plight, . . . VI. iv. 3. 6
life to *feele* that long for death had sought. . . . VI. xi. 45. 5
therby doth find, and plainly *feele,* . . . VII. vi. 1. 3
when I *feele* the bitter balefull smart, . . . *Am.* xxiv. 5
feele my flames augmented manifold! . . . *Am.* xxx. 8
Let them *feele* the utmost of your crueltyes; . . . *Am.* xlix. 9
Such fancies *feele* no love, but loose desyre. . . . *H.L.* 175
What hart can *feele* least touch of so sore launch, . . . *H.H.L.* 162
Then shalt thou *feele* thy spirit so possest, . . . *H.H.L.* 267

Feel—*Continued.*
But *feele* my wits to faile, and tongue to fold. . . . *H.H.B.* 7
And *feele* such joy and pleasure inwardly, . . . *H.H.B.* 264
Feeling. *See* **Self-feeling.**
Feeling the fit that him forewarnd to die, . . . *Ti.* 598
Ne *feeling* have in any earthly pleasure, . . . *Col.* 45
Her *feeling* speaches some compassion mov'd . . . I. v. 24. 6
Faire *feeling* words he wisely gan display, . . . I. vii. 38. 6
feeling wondrous comfort in her weaker eld: . . . I. x. 8. 9
strong effort Of *feeling* pleasures, . . . II. xi. 13. 8
feeling one close couched by her side, . . . III. i. 62. 1
His *feeling* wordes her feeble sence much pleased, . . . III. ii. 15. 1
Feeling her leape out of her loathed nest, . . . III. ii. 30. 3
feeling by his pulses beating rife . . . III. v. 31. 3
Those *feeling* words so neare the quicke did goe, . . . III. xi. 15. 7
Through secret *feeling* of his generous spright, . . . IV. iii. 14. 5
feeling life to fayle, it fell, . . . IV. iii. 20. 9
now *feeling* sommers might, . . . IV. iii. 23. 8
fell away, as *feeling* secret blame. . . . IV. v. 16. 7
nought *feeling,* ne nought fearing. . . . IV. vii. 8. 9
feeling him thus bite upon the bayt, . . . V. v. 42. 6
albe he wanted sence And sorrowes *feeling,* . . . V. vi. 9. 5
feeling ill Of his late fall, . . . VI. i. 35. 4
like an Hauke, which *feeling* her selfe freed . . . VI. iv. 19. 7
Feeling some curre behinde his heeles to bite, . . . VI. vi. 27. 6
feeling thence, no more her sorowes sadnesse, . . . *Am.* xxxix. 11
Feelingly. so *feelingly* he spake: . . . *Col.* 649
So *feelingly* her case she did complaine, . . . IV. xii. 5. 6
Feels. *feeles* the deepe delight that is in death, . . . *Frag.*
For whom so faire a Lady *feeles* so sore a wound!' . . . III. xi. 11. 9
Ne *feeles* the thornes and thickets pricke her tender toes. . . . IV. vii. 21. 9
feeles the warmth of sunny beames reflection, . . . IV. xii. 34. 7
Soone as he *feeles* it mollifide with heat, . . . V. v. 7. 8
Like to a flowre that *feeles* no heate of sunne, . . . VI. x. 44. 6
which who *feeles* not by sense . . . To flit still, . . . VII. vii. 22. 1
The gentle birde *feeles* no captivity . . . *Am.* lxv. 7
Then let thy flinty hart, that *feeles* no paine, . . . *H.H.L.* 246
Whose want too well now *feeles* my freendles case; . . . *Proth.* 140
Fee-simples. sell *fee-simples* in his Masters name, . . . *Hub.* 867
Feet. *See* **Horse-feet.**
with their *feete* uncleane the water fouled, . . . *Bel.*[1] x. 13
hundred vanquisht kings gronde at hir *feete,* . . . *Bel.*[1] xi. 9
Feete of a beare, a Lions throte she had. . . . *Rev.* i. 5
a sharped spyre . . . Ten *feete* each way . . . *Bel.* iii. 2
at his *feete* a bitch wolfe . . . *Bel.* ix. 9
with their villeine *feete* the streame did ray . . . *Bel.*[2] xii. 13
her *feete* Mount Viminall and Aventine doo meete. . . . *Ro.* iv. 13
now unnethes their *feete* could them uphold. . . . *S.C.* Ja. 6
Hellespont trampled with horses *feete,* . . . *Gn.* 49
An easie running verse with tender *feete.* . . . *Gn.* 53
Did learne to move their nimble-shifting *feete,* . . . *T.M.* 34
To fall before her *feete* at her beheast, . . . *Ti.* 73
One of his *feete* unwares from him did slide, . . . *Ti.* 544
Ne with his *feete* their silken leaves deface, . . . *Mui.* 175
Now in the same bathing his tender *feete;* . . . *Mui.* 182
up she tooke Her daintie *feete,* . . . *Mui.* 284
My wearie *feete* shall ever wandring be, . . . *D.* 457
Ne will I rest my *feete* for feeblenesse, . . . *D.* 460
His *feete* all bare, his beard all hoarie gray, . . . I. i. 29. 3
In stead thereof he kist her wearie *feet,* . . . I. iii. 6. 1
at her *feete* the Lyon watch doth keepe: . . . I. iii. 15. 4
All bare through peoples *feet* which thether traveiled. . . . I. iv. 2. 9
underneath her scornefull *feete* was layne A dreadfull Dragon I. iv. 10. 4
underneath their *feet,* all scattered lay Dead sculls . . . I. iv. 36. 8
They, . . . Doe kisse her *feete,* . . . I. vi. 12. 9
with their horned *feet* doe weare the ground . . . I. vi. 14. 3
underneath his filthy *feet* did tread The sacred thinges, . . . I. vii. 18. 6
his feeble *feet* for faintnesse reeld, . . . I. viii. 20. 7
Both *feet* and face one way are wont to lead. . . . I. viii. 31. 6
her *feete* most monstrous were in sight; . . . I. viii. 48. 5
free his *feet* that in the myre sticke fast? . . . I. ix. 39. 5
happy earth, Whereon thy innocent *feet* doe ever tread! . . . I. x. 9. 2
doen thy feeble *feet* unweeting hither stray? . . . I. x. 9. 9
when his *feet* encombred were, . . . I. x. 35. 6
he forst him to unty One of his grasping *feete,* . . . I. xi. 42. 9
His nigh forewearied feeble *feet* did slide, . . . I. xi. 45. 8
his *feet* their lawrell boughes did throw. . . . I. xii. 6. 4
all the floore was underneath their *feet* . . . I. xii. 13. 7
from his head no place appeared to his *feete.* . . . II. i. 5. 9
Espye a traveiler with *feet* surbet, . . . II. i. 22. 7
On goodly courser thondring with his *feet,* . . . II. iii. 11. 4
suffred not his wandring *feete* to slide; . . . II. iv. 2. 5
both his *feet* in fetters to an yron racke. . . . II. iv. 14. 9
Whose flying *feet* so fast their way applyde, . . . II. iv. 37. 3
underneath his *feete* The smouldring dust did . . . smoke, . . . II. v. 3. 3
at their *feet* her selfe most humbly feld, . . . II. vi. 32. 3
His feeble *feet* directed to the cry; . . . II. viii. 4. 5
at his *feet* . . . an armed corse did lye, . . . II. viii. 23. 7
underneath his *feet* soone made a purple plesh. . . . II. viii. 36. 9
wandring through the world with wearie *feet,* . . . II. x. 71. 3
Their *feet* unshod, their bodies wrapt in rags, . . . II. xi. 23. 4
Ne scarse his *feet* on ground were seene to tred: . . . II. xi. 26. 3
whose fiery *feete* did burne The verdant gras . . . III. i. 5. 5
So underneath her *feet* their swords they mard, . . . III. i. 30. 6
Her fearfull *feete* towards the bowre she mov'd, . . . III. i. 60. 2
surbate sore Their tender *feete* . . . III. iv. 34. 6
was bescracht and both his *feet* nigh lame. . . . III. v. 3. 9
I kisse thy blessed *feete.'* . . . III. v. 35. 9
flyes away of her owne *feete* afeard, . . . III. vii. 1. 3
apply His nimble *feet* to her conceived feare, . . . III. vii. 24. 6

Feet—*Continued.*
to her *feet* betooke her doubtfull sickernesse. . . . . . . III. vii. 25. 9
trampling *feete* upon the hollow lay Seemed to thunder, . . . III. viii. 15. 4
can withhold her wilfull wandring *feet;* . . . . III. ix. 7. 6
with their horned *feet* the greene gras wore, ... III. x. 45. 7
Upon his handes and *feete* he crept full light, ... III. x. 47. 2
He ran as fast as both his *feet* could beare, ... III. x. 53. 2
when he spedd His nimble *feet*, ... III. x. 55. 4
now so fast his *feet* he did apply, ... III. xi. 6. 5
underneath his *feet* was written thus, ... III. xi. 49. 1
with her feeble *feete* did move a comely pace. . . . . . . III. xii. 19. 9
When her weake *feete* could scarcely her sustaine, ... III. xii. 21. 6
as her eares, so eke her *feet* were odde, ... IV. i. 28. 6
either bare The other downe under their horses *feete*, . . . IV. i. 41. 8
I follow here the footing of thy *feete*, ... IV. ii. 34. 8
To which I boldly came upon my feeble *feete*. . . . . IV. vii. 17. 9
winged *feete* as nimble as the winde, ... IV. vii. 30. 2
There she alighting fell before her *feet*, ... IV. viii. 9. 5
He her beholding at her *feet* downe fell, ... IV. viii. 13. 1
tread downe under *feet*, ... IV. x. 2. 7
both her *feete* and legs together twyned . . . . IV. x. 40. 8
at the Idoles *feet* apart . . . . IV. x. 48. 7
Under the which her *feet* appeared plaine, ... IV. xi. 47. 5
Her silver *feet*, faire washt against this day: . . . . . . IV. xi. 47. 6
With golden hands and silver *feete* beside, ... V. ii. 10. 2
kneeling at his *feete* submissively: . . . . V. ii. 26. 5
eke her *feete*, those *feete* of silver trye, ... V. ii. 26. 7
backe againe they homeward turn their *feete;* . . . . V. iv. 51. 7
at her *feete* a Crocodile was rold, ... V. vii. 6. 8
lay Under the Idols *feete* in fearelesse bowre, ... V. vii. 15. 2
Him selfe before her *feete* he lowly threw, ... V. vii. 16. 2
under Isis *feete* doth sleepe for ever; . . . . V. vii. 22. 7
under his fierce horses *feet* have borne, ... V. viii. 31. 8
Fast did they fly as them their *feete* could beare . . . . . V. viii. 39. 1
Whylest kings and kesars at her *feet* did them prostrate. . . . V. ix. 29. 9
at her *feet* her sword was likewise layde, ... V. ix. 30. 6
round about before her *feet* there sate . . . . V. ix. 31. 1
underneath her *feete* . . . An huge great Lyon lay, ... V. ix. 33. 3
they fled As fast as *feete* could carry them away; . . . . . V. x. 36. 2
prostrated low Before his *feete* . . . . V. xi. 16. 2
Her Lions clawes he from her *feete* away did wipe. . . . . . V. xi. 27. 9
at her *feet* did fall, ... V. xii. 24. 6
Before his *feet* her selfe she did project; . . . . VI. i. 45. 2
And this his Ladie . . . On her faire *feet* . . . . VI. ii. 10. 3
Him seem'd his *feet* did fly and in their speed delight. . . . VI. iv. 19. 9
their sides were sore; their *feete* were lame. . . . . VI. v. 40. 9
Upon the ground with feeble *feete* he trode, ... VI. vi. 19. 5
falling lowly at his *feet* . . . . VI. vi. 31. 5
Him often scourg'd, and forst his *feete* to fynd: . . . . . VI. vii. 49. 5
Downe on his golden *feete* he often gazed, ... VI. viii. 26. 6
many *feete* fast thumping th' hollow ground, ... VI. x. 10. 4
underneath thy *feete* to place her prayse; . . . . VI. x. 28. 7
he it presented Before the *feete* of the faire Pastorell; . . . . VI. x. 36. 7
rearing up his former *feete* on hight, ... VI. xii. 29. 7
all the earth far underneath her *feete* . . . . VII. vii. 10. 1
fall lowly at her *feet;* And, with meeke . . . . *Am.* ii. 10
With bitter wounds through hands, through *feet*, and syde! *H.H.L.* 245
underneath his *feet* are to be found . . . . *H.H.B.* 180

Feign. *Cf.* **Fain,** *which in Spenser is sometimes not easily distinguished from* **Feign.**
Better it were a little to *feyne*, ... *S.C.* S. 137
it mens follies mote be forst to *fayne*, ... *S.C.* O. 75
truth, whose shape she well can *faine*, ... I. vii. 1. 5
for her humor fitting purpose *faine*, ... I. vii. 38. 7
With ydle force did *faine* them to withstand, ... I. xii. 35. 8
Full loth she seemd thereto, but yet did *faine*, ... II. i. 20. 8
Her purpose was not such as she did *faine*, ... II. i. 21. 1
both doe strive their fearefulnesse to *faine*. . . . . II. iii. 20. 6
some others *faine* To menage steeds, ... II. iv. 1. 8
greatly joyed merry tales to *faine*, ... II. vi. 6. 4
forcing it to *fayne*, him forth thence ledd, ... II. vii. 51. 2
However list her now her knowledge *fayne*, ... III. ii. 17. 2
men . . . in their foolish fancy *feigne* thee blinde, ... III. x. 4. 4
Yet was he meet, unless mine eye did *faine*, ... IV. vii. 15. 8
For courting fooles that curtesies would *faine*, ... VI. v. 38. 8
to *faine* A sodaine sickenesse . . . . VI. xi. 7. 7
Of sundrie things he purpose gan to *faine*, ... VI. xi. 39. 2
art thou yet alive, whom dead I long did *faine*?' . . . . . . VI. xii. 19. 9
which they *faine* That great Alcides whilome overthrew, . . . VI. xii. 32. 1
of his fellow gods that *faine* to be, ... VII. vii. 15. 2
Such as they *faine* Dan Cupid to have beene, ... VII. vii. 46. 7
were they so, as ye them *faine* to be, ... VII. vii. 49. 6
sundry wayes and fashions as clerkes *faine*, ... VII. vii. 55. 2
More then we men can *fayne!* . . . . *Epith.* 414
And were as faire as fabling wits do *fayne*, ... *H.H.B.* 216

Feigned. each thing *fained* ought more warie bee. . . . . . *Hub.* 495
He will not creepe, nor crouche with *fained* face, ... *Hub.* 727
All these through *fained* crimes he thrust adowne, ... *Hub.* 1186
With *fained* face, and watrie eyne halfe weeping, ... *Hub.* 1362
'All is but *fained*, and with oaker dide, ... *Ti.* 204
Through leasings lewd, and *fained* forgerie; . . . . *Col.* 696
semblance she did carrie under *feigned* hew. . . . . I. i. 46. 9
gan himselfe advise To . . . tempt her *faigned* truth. . . . . I. i. 50. 6
he runnes with *feigned* faithfull hast . . . . I. ii. 4. 1
with *faigned* paine The false witch did my wrathfull hand withhold: . . . . I. ii. 39. 7
Her seeming dead he fownd with *feigned* feare, ... I. ii. 45. 1
For feare, as seemd, or for some *feigned* losse: . . . . . . I. vi. 34. 8
Some feard, and fledd; some feard, and well it *faynd;* . . . . I. xii. 10. 1
fained cheare, as for the time behoves, ... II. ii. 34. 3

Feigned—*Continued.*
A mad man, or that *feigned* mad to bee, ... II. iv. 3. 5
Whom he had *feignd* th' abuser of my love to bee. . . . . . . II. iv. 27. 9
faynd to wash themselves incessantly, ... II. vii. 61. 6
Dissembled faire, and *faynd* to oversee. . . . . II. ix. 44. 3
all that *fained* is, as leasings, tales, ... II. ix. 51. 9
How ever finely she it *faind* to hyde. . . . . III. ii. 11. 5
Yet list the same efforce with *faind* gainesay; . . . . III. ii. 15. 8
Whatever foe had wrought, or frend had *faynd*, ... III. ii. 19. 5
Let us in *feigned* armes our selves disguize, ... III. iii. 53. 2
faynd to cheare his lady in dismay, ... III. viii. 15. 7
all his *fained* kindnes did detest, ... III. viii. 39. 4
The guilty cup she *fained* to mistake, ... III. ix. 31. 2
the Boaster from his loftie sell *Faynd* to alight, ... III. x. 38. 6
up remounted light, after *faind* to wend. . . . . III. x. 38. 9
that *fained* dreadfull flame, ... III. xii. 43. 2
for to hide her *fained* sex the better . . . . IV. i. 7. 3
Some thought that some enchantment *faygned* it; . . . . . . IV. i. 14. 5
Her *fayned* Paramour, her forced guest, ... IV. i. 36. 3
of *fayned* friendship which they vow'd afore. . . . . IV. ii. 18. 9
in close disguise Of *fayned* love, ... IV. ii. 30. 2
fayned still her former angry mood, ... IV. vi. 29. 8
Farre from all fraud or *fayned* blandishment; . . . . IV. x. 26. 7
hath *fained* That to her selfe that threasure appertained; . . V. iv. 13. 4
comming to this knight, she purpose *fayned*, ... V. v. 54. 1
her griefe with errour to beguyle, She *fayn'd* to count the time againe anew, ... V. vi. 5. 4
With *fayned* colours shading a true case; . . . . V. vii. 2. 7
under shew oftimes of *fayned* semblance . . . . V. ix. 22. 8
One time when he his weapon *faynd* to shift, ... V. xi. 7. 6
Ye will them all but *fayned* showes esteeme, ... VI. Pr. 4. 8
Yet were her words and lookes but false and *fayned*, ... VI. vi. 42. 1
Of few greene turfes an altar soone they *fayned*, ... VI. viii. 44. 8
The *fayned* friends, the unassured foes, ... *H.L.* 263
All other sights but *fayned* shadowes bee. . . . . *H.H.B.* 273

Feigning. oft *faining* to retire And oft him to assaile, . . . *Gn.* 306
That *feigning* dreame, and that faire-forged Spright, ... I. ii. 2. 2
So forth they rode, he *feining* seemely merth, ... I. ii. 27. 8
feigning then in every limb to quake . . . . II. i. 9. 3
Now *faining* dalliaunce and wanton sport, ... II. xii. 16. 3
in her *feigning* fancie did pourtray Him . . . . III. iv. 5. 7
As *fayning* choler which was turn'd to cold: . . . . IV. vi. 27. 2
Feigning full many a fond excuse to prate, ... IV. x. 14. 7
Some fearing fraud, some fraudulently *fayning*, ... IV. x. 43. 5
fayning to receive In her owne mouth the food . . . . V. v. 53. 1
the Prince, him *fayning* to embase, ... VI. vi. 20. 5
Fairer then fairest, in his *fayning* eye, ... *H.L.* 216
to his *fayning* fansie represent . . . . *H.L.* 254
Above that Idole of his *fayning* thought, ... *H.H.B.* 223

Feigns. Sometimes he falsely *faines* himselfe to sleepe, . . . II. v. 34. 4
She flyes; he *faines* to dy. . . . . III. vii. Arg.
ungracious crew which *faines* demurest grace. . . . . VII. vii. 35. 9
He *faines* himselfe, and doth his fortune blesse. . . . . . . *H.L.* 210
What heavens of joy then to himselfe he *faynes!* . . . . . . *H.L.* 240

Feining. *See* **Feigning.**

Feld(e). *See* **Felled.**

Felicities. Whilst heaven did favour his *felicities*, ... *Mui.* 21
their *felicities* The favourable heavens did not envy, ... I. vii. 43. 5

Felicity. all worlds *felicitie* . . . . *Bel.*[2] x. 7
at her owne *felicitie* did smile. . . . . *Van.* ix. 8
Usen we freely our *felicitie;* . . . . *S.C.* May 155
he therein had great *felicitie;* . . . . *Hub.* 706
Henceforth all worlds *felicitie* I hate. . . . . *Ti.* 574
What more *felicitie* can fall to creature . . . . *Mui.* 209
in hunting such *felicitie*, . . . he found, ... *As.* 79
Thou speakest thus gainst their *felicitie*, ... *Col.* 677
he . . . grudged at the great *felicitee* Of proud Lucifera, . . I. iv. 31. 8
vowed foe of my *felicity;* . . . . I. xii. 19. 3
Worthie of heven and hye *felicitie*, ... II. vii. 49. 5
raigned long in great *felicity*, ... II. x. 13. 2
With high renowme and great *felicity:* . . . . II. x. 36. 3
him succeede In kingdome, but not in *felicity:* . . . . III. iii. 31. 2
So life is losse, and death *felicity:* . . . . III. iv. 38. 7
Their goodly meriment and gay *felicity*. . . . . III. vi. 41. 9
Sporting him selfe in safe *felicity:* . . . . III. vi. 49. 4
As seeming plast in sole *felicity:* . . . . IV. ii. 11. 4
Envying my too great *felicity*, ... IV. viii. 16. 6
Might else have with *felicitie* bene crowned: . . . . V. v. 36. 7
in the midst of her *felicity*, ... V. vii. 14. 1
wish my lot were plast in such *felicitie*.' . . . . VI. ix. 19. 9
joyed long in close *felicity*, ... VI. x. 38. 6
live for ever in *felicity!* . . . . *Am.* lxviii. 8
sole aspect he counts *felicitye*. . . . . *H.L.* 217
Through feare of loosing his *felicitie*. . . . . *H.L.* 270
fully setteth his *felicitie;* . . . . *H.B.* 229
In full enjoyment of *felicitie*, ... *H.H.B.* 79
But in th' aspect of that *felicitie*, ... *H.H.B.* 284

Fell. All flaming downe she *fell* upon the plaine. . . . . . . *Bel.*[1] vi. 11
sodenly the Palme and Olive *fell*, ... *Bel.*[1] vii. 13
Sudden both Palme and Olive *fell* away, ... *Bel.*[2] ix. 13
downe she stricken *fell* with clap of thonder, ... *Bel.*[2] xv. 13
Most fierce and *fell* this woman seemde to me. . . . . *Rev.* ii. 11
Fell to the ground, and there untimely dide. . . . . *Pet.* i. 12
fell Boreas with sharpe blast Tossing huge tempests . . . . . *Ro.* xvi. 5
fell Erynnis, with hot burning tongs, ... *Ro.* xxiv. 5
her faire lockes *fell* from her loftie head, ... *Van.* vii. 11
downe to the earth he *fell* forthwith. . . . . *S.C.* F. 218
Fell headlong into a dell, ... *S.C.* Mar. 51
'It *fell* upon a holy eve, ... *S.C.* Au. 53
lordly love is such a Tyranne *fell*, ... *S.C.* O. 98

Fell—*Continued.*

fell all for nuts at strife? . . . *S.C.* D. 35
wrapt his scalie boughts with *fell* despight, . . . *Gn.* 255
beleeve that anie thing could please *Fell* Cerberus, . . . *Gn.* 440
Seeing his beautie, in love with it *fell*. . . . *Gn.* 680
Cruelly *fell* upon their flock in folde, . . . *Hub.* 335
passing foorth, as their adventures *fell*, . . . *Hub.* 359
woods, which he did lately *fell*, . . . *Hub.* 872
Whenas they came they *fell* at words, . . . *Hub.* 1019
the Princes pallaces *fell* fast To ruine . . . *Hub.* 1175
Then downe it *fell*, and low in ashes lay, . . . *Ti.* 502
downe hee *fell* into the deepe Abisse, . . . *Ti.* 545
all the rest downe shortlie *fell*, . . . *Ti.* 558
Upon them *fell*, and did unwares oppresse; . . . *Ti.* 572
with *fell* spight, Under the left wing stroke his weapon . . . *Mui.* 436
fell to ground for great extreamitie; . . . *D.* 185
'She *fell* away in her first ages spring, . . . *D.* 239
She *fell* away against all course of kinde. . . . *D.* 242
She *fel* away like fruit blowne downe with winde. . . . *D.* 244
To thinke to ground how that faire blossome *fell*. . . . *D.* 252
'Yet *fell* she not as one enforst to dye, . . . *D.* 253
Fell sodainly and faded under ground; . . . *D.* 481
with *fell* tooth accustomed to blood, . . . *As.* 118
as then occasion *fell*: . . . *Col.* 89
Nor outlawes *fell* affray the forest raunger. . . . *Col.* 319
so *fell* and puissant he grew, . . . *Col.* 808
'Assure your selfe, it *fell* not all to ground; . . . I. i. 54. 1
Now like a foxe, now like a dragon *fell*; . . . I. ii. 10. 6
both *fell* and furious, That, . . . Their steeds doe stagger, . . . I. ii. 15. 4
My dearest Lord *fell* from high honors staire . . . I. ii. 23. 7
With pittie calmd downe *fell* his angry mood. . . . I. iii. 8. 5
he . . . told her all that *fell*, in journey as she went. . . . I. iii. 32. 9
a darkesome clowd Upon him *fell*: . . . I. v. 13. 7
Fell from high Princes courtes, or Ladies bowres, . . . I. v. 51. 6
a greedy Wolfe, through honger *fell*, . . . I. vi. 10. 3
Thereby so fearlesse and so *fell* he grew, . . . I. vi. 25. 1
The Antelope, and Wolfe both fiers and *fell*; . . . I. vi. 26. 5
downe she *fell* for paine. . . . I. vi. 37. 4
they gan, both furious and *fell*, To thunder blowes, . . . I. vi. 43. 1
She *fell* to ground for sorrowfull regret, . . . I. vii. 20. 7
Then downe againe she *fell* unto the ground, . . . I. vii. 24. 1
wrought For this young Prince, when first to armes he *fell*; I. vii. 36. 7
So downe he *fell* before the cruell beast, . . . I. viii. 15. 1
with his puissaunce *fell* Had made his caytive thrall: . . . I. viii. 32. 7
With furious force and indignation *fell*; . . . I. viii. 39. 6
forward fare as their adventures *fell*: . . . I. ix. 2. 5
ever ready for your foeman *fell*: . . . I. xi. 2. 5
into his darke abysse all ravin *fell*. . . . I. xi. 12. 9
he stroke so furious and so *fell*, . . . I. xi. 24. 2
Upon his crest the hardned yron *fell*, . . . I. xi. 24. 4
Into the same the knight back overthrowen *fell*. . . . I. xi. 30. 9
that infernall Monster . . . with countenance *fell*, . . . I. xi. 31. 8
that holy water dew Wherein he *fell*, . . . I. xi. 36. 3
downe he *fell*, with dread of shame sore terrifide. . . . I. xi. 45. 9
on the ground still *fell*, . . . I. xi. 48. 3
Into that same he *fell*, . . . I. xi. 48. 9
downe he *fell*, and forth his life did breath, . . . I. xi. 54. 1
So downe he *fell*, . . . I. xi. 54. 3
downe he *fell*, as an huge rocky clift, . . . I. xi. 54. 5
downe he *fell*, and like an heaped mountaine lay. . . . I. xi. 54. 9
why with so fierce saliaunce, And *fell* intent, . . . II. i. 29. 7
themselves at discord *fell*, . . . II. ii. 20. 2
With horrible assault and fury *fell*, . . . II. ii. 20. 4
what cursed evil Spright, Or *fell* Erinnys, . . . II. ii. 29. 2
fell flatt to ground for feare, . . . II. iii. 6. 8
he from his loftie steed Downe *fell* . . . II. iii. 21. 3
Against him turning all his *fell* intent, . . . II. iv. 6. 6
poursewing my *fell* purpose, . . . II. iv. 31. 9
Griefe is a flood; and love a monster *fell*; . . . II. iv. 35. 3
With his bright blade did smite at him so *fell*, . . . II. v. 4. 2
glauncing *fell* On his horse necke . . . II. v. 4. 4
Their *fell* contention still increased more, . . . II. v. 22. 1
He then uprose, inflamd with *fell* despight, . . . II. v. 37. 8
Ready to drowne him selfe for *fell* despite: . . . II. vi. 43. 5
was the force so furious and so *fell*, . . . II. viii. 31. 1
He groveling *fell*, all gored in his gushing wound. . . . II. viii. 32. 9
By whose advise old Priams cittie *fell*, . . . II. ix. 48. 6
Into the which retourning backe he *fell*: . . . II. x. 11. 4
fell to vaine voluptuous disease: . . . II. x. 17. 5
blood of Henalois which therein *fell*. . . . II. x. 24. 5
through flight into fond mischief *fell*. . . . II. x. 26. 9
fell him selfe in fight: . . . II. x. 35. 5
fled asonder, and him *fell* before; . . . II. xi. 19. 3
to the ground the idle quarrell *fell*: . . . II. xi. 24. 8
Upon him *fell*, and lode upon him layd: . . . II. xi. 29. 5
Becomes more *fell*, and all . . . Treads down . . . II. xi. 33. 5
groveling to the ground he *fell*, . . . II. xi. 34. 9
his dead corse upon the flore *fell* nathemore. . . . II. xi. 37. 9
them enraged with *fell* surquedry: . . . II. xii. 39. 4
The which into an ample laver *fell*, . . . II. xii. 62. 3
Guyon drove so furious and *fell*, . . . III. i. 6. 2
Nigh a speares length behind his crouper *fell*; . . . III. i. 6. 7
Full of great envy and *fell* gealosy . . . III. i. 18. 2
fierce Bacchante seemd too *fell* and keene; . . . III. i. 45. 6
Some *fell* to daunce, some *fel* to hazardry, . . . III. i. 57. 1
with felonous despight And *fell* intent, . . . III. i. 65. 4
it *fell* into that Fairies mind . . . III. ii. 4. 4
the royall Infant *fell* Into her former fitt; . . . III. ii. 49. 1
Like a swift Otter, *fell* through emptinesse, . . . III. iii. 33. 7
with *fell* cruelty In their avenge . . . III. iii. 46. 8

Fell—*Continued.*

At last their wayes so *fell*, that they mote part: . . . III. iii. 62. 6
So *fell* proud Marinell upon the pretious shore. . . . III. iv. 17. 9
With so *fell* force, and villeinous despite, . . . III. v. 19. 2
with rigor *fell* Smote him . . . III. v. 23. 4
Downe on the ground his carkas groveling *fell*: . . . III. v. 23. 7
glauncing *fel* to ground, but him annoyed naught. . . . III. v. 24. 9
th' head *fell* backeward on the Continent; . . . III. v. 25. 7
mischief *fel* upon the meaners crowne. . . . III. v. 25. 8
from his steed he *fell* in deadly swowne: . . . III. v. 26. 3
a gentle slombring swowne Upon her *fell*, . . . III. vi. 7. 4
Without *fell* rancor or fond gealosy. . . . III. vi. 41. 6
Into misfortune *fell*, as ye did heare, . . . III. vi. 54. 8
with *fell* looke and hollow deadly gaze . . . III. vii. 7. 6
The quarry throwes to ground with *fell* despight, . . . III. vii. 39. 5
how he *fell* into the Gyaunts hands, . . . III. vii. 46. 8
with the Prince of Darkenes *fell* somewhyle . . . III. viii. 8. 3
Fell streight to ground in great astonishment. . . . III. viii. 12. 7
I would to heare desyre What to Aeneas *fell*; . . . III. ix. 40. 7
forth he rode as his adventure *fell*; . . . III. x. 38. 4
fell to ground half dedd. . . . III. x. 43. 9
wearie of their sport to sleepe they *fell*, . . . III. x. 49. 2
on the rockes he *fell* so flit and light, . . . III. x. 57. 5
Untroubled of vile feare or bitter *fell*. . . . III. xi. 2. 5
with *fell* woodnes he effierced was, . . . III. xi. 27. 4
turning to herselfe, his *fell* intent, . . . III. xii. 33. 3
to ground He *fell* halfe dead: . . . III. xii. 34. 2
The cruell steele . . . *Fell* softly forth, . . . III. xii. 38. 2
prostrate she *fell* unto the grownd. . . . III. xii. 38. 9
Before faire Britomart she *fell* prostrate, . . . III. xii. 39. 1
Centaures . . . That under great Alcides furie *fell*; . . . IV. i. 23. 5
did drive The noble Argonauts to outrage *fell*; . . . IV. i. 23. 7
So *fell* those two in spight of both their prydes; . . . IV. i. 42. 7
Did beare them both to *fell* avenges end, . . . IV. ii. 15. 2
They stemme ech other with so *fell* despight, . . . IV. ii. 16. 4
Have rays'd this cruell warre and outrage *fell*, . . . IV. ii. 24. 4
Yet from the wound no drop of bloud there *fell*, . . . IV. iii. 8. 6
enhaunce His haughtie courage to avengement *fell*: . . . IV. iii. 8. 8
so gave way unto his *fell* intent; . . . IV. iii. 18. 7
it *fell*, and deadly slept. . . . IV. iii. 20. 9
So thicke they *fell*, and forcibly were sent, . . . IV. iii. 26. 2
downe he *fell* as dead in all mens sight; . . . IV. iii. 30. 5
both at once *fell* dead upon the field, . . . IV. iii. 34. 8
Their wrathfull blades downe *fell* out of their hand, . . . IV. iii. 48. 4
friends profest are chaungd to foemen *fell*: . . . IV. iv. 1. 3
So much more sorely to the ground he *fell*, . . . IV. iv. 19. 6
as it *fell*, his steed he ready found; . . . IV. iv. 23. 3
By that the gloomy evening on them *fell*, . . . IV. iv. 25. 6
rudely tumbling downe under his horse-feete *fell*. . . . IV. iv. 30. 9
it loos'd And *fell* away, . . . IV. v. 16. 7
Shall else be told in order, as it *fell*. . . . IV. v. 28. 6
he to *fell* reveng was fully bent: . . . IV. v. 30. 9
the drouping night . . . Upon them *fell*, . . . IV. v. 32. 4
swell in every inner part For *fell* despight, . . . IV. vi. 7. 5
him saw approching neare With so *fell* rage, . . . IV. vi. 10. 4
With such *fell* greedines he her assayled, . . . IV. vi. 12. 6
Till on her horses hinder parts it *fell*; . . . IV. vi. 13. 6
cruell sword out of his fingers slacke *Fell* downe . . . IV. vi. 21. 6
At last *fell* humbly downe upon his knee, . . . IV. vi. 22. 2
With *fell* intent on him to bene ywroke; . . . IV. vi. 23. 3
Her hand *fell* downe, . . . IV. vi. 27. 4
She almost *fell* againe into a swound, . . . IV. vii. 9. 8
With *fell* despight her cruell arrowes tynde . . . IV. vii. 30. 7
on a day, by fortune as it *fell*, . . . IV. vii. 42. 1
Like as it *fell* to this unhappy boy, . . . IV. viii. 2. 1
There she alighting *fell* before her feet, . . . IV. viii. 9. 5
He her beholding at her feet downe *fell*, . . . IV. viii. 13. 1
To which they drew ere night upon them *fell*; . . . IV. viii. 23. 3
it *fell* with so despiteous dreare . . . IV. viii. 42. 5
as it *fell*, there was a gentle Squire . . . IV. viii. 50. 1
all full of *fell* despight, . . . IV. ix. 20. 3
Upon the sea to wreake his *fell* intent; . . . IV. ix. 23. 4
Cause of their discord and so *fell* debate . . . IV. ix. 24. 1
through lewd upbraide Of Ate and Duessa, they *fell* out; . . . IV. ix. 24. 6
a fresh desire Of *fell* revenge, . . . IV. ix. 29. 2
fell Into all filth and foule iniquitie, . . . V. i. 5. 6
It bit the earth for very *fell* despight, . . . V. ii. 18. 6
many wounded, As fortune *fell*; . . . V. iii. 6. 7
how *fell* ye in this state?' . . . V. iv. 28. 5
Like a *fell* Lionesse at him she flew, . . . V. iv. 39. 6
with *fell* intent And countenaunce fierce, . . . V. v. 5. 3
at her strooke with puissaunce fearefull *fell*: . . . V. v. 10. 7
downe she *fell* upon the grassie field . . . V. v. 11. 3
Through slipperie footing *fell* into the brooke, . . . V. v. 43. 3
For very *fell* despight which she conceived, . . . V. v. 47. 3
kicks, and squals, and shriekes for *fell* despight; . . . V. vi. 14. 5
nought The *fell* contagion may thereof restraine, . . . V. vii. 11. 8
proud Radigund, with *fell* despight, . . . V. vii. 32. 1
with most *fell* despight and deadly hate . . . V. viii. 18. 3
through *fell* tyranny He slaughtred had, . . . V. viii. 28. 7
fell Medea, when on Colchicke strand . . . V. viii. 47. 3
Is so exceeding furious and *fell* As wrong, . . . V. ix. 1. 2
like a stone it *fell* upon the land; . . . V. ix. 17. 8
Now at that instant, as occasion *fell*, . . . V. ix. 36. 1
this *fell* Tyrant, . . . Had left her now but five . . . V. x. 8. 1
after that his monstrous father *fell* Under Alcides club, . . . V. x. 11. 2
Fell straight about their neckes as they did kneele, . . . V. x. 20. 2
downe he *fell* upon his mother deare, . . . V. x. 35. 8
He brayd aloud for very *fell* despight; . . . V. xi. 8. 2
Downe streight to ground *fell* his astonisht steed, . . . V. xi. 9. 1

Fell—*Continued.*
Like a *fell* mastiffe through enraging heat, . . . V. xi. 12. 2
all the three attonce *fell* on the plaine, . . . V. xi. 14. 2
Full of *fell* ravin and fierce greedinesse; . . . V. xi. 24. 2
Then downe to ground *fell* that deformed Masse, . . . V. xi. 32. 1
(as good fortune *fell*) . . . V. xii. 4. 2
With dreadfull terror and with *fell* intent; . . . V. xii. 17. 2
With bitter rage and *fell* contention, . . . V. xii. 41. 3
where what him *fell* shall else be told. . . . V. xii. 43. 9
fell Chimaera, in her darkesome den, . . . VI. i. 8. 2
With so *fell* fury and dispiteous forse, . . . VI. i. 33. 6
did breake in speaches sharpe and *fell:* . . . VI. iii. 34. 9
Then North, then neither, but as fortune *fell:* . . . VI. iv. 25. 3
For *fell* despight to be so sorely crost; . . . VI. iv. 40. 4
by what traine She *fell* into that salvage villaines hand? . VI. v. 27. 8
Like a *fell* Lyon at him fiercely flew, . . . VI. vi. 22. 4
Upon them two they *fell* with might and maine, . . . VI. vi. 23. 3
whilest many underneath him *fell.* . . . VI. vi. 23. 9
He woxe nigh mad with wrath and *fell* despight, . . . VI. vi. 24. 8
Turnes him about with *fell* avengement: . . . VI. vi. 27. 7
to the ground he *fell* in senselesse swone: . . . VI. vi. 30. 7
Ne secretly from thought of *fell* revenge surceasse: . . . VI. vi. 43. 9
scattered all about *fell* on the flowre: . . . VI. vii. 8. 4
'Perdie,' (said he) 'in evill houre it *fell,* . . . VI. vii. 15. 1
Like a *fell* Lyon leaped to him light, . . . VI. vii. 25. 5
Fell flat to ground, ne word unto him sayd, . . . VI. vii. 25. 8
foule Infamie and *fell* Despight Gave evidence, . . . VI. vii. 34. 7
Fell into wretched woes, which she repented late. . . . VI. viii. 2. 9
for her sake *fell* into misery; . . . VI. viii. 3. 5
He in his necke had set his foote in *fell* disdaine. . . . VI. viii. 10. 9
fell to ground, like to a lumpe of durt; . . . VI. viii. 16. 8
at variaunce *fell* With those two Carles, . . . VI. viii. 31. 3
discoursing diversly Of sundry things as *fell,* . . . VI. ix. 12. 7
supper readie dight they to it *fell* . . . VI. ix. 17. 7
They *fell* to daunce: . . . VI. ix. 41. 5
for *fell* despight Of that displeasure, . . . VI. x. 18. 4
with *fell* clawes full of fierce gourmandize, . . . VI. x. 35. 4
to the ground astonished he *fell;* . . . VI. x. 36. 4
fell down with him in drerie swound. . . . VI. xi. 19. 9
Of carcases, which dying on her *fell.* . . . VI. xi. 20. 2
To stay their cruell hands from slaughter *fell,* . . . VI. xi. 20. 5
for very *fell* despight, . . . VI. xi. 25. 5
Fell all at ods, and fought through fury fierce and bold. . VI. xi. 30. 9
She unto him recounted all that *fell;* . . . VI. xii. 22. 2
made him almost mad for *fell* despight: . . . VI. xii. 31. 7
That place, from which by folly Titan *fell:* . . . VII. vi. 34. 3
But greedily her *fell* intent poursewth, . . . *Am.* xi. 7
the Furies *fell* Theyr snaky heads doe combe, . . . *Am.* lxxxv. 2
doest the Lions and *fell* Tigers tame, . . . *H.L.* 46
Hating the happie light from which they *fell.* . . . *H.H.L.* 91
fell from above Through pride, . . . *H.H.L.* 94
Sith purest Angels *fell* to be impure? . . . *H.H.L.* 98
Fell from the hope of promist heavenly place, . . . *H.H.L.* 122
How with most scornefull taunts, and *fell* despights, . . . *H.H.L.* 241
Felled. downe she on the plaine was *felde,* . . . *Bel.*[2] vii. 11
Her teeth out of her rotten gummes were *feld,* . . . I. viii. 47. 4
him so strongly stroke, that to the ground him *feld.* . . . I. xi. 28. 9
at their feet her selfe most humbly *feld,* . . . II. vi. 32. 3
high advaunced crests downe meekely *feld;* . . . II. xii. 40. 5
Their groves he *feld;* their gardins did deface; . . . II. xii. 83. 6
feld Great Ulfin thrise . . . III. iii. 55. 5
Yet mindfull how he late by one was *feld* . . . IV. i. 34. 4
Was with the force nigh *feld,* . . . IV. iii. 18. 9
So these two champions to the ground were *feld,* . . . IV. iv. 18. 6
having me, all wearie earst, downe *feld,* . . . IV. vi. 6. 8
Of butchers balefull hand to ground is *feld,* . . . VI. xii. 30. 8
them to hellish dungeons downe hast *feld.* . . . VII. vi. 27. 8
being lowe before her presence *feld* . . . VII. vii. 13. 7
An hatchet keene, with which he *felled* wood . . . VII. vii. 42. 6
Fellness. For very *felnesse* lowd he gan to weepe, . . . II. viii. 37. 5
Gnawing her nayles for *felnesse* and for yre, . . . IV. viii. 23. 8
in her thought did hide The *felnesse* of her heart, . . . V. vi. 18. 6
teare Her flesh for *felnesse,* which she inward hid: . . . V. xii. 32. 4
with more eager *felnesse* him pursew'd; . . . VI. iii. 50. 2
Fellow. every one did strive his *fellow* downe to throw. . . . II. vii. 47 .9
For pitie that ye want a *fellow* for your ayd.' . . . IV. i. 33. 9
a trembling dart, Whose *fellow* he before had sent . . . VI. ii. 6. 5
a slender dart, *Fellow* of this I beare, . . . VI. ii. 12. 7
when on ground they saw their *fellow* slaine, . . . VI. vi. 23. 1
when he saw his *fellow* lifelesse ly, . . . VI. vii. 10. 3
How both he and his *fellow* there in place Were vanquished, . VI. vii. 21. 4
Each gan his *fellow* solace and embrace . . . VI. viii. 37. 4
Fellow-furies. Doth urge her *fellow Furies* earnestlie . . . *Gn.* 423
Fellow-gods. of his *fellow gods* that faine to be, . . . VII. vii. 15. 2
Fellow-pagan. His other *fellow Pagan* which before him past. V. viii. 8. 9
Fellows. *See* **Playfellows.**
Two *fellowes* might no where be better fitted. . . . *Hub.* 50
Sixe of thy *fellowes* of the best array, . . . V. iv. 49. 7
Whom when his other *fellowes* saw, . . . V. x. 36. 1
Fellows'. *See* **Playfellows'.**
Fellow-servant. Of Phaedria, thine owne *fellow servaunt;* . . II. vi. 9. 8
To be her thrall, his *fellow-servant* vild: . . . III. vii. 17. 8
Fellow-shepherds. my *fellow Shepheards!* which do feed Your carelesse flocks . . . *D.* 519
ye, my *fellow shepheards,* . . . *Col.* 947
Fellowship. Piers, of *felowship,* tell us that saying: . . . *S.C.* May 172
would ye not poore *fellowship* expell, . . . *Hub.* 96
'Of *fellowship* (said then that bony Boy) . . . *Col.* 96
Whose *fellowship* seemd far unfitt for warlike swaine. . . . I. iv. 37. 9
of their lovely *fellowship* full glade, . . . III. x. 44. 8

Fellowship—*Continued.*
a joyous *fellowship* issewd Of Minstrales . . . III. xii. 5. 3
Was to that goodly *fellowship* restor'd, . . . IV. i. 15. 2
Now falne into their *fellowship* by chance: . . . IV. iv. 7. 4
For glorie vaine, their *fellowship* to lose, . . . IV. iv. 14. 5
To seeke by flight her *fellowship* t' eschew, . . . IV. viii. 56. 5
by his *fellowship* he colour might Both his estate and love . VI. x. 37. 8
Fellow-swains. tell your *fellow-swaines* That sad Alcyon dyde . *D.* 524
Felly. *Fellie* he hisseth, and doth fiercely stare, . . . *Gn.* 277
felly slewe Those warders strange, . . . *Hub.* 1370
Yet did she inly fret and *felly* burne, . . . *Mui.* 343
At them he gan to . . . *felly* gnarre, . . . I. v. 34. 6
does not so *felly* roste.' . . . II. vi. 50. 9
His Beast he *felly* prickt on either syde, . . . II. xi. 24. 3
charging him afresh thus *felly* him bespake. . . . IV. iii. 10. 9
he therewith so *felly* still did rave, . . . IV. vii. 28. 5
Like as a curre doth *felly* bite and teare . . . IV. viii. 36. 5
Fortune, envying good, hath *felly* frowned, . . . V. v. 36. 2
So both together, ylike *felly* bent, Like fiercely met. . . . V. viii. 7. 5
Whom when the Prince so *felly* saw to rage, . . . VI. vi. 39. 1
with their litle stings right *felly* fare; . . . VI. xi. 48. 4
a Tygre, . . . doth *felly* him oppresse. . . . *Am.* lvi. 4
Felon. What furie, or what feend with *felon* deeds . . . *T.M.* 45
a *felon* strong To many knights did daily worke disgrace; I. iii. 29. 3
'Now, *felon,* sure I read, . . . II. viii. 30. 2
freely read what wicked *felon* so Hath outrag'd you, . . . III. xi. 15. 2
the cursed *felon* high did reare His cruell hand . . . V. xii. 20. 2
Felonest. Those two were foes the *fellonest* on ground, . . . IV. ii. 32. 2
Felonous. Through *felonous* force of mine enemie.' . . . *S.C.* F. 156
He spide his foe with *felonous* intent, . . . *Gn.* 295
did acquite a murdrer *felonous;* . . . II. vii. 62. 7
with *felonous* despight And fell intent, . . . III. i. 65. 3
Twixt inward doole and *felonous* despight: . . . III. x. 17. 6
his *felonous* intent Returning disappointed his desire, . . . IV. vi. 11. 6
bit his lip for *felonous* despight, . . . IV. x. 33. 8
Felony. Abhorred bloodshed, and vile *felony,* . . . III. iv. 58. 3
Felt. in his headpeace he *felt* a sore payne: . . . *S.C.* May 242
griev'd as he had *felt* part of his paine; . . . *Hub.* 260
felt my heart nigh riven in my brest . . . *Ti.* 30
That stout Pendragon to his perill *felt,* . . . *Ti.* 104
I *felt* such anguish wound my feeble heart, . . . *Ti.* 482
Enfested grudge, the which his mother *felt,* . . . *Mui.* 354
have *felt* full many an heavie stowre. . . . I. iv. 46. 9
His chaunged powres at first them selves not *felt;* . . . I. vii. 6. 6
ghosts . . . Have *felt* the bitter dint of his avenging blade. . I. vii. 47. 9
when he . . . *felt* our feeble harts Embost with bale, . . . I. ix. 29. 1
never *felt* his imperceable brest So wondrous force . . . I. xi. 17. 7
each one *felt* secretly Himselfe thereby refte of his sences . I. xii. 39. 7
Which when he *felt* to move, he hoped faire . . . II. i. 43. 6
when he *felt* the folly of his Lord, . . . II. iii. 9. 3
Soone as Occasion *felt* her selfe untyde, . . . II. v. 19. 1
againe he armed *felt* his hond: . . . II. viii. 40. 6
had not yet *felt* Cupides wanton rage; . . . II. ix. 18. 2
never tasted grace, nor goodnes *felt;* . . . II. x. 7. 3
when he *felt* him dead, . . . II. xi. 42. 5
Yet life he saw, and *felt* his mighty mayne, . . . II. xi. 44. 4
She softely *felt* if any member moov'd, . . . III. i. 60. 7
Such secrete ease *felt* gentle Britomart, . . . III. ii. 15. 7
When feeble nature *felt* her selfe opprest, . . . III. ii. 29. 3
Shee softly *felt,* and rubbed busily, . . . III. ii. 34. 4
Which all that while shee *felt* to pant and quake, . . . III. ii. 42. 8
felt the crueltee Of his sharpe dartes . . . III. vi. 14. 4
felt in his old corage new delight To gin awake, . . . III. viii. 23. 4
the burning torment which he *felt;* . . . III. xi. 27. 3
felt the point of his hart-percing dart, . . . III. xi. 30. 2
As if no sorrow she ne *felt* ne drad; . . . III. xii. 18. 5
when she *felt* her selfe to be unbownd . . . III. xii. 38. 8
No word they spake, nor earthly thing they *felt,* . . . III. xii. 45. *or.* 8
where as their powre They *felt,* . . . IV. iii. 15. 5
him fild With double life and griefe; which when he *felt,* . IV. iii. 22. 3
Ne *felt* his blood to wast, . . . IV. iii. 29. 2
all unwares he *felt* an hideous sway . . . IV. iv. 31. 4
He *felt* his hart for very paine to quake, . . . IV. v. 44. 5
as if the steele had sence, And *felt* some ruth . . . IV. vi. 21. 7
when she *felt* Her selfe downe soust, . . . IV. vii. 9. 2
His stubborne heart, that never *felt* misfare, . . . IV. xii. 12. 4
feeble spirit inly *felt* refection: . . . IV. xii. 34. 5
when he *felt* him shrinke, . . . VI. i. 20. 8
When once he *felt* his foeman to relent, . . . VI. i. 21. 7
Now wanting them he *felt* himselfe so light, . . . VI. iv. 19. 6
not so well seene as *felt.* . . . VI. x. 42. 9
wondrous joy *felt* in her spirits thrall: . . . VI. xi. 44. 5
Had never joyance *felt* nor chearefull thought, . . . VI. xi. 45. 2
such passion . . . as this good Lady *felt,* . . . VI. xii. 21. 6
Female. Both male and *female* through commixture joynd: . . *Col.* 802
Ten thousand kindes of creatures, partly male And partly *femall,* . . . I. i. 21. 8
Both male and *female,* both under one name: . . . IV. x. 41. 7
Feminine. though graft in frailnesse *feminine.* . . . *Col.* 918
The one imperfect, mortall *foeminine,* . . . II. ix. 22. 4
the sister did in *feminine* And filthy lust exceede all woman-kinde, . . . III. xi. 4. 1
Feminity. onely mirrhor of *feminitie:* . . . *Col.* 513
yfostered to bee And trained up in trew *feminitee:* . . . III. vi. 51. 5
Fen. A monstrous beast ybredd in filthy *fen* He chose, . . . I. vii. 16. 8
flying fast as Roebucke through the *fen,* . . . II. x. 7. 5
he was fostred long in Stygian *fen,* . . . VI. i. 8. 4
Fence. was the *fence* thereof but weake and thin: . . . II. xii. 43. 4
Fenced. *fenst* himselfe about with many a flaming brand. . . V. viii. 35. 9
Fencible. all so faire and *fensible* withall; . . . II. ix. 21. 3

Fetched—*Continued.*
No fort so *fensible*, no wals so strong, . . . III. x. 10. 1
Fenny. With pype of *fennie* reedes doth him delight. . . . *Gn.* 112
Fens. moorish *fennes*, and marshes ever greene. . . . *Ti.* 140
Gnats . . . Out of the *fennes* of Allan doe arise, . . . II. ix. 16. 2
to those *fennes* for fastnesse she did fly, . . . V. x. 18. 8
Fens'. Nor the ranke grassie *fennes* delights untride. . . . *Mui.* 156
Fensible, Fenst. *See* **Fencible, Fenced.**
Feood, Feowe. *See* **Feud, Few.**
Ferce, -ly. *See* **Fierce, -ly.**
Fere. *See* **Fear.**
To yeeld Eurydice unto her *fere* . . . *Gn.* 463
faire Charissa to a lovely *fere* Was lincked, . . . I. x. 4. 8
Cambel tooke Cambina to his *fere*, . . . IV. iii. 52. 6
Stout Theseus and Pirithous his *feare* . . . IV. x. 27. 3
some fayre Franion, fit for such a *fere*, . . . V. iii. 22. 7
Then shalt thou take him to thy loved *fere*, . . . V. vii. 23. 5
To take Briana for his loving *fere* . . . VI. i. 43. 7
none she worthie thought to be her *fere*, . . . VI. vii. 29. 2
by his foolish *feare* Was holpen up, . . . VI. viii. 25. 8
By all meanes shund to match with any forrein *fere*. . . . VI. xii. 4. 9
Feres. I . . . Have trayned bene with many noble *feres* . . . VI. ii. 31. 4
Ferme. *See* **Farm.**
Ferramont. Which when the noble *Ferramont* espide, . . . IV. iv. 19. 1
With which so sore he *Ferramont* assaid, . . . IV. iv. 20. 7
Then did Sir *Ferramont* unto them shew His Lucida, . . . IV. v. 11. 6
Ferraugh. It was to weete the bold Sir *Ferraugh* hight, . . . IV. ii. 4. 5
Which *Ferrau* late from Braggadochio wonne: . . . IV. iv. 8. 2
Ferrex. Stout *Ferrex* and sterne Porrex him in prison threw. II. x. 34. 9
Ferry. forst to *ferrie* over Lethes river, . . . *Gn.* 338
him to *ferry* over that deepe ford. . . . II. vi. 4. 4
shee soone to hond Her *ferry* brought, . . . II. vi. 19. 5
To *ferry* that old man over the perlous foord. . . . II. vi. 19. 9
Did *ferry* him over the Idle lake: . . . II. xii. 17. 2
Ferryman. them awaited ready at the ford The *Ferriman*, . . . II. xi. 4. 2
that *Ferryman* With his stiffe oares . . . II. xii. 10. 1
'That may not bee,' said then the *Ferryman*, . . . II. xii. 11. 1
Fertile. His fattie waves doe *fertile* slime outwell, . . . I. i. 21. 3
overflowed all the *fertile* plaine, . . . I. xi. 48. 4
It was a chosen plott of *fertile* land, . . . II. vi. 12. 1
overflow With suddein fury all the *fertile* playne, . . . II. xi. 18. 6
The *fertile* Nile, which creatures new doth frame; . . . IV. xi. 20. 3
So *fertile* be the flouds in generation, . . . IV. xii. 1. 8
the countrie wherein I was bred, . . . *fertile* Lionesse . . . VI. ii. 30. 4
Fervent. *fervent* eyes to his destruction bent. . . . *Gn.* 296
Becomes more fierce and *fervent* in his gate; . . . *D.* 195
wave . . . Ne ever would through *fervent* sommer fade: . . . I. vii. 4. 7
when *fervent* sorrow slaked was, She up arose, . . . I. vii. 28. 1
Ne ever will their *fervent* fury slake, . . . I. ix. 8. 3
Their *fervent* appetites they quenched had, . . . I. xii. 15. 2
staring eyes sparckling with *fervent* fyre . . . II. vii. 37. 6
burning both with *fervent* fire . . . to understond, . . . II. ix. 60. 6
her essayd with many a *fervent* fit, . . . III. i. 34. 8
they slaked had the *fervent* heat Of appetite . . . III. i. 52. 1
Caried with *fervent* zeale: . . . IV. iv. 34. 3
fervent zeale Which I to him . . . did beare, . . . IV. viii. 55. 2
Claribell enraged rife With *fervent* flames, . . . IV. ix. 21. 4
To whom she bore most *fervent* love of late, . . . V. iv. 30. 3
The paynefull smith, with force of *fervent* heat, . . . *Am.* xxxii. 1
the more she *fervent* sees my fit, . . . *Am.* xxxii. 9
Let thy lifull heat not *fervent* be, . . . *Epith.* 118
Fervently. They all that charge did *fervently* apply . . . II. xi. 7. 6
Fervor. *fervour* of his flames somewhat adaw . . . V. ix. 35. 4
He gan his earnest *fervour* to augment, . . . V. ix. 46. 8
with thy furious *fervour* Thou doest afflict . . . *H.L.* 158
Fest. *See* **Feast.**
Festered. Ranckled so sore, and *festred* inwardly, . . . II. iv. 23. 3
He found that they had *festred* privily; . . . VI. vi. 5. 2
Festereth. inwardly it *festreth* sore, . . . *S.C.* Mar. 101
Festering. Inward corruption . . . *festring* sore did ranckle yett within, . . . I. x. 25. 4
Festival. honour in their *festivall* resort; . . . II. iii. 28. 4
ready dight with drapets *festivall*, . . . II. ix. 27. 3
brought a present joyfully . . . unto their *festivall*, . . . IV. xi. 33. 8
Fet. *See* **Fetched.**
Not Bilbo steele, nor brasse from Corinth *fet*, . . . *Mui.* 77
he was unhable them to *fett*, . . . II. ix. 58. 3
*Whom straunge adventure did from Britaine *fet*, . . . III. i. 8. 7
from the other fiftie soone the prisoner *fet*. . . . V. iii. 11. 9
From whom all earthly governance is *fet*. . . . *H.H.B.* 91
Fetch. *See* **Fet.**
To *fetchen* home May with their musicall: . . . *S.C.* May 28
left hys flocke to *fetch* a lasse, . . . *S.C.* Jul. 147
All as the shepheard that did *fetch* his dame . . . *S.C.* O. 28
They . . . daintie spices *fetch* from furthest Ynd, . . . I. v. 4. 6
sent with carefull diligence, To *fetch* a Leach, . . . I. x. 23. 7
Of whom all Faeryes spring, and *fetch* their lignage right. . . II. x. 71. 9
th' utmost sandy breach they shortly *fetch*, . . . II. xii. 21. 3
fetch from Faery Forreine ensamples . . . III. Pr. 1. 3
fetch their being from the sacred mould Of her immortall womb, . . . III. iv. 11. 8
All things from thence doe their first being *fetch*, . . . III. vi. 37. 1
To *fetch* from sea that ye at land lost late! . . . III. viii. 28. 4
fetch from heven thy great genealogie, . . . III. ix. 33. 7
her all Greece . . . Should *fetch* againe, . . . IV. xi. 19. 6
perforce with sword and targe Her forth to *fetch*, . . . IV. xii. 14. 8
By open force to *fetch* her quite away: . . . V. xi. 51. 2
Or stay till he his armes, . . . Might lightly *fetch*: . . . VI. ii. 19. 6
Fetched. *See* **Fet.**
fetcht from farre away, . . . *Mui.* 202

Fetched—*Continued.*
Sith she . . . Is *fetcht* fro me, . . . *D.* 439
precious odours *fetcht* from far away, . . . I. xii. 38. 4
Whence he it *fetcht* out of her native place, . . . III. v. 52. 4
In that same Gardin all the goodly flowres . . . Are *fetcht*: III. vi. 30. 4
From Lacedaemon *fetcht* the fayrest Dame . . . III. ix. 34. 7
Fettered. his foe *fettred* would release agayne, . . . II. v. 24. 8
Fetters. both his feet in *fetters* to an yron racke. . . . II. iv. 14. 9
loves his *fetters*, though they were of gold. . . . III. ix. 8. 5
Those yron *fetters* wherewith he was gyv'd, . . . V. iv. 35. 3
wrapt in *fetters* of a golden tresse, . . . V. viii. 1. 7
To covet *fetters*, though they golden bee! . . . *Am.* xxxvii. 14
Feud. Through mischievous debate and deadly *feood*, . . . IV. i. 26. 4
Feutred. *See* **Fewtered.**
Fever. in his lustlesse limbs, . . . A shaking *fever* raignd . . I. iv. 20. 8
Fever-fit. fayntnes . . . like a *fever fit* through all his bodie swelt. . . . I. vii. 6. 9
As if she had a *fever fitt*, . . . III. ii. 5. 4
Few. *Fewe* chymneis reeking you shall espye: . . . *S.C.* S. 117
Diggon on *fewe* such freends did ever lite. . . . *S.C.* S. 259
a *few* Now hold in hugger mugger . . . *Hub.* 138
a *few* have all, and all have nought, . . . *Hub.* 141
living they resigned quight For a *few* pence, . . . *Hub.* 574
full *few* which follow them, I see, . . . *Hub.* 637
few have found, and manie one hath mist! . . . *Hub.* 894
Some *few* beside this sacred skill esteme, . . . *T.M.* 583
Were but lost labour, that *few* would beleeve, . . . *Ti.* 90
With some *few* silver-dropping teares t' adorne; . . . *Ti.* 683
skill, though knowen yet to *few*; . . . *Col.* 401
that which thou mislikedst in a *few*.' . . . *Col.* 748
Not that these *few* lines can in them comprise . . . *Ded. Son.* xvi. 6
choosing out *few* words most horrible, . . . I. i. 37. 1
With whom he whoredome usd, that *few* did know, . . . I. iii. 18. 5
But *few* returned, having scaped hard, . . . I. iv. 3. 3
all the hinder partes, that *few* could spie, Were ruinous . . . I. iv. 5. 8
Wherein were closd *few* drops of liquor pure, . . . I. ix. 19. 3
So *few* there bee, That chose the narrow path, . . . I. x. 10. 3
Then with a *few* to walke the rightest way. . . . I. x. 10. 8
There wanted nought but *few* rites to be donne, . . . II. iv. 21. 5
blis . . . *few* gett, but many mis: . . . II. vii. 48. 9
being all defeated, save a *few*, . . . II. x. 55. 8
Few drops, more cleare then Nectar, . . . II. xii. 78. 4
ryding on forray *Few* dayes before, . . . III. iii. 58. 5
Few trickling teares she softly forth let fall, . . . III. vii. 9. 2
teares . . . in his eies, *few* drops of bitternesse. . . . III. x. 25. 9
these *few* words lett fly. . . . III. xi. 15. 9
Twixt both his hands *few* sparks he close did strayne, . . . III. xii. 9. 7
Great liking unto many, but true love to *feowe*. . . . III. xii. 13. 9
For fault of *few* that have abusd the same; . . . IV. Pr. 2. 5
Few men, but such as sober are and sage, . . . IV. iii. 43. 7
knowne to *few*, that Arthegall he hight, . . . IV. iv. 42. 8
By which *few* crooked sallowes grew in ranke: . . . IV. v. 33. 5
Onely *few* ruefull lookes unto her sent, . . . IV. viii. 13. 8
with *few* drops thereof did softly dew, Her wounds, . . . IV. viii. 20. 8
few plants, preserv'd through heavenly ayd, . . . IV. viii. 33. 3
few Could weenen whether they were false or trew: . . . IV. xi. 27. 4
in these *few* thousand yeares . . . V. Pr. 5. 4
with *few* sowces of his yron flale Dispersed all . . . V. iv. 24. 6
the Porter, skorning them so *few*, . . . V. iv. 37. 3
to make them seeme more *few*; . . . V. vi. 5. 7
with deepe sighes and singults *few*. . . . V. vi. 13. 9
In cyphers strange, that *few* could rightly read, . . . V. ix. 26. 3
Few perling drops from her faire lampes of light; . . . V. ix. 50. 7
soone as *few* drops of raine Thereon distill . . . V. xii. 13. 3
Atchiev'd so hard a quest, as *few* before; . . . VI. i. 5. 8
And from her sory hart *few* heavie words forth sight: . . . VI. ii. 42. 9
shedding *few* soft teares from tender eyne, . . . VI. v. 24. 3
few of them he left alive, . . . VI. vi. 24. 2
Of *few* greene turfes an altar soone they fayned, . . . VI. viii. 44. 8
closely did her wed, but knowne to *few*: . . . VI. xii. 5. 4
gave her doom in speeches *few*. . . . VII. vii. 57. 9
But that which fairest is, but *few* behold, . . . *Am.* xv. 13
Fewer. the *fewer* Woolves . . . The more bene the Foxes . . *S.C.* S. 154
Fewter. he his threatfull speare Gan *fewter*, . . . IV. vi. 10. 2
Fewtered. His speare he *feutred*, and at him it bore, . . . IV. iv. 45. 8
Feyne. *See* **Feign.**
Fiant. through his hand must passe the *Fiaunt*. . . . *Hub.* 1144
Fickle. Shall finde his state most *fickle* and unsure. . . . *Van.* xii. 14
I feare the *fickle* freakes,' . . . 'Of fortune false, . . . I. iv. 50. 1
ever *fickle* fortune rageth rife; . . . I. ix. 44. 8
Her *fickle* hart conceived hasty fyre, . . . III. i. 47. 6
His *fickle* mind full of inconstancie: . . . IV. i. 32. 5
flowring pride, so fading and so *fickle*, . . . VII. viii. 1. 8
Fickleness. in worlds *ficklenesse* Reposedst hope, . . . *D.* 150
Young knight . . . Beware of fraud, beware of *ficklenesse*, . I. iv. 1. 3
he was false, and fraught with *ficklenesse*, . . . I. iv. 25. 5
All flesh is frayle and full of *ficklenesse*, . . . VI. i. 41. 7
Fidelia. *Fidelia* and Speranza, virgins were; . . . I. x. 4. 6
the eldest, that *Fidelia* hight, . . . I. x. 12. 6
Fayre Una gan *Fidelia* fayre request, . . . I. x. 18. 3
his sinnes, . . . Made him forget all that *Fidelia* told. . . . I. x. 22. 5
to thy hand behight By wise *Fidelia*? . . . I. x. 50. 8
Fidelity. In shame of knighthood and *fidelitie*; . . . IV. vi. 8. 4
Fidessa. friendlesse, unfortunate, Now miserable I, *Fidessa*, I. ii. 26. 2
The false Duessa, now *Fidessa* hight, . . . I. ii. 44. 1
false Duessa . . . Called *Fidess'*, and so supposed to be, . . . I. iv. 2. 4
the faire *Fidessa*, loe! Is there possessed of the traytour vile; . . . I. iv. 42. 2
Lo! his *Fidessa*, to thy secret faith I flye.' . . . I. iv. 45. 9
faire *Fidessa*, . . . Returne from whence ye came, . . . I. iv. 51. 1

Fidessa—*Continued.*
The wanton loves of false *Fidessa* fayre, . . . I. vii. 26. 3
Thy neither friend nor foe, *Fidessa.'* . . . I. xii. 28. 9
this false woman that *Fidessa* hight, . . . I. xii. 32. 2
Fidessa hight the falsest Dame on grownd, . . . I. xii. 32. 3
Fidessa's. The false Duessa, cloked with *Fidessaes* name. . . . I. vii. 1. 9
Fie. *Fye* on thee, Diggon, . . . *S.C.* S. 150
"Fye, fye! deformed wight, . . . I. ii. 39. 1
fie on Fortune, mine avowed foe, . . . I. viii. 43. 3
To him said; *Fie, fie,* faint hearted Knight! . . . I. ix. 52. 6
'Fy, fy! false knight,' . . . IV. i. 51. 6
Fie on the man that did it first invent . . . IV. v. 18. 6
'Fie on such forgerie!' . . . V. xi. 56. 6
Fie on the pelfe for which good name is sold, . . . V. xi. 63. 6
Field. roming through the *field* with greedie rage . . . *Bel.*[2] vi. 6
Like as the seeded *field* greene grasse first showes, . . . *Ro.* xxx. 1
Whilome had bene the King of the *field,* . . . *S.C.* F. 108
to the *field* alone he speedeth, . . . *S.C.* F. 197
That he purchast of me in the playne *field:* . . . *S.C.* Au. 41
the flouret of the *field* doth fade, . . . *S.C.* N. 83
'The feeble flocks in *field* refuse their former foode, . . . *S.C.* N. 133
With shepheards swayne what ever fedde in *field;* . . . *S.C.* D. 44
Hector, the glorie of the Trojan *field:* . . . *Gn.* 516
Through everie *field* and forrest farre and nere, . . . *Hub.* 578
in *field* against them thrice prevailed; . . . *Ti.* 111
to sheild Achilles life from fate of Troyan *field.* . . . *Mui.* 64
The Goddesse selfe to chalenge to the *field,* . . . *Mui.* 270
Such as she oft is seene in warlicke *field:* . . . *Mui.* 323
in *field,* where-ever I did wend, . . . *D.* 127
every *field* and forest far away He sought, . . . *As.* 81
there lying on the *field,* . . . *As.* 183
What ever feeds in forest or in *field,* . . . *Col.* 820
Receive, dear Lord, in worth, the fruit of barren *field.* . . . *Ded. Son.* v. 14
The cruell markes of many' a bloody *fielde;* . . . I. i. 1. 4
'The Lyon, Lord of everie beast in *field,'* . . . I. iii. 7. 1
whilest him fortune favourd, fayre did thrive In bloudy *field;* I. iii. 37. 9
Ne ever wont in *field,* ne in round lists, to fight: . . . I. iii. 38. 9
He now, Lord of the *field,* . . . I. iii. 43. 5
The prowest knight that ever *field* did fight, . . . I. iv. 41. 7
Sowen in bloodie *field,* and bought with woe: . . . I. iv. 42. 5
I feare the . . . oddes of armes in *field.'* . . . I. iv. 50. 2
The faithfull knight in equall *field* . . . I. v. Arg.
now the pray of fowles in *field* he lyes, . . . I. v. 23. 3
The Sarazin, . . . soone him buckled to the *field.* . . . I. vi. 41. 9
A sea of blood . . . overflowed all the *field* arownd, . . . I. viii. 16. 8
downe he tumbled on the durtie *field,* . . . I. viii. 20. 4
the heavens, . . . Have made you master of the *field* . . . I. viii. 28. 2
from the *fielde* most cowardly doth fly! . . . I. x. 1. 5
wash thy hands from guilt of bloody *field:* . . . I. x. 60. 8
He bore a bloodie Crosse that quartred all the *field.'* . . . II. i. 18. 9
A flaming fire in midst of bloody *field,* . . . II. iv. 38. 3
'The lilly, Lady of the flowring *field,* . . . II. vi. 16. 1
soone prepard to *field,* his sword forth drew, . . . II. vi. 29. 3
Bad therefore I him deeme that thus lies dead on *field.'* . . . II. viii. 14. 9
in that same *field* victorious . . . II. x. 43. 7
overcame The wicked Gobbelines in bloody *field;* . . . II. x. 73. 2
Wel weened hee that *field* was then his owne, . . . II. xi. 35. 1
a Lion passant in a golden *field.* . . . III. i. 4. 9
shivering speare in bloody *field* first shooke, . . . III. i. 7. 3
deckt the azure *field* with her fayre pouldred skin. . . . III. ii. 25. 9
Til thou in open *fielde* adowne be smott: . . . III. ii. 46. 5
Against his Saxon foes in bloody *field* to fight. . . . III. iii. 29. 9
his proud foes discomfit in victorious *field.* . . . III. iii. 31. 9
that *field* . . . Shall Hevenfield be cald . . . III. iii. 38. 8
In the last *field* before Menevia, . . . III. iii. 55. 3
As ever man that bloody *field* did fight; . . . III. vii. 29. 5
where ever it in *field* was showne. . . . III. xi. 7. 9
speare and curtaxe both usd Priamond in *field.* . . . IV. ii. 42. 9
Assembled were in *field* the chalenge to define. . . . IV. iii. 3. 9
The *field* with listes was all about enclos'd, . . . IV. iii. 4. 1
For bloud to gush forth on the grassie *field;* . . . IV. iii. 9. 5
rushing forth into the emptie *field,* . . . IV. iii. 22. 7
both at once fell dead upon the *field,* . . . IV. iii. 34. 8
Marshals of the *field* Broke up the listes, . . . IV. iii. 35. 3
Shewing him selfe all ready for the *field.* . . . IV. iv. 17. 5
himselfe he soft withdrew Out of the *field,* . . . IV. iv. 25. 2
To range the *field,* and victorlike to raine, . . . IV. iv. 25. 4
There Satyrane Lord of the *field* he found, . . . IV. iv. 28. 1
So did these two through all the *field* their foes enforce. . . . IV. iv. 35. 9
none of them in *field* durst stand, . . . IV. iv. 43. 3
Into the Martian *field* adowne descended . . . IV. v. 6. 8
Eftsoones the others did the *field* recoure, . . . IV. ix. 25. 3
No flowre in *field,* that daintie odour throwes, . . . IV. x. 22. 3
A broken sword within a bloodie *field;* . . . V. i. 19. 8
too weake To aunswere his defiaunce in the *field,* . . . V. i. 24. 2
When Talus saw they all the *field* forsooke, . . . V. ii. 54. 7
into the *field* they came, . . . V. iii. 7. 2
overthrew, And chaced quite out of the *field,* . . . V. iii. 12. 6
So were they left Lords of the *field* alone: . . . V. iii. 12. 8
bore the Sunne brode blazed in a golden *field.* . . . V. iii. 14. 9
that his foe should him the *field* denie,) . . . V. iii. 32. 4
When thus the *field* was voided all away, . . . V. iv. 46. 1
try in equall *field* whether hath greater might. . . . V. iv. 48. 9
So forth into the *field* she marched thence, . . . V. v. 4. 7
The Trumpets sounded, and the *field* began; . . . V. v. 6. 1
downe she fell upon the grassie *field* . . . V. v. 11. 3
to her mercie him submitted in plaine *field.* . . . V. v. 16. 9
So being clad she brought him from the *field,* . . . V. v. 21. 1
if all fayle, yet farewell open *field;* . . . V. x. 24. 5
willing them forth to call Into the *field* . . . V. x. 31. 5

Field—*Continued.*
when he gave me armes in *field* to fight, . . . V. xi. 53. 3
made him oftentimes in *field* before me fall. . . . V. xi. 53. 9
losse of fame in disaventrous *field:* . . . V. xi. 55. 8
fights, And slaieth him in *field.* . . . V. xii. Arg.
with proud presumpteous gate Into the *field,* . . . V. xii. 14. 2
So stoutest knights doen oftentimes in *field.* . . . V. xii. 19. 5
menaced me from the *field* to beat, . . . VI. i. 40. 5
When to the *field* she went he with her went: . . . VI. ix. 34. 8
sith they twaine Long since had fought in *field:* . . . VI. xii. 11. 4
And reigneth over every beast in *field,* . . . *Am.* xx. 6
I goe lyke one that, having lost the *field,* . . . *Am.* lii. 2
nor in *field* nor bowre I her can fynd; . . . *Am.* lxxviii. 7
Yet *field* and bowre are full of her aspect: . . . *Am.* lxxviii. 8
Why doe not then the blossomes of the *field,* . . . *H.B.* 78
Great store of Flowers, the honour of the *field,* . . . *Proth.* 74
Fields. now these scorned *fields* bemone her fall, . . . *Ro.* xii. 13
Upon the naked *fields* in stackes he reares: . . . *Ro.* xxx. 8
sowing in th' Aemathian *fields* thy spight, . . . *Ro.* xxxi. 10
in *fields* where falls hem best. . . . *S.C.* Jun. 76
To raunge the *fields* with wide open throte. . . . *S.C.* S. 195
Walke in Elisian *fieldes* so free. . . . *S.C.* N. 179
Fayre *fieldes* and pleasaunt layes there bene; . . . *S.C.* N. 188
The *fieldes* ay fresh, the grasse ay greene. . . . *S.C.* N. 189
sundrie flowers in wilde *fieldes* gathered; . . . *Gn.* 132
The goodly *fields,* that earst so gay were dyde . . . *T.M.* 237
madest the forrests ring, And *fields* resownd, . . . *Ti.* 326
now in Elisian *fields* so free, . . . *Ti.* 332
Over the *fields,* in his franke lustinesse, . . . *Mui.* 148
to breath the freshing ayre In open *fields,* . . . *D.* 27
as I the *fields* did range . . . *D.* 106
Full carefully he kept them . . . In fairest *fields;* . . . *As.* 6
The *fields* with faded flowers did seem to mourne, . . . *Col.* 25
both woods and *fields* and floods revive, . . . *Col.* 29
the *fields* In which dame Cynthia her landheards fed; . . . *Col.* 276
Faire goodly *fields,* . . . *Col.* 278
From flocks and *fields,* to angels and to skie.' . . . *Col.* 619
former dayes Had in rude *fields* bene altogether spent, . . . *Col.* 669
only woond in *fields* and forests here:' . . . *Col.* 774
streams of purple blood new die the verdant *fields.* . . . I. ii. 17. 9
in fresh flowring *fields* themselves to sport: . . . I. iv. 37. 3
With pleasaunce of the breathing *fields* yfed, . . . I. iv. 38. 2
That all the *fieldes* rebellowed againe. . . . I. viii. 11. 4
Bulles, . . . fill the *fieldes* with troublous bellowing: . . . I. viii. 11. 8
The *fields,* the floods, the heavens, with one consent, . . . I. ix. 12. 8
Bryton *fieldes* with Sarazin blood bedyde, . . . I. xi. 7. 3
two broad Beacons, sett in open *fieldes,* . . . I. xi. 14. 3
The flowrs, the *fields,* and all that pleasaunt growes, . . . II. vi. 15. 2
The *fields* did laugh, the flowres did freshly spring, . . . II. vi. 24. 6
all the *fields* resounded with the ruefull cry. . . . II. viii. 3. 9
the *fieldes* of faire Scamander strowne With carcases . . . III. ix. 35. 6
the happie soules, which doe possesse Th' Elysian *fields* . . . IV. x. 23. 5
Through all the *fields* and vallies did before him flie. . . . V. iv. 44. 9
made smooth *fields* now full of flowres? . . . V. x. 23. 5
over all the *fields* themselves did muster, . . . V. xi. 58. 4
all about the *fields* like Squirrels hunt; . . . V. xi. 59. 3
The faire Serena . . . Wandred about the *fields,* . . . VI. iii. 23. 6
From thence into the open *fields* he fled, . . . VI. ix. 4. 1
In th' open *fields* an Infant left alone; . . . VI. ix. 14. 6
yet better so To lodge then in the salvage *fields* to rome. . . VI. ix. 16. 7
The *fields* my food, my flocke my rayment breed; . . . VI. ix. 20. 8
So being clad unto the *fields* he went . . . VI. ix. 37. 1
One day, as he did raunge the *fields* abroad, . . . VI. x. 5. 1
bearing it abrode Into the emptie *fields,* . . . VI. xii. 7. 2
She in the open *fields* had loosely layd . . . VI. xii. 16. 4
I seeke the *fields* with her late footing synd; . . . *Am.* lxxviii. 5
Fields'. gathered more store Of the *fields* honour . . . *Mui.* 123
Fiend. were it faerie, *feend,* or snake, . . . *S.C.* Mar. 76
What furie, or what *feend* with felon deeds . . . *T.M.* 45
Till that infernall *feend* . . . Forwasted all their land, . . . I. i. 5. 7
Whose corage when the *feend* perceivd to shrinke, . . . I. i. 22. 4
Here hauntes that *feend,* . . . I. xi. 2. 3
For dread of that huge *feend* . . . I. xi. 3. 3
Whom when the damned *feend* so fresh did spy, . . . I. xi. 35. 1
whenas the direfull *feend* She saw not stirre, . . . I. xi. 55. 5
'That cursed man, that cruel *feend* of hell, . . . II. vi. 50. 1
forth there lept An ugly *feend,* . . . II. vii. 26. 7
the *feend* his gnashing teeth did grate, . . . II. vii. 34. 1
every *feend* his busie paines applyde . . . II. vii. 35. 8
That dreadfull *feend,* which did behinde him wayt, . . . II. vii. 64. 4
hellish *feend* raysd up through divelish science. . . . II. xi. 39. 9
affraid of him as *feend* of hell. . . . III. iv. 47. 9
of that *feend* was rent without remorse: . . . III. vii. 31. 3
Fiercely he flew upon that wicked *feend,* . . . III. vii. 32. 2
Now like a Gyaunt; now like to a *feend;* . . . III. viii. 41. 2
when the wicked *feend* his Lord tormented, . . . IV. ii. 2. 2
The one a *feend,* the other an incarnate devill. . . . IV. ii. 3. 9
some *feend* This mischiefe framd . . . IV. vi. 17. 6
In sacrifize unto that cursed *feend;* . . . V. xi. 20. 4
A dreadfull *feend* with fowle deformed looke, . . . V. xi. 22. 5
She flew at him like to an hellish *feend,* . . . V. xi. 27. 2
then the *feend* her selfe more fiercely reard . . . V. xi. 30. 5
A dreadfull *feend,* of gods and men ydrad, . . . V. xii. 37. 8
that foule *feend,* who dayly doth attend . . . VI. iv. 31. 8
by whom that *feend* shold be fordonne. . . . VI. iv. 32. 9
no such beast they saw, Nor any wicked *feend* . . . VI. ix. 6. 2
when he saw the *feend,* . . . VI. x. 35. 2
fared like a *feend* right horrible in hew: . . . VI. xii. 31. 9
Fiendlike. neither would their *fiendlike* fury slacke, . . . IV. ix. 25. 5
Fiends. Much do I feare among such *fiends* to sit; . . . *Gn.* 381

Fiends—*Continued.*
approoved The *feends* to be too cruell and severe, ... *Gn.* 466
griesly *Feends* of hell him terrifie. . . . . *Gn.* 544
the cruell *fiends* of hell, ... *Gn.* 625
With fearfull *fiends,* that in deep darknes dwell. . . . . . *Ti.* 126
As one aghast with *feends* or damned sprights, ... I. ii. 4. 5
all the hellish brood Of *feends* infernall . . . . I. v. 32. 8
thousand *feends* that doe them endlesse paine . . . . . . I. ix. 49. 8
either hellish *feends,* or powres on hye: . . . . II. iii. 45. 5
As one affright With hellish *feends,* . . . . II. v. 37. 7
From other covetous *feends* it to defend, ... II. vii. 32. 4
By every fournace many *feendes* did byde, ... II. vii. 35. 6
More fitt emongst black *fiendes* then men to have his place. . II. vii. 41. 9
Against fowle *feendes* to ayd no militant! . . . . II. viii. 2. 5
as a man whom hellish *feendes* have frayd, ... II. viii. 46. 4
Infernall Hags, Centaurs, *feendes,* Hippodames, ... II. ix. 50. 8
companing with *feends* and filthy Sprights . . . . II. x. 8. 6
hideous shapes were like to *feendes* of hell, ... II. xi. 11. 3
Th' infernall *feends* with it he can asswage, ... II. xii. 41. 6
As one with vew of ghastly *feends* affright: . . . . III. ii. 29. 7
cruell *Feendes* should thee unwares devowre: . . . . III. iii. 8. 9
those *feends* may not their work forbeare, ... III. iii. 11. 4
The *feends* do quake when any him to them does name. . . . III. iii. 12. 9
the stubborne *feendes* he to his service bownd. . . . . . . III. iii. 14. 9
Dragons, and Minotaures, and *feendes* of hell, ... III. x. 40. 5
many dreadfull *feends* hath pointed to her gard. . . . . . . III. xi. 16. 9
Wherewith the hellish *fiends* he doth confound: . . . . . . IV. iii. 42. 7
like as one whom *feends* had made affrayd, ... V. iii. 18. 4
even the hellish *fiends* affrighted bee At sight thereof, ... VI. vi. 10. 4
sacrifizeth to th' infernall *feends:* . . . . VI. viii. 49. 4
Where with such damned *fiends* she should in darknesse dwell. VI. x. 43. 9
Doth make both Gods and hellish *fiends* affraid: . . . . . . VII. vi. 18. 3
for th' unruly *fiends* which they did feare; . . . . VII. vii. 3. 8
to provoke the yre Of damned *fiends,* . . . . *H.L.* 235

Fierce. *See* **Fiery-fierce.**
Most *fierce* and fell this woman seemde to me. . . . . *Rev.* ii. 11
this *fierce* hatefull beast and all hir traine . . . . *Rev.* iii. 13
Beres and Tygres, that maken *fiers* warre; . . . . *S.C.* Au. 28
more *fierce* in visage, and in pace, ... *Gn.* 269
Fierce Peleus, and the hardie Telamon, ... *Gn.* 482
Their match in glorie, mightie, *fierce,* and coy; . . . . . . *Gn.* 494
in ayde of that *fierce* fight, ... *Gn.* 505
Both *fierce* and furious in contention Encountred, ... *Gn.* 517
rushing with *fierce* might Out of his den, ... *Mui.* 434
Becomes more *fierce* and fervent in his gate; . . . . *D.* 195
Fierce warres and faithful loves shall moralize my song. . . I. Pr. 1. 9
As one for knightly giusts and *fierce* encounters fitt. . . . . I. i. 1. 9
he lept As Lyon *fierce* upon the flying pray, ... I. i. 17. 2
turning *fierce* her speckled taile advaunst, ... I. i. 17. 6
Lept *fierce* upon his shield, ... I. i. 18. 6
He thought have slaine her in his *fierce* despight; . . . . . I. i. 50. 3
Their horned fronts so *fierce* on either side . . . . I. ii. 16. 3
unmoved as a rocke, Both staring *fierce,* . . . . I. ii. 16. 8
in hope themselves to hide From the *fierce* heat, ... I. ii. 29. 9
So both to batteill *fierce* arraunged arre, ... I. ii. 36. 5
that disdainfull beast, Encountring *fierce,* . . . . I. iii. 19. 7
scorching flames of *fierce* Orions hound; . . . . I. iii. 31. 6
that proud Paynim forward came so *ferce* . . . . I. iii. 35. 1
her *fiers* servant . . . full greedy at him came, ... I. iii. 41. 1
him beside rides *fierce* revenging Wrath, Upon a Lion, ... I. iv. 33. 1
Enflam'd with fury and *fiers* hardy hed, ... I. iv. 38. 7
him rencountring *fierce,* . . . . I. iv. 39. 9
answerd he then *ferce,* 'I no whitt reck; . . . . I. iv. 50. 8
The knight was *fiers,* and full of youthly heat, ... I. v. 7. 4
a Gryfon . . . A Dragon *fiers* encountreth . . . . I. v. 8. 3
him before His father *fierce* of treason false accusd, ... I. v. 37. 8
High Caesar, great Pompey, and *fiers* Antonius. . . . . I. v. 49. 9
Till her unwares the *fiers* Sansloy did overtake: . . . . . . I. vi. 2. 9
The Antelope, and Wolfe both *fiers* and fell; . . . . I. vi. 26. 5
The pitteous pray of his *fiers* cruelty have bin. . . . . . . I. vii. 45. 9
The *fiers* threeforked engin, . . . highest trees hath rent, . . . I. viii. 9. 6
Encountring *fiers* with single sword in hand; . . . . I. viii. 12. 8
Duessa, full of . . . *fiers* disdaine to be affronted so, ... I. viii. 13. 2
the Gyaunt . . . Came hurtling in full *fiers,* . . . . I. viii. 17. 9
Shott many a dart at me with *fiers* intent; . . . . I. ix. 10. 8
The God of warre with his *fiers* equipage . . . . I. xi. 6. 7
The beast, impatient . . . of so *fierce* and forcible despight, . I. xi. 25. 7
him rencountring *fierce,* . . . . I. xi. 53. 4
with *fierce* yre And zealous haste . . . . II. i. 13. 1
seeing him from far so *fierce* to pricke, ... II. i. 26. 1
His *fierce* foe his steed could stay uneath, ... II. i. 27. 8
why with so *fierce* saliaunce, And fell intent, ... II. i. 29. 6
fiers fate did crop the blossome of his age. . . . . II. i. 41. 9
raging passion with *fierce* tyranny . . . . II. i. 57. 4
yonder is no game For thy *fiers* arrowes, ... II. iii. 35. 2
chaufd and fom'd with corage *fiers* and sterne, ... II. iii. 46. 8
prickt so *fiers,* that underneath his feete . . . . II. v. 3. 3
the rash assault and wrathful stowre Of his *fiers* foe, ... II. v. 10. 4
So both together *fiers* engrasped bee, ... II. v. 20. 8
Tho gan that villein wex so *fiers* and strong, ... II. v. 23. 1
When ever his *fiers* handes he free mote fynd: . . . . II. v. 28. 4
so *fiers* did play On th' others helmett, ... II. vi. 31. 5
Withhold your bloody handes from battaill *fierce;* . . . . . . II. vi. 33. 3
fiers Vulcans rage to tame, ... II. vii. 36. 5
that *fiers* Carle commaunding to forbeare, ... II. vii. 43. 2
found him *fiers* and bold.' . . . . II. viii. 13. 9
'Good or bad,' gan his brother *fiers* reply, ... II. viii. 15. 1
fiers Pyrochles, lacking his owne sword, ... II. viii. 19. 1
So ready dight *fierce* battaile to assay, ... II. viii. 22. 8
So *fierce* he laid about him, ... II. viii. 41. 1

Fierce—*Continued.*
salvage Bull, whom two *fierce* mastives bayt, ... II. viii. 42. 1
With his owne swerd he *fierce* at him did flye, ... II. viii. 47. 4
the *fierce* Northerne wind with blustring blast . . . . II. ix. 16. 8
being retourned late From his *fierce* warres, ... II. ix. 34. 8
in *fierce* contention, ... II. x. 11. 8
corage *fierce* that all men did affray, ... II. x. 15. 2
fierce Cundah gan shortly to envy . . . . II. x. 33. 2
most horrible of hew And *ferce* of force, ... II. xi. 13. 2
The *fierce* Spumador, trode them downe like docks; . . . . . II. xi. 19. 7
The *fierce* Spumador, borne of heavenly seed, ... II. xi. 19. 8
Upon a Tygre swift and *fierce* he rode, ... II. xi. 20. 4
fierce at him did ride, ... II. xi. 25. 2
thee *fierce* Fortune did so nearely drive, ... II. xi. 30. 8
Eft *fierce* retourning, ... II. xi. 36. 6
now awaking, *fierce* at them gan fly, ... II. xii. 84. 6
Full of disdainefull wrath he *fierce* uprose . . . . III. i. 9. 1
did darrayne *Fiers* battaill against one . . . . III. i. 20. 9
fierce Bacchante seemd too fell and keene; . . . . III. i. 45. 6
With so *fierce* furie and great puissaunce, ... III. iv. 16. 2
that *fierce* foster, which late fled away, ... III. v. 18. 5
Full of *fiers* fury and indignant hate . . . . III. v. 23. 3
more fresh And *fierce* he still appeard, ... III. vii. 32. 9
with the terrour of their *fierce* affret . . . . III. ix. 16. 3
That *fiers* youngmans unruly maystery; . . . . III. x. 2. 7
therewith *fierce* did stryke The raging billowes, ... III. xi. 40. 5
Both greedie *fiers* on other to be wroken: . . . . IV. ii. 21. 5
To whom *fierce* Atropos: 'Bold Fay; . . . . IV. ii. 49. 6
Carelesse of perill in their *fiers* affret, ... IV. iii. 6. 7
his poynant speare he *fierce* aventred . . . . IV. iii. 9. 1
So fresh he seemed and so *fierce* in sight: . . . . IV. iii. 23. 6
Till th' heat of his *fierce* furie he had spent; . . . . IV. iii. 26. 5
As two *fierce* Buls, that strive the rule to get . . . . IV. iv. 18. 3
So huge his hammer, and so *fierce* his heat, ... IV. v. 37. 7
Whereby the passion grew more *fierce* and faine, ... IV. vi. 33. 8
thrusting *fierce* into the thickest preace . . . . IV. ix. 32. 6
Ran *fierce* at me that fire glaunst from his horses hoofe. . . . IV. x. 9 .9
Fierce Eryx: and Alebius, ... IV. xi. 14. 7
Tygris *fierce,* whose streames of none may be withstood; . . IV. xi. 20. 9
with fell intent And countenaunce *fierce,* . . . . V. v. 5. 4
shun the dred despight Of her *fierce* wrath, ... V. v. 16. 2
To *fierce* avengement of that womans pride, ... V. vi. 18. 7
With like *fierce* minds, but meanings different; . . . . . . V. viii. 30. 2
under his *fierce* horses feet have borne, ... V. viii. 31. 8
gan with courage *fierce* addresse him to the fight. . . . . . . V. x. 31. 9
Full of fell ravin and *fierce* greedinesse; . . . . V. xi. 24. 2
he gan her with courage *fierce* assay, ... V. xi. 26. 6
But he was *fierce* and whot, ... VI. ii. 19. 6
with *fierce* fury . . . Upon him ran; . . . . VI. iv. 5. 3
his *fierce* steed that mote him much dismay: . . . . VI. iv. 6. 5
charged him so *fierce* and furiously, ... VI. v. 16. 5
Like a *fierce* Bull, that being busie bent . . . . VI. vi. 27. 4
With the *fierce* Lapithes which did them dismay, ... VI. x. 13. 5
with fell clawes full of *fierce* gourmandize, ... VI. x. 34. 5
fought through fury *fierce* and bold. . . . . VI. xi. 30. 9
fierce assayling him, with all their might . . . . VI. xi. 47. 8
fierce assailing forst him turne againe: . . . . VI. xii. 26. 2
Fayre cruell! why are ye so *fierce* and cruell? . . . . *Am.* xlix. 1

Fiercely. I saw a wasp, that *fiercely* him defide, ... *Van.* x. 7
For *fiercely* the good man at him did laye. . . . . *S.C.* F. 214
Fellie he hisseth, and doth *fiercely* stare, ... *Gn.* 277
Wherewith enrag'd he *fiercely* gan upstart, ... *Gn.* 289
he *fiercely* strake Whereas his temples . . . . *Gn.* 307
Upon those gates with force he *fiercely* flewe, ... *Hub.* 1369
Her yellow locks . . . She *fiersly* tore, ... *As.* 159
Snatcheth his sword, and *fiercely* to him flies; . . . . I. ii. 17. 2
strike so *fiercely,* that they do impresse . . . furrowes . . . . I. v. 6. 7
trampling the fine element would *fiercely* ramp. . . . . I. v. 28. 9
blowes, and *fiersly* to assaile Each other . . . . I. vi. 43. 2
Their gory sides fresh bleeding *fiercely* frett; . . . . I. vi. 44. 5
So *fiersly,* . . . They gan to fight retourne, ... I. vi. 45. 1
at him *fiersly* flew, ... I. viii. 6. 8
fiersely ran at him . . . . I. xi. 16. 2
fercely tooke his trenchand blade in hand, ... I. xi. 24. 1
did *fiercely* fall Upon his sunne-bright shield, ... I. xi. 40. 8
he *fiersly* did his foe assaile, ... I. xi. 42. 3
Against her snowy brest he *fiercely* bent, ... II. i. 11. 7
fercely unto battell sterne themselves prepar'd. . . . . . . II. ii. 19. 9
his lofty crest Did *fiercely* shake, ... II. iii. 35. 9
fiercely did menace: . . . . II. iii. 42. 8
strooke At him so *fiercely,* . . . . II. v. 6. 2
Fiercely approching to him lowdly cryde, ... II. v. 35. 3
therewithall he *fiersly* at him flew, ... II. vi. 29. 1
How without stop or stay he *fiersly* lept, ... II. vi. 42. 2
Both *fiercely* bent to have him disaraid; . . . . II. viii. 17. 3
full of anger *fiersly* to him cryde; . . . . II. viii. 31. 5
his balefull speare he *fiercely* bent . . . . II. viii. 32. 1
he *fiercely* gan approch, ... II. viii. 44. 3
they *fiercely* then begin to showre; . . . . II. viii. 48. 5
Fiersly at first those knights they did assayle, ... II. ix. 14. 1
chaste so *fiercely* after fearefull flight, ... II. x. 16. 5
him his foe more *fiercely* should poursew: . . . . II. xi. 27. 4
The Squyre arriving *fiercely* in his armes . . . . II. xi. 31. 1
Fiercely advaunst his valorous right arme, ... II. xi. 34. 7
rearing *fercely* their upstaring crests, ... II. xii. 39. 8
fiercely forward came withouten dread, ... III. i. 5. 8
His tyreling Jade he *fiersly* forth did push . . . . III. i. 17. 4
Wherewith enrag'd she *fiercely* at them flew, ... III. i. 66. 1
With his wide wings upon them *fiercely* fly, ... III. iii. 46. 6
after that wicked foster *fiercely* went: . . . . III. iv. 47. 4

Fiercely—*Continued.*
After that foster fowle he *fiercely* ridd . . . . III. v. 13. 4
Fiercely he flew upon that wicked feend, ... III. vii. 32. 2
Fiercely that straunger forward came: . . . . III. viii. 16. 1
pricked *fiercely* forward where she did him vew. . . . . . . III. xi. 4. 9
fiercely running to that Lady trew, ... III. xii. 32. 4
fiercely forth her mortall blade she drew, ... III. xii. 33. 8
So forth he *fiercely* prickt that one him scarce could see. . . IV. i. 35. 9
Fiercely forth prickt his steed . . . . IV. ii. 6. 7
Sir Blandamour, . . . thus *fiercely* him bespake: . . . . . IV. ii. 25. 2
Out of his headpeece Cambell *fiercely* reft, ... IV. iii. 12. 4
Rusht *fiercely* forth the battell to renew, ... IV. iii. 14. 6
they both together *fiercely* met, ... IV. iii. 15. 1
Against Cambello *fiercely* him addrest; . . . . IV. iii. 22. 8
fiercely each assayling gan afresh to fight. . . . . IV. iii. 35. 9
fiersly forth did ride. . . . . IV. iv. 17. 9
On whom remounting *fiercely* forth he rode, ... IV. iv. 23. 4
from one a weapon *fiercely* takes. . . . . IV. iv. 34. 9
Fiercely they followd on their bolde emprize, ... IV. iv. 36. 1
against her *fiercely* ran. . . . . IV. vi. 10. 2
Paridell and Druon *fiercely* laid At Scudamour, ... IV. ix. 30. 3
all at once at him gan *fiercely* flie, ... IV. ix. 33. 2
on his head-peece him so *fiercely* smit, ... V. iv. 39. 7
There her assayling *fiercely* fresh, ... V. iv. 41. 4
She *fiercely* towards him her selfe gan dight, ... V. iv. 43. 2
he gan *fiercely* her pursew. . . . . V. v. 7. 5
The Engin, *fiercely* flying forth, ... V. vi. 40. 4
Full *fiercely* layde the Amazon about, ... V. vii. 31. 1
her full *fiercely* chast In hope to have her overhent at last: . V. viii. 4. 4
So both together, ylike felly bent, Like *fiercely* met. . . . . V. viii. 7. 6
seeing him come still so *fiercely* on, ... V. viii. 9. 4
Wherewith full wroth he *fiercely* gan assay . . . . V. xi. 11. 4
more *fiercely* reard Uppon her wide great wings, ... V. xi. 30. 5
Like to a great Mill-damb forth *fiercely* gusht, ... V. xi. 31. 5
fiercely charged them with all his force: . . . . V. xii. 7. 2
He gan at him let drive more *fiercely* then afore. . . . . . V. xii. 22. 9
seeing him so *fiercely* towardes make, ... VI. i. 19. 2
he *fiercely* at him flew, ... VI. i. 20. 1
He *fiercely* him pursu'd, and pressed sore; . . . . VI. i. 21. 8
fiercely charging him with all his might, ... VI. iii. 25. 6
As *fiercely* . . . Chasing the gentle Calepine . . . . VI. iv. 2. 7
Upon the ground her selfe she *fiercely* threw, ... VI. v. 5. 1
Like a fell Lyon at him *fiercely* flew, ... VI. vi. 22. 4
With his sharpe sword he *fiercely* at him flew, ... VI. viii. 9. 2
gan *fiercely* fly Upon that Carle . . . . VI. viii. 12. 8
fiercely drawing forth his blade, ... VI. xi. 15. 7
the mad steele about doth *fiercely* fly, ... VI. xi. 16. 3
Fierceness. a courser . . . That through his *fiersnesse* fomed all with sweat, ... I. iii. 33. 4
at the last his *fiercenes* gan abate, ... III. vii. 35. 3
with like *fiercenesse* did ensew the chace, ... III. xi. 5. 2
Him forst, (maulgre) his *fercenes* to relent, ... III. xi. 26. 8
Did mitigate the *fiercenesse* of their mode, ... IV. iv. 5. 2
forestall Their furious encounter, and their *fiercenesse* pall. . V. iv. 5. 9
Fiercer. both milder beasts and *fiercer* foes . . . . *Bel.*[2] viii. 7
Their force is *fiercer* through infirmity . . . . II. xi. 1. 5
Fiercest. The fayrest kyne alive, but of the *fiercest* kynd: . . V. x. 9. 9
Fiers, -ly. *See* **Fierce, -ly.**
Fiery. tumbling through the ayre in *firie* fold, ... *Bel.*[2] vii. 10
The *firie* sunnes both one and other hous: . . . . *Ro.* x. 8
Ne durst againe his *fyrye* face out showe: . . . . *S.C.* Ap. 78
gates of hel, and *fyrie* furies forse, ... *S.C.* N. 164
The *fiery* Sun was mounted now on hight . . . . *Gn.* 65
Throwing his *firie* eyes on everie side, ... *Gn.* 270
Hyperions *fierie* childe Ascending . . . . *Mui.* 51
Phoebus *fiery* carre In hast was climbing . . . . I. ii. 1. 7
From *fiery* wheeles of his faire chariot Hurled his beame . . I. ii. 29. 4
That did presume his fathers *fyrie* wayne, ... I. iv. 9. 2
from their shields forth flyeth *firie* light, ... I. v. 7. 8
They . . . come to *fiery* flood of Phlegeton, ... I. v. 33. 3
to feed his *fyrie* lustfull eye, He snatcht the vele . . . . . I. vi. 4. 6
every head with *fyrie* tongue did flame, ... I. viii. 6. 3
With *firie* zeale he burnt in courage bold . . . . I. ix. 37. 4
Whom *fyrie* steele now burnt, that erst him armd; . . . . . . I. xi. 27. 8
steepe His *fierie* face in billowes of the west, ... I. xi. 31. 2
darted *fyrie* beames out of the same, ... II. iii. 23. 3
Moystened their *fierie* beames, with which she thrild . . . . II. xii. 78. 7
whose *fiery* feete did burne The verdant gras . . . . III. i. 5. 5
full of *firy* zele, him followed long, ... III. iv. 45. 8
Her *fyrie* eyes with furious sparkes did stare, ... III. vii. 39. 8
Shee sent at him one *fyrie* dart, ... III. ix. 28. 8
Is creasted all with lines of *firie* light, ... IV. i. 13. 8
Their *firie* steedes with so untamed forse . . . . IV. ii. 15. 1
from the same the *fierie* sparkles flasht, ... IV. iii. 25. 8
from his fearefull eyes two *fierie* beames, ... IV. viii. 39. 1
from her eies did flash out *fiery* light, ... V. vi. 38. 8
putting spurres unto her *fiery* beast, ... V. vi. 39. 2
his *fierie* teme Towards the westerne brim begins to draw, . . V. ix. 35. 1
Now when as Phoebus with his *fiery* waine . . . . VI. iii. 29. 1
his *fiery* eies, Like two great Beacons, ... VI. vii. 42. 1
lights the world forth from his *firie* carre. . . . . *H.B.* 112
dart at them their litle *fierie* launces; . . . . *H.B.* 241
Which from their faces dart out *fierie* light; . . . . *H.H.B.* 95
Fiery-bright. Darting their deadly arrowes, *fyry bright,* . . . *Am.* xvi. 7
Mounted in Phoebus charet *fierie bright,* . . . . V. iii. 19. 2
Fiery-fierce. steede, Pricked with wrath and *fiery fierce* disdaine, ... I. ii. 8. 4
Fiery-footed.
Sonne hath reared up His *fyerie-footed* teme, ... *S.C.* Jul. 18
Phoebus . . . Yett harnessed his *fyrie-footed* teeme, ... I. xii. 2. 2
Fiery-hot. pluck it out with pincers *fyrie whott,* . . . . . . I. x. 26. 8
Fiery-mouthed. the *firie-mouthed* steedes, which drew The Sunnes bright wayne . . . . V. viii. 40. 1
Fiery-red. bloodie eyes doo glister *firie red;* . . . . *Gn.* 350
His eies did hurle forth sparcles *fiery red,* . . . . I. iv. 33. 5
From flaming mouth bright sparckles *fiery redd,* . . . . . . I. vii. 31. 7
Fife. As merrie notes upon his rusticke *Fife,* . . . . *Gn.* 148
Fifth. Such one vile Envy was, that *fifte* in row did sitt. . . . I. iv. 32. 9
The *fift* had charge sick persons to attend, ... I. x. 41. 1
the *fift* troupe, most horrible of hew . . . . II. xi. 13. 1
Cruelly they assayed that *fift* Fort, ... II. xi. 13. 5
Against that same *fift* bulwarke they continued fight. . . . . II. xi. 13. 9
The *fift* Armeddan, skild in lovely layes; . . . . V. iii. 5. 7
Fifty. *fifty* sisters water in leke vessels draw. . . . . I. v. 35. 9
Dioclesians *fifty* daughters shene . . . . II. x. 8. 4
the Sea Nymphs . . . all which *fifty* are, ... IV. xi. 48. 5
he ere long the former *fiftie* bet, ... V. iii. 11. 8
from the other *fiftie* soone the prisoner fet. . . . . V. iii. 11. 9
Fight. *fight* against the Gods of heavenly berth, ... *Ro.* xii. 3
Perdie with Love thou diddest *fight;* . . . . *S.C.* Mar. 104
No deadly *fight* of warlick fleete doth feare; . . . . *Gn.* 124
Ida selfe, in ayde of that fierce *fight,* . . . . *Gn.* 505
He lately slue his dreadfull foe in *fight.* . . . . *Gn.* 648
Drawne into armes, and proofe of mortall *fight,* . . . . . . *Mui.* 4
Like as a warlike Brigandine, applyde To *fight,* . . . . . . *Mui.* 85
His forces faile, ne can no lenger *fight,* . . . . I. i. 22. 3
of your later *fight* ye all forwearied be; . . . . I. i. 32. 5
dull wearines of former *fight* Having yrockt asleepe his spright, ... I. i. 55. 4
Without regard of armes and dreaded *fight:* . . . . I. ii. 3. 6
As when two rams, . . . *Fight* for the rule . . . . I. ii. 16. 2
Ne ever wont in field, ne in round lists, to *fight:* . . . . . I. iii. 38. 9
Sansjoy doth chaleng him to *fight.* . . . . I. iv. Arg.
In equall lists they should the morrow next it *fight.* . . . . I. iv. 40. 9
The prowest knight that ever field did *fight,* . . . . I. iv. 41. 7
'what oddes can ever bee, Where both doe *fight* alike, ... I. iv. 50. 4
all for praise and honour he did *fight.* . . . . I. v. 7. 6
The wise Southsayer . . . telles of warres and mortall *fight.* . . I. v. 8. 9
ever lov'd to *fight* for Ladies right; . . . . I. vi. 20. 8
So long they *fight,* and full revenge pursue, ... I. vi. 44. 1
Then backe to *fight* againe, new breathed and entire. . . . . . I. vi. 44. 9
They gan to *fight* retourne, ... I. vi. 45. 2
So they to *fight;* . . . . I. vi. 47. 8
proofe he since hath made . . . in many a cruell *fight;* . . . . I. vii. 47. 7
Faire virgin, . . . Brings Arthure to the *fight:* . . . . I. viii. Arg.
To see what end of *fight* should him befall . . . . I. viii. 2. 9
Therewith the Gyant buckled him to *fight,* . . . . I. viii. 7. 1
With griping talaunts armd to greedy *fight,* . . . . I. viii. 48. 7
Doth soonest fall in disaventrous *fight,* . . . . I. ix. 11. 8
th' other for to *fight* With Unaes foe, ... I. ix. 20. 3
Ne bring him forth in face of dreadfull *fight,* . . . . I. ix. 20. 7
Is this the battaile which thou vauntst to *fight* . . . . I. ix. 52. 8
soone as it doth come to *fight* Against spirituall foes, ... I. x. 1. 3
yet he was unfitt for bloody *fight.* . . . . I. x. 2. 6
does free it selfe by *fight.* . . . . I. xi. 19. 9
her deare knight, who, weary of long *fight* . . . . I. xi. 50. 2
As if late *fight* had nought him damnifyde, ... I. xi. 52. 7
By forged treason or by open *fight,* . . . . II. i. 3. 3
chose for love to *fight.* . . . . II. ii. 18. 9
two brave knightes in bloody *fight* . . . . II. ii. 21. 3
being met In cruell *fight* . . . . II. ii. 22. 6
when Guyon came to part their *fight,* . . . . II. ii. 23. 8
Straunge sort of *fight,* three valiaunt knights to see . . . . II. ii. 26. 1
In fayre defence . . . was wont to *fight;* . . . . II. iv. 8. 4
stirre him up to strife and cruell *fight.* . . . . II. iv. 42. 7
he is all disposd to bloody *fight,* . . . . II. iv. 43. 7
With silly weake old woman that did (*thus to) *fight!* . . . . II. iv. 45. 5
Pyrochles does with Guyon *fight,* . . . . II. v. Arg.
On foot with him to matchen equall *fight:* . . . . II. v. 4. 8
he would algates with Pyrochles *fight,* . . . . II. v. 20. 2
From needlesse trouble of renewing *fight* . . . . II. v. 25. 2
glorious spoiles, purchast in perilous *fight:* . . . . II. v. 26. 3
for he would algates *fight:* . . . . II. v. 37. 9
care of vow'd revenge and cruell *fight,* . . . . II. vi. 8. 4
Disdeigning to be held so long in *fight.* . . . . II. vi. 30. 4
sith for me ye *fight,* . . . . II. vi. 33. 4
if for me ye *fight,* or me will serve, ... II. vi. 34. 1
full bent To prove extremities of bloody *fight,* . . . . II. vi. 36. 2
counseld him abstaine from perilous *fight;* . . . . II. vii. 42. 7
They for us *fight,* they watch and dewly ward, ... II. viii. 2. 6
lend The same to thee, against his lord to *fight;* . . . . . . II. viii. 21. 8
did he fall by treason, or by *fight?* . . . . II. viii. 24. 4
Wanting his sword when he on foot should *fight:* . . . . . . II. viii. 34. 2
Had reard him selfe againe to cruel *fight* . . . . II. viii. 34. 7
So did Prince Arthur beare himselfe in *fight,* . . . . II. viii. 48. 8
were enraunged ready still for *fight.* . . . . II. ix. 26. 5
He them defeated in victorious *fight,* . . . . II. x. 16. 4
fell him selfe in *fight:* . . . . II. x. 35. 5
ceased not the bloody *fight* for ought; . . . . II. x. 51. 5
though overcome in haplesse *fight,* . . . . II. x. 56. 8
having overcome The Romane legion in dreadfull *fight.* . . . . II. x. 60. 8
To see a cruell *fight* doen by the prince this day. . . . . . . II. xi. 4. 9
Against that same fift bulwarke they continued *fight.* . . . . II. xi. 13. 9
For her defence against that Carle to *fight,* . . . . II. xi. 16. 7
Whenas the Russian him in *fight* does chace) . . . . II. xi. 26. 8
freshly, as at first, prepard himselfe to *fight.* . . . . II. xi. 38. 9
Against this lifelesse shadow so to *fight:* . . . . II. xi. 44. 3
Rather for pleasure then for battery or *fight.* . . . . II. xii. 43. 9
The martiall brood accustomed to *fight:* . . . . III. i. 13. 5
for his trusty servaunts doth so strongly *fight.'* . . . . . . III. i. 29. 9
ever hope to match in equall *fight,* . . . . III. ii. 13. 8

Fight—*Continued.*
Against his Saxon foes in bloody field to *fight*. . . . . III. iii. 29. 9
Thrise shall he *fight* with them, and twise shall win; . . . . III. iii. 30. 6
whome hee lately brake . . . in victorious *fight*, ... III. iii. 52. 8
No whit lesse fayre then terrible in *fight*: . . . . III. iii. 56. 3
with his foes he could not come to *fight*. . . . . III. v. 20. 9
As ever man that bloody field did *fight*; . . . . III. vii. 29. 5
Her selfe to *fight* addrest, and threw her lode aside. . . . . III. vii. 38. 9
So ran the Geauntesse unto the *fight*, ... III. vii. 39. 7
semblaunce of faire *fight* did make, ... III. vii. 44. 8
Ne any may that Monster match in *fight*, ... III. vii. 52. 8
his late *fight* With Britomart so sore did him offend, ... III. x. 1. 7
how he with our foe may come to *fight*.' . . . . III. xi. 23. 4
Scudamour and Blandamour: Their *fight* and warlike deedes. . IV. i. Arg.
Scudamour her bought In perilous *fight* . . . . IV. i. 2. 2
A perilous *fight*, when he with force her brought . . . . . . IV. i. 2. 3
Ne list I for revenge provoke new *fight*, ... IV. i. 35. 3
through the bruses of his former *fight*, ... IV. i. 39. 8
my selfe will for you *fight*, ... IV. i. 40. 8
answere for thy wrong as shall fall out in *fight*.' . . . . . IV. ii. 13. 9
With murdrous weapons arm'd to cruell *fight*, ... IV. ii. 16. 2
Bidding them *fight* for honour of their love, ... IV. ii. 19. 6
There they, I weene, would *fight* untill this day, ... IV. ii. 20. 1
none of them durst undertake the *fight*; . . . . IV. ii. 40. 4
On horsebacke used Triamond to *fight*, ... IV. ii. 42. 4
For Canacee with Cambell for to *fight*. . . . . IV. iii. 3. 2
Right practicke was Sir Priamond in *fight*, ... IV. iii. 7. 1
him affronting soone, to *fight* was readie prest. . . . . . . IV. iii. 22. 9
Could stand on foot now to renew the *fight*: . . . . IV. iii. 23. 3
fiercely each assayling gan afresh to *fight*. . . . . IV. iii. 35. 9
eft them turned both againe to *fight*: . . . . IV. iii. 47. 3
he yet was sore of his late lucklesse *fight*. . . . . IV. iv. 3. 9
Yee shall her winne, as I have done, in *fight*: . . . . IV. iv. 9. 4
His person to emperill so in *fight*; . . . . IV. iv. 10. 6
When who so list to *fight* may *fight* his fill: . . . . IV. iv. 12. 6
so went forth to *fight*. . . . . IV. iv. 27. 9
Approved oft in many a perlous *fight*. . . . . IV. iv. 40. 5
That bore the Hebene speare, as wonne in *fight*. . . . . . . IV. v. 20. 5
Some proffer made with him for her to *fight*. . . . . IV. v. 27. 5
Scudamour and Arthegall Doe *fight* with Britomart: . . . . . IV. vi. Arg.
Whiles with long *fight* on foot he breathlesse was, ... IV. vi. 15. 2
Through toylesome heate and labour of her weary *fight*. . . . IV. vi. 19. 9
when in vaine to *fight* she oft assayd, ... IV. vi. 27. 6
Hath conquered you anew in second *fight*: . . . . IV. vi. 31. 3
Thereto the villaine used craft in *fight*; . . . . IV. vii. 26. 1
if it chaunst, (as needs it must in *fight*) . . . . IV. vii. 26. 6
yet he conquer'd not by bloudie *fight*, ... IV. viii. 47. 6
all afresh gan former *fight* renew. . . . . IV. ix. 26. 6
they long while continued in *fight*; . . . . IV. ix. 28. 1
had foyled . . . by wrongfull *fight* . . . . IV. ix. 36. 3
To *fight* with Hercules, that did advance . . . . IV. xi. 16. 5
much lesse him match in *fight*, ... V. i. 8. 7
it us'd in that great *fight* Against the Titans, ... V. i. 9. 5
by ordele, or by blooddy *fight*, ... V. i. 25. 3
Artegall . . . Does with the Pagan *fight*: . . . . V. ii. Arg.
on a Bridge he custometh to *fight*, ... V. ii. 7. 6
streight him selfe unto the *fight* addrest, ... V. ii. 12. 2
that use well knew To *fight* in water, ... V. ii. 13. 6
All sixe well-seene in armes, and prov'd in many a *fight*. . . V. iii. 5. 9
there all day continew'd cruell *fight*, ... V. iii. 7. 3
he chalenged the thiefe to *fight*: . . . . V. iii. 31. 6
With weapons in their hands as ready for to *fight*. . . . . . V. iv. 21. 9
Beholding all that womanish weake *fight*; . . . . V. iv. 25. 8
being overcome by her in *fight*, ... V. iv. 32. 6
ere she could joyne hand with him to *fight*, ... V. iv. 43. 5
mongst the rest the *fight* did untill evening last. . . . . . V. iv. 43. 9
Causd all her people to surcease from *fight*; . . . . V. iv. 45. 5
in single *fight* To try her Fortune, ... V. iv. 47. 6
to morrow I with him wil *fight*, ... V. iv. 48. 8
That he mote fresher be against the next daies *fight*. . . . V. iv. 51. 9
The last daies purpose of their vowed *fight*, ... V. v. 1. 6
till time they should begin the *fight*. . . . . V. v. 4. 9
Instead of Curiets and bases fit for *fight*. . . . . V. v. 20. 9
if she him wonne in *fight*. . . . . V. v. 23. 9
To *fight* with him, and goodly die her last. . . . . V. vi. 13. 3
Since that he was not forst, nor overcome in *fight*?' . . . . V. vi. 16. 9
Two Knights all armed ready for to *fight*; . . . . V. vi. 29. 2
On which Pollente with Artegall did *fight*. . . . . V. vi. 36. 7
Did forth issue all ready for the *fight*: . . . . V. vii. 27. 8
Whilest Fortune favourd her successe in *fight*: . . . . V. vii. 41. 7
against her still doth *fight*, ... V. viii. 20. 7
In the behalfe of wronged weake did *fight*: . . . . V. viii. 30. 8
takes the enterprize For Belgee for to *fight*: . . . . V. x. Arg.
th' armes and legs of three to succour him in *fight*. . . . . V. x. 8. 9
Hercules them all did overcome in *fight*. . . . . V. x. 10. 9
vanquished all ventrous knights in *fight*; . . . . V. x. 30. 4
gan with courage fierce addresse him to the *fight*. . . . . . V. x. 31. 9
Prince Arthure overcomes the great Gerioneo in *fight*: . . . . V. xi. Arg.
gan him selfe to *fight* on foote prepare: . . . . V. xi. 9. 4
when she saw that she was forst to *fight*, ... V. xi. 27. 1
With her unrighteous enemy to *fight*, ... V. xi. 39. 5
when he gave me armes in field to *fight*, ... V. xi. 53. 3
buckling him eftsoones unto the *fight*, ... V. xi. 57. 8
to trie the right Of fayre Irenaes cause in single *fight*: . . V. xii. 8. 9
With which he wont to *fight* to justifie his wrong: . . . . . V. xii. 14. 9
he had great skill in single *fight*: . . . . V. xii. 15. 5
gan him streight to buckle to the *fight*, ... V. xii. 16. 8
Calidore, that was well skild in *fight*, ... VI. i. 20. 5
Having late slaine her Seneschall in *fight*, ... VI. i. 29. 8
passing well expert in single *fight*, ... VI. i. 36. 4
prove the finall fortune of the *fight*; . . . . VI. i. 38. 4

Fight—*Continued.*
However strong and fortunate in *fight*, ... VI. i. 41. 3
to yeeld his Love, or else to *fight*: . . . . VI. ii. 18. 5
These goodly gilden armes which I have won in *fight*.' . . . VI. ii. 33. 9
For he durst not abide with Calidore to *fight*. . . . . VI. iii. 25. 9
To justifie thy fault gainst me in equall *fight*.' . . . . . . VI. iii. 35. 9
Unlesse that with his Lord he formerly did *fight*. . . . . . VI. iii. 38. 9
if he needes will *fight*, crave leave till morne, ... VI. iii. 41. 6
armes or weapon had he none to *fight*, ... VI. iv. 4. 1
proved oft in many perillous *fight*, ... VI. vi. 4. 3
Through many wounds, which lately he in *fight* Received had, . VI. vi. 20. 8
To *fight* with many foes about him ment, ... VI. vi. 27. 5
A wrongfull quarrell to maintaine by *fight*; . . . . VI. vi. 35. 6
slaine in so unequall *fight*: . . . . VI. vi. 37. 7
in former *fight* He of the Prince his life received . . . . . VI. vii. 2. 3
Which never yet they had approv'd in *fight*, ... VI. vii. 5. 5
Himselfe recovering was return'd to *fight*, ... VI. vii. 10. 2
Wearie of travell in his former *fight*, ... VI. vii. 19. 1
approved oft in *fight*, ... VI. viii. 14. 2
there gan a dreadfull *fight*. . . . . VI. xi. 47. 9
Such haughty mynds, enur'd to hardy *fight*, ... *Am.* xiv. 7
fresh against my selfe to *fight*. . . . . *Am.* xliv. 12
Drew millions more against their God to *fight*. . . . . *H.H.L.* 84

Fighting. nathemoe Was he abashed now, not *fighting* so; . . . II. iv. 8. 5
So wearie both of *fighting* had their fill, ... IV. iii. 36. 8
forced them from *fighting* to refraine, ... IV. iv. 25. 7
A tall young man, . . . *Fighting* on foot, ... VI. ii. 3. 8

Fights. The knight with that old Dragon *fights* . . . . I. xi. Arg.
Guyon . . . *Fights* with Cymochles, ... II. vi. Arg.
this brave knight, that for this vertue *fightes*, ... II. xii. 1. 6
Britomart *fightes* with many Knights; . . . . IV. ix. Arg.
Artegall *fights* with Radigund, ... V. v. Arg.
She *fights* with Radigund, ... V. vii. Arg.
He with the great Grantorto *fights*, ... V. xii. Arg.
Water *fights* With Fire, and Ayre with Earth, ... VII. vii. 25. 7
His cancred foes, his *fights*, his toyle, his strife, ... *H.H.L.* 234

Figure. Who list the Romane greatnes forth to *figure*, ... *Ro.* xxvi. 1
cast a *figure* for a Bishoprick; . . . . *Hub.* 511
Cannot your glorious pourtraict *figure* playne, ... III. Pr. 3. 7

Figured. Arachne *figur'd* how Jove did abuse Europa . . . . *Mui.* 277
could not find what sence it *figured*: . . . . III. xi. 50. 5
Had Deathes owne ymage *figurd* in her face, ... III. xii. 19. 6

Figures. Now turned into *figures* hideous, ... II. xii. 85. 4

Figuring. *Figuring* straunge characters of his art: . . . . . III. xii. 31. 2

Filch. To *filch* away sweet snatches of delight, ... *Epith.* 363

Filched. having *filcht* her bells, her up he cast . . . . . . III. x. 35. 7

File. Their handes they may not *file*. . . . . *S.C.* Jul. 192
Whose grosse defaults thy daintie pen may *file*, ... *Ded. Son.* xii.11
well could *file* his tongue as smooth as glas: . . . . I. i. 35. 7
'How ever, Sir, ye *fyle* Your courteous tongue . . . . III. ii. 12. 4
were it not ill fitting for this *file* . . . . VII. vi. 37. 1

Filed. *See* **Fair-filed.**
A *filed* toung, furnisht with tearmes of art, ... *Col.* 701
She lightly lept out of her *filed* bedd, ... III. i. 62. 2
On Fames eternall beadroll worthie to be *fyled*. . . . . IV. ii. 32. 9
In which the names of all loves folke were *fyled*, ... VI. vii. 33. 2
that which she hath *fylde* In her owne breast, ... VI. xi. 21. 3

Fill. Did *fill* with her renowmed nourslings praise . . . . . . *Ro.* x. 7
the heaven it selfe with her wide wonders *fill*. . . . . *Ro.* xxix. 8
fill the world with never dying fame! . . . . *Ro.* Env. 14
She shal be a Grace, To *fyll* the fourth place, ... *S.C.* Ap. 116
bedde, or bowre, both which I *fill* with cryes, ... *S.C.* Au. 167
Tho may we talke and tellen our *fill*, ... *S.C.* S. 53
a gulph . . . with his owne corps did *fill*, ... *Gn.* 605
whenas they feasted had their *fill*, ... *Hub.* 337
Pierce the dull heavens and *fill* the ayer wide, ... *T.M.* 118
fill the Scene with plaint, ... *T.M.* 153
fill with pleasure The listners eyes . . . . *T.M.* 177
All places with our pleasant notes to *fill*, ... *T.M.* 242
With fearfull howling do all places *fill*; . . . . *T.M.* 284
The schooles they *fill* with fond new fanglenesse, ... *T.M.* 327
fill their bookes with discipline of vice. . . . . *T.M.* 336
those that Love with leawdnes *fill*. . . . . *T.M.* 384
wont the world with famous acts to *fill*; . . . . *T.M.* 430
with deepe Oracles their verses *fill*: . . . . *T.M.* 562
when he hath both plaid and fed his *fill*, ... *Mui.* 205
fill with pleasance every wood and plaine. . . . . *D.* 56
with the same *fill* every hill and dale. . . . . *D.* 322
when as he piped had his *fill*, ... *Col.* 10
fill the same with store of timely wine. . . . . *Col.* 603
fill with stones, that all men may it know. . . . . *Col.* 635
And *fill* your mind with magnanimitee. . . . . *Ded. Son.* x. 12
Arrived there, the litle house they *fill*, ... I. i. 35. 1
Full envious that night so long his roome did *fill*: . . . . . I. ii. 1. 9
when they both had wept and wayld their *fill*, ... I. iii. 22. 6
his pride to *fill*, With foule reproches . . . Her . . . entertaines; I. iii. 43. 5
from backe and belly still did spare, To *fill* his bags, . . . I. iv. 28. 5
thousands moe the like that did that dongeon *fill*. . . . . . I. v. 50. 9
the heavens it doth *fill* With thundring noyse, ... I. vii. 13. 5
Bulles, . . . *fill* the fieldes with troublous bellowing: . . . I. viii. 11. 8
ay thereof her babes might sucke their *fill*; . . . . I. x. 30. 8
Those glistring armes that heven with light did *fill*, ... I. xi. 4. 8
all the ayre about with smoke and stench did *fill*. . . . . . I. xi. 13. 9
he doth *fill* The world with murdrous spoiles . . . . II. viii. 6. 3
gazing wonder they their mindes did *fill*; . . . . II. ix. 33. 3
all Which, him before, that sacred seate did *fill*, ... II. x. 76. 2
to the brim with Coltwood did it *fill*, ... III. ii. 49. 8
Bangor with massacred Martyrs *fill*, ... III. iii. 35. 6
Thus when they all had sorowed their *fill*, ... III. iv. 40. 1
her wombe did *fill* With hevenly seed, ... III. iv. 41. 5
of his sweetnesse takes her *fill*. . . . . III. vi. 46. 9

Fill—*Continued.*
having him embowelled To *fill* his hellish gorge, ... III. vii. 29. 2
Her garments gay with scales of fish that all did *fill*. . . . III. viii. 26. 9
On her faire face so did he feede his *fill*, ... III. ix. 27. 8
when of meats and drinks they had their *fill*, ... III. ix. 32. 1
all the forest did with horrour *fill*. . . . . III. x. 43. 4
I saw him sleepe with her all night his *fill*; . . . . IV. i. 49. 3
when at last she had beheld her *fill*, ... IV. ii. 49. 3
So wearie both of fighting had their *fill*, ... IV. iii. 36. 8
When who so list to fight may fight his *fill*: . . . . IV. iv. 12. 6
all the temple it did *fill* . . . . IV. x. 43. 9
therewith *fill* The coffers of her wicked threasury, ... V. ii. 9. 3
strove with puissance strong To *fill* the other scale . . . . V. ii. 46. 5
The sight whereof did all with gladnesse *fill*: . . . . V. iii. 15. 1
thought that she thereon could never gaze her *fill*. . . . . V. vii. 5. 9
all the Temple did with terrour *fill*; . . . . V. xi. 22. 8
Ere he had slept his *fill*, ... VI. i. 35. 3
all the woods with piteous plaints did *fill*, ... VI. iv. 18. 2
Use scanted diet, and forbeare your *fill*; . . . . VI. vi. 14. 7
to let her Sleepe out her *fill* . . . . VI. viii. 38. 2
did the ayre with terror *fill*, ... VI. viii. 46. 3
having fed his *fill*, ... VI. ix. 7. 6
there by her were poured forth at *fill*, ... VI. x. 5. 8
when they had flouted him their *fill*, ... VII. vi. 50. 1
those that all the other world do *fill*, ... VII. vii. 3. 4
What pen, what pencill, can expresse her *fill*? . . . . . . *Am.* xvii. 4
fill the world with her victorious prayse. . . . . *Am.* xxix. 14
singes, and feeds her *fill*. . . . . *Am.* lxv. 8
hart, that wont on your fayre eye To feed his *fill*, ... *Am.* lxxiii. 8
fill your selfe with those most joyous sights, ... *Am.* lxxxiii. 9
my glad mouth with her sweet prayses *fill*. . . . . *Am.* lxxxiv. 12
with such brightnesse whylest I *fill* my mind, ... *Am.* lxxxvii. 13
all the firmament doth *fill*; . . . . *Epith.* 142
thy spirits shall *fill* With sweete enragement of celestiall love, . *H.H.L.* 285
For of her fulnesse which the world doth *fill* They all partake, . *H.H.B.* 199
they gathered flowers to *fill* their flasket, ... *Proth.* 26
now had Flowers their *fill*, ... *Proth.* 55
Their wondring eyes to *fill*; . . . . *Proth.* 59
Filled. name of blasphemie *Filde* hir with pride. . . . . . *Rev.* ii. 4
With balmie odours *fil'd* th' ayre . . . . *Bel.*[2] xi. 4
With which he had those Romane spirits *fild*, ... *Ro.* xi. 6
his proude heart is *fild* with fretting ire: . . . . *Van.* x. 10
your silken hyde *Fil'd* with round flesh, ... *Hub.* 592
fild their mouthes with meeds of malefices: . . . . *Hub.* 1154
fild with treasure rackt with robberies; . . . . *Hub.* 1306
Fild with the wreaks of mortall miserie; . . . . *T.M.* 124
So all with rufull spectacles is *fild*, ... *T.M.* 163
her royal P'laces Be *fild* with praises . . . . *T.M.* 581
Are thereby *fild* with happie influence; . . . . *T.M.* 586
so plenteouslie Her lap she *filled* had, ... *Mui.* 141
Her blazed fame which all the world had *fil'd*, ... *Mui.* 266
Was *fil'd* with hope his purpose to obtaine: . . . . *Mui.* 396
th' ayre be *filled* (**fild*) with noyse of dolefull knells, . . . *D.* 335
She spoyld thereof, and *filled* with annoy. . . . . *As.* 162
being *fild* with furious insolence, ... *Col.* 622
Whose warlike prowesse . . . Hath *fild* sad Belgicke . . . . *Ded.Son.* xiv. 10
lewdnes *fild* him with reprochfull pain Of that foule evill, . . I. iv. 26. 6
Their mournefull charett, *fild* with rusty blood, ... I. v. 32. 2
He had . . . *fild* far landes with glorie of his might: . . . . I. vi. 20. 6
stony horrour all her sences *fild* With dying fitt, ... I. vi. 37. 3
fild her hidden caves with stormie yre, ... I. vii. 9. 5
masse of earthly slyme, . . . *fild* with sinfull cryme. . . . . I. vii. 9. 9
at him fiersly flew, with corage *fild*, ... I. viii. 6. 8
a cup of gold, With wine and water *fild* . . . . I. x. 13. 3
sownd . . . all the ayre with terror *filled* wyde, ... I. xi. 4. 2
thrise three tymes had *fild* her crooked hornes, ... II. i. 53. 3
the foolish man, *fild* with delight . . . . II. iii. 42. 2
fild with pleasures vayn, ... II. vi. 14. 2
Did feed his eyes, and *fild* his inner thought . . . . . . II. vii. 24. 4
all the chamber *filled* was with flyes . . . . II. ix. 51. 1
with all shame that sacred throne he *fild*. . . . . II. x. 21. 2
groveling to the ground he fell, and *fild* his place. . . . . II. xi. 34. 9
That all their sences *filled* with affright; . . . . II. xii. 2. 7
fild their sayles with feare: . . . . II. xii. 37. 2
hungry eies, which n'ote therewith be *fild*; . . . . II. xii. 78. 2
Vile rancour their rude harts had *fild* with such despight. . . III. v. 16. 9
fild his senses with abashment great; . . . . III. viii. 16. 7
whose noyaunce *fild* the fearefull sted . . . . III. xii. 2. 6
every wood . . . He *filld* with Hylas name; . . . . III. xii. 7. 9
faire Amoret, . . . was *fild* with new affright. . . . . III. xii. 44. 9
Fild with false rumors and seditious trouble, ... IV. i. 28. 3
fild the lookers on attonce with ruth and wonder. . . . . . . IV. iii. 15. 9
him *fild* With double life and griefe; . . . . IV. iii. 22. 2
filled were with rufull tine And secret feare, ... IV. iii. 37. 4
That stryfull hag with gealous discontent Had *fild*, ... IV. v. 30. 9
all his hairy brest with gory bloud was *fild*. . . . . IV. vii. 31. 9
fild With deepe disdaine . . . . IV. vii. 36. 2
inward grudge *fild* his heroicke brest: . . . . IV. ix. 32. 4
all the world have with their issue *fild*? . . . . IV. xi. 17. 2
Proteus house they *fild* even to the dore; . . . . IV. xii. 3. 3
filled all the house with feare and great uprore. . . . . . V. ii. 21. 9
fild his ballaunce full of idle toys: . . . . V. ii. 30. 8
Whereat her heart was *fild* with hope and drede, ... V. vi. 8. 7
fild with heavenly fury, thus he her behight. . . . . V. vii. 20. 9
fild with courage and with joyous glee, ... V. vii. 25. 4
all the grassie flore Was *fild* with bloud . . . . V. vii. 31. 6
nigh *fild* all the place, ... V. xi. 23. 2
his hart was inly child . . . and his thought with wonder *fild*. VI. ii. 4. 9
So full they *filled* every hill and Plaine; . . . . VII. vii. 4. 5
fild her wombe with fruitfull hope of nourishment. . . . . . VII. vii. 32. 9

Filled—*Continued.*
filled with the store Of that faire sight, ... *Am.* xxxv. 9
did daunt With their great deedes, and *fild* their childrens eares? *Com. Son.* iii. 4
al the world, *fil'd* with thy wide Alarmes, ... *Proth.* 158
Fillest. That *fillest* England with thy triumphes fame. . . . . *Proth.* 151
Fillet. From her fayre head her *fillet* she undight, ... I. iii. 4. 5
Filleth. with . . . piteous plaintes, she *filleth* his dull eares, . . I. iii. 44. 2
filleth all the sea with fome, ... IV. i. 42. 5
Fillets. Binde your *fillets* faste, ... *S.C.* Ap. 133
Filling. One with great bellowes gathered *filling* ayre, . . . II. vii. 36. 1
Fills. on the soft greene grasse feeding their *fills*, ... *Gn.* 78
all the ayre it *fills*, ... I. v. 16. 9
filles with flowres fayre Floraes painted lap: . . . . II. ii. 6. 5
Nations *filles* with awful dread, ... V. Pr. 11. 5
fills the darkned world with terror and dismay. . . . . . . VII. vii. 51. 9
Whose beautie *filles* the heavens with her light, ... *H.H.B.* 228
Of Gods high praise, that *filles* the brasen sky; . . . . . . *H.H.B.* 263
Filth. gathering also *filth* him to infest, ... *Van.* iv. 11
Forst with the *filth* his egs to fling away: . . . . *Van.* iv. 12
Deformd with *filth* and fowle iniquitie; . . . . *T.M.* 122
With brutishnesse and beastlie *filth* hath stained. . . . . . *T.M.* 270
Snake . . . Long fostred in the *filth* of Lerna lake: . . . . . I. vii. 17. 3
Whose secret *filth* good manners biddeth not be told. . . . . . I. viii. 46. 9
Their blood with secret *filth* infected hath, ... II. ii. 4. 7
Ne lets her waves with any *filth* be dyde; . . . . II. ii. 9. 8
the Monster *filth* did breede: . . . . II. iv. 35. 5
sparks, seed, drops, and *filth*, do thus delay; . . . . II. iv. 35. 6
filth wipe cleane away: . . . . II. iv. 35. 8
all the blood and *filth* away was washt; . . . . II. vi. 42. 8
mucky *filth* his braunching armes annoyes, ... II. vii. 15. 8
Delightes in *filth* and fowle incontinence: . . . . II. xii. 87. 7
fell Into all *filth* and foule iniquitie, ... V. i. 5. 7
powred out of her infernall sinke Most ugly *filth*; . . . . . V. xi. 31. 7
And from his face the *filth* that did it ray; . . . . VI. iv. 23. 5
ne *filth* mote therein drowne: . . . . VI. x. 7. 5
In which what *filth* and ordure did appeare, ... VI. xii. 24. 5
Filthiness. a greene gowne . . . underneath did hide his *filthinesse*; . . . I. iv. 25. 2
To hide her shame and loathly *filthinesse*, ... II. i. 22. 5
with their *filthinesse* Polluted this same gentle soyle . . . . II. x. 9. 1
Filthy. all the waves were stain'd with *filthie* hewe. . . . . *Van.* v. 12.
Two *filthie* blots in noble gentrie; . . . . *Hub.* 734
filthie brocage, and unseemly shifts, ... *Hub.* 851
With crudled blood and *filthie* gore deformed, ... *As.* 152
Most lothsom, *filthie*, foule, and full of vile disdaine. . . . . I. i. 14. 9
she spewd out of her *filthie* maw . . . . I. i. 20. 1
Her *filthie* parbreake all the place defiled has. . . . . I. i. 20. 9
Her body, full of *filthie* sin, ... I. i. 24. 7
A *filthy* foule old woman I did vew, ... I. ii. 40. 8
by his side rode loathsome Gluttony, . . . on a *filthie* swyne. . I. iv. 21. 2
Who rough, and blacke, and *filthy*, did appeare, ... I. iv. 24. 5
her abhorred face, so *filthy* and so fowle. . . . . I. v. 30. 9
A monstrous beast ybredd in *filthy* fen He chose, ... I. vii. 16. 8
underneath his *filthy* feet did tread The sacred thinges, ... I. vii. 18. 6
That her gay garments staynd with *filthy* gore, ... I. viii. 16. 7
all the floore (too *filthy* to be told) . . . . I. viii. 35. 5
a deepe descent, . . . breathed ever forth a *filthie* banefull smell. I. viii. 39. 9
nether darkenesse fowle, nor *filthy* bands, . . . his purpose could withhold, ... I. viii. 40. 1
head . . . Was overgrowne with scurfe and *filthy* scald; . . . . I. viii. 47. 3
filthy matter from them weld; . . . . I. viii. 47. 7
when they had . . . all her *filthy* feature open showne, ... I. viii. 49. 8
The *filthy* blottes of sin to wash away. . . . . I. x. 27. 7
Enwrapt in coleblacke clowds and *filthy* smoke, ... I. xi. 44. 8
Laid first his *filthie* hands on virgin cleene, ... II. i. 10. 4
Gan burne in *filthy* lust; . . . . II. iii. 42. 5
In ragged robes and *filthy* disaray; . . . . II. iv. 4. 2
glistring glosse, darkned with *filthy* dust, ... II. vii. 4. 3
companing with feends and *filthy* Sprights . . . . II. x. 8. 6
Of *filthy* lust, contrary unto kinde; . . . . III. ii. 40. 4
filthy lust inflame, ... III. iii. 1. 6
when she is nigh defild Of *filthy* wretch? . . . . III. viii. 27. 8
Ruffled and fowly raid with *filthy* soyle, ... III. viii. 32. 2
out of that same fishers *filthy* nest . . . . III. viii. 35. 7
A *filthy* blood, or humour rancorous, ... III. x. 59. 4
the sister did in feminine And *filthy* lust exceede all womankinde, ... III. xi. 4. 2
Her face most fowle and *filthy* was to see, ... IV. i. 27. 1
fingers *filthie* with long nayles unpared, ... IV. v. 35. 4
with *filthy* bloud The place there overflowne . . . . IV. vii. 32. 8
With *filthy* lockes about her scattered wide, ... IV. viii. 23. 7
Whose waters with his *filthy* bloud it stayned; . . . . V. ii. 19. 2
He did all to peeces breake, and foyle In *filthy* durt, ... V. xi. 33. 9
their faces Most foule and *filthie* were, ... V. xii. 28. 7
Through fowle commixture of his *filthy* blot; . . . . VI. i. 8. 3
Unmard with ragged mosse or *filthy* mud; . . . . VI. x. 7. 3
Let not one sparke of *filthy* lustfull fyre Breake out, ... *Am.* lxxxiii. 1
How ever fleshes fault it *filthy* make; . . . . *H.B.* 160
soyle, In which thou wallowest like to *filthy* swyne, ... *H.H.L.* 219
Filthy-feculent. both his handes, most *filthy feculent*, . . . II. vii. 61. 4
Final. Had framed for his *finall* overthroe. . . . . *Mui.* 424
To slaughter them, and worke their *finall* bale, ... *As.* 105
resolv'd to work his *finall* smart, ... I. ix. 51. 8
surrender late His life . . . unto *finall* fate. . . . . II. x. 13. 9
worke her *finall* bale. . . . . III. vii. 21. 9
Of *finall* peace and faire attonement . . . . V. viii. 21. 8
He should his flale to *final* execution bend. . . . . V. viii. 29. 9
with *finall* force them all he overcame. . . . . V. viii. 50. 9
prove the *finall* fortune of the fight; . . . . VI. i. 38. 4
It never rests till it have wrought his *finall* bane. . . . . . . VI. vi. 8. 9

Final—*Continued.*
That monstrous Beast by *finall* force to quell, VI. xii. 22. 7
Finally. *finally* the storme impetuous *Bel.*[2] xiii. 9
finally destroy Proud Priams towne. IV. xi. 19. 6
Find. *See* **Out-find.**
Shall *finde* his state most fickle and unsure *Van.* xii. 14
for the Kidde to *fynd:* *S.C.* May 289
so coole, as no where else I *fynde:* *S.C.* Jun. 5
Can nowhere *fynd* to shroude my lucklesse pate *S.C.* Jun. 16
Such favour couth he *fynd,* *S.C.* Jul. 138
Ne can I *find* salve for my sore: *S.C.* Au. 103
fynd no part 'Of pleasure past. *S.C.* Au. 168
Diggon should soone *find* favour and ease: *S.C.* S. 253
My head besprent with hoary frost I *fynd,* *S.C.* D. 135
The Foxe, that first this cause of griefe did *finde,* *Hub.* 51
hope thereof to *finde* due remedie? *Hub.* 57
In hope to *finde* there happier successe *Hub.* 658
with him far'd some better chaunce to *fynde* *Hub.* 942
Finde nothing worthie to be writ, *T.M.* 100
none more tragick matter I can *finde* *T.M.* 155
finde nought to busie me: *T.M.* 166
Find entertainment or in Court or Schoole; *T.M.* 410
finde worthie to commend For prize of value, *T.M.* 465
Upon the streaming rivers, sport to *finde;* *Mui.* 47
where shall I *finde* lamentable cryes, *Mui.* 411
Fit matter for his cares increase would *finde,* *D.* 3
My bed the ground that hardest I may *finde;* *D.* 377
in her workmanship no pleasure *finde,* *D.* 394
because I doo not *finde* My love with them, *D.* 423
cares *finde* quiet! *D.* 447
'To live I *finde* it deadly dolorous, *D.* 449
where ever thou doest *finde* the same, *As.* 195
a straunge shepheard chaunst to *find* me out, *Col.* 60
ought could *fynd* Worth harkening to, *Col.* 366
there professours *find* small maintenance, *Col.* 705
nor God nor man can *fynd* Defence, *Col.* 875
rymes . . . for their titles sake may *find* more grace *Ded. Son.* i. 14
They cannot *finde* that path, which first was showne, I. i. 10. 4
Till that some end they *finde,* I. i. 11. 2
Then forth I went his woefull corse to *find,* I. ii. 24. 6
How does He *find* in cruell hart to hate Her, I. iii. 7. 7
all that he by right or wrong could *find,* I. iii. 18. 1
an errant knight in armes ycled, And heathnish shield, . . . they new arrived *find:* I. iv. 38. 6
Scarse could he footing *find* in that fowle way, I. v. 53. 1
cryme in her could never creature *find;* I. vi. 2. 5
The wyld woodgods, . . . There *find* the virgin, I. vi. 9. 2
henceforth nothing faire but her on earth they *find* I. vi. 18. 9
A Satyre chaunst her wandring for to *finde;* I. vi. 22. 6
Go, *find* some other play-fellowes, I. vi. 28. 9
Why doe ye . . . liking *find* to gaze on earthly mould, I. vii. 22. 4
resolving him to *find* Alive or dead; I. vii. 28. 2
If then it *find* not helpe, and breeds despaire.' I. vii. 41. 6
my chaunce . . . There for to *find* a fresh unproved knight; I. vii. 47. 2
no where could he *find* that wofull thrall: I. viii. 37. 2
his foot could *find* no flore, I. viii. 39. 7
'what secret wound Could ever *find* to grieve the gentlest hart on ground?' I. ix. 7. 9
never vowd to rest till her I *fynd:* I. ix. 15. 8
where they *find* That cursed man, I. ix. 35. 1
Arrived there, the dore they *find* fast lockt, I. x. 5. 1
There they doe *finde* that godly aged Sire, I. x. 48. 1
whenas himselfe he gan to *fynd,* I. x. 68. 1
by force unwonted passage *fynd,* I. xi. 10. 7
mounting up, they *fynd* purveyaunce meet I. xii. 13. 5
That auncient Lord gan fit occasion *finde,* I. xii. 15. 3
shall *finde* friends, if need requireth soe I. xii. 28. 8
if yourselfe, Sir knight, ye faulty *fynd,* I. xii. 30. 7
'There did I *find,* or rather I was fownd I. xii. 32. 1
Ye shall him Archimago *find,* I ghesse, I. xii. 34. 8
who tries, shall *find* no lesse.' I. xii. 34. 9
Where ever he that godly knight may *fynd,* II. i. 2. 3
By certein signes . . . He may it *fynd;* II. Pr. 4. 3
A pleasing vaine of glory he did *fynd,* II. iii. 4. 5
Both feare and hope he in her face did *finde:* II. iii. 32. 5
Who seekes with painfull toile shall honor soonest *fynd:* II. iii. 40. 9
wisht me stay till I more truth should *fynd* II. iv. 22. 9
my engreeved mind could *find* no rest, II. iv. 23. 4
shal *find* no greater enimy II. v. 1. 3
Yet in himselfe some comfort he did *find,* II. v. 14. 7
When ever his fiers handes he free mote *fynd:* II. v. 28. 4
Whom bold Cymochles traveiling to *finde,* II. vi. 2. 1
pittie could *find* place, II. vi. 33. 2
Where ever that on ground they mote him *find:* II. viii. 11. 2
Yet no where can her *find:* II. ix. 7. 8
yet no where can her *find.'* II. ix. 38. 9
in the gardins of Adonis *fynd* A goodly creature II. x. 71. 4
Where she may *finde* the substance thin and light, III. i. 43. 3
'Mongst thousands good one wanton Dame to *find:* III. i. 49. 5
Could *find* no rest in such perplexed plight, III. i. 59. 5
Here have I cause in men just blame to *find,* III. ii. 1. 1
by record of antique times I *finde* III. ii. 2. 1
faire purpose gan to *find,* III. ii. 4. 2
read where I that faytour false may *find.'* III. ii. 13. 2
'perhaps ye should it better *find:* III. ii. 13. 5
sith it is uneath to *finde* his haunt, III. ii. 16. 2
For which no reason can *finde* remedy.' III. ii. 36. 2
Ne can my ronning sore *finde* remedee, III. ii. 39. 6
this affection nothing straunge I *finde;* III. ii. 40. 5
Short end of sorrowes they therby did *finde;* III. ii. 43. 8

Find—*Continued.*
To compas thy desire, and *find* that loved knight.' III. ii. 46. 9
Full many waies she sought, but none could *find,* III. iii. 5. 3
how shall she *finde* the man? III. iii. 25. 3
such as fittest she for love could *find,* III. iv. 5. 8
To *finde* some issue thence; III. v. 3. 2
how I may her *finde,* or where?' III. v. 6. 9
in her hart *finde* highest rowme III. v. 11. 3
To seeke his Lady where he mote her *finde;* III. v. 12. 2
those two vertues strove to *fynd* The higher place III. v. 55. 4
Infinite shapes of creatures men doe *fynd* III. vi. 8. 8
Yet no'te she *find* redresse for such despight: III. vi. 40. 7
To *finde* some refuge there, and rest her wearie syde III. vii. 5. 9
I now abrode have strayd, To *fynd* them out.' III. vii. 57. 5
hardly *finde* to aggravate her griefe; III. viii. 1. 8
parture of faire Florimell To *find* him forth: III. viii. 46. 6
Untill that it an issew forth may *finde:* III. ix. 15. 7
Cannot two fairer Cities *find* this day, III. ix. 51. 4
A fit occasion for his turne to *finde.* III. x. 4. 2
he was much afraid him selfe alone to *fynd* III. x. 41. 9
surpassed . . . In beastly use, all that I ever *finde:* (*I did ever *find*) III. xi. 4. 4
If goodnesse *find* no grace, III. xi. 9. 9
'If good *find* grace, and righteousnes reward, III. xi. 10. 1
could not *find* what sence it figured: III. xi. 50. 5
Shall *find* that all the workes IV. Pr. 3. 3
That shall you win more glory than ye here *find* gaines.' IV. ii. 27. 9
evermore, when she fit time could *fynd,* IV. ii. 53. 7
such as drinck, eternall happinesse do *fynd* IV. iii. 43. 9
Cannot *find* one this girdle to invest IV. v. 18. 5
Did *find* it fit withouten breach or let IV. v. 19. 5
no where could her *find,* nor tydings of her heare.' IV. vi. 36. 9
Till I her *find,* and wreake on him that did her reave.' IV. vi. 38. 9
new occasion fayld her more to *find,* IV. vi. 46. 2
in that place where I him thought to *find,* IV. vii. 18. 2
when she did *find* Her selfe so deckt, IV. viii. 7. 5
Where was her won, and how he mote her *find* IV. viii. 22. 4
such temperance is rare And hard to *finde,* IV. viii. 29. 7
'There did I *finde* mine onely faithfull frend IV. viii. 57. 1
in this storie *find* approved plaine; IV. ix. 3. 2
There did he *find* in her delitious boure IV. ix. 6. 1
there mote *find* to please it selfe withall; IV. x. 22. 7
Whom she besought to *find* some remedie, IV. xi. 6. 7
Such oddes I *finde* twixt those, and these V. Pr. 1. 5
Shall *find* that from the point V. Pr. 5. 3
Upon wyld beasts, which she in woods did *find* V. i. 7. 8
no where could they *finde* her, V. ii. 25. 1
The greater prowesse greater perils *find* V. iii. 9. 2
Great threasure sithence we did *finde* V. iv. 13. 2
all astonisht he him selfe did *find,* V. iv. 27. 3
thraldome *find* For lending life to me, V. v. 32. 4
well I may this weene by that I *fynd,* V. v. 41. 4
I him *find* to be too proudly fed: V. v. 50. 2
In case she might *finde* favour in his eye, V. v. 55. 2
find In her false hart his bondage to unbind, V. v. 56. 4
A thousand feares, that love-sicke fancies faine to *fynde* V. vi. 3. 9
shee in her heart did *find* Many vaine fancies V. vi. 7. 6
little good could *finde,* And much lesse honour V. vi. 32. 4
will my cares unfold, in hope to *find* Your aide V. vii. 19. 4
in hope to *find* some spoyle, V. ix. 9. 2
Yet could the Seneschals no entrance *find* V. x. 32. 6
The better to beguile whom she so fond did *finde* V. xi. 23. 9
Ne ought to answere thereunto did *find;* V. xi. 64. 3
what so Envie good or bad did *fynd* V. xii. 33. 4
Ne none can *find* but who was taught them by the Muse VI. *Pr.* 2. 9
in all Antiquity So faire a patterne *finde,* VI. *Pr.* 6. 2
in what place To *find* him out, VI. i. 7. 5
Untill a Mantle she for him doe *fynd* VI. i. 15. 4
And in the eyes of men great liking *find,* VI. ii. 2. 4
Tooke in foule scorne that I such fault did *find,* VI. ii. 11. 7
when as her he by no meanes could *find,* VI. ii. 21. 1
entreated, that they might *finde* favour VI. iii. 42. 9
where he mote *fynd* Some place of succour VI. iv. 26. 4
Find remedie unsought, which seeking cannot *fynd.'* VI. iv. 28. 9
Till she Prince Arthure *fynd;* VI. v. Arg.
wonderfull to *fynd* So milde humanity VI. v. 29. 8
'Let me therefore this favour for him *finde,* VI. v. 30. 1
Finde harbour fit to comfort her great neede; VI. v. 31. 4
Whether such grace were given her . . . I doe not *fynd:* VI. vi. 43. 3
To worke by wicked treason wayes doth *find,* VI. vii. 1. 8
the steele-head no stedfast hold could *fynd,* VI. vii. 10. 8
Him often scourg'd, and forst his feete to *fynd:* VI. vii. 49. 5
To eate the flesh of men whom they mote *fynde,* VI. viii. 36. 2
Whom by the Altar he doth sitting *find* VI. viii. 50. 2
He thus replyde: 'Now surely, syre, I *find,* VI. ix. 27. 3
Ne him could *find* to fancie in her brest: VI. ix. 40. 7
Nor any footing *fynde* for overgrowen gras: VI. x. 41. 9
she resolv'd no remedy to *fynde,* VI. xi. 8. 6
He mote perceive by signes which he did *fynd,* VI. xi. 27. 8
there did they *find* . . . The selfe same flocks VI. xi. 37. 1
There did they *find* . . . That Pastorell yet liv'd; VI. xi. 41. 5
therby did *find,* and plainly feele, VII. vi. 1. 3
nor *finde* like stuffe to that: VII. vii. 7. 5
find that all things stedfastnesse do hate VII. vii. 58. 2
Yet *find* I nought on earth, *Am.* ix. 3
For my sweet Saynt some service fit will *find* *Am.* xxii. 4
In one short houre I *find* by her undonne *Am.* xxiii. 8
Such labour like the Spyders web I *fynd,* *Am.* xxiii. 13
The powre thereof, which ofte in me I *find,* *Am.* xxviii. 5
The more I *fynd* their malice to increase *Am.* xliv. 14

Find—*Continued.*
when he by chance doth *find* A feeble beast, *Am.* lvi. 3
nor in field nor bowre I her can *fynd;* *Am.* lxxviii. 7
I *fynd* my selfe but fed with fancies vayne. *Am.* lxxviii. 12
To quench the flame which they in burning *fynd;* *H.L.* 102
Shall *find* by tryall, and confesse it then, *H.B.* 89
Whose utmost parts so beautifull I *fynd;* *H.H.B.* 108
All happie joy and full contentment *fynd.* *H.H.B.* 287
Findest. Thou *findest* faulte where nys to be found, *S.C.* May 144
Findeth. whoso else in pleasure *findeth* sense, *D.* 8
double gates he *findeth* locked fast, I. i. 40. 1
findeth dew effect or soone or late; III. iv. 27. 5
Finding. *finding* Kirkrapine there slayne, I. iii. 22. 3
Her nathelesse Th' enchaunter *finding* fit for his intents II. i. 22. 8
that brave steed there *finding* ready dight, II. iii. 4. 8
finding life not yet dislodged quight, II. viii. 9. 7
Finding in it fit ports for fishers trade, II. x. 6. 8
Finding the Nymph asleepe in secret wheare, III. iv. 19. 7
finding litle leasure her to wooe III. viii. 13. 3
finding not th' Hyena to be slayne, III. viii. 44. 4
finding him unable once to weld, IV. i. 37. 3
finding that the breath gan him to fayle, IV. i. 43. 5
Ate . . . *finding* now fit opportunity To stirre up strife IV. ii. 11. 7
finding no fit seat, the lifelesse corse it left. IV. iii. 21. 9
finding there fit solitary place For wofull wight, IV. vii. 38. 5
Finding no meanes how I might us enlarge, IV. viii. 61. 7
finding in the way the scattred scarfe, V. ii. 3. 3
finding there ready prest Sir Artegall, V. viii. 9. 1
comming to the place, and *finding* there Sir Artegall, V. xii. 12. 6
He, her not *finding*, both them thus nigh dead did leave. VI. ii. 43. 9
Finding where-as some wicked beast unware VII. vi. 48. 3
In *finding* fault with her too portly pride: *Am.* v. 2
Finding a tree alone all comfortlesse, Beats on it *Am.* lvi. 7
Finds. *Findes* all things needfull for contentment meeke, *Hub.* 911
Findes greater burthen of his miserie. *T.M.* 306
Griefe *findes* some ease by him that like does beare. *D.* 67
when all drownd in deadly sleepe he *findes,* I. i. 36. 6
Morpheus . . . drowned deepe In drowsie fit he *findes:* I. i. 40. 9
He oft *finds* med'cine who his griefe imparts, I. ii. 34. 4
Whom broad awake she *findes,* in troublous fitt, I. iv. 45. 1
Night . . . She *findes* forth comming I. v. 20. 4
There him he *findes* all sencelesse and aghast, I. ix. 23. 3
Guyon . . . *Fyndes* Mordant and Amavia slaine II. i. Arg.
He oft *finds* present helpe who does his griefe impart.' II. i. 46. 9
*for his revenge Atin Cymochles *finds.* II. v. Arg.
His owne woes author, who so bound it *findes,* II. v. 1. 8
Guyon *findes* Mamon in a delve II. vii. Arg.
Belphebe *findes* him almost dead, III. v. Arg.
Whom so she fittest *findes* to serve her lust, III. vii. 50. 4
Malbecco her poursewes; *Fynds* emongst Satyres, III. x. Arg.
Fond is the feare that *findes* no remedie: III. x. 3. 3
Britomart chaceth Ollyphant; *Findes* Scudamour distrest: III. xi. Arg.
Gainst which the pallid death *findes* no defence; V. xi. 45. 5
having thought long dead she *fyndes* alive, VI. xii. 21. 2
Fine. hundred pillers . . . of *fine* Diamant *Bel.*[1] ii. 3
shine all scaly with *fine* golden plates. *Bel.*[1] ii. 10
with *fine* perle and golde puft up in heart. *Rev.* ii. 7
with pencill *fine,* Fashion the pourtraicts *Ro.* xxv. 9
In *fine,* the steele had pierced his pitth, *S.C.* F. 217
he could shewe many a *fine* knack: *S.C.* May 286
teache her tread aloft in buskin *fine,* *S.C.* O. 113
'To make *fine* cages for the Nightingale, *S.C.* D. 79
his man Reynold, with *fine* counterfesaunce, *Hub.* 667
his *fine* feates and Courtly complement; *Hub.* 692
Supplanted by *fine* falshood and faire guile; *Hub.* 788
Thereto he could *fine* loving verses frame, *Hub.* 809
ye be *fine* and nimble it to doo; *Hub.* 1000
Through his *fine* handling, and his cleanly play, *Hub.* 1015
Fine Counterfesaunce, and unhurtfull Sport, *T.M.* 197
Wrought with faire pillours and *fine* imageries; *Ti.* 96
her *fine* corpes to a bag of venim grewe. *Mui.* 352
With *fine* small cords about it stretched wide, *Mui.* 359
Nor anie skil'd in loupes of fingring *fine,* *Mui.* 366
like a Crane his necke was long and *fyne* I. iv. 21. 5
trampling the *fine* element would fiercely ramp. I. v. 28. 9
no'te without an hound *fine* footing trace. II. *Pr.* 4. 5
to uphold His ydle humour with *fine* flattery. II. iii. 9. 8
No braunch whereon a *fine* bird did not sitt; II. vi. 13. 2
more smooth and *fine,* Then Jett or Marble II. ix. 24. 2
onely womanish *fine* forgery, II. xii. 28. 8
with daintie breach Of her *fine* fingers, II. xii. 56. 5
the rude And scorned partes were mingled with the *fine*) II. xii. 59. 2
diff'ring both in willes agreed in *fine:* II. xii. 59. 7
the *fine* nets, which oft we woven see II. xii. 77. 8
Of such malengine and *fine* forgerye, III. i. 53. 8
To finger the *fine* needle and nyce thread, III. ii. 6. 8
Girlonds of flowres . . . He *fine* would dight; III. vii. 17. 6
The same she tempred with *fine* Mercury III. viii. 6. 6
Through *fine* abusion of that Briton mayd; IV. i. 7. 2
to see their fatall *fine,* IV. iii. 37. 5
was framed all of silver *fine,* V. vii. 6. 2
With many deare delights bedecked *fyne.* *Am.* lxxi. 12
wicker basket, Made of *fine* twigs, *Proth.* 25
with *fine* Fingers cropt full feateously *Proth.* 27
Fined. Soone as the chaffe should in the fan be *fynd,* *S.C.* D. 125
Fine-fingered. The most *fine-fingred* workwoman on ground, *Mui.* 260
Finely. 'Lo! how *finely* the Graces can it foote *S.C.* Ap. 109
juggle *finely,* that became him well. *Hub.* 700
small cords . . . So *finely* sponne *Mui.* 360
How ever *finely* she it faind to hyde. III. ii. 11. 5

Finely—*Continued.*
Thus *finely* did he his false nets dispred, III. x. 9. 6
With golden foyle doth *finely* over-spred Some baser metall, IV. v. 15. 2
Fineness. For more *finenesse,* with a tawdrie lace. *S.C.* Ap. 135
Finesse. on his ragged shield was writ, *Salvagesse sans finesse,* IV. iv. 39. 9
Finest. with the *finest* silkes us to aray, *Hub.* 461
wont to feede with *finest* grasse that grew, *D.* 345
and *finest* sleights devise, *Col.* 694
Of every *finest* fingers touch affrayd; III. i. 61. 5
a garland doth compose Of *finest* flowers, VI. viii. 39. 8
her locks are *finest* Gold on ground; *Am.* xv. 11
Finger. To *finger* the fine needle and nyce thread, III. ii. 6. 8
Fingered. *See* **Fine-fingered, Rosy-fingered.**
Fingering. Nor anie skil'd in loupes of *fingring* fine, *Mui.* 366
Finger's. Of every finest *fingers* touch affrayd; III. i. 61. 5
Fingers. with daintie breach Of her fine *fingers,* II. xii. 56. 5
with unwearied *fingers* drawing out The lines of life, IV. ii. 48. 3
fingers filthie with long nayles unpared, IV. v. 35. 4
cruell sword out of his *fingers* slacke Fell downe IV. vi. 21. 5
with fine *Fingers* cropt full feateously *Proth.* 27
Finish. *Finish* the storie which thou hast begunne.' *Col.* 589
Well may she speede, and fairely *finish* her intent! I. xii. 42. 9
could not at least attend To *finish* it: II. x. 68. 6
Till they with mariage meet might *finish* that accord. IV. vi. 41. 9
that I it *finish* may. IV. vi. 47. 9
which I forbore To *finish* then, VI. ix. 2. 4
Finished. when he *finisht* hath as it should be, *Col.* 410
Finishing. Not *finishing* her Queene of Faery, *Am.* xxxiii. 3
Finny. with their *finny* oars the swelling sea did sheare. III. iv. 33. 9
Along the fomy waves driving his *finny* drove. III. viii. 29. 9
Fins. with his flaggie *finnes* doth seeme to sweepe *Van.* v. 4
their brode flaggy *finnes* no fome did reare, III. iv. 33. 6
Least they their *finnes* should bruze, III. iv. 34. 5
Fir. the *Firre* that weepeth still: I. i. 9. 2
Fir-bloom. Sweet is the *Firbloome,* *Am.* xxvi. 4
Fire. *See* **Lightning-fire.**
tombling through the aire in lompe of *fire,* *Bel.*[1] vi. 10
Of this faire *fire* the faire dispersed rayes *Bel.*[1] ix. 9
beast . . . shewde his force by *fire.* *Rev.* i. 12
pitilesse throwne downe in pit of *fire.* *Rev.* iii. 14
sudden flash of heavens *fire* out brast, *Pet.* iii. 11
Of this faire *fire* the scattered rayes *Bel.*[2] xi. 9
Did blowe new *fire,* *Ro.* xi. 7
As waves, as winde, as *fire,* spred over all, *Ro.* xvi. 13
Bearing the *fire* with which heaven doth us fray, *Ro.* xvii. 2
kindling *fire* within the hollow tree, *Van.* iv. 7
from his bloodie eyes doth sparkle *fire:* *Van.* x. 12
Whose naked Armes stretch unto the *fyre,* *S.C.* F. 171
A stepdame eke, as whott as *fyre,* *S.C.* Mar. 41
Wherewith they sette all the world on *fire;* *S.C.* S. 87
The raging *fyre* that kindled at his ray. *S.C.* D. 58
seeme to flame out flakes of flashing *fyre,* *Gn.* 263
as if on *fire* he fed; *Gn.* 346
Bett back the furie of the Trojan *fyre.* *Gn.* 496
th' one with *fire* and weapons did contend *Gn.* 521
my weake bodie, set on *fire* with griefe, *Hub.* 15
Thoughts halfe devine, full of the *fire* of love, *T.M.* 363
Such high conceipt of that celestiall *fire,* *T.M.* 391
the kindly *fire* Of lustfull yongth *Mui.* 33
The sea, the aire, the *fire,* the day, the night, *Mui.* 228
I hate the *fire,* because to nought it flyes; *D.* 404
the cold began to covet heat, And water *fire;* *Col.* 848
glorious *fire* it kindled in his hart; I. Pr. 3. 4
Oft *fire* is without smoke, I. i. 12. 4
full of *fire* and greedy hardiment, I. i. 14. 1
he burnt with gealous *fire;* I. ii. 5. 6
the flashing *fier* flies, . . . out of their burning shields; I. ii. 17. 7
when corage hott The *fire* of love, . . . First kindled I. ii. 35. 2
When nigh he drew . . . He burnt in *fire;* I. iii. 34. 3
inflames the skyen With *fire* not made to burne, I. iv. 9. 9
The shaking Palsey, and Saint Fraunces *fire,* I. iv. 35. 8
His suddein eye flaming with wrathfull *fyre,* I. v. 10. 2
to slake the heavenly *fire* that raged evermore. I. v. 40. 9
the world with sword and *fire* warrayd; I. v. 48. 2
turning wrathfull *fyre* to lustfull heat, I. vi. 3. 3
that divelish yron Engin . . . Conceiveth *fyre,* I. vii. 13. 5
love fresh coles unto her *fire* did lay; I. vii. 27. 5
harmeful head, thrise heated in the *fire,* I. vii. 37. 3
sithens silence lesseneth not my *fire,* I. ix. 8. 6
blow the *fire* which them to ashes brent: I. ix. 10. 6
hide the smoke that did his *fire* display, I. ix. 16. 4
fire and brimstone, which for ever shall remaine. I. ix. 49. 9
brought unto him swords, ropes, poison, *fire,* I. ix. 50. 6
burning starres and everliving *fire,* I. x. 50. 6
flashing *fire* about him shone: I. x. 53. 9
Did burne with wrath, and sparkled living *fyre:* I. xi. 14. 2
With *fire* and sword the region to invade: I. xi. 14. 6
flames of *fire* he threw forth from his large nosethril. I. xi. 22. 9
from his wide devouring oven sent A flake of *fire,* I. xi. 26. 4
With heat, toyle, wounds, armes, smart, and inward *fire,* I. xi. 28. 2
With fowle enfouldred smoake and flashing *fire,* I. xi. 40. 2
glauncing *fire* out of the yron plaid, I. xi. 42. 5
To save his body from the scorching *fire,* I. xi. 45. 4
in his eyes did rest Yet sparkling *fyre,* I. xii. 10. 8
The housling *fire* did kindle and provide, I. xii. 37. 4
kindling *fire* at her faire-burning eye, II. ii. 7. 6
his lustfull *fyre* To kindle oft assayd, II. iii. 23. 6
all on *fire* streight way, II. iv. 6. 5
threw forth sparkes of *fyre;* II. iv. 15. 6
with my heat kindled his cruell *fyre;* II. iv. 32. 8

Fire—*Continued.*
Wrath is a *fire;* and gealosie a weede; . . . . II. iv. 35. 2
The *fire* of sparkes, the weede of little seede, ... II. iv. 35. 4
A flaming *fire* in midst of bloody field, ... II. iv. 38. 3
round about him threw forth sparkling *fire,* . . . . II. v. 2. 6
added flame unto his former *fire,* . . . . II. v. 8. 4
she sought To kindle his quencht *fyre,* . . . . II. v. 19. 9
armd with *fire* more hardly he mote him withstond. . . . . II. v. 22. 9
Whereby close *fire* into his heart does creepe: . . . . II. v. 34. 7
his brother burns in furious *fyre.* . . . . II. vi. Arg.
With wrathfull *fire* his corage kindled bright, ... II. vi. 30. 7
'O! how I burne with implacable *fyre;* . . . . II. vi. 44. 2
his whott *fyre* burnes in mine entralles bright, ... II. vi. 50. 4
with the hidden *fire* too inly warmd. . . . . II. vi. 51. 5
kindled life-devouring *fire.'* . . . . II. vii. 17. 9
eyes sparckling with fervent *fyre* . . . . II. vii. 37. 6
Some rusty knifes, some staves in *fier* warmd: . . . . II. ix. 13. 7
It might breake out and set the whole on *fyre,* . . . . II. ix. 30. 2
they of living *fire* most subtilly Were made, ... II. ix. 46. 5
burning both with fervent *fire* . . . to understond, ... II. ix. 60. 6
seeth with secret *fire* eternally, ... II. x. 26. 3
stole *fire* from heven to animate His worke, ... II. x. 70. 7
Like as a *fire,* . . . At last breakes forth . . . . II. xi. 32. 1
Her fickle hart conceived hasty *fyre,* . . . . III. i. 47. 6
Like sparkes of *fire* which fall in sclender flex, ... III. i. 47. 7
The outward sparkes of her inburning *fire;* . . . . III. i. 53. 3
from like inward *fire* that outward smoke had steemd. . . . . III. i. 55. 9
through her bones the false instilled *fire* Did spred . . . . III. i. 56. 4
no usuall *fire,* no usuall rage Yt is, ... III. ii. 37. 3
Most sacred *fyre,* that burnest mightily . . . . III. iii. 1. 1
There shall a sparke of *fire,* . . . . III. iii. 48. 2
in brave sprite it kindles goodly *fire,* . . . . III. v. 1. 8
whose faire eyes, like lamps of quenched *fire,* . . . . III. v. 29. 3
shortly grew into outrageous *fire;* . . . . III. vii. 16. 2
So whot she burned in that lustfull *fyre;* . . . . III. vii. 49. 8
Broke into open *fire* and rage extreme; . . . . III. viii. 26. 5
To burn the same with unquenchable *fire,* . . . . III. ix. 17. 7
hearing them to call For *fire* in earnest, ... III. ix. 18. 3
He was not in the cities wofull *fyre* Consum'd, ... III. ix. 40. 8
saw the wicked *fire* so furiously Consume his hart, ... III. x. 14. 5
to her he turnd, And left the *fire;* . . . . III. x. 15. 2
A flaming *fire,* ymixt with smouldry smoke . . . . III. xi. 21. 6
neither may This *fire* be quencht by any witt or might, ... III. xi. 23. 7
Whom whenas Scudamour saw past the *fire* . . . . III. xi. 26. 1
like a *fire,* when he Aegin' assayd: . . . . III. xi. 35. 2
all the world with flashing *fire* brent; . . . . III. xi. 38. 5
set it all on *fire* by force unknowen, ... IV. ii. 1. 4
Did privily put coles unto his secret *fire.* . . . . IV. ii. 11. 9
behold the dreadfull sight Of flashing *fire,* . . . . IV. ii. 16. 8
fire did flash, like lightning after thunder, ... IV. iii. 15. 8
Like sparke of *fire* that from the andvile glode, ... IV. iv. 23. 5
wrought in Lemno with unquenched *fire:* . . . . IV. v. 4. 4
New matter added to his former *fire;* . . . . IV. vi. 11. 2
Whose *fire* were better turn'd to other flame; . . . . IV. vi. 32. 3
beath'd in *fire* for steele to be in sted. . . . . IV. vii. 7. 6
ever when he burnt in lustfull *fire,* . . . . IV. vii. 19. 8
what he was whose eyes did flame with *fire;* . . . . IV. viii. 46. 8
secret flakes of lustfull *fire* . . . . IV. viii. 48. 8
raging *fire* of love to womankind, ... IV. ix. 1. 6
Ran fierce at me that *fire* glaunst from his horses hoofe. . . . . IV. x. 9. 9
in their spirits kindling zealous *fire,* . . . . IV. x. 26. 8
fire devoure the ayre, and hell them quight, ... IV. x. 35. 6
All flaming with their sacrifices *fire,* . . . . IV. x. 38. 2
In generation seeke to quench their inward *fire.* . . . . IV. x. 46. 9
So would he of the *fire* one ballaunce make, ... V. ii. 31. 3
so did the *fire* the aire; . . . . V. ii. 32. 4
flakes of *fire,* bright as the sunny ray, ... V. v. 8. 3
all on *fire* ye would her surely weene; . . . . V. v. 8. 5
To feeding of her private *fire,* . . . . V. v. 53. 7
from the Altar all about did blow The holy *fire,* . . . . V. vii. 14. 5
fire to them did threat, ... V. xi. 12. 4
That mote thy kindled courage set on *fire,* . . . . VI. ii. 37. 3
sparkling *fire* out of his furious eyne, ... VI. v. 26. 2
The beames whereof did kindle lovely *fire* In th' harts . . . . VI. vii. 28. 8
His bloody vessels wash, and holy *fire* prepare. . . . . VI. viii. 39. 9
by the twinkling of their sacred *fire,* . . . . VI. viii. 48. 2
So for to quench his *fire* he did it more augment. . . . . VI. ix. 34. 9
she past the region of the ayre And of the *fire,* . . . . VII. vi. 7. 7
Kindle fresh sparks of that immortall *fire* . . . . VII. vii. 2. 4
'Last is the *fire;* . . . . VII. vii. 24. 1
Fire to Ayre, and th' Ayre to Water sheere, ... VII. vii. 25. 6
Water fights With *Fire,* . . . . VII. vii. 25. 8
Vesta, of the *fire* aethereall; . . . . VII. vii. 26. 4
hot July boyling like to *fire,* . . . . VII. vii. 36. 1
The light whereof hath kindled heavenly *fyre* . . . . *Am.* iii. 3
Is long ere it conceive the kindling *fyre;* . . . . *Am.* vi. 6
May kindle living *fire* within my brest. . . . . *Am.* vii. 12
full of the living *fire,* Kindled above . . . . *Am.* viii. 1
Nor to the *Fire;* for they consume not ever; . . . . *Am.* ix. 8
Proud Daphne, scorning Phoebus lovely *fyre,* . . . . *Am.* xxviii. 9
My love is lyke to yse, and I to *fyre;* . . . . *Am.* xxx. 1
fire, which all things melts, ... *Am.* xxx. 10
kindle *fyre* by wonderfull devyse! . . . . *Am.* xxx. 12
Did sacrifize unto the greedy *fyre.* . . . . *Am.* xlviii. 4
Not water; for her love doth burne like *fyre:* . . . . *Am.* lv. 6
Not *fyre:* for she doth friese with faint desire. . . . . *Am.* lv. 8
in her eyes the *fyre* of love does sparke. . . . . *Am.* lxxxi. 4
Let not one sparke of filthy lustfull *fyre* Breake out, ... *Am.* lxxxiii. 1
The sparkes whereof let kindle thine own *fyre,* . . . . *Am.* lxxxv. 9
gentle furie, kindled of thy *fire.* . . . . *H.L.* 28

Fire—*Continued.*
Kindled at first from heavens life-giving *fyre,* . . . . *H.L.* 65
The earth, the ayre, the water, and the *fyre,* . . . . *H.L.* 78
Ayre hated earth, and water hated *fyre,* . . . . *H.L.* 83
Through secret sparks of his infused *fyre,* . . . . *H.L.* 97
Some sparks remaining of that heavenly *fyre,* . . . . *H.L.* 107
Which at first blowing take not hastie *fyre;* . . . . *H.L.* 174
The flaming light of that celestiall *fyre* . . . . *H.L.* 186
Once kindled through that first conceived *fyre.* . . . . *H.L.* 203
stout Aeneas in the Trojane *fyre,* . . . . *H.L.* 232
seeking to aslake thy raging *fyre,* . . . . *H.B.* 4
The wondrous matter of my *fyre* to prayse. . . . . *H.B.* 7
darted *fyre* into my feeble ghost, ... *H.B.* 24
the thing . . . that kindleth lively *fyre,* . . . . *H.B.* 58
light proceedes, which kindleth lovers *fire,* . . . . *H.B.* 100
From light of his pure *fire;* . . . . *H.B.* 179
To warme your selves at my wide sparckling *fire,* . . . . *H.H.L.* 17
To deepest hell, and lake of damned *fyre,* . . . . *H.H.L.* 89
and set thee all on *fire* With burning zeale, ... *H.H.L.* 270
fire much more then ayre, . . . appeares more pure and fayre. *H.H.B.* 48
heaven then *fire,* appeares more pure and fayre. . . . . *H.H.B.* 49
Thunder, and lightning, and tempestuous *fyre,* . . . . *H.H.B.* 181
inflame The hearts of men with selfe-consuming *fyre* . . . . *H.H.B.* 275
Firebrand. shake and shiver Her flaming *fire-brond,* . . . . *Gn.* 343
Now brought to him a flaming *fyer brond,* . . . . II. v. 22. 6
a *firebrand* shee did tosse About her head, ... III. xii. 17. 6
Firebrand of hell, first tynd in Phlegeton, ... IV. ii. 1. 1
that foule blot, that hellish *fierbrand,* . . . . *H.B.* 169
Firebrands. With their bright *firebronds* me to terrifie. . . . . *Gn.* 424
Store of *firebronds* out of her nourseries . . . . *Gn.* 508
having quencht her burning *fier-brands,* . . . . III. xi. 47. 5
Fired. with sparks of hevenlie beautie *fired.* . . . . *Col.* 563
brasen Pillours never to be *fired,* . . . . *Ti.* 410
How he their heedelesse harts with love had *fir'd,* . . . . III. vi. 15. 4
The rest she *fyr'd,* for sport, or for despight: . . . . III. x. 12. 6
he the more with furious rage was *fyred,* . . . . IV. i. 54. 7
now his courage being throughly *fired,* . . . . IV. ix. 35. 1
At sight whereof his barbarous heart was *fired,* . . . . VI. xi. 4. 1
Then doe I die, as one with lightning *fyred.* . . . . *Am.* vii. 8
Fire-mouthed. that *fire-mouthed* Dragon, horrible and bright? I. ix. 52. 9
Fire's. the *fires* scorn'd furie to detest; . . . . *Gn.* 612
Fires. *See* **Bonfires, House-fires.**
be her selfe the matter of her *fires;* . . . . *Ro.* xxiii. 8
Cupid still emongest them kindled lustfull *fyres.* . . . . III. i. 39. 9
doth enlumine all these lesser *fyres,* . . . . V. Pr. 7. 2
Together strove, and kindled wrathfull *fires:* . . . . V. iv. 4. 5
Fire-spitting. seard In smythes *fire-spitting* forge, ... II. vii. 3. 9
Firm. if aught under heaven might *firme* endure. . . . . *Bel.*[2] xiv. 8
That which is *firme* doth flit and fall away, ... *Ro.* iii. 13
Made of some matter no lesse *firme* and strong? . . . . *Ro.* ix. 8
firme is fixt, and sendeth light from farre . . . . I. ii. 1. 4
Her love is *firme,* her care continuall, ... I. viii. 1. 5
no locke so *firme* and fast, But . . . flew open . . . . I. viii. 4. 8
as pledges *firme,* right hands together joynd. . . . . I. ix. 18. 9
an yron lock did fasten *firme* and strong. . . . . II. iv. 12. 9
Firme is thy faith, whom daunger never fro me drew. . . . . II. viii. 53. 9
Right *firme* and strong, ... II. ix. 55. 4
On *firme* foundation of true bountyhed: . . . . II. xii. 1. 5
not *firme* land, nor any certein wonne, ... II. xii. 11. 4
the fates are *firme,* And may not shrinck, ... III. iii. 25. 6
were for other causes *firme* and sound; . . . . III. vii. 60. 3
with so *firme* affection were allyde, ... IV. ii. 43. 2
there no substance was so *firme* and hard, ... V. i. 10. 6
with constant *firme* intent For zeale of Justice, ... V. ix. 49. 4
No faith so *firme,* no trust can be so strong, ... V. xii. 1. 8
Firme Chastity, that spight ne blemish dare: . . . . VI. x. 27. 5
Nothing doth *firme* and permanent appeare, ... VII. vii. 56. 2
with *firme* eyes affixt the ground still viewed. . . . . VII. vii. 57. 3
More *firme* and durable then steele or brasse, ... *H.H.B.* 153
Firmament. It seem'd her top the *firmament* did rayse, ... *Bel.*[2] xiv. 5
seemed to threat the *Firmament:* . . . . *S.C.* F. 117
The liquid clowdes, and lucid *firmament;* . . . . *Hub.* 1259
beautefie the shinie *firmament,* . . . . *Hub.* 1269
looke into the Christall *firmament:* . . . . *T.M.* 506
Alcides slew, and fixt in *firmament;* . . . . *D.* 166
As the wide compasse of the *firmament* . . . . *Ded. Son.* ix. 5
Through riven cloudes and molten *firmament;* . . . . I. viii. 9. 5
Was all disperst out of the *firmament,* . . . . III. i. 67. 8
with her pineons cleaves the liquid *firmament.* . . . . III. iv. 49. 9
tosse the deepes, and teare the *firmament,* . . . . IV. ix. 23. 7
left their scorched path yet in the *firmament.* . . . . V. viii. 40. 9
Being now placed in the *firmament,* . . . . VI. x. 13. 6
all the *firmament* doth fill; . . . . *Epith.* 142
Firmer. The harder wonne, the *firmer* will abide. . . . . *Am.* vi. 4
Firmest. wondrous faith, . . . Was *firmest* fixt . . . . I. ix. 17. 5
The *firmest* flint doth in continuance weare: . . . . *Am.* xviii. 4
Firmly. His breastplate first . . . he *firmely* bound, ... *Mui.* 58
were in love so *firmly* tide. . . . . *As.* 180
She held him fast, and *firmely* did upbeare, ... I. x. 35. 8
Thenceforth it *firmely* was established, ... II. xii. 13. 8
Both *firmely* armd for every hard assay, ... II. xii. 38. 8
had his furnitures not *firmely* tyde. . . . . III. i. 11. 8
firmely bound with faithfull band, ... III. iii. 27. 6
She *firmely* hath emprisoned for ay, ... III. vi. 48. 6
So *firmely* she had sealed up her brest. . . . . III. viii. 39. 5
sure a foole I doe him *firmely* hold, ... III. ix. 8. 4
firmely fixed did abide . . . . III. ix. 24. 3
by the tailes together *firmely* bound, ... IV. iii. 42. 4
firmely following her first intent, ... IV. viii. 50. 8
To whom his faith he *firmely* ment to hold, ... IV. viii. 53. 2

Firmly—*Continued.*
Upon his usuall beast it *firmely* bound, IV. ix. 4. 8
firmely fixt they were . . . their rights to try, V. iv. 6. 1
in th' Adamantine mould . . . so *firmely* was engraved, V. vi. 2. 7
For breach of faith to her, which he had *firmely* plight. V. vi. 12. 9
like a bulwarke *firmely* did abyde, V. x. 35. 4
Bynding himselfe most *firmely* to obay, VI. i. 44. 2
firmely stayd Upon the pillours of Eternity, VII. viii. 2. 3
with her owne goodwill hir *fyrmely* tyde. *Am.* lxvii. 12
captived are So *firmely,* that ye never may remove. *Am.* lxxi. 8
they *firmely* have remained, *H.L.* 92
th' Aire . . . *firmely* bounded On everie side, *H.H.B.* 38
Firms. Upon his card and compas *firmes* his eye, II. vii. 1. 6
First. Were *first* enclosures but of salvage soyle; *Ro.* xviii. 2
all things turne to their *first* being. *Ro.* xviii. 14
raynie cloud, *first* fed With earthly vapours *Ro.* xx. 1
which was *first* but shepheards shade, *Ro.* xx. 9
shall backe reverse To their *first* discord, *Ro.* xxii. 12
The seedes, of which all things at *first* were bred, *Ro.* xxii. 13
the which at *first* was spilt Upon your walls, *Ro.* xxiv. 12
though she owe her fall to the *first* winde, *Ro.* xxviii. 9
as the seeded field greene grasse *first* showes, *Ro.* xxx. 1
Well maist thou boast . . . That thou art *first,* *Ro.* xxxii. 13
Bellay, *first* garland of free Poesie *Ro.* Env. 1
This was the *first* sourse of shepheards sorowe, *S.C.* May 130
whilome was the *first* shepheard, *S.C.* Jul. 127
The *first* of all his cote, *S.C.* Jul. 162
tell me *first* of thy flocks estate. *S.C.* S. 24
That *first* the white beare to the stake did bring. *S.C.* O. 48
boughes with bloosmes that crowned were at *firste,* *S.C.* D. 103
let us turne to our *first* businesse. *Gn.* 64
first the high Palme trees, *Gn.* 190
Which *first* Triptoleme taught how to be sowne. *Gn.* 208
back to heaven, whence she was *first* conceived, *Hub.* 3
The Foxe, that *first* this cause of griefe did finde, *Hub.* 51
The Foxe . . . Gan *first* thus plaine *Hub.* 52
I meane my Gossip privie *first* to make.' *Hub.* 70
to resolve *first* hereupon.' *Hub.* 123
so by institution Ordained *first,* *Hub.* 145
that good man . . . *first* began T' enquire *Hub.* 244
returne from whence he *first* begun, *Hub.* 306
Whom they in civill manner *first* did greete, *Hub.* 362
First, therefore, when ye have . . . Your selfe attyred, *Hub.* 487
how shall we *first* come in, That after *Hub.* 643
Thus did the Ape at *first* him credit gaine, *Hub.* 689
first gan question, whether should assay *Hub.* 997
I Did *first* devise the plot *Hub.* 1036
the two *first* whome he encountred *Hub.* 1067
First . . . he pointed a strong gard, *Hub.* 1115
What time the Ape the kingdome *first* did gaine, *Hub.* 1207
The Foxe, *first* Author of that treacherie, *Hub.* 1379
those Armes *first* give To their Grandsyres, *T.M.* 95
First comming to the world with weeping eye, *T.M.* 159
love *first* gan you to torment, *T.M.* 374
as at *first* he sprong Out of th' Almighties bosome, *T.M.* 388
die forgot from whence at *first* they sprong, *T.M.* 443
How in his cradle *first* he fostred was; *T.M.* 500
from their *first* untill their utmost date, *Ti.* 45
him, that *first* was raisde for vertuous parts, *Ti.* 451
His breastplate *first,* *Mui.* 57
'She fell away in her *first* ages spring, *D.* 239
"Alcyon! ah, my *first* and latest love! *D.* 263
The which my soule *first* conquerd and possest *D.* 300
The *first* beginners of my endles care: *D.* 301
As the Great Judge at *first* did it ordaine, *D.* 363
the time that *first* the Nymph his mother *As.* 13
It *first* growes red, and then to blew doth fade, *As.* 185
since *first* on grassie greene Shepheards kept sheep, *As.* 209
first his sister that Clorinda hight, *As.* 211
after Tityrus *first* sung his lay, *Col.* 2
first since thy turning backe *Col.* 19
her good will he got her *first* to wedde. *Col.* 131
First into many parts his streame he shar'd, *Col.* 138
An island, which the *first* to west was showne. *Col.* 271
The *first,* to which we nigh approched, *Col.* 280
There did a loftie mount at *first* us greet, *Col.* 284
Unto that Goddesse grace me *first* enhanced, *Col.* 359
When *first* the fleecie cattell have begun *Col.* 606
shortly was of all the Gods the *first.* *Col.* 806
Then *first* gan heaven . . . For to appeare, *Col.* 855
her that *first* did stir that mortall stownd. *Col.* 878
demigods they be and *first* did spring From heaven, *Col.* 917
To these *first* labours needed furtheraunce. *Ded. Son.* ii. 14
that proud people, . . . didst *first* deface: *Ded. Son.* vi. 11
In the *first* season of my feeble age, *Ded. Son.* vii. 4
Mecaenas, . . . it *first* advaunst *Ded. Son.* xiii. 4
Who *first* my Muse did lift out of the flore, *Ded. Son.* xv. 6
cannot finde that path, which *first* was showne, I. i. 10. 4
Your *first* adventure: many such I pray, I. i. 27. 8
forst me at *first* to leave My fathers kingdom' I. i. 52. 1
in the *first* flowre of my freshest age, I. ii. 23. 1
corage hott The fire of love . . . *First* kindled I. ii. 35. 3
the *first,* . . . Was sluggish Idlenesse, the nourse of sin; I. iv. 18. 5
Such one was Idlenesse, *first* of this company. I. iv. 20. 9
More old then Jove, whom thou at *first* didst breede, I. v. 22. 3
That *first* the world with sword and fire warrayd, I. v. 48. 2
Yet *first* he cast by treatie, . . . Her to persuade I. vi. 3. 6
His chaunged powres at *first* them selves not felt; I. vii. 6. 6
the lampe of highest Jove, *First* made by him I. vii. 23. 2
If death it be, it is not the *first* wound I. vii. 25. 6

First—*Continued.*
For this young Prince, when *first* to armes he fell; I. vii. 36. 7
Him thought at *first* encounter to have slaine. I. viii. 7. 5
When corage *first* does creepe in manly chest, I. ix. 9. 2
Then *first* the cole of kindly heat appeares I. ix. 9. 3
adding new Feare to his *first* amazment, I. ix. 24. 2
Who *first* us greets, and after fayre areedes I. ix. 28. 6
The *first* of them, that eldest was and best, I. x. 37. 1
The *first* and chiefest of the seven, I. x. 44. 2
from the *first* unto the last degree, I. x. 45. 7
At their *first* presence grew agrieved sore, I. x. 49. 2
first thou must a season fast and pray, I. x. 52. 7
hong still on the shield, as it at *first* was pight. I. xi. 43. 9
The tree of life, the crime of our *first* fathers fall. I. xi. 46. 9
From that *first* tree forth flowd I. xi. 48. 1
in his *first* encounter, I. xi. 53. 1
From *first* to last in your late enterprise, I. xii. 17. 3
Laid *first* his filthie hands on virgin cleene, II. i. 10. 4
Since errant armes to sew he *first* began: II. ii. 17. 5
at his *first* arrivall them began . . . to pacifie, II. ii. 21. 8
The day that *first* doth lead the yeare around, II. ii. 42. 7
to court he cast t' advaunce his *first* degree. II. iii. 5. 9
Through fortune of his *first* adventure fayre, II. iii. 7. 2
The day that *first* of Priame she was seene, II. iii. 31. 7
When *first* I heard her horn sound II. iii. 44. 9
first the Hag did thrust away; II. iv. 6. 2
Must *first* begin, . . . *First* her restraine from her reprochfull blame II. iv. 11. 2, 3
Sir Guyon left his *first* emprise, II. iv. 12. 1
yet it better *first* I thought II. iv. 30. 4
wreake my wrath on him that *first* it wrought: II. iv. 30. 5
she did *first* offend, II. iv. 31. 5
Who *first* to rayse our house to honour did begin.' II. iv. 36. 9
to Guyon *first* He boldly spake; II. iv. 39. 1
Hard is his hap that *first* fals in his jeopardee.' II. iv. 43. 9
Him *first* saluted with a sturdy stroke: II. v. 3. 7
to her captive sonne yield his *first* libertee. II. v. 17. 9
is come to that same place where *first* she wefte. II. vi. 18. 9
first did teach the cursed steele to bight II. vi. 32. 8
First got with guile, and then preserv'd with dread, II. vii. 12. 3
'The antique world, in his *first* flowring youth, II. vii. 16. 1
The measure of her meane and naturall *first* need. II. vii. 16. 9
which sight at *first* him sore aghast. II. viii. 4. 9
The metall *first* he mixt with Medaewart, II. viii. 20. 5
First prayse of knighthood is fowle outrage to deface.' II. viii. 25. 9
when breath the body *first* doth leave; II. viii. 29. 2
sith I armes and knighthood *first* did plight, II. ix. 7. 2
Fiersly at *first* those knights they did assayle, II. ix. 14. 1
First she them led up to the Castle wall, II. ix. 21. 1
Those two the *first* and last proportions are; II. ix. 22. 3
The *first* of them could things to come foresee; II. ix. 49. 1
the *first* did in the forepart sit, II. ix. 49. 6
of this lands *first* conquest did devize, II. ix. 59. 7
first taught men a woman to obay: II. x. 20. 7
An happy man in his *first* dayes he was, II. x. 22. 1
first opened The bowels of wide Fraunce, II. x. 23. 6
taught her *first* how to be conquered; II. x. 23. 8
Who him at *first* well used every way; II. x. 30. 7
he *first* wore crowne of gold for dignity. II. x. 39. 9
First Gorboman, a man of vertuous life, II. x. 44. 3
Nought els but treason from the *first* this land did foyle. II. x. 48. 9
Lucius, That *first* received Christianity, II. x. 53. 4
of the Britons *first* crownd Soveraine. II. x. 58. 7
they which sought at *first* their helping hand, II. x. 65. 8
how *first* Prometheus did create A man, II. x. 70. 5
the *first* author of all Elfin kynd; II. x. 71. 2
The *first* and eldest, which that scepter swayd, II. x. 72. 4
Elfinan, who laid Cleopolis foundation *first* of all; II. x. 72. 8
The *first* troupe was a monstrous rablement II. xi. 8. 1
Snatcht *first* the one, and then the other Jade, II. xi. 31. 2
freshly, as at *first,* prepard himselfe to fight. II. xi. 38. 9
Give over to effect his *first* intent, II. xi. 41. 3
th' Earth his mother was, and *first* him bore, II. xi. 45. 2
First through the Euxine seas II. xii. 44. 9
as the Cyprian goddesse . . . did *first* appeare: II. xii. 65. 4
how sweetly shee Doth *first* peepe foorth II. xii. 74. 5
Ne more doth florish after *first* decay, II. xii. 75. 3
shivering speare in bloody field *first* shooke, III. i. 7. 3
They stayd not to avise who *first* should bee, III. i. 18. 3
First did it shew the bitter balefull stowre, III. i. 34. 7
When *first* her tender hart was with his beautie smit. III. i. 34. 9
The *first* of them by name Gardante hight, III. i. 45. 1
first she proov'd Whether she slept or wakte: III. i. 60. 5
About their Ladye *first* they flockt arownd; III. i. 64. 1
ykindled *first* above Emongst th' eternall spheres III. iii. 1. 2
of their *first* intent gan make new dout, III. iii. 14. 3
First entering, the dreadfull Mage there fownd III. iii. 14. 6
a sore evill . . . *First* rooting tooke; III. iii. 16. 6
First ill, and after ruled wickedly; III. iii. 46. 3
Carried her forward with her *first* intent: III. iv. 50. 5
he her *first* did breed III. iv. 59. 7
to his *first* poursuit him forward still doth call. III. v. 2. 9
First she him sought in Court, III. vi. 13. 1
there is the *first* seminary Of all things that are borne III. vi. 30. 4
thither they retourne where *first* they grew: III. vi. 33. 8
first was spoken by th' Almighty Lord, III. vi. 34. 5
As it at *first* created was of yore: III. vi. 36. 5
All things from thence doe their *first* being fetch, III. vi. 37. 1
ye *first* desire to learne What end III. vi. 54. 1
'The *first* which then refused me,' III. vii. 58. 1

Fit—*Continued.*
Fit time for him thence to depart it found, . . . IV. vi. 42. 4
A leman *fit* for such a lover deare: . . . IV. vii. 34. 5
framed speaches *fit* for his behoofe, . . . IV. vii. 37. 7
fit solitary place For wofull wight, . . . IV. vii. 38. 5
Who wondring much at that so sodaine *fit*, . . . IV. ix. 29. 6
'Fresh shadowes, *fit* to shroud from sunny ray; . . . IV. x. 24. 1
Whom seeing *fit*, and with no crime defilde, . . . V. i. 6. 4
Were worke *fit* for an Herauld, not for me: . . . V. iii. 3. 6
With divers fortune *fit* for such a game, . . . V. iii. 7. 4
some fayre Franion, *fit* for such a fere, . . . V. iii. 22. 7
Yet it to none of all their loynes would *fit*, . . . V. iii. 28. 4
Fit for such Ladies and such lovely knights; . . . V. iii. 40. 5
All sodainely enflam'd with furious *fit* . . . V. iv. 39. 5
beare with you both wine and juncates *fit*, . . . V. iv. 49. 8
Instead of Curiets and bases *fit* for fight. . . . V. v. 20. 9
drew him on with hope *fit* leasure to awayt. . . . V. v. 42. 9
Yet to awayt *fit* time she weened best, . . . V. v. 44. 8
with faire words, *fit* for the time and place, . . . V. v. 55. 6
none she found so *fit* to serve that turne, . . . V. vi. 6. 3
Such was this Ladies *fit* in her loves fond accusing. . . . V. vi. 14. 9
not, as women wont, in dolefull *fit* She was dismayd, . . . V. viii. 45. 6
the franticke *fit* Her burning tongue with rage inflamed hath, V. viii. 49. 1
fit matter for another song. . . . V. viii. 51. 9
Not *fit* mongst men that doe with reason mell, . . . V. ix. 1. 4
Fit for Adicia there to build her wicked bowre. . . . V. ix. 1. 9
Fit to catch hold of all that he could weld, . . . V. ix. 11. 3
Them entertayn'd, *fit* for their dignities, . . . V. x. 5. 4
To doe whatever he thought good or *fit*: . . . V. x. 13. 3
when *fit* occasion did betyde, . . . V. xi. 6. 4
Most squalid garments, *fit* for such a day; . . . V. xii. 12. 2
when as *fit* advantage he did spy, . . . V. xii. 20. 1
Meat *fit* for such a monsters monsterous dyeat: . . . V. xii. 31. 9
With whom those graces did so goodly *fit*: . . . VI. ii. 24. 7
sith now occasion *fit* Doth fall, . . . VI. ii. 33. 1
having both found *fit* occasion, . . . VI. iii. 8. 1
The pensive *fit* of her melancholie; . . . VI. iii. 9. 3
him seemed *fit* that wounded Knight To visite, . . . VI. iii. 14. 1
no place Of lodging *fit* for any errant Knight, . . . VI. iii. 38. 8
He gan in mind conceive a *fit* reliefe . . . VI. iv. 34. 4
Being now soft and *fit* them to embrace; . . . VI. iv. 35. 7
As to them seemed *fit* time to entertaine; . . . VI. v. 24. 7
Finde harbour *fit* to comfort her great neede; . . . VI. v. 31. 4
Somewhile with merry purpose, *fit* to please, . . . VI. v. 32. 7
He to that point *fit* speaches gan to frame, . . . VI. vi. 6. 2
Untill *fit* time and place he mote espy, . . . VI. vii. 3. 4
With shepheards hooke in hand, and *fit* attyre, . . . VI. ix. 13. 8
With such queint usage, *fit* for Queenes and Kings, . . . VI. ix. 35. 2
Colin Clout should pipe, as one most *fit*; . . . VI. ix. 41. 6
to the waters fall tuning their accents *fit*. . . . VI. x. 7. 9
as *fit* occasion forth them led; . . . VI. x. 30. 2
Fit to keepe sheepe, unfit for loves content: . . . VI. x. 37. 4
Renowmed hath with hymnes *fit* for a rurall skill. . . . VII. vi. 36. 9
my weaker wit with skill inspire, *Fit* for this turne; . . . VII. vii. 2. 3
(as *fit* for warlike stoures) . . . VII. vii. 28. 7
fit for harvests toyle, . . . VII. vii. 38. 5
His plough and harnesse *fit* to till the ground, . . . VII. vii. 43. 6
wondrous beauty *fit* to kindle love; . . . VII. vii. 45. 3
wings of gold *fit* to employ. . . . VII. vii. 46. 9
This holy season, *fit* to fast and pray, . . . *Am.* xxii. 1
For my sweet Saynt some service *fit* will find. . . . *Am.* xxii. 4
the more she fervent sees my *fit*, . . . *Am.* xxxii. 9
tost with troublous *fit* Of a proud love, . . . *Am.* xxxiii. 11
Fit medicines for my bodies best reliefe. . . . *Am.* l. 4
flowres . . . For damzels *fit* to decke their lovers bowres. . . . *Am.* lxiv. 4
on earth have found one *fit* for mate, . . . *Am.* lxvi. 6
What trophee then shall I most *fit* devize, . . . *Am.* lxix. 5
fit to entertayne The greatest Prince . . . *Am.* lxxvii. 3
Fit for the handmayd of the Faery Queene. . . . *Am.* lxxx. 14
Fit for so joyfull day: . . . *Epith.* 115
Fit for her selfe, adorning it with spoyle . . . *H.B.* 118
Their fleshy bowre, most *fit* for their delight, . . . *H.B.* 123
A pallace *fit* for such a virgin Queene. . . . *H.B.* 126
Fit to receive the seede of vertue strewed; . . . *H.B.* 138
In praise of that mad *fit* which fooles call love, . . . *H.H.L.* 9
most *fit* For so great powre and peerelesse majesty, . . . *H.H.B.* 185
daintie gemmes *Fit* to decke maydens bowres, . . . *Proth.* 15
Fit for so goodly stature, . . . *Proth.* 172
Fitly. want I words to speake it *fitly* forth: . . . *Col.* 625
In greene vine leaves he was right *fitly* clad, . . . I. iv. 22. 1
In his big base them *fitly* answered; . . . II. xii. 33. 2
To her this song most *fitly* is addrest, . . . IV. Pr. 4. 8
So *fitly* now here commeth next in place, . . . IV. v. 2. 1
That for another Canto will more *fitly* fall. . . . V. vii. 45. 9
Fits. Colin *fittes* such famous flight to scanne; . . . *S.C.* O. 88
So many furies and sharpe *fits* did haunt, . . . I. xi. 27. 4
how, or where, here *fits* not tell. . . . II. ii. 11. 9
Soone into other *fitts* he was transmewd, . . . II. iii. 37. 4
furious *fitts* at earst quite weren quaild: . . . II. iv. 14. 4
with sharpe *fits* thy tender hart oppresseth sore: . . . III. iii. 21. 9
sweete love gentle *fitts* emongst them throwes, . . . III. vi. 41. 5
with such unquiet *fits* Her selfe there close afflicted . . . V. vi. 15. 1
Sometimes I joy when glad occasion *fits*, . . . *Am.* liv. 5
here *fits* not well Olde woes, but joyes, to tell . . . *Proth.* 141
Fitted. Two fellowes might no where be better *fitted*. . . . *Hub.* 50
none should be out shut, sith all of loves were *fitted*. . . . IV. i. 12. 9
now himselfe he *fitted* had right well With two companions . . . IV. i. 32. 6
round about her tender wast it *fitted* well. . . . V. iii. 27. 9
Fitter. none *fitter* then this to applie. . . . *S.C.* F. 100
The *fytter* they my carefull case to frame: . . . *S.C.* Jun. 78

Fitter—*Continued.*
The forest wide is *fitter* to resound . . . *S.C.* Au. 159
Is not a *fitter* for this turne than yee: . . . *Hub.* 1002
Those now renew, as *fitter* for this place. . . . *T.M.* 378
borne to heaven, for heaven a *fitter* pray; . . . *D.* 164
Much *fitter* than the Lyon which with toyle Alcides slew, . . . *D.* 165
Fitter, perhaps, to thonder Martiall stowre, . . . *Ded.Son.* viii. 11
Proffer thy giftes, and *fitter* servaunts entertaine. . . . II. vii. 9. 9
forged showes, as *fitter* beene For courting fooles . . . VI. v. 38. 7
shortest night, when longest *fitter* weare: . . . *Epith.* 272
Fittest. devise A pasport for us both in *fittest* wize . . . *Hub.* 196
were *fittest* exercise Cattell to keep, . . . *Hub.* 282
Then *fittest* are these ragged rimes for mee, . . . *T.M.* 545
As *fittest* flowres to deck his mournfull hearse. . . . *As.* Interl. 228
two . . . *fittest* for to forge true-seeming lyes: . . . I. i. 38. 7
round about in *fittest* steades did place, . . . II. xi. 6. 2
such as *fittest* she for love could find, . . . III. iv. 5. 8
Whom so she *fittest* findes to serve her lust, . . . III. vii. 50. 4
Found it the *fittest* soyle for their abode, . . . III. ix. 49. 5
One prison *fittest* is to hold us two. . . . IV. xii. 10. 7
Whom she thought *fittest* for that businesse; . . . V. iv. 48. 2
The Blatant Beast the *fittest* meanes they found . . . VI. v. 14. 8
fittest is, that all contented rest With that they hold: . . . VI. ix. 29. 8
At length, when they occasion *fittest* found, . . . VI. xi. 42. 1
here falleth *fittest* to unfold Her antique race . . . VII. vi. 2. 1
as *fittest* for her game, . . . VII. vi. 39. 1
Fitteth. it *fitteth* best For Cupids man . . . IV. x. 54. 6
the use of armes, which . . . *fitteth* most . . . VI. ii. 32. 7
Fitting. *See* **Ill-fitting.**
fitting gestures to her purpose frame, . . . I. vii. 1. 6
for her humor *fitting* purpose faine, . . . I. vii. 38. 7
On which they lowly sitt, and *fitting* purpose frame. . . . I. xii. 13. 9
With spightfull speaches, *fitting* with her well; . . . V. v. 10. 4
What vertue is so *fitting* for a knight, . . . VI. ii. 1. 1
Drawne of two fishes, for the season *fitting*, . . . VII. vii. 43. 3
Five. *Five* joints thereof he hewd, . . . I. xi. 39. 9
Five sonnes he left, . . . II. x. 44. 1
all the sonnes of these *five* brethren raynd . . . II. x. 45. 6
The other *five five* sondry wayes he sett . . . II. xi. 7. 1
Against the *five* great Bulwarkes of that pyle, . . . II. xi. 7. 2
There those *five* sisters had continuall trade, . . . II. xii. 30. 8
'*Five* daies there be since he (they say) was slaine, . . . III. v. 10. 1
Of Alexander, and his Princes *five* . . . IV. i. 22. 8
Had left her now but *five* of all that brood: . . . V. x. 8. 2
Fix. On that bright Sunne of Glorie *fixe* thine eyes, . . . *H.H.B.* 139
Fixed. *See* **Fast-fixed, Infixed.**
While on this Lawrell *fixed* was mine eie, . . . *Pet.* iii. 8
all his minde on honour *fixed* is, . . . *Hub.* 771
Therein two deadly weapons *fixt* he bore, . . . *Mui.* 81
Alcides slew, and *fixt* in firmament; . . . *D.* 166
firme is *fixt*, and sendeth light from farre . . . I. ii. 1. 4
his eies be *fixt* before. . . . I. iii. 30. 8
wondrous faith . . . Was firmest *fixt* in myne extremest case. I. ix. 17. 5
with staring eyes *fixed* askaunce, . . . II. vii. 7. 5
fixed at his backe to cut his ayery wayes. . . . II. viii. 5. 9
fixed is On one that worthy may perhaps appeare; . . . III. ii. 42. 2
therein *fixt* his throne, . . . III. iii. 33. 6
firmely *fixed* did abide . . . III. ix. 24. 3
The worlds foundations from his centre *fixt*: . . . III. xii. 2. 4
evermore on Daunger *fixt* his eye, . . . III. xii. 12. 7
nothing could my *fixed* mind remove, . . . IV. vii. 16. 5
stedfast still her eyes did *fixed* rest, . . . IV. x. 49. 7
upon the Goddesse face Mine eye was *fixt*, . . . IV. x. 56. 2
firmely *fixt* they were . . . their rights to try, . . . V. iv. 6. 1
Yet in my truthes assurance I rest *fixed* fast.' . . . V. v. 38. 9
The eyes of all which thereon *fixed* beene, . . . VI. Pr. 6. 7
His poysnous point deepe *fixed* in his hart . . . VI. x. 31. 2
These marchants *fixed* eyes did so amaze, . . . VI. xi. 13. 6
To Joves faire palace *fixt* in heavens hight; . . . VII. vi. 15. 2
Their joy . . . Is *fixed* all on that which now they see; . . . *H.H.B.* 272
Fixeth. He thereon *fixeth* all his fantasie, . . . *H.B.* 228
Flag. A *flag* in her top-gallant, . . . *Van.* ix. 3
whose fethers, nothing flitt, Doe yet but *flagg*, . . . *Ded. Son.* ii. 8
Flaggy. with his *flaggie* finnes doth seeme to sweepe . . . *Van.* v. 4
His *flaggy* winges . . . Were like two sayles, . . . I. xi. 10. 1
their brode *flaggy* finnes no fome did reare, . . . III. iv. 33. 6
with his *flaggy* winges Beates downe both leaves and buds . . . III. vi. 39. 7
Flags. Amongst the *flags* and covert round about. . . . V. ii. 54. 6
faulcon . . . That *flags* awhile her fluttering wings beneath, . . . *H.H.B.* 27
Flail. in his hand an yron *flale* did hould, . . . V. i. 12. 8
with his iron *flale* at it let flie, . . . V. ii. 21. 2
layd on load with his huge yron *flaile*, . . . V. ii. 24. 2
when at them he with his *flaile* gan lay, . . . V. ii. 53. 5
with few sowces of his yron *flale* . . . V. iv. 24. 6
He with his yron *flaile* amongst them thondred, . . . V. v. 19. 2
to lay about With his rude yron *flaile*, . . . V. vi. 30. 2
He with his yron *flale* did thresh so thin, . . . V. vii. 35. 7
He should his *flale* to final execution bend, . . . V. viii. 29. 9
he with his yron *flayle* Gan drive at him . . . V. ix. 19. 2
mard the swinging of her *flaile*. . . . V. xi. 29. 6
With his huge *flaile* began to lay about; . . . V. xi. 47. 7
chiefly Talus with his yron *flayle*, . . . V. xi. 59. 4
Would her have chastiz'd with his yron *flaile*, . . . V. xii. 43. 3
Flake. from his wide devouring oven sent A *flake* of fire, . . . I. xi. 26. 4
as it had beene a *flake* Of lightning . . . III. ii. 5. 7
With his bright Tead that flames with many a *flake*, . . . *Epith.* 27
Flakes. seeme to flame out *flakes* of flashing fyre, . . . *Gn.* 263
Their fluttring arrowes, thicke as *flakes* of snow, . . . II. xi. 18. 2
casting secret *flakes* of lustfull fire . . . IV. viii. 48. 8
flakes of fire, bright as the sunny ray, . . . V. v. 8. 3

Flame. a kindled *flame,* Mounting like waves . . . . *Bel.*[1] ix. 1
shoure Gan quench the glystering *flame*. . . . . *Bel.*[1] ix. 12
Upon an hill a bright *flame* . . . Waving aloft . . . . *Bel.*[2] xi. 1
Of Sommers *flame,* nor of Winters threat, ... *S.C.* F. 20
seeme to *flame* out flakes of flashing fyre, ... *Gn.* 263
in his flesh endur'd the scorching *flame,* . . . . *Gn.* 607
quench the *flame* of furious despight, ... I. v. 14. 5
every head with fyrie tongue did *flame,* . . . . I. viii. 6. 3
The scorching *flame* sore swinged all his face, ... I. xi. 26. 6
In her faire eyes two living lamps did *flame,* . . . . II. iii. 23. 1
added *flame* unto his former fire, ... II. v. 8. 4
arm'd with raging *flame*. . . . . II. xi. 23. 9
Yt seemd thenchaunted *flame* which did Creusa wed. . . . . II. xii. 45. 9
as a cole to kindle fleshly *flame,* . . . . III. i. 50. 2
ne ought my *flame* relent, ... III. ii. 43. 4
Ne slake the fury of her cruell *flame,* . . . . III. ii. 52. 2
breake forth into bright burning *flame,* . . . . III. iii. 48. 6
Closely the wicked *flame* his bowels brent, ... III. vii. 16. 1
kindled heat that soone in *flame* forth brust: . . . . III. viii. 25. 4
seeing them resolvd indeed To *flame* the gates, ... III. ix. 18. 2
Shewing desire her inward *flame* to slake. . . . . III. ix. 31. 4
Gathred the Trojan reliques sav'd from *flame,* . . . . III. ix. 36. 8
all men busie to suppresse the *flame,* . . . . III. x. 16. 2
Assayld the *flame;* the which . . . gave place, ... III. xi. 25. 4
all the walles did seeme to *flame:* . . . . III. xi. 38. 6
made the sparckling waves . . . *flame* with gold; . . . . . III. xi. 41. 4
that fained dreadfull *flame,* . . . . III. xii. 43. 2
Ne in their frosen hearts feele kindly *flame;* . . . . IV. Pr. 2. 2
Whose fire were better turn'd to other *flame;* . . . . IV. vi. 32. 3
what he was whose eyes did *flame* with fire; . . . . IV. viii. 46. 8
quenched is with Cupids greater *flame:* . . . . IV. ix. 2. 2
odours rising from the altars *flame*. . . . . IV. x. 37. 3
My children and my people, burnt in *flame* . . . . V. xi. 19. 7
And *flame* forth honour in thy noble brest; . . . . VI. ii. 37. 4
his heart did inly *flame* With wrathfull fury . . . . VI. iii. 43. 4
for to shrowde in shade from Phoebus *flame,* . . . . VII. vi. 39. 3
His face with bashfull blood did *flame,* . . . . *Epig.* iii. 5
now t' asswage the force of this new *flame,* . . . . *H.L.* 8
To quench the *flame* which they in burning fynd; . . . . . *H.L.* 102
th' immortall *flame* Of heavenly light, ... *H.L.* 115
And kindled *flame* in all their inner parts, ... *H.L.* 124
Somewhat to slacke the rigour of my *flame?* . . . . *H.L.* 152
To reade my fault, and, wondring at my *flame,* . . . . . . *H.H.L.* 16
Kindled the *flame* of His consuming yre, ... *H.H.L.* 86

Flamed. So *flam'd* his eyne with rage and rancorous yre; . . I. xi. 14. 7
So easie was to quench his *flamed* minde . . . . II. vi. 8. 6
gave light, and *flamd* continually; . . . . II. ix. 46. 4
flam'd with zeale of vengeance inwardly, ... V. i. 14. 7

Flames. dew . . . gan quench those precious *flames;* . . . . *Bel.*[2] xi. 12
Nor the swift furie of the *flames* aspiring, ... *Ro.* xiii. 1
as ye see huge *flames* spred diverslie, ... *Ro.* xvi. 9
lightly slake The *flames* which love . . . . *S.C.* Jun. 86
shed his whirling *flames* on either side, ... *Gn.* 159
mouthes doo bay And barke out *flames,* . . . . *Gn.* 346
Flames, weapons, wounds, in Greeks fleete to have tynde. . *Gn.* 504
The Dorick *flames* consum'd the Iliack posts. . . . . *Gn.* 549
Where Phlegeton with quenchles *flames* doth burne; . . . . *Gn.* 622
As raging *flames* who striveth to suppresse.' . . . . I. ii. 34. 6
scorching *flames* of fierce Orions hound; . . . . I. iii. 31. 6
hurle not flashing *flames* upon that Paynim bold? . . . . . I. vi. 5. 9
Hurles forth his thundring dart . . . Enrold in *flames,* . . . I. viii. 9. 4
sparkes . . . troubled once, into huge *flames* will grow; . . I. ix. 8. 2
told, it *flames;* and, hidden, it does glow, ... I. ix. 8. 7
Those creeping *flames* by reason to subdew, ... I. ix. 9. 6
Beacons . . . Send forth their *flames* . . . . I. xi. 14. 4
flames of fire he threw forth from his large nosethril. . . . I. xi. 22. 9
Huge *flames* that dimmed all the hevens light, ... I. xi. 44. 3
Doth belch out *flames,* and rocks in peeces broke, ... I. xi. 44. 6
rend the ratling skyes with *flames* of fouldring heat. . . . II. ii. 20. 9
He hath a sword that *flames* like burning brond. . . . . . . II. iii. 18. 5
Burning in *flames,* yet no *flames* can I see, ... II. vi. 45. 3
'These *flames,* these *flames*' (he cryde) 'doe me torment.' . . II. vi. 49. 5
'What *flames,*' (quoth he), ... II. vi. 49. 6
'Harrow! the *flames* which me consume,' . . . . II. vi. 49. 8
avarice gan through his veines inspire His greedy *flames,* . . II. vii. 17. 9
it in *flames* of Aetna wrought apart, ... II. viii. 20. 7
Nourish the *flames* which they are warmd upon, ... II. x. 26. 5
Yt now devoures with *flames* and scorching heat, ... II. xi. 32. 8
wide nosethrils burnd With breathed *flames,* . . . . III. ix. 22. 4
'out of the *flames* for safegard fled, ... III. ix. 41. 2
she saw aloft appeare The Trojan *flames* . . . . III. x. 12. 8
To quench the *flames* which she had tyn'd before, ... III. x. 13. 3
Soone as the cruell *flames* yslaked were, ... III. x. 17. 1
Out of the *flames* which he had quencht whylere, ... III. x. 17. 3
So to her yold the *flames,* . . . . III. xi. 25. 9
bad the stubborne *flames* to yield him way: . . . . III. xi. 26. 4
forth in *flames* did fly. . . . . III. xii. 9. 9
Those dreadfull *flames* she also found delayd . . . . III. xii. 42. 7
Misdeeming sure that her those *flames* did burne; . . . . . III. xii. 45. 5
The furious *flames* of malice to asswage. . . . . IV. ii. 28. 4
Claribell enraged rife With fervent *flames,* . . . . IV. ix. 21. 4
Into outragious *flames* unwares did grow, ... V. vii. 14. 7
did streight devoure Both *flames* and tempest: . . . . V. vii. 15. 6
all the troublous stormes asswage And raging *flames,* . . . . V. vii. 23. 2
fervour of his *flames* somewhat adaw . . . . V. ix. 35. 4
inly burnt with *flames* most raging whot, ... VI. xi. 4. 2
dreadfull thunder-claps . . . With *flames* and flashing lights . VII. vii. 23. 9
and makes his *flames* to heaven aspire. . . . . *Am.* vi. 8
Burning in *flames* of pure and chast desyre: . . . . *Am.* xxii. 12
feele my *flames* augmented manifold! . . . . *Am.* xxx. 8

Flames—*Continued.*
all these *flames,* in which I fry, ... *Am.* xxxii. 5
With his bright Tead that *flames* with many a flake, ... *Epith.* 27
Through seas, through *flames,* . . . . *H.L.* 228

Flaming. All *flaming* downe she fell . . . . *Bel.*[1] vi. 11
The faithfull man with *flaming* countenaunce, ... *Rev.* iii. 2
All *flaming* downe she . . . was felde, ... *Bel.*[2] vii. 11
shake and shiver Her *flaming* fire-brond, ... *Gn.* 343
flaming mouthes of steedes, unwonted wilde, . . . to rayne: . I. iv. 9. 3
passion did . . . torment The *flaming* corage . . . . I. v. 1. 6
His suddein eye *flaming* with wrathfull fyre, ... I. v. 10. 2
Cerberus . . . lilled forth his bloody *flaming* tong: . . . . . I. v. 34. 4
From *flaming* mouth bright sparckles fiery redd, ... I. vii. 31. 7
beast; . . . threatned all his heades like *flaming* brandes. . . I. viii. 12. 6
Ne reard above the earth his *flaming* creast, ... I. xii. 2. 3
the morning starre . . . with *flaming* lockes bedight, ... I. xii. 21. 6
His *flaming* head did hasten for to steep, ... II. ii. 46. 3
A *flaming* fire in midst of bloody field, ... II. iv. 38. 3
With that he drew his *flaming* sword, ... II. v. 6. 1
Now brought to him a *flaming* fyer brond, ... II. v. 22. 6
Yet nought can quench mine inly *flaming* syde, ... II. vi. 44. 3
damned ghoste In *flaming* Phlegeton . . . . II. vi. 50. 9
More whott then Aetn', or *flaming* Mongiball . . . . II. ix. 29. 7
Now seeming *flaming* whott, ... II. ix. 39. 5
a blazing starre doth . . . *flaming* lockes dispredd, ... III. i. 16. 6
with her *flaming* sword about her layd, ... III. i. 66. 2
To seeke young men to quench her *flaming* thrust, ... III. vii. 50. 2
To dry them selves by Vulcanes *flaming* light, ... III. ix. 19. 8
A *flaming* fire, ymixt with smouldry smoke . . . . III. xi. 21. 6
His *flaming* furie sought to have assuaged . . . . IV. i. 54. 3
Shooting forth farre away two *flaming* streames, ... IV. viii. 39. 3
All *flaming* with their sacrifices fire, ... IV. x. 38. 2
both adorn'd with lampes of *flaming* light; . . . . V. iii. 19. 4
all the Temple put in jeopardy Of *flaming,* . . . . V. vii. 14. 9
So long as in his steedes the *flaming* breath did last. . . . . V. viii. 33. 9
fenst himselfe about with many a *flaming* brand. . . . . . . V. viii. 35. 9
All *flaming* with revenge and furious despight. . . . . V. viii. 46. 9
Above the earth upreard his *flaming* head, ... VI. i. 31. 2
With *flaming* sword in hand his terror more to breed. . . . . VI. vii. 11. 9
a thousand torches *flaming* bright Doe burne, ... *Epith.* 410
The *flaming* light of that celestiall fyre . . . . *H.L.* 186
bounded On everie side, with pyles of *flaming* brands, ... *H.H.B.* 39
Endure their Captains *flaming* head to see? . . . . *H.H.B.* 60
sparke Which darted is from Titans *flaming* head, ... *H.H.B.* 163

Flaminius. stout *Flaminius,* whose devotion Taught him . . . *Gn.* 611

Flank. her *flank* wide rended. . . . . *Bel.*[2] vi. 11
He smote his courser in the trembling *flanck,* . . . . II. iii. 6. 5
Which mote the feebled Britons strongly *flancke* . . . . . . IV. xi. 36. 3
Right in the *flanke* him strooke with deadly dreare, ... V. xii. 20. 5

Flanked. *flancked* both the bridges sides along, ... IV. x. 7. 4

Flaring. with rude *flaring* lockes About her eares, ... V. xii. 38. 8

Flash. *See* **Flush, Lightning-flash.**
sudden *flash* of heavens fire out brast, ... *Pet.* iii. 11
this brave monument with *flash* did rend. . . . . *Bel.*[2] iii. 14
fire did *flash,* like lightning after thunder, ... IV. iii. 15. 8
from her eies did *flash* out fiery light, ... V. vi. 38. 8

Flashed. he rudely *flasht* The waves about, ... II. vi. 42. 6
the rosy red *Flasht* through her face, ... III. ii. 5. 7
from the same the fierie sparkles *flasht,* . . . . IV. iii. 25. 8
through her eyes like sudden lightning *flashed,* . . . . . . V. v. 30. 3

Flashing. seeme to flame out flakes of *flashing* fyre, ... *Gn.* 263
the *flashing* fier flies, . . . out of their burning shields; . . . I. ii. 17. 7
While *flashing* beames do daze his feeble eyen, ... I. iv. 9. 6
With *flashing* thunderbolt ywounded sore: . . . . I. v. 40. 6
hurle not *flashing* flames upon that Paynim bold? . . . . . I. vi. 5. 9
amazd At *flashing* beames of that sunshiny shield, ... I. viii. 20. 2
flashing fire about him shone: . . . . I. x. 53. 9
fire, that *flashing* in his beard Him all amazd, ... I. xi. 26. 4
With fowle enfouldred smoake and *flashing* fire, ... I. xi. 40. 2
face The *flashing* blood with blushing did inflame, ... II. ix. 43. 3
all the world with *flashing* fire brent; . . . . III. xi. 38. 5
behold the dreadfull sight Of *flashing* fire, ... IV. ii. 16. 8
Out of her steely armes were *flashing* seene, ... V. v. 8. 4
the *flashing* Levin haps to light Uppon two stubborne oakes, . V. vi. 40. 1
dreadfull thunder-claps . . . With flames and *flashing* lights . VII. vii. 23. 9

Flasket. they gathered flowers to fill their *flasket,* . . . . . *Proth.* 26

Flat. Badde is the best; (this English is *flatt.*) . . . . *S.C.* S. 105
The woodborne people fall before her *flat,* . . . . I. vi. 16. 1
falling *flat* great humblesse he did make, ... I. xii. 25. 6
fell *flatt* to ground for feare, ... II. iii. 6. 8
To seize upon his foe *flatt* lying on the marle. . . . . . . II. xi. 33. 9
flat refusd to have adoe with mee, ... III. vii. 58. 3
evermore she him refused *flat,* . . . . III. viii. 39. 3
he *flat* refused To take me up . . . . VI. ii. 22. 2
Fell *flat* to ground, ne word unto him sayd, ... VI. vii. 25. 8

Flatling. Tho with her sword on him she *flatling* strooke, . . V. v. 18. 1

Flatly. They were in doubt, and *flatly* set abord. . . . . . . *Hub.* 324
flatly he of entrance was refusd. . . . . III. ix. 12. 6
whether thwart or *flatly* it did lyte, ... VI. vi. 30. 8

Flats. both from rocks and *flats* it selfe could wisely save. . II. vi. 5. 9

Flatter. when her listed she could fawne and *flatter;* . . . . VI. vi. 42. 6
When I doe praise her, say I doe but *flatter:* . . . . *Am.* lxxxiv. 2

Flatterer. all the fawning of the *flatterer*. . . . . III. viii. 38. 9

Flatteries. Bad counsels, prayses, and false *flatteries:* . . . . II. xi. 10. 8

Flattering. The *flattring* fruite is fallen to grownd before, . . *S.C.* D. 106
with smooth *flattering* Doo fawne on you, ... *Ti.* 200
when he saw his *flatt'ring* artes to fayle, ... I. vi. 5. 1
with faire countenance and *flattring* style . . . . II. i. 8. 5
Through his faire daughters face and *flattring* word. . . . . II. x. 66. 5
With *flattering* wordes he sweetly wooed her, ... III. viii. 38. 6

Flattering—*Continued.*
So her with *flattering* words he first assaid; . . . VII. vi. 43. 4
she with *flattring* smyles weake harts doth guyde Unto her love, *Am.* xlvii. 5
with false beauties *flattring* bait misled, . . . *H.H.B.* 290

Flattery. he hates fowle leasings, and vile *flatterie,* . . . *Hub.* 733
small gaines, but shameles *flatterie,* . . . *Hub.* 850
They feede the eares of fooles with *flattery,* . . . *T.M.* 323
to uphold His ydle humour with fine *flattery.* . . . II. iii. 9. 8
Some by close shouldring; some by *flatteree;* . . . II. vii. 47. 3
he loathd leasing and base *flattery,* . . . VI. i. 3. 8

Flavia. Ne thee lesse worthie, gentle *Flavia,* . . . *Col.* 572

Flaw. From that first *flaw* him selfe right well defended. . . . V. v. 6. 7

Flax. Like sparkes of fire which fall in sclender *flex,* . . . III. i. 47. 7
That he thereon should spin both *flax* and tow; . . . V. v. 23. 3

Fled. hys passing skil with him is *fledde,* . . . *S.C.* Jun. 91
All suddenly dismaid, . . . He *fled* abacke . . . *Gn.* 298
Out of the land is *fled* away and gone. . . . *Gn.* 360
Fled back to heaven, whence she was first conceived, . . . *Hub.* 3
They *fled* farre off, . . . *Hub.* 576
would have *fled* with terror all dismayde. . . . *Hub.* 956
the beasts therein *Fled* fast away . . . *Hub.* 1348
as one whose wits were reft, *Fled* here and there, . . . *Hub.* 1357
the false Foxe . . . *Fled* closely forth, . . . *Hub.* 1360
from beam to beame he *fled* All breathles, . . . *Hub.* 1373
From my unhappie neighborhood farre *fled,* . . . *Ti.* 146
Fled back too soone unto his native place; . . . *Ti.* 291
In bloodie streames foorth *fled* . . . *Mui.* 439
Revoked life, that would have *fled* away, . . . *D.* 188
Lookt for her knight, who far away was *fled,* . . . I. ii. 7. 7
from him *fled* away with all her powre; . . . I. ii. 20. 4
her pitcher downe she threw, And *fled* away: . . . I. iii. 11. 7
Full fast she *fled,* ne ever lookt behynd, . . . I. iii. 12. 1
the whiles the royall Mayd *Fledd* farre away, . . . I. vi. 47. 9
leaving all behind her *fled* away: . . . I. viii. 25. 6
Shee, . . . *Fled* to the wastfull wildernesse apace, . . . I. viii. 50. 3
as he *fledd* his eye was backward cast, . . . I. ix. 21. 5
Fledd fast away, halfe dead with dying feare; . . . I. ix. 30. 6
That bare-head knight . . . Would faine have *fled,* . . . I. ix. 34. 8
The cloudes before him *fledd* for terror great, . . . I. xi. 10. 8
Some feard, and *fledd;* some feard, and well it faynd; . . . I. xii. 10. 1
And now is *fled:* . . . II. i. 30. 9
As hynd from her, so she *fled* from her enimy. . . . II. ii. 7. 9
Both *fled* attonce, . . . II. iii. 19. 9
As through the flouring forrest rash she *fled,* . . . II. iii. 30. 7
So turned her about, and *fled* away apace. . . . II. iii. 42. 9
She *fled* away with ghastly dreriment, . . . II. iv. 31. 8
Eftsoones he *fled* away, and might no where be seene. . . . II. iv. 46. 9
Fledd fast away to tell his funerall . . . II. v. 25. 8
art thus fowly *fledd* from famous enimy?' . . . II. vi. 39. 9
The whiles false Archimage and Atin *fled* apace. . . . II. viii. 56. 9
A while they *fled,* but soone retournd againe . . . II. ix. 15. 1
in the chace was slaine of them that *fled,* . . . II. x. 57. 3
the sonnes of Constantine, which *fled,* . . . II. x. 67. 1
how the time was *fled* they quite forgate; . . . II. x. 77. 4
fast the land behynd them *fled* away. . . . II. xi. 4. 6
fled asonder, and him fell before; . . . II. xi. 19. 3
fled fast away for feare: . . . II. xi. 25. 6
as the winged wind his Tigre *fled,* . . . II. xi. 26. 1
yet he *fled* apace, . . . II. xi. 27. 1
nathemore forth *fled* his groning spright, . . . II. xi. 38. 8
the rest *Fled* all away . . . II. xii. 81. 7
fledd so fast that nothing mote him hold, . . . III. i. 15. 8
Still as she *fledd* her eye she backward threw, . . . III. i. 16. 1
from them *fled,* as light-foot hare from vew . . . III. iv. 46. 4
that way in which that Damozell Was *fledd* afore, . . . III. iv. 47. 9
That fearefull Ladie *fledd* from him, . . . III. iv. 50. 2
That fast she from him *fledd,* . . . III. iv. 51. 3
that fierce foster, which late *fled* away, . . . III. v. 18. 5
Out of her fleshly ferme *fled* to the place of paine. . . . III. v. 23. 9
he would have *fled* into the wood; . . . III. v. 25. 1
She *fled* into the wildernesse a space, . . . III. vi. 10. 3
Was from her *fled* as flit as ayery Dove, . . . III. vi. 11. 4
(So from her often he had *fled* away, . . . III. vi. 11. 6
in his frowardnes from her was *fled,* . . . III. vi. 20. 8
fledd so fast from that same foster stearne . . . III. vi. 54. 3
from Prince Arthure *fled* with wings of idle feare. . . . III. vi. 54. 9
So *fledd* fayre Florimell from her vaine feare, . . . III. vii. 1. 6
fled Ever alike, as if her former dred Were hard behind, . . . III. vii. 2. 4
Not halfe so fast the wicked Myrrha *fled* . . . III. vii. 26. 1
Fled fearfull Daphne on th' Aegaean strond, . . . III. vii. 26. 4
Florimell *fled* from that Monster yond, . . . III. vii. 26. 5
trembled like a lambe *fled* from the pray; . . . III. vii. 36. 6
Had she not *fled* into a secret mew, . . . III. viii. 4. 3
lefte his love to losse, and *fled* him selfe apace. . . . III. viii. 18. 9
with her *fled* away without abode. . . . III. viii. 19. 5
being *fled* into the fishers bote . . . III. viii. 21. 1
fledd From the sharpe hauke . . . III. viii. 33. 3
'out of the flames for safegard *fled,* . . . III. ix. 41. 2
He *fled* for feare of that he had misdonne, . . . III. ix. 48. 4
late he *fled* from his too earnest foe: . . . III. x. 23. 3
Malbecco . . . would have *fled* arere, . . . III. x. 23. 5
in hast he *fledd,* Ne ever looked back . . . III. x. 43. 6
High over hilles and over dales he *fledd,* . . . III. x. 55. 1
Still *fled* he forward, looking backward still; . . . III. x. 56. 1
a young man, the which *fled* From an huge Geaunt, . . . III. xi. 3. 3
the Gyaunt saw, . . . and from them *fled* apace: . . . III. xi. 5. 4
Long so she *fled,* and so he follow'd long; . . . IV. vii. 23. 1
fled away with ghastly dreriment, . . . IV. vii. 29. 8
Was *fled* to hell, surcharg'd with spoile and theft: . . . IV. vii. 32. 5
turnd her face, and *fled* away for evermore. . . . IV. vii. 36. 9

Fled—*Continued.*
who now is *fled* with shame.' . . . V. i. 15. 9
The whiles his guilefull groome was *fled* away, . . . V. iii. 38. 1
From which he lately had through reskew *fled:* . . . V. iv. 18. 8
They all were *fled* for feare; . . . V. vi. 35. 9
Fled fast into the towne, . . . V. vii. 34. 9
Yet *fled* she fast and both them farre outwent, . . . V. viii. 4. 6
fled from place to place. . . . V. viii. 36. 9
every place Where so he *fled,* . . . V. ix. 16. 5
they *fled* As fast as feete could carry them away; . . . V. x. 36. 1
Whose grudging ghost was thereout *fled* and past, . . . V. x. 37. 3
Streight th' other *fled* away, . . . V. x. 37. 7
Durst not abide, but *fled* away for feare, . . . V. x. 38. 3
when she *fled* into that covert greave, . . . VI. ii. 43. 8
and *fled* himselfe away for feare. . . . VI. iv. 7. 9
In following of him that *fled* so fast, . . . VI. iv. 9. 2
ere he *fled* he with his tooth impure Him heedlesse bit, . . . VI. v. 16. 8
They *fled,* and fast into the wood did get. . . . VI. v. 22. 7
fled Those evill tidings to their Lord to shew: . . . VI. vi. 24. 2
He *fled* from roome to roome, . . . VI. vi. 29. 6
fled away with all the speede she mought, . . . VI. vii. 50. 4
fled fast away, . . . VI. viii. 31. 4
Long thus she *fled,* . . . VI. viii. 32. 2
From thence into the open fields he *fled,* . . . VI. ix. 4. 1
why, when I them saw, *fled* they away from me?' . . . VI. x. 19. 9
Through cowherd feare he *fled* away . . . VI. x. 35. 3
Had from their maisters *fled,* . . . VI. xi. 39. 9
Fled from his wrath, . . . VI. xi. 49. 7
from them *fled* more fast Then any Deere, . . . VII. vi. 52. 4
every beast that to his den was *fled,* . . . *Am.* xl. 10
shadowes . . . Which all are *fled,* . . . *H.H.B.* 292

Flee. for succoure *flee* Under the shadow of his wing; . . . *To his Booke* 6
Nor elvish ghosts, nor gastly owles doe *flee.* . . . *S.C.* Jun. 24
Great whirlpooles which all fishes make to *flee;* . . . II. xii. 23. 7
do not in th' ayre more lightly *flee.* . . . II. xii. 77. 9
Yet did the smart remaine, though he himselfe did *flee.* . . . IV. v. 44. 9
fiends affrighted bee . . . and from her presence *flee:* . . . VI. vi. 10. 5

Fleece. Atcheived the golden *Fleece* in Colchid land, . . . *Ro.* x. 2
'Thou feeble flocke, whose *fleece* is rough and rent, . . . *S.C.* Ja. 43
so they han the *fleece,* . . . *S.C.* May 49
They han the *fleece,* and eke the flesh, . . . *S.C.* Jul. 189
the *fleece,* which him arayes, . . . *Gn.* 97
Whom golden *Fleece* did make an heavenly signe . . . *Gn.* 211
of their lambes, and of their woolly *fleece.* . . . *Hub.* 302
His goodly conquest of the golden *fleece,* . . . II. xii. 44. 6
All mindlesse of the Golden *fleece,* which made them strive. . . . IV. i. 23. 9
Forgetfull of the famous golden *fleece;* . . . *Am.* xliv. 3
a *fleece* of wooll, which privily The Latmian shepherd brought, . . . *Epith.* 379

Fleeced. *See* **Rich-fleeced.**

Fleeces. their flockes *fleeces* them to araye: . . . *S.C.* May 116

Fleecy. *See* **Golden-fleecy.**
I of your *fleecie* sheepe . . . would take on me the keep. . . . *Hub.* 289
the *fleecie* cattell have begun . . . to make their feast. . . . *Col.* 606
Their *fleecy* flowres they fearefully did steepe, . . . II. xii. 61. 8
Keeping their *fleecy* flockes as they were hyr'd, . . . III. vi. 15. 7
To helpe faire Pastorella home to drive Her *fleecie* flocke; . . . VI. ix. 15. 9
there by did keepe His *fleecie* flock . . . VI. xii. 9. 2

Fleer. common Courtiers love to gybe and *fleare* . . . *Hub.* 714

Fleet. No deadly fight of warlick *fleete* doth feare; . . . *Gn.* 124
Flames, weapons, wounds, in Greeks *fleete* to have tynde. . . . *Gn.* 504
seemd amid the surges for to *fleet,* . . . *Col.* 286
in frayle wood on Adrian gulf doth *fleet,* . . . II. vii. 14. 4
Islands, which doe *fleet* In the wide sea, . . . II. xii. 14. 3
How soone would yee assemble many a *fleete,* . . . III. viii. 28. 3
May her perhaps containe, that else would algates *fleet.'* . . . III. ix. 7. 9
till that likewise *fleet;* . . . IV. ix. 33. 8

Fleeting. Her words were like a streame of honny *fleeting,* . . . *Col.* 596

Flesh. warre upon the kings, and eate their *flesh.* . . . *Rev.* iii. 10
They han the fleece, and eke the *flesh,* . . . *S.C.* Jul. 189
So lost the Dogge the *flesh* in his mouth. . . . *S.C.* S. 61
We bene of *fleshe,* men as other bee, . . . *S.C.* S. 238
in his *flesh* endur'd the scorching flame, . . . *Gn.* 607
your silken hyde Fil'd with round *flesh,* . . . *Hub.* 592
flesh, a bubble-glas of breath, . . . *Ti.* 50
flesh delight In earthlie blis, . . . *Ti.* 527
the strong shackles of fraile *flesh,'* . . . *D.* 86
my *flesh* is numbd with feares: . . . *D.* 419
Full of great lumps of *flesh* . . . I. i. 20. 3
his grudging ghost did strive With the fraile *flesh;* . . . I. ii. 19. 8
they gan to . . . beat their brests, and naked *flesh* to teare: . . . I. iii. 22. 5
a dry dropsie through his *flesh* did flow, . . . I. iv. 23. 7
The cruell steele . . . doth bight In tender *flesh,* . . . I. v. 9. 4
My feareful *flesh* did tremble at their strife, . . . I. vi. 38. 6
'No faith so fast' . . . 'but *flesh* does paire.' . . . I. vii. 41. 8
'*Flesh* may empaire,' . . . 'but reason can repaire.' . . . I. vii. 41. 9
al his *flesh* shronk up like withered flowres. . . . I. viii. 41. 9
That makes frayle *flesh* to feare the bitter wave, . . . I. ix. 40. 5
Let every sinner die; Die shall all *flesh?* . . . I. ix. 47. 6
as superfluous *flesh* did rott, . . . I. x. 26. 6
rend his *flesh,* and his owne synewes eat. . . . I. x. 28. 3
pyn'd his *flesh* to keepe his body low and chast. . . . I. x. 48. 9
The steely head stuck fast still in his *flesh,* . . . I. xi. 22. 1
For he was *flesh:* (all *flesh* doth frayltie breed) . . . II. i. 52. 6
it may dwell In her sonnes *flesh,* . . . II. ii. 10. 8
Her face so faire as *flesh* it seemed not, . . . II. iii. 22. 1
inly bate Deepe in his *flesh,* . . . II. v. 7. 9
despiteously entayld Deepe in their *flesh,* . . . II. vi. 29. 8
teach the cursed steele to bight In his owne *flesh,* . . . II. vi. 32. 9
I, that am fraile *flesh* and earthly wight, . . . II. vii. 50. 3

Flesh—*Continued.*	
I can carve . . . His Lords owne *flesh.'*	II. viii. 22. 5
within his *flesh* Did breake the launce,	II. viii. 36. 6
through infirmity Of the fraile *flesh,*	II. xi. 1. 6
Flesh without blood, a person without spright,	II. xi. 40. 4
lov'd their native *flesh* against al kynd,	III. ii. 41. 3
had no powre in his soft *flesh* to bite.	III. v. 19. 5
The *flesh* therewith shee suppled and did steepe,	III. v. 33. 6
did in stocke of earthly *flesh* enrace,	III. v. 52. 5
in her pregnant *flesh* they shortly fructifide.	III. vi. 7. 9
with his teeth did teare His rugged *flesh,*	III. vii. 20. 5
feeds on wemens *flesh* as others feede on gras.	III. vii. 22. 9
Full many wounds in his corrupted *flesh*	III. vii. 32. 6
so fowly to devoure Her native *flesh*	III. vii. 49. 5
in his congealed *flesh* Infixt such secrete sting	III. viii. 25. 1
the Geaunts broode That fed on living *flesh,*	III. ix. 49. 9
in their *flesh* a griesly passage rend,	IV. ii. 15. 5
some celestiall shape that *flesh* did beare:	IV. v. 14. 7
to the tender *flesh* it went,	IV. vi. 15. 6
men . . . form'd of *flesh* and bone,	V. Pr. 2. 4
To teare his *flesh* in peeces for his sin:	V. iv. 37. 5
proud rebellious *flesh* to mortify:	V. vii. 9. 5
cruell steedes which he had fed With *flesh* of men,	V. viii. 28. 7
her owne deare *flesh* did teare:	V. viii. 47. 6
Offring to him in sinfull sacrifice The *flesh* of men,	V. x. 28. 7
Those he devoures, they say, both *flesh* and bone.	V. x. 29. 7
many wounds into his *flesh* it made,	V. xii. 19. 8
teare Her *flesh* for felnesse,	V. xii. 32. 4
All *flesh* is frayle and full of ficklenesse,	VI. i. 41. 7
their bad Stuard . . . Ne fed on *flesh,*	VI. iv. 14. 8
wound Made in his tender *flesh;*	VI. iv. 23. 9
none of them in his soft *flesh* did bite;	VI. v. 18. 7
To eate the *fleshe* of men whom they mote fynde,	VI. viii. 36. 2
of her dainty *flesh* they did devize To make a common feast,	VI. viii. 38. 8
his owne *flesh* he readie was to teare:	VI. xi. 25. 6
Do seize upon some beast whose *flesh* is bare,	VI. xi. 48. 2
if Gods should strive with *flesh* yfere,	VII. vi. 31. 7
Weake is th' assurance that weake *flesh* reposeth	*Am.* lviii. 1
All *flesh* is frayle, and all her strength unstayd,	*Am.* lviii. 5
frayle corruption, that doth *flesh* ensew.	*Am.* lxxix. 8
How then can sinfull *flesh* itselfe assure,	*H.H.L.* 97
In *flesh* at first the guilt committed was,	*H.H.L.* 141
Therefore in *flesh* it must be satisfyde;	*H.H.L.* 142
taking *flesh* of sacred virgins wombe,	*H.H.L.* 146
And them transport from *flesh* into the spright.	*H.H.B.* 259
Fleshed. therewith *flesht* upon him set anew,	VI. viii. 9. 7
Fleshes. They slue them, and upon their *fleshes* fed;	*Hub.* 318
made wide furrowes in their *fleshes* fraile,	I. vi. 43. 5
Fleshliness. soule assoyld from sinfull *fleshlinesse.*	*D.* 259
strong passion, or weake *fleshlinesse,*	II. iv. 2. 6
Fleshly. With *fleshly* follyes undefyled,	*S.C.* Jul. 155
Upon his *fleshly* corpse to make invasion:	*Hub.* 1090
to heaven went Out of this *fleshlie* gaole,	*Ti.* 296
see the end of pompe and *fleshlie* pride!	*Ti.* 543
how can fraile *fleshly* wight Forecast,	*Mui.* 226
Of *fleshlie* slime and fraile mortalitie;	*D.* 403
thousand other waies to bait his *fleshly* hookes.	I. iv. 25. 9
Ne *fleshly* brest can armed be so sownd,	I. ix. 11. 2
who most trustes in arme of *fleshly* might,	I. ix. 11. 6
'Come; come away, fraile, feeble, *fleshly* wight,	I. ix. 53. 1
What man is he, that boasts of *fleshly* might	I. x. 1. 1
never could the force of *fleshly* arme,	I. xi. 36. 6
feeble nature cloth'd with *fleshly* tyre.	II. i. 57. 3
th' eternall Lord in *fleshly* slime Enwombed was,	II. x. 50. 2
she was given all to *fleshly* lust,	III. i. 48. 5
as a cole to kindle *fleshly* flame,	III. i. 50. 2
Now ranckleth in this same fraile *fleshly* mould,	III. ii. 39. 3
So feeble is the powre of *fleshly* arme.	III. iv. 27. 6
Out of her *fleshly* ferme fled to the place of paine.	III. v. 23. 9
That is ingenerate in *fleshly* slime.	III. vi. 3. 5
That he with *fleshly* weeds would them attire:	III. vi. 32. 5
Fleshly corruption, nor mortall payne.	III. vi. 33. 4
In *fleshly* lust were mingled both yfere,	III. vii. 48. 8
Did wallow in all other *fleshly* myre,	III. vii. 49. 6
His wearie ghost assoyld from *fleshly* band	IV. iii. 13. 1
oppresst With *fleshly* weaknesse,	IV. v. 43. 3
fed on *fleshly* gore,	IV. vii. 5. 8
Therefore they mote not taste of *fleshly* food,	V. vii. 10. 1
Then, farewell *fleshly* force!	V. vii. 40. 9
Nothing on earth seemes fayre to *fleshly* sight,	*H.B.* 18
When she in *fleshly* seede is eft enraced,	*H.B.* 114
Their *fleshly* bowre, most fit for their delight,	*H.B.* 123
cryme Which was enrooted in all *fleshly* slyme.	*H.H.L.* 168
Whose glorious beames all *fleshly* sense doth daze	*H.H.L.* 278
this base world, subject to *fleshly* eye,	*H.H.B.* 23
Ne from thenceforth doth any *fleshly* sense, . . . remaine;	*H.H.B.* 267
Flesh's. Through *fleshes* frailtie, and deceipt of sin.	*T.M.* 492
Shall doffe her *fleshes* borrowd fayre attyre,	*Am.* xxvii. 6
How ever *fleshes* fault it filthy make;	*H.B.* 160
free from *fleshes* frayle infection.	*H.B.* 217
He downe descended, . . . in *fleshes* fraile attyre,	*H.H.L.* 137
Fleur-de-lis. Shall match with the fayre *flowre Delice.*	*S.C.* Ap. 144
The *flowre-deluce,* her lovely Paramoure,	II. vi. 16. 2
As fresh and fragrant as the *floure-deluce*	IV. i. 31. 7
all embost with Lyons and with *Flourdelice.*	V. ix. 27. 9
that faire Lady . . . *Flourdelis* hight,	V. xi. 49. 6
Flew. streight the spirite out of his senses *flew,*	*Gn.* 292
Upon those gates with force he fiercely *flewe,*	*Hub.* 1369
No gate . . . But with that percing noise *flew* open	I. viii. 4. 9
every dore of freewill open *flew.*	I. viii. 5. 3
Flew—*Continued.*	
at him fiersly *flew,*	I. viii. 6. 8
his shield, that covered was, open *flew;*	I. viii. 19. 2
Als *flew* his steed as he his bandes had brast,	I. ix. 21. 7
therewithall he fiersly at him *flew,*	II. vi. 29. 1
after him Owles and Night-ravens *flew,*	II. vii. 23. 3
all that els does horror breed, About them *flew,*	II. xii. 37. 2
flew about his heeles in wanton wize,	II. xii. 46. 8
her faire yellow locks behind her *flew,*	III. i. 16. 3
Wherewith enrag'd she fiercely at them *flew,*	III. i. 66. 1
through his haberjeon the forkehead *flew,*	III. v. 19. 3
Fiercely he *flew* upon that wicked feend,	III. vii. 32. 2
that yron wicket open *flew,*	III. xii. 3. 3
That brasen dore *flew* open,	III. xii. 29. 7
Like two mad mastiffes, each on other *flew,*	IV. ii. 17. 8
straight *flew* ope, and gave her way to ride.	IV. iii. 46. 3
flew away as lightly as the wind:	IV. viii. 7. 7
that sweet bird departing *flew* forthright,	IV. viii. 8. 7
Eftsoones she *flew* unto his fearelesse hand,	IV. viii. 12. 1
(so fast away he *flew*)	IV. viii. 40. 4
fame . . . *Flew* first abroad,	IV. x. 4. 2
flew A flocke of litle loves,	IV. x. 42. 1
They each at other tyrannously *flew;*	V. ii. 13. 2
streight the winged words out of his ballaunce *flew.*	V. ii. 44. 9
here and there before his presence *flew,*	V. ii. 53. 8
through the thickest like a Lyon *flew,*	V. iii. 8. 5
Like a fell Lionesse at him she *flew,*	V. iv. 39. 6
With her sharpe Cemitare at him she *flew,*	V. v. 9. 8
like mazed deare dismayfully they *flew.*	V. viii. 38. 9
thereon *flew* Like a wyld Gote,	V. ix. 15. 3
so furiously at him he *flew,*	V. xi. 5. 1
She *flew* at him like to an hellish feend,	V. xi. 27. 2
strongly *flew* With all her body at his head	V. xi. 30. 6
he fiercely at him *flew,*	VI. i. 20. 1
Ne time would give, . . . But at him *flew,*	VI. ii. 19. 8
And with mad moode againe upon him *flew,*	VI. iv. 6. 3
Like a fell Lyon at him fiercely *flew,*	VI. vi. 22. 4
With his sharpe sword he fiercely at him *flew,*	VI. viii. 9. 2
He *flew* upon him like a greedy kight	VI. viii. 28. 4
seeing Calidore, away he *flew,*	VI. xii. 25. 7
A gentle Bee . . . About him *flew*	*Epig.* iv. 4
Flex. *See* **Flax.**	
Flies. Tho gynne you, fond *flyes!* the cold to scorne,	*S.C.* F. 39
Of all the race of silver-winged *Flies*	*Mui.* 17
I hate the fire, because to nought it *flyes;*	*D.* 404
This lowly Muse, . . . *Flies* for like aide	*Ded. Son.* xiii. 8
Legions of Sprights, . . . like litle *flyes*	I. i. 38. 2
The Sarazin, . . . fiercely to him *flies;*	I. ii. 17. 2
the flashing fier *flies,* . . . out of their burning shields;	I. ii. 17. 7
all the ayre it fills, and *flyes* to heaven bright.	I. v. 16. 9
a ship, that *flyes* fayre under sayle,	I. vi. 1. 1
Sir Trevisan *flies* from Despeyre,	I. ix. Arg.
marveiles at himselfe stil as he *flies:*	I. xi. 34. 8
Atin to Cymochles for ayd *flyes.*	II. v. Arg.
in the aire their clustring army *flies;*	II. ix. 16. 4
all the chamber filled was with *flyes*	II. ix. 51. 1
fame now *flies,* that of a forreine foe He is yslaine,	III. v. 9. 8
He *flyes* about, and with his flaggy winges	III. vi. 39. 7
The witches sonne loves Florimell: She *flyes;*	III. vii. Arg.
flyes away of her owne feete afeard,	III. vii. 1. 3
Full fast she *flies,* and farre afore him goes,	IV. vii. 21. 8
Like foolish *flies* about an hony-crocke;	V. ii. 33. 3
He like a swarme of *flyes* them overthrew;	V. ii. 53. 6
With dreadfull force he *flies* at her bylive,	V. iv. 42. 6
flocking round about them, as a swarme Of *flyes*	V. xi. 58. 2
round about her flocke, like many *flies,*	VI. viii. 40. 2
Like as the wounded Whale to shore *flies* from the maine.	VI. x. 31. 9
flyes away as fast as he can hye,	VI. xi. 18. 8
How many *flyes* . . . Do seize upon some beast	VI. xi. 48. 1
my hart . . . *flyes* backe unto your sight.	*Am.* lxxiii. 8
In angry wize he *flyes* about,	*Epig.* iv. 9
Flight. With feeble *flight* venture to mount	*Bel.*[1] vi. 2
drove the Nimphs to *flight.*	*Bel.*[1] x. 14
rise, and with a larger *flight*	*Bel.* vii. 5
So long as Joves great Bird did make his *flight,*	*Ro.* xvii. 1
Through the maine sea making her merry *flight.*	*Van.* ix. 4
Such fond fantsies shall soone be put to *flight.*	*S.C.* Au. 22
So high to sore and make so large a *flight;*	*S.C.* O. 86
Colin fittes such famous *flight* to scanne;	*S.C.* O. 88
The hatefull darknes now had put to *flight;*	*Gn.* 69
They stole away, and tooke their hastie *flight,*	*Hub.* 339
in their speedie course and nimble *flight*	*Hub.* 621
With loftie *flight* above the earth he bounded,	*Ti.* 599
Two Angels, downe descending with swift *flight,*	*Ti.* 625
he so swift and nimble was of *flight,*	*Mui.* 41
In the wide aire to make her wandring *flight;*	*Mui.* 139
with good speed began to take his *flight.*	*Mui.* 147
With violent swift *flight* forth caried	*Mui.* 422
Such loftie *flight* base shepheard seemeth not,	*Col.* 618
Gorgon, . . . At which . . . Styx is put to *flight.*	I. i. 37. 9
a Gryfon . . . A Dragon fiers encountreth in his *flight,*	I. v. 8. 3
He by a privy Posterne tooke his *flight,*	I. v. 52. 7
he would him make . . . the Robuckes in *flight* to overtake,	I. vi. 24. 8
He forst to castle strong to take their *flight;*	I. vii. 44. 7
from whom make ye this hasty *flight?*	I. ix. 23. 8
with strong *flight* did forcibly divyde The yielding ayre,	I. xi. 18. 3
To trusse the pray too heavy for his *flight;*	I. xi. 19. 8
him rencountring fierce, as hauke in *flight,*	I. xi. 53. 4
From off the earth to take his aerie *flight.*	II. iii. 19. 5
grieved at her *flight;*	II. iii. 43. 2

Flight—*Continued.*
rage enforst my *flight;* . . . II. iv. 32. 1
whither with such hasty *flight* Art thou now bownd? . . . II. iv. 43. 2
After that varlets *flight,* . . . II. v. 2. 1
Gaz'd after him, as fowle escapt by *flight.* . . . II. viii. 9. 4
may not hope by *flight* to scape alive, . . . II. viii. 50. 3
many foes, whom straunger knightes to *flight* compell. . . . II. ix. Arg.
chaste so fiercely after fearefull *flight,* . . . II. x. 16. 5
through *flight* into fond mischief fell. . . . II. x. 26. 9
such as were through former *flight* preserv'd . . . II. x. 55. 5
in his *flight* the villein turn'd his face . . . II. xi. 26. 6
an innumerable *flight* Of harmefull fowles . . . II. xii. 35. 6
meet respect of honor putt to *flight:* . . . III. i. 48. 8
whenas all were put to shamefull *flight,* . . . III. i. 67. 1
the same was put to *flight;* . . . III. ii. 29. 5
Least afterwards it be too late to take thy *flight.'* . . . III. iv. 14. 9
nothing might relent her hasty *flight,* . . . III. iv. 49. 1
drive Their brother to reproch and shamefull *flight;* . . . III. v. 16. 6
in vaine was forst to turne his *flight,* . . . III. vii. 28. 5
did fall From her in *flight,* . . . III. vii. 31. 9
gan encrease his speed as she encreast her *flight.* . . . III. vii. 43. 9
to *flight* againe she did her take. . . . III. vii. 44. 9
liberty to frame their purpost *flight,* . . . III. x. 16. 5
Ne stayd his *flight* nor fearefull agony, . . . III. x. 56. 2
like a winged horse he tooke his *flight* . . . III. xi. 42. 7
He falleth nigh to ground, and scarse recovereth *flight.* . . . IV. iii. 19. 9
makes her feare a spur to hast her *flight:* . . . IV. vii. 22. 7
saw her forward still to make her *flight,* . . . IV. viii. 8. 2
To seeke by *flight* her fellowship t' eschew, . . . IV. viii. 56. 5
he was swift as swallow in her *flight,* . . . V. i. 20. 4
from the water to the land betooke his *flight.* . . . V. ii. 17. 9
with nimble *flight* Flowne at a flush of Ducks . . . V. ii. 54. 1
other wing, now made unmeete for *flight,* . . . V. v. 15. 3
She had not rid the mountenance of a *flight,* . . . V. vi. 36. 4
streight tooke his *flight* From that sad land . . . V. x. 11. 3
Had hid themselves, or taken further *flight:* . . . V. x. 19. 4
Whereto she ever list to make her hardy *flight.* . . . V. xi. 24. 9
Gainst which no *flight* nor rescue mote avayle, . . . V. xi. 59. 5
streight he tooke his *flight* Toward the Castle, . . . VI. i. 22. 3
I the measure of her *flight* doe search, . . . VI. ii. 32. 3
And to betake him selfe to fearefull *flight;* . . . VI. iii. 25. 8
But follow'd fast the Monster in his *flight:* . . . VI. iii. 26. 5
He had him overtaken in his *flight.* . . . VI. iv. 8. 6
freed From bels and jesses which did let her *flight,* . . . VI. iv. 19. 8
Thinking by speed to overtake his *flight;* . . . VI. v. 17. 2
when a cast of Faulcons make their *flight* . . . VII. vii. 9. 1
dooth oft refuse This too high *flight,* . . . VIII. vii. 1. 4
unto heaven forgets her former *flight.* . . . *Am.* lxxii. 8
Lyke as a byrd, . . . to it doth make his *flight:* . . . *Am.* lxxiii. 6
like fresh Eagle, make his hardie *flight* . . . *H.L.* 69
Till she her selfe for stronger *flight* can breath. . . . *H.H.B.* 28
Flight's. let them downe before his *flightes* end: . . . I. xi. 19. 4
Fling. Forst with the filth his egs to *fling* away: . . . *Van.* iv. 12
They cherelie chaunt, and rymes at randon *fling,* . . . *T.M.* 321
Flings. Or *flings* aloft, or treades downe in the flore, . . . II. viii. 42. 5
all their glory to the ground downe *flings,* . . . III. vi. 39. 5
Flint. Thy teares would make the hardest *flint* to flowe! . . . *S.C.* Jun. 114
'faire lady, hart of *flint* would rew The undeserved woes . . . I. ii. 26. 8
hart of *flint* asonder could have rifte; . . . II. vii. 23. 8
Headed with *flint,* and fethers bloody dide; . . . II. xi. 21. 4
The firmest *flint* doth in continuance weare: . . . *Am.* xviii. 4
she as steele and *flint* doth still remayne. . . . *Am.* xviii. 14
Flinty. Then let thy *flinty* hart, that feeles no paine, . . . *H.H.L.* 246
Flit. That which is firme doth *flit* and fall away, . . . *Ro.* iii. 13
with each storme does fall away, and *flit,* . . . *Ti.* 514
His choicefull sense with every change doth *flit:* . . . *Mui.* 159
They tarrie not, but *flit* and fall away, . . . *D.* 397
ere ye be aware will *flit* away; . . . *D.* 502
Forth-with her ghost out of her corps did *flit,* . . . *As.* 177
whose fethers, nothing *flitt,* Doe yet but flagg, . . . *Ded. Son.* ii. 7
on a sandie hill, that still did *flitt* And fall away, . . . I. iv. 5. 5
two dartes, exceeding *flit* And deadly sharp, . . . II. iv. 38. 7
the *flitt* barke, obaying to her mind, . . . II. vi. 20. 3
In Phaedrias *flitt* barck over that perlous shard. . . . II. vi. 38. 9
The life did *flit* away out of her nest, . . . II. vii. 66. 8
Such as in idle fantasies do *flit;* . . . II. ix. 50. 7
His falsed fayth, and love too lightly *flitt;* . . . II. xii. 44. 7
Therewith a while she her *flit* fancy fedd, . . . III. i. 56. 1
Was from her fled as *flit* as ayery Dove, . . . III. vi. 11. 4
her *flitt* palfrey did so well apply . . . III. vii. 24. 5
on the rockes he fell so *flit* and light, . . . III. x. 57. 5
Fearing least from her cage the wearie soule would *flit.* . . . III. xi. 12. 9
Now, like a stag; now, like a faulcon *flit:* . . . III. xi. 39. 8
I with that Squire agreede away to *flit,* . . . IV. vii. 17. 6
the Dove Would *flit* a litle forward, . . . IV. viii. 11. 2
ne once abacke did *flit,* . . . IV. ix. 29. 8
Thence doth by Huntingdon and Cambridge *flit,* . . . IV. xi. 34. 6
Ne doe their bodies only *flit* and fly, . . . VII. vii. 19. 7
which who feeles not by sense . . . To *flit* still, . . . VII. vii. 22. 3
when a dreadfull storme away is *flit,* . . . *Am.* xl. 7
Flits. when my joy to sorrow *flits,* I waile, . . . *Am.* liv. 7
Flitted. at last it *flitted* is, Whither the soules doe fly . . . I. ii. 19. 8
hardly he the *flitted* life does win . . . I. vii. 21. 7
Flitteth. he got faire Pegasus that *flitteth* in the ayre. . . . III. xi. 42. 9
Flitting. vaine worlds glorie, *flitting* too and fro, . . . *Pet.*[2] vii. 2
that is *flitting* doth abide and stay. . . . *Ro.* iii. 14
let the *flitting* aire my vaine words sever.' . . . *Gn.* 638
Her *flitting* parts, and element unsound, . . . I. xi. 18. 5
choose my *flitting* houres to spend, . . . II. vii. 33. 7
cleave The *flitting* skyes, like flying Pursuivant, . . . II. viii. 2. 4

Flitting—*Continued.*
flitting as the wavering wind After each beautie . . . IV. ii. 5. 2
flitting still doe flie, and still their places vary. . . . VII. vii. 21. 9
Ere *flitting* Time could wag his eyas wings . . . *H.H.L.* 24
Then th' Aire still *flitting,* but yet firmely bounded . . . *H.H.B.* 38
Float. on the dull waves did lightly *flote,* . . . II. vi. 38. 3
the rich furrowes *flote,* all quite fordonne: . . . III. vii. 34. 6
Long so she on the mighty maine did *flote,* . . . III. viii. 21. 3
Floated. *floted* in the midst of that great lake; . . . II. vi. 11. 4
Floating. *Floting* amid the sea in jeopardie, . . . *Col.* 273
On every side *floting* the floodes emong: . . . II. xii. 10. 7
By whom a little skippet *floting* did appeare. . . . II. xii. 14. 9
Did thrust the shallop from the *floting* strand: . . . III. vii. 27. 8
The fish, still *floting,* doe at randon range, . . . VII. vii. 21. 4
Europa *floting* through th' Argolick fluds: . . . VII. vii. 33. 4
As they came *floating* on the Christal Flood; . . . *Proth.* 57
Flock. All as his straying *flocke* he fedde: . . . *To his Booke* 10
Led forth his *flock,* that had bene long ypent: . . . *S.C.* Ja. 4
Tho to a hill his faynting *flocke* he ledde, . . . *S.C.* Ja. 11
'Thou feeble *flocke,* whose fleece is rough and rent, . . . *S.C.* Ja. 43
ever my *flocke* was my chiefe care, . . . *S.C.* F. 23
Seemeth thy *flocke* thy counsell can, . . . *S.C.* F. 77
a double eye, Ylike to my *flocke* and thine; . . . *S.C.* Mar. 39
Yougthes folke now *flocken* in every where, . . . *S.C.* May 9
on whom did attend A fayre *flocke* of Faeries, . . . *S.C.* May 32
What fallen the *flocke,* . . . *S.C.* May 49
Here wander may thy *flocke,* . . . *S.C.* Jun. 11
feede his *flocke* in fields . . . *S.C.* Jun. 76
Als for thy *flocke* and thee. . . . *S.C.* Jul. 8
Feeding the blessed *flocke* of Dan, . . . *S.C.* Jul. 51
shepheard great! That bought his *flocke* so deare, . . . *S.C.* Jul. 54
The *flocke* which he did keepe. . . . *S.C.* Jul. 132
left hys *flocke* to fetch a lasse, . . . *S.C.* Jul. 147
Of all my *flocke* there nis sike another, . . . *S.C.* Au. 38
The while my *flocke* did feede thereby; . . . *S.C.* Au. 59
Hey, ho, the fayre *flocke!* . . . *S.C.* Au. 118
Where is the fayre *flocke* . . . *S.C.* S. 9
wont to repayre Unto the *flocke,* . . . *S.C.* S. 187
when at even he came to the *flocke,* . . . *S.C.* S. 204
'Gather together ye my little *flocke,* . . . *S.C.* D. 145
My little *flock,* that was to me so liefe; . . . *S.C.* D. 146
his folded *flock* to keepe. . . . *S.C.* Env. 6
The whiles his *flock* their chawed cuds do eate. . . . *Gn.* 144
this Shepheards *flocke* Lay everie where, . . . *Gn.* 233
Gathering his straying *flocke,* . . . *Gn.* 319
lent to him the charge Of all his *flocke,* . . . *Hub.* 300
Cruelly fell upon their *flock* in folde, . . . *Hub.* 335
By whom the *flock* is rightly fed, and taught: . . . *Hub.* 442
My little *flocke* on westerne downes to keepe, . . . *D.* 100
As the least lamb in all my *flock* that went: . . . *D.* 126
She of my *flock* would take full warie keepe. . . . *D.* 133
'My little *flocke,* whom earst I lov'd so well, . . . *D.* 344
Did thether *flock* to see what they did heare. . . . *As.* 202
High on an hill, his *flocke* to vewen wide, . . . I. i. 23. 3
two rams, . . . Fight for the rule of the rich fleeced *flocke,* . . . I. ii. 16. 2
A seely Lamb far from the *flock* does take, . . . I. vi. 10. 4
the troupe of light-foot Naiades *Flocke* all about . . . I. vi. 18. 4
Amidst a *flock* of Damzelles fresh and gay, . . . II. v. 32. 4
how the fowles in aire Doe *flocke,* . . . II. vi. 28. 8
Whom all that folke . . . Doe *flock* about, . . . II. vii. 48. 6
round about him *flocke* impetuously, . . . II. xi. 18. 3
A *flocke* of litle loves, and sports, and joyes, . . . IV. x. 42. 2
Therefore the vulgar did about him *flocke,* . . . V. ii. 33. 1
round about her *flocke,* like many flies, . . . VI. viii. 40. 2
Fly like a *flocke* of doves before a Faulcons vew. . . . VI. viii. 49. 9
streight unto her litle *flocke* did fare: . . . VI. ix. 15. 2
To helpe faire Pastorella home to drive Her fleecie *flocke;* . . . VI. ix. 15. 9
After her *flocke* she in their fold had tyde: . . . VI. ix. 17. 6
The fields my food, my *flocke* my rayment breed; . . . VI. ix. 20. 8
to thee *flocke* to heare thy lovely layes! . . . VI. x. 19. 5
there by did keepe His fleecie *flock* . . . VI. xii. 9. 2
A *Flocke* of Nymphes I chaunced to espy, . . . *Proth.* 20
the foule . . . Gan *flock* about these twaine, . . . *Proth.* 120
Flocked. They *flocked* all about her bleeding wound, . . . I. i. 25. 7
all the hellish brood . . . *flockt* on every side, . . . I. v. 32. 8
Thus *flocked* all the folke him rownd about; . . . I. xii. 12. 1
fatall birds about them *flocked* were, . . . II. xii. 36. 2
About their Ladye first they *flockt* arownd; . . . III. i. 64. 1
after them a rude confused rout Of persons *flockt,* . . . III. xii. 25. 2
Her warlike maides about her *flockt* so fast, . . . V. iv. 43. 6
About him *flockt,* and hard at him did lay; . . . VI. i. 24. 2
Flocking. To feede youthes fancie, and the *flocking* fry, . . . *S.C.* O. 14
if the *flocking* Nymphes did folow Pan, . . . *S.C.* D. 47
flocking Persians did the Greeks affray; . . . *Gn.* 50
her faire damzels, *flocking* her arownd, . . . *Mui.* 116
manie Nymphes about them *flocking* round, . . . *Mui.* 295
Flocking together in confusde array; . . . V. xi. 43. 8
flocking round about them, as a swarme Of flyes . . . V. xi. 58. 1
flocking in great store Unto the cave gan preasse, . . . VI. xi. 46. 3
Flock's. Thy *flocks* father his corage hath lost. . . . *S.C.* F. 80
their *flockes* fleeces them to araye: . . . *S.C.* May 116
tell me first of thy *flocks* estate. . . . *S.C.* S. 24
That *flocks* grand Captaine and most trustie guide . . . *Gn.* 268
not a lambe of all their *flockes* supply . . . *Hub.* 316
my *flockes* father daily doth amend it. . . . VI. ix. 21. 8
Flocks. The whiles our *flockes* do graze about in sight, . . . *S.C.* Ap. 31
playen while their *flockes* be unfedde: . . . *S.C.* May 44
keepe both our *flockes* from straying. . . . *S.C.* May 173
fruictfull *flocks,* bene every where to see: . . . *S.C.* Jun. 22
Shepheards, which your *flocks* do feede, . . . *S.C.* Jun. 106

Flocks—*Continued.*	
ryse, ye blessed *Flocks,* and home apace,	*S.C.* Jun. 118
To feede theyr *flocks* at will,	*S.C.* Jul. 66
kept yfere The *flockes* of mighty Pan.	*S.C.* Jul. 144
loved their *flocks* to feede;	*S.C.* Jul. 166
What neede hem caren for their *flocks,*	*S.C.* Jul. 195
Their fasting *flockes* to keepe.	*S.C.* Jul. 200
of sike pastoures howe done the *flocks* creepe?	*S.C.* S. 140
doen so carefully theyr *flocks* tend.	*S.C.* S. 179
From soddein force theyr *flocks* for to gard.	*S.C.* S. 235
Whereon he earst had taught his *flocks* to feede,	*S.C.* O. 57
by your *flocks* on Kentish downes abyde,	*S.C.* N. 63
'The feeble *flocks* in field refuse their former foode,	*S.C.* N. 133
when our *flocks* into mischaunce mought fall,	*S.C.* D. 9
the *flocks,* which thou doest watch	*S.C.* D. 12
O *flocks!* O Faunes!	*Gn.* 145
fields resownd, and *flockes* to leap and daunce,	*Ti.* 326
flocks and shepheards caused to rejoyce.	*D.* 315
do feed Your carelesse *flocks* on hils	*D.* 520
all their *flocks* from feeding to refraine:	*Col.* 26
their *flocks,* devoyd of dangers feare,	*Col.* 54
Where be the *flockes* and heards, which she doth keep?	*Col.* 237
From *flocks* and fields, to angels and to skie.'	*Col.* 619
to draw their bleating *flocks* to rest.	*Col.* 955
with his sword disperst the raskall *flockes,*	II. xi. 19. 2
Keeping their fleecy *flockes* as they were hyr'd,	III. vi. 15. 7
A ravenous Wolfe amongst the scattered *flockes:*	V. xii. 38. 6
shepherds singing to their *flockes*	VI. ix. 4. 3
feend that mote offend Their happie *flockes,*	VI. ix. 6. 3
to their homes to hast Their tender *flocks,*	VI. ix. 13. 4
The whiles their *flockes* in shadowes shrouded bee,	VI. ix. 41. 4
drove away their *flocks;*	VI. x. 39. 9
wont the shepheards . . . feed an hundred *flocks,*	VI. xi. 26. 9
Some *flockes* of sheepe and shepheards to espy;	VI. xi. 36. 7
There did they find . . . The selfe same *flocks*	VI. xi. 37. 2
To hyre them well if they their *flockes* would keepe;	VI. xi. 40. 2
To keepe their *flockes* for litle hyre and chepe,	VI. xi. 40. 7
all those *flockes,* which they before Had reft from Meliboe	VI. xi. 51. 6
Flong. squallid Fortune, into basenes *flong,*	*T.M.* 543
dead mens bones, which round about were *flong;*	II. vii. 30. 7
He *flong* it from him;	II. viii. 49. 4
both flowres and girlonds far away Shee *flong,*	III. iv. 30. 2
despeyre she from her *flong.*	III. iv. 41. 9
friskt, and *flong* aloft, and louted low on knee.	V. iii. 34. 9
Flood. *See* **Water-flood.**	
a water, whose out gushing *flood*	*Bel.*[2] ix. 6
a brackish *flood* Of bitter teares,	*T.M.* 415
through the overflowing of the *flood*	*Ti.* 621
to match her with the neighbour *flood,*	*Col.* 122
A *floud* of poyson horrible and blacke,	I. i. 20. 2
They . . . come to fiery *flood* of Phlegeton,	I. v. 33. 3
made an open passage for the gushing *flood.*	I. ix. 36. 9
meetes a *flood* that doth his passage stay,	I. ix. 39. 3
wilt thy selfe not pas the *flood?*	I. ix. 39. 9
From which fast trickled forth a silver *flood,*	I. xi. 29. 4
Some wrestle, some do run, some bathe in christall *flood.*	I. xii. 7. 9
when stopped is the *flood.'*	II. iv. 11. 9
Griefe is a *flood;* and love a monster fell;	II. iv. 35. 3
The *flood* of drops, the Monster filth did breede:	II. iv. 35. 5
bent his hastie course towardes the ydle *flood.*	II. vi. 41. 9
The varlett saw, when to the *flood* he came,	II. vi. 42. 1
Fro me do flow into an ample *flood,*	II. vii. 8. 8
a blacke *flood,* which flow'd about it round.	II. vii. 56. 7
flood from mouth, Did fly abacke,	II. vii. 58. 6
a large lukewarme *flood,* Red as the Rose,	II. viii. 39. 1
Like Noyes great *flood,*	II. x. 15. 5
the silver *flood* Through every channell running	II. xii. 60. 3
th' one her selfe low ducked in the *flood,*	II. xii. 66. 3
by the grim *floud* of Cocytus slow,	III. iv. 55. 5
Right as he entring was into the *flood,*	III. v. 25. 3
he that strives to stop a suddein *flood,*	III. vii. 34. 1
the victour, through the *flood* Escaped hardly,	III. ix. 42. 8
As she sate carelesse by a cristall *flood*	IV. ii. 45. 4
when the *floud* is spent, then backe againe,	IV. iii. 27. 6
with the wasting of his vitall *flood,*	IV. iii. 28. 8
Thinking to hide the depth by troubling of the *flood.*	IV. vi. 29. 9
More great then th' eares of Elephants by Indus *flood.*	IV. vii. 6. 9
The place there overflowne seemd like a sodaine *flood.*	IV. vii. 32. 9
tempt the deepest *flood* To come	IV. x. 46. 5
Pactolus glistring with his golden *flood;*	IV. xi. 20. 8
Encloseth Corke with his devided *flood;*	IV. xi. 44. 4
Leapes forth into the *floud,*	V. ii. 8. 6
a trap was letten downe to fall Into the *floud:*	V. ii. 12. 7
There being both together in the *floud,*	V. ii. 13. 1
into the *flood* . . . adowne her cast,	V. ii. 27. 2
from their riven sides forth gushed like a *flood.*	VI. i. 37. 9
at the foote thereof a gentle *flud*	VI. x. 7. 1
a fayrer *flood* may no man see.	VII. vi. 40. 9
there flowed forth the Romane *Flood.*	VII. vii. 42. 9
through the *flood* before did softly slyde	VII. vii. 43. 4
lovely Daughters of the *Flood*	*Proth.* 21
floating on the Christal *Flood;*	*Proth.* 57
all the foule which in his *flood* did dwell	*Proth.* 119
Flood-gate. did the *floodgate* stop With his faire garment;	II. i. 43. 2
opened wide a red *floodgate.*	II. v. 7. 9
Floods. The *floddes* whereof shall them overflowe	*S.C.* May 94
flouds do gaspe, for dryed is theyr sourse,	*S.C.* N. 126
flouds of teares flowe in theyr stead	*S.C.* N. 127
'Some in the greedie *flouds* are sunke and drent;	*Gn.* 585
Let streaming *floods* their hastie courses stay,	*D.* 332
Floods—*Continued.*	
both woods and fields and *floods* revive,	*Col.* 29
Large *floods* of blood adowne their sides did raile;	I. vi. 43. 7
floods of blood could not them satisfie:	I. vi. 43. 8
The fields, the *floods,* the heavens, with one consent,	I. ix. 12. 8
Dry-shod to passe she parts the *flouds* in tway;	I. x. 20. 5
On every side floting the *floodes* emong:	II. xii. 10. 7
Helpe me to tell the names of all those *floods*	IV. xi. 10. 6
his neighbour *flouds* which nigh him dwell,	IV. xi. 30. 1
Sture, that parteth with his pleasant *floods*	IV. xi. 33. 3
The which in *floods* and fountaines doe appere,	IV. xi. 52. 8
So fertile be the *flouds* in generation,	IV. xii. 1. 8
Europa floting through th' Argolick *fluds:*	VII. vii. 33. 4
a rocke amidst the raging *floods;*	*Am.* lvi. 10
Floor. *See* **Chamber-floor.**	
The *floor* was Jaspis, and of Emeraude.	*Bel.*[1] ii. 11
The *floore* of Jasp and Emeraude	*Bel.*[2] ii. 11
to stomble at the threshold *flore:*	*S.C.* May 230
on the *flore* she saw the merchaundise	*S.C.* May 298
Who first my Muse did lift out of the *flore,*	*Ded. Son.* xv. 6
all the *floore* . . . Defiled was,	I. viii. 35. 5
his foot could find no *flore,*	I. viii. 39. 7
all the *floore* was . . . Bespredd with costly scarlott	I. xii. 13. 7
Both roofe, and *floore,* and walls, were all of gold,	II. vii. 29. 1
Or flings aloft, or treades downe in the *flore,*	II. viii. 42. 5
in the midst thereof upon the *floure*	II. ix. 34. 1
many Giaunts left on groning *flore:*	II. x. 10. 5
The one she slew upon the present *floure;*	II. x. 19. 5
his dead corse should fall upon the *flore;*	II. xi. 37. 8
his dead corse upon the *flore* fell nathemore.	II. xi. 37. 9
sitting on the *flore* the Hag she found	III. vii. 7. 2
as on the readie *flore* Of some Theatre,	III. xii. 3. 5
the *flore* to shrinke he did avyse;	III. xii. 10. 7
To rest he layd him downe upon the *flore,*	IV. v. 39. 3
spredding over all the *flore* alone,	IV. vii. 20. 7
he threw her rudely on the *flore,*	IV. vii. 28. 1
all the peece he shaked from the *flore,*	V. ii. 21. 8
all the grassie *flore* Was fild with bloud	V. vii. 31. 5
slew the Porter on the *flore.*	VI. i. 23. 9
There he that knight found lying on the *flore*	VI. ii. 40. 7
with their bloud did all the *flore* imbrew,	VI. v. 5. 3
scattered all about fell on the *flowre:*	VI. vii. 8. 4
And tread my life downe in the lowly *floure.*	*Am.* xx. 4
Flora. *Flora* now calleth forth eche flower,	*S.C.* Mar. 16
his Queene attone Was Lady *Flora,*	*S.C.* May 31
freshest *Flora* her with Yvie girlond crownd.	I. i. 48. 9
girlonds gay, That seemd as fresh as *Flora* in her prime;	I. iv. 17. 3
Flora's. filles with flowres fayre *Floraes* painted lap:	II. ii. 6. 5
all the ornaments of *Floraes* pride,	II. xii. 50. 5
Florentine. to that sad *Florentine* appeare,	*Bel.*[2] xiii. 2
Florimell. Fayre *Florimell* is chaced:	III. i. Arg.
Florimell of Arthure is Long followed,	III. iv. Arg.
Prince Arthur heares of *Florimell:*	III. v. Arg.
is ycleped *Florimell* the fayre,	III. v. 8. 7
Faire *Florimell* belov'd of many a knight,	III. v. 8. 8
he sets nought at all by *Florimell;*	III. v. 9. 5
fowre since *Florimell* the Court forwent,	III. v. 10. 2
Affrighted had the fairest *Florimell,*	III. v. 23. 2
That was, to weet, the goodly *Florimell;*	III. vi. 54. 5
The witches sonne loves *Florimell:*	III. vii. Arg.
So fledd fayre *Florimell* from her vaine feare,	III. vii. 1. 6
Florimell fled from that Monster yond,	III. vii. 26. 5
horse Whereon faire *Florimell* was wont to ride,	III. vii. 31. 2
wrong Which he supposed donne to *Florimell,*	III. vii. 35. 6
To tell what tydings of fayre *Florimell* became.	III. vii. 61. 9
The Witch creates a snowy Lady like to *Florimell;*	III. viii. Arg.
Another *Florimell,* in shape and looke	III. viii. 5. 8
Him selfe to fashion likest *Florimell,*	III. viii. 8. 6
garments gay, Which *Florimell* had left behind her late;	III. viii. 9. 2
fairest *Florimell* It was	III. viii. 19. 6
Florimell her selfe was far away,	III. viii. 20. 1
In such distresse and sad perplexity Was *Florimell,*	III. viii. 33. 9
Florimell with him unto his bowre he bore.	III. viii. 36. 9
Thither he brought the sory *Florimell,*	III. viii. 38. 1
suddein parture of faire *Florimell* To find him	III. viii. 46. 5
dead: . . . Henceforth for ever *Florimell* to bee;	III. viii. 47. 6
Blandamour winnes false *Florimell;*	IV. ii. Arg.
from Braggadocchio whilome reft The snowy *Florimell,*	IV. ii. 4. 7
the fayrest *Florimell* him seemed To him was fallen	IV. ii. 8. 3
Till seeing her, that *Florimell* did seme, In doubt	IV. ii. 17. 4
They said, it was for love of *Florimell.*	IV. ii. 22. 2
That fayrest *Florimell* was present there in place.	IV. ii. 22. 9
none alive but joy'd in *Florimell,*	IV. ii. 23. 2
That dare fro me thinke *Florimell* to take!'	IV. ii. 25. 4
Well knowne to appertaine to *Florimell,*	IV. ii. 25. 8
That chaleng'd ought in *Florimell,*	IV. ii. 28. 9
Satyrane makes a Turneyment For love of *Florimell:*	IV. iv. Arg.
For that rich girdle of faire *Florimell,*	IV. iv. 5. 8
It was to weete that snowy *Florimell,*	IV. iv. 8. 1
So *Florimell* with Ate forth was brought,	IV. iv. 10. 2
Florimell him fowly gan revile,	IV. iv. 11. 3
It was the same which lately *Florimel* had lost.	IV. iv. 15. 9
The Ladies for the girdle strive Of famous *Florimell:*	IV. v. Arg.
Shall fall the girdle of faire *Florimell:*	IV. v. 2. 5
Florimell, in her first ages flowre,	IV. v. 5. 7
thought he had the trew And very *Florimell,*	IV. v. 13. 8
Yet all were glad there *Florimell* to see,	IV. v. 14. 8
Yet thought that *Florimell* was not so faire as shee.	IV. v. 14. 9
Florimell her selfe in all mens vew She seem'd to passe:	IV. v. 15. 8
Florimell exceedingly did fret,	IV. v. 19. 7

Florimell—*Continued.*
Since with the rest she went not after *Florimell*. . . . IV. v. 28. 9
So whylome didst thou to faire *Florimell*, . . . IV. vii. 2. 1
false *Florimel* By Braggadochio lately was redeemed; . . . IV. ix. 20. 6
To let faire *Florimell* in bands remayne, . . . IV. xi. 1. 4
Marin for love of *Florimell* In languor wastes . . . IV. xii. Arg.
Florimell it was which wrought his paine, . . . IV. xii. 27. 8
unto her delivered *Florimell:* . . . IV. xii. 33. 2
Artegall heares of *Florimell*, . . . V. ii. Arg.
chiefly of the fairest *Florimell*, . . . V. ii. 2. 8
The spousals of faire *Florimell*, . . . V. iii. Arg.
So comes it now to *Florimell* by tourne, . . . V. iii. 1. 6
To chalenge all in right of *Florimell*, . . . V. iii. 4. 8
thether also came in open sight Fayre *Florimell*, . . . V. iii. 14. 2
then to him came fayrest *Florimell*, . . . V. iii. 15. 6
Then forth he brought his snowy *Florimele*, . . . V. iii. 17. 1
said, that surely *Florimell* it was, . . . V. iii. 17. 6
if it were not *Florimell* so tride, . . . V. iii. 17. 7
Florimell her selfe she then did pas. . . . V. iii. 17. 8
The more to be true *Florimell* he did surmize. . . . V. iii. 18. 9
Which didst that service unto *Florimell*. . . . V. iii. 21. 4
Is not (I wager) *Florimell* at all; . . . V. iii. 22. 6
he bad them *Florimell* forth call. . . . V. iii. 22. 9
Presented to the fayrest *Florimell*, . . . V. iii. 27. 8
Till *Florimell* about her fastned it. . . . V. iii. 28. 5
Whilest thus they busied were bout *Florimell*, . . . V. iii. 29. 1
Bold Marinell with *Florimell* the fayre, . . . V. iv. 3. 3
Florimell's. not so yellow thryse As *Florimells* fayre heare: . III. viii. 7. 8
this of *Florimels* unworthie paine . . . IV. i. 1. 5
For this was Dony, *Florimels* owne Dwarfe, . . . V. ii. 3. 1
Florimells owne girdle, from her reft . . . V. iii. 27. 4
Flote, -d, -ing. *See* **Float,** *etc.*
Flour. He had beene pouldred all as thin as *flowre:* . . . I. vii. 12. 4
he now had boulted all the *floure*, . . . II. iv. 24. 2
Flourdelice, Flourdelis. *See* **Fleur-de-lis.**
Floure. *See* **Floor, Flour, Flower.**
Flourish. may shee *florish* long In princely plight! . . . *S.C.* Ap. 48
florish in flowres of lusty-head: . . . *S.C.* May 204
flourish fayre In learned artes, . . . *Ti.* 269
in their daies most famouslie did *florish;* . . . *Ti.* 359
There learned arts do *florish* in great honor, . . . *Col.* 320
All these do *florish* in their sundry kynd, . . . *Col.* 452
florish faire above his equall peares: . . . II. viii. 5. 4
Doth *florish* in all beautie excellent; . . . II. xi. 2. 7
Ne more doth *florish* after first decay, . . . II. xii. 75. 3
She did it fayre dispred and let to *florish* fayre. . . . III. v. 51. 9
How ever gay their blossome or their blade Doe *flourish* now, . V. ii. 40. 5
flourish in all wealth and happinesse, . . . V. x. 11. 6
How-ever faire it *flourish* for a time, . . . VII. vii. 18. 2
Flourished. mongst all Cities *florished* much more. . . . *Ro.* xxviii. 14
the Romaine Empire . . . *florisht* most in might, . . . *Van.* xi. 2
faire it *florished* and long time stoud, . . . III. ix. 43. 8
Is often seene full freshly to have *florisht*, . . . IV. iii. 29. 7
when IRELAND *florished* in fame Of wealths . . . VII. vi. 38. 1
Flourishing. *flourishing* fresh leaves and blossomes did enwrap. II. iii. 30. 9
Flout. The whiles the foole did him revile and *flout*, . . . VI. viii. 11. 8
Flouted. when they had *flouted* him their fill, . . . VII. vi. 50. 1
Flow. *See* **Overflow.**
whilome from the Troyan blood did *flow*. . . . *Bel.*[2] v. 8
if on me some little drops would *flowe* . . . *S.C.* Jun. 93
Thy teares would make the hardest flint to *flowe!* . . . *S.C.* Jun. 114
The nombers *flowe* as fast as spring doth ryse. . . . *S.C.* O. 108
flouds of teares *flowe* in theyr stead . . . *S.C.* N. 127
alwayes *flow* to quench his thirstie heate. . . . *Gn.* 120
How he may *flow* in quiets matchles treasour, . . . *Gn.* 139
The Spartan Mirtle, whence sweet gumb does *flowe;* . . . *Gn.* 669
Large streames of honnie and sweete Nectar *flowe*, . . . *T.M.* 218
Not far from whence Sabrinaes streame doth *flow*, . . . *D.* 101
so huge streames of blood thereout did *flow*, . . . *As.* 122
the teares, that from her eyes did *flow*. . . . *As.* 192
the streames that, . . . *Flow* from thy fruitfull head, . . . *Ded.Son.* viii. 10
a dry dropsie through his flesh did *flow*, . . . I. iv. 23. 7
streames of blood down *flow;* . . . I. v. 9. 4
the waters, which from her did *flow*, . . . I. vii. 5. 6
Till living moysture into smoke do *flow*, . . . I. ix. 8. 4
fresh streames do *flow*, . . . II. ii. 9. 2
Fro me do *flow* into an ample flood, . . . II. vii. 8. 8
all my entrailes *flow* with poisnous gore, . . . III. ii. 39. 4
To doen his Nephew in all riches *flow;* . . . III. iv. 22. 2
a large streame of blood out of the wound did *flow*. . . . III. v. 21. 9
Her goodly lockes adowne her backe did *flow* . . . IV. xi. 46. 1
all about that rocke the sea did *flow:* . . . IV. xii. 15. 5
weigh the thought that from mans mind doth *flow:* . . . V. ii. 43. 4
Was fild with bloud which from their sides did *flow*, . . . V. vii. 31. 6
he in slights and jugling feates did *flow*, . . . V. ix. 13. 8
bathe in fountaines that do freshly *flowe* . . . VII. vi. 39. 4
every River still doth ebbe and *flowe;* . . . VII. vii. 20. 4
streames . . . stil do *flow*, and freshly still redound, . . . *H.H.L.* 165
From whom all guifts of wit and knowledge *flow*, . . . *H.H.B.* 9
Flowed. *See* **Overflowed.**
streames of blood foorth *flowed* on the gras. . . . *Ti.* 651
gore, Which *flowed* from his wounds in wondrous store. . . . I. viii. 24. 5
Forth *flowed* fresh A gushing river of blacke gory blood, . . . I. xi. 22. 3
flowd, as from a well, A trickling streame . . . I. xi. 48. 1
In wine and meats she *flowd* above the banck, . . . II. ii. 36. 6
a blacke flood, which *flow'd* about it round. . . . II. vii. 56. 7
Out of the wound the red blood *flowed* fresh, . . . II. viii. 36. 8
flowd from her lanck syde . . . III. ix. 21. 5
thousands like which *flowed* in his braine, . . . III. x. 8. 7
there *flowed* forth the Romane Flood. . . . VII. vii. 42. 9

Flower. *See* **Broom-flower, Fleur-de-lis.**
she languisht as the gathered *floure;* . . . *Pet.* vi. 9
bloosmes, wherewith your buds did *flowre;* . . . *S.C.* Ja. 34
Flora now calleth forth eche *flower*, . . . *S.C.* Mar. 16
Elisa . . . That blessed wight, The *flowre* of Virgins: . . . *S.C.* Ap. 48
the lasse, whose *flowre* is woxe a weede, . . . *S.C.* Jun. 109
The fayrest *floure* our gyrlond all emong . . . *S.C.* N. 75
Fresh Rhododaphne, and the Sabine *flowre*, . . . *Gn.* 673
whatsoever other *flowre* of worth, . . . *Gn.* 681
The *flowre* of wit, finde nought to busie me: . . . *T.M.* 166
those fresh buds, which wont so faire to *flowre*, . . . *T.M.* 249
faire *flower* of chastitie, . . . *Ti.* 251
every *flowre* and herbe there set in order: . . . *Mui.* 172
O that so faire a *flower* so soone should fade, . . . *D.* 237
Sith that my fairest *flower* is faded quight; . . . *D.* 494
Into one *flowre* that is both red and blew; . . . *As.* 184
He had a daughter fresh as *floure* of May, . . . *Col.* 106
Amyntas, *floure* of shepheards pride forlorne: . . . *Col.* 439
The *floure* of vertue and pure chastitie, . . . *Col.* 469
Phyllis, the *floure* of rare perfection, . . . *Col.* 544
The *flowre* of chevalry . . . Doth promise fruite . . . *Ded. Son.* x. 2
the chastest *flowre* that aye did spring On earthly braunch, . . I. i. 48. 4
in the first *flowre* of my freshest age, . . . I. ii. 23. 1
her . . . That was the *flowre* of faith and chastity: . . . I. iii. 23. 5
him destroy, That was the *flowre* of grace and chevalrye; . . I. iv. 45. 8
unto their God present That *flowre* of fayth . . . I. vi. 15. 5
'Fayre braunch of noblesse, *flowre* of chevalrie, . . . I. viii. 26. 7
'It was in freshest *flowre* of youthly yeares, . . . I. ix. 9. 1
So faire and fresh, as freshest *flowre* in May; . . . I. xii. 22. 1
Now in his freshest *flowre* of lusty-hed, . . . II. i. 41. 7
Doth beare the fayrest *flowre* in honourable seed. . . . II. iii. 10. 9
No daintie *flowre* or herbe that growes on grownd, . . . II. vi. 12. 6
Prince Arthur, *flowre* of grace and nobilesse, . . . II. viii. 18. 4
Shee is the *flowre* of grace and chastity . . . II. ix. 4. 3
in the *flowre* now of her freshest age; . . . II. ix. 18. 7
they Glorian call that glorious *flowre:* . . . II. x. 76. 8
through the Euxine seas bore all the *flowr* of Greece. . . . II. xii. 44. 9
In springing *flowre* the image of thy day. . . . II. xii. 74. 3
Of mortall life the leafe, the bud, the *flowre;* . . . II. xii. 75. 2
The fayre Adonis, turned to a *flowre;* . . . III. i. 34. 5
Now making girlonds of each *flowre* that grew, . . . III. i. 35. 4
Him to a dainty *flowre* she did transmew, . . . III. i. 38. 8
spred Abroad thy fresh youths fayrest *flowre*, . . . III. ii. 31. 7
he faded to a watry *flowre:* . . . III. ii. 45. 4
Rew, and Savine, and the *flowre* Of Camphora, . . . III. ii. 49. 5
whose *flowre* The girlond of her honour did adorne: . . . III. v. 51. 2
In Paradize whylome did plant this *flowre;* . . . III. v. 52. 3
it fayrest *Flowre* doth spyre, . . . III. v. 52. 8
With this fayre *flowre* your goodly girlonds dight . . . III. v. 53. 5
that faire *flowre* of beautie fades away, . . . III. vi. 38. 8
all about grew every sort of *flowre*, . . . III. vi. 45. 1
Sad Amaranthus, made a *flowre* but late, . . . III. vi. 45. 6
that faire Maide, the *flowre* of wemens pride; . . . III. vii. 31. 5
'Fayre Helene, *flowre* of beautie excellent, . . . III. ix. 35. 1
Britomart the *flowre* of chastity; . . . III. xi. 6. 2
fayrest *flowre* Wouldst gather faine, . . . IV. ii. 14. 3
Florimell, in her first ages *flowre*, . . . IV. v. 5. 7
Then did her glorious *flowre* wex dead and wan, . . . IV. viii. 32. 8
from that goodly glorious *flowre* proceed, . . . IV. viii. 33. 6
No *flowre* in field, that daintie odour throwes, . . . IV. x. 22. 3
had seene In their first *flowre*, . . . V. x. 7. 5
Amongst them all growes not a fayrer *flowre* . . . VI. Pr. 4. 1
Full glad . . . young Tristram grew; Like as a *flowre*, . . . VI. ii. 35. 7
when first the *flowre* Of beauty gan to bud, . . . VI. viii. 20. 1
fade Like to a *flowre* that feeles no heate of sunne, . . . VI. x. 44. 6
in his youthes freshest *flowre*, . . . VI. xii. 3. 5
with divers-colord *flowre* To decke hir selfe, . . . *Am.* iv. 11
faire *flowre!* in whom fresh youth doth raine, . . . *Am.* iv. 13
Fayre Venice, *flower* of the last worlds delight; . . . *Com. Son.* iv. 10
Venus . . . Fresh *flowre* of grace, . . . *H.B.* 282
O blessed Well of Love! O *Floure* of Grace! . . . *H.H.L.* 169
sweetest Season, when each *Flower* and weede . . . *Proth.* 68
flower of Chevalrie! . . . *Proth.* 150
Flowered. Whilome thy fresh spring *flowrd*, . . . *S.C.* Ja. 21
when *flowrd* my joyfull spring, . . . *S.C.* D. 19
Floweret. the *flouret* of the field doth fade, . . . *S.C.* N. 83
Flowereth. It *floureth* fresh, as it should never fayle? . . . *S.C.* N. 86
Flowerets. Where-with my fresh *flowretts* bene defast: . . . *S.C.* F. 182
fresh *flowrets* dight About her necke, . . . II. vi. 7. 4
Flowering. my *flowring* youth is foe to frost, . . . *S.C.* F. 31
With *flowring* blossomes to furnish the prime, . . . *S.C.* F. 167
flowring pride, opprest With early frosts, . . . *D.* 27
For ever with a *flowring* girlond crownd: . . . I. x. 54. 5
As through the *flouring* forrest rash she fled, . . . II. iii. 30. 7
Framed of wanton Yvie, *flouring* fayre, . . . II. v. 29. 3
'The lilly, Lady of the *flowring* field, . . . II. vi. 16. 1
'The antique world, in his first *flowring* youth, . . . II. vii. 16. 1
Does mow the *flowring* herbes and goodly things, . . . III. vi. 39. 4
shadie seates, and sundry *flowring* bankes, . . . IV. x. 25. 4
flowring pride, so fading and so fickle, . . . VII. viii. 1. 8
Flowers. On hearbs and *flowres* (*floures*[1]) she walked . . . *Pet.* vi. 3
the gay *floures* did offer to be eaten; . . . *Van.* ii. 6
The shepheards daughters to gather *flowres*, . . . *S.C.* F. 120
Seest how fresh my *flowers* bene spredde, . . . *S.C.* F. 129
Untimely my *flowres* forced to fall, . . . *S.C.* F. 177
florish in *flowres* of lusty-head: . . . *S.C.* May 204
The faded *flowres* her corse embrave. . . . *S.C.* N. 109
'The fragrant *flowres*, that in my garden grewe, . . . *S.C.* D. 109
To spil the *flowres* that should her girlond dight? . . . *S.C.* D. 114
sundrie *flowers* in wilde fieldes gathered; . . . *Gn.* 132

Flowers—*Continued.*
round about he taught sweete *flowres* to growe: . . . . *Gn.* 665
Full of sweete *flowres* and daintiest delights, ... *Ti.* 520
deckt with daintie *flowres,* . . . . *Ti.* 634
when *flowres* doo clothe the fruitful ground, ... *Mui.* 114
To gather *flowres* her forhead to array: . . . . *Mui.* 117
all those *flowres,* with which so plenteouslie . . . . *Mui.* 140
To feed on *flowres* and weeds of glorious feature, ... *Mui.* 213
a faire border wrought of sundrie *flowres,* . . . . *Mui.* 298
Let th' earth . . . bring foorth no *flowres,* . . . . *D.* 334
Gay chapelets of *flowers* and gyrlonds trim. . . . . *As.* 42
brought him presents, *flowers* if it were prime, ... *As.* 47
wont to be with *flowers* and gyrlonds dight, ... *As.* 153
As fittest *flowres* to deck his mournfull hearse. . . . . *As.* Interl. 228
The fields with faded *flowers* did seem to mourne, ... *Col.* 25
his flesh shronk up like withered *flowres.* . . . . I. viii. 41. 9
him . . . Who earst in *flowres* of freshest youth was clad. . . . . I. viii. 42. 4
deck with dainty *flowres* their brydall bed, ... I. x. 42. 3
her charet, all with *flowers* spred, ... I. xi. 51. 7
As fresh as *flowres* in medow greene doe grow . . . . I. xii. 6. 7
filles with *flowres* fayre Floraes painted lap: . . . . II. ii. 6. 5
In her rude heares sweet *flowres* themselves did lap, ... II. iii. 30. 8
all within with *flowres* was garnished, ... II. v. 29. 7
The *flowrs,* the fields, and all that pleasaunt growes, ... II. vi. 15. 2
the *flowres* did freshly spring, ... II. vi. 24. 6
deckt with *flowers* and herbars daintily: . . . . II. ix. 46. 2
With diverse *flowres* he daintily was deckt, ... II. xii. 49. 1
The painted *flowres,* the trees upshooting hye, ... II. xii. 58. 5
Their fleecy *flowres* they fearefully did steepe, ... II. xii. 61. 8
the faire *flowres* that decked him afore: . . . . III. iv. 17. 8
both *flowres* and girlonds far away Shee flong, ... III. iv. 30. 1
strowe with *flowres* the lamentable beare. . . . . III. iv. 42. 5
all the sweetest *flowers* that in the forrest grew: . . . . III. vi. 6. 9
In that same Gardin all the goodly *flowres,* . . . . III. vi. 30. 1
Lapped in *flowres* and pretious spycery, ... III. vi. 46. 5
Girlonds of *flowres* sometimes for her faire hed . . . . III. vii. 17. 5
mans wretched state, That *floures* so fresh at morne, ... III. ix. 39. 9
both in *flowres* doe live, ... III. xi. 37. 4
brings forth glorious *flowres* of fame, ... IV. Pr. 2. 7
flowres as fresh as May. . . . . IV. x. 37. 9
Out of her fruitfull lap aboundant *flowres;* . . . . IV. x. 45. 2
Unto her waste, with *flowres* bescattered, ... IV. xi. 46. 2
A Chapelet of sundry *flowers* she wore, ... IV. xi. 46. 6
made smooth fields now full of *flowres?* . . . . V. x. 23. 5
divers *flowres* distinct with rare delight, ... VI. iii. 23. 5
Deckt with greene boughes and *flowers* gay beseene: . . . . . VI. v. 38. 5
a garland doth compose Of finest *flowers,* . . . . VI. viii. 39. 8
deckt it all with *flowres* which they nigh hand obtayned. . . . VI. viii. 44. 9
a crowne Of sundry *flowres* with silken ribbands tyde, ... VI. ix. 7. 8
sweete *flowres* that far did smell . . . . VI. x. 14. 7
Out of her bowre, that many *flowers* strowes: . . . . VII. vi. 41. 5
Was dight with *flowers* that voluntary grew . . . . VII. vii. 10. 2
leaves of *flowres* That freshly budded . . . . VII. vii. 28. 2
all the fairest *flowres* and freshest buds . . . . VII. vii. 33. 7
throwing *flowres* out of her lap around: . . . . VII. vii. 34. 3
Deckt all with *flowres,* and wings of gold . . . . VII. vii. 46. 9
flowres, That dainty odours from them threw . . . . *Am.* lxiv. 2
Such fragrant *flowers* (**flowres*) doe give most odorous smell; *Am.* lxiv. 13
richly are displayd All sorts of *flowres,* . . . . *Am.* lxx. 3
woodbynd *flowers* and fragrant Eglantine; . . . . *Am.* lxxi. 10
All other fayre, lyke *flowres,* untymely fade. . . . . *Am.* lxxix. 14
let them eeke bring store of other *flowers,* . . . . *Epith.* 46
Be strewed with fragrant *flowers* all along, ... *Epith.* 50
Sprinckled with perle, and perling *flowres* atweene, ... *Epith.* 155
decke with *floures* thy altars well beseene. . . . . *H.L.* 293
Was paynted all with variable *flowers,* . . . . *Proth.* 13
they gathered *flowers* to fill their flasket, ... *Proth.* 26
the Nymphes, which now had *Flowers* their fill, ... *Proth.* 55
out of their baskets drew Great store of *Flowers,* . . . . *Proth.* 74
Tempes shore, Scattred with *Flowres,* . . . . *Proth.* 80
freshest *Flowres* which in that Mead they found, ... *Proth.* 84
Flowers'. *flowres* varietie With sundrie colours . . . . *Gn.* 109
Flowery. To dig up sods out of the *flowrie* grasse, ... *Gn.* 654
along the Lee, About whose *flowrie* bankes . . . . *Ti.* 136
flowrie bancks with silver liquor steepe; . . . . *D.* 102
sung by them with *flowry* gyrlonds crownd. . . . . *Col.* 643
With gilden hornes and *flowry* girlonds crownd, ... III. iv. 17. 2
by the *flowrie* marge Of a fresh streame . . . . IV. viii. 61. 5
Her *flowry* garlond tooke from her owne head, ... VI. ix. 42. 6
through the *flowry* Dales she tumbling downe . . . . VII. vi. 41. 6
lying on the *flowry* gras, ... *Epith.* 308
Floweth. Whence *floweth* Helicon, the learned well, ... *S.C.* Ap. 42
all the territories, Which Phison and Euphrates *floweth* by, . . I. vii. 43. 8
Flowing. *See* **Overflowing.**
Ran *flowing* all along the creekie shoare . . . . *Bel.*[1] vii. 7
Tho gan the streames of *flowing* wittes to cease, ... *S.C.* O. 71
all the way she wetts with *flowing* teares; . . . . I. iii. 44. 4
his *flowing* toung and troublous spright . . . . II. iii. 4. 6
flowing low and thick her cloth'd arownd, ... II. xii. 67. 4
Faire Ister, *flowing* from the mountaines hie: . . . . IV. xi. 20. 5
flowing fast to Rhy; . . . . IV. xi. 33. 2
flowing all from one, all one at last become. . . . . IV. xi. 43. 9
purple blood Yet *flowing* fresh, ... VI. iv. 12. 3
flowing from the beame Of thy bright starre, ... *H.B.* 55
Still *flowing* forth His goodnesse unto all, ... *H.H.L.* 100
Flown. *See* **Overflown.**
with nimble flight *Flowne* at a flush of Ducks . . . . V. ii. 54. 2
Flowre. *See* **Floor, Flour, Flower.**
Flows. *flowes* in pleasures and vaine pleasing toyes, ... II. v. 28. 8
here all plenty and all pleasure *flowes;* . . . . III. vi. 41. 4

Flows—*Continued.*
the tide, . . . *Flowes* up the Shenan with contrarie forse, . . IV. iii. 27. 2
underneath the same a river *flowes* . . . . V. ii. 8. 1
Through many woods and shady coverts *flowes,* . . . . VII. vi. 41. 7
Flung. *See* **Flong.**
Flush. With *flushe* [? flashe] stroke downe this noble monument. . . . . *Bel.*[1] iii. 14
Flowne at a *flush* of Ducks foreby the brooke, ... V. ii. 54. 2
How the red roses *flush* up in her cheekes, ... *Epith.* 226
Flushing. by the swift recourse of *flushing* blood . . . . . IV. vi. 29. 6
Flutter. Shall fly and *flutter* round about your bed, ... *Epith.* 359
Fluttered. Cupid selfe about her *fluttred* all in greene. . . . VII. vii. 34. 9
Fluttering. There may thy Muse display her *fluttryng* wing, *S.C.* O. 43
fluttering round about them still does sore: . . . . *Gn.* 406
Make thy selfe *fluttring* wings . . . . *U.V.* 2
Love, . . . light *fluttering* Upon the waves, ... *Mui.* 290
Fluttring among the Olives wantonly, ... *Mui.* 331
Fluttring about his ever-damned hedd, ... I. i. 38. 3
when *fluttring* wind does blow . . . . II. iii. 10. 3
Their *fluttring* arrowes, thicke as flakes of snow, ... II. xi. 18. 2
harmefull fowles about them *fluttering* cride, ... II. xii. 35. 7
fayntly *fluttering,* scarce his helmet raught, ... III. v. 24. 8
faulcon . . . That flags awhile her *fluttering* wings beneath, . . *H.H.B.* 27
Fly. Hereout did *flie* up to the throne of Gods, ... *Bel.*[1] ix. 6
Hereout up to the throne of Gods did *flie,* . . . . *Bel.*[2] xi. 6
Alas! by little ye to nothing *flie,* . . . . *Ro.* vii. 7
Whiles Jove at them his thunderbolts let *flie,* . . . . *Ro.* xii. 4
Whether they fare on foote, or *flie* aloft, ... *Ro.* xxiv. 3
The silly *Flie,* that no redresse did see, ... *Van.* iv. 5
fish . . . That makes the sea before his face to *flye,* . . . . . *Van.* v. 3
should my plaints . . . *Flye* to my love, ... *S.C.* Jun. 99
A shell-fish downe let *flye:* . . . . *S.C.* Jul. 224
I beate the bush, the byrds to them do *flye:* . . . . *S.C.* O. 17
flye backe to heaven apace. . . . . *S.C.* O. 84
as a thistle-downe in th' ayre doth *flie,* . . . . *Hub.* 634
Ne after everie tattling fable *flie;* . . . . *Hub.* 724
Else we may *flye;* . . . . *Hub.* 990
At sight of him, gan fast away to *flye;* . . . . *Hub.* 1069
bad him *flie* with never-resting speed . . . . *Hub.* 1247
He did uncase, and then away let *flie:* . . . . *Hub.* 1380
being driven hence, I thether *fly.* . . . . *T.M.* 528
fly forth unto my Love whersoever she be: . . . . *U.V.* 3
Fame with golden wings aloft doth *flie,* . . . . *Ti.* 421
The fresh yong *flie,* in whom the kindly fire . . . . *Mui.* 33
he along would *flie* Upon the streaming rivers, ... *Mui.* 46
So did this *flie* outstretch his fearefull hornes, ... *Mui.* 87
when them the gorgeous *Flie* had doft, ... *Mui.* 109
that *flie* them in her wings doth beare. . . . . *Mui.* 144
There he arriving round about doth *flie,* . . . . *Mui.* 169
unhappie happie *Flie,* Whose cruell fate . . . . *Mui.* 234
why he this *Flie* so maliced . . . . *Mui.* 257
At length, the foolish *Flie,* without foresight, ... *Mui.* 389
There the fond *Flie,* entangled, strugled long, ... *Mui.* 425
all times doo *flye* So fast away, ... *D.* 411
doth his trembling Muse but lowly *flie,* . . . . *Col.* 420
Doe yet but flagg, and lowly learne to *fly,* . . . . *Ded. Son.* ii. 8
'Fly, fly!' (quoth then The fearefull Dwarfe). . . . . I. i. 13. 8
Unto that Elfin knight he bad him *fly,* . . . . I. i. 46. 2
'My weaker yeares, . . . *Fly* to your fayth for succour . . . . I. i. 52. 6
so both away do *fly.* . . . . I. ii. 6. 9
of himselfe he ofte for feare . . . would *flie* away. . . . . . I. ii. 10. 8
at last it flitted is, Whither the soules doe *fly* . . . . I. ii. 19. 9
But *fly,* ah! *fly* far hence away, ... I. ii. 31. 4
Still seeking him, that from her still did *flye;* . . . . I. iii. 21. 8
Paynim . . . From whom her booteth not at all to *flie:* . . . I. iii. 40. 7
Lo! his Fidessa, to thy secret faith I *flye.'* . . . . I. iv. 45. 9
fly away for feare of fowle disgrace . . . . I. vi. 18. 7
she goes, to . . . seeke her spouse that from her still does *fly,* . I. vi. 22. 4
everie beast for feare of him did *fly,* and quake. . . . . I. vi. 24. 9
turning backe gan fast to *fly* away; . . . . I. vi. 28. 2
spoile her of her scarlot robe, and let her *fly.'* . . . . I. viii. 45. 9
That seemed from some feared foe to *fly,* . . . . I. ix. 21. 3
from the fielde most cowardly doth *fly!* . . . . I. x. 1. 5
As sparkles from the Andvile use to *fly,* . . . . I. xi. 42. 6
I to them for judgement just doe *fly,* . . . . I. xii. 27. 8
To *fly* the vengeaunce for his outrage dew: . . . . II. i. 25. 4
chaced her that fast from him did *fly;* . . . . II. ii. 7. 8
O! *fly* from wrath; *fly,* O my liefest Lord! . . . . II. ii. 30. 5
each bad other *flye:* . . . . II. iii. 19. 8
She could them nimbly move, and after *fly* apace. . . . . II. iii. 28. 9
fly away, or bide alone behinde; . . . . II. iii. 32. 4
cause one foot to *flye,* . . . . II. iii. 45. 4
gan her sonne to *flye* Full fast away, ... II. iv. 13. 6
round about a cloud of dust did *fly,* . . . . II. iv. 37. 4
Fly therefore, *fly* this fearefull stead anon, ... II. iv. 42. 8
'Fly, O Pyrochles! *fly* the dreadfull warre . . . . II. v. 16. 1
winged canvas with the wind to *fly:* . . . . II. vi. 5. 4
whither dost thou *flye* The shame and death, ... II. vi. 39. 6
Bidding his winged vessell fairely forward *fly:* . . . . II. vii. 1. 9
trembling Feare still to and fro did *fly,* . . . . II. vii. 22. 6
the fruit from hand . . . Did *fly* abacke, ... II. vii. 58. 7
far before a light-foote Page did *flie,* . . . . II. viii. 10. 4
from his saddle forced him to *fly;* . . . . II. viii. 33. 7
With his owne swerd he fierce at him did *flye,* . . . . II. viii. 47. 4
The clowdes, as thinges affrayd, before him *flye;* . . . . II. viii. 48. 3
'Fly, fly, good knights,' . . . *'fly* fast away, ... II. ix. 12. 1
Fly fast, and save your selves . . . . II. ix. 12. 3
Champions broke on them, that forst them *fly,* . . . . II. ix. 14. 6
him vanquisht she to *fly* constraind: . . . . II. x. 18. 5
as he to those woody hilles did *fly,* . . . . II. x. 33. 7

Fly—*Continued.*
twise renforst backe to their ships to *fly;* II. x. 48. 2
Rather then *fly,* or be captiv'd, II. x. 55. 9
at him let *fly* Their fluttring arrowes, II. xi. 18. 1
neither can he *fly,* nor other harme, II. xi. 34. 2
all the seas for feare doe seeme away to *fly.* II. xii. 3. 9
whiles they *fly* that Gulfes devouring jawes, II. xii. 4. 8
seem'd to *fly* for feare them to behold. II. xii. 25. 5
all that dreadfull Armie fast gan *flye* II. xii. 26. 8
through the sea resounding plaints did *fly:* II. xii. 27. 4
seemd with lively jollitee To *fly* about, II. xii. 60. 8
now awaking, fierce at them gan *fly,* II. xii. 84. 6
all spurd after, fast as they mote *fly,* III. i. 18. 4
Made them recoile, and *fly* from dredd decay, III. i. 21. 8
sleepe full far away from her did *fly:* III. ii. 28. 5
To doe the frosen cold away to *fly;* III. ii. 34. 5
Shall to the utmost mountaines *fly* apace. III. iii. 34. 4
With his wide wings upon them fiercely *fly,* III. iii. 46. 6
'*Fly* they, that need to *fly;* III. iv. 15. 2
ever from fayre Ladies love did *fly,* III. iv. 26. 6
Ile clip his wanton wings, that he no more shall *flye.*' III. vi. 24. 9
No need to bid her fast away to *flie:* III. vii. 24. 2
As it befell, that she could *flie* no more, III. vii. 25. 5
made her selfe more light away to *fly:* III. vii. 44. 4
The knight, him seeing *flie,* III. viii. 19. 1
To *fly* for succour to a little shed, III. ix. 11. 8
In speaking many false belgardes at her let *fly.* III. ix. 52. 9
ready seeing him with her to *fly,* III. x. 14. 2
her up he cast . . . lett her *fly* alone: III. x. 35. 8
The old man could not *fly,* but fell to ground III. x. 43. 9
hardly he with life away does *fly,* III. x. 53. 8
alwayes did their dread encounter *fly:* III. xi. 6. 4
these few words lett *fly.* III. xi. 15. 9
sparks . . . forth in flames did *fly.* III. xii. 9. 9
armes . . . clashing heard, he fast away did *fly,* III. xii. 12. 5
directly *fly* Unto her rest in Plutoes griesly land; IV. iii. 13. 2
With heapes of strokes, which he at him let *flie* IV. iii. 25. 4
So did one soule out of his bodie *flie* IV. iii. 30. 8
before they may to heaven *flie,* IV. iii. 44. 5
faine from themselves to *flie;* IV. iv. 47. 5
her pursu'd as fast as she did *flie:* IV. vii. 21. 7
forst him *flie* abacke, himselfe to save: IV. vii. 28. 4
Whom seeing *flie* she speedily poursewed IV. vii. 30. 1
A Squire came gallopping, as he would *flie,* IV. viii. 38. 2
all at once at him gan fiercely *flie,* IV. ix. 33. 2
makst the stormes to *flie;* IV. x. 44. 5
fain'd to *fly* for feare of being thrall; V. i. 22. 8
with his iron flale at it let *flie,* V. ii. 21. 2
Each one did *flie;* their hearts began to faile, V. ii. 24. 7
vaine it was to thinke from him to *flie;* V. iii. 38. 2
I heard report that farre abrode did *fly,* V. iv. 29. 4
Through all the fields and vallies did before him *flie.* V. iv. 44. 9
With fresh assault upon him she did *fly,* V. v. 14. 3
they gan to *flie,* V. vi. 30. 2
still from him as fast away did *flie,* V. viii. 6. 2
From whom she earst so fast away did *flie:* V. viii. 16. 3
made him backe againe as fast to *fly;* V. viii. 36. 3
Fast did they *fly* as them their feete could beare V. viii. 39. 1
To *fly* his stepdames loves outrageous, V. viii. 43. 3
He threw his burden downe, and fast away did *fly.* V. ix. 14. 9
to those fennes for fastnesse she did *fly,* V. x. 18. 8
When one in armes she saw, began to *fly;* V. x. 19. 6
Both man and beast doe *fly,* and succour doe inquyre. V. xi. 58. 9
made to *fly* like doves whom the Eagle doth affray. V. xii. 5. 9
By those which earst did *fly* away for feare, V. xii. 6. 5
Whom Calidore perceiving fast to *flie,* VI. i. 22. 6
'were not that thou wouldst *fly* VI. i. 28. 5
Bad him to *flie* with all the speed he could VI. i. 29. 4
Him seem'd his feet did *fly* and in their speed delight. VI. iv. 19. 9
He forced was to turne from him and *fly:* VI. v. 16. 7
flying still did ward, and warding *fly* away. VI. vi. 28. 9
he layd about, and made them fast to *flie.* VI. vi. 38. 9
gan fiercely *fly* Upon that Carle VI. viii. 12. 8
Fly like a flocke of doves before a Faulcons vew. VI. viii. 49. 9
he forced him to *flie.* VI. ix. 4. 9
the mad steele about doth fiercely *fly,* VI. xi. 16. 3
As if he did from some late daunger *fly,* VI. xi. 27. 5
So did he *fly* amongst them here and there, VI. xi. 49. 3
all the woods and dales, where he did *flie,* VII. vi. 52. 8
An humble suppliant loe! I lowely *fly,* VII. vii. 14. 2
Ne doe their bodies only flit and *fly,* VII. vii. 19. 7
flitting still doe *flie,* and still their places vary. VII. vii. 21. 9
Legions of loves with little wings did *fly;* *Am.* xvi. 6
On the Thessalian shore from him did *flie:* *Am.* xxviii. 10
fly no more, fayre Love, from Phebus chace, *Am.* xxviii. 13
let us . . . *fly* the faults with which we did offend. *Am.* lxii. 8
make him bond that bondage earst dyd *fly.* *Am.* lxv. 4
Sought not to *fly,* but fearelesse still did bide; *Am.* lxvii. 10
Drawne with sweet pleasures bayt, it back doth *fly,* *Am.* lxxii. 7
Breaking his prison, forth to you doth *fly.* *Am.* lxxiii. 4
joyous houres doe *fly* away too fast. *Am.* lxxxvi. 14
He tooke his wings and away did *fly.* *Epig.* i. 6
change thy cruelty, Or give like leave unto the *fly.*' *Epig.* iv. 20
the cruell boy . . . Would needs the *fly* pursue; *Epig.* iv. 22
The *Fly,* that I so much did scorne, Hath hurt me *Epig.* iv. 29
he the *fly* did mock. *Epig.* iv. 44
Forget their service and about her *fly,* *Epith.* 231
Shall *fly* and flutter round about your bed, *Epith.* 359
dare not to heaven *fly,* *H.L.* 181
Of the soare faulcon so I learne to *fly,* *H.H.B.* 26

Fly—*Continued.*
idle hopes, which still doe *fly* away, *Proth.* 8
Flyeth. from their shields forth *flyeth* firie light, I. v. 7. 8
Which having ended after him she *flyeth* swifte. II. vii. 23. 9
Flying. *See* **Fast-flying, High-flying.**
all is nought but *flying* vanitee! *Bel.* i. 11
Is now no more seen *flying,* nor alighting. *Ro.* xvii. 14
sittes not followe *flying* fame, *S.C.* Jun. 75
Cruell Agave, *flying* vengeance sore *Gn.* 172
Time, *flying* with winges swift, *Hub.* 308
th' Ape still *flying* he no where might get: *Hub.* 1372
monstrous error, *flying* in the ayre, *T.M.* 257
Toward those parts came *flying* carelesslie, *Mui.* 391
Like *flying* doves ye did before you chace; *Ded. Son.* vi. 9
he lept As Lyon fierce upon the *flying* pray, I. i. 17. 2
Still *flying* from his thoughts and gealous feare: I. ii. 12. 3
Phoebus, *flying* so most shamefull sight, I. vi. 6. 6
Una, . . . Fast *flying* from that Paynims greedy pray, I. vii. 20. 3
when the *flying* heavens he would affray; I. vii. 34. 4
Which *flying* fame throughout the world had spred, I. vii. 46. 2
Shee, *flying* fast from heavens hated face, . . . Fled I. viii. 50. 1
him . . . hardly he from *flying* forward stayd, I. ix. 23. 5
Halfe *flying* and halfe footing in his haste, I. xi. 8. 2
like mayne-yardes with *flying* canvas lynd; I. xi. 10. 5
With *flying* speede, . . . Came running in, I. xii. 24. 7
Orion, *flying* fast from hissing snake, II. ii. 46. 2
when the *flying* Libbard she did chace, II. iii. 28. 8
Whose *flying* feet so fast their way applyde, II. iv. 37. 3
cleave The flitting skyes, like *flying* Pursuivant, II. viii. 2. 4
to th' infernall shade Fast *flying,* II. viii. 45. 8
flying fast as Roebucke through the fen, II. x. 7. 5
his faire Leman *flying* through a brooke She overhent, II. x. 18. 8
flying from his guilt, by them was slayne; II. x. 67. 5
Stoupes at a *flying* heron with proud disdayne, II. xi. 43. 2
Flying from Junoes wrath and hard assay, II. xii. 13. 5
The *flying* ships with swiftnes to pursew: II. xii. 24. 4
Fast *flying* through this forest from her fo, III. v. 6. 2
All that same evening she in *flying* spent, III. vii. 2. 1
a mighty Giauntesse Fast *flying,* on a Courser III. vii. 37. 3
While she was *flying,* like a weary weft, V. iii. 27. 5
The Engin, fiercely *flying* forth, V. vi. 40. 4
A Damzell, *flying* on a palfrey fast V. viii. 4. 2
Gave way unto his horses speedie *flying,* V. viii. 32. 3
Ne could the Souldan them from *flying* stay V. viii. 38. 5
Flying from place to place with cowheard shame; V. viii. 50. 8
Flying from tree to tree, from wand to wand; V. ix. 17. 6
Did set uppon us *flying* both for feare; VI. i. 16. 4
Flying the fury of his bloudy will: VI. iii. 49. 4
flying still did ward, and warding fly away. VI. vi. 28. 9
untill the *flying* day Was farre forth spent, VI. ix. 12. 5
The false reports that *flying* tales doe beare, *H.L.* 261
Armies of Loves still *flying* too and fro, *H.B.* 240
Foal. As he had beene a *fole* of Pegasus his kynd. I. ix. 21. 9
Foam. Though eating hipps, and drinking watry *fome.* *Hub.* 948
The yron rowels into frothy *fome* he bitt. I. vii. 37. 9
their brode flaggy finnes no *fome* did reare, III. iv. 33. 6
filleth all the sea with *fome,* IV. i. 42. 5
Doth frie with *fome* above the surges hore. V. ii. 15. 8
he gan fret and *fome* out bloudy gore VI. xii. 31. 3
to thy home, Within the Westerne *fome:* *Epith.* 283
Foamed. a courser . . . That through his fiersnesse *fomed* all with sweat, I. iii. 33. 4
chaufd and *fom'd* with corage fiers and sterne, II. iii. 46. 8
His steed was bloody red, and *fomed* yre, II. v. 2. 8
drawne upon the waves that *fomed* him arownd. III. viii. 30. 9
fomed all about his bloody jawes: VI. xii. 29. 6
Foaming. His angry steede did chide his *foming* bitt, I. i. 1. 6
foming tarre, their bridles they would champ, I. v. 28. 8
wont in charett chace the *foming* bore: I. v. 37. 2
Where *foming* wrath their cruell tuskes they whett, I. vi. 44. 7
Chaufing and *foming* choler each against his fo. IV. iv. 29. 9
Foming with poyson round about her gils, V. xii. 36. 2
Foamy. *See* **Froth-foamy.**
river swift, whose *fomy* billowes *Bel.*² viii. 1
sweepe The *fomie* waves out of the dreadfull deep, *Van.* v. 5
with good speed the *fomie* billowes scowre: *Gn.* 564
In liquid waves to cut their *fomie* waie, *Ti.* 149
with her brest breaking the *fomy* wave, II. ii. 24. 8
in the *fomy* waves enrold, II. xii. 25. 4
sharply gan to spurne His *fomy* steed, III. i. 5. 5
Along the margent of the *fomy* shore, III. iv. 34. 4
Then gan he freshly pricke his *fomy* steed, III. iv. 48. 2
Along the *fomy* waves driving his finny drove. III. viii. 29. 9
the white *fomy* creame Did shine with silver, III. xi. 41. 4
Venus of the *fomy* sea was bred, IV. xii. 2. 2
Fodder. fedd on *fodder* to beguile her sight. III. xi. 42. 4
Foe. Daring the *foe* that cannot him defend: *Ro.* xiv. 8
my flowring youth is *foe* to frost, *S.C.* F. 31
All were it of my *foe,* then fonly pitied: *S.C.* May 58
Had lever my *foe* then my freend he be; *S.C.* May 167
Betraying him unto the traines of hys *foe.* *S.C.* May 200
He spide his *foe* with felonous intent, *Gn.* 295
To daunt his *foe* by ensample of the same. *Gn.* 608
He lately slue his dreadfull *foe* in fight. *Gn.* 648
after he had wonne th' Assyrian *foe,* *Hub.* 751
The *foe* of faire things, th' author of confusion, *Mui.* 244
His heart did earne against his hated *foe,* *Mui.* 254
feare of *foe* That hazarded his health, *Mui.* 377
Aragnoll (so his *foe* was hight) *Mui.* 385
the cursed cobweb, which his *foe* Had framed *Mui.* 423

Foes—*Continued.*
treasons could bewray, and *foes* convince: . . . III. ii. 21. 8
His manly face, that did his *foes* agrize, . . . III. ii. 24. 4
secrete *foes,* that him shall make in mischiefe fall. . . . III. iii. 28. 9
Against his Saxon *foes* in bloody field to fight. . . . III. iii. 29. 9
his proud *foes* discomfit in victorious field. . . . III. iii. 31. 9
to assist the Britons *fone.* . . . III. iii. 33. 9
on their Paynim *foes* avenge their ranckled ire. . . . III. iii. 36. 9
his *foes* shall feare, . . . III. iii. 45. 8
with his *foes* he could not come to fight. . . . III. v. 20. 9
With th' one his *foes* he threatned to invade, . . . III. xii. 11. 7
Some, of deare lovers *foes* perpetuall: . . . IV. i. 24. 5
all those knights, as their professed *fone,* . . . IV. ii. 28. 8
Those two were *foes* the fellonest on ground, . . . IV. ii. 32. 2
watcht on every side, of secret *foes* affrayd, . . . IV. ii. 36. 9
So mortall *foes* so friendly to agree, . . . IV. iii. 49. 7
deadly *foes* so faithfully affrended, . . . IV. iii. 50. 5
mortall *foes* doe turne to faithfull frends, . . . IV. iv. 1. 2
So did these two through all the field their *foes* enforce. . . . IV. iv. 35. 9
She came of her accord, in spight of all his *fone.* . . . IV. v. 26. 9
on his *foes* did worke full cruell wracke: . . . IV. ix. 25. 4
both his professed *fone:* . . . IV. ix. 30. 4
Of litle much, of *foes* she maketh friends, . . . IV. x. 34. 8
So Marinell by him was rescu'd from his *fone.* . . . V. iii. 12. 9
Defend thee from the vengeance of thy *fone;* . . . V. vi. 37. 7
raging flames, that many *foes* shall reare To hinder thee . . . V. vii. 23. 2
With which she used still to tye her *fone,* . . . V. vii. 28. 3
those deadly ends Of both her *foes* had seene, . . . V. viii. 10. 5
when they saw their *foes* dead out of doubt, . . . V. viii. 12. 3
asked her what were those two her *fone,* . . . V. viii. 16. 2
strongly beateth downe The malice of her *foes,* . . . V. viii. 17. 6
even to her *foes* her mercies multiply. . . . V. viii. 17. 9
Maugre so many *foes* which did withstand: . . . V. ix. 30. 5
when as *foes* enforst, or friends sought ayde, . . . V. ix. 30. 8
Her to defend against all forrein *foes* . . . V. x. 12. 4
For whom they wayted as his mortall *fone,* . . . V. xii. 37. 3
Though many *foes* did him maligne therefore, . . . VI. v. 12. 6
his three *foes* shrowded in guilefull shade . . . VI. v. 17. 8
So did that Squire his *foes* disperse and drive asonder. . . . VI. v. 19. 9
his three *foes* Sought to encompasse him . . . VI. v. 20. 1
in so great daunger set Mongst many *foes,* . . . VI. v. 22. 3
To fight with many *foes* about him ment, . . . VI. vi. 27. 5
Maintaine this evil use, thy *foes* thereby to foile. . . . VI. vi. 34. 9
left that salvage wight Amongst so many *foes,* . . . VI. vi. 37. 6
Fearelesse of *foes* that mote his peace molest; . . . VI. vii. 19. 4
Fearelesse of *foes,* or fortunes wrackfull yre . . . VI. ix. 27. 7
to low, to hie, To friends, to *foes;* . . . VI. x. 23. 9
How many of their friends were slaine, how many *fone.* . . . VI. xi. 20. 9
terrifide his *foes,* and armed him, . . . VI. xii. 26. 8
his old *foes* that once him sorely fear'd. . . . VII. vi. 15. 9
mote encheare his friends and *foes* mote terrifie. . . . VII. vi. 24. 9
need not feare the spight Of grudging *foes,* . . . *Am.* lix. 10
The fayned friends, the unassured *foes,* . . . *H.L.* 263
To free his *foes,* that from his heast had swerved! . . . *H.H.L.* 161
His cancred *foes,* his fights, his toyle, his strife, . . . *H.H.L.* 234
rod . . . With which he bruseth all his *foes* to dust, . . . *H.H.B.* 156
fruitfull issue . . . Which may your *foes* confound, . . . *Proth.* 105
Foes'. Then doe I more augment my *foes* despight; . . . *Am.* xliv. 10
Fog. suddeinly a grosse *fog* over-spred . . . II. xii. 34. 5
Like the faire Morning clad in misty *fog* . . . VI. xi. 3. 9
Foggy. by her hellish science raisd . . . A *foggy* mist . . . I. ii. 38. 5
A *foggy* mist had covered all the land; . . . I. iv. 36. 7
Phoebus, . . . His blushing face in *foggy* cloud implyes, . . . I. vi. 6. 7
When *foggy* mistes or cloudy tempests have . . . II. vii. 1. 3
a *foggy* mist hath overcast The face of heven, . . . III. iv. 13. 1
Like as the Moone in *foggie* winters night . . . V. v. 12. 8
like starres in *foggie* night. . . . VI. xi. 21. 9
Fogs. Black stormes and *fogs* are blowen up from farre, . . . *Gn.* 572
Foil. golden *foile* all over them displaid, . . . I. iv. 4. 4
both his foen with equall *foyle* to daunt. . . . II. iii. 13. 3
Nought els but treason from the first this land did *foyle.* . . . II. x. 48. 9
Yet all was forg'd and spred with golden *foyle,* . . . IV. ii. 29. 4
With golden *foyle* doth finely over-spred Some baser metall, . . . IV. v. 15. 2
so would hope him easily to *foyle.* . . . V. ix. 9. 5
he did all to peeces breake, and *foyle* In filthy durt, . . . V. xi. 33. 8
Maintaine this evil use, thy foes thereby to *foile.* . . . VI. vi. 34. 9
Foiled. Yet was she *foyld,* when as she me assailed. . . . *Ti.* 112
Arthure soone hath reskewed, And Paynim brethren *foyld.* . . . II. viii. Arg.
them late had *foyled* In open turney, . . . IV. ix. 36. 2
after that he had *foyled* The cruell Souldan, . . . V. ix. 2. 7
Foined. He hewd, and lasht, and *foynd,* . . . II. v. 9. 1
strooke, and *foynd,* and lasht outrageously, . . . II. viii. 47. 5
He stroke, he soust, he *foynd,* he hewd, he lasht, . . . IV. iii. 25. 6
She hewd, she *foynd,* she lasht, she laid on every side. . . . V. v. 6. 9
Fold. *See* **Sevenfold, Thousandfold, Twofold.**
tumbling through the ayre in firie *fold,* . . . *Bel.*[2] vii. 10
So faynt they woxe, and feeble in the *folde,* . . . *S.C.* Ja. 5
Cruelly fell upon their flock in *folde,* . . . *Hub.* 335
weaving straight a net with manie a *fold* . . . *Mui.* 357
wash faire Cynthiaes sheep, . . . And *fold* them up, . . . *Col.* 259
innocents trew, Which there were slaine as sheepe out of the *fold,* . . . I. viii. 35. 7
Shall he thy sins up in his knowledge *fold,* . . . I. ix. 47. 3
he his armes about her sides gan *fold,* . . . II. i. 46. 4
Eft to Cymochles twise so many *fold;* . . . II. viii. 41. 5
Great heapes of them, like sheepe in narrow *fold,* . . . IV. iii. 41. 4
After her flocke she in their *fold* had tyde: . . . VI. ix. 17. 6
every evening helping them to *fold:* . . . VI. ix. 37. 6
But feele my wits to faile, and tongue to *fold.* . . . *H.H.B.* 7
Folded. *See* **Double-folded, Many-folded.**

Folded—*Continued.*
his *folded* flocke to keepe. . . . *S.C.* Env. 6
With *folded* hands, and knees full lowly bent, . . . I. xi. 32. 6
Purfled upon with many a *folded* plight, . . . II. iii. 26. 5
Folding. *Folding* hir armes with thousand sighs . . . *Bel.*[1] viii. 2
Folding her armes to Heaven . . . *Bel.*[2] x. 2
Foldings. within their *fouldings* close enwrapped bee: . . . II. iii. 27. 9
Folds. to theyr *foldes* yeed at their owne leasure. . . . *S.C.* S. 145
Fast in theyr *folds* he did them locke, . . . *S.C.* S. 205
lette me in your *foldes* ye lock, . . . *S.C.* D. 147
all his *foldes* are now in length outstrained. . . . *Gn.* 280
taile . . . whose *folds* displaid Were stretcht now forth . . . I. i. 16. 3
An hatefull Snake, the which his taile uptyes In many *folds,* I. iv. 31. 5
His huge long tayle, wownd up in hundred *foldes,* . . . I. xi. 11. 1
Through all those *foldes* the steelehead passage wrought, . . . II. viii. 32. 7
The heardes out of their *foldes* were loosed quight, . . . III. x. 52. 8
to the *folds,* where sheepe at night doe seat, . . . VI. ix. 4. 7
Folk. (As most usen Ambitious *folke:*) . . . *S.C.* F. 161
Yougthes *folke* now flocken in every where, . . . *S.C.* May 9
When *folke* bene fat, and riches rancke, . . . *S.C.* Jul. 211
Thus flocked all the *folke* him rownd about; . . . I. xii. 12. 1
Whom all that *folke* . . . Doe flock about, . . . II. vii. 48. 5
th' inland *folke,* which sought him backe to drive, . . . III. ix. 42. 3
For Chian *folke* to pourtraict beauties Queene, . . . IV. v. 12. 7
Which late her *folke* had slaine, . . . V. vii. 25. 9
So sounded the retraite, and drew his *folke* away. . . . V. xii. 9. 9
triumphest in the piteous spoile Of these poore *folk,* . . . VI. vi. 25. 4
Wayting what tydings of her *folke* became. . . . VI. vi. 30. 3
In which the names of all loves *folke* were fyled, . . . VI. vii. 33. 2
So thou thy *folke* . . . Dost beare . . . *H.L.* 278
Folkmoot. To which *folke-mote* they all . . . Agreed to travell, IV. iv. 6. 1
Folk's. humid evening ill for sicke *folkes* cace; . . . III. ix. 26. 4
Folks. To see those *folkes* make such jovysaunce, . . . *S.C.* May 25
Follies. For Younkers, Palinode, such *follies* fitte, . . . *S.C.* May 17
My fancye eke from former *follies* move . . . *S.C.* Jun. 37
With fleshly *follyes* undefyled, . . . *S.C.* Jul. 155
it mens *follies* mote be forst to fayne, . . . *S.C.* O. 75
Sike *follies* nowe have gathered as too ripe, . . . *S.C.* D. 117
heares and sees the *follies* of the rest, . . . *Hub.* 725
fruitles *follies* and unsound delights. . . . *Hub.* 823
dare their *follies* forth so rashlie throwe, . . . *T.M.* 220
a burning hart he bare, Full of vaine *follies* . . . I. iv. 25. 4
Their wanton *follies* and light meriments: . . . II. v. 32. 6
Her dalliaunce he despis'd, and *follies* did forsake. . . . II. vi. 21. 9
Antickes, which their *follies* playd In the rich metall . . . III. xi. 51. 5
the Gods, that mortall *follies* vew, . . . VI. vii. 32. 1
to great ones such *follies* doe forgive; . . . VI. ix. 22. 2
I gan my *follies* to my selfe to plaine, . . . VI. ix. 25. 5
But all those *follies* now I do reprove, . . . *H.H.L.* 12
For who my passed *follies* now pursewes, . . . *H.H.L.* 20
Follow. sittes not *followe* flying fame, . . . *S.C.* Jun. 75
if the flocking Nymphes did *folow* Pan, . . . *S.C.* D. 47
But *followe* them farre off, . . . *S.C.* Env. 11
To *follow* Orpheus musicke through the land: . . . *Gn.* 452
froward fortune still to *follow* mee, . . . *Hub.* 66
drive to *follow* after their Belwether.' . . . *Hub.* 296
this good Sir did *follow* the plaine word, . . . *Hub.* 390
to *follow* any merrie motion. . . . *Hub.* 458
full few which *follow* them, I see, . . . *Hub.* 637
the yong lustie gallants he did chose To *follow,* . . . *Hub.* 798
Upon the payne that thereof *follow* may. . . . *Hub.* 1072
still did *follow* one unto the end, . . . I. i. 28. 5
him to *follow* was but fruitlesse paine: . . . I. ii. 8. 5
they ran, . . . To *follow* her that was the causer of their ill. I. iii. 22. 9
she did pray That plagues . . . Might . . . *follow* all the way, I. iii. 23. 8
Full many mischiefes *follow* cruell Wrath: . . . I. iv. 35. 1
my secret aide Shall *follow* you.' . . . I. iv. 51. 9
all the people *followe* with great glee, . . . I. v. 16. 7
Could not for sorrow *follow* him so fast; . . . I. vi. 40. 3
Inveigled him to *follow* her desires unmeete. . . . I. vii. 50. 9
foule shame him *follow* wher he went!' . . . II. i. 30. 9
Inflamed was to *follow* beauties pray, . . . II. ii. 7. 7
Did *follow* that ensample which he blam'd afore. . . . II. vi. 45. 9
give me leave to *follow* mine emprise.' . . . II. vii. 39. 6
He gan avize to *follow* him no more, . . . II. xi. 27. 6
Would not so lightly *follow* beauties chace, . . . III. i. 19. 2
he *follow* should his brethren bad, . . . III. v. 24. 5
*the bloudy tract they *follow* fast, . . . III. v. 37. 6
That Ladies all may *follow* her ensample dead. . . . III. v. 54. 9
We both are bownd to *follow* heavens beheasts, . . . III. vi. 22. 7
Did all the way him *follow* hard behynd; . . . III. x. 55. 6
Forst him eftsoones to *follow* other game, . . . III. xi. 38. 8
I *follow* here the footing of thy feete, . . . IV. ii. 34. 8
To *follow* that which he did long propound, . . . IV. vi. 42. 5
To *follow* his adventures first intent, . . . V. iv. 3. 6
To *follow* his old quest, . . . V. iv. 20. 9
thinking to *follow* fast His other fellow Pagan . . . V. viii. 8. 8
Yet still he him did *follow* every where, . . . V. viii. 33. 7
Can *follow* out those false footsteps of his, . . . V. ix. 6. 8
to *follow* him that was so swift and light. . . . V. ix. 15. 9
his yron man he sent To *follow* him; . . . V. ix. 16. 2
Calidore did *follow* him so fast, . . . VI. i. 23. 3
on his former way To *follow* his first quest, . . . VI. ii. 3. 6
passed forth to *follow* his first enterprize. . . . VI. vi. 44. 9
follow through the world where so he went, . . . VI. vii. 21. 8
store of cares doth *follow* riches store. . . . VI. ix. 21. 4
To *follow* sheepe and shepheards base attire: . . . VI. ix. 24. 4
Who now does *follow* the foule Blatant Beast, . . . VI. x. 1. 1
Whilest Calidore does *follow* that faire Mayd, . . . VI. x. 1. 2
yet his feare did *follow* him behynd: . . . VI. xi. 27. 6

Follow—*Continued.*
sith I needs must *follow* thy behest, . . . VII. vii. 2. 1
Followed. *followed* unto his palaice hye; . . . *Hub.* 1107
followed her make like turtle chaste, . . . *As.* 178
followd those which happie seemd to bee. . . . *Col.* 667
As if his feare still *followed* him behynd: . . . I. ix. 21. 6
Yet she still *followed* her former style, . . . II. vi. 22. 1
Him *followed* eke Sir Guyon evermore, . . . II. vii. 26. 3
There *follow'd* fast at hand two wicked Hags, . . . II. xi. 23. 2
Florimell of Arthure is Long *followed,* . . . III. iv. Arg.
full of firy zele, him *followed* long, . . . III. iv. 45. 8
Yet he her *followd* still . . . III. iv. 51. 5
Forthy the bloody tract they *followd* fast, . . . III. v. 37. 6
all the way him *followd* on the strand, . . . III. vii. 36. 7
Fayre Britomart so long him *followed,* . . . III. xi. 7. 1
Ne *followd* on so fast, . . . IV. iii. 32. 3
Fiercely they *followd* on their bolde emprize, . . . IV. iv. 36. 1
departed thence with speed, And *follow'd* them, . . . IV. v. 28. 3
Long so she fled, and so he *follow'd* long; . . . IV. vii. 23. 1
follow'd fast; but when he came in sight, . . . IV. vii. 37. 3
when long he *follow'd* had in vaine, . . . IV. vii. 38. 1
She *follow'd* her, and thought againe it to assay. . . . IV. viii. 10. 9
Them *follow'd* fast, and them reviled sore, . . . IV. viii. 35. 3
Him *follow'd* Yar, soft washing Norwitch wall, . . . IV. xi. 33. 6
'Which when his Ladie saw, she *follow'd* fast, . . . V. i. 18. 1
follow'd him with gladfull glee, . . . V. iii. 34. 8
followed was of him likewise full fast, . . . V. viii. 33. 8
As they were *follow'd* of their former feare. . . . V. viii. 39. 3
he *followd* him apace; . . . V. ix. 16. 5
Staide not . . . But *follow'd* fast the Monster . . . VI. iii. 26. 5
Through woods and hils he *follow'd* him so fast, . . . VI. iii. 26. 6
by the cry he *follow'd,* and pursewed fast. . . . VI. iv. 18. 9
He foot by foot him *followed* alway, . . . VI. vi. 28. 6
that angry foole Which *follow'd* her, . . . VI. vii. 39. 7
He *followed* fast, and chaced him so nie, . . . VI. ix. 4. 6
with restlesse paine and toile Him *follow'd* . . . VI. xii. 22. 9
like a fearefull dog him *followed* through the land. . . . VI. xii. 36. 9
Him through all Faery land he *follow'd* so, . . . VI. xii. 37. 1
They after *follow'd* all with shrill out-cry, . . . VII. vi. 52. 6
So they him *follow'd* till they weary were; . . . VII. vi. 53. 1
Followeth. him scourgeth that the bloud downe *followeth.* . . . VI. viii. 28. 9
Following. *folowing* th' example of hir damme: . . . *Bel.*[1] vi. 4
Following th' ensample of her mothers sight: . . . *Bel.*[2] vii. 4
For *following* that trade so base and vile; . . . *Hub.* 366
Phoebe fayre . . . was *following* the chace, . . . I. vii. 5. 2
With forced fury *following* his behest, . . . I. ix. 7. 5
Whose footsteps Bladud *following,* . . . II. x. 25. 6
Following the guydance of her blinded guest, . . . III. iv. 6. 8
firmely *following* her first intent, . . . IV. viii. 50. 8
following Dee, which Britons long ygone Did call divine, . . . IV. xi. 39. 3
following his chace in dewy morne, . . . V. viii. 43. 2
following that faire advantage fast, . . . VI. i. 39. 2
labour vaine In *following* of him that fled so fast, . . . VI. iv. 9. 2
with his whip, him *following* behynd, . . . VI. vii. 49. 4
may sing To ages *following* . . . *Proth.* 160
Follows. Such *followes* those whom fortune doth advaunce. . . . *Hub.* 1136
The same she *followes,* . . . I. iii. 10. 7
Her servile beast . . . *followes* her far off, . . . I. iii. 44. 7
she . . . *followes* other game and venery: . . . I. vi. 22. 5
feare them *followes* still . . . II. iii. 20. 3
Shee comes unsought, and shonned *followes* eke. . . . II. iv. 44. 3
Folly. Such *follie* great sorow to Niobe did breede: . . . *S.C.* Ap. 87
Sike mens *follie* I cannot compare . . . *S.C.* May 95
by his *foly* one did fall, . . . *S.C.* Jul. 67
Let thy *follye* be the priefe. . . . *S.C.* Au. 116
All places they with *follie* have possest, . . . *T.M.* 193
scornfull *Follie* with Contempt is crept, . . . *T.M.* 212
Blind Error, scornefull *Follie,* and base Spight, . . . *T.M.* 317
Pined with griefe of *folly* late repented: . . . *Mui.* 348
when he felt the *folly* of his Lord, . . . II. iii. 9. 3
A foe of *folly* and immodest toy, . . . II. vi. 37. 4
Bablers of *folly,* and blazers of cryme: . . . II. ix. 25. 6
Nath'lesse to thee thy *folly* I forgive; . . . III. iv. 37. 7
By which fraile youth is oft to *follie* led, . . . IV. Pr. 1. 6
made him selfe thensample of his *follie.* . . . IV. i. 36. 6
often did my *folly* fowle reprove: . . . IV. vii. 16. 4
folly seem'd to leave the thing undonne . . . IV. x. 53. 4
soone he gan such *folly* to forthinke againe. . . . IV. xii. 14. 9
To attribute their *folly* unto fate, . . . V. iv. 28. 2
I will a while with his first *folly* beare, . . . V. v. 48. 8
They have the price of their owne *folly* payd.' . . . V. viii. 23. 6
That place, from which by *folly* Titan fell: . . . VII. vi. 34. 3
Folly's. Deserves to taste his *follies* fruit, repented payne.' . . . II. v. 24. 9
on him selfe to wreake his *follies* owne despight. . . . IV. vii. 39. 9
He ment to make them know their *follies* prise, . . . IV. ix. 35. 2
To wrecke on them their *follies* hardyment: . . . V. iv. 24. 5
had receiv'd their *follies* worthy hire, . . . V. viii. 15. 3
So thought the Souldan, in his *follies* threat, . . . V. viii. 31. 5
for all his former *follies* meed, . . . VI. vii. 11. 8
late repentance through thy *follies* prief; . . . *H.H.B.* 293
Foltring. *See* **Faltering.**
Fome, *etc.* *See* **Foam,** *etc.*
Fon. Thou art a *fon* of thy love to boste; . . . *S.C.* F. 69
Sicker I hold him for a greater *fon,* . . . *S.C.* Ap. 158
Ah *fon!* now by thy losse art taught, . . . *S.C.* S. 68
Ah, *fon!* for love does teach him climbe . . . *S.C.* O. 91
Cuddy . . . thous a *fon,* . . . *Col.* 292
Fond. *See* **Fanded, Found.**
Tho gynne you, *fond* flyes! the cold to scorne, . . . *S.C.* F. 39
scorned bene dedes of *fond* foolerie. . . . *S.C.* May 62

Fond—*Continued.*
with *fond* termes, and witlesse words, . . . *S.C.* Jul. 35
Such *fond* fantsies shall soone be put to flight. . . . *S.C.* Au. 22
I was so *fonde* To leave the good, . . . *S.C.* S. 58
fond men doe all their dayes turmoyle. . . . *Gn.* 152
the *fond* Ape, himselfe uprearing hy . . . *Hub.* 663
'*Fond* Ape! (sayd then the Foxe) . . . *Hub.* 977
The schooles they fill with *fond* new fanglenesse, . . . *T.M.* 327
There the *fond* Flie, entangled, strugled long, . . . *Mui.* 425
fond man! that in worlds ficklenesse Reposedst hope, . . . *D.* 150
'And ye *fond* men! on fortunes wheele that ride, . . . *D.* 498
fond, that joyest in the woe thou hast! . . . I. ix. 39. 7
'well mote I shame to tell The *fond* encheason . . . II. i. 30. 2
fairly tempring, *fond* desire subdewd, . . . II. vi. 26. 6
'Are mortall men so *fond* and undiscreet . . . II. vii. 14. 7
through flight into *fond* mischief fell. . . . II. x. 26. 9
Foolish delights, and *fond* abusions, . . . II. xi. 11. 8
Of her *fond* favorites so nam'd amis, . . . II. xii. 69. 5
Great hazard were it, and adventure *fond,* . . . III. i. 10. 8
Out of her daughters hart *fond* fancies to reverse. . . . III. ii. 48. 9
'*Fond* Proteus, father of false prophecis! . . . III. iv. 37. 1
they more *fond* that credit to thee give! . . . III. iv. 37. 2
Without fell rancor or *fond* gealosy. . . . III. vi. 41. 6
shamefully reproved for his rudenes *fond.* . . . III. viii. 25. 9
Fond is the feare that findes no remedie: . . . III. x. 3. 3
Unquiet Care, and *fond* Unthriftyhead; . . . III. xii. 25. 4
'*Fond* knight,' (sayd she) . . . IV. i. 48. 3
such *fond* favours sparingly dispenst: . . . IV. ii. 9. 3
'*Fond* Squire,' full angry then sayd Paridell, . . . IV. ii. 22. 5
Ne ever was with *fond* affection moved, . . . IV. ii. 36. 3
'*Fond* dame, that deem'st of things divine As of humane, . . . IV. ii. 51. 5
Therefore this Fay I hold but *fond* and vaine, . . . IV. iii. 2. 1
Feigning full many a *fond* excuse to prate, . . . IV. x. 14. 7
False Labyrinthes, *fond* runners eyes to daze; . . . IV. x. 24. 8
to lerne So *fond* a lesson as to love againe: . . . V. v. 46. 4
Such was this Ladies fit in her loves *fond* accusing. . . . V. vi. 14. 9
The better to beguile whom she so *fond* did finde. . . . V. xi. 23. 9
will ye, *fond* Dame, attempted bee Unto a strangers love, . . . V. xi. 63. 1
could not chose but laugh at his *fond* game, . . . *Epig.* iv. 33
not, as *fond* men misdeeme, An outward shew . . . *H.B.* 90
Fonder. *fonder* then Cephisus foolish chyld, . . . III. ii. 44. 6
I, *fonder,* love a shade, the body far exyld.' . . . III. ii. 44. 9
Fondlings. to allure such *fondlings* . . . unto their owne decay: VI. vi. 42. 3
Fondly. her head she *fondly* would aguize With gaudy girlonds, II. vi. 7. 3
they *fondly* striv'd With th' Heliconian maides for maystery; II. xii. 31. 1
Great labour *fondly* hast thou hent in hand, . . . III. vii. 61. 2
Thereat th' old man did nought but *fondly* grin, . . . III. viii. 24. 6
Himselfe in thousand peeces *fondly* rent, . . . III. xi. 38. 4
That ye were runne so *fondly* far astray . . . V. iv. 26. 8
fondly feare to loose your liberty; . . . *Am.* lxv. 2
which *fondly* here admyre Faire seeming shewes, . . . *H.H.B.* 16
Fondness. their *fondnesse* inly I pitie: . . . *S.C.* May 38
Fondnesse it were for any, being free, . . . *Am.* xxxvii. 13
Fone. *See* **Foes.**
Fonly. rather be envied, . . . then *fonly* pitied: . . . *S.C.* May 58
Font. In cyphers strange, that few could rightly read, *Bon Font;* V. ix. 26. 4
Food. raunge abroad to seeke her *food,* . . . *Bel.*[2] vi. 5
My sheepe did leave theyr wonted *food,* . . . *S.C.* Au. 73
'The feeble flocks in field refuse their former *foode,* . . . *S.C.* N. 133
Content with any *food* that God doth send; . . . *Gn.* 140
The Oke, whose Acornes were our *foode,* . . . *Gn.* 206
Can no whit savour this celestiall *food,* . . . *T.M.* 591
starve, wanting my lively *foode:* . . . *U.V.* 17
I hate to tast, for *food* withholds my dying; . . . *D.* 416
Hurles forth his thundring dart with deadly *food* . . . I. viii. 9. 3
the object of his spight And deadly *food* he makes: . . . II. i. 3. 2
doen the heavens afford him vitall *food?* . . . II. i. 12. 3
Lo! here I now for want of *food* doe dye: . . . II. vii. 59. 7
weake and wan For want of *food* and sleepe, . . . II. vii. 65. 3
feed on shadowes whiles I die for *food,* . . . III. ii. 44. 3
Good both for erthly med'cine and for hevenly *food.* . . . III. iv. 40. 9
nor with commune *food,* As other wemens babes, . . . III. vi. 5. 8
Fruitfull of all thinges fitt for living *foode,* . . . III. ix. 49. 6
cursed seedes . . . yeeld her living *food:* . . . IV. i. 26. 2
Right fit to rend the *food* on which he fared. . . . IV. v. 35. 5
other *food* then that wilde forrest beares, . . . IV. vii. 41. 5
food which in her duresse she had found; . . . IV. viii. 19. 6
loath their wonted *food:* . . . IV. x. 46. 2
He might not with immortall *food* be fed, . . . IV. xii. 4. 3
Ne dayly *food* did take, ne nightly sleepe, . . . IV. xii. 19. 8
to receive In her owne mouthe the *food* ment for her chyld, . . V. v. 53. 2
Therefore they mote not taste of fleshly *food,* . . . V. vii. 10. 1
to his kyne for *food* assynd; . . . V. x. 9. 8
his lovely litle spoile Crying for *food* . . . VI. iv. 25. 8
Had for his *food* late gathered from the tree,) . . . VI. vii. 24. 5
The fields my *food,* my flocke my rayment breed; . . . VI. ix. 20. 8
your meane *food* shall be my daily feast, . . . VI. ix. 32. 3
Scarse yeelding her due *food* or timely rest, . . . VI. xi. 24. 5
My soules long-lacked *foode,* my heavens blis; . . . *Am.* i. 12
And also to sustayne thy selfe with *food.* . . . *Am.* ii. 8
a byrd, that in ones hand doth spy Desired *food,* . . . *Am.* lxxiii. 6
And last, the *food* of life, which now we have, . . . *H.H.L.* 194
Fool. is now lent to the *foole:* . . . *T.M.* 412
'Thou fearefull *foole,* Why takest not of that same fruite . . . II. vii. 63. 6
'*Foole!*' (sayd the Pagan) . . . II. viii. 52. 1
Enough to hold a *foole* in vaine delight. . . . III. viii. 10. 7
sure a *foole* I doe him firmely hold, . . . III. ix. 8. 4
prov'd himselfe most *foole* in what he seem'd most wise. . . . IV. ii. 9. 9
Whom she did put to death, deceived like a *foole.* . . . V. xi. 25. 9
a lewd *foole* her leading thorough dry and wet. . . . VI. vi. 16. 9

Fool—*Continued.*
Led by a Carle and *foole* which by her side did passe . . . . VI. vii. 27. 9
that angry *foole* Which follow'd her, ... VI. vii. 39. 6
that same *foole,* which most increast her paines, ... VI. vii. 44. 5
Ne ought that *foole* for pitty did him spare, ... VI. vii. 49. 3
the *foole,* which did that end awayte, Came running in; . . VI. viii. 11. 1
The whiles the *foole* did him revile and flout, ... VI. viii. 11. 8
To pitty him that list to play the *foole;* . . . . VI. viii. 21. 4
That huge great *foole* oppressing th' other Knight, ... VI. viii. 28. 2
Fooleries. make them merrie with their *fooleries;* . . . . . *T.M.* 320
Foolery. sike fancies weren *foolerie,* . . . . *S.C.* F. 211
scorned bene dedes of fond *foolerie.* . . . . *S.C.* May 62
Should Colin make judge of my *fooleree:* . . . . *S.C.* N. 28
Foolhappy. ne dares To joy at his *foolhappie* oversight: . . . I. vi. 1. 6
Foolhardice. with vaine *foolhardise* Daring the foe . . . . . . *Ro.* xiv. 7
reason with *foole-hardize* over ran; . . . . II. ii. 17. 7
Least thy *foolhardize* worke thy sad confusion.' . . . . II. iv. 42. 9
the third time shall rew his *foolhardise:* . . . . III. iii. 35. 7
Foolhardy. sooth to say, it is *foolhardie* thing, ... *Col.* 915
her *foolehardy* chyld Did come too neare, ... I. xii. 11. 1
in her *foolhardy* wit Conceiv'd a bold devise, ... III. iii. 52. 1
Had used beene of that *foolehardie* Squyre: . . . . III. v. 15. 8
Foolhardy as th' Earthes children, ... III. xi. 22. 8
for his hire to so *foole-hardy* dew, ... VII. vi. 45. 4
Foolish. he himselfe through *foolish* vanitie, ... *Van.* viii. 5
Ah, *foolish* Hobbinol! thy gyfts bene vayne; . . . . *S.C.* Ja. 59
Ah, *foolish* old man! I scorne thy skill, ... *S.C.* F. 51
made this *foolish* Brere wexe so bold, ... *S.C.* F. 124
Ah, *foolish* Boy! that is with love yblent: . . . . *S.C.* Ap. 155
to the Apes *folish* care, ... *S.C.* May 96
Kidde . . . Was too very *foolish* and unwise; . . . . *S.C.* May 175
'*Foolish* Foxe (said the Mule) . . . . *Hub.* 595
since the time that Phoebus *foolish* sonne Ythundered, ... *T.M.* 7
Through pompous pride, and *foolish* vanitie: . . . . *T.M.* 92
Whie then doo *foolish* men so much despize . . . . *T.M.* 145
Ne fearest *foolish* reprehension Of faulty men, ... *Com. Son.* i. 7
At length, the *foolish* Flie, without foresight, ... *Mui.* 389
'Cease, *foolish* man!' . . . . *D.* 71
Nought hast thou, *foolish* boy, seene in thy daies.' . . . . *Col.* 303
The *foolish* man, that pities . . . His mournefull plight, . . . I. v. 18. 7
'O *foolish* faeries sonne! . . . . I. vi. 47. 1
through his own *foolish* pride Or weaknes, ... I. viii. 1. 6
'hath thus distraught Thee, *foolish* man . . . . I. ix. 38. 2
O *foolish* men! why hast ye to your own decay?' . . . . . . I. x. 10. 9
the *foolish* man, fild with delight . . . . II. iii. 42. 2
To feede her *foolish* humour and vaine jolliment. . . . . . . II. vi. 3. 9
'*Foolish* old man,' said then the Pagan wroth, ... II. viii. 22. 1
eyes, That mad or *foolish* seemd: . . . . II. ix. 52. 7
Foolish delights, and fond abusions, ... II. xi. 11. 8
she your courage hath inclind Through *foolish* pitty, ... II. xii. 29. 2
we *foolish* men that prayse gin eke t' envy. . . . . III. ii. 2. 9
fonder then Cephisus *foolish* chyld, ... III. ii. 44. 6
O *foolish* physick, and unfruitfull paine, ... III. v. 42. 1
'But, *foolish* boy, what bootes thy service bace . . . . . . III. v. 47. 1
we scorne his *foolish* joy, ... III. vi. 24. 4
Foolish Narcisse, that likes the watry shore; . . . . III. vi. 45. 5
turning her feare to *foolish* wrath, ... III. vii. 8. 1
all hope wherewith he long had fedd His *foolish* malady, . . III. viii. 3. 9
'Thou *foolish* knight, that weenst with words . . . . III. viii. 17. 1
in their *foolish* fancy feigne thee blinde, ... III. x. 4. 4
Laught at his *foolish* labour spent in waste, ... III. x. 13. 4
The *foolish* man thereat woxe wondrous blith, ... III. x. 33. 1
The whiles her *foolish* garde, ... III. xi. 31. 5
'Both *foolish* knights! I can but laugh at both, ... IV. i. 47. 2
having cast him in a *foolish* trance, ... IV. ii. 9. 7
'Too *foolish* Paridell! that fayrest floure Wouldst gather faine, ... IV. ii. 14. 3
Like *foolish* flies about an hony-crocke; . . . . V. ii. 33. 3
'Thou *foolishe* Elfe,' (said then the Gyant wroth) . . . . . . V. ii. 37. 1
The *foolish* Kyte, led with licentious will, ... V. v. 15. 5
foolish Mayd! whyles heedlesse of the hooke . . . . V. v. 43. 1
by his *foolish* feare Was holpen up, ... VI. viii. 25. 8
'Then ceasse thy idle claime, thou *foolish* gerle; . . . . . . VII. vi. 34. 1
Foolish god Faunus . . . longed foolishly To see her naked . VII. vi. 42. 7
profest His *foolish* thought: A *foolish* Faune indeed, ... VII. vi. 46. 6
hookes, That from the *foolish* fish theyr bayts doe hyde: . . *Am.* xlvii. 4
fed On idle fancies of thy *foolish* thought, ... *H.H.B.* 289
Foolishly. so *foolishly* To come so farre . . . . *Hub.* 945
death for life exchanged *foolishlie:* . . . . VII. vi. 6. 4
longed *foolishly* To see her naked . . . . VII. vi. 42. 8
Fool's. a *fooles* talke to beare and to heare. . . . . *S.C.* May 141
Fools. *See* **Faint-heart-fools.**
knewe we, *fooles,* what it us bringes until, ... *S.C.* N. 185
They feede the eares of *fooles* with flattery, ... *T.M.* 323
they themselves for praise of *fooles* do sell, ... *Col.* 723
fooles, lovers, children, Dames. . . . . II. ix. 50. 9
Yet was admired much of *fooles,* women, and boys. . . . . . V. ii. 30. 9
usd to fish for *fooles* on the dry shore, ... V. ix. 11. 8
forged showes, as fitter beene For courting *fooles* . . . . . VI. v. 38. 8
fooles therefore They are which fortunes doe by vowes devize, VI. ix. 30. 7
T' entrap unwary *fooles* in their eternall bales. . . . . . . VI. x. 3. 9
In praise of that mad fit which *fooles* call love, ... *H.H.L.* 9
Foord. *See* **Ford.**
Foot. *See* **Dry-foot, Horse-foot, Lightfoot, Winged-foot.**
One *foote* on Thetis, th' other on the Morning, ... *Ro.* iv. 2
Whether they fare on *foote,* or flie aloft, ... *Ro.* xxiv. 3
Againe on *foote* to reare her pouldred corse. . . . . *Ro.* xxvii. 14
Whose *foote* in ground hath left but feeble holde, ... *Ro.* xxviii. 4
'Lo! how finely the Graces can it *foote* . . . . *S.C.* Ap. 109
They never sette *foote* in that same troade, ... *S.C.* S. 92

Foot—*Continued.*
the leane soules treaden under *foote,* . . . . *S.C.* S. 126
Unto the shifting of the shepheards *foote,* . . . . *S.C.* D. 116
With liquid *foote* doth slide downe easily. . . . . *Gn.* 24
chieflie joyes on *foote* them to beholde, ... *Hub.* 623
runne on *foote* a race, ... *Hub.* 744
Did ever after scorne on *foote* to goe. . . . . *Hub.* 752
treadeth under *foote* hir holie things, ... *T.M.* 569
This goodlie bridge, one *foote* not fastned well, ... *Ti.* 557
I sat . . . Under the *foote* of Mole, ... *Col.* 57
wisedome warnes, whilest *foot* is in the gate, ... I. i. 13. 4
hand or *foot* to stirr he strove in vaine. . . . . I. i. 18. 8
repining courage yields No *foote* to foe: . . . . I. ii. 17. 7
Under the steepe *foot* of a mountaine hore: . . . . I. iii. 10. 6
Under his Lordly *foot* him proudly hath suppresst. . . . . . I. iii. 19. 9
in *foote* and hand A grievous gout tormented him full sore, . I. iv. 29. 6
Where never *foote* of living wight did tread, ... I. vii. 50. 4
his *foot* could find no flore, ... I. viii. 39. 7
His dwelling . . . Under the *foot* of Rauran mossy hore, . . . I. ix. 4. 6
Thrise he assayd it from his *foote* to draw, ... I. xi. 41. 7
The other *foote,* fast fixed on his shield, ... I. xi. 43. 1
kist the ground whereon his *foot* was pight; . . . . I. xii. 25. 7
bound him hand and *foote* with yron chains; . . . . I. xii. 36. 2
fairely fare on *foot,* how ever loth: . . . . II. ii. 12. 3
So forth he far'd, as now befell, on *foot,* . . . . II. iii. 3. 1
His Palmer now shall *foot* no more alone. . . . . II. iii. 3. 5
rushed in on *foot* to ayd her . . . . II. iii. 3. 9
Streight at his *foot* in base humilitee, ... II. iii. 8. 8
nowhere could espye Tract of his *foot:* . . . . II. iii. 19. 7
cause one *foot* to flye, ... II. iii. 45. 4
on *foot* was forced for to yeed . . . . II. iv. 2. 3
such hideous puissaunce on *foot* to beare; . . . . II. v. 3. 9
On *foot* with him to matchen equall fight: . . . . II. v. 4. 8
on his brest his victor *foote* he thrust: . . . . II. v. 12. 6
He ran on *foot,* . . . . II. vi. 41. 3
Wanting his sword when he on *foot* should fight: . . . . . . II. viii. 34. 2
twise him forst his *foot* revoke. . . . . II. viii. 39. 9
both as swift on *foot* as chased Stags; . . . . II. xi. 23. 5
whosoever once hath fastened His *foot* thereon, ... II. xii. 12. 8
Ne did the other backe his *foote* returne, ... III. i. 5. 7
began to close With her on *foot,* . . . . III. i. 9. 4
Ne ever to them yielded *foot* of grownd, ... III. i. 21. 4
treading under *foote* her honest name: . . . . III. i. 50. 4
Ay joyning *foot* to *foot,* and syde to syde; . . . . III. i. 66. 8
Ne *foot* could further move. . . . . III. vii. 3. 8
on *foot* mote algates fare . . . . III. vii. 4. 1
Fast bounden hand and *foote* with cords of wire, ... III. vii. 37. 8
in *foote* doth beare A trembling Culver, ... III. vii. 39. 1
Unable to arise, or *foote* or hand to styre. . . . . III. vii. 45. 9
Shee strugled strongly both with *foote* and hand . . . . . . III. viii. 27. 3
that flowd . . . Downe to her *foot* with carelesse modestee. . III. ix. 21. 6
Upon whose stubborne neck, . . . She fastned hath her *foot;* III. ix. 45. 6
more bounteous creature never far'd On *foot* . . . . III. xi. 10. 4
hideous tayle his lefte *foot* did enfold, ... III. xi. 48. 7
Priamond on *foote* had more delight: . . . . IV. ii. 42. 5
horse and *foote* knew Diamond to wield: . . . . IV. ii. 42. 6
whilst his right *foot* did slyde. . . . . IV. iii. 18. 9
Could stand on *foot* now to renew the fight: . . . . IV. iii. 23. 3
that he should not long on *foote* endure, ... IV. iii. 32. 8
to alight on *foote* her algates did compell: . . . . IV. vi. 13. 9
Whiles with long fight on *foot* he breathlesse was, ... IV. vi. 15. 2
Himselfe by them on *foot* to succour them from feare. . . . IV. viii. 22. 9
With easie steps so soft as *foot* could stryde, ... IV. viii. 37. 2
annoyd The Prince on *foot,* not wonted so to fare; . . . . . IV. viii. 37. 6
Ne yeelded *foote,* ne once abacke did flit, ... IV. ix. 29. 8
Past forth on *foote,* . . . . IV. x. 15. 4
Hence fare on *foot,* till he an horse have gayned.' . . . . . . V. iii. 35. 6
Under my *foote* let each lay downe his sword; . . . . V. iv. 16. 7
in his necke Her proud *foote* setting, ... V. iv. 40. 3
Whom when he saw before his *foote* prostrated, ... V. v. 11. 6
Doth not your handmayds life at your *foot* lie?' . . . . V. v. 31. 6
One *foote* was set upon the Crocodile, ... V. vii. 7. 1
neither will one *foot,* till we that carle have hent.' . . . . . V. ix. 7. 9
the bold Prince was forced *foote* to give . . . . V. xi. 5. 6
gan him selfe to fight on *foote* prepare: . . . . V. xi. 9. 4
foot of man might sound the bottome plaine, ... V. xii. 5. 3
In these strange waies where never *foote* did use, ... VI. Pr. 2. 8
Both hand and *foote* unto a tree was bound; . . . . VI. i. 11. 4
To prove if better *foote* then horsebacke would ensew. . . . VI. i. 35. 9
ere he could recover *foote* againe, ... VI. i. 39. 1
save my life, which lot before your *foot* doth lay.' . . . . . VI. i. 39. 9
A tall young man, . . . Fighting on *foot,* . . . . VI. ii. 3. 8
a Ladie faire . . . Standing alone on *foot* . . . . VI. ii. 4. 2
To drive you so on *foot,* . . . . VI. ii. 15. 4
refused To take me up . . . But forst to trot on *foot,* . . . . VI. ii. 22. 5
Who was more light of *foote* and swift in chace, ... VI. iii. 25. 4
In travelling on *foote* so long a space, ... VI. iii. 29. 4
Not wont on *foote* with heavy armes to trace, ... VI. iii. 29. 5
hardly passable on *foote* it was; . . . . VI. iii. 30. 2
thou hast thy steed forlorne . . . So fare on *foote* . . . . . VI. iii. 32. 2
for thine owne defence, on *foote* alight . . . . VI. iii. 35. 8
He goth on *foote* all armed by her side, ... VI. iii. 46. 1
Where *foot* of living creature never trode, ... VI. iv. 13. 8
wont to . . . wend on *foot* for need, ... VI. iv. 19. 5
He could no path nor tract of *foot* descry, ... VI. iv. 24. 6
they ne might Endure to travell, nor one *foote* to frame: . . VI. v. 40. 8
As he unable were for very neede To move one *foote,* . . . . VI. vi. 19. 7
He *foot* by *foot* him followed alway, ... VI. vi. 28. 6
Ne would the Prince him ever *foot* forsake . . . . VI. vi. 29. 4
His *foot* he set on his vile necke, ... VI. vii. 26. 4

Foot—*Continued.*
When his *foote* slipt, . . . VI. vii. 48. 3
He in his necke had set his *foote* with fell disdaine. . . . VI. viii. 10. 9
least he should recover *foote* againe, . . . VI. viii. 17. 2
every *foote* did tremble which did tread, . . . VI. viii. 31. 8
Had traveld still on *foot* in heavie armes, . . . VI. viii. 47. 2
under *foot* doth tread The mightie ones, . . . VI. ix. 27. 8
at the *foote* thereof a gentle flud . . . VI. x. 7. 1
September marched, eeke on *foote*, . . . VII. vii. 38. 1
The whiles her *foot* she in my necke doth place, . . . *Am.* xx. 3
the ground whereas her *foot* shall tread, . . . *Epith.* 48
For feare the stones her tender *foot* should wrong, . . . *Epith.* 49
Footed. *See* **Fiery-footed, Wing-footed.**
Footing. In humble dales is *footing* fast, . . . *S.C.* Jul. 13
Have care for to pursue his *footing* light . . . *Gn.* 31
no *footing* now on earth appeares? . . . *Ti.* 65
alleies wide, With *footing* worne, and leading inward farr. . . I. i. 7. 8
to revoke The forward *footing* for an hidden shade: . . . I. i. 12. 8
gras, In which the tract of peoples *footing* was, . . . I. iii. 10. 5
she has A damzel spyde, slow *footing* her before, . . . I. iii. 10. 8
Scarse could he *footing* find in that fowle way, . . . I. v. 53. 1
as he forward moovd his *footing* old, . . . I. viii. 31. 3
Halfe flying and halfe *footing* in his haste, . . . I. xi. 8. 2
no'te without an hound fine *footing* trace. . . . II. Pr. 4. 5
by what meanes may I his *footing* tract?' . . . II. i. 12. 7
Ne had they *footing* found at last, . . . II. x. 48. 5
did her *footing* trace So sure and swiftly, . . . III. vii. 23. 7
Enforced them their forward *footing* to revoke. . . . III. xi. 21. 9
I follow here the *footing* of thy feete, . . . IV. ii. 34. 8
Stood still awhile, and his fast *footing* kept, . . . IV. iii. 20. 8
her *footing* to direct aright, . . . IV. xi. 25. 4
Through slipperie *footing* fell into the brooke, . . . V. v. 43. 3
where *footing* was so ill; . . . V. ix. 15. 7
them forbad to land, and *footing* did forstall. . . . V. xii. 4. 9
Guyde ye my *footing*, and conduct me well . . . VI. Pr. 2. 7
on his steede her did sustaine . . . soft *footing* her beside; . VI. iii. 28. 6
With a wyld man soft *footing* by his syde; . . . VI. vii. 6. 2
Nor any *footing* fynde for overgrowen gras: . . . VI. x. 41. 9
I seeke the fields with her late *footing* synd; . . . *Am.* lxxviii. 5
Footing's. no *footings* trace Nor wight appeard, . . . III. xi. 53. 5
ever troden was of *footings* trace: . . . IV. x. 21. 5
Footings'. They trampled have with their fowle *footings* trade, *T.M.* 275
Footman. this false *footman*, clokt with simplenesse, . . . I. xii. 34. 6
Foot-pace. all the way the Prince on *footpace* traced, . . . IV. viii. 34. 8
Footsteps. Whose *footsteps* Bladud following, . . . II. x. 25. 6
Can follow out those false *footsteps* of his, . . . V. ix. 6. 8
Foot-stool. they at her *foot-stoole* threw; . . . VII. vii. 10. 7
him, that at your *footstoole* humbled lies, . . . *Am.* xlix. 11
Before the *footestoole* of his Majestie . . . *H.H.B.* 142
For (*partial list*). *See* **All for, And for, But for, For ever, For to, Forwhy, Unlooked for.**
Now *for* a truth great Babylon is fallen. . . . *Rev.* ii. 14
For no such shadow shalbe had againe. . . . *Pet.* iii. 14
For if that time make ende of things . . . *Ro.* vii. 13
Tell me then, (*for* perhaps some one of you . . . *Ro.* xv. 9
For, in a people . . . Ambition is engendred . . . *Ro.* xxiii. 9
For th' auncient Plot of Rome, displayed plaine, . . . *Ro.* xxvi. 13
For if that time doo let thy glorie live, . . . *Ro.* xxxii. 11
For pale and wanne he was, . . . *S.C.* Ja. 8
albee rude Pan thou please, Yet *for* thou pleasest not . . . *S.C.* Ja. 68
For youngth is a bubble blown up with breath, . . . *S.C.* F. 87
to . . . snebbe the goode Oake, *for* he was old. . . . *S.C.* F. 126
What is he *for* a Ladde you so lament? . . . *S.C.* Ap. 17
let us homeward, *for* night draweth on, . . . *S.C.* Ap. 160
Ah! *for* love of that is to thee moste leefe, . . . *S.C.* S. 11
(Ah, *for* Colin, he whilome my joye!) . . . *S.C.* S. 177
for that her husbands daies She did prolong . . . *Gn.* 426
Saffron, sought *for* in Cilician soyle; . . . *Gn.* 671
for that my sense it greatly pleased, . . . *Hub.* 39
Both *for* because your griefe doth great appeare, . . . *Hub.* 73
Upon his tiptoes nicely . . . *For* making noyse, . . . *Hub.* 1010
For that the King did favour to them beare; . . . *Hub.* 1076
Not honored nor cared *for* of anie, . . . *T.M.* 225
The cause why he this Flie so maliced Was . . . *For* that his *Mui.* 259
deceive, *for* all his watchfull ward, . . . *Col.* 136
For that my selfe I do professe to be Vassall . . . *Col.* 466
The maker . . . *for* all his wondrous witt, Was nigh beguiled I. i. 45. 6
For her he hated as the hissing snake, . . . I. ii. 9. 8
knight was not *for* all his bragging bost; . . . I. iii. 24. 5
For unto knight there is no greater shame . . . I. iv. 1. 7
For that Hippolytus rent corse he did redresse. . . . I. v. 36. 9
Scarse could he footing find . . . *For* many corses, . . . I. v. 53. 2
Upon this dreadfull Beast . . . *for* more aw and dread. . . . I. vii. 18. 9
daunce *for* jollity, . . . I. vii. 32. 4
horrour . . . *For* ruth of gentle knight . . . I. viii. 39. 4
like would not *for* all this worldes wealth. . . . I. ix. 31. 4
Would safe depart, *for* all his subtile sleight, . . . I. ix. 54. 3
would not once have moved *for* the knight. . . . I. x. 49. 6
Cleopolis, *for* earthly frame, The fairest . . . I. x. 59. 2
Then *for* her sonne, . . . Madan was young, . . . II. x. 20. 1
to him gave *for* wife his daughter . . . II. x. 59. 4
for it is too long here to abide, I will deferre . . . IV. vii. 47. 8
she them all despiseth *for* great pride.' . . . V. ii. 10. 4
Yet *for* no bidding, nor *for* being shent, . . . VI. vi. 18. 8
For ere . . . Out of great Chaos . . . *H.L.* 57
For things hard gotten men more dearely deeme. . . . *H.L.* 168
For love is Lord of truth and loialtie, . . . *H.L.* 176
For love cannot endure a Paragone. . . . *H.L.* 251
For, through infusion of celestiall powre, . . . *H.B.* 50
For it is heavenly borne . . . *H.B.* 104

For—*Continued.*
For when the soule, the which derived was, . . . *H.B.* 106
For of the soule the bodie forme doth take; . . . *H.B.* 132
For soule is forme, and doth the bodie make. . . . *H.B.* 133
For all that faire is, is by nature good; . . . *H.B.* 139
For Love is a celestiall harmonie . . . *H.B.* 197
For all, that . . . do not love; . . . *H.B.* 208
for Love is not so light . . . *H.B.* 209
Forage. by his side his steed the grassy *forage* ate. . . . I. vii. 2. 9
from his loftie steed dismounting low Did let him *forage*. . . III. iv. 53. 7
Foray. A band of Britons, ryding on *forray* . . . III. iii. 58. 4
to *forray* the land, or scoure the deepe. . . . VI. xi. 40. 5
when all the theeves did rest, After a late *forray*, . . . VI. xi. 42. 3
whylome did *forray* The Nemaean forrest, . . . VII. vii. 36. 5
Forayed. dead now was their foe, which them *forrayed* late. I. xii. 3. 9
Forbade. them *forbad* to land, and footing did forstall. . . . V. xii. 4. 9
And entraunce boldly unto him *forbad*: . . . VI. iii. 38. 3
whom though he oft *forbad*, . . . VI. vi. 18. 7
Forbare. Yet nathemore the Giantesse *forbare*, . . . VII. vi. 13. 1
Forbear. to wrong holy eld did *forbeare*; . . . *S.C.* F. 206
doth *forbeare* His wonted songs, . . . *S.C.* Ap. 15
the fourth to *forbeare* is outragious: . . . *S.C.* May 133
Hardly *forbearen*, but have it they must: . . . *S.C.* May 135
With patience to *forbeare* the offred bowle? . . . *S.C.* May 139
my wombe her burdein would *forbeare*, . . . II. i. 53. 4
If I, or thou, dew vengeaunce doe *forbeare*, . . . II. i. 61. 7
Their deadly cruell discord to *forbeare*, . . . II. ii. 27. 8
Ne any evill meanes she did *forbeare*, . . . II. iv. 5. 8
did not *forbeare* Her honest merth . . . to partake; . . . II. vi. 21. 5
that fiers Carle commaunding to *forbeare*, . . . II. vii. 43. 2
Badd those same six *forbeare* that single enimy. . . . III. i. 22. 9
'Sir knight, these ydle termes *forbeare*; . . . III. ii. 16. 1
those feends may not their work *forbeare*, . . . III. iii. 11. 4
to *forbeare* The bloody batteill . . . III. iv. 24. 7
to her bed, which she was wont *forbeare*, . . . IV. i. 15. 8
His mightie indignation did *forbeare*; . . . IV. i. 45. 2
thrise he drew it backe; so did at last *forbeare*. . . . IV. i. 54. 9
to *forbeare* doth not forgive the det.' . . . IV. iii. 11. 5
made him oft, when he would strike, *forbeare*; . . . IV. vii. 27. 2
she did not her spightfull speach *forbeare*, . . . IV. viii. 36. 2
yet could she not *forbeare*. . . . V. vi. 4. 9
Use scanted diet, and *forbeare* your fill; . . . VI. vi. 14. 7
I must awhile *forbeare* to you to tell; . . . VI. vi. 17. 3
Boldly him bad such injurie *forbeare*; . . . VI. xi. 15. 2
Yet did he nought, for all that, him *forbeare*, . . . VI. xii. 33. 8
Forbears. every river eke his course *forbeares*, . . . III. ii. 32. 3
Forbid. *See* **Forbidden.**
detained bee For looking back, being *forbid* before: . . . *Gn.* 435
(which God *forbid!*) . . . IV. xi. 35. 2
love *forbid* him, that is life denayd; . . . IV. xii. 28. 7
Forbidden. *See* **Forbid, Late-forbidden.**
voyage rashly make By this *forbidden* way . . . III. iv. 14. 6
From all *forbidden* things his liking to withdraw. . . . IV. viii. 30. 9
him *forbidden*, who his heast observed: . . . V. xii. 43. 5
Into his Lords *forbidden* hall to passe? . . . VI. vi. 20. 4
Forbore. he that dreadfull deed *Forbore*, . . . *Hub.* 1239
the royall Beast *forbore* beleeving, . . . *Hub.* 1365
Ladies love as losse of time *forbore*: . . . I. v. 37. 4
His hand relented and the stroke *forbore*, . . . II. viii. 43. 4
them long *forbore*: . . . IV. ix. 34. 4
Yet still her blowes he bore, and her *forbore*, . . . V. v. 7. 1
I have *forbore* this duetie to fulfill; . . . V. v. 41. 3
All which nathlesse she for his love *forbore*; . . . V. v. 54. 8
That bloudie scutchin . . . have of late *forbore*, . . . V. xi. 54. 5
Him long *forbore*, and still his spirite spar'd, . . . VI. i. 20. 6
which I *forbore* To finish then, . . . VI. ix. 2. 3
Forborne. Carthage towres from spoile should be *forborne*, . . *Ro.* xxiii. 2
'*forborne* Your owne good shield in daungerous dismay? . . V. xi. 52. 1
Forby. 'he hence doth wonne, *Foreby* a fountaine, . . . I. vi. 39. 8
To reste him selfe *foreby* a fountaine syde, . . . I. vii. 2. 7
Hospitall, That was *foreby* the way, . . . I. x. 36. 2
Foreby that idle strond, . . . II. viii. 10. 8
castle, plaste *Foreby* a river . . . II. ix. 10. 4
He them encountred . . . *Foreby* the River . . . II. x. 16. 2
A goodly Lady did *foreby* them rush, . . . III. i. 15. 3
Foreby a narrow foord, . . . III. v. 17. 2
a flush of Ducks *foreby* the brooke, . . . V. ii. 54. 2
He tooke her up *forby* the lilly hand, . . . V. xi. 17. 1
We chaunst to come *foreby* a covert glade . . . VI. ii. 16. 3
Downe in a dale *forby* a rivers syde . . . VI. iii. 29. 6
Force. onely God surmountes the *force* of ty[me,] . . . *Bel.*[1] i. 13
savage beast, . . . shewde his *force* by fire, . . . *Rev.* i. 12
beast and Kings also Joinyng their *force* . . . *Rev.* iii. 12
With deadly *force* so in their cruell race . . . *Pet.* i. 8
heaven, that gan her *force* to feare. . . . *Ro.* xii. 12
Gods secure feare not her *force* at all. . . . *Ro.* xii. 14
Through felonous *force* of mine enemie.' . . . *S.C.* F. 156
From soddein *force* theyr flocks for to gard. . . . *S.C.* S. 235
gates of hel, and fyrie furies *forse*, . . . *S.C.* N. 164
from the *force* of Phoebus boyling ray, . . . *Gn.* 167
to defend The *force* of Vulcane . . . *Gn.* 524
feare he neede no *force* of enemie. . . . *Hub.* 1126
Upon those gates with *force* he fiercely flewe, . . . *Hub.* 1369
by *force* I conquered were Of hardie Saxons, . . . *Ti.* 113
feeble spirits in their *force* maintaine, . . . *D.* 438
Nor failing *force* to former strength restore: . . . *D.* 473
his new *force* to learne, . . . I. i. 3. 8
Add faith unto your *force*, and be not faint; . . . I. i. 19. 3
knitting all his *force*, got one hand free, . . . I. i. 19. 7
stroke at her with more then manly *force*, . . . I. i. 24. 6

Force—*Continued.*
with the sight amazd, forgat his furious *forse.* . . . I. iii. 5. 9
too weake and feeble was the *forse* Of salvage beast . . . I. iii. 42. 1
With greedy *force* each other doth assayle, . . . I. v. 6. 6
With greedy *force* he gan the fort assayle, . . . I. vi. 5. 3
His trembling hand he would him *force* to put Upon the Lyon I. vi. 24. 3
whom he had not taught To feare his *force:* . . . I. vi. 29. 5
with their *force* they perst both plate and maile, . . . I. vi. 43. 4
increasing more Their puissant *force,* . . . I. vi. 45. 3
With huge *force* and insupportable mayne, . . . I. vii. 11. 2
Him to his castle brought with hastie *forse,* . . . I. vii. 15. 8
The *force,* . . . In one alone left hand he now unites, . . . I. viii. 18. 1
With furious *force* and indignation fell; . . . I. viii. 39. 6
by *force* unwonted passage fynd, . . . I. xi. 10. 7
So wondrous *force* from hand of living wight; . . . I. xi. 17. 8
never could the *force* of fleshly arme, . . . I. xi. 36. 6
to his *force* to yielden it was faine; . . . I. xi. 37. 7
With ydle *force* did faine them to withstand, . . . I. xii. 35. 8
He pricked forth his puissant *force* to prove. . . . II. i. 50. 7
both with greedy *forse* Attonce upon him ran, . . . II. ii. 22. 1
with stiffe *force* shaking his mortall launce, . . . II. iii. 14. 4
adding more impetuous *forse,* . . . II. iv. 6. 3
His *force* was vaine, and strooke more often wyde, . . . II. iv. 7. 4
If wonted *force* and fortune doe me not much fayl.' . . . II. v. 5. 9
Ne deeme thy *force* by fortunes doome unjust, . . . II. v. 12. 8
nothing might sustaine his furious *forse:* . . . II. v. 23. 2
Is all his *force* forlorne, and all his glory donne? . . . II. v. 35. 9
Whom nether wind out of their seat could *forse* . . . II. vi. 20. 8
His prowd presumed *force* increased more, . . . II. vi. 30. 3
least *Force* or Fraud should unaware Breake in, . . . II. vii. 25. 3
weenest words or charms may *force* withstond: . . . II. viii. 22. 2
was the *force* so furious and so fell, . . . II. viii. 31. 1
He, swarving with the *force,* . . . II. viii. 36. 6
Assembling all his *force* and utmost might, . . . II. viii. 47. 3
Weake body wel is chang'd for minds redoubled *forse.* . . . II. ix. 55. 9
gathering *force* and corage valorous, . . . II. x. 18. 3
ruin'd wals he did reaedifye . . . gainst *force* of enimy, . . . II. x. 46. 5
Their *force* is fiercer through infirmity . . . II. xi. 1. 5
with incessaunt *force* and endlesse hate . . . II. xi. 6. 8
T' assayle with open *force* or hidden guyle, . . . II. xi. 7. 4
most horrible of hew And ferce of *force,* . . . II. xi. 13. 2
Nought feard theyr *force* that fortilage to win, . . . II. xii. 43. 5
neither guile nor *force* might it distraine. . . . II. xii. 82. 3
To weene your wrong by *force* to justify; . . . III. i. 25. 2
she of womans *force* did feare no harme; . . . III. iv. 27. 8
With so fell *force,* and villeinous despite, . . . III. v. 19. 2
strooke at him with *force* so violent, . . . III. v. 25. 4
having through incessant traveill spent His *force,* . . . III. vii. 3. 7
when his *force* gan faile his pace gan wex areare. . . . III. vii. 24. 9
we will by *force* it win, . . . III. ix. 9. 5
threatned him with *force* and punishment extreme: . . . III. ix. 10. 9
met Together with impetuous rage and *forse,* . . . III. x. 16. 2
with fowle *force* unto his will did drive; . . . III. x. 27. 7
to her yold the flames, and did their *force* revolt. . . . III. xi. 25. 9
Where *force* might not availe, there sleights . . . III. xii. 28. 1
with *force* her brought From twentie Knights . . . IV. i. 2. 3
set it all on fire by *force* unknowen, . . . IV. ii. 1. 4
with so untamed *forse* Did beare them both . . . IV. ii. 15. 1
in friendship for her sake To joyne your *force,* . . . IV. ii. 24. 7
to joyne in one With all their *force,* . . . IV. ii. 28. 7
met With dreadfull *force* and furious intent, . . . IV. iii. 6. 6
aventred With doubled *force* close underneath his shield, . . IV. iii. 9. 2
with the *force* it backward forced him to bow. . . . IV. iii. 11. 9
Was with the *force* nigh feld, . . . IV. iii. 18. 9
from his *force* seemes nought may it defend; . . . IV. iii. 19. 4
Flowes up the Shenan with contrarie *forse,* . . . IV. iii. 27. 2
proffer made by *force* her to reprize: . . . IV. iv. 8. 8
neither could the others *force* sustaine; . . . IV. iv. 18. 2
none his *force* were able to withstond, . . . IV. iv. 23. 8
doe breake by *force* Into an heard, . . . IV. iv. 35. 6
Could bide the *force* of that enchaunted speare, . . . IV. iv. 46. 4
(so much his *force* prevayled) . . . IV. vi. 12. 8
With dreadfull *force* falles on some steeple hie; . . . IV. vi. 14. 3
with the *force,* whiche in it selfe it bore, . . . IV. vi. 19. 2
mightie kingdomes of his *force* adred; . . . IV. viii. 47. 5
Gainst all that would it faine to *force* or wrong: . . . IV. x. 7. 5
Did neede to gard from *force,* . . . IV. xi. 3. 4
This Gyant found her and by *force* deflowr'd; . . . IV. xi. 42. 6
no man was affrayd Of *force,* . . . V. Pr. 9. 4
streight at him with all his *force* did go, . . . V. i. 21. 5
The maysterdome of each by *force* to gaine, . . . V. ii. 15. 4
In swimming be expert, through waters *force* to pas. . . . V. ii. 16. 9
force of stones which they did throw, . . . V. ii. 22. 7
He nigh them drew to stay th' avengers *forse,* . . . V. iii. 30. 7
by *force* or guile She doth subdue, . . . V. iv. 31. 1
With dreadfull *force* he flies at her bylive, . . . V. iv. 42. 6
To try her Fortune, and his *force* assay, . . . V. iv. 47. 7
The other it with *force* doth overthrow . . . V. vi. 40. 6
meaning to suppresse both forged guile And open *force:* . . . V. vii. 7. 4
having *force* increast through furious paine, . . . V. vii. 33. 6
Then, farewell fleshly *force!* . . . V. vii. 40. 9
he saw the hindmost . . . *force* him turne his face; . . . V. viii. 5. 7
him from *force* to let. . . . V. viii. 6. 9
With all their *force* to worke avengement strong . . . V. viii. 24. 6
threw A shivering dart with so impetuous *force,* . . . V. viii. 32. 6
She at her ran with all her *force* and might, . . . V. viii. 46. 8
with finall *force* them all he overcame. . . . V. viii. 50. 9
If not, we will it *force,* maugre your foe, . . . V. x. 24. 3
now by *force* extort out of her hand . . . V. x. 25. 3
with restlesse *force* Into his shield it readie passage found, . V. x. 33. 1

Force—*Continued.*
Ne to their *force* gave way, . . . V. x. 35. 3
By open *force* to fetch her quite away: . . . V. xi. 51. 2
she by *force* is still fro me detayned, . . . V. xi. 54. 8
fiercely charged him with all his *force:* . . . V. xii. 7. 2
with such *force* and furie violent . . . V. xii. 17. 5
With so fell fury and dispiteous *forse,* . . . VI. i. 33. 6
Thinking the utmost of their *force* to trie, . . . VI. i. 38. 3
by outragious *force* away did beare: . . . VI. iii. 18. 7
with fierce fury and with *force* infest . . . VI. iv. 5. 3
by no wize He could him *force* to loose, . . . VI. iv. 6. 9
having now no . . . *force* his shield to straine, . . . VI. iv. 7. 7
Here they of *force* (as fortune now did fall) . . . VI. iv. 15. 5
the beast . . . Upon him turned, and, with greedie *force* . . . VI. iv. 20. 6
by *force* could him destroy, . . . VI. v. 14. 3
his great *force* unable to endure, . . . VI. v. 16. 6
heaped strokes did round about him haile With so huge *force,* VI. v. 18. 4
With dreadfull *force* they all did him assaile, . . . VI. vi. 26. 1
Durst not the furie of his *force* abyde, . . . VI. vi. 28. 2
greater *force* there needs to maintaine wrong then right. . VI. vi. 35. 9
being carried with his *force* forthright . . . VI. vii. 7. 7
the first, whose *force* her first doth bring, . . . VI. vii. 9. 5
whether by *force,* or sleight, . . . they were away convayd? VI. vii. 34. 5
Compelling her, wher she would not, by *force,* . . . VI. vii. 44. 3
Till they him *force* the buxome yoke to beare: . . . VI. viii. 12. 4
Resolved in one t' assemble all his *force,* . . . VI. viii. 14. 8
Thereof by *force* to take their beastly pleasure: . . . VI. viii. 43. 6
That monstrous Beast by finall *force* to quell, . . . VI. xii. 22. 7
when the Beast saw he mote nought availe By *force,* . . . VI. xii. 33. 2
At last, when as he found his *force* to shrincke . . . VI. xii. 34. 1
she cast by *force* and tortious might Her to displace, . . . VII. vi. 10. 7
Whether by open *force,* or counsell wise: . . . VII. vi. 21. 8
Bending their *force* contrary to their face; . . . VII. vii. 35. 8
But then she seeks, . . . To *force* me live, . . . *Am.* xi. 12
The paynefull smith, with *force* of fervent heat, . . . *Am.* xxxii. 1
bend your *force* against your enemyes: . . . *Am.* xlix. 8
now t' asswage the *force* of this new flame, . . . *H.L.* 8
Ne ought so strong that may his *force* withstand, . . . *H.L.* 229
So torne and mangled with malicious *forse;* . . . *H.H.L.* 250

Forced. *forst* this hideous beast to open wide . . . *Van.* iii. 9
Forst with the filth his egs to fling away: . . . *Van.* iv. 12
His wide Abysse him *forced* forth to spewe, . . . *Van.* v. 10
Untimely my flowres *forced* to fall, . . . *S.C.* F. 177
Sore against my will was I *forst* to yield. . . . *S.C.* Au. 42
Such ill, as is *forced,* mought nedes be endured. . . . *S.C.* S. 139
it mens follies mote be *forst* to fayne, . . . *S.C.* O. 75
forst to ferrie over Lethes river, . . . *Gn.* 338
I, poore wretch, am *forced* to retourne . . . *Gn.* 618
Were *forst* their auncient houses to let lie, . . . *Hub.* 1178
then him waking, *forced* up to rize. . . . *Hub.* 1323
forst to overflow with brackish teares, . . . *T.M.* 29
To stay the steppe, ere *forced* to retrate. . . . I. i. 13. 5
with his trenchand blade . . . *forced* her to stay: . . . I. i. 17. 4
it *forst* him slacke His grasping hold, . . . I. i. 20. 4
he . . . Shooke him so hard, that *forced* him to speake. . . . I. i. 42. 6
owne deare sake *forst* me . . . to leave My fathers kingdom'— . I. i. 52. 1
he . . . *forced* him to stoupe upon his knee: . . . I. v. 12. 8
speed The fayre Duess' had *forst* him leave behind; . . . I. vi. 2. 2
Themselves . . . He *forst* to castle strong to take their flight I. vii. 44. 7
the Gyaunt . . . *forst* the knight retyre. . . . I. viii. 17. 9
her foundation *forst,* and feebled quight, . . . I. viii. 23. 4
With *forced* fury following his behest, . . . I. ix. 7. 5
he him *forst* to stay, . . . I. ix. 25. 4
forst, at last he made through silence suddein breach. . . . I. ix. 25. 9
him that would have *forced* me to dye? . . . I. ix. 26. 2
th' other *forst* him staye, and comforted in feare. . . . I. ix. 34. 9
forst him lay his hevenly thoughts aside; . . . I. x. 49. 3
he *forst* him to unty One of his grasping feete, . . . I. xi. 42. 8
forst him to retire A little backeward . . . I. xi. 45. 2
Now *forst* to yield, now forcing to invade; . . . II. ii. 25. 7
on foot was *forced* for to yeed . . . II. iv. 2. 3
with *forst* wind the fewell did inflame; . . . II. vii. 36. 2
Ne *forst* his rightful owner to offend; . . . II. viii. 21. 4
from his saddle *forced* him to fly; . . . II. viii. 33. 7
forced him his ground to traverse wyde, . . . II. viii. 35. 3
twise him *forst* his foot revoke. . . . II. viii. 39. 9
Champions broke on them, that *forst* them fly, . . . II. ix. 14. 6
forst their chiefetain, for his safeties sake, . . . II. x. 16. 6
their Syre . . . from Fraunce was *forced* to retyre. . . . II. x. 22. 9
Vortiger have (*om.) *forst* (*enforst) the kingdome to aband. . . . II. x. 65. 9
thereby *forst* his workemen to forsake, . . . III. iii. 10. 8
shall be *forst* to yield: . . . III. iii. 31. 6
through weaknesse he was *forst* at last To yield . . . III. v. 48. 2
her would *forced* have to have forlore Her former love . . III. vi. 53. 7
forst t' alight, on foot mote algates fare . . . III. vii. 4. 1
in vaine was *forst* to turne his flight, . . . III. vii. 28. 5
Him *forst* to leave his pray, . . . III. vii. 32. 4
Him *forst,* (maulgre) his fercenes to relent, . . . III. xi. 26. 8
Forst him eftsoones to follow other game, . . . III. xi. 38. 8
Her fayned Paramour, her *forced* guest, . . . IV. i. 36. 3
being *forst* his saddle soone to leave, . . . IV. i. 36. 4
forced him his shield to disadvaunce. . . . IV. iii. 8. 4
with the force it backward *forced* him to bow. . . . IV. iii. 11. 9
he was *forst* from daunger of the throwes Backe to retire, . IV. iii. 26. 3
His borrowed waters *forst* to redisbourse, . . . IV. iii. 27. 7
He *forced* was to strike, and save himselfe from teene. . . . IV. iii. 31. 9
forced them from fighting to refraine, . . . IV. iv. 25. 7
forced him to leave his loftie sell, . . . IV. iv. 30. 8
brute beasts, *forst* to refraine fro meat, . . . IV. iv. 47. 3

Forced—*Continued.*
forced them to seeke some covert bowre, . . . IV. v. 32. 5
forst to wake, He felt his hart for very paine to quake, . . . IV. v. 44. 4
she him *forced* backward to retreat, . . . IV. vi. 15. 3
Yet she it *forst* to have againe upheld, . . . IV. vi. 27. 1
forst him flie abacke, himselfe to save: . . . IV. vii. 28. 4
forst him backe with fowle dishonor to retreat. . . . IV. vii. 37. 9
uneath they *forced* were, . . . to relent, . . . IV. ix. 25. 7
forst to seeke my lifes deare patronnesse: . . . IV. x. 28. 8
she them *forced* hand to joyne in hand, . . . IV. x. 33. 2
he her quickly stayd, and *forst* to wend withall. . . . V. i. 22. 9
forced him, maulgre, it up to reare. . . . V. i. 29. 6
him *forst* forsake His horses backe . . . V. ii. 16. 1
he was *forced* to withdraw aside, . . . V. ii. 20. 7
forst the burden of their prize to stay. . . . V. iii. 11. 4
they were *forst*, through penurie and pyne, . . . V. v. 22. 6
Since that he was not *forst*, nor overcome in fight?' . . . V. vi. 16. 9
Yet being *forst* to abide the daies returning, . . . V. vi. 31. 3
shortly *forst* him to forsake The hight, . . . V. ix. 16. 6
forced it, the honour that is dew To God, to doe unto his Idole . . . V. x. 27. 8
the bold Prince was *forced* foote to give . . . V. xi. 5. 6
forst her turne againe in her despight To save her selfe, . . . V. xi. 26. 7
when she saw that she was *forst* to fight, . . . V. xi. 27. 1
forced him to throw it quite away, . . . V. xi. 46. 3
forced them, how ever strong and stout They were, . . . V. xi. 47. 4
forced to forgoe th' attempt remedilesse.' . . . V. xi. 51. 9
forced me to so infamous deed, . . . V. xi. 57. 4
forst at first those knights backe to retyre: . . . V. xi. 58. 6
of necessity His course of Justice he was *forst* to stay, . . . V. xii. 27. 4
refused To take me up . . . But *forst* to trot on foot, . . . VI. ii. 22. 5
charging him . . . *Forst* to forgoe his pray . . . VI. iii. 25. 7
But *forst* him gape and gaspe, . . . VI. iii. 26. 8
in his tender armes her *forced* up to stay. . . . VI. iii. 27. 9
That *forst* him backe recoyle and reele areare, . . . VI. iv. 5. 8
Ere long he overtooke and *forst* to stay; . . . VI. iv. 20. 2
He *forced* was to turne from him and fly: . . . VI. v. 16. 7
Was *forced* there to leave them both behynd . . . VI. v. 41. 3
forst him th' halter from his hand to loose, . . . VI. vii. 45. 7
Him often scourg'd, and *forst* his feete to fynd: . . . VI. vii. 49. 5
from the townes into the countrie *forsed*, . . . VI. ix. 3. 8
he *forced* him to flie. . . . VI. ix. 4. 9
fierce assailing *forst* him turne againe: . . . VI. xii. 26. 2
Jove, all fearlesse, *forc't* them to aby; . . . VII. vi. 24. 6
Was *forst* to yeeld my selfe . . . *Am.* xii. 10

Force's. prickt with courage, and thy *forces* pryde, . . . I. x. 66. 7
far above thy *forces* pitch to sore; . . . V. ii. 34. 4
asswage Their *forces* furie, and their terror slake; . . . V. xii. 8. 4

Forces. oft beheld the warlike Greekish *forces*, . . . *Gn.* 499
walls of Carthage vow'd, Trembling their *forces*, . . . *Gn.* 616
To tell my *forces*, matchable to none, . . . *Ti.* 89
With my great *forces* might compared bee: . . . *Ti.* 103
all his yongthly *forces* idly spent, . . . *Mui.* 431
her beastly bodie raizd With doubled *forces* . . . I. i. 18. 4
His *forces* faile, ne can no lenger fight: . . . I. i. 22. 3
daunted with theyr *forces* hideous, Their steeds doe stagger, I. ii. 15. 5
doest thy *forces* slake To after-send his foe, . . . I. v. 10. 8
Eftsoones his manly *forces* gan to fayle, . . . I. vii. 6. 4
all their *forces* spend Them selves in vaine: . . . I. viii. 21. 5
Knitt all his *forces*, . . . II. iv. 9. 7
oft his *forces* fayld, . . . II. iv. 14. 5
their *forces* gan to fayle, . . . II. ix. 14. 3
To joyne your force, their *forces* to repell . . . IV. ii. 24. 7
Having his *forces* all in one accrewed, . . . IV. vi. 18. 7
now their *forces* greatly were decayd, . . . IV. ix. 34. 1
all thy *forces* gather unto thee, . . . V. v. 34. 7
He all his *forces* streight to him did reare, . . . V. xii. 6. 7
Where singled *forces* faile, conjoynd may gaine. . . . VI. v. 14. 7
Their wounds recur'd, and *forces* reincreast, . . . VI. vi. 15. 7
Retourne agayne, my *forces* late dismayd, . . . *Am.* xiv. 1
Bring therefore all the *forces* that ye may, . . . *Am.* xiv. 9
with contrary *forces* to conspyre Each against other . . . *H.L.* 80

Forceth. *Forceth* it swell above his wonted mood, . . . III. vii. 34. 3
forceth further on, and striveth still . . . *H.L.* 247

Forcible. The beast, impatient . . . of so fierce and *forcible* despight, . . . I. xi. 25. 7

Forcibly. Into the Castle entred *forcibly*, . . . I. viii. 29. 4
with strong flight did *forcibly* divyde The yielding ayre, . . . I. xi. 18. 3
Yielded by him that held it *forcibly*: . . . II. iv. 40. 2
the sharpe steele, arriving *forcibly* On his broad shield, . . . II. v. 4. 3
with his naked hands him *forcibly* assayld. . . . II. xi. 41. 9
The stone-dead quarrey falls so *forciblye*, . . . II. xi. 43. 3
that Guest did beare her *forcibly*, . . . III. x. 13. 8
Forcibly driven with contrarie tydes, . . . IV. i. 42. 2
So thicke they fell, and *forcibly* were sent, . . . IV. iii. 26. 2
forcibly to ground they both together went. . . . IV. iv. 28. 9
Yet was the stroke so *forcibly* applide, . . . V. xi. 11. 1
with his club bet backe his brondyron bright So *forcibly*, VI. viii. 10. 5
Is *forcibly* kept downe, till he be throughly queld. . . . VI. xii. 30. 9
Did him suppresse, and *forcibly* subdew, . . . VI. xii. 31. 6

Forcing. *Forcing* with gyfts to winne his wanton heart. . . . *S.C.* Ap. 24
Now forst to yield, now *forcing* to invade; . . . II. ii. 25. 7
forcing it to fayne, him forth thence ledd, . . . II. vii. 51. 2
Forcyng to doe that did him fowle misseeme. . . . III. viii. 26. 7
Forcing in vaine the rest to her to tell; . . . V. vi. 11. 8

Ford. *See* **Water-ford.**
As men in Summer fearles passe the *foord* . . . *Ro.* xiv. 1
drave them to a *foord*, . . . *Gn.* 162
him to ferry over that deepe *ford*. . . . II. vi. 4. 4
To ferry that old man over the perlous *foord*. . . . II. vi. 19. 9

Ford—*Continued.*
he fownd in that dull *ford* The carefull servaunt . . . II. vi. 47. 8
them awaited ready at the *ford* The Ferriman, . . . II. xi. 4. 1
a covert glade, Foreby a narrow *foord*, . . . III. v. 17. 2
his passage through the *ford* to let. . . . III. v. 17. 9
through the *ford* to passen did assay; . . . III. v. 18. 4
labour'd long in that deepe *ford* . . . III. v. 19. 9
headlesse him into the *foord* he sent: . . . III. v. 25. 5
water of the *ford*, Or of the clouds, . . . III. vi. 34. 7
which way he through the *foord* mote pas: . . . VI. iii. 30. 4
themselves prepard thorough the *foord* to ride. . . . VI. iii. 30. 9
Through that same perillous *foord* . . . VI. iii. 31. 4
doth thus strongly ward the Castle of the *Ford?'* . . . VI. iii. 39. 9
Whom he did overthrow by yonder *foord;* . . . VI. iv. 29. 7

Fordo. that Tyrant to *fordoo*,) . . . V. xii. 3. 4

Fordone. charmes, A *fordonne* wight from dore of death mote raise, . . . I. v. 41. 8
many soules in dolours had *fordonne*: . . . I. x. 33. 7
his fraile thighes, nigh weary and *fordonne*, . . . I. x. 47. 8
To aide a virgin, desolate, *foredonne;* . . . I. x. 60. 4
many errant knightes hath fowle *fordonne;* . . . II. i. 51. 4
Whose wofull parents she hath wickedly *fordonne*.' . . . II. ii. 44. 9
'Least we unweeting hap to be *fordonne;* . . . II. xii. 11. 2
thy sad people, utterly *fordonne*, . . . III. iii. 34. 3
the rich furrowes flote, all quite *fordonne:* . . . III. vii. 34. 6
squiers make hast to helpe their Lords *fordonne*. . . . IV. iv. 38. 8
he sav'd the victour from *fordonne:* . . . IV. v. 7. 7
she had them both shamefully *fordonne*, . . . IV. ix. 28. 8
Which lawlesse men had formerly *fordonne:* . . . V. i. 2. 4
many errant Knights hath there *fordonne;* . . . V. ii. 4. 8
Where as so many knights had fouly bene *fordonne*. . . . V. x. 30. 9
by whom that feend shold be *fordonne*. . . . VI. iv. 32. 9
whose hart through feare was late *fordonne*, . . . VI. xi. 35. 5
Give leave to rest me being halfe *fordonne*, . . . *Am.* lxxx. 3

Fore. *See* **Tofore.**

Forecast. That is to come, let be *forecast:* . . . *S.C.* Mar. 59
how can fraile fleshly wight *Forecast*, . . . *Mui.* 227
Yet, wilfull man, he never would *forecast* . . . I. iv. 34. 8
mischiefe, which she did *forecast* . . . III. vii. 18. 4
as she had late *forecast*, . . . III. xii. 29. 8

Forecasting. *Fore-casting* how his foe he might annoy; . . . I. iv. 45. 2

Fore-damned. All desperate of his *fore-damned* spright, . . . III. x. 56. 8

Forefathers. their *forefathers*, famous over-all, Had founded . *Hub.* 1180
What bootes it then to come from glorious *Forefathers*, . . . *T.M.* 446

Forego, -ne. *See* **Forgo, -ne.**

Forehead. A grisly *forehed* and Saturnelike face. . . . *Bel.*[1] vii. 4
his broad *forhead* like two hornes divide, . . . *Gn.* 22
To gather flowres her *forhead* to array: . . . *Mui.* 117
thinking . . . to frame A girlond for her dainty *forehead* fit, I. ii. 30. 7
bayes His sweatie *forehead* in the breathing wynd, . . . I. vii. 3. 2
Her yvorie *forhead*, full of bountie brave, . . . II. iii. 24. 1
th' earth with his faire *forhead* strooke; . . . III. xi. 13. 7
The rugged *forehead*, that with grave foresight Welds kingdomes . . . IV. Pr. 1. 1
does beat her brest and *forhead* knockes. . . . V. xii. 38. 9
the crowne, which Ariadne wore Upon her yvory *forehead*, . . . VI. x. 13. 2
If Yvorie, her *forehead* Yvory weene; . . . *Am.* xv. 10
Her *forehead* yvory white, . . . *Epith.* 172
upon her *forhead* they behold . . . *H.B.* 253

Foreheads. to grace The learned *forheads*, . . . *T.M.* 82
Their frowning *forheades*, . . . all asyde doe lay; . . . I. vi. 11. 5
from the Sun their *forheads* fayr to shade; . . . III. iv. 29. 9
Their snowie *Foreheads* therewithall they crownd, . . . *Proth.* 86

Forehent. Doubleth her hast for feare to bee *for-hent*, . . . III. iv. 46. 8

Foreign. In *forrein* costes men sayd was plentye; . . . *S.C.* S. 28
Of *forreine* lands, of people different, . . . *Hub.* 765
a warlike equipage Of *forreine* beasts, . . . *Hub.* 1119
as he that perilous game In *forreine* soyle pursued . . . *As.* 92
As men use most to covet *forreine* thing.' . . . *Col.* 162
Desyrd of *forreine* foemen to be knowne, . . . I. vi. 29. 6
health to every *forreyne* nation: . . . II. x. 26. 7
unto him assembling *forreigne* might, . . . II. x. 35. 4
Against the *forreine* Morands he exprest; . . . II. x. 43. 8
Betrayd his countrey unto *forreine* spoyle. . . . II. x. 48. 8
neighbour Scots, and *forrein* Scatterlings . . . II. x. 63. 5
fetch from Faery *Forreine* ensamples . . . III. Pr. 1. 4
mightily defend Against their *forren* foe . . . III. iii. 23. 8
The powre of *forreine* Paynims which invade thy land. . . . III. iii. 27. 9
Which Uther with those *forrein* Pagans held, . . . III. iii. 55. 4
of a *forreine* foe He is yslaine, . . . III. v. 9. 8
many perilles past in *forreine* landes, . . . III. ix. 41. 8
it a wonder of the world is song In *forreine* landes; . . . III. ix. 45. 8
Attyr'd in *forraine* armes and straunge aray: . . . IV. vi. 9. 3
being carried farre from *forraine* lands. . . . V. iv. 5. 5
witnesse forth aright in *forrain* land, . . . V. ix. 37. 5
high alliance unto *forren* powre; . . . V. ix. 45. 6
from *forrein* land where they did dwell, . . . V. x. 6. 3
Her to defend against all *forrein* foes . . . V. x. 12. 4
Are not all places full of *forraine* powres? . . . V. x. 23. 2
away me to remove . . . Into some *forrein* land, . . . VI. ii. 29. 8
nature, which doth litle need Of *forreine* helpes . . . VI. ix. 20. 7
By all meanes shund to match with any *forrein* fere. . . . VI. xii. 4. 9
some beast of strange and *forraine* race . . . VII. vi. 28. 7
Thy country may be freed from *forraine* harmes; . . . *Proth.* 156

Foreigners. those *forreyners* which came from farre, . . . II. x. 65. 5

Forejudgment. seldome seene, *forejudgment* (**forejudgement*) proveth true. . . . *Mui.* 320

Forelay. *forelay* Athwart her snowy brest, . . . II. iii. 29. 5

Forelent. As if that life to losse they had *forelent*, . . . IV. iii. 6. 8

Fore-lifting. *Forelifting* up a-loft his speckled brest, . . . I. xi. 15. 2

For ever—*Continued.*
By like ensample mote *for ever* warned bee. — V. viii. 44. 9
From him to whom she was *for ever* bound: — VI. ii. 43. 7
That thou *for ever* doe those armes forsake, — VI. iii. 35. 5
And be *for ever* held a recreant Knight, — VI. iii. 35. 6
With whom he myndes *for ever* to remaine, — VI. x. 2. 5
In that still happy state *for ever* to abide. — VII. vi. 5. 9
The Wood-gods breed, which must *for ever* live: — VII. vi. 50. 4
though it live *for ever,* — VII. vii. 24. 1
new desire . . . that shall endure *for ever:* — *Am.* vi. 10
joy, her thrall *for ever* to remayne, — *Am.* xlii. 7
Yet live *for ever,* though against her will, — *Am.* xlviii. 13
May live *for ever* in felicity! — *Am.* lxviii. 8
Ye three Elizabeths! *for ever* live, — *Am.* lxxiv. 13
This day *for ever* to me holy is. — *Epith.* 249
That ye *for ever* it remember may. — *Epith.* 264
That happie port *for ever* to recure! — *H.L.* 298
Where they *for ever* should in bonds remaine — *H.H.L.* 125
Thy straying thoughts henceforth *for ever* rest. — *H.H.B.* 301
faultie guile *For ever* to assoile. — *Proth.* 100
Forewarn. Did him, they say, *forwarne* through sacred spell: — III. v. 9. 7
Forewarned. Feeling the fit that him *forewarnd* to die, — *Ti.* 598
Forewent. *See* **Forwent.**
Forgat. *See* **Forgot.**
with the sight amazd, *forgat* his furious forse. — I. iii. 5. 9
how the time was fled they quite *forgate;* — II. x. 77. 4
Yet on mount Thabor quite their wits *forgat,* — VII. vii. 7. 7
Forgate. *See* **Forgat.**
Forgave. The Prince soone hearkned, and his life *forgave.* — VI. vii. 12. 5
Forge. To face, to *forge,* to scoffe, to companie, — *Hub.* 506
two, . . . fittest for to *forge* true-seeming lyes: — I. i. 38. 7
the flashing fier flies, As from a *forge,* — I. ii. 17. 8
seard In smythes fire-spitting *forge,* — II. vii. 3. 9
As in the smoky *forge* it was compilde, — III. vii. 30. 5
So could she *forge* all colours, save the trew. — IV. i. 18. 5
Framed in goldsmithes *forge* with cunning hand: — IV. vi. 20. 4
all the villany That she could *forge* in her malicious head, — V. iv. 29. 8
he so crafty was to *forge* and face, — V. ix. 5. 4
Forged. *See* **Fair-forged, False-forged.**
They *forg'd* another, as for Clerkes booke-redd. — *Hub.* 358
'Whose *forged* beauty he did take . . . to have exceeded — I. ii. 36. 1
By *forged* treason or by open fight, — II. i. 3. 3
Her deeds were *forged,* — III. xii. 14. 8
Yet all was *forg'd* and spred with golden foyle, — IV. ii. 29. 4
with her *forged* beautie did seduce The hearts — IV. v. 11. 3
so *forged* things do fairest shew. — IV. v. 15. 9
With *forged* cause them falsely to defame; — IV. viii. 25. 7
meaning to suppresse both *forged* guile And open force: — V. vii. 7. 3
foule blaspheme that Queene for *forged* guyle, — V. ix. 25. 5
such *forged* showes, as fitter beene For courting fooles — VI. v. 38. 7
Oft interlacing many a *forged* lie, — VI. xii. 33. 5
Forgery. Through leasings lewd, and fained *forgerie;* — *Col.* 696
aboundance of an ydle braine . . . and painted *forgery,* — II. Pr. 1. 4
onely womanish fine *forgery,* — II. xii. 28. 8
Of such malengine and fine *forgerye,* — III. i. 53. 8
Out of the fore-side of their *forgerie,* — V. iii. 39. 2
'Fie on such *forgerie!'* — V. xi. 56. 6
it indeed is nought but *forgerie,* — VI. Pr. 5. 3
Forget. *forget* not what you be: — *Van.* xii. 12
never might his luckie scape *forget.* — *Gn.* 664
for feare her beads she did *forgett:* — I. iii. 14. 5
Whome great griefe made *forgett* the raines to hold — I. iv. 41. 3
Els had his sinnes, . . . Made him *forget* all — I. x. 22. 5
made him to *forget* His former payne, — II. v. 30. 8
Yet will I not forgoe, ne yet *forgett* — II. viii. 8. 3
both did *forget* The perilous present stownd — IV. ii. 15. 8
Now made *forget* their former cruell mood, — IV. iii. 39. 4
Selfe to *forget* to mind another is over-sight.' — IV. vii. 10. 9
shortly leave, and former love *forget.* — IV. viii. 53. 9
mighty hands *forget* their manlinesse; — V. viii. 1. 5
Forget his patience, and yeeld vengeaunce dew — V. xii. 42. 4
My tedious travell doe *forget* thereby; — VI. Pr. 1. 7
Whiles ye *forget* your former lay to sing, — *Epith.* 183
Forget their service and about her fly, — *Epith.* 231
That maketh them all worldly cares *forget,* — *H.H.B.* 265
Forgetful. *Forgetfull* of your former heavinesse; — *T.M.* 366
both stand senceless . . . *Forgetfull* of the hanging victory: — I. ii. 16. 6
Forgetfull of the hungry rage, — I. iii. 7. 4
Forgetfull of his owne that mindes an others cares. — I. v. 18. 9
Proud wemen, vaine, *forgetfull* of their yoke: — I. v. 50. 2
a dismayed Deare . . . *Forgetfull* of his safety, — III. xii. 17. 9
Forgetfull each to have bene ever others frend. — IV. ii. 14. 9
Forgetfull of her owne to minde his feares: — VI. iii. 12. 3
Forgetfull of the famous golden fleece; — *Am.* xliv. 3
man, *forgetfull* of his Makers grace — *H.H.L.* 120
Forgetfulness. In the *forgetfulnes* of sleepe — *Bel.* i. 3
die In foule *forgetfulnesse,* — *Ti.* 378
Forgeth. hande That *forgeth* thunder dartes for Jove — *Bel.*[1] iv. 11
Forgets. *Forgets* with wary warde them to awayt, — II. viii. 42. 3
She yet *forgets* that she of men was kynded: — V. v. 40. 8
unto heaven *forgets* her former flight. — *Am.* lxxii. 8
now *forgets* . . . His mothers heast to prove. — *Epig.* iv. 57
Forgetting. *forgetting* warres, he onely joyed In combats of sweet love, — V. v. 24. 8
Forgive. Ah, my liege Lord! *forgive* it unto mee, — *Mui.* 102
Forgive it me, faire Dames, sith lesse ye have not lefte. — *Ded.Son.*xvii.14
mote thy goodlyhed *forgive* it mee, — II. iii. 33. 7
Nath'lesse to thee thy folly I *forgive;* — III. iv. 37. 7
yet did his death *forgive.* — III. x. 7. 9
to forbeare doth not *forgive* the det.' — IV. iii. 11. 5

Forgive—*Continued.*
Which if ye please *forgive,* — V. viii. 13. 4
onely breath, sith that I did *forgive.'* — VI. vi. 36. 6
to great ones such follies doe *forgive;* — VI. ix. 22. 2
Forgiveth. God to us *forgiveth* every howre — I. x. 40. 6
Forgo. I wish I might this wearie life *forgoe,* — *Pet.*[2] vi. 5
nought feared they to *forgoe;* — *S.C.* May 110
Theyr yvory Luyts and Tamburins *forgoe,* — *S.C.* Jun. 59
kindly sleep . . . my feeble eyes *forgoe,* — *Hub.* 22
wishfull thing this sad life to *forgoe:* — *D.* 452
Forgoe that royal maides bequeathed care, — I. x. 63. 7
Sith Una now he algates must *forgoe,* — II. i. 2. 5
Yet will I not *forgoe,* ne yet forgett — II. viii. 8. 3
Then must he her *forgoe* with fowle defame, — III. i. 27. 2
could not stay, so fast she did *foregoe,* — III. v. 6. 5
Some, of sworne friends that did their faith *forgoe;* — IV. i. 24. 3
Ne her owne Amoret *forgoe* so light — IV. v. 20. 7
Both sire and friends and all for ever to *forgo.* — IV. vii. 16. 9
Forgoe the purchase of my gotten pray, — IV. viii. 62. 4
I neither can my love ne yet my life *forgo.'* — IV. ix. 39. 9
no intreatie would *forgoe* so glorious spoyle. — IV. x. 55. 9
not to *forgo* Those warlike weedes, — V. vi. 23. 6
forced to *forgoe* th' attempt remedilesse.' — V. xi. 51. 9
loosing soone his shield did it *forgoe;* — V. xii. 22. 7
forgoe This evill manner — VI. i. 27. 1
Forst to *forgoe* his pray — VI. iii. 25. 7
this Lady, . . . is ready to *forgo* the ghost; — VI. iii. 39. 4
For he would not his greedie grype *forgoe,* — VI. iv. 7. 3
If will; then she at will may will *forgoe.* — *Am.* xli. 4
Forgone. hath his sword through hard assay *forgone,* — II. iii. 12. 6
things *foregone* through many ages held, — II. ix. 56. 2
all *forgon,* They mote the better tend to their devotion. — V. vii. 9. 8
yet neither has *forgon* His horses backe, — V. viii. 9. 7
long since aside had . . . battell quite *forgone:* — V. xi. 37. 4
for his sake his deare life had *forgone;* — VI. vii. 18. 2
Forgot. *See* **Forgat.**
die *forgot* from whence at first they sprong, — *T.M.* 443
As they themselves shalbe *forgot* ere long. — *T.M.* 444
Deserving never here to be *forgot,* — *Ti.* 438
that waste, where I was quite *forgot.* — *Col.* 183
thou hast *forgot* Thy selfe, me seemes, — *Col.* 616
Shee has *forgott* how many a woeful stowre — I. iii. 30. 5
ne yet his vertues had *forgot:* — I. xi. 29. 9
He nought *forgott* how he whilome had sworne, — I. xii. 41. 6
Whiles in the bush he lay, not yett *forgott:* — II. iii. 43. 5
shortly he *forgot* the jeopardy, — II. x. 17. 3
hath so soone *forgot* the excellence Of his creation, — II. xii. 87. 2
In balefull night where all thinges are *forgot:* — III. vi. 47. 3
soone *forgot* his former sickely payne: — III. viii. 10. 3
forgot that whylome I heard tell From aged Mnemon; — III. ix. 47. 3
shortly she Malbecco has *forgott,* — III. x. 37. 1
he has quight *Forgot* he was a man, — III. x. 60. 9
his wound he soone *forgot,* — IV. iv. 33. 2
deviz'd some what to say, Which she *forgot,* — IV. vi. 45. 8
A wofull wretched maid, of God and man *forgot!* — IV. vii. 14. 9
all the raging seas for joy *forgot* to rore. — IV. xi. 23. 9
Ram . . . Hath now *forgot* where he was plast of yore, — V. Pr. 5. 8
through great fury both their skill *forgot,* — V. vii. 29. 4
They heare him not, they have *forgot* his lore, — V. viii. 39. 8
all obedience both to words and deeds They quite *forgot,* — V. viii. 41. 4
be *forgot* as it had never beene; — *Am.* xxvii. 7
Forgotten. *Forgotten* quite as they were never borne. — *Ti.* 182
Rather desires to be *forgotten* quight, — *D.* 89
My layes made of her shall not be *forgotten,* — *Col.* 642
of the wicked world *forgotten* quight, — IV. vii. 39. 6
Forhaile. *See* **Forhale.**
Forhale. Nought easeth the care that doth me *forhaile;* — *S.C.* S. 243
For(e)hed, -s. *See* **Forehead, -s.**
Forked. *See* **Three-forked.**
forkhed sting that death in it did beare, — *Van.* vi. 4
A twinne of *forked* trees — *Bel.* v. 14
Fork-head. backe rebownding left the *forckhead* keene: — II. iv. 46. 8
through his haberjeon the *forkehead* flew, — III. v. 19. 3
Forkhed. *See* **Forked.**
Forlent. Ladies love unto his Lord *forlent,* — III. iv. 47. 2
Forlore. *See* **Forlorn.**
banisht had my selfe, like wight *forlore,* — *Col.* 182
For ruth of gentle knight so fowle *forlore:* — I. viii. 39. 4
mortall life gan loath as thing *forlore,* — I. x. 21. 5
Where all the Nymphes have her unwares *forlore,* — II. iii. 31. 3
To save my Lord in wretched plight *forlore;* — II. vi. 48. 3
When ever they their heavenly bowres *forlore;* — II. xii. 52. 7
their charets they *forlore,* — III. iv. 34. 2
to all th' unworthy world *forlore* — III. v. 50. 8
her would forced have to have *forlore* Her former love — III. vi. 53. 7
Lightly she leaped, as a wight *forlore,* — III. vii. 25. 7
worldes of fancies . . . that now her quite *forlore:* — III. ix. 52. 5
in that wildernesse, of men *forlore,* — IV. vii. 39. 5
that wretched Greeke, that life *forlore,* — IV. x. 40. 5
go which way they list, their guide they have *forlore.* — V. viii. 39. 9
Is mine owne love, though me she have *forlore,* — V. xi. 49. 7
Whom when those knights so froward and *forlore* Beheld, — V. xi. 61. 8
implore To send her succour, being of all hope *forlore.* — VI. iv. 10. 9
Of his first quest, which he had long *forlore,* — VI. xii. 12. 2
Forlorn. *See* **Forlore.**
The weake, that hath the strong so oft *forlorne!* — *Van.* vi. 14
Thou weake, I wanne; thou leane, I quite *forlorne:* — *S.C.* Ja. 47
And am *forlorne,* (alas! why am I lorne?) — *S.C.* Ja. 62
art thou of thy loved lasse *forlorne?* — *S.C.* Ap. 4
Of fortune and of hope at once *forlorne.'* — *Hub.* 258

Forlorn—*Continued.*
Doo seeke to make us of the world *forlorne,* . . . *T.M.* 66
loath'd of losels as a thing *forlorne:* . . . *T.M.* 226
Have both desire of worthie deeds *forlorne,* . . . *T.M.* 437
of all Nations now I am *forlorne,* . . . *Ti.* 27
well he seemd to be sum wight *forlorne;* . . . *D.* 45
love had me *forlorne, forlorne* of me, . . . *Col.* 90
Amyntas, floure of shepheards pride *forlorne:* . . . *Col.* 439
The Willow, worne of *forlorne* Paramours; . . . I. i. 9. 3
Who now is left to keepe the *forlorne* maid . . . I. iii. 43. 1
two of three her Nephewes are so fowle *forlorne?* . . . I. v. 23. 9
The *forlorne* mayd did with loves longing burne, . . . I. vi. 22. 1
this man *forlorne,* And left to losse; . . . I. vii. 10. 5
The wofull Dwarfe . . . tooke up his *forlorne* weed; . . . I. vii. 19. 4
'The *forlorne* Maiden, whom your eies have seene . . . I. vii. 43. 1
ye, the *forlorne* reliques of his powre, . . . I. vii. 48. 1
Her, late *forlorne* and naked, he had found . . . II. i. 22. 1
Braggadocchio, . . . is of fayre Belphoebe fowle *forlorne.* . . . II. iii. Arg.
Is all his force *forlorne,* and all his glory donne? . . . II. v. 35. 9
His *forlorne* steed from him the victour wan: . . . II. vi. 41. 4
them that liv'd therin in state *forlorne:* . . . II. vii. 18. 3
wide Fraunce, a *forlorne* Dame, . . . II. x. 23. 7
was torne . . . and the roiall throne *forlorne.* . . . II. x. 36. 5
Late king, now captive; late lord, now *forlorne;* . . . III. iii. 42. 4
as wight *forlorne,* Long time she fostred up, . . . III. iv. 20. 3
Now lyest thou a lumpe of earth *forlorne;* . . . III. iv. 36. 7
'Great pitty sure that ye be so *forlorne* . . . III. vi. 21. 3
and wander wide . . . like a *forlorne* wefte; . . . III. x. 36. 3
he himselfe himselfe loath'd so *forlorne,* . . . III. x. 55. 7
So shamefully *forlorne* of womankynd, . . . III. x. 55. 8
theirs that have so cruell thee *forlorne!* . . . IV. viii. 15. 4
those six sad brethren, like *forlorne,* . . . IV. xi. 37. 1
Make meanes to win thy libertie *forlorne,* . . . V. v. 40. 2
They doe thy love *forlorne* in womens thraldome see. . . . V. vii. 21. 9
his faire limbs left in the woods *forlorne;* . . . V. viii. 43. 5
Whilest still she stands, as stonisht and *forlorne:* . . . V. xi. 29. 5
I my countrie have *forlorne,* . . . VI. ii. 27. 8
wretched life *forlorne* for vengement of his theft. . . . VI. iii. 18. 9
as thou hast thy steed *forlorne* with shame, . . . VI. iii. 32. 1
plight In which this Lady languisheth *forlorne,* . . . VI. iii. 41. 8
wend abrode, though feeble and *forlorne,* . . . VI. v. 7. 3
Treading downe earth as lothsome and *forlorne,* . . . *Am.* xiii. 11
Accoumpts my self her captive quite *forlorne.* . . . *Am.* xxix. 4
when as night hath us of light *forlorne,* . . . *Am.* lxxxvi. 7
they lye languishing like thrals *forlorne,* . . . *H.L.* 136

Form. All that Lysippus practike arte could *forme,* . . . *Ro.* xxix. 5
his rich attire and goodly *forme,* . . . *Van.* viii. 6
Much like an Angell in all *forme* and fashion. . . . *Col.* 615
a dull blast, that . . . with foule ugly *forme* did her disgrace: I. ii. 38. 8
T' adorne thy *forme* according thy desart, . . . II. iv. 26. 2
That houses *forme* within was rude and strong, . . . II. vii. 28. 1
mans body, both for powre and *forme,* . . . II. ix. 1. 3
had from hoggish *forme* him brought to naturall. . . . II. xii. 86. 9
whenas *forme* and feature it does ketch, . . . III. vi. 37. 3
when the life decayes and *forme* does fade, . . . III. vi. 37. 7
th' only *forme* and outward fashion; . . . III. vi. 38. 2
Which that same witch had in this *forme* engraft, . . . IV. ii. 10. 7
frame in earth, and *forme* of substance base, . . . IV. x. 21. 7
I doe not *forme* them to the common line . . . V. Pr. 3. 3
So did this Ladies goodly *forme* decay, . . . V. iii. 25. 8
changing all that *forme* of common-weale . . . V. vii. 42. 4
soone did make To leave his proper *forme,* . . . V. ix. 16. 9
gan her *forme* and feature to expresse, . . . VI. xi. 11. 8
other none such passion can contrive In perfect *forme,* . . . VI. xii. 21. 6
Unlike in *forme,* and chang'd by strange disguise: . . . VII. vii. 18. 8
newly fashion Unto a fairer *forme,* . . . *H.L.* 193
of the soule the bodie *forme* doth take; . . . *H.B.* 132
soule is *forme,* and doth the bodie make. . . . *H.B.* 133
A more refyned *forme,* . . . *H.B.* 214

Formal. Working her *formall* rowmes in wexen frame, . . . *S.C.* D. 68
chaunst with a *formall* Priest to meete, . . . *Hub.* 361
powred kindly heat and *formall* feature, . . . *Col.* 862

Formality. Holding a staffe in hand for mere *formalitee.* . . . II. xii. 48. 9

Formally. The skilfull Palmer *formally* did frame: . . . II. xii. 81. 5

Formed. How things she *formed* of a formelesse mas: . . . *T.M.* 502
As fairly *formd* as any star in skyes; . . . *As.* 188
formd so lively in each perfect part, . . . III. Pr. 1. 6
men . . . *form'd* of flesh and bone, . . . V. Pr. 2. 4
In sort as they were *formed* aunciently, . . . V. ii. 32. 8
of the earth they *formed* were of yore: . . . V. ii. 40. 3
Yet *form'd* by wondrous skill, and by His might, . . . *H.H.L.* 107

Former. Cooling againe his *former* kindled heate, . . . *Ro.* xi. 5
then returne to his *former* fall? . . . *S.C.* F. 14
My fancye eke from *former* follies move . . . *S.C.* Jun. 37
'The feeble flocks in field refuse their *former* foode, . . . *S.C.* N. 133
Equall in honour to the *former* crue, . . . *Gn.* 594
T' excuse his *former* treason and abusion, . . . *Hub.* 1363
Forgetfull of your *former* heavinesse; . . . *T.M.* 366
'Looke backe, who list, unto the *former* ages, . . . *Ti.* 57
Of *former* being in this mortall hous, . . . *Ti.* 354
for *former* vertues meede, . . . *Ti.* 398
Nath-lesse the Nymph her *former* liking held; . . . *Col.* 128
Nor failing force to *former* strength restore: . . . *D.* 473
I found much greater then the *former* fame; . . . *Col.* 334
former dayes Had in rude fields bene altogether spent, . . . *Col.* 668
being *former* foes, they wexed friends, . . . *Col.* 851
wearines of *former* fight Having yrockt asleepe his spright, . . . I. i. 55. 4
holding idely The broken reliques of their *former* cruelty. . . . I. ii. 16. 9
blast, that . . . Dimmed her *former* beauties shining ray, . . . I. ii. 38. 7
'Time and suffised fates to *former* kynd Shall us restore; . . . I. ii. 43. 8

Former—*Continued.*
on their *former* journey forward pas, . . . I. iii. 21. 3
trembling yet through feare of *former* hate. . . . I. vi. 9. 5
he recovered had his *former* hew; . . . I. ix. 20. 8
wrapped be in loves of *former* Dame, . . . I. xii. 30. 8
wary was the knight By tryall of his *former* harmes . . . II. i. 4. 7
transformed from his *former* skill, . . . II. i. 54. 4
added flame unto his *former* fire, . . . II. v. 8. 4
made him to forget His *former* payne, . . . II. v. 30. 9
Yet she still followed her *former* style, . . . II. vi. 22. 1
maystring them, renewd his *former* heat: . . . II. vii. 36. 6
great disparagment makes to his *former* might.' . . . II. viii. 29. 9
such as were through *former* flight preserv'd . . . II. x. 55. 5
Let them returned be unto their *former* state.' . . . II. xii. 85. 9
All were he wearie of his *former* paine; . . . III. i. 29. 4
Tho gan she to renew her *former* smart, . . . III. ii. 29. 8
the royall Infant fell Into her *former* fitt; . . . III. ii. 49. 2
Ere they to *former* rule restor'd shal bee, . . . III. iii. 44. 6
to *former* hew Hee turnd againe, . . . III. iii. 50. 8
Britomart kept on her *former* course, . . . III. iv. 5. 1
Her *former* sorrow into suddein wrath, . . . III. iv. 12. 6
To sorrow huge she turnd her *former* play, . . . III. iv. 30. 3
former feare of being fowly shent . . . III. iv. 50. 4
Where wicked ghosts doe waile their *former* sin. . . . III. v. 22. 4
the *former* chace Had undertaken after her, . . . III. v. 37. 1
Being through *former* bathing mollifide, . . . III. vi. 7. 6
Her *former* love and stedfast loialty, . . . III. vi. 53. 8
as if her *former* dred Were hard behind, . . . III. vii. 2. 5
backe returning to the *former* land, . . . III. vii. 61. 5
His *former* griefe with furie fresh reviv'd . . . III. viii. 3. 4
To make another like the *former* Dame, . . . III. viii. 5. 7
soone forgot his *former* sickely payne: . . . III. viii. 10. 3
he soone resinde His *former* suit, . . . III. xi. 5. 4
leave me to my *former* languishing? . . . III. xi. 24. 2
Much fayrer then the *former* was that roome, . . . III. xi. 51. 1
Restore unto her health and *former* state: . . . III. xii. 35. 6
who so list looke backe to *former* ages, . . . IV. Pr. 3. 1
So did they all their *former* strife accord; . . . IV. i. 15. 5
now had chang'd her *former* wonted hew; . . . IV. i. 18. 2
gan his *former* griefe renew. . . . IV. i. 38. 9
through the bruses of his *former* fight, . . . IV. i. 39. 8
of like *former* breaches Made in their friendship, . . . IV. ii. 12. 4
In whom he liv'd anew, of *former* life deprived. . . . IV. iii. 13. 9
Now made forget their *former* cruell mood, . . . IV. iii. 39. 4
forth upon his *former* voiage fared, . . . IV. v. 46. 2
New matter added to his *former* fire; . . . IV. vi. 11. 2
fayned still her *former* angry mood, . . . IV. vi. 29. 8
He by his *former* combate would not bide, . . . IV. vii. 29. 7
trembling every joynt through *former* feare; . . . IV. vii. 34. 2
him restore to *former* grace againe: . . . IV. vii. 47. 7
him receiv'd againe to *former* favours state. . . . IV. viii. 17. 9
though affide unto a *former* love, . . . IV. viii. 53. 1
former love forget. . . . IV. viii. 53. 9
I, that was not bent to *former* love . . . IV. viii. 60. 1
My *former* hardnesse first I faire excusd; . . . IV. viii. 60. 5
unto *former* liberty restore. . . . IV. ix. 8. 7
Resolved to pursue his *former* quest; . . . IV. ix. 17. 5
all afresh gan *former* fight renew. . . . IV. ix. 26. 6
I thereby my *former* love have lost; . . . IV. ix. 38. 2
all his *former* parts did earst appere: . . . IV. x. 20. 5
Marinells *former* wound is heald, . . . IV. xi. Arg.
his mothers *former* charge Gainst womens love, . . . IV. xii. 14. 5
that same *former* fatall wound of his . . . IV. xii. 22. 5
Ne *former* strength returne so suddenly, . . . IV. xii. 35. 4
unto his *former* journey he retourned: . . . V. ii. 28. 9
he ere long the *former* fiftie bet, . . . V. iii. 11. 8
saw my lands decay And *former* livelod fayle, . . . V. iv. 9. 7
gan renew her *former* cruelnesse: . . . V. v. 14. 4
all his *former* praise doth fowly spill: . . . V. vi. 1. 5
Gan her addresse unto her *former* way. . . . V. vi. 36. 3
after those two *former* rode apace . . . V. viii. 5. 2
As they were follow'd of their *former* feare. . . . V. viii. 39. 3
scornd all *former* law: . . . V. viii. 41. 4
Being returned to his *former* hew; . . . V. ix. 18. 8
To th' hearing of that *former* cause in hand . . . V. ix. 37. 2
His *former* fancies ruth he gan repent, . . . V. ix. 49. 2
in *former* age A Ladie of great worth . . . V. x. 7. 1
To graunt him that adventure for his *former* feat. . . . V. x. 15. 9
to his *former* journey him addrest; . . . V. xi. 35. 8
They turne afresh, and oft renew their *former* threat. . . . V. xi. 45. 9
all my *former* praise hath blemisht sore: . . . V. xi. 49. 4
My *former* shield I may resume againe: . . . V. xi. 56. 2
to release his *former* foule condition. . . . VI. i. 43. 9
recompence of all their *former* wrong. . . . VI. i. 47. 6
He now againe is on his *former* way . . . VI. ii. 3. 5
And Calidore forth passed to his *former* payne. . . . VI. ii. 38. 9
Gan freshly him addresse unto his *former* way. . . . VI. iii. 13. 9
discourse Of *former* daies mishap . . . VI. iii. 14. 9
His *former* malice to some new assay, . . . VI. iii. 47. 8
nigh tyrd with *former* chace, . . . VI. v. 21. 1
they to pitty turnd their *former* rage, . . . VI. v. 30. 8
her face and *former* parts professe A faire young Mayden, . . . VI. vi. 10. 6
according to the *former* token . . . VI. vi. 18. 1
As one that had no life him left through *former* feare. . . . VI. vi. 32. 9
in *former* fight He of the Prince his life received . . . VI. vii. 2. 3
nought abating of his *former* spight, . . . VI. vii. 10. 5
for all his *former* follies meed, . . . VI. vii. 11. 8
Wearie of travell in his *former* fight, . . . VI. vii. 19. 1
the *former* villaine, which did lead Her tyreling jade, . . . VI. vii. 40. 6
So fresh the image of her *former* dread, . . . VI. viii. 31. 6

Former—*Continued.*
His *former* quest, so full of toile and paine: . . . VI. x. 2. 2
scarcely yet from *former* feare exempted, . . . VI. x. 36. 8
Would not for ought be drawne to *former* drede, . . . VI. xi. 35. 6
all the stormes of fortunes *former* yre Were turnd, . . . VI. xii. 10. 4
Knowing his fatall hand by *former* feare; . . . VI. xii. 25. 8
rearing up his *former* feete on hight, . . . VI. xii. 29. 7
More then my *former* writs, . . . VI. xii. 41. 3
With hardned frosts of *former* winters ire, . . . VII. vii. 11. 4
Chaunge eke our mynds, and *former* lives amend; . . . *Am.* lxii. 6
unto heaven forgets her *former* flight . . . *Am.* lxxii. 8
againe enured His *former* cruelty . . . *Epig.* iv. 54
Whiles ye forget your *former* lay to sing, . . . *Epith.* 183
leave likewise your *former* lay to sing: . . . *Epith.* 313
Formerly. *Formerly* grounded and fast setteled . . . II. xii. 1. 4
formerly were bownd Up in one knott, . . . II. xii. 67. 2
A thousand charmes he *formerly* did prove, . . . III. xii. 31. 8
Whom *formerly* he had in battell wonne, . . . IV. iv. 8. 7
formerly Had knowne right well, . . . IV. viii. 10. 3
Which lawlesse men had *formerly* fordonne: . . . V. i. 2. 4
on the helmet smote him *formerlie*, . . . VI. i. 38. 8
Unlesse that with his Lord he *formerly* did fight . . . VI. iii. 38. 9
Formless. How things she formed of a *formelesse* mas: . . . *T.M.* 502
Form's. yield unto her *formes* direction, . . . *H.B.* 146
The which your *forms* first sourse may sympathize, . . . *H.B.* 192
Forms. monsters kinde In hundred *formes* to change . . . *Bel.*[2] viii. 10
death . . . to them appeares In thousand *formes*, . . . *Gn.* 584
he could take As many *formes* and shapes . . . I. ii. 10. 3
by those ugly *formes* weren pourtrayd . . . II. xi. 11. 7
The house of goodly *formes* and faire aspect, . . . III. vi. 12. 2
uncouth *formes*, which none yet ever knew: . . . III. vi. 35. 2
To chaunge her hew, and sondry *formes* to don, . . . III. vi. 38. 4
formes are variable, and decay . . . III. vi. 38. 6
him the Father of all *formes* they call: . . . III. vi. 47. 8
A thousand monstrous *formes* therein were made, . . . III. xi. 51. 7
love in thousand monstrous *formes* doth oft appeare . . . III. xi. 51. 9
Whatever *formes* ye list thereto apply, . . . VI. iv. 35. 6
her face . . . We changed see and sundry *formes* partake, . . . VII. vii. 50. 7
Such heavenly *formes* ought rather worshipt be, . . . *Am.* lxi. 13
Transported with celestiall desyre Of those faire *formes*, . . . *H.H.B.* 19
Forpass. Scarse can a Bishoprick *forpas* them by, . . . *Hub.* 519
Forpassed. One day, as hee *forpassed* by the plaine . . . III. x. 20. 5
Forpined. He was so wasted and *forpined* quight, . . . III. x. 57. 2
Forsaid. *forsayd* From places of delight, . . . *S.C.* Jul. 69
Forsake. yet Love she proudly did *forsake:* . . . *Pet.* vi. 4
Forsake your watry bowres, . . . *S.C.* Ap. 39
does the right way *forsake:* . . . *S.C.* May 165
Forsake the soyle that so doth thee bewitch: . . . *S.C.* Jun. 18
ere that life her lodging did *forsake*, . . . *D.* 260
But the ungodly ones he doth *forsake*, . . . *D.* 360
Hobbin desires, thou maist it not *forsake*;— . . . *Col.* 50
Him for to seeke, ne ever would *forsake*, . . . I. vi. 2. 8
The innocent pray in hast he does *forsake*; . . . I. vi. 10. 7
lively breath her sad brest did *forsake*; . . . I. vii. 20. 8
Assure your selfe I will you not *forsake*.' . . . I. vii. 52. 7
gives not rather cause it to *forsake*? . . . I. ix. 44. 5
he did them still *forsake* . . . I. xi. 24. 9
did her quite *forsake*; . . . II. iv. 13. 7
Her dalliaunce he despis'd, and follies did *forsake* . . . II. vi. 21. 9
the Prince would not *forsake* his sell, . . . II. viii. 31. 3
Ne stird, till hope of life did him *forsake:* . . . II. xi. 46. 8
all her vaine allurements did *forsake*; . . . II. xii. 17. 4
thereby forst his workemen to *forsake*, . . . III. iii. 10. 8
I here avow thee never to *forsake* . . . III. v. 11. 8
Dye rather, dye, then ever so faire love *forsake*!' . . . III. v. 47. 9
will I not *forsake* my forward way, . . . III. viii. 50. 4
But not so easie will I her *forsake*; . . . IV. ii. 14. 5
Her dearest love full loth so shortly to *forsake* . . . IV. vi. 42. 9
So loth she was his companie for to *forsake* . . . IV. vi. 45. 9
he will us quite *forsake* . . . V. Pr. 7. 9
him forst *forsake* His horses backe . . . V. ii. 16. 1
shortly forst him to *forsake* The hight, . . . V. ix. 16. 6
that thou for ever doe those armes *forsake*, . . . VI. iii. 35. 5
Ne would the Prince him ever foot *forsake* . . . VI. vi. 29. 4
What idle errand hast thou earths mansion to *forsake*?' . . . VII. vi. 25. 9
ne ever did their charge *forsake* . . . VII. vii. 45. 9
Forsaken. *Forsaken* Truth long seekes her love, . . . I. iii. Arg.
she, . . . all this while *Forsaken*, wofull, solitarie mayd, . . . I. iii. 3. 2
The wofull daughter and *forsaken* heyre . . . I. xii. 26. 3
To call backe life to her *forsaken* shop . . . II. i. 43. 7
now they lead him thence, of all *forsaken*, . . . V. iii. 9. 8
seeing then her selfe *forsaken* so, . . . V. iv. 10. 1
Whom now her keepers had *forsaken* quight . . . V. xi. 60. 2
Forsay. Sike worldly sovenance he must *forsay* . . . *S.C.* May 82
Forse, Forst. *See* **Force.**
Forslack. might *forslack* the charge to them foreshewed . . . VII. vii. 45. 5
Forslacked. Through other great adventures hethertoo Had it *forslackt:* . . . V. xii. 3. 6
If he for slouth *forslackt* so famous quest . . . VI. ix. 3. 5
that enterprize . . . *forslacked* had so sore; . . . VI. xii. 12. 5
Forslow. night with stealing steppes doe you *forsloe*, . . . *S.C.* Jun. 119
by no meanes my way I would *forslow* . . . IV. x. 15. 1
why she did her wonted course *forslowe*; . . . VII. vi. 16. 4
Forsook. Both christall wells and shadie groves *forsooke*, . . . *As.* 45
life *forsooke* his stubborne brest . . . I. iii. 42. 9
In haste *forsooke* their rurall meriment, . . . I. vi. 8. 2
'Thenceforth me desolate he quite *forsooke*, . . . I. vii. 50. 1
ne her right course for ought *forsooke* . . . III. iv. 44. 9
With great indignaunce he that sight *forsooke*, . . . III. xi. 13. 5
Yet she no whit dismayd her steed *forsooke*, . . . IV. vi. 14. 6

Forsook—*Continued.*
When Talus saw they all the field *forsooke*, . . . V. ii. 54. 7
as if her life *forsooke*, . . . V. v. 11. 4
joyous light the house of Jove *forsooke*; . . . V. vii. 8. 7
speare and shield . . . He quite *forsooke*, . . . VI. iv. 7. 9
till light the sky *forsooke* . . . VI. xi. 40. 9
also quite *forsooke* All those faire forrests . . . VII. vi. 54. 5
I all weary had the chace *forsooke*, . . . *Am.* lxvii. 6
Forspent. With hollow eyes and rawbone cheekes *forspent*, . . . IV. v. 34. 4
Forswat. Albee forswonck and *forswatt* I am . . . *S.C.* Ap. 99
Forswear. Shepheards delights he dooth them all *forsweare*; . . . *S.C.* Ap. 13
Forswonck. *See* **Forswunk.**
Forswore. sacred pledges he . . . *forswore!* . . . I. xii. 27. 4
Forswunk. Albee *forswonck* and forswatt I am . . . *S.C.* Ap. 99
Fort. The *Fort*, that Ladies hold in soveraigne dread . . . I. ii. 25. 4
Her to persuade that stubborne *fort* to yilde: . . . I. vi. 3. 7
With greedy force he gan the *fort* assayle, . . . I. vi. 5. 3
no *fort* can be so strong, . . . I. ix. 11. 1
fast imprisoned in sieged *fort* . . . I. xii. 4. 5
dying whylome did divide this *fort* . . . II. ii. 13. 3
cruell battry bend Gainst *fort* of Reason, . . . II. iv. 34. 8
Against the *forte* of reason evermore, . . . II. xi. 1. 3
All those against that *fort* did bend their batteries . . . II. xi. 10. 9
that same third *Fort*, that is the Smell, . . . II. xi. 11. 1
All those this sences *Fort* assayle incessantly . . . II. xi. 12. 9
Cruelly they assayed that fift *Fort*, . . . II. xi. 13. 5
No *fort* so fensible, no wals so strong, . . . III. x. 10. 1
leave his love in that sea-walled *fort* . . . IV. xii. 18. 5
Fortalice. Nought feard theyr force that *fortilage* to win, . . . II. xii. 43. 5
Forth (*partial list*). *See* **Far-forth, Setting-forth, Thence-forth, Whenceforth.**
threw *forth* a thousand rayes . . . *Bel.*[1] ii. 7
So many Neroes and Caligulaes Must still bring *forth* . . . *Bel.*[1] viii. 15
I saw the roote . . . send *forth* . . . *Bel.* v. 14
Who, . . . Pourd *foorth* a water, . . . *Bel.*[2] ix. 6
I saw a spring out of a rocke *forth* rayle, . . . *Bel.*[2] xii. 1
will likewise set *forth* The great Colosse, . . . *Ro.* ii. 9
like a corse drawne *forth* out of the tombe . . . *Ro.* v. 7
Brought *foorth* those signes . . . *Ro.* xv. 3
he *forth* is horld; . . . *Ro.* xx. 8
Powr'd vengeance *forth* . . . *Ro.* xxiv. 11
Who list the Romane greatnes *forth* to figure, . . . *Ro.* xxvi. 1
All that which Athens ever brought *forth* wise; . . . *Ro.* xxix. 9
may bring things better *forth* . . . *Van.* i. 14
His wide Abysse him forced *forth* to spewe, . . . *Van.* v. 10
asked who thee *forth* did bring, . . . *To his Booke* 8
Looking far *foorth* into the Ocean wide, . . . *Van.* ix. 1
A shepeheards boye . . . Led *forth* his flock, . . . *S.C.* Ja. 4
tel it not *forth:* . . . *S.C.* F. 239
Flora now calleth *forth* eche flower, . . . *S.C.* Mar. 16
With that sprong *forth* a naked swayne . . . *S.C.* Mar. 79
Yode *forth* abroade unto the greene wood, . . . *S.C.* May 178
Till fayrer Fortune shewe *forth* her head . . . *S.C.* S. 257
Or pricke them *forth* with pleasaunce . . . *S.C.* O. 23
'*Forth* was I ledde, . . . *S.C.* D. 61
Night *forth* from the darksome bowre . . . gan call, . . . *Gn.* 313
Throwes lightning *forth*, . . . *Gn.* 582
he gins to fashion *forth* a place; . . . *Gn.* 650
out of heavens windowes *forth* to looke, . . . *Hub.* 109
the Foxe *forth* toward them did goe; . . . *Hub.* 1074
fairly paced *forth* . . . *Hub.* 1264
Fled closely *forth*, . . . *Hub.* 1360
forth . . . unto his judgement brought, . . . *Hub.* 1376
he at last laid *forth* on balefull beare . . . *T.M.* 162
By which mans life . . . Was limned *forth*, . . . *T.M.* 202
blazon *foorth* an earthlie beauties praise . . . *T.M.* 369
fly *forth* unto my Love . . . *U.V.* 3
teares from her faire eyes *forth* railing: . . . *Ti.* 12
Which draw the dayes of men *forth* in extent; . . . *Ti.* 18
Whose meaning much I labored *foorth* to wreste, . . . *Ti.* 486
Then sets she *forth*, . . . *Mui.* 324
With violent swift flight *forth* caried . . . *Mui.* 422
foorth fled into the aire, . . . *Mui.* 439
calls *foorth* men unto their toylsome trade, . . . *D.* 485
he *foorth* did goe . . . *D.* 563
The dawning day *forth* comming from the East . . . *As.* 34
Did prick him *foorth* . . . *As.* 86
nor any *forth* can set, . . . *As.* 171
Stella . . . *Forth* darting beames of beautie . . . *As.* 190
From this day *forth* do call . . . *As.* 196
where, spreading *forth* at large, . . . *Col.* 111
'*Foorth* on our voyage . . . *Col.* 330
But call it *forth*, O call him *forth* . . . *Col.* 408
Faire spreading *forth* her leaves . . . *Col.* 545
the morning Sun, *Forth* looking . . . *Col.* 605
from a golden Censer *forth* doth rise, And throwing *forth* . . . *Col.* 609, 610
words to speake it fitly *forth* . . . *Col.* 625
In ampler wise it selfe will *forth* display . . . *Ded.Son.*xvi.14
Lay *forth* . . . The antique rolles, . . . I. Pr. 2. 3
forth unto the darksom hole he went, . . . I. i. 14. 3
whose folds . . . Were stretcht now *forth* at length . . . I. i. 16. 4
from a sacred fountaine welled *forth* . . . I. i. 34. 9
slyding softly *forth*, . . . I. i. 54. 9
rising *forth* out of her baser bowre, . . . I. ii. 7. 6
Forth spurred fast: . . . I. ii. 14. 8
He . . . forward *forth* did beare . . . I. ii. 45. 9
so *forth* told the story of her feare . . . I. iii. 25. 5
All hurtlen *forth*; . . . I. iv. 16. 3
from their shields *forth* flyeth firie light . . . I. v. 7. 8
Then *forth* she rose, . . . I. v. 19. 3

For to—*Continued.*
seemd amid the surges *for to* fleet, . . . *Col.* 286
fittest *for to* forge true-seeming lyes: . . . I. i. 38. 7
I cast *for to* compare . . . I. ii. 37. 3
It was a goodly heape *for to* behould, . . . I. iv. 5. 1
fire not made to burne, but fayrely *for to* shyne. . . . I. iv. 9. 9
Upon a Lion, loth *for to* be led; . . . I. iv. 33. 2
strive Himselfe with salves to health *for to* restore, . . . I. v. 40. 8
from one to other Ynd, Him *for to* seeke, . . . I. vi. 2. 8
chaunst her wandring *for to* finde; . . . I. vi. 22. 6
he suffred her *for to* retyre, . . . I. vi. 23. 5
To tempt the cause . . . *for to* bewray, . . . I. vii. 38. 8
cold beginneth *for to* creep, . . . I. vii. 39. 4
let me you intrete, *For to* unfold . . . I. vii. 40. 6
take delight . . . *for to* goe astray, . . . I. x. 10. 6
he gan *for to* abhore, . . . I. x. 21. 4
His office was the hungry *for to* feed, . . . I. x. 38. 2
if ye please *for to* discover plaine, . . . I. xii. 34. 7
All *for* their Ladies froward love *to* gaine . . . II. ii. 26. 4
disarmed *for to* be, . . . III. i. 42. 4

Fortold. *See* **Foretold.**

Forts. those small *forts* which ye were wont belay: . . . *Am.* xiv. 6

Fortunate. 'So happie are they, and so *fortunate,* . . . *Ti.* 393
O *fortunate* yong-man, . . . *Ti.* 433
Amaryllis, whether *fortunate* Or else unfortunate . . . *Col.* 564
However strong and *fortunate* in fight, . . . VI. i. 41. 3
Leading a life so free and *fortunate* . . . VI. ix. 19. 3
to tell of heavens King . . . his *fortunate* successe; . . . VII. vii. 1. 6

Fortune. Tossed with stormes of *fortune* variable! . . . *Pet.*[2] vi. 14
Be it by *fortune,* or by course of kinde, . . . *Ro.* ix. 3
Ne stroke on stroke of *fortune* variable, . . . *Ro.* xiii. 5
if that *fortune* chaunce you up to call . . . *Van.* xii. 11
Ne ever was to *Fortune* foeman, . . . *S.C.* F. 21
false *Fortune* such joy did him spight, . . . *S.C.* May 198
froward *fortune* doth ever availe: . . . *S.C.* S. 251
Till fayrer *Fortune* shewe forth her head. . . . *S.C.* S. 257
inconstant *fortune,* bent to ill, . . . *Gn.* 247
What God or *Fortune* would assist his might. . . . *Gn.* 301
whether God or *Fortune* made him bold . . . *Gn.* 302
valiant *fortune* made Dan Orpheus bolde; . . . *Gn.* 449
none whom *fortune* freely doth advaunce . . . *Gn.* 555
My *fortune* was, mongst manie others moe, . . . *Hub.* 13
froward *fortune* still to follow mee, . . . *Hub.* 66
To seeke my *fortune,* where I may it mend: . . . *Hub.* 88
Of *fortune* and of hope at once forlorne.' . . . *Hub.* 258
fortune doth you secret favour give.' . . . *Hub.* 594
if such *fortune* doo to us befall, . . . *Hub.* 617
if *fortune* thee in Court to live, . . . *Hub.* 631
Such followes those whom *fortune* doth advaunce. . . . *Hub.* 1136
Are heapt with spoyles of *fortune* . . . *T.M.* 161
squallid *Fortune,* into basenes flong, . . . *T.M.* 543
wicked *Fortune* faultles him misled, . . . *Mui.* 418
They her did praise, and my good *fortune* blesse. . . . *D.* 147
my *fortune* to deplore; . . . *D.* 475
With better *fortune* than did me succeed, . . . *D.* 521
By fate or *fortune* came unto the place, . . . *As.* 141
Of *fortune* and of envy uncomptrold, . . . *Col.* 662
'My weaker yeares, Captiv'd to *fortune* . . . I. i. 52. 5
fortune false betraide me to thy powre, . . . I. ii. 22. 5
his harder *fortune* was to fall Under my speare: . . . I. ii. 36. 6
whilest him *fortune* favourd, fayre did thrive In bloudy field; I. iii. 37. 8
I feare the fickle freakes,' . . . 'Of *fortune* false, . . . I. iv. 50. 2
Blaming of *Fortune,* which such trouble threw, . . . I. vi. 31. 5
'Tempestuous *fortune* hath spent all her spight, . . . I. vii. 25. 1
the breach Which love and *fortune* in her heart had wrought; I. vii. 42. 4
To wander where wilde *fortune* would me lead, . . . I. vii. 50. 2
Your *fortune* maister eke with governing . . . I. viii. 28. 3
fie on *Fortune,* mine avowed foe, . . . I. viii. 43. 3
ever fickle *fortune* rageth rife; . . . I. ix. 44. 8
The which good *fortune* doth to you present. . . . II. i. 16. 4
(hard *fortune* ye may ghesse) . . . II. i. 51. 1
Accusing *fortune,* and too cruell fate, . . . II. i. 56. 8
So *fortune* wrought, . . . II. iii. 3. 6
Through *fortune* of his first adventure fayre, . . . II. iii. 7. 2
'It was my *fortune* . . . To love a Lady . . . II. iv. 19. 1
What great despight doth *fortune* to thee beare, . . . II. iv. 25. 7
If wonted force and *fortune* doe me not much fayl.' . . . II. v. 5. 9
By *fortune* came, ledd with the troublous sowne: . . . II. vi. 47. 7
'Abide the *fortune* of thy present fate; . . . II. vii. 60. 2
Whom *fortune* hath already laid in lowest seat.' . . . II. viii. 27. 9
use thy *fortune* as it doth befall; . . . II. viii. 52. 2
happinesse Heven doth to me envy, and *fortune* favourlesse.' II. ix. 7. 9
'*Fortune,* the foe of famous chevisaunce, . . . II. ix. 8. 1
His life, and long good *fortune,* . . . II. x. 13. 9
whiles good *fortune* favoured her might, . . . II. x. 56. 6
thee fierce *Fortune* did so nearely drive, . . . II. xi. 30. 8
unto better *fortune* doth her selfe prepayre. . . . II. xi. 36. 9
shamefuller regrett For thy hard *fortune* . . . III. i. 8. 3
Whom *fortune* for her husband would allot: . . . III. ii. 23. 6
Other then my hard *fortune* to deplore, . . . III. ii. 39. 7
So was their *fortune* good, though wicked were their minde. III. ii. 43. 9
wicked *fortune* mine, though minde be good, . . . III. ii. 44. 1
better *fortune* thine, and better howre, . . . III. ii. 45. 5
thy good *fortune,* having fate obayd, . . . III. iii. 19. 7
Ne is thy fate, ne is thy *fortune* ill, . . . III. iii. 24. 6
to th' importunity Of froward *fortune* . . . III. iii. 31. 6
love it steres, and *fortune* rowes: . . . III. iv. 9. 5
fortune, Boteswaine, no assurance knowes; . . . III. iv. 9. 7
fayrest *fortune* to the Prince befell, . . . III. iv. 47. 6
he gan fowly wyte His wicked *fortune* . . . III. iv. 52. 8

Fortune—*Continued.*
froward *fortune,* and too forward Night, . . . III. v. 7. 4
now by *fortune* it was overflowne. . . . III. v. 17. 4
great grace or *fortune* thither brought Comfort . . . III. v. 27. 3
fortune all in equall launce doth sway, . . . III. vii. 4. 4
Driven to great distresse by *fortune* straunge, . . . III. viii. 20. 2
What *fortune* and his fate on him will lay; . . . III. x. 3. 2
I unwares this way by *fortune* straid, . . . III. x. 25. 5
now by *fortune* was arrived here, . . . III. x. 37. 4
Since so good *fortune* doth to you present So fayre a spoyle, IV. i. 5. 8
So *fortune* friends the bold:' . . . IV. ii. 7. 6
Did by great *fortune* get of her the sight, . . . IV. ii. 45. 3
to see the *fortune* of that fray, . . . IV. iii. 4. 7
Have by good *fortune* found some beasts fresh spoyle, . . . IV. iii. 16. 2
doubtfull *fortune* wavering to and fro, . . . IV. iii. 17. 7
Cambels fate that *fortune* did prevent; . . . IV. iii. 18. 5
With diverse *fortune* doubtfull to be deemed: . . . IV. iii. 28. 2
with no better *fortune* then the rest: . . . IV. iv. 21. 2
though some while *Fortune* from him withdrew, . . . IV. iv. 37. 7
with no better *fortune* then the rest afore. . . . IV. iv. 45. 9
by *fortune* . . . Upon his heavie eye-lids chaunst to fall, . . IV. v. 42. 1
'Ye gentle Knights, whom *fortune* here hath brought . . . IV. vi. 30. 2
on a day, by *fortune* as it fell, . . . IV. vii. 42. 1
what good *fortune* did to him afford; . . . IV. viii. 18. 7
by that meanes which *fortune* did unfold, . . . IV. viii. 53. 4
Till *fortune* did perforce it so decree: . . . IV. viii. 58. 8
With which my weaker patience *fortune* proves: . . . IV. viii. 63. 8
Amoret, whom *Fortune* by bequest Had left . . . IV. ix. 17. 7
By *fortune* in that place did chance to light: . . . IV. ix. 28. 3
by good *fortune* shortly him unseated. . . . IV. x. 10. 2
the which by *fortune* came Upon your seas, . . . IV. xii. 31. 3
The *fortune* of her life long time did feare: . . . V. ii. 3. 4
when as *fortune* all her spight hath showne, . . . V. iii. 1. 3
many wounded, As *fortune* fell; . . . V. iii. 6. 7
With divers *fortune* fit for such a game, . . . V. iii. 7. 4
Sir Guyon, as by *fortune* then befell, . . . V. iii. 29. 3
But what to them *Fortune* would justify: . . . V. iv. 6. 4
The portion of that good which *Fortune* gave her, . . . V. iv. 12. 7
Or God or *Fortune* unto me did throw, . . . V. iv. 14. 3
How *Fortune* will your ruin'd name repaire . . . V. iv. 34. 8
in single fight To try her *Fortune,* . . . V. iv. 47. 7
how *Fortune* would resolve that daungerous dout. . . . V. v. 5. 9
Was lately broken by some *fortune* ill; . . . V. v. 15. 4
Fortune, envying good, hath felly frowned, . . . V. v. 36. 2
It as a token of good *fortune* tooke. . . . V. vii. 8. 5
The course of all her *fortune* and posteritie. . . . V. vii. 12. 9
Whilest *Fortune* favourd her successe in fight: . . . V. vii. 41. 7
lowre Upon their blisse, and balefull *fortune* frowne: . . . V. x. 26. 7
The which good *Fortune* to him offred faire; . . . V. xi. 13. 5
To greet him the good *fortune* of his hand: . . . V. xi. 15. 4
(as good *fortune* fell) . . . V. xii. 4. 2
although good *Fortune* me befall, . . . VI. i. 6. 6
prove the finall *fortune* of the fight; . . . VI. i. 38. 4
thorough . . . *fortune* I my countrie have forlorne, . . . VI. ii. 27. 8
fortune hath this day Given to me the spoile . . . VI. ii. 33. 7
There to their *fortune* leave we them awhile, . . . VI. ii. 40. 1
Yet since it was his *fortune,* not his fault, . . . VI. iii. 21. 6
th' utmost end . . . Which that nights *fortune* . . . VI. iii. 44. 4
Till that, by *fortune* passing all foresight, . . . VI. iv. 2. 1
Here they of force (as *fortune* now did fall) . . . VI. iv. 15. 5
stone Which lay thereby (so *fortune* him did ayde) . . . VI. iv. 21. 3
Then North, then neither, but as *fortune* fell: . . . VI. iv. 25. 3
And by good *fortune* the plaine champion wonne: . . . VI. iv. 26. 3
And oft complayn'd of fate, and *fortune* oft defyde. . . . VI. iv. 26. 9
Lo! how good *fortune* doth to you present . . . VI. iv. 35. 3
What *fortune* to the Briton Prince did lite, . . . VI. vi. 17. 5
Fortune aunswerd not unto his call; . . . VI. viii. 10. 1
Fortune did not with his will conspire; . . . VI. viii. 15. 5
False *Fortune* did her safety betray . . . VI. viii. 34. 8
came by *fortune* blynde Whereas this Lady . . . lay. . . . VI. viii. 36. 7
The selfe same evening *fortune* hether drove, . . . VI. viii. 46. 8
In that same quest which *fortune* on him cast, . . . VI. ix. 2. 7
Found her by *fortune,* which to him befell, . . . VI. ix. 14. 5
For further *fortune* then I would inquire; . . . VI. ix. 24. 5
they to each such *fortune* doe diffuse, . . . VI. ix. 29. 4
each hath his *fortune* in his brest. . . . VI. ix. 29. 9
With stormes of *fortune* and tempestuous fate . . . VI. ix. 31. 5
'That my ill *fortune* did them hence displace; . . . VI. x. 20. 7
fortune, fraught with malice, . . . VI. x. 38. 7
Fortune, not with all this wrong Contented, . . . VI. xi. 2. 5
(as *Fortune* had ordayned) . . . VI. xi. 3. 3
Till *Fortune* would her captive bonds unbynde: . . . VI. xi. 8. 8
fortune now the victors meed did make: . . . VI. xi. 51. 4
take what *fortune,* time, and place would lend. . . . VII. vi. 23. 6
With guifts of body, *fortune,* and of mind. . . . *Am.* lxxiv. 4
He faines himselfe, and doth his *fortune* blesse. . . . *H.L.* 210
His faith, his *fortune,* in his breast he beares. . . . *H.L.* 224
Above the *fortune* of their first condition, . . . *H.H.L.* 81

Fortuned. It *fortuned* (as heavens had behight) . . . *Mui.* 241
It *fortuned* as he that perilous game . . . pursued . . . *As.* 91
It *fortuned,* out of the thickest wood A . . . Lyon rushed . I. iii. 5. 1
It *fortuned,* a noble warlike knight . . . to that forrest came I. vi. 20. 1
It *fortuned,* (as fayre it then befell) . . . I. xi. 29. 1
Upon the way him *fortuned* to meete, . . . II. i. 5. 6
'Him *fortuned* . . . To come, . . . II. i. 51. 1
It *fortuned,* forth faring on his way, . . . II. iv. 3. 1
One day it *fortuned* fayre Britomart, . . . III. ii. 22. 1
It *fortuned* (so time their turne did fitt) . . . III. iii. 58. 3
It *fortuned,* as they devised had: . . . III. v. 18. 1
It *fortuned,* faire Venus having lost Her little sonne, . . . III. vi. 11. 1

Fortuned—*Continued.*
It *fortuned* (high God did so ordaine) . . . . III. vii. 27. 1
It *fortuned,* whilest thus she stifly strove, ... III. viii. 29. 6
It *fortuned,* soone after they were gone, ... III. ix. 12. 1
in open place . . . He *fortun'd* her to meet, ... III. x. 6. 6
It *fortuned,* as they together far'd, ... III. x. 35. 1
It *fortuned* Belphebe with her peares, ... IV. vii. 23. 5
It *fortun'd* then, a solemne feast was there . . . . IV. xi. 8. 1
It *fortun'd,* whylest they were thus ill beset, ... V. iii. 10. 1
Amongst the which then *fortuned* to bee The noble Briton . V. x. 15. 1
It *fortun'd* then, that when the roules were red . . . . . . VI. vii. 33. 1
It *fortuned* one day, when Calidore Was hunting . . . . . VI. x. 39. 1
Fortuneless. disadventrous, and quite *fortunelesse;* . . . . . *Hub.* 100
Against all hard mishaps and *fortunelesse* misfare. . . . . IV. viii. 27. 9
Fortune's. that anie *fortunes* wreakes Could breake her course *Ro.* xxi. 7
fall through *fortunes* mutabilitie. . . . . *Gn.* 560
meane regard, and basest *fortunes* scorne, ... *Hub.* 60
they unto their *fortunes* change to tosse: . . . . *Hub.* 342
Fortunes freakes, is wisely taught to beare: . . . . *T.M.* 130
Feareles through his own fault or *Fortunes* spight . . . . . *T.M.* 303
The worlds sad spectacle, and *fortunes* scorne.' . . . . . . *Ti.* 28
maugre *fortunes* injurie, And times decay, ... *Ti.* 166
Ne feareth change of time, nor *fortunes* threate, ... *Ti.* 465
To be the pray of Tyme, and *Fortunes* spoyle! . . . . *Ti.* 516
'And ye fond men! on *fortunes* wheele that ride, ... *D.* 498
trust the guile of *fortunes* blandishment; . . . . *Col.* 671
Through envies snares, or *fortunes* freakes unkind. . . . . . I. iii. 1. 4
sithens *fortunes* guile, . . . hath now captived you, Returne . I. iv. 51. 1
forlorne Maiden, . . . The laughing stocke of *fortunes* mock-
eries, ... I. vii. 43. 2
So tossed was in *fortunes* cruell freakes: . . . . I. xii. 16. 8
Ne deeme thy force by *fortunes* doome unjust, ... II. v. 12. 8
She left him to his *fortunes* government, ... IV. vi. 46. 3
Fearelesse of *fortunes* chaunge or envies dread, ... IV. viii. 18. 3
terrifie from *Fortunes* faire adward: . . . . IV. x. 17. 5
well to beare The storme of *fortunes* frowne . . . . V. v. 38. 3
to his *fortunes* helpe make readie way?' . . . . V. v. 39. 4
seemes that *fortunes* headlong wheele Begins to turne, . . . V. x. 20. 7
Subject to *fortunes* chance, still chaunging new: . . . . . . VI. i. 41. 8
Fearelesse of foes and *fortunes* wrackfull yre . . . . VI. ix. 27. 7
The heavens of their *fortunes* fault accuse, ... VI. ix. 29. 2
all the stormes of *fortunes* former yre Were turnd, ... VI. xii. 10. 4
She in the open fields had loosely layd To *fortunes* spoile, . . VI. xii. 16. 5
blesse your *fortunes* fayre election. . . . . *Am.* lxxxiii. 14
Which death, or love, or *fortunes* wreck did rayse, ... *Epith.* 8
Fortunes. determined to seek Their *fortunes* farre abroad, . . . *Hub.* 48
everie streete Is full of *fortunes,* . . . . *Hub.* 91
he mongst Ladies could their *fortunes* read . . . . *Hub.* 698
The passed *fortunes,* which to thee befell . . . . *Col.* 33
fortunes tell, and read in loving bookes, ... I. iv. 25. 8
whose lives and *fortunes* bee . . . stil open layd, ... III. v. 36. 6
many *fortunes* prov'd in th' Ocean mayne, ... III. ix. 48. 8
Agreed to travell, and their *fortunes* try. . . . . IV. iv. 6. 4
many perils wonne, and many *fortunes* waide. . . . . IV. ix. 38. 9
Gan breake to him the *fortunes* of his love, ... VI. iii. 15. 2
to these happie *fortunes* cruell fate . . . . VI. iv. 30. 5
had in many *fortunes* tossed beene . . . . VI. vi. 3. 3
Till Mirabellaes *fortunes* I doe further say, ... VI. vii. 50. 9
sith your *fortunes* thus dispose, ... VI. viii. 29. 6
that my *fortunes* might transposed bee . . . . VI. ix. 28. 8
fooles therefore They are which *fortunes* doe by vowes devize, VI. ix. 30. 8
what straunge *fortunes* unto him befell, ... VI. ix. 46. 7
Fortuneth. How *fortuneth* this foule uncomely plight, ... VI. vii. 14. 8
Fortunize. Sith each unto himselfe his life may *fortunize.'* . . VI. ix. 30. 9
Forty. if the living yearly doo arise To *fortie* pound, ... *Hub.* 529
mighty man of God . . . Dwelt *forty* daies . . . . I. x. 53. 6
So did his *forty* yoemen, which there with him came. . . . VI. vi. 25. 9
longer unto me appeare, Then al those *fourty* . . . . *Am.* lx. 8
spheare of Cupid *fourty* yeares containes: . . . . *Am.* lx. 10
Forwandered. She . . . his *forwandred* steed unto him gott: . III. xi. 20. 6
Forwandering. A weary wight *forwandring* by the way; . . I. vi. 34. 3
Forward. both they *forward* went; . . . . *Hub.* 203
stoutly *forward* he his steps did straine, ... *Hub.* 241
with pleasure *forward* led, ... I. i. 8. 1
resolving *forward* still to fare, ... I. i. 11. 1
to revoke The *forward* footing for an hidden shade: . . . . . I. i. 12. 8
forward on his way . . . . I. i. 28. 7
He set her on her steede, and *forward* forth did beare . . . I. ii. 45. 9
on their former journey *forward* pas, ... I. iii. 21. 3
he *forward* gan advaunce . . . . I. iii. 25. 8
that proud Paynim *forward* came so ferce . . . . I. iii. 35. 1
he *forward* lasht the laesy teme, ... I. iv. 36. 3
forward forth doth pas, ... I. vii. 28. 3
as he *forward* moovd his footing old, ... I. viii. 31. 3
forward fare as their adventures fell: . . . . I. ix. 2. 5
Would not a while her *forward* course pursew, ... I. ix. 20. 6
Whom hardly he from flying *forward* stayd, ... I. ix. 23. 5
forward by that painfull way they pas . . . . I. x. 46. 1
glauncing by, foorth passed *forward* right. . . . . I. xi. 16. 5
Guyon *forward* gan his voyage make . . . . II. i. 34. 3
to attend awhile their *forward* steps they stay. . . . . II. i .35. 9
That *forward* paire she ever would asswage, ... II. ii. 38. 5
forward he his purpose gan pursew, ... II. ii. 45. 6
Their way they *forward* take . . . . II. vi. 11. 7
Bidding his winged vessell fairely *forward* fly: . . . . II. vii. 1. 9
They *forward* passe; . . . . II. vii. 31. 1
Thence *forward* he him ledd, ... II. vii. 35. 1
thence him *forward* ledd . . . . II. vii. 39. 9
Forward they passe, and strongly he them rowes, ... II. xii. 5. 1
passe on *forward:* so their way does ly, ... II. xii. 14. 2

Forward—*Continued.*
Yet stayd they not, but *forward* did proceed, ... II. xii. 37. 3
lookt still *forward* right, ... II. xii. 53. 4
nought regarding her displeasure, *forward* goth. . . . . . . II. xii. 57. 9
counseld well him *forward* thence did draw. . . . . II. xii. 69. 3
Yet swarved not, but kept their *forward* way . . . . II. xii. 76. 5
fiercely *forward* came withouten dread, ... III. i. 5. 8
stoutly *forward* came: . . . . III. i. 9. 4
when she saw them gone she *forward* went, ... III. i. 19. 6
Themselves they forth convaid, and passed *forward* right. . . III. iii. 61. 9
forward rode, and kept her ready way . . . . III. iv. 18. 2
Carried her *forward* with her first intent: . . . . III. iv. 50. 5
to his first poursuit him *forward* still doth call. . . . . . III. v. 2. 9
froward fortune, and too *forward* Night, ... III. v. 7. 4
His pace he freshly *forward* did advaunce, ... III. vii. 3. 3
of his *forward* hope deceived quight; . . . . III. vii. 28. 2
forward gallopt fast; . . . . III. vii. 38. 6
Fiercely that straunger *forward* came: . . . . III. viii. 16. 1
with the tide drove *forward* carelesly; . . . . III. viii. 21. 4
as they *forward* went, They spyde a knight . . . . III. viii. 44. 6
will I not forsake my *forward* way, ... III. viii. 50. 4
the night was *forward* spent, ... III. ix. 11. 3
They all agree, and *forward* them addresse: . . . . III. x. 40. 1
Then they march *forward* brave. . . . . III. x. 42. 9
Still fled he *forward,* looking backward still; . . . . III. x. 56. 1
pricked fiercely *forward* where she did him vew. . . . . . . III. xi. 4. 9
Enforced them their *forward* footing to revoke. . . . . . . III. xi. 21. 9
Her swords point directing *forward* right . . . . III. xi. 25. 3
forward with bold steps into the next roome went. . . . . . III. xi. 50. 9
as *forward* he did pace. . . . . III. xii. 15. 9
Her *forward* still with torture did constraine, ... III. xii. 21. 8
when th' one *forward* yode, The other backe retired . . . . IV. i. 28. 8
Sir Priamond, . . . himselfe did *forward* set. . . . . IV. iii. 6. 4
As fast as *forward* erst now backward to retrate. . . . . . . IV. iii. 26. 9
forward thence did pas Unto some resting place, ... IV. vi. 39. 3
saw her *forward* still to make her flight, ... IV. viii. 8. 2
the Dove Would flit a litle *forward,* . . . . IV. viii. 11. 2
So forth they yode, and *forward* softly paced, ... IV. viii. 34. 6
Th' one *forward* looking, ... IV. x. 12. 4
Whom he requir'd his *forward* hast to stay, ... V. ii. 2. 3
We on his first adventure may him *forward* send. . . . . . . V. iii. 40. 9
They pressed *forward,* entraunce to have made; . . . . V. iv. 38. 2
Yet stayed she not . . . but *forward* fared, ... V. vi. 38. 2
she *forward* went To seeke her love, ... V. vii. 24. 6
seeing her approch gan *forward* set . . . . V. viii. 6. 8
on his first adventure *forward* forth did ride. . . . . V. x. 17. 9
forward marched to a towne in sight. . . . . V. xii. 6. 3
still I *forward* trace.' . . . . VI. i. 7. 5
He with his speare, . . . Would thumpe her *forward* . . . . VI. ii. 10. 8
When *forward* we should fare . . . . VI. ii. 22. 2
She on her way cast *forward* to proceede, ... VI. v. 31. 2
Eftsoones they pricked forth with *forward* pryde, ... VI. vii. 6. 5
Then up he made him rise, and *forward* fare, ... VI. vii. 49. 1
So as they *forward* on their way did pas, ... VI. viii. 4. 1
Him hardly *forward* drew, ... VI. xi. 38. 3
Forwarned. Had not that charme from thee *forwarned* itt: . I. ii. 18. 4
Forwasted. that infernall feend . . . *Forwasted* all their land, I. i. 5. 8
their *forwasted* kingdom to repayre; . . . . I. xi. 1. 3
with great spoile and rage *Forwasted* all, ... II. x. 52. 8
Forwearied. *See* **Nigh-forwearied.**
of your later fight Ye all *forwearied* be; . . . . I. i. 32. 5
'*Forwearied* with my sportes, ... I. ix. 13. 1
of youre toyle . . . Ye both *forwearied* be: . . . . I. x. 17. 4
That he with worke may be *forwearied:* . . . . V. v. 50. 4
Forwent. nowe they bene to heaven *forewent,* . . . . *S.C.* Jul. 117
His wasted life her wearie lodge *forwent.* . . . . *As.* 174
fowre since Florimell the Court *forwent,* . . . . III. v. 10. 2
Whiles unawares his saddle he *forwent,* . . . . IV. vi. 11. 8
their well-knowen courses they *forwent;* . . . . V. viii. 40. 6
Forwhy. *for-why* no powre . . . in her did dwell: . . . . . . III. ii. 49. 2
for-why he found no way To enter in, ... IV. xii. 15. 3
For-why, he sayd, they all unequall were, ... V. ii. 32. 1
in vaine; *for-why* no remedy He saw . . . . VI. iii. 44. 1
for-why his Lord of old Did hate all errant Knights . . . . VI. vi. 21. 3
Forworn. A silly man, in simple weeds *forworne,* . . . . I. vi. 35. 1
Foster. a griesly *foster* forth did rush, ... III. i. 17. 2
after the foule *foster* Timias did strive. . . . . III. i. 18. 9
pursewing that same *foster* strong, ... III. iv. 45. 6
After that wicked *foster* fiercely went: . . . . III. iv. 47. 4
freed from that *foster* insolent, ... III. iv. 50. 7
A foule ill-favoured *foster,* . . . . III. v. 6. 3
After that *foster* fowle he fiercely ridd . . . . III. v. 13.4
that fierce *foster,* which late fled away, ... III. v. 18. 5
the *foster* with his long bore-speare . . . . III. v. 20. 1
fledd so fast from that same *foster* stearne . . . . III. vi. 54. 3
To stint all strife and *foster* friendly peace, ... IV. ii. 19. 2
Foster-child. Be to thy *foster Childe,* that from thy hand . . II. x. 69. 5
by this most sacred head Of my deare *foster childe,* . . . . III. ii. 33. 6
Foster-children. yeeld . . . Unto her *foster children,* . . . . *Gn.* 509
Fostered. How in his cradle first he *fostred* was; . . . . . . *T.M.* 500
Snake . . . Long *fostred* in the filth of Lerna lake: . . . . . I. vii. 17. 3
Long time she *fostred* up, ... III. iv. 20. 4
with them carried to be *fostered.* . . . . III. vi. 28. 2
yfostered to bee And trained up in trew feminitee: . . . . . III. vi. 51. 4
fostred up with bitter milke of tine, ... III. xi. 1. 4
Which she with her long *fostred* in that wood, ... IV. ii. 46. 1
Was *fostered* by those Graces, ... IV. v. 5. 8
sith I thee *fostred* first, ... V. v. 29. 4
he was *fostred* long in Stygian fen, ... VI. i. 8. 4
She should it cause be *fostred* under straunge attyre. . . . VI. xii. 6. 9

Foster-father. *foster father* of the Gyaunt dead; . . . I. viii. 31. 8
Fosters. Three *fosters* Timias wound; . . . III. v. Arg.
Fought. the Troyan Duke with Turnus *fought.* . . . *Bel.*[1] vii. 8
Fought with the bloudie Lapithaes at bord: . . . *Gn.* 42
with the Romanes *fought,* . . . *Ti.* 110
Fought, and in field against them thrice prevailed; . . . *Ti.* 111
He lightly left the foe with whom he *fought,* . . . I. viii. 15. 6
bitter battailes all are *fought?* . . . I. x. 62. 8
many bloody battailes *fought* in face, . . . I. x. 65. 3
many battailes *fought* and many fraies . . . II. iii. 38. 5
of renewing fight Already *fought,* . . . II. v. 25. 3
He *fought* great batteils with his salvage fone; . . . II. x. 10. 3
An army brought, and with him batteile *fought,* . . . II. x. 51. 2
Fought with Severus, and him overthrew, . . . II. x. 57. 2
those six, which lately with her *fought,* . . . III. i. 44. 1
cruell battailes, which he whilome *fought* . . . III. xi. 29. 6
oft for her in bloudie armes they *fought.* . . . IV. ii. 37. 5
Yet from thenceforth more warily he *fought,* . . . IV. iii. 32. 1
ever vanquisht all with whom he *fought;* . . . IV. viii. 48. 2
So long they *fought,* that all the grassie flore . . . V. vii. 31. 5
A Champion, that had with his Champion *fought,* . . . V. xi. 2. 3
That same is it which *fought* for you this day. . . . V. xi. 17. 6
Fought many battels without wound or losse; . . . V. xi. 53. 7
Slayne of that errant knight with whom he *fought;* . . . VI. vii. 16. 7
fought through fury fierce and bold. . . . VI. xi. 30. 9
sith they twaine Long since had *fought* in field: . . . VI. xii. 11. 4
Foul. What the *foule* evill hath thee so bestadde? . . . *S.C.* Au. 7
they bene like *foule* wagmoires overgrast, . . . *S.C.* S. 130
Fye on thee, Diggon, and all thy *foule* leasing! . . . *S.C.* S. 150
bridale torches *foule* Erynnis tynde; . . . *Gn.* 394
rustie horrour and *fowle* fashion; . . . *Gn.* 443
he hates *fowle* leasings, and vile flatterie, . . . *Hub.* 733
foule abuses both in realme and raine; . . . *Hub.* 1276
Each place abounding with *fowle* injuries, . . . *Hub.* 1305
Behold the *fowle* reproach and open shame, . . . *T.M.* 61
Deformd with filth and *fowle* iniquitie; . . . *T.M.* 122
the faire Scene with rudenes *foule* disguize. . . . *T.M.* 192
They trampled have with their *fowle* footings trade, . . . *T.M.* 275
fowle Goblins, and Shriekowles . . . *T.M.* 283
By him begotten of *fowle* infamy; . . . *T.M.* 316
With *fowle* reproach, and cruell banishment? . . . *T.M.* 426
die In *foule* forgetfulnesse, . . . *Ti.* 378
morning faire may bring *fowle* evening late, . . . *Mui.* 219
her faire face to *fowle* and loathsome hewe, . . . *Mui.* 351
Nor famous Ardeyn, nor *fowle* Arlo, is. . . . *As.* 96
wondrous wroth, for that so *foule* despight, . . . *Col.* 148
To thrust downe other into *foule* disgrace, . . . *Col.* 691
He is repayd with scorne and *foule* despite, . . . *Col.* 905
Defended from *foule* Envies poisnous bit. . . . *Ded. Son.* iii. 4
Foule Errour doth defeate: . . . I. i. Arg.
that infernall feend with *foule* uprore . . . I. i. 5. 7
To wish you backe returne with *foule* disgrace, . . . I. i. 13. 3
Most lothsom, filthie, *foule,* and full of vile disdaine. . . . I. i. 14. 9
Deformed monsters, *fowle,* and blacke as inke, . . . I. i. 22. 7
to all knighthood it is *foule* disgrace, . . . I. i. 31. 8
love with *foule* disdainefull spight He would not shend; . . . I. i. 53. 7
There lies he now with *foule* dishonor dead, . . . I. ii. 25. 5
Lyke a faire Lady, but did *fowle* Duessa hyde. . . . I. ii. 35. 9
a dull blast, that . . . with *foule* ugly forme did her disgrace . . . I. ii. 38. 8
A filthy *foule* old woman I did vew, . . . I. ii. 40. 8
they did seeme more *foule* and hideous, . . . I. ii. 41. 3
With *foule* reproches . . . Her vildly entertaines; . . . I. iii. 43. 6
having scaped hard, With balefull beggery, or *foule* disgrace; I. iv. 3. 4
lewdnes fild him with reprochfull pain Of that *foule* evill, . . . I. iv. 26. 7
Emongst the rest rode . . . The *foule* Duessa, . . . I. iv. 37. 5
Night, . . . in a *foule* blacke pitchy mantle clad, . . . I. v. 20. 3
two of three her Nephewes are so *fowle* forlorne.' . . . I. v. 23. 9
with her beares the *fowle* welfavourd witch. . . . I. v. 28. 2
her abhorred face, so filthy and so *fowle.* . . . I. v. 30. 9
name of native syre did *fowle* upbrayd, . . . I. v. 48. 7
The bold Semiramis . . . her *fowle* reproches spoke: . . . I. v. 50. 4
Scarse could he footing find in that *fowle* way, . . . I. v. 53. 1
after Archimagoes *fowle* defeat, . . . I. vi. 3. 1
he thinkes . . . Pholoe *fowle,* . . . I. vi. 15. 9
fly away for feare of *fowle* disgrace; . . . I. vi. 18. 7
With *foule* reprochfull words he boldly him defide. . . . I. vi. 40. 9
With *fowle* words tempring faire, . . . I. vii. 3. 9
bodie lay, All wallowd in his owne *fowle* bloody gore, . . . I. viii. 24. 4
gentle knight so *fowle* forlore; . . . I. viii. 39. 4
nether darkenesse *fowle,* nor filthy bands, . . . I. viii. 40. 1
so *fowle* deformed wight. . . . I. viii. 49. 2
such the sight Of *fowle* Duessa, . . . I. viii. 49. 5
In *fowle* reproch of knighthoodes fayre degree, . . . I. ix. 22. 6
wounding words, and termes of *foule* repriefe, . . . I. ix. 29. 4
With *fowle* enfouldred smoake and flashing fire, . . . I. xi. 40. 2
Who then would thinke . . . He could escape *fowle* death . . . I. xii. 36. 5
'Fayre Lady, through *fowle* sorrow ill bedight, . . . II. i. 14. 2
Death were too litle paine for such a *fowle* despight. . . . II. i. 17. 9
that same knight should doe so *foule* amis, . . . II. i. 19. 2
foule shame him follow wher he went!' . . . II. i. 30. 9
From *fowle* intemperaunce he ofte did stay, . . . II. i. 34. 8
Thus *fowle* to hasten your untimely date? . . . II. i. 44. 8
many errant knightes hath *fowle* fordonne; . . . II. i. 51. 4
Purged with drugs of *fowle* intemperaunce: . . . II. i. 54. 8
whether blott of *fowle* offence Might not be purgd . . . II. ii. 4. 1
that faire Una late *fowle* outraged, . . . II. ii. 18. 2
fowle revenging rage, and base contentious jarre. . . . II. ii. 30. 9
fowle deedes, too hideous to bee told, . . . II. ii. 44. 7
Braggadocchio, . . . is of fayre Belphoebe *fowle* forlorne. . . . II. iii. Arg.
mote him honour win to wreak so *foule* despight. . . . II. iii. 13. 9

Foul—*Continued.*
her feathers *fowle* disfigured . . . II. iii. 36. 7
'What *fowle* blott Is this to knight, . . . II. iii. 43. 7
In *fowle* reproch, and termes of vile despight, . . . II. iv. 5. 2
Her bitter rayling and *foule* revilement, . . . II. iv. 12. 5
fraught with *fowle* despight, . . . II. iv. 29. 1
did him deadly daunt, or *fowle* dismay; . . . II. iv. 40. 8
Engrost with mud which did them *fowle* agrise, . . . II. vi. 46. 7
griesly hew and *fowle* ill favour'd sight; . . . II. vii. 3. 5
'through *fowle* intemperaunce, Frayle men are oft captiv'd . . . II. vii. 15. 1
An ugly feend, more *fowle* then dismall day, . . . II. vii. 26. 7
Enwrapped in *fowle* smoke and clouds . . . II. vii. 28. 9
my soule was soyld with *fowle* iniquity.' . . . II. vii. 62. 9
Against *fowle* feendes to ayd us militant! . . . II. viii. 2. 5
That sire he *fowl* bespake: . . . II. viii. 12. 2
with *fowle* cowardize his carcas shame, . . . II. viii. 13. 4
'For knighthoods love doe not so *fowle* a deed, . . . II. viii. 16. 2
First prayse of knighthood is *fowle* outrage to deface.' . . . II. viii. 25. 9
when Cymochles saw the *fowle* reproch, . . . II. viii. 44. 1
none then it more *fowle* and indecent, . . . II. ix. 1. 5
they weened *fowle* reproch Was to them doen, . . . II. ix. 11. 1
all the liquour, which was *fowle* and waste, . . . II. ix. 32. 1
With *foule* repulse from Fraunce was forced . . . II. x. 22. 9
fowle Maleger doth deface. . . . II. xi. Arg.
So *fowle* and ugly, that exceeding feare . . . II. xi. 5. 8
a monstrous rablement Of *fowle* misshapen wightes, . . . II. xi. 8. 2
Slaunderous reproches, and *fowle* infamies. . . . II. xi. 10. 6
shame that ever should so *fowle* defects . . . II. xii. 23. 3
Clad in fayre weedes but *fowle* disordered, . . . II. xii. 55. 8
without *fowle* empeach, . . . II. xii. 56. 5
to see Him his nobility so *fowle* deface: . . . II. xii. 79. 4
Delightes in filth and *fowle* incontinence: . . . II. xii. 87. 7
For to revenge that *fowle* reprochefull shame, . . . III. i. 9. 2
after the *foule* foster Timias did strive. . . . III. i. 18. 9
Then must he her forgoe with *fowle* defame, . . . III. i. 27. 2
with *fowle* reproch To stirre up strife, . . . III. i. 64. 4
none of them *foule* mischiefe could eschew, . . . III. i. 66. 3
Late *foule* dishonour and reprochfull spight, . . . III. ii. 8. 8
her turne to *fowle* repriefe And sore reproch, . . . III. iii. 5. 7
Nor so *fowle* outrage doen by living men; . . . III. iii. 34. 6
Of whose *fowle* outrage they impatient, . . . III. iv. 45. 7
So deepe the deadly feare of that *foule* swaine . . . III. iv. 49. 2
'Night! thou *foule* Mother of annoyaunce sad, . . . III. iv. 55. 1
Fowle horror, and eke hellish dreriment: . . . III. iv. 58. 5
A *foule* ill-favoured foster, . . . III. v. 6. 3
After that foster *fowle* he fiercely ridd . . . III. v. 13. 4
cast t' avenge him of that *fowle* despight . . . III. v. 15. 3
his *foule* sore reduced to faire plight: . . . III. v. 41. 8
Whereof conceiving shame and *foule* disgrace, . . . III. vi. 10. 1
with *fowle* infamous blot, . . . III. vi. 13. 4
perceive In that *fowle* plight . . . III. vii. 46. 2
many hath to *foule* confusion brought. . . . III. vii. 48. 4
for feare of shame and *fowle* disgrace. . . . III. vii. 60. 5
thought that match a *fowle* disparagement: . . . III. viii. 12. 4
Forcyng to doe that did him *fowle* misseeme. . . . III. viii. 26. 7
knighthood *fowle* defaced by a faithlesse knight. . . . III. ix. 1. 9
To doe *fowle* death to die, . . . III. ix. 17. 9
his late fall and *fowle* indignity, . . . III. ix. 25. 2
for shame, so *fowle* reproch to shonne, . . . III. ix. 48. 5
the father of *fowle* gealosy, . . . III. x. 22. 5
with *fowle* force unto his will did drive; . . . III. x. 27. 7
Fowle Gealosy! that turnest love divine To joylesse dread, . . . III. xi. 1. 5
oft committed *fowle* Idolatree. . . . III. xi. 49. 5
he was *fowle,* ill-favoured, and grim, . . . III. xii. 15. 1
with *foule* outrages opprest. . . . III. xii. 41. 5
dread of shame and doubt of *fowle* dishonor . . . IV. i. 8. 6
Vile treason and *fowle* falshood hidden were, . . . IV. i. 17. 8
Her face most *fowle* and filthy was to see, . . . IV. i. 27. 1
by slight And *foule* advantage this good Knight dismayd, . . . IV. i. 44. 3
Whose Lord hath done my love this *foule* despight? . . . IV. i. 52. 8
Colour thy name with *foule* reproaches rust! . . . IV. i. 53. 7
with termes of *foule* despight, . . . IV. ii. 3. 3
Through that false witch, and that *foule* aged drevill; . . . IV. ii. 3. 8
Yet nigh approching he them *fowle* bespake, . . . IV. iv. 4. 1
On whom I waite to wreake that *foule* despight, . . . IV. vi. 5. 8
defiled with *foule* villanie The sacred pledge . . . IV. vi. 8. 2
the which it fairely blest From *foule* mischance; . . . IV. vi. 13. 5
often did my folly *fowle* reprove: . . . IV. vii. 16. 4
A *foule* and lothsome creature, did appeare, . . . IV. vii. 34. 4
forst him backe with *fowle* dishonor to retreat. . . . IV. vii. 37. 9
fowle rebuke and shame Be theirs . . . IV. viii. 15. 3
A *foule* and loathly creature sure in sight, . . . IV. viii. 24. 1
faire grew *foule,* and *foule* grew faire in sight; . . . IV. viii. 32. 5
that *fowle* rudenesse which did her deface; . . . IV. ix. 14. 3
They gan remember of the *fowle* upbraide, . . . IV. ix. 28. 5
gan first disswade From such *foule* outrage, . . . IV. ix. 34. 4
eke the love of Ladies *foule* defame; . . . IV. ix. 37. 5
ten thousand monsters *foule* abhor'd . . . IV. xi. 3. 8
most free from *fowle* despight, . . . IV. xi. 18. 8
fell Into all filth and *foule* iniquitie, . . . V. i. 5. 7
oppresst The faire Irena with his *foule* misdeede, . . . V. i. 13. 4
While she was flying . . . From that *foule* monster . . . V. iii. 27. 6
horrour of *fowle* death for Knight unfit, . . . V. iv. 25. 4
Voide of malitious mind or *foule* offence: . . . V. v. 33. 5
him to touch with falshoods *fowle* attaint, . . . V. vi. 12. 3
so great honour with so *fowle* reproch had blent. . . . V. vi. 18. 9
To be avenged for so *fowle* a deede, . . . V. vi. 31. 2
he falsely did revyle And *foule* blaspheme that Queene . . . V. ix. 25. 5
she it with *foule* abuse did marre; . . . V. ix. 38. 3
many other crimes of *foule* defame Against her brought, . . . V. ix. 43. 2

Foul—*Continued.*
Even *foule* Adulterie her face before, ... V. ix. 48. 8
Orthrus begotten by great Typhaon and *foule* Echidna . . . V. x. 10. 8
A dreadfull feend with *fowle* deformed looke, ... V. xi. 22. 5
fowle blasphemous speaches forth did cast, ... V. xi. 28. 2
Breathing out clouds of sulphure *fowle* and blacke, ... V. xi. 32. 2
'What *foule* disgrace is this To so faire Ladie, ... V. xi. 62. 1
With so *foule* blame as breach of faith once plight, ... V. xi. 62. 4
their faces Most *foule* and filthie were, ... V. xii. 28. 7
her *foule* heare Hung loose and loathsomely: . . . . V. xii. 29. 3
Her hands were *foule* and durtie, ... V. xii. 30. 1
of her owne *foule* entrayles makes her meat; . . . . V. xii. 31. 8
with unmanly guile And *foule* abusion, ... V. xii. 40. 4
Through *fowle* commixture of his filthy blot; . . . . VI. i. 8. 3
fowle upbrayd with faulty blame. . . . . VI. i. 24. 9
fowle entreaty him indignifyde, ... VI. i. 30. 5
The which shal nought to you but *foule* dishonor yearne. . . . VI. i. 40. 9
to release his former *foule* condition. . . . . VI. i. 43. 9
a Ladie faire . . . on foot in *foule* array; . . . . VI. ii. 4. 2
Tooke in *foule* scorne that I such fault did find, ... VI. ii. 11. 7
forst to trot on foot, and *foule* misused, ... VI. ii. 22. 5
I may avenge him of so *foule* despight.' . . . . VI. ii. 42. 6
in despight to be so *fowle* abused . . . . VI. iii. 33. 4
a rude churle, . . . accused Of *fowle* discourtesie, ... VI. iii. 33. 6
Because of one that wrought him *fowle* despight.' . . . . VI. iii. 40. 5
With wrathfull fury for so *foule* a shame, ... VI. iii. 43. 5
that *foule* feend, who dayly doth attend . . . . VI. iv. 31. 8
wrapt In sad misfortunes *foule* deformity . . . . VI. v. 1. 3
Ne ever shewed signe of *foule* disloyalty. . . . . VI. v. 9. 9
The *foule* discourt'sies and unknightly parts, ... VI. v. 33. 2
Begot of *foule* Echidna, ... VI. vi. 9. 9
Wrought to Sir Calepine so *foule* despight; . . . . VI. vi. 17. 7
with black dishonor And *foule* defame . . . . VI. vi. 25. 5
To shew such faintnesse and *foule* cowardize . . . . VI. vi. 35. 2
Bidding him turne againe, . . . *Foule* woman-wronger, ... VI. vii. 7. 3
How fortuneth this *foule* uncomely plight, ... VI. vii. 14. 8
Were vanquished, and put to *foule* disgrace; . . . . VI. vii. 21. 5
foule Infamie and fell Despight Gave evidence, ... VI. vii. 34. 7
Met her in such misseeming *foule* array; . . . . VI. vii. 39. 3
Yond Lady and her Squire with *foule* despight Abusde, ... VI. viii. 6. 3
Who now does follow the *foule* Blatant Beast, ... VI. x. 1. 1
Blew up a bitter storme of *foule* adversity. . . . . VI. x. 38. 9
With *foule* dishonour him mote blot therefore; . . . . VI. xii. 12. 7
yet that *foule* Beast . . . the more did tosse and teare, ... VI. xii. 24. 6
They mocke and scorne him, and him *foule* miscall; . . . . VII. vi. 49. 3
With every blast that bloweth, *fowle* or faire: . . . . VII. vii. 22. 8
The faire doth it prolong; the *fowle* doth it impaire. . . . . VII. vii. 22. 9
Scorn of base things, and sdeigne of *foule* dishonor: . . . . *Am.* v. 6
From feare of perrill and *foule* horror free. . . . . *Epith.* 322
deform'd with some *foule* imperfection. . . . . *H.B.* 147
goodly beautie, albe heavenly borne, Is *foule* abusd, ... *H.B.* 150
Loath that *foule* blot, ... *H.B.* 169
He was revyld, disgrast, and *foule* abused; . . . . *H.H.L.* 242
lampe . . . seemes *fowle*, and full of sinfull blame; . . . . *H.H.B.* 276
streame, . . . Seem'd *foule* to them, ... *Proth.* 48

Fouldering. rend the rathing skyes with flames of *fouldring* heat. . . . . II. ii. 20. 9

Fouldings. *See* **Foldings.**

Fouled. with their feete uncleane the water *fouled*, ... *Bel.*[1] x. 13
Altars *fouled*, and blasphemy spoke, ... VI. xii. 25. 3

Fouler. *See* **Fowler.**
nothing cleaner were . . . But rather *fowler* seemed . . . . II. vii. 61. 8
Fled all away for fear of *fowler* shame. . . . . II. xii. 81. 7

Foulest. best or fayrest, more Than worst or *fowlest*, ... *D.* 203
of the fayrest late, now made the *fowlest* place. . . . . II. xii. 83. 9
That is the greatest shame and *foulest* scorne, ... V. xi. 52. 3
Disloiall lust faire beauties *foulest* blame, ... *H.B.* 170

Foully. Turn'd to a Lapwing, *fowlie* them upbraydes, ... *Gn.* 405
How *fowlie* they their offices abus'd, ... *Hub.* 563
him *fowlie* did entreate; . . . . *Hub.* 922
ye my cousin Wolfe so *fowly* thwart, ... *Hub.* 1218
Rosalind of divers *fowly* blamed . . . . *Col.* 908
Faire knighthood *fowly* shamed, ... I. vi. 41. 3
The goddesse wroth gan *fowly* her disgrace, ... I. vii. 5. 5
taile, with dong all *fowly* dight; . . . . I. viii. 48. 4
that reprochfull fall right *fowly* he disdaynd; . . . . I. xi. 23. 9
her faire face with teares was *fowly* blubbered. . . . . II. i. 13. 9
The truncked beast fast bleeding did him *fowly* dight. . . . . II. v. 4. 9
fowly battered his comely corse, ... II. v. 23. 5
The famous name of knighthood *fowly* shend; . . . . II. vi. 35. 2
art thus *fowly* fledd from famous enimy?' . . . . II. vi. 39. 9
fowly blend, . . . the high heroicke spright, ... II. vii. 10. 5
he lived il that did thus *fowly* dye. . . . . II. viii. 12. 9
thousand Sar'zins *fowly* donne to dye.' . . . . II. viii. 18. 6
he to him leaped furiously, And *fowly* saide: . . . . II. viii. 33. 3
Both of their life and fame, for ever *fowly* blent. . . . . II. xii. 7. 9
fowly ras't, that none the signes might see: . . . . II. xii. 80. 4
Shall tread adowne, and doe him *fowly* dye; . . . . III. iii. 39. 8
former feare of being *fowly* shent . . . . III. iv. 50. 4
he gan *fowly* wyte His wicked fortune . . . . III. iv. 52. 7
Where they do wither, and are *fowly* mard: . . . . III. vi. 39. 6
so *fowly* to devoure Her native flesh . . . . III. vii. 49. 4
Ruffled and *fowly* raid with filthy soyle, ... III. viii. 32. 2
the faire welkin *fowly* overcast . . . . III. ix. 11. 4
his hore beard Was *fowly* dight, ... III. x. 52. 5
Florimell him *fowly* gan revile, ... IV. iv. 11. 3
He askt who had that Dame so *fouly* dight, ... V. i. 14. 8
fowly did array Withouten pitty of her goodly hew, ... V. ii. 25. 7
First he his beard did shave, and *fowly* shent, ... V. iii. 37. 5
all those Knights . . . she *fowly* doth entreate. . . . . V. iv. 31. 2

Foully—*Continued.*
all his former praise doth *fowly* spill: . . . . V. vi. 1. 5
Where as so many knights had *fouly* bene fordonne. . . . . V. x. 30. 9
Of all things, to dissemble, *fouly* may befall!' . . . . V. xi. 56. 9
Them *fouly* rent, and shamefully defaced had. . . . . V. xi. 60. 9
fouly rayle with all she could invent; . . . . V. xii. 40. 2
he *fouly* did to die. . . . . V. xii. 40. 9
That he gainst courtesie so *fowly* did default. . . . . VI. iii. 21. 9
Else had he surely there bene slaine, or *fowly* shent. . . . . VI. vii. 45. 9
so fayre beauty was so *fowly* shamed. . . . . *Am.* xli. 14

Foulness. like in *foulnesse* and deformity Unto that Monster, . V. xi. 25. 1

Found. *See* **New-found.**
greater was than can be *founde*, ... *Rev.* iv. 8
great riches as like cannot be *found* (*founde*[1])! . . . . *Pet.* ii. 14
Such was this Citie in her good daies *fownd*: . . . . *Ro.* vi. 4
Thou findest faulte where nys to be *found*, ... *S.C.* May 144
thy state, That Paradise hast *founde* . . . . *S.C.* Jun. 10
The vaunting Poets *found* nought worth a pease . . . . *S.C.* O. 69
yet alive art *founde?* . . . . *S.C.* D. 96
never *found* occasion for their tourne, ... *Hub.* 579
all the happinesse that heart desire, Is to be *found*: . . . . *Hub.* 610
here arriv'd, to see if like he *found*. . . . . *Hub.* 688
With all the thriftles games that may be *found*; . . . . *Hub.* 801
few have *found*, and manie one hath mist! . . . . *Hub.* 894
the Foxe, his copesmate he had *found*, ... *Hub.* 939
he *found*, where sleeping he did ly, ... *Hub.* 1320
all the gates he *found* fast lockt anon, ... *Hub.* 1350
Now without fruite or leaves are to be *found*. . . . . *T.M.* 252
vertue *found* So brave a Trompe, ... *Ti.* 433
Built all of richest stone that might bee *found*, ... *Ti.* 506
Two fairer beasts might not elswhere be *found*, ... *Ti.* 566
Emongst the rest a gentle Nymph was *found*, ... *Mui.* 118
all, that faire or pleasant may be *found*, ... *Mui.* 167
(as in stories it is written *found*) . . . . *Mui.* 258
neither most nor least I *found* miscaried . . . . *D.* 140
night without a Venus starre is *found*. . . . . *D.* 483
if in him *found* pity ever place, ... *As.* Pr. 17
Ne spight it selfe . . . *Found* ought in him, that she could say was ill. . . . . *As.* 24
in hunting such felicitie, . . . he *found*, ... *As.* 80
He *found* himselfe full greatly pleasd at it: . . . . *Col.* 71
I *found* much greater then the former fame; . . . . *Col.* 334
A gentler shepheard may no where be *found*: . . . . *Col.* 445
found I lyking in her royall mynd, ... *Col.* 454
of each, so as I *found*, to tell . . . . *Col.* 683
Nor honest mynd might there be *found* at all. . . . . *Col.* 734
all wemen are thy debtors *found*, ... *Col.* 901
Weening their wonted entrance to have *found* . . . . I. i. 25. 5
Having both *found* a new friend you to aid, ... I. ii. 27. 2
turning to his Lady, dead with feare her *fownd*. . . . . I. ii. 44. 9
Her seeming dead he *fownd* with feigned feare, ... I. ii. 45. 1
at length she *found* the troden gras, ... I. iii. 10. 4
Shee *found* them both in darksome corner pent; . . . . I. iii. 13. 5
Faery court, . . . Where noblest knights were to be *found* . . . I. iii. 28. 6
Such joy made Una, when her knight she *found*; . . . . I. iii. 32. 1
Whom when she *found*, as she him left in plight, ... I. v. 19. 7
she *found* the Faery knight Departed thence; . . . . I. v. 45. 3
Where he unwares the fairest Una *found*, ... I. vi. 30. 6
She *fownd* not in that perilous hous of Pryde, ... I. vii. 2. 2
Ere long she *fownd*, ... I. vii. 2. 6
If lesse then that I feare, more favour I have *found*.' . . . . I. vii. 25. 9
Found never help who never would his hurts impart.' . . . . I. vii. 40. 9
Whose gates he *fownd* fast shutt, ... I. viii. 3. 3
Where he with his Duessa dalliaunce *fownd*, ... I. viii. 5. 5
the Knight him at advantage *fownd*; . . . . I. viii. 10. 3
There all within full rich arayd he *found*, ... I. viii. 35. 1
he . . . key *found* not at all Emongst that bounch . . . . I. viii. 37. 4
He *found* the meanes that Prisoner up to reare; . . . . I. viii. 40. 6
store they *fownd* of al that dainty was and rare. . . . . I. viii. 50. 9
wound . . . Me hither brought by wayes yet never *found*, . . . I. ix. 7. 6
fort . . . unawares at disavantage *fownd*. . . . . I. ix. 11. 4
'When I awoke, and *found* her place devoyd, ... I. ix. 15. 1
Queene of Faeries! that hast *fownd*, Mongst many, one . . . I. ix. 16. 6
She *found* her selfe assayld with great perplexity; . . . . I. x. 22. 9
that deare Lord who oft thereon was *fownd*, ... I. x. 54. 4
thee a Ploughman all unweeting *fond*, ... I. x. 66. 3
The many favours I with thee have *fownd*, ... I. x. 67. 2
found no place his deadly point to rest. . . . . I. xi. 17. 4
ayre, which nigh too feeble *found* Her flitting parts, ... I. xi. 18. 4
his late wounded wing unserviceable *found*. . . . . I. xi. 25. 9
In all the world like was not to be *fownd*, ... I. xi. 47. 1
There did I find, or rather I was *fownd* . . . . I. xii. 32. 1
The Amazon huge river, now *found* trew? . . . . II. Pr. 2. 8
Where may that treachour . . . be *found*, ... II. i. 12. 6
Her, late forlorne and naked, he had *found* . . . . II. i. 22. 1
'Him so I sought; and so at last I *fownd*, ... II. i. 54. 1
him *found* not theare: . . . . II. ii. 11. 7
two brave knightes . . . he enraunged *fond*, ... II. ii. 21. 4
Might not be *found* a francker franion, ... II. ii. 37. 4
That may this day in all the world be *found*. . . . . II. ii. 42. 5
eke of surest steele that may be *fownd*, ... II. iii. 15. 8
Shall by to morrow by thy side be *fond*.' . . . . II. iii. 18. 7
wher-so they might be *found*, ... II. iii. 38. 6
wil be *found* with perill and with paine; . . . . II. iii. 41. 2
Long I her serv'd, and *found* her faithfull still, ... II. iv. 19. 6
'At last such grace I *found*, ... II. iv. 21. 1
There Atin *fownd* Cymochles sojourning, ... II. v. 28. 1
There he him *found* all carelesly displaid, ... II. v. 32. 1
the wanton Damsell *found* New merth . . . . II. vi. 6. 1
there it might be *fownd* To bud out faire, ... II. vi. 12. 8

Found—*Continued.*

where him she byding *fond* . . . . II. vi. 19. 5
Where drenched deepe he *fownd* . . . The carefull servaunt . . II. vi. 47. 8
long he yode, yet no adventure *found,* . . . . II. vii. 2. 6
he sitting *found* in secret shade An uncouth . . . wight, . . . II. vii. 3. 3
Fownd no defect in his Creators grace; . . . . II. vii. 16. 2
he *fownd* Fountaines of gold and silver . . . . II. vii. 17. 4
fownd A darkesome way, ... II. vii. 20. 6
found no place wher safe he shroud him might: . . . . II. vii. 22. 7
Ne ever could within one place be *fownd,* . . . . II. vii. 31. 6
sith thou hast *found* favour in mine eye, ... II. vii. 49. 7
By further search had passage *found* elsewhere; . . . . II. viii. 3. 4
the good Guyon he *found* slumbring fast . . . . II. viii. 4. 8
found him fiers and bold.' . . . . II. viii. 13. 9
them *fond* Emongst the shepeheard swaynes, ... II. viii. 40. 8
there eternall torment *found* For all the sinnes . . . . II. viii. 45. 8
goodly purpose they together *fond* . . . . II. viii. 56. 7
They *found* the gates fast barred long ere night, ... II. ix. 10. 8
With greater fury then before was *fownd,* . . . . II. ix. 15. 2
Diverse delights they *fownd* them selves to please; . . . . . . II. ix. 35. 1
not on ground mote like to this be *found:* . . . . II. ix. 45. 5
Th' ofspring of Elves and Faeryes there he *fond,* . . . . . . II. ix. 60. 4
Whom he at sea *found* wandring from their waies, ... II. x. 41. 7
for this Realme *found* many goodly layes, ... II. x. 42. 5
Ne had they footing *found* at last, ... II. x. 48. 5
all in peeces it was broken *fond,* . . . . II. xii. 57. 4
that which reft it no lesse faire was *fownd.* . . . . II. xii. 67. 7
bandes, which there they readie *found:* . . . . II. xii. 82. 5
He *fownd* him selfe dishonored so sore. . . . . III. i. 7. 4
tract of living creature none they *fownd,* . . . . III. i. 14. 8
Whom they *found* sitting on a sumptuous bed . . . . III. i. 41. 2
If any puffe of breath or signe of sence shee *fond.* . . . . . . III. i. 60. 9
whenas none she *fond,* . . . . III. i. 61. 1
fownd Their lady lying on the sencelesse grownd: . . . . III. i. 63. 4
many straunge adventures to bee *fond,* . . . . III. ii. 8. 3
Where now on earth, or how, he may be *fownd;* . . . . III. ii. 14. 2
'Was never such, but mote the like be *fownd,'* . . . . III. ii. 36. 3
blame Of her miscarriage should in her be *fond,* . . . . III. ii. 52. 8
That of no living wight he mote be *found,* . . . . III. iii. 7. 8
the dreadfull Mage there *fownd* Deepe busied . . . . III. iii. 14. 6
she *fond* Of diverse thinges discourses to dilate, ... III. iii. 62. 3
Florimell of Arthure is Long followed, but not *fond.* . . . . . III. iv. Arg.
Too trew the famous Marinell it *fownd,* . . . . III. iv. 29. 1
they *fownd* The lucklesse Marinell . . . . III. iv. 34. 8
Shee *fownd,* and brought it to her patient deare, ... III. v. 32. 8
How him in deadly case theyr Lady *fownd,* . . . . III. v. 38. 4
there she *found* him not; . . . . III. vi. 13. 2
many there she *found* which sore accus'd His falshood, . . . III. vi. 13. 3
Whereas she *found* the Goddesse with her crew, ... III. vi. 17. 2
fownd His feeble hart wide launched . . . . III. vi. 52. 8
she *found* A little cottage, ... III. vii. 6. 1
sitting on the flore the Hag she *found* . . . . III. vii. 7. 2
there *found* The fayrest creature . . . . III. vii. 13. 1
safety *fownd* at sea which she *fownd* not at land. . . . . . . III. vii. 27. 9
her golden girdle . . . he *fownd,* . . . . III. vii. 31. 9
found such favour in their loving hartes, ... III. vii. 55. 2
Till I so many other Dames had *fownd,* . . . . III. vii. 56. 4
All that I ever *fownd* so wisely stayd, ... III. vii. 57. 2
Whom I in countrey cottage *fownd* by chaunce: . . . . III. vii. 59. 2
'Safe her, I never any woman *found* . . . . III. vii. 60. 1
He *found* him not; for he had broke his band, ... III. vii. 61. 7
I *found* her golden girdle cast astray, ... III. viii. 49. 8
full of guests he *found* whyleare, ... III. ix. 13. 4
complaint Hath *fownd* another partner of your payne; . . . . . III. ix. 40. 2
weetlesse wandered . . . Ere rest he *fownd.* . . . . III. ix. 41. 7
'The Trojan Brute did first that citie *fownd,* . . . . III. ix. 46. 1
many fortunes prov'd . . . And great adventures *found,* . . . III. ix. 48. 9
Found it the fittest soyle for their abode, ... III. ix. 49. 5
when apart (if ever her apart) He *found,* . . . . III. x. 7. 2
To search her forth where so she might be *fond,* . . . . III. x. 19. 2
soone he shal be *fownd,* . . . . III. x. 32. 9
when he *found* it not, . . . became quite mad, ... III. x. 54. 3
at the last he *found* a cave with entrance small. . . . . III. x. 57. 9
Whereas no gate they *found* them to withhold, ... III. xi. 21. 3
went unto the dore . . . *fownd* it locked fast: . . . . III. xii. 27. 7
For many labours more then I have *found,* . . . . III. xii. 40. 3
vanisht utterly and cleane subverst She *found,* . . . . III. xii. 42. 4
Those dreadfull flames she also *found* delayd . . . . III. xii. 42. 7
More easie issew now then entrance late She *found;* . . . . . III. xii. 43. 2
There on the cold earth him now thrown she *found,* . . . . . III. xii. 43. *or.*6
Neither of them she *found* where she them lore: . . . . III. xii. 44. 4
found right safe assurance theare. . . . . IV. i. 15. 9
Yet many waies to enter may be *found,* . . . . IV. i. 20. 7
Albee in heart he like affection *fond,* . . . . IV. i. 34. 3
she, that is fayrest *found,* Shall have that golden girdle . . . IV. ii. 27. 1
Though now their acts be no where to be *found,* . . . . IV. ii. 32. 5
bore three such, three such not to be *fond!* . . . . IV. ii. 41. 6
There she them *found* all sitting round about, ... IV. ii. 48. 1
in warlike fresh aray Them *found* . . . . IV. ii. 53. 4
Have by good fortune *found* some beasts fresh spoyle, ... IV. iii. 16. 2
found rest Upon the brim of his brode-plated shield, ... IV. iii. 34. 5
since their dayes such lovers were not *found* elswhere. . . . . IV. iii. 52. 9
before them *found* in fresh aray Manie a brave knight . . . . IV. iv. 13. 7
as it fell, his steed he ready *found;* . . . . IV. iv. 23. 3
doubly him did grieve when so himselfe he *found.* . . . . . . IV. iv. 26. 9
There Satyrane Lord of the field he *found,* . . . . IV. iv. 28. 1
In vaine he sought, for there he *found* it not; . . . . IV. iv. 33. 4
There he in troupe *found* all that warlike crew, ... IV. iv. 33. 8
by his friend himselfe eke soone he *fond* . . . . IV. iv. 45. 3
There entring in, they *found* the goodman selfe . . . . . . IV. v. 34. 1

Found—*Continued.*

found himselfe on ground in great amazement. . . . . IV. vi. 11. 9
all his gealous feare he false had *found,* . . . . IV. vi. 28. 2
I *found* her not where I her left whyleare, ... IV. vi. 36. 6
Fit time for him thence to depart it *found,* . . . . IV. vi. 42. 4
her therewith full sore displeasd he *found,* . . . . IV. vi. 42. 7
she sundry purpose *found* . . . the time for to delay, ... IV. vi. 45. 1
Yet *found* they none. . . . . IV. vi. 47. 5
what guerdon hast thou *found* . . . . IV. vii. 1. 5
nothing *found* But darknesse and dread horrour . . . . IV. vii. 9. 6
where I him thought to find, There was I *found,* . . . . . . IV. vii. 18. 3
nought but darksome drerinesse she *found,* . . . . IV. vii. 33. 2
There she him *found* by that new lovely mate, ... IV. vii. 35. 3
found no ease of griefe nor hope of grace, ... IV. vii. 38. 2
he *found* this wretched man . . . . IV. vii. 43. 1
Amongst the rest a jewell rich he *found,* . . . . IV. viii. 6. 6
There *found* she her . . . Sitting in covert shade . . . . . . IV. viii. 9. 1
food which in her duresse she had *found;* . . . . IV. viii. 19. 6
At which he wondred much when all those signes he *fond.* . . IV. viii. 21. 9
entring in *found* none therein abide, ... IV. viii. 23. 4
Yet *found* no fault, but that the Hag did scold . . . . IV. viii. 28. 3
he *found* His head before him tombling . . . . IV. viii. 45. 4
him the more agreev'd I *found* thereby: . . . . IV. viii. 57. 5
'Thenceforth I *found* more favour at her hand, ... IV. viii. 61. 1
made it so to ride as it alive was *found.* . . . . IV. ix. 4. 9
he *found* great store of hoorded threasure, ... IV. ix. 12. 2
For every dram of hony therein *found* . . . . IV. x. 1. 4
The which I *found* sure lockt and chained fast. . . . . IV. x. 11. 3
fuming all with frankensence I *found* . . . . IV. x. 37. 2
This Gyant *found* her and by force deflowr'd; . . . . IV. xi. 42. 6
since he meanes *found* none, ... IV. xii. 12. 8
for-why he *found* no way To enter in, ... IV. xii. 15. 3
ne fraud in wight was to be *found:* . . . . V. Pr. 9. 4
Upon a day she *found* this gentle childe . . . . V. i. 6. 2
Mongst wicked men, in whom no truth she *found,* . . . . . . V. i. 11. 3
He *found* him selfe unwist so ill bestad, ... V. i. 22. 4
How she was *found* againe, and spousde to Marinell. . . . . . V. ii. 2. 9
then no ods at all in him he *fownd;* . . . . V. ii. 16. 5
At length *found* out whereas she hidden lay . . . . V. ii. 25. 5
mongst them al no change hath yet beene *found;* . . . . . . V. ii. 36. 4
For there is nothing lost, that may be *found* if sought. . . . . V. ii. 39. 9
Whom when so lewdly minded Talus *found,* . . . . V. ii. 49. 6
With whom great feast and goodly glee he *fond,* . . . . . . V. iv. 3. 4
readie to deserve what grace I *found.'* . . . . V. v. 42. 5
none she *found* so fit to serve that turne, ... V. vi. 6. 3
Yet *found* no place that could her liking please, ... V. vi. 7. 3
Yet *found* no easement in her troubled wits, ... V. vi. 15. 3
Each rowme she sought, but them all empty *fond.* . . . . . . V. vi. 35. 8
the Priestes she *found* full busily . . . . V. vii. 17. 7
therefore ought it have where ever she it *fond.* . . . . V. vii. 30. 9
Nath'lesse that stroke so cruell passage *found,* . . . . V. vii. 33. 1
by adventure *found* them faring so, ... V. viii. 15. 6
an hungry hound That hunting after game hath carrion *found,* V. viii. 36. 5
found No easie meanes according to his mind: . . . . V. viii. 42. 2
she of death was guiltie *found* by right, ... V. ix. 50. 4
There he her *found* in sorrow and dismay, ... V. x. 19. 1
Into his shield it readie passage *found,* . . . . V. x. 33. 2
when he *found* no more T'oppose against his powre . . . . . V. x. 38. 5
How that the Lady Belge now had *found* A Champion, ... V. xi. 2. 2
Whiles she alone is left, and thou here *found?* . . . . V. xi. 38. 6
Her halfe dismayd they *found* in doubtfull plight, ... V. xi. 60. 4
witnesse be Gerioneo *found,* . . . . V. xii. 2. 5
they *found* A ship all readie . . . . V. xii. 4. 1
they readie *found,* them to repell, Great hostes of men . . . V. xii. 4. 7
Ne ever any *found* his match in might; . . . . V. xii. 15. 4
That vertue should be plentifully *found,* . . . . VI. i. 1. 4
ne was there Lady *found* In Faery court, ... VI. i. 3. 1
by chaunce a comely Squire he *found,* . . . . VI. i. 11. 2
Ne wote I surely whether her he yet have *fond.'* . . . . . . VI. i. 16. 9
There he that knight *found* lying on the flore . . . . VI. ii. 40. 7
discourteous knight, . . . them in that shadow *found* . . . . VI. ii. 43. 2
having both *found* fit occasion, ... VI. iii. 8. 1
There he him *found* much better then he was; . . . . VI. iii. 14. 5
his Lady *found* In dolorous dismay . . . . VI. iii. 27. 2
he *found* That hardly passable on foote it was; . . . . VI. iii. 30. 1
There he this most discourteous craven *found,* . . . . VI. iv. 2. 6
There he that knight full sorely bleeding *found,* . . . . . . VI. iv. 9. 6
no herbe he *found* Which could redresse, ... VI. iv. 16. 8
wound Made in his tender flesh; but whole them all he *found.* VI. iv. 23. 9
Found nothing that he said unmeet nor geason, ... VI. iv. 37. 2
The Blatant Beast the fittest meanes they *found* . . . . . . VI. v. 14. 8
Of this wyld man, whom they full busie *found* . . . . VI. v. 25. 2
whether he alive be to be *found,* . . . . VI. v. 28. 7
He *found* that they had festred privily; . . . . VI. vi. 5. 2
He *found* the gate wyde ope, ... VI. vi. 19. 2
There he him *found* environed about With slaughtred bodies . VI. vi. 38. 1
There he him *found* in great astonishment, ... VI. vii. 14. 3
he *found* Whereas the Prince himselfe lay . . . . VI. vii. 18. 6
Then *found* he many missing of his crew, ... VI. vii. 34. 1
Serena, *found* of Salvages, ... VI. viii. Arg.
he plainely *found* It was his owne true groome, ... VI. viii. 27. 5
Found her by fortune, which to him befell, ... VI. ix. 14. 5
For so great kindnesse as he *found* that day . . . . VI. ix. 18. 5
There he a troupe of Ladies dauncing *found* . . . . VI. x. 10. 7
She *found* no meanes to barre him, ... VI. xi. 7. 7
Their Captaine there they cruelly *found* kild, ... VI. xi. 21. 1
They *found* that life did yet in her remaine: . . . . VI. xi. 22. 2
turne we backe to Calidore where we him *found.* . . . . VI. xi. 24. 9
Ne wight he *found* to whom he might complaine, ... VI. xi. 26. 1
Ne wight he *found* of whom he might inquire, ... VI. xi. 26. 2

Found—*Continued.*
there now not one he *found*. VI. xi. 26. 9
At length, when they occasion fittest *found*, VI. xi. 42. 1
When to the Cave they came, they *found* it fast; VI. xi. 43. 1
Ne lesse in hart rejoyced Calidore, When he her *found*; VI. xi. 45. 7
Mongst which he *found* a sword of better say, VI. xi. 47. 5
when he wrapped *found* Th' abandond spoyle, VI. xii. 9. 4
She *found* at last, by very certaine signes VI. xii. 20. 3
Through all estates he *found* that he had past, VI. xii. 23. 1
Where he him *found* despoyling all VI. xii. 23. 9
At last, when as he *found* his force to shrincke VI. xii. 34. 1
As I have *found* it registred of old VII. vi. 2. 3
Her sitting on an Ivory throne shee *found*, VII. vi. 9. 1
Where all the Gods she *found* in counsell close, VII. vi. 24. 2
none of all there-in more pleasure *found* Then Cynthia, VII. vi. 38. 6
No way he *found* to compasse his desire, VII. vi. 43. 1
Which too-too true that lands in-dwellers since have *found*. VII. vi. 55. 9
full her hand was *found*: VII. vii. 37. 5
their dew places *found*. VII. vii. 43. 9
riches that may farre be *found*: *Am.* xv. 6
Well worthy thou to have *found* better hyre, *Am.* xlviii. 5
(such grace I *found*,) *Am.* lxiv. 1
Could not on earth have *found* one fit for mate, *Am.* lxvi. 6
many thou hast pricked to the hart, That pitty never *found*: *Epig.* iv. 38
when he hath *found* favour to his will, *H.L.* 245
through unaptnesse in the substance *fownd*, *H.B.* 144
Before this worlds great frame, . . . *found* any being-place, *H.H.L.* 23
no jot Of loves dislike or pride was to be *found*, *H.H.L.* 34
underneath his feet are to be *found* *H.H.B.* 180
freshest Flowres which in that Mead they *found*, *Proth.* 84
Foundation. Upon the same to set *foundation* sure? *Ro.* xxiv. 14
shortly the *foundation* decaid, *Ti.* 500
so faire a mould Did on so weake *foundation* ever sitt: I. iv. 5. 4
her *foundation* forst, and feebled quight, I. viii. 23. 4
clift, Whose false *foundacion* waves have washt away, I. xi. 54. 6
Elfinan, who laid Cleopolis *foundation* first of all: II. x. 72. 8
On firme *foundation* of true bountyhed: II. xii. 1. 5
Even from the sole of his *foundation*, V. ii. 28. 2
Foundations. The weake *foundations* of this citie faire. *Bel.*[2] xiv. 14
her head, earth'd in her *foundations* deep, *Ro.* viii. 13
lose The worlds *foundations* from his centre fixt: III. xii. 2. 4
Founded. Had *founded* for the Kingdomes ornament, *Hub.* 1181
th' Earth, . . . *founded* Amid the Sea, *H.H.B.* 36
Foundering. through *foundring* or through sodein feare, IV. iv. 30. 3
Founders. There also some most famous *founders* were IV. xi. 15. 1
Foundest. with none of them thou favour *foundest*, *Col.* 461
since thou *foundst* such grace With Cynthia *Col.* 652
How many *fownd'st* thou such to put in thy record?' III. vii. 56. 9
Foundress. Albe Charissa were their chiefest *founderesse*. I. x. 44. 9
Fount. Yet dropping fresh out of the Indian *fount*, V. x. 16. 6
But that Eternall *Fount* of love and grace, *H.H.L.* 99
Fountain. the *fountaine*, where they sat around, *S.C.* Jun. 60
streame . . . from a sacred *fountaine* welled forth alway. I. i. 34. 9
'he hence doth wonne, Foreby a *fountaine*, I. vi. 39. 8
About the *fountaine* like a girlond made; I. vii. 4. 5
that fraile *fountain* which him feeble made, I. vii. 11. 8
Beside a bubling *fountaine* low she lay, II. i. 40. 2
secret vertues are infusd In every *fountaine*, II. ii. 5. 7
Here is the *fountaine* of the worldes good: II. vii. 38. 6
She is the *fountaine* of your modestee: II. ix. 43. 8
in the midst of all a *fountaine* stood, II. xii. 60. 1
Infinit streames continually did well Out of this *fountaine*, II. xii. 62. 2
seemd the *fountaine* in that sea did sayle upright. II. xii. 62. 9
bathe him in a *fountaine* by some covert glade: III. i. 35. 9
having vewed in a *fountaine* shere His face, III. ii. 44. 7
In a fresh *fountaine*, far from all mens vew, III. vi. 6. 6
Sitting beside a *fountaine* in a rew; III. vi. 17. 4
as a *fountaine* from her sweete lips went. III. vi. 25. 5
she at last came to a *fountaine* sheare, III. xi. 7. 2
men the more admyre their *fountaine* may; *H.B.* 186
Th' eternall *fountaine* of that heavenly beauty. *H.H.B.* 21
Fountains. poure foorth *fountaines* of incessant teares? *D.* 247
Fountaines of gold and silver to abownd, II. vii. 17. 5
The which in floods and *fountaines* doe appere, IV. xi. 52. 8
bathe in *fountaines* that do freshly flowe VII. vi. 39. 4
Fountain-side. Sate by the *fountaine side*, *Gn.* 238
did rest In secret shadow by a *fountaine side*: I. vi. 40. 6
he wearie sate . . . foreby a *fountaine syde*, I. vii. 2. 7
Four. Upon *foure* corners of the base *Bel.* iii. 9
To beare the frame, *foure* great Lyons *Bel.* iii. 10
He has them now *fowr* years besiegd to make them thrall. I. vii. 44. 9
Is not enough *fowre* quarters of a man, II. iii. 16. 6
fowre since Florimell the Court forwent, III. v. 10. 2
Which *four* great Hippodames did draw in temewise tyde. III. xi. 40. 9
foure of them the battell best beseemed, IV. ix. 20. 4
These *foure* were they from whom false Florimel IV. ix. 20. 6
So diversly these *foure* disposed were to love. IV. ix. 21. 9
From all *foure* parts of heaven doe rage full sore, IV. ix. 23. 6
Foure charged two, and two surcharged one; IV. ix. 30. 5
Foure times . . . he shifted hath V. Pr. 8. 5
every body two, and two she *foure* did read. VI. viii. 31. 9
these *fower* . . . To thousand sorts of Change we subject see: VII. vii. 25. 1
Four hundred. *fowr hundred* yeares And more had wasted, II. x. 62. 6
twise *fowre hundreth* yeares shalbe supplide, III. iii. 44. 5
Fourteen hundred. the terme of *fourteene hundred* yeres, V. Pr. 7. 5
Fourth. Wants not a *fourth* Grace, to make the daunce even? *S.C.* Ap. 113
She shal be a Grace, To fyll the *fourth* place, *S.C.* Ap. 116
the *fourth* to forbeare is outragious: *S.C.* May 133
Such one was Avarice, the *fourth* of this faire band. I. iv. 29. 9
The *fourth* appointed by his office was I. x. 40. 1

Fourth—*Continued.*
that *fourth* band which cruell battry bent II. xi. 12. 1
the *fourth* Bulwarke, that is the Taste, II. xi. 12. 2
The *fourth* was by that other knight dismayd, III. i. 29. 3
From the *fourth* howre of night untill the sixt; III. xii. 2. 7
The *fourth* Ecastor, of exceeding might; V. iii. 5. 6
that *fourth* Mayd, which there amidst them traced, VI. x. 25. 2
To be the *fourth* with those three other placed: VI. x. 25. 7
Fowl. *See* **Foul.**
the *foule* that shunnes the cherefull light *Bel.*[1] vi. 13
the *foule*, that doth the light dispise *Bel.*[2] vii. 13
the *foule*, that serves to beare the lightning, *Ro.* xvii. 13
when as the *Foule* was wroth, *Van.* iv. 13
gentle kinde as ever *Fowle* afore; *Ti.* 591
Sometime a *fowle*, sometime a fish in lake, I. ii. 10. 5
drave Far from that haunt all other chearefull *fowle*, I. ix. 33. 8
to contend With hardy *fowle* I. xi. 19. 6
As fearfull *fowle*, that long . . . her selfe hath hid, II. iii. 36. 1
Gaz'd after him, as *fowle* escapt by flight. II. viii. 9. 4
To which nor fish nor *fowle* did once approch, II. xii. 8. 3
The warie *fowle*, that spies him toward bend IV. iii. 19. 5
The trembling *foule* dismayd with dreadfull sight V. ii. 54. 3
hath seized for her share Uppon some *fowle* V. iv. 42. 5
Carried with wings of feare, like *fowle* aghast, V. viii. 4. 7
The warie *foule* his bill doth backward wring; VI. vii. 9. 4
all the *foule* . . . Gan flock about these twaine, *Proth.* 119
Fowler. Like as the *fouler* on his guilefull pype V. ix. 13. 1
Fowler's. The bird that knowes not the false *fowlers* call, III. i. 54. 8
Fowling-net. Entangled in a *fowling net*, *S.C.* Mar. 109
Fowls. made all other *Foules* his thralls to bee: *Van.* iv. 4
made him meat for wild *foules* of the ayre. *Gn.* 380
now the pray of *fowles* in field he lyes, I. v. 23. 3
Of *fowles* and beastes he made the piteous prayes, II. v. 26. 7
how the *fowles* in aire Doe flocke, II. vi. 28. 7
harmefull *fowles* about them fluttering cride, II. xii. 35. 7
For beasts and *foules* to feede upon for their repast. V. ix. 19. 9
Sitting like King of *fowles* in majesty and powre: VI. x. 6. 9
Ne have the watry *foules* a certaine grange VII. vii. 21. 7
a sight so fayre, Of *Fowles*, so lovely, *Proth.* 61
Fowls'. In his *Foules parley* durst not with it mel, VII. vii. 9. 5
Fowly. *See* **Foully.**
Fox. Will doe as did the *Foxe* by the Kidde. *S.C.* May 171
the *Foxe*, maister of collusion: *S.C.* May 219
the false *Foxe* came to the dore anone: *S.C.* May 236
Not as a *Foxe*, for then he had be kend, *S.C.* May 237
the *Foxe* him spyed; *S.C.* May 253
in came The false *Foxe*, *S.C.* May 279
the *Foxe* and th' Ape by him misguided; *Hub.* 38
The *Foxe* and th' Ape, disliking of their evill *Hub.* 46
The *Foxe*, that first this cause of griefe did finde, *Hub.* 51
The *Foxe* was glad, and quickly did agree: *Hub.* 102
'Now surely brother (said the *Foxe* anon) *Hub.* 124
(Said then the *Foxe*) *Hub.* 194
The *Foxe* him spying, bad the Ape him dight *Hub.* 233
this Curdog, . . . (Meaning the *Foxe*) *Hub.* 295
And the false *Foxe* his dog *Hub.* 304
The *Foxe* then counsel'd th' Ape *Hub.* 325
now the *Foxe* had gotten him a gowne, *Hub.* 353
Said then the *Foxe*: *Hub.* 403
The *Foxe* was well induc'd to be a Parson, *Hub.* 480
th' Ape and *Foxe* ere long so well them sped, *Hub.* 552
the *Foxe*, deep groning in his sprite, *Hub.* 588
'Foolish *Foxe* (said the Mule) *Hub.* 595
'Ay me! (said then the *Foxe*) *Hub.* 601
the slie *Foxe*, as like to be his groome, *Hub.* 661
this *Foxe* could not so closely hide His craftie feates, *Hub.* 919
the *Foxe*, his copesmate he had found, *Hub.* 939
him the *Foxe* with hardy words did stay, *Hub.* 957
'Fond Ape! (sayd then the *Foxe*) *Hub.* 977
the *Foxe* guilefull, and most covetous; *Hub.* 1022
'Nay (said the *Foxe*) *Hub.* 1033
the false *Foxe* him helped to array. *Hub.* 1063
unto them the *Foxe* alowd did cry, *Hub.* 1070
Till that the *Foxe* forth toward them did goe, *Hub.* 1074
sent the *Foxe* to them streightway, *Hub.* 1095
The subtile *Foxe* so well his message sayd, *Hub.* 1101
Strongly encorag'd by the crafty *Foxe*; *Hub.* 1104
Eftsones by counsell of the *Foxe* alone, *Hub.* 1112
Like as the *Foxe* did guide his graceles skill; *Hub.* 1128
the false *Foxe* most kindly plaid his part; *Hub.* 1137
The *Foxe* had promised of friendship store, *Hub.* 1206
(then said the *Foxe*) *Hub.* 1213
the *Foxe*, and his false blandishment: *Hub.* 1274
The wicked weed, which there the *Foxe* did lay, *Hub.* 1321
the false *Foxe*, when he the Lion heard, *Hub.* 1359
The *Foxe*, first Author of that treacherie, *Hub.* 1379
the whiles the *Foxe* is crept Into the hole, *Ti.* 216
Like as a wily *Foxe*, *Mui.* 401
Now like a *foxe*, now like a dragon fell; I. ii. 10. 6
Into a *Foxe* himselfe he first did tourne; V. ix. 17. 1
he him hunted like a *Foxe* full fast: V. ix. 17. 2
I hunt the *Fox*, VI. ix. 23. 1
Foxes. if *foxes* bene so crafty as so, *S.C.* May 312
The more bene the *Foxes* that here remaine. *S.C.* S. 155
Fox's. with the *Foxes* helpe them borne aside *Hub.* 1017
Done through the *Foxes* great oppressions, *Hub.* 1312
at her rompe she growing had behind A *foxes* taile, I. viii. 48. 4
Foy. *See* **Sansfoy.**
of them both did *foy* and tribute raise, II. x. 41. 4
Foynd. *See* **Foined.**

Fradubio. once a man, *Fradubio,* now a tree; . . . . I. ii. 33. 3
'Say on, *Fradubio,* . . . Quoth them the Knight; . . . . I. ii. 34. 1
The false Duessa, . . . Heard how in vaine *Fradubio* did lament, ... I. ii. 44. 2
Fraelissa. *Fraelissa* was as faire as faire mote bee, ... I. ii. 37. 8
Fragments. these olde *fragments* are for paternes borne: . . . *Ro.* xxvii. 8
Fragrant. 'The *fragrant* flowres, that in my garden grewe, . . *S.C.* D. 109
the *fragrant* Eglantine did spred His prickling armes, ... II. v. 29. 4
fragrant violets, and Paunces trim; . . . . III. i. 36. 8
As fresh and *fragrant* as the floure-deluce . . . . IV. i. 31. 7
fragrant odours they uppon her threw; . . . . VI. x. 14. 8
fragrant flowers doe give most odorous smell; . . . . *Am.* lxiv. 13
woodbynd flowers and *fragrant* Eglantine; . . . . *Am.* lxxi. 10
Be strewed with *fragrant* flowers all along, ... *Epith.* 50
Flowers . . . did *fragrant* odours yeild, ... *Proth.* 75
Fraight, -ed. *See* **Freight, -ed.**
Frail. buildes so stronglie on so *frayle* a soyle, ... *Ti.* 513
how can *fraile* fleshly wight Forecast, ... *Mui.* 226
the strong shackles of *fraile* flesh,' . . . . *D.* 86
Of fleshlie slime and *fraile* mortalitie; . . . . *D.* 403
was it but a wooden frame and *fraile,* . . . . *Col.* 216
us *fraile* men, his wretched vassals here, ... *Col.* 813
'My weaker yeares, Captiv'd to . . . *frayle* worldly feares, . . I. i. 52. 5
his grudging ghost did strive With the *fraile* flesh; . . . . . . I. ii. 19. 8
Both which *fraile* men doe oftentimes mistake, ... I. ii. 32. 7
my *frayle* eies these lines with teares do steepe, ... I. iii. 2. 3
whose glorious vew Their *frayle* amazed senses did confound: . I. iv. 7. 3
The yron walles to ward their blowes are weak and *fraile.* . . I. v. 6. 9
made wide furrowes in their fleshes *fraile,* . . . . I. vi. 43. 5
mightie strong was turnd to feeble *frayle.* . . . . I. vii. 6. 5
that *fraile* fountain which him feeble made, ... I. vii. 11. 8
That makes *frayle* flesh to feare the bitter wave, ... I. ix. 40. 5
Perceived him to waver, weake and *fraile,* . . . . I. ix. 49. 2
'Come; come away, *fraile,* feeble, fleshly wight, ... I. ix. 53. 1
his *fraile* thighes, nigh weary and fordonne, ... I. x. 47. 8
her strength recur'd from *fraile* infirmitis.' . . . . I. x. 52. 9
fraile affection did constraine His stout courage to stoupe, . . II. i. 42. 8
Els never should thy judgement be so *frayle* . . . . II. iii. 16. 4
How shall *frayle* pen descrive her heavenly face, ... II. iii. 25. 8
thine armes seem strong, but manhood *frayl:* . . . . II. v. 5. 6
Can call out of the bodies of *fraile* wightes; . . . . II. v. 27. 5
his *frayle* eye with spoyle of beauty feedes: . . . . II. v. 34. 3
For to allure *fraile* mind to carelesse ease: . . . . II. vi. 13. 6
with strong reason maistred passion *fraile,* . . . . II. vi. 40. 4
in *frayle* wood on Adrian gulf doth fleet, ... II. vii. 14. 4
Frayle men are oft captiv'd to covetise; . . . . II. vii. 15. 2
I, that am *fraile* flesh and earthly wight, ... II. vii. 50. 3
In *frayle* intemperaunce through sinfull bayt; . . . . II. vii. 64. 2
this *frayle* life of man, ... II. vii. 65. 4
fraile pen, with feare disparaged, ... II. x. 2. 8
through infirmity Of the *fraile* flesh, ... II. xi. 1. 6
Your stubborne hart t' affect with *fraile* infirmity. . . . . . II. xii. 28. 9
with which she thrild *Fraile* harts, ... II. xii. 78. 8
Sad, solemne, sowre, and full of fancies *fraile,* . . . . III. ii. 27. 5
Now ranckleth in this same *fraile* fleshly mould, ... III. ii. 39. 3
if the passion mayster thy *fraile* might, ... III. ii. 46. 6
Least his *fraile* senses were emperisht quight, ... III. vii. 20. 8
to deceive *Fraile* Ladies hart . . . . III. vii. 46. 4
Deepe indignation and compassion *frayle* . . . . III. viii. 31. 4
Fashioning . . . fancies evermore In her *fraile* witt, ... III. ix. 52. 5
The whiles the passing brightnes her *fraile* sences dazd. . . . III. xi. 49. 9
the *frayle* soule in deepe delight nigh drownd: . . . . III. xii. 6. 5
By which *fraile* youth is oft to follie led, ... IV. Pr. 1. 6
doth dayly grow Amongst *fraile* men, ... IV. i. 19. 3
pardon her besought his errour *frayle,* . . . . IV. vi. 22. 6
did *fraile* sense entice, ... IV. x. 22. 9
did him selfe from *fraile* impatience refraine. . . . . VI. i. 30. 9
All flesh is *frayle* and full of ficklenesse, ... VI. i. 41. 7
conceiving then great feare Of my *fraile* safetie, ... VI. ii. 29. 3
They fall too short of our *fraile* reckonings, ... VI. iii. 5. 4
To her *fraile* mansion of mortality: . . . . VI. iii. 28. 3
From things that stirre up *fraile* affection; . . . . VI. vi. 7. 7
'Speake, thou *fraile* woman, speake with confidence; . . . . . VII. vi. 25. 7
my *fraile* spirit . . . Lift up aloft, ... VII. vii. 1. 3
my *fraile* wit cannot devize to what It to compare, ... VII. vii. 7. 4
kindled heavenly fyre In my *fraile* spirit, ... *Am.* iii. 4
to lead *fraile* mindes to rest In chast desires, ... *Am.* viii. 7
mens *frayle* eyes, which gaze too bold, ... *Am.* xxxvii. 5
All flesh is *frayle,* . . . . *Am.* lviii. 5
my *fraile* fancy, fed with full delight, ... *Am.* lxxii. 9
my *frayle* thoughts too rashly led astray! . . . . *Am.* lxxvi. 6
permanent and free From *frayle* corruption, ... *Am.* lxxix. 8
Fraile men, whose eyes seek heavenly things to see, ... *H.L.* 118
free from fleshes *frayle* infection. . . . . *H.B.* 217
He downe descended, . . . in fleshes *fraile* attyre, ... *H.H.L.* 137
But we, *fraile* wights! whose sight cannot sustaine . . . . . . *H.H.B.* 120
Clear'd from grosse mists of *fraile* infirmities. . . . . *H.H.B.* 140
Frailness. though graft in *frailnesse* feminine. . . . . *Col.* 918
Frailty. Through fleshes *frailtie,* and deceipt of sin. . . . . . *T.M.* 492
Ne will I rest my limmes for *frailtie,* . . . . *D.* 461
(all flesh doth *frayltie* breed) . . . . II. i. 52. 6
Are bownd with commun bond of *frailtee,* . . . . III. v. 36. 8
To suppliants, through *frayltie* which offend: . . . . V. ix. 32. 4
Frame. On hill, a *frame* an hundred cubites hie . . . . *Bel.*[1] ii. 1
To beare the *frame,* foure great Lions . . . . *Bel.* iii. 10
a stately *frame,* An hundred cubits high . . . . *Bel.*[2] ii. 1
overthrew this *frame* with ruine great. . . . . *Bel.*[2] ii. 14
on sand was built the goodly *frame:* . . . . *Bel.*[2] xiv. 4
To *frame* this world that doth endure so long? . . . . *Ro.* ix. 6
dissolving his moist *frame,* . . . . *Ro.* xx. 7

Frame—*Continued.*
Well couth he tune his pipe and *frame* his stile: . . . . *S.C.* Ja. 10
Frame to thy songe their chereful cheriping, ... *S.C.* Jun. 55
my carefull case to *frame:* . . . . *S.C.* Jun. 78
bene thy Bagpypes renne farre out of *frame?* . . . . *S.C.* Au. 3
Soone as thou gynst to sette thy notes in *frame,* . . . . . . *S.C.* O. 25
Working her formall rowmes in wexen *frame,* . . . . *S.C.* D. 68
learnd of lighter timber cotes to *frame,* . . . . *S.C.* D. 77
wont to *frame* my pype . . . . *S.C.* D. 115
for thy worth *frame* some fit Poesie: . . . . *Gn.* 12
Ne wist what answere unto him to *frame,* . . . . *Hub.* 313
Thereto he could fine loving verses *frame,* . . . . *Hub.* 809
gan he to himselfe new shape to *frame;* . . . . *Hub.* 1266
those sweete wits, which wont the like to *frame,* . . . . . . *T.M.* 203
was it but a wooden *frame* and fraile, ... *Col.* 216
that *frame,* which us did beare; . . . . *Col.* 287
fit to *frame* an everlasting dittie, ... *Col.* 385
Her name Ile teach in knowen terms to *frame:* . . . . *Col.* 637
imperiall Majestie to *frame* In loftie numbers . . . . *Ded. Son.* xii. 7
thereof did verses *frame;* . . . . I. i. 37. 2
of those braunches greene to *frame* A girlond . . . . I. ii. 30. 6
fitting gestures to her purpose *frame,* . . . . I. vii. 1. 6
old man, . . . on a staffe his feeble steps did *frame,* . . . . . I. viii. 30. 3
he had charge my discipline to *frame,* . . . . I. ix. 5. 3
mortall life he learned had to *frame* . . . . I. x. 45. 8
Cleopolis, for earthly *frame,* The fairest peece . . . . I. x. 59. 2
On which they lowly sitt, and fitting purpose *frame.* . . . . I. xii. 13. 9
Therefore this craftie engine he did *frame,* . . . . II. i. 23. 7
wondrous strong by nature, and by skilfull *frame.* . . . . . . II. ii. 12. 9
she her selfe thus busily did *frame* . . . . II. ii. 16. 1
unto thee dew worship I may rightly *frame.'* . . . . II. iii. 33. 9
all his actions *frame,* . . . . II. v. 1. 2
quite disparted all the linked *frame,* . . . . II. viii. 44. 7
The *frame* thereof seemd partly circulare, ... II. ix. 22. 1
To vew her Castles other wondrous *frame:* . . . . II. ix. 44. 7
That Turrets *frame* most admirable was, ... II. ix. 45. 1
That goodly *frame* from ruine to sustaine: . . . . II. xi. 15. 5
that goodly *frame* of Temperaunce . . . . II. xii. 1. 1
The skilfull Palmer formally did *frame:* . . . . II. xii. 81. 5
To which her steps directly she did *frame.* . . . . III. i. 20. 3
Whereto that single knight did answere *frame:* . . . . III. i. 24. 1
Long were it to describe the goodly *frame,* . . . . III. i. 31. 1
hostes of men of meanest thinges could *frame,* . . . . III. iii. 12. 6
diverse plots did *frame* to maske in strange disguise. . . . . III. iii. 51. 9
To your faire selves a faire ensample *frame* . . . . III. v. 54. 1
She there deviz'd a wondrous worke to *frame,* . . . . III. viii. 5. 2
he could well his glozing speaches *frame* . . . . III. viii. 14. 4
whatso my feeble Muse can *frame* . . . . III. viii. 43. 2
skill his words to *frame* . . . . III. ix. 32. 7
liberty to *frame* Their purpost flight, ... III. x. 16. 4
all that fraud did *frame* To have efforst the love . . . . III. xii. 43. 7
To see their thrids so thin as spiders *frame,* . . . . IV. ii. 50. 8
This goodly counterfesaunce he did *frame:* . . . . IV. iv. 27. 4
by no meanes they could it thereto *frame,* . . . . IV. v. 16. 5
Frame thunderbolts for Joves avengefull threate. . . . . IV. v. 37. 4
To *frame* such subtile wire, so shinie cleare; . . . . IV. vi. 20. 6
Her mournefull notes full piteously did *frame,* . . . . IV. viii. 4. 2
causelesse crimes continually to *frame,* . . . . IV. viii. 25. 2
all the service of the bodie *frame,* . . . . IV. ix. 2. 7
whose goodly pride And costly *frame* . . . . IV. x. 16. 3
frame in earth, and forme of substance base, ... IV. x. 21. 7
much admyring that so goodly *frame,* . . . . IV. x. 31. 1
The fertile Nile, which creatures new doth *frame;* . . . . . . IV. xi. 20. 3
To whom the elder did this aunswere *frame:* . . . . V. iv. 7. 1
Which she against the dred Mercilla oft did *frame.* . . . . . . V. ix. 40. 9
of his owne vaine fancies thought did *frame:* . . . . V. xi. 19. 4
Which though I be not wise enough to *frame,* . . . . VI. iv. 34. 8
as he them best could *frame,* . . . . VI. v. 4. 3
they ne might Endure to travell, nor one foote to *frame:* . . . VI. v. 40. 8
He to that point fit speaches gan to *frame,* . . . . VI. vi. 6. 2
him selfe to battell he did *frame;* . . . . VI. vi. 25. 8
to recomfort him all comely meanes did *frame.* . . . . VI. x. 29. 9
all the worlds faire *frame* . . . She alter'd quite; . . . . . . VII. vi. 5. 5
You *frame* my thoughts, and fashion me within; . . . . *Am.* viii. 9
all the bodie to thy hest doest *frame,* . . . . *H.L.* 44
all that in this mortall *frame* Contained is, ... *H.L.* 113
An honourable Hymne I eke should *frame,* . . . . *H.B.* 10
Frame to themselves most beautifull and brave . . . . *H.B.* 122
Before this worlds great *frame,* . . . found any being-place, . . *H.H.L.* 22
looke on the *frame* Of this wyde universe, ... *H.H.B.* 30
Framed. was *framed* to endure The bit of balefull steele . . . *Mui.* 61
The which the Lemnian God *framde* craftily, ... *Mui.* 370
Had *framed* for his finall overthroe. . . . . *Mui.* 424
Yet I her *fram'd,* and wan so to my bent, ... *D.* 124
Of ought that *framed* is of mortall moulde, ... *D.* 493
The one faire *fram'd* of burnisht Yvory, ... I. i. 40. 2
fram'd of liquid ayre her tender partes, ... I. i. 45. 3
Faire Una *framed* words and count'naunce fitt; . . . . I. iii. 14. 7
that divelish yron Engin, . . . *framd* by Furies skill, ... I. vii. 13. 2
of Diamond perfect pure and cleene It *framed* was, ... I. vii. 33. 6
new matter *fram'd* Upon the old, ... II. v. 21. 2
Framed of wanton Yvie, flouring fayre, ... II. v. 29. 3
Some *framd* faire lookes, ... II. v. 33. 3
Trees, braunches, birds, and songs, were *framed* fitt . . . . . II. vi. 13. 5
of more worthy substance *fram'd* it was: . . . . II. ix. 23. 5
Of that same wood it *fram'd* was cunningly, ... II. xii. 41. 1
Yt *framed* was of precious yvory, ... II. xii. 44. 1
all of purest bullion *framed* were, ... III. i. 32. 6
His maker with her charmes had *framed* him so well. . . . . III. vii. 35. 9
Whose like on earth was never *framed* yit; . . . . III. viii. 5. 3

Framed—*Continued.*
This mischiefe *framd* for their first loves defeature, . . . IV. vi. 17. 7
Framed in goldsmithes forge with cunning hand: . . . IV. vi. 20. 4
framed speaches fit for his behoofe, . . . IV. vii. 37. 7
stately pillours *fram'd* after the Doricke guize. . . . IV. x. 6. 9
framed With endlesse cost . . . IV. x. 30. 6
And men . . . at first were *framed* Of earthly mould, . . . V. Pr. 2. 3
was *framed* all of silver fine, . . . V. vii. 6. 2
could be *fram'd* by workmans rare device; . . . V. ix. 27. 8
an Altar *framed* Of costly Ivory, . . . V. x. 28. 2
The flesh of men, to Gods owne likenesse *framed*, . . . V. x. 28. 7
(whether wicked fate so *framed* Or fault of men,) . . . VI. xii. 38. 7
Most happy letters! *fram'd* by skilfull trade, . . . *Am.* lxxiv. 1
song, thus *fram'd* in praise of thee. . . . *H.L.* 307

Frames. though your *frames* do for a time make warre . . . *Ro.* vii. 9
frames her house, in which she will be placed, . . . *H.B.* 117

France. first garland of free Poesie That *France* brought forth, *Ro.* Env. 2
In *Fraunce* and Ireland left a famous gage; . . . *Ded. Son.* xiv. 11
Whose father Hercules in *Fraunce* did quell, . . . II. x. 11. 7
their Syre . . . from *Fraunce* was forced to retyre. . . . II. x. 22. 9
first opened The bowels of wide *Fraunce*, . . . II. x. 23. 7
subjected *France* and Germany, . . . II. x. 40. 6
old Gall, that now is cleeped *France*, . . . IV. xi. 16. 4

Franchise. To whom the world this *franchise* ever yeelded, . . IV. ix. 37. 6

Franchisement. to worke Irenaes *franchisement*, . . . V. xi. 36. 4

Francis'. The shaking Palsey, and Saint *Fraunces* fire, . . . I. iv. 35. 8

Franion. Might not be found a francker *franion*, . . . II. ii. 37. 4
some fayre *Franion*, fit for such a fere, . . . V. iii. 22. 7

Frank. Ay, *francke* shepheard, how bene thy verses meint . *S.C.* N. 203
Thou hast it wonne, for it is of *franke* gift, . . . *Hub.* 531
Over the fields, in his *franke* lustinesse, . . . *Mui.* 148
Ten times so much be nombred *francke* and free.' . . . II. vii. 9. 5
More *franke* affection did to her afford. . . . IV. i. 15. 7
in joyous jolliment Of their *franke* loves, . . . VI. ii. 16. 6
In doing gentle deedes with *franke* delight, . . . VI. vii. 1. 2

Franker. Might not be found a *francker* franion, . . . II. ii. 37. 4

Frankincense. Ne *frankincens* he from Panchaea buyth: . . . *Gn.* 133
Matching the wealth of th' auncient *Frankincence;* . . . *Gn.* 674
Her thoughts are like the fume of *Franckincense*, . . . *Col.* 608
They all perfumde with *frankincense* divine, . . . I. xii. 38. 3
th' altars fume with *frankincense* arownd, . . . III. iv. 17. 4
fuming all with *frankensence* I found . . . IV. x. 37. 2

Franklin. Where them does meete a *francklin* faire and free, I. x. 6. 4

Frankly. *Franckly* each Paramor his leman knowes, . . . III. vi. 41. 7
frankely there their loves desire possesse; . . . IV. x. 28. 6
Thereto they both did *franckly* condiscend, . . . V. i. 25. 8

Frantic. she halfe *frantick*, having slaine her sonne, . . . *Gn.* 175
Cybeles *franticke* rites have made them mad: . . . I. vi. 15. 3
the Gyaunt . . . all enrag'd with smart and *frantick* yre, . . I. viii. 17. 8
'What *franticke* fit,' (quoth he) 'hath thus distraught Thee . I. ix. 38. 1
when the *frantick* fitt inflamd his spright, . . . II. iv. 7. 3
with which she doth enrage Her *frantick* sonne, . . . II. iv. 11. 5
sith love is *franticke* hight. . . . III. vii. 20. 9
With *franticke* passion and with furie fraught; . . . V. viii. 48. 7
the *franticke* fit Her burning tongue with rage inflamed hath, . V. viii. 49. 1

Fraud. ful of *fraude*, and guile, . . . *S.C.* May 127
Sperre the yate fast for feare of *fraude:* . . . *S.C.* May 224
the more bene fraight with *fraud* and spight, . . . *S.C.* S. 84
from the falsers *fraude* . . . to keepe. . . . *S.C.* Env. 6
Young knight . . . Beware of *fraud*, beware of ficklenesse, . I. iv. 1. 3
least Force or *Fraud* should unaware Breake in, . . . II. vii. 25. 3
all that *fraud* did frame . . . III. xii. 43. 7
Ne each of other feared *fraud* or tort, . . . IV. viii. 31. 3
Farre from all *fraud* or fayned blandishment; . . . IV. x. 26. 7
Some fearing *fraud*, some fraudulently fayning, . . . IV. x. 43. 5
ne *fraud* in wight was to be found: . . . V. Pr. 9. 4
like full of *fraud* and guile, . . . V. vi. 33. 2

Fraudulent. him doth chyde as false and *fraudulent*, . . . IV. xii. 23. 2

Fraudulently. Some fearing fraud, some *fraudulently* fayning, . IV. x. 43. 5

Fraught. his false hart, *fraught* with all treasons store, . . *Mui.* 395
Or *fraught* with envie that their galls do swell, . . . *Col.* 760
he was false, and *fraught* with ficklenesse, . . . I. iv. 25. 5
sad Una *fraught* with anguish sore, . . . I. vi. 45. 7
With windy Nitre and quick Sulphur *fraught*, . . . I. vii. 13. 3
fraught with rancour and engorged yre, . . . I. xi. 40. 5
fraught with fowle despight, . . . II. iv. 29. 1
fraught with great griefe And wrath, . . . II. viii. 33. 1
Glad was the knight, and with fresh courage *fraught*, . . . II. viii. 40. 5
forth together went with sorow *fraught*. . . . III. iv. 31. 7
Gardins of Adonis *fraught* With pleasures . . . III. vi. Arg.
From her sweete bowres, and beds with pleasures *fraught?* . III. vi. 20. 4
A wicked Spright, *yfraught* with fawning guyle . . . III. viii. 8. 1
great sackes with endlesse riches *fraught* . . . V. ii. 23. 4
Having the mindes of men with fury *fraught*, . . . V. vii. 11. 4
Then up she rose *fraught* with melancholy, . . . V. vii. 17. 5
the Souldan all with furie *fraught*, . . . V. viii. 28. 1
With franticke passion and with furie *fraught;* . . . V. viii. 48. 7
Therewith all *fraught* with fury and disdaine, . . . V. xi. 8. 1
Out of her poysnous entrails *fraught* with dire decay.' . . . V. xi. 20. 9
The other held a snake with venime *fraught*, . . . V. xii. 30. 5
fortune, *fraught* with malice, . . . VI. x. 38. 7
then the Captaine, *fraught* with more displeasure, . . . VI. xi. 14. 7
her wombe, unwist to wight, was *fraught*, . . . VI. xii. 6. 4
All were she *fraught* with pride and impudence, . . . VII. vi. 25. 2
Fayre soyle . . . *fraught* with store Of all that deare . . . *Am.* lxiii. 7
Fayre bosome! *fraught* with vertues richest tresure, . . . *Am.* lxxvi. 1
That all the world shold with his rimes be *fraught!* . . . *H.H.B.* 224
And senses *fraught* with such satietie, . . . *H.H.B.* 282

Fray. Bearing the fire with which heaven doth us *fray*, . . . *Ro.* xvii. 2
their service . . . To aide his friendes, or *fray* his enimies. . . I. i. 38. 5

Fray—*Continued.*
She . . . bad her knight addresse him to the *fray*, . . . I. ii. 14. 5
Disdaind to loose the meed he wonne in *fray;* . . . I. iv. 39. 8
the Paynim lay, . . . since his late luckelesse *fray*. . . . I. v. 29. 5
much rejoyced in their bloody *fray:* . . . I. vi. 48. 4
So diversly them selves in vaine they *fray;* . . . I. xii. 11. 7
Some troublous uprore or contentious *fray*, . . . II. iv. 3. 3
Goemot, whome in stout *fray* Corineus conquered, . . . II. x. 10. 8
When so him list his enimies to *fray;* . . . III. iii. 12. 7
when they were accorded from the *fray*, . . . III. ix. 17. 3
there the relicks of the drunken *fray*, . . . IV. i. 23. 1
to see the fortune of that *fray*, . . . IV. iii. 4. 7
By her subdewed in victorious *fray:* . . . V. v. 21. 5
He to her told the story of that *fray*, . . . V. vi. 30. 8
For her beginning a more fearefull *fray*, . . . V. viii. 10. 6
There then began a fearefull cruell *fray* . . . VI. i. 36. 1
To weet the cause of so uncomely *fray*, . . . VI. ii. 4. 4
When the bold Centaures made that bloudy *fray* . . . VI. x. 13. 4
who them sees would wonder at their *fray*, . . . VI. xi. 17. 7
when as he was dead, the *fray* gan ceasse; . . . VI. xi. 20. 3
but that his looks them *fray;* . . . *Am.* liii. 2
Fray us with things that be not: . . . *Epith.* 344

Frayed. The Lyon *frayed* them, him in to lett. . . . I. iii. 19. 3
as a man whom hellish feendes have *frayd*, . . . II. viii. 46. 4
could have *frayd* one with the very sight, . . . V. xii. 15. 7
He ran at him enraged, instead of being *frayde*. . . . VI. x. 35. 9

Fraying. Instead of *fraying*, they them selves did feare, . . II. xii. 40. 6

Frays. What *frayes* ye, that were wont to comfort me af-frayd?' . . . I. i. 52. 9
in vaine glorious *frayes* he litle did delight. . . . I. vi. 20. 9
many battailes fought and many *fraies* . . . II. iii. 38. 5
subdewde in equall *frayes* . . . II. v. 26. 5
stirre up bloudie *frayes*, . . . IV. i. 47. 8

Freaks. her ship, tost with so manie *freakes*, . . . *Ro.* xxi. 5
Fortunes *freakes*, is wisely taught to beare: . . . *T.M.* 130
Through envies snares, or fortunes *freakes* unkind. . . . I. iii. 1. 4
I feare the fickle *freakes*,' . . . 'Of fortune false, . . . I. iv. 50. 1
So tossed was in fortunes cruell *freakes:* . . . I. xii. 16. 8

Free. my *free* spirite might not . . . Be vext . . . *Pet.*[2] vii. 7
Bellay, first garland of *free* Poesie . . . *Ro.* Env. 1
Walke in Elisian fieldes so *free*. . . . *S.C.* N. 179
thou hast a *free* passeporte; . . . *S.C.* Env. 7
with pure brest from carefull sorrow *free*, . . . *Gn.* 107
Free from sad cares . . . *Gn.* 136
Free from all troubles and from worldly toyle, . . . *Gn.* 151
Alceste . . . *Free* from all care, . . . *Gn.* 426
Like two *free* men, . . . *Hub.* 160
Free men some beggers call, but they be *free*, . . . *Hub.* 161
wander *free* Where so us listeth, . . . *Hub.* 168
have the Gospell of *free* libertie.' . . . *Hub.* 478
In the wilde forrest raunging fresh and *free*. . . . *Hub.* 630
Free libertie to chaunt our charmes at will, . . . *T.M.* 244
Were wont to play, from all annoyance *free*, . . . *Ti.* 138
now in Elisian *fields* so free, . . . *Ti.* 332
strugled long, Himselfe to *free* thereout; . . . *Mui.* 426
as I the fields did range Fearelesse and *free*, . . . *D.* 107
old Palemon *free* from spight . . . *Col.* 396
knitting all his force, got one hand *free*, . . . I. i. 19. 7
he sate upon his courser *free*, . . . I. ii. 11. 8
One . . . Full strongly armd, and on a courser *free* . . . I. iii. 33. 3
the noble Prince . . . made himselfe *free* enterance. . . . I. viii. 34. 7
Raunging the forest wide on courser *free*, . . . I. ix. 12. 7
tellen *free* The secrete cause . . . I. ix. 25. 4
Sir Terwin . . . was both bold and *free*, . . . I. ix. 27. 4
free his feet that in the myre sticke fast? . . . I. ix. 39. 5
Where them does meete a francklin faire and *free*, . . . I. x. 6. 4
gave them ever *free*. . . . I. x. 43. 9
does *free* it selfe by fight. . . . I. xi. 19. 9
since mine he is, or *free* or bond, . . . I. xii. 28. 1
long captived soules from weary thraldome *free*. . . . II. i. 36. 9
To chaunge thy will, and set Occasion *free*, . . . II. v. 17. 8
to thee I yield them *free*.' . . . II. v. 18. 6
When ever his fiers handes he *free* mote fynd: . . . II. v. 28. 4
Ten times so much be nombred francke and *free*.' . . . II. vii. 9. 5
how more bold and *free* . . . II. xii. 74. 7
Now were they liegmen to this Ladie *free*, . . . III. i. 44. 8
In his *free* thought to build her sluggish nest, . . . III. v. 2. 2
The hevens so favorable were and *free*, . . . III. vi. 2. 2
From peril *free* he away her did beare; . . . III. vii. 24. 8
when hee saw him selfe *free* from poursute, . . . III. viii. 14. 1
to be *free* from hard restraynt and gealous feares. . . . III. ix. 4. 9
Each gan . . . weary armour *free*, . . . III. ix. 19. 7
False love! . . . Thou walkest *free*, . . . III. x. 4. 6
free from all mens reclame; . . . III. x. 16. 5
That did her win and *free* from chalenge set: . . . IV. i. 12. 4
Love is *free*, and led with selfe delight, . . . IV. i. 46. 8
Not all the gods can chaunge, nor Jove him self can *free!* . IV. ii. 51. 9
from feare of treason *free*, . . . IV. iii. 49. 4
I, who stood all fearelesse *free*, . . . IV. viii. 58. 6
All which he did from bitter bondage *free*, . . . IV. ix. 8. 6
The faire Poeana, he enlarged *free*, . . . IV. ix. 13. 2
hearke, ye gentle knights and Ladies *free*, . . . IV. x. 3. 6
in this joyous place they mote have joyance *free*. . . . IV. x. 23. 9
being *free* from feare and gealosye . . . IV. x. 28. 5
unlesse some heavenly powre her *free* . . . IV. xi. 1. 6
most *free* from fowle despight, . . . IV. xi. 18. 8
So had I rather to be thrall then *free;* . . . IV. xii. 10. 8
The which the prisoner points unto the *free!* . . . IV. xii. 11. 2
Together with her selfe in dowry *free;* . . . V. iv. 12. 8
Yet would she not thereto yeeld *free* accord . . . V. v. 27. 6

Free—*Continued.*
by his freedome get his *free* goodwill; V. v. 32. 8
That in and out thou mayst have passage *free.* V. v. 34. 5
if she would *free* him from that case, V. v. 55. 8
she did from thraldome *free,* V. vii. 43. 2
Prince Arthure and Sir Artegall *Free* Samient from feare: V. viii. Arg.
Most sacred wight, most debonayre and *free,* V. ix. 20. 7
none tydings bore Of Artegals arryvall her to *free,* V. xii. 11. 6
I, that knew my selfe from perill *free,* VI. i. 9. 7
shall it not her lockes, for raunsome fro me *free.'* VI. i. 19. 9
Sate with a knight . . . *free* from all gealous spyes. VI. ii. 16. 6
did *free* from feare Of a discourteous Knight, VI. iii. 18. 5
him selfe he thought from daunger *free,* VI. iii. 20. 6
From whom he meant to *free* him, if he might, VI. iv. 3. 8
whether *free* with him she now were, or in band? VI. v. 27. 9
Whom when the Salvage saw from daunger *free,* VI. vi. 40. 1
turne we now backe to that Ladie *free,* VI. vii. 27. 7
She was borne *free,* not bound to any wight, VI. vii. 30. 8
Leading a life so *free* and fortunate VI. ix. 19. 3
Simple and true, from convert malice *free;* VI. x. 24. 5
free from all that wite VI. xii. 41. 4
Fondnesse it were for any, being *free,* *Am.* xxxvii. 13
permanent and *free* From frayle corruption, *Am.* lxxix. 7
From feare of perrill and foule horror *free.* *Epith.* 322
And thou, fayre Hebe! and thou, Hymen *free!* *Epith.* 405
To let her live thus *free,* and me to dy. *H.L.* 154
free from fleshes frayle infection. *H.B.* 217
Like Gods with Nectar in their bankets *free;* *H.B.* 249
To *free* his foes, that from his heast had swerved! *H.H.L.* 161
But he our life hath left unto us *free,* *H.H.L.* 183
Free that was thrall, and blessed that was band; *H.H.L.* 184
And give thy selfe unto him full and *free,* *H.H.L.* 265
dowre, Which mighty God hath given to her *free,* *H.H.B.* 251
Free-born. sith then we are *free borne,* *Hub.* 133
Freed. eft, when ye count you *freed* from feare, *S.C.* F. 42
freed from bands of impacable fate, *Ti.* 395
The faire Andromeda from perill *freed:* *Ti.* 649
freed from wretched long imprisonment! *D.* 273
freed is from Cupids yoke by fate, *Col.* 566
his ghost, *freed* from repining strife, I. iii. 36. 5
he *freed* the Traveilers high-way, II. x. 39. 3
freed from that foster insolent, III. iv. 50. 7
I your vassall, by your prowesse *freed,* III. xii. 39. 7
eke fayre Amoret, now *freed* from feare, IV. i. 15. 6
Who, being *freed,* from one a weapon fiercely takes. IV. iv. 34. 9
sith you her *freed* fro thence IV. vi. 34. 7
from that time I from enchaunters theft Her *freed,* IV. vi. 35. 5
freed from feare and danger of that dismall wight. IV. vii. 33. 9
being *freed* from Proteus cruell band V. iii. 2. 1
he him selfe full lightly from him *freed,* V. xi. 9. 3
when that Knight from peril cleare was *freed,* V. xi. 48. 1
That yet my love may from their hands be *freed.'* V. xi. 57. 5
having *freed* Irena from distresse, V. xii. 27. 8
Whom from her Seneschall he lately *freed,* VI. i. 47. 4
God . . . had them *freed* from that deadly feare, VI. iv. 15. 3
like an Hauke, which feeling her selfe *freed* VI. iv. 19. 7
Serena, found of Salvages, By Calepine is *freed.* VI. viii. Arg.
Thy country may be *freed* *Proth.* 156
Freedom. My *freedome* lorne, my life he lefte to mone. *S.C.* D. 52
In the pride of his *freedome* principall: *Mui.* 380
Whose *freedom* shall thee turne to greatest scath! II. v. 18. 4
his exchange or *freedom* might be wrought. IV. viii. 58. 4
of their loves choise they might *freedom* clame, IV. ix. 37. 7
Could she her wished *freedome* fro me wooe: IV. x. 57. 5
Such thraldome or such *freedome* let it surely be. IV. xii. 10. 9
uncontrolled *freedome* to obtaine. V. ii. 33. 5
the heavens unjust, Spighting my happie *freedome,* V. v. 29. 8
by his *freedome* get his free goodwill; V. v. 32. 8
Life, *freedome,* grace, and gifts of great availe, V. v. 49. 3
his *freedome* to have gayned, V. v. 54. 3
her Dame his *freedome* did denye. V. v. 56. 9
Untill his owne true love his *freedome* gayned: V. v. 57. 8
they to *freedome* did retyre. VI. xii. 10. 5
Freeing. For *freeing* from their snares Irena thrall: V. xii. 37. 5
Freely. Usen we *freely* our felicitie; *S.C.* May 155
Thy lovely layes here mayst thou *freely* boste *S.C.* Jun. 13
none whom fortune *freely* doth advaunce *Gn.* 555
their owne happie chaunce Them *freely* offred, *Hub.* 963
freely up those royall spoyles he tooke, *Hub.* 1059
But *freely* doest, of what thee list, entreat, *Com. Son.* i. 9
all good, all grace there *freely* growes, *Col.* 324
'Yet shall they not escape so *freely* all, I. v. 26. 1
from her cursed foe thou have her *freely* quitt.' I. x. 63. 9
freely sprong out of the fruitfull grownd, I. xi. 47. 3
in a body which doth *freely* yeeld II. xi. 2. 1
As *freely* offering to be gathered; II. xii. 54. 6
freely read what wicked felon so Hath outrag'd you, III. xi. 15. 2
All is his justly that all *freely* dealth. IV. i. 6. 5
to her bed . . . Now *freely* drew, IV. i. 15. 9
if she should him *freely* set, IV. viii. 53. 8
all things *freely* grew V. Pr. 9. 7
his hart was *freely* plast. V. v. 46. 9
She *freely* gave that Castle for his paine, VI. i. 46. 7
not so *freely,* but that nathelesse He unto her a penance VI. vii. 37. 5
Unto your selfe I *freely* leave to chose, VI. viii. 29. 8
Right happy thou that mayst them *freely* see! VI. x. 19. 8
freely wend, Or at more ease continue there VI. xi. 6. 7
he *freely* drinks an health to all his peeres. VII. vii. 41. 9
He *freely* gave to be both rent and torne *H.H.L.* 150
That full and *freely* gave himselfe to thee. *H.H.L.* 266

Frees. Himselfe he *frees* by secret meanes unseene; II. i. 1. 8
She fights with Radigund, . . . And Artegall thence *frees.* V. vii. Arg.
Free will. None would choose goodnes of his owne *freewill.* *T.M.* 456
every dore of *freewill* open flew. I. viii. 5. 3
Of God; of grace; of justice; of *free-will;* I. x. 19. 6
lordeth in licentious blisse Of her *freewill,* *Am.* x. 4
Freeze. his fresh blood did *frieze* with fearefull cold, II. i. 42. 3
He gan to burne in rage, and *friese* in feare, V. xi. 2. 6
the Shepheard streight with jealousie did *frize.* VI. x. 33. 9
on his hoary beard his breath did *freese,* VII. vii. 31. 3
Not fyre: for she doth *friese* with faint desire. *Am.* lv. 8
Freezeth. The more she *frieseth* in her wilfull pryde; *Am.* xxxii. 10
Freezing. My life-bloud *friesing* with unkindly cold; *S.C.* Ja. 26
Now boyling hot, streight *friezing* deadly cold; VII. vii. 23. 3
Freight. the more bene *fraight* with fraud and spight, *S.C.* S. 84
all with suddein indignation *fraight,* I. xii. 35. 2
Freighted. With rich treasures this gay ship *fraighted* was: *Pet.* ii. 6
Frenne. So now his frend is chaunged for a *frenne.* *S.C.* Ap. 28
Frenzy. The swelling Splene, and *Frenzy* raging rife, I. iv. 35. 7
love to *frenzy* turnd, sith love is franticke hight. III. vii. 20. 9
Frequent. Gan more the same *frequent,* and further to invade. II. x. 6. 9
to resort To common haunts, and companies *frequent,* V. xii. 34. 7
Frequented. shepheard, . . . *Frequented* of these gentle Nymphes VI. x. 19. 4
Fresh. I saw a *fresh* spring rise out of a rocke, *Bel.*[1] x. 1
the *fresh* and lustie Lawrell tree, *Pet.* iii. 2
Whilome thy *fresh* spring flowrd, *S.C.* Ja. 21
Seest how *fresh* my flowers bene spredde, *S.C.* F. 129
Where-with my *fresh* flowretts bene defast: *S.C.* F. 182
When love-lads masken in *fresh* aray? *S.C.* May 2
a *fresh* bend Of lovely Nymphs. *S.C.* May 32
both *fresh* and lovely to see, *S.C.* May 183
should it nat yshend Your roundels *fresh,* *S.C.* Au. 140
Cuddie, *fresh* Cuddie, the liefest boye, *S.C.* Au. 195
It floureth *fresh,* as it should never fayle.' *S.C.* N. 86
The fieldes ay *fresh,* the grasse ay greene. *S.C.* N. 189
In the *fresh* shadowe did for them prepayre, *Gn.* 188
The Lilly *fresh,* and Violet belowe; *Gn.* 667
The purple Hyacinthe, and *fresh* Costmarie; *Gn.* 670
Fresh Rhododaphne, and the Sabine flowre, *Gn.* 673
To cloath her selfe in colours *fresh* and new, *Gn.* 684
In the wilde forrest raunging *fresh* and free. *Hub.* 630
all that els seemd faire and *fresh* *T.M.* 39
those *fresh* buds, which wont so faire to flowre, *T.M.* 249
The *fresh* yong flie, in whom the kindly fire *Mui.* 33
joy'd to range abroad in *fresh* attire, *Mui.* 37
Thus the *fresh* Clarion, being readie dight, *Mui.* 145
Fresh Costmarie, and breathfull Camomill, *Mui.* 195
her leafe was greene, and *fresh* her rinde, *D.* 240
He had a daughter *fresh* as floure of May, *Col.* 106
There fruitfull corne, faire trees, *fresh* herbage is, *Col.* 298
Faire spreading forth her leaves with *fresh* delight, *Col.* 545
with *fresh* clay did close the wooden wound: I. ii. 44. 8
girlonds gay, That seemd as *fresh* as Flora in her prime; I. iv. 17. 3
Phoebus, *fresh* as brydegrome to his mate, I. v. 2. 3
Their gory sides *fresh* bleeding fiercely frett; I. vi. 44. 5
love *fresh* coles unto her fire did lay; I. vii. 27. 5
There for to find a *fresh* unproved knight, I. vii. 47. 2
Forth gushed, like *fresh* water streame from riven rocke. I. viii. 10. 9
you, *fresh* budd of vertue springing fast, I. viii. 27. 1
that *fresh* bleeding wound, I. ix. 7. 3
With *fresh* desire his voyage to pursew; I. ix. 18. 4
blood . . . from his wound yet welled *fresh,* I. ix. 36. 7
to his *fresh* remembraunce did reverse The ugly vew I. ix. 48. 5
fresh encounter towardes him addrest; I. xi. 17. 2
Forth flowed *fresh* A gushing river of blacke gory blood, I. xi. 22. 3
As Eagle, *fresh* out of the ocean wave, I. xi. 34. 3
Whom when the damned feend so *fresh* did spy, I. xi. 35. 1
As *fresh* as flowres in medow greene doe grow I. xii. 6. 7
Diana in *fresh* sommers day Beholdes her nymphes I. xii. 7. 7
So faire and *fresh* that Lady shewd herselfe in sight. I. xii. 21. 9
So faire and *fresh,* as freshest flowre in May; I. xii. 22. 1
his *fresh* blood did frieze with fearefull cold, II. i. 42. 3
fresh streames do flow, II. ii. 9. 2
revive *Fresh* memory in me of that great Queene, II. ii. 40. 2
flourishing *fresh* leaves and blossomes did enwrap. II. iii. 30. 9
with *fresh* onsett he assayld, II. v. 11. 3
Amidst a flock of Damzelles *fresh* and gay, II. v. 32. 4
therein sate a Lady *fresh* and fayre, II. vi. 3. 1
fresh flowrets dight About her necke, II. vi. 7. 4
They spring, they bud, they blossome *fresh* and faire, II. vi. 15. 6
Out of the wound the red blood flowed *fresh,* II. viii. 36. 8
Glad was the knight, and with *fresh* courage fraught, II. viii. 40. 5
With so *fresh* hew uprysing him to see, II. viii. 54. 3
when againe They gave *fresh* charge, II. ix. 14. 3
was right faire and *fresh* as morning rose, II. ix. 36. 7
A man of yeares yet *fresh,* as mote appere, II. ix. 52. 3
with *fresh* corage on the victor servd: II. x. 55. 7
fresh begon That castle to assaile II. xi. 5. 3
then assayle him *fresh,* ere he could shift for more. II. xi. 27. 9
to him brought, *fresh* batteill to renew; II. xi. 28. 3
Out of his swowne arose, *fresh* to contend, II. xi. 35. 4
(For shee her weend a *fresh* and lusty knight,) III. i. 47. 3
spred Abroad thy *fresh* youths fayrest flowre, III. ii. 31. 7
In a *fresh* fountaine, far from all mens vew, III. vi. 6. 6
he is faire and *fresh* in face and guize III. vi. 23. 7
Th' one faire and *fresh,* the other old and dride. III. vi. 31. 7
As doth the lilly *fresh* before the sunny ray. III. vi. 38. 9
with *fresh* colours decke the wanton Pryme, III. vi. 42. 4
Fresh Hyacinthus, Phoebus paramoure III. vi. 45. 3

Fresh—*Continued.*
more *fresh* And fierce he still appeard, . . . III. vii. 32. 8
His former griefe with furie *fresh* reviv'd . . . III. viii. 3. 4
floures so *fresh* at morne, . . . III. ix. 39. 9
fresh Aurora had the shady damp . . . amoved . . . III. x. 1. 3
the *fresh* Swayne would not his leasure dwell, . . . III. x. 38. 7
The jolly Satyres, full of *fresh* delight, . . . III. x. 44. 3
With perfect peace and bandes of *fresh* accord, . . . III. x. 51. 4
She chearfull, *fresh,* and full of joyaunce glad, . . . III. xii. 18. 4
in her blood yet steeming *fresh* embayd: . . . III. xii. 21. 4
she, as morrow *fresh,* her selfe did reare . . . III. xii. 28. 8
As plaine as at the first when they were *fresh* and greene. . . . IV. i. 24. 9
As *fresh* and fragrant as the floure-deluce . . . IV. i. 31. 7
in warlike *fresh* aray Them found . . . IV. ii. 53. 3
on the other side, in *fresh* aray, Fayre Canacee . . . IV. iii. 4. 5
Have by good fortune found some beasts *fresh* spoyle, . . . IV. iii. 16. 2
So *fresh* he seemed and so fierce in sight: . . . IV. iii. 23. 6
As *fresh* as when it first was planted in the soyle. . . . IV. iii. 29. 9
he started up anon, . . . And *fresh* assayld his foe: . . . IV. iii. 31. 5
Faire Canacee, as *fresh* as morning rose, . . . IV. iii. 51. 7
That we may us reserve both *fresh* and strong . . . IV. iv. 12. 4
before them found in *fresh* aray Manie a brave knight . . . IV. iv. 13. 7
Rose in his strength, and gan her *fresh* assayle, . . . IV. vi. 16. 4
by the flowrie marge Of a *fresh* streame . . . IV. viii. 61. 6
all burning with a *fresh* desire . . . IV. ix. 29. 1
The Prince yet being *fresh* untoucht afore; . . . IV. ix. 34. 2
'*Fresh* shadowes, fit to shroud from sunny ray; . . . IV. x. 24. 1
flowres as *fresh* as May. . . . IV. x. 37. 9
he their sonne full *fresh* and jolly was, . . . IV. xi. 27. 1
Fresh Alimeda deckt with girlond greene; . . . IV. xi. 51. 1
There her assayling fiercely *fresh,* . . . V. iv. 41. 4
With *fresh* assault upon him she did fly, . . . V. v. 14. 3
so soone As she her face had wypt to *fresh* her blood: . . . V. v. 45. 7
with bloudie knyfe Yet dropping *fresh* in hand, . . . V. ix. 48. 3
of her widowhed Taking advantage, and her yet *fresh* woes, . . . V. x. 12. 2
Yet dropping *fresh* out of the Indian fount, . . . V. x. 16. 6
with *fresh* wonted grace Dispreds the glorie . . . V. xii. 13. 5
in *fresh* poyson steepe: . . . V. xii. 42. 8
But lov'd this *fresh* young Knight . . . VI. iii. 7. 5
Calidore rising up as *fresh* as day . . . VI. iii. 13. 8
out of an hill *fresh* gushing did appere. . . . VI. iii. 50. 9
purple blood Yet flowing *fresh,* . . . VI. iv. 12. 3
being *fresh* and full of youthly spright, . . . VI. vii. 5. 2
So *fresh* the image of her former dread, . . . VI. viii. 31. 6
full of *fresh* dismay, . . . VI. xi. 28. 3
Kindle *fresh* sparks of that immortall fire . . . VII. vii. 2. 4
Had in him kindled youthfull *fresh* desire, . . . VII. vii. 11. 7
fresh Aprill, full of lustyhed, . . . VII. vii. 33. 1
Fresh Love, that long hath slept . . . *Am.* iv. 6
faire flowre! in whom *fresh* youth doth raine, . . . *Am.* iv. 13
fresh against my selfe to fight. . . . *Am.* xliv. 12
Fresh Spring, the herald of loves mighty king, . . . *Am.* lxx. 1
Whose ymage yet I carry *fresh* in mynd. . . . *Am.* lxxviii. 4
fresh againe enured His former cruelty. . . . *Epig.* iv. 53
with *fresh* lusty-hed, Go to the bowre . . . *Epith.* 22
In theyr *fresh* garments trim. . . . *Epith.* 29
ye *fresh* boyes, that tend upon her groome, . . . *Epith.* 112
like *fresh* Eagle, make his hardie flight . . . *H.L.* 69
whose lampe doth yet remaine *Fresh* burning . . . *H.L.* 132
Venus . . . *Fresh* flowre of grace, . . . *H.B.* 282
The earth did *fresh* aray; . . . *Proth.* 69
So *fresh* they seem'd as day, . . . *Proth.* 70

Fresh-bleeding. *See* **Bleeding, Fresh.**

Fresher. turne we here . . . to gather *fresher* sprights, . . . V. iii. 40. 7
That he mote *fresher* be against the next daies fight. . . . V. iv. 51. 9

Freshest. Resembling Stella in her *freshest* yeares, . . . *As.* 189
freshest Flora her with Yvie girlond crownd. . . . I. i. 48. 9
in the first flowre of my *freshest* age, . . . I. ii. 23. 1
him. . . . Who earst in flowres of *freshest* youth was clad. . . . I. viii. 42. 4
'It was in *freshest* flowre of youthly yeares, . . . I. ix. 9. 1
She was a woman in her *freshest* age, . . . I. x. 30. 1
So faire and fresh, as *freshest* flowre in May; . . . I. xii. 22. 1
Now in his *freshest* flowre of lusty-hed, . . . II. i. 41. 7
man, Of wondrous beauty and of *freshest* yeares, . . . II. viii. 5. 2
in the flowre now of her *freshest* age; . . . II. ix. 18. 7
Now in the blossome of his *freshest* age. . . . III. vii. 46. 5
When as mans age was in his *freshest* prime, . . . V. Pr. 1. 3
in his youthes *freshest* flowre, . . . VI. xii. 3. 5
Did deck himselfe in *freshest* faire attire; . . . VII. vii. 11. 2
all the fairest flowres and *freshest* buds . . . VII. vii. 33. 7
freshest Flowres which in that Mead they found, . . . *Proth.* 84

Fresh-flowering. In a *fresh flowring* meadow lying lowe: . . . *Van.* ii. 4
in *fresh flowring* fields themselves to sport: . . . I. iv. 37. 3
The prayse of her *fresh flowring* Maydenhead; . . . III. v. 54. 6

Freshing. I walkt abroade to breath the *freshing* ayre . . . *D.* 26

Freshly. *freshly* bleeding of a grievous wounde. . . . *Rev.* i. 8
towards heaven *freshly* to arise . . . *Ro.* xvii. 11
the woodbine twigges that *freshly* bud; . . . *Gn.* 82
dreame gan *freshly* tosse his braine . . . I. i. 55. 6
his hurts, that yet still *freshly* bled. . . . I. v. 17. 3
bubbling wave did ever *freshly* well, . . . I. vii. 4. 6
freshly up arose the doughty knight, . . . I. xi. 52. 1
he saw himselfe so *freshly* reare, . . . I. xi. 52. 6
With heavie load on him they *freshly* gan to smight. . . . II. ii. 23. 9
Her mery fitt shee *freshly* gan to reare, . . . II. vi. 21. 2
the flowres did *freshly* spring, . . . II. vi. 24. 6
freshly, as at first, prepard himselfe to fight. . . . II. xi. 38. 9
Whom still he marked *freshly* to arize . . . II. xi. 44. 8
the downy heare Did now but *freshly* spring, . . . II. xii. 79. 9
her wound still inward *freshly* bledd, . . . III. i. 56. 3

Freshly—*Continued.*
Bee *freshly* kindled in the fruitfull Ile Of Mona, . . . III. iii. 48. 4
Then gan he *freshly* pricke his fomy steed, . . . III. iv. 48. 2
gan the battaile *freshly* to begin; . . . III. v. 22. 5
By tract of blood, which she had *freshly* seene . . . III. v. 28. 4
His pace he *freshly* forward did advaunce, . . . III. vii. 3. 3
In his proud furnitures she *freshly* dight, . . . III. vii. 18. 8
freshly bleeding forth her fainting spright, . . . III. xii. 20. 7
the trompets *freshly* blew. . . . IV. iii. 14. 9
Casts off his ragged skin and *freshly* doth him dight. . . . IV. iii. 23. 9
Is often seene full *freshly* to have florisht, . . . IV. iii. 29. 7
Gan *freshly* him addresse . . . VI. iii. 13. 9
bathe in fountaines that do *freshly* flowe . . . VII. vi. 39. 4
flowres That *freshly* budded . . . VII. vii. 28. 3
Then shall the new yeares joy forth *freshly* send, . . . *Am.* lxii. 9
streames . . . stil do flow, and *freshly* still redound, . . . *H.H.L.* 165

Freshness. th' open *freshnes* of the gentle aire, . . . III. viii. 11. 4

Fresh-renewed. She fedd her wound with *fresh renewed* bale. . . . I. vii. 28. 6

Fresh-springing. *fresh springing* wells, as christall neate, . . . *Gn.* 119

Fresh-steaming. with their bloud *fresh steeming* red, . . . VI. vi. 24. 7

Fret. To *fret* thy soule with crosses and with cares; . . . *Hub.* 903
Yet did she inly *fret* and felly burne, . . . *Mui.* 343
Their gory sides fresh bleeding fiercely *frett;* . . . I. vi. 44. 5
as doth an hidden moth The inner garment *frett,* . . . II. ii. 34. 8
To *frett* for anger or for griefe to mone? . . . II. iii. 3. 4
Eftsoones he gan to rage, and inly *frett,* . . . II. vi. 28. 3
Florimell exceedingly did *fret,* . . . IV. v. 19. 7
it encompast round as with a golden *fret.* . . . IV. xi. 27. 9
She gan thereat to *fret* and greatly grieve; . . . IV. xii. 26. 2
at her happinesse do *fret* and frowne; . . . V. viii. 17. 7
Then would she inly *fret,* and grieve, . . . V. xii. 32. 3
So did the Squire, the whiles the Carle did *fret* . . . VI. vii. 47. 7
he gan *fret* and fome out bloudy gore . . . VI. xii. 31. 3

Frets. nether spinnes nor cards, ne cares nor *fretts,* . . . II. vi. 16. 8

Fretted. skirt with gold Was *fretted* all about, . . . II. ix. 37. 2
round about *yfretted* all with gold, . . . III. ii. 25. 4
All *fretted* round with gold, and goodly wel beseene. . . . III. iii. 58. 9
He chauft, he griev'd, he *fretted,* and he sight, . . . VI. xi. 25. 7

Fretting. *See* **Heart-fretting.**
his proude heart is fild with *fretting* ire: . . . *Van.* x. 10
many mischiefes follow cruell Wrath: . . . *fretting* griefe, . . . I. iv. 35. 5

Friday. So semest thou like Good *Fryday* to frowne: . . . *S.C.* F. 30

Fried. boyld Her inward brest, and in her entrayles *fryde,* . . . V. v. 53. 8

Friend. So now his *frend* is chaunged for a frenne. . . . *S.C.* Ap. 28
Had lever my foe then my *freend* he be; . . . *S.C.* May 167
Bacchus fruite is *frend* to Phoebus wise; . . . *S.C.* O. 106
to me, my trustie *friend,* aread Thy councell: . . . *Hub.* 81
How saist thou (*friend*) have I not well discourst . . . *Hub.* 541
Suspition of *friend,* nor feare of foe . . . *Mui.* 377
or weenedst her thy *frend* . . . *D.* 151
Unpitied, unplaynd, of foe or *frend:* . . . *As.* 136
forward on his way (with God to *frend*) . . . I. i. 28. 7
Having both found a new *friend* you to aid, . . . I. ii. 27. 2
Better new *friend* then an old foe is said.' . . . I. ii. 27. 4
In stead of foe to wound my *friend* amis?' . . . I. iii. 39. 5
from his *frend* he seeldome knew his fo. . . . I. iv. 23. 5
By Dianes meanes, who was Hippolyts *frend,* . . . I. v. 39. 7
to ayde his *frend,* Againe his wonted angry weapon proov'd, . . . I. viii. 21. 2
As commonly as *frend* does with his *frend.* . . . I. x. 56. 5
thine owne nations *frend* And Patrone: . . . I. x. 61. 7
Thy neither *friend* nor foe, *Fidessa.'* . . . I. xii. 28. 9
so sterne and terrible in sight, That cheard his *friendes,* . . . II. i. 6. 4
Accourting each her *frend* with lavish fest: . . . II. ii. 16. 5
'My *friend,* hight Philemon, . . . II. iv. 20. 1
my falser *friend* did no less joyous deeme. . . . II. iv. 21. 9
To losse of love adjoyning losse of *frend,* . . . II. iv. 31. 2
Mars is Cupidoes *frend,* . . . II. vi. 35. 7
honour be defaste Of *friend* or foe, . . . III. i. 12. 5
Whatever foe had wrought, or *frend* had faynd, . . . III. ii. 19. 5
the hardy Mayd (with love to *frend*) . . . III. iii. 14. 5
Forgetfull each to have bene ever others *frend.* . . . IV. ii. 14. 9
Canacee gan wayle her dearest *frend.* . . . IV. iii. 35. 5
nought he car'd for *friend* or enemy, . . . IV. iv. 11. 8
unwares to wight And to his *friend* unwist, . . . IV. iv. 27. 7
Leading his *friend* away, . . . IV. iv. 33. 9
cast t' avenge the shame doen to his *freend:* . . . IV. iv. 45. 2
by his *friend* himselfe eke soone he fond . . . IV. iv. 45. 3
To bath their hands in bloud of dearest *freend,* . . . IV. vi. 17. 8
whether willed or nilled *friend* or foe, . . . IV. vii. 16. 6
'There did I finde mine onely faithfull *frend* . . . IV. viii. 57. 1
my *friend* that had her long refus'd, . . . IV. viii. 60. 2
Her captive lovers *friend,* young Placidas, . . . IV. viii. 63. 2
did me also *friend* in my retrate. . . . IV. x. 57. 9
Now hight Palemon, and is saylers *frend;* . . . IV. xi. 13. 6
as it mote a faithfull *friend* behove, . . . VI. iii. 15. 7
Unarm'd, as fearing neither foe nor *frend,* . . . VI. iv. 17. 4
Yet he them all refusd, though thankt her as a *frend;* . . . VI. iv. 39. 9
where is eke your *friend* which halfe it ought?' . . . VI. vii. 16. 5
to save his *friend* from jeopardy. . . . VI. viii. 12. 9
His life he steemed dearer then his *frend:* . . . VI. x. 35. 5
Sith in his powre she was to foe or *frend,* . . . VI. xi. 6. 4
make it more admyr'd of foe and *frend;* . . . *H.B.* 264

Friended. of the Muses ye may *friended* bee, . . . *Ti.* 366
me *friended* late In entrance, . . . IV. x. 57. 8
Of both beloved well, but litle *frended,* . . . V. v. 57. 7

Friendless. *friendlesse,* unfortunate, Now miserable I, Fidessa, I. ii. 26. 1
Whose want too well now feeles my *freendles* case; . . . *Proth.* 140

Friendly. *frendly* Faeries, met with many Graces, . . . *S.C.* Jun. 25
(with Phoebus *friendly* leave) . . . *Gn.* 52
The knights knitt *friendly* bands: . . . I. ix. Arg.

Friendly—*Continued.*
friendly each did others praise devize, . . . I. ix. 1. 7
entertaynes with *friendly* chearefull mood. . . . I. x. 32. 4
One day unto me came in *friendly* mood, . . . II. iv. 22. 4
Long they thus traveiled in *friendly* wise, . . . III. i. 14. 1
A *friendly* league of love perpetuall . . . III. iv. 4. 4
love and *friendly* aid Mongst gentle Knights to nourish . IV. i. 46. 3
To stint all strife and foster *friendly* peace, . . . IV. ii. 19. 2
In *friendly* sort that lasted but a while; . . . IV. ii. 29. 2
So mortall foes so *friendly* to agree, . . . IV. iii. 49. 7
to shut up all in *friendly* love, . . . IV. ix. 15. 1
With gentle words perswading them to *friendly* peace. . IV. ix. 32. 9
With that his wife in *friendly* wise to deale, . . . V. viii. 21. 2
Sweete semblaunt, *friendly* offices that bynde, . . . VI. x. 23. 5
usde him *friendly* for further intent, . . . VI. x. 37. 7
Friend's. greater crosse To see *frends* grave, . . . III. iv. 38. 9
purchase honour in his *friends* behalve, . . . IV. iv. 27. 3
cast t' avenge his *friends* indignity. . . . IV. iv. 28. 5
in remembrance of his *friends* late harme, . . . IV. iv. 35. 2
her error I abusd To my *friends* good . . . IV. viii. 60. 8
For his *friends* sake her offred favours scorne, . . . IV. ix. 3. 8
Friends. Great *freendes* and feeble foes: . . . *S.C.* Jul. 194
Diggon on fewe such *freends* did ever lite. . . . *S.C.* S. 259
there came to visite mee Some *friends,* . . . *Hub.* 18
being former foes, they wexed *friends,* . . . *Col.* 851
their service . . . To aide his *friendes,* or fray his enimies. . . I. i. 38. 5
fearefull *freends* weare out the wofull night, . . . I. iii. 20. 6
Nor wayld of *friends,* nor layd on groning beare, . . . I. v. 23. 4
truth . . . shall finde *friends,* . . . I. xii. 28. 8
That cheard his *friendes,* and did his foes amate: . . . II. i. 6. 4
Accord of *friendes,* consent of Parents sought, . . . II. iv. 21. 3
Others through *friendes;* others for base regard, . . . II. vii. 47. 4
open to their *friendes,* and closed to their foes. . . . II. ix. 23. 9
Lov'd of his *freends,* and of his foes eschewd: . . . II. x. 13. 3
murdred by the *freends* of Gratian. . . . II. x. 61. 5
frends to termes of gentle truce entize, . . . III. ii. 24. 5
With th' other he his *friends* ment to enwrap; . . . III. xii. 11. 8
the Ladie, ill of *friends* bestedded, . . . IV. i. 3. 7
Some, of sworne *friends* that did their faith forgoe; . . . IV. i. 24. 3
shortly *friends* them make: . . . IV. ii. 1. 9
So fortune *friends* the bold:' . . . IV. ii. 7. 6
Like faithfull *friends* thenceforth to joyne in one . . . IV. ii. 28. 6
plighted hands for ever *friends* to be. . . . IV. iii. 49. 5
mortall foes doe turne to faithfull *frends,* . . . IV. iv. 1. 2
friends profest are chaungd to foemen fell: . . . IV. iv. 1. 3
Both sire and *friends* and all for ever to forgo. . . . IV. vii. 16. 9
her *friends* with counsell sage Dissuaded her . . . IV. viii. 50. 4
zeale of *friends* combynd with vertues meet: . . . IV. ix. 1. 7
These paires of *friends* in peace and setled rest, . . . IV. ix. 17. 2
wonder was to see In *friends* profest, . . . IV. ix. 27. 7
Faint *friends* when they fall out most cruell fomen bee. . . IV. ix. 27. 9
Of litle much, of foes she maketh *friends,* . . . IV. x. 34. 8
her *frends* For her beginning a more fearefull fray, . . . V. viii. 10. 5
when as foes enforst, or *friends* sought ayde, . . . V. ix. 30. 8
from close *friends,* that dar'd not to appeare, . . . V. xii. 10. 8
to low, to hie, To *friends,* to foes; . . . VI. x. 23. 9
Ne stayeth leave to take before his *friends* doe dye. . . . VI. xi. 18. 9
How many of their *friends* were slaine, . . . VI. xi. 20. 9
Her father and her *friends* about her lying, . . . VI. xi. 23. 2
mote encheare his *friends,* and foes mote terrifie. . . . VII. vi. 24. 9
ne favour seek of *friends:* . . . *Am.* lix. 10
The fayned *friends,* the unassured foes, . . . *H.L.* 263
Friends'. with him to wend, gainst all her *friends* consent. IV. viii. 50. 9
Friendship. of such falsers *freendship* bene fayne. . . . *S.C.* May 305
(Both two sure bands in *friendship* to be tide) . . . *Hub.* 54
The Foxe had promised of *friendship* store, . . . *Hub.* 1206
after death all *friendship* doth decaie: . . . *Ti.* 207
of *friendship* I thee pray, . . . *Col.* 159
those two knights, fast *friendship* for to bynd, . . . I. ix. 18. 6
Doth nourish vertue, and fast *friendship* breeds, . . . II. ii. 31. 2
Saxon kinges his *friendship* shall intreat; . . . III. iii. 45. 3
Friendship professed with unfained hart. . . . III. iii. 62. 8
of *friendship* let me now you pray, . . . IV. i. 40. 2
former breaches Made in their *friendship,* . . . IV. ii. 12. 5
when we *friendship* first did sweare, . . . IV. ii. 13. 3
of fayned *friendship* which they vow'd afore. . . . IV. ii. 18. 9
ought in *friendship* for her sake To joyne your force, . . . IV. ii. 24. 6
Ne certes can that *friendship* long endure, . . . IV. ii. 29. 6
Profest to her true *friendship* and affection sweet. . . . IV. iii. 50. 9
friendship, which a faint affection breeds . . . IV. iv. 1. 8
in base mind nor *friendship* dwels nor enmity. . . . IV. iv. 11. 9
doth beget True love and faithfull *friendship,* . . . IV. vi. 46. 9
faithfull *friendship* doth them both suppresse, . . . IV. ix. 2. 3
these Squires true *friendship* more did sway . . . IV. ix. 3. 3
tyde In bands of *friendship,* . . . IV. x. 27. 8
Mother of blessed Peace and *Friendship* trew; . . . IV. x. 34. 2
Yet thus much *friendship* she to him did show, . . . V. v. 57. 1
Friendship's. true *friendships* bond Doth their long strife agree. . . . IV. iii. Arg.
friendships faultie guile For ever to assoile. . . . *Proth.* 99
Friese, -th, Friesing. *See* **Freeze,** *etc.*
Frieze. *See* **Freeze.**
Lastly, came Winter cloathed all in *frize,* . . . VII. vii. 31. 1
Friezes. Christall *frises,* . . . *Bel.*[1] iv. 3
the *fryses* christall, . . . *Bel.*[2] iv. 3
Friezing. *See* **Freezing.**
Frigate. worke and play About her little *frigot,* . . . II. vi. 7. 9
the hoare waters from his *frigot* ran, . . . II. xii. 10. 3
Fright. full of ghastly *fright* . . . Gan shut the dore. . . . I. iii. 12. 7
she waked full of fearefull *fright,* . . . V. vii. 16. 8

Fright—*Continued.*
in *fright* Uppon their wall good watch and ward did keepe. . . V. vii. 26. 5
Being alreadie dead with fearefull *fright:* . . . VI. viii. 45. 3
Frights. Whom suddenly he wakes with fearful *frights,* . . . I. ii. 4. 4
Frigot. *See* **Frigate.**
Fringe. Was hemd with golden *fringe.* . . . II. iii. 26. 9
Hemd all about with *fringe* of silver twine: . . . V. vii. 6. 5
Fringed. Their watchet mantles *frindgd* with silver rownd, . . III. iv. 40. 5
Frises. *See* **Friezes.**
Frisked. *friskt,* and flong aloft, and louted low on knee. . . V. iii. 34. 9
Frisks. beasts begin to play Their pleasant *friskes,* . . . IV. x. 46. 2
Frith. The Doune and eke the *Frith,* . . . IV. xi. 47. 9
Frivolous. To buy his Masters *frivolous* good will, . . . *Hub.* 889
Frize. *See* **Freeze, Frieze.**
Fro (*partial list*). *See* **To and fro.**
thou art beside thy wit, Furthest *fro* the marke, . . . *S.C.* May 307
'*Fro* thence I durst in derring-doe compare . . . *S.C.* D. 43
save my sheepe and me *fro* shame. . . . *S.C.* D. 78
reft *fro* me my sweete companion, And reft *fro* me my love, . *D.* 159, 160
which *fro* mine eyes do raine, . . . *D.* 376
Sith she . . . Is fetcht *fro* me, . . . *D.* 439
far be it . . . *fro* me, . . . *Col.* 464
mounts *fro* thence In rolling globes . . . *Col.* 610
convaid, And *fro* me hid: . . . I. ii. 24. 3
Far be it from your thought, and *fro* my wil, . . . I. iii. 28. 2
so sad sight *fro* me hyde. . . . I. vii. 22. 9
is the point of death now turnd *fro* mee, . . . I. ix. 26. 3
will I not *fro* mine own love remove, . . . III. i. 28. 3
Far *fro* my native soyle, . . . III. ii. 7. 8
fro me reft both life and light attone. . . . III. v. 7. 6
farre be such reproch *fro* mee! . . . III. v. 46. 3
Deliver her *fro* thence, . . . III. xi. 18. 9
too or *froe;* . . . III. xii. 12. 3
That dare *fro* me thinke Florimell to take!' . . . IV. ii. 25. 4
the tide, that comes *fro* th' Ocean mayne, . . . IV. iii. 27. 1
Fro love to hate, . . . IV. iii. 45. 6
beasts, forst to refraine *fro* meat, . . . IV. iv. 47. 3
Fro me the honour of that game did reare; . . . IV. vi. 6. 7
my love hath *fro* me reft, . . . IV. vi. 8. 1
long him *fro* my selfe removes?' . . . IV. viii. 63. 9
wished freedome *fro* me wooe: . . . IV. x. 57. 5
she by force is still *fro* me detayned, . . . V. xi. 54. 8
her lockes for raunsome *fro* me free.' . . . VI. i. 19. 9
fro me say, That . . . VI. iii. 41. 1
Ne Nature to or *fro* spake for a space, . . . VII. vii. 57. 2
acquit *fro* my continual smart; . . . *Am.* xlii. 6
life, which first *fro* me she reaved, . . . *H.B.* 279
Frock. Well decked in a *frocke* of gray, . . . *S.C.* Au. 65
Shee also dofte . . . her well-plighted *frock,* . . . III. ix. 21. 3
Frogs. *frogs,* bred in the slimie scowring . . . *Gn.* 229
loathly *frogs* and toades, which eyes did lacke, . . . I. i. 20. 7
todes and *frogs,* his pasture poysonous, . . . III. x. 59. 2
Yeeld me an hostry mongst the croking *frogs,* . . . V. x. 23. 8
th' unpleasant Quyre of *Frogs* still croking . . . *Epith.* 349
Frolic. To feast and *frollicke;* nathemore would she . . . IV. xiii. 13. 4
to *frolicke,* and to put away The pensive fit . . . VI. iii. 9. 2
Then Coridon woxe *frollicke,* that earst seemed dead. . . . VI. ix. 42. 9
Made him so *frollick* and so full of lust: . . . VII. vii. 39. 5
From (*partial list*).
Shaking the hill even *from* the bottome deepe, . . . *Bel.*[1] ii. 13
From whence arise diversitie of sects, . . . *Hub.* 388
from whence come yee; . . . *Hub.* 604
From whence he vewes, . . . *Hub.* 1228
From whence he never should be quit, . . . *Hub.* 1245
Could save the sonne of Thetis *from* to die; . . . *Ti.* 429
beame of beautie sparkled *from* above, . . . *Col.* 468
From thence he shootes his arrowes . . . *Col.* 811
none else *from* hence may us unbynd.' . . . I. ii. 43. 9
from whence when she him spyde, . . . I. iii. 26. 5
from thence arose away The mother . . . I. v. 44. 4
The everburning lamps *from* thence it braught, . . . I. vii. 18. 4
From whence the river Dee, . . . rolls . . . I. ix. 4. 7
He chose an halter *from* among the rest, . . . I. ix. 54. 4
from thence brought to his heavenly bowre. . . . I. x. 40. 9
Is not *from* hence the way, . . . I. x. 50. 4
From thence, far off he unto him did shew . . . I. x. 55. 1
sprong out *from* English race, . . . I. x. 60. 1
From thence a Faery thee unweeting reft, . . . I. x. 65. 6
From whence she might behold . . . I. xi. 5. 3
'*From* thence it comes, . . . II. ii. 10. 1
To tell *from* whence he came . . . II. ii. 39. 5
From off the earth . . . II. iii. 19. 5
'How hight he . . . and *from* whence?' . . . II. iv. 41. 1
but they *from* hence were sold; . . . II. vii. 54. 4
who shall let me now On this vile body *from* to wreak . . . II. viii. 28. 4
us . . . draw *from* on this journey to proceed.' . . . II. xii. 26. 5
each the other *from* to rise restraine; . . . II. xii. 64. 5
quite *from* off the earth . . . III. iii. 43. 9
forth issewd *from* under th' Altars smooke . . . V. xi. 22. 4
from th' Eternall Truth it doth proceed, . . . *H.H.B.* 174
country may be freed *from* forraine harmes; . . . *Proth.* 156
Front. *See* **Crest-front.**
hundred pillers . . . decking the *front,* . . . *Bel.*[1] ii. 3
The double *front* of a triumphall Arke: . . . *Bel.* iv. 4
Sterne face, and *front* full of Saturnlike awe . . . *Bel.*[2] ix. 4
So did that haughtie *front* . . . it selfe upreare . . . *Ro.* xii. 9
In whose high *front* was writ as doth ensue. . . . *Gn.* 686
blood-red billowes, like a walled *front,* . . . I. x. 53. 3
His snowy *front,* curled with golden heares, . . . II. viii. 5. 5
stout Despetto in his greater pryde Did *front* him, . . . VI. v. 20. 8

Fronting. pillours *fronting* faire the same, ... *Bel.*² ii. 3
Fronts. Their horned *fronts* so fierce on either side Doe meete, I. ii. 16. 3
Frorn. *See* **Frozen.**
My hart-blood is wel nigh *frorne,* . . . . *S.C.* F. 243
Frory. with his *frory* lips full softly kist, ... III. viii. 35. 2
Frory-hoar. An aged sire with head all *frory hore,* . . . . III. viii. 30. 3
Frost. now are clothd with mosse and hoary *frost,* . . . . . . *S.C.* Ja. 33
my flowring youth is foe to *frost,* . . . . *S.C.* F. 31
Clothed with cold, and hoary wyth *frost,* . . . . *S.C.* F. 79
The byting *frost* nipt his stalke dead, ... *S.C.* F. 231
My head besprent with hoary *frost* I fynd, ... *S.C.* D. 135
As hoary *frost* with spangles doth attire . . . . I. x. 48. 3
Ne suffred storme nor *frost* on them to fall, ... II. xii. 51. 3
sprinckled *frost* upon his deawy beard: . . . . III. viii. 30. 4
Frosts. opprest With early *frosts,* . . . . *D.* 28
With hardned *frosts* of former winters ire, ... VII. vii. 11. 4
Frosty. the *frosty* Night Her mantle black . . . gan overhaile: *S.C.* Ja. 74
browes, Full of wrinckles and *frostie* furrowes, ... *S.C.* F. 44
twinckling starres in *frostie* night; . . . . *H.B.* 257
Froth. newly borne Of th' Ocean's fruitfull *froth,* . . . . . . II. xii. 65. 4
Froth-foamy. the nimble thyes Of his *froth-fomy* steed, . . . I. xi. 23. 3
Frothy. The yron rowels into *frothy* fome he bitt. . . . . . I. vii. 37. 9
Ye might have seene the *frothy* billowes fry . . . . II. xii. 45. 1
Froughy. Of like not of the *frowie* fede, ... *S.C.* Jul. 111
Frounce. Some *frounce* their curled heare in courtly guise; I. iv. 14 .7
Froward. *froward* fortune doth ever availe: . . . . *S.C.* S. 251
haplesse rising of some *froward* starre, ... *Gn.* 570
froward fortune still to follow mee, ... *Hub.* 66
whom frowning *froward* fate Hath made sad witnesse . . . . II. i. 37. 1
All for their Ladies *froward* love to gaine, ... II. ii. 26. 4
those two *froward* sisters, their faire loves, ... II. ii. 34. 1
She scould, and frownd with *froward* countenaunce; . . . . II. ii. 35. 8
that same *froward* twaine would accorage, ... II. ii. 38. 7
to th' importunity Of *froward* fortune . . . . III. iii. 31. 6
froward fortune, and too forward Night, ... III. v. 7. 4
When so the *froward* skye began to lowre; . . . . III. v. 51. 7
With *froward* will doth set him selfe to weepe, ... V. vi. 14. 3
Whom when those knights so *froward* and forlore Beheld, . . V. xi. 61. 8
two of them still *froward* seem'd to bee, ... VI. x. 24. 7
Frowardness. in his *frowardnes* from her was fled, ... III. vi. 20. 8
Frowie. *See* **Froughy.**
Frown. So semest thou like Good Fryday to *frowne:* . . . . . *S.C.* F. 30
well to beare The storme of fortunes *frowne* . . . . V. v. 38. 3
at her happinesse do fret and *frowne;* . . . . V. viii. 17. 7
lowre Upon their blisse, and balefull fortune *frowne:* . . . . V. x. 26. 7
her *frowne* me drives away. . . . . *Am.* xxi. 12
Frowned. what evill starre On you hath *frownd,* . . . . I. viii. 42. 7
She scould, and *frownd* with froward countenaunce; . . . . II. ii. 35. 8
This *frownd,* that faund, ... II. ix. 35. 6
Fortune, envying good, hath felly *frowned,* . . . . V. v. 36. 2
she sternly *frownd* For high disdaine of such indignity, . . . V. vii. 28. 5
Thereat *frown'd* Coridon, and his lip closely bit. . . . . . . VI. ix. 41. 9
Frowning. Neede feare no chaunge of *frowning* fate; . . . . *S.C.* S. 71
Their *frowning* forheades, . . . all asyde doe lay; . . . . . . I. vi. 11. 5
whom *frowning* froward fate Hath made sad witnesse . . . . II. i. 37. 1
some part Thereof did in his *frouning* face appeare: . . . . IV. i. 45. 4
Frozen. *See* **Blood-frozen, Frorn, Heart-frozen.**
frosen horror ran through everie part. . . . . *Ti.* 483
pierce his *frosen* eares? . . . . *D.* 249
cold Have not all seized on your *frozen* hart, ... II. i. 46. 6
Shortly they reard out of her *frosen* swownd; . . . . III. i. 64. 3
To doe the *frosen* cold away to fly; . . . . III. ii. 34. 5
she did lye All night in old Tithonus *frozen* bed, ... III. iii. 20. 6
if life Yett in his *frosen* members did remaine; . . . . . . III. v. 31. 2
stir his *frosen* spright: . . . . III. viii. 23. 5
her faint hart was with the *frosen* cold Benumbd . . . . . III. viii. 34. 7
Ne in their *frosen* hearts feele kindly flame: . . . . IV. Pr. 2. 2
she to stones at length all *frosen* turne! . . . . *Am.* xxxii. 14
Fructified. in her pregnant flesh they shortly *fructifide.* . . . III. vi. 7. 9
Fruit. There growes lifes *fruite* unto the Churches good. . . . *Rev.* iv. 14
Renowm'd for *fruite* of famous progenie, ... *Ro.* vi. 6
His kiddes, his cracknelles, and his early *fruit.* . . . . . . *S.C.* Ja. 58
Nor for *fruict* nor for shadowe serves thy stocke; . . . . . . *S.C.* F. 128
Reapen the *fruite* thereof, ... *S.C.* May 65
Bacchus *fruite* is frend to Phoebus wise; . . . . *S.C.* O. 106
bringeth forth the *fruite* of sommers pryde; . . . . *S.C.* D. 74
promised of timely *fruite* such store, ... *S.C.* D. 104
The flattring *fruite* is fallen to grownd before, ... *S.C.* D. 106
season more secure Shall bring forth *fruit,* . . . . *Gn.* 10
yong plants, which wont with *fruit* t' abound, ... *T.M.* 251
Now without *fruite* or leaves are to be found. . . . . *T.M.* 252
the *fruit* of all your travailes toyle . . . . *Ti.* 515
Her long borne Infant, *fruit* of heavinesse, ... *D.* 32
She fel away like *fruit* blowne downe with winde. . . . . . *D.* 244
Or mellow *fruit* if it were harvest time. . . . . *As.* 48
Receive . . . The unripe *fruit* of an unready wit; . . . . . . *Ded. Son.* iii. 2
Receive . . . a simple taste Of the wilde *fruit* . . . . *Ded. Son.* v. 2
Receive, dear Lord, in worth, the *fruit* of barren field. . . . *Ded. Son.* v. 14
The flowre of chevalry . . . Doth promise *fruite* . . . . . . *Ded. Son.* x. 3
her kindly skil To bring forth *fruit,* . . . . I. iii. 28. 8
Bacchus merry *fruit* they did invent, ... I. vi. 15. 2
with timely *fruit* her belly sweld, And bore a boy . . . . . I. vi. 23. 3
trees, Whereon nor *fruit* nor leafe was ever seene, ... I. ix. 34. 2
Loaden with *fruit* and apples rosy redd, ... I. xi. 46. 2
like young *fruit* in May, ... II. iii. 29. 7
Deserves to taste his follies *fruit,* repented payne.' . . . . II. v. 24. 9
loaden all with *fruit* as thick as it might bee. . . . . II. vii. 53. 9
Their *fruit* were golden apples glistring bright, ... II. vii. 54. 1
planted there did bring forth *fruit* of gold; . . . . II. vii. 54. 7
Here also sprong that goodly golden *fruit,* . . . . II. vii. 55. 1

Fruit—*Continued.*
the *fruit* which grew upon the brincke; . . . . II. vii. 58. 5
the *fruit* from hand . . . Did fly abacke, ... II. vii. 58. 6
Why takest not of that same *fruite* of gold? . . . . II. vii. 63. 7
thou thy treasons *fruit* . . . shalt taste Right sowre, ... II. viii. 31. 8
with her right the riper *fruit* did reach, ... II. xii. 56. 2
the *fruit* more sweetnes did contayne, ... III. ii. 17. 7
Both leafe and *fruite,* both too untimely shed, ... III. ii. 31. 8
beareth *fruit* of honour and all chast desyre. . . . . III. v. 52. 9
Bacchus *fruit* out of the silver plate . . . . III. ix. 30. 3
Each other of loves bitter *fruit* despoile. . . . . III. xii. 47. *or.*2
Such is the powre of that same *fruit,* . . . . V. vii. 11. 7
great store of forrest *frute* . . . . VI. vii. 24. 4
That so rich *frute* should be from us bereft; . . . . VI. ix. 1. 7
last forth brought The *fruite* of joy and blisse, ... VI. ix. 45. 9
of his love he reapt the timely *frute,* . . . . VI. x. 38. 5
They fall to strokes, the *frute* of too much talke, ... VI. xi. 16. 2
twixt her paps, (like early *fruit* in May, ... *Am.* lxxvi. 9
Sweet *fruit* of pleasure, brought from Paradice . . . . *Am.* lxxvii. 11
Send us the timely *fruit* of this same night. . . . . *Epith.* 404
Fruitful. This peoples vertue yet so *fruitfull* was . . . . . . *Ro.* viii. 5
Which eare the *frutefull* graine doth shortly bring; . . . . . *Ro.* xxx. 4
France . . . though *fruitfull* of brave wits, ... *Ro.* Env. 2
Beside the *fruitfull* shore of muddie Nile, ... *Van.* iii. 1
fruictfull flocks, bene every where to see: . . . . *S.C.* Jun. 22
fruitefull Pales, and the forrest greene, ... *Gn.* 116
wilde greene woods and *fruitful* pastures minde; . . . . . . *Gn.* 637
Seemes that in *fruitfull* pastures ye doo live, ... *Hub.* 593
The *fruitfull* spawne of their ranke fantasies: . . . . *T.M.* 322
With *fruitfull* hope his aged breast he fed . . . . *Mui.* 25
when flowres doo clothe the *fruitful* ground, ... *Mui.* 114
A *fruitfull* Olyve tree, with berries spredd, ... *Mui.* 326
None fairer, nor more *fruitfull* to be red: . . . . *Col.* 279
There did our ship her *fruitfull* wombe unlade, ... *Col.* 288
There *fruitfull* corne, faire trees, fresh herbage is, ... *Col.* 298
load the braunches of the *fruitfull* vine; . . . . *Col.* 601
Out of the *fruitfull* wombe of their great mother. . . . . . . *Col.* 854
the streames that, . . . Flow from thy *fruitfull* head, ... *Ded. Son.* viii.10
The *fruitfull* Olive; . . . . I. i. 9. 8
creatures . . . of his *fruitful* seed; . . . . I. i. 21. 8
fruitfull cursed spawne of serpents small, ... I. i. 22. 6
Charissa, . . . left her *fruitfull* nest: . . . . I. x. 29. 8
hill, . . . Adornd with *fruitfull* Olives . . . . I. x. 54. 2
freely sprong out of the *fruitfull* grownd, ... I. xi. 47. 3
some hidden nest Of many Dragonettes, his *fruitfull* seede: . . I. xii. 10. 6
from whose *fruitfull* pap Their welheads spring, ... II. ii. 6. 2
nature them forth throwes Out of her *fruitfull* lap; . . . . . II. vi. 15. 5
earth out of her *fruitfull* woomb Throwes forth . . . . . . II. vii. 51. 6
Both faire and *fruitfull,* and the grownd dispred . . . . . . II. xii. 12. 2
newly borne Of th' Ocean's *fruitfull* froth, ... II. xii. 65. 4
fruitfull Ceres and Lyaeus fatt . . . . III. i. 51. 3
sacred Emperours, Thy *fruitfull* Ofspring, ... III. iii. 23. 2
overronne The *fruitfull* plaines, ... III. iii. 46. 8
Bee freshly kindled in the *fruitfull* Ile Of Mona, ... III. iii. 48. 4
Through influence of th' hevens *fruitfull* ray, ... III. vi. 6. 2
the *fruitfull* seades Of all things living, ... III. vi. 8. 3
It sited was in *fruitfull* soyle of old, ... III. vi. 31. 1
all the *fruitfull* spawne of fishes hew . . . . III. vi. 35. 7
The substaunces of natures *fruitfull* progenyes. . . . . III. vi. 36. 9
from their *fruitfull* sydes sweet gum did drop, ... III. vi. 43. 7
largely overflow the *fruitfull* plaine, ... III. vii. 34. 4
of the *fruitfull* liquor overflowne; . . . . III. ix. 30. 5
Fruitfull of all thinges fitt for living foode, ... III. ix. 49. 6
He turnd himselfe into a *fruitfull* vine, ... III. xi. 43. 8
fruitfull apples to have borne awhile, ... IV. iii. 29. 8
Out of her *fruitfull* lap abundant flowres; . . . . IV. x. 45. 2
all the Sea-gods and their *fruitfull* seede, ... IV. xi. 8. 2
The pleasant Boyne, the fishy *fruitfull* Ban, ... IV. xi. 41. 4
Whose *fruitfull* seede farre passeth those in land, ... IV. xii. 1. 3
with strong hand their *fruitful* rancknes did deface. . . . . V. i. 1. 9
forth she brought The *fruitfull* vine; . . . . V. vii. 11. 3
mother of a *frutefull* heritage, ... V. x. 7. 3
Yet seem'd the soyle both fayre and *frutefull* eft, ... VI. ix. 1. 5
did alite Upon the *fruitfull* earth, ... VII. vi. 20. 9
Out of her *fruitfull* bosome made to growe . . . . VII. vii. 8. 6
fild her wombe with *fruitfull* hope of nourishment. . . . . . VII. vii. 32. 9
Till they bring forth the *fruitfull* progeny; . . . . *Epith.* 403
Yet being . . . full of *fruitfull* love, ... *H.H.L.* 51
That *fruitfull* issue may to you afford, ... *Proth.* 104
Fruitfulest. *fruitfullest* Virginia who did ever vew? . . . . . II. Pr. 2. 9
Fruitful-headed. the *fruitfull-headed* beast, . . . Became stark blind, ... I. viii. 20. 1
Fruitfulness. The joyes whereof and happy *fruitfulnesse,* . . II. vi. 24. 3
Fruitless. loose thy labour and thy *fruitles* cost. . . . . . *Hub.* 636
fruitles follies and unsound delights. . . . . *Hub.* 823
him to follow was but *fruitlesse* paine: . . . . I. ii. 8. 5
Arriv'd wher they in erth their *fruitles* blood had sown. . . . I. vi. 45. 9
the world, whose joyes so *fruitlesse* are; . . . . I. x. 63. 2
Bid thee to them thy *fruitlesse* labors yield, ... II. vi. 16. 3
Refuse such *fruitlesse* toile, ... II. vi. 17. 9
he had long time sought with *fruitlesse* suit: . . . . II. vii. 55. 3
fruitlesse lives were under furrow sowne, ... III. ix. 35. 8
sow vaine sorrow in a *fruitlesse* eare, ... III. xi. 16. 2
'What is there ells but cease these *fruitlesse* paines, ... III. xi. 24. 1
'the *fruitlesse* end Of thy vaine boast, ... IV. i. 51. 1
on the ground their lives did strow, Like *fruitles* seede, . . . V. vii. 31. 9
two more of his armes did fall away, Like *fruitlesse* braunches, V. xi. 11. 8
fruitlesse worke is broken with least wynd. . . . . *Am.* xxiii. 14
my long *fruitlesse* stay In Princes Court, ... *Proth.* 6
Fruit's. seeme to labour under their *fruites* lode: . . . . . III. vi. 42. 6

Fruits. Sad be the sights, and bitter *fruites* of warre, II. ii. 30. 6
a gardin goodly garnished With hearbs and *fruits,* II. vii. 51. 5
Most famous *fruites* of matrimoniall bowre, III. iii. 3. 7
the *frutes* of the forrest was their feast; VI. iv. 14. 6
Laden with *fruits* that made him laugh, VII. vii. 30. 3
ripened *fruits* the which the earth had yold. VII. vii. 30. 9
Frustrate. *frustrate* all her paine, VII. vi. 48. 5
Fry. To feede youthes fancie, and the flocking *fry,* *S.C.* O. 14
Her heards be thousand fishes with their *frie,* *Col.* 242
Phlegeton, Whereas the damned ghosts in torments *fry,* I. v. 33. 4
them before the *fry* of children yong I. xii. 7. 1
frye in hartlesse griefe and dolefull tene: II. i. 58. 4
Ye might have seene the frothy billowes *fry* II. xii. 45. 1
Witnesse th' exceeding *fry* which there are fed, IV. xii. 2. 4
Doth *frie* with fome above the surges hore. V. ii. 15. 8
this off-scum of that cursed *fry* VII. vi. 30. 1
all these flames, in which I *fry,* *Am.* xxxii. 5
Fryses. *See* **Friezes.**
Fuel. with forst wind the *fewell* did inflame; II. vii. 36. 2
Fugitive. To seeke the *fugitive* both farre and nere. III. vi. 26. 4
Fugitives. He also gave to *fugitives* of Spayne, II. x. 41. 6
Fulfil. others pleasure to *fulfill.* II. iv. 19. 9
did like an halfe Theatre *fulfill:* II. xii. 30. 7
doe by all dew meanes thy destiny *fulfill.'* III. iii. 24. 9
I the same should faithfully *fulfill;* III. vii. 54. 7
so that he *fulfill* The penance IV. vi. 32. 5
to *fulfill* That which he doth with righteous doome decide, V. iv. 1. 3
which now she doth *fulfill.* V. iv. 30. 9
I have forbore this duetie to *fulfill;* V. v. 41. 3
I needes must by all meanes *fulfill* This penaunce, VI. viii. 30. 2
Fulfilled. The charme *fulfild,* dead suddeinly he downe did sincke. II. i. 55. 9
After she had nine moneths *fulfild* and gone: III. vi. 5. 5
Onely what needeth shall be here *fulfild,* IV. xi. 17. 7
In which her circles voyage is *fulfild,* *Am.* lx. 3
Fulgent. Her reliques *Fulgent* having gathered, II. x. 57. 1
Full (*partial list of adv.*). *See* **Bellyful.**
Sterne face, and front *full* of Saturnlike awe *Bel.*² ix. 4
browes, *Full* of wrinckles and frostie furrowes, *S.C.* F. 44
would make *full* faine; *S.C.* F. 67
ful of fraude, and guile, *S.C.* May 127
full of favour as kidde mought be. *S.C.* May 184
they bene false, and *full* of covetise, *S.C.* S. 82
They bene so grave and *full* of mayntenaunce. *S.C.* S. 169
This with *full* bit doth catch the utmost top *Gn.* 83
his beames *full* hott, *Gn.* 156
glauncing *full* dreadfullie, *Gn.* 262
everie streete Is *full* of fortunes, *Hub.* 91
full glad am I, *Hub.* 270
For a *full* complement of all their ill, *Hub.* 338
full few which follow them, *Hub.* 637
Full of the feared sight which late they sawe. *Hub.* 1110
Full of sad sights and sore Catastrophees; *T.M.* 158
I, whose joy was earst with Spirit *full* *T.M.* 289
Thoughts halfe devine, *full* of the fire of love, *T.M.* 363
bought *full* deere, *Ti.* 115
'His blessed spirite, *full* of power divine *Ti.* 288
Full of sweete flowres and daintiest delights, *Ti.* 520
Full of brave courage and bold hardyhed, *Mui.* 27
Full many a Ladie faire, in Court *full* oft *Mui.* 105
worke, *full* fit for kingly bowres; *Mui.* 300
full merrilie to pipe *D.* 55
' "Our daies are *full* of dolor and disease, *D.* 274
hideous monsters *full* of uglinesse; *D.* 340
Full many Maydens *As.* 37
Full litle faileth *As.* 135
all the day it standeth *full* of deow, *As.* 191
waile *full* many a sythe, *Col.* 23
My mind, *full* of my thoughts satietie, *Col.* 42
Full faine she lov'd, and was belov'd *full* faine *Col.* 116
full of inward feare, *Col.* 228
lies *full* low, *Col.* 434
Muse, *full* of high thoughts invention, *Col.* 446
Nor haughtie words most *full* of highest thoughts: *Col.* 716
All *full* of love, and love, and love my deare, *Col.* 777
voydnesse to seeke *full* satietie. *Col.* 850
full of fire and greedy hardiment, I. i. 14. 1
Most lothsom, filthie, foule, and *full* of vile disdaine. I. i. 14. 9
Full of great lumps of flesh I. i. 20. 3
Her vomit *full* of bookes and papers was, I. i. 20. 6
her body, *full* of filthie sin, I. i. 24. 7
creature, . . . *Full* of the makers guyle, I. i. 46. 7
Where that false couple were *full* closely ment I. ii. 5. 4
in wooden wals *full* faste, I. ii. 42. 8
Full of sad feare and ghastly dreriment, I. ii. 44. 4
Full fast she fled, I. iii. 12. 1
full of ghastly fright . . . Gan shut the dore. I. iii. 12. 7
Paynim forward came so . . . *full* of wrath, I. iii. 35. 2
her fiers servant, *full* of kingly aw And high disdaine, I. iii. 41. 1
goodly galleries far over laid, *Full* of faire windowes I. iv. 4. 8
Pecocks, . . . *full* of Argus eyes their tayles dispredden wide. I. iv. 17. 9
Full of diseases was his carcas blew, I. iv. 23. 6
a burning hart he bare, *Full* of vaine follies I. iv. 25. 4
coffers . . . With precious metall *full* as they might hold; I. iv. 27. 4
a kirtle of discolourd say . . . ypaynted *full* of eies; I. iv. 31. 2
No knight, but treachour *full* of false despight I. iv. 41. 5
for his sake have felt *full* many an heavie stowre. I. iv. 46. 9
The knight was fiers, and *full* of youthly heat, I. v. 7. 4
So long they fight, and *full* revenge pursue, I. vi. 44. 1
still he lay *full* low. I. vii. 12. 9

Full—*Continued.*
The proud Duessa, *full* of wrathfull spight, I. viii. 13. 1
Came hurtling in *full* fiers, I. viii. 17. 9
to the ground it doubleth him *full* low: I. viii. 18. 8
O fayrest virgin! *full* of heavenly light, I. ix. 17. 3
lookes *full* lowly cast, and gate *full* slow, I. x. 5. 6
a woman . . . *Full* of great love, I. x. 30. 5
His mind was *full* of spiritual repast, I. x. 48. 8
full many a lovely lay. I. x. 54. 9
sayles, in which the hollow wynd Is gathered *full,* I. xi. 10. 3
full of griefe and anguish vehement, I. xi. 26. 1
a silver flood, *Full* of great vertues, I. xi. 29. 5
knees *full* lowly bent, I. xi. 32. 6
To him assembled with one *full* consort, I. xii. 4. 7
they him layd *full* low in dungeon deepe, I. xii. 36. 1
In *full* content he there did long enjoy; I. xii. 41. 2
forth he fares, *full* of malicious mynd, II. i. 2. 1
Full loth she seemd II. i. 20. 8
full low Shee sight II. i. 47. 1
Full measured three quarters of her yeare, II. i. 53. 2
Full of disport, still laughing, loosely light, II. ii. 36. 2
ran away *full* light. II. iii. 4. 9
Her yvorie forhead, *full* of bountie brave, II. iii. 24. 1
full fayre aumayld: II. iii. 27. 5
her face ill-favourd, *full* of wrinckles old. II. iv. 4. 9
flye *Full* fast away, II. iv. 13. 7
when him ronning in *full* course he spyes, II. v. 10. 5
full low to lye; II. v. 12. 5
full of the stately tree II. v. 31. 2
Sterne was his looke, and *full* of stomacke vayne; II. vii. 41. 3
full of anger fiersly to him cryde; II. viii. 31. 5
full of princely bounty and great mind, II. viii. 51. 1
Full lively II. ix. 2. 9
full of grace and goodly modestee, II. xi. 18. 8
A carefull man, and *full* of comely guyse. II. ix. 31. 2
him *full* of melancholy did shew; II. ix. 52. 5
Of those that rowme was *full;* II. ix. 54. 1
all worm-eaten and *full* of canker holes. II. ix. 57. 9
their entrailles, *full* of quick Brimston, II. x. 26. 4
Without *full* point, or other Cesure right; II. x. 68. 3
Full large he was of limbe, II. xi. 20. 7
with a staffe, all *full* of litle snags, II. xi. 23. 7
Full litle wanted but he had him slaine, II. xi. 29. 6
taking his *full* course Until he came II. xi. 46. 5
his brave shield, *full* of old moniments, II. xii. 80. 3
Full of disdainefull wrath he fierce uprose III. i. 9. 1
Full of great envy and fell gealosy III. i. 18. 2
all was *full* of Damzels and of Squyres, III. i. 39. 6
shee was *full* of amiable grace III. i. 46. 1
full easely doth fall. III. i. 54. 9
Sad, solemne, sowre, and *full* of fancies fraile, III. ii. 27. 5
full far away . . . did flye III. ii. 28. 5
the *full* time, prefixt by destiny, III. iii. 40. 5
to their ready Steedes they clombe *full* light, III. iii. 61. 6
Strooke her *full* on the brest, III. iv. 15. 8
full of subtile sophismes, III. iv. 28. 7
full of bitter griefe and pensife thought, III. iv. 31. 5
full of firy zele, him followed long, III. iv. 45. 8
Till he had made amends, and *full* restore III. v. 18. 8
Full of fiers fury and indignant hate III. v. 23. 3
Full of soft passion and unwonted smart: III. v. 30. 8
The goodly Maide, *ful* of divinities III. v. 34. 7
the Damzell, *full* of doubtfull thought, III. vii. 8. 5
Full of sad feare and doubtfull agony III. vii. 32. 1
full of guests he found whyleare, III. ix. 13. 4
The jolly Satyres, *full* of fresh delight, III. x. 44. 3
There was he painted *full* of burning dartes, III. xi. 44. 8
harmony In *full* straunge notes III. xii. 6. 2
She chearfull, fresh, and *full* of joyaunce glad, III. xii. 18. 4
Full of sad signes, III. xii. 19. 7
Scudamore With her . . . Squire, both *full* of feare, III. xii. 44. 3
The barren ground was *full* of wicked weedes, IV. i. 25. 2
His fickle mind *full* of inconstancie: IV. i. 32. 5
He was *full* wo, and gan his former griefe renew. IV. i. 38. 9
with countenance sterne All *full* of wrath, IV. ii. 25. 2
courage *full* of haughtie hardiment, IV. ii. 39. 2
Stroke him . . . In th' arm-pit *full,* IV. iii. 33. 9
Blandamour *full* of vainglorious spright, IV. iv. 3. 6
Full of melancholie and sad misfare IV. vi. 2. 5
he was *full* bent to some mischievous deede. IV. vi. 2. 9
Against her rode, *full* of despiteous ire, IV. vi. 11. 4
full of wrath for that late stroke, IV. vi. 23. 1
So goodly grave, and *full* of princely aw, IV. vi. 33. 5
Pursuing that faire Lady *full* of feare: IV. vii. 24. 5
Full of sad anguish and in heavy case: IV. vii. 38. 4
Full of discomfort and disquiet plight, IV. viii. 8. 4
Full of sad powre, that poysnous bale did breede IV. viii. 39. 4
right hand In *full* avengement heaved up on hie, IV. viii. 43. 2
full of rage he gan to curse and sweare, IV. viii. 44. 2
Sixe they were all, all *full* of fell despight, IV. ix. 20. 3
Feigning *full* many a fond excuse IV. x. 14. 7
Full farre was I from thinking V. i. 15. 4
full of scorne to be commaunded so, V. i. 21. 2
full inly glad, V. ii. 3. 6
she is *full* faire, V. ii. 10. 1
fild his ballaunce *full* of idle toys: V. ii. 30. 8
with *full* satietie Of meates and drinkes V. iii. 4. 1
Radigund, *full* of heart-gnawing griefe V. iv. 47. 1
As the faire Moone in her most *full* aspect V. v. 3. 8
So she departed *full* of griefe and sdaine, V. v. 51. 6

Full—*Continued.*
like *full* of fraud and guile, ... V. vi. 33. 2
With *full* intent t' avenge that villany . . . . . V. vi. 35. 4
she waked *full* of fearefull fright, ... V. vii. 16. 8
Full fiercely layde . . . . . V. vii. 31. 1
After long travell of *full* twenty yeares, ... V. vii. 39. 6
followed was of him likewise *full* fast, ... V. viii. 33. 8
comming *full* before his horses vew, ... V. viii. 37. 8
all within it *full* of wyndings is . . . . . V. ix. 6. 6
like a Foxe *full* fast: . . . . . V. ix. 17. 2
All *full* of people making troublous din . . . . . V. ix. 23. 3
Are not all places *full* of forraine powres? . . . . . V. x. 23. 2
made smooth fields now *full* of flowres? . . . . . V. x. 23. 5
full lightly from him freed, ... V. xi. 9. 3
full wroth he fiercely gan . . . . . V. xi. 11. 4
Full of fell ravin and fierce greedinesse; . . . . . V. xi. 24. 2
Full loath . . . . . V. xi. 35. 6
full fayne And glad . . . . . V. xii. 9. 5
with eyes *full* sad and hart *full* sore, ... V. xii. 11. 7
all from him *full* lightly swept, ... VI. i. 24. 3
all *full* of wrath she thus replyde: . . . . . VI. i. 27. 6
uprose againe *full* light, ... VI. i. 34. 1
All flesh is frayle and *full* of ficklenesse, ... VI. i. 41. 7
comming forth yet *full* of late affray . . . . . VI. i. 44. 7
Wherewith he wroth, and *full* of proud disdaine, ... VI. ii. 11. 6
full of valour . . . . . VI. iii. 7. 8
A courteous Knight and *full* of faithfull trust; . . . . . VI. iii. 13. 2
Serena *full* of dolorous dismay, ... VI. iii. 45. 3
Full on the breast him strooke, ... VI. iv. 5. 7
Full like ere long . . . . . VI. v. 21. 4
whom they *full* busie found . . . . . VI. v. 25. 2
full faire did entertaine . . . . . VI. v. 38. 6
A faire young Mayden, *full* of comely glee; . . . . . VI. vi. 10. 7
A monstrous Dragon, *full* of fearefull uglinesse. . . . . . VI. vi. 10. 9
being fresh and *full* of youthly spright, ... VI. vii. 5. 2
did him smite *Full* in the shield . . . . . VI. vii. 8. 2
Full on his bever did him strike so sore, ... VI. vii. 8. 6
false Turpin was *full* glad and faine, ... VI. vii. 17. 1
he so *full* of indignation was, ... VI. vii. 26. 1
to the brim I have it *full* defrayd: . . . . . VI. viii. 24. 3
Of finest flowers, and with *full* busie care . . . . . VI. viii. 39. 8
slept *full* fast; . . . . . VI. viii. 47. 6
full fayre of face, ... VI. ix. 9. 1
His former quest, so *full* of toile and paine: . . . . . VI. x. 2. 2
with fell clawes *full* of fierce gourmandize, ... VI. x. 34. 5
full of fresh dismay, ... VI. xi. 28. 3
full of joy, streight forth she ran in hast . . . . . VI. xii. 16. 6
seemed to containe A *full* good pecke . . . . . VI. xii. 26. 6
full of grace and Majestie, ... VII. vi. 24. 8
Diana, *full* of indignation, ... VII. vi. 54. 1
So *full* they filled every hill and Plaine; . . . . . VII. vii. 4. 5
Great Nature, ever young, yet *full* of eld; . . . . . VII. vii. 13. 2
fresh Aprill, *full* of lustyhed, ... VII. vii. 33. 1
full her hand was found: . . . . . VII. vii. 37. 5
Then came October *full* of merry glee; . . . . . VII. vii. 39. 1
Made him so frollick and so *full* of lust: . . . . . VII. vii. 39. 5
Full of delightfull health and lively joy, ... VII. vii. 46. 8
full of the living fire, Kindled above . . . . . *Am.* viii. 1
my fraile fancy, fed with *full* delight, ... *Am.* lxxii. 9
Yet field and bowre are *full* of her aspect: . . . . . *Am.* lxxviii. 8
Still *full*, yet never satisfyde with it; . . . . . *H.L.* 199
After *full* joyance of their gentle game; . . . . . *H.L.* 291
my feeble breast, too *full* of thee? . . . . . *H.B.* 3
Yet being . . . *full* of fruitfull love, ... *H.H.L.* 51
though not in powre so great, Yet *full* of beautie, ... *H.H.L.* 54
And give thy selfe unto him *full* and free, ... *H.H.L.* 265
That *full* and freely gave himselfe to thee. . . . . . *H.H.L.* 266
In *full* enjoyment of felicitie, ... *H.H.B.* 79
lampe . . . Thenceforth seemes fowle, and *full* of sinfull blame; *H.H.B.* 276
So *full* their eyes are of that glorious sight, ... *H.H.B.* 281
All happie joy and *full* contentment fynd. . . . . . *H.H.B.* 287
cropt *full* feateously . . . . . *Proth.* 27

Fuller. feedes him once the *fuller* by a graine? . . . . . *S.C.* O. 34

Fullness. Their bellies swolne he saw with *fulnesse* burst, . . I. i. 26. 5
sappy liquor, that with *fulnesse* sweld, ... II. xii. 56. 3
Fed on the *fulnesse* of that chearefull glaunce, ... *Am.* xxxix. 12
For of her *fulnesse* which the world doth fill They all partake, . *H.H.B.* 199

Fully. Thrise three Moones bene *fully* spent . . . . . *S.C.* S. 20
light Out of the ruddy East was *fully* reard, ... III. x. 52. 7
he to fell reveng was *fully* bent: . . . . . IV. v. 30. 9
fully bent her That battells utmost triall to adventer. . . . . V. v. 5. 4
right *fully* bent To fierce avengement . . . . . V. vi. 18. 6
Their tender flocks, now being *fully* fed, ... VI. ix. 13. 4
And *fully* setteth his felicitie; . . . . . *H.B.* 229

Fulmined. a flake Of lightning through bright heven *fulmined:* III. ii. 5. 8

Fume. Her thoughts are like the *fume* of Franckincence, . . . *Col.* 608
th' altars *fume* with frankincense arownd, ... III. iv. 17. 4
fume in his disdainefull mynd the more, ... VI. vii. 47. 8

Fumed. how he *fum'd*, and sweld, and rag'd, and panted; . . *Hub.* 1340

Fumeth. Nought else but smoke, and *fumeth* soone away; . . *Col.* 720

Fuming. *fuming* all with frankensence I found . . . . . IV. x. 37. 2

Funeral. Rome now of Rome is th' onely *funerall*, ... *Ro.* iii. 9
The moniment of whose sad *funerall*, ... *Ti.* 117
In *funerall* complaints and waylfull tyne, ... *Mui.* 12
the Cypresse *funerall;* . . . . . I. i. 8. 9
The Lady, . . . Staid not to waile his woefull *funerall*, ... I. ii. 20. 3
many corses . . . lay Without remorse or decent *funerall;* . . I. v. 53. 4
to tell his *funerall* Unto his brother, ... II. v. 25. 8
wandring ghost that wanted *funerall*, ... II. xi. 39. 7

Funsheon. shee had out of measure Long lov'd the *Fanchin*, . VII. vi. 44. 4

Funsheon—*Continued.*
Of her beloved *Fanchin* did obtaine, ... VII. vi. 53. 5
Till with the *Fanchin* she her selfe do wed, ... VII. vi. 53. 8

Funsheon's. No whit inferiour to thy *Fanchins* (**Funchins*)
praise, ... *Col.* 301

Fur. could make a jolly hole in theyr *furre:* . . . . . *S.C.* S. 165

Furies. *See* **Fellow-furies.**
furies rules, and Tartare tempereth. . . . . . *Hub.* 1294
mourning altars . . . The black infernall *Furies* doen aslake: . I. iii. 36. 8
dreadfull *Furies*, which their chaines have brast, ... I. v. 31. 8
Infernall *furies* with their chaines untyde. . . . . . I. ix. 24. 5
So many *furies* and sharpe fits did haunt, ... I. xi. 27. 4
thousand *furies* wait on wrathfull sword; . . . . . II. ii. 30. 7
rule the *Furyes* when they most doe rage. . . . . . II. xii. 41. 8
by infernall *furies* nourished; . . . . . IV. i. 26. 8
first tynd in Phlegeton, By thousand *furies*, ... IV. ii. 1. 2
Him selfe he bent their *furies* to abate, ... IV. ix. 34. 6
the *Furies* fell Theyr snaky heads doe combe, ... *Am.* lxxxv. 2

Furies'. gates of hel, and fyrie *furies* forse, ... *S.C.* N. 164
fed with *Furies* milke for sustenaunce . . . . . *T.M.* 261
that divelish yron Engin, . . . framd by *Furies* skill, ... I. vii. 13. 2
With hellish feends, or *Furies* mad uprore, ... II. v. 37. 7
other like infernall *furies* kinde; . . . . . V. xi. 23. 6

Furious. beating downe these walls with *furious* mood . . . *Ro.* xi. 11
The *furious* squadrons downe to ground did fall, ... *Ro.* xii. 6
home him hasted with *furious* heate, ... *S.C.* F. 193
from th' Argolick ships with *furious* yre . . . . . *Gn.* 495
Both fierce and *furious* in contention Encountred, ... *Gn.* 517
being fild with *furious* insolence, ... *Col.* 622
Halfe *furious* unto his foe he came, ... I. i. 24. 3
he . . . would have slaine them in his *furious* ire, ... I. ii. 5. 8
both fell and *furious*, That, . . . Their steeds doe stagger, . . I. ii. 15. 4
with the sight amazd, forgat his *furious* forse. . . . . . I. iii. 5. 9
open breakes the dore in *furious* wize, ... I. iii. 19. 5
when the *furious* fitt was overpast, ... I. iv. 34. 6
quench the flame of *furious* despight, ... I. v. 14. 5
they gan, both *furious* and fell, To thunder blowes, ... I. vi. 43. 1
The ydle stroke, enforcing *furious* way, ... I. viii. 8. 2
at his foe with *furious* rigor smites, ... I. viii. 18. 5
With *furious* force and indignation fell; . . . . . I. viii. 39. 6
Fayre Goddesse, lay that *furious* fitt asyde, ... I. xi. 7. 1
Exceeding rage enflam'd the *furious* Beast, ... I. xi. 17. 5
Trebly augmented was his *furious* mood . . . . . I. xi. 22. 7
he stroke so *furious* and so fell, ... I. xi. 24. 2
they mingled were in *furious* armes, ... II. ii. 27. 1
furious fitts at earst quite weren quaild: . . . . . II. iv. 14. 4
that *furious* beast His precious horne . . . Strikes in the stocke, II. v. 10. 6
nothing might sustaine his *furious* forse: . . . . . II. v. 23. 2
his brother burns in *furious* fyre. . . . . . II. vi. Arg.
Furious ever I thee knew to bee, ... II. vi. 49. 3
settle patience in so *furious* heat? . . . . . II. viii. 27. 6
was the force so *furious* and so fell, ... II. viii. 31. 1
Three times more *furious* and more puissaunt, ... II. viii. 34. 8
At last breakes forth with *furious* unrest, ... II. xi. 32. 5
Her mighty charmes, her *furious* loving fitt; . . . . . II. xii. 44. 5
Guyon drove so *furious* and fell, ... III. i. 6. 2
Her fyrie eyes with *furious* sparkes did stare, ... III. vii. 39. 8
with his *furious* blast . . . . . III. ix. 15. 8
he the more with *furious* rage was fyred, ... IV. i. 54. 7
The outrage of his *furious* fit relented. . . . . . IV. ii. 2. 4
The *furious* flames of malice to asswage. . . . . . IV. ii. 28. 4
With dreadfull force and *furious* intent, ... IV. iii. 6. 6
passing forth with *furious* affret, ... IV. iii. 11. 7
They from them selves gan turne their *furious* ire, ... IV. ix. 29. 3
with *furious* might All th' East . . . did over-ronne, ... V. i. 2. 1
those Damzells did forestall Their *furious* encounter, ... V. iv. 5. 9
All sodainely enflam'd with *furious* fit . . . . . V. iv. 39. 5
She . . . on him ran With *furious* rage, ... V. v. 6. 4
when calmed was her *furious* heat, ... V. v. 47. 8
having force increast through *furious* paine, ... V. vii. 33. 6
All flaming with revenge and *furious* despight. . . . . . V. viii. 46. 9
Nor all the Moenades so *furious* were, ... V. viii. 47. 8
with *furious* bit Snatching at every thing . . . . . V. viii. 49. 3
Is so exceeding *furious* and fell As wrong, ... V. ix. 1. 2
ryven quight Out of their breasts with *furious* despight: . . . V. x. 32. 5
With that all mad and *furious* he grew, ... V. xi. 12. 1
To save him selfe from those his *furious* heats, ... V. xi. 13. 3
both inflam'd with *furious* despight; . . . . . VI. i. 36. 5
Sparkling fire out of his *furious* eyne, ... VI. v. 26. 2
He to him turnd with *furious* intent, ... VI. vi. 27. 2
fared like a *furious* wyld Beare, ... VI. xi. 25. 8
with thy *furious* fervour Thou does afflict . . . . . *H.L.* 158

Furiously. both eftsoones upstarted *furiously*, ... II. viii. 18. 8
he to him leaped *furiously*, ... II. viii. 33. 2
furiously Hurling his sword away . . . . . III. vii. 33. 5
saw the wicked fire so *furiously* Consume his hart, ... III. x. 14. 5
begonne His stolen steed to thunder *furiously*, ... III. x. 33. 6
So *furiously* they met, that either bare The other downe . . . IV. i. 41. 7
So *furiously* each other did assayle, ... IV. ii. 18. 1
So *furiously* they both together met, ... IV. iv. 18. 1
seeing him come on so *furiously*, ... IV. iv. 28. 7
therewithall at him right *furiously* she strooke. . . . . . IV. vi. 14. 9
So *furiously* she strooke in her first heat, ... IV. vi. 15. 1
So *furiously* that, ere he wist, ... IV. viii. 45. 4
they much more *furiously* gan fare, ... IV. ix. 27. 1
so *furiously* at him he flew, ... V. xi. 5. 1
charged him so fierce and *furiously*, ... VI. v. 16. 5

Furlong's. both a *furlongs* mountenaunce Retird their steeds, . III. viii. 18. 5

Furlongs. three *furlongs* does but litle lacke; . . . . . I. xi. 11. 7
carried him perforse Above three *furlongs*, ... II. xi. 46. 5

Furnace. From his infernall *fournace* forth he threw Huge flames I. xi. 44. 2
By every *fournace* many feendes did byde, II. vii. 35. 6
a mightie *fornace,* burning whott, II. ix. 29. 6
nosethrils burnd . . . like to a *furnace* redd, III. ix. 22. 4
Furnaces. hundred *fournaces* all burning bright: II. vii. 35. 5
Furniment. in a charet of straunge *furniment* IV. iii. 38. 4
Furnish. With flowring blossomes to *furnish* the prime, *S.C.* F. 167
by his shifts his Master *furnish* can. *Hub.* 918
Furnished. A filed toung, *furnisht* with tearmes of art, *Col.* 701
bravely *furnished* as ship might bee, II. xii. 19. 3
Unfitly *furnisht* with thy bag and booke, III. x. 24. 7
Furniture. some *furniture* about her steed To be disordred VI. v. 10. 2
Furnitures. theretoo gan his *furnitures* prepare. *Mui.* 56
had his *furnitures* not firmely tyde. III. i. 11. 8
In his proud *furnitures* she freshly dight, III. vii. 18. 8
As each one had his *furnitures* deviz'd. V. iii. 4. 5
Furor. Guyon does *Furor* bind in chaines, II. iv. Arg.
That same is *Furor,* II. iv. 10. 6
whoso will raging *Furor* tame, II. iv. 11. 1
when as Guyon *Furor* had captivd, II. iv. 16. 1
soone as *Furor* was enlargd, II. v. 19. 8
Furor, oh! *Furor* hath me thus bedight: II. vi. 50. 2
Furor's. Pyrochles . . . *Furors* chayne untyes, II. v. Arg.
more thereby increased *Furors* might, II. v. 22. 2
Furrow. three yardes deepe a *furrow* up did throw. I. viii. 8. 6
in an heaped *furrow* did thee hyde; I. x. 66. 2
fruitlesse lives were under *furrow* sowne, III. ix. 35. 8
Backe to the *furrow* which I lately left. VI. ix. 1. 2
I lately left a *furrow,* one or twayne, Unplough'd, VI. ix. 1. 3
Furrow's. yokes assoyle At this same *furrowes* end, III. xii. 47. *or.*6
turne we here to this faire *furrowes* end V. iii. 40. 6
Furrows. browes, Full of wrinckles and frostie *furrowes,* *S.C.* F. 44
Furrows'. Quenching the gasping *furrowes* thirst with rayne? *S.C.* Ap. 6
in my face deepe *furrowes* eld hath pight: *S.C.* D. 134
impresse Deepe dinted *furrowes* in the battred mayle: I. v. 6. 8
they . . . made wide *furrowes* in their fleshes fraile, I. vi. 43. 5
the rich *furrowes* flote, all quite fordonne: III. vii. 34. 6
Further. Ne *further* seeke to glose *Gn.* Ded. 10
and not be *further* vext. *Gn.* Ded. 12
would he *further* none but for availe; *Hub.* 1204
bad him stay at ease till *further* preeving. *Hub.* 1366
Upon that famous Rivers *further* shore, *Ti.* 589
tell on *further,* Colin, as befell *Col.* 176
'But say on *further* . . . The rest *Col.* 328
with-hold, till *further* tryall made.' I. i. 12. 6
How he may worke unto her *further* smarts; I. ii. 9. 7
she bad him tellen plaine The *further* processe I. vi. 37. 8
He hearkned, and did stay from *further* harmes, I. vii. 15. 1
Perswade us dye, to stint all *further* strife: I. ix. 29. 8
further from it daily wanderest: I. ix. 40. 3
The *further* he doth goe, the *further* he doth stray. I. ix. 43. 9
doe no *further* goe, no *further* stray, I. ix. 44. 1
For feare of *further* harme, II. iv. 39. 4
Forthwith directed to that *further* strand; II. vi. 38. 2
him forward ledd him *further* to entise. II. vii. 39. 9
They made the *further* shore resounden wide. II. vii. 57. 6
He lookt a litle *further,* II. vii. 61. 1
By *further* search had passage found elsewhere; II. viii. 3. 4
further way It made, II. viii. 38. 6
and *further* to invade. II. x. 6. 9
it no *further* went, But to the ground II. xi. 24. 7
But to occasion him to *further* talke, III. ii. 12. 1
ne *further* fastned not, But went her way; III. ii. 26. 2
Stoutly foorth stepping on the *further* shore, III. v. 18. 6
Ne foot could *further* move. III. vii. 3. 8
bide him batteill without *further* treat. III. viii. 16. 5
The which to let you weet will *further* time requyre. III. viii. 52. 9
Thence to depart for *further* aide t' enquire: III. xii. 45. 8
Ne stayed *further* newes thereof to learne, IV. x. 9. 3
Excludes from fairest hope withouten *further* triall. IV. x. 17. 9
Perhaps I may all *further* quarrell end, V. i. 25. 6
further did uncomely speaches crake. V. iii. 16. 7
further right by tokens to descrie, V. iii. 32. 5
That *further* mayd, hight Philtera the faire, V. iv. 8. 7
broke his sword, for feare of *further* harmes, V. v. 21. 8
this *further* purpose to him shope. V. v. 39. 9
gan the other *further* to devize V. vi. 20. 7
Till to the Bridges *further* end she past; V. vi. 39. 6
passing litle *further,* V. ix. 21. 3
Had hid themselves, or taken *further* flight: V. x. 19. 4
She humbly thankt him . . . And *further* sayd: V. xi. 18. 2
Sir Calidore . . . *further* gan inquire VI. ii. 13. 6
and *further* gan devize VI. iii. 8. 8
Stood on the *further* bancke beholding him; VI. iii. 34. 2
And like in time to *further* ill to grow, VI. iv. 30. 8
whose covert stopt his *further* sight: VI. v. 17. 7
did from *further* violence restraine, VI. v. 27. 4
further could not pas Through feeblenesse, VI. v. 31. 8
'Yet *further* hast thou heaped shame to shame, VI. vi. 34. 1
Till Mirabellaes fortunes I doe *further* say. VI. vii. 50. 9
For *further* fortune then I would inquire; VI. ix. 24. 5
usde him friendly for *further* intent, VI. x. 37. 7
further then she willing was he prest, VI. xi. 7. 6
in his mind had closely made A *further* purpose, VI. xi. 38. 8
Tho *further* asking her of sundry things, VI. xii. 20. 1
'Cease therefore, daughter, *further* to aspire, VII. vii. 59. 1
further seemes his terme still to extend, *Am.* lxxxvi. 11
we cease your *further* prayse to sing; *Epith.* 407
they seeke onely, without *further* care, *H.L.* 101

Further—*Continued.*
forceth *further* on, and striveth still *H.L.* 247
as every thing . . . *further* is from earth, *H.H.B.* 45
Looke thou no *further,* but affixe thine eye *H.H.B.* 50
Furtherance. To these first labours needed *furtheraunce.* *Ded. Son.* ii. 14
for *furtherance* of his guile, II. iv. 25. 1
Furthest. *Furthest* fro the marke, *S.C.* May 307
Furthest from end then, when they neerest weene, I. i. 10. 6
furthest from her hope, when most she weened nye. I. iii. 21. 9
daintie spices fetch from *furthest* Ynd, I. v. 4. 6
they be come unto the *furthest* part; I. v. 36. 4
The *furthest* North that did to them appeare: III. ix. 49. 3
doome . . . That *furthest* Nations filles with awful dread, V. Pr. 11. 5
furthest from the skie And from the earth, VI. vi. 11. 2
Fury. breathing *furie* from his inward gall *Bel.*[2] xiv. 11
for your antique *furie* here doo call, *Ro.* i. 12
Emongst themselves with cruell *furie* striving, *Ro.* x. 11
Nor the swift *furie* of the flames aspiring, *Ro.* xiii. 1
If the blinde *furie,* which warres breedeth oft, *Ro.* xxiv. 1
Thou onely cause, O Civill *furie!* art, *Ro.* xxxi. 9
the wilde beasts their *furie* did withhold, *Gn.* 451
Bett back the *furie* of the Trojan fyre. *Gn.* 496
the fires scorn'd *furie* to detest; *Gn.* 612
What *furie,* or what feend with felon deeds *T.M.* 45
Enflam'd with *fury* . . . He seemd in hart to harbour thoughts unkind, I. iv. 38. 7
Commaunded them their *fury* to refraine; I. iv. 40. 7
with so' exceeding *furie* at him strake, I. v. 12. 7
what *fury* mad Hath thee incenst I. vi. 47. 1
he gan . . . towardes him with dreadfull *fury* praunce; I. vii. 11. 3
With forced *fury* following his behest, I. ix. 7. 5
Ne ever will their fervent *fury* slake, I. ix. 8. 3
with bold *furie* armes the weakest hart: II. i. 57. 8
With horrible assault and *fury* fell, II. ii. 20. 4
suppressing *fury* mad, They gan abstaine II. ii. 28. 7
It's eath his ydle *fury* to aswage, II. iv. 11. 7
with horrible affright And hellish *fury* II. iv. 30. 2
such agony As griefe and *fury* unto me did bring; II. iv. 33. 4
Yet nathemore did it his *fury* stint, II. v. 8. 3
What hellish *fury* hath at earst thee hent? II. vi. 49. 2
With greater *fury* then before was fownd; II. ix. 15. 2
overflow With suddein *fury* all the fertile playne, II. xi. 18. 6
those wild-beasts that rag'd with *furie* mad; II. xii. 84. 5
Ne slake the *fury* of her cruell flame, III. ii. 52. 2
'He in his *furie* all shall overronne, III. iii. 34. 1
marching forth with *fury* insolent III. iii. 38. 3
will hevens *fury* never slake, III. iii. 43. 5
the *fury* past, to former hew Hee turnd againe, III. iii. 50. 8
With so fierce *furie* and great puissaunce, III. iv. 16. 2
Full of fiers *fury* and indignant hate III. v. 23. 3
Asswage the *fury* which his entrails teares: III. vii. 21. 4
His former griefe with *furie* fresh reviv'd III. viii. 3. 4
Ne ought your burning *fury* mote abate; III. viii. 28. 7
With extreme *fury* he became quite mad, III. x. 54. 5
what *furie* furst Brought thee from balefull house of Proserpine, III. xi. 1. 1
Troden in dust with *fury* insolent, III. xi. 52. 8
Next him went Griefe and *Fury,* III. xii. 16. 1
Fury was full ill appareiled In rags, III. xii. 17. 1
From her, to whom his *fury* first he ment, III. xii. 33. 1
under great Alcides *furie* fell; IV. i. 23. 5
His flaming *furie* sought to have assuaged IV. i. 54. 3
with the *furie* of their owne affret IV. ii. 15. 6
with such *furie* backe at him it heft, IV. iii. 12. 5
Till th' heat of his fierce *furie* he had spent; IV. iii. 26. 5
some hellish *furie* or some feend IV. vi. 17. 6
neither would their fiendlike *fury* slacke, IV. ix. 25. 5
Soone as with *fury* thou doest them inspire, IV. x. 46. 8
Ne other end their *fury* would afford, V. iv. 6. 3
Having the mindes of men with *fury* fraught, V. vii. 11. 4
fild with heavenly *fury,* thus he her behight. V. vii. 20. 9
through great *fury* both their skill forgot, V. vii. 29. 4
she his *fury* willed him to slake: V. vii. 36. 7
the Souldan all with *furie* fraught, V. viii. 28. 1
Such was the *furie* of these head-strong steeds, V. viii. 41. 1
With franticke passion and with *furie* fraught; V. viii. 48. 7
Therewith all fraught with *fury* and disdaine, V. xi. 8. 1
asswage Their forces *furie,* and their terror slake; V. xii. 8. 4
with such force and *furie* violent V. xii. 17. 5
goodly *fury* into them infuse, VI. Pr. 2. 6
Such was the *fury* of this hellish Beast, VI. xii. 32. 6
With so fell *fury* and dispiteous forse, VI. i. 33. 6
his heart did inly flame With wrathfull *fury* VI. iii. 43. 5
Flying the *fury* of his bloudy will: VI. iii. 49. 4
with fierce *fury* . . . Upon him ran; VI. iv. 5. 3
with greedie force And *furie* to be crossed in his way, VI. iv. 20. 7
Durst not the *furie* of his force abyde, VI. vi. 28. 2
fought through *fury* fierce and bold. VI. xi. 30. 9
Such was the *fury* of this hellish Beast, VI. xii. 32. 6
me with heavenly *fury* doth inspire, *Am.* lxxxiv. 11
my feeble breast inspire With gentle *furie,* *H.L.* 28
What wontlesse *fury* dost thou now inspire *H.B.* 2
Future. No signe of storme, no feare of *future* paine, *Gn.* 565
Whose praises I to *future* age doo sing; *Ti.* 277
With fruitfull hope . . . Of *future* good, *Mui.* 26
Litle wist he his fatall *future* woe, *Mui.* 381
Whose *future* woes so plaine he fashioned; III. iii. 43. 3
when thy glory shall be farre displayd To *future* age, VI. x. 28. 9
Fylde. *See* **Filed.**
Fynd. *See* **Find, Fined.**

G

Gage. have in *gage* The Primitias of your Parsonage: . . . *Hub.* 517
In *gage* for his gay Masters hopelesse dett: . . . *Hub.* 865
nothing ever may redeeme, . . . so sure a *gage,* . . . *Ded. Son.* vii. 7
In Fraunce and Ireland left a famous *gage;* . . . *Ded.Son.* xiv.11
that same envious *gage* Of victors glory . . . I. iv. 39. 5
To reave by strength the griped *gage* away: . . . I. xi. 41. 6
That could her purchase with his lives adventur'd *gage.* . . . IV. iii. 4. 9
Out of his hands could not redeeme her *gage,* . . . IV. viii. 50. 7
Gaged. As if their lives had in his hand beene *gagd;* . . . II. iii. 14. 3
Gain. to thinke How great sport they *gaynen* . . . *S.C.* May 36
get all the *gayne,* . . . *S.C.* May 50
lived with little *gayne:* . . . *S.C.* Jul. 128
for such, as of guile maken *gayne,* . . . *S.C.* S. 34
who will seeke for unknowne *gayne,* . . . *S.C.* S. 72
little good hath got, and much lesse *gayne.* . . . *S.C.* O. 10
The glory eke much greater then the *gayne:* . . . *S.C.* O. 20
Much greater gyfts for guerdon thou shalt *gayne,* . . . *S.C.* N. 45
all my hoped *gaine* is turnd to scathe: . . . *S.C.* D. 100
seeke some other way to *gaine* by giving, . . . *Hub.* 350
Thus did the Ape at first him credit *gaine,* . . . *Hub.* 689
Not so much for to *gaine,* or for to raise . . . *Hub.* 774
may be matter meete to *gaine* him praise: . . . *Hub.* 779
vaine to seeke, Or hope to *gaine,* . . . *Hub.* 913
great he was in grace, and rich through *gaine.* . . . *Hub.* 1200
What time the Ape the kingdome first did *gaine,* . . . *Hub.* 1207
without gifts or *gaine;* . . . *T.M.* 82
greatest ones did sue to *gaine* his grace; . . . *Ti.* 186
who so els did goodnes by him *gaine,* . . . *Ti.* 232
Such one King Edmond, but was rent for *gaine.* . . . *Ti.* 418
Bold men, presuming life for *gaine* to sell, . . . *Col.* 209
glad to *gain* such favour, gan devise, . . . I. vi. 32. 8
To *gayne* so goodly guerdon as she spake: . . . I. vii. 15. 2
Of that great Queene may well *gaine* worthie grace, . . . I. ix. 17. 7
she was inly glad her purpose so to *gaine.* . . . II. i. 20. 9
All for their Ladies froward love to *gaine,* . . . II. ii. 26. 4
Ill by ensample good doth often *gayne.'* . . . II. ii. 45. 5
if thou meane her love to *gayn.* . . . II. vi. 28. 6
them that covet such eye-glutting *gaine* . . . II. vii. 9. 8
sometimes with hope of *gayn,* . . . II. xi. 14. 8
'So may ye *gaine* to you full great renowme . . . III. v. 11. 1
Which if thou *gaine,* I shal be well apayd. . . . III. v. 36. 5
glad by any meanes her grace to *gaine,* . . . III. vii. 54. 1
for faire ladies love and glories *gaine,* . . . III. ix. 37. 7
without regard of *gaine* or scath, . . . IV. ii. 11. 3
God send you better *gaine!'* . . . IV. ii. 6. 5
gaine a feastfull guerdon of their toyle, . . . IV. iii. 16. 4
He sends the sea his owne with double *gaine,* . . . IV. iii. 27. 8
that could so goodly riches *gaine,* . . . IV. iv. 16. 8
that glorious prize to *gaine.* . . . IV. iv. 26. 5
Who was right glad to *gaine* so goodly meed: . . . IV. v. 22. 2
Death is to him . . . Both grace and *gaine;* . . . IV. vii. 11. 8
rule to himselfe did *gaine* Of many Nations . . . IV. viii. 47. 3
That enterprize for greatest glories *gayne.* . . . IV. ix. 4. 5
such *gaine* was gotten deare. . . . IV. ix. 30. 9
she her love to him would shortly *gaine.* . . . IV. xii. 27. 6
the fairer love to *gaine,* . . . V. i. 24. 8
The maysterdome of each by force to *gaine,* . . . V. ii. 15. 4
In hope by him great benefite to *gaine,* . . . V. ii. 33. 4
The Fayrie, glad to *gaine* his libertie, . . . V. v. 55. 4
May you in heaven immortall guerdon *gaine* . . . V. x. 21. 4
much to *gaine,* a litle for to yield: . . . V. xii. 19. 4
That shall you glory *gaine* More then his love, . . . VI. i. 27. 4
Doth best become and greatest grace doth *gaine:* . . . VI. ii. 2. 8
So fare on foote till thou another *gayne,* . . . VI. iii. 32. 2
When ought he did, that did their lyking *gaine.* . . . VI. iv. 16. 5
Where singled forces faile, conjoynd may *gaine.* . . . VI. v. 14. 7
his two knights Doe *gaine* their treasons meed: . . . VI. vii. Arg.
ere he recovery could *gaine,* . . . VI. viii. 10. 8
her companie to *gaine,* . . . VI. ix. 34. 7
Long time had lov'd, and hop'd her love to *gaine,* . . . VI. ix. 38. 2
the guerdon of his love to *gaine;* . . . VI. x. 2. 4
through that small favours *gaine,* . . . VI. xi. 7. 5
Rule and dominion to her selfe to *gaine;* . . . VII. vi. 4. 2
Thinks of her Dairy to make wondrous *gaine,* . . . VII. vi. 48. 2
I doo complaine, . . . that justice I may *gaine.* . . . *Am.* xii. 14
seeke most pretious things to make your *gain;* . . . *Am.* xv. 2
That endlesse pleasure shall unto me *gaine!* . . . *Am.* xxvi. 14
All sorrowes short that *gaine* eternall blisse. . . . *Am.* lxiii. 14
loosing one, two liberties ye *gayne,* . . . *Am.* lxv. 3
Bring home with you the glory of her *gaine* . . . *Epith.* 244
please her best, and grace unto him *gaine;* . . . *H.L.* 222
To live thus happie as her grace to *gaine.* . . . *H.L.* 244
Had it beene wrong to aske his owne with *gaine?* . . . *H.H.L.* 180
Their joy, their comfort, their desire, their *gaine,* . . . *H.H.B.* 271
Gained. Fayth of my soule, I deeme ech have *gayned:* . . . *S.C.* Au. 131
his man Raynolds purchase which he *gain'd.* . . . *Hub.* 854
the man . . . thorough grace hath *gained* victory: . . . I. x. 1. 7
shortly *gaynd* that losse exceeded farre. . . . II. v. 15. 5
whenas hee In Nemus *gayned* goodly victoree: . . . II. v. 31. 5
Till aged Hely by dew heritage it *gaynd.* . . . II. x. 45. 9
At last of her far off he *gained* vew. . . . III. iv. 48. 1
th' other litle *gained* by the lone, . . . IV. ix. 30. 7
till he an horse have *gayned.'* . . . V. iii. 35. 6
No fayrer conquest then that with goodwill is *gayned.* . . . V. v. 17. 9
For feare her mistresse shold have knowledge *gayned;* . . . V. v. 44. 4
his freedome to have *gayned,* . . . V. v. 54. 3
Untill his owne true love his freedome *gayned:* . . . V. v. 57. 8

Gained—*Continued.*
As she had got thereby and *gayned* a great stake. . . . V. xii. 32. 9
The which in all mens liking *gayned* place, . . . VI. i. 3. 4
to her selfe to have *gained* The kingdome of the Night, . . . VII. vi. 10. 8
how litle glory ye have *gayned* . . . *Am.* xxxvi. 10
Where oft I *gayned* giftes and goodly grace . . . *Proth.* 138
Gainest. So mak'st thou kings, and *gaynest* wrongfull government. . . . II. vii. 13. 9
Gaineth. A little well is lent that *gaineth* more withall. . . . VI. xi. 6. 9
Gainful. either for some *gainfull* benefit, . . . *Hub.* 639
Gains. sure his honestie Got him small *gaines,* . . . *Hub.* 850
to be instruments of others *gaines.* . . . *Col.* 706
greater conquest of hard love he *gaynes,* . . . I. vi. 3. 8
The knight . . . *gayns* Most glorious victory. . . . I. xi. Arg.
That shall you win more glory than ye here find *gaines.'* . . . IV. ii. 27. 9
Loose so immortall glory, and so endlesse *gaines.* . . . IV. xi. 22. 9
Which he atchieved to his owne great *gaines,* . . . VI. ix. 2. 8
by such trafficke after *gaines* to hunt, . . . VI. xi. 9. 4
Gainsaid. none *gainsaid,* nor none did him envie. . . . *Mui.* 152
She stood astonied long, ne ought *gainesaid;* . . . *Mui.* 339
yeelding soft, in that she nought *gainsaid,* . . . I. ii. 27. 7
her two other sisters . . . Her lowd *gainsaid,* . . . II. ii. 28. 2
whiles she no whit *gainesayd:* . . . V. xi. 64. 8
he had good right gaynst all that it *gainesayd.* . . . VI. ii. 18. 9
Gainsay. Yet list the same efforce with faind *gainesay;* . . . III. ii. 15. 8
Dy, if thou it *gainesay:* . . . III. viii. 12. 9
The fearefull Chorle durst not *gainesay* nor dooe, . . . III. viii. 13. 1
loth, yet durst he not *gainesay,* . . . III. x. 23. 8
I glad did not *gaine say* nor strive, . . . IV. viii. 56. 8
To which the Lion strongly doth *gainesay,* . . . V. vii. 30. 7
Gainsaying. with him went without *gaine-saying* more. . . . V. vi. 22. 3
Gainst (*partial list*).
cleare as Christall *gainst* the Sunnie beames, . . . *Bel.*[2] xii. 2
make warre *Gainst* time, . . . *Ro.* vii. 10
opposing *gainst* her might, . . . *Ro.* xviii. 11
'*Gainst* which the noble sonne of Telamon . . . *Gn.* 513
gainst whom appeard anon Hector, . . . *Gn.* 515
speakest thus *gainst* their felicitie, . . . *Col.* 677
advaunst His cursed hand *gainst* God, . . . I. v. 47. 9
To her yeeld passage *gainst* his Lord to goe, . . . I. viii. 13. 7
happie victory *Gainst* him, . . . I. xii. 4. 4
gainst the craggy clifts did loudly rore, . . . III. iv. 7. 5
gainst tyde and winde: . . . III. iv. 9. 8
looking still askaunce *Gainst* Britomart, . . . III. ix. 27. 4
for a Lady *gainst* a faithlesse knight: . . . III. x. 28. 5
Gainst whom he alwayes bent . . . III. xii. 12. 8
Gainst all that truth or vertue doe professe; . . . IV. viii. 24. 7
ye plaine, *Gainst* one . . . IV. xii. 30. 3
damn'd her sonnes which *gainst* them did rebell, . . . V. vii. 10. 8
Gainst tortious powre and lawlesse regiment, . . . V. viii. 30. 7
That he *gainst* courtesie so fowly did default. . . . VI. iii. 21. 9
To justifie thy fault *gainst* me in equall fight.' . . . VI. iii. 35. 9
his tongue doth whet *Gainst* all, . . . VI. vi. 12. 4
Gainst errant Knights and Ladies . . . VI. vi. 34. 5
gainst the cold hard earth so sore him strake, . . . VI. vii. 11. 4
began to reare *Gainst* all the Gods, . . . VII. vi. 1. 9
Gaynst such strong castles needeth greater might . . . *Am.* xiv. 5
raging floods; *Gaynst* which, a ship, . . . *Am.* lvi. 11
Gainstrive. He may them catch unable to *gainestrive,* . . . IV. vii. 12. 7
Gainstriving. him *gainstriving* nought at all prevaild; . . . II. iv. 14. 2
Gait. scarse thy legs uphold thy feeble *gate.'* . . . *Hub.* 600
Goe but a lowly *gate* . . . *S.C.* Env. 8
gently to them bowing in his *gate,* . . . *Hub.* 1084
Becomes more fierce and fervent in his *gate;* . . . *D.* 195
Came ramping forth with proud presumpteous *gate,* . . . I. viii. 12. 5
old man, . . . guyde his wearie *gate* both too and fro, . . . I. viii. 30. 4
all hory gray, With . . . *gate* full slow, . . . I. x. 5. 6
Stood gaping at their *gate,* and wondred them to see. . . . III. iv. 32. 9
to yonder castle turne your *gate.'* . . . III. viii. 51. 9
That by his *gate* might easily appeare; . . . III. xii. 8. 6
Who came at length with proud presumpteous *gate* . . . V. xii. 14. 1
Galage. *See* **Galosh.**
Galathea. Ne lesse praise-worthie *Galathea* seemes, . . . *Col.* 516
Faire *Galathea* with bright shining beames, . . . *Col.* 518
snowy neckd Doris, and milkewhite *Galathaea:* . . . IV. xi. 49. 9
Gale. At last blow up some gentle *gale* of ease, . . . III. iv. 10. 3
Galene. Light Doto, wanton Glauce, and *Galene* glad: . . . IV. xi. 48. 9
Galingale. Embathed Balme, and chearfull *Galingale,* . . . *Mui.* 194
Gall. *See* **Gaul.**
breathing furie from his inward *gall* . . . *Bel.*[2] xiv. 11
Of Hony and of *Gaule* in love . . . *S.C.*Mar.Emb.3
The Honye is much, but the *Gaule* is more. . . . *S.C.*Mar.Emb.4
I pray thee, *gall* not my old griefe: . . . *S.C.* S. 12
O *gall* of all good heartes! . . . *Ti.* 449
Sweet without sowre, and honny without *gall:* . . . *As.* 26
His *gall* did grate for griefe and high disdaine; . . . I. i. 19. 6
And wast his inward *gall* with deepe despight, . . . I. ii. 6. 4
With fowle words tempring faire, soure *gall* with hony sweet. I. vii. 3. 9
trees of bitter *Gall,* and Heben sad; . . . II. vii. 52. 2
did consume his *gall* with anguish sore: . . . III. x. 18. 2
Corrupts the stomacke with *gall* vitious, . . . III. x. 59. 7
nought but *gall* and venim comprehended, . . . IV. i. 27. 4
bitter *gall* away to chace, . . . IV. iii. 43. 3
heart did almost rend in tway, For very *gall,* . . . IV. iv. 22. 8
Pouring out streames of poyson and of *gall* . . . IV. viii. 24. 6
love with *gall* and hony doth abound; . . . IV. x. 1. 2
A pound of *gall* doth over it redound: . . . IV. x. 1. 5

Gall—*Continued.*
How ever it his noble heart did *gall* . . . V. v. 26. 3
She gan to storme, and rage, and rend her *gall,* . . . V. v. 47. 2
by her tempred without griefe or *gall,* . . . V. x. 4. 5
vexeth so that makes her eat her *gall;* . . . V. xii. 31. 5
had no courage, or else had no *gall.* . . . VI. iii. 36. 5
pours his poysnous *gall* forth . . . VI. vi. 12. 5
choked be with overflowing *gall.* . . . *Am.* xliii. 4
eates the hart and feedes upon the *gall,* . . . *H.L.* 268
Gallant. *See* **Stoop-gallant, Top-gallant.**
wisely did maintaine With *gallant* showe, . . . *Hub.* 691
gallant shew to be in greatest gree, . . . II. iii. 5. 8
this *gallant* with his goodly crew . . . IV. i. 33. 1
Gallantry. plaine attire such glorious *gallantry* Disdaines . . . *Col.* 729
Gallants. the yong lustie *gallants* he did chose To follow, . . . *Hub.* 797
Galled. The more it *gauld* and griev'd him night and day, . . . IV. v. 31. 8
Galleries. Sure gates, sweete gardens, stately *galleries,* . . . *Ti.* 95
goodly *galleries* far over laid, Full of faire windowes . . . I. iv. 4. 7
Galles. *See* **Gauls.**
Gallop. An armed knight towards them *gallop* fast, . . . I. ix. 21. 2
With hasty *gallop* towards her did ryde. . . . III. iv. 12. 3
Galloped. forward *gallopt* fast; . . . III. vii. 38. 6
Galloping. A Squire came *gallopping,* as he would flie, . . . IV. viii. 38. 2
Gallows. on a *gallowes* bleak Shall give th' enchaunter his unhappy hire. . . . III. iii. 36. 5
Gallows-tree. Saves Terpine from the *gallow tree,* . . . V. iv. Arg.
ready for the *gallow-tree* prepard: . . . V. iv. 22. 4
At length him nayled on a *gallow-tree,* . . . *H.H.L.* 153
Gallows-trees. hong their conquerd armes . . . On *gallow trees,* II. v. 26. 9
Galls. fraught with envie that their *galls* do swell, . . . *Col.* 760
Galosh. my *galage* growne fast to my heele: . . . *S.C.* F. 244
if thy *galage* once sticketh fast, . . . *S.C.* S. 131
Game. *See* **Laughing-game, May-game, Scoffing-game.**
Love . . . is abroad at his *game.* . . . *S.C.* Mar. 27
Tell me, Perigot, what shalbe the *game,* . . . *S.C.* Au. 1
gather nuttes to make me Christmas *game,* . . . *S.C.* D. 26
Of Lovers Miseries which maketh his bloodie *game?* . . . *Tetrasticon* 2
me no man bewaileth, but in *game,* . . . *Ti.* 162
as he that perilous *game* In forreine soyle pursued . . . *As.* 91
she . . . followes other *game* and venery: . . . I. vi. 22. 5
In these and like delightes of bloody *game* . . . I. vi. 29. 1
crowned her twixt earnest and twixt *game:* . . . I. xii. 8. 7
So can he turne his earnest unto *game,* . . . II. i. 31. 1
To seeke her *game:* . . . II. iii. 31. 5
yonder is no *game* . . . II. iii. 35. 1
Such cruell *game* my scarmoges disarmes. . . . II. vi. 34. 5
with court and goodly *game* . . . II. ix. 44. 4
makes his *game* The flying ships with swiftnes to pursew: . . . II. xii. 24. 3
minding nought but lustfull *game,* . . . II. xii. 81. 2
At tilt or tourney, or like warlike *game,* . . . III. ii. 9. 8
After late chace of their embrewed *game,* . . . III. vi. 17. 3
Forst him eftsoones to follow other *game,* . . . III. xi. 38. 8
turning all to *game* And pleasaunt bord, . . . IV. iv. 13. 1
Assembled for to get the honour of that *game.* . . . IV. iv. 13. 9
Far'd like a lyon in his bloodie *game,* . . . IV. iv. 41. 5
Fro me the honour of that *game* did reare; . . . IV. vi. 6. 7
With divers fortune fit for such a *game,* . . . V. iii. 7. 4
of his *game* she soone enwombed grew, . . . V. vii. 16. 5
an hungry hound That hunting after *game* hath carrion found, V. viii. 36. 5
When he did raunge the wood for salvage *game,* . . . VI. v. 15. 2
Did chalenge Calidore to wrestling *game;* . . . VI. ix. 43. 6
Another quest, another *game* in vew He hath, . . . VI. x. 2. 3
as fittest for her *game,* . . . VII. vi. 39. 1
Seeing the *game* from him escapt away, . . . *Am.* lxvii. 2
'Twixt earnest and twixt *game:* . . . *Epig.* iv. 12
could not chose but laugh at his fond *game,* . . . *Epig.* iv. 33
Making their cruell rage thy scornefull *game,* . . . *H.L.* 47
After full joyance of their gentle *game;* . . . *H.L.* 291
Games. With all the thriftles *games* that may be found; . . . *Hub.* 801
pledges, as the spoiles of my victorious *games.* . . . III. vii. 54. 9
seeing both bent to so bloudy *games,* . . . IV. ii. 20. 4
To practise *games* and maisteries to try, . . . VI. ix. 43. 2
Whether it were to caroll, . . . or *games* to exercize, . . . VI. x. 33. 6
Gamesome. *gamesom* merth to grievous dreriment: . . . III. iv. 30. 4
of her shame to make a *gamesome* jest; . . . VII. vi. 51. 3
Gan. *See* **Gan.**
shoure *Gan* quench the glystering flame. . . . *Bel.*[1] ix. 12
By more and more she *gan* . . . t' assure (trust[1]) . . . *Bel.* vii. 3
Which *gan* assaile this ship . . . *Bel.* xiii. 7
dew . . . *gan* quench those precious flames; . . . *Bel.*[2] xi. 12
The skie *gan* everie where to overcast, . . . *Pet.* iii. 9
Then *gan* that Nation, th' earths new Giant brood, . . . *Ro.* xi. 9
heaven, that *gan* her force to feare. . . . *Ro.* xii. 12
shortly *gan* all other beasts to scorne. . . . *Van.* viii. 8
The nations *gan* their soveraigntie disdaine, . . . *Van.* xi. 3
I *gan* in my engrieved brest To scorne . . . *Van.* xii. 5
the welked Phoebus *gan* availe His weary waine; . . . *S.C.* Ja. 73
Her mantle black through heaven *gan* overhaile: . . . *S.C.* Ja. 75
With painted words tho *gan* this proude weede . . . *S.C.* F. 160
eftsones Winter *gan* to approche; . . . *S.C.* F. 225
Now *gan* he repent his pryde to late; . . . *S.C.* F. 229
Some *gan* to gape for greedie governaunce, . . . *S.C.* May 121
Tho *gan* shepheards swaines to looke aloft, . . . *S.C.* May 124
his wreathed hornes *gan* newly sprout: . . . *S.C.* May 186
with that *gan* weepe, . . . *S.C.* May 189
gan his newe-budded beard to stroke. . . . *S.C.* May 214
(then *gan* he crye) . . . *S.C.* May 255
lowdly she *gan* to call Her Kidde; . . . *S.C.* May 296
after vertue *gan* for age to stoope, . . . *S.C.* O. 67
Tho *gan* the streames of flowing wittes to cease, . . . *S.C.* O. 71

Gan—*Continued.*
gan to shoote agayne, . . . *S.C.* O. 74
Thus *gan* he make of love his piteous mone. . . . *S.C.* D. 6
'Tho *gan* my lovely Spring bid me farewel, . . . *S.C.* D. 55
His little Goats *gan* drive out of their stalls, . . . *Gn.* 71
Into the highest top of heaven *gan* clime, . . . *Gn.* 157
gan the shepheard gather into one His stragling Goates, . . . *Gn.* 161
Wherewith enrag'd he fiercely *gan* upstart, . . . *Gn.* 289
streight about him *gan* beholde What God . . . *Gn.* 300
Night . . . her teemed steedes *gan* call, . . . *Gn.* 314
laesie Vesper . . . *gan* proceede withall; . . . *Gn.* 316
in sad tearmes *gan* sorrowfully weepe, . . . *Gn.* 325
Gan first thus plaine his case . . . *Hub.* 52
Eftsoones the Ape himselfe *gan* up to reare, . . . *Hub.* 237
With that the husbandman *gan* him avize, . . . *Hub.* 281
they *gan* to be descryed Of everie one, . . . *Hub.* 345
with reproachfull tearmes *gan* them revile, . . . *Hub.* 365
Gan at the length them to rebuke againe, . . . *Hub.* 397
The Priest *gan* wexe halfe proud to be so praide, . . . *Hub.* 413
of the Priest eftsoones *gan* to enquire, . . . *Hub.* 481
he through pride and fatnes *gan* despise Their meanesse; . . . *Hub.* 586
Then *gan* this craftie couple to devize, . . . *Hub.* 655
gan the Courtiers gaze on everie side, . . . *Hub.* 669
By secrete meanes *gan* of his state enquire, . . . *Hub.* 681
gan To growe into great lacke, . . . *Hub.* 926
all men him uncased *gan* deride, . . . *Hub.* 930
Now *gan* some courage unto him to take, . . . *Hub.* 994
first *gan* question, whether should assay . . . *Hub.* 997
faintly *gan* into his worke to enter, . . . *Hub.* 1006
At sight of him, *gan* fast away to flye; . . . *Hub.* 1069
Gan to provide for all things in assurance, . . . *Hub.* 1113
gan he rule and tyrannize at will, . . . *Hub.* 1127
Then *gan* he to himselfe new shape to frame; . . . *Hub.* 1266
He *gan* enquire of some in secret wize, . . . *Hub.* 1272
The Lion looking up *gan* him avize, . . . *Hub.* 1324
Thereat enraged, soone he *gan* upstart, . . . *Hub.* 1333
for his rough hide He *gan* to reach, . . . *Hub.* 1336
he *gan* full terribly to rore, . . . *Hub.* 1337
Then *gan* she wofully to waile, . . . *T.M.* 169
first *gan* you to torment, . . . *T.M.* 374
she lowdly *gan* to waile and shrike, . . . *T.M.* 475
Gan faile, and all the rest downe shortlie fell, . . . *Ti.* 558
theretoo *gan* his furnitures prepare. . . . *Mui.* 56
Lord! how he *gan* for to bestirre him tho, . . . *Mui.* 252
Then *gan* she greatly to lament and weepe. . . . *Mui.* 288
Then *gan* the Goddesse bright Her selfe . . . to dight. . . . *Mui.* 303
steeds . . . *gan* water in the west, . . . *D.* 25
gan to cast how I her compasse might, . . . *D.* 115
Therewith he *gan* afresh to waile and weepe, . . . *D.* 169
Then *gan* I him to comfort all my best, . . . *D.* 190
gan him to recomfort as I might. . . . *D.* 546
Gan dight themselves t' expresse . . . *As.* Interl. 225
gan thus to him areed. . . . *Col.* 15
they all *gan* throng about him neare, . . . *Col.* 52
gan a gentle bonylasse to speake, . . . *Col.* 172
He *gan* to cast great lyking to my lore, . . . *Col.* 180
she thenceforth therein *gan* take delight; . . . *Col.* 361
gan by litle learne to love each other: . . . *Col.* 852
gan heaven out of darknesse dread For to appeare, . . . *Col.* 855
Next *gan* the earth to shew her naked head, . . . *Col.* 857
Thenceforth they *gan* each one his like to love, . . . *Col.* 863
Therewith enrag'd she loudly *gan* to bray, . . . I. i. 17. 5
Whereat he *gan* to stretch; . . . I. i. 42. 5
The Sprite then *gan* more boldly him to wake, . . . I. i. 43. 1
whereat he *gan* to quake, . . . I. i. 43. 3
He . . . *gan* himselfe advise To prove his sense, . . . I. i. 50. 5
That troublous dreame *gan* freshly tosse his braine . . . I. i. 55. 6
messengers of hell, . . . *gan* tel Their bootelesse paines, . . . I. ii. 2. 3
wicked maister, . . . *gan* threaten hellish paine, . . . I. ii. 2. 6
guest, . . . *gan* now to take more sound repast; . . . I. ii. 4. 3
Then *gan* she wail and weepe to see that woeful stowre. . . . I. ii. 7. 9
The knight of the Redcrosse, . . . *Gan* fairely couch his speare, I. ii. 15. 3
the sleeping spark Of native vertue *gan* eftsoones revive; . . . I. ii. 19. 2
after her as hastily *gan* scowre, . . . I. ii. 20. 5
Melting in teares, then *gan* shee thus lament. . . . I. ii. 22. 1
from her most beastly companie I *gan* refraine, . . . I. ii. 41. 6
with pale and deadly hew, At last she up *gan* lift: . . . I. ii. 45. 6
Her hart *gan* melt in great compassion; . . . I. iii. 6. 8
approching she to her *gan* call, . . . I. iii. 11. 1
full of ghastly fright . . . *Gan* shut the dore. . . . I. iii. 12. 8
she *gan* them pray, That in their cotage small . . . I. iii. 14. 8
For anguish great they *gan* to rend their heare, . . . I. iii. 22. 4
they *gan* loudly bray, With hollow houling, . . . I. iii. 23. 1
Therewith she *gan* her passion to renew, . . . I. iii. 25. 1
he forward *gan* advaunce His fair enchaunted steed, . . . I. iii. 25. 8
She . . . towards him *gan* ride: . . . I. iii. 26. 7
He . . . *gan* eftsoones prepare Himselfe to batteill . . . I. iii. 34. 3
hope of new good hap he *gan* to feele; . . . I. iii. 34. 8
in haste his helmet *gan* unlace, . . . I. iii. 37. 1
Therewith they *gan* to hurtlen greedily, . . . I. iv. 40. 1
the golden Orientall gate . . . *gan* to open fayre; . . . I. v. 2. 2
lowd to him *gan* call The false Duessa, . . . I. v. 11. 8
Out of his swowning dreame he *gan* awake; . . . I. v. 12. 2
his heavie hand he high *gan* reare, . . . I. v. 13. 5
they . . . softly *gan* embalme on everie side: . . . I. v. 17. 5
the witches speach she *gan* to heare, . . . I. v. 21. 7
She stayd; and foorth Duessa *gan* proceede: . . . I. v. 22. 1
At them he *gan* to reare his bristles strong, . . . I. v. 34. 5
gan to him discover all his harmes, . . . I. v. 41. 5
His cunning hand *gan* to his wounds to lay, . . . I. v. 44. 2

Gan—*Continued.*

Then *gan* her beautie shyne as brightest skye,	I. vi. 4. 8
With greedy force he *gan* the fort assayle,	I. vi. 5. 3
got his ready steed, and fast away *gan* ryde.	I. vi. 8. 9
till to ryper yeares he *gan* aspyre,	I. vi. 23. 7
turning backe *gan* fast to fly away;	I. vi. 28. 2
then to him these womanish words *gan* say:	I. vi. 28. 5
Gan her admire, and her sad sorrowes rew,	I. vi. 31. 4
glad to gain such favour, *gan* devise,	I. vi. 32. 8
towards him they *gan* in haste to ride,	I. vi. 34. 4
he them spying *gan* to turne aside	I. vi. 34. 7
Una *gan* to aske, if ought he knew,	I. vi. 36. 4
Then *gan* the Pilgrim thus:	I. vi. 38. 1
Therewith they *gan*, . . . To thunder blowes,	I. vi. 43. 1
They *gan* to fight retourne,	I. vi. 45. 2
he *gan* revive the memory Of his leud lusts,	I. vi. 46. 2
The witch approching *gan* him fayrely greet,	I. vii. 3. 6
Unkindnesse past, they *gan* of solace treat,	I. vii. 4. 1
The goddesse wroth *gan* fowly her disgrace,	I. vii. 5. 5
Eftsoones his manly forces *gan* to fayle,	I. vii. 6. 4
crudled cold his corage *gan* assayle,	I. vii. 6. 7
Th' Elfe . . . his unready weapons *gan* in hand to take.	I. vii. 7. 9
he *gan* advaunce With huge force	I. vii. 11. 1
Duessa loud to him *gan* crye,	I. vii. 14. 4
Then *gan* the Dwarfe the whole discourse declare;	I. vii. 26. 1
With lovely court he *gan* her entertaine;	I. vii. 38. 2
Faire feeling words he wisely *gan* display,	I. vii. 38. 6
Wherewith enmovd, these bleeding words she *gan* to say.	I. vii. 38. 9
Ere she had ended all she *gan* to faint:	I. vii. 52. 1
That when the carefull knight *gan* well avise,	I. viii. 15. 5
He . . . to the beast *gan* turne his enterprise,	I. viii. 15. 7
Unto the Gyaunt lowdly she *gan* call;	I. viii. 20. 8
Then *gan* he lowdly through the house to call;	I. viii. 29. 6
gentle Una thus to him *gan* say:	I. ix. 16. 5
The golden Sunne his glistring head *gan* shew,	I. ix. 18. 2
as they traveild, lo! they *gan* espy	I. ix. 21. 1
hopelesse, hartlesse, *gan* the cunning thiefe Perswade us dye,	I. ix. 29. 7
Then *gan* the villein him to overcraw,	I. ix. 50. 5
Thus as they *gan* of sondrie thinges devise,	I. x. 12. 1
They, seeing Una, towardes her *gan* wend,	I. x. 15. 1
goodly *gan* discourse of many a noble gest.	I. x. 15. 9
a Groome, . . . *gan* despoile Of puissant armes,	I. x. 17. 7
Fayre Una *gan* Fidelia fayre request,	I. x. 18. 3
wretched world he *gan* for to abhore,	I. x. 21. 4
mortall life *gan* loath as thing forelore,	I. x. 21. 5
he *gan* apply relief	I. x. 24. 4
Gan him instruct in everie good behest,	I. x. 33. 3
when his feet . . . *gan* to shrinke,	I. x. 35. 7
his fraile thighes . . . *Gan* faile;	I. x. 47. 9
Whereat he wondred much, and *gan* enquere,	I. x. 56. 6
whenas himselfe he *gan* to fynd,	I. x. 68. 1
gan him desyre Of her adventure myndfull for to bee.	I. x. 68. 7
High time now *gan* it wex	I. xi. 1. 1
her knight she *gan* to cheare,	I. xi. 1. 5
Eftsoones he *gan* advance his haughty crest,	I. xi. 15. 5
The knight *gan* fayrely couch his steady speare,	I. xi. 16. 1
gan his sturdy sterne about to weld,	I. xi. 28. 8
gan the golden Phoebus for to steepe His fierie face	I. xi. 31. 1
Gan high advaunce his broad discoloured brest	I. xi. 31. 7
gan to highest God entirely pray	I. xi. 32. 4
The morrow next *gan* earely to appeare,	I. xi. 33. 1
ere the morrow next *gan* reare Out of the sea	I. xi. 33. 3
Then *gan* he tosse aloft his stretched traine,	I. xi. 37. 5
the drouping day-light *gan* to fade,	I. xi. 49. 5
gan to shade The face of earth	I. xi. 49. 7
for his safetie *gan* devoutly pray,	I. xi. 50. 8
The joyous day *gan* early to appeare;	I. xi. 51. 1
Aurora from the deawy bed . . . *gan* herselfe to reare	I. xi. 51. 3
He woxe dismaid, and *gan* his fate to feare:	I. xi. 52. 8
to his Lord and Lady lowd *gan* call,	I. xii. 2. 8
Then *gan* triumphant Trompets sownd on hye,	I. xii. 4. 1
to her gossibs *gan* in counsell say;	I. xii. 11. 4
That auncient Lord *gan* fit occasion finde,	I. xii. 15. 3
Thus *gan* to say—	I. xii. 24. 6
He *gan* renew the late forbidden bains,	I. xii. 36. 7
Then *gan* they sprinckle all the posts with wine,	I. xii. 38. 1
He *gan* to weave a web of wicked guyle,	II. i. 8. 4
He . . . his percing speach *gan* paynt:	II. i. 9. 5
she *gan* appease Her voluntarie paine,	II. i. 16. 8
His warlike armes about him *gan* embrace,	II. i. 26. 2
He *gan* rencounter him in equall race.	II. i. 26. 5
that warriour *gan* abace His threatned speare,	II. i. 26. 7
Then Guyon forward *gan* his voyage make	II. i. 34. 3
His hart *gan* wexe as starke as marble stone,	II. i. 42. 2
At last his mighty ghost *gan* deepe to grone,	II. i. 42. 5
then *gan* softly feel Her feeble pulse,	II. i. 43. 3
shee *gan* to breath out living aire.	II. i. 43. 9
he perceiving greatly *gan* rejoice,	II. i. 44. 1
her dim eie-lids she up *gan* reare,	II. i. 45. 1
he his armes about her sides *gan* fold,	II. i. 46. 4
Then meanes I *gan* devise for his deliveraunce.	II. i. 54. 9
gan devoutly sweare;	II. i. 61. 4
The litle babe . . . *Gan* smyle on them,	II. ii. 1. 6
Whom thus at gaze the Palmer *gan* to bord	II. ii. 5. 1
Gan with new rage their shieldes to hew	II. ii. 23. 7
on him they freshly *gan* to smight.	II. ii. 23. 9
They *gan* abstaine from dint of direfull stroke,	II. ii. 28. 8
forward he his purpose *gan* pursew,	II. ii. 45. 6
Gan cleare the deawy ayre	II. iii. 1. 4
Now *gan* his hart all swell in jollity.	II. iii. 5. 1

Gan—*Continued.*

He *gan* to hope of men to be receiv'd	II. iii. 5. 5
his pitious handes *gan* reare.	II. iii. 6. 9
this liegeman *gan* to wexe more bold,	II. iii. 9. 2
In his owne kind he *gan* him selfe unfold;	II. iii. 9. 4
coming close to Trompart *gan* inquere	II. iii. 12. 1
that boaster *gan* to quake,	II. iii. 18. 8
Now little *gan* to swell,	II. iii. 29. 8
towards *gan* a deadly shafte advaunce,	II. iii. 34. 5
He *gan* himselfe to vaunt:	II. iii. 37. 2
Gan burne in filthy lust;	II. iii. 42. 5
gan to ride As one unfitt therefore,	II. iii. 46. 3
With beastly brutish rage *gan* him assay,	II. iv. 6. 7
gan soone unbrace His grasping hold:	II. iv. 9. 7
Then *gan* her sonne to flye Full fast away,	II. iv. 13. 6
He *gan* to comfort,	II. iv. 16. 6
Being at last recured, he *gan* inquyre	II. iv. 16. 7
Then *gan* the Palmer thus;	II. iv. 34. 1
gan to grind His grated teeth	II. v. 14. 2
gan to breake the bands of their captivitee.	II. v. 18. 9
Now *gan* Pyrochles wex as wood as hee,	II. v. 20. 6
Tho *gan* that villein wex so fiers and strong,	II. v. 23. 1
gan him dight to succour his distresse,	II. v. 24. 2
Her mery fitt shee freshly *gan* to reare,	II. vi. 21. 2
Such as he saw she *gan* him lay before,	II. vi. 24. 4
Gan him avize, howe ill did him beseme	II. vi. 27. 4
Eftsoones he *gan* to rage, and inly frett,	II. vi. 28. 3
forth she *gan* proceede:	II. vi. 33. 6
Yet at her speach their rages *gan* relent,	II. vi. 36. 3
Streight *gan* he him revyle,	II. vi. 39. 3
gan exceed The measure of her meane	II. vii. 16. 8
gan a cursed hand the quiet wombe	II. vii. 17. 1
avarice *gan* through his veines inspire	II. vii. 17. 8
His harmefull club he *gan* to hurtle hye,	II. vii. 42. 3
Who likewise *gan* himselfe to batteill dight,	II. vii. 42. 5
he *gan* inquire, What meant that preace	II. vii. 48. 1
Then *gan* the cursed wretch alowd to cry,	II. vii. 60. 6
vitall powres *gan* wexe both weake and wan	II. vii. 65. 2
Gan sucke this vitall ayre into his brest,	II. vii. 66. 6
he *gan* display His painted nimble wings,	II. viii. 8. 8
With trembling hand his troubled pulse *gan* try;	II. viii. 9. 6
'Good or bad,' *gan* his brother fiers reply,	II. viii. 15. 1
th' other brother *gan* his helme unlace,	II. viii. 17. 2
gan themselves prepare to batteill greedily.	II. viii. 18. 9
The want thereof now greatly *gan* to plaine,	II. viii. 19. 2
he *gan* spy Where at his feet,	II. viii. 23. 6
Pyrochles *gan* reply the second tyme,	II. viii. 30. 1
Horribly then he *gan* to rage and rayle,	II. viii. 37. 1
For very felnesse lowd he *gan* to weepe,	II. viii. 37. 5
his deare hart the picture *gan* adore;	II. viii. 43. 5
he fiercely *gan* approch,	II. viii. 44. 3
when this breathlesse woxe, that batteil *gan* renew.	II. viii. 47. 9
His shining Helmet he *gan* soone unlace,	II. viii. 52. 8
gan he to discourse the whole debate,	II. viii. 54. 6
gan Sir Guyon all the story shew	II. ix. 9. 5
Phoebus *gan* decline in haste His weary wagon	II. ix. 10. 1
the Squire *gan* nigher to approch,	II. ix. 11. 3
their forces *gan* to fayle,	II. ix. 14. 3
they *gan* dispose Themselves to court,	II. ix. 36. 4
as they *gan* his Library to vew,	II. ix. 59. 3
Gan more the same frequent,	II. x. 6. 9
gan abhorre her broods unkindly crime,	II. x. 9. 4
The eldest, Gonorill, *gan* to protest	II. x. 28. 1
His daughter *gan* despise his drouping day,	II. x. 30. 4
The wretched man *gan* then avise too late,	II. x. 31. 1
gan the bloody brethren both to raine;	II. x. 33. 1
fierce Cundah *gan* shortly to envy His brother Morgan,	II. x. 33. 2
gan Carausius tirannize anew,	II. x. 57. 5
gan this Realme renew her passed prime:	II. x. 58. 8
gan the Hunnes and Picts invade this land,	II. x. 61. 6
he eftsoones *gan* launch his barke forthright.	II. xi. 4. 4
soone as Titan *gan* his head exault,	II. xi. 9. 4
now it *gan* to threaten neare decay:	II. xi. 14. 5
Gan her recomfort from so sad affright,	II. xi. 16. 5
He *gan* avize to follow him no more,	II. xi. 27. 6
gan him selfe to second battaill bend,	II. xi. 35. 5
the Carle as fast *Gan* heap huge strokes on him,	II. xi. 43. 9
Forthy he *gan* some other wayes advize,	II. xi. 44. 6
she in merry sort Them *gan* to bord,	II. xii. 16. 2
the Palmer *gan* full bitterly Her to rebuke	II. xii. 16. 5
all that dreadfull Armie fast *gan* flye	II. xii. 26. 8
shortly *gan* descry The land	II. xii. 34. 3
at last the weather *gan* to cleare,	II. xii. 37. 5
somewhat *gan* relent his earnest pace;	II. xii. 65. 8
His stubborne brest *gan* secret pleasaunce to embrace.	II. xii. 65. 9
gan all the quire of birdes	II. xii. 76. 1
now awaking, fierce at them *gan* fly,	II. xii. 84. 6
He them espying *gan* him selfe prepare,	III. i. 4. 7
sharply *gan* to spurne His fomy steed,	III. i. 5. 4
he *gan* to feare His toward perill,	III. i. 9. 6
gan fayre perswade Not to provoke misfortune,	III. i. 10. 1
Tho *gan* she myldly of them to inquyre	III. i. 23. 8
each *gan* diversely devize.	III. i. 33. 9
Shee greatly *gan* enamoured to wex	III. i. 47. 4
Gan choose his Dame with *Bascimano* gay,	III. i. 56. 8
she *gan* her selfe despoile,	III. i. 58. 6
afterwardes they *gan* . . . To stirre up strife,	III. i. 64. 4
Gan coyne streight lawes to curb their liberty:	III. ii. 2. 6
faire purpose *gan* to find,	III. ii. 4. 2
much more straungely *gan* to love his sight,	III. ii. 18. 2

Gan—*Continued.*

she *gan* againe Her to bethinke . . . III. ii. 22. 8
Ruffed of love, *gan* lowly to availe; . . . III. ii. 27. 2
Tho *gan* she to renew her former smart, . . . III. ii. 29. 8
of their first intent *gan* make new dout, . . . III. iii. 14. 3
Therewith th' Enchaunter softly *gan* to smyle . . . III. iii. 17. 1
then his spirite thus *gan* foorth display: . . . III. iii. 21. 5
gan with sharpe repriefe Her to restraine, . . . III. iv. 11. 4
The which his mother seeing *gan* to feare . . . III. iv. 24. 4
They softly *gan* to search his griesly wownd: . . . III. iv. 40. 2
Then *gan* he freshly pricke his fomy steed, . . . III. iv. 48. 2
he *gan* fowly wyte His wicked fortune . . . III. iv. 52. 7
by the way he greatly *gan* complaine . . . III. v. 12. 3
His coward courage *gan* emboldned bee, . . . III. v. 15. 2
Forthwith themselves . . . they *gan* arme bylive, . . . III. v. 16. 2
Tho *gan* the battaile freshly to begin; . . . III. v. 22. 5
with sterne horror backward *gan* to start; . . . III. v. 30. 6
He up *gan* lifte toward the azure skies, . . . III. v. 34. 4
gan ransack fast His inward partes, . . . III. v. 48. 4
fayre Belphoebe *gan* to feare, . . . III. v. 49. 1
She *gan* avize where els he mote him hyde: . . . III. vi. 16. 2
Goodly she *gan* faire Cytherea greet, . . . III. vi. 20. 1
Thereat Diana *gan* to smile, . . . III. vi. 21. 1
gan relent What shee had said; . . . III. vi. 25. 2
gan recomfort her in her rude wyse, . . . III. vii. 10. 1
gan she gather up her garments rent, . . . III. vii. 11. 1
Softly at last he *gan* his mother aske, . . . III. vii. 14. 1
Was greatly woe begon, and *gan* to feare . . . III. vii. 20. 7
when his force *gan* faile his pace *gan* wex areare. . . . III. vii. 24. 9
now she *gan* approch to the sea shore, . . . III. vii. 25. 4
at the last his fiercenes *gan* abate, . . . III. vii. 35. 3
gan encrease his speed as she encreast her flight. . . . III. vii. 43. 9
the good Sir Satyrane *gan* awake . . . III. vii. 45. 1
he *gan* to make Exceeding mone, . . . III. vii. 45. 3
after *gan* inquire his parentage, . . . III. vii. 46. 7
She *gan* for me devise a grievous punishment; . . . III. vii. 55. 9
Who seeing her *gan* streight upstart, . . . III. viii. 9. 8
He *gan* make gentle purpose to his Dame . . . III. viii. 14. 2
the drie withered stocke it *gan* refresh, . . . III. viii. 25. 3
now he strength *gan* adde unto his will, . . . III. viii. 26. 6
comming nigh, eftsoones he *gan* to gesse, . . . III. viii. 45. 3
Gan first inquire of tydinges farre abrode, . . . III. viii. 45. 8
his hew *Gan* greatly chaunge . . . III. viii. 48. 2
that young Squyre *Gan* them informe the cause, . . . III. viii. 52. 7
Thereat Sir Satyrane *gan* smyle, . . . III. ix. 6. 6
welkin . . . *Gan* blowen up a bitter stormy blast, . . . III. ix. 11. 5
he *gan* to wex exceeding wroth, . . . III. ix. 13. 6
drew he his bright sword, and *gan* about him throw. . . . III. ix. 16. 9
Against that Castles Lord they *gan* conspire, . . . III. ix. 17. 4
Each *gan* undight Their garments wett, . . . III. ix. 19. 6
Gan causen why she could not come in place; . . . III. ix. 26. 2
when both nations *gan* to strive . . . III. ix. 43. 3
He *gan* devise how her he reskew mought: . . . III. x. 18. 8
Till drouping Phoebus *gan* to hyde his golden hedd. . . . III. x. 45. 9
up they *gan* their mery pypes to trusse, . . . III. x. 46. 1
gan the humid vapour shed the grownd With perly deaw, . III. x. 46. 5
gan he her perswade to leave that . . . life, . . . III. x. 51. 1
up *gan* looke, And seeing . . . a stranger knight, . . . III. xi. 13. 2
gan apply Fit medcine to his griefe, . . . III. xi. 13. 8
he likewise *gan* assay . . . III. xi. 26. 2
sad shadowes *gan* the world to hyde . . . III. xi. 55. 3
By lively actions he *gan* bewray Some argument . . . III. xii. 4. 5
it *gan* againe to play, . . . III. xii. 6. 8
fading vitall powres *gan* to fade, . . . III. xii. 21. 7
gan streight to over-looke Those cursed leaves, . . . III. xii. 36. 1
That horrour *gan* the virgins hart to perse, . . . III. xii. 36. 5
Anon she *gan* perceive the house to quake, . . . III. xii. 37. 1
that mightie chaine, . . . adowne *gan* fall, . . . III. xii. 37. 8
gentle spright Now *gan* to feede on hope, . . . III. xii. 44. 7
gan advize with her old Squire, . . . III. xii. 45. 6
every one *gan* grow in secret dout . . . IV. i. 14. 3
gan with passion great . . . privately bemone. . . . IV. i. 16. 3
gan his former griefe renew. . . . IV. i. 38. 9
gan him selfe prepare Him to receive . . . IV. i. 41. 5
finding that the breath *gan* him to fayle, . . . IV. i. 43. 5
gan thereat to triumph without victorie. . . . IV. i. 50. 9
His hart with secret envie *gan* to swell, . . . IV. ii. 7. 8
gan this bitter answere to him make: . . . IV. ii. 14. 2
they *gan* their shivering speares to shake, . . . IV. ii. 14. 7
Then, turning to those Knights, he *gan* anew: . . . IV. ii. 24. 1
gan therefore close spight to him to beare; . . . IV. ii. 26. 5
They *gan* abate the rancour of their rage, . . . IV. ii. 28. 2
she *gan* to dout Their safetie; . . . IV. ii. 46. 6
Lachesis thereat *gan* to repine, . . . IV. ii. 51. 4
for want of breath *gan* to abate, . . . IV. iii. 26. 6
He *gan* to faint toward the battels end, . . . IV. iii. 32. 7
Canacee *gan* wayle her dearest frend. . . . IV. iii. 35. 5
fiercely each assayling *gan* afresh to fight. . . . IV. iii. 35. 9
Eftsoones out of her Coch she *gan* availe, . . . IV. iii. 46. 4
teares *gan* shed amaine, . . . IV. iii. 47. 5
They all *gan* shout aloud, . . . IV. iii. 49. 9
In lovely wise she *gan* that Lady greet, . . . IV. iii. 50. 6
gan their shields addresse them selves afore: . . . IV. iv. 4. 8
gan to treate of deeds of armes abrode, . . . IV. iv. 5. 4
Which th' other seeing *gan* his course relent, . . . IV. iv. 7. 1
Which scornefull offer Blandamour *gan* soone despize; . . . IV. iv. 8. 9
At which they all *gan* laugh full merrily: . . . IV. iv. 10. 3
At which his vaine excuse they all *gan* smile, . . . IV. iv. 11. 1
Florimell him fowly *gan* revile, . . . IV. iv. 11. 3
he *gan* to gather up around His weapons . . . IV. iv. 23. 1

Gan—*Continued.*

gan the part of Chalengers anew To range the field, . . . IV. iv. 25. 3
The morrow next the Turney *gan* anew: . . . IV. iv. 26. 1
much he *gan* his glorie to envy, . . . IV. iv. 28. 4
every one *gan* shun his dreadfull sight, . . . IV. iv. 41. 8
each of other *gan* inquire his name. . . . IV. iv. 42. 3
Till evening that the Sunne *gan* downward bend. . . . IV. iv. 43. 6
shrilling trompets loudly *gan* to bray, . . . IV. iv. 48. 5
He lowdly *gan* to laugh, and thus to jest; . . . IV. v. 18. 2
Thereat all Knights *gan* laugh, and Ladies lowre: . . . IV. v. 19. 1
Whereat the rest *gan* greatly to envie, . . . IV. v. 19. 6
about her body *gan* it tie. . . . IV. v. 19. 9
He *gan* to cast how to appease the same, . . . IV. v. 25. 2
feare His ydle braine *gan* busily molest, . . . IV. v. 43. 7
Gan towards them to pricke with eger speede, . . . IV. vi. 2. 8
his speare he *gan* abase And voide his course: . . . IV. vi. 3. 4
Tho *gan* he swell in every inner part . . . IV. vi. 7. 4
he his threatfull speare *Gan* fewter, . . . IV. vi. 10. 2
her selfe she lightly *gan* To dight, . . . IV. vi. 10. 4
Rose in his strength, and *gan* her fresh assayle, . . . IV. vi. 16. 4
She *gan* eftsoones it to her mind to call . . . IV. vi. 26. 4
Therewith her wrathfull courage *gan* appall, . . . IV. vi. 26. 7
themselves *gan* there assemble; . . . IV. vi. 29. 5
When Glauce thus *gan* wisely all upknit: . . . IV. vi. 30. 1
eft *gan* into tender teares to melt. . . . IV. vii. 9. 5
Gan dight him selfe unto his wonted sinne; . . . IV. vii. 20. 8
Of whom she *gan* enquire of her estate, . . . IV. vii. 34. 8
Saluting him *gan* into speach to fall, . . . IV. vii. 43. 8
she *gan* mone his undeserved smart, . . . IV. viii. 3. 8
gan to her her mournfull plaint to make, . . . IV. viii. 9. 6
her inburning wrath she *gan* abate, . . . IV. viii. 17. 8
he *gan* to rew The evill case . . . IV. viii. 20. 1
He *gan* of them inquire, . . . IV. viii. 21. 2
gan from their eye-lids chace The drowzie humour . . . IV. viii. 34. 3
he *gan* enquire his cause of dread: . . . IV. viii. 41. 4
as he *gan* the same to him aread, . . . IV. viii. 41. 5
full of rage he *gan* to curse and sweare, . . . IV. viii. 44. 2
gan the Prince at leasure to inquire . . . IV. viii. 46. 6
Gan blame me much for being so untrew . . . IV. viii. 56. 4
gan he all this storie to renew, . . . IV. viii. 64. 1
He *gan* advise how best he mote darrayne That enterprize . IV. ix. 4. 4
Then *gan* she loudly cry, and weepe, and waile, . . . IV. ix. 7. 6
Gan both envy, and bitterly to ban; . . . IV. ix. 9. 7
gan they ransacke that same Castle strong, . . . IV. ix. 12. 1
gan they change their sides, . . . IV. ix. 26. 1
all afresh *gan* former fight renew. . . . IV. ix. 26. 6
they much more furiously *gan* fare, . . . IV. ix. 27. 1
They *gan* remember of the fowle upbraide, . . . IV. ix. 28. 5
They from them selves *gan* turne their furious ire, . . . IV. ix. 29. 3
all at once at him *gan* fiercely flie, . . . IV. ix. 33. 2
them with speaches milde *gan* first disswade . . . IV. ix. 34. 3
he *gan* him selfe advise To stay his hand, . . . IV. ix. 35. 5
who all that passed *gan* repeat: . . . IV. ix. 35. 9
So *gan* the rest him likewise to require, . . . IV. ix. 41. 1
gan avise To winne me honour . . . IV. x. 4. 3
With all my might I *gan* to lay about: . . . IV. x. 19. 7
the glaive . . . He *gan* forthwith t' avale, . . . IV. x. 19. 9
gan their endlesse happinesse envye, . . . IV. x. 28. 4
my hart *gan* throb . . . IV. x. 53. 1
She *gan* afresh thus to renew her wretched case. . . . IV. xii. 8. 9
gan he make him tread his steps anew, . . . IV. xii. 13. 8
Now *gan* he in his grieved minde devise, . . . IV. xii. 14. 1
Then *gan* he thinke, . . . IV. xii. 14. 7
soone he *gan* such folly to forthinke againe. . . . IV. xii. 14. 9
Backe to him selfe he *gan* returne the blame, . . . IV. xii. 16. 2
every one *gan* homeward to resort: . . . IV. xii. 18. 2
He *gan* record the lamentable stowre, . . . IV. xii. 19. 3
in short space his wonted chearefull hew *Gan* fade, . . . IV. xii. 20. 2
gan her heart to faint, and quake, and earne, . . . IV. xii. 24. 4
She *gan* thereat to fret and greatly grieve; . . . IV. xii. 26. 2
gan first to scold And chyde at him . . . IV. xii. 26. 3
afterwards she *gan* him soft to shrieve, . . . IV. xii. 26. 5
She *gan* afresh to chafe, and grieve in every vaine. . . . IV. xii. 27. 9
rather *gan* in troubled mind devize . . . IV. xii. 28. 8
His cheared heart eftsoones away *gan* chace Sad death, . . . IV. xii. 34. 3
when the world with sinne *gan* to abound, . . . V. i. 11. 1
on him catching hold *gan* loud to crie, . . . V. i. 18. 2
He gently *gan* him to demaund of all . . . V. i. 23. 3
sternly *gan* repine at his beheast; . . . V. i. 29. 2
gan of sundry newes his store to tell, . . . V. ii. 2. 6
When as they to the passage *gan* to draw, . . . V. ii. 11. 4
as his head he *gan* a litle reare . . . V. ii. 18. 3
gan entreat that iron man below . . . V. ii. 22. 5
Artegall him fairely *gan* asswage, . . . V. ii. 47. 3
They *gan* to gather in tumultuous rout, . . . V. ii. 51. 3
They *gan* with all their weapons him assay, . . . V. ii. 53. 2
when at him he with his flaile *gan* lay, . . . V. ii. 53. 5
To deedes of armes . . . They *gan* themselves addresse, . . . V. iii. 4. 4
goodly *gan* to greet his brave emprise, . . . V. iii. 15. 7
gan inquire how was that steed bereaved, . . . V. iii. 30. 8
all that piteous storie . . . to him *gan* tell; . . . V. iii. 31. 3
the proud boaster *gan* his doome upbrayd, . . . V. iii. 35. 7
All *gan* to jest and gibe full merilie . . . V. iii. 39. 4
Gan to repent that she had beene so mad . . . V. iv. 11. 4
They round about him *gan* to swarme apace, . . . V. iv. 23. 7
She fiercely towards him her selfe *gan* dight, . . . V. iv. 43. 2
he *gan* fiercely her pursew. . . . V. v. 7. 5
Thereat she *gan* to triumph with great boast, . . . V. v. 10. 1
his great hart *gan* inwardly to swell . . . V. v. 10. 5
gan renew her former cruelnesse: . . . V. v. 14. 4

Gan—*Continued.*
Gan cast a secret liking to this captive straunge. V. v. 26. 9
She *gan* to stoupe, and her proud mind convert V. v. 28. 7
she *gan* unfold The cause of her conceived maladie, V. v. 31. 7
gan to doubt least she him sought t' appeach Of treason, V. v. 37. 3
gan thenceforth to cast affection, V. v. 43. 7
Gan to demaund of her some tydings good, V. v. 45. 2
Therewith she *gan* at first to change her mood, V. v. 45. 4
Tho *gan* she tell her all that she had donne, V. v. 45. 8
She *gan* to storme, and rage, and rend her gall, V. v. 47. 2
She chang'd that threatfull mood, and mildly *gan* entreat: V. v. 47. 9
She *gan* to cast in her misdoubtfull mynde A thousand feares, V. vi. 3. 8
gan enquire of him with mylder mood V. vi. 15. 6
he *gan* at large to her dilate The whole discourse V. vi. 17. 1
gan gently her salute With curteous words, V. vi. 20. 1
Then *gan* the other further to devize Of things abrode, V. vi. 20. 7
they *gan* to flie, V. vi. 30. 2
Gan her addresse unto her former way. V. vi. 36. 3
These vile reproches *gan* unto her speake: V. vi. 37. 3
He *gan* to threaten her likewise to eat, V. vii. 15. 8
gan for grace and love of her to seeke; V. vii. 16. 3
Then *gan* she to declare the whole discourse V. vii. 20. 1
Her heart *gan* grudge for very deepe despight V. vii. 37. 8
gan forward set To save her from her feare, V. viii. 6. 8
They stayd their hands, when she thus *gan* to speake: V. viii. 11. 1
Eftsoones they *gan* their wrothfull hands to hold, V. viii. 12. 4
Then Artegall *gan* of the Prince enquire, V. viii. 15. 1
gan eftsoones devize to be aveng'd for it. V. viii. 45. 9
their harts *gan* earne To understand V. ix. 7. 1
Gan to advize what best were to be done. V. ix. 8. 5
Gan weepe and wayle, as if great griefe had her affected. V. ix. 9. 9
He *gan* with guilefull words her to perswade V. ix. 12. 5
Gan forth to lay his bayte her to beguyle, V. ix. 12. 8
Then *ganne* it runne away incontinent, V. ix. 18. 7
he with his yron flayle *Gan* drive at him V. ix. 19. 3
softly royne, when salvage choler *gan* redound. V. ix. 33. 9
Her selfe eftsoones she *gan* convert againe: V. ix. 37. 3
He *gan* that Ladie strongly to appele V. ix. 39. 5
First *gan* he tell how this . . . Duessa hight; V. ix. 40. 1
Then *gan* Authority her to appose V. ix. 44. 1
Next *gan* Religion gainst her to impute High Gods beheast, V. ix. 44. 5
Then *gan* the Peoples cry and Commons sute V. ix. 44. 7
for great ruth his courage *gan* relent: V. ix. 46. 6
He *gan* his earnest fervour to augment, V. ix. 46. 8
He *gan* t' efforce the evidence anew, V. ix. 47. 1
His former fancies ruth he *gan* repent, V. ix. 49. 2
he *gan* forth from that howre To stirre up strife V. x. 13. 4
humbly *gan* that mightie Queene entreat V. x. 15. 8
Himselfe unto his journey *Gan* prepare, V. x. 16. 2
Upon his voyage forth he *gan* to fare V. x. 17. 5
She *gan* take hart and looke up joyfully; V. x. 19. 8
feeble spirits, that *gan* faint and reele, V. x. 20. 5
Gan to recomfort her all that he might, V. x. 22. 3
To which when now they *gan* approch in sight, V. x. 30. 7
gan with courage fierce addresse him to the fight. V. x. 31. 9
her *gan* cheare with what she there had vewed, V. x. 38. 8
He *gan* to burne in rage, V. xi. 2. 6
with his huge great yron axe *gan* hew V. xi. 5. 3
He *gan* to watch the wielding of his hand, V. xi. 7. 2
Gan into one assemble all the might Of all his hands, V. xi. 8. 4
gan him selfe to fight on foote prepare: V. xi. 9. 4
Wherewith full wroth he fiercely *gan* assay V. xi. 11. 4
gan to chaufe and sweat, V. xi. 12. 7
his heart *gan* earne For great desire V. xi. 21. 1
he *gan* him selfe streightway Thereto addresse, V. xi. 21. 4
he *gan* her with courage fierce assay, V. xi. 26. 6
With that aloude she *gan* to bray and yell, V. xi. 28. 1
Then *gan* she cry much louder then afore, V. xi. 30. 1
She *gan* rejoyce and shew triumphant chere, V. xi. 33. 2
Gan shout aloud, that unto heaven it rong; V. xi. 34. 2
Whom by his name saluting, thus he *gan*: V. xi. 38. 1
Them also *gan* assaile with outrage bold, V. xi. 47. 3
Of whom Sir Artegall *gan* then enquire V. xi. 48. 6
to his voyage *gan* againe proceed; V. xi. 65. 8
To the sea-shore he *gan* his way apply, V. xii. 3. 8
gan him streight to buckle to the fight, V. xii. 16. 8
He *gan* at him let drive more fiercely then afore. V. xii. 22. 9
Then th' other comming neare *gan* him revile, V. xii. 40. 1
To whom Sir Artegall *gan* to expresse VI. i. 5. 3
gan to drive at him more hard. VI. i. 20. 9
His heart *gan* faint, VI. i. 22. 3
he for dread of death *gan* loude to crie VI. i. 22. 8
with uncomely shame *Gan* him salute, VI. i. 24. 9
gan t' augment her bitternesse much more; VI. i. 32. 2
gan to stretch his limbs; VI. i. 35. 4
courage chill Kindling afresh, *gan* battell to renew, VI. i. 35. 8
I . . . *gan* to blame him for such cruelty VI. ii. 11. 3
Sir Calidore . . . further *gan* inquire VI. ii. 13. 6
He inly *gan* her lover to envy, VI. ii. 17. 2
He . . . in that rage *gan* rove VI. ii. 20. 7
There *gan* he me to curse VI. ii. 21. 4
Him much more now then earst he *gan* admire VI. ii. 34. 2
His mightie hart their mournefull case *gan* rew, VI. ii. 41. 8
The Ladie, . . . *Gan* reare her eyes VI. ii. 42. 8
he *gan* of her demand, What manner wight he was, VI. ii. 44. 2
Then *gan* Sir Calidore to ghesse streightway, VI. ii. 45. 1
Whereof she now bethinking, *gan* t' advize VI. iii. 8. 6
and further *gan* devize VI. iii. 8. 8
when day *gan* to uplooke, VI. iii. 11. 1
He also *gan* uplooke VI. iii. 11. 2

Gan—*Continued.*
conspiring *gan* to intimate Each others griefe VI. iii. 12. 4
Gan freshly him addresse VI. iii. 13. 9
Gan breake to him the fortunes of his love, VI. iii. 15. 2
His long adventures *gan* to him relate, VI. iii. 22. 8
the Knight, . . . *Gan* him entreat VI. iii. 38. 5
Gan cry aloud with horrible affright, VI. iv. 8. 8
He *gan* in mind conceive a fit reliefe VI. iv. 34. 4
Gan teare her hayre, and all her garments rent, VI. v. 4. 8
gan himselfe addresse to take her part. VI. v. 8. 3
Those warlike armes . . . he *gan* eftsoones prepare, VI. v. 8. 5
Out of their ambush broke, and *gan* him to invade. VI. v. 17. 9
He *gan* to shrinke and somewhat to give place, VI. v. 21. 3
Whence soone upstarting much he *gan* repine, VI. v. 26. 5
Then *gan* the Prince of her for to demand VI. v. 27. 6
now her wounds corruption *gan* to breed: VI. v. 31. 5
Now *gan* to faint, and further could not pas VI. v. 31. 8
gan them selves to dight Unto their journey; VI. v. 40. 5
The inner parts now *gan* to putrify, VI. vi. 5. 4
He to that point fit speaches *gan* to frame, VI. vi. 6. 2
him against his powre *gan* to prepare; VI. vi. 27. 3
Gan him recomfort and from ground to reare: VI. vi. 32. 6
He *gan* bethinke him in what perilous plight VI. vi. 37. 4
He *gan* devize to be aveng'd anew VI. vii. 2. 6
Gan to complaine of great discourtesie, VI. vii. 4. 3
plainely *gan* to him declare the case VI. vii. 21. 2
He *gan* to him object his haynous crime, VI. vii. 26. 7
Her stubborne hart . . . *Gan* stoupe; VI. vii. 36. 8
they *gan* augment Their cruelty, VI. viii. 4. 6
approching thus he *gan* to say: VI. viii. 7. 3
gan fiercely fly Upon that Carle VI. viii. 12. 8
still suppressing, *gan* of her inquire, VI. viii. 18. 3
when first the flowre Of beauty *gan* to bud, VI. viii. 20. 2
Gan him to hale, and teare, and scratch, and bite; VI. viii. 28. 7
Then thus the Prince *gan* say: VI. viii. 29. 5
Each *gan* his fellow solace and embrace VI. viii. 37. 4
Then *gan* they to devize what course to take; VI. viii. 37. 6
some of them *gan* mongst themselves devize VI. viii. 43. 5
Gan mutter close a certaine secret charme, VI. viii. 45. 6
Which doen, he *gan* aloft t' advance his arme, VI. viii. 45. 8
Then *gan* the bagpypes and the hornes to shrill VI. viii. 46. 1
Her deawy humour *gan* on th' earth to shed, VI. ix. 13. 2
Gan greatly thanke his host and his good wife; VI. ix. 18. 6
Gan highly to commend the happie life VI. ix. 18. 8
I *gan* my follies to my selfe to plaine, VI. ix. 25. 5
Tho *gan* that shepheard thus for to dilate: VI. x. 21. 1
now *gan* afresh to rancle sore, VI. x. 31. 3
Gan cry to them aloud to helpe her VI. x. 34. 9
From that day forth she *gan* him to affect, VI. x. 37. 1
Gan to inquire for that faire shepherdesse, VI. xi. 11. 6
gan her forme and feature to expresse, VI. xi. 11. 8
when as he was dead, the fray *gan* ceasse; VI. xi. 20. 3
lighting candles new, *gan* search anone, VI. xi. 20. 8
His hart *gan* fayle, VI. xi. 37. 9
Of sundrie things he purpose *gan* to faine, VI. xi. 39. 2
gan aloud for Pastorell to call, VI. xi. 44. 2
in great store Unto the cave *gan* preasse, VI. xi. 46. 4
with all their might *Gan* all upon him lay: VI. xi. 47. 9
there *gan* a dreadfull fight. VI. xi. 47. 9
He her *gan* to recomfort all he might VI. xi. 50. 2
She forth *gan* lay unto the open light The litle babe, VI. xii. 7. 4
Untill the Damzell *gan* to wex more sound and strong. VI. xii. 11. 9
Tho *gan* Sir Calidore him to advize Of his first quest, VI. xii. 12. 1
she *gan* to cast In her conceiptfull mynd VI. xii. 16. 1
gan to question streight, how she it knew? VI. xii. 18. 2
he *gan* fret and fome out bloudy gore VI. xii. 31. 3
he *gan* his hundred tongues apply, VI. xii. 33. 2
She *gan* to cast in her ambitious thought VII. vi. 7. 3
She *gan* to burne in her ambitious spright, VII. vi. 10. 5
Gan call to him aloud with all their might VII. vi. 15. 4
straight *gan* cast their counsell grave and wise. VII. vi. 22. 6
gan now advise What course were best to take VII. vi. 22. 8
in his soveraine throne *gan* straight dispose Himselfe, VII. vi. 24. 7
They *gan* to cast what penaunce him to give. VII. vi. 50. 2
gan examine him in straighter sort, VII. vi. 51. 4
Thus *gan* her plaintif Plea with words to amplifie: VII. vii. 13. 9
thus *gan* the Titanesse: VII. vii. 47. 1
Then thus *gan* Jove: VII. vii. 48. 1
Love . . . *Gan* reare his head, *H.L.* 63
He *gan* to move out of his idle seate; *H.L.* 66
he *gan* to mount up hyre, *H.L.* 68
through the world his way he *gan* to take, *H.L.* 74
gan to raunge them selves in huge array, *H.L.* 79
That they *gan* cast their state how to increase *H.H.L.* 80
all the foule . . . *Gan* flock about these twaine, *Proth.* 120

Gang. She mought ne *gang* on the greene. *S.C.* Mar. 57
let hem *gange* alone a Gods name; *S.C.* S. 100
they *gang* in more secrete wise, *S.C.* S. 156

Ganges. By Nyle, or *Gange*, or Tygre, or Euphrate; *Ro.* xxxi. 4
Great *Ganges*, and immortall Euphrates, IV. xi. 21. 1

Gaol. *See* **Jail.**

Gape. Some gan to *gape* for greedie governaunce, *S.C.* May 121
Seeing the gored woundes to *gape* so wyde, I. v. 9. 8
greedy gulfe does *gape*, I. xi. 21. 5
his wide mouth did *gape* With huge great teeth, IV. vii. 5. 5
But forst him *gape* and gaspe, VI. iii. 26. 8

Gaped. his deepe devouring jawes Wyde *gaped*, I. xi. 12. 8
the gate of Hell, which *gaped* wide, II. vii. 24. 6
gaped still as coveting to drinke II. vii. 58. 2
gaped like a gulfe when he did gerne; V. xii. 15. 8

Gapes. Offring to fall into each mouth that *gapes,* . . . . . . *Col.* 602
Gaping. *See* **Wide-gaping.**
the *gaping* earth devoure The spring, the place, ... *Pet.* iv. 10
beasts with deep mouthes *gaping* direfull . . . . *Col.* 202
With *gaping* mouth at her ran greedily, ... I. iii. 5. 5
With *gaping* jawes full greedy at him came, ... I. iii. 41. 4
A sea of blood gusht from the *gaping* wownd, ... I. viii. 16. 6
gaping wyde, He thought . . . him to have swallowd . . . . I. xi. 53. 1
upon with *gaping* wonderment; . . . . I. xii. 9. 5
gaping wide to swallow them alyve . . . . II. xii. 5. 7
all attonce, *gaping* full greedily, ... II. xii. 39. 7
Stood *gaping* at their gate, and wondred them to see. . . . . III. iv. 32. 9
greedily long *gaping* at the sight, ... III. vii. 28. 4
ten thousand monsters . . . *gaping* griesly, all begor'd. . . . IV. xi. 3. 9
the Crocodile, . . . *gaping* greedy wide . . . . V. vii. 15. 5
the beast enrag'd . . . *Gaping* full wyde, ... VI. iv. 20. 8
and thrust it all attone Into his *gaping* throte, ... VI. iv. 21. 5
Gar. To stirre up strife, and *garre* them disagree: . . . . . . II. v. 19. 7
Gard, -ed. *See* **Guard, -ed.**
Gardante. The first of them by name *Gardante* hight, ... III. i. 45. 1
one of those sixe knights, *Gardante* hight, ... III. i. 65. 1
Garden. 'The fragrant flowres, that in my *garden* grewe, . . . *S.C.* D. 109
could this *gardine* staine. . . . . *Ti.* 525
Since that I saw this *gardine* wasted quite, ... *Ti.* 529
Grewe in this *Gardin,* . . . . *Mui.* 202
this *gardin,* where yong Clarion Was wont to solace him, . . *Mui.* 242
a *gardin* goodly garnished With hearbs and fruits, ... II. vii. 51. 4
The *Gardin* of Proserpina this hight; . . . . II. vii. 53. 1
the utmost bound Of this great *gardin,* . . . . II. vii. 56. 5
He of this *Gardin* had the governall, ... II. xii. 48. 7
This *Gardin* to adorne with all variety. . . . . II. xii. 59. 9
The *Gardin* of Adonis, far renowmd by fame. . . . . III. vi. 29. 9
In that same *Gardin* all the goodly flowres, ... III. vi. 30. 1
They in that *Gardin* planted bee agayne, ... III. vi. 33. 2
That in the *Gardin* of Adonis springs, ... III. vi. 39. 2
When walking through the *Gardin* them she saw, ... III. vi. 40. 6
All that in this delightfull *Gardin* growes . . . . III. vi. 41. 2
in the Princes *gardin* daily wrought: . . . . VI. ix. 24. 8
a *gardin* of sweet flowres, ... *Am.* lxiv. 2
brought . . . By Love himselfe, and in his *garden* plaste. . . *Am.* lxxvii. 12
Gardener. Ne needs there *Gardiner* to sett or sow, ... III. vi. 34. 1
Garden's. told that *gardins* pleasures in their caroling. . . . II. vi. 24. 9
Gardens. Sure gates, sweete *gardens,* stately galleries, ... *Ti.* 95
To the gay *gardins* his unstaid desire Him wholly caried, . . *Mui.* 161
in the *gardens* of Adonis nurst: . . . . *Col.* 804
Did in the *gardins* of Adonis fynd . . . . II. x. 71. 4
Their groves he feld; their *gardins* did deface; . . . . II. xii. 83. 6
The *Gardins* of Adonis fraught With pleasures . . . . III. vi. Arg.
walke about her *gardens* of delight, ... IV. viii. 54. 3
Garden-side. drenched lay full deepe under the *Garden side.* . II. vii. 57. 9
Garland. *See* **Ivy-garland, Laurel-garland, Olive-garland.**
Bellay, first *garland* of free Poesie . . . . *Ro.* Env. 1
her *garland* so much honoured . . . . *Van.* vii. 9
The fayrest floure our *gyrlond* all emong . . . . *S.C.* N. 75
for her *girlond* Olive braunches beare, ... *S.C.* N. 144
To spil the flowres that should her *girlond* dight? . . . . . *S.C.* D. 114
Realmes chiefe strength and *girlond* of the crowne. . . . . . *Hub.* 1185
That is the *girlond* of Nobilitie. . . . . *T.M.* 84
that Citie, which the *garland* wore Of Britaines pride, . . . *Ti.* 36
with rosie *garland* crownd! . . . . *D.* 312
like faire Phebes *garlond* shining new, ... *Col.* 342
courts chief *garlond* with all vertues dight, ... *Col.* 499
Whose *girland* now is set in highest place, ... *Ded. Son.* xiii. 2
Wherewith that courtly *garlond* most ye grace . . . . . . *Ded. Son.* xvi. 4
thinking . . . to frame A *girlond* for her dainty forehead fit, . I. ii. 30. 7
A Rosy *girlond* was the victors meede. . . . . I. ii. 37. 5
greene boughes . . . About the fountaine like a *girlond* made; I. vii. 4. 5
never any could that *girlond* win, ... I. vii. 45. 6
For ever with a flowring *girlond* crownd: . . . . I. x. 54. 5
on her head they sett a *girlond* greene, ... I. xii. 8. 6
crowned with a *garland* of sweete Rosiere. . . . . II. ix. 19. 9
they still the *girlond* bore away; . . . . III. ii. 2. 4
every one did teare her *girlond* from her crowne. . . . . . . III. iv. 30. 9
The *girlond* of her honour did adorne: . . . . III. v. 51. 3
Whiles all her Nymphes did like a *girlond* her enclose. . . . III. vi. 19. 9
like a *girlond* compassed the hight; . . . . III. vi. 43. 6
Helene, . . . *girlond* of the mighty Conquerours, ... III. ix. 35. 2
breaking quite his *garlond* ever greene, ... III. xi. 37. 8
Fresh Alimeda deckt with *girlond* greene; . . . . IV. xi. 51. 1
To whom that day they should the *girlond* yield, ... V. iii. 14. 6
To make a *garland* to adorne her hed, ... VI. iii. 23. 8
The Priest him selfe a *garland* doth compose . . . . VI. viii. 39. 7
Environ'd with a *girland,* . . . Of lovely lasses; . . . . . . VI. ix. 8. 3
Her flowry *garlond* tooke from her owne head, ... VI. ix. 42. 6
A *garland* was the meed of victory: . . . . VI. ix. 43. 4
like a *girlond* did in compasse stemme: . . . . VI. x. 12. 5
Crownd with a rosie *girlond* . . . . VI. x. 14. 5
as a *girlond* seemes to deck the locks . . . . VII. vi. 41. 3
He with an Oaken *girlond* now did tire, ... VII. vii. 11. 5
a *girlond* well beseene He wore, ... VII. vii. 29. 4
is comming forth with *girland* crouned. . . . . *Am.* xix. 4
*And having all your heads with *girland* crownd, ... *Epith.* 13
bring in hand Another gay *girland,* . . . . *Epith.* 42
being crowned with a *girland* greene, ... *Epith.* 157
the *garland* of your glorie marre, ... *H.B.* 174
Garlands. *See* **Laurel-garlands.**
To peinct their *girlonds* with his colowres; . . . . *S.C.* F. 121
girlonds of roses, and Sopps in wine. . . . . *S.C.* May 14
Dight gaudy *Girlonds* was my common trade, ... *S.C.* Jun. 45
girt in *girlonds* of wild Yvie twine, ... *S.C.* O. 111

Garlands—*Continued.*
The gaudie *girlonds* deck her grave, ... *S.C.* N. 108
deckt . . . With manie *garlands* for his victories, ... *Ti.* 653
Gay chapelets of flowers and *gyrlonds* trim. . . . . *As.* 42
wont to be with flowers and *gyrlonds* dight, ... *As.* 153
sung by them with flowry *gyrlonds* crownd. . . . . *Col.* 643
she comes, . . . Adorned all with gold and *girlonds* gay, . . . I. iv. 17. 2
The comely virgins came, with *girlands* dight, ... I. xii. 6. 6
all the people decke with *girlands* greene, ... II. iii. 28. 3
her head she fondly would aguize With gaudy *girlonds,* . . . II. vi. 7. 4
Now making *girlonds* of each flowre that grew, ... III. i. 35. 4
With gilden hornes and flowry *girlonds* crownd, ... III. iv. 17. 2
Gay *girlonds* from the Sun their forheads fayr to shade; . . . III. iv. 29. 9
both flowres and *girlonds* far away Shee flong, ... III. iv. 30. 1
With this fayre flowre your goodly *girlonds* dight . . . . . III. v. 53. 5
decks the *girlonds* of her Paramoures, ... III. vi. 30. 3
Girlonds of flowres sometimes for her faire hed . . . . . . III. vii. 17. 5
Faire Helenore with *girlonds* all bespredd, ... III. x. 44. 5
their proud *girlonds* of tryumphant bayes . . . . III. xi. 52. 7
Their *girlonds* rent, their bowres despoyled all; . . . . . . IV. i. 24. 7
All deckt with crownes, and chaynes, and *girlands* gay, ... IV. x. 37. 6
Both *girlonds* of his Saints against their foes offence. . . . . IV. x. 51. 9
Crowned with *girlonds* of immortall baies; . . . . V. xi. 34. 6
garnished with *garlonds* goodly dight . . . . VII. vii. 33. 6
having all your heads with *girlands* crownd, ... *Epith.* 13
Al with gay *girlands* goodly wel beseene. . . . . *Epith.* 40
all the pillours deck with *girlands* trim, ... *Epith.* 207
two *Garlands* bound Of freshest Flowres . . . . *Proth.* 83
Garment. A *garment* better than of wooll or heare. . . . . *Hub.* 474
by her cleanly *garment* catching hold, Her from her Palfrey pluckt, ... I. iii. 40. 8
His *garment,* . . . With thornes together pind . . . . I. ix. 36. 1
him the poysoned *garment* did enchaunt, ... I. xi. 27. 5
a *garment* she did weare All lilly white, ... I. xii. 22. 6
did the floodgate stop With his faire *garment;* . . . . II. i. 43. 3
as doth an hidden moth The inner *garment* frett, ... II. ii. 34. 8
all her *garment* blew, ... II. ix. 40. 5
His looser *garment* to the ground did fall, ... II. xii. 46. 7
With her soft *garment* wipes away the gore . . . . III. i. 38. 5
His *garment* nether was of silke nor say, ... III. xii. 8. 1
His *garment* was disguysed very vayne, ... III. xii. 9. 5
Rude was his *garment,* and to rags all rent, ... IV. v. 35. 1
ne other *garment* wore, For all his haire was like a *garment* . IV. vii. 7. 2, 3
his *garment,* to be thereto meet, ... IV. vii. 40. 1
with her *garment* covering him from sight, ... VI. vi. 31. 3
their upper *garment* which they weare; . . . . VI. vi. 34. 7
Her *garment* was so bright and wondrous sheene, ... VII. vii. 7. 3
In *garment* all of gold downe to the ground; . . . . VII. vii. 37. 2
Garments. Where sate a gentle Lady . . . With *garments* rent, II. i. 13. 6
(As *garments* doen, which wexen old above,) . . . . *S.C.* Jun. 39
A simple husbandman in *garments* gray; . . . . *Hub.* 228
to weare *garments* base of wollen twist, ... *Hub.* 460
Good *garments* for their service should deserve; . . . . . . *Hub.* 468
in those his *garments* olde; . . . . *Hub.* 928
garments gathered neare; . . . . *Mui.* 284
Seeme greatest, when their *garments* are most gay. . . . . . *Col.* 722
in *garments* gilt And gorgeous gold arayd, ... I. v. 26. 7
That her gay *garments* staynd with filthy gore, ... I. viii. 16. 7
often tore Her guiltlesse *garments* . . . . I. x. 28. 6
In which were not rich tyres, nor *garments* gay, ... I. x. 39. 2
with their *garments* strowes the paved street; . . . . I. xii. 13. 4
With *garments* rent, and heare discheveled, ... II. i. 13. 6
That all her goodly *garments* staind arownd, ... II. i. 39. 8
In goodly *garments* that her well became, ... II. ii. 14. 7
garments loose that seemd unmeet for womanhed. . . . . . . II. xii. 55. 9
Her *garments* all were wrought of beaten gold, ... III. i. 15. 6
her *garments* loose Upgath'ring, ... III. vi. 19. 6
gan she gather up her *garments* rent, ... III. vii. 11. 1
Him shaped thus she deckt in *garments* gay, ... III. viii. 9. 1
Her *garments* gay with scales of fish that all did fill. . . . . III. viii. 26. 9
Each gan undight Their *garments* wett, ... III. ix. 19. 7
al yclad in *garments* light . . . . III. x. 21. 6
Yclad in costly *garments* fit for tragicke Stage. . . . . . . III. xii. 3. 9
from her backe her *garments* she did teare, ... III. xii. 17. 4
all her silken *garments* did with bloud bestaine. . . . . . . IV. vii. 27. 9
clothed all in *garments* made of line, ... V. vii. 6. 4
Sate goodly Temperance in *garments* clene, ... V. ix. 32. 8
on her selfe did dight Most squalid *garments,* . . . . V. xii. 12. 2
their *garments* yet, Being all rag'd and tatter'd, ... V. xii. 28. 7
all her *garments* from her snowy brest, ... VI. i. 17. 7
That all his *garments* and the grasse in vermeill dyde. . . . VI. ii. 40. 9
Gan teare her hayre, and all her *garments* rent, ... VI. v. 4. 8
his *garments* so did daze their eyes. . . . . VII. vii. 7. 9
all his *garments* he had cast away. . . . . VII. vii. 36. 2
In theyr fresh *garments* trim. . . . . *Epith.* 29
Garnished. His head was *garnisht* with the Laurel . . . . . *Bel.*[1] vii. 12
head with Lawrell *garnisht* was about. . . . . *Bel.*[2] ix. 12
Descendeth *garnisht* as a loved spouse. . . . . *Rev.* iv. 4
a Persian mitre . . . with crowns and owches *garnished,* . . . I. ii. 13. 5
till at last they see A goodly building bravely *garnished;* . . . I. iv. 2. 6
all within with flowres was *garnished,* . . . . II. v. 29. 7
a gardin goodly *garnished* With hearbs and fruits, ... II. vii. 51. 4
with brave bauldrick *garnished.* . . . . III. iii. 59. 9
garnisht all with gold upon the blade . . . . V. i. 10. 3
garnished with garlonds goodly dight . . . . VII. vii. 33. 6
Garnisht with heavenly guifts of high degree, ... *Epith.* 187
Garnishing. goodly personage And noble deeds, each other *garnishing,* . . . . *Ded. Son.* vi. 2
Garrison. There eke he placed a strong *garrisone,* . . . . . . V. x. 30. 1
Gars. Tell me, good Hobbinoll, what *garres* thee greete? . . . *S.C.* Ap. 1

Gars—*Continued.*
Their ill haviour *garres* men missay . . . *S.C.* S. 106
Gash. made a large And open *gash* therein: . . . II. v. 6. 5
Gasp. flouds do *gaspe,* for dryed is theyr sourse, . . . *S.C.* N. 126
But forst him gape and *gaspe,* . . . VI. iii. 26. 8
that made him grone And *gaspe* for breath, . . . VI. iv. 21. 6
Gasping. Quenching the *gasping* furrowes thirst with rayne? *S.C.* Ap. 6
Gastful, Gastly. *See* **Ghastful, Ghastly.**
Gat. *See* **Got.**
ye thereby much greater glory *gate,* . . . *Am.* lxvi. 9
all the good that ever yet I *gat:* . . . III. v. 7. 3
Gate. *See* **Back-gate, Castle-gate, City-gate, Flood-gate, Gait, Gat, Goat, Hell-gate, Temple-gate, Town-gate.**
Eche *gate* was of an orient perfect pearle, . . . *Rev.* iv. 10
Sperre the *yate* fast . . . *S.C.* May 224
to his *Gate* he pointed a strong gard, . . . *Hub.* 1115
some ungracious blast, out of the *gate* Of Aeoles raine, . . . *Mui.* 419
wisedome warnes, whilest foot is in the *gate,* . . . I. i. 13. 4
the golden Orientall *gate* Of greatest heaven . . . I. v. 2. 1
No *gate* so strong, no locke so firme . . . I. viii. 4. 8
The same before the Geaunts *gate* he blew, . . . I. viii. 5. 1
He badd to open wyde his brasen *gate,* . . . I. xii. 3. 6
Before her *gate* high God did Sweate ordaine, . . . II. iii. 41. 5
That to the *gate* of Hell . . . Was next adjoyning, . . . II. vii. 24. 6
a broad *gate* all built of beaten gold: . . . II. vii. 40. 2
The *gate* was open; . . . II. vii. 40. 3
to the *gate* directly did incline . . . II. ix. 24. 7
Nor wight nor word mote passe out of the *gate,* . . . II. ix. 25. 3
built that *gate* which of his name is hight, . . . II. x. 46. 6
Whom nought regarding they kept on their *gate,* . . . II. xii. 17. 3
the *gate* was wrought of substaunce light, . . . II. xii. 43. 8
more might in that goodly *gate* Be red, . . . II. xii. 46. 1
he came unto another *gate;* . . . II. xii. 53. 6
No *gate,* but like one, . . . II. xii. 53. 7
faire before the *gate* a spatious playne, . . . III. i. 20. 6
She then the Cities sought from *gate* to *gate,* . . . III. vi. 14. 1
they agayn returne backe by the hinder *gate.* . . . III. vi. 32. 9
The which beside the *gate* for swyne was ordered. . . . III. ix. 11. 9
Hygate . . . by West, And Overt *gate* by North: . . . III. ix. 46. 3
Whereas no *gate* they found them to withhold, . . . III. xi. 21. 3
chokt the porch of that enchaunted *gate* . . . III. xii. 43. 3
every houre they knocke at deathes *gate?* . . . IV. iii. 1. 7
the *gate* to him unbard; . . . IV. ix. 5. 8
to the Bridges utter *gate* I came; . . . IV. x. 11. 2
Behinde the *gate* that none her might espy; . . . IV. x. 13. 2
streight he closd the *gate:* . . . IV. x. 14. 4
'Thence forth I passed to the second *gate,* . . . IV. x. 16. 1
The *Gate* of Good Desert, . . . IV. x. 16. 2
unto Venus grace the *gate* doth open right. . . . IV. x. 35. 9
gathering them unto her citties *gate,* . . . V. iv. 45. 6
there without the *gate,* . . . V. vii. 26. 1
pressing through the preace unto the *gate,* . . . V. vii. 35. 3
hindmost in the *gate* he overhent, . . . V. x. 36. 6
laboured fast To sperre the *gate;* . . . V. x. 37. 2
The *gate* soone opened to receive him in; . . . VI. i. 23. 2
arriving with the fall of day Drew to the *gate,* . . . VI. iii. 37. 8
the rude Porter . . . Did shut the *gate* . . . VI. iii. 38. 2
That here is at his *gate* an errant Knight, . . . VI. iii. 41. 2
He found the *gate* wyde ope, . . . VI. vi. 19. 2
did them porters make Of heavens *gate* . . . VII. vii. 45. 7
New yeare, forth looking out of Janus *gate,* . . . *Am.* iv. 1
The *gate* with pearles and rubyes richly dight; . . . *Am.* lxxxi. 10
Gates. *See* **Goats, Temple-gates.**
Square was this Citie, and twelve *gates* it had. . . . *Rev.* iv. 9
The griesly *gates* of his devouring hell, . . . *Van.* iii. 10
gates of hel, and fyrie furies forse, . . . *S.C.* N. 164
standing by the *gates* in strange disguize, . . . *Hub.* 1271
all the *gates* he found fast lockt anon, . . . *Hub.* 1350
Upon those *gates* with force he fiercely flewe, . . . *Hub.* 1369
Sure *gates,* sweete gardens, stately galleries, . . . *Ti.* 95
'The sevenfold yron *gates* of grislie Hell, . . . *Ti.* 372
double *gates* he findeth locked fast, . . . I. i. 40. 1
still to all the *gates* stood open wide: . . . I. iv. 6. 2
Whose *gates* he fownd fast shutt, . . . I. viii. 3. 3
Their *gates* to all were open evermore, . . . I. x. 36. 6
All these before the *gates* of Pluto lay, . . . II. vii. 24. 1
They found the *gates* fast barred long ere night, . . . II. ix. 10. 8
Therein two *gates* were placed seemly well: . . . II. ix. 23. 1
he behight Those *gates* to be unbar'd, . . . II. xi. 17. 4
double *gates* it had which opened wide, . . . III. vi. 31. 5
to the *gates* they goe To burn the same . . . III. ix. 17. 6
seeing them resolvd indeed To flame the *gates,* . . . III. ix. 18. 2
Hard by the *gates* of hell her dwelling is; . . . IV. i. 20. 1
Did beat uppon the *gates* to enter in; . . . V. iv. 37. 2
She bad that streight the *gates* should be unbard, . . . V. iv. 37. 8
Soone as the *gates* were open to them set, . . . V. iv. 38. 1
Then caused he the *gates* be opened wyde; . . . V. viii. 51. 1
Whose silver *gates* . . . she entred, . . . VII. vi. 8. 5
beating at his *gates* full earnestly, . . . VII. vi. 15. 3
Gather. As they which gleane, the reliques use to *gather,* . . . *Ro.* xxx. 13
The shepheards daughters to *gather* flowres, . . . *S.C.* F. 120
When Damsines I *gether,* . . . *S.C.* Ap. 152
To *gather* May bus-kets and smelling brere: . . . *S.C.* May 10
gather nuttes to make me Christmas game, . . . *S.C.* D. 26
'*Gather* together ye my little flocke, . . . *S.C.* D. 145
gan the shepheard *gather* into one His stragling Goates, . . . *Gn.* 161
live like Lords of that which they doo *gather,* . . . *Hub.* 164
Or care to overlooke, or trust to *gather,* . . . *Hub.* 279
will serve my sheepe to *gather,* . . . *Hub.* 295
Then was high time their wits about to *geather.* . . . *Hub.* 570

Gather—*Continued.*
To *gather* flowres her forhead to array: . . . *Mui.* 117
Go, *gather* up the reliques of thy race; . . . I. v. 24. 2
stayd, To *gather* breath in many miseryes. . . . I. vi. 19. 4
Gather therefore the Rose whilest yet is prime, . . . II. xii. 75. 6
Gather the Rose of love whilest yet is time, . . . II. xii. 75. 8
his wound did *gather,* and grow hole, . . . III. v. 43. 1
gan she *gather* up her garments rent, . . . III. vii. 11. 1
all their goodly heardes did *gather* rownd; . . . III. x. 46. 2
fayrest floure Wouldst *gather* faine, . . . IV. ii. 14. 4
he gan to *gather* up around His weapons . . . IV. iv. 23. 1
laugh aloud, and *gather* great delight. . . . IV. vii. 26. 9
They gan to *gather* in tumultuous rout, . . . V. ii. 51. 3
turne we here . . . to *gather* fresher sprights, . . . V. iii. 40. 7
all thy forces *gather* unto thee, . . . V. v. 34. 7
he nould let him breath, nor *gather* spright, . . . VI. iii. 26. 7
went To the greene wood to *gather* strawberies, . . . VI. x. 34. 2
gather to myselfe new breath awhile. . . . *Am.* lxxx. 4
Gathered. she languisht as the *gathered* floure; . . . *Pet.* vi. 9
flames . . . *Gathered* in one up to the heavens to spyre, . . . *Ro.* xvi. 10
earthly vapours *gathered* in the ayre, . . . *Ro.* xx. 2
as they had bene *gathered* long; . . . *S.C.* D. 110
Sike follies nowe have *gathered* as too ripe, . . . *S.C.* D. 117
sundrie flowers in wilde fieldes *gathered;* . . . *Gn.* 132
gathered more store Of the fields honour . . . *Mui.* 122
garments *gathered* neare; . . . *Mui.* 284
That the worlds pride seemes *gathered* there to bee. . . . *Ded.Son.*xvii. 12
kindling rage her selfe she *gathered* round, . . . I. i. 18. 2
all . . . *Gathred* themselves about her body round, . . . I. i. 25. 4
Is *gathered* full, and worketh speedy way; . . . I. xi. 10. 3
Could *gathered* be through all the world arownd, . . . II. vii. 31. 8
One with great bellowes *gathered* filling ayre, . . . II. vii. 36. 1
Gathered the Princes of the people loose . . . II. x. 37. 6
Her reliques Fulgent having *gathered,* . . . II. x. 57. 1
that lame Hag . . . *gathered* them againe, . . . II. xi. 28. 2
As freely offering to be *gathered;* . . . II. xii. 54. 6
Had *gathered* Rew, and Savine, . . . III. ii. 49. 5
Which she had *gathered* in a shady glade . . . III. viii. 6. 3
Gathred the Trojan reliques sav'd from flame, . . . III. ix. 36. 8
His armes, . . . She *gathered* up and did about him dresse, . III. xi. 20. 5
great riches, *gathered* manie a day, . . . IV. i. 29. 5
The which that tyrant *gathered* had by wrong . . . IV. ix. 12. 3
Full many people *gathered* in a crew; . . . V. ii. 29. 5
gathered unto her her troubled wit, . . . V. viii. 45. 8
lay aside this griefe, Which ye have *gathered* . . . VI. ii. 46. 2
Had for his food late *gathered* from the tree,) . . . VI. vii. 24. 5
Gathered him selfe together soone againe, . . . VI. vii. 46. 2
each his sundrie sheepe with severall care *Gathered* together, . VI. ix. 15. 5
all . . . Devized to worke delight was *gathered* there, . . . VI. x. 5. 7
In whom so many Graces *gathered* are, . . . VI. x. 27. 2
from all the brookes thereby Had *gathered,* . . . VII. vii. 10. 7
they *gathered* flowers to fill their flasket, . . . *Proth.* 26
They *gathered* some; . . . *Proth.* 30
Gathereth. Of all the which he *gathereth* what is fit . . . *Hub.* 789
Gathering. *gathering* also filth him to infest, . . . *Van.* iv. 11
limbs, with lightening rent, They, *gathering* up, . . . *Gn.* 200
Gathering his straying flocke, . . . *Gn.* 319
gathering unto him a ragged rout . . . *T.M.* 267
in *gathering* Into her lap the children of the spring. . . . *Mui.* 127
Whereof the Goddesse *gathering* jealous feare, . . . *Mui.* 129
gathering up the reliques of his smart, . . . I. v. 39. 6
gathering up himselfe out of the mire . . . I. xi. 40. 7
gathering force and corage valorous, . . . II. x. 18. 3
such as were through former flight preserv'd *Gathering* againe, II. x. 55. 6
th' Infants tutors *gathering* to feare, . . . II. x. 64. 4
gathering him rownd about more neare, . . . III. i. 23. 3
Gathering sweete daffadillyes, to have made Gay girlonds . III. iv. 29. 8
Whilest he to *gathering* of the gold did fall: . . . V. ii. 23. 8
gathering them unto her citties gate, . . . V. iv. 45. 6
Yet *gathering* spirit of her natures pride, . . . VII. vi. 26. 2
Thence *gathering* plumes of perfect speculation, . . . *H.H.B.* 134
Gathers. thereof *gathers* for himselfe the best. . . . *Hub.* 726
Gaudy. Ylike as others, girt in *gawdy* greene? . . . *S.C.* May 4
Dight *gaudy* Girlonds was my common trade, . . . *S.C.* Jun. 45
The *gaudie* girlonds deck her grave, . . . *S.C.* N. 108
her head she fondly would aguize With *gaudy* girlonds, . . II. vi. 7. 4
Gaul. old *Gall,* that now is cleeped France, . . . IV. xi. 16. 4
Gauld. *See* **Galled.**
Gaule. *See* **Gall.**
Gauls. The *Galles* were, by corrupting of a mayde, . . . *Van.* xi. 6
Gauntlet. threw his *gauntlet,* as a sacred pledge . . . I. iv. 43. 1
Gave. The mightie Dragon *gave* to hir his power. . . . *Rev.* i. 6
thilke God, that *gave* him that good, . . . *S.C.* May 85
Love they him called that *gave* me checkmate, . . . *S.C.* D. 53
Nereis to the Seas a token *gave,* . . . *Gn.* 567
she *gave* like blessing to each creture, . . . *Hub.* 146
to those ashes *gave* a second life, . . . *Ti.* 669
Gave her the fatall wound of deadlie smart, . . . *D.* 158
gave that name unto that pleasant vale; . . . *Col.* 107
Who ever *gave* more honourable prize . . . *Ded. Son.* xiv. 1
adventure . . . That greatest Gloriana to him *gave,* . . . I. i. 3. 2
to the Dwarfe a while his needlesse spere he *gave.* . . . I. i. 11. 9
The one of them he *gave* a message . . . I. i. 38. 8
which her lavish lovers to her *gave.* . . . I. ii. 13. 6
I would not yeeld that to Sansfoy I *gave.* . . . I. iv. 47. 9
He *gave* her gold and purple pall to weare, . . . I. vii. 16. 3
he *gave* in charge unto his Squyre, That scarlot whore . . . I. viii. 29. 1
those two knights . . . *Gave* goodly gifts, . . . I. ix. 18. 8
Prince Arthur *gave* a boxe of Diamond sure, . . . I. ix. 19. 1
the Redcrosse knight him *gave* A booke, . . . I. ix. 19. 6

Gave—*Continued.*
gave it him in hand: . . . . I. ix. 51. 3
Almightie God her *gave* such powre and puissaunce great. . . I. x. 20. 9
wise Speranza *gave* him comfort sweet, ... I. x. 22. 1
the carefull charge of him she *gave,* . . . . I. x. 34. 6
he . . . *gave* All in his hand, ... I. x. 42. 7
He did supply their want, and *gave* them ever free. . . . . I. x. 43. 9
Georgos he thee *gave* to name; . . . . I. x. 66. 6
thens departing *gave* for his paynes hyre . . . . I. x. 68. 5
Life and long health that gracious ointment *gave,* . . . . I. xi. 48. 6
sacred pledges he both *gave,* and had, ... I. xii. 27. 3
after *gave* a grone so deepe and low . . . . II. i. 38. 3
to the Palmer *gave* to beare; . . . . II. ii. 11. 2
Gave him great ayd, and made him more inclynd: . . . . II. iii. 4. 7
Of deadly drugs I *gave* him drinke anon, ... II. iv. 30. 8
'Feare *gave* her winges, ... II. iv. 32. 1
that she *gave* into his hond, ... II. v. 22. 8
Gave wondrous great contentment to the knight, ... II. vi. 8. 2
Ne *gave* him leave to bid that aged sire Adieu; . . . . II. vi. 20. 5
to that Damsell thankes *gave* for reward. . . . . II. vi. 38. 6
hidden vertue to it *gave.* . . . . II. viii. 20. 9
Gave signes of grudge and discontentment vaine. . . . . II. viii. 23. 5
Gave him great hart and hope of victory. . . . . II. viii. 39. 4
when againe They *gave* fresh charge, ... II. ix. 14. 3
gave light, and flamd continually; . . . . II. ix. 46. 4
He also *gave* to fugitives of Spayne, ... II. x. 41. 6
to him *gave* for wife his daughter bright, ... II. x. 59. 4
his daughter deare He *gave* in wedlocke . . . . II. x. 61. 2
How much to her we owe, that all us *gave;* . . . . II. x. 69. 8
gave unto us all what ever good we have. . . . . II. x. 69. 9
grownd he *gave,* and lightly lept areare: . . . . II. xi. 36. 5
gave against his mother earth a gronefull sownd. . . . . II. xi. 42. 9
blushing to her laughter *gave* more grace, ... II. xii. 68. 2
scarse them leasure *gave* her passing to behold. . . . . III. i. 15. 9
With which fayre Britomart *gave* light unto the day. . . . . III. i. 43. 9
eke the Redcrosse knight *gave* her good ayd, ... III. i. 66. 7
gave unto king Ryence for his gard, ... III. ii. 21. 2
she *gave* him warning every day . . . . III. iv. 26. 1
Thy life she *gave,* thy life she doth deserve: . . . . III. v. 46. 8
The rest upon her person *gave* attendance great. . . . . III. vi. 17. 9
gave it streight in charge . . . . III. vii. 23. 1
fear *gave* her wings, and need her corage taught. . . . . III. vii. 26. 9
Whom Venus to him *gave* for meed of worthinesse; . . . . III. ix. 34. 9
Gave them safe conduct, till to end they came. . . . . III. x. 16. 7
the flame; the which eftsoones *gave* place, ... III. xi. 25. 4
gave him being, commune to them twayne: . . . . III. xii. 9. 4
gave her leave at pleasure forth to passe. . . . . III. xii. 43. 6
so *gave* way unto his fell intent; . . . . IV. iii. 18. 7
straight flew ope, and *gave* her way to ride. . . . . IV. iii. 46. 3
That girdle *gave* the vertue of chast love, ... IV. v. 3. 1
gave place to kindly rest, ... IV. v. 43. 4
for advantage ground unto him *gave,* . . . . IV. vii. 28. 7
that cruell stroke Which Britomart him *gave,* . . . . IV. xi. 5. 9
Which steely brand . . . She *gave* unto him, ... V. i. 9. 2
The portion of that good which Fortune *gave* her, ... V. iv. 12. 7
gave them gifts and things of deare delight. . . . . V. iv. 51. 6
in his hand a distaffe to him *gave,* . . . . V. v. 23. 2
one thought, That *gave* none other place. . . . . V. vi. 21. 4
gave to them great living and large fee: . . . . V. vii. 43. 4
Gave unto her great comfort and reliefe; . . . . V. vii. 44. 7
Unto his horses *gave* his guests for meat, ... V. viii. 31. 2
Gave way unto his horses speedie flying, ... V. viii. 32. 3
gave him great ayde: . . . . V. ix. 5. 3
gave beginning to her woe and wretchednesse. . . . . V. x. 11. 9
gave him soveraine powre . . . . V. x. 13. 2
gave him roiall giftes and riches rare, ... V. x. 17. 2
Gave leave unto his ghost . . . To wander in the griesly shades . V. x. 33. 5
Ne to their force *gave* way, ... V. x. 35. 3
Albe that it most safety to him *gave,* . . . . V. xi. 46. 5
when he *gave* me armes in field to fight, ... V. xi. 53. 3
when he gave me armes . . . *Gave* me a shield, ... V. xi. 53. 4
ne *gave* him longer day: . . . . V. xii. 9. 8
She freely *gave* that Castle for his paine, ... VI. i. 46. 7
gave them straight unto that Squire againe, ... VI. i. 47. 3
foule Infamie and fell Despight *Gave* evidence, ... VI. vii. 34. 8
gave his foe good hope of victory: . . . . VI. viii. 9. 6
way to them he *gave* forth right to pas; . . . . VI. viii. 14. 3
they all *gave* one consent . . . . VI. viii. 38. 4
gave him for to feed . . . . VI. ix. 7. 3
Gave it to Coridon, and said he wonne it well. . . . . VI. ix. 44. 9
better tearmes . . . Which *gave* him hope, ... VI. xi. 7. 3
gently waking them *gave* them the time of day. . . . . VI. xi. 38. 9
ye to me *gave* A little mayde, ... VI. xii. 17. 6
the Gods, that *gave* good eare To her bold words, ... VII. vi. 28. 1
equall *gave* to each as Justice duly scann'd. . . . . VII. vii. 38. 9
gave her doome in speeches few. . . . . VII. vii. 57. 9
the bay, which I unto her *gave,* . . . . *Am.* xxix. 3
one disparagement they to you *gave,* . . . . *Am.* lxvi. 3
The first my being to me *gave* by kind, ... *Am.* lxxiv. 5
He *gave* as their inheritance to hold, ... *H.H.L.* 61
He freely *gave* to be both rent and torne . . . . *H.H.L.* 150
He *gave* us life, he it restored lost; . . . . *H.H.L.* 181
Who first to us our life and being *gave,* . . . . *H.H.L.* 191
That full and freely *gave* himselfe to thee. . . . . *H.H.L.* 266
That to me *gave* this Lifes first native sourse, ... *Proth.* 129
Gavest. for his sake thy life thou *gavest.'* . . . . V. vii. 32. 6
Gay. With rich treasures this *gay* ship fraighted was: . . . . *Pet.* ii. 6
Renewes herselfe with buildings rich and *gay;* . . . . *Ro.* xxvii. 11
the *gay* floures did offer to be eaten; . . . . *Van.* ii. 6
more for thrift did care than for *gay* clothing: . . . . *Hub.* 231

Gay—*Continued.*
Gay without good is good hearts greatest loathing. . . . . *Hub.* 232
That before God we may appeare more *gay,* . . . . *Hub.* 462
so goodly and so *gay* In your attyres, ... *Hub.* 590
In gage for his *gay* Masters hopelesse dett: . . . . *Hub.* 865
wont to be the glorie of *gay* wits, ... *T.M.* 182
fields, that earst so *gay* were dyde In colours . . . . *T.M.* 237
thy *gay* Sonne, that winged God of Love, ... *T.M.* 401
all that in this world is great or *gaie* . . . . *Ti.* 55
To the *gay* gardins his unstaid desire Him wholly caried, . . . *Mui.* 161
Gay chapelets of flowers and gyrlonds trim. . . . . *As.* 42
Seeme greatest, when their garments are most *gay.* . . . . *Col.* 722
Unlesse that some *gay* Mistresse badge he beares: . . . . *Col.* 780
In whose great shield was writ with letters *gay* . . . . I. ii. 12. 7
others trimly dight Their *gay* attyre; . . . . I. iv. 14. 9
she comes, . . . Adorned all with gold and girlonds *gay,* . . . I. iv. 17. 2
Greatly advauncing his *gay* chevalree: . . . . I. v. 16. 5
an horne . . . in twisted gold And tasselles *gay.* . . . . I. viii. 3. 7
That her *gay* garments staynd with filthy gore, ... I. viii. 16. 7
In which were not rich tyres, nor garments *gay,* . . . . I. x. 39. 2
deckt himselfe with fethers youthly *gay,* . . . . I. xi. 34. 5
Gay steed with spurs did pricke, ... II. i. 49. 9
These two *gay* knights, vowd to so diverse loves, ... II. ii. 19. 1
in court *gay* portaunce he perceiv'd, ... II. iii. 5. 7
at her backe a bow and quiver *gay,* . . . . II. iii. 29. 2
Great glory and *gay* spoile, sure hast thou gott, ... II. iv. 45. 6
Amidst a flock of Damzelles fresh and *gay,* . . . . II. v. 32. 4
that *gay* payre, issewing on the shore, ... II. vi. 11. 6
Faire shields, *gay* steedes, bright armes be my delight; . . . II. vii. 10. 8
a woman, gorgeous *gay* And richly cladd . . . . II. vii. 44. 6
With his *gay* Squyre issewing did espye, ... II. xi. 17. 8
Gan choose his Dame with *Bascimano gay,* . . . . III. i. 56. 8
Gay girlonds from the Sun their forheads fayr to shade; . . III. iv. 29. 9
your *gay* sonne, that gives ye so good ayd . . . . III. vi. 21. 4
Their goodly meriment and *gay* felicity. . . . . III. vi. 41. 9
Him shaped thus she deckt in garments *gay,* . . . . III. viii. 9. 1
Her garments *gay* with scales of fish that all did fill. . . . III. viii. 26. 9
Her golden locks, that were in trammells *gay* Upbounden, . . III. ix. 20. 4
However *gay* and goodly be the style, ... IV. ii. 29. 7
All deckt with crownes, and chaynes, and girlands *gay,* . . . IV. x. 37. 6
That her *gay* clothes did in discolour die. . . . . V. i. 14. 5
How ever *gay* their blossome or their blade Doe flourish now, . V. ii. 40. 4
Dispreds the glorie of her leaves *gay;* . . . . V. xii. 13. 6
Yet is that glasse so *gay,* that it can blynd . . . . VI. Pr. 5. 6
'To them that list the worlds *gay* showes I leave, ... VI. ix. 22. 1
all this worlds *gay* showes, which we admire, ... VI. ix. 27. 4
Al with *gay* girlands goodly wel beseene. . . . . *Epith.* 40
bring in hand Another *gay* girland, ... *Epith.* 42
Gay-beseen. Deckt with greene boughes and flowers *gay beseene:* . . . . VI. v. 38. 5
That goodly Idoll, now so *gay beseene,* . . . . *Am.* xxvii. 5
Gayne, -n. *See* **Gain.**
Gay-painted. She her *gay painted* plumes disorderid; . . . . II. iii. 36. 4
Gay-seeming. this vile world and these *gay-seeming* things; *H.H.B.* 299
Gaze. thrust out his golden hedde, Upon her to *gaze:* . . . . *S.C.* Ap. 74
gan the Courtiers *gaze* on everie side, ... *Hub.* 669
lifted up above the worldes *gaze,* . . . . *T.M.* 587
people, . . . Doe ride each other upon her to *gaze:* . . . . I. iv. 16. 8
flockt . . . To *gaze* on erthly wight . . . . I. v. 32. 9
Leave off their worke, . . . To *gaze* on them; . . . . I. v. 36. 3
Why doe ye . . . liking find to *gaze* on earthly mould, ... I. vii. 22. 4
Whom thus at *gaze* the Palmer gan to bord . . . . II. ii. 5. 1
with fell looke and hollow deadly *gaze* . . . . III. vii. 7. 6
round about themselves awhile did *gaze;* . . . . IV. ii. 17. 3
That men on him the more might *gaze* alone. . . . . IV. iv. 14. 6
Low looking dales, disloignd from common *gaze;* . . . . IV. x. 24. 6
thought that she thereon could never *gaze* her fill. . . . . V. vii. 5. 9
They ceast their clamors upon them to *gaze;* . . . . V. ix. 24. 1
that goodly glorious *gaze* . . . . VI. x. 4. 1
A while on her they greedily did *gaze,* . . . . VI. xi. 13. 8
So did their ghastly *gaze* bewray their hidden feares. . . . . VII. vi. 28. 9
rash eies which *gaze* on her so wide, ... *Am.* v. 7
I unwarily did *gaze* On those fayre eyes, ... *Am.* xvi. 1
having it, they *gaze* on it the more; . . . . *Am.* xxxv. 6
mens frayle eyes, that *gaze* too bold, ... *Am.* xxxvii. 5
To let them *gaze,* whylest he on them may pray: . . . . *Am.* liii. 4
When others *gaze* upon theyr shadowes vayne, ... *Am.* lxxxvii. 6
Upon her so to *gaze,* . . . . *Epith.* 182
all earthes glorie, on which men do *gaze,* . . . . *H.H.L.* 275
The greatest wisards which thereon do *gaze.* . . . . *H.H.B.* 168
ceasse to *gaze* on matter of thy grief: . . . . *H.H.B.* 294
Gazed. *gazd* on her as they were wood, ... *S.C.* Au. 75
Still as I *gazed,* I beheld where stood A Knight . . . . *Ti.* 645
on whom while so he *gazd,* . . . . I. i. 26. 3
gazd upon with gaping wonderment; . . . . I. xii. 9. 5
Gaz'd after him, as fowle escapt by flight. . . . . II. viii. 9. 4
So as they *gazed* after her a whyle, ... III. i. 17. 1
one, which hath *gaz'd* On the bright Sunne unwares, ... III. vii. 13. 6
ever more and more upon it *gazd,* . . . . III. xi. 49. 8
gazed on their harmes, not pittying their estate. . . . . IV. ii. 20. 9
He *gazed* still upon that snowy mayd; . . . . V. iii. 18. 7
He *gaz'd* about and stared horriblie, ... VI. vii. 42. 8
Downe on his golden feete he often *gazed,* . . . . VI. viii. 26. 6
on her uncouth habit and sterne looke still *gazed.* . . . . VII. vi. 13. 9
Gazeful. beheld with *gazefull* eye, ... IV. x. 28. 2
The ravisht harts of *gazefull* men . . . . *H.B.* 12
Then looke, who list thy *gazefull* eyes to feed . . . . *H.H.B.* 29
Gazement. Covered from peoples *gazement* with a vele: . V. iii. 17. 3
Gazer. Like lightening flash that hath the *gazer* burned, . . V. viii. 38. 1
Gazer's. *gazers* sence with double pleasure fed, ... II. iii. 22. 8

Gazers. *See* **Star-gazers.**
To make the bayte her *gazers* to embrew: . . . *Am.* liii. 11
So many *gazers* as on her do stare, . . . *Epith.* 160
Gazers'. Great ruth in all the *gazers* harts did grow, . . . I. v. 9. 7
Ne rov'd at randon, after *gazers* guyse, . . . IV. x. 49. 8
Gazing. blinde his *gazing* eye; . . . *Gn.* 100
gazing ghastly on, (for feare and yre . . . *Gn.* 310
The kingly beast upon her *gazing* stood: . . . I. iii. 8. 4
By them they passe, all *gazing* on them round, . . . I. iv. 7. 1
the which, . . . The gods stand *gazing* on, . . . I. iv. 17. 6
earely waite him many a *gazing* eye, . . . I. v. 3. 2
old Sylvanus . . . *gazing* stood . . . I. vi. 16. 4
He would them *gazing* blind, or turne to other hew. . . . I. vii. 35. 9
As he thereon stood *gazing*, . . . I. x. 56. 1
with rare delight And *gazing* wonder . . . II. ix. 33. 3
Gazing awhile at his unwonted guise; . . . II. xii. 66. 2
On which when *gazing* him the Palmer saw, . . . II. xii. 69. 1
gazing each on other nought bespake. . . . III. vi. 27. 6
they all on her, Stood *gazing*, . . . III. ix. 23. 4
ne could satisfy . . . with *gazing* a long space: . . . III. xi. 53. 4
gazing on that Chambers ornament, . . . III. xii. 29. 2
there among Stood *gazing*, . . . IV. iii. 37. 4
All on her *gazing* wisht, and vowd, and prayd, . . . IV. v. 26. 3
long *gazing* thereupon, At last fell humbly downe . . . IV. vi. 22. 1
over him she there long *gazing* stood, . . . IV. vii. 32. 6
Thus *gazing* long at them much wondred he; . . . IV. ix. 11. 8
thereuppon long while stood *gazing* still, . . . V. vii. 5. 8
there stood *gazing* from the Citties wall . . . V. xi. 15. 6
gazing still on others stands. . . . VI. ix. 11. 9
So stood he still long *gazing* thereupon, . . . VI. ix. 12. 1
Gealous, Gealosy. *See* **Jealous, -y.**
Gear. Aray thyselfe in her most gorgeous *geare*, . . . II. iv. 26. 8
unknowen *geare* And uncouth fashion, . . . IV. xi. 45. 2
Thus goe they both together to their *geare*, . . . V. viii. 30. 1
Ere he were throughly buckled to his *geare*, . . . V. xi. 10. 2
That to Sir Calidore was easie *geare;* . . . VI. iii. 6. 5
unable to support So huge a burden on such broken *geare*, . . . VI. viii. 16. 7
spat out poyson, and gore-bloudy *gere*, . . . VI. xii. 28. 3
Geare. *See* **Jeer.**
Gears. spoyling all her *geares* and goodly ray . . . V. ii. 50. 4
Geason. this age, in which all good is *geason*, . . . *Van.* i. 5
it to Leaches seemed strange and *geason*. . . . *Hub.* 12
Found nothing that he said unmeet nor *geason*, . . . VI. iv. 37. 2
Geather. *See* **Gather.**
Geaunt, -ess, -s. *See* **Giant, -ess, -s.**
Gehon's. *Gehons* golden waves doe wash continually: . . . I. vii. 43. 9
Gelded. *See* **Gelt.**
Gelly-blood. *See* **Jelly-blood.**
Gelosy. *See* **Jealosy.**
Gelt. *See* **Gelded, Gilt.**
it must be *gelt* in privitie. . . . *Hub.* 520
like a ghastly *Gelt* whose wits are reaved, . . . IV. vii. 21. 3
Some would have *gelt* him; . . . VII. vi. 50. 3
Gem. as a precious *gemme* Amidst a ring . . . VI. x. 12. 7
Gems. a tyre of gold, Adornd with *gemmes* . . . I. x. 31. 6
Her selfe adorn'd with *gems* and jewels manifold. . . . V. vii. 13. 9
Adorned all with *gemmes* of endlesse price, . . . V. ix. 27. 6
And with ten thousand *gemmes* of shyning gold,) . . . *H.H.L.* 60
all with *gemmes* and jewels gorgeously Adornd,. . . *H.H.B.* 187
meades adornd with daintie *gemmes* . . . *Proth.* 14
Genealogy. fetch from heven thy great *genealogie*, . . . III. ix. 33. 7
General. That men may thinke of you in *generall*, . . . *Hub.* 647
prizde with slaughter of their *Generall;* . . . *Ti.* 116
the blame . . . is too *generall*, . . . *Col.* 732
'Blame is . . . more blamelesse *generall*, . . . *Col.* 749
Were by them slaine by *generall* consent: . . . VI. xi. 31. 5
Yet is she chang'd in part, and eeke in *generall:* . . . VII. vii. 17. 9
Of all the which demand in *generall*, . . . VII. vii. 27. 5
Generation. *generation* of all That lives, . . . II. xii. 47. 3
Great father he of *generation* Is rightly cald, . . . III. vi. 9. 1
In *generation* seeke to quench their inward fire. . . . IV. x. 46. 9
So fertile be the flouds in *generation*, . . . IV. xii. 1. 8
generation goodly dost enlarge, . . . *Epith.* 384
Generous. *generous* stout courage did inspyre, . . . III. iii. 57. 4
Through secret feeling of his *generous* spright, . . . IV. iii. 14. 5
fyre Which kindleth love in *generous* desyre, . . . *H.L.* 187
Genial. The bridale bowre and *geniall* bed remaine, . . . *Epith.* 399
Genius. th' auncient *Genius* of that Citie brent: . . . *Ti.* 19
They in that place him *Genius* did call: . . . II. xii. 47. 1
Old *Genius* the porter of them was, . . . III. vi. 31. 8
Old *Genius*, the which a double nature has. . . . III. vi. 31. 9
And thou, glad *Genius!* in whose gentle hand . . . *Epith.* 398
Gent. 'Well worthy impe,' said then the Lady *gent*, . . . I. ix. 6. 1
He lov'd, as was his lot, a Lady *gent*, . . . I. ix. 27. 6
A knight had wrought against a Ladie *gent;* . . . II. i. 30. 6
till Genuissa *gent* Persuaded him to ceasse, . . . II. x. 52. 8
the prowest and most *gent*, . . . II. xi. 17. 5
they all seemed courteous and *gent*, . . . III. i. 44. 4
Was usd of knightes and Ladies seeming *gent:* . . . III. i. 67. 6
the Prince and Faery *gent*, . . . III. iv. 45. 4
Having farre off espyde a Tassell *gent*, . . . III. iv. 49. 6
for love of knighthood *gent*, . . . III. v. 10. 5
The Lady *gent* Thereat was suddein strook . . . III. vii. 3. 8
Ladies, knights, and Damsels *gent*, . . . III. xi. 46. 1
In th' hearing of full many Knights and Ladies *gent*. . . . V. x. 14. 9
a Ladie *gent* Sate with a knight . . . VI. ii. 16. 4
Gentilesse. man, that . . . neither *gentlesse* knew, . . . VI. iv. 3. 2
Gentility. far expell All civile usage and *gentility*, . . . III. vi. 1. 8
Gentle. the *gentle* sounding of the waters fall: . . . *Pet.*[1] iv. 7
pincht the haunches of that (this[1]) *gentle* beast, . . . *Pet.* i. 9

Gentle—*Continued.*
Ye *gentle* Shepheards, which your flocks do feede, . . . *S.C.* Jun. 106
The *gentle* shepheard satte beside a springe, . . . *S.C.* D. 1
with *gentle* mood Of Poets Prince, . . . *Gn.* 17
With *gentle* murmure of the breathing ayre, . . . *Gn.* 186
a *gentle* murmure sent; . . . *Gn.* 228
gentle slumbring sleep oppressed him . . . *Gn.* 239
the right *gentle* minde would bite his lip, . . . *Hub.* 711
The canker worme of everie *gentle* brest; . . . *Hub.* 736
with Loves, and Ladies *gentle* sports, . . . *Hub.* 757
love of letters did inspire Their *gentle* wits, . . . *Hub.* 830
The foes of learning and each *gentle* thought; . . . *T.M.* 64
The *gentle* minds, in midst of worldlie smarts: . . . *T.M.* 136
Marring my joyous *gentle* dalliaunce. . . . *T.M.* 186
that same *gentle* Spirit, . . . *T.M.* 217
gentle mindes with lewd delights distaine; . . . *T.M.* 334
some one perhaps of *gentle* kin, . . . *T.M.* 345
Ye *gentle* Spirits, breathing from above, . . . *T.M.* 361
that *gentle* River for great griefe Of my mishaps, . . . *Ti.* 141
'Most *gentle* spirite, breathed from above . . . *Ti.* 281
cared not to cherishe No *gentle* wits, . . . *Ti.* 363
the *gentle* Squire, to entertaine His fayre Belphoebe, . . . *Ti.* 524
gentle kinde as ever Fowle afore; . . . *Ti.* 591
With *gentle* calme the world had quieted, . . . *Mui.* 50
ward his *gentle* corpes from cruell wound; . . . *Mui.* 60
Emongst the rest a *gentle* Nymph was found, . . . *Mui.* 118
Then stay, Alcyon, *gentle* shepheard! . . . *D.* 68
all my joy was on my *gentle* sheepe, . . . *D.* 104
Hearken, ye *gentle* shepheards, to my song, . . . *As.* Pr. 5
A *gentle* shepheard borne in Arcady, . . . *As.* 1
With *gentle* usage and demeanure myld: . . . *As.* 20
another swaine Of *gentle* wit . . . *As.* Interl. 218
gan a *gentle* bonylasse to speake, . . . *Col.* 172
Whose *gentle* spright for Daphnes death . . . *Col.* 386
ingratefull to each *gentle* mayd, . . . *Col.* 462
That I of *gentle* Mayds should ill deserve! . . . *Col.* 465
Ne thee lesse worthie, *gentle* Flavia, . . . *Col.* 572
Ne is there place for any *gentle* wit, . . . *Col.* 707
not any *gentle* wit of name Nor honest mynd . . . *Col.* 733
despite, That yrkes each *gentle* heart which it doth heare.' . . . *Col.* 906
Receive, most noble Lord, in *gentle* gree, . . . *Ded. Son.* iii. 1
dwel . . . *gentle* Nymphes, delights of learned wits; . . . *Ded. Son.* v. 10
to . . . sing of Knights and Ladies *gentle* deeds; . . . I. Pr. 1. 5
Mart, In loves and *gentle* jollities arraid, . . . I. Pr. 3. 8
A *gentle* Knight was pricking on the plaine, . . . I. i. 1. 1
As *gentle* shepheard in sweete eventide, . . . I. i. 23. 1
Care . . . Who oft is wont to trouble *gentle* Sleepe. . . . I. i. 40. 6
With *gentle* blandishment and lovely looke, . . . I. i. 49. 8
Tho can she weepe, to stirre up *gentle* ruth . . . I. i. 50. 8
Much griev'd to thinke that *gentle* Dame so light, . . . I. i. 55. 2
sore grieved in her *gentle* brest, . . . I. ii. 8. 8
Which to expresse he bends his *gentle* wit: . . . I. ii. 30. 5
it was my lott To love this *gentle* Lady, . . . I. ii. 35. 4
nigh he drew unto this *gentle* payre, . . . I. iii. 34. 1
A *gentle* Husher, Vanitie by name, Made rowme, . . . I. iv. 13. 3
With *gentle* wordes he can her fayrely greet, . . . I. iv. 46. 1
slew with glauncing dart amisse A *gentle* Hynd, . . . I. vi. 17. 6
During which time her *gentle* wit she plyes . . . I. vi. 19. 5
make proofe of her cruelty On *gentle* Dame, . . . I. vi. 31. 7
The *gentle* virgin, left behinde alone, . . . I. vi. 33. 3
Hereof this *gentle* knight unweeting was; . . . I. vii. 6. 1
A *gentle* youth, his dearely loved Squire, . . . I. vii. 37. 1
'Ah Lady deare,' quoth then the *gentle* knight, . . . I. vii. 40. 1
horrour ran through every joynt, For ruth of *gentle* knight . . . I. viii. 39. 4
upbrought in *gentle* thewes and martiall might. . . . I. ix. 3. 9
the river Dee . . . His tombling billowes rolls with *gentle* rore; . . . I. ix. 4. 8
gentle Una thus to him gan say: . . . I. ix. 16. 5
'Thine, O! then,' said the *gentle* Redcrosse knight, . . . I. ix. 17. 1
Him yett againe . . . bespake The *gentle* knight; . . . I. ix. 24. 7
Whenas the *gentle* Redcrosse knight did vew, . . . I. ix. 37. 3
There fayrely them receives a *gentle* Squyre, . . . I. x. 7. 1
there sate a *gentle* payre, Of turtle doves, . . . I. x. 31. 8
Up rose the *gentle* virgin from her place, . . . I. xi. 33. 5
gentle Una saw the second fall Of her deare knight, . . . I. xi. 50. 1
never *gentle* knight . . . So tossed was . . . I. xii. 16. 7
did throw This *gentle* knight into so great distresse, . . . I. xii. 33. 8
Where sate a *gentle* Lady all alone, . . . II. i. 13. 5
Eftsoone she said; 'Ah! *gentle* trustie Squyre, . . . II. i. 17. 1
the man, that ever would deceave A *gentle* Lady, . . . II. i. 17. 8
Or ever *gentle* Damzell so abuse: . . . II. i. 19. 3
well ye worthy bene for worth and *gentle* thewes.' . . . II. i. 33. 9
As *gentle* Hynd, . . . forth her bleeding life does raine, . . . II. i. 38. 6
The *gentle* knight her soone with carefull paine Uplifted . . . II. i. 46. 1
all that *gentle* noriture ensu'th; . . . II. iii. 2. 5
without desert of *gentle* deed And noble worth, . . . II. iii. 10. 6
a science Proper to *gentle* blood: . . . II. iv. 1. 8
would abuse so *gentle* Dame! . . . II. iv. 20. 9
there trickled softly downe A *gentle* streame, . . . II. v. 30. 2
That *gentle* Lady did to him impart: . . . II. vi. 26. 5
lovely peace, and *gentle* amity, . . . II. vi. 35. 3
Of courteous clemency in *gentle* hart. . . . II. vi. 36. 6
with uncomely weedes the *gentle* wave accloyes. . . . II. vii. 15. 9
'Gramercy, Mammon,' (said the *gentle* knight) . . . II. vii. 50. 1
gentle Knight, That doth against the dead . . . II. viii. 29. 6
him the Prince with *gentle* court did bord: . . . II. ix. 2. 5
was shee woo'd of many a *gentle* knight, . . . II. ix. 18. 3
gentle court and gracious delight Shee to them made, . . . II. ix. 20. 3
As if some pensive thought constraind her *gentle* spright. . . . II. ix. 36. 9
'*Gentle* Madame, why beene ye thus dismayd, . . . II. ix. 37. 5
Another Damsell of that *gentle* crew, . . . II. ix. 40. 2

Gentle—*Continued.*
Polluted this same *gentle* soyle long time; . . . II. x. 9. 2
gentle Alma, seeing it so late, . . . II. x. 77. 5
Had not his *gentle* Squire beheld his paine, . . . II. xi. 29. 8
'O thou fayre sonne of *gentle* Faery, . . . II. xii. 32. 3
Which outrage when those *gentle* knights did see, . . . III. i. 18. 1
of many a *gentle* knight, . . . III. i. 31. 6
in each *gentle* hart desire of honor breeds. . . . III. i. 49. 9
rudely sdeigne a *gentle* harts request, . . . III. i. 55. 4
every knight, and every *gentle* Squire, . . . III. i. 56. 7
t' upbrayd A *gentle* knight with so unknightly blame; . . . III. ii. 9. 6
It ill beseemes a knight of *gentle* sort, . . . III. ii. 12. 6
Such secrete ease felt *gentle* Britomart, . . . III. ii. 15. 7
frends to termes of *gentle* truce entize, . . . III. ii. 24. 5
love, that is in *gentle* brest begonne, . . . III. ii. 51. 7
At last blow up some *gentle* gale of ease, . . . III. iv. 10. 3
Timias, the Princes *gentle* Squyre, . . . III. iv. 47. 1
Was earst impressed in her *gentle* spright. . . . III. iv. 49. 3
gentle Sleepe envyde him any rest: . . . III. iv. 54. 1
Served a *gentle* Lady of great sway . . . III. v. 4. 5
The *gentle* Squyre came ryding that same way, . . . III. v. 18. 2
'Ah! *gentle* Squire, Nor Goddesse I, nor Angell; . . . III. v. 36. 1
seemd to plaine With *gentle* murmure . . . III. v. 39. 9
In *gentle* Ladies breste and bounteous race Of woman kind . . . III. v. 52. 7
gentle sprite deforme with rude rusticity. . . . III. vi. 1. 9
a *gentle* slombring swowne Upon her fell, . . . III. vi. 7. 3
the *gentle* Shepheard swaynes, . . . III. vi. 15. 6
Spare, *gentle* sister, with reproch my paine to eeke; . . . III. vi. 22. 9
With sugred words and *gentle* blandishment, . . . III. vi. 25. 4
sweete love *gentle* fitts emongst them throwes, . . . III. vi. 41. 5
to their senses vyld Her *gentle* speach applyde, . . . III. vii. 15. 4
That *gentle* Lady whom I love and serve, . . . III. vii. 53. 6
I might doe service unto *gentle* Dames, . . . III. vii. 54. 6
'Ah! *gentle* Squyre,' (quoth he) . . . III. vii. 56. 8
This *gentle* Damzell, whom I write upon, . . . III. viii. 1. 4
with *gentle* countenaunce, retain'd Enough . . . III. viii. 10. 6
th' open freshnes of the *gentle* aire, . . . III. viii. 11. 4
He gan make *gentle* purpose to his Dame . . . III. viii. 14. 2
there with many *gentle* termes her faire besought. . . . III. viii. 35. 9
'Ah! *gentle* knight,' . . . 'Thy labour all is lost, . . . III. viii. 47. 1
fast goodwill, with *gentle* courtesyes, . . . III. ix. 7. 7
'entreat The man by *gentle* meanes . . . III. ix. 9. 2
shewd her selfe in all a *gentle* courteous Dame, . . . III. ix. 26. 9
Purpose was moved by that *gentle* Dame . . . III. ix. 32. 2
The *gentle* Lady, loose at randon lefte, . . . III. x. 36. 1
'Ah *gentle* knight! . . . III. xi. 14. 1
thrald your *gentle* make. . . . III. xi. 15. 3
gentle Ladyes helplesse misery: . . . III. xi. 18. 6
gentle pangues, with which he maked meeke The mightie Mars, III. xi. 44. 2
she was *gentle* and of milde aspect, . . . III. xii. 14. 3
'*Gentle* Dame, reward enough I weene, . . . III. xii. 40. 2
no lesse griefe endured for your *gentle* sake.' . . . III. xii. 40. 9
gentle spright Now gan to feede on hope, . . . III. xii. 44. 6
Was much empassiond in her *gentle* sprite, . . . III. xii. 46. *or.*7
through her *gentle* deed Was . . . restor'd, . . . IV. i. 15. 1
'Ah *gentle* knight!' then false Duessa sayd, . . . IV. i. 46. 1
love and friendly aid Mongst *gentle* knights to nourish . . . IV. i. 46. 4
'Ah *gentle* Knights!' (quoth he) 'how may that bee, . . . IV. ii. 22. 3
twixt themselves did *gentle* purpose make, . . . IV. ii. 30. 7
All which when *gentle* Canacee beheld, . . . IV. iii. 50. 1
To joyous feast and other *gentle* play, . . . IV. iv. 48. 7
the *gentle* Amoret Likewise assayd . . . IV. v. 19. 2
her lover long miswent, The *gentle* Scudamour, . . . IV. v. 30. 7
When *gentle* sleepe his heavie eyes would close; . . . IV. v. 40. 2
pyning anguish hid in *gentle* hart, . . . IV. vi. 1. 2
'Ah, *gentle* Scudamour! unto your grace I me submit, . . . IV. vi. 3. 7
'Ye *gentle* Knights, whom fortune here hath brought . . . IV. vi. 30. 2
did lay Continuall siege unto her *gentle* hart; . . . IV. vi. 40. 4
whose *gentle* hart Thou martyrest . . . IV. vii. 2. 4
It was my lot to love a *gentle* swaine, . . . IV. vii. 15. 6
that same *gentle* Squire arriv'd in place . . . IV. vii. 24. 3
Which drery sight the *gentle* Squire espying . . . IV. vii. 25. 1
She left the *gentle* Squire with Amoret: . . . IV. vii. 35. 2
he whilome some *gentle* swaine had beene, . . . IV. vii. 45. 6
The *gentle* Squire recovers grace, . . . IV. viii. Arg.
to this *gentle* Squire did happen late, . . . IV. viii. 1. 2
this *gentle* bird to him did use . . . IV. viii. 5. 1
Her *gentle* Squire through her displeasure did pertake. . . . IV. viii. 9. 9
No service lothsome to a *gentle* kind, . . . IV. viii. 22. 7
These *gentle* Ladies will misdeeme too light . . . IV. viii. 29. 4
This *gentle* crew gan from their eye-lids chace . . . IV. viii. 34. 3
a *gentle* Squire That lov'd a Ladie . . . IV. viii. 50. 1
the *gentle* hart should most assured bind. . . . IV. ix. 1. 9
To yeeld strong succour to that *gentle* swayne, . . . IV. ix. 4. 2
Britomart and *gentle* Scudamour; . . . IV. ix. 22. 2
With *gentle* words perswading them to friendly peace. . . . IV. ix. 32. 9
to see that *gentle* maide so tost!' . . . IV. ix. 38. 5
this *gentle* crew Is now so well accorded . . . IV. ix. 40. 4
hearke, ye *gentle* knights and Ladies free, . . . IV. x. 3. 6
Soft rombling brookes, that *gentle* slomber drew; . . . IV. x. 24. 4
she in *gentle* wise me entertayned, . . . IV. x. 36. 2
Holding her hand upon her *gentle* hart; . . . IV. x. 51. 2
many a *gentle* Muse and many a learned wit. . . . IV. xi. 34. 9
The first the *gentle* Shure . . . IV. xi. 43. 1
with their boughes the *gentle* plants did beat: . . . V. i. 1. 5
Upon a day she found this *gentle* childe . . . V. i. 6. 2
Much did his words the *gentle* Ladie quell, . . . V. iii. 16. 8
A *gentle* Faulcon sitting on an hill, . . . V. v. 15. 2
Doth beat upon the *gentle* bird in vaine, . . . V. v. 15. 6
This *gentle* knight himselfe so well behaved, . . . V. vi. 2. 2

Gentle—*Continued.*
'Ah *gentle* Knights! what meane ye thus . . . V. viii. 11. 2
Thence forth they passed with that *gentle* Mayd . . . V. ix. 20. 1
The *gentle* knights rejoyced much to heare The prayses . . . V. ix. 21. 1
forth he gan to fare With those two *gentle* youthes, . . . V. x. 17. 6
Much was the Ladie in her *gentle* mind Abasht . . . V. xi. 64. 1
Both noble armes and *gentle* curtesie. . . . VI. i. 26. 8
As then the guize was for each *gentle* swayne: . . . VI. ii. 6. 3
'What meanes this, *gentle* Swaine, . . . VI. ii. 7. 2
aread, thou *gentle* chyld, wherefore . . . VI. ii. 8. 8
turning backe unto that *gentle* boy, . . . VI. ii. 24. 1
'Faire *gentle* swayne, and yet as stout as fayre, . . . VI. ii. 25. 1
Have trayned bene . . . In *gentle* thewes . . . VI. ii. 31. 5
Which ye have gathered to your *gentle* hart . . . VI. ii. 46. 2
The *gentle* minde by *gentle* deeds is knowne: . . . VI. iii. 1. 2
gentle bloud will *gentle* manners breed; . . . VI. iii. 2. 2
The *gentle* Aladine did earst invade, . . . VI. iii. 8. 4
With which his *gentle* words and goodly wit . . . VI. iii. 22. 1
Allur'd with myldnesse of the *gentle* wether . . . VI. iii. 23. 3
Chasing the *gentle* Calepine around, . . . VI. iv. 2. 8
O what an easie thing is to descry The *gentle* bloud, . . . VI. v. 1. 2
Yet will it shew some sparkes of *gentle* mynd, . . . VI. v. 1. 8
Yet shewd some token of his *gentle* blood . . . VI. v. 2. 5
By *gentle* usage of that wretched Dame: . . . VI. v. 2. 6
So milde humanity and perfect *gentle* mynd. . . . VI. v. 29. 9
Some goodly person, and of *gentle* race, . . . VI. v. 36. 7
Ne yet that *gentle* Squire, . . . VI. v. 39. 7
Like as the *gentle* hart it selfe bewrayes . . . VI. vii. 1. 1
In doing *gentle* deedes with franke delight, . . . VI. vii. 1. 2
The *gentle* Prince not farre away they spyde, . . . VI. vii. 6. 7
the *gentle* knight Would not be tempted . . . VI. vii. 23. 1
In th' harts of many a knight, and many a *gentle* squire. . . . VI. vii. 28. 9
the *gentle* Squire, with faire Serene, . . . VI. vii. 39. 2
His *gentle* heart with indignation sweld, . . . VI. vii. 45. 3
to his *gentle* mynd Was much more grievous . . . VI. vii. 49. 7
Ye *gentle* Ladies, in whose soveraine powre . . . VI. viii. 1. 1
after thraldome of the *gentle* Squire, . . . VI. viii. 3. 1
I was belov'd of many a *gentle* Knight, . . . VI. viii. 20. 5
It was his owne true groome, the *gentle* Squire, . . . VI. viii. 27. 6
When first the *gentle* Squire at variaunce fell . . . VI. viii. 31. 3
Great travell hath the *gentle* Calidore . . . endured, . . . VI. ix. 2. 1
tooke their *gentle* offer: . . . VI. ix. 7. 2
The *gentle* knight, as he that did excell In courtesie . . . VI. ix. 18. 3
Thus did the *gentle* knight himselfe abeare . . . VI. ix. 45. 1
at the foote thereof a *gentle* flud . . . VI. x. 7. 1
Frequented of these *gentle* Nymphes alwayes, . . . VI. x. 19. 4
That we likewise should mylde and *gentle* be; . . . VI. x. 24. 2
gentle Shepheard, pardon thou my shame, . . . VI. x. 29. 6
taking leave of that same *gentle* Swaine, . . . VI. x. 32. 1
The *gentle* heart scornes base disparagement. . . . VI. x. 37. 5
Which with those *gentle* shepherds here I wont to lead.' . . . VI. xi. 32. 9
Her *gentle* hart . . . Began some smacke of comfort new to tast, VI. xi. 45. 1
delayd This *gentle* knight from sewing his first quest, . . . VI. xii. 2. 2
For never more defaming *gentle* Knight, . . . VI. xii. 34. 6
Ne spareth he the *gentle* Poets rime; . . . VI. xii. 40. 8
(in whose *gentle* spright, The pure well head of Poesie did dwell) . . . VII. vii. 9. 3
Ah, *gentle* Mole! such joyance hath thee well beseene. . . . VII. vii. 11. 9
the joyous oyle, whose *gentle* gust Made him so frollick . . . VII. vii. 39. 4
to kindle new desire In *gentle* brest, . . . *Am.* vi. 10
your *gentle* brest inspire With sweet infusion, . . . *Am.* xxviii. 6
Such is the powre of love in *gentle* mind, . . . *Am.* xxx. 13
The *gentle* birde feeles no captivity . . . *Am.* lxv. 7
The *gentle* deare returnd the selfe-same way, . . . *Am.* lxvii. 7
peace shall see Betweene the Spyder and the *gentle* Bee. . . . *Am.* lxxi. 14
the trew fayre, that is the *gentle* wit, . . . *Am.* lxxix. 3
To beare the message of her *gentle* spright. . . . *Am.* lxxxi. 12
Attempt to work her *gentle* mindes unrest: . . . *Am.* lxxxiii. 4
A *gentle* Bee, with his loud trumpet murm'ring, . . . *Epig.* iv. 3
Breake *gentle* sleepe with misconceived dout. . . . *Epith.* 337
And thou, glad Genius! in whose *gentle* hand . . . *Epith.* 398
to overspred Me with the shadow of thy *gentle* wing, . . . *H.L.* 20
my feeble breast inspire With *gentle* furie, . . . *H.L.* 28
that monster placed In *gentle* love, . . . *H.L.* 272
After full joyance of their *gentle* game; . . . *H.L.* 291
That is a signe to know the *gentle* blood. . . . *H.B.* 140
many a *gentle* mynd Dwels in deformed tabernacle . . . *H.B.* 141
gentle Love, that loiall is and trew, . . . *H.B.* 176
Should in loves *gentle* band combyned bee . . . *H.B.* 205
Ah! *gentle* Muse! thou art too weake and faint . . . *H.H.B.* 230
A *gentle* spirit, that lightly did delay . . . *Proth.* 3
the *gentle* streame, the which them bare, . . . *Proth.* 47
'Ye *gentle* Birdes! the worlds faire ornament, . . . *Proth.* 91
Joy may you have, and *gentle* hearts content . . . *Proth.* 94
gentle Eccho . . . Their accents did resound. . . . *Proth.* 112
Two *gentle* Knights of lovely face and feature, . . . *Proth.* 169

Gentleman. some good *Gentleman,* that hath the right . . . *Hub.* 525
the Ape anon Himselfe had cloathed like a *Gentleman,* . . . *Hub.* 660
A noble *Gentleman* of high regard, . . . *Hub.* 685
when this Courtly *Gentleman* with toyle Himselfe hath wearied, *Hub.* 753

Gentleness. *gentlenesse* of spright And manners mylde . . . VI. i. 2. 3
wroth Against her Knight, her *gentlenesse* refused, . . . VI. iii. 33. 2

Gentler. A *gentler* shepheard may no where be found: . . . *Col.* 445

Gentlesse. *See* **Gentilesse.**

Gentlest. Of *gentlest* race that ever shepheard bore, . . . *As.* 2
The *gentlest* shepheardesse that lives this day, . . . *As.* 212
to grieve the *gentlest* hart on ground?' . . . I. ix. 7. 9
The *gentlest* knight, that ever . . . with spurs did pricke, . . . II. i. 49. 8
Ah! *gentlest* knight, that ever armor bore, . . . III. i. 7. 5
as it falleth, in the *gentlest* harts . . . III. ii. 23. 1

Gentlest—*Continued.*
Now God thee keepe, thou *gentlest* squire alive, III. v. 26. 6
I enjoyd the *gentlest* Dame alive; III. x. 27. 2
'Ah! *gentlest* knight alive,' III. xi. 19. 1
was the conquest of the *gentlest* Knight VI. x. 40. 8
Gentle-warbling. The simple ayre, the *gentle warbling* wynde, *S.C.* Jun. 4
The *gentle warbling* wind low answered to all. II. xii. 71. 9
Gently. But *gently* tooke that ungently came; *S.C.* F. 22
gently to them bowing in his gate, *Hub.* 1084
romble *gently* downe with murmur soft, *T.M.* 26
To whom the shepheard *gently* answered thus; *Col.* 36
The same aboord us *gently* did receave, *Col.* 224
a christall streame did *gently* play, I. i. 34. 8
gently grenning, . . . To comfort her; I. vi. 11. 7
through the trembling leaves full *gently* playes, I. vii. 3. 3
gently askt, where all the people bee, I. viii. 32. 3
gently come into my feeble brest; I. xi. 6. 1
Come *gently,* but not with that mightie rage, I. xi. 6. 2
gently answered, They entraunce did desire II. ix. 11. 9
to her *gently* said: II. ix. 41. 9
Gently attempred, and disposd so well, II. xii. 51. 8
him to sleepe she *gently* would perswade, III. i. 35. 8
them of patience *gently* prayd. III. ix. 10. 7
He *gently* gan him to demaund of all V. i. 23. 3
he *gently* did desyre To stay her stroks, V. v. 16. 5
gan *gently* her salute With curteous words, V. vi. 20. 1
Her chearing up, thus *gently* to her sayd: VI. iv. 27. 7
gently waking them gave them the time of day. VI. xi. 38. 9
for my faults ye will me *gently* beat. *Am.* xxiv. 14
him take, and in your bosome bright *Gently* encage, *Am.* lxxiii. 10
Gentry. Two filthie blots in noble *gentrie;* *Hub.* 734
Genuissa. to him allide His daughter *Genuiss'* in marriage: II. x. 52. 4
till *Genuissa* gent Persuaded him to ceasse, II. x. 52. 8
Geoffrey. old Dan *Geffrey* . . . durst not with it mel, VII. vii. 9. 3
George. Saint *George* himselfe ye would have deemed him I. ii. 11. 9
The true Saint *George,* was wandred far away, I. ii. 12. 2
thou *Saint George* shalt called bee, *Saint George* of mery *England,* I. x. 61. 8, 9
Georgos. *Georgos* he thee gave to name; I. x. 66. 6
Gerioneo, -s. *See* **Geryoneo, -'s.**
Gerle. *See* **Girl.**
German. Then was the *Germane* Raven in disguise *Ro.* xvii. 9
sluggish *german,* doest thy forces slake I. v. 10. 8
Thyselfe thy message do to *german* deare; I. v. 13. 2
th' English Bath, and eke the *German* Spau; I. xi. 30. 7
Which when his *german* saw, II. viii. 46. 1
Germans. Those *germans* did subdew all Germany, II. x. 22. 7
Germany. Those germans did subdew all *Germany,* II. x. 22. 7
subjected France and *Germany,* II. x. 40. 6
He sent to *Germany* straunge aid to reare; II. x. 64. 7
Gerne. *See* **Girn.**
Geryon. borne and bred Of Gyants race, the sonne of *Geryon;* V. x. 9. 2
The image of his monstrous parent *Geryone.* V. x. 13. 9
Geryoneo. His sonne was this *Geryoneo* hight; V. x. 11. 1
Prince Arthure overcomes the great *Gerioneo* in fight: V. xi. Arg.
witnesse be *Gerioneo* found, V. xii. 2. 5
Geryoneo's. *Gerioneos* Seneschall He slayes V. x. Arg.
Gesippus. Myld Titus and *Gesippus* without pryde; IV. x. 27. 5
Gesse. *See* **Guess.**
Gest. thought of honor, nor brave *gest,* *Hub.* 978
goodly gan discourse of many a noble *gest.* I. x. 15. 9
famous far abroad for warlike *gest,* II. ii. 16. 7
of his name and memorable *gest* II. x. 12. 4
his Heroicke grace and honorable *gest.* III. ii. 24. 9
her prowd portaunce and her princely *gest,* III. ii. 27. 3
Ne how to speake, ne how to use his *gest;* III. viii. 8. 7
Each labouring t' advance the others *gest,* IV. iv. 36. 7
To winne me honour by some noble *gest,* IV. x. 4. 4
Gests. The Porter eke to her did lout with humble *gestes.* II. ix. 26. 9
memorable *gestes* Of famous Wisards II. ix. 53. 3
their brave *gestes* and prowesse martiall: III. ii. 1. 6
By signes, by lookes, and all his other *gests;* VI. iv. 14. 3
Gestures. fitting *gestures* to her purpose frame, I. vii. 1. 6
Get. *get* all the gayne, *S.C.* May 50
would they take no paines to *get* their living, *Hub.* 349
way for one that is unlern'd Living to *get,* *Hub.* 536
Needes anie more to learne to *get* a living?' *Hub.* 544
th' Ape still flying he no where might *get:* *Hub.* 1372
thorough daily care To *get,* . . . his owne, I. iv. 28. 8
ere he could . . . *gett* his shield, I. vii. 8. 2
blis . . . few *gett,* but many mis: II. vii. 48. 9
To *get* a snatch when turned is his face. III. i. 22. 5
mickle fame Did *get* through great adventures III. iv. 20. 6
To *get* small thankes, and therewith many blames, III. vii. 61. 3
Did by great fortune *get* of her the sight, IV. ii. 45. 3
with her alwaies ride, till he another *get.'* IV. iv. 9. 9
Assembled for to *get* the honour of that game. IV. iv. 13. 9
strive the rule to *get* Of all the heard, IV. iv. 18. 3
in hope themselves to *get* her: IV. v. 21. 2
In great displeasure that he could not *get* her. IV. v. 21. 7
Where they might tydings *get* of her estate; IV. vi. 47. 4
handling soft the hurts which she did *get;* IV. vii. 35. 7
To win her grace his libertie to *get:* IV. viii. 53. 6
whether should the honor *get.* V. iii. 24. 4
by his freedome *get* his free goodwill; V. v. 32. 8
Which if I might by your good office *get,* V. v. 42. 3
to *get* Succour against her greedy enimy: V. viii. 6. 6
brought the pillage home, whence none could *get* it out. V. ix. 4. 9
Long while he tug'd and strove to *get* it out, V. xii. 22. 1
a trotting Stalion *get* An ambling Colt, VI. iii. 1. 6

Get—*Continued.*
did inquere After adventures, where they mote them *get.* VI. v. 11. 6
They fled, and fast into the wood did *get.* VI. v. 22. 7
To spy where he may some advauntage *get,* VI. vii. 47. 5
stryving each to *get* The greatest portion VI. xi. 17. 3
he would undertake for this to *get* her To be his Love, VII. vi. 44. 5
Out of her bands ye by no meanes shall *get.* *Am.* xxxvii. 12
Onely my paines wil be the more to *get* her; *Am.* li. 13
to *get* his love retyre; *H.L.* 235
fruitfull love, that loves to *get* Things like himselfe, *H.H.L.* 51
Getteth. The Nymph, his mother, *getteth* her IV. xii. Arg.
Getting. Vaine Braggadocchio, *getting* Guyons horse, II. iii. Arg.
Ghastful. Here will I dwell apart In *gastfull* grove *S.C.* Au. 170
Ghastliness. let *ghastlinesse* And drery horror dim the chearfull light, *D.* 327
her horn sound with such *ghastlinesse.* II. iii. 44. 9
Ghastly. Nor elvish ghosts, nor *gastly* owles doe flee. *S.C.* Jun. 24
The *ghastlie* Owle her grievous ynne doth keepe. *S.C.* D. 72
gazing *ghastly* on, (for feare and yre *Gn.* 310
to worke more *ghastly* feares. *Gn.* 584
Of ghostly darkenes, and of *gastlie* dreed; *T.M.* 532
On which the clowde of *ghastly* night did sit, *D.* 305
as *ghastly* dreadfull, as it seemes, *Col.* 208
Full of sad feare and *ghastly* dreriment, I. ii. 44. 4
full of *ghastly* fright . . . Gan shut the dore. I. iii. 12. 7
the *ghastly* owle, With drery shriekes I. v. 30. 6
A ruefull spectacle of death and *ghastly* drere. I. viii. 40. 9
the *ghastly* Owle, Shrieking his balefull note, I. ix. 33. 6
scratcht her face with *ghastly* dreriment; II. i. 15. 5
As *ghastly* bug, does greatly them affeare: II. iii. 20. 5
She fled away with *ghastly* dreriment, II. iv. 31. 8
a dead mans skull, that seemd a *ghastly* sight. II. xi. 22. 9
Through *ghastly* horror and eternall shade: II. xii. 41. 5
they did unmanly looke, And stared *ghastly;* II. xii. 86. 4
Through suddein feare and *ghastly* drerihedd, III. i. 62. 5
As one with vew of *ghastly* feends affright: III. ii. 29. 7
not of nought these suddein *ghastly* feares III. ii. 31. 1
such *ghastly* noyse of yron chaines III. iii. 9. 2
other *ghastly* spectacle dismayd, III. iii. 50. 3
With nought but *ghastly* lookes him answered; III. vii. 14. 6
saw the *ghastly* fit III. xi. 12. 6
With *ghastly* looks and dreadfull drerihead; III. xii. 17. 3
like a *ghastly* Gelt whose wits are reaved, IV. vii. 21. 3
fled away with *ghastly* dreriment, IV. vii. 29. 8
It made her . . . stare with *ghastly* eye. V. iv. 41. 9
sternely him beheld with grim and *ghastly* looke. V. xi. 12. 9
Was with his *ghastly* count'nance nothing queld; V. xii. 16. 7
rising up at last in *ghastly* wize, VI. vi. 32. 7
Which when she sees with *ghastly* grieffull eies, VI. viii. 40. 5
So did their *ghastly* gaze bewray their hidden feares. VII. vi. 28. 9
Ghesse, Ghest, Ghesseth. *See* **Guess,** *etc.*
Ghost. a *ghost* appeare before mine eyes *Bel.*[1] i. 5
all astonned with this nightly *ghost,* *Bel.*[1] vii. 1
Then did a *Ghost* before mine eyes appeare, *Bel.*[2] i. 5
all astonied with this mighty *ghoast,* *Bel.*[2] ix. 1
my poore wretched *ghost* Is forst to ferrie *Gn.* 337
thou art he whom my poore *ghost* complaines *Gn.* 630
grieve my *ghost,* that ill mote him behove, *D.* 265
to her *ghost* doo service day by day. *D.* 371
Forth-with her *ghost* out of her corps did flit, *As.* 177
his grudging *ghost* did strive With the fraile flesh; I. ii. 19. 7
'What voice of damned *Ghost* from Limbo lake, I. ii. 32. 5
'Nor damned *Ghost,'* . . . to thee these words doth speake; I. ii. 33. 1
Henceforth his *ghost* . . . may passen over Lethe lake; I. iii. 36. 5
greeved *ghost* for vengeance deep do grone: I. iv. 49. 7
Goe, guiltie *ghost,* to him my message make, I. v. 11. 3
Then gins her grieved *ghost* thus to lament and mourne: I. vii. 21. 9
At last his mighty *ghost* gan deepe to grone, II. i. 42. 5
damned *ghoste* In flaming Phlegeton II. vi. 50. 8
to doen outrage to a sleeping *ghost;* II. viii. 26. 2
tombling downe on ground, Breathd out his *ghost,* II. viii. 45. 7
like a *ghost* he seem'd II. xi. 20. 9
wandring *ghost* that wanted funerall, II. xi. 39. 7
She shortly like a pyned *ghost* became III. ii. 52. 5
Like to a *ghost,* that lately is reviv'd III. vii. 14. 7
Let forth his wearie *ghost,* IV. iii. 12. 9
His wearie *ghost* assoyld from fleshly band IV. iii. 13. 1
halfe affeard . . . as he some *ghost* had seene, IV. iii. 31. 6
like a pined *ghost* he soone appeares: IV. vii. 41. 4
Like *ghost* late risen from his grave agryz'd, IV. viii. 12. 7
the *ghost* would rive Out of their wretched corses, IV. ix. 22. 8
my weary *ghost,* with griefe outworne, IV. xii. 8. 1
Like ruefull *ghost,* IV. xii. 20. 9
leave unto his *ghost* . . . To wander in the griesly shades V. x. 33. 5
Whose grudging *ghost* was thereout fled and past, V. x. 37. 3
her he deemes already but a damned *ghoste.'* V. xi. 42. 9
this Lady, . . . is ready to forgo the *ghost;* VI. iii. 39. 4
Like troubled *ghost,* did dreadfully appeare, VI. vi. 32. 8
darted fyre into my feeble *ghost,* *H.B.* 24
Ghostly. Ye may me trust as your owne *ghostly* father.' *Hub.* 280
By that he ended had his *ghostly* sermon, *Hub.* 479
in loathsome den Of *ghostly* darkenes, *T.M.* 532
Ghosts. Ye pallid spirits, and ye ashie *ghoasts,* *Ro.* xv. 1
Nor elvish *ghosts,* nor gastly owles doe flee. *S.C.* Jun. 24
Up, grieslie *ghostes!* *S.C.* N. 55
Where wretched *ghosts* sit wailing evermore. *Gn.* 384
With which the damned *ghosts* he governeth, *Hub.* 1293
grisly *Ghosts,* to heare the dolefull teene. *D.* 21
The trembling *ghosts* with sad amazed mood, I. v. 32. 5
Phlegeton, Whereas the damned *ghosts* in torments fry, I. v. 33. 4

Ghosts—*Continued.*
The groning *ghosts* of many one dismaide . . . . I. vii. 47. 8
all about it wandring *ghostes* did wayle and howle. . . . . . I. ix. 33. 9
The damned *ghosts* that doe in torments waile, ... I. ix. 49. 7
they to direfull death their groning *ghosts* did send. . . . . II. xi. 15. 9
Through which the damned *ghosts* doen often creepe . . . . II. xii. 6. 5
Where wicked *ghosts* doe waile their former sin. . . . . . . III. v. 22. 4
what *ghosts* there under ground Lay hid . . . . IV. vii. 33. 5
damned *ghosts* which dwell For aye in darkenesse, ... VI. xii. 35. 7
damned *ghosts*, cald up with mighty spels, ... *Epith.* 347
Giambeux. *See* **Jambeux.**
Giant. that Nation, th' earths new *Giant* brood, ... *Ro.* xi. 9
the *Geaunt* has not such a weight, ... *S.C.* May 142
Soone after this a *Giaunt* came in place, ... *Ti.* 533
The Redcrosse knight is . . . By *Gyaunt* proud opprest: . . . I. vii. Arg.
An hideous *Geaunt*, horrible and hye, ... I. vii. 8. 4
The *Geaunt* strooke so maynly mercilesse, ... I. vii. 12. 1
So daunted when the *Geaunt* saw the knight, ... I. vii. 14. 1
The lucklesse conflict with the *Gyaunt* stout, ... I. vii. 26. 8
his foe, a *Gyaunt* huge and tall; . . . . I. vii. 51. 2
Arthure . . . slayes the *Gyaunt*, ... I. viii. Arg.
The *Gyaunt* selfe, dismaied with that sownd, ... I. viii. 5. 4
Therewith the *Gyant* buckled him to fight, ... I. viii. 7. 1
Had not the *Gyaunt* soone her succoured; . . . . I. viii. 17. 7
Which when the *Gyaunt* spyde with staring eye, ... I. viii. 19. 6
Unto the *Gyaunt* lowdly she gan call; . . . . I. viii. 20. 8
body, which the *Gyaunt* bore, Was vanisht quite; . . . . . . I. viii. 24. 7
foster father of the *Gyaunt* dead; . . . . I. viii. 31. 8
Like an huge *Gyant* of the Titans race; . . . . II. vii. 41. 6
the Nimphe that bore A *gyaunt* babe . . . . II. xii. 52. 3
How like a *Gyaunt* in each manly part . . . . III. iii. 32. 3
Now like a *Gyaunt*; now like to a feend; . . . . III. viii. 41. 2
fled From an huge *Geaunt*, ... III. xi. 3. 4
Whom when the *Gyaunt* saw, he soone . . . fled apace: . . . . III. xi. 5. 3
He like a monstrous *Gyant* seem'd in sight, ... IV. v. 37. 1
An hideous *Giant*, dreadfull to behold, ... IV. x. 16. 6
Which that great *Gyant* Blomius begot . . . . IV. xi. 42. 2
This *Gyant* found her and by force deflowr'd; . . . . IV. xi. 42. 6
There they beheld a mighty *Gyant* . . . . V. ii. 30. 1
'Thou foolishe Elfe,' (said then the *Gyant* wroth) . . . . . . V. ii. 37. 1
Therewith the *Gyant* much abashed sayd, ... V. ii. 44. 1
then the *Gyant* strove with puissance strong . . . . V. ii. 46. 4
downe the cliffe the wretched *Gyant* tumbled; . . . . V. ii. 50. 6
Whereof when as the *Gyant* was aware, ... V. xi. 9. 5
The which this *Gyant* reared first on hie, ... V. xi. 19. 3
Like to a *Giant* for his monstrous hight, ... V. xii. 15. 2
From a great *Gyant*, called Cormoraunt, ... VI. iv. 29. 6
this proud *gyant* should with brave emprize Quite overthrow VI. iv. 33. 4
rather like a *Gyant* monstruous: . . . . VI. vii. 41. 4
Giantess. He spide far off a mighty *Giauntesse* . . . . III. vii. 37. 2
So ran the *Geauntesse* unto the fight, ... III. vii. 39. 7
'That *Geauntesse* Argante is behight, ... III. vii. 47. 2
that bold knight, whom ye pursuing saw That *Geauntesse*, . III. vii. 52. 2
Of an huge *Geauntesse* whylome was bred, ... IV. viii. 47. 2
Yet nathemore the *Giantesse* forbare, ... VII. vi. 13. 1
Giantlike. sate thereby, with *gyantlike* resemblance, ... V. ix. 22. 6
Giant's. Thrall to that *Gyaunts* hatefull tyranny: . . . . I. viii. 2. 5
The same before the *Geaunts* gate he blew, ... I. viii. 5. 1
Such was this *Gyaunts* fall, ... I. viii. 23. 8
saves the Squyre of Dames From *Gyaunts* tyranny. . . . . . III. vii. Arg.
how he fell into the *Gyaunts* hands, ... III. vii. 46. 8
This *Gyants* sonne, that lies there on the laire . . . . IV. viii. 51. 5
'This *Gyants* daughter came upon a day . . . . IV. viii. 52. 1
Giants. The *Giants* old should once again uprise, ... *Ro.* iv. 6
the *Giaunts* did the Gods assay; . . . . *Ro.* xvii. 4
of *Giaunts*, hard to be beleeved; . . . . *Hub.* 31
hideous *Giaunts*, and halfe beastly men, ... II. x. 7. 2
They brought forth *Geaunts*, ... II. x. 8. 8
many *Giaunts* left on groning flore: . . . . II. x. 10. 5
Elfar, who two brethren *gyauntes* kild, ... II. x. 73. 5
those two brethren *Gyauntes* did defend The walles . . . . . II. xi. 15. 6
From slaughter of the *Giaunts* conquered; . . . . III. ix. 22. 2
in that same day when Jove those *Gyants* quelled: . . . . . V. i. 9. 9
Even the bloud of *Gyants*, which were slaine . . . . V. vii. 10. 4
he was descended of the hous Of those old *Gyants*, ... VI. vii. 41. 6
Giants'. When *Giants* bloud did staine Phlegraean ground. . . *Gn.* 40
an huge nation of the *Geaunts* broode . . . . III. ix. 49. 8
they say that he was borne and bred Of *Gyants* race, ... V. x. 9. 2
Gibbet. Uppon that *gibbet*, which is there behind, ... V. iv. 32. 3
Gibe. common Courtiers love to *gybe* and fleare . . . . *Hub.* 714
when he saw her toy, and *gibe*, and geare, ... II. vi. 21. 7
All gan to jest and *gibe* full merilie . . . . V. iii. 39. 4
Gift. rest the *gift* of Gods . . . . *Bel.*[1] i. 1
Thou hast it wonne, for it is of franke *gift*, ... *Hub.* 531
th' heavenly *gift* of wisedomes influence, ... *T.M.* 86
everie *gift*, and everie goodly meed, ... *Col.* 592
Vouchsafe in worth this small *guift* to receave, ... *Ded. Son.* vii. 8
But other some, by *guifte* of later grace, ... II. ii. 6. 6
massy gold of glorious *guifte*, ... II. vii. 28. 4
'Foole!' . . . 'I thy *gift* defye, ... II. viii. 52. 1
So shall you by one *gift* save all us three alive.' . . . . . . IV. xii. 31. 9
To seeke for succour of this Ladies *gieft*; . . . . V. x. 14. 7
Delivered hath into your hands by *gift*, ... VI. viii. 1. 5
He would commend his *guift*, ... VI. ix. 40. 5
Gifts. heaven whence all good *gifts* do come, ... *Bel.*[2] i. 8
His clownish *gifts* and curtsies I disdaine, ... *S.C.* Ja. 57
Ah, foolish Hobbinol! thy *gyfts* bene vayne; . . . . *S.C.* Ja. 59
Forcing with *gyfts* to winne his wanton heart. . . . . *S.C.* Ap. 24
Much greater *gyfts* for guerdon thou shalt gayne, ... *S.C.* N. 45
Their memories, their singings, and their *gifts*, ... *Hub.* 454

Gifts—*Continued.*
some good Ladies *gifts*: . . . . *Hub.* 852
without *gifts* or gaine; . . . . *T.M.* 82
Deignd to behold me and their *gifts* bestowe, ... *Ti.* 81
the heavens powrde all their *gifts* upon her. . . . . *Ti.* 280
Ne for their *gifts* unworthie of his wit, ... *As.* 51
God his *gifts* there plenteously bestowes, ... *Col.* 326
All heavenly *gifts* and riches locked are; . . . . *Col.* 489
those two knights . . . Gave goodly *gifts*, ... I. ix. 18. 8
princely *gifts* of yvory and gold, ... I. xii. 12. 6
To them that covet . . . Proffer thy *giftes*, ... II. vii. 9. 9
The *guifts* of soveraine bounty did embrace: . . . . II. vii. 16. 4
with *guifts* his Lord Cadwallin pacify. . . . . III. iii. 39. 9
ful of divinities And *gifts* of heavenly grace, ... III. v. 34. 8
all the *gifts* of grace and chastitee . . . . III. vi. 2. 5
offered faire *guiftes* t' allure her sight; . . . . III. viii. 38. 7
will not use his *gifts* for thanklesse nigardise.' . . . . IV. viii. 15. 9
through *gifts*, or guile, or such like waies, ... IV. x. 18. 8
thousand pretious *gifts* worth many a pound, ... IV. x. 37. 7
Both *gifts* of God, not gotten but from thence, ... IV. x. 51. 8
neither *gifts* nor graces kind . . . . IV. xi. 2. 7
She did allure with *gifts* and speaches milde . . . . V. i. 6. 5
gave them *gifts* and things of deare delight. . . . . V. iv. 51. 6
Life, freedome, grace, and *gifts* of great availe, ... V. v. 49. 3
royall *gifts* of gold and silver wrought . . . . V. vii. 24. 4
gave him roiall *giftes* and riches rare, ... V. x. 17. 2
With golden *giftes* and many a guilefull word . . . . V. xi. 50. 4
O! who may not with *gifts* and words be tempted? . . . . . V. xi. 50. 6
For *guiftes* of gold or any worldly glee, ... V. xi. 63. 3
deckt with wondrous *giftes* of natures grace, ... VI. vii. 28. 5
Adornd with goodly *gifts* of beauties grace, ... VI. viii. 2. 2
Nature me endu'd with plenteous dowre Of all her *gifts*, . . VI. viii. 20. 4
most of all those three did her with *gifts* endew. . . . . . . VI. x. 14. 9
Those three to men all *gifts* of grace do graunt; . . . . . . VI. x. 15. 4
'These three men all gracious *gifts* bestow, ... VI. x. 23. 1
a goddesse graced With heavenly *gifts* . . . . VI. x. 25. 5
With looks, with words, with *gifts* he oft her wowed, ... VI. xi. 4. 8
through grace Or secret *guifts*, ... VI. xii. 6. 2
pleasing *gifts* for her purvaid, ... VII. vi. 43. 5
so goodly *giftes* of beauties grace! . . . . *Am.* xxxi. 2
all her natures goodly *guifts* are lost: . . . . *Am.* xli. 8
Each of which did her with theyr *guifts* adorne; . . . . . . *Am.* lxi. 8
With *guifts* of body, fortune, and of mind. . . . . *Am.* lxxiv. 4
Garnisht with heavenly *guifts* of high degree, ... *Epith.* 187
From whom all *guifts* of wit and knowledge flow, ... *H.H.B.* 9
Where oft I gayned *giftes* and goodly grace . . . . *Proth.* 138
Two gentle Knights . . . With *gifts* of wit, ... *Proth.* 171
Gilded. *See* **Gilden.**
Gilden. a Bull . . . With *gilden* hornes embowed like the Moone, ... *Van.* ii. 3
A *gilden* towre, which shone exceedinglie; . . . . *Van.* viii. 4
His *gylden* quiver at his backe, ... *S.C.* Mar. 82
embayld In *gilden* buskins of costly Cordwayne, ... II. iii. 27. 3
With *gilden* hornes and flowry girlonds crownd, ... III. iv. 17. 2
Her bow and *gilden* quiver lying him beside. . . . . III. v. 34. 9
These goodly *gilden* armes which I have won . . . . VI. ii. 33. 9
of stature large, Clad all in *gilden* armes, ... VI. ii. 44. 7
His hornes were *gilden* all with golden studs, ... VII. vii. 33. 5
Gills. Foming with poyson round about her *gils*, ... V. xii. 36. 2
Gillyflowers. 'Bring hether the Pincke . . . With *Gelliflowres*; *S.C.* Ap. 137
Her lips did smell lyke unto *Gillyflowers*; . . . . *Am.* lxiv. 5
Gilt. I wonne her with a gyrdle of *gelt*, ... *S.C.* F. 65
The knotted rush-ringes, and *gilte* Rosemaree? . . . . *S.C.* N. 116
in garments *gilt* And gorgeous gold arayd, ... I. v. 26. 7
though richly *guilt*, ... II. ix. 45. 8
With scutchins *gilt* and banners broad displayd; . . . . IV. iii. 5. 6
all the pillours of the one were *guilt*, ... IV. x. 5. 8
A *guilt* engraven morion he did weare: . . . . VII. vii. 28. 8
Gin. These bitter blasts never *ginne* tasswage? . . . . *S.C.* F. 2
Tho *gynne* you, fond flyes! the cold to scorne, ... *S.C.* F. 39
Gynne when ye lyst, ... *S.C.* Au. 51
now unto despaire I *gin* to growe, ... *Hub.* 79
subtil *gin*, The which the Lemnian God framde . . . . *Mui.* 369
Typhoeus joynts were stretched on a *gin*; . . . . I. v. 35. 7
gin to pittie her unhappie state: . . . . I. vi. 9. 7
Then *gin* the blustring brethren boldly threat . . . . I. xi. 21. 7
through treason and deceiptfull *gin*, ... II. iii. 13. 7
we foolish men that prayse *gin* eke t' envy. . . . . III. ii. 2. 9
From their long vassalage *gin* to respire, ... III. iii. 36. 8
Busie (as seem'd) about some wicked *gin*: . . . . III. vii. 7. 3
To *gin* awake, and stir his frosen spright: . . . . III. viii. 23. 5
the great waters *gin* apace to swell, ... III. viii. 24. 2
'yet now I *gin* new life to feele; . . . . V. x. 20. 4
when I *gin* to feele decay of might, ... VI. Pr. 1. 8
in some snare or *gin* set close behind, Entrapped him, ... VII. vi. 48. 6
Then *gin* I thinke on that which Nature sayd, ... VII. viii. 2. 1
how the Minstrils *gin* to shrill aloud . . . . *Epith.* 129
Ginneth. the bright Sunne *gynneth* to dismount; . . . . *S.C.* May 315
Now *gynneth* this roundelay. . . . . *S.C.* Au. 56
By vew of her he *ginneth* to revive His ancient love, ... I. vi. 17. 1
Gins. *gins* Bartas hie to rayse His heavenly Muse, ... *Ro.* Env. 11
The grasse nowe *ginnes* to be refresht, ... *S.C.* Mar. 10
Now *gynnes* to mizzle, ... *S.C.* N. 208
gins straight to prepare The weapons, ... *Gn.* 275
Eftsoones he *gins* to fashion forth a place; . . . . *Gn.* 650
Now *ginnes* to shoote up fast, ... *Ti.* 269
all his *gins*, that him entangle might; . . . . *Mui.* 387
As when old father Nilus *gins* to swell . . . . I. i. 21. 1
when his later spring *gins* to avale, ... I. i. 21. 5
ruddy Phebus *gins* to welke in west, ... I. i. 23. 2

Gins—*Continued.*
Then *gins* her grieved ghost thus to lament and mourne: . . I. vii. 21. 9
She *gins* her feathers . . . Prowdly to prune, ... II. iii. 36. 7
Now *ginnes* that goodly frame of Temperaunce . . . . II. xii. 1. 1
sith the Sunne now *ginnes* to slake his beames . . . . III. viii. 51. 3
her Gorgonian shield *gins* to untye . . . . III. ix. 22. 8
she *gins* to mend her pace, ... IV. vii. 22. 6
gins to spread his leafe before the faire sunshine. . . . . . IV. xii. 34. 9
Gins to abate the brightnesse of his beme, ... V. ix. 35. 3
Like as a tender Rose . . . *Gins* to looke up, ... V. xii. 13. 5
now *ginnes* to despize The good Sir Bruin . . . . VI. iv. 33. 5
Phoebus *gins* to shew his glorious hed. . . . . *Epith.* 77
Ginst. Soone as thou *gynst* to sette thy notes in frame, ... *S.C.* O. 25
Gipsy. like a *Gipsen,* or a Juggeler, ... *Hub.* 86
Gird. *gird* in your waste, ... *S.C.* Ap. 134
Manie great bandogs which her *gird* about: . . . . *Gn.* 540
about her middle small They thought to *gird,* . . . . IV. v. 16. 4
Girded. *See* **Girt.**
girded with a belt of twisted brake: . . . . II. xi. 22. 7
Girding. It would have cleft him to the *girding* place; . . IV. viii. 43. 8
Girdle. I wonne her with a *gyrdle* of gelt, ... *S.C.* F. 65
her golden *girdle,* which did fall From her in flight, ... III. vii. 31. 8
retourning spyde Tyde with her golden *girdle;* . . . . III. viii. 2. 7
I found her golden *girdle* cast astray, ... III. viii. 49. 8
Satyran a *girdle* did uptake . . . . IV. ii. 25. 7
Shall have that golden *girdle* for reward; . . . . IV. ii. 27. 2
For that rich *girdle* of faire Florimell, ... IV. iv. 5. 8
A gorgeous *girdle,* curiously embost . . . . IV. iv. 15. 6
The Ladies for the *girdle* strive Of famous Florimell: . . . . IV. v. Arg.
Shall fall the *girdle* of faire Florimell: . . . . IV. v. 2. 5
That *girdle* gave the vertue of chast love, ... IV. v. 3. 1
Dame Venus *girdle,* by her steemed deare . . . . IV. v. 3. 7
Cannot find one this *girdle* to invest. . . . . IV. v. 18. 5
th' emptie *girdle* which about her wast was wrought. . . . . V. iii. 24. 9
Florimells owne *girdle,* from her reft . . . . V. iii. 27. 4
Girdle's. Likewise assayd to prove that *girdles* powre; . . . . IV. v. 19. 3
Girl. 'Then ceasse thy idle claime, thou foolish *gerle;* . . . . VII. vi. 34. 1
Girland, Girlond, -s. *See* **Garland, -s.**
Girn. gaped like a gulfe when he did *gerne;* . . . . V. xii. 15. 8
Girt. *See* **Girded.**
Ylike as others, *girt* in gawdy greene? . . . . *S.C.* May 4
Ygyrt with belts of glitterand gold, ... *S.C.* Jul. 177
girt in girlonds of wild Yvie twine, ... *S.C.* O. 111
fiends of hell *Girt* with long snakes, ... *Gn.* 626
the puissant brood Of golden *girt* Alcmena, ... *Ti.* 380
with yvie twyne his waste is *girt* about. . . . . I. vi. 14. 9
girt in with two walls on either side; . . . . III. vi. 31. 2
her small waste *girt* rownd with yron bands . . . . III. xii. 30. 8
Giust. To *giust* with that brave straunger knight a cast, . . . III. x. 35. 4
them against came all that list to *giust,* . . . . V. iii. 6. 1
Giusted. So foorth they went, and both together *giusted;* . . IV. i. 11. 1
Giusts. sing of bloody Mars, of wars, of *giusts;* . . . . *S.C.* O. 39
As one for knightly *giusts* and fierce encounters fitt. . . . . I. i. 1. 9
Paridell *giusts* with Britomart; . . . . III. ix. Arg.
solemne feasts and *giusts* ordain'd therefore: . . . . V. iii. 2. 6
Give. *See* **Overgive.**
Wolfe did *give* sucke To two yong babes. . . . . *Bel.*[1] vii. 9
my Lute, whom Phoebus deignd to *give,* . . . . *Ro.* xxxii. 9
give a second life to dead decayes! . . . . *Ro.* Env. 6
can to other *give* eternall dayes: . . . . *Ro.* Env. 8
never *give* trust to his trecheree: . . . . *S.C.* May 222
Queene-apples unrype, To *give* my Rosalind; . . . . *S.C.* Jun. 44
I shall thee *give* yond Cosset . . . . *S.C.* N. 42
give him curds and clouted Creame. . . . . *S.C.* N. 99
(God *give* them paine!) . . . . *Hub.* 304
none would *give,* but all men would them wyte: . . . . *Hub.* 348
Such grace did God unto his creatures *give.* . . . . *Hub.* 402
fortune doth you secret favour *give.'* . . . . *Hub.* 594
To spend, to *give,* to want, to be undonne. . . . . *Hub.* 906
Nought suffered he the Ape to *give* or graunt, ... *Hub.* 1143
to *give* largely to the boxe refused. . . . . *Hub.* 1224
did those Armes first *give* To their Grandsyres, ... *T.M.* 95
Such grace the heavens doo to my verses *give.* . . . . *Ti.* 259
unto men eternitie do *give;* . . . . *Ti.* 367
how can mortall immortalitie *give?* . . . . *Ti.* 413
Give leave to him . . . to lament His losse, ... *Ti.* 676
give unto my heavie eyes A well of teares, ... *Mui.* 409
to *give* them light Which dwell in darknes, ... *D.* 478
Such grace sometimes shall *give* me some reliefe, ... *Col.* 945
But, sith thou maist not so, *give* leave a while . . . . . . *Ded. Son.* xii. 9
Ne spared he to *give* her gold and rings; . . . . I. iii. 18. 8
foolish man, so rash a doome to *give?* . . . . I. ix. 38. 2
Is then unjust to each his dew to *give?* . . . . I. ix. 38. 7
His office was to *give* entertainement . . . . I. x. 37. 4
His office was the . . . thristy *give* to drinke; . . . . I. x. 38. 3
some he would *give* to the pore. . . . . I. x. 38. 9
if that no spare clothes to *give* he had, ... I. x. 39. 8
warning *give* that enimies conspyre . . . . I. xi. 14. 5
'Fayre sonne, God *give* you happy chaunce, ... II. i. 31. 7
So courteous conge both did *give* and take, ... II. i. 34. 1
So *give* me leave to rest.' . . . . II. i. 37. 9
Take not away, now got, which none would *give* to me.' . . . II. i. 47. 9
give death to him that death does *give,* . . . . II. i. 55. 4
I *give* thee life: . . . . II. iii. 8. 5
give you eke good helpe to their decay, ... II. iii. 15. 2
Give no ods to your foes, ... II. iii. 15. 4
To which right wel the wise doe *give* that name, ... II. v. 1. 5
love does *give* his sweet Alarmes Without bloodshed, ... II. vi. 34. 7
O Atin! helpe to me last death to *give.'* . . . . II. vi. 45. 5
give me leave to follow mine emprise.' . . . . II. vii. 39. 6

Give—*Continued.*
Of grace I pray thee, *give* to eat and drinke to mee!' . . . . II. vii. 59. 9
More glory thought to *give* life then decay, ... II. viii. 51. 4
Who now shall *give* unto me words and sound . . . . II. x. 1. 1
Give over to effect his first intent, ... II. xi. 41. 3
Thereof she usd to *give* to drinke to each, ... II. xii. 56. 7
'Great ayd thereto his mighty puissaunce . . . shall *give* . III. iii. 28. 2
Shall *give* th' enchaunter his unhappy hire. . . . . III. iii. 36. 6
Her to restraine, and *give* her good reliefe . . . . III. iv. 11. 5
they more fond that credit to the *give!* . . . . III. iv. 37. 2
Because I could not *give* her many a Jane.' . . . . III. vii. 58. 4
but if she Mercie would him *give,* . . . . III. x. 7. 8
Peece, that unto parley eare will *give,* . . . . III. x. 10. 5
every Satyre first did *give* a busse To Hellenore; . . . . . III. x. 46. 3
To *give* him the reward for such vile outrage dew. . . . . . III. xii. 33. 9
So both together *give* a new allarme, ... IV. iv. 35. 4
for her loves first hire *Give* it to her, ... IV. v. 4. 6
yet he her made To *give* him ground, ... IV. vi. 12. 8
inforced to *give* place Unto the passion . . . . IV. xii. 8. 6
'Unto yourselfe,' said they, 'we *give* our word, ... V. iv. 16. 4
Ne doth she *give* them other thing to eat . . . . V. iv. 31. 7
Give her great comfort and some harts content. . . . . . . V. v. 35. 3
Give him more labour, ... V. v. 50. 3
I resolve this siege not to *give* over, ... V. v. 51. 4
So blesse thee God, and *give* thee joyance of thy dreame!' . V. vii. 23. 9
the bold Prince was forced foote to *give* . . . . V. xi. 5. 6
What guerdon can I *give* thee for thy paine, ... V. xi. 16. 8
way did *give* unto their gracelesse speed: . . . . V. xii. 18. 4
Wilt *give* thy beard, though it but little bee? . . . . VI. i. 19. 8
Ne time would *give,* nor any termes aby, ... VI. ii. 19. 7
To *give* faire colour to that Ladies cause . . . . VI. iii. 16. 9
He gan to shrinke and somewhat to *give* place, ... VI. v. 21. 3
Give salves to every sore, but counsell to the minde. . . . VI. vi. 5. 9
he them away did *give,* . . . . VI. vi. 36. 8
he did him constraine To *give* him ground, ... VI. vii. 46. 6
Whether more wary were to *give* or ward the blow. . . . . . VI. viii. 13. 9
ne did *give* Them selves to any trade, ... VI. viii. 35. 4
Coridon most helpe did *give.* . . . . VI. ix. 15. 9
Give leave awhyle, good father, in this shore To rest . . . VI. ix. 31. 3
I shall You well reward, and golden guerdon *give,* . . . . . VI. ix. 32. 6
Whereof her name ye then to her did *give.* . . . . VI. xii. 18. 6
her need *give* lone Of her faire light . . . . VII. vi. 11. 7
They gan to cast what penaunce him to *give.* . . . . VII. vi. 50. 2
most agreed, and did this sentence *give,* . . . . VII. vi. 50. 7
him, . . . With mercifull regard *give* mercy too. . . . . . . *Am.* xlix. 12
flowers doe *give* most odorous smell; . . . . *Am.* lxiv. 13
That three such graces did unto me *give.* . . . . *Am.* lxxiv. 14
Give leave to rest me being halfe fordonne, ... *Am.* lxxx. 3
give leave to me . . . To sport my muse, ... *Am.* lxxx. 9
change thy cruelty, Or *give* like leave unto the fly.' . . . . *Epig.* iv. 20
Why blush ye, love, to *give* to me your hand, ... *Epith.* 238
One drop of grace at length will to me *give,* . . . . *H.B.* 277
And *give* me words equall unto my thought, ... *H.H.L.* 48
Knowing that, whatsoere to them we *give,* . . . . *H.H.L.* 209
We *give* to him by whom we all doe live. . . . . *H.H.L.* 210
And *give* thy selfe unto him full and free, ... *H.H.L.* 265
Given. Let that rowme to my Lady be *yeven:* . . . . *S.C.* Ap. 114
shaming to have *given* so great head To his off-spring, . . . *Ro.* xi. 1
in a people *given* all to ease, ... *Ro.* xxiii. 9
given like cause with thee to waile . . . . *D.* 66
reliefe, Which *given* was to them for good intents: . . . . . I. iii. 17. 4
Great grace that old man to him *given* had; . . . . I. x. 47. 1
this grace I have Me *given* . . . . II. iii. 45. 2
Was *given* all to lust and loose living, ... II. v. 28. 3
she was *given* all to fleshly lust, ... III. i. 48. 5
To whom sweet Poets verse hath *given* endlesse date. . . . . III. vi. 45. 9
To Britomart was *given* by good right; . . . . IV. v. 8. 3
she *given* is to vaine delight, ... IV. viii. 49. 8
such grace is *given* them from above, ... IV. x. 2. 1
long *given* him in vaine: . . . . IV. xii. 14. 6
though unto his will she *given* were, ... IV. xii. 15. 6
Faith may be *given,* it is by them told . . . . V. Pr. 8. 3
from the most that some were *given* to the least? . . . . . V. ii. 37. 9
The charge of Justice *given* was in trust, ... V. iv. 2. 2
nought was *given* them to sup or dyne, ... V. v. 22. 8
he had *given* streight commaundement . . . . V. xii. 10. 3
unrighteous ire . . . had *given* him his owne due hire? . . . VI. ii. 13. 9
fortune hath this day *Given* to me the spoile . . . . VI. ii. 33. 8
woundes the which the Blatant Beast Had *given* them, . . . VI. v. 39. 9
thy life unto this Ladie fayre I *given* have, ... VI. vi. 36. 2
Whether such grace were *given* her by kynd, ... VI. vi. 43. 1
Given to Calidore as his due right; . . . . VI. ix. 44. 7
why hath nature . . . *Given* so goodly giftes . . . . *Am.* xxxi. 2
A dreadfull countenaunce she *given* hath; . . . . *Am.* xxxi. 6
dowre, Which mighty God hath *given* to her free, ... *H.H.B.* 251
Gives. Colin them *gives* to Rosalind againe. . . . . *S.C.* Ja. 60
as the springe *gives* place to elder time, ... *S.C.* D. 73
gives the fruit of all your travailes toyle . . . . *Ti.* 515
to her selfe she *gives* her Aegide shield, ... *Mui.* 321
gives to their professors stipends large. . . . . *Col.* 746
their praise, Which *gives* them life, ... *Ded. Son.* iv. 11
Vertue *gives* her selfe light . . . . I. i. 12. 9
Untroubled night, . . . *gives* counsell best.' . . . . I. i. 33. 3
will to might *gives* greatest aid.' . . . . I. vii. 41. 4
gives not rather cause it to forsake? . . . . I. ix. 44. 5
To him that *gives* thee life and liberty; . . . . II. v. 13. 6
your gay sonne, that *gives* ye so good ayd . . . . III. vi. 21. 4
Therfore needs mote he live, that living *gives* to all. . . . III. vi. 47. 9
death and life attonce unto him *gives,* . . . . III. x. 60. 3
getteth her And *gives* to him for wife. . . . . IV. xii. Arg.

Gives—*Continued.*
He *gives* to this, from that he takes away, ... V. ii. 41. 8
'Whats this (quoth he) that *gives* so great a voyce . . . . . *Epig.* iv. 7
Gives me great hope of your relenting mynd: . . . . *Am.* xxviii. 2
Givest. To learned wits *givest* courage worthily, ... *Gn.* 36
Giveth. God *giveth* good for none other end. . . . . *S.C.* May 72
It *giveth* name unto that auncient Cittie, ... *Col.* 112
giveth comfort to her courage cold: . . . . VI. iv. 1. 5
vertue . . . *giveth* lawes alone, ... *Epith.* 195
the thing which *giveth* pleasant grace . . . . *H.B.* 57
Giving. *See* **Life-giving, Light-giving.**
Giving accompt of th' annuall increce . . . . *Hub.* 301
seeke some other way to gaine by *giving,* . . . . *Hub.* 350
To him that hath a whit of Natures *giving?* . . . . *Hub.* 418
giving hastie credit to th' accuser, ... *Mui.* 135
giving warning of th' unwonted sound, ... I. v. 30. 8
Giving the bridle to her wanton will, ... III. i. 50. 3
Giving her dearest children one by one Unto a dreadfull Monster . . . . V. x. 13. 6
So shall you live, by *giving* life to me. . . . . *Am.* xlix. 14
Glad. the messenger of tidings *glad;* . . . . *Bel.*[2] xiv. 3
my *glad* hart thereat did much rejoyce. . . . . *Pet.*[2] iv. 8
wont to make the jolly shepeheards *gladde,* . . . . *S.C.* Au. 9
Both seeming now full *glad* and joyeous . . . . *Gn.* 483
The Foxe was *glad,* and quickly did agree: . . . . *Hub.* 102
'Good Sir, full *glad* am I, To take what paines . . . . . . *Hub.* 270
The Ape was *glad* to end the strife so light, ... *Hub.* 1056
the *glad* marchant, that does vew from ground His ship . . . I. iii. 32. 3
Right *glad* with him to have increast their crew; . . . . . . I. iv. 15. 2
when he heard of harme he wexed wondrous *glad.* . . . . . I. iv. 30. 9
all . . . gently grenning, shew a semblance *glad* . . . . . . I. vi. 11. 7
all as *glad* as birdes of joyous Pryme, ... I. vi. 13. 5
Far off he wonders what them makes so *glad;* . . . . I. vi. 15. 1
Glad of such lucke, the . . . mayd Did her content . . . . I. vi. 19. 1
glad to gain such favour, gan devise, ... I. vi. 32. 8
to see him made her *glad,* . . . . I. viii. 42. 2
His owne cote he would . . . distribute *glad.* . . . . I. x. 39. 9
The watchman wayting tydings *glad* to heare; . . . . I. xi. 3. 7
Glad signe of victory and peace in all their land. . . . . . . I. xii. 5. 9
she was inly *glad* her purpose so to gaine. . . . . II. i. 20. 9
ever of their loves they would be *glad:* . . . . II. ii. 28. 4
glad t' embosome his affection vile, ... II. iv. 25. 3
wondrous *glad,* out of the path Did lightly leape, ... II. v. 18. 7
She no lesse *glad* then he desirous was . . . . II. vi. 37. 1
with *glad* thankes, and unreproved truth, ... II. vii. 16. 3
Socrates; who, thereof quaffing *glad,* Pourd out his life . . II. vii. 52. 7
'*glad* and faine Beteeme to you this sword, ... II. viii. 19. 5
Glad was the knight, and with fresh courage fraught, . . . II. viii. 40. 5
right *glad* he grew, ... II. viii. 53. 6
The Palmer, *glad* With so fresh hew . . . . II. viii. 54. 2
with her bounty and *glad* countenaunce Doth blesse . . . . . II. ix. 5. 4
maketh every creature *glad,* . . . . II. xi. 3. 4
The royall Maid woxe inly wondrous *glad,* . . . . III. ii. 11. 1
conceiving hope of comfort *glad,* . . . . III. iii. 51. 3
Sad life worse then *glad* death; . . . . III. iv. 38. 8
To scorne the joy that Jove is *glad* to seeke: . . . . III. vi. 22. 6
As *glad* of that small rest as Bird of tempest gon. . . . . . III. vii. 10. 9
glad by any meanes her grace to gaine, ... III. vii. 54. 1
am I *glad* that here I now in safety ame. . . . . III. viii. 23. 9
Paridell, . . . being *glad* of so fitte tide . . . . III. ix. 32. 8
of their lovely fellowship full *glade,* . . . . III. x. 44. 8
Ne ought but deare Bisaltis ay could make him *glad.* . . . . III. xi. 41. 9
She chearefull, fresh, and full of joyaunce *glad,* . . . . . . III. xii. 18. 4
He, *glad* of life, that lookt for death . . . . III. xii. 35. 8
glad to rest withall. . . . . IV. ii. 21. 9
Glad man was he to see that joyous sight, ... IV. ii. 23. 1
full *glad* for thirst, ech drunk an harty draught; . . . . . . IV. iii. 48. 9
Instead of strokes, each other kissed *glad,* . . . . IV. iii. 49. 3
Yet all were *glad* there Florimell to see, ... IV. v. 14. 8
They were full *glad,* in hope themselves to get her: . . . . . IV. v. 21. 2
Who was right *glad* to gaine so goodly meed: . . . . IV. v. 22. 2
Full *glad* of so good end, ... IV. vi. 25. 3
Scudamour, now woxen inly *glad* . . . . IV. vi. 28. 1
as seeming wondrous *glad,* . . . . IV. vii. 24. 8
how he wexed *glad* When he it heard, ... IV. vii. 46. 7
ne once shew'd countenance *glad,* . . . . IV. viii. 2. 7
he woxe full *glad* To see his foe . . . . IV. viii. 46. 1
I *glad* did not gaine say nor strive, ... IV. viii. 56. 8
whose great desire He *glad* to satisfie, ... IV. ix. 41. 4
Ne ought on earth that merry is and *glad,* . . . . IV. x. 47. 3
Light Doto, wanton Glauce, and Galene *glad:* . . . . IV. xi. 48. 9
he was full inly *glad,* . . . . V. ii. 3. 6
Bracidas and Lucy were right *glad,* . . . . V. iv. 20. 3
They left behind them, *glad* to be so quit: . . . . V. iv. 25. 2
Glad from his companie to be so sondred; . . . . V. v. 19. 4
The Fayrie, *glad* to gaine his libertie, ... V. v. 55. 4
Was *glad* to yeeld unto his good request, ... V. vi. 22. 2
As *glad* to heare of armes, ... V. vii. 25. 5
as nothing *glad* To have beheld a spectacle so bad; . . . . V. vii. 38. 4
joyd much in his semblance *glad.* . . . . V. vii. 41. 9
glad of spoyle and ruinous decay, ... V. ix. 47. 6
Whereof she *glad,* . . . Him entertayn'd . . . . V. x. 12. 6
Out of the pleasant soyle and cities *glad,* . . . . V. x. 18. 5
Yet *glad* at last to make most base submission, ... V. x. 27. 4
Whom when he saw on ground, he was full *glad,* . . . . . . V. xi. 32. 6
full fayne And *glad* he was the slaughter so to stay; . . . . V. xii. 9. 6
neither *glad* nor sorie for their sight; . . . . V. xi. 60. 5
Glad to be quit from that proud Tyrants awe, ... V. xii. 24. 3
I am right *glad* To heare these tidings, ... VI. i. 10. 2
Whereof she now more *glad* then sory earst, ... VI. i. 45. 1

Glad—*Continued.*
So all returning to the Castle *glad,* . . . . VI. i. 46. 1
I yet *glad* to beare the packe . . . . VI. ii. 21. 7
Full *glad* and joyous then young Tristram grew; . . . . . . VI. ii. 35. 6
'*Glad* would I surely be, . . . To have thy presence . . . . . VI. ii. 37. 1
though she were right *glad* so rid to bee . . . . VI. iv. 10. 1
Glad of that easement, though it were but small; . . . . . VI. iv. 15. 7
Right *glad* was Calepine to bee so rid . . . . VI. iv. 38. 1
Ne she lesse *glad;* for she so wisely did, ... VI. iv. 38. 3
Whereof exceeding *glad* he to him drew, ... VI. v. 23. 3
Were *glad* to heare of that adventure new, ... VI. vii. 5. 3
glad of life, and willing eke to wreake The guilt on him . . VI. vii. 13. 6
Thereof false Turpin was full *glad* and faine, ... VI. vii. 17. 1
may her feeble leaves with comfort *glade*— . . . . VI. x. 44. 7
Whereof right *glad* they seem'd, ... VI. xi. 40. 1
Whereof they both full *glad* and blyth did rest, ... VI. xi. 41. 8
full *glad* That he had banisht hunger, ... VII. vii. 30. 3
His Saviour's birth his mind so much did *glad.* . . . . VII. vii. 41. 4
Sometimes I joy when *glad* occasion fits, ... *Am.* liv. 5
my *glad* mouth with her sweet prayses fill. . . . . *Am.* lxxxiv. 12
As joying in the sight Of these *glad* many, ... *Epith.* 294
And thou, *glad* Genius! in whose gentle hand . . . . *Epith.* 398
by signes his *glad* affection show, ... *Proth.* 117
Gladded. Which sight much *gladed* me; . . . . *Col.* 266
Glade. *See* **Glad.**
they spide, how, in a gloomy *glade,* . . . . *Hub.* 951
with greene boughes decking a gloomy *glade,* . . . . I. vii. 4. 4
as in a hollow *glade,* Those glaring lampes were sett . . . . I. xi. 14. 8
At last he came unto a gloomy *glade,* . . . . II. vii. 3. 1
bathe him in a fountaine by some covert *glade:* . . . . . . III. i. 35. 9
none durst passen through that perilous *glade:* . . . . . . III. iv. 21. 5
Within that wood there was a covert *glade,* . . . . III. v. 17. 1
Where was their dwelling, in a pleasant *glade* . . . . III. v. 39. 2
a shady *glade* Of the Riphoean hils, ... III. viii. 6. 3
Thrust to an Hynd within some covert *glade,* . . . . IV. vi. 12. 4
chose out a gloomy *glade,* Where hardly eye mote see . . . IV. vii. 38. 6
We chaunst to come foreby a covert *glade* . . . . VI. ii. 16. 3
They met together in that respect lucklesse *glade;* . . . . VI. iii. 8. 2
Farre in the forrest, by a hollow *glade* . . . . VI. iv. 13. 5
at length unto a woody *glade* He came, ... VI. v. 17. 6
Glades. round about me heapt in darksome *glades;* . . . . *Gn.* 372
Gladful. Of his successe and *gladfull* victory: . . . . III. iii. 59. 4
Some *gladfull* newes and sure intelligence, ... IV. vi. 34. 4
follow'd him with *gladfull* glee, ... V. iii. 34. 8
Spending their joyous dayes and *gladfull* nights, ... V. iii. 40. 2
to whom she straight did hie With *gladfull* hast, ... V. viii. 6. 6
The *gladfull* blessing of posteritie, ... VI. iv. 31. 3
Lord! what *gladfull* glee They made . . . . VI. viii. 37. 1
making *gladfull* glee, ... VI. x. 10. 8
With *gladfull* speaches and with lovely cheare; . . . . VI. xi. 50. 3
Gladfulness. all his *gladfulnes,* and kingly joyaunce. . . . *Mui.* 208
Gladliest. *gladliest* I of your fleecie sheepe . . . would take . *Hub.* 289
Gladly. '*Gladly* (said he) what ever such like paine . . . . *Hub.* 287
gladly did them guide, till to the Hall they came. . . . . . I. x. 6. 9
gladly graunted their desire. . . . . II. ix. 60. 9
Upon them *gladly* would have prov'd his might, ... IV. iv. 3. 8
She *gladly* graunted it: . . . . V. x. 16. 1
his heasts did *gladly* heare, ... VI. i. 43. 2
The noble ympe, . . . It *gladly* did accept, ... VI. ii. 38. 7
Ne would I *gladly* combate with mine host, ... VI. iii. 39. 5
She *gladly* did of that same babe accept, ... VI. iv. 37. 6
The which full *gladly* they did take in gree, ... VI. v. 39. 3
Did *gladly* hearken to his grave beheast, ... VI. vi. 15. 2
The knight full *gladly* soone agreed thereto, ... VI. ix. 16. 8
As meanes of blisse I *gladly* wil embrace; . . . . *Am.* xxv. 12
slaying him that would live *gladly* yours! . . . . *Am.* lvii. 12
Gladness. I goe with *gladnesse* to my wished rest, ... *D.* 282
With sober *gladnesse* and myld modestie; . . . . I. viii. 26. 5
wondrous *gladnes* to her hart applyde. . . . . III. viii. 2. 9
The sight whereof did all with *gladnesse* fill. . . . . V. iii. 15. 1
signes of *gladnesse* all did shew. . . . . V. iii. 23. 9
went forth his *gladnesse* to partake With Belge, ... V. xi. 32. 7
me revived with hart-robbing *gladnesse.* . . . . *Am.* xxxix. 8
disdayne Of all worlds *gladnesse,* . . . . *Am.* lii. 12
Gladsome. tree . . . throw forth his *gladsome* shade, ... *Bel.*[1] v. 2
tree . . . to spread his *gladsome* gleame, ... *Bel.*[2] v. 2
great mirth and *gladsome* glee. . . . . *Gn.* 184
meanes of *gladsome* solace to devise: . . . . *Hub.* 20
From highest heven in *gladsome* companee, ... I. x. 56. 3
Where *gladsome* Guyon salied forth to land, ... II. vi. 38. 5
Unto the *gladsome* port of her intent. . . . . III. iv. 10. 5
Thence to depart with glee and *gladsome* chere. . . . . . . IV. iii. 51. 3
with great joyance and with *gladsome* glee . . . . IV. viii. 59. 6
gladsome countenaunce nor pleasaunt glee; . . . . IV. ix. 13. 5
rest her selfe as in a *gladsome* port, ... VI. x. 9. 4
the new yeares joy . . . send, Into the glooming world, his *gladsome* ray: . . . . *Am.* lxii. 10
Glaive. laying both his hands upon his *glave,* . . . . IV. vii. 28. 2
the *glaive* which he did wield . . . . IV. x. 19. 8
Glaives. With bils and *glayves* making a dreadfull luster, . . V. xi. 58. 5
Achilles preassing through the Phrygian *glaives,* . . . . . . *H.L.* 233
Glamorgan. woody hilles . . . hight of him *Glamorgan,* . . . . II. x. 33. 8
Glance. *See* **Eye-glance.**
The *glaunce* into my heart did glide; . . . . *S.C.* Au. 93
through the *glaunce* Of envies dart, ... *Gn.* 557
Most like Alcyon seeming at a *glaunce;* . . . . *D.* 53
soone as on that knight his eye did *glaunce,* . . . . II. i. 31. 4
Unto the bush her eye did suddein *glaunce,* . . . . II. iii. 34. 2
as the Sunny beames do *glaunce* and glide . . . . II. v. 2. 4
as swift as *glaunce* of eye, A litle Gondelay, ... II. vi. 2. 6

Glance—*Continued.*
Did roll too lightly, and too often *glaunce*, III. i. 41. 8
Still did he rove at her with crafty *glaunce* III. i. 50. 6
eternall providence, that has Guyded thy *glaunce*, III. iii. 24. 5
The wicked steele through his left side did *glaunce*. III. iv. 16. 5
Whom having slain through luckles arrowes *glaunce*, III. ix. 48. 3
with unluckie *glaunce* Through Cambels shoulder it unwarely went, IV. iii. 8. 2
His roving eie did on the Lady *glaunce* IV. iv. 7. 7
it on the church doth *glance*, IV. vi. 14. 4
The *glaunce* whereof their dimmed eies would daze, VI. x. 4. 3
Fed on the fulnesse of that chearefull *glaunce*, *Am.* xxxix. 11
Ne one light *glance* of sensuall desyre *Am.* lxxxiii. 3
some *glance* doth in mine eie remayne, *Am.* lxxxvii. 8
suffers not one looke to *glaunce* awry, *Epith.* 236
Glanced. *See* **Yglanced.**
The stroke . . . from her head unto her shoulder *glaunst*. I. i. 17. 9
thence it *glaunst* Adowne her backe, IV. vi. 13. 3
thence forth *glaunst* Adowne in vaine, IV. vi. 19. 3
Ran fierce at me that fire *glaunst* from his horses hoofe. IV. x. 9. 9
being carried with his force forthright *Glaunst* swiftly by; VI. vii. 7. 8
Glances. *See* **Eye-glances.**
closely eide . . . that *glaunces* might not glide: III. ix. 27. 5
Glanceth. *Glaunceth* from Phoebus face forthright, *S.C.* Au. 83
Glancing. *See* **Wide-glancing.**
She rovde at me with *glauncing* eye, *S.C.* Au. 79
the *glauncing* rayes Of precious stones, *Gn.* 101
his bright eyes, *glauncing* full dreadfullie, *Gn.* 262
glauncing downe his shield from blame him fairly blest. I. ii. 18. 9
slew with *glauncing* dart amisse A gentle Hynd, I. vi. 17. 5
armour . . . Like *glauncing* light of Phoebus brightest ray; I. vii. 29. 5
since that *glauncing* sight, He hath no powre to hurt, I. viii. 21. 6
steele, . . . *glauncing* by, foorth passed forward right. I. xi. 16. 5
glauncing from his scaly necke I. xi. 20. 6
glauncing fire out of the yron plaid, I. xi. 42. 5
glauncing fell On his horse necke II. v. 4. 4
glauncing on his helmet, II. v. 6. 4
faire lookes, *glancing* like evening lights; II. v. 33. 3
glauncing downe would not his owner byte; II. viii. 38. 4
Glauncing unwares in charmed looking glas, III. iii. 24. 2
glauncing fel to ground, but him annoyed naught. III. v. 24. 9
glauncing on the tempred metall, III. vii. 40. 8
she saw with sodaine *glauncing* eye, IV. vii. 36. 1
glauncing downe his thigh the purple bloud forth drew. V. v. 9. 9
The *glauncing* sparkles through her bever glared, V. vi. 38. 7
glauncing on her shoulder-plate it bit Unto the bone, V. vii. 33. 2
glauncing by deceiv'd him of that he desynd. VI. vii. 10. 9
Glauncing askew, as if his enemies He scorned VI. vii. 42. 3
I mote perceive how, in her *glauncing* sight, *Am.* xvi. 5
glancing through the eyes with countenance coy *H.L.* 122
Glared. The glauncing sparkles through her bever *glared*, V. vi. 38. 7
eies, Like two great Beacons, *glared* bright and wyde, VI. vii. 42. 2
Glaring. *glaring* lampes were sett that made a dreadfull shade. I. xi. 14. 9
Glass. *See* **Bubble-glass, Crystal-glass, Hour-glass, Looking-glass.**
out of his packe a *glasse* he tooke, *S.C.* May 274
for the love of the *glasse* he did see. *S.C.* May 283
as a *glasse* upon the water shone, *Ti.* 220
well could file his tongue as smooth as *glas*: I. i. 35. 7
all embrewd in blood his eyes did shine as *glas*. I. vii. 17. 9
linger till the *glas* be all out ronne? I. ix. 47. 8
this bright Angels towre quite dims that towre of *glas*.' I. x. 58. 9
Like to the world itselfe, and seemd a world of *glas*. III. ii. 19. 9
Ybuilded all of *glasse*, by Magicke powre, III. ii. 20. 7
in that enchaunted *glasse* she saw; IV. vi. 26. 6
like to christall glasse, Yet *glasse* was not, IV. x. 39. 7
likest *glasse* did seeme. IV. x. 39. 9
see not perfect things but in a *glas*: VI. Pr. 5. 5
Yet is that *glasse* so gay, that it can blynd VI. Pr. 5. 6
Ne could be seene but like an image in a *glass*. VII. vii. 6. 9
Nor unto *Glasse*; such basenesse mought offend her. *Am.* ix. 12
in your *glasse* . . . Your goodly selfe for evermore to vew: *Am.* xlv. 1
Glasses. bells, and babes, and *glasses*, in hys packe: *S.C.* May 240
Glassy. upon the *glassy* See A bridge of bras, II. x. 73. 8
Such was the *glassy* globe that Merlin made, III. ii. 21. 1
Glauce. Her aged Nourse, whose name was *Glauce* hight, III. ii. 30. 2
That when old *Glauce* saw, III. ii. 52. 7
Old *Glauce* cast to cure this Ladies griefe; III. iii. 5. 2
Then *Glauce* thus: 'Let not it thee offend, III. iii. 15. 6
'*Glauce*, what needes this colourable word III. iii. 19. 3
'But read,' (saide *Glauce*) 'thou Magitian, III. iii. 25. 1
old *Glauce* thither led Faire Britomart, III. iii. 59. 6
old *Glauce* gan with sharpe repriefe Her to restraine, III. iv. 11. 4
lookt on *Glauce* grim; IV. i. 50. 3
He for revenge had guiltlesse *Glauce* slaine: IV. i. 52. 4
Such us'd wise *Glauce* to that wrathfull knight, IV. ii. 3. 1
For ought that *Glauce* could or doe or say. IV. v. 31. 6
Glauce, seeing all that chaunced there, IV. vi. 25. 1
when *Glauce* thus gan wisely all upknit: IV. vi. 30. 1
Till *Glauce* thus: 'Faire Sir, be nought dismayd IV. vi. 37. 6
Light Doto, wanton *Glauce*, and Galene glad: IV. xi. 48. 9
Glauconome. seeming still to smile, *Glauconome*, IV. xi. 50. 8
Glaucus. *Glaucus*, that wise southsayes understood; IV. xi. 13. 3
Glave. *See* **Glaive.**
Gleam. tree . . . to spread his gladsome *gleame*, *Bel.*[2] v. 2
Gleams. like sunny beames, . . . shewe their golden *gleames*, III. ix. 20. 8
Mongst which crept litle Angels through the glittering *gleames*. V. ix. 28. 9
Glean. As they which *gleane*, the reliques use to gather, *Ro.* xxx. 13
Glee. all this *glee* had no continuaunce: *S.C.* F. 224

Glee—*Continued.*
the Kidde made him good *glee*, *S.C.* May 282
'Now leave, ye shepheards boyes, your merry *glee*; *S.C.* D. 139
long lasting life with joyous *glee*, *Gn.* 59
great mirth and gladsome *glee*. *Gn.* 184
Then made they revell route and goodly *glee*; *Hub.* 558
all that goodly *glee*, *T.M.* 181
all the people followe with great *glee*, I. v. 16. 7
'Most goodly *glee* . . . She to me made, I. ix. 14. 1
nor for gold nor *glee* will I abyde By you, I. ix. 32. 7
entertaines with comely courteous *glee*; I. x. 6. 5
him salute with well beseeming *glee*; I. x. 15. 7
The whiles the other Ladies mind theyr mery *glee*. II. viii. 6. 9
they were entertaynd with courteous And comely *glee* III. i. 31. 5
Their goodly entertainement and great *glee*. III. i. 42. 2
Thence to depart with *glee* and gladsome chere. IV. iii. 51. 3
in her joyous *glee*, To view the thrals IV. viii. 52. 2
with great joyance and with gladsome *glee* IV. viii. 59. 6
gladsome countenaunce nor pleasaunt *glee*; IV. ix. 13. 5
follow'd him with gladfull *glee*, V. iii. 34. 8
With whom great feast and goodly *glee* he fond, V. iv. 3. 4
fild with courage and with joyous *glee*, V. vii. 25. 4
For guiftes of gold or any worldly *glee*, V. xi. 63. 3
goodly *glee* and feast to them she made, VI. i. 46. 3
no meanes to comfort, nor procure her *glee*. VI. iii. 43. 9
A faire young Mayden, full of comely *glee*; VI. vi. 10. 7
With all the courteous *glee* and goodly feast VI. vi. 41. 4
Lord! what gladfull *glee* They made VI. viii. 37. 1
Were met to make their sports and merrie *glee*, VI. ix. 41. 2
making gladfull *glee*, VI. x. 10. 8
this way comming from feastfull *glee* VI. x. 22. 4
Then came October full of merry *glee*; VII. vii. 39. 1
Glen. woes the Widdowes daughter of the *glenne*; *S.C.* Ap. 26
There in a gloomy hollow *glen* III. vii. 6. 1
Glib. With heary *glib* deform'd and meiger face, IV. viii. 12. 6
Glide. The glaunce into my heart did *glide*; *S.C.* Au. 93
the stiffe beame . . . did *glyde* Close under his left wing, I. xi. 20. 6
as the Sunny beames do glaunce and *glide* V. ii. 4
closely eide . . . that glaunces might not *glide*: III. ix. 27. 5
secretly did *glyde* Into his heart, III. ix. 29. 4
Stayd not, till through his curat it did *glyde*, V. viii. 34. 8
The sweete eye-glaunces, that like arrowes *glide*; *Am.* xvii. 9
Glided. *See* **Glode.**
Glider. Hey, ho, the *glyder*! *S.C.* Au. 94
Glides. Through both whose borders swiftly downe it *glides*. IV. xi. 31. 3
Gliding. *glyding* through the ayre lights all the heavens darke. VI. vii. 7. 9
Glimpse. Whom soone as Talus spide by *glims* of night, V. vi. 29. 5
by th' uncertaine *glims* of starry night, VI. viii. 48. 1
Seene but a *glims* of this which I pretend, *H.H.B.* 221
Glister. bloodie eyes doo *glister* firie red; *Gn.* 350
Yet through that darksome vale do *glister* bright; *Col.* 495
the bright *glister* of their beames cleare III. i. 32. 8
it did *glister* like the golden sand, IV. vi. 20. 7
beames, which then did *glyster* fayre; *Proth.* 4
Glistered. golden aygulets, that *glistred* bright II. iii. 26. 7
glistred all with gold and glorious shew, III. i. 41. 3
Glistereth. that *glistreth* bright With burning starres I. x. 50. 5
His glorious face! which *glistereth* else so bright, *H.H.B.* 118
Glistering. *See* **Bright-glistering.**
shoure Gan quench the *glystering* flame. *Bel.*[1] ix. 12
his golden Charet *glistering* light; *Gn.* 67
Ne *glistering* of golde, *Gn.* 99
Upon his head his *glistering* Burganet, *Mui.* 73
His glorious colours, and his *glistering* eies. *Mui.* 336
his *glistring* armor made A litle glooming light, I. i. 14. 4
Queene . . . In *glistring* gold and perelesse pretious stone; I. iv. 8. 6
Phoebus . . . hurld his *glistring* beams through gloomy ayre. I. v. 2. 5
so exceeding shone his *glistring* ray, I. vii. 34. 5
The golden Sunne his *glistring* head gan shew, I. ix. 18. 2
with his *glistring* armes does ill agree; I. ix. 22. 8
Those *glistring* armes that heven with light did fill, I. xi. 4. 8
glistring glosse, darkned with filthy dust, II. vii. 4. 3
Glistring in armes and battailous aray, II. vii. 37. 2
as in *glistring* glory she did sitt, II. vii. 46. 1
Their fruit were golden apples *glistring* bright, II. vii. 54. 1
all armed bright In *glistring* steele, II. ix. 26. 3
Glistring in armes and warlike ornament, II. xi. 24. 2
the *glistring* walles were hong With warlike spoiles III. xi. 52. 1
her *glistring* helmet she unlaced; IV. i. 13. 1
Pactolus *glistring* with his golden flood; IV. xi. 20. 8
In *glistering* armes right goodly well-beseene, V. viii. 29. 4
Glistring like gold amongst the plights enrold, V. ix. 28. 7
All *glistring* glorious in their Makers light. *H.H.L.* 56
All sowd with *glistring* stars more thicke then grasse, *H.H.B.* 53
Glisters. his Adamants with which he shines And *glisters* wide, IV. xi. 31. 8
Glitterand. *See* **Glittering.**
Ygyrt with belts of *glitterand* gold, *S.C.* Jul. 177
Her glorious *glitterand* light doth all mens eies amaze. I. iv. 16. 9
His *glitterand* armour shined far away, I. vii. 29. 4
Soone as those *glitterand* armes he did espye, II. vii. 42. 1
Eftsoones himselfe in *glitterand* armes he dight, II. xi. 17. 1
Glittering. *See* **Glitterand.**
Upon the *glyttering* wave doth playe, *S.C.* Au. 91
A trophee of his *glittering* spoyles and treasure, *Gn.* 127
His *glittering* breast he lifteth up on hie, *Gn.* 258
his owne armes when *glittering* he did spy III. xii. 12. 4
the waves, *glittering* like Christall glas, IV. xi. 27. 3
glittering spangs that did like starres appeare, IV. xi. 45. 5
crept litle Angels through the *glittering* gleames. V. ix. 28. 9

Globe. fall, that seemd to shake The stedfast *globe* of earth, . . . I. viii. 23. 9
Such was the glassy *globe* that Merlin made, . . . III. ii. 21. 1
Globes. In rolling *globes* up to the vauted skies. . . . *Col.* 611
Glode. Like sparke of fire that from the andvile *glode,* . . . IV. iv. 23. 5
Gloom. at last I see it *gloome,* . . . *Epith.* 285
Glooming. the *glooming* skies Warnd them . . . *Col.* 954
A litle *glooming* light, much like a shade; . . . I. i. 14. 5
Phoebus in the *glooming* East . . . I. xii. 2. 1
Now *glooming* sadly, so to cloke her matter; . . . VI. vi. 42. 8
the new yeares joy . . . send, Into the *glooming* world, . . . *Am.* lxii. 10
Gloomy. they spide, how, in a *gloomy* glade, . . . *Hub.* 951
In *gloomie* evening, when the wearie Sun, . . . *D.* 22
Phoebus . . . hurld his glistring beams through *gloomy* ayre. . I. v. 2. 5
with greene boughes decking a *gloomy* glade, . . . I. vii. 4. 4
At last he came unto a *gloomy* glade, . . . II. vii. 3. 1
A *gloomy* grove of mirtle trees did rise, . . . III. vi. 43. 3
There in a *gloomy* hollow glen . . . III. vii. 6. 1
th' Earthes *gloomy* shade Did dim the brightnesse . . . III. x. 46. 6
Like as a *gloomie* cloud, . . . IV. i. 45. 5
By that the *gloomy* evening on them fell, . . . IV. iv. 25. 6
chose out a *gloomy* glade, . . . IV. vii. 38. 6
to the *gloomy* world itselfe bewray'd: . . . IV. x. 52. 7
Did underneath them make a *gloomy* shade, . . . VI. iv. 13. 7
Gloriana. adventure . . . That greatest *Gloriana* to him gave, I. i. 3. 2
Forthwith to court of *Gloriane* I sped, . . . I. vii. 46. 5
Gloriane, great Queene of glory bright, . . . I. vii. 46. 6
Elfin Emperours, Till time of *Gloriane.* . . . II. x. Arg.
they *Glorian* call that glorious flowre: . . . II. x. 76. 8
Long mayst thou, *Glorian,* live . . . II. x. 76. 9
either *Gloriana* let her chuse, . . . III. Pr. 5. 7
his avowed quest, Which he had undertane to *Gloriane;* . . V. viii. 3. 3
Appointed by that mightie Faerie Prince, Great *Gloriane,* . V. xii. 3. 4
Great *Gloriana,* greatest Majesty! . . . VI. x. 28. 3
Gloriana's. (Save onely *Glorianaes* heavenly hew, . . . VI. x. 4. 7
Glories. *glories* most in mortall miseries, . . . *D.* 152
Does all their deedes deface, and dims their *glories* all. . . III. ii. 1. 9
Glorified. with sweete Poets verse be *glorifide.* . . . *Ti.* 427
Progeny; . . . By whose endevours they are *glorifide,* . . . *Ded. Son.* iv. 8
on knight so goodly *glorifyde,* . . . III. ii. 11. 4
Admir'd of all the people and much *glorifide.* . . . IV. iii. 51. 9
With great successe, that her hath *glorifide,* . . . V. iv. 33. 7
With tryumph entertayn'd and *glorifyde,* . . . V. viii. 51. 3
Glorify. the wilde beasts whom armes did *glorifie,* . . . *Hub.* 1184
Whose merits they to *glorifie* do chose. . . . *Ti.* 371
him, whom all the world did *glorifie:* . . . *Ti.* 663
hable . . . her name to *glorifie.* . . . *Col.* 379
That warlike feats doest highest *glorifie.* . . . II. iii. 38. 3
Oxford, thine doth Thame most *glorify.* . . . IV. xi. 26. 9
through the world thereby should *glorifie* his name. . . . VI. xii. 12. 9
Glorious. *See* **Vainglorious.**
An Hydra was of warriours *glorious,* . . . *Ro.* x. 6
What bootes it then to come from *glorious* Forefathers, . . . *T.M.* 445
Admirers of her *glorious* excellence; . . . *T.M.* 584
To feed on flowres and weeds of *glorious* feature, . . . *Mui.* 213
His *glorious* colours, and his glistering eies. . . . *Mui.* 336
in remembrance of that *glorious* bright, . . . *Col.* 46
plaine attire such *glorious* gallantry Disdaines . . . *Col.* 729
comprise Those *glorious* ornaments of hevenly grace, . . . *Ded. Son.* xvi. 7
glorious fire it kindled in his hart; . . . I. Pr. 3. 4
that true *glorious* type of thine, . . . I. Pr. 4. 7
For whose sweete sake that *glorious* badge he wore, . . . I. i. 2. 3
(That greatest *Glorious* Queene of Faery lond) . . . I. i. 3. 3
In so ritch weedes, and seeming *glorious* show, . . . I. ii. 21. 5
whose *glorious* vew Their frayle amazed senses did confound: I. iv. 7. 2
To dim the brightnesse of her *glorious* throne, . . . I. iv. 8. 8
Her *glorious* glitterand light doth all mens eies amaze. . . . I. iv. 16. 9
hart that . . . is with childe of *glorious* great intent, . . . I. v. 1. 2
haughtie Helmet . . . Both *glorious* brightnesse and great terrour bredd: . . . I. vii. 31. 2
that most *glorious* house, that glistreth bright . . . I. x. 50. 5
The knight . . . gayns Most *glorious* victory. . . . I. xi. Arg.
glorious light of her sunshyny face, . . . I. xii. 23. 2
enrolled is your *glorious* name In heavenly Regesters . . . II. i. 32. 3
be these the parts Of *glorious* knighthood, . . . II. ii. 29. 6
Great and most *glorious* virgin Queene alive, . . . II. ii. 40. 3
great or *glorious* in mortall eye, . . . II. ii. 41. 4
So *glorious* mirrhour of celestiall grace, . . . II. iii. 25. 6
glorious spoiles, purchast in perilous fight: . . . II. v. 26. 3
massy gold of *glorious* guifte, . . . II. vii. 28. 4
so *glorious* bayte Would tempt his guest . . . II. vii. 34. 3
the trew lively-head Of that most *glorious* visage . . . II. ix. 3. 4
they Glorian call that *glorious* flowre: . . . II. x. 76. 8
greatest and most *glorious* thing on ground . . . II. xi. 30. 1
Cannot your *glorious* pourtraict figure playne, . . . III. Pr. 3. 7
Did sparckle forth great light, and *glorious* did appeare. . III. i. 32. 9
glistred all with gold and *glorious* shew, . . . III. i. 41. 3
Ne in so *glorious* spoile themselves embosse: . . . III. i. 64. 8
My *glorious* Soveraines goodly auncestrye, . . . III. iii. 4. 7
glorious Features of beautie, and all shapes select, . . . III. vi. 12. 3
to rest in *glorious* victorye. . . . III. ix. 22. 9
Her goodly personage and *glorious* hew, . . . III. ix. 23. 6
What boots it boast thy *glorious* descent, . . . III. ix. 33. 6
brings forth *glorious* flowres of fame, . . . IV. Pr. 2. 7
Made him seeme happie for so *glorious* theft; . . . IV. ii. 4. 8
Ne desperate of *glorious* victorie; . . . IV. iii. 25. 2
hearts quite robbed with so *glorious* sight, . . . IV. iv. 16. 5
that *glorious* prize to gaine. . . . IV. v. 26. 5
That *glorious* belt did in it selfe containe, . . . IV. v. 2. 8
Then did her *glorious* flowre wex dead and wan, . . . IV. viii. 32. 8
from that goodly *glorious* flowre proceed, . . . IV. viii. 33. 6

Glorious—*Continued.*
though sweet love to conquer *glorious* bee, . . . IV. x. 3. 8
no intreatie would forgoe so *glorious* spoyle. . . . IV. x. 55. 9
That *glorious* spoyle of beautie with me lead, . . . IV. x. 58. 3
that same great *glorious* lampe of light, . . . V. Pr. 7. 1
makes them like himselfe in *glorious* sight . . . V. Pr. 10. 7
The *glorious* picture vanisheth away, . . . V. iii. 25. 6
what a *glorious* shew he made in all their sights. . . . V. iii. 39. 9
beautie is more *glorious* bright and clere, . . . VI. vii. 29. 7
that goodly *glorious* gaze . . . VI. x. 4. 1
they their *glorious* Lord in strange disguise Transfigur'd sawe; VII. vii. 7. 8
The *glorious* pourtraict of that Angels face, . . . *Am.* xvii. 1
In which her *glorious* ymage placed is; . . . *Am.* xxii. 6
decke her head with *glorious* bayes, . . . *Am.* xxix. 13
that same *glorious* beauties ydle boast . . . *Am.* xli. 9
The *glorious* image of the Makers beautie, . . . *Am.* lxi. 1
Most *glorious* Lord of lyfe! . . . *Am.* lxviii. 1
The happy purchase of my *glorious* spoile, . . . *Am.* lxix. 13
in the hevens wryte your *glorious* name. . . . *Am.* lxxv. 12
turne to nought and loose that *glorious* hew; . . . *Am.* lxxix. 6
enchased Your *glorious* name in golden moniment. . . . *Am.* lxxxii. 8
Phoebus gins to shew his *glorious* hed. . . . *Epith.* 77
glorious lampe of love! . . . *Epith.* 288
for the guerdon of theyr *glorious* merit, . . . *Epith.* 421
Beauties *glorious* beame. . . . *H.L.* 116
The Sunne more bright and *glorious* doth appeare; . . . *H.L.* 277
All glistring *glorious* in their Makers light. . . . *H.H.L.* 56
Next to Himselfe in *glorious* degree, . . . *H.H.L.* 93
In which he reigned with his *glorious* syre, . . . *H.H.L.* 135
O *glorious* Morning-Starre! O Lampe of Light! . . . *H.H.L.* 170
Whose *glorious* beames all fleshly sense doth daze . . . *H.H.L.* 278
So full their eyes are of that *glorious* sight, . . . *H.H.B.* 281
And *glorious* images in heaven wrought, . . . *H.H.B.* 3
Whence they doe still behold the *glorious* face . . . *H.H.B.* 80
His *glorious* face! which glistereth else so bright, . . . *H.H.B.* 118
all about him sheddeth *glorious* light: . . . *H.H.B.* 161
More excellent, more *glorious,* more divine, . . . *H.H.B.* 171
beautie . . . Sparkled on her from Gods owne *glorious* face, . *H.H.B.* 207
great Elisaes *glorious* name may ring . . . *Proth.* 157
Gloriously. In goodly colours *gloriously* arrayd; . . . *Am.* lxx. 4
Glory. She seemde with *glorie* of the scarlet faire, . . . *Rev.* ii. 6
auncient *glory* (*glorie*[1]) of the Romaine peares (lordes[1]). . *Bel.* iv. 8
the great (*om.*[1]) *glorie* (*glory*[1]) and the auncient praise, . *Bel.* x. 6
trustles state Of vaine worlds *glorie,* . . . *Pet.*[2] vii. 2
Your *glorie,* fairest of all earthly thing! . . . *Ro.* i. 14
Mausolus worke will be the Carians *glorie;* . . . *Ro.* ii. 7
th' heavens in *glorie* triumpht over all: . . . *Ro.* xii. 8
The Romane triumphs *glorie* to beholde . . . *Ro.* xiv. 12
if that time doo let thy *glorie* live, . . . *Ro.* xxxii. 11
Let therefore nought, that great is, therein *glorie,* . . . *Van.* viii. 13
all his *glory* in his cruell clawes. . . . *Van.* x. 6
The *glory* eke much greater then the gayne: . . . *S.C.* O. 20
the *glorie* bee Of the Pierian streames, . . . *Gn.* 25
Let everlasting lightsome *glory* strive, . . . *Gn.* 55
Their match in *glorie,* mightie, fierce, and coy; . . . *Gn.* 494
Hector, the *glorie* of the Trojan field: . . . *Gn.* 516
The *glorie* of the stock of Tantalus, . . . *Gn.* 546
Resembling Aarons *glorie* in his place: . . . *Hub.* 463
Tickled with *glorie* and rash covetise: . . . *Hub.* 996
in his new *glory* sheene. . . . *Hub.* 1066
wont to be the *glorie* of gay wits, . . . *T.M.* 182
His love, his truth, his *glorie,* and his might, . . . *T.M.* 513
'O vaine worlds *glorie!* . . . *Ti.* 43
'He now is dead, and all his *glorie* gone, . . . *Ti.* 218
sits in highest seate Of this worlds *glorie,* . . . *Ti.* 464
In *glorie,* or in greatnes to excell, . . . *Ti.* 555
glorie of the world your high thoughts scorne, . . . *Ti.* 681
'She is the Rose, the *glorie* of the day, . . . *D.* 232
in a moment loose their grace and *glorie.* . . . *D.* 497
Whose *glorie* greater then my simple thought, . . . *Col.* 333
To end thy *glorie* which he hath begun: . . . *Col.* 409
Excelling most in *glorie* and great light: . . . *Col.* 497
glorie that in simple eie Seeme greatest, . . . *Col.* 721
That her bright *glorie* else hath much defamed. . . . *Col.* 910
th' antique *glory* of thine auncestry . . . *Ded. Son.* iii. 6
that Emperesse, The worlds sole *glory* . . . *Ded. Son.* xi. 4
that most Heroicke spirit, . . . the *glory* of our daies, . . . *Ded. Son.* xv. 2
Armory, Wherein ye have great *glory* wonne this day, . . . I. i. 27. 6
to compare Whether in beauties *glorie* did exceede: . . . I. ii. 37. 4
Proud of such *glory* . . . He leaves the welkin way . . . I. iv. 9. 5
the stout Faery . . . Thought all their *glorie* vaine . . . I. iv. 15. 7
that same envious gage Of victors *glory* . . . I. iv. 39. 6
to augment the *glorie* of his guile, His dearest love, . . . I. iv. 42. 1
Th' eternall brood of *glorie* excellent: . . . I. v. 1. 4
The conquest yours; I yours; the shield, and *glory* yours.' . . I. v. 14. 9
He had . . . fild far landes with *glorie* of his might: . . . I. vi. 20. 6
Gloriane, great Queene of *glory* bright, . . . I. vii. 46. 6
glory does to them for guerdon graunt: . . . I. x. 59. 8
How dare I thinke such *glory* to attaine?' . . . I. x. 62. 2
feeble eyes your *glory* may behold, . . . II. Pr. 5. 3
he hath great *glory* wonne, . . . II. i. 19. 9
spred his *glory* through all countryes wide. . . . II. i. 35. 4
My Soveraine, Whose *glory* is in gracious deeds, . . . II. ii. 43. 6
A pleasing vaine of *glory* he did fynd, . . . II. iii. 4. 5
Great *glory* and gay spoile, sure hast thou gott, . . . II. iv. 45. 6
Is all his force forlorne, and all his *glory* donne? . . . II. v. 35. 9
Of love they ever greater *glory* bore . . . II. vi. 35. 6
whom I lust do heape with *glory* and renowne?' . . . II. vii. 11. 9
His *glory* did enhaunce, and pompous pryde display. . . . II. vii. 44. 9
as in glistring *glory* she did sitt, . . . II. vii. 46. 1

Glory—*Continued.*
goodly was their *glory* to behold; . . . II. vii. 54. 2
More *glory* thought to give life then decay, . . . II. viii. 51. 4
Whose *glory* shineth as the morning starre, . . . II. ix. 4. 6
Through great desire of *glory* and of fame; . . . II. ix. 38. 7
Conceive such soveraine *glory* and great bountyhed? . . . II. x. 2 .9
the *glory* of her sex, . . . II. x. 20. 6
no moniment of Brutus, nor of Britons *glorie* auncient. . . . II. x. 36. 9
Great was his power and *glorie* . . . II. x. 76. 1
Long mayst thou, Glorian, live in *glory* and great powre! . II. x. 76. 9
Revivyng thought of *glory* and of fame, . . . II. xi. 31. 8
Where is the Antique *glory* now become, . . . III. iv. 1. 1
To hunt for *glory* and renowmed prayse. . . . III. i. 3. 3
for *glorie* of great valiaunce, . . . III. iv. 3. 3
to advaunce his name and *glory* more, . . . III. iv. 21. 6
That mortall men her *glory* should admyre. . . . III. v. 52. 6
Your *glory* sett to chace the salvage beasts, . . . III. vi. 22. 2
all their *glory* to the ground downe flings, . . . III. vi. 39. 5
His *glory* did repose, and credit did maintaine. . . . III. viii. 11. 9
Most vertuous virgin! *glory* be thy meed, . . . III. viii. 42. 6
doth blend The shyning *glory* of your soveraine light; . . . III. ix. 1. 8
Their ofspring hath . . . later *glory* shent? . . . III. ix. 33. 9
The *glory* of the later world to spring, . . . III. ix. 44. 2
in all *glory* and gieat enterprise, . . . III. ix. 44. 8
Ne in small meares containe his *glory* great, . . . III. ix. 46. 8
So shall your *glory* bee advaunced mach, . . . III. x. 28. 5
Fame is my meed, and *glory* vertues pay: . . . III. x. 31. 7
Even immortal prayse and *glory* wyde, . . . III. xii. 39. 6
all their *glory* quite decayd; . . . III. xii. 42. 4
with great *glorie* both the shield of love . . . he brought away, . . . IV. i. 2. 6
That shall you win more *glory* than ye here find gaines.' . . . IV. ii. 27. 9
For *glorie* vaine, their fellowship to lose, . . . IV. iv. 14. 5
much he gan his *glorie* to envy, . . . IV. iv. 28. 4
A stranger knight, that did his *glorie* shend: . . . IV. iv. 43. 8
That many wish to win for *glorie* vaine, . . . IV. v. 2. 6
What *glorie,* or what guerdon hast thou found . . . IV. vii. 1. 5
Loose so immortall *glory,* and so endlesse gaines. . . . IV. xi. 22. 9
Whose *glorie* is to aide all suppliants pore, . . . V. i. 4. 6
Their greatest *glory* for their rightfull deedes, . . . V. ii. 1. 6
To tell the *glorie* of the feast that day, . . . V. iii. 3. 1
'By which that *glorie* gotten doth appeare . . . V. iii. 22. 4
her *glory* to partake; . . . V. vii. 36. 2
her *glorie* to commend, . . . V. ix. 32. 7
Dispreds the *glorie* of her leaves gay; . . . V. xii. 13. 6
eke her champions *glorie* sounded overall. . . . V. xii. 24. 9
That shall you *glory* gaine More then his love, . . . VI. i. 27. 4
he grace and *glory* wonne alwaies, . . . VI. vi. 4. 4
Love hath the *glory* of his kingdome left, . . . VI. viii. 1. 2
thighes, whose *glorie* did appeare Like a triumphal Arch, . VI. viii. 42. 7
Reaping eternall *glorie* of his restlesse paines. . . . VI. ix. 2. 9
daily doe behold The *glorie* of the great . . . VI. ix. 28. 2
'Sunne of the world, great *glory* of the sky, . . . VI. x. 28. 1
when thy *glory* shall be farre displayd To future age, . . . VI. x. 28. 8
th' onely *glory* of his might. . . . VI. x. 40. 9
Where Cynthia raignes in everlasting *glory,* . . . VII. vi. 8. 2
t' envie her that in such *glory* raigned. . . . VII. vi. 10. 6
Bellona, whose great *glory* thou doost spight, . . . VII. vi. 32. 5
this worlds worthlesse *glory* to embase, . . . *Am.* xvii. 3
But taketh *glory* in her cruelnesse. . . . *Am.* xx. 12
all worlds *glorie* is but drosse uncleane, . . . *Am.* xxvii. 2
To sing the *glory* of their famous deedes. . . . *Am.* xxix. 8
All this worlds *glory* seemeth vayne to me, . . . *Am.* xxxv. 13
how little *glory* ye have gayned . . . *Am.* xxxvi. 10
And greater *glory* thinke, to save then spill. . . . *Am.* xlix. 4
glory thinke to make these cruel stoures. . . . *Am.* lvii. 10
what *glory* can be got, In slaying him . . . *Am.* lvii. 11
much greater *glory* gate, . . . *Am.* lxvi. 9
Resembling heavens *glory* in her light, . . . *Am.* lxxii. 6
To speake her prayse and *glory* excellent, . . . *Am.* lxxiv. 11
Bring home with you the *glory* of her gaine . . . *Epith.* 244
to receive the triumph of your *glorie,* . . . *H.L.* 34
Who can expresse the *glorie* of thy might? . . . *H.L.* 49
Certes small *glory* doest thou winne hereby, . . . *H.L.* 153
herein eke thy *glory* seemeth more, . . . *H.L.* 162
thy blisse, and heavens *glorie.* . . . *H.L.* 279
your bright *glorie* darkned quight; . . . *H.B.* 165
the garland of your *glorie* marre, . . . *H.B.* 174
In endlesse *glorie* and immortall might, . . . *H.H.L.* 37
Where they behold the *glorie* of his light, . . . *H.H.L.* 69
Eternall King of *Glorie,* Lord of Might, . . . *H.H.L.* 172
The *glory* of our heavenly riches lay, . . . *H.H.L.* 229
all earthes *glorie,* on which men do gaze, . . . *H.H.L.* 275
Th' Idee of his pure *glorie* present still Before thy face, . *H.H.L.* 284
That with the *glorie* of so goodly sight . . . *H.H.B.* 15
The *glory* of that Majestie Divine, . . . *H.H.B.* 124
On that bright Sunne of *Glorie* fixe thine eyes, . . . *H.H.B.* 139
With the great *glorie* of that wondrous light . . . *H.H.B.* 176
the worlds faire ornament, And heavens *glorie,* . . . *Proth.* 92
a noble Peer, Great Englands *glory,* . . . *Proth.* 146

Glory's. for faire ladies love and *glories* gaine, . . . III. ix. 37. 7
That enterprize for greatest *glories* gayne. . . . IV. ix. 4. 5
is ought so bright And beautifull as *glories* beames appeare, V. xi. 62. 8
Her *glories* pride that none may it repayre. . . . *Am.* lviii. 8

Glose. *See* **Gloze.**

Gloss. glistring *glosse,* darkned with filthy dust, . . . II. vii. 4. 3
He much more goodly *glosse* thereon doth shed . . . IV. v. 15. 5

Glove. hery with hymnes thy lasses *glove;* . . . *S.C.* F. 62

Glow. told, it flames; and, hidden, it does *glow,* . . . I. ix. 8. 7
downe both sides two wide long eares did *glow,* . . . IV. vii. 6. 7

Gloze. seeke to *glose* upon the text; . . . *Gn. Ded.* 10

Glozing. he could well his *glozing* speaches frame . . . III. viii. 14. 4

Glued. *Glewed* togither with some subtile matter. . . . *Col.* 217

Glutted. with the weedes be *glutted.* . . . *S.C.* Jul. 112
with many a Lambe had *glutted* his gulfe, . . . *S.C.* S. 185
with your carkasses wild beasts be *glutted.* . . . *D.* 350

Glutting. *See* **Eye-glutting.**

Glutton. He casts his *glutton* sense to satisfie, . . . *Mui.* 179

Gluttony. *Gluttonie,* malice, pride, and covetize, . . . *Hub.* 1309
by his side rode loathsome *Gluttony,* . . . I. iv. 21. 1
Such one was *Gluttony,* the second of that crew. . . . I. iv. 23. 9
For Steward was excessive *Gluttony,* . . . I. iv. 43. 7

Gnar. he gan to reare his bristles strong, And felly *gnarre,* . I. v. 34. 6

Gnash. teeth he still did grind And grimly *gnash,* . . . II. iv. 15. 4
both did *gnash* their teeth, and both did threten life. . . . II. vii. 21 .9

Gnashed. he *gnasht* his teeth to see Those heapes of gold . I. iv. 31. 6
gnasht his yron tuskes at that displeasing sight. . . . IV. x. 33. 9
gnashed with his teeth, . . . V. ii. 18. 7
gnasht his teeth, and his head at him shooke, . . . V. xi. 12. 8

Gnashing. the feend his *gnashing* teeth did grate, . . . II. vii. 34. 1
with *gnashing* teeth did bite The bitter earth, . . . III. v. 22. 1
Gnashing his cruell teeth at him in vaine, . . . VI. iv. 22. 8
Gnashing his grinded teeth with griesly looke, . . . VI. v. 26. 1

Gnat. A *Gnat,* unto the sleepie Shepheard went; . . . *Gn.* 283
The Image of that *Gnat* appeard to him, . . . *Gn.* 324
To thee, small *Gnat,* in lieu of his life saved; . . . *Gn.* 687

Gnat's. May by this *Gnatts* complaint be easily knowen. . . . *Gn. Ded.* 14
excuse This *Gnats* small Poeme, . . . *Gn.* 5
lighter seeme than this *Gnats* idle name. . . . *Gn.* 8
that *Gnats* death, which deeply was imprest, . . . *Gn.* 645

Gnats. A cloud of cumbrous *gnattes* doe him molest, . . . I. i. 23. 5
As when a swarme of *Gnats* at eventide . . . II. ix. 16. 1

Gnaw. disdaine and rancour, which did *gnaw* His hart . . . II. viii. 50. 7
Another in her teeth did *gnaw* a rush; . . . II. ix. 35. 8
gnaw his gealous hart, . . . IV. vi. 7. 5

Gnawed. On which she fed and *gnawed* hungrily, . . . V. xii. 30. 6

Gnawing. *See* **Heart-gnawing.**
The *gnawing* envie, the hart-fretting feare, . . . *H.L.* 259
'The *gnawing* anguish, and sharp gelosy, . . . II. iv. 23. 1
gnawing Gealosy, . . . his bitter lips did bight; . . . II. vii. 22. 4
Gnawing her nayles for felnesse and for yre, . . . IV. viii. 23. 8

Gnawn. *See* **Half-gnawn.**

Gnidus. *See* **Cnidus.**

Go. *See* **Ago, Outgo, Overgo.**
Goe, little booke! . . . *To his Booke* 1
I cast to *goe* a shooting. . . . *S.C.* Mar. 63
Ladyes of the lake behight, That unto her *goe.* . . . *S.C.* Ap. 121
time, I gesse, homeward to *goe:* . . . *S.C.* Jun. 117
Theyr good is with them *goe:* . . . *S.C.* Jul. 118
if you *goe* nye, . . . *S.C.* S. 116
Is faded quite, and into dust *ygoe.* . . . *S.C.* N. 76
Goe, lyttle Calender! . . . *S.C.* Env. 7
Goe but a lowly gate . . . *S.C.* Env. 8
fayre Naiades, *Go* too, . . . *Gn.* 27
Go ye with them, *go,* cursed damosells, . . . *Gn.* 393
durst those lowest shadowes *goe* to see, . . . *Gn.* 438
boldlie doth amongst the boldest *go;* . . . *Hub.* 666
Did ever after scorne on foote to *goe.* . . . *Hub.* 752
Whilst through the forest rechlesse they did *goe,* . . . *Hub.* 950
Till that the Foxe forth toward them did *goe,* . . . *Hub.* 1074
Unto the King so rash ye may not *goe;* . . . *Hub.* 1214
now thou maist *go* pack; . . . *T.M.* 398
May now *goe* prune his plumes . . . *T.M.* 402
Go beg with us, and be companions still, . . . *T.M.* 407
So wailing backe *go* to their wofull toomb. . . . *Ti.* 49
'"I *goe,* and long desired have to *goe;* . . . *D.* 281
I *goe* with gladnesse to my wished rest, . . . *D.* 282
'"Yet, ere I *goe,* a pledge I leave with thee . . . *D.* 288
round about doth *goe* Like a Mill-wheele . . . *D.* 431
under ground to *goe* to give them light . . . *D.* 478
without taking leave he foorth did *goe* . . . *D.* 563
how we rashly *go* To serve that God, . . . *Col.* 797
he was . . . unhable once to stirre or *go;* . . . I. iv. 23. 2
well he could not touch, nor *goe,* nor stand. . . . I. iv. 29. 8
Duessa . . . to hell does *goe.* . . . I. v. Arg.
'*Goe,* caytive Elfe, him quickly overtake, . . . I. v. 11. 1
Goe, guiltie ghost, to him my message make, . . . I. v. 11. 3
'*Goe* now, proud Miscreant, . . . I. v. 13. 1
Goe say, his foe thy shield with his doth beare.' . . . I. v. 13. 4
Go, gather up the reliques of thy race; . . . I. v. 24. 2
Or else *goe* them avenge, . . . I. v. 24. 3
Lo! now I *goe* with thee.' . . . I. v. 27. 9
Goe to then, O thou . . . sonne Of great Apollo! . . . I. v. 43. 6
Go, find some other play-fellowes, . . . I. vi. 28. 9
To her yeeld passage gainst his Lord to *goe,* . . . I. viii. 13. 7
They let her *goe* at will, and wander waies unknowne. . . . I. viii. 49. 9
The further he doth *goe,* the further he doth stray. . . . I. ix. 43. 9
doe no further *goe,* no further stray, . . . I. ix. 44. 1
To come and *goe* with tidings from the heart, . . . I. ix. 51. 6
With many rather for to *goe* astray. . . . I. x. 10. 6
The eldest did against the youngest *goe,* . . . II. ii. 13. 8
Withouten which she could not *goe* upright; . . . II. iv. 5. 7
They *goe* abord, And he eftsoones gan launch . . . II. xi. 4. 3
go to see that dreadful place. . . . III. iii. 8. 2
'*Goe,* Dame; *goe,* seeke your boy, . . . III. vi. 24. 2
Doth it consume and into nothing *goe,* . . . III. vi. 37. 8
A womans will, which is disposd to *go* astray. . . . III. ix. 6. 9
to the gates they *goe* To burn the same . . . III. ix. 17. 6
besought Them *go* to rest. . . . III. ix. 53. 9
ever faine he towards them would *goe,* . . . III. x. 22. 1

Go—*Continued.*
let us *goe* to seeke my dearest Dame, ... III. x. 39. 5
Those feeling words so neare the quicke did *goe,* . . . . . III. xi. 15. 7
where ever thou do *go* or ryde, ... IV. i. 51. 8
warded, or avoyded and let *goe,* . . . . . IV. iii. 17. 4
As two wild Boares together grapling *go,* . . . . . IV. iv. 29. 8
so in to *goe,* . . . . . IV. x. 19. 3
Sometime with tender teares to let her *goe,* . . . . . IV. x. 57. 2
unto great king Neptune selfe did *goe,* . . . . . IV. xii. 29. 4
straight at him with all his force did *go,* . . . . . V. i. 21. 5
So did this Ladies goodly forme decay, And into nothing *goe,* V. iii. 25. 9
'*Goe,* damzell, quickly, doe thy selfe addresse . . . . . V. iv. 48. 4
Goe thou unto that stranger Faery Knight, ... V. iv. 48. 6
Goe streight, and take with thee . . . Sixe of thy fellowes . V. iv. 49. 6
Goe now, Clarinda; . . . . . V. v. 34. 6
Thus *goe* they both together to their geare, ... V. viii. 30. 1
Yet could the Prince not nigh unto him *goe,* . . . . . V. viii. 37. 3
go which way they list, their guide they have forlore. . . . . V. viii. 39. 9
they overcommen Agree to *goe* with her; . . . . . V. ix. 4. 2
whether shall I *goe?* . . . . . V. x. 23. 1
'Nathlesse,' (said he) 'deare Ladie, with me *goe;* . . . . . V. x. 24. 1
The trompets sound, and they together *goe* . . . . . V. xii. 17. 1
He . . . Would thumpe her forward and inforce to *goe,* . . . VI. ii. 10. 8
Chyld Tristram prayd that he with him might *goe* . . . . . VI. ii. 36. 3
'But *go* thy waies to him, and fro me say, ... VI. iii. 41. 1
with medicine To *goe* about to salve such kynd of sore, . . . VI. vi. 13. 2
home with him did *go.* . . . . . VI. ix. 16. 9
toward them did *go.* . . . . . VI. x. 17. 9
good should from us *goe,* then come, in greater store. . . . VI. x. 24. 9
So forth they *goe* together . . . . . VI. xi. 36. 1
all the people, where so he did *go,* . . . . . VI. xii. 37. 3
Go seek he out that Alane where he may be sought. . . . . VII. vii. 9. 9
I *goe* lyke one that, . . . Is prisoner . . . . . *Am.* lii. 2
Goe to my love, where she is carelesse layd, ... *Am.* lxx. 5
Lackyng my love, I *go* from place to place, ... *Am.* lxxviii. 1
Goe visit her in her chast bowre of rest . . . . . *Am.* lxxxiii. 7
Go to the bowre of my beloved love, ... *Epith.* 23
backe againe they *go,* . . . . . *H.B.* 242

Goale. *See* **Jail.**

Goat. The *Gate* her dame . . . Yode forth . . . . . *S.C.* May 177
So schooled the *Gate* her wanton sonne, ... *S.C.* May 227
rode lustfull Lechery Upon a bearded *Gote,* (*Goat*) . . . . I. iv. 24. 2
like a *Gote* emongst the Gotes did rush; . . . . . III. x. 47. 3
thereon flew Like a wyld *Gote,* . . . . . V. ix. 15. 4
like a wilde *goate* round about did chace . . . . . VI. iii. 49. 3
from the *Goat* her kidde, how to convay: . . . . . VI. ix. 23. 4
Upon a shaggy-bearded *Goat* he rode, ... VII. vii. 41. 5

Goatherd. Is not thilke same a *goteheard* prowde, ... *S.C.* Jul. 1
As *Goteherd* prowd, that, sitting hye, ... *S.C.* Jul. 103

Goatherds. they dwell (As *goteheards* wont) upon a hill, . *S.C.* Jul. 47

Goatish. through likenesse of his *gotish* beard, ... III. x. 47. 6
by his *goatish* beard some did him haile: . . . . . VII. vi. 49. 5

Goats. Teribinth, good for *Gotes:* . . . . . *S.C.* Jul. 86
if they with thy *Gotes* should yede, ... *S.C.* Jul. 109
when my *Gates* shall han their bellies layd, ... *S.C.* O. 119
His little *Goats* gan drive out of their stalls, ... *Gn.* 71
There his milk-dropping *Goats* be His delight, ... *Gn.* 115
gan the shepheard gather into one His stragling *Goates,* . . . *Gn.* 162
To milk their *gotes,* and make them cheese . . . . . III. x. 36. 8
The whiles their *Gotes* upon the brouzes fedd, ... III. x. 45. 8
like a Gote emongst the *Gotes* did rush; . . . . . III. x. 47. 3
like wyld *Goates* them chaced all about, ... V. viii. 50. 7

Gobbelines. *See* **Goblins.**

Gobbet. Then from her mouth the *gobbet* she does take, . . . V. xii. 39. 1

Gobbets. great lumps of flesh and *gobbets* raw, ... I. i. 20. 3
In which yett trickling blood, and *gobbets* raw, ... I. xi. 13. 3

Goblins. *See* **Hobgoblins.**
fowle *Goblins,* and Shriekowles . . . . . *T.M.* 283
overcame The wicked *Gobbelines* in bloody field; . . . . . II. x. 73. 2

God. *See* **Good, Money-god, Sea-god, Wood-god.**
onely *God* surmountes the force of ty[me,] . . . . . *Bel.*[1] i. 13
In *God* alone do stay my confidence. . . . . . *Bel.*[1] i. 14
The worde of *God* made him a noble name. . . . . . *Rev.* iii. 4
the bright abode Of *God* and men. . . . . . *Rev.* iv. 6
For he shall be their *God,* . . . . . *Rev.* iv. 6
Sith onely *God* surmounts all times decay, ... *Bel.*[2] i. 13
In *God* alone my confidence do stay. . . . . . *Bel.*[2] i. 14
faire as mote the greatest *god* delite; . . . . . *Pet.* i. 5
Nor swelling streames of that *God* snakie-paced, ... *Ro.* xiii. 10
God might not endure . . . to set foundation sure? . . . . . *Ro.* xxiv. 13
Pan, thou shepheards *God* that once didst love, ... *S.C.* Ja. 17
Ah, *God!* that love should breede both joy and payne! . . . *S.C.* Ja. 54
'O, my liege Lord! the *God* of my life! . . . . . *S.C.* F. 150
(There shrouded was the little *God*) . . . . . *S.C.* Mar. 68
*Is graunted scarce to *God* above. . . . . . *S.C.* Mar. 120
Which Pan, the shepheards *God,* of her begot: . . . . . *S.C.* Ap. 51
their *God* his good does them send, ... *S.C.* May 64
God giveth good for none other end. . . . . . *S.C.* May 72
thilke *God,* that gave him that good, ... *S.C.* May 85
God wote, such cause hath she none) . . . . . *S.C.* May 98
The shepheards *Gods* so wel them guided, ... *S.C.* May 113
'*God* blesse thee, poore Orphane! . . . . . *S.C.* May 191
The *God* of shepheards, Tityrus, is dead, ... *S.C.* Jun. 81
God shield, man, that I should clime, ... *S.C.* Jul. 9
wonned not the great *God* Pan Upon Mount Olivet, ... *S.C.* Jul. 49
To Kerke the narre, from *God* more farre, ... *S.C.* Jul. 97
(thanked be *God* therefore) . . . . . *S.C.* Jul. 169
So hath theyr *god* them blist; . . . . . *S.C.* Jul. 174
Shepheards sich, *God* mought us many send, ... *S.C.* S. 178
God shield, man, he should so ill have thrive, ... *S.C.* S. 226

God—*Continued.*
were Hobbinoll as *God* mought please, ... *S.C.* S. 252
Ah, Hobbinoll! *God* mought it thee requite; . . . . . *S.C.* S. 258
'O soveraigne Pan! thou *god* of shepheards all, ... *S.C.* D. 7
The shepheards *God* (perdie *God* was he none) . . . . . *S.C.* D. 50
dauncing all in companie, Adorne that *God:* . . . . . *Gn.* 28
Of him his *God* is worshipt with his sythe, ... *Gn.* 129
Content with any food that *God* doth send; . . . . . *Gn.* 140
What *God* or Fortune would assist his might. . . . . . *Gn.* 301
whether *God* or Fortune made him bold . . . . . *Gn.* 302
(*God* give them paine!) . . . . . *Hub.* 304
And yet (*God* wote) small oddes I often see . . . . . *Hub.* 373
little els (*God* wote) could thereof skill; . . . . . *Hub.* 381
hatefull heresies, of *God* abhor'd: . . . . . *Hub.* 389
An easie life, and fit high *God* to please. . . . . . *Hub.* 395
Such grace did *God* unto his creatures give. . . . . . *Hub.* 402
God it is that feedes them with his grace, ... *Hub.* 437
All shalbe taught of *God.* . . . . . *Hub.* 440
That before *God* we may appeare more gay, ... *Hub.* 462
hath a zealous disposition To *God,* . . . . . *Hub.* 492
manie eke of them (*God* wote) are driven . . . . . *Hub.* 539
mocke high *God* himselfe, whom they professe? . . . . . *Hub.* 843
what car'd he for *God,* or godlinesse? . . . . . *Hub.* 844
That curse *God* send unto mine enemie! . . . . . *Hub.* 914
Let *God* . . . care for the manie, ... *Hub.* 1195
the *God* of goodly Arts: . . . . . *T.M.* 58
God himselfe for wisedome most is praised, ... *T.M.* 89
men to *God* thereby are nighest raised. . . . . . *T.M.* 90
thy gay Sonne, that winged *God* of Love, ... *T.M.* 401
what to man, and what to *God,* wee owe. . . . . . *T.M.* 504
the blindfoulded pretie *God,* that feathered Archer, ... *Tetrasticon* 1
Living, on *God* and on thy selfe relie; . . . . . *Ti.* 209
hope of heaven, and heart to *God* inclinde; . . . . . *Ti.* 585
The Archer *God,* the sonne of Cytheree, ... *Mui.* 98
none, except a *God,* or *God* him guide, ... *Mui.* 223
Before them stands the *God* of Seas in place, ... *Mui.* 313
The which the Lemnian *God* framde craftily, ... *Mui.* 370
God his gifts there plenteously bestowes, ... *Col.* 326
I weened sure he was our *God* alone, ... *Col.* 773
that *God,* that is so greatly dred; . . . . . *Col.* 798
of that *God* the Priest thou shouldest bee, ... *Col.* 832
nor *God* nor man can fynd Defence, ... *Col.* 875
A monster vile, whom *God* and man does hate: . . . . . I. i. 13. 7
God helpe the man so wrapt in Errours . . . traine! . . . . I. i. 18. 9
forward on his way (with *God* to frend) . . . . . I. i. 28. 7
highest *God,* the Lord of life and light: . . . . . I. i. 37. 6
The *God* obayde; and, calling forth . . . A diverse Dreame . I. i. 44. 1
the blind *God* that doth me thus amate, ... I. i. 51. 4
He . . . cared not for *God* or man a point. . . . . . I. ii. 12. 9
ever most adord As the *God* of my life? . . . . . I. iii. 7. 9
of his wicked pelfe his *God* he made, ... I. iv. 27. 6
him as onely *God* to call upon; . . . . . I. v. 47. 3
Antiochus, the which advaunst His cursed hand gainst *God,* . I. v. 47. 9
scornd of *God* and man, a shamefull death he dide. . . . . I. v. 48. 9
unto their *God* present That flowre of fayth . . . . . I. vi. 15. 4
The *God* himselfe, . . . Stood long amazd, ... I. vi. 15. 6
blessed sprites, . . . To *God* for vengeance cryde continually; I. viii. 36. 7
Their *God* . . . Shott many a dart . . . . . I. ix. 10. 7
We met that villen, (*God* from him me blesse!) . . . . . I. ix. 28. 3
God you never let his charmed speaches heare!' . . . . . I. ix. 30. 9
thankt be *God,* and her encrease so evermore!' . . . . . I. x. 16. 9
Of *God;* of grace; of justice; of freewill; . . . . . I. x. 19. 6
Almightie *God* her gave such powre and puissaunce great. . . I. x. 20. 9
The grace of *God* he layd up still in store, ... I. x. 38. 6
The images of *God* in earthly clay; . . . . . I. x. 39. 7
God to us forgiveth every howre . . . . . I. x. 40. 6
Ah, dearest *God,* me graunt, ... I. x. 42. 9
Of *God* and goodnes was his meditation. . . . . . I. x. 46. 9
God he often saw from heavens hight: . . . . . I. x. 47. 2
Such one as that same mighty man of *God,* . . . . . I. x. 53. 2
writt in stone . . . by the hand of *God,* . . . . . I. x. 53. 7
The new Hierusalem, that *God* has built . . . . . I. x. 57. 2
More dear unto their *God* then younglings to their dam.' . . I. x. 57. 9
'so *God* me grace, ... I. x. 64. 1
The *God* of warre with his fiers equipage . . . . . I. xi. 6. 7
I this man of *God* his godly armes may blaze. . . . . . I. xi. 7. 9
gan to highest *God* entirely pray . . . . . I. xi. 32. 4
(eternall *God* that chaunce did guide) . . . . . I. xi. 45. 6
Great *God* it planted in that blessed stedd . . . . . I. xi. 46. 7
God she praysd, and thankt her faithfull knight, ... I. xi. 55. 8
well arrived are, (high *God* be blest!) . . . . . I. xii. 17. 8
High *God* be witnesse that I guiltlesse ame; . . . . . I. xii. 30. 6
Would *God!* thy selfe now present were in place . . . . . II. i. 9. 8
God ye speed and send you good successe, ... II. i. 25. 6
'Fayre sonne, *God* give you happy chaunce, ... II. i. 31. 7
God guide thee, Guyon, well to end thy warke, ... II. i. 32. 8
'Such and such evil *God* on Guyon reare, ... II. i. 61. 5
high *God* . . . Imprinted had that token . . . . . II. ii. 4. 3
Before her gate high *God* did Sweate ordaine, ... II. iii. 41. 5
the blinded *god* his lustfull fyre To kindle . . . . . II. iii. 23. 6
Ah *God!* what horrour and tormenting griefe . . . . . II. iv. 28. 6
'*God* of the world and worldlings I me call, ... II. vii. 8. 1
Great Mammon, greatest *god* below the skye, ... II. vii. 8. 2
Eternall *God* thee save from such decay! . . . . . II. vii. 34. 7
As if the highest *God* defy he would: . . . . . II. vii. 40. 5
The *God,* though loth, yet was constraynd t' obay; . . . . . II. vii. 66. 1
highest *God* that loves his creatures so, ... II. viii. 1. 6
why should hevenly *God* to men have such regard? . . II. viii. 2. 9
'The charge, which *God* doth unto me arrett, ... II. viii. 8. 1
So streightly *God* doth judge. . . . . . II. viii. 29. 6

God's—*Continued.*
Those for *Gods* sake his dewty was to entertaine. . . . . . . I. x. 37. 9
The wondrous workmanship of *Gods* owne mould, ... I. x. 42. 6
For *Gods* deare love be not so wilfull bent, ... II. i. 16. 2
Of all *Gods* workes which doe this worlde adorne, ... II. ix. 1. 1
Of *Gods* high praise, and of their loves sweet teene, ... III. v. 40. 4
Such as the Angels weare before *Gods* tribunall! . . . . . . III. v. 53. 9
by *Gods* grace, and her good heedinesse, ... V. vi. 34. 6
Next gan Religion gainst her to impute High *Gods* beheast, . V. ix. 44. 6
The flesh of men, to *Gods* owne likenesse framed, ... V. x. 28. 7
her selfe she wholy recommended To *Gods* sole grace, ... VI. iv. 10. 8
And sit in *Gods* owne seat without commission; . . . . . . *H.H.L.* 82
Angels and Archangels, which attend On *Gods* owne person, . *H.H.B.* 98
beautie . . . Sparkled on her from *Gods* owne glorious face, . *H.H.B.* 207
Of *Gods* high praise, that filles the brasen sky; . . . . . . *H.H.B.* 263

Gods. *See* **Fellow-gods, Sea-gods, Wood-gods.**
rest the gift of *Gods* . . . . *Bel.*[1] i. 1
The place where is the temple of the *Gods*, ... *Bel.*[1] vi. 8
erst of *Gods* and man I worshipt was? . . . . *Bel.*[1] viii. 8
flie up to the throne of *Gods*, ... *Bel.*[1] ix. 6
In majestie she seemde to matche the *Gods*. . . . . *Bel.*[1] xi. 6
Gods and men my honour up did raise? . . . . *Bel.*[2] x. 8
up to the throne of *Gods* did flie, ... *Bel.*[2] xi. 6
Did seeme to match the *Gods* in Majestie. . . . . *Bel.*[2] xv. 6
Proud that so manie *Gods* she brought to light; . . . . . . *Ro.* vi. 3
So did the *Gods* by heavenly doome decree, ... *Ro.* vi. 11
Ye cruell starres, and eke ye *Gods* unkinde, ... *Ro.* ix. 1
fight against the *Gods* of heavenly berth, ... *Ro.* xii. 3
Gods secure feare not her force at all. . . . . *Ro.* xii. 14
Nor wrath of *Gods*, nor spight of men unstable, ... *Ro.* xiii. 7
the Giaunts did the *Gods* assay; . . . . *Ro.* xvii. 4
'Ye *Gods* of love, that pitie lovers payne, ... *S.C.* Ja. 13
(If any *gods* the paine of lovers pitie) . . . . *S.C.* Ja. 14
Is graunted scarce to *Gods* above. *S.C.*Mar.Emb.2
cruell fate And angry *Gods* pursue . . . . *S.C.* Jun. 15
why weary we the *Gods* with playnts, ... *S.C.* N. 173
There lives shee with the blessed *Gods* in blisse, ... *S.C.* N. 194
honor now of highest *gods* she is, ... *S.C.* N. 197
did the bankets of the *Gods* bewray, ... *Gn.* 386
scorning to the sacred *Gods* to pray, ... *Gn.* 390
Heare, thou great Father of the *Gods* on hie, ... *T.M.* 55
What wrath of *Gods*, or wicked influence . . . . *T.M.* 481
with the *Gods*, . . . On Nectar and Ambrosia do feede. . . . . *Ti.* 398
Twelve *Gods* doo sit around in royall state, ... *Mui.* 307
Each of the *Gods*, by his like visnomie . . . . *Mui.* 310
all the *Gods*, which saw his wondrous might, ... *Mui.* 318
That all the *Gods* admir'd: . . . . *Mui.* 327
all the *Gods* with common mockerie Might laugh . . . . . . *Mui.* 372
as the mother of the *Gods*, that sought For faire Eurydice, . . *D.* 463
The *gods*, which all things see, this same beheld, ... *As.* 181
him the greatest of the *Gods* we deeme, ... *Col.* 799
shortly was of all the *Gods* the first. . . . . *Col.* 806
Through judgement of the *gods* to been ywroken, ... *Col.* 921
the which, . . . The *gods* stand gazing on, ... I. iv. 17. 6
that great house of *Gods* caelestiall, ... I. v. 22. 4
what of *gods* then boots it to be borne, ... I. v. 23. 6
to the hous of hevenly *gods* it raught: . . . . I. vii. 18. 2
doe the temple of the *Gods* support, ... II. iii. 28. 2
To weete which of the *gods* I shall thee name, ... II. iii. 33. 8
From whence the *gods* have her for envy thrust: . . . . . . II. vii. 49. 6
Apple . . . emongst the *gods* false Ate threw; . . . . II. vii. 55. 5
Accusing highest Jove and *gods* ingrate; . . . . II. vii. 60. 7
Cursing his *Gods*, and him selfe damning deepe: . . . . II. viii. 37. 2
all the *Gods* admird his lofty note. . . . . II. x. 3. 5
Ida, where the *Gods* lov'd to repayre, ... II. xii. 52. 6
In which the *Gods* doe dwell eternally; . . . . III. iv. 43. 5
(Black Herebus, thy husband, is the foe Of all the *Gods*,) . . III. iv. 55. 8
whose sad annoy The *Gods* doe dread, ... III. vi. 24. 8
Yet pitty often did the *gods* relent, ... III. vi. 40. 1
hid from the world, and from the skill Of Stygian *Gods*, . . . III. vi. 46. 7
With many of the *Gods* in company . . . . III. vi. 49. 2
Pleasure, that doth both *gods* and men aggrate, ... III. vi. 50. 8
angry *Gods* and cruell skie . . . . III. ix. 33. 4
the which made Batteill against the *Gods*, ... III. xi. 22. 9
fought Gainst all the *Gods* . . . . III. xi. 29. 7
Unto the Victor of the Gods this bee: . . . . III. xi. 49. 2
Farre from the view of *gods* and heavens bliss, ... IV. ii. 47. 8
Not all the *gods* can chaunge, ... IV. ii. 51. 9
As one in feare the Stygian *gods* t' offend, ... IV. iii. 32. 2
Devized by the *Gods*, for to asswage Harts grief, ... IV. iii. 43. 2
Are by the *Gods* to drinck thereof assynd; . . . . IV. iii. 43. 8
there made *gods*, though borne of mortall berth, ... IV. iii. 44. 3
Before that they in blisse amongst the *Gods* were plaste. . . IV. iii. 44. 9
all the *gods* did mone her miserable case. . . . . IV. vii. 30. 9
named To all the heathen *Gods*, ... IV. x. 30. 9
The joy of *Gods* and men, ... IV. x. 44. 2
Old Styx the Grandame of the *Gods*, ... IV. xi. 4. 5
for the *Gods* in Proteus house be made: . . . . IV. xi. 9. 2
that great banquet of the watry *Gods*, ... IV. xi. 10. 8
could the ledden of the *gods* unfold; . . . . IV. xi. 19. 2
Like as the mother of the *Gods*, ... IV. xi. 28. 1
Of *Gods*, of Nymphs, of rivers, yet unred; . . . . IV. xii. 2. 7
The manner of the *Gods* when they at banquet be. . . . . . . IV. xii. 3. 9
Ne with th' eternall *Gods* to bancket come; . . . . IV. xii. 4. 4
'Ye *Gods* of seas, if any *Gods* at all Have care of right, . . . IV. xii. 9. 1
leaving watry *gods*, as booting nought, ... IV. xii. 25. 2
place deserved with the *Gods* on hy. . . . . V. ii. 1. 7
With which the *Gods* themselves are mylder made: . . . . . . V. v. 49. 4
That *Gods* and men doe equally adore, ... V. vii. 1. 2
doth true justice deale To his inferiour *Gods*, ... V. vii. 1. 7

Gods—*Continued.*
the earth . . . Wroth with the *Gods*, ... V. vii. 10. 7
To make new warre against the *Gods* againe. . . . . V. vii. 11. 6
Can from th' immortall *Gods* ought hidden bee? . . . . V. vii. 21. 6
blasphemies forth threw Against his *Gods*, ... V. xi. 12. 4
A dreadfull feend, of *gods* and men ydrad, ... V. xii. 37. 8
by the *Gods* with paine Planted in earth, ... VI. Pr. 3. 5
For love amongst the woodie *Gods* to dwell) . . . . VI. ii. 26. 3
thought that those brave imps were sowen Here by the *Gods*, VI. iv. 36. 8
Whom *Gods* doe hate, and heavens abhor to see; . . . . . . VI. vi. 10. 2
'To her the *Gods* . . . appointed have her place . . . . VI. vi. 11. 1
What could the *Gods* doe more, ... VI. vii. 31. 9
the *Gods*, that mortall follies vew, ... VI. vii. 32. 1
so sacred threasure Vow'd to the *gods:* . . . . VI. viii. 43. 9
as well of *Gods* as Men To be the Soveraine. . . . . VII. vi. Arg.
her selfe began to reare Gainst all the *Gods*, ... VII. vi. 1. 9
by her disposed diversly To *Gods* and men, ... VII. vi. 3. 6
(which none yet durst Of *Gods* or men to alter . . . . VII. vi. 5. 6
unto *Gods*, whose state she did maligne, ... VII. vi. 11. 6
unto the king of *Gods* to plaine. . . . . VII. vi. 14. 9
The father of the *Gods* . . . . VII. vi. 15. 6
make both *Gods* and hellish fiends affraid: . . . . VII. vi. 18. 3
With all the *Gods* about him congregate: . . . . VII. vi. 19. 5
whil'st the *Gods* . . . Were troubled, ... VII. vi. 23. 1
the *Gods* she found in counsell close, ... VII. vi. 24. 2
Grand-mother magnifide Of all the *Gods*, ... VII. vi. 26. 6
I greater am . . . Then all the *Gods*, ... VII. vi. 26. 9
the *Gods*, that gave good eare . . . . VII. vi. 28. 1
tall as any there Of all the *Gods*, ... VII. vi. 28. 4
if *Gods* should strive with flesh yfere, ... VII. vi. 31. 7
behight Father of *Gods* and men . . . . VII. vi. 35. 5
The *gods* then us'd . . . Oft to resort there-to, ... VII. vi. 38. 4
With whom the woody *Gods* did oft consort, ... VII. vi. 39. 8
The *gods* assembled all on Arlo Hill; . . . . VII. vii. 3. 2
Then any of the *gods* or Powers on hie: . . . . VII. vii. 5. 4
since the day That all the *gods* whylome assembled were . . VII. vii. 12. 2
all the *gods* were ravisht with delight . . . . VII. vii. 12. 8
gods no more then men thou doest esteeme; . . . . VII. vii. 15. 8
even the *gods* to thee, as men to *gods*, do seeme. . . . . . VII. vii. 15. 9
These *gods* do claime the worlds whole soverainty, ... VII. vii. 16. 2
mauger Jove, and all his *gods* beside, ... VII. vii. 17. 1
these, that *Gods* themselves do call, ... VII. vii. 26. 2
heavens gate (whence all the *gods* issued) . . . . VII. vii. 45. 7
them we *gods* do rule, and in them also thee. . . . . VII. vii. 48. 9
all the *Gods* in councell did agree . . . . *Am.* xxiv. 9
the *gods*, in theyr revengefull yre, ... *Am.* xxviii. 11
all the *gods* he threats with thundring dart: . . . . *Am.* xxxix. 4
suffrest neyther *gods* in sky, Nor men in earth, to rest: . . . *Epig.* iv. 15
ye high heavens, the temple of the *gods*, ... *Epith.* 409
Victor of *gods*, subduer of mankynd, ... *H.L.* 45
Ah, *Gods!* that ever ye that monster placed . . . . *H.L.* 271
lie like *Gods* in yvorie beds arayd, ... *H.L.* 285
name then would I raise Bove all the *gods*, ... *H.L.* 304
Like *Gods* with Nectar in their bankets free; . . . . *H.B.* 249

Gods'. *See* **Sea-gods'.**
she raught the *Gods* owne mansions: . . . . *Bel.*[2] vii. 8
Seeking to kisse her, brok'st the *Gods* decree, ... *Gn.* 471
whether through the *Gods* decree, ... *Gn.* 569
wonts to decke the *Gods* immortall crew . . . . *Hub.* 1268
As for the *gods* owne principality, ... VII. vii. 16. 5

Goemagot, Goemot. *See* **Gogmagog.**

Goes. He to his studie *goes;* . . . . I. i. 36. 7
to the wood she *goes*, to serve her turne, ... I. vi. 22. 3
when the oyle is spent, The light *goes* out, ... II. x. 30. 2
Full fast she flies, and farre afore him *goes*, ... IV. vii. 21. 8
He where he list *goes* loose, ... IV. xii. 11. 4
She *goes* to seeke him, ... V. vi. Arg.

Goeth. he *goeth* to that soveraine Queene; . . . . I. v. 16. 1
nought regarding her displeasure, forward *goth*. . . . . . . II. xii. 57. 9
with whom now she *goth* In lovely wise, ... IV. i. 47. 5
upon them *goth* As on the ground, ... IV. xi. 14. 5
each estate quite out of order *goth?* . . . . V. ii. 37. 3
some doe say it *goeth* downe to hell: . . . . V. ix. 6. 5
with presumpteous powre against that knight streight *go'th*. VI. ii. 17. 9
And carelesly into the river *goth*, ... VI. iii. 33.3
forth on his journey *goth*. . . . . VI. iii. 45. 9
He *goth* on foote all armed by her side, ... VI. iii. 46. 1

Gogh. *See* **Y scuith gogh.**

Gogmagog. besprincled with the gore Of mighty *Goemot*, . . . II. x. 10. 8
the great *Goemagot* of strong Corineus, ... III. ix. 50. 3

Gold. an hundred steps of purest *golde*. . . . . *Bel.*[1] ii. 8
the bases were of richest *golde*, ... *Bel.*[1] iv. 2
with fine perle and *golde* puft up in heart. . . . . *Rev.* ii. 7
The houses *golde*, the pavement precious stone. . . . . . . *Rev.* iv. 11
Golde was the parget; . . . . *Bel.* ii. 9
foure great Lyons of *gold* (*golde*[1]) . . . . *Bel.* iii. 10
shine all scaly with great plates of *golde;* . . . . *Bel.*[2] ii. 10
The sailes of *golde*, of silke the tackle were: . . . . *Pet.* ii. 3
As snowe and *golde* together had been wrought: . . . . *Pet.* vi. 6
shields of brasse that shone like burnisht *golde*, ... *Van.* vi. 3
Ygyrt with belts of glitterand *gold*, ... *S.C.* Jul. 177
So you may buye *golde* to deere. . . . . *S.C.* Au. 108
golde, which underlayes The summer beames, ... *Gn.* 99
paint with pallid greene her buds of *gold*. . . . . *Gn.* 222
On everie side did shine like scalie *golde*. . . . . *Gn.* 261
this might better be the world of *gold;* . . . . *Hub.* 152
without *golde* now nothing wilbe got, ... *Hub.* 153
Enchaste with chaine and circulet of *golde*. . . . . *Hub.* 624
To register, and sound in trump of *gold*, ... *T.M.* 98
her yeolow locks, like wyrie *gold* . . . . *Ti.* 10

Gold—*Continued.*
Adornd with purest *golde* and precious stone; *Ti.* 86
I saw an Image, all of massie *gold,* *Ti.* 491
Then did I see a Bridge, made all of *golde,* *Ti.* 547
Made of *golde* and costlie yvorie, *Ti.* 605
Adorned all with costly cloth of *gold,* *Ti.* 632
Lastly I saw an Arke of purest *golde* *Ti.* 659
pearles of Ynde, or *gold* of Opher, *Col.* 490
Then got he bow and shafts of *gold* and lead, *Col.* 807
Purfled with *gold* and pearle of rich assay; I. ii. 13. 3
Ne spared he to give her *gold* and rings; I. iii. 18. 8
Queene . . . In glistring *gold* and perelesse pretious stone; I. iv. 8. 6
she comes, . . . Adorned all with *gold* and girlonds gay, I. iv. 17. 2
Avarice . . . did ride, Uppon a Camell loaden all with *gold;* I. iv. 27. 2
he gnasht his teeth to see Those heapes of *gold* I. iv. 31. 7
Adornd with *gold* and jewels shining cleare, I. v. 21. 2
in garments gilt And gorgeous *gold* arayd, I. v. 26. 8
He gave her *gold* and purple pall to weare, I. vii. 16. 3
hilts were burnisht *gold,* and handle strong Of mother perle; I. vii. 30. 8
His haughtie Helmet, horrid all with *gold,* I. vii. 31. 1
With sprincled pearle and *gold* full richly drest, I. vii. 32. 3
an horne . . . in twisted *gold* And tasselles gay. I. viii. 3. 6
With royall arras, and resplendent *gold,* I. viii. 35. 2
a boxe . . . Embowd with *gold* and gorgeous ornament, I. ix. 19. 2
nor for *gold* nor glee will I abyde By you, I. ix. 32. 7
in her right hand bore a cup of *gold,* I. x. 13. 2
on her head she wore a tyre of *gold,* I. x. 31. 5
nor would for *gold* or fee Be wonne I. x. 43. 6
princely gifts of yvory and *gold,* I. xii. 12. 6
With silkin curtens and *gold* coverletts, II. vi. 16. 6
His yron cote . . . Was underneath enveloped with *gold;* II. vii. 4. 2
Great heapes of *gold* that never could be spent; II. vii. 5. 2
Fountaines of *gold* and silver to abownd, II. vii. 17. 5
life for *gold* engage. II. vii. 18. 5
so much *gold* Thou canst preserve II. vii. 20. 3
massy *gold* of glorious guifte, II. vii. 28. 4
Both roofe, and floore, and walls, were all of *gold,* II. vii. 29. 1
a broad gate all built of beaten *gold:* II. vii. 40. 2
She held a great *gold* chaine ylincked well, II. vii. 46. 2
planted there did bring forth fruit of *gold;* II. vii. 54. 7
Why takest not of that same fruite of *gold?* II. vii. 63. 7
gold al is not that doth golden seeme; II. viii. 14. 5
Braunched with *gold* and perle most richly wrought, II. ix. 19. 4
skirt with *gold* Was fretted all about, II. ix. 37. 1
he first wore crowne of *gold* for dignity. II. x. 39. 9
otherwhiles, with *gold* besprinkeled, II. xii. 45. 8
some were of burnisht *gold,* II. xii. 55. 1
In her left hand a Cup of *gold* she held, II. xii. 56. 1
of purest *gold* was spred A trayle of yvie II. xii. 61. 1
Her garments all were wrought of beaten *gold,* III. i. 15. 6
glistred all with *gold* and glorious shew, III. i. 41. 3
with *gold* and Ermines faire enveloped. III. i. 59. 9
round about yfretted all with *gold,* III. ii. 25. 4
That fame in tromp of *gold* eternally displayes. III. iii. 3. 9
All fretted round with *gold,* and goodly wel beseene. III. iii. 58. 9
would not stay For *gold,* or perles, or pretious stones, III. iv. 18. 8
Gold, amber, yvorie, perles, owches, rings, III. iv. 23. 5
'Royally clad' (quoth he) 'in cloth of *gold,* III. v. 5. 2
The one of yron, the other of bright *gold,* III. vi. 31. 3
loves his fetters, though they were of *gold.* III. ix. 8. 5
goodly arras . . . Woven with *gold* and silke, III. xi. 28. 3
made the sparckling waves . . . flame with *gold;* III. xi. 41. 4
there stood an Image all alone Of massy *gold,* III. xi. 47. 5
Some headed with sad lead, some with pure *gold;* III. xi. 48. 4
with pure *gold* it all was overlayd, III. xi. 51. 4
her fayre lockes were woven up in *gold:* III. xii. 13. 4
Without adorne of *gold* or silver bright, III. xii. 20. 2
With *gold* and many a gorgeous ornament, IV. iii. 38. 7
Bearing that precious relicke in an arke Of *gold,* IV. iv. 15. 3
Unto the vulgar for good *gold* insted, IV. v. 15. 4
perfect *gold* surmounts the meanest brasse. IV. ix. 2. 9
all her gowne Enwoven was with *gold,* IV. x. 31. 9
Nor shining *gold,* nor mouldring clay it was; IV. x. 39. 5
With nimble wings of *gold* and purple hew; IV. x. 42. 3
quaile in conquest of that land of *gold.* IV. xi. 22. 5
garnisht all with *gold* upon the blade V. i. 10. 3
Whilest he to gathering of the *gold* did fall: V. ii. 23. 8
whereas she hidden lay Under an heape of *gold.* V. ii. 25. 6
her suppliant hands, those hands of *gold,* V. ii. 26. 6
Basted with bends of *gold* on every side, V. v. 3. 2
His Lyons skin chaungd to a pall of *gold,* V. v. 24. 7
all dispred With shining *gold,* V. vii. 5. 5
Uppon her head she wore a Crowne of *gold;* V. vii. 6. 6
Moone-like Mitre to a Crowne of *gold;* V. vii. 13. 6
royall gifts of *gold* and silver wrought V. vii. 24. 4
all their tops bright glistering with *gold,* V. ix. 21. 7
Upon a throne of *gold* full bright and sheene, V. ix. 27. 5
Not of rich tissew, nor of cloth of *gold,* V. ix. 28. 2
Glistring like *gold* amongst the plights enrold, V. ix. 28. 7
There he that Idoll saw of massy *gold* V. xi. 21. 8
For guiftes of *gold* or any worldly glee, V. xi. 63. 3
Dearer is love then life, and fame then *gold;* V. xi. 63. 8
to thinke *gold* that is bras; VI. Pr. 5. 7
taking from her hand a ring of *gould,* VI. i. 29. 2
Pinckt upon *gold,* and paled part per part, VI. ii. 6. 2
So forth he drew much *gold,* and toward him it drive. VI. ix. 32. 9
offred store of *gold:* VI. xi. 14. 6
In garment all of *gold* downe to the ground; VII. vii. 37. 2
wings of *gold* fit to employ. VII. vii. 46. 9
If *Gold,* her locks are finest *Gold* on ground; *Am.* xv. 11

Gold—*Continued.*
under a net of *gold;* *Am.* xxxvii. 2
which is *gold,* or heare, may scarse be told? *Am.* xxxvii. 4
And with ten thousand gemmes of shyning *gold,*) *H.H.L.* 60
on her head a crowne of purest *gold* Is set, *H.H.B.* 190
Golden. shine all scaly with fine *golden* plates. *Bel.*[1] ii. 10
With *golden* wings in habite of a Nymph. *Bel.*[1] iv. 6
Renting hir faire visage and *golden* haire, *Bel.*[1] viii. 4
sodain dropping of a *golden* shoure *Bel.*[1] ix. 11
shining land, That *golden* Pactol drives *Bel.*[1] x. 4
in this *golden* vessel couched weare The ashes *Bel.* iii. 7
outraging her cheekes and *golden* haire, *Bel.*[2] x. 3
bottome yeallow, like the *golden* grayle *Bel.*[2] xii. 3
With purple wings, and crest of *golden* hewe; *Pet.* v. 2
Atcheived the *golden* Fleece in Colchid land, *Ro.* x. 2
'I sawe Phoebus thrust out his *golden* hedde, *S.C.* Ap. 73
To crowne her *golden* locks: *S.C.* Jun. 46
betweene the Cuppe And *golden* Diademe: *S.C.* Jul. 20
The *golden* ofspring of Latona pure, *Gn.* 13
his *golden* Charet glistering light; *Gn.* 67
Whom *golden* Fleece did make an heavenly signe; *Gn.* 211
Vesper in his timely howre From *golden* Oeta *Gn.* 316
That was the *golden* age of Saturne old, *Hub.* 151
So well his *golden* Circlet him beseemeth. *Hub.* 627
The *golden* brood of great Apolloes wit, *T.M.* 2
all her Sisters rent their *golden* heares, *T.M.* 111
golden Trompet of eternitie, *T.M.* 458
now I will my *golden* Clarion rend, *T.M.* 463
do those men in *golden* thrones repose, *Ti.* 370
the puissant brood Of *golden* girt Alcmena, *Ti.* 380
Fame with *golden* wings aloft doth flie, *Ti.* 421
so silken soft And *golden* faire, *Mui.* 108
In whose brave mynd, as in a *golden* cofer, *Col.* 488
from a *golden* Censer forth doth rise, *Col.* 609
With price whereof they buy a *golden* bell, *Col.* 725
To tast the streames that, like a *golden* showre, *Ded. Son.* viii. 9
hath writ her owne record In *golden* verse, *Ded. Son.* xii. 4
For thereunto doth need a *golden* quill, *Ded.Son.*xvi.10
Whose bridle rung with *golden* bels and bosses brave. I. ii. 13. 9
golden Phoebus, . . . Hurled his beame so scorching I. ii. 29. 3
golden foile all over them displaid, I. iv. 4. 4
strove to match, . . . Great Junoes *golden* chayre; I. iv. 17. 5
the *golden* Orientall gate Of greatest heaven I. v. 2. 1
buckled with a *golden* tong. I. vii. 30. 9
a Dragon . . . over all did spredd His *golden* winges: I. vii. 31. 5
Phoebus *golden* face it did attaint, I. vii. 34. 6
Gehons *golden* waves doe wash continually: I. vii. 43. 9
Then tooke the angrie witch her *golden* cup, I. viii. 14. 1
Her *golden* cup she cast unto the ground, I. viii. 25. 2
golden chayne, wherewith yfere The vertues linked are I. ix. 1. 1
The *golden* Sunne his glistring head gan shew, I. ix. 18. 2
writt with *golden* letters rich and brave: I. ix. 19. 8
tore Her guiltlesse garments and her *golden* heare, I. x. 28. 6
gan the *golden* Phoebus for to steepe His fierie face I. xi. 31. 1
Her *golden* locks for hast were loosely shed I. xi. 51. 5
Her looser *golden* lockes he rudely rent, II. i. 11. 5
Her *golden* lockes most cruelly she rent, II. i. 15. 4
'with *golden* squire . . . can measure out a meane; II. i. 58. 1
The face of *golden* Meane: II. ii. Arg.
He left his loftie steed with *golden* sell II. ii. 11. 6
Her *golden* lockes she roundly did uptye II. ii. 15. 7
rode in *golden* sell with single spere, II. iii. 12. 3
besprinckled was throughout With *golden* aygulets, II. iii. 26. 7
Was hemd with *golden* fringe. II. iii. 26. 9
All bard with *golden* bendes, II. iii. 27. 4
Knit with a *golden* bauldricke, II. iii. 29. 5
Her yellow lockes, crisped like *golden* wyre, II. iii. 30. 1
idle offers of thy *golden* fee; II. vii. 9. 7
his busy paines applyde To melt the *golden* metall, II. vii. 35. 9
he himselfe was all of *golden* mould, II. vii. 40. 7
Many great *golden* pillours did upbeare The massy roofe, II. vii. 43. 5
Their fruit were *golden* apples glistring bright, II. vii. 54. 1
Here also sprong that goodly *golden* fruit, II. vii. 55. 1
Here eke that famous *golden* Apple grew, II. vii. 55. 4
they with *golden* pineons cleave The flitting skyes, II. viii. 2. 3
His snowy front, curled with *golden* heares, II. viii. 5. 5
gold al is not that doth *golden* seeme; II. viii. 14. 5
Her yellow *golden* heare Was trimly woven II. ix. 19. 6
Elfiline enclosd it with a *golden* wall. II. x. 72. 9
His goodly conquest of the *golden* fleece, II. xii. 44. 6
th' yvorie in *golden* mantle gownd: II. xii. 67. 5
a Lion passant in a *golden* field. III. i. 4. 9
with that *golden* chaine of concord tyde. III. i. 12. 8
To crowne his *golden* lockes with honour dew; III. i. 35. 5
all the gravell mixt with *golden* owre: III. iv. 18. 6
now the *golden* Hesperus Was mounted high III. iv. 51. 6
Her *golden* lockes, that late in tresses bright Embreaded were III. vi. 18. 6
With *golden* wreath and gorgeous ornament; III. vii. 11. 3
her *golden* girdle, which did fall From her in flight, III. vii. 31. 8
The *golden* ribband, which that virgin wore III. vii. 36. 1
Tyde with her *golden* girdle; III. viii. 2. 7
With *golden* wyre to weave her curled head; III. viii. 7. 6
golden wyre was not so yellow III. viii. 7. 7
I found her *golden* girdle cast astray, III. viii. 49. 8
Her *golden* locks, that were in trammells gay Upbounden, III. ix. 20. 4
shewe their *golden* gleames, III. ix. 20. 8
inly tickled with that *golden* vew. III. x. 30. 3
all that *golden* pray, . . . I loath III. x. 31. 4
Till drouping Phoebus gan to hyde his *golden* hedd. III. x. 45. 9
that doth his *golden* wings embay In blessed Nectar III. xi. 2. 3

Golden—*Continued.*
into a *golden* showre Him selfe he chaung'd, . . . III. xi. 31. 1
Whenas the God to *golden* hew him selfe transfard. . . . III. xi. 31. 9
The God himselfe rending his *golden* heare, . . . III. xi. 37. 7
Ease, on his robe in *golden* letters cyphered. . . . III. xii. 4. 9
her *golden* lockes, that were upbound . . . IV. i. 13. 2
The *golden* Apple, cause of all their wrong, . . . IV. i. 22. 5
All mindlesse of the *Golden* fleece, which made them strive. . . IV. i. 23. 9
that great *golden* chaine quite to divide, . . . IV. i. 30. 8
With *golden* words and goodly countenance, . . . IV. ii. 9. 2
Shall have that *golden* girdle for reward; . . . IV. ii. 27. 2
Yet all was forg'd and spred with *golden* foyle, . . . IV. ii. 29. 4
Combing her *golden* lockes, as seemd her good; . . . IV. ii. 45. 5
Her *golden* cup to them for drinke she raught, . . . IV. iii. 48. 8
Him needeth sure a *golden* pen, I weene, . . . IV. v. 12. 2
With *golden* foyle doth finely over-spred Some baser metall, . . IV. v. 15. 2
golden belt by doome of all Graunted to her, . . . IV. v. 16. 1
Like to a *golden* border did appeare, . . . IV. vi. 20. 3
it did glister like the *golden* sand, . . . IV. vi. 20. 7
with a litle *golden* chaine about it bound. . . . IV. viii. 6. 9
hangd on high with *golden* ribbands laced; . . . IV. x. 8. 5
With *golden* letters goodly well enchaced; . . . IV. x. 8. 7
Pactolus glistring with his *golden* flood; . . . IV. xi. 20. 8
it encompast round as with a *golden* fret. . . . IV. xi. 27. 9
from the *golden* age, that first was named, . . . V. Pr. 2. 1
With *golden* hands and silver feete beside, . . . V. ii. 10. 2
bore the Sunne brode blazed in a *golden* field. . . . V. iii. 14. 9
Artegall that *golden* belt uptooke, . . . V. iii. 27. 1
th' one hand seizing on his *golden* bit, . . . V. iii. 29. 6
As he with *golden* saddle is arayd, . . . V. iii. 35. 4
wrapt in fetters of a *golden* tresse, . . . V. viii. 1. 7
With *golden* giftes and many a guilefull word . . . V. xi. 50. 4
Downe on his *golden* feete he often gazed, . . . VI. viii. 26. 6
rends her *golden* locks, and snowy brests embrew. . . . VI. viii. 40. 9
I shall You well reward, and *golden* guerdon give, . . . VI. ix. 32. 6
What time the *golden* apple was unto him brought. . . . VI. ix. 36. 9
nor her *golden* haire Into their comely tresses dewly drest, . . VI. xii. 15. 3
lifting up her *golden* wand, . . . VII. vi. 13. 4
His hornes were gilden all with *golden* studs, . . . VII. vii. 33. 5
her *golden* tresses She doth attyre . . . *Am.* xxxvii. 1
entangle in that *golden* snare; . . . *Am.* xxxvii. 6
To covet fetters, though they *golden* bee! . . . *Am.* xxxvii. 14
Forgetfull of the famous *golden* fleece; . . . *Am.* xliv. 3
they are lyke but unto *golden* hookes, . . . *Am.* xlvii. 3
the fayre tresses of your *golden* hayre,) . . . *Am.* lxxiii. 3
Twoo *golden* apples of unvalewd price; . . . *Am.* lxxvii. 6
her fayre *golden* heares . . . ye waving chance to marke; . . *Am.* lxxxi. 1
enchased Your glorious name in *golden* moniment. . . . *Am.* lxxxii. 8
Her worth is written with a *golden* quill, . . . *Am.* lxxxiv. 10
His *golden* beame upon the hils doth spred, . . . *Epith.* 20
Her long loose yellow locks lyke *golden* wyre, . . . *Epith.* 154
Doe lyke a *golden* mantle her attyre; . . . *Epith.* 156
the bright evening-star with *golden* creast Appeare . . . *Epith.* 286
On *golden* plumes up to the purest skie, . . . *H.L.* 178
That *golden* wyre, those sparkling stars so bright, . . . *H.B.* 97
Love, lift me up upon thy *golden* wings, . . . *H.H.L.* 1
Cherubins, Which all with *golden* wings are overdight, . . . *H.H.B.* 93
Hesper, when his *golden* hayre . . . he hath bathed fayre, . . . *Proth.* 164

Golden-fleecy. For that same *golden fleecy* Ram, . . . V. Pr. 5. 6

Gold's. hundred steps of Afrike *golds* enchase: . . . *Bel.*[2] ii. 8

Golds. With Roses dight and *Goolds* and Daffadillies; . . . *Col.* 339

Goldsmith. As guilefull *Goldsmith* that by secret skill . . . IV. v. 15. 1

Goldsmith's. Framed in *goldsmithes* forge with cunning hand: IV. vi. 20. 4
goldsmithes cunning could not understand . . . IV. vi. 20. 5

Gondola. A litle *Gondelay*, bedecked trim . . . II. vi. 2. 7
There her small *Gondelay* her port did make, . . . II. vi. 11. 5

Gone. *See* **Go, Outgone, Overgone, Ygo.**
To see such pleasures *gon* so suddenly. . . . *Pet.*[2] iv. 14
When these sad sights were overpast and *gone*, . . . *Van.* xii. 1
after shee was *gone*, . . . *S.C.* May 235
her Kidde shee knewe well was *gone:* . . . *S.C.* May 300
yts time to be *gone*. . . . *S.C.* Au. 198
Now she is *gone* that safely did hem keepe: . . . *S.C.* N. 137
'Dido is *gone* afore; . . . *S.C.* N. 193
Out of the land is fled away and *gone*. . . . *Gn.* 360
O! all is *gone;* . . . *T.M.* 181
As if shee all to water would have *gone;* . . . *T.M.* 596
by my foes are now all spent and *gone;* . . . *Ti.* 88
'They all are *gone*, and all with them is *gone;* . . . *Ti.* 155
He now is *gone*, . . . *Ti.* 216
'He now is dead, and all his glorie *gone*, . . . *Ti.* 218
suddeinly both bed and all was *gone*, . . . *Ti.* 643
My Lyonesse (ah, woe is mee!) is *gon!* . . . *D.* 161
he quite is *gone*, Amyntas quite is *gone*, . . . *Col.* 433, 434
after Astrofell is dead and *gone:* . . . *Col.* 449
suddain all were *gone*. . . . I. i. 15. 9
when Satyres all were *gone* . . . I. vi. 33. 1
Dead sculls and bones of men whose life had *gone* astray. . . I. iv. 36. 9
their griefe is with them *gone:* . . . I. iv. 49. 2
And zealous haste away is quickly *gone* . . . II. i. 13. 2
Sith his good steed is lately from him *gone;* . . . II. iii. 3. 2
*Sometimes she laught, that nigh her breth was *gone*, . . . II. vi. 3. 4
all so soone as Guyon thence was *gon* . . . II. xi. 5. 1
when she saw them *gone* she forward went, . . . III. i. 19. 6
Taketh his nimble winges, and soone away is *gone*.' . . . III. i. 25. 9
The worde *gone* out she backe againe would call, . . . III. ii. 9. 1
After she had nine moneths fulfild and *gone:* . . . III. vi. 5. 5
As glad of that small rest as Bird of tempest *gon*. . . . III. vii. 10. 9
well they kent That their fayre guest was *gone*, . . . III. vii. 19. 8
after her are *gone* All the brave knightes . . . III. viii. 46. 6

Gone—*Continued.*
soone after they were *gone*, . . . III. ix. 12. 1
So beene they *gone* yfere, . . . III. x. 16. 8
whiles Jove to earth is *gone*.' . . . III. xi. 35. 9
when as she her selfe was lost and *gone*, . . . IV. ii. 26. 1
That was the Salvage Knight: but he was *gone*, . . . IV. v. 21. 6
so soone as they perceiv'd That she was *gone*, . . . IV. v. 28. 2
thought she wandred was, or *gone* astray: . . . IV. vi. 36. 7
none Equall to this, where ever I have *gone*. . . . IV. vii. 14. 5
When I was *gone*, soone after me she sent . . . V. viii. 23. 2
he farre was *gone* and past: . . . V. viii. 33. 6
Ne none can backe returne that once are *gone* amis. . . . V. ix. 6. 9
sith that he is *gone* irrevocable, . . . VI. ii. 15. 1
repentaunce for things past and *gon*. . . . VI. viii. 24. 5
Although his quest were farre afore him *gon:* . . . VI. ix. 12. 3
cleane were *gone*, which way he never knew; . . . VI. x. 18. 3
being *gone*, none can them bring in place, . . . VI. x. 20. 4
Sith they that were the cause of all were *gone:* . . . VI. xi. 20. 6
is of late far out of order *gone*. . . . VII. vii. 51. 4
Now it is night, ye damsels may be *gon*, . . . *Epith.* 311

Goneril. The eldest, *Gonorill*, gan to protest . . . II. x. 28. 1
A private life ledd in Albania With *Gonorill*, . . . II. x. 29. 8

Good. *See* **Good day, Goodwill.**
growes lifes fruite unto the Churches *good*. . . . *Rev.* iv. 14
heaven whence all *good* gifts do come, . . . *Bel.*[2] i. 8
Such was this Citie in her *good* daies fownd: . . . *Ro.* vi. 4
All the *good* hap of th' oldest times afore, . . . *Ro.* xix. 6
In which all *good* and evill was enclosed, . . . *Ro.* xix. 10
this age, in which all *good* is geason, . . . *Van.* i. 5
Griefe of *good* mindes, to see goodnesse disgraced! . . . *Van.* i. 8
Proud of his highest service, and *good* hap, . . . *Van.* iv. 3
From *good* to badd, and from badde to worse, . . . *S.C.* F. 12
So semest thou like *Good* Fryday to frowne: . . . *S.C.* F. 30
Cuddie, I wote thou kenst little *good*, . . . *S.C.* F. 85
What ever that *good* old man bespake. . . . *S.C.* F. 97
to scold And snebbe the *good* Oake, . . . *S.C.* F. 126
Submitting me to your *good* sufferance, . . . *S.C.* F. 187
the *good* man noulde stay his leasure, . . . *S.C.* F. 192
fiercely the *good* man at him did laye. . . . *S.C.* F. 214
(But now I trowe can better *good*,) . . . *S.C.* Mar. 56
Tell me, *good* Hobbinoll, what garres thee greete? . . . *S.C.* Ap. 1
their God his *good* does them send, . . . *S.C.* May 64
their *good* is ygoe, . . . *S.C.* May 67
Good is no *good*, but if it be spend; . . . *S.C.* May 71
God giveth *good* for none other end. . . . *S.C.* May 72
thilke God, that gave him that *good*, . . . S.C. May 85
So often times, when as *good* is meant, . . . *S.C.* May 101
her dame, that had *good* reason, . . . *S.C.* May 177
what shee thought *good:* . . . *S.C.* May 179
That some *good* body woulde once pitie mee!' . . . *S.C.* May 248
'Ah, *good* young maister!' . . . *S.C.* May 255
the Kidde made him *good* glee, . . . *S.C.* May 282
Teribinth, *good* for Gotes: . . . *S.C.* Jul. 86
Theyr *good* is with them goe: . . . *S.C.* Jul. 118
(Mought they *good* sheepeheards bene?) . . . *S.C.* Jul. 178
Here is a great deale of *good* matter Lost . . . *S.C.* Jul. 205
Ah! *good* Algrind! his hap was ill, . . . *S.C.* Jul. 229
Never knew I lovers sheepe in *good* plight: . . . *S.C.* Au. 20
With mery thing its *good* to medle sadde. . . . *S.C.* Au. 144
maken a Mart of theyr *good* name: . . . *S.C.* S. 37
To leave the *good*, that I had in hande, . . . *S.C.* S. 59
Ne in *good* nor goodnes taken delight, . . . *S.C.* S. 85
ought of the gotten *good* to restore: . . . *S.C.* S. 129
he call hem at theyr *good* choyce; . . . *S.C.* S. 143
not *good* Dogges hem needeth to chace, . . . *S.C.* S. 166
When the *good* old man used to sleepe. . . . *S.C.* S. 189
Too *good* for him had bene a great deale worse; . . . *S.C.* S. 213
good Hobbinoll, mought I thee praye Of ayde . . . *S.C.* S. 246
little *good* hath got, . . . *S.C.* O. 10
What *good* thereof to Cuddie can arise? . . . *S.C.* O. 18
to restraine The lust . . . with *good* advice, . . . *S.C.* O. 22
Reliven not for any *good*. . . . *S.C.* N. 89
to weete whats *good* or ill, . . . *S.C.* N. 183
A *good* old shepheard, Wrenock was his name, . . . *S.C.* D. 41
Adieu, *good* Hobbinoll, that was so true, . . . *S.C.* D. 155
good men, of whom thou oft are blest; . . . *Gn.* 62
whence no *good* commeth by; . . . *Gn.* 102
In steed of *good*, hastning his cruel fate. . . . *Gn.* 328
boasts his *good* event . . . *Gn.* 534
with *good* speed the fomie billowes scowre: . . . *Gn.* 564
His worke he shortly to *good* purpose brought, . . . *Gn.* 655
Amongst the rest a *good* old woman was, . . . *Hub.* 33
advaunced, For my *good* parts; . . . *Hub.* 64
I likewise have wasted much *good* time, . . . *Hub.* 75
Abroad, where change is, *good* may gotten bee.' . . . *Hub.* 101
all the rest doo rob of *good* and land. . . . *Hub.* 140
Sildome but some *good* commeth ere the end.' . . . *Hub.* 172
Withouten pasport or *good* warrantye, . . . *Hub.* 186
A *good* yeoman he was of honest place, . . . *Hub.* 230
Gay without *good* is *good* hearts greatest loathing. . . . *Hub.* 232
As if *good* service he were fit to doo; . . . *Hub.* 239
that *good* man, Seeing them . . . *Hub.* 243
in long service lost both limbs and *good;* . . . *Hub.* 248
'*Good* Sir, full glad am I, . . . *Hub.* 270
men of *good* deserving . . . *Hub.* 369
this *good* Sir did follow the plaine word, . . . *Hub.* 390
no *good* trade of life did entertaine, . . . *Hub.* 398
some *good* course that we might undertake; . . . *Hub.* 411
In the meane-time to live in *good* estate, . . . *Hub.* 427
Good garments for their service should deserve; . . . *Hub.* 468

Good—*Continued.*

Much *good* deep learning one thereout may reed; . . . . . . *Hub.* 484
some *good* Gentleman, that hath the right . . . . *Hub.* 525
The Priest him wisht *good* speed, ... *Hub.* 550
Newes may perhaps some *good* unweeting beare.' . . . . *Hub.* 606
with a *good* bold face, ... *Hub.* 645
good Courtiers may ye bee!' . . . . *Hub.* 653
The which in Court him served to *good* stead; . . . . . . *Hub.* 697
To heare the Javell so *good* men to nip; . . . . *Hub.* 712
backbite Anies *good* name for envie or despite: . . . . . . *Hub.* 720
some *good* Ladies gifts: . . . . *Hub.* 852
had not power to doo him *good* or ill. . . . . *Hub.* 890
To loose *good* dayes, that might be better spent; . . . . . *Hub.* 897
In case the *good* . . . they would wisely take. . . . . . . *Hub.* 962
he askt how *good* might growe . . . . *Hub.* 965
(if we thinke *good*) . . . . *Hub.* 970
deare brother, take *good* hart, ... *Hub.* 1003
it *good* sport had been him to have eyde: . . . . *Hub.* 1013
did he *good* to none, to manie ill, ... *Hub.* 1197
seeke with slaunder his *good* name to blot; . . . . *Hub.* 1219
surcease, *good* Dame, and hence depart.' . . . . *Hub.* 1221
good men blame, and losels magnify. . . . . *T.M.* 324
As heretofore of *good*, so now of ill. . . . . *T.M.* 408
if *good* were not praised more than ill, ... *T.M.* 455
Lifting the *Good* up to high Honours seat, ... *Com. Son.* i. 11
Thy father, that *good* Earle of rare renowne, ... *Ti.* 261
Whose great *good* deeds, in countrey and in towne, ... *Ti.* 263
So life exchanging for his countries *good*. . . . . *Ti.* 301
in this halfe happie I doo read *Good* Melibae, ... *Ti.* 436
O gall of all *good* heartes! . . . . *Ti.* 449
Exceeding all this baser worldes *good:* . . . . *Ti.* 620
With fruitfull hope . . . Of future *good,* . . . . *Mui.* 26
with *good* speed began to take his flight. . . . . *Mui.* 147
Cummin *good* for eyes, ... *Mui.* 188
Sharpe Isope, *good* for greene wounds remedies, ... *Mui.* 190
whatso else of vertue *good* or ill . . . . *Mui.* 201
al *good* things with venemous tooth devowres, ... *Mui.* 302
his gins . . . Drest in *good* order . . . . *Mui.* 388
So carefull was for them, and for my *good,* . . . . *D.* 138
They her did praise, and my *good* fortune blesse. . . . . . *D.* 147
at all complaine My *good* to heare, ... *D.* 280
'The *good* and righteous he away doth take, ... *D.* 358
spight it selfe, that all *good* things doth spill, ... *As.* 23
Had not *good* hap those shepheards thether led. . . . . . . *As.* 144
of *good* passed newly to discus, ... *Col.* 38
her old sire more carefull of her *good,* . . . . *Col.* 120
with hope of *good,* and hate of ill, ... *Col.* 192
No ravenous wolves the *good* mans hope destroy . . . . . . *Col.* 318
For end, all *good,* all grace there freely growes, ... *Col.* 324
good Harpalus, now woxen aged . . . . *Col.* 380
selfe-regard of private *good* or ill . . . . *Col.* 682
Vouchsafe from him this token in *good* worth to take. . . . *Ded. Son.* xv. 14
At that *good* knight so cunningly didst rove, ... I. Pr. 3. 3
The Aspine *good* for staves; . . . . I. i. 8. 9
Making . . . eke her hurt their *good*. . . . . I. i. 25. 9
seemde best the person to put on Of that *good* knight, ... I. ii. 11. 2
this *good* knight, . . . him thither hastly got: . . . . . . I. ii. 29. 1
the *good* knight, . . . The bleeding bough did thrust into the ground, ... I. ii. 44. 3
reliefe, Which given was to them for *good* intents: . . . . . I. iii. 17. 4
Good cause of mine excuse, ... I. iii. 29. 6
hope of new *good* hap he gan to feele; . . . . I. iii. 34. 8
hee . . . scarse *good* morsell all his life did taste, ... I. iv. 28. 3
He hated all *good* workes and vertuous deeds, ... I. iv. 32. 1
death it was, when any *good* he saw; . . . . I. iv. 30. 7
So every *good* to bad he doth abuse; . . . . I. iv. 32. 5
that *good* knight would not so nigh repaire, ... I. iv. 37. 7
good successes which their foes ensew: . . . . I. v. 25. 3
Good cause he had to hasten thence away; . . . . I. v. 45. 6
That *good* knight of the Redcrosse to have slain: . . . . . . I. vi. 41. 4
she chaunced by *good* hap to meet . . . . I. vii. 29. 1
'Faire Sir, I hope *good* hap hath brought You . . . . . . I. vii. 42. 5
'Yt was my chaunce (my chaunce was faire and *good*) . . . I. vii. 47. 1
O! heavie record of the *good* Redcrosse, ... I. vii. 48. 8
penaunce pay Of treble *good: good* growes of evils priefe.' . . I. viii. 43. 6
th' only *good* that growes of passed feare Is to be wise, . . . I. viii. 44. 5
Whose secret filth *good* manners biddeth not be told. . . . . I. viii. 46. 9
this *good* Prince redeemd the Redcrosse knight . . . . . . I. ix. 1. 9
Least so great *good* . . . Should die unknown, ... I. ix. 2. 8
Most envious man, that grieves at neighbours *good;* . . . . I. ix. 39. 6
good lucke prolonged hath thy date, ... I. ix. 45. 7
all the *good* is Gods, both power and eke will. . . . . . . I. x. 1. 9
all the day in doing *good* and godly deedes. . . . . I. x. 3. 9
knew his *good* to all of each degree, ... I. x. 7. 5
this *good* knight his way with me addrest, ... I. x. 11. 3
'Deare dame, And you, *good* Sir, ... I. x. 17. 2
Una her besought, to be so *good* . . . . I. x. 32. 5
Gan him instruct in everie *good* behest, ... I. x. 33. 3
in every *good* behest . . . Shee him instructed . . . . . . I. x. 45. 3
'That word shall I,' (said he) 'avouchen *good,* . . . . . . I. x. 64. 8
Great thankes, and goodly meed, to that *good* syre . . . . . I. x. 68. 4
Full of great vertues, and for med'cine *good:* . . . . I. xi. 29. 5
in that soile, where all *good* things did grow, ... I. xi. 47. 2
eftsoones did know Both *good* and ill, ... I. xi. 47. 8
this faery knight, The *good* Sir Guyon, ... II. Pr. 5. 8
to all *good* he enimy was still. . . . . II. i. 5. 5
knighthood tooke of *good* Sir Huons hand, ... II. i. 6. 8
The which *good* fortune doth to you present. . . . . II. i. 16. 4
he surely is A right *good* knight, ... II. i. 19. 5
make you *good* amendment for the same: . . . . II. i. 20. 4

Good—*Continued.*

all he did was to deceive *good* knights, ... II. i. 23. 1
God ye speed and send you *good* successe, ... II. i. 25. 6
when the *good* Sir Guyon did behold, ... II. i. 42. 1
this dead corpse . . . the *good* Sir Mortdant was: . . . . . . II. i. 49. 9
good Sir Guyon could uneath . . . . II. i. 56. 5
'death is an equall doome To *good* and bad, ... II. i. 59. 2
by *good* prayers, or by other hap, ... II. ii. 6. 7
not so *good* of deedes as great of name, ... II. ii. 17. 3
Ill by ensample *good* doth often gayne.' . . . . II. ii. 45. 5
Sith his *good* steed is lately from him gone; . . . . II. iii. 3. 2
give you eke *good* helpe to their decay. . . . . II. iii. 15. 2
All *good* and honour might therein be red, ... II. iii. 24. 5
envying my toward *good,* . . . . II. iv. 22. 2
staynd their prayses with thy least *good* part; . . . . II. iv. 26. 4
Honour, estate, and all this worldes *good,* . . . . II. vii. 8. 6
Here is the fountaine of the worldes *good:* . . . . II. vii. 38. 6
the *good* Guyon he found slumbring fast . . . . II. viii. 4. 8
Ne all *good* knights that shake well speare and shield. . . . II. viii. 14. 6
'*Good* or bad,' gan his brother fiers reply, ... II. viii. 15. 1
And of that shield, more worthy of *good* knight; . . . . . . II. viii. 15. 8
His owne *good* sword Morddure, ... II. viii. 30. 7
robbed mee Of my *good* sword and shield?' . . . . II. viii. 54. 2
Good turnes be counted as a servile bond . . . . II. viii. 56. 2
'Fly fly, *good* knights,' (said he) . . . . II. ix. 12. 1
many *good* knights slaine . . . . II. ix. 12. 9
in *good* order, and with dew regard; . . . . II. ix. 25. 4
Not *good* nor serviceable elles for ought, ... II. ix. 32. 2
Greece, the Nourse of all *good* arts, ... II. ix. 48. 1
His life, and long *good* fortune, ... II. x. 13. 9
endlesse moniments of his great *good:* . . . . II. x. 46. 3
Good Claudius, that next was Emperour, ... II. x. 51. 1
Then Coyll; and after him *good* Lucius, ... II. x. 53. 3
This *good* king shortly without issew dide, ... II. x. 54. 1
Not with so *good* successe as shee deserv'd; . . . . II. x. 55. 2
whiles *good* fortune favoured her might, ... II. x. 56. 6
gave unto us all what ever *good* we have. . . . . II. x. 69. 9
So fast as his *good* Courser could him beare; . . . . II. xi. 25. 8
His owne *good* sword Mordure, ... II. xi. 41. 6
his *good* Squyre, him helping up with speed, ... II. xi. 48. 7
of our safety *good* heede to take; . . . . II. xii. 17. 7
a God . . . Did wisely make, and *good* Agdistes call; . . . . . II. xii. 48. 2
The foe of life, that *good* envyes to all, ... II. xii. 48. 4
good Sir Guyon deare besought The Prince of grace . . . . . III. i. 5. 1
By such *good* meanes he him discounselled . . . . III. i. 11. 1
'Mongst thousands *good* one wanton Dame to find: . . . . . . III. i. 49. 5
eke the Redcrosse knight gave her *good* ayd, ... III. i. 66. 7
So was their fortune *good,* though wicked were their minde. . III. ii. 43. 9
wicked fortune mine, though minde be *good,* . . . . III. ii. 44. 1
thy *good* fortune, having fate obayd, ... III. iii. 19. 7
Yet ought mens *good* endevours them confirme, ... III. iii. 25. 8
Against the *good* king Oswald, ... III. iii. 38. 4
Ne shall the *good* Cadwallader . . . be hable it to remedy, . . III. iii. 40. 3
good king Uther now doth make Strong warre . . . . III. iii. 52. 5
(need makes *good* schollers) . . . . III. iii. 53. 3
give her *good* reliefe . . . . III. iv. 11. 5
They pourd in soveraine balme and Nectar *good,* . . . . . . III. iv. 40. 8
Good both for erthly med'cine and for hevenly food. . . . . III. iv. 40. 9
good Sir, tell out of hand.' . . . . III. v. 4. 9
all the *good* that ever yet I gat: . . . . III. v. 7. 3
By your *good* counsell, or bold hardiment, ... III. v. 10. 7
Do one or other *good,* . . . . III. v. 10. 9
Of all *good* Ladies through the worlde . . . . III. v. 11. 2
The want of his *good* Squire . . . . III. v. 12. 4
gives ye so *good* ayd . . . . III. vi. 21. 4
A laesy loord, for nothing *good* to donne, ... III. vii. 12. 3
It was to weete the *good* Sir Satyrane, ... III. vii. 30. 1
the *good* Sir Satyrane gan awake . . . . III. vii. 45. 1
Gainst natures law and *good* behaveoure; . . . . III. vii. 49. 2
Three hundred pledges for my *good* desartes, ... III. vii. 55. 4
thrice three hundred thanks for my *good* partes, ... III. vii. 55. 5
good man, sith far in sea we bee, ... III. viii. 24. 1
he, that never *good* nor maners knew, ... III. viii. 26. 1
but God turne the same to *good* sooth-say, ... III. viii. 50. 2
never let th' ensample of the bad Offend the *good;* . . . . . III. ix. 2. 2
good by paragone Of evill, may more notably be rad, ... III. ix. 2. 2
The *good* man selfe, which then the Porter playd, ... III. ix. 10. 2
hardly praisd his wedlock *good,* . . . . III. ix. 42. 9
'*Good* Sir, let not my rudenes be no breach . . . . III. x. 25. 3
'take *good* hart, And tell thy griefe, ... III. x. 26. 1
al *good* knghts, that armes doe bear this day, ... III. x. 27. 8
every one as commune *good* her handeled. . . . . III. x. 36. 9
litle *good* of him is to be got, ... III. x. 39. 3
Ne ever looked back for *good* or ill; . . . . III. x. 43. 7
hast thou, Lord, of *good* mens cause no heed? . . . . III. xi. 9. 6
What booteth then the *good* and righteous deed, ... III. xi. 9. 8
'If *good* find grace, and righteousnes reward, ... III. xi. 10. 1
hevenly grace some *goode* reliefe You send, ... III. xi. 14. 3
nor signe of her *good* speed, ... III. xii. 45. 3
under maske of beautie and *good* grace . . . . IV. i. 17. 7
To hurt *good* knights, ... IV. i. 31. 3
Good lucke presents you with yond lovely mayd, ... IV. i. 33. 8
made *good* semblance to his companie, ... IV. i. 38. 2
Ye will me now with like *good* turne repay, ... IV. i. 40. 5
And foule advantage this *good* Knight dismayd, ... IV. i. 44. 3
old and crooked and not *good* for ought. . . . . IV. ii. 3. 5
good fortune doth to you present So fayre a spoyle, ... IV. ii. 5. 8
wicked Time that all *good* thoughts doth waste, ... IV. ii. 33. 1
Combing her golden lockes, as seemd her *good;* . . . . . . IV. ii. 45. 5
Have by *good* fortune found . . . . IV. iii. 16. 2

Good—*Continued.*
with so *good* wariment . . . IV. iii. 17. 3
T'obey their riders hest, as seemed *good*. . . . IV. iii. 39. 5
Without regard of *good*, . . . IV. iv. 1. 9
To Britomart was given by *good* right; . . . IV. v. 8. 3
Unto the vulgar for *good* gold insted, . . . IV. v. 15. 4
Full glad of so *good* end, . . . IV. vi. 25. 3
An happie life with grace and *good* accord, . . . IV. viii. 18. 2
what *good* fortune did to him afford; . . . IV. viii. 18. 7
steale away the crowne of their *good* name: . . . IV. viii. 25. 4
all that on him lookt without *good* heed, . . . IV. viii. 39. 5
her error I abusd To my friends *good* . . . IV. viii. 60. 8
with *good* thewes and speaches well applyde . . . IV. ix. 14. 6
Then *good* Sir Claribell him thus bespake: . . . IV. ix. 40. 1
by *good* fortune shortly him unseated. . . . IV. x. 10. 2
The Gate of *Good* Desert, . . . IV. x. 16. 2
As every one had cause of *good* or ill. . . . IV. x. 43. 6
in order seemly *good* Did on the Thamis attend, . . . IV. xi. 44. 7
When *good* was onely for it selfe desyred, . . . V. Pr. 3. 6
both to *good* and bad he dealeth right, . . . V. Pr. 10. 4
Nor tooke away his love, but his owne proper *good*. . . . V. i. 23. 9
The spoile of peoples evil gotten *good*, . . . V. ii. 27. 7
Were it not *good* that wrong were then surceast, . . . V. ii. 37. 8
well they hoped to have got great *good*, . . . V. ii. 51. 6
His owne *good* steed, . . . V. iii. 29. 5
lewdnes blotteth *good* deserts with blame. . . . V. iii. 38. 9
with faire words, but words did little *good*, . . . V. iv. 4. 8
through my good endevour . . . did helpe . . . V. iv. 12. 2
that *good* which Fortune gave her, . . . V. iv. 12. 7
what so *good* or ill . . . I hold mine owne, . . . V. iv. 14. 2
Yet my *good* lucke he shall not likewise pray, . . . V. iv. 14. 8
Known by *good* markes and perfect *good* espiall: . . . V. iv. 15. 8
By what *good* right doe you withhold this day?' . . . V. iv. 17. 5
'Your right is *good*,' (sayd he) . . . V. iv. 17. 8
'Your right is *good*,' (sayd he) . . . V. iv. 18. 8
for such *good* him recompence with ill? . . . V. v. 32. 6
with sure promise of her *good* endevour . . . V. v. 35. 2
Fortune, envying *good*, hath felly frowned, . . . V. v. 36. 2
That will not take the offer of *good* hope, . . . V. v. 39. 6
Which if I might by your *good* office get, . . . V. v. 42. 3
Gan to demaund of her some tydings *good*, . . . V. v. 45. 2
Who will not stoupe with *good* shall be made stoupe with harme. . . . V. v. 49. 9
by all *good* means he might, deserve such grace. . . . V. v. 55. 9
tell what ever it be, *good* or bad, . . . V. vi. 10. 2
never word did say Nor *good* nor bad, . . . V. vi. 18. 4
To lodge with him that night, unles *good* cause empeach. . . V. vi. 21. 9
Was glad to yeeld unto his *good* request, . . . V. vi. 22. 2
little *good* could finde, And much lesse honour . . . V. vi. 32. 4
by Gods grace, and her *good* heedinesse, . . . V. vi. 34. 6
It as a token of *good* fortune tooke. . . . V. vii. 8. 5
Uppon their wall *good* watch and ward did keepe. . . . V. vii. 26. 6
her *good* Knights, of which so brave a band Serves her . . . V. viii. 18. 6
thankt be God, and your *good* hardiment, . . . V. viii. 23. 5
his *good* steed . . . Durst not endure their sight, . . . V. viii. 36. 7
To doe whatever he thought *good* or fit: . . . V. x. 13. 3
Good hart in evils doth the evils much amend. . . . V. x. 22. 9
The which *good* Fortune to him offred faire; . . . V. xi. 13. 5
To greet him the *good* fortune . . . V. xi. 15. 4
'Haile, *good* Sir Sergis, . . . V. xi. 38. 2
'forborne Your owne *good* shield . . . V. xi. 52. 2
By a *good* knight, . . . V. xi. 53. 2
the pelfe for which *good* name is sold, . . . V. xi. 63. 6
(as *good* fortune fell) . . . V. xii. 4. 2
if she hapt of any *good* to heare, . . . V. xii. 32. 1
what so Envie *good* or bad did fynd . . . V. xii. 33. 4
mens *good* name to have bereaved. . . . V. xii. 33. 9
whatsoever *good* by any sayd . . . V. xii. 34. 1
To hearke what any one did *good* report, . . . V. xii. 34. 8
To throw amongst the *good* which others had disprad. . . . V. xii. 36. 9
the *good* successe Which ye have had . . . VI. i. 5. 1
good direction how to enter in, . . . VI. i. 6. 3
although *good* Fortune me befall, . . . VI. i. 6. 6
Good Knights and Ladies true, . . . VI. i. 7. 9
for hyre of his *good* deede, . . . VI. i. 47. 2
ought they well to know Their *good*; . . . VI. ii. 1. 7
praise likewise deserve *good* thewes . . . VI. ii. 2. 9
he had *good* right gaynst all that it gainesayd. . . . VI. ii. 18. 9
He burst into these wordes, as to him seemed *good*: . . . VI. ii. 24. 9
Tristram . . . the onely heire Of *good* king Meliogras . . . VI. ii. 28. 2
good Sir, sith now occasion fit Doth fall, . . . VI. ii. 33. 1
And turne we backe to *good* Sir Calidore; . . . VI. ii. 40. 2
that whilome that *good* Poet sayd, . . . VI. iii. 1. 1
did that *good* old Knight Temper his griefe, . . . VI. iii. 6. 1
hazard she at earst had made Of her *good* fame; . . . VI. iii. 8. 8
But Calidore with all *good* courtesie . . . VI. iii. 9. 1
When Calidore in seemly *good* array . . . VI. iii. 9. 7
next after life, he tendered her *good*. . . . VI. iii. 11. 9
And by *good* fortune the plaine champion wonne: . . . VI. iv. 26. 3
The *good* Sir Bruin growing farre in yeares, . . . VI. iv. 33. 6
Lo! how *good* fortune doth to you present . . . VI. iv. 35. 3
Ne ever saw faire guize, ne learned *good*, . . . VI. v. 2. 4
he lacked had The *good* Sir Calepine, . . . VI. v. 3. 2
otherwhile with *good* encouragement . . . VI. v. 32. 8
goodly person, . . . That could his *good* to all; . . . VI. v. 36. 8
In that *good* Hermits charge; . . . VI. v. 41. 4
tongue doth whet Gainst all, both *good* and bad, . . . VI. vi. 12. 4
sith we need *good* counsell,' . . . VI. vi. 13. 8
'Aread, *good* Sire, some counsell . . . VI. vi. 13. 9
Of that *good* Hermite both they tooke their leave, . . . VI. vi. 15. 8

Good—*Continued.*
how to please the minds of *good* and ill, . . . VI. vi. 41. 8
her *good* dayes in dolorous disgrace: . . . VI. vii. 38. 4
gave his foe *good* hope of victory: . . . VI. viii. 9. 6
The *good* Sir Calepine, her owne true Knight, . . . VI. viii. 33. 2
For joy of such *good* hap by heavenly grace. . . . VI. viii. 37. 5
day, that doth discover bad and *good*, . . . VI. viii. 51. 7
Then came to them a *good* old aged syre, . . . VI. ix. 13. 6
Meliboee (so hight that *good* old man) . . . VI. ix. 16. 1
thanke his host and his *good* wife; . . . VI. ix. 18. 6
'It is the mynd that maketh *good* or ill, . . . VI. ix. 30. 1
Give leave awhyle, *good* father, . . . VI. ix. 31. 3
the *good* man . . . did thrust it farre away, . . . VI. ix. 33. 1
farre From malicing, or grudging his *good* houre, . . . VI. ix. 39. 7
good should from us goe, . . . VI. x. 24. 9
forth the *good* old Meliboe was brought, . . . VI. xi. 11. 1
Old Meliboe and his *good* wife withall . . . VI. xi. 31. 6
Whereof was Lord the *good* Sir Bellamoure; . . . VI. xii. 3. 4
such passion . . . as this *good* Lady felt, . . . VI. xii. 21. 6
seemed to containe A full *good* pecke . . . VI. xii. 26. 6
Of *good* and bad alike, . . . VI. xii. 28. 6
The *good* Sir Pelleas him tooke in hand, . . . VI. xii. 39. 6
Nature had establisht first In *good* estate, . . . VII. vi. 5. 3
wrong of right, and bad of *good* did make . . . VII. vi. 6. 3
Good on-set boads *good* end. . . . VII. vi. 23. 9
that gave *good* eare To her bold words, . . . VII. vi. 28. 1
to be her debter For many moe *good* turnes . . . VII. vi. 44. 8
From *good* to bad, from bad to worst of all: . . . VII. vii. 19. 6
Chose rather to be praysd for dooing *good*, . . . *Am.* xxxviii. 13
And speake her *good*, though she requite it ill. . . . *Am.* xlviii. 14
Good shames to be to ill an instrument! . . . *Am.* liii. 12
Set all your things in seemely *good* aray, . . . *Epith.* 114
what ye do, albe it *good* or ill. . . . *Epith.* 367
all that faire is, is by nature *good*; . . . *H.B.* 139
Nothing so *good*, but that . . . May be corrupt, . . . *H.B.* 157
How can we thee requite for all this *good*? . . . *H.H.L.* 174
Offending none, and doing *good* to all, . . . *H.H.L.* 237
For all thats *good* is beautifull and faire. . . . *H.H.B.* 133
Good day. Diggon Davie! I bidde her *god day*; . . . *S.C.* S. 1
Goodlihead. Craving your *goodlihead* to aswage . . . *S.C.* F. 184
So be your *goodlihead* doe not disdayne . . . *S.C.* May 270
mote thy *goodlyhed* forgive it mee, . . . II. iii. 33. 7
pleased with that seeming *goodly-hed*, . . . III. ii. 38. 8
That in thy face appeares and gratious *goodlyhead*. . . . VI. ii. 25. 9
Goodly. Many a spoile, and many *goodly* signes, . . . *Bel.*[1] v. 6
many a spoyle, and many a *goodly* show, . . . *Bel.*[2] v. 6
on sand was built the *goodly* frame: . . . *Bel.*[2] xiv. 4
death shall spoyle your *goodly* features. . . . *Pet.*[2] vii. 14
all his *goodly* feature . . . nought him pleased: . . . *Van.* ii. 12
High on a hill a *goodly* Cedar grewe, . . . *Van.* vii. 1
To see so *goodly* thing so soone decayed. . . . *Van.* vii. 14
his rich attire and *goodly* forme, . . . *Van.* viii. 6
A *goodly* ship with banners bravely dight, . . . *Van.* ix. 2
A *goodly* Oake sometime had it bene, . . . *S.C.* F. 103
over them spred a *goodly* wild vine, . . . *S.C.* Au. 29
"There also *goodly* Agamemnon bosts, . . . *Gn.* 545
Whom ye in *goodly* seates may placed see, . . . *Gn.* 595
manie honest men . . . grow to *goodly* prize. . . . *Hub.* 420
Then made they revell route and *goodly* glee; . . . *Hub.* 558
The Mule all deckt in *goodly* rich aray, . . . *Hub.* 582
so *goodly* and so gay In your attyres, . . . *Hub.* 590
the God of *goodly* Arts: . . . *T.M.* 58
all that *goodly* glee, . . . *T.M.* 181
With seasoned wit and *goodly* pleasance graced, . . . *T.M.* 200
The *goodly* fields, that earst so gay were dyde . . . *T.M.* 237
what ever thing is *goodly* thought, . . . *T.M.* 405
The *goodly* off-spring of Joves progenie, . . . *T.M.* 429
Have mard the face of *goodly* Poesie, . . . *T.M.* 557
As for those many *goodly* matters leaft I for others. . . . *Ex Tempore* 2
Nigh where the *goodly* Verlame stood . . . *Ti.* 3
'High towers, faire temples, *goodly* theaters, . . . *Ti.* 92
In learned artes, and *goodlie* governaunce, . . . *Ti.* 270
thy husbands sister die, That *goodly* Ladie, . . . *Ti.* 275
This *goodlie* bridge . . . Gan faile, . . . *Ti.* 557
the *goodlie* criew Of white Strimonian brood . . . *Ti.* 592
Therein a *goodly* Virgine sleeping lay; . . . *Ti.* 636
So many *goodly* colours doth containe. . . . *Mui.* 96
A *goodly* worke, full fit for kingly bowres; . . . *Mui.* 300
'Much was I moved at so *goodly* sight, . . . *D.* 113
That men admire in *goodlie* womankinde, . . . *D.* 212
Faire *goodly* fields, . . . *Col.* 278
seemed to be a *goodly* pleasant lea: . . . *Col.* 283
most *goodly* rivers there appeare, . . . *Col.* 300
'They all (quoth he) me graced *goodly* well, . . . *Col.* 485
goodly beames though they be overdight . . . *Col.* 493
Through the myld temperance of her *goodly* raies. . . . *Col.* 551
like a *goodly* beacon high addrest, . . . *Col.* 562
those *goodly* favours Bestowd on thee, . . . *Col.* 585
everie gift, and everie *goodly* meed, . . . *Col.* 592
All *goodly* bountie and true honour sits. . . . *Ded. Son.* v. 12
And ye, brave Lord, whose *goodly* personage . . . *Ded. Son.* vi. 1
As *goodlie* well ye shew'd in late assaies, . . . *Ded. Son.* x. 8
Bids me, . . . to adore His *goodly* image, . . . *Ded. Son.* xv. 9
The maker selfe, . . . Was nigh beguiled with so *goodly* sight. . . I. i. 45. 7
A *goodly* Lady clad in scarlot red, . . . I. ii. 13. 2
they came at last Where grew two *goodly* trees, . . . I. ii. 28. 3
pleasaunce each to other makes, With *goodly* purposes, . . . I. ii. 30. 2
till at last they see A *goodly* building bravely garnished; . . . I. iv. 2. 6
goodly galleries far over laid, Full of faire windowes . . . I. iv. 4. 7
It was a *goodly* heape for to behould, . . . I. iv. 5. 1

Goodly—*Continued.*

A gentle Husher . . . *goodly* brought them	I. iv. 13. 5
Goodly they all that knight doe entertayne,	I. iv. 15. 1
So forth they marchen in this *goodly* sort,	I. iv. 37. 1
Greeting him *goodly* with new victorie,	I. v. 15. 8
she accepts with thankes and *goodly* gree,	I. v. 16. 4
His *goodly* corps, . . . Was quite dismembred,	I. v. 38. 6
Thenceforth he kept her *goodly* company,	I. vi. 31. 8
goodly court he made still to his Dame,	I. vii. 7. 1
To gayne so *goodly* guerdon as she spake:	I. vii. 15. 2
A *goodly* knight, faire marching by the way,	I. vii. 29. 2
A *goodly* person, and could menage faire His stubborne steed	I. vii. 37. 5
His *goodly* reason, and well-guided speach,	I. vii. 42. 1
calmd his wrath with *goodly* temperance.	I. viii. 34. 5
O *goodly* golden chayne, wherewith yfere The vertues linked are	I. ix. 1. 1
The verdant gras my couch did *goodly* dight,	I. ix. 13. 3
'Most *goodly* glee . . . She to me made,	I. ix. 14. 1
those two knights . . . Gave *goodly* gifts,	I. ix. 18. 8
well upbrought In *goodly* thewes, and godly exercise:	I. x. 4. 4
Each *goodly* thing is hardest to begin;	I. x. 6. 1
The auncient Dame Him *goodly* greeted	I. x. 11. 6
two most *goodly* virgins came in place,	I. x. 12. 2
goodly gan discourse of many a noble gest.	I. x. 15. 9
forth him ledd Into a *goodly* lodge,	I. x. 17. 7
wonder was to heare her *goodly* speach:	I. x. 19. 7
With *goodly* counsell and advisement right;	I. x. 23. 5
With *goodly* grace and comely personage,	I. x. 30. 3
A little path . . . to a *goodly* Citty led his vew,	I. x. 55. 3
Great thankes, and *goodly* meed,	I. x. 68. 4
That erst him *goodly* armd, now most of all him harmd.	I. xi. 27. 9
There grew a *goodly* tree him faire beside,	I. xi. 46. 1
before did march a *goodly* band Of tall young men,	I. xii. 5. 6
such as she was, a *goodly* maiden Queene.	I. xii. 8. 9
that hoarie king, . . . Him *goodly* greetes,	I. xii. 12. 5
What needes me tell their feast and *goodly* guize,	I. xii. 14. 1
Then stepped forth the *goodly* royall Mayd,	I. xii. 33. 1
great rule of Temp'raunce *goodly* doth appeare.	II. Pr. 5. 9
A *goodly* knight, all armd in harnesse meete,	II. i. 5. 8
Goodly comportaunce each to other beare,	II. i. 29. 3
I know your *goodly* governaunce,	II. i. 29. 8
turne his earnest unto game, Through *goodly* handling	II. i. 31. 2
Wherewith above all knights ye *goodly* seeme aguizd!	II. i. 31. 9
That all her *goodly* garments staind arownd,	II. i. 39. 8
Seemd to have beene a *goodly* personage,	II. i. 41. 6
goodly counsell, that for wounded hart Is meetest med'cine,	II. i. 44. 2
the Palmer gan to bord With *goodly* reason,	II. ii. 5. 2
with golden sell And *goodly* gorgeous barbes,	II. ii. 11. 7
In *goodly* garments that her well became,	II. ii. 14. 7
She led him up into a *goodly* bowre,	II. ii. 15. 1
them began With *goodly* meanes to pacifie,	II. ii. 21. 9
With sober grace and *goodly* carriage:	II. ii. 38. 2
On *goodly* courser thondring with his feet,	II. iii. 11. 4
A *goodly* Ladie clad in hunters weed,	II. iii. 21. 7
Through *goodly* mixture of complexions dew;	II. iii. 22. 4
when her *goodly* visage he beheld,	II. iii. 37. 1
fayre defence and *goodly* menaging Of armes	II. iv. 8. 3
it the *goodly* peace of staied mindes Does overthrow,	II. v. 1. 6
whenas hee In Nemus gayned *goodly* victoree:	II. v. 31. 5
Guyon in them all shewes *goodly* maysteries.	II. vi. 1. 9
Holding in hand a *goodly* arming sword,	II. vi. 47. 6
'That *goodly* one . . . my daughter is:	II. vii. 48. 4
a gardin *goodly* garnished With hearbs and fruits,	II. vii. 51. 4
a thick Arber *goodly* over-dight,	II. vii. 53. 3
Next thereunto did grow a *goodly* tree,	II. vii. 53. 6
goodly was their glory to behold;	II. vii. 54. 2
Here also sprong that *goodly* golden fruit,	II. vii. 55. 1
So *goodly* did beguile the Guyler of his pray.	II. vii. 64. 9
with his *goodly* sisters, Graces three:	II. viii. 6. 6
that straunger knight . . . *goodly* salued them;	II. viii. 23. 2
goodly purpose they together fond	II. viii. 56. 7
on your shield, so *goodly* scord,	II. ix. 2. 7
Whenas they spide a *goodly* castle,	II. ix. 10. 3
a *goodly* traine Of Squires and Ladies	II. ix. 17. 7
full of grace and *goodly* modestee,	II. ix. 18. 8
Goodly shee entertaind those noble knights,	II. ix. 20. 1
So *goodly* workemanship should not endure.	II. ix. 21. 8
All which compacted made a *goodly* Diapase.	II. ix. 22. 9
There added was by *goodly* ordinaunce	II. ix. 30. 3
goodly order and great workmans skill	II. ix. 33. 1
soone into a *goodly* Parlour brought,	II. ix. 33. 6
with court and *goodly* game	II. ix. 44. 4
Two *goodly* Beacons, set in watches stead,	II. ix. 46. 3
His *goodly* reason and grave personage,	II. ix. 54. 7
for this Realme found many *goodly* layes,	II. x. 42. 5
goodly well long time it governed;	II. x. 47. 4
in all godly thewes and *goodly* praise	II. x. 59. 6
A *goodly* creature, whom he deemd in mynd	II. x. 71. 5
All happy peace and *goodly* government	II. xi. 2. 4
Attempred *goodly* well for health and for delight.	II. xi. 2. 9
That *goodly* frame from ruine to sustaine:	II. xi. 15. 5
ginnes that *goodly* frame of Temperaunce	II. xii. 1. 1
a *goodly* Ship did see	II. xii. 19. 1
Goodly it was enclosed rownd about,	II. xii. 43. 1
His *goodly* conquest of the golden fleece,	II. xii. 44. 6
more might in that *goodly* gate Be red,	II. xii. 46. 1
goodly beautifide With all the ornaments	II. xii. 50. 4
being *goodly* dight With bowes and braunches,	II. xii. 53. 7
It was her guise all Straungers *goodly* so to greet.	II. xii. 56. 9
Most *goodly* it with curious ymageree Was overwrought,	II. xii. 60. 5
Some *goodly* swayne of honorable place,	II. xii. 79. 2

Goodly—*Continued.*

Ne ought their *goodly* workmanship might save Them	II. xii. 83. 3
on his arme addresse his *goodly* shield	III. i. 4. 8
Through *goodly* temperaunce and affection chaste;	III. i. 12. 2
So *goodly* all agreed they forth yfere did ryde.	III. i. 12. 9
O! *goodly* usage of those antique tymes,	III. i. 13. 1
A *goodly* Lady did foreby them rush,	III. i. 15. 3
in hope to win thereby Most *goodly* meede,	III. i. 18. 8
That Castle was most *goodly* edifyde,	III. i. 20. 4
Long were it to describe the *goodly* frame,	III. i. 31. 1
So was that chamber clad in *goodly* wize:	III. i. 39. 1
Their *goodly* entertainement and great glee.	III. i. 42. 2
so did let her *goodly* visage to appere.	III. i. 42. 9
goodly taught to tilt and turnament:	III. i. 44. 7
All were faire knights, and *goodly* well beseene;	III. i. 45. 8
on knight so *goodly* glorifyde,	III. ii. 11. 4
My glorious Soveraines *goodly* auncestrye,	III. iii. 4. 7
If ay more *goodly* creature thou didst see?	III. iii. 32. 2
Howell Dha shall *goodly* well indew	III. iii. 45. 4
persuade The warlike minds to learne her *goodly* lore,	III. iii. 49. 4
A *goodly* Armour, and full rich aray,	III. iii. 58. 7
All fretted round with gold, and *goodly* wel beseene.	III. iii. 58. 9
all her *goodly* deedes doe well declare.	III. iv. 3. 5
her *goodly* shield addressing fayre,	III. iv. 14. 1
to win so *goodly* pray.	III. iv. 46. 9
cursed night that reft from him so *goodly* scope.	III. iv. 52. 9
in brave sprite it kindles *goodly* fire,	III. v. 1. 8
The *goodly* ornaments of beautie bright;	III. v. 8. 6
The *goodly* Maide, ful of divinities	III. v. 34. 7
they saw that *goodly* boy with blood Defowled,	III. v. 38. 1
With this fayre flowre your *goodly* girlonds dight,	III. v. 53. 5
Tempred with grace and *goodly* modesty,	III. v. 55. 3
It were a *goodly* storie to declare	III. vi. 5. 1
The house of *goodly* formes and faire aspect,	III. vi. 12. 2
Goodly she gan faire Cytherea greet,	III. vi. 20. 1
as a fountaine . . . welled *goodly* forth,	III. vi. 25. 6
To be upbrought in *goodly* womanhed;	III. vi. 28. 7
In that same Gardin all the *goodly* flowres,	III. vi. 30. 1
Does mow the flowring herbes and *goodly* things,	III. vi. 39. 4
Their *goodly* meriment and gay felicity.	III. vi. 41. 9
In all the lore of love, and *goodly* womanhead.	III. vi. 51. 9
many one Admyrd her *goodly* haveour,	III. vi. 52. 8
That was, to weet, the *goodly* Florimell;	III. vi. 54. 5
vouchsafed to embace Her *goodly* port,	III. vii. 15. 3
Yt was a *goodly* Swaine, and of great might,	III. vii. 29. 4
t' advance thy *goodly* chastitee	III. viii. 43. 3
ought your *goodly* patience offend,	III. ix. 1. 5
Her *goodly* personage and glorious hew,	III. ix. 23. 6
Out of the *goodly* heven amoved quight,	III. x. 1. 4
louted low, and greeted *goodly* well;	III. x. 37. 9
The silly man . . . Saw all this *goodly* sport,	III. x. 45. 2
all their *goodly* heardes did gather rownd;	III. x. 46. 2
goodly arras of great majesty,	III. xi. 28. 2
To search each secrete of that *goodly* sted,	III. xi. 50. 2
The *goodly* ordinaunce of this rich Place,	III. xi. 53. 2
Minstrales making *goodly* meriment,	III. xii. 5. 4
paynted plumes in *goodly* order dight,	III. xii. 8. 2
Goodly adorned and exceeding faire:	III. xii. 14. 5
did survay his *goodly* company;	III. xii. 23. 3
goodly well advaunce that *goodly* well was tryde.'	III. xii. 39. 9
those *goodly* rowmes, which erst She saw	III. xii. 42. 1
Was to that *goodly* fellowship restor'd,	IV. i. 15. 2
made full *goodly* joyance to her new-found mate.	IV. i. 31. 9
this gallant with his *goodly* crew	IV. i. 33. 1
had a *goodly* Ladie by his side,	IV. ii. 4. 3
With golden words and *goodly* countenance,	IV. ii. 9. 2
However gay and *goodly* be the style,	IV. ii. 29. 7
two Ladies of most *goodly* hew,	IV. ii. 30. 6
rul'd her thoughts with *goodly* governement,	IV. ii. 36. 4
she was right faire, . . . and of *goodly* stature:	IV. ii. 44. 7
In brave aray and *goodly* amenance,	IV. iii. 5. 5
Thus when they all accorded *goodly* were,	IV. iii. 51. 1
that could so *goodly* riches gaine,	IV. iv. 16. 8
This *goodly* counterfesaunce he did frame:	IV. iv. 27. 4
brought with her from thence that *goodly* belt away.	IV. v. 5. 9
That *goodly* belt was Cestus hight by name,	IV. v. 6. 1
To tell the feature of each *goodly* face:	IV. v. 12. 3
He much more *goodly* glosse thereon doth shed	IV. v. 15. 5
Who was right glad to gaine so *goodly* meed:	IV. v. 22. 2
To spoyle so *goodly* workmanship of nature,	IV. vi. 17. 4
So *goodly* grave, and full of princely aw,	IV. vi. 33. 5
Where *goodly* solace was unto them made,	IV. vi. 39. 6
goodly grace she him did shew:	IV. viii. 6. 5
from that *goodly* glorious flowre proceed,	IV. viii. 33. 6
though she were most faire, and *goodly* dyde,	IV. ix. 14. 8
goodly learned had of yore	IV. ix. 19. 2
To whom the Prince thus *goodly* well replied:	IV. ix. 37. 1
It was a bridge ybuilt in *goodly* wize	IV. x. 6. 6
With golden letters *goodly* well enchaced;	IV. x. 8. 7
beholding all the way The *goodly* workes,	IV. x. 15. 5
whose *goodly* pride And costly frame	IV. x. 16. 2
goodly workmanship farre past all other	IV. x. 29. 8
much admyring that so *goodly* frame,	IV. x. 31. 1
next to her sate *goodly* Shamefastnesse,	IV. x. 50. 1
darted forth delights the which her *goodly* graced.	IV. x. 50. 9
in the midst of them a *goodly* mayd	IV. x. 52. 2
For *goodly* triumph and great jollyment,	IV. xi. 12. 4
The eares and hearts of all that *goodly* crew,	IV. xi. 23. 5
The noble Thamis, with all his *goodly* traine;	IV. xi. 24. 3
Cambridge or Oxford, Englands *goodly* beames.	IV. xi. 35. 6

Goodly—*Continued.*
the *goodly* Barow which doth hoord . . . IV. xi. 43. 5
Her *goodly* lockes adowne her backe did flow . . . IV. xi. 46. 1
All *goodly* damzels, deckt with long greene haire, . . . IV. xi. 48. 2
Joyous Thalia, *goodly* Amphitrite, . . . IV. xi. 49. 2
gold upon the blade In *goodly* wise, . . . V. i. 10. 4
Having great Lordships got and *goodly* farmes, . . . V. ii. 5. 7
She ment him to corrupt with *goodly* meede; . . . V. ii. 23. 3
Withouten pitty of her *goodly* hew, . . . V. ii. 25. 8
In *goodly* measure by their Makers might; . . . V. ii. 35. 2
spoyling all her geares and *goodly* ray . . . V. ii. 50. 4
The *goodly* service, the devicefull sights, . . . V. iii. 3. 2
goodly gan to greet his brave emprise, . . . V. iii. 15. 7
Ne of that *goodly* hew remayned ought, . . . V. iii. 24. 8
Her *goodly* bow, which paints the liquid ayre, . . . V. iii. 25. 3
So did this Ladies *goodly* forme decay, . . . V. iii. 25. 8
With whom great feast and *goodly* glee he fond, . . . V. iv. 3. 4
With whom a *goodly* doure I should have got, . . . V. iv. 8. 8
Both *goodly* portions, but of both the better she. . . . V. iv. 12. 9
A *goodly* citty and a mighty one, . . . V. iv. 35. 8
them *goodly* well did greete, . . . V. iv. 51. 2
He saw . . . A miracle of natures *goodly* grace . . . V. v. 12. 3
Both *goodly* meede of him it purchase may, . . . V. v. 33. 8
To fight with him, and *goodly* die her last. . . . V. vi. 13. 3
For he, their host, them *goodly* well did cheare, . . . V. vi. 22. 8
There she received was in *goodly* wize . . . V. vii. 4. 1
Whose *goodly* building when she did behould, . . . V. vii. 5. 3
In glistering armes right *goodly* well-beseene, . . . V. viii. 29. 4
goodly seem'd t' adorne her royall state; . . . V. ix. 31. 3
Sate *goodly* Temperance in garments clene, . . . V. ix. 32. 8
with *goodly* chere Them entertayn'd, . . . V. x. 5. 3
Even seventeene *goodly* sonnes; . . . V. x. 7. 4
Both *goodly* Castle, and both *goodly* Towne, . . . V. x. 26. 5
with right humble thankes him *goodly* greeting . . . V. x. 39. 1
thankes for their so *goodly* deed, . . . V. xi. 48. 3
goodly light then Phoebus lampe doth shine more cleare? . V. xi. 62. 9
goodly fury into them infuse, . . . VI. Pr. 2. 6
The *goodly* praise of Princely curtesie, . . . VI. Pr. 6. 3
Right so from you all *goodly* vertues well . . . VI. Pr. 7. 6
of all *goodly* manners is the ground, . . . VI. i. 1. 5
so *goodly* as ye can devize, . . . VI. i. 5. 7
both tooke *goodly* leave, and parted severall. . . . VI. i. 10. 9
calm'd his wrathfull heat With *goodly* patience, . . . VI. i. 40. 3
goodly glee and feast to them she made, . . . VI. i. 46. 3
some so *goodly* gratious are by kind, . . . VI. ii. 2. 2
and saw to bee A *goodly* youth . . . VI. ii. 5. 2
With whom those graces did so *goodly* fit: . . . VI. ii. 24. 7
These *goodly* gilden armes which I have won . . . VI. ii. 33. 9
despoyling . . . Of all those *goodly* implements . . . VI. ii. 39. 2
his gentle words and *goodly* wit . . . VI. iii. 22. 1
Therefore inclyning to his *goodly* reason, . . . VI. iv. 37. 4
And it in *goodly* thewes so well upbrought, . . . VI. iv. 38. 7
Some *goodly* person, and of gentle race, . . . VI. v. 36. 7
from his craven bodie torne Those *goodly* armes, . . . VI. vi. 36. 8
With all the courteous glee and *goodly* feast . . . VI. vi. 41. 4
for their paines obtaine of him a *goodly* meed. . . . VI. vii. 4. 9
praise the feature of her *goodly* face; . . . VI. vii. 28. 7
nought regarding her so *goodly* hew, . . . VI. vii. 32. 3
Wasting her *goodly* hew in heavie teares, . . . VI. vii. 38. 3
Adornd with *goodly* gifts of beauties grace, . . . VI. viii. 2. 2
being naked, . . . The *goodly* threasures of nature appeare: . VI. viii. 41. 7
Her *goodly* thighes, whose glorie did appeare . . . VI. viii. 42. 7
a girland, *goodly* graced, Of lovely lasses; . . . VI. ix. 8. 3
that *goodly* glorious gaze . . . VI. x. 4. 1
with her *goodly* presence all the rest much graced. . . . VI. x. 12. 9
Such was the beauty of this *goodly* band, . . . VI. x. 14. 1
dayes Here leadest in this *goodly* merry-make, . . . VI. x. 19. 3
waste her *goodly* beauty, . . . VI. x. 44. 5
Deviz'd all *goodly* meanes . . . VI. xi. 50. 6
Both whom they *goodly* well did entertaine; . . . VI. xii. 11. 1
th' Images, for all their *goodly* hew, Did cast to ground, . . . VI. xii. 25. 4
All fairely deckt with heavens *goodly* storie; . . . VII. vi. 8. 4
The *goodly* building of her Palace bright, . . . VII. vi. 10. 2
those Woods, and all that *goodly* Chase . . . VII. vi. 55. 7
With *goodly* port and gracious Majesty, . . . VII. vii. 5. 2
garnished with garlonds *goodly* dight . . . VII. vii. 33. 6
The *goodly* Sun encompast all with beames bright. . . . VII. vii. 44. 9
So Venus eeke, that *goodly* Paragone, . . . VII. vii. 51. 5
her faire countenance, like a *goodly* banner, . . . *Am.* v. 11
th' ymage of their *goodly* light. . . . *Am.* ix. 4
that proud port, which her so *goodly* graceth, . . . *Am.* xiii. 1
Most *goodly* temperature ye may descry; . . . *Am.* xiii. 4
rare perfection of each *goodly* part; . . . *Am.* xxiv. 2
That *goodly* Idoll, now so gay beseene, . . . *Am.* xxvii. 5
so *goodly* giftes of beauties grace! . . . *Am.* xxxi. 2
Thrugh the broad world doth spred his *goodly* ray; . . . *Am.* xl. 8
all her natures *goodly* guifts are lost: . . . *Am.* xli. 8
Your *goodly* selfe for evermore to vew: . . . *Am.* xlv. 2
The *goodly* ymage of your visnomy, . . . *Am.* xlv. 11
with the *goodly* semblant of her hew, . . . *Am.* liii. 6
Her *goodly* bosome, lyke a Strawberry bed; . . . *Am.* lxiv. 9
to see a beast so wyld, So *goodly* wonne, . . . *Am.* lxvii. 14
In *goodly* colours gloriously arrayd; . . . *Am.* lxx. 4
A *goodly* table of pure yvory, . . . *Am.* lxxvii. 2
cloud of pryde, that oft doth dark Her *goodly* light, . . . *Am.* lxxxi. 8
since ye deignd so *goodly* to relent . . . *Am.* lxxxii. 9
Al with gay girlands *goodly* wel beseene. . . . *Epith.* 40
So *goodly* all agree, with sweet consent, . . . *Epith.* 83
now shew theyr *goodly* beams . . . *Epith.* 94
Her *goodly* eyes lyke Saphyres shining bright, . . . *Epith.* 171

Goodly—*Continued.*
the pure snow, with *goodly* vermill stayne . . . *Epith.* 227
Are governed with *goodly* modesty, . . . *Epith.* 235
Behold how *goodly* my faire love does ly, . . . *Epith.* 305
generation *goodly* dost enlarge, . . . *Epith.* 384
Be unto her a *goodly* ornament, . . . *Epith.* 432
his *goodly* face long hidden was . . . *H.L.* 59
lend him light from her owne *goodly* ray; . . . *H.L.* 73
tempering *goodly* well Their contrary dislikes . . . *H.L.* 85
things that are contained Within this *goodly* cope, . . . *H.L.* 95
He is enlumind with that *goodly* light, . . . *H.L.* 108
Unto like *goodly* semblant to aspyre; . . . *H.L.* 109
he before his eyes had plast A *goodly* Paterne, . . . *H.B.* 32
goodly temp'rament Of pure complexions, . . . *H.B.* 66
that same *goodly* hew of white and red, . . . *H.B.* 92
Shall turne to dust, and loose their *goodly* light. . . . *H.B.* 98
goodly beautie, albe heavenly borne, . . . *H.B.* 149
adde more brightnesse to your *goodly* hew, . . . *H.B.* 178
Through contemplation of those *goodly* sights, . . . *H.H.B.* 2
That with the glorie of so *goodly* sight . . . *H.H.B.* 15
beautie . . . more increast by her owne *goodly* grace, . . . *H.H.B.* 208
Angels, which her *goodly* face behold . . . *H.H.B.* 232
Nymphes . . . With *goodly* greenish locks, . . . *Proth.* 22
two Swannes of *goodly* hewe . . . *Proth.* 37
upon those *goodly* Birds they threw . . . *Proth.* 76
Where oft I gayned giftes and *goodly* grace . . . *Proth.* 138
were *goodly* to bee seene Two gentle Knights . . . *Proth.* 168
Fit for so *goodly* stature, . . . *Proth.* 172

Goodman. Him rested the *goodman* on the lea, . . . *S.C.* F. 158
The *goodman* granted, doubting nought their deeds, . . . *Hub.* 328
There entring in, they found the *goodman* selfe . . . IV. v. 34. 1
The *goodman* of this house was Dolon hight; . . . V. vi. 32. 1

Goodness. Griefe of good mindes, to see *goodnesse* disgraced! . *Van.* i. 8
but your *goodnes* the same recure, . . . *S.C.* F. 154
Ne in good nor *goodnes* taken delight, . . . *S.C.* S. 85
None would choose *goodnes* of his owne freewill. . . . *T.M.* 456
who so els did *goodnes* by him gaine, . . . *Ti.* 232
He grew up fast in *goodnesse* and in grace, . . . *As.* 17
great Cynthiaes *goodnesse*, and high grace, . . . *Col.* 588
Of God and *goodnes* was his meditation. . . . I. x. 46. 9
never tasted grace, nor *goodnes* felt; . . . II. x. 7. 3
in heven, whereas all *goodnes* is, . . . III. ix. 2. 6
If *goodnesse* find no grace, . . . III. xi. 9. 9
Her nature is all *goodnesse* to abuse, . . . IV. viii. 25. 1
all the world with *goodnesse* did abound: . . . V. Pr. 9. 2
High God, whose *goodnesse* he despaired quight, . . . V. ii. 18. 8
thence all *goodnesse* he bereft, . . . VI. xii. 23. 5
seeke by grace and *goodnesse* to obtaine That place, . . . VII. vi. 34. 2
in fame Of wealths and *goodnesse*, far above the rest . . . VII. vi. 38. 2
Still flowing forth His *goodnesse* unto all, . . . *H.H.L.* 100
His *goodnesse*, which his beautie doth declare; . . . *H.H.B.* 132

Goods. Consumed had their *goods* and thriftlesse howres, . . . I. v. 51. 8
thou didst these *goods* bereave From rightfull owner . . . II. vii. 19. 3
His dayes, his *goods*, his bodie, he did spend: . . . II. xii. 80. 8
had gotten a great pray Of Saxon *goods*; . . . III. iii. 58. 6
suffer wreck both of her selfe and *goods*. . . . *Am.* lvi. 12

Goodwill. Shee deignes not my *good will*, . . . *S.C.* Ja. 63
To buy his Masters frivolous *good will*, . . . *Hub.* 889
her *good will* he got her first to wedde. . . . *Col.* 131
But to make humble present of *good will*: . . . *Ded. Son.* xvi.12
chose in Faery court, of meere *goodwil*, . . . I. iii. 28. 5
More then *goodwill* to me attribute nought; . . . II. i. 33. 4
With right hands plighted, pledges of *good will*. . . . II. i. 34. 2
Scorne the faire offer of *good will* profest; . . . III. i. 55. 2
fast *goodwill*, with gentle courtesyes, . . . III. ix. 7. 7
No fayrer conquest then that with *goodwill* is gayned. . . . V. v. 17. 9
by his freedome get his free *goodwill*; . . . V. v. 32. 8
with her owne *good will*, . . . V. xi. 49. 9
well she knew the wayes to win *good will* . . . VI. vi. 41. 6
thankes to you for your *good will*.' . . . VI. viii. 30. 5
courtesie amongst the rudest breeds *Good will* . . . VI. ix. 45. 6
simple truth, and mutuall *good-will*, . . . *Am.* lxv. 11
I . . . with her owne *goodwill* hir fyrmely tyde. . . . *Am.* lxvii. 12

Goody. 'Soft, *Gooddie* Sheepe! (then said the Foxe) . . . *Hub.* 1213

Goord. *See* **Gourd.**

Goose. Had not a *Goose* the treachery bewrayde; . . . *Van.* xi. 8
a *Goose* great Rome from ruine stayde, . . . *Van.* xi. 9

Gorbodue. Kinmarke did rayne, And *Gorbogud*, . . . II. x. 34. 6

Gorbogud. *See* **Gorbodue.**

Gorboman. First *Gorboman*, a man of vertuous life, . . . II. x. 44. 3

Gorbonianus. *See* **Gorboman.**

Gore. Like two sharpe speares his enemies to *gore*: . . . *Mui.* 83
With crudled blood and filthie *gore* deformed, . . . *As.* 152
with their drery wounds, and bloody *gore*, . . . I. vi. 45. 5
That her gay garments staynd with filthy *gore*, . . . I. viii. 16. 7
bodie lay, All wallowd in his owne fowle bloody *gore*, . . . I. viii. 24. 4
swoln with wrath and poyson, and with bloody *gore*; . . . I. xi. 8. 9
the cleane waves with purple *gore* did ray: . . . II. i. 40. 4
His guiltie handes from bloody *gore* to cleene. . . . II. ii. 3. 4
soyld with durtie *gore*, . . . II. vi. 41. 7
besprincled with the *gore* Of mighty Goemot, . . . II. x. 10. 7
Fayre Daphne Phoebus hart with love did *gore*; . . . II. xii. 52. 5
With her soft garment wipes away the *gore* . . . III. i. 38. 5
it was seene To *gore* her side; . . . III. i. 65. 6
all my entrailes flow with poisnous *gore*, . . . III. ii. 39. 4
He tombled on an heape, and wallowd in his *gore*. . . . III. iv. 16. 9
with his streaming *gore* Distaincs the pillours . . . III. iv. 17. 6
all in *gore* And cruddy blood enwallowed . . . III. iv. 34. 7
wallowd all in his owne *gore*. . . . III. v. 26. 5
in whose purple *gore* Me seemes I see Amintas wretched fate, . III. vi. 45. 7

Gore—*Continued.*
all their armours staynd with bloudie *gore;* IV. ii. 18. 6
rape Of men and beasts; and fed on fleshly *gore,* IV. vii. 5. 8
all in *gore* They trode, V. vii. 31. 7
Enwallow'd in his owne blacke bloudy *gore,* V. xi. 14. 6
The bloudie *gore* and poyson dropping lothsomely. V. xii. 30. 9
lake Of bloudy *gore* congeal'd about them stood, VI. i. 37. 8
Betwixt his bloodie jawes, besprinckled all with *gore.* VI. iv. 17. 9
he bathed lay in his owne bloody *gore.* VI. vii. 8. 9
To see him so bedight with bloodie *gore,* VI. vii. 14. 4
he gan fret and fome out bloudy *gore* VI. xii. 31. 3
Gore blood. forth gusht a stream of *gore blood* thick, II. i. 39. 7
the *gore-bloud* thence gushing grievously V. xii. 20. 6
All in *gore bloud* there tumbled on the ground, VI. iii. 27. 4
Gore-bloody. spat out poyson, and *gore-bloudy* gere, VI. xii. 28. 3
Gored. from his *gored* wound a well of bloud did gush. I. iii. 35. 9
Seeing the *gored* woundes to gape so wyde, I. v. 9. 8
Out of her *gored* wound the cruell steel II. i. 43. 1
gor'd with many a wownd, II. iv. 3. 8
purple robe *gored* with many a wound, II. vii. 13. 7
He groveling fell, all *gored* in his gushing wound. II. viii. 32. 9
the wyde wound, . . . and riven bowels *gor'd,* III. xii. 38. 4
Gorge. he grypt her *gorge* with so great paine, I. i. 19. 8
most like a brutish beast, He spued up his *gorge,* I. iv. 21. 9
Out of his stinking *gorge* forth steemed still, I. xi. 13. 8
having him embowelled To fill his hellish *gorge,* III. vii. 29. 2
did gripe his *gorge* so fast, VI. iv. 22. 4
Gorged. That which I eate did I joy, and that which I greedily *gorged,* *Ex Tempore* 1
Gorgeous. when them the *gorgeous* Flie had doft, *Mui.* 109
most brave embellished With royall robes and *gorgeous* array, I. iv. 8. 4
in garments gilt And *gorgeous* gold arayd, I. v. 26. 8
His *gorgeous* ryder from her loftie sted Would have cast downe, I. viii. 17. 5
a boxe . . . Embowd with gold and *gorgeous* ornament, I. ix. 19. 2
with golden sell And goodly *gorgeous* barbes, II. ii. 11. 7
Aray thyselfe in her most *gorgeous* geare, II. iv. 26. 8
a woman, *gorgeous* gay And richly cladd II. vii. 44. 6
With golden wreath and *gorgeous* ornament; III. vii. 11. 3
With gold and many a *gorgeous* ornament, IV. iii. 38. 7
A *gorgeous* girdle, curiously embost IV. iv. 15. 6
Gorgeously. Adorn'd with bells and bosses *gorgeouslie* *Van.* viii. 2
all with gemmes and jewels *gorgeously* Adornd, *H.H.B.* 187
Gorget. His weasand-pipe it through his *gorget* cleft. IV. iii. 12. 7
Gorgon. Great *Gorgon,* prince of darknes and dead night: I. i. 37. 8
Gorgonian. her *Gorgonian* shield gins to untye III. ix. 22. 8
Gorlois. 'But sooth he is the sonne of *Gorlois,* III. iii. 27. 1
Gormandize. To make a common feast, and feed with *gurmandize.* VI. viii. 38. 9
with fell clawes full of fierce *gourmandize,* VI. x. 34. 5
Gormond. Great *Gormond,* having with huge mightinesse Ireland subdewd, III. iii. 33. 5
Gory. out of whose rifte there came Smal drops of *gory* bloud, I. ii. 30. 9
Their *gory* sides fresh bleeding fiercely frett; I. vi. 44. 5
A gushing river of blacke *gory* blood, I. xi. 22. 4
from his *gory* sydes the blood did gush. III. i. 17. 7
all his hairy brest with *gory* bloud was fild. IV. vii. 31. 9
nought mote slake Their greedy vengeaunces but *goary* blood, VI. i. 37. 6
Goshawk. a *Goshauke,* that in foote doth beare A trembling Culver, III. vii. 39. 1
by chaunce hath spide A *Goshauke,* V. iv. 42. 4
Gospel. have the *Gospell* of free libertie.' *Hub.* 478
Gossip. 'Neighbour Ape, and my *Gossip* eke beside, *Hub.* 53
I meane my *Gossip* privie first to make.' *Hub.* 70
'Ah! my deare *Gossip,* *Hub.* 71
'Right well, deere *Gossip,* ye advized have, *Hub.* 193
Gossips. to her *gossibs* gan in counsell say; I. xii. 11. 4
Got. *See* **Gotten.**
A Biggen he had *got* about his brayne, *S.C.* May 241
with great cold he had *gotte* the gout, *S.C.* May 244
little good hath *got,* *S.C.* O. 10
well hast thow it *gotte.* *S.C.* N. 206
without golde now nothing wilbe *got,* *Hub.* 153
sure his honestie *Got* him small gaines, *Hub.* 850
so he *got* it, little did he pas. *Hub.* 1150
hath a Poet *got* To sing his living praises *Ti.* 436
her good will he *got* her first to wedde. *Col.* 131
Then *got* he bow and shafts of gold and lead, *Col.* 807
knitting all his force, *got* one hand free, I. i. 19. 7
For the coole shade him thither hastly *got:* I. ii. 29. 2
to her snowy Palfrey *got* agayne, I. iii. 8. 8
stelths, and pillage . . . *got* abroad by purchas criminall. I. iii. 16. 9
got his ready steed, and fast away gan ryde. I. vi. 8. 9
before that cursed Dragon *got* That happy land, I. xi. 29. 6
fast it stucke, ne would thereout be *gott:* I. xi. 38. 7
Take not away, now *got,* which none would give to me.' II. i. 47. 9
So to his steed he *gott,* and gan to ride II. iii. 46. 3
Great glory and gay spoile, sure hast *gott,* II. iv. 45. 6
First *got* with guile, and then preserv'd with dread, II. vii. 12. 3
I know it well be *gott;* II. vii. 19. 2
those which Hercules . . . *Got* from great Atlas daughters, II. vii. 54. 6
fruit, With which Acontius *got* his lover trew, II. vii. 55. 2
So long as any thing it in the caudron *gott.* II. ix. 29. 9
In meed of these great conquests by them *gott,* II. x. 12. 1
by him Caesar *got* the victory, II. x. 49. 1
got large portions of land, II. x. 65. 6
The growing evill, ere it strength have *gott,* III. ii. 46. 2
when in none of all these she him *got,* III. vi. 16. 1
On faire Oenone *got* a lovely boy, III. ix. 36. 4
litle good of him is to be *got,* III. x. 39. 3
She . . . his forwandred steed unto him *gott:* III. xi. 20. 6

Got—*Continued.*
On whom he *got* faire Pegasus that flitteth in the ayre. III. xi. 42. 9
Signe of nigh battaill, or *got* victory: III. xii. 1. 6
shar'd to them the spoiles that he had *got* alive. IV. i. 22. 9
He woxe full blithe, as he had *got* thereby, IV. i. 50. 8
Having so peerelesse paragon *ygot:* IV. ii. 8. 2
Got these three lovely babes, IV. ii. 45. 9
having now misfortune *got* for guide. IV. iv. 24. 4
Cambello it away before had *got.* IV. iv. 33. 5
Under Slewbloome in shady grove was *got,* IV. xi. 42. 5
those great Heroes *got* thereby Their greatest glory V. ii. 1. 5
Having great Lordships *got* and goodly farmes, V. ii. 5. 7
well they hoped to have *got* great good, V. ii. 51. 6
With whom a goodly doure I should have *got,* V. iv. 8. 8
Which having *got,* he gan . . . To stirre up strife V. x. 13. 4
He wox right blyth, as he had *got* thereby, V. xi. 9. 6
As she had *got* thereby and gayned a great stake. V. xii. 32. 9
His steede, . . . Well as she could she *got,* and did bedight; VI. v. 7. 6
Which having *got,* he used without crime VI. ix. 46. 3
Of all the other pray which they had *got,* VI. xi. 4. 4
got into the world at liberty againe. VI. xii. 38. 9
easie things, that may be *got* at will, *Am.* xxvi. 11
what glory can be *got,* In slaying him *Am.* lvii. 11
having *got* it, may it more esteeme; *H.L.* 167
Gote, Gotish, Gotes. *See* **Goat, Goatish, Goats.**
Goth. *See* **Goeth.**
Gothic. Into the *Gothicke* colde hot rage instil'd. *Ro.* xi. 8
Gotten. *See* **Evil-gotten, Got, Ill-gotten, Long-gotten.**
ought of the *gotten* good to restore: *S.C.* S. 129
Abroad, where change is, good may *gotten* bee.' *Hub.* 101
now the Foxe had *gotten* him a gowne, *Hub.* 353
without reward Livings in Court be *gotten,* *Hub.* 514
gotten was but hate. II. ii. 26. 5
traveillers, whom *gotten* they did kill. II. xii. 31. 9
he by an Elfe was *gotten* of a Fay: III. iii. 26. 9
had *gotten* a great pray Of Saxon goods; III. iii. 58. 5
he has *gotten* to a forrest neare, III. xi. 6. 6
by thee *gotten* From thy sweete smyling mother IV. Pr. 5. 6
'Unworthy life, that love with guile hast *gotten;* IV. i. 51. 7
of your *gotten* spoyle their owne triumph to make.' IV. ii. 24. 9
saves his *gotten* pray: IV. vii. 25. 7
Forgoe the purchase of my *gotten* pray, IV. viii. 62. 4
such gaine was *gotten* deare. IV. ix. 30. 9
Both gifts of God, not *gotten* but from thence, IV. x. 51. 8
that she *gotten* had So faire a wife IV. xii. 33. 6
gotten by her slight And earnest search, V. i. 9. 2
'By which that glorie *gotten* doth appeare. V. iii. 22. 4
As if the prize she *gotten* had almost, V. v. 10. 3
With which whylome he *gotten* had great fame: V. v. 20. 5
As either might for wealth have *gotten* bene, V. ix. 27. 7
unto themselves they *gotten* had A monster, V. xii. 37. 6
his late conquest which he *gotten* had: VI. i. 4. 5
there should to him a sonne Be *gotten,* not begotten; VI. iv. 32. 7
the conquest of his might, *Gotten* by spoyle VI. v. 9. 5
Gotten great worship in this worldes sight: VI. vi. 35. 8
After he *gotten* had with busie paine VI. vi. 38. 7
glorious spoile, *gotten* at last with labour *Am.* lxix. 14
things hard *gotten* men more dearely deeme. *H.L.* 168
Gourd. mosse as greene as any *goord,* *Gn.* 164
Gout. with great cold he had gotte the *gout.* *S.C.* May 244
in foote and hand A grievous *gout* tormented him full sore, I. iv. 29. 7
Govern. counselled faire Alma how to *governe* well. II. ix. 48. 9
yield her rowme to day that can it *governe* well.' III. iv. 60. 9
them *governe* wisely well, III. xi. 2. 7
Governail. He of this Gardin had the *governall,* II. xii. 48. 7
Governance. Some gan to gape for greedie *governaunce,* *S.C.* May 121
for wise and civill *governaunce.* *Hub.* 782
In learned artes, and goodlie *governaunce,* *Ti.* 270
That is regardles of his *governaunce.* *Mui.* 384
For her great worth and noble *governance;* *Col.* 503
I know your goodly *governaunce,* II. i. 29. 8
through wise handling and faire *governaunce,* II. i. 54. 6
Unworthy of faire Ladies comely *governaunce.* II. ii. 35. 9
Had he had *governaunce* it well to guyde; II. iv. 7. 2
guyde thy waies with warie *governaunce,* II. iv. 36. 4
shortly brought to civile *governaunce,* II. x. 38. 8
by Palmers *governaunce,* Passing through perilles great, II. xii. Arg.
From whom all earthly *governance* is fet. *H.H.B.* 91
Governed. so well, they say, It *governd* was, I. x. 3. 4
goodly well long time it *governed;* II. x. 47. 4
his sage Palmer that him *governed;* II. xii. 38. 5
Are *governed* with goodly modesty, *Epith.* 235
Governeth. With which the damned ghosts he *governeth,* *Hub.* 1293
Governing. his weake steps *governing* . . . on cypresse stadle stout, I. vi. 14. 7
Your fortune maister eke with *governing,* I. viii. 28. 3
under her *governing.* III. ix. 44. 5
Government. Mayst witnesse well, by thy ill *governement,* *S.C.* Ja. 45
Of kingdomes change, of divers *gouvernment,* (**government*) *Hub.* 766
government of state Will without wisedome soone be ruinate. *Hub.* 1039
ye shall have both crowne and *government,* *Hub.* 1050
of the King, and of his *government,* *Hub.* 1273
grow to height of kingdomes *government,* *T.M.* 76
The burdein of this kingdomes *governement,* *Ded. Son.* ix. 4
of his hands he had no *governement,* I. iv. 34. 4
I them warded all with wary *government.* I. ix. 10. 9
Of all the house had charge and *governement,* I. x. 37. 2
So mak'st thou kings, and gaynest wrongfull *government.* II. vii. 13. 9
Whiles it is kept in sober *government;* II. ix. 1. 4
their quiet *government* annoyd; II. x. 14. 8

Government—*Continued.*
All happy peace and goodly *government* . . . . II. xi. 2. 4
to the Saxons over-give their *government*. . . . . III. iii. 41. 9
rul'd her thoughts with goodly *governement,* . . . . IV. ii. 36. 4
She lesse esteem'd then th' others vertuous *government*. . . . IV. v. 20. 9
She left him to his fortunes *government,* . . . . IV. vi. 46. 3
that great yron groome, his gard and *government*. . . . . . V. iv. 3. 9
The true guide of his way and vertuous *government*. . . . . V. viii. 3. 9
did rebell gainst lawfull *government;* . . . . V. xii. 26. 8
Governments. Till it reduced was to one mans *governments*. . II. ix. 59. 9
maintaynd With mightie deedes their sondry *governments;* . . II. x. 74. 4
Gown. now the Foxe had gotten him a *gowne,* . . . . *Hub.* 353
In a greene *gowne* he clothed was full faire, ... I. iv. 25. 1
Lo! to that shore one in an auncient *gowne,* . . . . II. vi. 47. 4
all her *gowne* Enwoven was with gold, ... IV. x. 31. 8
Gowned. Th' olde honour of the people *gowned* long. . . . . *Ro.* xxxii. 14
Without a *gowned* beast him fast beside, ... *Hub.* 749
sage and sober peres, all gravely *gownd;* . . . . I. xii. 5. 5
th' yvorie in golden mantle *gownd:* . . . . II. xii. 67. 5
Gowns. with their *gownes* their gravitie maintaine. . . . . *Hub.* 838
Grace. All heavenly *grace* and vertue shrined is, ... *Pet.*[2] vii. 10
So sprong her *grace* Of heavenly race, ... *S.C.* Ap. 52
Her heavenly haveour, her princely *grace,* . . . . *S.C.* Ap. 66
Wants not a fourth *Grace,* to make the daunce even? . . . . *S.C.* Ap. 113
She shal be a *Grace,* To fyll the fourth place, ... *S.C.* Ap. 115
To adorne her *grace:* . . . . *S.C.* Ap. 130
The old lineaments of his fathers *grace*. . . . . *S.C.* May 212
faithlesse Rosalind and voide of *grace,* . . . . *S.C.* Jun. 115
Through Venus *grace,* and vertues cariage. . . . . *Gn.* 488
Such *grace* did God unto his creatures give. . . . . *Hub.* 402
God it is that feedes them with his *grace,* . . . . *Hub.* 437
read (faire Sir, of *grace*) . . . . *Hub.* 604
the highest now in *grace* Be the wilde beasts, ... *Hub.* 619
Thinking that their disgracing did him *grace:* . . . . *Hub.* 708
Not so much for to gaine, . . . as for his *grace,* . . . . . . *Hub.* 775
To have thy Princes *grace,* yet want her Peeres; . . . . . . *Hub.* 901
So great he was in *grace,* and rich through gaine. . . . . . *Hub.* 1200
to *grace* The learned forheads, ... *T.M.* 81
Before your Loves did take you unto *grace;* . . . . *T.M.* 377
Doth borrow *grace,* the fancie to aggrate; . . . . *T.M.* 406
Is ignorance, the enemy of *grace,* . . . . *T.M.* 497
greatest ones did sue to gaine his *grace;* . . . . *Ti.* 186
Such *grace* the heavens doo to my verses give. . . . . *Ti.* 259
influence of all celestiall *grace,* . . . . *Ti.* 289
Some one, that would with *grace* be gratifide, ... *Mui.* 110
'In puresse and in all celestiall *grace,* . . . . *D.* 211
in a moment loose their *grace* and glorie. . . . . *D.* 497
Hath farre exiled from your Ladies *grace,* . . . . D. 506
He grew up fast in goodnesse and in *grace,* . . . . *As.* 17
in his *grace* did boast you most to bee! . . . . *As.* 130
move to take him to her *grace* againe. . . . . *Col.* 175
grace was great, and bounty most rewardfull. . . . . *Col.* 187
all good, all *grace* there freely growes, ... *Col.* 324
Had people *grace* it gratefully to use: . . . . *Col.* 325
let us heare what *grace* she shewed thee. . . . . *Col.* 356
Unto that Goddesse *grace* me first enhanced, ... *Col.* 359
The pearle of peerlesse *grace* and modestie: . . . . *Col.* 471
say, who else vouchsafed thee of *grace?'* . . . . *Col.* 484
great Cynthia her in chiefest *grace* Doth hold, ... *Col.* 500
She is the blosome of *grace* and curtesie, ... *Col.* 528
great Cynthiaes goodnesse, and high *grace,* . . . . *Col.* 588
since thou foundst such *grace* With Cynthia . . . . *Col.* 652
of their *grace* us dignifie: . . . . *Col.* 818
when he list shew *grace,* Does graunt them *grace* . . . . . *Col.* 881, 882
so much *grace* let her vouchsafe to grant . . . . *Col.* 939
Such *grace* shall be some guerdon for the griefe, ... *Col.* 943
Such *grace* sometimes shall give me some reliefe, ... *Col.* 945
rymes . . . for their titles sake may find more *grace*. . . . . *Ded. Son.* i. 14
that Emperesse, . . . her sexes *grace:* . . . . *Ded. Son.* xi. 4
Mecaenas, . . . It first advaunst to great Augustus *grace,* . . *Ded. Son.* xiii. 4
And native beauty deck with hevenlie *grace:* . . . . *Ded. Son.* xv. 12
Wherewith that courtly garlond most ye *grace* . . . . *Ded. Son.* xvi. 4
comprise Those glorious ornaments of hevenly *grace,* . . . . *Ded. Son.* xvi. 7
Mirrour of *grace* and Majestie divine, ... I. Pr. 4. 2
To winne him worshippe, and her *grace* to have, ... I. i. 3. 4
Did never mortall eye behold such heavenly *grace*. . . . . . I. iii. 4 .9
Ne other *grace* vouchsafed them to showe . . . . I. iv. 14. 3
him destroy, That was the flowre of *grace* and chevalrye; . . . I. iv. 45. 8
so true-seeming *grace* It carried, ... I. v. 27. 4
never past, That backe retourned without heavenly *grace;* . . . I. v. 31. 7
From lawlesse lust by wondrous *grace* . . . . I. vi. Arg.
when they vewed have her heavenly *grace,* . . . . I. vi. 18. 5
were not hevenly *grace* that did him blesse, ... I. vii. 12. 3
Who her as willingly to *grace* did take, ... I. vii. 15. 4
Were not that heavenly *grace* doth him uphold, ... I. viii. 1. 3
Of that great Queene may well gaine worthie *grace,* . . . . . I. ix. 17. 7
A worke of wondrous *grace,* and hable soules to save. . . . . I. ix. 19. 9
had not greater *grace* Me reft from it, ... I. ix. 26. 8
Of *grace* do me unto his cabin guyde.' . . . . I. ix. 32. 3
'will ryde Against my liking backe to doe you *grace:* . . . . I. ix. 32. 6
Is not great *grace* to helpe him over past. . . . . I. ix. 39. 4
Where justice growes, there grows eke greater *grace,* . . . . . I. ix. 53. 6
the man . . . thorough *grace* hath gained victory: . . . . . . I. x. 1. 7
she up arose with seemely *grace,* . . . . I. x. 8. 4
What *grace* hath thee now hither brought this way? . . . . . . I. x. 9. 8
With countenance demure, and modest *grace,* . . . . I. x. 12. 4
Of God; of *grace;* of justice; of freewill; . . . . I. x. 19. 6
To such perfection of all hevenly *grace,* . . . . I. x. 21. 3
With goodly *grace* and comely personage, ... I. x. 30. 3
thristy give to drinke; a worke of *grace*. . . . . I. x. 38. 3

Grace—*Continued.*
The *grace* of God he layd up still in store, ... I. x. 38. 6
Great *grace* that old man to him given had; . . . . I. x. 47. 1
Well worthy doest thy service for her *grace,* . . . . I. x. 60. 3
'Unworthy wretch,' (quoth he) 'of so great *grace,* . . . . . . I. x. 62. 1
'so God me *grace,* . . . . I. x. 64. 1
added *grace* unto her excellence: . . . . I. xii. 24. 4
thy sight could win thee *grace*. . . . . II. i. 9. 9
But other some, by guifte of later *grace,* . . . . II. ii. 6. 6
To rest themselves, and *grace* to reconcile. . . . . II. ii. 33. 5
With sober *grace* and goodly carriage: . . . . II. ii. 38. 2
with bold *grace,* and comely gravity, ... II. ii. 39. 7
In her the richesse of all heavenly *grace* . . . . II. ii. 41. 1
everie one her with a *grace* endowes, ... II. iii. 25. 4
So glorious mirrhour of celestiall *grace,* . . . . II. iii. 25. 6
with stately *grace* and princely port . . . . II. iii. 28. 5
when she herselfe would *grace;* . . . . II. iii. 28. 6
this *grace* I have Me given . . . . II. iii. 45. 1
'At last such *grace* I found, ... II. iv. 21. 1
wanted *grace* in utt'ring of the same, ... II. vi. 6. 8
to me this *grace* Both yield, ... II. vi. 33. 4
'The antique world . . . Fownd no defect in his Creators *grace;* II. vii. 16. 2
If then thee list my offred *grace* to use, ... II. vii. 18. 6
Such *grace* now to be happy is before thee laid.' . . . . . . II. vii. 32. 9
'Certes,' (sayd he) 'I n'ill thine offred *grace,* . . . . II. vii. 33. 1
so great *grace* and offred high estate; . . . . II. vii. 50. 2
Of *grace* I pray thee, give to eat and drinke to mee!' . . . . II. vii. 59. 9
O! th' exceeding *grace* Of highest God . . . . II. viii. 1. 5
An armed knight, of bold and bounteous *grace,* . . . . II. viii. 17. 5
Prince Arthur, flowre of *grace* and nobilesse, ... II. viii. 18. 4
hope of helpe and timely *grace,* . . . . II. viii. 25. 6
he so wilfully refused *grace;* . . . . II. viii. 52. 6
incontinent Doth loose his dignity and native *grace:* . . . . II. ix. 1. 8
Shee is the flowre of *grace* and chastity . . . . II. ix. 4. 3
grace of earthly Prince so soveraine, ... II. ix. 6. 2
full of *grace* and goodly modestee, ... II. ix. 18. 8
to her homage made with humble *grace:* . . . . II. ix. 36. 3
the strong passion mard her modest *grace,* . . . . II. ix. 43. 4
never tasted *grace,* nor goodnes felt; . . . . II. x. 7. 3
heavenly *grace* so plenteously displayd! . . . . II. x. 50. 6
Received is to *grace* and new accord, ... II. x. 66. 4
Ne like in *grace,* ne like in learned skill; . . . . II. x. 76. 7
had not *grace* thee blest, ... II. xi. 30. 9
blushing to her laughter gave more *grace,* . . . . II. xii. 68. 2
A sweet regard and amiable *grace,* . . . . II. xii. 79. 5
besought The Prince of *grace* to let him ronne that turne. . . III. i. 5. 2
Without regard of *grace* or comely amenaunce. . . . . III. i. 41. 9
shee was full of amiable *grace* . . . . III. i. 46. 1
his Heroicke *grace* and honorable gest. . . . . III. ii. 24. 9
of *grace* I pray, Pitty our playnt, ... III. iii. 21. 2
thy great *grace* and my great jeopardee, ... III. iv. 10. 8
great *grace* or fortune thither brought Comfort . . . . III. v. 27. 3
ful of divinities And gifts of heavenly *grace* . . . . III. v. 34. 8
'what *grace* is this That thou hast shewed to me . . . . . . III. v. 35. 1
To make ensample of his heavenly *grace,* . . . . III. v. 52. 2
Tempred with *grace* and goodly modesty, ... III. v. 55. 3
all the gifts of *grace* and chastitee . . . . III. vi. 2. 5
The heritage of all celestiall *grace;* . . . . III. vi. 4. 7
Of *grace* and beautie noble Paragone, ... III. vi. 52. 2
quite devourd her beauties scornefull *grace*. . . . . III. vii. 23. 5
glad by any meanes her *grace* to gaine, ... III. vii. 54. 1
of voluntary *grace* And soveraine favor . . . . III. viii. 29. 2
Shee came in presence with right comely *grace,* . . . . III. ix. 26. 7
If goodnesse find no *grace,* . . . . III. xi. 9. 9
'If good find *grace,* and righteousnes reward, ... III. xi. 10. 1
if that hevenly *grace* some goode reliefe You send, ... III. xi. 14. 3
in that horror shewd a seemely *grace,* . . . . III. xii. 19. 8
under maske of beautie and good *grace* . . . . IV. i. 17. 7
Sith she her selfe was of his *grace* indigne; . . . . IV. i. 30. 5
by that her outward *grace* . . . . IV. ii. 22. 8
Nepenthe is a drinck of soverayne *grace,* . . . . IV. iii. 43. 1
Disgracing them, him selfe thereby to *grace,* . . . . IV. iv. 4. 2
The controverse of beauties soveraine *grace;* . . . . IV. v. 2. 3
unto your *grace* I me submit, ... IV. vi. 3. 7
Graunt him your *grace;* . . . . IV. vi. 32. 5
Death is to him . . . Both *grace* and gaine; . . . . IV. vii. 11. 8
evermore, when he did *grace* entreat, ... IV. vii. 37. 6
found no ease of griefe nor hope of *grace,* . . . . IV. vii. 38. 2
him restore to former *grace* againe: . . . . IV. vii. 47. 7
The gentle Squire recovers *grace,* . . . . IV. viii. Arg.
goodly *grace* she him did shew: . . . . IV. viii. 6. 5
wisht it were in her to doe him any *grace*. . . . . IV. viii. 12. 9
The *grace* of his Creator doth despise, ... IV. viii. 15. 8
An happie life with *grace* and good accord, ... IV. viii. 18. 2
To win her *grace* his libertie to get: . . . . IV. viii. 53. 6
By her committed be, of speciall *grace,* . . . . IV. viii. 54. 7
the Prince, through his well wonted *grace,* . . . . IV. ix. 14. 1
suuch *grace* is given them from above, ... IV. x. 2. 1
Unworthy they of *grace,* . . . . IV. x. 17. 8
she was of such *grace* and vertuous might, ... IV. x. 33. 6
unto Venus *grace* the gate doth open right. . . . . IV. x. 35. 9
Queene of beautie and of *grace,* . . . . IV. x. 44. 1
Shyning with beauties light and heavenly vertues *grace*. . . . IV. x. 52. 9
with amiable *grace* To laugh at me, ... IV. x. 56. 3
Adorn'd with honor and all comely *grace:* . . . . V. iii. 23. 2
He saw, . . . A miracle of natures goodly *grace* . . . . V. v. 12. 3
him entreat for *grace* that had procur'd her paine. . . . . . V. v. 28. 9
of princely *grace* to be inclyn'd thereto. . . . . V. v. 41. 9
readie to deserve what *grace* I found.' . . . . V. v. 42. 5
Life, freedome, *grace,* and gifts of great availe, ... V. v. 49. 3

Grace—*Continued.*
by all good means he might, deserve such *grace*. . . . V. v. 55. 9
by Gods *grace*, and her good heedinesse, . . . V. vi. 34. 6
Justice was a God of soveraine *grace*, . . . V. vii. 2. 2
gan for *grace* and love of her to seeke; . . . V. vii. 16. 3
soveraine *grace*, with which her royall crowne She doth support, V. viii. 17. 4
Dealing with Justice with indifferent *grace*, . . . V. ix. 36. 4
through high heavens *grace*, . . . V. ix. 42. 1
From thence pour'd down on men by influence of *grace*. . . . V. x. 1. 9
She humbly thankt him for that wondrous *grace*, . . . V. xi. 18. 1
'Ten daies,' (quoth he) 'he graunted hath of *grace*, . . . V. xi. 42. 3
with fresh wonted *grace* Dispreds the glorie . . . V. xii. 13. 5
with the greatest purchast greatest *grace:* . . . VI. i. 3. 5
Doth best become and greatest *grace* doth gaine; . . . VI. ii. 2. 8
A goodly youth of amiable *grace*, . . . VI. ii. 5. 2
recommended To Gods sole *grace*, . . . VI. iv. 10. 8
of her *grace* did stand againe assured, . . . VI. v. 12. 3
With stayed steps and grave beseeming *grace:* . . . VI. v. 36. 5
he *grace* and glory wonne alwaies, . . . VI. vi. 4. 4
her bowd Upon her knee, intreating him for *grace*, . . . VI. vi. 31. 6
Whether such *grace* were given her by kynd, . . . VI. vi. 43. 1
deckt with wondrous giftes of natures *grace*, . . . VI. vii. 28. 5
Adornd with goodly gifts of beauties *grace*, . . . VI. viii. 2. 2
For joy of such good hap by heavenly *grace*. . . . VI. viii. 37. 5
since by *grace* of God she there was sent, . . . VI. viii. 38. 5
Which she did more augment with modest *grace* . . . VI. ix. 9. 3
most in Pastorellaes *grace* did sit: . . . VI. ix. 41. 8
him to *grace*, Her flowry garlond tooke . . . VI. ix. 42. 5
Was favoured and to her *grace* commended. . . . VI. ix. 46. 6
how he may be relieved With *grace* from her, . . . VI. x. 1. 9
Those three to men all gifts of *grace* do graunt; . . . VI. x. 15. 4
Thy love is there advaunst to be another *Grace*. . . . VI. x. 16. 9
But whom they of them selves list so to *grace*.' . . . VI. x. 20. 5
graced her so much to be another *Grace*. . . . VI. x. 26. 9
'Another *Grace* she well deserves to be, . . . VI. x. 27. 1
with such courtesie doth *grace*, . . . VI. x. 27. 6
if any *grace* chaunst to arize To him, . . . VI. x. 33. 8
through *grace* Or secret guifts, . . . VI. xii. 6. 1
what mortall hand or heavens *grace* . . . VI. xii. 8. 7
full of *grace* and Majestie, . . . VII. vi. 24. 8
marked well her *grace*, . . . VII. vi. 28. 2
could the greatest wrath soone turne to *grace*, . . . VII. vi. 31. 3
seeke by *grace* and goodnesse to obtaine That place, . . . VII. vi. 34. 2
ungracious crew which faines demurest *grace*. . . . VII. vii. 35. 9
Pardon for thee, and *grace* for me, intreat: . . . *Am.* ii. 12
In vaine I seeke and sew to her for *grace*, . . . *Am.* xx. 1
appeare t' adorne her beauties *grace?* . . . *Am.* xxi. 4
A close intent at last to shew me *grace;* . . . *Am.* xxv. 10
so goodly giftes of beauties *grace!* . . . *Am.* xxxi. 2
Lodwick, this of *grace* to me aread; . . . *Am.* xxxiii. 5
Make peace therefore, and graunt me timely *grace*, . . . *Am.* lvii. 13
to kisse her lyps, (such *grace* I found,) . . . *Am.* lxiv. 1
Adornd with beautyes *grace* and vertues store? . . . *Epith.* 170
ere thou doest them unto *grace* restore, . . . *H.L.* 164
heavens such happie *grace* did to him lend, . . . *H.L.* 213
please her best, and *grace* unto him gaine; . . . *H.L.* 222
To live thus happy as her *grace* to gaine. . . . *H.L.* 244
whose soverayne *grace* and kindly dewty . . . *H.B.* 17
Some deaw of *grace* into my withered hart, . . . *H.B.* 27
pleasant *grace* To all things faire, . . . *H.B.* 57
chearefull *grace* and amiable sight; . . . *H.B.* 131
still preserve your first informed *grace*, . . . *H.B.* 167
One drop of *grace* at length will to me give, . . . *H.B.* 277
Venus . . . Fresh flowre of *grace*, . . . *H.B.* 282
Eternall spring of *grace* and wisedome trew, . . . *H.H.L.* 44
Yet being pregnant still with powrefull *grace*, . . . *H.H.L.* 50
But that Eternall Fount of love and *grace*, . . . *H.H.L.* 99
man, forgetfull of his Makers *grace* . . . *H.H.L.* 120
O blessed Well of Love! O Floure of *Grace!* . . . *H.H.L.* 169
His *grace*, his doome, his mercy, and his might, . . . *H.H.B.* 111
And shew himselfe in th' image of his *grace*, . . . *H.H.B.* 114
beautie . . . more increast by her owne goodly *grace*, . . . *H.H.B.* 208
Of all on earth whom God so much doth *grace* . . . *H.H.B.* 240
Where oft I gayned giftes and goodly *grace* . . . *Proth.* 138
Graced. With seasoned wit and goodly pleasance *graced*, . . . *T.M.* 200
'They all (quoth he) me *graced* goodly well, . . . *Col.* 485
The shield of Love, whose guerdon me hath *graced*, . . . IV. x. 8. 4
darted forth delights the which her goodly *graced*. . . . IV. x. 50. 9
a girland, goodly *graced*, Of lovely lasses; . . . VI. ix. 8. 3
wish th' heavens so much had *graced* mee, . . . VI. ix. 28. 6
all he could he *graced* him with her, . . . VI. ix. 39. 8
With her goodly presence all the rest much *graced*. . . . VI. x. 12. 9
a goddesse *graced* With heavenly gifts . . . VI. x. 25. 4
graced her so much to be another Grace. . . . VI. x. 26. 9
To tell her how the heavens had her *graste* . . . VI. xii. 16. 8
had the equall hevens so much you *graced* . . . *Am.* lxxxii. 5
According as the heavens have her *graced*, . . . *H.B.* 116
Graceful. Whom ye thought worthy of your *gracefull* rymes, . *Epith.* 3
Graceless. if for *gracelesse* greefe I dye, . . . *S.C.* Au. 113
Hey, ho, *gracelesse* griefe! . . . *S.C.* Au. 114
Like as the Foxe did guide his *graceles* skill; . . . *Hub.* 1128
gracelesse men them greatly do abuse.' . . . *Col.* 327
'This *gracelesse* man, for furtherance of his guile, . . . II. iv. 25. 1
Ungratious children of one *gracelesse* syre, . . . III. v. 15. 6
Much was he grieved with that *gracelesse* chaunce; . . . IV. iii. 8. 5
saw that boasters pride and *gracelesse* guile, . . . V. iii. 20. 3
way did give unto their *gracelesse* speed: . . . V. xii. 18. 4
Graces. 'Lo! how finely the *Graces* can it foote . . . *S.C.* Ap. 109
frendly Faeries, met with many *Graces*, . . . *S.C.* Jun. 25
maske in mirth with *Graces* well beseene? . . . *T.M.* 180

Graces—*Continued.*
The true Pandora of all heavenly *graces*, . . . *T.M.* 578
be heavenly *graces* there, . . . *Col.* 306
'Both heaven and heavenly *graces* do . . . abound . . . *Col.* 308
There, in deede, dwel faire *Graces* many one, . . . *Ded. Son.* v. 9
the *Graces* seemed all to sing, . . . dauncing all around; . . I. i. 48. 7
Upon her eyelids many *Graces* sate, . . . II. iii. 25. 1
unto none my *graces* do envye: . . . II. vii. 8. 4
with his goodly sisters, *Graces* three: . . . II. viii. 6. 6
so great *graces* as ye have me shewd, . . . II. viii. 55. 8
all the *Graces* rockt her cradle being borne. . . . III. vi. 2. 9
She with the pleasant *Graces* wont to play. . . . IV. v. 5. 6
Was fostered by those *Graces*, . . . IV. v. 5. 8
neither gifts nor *graces* kind . . . IV. xi. 2. 7
With whom those *graces* did so goodly fit: . . . VI. ii. 24. 7
Calidore sees the *Graces* daunce . . . VI. x. Arg.
with the *Graces* there to play and sport; . . . VI. x. 9. 5
Those were the *Graces*, daughters of delight, . . . VI. x. 15. 1
They all are *Graces* which on her depend, . . . VI. x. 21. 6
the *Graces*, that here wont to dwell, . . . VI. x. 26. 7
In whom so many *Graces* gathered are, . . . VI. x. 27. 2
sweetly doe appeare An hundred *Graces* . . . *Am.* xl. 4
That three such *graces* did unto me give. . . . *Am.* lxxiv. 14
still throw betweene Some *graces* to be seene; . . . *Epith.* 107
let the *Graces* daunce unto the rest, . . . *Epith.* 257
A thousand *Graces* masking in delight; . . . *H.B.* 254
Graceth. that proud port, which her so goodly *graceth*, . . . *Am.* xiii. 1
Gracing. Some shew of favour, by him *gracing* small, . . . VI. xi. 6. 6
Gracious. in lieu of paines so *gracious*, . . . *Gn.* 333
Use them but well, with *gracious* clemencye, . . . *Hub.* 1080
What to be great? what to be *gracious?* . . . *Ti.* 352
Thy *gracious* Soverains praises to compile, . . . *Ded. Son.* xii. 6
But with remembraunce of your *gracious* name, . . . *Ded. Son.* xvi. 3
who with *gratious* bread the hungry feeds, . . . I. iv. 32. 3
speach, So deepe did settle in her *gracious* thought, . . . I. vii. 42. 2
To be both *gratious* and eke liberall: . . . I. x. 34. 5
Poore prisoners to relieve with *gratious* ayd, . . . I. x. 40. 2
Life and long health that *gracious* ointment gave, . . . I. xi. 48. 6
Themselves to ground with *gracious* humblesse bent, . . . I. xii. 8. 3
'Ye bene right hard amated, *gratious* Lord, . . . II. ii. 5. 3
gratious womanhood, and gravitie, . . . II. ii. 15. 5
Her *gracious* words their rancour did appall, . . . II. ii. 32. 1
My Soveraine, Whose glory is in *gracious* deeds, . . . II. ii. 43. 6
she to him her *gracious* speach renewd: . . . II. iii. 37. 5
gratious to that Lady as to mee; . . . II. iv. 20. 4
by whose most *gratious* ayd I live this day, . . . II. viii. 55. 5
Whom *gracious* lott and thy great valiaunce . . . II. ix. 5. 2
gentle court and *gracious* delight Shee to them made, . . . II. ix. 20. 3
Soone as the *gracious* Alma came in place, . . . II. ix. 36. 1
The *gratious* Numa of great Britany; . . . II. x. 39. 6
a *gracious* servaunt pictured His Cynthia, . . . III. Pr. 4. 5
glee of many *gratious* Faire Ladies, . . . III. i. 31. 5
From her faire eyes and *gratious* countenaunce. . . . III. v. 42. 6
Thy life she saved by her *gratious* deed; . . . III. v. 45. 3
She, *gratious* Lady, yet no paines did spare . . . III. v. 50. 1
Through *gratious* regard of her faire eye, . . . III. ix. 25. 4
a kindly pride Of *gratious* speach . . . III. ix. 32. 7
I graunt to thy great misery *Gratious* respect; . . . III. x. 32. 2
So proov'd it eke that *gratious* God of wine, . . . III. xi. 43. 6
Yield you in lieu of this your *gracious* deed? . . . III. xii. 39. 4
Much more of price and of more *gratious* powre, . . . IV. iii. 45. 1
to my wound her *gratious* help impart. . . . IV. x. 48. 5
She her besought of *gratious* redresse. . . . V. i. 4. 4
more my *gratious* mercie by this wize, . . . V. v. 48. 7
Unto the presence of that *gratious* Queene; . . . V. ix. 27. 2
unto *gratious* great Mercilla call For ayde . . . V. x. 14. 3
comely guize withall And *gracious* speach, . . . VI. i. 2. 6
some so goodly *gratious* are by kind, . . . VI. ii. 2. 2
That in thy face appeares and *gratious* goodlyhead. . . . VI. ii. 25. 9
There they awhile some *gracious* speaches spent, . . . VI. v. 24. 6
'These three on men all *gracious* gifts bestow, . . . VI. x. 23. 1
Have Jove thy *gracious* Lord and Soveraine.' . . . VII. vi. 34. 5
With goodly port and *gracious* Majesty, . . . VII. vii. 5. 2
Graciously. favour my beginnings *graciously;* . . . *Gn.* 38
vouchsafe . . . *gratiously* to heare: . . . II. Pr. 5. 8
Graffed. *graffed* to the ground is my breche: . . . *S.C.* F. 242
From heaven, though *graft* in frailnesse feminine . . . *Col.* 918
Graft. *See* **Graffed.**
Grail. bottome yeallow, like the golden *grayle* . . . *Bel.*[2] xii. 3
lying downe upon the sandie *graile*, . . . I. vii. 6. 2
brought with him the holy *grayle*, . . . II. x. 53. 8
all his bones as small as sandy *grayle* He broke, . . . V. xi. 26. 2
Grain. Which eare the frutefull *graine* doth shortly bring; . . *Ro.* xxx. 4
As halfe unwilling to cutte the *graine;* . . . *S.C.* F. 204
feedes him once the fuller by a *graine?* . . . *S.C.* O. 34
her coulours, died deepe in *graine*, . . . I. vii. 1. 4
All armd with ragged snubbes and knottie *graine*, . . . I. viii. 7. 4
Like crimsin dyde in *grayne:* . . . *Epith.* 228
Gramercy. *'Gramercy*, Mammon,' (said the gentle Knight) . . II. vii. 50. 1
'Gramercy Sir,' said he; but mote I weete . . . II. ix. 9. 1
Grand. That flocks *grand* Captaine and most trustie guide . . *Gn.* 268
Grandam. Old Styx the *Grandame* of the Gods, . . . IV. xi. 4. 5
Grandams. No leasing new, nor *Grandams* fable stale, . . . *Col.* 102
Grandfathers. *See* **Great-grandfathers.**
Striving in power their *grandfathers* to passe, . . . *Ro.* viii. 7
Grandmother. *See* **Great-grandmother.**
'O! thou most auncient *Grandmother* of all. . . . I. v. 22. 2
Of her that is *Grand-mother* magnifide Of all the Gods, . . . VII. vi. 26. 5
This great *Grandmother* of all creatures bred, . . . VII. vii. 13. 1
Grandsire. *See* **Great-grandsire.**

Grandsire—*Continued.*
if that my *Grandsire* me sayd be true, . . . *S.C.* May 268
Great Romulus, the *Grandsyre* of them all; . . . I. v. 49. 5
from the *grandsyre* to the Nephewes sonne, . . . II. viii. 29. 3
Thy *Grandsire* Nereus promist to adorne? . . . III. iv. 36. 5
Grandsire's. 'He, noble bud, his *Grandsires* livelie hayre, . . . *Ti.* 267
Grandsires. did those Armes first give To their *Grandsyres,* *T.M.* 96
Grange. Ne have the watry foules a certaine *grange* . . . VII. vii. 21. 7
Grant. *See* **Granta.**
Nought suffered he the Ape to give or *graunt,* . . . *Hub.* 1143
graunt his boone that most desires to dye. . . . *D.* 357
Does *graunt* them grace . . . *Col.* 882
so much grace let her vouchsafe to *grant* . . . *Col.* 939
Ah, dearest God, me *graunt,* . . . I. x. 42. 9
glory does to them for guerdon *graunt:* . . . I. x. 59. 8
Great favour I thee *graunt* . . . II. iii. 7. 9
Life will I *graunt* thee for thy valiaunce, . . . II. viii. 51. 8
The God did *graunt* his daughters deare demaund, . . . III. iv. 22. 1
other offices for mother meet They would not *graunt*— . . . III. iv. 39. 7
I *graunt* to thy great misery Gratious respect; . . . III. x. 32. 1
her besought To *graunt* her boone, . . . IV. ii. 50. 2
Graunt this; that when ye shred with fatall knife His line, IV. ii. 52. 3
To *graunt* unto those warriours truce a whyle; . . . IV. vi. 25. 7
Graunt him your grace; . . . IV. vi. 32. 5
graunt more scope to me to walke at large. . . . IV. viii. 61. 4
O *graunt* that of my love at last I may not misse!" . . . IV. x. 47. 9
Besought her to *graunt* ease unto my smart, . . . IV. x. 48. 4
To *graunt* to her her sonnes life, . . . IV. xii. 29. 7
If I should *graunt* that I have doen the same, . . . V. i. 15. 6
To *graunt* him that adventure for his former feat. . . . V. x. 15. 9
I will it *graunt,* your hopelesse life to save, . . . VI. i. 42. 5
I may not *graunt* that ye so greatly prayde. . . . VI. ii. 37. 9
Have not vouchsaft to *graunt* unto us twaine . . . VI. iv. 31. 2
Ne lodging would to any of them *graunt;* . . . VI. vi. 21. 5
As *graunt* me live in like condition; . . . VI. ix. 28. 7
Those three to men all gifts of grace do *graunt;* . . . VI. x. 15. 4
To *graunt* him favour or afford him love: . . . VI. xi. 5. 4
grant me that Saboaths sight. . . . VII. viii. 2. 9
Which if she *graunt,* then live, and my love cherish: . . . *Am.* ii. 13
To *graunt* small respit to my restlesse toile; . . . *Am.* xi. 6
till she vouchsafe to *grawnt* me rest; . . . *Am.* xxxiii. 13
Make peace therefore, and *graunt* me timely grace, . . . *Am.* lvii. 13
grant that we . . . May live for ever in felicity! . . . *Am.* lxviii. 6
Grant that it may be so. . . . *Epith.* 406
graunt, O great Soveraine! . . . *H.B.* 274
Granta. The Cle, the Were, the *Grant,* the Sture, the Rowne. . . . IV. xi. 34. 5
Granted. Is *graunted* scarce to Gods above. . . . *S.C.*Mar.Emb.2
The goodman *granted,* doubting nought their deeds, . . . *Hub.* 328
when he saw no entraunce to him *graunted,* . . . *Hub.* 1367
She *graunted;* and that knight so much agraste, . . . I. x. 18. 7
Shee *graunted;* and, them leading forth, . . . II. ix. 20. 9
gladly *graunted* their desire. . . . II. ix. 60. 9
He *graunted:* then the Faery quickly raught . . . III. i. 5. 3
She *graunted;* and then in they all together far'd. . . . III. i. 30. 9
They *graunted* it; and then that carefull Fay Departed . . . IV. ii. 53. 1
Graunted to her, as to the fayrest Dame. . . . IV. v. 16. 2
Her *graunted* love, but with affection cold, . . . IV. viii. 53. 5
Prince Arthur *graunted* had To yeeld . . . IV. ix. 4. 1
He *graunted* it: . . . IV. xii. 32. 1
She gladly *graunted* it: . . . V. x. 16. 1
'Ten daies,' (quoth he) 'he *graunted* hath of grace, . . . V. xi. 42. 3
To whom his life he *graunted* for her love, . . . VI. vi. 37. 3
Granting. Which Clotho *graunting* shewed her the same. . . . IV. ii. 50. 6
Grantorto. a strong tyrant . . . *Grantorto* was his name. . . . V. i. 3. 9
Surprized was, and to *Grantorto* brought, . . . V. xi. 39. 8
a Tyrant, which *Grandtorto* hight, . . . V. xi. 50. 3
Therewith *Grandtorto* selfe I did appall, . . . V. xi. 53. 8
He with the great *Grantorto* fights, . . . V. xii. Arg.
so be now *Grantorto,* . . . V. xii. 2. 8
Which message when *Grantorto* heard, . . . V. xii. 9. 5
Grandtorto . . . he fouly did to die. . . . V. xii. 40. 8
Grantorto's. *Grantortoes* worthy punishment. . . . V. xi. 36. 5
Grapes. Her deeds were like great clusters of ripe *grapes,* . . . *Col.* 600
into her faire bosome made his *grapes* decline. . . . III. xi. 43. 9
Grapplement. With their rude handes and gryesly *graplement;* II. xi. 29. 3
Grapples. Amongst the yron hookes and *graples* keene . . . V. viii. 42. 6
Grappling. As two wild Boares together *grapling* go, . . . IV. iv. 29. 8
Graseth, Grasing. *See* **Grazeth, Grazing.**
Grasping. Knitting his wanton armes with *grasping* hold, . . . *Gn.* 218
it forst him slacke His *grasping* hold, . . . I. i. 20. 5
he forst him to unty One of his *grasping* feete, . . . I. xi. 42. 9
gan soone unbrace His *grasping* hold: . . . II. iv. 9. 8
Grasps. All that the Ocean *graspes* in his long armes; . . . *Ro.* xxvi. 6
Grass. Like as the seeded field greene *grasse* first showes, . . . *Ro.* xxx. 1
Then from greene *grasse* into a stalke doth spring, . . . *Ro.* xxx. 2
Up to his eares the verdant *grasse* did growe, . . . *Van.* ii. 5
The *grasse* nowe ginnes to be refresht, . . . *S.C.* Mar. 10
the grownd with *grasse,* . . . *S.C.* May 7
The fieldes ay fresh, the *grasse* ay greene. . . . *S.C.* N. 189
Where thickest *grasse* did cloath the open hills. . . . *Gn.* 74
on the soft greene *grasse* feeding their fills, . . . *Gn.* 78
On the soft *grasse* his limbs doth oft display, . . . *Gn.* 108
To dig up sods out of the flowrie *grasse,* . . . *Gn.* 654
Sith now I am but weedes and wastfull *gras?* . . . *Ti.* 42
streames of blood foorth flowed on the *gras.* . . . *Ti.* 651
softly tread The tender *grasse,* . . . *D.* 312
wont to feede with finest *grasse* that grew, . . . *D.* 345
Upon the perled *grasse* to make their feast. . . . *Col.* 607
creeping sought way in the weedy *gras:* . . . I. i. 20. 8
on the *grasse* her dainty limbs did lay . . . I. iii. 4. 3

Grass—*Continued.*
at length she found the troden *gras,* . . . I. iii. 10. 4
The verdant *gras* my couch did goodly dight, . . . I. ix. 13. 3
nought but pressed *gras* where she had lyen, . . . I. ix. 15. 2
there lay upon the *gras* A dreary corse, . . . I. ix. 36. 4
often bounding on the brused *gras,* . . . I. xi. 15. 3
upon the soiled *gras* The dead corse of an armed knight . . . II. i. 41. 1
on greene *gras* Gay steed with spurs did pricke, . . . II. i. 49. 8
whose fiery feete did burne The verdant *gras* . . . III. i. 5. 6
the greene *grasse* that groweth they shall bren, . . . III. iii. 34. 8
feeds on wemens flesh as others feede on *gras.* . . . III. vii. 22. 9
with their horned feet the greene *gras* wore, . . . III. x. 45. 7
wilfully him throwing on the *gras* . . . III. xi. 27. 5
hidden snares Through the greene *gras* . . . III. xi. 28. 9
With pearly dew sprinkling the morning *grasse:* . . . IV. v. 45. 5
pour'd the purple bloud forth on the *gras;* . . . IV. vi. 15. 7
That all his garments and the *grasse* in vermeill dyde. . . . VI. ii. 40. 9
as he lay upon the humbled *gras,* . . . VI. vii. 26. 3
Upon the *grasse* her selfe adowne she layd; . . . VI. viii. 34. 3
they them selves did place Upon the *grasse,* . . . VI. viii. 39. 2
Nor any footing fynd for overgrowen *gras:* . . . VI. x. 41. 9
on the soft And downy *grasse* her dainty limbes to lay . . . VII. vi. 42. 4
lying on the flowry *gras,* . . . *Epith.* 308
All sowd with glistring stars more thicke then *grasse,* . . . *H.H.B.* 53
Grassed. *See* **Overgrassed.**
Grasshopper. Such pleasaunce makes the *Grashopper* so poore, *S.C.* O. 11
Grasshoppers. shrill *grashoppers* chirped them around; . . . *Gn.* 231
Grassy. 'See, where she sits upon the *grassie* greene, . . . *S.C.* Ap. 55
The *grassye* ground with daintye Daysies dight, . . . *S.C.* Jun. 6
playing on the *grassy* greene, . . . *Gn.* 177
looslie on the *grassie* greene dispredd, . . . *Gn.* 242
He soft arrived on the *grassie* plaine, . . . *Hub.* 1263
Nor the ranke *grassie* fennes delights untride. . . . *Mui.* 156
I spied playing on the *grassie* playne . . . *D.* 110
About the *grassie* bancks of Haemony . . . *As.* 3
since first on *grassie* greene Shepheards kept sheep, . . . *As.* 209
by his side his steed the *grassy* forage ate. . . . I. vii. 2. 9
Pourd out in loosnesse on the *grassy* grownd, . . . I. vii. 7. 2
into a deepe sanguine dide the *grassy* grownd. . . . II. i. 39. 9
layd him downe upon a *grassy* playn; . . . II. vi. 14. 4
grassy greene of delectable hew; . . . II. xii. 12. 3
fayre *grassy* grownd Mantled with greene, . . . II. xii. 50. 3
Downe himselfe he layd Upon the *grassy* ground . . . III. iv. 53. 8
besprinckled all the *grassy* greene: . . . III. v. 28. 5
Upon the *grassy* ground her selfe she layd . . . III. vi. 7. 2
a knight all wallowed Upon the *grassy* ground, . . . III. xi. 7. 4
For bloud to gush forth on the *grassie* field; . . . IV. iii. 9. 5
downe she fell upon the *grassie* field . . . V. v. 11. 3
all the *grassie* flore Was fild with bloud . . . V. vii. 31. 5
Loosely displayd upon the *grassie* ground, . . . VI. vii. 18. 8
Graste. *See* **Graced.**
Grate. His gall did *grate* for griefe and high disdaine; . . . I. i. 19. 6
in the same a little *grate* was pight, . . . I. viii. 37. 6
for griefe his hart did *grate,* . . . II. i. 56. 6
the feend his gnashing teeth did *grate,* . . . II. vii. 34. 1
chiefely Paridell his hart did *grate* . . . III. ix. 14. 5
Her heart for rage did *grate,* . . . V. iv. 37. 7
Grated. gan to grind His *grated* teeth . . . II. v. 14. 3
Grateful. goodly gifts, the signes of *gratefull* mynd, . . . I. ix. 18. 8
eke with *gratefull* service me right well apay. . . . V. v. 33. 9
Her selfe most *gratefull* shew'd, . . . V. viii. 23. 9
Gratefully. Had people grace it *gratefully* to use: . . . *Col.* 325
Gratian. murdred by the freends of *Gratian.* . . . II. x. 61. 5
Gratified. Some one, that would with grace be *gratifide,* . . . *Mui.* 110
all new-come guests he *gratyfide:* . . . II. xii. 49. 5
Grating. Grinding his teeth, and *grating* his great hart; . . . *Hub.* 1334
Grave. Corinth skil'd in curious workes to *grave;* . . . *Ro.* xxix. 4
They bene so *grave* and full of mayntenaunce. . . . *S.C.* S. 169
The gaudie girlonds deck her *grave,* . . . *S.C.* N. 108
afterwards with *grave* advizement said: . . . *Hub.* 176
through wise speaches and *grave* conference . . . *Hub.* 791
hell, and darkenesse, and the grislie *grave,* . . . *T.M.* 496
have in mine owne bowels made my *grave,* . . . *Ti.* 26
these wofull layes, On my *grave* written, . . . *D.* 537
Oft from those *grave* affaires were wont abstaine, . . . *Ded. Son.* i. 5
To menage of most *grave* affaires is bent; . . . *Ded. Son.* ix. 2
And wipe their faults out of your censure *grave.* . . . *Ded. Son.* ix. 14
He, . . . his mother earth did kis, Greeting his *grave:* . . . I. ii. 19. 7
whom he . . . slew, and brought to shamefull *grave:* . . . I. iv. 47. 6
pourtrahed With natures pen, in ages *grave* degree, . . . I. viii. 33. 8
His dwelling . . . Darke, dolefull, dreary, like a greedy *grave,* I. ix. 33. 4
layes the soule to sleepe in quiet *grave?* . . . I. ix. 40. 7
Through wisedome of a matrone *grave* . . . I. x. 3. 5
'Thrise happy man,' said then the father *grave,* . . . I. x. 51. 1
The sencelesse corse appointed for the *grave:* . . . I. xi. 48. 8
with utt'rance *grave,* and count'nance sad, . . . I. xii. 15. 7
with great wisedome and *grave* eloquence . . . I. xii. 24. 5
well ye wote by *grave* intendiment, . . . I. xii. 31. 3
he threw Into the *grave,* . . . II. i. 61. 4
boast to swallow her in greedy *grave;* . . . II. ii. 24. 6
the Palmer, by his *grave* restraynt, Him stayd . . . II. v. 24. 3
'Not one, nor other,' sayd the Palmer *grave,* . . . II. viii. 24. 6
His goodly reason and *grave* personage, . . . II. ix. 54. 7
Ne him committ to *grave* terrestriall, . . . II. xi. 45. 8
In th' huge abysse of his engulfing *grave,* . . . II. xii. 5. 8
greater crosse To see frends *grave,* . . . III. iv. 38. 9
dead the *grave* self to engrosse. . . . III. iv. 38. 9
Ne privy bee unto your treasures *grave.'* . . . III. x. 42. 8
a *grave* personage That in his hand a braunch of laurell bore, III. xii. 3. 6
with *grave* foresight Welds kingdomes causes . . . IV. Pr. 1. 1

Grave—*Continued.*
So goodly *grave,* and full of princely aw, . . . IV. vi. 33. 5
Like ghost late risen from his *grave* agryz'd, . . . IV. viii. 12. 7
came Many *grave* persons that against her pled. . . . V. ix. 43. 6
With stayed steps and *grave* beseeming grace: . . . VI. v. 36. 5
Did gladly hearken to his *grave* beheast, . . . VI. vi. 15. 2
straight gan cast their counsell *grave* and wise. . . . VII. vi. 22. 6
Grave-clothes. like a ghost he seem'd whose *grave-clothes* were unbound: . . . II. xi. 20. 9
Gravel. all the *gravell* mixt with golden owre: . . . III. iv. 18. 6
Gravely. A noble crew . . . all *gravely* gownd; . . . I. xii. 5. 5
Graven. With curious Corbes and pendants *graven* faire, . . . IV. x. 6. 7
Graver. Aread in *graver* wise what I demaund of thee.' . . . I. viii. 33. 9
graver countenance then all the rest; . . . IV. x. 49. 2
Gravest. To be the greatest and the *gravest* wight, . . . V. vii. 18. 5
Gravity. There thou must walke in sober *gravitee,* . . . *Hub.* 496
with their gownes their *gravitie* maintaine. . . . *Hub.* 838
His reverend heares and holy *gravitee* . . . I. viii. 32. 1
gratious womanhood, and *gravitie,* . . . II. ii. 15. 5
with bold grace, and comely *gravity,* . . . II. ii. 39. 7
Whose hoary locks great *gravitie* did crowne, . . . II. vi. 47. 5
Gray. now the *gray* mosse marred his rine; . . . *S.C.* F. 111
Well decked in a frocke of *gray,* . . . *S.C.* Au. 65
Hey, ho, *gray* is greete! . . . *S.C.* Au. 66
the greene in *gray* is tinct; . . . *S.C.* N. 107
A simple husbandman in garments *gray;* . . . *Hub.* 228
The wholesome Saulge, and Lavender still *gray,* . . . *Mui.* 187
(Mole hight that mountain *gray* . . . *Col.* 104
His feete all bare, his beard all hoarie *gray,* . . . I. i. 29. 3
Where grew two goodly trees, . . . with *gray* mosse overcast; I. ii. 28. 4
He was an aged syre, all hory *gray,* . . . I. x. 5. 5
he hath lefte his plumes all hory *gray,* . . . I. xi. 34. 4
Of rypest yeares, and heares all hoarie *gray,* . . . II. i. 7. 3
under him a *gray* steede he did wield, . . . II. i. 18. 6
loathly were and hoarie *gray,* . . . II. iv. 4. 5
did staine And the *gray* Ocean into purple dy: . . . II. x. 48. 4
on a Courser dapled *gray,* . . . III. vii. 37. 3
With head all hoary, and his beard all *gray,* . . . IV. xi. 25. 8
The chaulky Kenet, and the Thetis *gray,* . . . IV. xi. 29. 5
waters *gray* By faire Kilkenny and Rosseponte boord; . . . IV. xi. 43. 3
made him change his *gray* attire to greene: . . . VII. vii. 11. 8
now round, now bright, now browne and *gray;* . . . VII. vii. 50. 8
Gray-eyed. The *gray-eyde* Doris; . . . IV. xi. 48. 5
Grayle. *See* **Grail.**
Graze. The whiles our flockes do *graze* about in sight, . . . *S.C.* Ap. 31
Letting their steedes to *graze* upon the greene. . . . VI. v. 38. 2
Grazeth. sike mischiefe *graseth* hem emong, . . . *S.C.* S. 113
Grazing. Whiles he had keeping of his *grasing* steed. . . . I. vii. 19. 2
Sitting in shade beside his *grazing* steede; . . . IV. vi. 2. 6
Great. the *great* Typhaeus sister . . . *Bel.*[1] xi. 4
With so *great* noyse I start . . . *Bel.*[1] xi. 14
O *great* misfortune, O *great* griefe, . . . *Pet.*[1] ii. 10
great Babylon is fallen. . . . *Rev.* ii. 14
that *great* rivers banck, that runnes by Rome; . . . *Bel.* i. 6
under this *great* temple . . . *Bel.* i. 10
To beare the frame, foure *great* Lyons . . . *Bel.* iii. 10
So *great* riches as like cannot be found! . . . *Pet.* ii. 14
foorthwith in *great* despight he dide, . . . *Pet.* v. 11
shine all scaly with *great* plates of golde; . . . *Bel.*[2] ii. 10
overthrew this frame with ruine *great.* . . . *Bel.*[2] ii. 14
the roote in *great* disdaine . . . send forth . . . *Bel.*[2] v. 13
the ground-work of an old *great* wall; . . . *Bel.*[2] viii. 2
the *great* glorie and the auncient praise, . . . *Bel.*[2] x. 6
suddenly arose a tempest *great,* . . . *Bel.*[2] xiii. 5
I thus mazed was with *great* affray, . . . *Bel.*[2] xv. 11
with *great* noyse I wakte . . . *Bel.*[2] xv. 14
O, how *great* ruth, and sorrowfull assay, . . . *Pet.*[2] ii. 11
Great Babylon her haughtie walls will praise, . . . *Ro.* ii. 1
the storie Of Joves *great* Image . . . *Ro.* ii. 6
The *great* Colosse, erect to Memorie; . . . *Ro.* ii. 10
her *great* spirite . . . is in the same enwombed; . . . *Ro.* v. 10
rejoyned to the spirite Of this *great* masse, . . . *Ro.* v. 11
more than that *great* Phrygian mother . . . *Ro.* vi. 5
onely Rome could make *great* Rome to tremble: . . . *Ro.* vi. 10
shaming to have given so *great* head To his off-spring, . . . *Ro.* xi. 1
In a *great* mountaine heap't with hideous noyse, . . . *Ro.* xvi. 2
So long as Joves *great* Bird did make his flight, . . . *Ro.* xvii. 1
their rule of yearely Presidents Grew *great,* . . . *Ro.* xviii. 8
sixe months greater a *great* deele; . . . *Ro.* xviii. 8
rose to so *great* might, . . . *Ro.* xviii. 9
Rome, in the time of her *great* ancesters, . . . *Ro.* xix. 7
their *great* sinnes, the causers of their paine, . . . *Ro.* xix. 13
With his *great* bellie spreds the dimmed world, . . . *Ro.* xx. 6
not able to beare so *great* weight, . . . *Ro.* xx. 12
If too *great* winde against the port him drive, . . . *Ro.* xxi. 13
Shall in *great* Chaos wombe againe be hid. . . . *Ro.* xxii. 14
By paterne of *great* Virgils spirit divine! . . . *Ro.* xxv. 11
He that hath seene a *great* Oke drie and dead, . . . *Ro.* xxviii. 1
O mervelous *great* change! . . . *Ro.* xxix. 12
So by the small the *great* is oft diseased. . . . *Van.* ii. 14
(O *great* ruth for the same!) . . . *Van.* vii. 10
Let therefore nought, that *great* is, therein glorie, . . . *Van.* viii. 13
Should able be so *great* an one to wring. . . . *Van.* ix. 14
a Goose *great* Rome from ruine stayde, . . . *Van.* xi. 9
To see so *great* things by so small distrest . . . *Van.* xii. 4
To scorne all difference of *great* and small, . . . *Van.* xii. 6
So spake this bold brere with *great* disdaine: . . . *S.C.* F. 139
Such follie *great* sorow to Niobe did breede: . . . *S.C.* Ap. 87
Great pittie is, he be in such taking, . . . *S.C.* Ap. 156
to thinke How *great* sport they gaynen . . . *S.C.* May 36

Great—*Continued.*
When *great* Pan account of shepeherdes shall aske. . . . *S.C.* May 54
the *great* care I have of thy health . . . *S.C.* May 215
with *great* cold he had gotte the gout. . . . *S.C.* May 244
Asked the cause of his *great* distresse, . . . *S.C.* May 260
made *great* mone. . . . *S.C.* May 301
Great clymbers fall unsoft. . . . *S.C.* Jul. 12
wonned not the *great* God Pan Upon mount Olivet, . . . *S.C.* Jul. 49
O blessed sheepe! O shepheard *great!* . . . *S.C.* Jul. 53
They han *great* stores and thriftye stockes, . . . *S.C.* Jul. 193
Great freendes and feeble foes: . . . *S.C.* Jul. 194
Here is a *great* deale of good matter Lost . . . *S.C.* Jul. 205
He is a shepheard *great* in gree, . . . *S.C.* Jul. 215
that *great* Pan bought with deare borrow, . . . *S.C.* S. 96
For feare of raungers and the *great* hunt, . . . *S.C.* S. 159
We han *great* Bandogs will teare their skinne. . . . *S.C.* S. 163
Mischiefe light on him, and Gods *great* curse! . . . *S.C.* S. 212
Too good for him had bene a *great* deale worse; . . . *S.C.* S. 213
great Augustus long ygoe is dead, . . . *S.C.* O. 62
Dido! the *greate* shepehearde his daughter sheene. . . . *S.C.* N. 38
greate shepheard, Lobbin, how *great* is thy griefe! . . . *S.C.* N. 113
Whether rejoyce or weepe for *great* constrainte. . . . *S.C.* N. 205
you (*great* Lord) the causer of my care, . . . *Gn. Ded.* 2
ornament of *great* Joves progenie, . . . *Gn.* 14
O! the *great* happines, which shepheards have, . . . *Gn.* 89
As the *great* Ocean doth himselfe divide. . . . *Gn.* 160
great mirth and gladsome glee. . . . *Gn.* 184
The *great* Argoan ships brave ornament, . . . *Gn.* 210
An huge *great* Serpent, all with speckles pide, . . . *Gn.* 250
murdred troupes upon *great* heapes to lay. . . . *Gn.* 400
beside the honourable band Of *great* Heroes . . . *Gn.* 480
Great Nereus his daughter and his joy. . . . *Gn.* 492
that *great* warre, which Trojanes oft behelde? . . . *Gn.* 498
As the *great* clap of thunder . . . *Gn.* 519
'Againe *great* dole on either partie grewe, . . . *Gn.* 529
Manie *great* bandogs which her gird about: . . . *Gn.* 540
because your griefe doth *great* appeare, . . . *Hub.* 73
As pausing in *great* doubt, awhile he staid, . . . *Hub.* 175
we shall ronne Into *great* daunger, . . . *Hub.* 184
how to scape *great* punishment, . . . *Hub.* 314
the charge is wondrous *great,* . . . *Hub.* 431
Ne is the paines so *great,* but beare ye may, . . . *Hub.* 446
not so *great,* as it was wont of yore, . . . *Hub.* 447
other *great* one in the worldes eye, . . . *Hub.* 490
to be a beetle-stock Of thy *great* Masters will, . . . *Hub.* 508
they, that are *great* Clerkes, have nearer wayes, . . . *Hub.* 537
Ye a *great* master are in your degree: . . . *Hub.* 546
Great thankes I yeeld you for your discipline, . . . *Hub.* 547
As if he were some *great* Magnifico, . . . *Hub.* 665
he therein had *great* felicitie; . . . *Hub.* 706
being one of *great* regard In Court, . . . *Hub.* 885
To growe into *great* lacke, . . . *Hub.* 927
he driven was to *great* distresse, . . . *Hub.* 933
So *great* he was in grace, and rich through gaine. . . . *Hub.* 1200
he sdeignfully it scorn'd In his *great* heart, . . . *Hub.* 1235
Done through the Foxes *great* oppressions, . . . *Hub.* 1312
Grinding his teeth, and grating his *great* hart; . . . *Hub.* 1334
The golden brood of *great* Apolloes wit, . . . *T.M.* 2
Heare, thou *great* Father of the Gods on hie, . . . *T.M.* 55
whom thou, *great* Jove, by doome unjust . . . *T.M.* 69
great revenues all in sumptuous pride They spend, . . . *T.M.* 469
There we behold the heavens *great* Hierarchie, . . . *T.M.* 507
Ne fawnest for the favour of the *great;* . . . *Com. Son.* i. 6
Like a *great* Lord of peerelesse liberty; . . . *Com. Son.* i. 10
With so *great* labour and long lasting paine, . . . *Ti.* 53
all that in this world is *great* or gaie . . . *Ti.* 55
great warriors, which did overcome The world . . . *Ti.* 61
where is that same *great* seven-headded beast, . . . *Ti.* 71
With my *great* forces might compared bee: . . . *Ti.* 103
for *great* griefe Of my mishaps, . . . *Ti.* 141
Yet it is comfort in *great* languishment, . . . *Ti.* 159
through the *great* outrage Of her owne people . . . *Ti.* 172
Whose *great* good deeds, in countrey and in towne, . . . *Ti.* 263
What to be *great?* what to be gracious? . . . *Ti.* 352
'How manie *great* ones may remembred be, . . . *Ti.* 358
raised they the puissant brood . . . for *great* merite, . . . *Ti.* 380
'Such one Mausolus made, the worlds *great* wonder, . . . *Ti.* 414
'Those two be those two *great* calamities, . . . *Ti.* 442
did grieve the noble spright . . . with *great* indignities, . . . *Ti.* 444
Not that *great* Idoll might with this compaire, . . . *Ti.* 495
Was (O *great* pitie!) built of brickle clay, . . . *Ti.* 499
that *great* Towre, which is so much renownd . . . *Ti.* 509
that *great* Arche, which Trajan edifide, . . . *Ti.* 551
for *great* sorrow of their sudden fate, . . . *Ti.* 573
Which th' ashes seem'd of some *great* Prince to hold, . . . *Ti.* 661
Betwixt two mightie ones of *great* estate, . . . *Mui.* 3
By his *great* lookes and power Imperiall. . . . *Mui.* 312
With griefe of mournefull *great* mishap opprest, . . . *D.* 2
fell to ground for *great* extreamitie; . . . *D.* 185
with her she reft *Great* hope, . . . *D.* 221
unto the bridale feast Of his *great* Lord, . . . *D.* 269
As the *Great* Judge at first did it ordaine, . . . *D.* 363
he of them *great* troups did soone entrap. . . . *As.* 100
how *great* a losse Had all the shepheards . . . *Col.* 16
ragged ruines breed *great* ruth and pittie . . . *Col.* 114
In *great* avenge did roll downe from his hill . . . *Col.* 149
Of *great* unkindnesse, and of usage hard, . . . *Col.* 165
could *great* Cynthiaes sore displeasure breake, . . . *Col.* 174
He gan to cast *great* lyking to my lore, . . . *Col.* 180
great dislyking to my lucklesse lot, . . . *Col.* 181

Great—*Continued.*

grace was *great,* and bounty most rewardfull. . . . *Col.* 187
Behold! an huge *great* vessell to us came, . . . *Col.* 213
a *great* shepheardesse, that Cynthia hight, . . . *Col.* 234
There learned arts do florish in *great* honor, . . . *Col.* 320
not by measure of her owne *great* mynd, . . . *Col.* 364
shee That is so *great* a shepheardesse her selfe, . . . *Col.* 369
There eke is Palin worthie of *great* praise, . . . *Col.* 392
Excelling most in glorie and *great* light: . . . *Col.* 497
great Cynthia her in chiefest grace Doth hold, . . . *Col.* 500
For her *great* worth and noble governance; . . . *Col.* 503
Best knowne by bearing up *great* Cynthiaes traine: . . . *Col.* 509
great Cynthiaes goodnesse, and high grace, . . . *Col.* 588
Her deeds were like *great* clusters of ripe grapes, . . . *Col.* 600
her *great* excellence Lifts me . . . *Col.* 620
so *great* enemies as of them bee, . . . *Col.* 844
Out of the fruitfull wombe of their *great* mother. . . . *Col.* 854
How *great* a guilt upon your heads ye draw, . . . *Col.* 928
This simple trophe of her *great* conquest.'— . . . *Col.* 951
So you, *great* Lord, that with your counsell sway . . . *Ded. Son.* i. 9
Mecaenas, . . . It first advaunst to *great* Augustus grace, . . . *Ded. Son.* xiii. 4
That are the *great* Mecaenas of this age, . . . *Ded. Son.* xiii. 9
Great Ladie of the greatest Isle, . . . I. Pr. 4. 3
Upon a *great* adventure he was bond, . . . I. i. 3. 1
when he heard, in *great* perplexitie, . . . I. i. 19. 5
he grypt her gorge with so *great* paine, . . . I. i. 19. 8
Full of *great* lumps of flesh . . . I. i. 20. 3
Armory, Wherein ye have *great* glory wonne this day, . . . I. i. 27. 6
no . . . wight May ever passe, but thorough *great* distresse.' . . . I. i. 32. 3
Great Gorgon, prince of darknes and dead night; . . . I. i. 37. 8
this *great* passion of unwonted lust, . . . I. i. 49. 1
The guilefull *great* Enchaunter parts . . . I. ii. Arg.
Retourning to his bed in torment *great,* . . . I. ii. 6. 1
In whose *great* shield was writ with letters gay . . . I. ii. 12. 7
O, how *great* sorrow my sad soule assaid! . . . I. ii. 24. 5
He in *great* passion al this while did dwell, . . . I. ii. 26. 5
For danger *great,* . . . I saw before mine eyes, . . . I. ii. 41. 8
I . . . Feele my hart perst with so *great* agony, . . . I. iii. 1. 8
Her angels face, As the *great* eye of heaven, . . . I. iii. 4. 7
Her hart gan melt in *great* compassion; . . . I. iii. 6. 8
For anguish *great* they gan to rend their heare, . . . I. iii. 22. 4
so *great* was the puissance of his push, . . . I. iii. 35. 6
Great troupes of people traveild thetherward . . . I. iv. 3. 1
But full *great* pittie, that so faire a mould . . . I. iv. 5. 3
To prove the wide report of her *great* Majestee. . . . I. iv. 13. 9
Thought . . . that *great* Princesse too exceeding prowd, . . . I. iv. 15. 8
strove to match, . . . *Great* Junoes golden chayre; . . . I. iv. 17. 5
he . . . grudged at the *great* felicitee Of proud Lucifera, . . . I. iv. 31. 8
that *great* Queene, . . . Commaunded them their fury to refraine; . . . I. iv. 40. 5
Whome *great* griefe made forgett the raines to hold . . . I. iv. 41. 3
hart that . . . is with childe of glorious *great* intent, . . . I. v. 1. 2
The Sarazin . . . heaped blowes like yron hammers *great;* . . . I. v. 7. 2
Great ruth in all the gazers harts did grow, . . . I. v. 9. 7
all the people followe with *great* glee, . . . I. v. 16. 7
that *great* house of Gods caelestiall, . . . I. v. 22. 4
who shall not *great* Nightes children scorne, . . . I. v. 23. 8
chaunge in that *great* mothers face: . . . I. v. 24. 7
by my ruines thinkes to make them *great:* . . . I. v. 25. 8
To make one *great* by others losse is bad excheat. . . . I. v. 25. 9
O thou far renowmed sonne Of *great* Apollo! . . . I. v. 43. 7
Great pains, and greater praise, both never to be donne.' . . . I. v. 43. 9
There was that *great* proud king of Babylon, . . . I. v. 47. 1
through his *great* richesse store; . . . I. v. 47. 7
them long time before, *great* Nimrod was, . . . I. v. 48. 1
Great Romulus, the Grandsyre of them all; . . . I. v. 49. 5
High Caesar, *great* Pompey, and fiers Antonius. . . . I. v. 49. 9
many corses, like a *great* Lay-stall, . . . I. v. 53. 2
al through that *great* Princesse pride did fall, . . . I. v. 53. 5
cryes, The last vaine helpe of wemens *great* distresse, . . . I. vi. 6. 3
Great maistresse of her art was that false Dame, . . . I. vii. 1. 8
So growen *great,* through arrogant delight . . . I. vii. 10. 1
'O *great* Orgoglio! greatest under skye, . . . I. vii. 14. 5
that renowmed Snake Which *great* Alcides in Stremona slew, . . . I. vii. 17. 2
seven *great* heads out of his body grew, . . . I. vii. 17. 7
with them all departes to tell his *great* distresse. . . . I. vii. 19. 9
Helmet . . . glorious brightnesse and *great* terrour bredd: . . . I. vii. 31. 2
'Well may I ween your griefe is wondrous *great;* . . . I. vii. 40. 2
wondrous *great* griefe groneth in my spright, . . . I. vii. 40. 3
'*great* griefe will not be tould, . . . I. vii. 41. 1
An huge *great* Dragon, horrible in sight, . . . I. vii. 44. 2
Gloriane, *great* Queene of glory bright, . . . I. vii. 46. 6
my cause of griefe, more *great* then may be told.' . . . I. vii. 51. 9
'Certes, Madame, ye have *great* cause of plaint; . . . I. vii. 52. 3
Wyde wonders . . . Of that same hornes *great* vertues . . . I. viii. 3. 8
As *great* a noyse, as when . . . complaine, . . . I. viii. 11. 5
That to have heard *great* horror would have bred; . . . I. viii. 17. 2
Through *great* impatience of his grieved hed, . . . I. viii. 17. 4
That huge *great* body, which the Gyaunt bore, . . . I. viii. 24. 7
he himselfe with greedie *great* desyre Into the Castle entred . . . I. viii. 29. 3
great Orgoglio with his puissaunce fell . . . I. viii. 32. 7
sprites, . . . with *great* griefe were often heard to grone, . . . I. viii. 36. 8
Least so *great* good . . . Should die unknown, . . . I. ix. 2. 8
'Thither the *great* magicien Merlin came, . . . I. ix. 5. 1
Before their rage grew to so *great* unrest, . . . I. ix. 9. 7
chaunge of hew *great* passion did bewray; . . . I. ix. 16. 2
Of that *great* Queene may well gaine worthie grace, . . . I. ix. 17. 7
Is not *great* grace to helpe him over past, . . . I. ix. 39. 4
All those *great* battels, which thou boasts to win . . . I. ix. 43. 3
In word and deede that shewd *great* modestee, . . . I. x. 7. 4

Great—*Continued.*

As might become a Squyre so *great* persons to greet. . . . I. x. 7. 9
great hostes of men she could dismay; . . . I. x. 20. 4
Almightie God her gave such powre and puissaunce *great.* . . . I. x. 20. 9
his sinnes, so *great* and manifold, . . . I. x. 22. 4
She found her selfe assayld with *great* perplexity; . . . I. x. 22. 9
had *great* insight In that disease . . . I. x. 23. 7
his torment often was so *great,* That . . . he would cry . . . I. x. 28. 1
a woman . . . Full of *great* love, . . . I. x. 30. 5
Shee him instructed with *great* industree. . . . I. x. 45. 5
Great grace that old man to him given had; . . . I. x. 47. 1
eien . . . through *great* age had lost their kindly sight, . . . I. x. 47. 4
The Citty of the *greate* king hight it well, . . . I. x. 55. 8
with *great* joy into that Citty wend, . . . I. x. 56. 4
great Cleopolis . . . The fairest citty was . . . I. x. 58. 2
this *great* Citty that does far surpas, . . . I. x. 58. 8
'Unworthy wretch,' (quoth he) 'of so *great* grace, . . . I. x. 62. 1
Great thankes, and goodly meed, . . . I. x. 68. 4
he lay upon the sunny side Of a *great* hill, . . . I. xi. 4. 6
himselfe like a *great* hill: . . . I. xi. 4. 6
hartes of *great* Heroes doest enrage, . . . I. xi. 6. 4
Twixt that *great* faery Queene and Paynim king, . . . I. xi. 7. 4
The cloudes before him fledd for terror *great,* . . . I. xi. 10. 8
As for *great* joyance of his newcome guest. . . . I. xi. 15. 4
To be avenged of so *great* despight; . . . I. xi. 17. 6
To beare so *great* a weight: . . . I. xi. 18. 6
that *great* Champion of the antique world, . . . I. xi. 27. 1
Full of *great* vertues, and for med'cine good: . . . I. xi. 29. 5
Great woe and sorrow did her soule assay, . . . I. xi. 32. 2
she had *great* doubt of his safety, . . . I. xi. 33. 8
great vertues over-all were redd; . . . I. xi. 46. 4
Great God it planted in that blessed stedd . . . I. xi. 46. 7
Did grone, as feeble so *great* load to lift; . . . I. xi. 54. 4
rolling downe *great* Neptune doth dismay: . . . I. xi. 54. 8
atchievde so *great* a conquest by his might. . . . I. xi. 55. 9
Rejoycing at the fall of that *great* beast, . . . I. xii. 4. 8
costly scarlott of *great* name, . . . I. xii. 13. 8
Great pleasure, mixt with pittiful regard, . . . I. xii. 16. 1
great beene the evils which ye bore . . . I. xii. 17. 2
Backe to retourne to that *great* Faery Queene, . . . I. xii. 18. 6
with *great* wisedome and grave eloquence . . . I. xii. 24. 5
With flying speede, and seeming *great* pretence, . . . I. xii. 24. 7
falling flat *great* humblesse he did make, . . . I. xii. 25. 6
that *great* Emperour of all the West; . . . I. xii. 26. 4
still he sate . . . As in *great* muse, . . . I. xii. 29. 4
throw This gentle knight into so *great* distresse, . . . I. xii. 33. 8
made *great* feast to solemnize that day: . . . I. xii. 38. 2
all the house did sweat with *great* aray: . . . I. xii. 38. 5
Great joy was made that day of young and old, . . . I. xii. 40. 1
through hardy enterprize Many *great* Regions are discovered, II. Pr. 2. 4
in this antique ymage thy *great* auncestry. . . . II. Pr. 4. 9
great rule of Temp'raunce goodly doth appeare. . . . II. Pr. 5. 9
that seeke with warlike spoyle, And *great* atchiev'ments, . . . II. i. 8. 8
that seeke . . . *great* your selfe to make, . . . II. i. 8. 8
the earth, *great* mother of us all, . . . II. i. 10. 6
Great pitty is to see you thus dismayd, . . . II. i. 14. 3
Either for grievous shame, or for *great* teene, . . . II. i. 15. 8
he hath *great* glory wonne, . . . II. i. 19. 9
Great cause, I weene, you guided, . . . II. i. 29. 9
As Lion, grudging in his *great* disdaine, . . . II. i. 42. 6
herselfe, in *great* despight, She groveling threw to ground, . . . II. i. 45. 8
through danger and *great* dreed. . . . II. i. 52. 9
For all so *great* shame after death I weene, . . . II. i. 59. 8
The *great* earthes wombe they open to the sky, . . . II. i. 60. 2
him into *great* amaz'ment drove, . . . II. ii. 3. 8
through the *great* contagion direful deadly stonck. . . . II. ii. 4. 9
of your ignorance *great* merveill make, . . . II. ii. 5. 4
from their sourse indewd By *great* Dame Nature, . . . II. ii. 6. 2
not so good of deedes as *great* of name, . . . II. ii. 17. 3
with amazement *great* Did rend the ratling skyes . . . II. ii. 20. 8
Wondrous *great* prowesse and heroick worth He shewd . . . II. ii. 25. 3
revive Fresh memory in me of that *great* Queene, . . . II. ii. 40. 2
Great and most glorious virgin Queene alive, . . . II. ii. 40. 3
great or glorious in mortall eye, . . . II. ii. 41. 4
men, beholding so *great* excellence . . . II. ii. 41. 6
As th' Idole of her makers *great* magnificence. . . . II. ii. 41. 9
all unfitt for so *great* purpose, . . . II. ii. 43. 9
Gave him *great* ayd, . . . II. iii. 4. 7
of him selfe *great* hope and help conceiv'd, . . . II. iii. 5. 2
To him avaunting in *great* bravery, . . . II. iii. 6. 3
Great favour I thee graunt . . . II. iii. 7. 9
'He is a *great* adventurer,' . . . II. iii. 12. 5
great sure shal be thy meed, . . . II. iii. 14. 6
dead through *great* affright . . . II. iii. 19. 7
seemd to be a woman of *great* worth, . . . II. iii. 21. 8
write the battailes of his *great* godhed: . . . II. iii. 24. 4
Did shew her selfe in *great* triumphant joy, . . . II. iii. 31. 8
her *great* words did appall My feeble corage, . . . II. iii. 44. 5
great difference Betweene the vulgar and the noble seed, . . . II. iv. 1. 2
Drew . . . A handsom stripling with *great* crueltee, . . . II. iv. 3. 7
The noble Guyon, mov'd with *great* remorse, . . . II. iv. 6. 1
his *great* yron teeth he still did grind . . . II. iv. 15. 3
more for ranck despight then for *great* paine, . . . II. iv. 15. 7
To love a Lady fayre of *great* degree, . . . II. iv. 19. 2
What *great* despight doth fortune to thee beare, . . . II. iv. 25. 7
The knight at his *great* boldnesse wondered; . . . II. iv. 39. 6
A knight of wondrous powre and *great* assay, . . . II. iv. 40. 6
Great cause, that carries thee so swifte and light.' . . . II. iv. 43. 4
Great glory and gay spoile, sure hast thou gott, . . . II. iv. 45. 6
through *great* constraint He made him stoup . . . II. v. 11. 5

Great—*Continued.*
in Princes courts to worke *great* scath and hindrance: V. ix. 22. 9
An huge *great* Lyon lay, V. ix. 33. 4
The tryall of a *great* and weightie case, V. ix. 36. 7
A Ladie of *great* countenance and place, V. ix. 38. 2
The peoples *great* compassion unto her allure. V. ix. 38. 9
That false Duessa, which had wrought *great* care V. ix. 40. 3
Great ruth through her misfortunes tragicke stowre; V. ix. 45. 8
for *great* ruth his courage gan relent: V. ix. 46. 6
This well I wote, that sure she is as *great*, V. x. 1. 5
if that Vertue be of so *great* might V. x. 2. 1
What heavenly Muse shall thy *great* honour rayse V. x. 3. 3
Both doing and receiving curtesies Of that *great* Ladie, V. x. 5. 3
Wrapt in *great* dolours and in deadly feares V. x. 6. 7
A Ladie of *great* worth and wealth had beene, V. x. 7. 2
For his huge powre and *great* oppression, V. x. 9. 4
Orthrus begotten by *great* Typhaon And foule Echidna V. x. 10. 7
unto gratious *great* Mercilla call For ayde V. x. 14. 3
He stepped forth with courage bold and *great*, V. x. 15. 6
Then taking humble leave of that *great* Queene, V. x. 17. 1
For so *great* travell as you doe sustaine! V. x. 21. 5
As three *great* Culverings for battrie bent, V. x. 34. 6
Ne to their force gave way, that was *great* wonder; V. x. 35. 3
For so *great* prowesse as he there had proved, V. x. 39. 2
With *great* admiraunce inwardly was moved, V. x. 39. 4
Prince Arthure overcomes the *great* Gerioneo in fight: V. xi. Arg.
with his huge *great* yron axe gan hew V. xi. 5. 3
Thereto a *great* advauntage eke he has V. xi. 6. 1
hell unto him selfe with horrour *great*. V. xi. 12. 5
There stands an Idole of *great* note and name, V. xi. 19. 2
For *great* desire that Monster to assay, V. xi. 21. 2
An huge *great* Beast it was, V. xi. 23. 1
seem'd to be of infinite *great* strength: V. xi. 23. 3
backe she would have turnd for *great* affright: V. xi. 26. 5
more fiercely reard Uppon her wide *great* wings, V. xi. 30. 6
Like to a *great* Mill-damb forth fiercely gusht, V. xi. 31. 5
Making *great* feast and joyous merriment, V. xi. 35. 2
their numbers are so *great*, V. xi. 45. 6
yeeld *great* thankes for their so goodly deed, V. xi. 48. 3
oft I driven am to *great* distresse, V. xi. 51. 8
Unto her ran with greedie *great* desyre, V. xi. 61. 2
The which they troubled had with *great* turmoyle. V. xi. 65. 5
He with the *great* Grantorto fights, V. xii. Arg.
Appointed by that mightie Faerie Prince, *Great* Gloriane, V. xii. 3. 4
Through other *great* adventures hethertoo Had it forslackt: V. xii. 3. 5
Great hostes of men in order martiall, V. xii. 4. 8
All armed in a cote of yron plate Of *great* defence V. xii. 14. 4
he had *great* skill in single fight: V. xii. 15. 5
thereon seizing tooke no *great* effect; V. xii. 21. 7
then would she make *Great* cheare, V. xii. 32. 7
in anothers losse *great* pleasure take, V. xii. 32. 8
As she had got thereby and gayned a *great* stake. V. xii. 32. 9
take *great* joy to publish it to many, V. xii. 35. 3
Great skill it is such duties timely to bestow. VI. ii. 1. 9
great helpe dame Nature selfe doth lend; VI. ii. 2. 1
And in the eyes of men *great* liking find, VI. ii. 2. 4
his hart was inly child With *great* amazement, VI. ii. 4. 9
'Perdie *great* blame' . . . a wight unarm'd to wrong: VI. ii. 8. 6
He with his speare, that was to him *great* blame, VI. ii. 10. 7
I . . . wish thee grow in worship and *great* weale; VI. ii. 26. 7
conceiving then *great* feare Of my fraile safetie, VI. ii. 29. 2
that wounded Knight in his *great* need, VI. iii. 2. 5
And borne *great* sway in armes amongst his peares; VI. iii. 3. 3
sought her to affy To a *great* pere; VI. iii. 7. 3
How *great* a hazard she at earst had made VI. iii. 8. 7
And in his wide *great* mouth away her bare VI. iii. 24. 4
the blood ensew'd In *great* aboundance, VI. iii. 50. 8
his life . . . was certes in *great* jeopardy, VI. iii. 51. 5
He made *great* mone after his salvage mood; VI. iv. 12. 4
From a *great* Gyant, called Cormoraunt, VI. iv. 29. 6
his *great* force unable to endure, VI. v. 16. 6
seeing one in so *great* daunger set VI. v. 22. 2
Finde harbour fit to comfort her *great* neede; VI. v. 31. 4
So all that night they past in *great* disease, VI. v. 40. 1
great affaires in mynd Would not permit VI. v. 41. 1
in the mindes of men had *great* insight; VI. vi. 3. 6
Now left alone in *great* extremity; VI. vi. 16. 3
Would not her leave alone in her *great* need. VI. vi. 16. 5
The people of the house rose forth in *great* uprore. VI. vi. 22. 9
did rattle like to haile In a *great* tempest; VI. vi. 26. 4
with *great* affright She starting up VI. vi. 31. 1
Gotten *great* worship in this worldes sight: VI. vi. 35. 8
Gan to complaine of *great* discourtesie, VI. vii. 4. 3
Great treason to him meant, his life to reave. VI. vii. 12. 4
for promise of *great* meed, VI. vii. 12. 7
There he him found in *great* astonishment, VI. vii. 14. 3
Great shame in lieges blood to be embrew'd! VI. vii. 23. 6
great store of forrest frute VI. vii. 24. 4
She was a Ladie of *great* dignitie, VI. vii. 28. 1
In *great* displeasure wild a Capias Should issue forth VI. vii. 35. 4
sib to *great* Orgolio, VI. vii. 41. 8
eies, Like two *great* Beacons, glared bright and wyde, VI. vii. 42. 2
could no lenger beare so *great* abuse VI. vii. 45. 4
Ne could with seeing satisfie his *great* desire. VI. viii. 27. 9
That huge *great* foole oppressing th' other Knight, VI. viii. 28. 2
A *great* adventure, which did him from them devide. VI. viii. 30. 9
endured for her sake *Great* perill of his life, VI. viii. 33. 9
that were too *great* a shame, VI. ix. 1. 6
Besides the *great* dishonour and defame, VI. ix. 1. 8
Great travell hath the gentle Calidore . . . endured, VI. ix. 2. 1

Great—*Continued.*
Which he atchieved to his owne *great* gaines, VI. ix. 2. 8
For so *great* kindnesse as he found that day VI. ix. 18. 5
to *great* ones such follies doe forgive; VI. ix. 22. 2
his speach, that wrought him *great* content, VI. ix. 26. 5
daily doe behold The glorie of the *great* VI. ix. 28. 2
Now loath *great* Lordship and ambition; VI. ix. 28. 5
worke his foe *great* shame. VI. ix. 43. 9
made *great* mone for that unhappy turne: VI. x. 18. 6
'Sunne of the world, *great* glory of the sky, VI. x. 28. 1
Great Gloriana, greatest Majesty! VI. x. 28. 3
Would be on earth too *great* a blessednesse, VI. xi. 1. 4
with *great* rage he stoutly doth denay; VI. xi. 15. 6
I onely scapt through *great* confusione VI. xi. 32. 3
His hart quite deaded was with anguish *great*, VI. xi. 33. 2
Where shortly they in *great* acquaintance grew, VI. xi. 41. 3
faire Pastorell through *great* affright Was almost dead, VI. xi. 43. 7
in *great* store Unto the cave gan preasse, VI. xi. 46. 3
Fayre Pastorella by *great* hap Her parents understands. VI. xii. Arg.
farre renound For his *great* riches VI. xii. 4. 3
he grew In so *great* rage VI. xii. 5. 6
resolving to returne in hast Unto so *great* atchievement, VI. xii. 13. 2
for *great* desire Rent up her brest, VI. xii. 19. 3
That *great* Alcides whilome overthrew, VI. xii. 32. 2
thereunto a *great* long chaine he tight, VI. xii. 34. 8
He growen is so *great* and strong of late, VI. xii. 40. 4
many of them afterwards obtain'd *Great* power VII. vi. 3. 2
Of her *great* power, to many ones *great* paine, VII. vi. 4. 7
All ran together with a *great* out-cry VII. vi. 15. 1
they suddaine all arose In *great* amaze, VII. vi. 24. 5
halfe confused with his *great* commaund, VII. vi. 26. 1
great Earth, *great* Chaos child; VII. vi. 26. 6
great Prometheus tasting of our ire, VII. vi. 29. 7
Bellona, whose *great* glory thou doost spight, VII. vi. 32. 5
Before *great* Natures presence should appeare, VII. vi. 36. 3
for *great* joy of some-what he did spy, VII. vi. 46. 3
Then forth issewed (*great* goddesse) *great* dame Nature VII. vii. 5. 1
Was never so *great* joyance VII. vii. 12. 1
This *great* Grandmother of all creatures bred, VII. vii. 13. 1
Great Nature, ever young, yet full of eld; VII. vii. 13. 2
'To thee, O greatest Goddesse, onely *great!* VII. vii. 14. 1
the Earth (*great* mother of us all) VII. vii. 17. 6
Now like *great* Hills, and streight like sluces VII. vii. 20. 9
by Dianaes doom unjust Slew *great* Orion; VII. vii. 39. 8
merry feasting which he made And *great* bonfires, VII. vii. 41. 3
Upon an huge *great* Earth-pot steane he stood, VII. vii. 42. 8
within this wide *great* Universe VII. vii. 56. 1
that *great* Sabaoth God, VII. viii. 2. 9
doth burne, it doth divide *Great* heat, *Am.* vi. 8
Great shame it is to leave, like one afrayd, *Am.* xiv. 3
Gives me *great* hope of your relenting mynd: *Am.* xxviii. 2
her *great* triumph, which my skill exceeds, *Am.* xxix. 11
her cold so *great* Is not dissolv'd *Am.* xxx. 2
Great wrong I doe, *Am.* xxxiii. 1
Great shame it is, thing so divine in view, *Am.* liii. 9
great deeds and valarous emprize. *Am.* lxix. 4
'Whats this (quoth he) that gives so *great* a voyce *Epig.* iv. 7
how *great* the smart Of those whom thou dost wound: *Epig.* iv. 35
let them make *great* store of bridale poses, *Epith.* 45
When he begot the *great* Tirynthian groome: *Epith.* 329
great Juno! which with awful might *Epith.* 390
Heroes, which their world did daunt With their *great* deedes, *Com. Son.* iii. 4
Admire their statues, their Colossoes *great:* *Com. Son.* iii. 6
Matchable to the greatest of those *great;* *Com.Son.* iii. 10
Great both by name, and *great* in power and might, *Com.Son.* iii. 11
shewing, by their heapes, how *great* they were. *Com. Son.* iv. 8
The wondrous triumphs of my *great* god-hed: *H.L.* 18
Great God of Might, that reignest in the mynd, *H.L.* 43
in their roring taking *great* delight; *H.L.* 48
When thy *great* mother Venus first thee bare, *H.L.* 52
Out of *great* Chaos ugly prison crept, *H.L.* 58
Through all that *great* wide wast, *H.L.* 70
The worlds *great* Parent, *H.L.* 156
Thou in me kindlest much more *great* desyre, *H.B.* 5
great Goddesse! Queene of Beauty, *H.B.* 15
this worlds *great* Workmaister *H.B.* 29
out of that *great* immortall Spright, *H.B.* 107
O *great* Beauties Queene, *H.B.* 267
Adore the powre of thy *great* Majestie, *H.B.* 271
graunt, O *great* Soveraine! *H.B.* 274
great Goddesse of my life, *H.B.* 282
Before this worlds *great* frame, . . . found any being-place, *H.H.L.* 22
His second brood, though not in powre so *great*, *H.H.L.* 53
Till that *great* Lord of Love, which him at first *H.H.L.* 127
Him first to love *great* right and reason is, *H.H.L.* 190
Yet being malist both of *great* and small. *H.H.L.* 238
ravisht with devouring *great* desire Of his deare selfe, *H.H.L.* 268
to bethinke how *great* that beautie is, *H.H.B.* 107
Ne dare looke . . . On the dred face of that *great* Deity, *H.H.B.* 145
And the *great* Dragon strongly doth represse, *H.H.B.* 157
With the *great* glorie of that wondrous light *H.H.B.* 176
most fit For so *great* powre and peerelesse majesty, *H.H.B.* 186
As their *great* Maker did at first ordaine, *H.H.B.* 201
out of their baskets drew *Great* store of Flowers, *Proth.* 74
I gayned giftes and goodly grace Of that *great* Lord, *Proth.* 139
a noble Peer, *Great* Englands glory, *Proth.* 146
great Elisaes glorious name may ring *Proth.* 157
With a *great* traine ensuing. *Proth.* 167

Greater. Hir brightnesse *greater* was than can be founde, *Rev.* iv. 8
if she should *greater* growe, *Ro.* iv. 5

Greater—*Continued.*
sixe months *greater* a great deele; . . . . . . *Ro.* xviii. 8
Sicker I hold him for a *greater* fon, ... *S.C.* Ap. 158
The fame whereof doth dayly *greater* growe. . . . . . *S.C.* Jun. 92
The walled townes doe worke my *greater* woe; . . . . . . *S.C.* Au. 158
Seemeth ay *greater* when it is farre: . . . . . . *S.C.* S. 77
The glory eke much *greater* then the gayne: . . . . . . *S.C.* O. 20
Much *greater* gyfts for guerdon thou shalt gayne, ... *S.C.* N. 45
tryed time yet taught me *greater* thinges; . . . . . . *S.C.* D. 85
Ere the breme Winter breede you *greater* griefe. . . . . . . *S.C.* D. 148
He is with *greater* matter busied Than a Lambe, ... *Hub.* 1215
Findes *greater* burthen of his miserie. . . . . . . *T.M.* 306
neither could the others *greater* might . . . endure; . . . . . . *Mui.* 6
her worthinesse Much *greater* than the rude report . . . . . . *D.* 146
Much *greater* then that frame, ... *Col.* 287
glorie *greater* then my simple thought, ... *Col.* 333
I found much *greater* then the former fame; . . . . . . *Col.* 334
there is no *greater* shame Then . . . inconstancie in love: . . I. iv. 1. 7
each others *greater* pride does spight. . . . . . . I. iv. 14. 9
a dry dropsie . . . Which by misdiet daily *greater* grew. . . I. iv. 23. 8
Great pains, and *greater* praise, both never to be donne.' . . I. v. 43. 9
greater conquest of hard love he gaynes, ... I. vi. 3. 8
Which *greater* grew the more she did contend, ... I. vii. 27. 3
greater love, the *greater* is the losse. . . . . . . I. vii. 27. 6
griefe' . . . 'does *greater* grow displaid,' . . . . . . I. vii. 41. 5
all still shronke, and still he *greater* grew: . . . . . . I. vii. 45. 7
had not *greater* grace Me reft from it, ... I. ix. 26. 8
'The lenger life, I wote, the *greater* sin; . . . . . . I. ix. 43. 1
The *greater* sin, the *greater* punishment: . . . . . . I. ix. 43. 2
Where justice growes, there grows eke *greater* grace, ... I. ix. 53. 6
his baptized hands now *greater* grew, ... I. xi. 36. 4
his wrong with *greater* puissance maintaine.' . . . . . . II. i. 14. 9
shal find no *greater* enimy . . . . . . II. v. 1. 3
Of love they ever *greater* glory bore . . . . . . II. vi. 35. 6
Ne suffred them to ryse or *greater* grow; . . . . . . II. vii. 47. 8
With *greater* fury then before was fownd; . . . . . . II. ix. 15. 2
Regan *greater* love to him profest Then all the world, ... II. x. 28. 3
Much *greater* griefe and shamefuller regrett . . . . . . III. i. 8. 2
to refraine From chase of *greater* beastes, ... III. i. 37. 7
yett in armes Noctante *greater* grew: . . . . . . III. i. 45. 7
is by name The *greater* Brytayne, ... III. ii. 7. 9
great care she tooke, and *greater* feare, ... III. iii. 5. 6
greater crosse To see frends grave, ... III. iv. 38. 8
'Troy, . . . whilome far much *greater* then thy fame, ... III. ix. 33. 3
Thereto her feare was made so much the *greater* . . . . . . IV. i. 7. 1
Cambell still more strong and *greater* grew, ... IV. iii. 29. 1
Whether of them in her should have the *greater* share. . . . IV. iii. 39. 9
greater love to me then her he did professe. . . . . . . IV. viii. 57. 9
quenched is with Cupids *greater* flame: . . . . . . IV. ix. 2. 2
'a *greater* wrong remaines: . . . . . . IV. ix. 38. 1
is the paine thereof much *greater* then the fee. . . . . . . IV. x. 3. 9
often tride In *greater* perils . . . . . . IV. x. 18. 2
towards th' end grew *greater* in his might, ... V. ii. 17. 6
how canst thou those *greater* secrets know, ... V. ii. 43. 7
Whether of them the *greater* were attone; . . . . . . V. ii. 48. 8
The *greater* prowesse *greater* perils find. . . . . . . V. iii. 9. 2
Isle, that *greater* bredth now beares. . . . . . . V. iv. 7. 9
A Princesse of great powre and *greater* pride, ... V. iv. 33. 4
try in equall field whether hath *greater* might. . . . . . . V. iv. 48. 9
So much the *greater* still her anguish grew, ... V. v. 28. 1
greater shame t' abide so great misprize, ... V. v. 48. 4
that his guilt the *greater* may appeare, ... V. v. 48. 6
lay upon him, for his *greater* dread, Cold yron chaines . . . V. v. 50. 7
As it is *greater* prayse to save then spill, ... V. x. 2. 8
Much *greater* then was ever in her weeting, ... V. x. 39. 3
nought was terrifide, but *greater* courage tooke. . . . . . . V. xi. 28. 9
He *greater* grew, and gan to drive at him more hard. . . . VI. i. 20. 9
No *greater* shame to man then inhumanitie. . . . . . . VI. i. 26. 9
others that have *greater* skill . . . cannot attaine; . . . . . VI. ii. 2. 5
unfit For . . . worke of *greater* care, ... VI. ii. 9. 3
I never saw in any *greater* hope appeare.' . . . . . . VI. ii. 26. 9
you to reward with *greater* dignitie.' . . . . . . VI. ii. 34. 9
as if his *greater* pryde Did scorne the challenge . . . . . . VI. iii. 36. 3
stout Despetto in his *greater* pryde Did front him, ... VI. v. 20. 7
greater force there needs to maintaine wrong then right. . . VI. vi. 35. 9
for *greater* infamie, ... VI. vii. 27. 1
Least unto me betide a *greater* ill; . . . . . . VI. viii. 30. 4
good should from us goe, then come, in *greater* store. . . . . VI. x. 24. 9
greater mischiefe on her threw, ... VI. xi. 2. 6
sorrowes heapt on her in *greater* throng; . . . . . . VI. xi. 2. 7
For his great riches and his *greater* might: . . . . . . VI. xii. 4. 3
thousand heads, . . . in *greater* number grew. . . . . . . VI. xii. 32. 5
I *greater* am in bloud . . . Then all the Gods, ... VII. vi. 26. 8
whither doost thou now, thou *greater* Muse, Me . . . bring, . VII. vii. 1. 1
Being far *greater* and more tall of stature . . . . . . VII. vii. 5. 3
Till *greater* then my wombe thou woxen art: . . . . . . *Am.* ii. 4
needeth *greater* might Then those small forts . . . . . . *Am.* xiv. 5
A *greater* craftesmans hand thereto doth neede, ... *Am.* xvii. 13
greater they might be, That *greater* meede at last may turne
to mee. . . . . . . *Am.* xxv. 13, 14
my proud one doth worke the *greater* scath, ... *Am.* xxxi. 9
And *greater* glory thinke, to save then spill. . . . . . . *Am.* xlix. 4
having her, my joy wil be the *greater*. . . . . . . *Am.* li. 14
seemd the longer for my *greater* paines. . . . . . . *Am.* lx. 12
thereby much *greater* glory gate, ... *Am.* lxvi. 9
your light . . . in my darknesse, *greater* doth appeare, . . . *Am.* lxvi. 12

Greater-learned. Some *greater learned* wit will magnifie: . . *Ro.* ii. 12

Greatest. faire as mote the *greatest* god delite; . . . . . . *Pet.* i. 5
when thou wast in *greatest* hight, ... *Ro.* xxxi. 12
should *greatest* things the least disdaine, ... *Van.* iii. 13

Greatest—*Continued.*
'Lo! how the least the *greatest* may reprove.' . . . . . . *Van.* iv. 14
Sith that the *greatest* often are oppresst, ... *Van.* xii. 7
Gay without good is good hearts *greatest* loathing. . . . . . *Hub.* 232
now in Court doth beare the *greatest* sway, ... *Hub.* 616
greatest ones did sue to gaine his grace; . . . . . . *Ti.* 186
Of *greatest* ones he, *greatest* in his place, ... *Ti.* 187
Sith time doth *greatest* things to ruine bring? . . . . . . *Ti.* 556
I, poore swaine, of many, *greatest* crosse! . . . . . . *Col.* 18
in simple eie Seeme *greatest*, when their garments are most
gay. . . . . . . *Col.* 722
him the *greatest* of the Gods we deeme, ... *Col.* 799
Great Ladie of the *greatest* Isle, ... I. Pr. 4. 3
adventure . . . That *greatest* Gloriana to him gave, ... I. i. 3. 2
(That *greatest* Glorious Queene of Faery lond) . . . . . . I. i. 3. 3
Whose greedy lust did lacke in *greatest* store; . . . . . . I. iv. 29. 2
Devizing how that . . . turnament With *greatest* honour he
atchieven might: . . . . . . I. v. 1. 8
the golden Orientall gate Of *greatest* heaven . . . . . . I. v. 2. 2
The *greatest* Earth his uncouth mother was, ... I. vii. 9. 1
'O great Orgoglio! *greatest* under skye, ... I. vii. 14. 5
counsell mitigates the *greatest* smart: . . . . . . I. vii. 40. 8
will to might gives *greatest* aid.' . . . . . . I. vii. 41. 4
That *greatest* Princes presence might behold. . . . . . . I. viii. 35. 4
'Thou, wretched man, of death hast *greatest* need, ... I. ix. 45. 1
gallant shew to be in *greatest* gree, ... II. iii. 5. 8
Whose freedom shall thee turne to *greatest* scath! . . . . . II. v. 18. 4
Him to aggrate, and *greatest* pleasures shew: . . . . . . II. v. 33. 2
Great Mammon, *greatest* god below the skye, ... II. vii. 8. 2
There mournfull Cypresse grew in *greatest* store, ... II. vii. 52. 1
three the chiefest and of *greatest* powre, ... II. ix. 47. 7
greatest and most glorious thing on ground . . . . . . II. xi. 30. 1
in time of *greatest* storme; . . . . . . II. xii. 24. 6
greatest Princes liking it mote well delight. . . . . . . III. v. 40. 9
greatest shame was to that maiden twin, ... III. vii. 49. 3
Doest conquer *greatest* conquerors on ground, ... IV. vii. 1. 2
Him to recomfort in his *greatest* care, ... IV. viii. 5. 4
greatest Princes court would welcome fayne; . . . . . . IV. viii. 27. 2
for *greatest* glories gayne. . . . . . . IV. ix. 4. 5
Their *greatest* glory for their rightfull deedes, ... V. ii. 1. 6
the *greatest* prayse redounded To Marinell, ... V. iii. 6. 8
Thereof make tryall in my *greatest* need. . . . . . . V. v. 29. 6
To be the *greatest* and the gravest wight, ... V. vii. 18. 5
With hope of helpe in that her *greatest* neede. . . . . . . V. x. 22. 5
That is the *greatest* shame and foulest scorne, ... V. xi. 52. 3
Whose sight to her is *greatest* crosse may fall, ... V. xii. 31. 4
with the *greatest* purchast *greatest* grace: . . . . . . VI. i. 3. 5
Doth best become and *greatest* grace doth gaine: . . . . . . VI. ii. 2. 8
To shew such faintnesse . . . Is *greatest* shame; . . . . . . VI. vi. 35. 3
Words sharpely wound, but *greatest* griefe of scorning growes. VI. vii. 49. 9
The *greatest* shame that ever eye yet saw, ... VI. viii. 6. 2
Hath not enough, but wants in *greatest* store, ... VI. ix. 30. 4
Great Gloriana, *greatest* Majesty! . . . . . . VI. x. 28. 3
The *greatest* portion of the greedie pray, ... VI. xi. 17. 4
could the *greatest* wrath soone turne to grace, ... VII. vi. 31. 3
'To thee, O *greatest* Goddesse, onely great! . . . . . . VII. vii. 14. 1
Of which the *greatest* part is due to me, ... VII. vii. 15. 4
raign and bear the *greatest* sway; . . . . . . VII. vii. 47. 4
judge then, (O thou *greatest* goddesse trew) . . . . . . VII. vii. 56. 6
In all things else she beares the *greatest* sway: . . . . . . VII. viii. 1. 5
to entertayne The *greatest* Prince . . . . . . *Am.* lxxvii. 4
even the *greatest* did not greatly scorne . . . . . . *Epith.* 4
Matchable to the *greatest* of those great; . . . . . . *Com.Son.* iii. 10
Whom *greatest* Princes sought on lowest knee. . . . . . . *H.H.L.* 231
amaze The *greatest* wisards which thereon do gaze. . . . . . *H.H.B.* 168

Great-grandfathers. Thy fathers and *great Grandfathers* of old, II. x. 4. 6

Great-grandmother. the quiet wombe Of his *great Grand-mother* . . . . . . II. vii. 17. 2

Great-grandsire. From my *great Grandsire* Titan unto mee
Deriv'd . . . . . . VII. vii. 16. 8

Great-lamenting. with *great lamenting* paine, . . . she filleth
his dull eares, ... I. iii. 44. 1

Greatly. My spright was *greatly* moved . . . . . . *Van.* xii. 2
Greatly aghast . . . . . . *S.C.* F. 157
Willye is not *greatly* overgone, ... *S.C.* Au. 127
my sense it *greatly* pleased, ... *Hub.* 39
they *greatly* him mistooke. . . . . . . *Hub.* 704
his heart was *greatly* eased. . . . . . . *Hub.* 710
griefe thereof my spirite *greatly* pained. . . . . . . *Ti.* 560
gan she *greatly* to lament and weepe. . . . . . . *Mui.* 288
He found himselfe full *greatly* pleasd at it: . . . . . . *Col.* 71
gracelesse men them *greatly* do abuse.' . . . . . . *Col.* 327
that God, that is so *greatly* dred; . . . . . . *Col.* 798
To thee are all true lovers *greatly* bound. . . . . . . *Col.* 899
greatly shunned manly exercise; . . . . . . I. iv. 20. 2
Greatly advauncing his gay chevalree: . . . . . . I. v. 16. 5
She *greatly* grew amazed at the sight, ... I. v. 21. 3
Una *greatly* with those newes distrest. . . . . . . I. vii. Arg.
death after life, does *greatly* please.' . . . . . . I. ix. 40. 9
greatly joy each other for to see: . . . . . . I. x. 15. 4
Whose sight my feeble soule doth *greatly* cheare: . . . . . . I. xi. 3. 5
The king was *greatly* moved at her speach; . . . . . . I. xii. 35. 1
he perceiving *greatly* gan rejoice, ... II. i. 44. 1
Th' enchaunter *greatly* joyed . . . . . . II. iii. 13. 1
does *greatly* them affeare: . . . . . . II. iii. 20. 5
Ne car'd he *greatly* for her presence vayne, ... II. iii. 43. 6
greatly joyous seemed for my sake, ... II. iv. 20. 3
The knight was *greatly* moved at his playnt, ... II. v. 24. 1
greatly joyed merry tales to faine, ... II. vi. 6. 4
The want thereof now *greatly* gan to plaine, ... II. viii. 19. 2

Greatly—*Continued.*
since it *greatly* did decay . . . II. x. 53. 9
Thereat they *greatly* were dismayd, . . . II. xii. 35. 1
Repyned *greatly,* and did him miscall . . . II. xii. 86. 8
His daedale hand would faile and *greatly* faynt, . . . III. Pr. 2. 4
Of the faire Alma *greatly* were procur'd . . . III. i. 1. 5
They *greatly* wondred whence so sumptuous guize . . . III. i. 33. 8
Shee *greatly* gan enamoured to wex . . . III. i. 47. 4
Hart that is inly hurt is *greatly* eased With hope . . . III. ii. 15. 3
So *greatly* his commandement they feare, . . . III. iii. 11. 5
they grew *Greatly* confused in behaveoure . . . III. iii. 50. 7
by the way he *greatly* gan complaine . . . III. v. 12. 3
her expectation *greatly* was deceav'd . . . III. v. 28. 9
The sight whereof did *greatly* him adaw, . . . III. vii. 13. 4
Was *greatly* woe begon, and gan to feare . . . III. vii. 20. 7
of her safety *greatly* grew afrayd . . . III. vii. 25. 3
Greatly he grew enrag'd, . . . III. vii. 33. 5
'Thy labour all is lost, I *greatly* dread, . . . III. viii. 47. 2
his hew Gan *greatly* chaunge . . . III. viii. 48. 2
'Thy offers base I *greatly* loth, . . . III. x. 29. 6
Greatly thereat was Britomart dismayd, . . . III. xi. 22. 1
The warlike Mayd . . . Did *greatly* wonder; . . . III. xi. 53. 3
Do *greatly* stand amaz'd at such unwonted wonder . . . IV. ii. 16. 9
Thereat did *greatly* grudge, . . . IV. ii. 26. 3
To hasten *greatly* to his parties ayd, . . . IV. iv. 20. 2
thereat *greatly* grudged Arthegall, . . . IV. v. 9. 1
Whereat the rest gan *greatly* to envie, . . . IV. v. 19. 6
Yet at her choice they all did *greatly* muse . . . IV. v. 21. 3
Blandamour thereat full *greatly* grudged, . . . IV. v. 22. 3
Whence neither *greatly* hasted to arise, . . . IV. vi. 10. 8
Did *greatly* solace his engrieved mind . . . IV. viii. 7. 4
he *greatly* did desire To know . . . IV. viii. 22. 1
now their forces *greatly* were decayd, . . . IV. ix. 34. 1
She gan thereat to fret and *greatly* grieve; . . . IV. xii. 26. 2
Which when he saw he *greatly* grew in rage, . . . V. ii. 47. 1
of the meane he *greatly* did misleeke . . . V. ii. 49. 5
greatly it desir'd of her to learne, . . . V. ix. 7. 3
She comming forth, . . . was *greatly* queld, . . . V. xi. 26. 3
Whereat Sir Calidore . . . *greatly* joy'd . . . VI. ii. 36. 7
I may not graunt that ye so *greatly* prayde . . . VI. ii. 37. 9
To make abode that night he *greatly* was besought . . . VI. iii. 2. 9
Let none therefore . . . Too *greatly* grieve . . . VI. iii. 5. 9
his lovely litle spoile . . . did *greatly* him offend: . . . VI. iv. 25. 8
now the same he *greatly* doth forthinke . . . VI. iv. 32. 5
Was *greatly* growne in love of that brave pere,) . . . VI. v. 41. 8
Gan *greatly* thanke his host and his good wife; . . . VI. ix. 18. 6
Calidore he *greatly* did mistake, . . . VI. ix. 44. 1
Ne certes mote he *greatly* blamed be . . . VI. x. 3. 1
did her *greatly* like, and did her *greatly* praize . . . VI. xi. 13. 9
Yet *greatly* did the Beast repine . . . VI. xii. 36. 1
even the greatest did not *greatly* scorne . . . *Epith.* 4

Greatness. To shewe the *greatnesse* of the stately race, . . . *Bel.*[1] v. 7
Which that brave races *greatnes* did attest, . . . *Bel.*[2] v. 7
Tombes of her *greatnes* which did threate the skies: . . . *Ro.* iv. 8
In case thy *greatnes* he can gesse in harte, . . . *Ro.* v. 3
Whose *greatnes* by the *greatnes* of none other, . . . *Ro.* vi. 7
Who list the Romane *greatnes* forth to figure, . . . *Ro.* xxvi. 1
To *greatnes* growne, through long prosperitie, . . . *Ro.* xxxi. 13
That did so much in his owne *greatnesse* trust . . . *Van.* vi. 12
all his *greatnes* vapoured to nought, . . . *Ti.* 219
In glorie, or in *greatnes* to excell, . . . *Ti.* 555
Such *greatnes* I cannot compare to ought: . . . *Col.* 335
to increase his wondrous *greatnes* more, . . . I. xi. 8. 8
Like belles in *greatnesse* orderly succeed, . . . IV. v. 36. 8

Great-tormenting. let her weet The *great tormenting* griefe . . . IV. viii. 9. 8

Greave. fast closed in some hollow *greave,* . . . III. x. 42. 3
when she fled into that covert *greave,* . . . VI. ii. 43. 8

Grecian. Who of the *Grecian* Libbard now ought heares, . . . *Ti.* 68

Gree. He is a shepheard great in *gree,* . . . *S.C.* Jul. 215
Receive, most Noble Lord, in gentle *gree,* . . . *Ded. Son.* iii. 1
she accepts with thankes and goodly *gree,* . . . I. v. 16. 4
gallant shew to be in greatest *gree,* . . . II. iii. 5. 8
her besought to take it well in *gree,* . . . V. vi. 21. 7
The which full gladly they did take in *gree,* . . . VI. v. 39. 3

Greece. *Greece* will the olde Ephesian buildings blaze, . . . *Ro.* ii. 3
The same yet vaunting *Greece* will tell the storie . . . *Ro.* ii. 5
All that which *Greece* their temples to embrave . . . *Ro.* xxix. 2
all the brood of *Greece* so highly praised, . . . *Col.* 413
They bring them wines of *Greece* and Araby, . . . I. v. 4. 5
Greece, the Nourse of all good arts, . . . II. ix. 48. 1
ransackt *Greece* wel tryde, when they were wroth; . . . II. x. 40. 5
through the Euxine seas bore all the flowr of *Greece* . . . II. xii. 44. 9
the fayrest Dame That ever *Greece* did boast, . . . III. ix. 34. 8
when strife was growen Amongst those famous ympes of *Greece,* . . . IV. ii. 1. 8
her all *Greece* with many a champion bold Should fetch againe, . . . IV. xi. 19. 5
those renoumed noble Peres of *Greece,* . . . *Am.* xliv. 1

Greedily. That which I eate did I joy, and that which I *greedily* gorged, . . . *Ex Tempore* 1
on their pleasures *greedily* doth pray . . . *Mui.* 204
seized *greedelie* On the resistles pray; . . . *Mui.* 435
Full *greedily* into the heard he thrust, . . . *As.* 104
at her ran *greedily,* To have attonce devourd . . . I. iii. 5. 5
they gan to hurtlen *greedily,* . . . I. iv. 40. 1
cruell steele so *greedily* doth bight In tender flesh, . . . I. v. 9. 3
To see their blades so *greedily* imbrew, . . . I. vi. 38. 7
gan themselves prepare to batteill *greedily* . . . II. viii. 18. 9
In which whenas he *greedily* did looke, . . . II. ix. 60. 3
all attonce, gaping full *greedily,* . . . II. xii. 39. 7
greedily depasturing delight; . . . II. xii. 73. 4

Greedily—*Continued.*
greedily long gaping at the sight, . . . III. vii. 28. 4
Unto his reskew ran, and *greedily* him spedd . . . III. vii. 30. 9
behinde The fearefull boy so *greedily* poursew, . . . III. xi. 4. 6
a Deare, that *greedily* embayes In the cool soile, . . . III. xii. 44. *or.* 7
The which whyleare she was so *greedily* Devouring, . . . V. xii. 39. 2
greedily him griping his avengement stayd . . . VI. v. 26. 9
A while on her they *greedily* did gaze, . . . VI. xi. 13. 8
Whom catching *greedily,* for great desire Rent up her brest, . . . VI. xii. 19. 3
But *greedily* her fell intent poursewth, . . . *Am.* xi. 7

Greediness. eger *greedinesse* through every member thrild . . . I. viii. 6. 9
the Gulfe of *Greedinesse,* they say, . . . II. xii. 3. 4
yield herselfe to spoile of *greedinesse:* . . . III. vii. 25. 6
With such fell *greedines* he her assayled, . . . IV. vi. 12. 6
Both challenge it with equall *greedinesse:* . . . V. vii. 30. 3
Full of fell ravin and fierce *greedinesse;* . . . V. xi. 24. 2
a Tygre, that with *greedinesse* Hunts after bloud; . . . *Am.* lvi. 2

Greedy. roming through the field with *greedie* rage . . . *Bel.*[2] vi. 6
Within the gulfe of *greedie* Nereus . . . *Bel.*[2] xiii. 11
cram'd with guiltles blood and *greedie* pray . . . *Van.* iii. 4
Some gan to gape for *greedie* governaunce, . . . *S.C.* May 121
rend the *greedie* mindes of covetous men, . . . *Gn.* 95
No *greedy* riches knowes nor bloudie strife, . . . *Gn.* 123
greedie Scilla, under whom there bay Manie great bandogs . . . *Gn.* 539
'Some in the *greedie* flouds are sunke and drent; . . . *Gn.* 585
beguile Their *greedie* mouthes of the expected spoyle; . . . *Hub.* 1286
overran the East with *greedie* powre, . . . *Ti.* 69
after *greedie* spoyle of bloud to crave: . . . *Ti.* 565
Greedie of mischiefe, ranging all about, . . . *D.* 157
with *greedie* listfull eares, . . . *Col.* 7
full of fire and *greedy* hardiment, . . . I. i. 14. 1
Lyon . . . Hunting full *greedy* after salvage blood . . . I. iii. 5. 3
With gaping jawes full *greedy* at him came, . . . I. iii. 41. 4
greedy Avarice by him did ride, . . . I. iv. 27. 1
Whose *greedy* lust did lacke in greatest store; . . . I. iv. 29. 2
With *greedy* force each other doth assayle, . . . I. v. 6. 6
with *greedy* eye He sought all round about, . . . I. v. 15. 1
With *greedy* force he gan the fort assayle, . . . I. vi. 5. 3
As when a *greedy* Wolfe, through honger fell, . . . I. vi. 10. 3
More *greedy* they of newes fast towards him do crosse . . . I. vi. 34. 9
Una, . . . Fast flying from that Paynims *greedy* pray, . . . I. vii. 20. 3
all the crest a Dragon did enfold With *greedie* pawes, . . . I. vii. 31. 4
he himselfe with *greedie* great desyre Into the Castle entred . . . I. viii. 29. 3
With griping talaunts armd to *greedy* fight, . . . I. viii. 48. 7
Darke, dolefull, dreary, like a *greedy* grave, . . . I. ix. 33. 4
greedy gulfe does gape, . . . I. xi. 21. 5
from Cerberus *greedy* jaw To plucke a bone, . . . I. xi. 41. 4
both with *greedy* forse Attonce upon him ran, . . . II. ii. 22. 1
boast to swallow her in *greedy* grave; . . . II. ii. 24. 6
if to thy great mind, or *greedy* vew, . . . II. vii. 9. 3
avarice gan through his veines inspire His *greedy* flames, . . . II. vii. 17. 9
Threatning with *greedy* gripe to doe him dye, . . . II. vii. 27. 7
griev'd so long to lacke his *greedie* pray; . . . II. vii. 34. 2
'Nay, nay, thou *greedy* Tantalus,' . . . II. vii. 60. 1
satisfy The *greedy* hunger of revenging yre, . . . II. viii. 15. 4
With *greedy* pace forth rushing . . . II. ix. 14. 9
O! the *greedy* thirst of royall crowne, . . . II. x. 35. 1
With *greedie* malice and importune toyle, . . . II. xi. 7. 7
Some mouth'd like *greedy* Oystriges; . . . II. xi. 12. 4
Still as the *greedy* knight nigh to him drew; . . . II. xi. 27. 2
streame more violent and *greedy* growes: . . . II. xii. 5. 3
greedy Rosmarines with visages deforme . . . II. xii. 24. 9
th' amarous sweet spoiles to *greedy* eyes revele . . . II. xii. 64. 9
Had in his *greedy* gulfe devoured deepe, . . . III. iv. 22. 6
Infixt such secrete sting of *greedy* lust, . . . III. viii. 25. 2
hayle The *greedy* villein from his hoped pray, . . . III. viii. 31. 6
With *greedy* jawes her ready for to teare: . . . III. viii. 33. 7
greedy eares her weake hart from her bore; . . . III. ix. 52. 7
With *greedy* will and envious desire, . . . III. xi. 26. 3
ne could satisfy Her *greedy* eyes . . . III. xi. 53. 4
Both *greedie* fiers on other to be wroken: . . . IV. ii. 21. 5
a Vulture *greedie* of his pray, . . . IV. iii. 19. 1
greedy Wolves doe breake by force Into an heard, . . . IV. iv. 35. 6
Amoret rapt by *greedie* lust Belphebe saves . . . IV. vii. Arg.
Whilest he on him was *greedy* to be wroke, . . . IV. vii. 26. 7
through it thrild His *greedy* throte, . . . IV. vii. 31. 7
For ought will from his *greedie* pleasure spare: . . . IV. viii. 29. 8
greedy hold of that his bloudy feast: . . . IV. ix. 31. 8
greedy seas doe in the spoile of life delight . . . IV. xii. 6. 9
Did stay a while their *greedy* bickerment, . . . V. iv. 6. 8
from her griping pounce the *greedy* prey doth rive . . . V. iv. 42. 9
like a *greedie* Beare unto her pray, . . . V. v. 9. 7
Her wrathfull hand from *greedy* vengeance to have stayd . . . V. v. 14. 9
they together run With *greedy* rage, . . . V. vii. 29. 2
to get Succour against her *greedy* enimy: . . . V. viii. 6. 7
like hound full *greedy* of his pray, . . . V. viii. 7. 1
Till he himselfe was made their *greedie* pray, . . . V. viii. 31. 3
running unto them with *greedy* joyes, . . . V. x. 20. 1
greedy t' understand To whether should the victory befall, . . . V. xi. 15. 7
Strongly he strove out of her *greedy* gripe To loose his shield, . . . V. xi. 27. 6
Unto her ran with *greedie* great desyre, . . . V. xi. 61. 2
running all with *greedie* joyfulnesse To faire Irena, . . . V. xii. 24. 5
nought mote slake Their *greedy* vengeaunces . . . VI. i. 37. 6
Tristram, . . . Long fed his *greedie* eyes . . . VI. ii. 39. 3
greedy to avenge that vile despight, . . . VI. iii. 45. 7
Pursuing him apace with *greedy* speede; . . . VI. iii. 46. 7
For he would not his *greedie* grype forgoe, . . . VI. iv. 7. 3
the beast . . . Upon him turned, and, with *greedie* force . . . VI. iv. 20. 6
plucke the pray oftimes out of their *greedy* hould . . . VI. v. 15. 9
He flew upon him like a *greedy* kight . . . VI. viii. 28. 4

Greedy—*Continued.*
with *greedy* eare Hong still upon his melting mouth attent; . VI. ix. 26. 1
with delight his *greedy* fancy fed . . . . . . VI. x. 30. 4
greedy mouth wide gaping like hell-gate, ... VI. x. 34. 6
The greatest portion of the *greedie* pray, ... VI. xi. 17. 4
My hungry eyes, through *greedy* covetize . . . . . . *Am.* xxxv. 1
He forth was thrown into the *greedy* seas; . . . . . . *Am.* xxxviii. 2
Did sacrifize unto the *greedy* fyre. . . . . . . *Am.* xlviii. 4
greedy pikes which use therein to feed; . . . . . . *Epith.* 58
greedy pleasure, carelesse of your toyes, ... *Epith.* 365
ye that wont with *greedy* vaine desire . . . . . . *H.H.L.* 15
Did puffe them up with *greedy* bold ambition, ... *H.H.L.* 79
Greedy-wide. gaping *greedy wide* did streight devoure Both flames and tempest: . . . . . . V. vii. 15. 5
Greek. Ne yet of Latine, ne of *Greeke,* . . . . . . *Hub.* 386
paines far passing that long wandring *Greeke,* . . . . . . I. iii. 21. 5
Greeke and Asian rivers stayned with their blood. . . . . . . III. iii. 22. 9
that wretched *Greeke,* that life forlore, ... IV. x. 40. 5
Greekish. oft beheld the warlike *Greekish* forces, ... *Gn.* 499
famous light of all the *Greekish* hosts; . . . . . . *Gn.* 547
made a lake Of *Greekish* blood . . . . . . III. iv. 2. 6
Greeks. as at Troy most dastards of the *Greekes* . . . . . . *Ro.* xiv. 9
flocking Persians did the *Greeks* affray; . . . . . . *Gn.* 50
the *Greekes* themselves, more dolorous, ... *Gn.* 550
many noble *Greekes* and Trojans made to bleed. . . . . . . II. vii. 55. 9
young Hectors blood by cruell *Greekes* was spilt. . . . . . . II. ix. 45. 9
after *Greekes* did Priams realme destroy, ... III. ix. 36. 7
Greeks and Trojans which therein did die; . . . . . . IV. xi. 20. 7
Greeks'. Flames, weapons, wounds, in *Greeks* fleete to have tynde. . . . . . . *Gn.* 504
With zelous envy of *Greekes* cruell fact . . . . . . III. ix. 38. 5
Green. *See* **Evergreen, Lincoln green.**
faire *greene* Laurel witherd up and dide. . . . . . . *Bel.*[1] vii. 14
conquerours bedecked with his *greene,* . . . . . . *Bel.*[2] v. 3
faire *greene* Lawrell branch did quite decay. . . . . . . *Bel.*[2] ix. 14
Like as the seeded field *greene* grasse first showes, ... *Ro.* xxx. 1
Then from *greene* grasse into a stalke doth spring, ... *Ro.* xxx. 2
crowing in pypes made of *greene* corne, ... *S.C.* F. 40
were thy yeares *greene,* as now bene myne, ... *S.C.* F. 59
There grewe an aged Tree on the *greene,* . . . . . . *S.C.* F. 102
With Leaves engrained in lusty *greene;* . . . . . . *S.C.* F. 131
She mought ne gang on the *greene.* . . . . . . *S.C.* Mar. 57
'See, where she sits upon the grassie *greene,* . . . . . . *S.C.* Ap. 55
Bay leaves betweene, And primroses *greene,* . . . . . . *S.C.* Ap. 62
'Ye shepheards daughters, that dwell on the *greene,* . . . . . . *S.C.* Ap. 127
Ylike as others, girt in gawdy *greene?* . . . . . . *S.C.* May 4
the Woods With *greene* leaves, ... *S.C.* May 8
in a Kirtle of *greene* saye, ... *S.C.* Au. 67
The *greene* is for maydens meete. . . . . . . *S.C.* Au. 68
the *greene* in gray is tinct; . . . . . . *S.C.* N. 107
that were wont *greene* bayes to weare, ... *S.C.* N. 146
The fieldes ay fresh, the grasse ay *greene.* . . . . . . *S.C.* N. 189
Hearken awhile, from thy *greene* cabinet, ... *S.C.* D. 17
groves, with *green* leaves dight. . . . . . . *Gn.* 32
on the soft *greene* grasse feeding their fills, ... *Gn.* 78
fruitefull Pales, and the forrest *greene,* . . . . . . *Gn.* 116
playing on the grassy *greene,* . . . . . . *Gn.* 177
paint with pallid *greene* her buds of gold. . . . . . . *Gn.* 222
looslie on the grassie *greene* dispredd, ... *Gn.* 242
By that same River lurking under *greene,* . . . . . . *Gn.* 649
A little mount, of *greene* turffs edifide; . . . . . . *Gn.* 660
Oxeye still *greene,* and bitter Patience; . . . . . . *Gn.* 678
The woods, the rivers, and the medowes *green,* . . . . . . *Mui.* 153
Sharpe Isope, good for *greene* wounds remedies, ... *Mui.* 190
I her caught disporting on the *greene,* . . . . . . *D.* 118
Whil'st yet her leafe was *greene,* . . . . . . *D.* 240
since first on grassie *greene* Shepheards kept sheep, ... *As.* 209
the cooly shade Of the *greene* alders . . . . . . *Col.* 59
their *greene* leaves, . . . Made a calme shadowe . . . . . . I. ii. 28. 5
thinking of those braunches *greene* to frame A girlond . . . . . . I. ii. 30. 6
In *greene* vine leaves he was right fitly clad, ... I. iv. 22. 1
In a *greene* gowne he clothed was full faire, ... I. iv. 25. 1
She is ybrought unto a paled *greene,* . . . . . . I. v. 5. 3
with *greene* braunches strowing all the ground, ... I. vi. 13. 8
with *greene* boughes decking a gloomy glade, ... I. vii. 4. 4
an almond tree ymounted hye On top of *greene* Selinis . . . . . . I. vii. 32. 6
His dwelling is low in a valley *greene,* . . . . . . I. ix. 4. 5
carcases were scattred on the *greene,* . . . . . . I. ix. 34. 5
like a leafe of Aspin *greene,* . . . . . . I. ix. 51. 4
As fresh as flowres in medow *greene* doe grow . . . . . . I. xii. 6. 7
on her head they sett a girlond *greene,* . . . . . . I. xii. 8. 6
with *greene* mosse cov'ring her nakednesse . . . . . . II. i. 22. 4
on *greene* gras Gay steed with spurs did pricke, ... II. i. 49. 8
they come unto a forrest *greene,* . . . . . . II. iii. 20. 1
all the people decke with girlands *greene,* . . . . . . II. iii. 28. 3
Of swift Eurotas, or on Cynthus *greene,* . . . . . . II. iii. 31. 2
did an Arber *greene* dispred, ... II. v. 29. 2
The *greene* shield dyde in dolorous vermell? . . . . . . II. x. 24. 7
grassy *greene* of delectable hew; . . . . . . II. xii. 12. 3
fayre grassy grownd Mantled with *greene,* . . . . . . II. xii. 50. 4
That speare enchaunted was which layd thee on the *greene.* . . III. i. 7. 9
a spatious playne, Mantled with *greene,* . . . . . . III. i. 20. 7
the *greene* grasse that groweth they shall bren, ... III. iii. 34. 8
besprinckled all the grassy *greene:* . . . . . . III. v. 28. 5
Planted with mirtle trees and laurells *greene,* . . . . . . III. v. 40. 2
with their horned feet the *greene* gras wore, ... III. x. 45. 7
hidden snares Through the *greene* gras . . . . . . III. xi. 28. 9
As plaine as at the first when they were fresh and *greene.* . . IV. i. 24. 9
His wast was with a wreath of yvie *greene* Engirt about, . . . IV. vii. 7. 1
damzels, deckt with long *greene* haire, ... IV. xi. 48. 2

Green—*Continued.*
Fresh Alimeda deckt with girlond *greene;* . . . . . . IV. xi. 51. 1
on the *greene* The Briton Prince him readie did awayte, . . . V. viii. 29. 2
scattred all about, and strow'd upon the *greene.* . . . . . . V. viii. 42. 9
before this Castle *greene* Built a faire Chappell, ... V. x. 28. 1
in a woodmans jacket . . . Of Lincolne *greene,* . . . . . . VI. ii. 5. 7
Of all that raungeth in the forrest *greene,* . . . . . . VI. ii. 31. 8
Letting their steedes to graze upon the *greene.* . . . . . . VI. v. 38. 2
Deckt with *greene* boughes and flowers gay beseene: . . . . . . VI. v. 38. 5
Of few *greene* turfes an altar soone they fayned, ... VI. viii. 44. 8
Yclad in home-made *greene* that her owne hands had dyde. . . VI. ix. 7. 9
He durst not enter into th' open *greene,* . . . . . . VI. x. 11. 1
sitting downe by them upon the *greene,* . . . . . . VI. xi. 39. 1
made him change his gray attire to *greene:* . . . . . . VII. vii. 11. 8
a thin silken cassock coloured *greene,* . . . . . . VII. vii. 29. 2
he in forrest *greene* Had hunted late . . . . . . VII. vii. 29. 7
Cupid selfe about her fluttred all in *greene.* . . . . . . VII. vii. 34. 9
jolly June, arrayd All in *greene* leaves, ... VII. vii. 35. 2
Both of the rivers and the forrests *greene,* . . . . . . *Epith.* 38
being crowned with a girland *greene,* . . . . . . *Epith.* 157
Greenish. Flocke of Nymphes . . . With goodly *greenish* locks, *Proth.* 22
Greenwood. Lawrell tree, Amidst (Amidde[1]) the yong *greene* (*grene*[1]) *wood;* . . . . . . *Pet.* iii. 3
to the *greene Wood* they speeden hem . . . . . . *S.C.* May 27
Yode forth abroade unto the *greene wood,* . . . . . . *S.C.* May 178
The gentle Lady, . . . The *greene-wood* long did walke, . . . III. x. 36. 2
'No tree . . . in *greenewood* growes, ... IV. x. 22. 1
as they all three together went To the *greene wood* . . . . . . VI. x. 34. 2
Greenwood's. as under *greene woodes* syde He lately heard . . II. iii. 3. 6
Under the *greenewoods* side in sorie plight, ... VI. iv. 39. 2
Greenwoods. wilde *greene woods* and fruitful pastures minde; . *Gn.* 637
Greet. Tell me, good Hobbinoll, what garres thee *greete?* . . . *S.C.* Ap. 1
Hey, ho, gray is *greete!* . . . . . . *S.C.* Au. 66
Whom they in civill manner first did *greete,* . . . . . . *Hub.* 362
larke . . . with her song doth *greet* The dawning day . . . . *As.* 33
There did a loftie mount at first us *greet,* . . . . . . *Col.* 284
His Lady, . . . Approcht in hast to *greet* his victorie; . . . . I. i. 27. 2
With gentle wordes he can her fayrely *greet,* . . . . . . I. iv. 46. 1
The witch approching gan him fayrely *greet,* . . . . . . I. vii. 3. 6
Came running fast to *greet* his victorie, ... I. viii. 26. 4
As might become a Squyre so great persons to *greet.* . . . . . I. x. 7. 9
The knight and Una entring fayre her *greet,* . . . . . . I. x. 32. 1
doen upreare Their bevers bright each other for to *greet;* . . II. i. 29. 2
he never staid to *greete,* . . . . . . II. v. 3. 1
It was her guise all Straungers goodly so to *greet.* . . . . . II. xii. 56. 9
Goodly she gan faire Cytherea *greet,* . . . . . . III. vi. 20. 1
I *greet* you well Your countrey kin; . . . . . . III. ix. 51. 6
This happie day I have to *greete* you well, ... IV. ii. 23. 5
In lovely wise she gan that Lady *greet,* . . . . . . IV. iii. 50. 6
To *greet* his guerdon unto every knight, ... V. iii. 14. 3
goodly gan to *greet* his brave emprise, ... V. iii. 15. 7
them goodly well did *greete,* . . . . . . V. iv. 51. 2
To *greet* him the good fortune of his hand: . . . . . . V. xi. 15. 4
He drawing neare began to *greete* them faire, ... V. xi. 48. 2
he did not stay To *greet* him first, ... VI. xi. 28. 2
Greeted. The auncient Dame Him goodly *greeted* . . . . . . I. x. 11. 6
louted low, and *greeted* goodly well; . . . . . . III. x. 37. 9
Now when they saw it falne, they eke him *greeted* all. . . . . V. xi. 15. 9
Greeting. He, . . . his mother earth did kis, *Greeting* his grave: I. ii. 19. 7
Heralds . . . *Greeting* him goodly with new victorie, ... I. v. 15. 8
Who, well them *greeting,* humbly did requight, ... I. x. 49. 8
Her *greeting* . . . in these sad lines addrest . . . . . . I. xii. 26. 2
The Championesse them *greeting,* as she could, ... V. vii. 5. 1
with right humble thankes him goodly *greeting* . . . . . . V. x. 39. 1
The villaine, wroth for *greeting* him so sore, ... VI. vii. 46. 1
first him *greeting,* thus unto him spake: . . . . . . VI. x. 19. 1
Greets. A man of hell . . . Who first us *greets,* . . . . . . I. ix. 28. 6
Him goodly *greetes,* and fayre does entertayne . . . . . . I. xii. 12. 5
Greislie, Gren, Greve. *See* **Grisly, Grin, Grieve.**
Grew. *See* **Overgrew.**
their rule of yearely Presidents *Grew* great, ... *Ro.* xviii. 8
Uprising by degrees, *grewe* to such height, ... *Ro.* xx. 10
So *grew* the Romane Empire by degree, ... *Ro.* xxx. 9
High on a hill a goodly Cedar *grewe,* . . . . . . *Van.* vii. 1
There *grewe* an aged Tree on the greene, ... *S.C.* F. 102
Hard by his side *grewe* a bragging Brere, ... *S.C.* F. 115
'The fragrant flowres, that in my garden *grewe,* . . . . . . *S.C.* D. 109
them amongst the wicked Lotos *grew,* . . . . . . *Gn.* 193
Here also *grew* the rougher rinded Pine, ... *Gn.* 209
Emongst the rest the clambring Yvie *grew,* . . . . . . *Gn.* 217
'Againe great dole on either partie *grewe,* . . . . . . *Gn.* 529
Grewe in this Gardin, fetcht from farre away, ... *Mui.* 202
She *grew* to hideous shape of dryrihed, ... *Mui.* 347
her fine corpes to a bag of venim *grewe.* . . . . . . *Mui.* 352
feede with finest grasse that *grew,* . . . . . . *D.* 345
He *grew* up fast . . . . . . *As.* 17
sung so long untill quite hoarse he *grew.* . . . . . . *Col.* 399
so fell and puissant he *grew,* . . . . . . *Col.* 808
for my sake unknowne such griefe unto you *grew.* . . . . . . I. i. 53. 9
they came at last Where *grew* two goodly trees, ... I. ii. 28. 3
lawlesse riotise, By which he *grew* to grievous malady; . . . I. iv. 20. 6
a dry dropsie . . . Which by misdiet daily greater *grew.* . . . I. iv. 23. 8
She greatly *grew* amazed at the sight, ... I. v. 21. 3
Thereby so fearlesse and so fell he *grew,* . . . . . . I. vi. 25. 1
seven great heads out of his body *grew,* . . . . . . I. vii. 17. 7
greater *grew* the more she did contend, ... I. vii. 27. 3
all still shronke, and still he greater *grew:* . . . . . . I. vii. 45. 7
Before their rage *grew* to so great unrest, ... I. ix. 9. 7
The faithfull knight now *grew* . . . . . . I. x. 21. 1
At their first presence *grew* agrieved sore, ... I. x. 49. 2

Grew—*Continued.*
his baptized hands now greater *grew*, I. xi. 36. 4
There *grew* a goodly tree him faire beside, I. xi. 46. 1
Another like faire tree eke *grew* thereby, I. xi. 47. 6
Grew all afore, and loosely hong unrold; II. iv. 4. 6
There mournfull Cypresse *grew* in greatest store, II. vii. 52. 1
On earth like never *grew*, II. vii. 54. 3
Here eke that famous golden Apple *grew*, II. vii. 55. 4
the fruit which *grew* upon the brincke; II. vii. 58. 5
right glad he *grew*, II. viii. 53. 6
Gorbogud, till far in years he *grew*: II. x. 34. 6
great trouble in the kingdome *grew*, II. x. 54. 2
Grew great, and got large portions of land, II. x. 65. 6
Of these a mighty people shortly *grew*, II. x. 72. 1
shortly *grew* into so great quantitie, II. xii. 62. 4
nigh he breathlesse *grew*, III. i. 21. 3
girlonds of each flowre that *grew*, III. i. 35. 4
in that cloth was wrought as if it lively *grew*. III. i. 38. 9
yett in armes Noctante greater *grew*: III. i. 45. 7
Eftsoones shee *grew* to great impatience, III. i. 48. 1
they *grew* Greatly confused in behaveoure. III. iii. 50. 6
Grew pensive through that amarous discourse, III. iv. 5. 3
he wondrous pensive *grew* in minde, III. v. 12. 5
shee *grew* Full of soft passion III. v. 30. 7
all the sweetest flowers that in the forrest *grew*: III. vi. 6. 9
thither they retourne where first they *grew*: III. vi. 33. 8
all about *grew* every sort of flowre, III. vi. 45. 1
when she to perfect ripenes *grew*, III. vi. 52. 1
She *grew* familiare in that desert place. III. vii. 15. 5
shortly *grew* into outrageous fire; III. vii. 16. 2
of her safety greatly *grew* afrayd. III. vii. 25. 3
Greatly he *grew* enrag'd, III. vii. 33. 5
With thought whereof exceeding mad he *grew*, III. viii. 4. 1
of the antique Trojan stocke there *grew* Another plant, III. ix. 47. 6
Exceeding wroth therewith the virgin *grew*, III. xii. 33. 6
fostred . . . Till that to ripenesse of mans state they *grew*: IV. ii. 46. 2
Upon which ground this same great battell *grew*, IV. ii. 54. 6
Cambell still more strong and greater *grew*, IV. iii. 29. 1
By which few crooked sallowes *grew* in ranke: IV. v. 33. 5
Whereby the passion *grew* more fierce and faine, IV. vi. 33. 8
faire *grew* foule, and foule *grew* faire in sight; IV. viii. 32. 5
the sting which in her tongs end *grew*. IV. viii. 36. 9
there was planted, or *grew* naturall: IV. x. 22. 5
she her selfe likewise divinely *grew*; IV. x. 34. 4
His cheeke-bones raw, and eie-pits hollow *grew*, IV. xii. 20. 3
all things freely *grew* out of the ground: V. Pr. 9. 7
the wicked seede of vice . . . shortly *grew* full great, V. i. 1. 4
towards th' end *grew* greater in his might, V. ii. 17. 6
Which when he saw he greatly *grew* in rage, V. ii. 47. 1
halfe enrag'd she *grew*, V. v. 9. 6
So much the greater still her anguish *grew*, V. v. 28. 1
right discontent In minde he *grew*, V. vi. 24. 2
of his game she soone enwombed *grew*, V. vii. 16. 5
With that all mad and furious he *grew*, V. xi. 12. 1
with the sting which in her vile tongue *grew* V. xii. 42. 7
nurst, Till it to ripenesse *grew*, VI. Pr. 3. 9
Till he to perfect ripenesse *grew*; VI. i. 8. 5
He greater *grew*, and gan to drive at him more hard. VI. i. 20. 9
But still his passion *grew* more violent VI. ii. 21. 9
Full glad and joyous then young Tristram *grew*; VI. ii. 35. 6
With that the wyld man more enraged *grew*, VI. iv. 6. 1
for exceeding griefe which inly *grew* VI. iv. 40. 1
eftsoones he all enraged *grew*, VI. vi. 22. 2
she thereof *grew* proud and insolent, VI. vii. 29. 1
like one halfe entraunced *grew*. VI. ix. 26. 9
Where shortly they in great acquaintance *grew*, VI. xi. 41. 3
he *grew* In so great rage VI. xii. 5. 5
The litle purple rose which thereon *grew*, VI. xii. 18. 5
thousand heads, the which . . . in greater number *grew*. VI. xii. 32. 5
Was dight with flowers that voluntary *grew* VII. vii. 10. 2
Of every sort, which in that Meadow *grew*, *Proth.* 29

Gride. All as I were through the body *gryde*: *S.C.* F. 4
Therewith my soule was sharply *gryde*, *S.C.* Au. 95
With brandisht tongue the emptie aire did *gride*, *Gn.* 254
through his thigh the mortall steele did *gryde*: II. viii. 36. 5
in minde to *gride* The loathed leachour. III. i. 62. 3
love hath *gryde* My feeble brest of late, III. ii. 37. 8
Into his heart, which it did sorely *gryde*. III. ix. 29. 5
Such was the wound that Scudamour did *gride*, IV. vi. 1. 8

Grided. *See* **Gride.**

Grief. nought in this worlde but *griefe* endures. *Bel.*[1] iii. 12
O great misfortune, O great *griefe*, *Pet.*[1] ii. 10
nothing doth endure, But bitter *griefe* *Pet.* vi. 12
Griefe of good mindes, to see goodnesse disgraced! *Van.* i. 8
yeelded, with shame and *greefe* adawed, *S.C.* F. 141
And waked againe with *griefe*; *S.C.* Mar. 48
if for gracelesse *greefe* I dye, *S.C.* Au. 113
Hey, ho, gracelesse *griefe*! *S.C.* Au. 114
I pray thee, gall not my old *griefe*: *S.C.* S. 12
how great is thy *griefe*! *S.C.* N. 113
Ere the breme Winter breede you greater *griefe*. *S.C.* D. 148
griefe enough it is to grieved wight *Gn. Ded.* 11
my weake bodie, set on fire with *griefe*, *Hub.* 15
The Foxe, that first this cause of *griefe* did finde, *Hub.* 51
because your *griefe* doth great appeare, *Hub.* 73
Can *griefe* then enter into heavenly harts, *T.M.* 47
naught on earth her *griefe* might pacifie; *T.M.* 356
for great *griefe* Of my mishaps, *Ti.* 141
'O *griefe* of griefes! *Ti.* 449
do my soule with inward *griefe* infest: *Ti.* 460

Grief—*Continued.*
nigh with *griefe* thereof my heart was brust. *Ti.* 518
griefe thereof my spirite greatly pained. *Ti.* 560
all is vanitie and *griefe* of minde, *Ti.* 583
Pined with *griefe* of folly late repented: *Mui.* 348
mournfull tunes enough my *griefe* to show? *Mui.* 412
With *griefe* of mournefull great mishap opprest, *D.* 2
Griefe findes some ease by him that like does beare. *D.* 67
since so much thou seemst to rue my *griefe*, *D.* 92
All were my self, through *griefe*, in deadly drearing. *D.* 189
Leaving behind them nought but *griefe* of minde, *D.* 398
With inward anguish and great *griefe* opprest: *As.* 206
Such grace shall be some guerdon for the *griefe*, *Col.* 943
His gall did grate for *griefe* and high disdaine; I. i. 19. 6
for my sake unknowne such *griefe* unto you grew. I. i. 53. 9
Will was his guide, and *griefe* led him astray. I. ii. 12. 4
He oft finds med'cine who his *griefe* imparts, I. ii. 34. 4
many mischiefes follow cruell Wrath: . . . fretting *griefe*. I. iv. 35. 5
Whome great *griefe* made forgett the raines to hold I. iv. 41. 3
Cause of my new *griefe*, cause of my new joy; I. iv. 45. 5
their *griefe* is with them gone: I. iv. 49. 2
sweet musicke . . . Him to beguile of *griefe* I. v. 17. 8
in false *griefe* hyding his harmefull guile, I. v. 18. 5
For *griefe* whereof the lad n'ould after joy, I. vi. 17. 8
The further processe of her hidden *griefe*: I. vi. 37. 8
rip up *griefe* where it may not availe: I. vii. 39. 8
'Well may I ween your *griefe* is wondrous great; I. vii. 40. 2
wondrous great *griefe* groneth in my spright, I. vii. 40. 3
'great *griefe* will not be tould, I. vii. 41. 1
griefe' . . . 'does greater grow displaid,' I. vii. 41. 5
to inquere the secrets of my *griefe*, I. vii. 42. 6
This is my cause of *griefe*, I. vii. 51. 9
Such percing *griefe* her stubborne hart did wound, I. viii. 25. 4
sprites, . . . with great *griefe* were often heard to grone, I. viii. 36. 8
Had no delight to treaten of his *griefe*; I. viii. 43. 8
Embost with bale, and bitter byting *griefe*, I. ix. 29. 2
Could hardly him intreat to tell his *grief*: I. x. 24. 2
full of *griefe* and anguish vehement, I. xi. 26. 1
The *griefe* thereof him wondrous sore diseasd, I. xi. 38. 8
For *griefe* thereof and divelish despight, I. xi. 44. 1
appease your *griefe* and heavy plight, II. i. 14. 5
now exceeding *griefe* him overcame, II. i. 23. 5
Let one word fall that may your *grief* unfold, II. i. 46. 7
He oft finds present helpe who does his *griefe* impart.' II. i. 46. 9
die with you in sorrow, and partake your *griefe*.' II. i. 48. 9
for *griefe* his hart did grate, II. i. 56. 6
frye in hartlesse *griefe* and dolefull tene: II. i. 58. 4
To frett for anger, or for *griefe* to mone? II. iii. 3. 4
what horrour and tormenting *griefe* II. iv. 28. 6
'Thus heaping crime on crime, and *griefe* on *griefe*, II. iv. 31. 1
such agony As *griefe* and fury unto me did bring; II. iv. 33. 4
Wrath, gelosy, *griefe*, love, this Squyre have laide thus low. II. iv. 34. 9
'Wrath, gealosie, *griefe*, love, do thus expell: II. iv. 35. 1
Griefe is a flood; and love a monster fell; II. iv. 35. 3
So shall wrath, gealosy, *griefe*, love, die and decay.' II. iv. 35. 9
for *grief* of mind That he . . . was conquered: II. v. 14. 5
griefe and wrath, that be her enemies II. vi. 1. 6
his *griefe* He knew right well, II. vi. 51. 1
Leaving behind them *griefe* and heavinesse: II. vii. 12. 5
fraught with great *griefe* And wrath, II. viii. 33. 1
prickt with guiltie shame And inward *griefe*, II. viii. 44. 3
All pleasaunce was to them *griefe* and annoy: II. ix. 35. 5
herselfe for *griefe* did kill; II. xii. 52. 3
Much greater *griefe* and shamefuller regrett III. i. 8. 2
With sighes, and sobs, and plaints, and piteous *griefe*, III. i. 53. 2
by long triall of the inward *griefe* III. i. 54. 3
Like an huge Aetn' of deepe engulfed *gryefe*, III. ii. 32. 6
to ease thy *griefe* And win thy will: III. ii. 33. 6
rather doth my helpelesse *griefe* augment; III. ii. 43. 5
to cure this Ladies *griefe*; III. iii. 5. 2
'Sith then thou knowest all our *griefe*, III. iii. 21. 1
Both for his *griefe*, and for her peoples sake, III. iii. 43. 2
'Huge sea of sorrow and tempestuous *griefe*, III. iv. 8. 1
She shut up all her plaint in privy *griefe* III. iv. 11. 2
The mist of *griefe* dissolv'd did into vengeance powre. III. iv. 13. 9
full of bitter *griefe* and pensife thought, III. iv. 31. 5
Exceeding *griefe* that wound in him empight, III. v. 20. 8
hardly finde to aggravate her *griefe*; III. viii. 1. 8
His former *griefe* with furie fresh reviv'd III. viii. 3. 4
Dye had she rather in tormenting *griefe* III. viii. 42. 3
to her he sought to intimate His inward *griefe*, III. ix. 30. 2
Into huge waves of *griefe* and gealosye III. x. 17. 4
Long thus he chawd the cud of inward *griefe*, III. x. 18. 1
Ne *griefe* might not his love to him restore, III. x. 18. 7
tell thy *griefe*, if any hidden lye: III. x. 26. 2
Ne word he had to speake his *griefe* to tell, III. x. 37. 8
Griefe, and despight, and gealosy, and scorne, III. x. 55. 5
through privy *griefe* and horrour vaine, III. x. 60. 7
gan apply Fit medcine to his *griefe*, III. xi. 13. 9
deepe conceived *griefe* Well seemes t' exceede the powre of patience, III. xi. 14. 1
For *griefe* whereof, ye mote have . . . seene III. xi. 37. 6
Next him went *Griefe* and Fury, III. xii. 16. 1
Griefe all in sable sorrowfully clad, III. xii. 16. 2
no lesse *griefe* endured for your gentle sake.' III. xii. 40. 9
with wondrous *griefe* of mynd And shame, IV. i. 37. 6
gan his former *griefe* renew. IV. i. 38. 9
his heart Was thrild with inward *griefe*: IV. i. 49. 7
him fild With double life and *griefe*; IV. iii. 22. 3
Devized by the Gods, for to aswage Harts *grief*, IV. iii. 43. 3

Grief—*Continued.*
So much the more her *griefe,* the more her toyle: IV. v. 30. 1
Yet neither toyle nor *griefe* she once did spare, IV. v. 30. 2
What equall torment to the *griefe* of mind IV. vi. 1. 1
she waked out of dread Streight into *griefe,* IV. vii. 9. 4
seekes to know anothers *griefe* in vaine, IV. vii. 10. 7
found no ease of *griefe* nor hope of grace, IV. vii. 38. 2
As one with *griefe* and anguishe overcum, IV. vii. 44. 4
let her weet The great tormenting *griefe* IV. viii. 9. 8
through inward *griefe* or wilfull scorne IV. viii. 15. 5
wound the soule it selfe with *griefe* unkind; IV. viii. 26. 7
most she touched was with *griefe* entire IV. ix. 13. 8
Sith love was first the ground of all her *griefe,* IV. ix. 15. 2
piteously complaind her carefull *grieffe,* IV. xii. 5. 3
hoping *griefe* may lessen being told, IV. xii. 6. 3
my weary ghost, with *griefe* outworne, IV. xii. 8. 1
even for *griefe* of minde he oft did grone, IV. xii. 12. 6
To see an helplesse evill double *griefe* doth lend. IV. xii. 21. 9
grief unknowne, which he could not discerne: IV. xii. 24. 2
Thinking to have her *griefe* by death bereaved: V. iv. 10. 4
Radigund, full of heart-gnawing *griefe* V. iv. 47. 1
So she departed full of *griefe* and sdaine, V. v. 51. 6
her *griefe* with errour to beguyle, V. vi. 5. 3
With sodaine stounds of wrath and *griefe* attone; V. vi. 17. 6
Chawing the cud of *griefe* and inward paine, V. vi. 19. 2
With inward *griefe* and malice did against them swell. V. vii. 10. 9
For his departure, her new cause of *griefe:* V. vii. 44. 2
as if great *griefe* had her affected; V. ix. 9. 9
Griefe did plead, and many teares forth powre. V. ix. 45. 9
by her tempred without *griefe* or gall, V. x. 4. 5
let not your *griefe* empeach To tell VI. ii. 42. 2
'Therefore, faire Lady, lay aside this *griefe,* VI. ii. 46. 1
did that good old Knight Temper his *griefe,* VI. iii. 6. 2
gan to intimate Each others *griefe* VI. iii. 12. 5
'Sith then ye needs will know the *griefe* I hoord, VI. iv. 29. 2
this my cause of *griefe* to you appeares; VI. iv. 33. 8
With tender ruth for her unworthy *griefe;* VI. iv. 34. 2
for exceeding *griefe* which inly grew VI. iv. 40. 1
whose *griefe* through suffraunce sore increast. VI. v. 39. 9
Words sharpely wound, but greatest *griefe* of scorning growes. VI. vii. 49. 9
after *griefe* awhile had had his course, VI. xi. 34. 1
Calidore recomforting his *griefe,* VI. xi. 38. 1
chiefly Calidore, whom *griefe* had most possest. VI. xi. 41. 9
lovely light to cleare my cloudy *grief,* *Am.* xxxiv. 12
griefe renew, and passions doe awake *Am.* xliv. 11
she, all carelesse of his *griefe* *Am.* xlviii. 9
Of my harts wound, and of my bodies *griefe;* *Am.* l. 2
faine my *griefe* with chaunges to beguile, *Am.* lxxxvi. 10
he weeping came, And of his *griefe* complayned: *Epig.* iv. 32
drinketh up the lyfe . . . with consuming *griefe.* *H.L.* 126
recure my harts long pyning *griefe,* *H.B.* 285
ceasse to gaze on matter of thy *grief:* *H.H.B.* 294
Grieffull. with passion great And *griefull* pittie IV. i. 16. 4
Which when she sees with ghastly *grieffull* eies, VI. viii. 40. 5
Grief's. 'This *griefes* deepe wound I would to thee disclose, V. v. 30. 7
Griefs. 'Resort of people doth my *greefs* augment, *S.C.* Au. 157
'O griefe of *griefes!* *Ti.* 449
double *griefs* afflict concealing harts, I. ii. 34. 5
Griefull. *See* **Grieffull.**
Griesie, Griesly. *See* **Grisy, Grisly.**
Grievance. this world doth nought but *grievance* hold! *Bel.*[2] iii. 12
stoope-gallaunt Age, the hoste of *Greevaunce.* *S.C.* F. 90
praying to be garded from *greevance.'* *S.C.* F. 188
In playner wise to tell her *grievance* she begonne. III. i. 52. 9
Through *grievaunce* of his late received wound, IV. iv. 26. 8
such a sore, that doth her *grievance* hide, IV. vi. 1. 6
Grieve. ever since my hart did *greve,* *S.C.* Au. 123
grieve that my remembrance quite is raced Out *Ti.* 177
did *grieve* the noble spright Of Salomon *Ti.* 443
the earth did *grieve* exceedingly, *Ti.* 671
grieve my ghost, that ill mote him behove, *D.* 265
wound Could ever find to *grieve* the gentlest hart on ground?' I. ix. 7. 9
at their second sister grutch And inly *grieve,* II. ii. 34. 7
Did see and *grieve* at his bold fashion; II. ii. 37. 7
to recover right for such as wrong did *grieve.* III. i. 3. 9
Let not thee *grieve* dismounted to have beene, III. i. 7. 6
if it should not *grieve* you III. ix. 40. 5
doubly did him *grieve* when so himselfe he found. IV. iv. 26. 9
They have him taken captive, though it *grieve* him sore. IV. iv. 32. 9
She gan thereat to fret and greatly *grieve;* IV. xii. 26. 2
grieve in every vaine. IV. xii. 27. 9
Whose nature is to *grieve* and grudge at all V. xii. 31. 2
Then would she inly fret, and *grieve,* V. xii. 32. 3
Let none therefore . . . Too greatly *grieve* VI. iii. 5. 9
As if it them should *grieve* to see his punishment. VI. viii. 4. 9
Ne once my minds unmoved quiet *grieve;* VI. ix. 22. 7
the nights they *grieve* and grone, *H.L.* 129
th' evils which poore lovers *greeve.* *H.L.* 258
Grieved. griefe enough it is to *grieved* wight *Gn. Ded.* 11
His inly *grieved* minde full sore opprest; *Gn.* 643
Was *griev'd* as he had felt part of his paine; *Hub.* 260
he saw, that sorely *griev'd* his hart, *Hub.* 1304
My thought returned *greeved* home againe, *Ti.* 478
sight thereof much *griev'd* my pensive thought. *Ti.* 623
I sore *griev'd* to see his wretched case. *D.* 553
Much *griev'd* to thinke that gentle Dame so light, I. i. 55. 2
sore *grieved* in her gentle brest, I. ii. 8. 8
greevd to thinke how foe did him destroy, I. iv. 45. 7
greeved ghost for vengeance deep do grone: I. iv. 49. 7
Then gins her *grieved* ghost thus to lament and mourne: I. vii. 21. 9

Grieved—*Continued.*
Through great impatience of his *grieved* hed, I. viii. 17. 4
Their God himselfe, *grievd* at my libertie, I. ix. 10. 7
Greevd with remembrance of his wicked wayes, I. x. 21. 6
that disease of *grieved* conscience, I. x. 23. 8
Faynt, wearie, sore, emboyled, *grieved,* brent, I. xi. 28. 1
grieved mindes, which choler did englut, II. ii. 23. 5
grieved at her flight; II. iii. 43. 2
dismayd . . . Pyrochles was, and *grieved* eke entyre; II. v. 8. 2
The varlet at his plaint was *grieved* so sore, II. vi. 45. 6
griev'd so long to lacke his greedie pray; II. vii. 34. 2
nought him *griev'd* to beene from rule deposed downe. II. x. 29. 9
her seeming *griev'd* Out of her heavie swowne not to awake III. vi. 27. 7
Saw all this goodly sport, and *grieved* sore; III. x. 45. 2
it *grieved* him full sore, IV. i. 39. 7
Much was he *grieved* with that gracelesse chaunce; IV. iii. 8. 5
The more it gauld and *griev'd* him night and day, IV. v. 31. 8
long time his *grieved* hart did wound, IV. vi. 28. 5
grieved was for losse both of her sire, IV. ix. 13. 6
Now gan he in his *grieved* minde devise, IV. xii. 14. 1
griev'd her more that she it could not mend: IV. xii. 21. 8
If ought lay hidden in his *grieved* thought, IV. xii. 24. 8
grieved to restore the pledge he did possesse. IV. xii. 32. 9
Griev'd to the soule, and groning inwardly, V. iv. 22. 8
Restlesse, recomfortlesse, with heart deepe *grieved,* V. vi. 24. 6
Much was he *grieved* with that haplesse throe, V. viii. 35. 1
grieved sore that . . . she had Fallen into that Tyrants hand V. xi. 40. 8
Doe it disclose to ease your *grieved* spright: VI. iv. 28. 7
'But most my Lord is *grieved* herewithall, VI. iv. 32. 1
much *griev'd* against that straunger knight, VI. vii. 20. 6
groning sore from *grieved* hart entire VI. viii. 48. 7
that sore she *griev'd* to see, VI. xi. 23. 1
He chauft, he *griev'd,* he fretted, and he sight, VI. xi. 25. 7
Melt into teares, and grone in *grieved* thought. *H.H.L.* 252
Grieves. Most envious man, that *grieves* at neighbours good; I. ix. 39. 6
what were they all, whose lacke thee *grieves* so sore?' VI. x. 20. 9
how ever it him *greeves,* VI. xi. 15. 3
Grieveth. much it *grieveth* me to thinke thereon. *Pet.* i. 3
in minde, the which most *grieveth* me, VI. v. 28. 3
Grieving. inlie *greeving* in my groning brest, *Ti.* 484
Grievous. O *grevous* chaunge! *Bel.*[1] ix. 12
freshly bleeding of a *grievous* wounde. *Rev.* i. 8
(O *grievous* chance!) *Bel.*[2] xi. 12
The ghastlie Owle her *grievous* ynne doth keepe. *S.C.* D. 72
Began her *grievous* plaint, as doth ensew. *T.M.* 114, 174, 234, 300, 420
With shrikes and groanes and *grievous* agonie. *T.M.* 358
lawlesse riotise, By which he grew to *grievous* malady; I. iv. 20. 6
in foote and hand A *grievous* gout tormented him full sore, I. iv. 29. 7
The sad earth, . . . Did grone full *grievous* I. viii. 8. 8
Whose *grievous* fall when false Duessa spyde, I. viii. 25. 1
'The things, that *grievous* were to doe, or beare, I. viii. 44. 2
the *grievous* smart which him did wring, I. xi. 39. 2
Either for *grievous* shame, or for great teene, II. i. 15. 8
playnd of *grievous* outrage, II. i. 30. 5
did complaine Of *grievous* mischiefes II. ii. 43. 3
In joyous pleasure then in *grievous* paine; II. vi. 1. 2
oftentimes great grones, and *grievous* stownds, III. iii. 9. 6
thought so to beguile her *grievous* smart; III. iv. 6. 2
so her smart was much more *grievous* bredd, III. iv. 6. 3
gamesom merth to *grievous* dreriment: III. iv. 30. 4
did the best His *grievous* hurt to guarish, III. v. 41. 6
She gan for me devise a *grievous* punishment; III. vii. 55. 9
wrap in *grievous* woe. III. ix. 17. 9
seemd more *grievous* then it was before. III. x. 18. 5
did the rest with *grievous* sighes suppresse, III. x. 25. 8
she heard with *grievous* throb Him grone, III. xi. 8. 6
made it seeme to feele her *grievous* paine, IV. xii. 5. 8
On whom he did inflict most *grievous* punishment. V. xii. 26. 9
Ne sparing him the more for all his *grievous* wound. VI. iv. 2. 9
for *grievous* paine Of their late woundes, VI. v. 39. 7
Was much more *grievous* then the others blowes: VI. vii. 49. 8
Grievously. a large lukewarme flood, . . . thence gushed *grievously;* II. viii. 39. 2
grudged *grievously* To house a guest III. x. 2. 2
the gore-bloud thence gushing *grievously* V. xii. 20. 6
Griffin. As when a *Gryfon,* seized of his pray, I. v. 8. 2
Griffins. as *Griffons,* Minotaures, Crocodiles, *Hub.* 1123
others like *Gryphons* dreare; II. xi. 8. 4
Griffith. *Griffyth* Conan also shall upreare His dreaded head, III. iii. 45. 6
Grim. With greislie countenaunce and visage *grim,* *Gn.* 326
There *grim* Persephone, encountring mee, *Gn.* 422
Like a *grimme* Lyon rushing *Mui.* 434
yet quakes . . . to see the Lyon looke so *grim.* I. vi. 10. 9
with *grim* looke And count'naunce sterne, II. v. 14. 1
over them sad horror with *grim* hew II. vii. 23. 1
With hoary lockes all loose, and visage *grim;* II. xi. 23. 3
by the *grim* floud of Cocytus slow, III. iv. 55. 5
looked *grim,* And faynd to cheare his lady III. viii. 15. 6
more for feare of his *grim* sight, III. viii. 32. 8
he was fowle, ill favoured, and *grim,* III. xii. 15. 1
lookt on Glauce *grim;* IV. i. 50. 3
Of two *grim* lyons, taken from the wood, IV. iii. 39. 2
at first espiall Of his *grim* face, IV. x. 17. 7
brought he forth with griesly *grim* aspect Abhorred Murder, V. ix. 48. 1
sternely him beheld with *grim* and ghastly looke. V. xi. 12. 9
Looking . . . with count'nance *grim,* VI. iii. 34. 7
Appearing like the mouth of Orcus griesly *grim:* VI. xii. 26. 9
Death with most *grim* and griesly visage seene, VII. vii. 46. 2
grim Sir Saturne oft doth spare His sterne aspect, VII. vii. 52. 7

Grimly. teeth he still did grind And *grimly* gnash, ... II. iv. 15. 4
Grin. *See* **Girn.**
Thereat th' old man did nought but fondly *grin,* . . . . . III. viii. 24. 6
Her heart for rage did grate, and teeth did *grin.* . . . . . V. iv. 37. 7
Tygres, that did seeme to *gren* And snar at all . . . . . VI. xii. 27. 6
Grind. *See* **Grinded, Grinned.**
his great yron teeth he still did *grind* . . . . . II. iv. 15. 3
gan to *grind* His grated teeth . . . . . II. v. 14. 2
Grinded. Gnashing his *grinded* teeth with griesly looke, . . . VI. v. 26. 1
Grinding. *Grinding* his teeth, and grating his great hart; . . *Hub.* 1334
Grinned. He *grind,* hee bit, he scratcht, he venim threw, . . VI. xii. 31. 8
Grinning. all . . . gently *grenning,* shew a semblance glad . . I. vi. 11. 7
by his *grenning* laughter mote farre off be rad. . . . . . IV. vii. 24. 9
grinning griesly, did against him weld His deadly weapon . V. xii. 16. 4
Gripe. Did *grype* your hearts with noysome rage imbew'd, . . *Ro.* xxiv. 6
Threatning with greedy *gripe* to doe him dye, ... II. vii. 27. 7
Strongly he strove out of her greedy *gripe* To loose his shield, . V. xi. 27. 6
For he would not his greedie *grype* forgoe, ... VI. iv. 7. 3
did *gripe* his gorge so fast, ... VI. iv. 22. 4
Griped. he *grypt* her gorge with so great paine, ... I. i. 19. 8
From Lyons clawes to pluck the *gryped* pray. . . . . . I. vi. 7. 4
grypt it fast withall. . . . . I. xi. 40. 9
To reave by strength the *griped* gage away: . . . . . I. xi. 41. 6
Him sternly *grypt,* and hailing to and fro, ... II. iv. 8. 7
Uppon his iron coller *griped* fast, ... V. ii. 14. 4
Having both sides through *grypt* with griesly wound. . . . VI. iii. 27. 5
Griping. from his *griping* pawes He hath his shield redeemd, . I. iii. 41. 8
With *griping* talaunts armd to greedy fight, ... I. viii. 48. 7
He so disseized of his *gryping* grosse, ... I. xi. 20. 1
from her *griping* pounce the greedy prey doth rive. . . . . V. iv. 42. 9
whilest in hand it *gryping* hard he hent, ... V. ix. 18. 4
greedily him *griping* his avengement stayd. . . . . . VI. v. 26. 9
Gripple. he gnasht his teeth . . . with *griple* Covetyse; . . . I. iv. 31. 7
Ne ever Artegall his *griple* strong . . . wold slacke, ... V. ii. 14. 8
Tho on his shield he *gripple* hold did lay, ... VI. iv. 6. 7
Grisly. A *grisly* forehed and Saturnelike face. . . . . . *Bel.*[1] vii. 4
wall, . . . cover'd all with *griesly* shadowes, ... *Bel.*[2] viii. 3
The *griesly* (**greisly*) gates of his devouring hell, ... *Van.* iii. 10
Up, *grieslie* ghostes! . . . . *S.C.* N. 55
The *grieslie* Tode-stoole growne there . . . . *S.C.* D. 69
With *greislie* countenaunce and visage grim, ... *Gn.* 326
griesly Feends of hell him terrifie. . . . . *Gn.* 544
With hollow browes and *greisly* countenaunce, ... *T.M.* 185
hell, and darkenesse, and the *grislie* grave, ... *T.M.* 496
greislie shades, such as doo haunt in hell . . . . . . *Ti.* 125
'The sevenfold yron gates of *grislie* Hell, ... *Ti.* 372
Which when the *greisly* tyrant did espie, ... *Mui.* 433
grisly Ghosts, to heare the dolefull teene. . . . . . . *D.* 21
No *griesly* famine, nor no raging sweard, ... *Col.* 314
He bad awake blacke Plutoes *griesly* Dame; . . . . . . I. i. 37. 4
Of *griesly* Pluto she the daughter was, ... I. iv. 11. 1
griesly Night, with visage deadly sad, ... I. v. 20. 1
her darke *griesly* looke them much dismay: . . . . . . I. v. 30. 5
other *griesly* thing that him aghast. . . . . I. ix. 21. 4
like the *griesly* mouth of hell, ... I. xi. 12. 8
A cruell knife that made a *griesly* wownd, ... II. i. 39. 6
*The slouthfull wave of that great *griesly* lake; . . . . . II. vi. 18. 7
griesly hew and fowle ill favour'd sight; . . . . . . II. vii. 3. 5
streight did lead to Plutoes *griesly* rayne. . . . . . . II. vii. 21. 4
Through *griesly* shadowes by a beaten path, ... II. vii. 51. 3
With their rude handes and *gryesly* graplement; . . . . . II. xi. 29. 3
that *grisely* mouth did see Sucking the seas . . . . . . II. xii. 6. 1
The *griesly* Wasserman, that makes his game . . . . . . II. xii. 24. 3
sore annoyed, groping in that *griesly* night. . . . . . II. xii. 35. 9
Whose hideous horror . . . Full *griesly* seemd: . . . . . III. i. 14. 7
a *griesly* foster forth did rush, ... III. i. 17. 2
all the *griesly* Monsters of the See . . . . III. iv. 32. 8
They softly gan to search his *griesly* wownd: . . . . . III. iv. 40. 2
griesly shadowes covered heaven bright, ... III. iv. 52. 2
The state of life out of the *griesly* shade. . . . . . III. vi. 37. 5
with *griesly* hate And dreadfull horror . . . . III. xi. 21. 7
Straunge horrour to deforme his *griesly* shade: . . . . . III. xii. 11. 4
in their flesh a *griesly* passage rend, ... IV. ii. 15. 5
the thrid By *griesly* Lachesis was spun . . . . IV. ii. 48. 6
fly Unto her rest in Plutoes *griesly* land; . . . . . . IV. iii. 13. 3
therein made a very *griesly* wound, ... IV. iv. 24. 6
Full blacke and *griesly* did his face appeare, ... IV. v. 34. 6
espies that *griesly* wight Approching nigh, ... IV. vii. 22. 5
He let to grow and *griesly* to concrew, ... IV. vii. 40. 5
ten thousand monsters . . . gaping *griesly,* all begor'd. . . . IV. xi. 3. 9
it bit Unto the bone, and made a *griesly* wound, ... V. vii. 33. 3
made a *griesly* wound in his enriven side. . . . . . . V. viii. 34. 9
brought he forth with *griesly* grim aspect Abhorred Murder, . V. ix. 48. 1
To wander in the *griesly* shades of night. . . . . . . V. x. 33. 6
grinning *griesly,* did against him weld His deadly weapon . . V. xii. 16. 4
ill favour'd Hags he met, . . . Two *griesly* creatures: . . . . V. xii. 28. 6
Having both sides through grypt with *griesly* wound. . . . VI. iii. 27. 5
Gnashing his grinded teeth with *griesly* looke, ... VI. v. 26. 1
griesly wounds that him appalled sore; . . . . VI. vii. 14. 5
kept with gard Of *griesly* theeves, ... VI. x. 43. 8
in the horror of the *griesly* night, ... VI. xi. 16. 6
Appearing like the mouth of Orcus *griesly* grim: . . . . . VI. xii. 26. 9
tell To *griesly* Pluto what on earth was donne, ... VI. xii. 35. 6
Death with most grim and *griesly* visage seene, ... VII. vii. 46. 2
griesly vultures, make us once affeard: . . . . *Epith.* 348
Grisy. His *griesie* lockes, long growen and unbound, ... I. ix. 35. 4
The slouthfull wave of that great *griesy* lake: . . . . . . II. vi. 18. 7
Was, as the rest, a *grysie* rablement; . . . . II. xi. 12. 3
ere the grosse Earthes *gryesy* shade Was all disperst . . . . III. i. 67. 7
Led of two *grysie* Villeins, ... III. xii. 19. 2

Groan. I heard the tronck to *grone;* . . . . *Bel.* v. 12
th' earth under her childrens weight did *grone,* . . . . . . *Ro.* xii. 7
inly deepe did *grone,* . . . . *D.* 48
greeved ghost for vengeance deep do *grone:* . . . . . . I. iv. 49. 7
The sad earth, . . . Did *grone* full grievous . . . . I. viii. 8. 8
sprites, . . . with great griefe were often heard to *grone,* . . . I. viii. 36. 8
him underneath Did *grone,* . . . . I. xi. 54. 4
after gave a *grone* so deepe and low . . . . II. i. 38. 3
At last his mighty ghost gan deepe to *grone,* . . . . . . II. i. 42. 5
He lately heard that dying Lady *grone,* . . . . II. iii. 3. 7
That speare is him enough to doen a thousand *grone.'* . . . . II. iii. 12. 9
made his spright to *grone* full piteous; . . . . II. xi. 38. 7
she heard with grievous throb Him *grone,* . . . . III. xi. 8. 7
oft to *grone* with billowes beating from the maine: . . . . . IV. xii. 5. 9
even for griefe of minde he oft did *grone,* . . . . . . IV. xii. 12. 6
that made him *grone* And gaspe for breath, ... VI. iv. 21. 5
Full many a night for her did sigh and *grone:* . . . . . . VI. ix. 10. 4
the nights they grieve and *grone,* . . . . *H.L.* 129
Melt into teares, and *grone* in grieved thought. . . . . . *H.H.L.* 252
Groaned. hundred vanquisht kings *gronde* at hir feete, ... *Bel.*[1] xi. 9
Long having deeply *gron'd* these Visions sad, ... *Bel.*[2] xiv. 1
The blocke oft *groned* under the blow, ... *S.C.* F. 215
layd him downe, and *groned,* . . . . *S.C.* May 246
The ground eke *groned* under him for dreed: . . . . . . I. vii. 8. 6
and *groaned* inwardly, To thinke of this ill state . . . . . VI. iii. 11. 5
Full many a one for me deepe *groand* and sight, ... VI. viii. 20. 7
Groaneth. wondrous great griefe *groneth* in my spright, . . . I. vii. 40. 3
groneth out his utmost grudging spright . . . . II. v. 36. 7
Groanful. gave against his mother earth a *gronefull* sownd. . II. xi. 42. 9
Groaning. *See* **Deepe-groaning.**
the Foxe, deep *groning* in his sprite, ... *Hub.* 588
inlie greeving in my *groning* brest, ... *Ti.* 484
their Parent deare . . . *Groning* full deadly, ... I. i. 25. 3
groning deep; 'Nor damned Ghost,' (quoth he,) . . . . . . I. ii. 33. 1
Nor wayld of friends, nor layd on *groning* beare, ... I. v. 23. 4
The *groning* ghosts of many one dismaide . . . . I. vii. 47. 8
groning deepe, thus answerd him againe; . . . . II. vii. 59. 3
many Giaunts left on *groning* flore: . . . . II. x. 10. 5
they to direfull death their *groning* ghosts did send. . . . . II. xi. 15. 9
nathemore forth fled his *groning* spright, ... II. xi. 38. 8
life recur'd agayne, And, *groning* inly deepe, ... III. v. 34. 2
Some litle whispering, and soft *groning* sound. . . . . . IV. vii. 33. 4
left them *groning* there upon the plaine: . . . . IV. x. 10. 6
inly *groning* deepe and sighing oft, ... IV. x. 48. 3
Griev'd to the soule, and *groning* inwardly, ... V. iv. 22. 8
sent His *groning* soule unto her place of punishment. . . . . V. x. 36. 9
There she long groveling and deepe *groning* lay, ... VI. v. 5. 6
groning sore from grieved hart entire . . . . VI. viii. 48. 7
Groanings. His ruefull shriekes and *gronings,* . . . . . . I. x. 28. 5
Groans. With shrikes and *groanes* and grievous agonie. . . . . *T.M.* 358
here no tunes, save sobs and *grones,* shall ring. . . . . . . *D.* 14
she does lament . . . And sighes, and *grones,* . . . . . . I. iii. 15. 7
oftentimes great *grones,* and grievous stownds, ... III. iii. 9. 6
Groined. Beares, that *groynd* continually; . . . . VI. xii. 27. 5
Gronde. *See* **Groaned.**
Grone, -d, *etc.* *See* **Groan, -d,** *etc.*
Groom. *See* **Bridegroom, Herd-groom.**
the slie Foxe, as like to be his *groome,* . . . . *Hub.* 661
(a jolly *groome* was he, ... *Col.* 12
Then called she a *Groome,* that forth him ledd . . . . . . I. x. 17. 6
the bushy Teade a *groome* did light, ... I. xii. 37. 6
'Hayle, *Groome!* didst not thou see a bleeding Hynde, ... II. iii. 32. 7
it was a *groome* of base degree, ... II. iv. 24. 3
Disguised like that *groome* of base degree, ... II. iv. 27. 8
Straying alone withouten *groome* or guide: . . . . III. x. 36. 5
she left her *groome* An yron man, ... V. i. 12. 1
Thereto he hath a *groome* of evill guize, ... V. ii. 6. 6
The whiles his guilefull *groome* was fled away, ... V. iii. 38. 1
that great yron *groome,* his gard and government. . . . . . V. iv. 3. 9
it was Talus, Artegall his *groome:* . . . . V. vi. 8. 6
The *groome* went streight way in, ... VI. iii. 42. 1
Which answer when the *groome* returning brought . . . . . VI. iii. 43. 3
she did th' assistance need Of this her *groome;* . . . . . . VI. v. 10. 5
Ere long to him a homely *groome* there came, ... VI. vi. 20. 1
It was his owne true *groome,* the gentle Squire, ... VI. viii. 27. 6
ye fresh boyes, that tend upon her *groome,* . . . . *Epith.* 112
When he begot the great Tirynthian *groome:* . . . . *Epith.* 329
Grooms. *See* **Herd-grooms, Shepherd-grooms.**
When shepheardes *groomes* han leave to playe, ... *S.C.* Mar. 62
One of those *groomes* (a jolly groome was he, ... *Col.* 12
Beware therefore, ye *groomes,* . . . . *Col.* 925
many *Groomes* and Squyres ready were . . . . II. xi. 49. 1
All sixe strong *groomes,* but one then other more; . . . . . IV. v. 36. 5
on either side she was sustained Of two smal *grooms,* . . . . IV. xi. 25. 2
Where *groomes* awayted her to have undrest; . . . . V. vi. 23. 3
they themselves were evill *groomes,* they sayd, ... VI. xi. 40. 3
Grope. made me bold, In bitter hyve to *grope* for honny: . . *Epig.* i. 4
Groping. sore annoyed, *groping* in that griesly night. . . . . II. xii. 35. 9
Grose. *See* **Gross.**
Gross. *grose* disease Soone growes through humours superfluitie. *Ro.* xxiii. 11
by much wrestling to leese the *grosse.* . . . . *S.C.* S. 135
Whose *grosse* defaults thy daintie pen may file, ... *Ded. Son.* xii. 11
He so disseized of his gryping *grosse,* . . . . I. xi. 20. 1
suddeinly a *grosse* fog over-spred . . . . II. xii. 34. 5
ere the *grosse* Earthes gryesy shade Was all disperst . . . . . III. i. 67. 7
full *grosse* and fat As fed with lard, ... VII. vii. 40. 1
the *grosse* matter of this earthly myne . . . . *H.B.* 46
grosse matter by a soveraine might Tempers . . . . *H.B.* 124
Clear'd from *grosse* mists of fraile infirmities. . . . . . . *H.H.B.* 140
Ground. *See* **Underground.**

Ground—*Continued.*

Fell to the *ground* (*grounde*[1]), and there . . . dide. *Pet.* i. 12
The furious squadrons downe to *ground* did fall, *Ro.* xii. 6
Be it where the yerely starre doth scorch the *ground,* *Ro.* xxvi. 7
Whose foote in *ground* hath left but feeble holde, *Ro.* xxviii. 4
halfe disbowel'd lies above the *ground,* *Ro.* xxviii. 5
'Thou barrein *ground,* whome winters wrath hath wasted, *S.C.* Ja. 19
Thy wast bignes but combers the *grownd,* *S.C.* F. 133
Of custome for to survewe his *grownd,* *S.C.* F. 145
His wonderous weight made the *ground* to quake, *S.C.* F. 219
graffed to the *ground* is my breche: *S.C.* F. 242
Strowe me the *ground* with Daffadowndillies, *S.C.* Ap. 140
the *grownd* with grasse, *S.C.* May 7
buildest strong warke upon a weake *ground:* *S.C.* May 145
The grassye *ground* with daintye Daysies dight, *S.C.* Jun. 6
thou hast measured much *grownd,* *S.C.* S. 21
I cast to have lorne this *grounde:* *S.C.* S. 57
The flattring fruite is fallen to *grownd* before, *S.C.* D. 106
When Giants bloud did staine Phlegraean *ground.* *Gn.* 40
sleep oppressed him Displaid on *ground,* *Gn.* 240
The joyous Spring out of the *ground* brings forth, *Gn.* 683
looke lowly on the *ground,* *Hub.* 498
costly trappings that to *ground* downe hung. *Hub.* 584
seene the manners of all beasts on *ground;* *Hub.* 687
May we his Crowne and Mace take from the *ground,* *Hub.* 968
their olde Castles to the *ground* to fall, *Hub.* 1179
As if it quite were riven from the *ground,* *Hub.* 1354
Bee now become most wretched wightes on *ground.* *T.M.* 312
placed on a plot of sandie *ground:* *Ti.* 508
what can long abide above this *ground* *Ti.* 568
when flowres doo clothe the fruitful *ground,* *Mui.* 114
The most fine-fingred workwoman on *ground,* *Mui.* 260
with her weapon dredd She smote the *ground,* *Mui.* 325
The wretchedst man that treades this day on *ground?'* *D.* 63
they, that live on *ground,* *D.* 87
fell to *ground* for great extreamitie; *D.* 185
To thinke to *ground* how that faire blossome fell. *D.* 252
My bed the *ground* that hardest I may finde; *D.* 377
As if againe he would have fallen to *ground;* *D.* 543
in the *ground* each where will it engrosse, *Col.* 634
having ended, he from *ground* did rise, *Col.* 952
as she lay upon the durtie *ground,* I. i. 15. 1
her beastly bodie raizd . . . high above the *ground:* I. i. 18. 4
their Parent deare They saw . . . falling to the *ground,* I. i. 25. 2
to the *ground* his eyes were lowly bent, I. i. 29. 6
'Assure your selfe, it fell not all to *ground;* I. i. 54. 1
The fearefull shepheard, . . . shund th' unlucky *ground.* I. ii. 28. 9
knight, . . . The bleeding bough did thrust into the *ground,* I. ii. 44. 6
the glad marchant, that does vew from *ground* His ship I. iii. 32. 3
He, tombling rudely downe, to *ground* did rush, I. iii. 35. 8
all the while she stood upon the *ground,* I. v. 30. 1
So from the *ground* she fearelesse doth arise, I. vi. 13. 3
with greene braunches strowing all the *ground,* I. vi. 13. 8
with their horned feet doe weare the *ground,* I. vi. 14. 3
Pourd out in loosnesse on the grassy *grownd,* I. vii. 7. 2
The *ground* eke groned under him for dreed: I. vii. 8. 6
prowdly threw to *ground,* as things of naught; I. vii. 18. 5
She fell to *ground* for sorrowfull regret, I. vii. 20. 7
Then downe againe she fell unto the *ground,* I. vii. 24. 1
ne ever . . . Had throwne to *ground* the unregarded right: I. vii. 47. 5
all the castle quaked from the *grownd,* I. viii. 5. 2
The ydle stroke, . . . Did fall to *ground,* I. viii. 8. 4
His boystrous club, so buried in the *grownd,* I. viii. 10. 1
his left arme, . . . Did fall to *ground,* I. viii. 10. 7
over shoes in blood he waded on the *grownd.* I. viii. 16. 9
to the *ground* it doubleth him full low: I. viii. 18. 8
For to have slain the man, that on the *ground* did lye. I. viii. 19. 9
as a Castle, . . . Is undermined from the lowest *ground,* I. viii. 23. 3
Her golden cup she cast unto the *ground,* I. viii. 25. 2
three Moones . . . have been thrice hid underneath the *ground,* I. viii. 38. 7
to grieve the gentlest hart on *ground?'* I. ix. 7. 9
Nothing is sure that growes on earthly *ground;* I. ix. 11. 5
True loves are often sown, but seldom grow on *ground.'* I. ix. 16. 9
That cursed man, low sitting on the *ground,* I. ix. 35. 2
threw it to the *ground,* enraged rife, I. ix. 52. 5
adowne he looked to the *grownd* I. x. 67. 5
seemd uneath to shake the stedfast *ground.* I. xi. 4. 3
horse and man to *ground* did rush. I. xi. 16. 9
Himselfe up high he lifted from the *ground,* I. xi. 18. 2
comming down to *ground,* does free it selfe I. xi. 19. 9
to the *ground* he is . . . constraynd To throw his ryder; I. xi. 23. 6
with his winges to stye above the *ground;* I. xi. 25. 8
him so strongly stroke, that to the *ground* him feld. I. xi. 28. 9
freely sprong out of the fruitfull *grownd,* I. xi. 47. 3
on the *ground* still fell, I. xi. 48. 3
Arayd in antique robes downe to the *grownd,* I. xii. 5. 2
Themselves to *ground* with gracious humblesse bent, I. xii. 8. 3
Stretcht on the *ground* in monstrous large extent, I. xii. 9. 7
kist the *ground* whereon his foot was pight; I. xii. 25. 7
Fidessa hight the falsest Dame on *grownd,* I. xii. 32. 3
on the *ground* herselfe prostrating low, I. xii. 33. 2
drew her on the *ground;* II. i. 11. 6
into a deepe sanguine dide the grassy *grownd.* II. i. 39. 9
herselfe, . . . She groveling threw to *ground,* II. i. 45. 9
In number of the noblest knightes on *ground;* II. ii. 42. 2
fell flatt to *ground* for feare, II. iii. 6. 8
they be two the prowest knights on *grownd,* II. iii. 15. 6
Downe fell to *grownd,* II. iii. 21. 3
Drew by the heare along upon the *ground* II. iv. 3. 6
to the *ground* her threw: II. iv. 12. 4

Ground—*Continued.*

Then him to *ground* he cast, II. iv. 14. 7
Lying on *ground,* all soild with blood and myre: II. iv. 16. 4
streight on *grownd* made him full low to lye; II. v. 12. 5
He cast him downe to *ground,* II. v. 23. 3
Whiles sad Pyrochles lies on sencelesse *ground,* II. v. 36. 6
No daintie flowre or herbe that growes on *grownd,* II. vi. 12. 6
To shed your lives on *ground?* II. vi. 32. 7
still he traveild through wide wastfull *ground,* II. vii. 2. 8
Witnesse the guiltlesse blood pourd oft on *ground,* II. vii. 13. 4
deep descended through the hollow *grownd,* II. vii. 20. 8
all the *grownd* with sculs was scattered, II. vii. 30. 6
tree, So fayre and great that shadowed all the *ground,* II. vii. 56. 2
Where ever that on *ground* they mote him find: II. viii. 11. 2
to *ground* He groveling fell, II. viii. 32. 8
forced him his *ground* to traverse wyde, II. viii. 35. 3
He, tombling downe on *ground,* II. viii. 45. 6
carcases on *ground* were horribly prostrate. II. viii. 54. 9
overronne, to tread them to the *grownd:* II. ix. 15. 5
yclad in red Downe to the *ground,* II. ix. 27. 6
Unto the *grownd* she cast her modest eye, II. ix. 41. 2
it survewd as hils doen lower *ground;* II. ix. 45. 4
not on *ground* mote like to this be found: II. ix. 45. 5
from *ground* My lowly verse may loftily arise, II. x. 1. 3
being eight lugs of *grownd,* II. x. 11. 3
his long legs nigh raught unto the *ground.* II. xi. 20. 6
to the *ground* the idle quarrell fell: II. xi. 24. 8
Ne scarse his feet on *ground* were seene to tred: II. xi. 26. 3
greatest and most glorious thing on *ground* II. xi. 30. 1
groveling to the *ground* he fell, II. xi. 34. 9
grownd he gave, and lightly lept areare: II. xi. 36. 5
kest The lumpish corse unto the sencelesse *grownd;* II. xi. 42.6
Therefore to *ground* he would him cast no more, II. xi. 45. 7
the *grownd* dispred With grassy greene II. xii. 12. 2
His looser garment to the *ground* did fall, II. xii. 46. 7
fayre grassy *grownd* Mantled with greene, II. xii. 50. 3
The cup to *ground* did violently cast, II. xii. 57. 3
the most daintie Paradise on *ground* II. xii. 58. 1
Such as attonce might not on living *ground,* II. xii. 70. 3
brought to *grownd* that never wast before; III. i. 7. 7
Ne ever to them yielded foot of *grownd,* III. i. 21. 4
For I love one, the truest one on *grownd,* III. i. 24. 6
Ne did she stay till three on *ground* she layd III. i. 29. 1
fownd Their lady lying on the sencelesse *grownd:* III. i. 63. 5
low underneath the *ground,* In a deepe delve, III. iii. 7. 6
writing straunge characters in the *grownd,* III. iii. 14. 8
him perforce unto the *ground* it bore. III. iii. 60. 7
Distaines the pillours and the holy *grownd,* III. iv. 17. 7
Their tender feete upon the stony *grownd:* III. iv. 34. 6
spredding on the *grownd* Their watchet mantles III. iv. 40. 4
Downe himselfe he layd Upon the grassy *ground* III. iv. 53. 8
He is yslaine, which is the *ground* of all our woe. III. v. 9. 9
Downe on the *ground* his carkas groveling fell: III. v. 23. 7
glauncing fel to *ground,* but him annoyed naught. III. v. 24. 9
His locks, like faded leaves fallen to *grownd,* III. v. 29. 5
Upon the grassy *ground* her selfe she layd III. vi. 7. 2
all their glory to the *ground* downe flings, III. vi. 39. 5
all the *ground,* with pretious deaw bedight, III. vi. 43. 8
all fayre Ladies that doe live on *grownd.* III. vi. 52. 6
Lightly upstarted from the dustie *ground,* III. vii. 7. 5
Sate downe upon the dusty *ground* anon; III. vii. 10. 8
Sitting beside his mother on the *ground;* III. vii. 13. 3
The quarry throwes to *ground* with fell despight, III. vii. 39. 5
Fell streight to *ground* in great astonishment. III. viii. 12. 7
The fairest wight on *ground,* and most of men esteem'd. III. viii. 13. 9
fals to *ground* to seeke for succor theare, III. viii. 33. 5
They rudely drove to *ground* both man and horse, III. ix. 16. 4
cast himselfe on *ground* her fast besyde: III. x. 7. 5
bearing with him treasure . . . The rest he leaves in *ground:* III. x. 19. 4
to the *ground* him meekely made to bowe, III. x. 24. 3
Trompart, lowly to the *grownd* inclinde, III. x. 30. 7
buried in the *ground* from jeopardy, III. x. 42. 4
fell to *ground* half dedd. III. x. 43. 9
shed the *grownd* With perly deaw, III. x. 46. 5
a knight all wallowed Upon the grassy *ground,* III. xi. 7. 4
His face upon the *grownd* did groveling ly, III. xi. 8. 1
Unworthy wretch to tread upon the *ground,* III. xi. 11. 8
spoiles wherewith he all the *ground* did strow, III. xi. 45. 7
to *ground* He fell halfe dead: III. xii. 34. 1
prostrate she fell unto the *grownd.* III. xii. 38. 9
Britomart, uprearing her from *grownd,* III. xii. 40. 1
himself he reared light from *ground.* III. xii. 43. *or.*9
The barren *ground* was full of wicked weedes, IV. i. 25. 2
the rest him seeing lie on *ground* Ran hastily, IV. i. 43. 3
Upon the *ground* awhile in slomber lay; IV. ii. 7. 2
Each other horse and man to *ground* did send; IV. ii. 15. 7
all the *ground* with purple bloud was sprent, IV. ii. 18. 5
of those Knights, who is most stout on *ground,* IV. ii. 27. 3
Those two were foes the fellonest on *ground,* IV. ii. 32. 2
Upon which *ground* this same great battell grew, IV. ii. 54. 6
Whom when on *ground* his brother next beheld, IV. iii. 14. 1
He falleth nigh to *ground,* IV. iii. 19. 9
So these two champions to the *ground* were feld, IV. iv. 18. 6
So much more sorely to the *ground* he fell, IV. iv. 19. 6
horse and man to *ground* he quite did beare, IV. iv. 20. 8
Gainst whom none able was to stand on *ground;* IV. iv. 28. 3
forcibly to *ground* they both together went. IV. iv. 28. 9
In hope to take him prisoner, where he stood on *ground.* IV. iv. 31. 9
seemed some blacksmith dwelt in that desert *ground.* IV. v. 33. 9
to the *ground* she smote both horse and man; IV. vi. 10. 7

Growing—*Continued.*
growing he his owne perfection wrought, *Col.* 805
tree, High *growing* on the top of rocky clift, I. viii. 22. 6
at her rompe she *growing* had behind A foxes taile, I. viii. 48. 3
represse The *growing* evill, ere it strength have gott, III. ii. 46. 2
Great matter *growing* of beginning small, IV. ii. 54. 7
through long sufferance *growing* now more great, IV. vi. 16. 3
The good Sir Bruin *growing* farre in yeares, VI. iv. 33. 6
Grown. *See* **Long-grown, New-grown, Overgrown.**
To greatnes *growne,* through long prosperitie, *Ro.* xxxi. 13
my galage *growne* fast to my heele: *S.C.* F. 244
The grieslie Tode-stoole *growne* there mought I se, *S.C.* D. 69
So *growen* great, through arrogant delight I. vii. 10. 1
growne old In cunning sleightes II. iii. 9. 5
He now was *growne* right wise and wondrous sage: II. ix. 54. 5
So seemd those two, as *growne* together quite, III. xii. 46. *or.*5
weedes, . . . Now *growen* great, at first of little seedes, IV. i. 25. 4
when to ripenesse due they *growen* arre, IV. i. 25. 6
when strife was *growen* Amongst those famous ympes of Greece, IV. ii. 1. 7
with which *growen* great, And swolne with pride V. vii. 15. 6
where I have wond thus long . . . now *growen* to stature strong. VI. ii. 30. 9
Of what degree and what race he is *growne:* VI. iii. 1. 5
Was greatly *growne* in love of that brave pere,) VI. v. 41. 8
being *growen* strong it forth doth bring Sorrow, VI. vi. 8. 5
He *growen* is so great and strong of late, VI. xii. 40. 4
Grows. *See* **Forth-grows.**
There *growes* lifes fruite unto the Churches good. *Rev.* iv. 14
Soone *growes* through humours superfluitie. *Ro.* xxiii. 12
Here *growes* Melampode every where, *S.C.* Jul. 85
It first *growes* red, and then to blew doth fade, *As.* 185
all good, all grace there freely *growes,* *Col.* 324
good *growes* of evils priefe.' I. viii. 43. 6
th' only good that *growes* of passed feare I. viii. 44. 5
Nothing is sure that *growes* on earthly grownd; I. ix. 11. 5
Where justice *growes,* there *grows* eke greater grace, I. ix. 53. 6
flowre or herbe that *growes* on grownd, II. vi. 12. 6
The flowrs, the fields, and all that pleasaunt *growes,* II. vi. 15. 2
It *growes* a Monster, and incontinent II. ix. 1. 7
streame more violent and greedy *growes:* II. xii. 5. 3
All that in this delightfull Gardin *growes* III. vi. 41. 2
'No tree . . . in greenewood *growes,* IV. x. 22. 1
once amisse *growes* daily wourse and wourse: V. Pr. 1. 9
Amongst them all *growes* not a fayrer flowre VI. Pr. 4. 1
but greatest griefe of scorning *growes.* VI. vii. 49. 9
The litle that I have *growes* dayly more VI. ix. 21. 5
On which a grove of Oakes high-mounted *growes,* VII. vi. 41. 2
Sweet is the Rose, but *growes* upon a brere; *Am.* xxvi. 1
harder *growes* the more I her intreat! *Am.* xxx. 4
harder *growes,* the harder she is smit *Am.* xxxii. 11
so still more cleare And faire it *growes,* *H.H.B.* 46
Grudge. mindfull of that olde Enfested *grudge,* *Mui.* 354
signes of *grudge* and discontentment vaine. II. viii. 23. 5
Ne was there outward breach, nor *grudge* in hart, II. x. 14. 7
grudge in so streight prison to be prest, II. xi. 32. 4
In him bewraid great *grudge* and maltalent: III. iv. 61. 8
inly *grudge* at him that he had sped so well. IV. ii. 7. 9
Full many knights, . . . Thereat did greatly *grudge,* IV. ii. 26. 3
inward *grudge* fild his heroicke brest: IV. ix. 32. 4
Her heart gan *grudge* for very deepe despight V. vii. 37. 8
Whose nature is to grieve and *grudge* at all V. xii. 31. 2
Thought sure t' avenge his *grudge,* VI. ix. 43. 9
in his spright Did inly *grudge,* VII. vi. 35. 8
Grudged. *grudged* at the great felicitee Of proud Lucifera, I. iv. 31. 8
grudg'd to see the counterfet should shame The thing III. viii. 5. 5
grudged grievously To house a guest III. x. 2. 2
thereat greatly *grudged* Arthegall, IV. v. 9. 1
Blandamour thereat full greatly *grudged,* IV. v. 22. 3
not the stately Severne *grudg'd* at all, IV. xi. 30. 6
Grudgeful. rayle at them with *grudgefull* discontent, IV. viii. 28. 4
Grudging. Ne dyde with dread and *grudging* discontent, *D.* 254
his *grudging* ghost did strive With the fraile flesh; I. ii. 19. 7
As Lion, *grudging* in his great disdaine, II. i. 42. 6
groneth out his utmost *grudging* spright II. v. 36. 7
Sir Guyon, *grudging* not so much his might II. vi. 30. 5
Whose *grudging* ghost was thereout fled and past, V. x. 37. 3
malicing, or *grudging* his good houre, VI. ix. 39. 7
feare the spight Of *grudging* foes, *Am.* lix. 10
Grutch. both did at their second sister *grutch* II. ii. 34. 6
Gryde. *See* **Gride, Grided.**
Gryesy. *See* **Grisy.**
Gryll. hight *Grylle* by name, II. xii. 86. 7
Let *Gryll* be *Gryll,* and have his hoggish minde; II. xii. 87. 8
Gryphon, Grypt. *See* **Griffin, Griped.**
Gualsever. yet thereof *Gualsever* they doe call: IV. xi. 36. 5
Guard. *See* **Safe-guard.**
From soddein force theyr flocks for to *gard.* *S.C.* S. 235
to his Gate he pointed a strong *gard,* *Hub.* 1115
through the *gard,* which never him descride, *Hub.* 1301
The Lyon . . . a strong *gard* Of her chast person, I. iii. 9. 2
Her faithfull *gard* remov'd, her hope dismaid, I. iii. 43. 3
Eftsoones the *Gard* . . . Attacht that faytor false, I. xii. 35. 4
spoile the treasure there in *gard:* II. vii. 25. 4
With a strong *gard,* all reskew to prevent, III. i. 2. 3
gave unto king Ryence for his *gard,* III. ii. 21. 2
many dreadfull feends hath pointed to her *gard.* III. xi. 16. 9
The whiles her foolish *garde,* III. xi. 31. 5
Against all those that chalenge it to *gard* IV. ii. 27. 7
Did neede to *gard* from force, IV. xi. 3. 4
The other stayd behind to *gard* the pray: V. iii. 11. 7
that great yron groome, his *gard* and government. V. iv. 3. 9

Guard—*Continued.*
t' advize . . . how himselfe to *gard,* VI. iv. 5. 2
gard her to defend from bold oppressors might. VI. v. 7. 9
Did warne his rider be upon his *gard;* VI. v. 21. 7
kept with *gard* Of griesly theeves, VI. x. 43. 7
Guarded. praying to be *garded* from greevance.' *S.C.* F. 188
Guarded of many which did her defend: V. ii. 20. 3
she came . . . *Guarded* with many Damzels V. v. 4. 3
all that while her life she safely *garded;* V. v. 8. 8
Guardian. As *Guardian* and Steward of the rest. I. x. 37. 3
Guarish. did the best His grievous hurt to *guarish,* III. v. 41. 6
Guarished. all his wounds, and all his bruses *guarisht;* IV. iii. 29. 5
Guendolen. quite his hart from *Guendolene* remov'd, II. x. 17. 8
From *Guendolene* his wife, II. x. 17. 9
stout *Guendolen;* Renowmed Martia; III. iii. 54. 8
Guerdon. Much greater gyfts for *guerdon* thou shalt gayne, *S.C.* N. 45
Where then is now the *guerdon* of my paine? *Gn.* 356
Such grace shall be some *guerdon* for the griefe, *Col.* 943
him, who has the *guerdon* of his guile, I. iii. 40. 3
To gayne so goodly *guerdon* as she spake: I. vii. 15. 2
glory does to them for *guerdon* graunt: I. x. 59. 8
Till guiltie blood her *guerdon* doe obtayne!' II. i. 61. 8
Thy carcas for their pray, the *guerdon* of thy payn.' II. vi. 28. 9
Great *guerdon,* well I wote, should you remaine, II. ix. 6. 7
Your worthy paine shall wel reward with *guerdon* rich.' III. x. 28. 9
gaine a feastfull *guerdon* of their toyle, IV. iii. 16. 4
What glorie, or what *guerdon* hast thou found IV. vii. 1. 5
every day, for *guerdon* of her song, IV. viii. 5. 6
The shield of Love, whose *guerdon* me hath graced, IV. x. 8. 4
for *guerdon* of my paine, IV. x. 10. 8
To greet his *guerdon* unto every knight, V. iii. 14. 3
May you in heaven immortall *guerdon* gaine V. x. 21. 4
What *guerdon* can I give thee for thy paine, V. xi. 16. 8
That thankfull *guerdon* may to you repay.' VI. ii. 38. 5
I shall You well reward, and golden *guerdon* give, VI. ix. 32. 6
the *guerdon* of his love to gaine; VI. x. 2. 4
for the *guerdon* of theyr glorious merit, *Epith.* 421
But love of us, for *guerdon* of thy paine: *H.H.L.* 177
Guess. In case thy greatnes he can *gesse* in harte, *Ro.* v. 3
time, I *gesse,* homeward to goe: *S.C.* Jun. 117
The base-borne brood of blindnes cannot *gesse,* *T.M.* 392
names I cannot readily now *ghesse:* *Col.* 740
Ye shall him Archimago find, I *ghesse,* I. xii. 34. 8
(hard fortune ye may *ghesse*) II. i. 51. 1
comming nigh, eftsoones he gan to *gesse,* III. viii. 45. 3
well she wist not what by them to *gesse:* IV. i. 7. 6
ghesse the man to be dismayd with gealous dread. IV. v. 45. 9
could not *ghesse* The cause IV. vii. 45. 2
Aemylia well he lov'd, as I mote *ghesse,* IV. viii. 57. 8
It seem'd a second paradise to *ghesse,* IV. x. 23. 2
Then gan Sir Calidore to *ghesse* streightway, VI. ii. 45. 1
Ne by inquirie learne, nor *ghesse* by ayme; VI. iv. 24. 7
Guessed. soone he came, as he the place had *ghest,* I. vi. 40. 4
He *ghest* his nature by his countenance, I. viii. 34. 4
Whom at the first he *ghessed* by his looke, V. i. 20. 8
Yet whether side was victor note be *ghest:* V. iii. 7. 6
chiefly by that yron page he *ghest,* V. vi. 34. 3
they streightway *ghest* That it was she VI. i. 17. 2
Guesseth. Their harts she *ghesseth* by their humble guise, I. vi. 13. 1
Guest. Forthwith he runnes . . . Unto his *guest,* I. ii. 4. 2
that good knight, his late beguiled *guest:* I. ii. 11. 2
when the carle . . . saw his *guest* Would safe depart, I. ix. 54. 2
fayre Una brought this unacquainted *guest.* I. x. 29. 9
As for great joyance of his newcome *guest.* I. xi. 15. 4
to demaund of his renowmed *guest:* I. xii. 15. 6
thy daughter linck . . . to that new unknowen *guest:* I. xii. 26. 7
With doubtfull eyes fast fixed on his *guest:* I. xii. 29. 6
to entertaine her new-come *guest,* II. ii. 16. 2
Her selfe to cherish, and her *guest* to cheare. II. vi. 21. 4
Well hoped hee, ere long that hardy *guest,* II. vii. 27. 1
tempt his *guest* to take thereof assay; II. vii. 34. 4
lurking from the vew of covetous *guest,* II. xii. 55. 4
to wooe a wandring *guest,* III. i. 55. 7
Unto their bowres to guyden every *guest.* III. i. 58. 4
Following the guydance of her blinded *guest,* III. iv. 6. 8
well they kent That their fayre *guest* was gone, III. vii. 19. 8
To house a *guest* that would be needes obayd, III. x. 2. 3
that *Guest* did beare her forcibly, III. x. 13. 8
Her fayned Paramour, her forced *guest,* IV. i. 36. 3
not meet for any *guest,* IV. v. 32. 8
at sent of stranger *guest,* IV. v. 41. 7
he weend that this his present *guest* Was Artegall, V. vi. 34. 1
Did closely harbour such a jealous *guest*) V. vii. 27. 5
'Not that the burden of so bold a *guest* Shall chargefull be, VI. ix. 32. 1
With lustfull eyes beheld that lovely *guest,* VI. xi. 3. 7
doth not the blinded *guest* Shoot out his darts *Am.* viii. 5
Guests. Unto their lodgings then his *guestes* he riddes: I. i. 36. 5
Archimago, when his *guests* He saw divided I. ii. 9. 1
whose care Was *guests* to welcome, I. x. 44. 3
Those *guestes,* beguyled, did beguyle their eyes II. ii. 46. 6
as Alma passed with her *guestes,* II. ix. 26. 6
he did bestow Both *guestes* and meate, II. ix. 28. 4
forth ledd her *guestes* anone II. ix. 28. 8
Whom Alma having shewed to her *guestes,* II. ix. 53. 1
to her *guestes* doth bounteous banket dight, II. xi. 2. 8
Ran towards to devoure those unexpected *guests.* II. xii. 39. 9
their entred *guestes* to keep within, II. xii. 43. 2
all new-come *guests* he gratyfide: II. xii. 49. 5
full of *guests* he found whyleare, III. ix. 13. 4
Sclaunder her *guests* doth staine: IV. viii. Arg.

Guests—*Continued.*
that Hag, unmeet to host such *guests,* . . . . IV. viii. 27. 1
Unto his horses gave his *guests* for meat, ... V. viii. 31. 2
To cheare his *guests* whom he had stayd that night, ... VI. iii. 6. 3
Thether he brought these unacquainted *guests,* . . . . VI. iv. 14. 1
My thoughts the *guests,* which would thereon have fedd. . . . *Am.* lxxvii. 14
Guidance. Nor *guidaunce* of herselfe in her did dwell: . . . . III. ii. 49. 3
Following the *guydance* of her blinded guest, ... III. iv. 6. 8
Guide. That flocks grand Captaine and most trustie *guide* . . *Gn.* 268
Like as the Foxe did *guide* his graceles skill; . . . . *Hub.* 1128
none, except a God, or God him *guide,* . . . . *Mui.* 223
Will was his *guide,* and griefe led him astray. . . . . I. ii. 12. 4
the first, that all the rest did *guyde,* Was sluggish Idlenesse, . I. iv. 18. 5
lampe . . . First made by him mens wandring wayes to *guyde,* . I. vii. 23. 2
For whose deliverance she this Prince doth thither *guyd.* . . . I. viii. 1. 9
guyde his wearie gate both too and fro, ... I. viii. 30. 4
Of grace do me unto his cabin *guyde.*' . . . . I. ix. 32. 4
gladly did them *guide,* till to the Hall they came. . . . . . . I. x. 6. 9
his weaker wandring steps to *guyde,* . . . . I. x. 34. 1
his toylesome teme that way did *guyde,* . . . . I. x. 66. 4
(eternall God that chaunce did *guide*) . . . . I. xi. 45. 6
his aged *Guide* in presence came; . . . . II. i. 31. 3
God *guide* thee, Guyon, well to end thy warke, ... II. i. 32. 8
Sir Guyon with his faithful *guyde* . . . . II. ii. 1. 1
that blacke Palmer, his most trusty *guide,* . . . . II. iv. 2. 4
Had he had governaunce it well to *guyde;* . . . . II. iv. 7. 2
guyde thy waies with warie governaunce, ... II. iv. 36. 4
Withouten oare or Pilot it to *guide,* . . . . II. vi. 5. 3
where him she byding fond With his sad *guide:* . . . . II. vi. 19. 6
Guyon was loath to leave his *guide* behind, ... II. vi. 20. 1
Guyon having lost his trustie *guyde,* . . . . II. vii. 2. 1
Into the world to *guyde* him backe, ... II. vii. 65. 9
I labour would to *guide* you through al Faery land.' . . . . . II. ix. 8. 9
Upon his voyage with his trustie *guyde,* . . . . II. xi. 5. 2
Unto their bowres to *guyden* every guest. . . . . III. i. 58. 4
guyde the heavenly causes to their constant terme. . . . . . III. iii. 25. 9
the place, to which her hope did *guyde,* . . . . III. vii. 5. 8
to *guide* the cock-bote well, ... III. viii. 24. 4
Straying alone withouten groome or *guide:* . . . . III. x. 36. 5
bold to *guide* the charet of the Sunne, ... III. xi. 38. 3
having now misfortune got for *guide.* . . . . IV. iv. 24. 4
making blind love her *guide.* . . . . IV. v. 29. 5
Ne wight him to attend, or way to *guide,* . . . . IV. vi. 44. 6
Withouten comfort and withouten *guide,* . . . . IV. vii. 2. 8
drew thereto, making her eare her *guide:* . . . . IV. vii. 29. 4
In th' end she her unto that place did *guide,* . . . . IV. viii. 11. 8
what evill *guide* Them thether brought, ... IV. viii. 21. 2
steadie hand was faine his steede to *guyde,* . . . . IV. viii. 37. 7
To *guide* the beast that did his maister beare, ... IV. ix. 5. 4
'Now by my life,' (sayd he) 'and God to *guide,* . . . . V. ii. 10. 5
Al which the heavens containe, and in their courses *guide.* . . V. ii. 35. 9
nimbly did him dight to *guide* the way . . . . V. iv. 35. 5
bad Talus *guide* her on. . . . . V. vi. 17. 9
To seeke her Knight, as Talus her did *guide.* . . . . V. vi. 18. 2
Your aide to *guide* me out of errour blind.' . . . . V. vii. 19. 5
The true *guide* of his way and vertuous government. . . . . . V. viii. 3. 9
go which way they list, their *guide* they have forlore. . . . . V. viii. 39. 9
I would you *guyde* directly to the place.' . . . . V. ix. 7. 7
With those two gentle youthes, which him did *guide* . . . . . V. x. 17. 6
The waies, through which my weary steps I *guyde* . . . . . . VI. Pr. 1. 1
Guyde ye my footing, and conduct me well . . . . VI. Pr. 2. 7
withouten *guyde* Or good direction . . . . VI. i. 6. 2
he, that could his wrath full wisely *guyde,* . . . . VI. i. 30. 7
To which he meant his weary steps to *guyde,* . . . . VI. iii. 29. 8
Withouten *guide* her to conduct aright, ... VI. v. 7. 8
To *guide* mens labours, ... VI. v. 40. 3
As women wont their guilefull wits to *guyde,* . . . . VI. vi. 43. 2
better able it to *guide* alone; . . . . VII. vi. 11. 4
And eke his learned hand at pleasure *guide,* . . . . *Am.* xvii. 6
Whenas a storme hath dimd her trusty *guyde,* . . . . *Am.* xxxiv. 3
she . . . weake harts doth *guyde* Unto her love, ... *Am.* xlvii. 5
Yet wanting light to *guide* his wandring way, ... *H.L.* 71
Thou art his god, thou art his mightie *guyde,* . . . . *H.L.* 225
My *guide,* my God, my victor, and my king: . . . . *H.L.* 305
Guided. *See* **Well-guided.**
The shepheards God so wel them *guided,* . . . . *S.C.* May 113
as that same shepheard still us *guyded,* . . . . *Col.* 331
It governd was, and *guided* evermore, ... I. x. 3. 4
Great cause, I weene, you *guided,* . . . . II. i. 29. 9
his blacke Palmer, that him *guided* still: . . . . II. i. 34. 4
Still he him *guided* over dale and hill, ... II. i. 34. 5
eternall providence, that has *Guyded* thy glaunce, ... III. iii. 24. 5
what unwonted path Had *guided* her, ... III. vii. 8. 4
never thoght one thing, but doubly stil was *guided.* . . . . . IV. i. 27. 9
All being *guided* by Sir Artegall: . . . . IV. vi. 39. 5
guyded through th' ayrie wyde By some bad spirit . . . . . . V. viii. 34. 6
Them *guyded* through the throng, ... V. ix. 23. 9
were *guyded* by degree Unto the presence of that gratious Queene; . . . . V. ix. 27. 1
Guides. To sinfull hous of Pryde Duessa *Guydes* . . . . I. iv. Arg.
he Guyon *guydes* an uncouth way . . . . II. i. 24. 1
Guidest. *guydest* lovers through the nights sad dread, ... *Epith.* 290
Guiding. When such an one had *guiding* of the way, ... I. iv. 19. 8
forth they went, the Dwarfe them *guiding* ever right. . . . . I. vii. 52. 9
Guild. As it some *Gyeld* or solemne Temple weare. . . . . . . II. vii. 43. 4
Guile. ful of fraude, and *guile,* . . . . *S.C.* May 127
for such, as of *guile* maken gayne, ... *S.C.* S. 34
lying all at ease from *guile* or spight, ... *Gn.* 111
Abusing manie through their cloaked *guile,* . . . . *Hub.* 344
Supplanted by fine falshood and faire *guile;* . . . . *Hub.* 788

Guile—*Continued.*
an usurping Ape, with *guile* suborn'd, ... *Hub.* 1233
punished for their presumptuous *guile.* . . . . *Hub.* 1256
trust the *guile* of fortunes blandishment; . . . . *Col.* 671
creature, . . . Full of the makers *guyle,* . . . . I. i. 46. 7
What not by right she cast to win by *guile;* . . . . I. ii. 38. 3
him, who has the guerdon of his *guile,* . . . . I. iii. 40. 3
who through *guile* hath slayn The prowest knight . . . . I. iv. 41. 6
to augment the glorie of his *guile,* His dearest love, ... I. iv. 42. 1
sithens fortunes *guile,* . . . Hath now captived you, Returne . . I. iv. 51. 1
in false griefe hyding his harmefull *guile,* . . . . I. v. 18. 5
he . . . Her constant hart did tempt with diverse *guile:* . . . I. vi. 4. 3
hast with knightlesse *guile,* . . . Faire knighthood fowly shamed, I. vi. 41. 2
blent My name with *guile* and traiterous intent: . . . . I. vi. 42. 5
The guiltlesse man with *guile* to entertaine? . . . . I. vii. 1. 7
That conning Architect of cancred *guyle,* . . . . II. i. 1. 1
He gan to weave a web of wicked *guyle,* . . . . II. i. 8. 4
To cloke her *guile* with sorrow and sad teene; . . . . II. i. 21. 7
for furtherance of his *guile,* . . . . II. iv. 25. 1
So hast thou oft with *guile* thine honor blent; . . . . II. v. 5. 7
litle may such *guile* thee now avayl, ... II. v. 5. 8
First got with *guile,* and then preserv'd with dread, ... II. vii. 12. 3
bloodguiltinesse or *guile* them blott.' . . . . II. vii. 19. 5
T' assayle with open force or hidden *guyle,* . . . . II. xi. 7. 4
neither *guile* nor force might it distraine. . . . . II. xii. 82. 3
Who meanes no *guile* be guiled soonest shall, ... III. i. 54. 6
she to him dissembled womanish *guyle,* . . . . III. iii. 17. 3
yfraught with fawning *guyle* And fayre resemblance . . . . . . III. viii. 8. 1
womans subtiltyes Can *guylen* Argus, ... III. ix. 7. 3
with humble pride and pleasing *guile:* . . . . III. x. 9. 3
'Unworthy life, that love with *guile* hast gotten; . . . . . . IV. i. 51. 7
under it hidde hate and hollow *guyle.* . . . . IV. ii. 29. 5
Ne then of *guile* had made experiment; . . . . IV. viii. 30. 4
through gifts, or *guile,* or such like waies, ... IV. x. 18. 8
Most voide of *guile,* most free from fowle despight, ... IV. xi. 18. 8
saw that boasters pride and gracelesse *guile,* . . . . V. iii. 20. 3
by force or *guile* She doth subdue, ... V. iv. 31. 1
Artegall . . . is subdewd by *guile:* . . . . V. v. Arg.
with *guyle* My heart at first betrayd, ... V. vi. 25. 1
like full of fraud and *guile,* . . . . V. vi. 33. 2
meaning to suppresse both forged *guile* And open force: . . . V. vii. 7. 3
To keepe out *guyle,* and malice, and despight, ... V. ix. 22. 7
foule blaspheme that Queene for forged *guyle,* . . . . V. ix. 25. 5
Through avarice, or powre, or *guile,* or strife, ... V. xi. 1. 3
Ay me, that ever *guyle* in wemen was invented! . . . . V. xi. 50. 9
with unmanly *guile* And foule abusion, ... V. xii. 40. 3
not with manhood, but with *guile* Maintaine this evil use, . . VI. vi. 34. 8
without *guile* Or false dissemblaunce . . . . VI. x. 24. 3
What *guyle* is this, ... *Am.* xxxvii. 1
Consume thee quite, that didst with *guile* conspire . . . . . . *Am.* lxxxv. 11
friendships faultie *guile* For ever to assoile. . . . . *Proth.* 99
Guiled. Who meanes no guile be *guiled* soonest shall, ... III. i. 54. 6
Guileful. the Foxe *guilefull,* and most covetous; . . . . . . *Hub.* 1022
To which him needs a *guilefull* hollow hart, ... *Col.* 699
The *guilefull* great Enchaunter parts . . . . I. ii. Arg.
Or *guilefull* spright wandring in empty aire, ... I. ii. 32. 6
'Nor *guileful* sprite to thee these words doth speake; . . . . I. ii. 33. 2
To thinke how she through *guyleful* handeling, ... I. iii. 2. 4
on those *guilefull* . . . eyes . . . The cloude of death did sit. . I. iii. 39. 7
whom he with *guilefull* snare Entrapped slew, ... I. iv. 47. 5
O! never, Sir, desire to try his *guilefull* traine.' . . . . . . I. ix. 31. 9
her *guilefull* bayt She will embosome deeper in your mind, . . II. xii. 29. 2
Through *guilefull* semblants which he makes us see: . . . . . . II. xii. 48. 6
Britomart would not such *guilfull* message know. . . . . III. i. 51. 9
By false illusion of a *guilefull* Spright . . . . III. iii. 13. 4
As *guilefull* Goldsmith that by secret skill . . . . IV. v. 15. 1
With *guilefull* love did secretly agree . . . . IV. vii. 15. 4
The whiles his *guilefull* groome was fled away, ... V. iii. 38. 1
some *guilefull* traine did weave, ... V. v. 37. 4
with *guilefull* call Did cast for to allure . . . . V. v. 52. 8
with *guilefull* words her to perswade To banish feare; . . . . V. ix. 12. 5
on his *guilefull* pype Charmes to the birds . . . . V. ix. 13. 1
By *guilefull* treason and by subtill slight . . . . V. xi. 39. 7
With golden giftes and many a *guilefull* word . . . . V. xi. 50. 4
Ere that I in her *guilefull* traines was well expert. . . . . . . VI. i. 12. 9
his three foes shrowded in *guilefull* shade . . . . VI. v. 17. 8
As women wont their *guilefull* wits to guyde, ... VI. vi. 43. 2
By unjust And *guilefull* meanes, ... VII. vi. 27. 4
In the close covert of her *guilefull* eyen, ... *Am.* xii. 7
stare Henceforth too rashly on that *guilefull* net, ... *Am.* xxxvii. 10
ye have theyr *guylefull* traynes well tryde: . . . . *Am.* xlvii. 2
Guilefully. for holding *guilefully* away Ulysses men, ... *Gn.* 194
to my foe hath *guilefully* consented: . . . . V. xi. 50. 8
Guiler. So goodly did beguile the *Guyler* of his pray. . . . . II. vii. 64. 9
Guilers. Where those two *guilers* with Malbecco were. . . . . III. x. 37. 5
Guilt. *See* **Gilt.**
whose unappeased *guilt* Powr'd vengeance forth . . . . *Ro.* xxiv. 10
Yet was the *guilt* thereof, Orpheus, in thee. . . . . *Gn.* 436
Least that the world thee dead accuse of *guilt,* . . . . *D.* 82
How great a *guilt* upon your heads ye draw, ... *Col.* 928
some shall pay the price of others *guilt;* . . . . I. v. 26. 2
for want of faith, or *guilt* of sin, ... I. vii. 45. 8
To wreake the *guilt* of mortall sins is bent, ... I. viii. 9. 2
the dart of sinfull *guilt* the soule dismayes. . . . . I. x. 21. 9
His chosen people, purg'd from sinful *guilt* . . . . I. x. 57. 4
wash thy hands from *guilt* of bloody field: . . . . I. x. 60. 8
guilt of sinfull crimes cleane wash away; . . . . I. xi. 30. 2
washt away his *guilt* with guilty potion. . . . . II. iv. 30. 9
Why should not that dead carrion satisfye The *guilt* . . . . . II. viii. 28. 7
vengeaunce utterly the *guilt* bereave: . . . . II. viii. 29. 5

Guilt—*Continued.*
To purge away the *guilt* of sinfull crime. . . . . II. x. 50. 4
flying from his *guilt*, by them was slayne; . . . . II. x. 67. 5
No *guilt* in you, but in the tyranny of love. . . . . III. ii. 40. 9
to accursed fate, The *guilt* I doe ascribe: . . . . III. iv. 37. 9
The privie *guilt* whereof makes him alway Suspect her truth, . III. ix. 5. 3
lay on heaven the *guilt* of their owne crimes. . . . . V. iv. 28. 3
that his *guilt* the greater may appeare, ... V. v. 48. 6
'Neither will I Him charge with *guilt*, ... VI. ii. 14. 4
To wreake on me the *guilt* of his owne wrong: . . . . VI. ii. 21. 6
willing eke to wreake The *guilt* on him . . . . VI. vii. 13. 7
by force, . . . Or their owne *guilt*, they were away convayd? VI. vii. 34. 6
their *guilt* to hyde: . . . . VI. viii. 44. 7
In flesh at first the *guilt* committed was, ... *H.H.L.* 141
And clense the *guilt* of that infected cryme . . . . *H.H.L.* 167
Guiltiness. *See* **Blood-guiltiness.**
Guiltless. cram'd with *guiltles* blood and greedie pray . . . . *Van.* iii. 4
Each place defilde with blood of *guiltles* beasts, ... *Hub.* 1307
his pure streames with *guiltles* blood oft stained; . . . . . *Ti.* 145
powre forth th' offring of his *guiltles* blood: . . . . *Ti.* 300
ruefull plaints, me bidding *guiltlesse* blood to spare?' . . . . I. ii. 32. 9
The *guiltlesse* man with guile to entertaine? . . . . I. vii. 1. 7
With blood of *guiltlesse* babes, and innocents . . . . I. viii. 35. 6
often tore Her *guiltlesse* garments . . . . I. x. 28. 6
High God be witnesse that I *guiltlesse* ame; . . . . I. xii. 30. 6
Witnesse the *guiltlesse* blood pourd oft on ground, ... II. vii. 13. 4
Albe her *guiltlesse* conscience her cleard, ... III. vi. 10. 2
He for revenge had *guiltlesse* Glauce slaine: . . . . IV. i. 52. 4
With which she *guiltlesse* persons may accuse, ... IV. viii. 25. 3
of all he *guiltlesse* stood, ... V. i. 23. 6
In *guiltlesse* blood of many an innocent: . . . . V. xii. 40. 7
and *guiltlesse* innocent Of blame, ... VI. iii. 18. 3
Whose share, her *guiltlesse* bloud, they would present; . . . . VI. viii. 38. 7
Shames not to be with *guiltlesse* bloud defylde, ... *Am.* xx. 11
blam'd for spilling *guiltlesse* blood. . . . . *Am.* xxxviii. 14
Guilty. Ne Afrike thereof *guiltie* is, nor Spaine, ... *Ro.* xxxi. 5
the *guiltie* blood Which she . . . had shed before; . . . . . . *Gn.* 173
wretched boy, they slew with *guiltie* blades; . . . . *Gn.* 403
Untill he quite him of this *guiltie* blame. . . . . *Ti.* 230
guiltie hands of enemies . . . . *Ti.* 299
bitter anguish of his *guilty* sight, ... I. ii. 6. 2
'O! spare with *guilty* hands to teare My tender sides . . . . . I. ii. 31. 2
He lives that . . . *guiltie* Elfin blood shall sacrifice in hast.' . I. iv. 49. 9
Goe, *guiltie* ghost, to him my message make, ... I. v. 11. 3
maintain Thy *guilty* wrong, or els thee *guilty* yield.' . . . . I. vi. 41. 6
manly hands imbrewd in *guilty* blood Had never beene, . . . I. vii. 47. 3
his owne *guiltie* mind, deserving death. . . . . I. ix. 38. 6
guilty be of thine impietie? . . . . I. ix. 47. 4
Witnesse . . . *guilty* heavens of his bold perjury; . . . . . . I. xii. 27. 6
My conscience cleare with *guilty* bands would bynd? . . . . . I. xii. 30. 5
As heven accusing *guilty* of her death, ... II. i. 49. 2
Till *guiltie* blood her guerdon doe obtayne!' . . . . II. i. 61. 8
His *guiltie* handes from bloody gore to cleene. . . . . II. ii. 3. 4
washt away his guilt with *guilty* potion. . . . . II. iv. 30. 9
prickt with *guiltie* shame And inward griefe, ... II. viii. 44. 2
under the blacke vele of *guilty* Night, ... III. i. 59. 7
The *guilty* cup she fained to mistake, ... III. ix. 31. 2
guilty Dread Of heavenly vengeaunce; . . . . III. xii. 25. 7
die *guiltie* of the blame The which another did, ... V. i. 15. 8
rather *guilty* chose himselfe to yield: . . . . V. i. 24. 5
the streame washt away her *guilty* blood. . . . . V. ii. 27. 5
'Ye *guilty* eyes,' (sayd she) 'the which with guyle . . . . . . V. vi. 25. 1
through his owne *guilty* wile: . . . . V. vi. 33. 5
there with *guiltie* bloudshed charged ryfe: . . . . V. ix. 48. 4
So was she *guiltie* deemed of them all. . . . . V. ix. 49. 6
she of death was *guiltie* found by right, ... V. ix. 50. 4
hast with *guilty* hand Murdred my men, ... VI. i. 25. 2
In haste forth started from the *guilty* brooke; . . . . VII. vi. 47. 2
Their quiet heads, devoyd of *guilty* shame, ... *H.L.* 290
through *guilty* shame May be corrupt, ... *H.B.* 157
Guintellius, Guinthelinus, Guintolinus. *See* **Guitheline.**
Guise. After th' Ionicke, Atticke, Doricke *guise*; . . . . *Ro.* xxix. 3
After his *guize* did cast abroad to fare: . . . . *Mui.* 55
half enraged at her shamelesse *guise*, ... I. i. 50. 2
Some frounce their curled heare in courtly *guise*; . . . . . . I. iv. 14. 7
through evill *guise*, A shaking fever raignd continually. . . . I. iv. 20. 7
Their hearts she ghesseth by their humble *guise*, ... I. vi. 13. 1
the maister of his *guise*, Did often tremble at his horrid vew; . I. vi. 25. 2
Him goodly greeted in her modest *guyse*, ... I. x. 11. 6
What needes me tell their feast and goodly *guize*, ... I. xii. 14. 1
rich arayd, and yet in modest *guize*, ... II. ii. 14. 6
as was her wonted *guize*, ... II. vi. 21. 1
noise of armes, or vew of martiall *guize*, ... II. vi. 25. 8
A carefull man, and full of comely *guyse*. . . . . II. ix. 31. 2
To swell above the measure of his *guise*, ... II. xii. 21. 8
It was her *guise* all Straungers goodly so to greet. . . . . . II. xii. 56. 9
Gazing awhile at his unwonted *guise*; . . . . II. xii. 66. 2
whence so sumptuous *guize* Might be maintaynd, ... III. i. 33. 8
As whylome was the antique worldes *guize*, ... III. i. 39. 3
he is faire and fresh in face and *guize* . . . . III. vi. 23. 7
After the Persian Monarks antique *guize*, ... IV. iii. 38. 8
his uncouth *guise* and usage quaint . . . . IV. vii. 45. 1
stately pillours fram'd after the Doricke *guize*. . . . . IV. x. 6. 9
Ne rov'd at randon, after gazers *guyse*, ... IV. x. 49. 8
Thereto he hath a groome of evill *guize*, ... V. ii. 6. 6
termes to entertaine of common *guize*, ... V. vi. 20. 4
linnen stole after those Priestes *guize*, ... V. vii. 13. 3
The more t' aggrate his God with such his blouddy *guize*. . . V. xi. 19. 9
comely *guize* withall And gracious speach, ... VI. i. 2. 5
As then the *guize* was for each gentle swayne: . . . . VI. ii. 6. 3

Guise—*Continued.*
Ne ever saw faire *guize*, ne learned good, ... VI. v. 2. 4
his Dame, him seeing in such *guize*, ... VI. vi. 32. 5
Did litle whit regard his courteous *guize*, ... VI. ix. 35. 6
He much was troubled at that straungers *guize*, ... VI. ix. 38. 3
Guitheline. After him raigned *Guitheline* his hayre, ... II. x. 42. 1
Guizor. His name was *Guizor*; . . . . V. vi. 33. 6
appease the spright Of *Guizor* by thee slaine, ... V. vi. 37. 9
Gulf. Within the *gulfe* of greedie Nereus. . . . . *Bel.*[2] xiii. 11
with many a Lambe had glutted his *gulfe*, ... *S.C.* S. 185
a *gulph* most hideous Amidst the Towne . . . . *Gn.* 604
Bold men . . . Dare tempt that *gulf*, ... *Col.* 210
yawning *gulfe* of deepe Avernus hole. . . . . I. v. 31. 3
From surging *gulf* two Monsters streight were brought, . . . I. v. 38. 3
greedy *gulfe* does gape, ... I. xi. 21. 5
Island, that doth ronne And stray in perilous *gulfe*, ... II. i. 51. 6
in frayle wood on Adrian *gulf* doth fleet, ... II. vii. 14. 4
That is the *Gulfe* of Greedinesse, they say; . . . . II. xii. 3. 4
Untill they nigh unto that *Gulfe* arryve, ... II. xii. 5. 2
Had in his greedy *gulfe* devoured deepe, ... III. iv. 22. 6
gaped like a *gulfe* when he did gerne; . . . . V. xii. 15. 8
Gulfing. deep Charybdis *gulphing* in and out: . . . . *Gn.* 542
Gulf's. whiles they fly that *Gulfes* devouring jawes, ... II. xii. 4. 8
Gulls. *See* **Sea-gulls.**
Gum. The Spartan Mirtle, whence sweet *gumb* does flowe; . . *Gn.* 669
from their fruitfull sydes sweet *gum* did drop, ... III. vi. 43. 7
Gums. Her teeth out of her rotten *gummes* were feld, ... I. viii. 47. 4
Gurgiunt. *Gurgiunt,* (*Gurgunt) great Belinus sonne, ... II. x. 41. 1
Gurgustus. Next great *Gurgustus,* then faire Caecily, ... II. x. 34. 3
Gurmond. *See* **Gormond.**
Gush. from his gored wound a well of bloud did *gush*. . . . . I. iii. 35. 9
When the hart blood should *gush* out of his chest, ... II. xi. 37. 7
from his gory sydes the blood did *gush*. . . . . III. i. 17. 7
readie way did yield For bloud to *gush* forth . . . . IV. iii. 9. 5
forth would breake, and *gush* in great excesse, ... IV. viii. 24. 5
Gushed. cole-black blood forth *gushed* from her corse. . . . . I. i. 24. 9
Large streames of blood . . . Forth *gushed*, ... I. viii. 10. 9
A sea of blood *gusht* from the gaping wownd, ... I. viii. 16. 6
forth *gusht* a stream of gore blood thick, ... II. i. 39. 7
a large lukewarme flood . . . thence *gushed* grievously; . . . II. viii. 39. 2
the blood forth *gusht* in so great store, ... III. v. 26. 4
A streame of coleblacke bloud thence *gusht* amaine, ... IV. vii. 27. 8
gushed through their armes, that all in gore They trode, . . . V. vii. 31. 7
Like to a great Mill-damb forth fiercely *gusht*, ... V. xi. 31. 5
from their riven sides forth *gushed* like a flood. . . . . . . VI. i. 37. 9
in teares, which *gushed* fast Like many water streames, . . . VI. viii. 19. 1
Gushing. *See* **Outgushing.**
he saw . . . bowels *gushing* forth: . . . . I. i. 26. 6
made an open passage for the *gushing* flood. . . . . I. ix. 36. 9
A *gushing* river of blacke gory blood, ... I. xi. 22. 4
He groveling fell, all gored in his *gushing* wound. . . . . . . II. viii. 32. 9
the gore-bloud thence *gushing* grievously, ... V. xii. 20. 6
as a well . . . out of an hill fresh *gushing* . . . . VI. iii. 50. 9
full of fresh dismay, And *gushing* forth in teares, ... VI. xi. 28. 4
Gust. the joyous oyle, whose gentle *gust* Made him so frollick . VII. vii. 39. 4
Gut. loose like an emptie *gut*; . . . . *Hub.* 212
Guylen. *See* **Guile.**
Guyon. this faery knight, The good Sir *Guyon*, ... II. Pr. 5. 8
Guyon, by Archimage abusd, ... II. i. Arg.
by my head,' (saide *Guyon*) 'much I muse, ... II. i. 19. 1
he *Guyon* guydes an uncouth way . . . . II. i. 24. 1
'Ah! deare Sir *Guyon*, well becommeth you, ... II. i. 28. 3
'Now mote I weet, Sir *Guyon*, ... II. i. 29. 6
God guide thee, *Guyon*, well to end thy warke, ... II. i. 32. 8
Then *Guyon* forward gan his voyage make . . . . II. i. 34. 3
when the good Sir *Guyon* did behold, ... II. i. 42. 1
Sir *Guyon* could uneath From teares abstayne; . . . . II. i. 56. 5
Sir *Guyon* . . . Bynempt a sacred vow, ... II. i. 60. 8
'Such and such evil God on *Guyon* reare, ... II. i. 61. 5
when Sir *Guyon* with his faithful guyde . . . . II. ii. 1. 1
when Sir *Guyon* saw, all were he wroth, ... II. ii. 12. 1
when *Guyon* came to part their fight, ... II. ii. 23. 8
She *Guyon* deare besought of curtesie To tell . . . . II. ii. 39. 4
Sir *Guyon*, mindfull of his vow yplight, ... II. iii. 1. 5
with *Guyon* knitt in one consent, ... II. iii. 11. 8
The ill . . . he now to *Guyon* ment. . . . . II. iii. 11. 9
By *Guyon*, and by that false Redcrosse knight; . . . . II. iii. 13. 6
Guyon does Furor bind in chaines, ... II. iv. Arg.
The noble *Guyon*, mov'd with great remorse, ... II. iv. 6. 1
O *Guyon!* never thinke that so . . . . II. iv. 10. 2
Sir *Guyon* left his first emprise, ... II. iv. 12. 1
Guyon after him in hast did hye, ... II. iv. 13. 8
when as *Guyon* Furor had captivd, ... II. iv. 16. 1
Said *Guyon*; 'Squyre, sore have ye beene diseasd, ... II. iv. 33. 8
'Unlucky Squire,' (saide *Guyon*) . . . take heede . . . . II. iv. 36. 1
to *Guyon* first He boldly spake; . . . . II. iv. 39. 1
'How hight he then,' (sayd *Guyon*) . . . . II. iv. 41. 1
Said *Guyon*: 'let that message to thy Lord be brought.' . . . II. iv. 44. 9
Pyrochles does with *Guyon* fight, ... II. v. Arg.
on the plaine fast pricking *Guyon* spide One . . . . II. v. 2. 2
It booted nought Sir *Guyon*, ... II. v. 3. 8
Exceeding wroth was *Guyon* at that blow, ... II. v. 7. 1
Guyon, in the heat of all his strife, ... II. v. 9. 5
With such faire sleight him *Guyon* often fayld, ... II. v. 11. 1
Whom *Guyon* seeing stoup, poursewed fast . . . . II. v. 12. 1
Eftsoones his cruel hand Sir *Guyon* stayd, ... II. v. 13. 1
Which *Guyon* marking said; 'Be nought agriev'd, ... II. v. 15. 1
Thereat Sir *Guyon* smylde; . . . . II. v. 18. 1
streight defyde Both *Guyon* and Pyrochles; . . . . II. v. 19. 4
Guyon standing by their uncouth strife does see. . . . . . . II. v. 20. 9

Guyon—*Continued.*
Guyon much disdeigned so loathly sight . . . II. v. 23. 6
'Help, O Sir *Guyon!* helpe, . . . II. v. 23. 8
Guyon obayd: So him away he drew . . . II. v. 25. 1
Guyon is of immodest Merth Led into loose desyre; . . . II. vi. Arg.
Guyon in them all shewes goodly maysteries. . . . II. vi. 1. 9
By this time was the worthy *Guyon* brought . . . II. vi. 19. 1
Guyon was loath to leave his guide behind, . . . II. vi. 20. 1
whenas *Guyon* of that land had sight, . . . II. vi. 22. 5
in the way he with Sir *Guyon* mett, . . . II. vi. 28. 1
Sir *Guyon*, grudging not so much his might . . . II. vi. 30. 5
Where gladsome *Guyon* salied forth to land, . . . II. vi. 38. 5
sober *Guyon*, hearing him so rayle, . . . II. vi. 40. 2
Guyon findes Mamon in a delve . . . II. vii. Arg.
Guyon . . . proceedes Yet on his way, . . . II. vii. 2. 1
Soone as he *Guyon* saw, . . . II. vii. 6. 1
Guyon, lightly to him leaping, . . . II. vii. 6. 6
Him followed eke Sir *Guyon* evermore, . . . II. vii. 26. 3
They forward passe; ne *Guyon* yet spoke word, . . . II. vii. 31. 1
Which whenas *Guyon* saw, . . . II. vii. 48. 1
Sir *Guyon*, layd in swowne, . . . II. viii. Arg.
the while that *Guyon* did abide In Mamons house, . . . II. viii. 3. 1
Where *Guyon* lay in traunce; . . . II. viii. 3. 6
the good *Guyon* he found slumbring fast . . . II. viii. 4. 8
he which earst them combatted was *Guyon* bold. . . . II. viii. 10. 9
seven fold shield, which he from *Guyon* brought, . . . II. viii. 32. 5
Sir *Guyon* from his traunce awakt, . . . II. viii. 53. 1
Prince recov'ring his stolne sword, And *Guyon* his lost shield, . II. ix. 2. 3
Said *Guyon*, 'Noble Lord, what meed so great, . . . II. ix. 6. 1
'Seldom' (said *Guyon*) 'yields to vertue aide, . . . II. ix. 8. 2
gan Sir *Guyon* all the story shew . . . II. ix. 9. 5
So long as *Guyon* with her commoned, . . . II. ix. 41. 1
Guyon mervayld at her uncouth cace; . . . II. ix. 43. 5
Sir *Guyon* chaunst eke on another booke, . . . II. ix. 60. 1
Guyon all this while his booke did read, . . . II. x. 70. 1
Sir *Guyon*, in bright armour clad, . . . II. xi. 3. 5
all so soone as *Guyon* thence was gon . . . II. xi. 5. 1
Guyon, by Palmers governaunce, Passing through perilles great, II. xii. Arg.

Guyon—*Continued.*
Which *Guyon* hearing . . . II. xii. 28. 1
to *Guyon*, as he passed by, . . . II. xii. 32. 1
forth the noble *Guyon* sallied, . . . II. xii. 38. 4
So did he eke Sir *Guyon* passing by; . . . II. xii. 49. 6
Much wondred *Guyon* at the fayre aspect . . . II. xii. 53. 1
she to *Guyon* offred it to tast, . . . II. xii. 57. 1
As *Guyon* hapned by the same to wend, . . . II. xii. 63. 5
Whom such when *Guyon* saw, . . . II. xii. 65. 7
Guyon broke downe with rigour pittilesse; . . . II. xii. 83. 2
Then *Guyon* askt, what meant those beastes . . . II. xii. 84. 9
Saide *Guyon;* 'See the mind of beastly man, . . . II. xii. 87. 1
Guyon encountreth Britomart: . . . III. i. Arg.
good Sir *Guyon* deare besought The Prince of grace . . . III. i. 5. 1
Guyon drove so furious and fell, . . . III. i. 6. 2
Guyon selfe, ere well he was aware, . . . III. i. 6. 6
The Prince and *Guyon* equally bylive Her selfe pursewd, . . . III. i. 18. 6
She, traveiling with *Guyon*, . . . III. ii. 4. 1
Sir *Guyon*, as by fortune then befell, . . . V. iii. 29. 3
Guyon would him algates have perforse, . . . V. iii. 30. 4
'If that' (said *Guyon*) 'may you satisfie, . . . V. iii. 32. 7
Untill that *Guyon* selfe unto him spake, . . . V. iii. 34. 2
'Lo there! Sir *Guyon*, take to you the steed, . . . V. iii. 35. 3
Guyon did his choler pacify, . . . V. iii. 36. 5
Guyon's. Vaine Braggadocchio, getting *Guyons* horse, . . . II. iii. Arg.
bashed not For *Guyons* lookes, . . . II. iv. 37. 9
Under Sir *Guyons* puissaunt stroke to fall, . . . II. v. 25. 6
Cymochles sword on *Guyons* shield yglaunst, . . . II. vi. 31. 3
Guyons angry blade so fiers did play . . . II. vi. 31. 5
Guyons shield about his wrest he bond: . . . II. viii. 22. 7
Sir *Guyons* sword he lightly to him raught, . . . II. viii. 40. 2
(Who *Guyons* shield cast ever him before, . . . II. viii. 43. 2
Guyons senses softly tickeled, . . . II. xii. 33. 7
Gyeld. *See* **Guild.**
Gyre. hurtle rownd in warlike *gyre*, . . . II. v. 8. 7
Perforce disparted their compacted *gyre*, . . . III. i. 23. 6
Gyrlond, -s. *See* **Garland, -s.**
Gyved. Those yron fetters wherewith he was *gyv'd*, . . . V. iv. 35. 3

H

Habergeon. her Maides attyre To turne into a massy *habergeon*, III. iii. 57. 8
through his *haberjeon* the forkehead flew, . . . III. v. 19. 3
His mayled *haberjeon* she did undight, . . . III. v. 31. 8
Shee also dofte her heavy haberjeon, . . . III. ix. 21. 1
His *haberjeon*, his helmet, and his speare: . . . III. xi. 7. 5
Through shield and mayle and *haberjeon* did wend, . . . IV. ii. 15. 4
She wore for her defence a mayled *habergeon*. . . . V. v. 2. 9
Both through his *haberjeon* and eke his corse; . . . V. x. 33. 3
Habergeons. Their mightie strokes their *haberjeons* dismayld, . II. vi. 29. 5
Habiliment. Straunge Lady in so straunge *habiliment*, . . . I. vi. 30. 7
Habiliments. Both their *habiliments* unto them tooke, . . . *Hub.* 110
He . . . spoild the Priests of their *habiliments;* . . . I. iii. 17. 7
sad *habiliments* right well beseene: . . . I. xii. 5. 3
Her nathelesse Th' enchaunter . . . deckt with dew *habiliments*. II. i. 22. 9
disaray Her upper partes of meet *habiliments*, . . . II. v. 32. 8
To clad his corpse with meete *habiliments*, . . . VI. iv. 4. 5
Hability, Hable. *See* **Ability, Able,** *etc.*
Habit. With golden wings in *habite* of a Nymph. . . . *Bel.*[1] iv. 6
In some straunge *habit*, after uncouth wize; . . . *Hub.* 84
sluggish Idlenesse, . . . Arayd in *habit* blacke, . . . I. iv. 18. 8
the Palmer eke in *habit* sad . . . II. xi. 3. 7
on her uncouth *habit* and sterne looke still gazed. . . . VII. vi. 13. 9
it the fairer bodie doth procure To *habit* in, . . . *H.B.* 130
Habitance. That here in desert hast thine *habitaunce*, . . . II. vii. 7. 2
Hacked. they now *hackt* and hewd . . . V. vii. 29. 9
Hacqueton. *See* **Haqueton.**
Had (*partial list of auxiliary*).
Feete of a beare, a Lions throte she *had*. . . . *Rev.* i. 5
Square was this Citie, and twelve gates it *had*. . . . *Rev.* iv. 9
no such shadow shalbe *had* againe. . . . *Pet.* iii. 14
Heaven *had* not feare of that presumptuous might, . . . *Ro.* xvii. 3
Had all the world in armes against her bent, . . . *Ro.* xxi. 6
O that I *had* the Thracian Poets harpe, . . . *Ro.* xxv. 1
that I *had* Amphions instrument, . . . *Ro.* xxv. 5
All that which Asie ever *had* of prise, . . . *Ro.* xxix. 11
all this glee *had* no continuaunce: . . . *S.C.* F. 224
bowe and shafts as then none *had*, . . . *S.C.* Mar. 113
I . . . *had* rather be envied, . . . *S.C.* May 57
When shepeheards *had* none inheritaunce, . . . *S.C.* May 105
Had lever my foe then my freend he be; . . . *S.C.* May 167
her dame, that *had* good reason, . . . *S.C.* May 177
she *had* a motherly care . . . *S.C.* May 180
Such end *had* the Kidde, . . . *S.C.* May 302
This *had* a brother . . . *S.C.* Jul. 161
To leave the good, that I *had* in hande, . . . *S.C.* S. 59
they *had* be better come at their cal; . . . *S.C.* S. 146
Never *had* shepheard so kene a kurre, . . . *S.C.* S. 182
For beauties prayse and pleasaunce *had* no peere; . . . *S.C.* N. 94
I of doubted daunger *had* no feare: . . . *S.C.* D. 22
choise I *had* to choose my wandring waye, . . . *S.C.* D. 62
hardie will he *had* To overcome, . . . *Gn.* 303
not a lambe . . . *Had* they to shew; . . . *Hub.* 317
they more subtill meaning *had* than he; . . . *Hub.* 330
askt what license, or what Pas they *had?* . . . *Hub.* 367
Of such deep learning little *had* he neede, . . . *Hub.* 385
Seeing the world . . . *Had* wayes enough . . . *Hub.* 401
he therein *had* great felicitie; . . . *Hub.* 706
fee-simples . . . Which he *had* never, . . . *Hub.* 868

had not power to doo him good or ill. . . . *Hub.* 890
Of men of armes he *had* but small regard, . . . *Hub.* 1189
th' *Apes* long taile (which then he *had*) . . . *Hub.* 1381
For her departure, *had* no word to say; . . . *Ti.* 474
Suspition of friend, nor feare of foe . . . *had* he at all, . . . *Mui.* 378
No chace so hard, but he therein *had* skill. . . . *As.* 84
matcht with such courage as he *had*, . . . *As.* 85
where were ye, when he of you *had* need, . . . *As.* 131
how great a losse *Had* all the shepheards nation . . . *Col.* 17
He *had* a daughter fresh as floure of May, . . . *Col.* 106
had it armes and wings, . . . *Col.* 218
Poets wits are *had* in peerlesse price: . . . *Col.* 321
Had people grace it gratefully to use: . . . *Col.* 325
man, that *had* the sparke of reasons might . . . *Col.* 867
who can tell what cause *had* that faire Mayd . . . *Col.* 911
soveraine hope which in his helpe he *had*. . . . I. i. 2. 6
Seemed in heart some hidden care she *had*, . . . I. i. 4. 8
by his belt his booke he hanging *had:* . . . I. i. 29. 4
that olde man of pleasing wordes *had* store, . . . I. i. 35. 6
arts, That *had* such might over true meaning harts: . . . I. ii. 9. 5
Hee *had* a faire companion of his way, . . . I. ii. 13. 1
a knight . . . That *had* a like faire Lady . . . I. ii. 35. 8
rightfull kingdome she *had* none at all, . . . I. iv. 12. 3
of devotion he *had* little care, . . . I. iv. 19. 3
When such an one *had* guiding of the way, . . . I. iv. 19. 8
he . . . on his head an yvie girland *had*, . . . I. iv. 22. 3
childe ne kinsman living *had* he none To leave them to; . . . I. iv. 28. 6
Whose need *had* end, but no end covetise; . . . I. iv. 29. 3
Who *had* enough, yett wished ever more; . . . I. iv. 29. 5
he . . . wept, that cause of weeping none he *had*, . . . I. iv. 30. 8
of his hands he *had* no governement, . . . I. iv. 34. 4
if that either to that shield *had* right, . . . I. iv. 40. 8
she in hell and heaven *had* power equally. . . . I. v. 34. 9
Good cause he *had* to hasten thence away; . . . I. v. 45. 6
ne joynt to move, she *had;* . . . I. vi. 11. 2
Venus never *had* so sober mood: . . . I. vi. 16. 7
Therion, . . . Who *had* more joy to raunge the forrest wyde, . I. vi. 21. 7
Such joy he *had* their stubborne harts to quell, . . . I. vi. 26. 7
Were it not better I that Lady *had* . . . I. vi. 47. 3
he *had* keeping of his grasing steed, . . . I. vii. 19. 2
No magicke arts hereof *had* any might, . . . I. vii. 35. 1
'Well hoped I, and faire beginnings *had*, . . . I. vii. 49. 1
No powre he *had* to stirre, . . . I. viii. 15. 4
Had no delight to treaten of his griefe; . . . I. viii. 43. 8
at her rompe she growing *had* behind A foxes taile, . . . I. viii. 48. 3
he *had* charge my discipline to frame, . . . I. ix. 5. 3
lever *had* I die then see . . . I. ix. 32. 9
by him *had* many pledges dere. . . . I. x. 4. 9
the which *had* great insight In that disease . . . I. x. 23. 7
med'cines, which *had* passing prief; . . . I. x. 24. 5
Of all the house *had* charge and governement, . . . I. x. 37. 2
He *had* enough; . . . I. x. 38. 8
had he lesse, yet some he would give to the pore. . . . I. x. 38. 9
The third *had* of their wardrobe custody, . . . I. x. 39. 1
if that no spare clothes to give he *had*, . . . I. x. 39. 8
The fift *had* charge sick persons to attend, . . . I. x. 41. 1
The sixt *had* charge of them now being dead, . . . I. x. 42. 1
The seventh . . . *Had* charge the tender Orphans . . . I. x. 43. 2

Had—*Continued.*
sacred pledges he both gave, and *had*, . . . I. xii. 27. 3
Eftsoones of him *had* perfect cognizaunce, . . . II. i. 31. 5
To kindle oft assayd, but *had* no might; . . . II. iii. 23. 7
Had he *had* governaunce it well to guyde; . . . II. iv. 7. 2
beckned him, the last help she *had* left; . . . II. iv. 13. 3
sometimes *had* the worse, and lost by warre, . . . II. v. 15. 4
of his way he *had* no sovenaunce, . . . II. vi. 8. 3
whenas Guyon of that land *had* sight, . . . II. vi. 22. 5
had both life and sence, . . . II. vii. 40. 8
they shall soone be *had*.' . . . II. viii. 54. 5
The rest *had* severall offices assynd; . . . II. ix. 31. 6
Great wonder *had* the knight . . . II. ix. 41. 8
He *had* a sharpe foresight . . . II. ix. 49. 8
Great pleasure *had* those straunger knightes . . . II. ix. 54. 6
Corineus *had* that Province utmost west . . . II. x. 12. 2
Canute *had* his portion from the rest, . . . II. x. 12. 7
Albanact *had* all the Northerne part, . . . II. x. 14. 2
had no issue male him to succeed, . . . II. x. 27. 2
long *had* in great renowne, . . . II. x. 29. 8
had to wife Dame Mertia the fayre, . . . II. x. 42. 3
He *had* two sonnes, . . . II. x. 46. 1
The one of which *had* two heades, . . . II. x. 73. 6
some *had* wings, and some *had* clawes to teare: . . . II. xi. 8. 5
every one of them *had* Lynces eyes; . . . II. xi. 8. 6
the one her other legge *had* lame, . . . II. xi. 23. 6
she *had* cause to busie them withall; . . . II. xii. 15. 3
There those five sisters *had* continuall trade, . . . II. xii. 30. 8
Such vertue in his staffe *had* eke this Palmer sage. . . . II. xii. 41. 9
He of this Gardin *had* the governall, . . . II. xii. 48. 7
yet the vanquished *had* no despight. . . . III. i. 13. 7
what reward *had* he that overcame?' . . . III. i. 27. 7
had never priefe Of such malengine . . . III. i. 53. 7
she sighing softly *had* no powre To speake . . . III. ii. 5. 1
As if she *had* a fever fitt, . . . III. ii. 5. 4
It vertue *had* to shew in perfect sight . . . III. ii. 19. 1
Though straunge beginning *had*, . . . III. ii. 42. 2
For Merlin *had* in Magick more insight . . . III. iii. 11. 8
all that els *had* puissaunce, . . . III. iv. 3. 1
'What *had* th' eternall Maker need of thee . . . III. iv. 56. 1
had no powre in his soft flesh to bite. . . . III. v. 19. 5
load upon him layd his life for to have *had*. . . . III. v. 22. 9
shee of herbes *had* great intendiment, . . . III. v. 32. 3
double gates it *had* which opened wide, . . . III. vi. 31. 5
Ne *had* one word to speake for great amaze, . . . III. vii. 7. 8
This wicked woman *had* a wicked sonne, . . . III. vii. 12. 1
had he not the hart, nor hardiment, . . . III. vii. 16. 3
chastitee *Had* lodging in so meane a maintenaunce; . . . III. vii. 59. 4
deedes of armes *had* ever in despaire, . . . III. viii. 11. 7
had no regard Him to poursew, . . . III. viii. 19. 1
Dye *had* she rather . . . III. viii. 42. 3
rather *had* he dy . . . III. ix. 14. 8
when of meats and drinks they *had* their fill, . . . III. ix. 32. 1
meant to ravish her, that rather *had* to dy. . . . III. x. 13. 9
The loving couple . . . leasure *had* and liberty . . . III. x. 16. 4
Ne word he *had* to speake his griefe to tell, . . . III. x. 37. 8
winges it *had* with sondry colours dight, . . . III. xi. 47. 6
As if in minde he somewhat *had* to say; . . . III. xii. 4. 2
at his backe a brode Capuccio *had*, . . . III. xii. 10. 3
A paire of Pincers in his hand he *had*, . . . III. xii. 16. 5
an angry Waspe th' one in a viall *had*, . . . III. xii. 18. 7
Die *had* she lever . . . IV. i. 6. 8
hee, Which *had* no love nor lemman . . . IV. i. 9. 8
ech of them *had* ryding by his side A Ladie, . . . IV. i. 17. 3
He *had* small lust to buy his love so deare, . . . IV. i. 34. 6
Ne word *had* he to speake for great dismay, . . . IV. i. 50. 2
Knight That *had* a goodly Ladie by his side, . . . IV. ii. 4. 3
But Paridell, that *had* too late a tryall . . . IV. ii. 6. 1
each not farre behinde him *had* his make, . . . IV. ii. 30. 5
Had power to staunch al wounds . . . IV. ii. 39. 9
Priamond on foote *had* more delight; . . . IV. ii. 42. 5
Their mother . . . *had* full blessed hap . . . IV. ii. 43. 8
a Fay, and *had* the skill Of secret things, . . . IV. ii. 44. 1
Now this the better *had*, now *had* his fo; . . . IV. iii. 28. 3
So wearie both of fighting *had* their fill, . . . IV. iii. 36. 8
For that *had* might to change the hearts . . . IV. iii. 45. 5
(for small delight They *had* . . . IV. iii. 47. 2
Triamond *had* Canacee to wife, . . . IV. iii. 52. 4
Sith each of them his Ladie *had* him by, . . . IV. iv. 6. 2
Which Blandamour *had* riding by his side: . . . IV. iv. 7. 8
had no will To hasten greatly . . . IV. iv. 20. 1
litle lust he *had* to rise againe: . . . IV. iv. 44. 6
all the rest which *had* the best afore, . . . IV. v. 8. 6
thought he *had* the trew And very Florimell, . . . IV. v. 13. 7
Ne better *had* he, ne for better cared: . . . IV. v. 35. 2
he *had* sixe servants prest, . . . IV. v. 36. 1
as if the steele *had* sence, . . . IV. vi. 21. 6
Ne care he *had*, ne pittie of the pray, . . . IV. vii. 8. 4
Then loyall love *had* royall regiment, . . . IV. viii. 30. 7
her Dwarfe, which *had* me in his charge, . . . IV. viii. 61. 2
cause of feare, sure, *had* she none . . . IV. ix. 19. 1
sometimes Paridell and Blandamour The better *had*, . . . IV. ix. 25. 2
Doubt, that *had* a double face, . . . IV. x. 12. 3
As every one *had* cause of good or ill. . . . IV. x. 43. 6
hundred mouthes, and voice of brasse I *had*, . . . IV. xi. 9. 7
All which she there on her attending *had*: . . . IV. xi. 48. 6
So *had* I rather to be thrall then free; . . . IV. xii. 10. 8
As to his memory they *had* recourse; . . . V. ii. 2. 7
if time he *had*, He would be there . . . V. ii. 3. 8
the Paynim . . . great advantage *had*, . . . V. ii. 13. 6

Had—*Continued.*
Uncertaine whether *had* the better side; . . . V. ii. 17. 2
If ought he *had* the same to counterpoys; . . . V. ii. 30. 6
The second *had* to name Sir Bellisont, . . . V. iii. 5. 3
None was debard, but all *had* leave that lust. . . . V. iii. 6. 3
Whom Trompart *had* in keeping there beside, . . . V. iii. 17. 2
Such power it *had*, that to no womans wast . . . V. iii. 28. 6
rather *had* to lose then trie in armes his right. . . . V. iii. 31. 9
Had neede have mightie hands . . . V. iv. 1. 3
each one *had* his right. . . . V. iv. 20. 6
little *had* for his excuse to say, . . . V. iv. 27. 4
might have *had* of life or death election: . . . V. v. 26. 5
little lust *had* she to talke of ought, . . . V. vi. 21. 1
He *had* three sonnes, . . . V. vi. 33. 1
To shew that she *had* powre . . . V. vii. 6. 7
As well as to her minde it *had* recourse. . . . V. vii. 20. 3
as his proud wife of her *had* sight, . . . V. viii. 26. 5
Of which he *had* with him abundant store . . . V. viii. 34. 2
had to name The Kingdomes Care, . . . V. ix. 43. 7
The woefull widow *had* no meanes now left, . . . V. x. 14. 2
when her owne two sonnes she *had* in sight, . . . V. x. 19. 7
To which they *had* no right, . . . V. xi. 3. 9
of a Mayd she *had* the outward face, . . . V. xi. 23. 7
Thereto the body of a dog she *had*, . . . V. xi. 24. 1
he *had* great skill in single fight: . . . V. xii. 15. 5
Or harme that any *had*, . . . V. xii. 32. 6
A distaffe in her other hand she *had*, . . . V. xii. 36. 6
whenas each of other *had* a sight, . . . VI. i. 4. 6
the good successe Which ye have *had* . . . VI. i. 5. 2
none afore . . . I have *had*; . . . VI. i. 10. 4
had now her self in hould, . . . VI. i. 29. 7
by his side his hunters horne he hanging *had*. . . . VI. ii. 5. 9
Or *had* no courage, or else *had* no gall. . . . VI. iii. 36. 5
the rude Porter that no manners *had* . . . VI. iii. 38. 1
Yet *had* no meanes to comfort, nor procure her glee. . . . VI. iii. 43. 9
Yet armes or weapon *had* he none to fight, . . . VI. iv. 4. 1
For other language *had* he none, nor speach, . . . VI. iv. 11. 6
in the mindes of men *had* great insight; . . . VI. vi. 3. 6
As one that *had* no life him left . . . VI. vi. 32. 9
her beautie *had* such soveraine might, . . . VI. vii. 31. 6
Ne powre *had* to withstand, . . . VI. vii. 48. 9
Ne any will *had* thence to move away, . . . VI. ix. 12. 2
for other he *had* none; . . . VI. ix. 14. 8
thence he *had* no will away to fare, . . . VI. x. 30. 8
He *had* no weapon but his shepheards hooke . . . VI. x. 36. 1
They spoyld old Melibee of all he *had*, . . . VI. x. 40. 2
had the chiefe commaund of all the rest, . . . VI. xi. 3. 5
With which none *had* to doe, . . . VI. xi. 12. 4
after griefe awhile had *had* his course, . . . VI. xi. 34. 1
The rosie marke . . . That litle Infant *had*, . . . VI. xii. 15. 7
had to her that soveraigne seat By highest Jove assign'd, . . . VII. vi. 12. 1
He *had* his ploughing-share and coulter ready tyde. . . . VII. vii. 39. 9
yet *had* he by his side His plough . . . VII. vii. 43. 5
Never *had* man more joyfull day then this, . . . *Epith.* 246
each one *had* a little wicker basket, . . . *Proth.* 24
the Nymphes, which now *had* Flowers their fill, . . . *Proth.* 55

Had-I-wist. to sue for *had ywist*, . . . *Hub.* 893

Hadst. Such cause of mourning never *hadst* afore; . . . *S.C.* N. 54
Dead . . . thou *haddest* bin, . . . I. ii. 18. 3

Haemony. About the grassie bancks of *Haemony* . . . *As.* 3

Haemus. From top of *Hemus* by him heaped hye;) . . . III. ix. 22. 6
On *Haemus* hill in their divine array, . . . VII. vii. 12. 3

Hag. 'The divelish *hag* . . . Perceiv'd my thought; . . . I. ii. 42. 1
A loathly, wrinckled *hag*, ill favoured, old, . . . I. viii. 46. 8
that lame *Hag*, . . . II. xi. 28. 1
That other *Hag* did far away espye . . . II. xi. 28. 8
him behynd a wicked *Hag* did stalke, . . . II. iv. 4. 1
first the *Hag* did thrust away; . . . II. iv. 6. 2
the *Hag*, with many a bitter threat, . . . II. iv. 9. 3
that same *Hag*, his aged mother, hight Occasion; . . . II. iv. 10. 8
sitting on the flore the *Hag* she found . . . III. vii. 7. 2
that vile *Hag* . . . was much moved . . . III. vii. 9. 8
such whenas the wicked *Hag* did vew, . . . III. vii. 11. 4
that vile *hag*, or her uncivile sonne; . . . III. vii. 19. 6
that accursed *Hag*, her hostesse late, . . . III. viii. 2. 1
Such was that *hag* which with Duessa roade; . . . IV. i. 31. 1
'Vile *hag!*' (sayd Scudamour) why dost thou lye, . . . IV. i. 48. 1
as that *Hag* him teaches: . . . IV. ii. 12. 5
Together with this *Hag* beside her set, . . . IV. iv. 9. 6
he shall have the *Hag* that is ybet, . . . IV. iv. 9. 8
such an *Hag*, that seemed worse then nought, . . . IV. iv. 10. 5
whether shall have the *Hag*, or hold the Lady still.' . . . IV. iv. 12. 9
That stryfull *hag* with gealous discontent . . . IV. v. 30. 8
how that *Hag* his love abused had . . . IV. vi. 28. 3
the *Hag*, there with her mewed, . . . IV. vii. 34. 3
Such was that *Hag*, unmeet to host such guests, . . . IV. viii. 27. 1
the *Hag* did scold And rayle at them . . . IV. viii. 28. 3
That shamefull *Hag*, the slaunder of her sexe, . . . IV. viii. 35. 2
He brought forth that old *hag* of hellish hew, . . . V. ix. 47. 3
A wicked *hag*, and Envy selfe excelling In mischiefe; . . . V. xii. 35. 7

Haggard. *hagard* hauke, presuming to contend With hardy fowle . . . I. xi. 19. 5

Hags. hellish *hags* had met upon the way; . . . *D.* 566
Infernall *Hags*, Centaurs, feendes, Hippodames, . . . II. ix. 50. 8
There follow'd fast at hand two wicked *Hags*, . . . II. xi. 23. 2
Which when those wicked *Hags* from far did spye, . . . II. xi. 47. 1
two old ill favour'd *Hags* he met, . . . V. xii. 28. 4
Such were these *Hags*, and so unhandsome drest: . . . V. xii. 38. 1
those *hags* them selves did paine To sharpen him, . . . V. xii. 41. 8

Hail. *See* **All-hail, Hale.**

Hail—*Continued.*
In raine, or snowe, or *haile,* he forth is horld; . . . *Ro.* xx. 8
haile, and harmful showres, . . . *Gn.* 582
neither car'd for wynd, nor *haile,* nor raine, . . . *Col.* 221
'*Hayle,* Groome! didst not thou see a bleeding Hynde, . . . II. iii. 32. 7
Upon his shield their heaped *hayle* he bore, . . . II. xi. 19. 1
With showre and *hayle* so horrible and dred, . . . III. ix. 11. 6
As thicke as *hayle* forth poured from the skie: . . . IV. iii. 25. 5
Heaping huge strokes as thicke as showre of *hayle,* . . . IV. vi. 16. 5
raine, and *haile* and sleet, . . . IV. ix. 33. 6
'*Haile,* good Sir Sergis, truest Knight alive . . . V. xi. 38. 2
'*Haile,* noblest Knight Of all . . . VI. i. 4. 8
heaped strokes did round about him *haile* . . . VI. v. 18. 3
on his shield did rattle like to *haile* . . . VI. vi. 26. 3
'*Haile,* jolly shepheard, . . . VI. x. 19. 2
Rayne, *haile,* and snowe do pay them sad penance, . . . VII. vii. 23. 7
Hailed. As thicke as it had *hayled*. . . . *S.C.* Mar. 87
Then him to ground he cast, and rudely *hayld,* . . . II. iv. 14. 7
arrowes *haild* so thicke, that they could not abide. . . . V. iv. 38. 9
Hailing. th' *hayling* darts of heaven beating hard. . . . *Mui.* 80
hailing to and fro, . . . II. iv. 8. 7
Hainault. warreyd on Brunchild In *Henault,* . . . II. x. 21. 8
Hainous. *See* **Heinous.**
Hair. and side did hang his *hair,* . . . *Bel.*[1] vii. 3
Renting hir faire visage and golden *haire,* . . . *Bel.*[1] viii. 4
outraging her cheekes and golden *haire,* . . . *Bel.*[2] x. 3
fayre Aurora, with her rosie *heare,* . . . *Gn.* 68
A garment better than of wooll or *heare*. . . . *Hub.* 474
Of milde aspect, and *haire* as soft as silke, . . . *Ti.* 563
Did rend his *haire,* and beat his blubbred face, . . . *D.* 551
Astond he stood, and up his *heare* did hove; . . . I. ii. 31. 8
For anguish great they gan to rend their *heare,* . . . I. iii. 22. 4
cry, and curse, and raile, and rend her *heare,* . . . I. iii. 25. 2
Some frounce their curled *heare* in courtly guise; . . . I. iv. 14. 7
whose rugged *heare* . . . Was like the person selfe . . . I. iv. 24. 2
Phoebus . . . Came dauncing forth, shaking his deawie *hayre,* I. v. 2. 4
his rash syre began to rend His *heare,* . . . I. v. 39. 5
tore Her guiltlesse garments and her golden *heare,* . . . I. x. 28. 6
With garments rent, and *heare* discheveled, . . . II. i. 13. 6
he cutt a lock of all their *heare,* . . . II. i. 61. 2
*As ghastly bug their *haire* on end does reare: . . . II. iii. 20. 5
Drew by the *heare* along upon the grownd . . . II. iv. 3. 6
Her yellow golden *heare* Was trimly woven . . . II. ix. 19. 6
A daintie damsell dressing of her *heare,* . . . II. xii. 14. 8
their yellow *heare* Christalline humor dropped downe apace. . II. xii. 65. 5
the downy *heare* Did now but freshly spring, . . . II. xii. 79. 8
did teare His rugged flesh, and rent his ragged *heare;* . . . III. vii. 20. 5
not so yellow thryse As Florimells fayre *heare:* . . . III. viii. 7. 8
With upstart *haire* and staring eyes dismay, . . . III. x. 54. 8
The God himselfe rending his golden *heare,* . . . III. xi. 37. 7
her bright browes were deckt with borrowed *haire;* . . . III. xii. 14. 7
from her head ofte rente her snarled *heare:* . . . III. xii. 17. 5
With rugged beard, and hoarie shagged *heare,* . . . IV. v. 34. 8
round about the same her yellow *heare,* . . . IV. vi. 20. 1
overgrowne with *haire,* that could awhape An hardy hart; . IV. vii. 5. 4
all his *haire* was like a garment seene; . . . IV. vii. 7. 3
All overgrowen with rude and rugged *haire;* . . . IV. vii. 43. 4
rent his *haire* and scratcht his face for paine. . . . IV. viii. 46. 5
As with a robe, with her owne silver *haire,* . . . IV. xi. 11. 8
Did tricle downe her *haire,* . . . IV. xi. 46. 8
damzels, deckt with long greene *haire,* . . . IV. xi. 48. 2
She to them runnes in hast, and her *haire* rends, . . . V. viii. 10. 7
The morrow next appear'd with purple *hayre* . . . V. x. 16. 5
her foule *heare* Hung loose and loathsomely: . . . V. xii. 29. 3
Hayling that mayden by the yellow *heare,* . . . VI. i. 17. 6
the hope that to my hoary *heare* Thou brings? . . . VI. iii. 4. 7
Gan teare her *hayre,* and all her garments rent, . . . VI. v. 4. 8
nor her golden *haire* Into their comely tresses dewly drest, . VI. xii. 15. 3
which is gold, or *heare,* may scarse be told? . . . *Am.* xxxvii. 4
the fayre tresses of your golden *hayre,*) . . . *Am.* lxxiii. 3
Hesper, when his golden *hayre* In th' Ocean billowes . . . *Proth.* 164
Haire. *See* **Heir.**
Hairs. mowes The waving lockes of those faire yeallow *heares,* *Ro.* xxx. 6
draweth newe delightes with hoary *heares*. . . . *S.C.* Jun. 40
all her Sisters rent their golden *heares*. . . . *T.M.* 111
on his craven crest A bounch of *heares* . . . I. ii. 11. 6
A bounch of *heares* discolourd diversly, . . . I. vii. 32. 2
His reverend *heares* and holy gravitee . . . I. viii. 32. 1
curld uncombed *heares* Upstaring stiffe, . . . I. ix. 22. 2
Of rypest yeares, and *heares* all hoarie gray, . . . II. i. 7. 3
that no looser *heares* Did out of order stray . . . II. ii. 15. 8
In her rude *heares* sweet flowres themselves did lap, . . . II. iii. 30. 8
His snowy front, curled with golden *heares,* . . . II. viii. 5. 5
Staring with hollow eies, and stiffe upstanding *heares*. . . II. ix. 13. 9
taking thrise three *heares* from off her head, . . . III. ii. 50. 1
knocke his head, and rend his rugged *heares,* . . . IV. viii. 4. 8
many scarres and many hoary *heares,* . . . V. vii. 39. 8
her fayre golden *heares* . . . ye waving chance to marke; . *Am.* lxxxi. 1
Hairy. An *hairie* hide of some wilde beast, . . . *Mui.* 66
His broad outstretched hornes, his *hayrie* thies, . . . *Mui.* 335
doth farre outcast His *hearie* beames, . . . III. i. 16. 6
all his *hairy* brest with gory bloud was fild. . . . IV. vii. 31. 9
With *heary* glib deform'd and meiger face, . . . IV. viii. 12. 6
Hale. *See* **Hearty-hale.**
they bene *hale* enough, . . . *S.C.* Jul. 107
all heedlesse of his dearest *hale,* . . . *As.* 103
streight did he *hayle* The greedy villein . . . III. viii. 31. 5
See, how they doe the Lady *hale* and draw! . . . VI. viii. 6. 7
Gan him to *hale,* and teare, and scratch, and bite; . . . VI. viii. 28. 7
by his goatish beard some did him *haile:* . . . VII. vi. 49. 5

Haled. rudely *hayld* her forth without remorse, . . . V. ii. 26. 3
But *hayld* and puld with all his might and maine, . . . VI. iv. 7. 4
Hales. with both his hands unto him *hayles* The resty raynes, V. viii. 39. 5
Half. *halfe* disbowel'd lies . . . *Ro.* xxviii. 5
the pensife boy, *halfe* in despight, Arose, . . . *S.C.* Ja. 76
As *halfe* unwilling . . . *S.C.* F. 204
forth shee yode, thereat *halfe* aghast: . . . *S.C.* May 233
halfe with shame confound . . . *S.C.* Jun. 63
halfe in doubt he opened the dore, . . . *S.C.* S. 220
ere they were *halfe* mellow ripe; . . . *S.C.* D. 107
Now had the Sun *halfe* heaven overgone, . . . *Gn.* 165
she *halfe* frantick, having slaine her sonne, . . . *Gn.* 175
ere the yeare have *halfe* his course out-run, . . . *Hub.* 305
The Priest gan wexe *halfe* proud . . . *Hub.* 413
ne *halfe* so streight and sore. . . . *Hub.* 448
Ne suffer it to house there *halfe* a day. . . . *Hub.* 828
watrie eyne *halfe* weeping, . . . *Hub.* 1362
all Apes but *halfe* their eares have left, . . . *Hub.* 1383
Thoughts *halfe* devine, . . . *T.M.* 363
vainly thinke your selves *halfe* happie then, . . . *Ti.* 199
in this *halfe* happie I doo read Good Melibae, . . . *Ti.* 435
Not *halfe* so manie sundrie colours . . . *Mui.* 92
halfe in doubt, because of his disguize, . . . *D.* 57
(saide he, *halfe* wrothfully) . . . *D.* 71
yet would live with heart *halfe* stonie cold, . . . *Col.* 206
This sun would faile me ere I *halfe* had ended: . . . *Col.* 579
ugly monster . . . *Halfe* like a serpent horribly displaide, . I. i. 14. 7
th' other *halfe* did womans shape retaine, . . . I. i. 14. 8
Halfe furious unto his foe he came, . . . I. i. 24. 3
Halfe angrie asked him, for what he came. . . . I. i. 43. 5
as *halfe* blushing offred him to kis, . . . I. i. 49. 7
half enraged at her shamelesse guise, . . . I. i. 50. 2
Halfe mad through malice . . . I. iii. 22. 8
halfe ashamed wondred at the sight: . . . I. iii. 38. 6
halfe loth to looke so lowe, . . . I. iv. 14. 1
The Marriner yet *halfe* amazed stares . . . I. vi. 1. 4
The mightie trunck, *halfe* rent with ragged rift, . . . I. viii. 22. 8
halfe dead with dying feare; . . . I. ix. 30. 6
The mossy braunches of an Oke *halfe* ded. . . . I. x. 48. 4
Halfe flying and *halfe* footing in his haste, . . . I. xi. 8. 2
Halfe dead through feare, . . . I. xii. 11. 3
sayd then the knight *halfe* wroth, . . . II. i. 11. 1
lay, *halfe* dead, *halfe* quick; . . . II. i. 39. 4
halfe discontent, mote nathelesse Himselfe appease, . . . II. vi. 24. 1
Joves dreaded thunder light Does scorch not *halfe* so sore, . . . II. vi. 50. 8
halfe in disdaineful wise, . . . II. ix. 38. 1
an old old man, *halfe* blind, . . . II. ix. 55. 5
hideous Giaunts, and *halfe* beastly men, . . . II. x. 7. 2
The Prince him selfe *halfe* seemed to offend; . . . II. x. 68. 7
halfe unwilling from their bookes them brought, . . . II. x. 77. 8
halfe the steele behind his backe did rest; . . . II. xi. 37. 5
Halfe in amaze with horror hideous, . . . II. xi. 38. 4
halfe in rage to be deluded thus, . . . II. xi. 38. 5
did like an *halfe* Theatre fulfill: . . . II. xii. 30. 7
th' upper *halfe* their hew retayned still, . . . II. xii. 31. 6
Art, as *halfe* in scorne Of niggard Nature, . . . II. xii. 50. 6
th' eternall lampes . . . were *halfe* yspent, . . . III. i. 57. 7
the Dame, *halfe* dedd Through suddein feare . . . III. i. 62. 4
Halfe armd and *halfe* unarmd, . . . III. i. 63. 3
Th' old woman wox *half* blanck those wordes to heare, . . . III. iii. 17. 8
suddein fitt, and *halfe* extatick stoure, . . . III. iii. 50. 5
Halfe of thy dayes doest lead in horrour hideous. . . . III. iv. 55. 9
as *halfe* in great disdaine, . . . III. iv. 61. 5
woxe *halfe* wroth against her damzels slacke, . . . III. vi. 19. 3
To whom *halfe* weeping she thus answered; . . . III. vi. 20. 6
Not *halfe* so fast the wicked Myrrha fled . . . III. vii. 26. 1
Nor *halfe* so fast to save her maydenhed . . . III. vii. 26. 3
being but *halfe* twin of that berth: . . . III. vii. 47. 9
As if the word so spoken were *halfe* donne, . . . III. x. 33. 2
fell to ground *half* dedd. . . . III. x. 43. 9
to ground He fell *halfe* dead: . . . III. xii. 34. 2
Twixt dolour and despight *halfe* desperate, . . . III. xii. 43. *or.*3
Britomart, *halfe* envying their blesse, . . . III. xii. 46. *or.*6
Whose scoffed words he taking *halfe* in scorne, . . . IV. ii. 6. 6
The other *halfe,* behind yet sticking fast, . . . IV. iii. 12. 3
Then he *halfe* vanquisht, then the other seemed, . . . IV. iii. 28. 4
halfe affeard Of th' uncouth sight, . . . IV. iii. 31. 5
Triamond, *halfe* wroth to see him staid, . . . IV. iv. 20. 5
snatching from her hand *halfe* angrily The belt . . . IV. v. 19. 8
The Prince *halfe* rapt began on her to dote; . . . IV. ix. 6. 7
halfe angry therewithall. . . . IV. x. 11. 9
were they brethren both of *halfe* the blood, . . . IV. x. 32. 3
'By her I entring *half* dismayed was; . . . IV. x. 36. 1
he was *halfe* mortall, . . . IV. xii. 4. 1
halfe dead did hide her selfe for feare. . . . V. ii. 24. 9
Of which th' one *halfe* upon himselfe did set, . . . V. iii. 11. 6
but *halfe* seene his ugly visnomie, . . . V. iv. 11. 3
their Queene her selfe, *halfe* like a man, . . . V. iv. 36. 8
Through vengeful wrath and sdeignfull pride *half* mad; . . . V. iv. 43. 3
Halfe of her shield he shared quite away, . . . V. v. 9. 2
halfe her side it selfe did naked show, . . . V. v. 9. 3
halfe enrag'd she grew, . . . V. v. 9. 6
she turn'd her head, as *halfe* abashed, . . . V. v. 30. 1
As one adaw'd, and *halfe* confused stood; . . . V. v. 45. 5
ere they were *halfe* ded . . . V. viii. 28. 8
with unwonted terror *halfe* affray, . . . V. ix. 24. 4
made him stagger and stand *halfe* agast, . . . V. xi. 28. 7
Sir Burbon, blushing *halfe* for shame: . . . V. xi. 52. 6
Her *halfe* dismayd they found in doubtfull plight, . . . V. xi. 60. 4
Artegall, returning yet *halfe* sad . . . VI. i. 4. 4

Half—*Continued.*
when her he mist, He woxe *halfe* mad; . . . . . VI. ii. 20. 7
(quoth he *halfe* wrothfully) . . . . . VI. vii. 16. 1
where is eke your friend which *halfe* it ought?' . . . . . VI. vii. 16. 5
how could her love make *half* amends therefore? . . . . . VI. vii. 38. 9
like one *halfe* entraunced grew. . . . . . VI. ix. 26. 9
gave him hope, and did him *halfe* perswade, ... VI. xi. 7. 3
halfe enraged at that ruefull sight; . . . . . VI. xi. 25. 4
being *halfe* dismayd, ... VI. xii. 16. 7
halfe confused with his great commaund, ... VII. vi. 26. 1
I in hand her yet *halfe* trembling tooke, ... *Am.* lxvii. 11
Give leave to rest me being *halfe* fordonne, ... *Am.* lxxx. 3
Halfen. he Malbeccoes *halfen* eye did wyle; . . . . . III. x. 5. 2
His *halfen* eye he wiled wondrous well, ... III. x. 5. 3
Halfendeal. hevenly lampes were *halfendeale* ybrent: . . . . . III. ix. 53. 5
Half-gnawn. even that *halfe-gnawen* snake, ... V. xii. 39. 3
Half-horsy. th' *halfe-horsy* people, Centaures hight, ... *Gn.* 41
Halidom. sure, and by my *hallidome*, (quoth he) . . . . . *Hub.* 545
Halimeda. Fresh *Alimeda* deckt with girlond greene; . . . . . IV. xi. 51. 1
Haling. *Hayling* that mayden by the yellow heare, ... VI. i. 17. 6
Haling her palfrey by the hempen raines: . . . . . VI. vii. 44. 4
Scourging and *haling* him more vehement; . . . . . VI. viii. 4. 8
Hall. *See* **Castle-hall, Judgement-hall.**
Merily masking both in bowre and *hall*. . . . . . *As.* 28
purchace highest rowmes in bowre and *hall:* . . . . . *Col.* 726
Thence to the *hall*, which was . . . With rich array . . . dight. I. iv. 6. 5
The heapes of people, thronging in the *hall*, ... I. iv. 16. 7
Feasting and courting both in bowre and *hall;* . . . . . I. iv. 43. 6
forth he comes into the commune *hall;* . . . . . I. v. 3. 1
Which wast begot in Daemogorgons *hall*, ... I. v. 22. 5
nor wight was seene in bowre or *hall*. . . . . . I. viii. 29. 9
gladly did them guide, till to the *Hall* they came. . . . . . I. x. 6. 9
All in the open *hall* amazed stood . . . . . I. xii. 25. 1
Thence she them brought into a stately *Hall*, ... II. ix. 27. 1
through the *Hall* there walked to and fro . . . . . II. ix. 28. 1
in her fathers *hall* . . . in that enchaunted glasse she saw; IV. vi. 26. 5
dayly feasting both in bowre and *hall*, ... IV. vi. 39. 7
He comes to Proteus *hall*, ... IV. xi. Arg.
All these together marched toward Proteus *hall*. . . . . . IV. xi. 39. 9
Came to the open *hall* to listen . . . . . V. iii. 13. 8
thether also came . . . into the common *hall*, ... V. iii. 14. 2
Thereof great hurly-burly moved was Throughout the *hall* . V. iii. 30. 2
drawing him out of the open *hall* . . . . . V. iii. 37. 3
She heard a wondrous noise below the *hall:* . . . . . V. vi. 27. 5
they passing in Went up the *hall*, ... V. ix. 23. 2
The marshall of the *hall* to them did come, ... V. ix. 23. 7
ran into the *Hall*, where he did weene Him selfe to save; . V. x. 37. 8
well beseemeth that in Princes *hall* . . . . . VI. i. 1. 3
passing forth into the *hall* he came, ... VI. i. 24. 6
Ne stayd, till that he came into the *hall;* . . . . . VI. vi. 19. 3
Into his Lords forbidden *hall* to passe? . . . . . VI. vi. 20. 4
this your cabin both my bowre and *hall:* . . . . . VI. ix. 32. 4
Hallidome. *See* **Halidom.**
Halloo. Yet did she not lament with loude *alew*, ... V. vi. 13. 8
Hallow. A table . . . I avow to *hallow* unto thee!' . . . . . III. iv. 10. 9
Hallowed. often *halowed* with holy-water dewe: . . . . . *S.C.* F. 210
Hallowing. with a sheepe, The Altars *hallowing*. . . . . . *S.C.* Jul. 136
Whooping and *hallowing* on every part, ... VI. viii. 40. 3
Halsed. lovely *haulst*, from feare of treason free, ... IV. iii. 49. 4
Halter. He chose an *halter* from among the rest, ... I. ix. 54. 4
round about his necke an *halter* tight, ... V. iv. 22. 3
forst him th' *halter* from his hand to loose, ... VI. vii. 45. 7
Ham. Below her *ham* her weed did somewhat trayne, ... II. iii. 27. 1
short tucked for light motion Up to her *ham;* . . . . . V. v. 2. 7
Hamadryads. faire *Hamadryades*, Her to behold do thither runne . . . . . I. vi. 18. 1
Hammer. So huge his *hammer*, and so fierce his heat, ... IV. v. 37. 7
Hammers. heaped blowes like yron *hammers* great; . . . . . I. v. 7. 2
when heavy *hammers* on the wedge are swaid: . . . . . I. xi. 42. 7
they heard the sound Of many yron *hammers* . . . . . IV. v. 33. 7
With huge great *hammers*, that did never rest . . . . . IV. v. 36. 3
So likewise did the *hammers* which they bore, ... IV. v. 36. 7
Hammers'. *hammers* sound his senses did molest, ... IV. v. 41. 2
Han. *See* **Have.**
Hand. *See* **Left hand, Nigh hand, Right hand, Underhand, White-hand.**
made by his owne skilfull *hande* . . . . . *Bel.*[1] iv. 10
One *hand* on Scythia, th' other on the More, ... *Ro.* iv. 3
Doth yet himselfe with fatall *hand* enforce, ... *Ro.* xxvii. 13
Didst arme thy *hand* against thy proper hart; . . . . . *Ro.* xxxi. 11
Was not I planted of thine owne *hand*, ... *S.C.* F. 165
His harmefull Hatchet he hent in *hand*, ... *S.C.* F. 195
With bowe and bolts in either *hand*, ... *S.C.* Mar. 65
All for Elisa in her *hand* to weare? . . . . . *S.C.* Ap. 105
In evill houre thou hentest in *hond* . . . . . *S.C.* Jul. 37
To leave the good, that I had in *hande*, ... *S.C.* S. 59
Unwisely weaves, that takes two webbes in *hand*. . . . . . *S.C.* O. 102
with his *hand* him rashly bruzing slewe . . . . . *Gn.* 290
each with brothers bloudie *hand* was slaine. . . . . . *Gn.* 416
hold in hugger mugger in their *hand*, ... *Hub.* 139
not with kissed *hand* belowe the knee, ... *Hub.* 730
dare his hardy *hand* to those outstretch, ... *Hub.* 974
the worke of your nimble *hand*, ... *Hub.* 1035
through his *hand* must passe the Fiaunt. . . . . . *Hub.* 1144
high Jove, in whose almightie *hand* . . . . . *Hub.* 1225
in his *hand* He tooke Caduceus, ... *Hub.* 1291
reatch his *hand* into his enemies hoast. . . . . . *Ti.* 542
woven even now Of Joves owne *hand*, ... *Mui.* 236
Jaakob staffe in *hand* devoutlie crost, ... *D.* 41
bring to *hand* that yet had never beene; . . . . . *D.* 116

Hand—*Continued.*
he tooke in *hond* My pipe, ... *Col.* 72
To have in her commandement at *hand*.' . . . . . *Col.* 263
Enforst to seeke some covert nigh at *hand*, ... I. i. 7. 1
nought aghast, his mightie *hand* enhaunst: . . . . . I. i. 17. 8
hand or foot to stirr he strove in vaine. . . . . . I. i. 18. 8
knitting all his force, got one *hand* free, ... I. i. 19. 7
He stayde his *hand;* and gan himselfe advise . . . . . I. i. 50. 5
he suddenly up start With sword in *hand*, ... I. ii. 5. 2
His foe was nigh at *hand*. . . . . . I. ii. 14. 6
Astonied with the stroke of their owne *hand*, ... I. ii. 15. 8
'Whose forged beauty he did take in *hand* . . . to have exceeded . . . . . I. ii. 36. 1
The false witch did my wrathfull *hand* withhold: . . . . . I. ii. 39. 8
Truth . . . fals in *hand* of leachour . . . . . I. iii. Arg.
To weet if dwelling place were nigh at *hand;* . . . . . I. iii. 11. 2
His bleeding hart is in the vengers *hand;* . . . . . I. iii. 20. 2
hee durst not show Him selfe too nigh at *hand*, ... I. iii. 26. 4
Una cride, 'O! hold that heavie *hand*, ... I. iii. 37. 2
His hasty *hand* he doth amased hold, ... I. iii. 38. 5
Left in the *hand* of that same Paynim bold, ... I. iii. 40. 6
mightie corse, As ever wielded speare in warlike *hand*, . . I. iii. 42. 4
Through highest heaven with weaker *hand* to rayne: . . . . . I. iv. 9. 4
in her *hand* she held a mirrhour bright, ... I. iv. 10. 6
in his *hand* his Portesse still he bare, ... I. iv. 19. 1
he . . . in his *hand* did beare a bouzing can, ... I. iv. 22. 6
in his *hand* a burning hart he bare, ... I. iv. 25. 3
in foote and *hand* A grievous gout tormented him full sore, . I. iv. 29. 6
in his *hand* a burning brond he hath, ... I. iv. 33. 3
on his dagger still his *hand* he held, ... I. iv. 33. 8
after all, . . . Rode Sathan with a smarting whip in *hand*, . I. iv. 36. 2
That brothers *hand* shall dearely well requight, ... I. iv. 42. 6
his heavie *hand* he high gan reare, ... I. v. 13. 5
His cunning *hand* gan to his wounds to lay, ... I. v. 44. 2
Antiochus, the which advaunst His cursed *hand* gainst God, . I. v. 47. 9
His trembling *hand* he would him force to put Upon the Lyon I. vi. 24. 3
in his *hand* a Jacobs staffe, ... I. vi. 35. 7
Th' Elfe . . . his unready weapons gan in *hand* to take. . . I. vii. 7. 9
His heavie *hand* he heaved up on hye, ... I. vii. 14. 2
O! hold thy mortall *hand* for Ladies sake; . . . . . I. vii. 14. 6
Encountring fiers with single sword in *hand;* . . . . . I. viii. 12. 8
Pupill fitt for such a Tutors *hand!* . . . . . I. ix. 6. 2
gave it him in *hand:* his *hand* did quake . . . . . I. ix. 51. 3
He lifted up his *hand*, that backe againe did start. . . . . . I. ix. 51. 9
Out of his *hand* she snatcht the cursed knife, ... I. ix. 52. 4
in her other *hand* she fast did hold . . . . . I. x. 13. 7
Amendment readie still at *hand* did wayt, ... I. x. 26. 7
taking by the *hand* that Faeries sonne, ... I. x. 33. 2
by the *hand* him beares Forth . . . . . I. x. 35. 1
he . . . gave All in his *hand*, ... I. x. 42. 8
the keies are to thy *hand* behight . . . . . I. x. 50. 7
staggering steps thy steady *hand* doth lead, ... I. x. 51. 2
writt in stone . . . by the *hand* of God, ... I. x. 53. 7
Who did her cause into thy *hand* committ, ... I. x. 63. 8
with mightie *hand* . . . High reard their royall throne . . I. x. 65. 2
the dreadful Beast drew nigh to *hand*, ... I. xi. 8. 1
So wondrous force from *hand* of living wight; . . . . . I. xi. 17. 8
fercely tooke his trenchand blade in *hand*, ... I. xi. 24. 1
Great God it planted . . . With his Almighty *hand*, ... I. xi. 46. 8
Behold! I see the haven nigh at *hand* . . . . . I. xii. 1. 1
out of *hond* Proclaymed joy and peace . . . . . I. xii. 3. 7
now they laurell braunches bore in *hand*, ... I. xii. 5. 8
scratch my sonne, or rend his tender *hand?*' . . . . . I. xii. 11. 6
Withhold . . . your hasty *hond* From knitting league . . . . I. xii. 28. 3
often semblaunce made to scape out of their *hand*. . . . . . I. xii. 35. 9
bound him *hand* and foote with yron chains; . . . . . I. xii. 36. 2
Possessed of his Ladies hart and *hand;* . . . . . I. xii. 40. 7
knighthood tooke of good Sir Huons *hand*, ... II. i. 6. 8
Whose hastie *hand* so far from reason strayd, ... II. i. 28. 5
Who made my *hand* the organ of his might: . . . . . II. i. 33. 3
cursed *hand*, hath plaid this cruell part, ... II. i. 44. 7
this babes bloody *hand* May not be clensd . . . . . II. ii. 10. 1
To weet what dreadfull thing was there in *hond*, ... II. ii. 21. 2
hold your dead-doing *hand*,' . . . . . II. iii. 8. 1
As if their lives had in his *hand* beene gagd; . . . . . II. iii. 14. 3
'That shall I shortly purchase to your *hond;* . . . . . II. iii. 18. 2
in her *hand* a sharpe bore-speare she held, ... II. iii. 29. 1
'O! stay thy *hand;* . . . . . II. iii. 35. 1
Those deadly tooles which in her *hand* she held, ... II. iii. 37. 3
with solemne oath and plighted *hand* Assurd, ... II. iv. 23. 8
With wrathfull *hand* I slew her innocent, ... II. iv. 29. 4
in his *hand* two dartes, ... II. iv. 38. 7
Eftsoones his cruel *hand* Sir Guyon stayd, ... II. v. 13. 1
that she gave into his *hond*. . . . . . II. v. 22. 8
by Natures cunning *hand* Bene choycely picked out . . . . . II. vi. 12. 3
shee soone to *hond* Her ferry brought, ... II. vi. 19. 4
ever held his *hand* upon his hart; . . . . . II. vi. 26. 2
What coward *hand* shall doe thee next to dye, ... II. vi. 39. 8
Holding in *hand* a goodly arming sword, ... II. vi. 47. 6
Helpe with thy *hand*, or with thy counsell sage: . . . . . II. vi. 48. 4
His *hand* that trembled as one terrifyde; . . . . . II. vii. 6. 7
gan a cursed *hand* the quiet wombe . . . . . II. vii. 17. 1
ne *hand* these handled not; . . . . . II. vii. 19. 7
The one in *hand* an yron whip did strayne, ... II. vii. 21. 7
If ever covetous *hand*, or lustfull eye, ... II. vii. 27. 2
Mammon did his hasty *hand* withhold, ... II. vii. 42. 6
stretching forth his *hand* . . . . . II. vii. 58. 4
the fruit from *hand* . . . Did fly abacke, ... II. vii. 58. 6
evill is at *hand* him to offend.' . . . . . II. viii. 8. 7
With trembling *hand* his troubled pulse gan try; . . . . . II. viii. 9. 6

Hand—*Continued.*

wrathfull *hand* wrought not her owne desire? II. viii. 15. 5
rude *hand* upon his shield he laid, II. viii. 17. 1
out of his *hond* . . . he rudely snatcht away, II. viii. 22. 5
doth against the dead his *hand* upheave, II. viii. 29. 7
his *hand,* more sad then lomp of lead, II. viii. 30. 5
thy cruell *hond,* That twise hath spedd; II. viii. 37. 6
againe he armed felt his *hond:* II. viii. 40. 6
back againe turning his busie *hond,* II. viii. 41. 6
His *hand* relented and the stroke forbore, II. viii. 43. 4
may Thy cursed *hand* so cruelly have swayd II. viii. 46. 7
read, what wicked *hand* hath robbed mee II. viii. 54. 1
withstond Oppressours powre by armes and puissant *hond?* II. viii. 56. 5
hard adventure which I have in *hand,* II. ix. 8. 8
in his *hand* a white rod menaged: II. ix. 27. 7
in her *hand* a Poplar braunch did hold: II. ix. 37. 3
yvory Which cunning Craftesman *hand* hath overlayd II. ix. 41. 6
There chaunced to the Princes *hand* to rize II. ix. 59. 5
As it delivered was from *hond* to *hond:* II. ix. 60. 5
In her owne *hand* the crowne she kept in store, II. x. 20. 3
with most cruell *hand* him murdred pittilesse. II. x. 35. 9
they overran all parts with easy *hand.* II. x. 61. 9
they which sought at first their helping *hand,* II. x. 65. 8
As if the rest some wicked *hand* did rend, II. x. 68. 4
from thy *hand* Did commun breath and nouriture receave. II. x. 69. 5
in his *hand* a bended bow was seene, II. xi. 21. 1
There follow'd fast at *hand* two wicked Hags, II. xi. 23. 2
often need the helpe of weaker *hand;* II. xi. 30. 2
With stedfast *hand* upon his horse did stay, II. xi. 48. 8
Sir Palmer, keepe an even *hand,* II. xii. 18. 3
hard at *hand* they spy II. xii. 18. 5
defects From her most cunning *hand* escaped bee; II. xii. 23. 4
Holding a staffe in *hand* for mere formalitee, II. xii. 48. 9
taking it out of her tender *hond,* II. xii. 57. 2
His daedale *hand* would faile and greatly faynt, III. Pr. 2. 4
To loose long gotten honour with one evill *hond.* III. i. 10. 9
in his clownish *hand* a sharp bore speare he shooke. III. i. 17. 9
with cunning *hand* was pourtrahed The love of Venus III. i. 34. 3
Dare not for dread his hardy *hand* expose, III. i. 46. 8
with her softe *hand* She softely felt III. i. 60. 6
Carados her *hand* withheld From rash revenge, III. iii. 55. 7
That mortall speare she in her *hand* did take, III. iv. 14. 2
Through heavy stroke of Britomartis *hond.* III. iv. 29. 4
Not this the worke of womans *hand* ywis, III. iv. 37. 3
Cursed the *hand* that did so deadly smight III. iv. 44. 4
good Sir, tell out of *hand.'* III. v. 4. 9
His bootelesse bow in feeble *hand* upcaught, III. v. 24. 6
From dread of her revenging fathers *hond;* III. vii. 26. 2
he tooke in *hand,* And with it bownd the beast, III. vii. 36. 2
Fast bounden *hand* and foote with cords of wire, III. vii. 37. 8
She caught in *hand* an huge great yron mace, III. vii. 40. 1
on his collar laying puissaunt *hand,* III. vii. 43. 1
when him at *hand* she did espy, III. vii. 44. 7
Unable to arise, or foote or *hand* to styre. III. vii. 45. 9
Great labour fondly hast thou hent in *hand,* III. vii. 61. 2
In *hand* she boldly tooke To make another III. viii. 5. 6
his rough *hond* Where ill became him III. viii. 25. 6
Shee strugled strongly both with foote and *hand* III. viii. 27. 3
rough Masons *hand* with engines keene III. viii. 37. 6
hand should dare for to engore Her noble blood? III. viii. 48. 8
when so of his *hand* the pledge she raught, III. ix. 31. 1
sewd At *hand* with humble pride III. x. 9. 3
So takes in *hond* To seeke her III. x. 19. 4
Why then is Busirane with wicked *hand* Suffred, III. xi. 10. 7
Perhaps this *hand* may helpe to ease your woe, III. xi. 15. 4
powre of *hand,* nor skill of learned brest, III. xi. 16. 3
both are of thy haplesse *hand* extinct, III. xi. 37. 3
in his *hand* a braunch of laurell bore, III. xii. 3. 7
to the vulgare beckning with his *hand,* III. xii. 4. 3
in his *hand* a windy fan did beare, III. xii. 8. 8
A net in th' one *hand,* III. xii. 11. 5
in her *hand* did hold An holy-water-sprinckle, III. xii. 13. 5
alwaies in her *hand* two clewes of silke she twynd. III. xii. 14. 9
A paire of Pincers in his *hand* he had, III. xii. 16. 5
(The work of cruell *hand*) III. xii. 20. 8
Shame burning brond-yrons in her *hand* did hold: III. xii. 24. 8
His cursed *hand* withheld, III. xii. 32. 9
Therewith she stayd her *hand,* III. xii. 34. 8
slack her threatfull *hand* for daungers dout; III. xii. 37. 4
laid the noble Championesse strong *hond* Upon th' enchaunter III. xii. 41. 3
the lovely paire drew nigh to *hond:* IV. i. 34. 1
Why doth mine *hand* from thine avenge abstaine, IV. i. 52. 7
thrise his *hand* to kill her did upreare, IV. i. 54. 8
did take His silver Harpe in *hand* IV. ii. 1. 9
This *hand* her wonne, this *hand* shall her defend.' IV. ii. 14. 6
as they now approched nigh at *hand,* IV. ii. 31. 1
These three that hardie chalenge tooke in *hand,* IV. iii. 3. 1
in his *hand* nought but the troncheon left; IV. iii. 12. 2
seeing it at *hand,* he swarv'd asyde, IV. iii. 18. 6
his mightie *hand* He heav'd on high, IV. iii. 33. 1
Stroke him, as he his *hand* to strike upreard, IV. iii. 33. 8
in her other *hand* a cup she hild, IV. iii. 42. 8
Their wrathfull blades downe fell out of their *hand,* IV. iii. 48. 4
Then tooke the bold Sir Satyrane in *hand.* IV. iv. 17. 1
went away sore wounded of his haplesse *hand.* IV. iv. 21. 9
So dreadfull were his strokes, so deadly was his *hond.* IV. iv. 23. 9
ere his *hand* he reard, he overthrew Seven Knights, IV. iv. 41. 1
Till by mishap he in his foemens *hand* did light. IV. v. 7. 9
snatching from her *hand* halfe angrily The belt IV. v. 19. 8
This *hand* may helpe, or succour ought supplie, IV. vi. 8. 7

Hand—*Continued.*

Ah, cruell *hand!* and thrise more cruell hart, IV. vi. 16. 8
At last his lucklesse *hand* he heav'd on hie, IV. vi. 18. 6
Framed in goldsmithes forge with cunning *hand:* IV. vi. 20. 4
as his *hand* he up againe did reare, IV. vi. 21. 1
felt some ruth or sence his *hand* did lacke, IV. vi. 21. 7
All that long while upheld her wrathfull *hand,* IV. vi. 23. 2
her enhaunced *hand* she downe can soft withdraw. IV. vi. 26. 9
Her *hand* fell downe, IV. vi. 27. 4
womans *hand* Hath conquered you IV. vi. 31. 2
Like to a stubborne steede whom strong *hand* would restraine. IV. vi. 33. 9
in his *hand* a tall young oake he bore, IV. vii. 7. 4
he his *hand* so carefully did beare, IV. vii. 27. 5
scarse the Squire his *hand* could once upreare, IV. vii. 28. 6
With bow in *hand* and arrowes ready bent, IV. vii. 29. 6
of his owne rash *hand* one wound was to be seene. IV. vii. 35. 9
held her wrathfull *hand* from vengeance sore: IV. vii. 36. 6
With ready *hand* it to have reft away; IV. viii. 10. 6
Eftsoones she flew unto his fearelesse *hand,* IV. viii. 12. 1
untide . . . by Virgins *hond;* IV. viii. 21. 6
steadie *hand* was faine his steede to guyde, IV. viii. 37. 7
ere his *hand* he could recure againe IV. viii. 45. 1
'Thenceforth I found more favour at her *hand,* IV. viii. 61. 1
nigh at *hand* Those Ladies two, IV. viii. 62. 6
in a mighty *hond* Her person . . . did remaine, IV. ix. 18. 2
gan him selfe advise To stay his *hand,* IV. ix. 35. 6
she them forced *hand* to joyne in *hand,* IV. x. 33. 2
Holding her *hand* upon her gentle hart; IV. x. 51. 2
by the lilly *hand* her labour'd up to reare. IV. x. 53. 9
The pledge of faith, her *hand,* engaged held IV. x. 55. 7
to lay *hand* on her not one of all them daring. IV. x. 56. 9
of a womans *hand* it was ywroke, IV. xi. 5. 6
what an endlesse worke have I in *hand,* IV. xii. 1. 1
Whom she receiving by the lilly *hand,* IV. xii. 33. 3
with strong *hand* their fruitful rancknes did deface. V. i. 1. 9
Did with strong *hand* withhold; V. i. 3. 9
bide the horror of his wreakfull *hand,* V. i. 8. 8
in his *hand* an yron flale did hould, V. i. 12. 8
whether his owne *hand,* or whether other wight? V. i. 14. 9
That did his *hand* in Ladies bloud embrew, V. i. 16. 4
rather of his *hand* besought to die. V. i. 18. 4
keepes a Bridges passage by strong *hond,* V. ii. 4. 7
With bright Chrysaor in his cruell *hand,* V. ii. 18. 2
curst the *hand* which did that vengeance on him dight. V. ii. 18. 9
Of Justice, which in Talus *hand* did lye; V. ii. 26. 2
An huge great paire of ballance in his *hand,* V. ii. 30. 3
In vaine therefore doest thou now take in *hand* V. ii. 42. 5
by misfortune in his *hand* did fall.' V. iii. 22. 8
th' one *hand* seizing on his golden bit, V. iii. 29. 6
one did take The horse in *hand* V. iii. 33. 2
thrise did lay his *hand* upon his sword; V. iii. 36. 3
Which long agoe he taken had in *hond:* V. iv. 3. 7
this maides with whom I fastned *hand,* V. iv. 15. 7
So each of them layd downe his sword out of his *hand.* V. iv. 16. 9
plucked quite from all possessors *hand,* V. iv. 19. 3
on womankinde His mighty *hand* to shend, V. iv. 24. 4
She causeth them be hang'd up out of *hand;* V. iv. 32. 4
ere she could joyne *hand* with him to fight, V. iv. 43. 5
Cursing his *hand* that had that visage mard: V. v. 13. 4
No *hand* so cruell, nor no hart so hard, V. v. 13. 5
Her wrathful *hand* from greedy vengeance to have stayd. V. v. 14. 9
in his *hand* a distaffe to him gave, V. v. 23. 2
T' obay the heasts of mans well-ruling *hand.* V. v. 25. 4
Not by strong *hand* compelled thereunto, V. vi. 16. 4
as next to *hand* did light, V. vi. 20. 8
in his *hand* his thresher ready keight. V. vi. 29. 7
So well as could with cunning *hand* be wrought, V. vii. 6. 3
in her other *hand* She stretched forth a long white sclender wand. V. vii. 7. 4
ere they reared *hand* the Amazone Began V. vii. 28. 1
she to hunt the beast first tooke in *hond;* V. vii. 30. 8
Suffring my *hand* against my heart to stray; V. viii. 13. 3
to his part allures, and bribeth under *hand.* V. viii. 18. 9
being wounded of the huntsmans *hand* V. viii. 35. 6
With knife in *hand,* V. viii. 46. 3
with knife in *hand* She threw her husbands murdred infant V. viii. 47. 1
Did stay her cruell *hand* ere she her raught; V. viii. 48. 2
So light of *hand,* and nymble of his pace, V. ix. 5. 5
Which when the Damzell neare at *hand* did spy, V. ix. 8. 3
in his *hand* an huge long staffe he held, V. ix. 11. 1
he then tooke it up, and held fast in his *hand.* V. ix. 17. 9
whilest in *hand* it gryping hard he hent, V. ix. 18. 4
Holding a Scepter in her royall *hand,* V. ix. 30. 2
To th' hearing of that former cause in *hand* V. ix. 37. 2
with bloudie knyfe Yet dropping fresh in *hand,* V. ix. 48. 3
now by force extort out of her *hand* V. x. 25. 3
would his doings justifie with his owne *hand.* V. xi. 4. 9
his weapon shift from side to syde, From *hand* to *hand;* V. xi. 6. 6
He gan to watch the wielding of his *hand,* V. xi. 7. 2
chang'd from *hand* to *hand,* V. xi. 7. 7
To greet him the good fortune of his *hand:* V. xi. 15. 4
He tooke her up forby the lilly *hand,* V. xi. 17. 1
reave out of the *hand* that did it hend: V. xi. 27. 5
Fallen into that Tyrants *hand* and usage bad. V. xi. 40. 9
long having since Taken in *hand* th' exploit, V. xii. 3. 2
As thicke as doth the seede after the sowers *hand.* V. xii. 7. 9
in his *hand* an huge Polaxe did beare, V. xii. 14. 7
His deadly weapon which in *hand* he held: V. xii. 16. 5
high did reare His cruell *hand* to smite him mortally, V. xii. 20. 3
A distaffe in her other *hand* she had, V. xii. 36. 6

Hand—*Continued.*
Both *hand* and foote unto a tree was bound; VI. i. 11. 4
What cruell *hand* thy wretched thraldome wrought, VI. i. 12. 3
little bootes against him *hand* to reare. VI. i. 16. 5
with *hand* unblest Hayling that mayden VI. i. 17. 5
hast with guilty *hand* Murdred my men, VI. i. 25. 2
taking from her *hand* a ring of gould, VI. i. 29. 2
alive or dead Her foe deliver up into her *hand:* VI. i. 31. 6
tooke in *hand* her quarrell to maintaine; VI. i. 33. 2
his mortall *hand* a while he stayd; VI. i. 40. 1
unto his *hand* in chase did happen neare. VI. ii. 6. 9
Why hath thy *hand* . . . it selfe embrewed In blood VI. ii. 7. 3
He with strong *hand* downe from his steed me throw'th VI. ii. 17. 8
with carefull *hand* . . . To wype his wounds, VI. ii. 41. 4
what cruell *hand* hath thus arayd This knight VI. ii. 42. 3
Which had this outrage wrought with wicked *hand*. VI. ii. 44. 4
With speare in th' one *hand* VI. iii. 33. 8
his long speare So nigh at *hand*, VI. iv. 7. 7
catching up in *hand* a ragged stone VI. iv. 21. 2
And quietly doth hold it in his *hand*, VI. iv. 30. 3
sternely with strong *hand* he from his handling kept. VI. v. 25. 9
laying *hand* upon his wrathfull blade VI. v. 26. 6
it perceiving *hand* upon him layd, VI. v. 26. 8
by what traine She fell into that salvage villaines *hand?* VI. v. 27. 8
No wound, which warlike *hand* of enemy Inflicts VI. vi. 1. 1
rude *hand* on him did lay, To thrust him out of dore VI. vi. 21. 8
He stayd his second strooke, and did his *hand* abase. VI. vi. 31. 9
slaughtred bodies which his *hand* had slaine, VI. vi. 38. 2
Approching to him neare, his *hand* he stayd, VI. vi. 39. 2
streight he held his *hand* at his commaundement. VI. vi. 40. 9
With flaming sword in *hand* his terror more to breed. VI. vii. 11. 9
throwing downe his load out of his *hand*, VI. vii. 24. 3
in his *hand* a mighty yron club he bore. VI. vii. 43. 9
having in his *hand* a whip, Her therewith yirks; VI. vii. 44. 6
forst him th' halter from his *hand* to loose, VI. vii. 45. 7
Till heavy *hand* the Carle upon him layd, VI. vii. 48. 6
as his *hand* was heaved up on hight, VI. viii. 10. 2
His dreadfull *hand* he heaved up aloft, VI. viii. 15. 1
He staide his *hand* according her desire, VI. viii. 18. 1
his cruell *hand* to stay, VI. viii. 29. 2
Then to the rest his wrathfull *hand* he bends; VI. viii. 49. 5
With shepheards hooke in *hand*, and fit attyre, VI. ix. 13. 8
night arrived hard at *hand*, VI. ix. 16. 3
in his *hand* he tooke . . . a shepheards hooke; VI. ix. 36. 4
In his strong *hand* their rugged teats to hold, VI. ix. 37. 8
who so hardie *hand* on her doth lay, VI. xi. 15. 8
At length espyes at *hand* the happie cost, VI. xi. 44. 8
Still slew the formost that came first to *hand* VI. xi. 46. 8
what mortall *hand* or heavens grace VI. xii. 8. 7
Knowing his fatall *hand* by former feare; VI. xii. 25. 8
Of butchers balefull *hand* to ground is feld, VI. xii. 30. 8
trembled underneath his mighty *hand*, VI. xii. 36. 8
The good Sir Pelleas him tooke in *hand*, VI. xii. 39. 6
Hecate, in whose almighty *hand* He plac't all rule VII. vi. 3. 3
an hory Old aged Sire, with hower-glasse in *hand*, VII. vi. 8. 6
raught forth her *hand* To pluck her downe VII. vi. 13. 2
his burning levin-brond in *hand* he tooke. VII. vi. 30. 9
He staid his *hand;* VII. vi. 31. 5
in his *hand* a javelin he did beare, VII. vii. 28. 6
in his *hand* he bore A boawe and shaftes, VII. vii. 29. 6
in his *hand* a sickle he did holde, VII. vii. 30. 8
Yet in his *hand* a spade he also hent, VII. vii. 32. 6
led a lovely Mayd Forth by the lilly *hand*, VII. vii. 37. 4
full her *hand* was found: VII. vii. 37. 5
In his one *hand* . . . He held a knife-hook; VII. vii. 38. 5
in th' other *hand* A paire of waights, VII. vii. 38. 6
in his *hand* a broad deepe boawle he beares, VII. vii. 41. 8
held in *hand* a mace, VII. vii. 44. 5
And eke his learned *hand* at pleasure guide, *Am.* xvii. 6
A greater craftesmans *hand* thereto doth neede, *Am.* xvii. 13
in *hand* my tunelesse harp I take, *Am.* xliv. 9
whom too cruell *hand* Did make the matter *Am.* xlviii. 1
With plenteous *hand* by heaven upon you thrown; *Am.* lxvi. 2
I in *hand* her yet halfe trembling tooke, *Am.* lxvii. 11
a byrd, that in ones *hand* doth spy Desired food, *Am.* lxxiii. 5
Agayne, I wrote it with a second *hand;* *Am.* lxxv. 3
in his *hand* . . . Him caught *Epig.* iv. 23
on it he hasty *hand* did lay, *Epig.* iv. 25
bring in *hand* Another gay girland, *Epith.* 41
Why blush ye, love, to give to me your *hand*, *Epith.* 238
And thou, *glad* Genius! in whose gentle *hand* *Epith.* 398
With which thou armest his resistlesse *hand*. *H.L.* 230
made Of that selfe mould, and that selfe Makers *hand*, *H.H.L.* 198
in her *hand* a scepter she doth hold, *H.H.B.* 192

Handed. *See* **Bloody-handed, Lily-handed, Nimbler-handed.**

Handle. perhaps ye things may *handle* soe, *Hub.* 641
best can *handle* his deceitfull wit *Col.* 693
His cruell wounds . . . They . . . *handle* softly, I. v. 29. 8
hilts were burnisht gold, and *handle* strong Of mother perle; I. vii. 30. 8
that they might him *handle* more at will, III. iv. 40. 3
Triamond to *handle* speare and shield, IV. ii. 42. 8
likewise Should *handle* as the rest of her allies, VII. vi. 30. 5
those lilly hands, . . . Shall *handle* you, *Am.* i. 3

Handled. afterwards I *handled* her so fayre, *D.* 120
his soveraine Dame So rudely *handled* by her foe he saw, I. iii. 41. 3
Ne tong did tell, ne hand these *handled* not; II. vii. 19. 7
eke the Prince like treaty *handeled*, III. i. 11. 3
every one as commune good her *handeled*. III. x. 36. 9
To be captiv'd and *handled* as he list, VI. viii. 13. 2

Handling. throgh their owne faire *handling* wisely wroght, *Hub.* 554

Handling—*Continued.*
Through his fine *handling*, and his cleanly play, *Hub.* 1015
To thinke how she through guyleful *handeling*, I. iii. 2. 4
the heavens, and your faire *handeling*, Have made you master I. viii. 28. 1
turne his earnest unto game, Through goodly *handling* II. i. 31. 2
through wise *handling* and faire governaunce, II. i. 54. 6
His rude assault and rugged *handeling* II. iv. 8. 1
Through wounds, and strokes, and stubborne *handeling*, II. iv. 33. 2
By their faire *handling*, III. ix. 31. 9
handling soft the hurts which she did get; IV. vii. 35. 7
Through stubborne *handling* of her love-sicke hart; V. v. 28. 2
Handling and turning them a thousand wayes: VI. ii. 39. 5
sternely with strong hand it from his *handling* kept. VI. v. 25. 9
Whose cruell *handling* when that Squire beheld, VI. vii. 45. 1
so hard *handling* those which best thee serve, *H.L.* 163

Handmaid. Did court the *handmayd* of my Lady deare, II. iv. 25. 2
Her faultie *Handmayd*, which that bale did breede, II. iv. 29. 8
great Dame Natures *handmaide* chearing every kind. III. iv. 56. 9
she did call Her nearest *handmayd*, V. v. 29. 2
To make one minime of thy poore *handmayd*, VI. x. 28. 6
Delivered to her *handmayd*, VI. xii. 6. 8
her owne *handmayd*, that Melissa hight, VI. xii. 14. 8
Fit for the *handmayd* of the Faery Queene. *Am.* lxxx. 14

Handmaid's. Doth not your *handmayds* life at your foot lie?' V. v. 31. 6

Handmaids. On her two pretty *handmaides* did attend, IV. xi. 47. 1
the Graces, . . . *Handmaides* of Venus, VI. x. 15. 2
ye three *handmayds* of the Cyprian Queene, *Epith.* 103
thousands more Thy *handmaides* be, *H.B.* 261

Hands. Why have your *hands* long sithence traveiled *Ro.* ix. 5
these old Romane works, built with your *hands*, *Ro.* xv. 13
That which no *hands* can evermore compyle. *Ro.* xxv. 14
Till that Barbarian *hands* it quite did spill, *Ro.* xxx. 10
Their *handes* they may not file. *S.C.* Jul. 192
blood Which she with cursed *hands* had shed before; *Gn.* 174
fortunes read Out of their *hands*, *Hub.* 699
wring Her wretched *hands* *T.M.* 170
with *hands* uncleane Dares to pollute *T.M.* 567
guiltie *hands* of enemies *Ti.* 299
whose sad *hands* Doo weave the direfull threds *D.* 16
Which in your noble *hands* for pledge I leave *Ded. Son.* vii. 9
with his clownish *hands* their tender wings He brusheth I. i. 23. 8
Wringing her *hands*, in wemens pitteous wise, I. i. 50. 7
Into the *hands* of hys accursed fone, I. ii. 23. 8
'O! spare with guilty *hands* to teare My tender sides I. ii. 31. 2
he . . . lickt her lilly *hands* with fawning tong, I. iii. 6. 2
quaking *hands*, and other signes of feare: I. iii. 12. 6
of his *hands* he had no governement, I. iv. 34. 4
Shouting, and clapping all their *hands* on hight, I. v. 16. 8
manly *hands* imbrewd in guilty blood Had never beene, I. vii. 47. 3
(Entire affection hateth nicer *hands*) I. viii. 40. 3
How to advaunce with favourable *hands*, I. ix. 1. 8
as pledges firme, right *hands* together joynd. I. ix. 18. 9
wash thy *hands* from guilt of bloody field: I. x. 60. 8
fame, That warlike *handes* ennoblest with immortall name; I. xi. 5. 9
With folded *hands*, and knees full lowly bent, I. xi. 32. 6
his baptized *hands* now greater grew, I. xi. 36. 4
in their *handes* sweet Timbrels all upheld on hight. I. xii. 6. 9
to his *handes* that writt he did betake, I. xii. 25. 8
Bad on that Messenger rude *hands* to reach. I. xii. 35. 3
His owne two *hands* the holy knotts did knitt, I. xii. 37. 1
His owne two *hands*, for such a turne most fitt, I. xii. 37. 3
out of caytives *handes* Himselfe he frees II. i. 1. 7
Whom his victorious *handes* did earst restore II. i. 2. 6
Laid first his filthie *hands* on virgin cleene, II. i. 10. 4
Wringing her *handes*, and making piteous mone: II. i. 13. 7
With right *hands* plighted, pledges of good will. II. i. 34. 2
Thy litle *hands* embrewd in bleeding brest II. i. 37. 8
in her streaming blood he did embay His litle *hands*, II. i. 40. 8
With feeble *hands* then stretched forth on hye, II. i. 49. 1
Babes bloody *handes* may not be clensd: II. ii. Arg.
His guiltie *handes* from bloody gore to cleene. II. ii. 3. 4
still the litle *hands* were bloody seene: II. ii. 3. 7
more to mighty *hands* then rightfull cause doth trust. II. ii. 29. 9
his pitious *handes* gan reare. II. iii. 6. 9
Forth creeping on his caitive *hands* and thies; II. iii. 35. 7
His mighty *hands* did on the madman lay, II. iv. 6. 4
With her two crooked *handes* she signes did make, II. iv. 13. 2
both her *handes* fast bound unto a stake, II. iv. 13. 5
both his *hands* fast bound behind his backe, II. iv. 14. 8
My hart, my *handes*, mine eies, and all assayd! II. iv. 28. 7
mortall *hands* may not withstand his might, II. iv. 42. 2
To ridd a wretched man from *handes* of hellish wight!' II. v. 23. 9
When ever his fiers *handes* he free mote fynd: II. v. 28. 4
Both of them high attonce their *handes* enhaunst, II. vi. 31. 1
Withold your bloody *handes* from battaill fierce; II. vi. 33. 3
The mightie martiall *handes* doe most commend: II. vi. 35. 5
that ought those puissant *hands* may marre: II. vi. 44. 8
Weake *handes*, but counsell is most strong in age'. II. vi. 48. 5
His cole-blacke *hands* did seeme to have ben seard II. vii. 3. 8
both his *handes*, most filthy feculent, II. vii. 61. 4
my *handes* I washt in purity, II. vii. 62. 8
living *handes* immortalizd his name. II. viii. 13. 5
her attaching thought her *hands* to tye; II. xi. 28. 6
With their rude *handes* and gryesly graplement; II. xi. 29. 3
Having off-shakt them and escapt their *hands*, II. xi. 33. 4
his *hands* Discharged of his bow II. xi. 33. 7
with his naked *hands* him forcibly assayld. II. xi. 41. 9
up he caught him twixt his puissant *hands*, II. xi. 46. 1
Impotence with her owne wilfull *hands* II. xi. 47. 7

Hands—*Continued.*
did them selves into their *hands* incline, II. xii. 54. 5
holy Church with faithlesse *handes* deface, III. iii. 34. 2
Al holding crosses in their *hands* on hye, III. iii. 38. 6
our weake *hands* . . . teach III. iii. 53. 3
up him taking in their tender *hands,* III. iv. 42. 1
A forest-bill, which both his *hands* did strayne; III. v. 21. 5
atweene her lilly *handes* twaine III. v. 33. 3
how he fell into the Gyaunts *hands,* III. vii. 46. 8
Her up betwixt his rugged *hands* he reard, III. viii. 35. 1
To save his people sad from victours vengefull *handes.* III. ix. 41. 9
As Hellene, . . . Did clap her *hands,* III. x. 12. 9
Upon his *handes* and feete he crept full light, III. x. 47. 2
he the powre of chaste *hands* might not beare, III. xi. 6. 3
Twixt both his *hands* few sparks he close did strayne, III. xii. 9. 7
both whose *hands* Were bounden fast, III. xii. 30. 6
Likewise unequall were her *handes* twaine; IV. i. 29. 1
To stay their *hands,* till he awhile had spoken; IV. ii. 21. 2
they at last their wrothfull *hands* let fall, IV. ii. 21. 8
plighted *hands* for ever friends to be. IV. iii. 49. 5
in their *hands* their idle troncheons held, IV. iv. 18. 8
With blistred *hands* emongst the cinders brent, IV. v. 35. 3
with *hands* impure To spoyle so goodly workmanship IV. vi. 17. 3
To bath their *hands* in bloud of dearest freend, IV. vi. 17. 8
laying both his *hands* upon his glave, IV. vii. 28. 2
Out of his *hands* could not redeeme her gage, IV. viii. 50. 7
they for nought their cruell *hands* would stay, IV. ix. 31. 3
she holds them with her blessed *hands.* IV. x. 35. 7
With golden *hands* and silver feete beside, V. ii. 10. 2
In whose right *hands* great power is contayned, V. ii. 19. 7
Still holding up her suppliant *hands* on hye, V. ii. 26. 4
her suppliant *hands,* those *hands* of gold, V. ii. 26. 6
loth he was his noble *hands* t' embrew V. ii. 52. 4
Had neede have mightie *hands* V. iv. 1. 3
bent against them selves their cruell *hands;* V. iv. 5. 7
With weapons in their *hands* as ready for to fight. V. iv. 21. 9
With both his *hands* behinde him pinnoed hard, V. iv. 22. 2
That he of womens *hands* so base a death should dy. V. iv. 22. 9
Meaning on him their cruell *hands* to lay, V. iv. 23. 8
Standing with emptie *hands* all weaponlesse, V. v. 14. 2
when they thought on Talus *hands* to lay, V. v. 19. 1
what their *hands* could earne by twisting linnen twyne. V. v. 22. 9
apply His mightie *hands* the distaffe vile to hold V. v. 24. 4
mighty *hands* forget their manlinesse; V. viii. 1. 5
Crying to them their cruell *hands* to stay, V. viii. 10. 8
They stayd their *hands,* when she thus gan to speake: V. viii. 11. 1
Eftsoones they gan their wrothfull *hands* to hold, V. viii. 12. 4
with both his *hands* unto him hayles The resty raynes, V. viii. 39. 5
she did at last commit All to his *hands,* V. x. 13. 2
Through his three double *hands* thrise multiplyde, V. xi. 6. 2
Gan into one assemble all the might Of all his *hands,* V. xi. 8. 5
holding up her wretched *hands* To him for aide, V. xi. 44. 8
That yet my love may from their *hands* be freed.' V. xi. 57. 5
Her *hands* were foule and durtie, V. xii. 30. 1
both their *hands* on hie At once did heave VI. i. 38. 1
her did sustaine With carefull *hands,* VI. iii. 28. 6
Kissing his *hands,* and crouching to the ground; VI. iv. 11. 5
Now wringing both his wretched *hands* in one, VI. v. 4. 4
holding up his *hands,* with silence mercie prayd. VI. vii. 25. 9
with cursed *hands* uncleane Whipping her horse, VI. vii. 39. 7
Led in a rope which both his *hands* did bynd; VI. vii. 49. 2
Delivered hath into your *hands* by gift, VI. viii. 1. 5
Abide, and from them lay your loathly *hands,* VI. viii. 7. 8
Laide heavy *hands* on him and held so strayte, VI. viii. 11. 3
all bootes not; they *hands* upon her lay: VI. viii. 41. 1
He first her *hands* beginneth to unbind, VI. viii. 50. 5
Yclad in home-made greene that her owne *hands* had dyde. VI. ix. 7. 9
out of his cruell *hands;* VI. ix. 11. 8
Whylest everie one with helping *hands* did strive, VI. ix. 15. 6
To stay their cruell *hands* from slaughter fell, VI. xi. 20. 5
Wringing her *hands,* and ruefully loud crying? VI. xi. 23. 7
Then all attonce their *hands* upon Molanna laid. VII. vi. 51. 9
those lilly *hands,* Which hold my life *Am.* i. 1
to yeeld my selfe into their *hands;* *Am.* xii. 10
her faire *hands* are Silver sheene: *Am.* xv. 12
in bloody bath . . . her cruell *hands* embrew. *Am.* xxxi. 12
whylst her bloody *hands* them slay, Her eyes looke lovely, *Am.* xlvii. 9
blesseth her with his two happy *hands,* *Epith.* 225
He freely gave to be both rent and torne Of cruell *hands,* *H.H.L.* 151
With bitter wounds through *hands,* through feet, and syde! *H.H.L.* 245
th' Aire . . . Never consum'd, nor quencht with mortall *hands;* *H.H.B.* 40

Hands'. with his owne *hands* might, VI. viii. 10. 5

Handsel. It dearely shall aby, and death for *handsell* pay. VI. xi. 15. 9

Handsome. In stead of them a *handsome* bat he held, *Hub.* 217
like a *handsome* swaine it him became. *Hub.* 242
in *handsome* wise Your selfe attyred, *Hub.* 487
Drew by the heare . . . A *handsom* stripling II. iv. 3. 7
for want of *handsome* time and place, III. vii. 60. 4
Hope in ranke, a *handsome* Mayd, III. xii. 13. 1

Handsomely. He would have slipt the coller *handsomly,* *Hub.* 269

Handwriting. grace . . . that accurst *hand-writing* doth deface. I. ix. 53. 8

Handy. to his *handy* swimming him betake. V. ii. 16. 3

Hang. and side did *hang* his hair, *Bel.*[1] vii. 3
Like wailefull widdowes *hangen* their crags; *S.C.* F. 82
hang theyr heads as they would learne to weepe; *S.C.* N. 134
Here will I *hang* my pype upon this tree: *S.C.* D. 141
snakes . . . *hang* in heapes, that horribly affray, *Gn.* 349
eke behind His scrip did *hang,* I. vi. 35. 9
stubs of trees . . . Did *hang* upon the ragged rocky knees; I. ix. 34. 3
Another harnesse which did *hang* thereby III. iii. 61. 2

Hang—*Continued.*
Did *hang* in long suspence what would ensew, VII. vii. 57. 6
Bynd up the locks the which *hang* scatterd light, *Epith.* 62

Hanged. his shield is *hangd* with bloody hew; I. v. 5. 8
here thy shield is *hangd* for victors hyre? I. v. 10. 7
stubs of trees . . . On which had many wretches *hanged* beene, I. ix. 34. 4
His chamber all was *hangd* about with rolls II. ix. 57. 6
King Ryence caused to be *hanged* hy III. iii. 59. 2
hangd on high with golden ribbands laced; IV. x. 8. 5
She causeth them be *hang'd* up out of hand; V. iv. 32. 4
Where he full shamefully was *hanged* by the hed. V. v. 18. 9
she causd his warlike armes Be *hang'd* on high, V. v. 21. 7
The spoiles of Princes *hang'd* which were in battel won. VI. viii. 42. 9

Hanging. *See* **Overhanging.**
side-long beard, and locks down *hanging* loast, *Bel.*[2] ix. 3
hanging heads did seeme his carefull case to weepe. *S.C.* Ja. 78
th' Ape a cassocke sidelong *hanging* downe; *Hub.* 354
by his belt his booke he *hanging* had: I. i. 29. 4
both stand sencelesse . . . Forgetfull of the *hanging* victory: I. ii. 16. 6
His sandy lockes, long *hanging* downe behind, II. v. 14. 4
bounches *hanging* downe seemd to entice II. xii. 54. 3
Downe *hanging* his dull head with heavy chere, III. xii. 16. 3
hanging downe his heavy countenaunce; III. xii. 18. 3
like a wide deepe poke, downe *hanging* low, IV. vii. 6. 2
Under the *hanging* of an hideous clieffe IV. xii. 5. 1
next her selfe her righteous ballance *hanging* bee. V. i. 11. 9
hanging down her head with heavie cheare, V. xi. 64. 4
by his side his hunters horne he *hanging* had. VI. ii. 5. 9
hanging up his armes and warlike spoyle, VI. v. 37. 8
hanging downe his head, did like a Mome appeare. VII. vi. 49. 9

Hania. Let Scaldis tell, and let tell *Hania,* II. x. 24. 1

Hannibal. Stout Scipio, and stubborne *Hanniball;* I. v. 49. 7

Hap. Where all worldes *hap* was reposed, *Bel.*[1] viii. 7
All the good *hap* of th' oldest times afore, *Ro.* xix. 6
Proud of his highest service, and good *hap,* *Van.* iv. 3
Ah! good Algrind! his *hap* was ill, *S.C.* Jul. 229
Hard is our *hap,* *Hub.* 170
evill *hap* Unworthy in such wretchednes doth wrap, *Hub.* 601
(O sad *hap,* and howre unfortunate!) *Mui.* 421
the Shepheards, which my *hap* did heare, *D.* 141
if any nycer wit Shall *hap* to heare, *As.* Pr. 14
Had not good *hap* those shepheards thether led. *As.* 144
fly, . . . Least to you *hap* that happened to me heare, I. ii. 31. 5
The heavie *hap* which on them is alight; I. iii. 20. 8
hope of new good *hap* he gan to feele; I. iii. 34. 8
helplesse *hap* it booteth not to mone. I. iv. 49. 5
she chaunced by good *hap* to meet A goodly knight, I. vii. 29. 1
'Faire Sir, I hope good *hap* hath brought You I. vii. 42. 5
empty sides . . . Could make a stony hart his *hap* to rew; I. viii. 41. 5
by good prayers, or by other *hap,* II. ii. 6. 7
to taken heed Of what might *hap.* II. iii. 21. 6
whether art it were or heedlesse *hap,* II. iii. 30. 6
'what man can shun the *hap,* II. iv. 17. 2
Hard is his *hap* that first fals in his jeopardee.' II. iv. 43. 9
'Least wee unweeting *hap* to be fordonne; II. xii. 11. 2
sad sorow and disdaine Of his hard *hap* III. iv. 54. 3
Their mother . . . had full blessed *hap* IV. ii. 43. 8
if I *hap* to fayle, you shall recure my right.' IV. vi. 9. 9
In Princes Court doe *hap* to sprout againe, IV. viii. 33. 4
pant with hope of that adventures *hap:* IV. x. 9. 2
I them both with equall *hap* defeated. IV. x. 10. 4
Cares not what evils *hap* to wretched wight; IV. xii. 6. 8
What evil *hap* to Marinell betid, V. iii. 10. 6
That made them grow so high t' all honorable *hap.'* VI. iv. 36. 9
How ever by hard *hap* he hether came, VI. v. 2. 8
For joy of such good *hap* by heavenly grace. VI. viii. 37. 5
destiny Or other dyrefull *hap* from heaven or hell VI. xi. 29. 8
Fayre Pastorella by great *hap* Her parents understands. VI. xii. Arg.
A gentle Bee . . . About him flew by *hap.* *Epig.* iv. 4
Till which we cease our hopefull *hap* to sing; *Epith.* 388

Hapless. For ruth and pitie of so *haples* plight: *Pet.*[2] v. 13
The *haplesse* mischiefe that has thee hent; *S.C.* S. 249
haplesse rising of some froward starre, *Gn.* 570
never didst thou heare more *haplesse* fate. *D.* 98
Much seemed he to mone her *haplesse* chaunce, I. iii. 25. 6
Who *haplesse,* and eke hopelesse, . . . Did to him pace I. vii. 11. 4
'Ensample make of him your *haplesse* joy, I. ix. 12. 1
That I may tell this *haplesse* history?' I. ix. 26. 4
though overcome in *haplesse* fight, II. x. 56. 8
full many had with *haplesse* doole Beene suncke, II. xii. 20. 3
What stony hart, that heares thy *haplesse* fate, III. ix. 39. 6
both are of thy *haplesse* hand extinct, III. xi. 37. 3
went away sore wounded of his *haplesse* hand. IV. iv. 21. 9
by what *haplesse* fate Or hard misfortune IV. vi. 47. 5
Unweeting of thine owne like *haplesse* plight: IV. vii. 10. 8
through that *haplesse* wound IV. viii. 19. 8
'Sir Turpine! *haplesse* man, what make you here? V. iv. 26. 1
'Most *haplesse* well ye may Me justly terme, V. iv. 27. 5
him captived hath in *haplesse* woe.' V. vi. 11. 3
Much was he grieved with that *haplesse* throe, V. viii. 35. 1
'My *haplesse* case Is not occasiond VI. i. 12. 5
with the horrour of her *haplesse* care VI. iii. 24. 7
There-on an heavy *haplesse* curse did lay; VII. vi. 55. 3
state In which he stood before his *haplesse* fate. *H.H.L.* 140

Haply. No: but *happely* I hym spyde, *S.C.* Mar. 31
Least that the Poplar *happely* should rew *Gn.* 219
least he my Loove *happely* chaunce to beholde. *Tetrasticon* 4
haply in her hart finde highest rowme III. v. 11. 3

Happed. if she *hapt* of any good to heare, V. xii. 32. 1
wretched sorrowes, which have often *hapt!* VI. v. 1. 4

Happely. *See* **Haply, Happily.**
Happen. ought may *happen,* . . . *S.C.* May 104
What did of late chaunce *happen* (*om.) to the Lyon stearne, *Hub.* 1250
May *happen* unto the most happiest wight; . . . *D.* 517
When as my hearse shall *happen* to your sightes, . . . *D.* 528
Into the which hereafter thou maist *happen* fall. . . . I. ix. 45. 9
if thou ever *happen* that same way To traveill, . . . III. iii. 8. 1
he feareth evill *happen* may; . . . III. x. 3. 5
to this gentle Squire did *happen* late, . . . IV. viii. 1. 2
Should *happen* this with living eye to see, . . . IV. x. 23. 6
That his decay should *happen* by a mayd. . . . IV. xii. 28. 5
unto his hand in chase did *happen* neare. . . . VI. ii. 6. 9
Happened. strange things *happened* (*hapned*[1]) me to see, . . *Pet.* i. 2
fly, . . . Least to you hap that *happened* to me heare, . . . I. ii. 31. 5
By that which lately *hapned* Una saw . . . I. x. 2. 1
Whom passing by she *happened* to meet: . . . II. xii. 56. 8
As Guyon *hapned* by the same to wend, . . . II. xii. 63. 5
Who all to her at large, as *hapned,* did relate. . . . IV. vii. 34. 9
all the accident there *hapned* plaine, . . . IV. viii. 46. 7
Tydings of all which there had *hapned* on the land. . . . IV. viii. 62. 9
It is so *hapned* that the heavens unjust, . . . V. v. 29. 7
Happier. In hope to finde there *happier* successe. . . . *Hub.* 658
Happiest. Harvey, the happy above *happiest* men . . . *Com. Son.* i. 1
May happen unto the most *happiest* wight; . . . *D.* 517
Happily. might I *happily* Unto you bring, . . . I. xi. 3. 8
Of other worldes he *happily* should heare, . . . II. Pr. 3. 8
had it not *happily* found rest . . . IV. iii. 34. 5
Betwixt him and his hurt bene *happily,* . . . IV. viii. 43. 7
Artegall, arriving *happily,* . . . V. iv. 6. 7
where *happily* he spide A rout of many people . . . V. iv. 21. 2
In which she wont to harbour *happily:* . . . V. x. 18. 6
Least ye therefore mote *happily* me blame, . . . V. xi. 52. 8
That had to any *happily* betid, . . . V. xii. 32. 2
Happiness. Sith so small thing his *happines* may varie. . . . *Van.* viii. 14
Live thou for ever in all *happinesse!* . . . *Gn.* 63
O! the great *happines,* which shepheards have, . . . *Gn.* 89
all the *happinesse* that heart desire, . . . *Hub.* 609
One joyous howre in blisfull *happines,* . . . *Hub.* 983
O soveraigne Lord! O soveraigne *happinesse,* . . . *T.M.* 515
Such *happinesse* have they . . . *T.M.* 517
Whose *happines* the heavens envying, . . . *Ti.* 24
Taste no one hower of *happines* or merth; . . . *Ti.* 46
where thou dost that *happines* enjoy, . . . *Ti.* 306
hath no hope of *happinesse* or blis. . . . *Ti.* 357
All *happinesse* in Hebes silver bowre, . . . *Ti.* 384
In state of blis, or stedfast *happinesse?* . . . *Ti.* 569
To live in heaven where *happines* is rife: . . . *Ti.* 670
Who rests not pleased with such *happines,* . . . *Mui.* 215
of all *happines* hath us deprived. . . . *Mui.* 416
'Long thus I joyed in my *happinesse,* . . . *D.* 148
Wherein eternall peace and *happinesse* doth dwell. . . . I. x. 55. 9
Affyaunce made, my *happinesse* begonne, . . . II. iv. 21. 4
Another *happines,* another end. . . . II. vii. 33. 4
such *happinesse* Heven doth to me envy, . . . II. ix. 7. 8
none does others *happinesse* envye; . . . II. xii. 58. 4
men of *happinesse* deprive. . . . III. iv. 57. 9
Such *happinesse* did, maulgre, to me spight, . . . III. v. 7. 5
courtly blis and wonted *happinesse,* . . . III. viii. 20. 8
to her selfe oft wisht like *happinesse:* . . . III. xii. 46. *or.*8
such as drinck, eternall *happinesse* do fynd. . . . IV. iii. 43. 9
I never joyed *happinesse* nor rest; . . . IV. ix. 39. 3
They soone would loath their lesser *happinesse,* . . . IV. x. 23. 7
gan their endlesse *happinesse* envye, . . . IV. x. 28. 4
strength and wealth and *happinesse* she lends, . . . IV. x. 34. 6
at her *happinesse* do fret and frowne; . . . V. viii. 17. 7
flourish in all wealth and *happinesse,* . . . V. x. 11. 6
certes I your *happinesse* envie, . . . VI. ix. 19. 8
now have prov'd what *happinesse* ye hold . . . VI. ix. 28. 3
here on earth is no sure *happinesse,* . . . VI. xi. 1. 7
Thenceforth they joy'd in *happinesse* together, . . . VI. xii. 10. 6
Hart need not wish none other *happinesse,* . . . *Am.* lxxii. 13
which they may long possesse With lasting *happinesse,* . . . *Epith.* 419
Ne ever should their *happinesse* decay, . . . *H.H.L.* 76
All joy, all blisse, all *happinesse,* have place; . . . *H.H.B.* 243
have thou . . . endlesse *happinesse* of thine owne name . . . *Proth.* 153
Happy. *See* **Foolhappy.**
shortly turne unto my *happie* rest, . . . *Pet.*[2] vii. 6
Live, *happie* spirits, th' honour of your name, . . . *Ro.* Env. 13
O *happy* Hobbinoll! I blesse thy state, . . . *S.C.* Jun. 9
sike *happy* cheere is turnd to heavie chaunce, . . . *S.C.* N. 103
O *happye* herse! . . . *S.C.* N. 170
O *happy* herse! . . . *S.C.* N. 180,190, 200
let an *happie* roome remaine for thee . . . *Gn.* 57
who can lead, then, a more *happie* life . . . *Gn.* 121
to the seates of *happie* soules admitted: . . . *Gn.* 478
Renown'd in choyce of *happie* marriage . . . *Gn.* 487
happie winde and weather entertaine, . . . *Gn.* 563
thrice *happie* then Was the condition of mortall men. . . . *Hub.* 149
their owne *happie* chaunce Them freely offred, . . . *Hub.* 962
Are thereby fild with *happie* influence; . . . *T.M.* 586
Harvey, the *happy* above happiest men . . . *Com. Son.* i. 1
vainly thinke your selves halfe *happie* then, . . . *Ti.* 199
'He, whilest he lived, *happie* was through thee, . . . *Ti.* 246
being dead, is *happie* now much more; . . . *Ti.* 247
Have purchast him in heaven an *happie* crowne, . . . *Ti.* 264
out of her *happie* womb did bring The sacred brood . . . *Ti.* 278
ere his *happie* soule to heaven went . . . *Ti.* 295
That *happie* there I maie thee alwaies see. . . . *Ti.* 308
O, *happie* were those dayes, thrice *happie* were! . . . *Ti.* 329

Happy—*Continued.*
now, more *happie* thou, and wretched wee . . . *Ti.* 330
'So *happie* are they, and so fortunate, . . . *Ti.* 393
in this halfe *happie* I doo read Good Melibae, . . . *Ti.* 435
who can him assure of *happie* day, . . . *Mui.* 218
unhappie *happie* Flie, Whose cruell fate . . . *Mui.* 234
May come their *happie* quiet to molest; . . . *D.* 284
How *happie* was I then, and wretched now! . . . *D.* 308
'How *happie* was I when I saw her . . . *D.* 309
'And ye, more *happie* Lovers! which enjoy . . . *D.* 512
he was not so *happie* as the rest. . . . *As.* 12
Thrise *happie* she, whom he to praise did chose. . . . *As.* 36
Full *happie* man (misweening much) was hee, . . . *As.* 101
all *happie* peace and plenteous store . . . *Col.* 310
'Thrise *happie* Mayd, . . . *Col.* 480
Thrise *happie* do I hold thee, noble swaine, . . . *Col.* 552
Why didst thou ever leave that *happie* place, . . . *Col.* 654
'*Happie* indeed (said Colin) I him hold, . . . *Col.* 660
still are wont most *happie* states t' annoy: . . . *Col.* 663
followd those which *happie* seemd to bee. . . . *Col.* 667
'Faire knight, borne under *happie* starre, . . . I. i. 27. 3
'O! who is that, which bringes me *happy* choyce Of death, . I. viii. 38. 3
'O *happy* Queene of Faeries! . . . I. ix. 16. 6
not so *happy* as mote *happy* bee: . . . I. ix. 27. 5
happy ease, which thou doest want and crave, . . . I. ix. 40. 2
her embracing, said; 'O *happy* earth, . . . I. x. 9. 1
bid her joy of that her *happy* brood; . . . I. x. 32. 2
'Thrise *happy* man,' said then the father grave, . . . I. x. 51. 1
before that cursed Dragon got *That* happy land, . . . I. xi. 29. 7
happy life to all which thereon fedd, . . . I. xi. 46. 5
their new joy, and *happie* victory . . . I. xii. 4. 3
'the troubler of my *happy* peace, . . . I. xii. 19. 2
Thrise *happy* man the knight himselfe did hold, . . . I. xii. 40. 6
happy land of Faery, Which I so much doe vaunt, . . . II. Pr. 1. 7
As wetherbeaten ship arryv'd on *happie* shore. . . . II. i. 2. 9
'Fayre sonne, God give you *happy* chaunce, . . . II. i. 31. 7
home ye may report thrise *happy* newes; . . . II. i. 33. 8
Thrise *happy* man, who fares them both atweene! . . . II. i. 58. 5
So *happy* peace they made and faire accord. . . . II. iii. 9. 1
happy blis And all delight does raigne, . . . II. iii. 39. 4
Unto her *happy* mansion attaine: . . . II. iii. 41. 4
Happy! who can abstaine, . . . II. iv. 44. 4
The joyes whereof and *happy* fruitfulnesse, . . . II. vi. 24. 3
more *happy* he then wise, . . . II. vi. 46. 4
Like Angels life was then mens *happy* cace; . . . II. vii. 16. 5
Such grace now to be *happy* is before thee laid.' . . . II. vii. 32. 9
Ne to be made so *happy* doe intend: . . . II. vii. 33. 2
'Thrise *happy* man,' (said then the Briton knight) . . . II. ix. 5. 1
An *happy* man in his first dayes he was, . . . II. x. 22. 1
happy father of faire progeny: . . . II. x. 22. 2
Next him king Leyr in *happie* peace long raynd, . . . II. x. 27. 1
O joyous memorie of *happy* time, . . . II. x. 50. 5
Nath'lesse the same enjoyed but short *happy* howre: . . . II. x. 57. 9
All *happy* peace and goodly government . . . II. xi. 2. 4
all his labor brought to *happy* end; . . . II. xi. 35. 2
Nothing on earth mote alwaies *happy* beene: . . . III. i. 10. 7
Happy this Realme, had it remayned ever since! . . . III. ii. 21. 9
Yet shall he long time warre with *happy* speed, . . . III. iii. 31. 3
each to assay Whether more *happy* were . . . III. iv. 46. 9
Should *happy* bee, and have immortall blis: . . . III. vi. 41. 3
in stedfast love and *happy* state . . . III. vi. 50. 6
Extremely joyed in so *happy* sight, . . . III. viii. 10. 2
next to none after that *happy* day, . . . III. viii. 13. 7
each take *happy* chaunce.' . . . III. viii. 18. 4
wicked Sprightes did fall from *happy* blis; . . . III. ix. 2. 8
spare thy *happy* daies, . . . III. xi. 19. 5
Made him seeme *happie* for so glorious theft; . . . IV. ii. 4. 8
'Lo! sluggish Knight, the victors *happie* pray! . . . IV. ii. 7. 5
To him was fallen for his *happie* lot, . . . IV. ii. 8. 4
This *happie* day I have to greete you well, . . . IV. ii. 23. 5
Long may you live in health and *happie* state!' . . . IV. ii. 23. 8
Then pardon, O most sacred *happie* spirit! . . . IV. ii. 34. 1
Most confidence and hope of *happie* speed, . . . IV. ii. 39. 6
Borne of one mother in one *happie* mold, . . . IV. ii. 41. 3
Borne at one burden in one *happie* morne; . . . IV. ii. 41. 4
Thrise *happie* mother, and thrise *happie* morne, . . . IV. ii. 41. 5
he that *happie* seemes, and least in payne, . . . IV. iii. 1. 8
none did ever see More *happie* creatures . . . IV. iii. 2. 5
The which Rinaldo drunck in *happie* howre, . . . IV. iii. 45. 3
With whom he ledd a long and *happie* life; . . . IV. iii. 52. 5
Thrise *happie* Ladie, and thrise *happie* knight, . . . IV. iv. 16. 7
So nought may be esteemed *happie* till the end. . . . IV. iv. 43. 9
joyd in *happy* peace, . . . IV. vii. 15. 3
An *happie* life with grace and good accord, . . . IV. viii. 18. 2
the *happie* soules, which doe possesse Th' Elysian fields . . . IV. x. 23. 4
never tasted blis Nor *happie* howre, . . . IV. x. 28. 2
with *happy* eye I spyde . . . IV. x. 48. 6
So ever loose, so ever *happy* be! . . . IV. xii. 11. 5
where so loose or *happy* that thou art, . . . IV. xii. 11. 6
what on earth can alwayes *happie* stand? . . . V. iii. 9. 1
the heavens unjust, Spighting my *happie* freedome, . . . V. v. 29. 8
'Mongst many which maligne her *happy* state, . . . V. viii. 18. 1
With which high God had blest her *happie* land, . . . V. ix. 30. 4
More *happie* mother would her surely weene . . . V. x. 7. 7
happy man,' (sayd then Sir Calidore) . . . VI. i. 5. 6
to these *happie* fortunes cruell fate . . . VI. iv. 30. 5
To *happie* blisse he was full high uprear'd, . . . VI. v. 12. 4
from the high degree of *happy* state Fell . . . VI. viii. 2. 8
feend that mote offend Their *happie* flockes, . . . VI. ix. 6. 3
to commend the *happie* life Which Shepheards lead, . . . VI. ix. 18. 8

Happy—*Continued.*
'How much' (sayd he) 'more *happie* is the state . . . . . . VI. ix. 19. 1
'If *happie,* then it is in this intent, ... VI. ix. 20. 2
maketh wretch or *happie,* rich or poore; . . . . . . VI. ix. 30. 2
The *happy* peace which there doth overflow, ... VI. x. 3. 4
Right *happy* thou that mayst them freely see! . . . . . . VI. x. 19. 8
'Not I so *happy* . . . As thou unhappy, ... VI. x. 20. 1
At length espyes at hand the *happie* cost, ... VI. xi. 44. 8
In that still *happy* state for ever to abide. . . . . . . VII. vi. 5. 9
all the heavenly crew Of *happy* wights, ... VII. vi. 14. 4
Happy, ye leaves! when as those lily hands, ... *Am.* i. 1
And *happy* lines! on which, with starry light, ... *Am.* i. 5
happy rymes! bath'd in the sacred brooke . . . . . . *Am.* i. 9
Thrise *happie* she! that is so well assured . . . . . . *Am.* lix. 1
Most *happy* she, that most assur'd doth rest; . . . . . . *Am.* lix. 13
he most *happy,* who such one loves best. . . . . . . *Am.* lix. 14
the *happy* shore, In which I hope . . . to arryve: . . . . . . *Am.* lxiii. 5
Most *happy* he! that can at last atchyve . . . so sweet a rest; *Am.* lxiii. 9
those *happy* blessings, which ye have . . . . . . *Am.* lxvi. 1
The *happy* purchase of my glorious spoile, ... *Am.* lxix. 13
Most *happy* letters! . . . With which that *happy* name was first desynd, ... *Am.* lxxiv. 1, 2
which three times thrise *happy* hath me made, ... *Am.* lxxiv. 3
Sweet thoughts! I envy your so *happy* rest, ... *Am.* lxxvi. 13
blesseth her with his two *happy* hands, ... *Epith.* 225
happy influence upon us raine, ... *Epith.* 416
Thrise *happie* man! . . . . . . *H.L.* 209
thus farre *happie* he himselfe doth weene, ... *H.L.* 212
heavens such *happie* grace did to him lend, ... *H.L.* 213
To live thus *happie* as her grace to gaine. . . . . . . *H.L.* 244
all delight and joyous *happie* rest, ... *H.L.* 281
That *happie* port for ever to recure! . . . . . . *H.L.* 298
Hating the *happie* light from which they fell. . . . . . . *H.H.L.* 91
him restore unto that *happie* state . . . . . . *H.H.L.* 139
Faire is the heaven where *happy* soules have place, ... *H.H.B.* 78
But who so may, thrise *happie* man him hold, ... *H.H.B.* 239
All *happie* joy and full contentment fynd. . . . . . . *H.H.B.* 287
whom this *happie* hower Doth leade . . . . . . *Proth.* 92

Haps. Through manie *haps,* which needs not here to tell, . . . *Hub.* 360
The hard adventures and strange *haps* to tell, ... IV. v. 28. 8
haps to light Uppon two stubborne oakes, ... V. vi. 40. 1
What *haps* to day to me to morrow may to you. . . . . . . VI. i. 41. 9
Oftimes it *haps* that sorrowes of the mynd . . . . . . VI. iv. 28. 8

Haqueton. on his *hacqueton* did lyte, ... II. viii. 38. 7

Harbinger. sleepe (the *harbenger* of wearie wights) . . . . *D.* 470

Harbor. where *harbrough* nis to see, ... *S.C.* Jun. 19
Faire *harbour* that them seems, ... I. i. 7. 9
He seemd in hart to *harbour* thoughts unkind, ... I. iv. 38. 8
more heavy plight Then that I . . . *harbour* in mine hart: . . I. vii. 25. 4
such as want of *harbour* did constraine: . . . . . . I. x. 37. 8
Did closely *harbour* such a jealous guest) . . . . . . V. vii. 27. 5
In which she wont to *harbour* happily: . . . . . . V. x. 18. 6
harbour here in safety from those ravenous dogs.' . . . . . . V. x. 23. 9
Some place shall us receive and *harbour* yield; . . . . . . V. x. 24. 2
For his sicke charge some *harbour* there to seeke; . . . . . . VI. iii. 37. 6
a ship . . . Now farre from *harbour* likely to be lost, ... VI. iv. 1. 3
Finde *harbour* fit to comfort her great neede; . . . . . . VI. v. 31. 4
The sacred *harbour* of that hevenly spright; . . . . . . *Am.* lxxvi. 4

Harbored. Left for sweete Muses to be *harboured,* . . . . *Ded. Son.* v. 7
Should *harbour'd* be and all those Woods deface, ... VII. vi. 55. 5
have *harbourd* since their first descent . . . . . . *H.B.* 201

Harbors. Sweete quiet *harbours* in his harmeless head, ... *Gn.* 134
Regard of honour *harbours* more than ought, ... *Hub.* 718
The noble hart that *harbours* vertuous thought, ... I. v. 1. 1

Harbrough. *See* **Harbor.**

Hard. *See* **Heard.**
harde by a violent streame, ... *Bel.*[1] xi. 7
Hard by a rivers side . . . . . . *Bel.* x. 1
makes me wayle so *hard* (*harde*[1]) a destenie. . . . . . . *Pet.* i. 14
Was this (ye Romans) your *hard* destinie, ... *Ro.* xxiv. 9
Hard by his side grewe a bragging Brere, ... *S.C.* F. 115
with her *hard* hold, and straight embracing, ... *S.C.* May 99
leave to live *hard,* and learne to ligge soft: . . . . . . *S.C.* May 125
is *hard* to asswage: . . . . . . *S.C.* May 137
a yong alder *hard* beside him pight, ... *Gn.* 299
Its *hard* to read: . . . . . . *Gn.* 303
Through their *hard* barke his silver sound receav'd. . . . . . . *Gn.* 456
of Giaunts, *hard* to be beleeved; . . . . . . *Hub.* 31
disliking of their evill And *hard* estate, ... *Hub.* 47
the Ape, beginning well to wey This *hard* adventure, ... *Hub.* 113
Hard is our hap, ... *Hub.* 170
husbands life is labourous and *hard?* . . . . . . *Hub.* 266
Its an *hard* case, when men of good deserving . . . . . . *Hub.* 369
Livings in court be gotten, though full *hard;* . . . . . . *Hub.* 514
to compas anie sute not *hard,* . . . . . . *Hub.* 886
That none might enter but with issue *hard:* . . . . . . *Hub.* 1116
kept them lowe, and streigned verie *hard.* . . . . . . *Hub.* 1190
th' hayling darts of heaven beating *hard.* . . . . . . *Mui.* 80
that any should bemone My *hard* mishap, ... *D.* 76
No chace so *hard,* but he therein had skill. . . . . . . *As.* 84
Of great unkindnesse, and of usage *hard,* . . . . . . *Col.* 165
being to that swaine too cruell *hard,* . . . . . . *Col.* 909
hard by a forests side, ... I. i. 34. 2
he againe Shooke him so *hard,* . . . . . . I. i. 42. 6
You, whom my *hard* avenging destinie Hath made judge . . . I. i. 51. 8
On silly Dame, subject to *hard* mischaunce, ... I. ii. 21. 3
So *hard* the discord was to be agreede. . . . . . . I. ii. 37. 7
a faythfull mate Of her sad troubles and misfortunes *hard:* . . I. iii. 9. 4
what *hard* mishap is this, That hath thee hether brought . . I. iii. 39. 2
few returned, having scaped *hard,* . . . . . . I. iv. 3. 3

Hard—*Continued.*
greater conquest of *hard* love he gaynes, ... I. vi. 3. 8
he would learne The Lyon stoup to him . . . (A lesson *hard*) . I. vi. 25. 8
famous *harde* atchievements still pursew; . . . . . . I. vii. 45. 5
by *hard* meanes enforcing her to stay, ... I. viii. 25. 8
'Full *hard* it is,' (quoth he) . . . . . . I. ix. 6. 6
his sinewes woxen weake and raw, Through . . . *hard* constraint, I. x. 2. 4
Wherein darke things were writt, *hard* to be understood. . . . I. x. 13. 9
whether dread did dwell . . . is *hard* to tell. . . . . . I. x. 14. 5
'Unhappy falls that *hard* necessity,' . . . . . . I. xii. 19. 1
through perils straunge and *hard,* . . . . . . I. xii. 31. 8
Of late most *hard* achiev'ment by you donne, ... II. i. 32. 2
Through many *hard* assayes which did betide; . . . . . . II. i. 35. 2
(*hard* fortune ye may ghesse) . . . . . . II. i. 51. 1
Hard help at need! So deare thee, babe, I bought; . . . . II. i. 53. 8
'Ye bene right *hard* amated, ... II. ii. 5. 3
hath his sword through *hard* assay forgone, ... II. iii. 12. 6
oft approv'd in many *hard* assay; . . . . . . II. iii. 15. 7
What *hard* mishap him brought to such distresse, ... II. iv. 16. 8
'here comes, and is *hard* by, A knight . . . . . . II. iv. 40. 5
Hard is his hap that first fals in his jeopardee.' . . . . . . II. iv. 43. 9
Those that were low themselves held others *hard,* . . . . . . II. vii. 47. 7
thy faithfull aide in *hard* assay, ... II. viii. 7. 4
cleaving the *hard* steele, did deepe invade . . . . . . II. viii. 45. 4
hard adventure which I have in hand, ... II. ix. 8. 8
Him selfe addrest to that adventure *hard:* . . . . . . II. xi. 3. 8
many *hard* Atchievement wrought, ... II. xi. 15. 3
Flying from Junoes wrath and *hard* assay, ... II. xii. 13. 5
hard at hand they spy . . . . . . II. xii. 18. 5
Both firmely armd for every *hard* assay, ... II. xii. 38. 8
Right *hard* it was for wight which did it heare, ... II. xii. 70. 5
So *hard* a workemanship adventure darre, ... III. Pr. 2. 8
for witnes of his *hard* assay . . . . . . III. i. 2. 5
many *hard* adventures did atchieve; . . . . . . III. i. 3. 6
shamefuller regrett For thy *hard* fortune . . . . . . III. i. 8. 3
there so *hard* besett . . . . . . III. i. 8. 5
Seeking adventures *hard,* to exercise Their puissaunce, . . . III. i. 14. 3
'Perdy,' (said Britomart) 'the choise is *hard;* . . . . . . III. i. 27. 6
To hunt out perilles and adventures *hard,* . . . . . . III. ii. 7. 2
That man to *hard* conditions to bind, ... III. ii. 13. 7
Other then my *hard* fortune to deplore, ... III. ii. 39. 7
Should of his dearest daughters *hard* misfortune heare. . . . III. iii. 5. 9
The *hard* beginne that meetes thee in the dore, ... III. iii. 21. 8
How to effect so *hard* an enterprize, ... III. iii. 51. 6
t' atchieve an *hard* emprize; . . . . . . III. iii. 53. 7
Some *hard* mishap in hazard of his life. . . . . . . III. iv. 24. 6
A lesson too too *hard* for living clay . . . . . . III. iv. 26. 3
the *hard* rocks could scarse from tears refraine; . . . . . . III. iv. 35. 7
the *hard* steele his pillow. . . . . . . III. iv. 53. 9
sad sorow and disdaine Of his *hard* hap . . . . . . III. iv. 54. 3
till him oppressed *hard* The heavie plague . . . . . . III. v. 14. 8
Ne ever pitty may relent his malice *hard.* . . . . . . III. vi. 39. 9
as if her former dred Were *hard* behind, ... III. vii. 2. 6
Need teacheth her this lesson *hard* and rare, ... III. vii. 4. 3
brought she was now to so *hard* constraint, ... III. vii. 10. 7
Her *hard* pursewd, and sought for to suppresse. . . . . . . III. vii. 37. 5
on his helmet martelled so *hard* . . . . . . III. vii. 42. 3
used her so *hard* To reave her honor, ... III. viii. 14. 8
What *hard* misfortune brought me to this same; . . . . . . III. viii. 23. 8
Hard is to teach an old horse amble trew: . . . . . . III. viii. 26. 3
to be free from *hard* restraynt and gealous feares. . . . . . III. ix. 4. 9
with watch and *hard* restraynt . . . . . . III. ix. 6. 8
Did all the way him follow *hard* behynd; . . . . . . III. x. 55. 6
to compasse Philliras *hard* love, ... III. xi. 43. 7
shrunck when *hard* thereon he lay. . . . . . . III. xii. 10. 9
whose names is *hard* to read: . . . . . . III. xii. 25. 2
both fitt for *hard* emprize: . . . . . . III. xii. 28. 2
That seem'd full *hard* t' accord two things . . . . . . IV. i. 11. 9
of their loves did treat, And *hard* adventures, ... IV. i. 16. 2
Hard by the gates of hell her dwelling is; . . . . . . IV. i. 20. 1
whether were more false full *hard* it is to tell. . . . . . . IV. i. 32. 9
hard it was to weene which harder were. . . . . . . IV. iii. 7. 5
In quyent disguise, full *hard* to be descride: . . . . . . IV. iv. 39. 3
So *hard* this Idole was to be ared, ... IV. v. 15. 7
The *hard* adventures and strange haps to tell, ... IV. v. 28. 8
bound Upon an *hard* adventure . . . . . . IV. vi. 42. 3
by what haplesse fate Or *hard* misfortune . . . . . . IV. vi. 47. 6
had it bene right *hard* him to withstand, ... IV. vii. 25. 8
His *hard* mishap in dolor to deplore, ... IV. vii. 39. 7
what heavens *hard* disgrace, Or wrath of cruell wight . . . IV. viii. 14. 7
Against all *hard* mishaps and fortunelesse misfare. . . . . IV. viii. 27. 9
rare And *hard* to finde, ... IV. viii. 29. 7
More *hard* for hungry steed t' abstaine . . . . . . IV. viii. 29. 9
all the way from trotting *hard* to spare; . . . . . . IV. viii. 37. 8
hard behind his backe his foe was prest, ... IV. viii. 41. 6
hard unto his crowne The shield it drove, ... IV. viii. 42. 6
An *hard* mishap and disaventrous case . . . . . . IV. viii. 51. 3
Hard is the doubt, and difficult to deeme, ... IV. ix. 1. 1
Of two full *hard* to read the harder theft: . . . . . . IV. ix. 36. 6
Britomart did him importune *hard* . . . . . . IV. ix. 41. 2
My *hard* mishaps that ye may learne to shonne; . . . . . . IV. x. 3. 7
on that *hard* adventure forth I went, ... IV. x. 5. 1
shew of perill *hard* . . . . . . IV. x. 17. 4
in *hard* assaies Were cowards knowne, ... IV. x. 18. 6
the things which come through *hard* distresse. . . . . . . IV. x. 28. 9
'The cause . . . Was *hard* to know, ... IV. x. 41. 2
in thoughts lesse *hard* and bold, ... IV. xi. 22. 4
count the starres on hye, Or ought more *hard,* . . . . . . IV. xi. 53. 3
his *hard* rocky hart for no entreating Will yeeld, ... IV. xii. 7. 3
To come of him for using her so *hard,* . . . . . . IV. xii. 12. 3

Hard—*Continued.*
An *hard* adventure, which did then befall, . . . V. i. 3. 4
there no substance was so firme and *hard,* . . . V. i. 10. 6
wend with him on his adventure *hard;* . . . V. i. 30. 5
A noble Knight, and tride in *hard* assayes; . . . V. iii. 5. 2
With both his hands behinde him pinnoed *hard,* . . . V. iv. 22. 2
falne on you by heavens *hard* direction . . . V. iv. 26. 7
Through *hard* adventures deedes of armes to try, . . . V. iv. 29. 2
No hand so cruell, nor no hart so *hard,* . . . V. v. 13. 5
So *hard* it is to be a womans slave. . . . V. v. 23. 5
'Bound unto me but not with such *hard* bands . . . V. v. 33. 1
Let him lodge *hard,* and lie in strawen bed, . . . V. v. 50. 5
least some *hard* mishap Had him misfalne . . . V. vi. 4. 1
by *hard* mishap doth lie In wretched bondage, . . . V. vi. 10. 6
with *hard* enduraunce had Heard to the end, . . . V. vi. 17. 4
bake their sides uppon the cold *hard* stone, . . . V. vii. 9. 3
whilest in hand it gryping *hard* he hent, . . . V. ix. 18. 4
on both sides was then debating *hard;* . . . V. ix. 36. 8
rare in-sight *hard* matters to revele; . . . V. ix. 39. 2
her selfe did hyde from his *hard* tyranny. . . . V. x. 18. 9
orders new Imposd on it with many a *hard* condition, . . . V. x. 27. 7
the Prince *hard* preased in betweene, . . . V. x. 37. 6
Hard is the case the which ye doe complaine; . . . V. xi. 55. 2
Yet not so *hard* (for nought so *hard* may light . . . V. xi. 55. 3
Uppon an *hard* adventure sore bestad, . . . VI. i. 4. 2
Atchiev'd so *hard* a quest, as few before; . . . VI. i. 5. 8
what *hard* mishap thee brought . . . VI. i. 12. 1
uppon yond rocky hill, *Hard* by a streight, . . . VI. i. 13. 2
gan to drive at him more *hard.* . . . VI. i. 20. 9
hard at him did lay; . . . VI. i. 24. 2
Full on the breast him strooke, so strong and *hard* . . . VI. iv. 5. 7
And held the same so *hard,* . . . VI. iv. 6. 8
An *hard* adventure with unhappie end, . . . VI. iv. 17. 7
How ever by *hard* hap he hether came, . . . VI. v. 2. 8
Now beating his *hard* head upon a stone, . . . VI. v. 4. 5
Bout which whilest he was busied thus *hard,* . . . VI. v. 11. 1
Full like ere long to have escaped *hard;* . . . VI. v. 21. 4
gainst the cold *hard* earth so sore him strake, . . . VI. vii. 11. 4
So *hard* a taske as life for hyre to sell; . . . VI. vii. 15. 3
Through such her stubborne stifnesse and *hard* hart, . . . VI. vii. 31. 1
abide the death that *hard* before you stands.' . . . VI. viii. 7. 9
For penaunce of my proud and *hard* rebellious hart. . . . VI. viii. 19. 9
night arrived *hard* at hand, . . . VI. ix. 16. 3
To Merchants, which them kept in bondage *hard,* . . . VI. x. 43. 5
Putting his puissaunce forth, pursu'd so *hard,* . . . VI. xii. 30. 3
So *hard* it is for any living wight . . . VII. vii. 9. 1
So *hard* it is to kindle new desire . . . *Am.* vi. 9
Yet cannot I, . . . soften her *hard* hart; . . . *Am.* xviii. 6
to so *hard* a hart Given so goodly giftes . . . *Am.* xxxi. 1
Her hart more *harde* then yron . . . *Am.* xxxii. 6
hard t' atchieve and bring to end. . . . *Am.* li. 8
Ne ought so *hard,* but he, . . . Mote soften it . . . *Am.* li. 9
Fayre be ye sure, but *hard* and obstinate, . . . *Am.* lvi. 9
By so *hard* handling those . . . *H.L.* 163
things *hard* gotten men more dearely deeme. . . . *H.L.* 168
So *hard* those heavenly beauties be enfyred . . . *H.L.* 169
the *hard* diamond which them both doth passe. . . . *H.H.B.* 154

Hard-avenging. *See* **Avenging, Hard.**

Harden. That fire . . . should *harden* yse; . . . *Am.* xxx. 10

Hardened. Upon his crest the *hardned* yron fell, . . . I. xi. 24. 4
his more *hardned* crest was armd so well, . . . I. xi. 24. 5
the revenging steele . . . *hardned* with that holy water dew . . . I. xi. 36. 2
hardned more with my aboundant teares: . . . IV. xii. 7. 5
Their *hardned* hearts, enur'd to bloud and cruelty. . . . V. viii. 1. 9
With *hardned* frosts of former winters ire, . . . VII. vii. 11. 4
if in your *hardned* brest ye hide . . . *Am.* xxv. 9

Hardens. She laughes, and *hardens* evermore her hart. . . . *Am.* liv. 12

Harder. his *harder* fortune was to fall Under my speare: . . . I. ii. 36. 6
His *harder* hyde would nether perce nor bight, . . . I. xi. 16. 4
Nor *harder* was from Cerberus greedy jaw To plucke a bone, . . . I. xi. 41. 4
A *harder* lesson to learne Continence . . . II. vi. 1. 1
With *harder* meanes he cast her to subdew, . . . III. viii. 40. 7
discord *harder* is to end then to begin. . . . IV. i. 20. 9
(The *harder* it to make them well agree) . . . IV. ii. 38. 4
hard it was to weene which *harder* were. . . . IV. iii. 7. 5
Of two full hard to read the *harder* theft: . . . IV. ix. 36. 6
That *harder* may be ended, then begonne: . . . IV. x. 3. 4
The *harder* wonne, the firmer will abide. . . . *Am.* vi. 4
harder growes the more I her intreat! . . . *Am.* xxx. 4
harder growes, the *harder* she is smit . . . *Am.* xxxii. 11

Hardest. make the *hardest* flint to flowe! . . . *S.C.* Jun. 114
My bed the ground that *hardest* I may finde; . . . *D.* 377
hardest heart would bleede to hear their piteous mone. . . . I. viii. 36. 9
Each goodly thing is *hardest* to begin; . . . I. x. 6. 1
the *hardest* hart of stone Would hardly finde . . . III. viii. 1. 7
hardest marble weares; . . . IV. xii. 7. 2
men . . . Are now transformed into *hardest* stone; . . . V. Pr. 2. 5
The *hardest* steele, in tract of time doth teare: . . . *Am.* xviii. 2
The *hardest* yron soone doth mollify; . . . *Am.* xxxii. 2
ymages Of *hardest* marble are of purpose made, . . . *Am.* li. 2

Hardihead. Puft up with pride of Romane *hardiehead,* . . . *Ro.* xi. 3
Crave pardon for my *hardyhedde.* . . . *To his Booke* 12
Full of brave courage and bold *hardyhed,* . . . *Mui.* 27
Enflam'd with fury and fiers *hardy hed,* . . . I. iv. 38. 7

Hardily. nought they feard, but past on *hardily,* . . . II. xii. 39. 5
full of fire and greedy *hardiment,* . . . I. i. 14. 1

Hardiment. prickt forth . . . heat of *hardiment,* . . . I. ix. 12. 6
mercie, Lord, For mine offence and heedelesse *hardiment,* . . . II. i. 27. 2
Hardly could he endure his *hardiment,* . . . II. ii. 37. 8
To make more triall of his *hardiment,* . . . III. i. 2. 8

Hardiment—*Continued.*
With steadfast corage and stout *hardiment:* . . . III. i. 19. 8
By your good counsell, or bold *hardiment,* . . . III. v. 10. 7
had he not the hart, nor *hardiment,* . . . III. vii. 16. 3
in his port appeared manly *hardiment.* . . . III. viii. 44. 9
straunge affaires, and noble *hardiment,* . . . III. ix. 53. 2
courage full of haughtie *hardiment,* . . . IV. ii. 39. 2
Met him mid-way with equall *hardiment,* . . . IV. iv. 28. 8
Whom he assayld with dreadlesse *hardiment,* . . . V. iii. 11. 3
To wrecke on them their follies *hardyment:* . . . V. iv. 24. 5
thankt be God, and your good *hardiment,* . . . V. viii. 23. 5
thy love, for lacke of *hardiment,* . . . hast shamed . . . VI. vi. 33. 7
in his hand, with heedlesse *hardiment,* Him caught . . . *Epig.* iv. 23

Hardiness. his too haughtie *hardines* might reare Some hard mishap . . . III. iv. 24. 5
with great *hardinesse* Her hard pursewd, . . . III. vii. 37. 4
through great prowesse and bold *hardinesse,* . . . III. ix. 34. 6
At whose strange sight and haughty *hardinesse* He wondred . . . VII. vi. 17. 4

Hardize. *See* **Foolhardice.**

Hardly. *Hardly* forbearen, but have it they must: . . . *S.C.* May 135
Hardly my selfe escaped thilke payne, . . . *S.C.* S. 66
Hardly, naythles, were they restrayned so, . . . *Hub.* 1073
hardly did refraine, But that with thunder bolts . . . *Hub.* 1235
Of rustick muse full *hardly* to be betterd. . . . *D.* 231
he . . . *hardly* was restreined of that aged sire. . . . I. ii. 5. 9
Which *hardly* doen, at length she gan them pray, . . . I. iii. 14. 8
She *hardly* yet perswaded was to stay, . . . I. vi. 28. 4
So *hardly* he the flitted life does win . . . I. vii. 21. 7
Whom *hardly* he from flying forward stayd, . . . I. ix. 23. 5
Could *hardly* him intreat to tell his grief: . . . I. x. 24. 2
hardly could bee hurt who was already stong. . . . II. i. 3. 9
fish . . . new bait wil *hardly* byte. . . . II. i. 4. 9
Hardly could he endure his hardiment, . . . II. ii. 37. 8
more *hardly* he mote him withstond. . . . II. v. 22. 9
With some late perill which he *hardly* past, . . . III. v. 3. 4
full *hardly* was assayd Of deadly daunger, . . . III. v. 13. 1
hardly finde to aggravate her griefe; . . . III. viii. 1. 8
Escaped *hardly, hardly* praisd his wedlock good. . . . III. ix. 42. 9
hardly he with life away does fly, . . . III. x. 53. 8
hardly of her chearefull speech Did comfort take, . . . IV. vi. 38. 1
hardly could he come the carle to touch, . . . IV. vii. 27. 3
Where *hardly* eye mote see bright heavens face . . . IV. vii. 38. 7
By which I *hardly* past with much adoe: . . . IV. x. 57. 7
the Bull hath . . . So *hardly* butted . . . V. Pr. 6. 2
Can *hardly* but by Sacrament be tride, . . . V. i. 25. 2
That yron heart it *hardly* could sustaine: . . . VI. i. 30. 6
he found That *hardly* passable on foote it was; . . . VI. iii. 30. 2
Albe the wyld-man *hardly* would refraine. . . . VI. v. 27. 5
hardly one could know . . . VI. viii. 13. 8
but *hardly* seene by candle-light, . . . VI. xi. 13. 2
Him *hardly* forward drew, . . . VI. xi. 38. 3
Yet as it was, I *hardly* scap't with paine. . . . *Am.* xvi. 14
Within my hart, though *hardly* it can shew . . . *Am.* xlv. 5
stormes and tempests . . . Which *hardly* I endured . . . *Am.* lxiii. 2
What brave exploit, what perill *hardly* wrought, . . . *H.L.* 220

Hardness. mickle want and *hardnesse* suffered; . . . *Hub.* 944
Whose utmost *hardnesse* I before had tryde, . . . *Col.* 673
Enur'd to *hardnesse* and to homely fare, . . . IV. viii. 27. 6
My former *hardnesse* first I faire excusd; . . . IV. viii. 60. 5
Let him feele *hardnesse* of thy heavie arme: . . . V. v. 49. 8
cruelty and *hardnesse* from you chace, . . . VI. viii. 2. 4
Her *hardnes* blame, which I should more commend? . . . *Am.* li. 6

Hardy. *See* **Foolhardy.**
hardie will he had To overcome, . . . *Gn.* 303
Fierce Peleus, and the *hardie* Telamon, . . . *Gn.* 482
him the Foxe with *hardy* words did stay, . . . *Hub.* 957
dare his *hardy* hand to those outstretch, . . . *Hub.* 974
by force I conquered were Of *hardie* Saxons, . . . *Ti.* 114
Both wise and *hardie,* (too *hardie,* alas!) . . . *As.* 72
The one upon his *hardie* head him plaste, . . . I. i. 47. 3
to contend With *hardy* fowle . . . I. xi. 19. 6
him in *hardy* battayle overcame, . . . I. xii. 20. 4
through *hardy* enterprize Many great Regions are discovered, . . . II. Pr. 2. 3
Was hight Sir Huddibras, an *hardy* man; . . . II. ii. 17. 2
For his bold feates and *hardy* confidence, . . . II. iv. 41. 3
'*Hardy* Elfe, . . . I read thee rash . . . II. vii. 7. 6
Well hoped hee, ere long that *hardy* guest, . . . II. vii. 27. 1
Since he this *hardy* enterprize began: . . . II. vii. 65. 7
hardy Nennius, whom he yet did slay, . . . II. x. 49. 4
he was not so *hardy* to abide That bitter stownd, . . . II. xi. 25. 4
Dare not for dread his *hardy* hand expose, . . . III. i. 46. 8
For *hardie* thing it is, to weene by might . . . III. ii. 13. 6
the *hardy* Mayd (with love to frend) . . . III. iii. 14. 5
with *hardy* enterprise Shall backe repulse the valiaunt Brockwell . . . III. iii. 35. 4
That stroke the *hardy* Squire did sore displease, . . . III. v. 19. 6
He from such *hardy* boldnesse was restraynd, . . . III. v. 44. 8
her the *hardy* knight pursewd so nye . . . III. vii. 44. 5
of the *hardie* Britomarts successe: . . . III. xii. 43. *or.*5
These three that *hardie* chalenge tooke in hand, . . . IV. iii. 3. 1
the *hardy* Satyrane Appear'd in place, . . . IV. iv. 26. 2
could awhape An *hardy* hart; . . . IV. vii. 5. 5
much renound For noble courage and for *hardie* race, . . . V. viii. 36. 8
mote appall An *hardie* courage, . . . V. ix. 33. 5
to make her *hardy* flight. . . . V. xi. 24. 9
The *hardy* boy . . . Upon him set, . . . VI. v. 16. 1
who so *hardie* hand on her doth lay, . . . VI. xi. 15. 8
when the *hardy* Titanesse beheld . . . VII. vi. 10. 1
wote thou this, thou *hardy* Titanesse, . . . VII. vi. 33. 1
Such haughty mynds, enur'd to *hardy* fight, . . . *Am.* xiv. 7

Hardy—*Continued.*
like fresh Eagle, make his *hardie* flight . . . *H.L.* 69
Hare. hunt the hartlesse *hare* til shee were tame. . . . *S.C.* D. 28
from them fled, as light-foot *hare* from vew . . . III. iv. 46. 4
Hark. *Harke* then, ye jolly shepheards, to my song.' . . . *Col.* 51
That she may *hearke* to love, . . . IV. Pr. 5. 9
List not to *hearke,* but made this faire denyall: . . . IV. ii. 6. 3
hearke, ye gentle knights and Ladies free, . . . IV. x. 3. 6
So well that Leach did *hearke* to her request, . . . IV. xi. 7. 1
Yet nould she *hearke,* . . . V. v. 16. 7
To *hearke* what any one did good report, . . . V. xii. 34. 8
Hark! how the cheerefull birds do chaunt . . . *Epith.* 78
Harke! how the Minstrils gin to shrill aloud . . . *Epith.* 129
Harlot. Saying, that *harlott* she too lately knew, . . . I. iii. 25. 3
Harlot's. hide Thy maisters shame, in *harlots* bondage tide: . V. vi. 11. 5
Harm. (Ay little helpe to *harme* there needeth!) . . . *S.C.* F. 198
Harme may come of melling. . . . *S.C.* Jul. 208
without *harme* us farre away did beare, . . . *Col.* 225
when he heard of *harme* he wexed wondrous glad. . . . I. iv. 30. 9
Late learnd what *harme* to hasty trust ensu'th. . . . I. vi. 12. 4
could never wight him *harme* By subtilty, . . . I. xi. 36. 8
For feare of further *harme,* . . . II. iv. 39. 4
whence should come that *harme,* . . . II. iv. 40. 3
Though otherwise it did him litle *harme:* . . . II. v. 7. 4
neither can he fly, nor other *harme,* . . . II. xi. 34. 2
could doe *harme,* yet could not harmed bee, . . . II. xi. 40. 6
she of womans force did feare no *harme;* . . . III. iv. 27. 8
in remembrance of his friends late *harme,* . . . IV. iv. 35. 2
'Small *harme* it were For any knight . . . IV. vi. 4. 1
before the *harme* came neare: . . . IV. viii. 42. 4
For feare of *harme* that might lie hidden there; . . . IV. x. 20. 2
Who will not stoupe with good shall be made stoupe with *harme.* . . . V. v. 49. 9
of ill that any did, Or *harme* that any had, . . . V. xii. 32. 6
by discovering my estate, *Harme* may arise . . . VI. ii. 27. 3
Harmed. ne might his corse bee *harmd* With dint of swerd, . I. xi. 9. 3
That erst him goodly armd, now most of all him *harmd.* . . . I. xi. 27. 9
he slumbred fearing not be *harmd:* . . . II. vi. 14. 8
Of every place that was with bruzing *harmd,* . . . II. vi. 51. 4
could doe harme, yet could not *harmed* bee, . . . II. xi. 40. 6
Some fearing shriekt, some being *harmed* hould, . . . IV. iii. 41. 7
glaunst Adowne in vaine, ne *harm'd* her any more. . . . IV. vi. 19. 4
th' other two well likely to have *harmed.* . . . V. iv. 36. 5
Harmful. His *harmefull* Hatchet he hent in hand, . . . *S.C.* F. 195
haile, and *harmful* showres, . . . *Gn.* 582
bitter-breathing windes with *harmfull* blast, . . . *Ti.* 405
in false griefe hyding his *harmefull* guile, . . . I. v. 18. 5
harmeful head, thrise heated in the fire, . . . I. vii. 37. 3
harmefull pestilence, So sore him noyd, . . . I. xi. 45. 1
His *harmefull* club he gan to hurtle hye, . . . II. vii. 42. 3
hurling up his *harmefull* blade on hy, . . . II. viii. 33. 5
harmefull fowles about them fluttering cride, . . . II. xii. 35. 7
the biting of that *harmefull* Beast . . . VI. vi. 15. 5
Harmless. Sweete quiet harbours in his *harmeless* head, . . . *Gn.* 134
Harmony. In stead of them, and their sweet *harmonie,* . . . *D.* 15
With hungrie eares to heare his *harmonie:* . . . *Col.* 53
Joying to heare the birdes sweete *harmony,* . . . I. i. 8. 2
Chaunted alowd their chearefull *harmonee,* . . . II. v. 31. 7
a straunge kinde of *harmony,* . . . II. xii. 33. 6
there consorted in one *harmonee;* . . . II. xii. 70. 8
Musicke did divide Her looser notes with Lydian *harmony;* . . III. i. 40. 2
a most delitious *harmony* . . . was sweetly heard . . . III. xii. 6. 1
Love is a celestiall *harmonie* . . . *H.B.* 197
Harms. their buds, that perish through their *harmes.* . . . *T.M.* 78
gan to him discover all his *harmes,* . . . I. v. 41. 5
He hearkned, and did stay from further *harmes,* . . . I. vii. 15. 1
Such helplesse *harmes* yts better hidden keep, . . . I. vii. 39. 7
wary was the knight By tryall of his former *harmes* . . . II. i. 4. 7
in pitty of their *harmes,* . . . II. ii. 27. 3
doolefull sorrow heape with deadly *harmes:* . . . II. vi. 34. 4
His chiefest letts and authors of his *harmes,* . . . II. xi. 31. 3
whereas all the plagues and *harmes* abound . . . IV. i. 20. 2
gazed on their *harmes,* not pittying their estate. . . . IV. ii. 20. 9
by their many wounds and carelesse *harmes,* . . . IV. iv. 38. 3
on their common *harmes* together did devise. . . . IV. vi. 10. 9
how their *harmes* befell? . . . IV. viii. 21. 3
that doth to travellers such *harmes?'* . . . V. ii. 5. 2
broke his sword, for feare of further *harmes,* . . . V. v. 21. 8
Ne ought was feared of his certaine *harmes:* . . . VI. viii. 47. 4
house-fyres, nor lightnings helpelesse *harmes,* . . . *Epith.* 340
freed from forraine *harmes;* . . . *Proth.* 156
Harness. A goodly knight, all armd in *harnesse* meete, . . . II. i. 5. 8
Another *harnesse* which did hang thereby . . . III. iii. 61. 2
Eftsoones the people all to *harnesse* ran, . . . V. iv. 36. 6
His plough and *harnesse* fit to till the ground, . . . VII. vii. 43. 6
Harness-bearing. Joves *harnesse-bearing* Bird from hye . . . II. xi. 43. 1
Harnessed. yron charet . . . Already *harnessed* for journey new, I. v. 20. 7
Phoebus . . . Yett *harnessed* his fyrie-footed teeme, . . . I. xii. 2. 2
Harp. O that I had the Thracian Poets *harpe,* . . . *Ro.* xxv. 1
Playing on yvorie *harp* with silver strong. . . . *Gn.* 16
an *Harpe* stroong all with silver twyne, . . . *Ti.* 604
whylome seemed to have been The *Harpe* . . . *Ti.* 607
But was th' *Harpe* of Philisides now dead. . . . *Ti.* 609
The *Harpe* well knowne beside the Northern Beare. . . . *Ti.* 616
did take His silver *Harpe* in hand . . . IV. ii. 1. 9
playing on his *harpe,* . . . IV. xi. 23. 4
the sweet musick, which his *harp* did make, . . . *Am.* xxxviii. 3
Orpheus with his *harp* theyr strife did bar. . . . *Am.* xliv. 4
when in hand my tunelesse *harp* I take, . . . *Am.* xliv. 9
Harpalus. good *Harpalus,* now woxen aged . . . *Col.* 380
Harpies. The hellish *Harpyes,* prophets of sad destiny. . . . II. xii. 36. 9
Harp's. So meane *Harpes* worke may chalenge for her meed? . *Ro.* xxxii. 4
Harrow. *'Harrow* now out, and well away!' he cryde, . . . II. vi. 43. 6
'Harrow! the flames which me consume,' . . . II. vi. 49. 8
Harrow and well away! . . . II. viii. 46. 8
Harrowed. he, that *harrowd* hell with heavie stowre, . . . I. x. 40. 8
having *harrowd* hell, didst bring away Captivity . . . *Am.* lxviii. 3
Hart, -en, -ened. *See* **Heart, -en, -ened.**
Harts. measured by his weed, . . . As *harts* by hornes, . . . *Col.* 712
all *harts* that hornes the highest beares; . . . *Col.* 714
Some having heads like *Harts,* . . . II. xi. 10. 4
Harvest. Well mought it beseme any *harvest* Queene. . . . *S.C.* Au. 36
Thus is my *harvest* hastened all to rathe; . . . *S.C.* D. 98
My *harvest,* wast, my hope away dyd wipe. . . . *S.C.* D. 108
My *harveste* hasts to stirre up Winter sterne, . . . *S.C.* D. 129
Or mellow fruit if it were *harvest* time. . . . *As.* 48
Who reapes the *harvest* sowen by his foe, . . . I. iv. 42. 4
There is continuall Spring, and *harvest* there Continuall, . . . III. vi. 42. 1
Should reap the *harvest* ere it ripened were: . . . VI. ix. 38. 6
Whose *harvest* seemd to hasten now apace,) . . . *Am.* lxxvi. 10
Harvest-hope. of all my *harvest-hope* I have Nought reaped *S.C.* D. 121
Harvest's. heavy laden with the spoyle Of *harvests* riches, . VII. vii. 38. 3
fit for *harvests* toyle, . . . VII. vii. 38. 5
Harvey. *Harvey,* the happy above happiest men . . . *Com. Son.* i. 1
Harwich. Clare and *Harwitch* both doth beautify: . . . IV. xi. 33. 5
Has (*partial list of auxiliary*). *See* **Nas.**
the Geaunt *has* not such a weight, . . . *S.C.* May 142
what peace *has* the Lion with the Lambe? . . . *S.C.* May 169
Here *has* the salt Medway his sourse, . . . *S.C.* Jul. 79
Areede uprightly who *has* the victorye . . . *S.C.* Au. 130
He *has* a Dogge to byte or to barke; . . . *S.C.* S. 181
The Nimph, which of that water course *has* charge, . . . *Col.* 109
whereof the name it *has,* . . . *Col.* 282
The noblest mind the best contentment *has.* . . . I. i. 35. 4
He that the wild West under his rule *has,* . . . I. ii. 22. 8
him, who *has* the guerdon of his guile, . . . I. iii. 40. 3
where that same wicked wight His dwelling *has,* . . . I. ix. 33. 2
For all so many weekes as the yeare *has,* . . . II. x. 22. 3
Old Genius, the which a double nature *has.* . . . III. vi. 31. 9
has no skill of Court nor courtesie, . . . III. ix. 3. 6
has full large to live and spend at libertie. . . . III. ix. 3. 9
far unlike conditions *has;* . . . III. ix. 4. 7
each Knight, that use of perill *has,* . . . V. ii. 16. 8
So feeble skill of perfect things the vulgar *has.* . . . V. iii. 17. 9
Tyrant, who invaded *has* Her land, . . . alas! . . . V. x. 6. 8
Thereto a great advauntage eke he *has* . . . V. xi. 6. 1
of a man, they say, It *has* the voice, . . . V. xi. 20. 7
Hask. taken up his ynne in Fishes *haske.* . . . *S.C.* N. 16
Hast (*partial list of auxiliary*). *See* **Haste.**
That long *hast* traveld, . . . *Ro.* Env. 4
Where *hast* thou coverture? . . . *S.C.* Jul. 26
sith thys hyll Thou *hast* such doubt to climbe. . . . *S.C.* Jul. 232
Now say on, Diggon, what ever thou *hast.* . . . *S.C.* S. 55
of their maisters *hast* no lesse regarde . . . *S.C.* D. 11
hast thy deathes wound? . . . *S.C.* D. 95
Goe, lyttle Calendar! thou *hast* a free passeporte; . . . *S.C.* Env. 7
'Colin, my liefe, . . . *Hast* made us all so blessed . . . *Col.* 21
*That us late dead, *hast* made againe alive: . . . *Col.* 31
Hast sole possession in so chaste a brest! . . . *Col.* 555
fond, that joyest in the woe thou *hast!* . . . I. ix. 39. 7
'Thou, wretched man, of death *hast* greatest need, . . . I. ix. 45. 1
In heavenly mercies *hast* thou not a part? . . . I. ix. 53. 4
here in desert *hast* thine habitaunce, . . . II. vii. 7. 2
over mortall mindes *hast* so great might, . . . III. ii. 2
retyre, whiles thou *hast* might, . . . III. iv. 14. 8
hast thou, Lord, of good mens cause no heed? . . . III. xi. 9. 6
What idle errand *hast* thou . . . VII. vi. 25. 9
Vayne man, quod I, that *hast* but little priefe . . . *Am.* l. 5
sith of wemens labours thou *hast* charge, . . . *Epith.* 383
Haste. Yts time to *hast* us homeward. . . . *S.C.* Mar. 117
ranne awaye with him in all *hast.* . . . *S.C.* May 293
though one fall through heedlesse *hast,* . . . *S.C.* Jul. 15
balefull barking bringes in *hast* Pyne, . . . *S.C.* Jul. 23
now at earst the dirke night doth *hast.* . . . *S.C.* S. 6
Make *hast,* ye shepheards, thether to revert: . . . *S.C.* N. 191
after Winter dreerie death does *hast.* . . . *S.C.* D. 144
in *hast,* disroabed as he was, . . . *Hub.* 1343
after him did make untimely *haste:* . . . *As.* 176
His Lady, . . . Approcht in *hast* to greet his victorie; . . . I. i. 27. 2
the dreame he bore In *hast* unto his Lord, . . . I. i. 44. 9
well instructed, to their worke they *haste;* . . . I. i. 47. 1
Phoebus fiery carre In *hast* was climbing . . . I. ii. 1. 8
he runnes with feigned faithfull *hast* . . . I. ii. 4. 1
in *haste* his helmet gan unlace, . . . I. iii. 37. 1
How many mischieves should ensue his heedlesse *hast.* . . . I. iv. 34. 9
He lives that . . . guiltie Elfin blood shall sacrifice in *hast.'* . I. iv. 49. 9
In *haste* Duessa from her place arose, . . . I. v. 14. 1
In *haste* forsooke their rurall meriment, . . . I. vi. 8. 2
The innocent pray in *hast* he does forsake; . . . I. vi. 10. 7
towards him they gan in *haste* to ride, . . . I. vi. 34. 4
Therewith the knight thence marched forth in *hast,* . . . I. vi. 40. 1
catching up in *hast* his three-square shield . . . I. vi. 41. 8
Hath thee incenst to *hast* thy dolefull fate? . . . I. vi. 47. 2
In *hast* came rushing forth from inner bowre, . . . I. viii. 5. 6
To come unto his wished home in *haste.* . . . I. ix. 39. 2
O foolish men! why *hast* ye to your own decay? . . . I. x. 10. 9
Halfe flying and halfe footing in his *haste.* . . . I. xi. 8. 2
Her golden locks for *hast* were loosely shed . . . I. xi. 51. 5
with fierce yre And zealous *haste* . . . II. i. 13. 2
Whereto he drew in *hast* . . . II. iv. 3. 4

Haste—*Continued.*
Guyon after him in *hast* did hye, . . . II. iv. 13. 8
he in *hast* approched to the shore, . . . II. vi. 48. 9
in great affright And *haste* he rose . . . II. vii. 6. 2
voyce, That bad him come in *haste*. . . . II. viii. 4. 4
Phoebus gan decline in *haste* His weary wagon . . . II. ix. 10. 1
in *haste* he yode The cause to weet, . . . II. xi. 20. 2
for him in *hast* did send; . . . III. iii. 10. 7
sent in *haste* for Tryphon, . . . III. iv. 43. 7
Doubleth her *hast* for feare to bee for-hent, . . . III. iv. 49. 8
With no lesse *hast*, and eke with no lesse dreed, . . . III. iv. 50. 1
O Titan! *hast* to reare thy joyous waine; . . . III. iv. 60. 3
made more *haste* the life to have bereav'd; . . . III. v. 28. 8
Into the woods thenceforth in *haste* shee went, . . . III. v. 32. 1
for hindring of her *haste*, . . . III. vi. 18. 7
Nor wearinesse to slack her *hast*, . . . III. vii. 2. 4
Went forth in *haste*, and did her footing trace . . . III. vii. 23. 7
in *haste* He lefte his captive Beast . . . III. vii. 38. 1
His charett swifte in *hast* he thither steard, . . . III. viii. 30. 7
Mote not mislike you also to abate Your zealous *hast*, . . . III. viii. 51. 7
The whiles her husband ran with sory *haste* . . . III. x. 13. 2
in *hast* he fledd, Ne ever looked back . . . III. x. 43. 6
His wicked bookes in *hast* he overthrew, . . . III. xii. 32. 2
came forth in *hast* to take his part, . . . IV. iii. 40. 8
For *hast* did over-runne, in dust enrould: . . . IV. iii. 41. 5
In *hast* she from her lofty chaire descended, . . . IV. iii. 50. 2
neither could in *hast* themselves againe upreare. . . . IV. iv. 20. 9
squiers make *hast* to helpe their Lords fordonne. . . . IV. iv. 38. 8
Ran forth in *hast* with hideous outcry, . . . IV. vii. 21. 4
makes her feare a spur to *hast* her flight: . . . IV. vii. 22. 7
hast to crosse him by the nearest way, . . . IV. vii. 25. 2
She ran in *hast* his life to have bereft; . . . IV. vii. 32. 2
Therewith she rose in *hast*, . . . IV. viii. 10. 5
Therefore to Tryphon she againe doth *hast*, . . . IV. xii. 23. 1
Unto the shinie heaven in *haste* she hide, . . . IV. xii. 25. 3
Whom he requir'd his forward *hast* to stay, . . . V. ii. 2. 3
He saw no way but close with him in *hast*; . . . V. ii. 14. 2
to whom he straight did hie With gladfull *hast*, . . . V. viii. 6. 6
She to them runnes in *hast*, . . . V. viii. 10. 7
Nathelesse him selfe he armed all in *hast*, . . . V. xi. 3. 1
She towards him in *hast* her selfe did draw . . . V. xi. 15. 3
a Dwarfe she cald to her in *hast*, . . . VI. i. 29. 1
The Dwarfe his way did *hast*, . . . VI. i. 30. 1
he ran with zealous *haste* To rescue th' infant, . . . VI. iv. 18. 6
Came forth in *hast*; . . . VI. vi. 24. 5
descending backe in *haste* he sought If yet he were alive, . . . VI. vi. 37. 8
Himselfe in *hast* he arm'd, . . . VI. vii. 2. 9
if ye list to *haste* a litle more, . . . VI. vii. 6. 3
I forbore To finish then, for other present *hast*. . . . VI. ix. 2. 4
shepheards to their homes to *hast* Their tender flocks, . . . VI. ix. 13. 3
ran in *hast* To reskue her; . . . VI. x. 35. 1
resolving to returne in *hast* . . . VI. xii. 13. 1
forth she ran in *hast* Unto her mistresse, . . . VI. xii. 16. 6
forth in *hast* ran to the straunger Mayd; . . . VI. xii. 19. 2
Ran forth in *haste* . . . VII. vi. 14. 9
In *haste* forth started . . . VII. vi. 47. 2
Make *hast*, therefore, sweet love, . . . *Am.* lxx. 13
Hast thee, O fayrest Planet, to thy home, . . . *Epith.* 282
the Nymphes, . . . Ran all in *haste* . . . *Proth.* 56
Hasted. after *hasted* Thy sommer prowde, . . . *S.C.* Ja. 21
home him *hasted* with furious heate, . . . *S.C.* F. 193
Whence neither greatly *hasted* to arise, . . . IV. vi. 10. 8
turn'd abacke, and to retyre him *hasted* . . . VI. vi. 28. 3
Hasten. home they *hasten* the postes to dight, . . . *S.C.* May 11
Good cause he had to *hasten* thence away; . . . I. v. 45. 6
Thus fowle to *hasten* your untimely date? . . . II. i. 44. 8
His flaming head did *hasten* for to steep, . . . II. ii. 46. 3
To *hasten* greatly to his parties ayd, . . . IV. iv. 20. 2
Whose harvest seemd to *hasten* now apace,) . . . *Am.* lxxvi. 10
Hastened. Sorrowe ne neede be *hastened* on, . . . *S.C.* May 152
Thus is my harvest *hastened* all to rathe; . . . *S.C.* D. 98
He rousd himselfe full blyth, and *hastned* them untill. . . . I. xi. 4. 9
Hastening. Tyber *hastning* to his fall . . . *Ro.* iii. 11
In steed of good, *hastning* his cruell fate. . . . *Gn.* 328
Hastely. Tho pumie stones I *hastly* hent . . . *S.C.* Mar. 89
Renne after *hastely* thy silver sound; . . . *S.C.* Jun. 61
informe his Master *hastely*, . . . *Hub.* 880
For the coole shade him thither *hastly* got: . . . I. ii. 29. 2
hither *hastly* sent Vespasian, . . . II. x. 52. 6
Trompart, ronning *hastely*, him did stay, . . . III. x. 23. 6
Hastes. My harveste *hasts* to stirre up Winter sterne, . . . *S.C.* D. 129
Hastily. To Morpheus house doth *hastily* repaire. . . . I. i. 39. 3
Then up he rose, and clad him *hastily*: . . . I. ii. 6. 8
Who after her as *hastily* gan scowre, . . . I. ii. 20. 5
lefte the doubtfull battell *hastily*, . . . I. vi. 46. 4
she *hastily* did draw Her dreadfull beast; . . . I. viii. 12. 3
A varlet ronning towardes *hastily*, . . . II. iv. 37. 2
That nothing should him *hastily* awake. . . . II. vi. 18. 4
O, come *hastily!*' . . . II. viii. 3. 8
she to him ran *hastily*; . . . II. xi. 28. 9
As fayre Aurora, rysing *hastily*, . . . III. iii. 20. 4
with it ronning *hast'ly* to her sonne, . . . III. viii. 3. 1
hastily remounting to his steed . . . III. ix. 15. 1
Ran *hastily*, to weete what did him ayle. . . . IV. i. 43. 4
To whom his course he *hastily* applide, . . . V. iv. 21. 4
Hastily bent that enterprise to heare, . . . V. x. 15. 4
crie Unto the ward to open to him *hastilie*. . . . VI. i. 22. 9
To whom himselfe he *hastily* did draw . . . VI. ii. 4. 3
Hastily starting up, . . . Ran after fast . . . VI. iii. 24. 8
Hasting. Hasting to raunch the arrow out, . . . *S.C.* Au. 97

Hasting—*Continued.*
hasting towards him gan fayre perswade . . . III. i. 10. 1
hasting Prime did make them burgein round. . . . VII. vii. 43. 8
Hasty. catching *hastie* holde Of a yong alder . . . *Gn.* 298
eke the Moone her *hastie* steedes did stay, . . . *Gn.* 457
They stole away, and tooke their *hastie* flight, . . . *Hub.* 339
giving *hastie* credit to th' accuser, . . . *Mui.* 135
Let streaming floods their *hastie* courses stay, . . . *D.* 332
which doe byte their *hasty* supper best; . . . I. i. 23. 4
hastie heat tempring with sufferance wise, . . . I. i. 50. 4
One pricking towards them with *hastie* heat, . . . I. iii. 33. 2
His *hasty* hand he doth amased hold, . . . I. iii. 38. 5
Trembling through *hasty* rage when choler in him sweld. . . . I. iv. 33. 9
hasty tong that did offend: . . . I. v. 39. 5
hastie speed The fayre Duess' had forst him leave behind; . . . I. vi. 2. 1
Late learnd what harme to *hasty* trust ensu'th. . . . I. vi. 12. 4
Him to his castle brought with *hastie* forse, . . . I. vii. 15. 8
Her *hastie* ruine does more heavie make, . . . I. viii. 23. 6
to him she ran With *hasty* joy: . . . I. viii. 42. 2
from whom make ye this *hasty* flight? . . . I. ix. 23. 8
'With which sad instrument of *hasty* death, . . . I. ix. 30. 1
She would commaund the *hasty* Sunne to stay, . . . I. x. 20. 2
Uprose with *hasty* joy, and feeble speed, . . . I. xii. 3. 1
wondred at his breathlesse *hasty* mood: . . . I. xii. 25. 3
Withhold . . . your *hasty* hond From knitting league with him, I. xii. 28. 3
Whose *hastie* hand so far from reason strayd, . . . II. i. 28. 5
suffred not in wrath his *hasty* steps to stray. . . . II. i. 34. 9
whither with such *hasty* flight Art thou now bownd? . . . II. iv. 43. 2
hasty wroth, and heedlesse hazardry, . . . II. v. 13. 8
Him *hasty* to arise. . . . II. v. 37. 6
Appease his heat, or *hastie* passage stay; . . . II. v. 38. 4
The *hasty* heat of his avowd revenge delayd. . . . II. vi. 40. 9
bent his *hastie* course towardes the ydle flood. . . . II. vi. 41. 9
Mammon did his *hasty* hand withhold, . . . II. vii. 42. 6
So *hasty* heat soone cooled to subdew: . . . II. viii. 47. 8
Her fickle hart conceived *hasty* fyre, . . . III. i. 47. 6
With *hasty* gallop towards her did ryde. . . . III. iv. 12. 3
nothing might relent her *hasty* flight, . . . III. iv. 49. 1
ever *hasty* Night he blamed bitterlie. . . . III. iv. 54. 9
to her ran with *hasty* egernesse, . . . III. xii. 44. *or.*6
when as he saw her *hastie* heat Abate, . . . IV. vi. 16. 1
He chaunst to meet a Dwarfe in *hasty* course, . . . V. ii. 2. 2
One comming towards her with *hasty* speede. . . . V. vi. 8. 2
on it he *hasty* hand did lay, . . . *Epig.* iv. 25
cutting off through *hasty* accidents, . . . *Epith.* 429
Which at first blowing take not *hastie* fyre; . . . *H.L.* 174
Hat. on his head his dreadfull *hat* he dight, . . . *Hub.* 1279
Hatched. courd it tenderly, As chicken newly *hatcht*, . . . II. viii. 9. 9
Hatchet. His harmefull *Hatchet* he hent in hand, . . . *S.C.* F. 195
An *hatchet* keene, with which he felled wood . . . VII. vii. 42. 6
Hatchet's. the *hatchets* slight Hath pruned from the native tree, . . . V. xi. 11. 8
Hate. I *hate* the house, since thence my love did part, . . . *S.C.* Au. 161
better mought they have behote him *Hate*. . . . *S.C.* D. 54
hating those that *hate*; . . . *Hub.* 428
without strife or *hate*, Findes all things needfull . . . *Hub.* 910
such as *hate* the honour of our name, . . . *T.M.* 63
he light and heaven does *hate*: . . . *T.M.* 190
Henceforth all worlds felicitie I *hate*. . . . *Ti.* 574
Through prowd ambition and hart-swelling *hate*, . . . *Mui.* 5
'Hencefoorth I *hate* what ever Nature made, . . . *D.* 393
'I *hate* the heaven, because it doth withhold . . . *D.* 400
I *hate* the earth, because it is the mold . . . *D.* 402
I *hate* the fire, because to nought it flyes; . . . *D.* 404
I *hate* the Ayre, because sighes of it be; . . . *D.* 405
I *hate* the Sea, because it teares supplyes. . . . *D.* 406
'I *hate* the day, because it lendeth light . . . *D.* 407
I *hate* the darknesse and the drery night, . . . *D.* 409
I *hate* all times, because, all times doo flye . . . *D.* 411
'I *hate* to speake, my voyce is spent . . . *D.* 414
I *hate* to heare, lowd plaints have duld mine eares; . . . *D.* 415
I *hate* to tast, for food withholds my dying; . . . *D.* 416
I *hate* to see, mine eyes are dimd with teares; . . . *D.* 417
I *hate* to smell, no sweet on earth is left; . . . *D.* 418
I *hate* to feele, my flesh is numbd with feares: . . . *D.* 419
'I *hate* all men, and shun all womankinde; . . . *D.* 421
life I *hate*, because it will not last; . . . *D.* 425
death I *hate*, because it life doth marre; . . . *D.* 426
all I *hate* that is to come or past. . . . *D.* 427
'So all the world, and all in it I *hate*, . . . *D.* 428
with hope of good, and *hate* of ill, . . . *Col.* 192
A monster vile, whom God and man does *hate*: . . . I. i. 13. 7
For hoped love to winne me certaine *hate?* . . . I. i. 51. 5
to *hate* Her, that him lov'd, . . . I. iii. 7. 7
sitting high, for lowly she did *hate*: . . . I. iv. 10. 3
Her love she turnd to *hate*, . . . I. v. 37. 7
trembling yet through feare of former *hate*. . . . I. vi. 9. 5
Most sencelesse man he, that himselfe doth *hate*, . . . I. vi. 47. 5
head . . . as in *hate* of honorable eld, Was overgrowne with scurfe . . . I. viii. 47. 2
th' antique world excesse and pryde did *hate*: . . . I. xii. 14. 8
Each other does envy with deadly *hate*, . . . II. ii. 19. 2
love to gaine, Which gotten was but *hate*. . . . II. ii. 26. 5
Disloyall Treason, and hart-burning *Hate*; . . . II. vii. 22. 3
with incessant force and endlesse *hate* . . . II. xi. 6. 8
Such as by nature men abhorre and *hate*; . . . II. xii. 36. 3
Such love is *hate*, and such desire is shame. . . . III. i. 50. 5
His mother bad him womens love to *hate*, . . . III. iv. 27. 7
they that dye doe nether love nor *hate*: . . . III. iv. 37. 6
all that lewdnesse love doe *hate* the light to see. . . . III. iv. 58. 9

Hate—*Continued.*
Full of fierce fury and indignant *hate* III. v. 23. 3
Shall I then *hate* her that from deathes dore Me brought? III. v. 46. 2
with griesly *hate* And dreadfull horror III. xi. 21. 7
did not seeke t' appease their deadly *hate*. IV. ii. 20. 8
under it hidde *hate* and hollow guyle. IV. ii. 29. 5
to change the hearts of men Fro love to *hate,* IV. iii. 45. 6
mov'd Belphebe her no lesse to *hate,* IV. vii. 34. 6
The one of them hight Love, the other *Hate.* IV. x. 32. 6
Hate was the elder, Love the younger brother; IV. x. 32. 7
'The cause, they say, of this her cruell *hate* V. iv. 30. 1
His father Dolon had . . . shewd his cankred *hate.* V. vi. 33. 9
with most fell despight and deadly *hate* V. viii. 18. 3
Whom Gods doe *hate,* and heavens abhor to see; VI. vi. 10. 2
his Lord of old Did *hate* all errant Knights VI. vi. 21. 4
For all that shame, which kindled inward *hate:* VI. vii. 2. 7
from you turne the love of men to *hate:* VI. viii. 2. 6
all things stedfastnesse do *hate* And changed be; VII. vii. 58. 2
Degendering to *hate,* fell from above *H.H.L.* 94
Hated. His heart did earne against his *hated* foe, *Mui.* 254
light she *hated* as the deadly bale, I. i. 16. 7
her he *hated* as the hissing snake, I. ii. 9. 8
He *hated* all good workes and vertuous deeds, I. iv. 32. 1
she all day did hide her *hated* hew. I. v. 20. 5
evermore she *hated,* never lov'd: I. v. 24. 9
'O lightsome day! . . . Henceforth thy *hated* face for ever hyde, I. vii. 23. 4
Shee, flying fast from heavens *hated* face, . . . Fled I. viii. 50. 1
Cupids wanton snare As hell she *hated;* I. x. 30. 6
Whom mortally he *hated* evermore, IV. i. 39. 4
as the death he *hated* such despight, V. iii. 31. 8
as if such use they *hated.* V. vii. 29. 9
That recreant knight, whose *hated* life I sought? VI. vii. 16. 4
much she *hated* sight of living eye. VII. vi. 42. 6
Ayre *hated* earth, and water *hated* fyre, *H.L.* 83
Hateful. this fierce *hatefull* beast and all hir traine *Rev.* iii. 13
The *hatefull* darknes now had put to flight; *Gn.* 69
hatefull heresies, of God abhor'd: *Hub.* 389
Had lately built his *hatefull* mansion; *Mui.* 246
Where hidden was his *hatefull* enemie. *Mui.* 392
He raft her *hatefull* heade without remorse: I. i. 24. 8
in his bosome secretly there lay An *hatefull* Snake, I. iv. 31. 4
Thrall to that Gyaunts *hatefull* tyranny: I. viii. 2. 5
wreake on them their hainous *hatefull* deed.' II. iii. 14. 9
The *hatefull* messengers of heavy things, II. vii. 23. 4
staynes his snowy skin with *hatefull* hew: III. i. 38. 6
In *hatefull* darknes and in deepe horrore, III. vi. 36. 7
Hatefull both to him selfe and every wight; III. x. 60. 6
O *hatefull* hellish Snake! III. xi. 1. 1
With *hatefull* thoughts to languish and to pine, III. xi. 1. 7
with hideous And *hatefull* outrage long him chaced III. xi. 3. 5
In perfect love, devoide of *hatefull* strife, IV. iii. 52. 2
there were none her *hatefull* words to heare. IV. viii. 36. 4
to his *hatefull* foe He mote not come V. viii. 35. 3
spake licentious words and *hatefull* things VI. xii. 28. 5
did him compell To see the *hatefull* sunne, VI. xii. 35. 5
Hates. He *hates* fowle leasings, and vile flatterie, *Hub.* 733
harts deep sorrow *hates* both life and light. *D.* 91
Tounge *hates* to tell the rest that eye to see abhord.' II. i. 11. 9
Hateth. Shepheards devise she *hateth* as the snake, *S.C.* Ja. 65
(Entire affection *hateth* nicer hands) I. viii. 40. 3
To shew how sore bloodguiltinesse he *hat'th;* II. ii. 4. 5
Hath (*partial list of auxiliary*).
onely Rome of Rome *hath* victorie; *Ro.* iii. 10
such sight *hath* bred my bane. *S.C.* Ja. 53
hath he skill to make so excellent, *S.C.* Ap. 19
Yet *hath* so little skill to brydle love? *S.C.* Ap. 20
such cause *hath* she none) *S.C.* May 98
To him that *hath* a whit of Natures giving? *Hub.* 418
the charge is wondrous great, . . . and *hath* an heavie threat.' *Hub.* 432
hath a zealous disposition To God, *Hub.* 491
some good Gentleman, that *hath* the right *Hub.* 525
hath not seene that heavens portracture. *Hub.* 611
such as *hath* a Reynold to his man, *Hub.* 917
hath no hope of happinesse or blis. *Ti.* 357
she *hath* praises in all plenteousnesse *D.* 227
the shepheard which *hath* charge in chief, *Col.* 244
Religion *hath* lay powre to rest upon her, *Col.* 322
hath so many shepheards in her fee, *Col.* 370
'what *hath* ye thus dismayd? I. i. 52. 8
true love *hath* no powre To looken backe; I. iii. 30. 7
in his hand a burning brond he *hath,* I. iv. 33. 3
dreaded Night in brightest day *hath* place, I. v. 24. 4
He *hath* no powre to hurt, I. viii. 21. 7
What *hath* poore Virgin I. viii. 27. 3
what *hath* life that may it loved make, I. ix. 44. 4
who *hath* skill them rightly to have chusd, II. ii. 5. 8
Hath great or glorious in mortall eye, II. ii. 41. 4
He *hath* a sword that flames like burning brond. II. iii. 18. 5
Whose soveraine beautie *hath* no living pere; III. i. 26. 3
Another arrow *hath* your lovers hart to hit.' III. ii. 35. 9
No shadow but a body *hath* in powre: III. ii. 45. 7
More neede of leach-crafte *hath* your Damozell, III. iii. 17. 5
She *hath* the leading of a Martiall And mightie people, III. iii. 56. 4
Love, my lewd Pilott, *hath* a restlesse minde; III. iv. 9. 6
hath the charge of Neptunes mighty heard; III. viii. 30. 2
he, the tyrant, which her *hath* in ward III. xi. 16. 6
Whom he that *hath* were loth to lose so light, IV. iv. 9. 2
Which *hath* in charge the ingate of the yeare: IV. x. 12. 6
she *hath* both kinds in one, IV. x. 41. 6
Where she *hath* now an everlasting place V. i. 11. 5

Hath—*Continued.*
Thereto he *hath* a groome of evill guize, V. ii. 6. 6
try in equall field whether *hath* greater might. V. iv. 48. 9
Such wondrous powre *hath* wemens faire aspect V. viii. 2. 8
neither *hath* religion nor fay, V. viii. 19. 7
each *hath* his fortune in his brest. VI. ix. 29. 9
some, that *hath* abundance at his will, VI. ix. 30. 3
Hath not enough, but wants in greatest store, VI. ix. 30. 4
other, that *hath* litle, askes no more, VI. ix. 30. 5
Another quest, another game in vew He *hath,* VI. x. 2. 4
what *hath* all that goodly glorious gaze VI. x. 4. 1
All paine *hath* end, and every war *hath* peace; *Am.* xi. 13
on earth nought *hath* enduraunce. *Am.* lviii. 12
Hath white and red in it such wondrous powre, *H.B.* 71
hath in it the more of heavenly light, *H.B.* 128
shew what wondrous powre your beauty *hath,* *H.B.* 286
Ne *hath* their day, ne *hath* their blisse, an end, *H.H.L.* 74
Whose smile, they say, *hath* vertue to remove *Proth.* 98
Hating. Ne rust of age *hating* continuance, *Ro.* xiii. 6
hating those that hate; *Hub.* 428
as *hating* life and light. II. i. 45. 9
Hating the happie light from which they fell. *H.H.L.* 91
Hatred. wrath and *hatred* warely to shonne, I. x. 33. 5
wrath . . . That drew on men Gods *hatred* I. x. 33. 6
this doth *hatred* make in love to brenne, IV. iii. 45. 7
hatred, murther, treason, and despight, IV. x. 20. 6
Albe that *Hatred* was thereto full loth, IV. x. 33. 3
Hatred would my entrance have restrayned, IV. x. 36. 4
She turn'd her love to *hatred* manifold, V. iv. 30. 7
Hauberk. on the *haubergh* stroke the Prince so sore, II. viii. 44. 6
through his mayled *hauberque,* III. iv. 16. 4
through the seame, which did his *hauberk* close, IV. iii. 30. 3
Hauberks. Their . . . speres were broke, and *hauberques* rent, III. xi. 52. 6
Ne helmets bright ne *hawberks* strong did spare, IV. ix. 27. 3
Haught. courage *haught* Desyrd of forreine foemen to be knowne, I. vi. 29. 5
Or through support of count'nance proud and *hault,* VI. ii. 23. 8
Haughty. the most *haughtie* mountaines hight, *Bel.*[2] vii. 7
Great Babylon her *haughtie* walls will praise, *Ro.* ii. 1
So did that *haughtie* front . . . it selfe upreare *Ro.* xii. 9
These *haughtie* heapes, these palaces of olde, *Ro.* xxvii. 3
so his *hauty* hornes did he weld.' *S.C.* May 206
Nor *haughtie* words most full of highest thoughts: *Col.* 716
at his *haughty* helmet making mark, I. ii. 19. 3
Duessa . . . highly honourd in his *haughtie* eye: I. vii. 16. 2
haughtie Helmet, horrid all with gold, I. vii. 31. 1
lett downe that *haughtie* string, I. xi. 7. 7
Eftsoones he gan advance his *haughty* crest, I. xi. 15. 5
The knight emboyling in his *haughtie* hart II. iv. 9. 6
he smote his *haughty* crest so hye, II. v. 12. 4
That hath so many *haughty* conquests wonne? II. v. 35. 8
Smote him so hugely on his *haughtie* crest, II. viii. 33. 6
Equall unto this *haughty* enterprise? II. x. 1. 2
too *haughtie* hardines might reare Some hard mishap III. iv. 24. 5
haughtie courage soften, IV. Pr. 5. 8
courage full of *haughtie* hardiment, IV. ii. 39. 2
did the more enhaunce His *haughtie* courage IV. iii. 8. 8
haughtie spirits meekely to adaw, IV. vi. 26. 8
that warriouresse with *haughty* crest Did forth issue V. vii. 27. 7
he streightway with *haughtie* choler burned, VI. ii. 12. 3
At whose strange sight and *haughty* hardinesse He wondred VII. vi. 17. 4
when the *haughty* Titanesse beheld, VII. vi. 25. 1
Such *haughty* mynds, enur'd to hardy fight, *Am.* xiv. 7
to the heaven her *haughty* lookes aspire: *Am.* lv. 11
Up to your *haughty* pallaces may mount; *Epith.* 420
Haulst. *See* **Halsed.**
Hault. *See* **Haught.**
Haunch. Whose right *haunch* earst my stedfast arrow strake? II. iii. 32. 8
Haunches. pincht the *haunches* of that (this[1]) gentle beast, *Pet.* i. 9
Haunt. Sylvanes *haunten* rathe; *S.C.* Jul. 78
dare To come unto his *haunt;* *Gn.* 274
doo thou *haunt* the soft downe-rolling river, *Gn.* 636
Poore suters, that in Court did *haunt* some while; *Hub.* 878
greislie shades, such as doo *haunt* in hell *Ti.* 125
There now *haunt* yelling Mewes *Ti.* 133
All these, and many evils moe *haunt* ire, I. iv. 35. 6
drave Far from that *haunt* all other chearefull fowle, I. ix. 33. 8
beseemes all knights . . . that same to *haunt,* I. x. 59. 6
So many furies and sharpe fits did *haunt,* I. xi. 27. 4
Where many Mermayds *haunt* II. xii. 17. 9
sweet Parnasse, the *haunt* of Muses fayre; II. xii. 52. 8
sith it is uneath to finde his *haunt,* III. ii. 16. 2
where most he us'd Whylome to *haunt,* III. vi. 13. 2
With many of the gods in company Which thither *haunt,* III. vi. 49. 3
that wastefull wildernesse Huge monsters *haunt,* III. x. 40. 4
Did hate all errant Knights which there did *haunt,* VI. vi. 21. 4
are wont to *haunt* Uppon this hill, VI. x. 15. 2
Haunted. carrion Crowes . . . That in our Peere-tree *haunted:* *S.C.* Mar. 111
Haunts. Here *hauntes* that feend, and does his dayly spoyle; I. xi. 2. 3
To search the secret *haunts* of Dianes company. III. vi. 16. 9
she used often to resort To common *haunts,* V. xii. 34. 7
Have (*partial list of auxiliary*).
Sith I *have* seene so faire a thing *Bel.*[1] iv. 13
all things which beneath the Moone *have* being *Ro.* ix. 10
Thy Ewes, that wont to *have* blowen bags, *S.C.* F. 81
Thomalin, *have* no care for-thy; *S.C.* Mar. 37
My selfe will *have* a double eye, *S.C.* Mar. 38
For als at home I *have* a syre, *S.C.* Mar. 40
She shoulde *have* neede no more spell; *S.C.* Mar. 54
When shepheardes groomes *han* leave to playe, *S.C.* Mar. 62

Have—*Continued.*

to *have* the overthrowe . . . *S.C.* Ap. 81
so they *han* the fleece, . . . *S.C.* May 49
have it they must: . . . *S.C.* May 135
what concord *han* light and darke sam? . . . *S.C.* May 168
Of my old age *have* this one delight, . . . *S.C.* May 202
the great care I *have* of thy health . . . *S.C.* May 216
Such pierlesse pleasures *have* we . . . *S.C.* Jun. 32
of them *han* theyr name. . . . *S.C.* Jul. 40
Here *han* the holy Faunes recourse, . . . *S.C.* Jul. 77
the sayncts Which *han* be dead . . . *S.C.* Jul. 116
Theyr sheepe *han* crustes, . . . *S.C.* Jul. 187
They *han* the fleece, and eke the flesh, . . . *S.C.* Jul. 189
They *han* great stores and thriftye stockes, . . . *S.C.* Jul. 193
They *han* fatte kernes, . . . *S.C.* Jul. 199
Sike syrlye shepheards *han* we none, . . . *S.C.* Jul. 203
Thou medlest more then shall *have* thanke, . . . *S.C.* Jul. 209
I fear me, thou *have* a squint eye: . . . *S.C.* Au. 129
They boast they *han* the devill at commaund, . . . *S.C.* S. 94
aske hem therefore what they *han* paund: . . . *S.C.* S. 95
We *han* great Bandogs will teare their skinne. . . . *S.C.* S. 163
They *han* the pleasure, . . . *S.C.* O. 16
when my Gates shall *han* their bellies layd, . . . *S.C.* O. 119
Cuddie shall *have* a Kidde to store his farme. . . . *S.C.* O. 120
Matter of myrth now shalt thou *have* no more; . . . *S.C.* N. 56
dewed with teares they *han* be ever among. . . . *S.C.* D. 112
Have care for to pursue his footing light . . . *Gn.* 31
O! the great happines, which shepheards *have,* . . . *Gn.* 89
Calling in vaine for rest, and can *have* none. . . . *Gn.* 392
deserve to *have* small faults remitted, . . . *Gn.* 474
worse than that I *have* I cannot meete. . . . *Hub.* 89
a few *have* all, and all *have* nought, . . . *Hub.* 141
have no wit to live withouten toyle; . . . *Hub.* 158
if that anie other place you *have,* . . . *Hub.* 277
We *have* not yet the tract of anie troad, . . . *Hub.* 406
may *have* lying by our sides Our lovely Lasses, . . . *Hub.* 475
have the Gospell of free libertie.' . . . *Hub.* 478
have in gage The Primitias of your Parsonage: . . . *Hub.* 517
then his yongest sonne Shall twentie *have,* . . . *Hub.* 530
they, that are great Clerkes, *have* nearer wayes, . . . *Hub.* 537
To *have* thy Princes grace, . . . *Hub.* 901
To *have* thy asking, . . . *Hub.* 902
to *have* the rayne Twixt them divided . . . *Hub.* 1023
ye shall *have* both crowne and government, . . . *Hub.* 1050
so his rule might lenger *have* endurance. . . . *Hub.* 1114
Ne would he anie let to *have* accesse . . . *Hub.* 1201
all Apes but halfe their eares *have* left, . . . *Hub.* 1383
succeeding ages *have* no light Of things forepast, . . . *T.M.* 103
Because I nothing noble *have* to sing. . . . *T.M.* 108
Because that mourning matter I *have* none. . . . *T.M.* 168
hold by wrong that wee should *have* by right. . . . *T.M.* 318
to *have* the auncestrie . . . memorizde anew; . . . *T.M.* 439
mortall men *have* powre to deifie: . . . *T.M.* 460
It is the onelie comfort which they *have,* . . . *T.M.* 494
Such happinesse *have* they . . . *T.M.* 517
shame and sorrow and accursed case *Have* they . . . *T.M.* 520
By those which *have* no skill to rule them right, . . . *T.M.* 551
comfort can I, wretched creature, *have?* . . . *Ti.* 23
'Name *have* I none (quoth she) . . . *Ti.* 34
if I might of her *have* sight. . . . *Ti.* 476
salvage nature seemed not to *have,* . . . *Ti.* 564
till thou *have* to my trustie eare Committed . . . *D.* 69
well did hope my joy would *have* no end, . . . *D.* 149
heavenly spirits *have* compassion On mortall men, . . . *D.* 384
Sith all my sorrow should *have* end thereby, . . . *D.* 446
they shall *have* no long endurance, . . . *D.* 501
Ne feeling *have* in any earthly pleasure, . . . *Col.* 45
Have in the Ocean charge to me assignd; . . . *Col.* 253
To *have* in her commandement at hand.' . . . *Col.* 263
know how to *have* donne. . . . *Col.* 591
'Cause *have* I none . . . *Col.* 680
arts of schoole *have* there small countenance, . . . *Col.* 703
highest lookes *have* not the highest mynd, . . . *Col.* 715
So hie her thoughts as she her selfe *have* place, . . . *Col.* 937
In this same Pageaunt *have* a worthy place, . . . *Ded. Son.* vi. 6
have your deserved place High . . . *Ded. Son.* xi. 2
Here eke of right *have* you a worthie place, . . . *Ded. Son.* xi. 5
desird Of all the fairest Maides to *have* the vew. . . . *Ded.Son.* xvii. 4
To winne him worshippe, and her grace to *have,* . . . I. i. 3. 4
In charmes and magick to *have* wondrous might, . . . I. iii. 38. 8
Abyde, till I have told the message which I *have.'* . . . I. v. 21. 9
shall *have* their deadly meed.' . . . I. vii. 23. 9
Madame, ye *have* great cause of plaint, . . . I. vii. 52. 3
What if some little payne the passage *have,* . . . I. ix. 40. 4
Are written sure, and *have* their certein date. . . . I. ix. 42. 5
If any strength we *have,* it is to ill, . . . I. x. 1. 8
To *have* her knight into her schoolehous plaste, . . . I. x. 18. 4
O man! *have* mind of that last bitter throw; . . . I. x. 41. 8
Should *have* mine onely daughter to his Dame, . . . I. xii. 20. 5
All wrongs *have* mendes, . . . II. i. 20. 5
'Joy may you *have,* and everlasting fame, . . . II. i. 32. 1
of her love too lavish: (litle *have* she thanck!) . . . II. ii. 36. 9
this grace I *have* Me given by eternall destiny, . . . II. iii. 45. 1
For it was taught the way which she would *have,* . . . II. vi. 5. 8
What bootes it al to *have,* and nothing use? . . . II. vi. 17. 6
Such powre *have* pleasing wordes: . . . II. vi. 36. 5
When foggy mistes or cloudy tempests *have* . . . yblent, . . . II. vii. 1. 3
If thee list not, leave *have* thou to refuse: . . . II. vii. 18. 8
to be Lord of those that riches *have,* . . . II. vii. 33. 8
them to *have* myselfe, and be their servile sclave.' . . . II. vii. 33. 9

Have—*Continued.*

All that I need I *have:* . . . II. vii. 39. 3
To covet more then I *have* cause to use? . . . II. vii. 39. 4
More fitt emongst black fiendes then men to *have* his place. . . II. vii. 41. 9
to remove the same I *have* no might: . . . II. vii. 50. 8
why should hevenly God to men *have* such regard? . . . II. viii. 2. 9
fiercely bent to *have* him disaraid; . . . II. viii. 17. 3
Words, well dispost, *Have* secrete powre . . . II. viii. 26. 8
hard adventure which I *have* in hand, . . . II. ix. 8. 8
Here may ye not *have* entraunce, . . . II. ix. 12. 4
have three years sought one, yet no where can her find.' . . . II. ix. 38. 9
Ne did it then deserve a name to *have,* . . . II. x. 6. 1
To *have* a pere in part of soverainty; . . . II. x. 33. 4
gave unto us all what ever good we *have.* . . . II. x. 69. 9
Let Gryll be Gryll, and *have* his hoggish minde; . . . II. xii. 87. 8
In case he *have* no Lady nor no love, . . . III. i. 26. 8
'But if he *have* a Lady or a Love, . . . III. i. 27. 1
have our Ladies love for his reward. . . . III. i. 27. 9
'Therefore aread, Sir, if thou *have* a love.' . . . III. i. 28. 1
Love *have* I sure, '(quoth she)' but Lady none; . . . III. i. 28. 2
Full easy was for her to *have* beliefe, . . . III. i. 54. 1
Here *have* I cause in men just blame to find, . . . III. ii. 1. 1
Joy thereof *have* thou, and eternall blis!' . . . III. ii. 42. 5
Can *have* no ende nor hope of my desire, . . . III. ii. 44. 2
helpe may *have* elsewhere, . . . III. iii. 17. 6
of a woman he should *have* much ill; . . . III. iv. 25. 8
of her errour straunge I *have* great ruth . . . III. v. 7. 9
Should happy bee, and *have* immortall blis: . . . III. vi. 41. 3
flat refusd to *have* adoe with mee, . . . III. vii. 58. 3
Have care, I pray, to guide the cock-bote well, . . . III. viii. 24. 4
of his lady they might *have* the sight . . . III. ix. 25. 8
least doubt of us ye *have,* . . . III. x. 42. 6
That his swift charet might *have* passage wyde . . . III. xi. 40. 8
either he should neither of them *have,* or both. . . . IV. i. 10. 9
'I saw him *have* your Amoret at will; . . . IV. i. 49. 1
This happie day I *have* to greete you well, . . . IV. ii. 23. 5
she . . . Shall *have* that golden girdle for reward; . . . IV. ii. 27. 2
makes it seeme to *have* some other sourse; . . . IV. iii. 27. 5
Desirous both to *have* the battell donne; . . . IV. iii. 36. 5
Whether of them in her should *have* the greater share. . . . IV. iii. 39. 9
who so winnes her may her *have* by right: . . . IV. iv. 9. 7
he shall *have* the Hag that is ybet, . . . IV. iv. 9. 8
Whether shall *have* the Hag, . . . IV. iv. 12. 9
'Great cause of sorrow certes, Sir, ye *have;* . . . IV. vi. 38. 6
have the sterne remembrance wypt away . . . IV. viii. 1. 8
That none mote *have* accesse, . . . IV. x. 6. 4
they mote *have* joyance free. . . . IV. x. 23. 9
what an endlesse worke *have* I in hand, . . . IV. xii. 1. 1
if any Gods at all *Have* care of right, . . . IV. xii. 9. 2
such was he of whom I *have* to tell, . . . V. i. 3. 1
For all we *have* is his: . . . V. ii. 41. 9
Guyon would him algates *have* perforse, . . . V. iii. 30. 4
Another, that would seeme to *have* more wit, . . . V. iii. 33. 6
Had neede *have* mightie hands . . . V. iv. 1. 3
this of Artegall, which here we *have* to say. . . . V. iv. 2. 9
That in and out thou mayst *have* passage free. . . . V. v. 34. 5
Equity, Whereof I *have* to treat here presently: . . . V. vii. 3. 5
therefore ought it *have* where ever she it fond. . . . V. vii. 30. 9
With hope of her some wishfull boot to *have.* . . . V. ix. 10. 3
with her purple pall Would *have* the passion hid, . . . V. ix. 50. 9
meriteth to *have* as high a place, . . . V. x. 1. 6
What else they *have* is all the Tyrants fee; . . . V. x. 29. 8
before that tide None can *have* tidings . . . V. xi. 42. 5
if I live till those ten daies *have* end, . . . V. xi. 43. 2
Assure your selfe, Sir Knight, she shall *have* ayd, . . . V. xi. 43. 3
Yet can I not my love *have* nathemore, . . . V. xi. 54. 7
the keeping *have* of learnings threasures . . . VI. Pr. 2. 3
did seeme a thousand tongues to *have,* . . . VI. i. 9. 3
ye *have* much adoe to deale withall.' . . . VI. i. 10. 8
tell, if thou *have* it knowne.' . . . VI. i. 14. 4
How can he mercy ever hope to *have?* . . . VI. i. 42. 2
For knights and all men this by nature *have,* . . . VI. ii. 14. 8
'Glad would I surely be, . . . To *have* thy presence . . . VI. ii. 37. 2
My life will by his death *have* lamentable end. . . . VI. viii. 17. 9
if ye list *have* liberty ye may; . . . VI. viii. 29. 7
doe my selfe with that I *have* content; . . . VI. ix. 20. 5
They, that *have* much, feare much to loose thereby, . . . VI. ix. 21. 3
The litle that I *have* growes dayly more . . . VI. ix. 21. 5
What *have* I, but to praise th' Almighty . . . VI. ix. 21. 9
Litle for him to *have* one silly lasse; . . . VI. xi. 12. 6
Whose heavy tydings now I *have* to tell. . . . VI. xi. 31. 3
The same againe if now ye list to *have,* . . . VI. xii. 17. 8
Have Jove thy gracious Lord and Soveraine.' . . . VII. vi. 34. 5
Ne *have* the watry foules a certaine grange . . . VII. vii. 21. 7
So many turning cranks these *have,* . . . VII. vii. 52. 9
each of you, That vertue *have* or this . . . VII. vii. 54. 7
Nor to the Starres; for they *have* purer sight; . . . *Am.* ix. 7
when shall these wearie woes *have* end, . . . *Am.* xxxvi. 1
Is it because your eyes *have* powre to kill? . . . *Am.* xlix. 2
then my body shall *have* shortly ease: . . . *Am.* l. 11
when shall I *have* peace with you? . . . *Am.* lvii. 1
here on earth to *have* such hevens blisse. . . . *Am.* lxxii. 14
when will this long weary day *have* end, . . . *Epith.* 278
Thy tyred steedes long since *have* need of rest. . . . *Epith.* 284
Their being *have,* and dayly are increast . . . *H.L.* 96
soules, which *have* The most resemblance . . . *H.B.* 120
every one doth seeke and sew to *have* it, . . . *H.B.* 153
the food of life, which now we *have,* . . . *H.H.L.* 194
Where they shall *have* like heritage of land, . . . *H.H.L.* 200
All joy, all blisse, all happinesse, *have* place; . . . *H.H.B.* 243

Have—*Continued.*
Joy may you *have,* and gentle hearts content . . . . *Proth.* 94
Where now the studious Lawyers *have* their bowers, ... *Proth.* 134
Joy *have* thou of thy noble victorie, ... *Proth.* 152
Haven. Behold! I see the *haven* nigh at hand . . . . I. xii. 1. 1
to the wished *haven* bring thy weary barke!' . . . . II. i. 32. 9
Far from the hoped *haven* of reliefe, ... III. iv. 8. 3
Shut up her *haven,* mard her marchants trade, ... V. x. 25. 6
Having (*partial list of auxiliary*).
having all parts in their power, ... *Ro.* viii. 9
Nought *having,* nought feared they to forgoe; . . . . *S.C.* May 110
With horrid sound though *having* little sence, ... *T.M.* 554
having none to let, to wood did wend. . . . . *As.* 126
Having his Amaryllis left to mone. . . . . *Col.* 435
In vaine he seekes that *having* cannot hold. . . . . I. vi. 33. 7
having not complaine, and *having* it upbrayd?' . . . . . . II. vii. 14. 9
Some *having* heads like Harts, ... II. xi. 10. 4
having at a bay The salvage beast . . . . III. i. 22. 1
Having a keeper still with him in place; . . . . IV. viii. 54. 4
having in companie This lucklesse Ladie . . . . V. i. 16. 8
long *having* since Taken in hand th' exploit, ... V. xii. 3. 1
having soone his armes about him dight, ... VI. i. 32. 6
having now no use of his long speare . . . . VI. iv. 7. 6
having in his hand a whip, Her therewith yirks; . . . . . VI. vii. 44. 6
a Mastiffe *having* at a bay A salvage Bull, ... VI. vii. 47. 1
having small yet doe I not complaine Of want, ... VI. ix. 20. 3
nought *having* dout Of that was doen, ... VI. xi. 46. 4
having, pine; and, *having* not, complaine. . . . . *Am.* xxxv. 4
having it, they gaze on it the more; . . . . *Am.* xxxv. 6
having her, my joy will be the greater. . . . . *Am.* li. 14
having yet in his deducted spright . . . . *H.L.* 106
Havior. Her heavenly *haveour,* her princely grace, ... *S.C.* Ap. 66
Their ill *haviour* garres men missay . . . . *S.C.* S. 106
Ne in her speach, ne in her *haviour,* . . . . II. ii. 15. 3
many one Admyrd her goodly *haveour,* . . . . III. vi. 52. 8
With comely *haveour* and count'nance sage, ... III. xii. 3. 8
Havoc. he amongst them cruell *havocke* makes, ... IV. iv. 34. 6
Whom with sore *havocke* soone they overthrew, ... V. iii. 12. 5
Made cruell *havocke* of the baser crew, ... V. xi. 59. 6
Of whom he makes such *havocke* and such hew, ... VI. viii. 49. 6
mongst them stalke, And makes huge *havocke,* . . . . . . VI. xi. 16. 8
such spoile, such *havocke,* and such theft He wrought, . . . VI. xii. 23. 4
Hawk. *See* **Eyas-hawk.**
hagard *hauke,* presuming to contend With hardy fowle . . . . I. xi. 19. 5
him rencountring fierce, as *hauke* in flight, ... I. xi. 53. 4
For dread of soring *hauke* her selfe hath hid, ... II. iii. 36. 2
the sharpe *hauke* which her attached neare, ... III. viii. 33. 4
'Ne is there *hauke* which mantleth her on pearch, ... VI. ii. 32. 1
like an *Hauke,* which feeling her selfe freed . . . . VI. iv. 19. 7
in their tops the soring *hauke* did towre, ... VI. x. 6. 8
Hawthorn. Seest not thilke same *Hawthorne* studde, ... *S.C.* Mar. 13
With *Hawthorne* buds, and swete Eglantine, ... *S.C.* May 13
Hay. under the cocked *hay.* . . . . *S.C.* N. 12
he is old, and withered like *hay,* . . . . III. ix. 5. 1
In simple cratch, wrapt in a wad of *hay,* . . . . *H.H.L.* 226
Hay-de-guys. With *Heydeguyes,* and trimly trodden traces, . *S.C.* Jun. 27
Hayld, Hayle. *See* **Hailed, Haled, Hail,** *etc.*
Haynous, Hayre. *See* **Heinous, Heir.**
Hazard. Great *hazard* were it, and adventure fond, ... III. i. 10. 8
Some hard mishap in *hazard* of his life. . . . . III. iv. 24. 6
seeke els without *hazard* of thy hedd.' . . . . III. viii. 17. 6
life to *hazard* for faire Ladies looke; . . . . IV. ii. 40. 6
he her must hurt, or *hazard* neare: . . . . IV. vii. 27. 4
How great a *hazard* she at earst had made . . . . VI. iii. 8. 7
Hazarded. feare of foe That *hazarded* his health, ... *Mui.* 378
How to save hole her *hazarded* estate; . . . . VI. iii. 12. 7
Hazardize. Her selfe had ronne into that *hazardize;* . . . . II. xii. 19. 5
Hazardry. hasty wroth, and heedlesse *hazardry,* . . . . II. v. 13. 8
Some fell to daunce, some fel to *hazardry,* . . . . III. i. 57. 1
Hazel. like an *hazell* wand it quivered and quooke. . . . . . VI. vii. 24. 9
He (*partial list*).
He bade me upwarde unto heaven looke. . . . . *Bel.*[1] i. 8
He is the Shepheard, and the Priest is *hee;* . . . . *Hub.* 443
'Old father Mole, . . . *He* had a daughter . . . . *Col.* 106
Did not *he* all create To die againe? . . . . I. ix. 42. 2
'Is not *he* just, that all this doth behold . . . . I. ix. 47. 1
Head. *See* **Barehead, Fork-head, Godhead, Goodlihead, Hardihead, Jollyhead, Lustihead, Overhead, Pike-head, Sharp-head, Steel-head, Well-head.**
His *head* was garnisht with the Laurel . . . . *Bel.*[1] vii. 12
Hir *head* . . . with a morian armed, ... *Bel.*[1] xi. 5
His *head* did shine with crounes set therupon. . . . . *Rev.* iii. 3
head with Lawrell garnisht was about. . . . . *Bel.*[2] ix. 12
Whose *head* . . . with a morion hidd, ... *Bel.*[2] xv. 5
Upon her *head* he heapt Mount Saturnal, ... *Ro.* iv. 9
her *head,* earth'd in her foundations deep, ... *Ro.* viii. 13
shaming to have given so great *head* To his off-spring, . . . *Ro.* xi. 1
cloud, . . . to steepe his *hed,* Doth plonge himselfe . . . . *Ro.* xx. 3
Lifting to heaven her aged hoarie *head,* . . . . *Ro.* xxviii. 3
her faire lockes fell from her loftie *head,* . . . . *Van.* vii. 11
sicker thy *head* veray tottie is, ... *S.C.* F. 55
The watrie wette weighed downe his *head,* . . . . *S.C.* F. 232
utter his tender *head?* . . . . *S.C.* Mar. 15
Upon her *head* a Cremosin coronet, ... *S.C.* Ap. 59
'I sawe Phoebus thrust out his golden *hedde,* . . . . *S.C.* Ap. 73
His Vellet *head* began to shoote out, ... *S.C.* May 185
so thy father his *head* upheld, ... *S.C.* May 205
was the soveraigne *head* Of shepheards all . . . . *S.C.* Jun. 83
the spring was in his learned *hedde,* . . . . *S.C.* Jun. 94
weening hys whyte *head* was chalke, ... *S.C.* Jul. 223

Head—*Continued.*
A chapelet on her *head* she wore, ... *S.C.* Au. 69
I left the *head* in my hart-roote, ... *S.C.* Au. 99
sithence I sawe thy *head* last, ... *S.C.* S. 19
Till fayrer Fortune shewe forth her *head.* . . . . *S.C.* S. 257
hold up thy heavye *head,* . . . . *S.C.* O. 1
The vaunted verse a vacant *head* demaundes, ... *S.C.* O. 100
My *head* besprent with hoary frost I fynd, ... *S.C.* D. 135
Sweete quiet harbours in his harmeless *head,* . . . . *Gn.* 134
weighing down his drouping drowsie *hedd,* . . . . *Gn.* 244
with proud vaunt his *head* aloft doth holde; . . . . *Gn.* 259
Ten thousand snakes cralling about his *hed* . . . . *Gn.* 348
two is better than one *head.'* . . . . *Hub.* 82
Upon his *head* an old Scotch cap he wore, ... *Hub.* 209
upon his *head* The Crowne, ... *Hub.* 1061
the Lambes owne mothers *hed.* . . . . *Hub.* 1216
on his *head* his dreadfull hat he dight, ... *Hub.* 1279
That on his *head* he wore, and in his hand . . . . *Hub.* 1291
From underneath his *head* he tooke away, ... *Hub.* 1322
thy kingdome from thy *head* is rent, ... *Hub.* 1329
all comfortlesse doth hide her chearlesse *head* . . . . . . *T.M.* 239
Upon his *head* his glistering Burganet, ... *Mui.* 73
A burning Teade about his *head* did move, ... *Mui.* 293
steelhed speare, and morion on her *hedd,* . . . . *Mui.* 322
perforce him drove on *hed,* . . . . *Mui.* 420
had it armes and wings, and *head* and taile, ... *Col.* 218
With hoary *head* and deawy dropping beard, ... *Col.* 250
Upon a virgin brydes adorned *head,* . . . . *Col.* 338
Next gan the earth to show her naked *head,* . . . . *Col.* 857
the streames that, . . . Flow from thy fruitfull *head,* . . . . *Ded.Son.* viii. 10
hurling her hideous taile About her cursed *head;* . . . . . . I. i. 16. 3
The stroke . . . from her *head* unto her shoulder glaunst. . . . I. i. 17. 9
He raft her hatefull *heade* without remorse: . . . . I. i. 24. 8
flyes Fluttring about his ever-damned *hedd,* . . . . I. i. 38. 3
Cynthia . . . doth steepe In silver deaw his ever-drouping *hed,* I. i. 39. 8
lifting up his lompish *head,* . . . . I. i. 43. 4
His heavie *head,* devoide of careful carke; . . . . I. i. 44. 4
The one upon his hardie *head* him plaste, ... I. i. 47. 3
like a Persian mitre on her *hed* Shee wore, ... I. ii. 13. 4
I warne thee . . . hide thy *head.'* . . . . I. ii. 18. 6
So hugely stroke, that it . . . cleft his *head.* . . . . I. ii. 19. 5
From her fayre *head* her fillet she undight, ... I. iii. 4. 5
when he sees his age, And hoarie *head* of Archimago old, . . . I. iii. 38. 4
Scarse could he once uphold his heavie *hedd,* . . . . I. iv. 19. 5
he . . . on his *head* an yvie girland had, ... I. iv. 22. 3
a burning brond . . . The which he brandisheth about his *hed:* I. iv. 33. 4
He gave her . . . triple crowne set on her *head* full hye, . . . I. vii. 16. 4
this dreadfull Beast with sevenfold *head* . . . . I. vii. 18. 8
stone . . . Shapt like a Ladies *head,* exceeding shone, ... I. vii. 30. 3
his dreadfull hideous *hedd,* Close couched on the bever, . . . I. vii. 31. 5
harmeful *head,* thrise heated in the fire, ... I. vii. 37. 3
every *head* with fyrie tongue did flame, ... I. viii. 6. 3
every *head* was crowned on his creast, ... I. viii. 6. 4
Through great impatience of his grieved *hed,* . . . . I. viii. 17. 4
His sparkling blade about his *head* he blest, ... I. viii. 22. 3
How ill it sits with that same silver *hed,* . . . . I. viii. 33. 5
Her crafty *head* was altogether bald, ... I. viii. 47. 1
The golden Sunne his glistring *head* gan shew, ... I. ix. 18. 2
they might perceive his *head* To bee unarmd, ... I. ix. 22. 1
to redeeme thy woefull parents *head* From tyrans rage . . . . I. x. 9. 4
beames . . . round about her *head* did shine . . . . I. x. 12. 9
on her *head* she wore a tyre of gold, ... I. x. 31. 5
that sacred hill, whose *head* full hie, ... I. x. 54. 1
his most hideous *head* my tongue to tell Does tremble; . . . I. xi. 12. 6
The steely *head* stuck fast still in his flesh, ... I. xi. 22. 1
The same advauncing high above his *head,* . . . . I. xi. 38. 1
on her *head* they sett a girlond greene, ... I. xii. 8. 6
from his *head* no place appeared to his feete. . . . . II. i. 5. 9
hid her visage, and her *head* downe bent, ... II. i. 15. 7
by my *head,'* (saide Guyon) 'much I muse, ... II. i. 19. 1
from so heavie sight his *head* did wreath, ... II. i. 56. 7
His flaming *head* did hasten for to steep, ... II. ii. 46. 3
To hide his coward *head* . . . . II. iii. 21. 4
from the *head* the body sundred quight. . . . . II. v. 4. 6
her *head* she fondly would aguize . . . . II. vi. 7. 3
laying his *head* disarmd In her loose lap, ... II. vi. 14. 6
bared all his *head* unto the bone; . . . . II. vi. 31. 8
His *head* and beard with sout were ill bedight, ... II. vii. 3. 7
lifting up his *head,* him answerd thus; . . . . II. vii. 62. 2
Beside his *head* there satt a faire young man, ... II. viii. 5. 1
Uplifting high, . . . to cleave his *head.* . . . . II. viii. 30. 7
Have cleft his *head* in twaine, ... II. viii. 33. 9
breake the launce, and let the *head* abyde. . . . . II. viii. 36. 7
did deepe invade Into his *head,* . . . . II. viii. 45. 5
Beare ye the picture of that Ladies *head?* . . . . II. ix. 2. 8
Ne other tire she on her *head* did weare, ... II. ix. 19. 8
abasht for shame Held downe her *head,* . . . . II. ix. 43. 2
Realmes defence, Did *head* against them make . . . . II. x. 15. 9
made he *head* against his enimies, ... II. x. 38. 1
soone as Titan gan his *head* exault, ... II. xi. 9. 4
Upon his *head* he wore an Helmet light, ... II. xi. 22. 8
her adorned *hed* . . . forth to advaunce, ... II. xii. 1. 2
Whose sleepie *head* she in her lap did soft dispose. . . . . . II. xii. 76. 9
bent his dreadful speare against the others *head.* . . . . . . III. i. 5. 9
her soft arme lay underneath his *hed,* . . . . III. i. 36. 3
her bright *hed* Discovers to the world discomfited: . . . . . III. i. 43. 4
Then I avow, by this most sacred *head* . . . . III. ii. 33. 5
taking thrise three heares from off her *head,* . . . . III. ii. 50. 1
from the *head* Of his coosen Constantius, ... III. iii. 29. 4
crowne with martiredome his sacred *head:* . . . . III. iii. 39. 4

Head—*Continued.*
shall upreare His dreaded *head*, . . . III. iii. 45. 7
from the Daniske Tyrants *head* shall rend . . . III. iii. 47. 6
Decline her *head*, and touch her crouper with her crown. . . . III. iv. 15. 9
ere the morrow did upreare His deawy *head* . . . III. iv. 61. 4
he would have hid His shamefull *head* . . . III. v. 13. 8
to the chin he clefte his *head* in twaine. . . . III. v. 23. 6
th' *head* fell backeward on the Continent; . . . III. v. 25. 7
from his *head* his heavy burganet did light. . . . III. v. 31. 9
Girlonds of flowres sometimes for her faire *hed* . . . III. vii. 17. 5
in his Scutchin bore a Satyres *hedd*. . . . III. vii. 30. 6
With golden wyre to weave her curled *head;* . . . III. viii. 7. 6
seeke els without hazard of thy *hedd*.' . . . III. viii. 17. 6
An aged sire with *head* all frory hore, . . . III. viii. 30. 3
loosd her helmet from her lofty *hedd*, . . . III. ix. 22. 7
whose *hedd* Empoisned was with privy lust . . . III. ix. 28. 8
Ne he twixt heven and earth shall hide his *hedd*, . . . III. x. 32. 8
He in a bush did hyde his fearefull *hedd*. . . . III. x. 44. 2
Phoebus gan to hyde his golden *hedd*. . . . III. x. 45. 9
up his *head* he reared easily, . . . III. xi. 15. 8
Did beat and bounse his *head* and brest ful sore: . . . III. xi. 27. 6
his hoarie *hed* Dropped with brackish deaw: . . . III. xi. 40. 3
hong adowne his *head* . . . III. xi. 41. 7
Downe hanging his dull *head* with heavy chere, . . . III. xii. 16. 3
from his shoulders quite his *head* he reft: . . . IV. iii. 20. 6
a firebrand she did tosse About her *head*, . . . III. xii. 17. 7
left the *head* behinde: . . . IV. iii. 10. 7
from his shoulders quite his *head* he reft: . . . IV. iii. 20. 6
in his *head* an hideous wound imprest: . . . IV. iii. 34. 4
thus he sharply sayd: 'Now, by my *head*, . . . IV. vi. 7. 6
knocke his *head*, and rend his rugged heares, . . . IV. viii. 4. 8
dreadfull weapon aymed at his *head*, . . . IV. viii. 41. 7
Over his *head* before the harme came neare: . . . IV. viii. 42. 4
found His *head* before him tombling . . . IV. viii. 45. 5
having ympt the *head* to it agayne, . . . IV. ix. 4. 7
on her *head* a crowne She wore, . . . IV. x. 31. 6
whose *head* and tail were fast combyned. . . . IV. x. 40. 9
sad Asopus, comely with his hoarie *head*. . . . IV. xi. 14. 9
With *head* all hoary, and his beard all gray, . . . IV. xi. 25. 8
on his *head* like to a Coronet He wore, . . . IV. xi. 27. 6
on her *hed* A Chapelet of sundry flowers . . . IV. xi. 46. 5
Liftes up his *head* that did before decline, . . . IV. xii. 34. 8
at one stroke cropt off her *head* with scorne, . . . V. i. 18. 6
Beare for his penaunce that same Ladies *head*, . . . V. i. 26. 8
He chose with shame to beare that Ladies *head:* . . . V. i. 27. 8
beare the burden of defame, Your owne dead Ladies *head*, . . . V. i. 28. 9
To beare that Ladies *head* before his breast, . . . V. i. 29. 4
as his *head* he gan a litle reare . . . V. ii. 18. 3
his blasphemous *head* . . . He pitcht upon a pole . . . V. ii. 19. 3
none Against them durst his *head* to perill shew. . . . V. iii. 12. 7
face was covered, and his *head* was bar'd, . . . V. iv. 22. 5
villany That she could forge in her malicious *head*, . . . V. iv. 29. 8
at his *head* did levell, . . . V. iv. 40. 3
both *head* and helmet to have raced. . . . V. v. 11. 9
Where he full shamefully was hanged by the *hed*. . . . V. v. 18. 9
With that she turn'd her *head*, . . . V. v. 30. 1
Uppon her *head* she wore a Crowne of gold; . . . V. vii. 6. 6
deckt with Mitre on her *hed* . . . V. vii. 13. 2
both *head* and helmet cleft. . . . V. vii. 34. 6
She turnd her *head* aside, . . . V. vii. 38. 4
on his *head* unhappily he pight, . . . V. viii. 8. 2
high over his *head* There written was . . . V. ix. 26. 1
a sage old Syre, . . . with a white silver *hed*, . . . V. ix. 43. 8
lighting on his horses *head* him quite did mall. . . . V. xi. 8. 9
his *head* at him shooke, . . . V. xi. 12. 8
strongly flew With all her body at his *head* . . . V. xi. 30. 7
hanging down her *head* with heavie cheare, . . . V. xi. 64. 4
nigh withered was, And hung the *head*, . . . V. xii. 13. 3
on his *head* a steele cap he did weare . . . V. xii. 14. 5
stouped oft his *head* from shame to shield: . . . V. xii. 19. 2
No shame to stoupe, ones *head* more high to reare; . . . V. xii. 19. 3
He stroke him with Chrysaor on the *hed*, . . . V. xii. 23. 2
reft his *head* to ease him of his paine. . . . V. xii. 23. 9
with th' one of which she scratcht Her cursed *head*, . . . V. xii. 30. 4
from her *head* her lockes he nigh did teare, . . . VI. i. 17. 8
cleft his *head* asunder to his chin. . . . VI. i. 23. 5
Above the earth upreard his flaming *head*, . . . VI. i. 31. 2
on his *head* an hood with aglets sprad, . . . VI. ii. 5. 8
crowne which should my *head* by right adorne) . . . VI. ii. 27. 9
tooke with him the *head*, the signe of shame. . . . VI. iii. 17. 6
he shew'd his *head* there left, . . . VI. iii. 18. 8
To make a garland to adorne her *hed*, . . . VI. iii. 23. 8
Uprear'd her *head* to see that chearefull sight. . . . VI. iii. 45. 5
hide his *head* from heavens spight, . . . VI. iv. 39. 4
Now beating his hard *head* upon a stone, . . . VI. v. 4. 5
with his fist unwares on th' *head* he strooke, . . . VI. v. 26. 3
So hideous is her shape, so huge her *hed*, . . . VI. vi. 10. 3
with his fist unwares on th' *head* he strooke, . . . VI. v. 26. 3
on his *head* a roll of linnen plight, . . . VI. vii. 43. 5
did his *head* for bashfulnesse abase, . . . VI. viii. 5. 5
His *head* meant from his shoulders to have swept. . . . VI. viii. 17. 3
Whose silver lockes bedeckt his beard and *hed*, . . . VI. ix. 13. 7
Her flowry garlond tooke from her owne *head*, . . . VI. ix. 42. 6
hewing off his *head*, . . . VI. x. 36. 6
he his face, his *head*, his brest did beat, . . . VI. xi. 33. 4
That is the highest *head* (in all mens sights) . . . VII. vi. 36. 7
hanging downe his *head*, did like a Mome appeare. . . . VII. vi. 49. 9
Her *head* and face was hid that mote to none appeare. . . . VII. vii. 5. 9
his high *head*, that seemeth alwayes hore . . . VII. vii. 11. 3
on his *head* . . A guilt engraven morion . . . VII. vii. 28. 7

Head—*Continued.*
on his *head* a girlond . . . He wore, . . . VII. vii. 29. 4
Upon his *head* a wreath . . . he bore; . . . VII. vii. 30. 6
decke her *head* with glorious bayes, . . . *Am.* xxix. 13
Sufficient worke for one mans simple *head*, . . . *Am.* xxxiii. 7
to the light lift up theyr drouping *hed*. . . . *Am.* xl. 12
Within a bush his dreadfull *head* doth hide, . . . *Am.* liii. 3
catching hold on thine owne wicked *hed*, . . . *Am.* lxxxv. 10
Cupid lay, His quiver by his *head:* . . . *Epig.* ii. 3
Phoebus gins to shew his glorious *hed*. . . . *Epith.* 77
More bright then Hesperus his *head* doth rere. . . . *Epith.* 95
lyke to those which red Medusaes mazeful *hed*. . . . *Epith.* 190
Love . . . Gan reare his *head*, . . . *H.L.* 63
Endure their Captains flaming *head* to see? . . . *H.H.B.* 60
sparke Which darted is from Titans flaming *head*, . . . *H.H.B.* 163
on her *head* a crowne of purest gold Is set, . . . *H.H.B.* 190

Headed. *See* **Fruitful-headed, Ill headed, Iron-headed, Maiden - headed, Many - headed, Seven - headed, Spring-headed, Steel-headed, Two-headed.**
Headed with yre and vengeable despight. . . . II. iv. 46. 2
some were *Headed* like Owles, . . . II. xi. 8. 3
Headed with flint, and fethers bloody dide; . . . II. xi. 21. 4
A cruell shaft, *headed* with deadly ill, . . . III. v. 20. 4
arrowes . . . Some *headed* with sad lead, . . . III. xi. 48. 4

Headland. An high *headland* thrust far into the sea, . . . *Col.* 281

Headless. So vainely tadvaunce thy *headlesse* hood; . . . *S.C.* F. 86
headlesse his unweldy bodie lay, . . . I. viii. 24. 3
left his *headlesse* body bleeding all the place. . . . II. viii. 52. 9
headlesse him into the foord he sent: . . . III. v. 25. 5
The *headlesse* tronke, as heedlesse of that stower, Stood still . IV. iii. 20. 7
Were much amaz'd the *headlesse* tronke to see Stand up . . . IV. iii. 21. 2
lies there on the laire An *headlesse* heape, . . . IV. viii. 51. 6
That *headlesse* tyrants tronke he reard from ground, . . . IV. ix. 4. 6
An *headlesse* Ladie lying him beside . . . V. i. 14. 3
This lucklesse Ladie which now here doth *headlesse* lie. . . . V. i. 16. 9

Headlong. Fell *headlong* into a dell, . . . *S.C.* Mar. 51
Nor bounds nor banks his *headlong* ruine may sustayne. . . . II. xi. 18. 9
Hedlong her selfe did cast into that lake; . . . II. xi. 47. 6
All destitute of helpe doth *headlong* fall; . . . V. ii. 8. 4
Into the Sea her selfe did *headlong* throw, . . . V. iv. 10. 3
Alreadie seemes that fortunes *headlong* wheele Begins to turne, V. x. 20. 7
Who then can thinke their *hedlong* ruine to recure? . . . V. x. 26. 9

Head-piece. in his *headpeace* he felt a sore payne: . . . *S.C.* May 242
Out of his *headpeece* Cambell fiercely reft, . . . IV. iii. 12. 4
him did rap Upon his *headpeece* . . . IV. v. 42. 4
on his *head-peece* him so fiercely smit, . . . V. iv. 39. 7

Head-purging. Veyne-healing Verven, and *hed-purging* Dill, . *Mui.* 197

Heads. *See* **Well-heads.**
seven springing *heds* of monstrous crimes, . . . *Bel.*[1] viii. 13
seven *heads*, ten crounes, ten hornes did beare, . . . *Rev.* i. 2
One of hir *heads* yet there I did espie, . . . *Rev.* i. 7
seven *heads* I saw, Ten hornes . . . *Rev.* ii. 4
a strange beast with seven *heads* . . . *Bel.*[2] viii. 5
seven *heads*, budding monstrous crimes . . . *Bel.*[2] x. 12
hanging *heads* did seeme his carefull case to weepe. . . . *S.C.* Ja. 78
Ylike as a Monster of many *heads;* . . . *S.C.* S. 121
hang theyr *heads* as they would learne to weepe; . . . *S.C.* N. 134
high shoote up their *heads* into the skyes. . . . *Gn.* 192
How great a guilt upon your *heads* ye draw, . . . *Col.* 928
Those prudent *heads*, that with theire counsels wise . . . *Ded. Son.* i. 1
burning blades about their *heades* doe blesse, . . . I. v. 6. 4
dreadfull Cerberus His three deformed *heads* did lay along, . . I. v. 34. 2
many *heades* . . . Did breed him endlesse labor to subdew. I. vii. 17. 4
seven great *heads* out of his body grew, . . . I. vii. 17. 7
beast; . . . threatned all his *heades* like flaming brandes. . . . I. viii. 12. 6
Stroke one of those deformed *heades* so sore, . . . I. viii. 16. 2
two hils, whose high *heads* overplast . . . II. i. 24. 4
from whose two *heads* . . . fresh streames do flow, . . . II. ii. 9. 1
whose *heads* were dight In poyson . . . II. iv. 38. 8
The one of which had two *heades*, . . . II. x. 73. 6
Some having *heads* like Harts, . . . II. xi. 10. 4
crowne your *heades* with heavenly coronall, . . . III. v. 53. 8
in his shield . . . the *heads* of many broken speares; . . . IV. i. 48. 9
Where they might hide their *heads* in quiet rest, . . . IV. v. 32. 6
Bearing his sixe deformed *heads* on hye, . . . IV. xi. 32. 2
on their *heads* . . . They wore rich Mitres . . . V. vii. 4. 5
their *heads* from death to hide, . . . VI. xi. 49. 8
labourd long in vaine To crop his thousand *heads*, . . . VI. xii. 32. 4
Did seeme to bow their bloosming *heads* full lowe . . . VII. vii. 8. 8
they therewith doe Poetes *heads* adorne, . . . *Am.* xxix. 7
the Furies fell Theyr snaky *heads* doe combe, . . . *Am.* lxxxv. 3
having all your *heads* with girlands crownd, . . . *Epith.* 13
in her snowy bosome boldly lay Their quiet *heads*, . . . *H.L.* 290

Head-stall. Him by the bright embrodered *hed-stall* tooke; . V. iii. 33. 7

Headstrong. Such was the furie of these *head-strong* steeds, . V. viii. 41. 1

Heal. The next to *heale* theyr throtes. . . . *S.C.* Jul. 88
Aesculape . . . by his art Did *heale* them all againe, . . . I. v. 39. 9
That any wownd could *heale* incontinent. . . . I. ix. 19. 5
that gracious ointment . . . deadly wounds could *heale*, . . . I. xi. 48. 7
Did *heale* his woundes, and scorching heat alay; . . . I. xi. 50. 6
Hable to *heale* the sicke, and to revive the ded. . . . II. iii. 22. 9
How she might *heale* her sonne whose senses were decayd. . . . III. viii. 4. 9
he there sojourned his woundes to *heale;* . . . III. x. 5. 6
Him to refresh, and her late wounds to *heale:* . . . V. vii. 42. 2
all the passions *heale* which wound the weaker spright. . . . VI. vi. 3. 9
in your selfe your onely hope doth lie To *heale* your selves, . . VI. vi. 7. 2
with one salve, both hart and body *heale*. . . . *Am.* l. 14
al my wounds wil *heale* in little space. . . . *Am.* lvii. 14
To *heale* the sores of sinfull soules unsound, . . . *H.H.L.* 166

Healed. wounds . . . handle softly till they can be *heald:* . I. v. 29. 8

Healed—*Continued.*
his woundes wyde Not throughly *heald* . . . I. v. 45. 5
infected sin, Not purg'd nor *heald,* . . . I. x. 25. 3
All *healed* of his hurts and woundes wide, . . . I. xi. 52. 2
Least that his wound were inly well not *heald,* . . . III. v. 49. 2
Untill that they their wounds well *healed* had, . . . IV. vi. 39. 8
Marinells former wound is *heald,* . . . IV. xi. Arg.
Whyleare by Tryphon was not throughly *healed,* . . . IV. xii. 22. 6
the biting . . . Was throughly *heal'd.* . . . VI. vi. 15. 6
Healing. *See* **Vein-healing.**
Heals. *heales* up one, and makes another wound! . . . III. v. 42. 2
The Hermite *heales* both Squire and dame . . . VI. vi. Arg.
Health. the great care I have of thy *health* . . . *S.C.* May 216
It is a signe of *helth.* . . . *S.C.* Jul. 212
his vowed life to spill For Countreyes *health,* . . . *Gn.* 604
feare of foe That hazarded his *health,* . . . *Mui.* 378
strive Himselfe with salves to *health* for to restore, . . . I. v. 40. 8
Both carelesse of his *health,* and of his fame; . . . I. vii. 7. 3
to spoyle the Castle of his *health?'* . . . I. ix. 31. 2
wants she *health,* or busie is elswhere?' . . . I. x. 16. 3
they did to *health* restore The man . . . I. x. 27. 8
Life and long *health* that gracious ointment gave, . . . I. xi. 48. 6
his owne *health* remembring now no more, . . . II. vi. 45. 8
him restor'd to *helth* that would have algates dyde. . . . II. vi. 51. 9
health to every forreyne nation: . . . II. x. 26. 7
Attempred goodly well for *health* and for delight. . . . II. xi. 2. 9
his hart woxe sore, and *health* decayd: . . . III. v. 43. 2
Her crased *helth,* her late recourse to rest, . . . III. ix. 26. 3
Restore unto her *health* and former state: . . . III. xii. 35. 6
her lives Lord and patrone of her *health* . . . IV. i. 6. 2
Long may you live in *health* and happie state!' . . . IV. ii. 23. 8
of her *health* when Artegall did heare, . . . V. ii. 3. 5
If therefore *health* ye seeke, observe this one: . . . VI. vi. 7. 5
If that no salves may us to *health* restore? . . . VI. vi. 13. 7
in that villaines *health* her safety lies; . . . VI. viii. 18. 5
he freely drinks an *health* to all his peeres. . . . VII. vii. 41. 9
Full of delightfull *health* and lively joy, . . . VII. vii. 46. 8
Healthful. him restor'd to *healthfull* state againe: . . . IV. xi. 7. 4
Heame. *See* **Home.**
Heap. barbarous villaines in disordred *heape,* . . . *Bel.*[1] v. 10
They *heapen* hylles of wrath; . . . *S.C.* Jul. 202
An *heape* of earth he hoorded up on hie, . . . *Gn.* 657
There now is but an *heap* of lyme and sand, . . . *Ti.* 129
did a stately *heape* of stones upreare, . . . *Col.* 285
It was a goodly *heape* for to behould, . . . I. iv. 5. 1
in his lap an *heap* of coine he told; . . . I. iv. 27. 5
Whose shield he beares renverst, the more to *heap* disdayn. . . . I. iv. 41. 9
All these together in one *heape* were throwne, . . . I. v. 49. 1
with bloodguiltinesse to *heape* offence, . . . II. ii. 30. 3
To *heape* more vengeance on that wretched wight: . . . II. iv. 5. 4
doolefull sorrow *heape* with deadly harmes: . . . II. vi. 34. 4
whom I lust do *heape* with glory and renowne?' . . . II. vii. 11. 9
the Carle as fast Gan *heap* huge strokes on him, . . . II. xi. 43. 9
He tombled on an *heape,* and wallowd in his gore. . . . III. iv. 16. 9
Did *heape* on her new waves of weary wretchednesse. . . . III. viii. 20. 9
To *heape* on him dew vengeaunce for his hire. . . . III. ix. 17. 5
an huge *heape* of singultes did oppresse His strugling soule, . . . III. xi. 12. 1
rolled on an *heape,* lay still in swound . . . IV. i. 43. 1
on an *heape* were tumbled horse and man: . . . IV. iv. 19. 7
lies there on the laire An headlesse *heape,* . . . IV. viii. 51. 6
whereas she hidden lay Under an *heape* of gold. . . . V. ii. 25. 6
Whom heaven would *heape* with blis, . . . *Epith.* 247
Heaped. Upon her head he *heapt* Mount Saturnal, . . . *Ro.* iv. 9
the children of the earth *Heapt* hils on hils . . . *Ro.* xii. 2
heaped was On these seven Romane hils, . . . *Ro.* xii. 9
Now to become nought els but *heaped* sands? . . . *Ro.* xv. 14
In a great mountaine *heap't* with hideous noyse, . . . *Ro.* xvi. 2
heaped snowe burdned him so sore, . . . *S.C.* F. 233
round about me *heapt* in darksome glades; . . . *Gn.* 372
Are *heapt* with spoyles of fortune . . . *T.M.* 161
heaped spoyles of bleeding harts to see, . . . *Mui.* 100
A world of waters *heaped* up on hie, . . . *Col.* 197
The Sarazin . . . *heaped* blowes like yron hammers great; . . . I. v. 7. 2
With *heaped* strokes more hugely then before; . . . I. vi. 45. 4
hart, . . . *heaped* with so huge misfortunes, . . . I. vii. 39. 3
heaped hight Her hastie ruine does more heavie make, . . . I. viii. 23. 5
High *heaped* up with huge iniquitee, . . . I. ix. 46. 4
in an *heaped* furrow did thee hyde; . . . I. x. 66. 2
like an *heaped* mountaine lay. . . . I. xi. 54. 9
Heaped together in rude rablement, . . . I. xii. 9. 2
fate That *heaped* on him so many wrathfull wreakes; . . . I. xii. 16. 6
Here *heaped* up with termes of love unkynd, . . . I. xii. 30. 4
They *heapt* huge strokes the scorned life to quell, . . . II. ii. 20. 5
In chiefe degree are *heaped* up on hye: . . . II. ii. 41. 2
From sea to sea he *heapt* a mighty mound, . . . II. x. 63. 8
Upon his shield their *heaped* hayle he bore, . . . II. xi. 19. 1
Sorrow is *heaped* in thy hollow chest, . . . III. ii. 32. 7
his *heaped* waves he did command . . . III. iv. 22. 3
upon that shore there *heaped* was Exceeding riches . . . III. iv. 23. 1
her bowre Is built of hollow billowes *heaped* hye, . . . III. iv. 43. 2
he perforce him held, and strokes upon him *hept.* . . . III. vii. 33. 9
heaped hils on hight To scale the skyes . . . III. vii. 47. 4
From top of Hemus by him *heaped* hye;) . . . III. ix. 22. 6
angry Gods . . . Upon thee *heapt* a direfull destinie; . . . III. ix. 33. 5
heap'd together with the vulgar sort, . . . III. xi. 46. 2
Which she with wrongs hath *heaped* up so hy . . . V. ii. 9. 5
that rout . . . *heaped* strokes so fast on every side, . . . V. iv. 38. 8
cruell heavens have *heapt* an heavy fate; . . . V. v. 36. 3
Her selfe most gratefull shew'd, and *heaped* thanks repayd. . . . V. viii. 23. 9
heaped strokes did round about him haile . . . VI. v. 18. 3

Heaped—*Continued.*
'Yet further hast thou *heaped* shame to shame, . . . VI. vi. 34. 1
sorrowes *heapt* on her in greater throng; . . . VI. xi. 2. 7
Heaping. *Heaping* up waves of welth and woe, . . . *S.C.* May 93
'Thus *heaping* crime on crime, . . . II. iv. 31. 1
heaping stroakes which thereon soused sore: . . . IV. v. 36. 4
Heaping huge strokes as thicke as showre of hayle, . . . IV. vi. 16. 5
heaping stormes of trouble on them daily more? . . . IV. vii. 1. 9
Heaps. These *heapes* of stones, these old wals, . . . *Ro.* xviii. 1
These haughtie *heapes,* these palaces of olde, . . . *Ro.* xxvii. 3
snakes . . . hang in *heapes,* that horribly affray, . . . *Gn.* 349
murdred troupes upon great *heapes* to lay. . . . *Gn.* 400
Heapes of huge wordes uphoorded hideously, . . . *T.M.* 553
by her *heaps* her hugenesse testifies. . . . *Ti.* 77
Huge *heapes* of mudd he leaves, . . . I. i. 21. 6
The *heapes* of people, . . . Doe ride each other . . . I. iv. 16. 7
he gnasht his teeth to see Those *heapes* of gold . . . I. iv. 31. 7
Great *heapes* of gold that never could be spent; . . . II. vii. 5. 2
*these rich *heapes* of wealth doest hide apart . . . II. vii. 7. 3
To trouble my still seate, and *heapes* of pretious pelfe. . . . II. vii. 7. 9
To hoord up *heapes* of evill gotten masse, . . . III. ix. 4. 2
sore bestedde With *heapes* of strokes, . . . IV. iii. 25. 4
Great *heapes* of them, like sheepe in narrow fold, . . . IV. iii. 41. 4
Great *heapes* of salmons in his deepe bosome: . . . IV. xi. 43. 6
in great *heapes* them circled all about, . . . V. v. 5. 8
th' *heapes* of those which he did wound and slay, . . . V. v. 19. 6
the *heapes* which he did make Of slaughtred carkasses, . . . V. vii. 36. 4
All on confused *heaps* themselves assay, . . . VI. xi. 17. 5
shewing, by their *heapes,* how great they were. . . . *Com. Son.* iv. 8
Hear. to *heare* a noise alluring slepe . . . *Bel.*[1] x. 7
to *heare* novells of his devise; . . . *S.C.* F. 95
That it a heaven is to *heare.* . . . *S.C.* Ap. 108
a fooles talke to beare and to *heare.* . . . *S.C.* May 141
to *heare* thy rymes and roundelayes, . . . *S.C.* Jun. 49
to *heare* a doolefull verse Of Rosalend . . . *S.C.* Au. 140
him to *heare,* or matter of his deede. . . . *S.C.* Au. 148
my cryes . . . You *heare* all night, . . . *S.C.* Au. 177
my nightly cryes Ye *heare* apart, . . . *S.C.* Au. 190
Tityrus, I *heare,* . . . left his Oaten reede, . . . *S.C.* O. 55
the Heavens did quake his verse to *here.* . . . *S.C.* O. 60
(so be thou deigne to *heare* Rude ditties, . . . *S.C.* D. 13
delay Thy nightly course, to *heare* his melodie? . . . *Gn.* 460
Heare, then, my paine and inward agonie. . . . *Hub.* 58
ye shall shortly *heare.'* . . . *Hub.* 549
what of tidings you abroad doo *heare?* . . . *Hub.* 605
To *heare* the Javell so good men to nip; . . . *Hub.* 712
At everie thing which they *heare* spoken ill, . . . *Hub.* 715
To *heare* their doome, and sad ensample see. . . . *Hub.* 1378
thether came to *heare* their musick sweet, . . . *T.M.* 32
Heare, thou great Father of the Gods on hie, . . . *T.M.* 55
Heare, and behold the miserable state Of us, . . . *T.M.* 59
they him *heare,* and they him highly prayse. . . . *T.M.* 414
tell hir, I can *heare* no mirth. . . . *U.V.* 9
her to *heare* I feele my feeble spright Robbed of sense, . . . *Ti.* 320
To runne thy shrill Arcadian Pipe to *heare:* . . . *Ti.* 328
doost *heare* their heavenlie layes, . . . *Ti.* 335
they *heare* thine, and thine doo better praise. . . . *Ti.* 336
Of whome no word we *heare,* . . . *Ti.* 360
grisly Ghosts, to *heare* the dolefull teene. . . . *D.* 21
Hath made fit mate thy wretched case to *heare,* . . . *D.* 65
'To seeke to *heare* that which cannot be tolde, . . . *D.* 72
never didst thou *heare* more haplesse fate. . . . *D.* 98
the Shepheards, which my hap did *heare,* . . . *D.* 141
at all complaine My good to *heare,* . . . *D.* 280
heavens refuse to *heare* a wretches cry; . . . *D.* 355
I hate to *heare,* lowd plaints have duld mine eares; . . . *D.* 415
When ye doo *heare* me in that desert place . . . *D.* 508
When ye doo *heare* my sorrowfull annoy, . . . *D.* 514
when ye *heare* that I am dead or slaine, . . . *D.* 523
if any nycer wit Shall hap to *heare,* . . . *As.* Pr. 14
To *heare* the charmes of his enchanting skill; . . . *As.* 46
Did thether flock to see what they did *heare.* . . . *As.* 202
With hungrie eares to *heare* his harmonie: . . . *Col.* 53
'*Heare* then (quoth he) the tenor of my tale, . . . *Col.* 100
I do covet most the same to *heare,* . . . *Col.* 161
let us *heare* what grace she shewed thee, . . . *Col.* 356
it desir'd at timely houres to *heare,* . . . *Col.* 362
To *heare* thee sing, a simple silly Elfe? . . . *Col.* 371
When as ye *heare* her memory renewed, . . . *Col.* 645
yrkes each gentle heart which it doth *heare.'* . . . *Col.* 906
see And *heare* the languors of my too long dying, . . . *Col.* 948
The which to *heare* vouchsafe, O dearest dread, . . . I. Pr. 4. 9
Joying to *heare* the birdes sweete harmony, . . . I. i. 8. 2
if of . . . homebredd evil ye desire to *heare,* . . . I. i. 31. 2
his dull eares to *heare* what shee did tell; . . . I. ii. 26. 7
She could not *heare,* nor speake, nor understand; . . . I. iii. 11. 4
the witches speach she gan to *heare,* . . . I. v. 21. 7
If old Aveugles sonnes so evil *heare?* . . . I. v. 23. 7
none can breath, nor see, nor *heare* at will, . . . I. vii. 13. 7
thus I *heare* you of your sorrowes treat. . . . I. vii. 40. 4
heare the story sad, which I shall tell you briefe. . . . I. vii. 42. 9
O *heare,* how piteous he to you for ayd does call!' . . . I. viii. 28. 9
bleede to *hear* their piteous mone. . . . I. viii. 36. 9
Ne living man like wordes did ever *heare,* . . . I. ix. 14. 7
God you never let his charmed speaches *heare!'* . . . I. ix. 30. 9
heare the wisedom of her wordes divine. . . . I. x. 18. 6
wonder was to *heare* her goodly speach: . . . I. x. 19. 7
The watchman wayting tydings glad to heare, . . . I. xi. 3. 7
So shaked he, that horror was to *heare:* . . . I. xi. 9. 7
Of other worldes he happily should *heare,* . . . II. Pr. 3. 8

Hear—*Continued.*

The brave adventures of this faery knight . . . to *heare*; . . . II. Pr. 5. 8
he hath great glory wonne, as I *heare* tell. . . . II. i. 19. 9
'*Heare* then, O man! the sorrowes . . . II. i. 49. 5
to her just conditions of faire peace to *heare*. . . . II. ii. 27. 9
to *heare* of straunge adventures to be told. . . . II. ii. 42. 9
whistling wind they *heare*, . . . II. iii. 20. 4
She list not *heare*, but her disports poursewd, . . . II. vi. 26. 8
all the forest quakes to *heare* him rore: . . . II. viii. 42. 7
quite ravisht with delight to *heare* . . . II. x. 69. 1
Like did he never *heare*, like did he never see. . . . II. xi. 40. 9
let him *heare* some part of their rare melody. . . . II. xii. 33. 9
hard it was for wight which did it *heare*, . . . II. xii. 70. 5
wonder was to *heare* their trim consort. . . . III. i. 40. 6
To *heare* her Love so highly magnifyde; . . . III. ii. 11. 2
of his dearest daughters hard misfortune *heare*. . . . III. iii. 5. 9
brasen Caudrons thou shalt rombling *heare*, . . . III. iii. 9. 3
wox half blanck those wordes to *heare*, . . . III. iii. 17. 8
To *heare* so often, in that royall hous, . . . III. iii. 54. 2
boastfull men so oft abasht to *heare*? . . . III. iv. 1. 7
To *heare* the warlike feates . . . III. iv. 2. 4
wondrous ruth to all that shall it *heare*: . . . III. v. 6. 8
she everywhere mote *heare* Complayning, . . . III. vi. 13. 6
Into misfortune fell, as ye did *heare*, . . . III. vi. 54. 8
Each shade she saw, and each noyse she did *heare*, . . . III. vii. 1. 8
most lament For her depart, that ever man did *heare*: . . . III. vii. 20. 2
his hart did grate To *heare* him threaten . . . III. ix. 14. 6
I would to *heare* desyre What to Aeneas fell; . . . III. ix. 40. 6
Vouchsafe with mild regard a wretches cace to *heare*.' . . . III. x. 26. 9
prayd her wake to *heare* him plaine. . . . III. x. 49. 6
In signe of silence, as to *heare* a play, . . . III. xii. 4. 4
She much was cheard to *heare* him mentiond, . . . III. xii. 41. 1
that she may the better deigne to *heare*, . . . IV. Pr. 5. 1
Which when as Scudamour did *heare*, . . . IV. i. 49. 6
heare the ordenance thonder, . . . IV. ii. 16. 8
Content to *heare* him speake, . . . IV. ii. 21. 9
Like to the Northern winde, that none could *heare*: . . . IV. v. 38. 8
Desiring of his Amoret to *heare* . . . IV. vi. 34. 3
no where could her find, nor tydings of her *heare*.' . . . IV. vi. 36. 9
dismayd With needlesse dread, till certaintie ye *heare*; . . . IV. vi. 37. 7
pittie is to *heare* the perils which she tride. . . . IV. vii. 2. 9
The hideous noise of their huge strokes did *heare*, . . . IV. vii. 29. 3
Seeking adventures where he mote *heare* tell; . . . IV. vii. 42. 3
there were none her hatefull words to *heare*. . . . IV. viii. 36. 4
sigh full sore to *heare* the miserie . . . IV. viii. 64. 4
That none might *heare* the sorrow of my hart, . . . IV. x. 48. 2
count my cares when none is nigh to *heare*, . . . IV. xii. 6. 2
listening if he mote her *heare* againe, . . . IV. xii. 17. 4
soone as she did *heare* . . . IV. xii. 27. 7
of her health when Artegall did *heare*, . . . V. ii. 3. 5
'Within three daies,' (quoth he) 'as I do *here*, . . . V. ii. 4. 1
All which when Artegall did see and *heare*, . . . V. ii. 33. 6
turn'd aside for shame to *heare* what he did tell. . . . V. iii. 16. 9
To *heare* the piteous beast pleading her plaintiffe cause. . . . V. iv. 40. 9
since she no ill did *heare*, . . . V. vi. 4. 8
ought to *heare* that mote delightfull bee: . . . V. vi. 21. 2
As glad to *heare* of armes, . . . V. vii. 25. 5
sore engriev'd to *heare*, . . . V. vii. 32. 7
Untill they both doe *heare* what she to them will say. . . . V. viii. 10. 9
They *heare* him not, they have forgot his lore, . . . V. viii. 39. 8
Crying to them in vaine that nould his crying *heare*. . . . V. viii. 41. 9
The gentle knights rejoyced much to *heare* The prayses . . . V. ix. 21. 1
Where they mote *heare* the matter throughly scand . . . V. ix. 37. 7
Though plaine she saw, by all that she did *heare*, . . . V. ix. 50. 3
Hastily bent that enterprise to *heare*, . . . V. x. 15. 4
Did quake to *heare*, and nigh asunder brast: . . . V. xi. 28. 5
tidings sad Did much abash Sir Artegall to *heare*, . . . V. xi. 40. 7
no redemption nigh she did nor *heare* nor see. . . . V. xii. 11. 9
if she hapt of any good to *heare*, . . . V. xii. 32. 1
I am right glad To *heare* these tidings, . . . VI. i. 10. 3
'A shamefull use as ever I did *heare*,' . . . VI. i. 14. 1
his heasts did gladly *heare*, . . . VI. i. 43. 2
more enforst my paine, the more my plaints to *heare*. . . . VI. ii. 22. 9
And *heare* th' adventure of her late mischaunce; . . . VI. iii. 19. 2
The dastard, that did *heare* him selfe defyde, . . . VI. iii. 36. 1
To take the ayre and *heare* the thrushes song, . . . VI. iv. 17. 3
Whom pityting to *heare* so sore complaine, . . . VI. iv. 23. 3
So lewdly had abusde, as ye did lately *heare*. . . . VI. vi. 17. 9
To erect this wicked custome, which I *heare* . . . VI. vi. 34. 4
Were glad to *heare* of that adventure new, . . . VI. vii. 5. 3
none is nigh to *heare* that will her rew, . . . VI. viii. 40. 8
to thee flocke to *heare* thy lovely layes! . . . VI. x. 19. 5
who sees not would be affrayd to *heare*: . . . VI. xi. 17. 8
but could no tydings *heare*: . . . VI. xi. 26. 5
Whose like he never once did speake, nor *heare*, . . . VI. xii. 33. 6
Ne ought he said, what ever he did *heare*, . . . VII. vi. 49. 8
According as thy selfe doest see and *heare*, . . . VII. vii. 56. 7
once vouchsafe my plaint to *heare*, . . . *Am.* xviii. 7
would not *heare*, when he to her complayned . . . *Am.* xlviii. 11
To *heare* theyr names sung in your simple layes, . . . *Epith.* 5
all the Nymphes that you can *heare* . . . *Epith.* 37
But blush to *heare* her prayses sung . . . *Epith.* 163
And *heare* such heavenly notes and carolings, . . . *H.H.B.* 262

Heard. *See* **Herd.**

I *heard* (*hearde*[1]) the tronck to grone; . . . *Bel.* v. 12
I *heard* a busie bustling. . . . *S.C.* Mar. 69
But then *heard* no more rustling: . . . *S.C.* Mar. 72
For once I *heard* my father say, . . . *S.C.* Mar. 106
Well *heard* Kiddie al this sore constraint, . . . *S.C.* May 249
I *heard* that Pan with Phoebus strove, . . . *S.C.* Jun. 68

Heard—*Continued.*

(as I have *heard* Old Algrind often sayne) . . . *S.C.* Jul. 125
sike a roundle never *heard* I none: . . . *S.C.* Au. 125
The honest man, that *heard* him thus complaine, . . . *Hub.* 259
Whenas the Ape him *hard* so much to talke . . . *Hub.* 267
evermore he *heard* each one complaine . . . *Hub.* 1275
the false Foxe, when he the Lion *heard*, . . . *Hub.* 1359
Was ever *heard* such wayling in this place. . . . *T.M.* 18
now no pastorall is to bee *hard*. . . . *T.M.* 282
Their names shall of the later age be *heard*, . . . *Ti.* 348
at last I *heard* a voyce, . . . *Ti.* 580
all the way most heavenly noyse was *heard* . . . *Ti.* 612
I *heard* a voyce that called farre away, . . . *Ti.* 638
(as they *heard* before) . . . *Mui.* 126
having *hard* Her blazed fame . . . *Mui.* 265
'Let Bagpipe never more be *heard* to shrill, . . . *D.* 323
The heaviest plaint that ever I *heard* sound, . . . *D.* 541
The mournfulst verse that ever man *heard* tell: . . . *As.* Pr. 8
Where store he *heard* to be of salvage pray. . . . *As.* 94
Was *heard* to sound as she was wont on hye, . . . *Col.* 20
The woods were *heard* to waile full many a sythe, . . . *Col.* 23
when he *heard* the musicke which I made, . . . *Col.* 70
No wayling there nor wretchednesse is *heard*, . . . *Col.* 312
what ever thou hast *heard* to be . . . praysd . . . *Col.* 568
I have often *heard* Faire Rosalind . . . fowly blamed . . . *Col.* 907
oft I *heard* it spoken, How one, . . . *Col.* 919
That when he *heard*, in great perplexitie, . . . I. i. 19. 5
Long way he traveiled before he *heard* of ought. . . . I. i. 28. 9
No other noyse, . . . Might there be *heard*; . . . I. i. 41. 8
Therewith a piteous yelling voice was *heard*, . . . I. ii. 31. 1
Heard how in vaine Fradubio did lament, . . . I. ii. 44. 2
when he *heard* of harme he wexed wondrous glad. . . . I. iv. 30. 9
Soone as the Faerie *heard* his Ladie speake, . . . I. v. 12. 1
when they *heard* that pitteous strained voice, . . . I. vi. 8. 1
warres, nor new adventures, none he *herd*. . . . I. vi. 36. 3
heard abroad of that her champion trew, . . . I. vi. 36. 5
at the last he *heard* a dreadfull sownd, . . . I. vii. 7. 4
She *heard* with patience all unto the end, . . . I. vii. 27. 1
when he *heard* her answers loth, . . . I. vii. 38. 3
Was never wight that *heard* that shrilling sownd, . . . I. viii. 4. 1
Three miles it might be easy *heard* arownd, . . . I. viii. 4. 3
That when his deare Duessa *heard*, . . . I. viii. 12. 1
That to have *heard* great horror would have bred; . . . I. viii. 17. 2
Nor voice was *heard*, nor wight was seene . . . I. viii. 29. 9
sprites, . . . with great griefe were often *heard* to grone, . . . I. viii. 36. 8
when that Champion *heard*, . . . his hart was thrilled sore; I. viii. 39. 1
Ay wont to laugh when them I *heard* to cry, . . . I. ix. 10. 5
never rest, Till I that treachours art have *heard* . . . I. ix. 32. 2
they *heard* a roaring hideous sownd, . . . I. xi. 4. 1
He lowdly brayd, that like was never *heard*; . . . I. xi. 26. 2
they his pittifull adventures *heard*; . . . I. xii. 16. 3
there was an heavenly noise *Heard* sownd . . . I. xii. 39. 2
Who ever *heard* of th' Indian Peru? . . . II. Pr. 2. 6
when she *heard*, . . . II. i. 15. 1
When she her Squyre *heard* speake, . . . II. i. 16. 8
when he *heard* him speake, . . . II. i. 28. 1
They *heard* a rueful voice, . . . II. i. 35. 7
when that warriour *heard*, dismounting straict . . . II. i. 39. 1
Whom when I *heard* to beene so ill bestad, . . . II. i. 52. 7
The goddesse *heard*; . . . II. ii. 8. 6
when they *heard* How . . . straunge knight arrived . . . II. ii. 19. 6
He lately *heard* that dying Lady grone, . . . II. iii. 3. 7
At last they *heard* a horne . . . II. iii. 20. 7
through the thicke they *heard* one rudely rush, . . . II. iii. 21. 1
When first I *heard* her horn sound . . . II. iii. 44. 9
when earst that horne I *heard*, . . . II. iii. 45. 6
'Which when I *heard*, . . . II. iv. 30. 1
That when the varlett *heard* and saw, . . . II. iv. 45. 1
when far off Cymochles *heard* and saw, . . . II. vi. 4. 1
Which when as Archimago *heard*, . . . II. vi. 51. 1
suddeinly He *heard* a voyce . . . II. viii. 3. 7
Againe he *heard* a more efforced voyce, . . . II. viii. 4. 3
when he *heard*, and saw the tokens trew, . . . II. viii. 55. 1
His larumbell might lowd and wyde be *hard* . . . II. ix. 25. 7
Which when the Romanes *heard*, . . . II. x. 59. 1
When as their Capteine *heard*, . . . II. xi. 20. 2
An hideous roring far away they *heard*, . . . II. xii. 2. 6
as they went they *heard* a rueful cry . . . II. xii. 27. 2
they *heard* an hideous bellowing . . . II. xii. 39. 1
Eftsoones they *heard* a most melodious sound, . . . II. xii. 70. 1
might not . . . be *heard* elsewhere: . . . II. xii. 70. 4
whence that Musick seemed *heard* to bee, . . . II. xii. 72. 1
The constant payre *heard* all that he did say, . . . II. xii. 76. 4
he it knew at home before he *hard* Tydings thereof, . . . III. ii. 21. 4
heavy tidings *heard*, whereas she playd . . . III. iv. 29. 6
She sweetely *heard* complaine, . . . III. vi. 15. 8
tell me, if that ye my sonne have *heard* . . . III. vi. 23. 1
when those pittifull outcries he *heard* . . . III. viii. 30. 5
Which wordes when Paridell had *heard*, . . . III. viii. 48. 1
the noble Britomart *heard* tell . . . III. ix. 38. 1
She *heard* that she was lineally extract; . . . III. ix. 38. 7
forgot that whylome I *heard* tell . . . III. ix. 47. 3
so *heard* I say Old Mnemon. . . . III. ix. 51. 5
They *heard* a noyse of many bagpipes shrill, . . . III. x. 43. 2
none of all the Satyres him espyde or *heard*. . . . III. x. 47. 9
Nine times he *heard* him come aloft ere day, . . . III. x. 48. 5
she *heard* with grievous throb Him grone, . . . III. xi. 8. 6
Which when she *heard*, and saw the ghastly fit . . . III. xi. 12. 6
She *heard* a shrilling Trompet sound alowd, . . . III. xii. 1. 5
harmony . . . was sweetly *heard* to sound, . . . III. xii. 6. 2

Heard—*Continued.*
armes . . . glittering he did spy Or clashing *heard*, . . . III. xii. 12. 5
Soone as he *heard*, himself he reared . . . from ground. . . . III. xii. 43. *or.*9
Als as she double spake, so *heard* she double, . . . IV. i. 28. 1
So stood Sir Scudamour when this he *heard*, . . . IV. i. 50. 1
for the words which she *heard* say, . . . IV. i. 50. 4
When they the reason of his words had *hard*, . . . IV. ii. 28. 1
The wicked weapon *heard* his wrathfull vow, . . . IV. iii. 11. 6
All suddenly they *heard* a troublous noyes, . . . IV. iii. 37. 6
they *heard* the sound Of many yron hammers . . . IV. v. 33. 6
When Scudamour *heard* mention of that speare, . . . IV. vi. 7. 1
Soone as she *heard* the name of Artegall, . . . IV. vi. 29. 1
When Scudamour those heavie tydings *heard*, . . . IV. vi. 37. 1
she *heard* One rushing forth . . . IV. vii. 4. 3
Britomart *heard* not the shrilling sound, . . . IV. vii. 4. 8
she *heard* some one close by her side Sighing . . . IV. vii. 10. 1
how he wexed glad When he it *heard*, . . . IV. vii. 46. 8
Him seemed oft he *heard* his owne right name. . . . IV. viii. 4. 5
When so he *heard* her say, . . . IV. viii. 16. 1
never *heard* one word Of tydings . . . IV. viii. 18. 5
Which Ladies love, I *heard*, had never wonne . . . IV. x. 53. 7
Then was there *heard* a most celestiall sound . . . IV. xi. 23. 1
He *heard* the lamentable voice of one, . . . IV. xii. 5. 2
All which complaint when Marinell had *heard*, . . . IV. xii. 12. 1
(as ye have *heard* whyleare) . . . V. ii. 3. 2
as ye *heard* afore. . . . V. iii. 13. 5
I *heard* report that farre abrode did fly, . . . V. iv. 29. 4
Which when as Radigund there comming *heard*, . . . V. iv. 37. 6
In sort as ye have *heard* the same of late: . . . V. vi. 17. 3
with hard enduraunce had *Heard* to the end, . . . V. vi. 17. 5
She *heard* a wondrous noise below the hall: . . . V. vi. 27. 5
It was not long before she *heard* the sound . . . V. vi. 28. 6
All which when he unto the end had *heard*, . . . V. vii. 20. 4
All which when she unto the end had *heard*, . . . V. vii. 24. 1
Which when the other *heard*, she sternly frownd . . . V. vii. 28. 5
Whom when they *heard* so say, they lookt about . . . V. viii. 12. 1
having throughly *heard* and seene Al those great wrongs, . . . V. viii. 24. 1
Which when those knights had *heard*, . . . V. ix. 7. 1
to be *heard* The tryall of a . . . case, . . . V. ix. 36. 6
All which when as the Prince had *heard* and seene, . . . V. ix. 49. 1
When they had seene and *heard* her doome . . . V. x. 4. 3
sith he *heard* but one that did appeare, . . . V. xi. 2. 8
Which when the Prince *heard* tell, . . . V. xi. 21. 1
all the people there without it *heard*, . . . V. xi. 30. 2
Which message when Grantorto *heard*, . . . V. xii. 9. 5
if she *heard* of ill that any did, . . . V. xii. 32. 5
whatsoever good by any sayd Or doen she *heard*, . . . V. xii. 34. 2
if that any ill she *heard* of any, . . . V. xii. 35. 1
they *heard* a ruefull shrieke . . . VI. i. 17. 1
when well Sir Calidore had *heard*, . . . VI. ii. 34. 1
Came to the place whereas ye *heard* afore . . . VI. ii. 40. 4
At length he *heard* under the forrests syde A voice, . . . VI. iv. 26. 6
Which when he *heard*, he inly touched was . . . VI. iv. 34. 1
(as ye *heard*) . . . VI. v. 12. 2
he in the forrest *heard* A trampling steede, . . . VI. v. 21. 5
Which when as Cupid *heard*, he wexed wroth; . . . VI. vii. 33. 6
All which when Cupid *heard*, . . . VI. vii. 35. 3
as earst you *heard*, . . . VI. viii. 31. 2
sound Of a shrill pipe he playing *heard* . . . VI. x. 10. 3
Knowing his voice, although not *heard* long sin, . . . VI. xi. 44. 3
I will rehearse that whylome I *heard* say, . . . VII. vi. 1. 7
when this he *heard*, Was troubled much . . . VII. vi. 15. 6
running straight where-as she *heard* his voice, . . . VII. vi. 47. 3
No word was *heard* of her that most it ought; . . . *Am.* xix. 10
Be *heard* all night within, nor yet without: . . . *Epith.* 335
Let not the shriech Oule nor the Storke be *heard*, . . . *Epith.* 345

Heardest. Sike a song never *heardest* thou . . . *S.C.* Au. 50

Heare, -s, Heary. *See* **Hair, -s, -y.**

Hearer. carefull pipe may make the *hearer* rew: . . . *Col.* 397

Hearer's. Hable to melt the *hearers* heart unweeting, . . . *Col.* 598

Hearers'. salt teares bedeawd the *hearers* cheaks. . . . I. xii. 16. 9

Hearest. careles *hear'st* my intollerable cares. . . . *Gn.* 632
Save as thou seest or *hearst*. . . . II. viii. 14. 3

Hearing. *hearing* them so heavily lament, . . . *T.M.* 35
Which *hearing*, his rash syre began to rend His heare, . . . I. v. 39. 4
The Sarazin, this *hearing*, rose amain, . . . I. vi. 41. 7
By *hearing* her, and by her sisters lore, . . . I. x. 21. 2
hearing evermore His ruefull shriekes . . . I. x. 28. 4
sober Guyon, *hearing* him so rayle, . . . II. vi. 40. 2
The second Bulwarke was the *Hearing* sence, . . . II. xi. 10. 1
Which Guyon *hearing* . . . II. xii. 28. 1
Malbecco, . . . *hearing* them to call For fire in earnest, . . . III. ix. 18. 2
The wretched man *hearing* her call for ayd, . . . III. x. 14. 1
Hearing him those same bloody lynes reherse; . . . III. xii. 36. 7
Unto his cave farre from all peoples *hearing*, . . . IV. vii. 8. 8
farre from *hearing* of my heavy plight; . . . IV. xii. 6. 6
Which Artegall well *hearing*, . . . V. iii. 32. 1
hearing pleas of people meane and base: . . . V. ix. 36. 5
To th' *hearing* of that former cause in hand . . . V. ix. 37. 2
In th' *hearing* of full many Knights and Ladies gent. . . . V. x. 14. 9
Talus, *hearing* her so lewdly raile, . . . V. xii. 43. 1
hearing th' answeres of his pregnant wit, . . . VI. ii. 24. 4
The Ladie, *hearing* his so courteous speach, . . . VI. ii. 42. 7
hearing how his people badly sped, . . . VI. vi. 24. 4
Which Coridon first *hearing* ran in hast . . . VI. x. 35. 1
Hearing the holy priest that to her speakes, . . . *Epith.* 224

Hearke. *See* **Hark.**

Hearken. Now listen a while and *hearken* the end. . . . *S.C.* F. 101
Hearken awhile, from thy greene cabinet, . . . *S.C.* D. 17
Then *harken* well till it to ende bee brought, . . . *D.* 97

Hearken—*Continued.*
Hearken, ye gentle shepheards, to my song, . . . *As.* Pr. 5
hearken to the sober speaches which she spoke . . . II. ii. 28. 9
They to him *hearken*, as beseemeth meete, . . . II. xii. 14. 1
ill it were to *hearken* to her cry, . . . II. xii. 28. 6
soone compeld to *hearken* unto peace. . . . III. i. 23. 7
hearken to his lore, and all his counsell hyde. . . . III. x. 50. 9
So litle did they *hearken* to her sweet beheast. . . . IV. ix. 31. 9
Did gladly *hearken* to his grave beheast, . . . VI. vi. 15. 2
'*Harken* to mee awhile, yee heavenly Powers! . . . VII. vi. 20. 1
hearken to the birds love-learned song, . . . *Epith.* 88

Hearkened. He *hearkned*, and did stay from further harmes, . . . I. vii. 15. 1
He *hearkned* to his reason, . . . II. ii. 11. 1
Him *hearkned* to, and soone her selfe arayd, . . . II. iv. 27. 2
The merry mariner unto his word Soone *hearkned*, . . . II. vi. 4. 6
He *hearkned*, and his armes about him tooke, . . . II. xii. 38. 1
hearkned now and then Some litle whispering, . . . IV. vii. 33. 3
Her wisedome did admire, and *hearkned* to her loring. . . . V. vii. 42. 9
The Prince soone *hearkned*, and his life forgave. . . . VI. vii. 12. 5
The Infant *hearkned* wisely to her tale, . . . VI. viii. 25. 1

Hearkening. ought could fynd Worth *harkening* to, . . . *Col.* 367
To which all *harkning* did a while aswage Their forces furie, . . . V. xii. 8. 3
hearkning to that voice, . . . VI. i. 19. 1
To whose wise read she *hearkning* sent me streight . . . VI. ii. 30. 7
The Ladie, *hearkning* to his senseful speach, . . . VI. iv. 37. 1

Hears. *heares* and sees the follies of the rest, . . . *Hub.* 725
Who of the Grecian Libbard now ought *heares*, . . . *Ti.* 68
Whence he them *heares*; and, when he list shew grace, . . . *Col.* 881
he, enrag'd with rancor, nothing *heares*. . . . I. iii. 44. 5
The whistler shrill, that whoso *heares* doth dy; . . . II. xii. 36. 8
Whereso he *heares* that any doth confownd Them . . . III. ii. 14. 7
Prince Arthur *heares* of Florimell: . . . III. v. Arg.
So strong is passion that no reason *heares*. . . . III. vii. 21. 5
What stony hart, that *heares* thy haplesse fate, . . . III. ix. 39. 6
Tell what thou saw'st, maulgre who so it *heares*.' . . . IV. i. 48. 6
when my piteous plaints he *heares*, . . . IV. xii. 7. 4
some pit, where she him *heares* complaine, . . . IV. xii. 17. 7
Artegall *heares* of Florimell, . . . V. ii. Arg.
who so *heares* her heavinesse, would rew . . . VI. xi. 2. 8

Hearse. O heavie (heavy) *herse!* . . . *S.C.* N. 60, 70, 80, 90, 100, 110,120,130, 140,150,160
O happye *herse!* . . . *S.C.* N. 170,180, 190, 200
to decke thy sable *Herse*. . . . *Ti.* 679
When as my *hearse* shall happen to your sightes, . . . *D.* 528
As fittest flowres to deck his mournfull *hearse*. . . . *As.* Interl. 228
To decke his *herce*, and trap his tomb-blacke steed.' . . . II. viii. 16. 7
'What *herce* or steed' . . . 'should he have dight, . . . II. viii. 16. 8
from the holy *herse* Her love-sicke hart . . . did steale; . . . III. ii. 48. 6
Beene they all dead, and laide in dolefull *herse*, . . . III. iv. 1. 8

Heart. *See* **Faint-heart-fools.**
sight wherof dyd make my *heart* rejoyce. . . . *Pet.*[1] iv. 8
my *heart* yet burnes in paine. . . . *Pet.*[1] v. 12
puft up in *heart*. . . . *Rev.* ii. 7
aggreeves my *hart* (*heart*[1]) even to this houre, . . . *Pet.* iv. 12
All pleasure . . . for which mans *hart* could long; . . . *Bel.*[2] xii. 6
my glad *hart* thereat did much rejoyce. . . . *Pet.*[2] iv. 8
yet my *heart* burnes in exceeding paine, . . . *Pet.*[2] v. 12
In case thy greatnes he can gesse in *harte*, . . . *Ro.* v. 3
Didst arme thy hand against thy proper *hart;* . . . *Ro.* xxxi. 11
his proude *heart* is fild with fretting ire: . . . *Van.* x. 10
'Such rage as winters reigneth in my *heart*, . . . *S.C.* Ja. 25
cruddles the blood and pricks the *harte:* . . . *S.C.* F. 46
Forcing with gyfts to winne his wanton *heart*. . . . *S.C.* Ap. 24
Made my *heart* after the pype to daunce: . . . *S.C.* May 26
carefull thoughts in her *heart* did creepe) . . . *S.C.* May 190
a sigh had nigh rent her *heart* in twaine) . . . *S.C.* May 194
A thrilling throbbe from her *hart* did aryse, . . . *S.C.* May 208
which love within his *heart* had bredd, . . . *S.C.* Jun. 86
pierce her *heart* with poynt of worthy wight, . . . *S.C.* Jun. 100
she the truest shepheards *hart* made bleede, . . . *S.C.* Jun. 111
when the *hart* is ill assayde, . . . *S.C.* Au. 5
So love into thy *hart* did streame: . . . *S.C.* Au. 84
The glaunce into my *heart* did glide; . . . *S.C.* Au. 93
ever since my *hart* did greve, . . . *S.C.* Au. 123
sorrow close shrouded in *hart*, . . . *S.C.* S. 15
such eeking hath made my *hart* sore. . . . *S.C.* S. 31
with cleane minde, and *heart* sincere, . . . *Gn.* 122
In quiet rest his molten *heart* did steep, . . . *Gn.* 245
all the happinesse that *heart* desire, . . . *Hub.* 609
his *heart* was greatly eased. . . . *Hub.* 710
To eate thy *heart* through comfortlesse dispaires; . . . *Hub.* 904
deare brother, take good *hart*, . . . *Hub.* 1003
So went the Sheepe away with heavie *hart:* . . . *Hub.* 1222
he sdeignfully it scorn'd In his great *heart*, . . . *Hub.* 1235
he saw, that sorely griev'd his *hart*, . . . *Hub.* 1304
Grinding his teeth, and grating his great *hart;* . . . *Hub.* 1334
could have made a stonie *heart* to weep; . . . *T.M.* 110
deignes to pitie a perplexed *hart;* . . . *T.M.* 424
felt my *heart* nigh riven in my brest . . . *Ti.* 30
Him true in *heart* and trustie to you trow. . . . *Ti.* 203
I felt such anguish wound my feeble *heart*, . . . *Ti.* 482
nigh with griefe thereof my *heart* was brust. . . . *Ti.* 518
hope of heaven, and *heart* to God inclinde; . . . *Ti.* 585
(Whilst oft his *heart* did melt in tender teares) . . . *Mui.* 30
Before his noble *heart* he firmely bound, . . . *Mui.* 58
His *heart* did earne against his hated foe, . . . *Mui.* 254

Heart—*Continued.*

His *heart* with vengefull malice inly swelt; . . . *Mui.* 356
his false *hart,* fraught with all treasons store, . . . *Mui.* 395
stroke his weapon slie Into his *heart,* . . . *Mui.* 438
As if his *heart* in peeces would have rent. . . . *D.* 49
reft fro me my love, my life, my *hart:* . . . *D.* 160
to a beast his noble *hart* embase, . . . *D.* 180
'What *hart* so stony hard but that would weepe, . . . *D.* 246
accents, which like swords Did wound my *heart,* . . . *D.* 298
to breed Compassion in a countrey lasses *hart* . . . *As.* Pr. 4
For her that did his *heart* with love inflame. . . . *As.* 40
he whose *heart* like sorrow did invade. . . . *As.* 172
'Fearful much more . . . then *hart* can fear: . . . *Col.* 201
yet would live with *heart* halfe stonie cold, . . . *Col.* 206
can empierce a Princes mightie *hart.* . . . *Col.* 431
To her my *heart* I nightly martyrize: . . . *Col.* 473
My thought, my *heart,* my love, my life is shee, . . . *Col.* 476
seald up in the threasure of her *hart.* . . . *Col.* 571
Hable to melt the hearers *heart* unweeting, . . . *Col.* 598
To which him needs a guilefull hollow *hart,* . . . *Col.* 699
with chaste *heart* to honor him alway: . . . *Col.* 888
despite, That yrkes each gentle *heart* which it doth heare.' . *Col.* 906
glorious fire it kindled in his *hart;* . . . I. Pr. 3. 4
his *hart* did earne To prove his puissance . . . I. i. 3. 6
Seemed in *heart* some hidden care she had, . . . I. i. 4. 8
nigh his manly *hart* did melt away, . . . I. i. 47. 5
that false winged boy Her chaste *hart* had subdewd . . . I. i. 47. 9
Her swollen *hart* her speech seemd to bereave, . . . I. i. 52. 3
all so deare as life is to my *hart,* I deeme your love, . . . I. i. 54. 2
He . . . did his stout *heart* eat, . . . I. ii. 6. 3
prickte with pride And hope to winne his Ladies *hearte* . . . I. ii. 14. 7
Did much emmove his stout heroicke *heart;* . . . I. ii. 21. 6
'faire lady, *hart* of flint would rew The undeserved woes . . . I. ii. 26. 8
I . . . Feele my *hart* perst with so great agony, . . . I. iii. 1. 8
Her *hart* gan melt in great compassion; . . . I. iii. 6. 8
How does he find in cruell *hart* to hate Her, . . . I. iii. 7. 7
in close *hart* shutting up her payne, . . . I. iii. 8. 6
His bleeding *hart* is in the vengers hand; . . . I. iii. 20. 2
ought . . . That should as death unto my deare *heart* light: . I. iii. 27. 5
Cruell revenge, which he in *hart* did hyde; . . . I. iii. 33. 8
he . . . launcht his Lordly *hart:* . . . I. iii. 42. 8
stony *hart* could riven have in twaine; . . . I. iii. 44. 3
Least . . . rash misweening doe thy *hart* remove: . . . I. iv. 1. 6
in his hand a burning *hart* he bare, . . . I. iv. 25. 3
He seemd in *hart* to harbour thoughts unkind, . . . I. iv. 38. 8
bad say on the secrete of her *hart:* . . . I. iv. 46. 2
in eternal woes my weaker *hart* Have wasted, . . . I. iv. 46. 7
The noble *hart* that harbours vertuous thought, . . . I. v. 1. 1
Her feeling speaches some compassion moved In *hart,* . . . I. v. 24. 7
pitty in her *hart* was never prov'd Till then, . . . I. v. 24. 8
Croesus, that enhaunst His *hart* too high . . . I. v. 47. 7
he . . . Her constant *hart* did tempt with diverse guile: . . I. vi. 4. 3
burnt his beastly *hart* t' efforce her chastitye. . . . I. vi. 4. 9
Such fearefull fitt assaid her trembling *hart,* . . . I. vi. 11. 1
her deare *heart* with anguish did torment, . . . I. vi. 32. 4
That cruell word her tender *hart* so thrild, . . . I. vi. 37. 1
might her pitteous *hart* be seene to pant and quake. . . . I. vii. 20. 9
dead was his *hart* within, . . . I. vii. 21. 2
recovering *hart,* he does begin To rubb her temples, . . . I. vii. 21. 4
let the stony dart of sencelesse cold Perce to my *hart,* . . . I. vii. 22. 8
more heavy plight Then that I . . . harbour in mine *hart:* . I. vii. 25. 4
sorrowfull assay . . . almost rent her tender *hart* in tway; . I. vii. 27. 4
he knew Some secret sorrow did her *heart* distraine; . . . I. vii. 38. 4
hart, so plungd in sea of sorrowes deep, . . . I. vii. 39. 2
in my *heart* his yron arrow steep, . . . I. vii. 39. 5
you intrete, For to unfold the anguish of your *hart:* . . . I. vii. 40. 6
the breach Which love and fortune in her *heart* had wrought; I. vii. 42. 4
stoutest *heart,* I weene, could cause to quake: . . . I. vii. 52. 4
wondrous anguish in his *hart* it wrought, . . . I. viii. 15. 8
Such percing griefe her stubborne *hart* did wound, . . . I. viii. 25. 4
hardest *heart* would bleede to hear their piteous mone. . . . I. viii. 36. 9
with percing point Of pitty deare his *hart* was thrilled sore; I. viii. 39. 2
empty sides . . . Could make a stony *hart* his hap to rew; . I. viii. 41. 5
ensample hath this lesson deare Deepe written in my *heart* . I. viii. 44. 8
'what secret wound Could ever find to grieve the gentlest *hart* on ground?' . . . I. ix. 7. 9
slombring soft my *hart* did steale away, . . . I. ix. 13. 6
Was never *hart* so ravisht with delight, . . . I. ix. 14. 6
nathemore . . . Could his blood frosen *hart* emboldened bee, . I. ix. 25. 7
His subtile tong . . . mealt'h Into the *heart,* . . . I. ix. 31. 6
cold that makes the *hart* to quake, . . . I. ix. 44. 7
as a swords poynt through his *hart* did perse, . . . I. ix. 48. 2
To come and goe with tidings from the *heart,* . . . I. ix. 51. 6
Ne let vaine words bewitch thy manly *hart,* . . . I. ix. 53. 2
Her *heart* with joy unwonted inly sweld, . . . I. x. 8. 8
whether dread did dwell Or anguish in her *hart,* . . . I. x. 14. 5
rayse againe to life the *hart* that she did thrill. . . . I. x. 19. 9
sinfull horror workes in wounded *hart,* . . . I. x. 23. 3
sharp Remorse his *hart* did prick and nip, . . . I. x. 27. 3
Hart cannot thinke what outrage . . . I. xi. 40. 1
Possessed of his Ladies *hart* and hand; . . . I. xii. 40. 7
His *heart* did seeme to melt in pleasures manifold. . . . I. xii. 40. 9
as if her *hart* with sorrow had transfixed beene: . . . II. i. 15. 9
seemd her tender *heart* was rent in twaine, . . . II. i. 38. 4
Which shee increased with her bleeding *hart,* . . . II. i. 40. 3
His *hart* gan wexe as starke as marble stone, . . . II. i. 42. 2
goodly counsell, that for wounded *hart* Is meetest med'cine, . II. i. 44. 2
cold Have not all seized on your frozen *hart,* . . . II. i. 46. 6
The bitter pangs that doth your *heart* infest. . . . II. i. 48. 5
for griefe his *hart* did grate, . . . II. i. 56. 6

Heart—*Continued.*

with bold furie armes the weakest *hart:* . . . II. i. 57. 8
ruth emperced deepe In that knightes *hart,* . . . II. ii. 1. 9
Now gan his *hart* all swell in jollity, . . . II. iii. 5. 1
appall My feeble corage, and my *heart* oppresse, . . . II. iii. 44. 6
The knight emboyling in his haughtie *hart* . . . II. iv. 9. 6
With *hart* then throbbing, . . . II. iv. 17. 1
My *hart,* my handes, mine eies, and all assayd! . . . II. iv. 28. 7
wel nigh molt his *hart* in raging yre: . . . II. v. 8. 5
Ne let thy stout *hart* melt in pitty vayne: . . . II. v. 24. 6
Whereby close fire into his *heart* does creepe: . . . II. v. 34. 7
all that might his constant *hart* Withdraw . . . II. vi. 25. 5
ever held his hand upon his *hart;* . . . II. vi. 26. 2
In slouthfull sleepe his molten *hart* to steme, . . . II. vi. 27. 5
Of courteous clemency in gentle *hart.* . . . II. vi. 36. 6
Though somewhat moved in his mightie *hart,* . . . II. vi. 40. 3
his deepe wounded *hart* in two did rive; . . . II. vi. 45. 7
That noble *heart* as great dishonour doth despize. . . . II. vii. 12. 9
hart of flint asonder could have rifte; . . . II. vii. 23. 8
Gave him great *hart* and hope of victory. . . . II. viii. 39 .4
his deare *hart* the picture gan adore; . . . II. viii. 43. 5
the stony feare Ran to his *hart,* . . . II. viii. 46. 2
disdaine and rancour, which did gnaw His *hart* . . . II. viii. 50. 8
His *hart* with great affection was embayd, . . . II. viii. 55. 2
in the secret of your *hart* close lyes, . . . II. ix. 42. 4
Ne was there outward breach, nor grudge in *hart,* . . . II. x. 14. 7
quite his *hart* from Guendolene remov'd, . . . II. x. 17. 8
trembling terror did his *hart* apall; . . . II. xi. 39. 2
So ryv'd her trembling *hart,* and wicked end did make. . . II. xi. 47. 9
Your stubborne *hart* t' affect with fraile infirmity. . . . II. xii. 28. 9
Fayre Daphne Phoebus *hart* with love did gore; . . . II. xii. 52. 5
all that might his melting *hart* entyse . . . II. xii. 66. 7
Need but behold the pourtraict of her *hart;* . . . III. Pr. 1. 8
When first her tender *hart* was with his beautie smit. . . . III. i. 34. 9
So did she steale his heedelesse *hart* away, . . . III. i. 37. 1
Her fickle *hart* conceived hasty fyre, . . . III. i. 47. 6
in each gentle *hart* desire of honor breeds. . . . III. i. 49. 9
her false eies, that at her *hart* did ayme, . . . III. i. 50. 7
imperious love her *hart* did vexe, . . . III. i. 54. 4
she affixed had Her *heart* on knight . . . III. ii. 11. 4
softly sunck into her molten *hart:* . . . III. ii. 15. 2
Hart that is inly hurt is greatly eased With hope . . . III. ii. 15. 3
thinke of that fayre visage written in her *hart.* . . . III. ii. 29. 9
To let the secret of her *hart* to her appeare. . . . III. ii. 34. 9
Another arrow hath your lovers *hart* to hit.' . . . III. ii. 35. 9
sucks the blood which from my *hart* doth bleed: . . . III. ii. 37. 5
yield your *heart* whence ye cannot remove? . . . III. ii. 40. 8
Nor so did Biblis spend her pining *hart;* . . . III. ii. 41. 2
(welfare thy *heart,* my deare!) . . . III. ii. 42. 1
Her love-sicke *hart* to other thoughts did steale; . . . III. ii. 48. 7
Out of her daughters *hart* fond fancies to reverse. . . . III. ii. 48. 9
with sharpe fits thy tender *hart* oppresseth sore: . . . III. iii. 21. 9
Friendship professed with unfained *hart.* . . . III. iii. 62. 8
the deepe wound more deep engord her *hart,* . . . III. iv. 6. 4
to an heavy *hart* Thou art the roote . . . of bitter cares, . III. iv. 57. 1
Panting for breath, and almost out of *hart,* . . . III. v. 4. 1
in her *hart* finde highest rowme . . . III. v. 11. 3
The point of pitty perced through her tender *hart.* . . . III. v. 30. 9
hurt his *hart,* the which before was sound, . . . III. v. 42. 4
his *hart* woxe sore, and health decayd: . . . III. v. 43. 2
neither blood in face nor life in *hart* It left, . . . III. v. 48. 6
Yet never he his *hart* to her reveald; . . . III. v. 49. 7
can restore A love-sick *hart,* . . . III. v. 50. 7
upbrayd A dolefull *heart* with so disdainfull pride: . . . III. vi. 21. 8
Her *hart* was pierst with pitty at the sight, . . . III. vi. 40. 5
His feeble *hart* wide launched with loves cruel wownd. . . III. vi. 52. 9
To whom her loving *hart* she linked fast . . . III. vi. 53. 3
none so bestiall Nor salvage *hart,* . . . III. vii. 9. 6
had he not the *hart,* nor hardiment, . . . III. vii. 16. 3
deceive Fraile Ladies *hart* with loves consuming rage, . . . III. vii. 46. 4
My *heart* doth melt with meere compassion, . . . III. viii. 1. 2
the hardest *hart* of stone Would hardly finde . . . III. viii. 1. 7
Had so enranckled her malitious *hart,* . . . III. viii. 2. 2
wondrous gladnes to her *hart* applyde. . . . III. viii. 2. 9
would have algates riv'd The *hart* out of his brest: . . . III. viii. 3. 6
compassion frayle Into his *hart* attonce: . . . III. viii. 31. 5
Her *heart* nigh broken was with weary toyle, . . . III. viii. 32. 4
her faint *hart* was with the frosen cold Benumbd . . . III. viii. 34. 7
In th' *heart* of every honourable Dame, . . . III. viii. 43. 5
the burning *hart* which on his brest He bare, . . . III. viii. 45. 4
chiefely Paridell his *hart* did grate . . . III. ix. 14. 5
to the wound his weake *heart* opened wyde: . . . III. ix. 29. 2
secretly did glyde Into his *heart,* . . . III. ix. 29. 5
What stony *hart,* that heares thy haplesse fate, . . . III. ix. 39. 6
greedy eares her weake *hart* from her bore; . . . III. ix. 52. 7
did eke beguyle, Both eyes and *hart* attonce, . . . III. x. 5. 5
all the sleights unbosomd in his *hart:* . . . III. x. 7. 3
she her love and *hart* hath wholy sold To him, . . . III. x. 11. 2
saw the wicked fire so furiously Consume his *hart,* . . . III. x. 14. 6
ever his faint *hart* much earned at the sight: . . . III. x. 21. 9
'take good *hart,* And tell thy griefe, . . . III. x. 26. 1
That chearful word his weak *heart* much did cheare, . . . III. x. 26. 6
That dreadfull sound the bosters *hart* did thrill . . . III. x. 43. 5
did his *hart* with bitter thoughts engore, . . . III. x. 45. 4
all his *hart* with gealosy did swell; . . . III. x. 48. 6
doth with curelesse care consume the *hart,* . . . III. x. 59. 6
mak'st the loving *hart* With hatefull thoughts to languish . III. xi. 1. 6
as if his *hart* were peeces made, . . . III. xi. 8. 7
pitty did the Virgins *hart* of patience rob. . . . III. xi. 8. 9
the sharpe steele doth rive her *hart* in tway, . . . III. xi. 11. 4

Heart—*Continued.*
eates the *hart* and feedes upon the gall, . . . *H.L.* 268
Some deaw of grace into my withered *hart*, . . . *H.B.* 27
it can pierce through th' eyes unto the *hart*, . . . *H.B.* 72
My trembling *hart* in her eternall chaine, . . . *H.B.* 276
pierst the piteous *hart* Of that deare Lord . . . *H.H.L.* 156
What *hart* can feele least touch of so sore launch, . . . *H.H.L.* 162
Then let thy flinty *hart*, that feeles no paine, . . . *H.H.L.* 246
With all thy *hart*, with all thy soule and mind, . . . *H.H.L.* 260
Heart-binding. that of Amorets *hart-binding* chaine, . . . IV. i. 1. 4
Heart-blood. My *hart-blood* is wel nigh frorne, . . . *S.C.* F. 243
my *heart-blood* dropping weares, . . . *D.* 251
When the *hart blood* should gush out of his chest, . . . II. xi. 37. 7
lay bleding out his *hart-blood* neare. . . . III. v. 32. 9
With point of steele that close his *hartbloud* spild, . . . IV. iii. 22. 5
Heart-breaking. Making your musick of *hart-breaking* mone. *T.M.* 6
Heart-burning. Disloyall Treason, and *hart-burning* Hate; . . II. vii. 22. 3
through long languour and *hart-burning* brame, . . . III. ii. 52. 4
Hearted. *See* **Faint-hearted, Vile-hearted.**
Hearten. *Harten* against her selfe her conquer'd spoile, . . . *Ro.* xxii. 6
Heartened. seeing them through suffrance *hartned* more, . . . IV. ix. 34. 5
Heart-fretting. In such disquiet and *hart-fretting* payne . . . IV. v. 45. 1
The gnawing envie, the *hart-fretting* feare, . . . *H.L.* 259
Heart-frozen. delayd by her *hart-frosen* cold; . . . *Am.* xxx. 6
Heart-gnawing. Radigund, full of *heart-gnawing* griefe . . . V. iv. 47. 1
Heartless. hunt the *hartlesse* hare til shee were tame. . . . *S.C.* D. 28
All suddenly dismaid, and *hartles* quight, . . . *Gn.* 297
all within were dead and *hartles* left: . . . *Hub.* 1355
Like *hartlesse* deare, dismayd with thunders sound. . . . *Col.* 9
Then *hartlesse* quite, and full of inward feare, . . . *Col.* 228
With stony eyes and *hartlesse* hollow hew, . . . I. ix. 24. 3
hopelesse, *hartlesse,* gan the cunning thiefe . . . I. ix. 29. 7
frye in *hartlesse* griefe and dolefull tene: . . . II. i. 58. 4
The *hartlesse* Hynd and Robucke to dismay, . . . II. ii. 7. 4
Such when as *hartlesse* Trompart her did vew, . . . II. iii. 32. 1
He seemed breathlesse, *hartlesse,* faint, and wan; . . . II. vi. 41. 5
Was at his backe with *heartlesse* hedinesse, . . . VI. vi. 26. 7
Heartly. (Thereat full *hartely* laughed Satyrane.) . . . III. vii. 58. 5
Heart-murdering. Direfull impatience, and *hart-murdring* love: II. v. 16. 4
Thereto compelled through *hart-murdring* paine; . . . V. v. 30. 8
Heart-piercing. felt the point of his *hart-percing* dart, . . . III. xi. 30. 2
Heart-quelling. faire Venus, . . . With her *heart-quelling* Sonne *Proth.* 97
Heart-robbing. Drawne with the powre of an *heart-robbing* eye, . . . V. viii. 1. 6
me revived with *hart-robbing* gladnesse. . . . *Am.* xxxix. 8
Heart-root. I left the head in my *hart-roote,* . . . *S.C.* Au. 99
kydst not ene to cure thy sore *hart-roote,* . . . *S.C.* D. 93
Heart's. Gay without good is good *hearts* greatest loathing. . . *Hub.* 232
Therefore I mourne with deep *harts* sorrowing, . . . *T.M.* 107
to thee sings with deep *harts* sorrowing, . . . *Ti.* 318
harts deep sorrow hates both life and light. . . . *D.* 91
my *hearts* eternall threasure. . . . *Col.* 47
rudely sdeigne a gentle *harts* request; . . . III. i. 55. 4
choicest med'cine for sick *harts* reliefe: . . . III. iii. 5. 5
Her dearest sonne, her dearest *harts* delight: . . . III. iv. 44. 5
Devized by the Gods, for to asswage *Harts* grief, . . . IV. iii. 43. 3
woxe nigh mad for very *harts* despight, . . . IV. v. 27. 2
neither showed to other their *hearts* privity. . . . IV. ix. 19. 9
Give her great comfort and some *harts* content. . . . V. v. 35. 3
from thy tongue thy *hearts* intent doth hold.' . . . V. vi. 10. 3
Made kill her selfe for very *hearts* despight . . . V. xi. 25. 4
hearts dismay and inward dolour queld, . . . VI. i. 18. 3
(Being his *harts* owne wish,) . . . VI. ix. 16. 9
to insinuate his *harts* desire, . . . VI. ix. 27. 2
Wrapped in wretched cares and *hearts* unrest, . . . VI. xi. 3. 2
Written with teares in *harts* close-bleeding book. . . . *Am.* i. 8
thou wrongest my deare *harts* desire, . . . *Am.* v. 1
her deep wit, that true *harts* thought can spel, . . . *Am.* xliii. 13
Of my *harts* wound, and of my bodies griefe; . . . *Am.* l. 2
Her *harts* desire with most contentment please. . . . *Am.* lxxii. 12
this the worke of *harts* astonishment. . . . *Am.* lxxxi. 14
His *harts* enshrined saint, his heavens queene, . . . *H.L.* 215
may recure my *harts* long pyning griefe, . . . *H.B.* 285
Joy may you have, and gentle *hearts* content . . . *Proth.* 94
Hearts. griefe, that dothe our *hearts* anoy. . . . *Pet.*[1] vi. 12
Wonts not t' enrage the *hearts* of equall beasts, . . . *Ro.* xxiv. 2
Did grype your *hearts* with noysome rage imbew'd, . . . *Ro.* xxiv. 6
when their *false* harts bene hidde, . . . *S.C.* May 170
sad cares that rich mens *hearts* devowre. . . . *Gn.* 136
Brings downe the stowtest *hearts* to lowest state; . . . *Hub.* 255
the *harts* of all his enemyes; . . . *Hub.* 1296
Roaring yet lowder that all *harts* it daunted, . . . *Hub.* 1368
Can griefe then enter into heavenly *harts,* . . . *T.M.* 47
In th' *hearts* of men to rule them carefully, . . . *T.M.* 314
The noble *hearts* to pleasures they allure, . . . *T.M.* 331
launch your *hearts* with lamentable wounds . . . *T.M.* 375
O gall of all good *heartes!* . . . *Ti.* 449
Such rancour in the *harts* of mightie men? . . . *Mui.* 16
heaped spoyles of bleeding *harts* to see, . . . *Mui.* 100
they in secret *harts* envying sore, . . . *Mui.* 124
with your loves do their rude *hearts* possesse, . . . *D.* 527
you whose softened *hearts* it may empierse . . . *As.* Pr. 9
all mens *hearts* . . . He stole away, . . . *As.* 21
To prove that death their *hearts* cannot divide, . . . *As.* 179
Belov'd of high and low with faithfull *harts.* . . . *Col.* 531
my dread Lord, that doest liege *hearts* possesse, . . . *Col.* 793
With humble *hearts* to heaven uplifted hie, . . . *Col.* 816
ye . . . in subdued *harts* do tyranyse; . . . *Ded. Son.* xvi. 9
had such might over true meaning *harts;* . . . I. ii. 9. 5
double griefs afflict concealing *harts,* . . . I. ii. 34. 5

Hearts—*Continued.*
joyd weake wemens *hearts* to tempt, and prove, . . . I. iv. 26. 4
So been they parted both, with *harts* on edge . . . I. iv. 43. 3
Great ruth in all the gazers *harts* did grow, . . . I. v. 9. 7
Their *harts* she ghesseth by their humble guise, . . . I. vi. 13. 1
Such joy he had their stubborne *harts* to quell, . . . I. vi. 26. 7
peoples *hartes* with awfull terror tye, . . . I. vii. 16. 7
suddeine horrour to faint *hartes* did show; . . . I. vii. 31. 8
Th' eternall bale of heavie wounded *harts:* . . . I. viii. 14. 5
when he . . . felt our feeble *harts* Embost with bale, . . . I. ix. 29. 1
hartes of great Heroes doest enrage, . . . I. xi. 6. 4
in your noble *harts* Her hellish brond hath kindled . . . II. ii. 29. 2
Love, that two *harts* makes one, . . . II. iv. 19. 8
word so deepe did in their *harts* impresse, . . . II. viii. 18. 7
with sweet science mollifide their stubborne *harts.* . . . II. x. 25. 9
all mens *harts* in dew obedience held; . . . II. x. 32. 5
with which she thrild Fraile *harts,* . . . II. xii. 78. 8
Could judge what paines doe loving *harts* perplexe. . . . III. i. 54. 5
as it falleth, in the gentlest *harts* . . . III. ii. 23. 1
With lighter *hearts* unto their home retird; . . . III. iii. 51. 4
Vile rancour their rude *harts* had fild with such despight. . . III. v. 16. 9
Their wofull *harts* he wounded had . . . III. vi. 13. 8
How he their heedelesse *harts* with love had fir'd, . . . III. vi. 15. 4
in the wofull *harts* Of many wretches . . . III. vi. 49. 6
found such favour in their loving *hartes,* . . . III. vii. 55. 2
he many weake *harts* had subdewd Of yore, . . . III. x. 9. 7
On which their eies and *harts* were wholly sett, . . . III. x. 34. 6
your kingdomes make In th' *harts* of men, . . . III. xi. 2. 7
Ne in their frosen *hearts* feele kindly flame; . . . IV. Pr. 2. 2
none . . . to them tydings tell that mote their *harts* delight. IV. i. 16. 9
vertue is the band that bindeth *harts* most sure. . . . IV. ii. 29. 9
Smart daunts not mighty *harts,* . . . IV. iii. 8. 9
all mens eyes and *hearts* . . . filled were with rufull tine . IV. iii. 37. 3
to change the *hearts* of men Fro love to hate, . . . IV. iii. 45. 5
as if their *hearts* did faile, . . . IV. iii. 48. 3
hearts quite robbed with so glorious sight, . . . IV. iv. 16. 5
able was weake *harts* away to steale. . . . IV. v. 10. 5
did seduce The *hearts* of some . . . IV. v. 11. 4
setst thy kingdome in the captive *harts* Of Kings . . . IV. vii. 1. 3
could have perst the *hearts* of Tigres and of Beares. . . . IV. viii. 4. 9
into their *harts* and parts entire. . . . IV. viii. 48. 9
faint *hearts,* at first espiall . . . IV. x. 17. 6
luring baytes oftimes doe heedlesse *harts* entyse. . . . IV. x. 49. 9
O men! which boast your strong And valiant *hearts,* . . . IV. xi. 22. 4
The eares and *hearts* of all that goodly crew, . . . IV. xi. 23. 5
their *hearts* began to faile, . . . V. ii. 24. 7
their faint *harts* with senselesse horrour queld, . . . V. iii. 26. 3
proudest *harts* base love hath blynded.' . . . V. v. 40. 9
The skill whereof to Princes *hearts* he doth reveale, . . . V. vii. 1. 9
Their hardned *hearts,* enur'd to bloud and cruelty. . . . V. viii. 1. 9
their *harts* gan earne To understand . . . V. ix. 7. 1
did steale mens *hearts* away: . . . VI. i. 2. 6
Their *hearts* were sicke; their sides were sore; . . . VI. v. 40. 9
in signe Of servile yoke, that nobler *harts* repine: . . . VI. vii. 26. 5
did kindle lovely fire In th' *harts* of many a knight, . . . VI. vii. 28. 9
th' *hearts* of men, as your eternall dowre, . . . VI. viii. 1. 3
the winged God that woundeth *harts* . . . VI. viii. 22. 1
could so meekly make proud *hearts* avale, . . . VI. viii. 25. 3
humbled *harts* brings captive unto thee, . . . *Am.* x. 7
craftily enfold Theyr weaker *harts,* . . . *Am.* xxxvii. 8
she . . . weake *harts* doth guyde Unto her love, . . . *Am.* xlvii. 5
thou madest many *harts* to bleed . . . *H.L.* 12
Prepare your selves, and open wide your *harts* . . . *H.L.* 33
sterve their *harts* that needeth nourture most, . . . *H.L.* 39
Rest not till they have pierst the trembling *harts,* . . . *H.L.* 123
The ravisht *harts* of gazefull men . . . *H.B.* 12
robs the *harts* of those which it admyre; . . . *H.B.* 61
likely *harts* composd of starres concent, . . . *H.B.* 198
in mens *harts* thou mayst thy throne enstall, . . . *H.B.* 265
The *hearts* of men, . . . may lift themselves up hyer, . . . *H.H.B.* 16
inflame The *hearts* of men with selfe-consuming fyre . . . *H.H.B.* 275
Let endlesse Peace your steadfast *hearts* accord, . . . *Proth.* 101
Hearts'. lovers lincked in true *harts* consent, . . . IV. x. 26. 4
Heart-sore. His onely *hart-sore,* and his onely foe; . . . II. i. 2. 4
Heart-strings. tree, . . . Whose *hartstrings* with keene steele nigh hewen be; . . . I. viii. 22. 7
hart-strings of an Aegle ryv'd. . . . II. x. 70. 9
Her hart did leape, and all her *hart-strings* tremble, . . . IV. vi. 29. 2
all her *hart-strings* brast, . . . VI. xi. 22. 8
Heart-swelling. Through prowd ambition and *hart-swelling* hate, . . . *Mui.* 5
Heart-thrilling. to him threatned his *hart-thrilling* speare: II. iii. 6. 6
To yield wide way to his *hart-thrilling* brond; . . . II. viii. 41. 8
with *hart-thrilling* throbs and bitter stowre, . . . III. ii. 5. 3
with her *hart-thrilling* eies To make a truce, . . . *Am.* xii. 1
Heart-wounding. vainely did expownd To be *hart-wownding* love, . . . III. iv. 28. 4
Hearty. Ne may thee help the manie *hartie* vow, . . . *Mui.* 237
nathemore by his bold *hartie* speach . . . I. ix. 25. 6
With *hartie* wordes her knight she gan to cheare, . . . I. xi. 1. 5
Her *harty* wordes so deepe into the mynd . . . sunke, . . . III. iii. 57. 1
ech drunk an *harty* draught; . . . IV. iii. 48. 9
Hearty-hale. Sound Savorie, and Bazil *hartie-hale,* . . . *Mui.* 198
Heat. *See* **Summer's-heat.**
Cooling againe his former kindled *heate,* . . . *Ro.* xi. 5
Yet never complained of cold nor *heate,* . . . *S.C.* F. 19
home him hasted with furious *heate,* . . . *S.C.* F. 193
Agaynst his cruell scortching *heate,* . . . *S.C.* Jul. 25
Were not better to shunne the scortching *heate?* . . . *S.C.* Au. 48
heate of heedlesse lust me so did sting, . . . *S.C.* D. 21

Heat—*Continued.*
A comett stird up that unkindly *heate,* . . . *S.C.* D. 59
alwayes flow to quench his thirstie *heate.* . . . *Gn.* 120
In some coole shadow from the scorching *heat,* . . . *Gn.* 143
There from the boyling *heate* himselfe to hide: . . . *Gn.* 252
having doft for *heate* his dreadfull hide: . . . *Hub.* 954
Through him the cold began to covet *heat,* . . . *Col.* 847
powred kindly *heat* and formall feature, . . . *Col.* 862
hastie *heat* tempring with sufferance wise, . . . I. i. 50. 4
in hope themselves to hide From the fierce *heat,* . . . I. ii. 29. 9
though a tree I seme, yet cold and *heat* me paines.' . . . I. ii. 33. 9
One pricking towards them with hastie *heat,* . . . I. iii. 33. 2
other clothes he could not weare for *heate;* . . . I. iv. 22. 2
spices . . . To kindle *heat* of corage privily; . . . I. v. 4. 7
The knight was fiers, and full of youthly *heat,* . . . I. v. 7. 4
turning wrathfull fyre to lustfull *heat,* . . . I. vi. 3. 3
shade, Which shielded them against the boyling *heat,* . . . I. vii. 4. 3
This nymph, quite tyr'd with *heat* of scorching ayre, . . . I. vii. 5. 3
Then first the cole of kindly *heat* appeares . . . I. ix. 9. 3
prickt forth with . . . *heat* of hardiment, . . . I. ix. 12. 6
With *heat,* toyle, wounds, armes, smart, and inward fire, . . . I. xi. 28. 2
The *heate* whereof, and harmefull pestilence, . . . I. xi. 45. 1
Did heale his woundes, and scorching *heat* alay; . . . I. xi. 50. 6
rend the ratling skyes with flames of fouldring *heat.* . . . II. ii. 20. 9
for *heat* of scorching aire, . . . II. iii. 26. 3
with my *heat* kindled his cruell fyre; . . . II. iv. 32. 8
Guyon, in the *heat* of all his strife, . . . II. v. 9. 5
Therein did often quench his thristy *heat,* . . . II. v. 30. 6
ne sweete entreaties, might Appease his *heat,* . . . II. v. 38. 4
The hasty *heat* of his avowd revenge delayd. . . . II. vi. 40. 9
maystring them, renewd his former *heat:* . . . II. vii. 36. 6
from open *heat* Her selfe to shroud, . . . II. vii. 53. 4
better reason will aswage The rash revengers *heat.* . . . II. viii. 26. 7
settle patience in so furious *heat?* . . . II. viii. 27. 6
So hasty *heat* soone cooled to subdew: . . . II. viii. 47. 8
to delay the *heat,* least by mischaunce . . . II. ix. 30. 1
Yt now devoures with flames and scorching *heat,* . . . II. xi. 32. 8
Nor scorching *heat,* nor cold intemperate, . . . II. xii. 51. 5
As faint through *heat,* or dight to pleasant sin; . . . II. xii. 77. 2
they slaked had the fervent *heat* Of appetite . . . III. i. 52. 1
She bath'd her brest the boyling *heat* t' allay; . . . III. vi. 6. 7
tempred right With *heate* and humour, . . . III. vi. 9. 5
Others lay shaded from the scorching *heat,* . . . III. vi. 17. 8
After her *heat* the breathing cold to taste: . . . III. vi. 18. 5
kindled *heat* that soone in flame forth brust: . . . III. viii. 25. 4
From scorching *heat* her daintie limbes to shade; . . . III. xi. 32. 5
What time the dayes with scorching *heat* abound, . . . IV. i. 13. 7
Till th' *heat* of his fierce furie he had spent; . . . IV. iii. 26. 5
when raging *heat* Doth burne the earth . . . IV. iv. 47. 1
So huge his hammer, and so fierce his *heat,* . . . IV. v. 37. 7
So furiously she strooke in her first *heat,* . . . IV. vi. 15. 1
when as he saw her hastie *heat* Abate, . . . IV. vi. 16. 1
Through toylesome *heate* and labour . . . IV. vi. 19. 9
As blasted bloosme through *heat* doth languish . . . IV. viii. 2. 9
hard to finde, that *heat* of youthfull spright . . . IV. viii. 29. 7
mollifie, and calme her raging *heat:* . . . IV. ix. 14. 7
the cause of their so cruell *heat* . . . IV. ix. 35. 8
inspired with heroicke *heat,* . . . V. i. 1. 7
Her snowy substance melted as with *heat,* . . . V. iii. 24. 7
Soone as he feeles it mollifide with *heat,* . . . V. v. 7. 8
when calmed was her furious *heat,* . . . V. v. 47. 8
in his first rages *heat,* . . . V. viii. 31. 7
Like a fell mastiffe through enraging *heat,* . . . V. xi. 12. 2
a Steare, in *heat* of sommers day, . . . VI. i. 24. 4
having somewhat calm'd his wrathfull *heat* . . . VI. i. 40. 2
With such faire words she did their *heat* asswage, . . . VI. v. 30. 6
Layes of sweete love and youthes delightfull *heat:* . . . VI. ix. 4. 4
Offred him drinke to quench his thirstie *heat,* . . . VI. ix. 6. 8
a flowre that feeles no *heate* of sunne, . . . VI. x. 44. 6
Like lyfull *heat* to nummed senses brought, . . . VI. xi. 45. 4
To lose their *heat* and shortly to decay; . . . VII. vii. 24. 4
it doth divide Great *heat,* and makes . . . *Am.* vi. 8
my exceeding *heat* Is not delayd . . . *Am.* xxx. 5
The paynefull smith, with force of fervent *heat,* . . . *Am.* xxxii. 1
Let thy lifull *heat* not fervent be, . . . *Epith.* 118
He somewhat loseth of his *heat* and light, . . . *Epith.* 268
taking to him wings of his owne *heate,* . . . *H.L.* 64
I have in th' *heat* of youth made heretofore, . . . *H.H.L.* 10
Sith now that *heat* is quenched, quench my blame, . . . *H.H.L.* 18

Heated. harmeful head, thrise *heated* in the fire, . . . I. vii. 37. 3
his limbes with labor *heated* sore. . . . VII. vii. 29. 9

Heath. now entombed lies at Stoneheng by the *heath.* . . . II. x. 67. 9

Heathen. comes unto the place where th' *Hethen* knight . . . I. v. 19. 4
named To all the *heathen* Gods, . . . IV. x. 30. 9
All other Idoles which the *heathen* adore, . . . IV. x. 40. 2

Heathenish. *heathnish* shield, wherein with letters red, Was writt *Sansjoy,* . . . I. iv. 38. 5

Heats. enraged *heates,* Here heaped up . . . I. xii. 30. 3
To save him selfe from those his furious *heats,* . . . V. xi. 13. 3

Heave. both their hands on hie At once did *heave* . . . VI. i. 38. 2

Heaved. *See* **Heft.**
His heavie hand he *heaved* up on hye, . . . I. vii. 14. 2
His weapon huge, that *heaved* was on hye . . . I. viii. 19. 8
Diamond, . . . *heav'd* his murdrous axe at him . . . IV. iii. 17. 9
his mightie hand He *heav'd* on high, . . . IV. iii. 33. 2
At last his lucklesse hand he *heav'd* on hie, . . . IV. vi. 18. 6
right hand In full avengement *heaved* up on hie, . . . IV. viii. 43. 2
heaved them on hight, . . . V. xi. 8. 5
as his hand was *heaved* up on hight, . . . VI. viii. 10. 2
His dreadfull hand he *heaved* up aloft, . . . VI. viii. 15. 1

Heaven. He bade me upwarde unto *heaven* looke. . . . *Bel.*[1] i. 8
A sodaine tempest from the *heaven,* . . . *Bel.*[1] iii. 13
no more see faire thing under *heaven,* . . . *Bel.*[1] iv. 12
With feeble flight venture to mount to *heaven,* . . . *Bel.*[1] vi. 2
hir armes with thousand sighs to *heaven,* . . . *Bel.*[1] viii. 2
flame, Mounting like waves . . . to *heaven,* . . . *Bel.*[1] ix. 2
She climbed up to *heaven* in the smoke. . . . *Bel.*[1] ix. 8
An Angell then descending downe from *Heaven,* . . . *Rev.* ii. 12
from the *heaven* on horses white, . . . *Rev.* iii. 6
I saw new Earth, new *Heaven,* . . . *Rev.* iv. 1
heaven whence all good gifts do come, . . . *Bel.*[2] i. 8
a tempest from the *heaven* descend, . . . *Bel.*[2] iii. 13
her armes to *Heaven* with thousand throbs, . . . *Bel.*[2] x. 2
in the smoake she unto *heaven* did stie. . . . *Bel.*[2] xi. 8
if aught under *heaven* might firme endure. . . . *Bel.*[2] xiv. 8
Both *heaven* and earth in roundnesse compassing; . . . *Ro.* iv. 4
what ever nature, arte, And *heaven* could doo, . . . *Ro.* v. 2
you to see doth th' *heaven* it selfe appall; . . . *Ro.* vii. 6
The lowest earth join'd to the *heaven* hie; . . . *Ro.* viii. 8
Heaven envious, and bitter stepdame Nature! . . . *Ro.* ix. 2
lift her loftie face Against the *heaven,* . . . *Ro.* xii. 12
Bearing the fire with which *heaven* doth us fray, . . . *Ro.* xvii. 2
Heaven had not feare of that presumptuous might, . . . *Ro.* xvii. 3
That antique horror, which made *heaven* adredd. . . . *Ro.* xvii. 8
towards *heaven* freshly to arise . . . *Ro.* xvii. 11
th' *heaven* it selfe, opposing gainst her might, . . . *Ro.* xviii. 11
All that is perfect, which th' *heaven* beautefies; . . . *Ro.* xix. 1
Caried to *heaven,* from sinfull bondage losed; . . . *Ro.* xix. 12
Lifting to *heaven* her aged hoarie head, . . . *Ro.* xxviii. 3
the *heaven* it selfe with her wide wonders fill. . . . *Ro.* xxix. 8
If under *heaven* anie endurance were, . . . *Ro.* xxxii. 5
Her mantle black through *heaven* gan overhaile: . . . *S.C.* Ja. 75
That it a *heaven* is to heare. . . . *S.C.* Ap. 108
reigne with the rest in *heaven.* . . . *S.C.* Ap. 117
the hills bene nigher *heven,* . . . *S.C.* Jul. 89
Of *Heaven* to demen so; . . . *S.C.* Jul. 94
nowe they bene to *heaven* forewent, . . . *S.C.* Jul. 117
they con to *heaven* the high-way, . . . *S.C.* S. 90
So mought our Cuddies name to *heaven* sownde. . . . *S.C.* O. 54
flye backe to *heaven* apace. . . . *S.C.* O. 84
Dido nis dead, but into *heaven* hent. . . . *S.C.* N. 169
I learned als the signes of *heaven* to ken, . . . *S.C.* D. 83
Into the highest top of *heaven* gan clime, . . . *Gn.* 157
Now had the Sun halfe *heaven* overgone, . . . *Gn.* 165
none . . . Himselfe therefore to *heaven* should elevate; . . . *Gn.* 556
Fled back to *heaven,* whence she was first conceived, . . . *Hub.* 3
everie sound that under *heaven* blew; . . . *Hub.* 1011
Whatso the *heaven* in his wide vawte containes, . . . *Hub.* 1229
he light and *heaven* does hate: . . . *T.M.* 190
Bacchus and Hercules I raisd to *heaven,* . . . *T.M.* 461
towards *heaven* shee seemd on high to weld. . . . *Ti.* 14
All things doo change that under *heaven* abide, . . . *Ti.* 206
Have purchast him in *heaven* an happie crowne, . . . *Ti.* 264
Worthie of *heaven* it selfe, . . . *Ti.* 287
ere his happie soule to *heaven* went . . . *Ti.* 295
raised they the puissant brood . . . To highest *heaven,* . . . *Ti.* 383
To shew in *Heaven* his brightnes orient; . . . *Ti.* 389
with Pyramides to *heaven* aspired, . . . *Ti.* 408
assay To mount to *heaven,* . . . *Ti.* 426
With showres of *heaven* and tempests worne away; . . . *Ti.* 501
hope of *heaven,* and heart to God inclinde; . . . *Ti.* 585
out of sight to highest *heaven* mounted, . . . *Ti.* 600
So now in *heaven* a signe it doth appeare, . . . *Ti.* 615
straight to *heaven* him bore, . . . *Ti.* 657
From *heaven* descending to appease their strife, . . . *Ti.* 667
To live in *heaven* where happines is rife: . . . *Ti.* 670
by lacke of thee to *heaven* hent, . . . *Ti.* 677
unto *heaven* let your high minde aspire, . . . *Ti.* 685
Whilst *heaven* did favour his felicities, . . . *Mui.* 21
high in *heaven* Hyperions fierie childe . . . *Mui.* 51
th' hayling darts of *heaven* beating hard. . . . *Mui.* 80
ne *heaven* doth shine so bright, . . . *Mui.* 93
borne to *heaven,* for *heaven* a fitter pray; . . . *D.* 164
Will honour *heaven,* or heavenlie powers adore, . . . *D.* 198
Yet shee in purenesse *heaven* it selfe did pas. . . . *D.* 210
'I hate the *heaven,* because it doth withhold . . . *D.* 400
in ought under *heaven* repose assurance, . . . *D.* 499
nought but sea and *heaven* to us appeare. . . . *Col.* 227
is theyr *heaven* likewise there all one? . . . *Col.* 305
if like *heaven,* be heavenly graces there, . . . *Col.* 306
'Both *heaven* and heavenly graces do . . . abound . . . *Col.* 308
Her name to eccho unto *heaven* hie. . . . *Col.* 483
taking up to *heaven,* him godded new. . . . *Col.* 810
With humble hearts to *heaven* uplifted hie, . . . *Col.* 816
gan *heaven* out of darknesse dread For to appeare, . . . *Col.* 855
first did spring From *heaven,* . . . *Col.* 918
th' unkindly Impes, of *heaven* accurst, . . . I. i. 26. 2
The Sunne, that measures *heaven* all day long, . . . I. i. 32. 8
He . . . cursed *heven;* . . . I. i. 37. 5
Shall I accuse . . . mightie causes wrought in *heaven* above, . . . I. i. 51. 3
Her angels face, As the great eye of *heaven,* . . . I. iii. 4. 7
blustring breath of *Heaven,* that none can bide, . . . I. iii. 31. 5
every breath of *heaven* shaked itt: . . . I. iv. 5. 7
Through highest *heaven* with weaker hand to rayne: . . . I. iv. 9. 4
Looking to *heaven,* for earth she did disdayne, . . . I. iv. 10. 2
thundring Jove, that high in *heaven* doth dwell . . . I. iv. 11. 5
the golden Orientall gate Of greatest *heaven* . . . I. v. 2. 2
all the ayre it fills, and flyes to *heaven* bright. . . . I. v. 16. 9
to the Easterne coast of *heaven* makes speedy way: . . . I. v. 19. 9
she in hell and *heaven* had power equally. . . . I. v. 34. 9

Heaven—*Continued.*
daring tempt the Queene of *heaven* to sin; . . . I. v. 35. 2
thrust from *heaven* dew, . . . I. v. 42. 5
From hope of *heaven* hath thee excluded quight, . . . I. v. 43. 2
dawning light Discovered had the world to *heaven* wyde, . . . I. v. 52. 6
everie little breath that under *heaven* is blowne. . . . I. vii. 32. 9
From every coast that *heaven* walks about . . . I. vii. 45. 3
what ever thing is donne In *heaven* and earth? . . . I. ix. 42. 2
that all this doth behold From highest *heven*, . . . I. ix. 47. 2
Caelia men did her call, as thought From *heaven* to come, . . . I. x. 4. 2
broad-blazed fame, That up to *heven* is blowne.' . . . I. x. 11. 5
ever up to *heven*, . . . Her stedfast eyes were bent, . . . I. x. 14. 8
to *heaven* she teacheth him the ready path. . . . I. x. 33. 9
high *heaven* to attaine? . . . I. x. 50. 3
Who better can the way to *heaven* aread . . . I. x. 51. 4
descend From highest *heven* . . . I. x. 56. 3
she is hevenly borne, and *heaven* may justly vaunt. . . . I. x. 59. 9
path . . . after all to *heaven* shall thee send; . . . I. x. 61. 2
the way that does to *heaven* bownd!' . . . I. x. 67. 4
High *heven* behold the tedious toyle . . . I. xi. 1. 9
Those glistring armes that *heven* with light did fill, . . . I. xi. 4. 8
with their horror *heven* and earth did ring; . . . I. xi. 7. 5
al the land with stench and *heven* with horror choke. . . . I. xi. 44. 9
high her burning torch set up in *heaven* bright. . . . I. xi. 49. 9
From *heven* high to chace the chearelesse darke; . . . I. xi. 51. 8
sent to *heven* the ecchoed report Of their new joy, . . . I. xii. 4. 2
Lifting to *heven* her everlasting fame: . . . I. xii. 8. 5
that victorious man, Whom all admired as from *heaven* sent, . . . I. xii. 9. 4
heven thee deignes to hold in living state, . . . II. i. 37. 3
As *heven* accusing guilty of her death, . . . II. i. 49. 2
cover'd *heaven* with hideous dreriment, . . . II. vii. 1. 5
upper end to highest *heven* was knitt, . . . II. vii. 46. 3
Worthie of *heven* and hye felicitie, . . . II. vii. 49. 5
eke blaspheming *heaven* bitterly, . . . II. vii. 60. 8
And is there care in *heaven?* . . . II. viii. 1. 1
such happinesse *Heven* doth to me envy, . . . II. ix. 7. 9
even *heven* rejoyced her sweete face to see. . . . II. ix. 18. 9
Like highest *heaven* compassed around, . . . II. ix. 45. 2
In whose sad time blood did from *heaven* rayne. . . . II. x. 34. 2
stole fire from *heven* to animate His worke, . . . II. x. 70. 7
The windowes of bright *heaven* opened had, . . . II. xi. 3. 2
a flake Of lightning through bright *heven* fulmined: . . . III. ii. 5. 8
Under what coast of *heaven* the man did dwell, . . . III. iii. 6. 5
heven it selfe shall their successe envy, . . . III. iii. 40. 7
to be in *heaven* enrold. . . . III. iv. 11. 9
a foggy mist hath overcast The face of *heven*, . . . III. iv. 13. 2
Was mounted high in top of *heaven* sheene, . . . III. iv. 51. 7
griesly shadowes covered *heaven* bright, . . . III. iv. 52. 2
wast begot in *heaven*, . . . III. iv. 55. 3
Which darknesse shall subdue and *heaven* win: . . . III. iv. 59. 6
the Titans which did make Warre against *heven*, . . . III. vii. 47. 4
So made him thinke him selfe in *heven* that was in hell. . . . III. viii. 19. 9
cride to *heven*, from humane helpe exild. . . . III. viii. 27. 5
Both light of *heven* and strength of men relate: . . . III. viii. 51. 8
in *heven*, whereas all goodnes is, . . . III. ix. 2. 6
fetch from *heven* thy great genealogie, . . . III. ix. 33. 7
the shady damp Out of the goodly *heven* amoved quight, . . . III. x. 1. 4
Ne he twixt *heven* and earth shall hide his hedd, . . . III. x. 32. 8
As if he *heaven* and hell would over-ronne, . . . III. x. 33. 7
Whiles that from *heaven* he suffered exile. . . . III. xi. 39. 5
High *heven* beholdes sad lovers nightly theeveryes. . . . III. xi. 45. 9
*discolourd bow she spreds through *heaven* . . . III. xi. 47. 9
ycovered had Fayre *heaven* with an universall clowd, . . . III. xii. 1. 2
Prince of peace from *heaven* blest. . . . IV. Pr. 4. 9
before they may to *heaven* flie, . . . IV. iii. 44. 5
They all gan shout aloud, that all the *heaven* rings. . . . IV. iii. 49. 9
conquerd sea and land, And *heaven* it selfe, . . . IV. vi. 31. 5
lovers *heaven* must passe by sorrowes hell.' . . . IV. vi. 32. 7
twenty daies . . . have past through *heven* sheene, . . . IV. vii. 13. 2
'If *heaven*, then none may it redresse or blame, . . . IV. viii. 15. 1
heaven, first author of my languishment, . . . IV. viii. 16. 5
From all foure parts of *heaven* doe rage full sore, . . . IV. ix. 23. 6
I thought there was none other *heaven* then this; . . . IV. x. 28. 3
the *heaven* is in his course contained. . . . IV. x. 35. 1
rould in clouds to *heaven* did aspire, . . . IV. x. 38. 4
those rolles, layd up in *heaven* above, . . . IV. xi. 10. 3
heaven, that unto all lends equall eare, . . . IV. xii. 6. 5
Unto the shinie *heaven* in haste she hide, . . . IV. xii. 25. 3
whylome rebelled Gainst highest *heaven:* . . . V. i. 9. 7
Return'd to *heaven*, whence she deriv'd her race; . . . V. i. 11. 4
Then would he ballaunce *heaven* and hell together, . . . V. ii. 31. 5
weigh the winde that under *heaven* doth blow; . . . V. ii. 43. 2
so soone as morrow light Appear'd in *heaven*, . . . V. iii. 7. 2
lay on *heaven* the guilt of their owne crimes. . . . V. iv. 28. 3
lampe of lightsome day Up-lifted in the porch of *heaven* hie: V. vii. 17. 4
Nought under *heaven* so strongly doth allure The sence of man, V. viii. 1. 1
shone as bright as doth the *heaven* sheene: . . . V. viii. 29. 5
May you in *heaven* immortall guerdon gaine . . . V. x. 21. 4
Gan shout aloud, that unto *heaven* it rong; . . . V. xi. 34. 2
did warres darraine Against the *heaven* in order battailous, . VI. vii. 41. 7
Through the bright *heaven* doth her beams display, . . . VI. x. 13. 7
a goddesse . . . from *heven* first enraced? . . . VI. x. 25. 5
Liker to *heaven* then mortall wretchednesse: . . . VI. xi. 1. 5
up to *heaven* his eyes fast-streming threw: . . . VI. xi. 28. 6
what destiny Or other dyrefull hap from *heaven* or hell . . . VI. xi. 29. 8
That makes both *heaven* and earth to tremble at her pride. . . VII. vi. 3. 9
if from *heaven* it were, then to arrest The Author, . . . VII. vi. 16. 8
even the highest Powers of *heaven* to check) . . . VII. vi. 22. 4
though wrongfully from *heaven* exil'd. . . . VII. vi. 26. 9

Heaven—*Continued.*
In this bold sort to *Heaven* claime to make, . . . VII. vi. 29. 3
(Such sway doth beauty even in *Heaven* beare) . . . VII. vi. 31. 4
art yborne of *heaven* and heavenly Sire, . . . VII. vii. 2. 7
Can tell things doen in *heaven* so long ygone, . . . VII. vii. 2. 8
heaven it selfe by heritage in Fee: . . . VII. vii. 15. 5
heaven and earth I both alike do deeme, . . . VII. vii. 15. 6
Sith *heaven* and earth are both alike to thee, . . . VII. vii. 15. 7
When any winde doth under *heaven* blowe; . . . VII. vii. 20. 7
was to *heaven* extold. . . . VII. vii. 37. 9
all things else that under *heaven* dwell . . . VII. vii. 48. 2
and makes his flames to *heaven* aspire. . . . *Am.* vi. 8
and thinke how she to *heaven* may clime; . . . *Am.* xiii. 10
Into this sinfull world from *heaven* to send; . . . *Am.* xxiv. 10
from *heaven* most hideous stormes are sent, . . . *Am.* xlvi. 3
Whom then shall I, or *heaven* or her, obay? . . . *Am.* xlvi. 5
But as she will, . . . My lower *heaven*, . . . *Am.* xlvi. 8
to the *heaven* her haughty lookes aspire: . . . *Am.* lv. 11
sith so *heaven* ye lykened are the best, . . . *Am.* lv. 13
blessings . . . by *heaven* upon you thrown; . . . *Am.* lxvi. 2
high worths . . . Ne but in *heaven* matchable . . . *Am.* lxvi. 7
unto *heaven* forgets her former flight. . . . *Am.* lxxii. 8
Ne thinks of other *heaven*, . . . *Am.* lxxii. 11
when as day the *heaven* doth adorne, . . . *Am.* lxxxvi. 5
ought that under *heaven* doth hove . . . *Am.* lxxxviii. 9
Whom *heaven* would heape with blis, . . . *Epith.* 247
all the host of *heaven* in rankes doost lead, . . . *Epith.* 289
walkes about high *heaven* al the night? . . . *Epith.* 375
huge Pyramids, which do *heaven* threat. . . . *Com. Son.* iii. 8
dare not to *heaven* fly, . . . *H.L.* 181
through *heaven* and hell thou makest way . . . *H.L.* 236
thou doest thy entrance make Unto thy *heaven*, . . . *H.L.* 274
in *heaven*, that no man may it see . . . *H.B.* 38
those whom *heaven* did at first ordaine, . . . *H.B.* 206
(Not this round *heaven*, which we from hence behold, . . . *H.H.L.* 58
And glorious images in *heaven* wrought, . . . *H.H.B.* 3
heaven then fire, appeares more pure and fayre. . . . *H.H.B.* 49
Faire is the *heaven* where happy soules have place, . . . *H.H.B.* 78
Yet fairer is that *heaven*, in which doe raine . . . *H.H.B.* 85
Both *heaven* and earth obey unto her will, . . . *H.H.B.* 197
Heavenfield. Shall *Hevenfield* be cald to all posterity. . . . III. iii. 38. 9
Heavenly. *heavenly* branches did I see arise . . . *Pet.* iii. 1
of some *heavenly* wight I had the vewe; . . . *Pet.* v. 4
All *heavenly* grace and vertue shrined is, . . . *Pet.*[2] vii. 10
Ye *heavenly* spirites, whose ashie cinders lie . . . *Ro.* i. 1
So did the Gods by *heavenly* doome decree, . . . *Ro.* vi. 11
fight against the Gods of *heavenly* berth, . . . *Ro.* xii. 3
Their *heavenly* vertues from these woes assoyling, . . . *Ro.* xix. 11
gins Bartas hie to rayse His *heavenly* Muse, . . . *Ro.* Env. 12
So sprong her grace Of *heavenly* race, . . . *S.C.* Ap. 53
Her *heavenly* haveour, her princely grace, . . . *S.C.* Ap. 66
heavenly ranks, where blessed soules do rest; . . . *Gn.* 58
Up to the *heavenly* towers, . . . *Gn.* 66
Whom golden Fleece did make an *heavenly* signe; . . . *Gn.* 211
all the *heavenly* powres Conspire in one . . . *Gn.* 578
The bread of life powr'd downe from *heavenly* place. . . . *Hub.* 438
the *heavenly* noyses Of their sweete instruments . . . *T.M.* 19
Can griefe then enter into *heavenly* harts? . . . *T.M.* 47
th' *heavenly* gift of wisdomes influence, . . . *T.M.* 86
When th' *heavenlie* light of knowledge is put out, . . . *T.M.* 488
ignorance . . . mindes of men borne *heavenlie* doth debace. . . *T.M.* 498
The precepts of my *heavenlie* discipline; . . . *T.M.* 518
To make men *heavenly* wise through humbled will. . . . *T.M.* 522
contemplation of things *heavenlie* wrought: . . . *T.M.* 526
The true Pandora of all *heavenly* graces, . . . *T.M.* 578
her eternize with their *heavenlie* writs! . . . *T.M.* 582
Playing alone carelesse on hir *heavenlie* Virginals. . . . *U.V.* 6
Unto his *heavenlie* maker to present His bodie, . . . *Ti.* 297
doost heare their *heavenlie* layes, . . . *Ti.* 335
that blessed throng Of *heavenlie* Poets and Heroes . . . *Ti.* 341
There stood a snowie Swan of *heavenly* hiew, . . . *Ti.* 590
Where now he is become an *heavenly* signe, . . . *Ti.* 601
all the way most *heavenly* noyse was heard . . . *Ti.* 612
In which all *heavenly* treasures locked are. . . . *Ti.* 630
Dan Perseus, borne of *heavenly* seed, . . . *Ti.* 648
as ye be of *heavenlie* off-spring borne, . . . *Ti.* 684
by her *heavenly* might, . . . *Mui.* 137
Will honour heaven, or *heavenlie* powers adore, . . . *D.* 198
her with *heavenly* hymnes doth deifie, . . . *D.* 230
when she list advance her *heavenly* voyce, . . . *D.* 313
heavenly spirits have compassion On mortall men, . . . *D.* 384
an hundred Nymphs all *heavenly* borne, . . . *Col.* 256
be *heavenly* graces there, . . . *Col.* 306
'Both heaven and *heavenly* graces do . . . abound . . . *Col.* 308
All *heavenly* gifts and riches locked are; . . . *Col.* 489
with sparks of *hevenlie* beautie fired. . . . *Col.* 563
Emongst the seats of Angels *heavenly* wrought, . . . *Col.* 614
of divine regard and *heavenly* hew, . . . *Col.* 933
crownd with lasting baies Of *hevenlie* blis . . . *Ded. Son.* xv. 5
And native beauty deck with *hevenlie* grace: . . . *Ded. Son.* xv. 12
comprise Those glorious ornaments of *hevenly* grace, . . . *Ded. Son.* xvi. 7
O Goddesse *heavenly* bright! . . . I. Pr. 4. 1
Did never mortall eye behold such *heavenly* grace. . . . I. iii. 4. 9
At last, . . . Arose the virgin, borne of *heavenly* brood, . . . I. iii. 8. 7
you, my liefe, yborn of *hevenly* berth. . . . I. iii. 28. 9
most *heavenly* melody . . . sweet musicke did divide, . . . I. v. 17. 6
creature never past, That backe retourned without *heavenly* grace; . . . I. v. 31. 7
And slake the *heavenly* fire that raged evermore. . . . I. v. 40. 9
Ah heavens! that doe . . . *heavenly* virgin thus outraged see, . I. vi. 5. 7

Heaven's—*Continued.*
those same antique Peres, the *hevens* brood, . . . III. iii. 22. 8
will *hevens* fury never slake, . . . III. iii. 43. 5
We both are bownd to follow *heavens* beheasts, . . . III. vi. 22. 7
From *heavens* blis and everlasting rest: . . . III. viii. 8. 4
appeare . . . flames and reach to *hevens* hight, . . . III. x. 12. 8
Jove . . . leaving *heavens* kingdome, . . . III. xi. 30. 3
When her discolourd bow she spreds through *hevens* hight. . . III. xi. 47. 9
Farre from the view of gods and *heavens* bliss, . . . IV. ii. 47. 8
So soone as *heavens* window shewed light, . . . IV. iii. 3. 7
by this *heavens* light, I vow you dead or living not to leave, . IV. vi. 38. 7
Where hardly eye mote see bright *heavens* face . . . IV. vii. 38. 7
what *heavens* hard disgrace, Or wrath of cruell wight . . . IV. viii. 14. 7
soone as day discovered *heavens* face . . . IV. viii. 34. 1
falne on you by *heavens* hard direction . . . V. iv. 26. 7
The worke of *heavens* will surpasseth humaine thought.' . . . V. iv. 27. 9
well to beare The storme of fortunes frowne or *heavens* threat, . V. v. 38. 3
by *heavens* high decree, . . . V. viii. 44. 6
through high *heavens* grace, . . . V. ix. 42. 1
Long shut up in the bud from *heavens* vew, . . . VI. ii. 35. 8
Or house to hide his head from *heavens* spight, . . . VI. iv. 39. 4
Tell me what worlds despight, or *heavens* yre, . . . VI. v. 23. 7
what mortall hand or *heavens* grace . . . VI. xii. 8. 7
strive With Saturnes sonne for *heavens* regiment; . . . VII. vi. 2. 7
All fairely deckt with *heavens* goodly storie; . . . VII. vi. 8. 4
Bade her attonce from *heavens* coast to pack, . . . VII. vi. 12. 8
To Joves faire palace fixt in *heavens* hight; . . . VII. vi. 15. 2
To thrust . . . eke our selves from *heavens* high Empire, . . . VII. vi. 21. 4
May challenge ought in *Heavens* interesse; . . . VII. vi. 33. 3
to tell of *heavens* King . . . his fortunate successe; . . . VII. vii. 1. 5
him of *heavens* Empire sought to dispossesse? . . . VII. vii. 1. 9
did them porters make Of *heavens* gate . . . VII. vii. 45. 7
that Angels blessed looke, . . . my *heavens* blis; . . . *Am.* i. 12
Resembling *heavens* glory in her light, . . . *Am.* lxxii. 6
here on earth to have such *hevens* blisse. . . . *Am.* lxxii. 14
face long hidden was From *heavens* view, . . . *H.L.* 60
Kindled at first from *heavens* life-giving fyre, . . . *H.L.* 65
Their lives they loath, and *heavens* light disdaine; . . . *H.L.* 130
His harts enshrined saint, his *heavens* queene, . . . *H.L.* 215
thy blisse, and *heavens* glorie. . . . *H.L.* 279
from the top of purest *heavens* hight . . . *H.B.* 109
lively images of *heavens* light, . . . *H.B.* 163
From this base world unto thy *heavens* hight, . . . *H.H.L.* 2
Unto the God of Love, high *heavens* king. . . . *H.H.L.* 7
From *heavens* hight, to which they did aspyre, . . . *H.H.L.* 88
that faire love of mightie *heavens* King; . . . *H.H.B.* 235
beauties bright, That shone as *heavens* light, . . . *Proth.* 52
the worlds faire ornament, And *heavens* glorie, . . . *Proth.* 92

Heavens. th' inconstance of the *heavens:* . . . *Bel.*[1] xi. 3
I saw the *heavens* warre against hir tho, . . . *Bel.*[1] xi. 12
the *heavens* still wavering thus, . . . *Bel.*[2] xv. 3
I saw the *heavens* in warre against her rize: . . . *Bel.*[2] xv. 12
did her courage to the *heavens* advaunce. . . . *Ro.* vi. 14
th' *heavens* in glorie triumpht over all: . . . *Ro.* xii. 8
flames . . . Gathered in one up to the *heavens* to spyre, . . . *Ro.* xvi. 10
th' *heavens* looked lovely all the while, . . . *Van.* ix. 6
the *Heavens* did quake his verse to here. . . . *S.C.* O. 60
The *heavens* doe melt in teares without remorse; . . . *S.C.* N. 131
thunder which doth ryve The ratling *heavens,* . . . *Gn.* 520
The *heavens* on everie side enclowded bee: . . . *Gn.* 571
The billowes striving to the *heavens* to reach, . . . *Gn.* 575
th' *heavens* striving them for to impeach. . . . *Gn.* 576
with shrilling cryes Pierce the dull *heavens* . . . *T.M.* 118
Till please the *heavens* affoord me remedy. . . . *T.M.* 294
Whose happines the *heavens* envying, . . . *Ti.* 24
whilst *heavens* with equall vewe Deignd to behold me . . . *Ti.* 80
Such grace the *heavens* doo to my verses give. . . . *Ti.* 259
the *heavens* powrde all their gifts upon her. . . . *Ti.* 280
nigh unto the *Heavens* in height upreared, . . . *Ti.* 507
Seemed the *heavens* with the earth did disagree, . . . *Ti.* 664
all the *heavens* on lower creatures smilde, . . . *Mui.* 53
whatso *heavens* in their secret doome Ordained have, . . . *Mui.* 225
It fortuned (as *heavens* had behight) . . . *Mui.* 241
To carelesse *heavens* I doo daylie call; . . . *D.* 354
heavens refuse to heare a wretches cry; . . . *D.* 355
th' *heavens* with long languor pacifide, . . . *D.* 388
The image of the *heavens* in shape humane.' . . . *Col.* 351
Before that angry *heavens* list to lowre, . . . I. ii. 22. 4
both . . . souce so sore that they the *heavens* affray; . . . I. v. 8. 7
Ah *heavens!* . . . How can ye vengeance just so long withhold, I. vi. 5. 6
the *heavens* it doth fill With thundring noyse, . . . I. vii. 13. 5
when the flying *heavens* he would affray; . . . I. vii. 34. 4
their felicities The favourable *heavens* did not envy, . . . I. vii. 43. 6
ye *heavens,* that all things right esteeme, . . . I. vii. 49. 7
the *heavens,* . . . Have made you master of the field . . . I. viii. 28. 1
The fields, the floods, the *heavens,* with one consent, . . . I. ix. 12. 8
all the *hevens* stood still . . . I. xi. 10. 9
Witnesse . . . guilty *heavens* of his bold perjury; . . . I. xii. 27. 6
What *hevens?* what altars? . . . I. xii. 30. 3
Witnes, ye *heavens,* whom she in vaine to help did call. . . II. i. 10. 9
doen the *heavens* afford him vitall food?' . . . II. i. 12. 3
if that carelesse *hevens,*' (quoth she) 'despise . . . II. i. 36. 1
hevens just with equall brow Vouchsafed . . . II. i. 50. 3
the *Heavens* alwayes joviall . . . II. xii. 51. 1
'The man, whom *heavens* have ordaynd . . . III. iii. 26. 1
th' *heavens* have decreed to displace The Britons . . . III. iii. 41. 7
'But if the *heavens* did his dayes envie, . . . III. iv. 39. 1
To her to whom the *hevens* doe serve and sew? . . . III. v. 47. 2
The *hevens* so favorable were and free, . . . III. vi. 2. 2
the *heavens,* of voluntary grace . . . III. viii. 29. 2

Heavens—*Continued.*
The *hevens* such crueltie abhore.' . . . III. viii. 48. 9
now the *hevens* obey to me alone, . . . III. xi. 35. 8
ungodly trade The *heavens* abhorre, . . . IV. vii. 12. 4
But if the *heavens* helpe to redresse her wrong, . . . IV. vii. 23. 3
heavens laugh, and al the world shews joyous cheare. . . . IV. x. 44. 9
For who so list into the *heavens* looke, . . . V. Pr. 5. 1
Al which the *heavens* containe, . . . V. ii. 35. 9
day forth dawning . . . Nights humid curtaine from the *heavens* withdrew, . . . V. v. 1. 2
Unlesse the *heavens* them lift to lawfull soveraintie. . . . V. v. 25. 9
the *heavens* unjust . . . have agreed To thrall my looser life, . V. v. 29. 7
cruell *heavens* hath heapt an heavy fate; . . . V. v. 36. 3
hevens themselves . . . rul'd by righteous lore Of highest Jove, V. vii. 1. 4
O ye *Heavens,* defend! and turne away From her . . . V. viii. 19. 5
bringing light into the *heavens* fayre, . . . V. x. 16. 7
Till that th' offended *heavens* list to lowre Upon their blisse, . V. x. 26. 6
witnesse unto me, ye *heavens!* . . . V. xi. 41. 6
'For th' *heavens,* envying our prosperitie, . . . VI. iv. 31. 1
Whom Gods doe hate, and *heavens* abhor to see; . . . VI. vi. 10. 2
whose tempestuous rage Makes th' *heavens* tremble . . . VI. vi. 11. 9
glyding through the ayre lights all the *heavens* darke. . . . VI. vii. 7. 9
Yet *heavens* them selves, that favour feeble rights, . . . VI. viii. 18. 8
'Nor *heavens,* nor men, can me . . . Deliver . . . VI. viii. 19. 5
had through the *heavens* wyde By this dispred, . . . VI. viii. 44. 5
wish th' *heavens* so much had graced mee, . . . VI. ix. 28. 6
The *heavens* of their fortunes fault accuse, . . . VI. ix. 29. 2
Oft cursing th' *heavens,* that so cruell were To her, . . . VI. xi. 33. 6
To tell her how the *heavens* had her graste . . . VI. xii. 16. 8
eke the *heavens,* and all the heavenly crew . . . VII. vi. 14. 3
Witnesse, ye *Heavens,* the truth of all that I have teld!' . . . VII. vi. 27. 9
Have wonne the Empire of the *Heavens* bright; . . . VII. vi. 33. 7
Shouting as they the *heavens* would have brast; . . . VII. vi. 52. 7
The *heavens* know best what is the best for me . . . *Am.* xlvi. 6
ye high *hevens,* that all this sorowe see, . . . *Am.* xlvi. 9
in the *heavens* wryte your glorious name. . . . *Am.* lxxv. 12
had the equall *hevens* so much you graced . . . *Am.* lxxxii. 5
even to the *heavens* theyr shouting shrill Doth reach, . . . *Epith.* 141
ye high *heavens,* the temple of the gods, . . . *Epith.* 409
heavens such happie grace did to him lend, . . . *H.L.* 213
What *heavens* of joy then to himselfe he faynes! . . . *H.L.* 240
According as the *heavens* have her graced, . . . *H.B.* 116
For farre above these *heavens,* which here we see, . . . *H.H.B.* 64
And as these *heavens* still by degrees arize, . . . *H.H.B.* 71
Whose beautie filles the *heavens* with her light, . . . *H.H.B.* 228
Which decke the Bauldricke of the *Heavens* bright; . . . *Proth.* 173

Heavens'. *See* **Heaven's.**
Thrice having seene under the *heavens* veale . . . *Ro.* i. 9
beares on his shoulders the *heavens* height. . . . *S.C.* May 143
There we behold the *heavens* great Hierarchie, . . . *T.M.* 507
The worlds late wonder, and the *heavens* new joy; . . . *Ti.* 303
now art made the *heavens* ornament, . . . *Ti.* 674
that most Heroicke spirit, The *hevens* pride, . . . *Ded. Son.* xv. 2
Since I the *heavens* chearefull face did vew. . . . I. viii. 38. 8
Huge flames that dimmed all the *hevens* light, . . . I. xi. 44. 3
Through influence of th' *hevens* fruitfull ray . . . III. vi. 6. 2
before the *heavens* fairest light . . . was fully reard, . . . III. x. 52. 6
the *heavens* revolution Is wandred farre . . . V. Pr. 4. 6
The *heavens* bright-shining baudricke to enchace; . . . V. i. 11. 7
Their sound did reach unto the *heavens* hight: . . . V. v. 4. 6
Sith shady dampe had dimd the *heavens* reach, . . . V. vi. 21. 8
T' attempt the empire of the *heavens* hight, . . . VII. vi. 7. 4
Made of the *heavens* substance, . . . VII. vi. 10. 3
The *Heavens* Herald staid not to reply, . . . VII. vi. 19. 1
Sought to assaile the *heavens* eternall towers, . . . VII. vi. 20. 3
thou, Jove, injuriously hast held The *Heavens* rule . . . VII. vi. 27. 7
though she all unworthy were Of the *Heav'ns* Rule; . . . VII. viii. 1. 4
As King and Queene, the *heavens* Empire sway; . . . *H.H.B.* 56
up to the *heavens* hight. . . . *H.L.* 189
To them the *heavens* illimitable hight . . . *H.H.L.* 57

Heaviest. The *heaviest* plaint that ever I heard sound, . . . *D.* 541

Heavily. he *heavily* departed With piteous crie, . . . *Gn.* 639
hearing them so *heavily* lament, . . . *T.M.* 35
Like *heavily* lamenting from them went. . . . *T.M.* 36
of sorrowe *heavilie* can sing; . . . *D.* 12
charged *heavily* Of hardy Nennius, . . . II. x. 49. 3

Heaviness. pittying hys *heavinesse,* . . . *S.C.* May 259
endles paines and hideous *heavinesse* . . . *Gn.* 371
Was turned now to dismall *heavinesse,* . . . *T.M.* 41
Ah, wretched world! the house of *heavinesse,* . . . *T.M.* 123
Forgetfull of your former *heavinesse;* . . . *T.M.* 366
Her long borne Infant, fruit of *heavinesse,* . . . *D.* 32
To make the image of true *heavinesse:* . . . *D.* 329
Ne will I rest mine eyes for *heavinesse.* . . . *D.* 462
burning blades . . . The instruments of wrath and *heavinesse.* . I. v. 6. 5
Una, with huge *heavinesse* oppress, . . . I. vi. 40. 2
The rueful moniments of *heavinesse;* . . . I. vii. 19. 8
Leaving behind them griefe and *heavinesse:* . . . II. vii. 12. 5
In wilfull anguish and dead *heavinesse,* . . . III. xii. 43. *or.*7
tempred for the time her present *heavinesse.* . . . V. vii. 44. 9
He tooke his leave of her there left in *heavinesse.* . . . V. xii. 27. 9
who so heares her *heavinesse,* would rew . . . VI. xi. 2. 8

Heavy. From heavens hight into mens *heavy* eyes, . . . *Bel.*[2] i. 2
Hey, ho, *heavie* cheere! . . . *S.C.* Au. 106
Then listneth ech unto my *heavy* laye, . . . *S.C.* Au. 149
hold up thy *heavye* head, . . . *S.C.* O. 1
O *heavie* herse! . . . *S.C.* N. 60, 70, 80, 90, 100, 110, 120, 130, 140, 150, 160

Heavy—*Continued.*
sike happy cheere is turnd to *heavie* chaunce, . . . *S.C.* N. 103
now morne with *heavy* cheare, . . . *S.C.* N. 151
soone ensued them with *heavie* stowre. . . . *Gn.* 566
the sloathfull fit . . . Had left the *heavie* Shepheard, . . . *Gn.* 642
All were my spirite *heavie* and diseased, . . . *Hub.* 40
the charge . . . hath an *heavie* threat.' . . . *Hub.* 432
So went the Sheepe away with *heavie* hart: . . . *Hub.* 1222
lying reastlesse in *heavy* bedde, . . . *U.V.* 4
who will bewaile my *heavy* chaunce? . . . *U.V.* 19
Much was I troubled in my *heavie* spright, . . . *Ti.* 575
give unto my *heavie* eyes A well of teares, . . . *Mui.* 409
What-ever man be he whose *heavie* minde, . . . *D.* 1
even their *heavie* song would breede delight; . . . *D.* 13
Downe to the earth his *heavie* eyes were throwne, . . . *D.* 46
I will to thee this *heavie* case relate: . . . *D.* 96
I for pittie of his *heavie* plight . . . *D.* 170
with wofull *heavie* thought; . . . *D.* 465
Thus when he ended had his *heavie* plaint, . . . *D.* 540
the light to mount on hie, And th' *heavie* downe to peize; . . *Col.* 849
heavie sate upon her palfrey slow; . . . I. i. 4. 7
His *heavie* head, devoide of careful carke; . . . I. i. 44. 4
on his backe a *heavy* load he bare . . . I. iii. 16. 7
The *heavie* hap which on them is alight; . . . I. iii. 20. 8
Una cride, 'O! hold that *heavie* hand, . . . I. iii. 37. 2
Scarse could he once uphold his *heavie* hedd, . . . I. iv. 19. 5
have felt full many an *heavie* stowre. . . . I. iv. 46. 9
his *heavie* hand he high gan reare, . . . I. v. 13. 5
they . . . brought the *heavy* corse with easy pace . . . I. v. 31. 2
lastly thrown themselves into these *heavy* stowres. . . . I. v. 51. 9
His *heavie* hand he heaved up on hye, . . . I. vii. 14. 2
more *heavy* plight Then that I feele, . . . I. vii. 25. 3
O! *heavie* record of the good Redcrosse, . . . I. vii. 48. 8
his *heavy* sway So deepely dinted in the driven clay, . . . I. viii. 8. 4
Th' eternall bale of *heavie* wounded harts: . . . I. viii. 14. 5
The stroke upon his shield so *heavie* lites, . . . I. viii. 18. 7
Her hastie ruine does more *heavie* make, . . . I. viii. 23. 6
all that noyd his *heavie* spright . . . I. x. 24. 3
he, that harrowd hell with *heavie* stowre, . . . I. x. 40. 8
To trusse the pray too *heavy* for his flight; . . . I. xi. 19. 8
When *heavy* hammers on the wedge are swaid: . . . I. xi. 42. 7
appease your griefe and *heavy* plight, . . . II. i. 14. 5
from so *heavie* sight his head did wreath, . . . II. i. 56. 7
An *heavie* load, himselfe did lightly reare; . . . II. ii. 11. 4
With *heavie* load on him they freshly gan to smight. . . . II. ii. 23. 9
When late he saw his Lord in *heavie* plight . . . II. v. 25. 5
The hatefull messengers of *heavy* things, . . . II. vii. 23. 4
heavy ruine they did seeme to threatt; . . . II. vii. 28. 6
Behold this *heavy* sight, thou reverend Sire! . . . II. viii. 7. 6
cloudes of deadly night . . . his *heavy* eylids cover'd have, . . II. viii. 24. 8
Through *heavy* stroke of Britomartis hond. . . . III. iv. 29. 4
heavy tidings heard, . . . III. iv. 29. 6
Lamenting his mishap and *heavy* plight; . . . III. iv. 44. 2
Sister of *heavie* death, and nourse of woe, . . . III. iv. 55. 2
to an *heavy* hart Thou art the roote and nourse of bitter cares, III. iv. 57. 1
With *heavy* look and lumpish pace, . . . III. iv. 61. 7
The *heavie* plague that for such leachours is prepard. . . . III. v. 14. 9
Saw never living eie more *heavy* sight, . . . III. v. 30. 1
from his head his *heavy* burganet did light. . . . III. v. 31. 9
reskewed out of the *heavy* stownd. . . . III. v. 38. 5
Out of her *heavie* swowne not to awake . . . III. vi. 27. 8
the *heavy* trees they clyme, . . . III. vi. 42. 5
Shee also dofte her *heavy* haberjeon, . . . III. ix. 21. 1
lament The *heavie* losse of their brave Paramours, . . . III. ix. 35. 4
With this sad hersall of his *heavy* stresse . . . III. xi. 18. 1
ne let sleepe oppresse Her *heavy* eyes . . . III. xi. 55. 7
Downe hanging his dull head with *heavy* chere, . . . III. xii. 16. 3
hanging downe his *heavy* countenaunce; . . . III. xii. 18. 3
Though sad and sorie for so *heavy* sight, . . . IV. iii. 14. 2
falling *heavie* on Cambelloes crest, . . . IV. iii. 34. 2
heavy heart with comfort doth rejoyce. . . . IV. iii. 45. 8
laying on them *heavy* lode, . . . IV. iv. 23. 7
When gentle sleepe his *heavie* eyes would close; . . . IV. v. 40. 2
Upon his *heavie* eye-lids chaunst to fall, . . . IV. v. 42. 2
up he rose, like *heavie* lumpe of lead, . . . IV. v. 45. 6
When Scudamour those *heavie* tydings heard, . . . IV. vi. 37. 1
backe returned with right *heavie* mind . . . IV. vi. 46. 4
With Beares and Tygers taking *heavie* part, . . . IV. vii. 2. 7
heavie sleepe the eye-lids did surprise Of Britomart, . . . IV. vii. 3. 7
to rue the others *heavy* cheare; . . . IV. vii. 34. 7
Full of sad anguish and in *heavy* case: . . . IV. vii. 38. 4
heavie armes which sore annoyd The Prince . . . IV. viii. 37. 5
despiteous dreare And *heavie* sway, . . . IV. viii. 42. 6
In *heavy* plight and sad perplexitie; . . . IV. viii. 57. 2
She bad to lighten my too *heavie* band, . . . IV. viii. 61. 3
auncient *heavy* burden which he bore . . . IV. xi. 26. 3
farre from hearing of my *heavy* plight; . . . IV. xii. 6. 6
'Which is' (sayd he) 'more *heavy* then in weight, . . . V. ii. 44. 5
with full *heavy* heart with them he far'd, . . . V. iv. 22. 7
cruell heavens have heapt an *heavy* fate; . . . V. v. 36. 3
Let him feele hardnesse of thy *heavie* arme: . . . V. v. 49. 8
with sweete rest her *heavy* eyes did close, . . . V. vii. 12. 3
as she prest on him with *heavy* sway, . . . V. xi. 31. 1
hanging down her head with *heavie* cheare, . . . V. xi. 64. 4
The *heavy* Mayd, to whom none tydings bore . . . V. xii. 11. 5
He sorely punished with *heavie* payne; . . . V. xii. 25. 7
The *heavy* burden of whose dreadfull might . . . VI. i. 22. 1
With *heavie* eyne, from teares uneath refrayning, . . . VI. ii. 41. 7
And from her sory hart few *heavie* words forth sight: . . . VI. ii. 42. 9
Not wont on foote with *heavy* armes to trace, . . . VI. iii. 29. 5

Heavy—*Continued.*
Well then him chaunst his *heavy* armes to want, . . . VI. iv. 19. 1
Wasting her goodly hew in *heavie* teares, . . . VI. vii. 38. 3
Till *heavy* hand the Carle upon him layd, . . . VI. vii. 48. 6
Laide *heavy* hands on him and held so strayte, . . . VI. viii. 11. 3
Had traveld still on foot in *heavie* armes, . . . VI. viii. 47. 2
Whose *heavy* tydings now I have to tell. . . . VI. xi. 31. 3
left in *heavy* care Through daily mourning . . . VI. xii. 14. 4
nathemore his *heavy* load releast, . . . VI. xii. 32. 8
There-on an *heavy* haplesse curse did lay; . . . VII. vi. 55. 3
with his *heavy* sledge he can it beat, . . . *Am.* xxxii. 3
prisoner led away with *heavy* hart, . . . *Am.* lii. 3
cheare you your *heavy* spright, . . . *Am.* lxii. 13
the native might Of *heavie* earth, . . . *H.L.* 189
Heavy-clouded. Lift up to him thy *heavie clouded* eyne, . . . *H.H.L.* 222
Heavy-laden. *heavy laden* with the spoyle Of harvests riches, VII. vii. 38. 2
Hebe. And thou, fayre *Hebe!* and thou, Hymen free! . . . *Epith.* 405
Hercules and *Hebe,* and the rest Of Venus dearlings, . . . *H.L.* 283
Heben(e). *See* **Ebon.**
Hebe's. All happinesse in *Hebes* silver bowre, . . . *Ti.* 384
Hebrus. represse The streames of *Hebrus* with his songs, . . . *Gn.* 181
Ne can Cephise, nor *Hebrus,* match this well: . . . I. xi. 30. 8
Hecate. the dreaded name Of *Hecate:* . . . I. i. 43. 3
Hecate, in whose almighty hand He plac't all rule . . . VII. vi. 3. 3
Hector. Did brave about the corpes of *Hector* colde; . . . *Ro.* xiv. 10
Whilst *Hector* raged with outragious minde, . . . *Gn.* 503
Hector, the glorie of the Trojan field: . . . *Gn.* 516
Having the blood of vanquisht *Hector* shedd, . . . *Gn.* 527
Hector's. young *Hectors* blood by cruell Greekes was spilt. . . II. ix. 45. 9
Heder. He would have devoured both *hidder* and shidder. . . *S.C.* S. 211
Hedge. To *hedge,* to ditch, to thrash, to thetch, to mowe? . . *Hub.* 264
Ne *hedge* ne ditch his readie passage brake; . . . II. xi. 26. 5
Nor *hedge,* nor ditch, nor hill, nor dale she staies, . . . IV. vii. 22. 1
Hedgehog. Into a *Hedgehogge* all unwares it went, . . . V. ix. 18. 5
Hedges. Like loathsome lazars, by the *hedges* lay. . . . I. iv. 3. 6
Heed. Warning all other to take *heede.* . . . *S.C.* Ap. 90
How, but, with *heede* and watchfullnesse, . . . *S.C.* S. 230
badd thereof take *heed;* . . . I. xii. 10. 8
So kept she them in order, and her selfe in *heed.* . . . II. ii. 38. 9
to taken *heed* Of what might hap. . . . II. iii. 21. 5
Henceforth take *heede* of that thou now hast past, . . . II. iv. 36. 3
Upon him lightly leaping without *heed* . . . II. viii. 49. 5
of our safety good *heede* to take; . . . II. xii. 17. 7
of each turning still kept wary *heed:* . . . III. iv. 48. 5
hast thou, Lord, of good mens cause no *heed?* . . . III. xi. 9. 6
ere she backe could turne to taken *heed,* . . . IV. vii. 4. 5
all that on him lookt without good *heed,* . . . IV. viii. 39. 5
his hindparts, whereof *heed* I tooke, . . . IV. x. 20. 3
with right wary *heede,* . . . V. vi. 31. 4
he chaunst far off to *heed* A Damzell, . . . V. viii. 4. 1
with warie *heed* He shund his strokes, . . . V. xii. 18. 2
Through that same perillous foord with better *heede,* . . . VI. iii. 31. 4
for lacke of *heed* Now gan to faint, . . . VI. v. 31. 7
For want of taking *heede* unto the same, . . . VI. vi. 2. 4
Take *heed,* therefore, myne eyes, . . . *Am.* xxxvii. 9
with carefull *heed* The silver scaly trouts doe tend . . . *Epith.* 56
Heedful. by wrestling to wex strong and *heedfull,* . . . *Hub.* 746
th' *heedful* Boteman strongly forth did stretch His brawnie armes, . . . II. xii. 21. 1
had he not it shun'd with *heedfull* vew, . . . V. viii. 32. 7
had he not foreseene with *heedfull* vew, . . . V. xi. 30. 8
Heediness. by Gods grace, and her good *heedinesse,* . . . V. vi. 34. 6
Was at his backe with heartlesse *heedinesse,* . . . VI. vi. 26. 7
Heedless. though one fall through *heedlesse* hast, . . . *S.C.* Jul. 15
heate of *heedlesse* lust me so did sting, . . . *S.C* D. 21
As in avengement of his *heedles* smart, . . . *Gn.* 291
all *heedlesse* of his dearest hale, . . . *As.* 103
How many mischieves should ensue his *heedlesse* hast. . . . I. iv. 34. 9
mercie, Lord, For mine offence and *heedelesse* hardiment, . . . II. i. 27. 2
whether art it were or *heedlesse* hap, . . . II. iii. 30. 6
hasty wroth, and *heedlesse* hazardry, . . . II. v. 13. 8
I read thee rash and *heedlesse* of thy selfe, . . . II. vii. 7. 8
So did she steale his *heedelesse* hart away, . . . III. i. 37. 1
How he their *heedelesse* harts with love had fir'd, . . . III. vi. 15. 4
'Pardon, I pray, my *heedlesse* oversight, . . . III. ix. 47. 2
every man, Surcharg'd with wine, were *heedlesse* and ill-hedded, IV. i. 3. 4
with the shocke of their owne *heedlesse* might . . . IV. ii. 16. 5
The headlesse tronke, as *heedlesse* of that stower, . . . IV. iii. 20. 7
luring baytes oftimes doe *heedlesse* harts entyse. . . . IV. x. 49. 9
heedlesse of the hooke . . . V. v. 43. 1
he with his tooth impure Him *heedlesse* bit, . . . VI. v. 16. 9
The whyles they strike at him with *heedlesse* might, . . . VI. vii. 9. 3
in his hand, with *heedlesse* hardiment, Him caught . . . *Epig.* iv. 23
Heedy. *heedy* shepheards to discerne their face; . . . *S.C.* S. 167
That they the whiles may take lesse *heedie* keepe . . . V. ix. 13. 3
Heel. A stinging serpent by the *heele* her caught; . . . *Pet.* vi. 8
stopt her course, and held her by the *heele,* . . . *Van.* ix. 11
my galage growne fast to my *heele:* . . . *S.C.* F. 244
he . . . hit me running in the *heele:* . . . *S.C.* Mar. 97
His hinder *heele* was wrapt in a clout, . . . *S.C.* May 243
bent his speare, and spurd his horse with yron *heele.* . . . I. iii. 34. 9
from her shoulder to her *heele* downe raught; . . . II. ix. 19. 2
it raught Downe to her lowest *heele;* . . . V. v. 2. 8
Heeled. *See* **Winged-heeled.**
Heeling. his hose broken high above the *heeling,* . . . *Hub.* 213
Heels. with his winged *heeles* did tread the wynd, . . . I. ix. 21. 8
flew about his *heeles* in wanton wize, . . . II. xii. 46. 8
Her golden locks, . . . raught unto her *heeles;* . . . III. ix. 20. 6
golden lockes, . . . unto her *heeles* downe traced, . . . IV. i. 13. 3
with his *heeles* so sorely he him strake, . . . V. iii. 33. 3

Heels—*Continued.*
Feeling some curre behinde his *heeles* to bite, ... VI. vi. 27. 6
Unto his *heeles* himselfe he did betake, ... VI. vi. 29. 2
He by the *heeles* him hung upon a tree, ... VI. vii. 27. 2

Heft. *See* **Heaved.**
Inflam'd with wrath, his raging blade he *hefte,* . . . . I. xi. 39. 6
with such furie backe at him it *heft,* . . . . IV. iii. 12. 5

Height. up unto his *hight* (*height*[1]), ... *Bel.* iii. 3
From heavens *hight* into mens heavy eyes, ... *Bel.*[2] i. 2
With feeble wings assay to mount on *hight;* . . . . *Bel.*[2] vii. 2
the most haughtie mountaines *hight,* . . . . *Bel.*[2] vii. 7
no time should so low embase their *hight,* . . . . *Ro.* viii. 12
Uprising by degrees, grewe to such *height,* . . . . *Ro.* xx. 10
Her length, her breadth, her deepnes, or her *hight;* . . . . *Ro.* xxvi. 4
when thou wast in greatest *hight,* . . . . *Ro.* xxxi. 12
Throughly rooted, and of wonderous *hight;* . . . . *S.C.* F. 107
beares on his shoulders the heavens *height.* . . . . *S.C.* May 143
systers nine, which dwell on Parnasse *hight,* . . . . *S.C.* Jun. 28
affrayd To clime this hilles *height.* . . . . *S.C.* Jul. 72
is enstalled nowe in heavens *hight.* . . . . *S.C.* N. 177
The fiery Sun was mounted now on *hight* . . . . *Gn.* 65
both eares pared of their *hight;* . . . . *Hub.* 1382
grow to *height* (**hight*) of kingdomes government, ... *T.M.* 76
nigh unto the Heavens in *height* upreared, ... *Ti.* 507
lowly thoughts lift up to heavens *hight,* . . . . *T.M.* 459
To view the workmanship of heavens *hight:* . . . . *Mui.* 45
Lift up thy notes unto their wonted *height,* . . . . *Col.* 390
daring not too rashing mount on *hight,* . . . . *Col.* 421
clapping all their hands on *hight,* . . . . I. v. 16. 8
The *hight* of three the tallest sonnes of mortall seed. . . . . I. vii. 8. 9
lifting up his dreadfull club on *hight,* . . . . I. viii. 7. 3
heaped *hight* Her hastie ruine does more heavie make, ... I. viii. 23. 5
a cup . . . fild up to the *hight,* . . . . I. x. 13. 3
backward turne his course from hevens *hight:* . . . . I. x. 20. 3
God he often saw from heavens *hight:* . . . . I. x. 47. 2
to what end they clomb that tedious *hight?* . . . . I. x. 49. 9
sweet Timbrels all upheld on *hight.* . . . . I. xii. 6. 9
Far passing th' *hight* of men terrestriall, ... II. vii. 41. 5
doth it selfe stretch forth to hevens *hight,* . . . . II. x. 2. 5
depth exceeded not three cubits *hight,* . . . . II. xii. 62. 6
So is his soveraine honour raisde to hevens *hight.'* . . . . . III. ii. 14. 9
Betwixt the lowest earth and hevens *hight,* . . . . III. ii. 19. 3
to hevens *hight* forth stretched bee: . . . . III. iii. 22. 4
like a girlond compassed the *hight;* . . . . III. vi. 43. 6
having spide on *hight* An Eagle . . . . III. vii. 39. 2
Upon the top of Mount Olympus *hight,* . . . . III. vii. 41. 5
heaped hils on *hight* To scale the skyes . . . . III. vii. 47. 4
Another plant, that raught to wondrous *hight,* . . . . III. ix. 47. 7
appeare . . . flames and reach to hevens *hight,* . . . . . . III. x. 12. 8
through the helpe of his faire hornes on *hight,* . . . . . . III. x. 47. 4
To looke adowne, or upward to the *hight:* . . . . III. x. 56. 6
When her discolourd bow she spreds through hevens *hight.* . . . III. xi. 47. 9
Whose *hight* all Ephesus did oversee, ... IV. x. 30. 2
learned Ptolomaee his *hight* did take, ... V. Pr. 7. 6
since the time they first tooke the Sunnes *hight,* . . . . . . V. Pr. 8. 4
Bold Radigund with sound of trumpe on *hight,* . . . . V. iv. 45. 4
Their sound did reach unto the heavens *hight:* . . . . V. v. 4. 6
Which when his Ladie from the castles *hight* Beheld, ... V. viii. 45. 4
shortly forst him to forsake The *hight,* . . . . V. ix. 16. 7
heaved them on *hight,* . . . . V. xi. 8. 5
Like to a Giant for his monstrous *hight,* . . . . V. xii. 15. 2
Exceeding all the rest in powre and *hight;* . . . . VI. v. 13. 7
with reprochfull words him thus bespake on *hight.* . . . . . VI. vi. 24. 9
as his hand was heaved up on *hight,* . . . . VI. viii. 10. 2
was bordered with a wood Of matchlesse *hight,* . . . . VI. x. 6. 3
with equall *hight* Did seeme to overlooke the lowly vale: . . . VI. x. 8. 7
sound Of a shrill pipe he playing heard on *hight,* . . . . . . VI. x. 10. 3
rearing up his former feete on *hight,* . . . . VI. xii. 29. 7
T' attempt the empire of the heavens *hight,* . . . . VII. vi. 7. 4
With thousand Crystall pillors of huge *hight,* . . . . VII. vi. 10. 4
faire palace fixt in heavens *hight;* . . . . VII. vi. 15. 2
Day did beare upon his scepters *hight* The goodly Sun . . . . VII. vii. 44. 8
This day the sunne is in his chiefest *hight,* . . . . *Epith.* 265
up to the heavens *hight.* . . . . *H.L.* 189
from the top of purest heavens *hight* . . . . *H.B.* 109
From this base world unto thy heavens *hight,* . . . . *H.H.L.* 2
To them the heavens illimitable *hight* . . . . *H.H.L.* 57
From heavens *hight,* to which they did aspyre, ... *H.H.L.* 88
heavens, . . . infinite in largenesse and in *hight,* . . . . . *H.H.B.* 67

Heights. upon the highest *hights* Of Arlo-hill . . . . VII. vi. 36. 5
fairest Hill That was in all this holy Islands *hights*) . . . . VII. vi. 37. 7

Heinous. almost it did *haynous* violence . . . . II. i. 28. 6
wreake on them their *hainous* hatefull deed.' . . . . II. iii. 14. 9
breathes out wrath and *hainous* crueltee: . . . . II. iv. 43. 8
That am the authour of this *hainous* deed, ... II. vi. 33. 8
worke so *hainous* tort, ... III. ii. 12. 8
endured sore Sore trouble of an *hainous* enimy, ... III. vi. 53. 6
He cast to punish for his *hainous* fault: . . . . III. viii. 36. 3
As may be worthy of his *haynous* sin.' . . . . III. ix. 9. 7
Of many *haynous* crymes by her enured; . . . . V. ix. 39. 6
Strongly did Zele her *haynous* fact enforce, ... V. ix. 43. 1
Which *haynous* sight when Calidore beheld, ... VI. i. 18. 1
He gan to him object his *haynous* crime, ... VI. vii. 26. 7

Heir. With them it sits to care for their *heire,* . . . . . . *S.C.* May 77
To deck her Dame, and enrich her *heyre;* . . . . *S.C.* S. 115
'He, noble bud, his Grandsires livelie *hayre,* . . . . *Ti.* 267
Clarion, the eldest sonne and *haire* Of Muscaroll; . . . . . . *Mui.* 22
For being borne an auncient Lions *haire,* . . . . *D.* 122
Which of their praises have left you the *haire;* . . . . *Ded. Son.* x. 4
'He, . . . betrothed me unto the onely *haire* . . . . I. ii. 23. 2

Heir—*Continued.*
That I was sonne and *heire* unto a king, ... I. ix. 5. 8
His onely daughter and his only *hayre;* (**heyre*) . . . . . I. xii. 21. 3
The wofull daughter and forsaken *heyre* (**heire*) . . . . . I. xii. 26. 3
in his crown he counted her no *hayre,* . . . . II. x. 28. 8
After him raigned Guitheline his *hayre,* . . . . II. x. 42. 1
him with her made of his kingdome *heyre,* . . . . II. x. 61. 3
left none *heire* them to withstand, ... II. x. 61. 8
Being his onely daughter and his *hayre;* . . . . III. ii. 22. 4
She, Angel-like, the *heyre* of ancient kings . . . . V. ix. 29. 7
Tristram . . . the onely *heire* Of good King Meliogras . . . . VI. ii. 28. 1
begot, Like to it selfe his eldest sonne and *heire,* . . . . . . *H.H.L.* 31

Heir-apparent. of my kingdome *heyre apparaunt* bee: . . . . I. xii. 20. 6

Heirs. such as claymd themselves Brutes rightfull *hayres,* . . II. x. 37. 5
So that for want of *heires* it to defend, ... VI. iv. 31. 6

Held. *See* **Upheld.**
Since of all workmen *helde* in reckning best; . . . . *Ro.* xxvii. 7
stopt her course, and *held* her by the heele, ... Van. ix. 11
In stead of them a handsome bat he *held,* . . . . *Hub.* 217
Then was shee *held* in soveraigne dignitie, ... *T.M.* 563
In her right hand a broken rod she *held,* . . . . *Ti.* 13
Whom England high in count of honour *held,* . . . . *Ti.* 185
scarce the skin the strong contagion *helde.* . . . . *Mui.* 256
Ne will be *helde* in anie stedfast plight, ... *D.* 496
deare did entertaine, . . . and *held* in passing price, ... *As.* Interl. 220
Nath-lesse the Nymph her former liking *held;* . . . . *Col.* 128
all the world in their subjection *held;* . . . . I. i. 5. 6
in her hand she *held* a mirrhour bright, ... I. iv. 10. 6
on his dagger still his hand he *held,* . . . . I. iv. 33. 8
there he *held* Her captive to his sensuall desyre, ... I. vi. 23. 1
hope . . . That earst us *held* in love of lingring life; . . . . I. ix. 29. 6
She *held* him fast, and firmely did upbeare, ... I. x. 35. 8
a sharpe bore-speare she *held,* . . . . II. iii. 29. 1
Those deadly tooles which in her hand she *held,* . . . . II. iii. 37. 3
in his hand two dartes . . . he *held,* . . . . II. iv. 38. 8
Yielded by him that *held* it forcibly: . . . . II. iv. 40. 2
ever *held* his hand upon his hart; . . . . II. vi. 26. 2
Disdeigning to bee *held* so long in fight. . . . . II. vi. 30. 4
In his right hand an yron club he *held,* . . . . II. vii. 40. 6
She *held* a great gold chaine ylincked well, ... II. vii. 46. 2
Those that were low themselves *held* others hard, ... II. vii. 47. 7
abasht for shame *Held* downe her head, ... II. ix. 43. 2
things foregone through many ages *held,* . . . . II. ix. 56. 2
They *held* this land, ... II. x. 9. 1
all mens harts in dew obedience *held;* . . . . II. x. 32. 5
Held on his course with stayed stedfastnesse, ... II. xii. 29. 6
In her left hand a Cup of gold she *held,* . . . . II. xii. 56. 1
So *held* them under fast; . . . . II. xii. 81. 6
Which Uther with those forrein Pagans *held,* . . . . III. iii. 55. 4
he perforce him *held,* and strokes upon him hept. . . . . . . III. vii. 33. 9
him he *held,* and did through might amate. . . . . III. vii. 35. 1
So long he *held* him, and him bett so long, ... III. vii. 35. 2
'Sir, him wise I never *held,* . . . . IV. i. 34. 7
Sad Clotho *held* the rocke, ... IV. ii. 48. 5
in her other hand a cup she *hild,* . . . . IV. iii. 42. 8
in their hands their idle troncheons *held,* . . . . IV. iv. 18. 8
in an open Turney lately *held,* . . . . IV. vi. 6. 6
He *held* the Lady forth before him right, ... IV. viii. 26. 3
held her wrathfull hand from vengeance sore: . . . . IV. vii. 36. 6
Held vertue for it selfe in soveraine awe: . . . . IV. viii. 30. 6
He her unwares attacht, and captive *held* by might. . . . . . . IV. ix. 6. 9
forth to bring those thrals which there he *held.* . . . . IV. ix. 8. 3
him embracing fast betwixt them *held,* . . . . IV. ix. 9. 3
The pledge of faith, her hand, engaged *held* . . . . IV. x. 55. 7
in small compasse *hild?* . . . . IV. xi. 17. 4
Though vertue then were *held* in highest price, ... V. i. 1. 1
For his great justice, *held* in high regard, ... V. i. 30. 2
had he not bene *held,* he nought had fayld of it. . . . . V. iii. 29. 9
of him requere That Damsell whom he *held* . . . . V. viii. 27. 9
in his hand an huge long staffe he *held,* . . . . V. ix. 11. 1
tooke it up, and *held* fast in his hand. . . . . V. ix. 17. 9
His deadly weapon which in hand he *held:* . . . . V. xii. 16. 5
The other *held* a snake with venime fraught, ... V. xii. 30. 5
In his right hand he *held* a trembling dart, ... VI. ii. 6. 4
And in his left he *held* a sharpe bore-speare, ... VI. ii. 6. 6
And be for ever *held* a recreant Knight, ... VI. iii. 35. 6
And *held* the same so hard, ... VI. iv. 6. 8
streight he *held* his hand at his commaundement. . . . . VI. vi. 40. 9
Laide heavy hands on him and *held* so strayte, ... VI. viii. 11. 3
Whom with his weight unweldy downe he *held,* . . . . VI. viii. 28. 3
religion *held* even theeves in measure. . . . . VI. viii. 43. 9
She long so *held,* and softly weeping sayd; . . . . VI. xii. 19. 7
His shield he on him threw, and fast downe *held:* . . . . . . VI. xii. 30. 6
did rage and rore To be downe *held,* . . . . VI. xii. 31. 2
hast *held* The Heavens rule . . . . VII. vi. 27. 6
In his right hand a tipped staffe he *held,* . . . . VII. vii. 31. 6
In his one hand . . . He *held* a knife-hook; . . . . VII. vii. 38. 6
held in hand a mace, ... VII. vii. 44. 5

Helen. one, that fairest *Helene* did revile, ... *Col.* 920
had of her fayre *Helen* for his meed, ... II. vii. 55. 8
Fayre *Helena,* the fairest living wight; . . . . II. x. 59. 5
'Fayre *Helene,* flowre of beautie excellent, ... III. ix. 35. 1
As *Hellene,* when she saw aloft appeare . . . . III. x. 12. 7
This second *Helene,* fayre Dame Hellenore, ... III. x. 13. 1

Helena. *See* **Helen.**

Helice. My *Helice,* the lodestar of my lyfe, ... *Am.* xxxiv. 10

Helicon. Whence floweth *Helicon,* the learned well, ... *S.C.* Ap. 42
Beside the silver Springs of *Helicone,* . . . . *T.M.* 5
The sacred springs of horsefoot *Helicon,* . . . . *T.M.* 271
Not one Parnassus nor one *Helicone,* . . . . *Ded. Son.* v. 6

Helicon—*Continued.*
Of *Helicon,* whence she derived is; . . . *Am.* i. 10
Heliconian. the love which thou doest beare To th' *Heliconian* ymps, . . . *Ded. Son.* iii. 11
striv'd With th' *Heliconian* maides for maystery; . . . II. xii. 31. 2
Helie. *See* **Hely.**
Hell. *See* **Rake-hell.**
May reach from hence to depth of darkest *hell,* . . . *Ro.* i. 6
The griesly gates of his devouring *hell,* . . . *Van.* iii. 10
gates of *hel,* and fyrie furies forse, . . . *S.C.* N. 164
The Queene of *hell* to move as easily, . . . *Gn.* 462
If *Hell* at least . . . Knew how to pardon, . . . *Gn.* 475
griesly Feends of *hell* him terrifie. . . . *Gn.* 544
the cruell fiends of *hell,* . . . *Gn.* 625
What *hell* it is in suing long to bide: . . . *Hub.* 896
had him slaine, And driven downe to *hell,* . . . *Hub.* 1237
hell, and darkenesse, and the grislie grave, . . . *T.M.* 496
greislie shades, such as doo haunt in *hell,* . . . *Ti.* 125
'The sevenfold yron gates of grislie *Hell,* . . . *Ti.* 372
waies unknowne, waies leading down to *hell.* . . . *Col.* 211
when those accursed messengers of *hell,* . . . Came . . . I. ii. 2. 1
sad Proserpina, the Queene of *hell;* . . . I. iv. 11. 2
unto *hell* him selfe for money sold; . . . I. iv. 27. 7
Duessa . . . to *hell* does goe. . . . I. v. Arg.
an entraunce . . . Descends to *hell:* . . . I. v. 31. 6
she in *hell* and heaven had power equally. . . . I. v. 34. 9
unto *hell* did thrust him downe alive, . . . I. v. 40. 5
wrought In deepest *Hell,* and framd by Furies skill, . . . I. vii. 13. 2
a deepe descent, as darke as *hell,* . . . I. viii. 39. 8
A man of *hell* that calls himselfe Despayre; . . . I. ix. 28. 5
Cupids wanton snare As *hell* she hated; . . . I. x. 30. 6
his spright Had past the paines of *hell* . . . I. x. 32. 9
he, that harrowd *hell* with heavie stowre, . . . I. x. 40. 8
sin, and *hell,* and death, doe most dismay . . . I. x. 41. 4
like the griesly mouth of *hell,* . . . I. xi. 12. 8
'That cursed man, that cruel feend of *hell,* . . . II. vi. 50. 1
That to the gate of *Hell* . . . Was next adjoyning, . . . II. vii. 24. 6
lower part did reach to lowest *Hell;* . . . II. vii. 46. 4
hideous shapes were like to feendes of *hell,* . . . II. xi. 11. 3
seemd more horrible then *hell* to bee, . . . II. xii. 6. 3
affraid of him as feend of *hell.* . . . III. iv. 47. 9
thrust downe to *hell* below, . . . III. iv. 55. 4
Chace her away, from whence she came, to *hell:* . . . III. iv. 60. 6
So made him thinke him selfe in heven that was in *hell.* . . . III. viii. 19. 9
As if he heaven and *hell* would over-ronne, . . . III. x. 33. 7
Dragons, and Minotaures, and feendes of *hell,* . . . III. x. 40. 5
paines in love, or punishments in *hell:* . . . III. xii. 26. 5
Hard by the gates of *hell* her dwelling is; . . . IV. i. 20. 1
sent away So many centaures drunken soules to *hell,* . . . IV. i. 23. 4
Firebrand of *hell,* first tynd in Phlegeton, . . . IV. ii. 1. 1
lovers heaven must passe by sorrowes *hell.'* . . . IV. vi. 32. 7
he in *hell* doth lie, That lives a loathed life, . . . IV. vii. 11. 8
Was fled to *hell,* surcharg'd with spoile and theft: . . . IV. vii. 32. 5
fire devoure the ayre, and *hell* them quight, . . . IV. x. 35. 6
Like to the balefull house of lowest *hell,* . . . IV. xi. 4. 3
lowest *hell,* to which I lie most neare, . . . IV. xii. 6. 7
Then would he ballaunce heaven and *hell* together, . . . V. ii. 31. 5
some doe say it goeth downe to *hell:* . . . V. ix. 6. 5
fire to them did threat, And *hell* unto him selfe . . . V. xi. 12. 5
swarmes of damned soules to *hell* he sends: . . . VI. viii. 49. 7
she thought her self in *hell,* . . . VI. x. 43. 8
what destiny Or other dyrefull hap from heaven or *hell* . . . VI. xi. 29. 8
Brought forth with him the dreadfull dog of *hell,* . . . VI. xii. 35. 2
Him to attache, and downe to *hell* to throwe; . . . VII. vi. 16. 7
thunder-drive to *hell?'* . . . VII. vi. 30. 6
having harrowd *hell,* didst bring away Captivity . . . *Am.* lxviii. 3
all the plagues, and horrid paines, of *hell* . . . *Am.* lxxxv. 5
through heaven and *hell* thou makest way . . . *H.L.* 236
make a lovers life a wretches *hell.* . . . *H.L.* 265
To deepest *hell,* and lake of damned fyre, . . . *H.H.L.* 89
In that deepe horror of despeyred *hell,* . . . *H.H.L.* 130
Hell-born. like the *hell-borne* Hydra, . . . VI. xii. 32. 1
Hell-bred. The *hell-bred* beast threw forth unto the skies, . . . I. xi. 40. 3
Hell-dreaded. By his deepe science and *hell-dreaded* might, . . . III. ii. 18. 7
Hell-gate. Here Sleep, ther Richesse, and *Hel-gate* them both betwext. . . . II. vii. 25. 9
greedy mouth wide gaping like *hell-gate,* . . . VI. x. 34. 6
Helle. like a Ram, faire *Helle* to pervart, . . . III. xi. 30. 5
Ram, which bore Phrixus and *Helle* . . . V. Pr. 5. 7
Hellebore. Dead sleeping Poppy, and black *Hellebore;* . . . II. vii. 52. 3
Hellenore. 'Malbecco he, and *Hellenore* she hight; . . . III. ix. 6. 1
Upon his lips hong faire Dame *Hellenore* . . . III. ix. 52. 2
Paridell rapeth *Hellenore:* . . . III. x. Arg. 1
This second Helene, fayre Dame *Hellenore,* . . . III. x. 13. 1
asked him for *Hellenore:* . . . III. x. 38. 1
Faire *Helenore* with girlonds all bespredd, . . . III. x. 44. 5
To see th' unkindnes of his *Hellenore.* . . . III. x. 45. 5
every Satyre first did give a busse To *Hellenore;* . . . III. x. 46. 4
Hellenore's. *Hellenors* both eyes did eke beguyle, . . . III. x. 5. 4
Hellespont. *Hellespont* trampled with horses feete, . . . *Gn.* 49
In th' *Hellespont* being nigh drowned all. . . . *Gn.* 552
The same which over *Hellespontus* swam; . . . VII. vii. 32. 5
Hellish. His musicks might the *hellish* hound did tame. . . . *S.C.* O. 30
Image of *hellish* horrour, Ignorance, . . . *T.M.* 259
hellish hags had met upon the way; . . . *D.* 566
She poured forth out of her *hellish* sinke . . . I. i. 22. 5
wicked maister, . . . gan threaten *hellish* paine, . . . I. ii. 2. 6
by her *hellish* science raisd . . . A foggy mist . . . I. ii. 38. 4
cole blacke steedes yborne of *hellish* brood, . . . I. v. 20. 8
all the *hellish* brood Of feends infernall . . . I. v. 32. 7

Hellish—*Continued.*
hellish anguish did his soule assaile; . . . I. ix. 49. 4
doth quench the brond of *hellish* smart, . . . I. ix. 53. 7
he from *hellish* entrailes did expire. . . . I. xi. 45. 5
Her *hellish* brond hath kindled with despight, . . . II. ii. 29. 3
either *hellish* feends, or powres on hye: . . . II. iii. 45. 5
with horrible affright And *hellish* fury . . . II. iv. 30. 2
To ridd a wretched man from handes of *hellish* wight!' . . . II. v. 23. 9
As one affright With *hellish* feends, . . . II. v. 37. 7
What *hellish* fury hath at earst thee hent? . . . II. vi. 49. 2
Outrageous wrong, and *hellish* covetize, . . . II. vii. 12. 8
dipped in the bitter wave Of *hellish* Styx, . . . II. viii. 20. 9
as a man whom *hellish* feendes have frayd, . . . II. viii. 46. 4
hellish feend raysd up through divelish science. . . . II. xi. 39. 9
The *hellish* Harpyes, prophets of sad destiny. . . . II. xii. 36. 9
Fowle horror, and eke *hellish* dreriment: . . . III. iv. 55. 5
her divelish deedes And *hellish* arts . . . III. vii. 6. 8
To fill his *hellish* gorge, . . . III. vii. 29. 2
O hatefull *hellish* Snake! . . . III. xi. 1. 1
she at first was borne of *hellish* brood, . . . IV. i. 26. 7
Wherewith the *hellish* fiends he doth confound: . . . IV. iii. 42. 7
some *hellish* furie or some feend . . . IV. vi. 17. 6
Of this accursed Carle of *hellish* kind, . . . IV. vii. 18. 4
ere unto his *hellish* den he raught, . . . IV. vii. 31. 2
He brought forth that old hag of *hellish* hew, . . . V. ix. 47. 3
Horrible, hideous, and of *hellish* race, . . . V. xi. 23. 4
She flew at him like to an *hellish* feend, . . . V. xi. 27. 2
'It is a Monster bred of *hellishe* race,' . . . VI. i. 7. 7
such hurts are *hellish* paine. . . . VI. vi. 1. 9
that same beast was bred of *hellish* strene, . . . VI. vi. 9. 7
even the *hellish* fiends affrighted bee At sight thereof, . . . VI. vi. 10. 4
This *hellish* Dog, that hight the Blatant Beast; . . . VI. vi. 12. 2
Whylest thus she in these *hellish* dens remayned, . . . VI. xi. 3. 1
Unto their *hellish* den those theeves them brought; . . . VI. xi. 41. 2
Such was the fury of this *hellish* Beast, . . . VI. xii. 32. 6
Doth make both Gods and *hellish* fiends affraid: . . . VII. vi. 18. 3
them to *hellish* dungeons downe hast feld. . . . VII. vi. 27. 8
O how doth it torment . . . with more then *hellish* paine! . . . *H.L.* 253
Loath that foule blot, that *hellish* fierbrand, . . . *H.B.* 169
Hell-mouth. did the house of Richesse from *hell-mouth* divide. . . . II. vii. 24. 9
Helm. Withouten *helme* or Pilot her to sway: . . . *T.M.* 142
there sate a knight with *helme* unlaste, . . . II. i. 24. 7
to them does the steddy *helme* apply, . . . II. vii. 1. 8
th' other brother gan his *helme* unlace, . . . II. viii. 17. 2
would have unlast His *Helme,* . . . VI. i. 39. 6
Helmet. at his haughty helmet making mark, . . . I. ii. 19. 3
in haste his *helmet* gan unlace, . . . I. iii. 37. 1
rending up his *helmet,* would Have slayne him streight; . . . I. iii. 38. 2
catching up in hast his . . . shining *helmet,* . . . I. vi. 41. 9
haughtie *Helmet,* horrid all with gold, . . . I. vii. 31. 1
pillow was my *helmett* fayre displayd; . . . I. ix. 13. 4
thought his armes to leave, and *helmet* to unlace. . . . I. xi. 26. 9
glauncing on his *helmet,* . . . II. v. 6. 4
so fiers did play On th' others *helmett,* . . . II. vi. 31. 6
His shining *Helmet* he gan soone unlace, . . . II. viii. 52. 8
Upon his head he wore an *Helmet* light, . . . II. xi. 22. 8
on her dight Her *Helmet,* . . . III. iv. 12. 5
fayntly fluttering, scarce his *helmet* raught, . . . III. v. 24. 8
on his *helmet* martelled so hard . . . III. vii. 42. 3
loosd her *helmet* from her lofty hedd, . . . III. ix. 22. 7
His haberjeon, his *helmet,* and his speare: . . . III. xi. 7. 5
her glistring *helmet* she unlaced; . . . IV. i. 13. 1
doft his *helmet,* and undid his mayle: . . . IV. i. 43. 7
The wicked stroke upon her *helmet* chaunst, . . . IV. vi. 19. 1
Upon her *helmet* he againe her strooke, . . . V. v. 11. 2
her sunshynie *helmet* soone unlaced, . . . V. v. 11. 8
Thinking at once both head and *helmet* to have raced. . . . V. v. 11. 9
Which when she saw her *helmet* she unlaste, . . . V. vii. 8. 8
She her so rudely on the *helmet* smit . . . V. vii. 33. 7
She with one stroke both head and *helmet* cleft. . . . V. vii. 34. 6
on the *helmet* smote him formerlie, . . . VI. i. 38. 8
His shield, his *helmet,* and his curats bare; . . . VI. v. 8. 7
Helmets. hewen *helmets* deepe shew marks of eithers might. . . . I. v. 7. 9
mighty brawned bowrs Were wont to . . . *helmets* hew, . . . I. viii. 41. 7
Hewing and slashing shields and *helmets* bright, . . . IV. iv. 41. 6
Ne *helmets* bright ne hawberks strong did spare, . . . IV. ix. 27. 3
Helms. *helmes* unbruzed wexen dayly browne. . . . *S.C.* O. 42
mailes did rash, and *helmes* did hew. . . . IV. ii. 17. 9
Rashing off *helmes,* and ryving plates asonder, . . . V. iii. 8. 6
They hew'd their *helmes,* and plates asunder brake, . . . VI. i. 37. 4
Help. (Ay little *helpe* to harme there needeth!) . . . *S.C.* F. 198
Helpe me to blaze Her worthy praise, . . . *S.C.* Ap. 43
To *helpen* the Ladyes their Maybush beare!) . . . *S.C.* May 34
What *helpe?* her Kidde . . . was gone: . . . *S.C.* May 300
Helpe me, ye banefull byrds, . . . *S.C.* Au. 173
times delay new hope of *helpe* still breeds. . . . *Hub.* 327
the best *helpe,* which chiefly him sustain'd, . . . *Hub.* 853
with the Foxes *helpe* them borne aside . . . *Hub.* 1017
So seeke we *helpe* our sorrow to redresse, . . . *T.M.* 351
Ne may thee *help* the manie hartie vow, . . . *Mui.* 237
Helpe, O thou Tragick Muse! . . . *Mui.* 413
Help me to wayle my miserable case, . . . *D.* 510
Helpe, O ye shepheards, *helpe* ye all in this, . . . *Col.* 436
Helpe Amaryllis this her losse to mourne: . . . *Col.* 437
Helpe then, O holy virgin! . . . I. Pr. 2. 1
O, *helpe* thou my weake wit, . . . I. Pr. 2. 9
soveraine hope which in his *helpe* he had. . . . I. i. 2. 6
God *helpe* the man so wrapt in Errours endlesse traine! . . . I. i. 18. 9
cryes, The last vaine *helpe* of wemens great distresse, . . . I. vi. 6. 3
Found never *help* who never would his hurts impart.' . . . I. vii. 40. 9

Help—*Continued.*
If then it find not *helpe,* and breeds despaire.' . . . I. vii. 41. 6
'O! *helpe,* Orgoglio; *helpe!* or els we perish all.' . . . I. viii. 20. 9
Is not great grace to *helpe* him over past . . . I. ix. 39. 4
helpe the helpelesse pore: . . . I. x. 3. 7
by her *helpe* the top at last he wonne. . . . I. x. 47. 9
Witnes, ye heavens, whom she in vaine to *help* did call. . . . II. i. 10. 9
help never comes too late.' . . . II. i. 44. 9
He oft finds present *helpe* who does his griefe impart.' . . . II. i. 46. 9
Hard *help* at need! So deare thee, babe, I bought; . . . II. i. 53. 8
of him selfe great hope and *help* conceiv'd, . . . II. iii. 5. 2
give you eke good *helpe* to their decay. . . . II. iii. 15. 2
beckned him, the last *help* she had left; . . . II. iv. 13. 3
he that last left *helpe* away did take, . . . II. iv. 13. 4
if she had her least *helpe* to thee lent, . . . II. iv. 26. 1
'*Help,* O Sir Guyon! *helpe,* . . . II. v. 23. 8
Calling thy *help* in vaine . . . II. v. 36. 9
O Atin! *helpe* to me last death to give.' . . . II. vi. 45. 5
lowdly cald; '*Help, helpe!* O Archimage! . . . II. vi. 48. 2
Helpe with thy hand, or with thy counsell sage: . . . II. vi. 48. 4
helpe, he saw, he needed more Then pitty, . . . II. vi. 48. 8
hope of *helpe* and timely grace, . . . II. viii. 25. 6
by the *helpe* of Vortimere his sonne, . . . II. x. 66. 1
often need the *helpe* of weaker hand; . . . II. xi. 30. 2
when she saw no *helpe* might him restore, . . . III. i. 38. 7
helpe may have elsewhere, . . . III. iii. 17. 6
O! who shal *helpe* me to lament and mourne . . . III. iii. 42. 7
unable to withstand Or *helpe* himselfe; . . . III. vii. 43. 4
cride to heven, from humane *helpe* exild. . . . III. viii. 27. 5
call alowd for *helpe,* ere *helpe* were past; . . . III. x. 13. 7
through the *helpe* of his faire hornes on hight, . . . III. x. 47. 4
seemd no *help* for him was left in living sight. . . . III. x. 56. 9
Perhaps this hand may *helpe* to ease your woe, . . . III. xi. 15. 4
squiers make hast to *helpe* their Lords fordonne. . . . IV. iv. 38. 8
In no lesse neede of *helpe* then him he weend. . . . IV. iv. 45. 4
This hand may *helpe,* or succour ought supplie, . . . IV. vi. 8. 7
'Through *helpe*' (quoth she) 'of this old woman here . . . IV. vii. 19. 6
But-if the heavens *helpe* to redresse her wrong, . . . IV. vii. 23. 3
to my wound her gratious *help* impart. . . . IV. x. 48. 5
At last to Tryphon she for *helpe* did hie, . . . IV. xi. 6. 5
Helpe, therefore, O! thou sacred imp of Jove . . . IV. xi. 10. 1
Helpe me to tell the names of all those floods . . . IV. xi. 10. 6
All destitute of *helpe* doth headlong fall; . . . V. ii. 8. 4
did *helpe* to save her. . . . V. iv. 12. 4
he that *helpe* from her against her will discarded. . . . V. v. 8. 9
to his fortunes *helpe* make readie way?' . . . V. v. 39. 4
for *helpe* aloud in earnest cride: . . . V. ix. 12. 3
Crying for *helpe* aloud: . . . V. ix. 14. 6
Crying in vaine for *helpe,* when *helpe* was past: . . . V. ix. 19. 6
With hope of *helpe* in that her greatest neede . . . V. x. 22. 5
it was she the which for *helpe* did seeke. . . . VI. i. 17. 3
great *helpe* dame Nature selfe doth lend; . . . VI. ii. 2. 1
the onely *helpe* now left them . . . VI. iii. 12. 8
As if his cry did meane for *helpe* to call, . . . VI. iv. 18. 3
quite they seem'd past *helpe* of surgery; . . . VI. vi. 5. 5
in your selfe your onely *helpe* doth lie . . . VI. vi. 7. 1
'What hope of *helpe* doth then for us remaine, . . . VI. vi. 13. 6
To *helpe* faire Pastorella home to drive Her fleecie flocke; . . . VI. ix. 15. 8
Coridon most *helpe* did give. . . . VI. ix. 15. 9
Gan cry to them aloud to *helpe* her . . . VI. x. 34. 9
Would for the wretched infants *helpe* provyde; . . . VI. xii. 8. 8
ere he new *helpe* could call, . . . VI. xii. 30. 5
Helpe me mine owne loves prayses to resound; . . . *Epith.* 14
To *helpe* to decke her, and to *help* to sing, . . . *Epith.* 72
Helpe quickly her to dight: . . . *Epith.* 97
Helpe to addorne my beautifullest bride: . . . *Epith.* 105

Helped. *See* **Holpen.**
the false Foxe him *helped* to array. . . . *Hub.* 1063
You to have *helpt* I hold my selfe yet blest.' . . . I. ix. 7. 7
her mis-shape much *helpt;* . . . V. xii. 29. 3
helped through the swiftnesse of his steed, . . . VI. iv. 8. 5

Helping. they which sought at first their *helping* hand, . . . II. x. 65. 8
his good Squyre, him *helping* up with speed, . . . II. xi. 48. 7
Whylest everie one with *helping* hands did strive, . . . VI. ix. 15. 6
every evening *helping* them to fold: . . . VI. ix. 37. 6

Helpless. *helplesse* hap it booteth not to mone. . . . I. iv. 49. 5
Such *helplesse* harmes yts better hidden keep, . . . I. vii. 39. 7
helpe the *helpelesse* pore: . . . I. x. 3. 7
helplesse what may it boot To frett for anger, . . . II. iii. 3. 3
on this rock are rent, and sunck in *helples* wawes.' . . . II. xii. 4. 9
rather doth my *helpelesse* griefe augment; . . . III. ii. 43. 5
gentle Ladyes *helplesse* misery: . . . III. xi. 18. 6
To see an *helplesse* evill double griefe doth lend. . . . IV. xii. 21. 9
So miserably him all *helpelesse* slew, . . . VI. vi. 22. 7
house-fyres, nor lightnings *helpelesse* harmes, . . . *Epith.* 340

Helps. she sought for *helps* to cloke her crime withall. . . . II. vii. 45. 9
when all other *helpes* she saw to faile, . . . III. vii. 21. 6
all other *helpes* were past. . . . VI. iii. 12. 9
nature, which doth litle need Of forreine *helpes* . . . VI. ix. 20. 7
Then all their *helpes* they busily applyde . . . VI. xi. 22. 3

Hely. Till aged *Hely* by dew heritage it gaynd. . . . II. x. 45. 9

Hem. *See* **Them.**
to the greene Wood they speeden *hem* all, . . . *S.C.* May 27
blamest *hem* much . . . *S.C.* May 147
such end, perdie, does all *hem* remayne, . . . *S.C.* May 304
With holy water they doen *hem* all drench. . . . *S.C.* S. 89
not good Dogges *hem* needeth to chace, . . . *S.C.* S. 166
How mought we, Diggon, *hem* be-hold? . . . *S.C.* S. 229
better learne of *hem* that learned bee, . . . *S.C.* N. 29
safely did *hem* keepe: . . . *S.C.* N. 137

Hem—*Continued.*
the rest them round about did *hemme,* . . . VI. x. 12. 4

Hemmed. round about with mightie white rocks *hemd,* . . . *Col.* 274
Was *hemd* with golden fringe. . . . II. iii. 26. 9
Hemd in with waters like a wall in sight, . . . V. ii. 35. 7
All clad in linnen robes with silver *hemd;* . . . V. vii. 4. 4
Hemd all about with fringe of silver twine: . . . V. vii. 6. 5

Hempen. About his neck an *hempen* rope he weares, . . . I. ix. 22. 7
Haling her palfrey by the *hempen* raines: . . . VI. vii. 44. 4
with an *hempen* cord He like a dog was led . . . VI. viii. 5. 3

Hems. Whose rutty Bancke, the which his River *hemmes* . . . *Proth.* 12

Hemus. *See* **Haemus.**

Henalois. blood of *Henalois* which therein fell. . . . II. x. 24. 5

Henault. *See* **Hainault.**

Hence (*partial list*).
May reach from *hence* to depth . . . *Ro.* i. 6
soone I rede thee *hence* remove, . . . *S.C.* F. 137
twincling starres the daylight *hence* chase. . . . *S.C.* Ap. 161
Hence with the Nightingale will I take part, . . . *S.C.* Au. 183
and *hence* depart.' . . . *Hub.* 1221
From *hence* wee mount aloft . . . *T.M.* 505
being driven *hence,* . . . *T.M.* 528
banisht farre away from *hence;* . . . *D.* 10
she parted *hence,* . . . *D.* 220
Whilest thou wast *hence,* . . . *Col.* 22
that thee did *hence* dissuade.' . . . *Col.* 177
'Far *hence* . . . in wastfull wildernesse . . . I. i. 32. 1
fly far *hence* away, . . . I. ii. 31. 4
borne him *hence* to Plutoes balefull bowres: . . . I. v. 14. 8
'Not far away,' (quoth he) 'he *hence* doth wonne, . . . I. vi. 39. 7
'*hence* shall I never rest, . . . I. ix. 32. 1
soule departing *hence* away. . . . I. x. 41. 5
hence began, And planted there did bring forth . . . II. vii. 54. 6
let us *hence* depart . . . II. xii. 87. 9
recount from *hence* My glorious . . . III. iii. 4. 6
Hence farre away we will blyndfolded ly, . . . III. x. 42. 7
Deliver *hence* out of this dungeon strong, . . . IV. xii. 9. 4
how far *hence* Is he, . . . V. ii. 5. 1
Hence fare on foot, . . . V. iii. 35. 6
where and how far *hence* does she abide?' . . . V. iv. 33. 2
from *hence* Their sound did reach . . . V. v. 4. 5
where is he thy Lord, and how far *hence?* . . . V. vi. 9. 2
not far *hence* doth wone, . . . V. viii. 16. 7
'Not farre from *hence,* uppon yond rocky hill, . . . VI. i. 13. 1
And how ye may him *hence,* . . . Convay . . . VI. ii. 46. 5
ne ever knighthood dare *Hence* to professe; . . . VI. vi. 36. 4
my ill fortune did them *hence* displace; . . . VI. x. 20. 7
caried us from *hence;* . . . VI. xi. 30. 5
(Not this round heaven, which we from *hence* behold, . . . *H.H.L.* 58

Henceforth. And will *henceforth* immortalize no more; . . . *T.M.* 464
Henceforth all worlds felicitie I hate. . . . *Ti.* 574
'What man *henceforth* that breatheth . . . *D.* 197
cease *henceforth* things kindly forth to bring, . . . *D.* 339
Feede ye *hencefoorth* on bitter Astrofell . . . *D.* 346
'*Hencefoorth* I hate what ever Nature made, . . . *D.* 393
'*Hencefoorth* mine eyes shall never more behold . . . *D.* 491
I pray, And *henceforth* ever wish . . . I. i. 27. 9
'*Henceforth* in safe assuraunce may ye rest, . . . I. ii. 27. 1
Henceforth his ghost, freed from repining strife, . . . I. iii. 36. 5
henceforth nothing faire but her on earth they find . . . I. vi. 18. 9
Henceforth thy hated face for ever hyde, . . . I. vii. 23. 4
'*Henceforth,* Sir knight, take to you wonted strength, . . . I. viii. 45. 1
henceforth, bee at your keeping well, . . . I. xi. 2. 4
why should ever I *henceforth* desyre . . . II. i. 17. 3
Henceforth take heede of that thou now hast past, . . . II. iv. 36. 3
henceforth by this daies ensample trow, . . . II. v. 13. 7
him *henceforth* the same can save no more; . . . II. viii. 43. 7
Ne feareth he *henceforth* that foe of his, . . . III. vi. 48. 3
dead, . . . *Henceforth* for ever Florimell to bee; . . . III. viii. 47. 6
But weete *henceforth,* that all . . . I loath . . . III. x. 31. 4
Henceforth, faire Lady, comfort to you take, . . . III. xii. 40. 6
Henceforth may not disdaine . . . IV. vi. 31. 2
Ne *henceforth* be rebellious unto love, . . . IV. vi. 31. 6
henceforth he oft shall hungry sit.' . . . V. iv. 49. 9
henceforth in batteilous array I may beare armes, . . . VI. ii. 33. 5
from *henceforth* he meanes no more to sew . . . VI. x. 2. 1
how ye doe stare *Henceforth* too rashly . . . *Am.* xxxvii. 10
Dare not *henceforth,* . . . T' accuse of pride, . . . *Am.* lxi. 3
henceforth some pitty take, . . . *Epig.* iv. 39
Thy straying thoughts *henceforth* for ever rest. . . . *H.H.B.* 301

Hend. reave out of the hand that did it *hend:* . . . V. xi. 27. 5

Henge. *See* **Hinge.**

Hengist. their Capitayns, which hight *Hengist* and Horsus, . . . II. x. 65. 2
Hengist, seeming sad for that was donne, . . . II. x. 66. 3
Hengist eke soon brought to shamefull death. . . . II. x. 67. 6

Hent. *See* **Forehent, Overhent.**
His harmefull Hatchet he *hent* in hand, . . . *S.C.* F. 195
pumie stones I hastly *hent* And threwe; . . . *S.C.* Mar. 89
The haplesse mischiefe that has thee *hent;* . . . *S.C.* S. 249
Dido nis dead, but into heaven *hent.* . . . *S.C.* N. 169
by lacke of thee to heaven *hent,* . . . *Ti.* 677
The whiles soft death away her spirit *hent,* . . . *D.* 258
The litle babe up in his armes he *hent;* . . . II. ii. 1. 4
fast her *hent* By the hoare lockes . . . II. iv. 12. 2
What hellish fury hath at earst thee *hent?* . . . II. vi. 49. 2
his well proved weapons to him *hent;* . . . II. xi. 17. 2
Great labour fondly hast thou *hent* in hand, . . . III. vii. 61. 2
For losse of his deare love by Neptune *hent,* . . . IV. ix. 23. 2
Talus by the backe the boaster *hent,* . . . V. iii. 37. 2
neither will one foot, till we that carle have *hent.'* . . . V. ix. 7. 9

Hent—*Continued.*
whilest in hand it gryping hard he *hent*, . . . V. ix. 18. 4
all the captives, which they here had *hent*, . . . VI. xi. 31. 4
Yet in his hand a spade he also *hent*, . . . VII. vii. 32. 6
Hentest. In evill houre thou *hentest* in hond . . . *S.C.* Jul. 37
Hept. *See* **Heaped.**
Her (*partial list*). folowing th' example of *hir* damme: . . . *Bel.*[1] vi. 4
Her length, *her* breadth, *her* deepnes, or *her* hight; . . . *Ro.* xxvi. 4
And layen *her* faults the world beforne, . . . *S.C.* May 160
I bidde *her* god day; Or Diggon *her* is Or . . . *S.C.* S. 1, 2
Her was *her*, while it was daye-light, . . . *S.C.* S. 3
But now *her* is a most wretched wight: . . . *S.C.* S. 4
robben one another, And . . . beguile *her* brother; . . . *S.C.* S. 39
Dares to pollute *her* hidden mysterie; . . . *T.M.* 568
treadeth under foote *hir* holie things, . . . *T.M.* 569
If at *hir* Virginals, tell *hir*, I can heare . . . *U.V.* 9
Crept forth like wormes out of *her* slimie nature. . . . *Col.* 860
from *her* settled seat, The house was raysd, . . . II. ii. 20. 6
Her seem'd, as she was doing sacrifize . . . V. vii. 13. 1
when *her* listed she could . . . VI. vi. 42. 6
Hands that houlds my life in *hir* deaddoing might . . . *Am.*[1] 1. 2
Thou doest emmarble the proud hart of *her* . . . *H.L.* 139
Herald. Were worke fit for an *Herauld*, not for me: . . . V. iii. 3. 6
Till he an *Herauld* cald, and to him spake, . . . V. xii. 8. 5
The Heavens *Herald* staid not to reply, . . . VII. vi. 19. 1
Spring, the *herald* of loves mighty king, . . . *Am.* lxx. 1
Heralds. running *Heralds* humble homage made, . . . I. v. 15. 7
To Marinell, whose name the *Heralds* loud resounded. . . . V. iii. 6. 9
Herb. whatso other *hearb* of lovely hew, . . . *Gn.* 682
every flowre and *herbe* there set in order: . . . *Mui.* 172
Now sucking of the sap of *herbe* most meete, . . . *Mui.* 180
That *hearbe* of some Starlight is cald by name, . . . *As.* 193
No daintie flowre or *herbe* that growes on grownd, . . . II. vi. 12. 6
A certaine *herbe* from thence unto him brought, . . . VI. iv. 12. 6
that same Ladies hurt no *herbe* he found . . . VI. iv. 16. 8
Herbage. There fruitfull corne, faire trees, fresh *herbage* is, . *Col.* 298
Herbars. *See* **Arbors.**
Herbs. On *hearbs* (*herbes*[1]) and flowres she walked . . . *Pet.* vi. 3
The power of *herbs*, both which can hurt and ease, . . . *S.C.* D. 88
The hidden powre of *herbes*, and might of Magick spel? . . . I. ii. 10. 9
With wicked *herbes* and oyntments did besmeare My body . . I. ii. 42. 3
If either salves, or oyles, or *herbes*, or charmes . . . I. v. 41. 7
he balmes and *herbes* thereto applyde, . . . II. vi. 51. 6
a gardin goodly garnished With *hearbs* and fruits, . . . II. vii. 51. 5
Nor *herbes*, nor charmes, nor counsel, . . . III. iii. 5. 4
To seeke for *hearbes* that mote him remedy; . . . III. v. 32. 2
shee of *herbes* had great intendiment, . . . III. v. 32. 3
Does mow the flowring *herbes* and goodly things, . . . III. vi. 39. 4
With *herbs*, with charms, with counsel, and with teares; . . III. vii. 21. 2
tears, nor charms, nor *herbs*, nor counsell, . . . III. vii. 21. 3
In power of *herbes*, and tunes of beasts and burds; . . . IV. ii. 35. 6
many *herbes* did use. . . . IV. xi. 6. 3
In seeking . . . For *herbes* to dresse their wounds; . . . VI. iv. 16. 4
Hercean. Some scattred on the *Hercaean* shores unknowne; . . *Gn.* 588
Hercules. an hundred such as *Hercules*, . . . *Bel.*[1] viii. 12
Of hundred *Hercules* to be assaide, . . . *Bel.*[2] x. 11
there being then not living An *Hercules* . . . *Ro.* x. 10
Bacchus and *Hercules* I raisd to heaven, . . . *T.M.* 461
those which *Hercules*, with conquest bold Got . . . II. vii. 54. 5
Whose father *Hercules* in Fraunce did quell, . . . II. x. 11. 7
great *Hercules* and Hyllus deare . . . IV. x. 27. 1
Hercules, that did advance To vanquish all the world . . . IV. xi. 16. 5
Next *Hercules* his like ensample shewed, . . . V. i. 2. 6
That whylome hath of *Hercules* bene told, . . . V. v. 24. 2
Hercules them all did overcome in fight. . . . V. x. 10. 9
apples . . . Far passing those which *Hercules* came by, . . . *Am.* lxxvii. 7
Hercules and Hebe, and the rest Of Venus dearlings, . . . *H.L.* 283
Hercules'. *Hercules* two pillors . . . Did make to quake . . . *Proth.* 148
Herd. *See* **Heard.**
Whose straying *heard* them selfe doth shrowde . . . *S.C.* Jul. 3
he his *heard* back from that water foord Drave, . . . *Gn.* 166
Full greedily into the *heard* he thrust, . . . *As.* 104
The whiles the captive *heard* his nets did rend, . . . *As.* 125
heard Of stinking Seales and Porcpisces . . . *Col.* 248
when in Cymbrian plaine An *heard* of Bulles, . . . complaine, I. viii. 11. 6
Like as an Hynd forth singled from the *heard*, . . . III. vii. 1. 1
hath the charge of Neptunes mighty *heard;* . . . III. viii. 30. 2
with his staffe, that drives his *heard* astray, . . . III. viii. 31. 8
home he marcht emongst the horned *heard*, . . . III. x. 47. 8
then turnd to the *heard*, . . . III. x. 52. 2
strive the rule to get Of all the *heard*, . . . IV. iv. 18. 4
doe breake by force Into an *heard*, . . . IV. iv. 35. 7
Ne was there *heard* . . . But did her honour; . . . VI. ix. 10. 1
Like as a Lion mongst an *heard* of dere, . . . VI. xi. 49. 1
Herd-groom. That shall yonder *heardgrome*, . . . *S.C.* Au. 45
Herdgrome, I fear me, thou have a squint eye: . . . *S.C.* Au. 129
Ne can Willye wite the witelesse *herdgroome.* . . . *S.C.* Au. 136
Herd-grooms. So loytring live you little *heardgroomes*, . . . *S.C.* F. 35
they were poore *heardgroomes*, . . . VI. xi. 39. 8
Herds. *See* **Land-herds.**
lukewarm blood Of the small *heards*, . . . *Bel.*[2] vi. 8
Your carefull *heards* with cold bene annoied: . . . *S.C.* F. 48
the *herds* Of ravenous wilde beasts, . . . *Hub.* 1284
Where be the flockes and *heards*, which she doth keep? . . . *Col.* 237
surges hie, On which faire Cynthia her *heards* doth feed: . . *Col.* 241
Her *heards* be thousand fishes with their frie, . . . *Col.* 242
the whole assembly of those *heards* Moov'd at his speech, . . *Col.* 648
all their goodly *heardes* did gather rownd; . . . III. x. 46. 2
The *heardes* out of their foldes were loosed quight, . . . III. x. 52. 8
Whereas the *Heardes* were keeping of their neat, . . . VI. ix. 4. 2

Herds—*Continued.*
evermore his speach he did apply To th' *heards*, . . . VI. ix. 12. 9
for want of *heards*, themselves then kept. . . . VI. xi. 37. 5
Unwont with *heards* to watch, . . . VI. xi. 40. 4
Here (*partial list*). *See* **Hear.**
which for Rome in Rome *here* seekest, . . . *Ro.* iii. 1
here above him secretly doth hide) . . . *Ro.* xv. 10
All that . . . Was *here* to see. . . . *Ro.* xxix. 12
The while they *here* liven at ease . . . *S.C.* May 66
Lo! Collin, *here* the place . . . *S.C.* Jun. 1
what wants me *here* to worke delyte? . . . *S.C.* Jun. 3
Here no night-ravenes lodge, . . . *S.C.* Jun. 23
Here han the holy Faunes recourse, . . . *S.C.* Jul. 77
Here growes Melampode . . . *S.C.* Jul. 85
Here is a great deale of good matter . . . *S.C.* Jul. 205
Here will I dwell apart . . . *S.C.* Au. 169
That *here* by there I whilome usd to keepe, . . . *S.C.* S. 63
While *here* on earth she did abyde. . . . *S.C.* N. 199
Here will I hang my pype . . . *S.C.* D. 141
Ne let the sacred Sisters *here* be hight, . . . *D.* 11
So will I travell whilest I tarrie *heere* . . . *D.* 466
Least to you hap that happened to me *heare*, . . . I. ii. 31. 5
here thy shield is hangd for victors hyre? . . . I. v. 10. 7
Here take thy lovers token on thy pate.' . . . I. vi. 47. 7
he hath left you *heare* . . . I. vi. 48. 5
'Such then,' . . . 'as she seemeth *here*, . . . I. viii. 49. 3
die at ease, that liveth *here* uneath? . . . I. ix. 38. 9
errant knight to see *Here* in this place; . . . I. x. 10. 2
let me *heare* for aie in peace remaine, . . . I. x. 63. 3
Here hauntes that feend, . . . I. xi. 2. 3
what enraged heates, *Here* heaped up . . . I. xii. 30. 4
Suffice it *heare* by signes to understand . . . I. xii. 40. 4
Which we far off will *here* abide to vew.' . . . II. i. 25. 7
how, or where, *here* fits not tell. . . . II. ii. 11. 9
That *here* in desert hast thine habitaunce, . . . II vii. 7. 2
Here Sleep, ther Richesse, . . . II. vii. 25. 9
'Loe! *here* the worldes blis: loe! *here* the end, . . . II. vii. 32. 7
Lo! Tantalus, I *here* tormented lye: . . . II. vii. 59. 5
here I now for want of food doe dye: . . . II. vii. 59. 7
Here may ye not have entraunce, . . . II. ix. 12. 4
Here, there, and every where, . . . III. i. 66. 5
'What monstrous enmity provoke we *heare?* . . . III. xi. 22. 7
Tracing and traversing, now *here*, now there; . . . IV. vii. 28. 8
here thy Artegall. . . . V. Pr. 11. 9
in my way, a little *here* beyond, . . . V. ii. 4. 5
haplesse man, what make you *here?* . . . V. iv. 26. 1
That *here* on earth is no sure happinesse, . . . VI. xi. 1. 7
nothing knew Of all that chaunced *heere*, . . . VII. vi. 14. 2
doth lighten all that *here* we see. . . . *Am.* ix. 14
But *here* on earth to have such hevens blisse. . . . *Am.* lxxii. 14
Be also present *heere;* . . . *Epith.* 71
here fits not well Olde woes, . . . *Proth.* 141
Hereafter. *Hereafter*, when as season more secure . . . *Gn.* 9
Hereafter many yeares . . . *Gn.* 61
Why will *hereafter* anie flesh delight . . . *Ti.* 527
Now praysd, *hereafter* deare thou shalt repent; . . . I. ix. 43. 5
Into the which *hereafter* thou maist happen fall. . . . I. ix. 45. 9
Least thou perhaps *hereafter* wish, . . . II. vii. 38. 9
whose like *hereafter* seldome may, . . . VI. ii. 33. 2
That it *hereafter* may you not repent, . . . *Am.* lxxiii. 13
Here and there. Like Swallow swift I wandred *here and there;* . . . *S.C.* D. 20
after that long straied *here and there*, . . . *Hub.* 577
th' Ape himselfe, . . . Fled *here and there*, . . . *Hub.* 1357
Yet *here, and there*, and every where, unwares . . . III. xi. 28. 6
in the ydle ayre he mov'd still *here and theare.* . . . III. xii. 8. 9
About her head, still roming *here and there;* . . . III. xii. 17. 7
At puffe of every storme doth stagger *here and theare.* . . IV. iii. 9. 9
and turneyed *here and theare*, . . . IV. iv. 30. 1
So, as they coursed *here and there*, it chaunst . . . IV. vi. 13. 1
here and there and round about doth stie, . . . IV. ix. 33. 5
here and there were pleasant arbors pight, . . . IV. x. 25. 3
sprinckled *here and theare* With glittering spangs . . . IV. xi. 45. 4
In this sad plight he walked *here and there*, . . . IV. xii. 17. 1
hid them selves in corners *here and there;* . . . V. ii. 24. 8
here and there before his presence flew, . . . V. ii. 53. 8
here and there like scattred sheepe they lay: . . . V. vi. 30. 6
From side to side they tost him *here and there*, . . . V. viii. 41. 8
here and there shooting forth silver streames, . . . V. ix. 28. 8
her, thus loosely wandring *here and there*, . . . VI. iii. 24. 3
So did he fly amongst them *here and there*, . . . VI. xi. 49. 3
the Monckes he chaced *here and there* . . . VI. xii. 24. 2
them amongst were mingled *here and there* . . . VI. xii. 28. 1
wandring *here and there* all desolate, . . . *Am.* lxxxviii. 7
Hereat. be nought *hereat* dismayd, . . . I. xii. 31. 2
Herebefore. *here before* a perlous passage lyes, . . . II. xii. 17. 8
Herebus. *See* **Erebus.**
Hereby. *Hereby* I learned have not to despise . . . *Van.* v. 13
Whose praise *hereby* no whit impaired is, . . . *Col.* 755
daunger, which *hereby* doth dwell, . . . I. i. 31. 1
his cruell foes, that stand *hereby*, . . . II. viii. 25. 1
Let all that live *hereby* be counselled . . . II. xii. 9. 8
as I in solace sate *hereby* . . . V. i. 16. 6
a mighty man, which wonnes *hereby*, (*here by) . . . V. viii. 18. 2
in this Church *hereby* There stands . . . V. xi. 19. 1
small glory doest thou winne *hereby*, . . . *H.L.* 153
Herein. *herein* I tooke my chiefe delight, . . . *Pet.* iv. 9
Be therefore counselled *herein* . . . *Hub.* 985
her plaint, as doth *herein* ensew. . . . *T.M.* 480
thou thy selfe *herein* shalt also live: . . . *Ti.* 258

Herein—*Continued.*
plaint *herein* exprest, ... D. 4
many doe partake *Herein;* . . . . . . IV. ii. 25. 6
herein most exprest, ... V. Pr. 10. 3
Herein the noblesse of this knight exceedes, ... V. ii. 1. 8
herein doest all earthly Princes pas? . . . . . . V. x. 3. 2
herein eke thy glory seemeth more, ... *H.L.* 162
Hereof. *Hereof* when tydings far abroad did passe, ... *As.* 199
Hereof this gentle knight unweeting was; . . . . . . I. vii. 6. 1
No magicke arts *hereof* had any might, ... I. vii. 35. 1
Newes *hereof* . . . . . . II. ii. 16. 3
The roofe *hereof* . . . . . . II. ix. 46. 1
Tydings *hereof* . . . . . . III. iv. 19. 2
To drincke *hereof,* . . . . . . IV. iii. 44. 6
did those olde Heroes *hereof* taste, ... IV. iii. 44. 8
To whom the right *hereof* it selfe hath sold, ... IV. xi. 22. 7
for recompence *hereof* . . . . . . VI. ix. 32. 5
in regard *hereof* . . . . . . VI. x. 9. 9
Hereout. *Hereout* up to the throne of Gods did flie, ... *Bel.* xi. 6
Heresies. hatefull *heresies,* of God abhor'd: . . . . . . *Hub.* 389
them of crimes and *heresies* accus'd, ... *Hub.* 564
Heresy. Yet *heresy* nor treason didst conspire, ... *Am.* xlviii. 7
Heretics. so bad end for *hereticks* ordayned; . . . . . . *Am.* xlviii. 6
Hereto. *Hereto,* the hills bene nigher heven, ... *S.C.* Jul. 89
No Muses aide me needes *heretoo* to call; . . . . . . *Hub.* 43
Approach *hereto;* . . . . . . *D.* 19
my lucklesse lott doth me constrayne *Hereto* perforce. . . . III. Pr. 3. 5
Heretofore. As *heretofore* of good, so now of ill. . . . . . . *T.M.* 408
accounted *heretofore* The learneds meed . . . . . . *T.M.* 411
Well knowne, and far renowmed *heretofore,* . . . . . . V. xi. 49. 2
tempests . . . Which hardly I endured *heretofore,* . . . . . . *Am.* lxiii. 2
I have in th' heat of youth made *heretofore,* . . . . . . *H.H.L.* 10
Hereupon. to resolve first *hereupon.'* . . . . . . *Hub.* 123
hereupon an oath unto me plight.' . . . . . . *Hub.* 1055
Herewith. Therefore *herewith* doo not your selfe dismay; . . *Hub.* 445
be not *herewith* dismaid, ... II. ix. 8. 5
Cupid, not *herewith* content, ... III. xi. 38. 7
Herewithal. 'But most my Lord is grieved *herewithall,* . . . VI. iv. 32. 1
Heried. for Apolloes temple highly *herried.'* . . . . . . II. xii. 13. 9
With thousand blessings she is *heried.* . . . . . . III. i. 43. 7
Heritage. Enaunter their *heritage* doe impaire. . . . . . . *S.C.* May 78
Let us our fathers *heritage* divide, ... *Hub.* 136
From our owne native *heritage* exilde, ... *T.M.* 341
she had none . . . Ne *heritage* of native soveraintie; . . . I. iv. 12. 4
Enjoyd an *heritage* of lasting peace, ... II. x. 25. 2
Till aged Hely by dew *heritage* it gaynd. . . . . . . II. x. 45. 9
did share The *heritage* of all celestiall grace; . . . . . . III. vi. 4. 7
from the *heritage,* which she did clame, ... V. i. 3. 8
To hinder thee from the just *heritage* . . . . . . V. vii. 23. 3
mother of a frutefull *heritage,* . . . . . . V. x. 7. 3
In th' *heritage* of our unhappie paine: . . . . . . VI. iv. 31. 5
chalenge th' *heritage* of this our skie; . . . . . . VII. vi. 30. 3
heaven it selfe by *heritage* in Fee: . . . . . . VII. vii. 15. 5
that to be My *heritage* Jove's selfe cannot denie, ... VII. vii. 16. 7
Where they shall have like *heritage* of land, ... *H.H.L.* 200
Hermaphrodite. they had beene that faire *Hermaphrodite,* . III. xii. 46. *or.* 2
Hermes. To whom when *Hermes* had his message told, . . . VII. vi. 19. 6
Hermes'. thogh she nought did reck Of *Hermes* message, . . . VII. vi. 22. 8
(After returne of *Hermes* Embassie) . . . . . . VII. vi. 23. 2
Hermit. the *Hermite* dewly wont to say His holy thinges . I. i. 34. 6
Weening therein some holy *Hermit* lay, ... IV. vii. 42. 7
his Squyre, With th' *Hermit* leaves behynd. . . . . . . VI. v. Arg.
Therein the *Hermite,* which his life here led . . . . . . VI. v. 35. 5
Whom when the *Hermite* present saw in place, ... VI. v. 36. 2
The *Hermite* heales both Squire and dame . . . . . . VI. vi. Arg.
Howbe that carefull *Hermite* did his best, ... VI. vi. 2. 6
Of that good *Hermite* both they tooke their leave, ... VI. vi. 15. 8
Hermitage. A little lowly *Hermitage* it was, ... I. i. 34. 1
eke a litle *Hermitage* thereby, ... I. x. 46. 4
By which a little *Hermitage* there lay, ... VI. v. 34. 8
He thence them led into his *Hermitage,* . . . . . . VI. v. 38. 1
He tooke him selfe unto this *Hermitage,* . . . . . . VI. vi. 4. 8
Hermit's. In that good *Hermits* charge; . . . . . . VI. v. 41. 4
Herneshaw. *See* **Heronsew.**
Heroes. beside the honourable band Of great *Heroes* . . . . *Gn.* 480
Here manie other like *Heroes* bee. . . . . . . *Gn.* 593
the auncestrie Of th' old *Heroes* . . . . . . *T.M.* 440
throng Of heavenlie Poets and *Heroes* strong. . . . . . . *Ti.* 341
ensample to the present age Of th' old *Heroes,* . . . . . . *Ded. Son.* vi. 4
hartes of great *Heroes* doest enrage, ... I. xi. 6. 4
one of th' old *Heroes* seemes to bee! . . . . . . III. iii. 32. 5
brave exploits which great *Heroes* wonne, ... IV. Pr. 3. 4
So did those olde *Heroes* hereof taste, ... IV. iii. 44. 8
By whom those old *Heroes* wonne such fame; . . . . . . IV. xi. 13. 2
those great *Heroes* got thereby Their greatest glory . . . . V. ii. 1. 5
ancient monuments of mightie peeres, And old *Heroes,* . . . *Com. Son.* iii. 3
Heroic. Whose living praises in *heroick* style, ... *T.M.* 431
lifting up her brave *heroick* thought . . . . . . *Ti.* 109
Who lives that can match that *heroick* song, ... *Col.* 404
make more famous memory Of thine *Heroicke* parts, ... *Ded. Son.* ii. 12
In loftie numbers and *heroicke* stile. . . . . . . *Ded. Son.* xii. 8
Remembraunce of that most *Heroicke* spirit, ... *Ded. Son.* xv. 1
Her humblesse low, . . . Did much emmove his stout *heroicke*
heart; . . . . . . I. ii. 21. 6
Wondrous great prowesse and *heroick* worth He shewd . . II. ii. 25. 3
low abase the high *heroicke* spright, ... II. vii. 10. 6
his *Heroicke* grace and honorable gest. . . . . . . III. ii. 24. 9
The higher place in her *Heroick* mynd: . . . . . . III. v. 55. 5
'What huge *heroicke* magnanimity . . . . . . III. xi. 19. 2
With warlike numbers and *Heroicke* sound, ... IV. ii. 32. 7

Heroic—*Continued.*
inward grudge fild his *heroicke* brest: . . . . . . IV. ix. 32. 4
inspired with *heroicke* heat, ... V. i. 1. 7
Or surely borne of some *Heroicke* sead, ... VI. ii. 25. 8
Heroically. Doth like himselfe *Heroically* sound. . . . . . . *Col.* 447
Heron. Stoupes at a flying *heron* with proud disdayne, . . II. xi. 43. 2
Strikes at an *Heron* with all his bodies sway, ... IV. iii. 19. 3
Heronsew. At an *Herneshaw,* that lyes aloft on wing, . . . VI. vii. 9. 2
Hero's. stirredst up th' *Heroes* high intents, ... III. iii. 2. 8
Herried. *See* **Heried.**
Hers (*partial list*).
And I *hers* ever onely, ... *Col.* 477
hers I die, ... *Col.* 950
Venus *hers* thence far away convayd, ... III. vi. 28. 6
th' one in a viall had, Th' other in *hers* an . . . . . . III. xii. 18. 8
To you that ornament of *hers* pertaines . . . . . . IV. ii. 27. 6
My knight *hers* . . . to daunger drove, ... VI. ii. 20. 5
One of his shafts she stole away. And one of *hers* did . . . *Epig.* ii. 5
Hersall. With this sad *hersall* of his heavy stresse . . . . III. xi. 18. 1
Herself (*partial list*).
hath tam'd *herselfe* at last; . . . . . . *Ro.* iii. 7
Queene of land and sea *her selfe* she made . . . . . . *Ro.* xx. 11
As envying *her selfe,* that too exceeding shone: . . . . . . I. iv. 8. 9
Cleopatra . . . *her selfe* did stoutly kill; . . . . . . I. v. 50. 8
She found *her selfe* assayld with great perplexity; . . . . I. x. 22. 9
In sumptuous tire she joyd *her selfe* to pranck, ... II. ii. 36. 8
So kept she them in order, and *her selfe* in heed. . . . . II. ii. 38. 9
Ceasse then, myne eyes, to seeke *her selfe* to see; . . . . . *Am.* lxxxviii. 13
Hery. *hery* with hymnes thy lasses glove; . . . . . . *S.C.* F. 62
Nor Pan to *herye,* nor with love to playe; . . . . . . *S.C.* N. 10
Hesperus. At last faire *Hesperus* . . . Had spent his lampe, I. ii. 6. 6
stone . . . shone, Like *Hesperus* emongst the lesser lights, . . I. vii. 30. 4
now the golden *Hesperus* Was mounted high . . . . . . III. iv. 51. 6
More bright then *Hesperus* his head doth rere. . . . . . . *Epith.* 95
Radiant *Hesper,* when his golden hayre . . . he hath bathed . *Proth.* 164
Hest. T' obey their riders *hest,* as seemed good. . . . . . . IV. iii. 39. 5
durst withstand His dreadfull *heast,* . . . . . . V. i. 8. 7
him forbidden, who his *heast* observed: . . . . . . V. xii. 43. 5
Regarding nought religion, nor their holy *heast.* . . . . . VI. xii. 24. 9
forgets . . . His mothers *heast* to prove. . . . . . . *Epig.* iv. 58
all the bodie to thy *hest* doest frame, ... *H.L.* 44
To free his foes, that from his *heast* had swerved! . . . . . *H.H.L.* 161
Hests. The sacred thinges, and holy *heastes* foretaught. . . I. vii. 18. 7
she that hight of many *heastes* Polynome; . . . . . . IV. xi. 50. 9
T' obay the *heasts* of mans well-ruling hand . . . . . . V. v. 25. 4
his *heasts* did gladly heare, ... VI. i. 43. 2
As if he long had to his *heasts* bene trayned. . . . . . . VI. vi. 39. 6
him that doeth thy lovely *heasts* despize, ... *H.L.* 160
Heven, -ly, -field. *See* **Heaven,** *etc.*
Hew. *See* **Hue.**
mighty brawned bowrs Were wont to . . . helmets *hew,* . . . I. viii. 41. 7
Gan with new rage their shieldes to *hew* . . . . . . II. ii. 23. 7
mailes did rash, and helmes did *hew.* . . . . . . IV. ii. 17. 9
with his huge great yron axe gan *hew* . . . . . . V. xi. 5. 3
Of whom he makes such havocke and such *hew,* . . . . . . VI. viii. 49 .6
all that nere him came did *hew* and slay, ... VI. xi. 49. 4
Hewed. a large share it *hewd* out of the rest, ... I. ii. 18. 8
Five joints thereof he *hewd,* . . . . . . I. xi. 39. 9
made such way that *hewd* it quite in twaine; . . . . . . I. xi. 43. 7
He *hewd,* and lasht, and foynd, ... II. v. 9. 1
He stroke, he soust, he foynd, he *hewd,* he lasht, ... IV. iii. 25. 6
She *hewd,* she foynd, she lasht, she laid on every side. . . V. v. 6. 9
Which they now hackt and *hewd* as if such use they hated. . V. vii. 29. 9
They *hew'd* their helmes, and plates asunder brake, ... VI. i. 37. 4
Hewing. Which *hewing* quite asunder, ... II. viii. 38. 6
Hewing and slashing at their idle shades; . . . . . . II. ix. 15. 8
Hewing and slashing shields and helmets bright, ... IV. iv. 41. 6
hewing off his head, ... VI. x. 36. 6
Hewn. *hewen* helmets (*helmets *hewen*) deepe shew marks of
eithers might. . . . . . I. v. 7. 9
Hewen out of Adamant rocke with engines keene, ... I. vii. 33. 7
Whose hartstrings with keene steele nigh *hewen* be; . . . . I. viii. 22. 7
Lyke an huge cave *hewne* out of rocky clifte, ... II. vii. 28. 2
Of *hewen* stone the porch was fayrely wrought, ... II. ix. 24. 1
Hewen underneath that Mount, ... III. vi. 48. 9
all the *hewen* stones thereof defaced, ... V. ii. 28. 3
Is wondrous strong and *hewen* farre under ground, ... V. ix. 6. 3
Heydeguyes. *See* **Hay-de-guys.**
Hey-ho. *Hey, ho,* . . . . . . *S.C.* Au. 54, 58, 62, 66, 70, 74, 78, 82, 86, 90, 94, 98, 102, 106, 110, 114, 118, 122
Heyre. *See* **Heir.**
Hid. *See* **Hidden.**
head, full bravely with a morion *hidd,* . . . . . . *Bel.*[2] xv. 5
Shall in great Chaos wombe againe be *hid.* . . . . . . *Ro.* xxii. 14
when their false harts bene *hidde,* . . . . . . *S.C.* May 170
Shall die in darknesse, and lie *hid* in slime: . . . . . . *T.M.* 106
from commune vew Their fairer parts are *hid,* . . . . . . *Ded. Son.* ix. 11
The danger *hid,* the place unknowne and wilde, ... I. i. 12. 3
'His blessed body, . . . Was afterward, . . . fro me *hid:* . . . I. ii. 24. 3
'Her neather partes misshapen, . . . Were *hidd* in water, . . I. ii. 41. 2
Who all that while lay *hid* in secret shade. . . . . . . I. v. 15. 4
three Moones . . . have been thrice *hid* underneath the ground, I. viii. 38. 7
His griesie lockes . . . *hid* his face, ... I. ix. 35. 6
Let nought be *hid* from me that ought to be exprest. . . . . I. xii. 29. 9
hid her visage, and her head downe bent, ... II. i. 15. 7
For dread of soring hauke her selfe hath *hid,* . . . . . . II. iii. 36. 2

Hid—*Continued.*
I *hid* my selfe from it, . . . II. iii. 45. 8
the *hid* treasures in her sacred tombe . . . II. vii. 17. 3
hid in *darkenes,* that none could behold . . . II. vii. 29. 3
The rest *hidd* underneath him more desirous made. . . . II. xii. 66. 9
So *hidd* in lockes and waves from lookers theft, . . . II. xii. 67. 8
hid no whit her alablaster skin, . . . II. xii. 77. 5
in his ashes raked up and *hid,* . . . III. iii. 48. 3
he would have *hid* His shamefull head . . . III. v. 13. 7
By her *hid* from the world, . . . III. vi. 46. 6
Downe in her lap she *hid* her face, . . . III. viii. 32. 9
in th' earthes hollow caves hath long ben *hid* . . . III. ix. 15. 3
his closet . . . where all his wealth Lay *hid;* . . . III. x. 12. 4
faining to be *hidd* from envious eye; . . . III. xi. 28. 5
walkte each where for feare of *hid* mischaunce, . . . III. xii. 15. 7
golden foyle, That under it *hidde* hate . . . IV. ii. 29. 5
The lines of life, from living knowledge *hid*. . . . IV. ii. 48. 4
pyning anguish *hid* in gentle hart, . . . IV. vi. 1. 2
Lay *hid* in horrour of eternall night? . . . IV. vii. 33. 6
all their sundry kinds, and all their *hid* abodes. . . . IV. xi. 10. 9
shall see Stamford, though now homely *hid,* . . . IV. xi. 35. 4
hid them selves in corners here and there; . . . V. ii. 24. 8
hid themselves in holes and bushes from his vew. . . . V. ii. 53. 9
change his shield with him, to be the better *hid*. . . . V. iii. 10. 9
Would have the passion *hid,* and up arose . . . V. ix. 50. 9
Had *hid* themselves, or taken further flight: . . . V. x. 19. 4
teare Her flesh for felnesse, which she inward *hid:* . . . V. xii. 32. 4
his Ladie, . . . closely *hid* her selfe . . . VI. ii. 20. 4
To some *hid* end to make more easie way, . . . VI. vi. 42. 2
To this attempt to wreake his *hid* despight, . . . VI. vii. 12. 8
Shame would be *hid*. . . . VI. viii. 5. 7
All those faire forrests about Arlo *hid;* . . . VII. vi. 54. 6
Her head and face was *hid* . . . VII. vii. 5. 9
His throne is . . . *hid* in his owne brightnesse . . . *H.H.B.* 178

Hidden. *See* **Hid.**
kydst the *hidden* kinds of many a wede, . . . *S.C.* D. 92
Dares to pollute her *hidden* mysterie; . . . *T.M.* 568
Feareles of foes and *hidden* jeopardie, . . . *Mui.* 251
Where *hidden* was his hatefull enemie. . . . *Mui.* 392
To let thy fame lie so in *hidden* shade: . . . *Col.* 407
The antique rolles, which there lye *hidden* still, . . . I. Pr. 2. 4
Seemed in heart some *hidden* care she had, . . . I. i. 4. 8
to revoke The forward footing for an *hidden* shade: . . . I. i. 12. 8
Silly old man, that lives in *hidden* cell, . . . I. i. 30. 6
all this while, with charmes and *hidden* artes, . . . I. i. 45. 1
seeming to mistrust Some secret ill, or *hidden* foe . . . I. i. 49. 4
Shall I accuse the *hidden* cruell fate, . . . I. i. 51. 2
who can tell The *hidden* powre of herbes, . . . I. ii. 10. 9
The *hidden* cause of their captivitie; . . . I. v. 46. 3
As when a ship, . . . An *hidden* rocke escaped hath . . . I. vi. 1. 2
The further processe of her *hidden* griefe: . . . I. vi. 37. 8
fild her *hidden* caves with stormie yre, . . . I. vii. 9. 5
Such helplesse harmes yts better *hidden* keep, . . . I. vii. 39. 7
from mee are *hidden* yitt; . . . I. ix. 3. 4
told, it flames; and, *hidden,* it does glow, . . . I. ix. 8. 7
creeping close, as Snake in *hidden* weedes, . . . I. ix. 28. 8
some *hidden* nest Of many Dragonettes, . . . I. xii. 10. 5
have from wisest ages *hidden* beene; . . . II. Pr. 3. 2
or *hidden* danger did entrap; . . . II. i. 26. 9
as doth an *hidden* moth The inner garment frett, . . . II. ii. 34. 7
hidden lyes unwares him to surpryse? . . . II. iv. 17. 3
with the *hidden* fire too inly warmd. . . . II. vi. 51. 5
hidden vertue to it gave. . . . II. viii. 20. 9
T' assayle with open force or *hidden* guyle, . . . II. xi. 7. 4
a whirlepoole of *hidden* jeopardy; . . . II. xii. 18. 2
great Tethys bosome, where they *hidden* lye. . . . II. xii. 26. 9
Worse is the daunger *hidden* then descride. . . . II. xii. 35. 5
Into his *hidden* nett full easely doth fall. . . . III. i. 54. 9
Lay *hidden* in the bottome of the pot. . . . III. ii. 26. 5
Unwares the *hidden* hooke with baite I swallowed. . . . III. ii. 38. 9
Were from him *hidden,* or unknowne of yore. . . . III. iii. 15. 5
More *hidden* are then Sunne in cloudy vele; . . . III. iii. 19. 6
there *hidden* lye Light-shonning thefte, . . . III. iv. 58. 1
out of her *hidden* cave she cald . . . III. vii. 22. 1
tell thy griefe, if any *hidden* lye; . . . III. x. 26. 2
hidden snares Through the greene gras . . . III. xi. 28. 8
Vile treason and fowle falshood *hidden* were, . . . IV. i. 17. 8
By wondrous skill and many *hidden* wayes . . . IV. ii. 47. 3
hidden love t' appeare. . . . IV. iii. 46. 9
Sends forth the winds out of his *hidden* threasure . . . IV. ix. 23. 3
harme that might lie *hidden* there; . . . IV. x. 20. 2
tell their *hidden* race, . . . IV. xi. 40. 8
If ought lay *hidden* in his grieved thought, . . . IV. xii. 24. 8
found out whereas she *hidden* lay . . . V. ii. 25. 5
wyder made the wound of th' *hidden* dart. . . . V. v. 28. 5
Whose *hidden* drift he could not well perceive; . . . V. v. 37. 2
Can from th' immortall Gods ought *hidden* bee? . . . V. vii. 21. 6
roiall pompe, which there long *hidden* lay, . . . V. viii. 51. 5
full of wyndings is And *hidden* wayes, . . . V. ix. 6. 7
then came Daunger, threatning *hidden* dread . . . V. ix. 45. 5
out of an *hidden* shade There forth issewd . . . V. xi. 22. 3
could reveale All *hidden* crimes, . . . V. xii. 26. 6
it in silver bowre does *hidden* ly . . . VI. Pr. 3. 3
the wood, where so he wist She *hidden* was, . . . VI. ii. 20. 9
Without suspect of ill or daungers *hidden* dred. . . . VI. iii. 23. 9
Sir Calepine himselfe away had *hidden* it. . . . VI. v. 8. 9
ghastly gaze bewray their *hidden* feares. . . . VII. vi. 28. 9
couldst not hold thy selfe so *hidden* blest, . . . VII. vi. 46. 7
A wicked ambush which lay *hidden* long . . . *Am.* xii. 6
Through *hidden* perils round about me plast; . . . *Am.* xxxiv. 8

Hidden—*Continued.*
false whispers, breeding *hidden* feares, . . . *Epith.* 336
face long *hidden* was From heavens view, . . . *H.L.* 59
Even heavenly riches, which there *hidden* ly . . . *H.H.B.* 248

Hidder. *See* **Heder.**

Hide. some one of you . . . secretly doth *hide*) . . . *Ro.* xv. 10
Through his faire *hide* his angrie sting did threaten, . . . *Van.* ii. 11
Safe in his dreadles den him thought to *hide:* . . . *Van.* x. 4
The kene cold blowes through my beaten *hyde,* . . . *S.C.* F. 3
Where in a bush he did him *hide,* . . . *S.C.* Mar. 32
by the *hyde* the Wolfe Lowder caught; . . . *S.C.* S. 223
There from the boyling heate himselfe to *hide:* . . . *Gn.* 252
your silken *hyde* Fil'd with round flesh, . . . *Hub.* 591
flesh, that everie bone doth *hide*. . . . *Hub.* 592
could not so closely *hide* His craftie feates, . . . *Hub.* 919
having doft for heate his dreadfull *hide:* . . . *Hub.* 954
for his rough *hide* He gan to reach, . . . *Hub.* 1335
To *hide* himselfe from his owne feared thought. . . . *Hub.* 1358
better farre it were to *hide* their names, . . . *T.M.* 101
All comfortlesse doth *hide* her chearlesse head . . . *T.M.* 239
Where doth she all that wondrous welth nowe *hide?* . . . *Ti.* 75
in it did most precious treasure *hide,* . . . *Ti.* 619
An hairie *hide* of some wilde beast, . . . *Mui.* 66
The engines which in them sad death doo *hyde:* . . . *Mui.* 86
but the same did *hide* Under a vele, . . . I. i. 4. 3
Did spred so broad, that heavens light did *hide,* . . . I. i. 7. 5
I warne thee . . . *hide* thy head.' . . . I. ii. 18. 6
in hope themselves to *hide* From the fierce heat, . . . I. ii. 29. 8
Lyke a faire Lady, but did fowle Duessa *hyde*. . . . I. ii. 35. 9
having tand his tawney *hide* With . . . breath of Heaven, . . . I. iii. 31. 4
Cruell revenge, which he in hart did *hyde;* . . . I. iii. 33. 8
a greene gowne . . . underneath did *hide* his filthinesse; . . . I. iv. 25. 2
she all day did *hide* her hated hew. . . . I. v. 20. 5
let eternall night so sad sight fro me *hyde*. . . . I. vii. 22. 9
'O lightsome day! . . . thy hated face for ever *hyde,* . . . I. vii. 23. 4
From living eies her open shame to *hide,* . . . I. viii. 50. 4
hide the smoke that did his fire display, . . . I. ix. 16. 4
in an heaped furrow did thee *hyde;* . . . I. x. 66. 2
His harder *hyde* would nether perce nor bight, . . . I. xi. 16. 4
Wherewith her heavenly beautie she did *hide,* . . . I. xii. 22. 4
sacred lamp in secret chamber *hide,* . . . I. xii. 37. 7
To *hide* her shame and loathly filthinesse, . . . II. i. 22. 5
To *hide* his coward head . . . II. iii. 21. 4
ne thinkes how erst she did her *hide*. . . . II. iii. 36. 9
Into the hollow earth, them there to *hide*. . . . II. vii. 6. 5
these rich hils of welth doest *hide* apart . . . II. vii. 7. 3
So huge a masse and *hide* from heavens eie? . . . II. vii. 20. 2
shame his ugly face did *hide* from living eye. . . . II. vii. 22. 9
the river, which the same did *hyde;* . . . II. vii. 61. 3
with faire semblaunt sought to *hyde* the breach, . . . II. ix. 39. 3
Without or robe or rag to *hide* his shame: . . . II. x. 58. 3
all the land they under them did *hyde;* . . . II. xi. 5. 7
Such as the Indians in their quivers *hide:* . . . II. xi. 21. 5
ne car'd to *hyde* Their dainty partes . . . II. xii. 63. 8
Did use to *hide,* and plaine apparaunce shonne) . . . III. i. 52. 8
How ever finely she it faind to *hyde*. . . . III. ii. 11. 5
since thy faithful zele lets me not *hyde* My crime, . . . III. ii. 37. 6
She gan avize where els he mote him *hyde:* . . . III. vi. 16. 2
So may he long him selfe full easie *hide;* . . . III. vi. 23. 6
hellish arts from people she might *hide,* . . . III. vii. 6. 8
haberjeon, . . . the faire feature of her limbs did *hyde;* . . . III. ix. 21. 2
All his demeasnure from his sight did *hide:* . . . III. ix. 27. 7
they lay in wait, or els them selves did *hide*. . . . III. x. 20. 9
In lofty looks to *hide* an humble minde, . . . III. x. 30. 2
Ne he twixt heven and earth shall *hide* his hedd, . . . III. x. 32. 8
He in a bush did *hyde* his fearefull hedd. . . . III. x. 44. 2
Till drouping Phoebus gan to *hyde* his golden hedd. . . . III. x. 45. 9
hearken to his lore, and all his counsell *hyde*. . . . III. x. 50. 9
sad shadowes gan the world to *hyde* . . . III. xi. 55. 3
for to *hide* her fained sex the better . . . IV. i. 7. 3
glosse thereon doth shed To *hide* his falshood, . . . IV. v. 15. 6
Where they might *hide* their heads in quiet rest, . . . IV. v. 32. 6
such a sore, that doth her grievance *hide,* . . . IV. vi. 1. 6
Thinking to *hide* the depth by troubling of the flood. . . . IV. vi. 29. 9
To *hide* her wound, that none might it perceive: . . . IV. vi. 40. 8
To *hide* th' intent which in my heart did lurke, . . . IV. vii. 17. 3
To *hide* the metall, . . . IV. xi. 45. 7
eke their dame halfe dead did *hide* her self for feare. . . . V. ii. 24. 9
Doe *hide* themselves from her astonying looke . . . V. ii. 54. 5
To *hide* the blush which in her visage rose . . . V. v. 30. 2
The more that she it sought to cover and to *hyde*. . . . V. v. 53. 9
'The tidings sad, That I would *hide,* . . . V. vi. 10. 5
badly doest thou *hide* Thy maisters shame, . . . V. vi. 11. 4
in her thought did *hide* The felnesse of her heart, . . . V. vi. 18. 5
I will not seeke the same from you to *hide;* . . . V. vii. 19. 3
To *hide* thy state from being understood? . . . V. vii. 21. 5
there her selfe did *hyde* from his hard tyranny. . . . V. x. 18. 9
To *hide* the horrour which did lurke behinde, . . . V. xi. 23. 8
Or house to *hide* his head from heavens spight, . . . VI. iv. 39. 4
there thinking him to *hyde:* . . . VI. vi. 28. 4
their guilt to *hyde:* . . . VI. viii. 44. 7
whilst darknes him doth *hide,* . . . VI. xi. 18. 7
their heads from death to *hide,* . . . VI. xi. 49. 8
Behind the bushes, where she did her *hyde,* . . . VI. xii. 8. 6
To *hide* the terror of her uncouth hew . . . VII. vii. 6. 2
Him slew, and with his *hide* did him array. . . . VII. vii. 36. 7
if in your hardned brest ye *hide* A close intent . . . *Am.* xxv. 9
hookes, That from the foolish fish theyr bayts doe *hyde:* . . . *Am.* xlvii. 4
his spotted *hyde* Doth please all beasts, . . . *Am.* liii. 1
Within a bush his dreadfull head doth *hide,* . . . *Am.* liii. 3

Hideous. a naked rout of Faunes With *hideous* cry . . . . *Bel.*[1] x. 12
An *hideous* bodie big and strong . . . . *Bel.* ix. 2
with *hideous* outcrie, A troupe of Satyres . . . . *Bel.*[2] xii. 11
In a great mountaine heap't with *hideous* noyse, ... *Ro.* xvi. 2
forst this *hideous* beast to open wide . . . . *Van.* iii. 9
An *hideous* Dragon, dreadfull to behold, ... *Van.* vi. 1
The scalie backe of that most *hideous* snake . . . . *Gn.* 305
endles paines and *hideous* heavinesse . . . . *Gn.* 371
a gulph most *hideous* Amidst the Towne . . . . *Gn.* 604
She grew to *hideous* shape of dryrihed, ... *Mui.* 347
hideous monsters full of uglinesse; . . . . *D.* 340
Horrible, *hideous*, roaring with hoarse crie.' . . . . *Col.* 199
angry Jove an *hideous* storme of raine Did poure . . . . I. i. 6. 6
hurling her *hideous* taile About her cursed head; . . . . I. i. 16. 2
daunted with theyr forces *hideous*, Their steeds doe stagger, . I. ii. 15. 5
they did seeme more foule and *hideous*, ... I. ii. 41. 3
A dreadfull Dragon with an *hideous* trayne, ... I. iv. 10. 5
With *hideous* horror both together smight, ... I. v. 8. 6
Ah heavens! that doe this *hideous* act behold, ... I. vi. 5. 6
An *hideous* Geaunt, horrible and hye, ... I. vii. 8. 4
his dreadfull *hideous* hedd, Close couched on the bever, . . I. vii. 31. 5
Ne shame he thought to shonne so *hideous* might: . . . . I. viii. 8. 1
his *hideous* club aloft he dites, ... I. viii. 18. 4
they heard a roaring *hideous* sownd, ... I. xi. 4. 1
his most *hideous* head my tongue to tell Does tremble; . . . I. xi. 12. 6
His *hideous* tayle then hurled he about, ... I. xi. 23. 1
fowle deedes, too *hideous* to bee told, ... II. ii. 44. 7
such *hideous* puissaunce on foot to beare; . . . . II. v. 3. 9
cover'd heaven with *hideous* dreriment, ... II. vii. 1. 5
With *hideous* strokes and importable powre, ... II. viii. 35. 2
hideous Giaunts, and halfe beastly men, ... II. x. 7. 2
that huge sonne of *hideous* Albion, ... II. x. 11. 6
(O *hideous* hunger of dominion!) . . . . II. x. 47. 9
hideous shapes were like to feendes of hell, ... II. xi. 11. 3
hideous Ordinaunce Upon the Bulwarkes cruelly did play, . . II. xi. 14. 3
Halfe in amaze with horror *hideous*, ... II. xi. 38. 4
An *hideous* roring far away they heard, ... II. xii. 2. 6
'On thother syde an *hideous* Rocke is pight . . . . II. xii. 4. 1
an *hideous* hoast arrayd Of huge Sea monsters, ... II. xii. 22. 8
an *hideous* bellowing Of many beasts, ... II. xii. 39. 1
Now turned into figures *hideous*, ... II. xii. 85. 4
hideous horror and sad trembling sownd, ... III. i. 14. 6
It is an *hideous* hollow cave . . . . III. iii. 8. 3
Halfe of thy dayes doest lead in horrour *hideous*. . . . . III. iv. 55. 9
An *hideous* beast of horrible aspect, ... III. vii. 22. 2
quaked under their so *hideous* masse; . . . . III. ix. 50. 6
with *hideous* And hatefull outrage long him chaced . . . . III. xi. 3. 4
hideous tayle his lefte foot did enfold, ... III. xi. 48. 7
an *hideous* storme of winde arose, ... III. xii. 2. 1
doth beare An *hideous* storme, ... IV. i. 45. 6
Demogorgon, . . . The *hideous* Chaos keepes, ... IV. ii. 47. 9
could once sustaine the *hideous* stowre, ... IV. iii. 15. 5
in his head an *hideous* wound imprest: . . . . IV. iii. 34. 4
meete with so *hideous* maine, ... IV. iv. 18. 4
all unwares he felt an *hideous* sway . . . . IV. iv. 31. 4
Ran forth in hast with *hideous* outcry, ... IV. vii. 21. 4
The *hideous* noise of their huge strokes did heare, ... IV. vii. 29. 3
An *hideous* Giant, dreadfull to behold, ... IV. x. 16. 6
Under the hanging of an *hideous* clieffe . . . . IV. xii. 5. 1
An *hideous* tempest seemed from below To rise . . . . V. vii. 14. 2
Like to an *hideous* storme, which nothing may empeach. . . . V. vii. 35. 9
An *hideous* monster doth in darknesse lie, ... V. x. 29. 3
An *hideous* monster that doth it defend, ... V. xi. 20. 2
Horrible, *hideous*, and of hellish race, ... V. xi. 23. 4
Of stature huge and *hideous* he was, ... V. xii. 15. 1
layd On *hideous* strokes . . . . VI. i. 20. 2
So *hideous* is her shape, so huge her hed, ... VI. vi. 10. 3
doth lie In *hideous* horrour and obscurity, ... VI. vi. 11. 5
eeke of person huge and *hideous*, ... VI. vii. 41. 2
from heaven most *hideous* stormes are sent, ... *Am.* xlvi. 3
Hideously. Heapes of huge wordes uphoorded *hideously*, . . . *T.M.* 553
therewith stroke at her so *hideouslie*, ... IV. vi. 18. 8
thundred strokes thereon so *hideouslie*, ... V. ii. 21. 7
gan hew So *hideously* uppon his armour bright, ... V. xi. 5. 4
Hides. Phoebus, . . . *hydes* for shame. . . . . I. vi. 6. 8
Hiding. Under blacke stole *hyding* her bayted hooke; . . . . I. i. 49. 6
in false griefe *hyding* his harmefull guile, ... I. v. 18. 5
With smoake and sulphur *hiding* all the place, ... I. v. 31. 5
Hie. *Hye* thee home, shepheard, ... *S.C.* F. 246
'Ye shepheards daughters, . . . *Hye* you there apace: . . . . *S.C.* Ap. 128
I hold it best for us home to *hye*. . . . . *S.C.* May 317
hye we homeward fast. . . . . *S.C.* N. 208
Guyon after him in hast did *hye*, ... II. iv. 13. 8
At last to Tryphon she for helpe did *hie*, ... IV. xi. 6. 5
to whom she straight did *hie* With gladfull hast, ... V. viii. 6. 5
him selfe did faster *hye* To reskue him, ... VI. v. 22. 3
flyes away as fast as he can *hye*, ... VI. xi. 18. 8
Hied. Home when the doubtfull Damme had her *hyde*, ... *S.C.* May 294
Whom to poursue the Infant after *hide* . . . . II. xi. 25. 7
Unto the shinie heaven in haste she *hide*, ... IV. xii. 25. 3
Hierarchy. There we behold the heavens great *Hierarchie*, . . *T.M.* 507
Hierusalem. *See* **Jerusalem.**
Hies. then each to rest him *hyes*. . . . . II. ii. 46. 9
Hiest. *See* **Highest.**
Hiew. *See* **Hue.**
High. So *hie* as mought an Archer reache with sight. . . . *Bel.*[1] iii. 4
set on *hie* upon triumphing chaire, ... *Bel.*[1] iv. 7
the roote in *hie* disdaine Sende forth . . . . *Bel.*[1] v. 13
The holy Citie of the Lorde, from *hye* . . . . *Rev.* iv. 3
frame, An hundred cubits *high* (*hie*[1]) . . . . *Bel.* ii. 2

High—*Continued.*
On *high* hills top I saw a stately frame . . . . *Bel.*[2] ii. 1
in triumphant chayre was set on *hie*, ... *Bel.*[2] iv. 7
did raise a Trophee *hie*; . . . . *Bel.*[2] xv. 8
sharped steeples *high* shot up in ayre; . . . . *Ro.* ii. 2
She, whose *high* top above the starres did sore, ... *Ro.* iv. 1
In her swifte charret with *high* turrets crownde, ... *Ro.* vi. 2
The lowest earth join'd to the heaven *hie*; . . . . *Ro.* viii. 8
these arcks, these baths, these temples *hie*; . . . . *Ro.* xxvii. 4
gins Bartas *hie* to rayse His heavenly Muse, ... *Ro.* Env. 11
High on a hill a goodly Cedar grewe, ... *Van.* vii. 1
As doen *high* Towers in an earthquake: . . . . *S.C.* F. 6
sitting *hye*, Upon the Mountaine sayles. . . . . *S.C.* Jul. 103
An Eagle sored *hye*, ... *S.C.* Jul. 222
Sitting upon a hill so *hye*, ... *S.C.* Au. 57
Hey, ho, the *high* hyll! . . . . *S.C.* Au. 58
So *high* to sore . . . . *S.C.* O. 86
mount as *high*, and sing as soote . . . . *S.C.* O. 90
love does teach him climbe so *hie*, ... *S.C.* O. 91
their *high* steppes adore: . . . . *S.C.* Env. 11
To an *high* mountaines top he with them went, ... *Gn.* 73
clambring through the hollow cliffes on *hy* . . . . *Gn.* 79
high doth overlooke Her owne like image . . . . *Gn.* 87
the *high* Palme trees, with braunches faire, ... *Gn.* 190
high shoote up their heads into the skyes. . . . . *Gn.* 192
coveting, with his *high* tops extent, ... *Gn.* 212
His glittering breast he lifteth up on *hie*, ... *Gn.* 258
An heape of earth he hoorded up on *hie*, ... *Gn.* 657
In whose *high* front was writ as doth ensue. . . . . *Gn.* 686
losels lifted up on *high*, ... *Hub.* 67
*losels lifted *high*, where I did looke, ... *Hub.* 67
his hose broken *high* above the heeling, ... *Hub.* 213
on his shoulders *high* his bat to beare, ... *Hub.* 238
An easie life, and fit *high* God to please. . . . . *Hub.* 395
he that serves the Lord of hoasts most *high*, ... *Hub.* 469
Then was *high* time their wits about to geather. . . . . *Hub.* 570
himselfe uprearing *hy* Upon his tiptoes, ... *Hub.* 663
A noble Gentleman of *high* regard, ... *Hub.* 685
to raise Himselfe to *high* degree, ... *Hub.* 775
mocke *high* God himselfe, ... *Hub.* 843
followed unto his palaice *hye*; . . . . *Hub.* 1107
high Jove, in whose almightie hand . . . . *Hub.* 1225
Sitting one day within his turret *hye*, ... *Hub.* 1227
Heare, thou great Father of the Gods on *hie*, ... *T.M.* 55
Such *high* conceipt of that celestiall fire, ... *T.M.* 391
with humble minde and *high* insight, ... *T.M.* 511
Princes and *high* Priests . . . . *T.M.* 560
Lifting the Good up to *high* Honours seat, ... *Com. Son.* i. 11
towards heaven shee seemd on *high* to weld. . . . . *Ti.* 14
'*High* towers, faire temples, goodly theaters, ... *Ti.* 92
'Where my *high* steeples whilom usde to stand, ... *Ti.* 127
Whom England *high* in count of honour held, ... *Ti.* 185
Placed on *high* upon an Altare faire, ... *Ti.* 492
Upon a brazen pillour standing *hie*, ... *Ti.* 660
glorie of the world your *high* thoughts scorne, ... *Ti.* 681
unto heaven let your *high* minde aspire, ... *Ti.* 685
high in heaven Hyperions fierie childe . . . . *Mui.* 51
heard to sound as she was wont on *hye*, ... *Col.* 20
her father, sitting still on *hie*, ... *Col.* 132
A world of waters heaped up on *hie*, ... *Col.* 197
'These be the hills (quoth he) the surges *hie*, ... *Col.* 240
An *high* headland thrust far into the sea, ... *Col.* 281
Muse, full of *high* thoughts invention, ... *Col.* 446
Her name to eccho unto heaven *hie*. . . . . *Col.* 483
For *high* desert, advaunst to that degree. . . . . *Col.* 527
Belov'd of *high* and low with faithfull harts. . . . . *Col.* 531
like a goodly beacon *high* addrest, ... *Col.* 562
Right noble Nymphs, and *high* to be commended: . . . . *Col.* 577
great Cynthiaes goodnesse, and *high* grace, ... *Col.* 588
thou hast forgot Thy selfe, . . . to mount so *hie*: . . . . *Col.* 617
service *high* so basely they ensew, ... *Col.* 767
With humble hearts to heaven uplifted *hie*, ... *Col.* 816
that *high* powre, wherewith thou art possest. . . . . *Col.* 826
the light to mount on *hie*, And th' heavie downe . . . . *Col.* 848
to my selfe the blame that lookt so *hie*: . . . . *Col.* 936
So *hie* her thoughts as she her selfe have place, ... *Col.* 937
In whose *high* thoughts Pleasure hath built her bowre, . . . *Ded. Son.* viii. 6
For honor of your name and *high* descent. . . . . *Ded. Son.* x. 14
High in the favour of that Emperesse, ... *Ded. Son.* xi. 3
And for your owne *high* merit in like cace: . . . . *Ded. Son.* xi. 7
the trees so straight and *hy*, ... I. i. 8. 5
her beastly bodie raizd . . . *high* above the ground: . . . . I. i. 18. 4
His gall did grate for . . . *high* disdaine; . . . . I. i. 19. 6
High on an hill, his flocke to vewen wide, ... I. i. 23. 3
trickling streame from *high* rock tumbling downe, ... I. i. 41. 2
the *high* hils Titan discovered, ... I. ii. 7. 4
He that . . . *high* hath set his throne where Tiberis doth pas. I. ii. 22. 9
My dearest Lord fell from *high* honors staire . . . . I. ii. 23. 7
Phoebus, now ymounted *hie*, ... I. ii. 29. 3
when Aldeboran was mounted *hye* . . . . I. iii. 16. 1
her fiers servant, full of kingly aw And *high* disdaine, . . I. iii. 41. 2
Whose wals were *high*, but nothing strong nor thick, ... I. iv. 4. 3
High lifted up were many loftie towres, ... I. iv. 4. 6
on a sandie hill, . . . it mounted was full *hie*, ... I. iv. 5. 6
High above all a cloth of State was spred, ... I. iv. 8. 1
sitting *high*, for lowly she did hate: . . . . I. iv. 10. 3
Jove, that *high* in heaven doth dwell . . . . I. iv. 11. 5
the lowest stayre Of her *high* throne; . . . . I. iv. 13. 6
when she does ride To Joves *high* hous . . . . I. iv. 17. 7
they . . . clash their shields, and shake their swerds on *hy*, . I. iv. 40. 3

High—*Continued.*
upon eternall paine Of *high* displeasure that ensewen might, I. iv. 40. 6
A shrilling trompett sownded from on *hye,* . . . I. v. 6. 1
his heavie hand he *high* gan reare, . . . I. v. 13. 5
At last the trumpets Triumph sound on *hie;* . . . I. v. 15. 6
shyning lampes in Joves *high* house were light; . . . I. v. 19. 2
ghosts . . . Cursing *high* Jove, . . . I. v. 33. 6
enhaunst His hart too *high* . . . I. v. 47. 7
High Caesar, great Pompey, and fiers Antonius. . . . I. v. 49. 9
Fell from *high* Princes courtes, or Ladies bowres, . . . I. v. 51. 6
An hideous Geaunt, horrible and *hye,* . . . I. vii. 8. 4
arrogant delight Of th' *high* descent whereof he was yborne, I. vii. 10. 2
His heavie *hand* he heaved up on hye, . . . I. vii. 14. 2
triple crowne set on her head full *hye,* . . . I. vii. 16. 4
High over hills, and lowe adowne the dale, . . . I. vii. 28. 8
ymounted *hye* On top of greene Selinis . . . I. vii. 32. 5
Nigh to a castle builded strong and *hye:* . . . I. viii. 2. 2
Duessa came, *High* mounted on her many headed beast, . . . I. viii. 6. 2
Inflamd with scornefull wrath and *high* disdaine, . . . I. viii. 7. 2
high advauncing his blood-thirstie blade, . . . I. viii. 16. 1
His weapon huge, that heaved was on *hye* . . . I. viii. 19. 8
the Prince, . . . threatning *high* his dreadfull stroke, . . . I. viii. 22. 2
aged tree, *High* growing on the top of rocky clift, . . . I. viii. 22. 6
as a Castle, reared *high* and round, . . . I. viii. 23. 1
he that *high* does sit, and all things see . . . I. viii. 27. 6
what *high* intent, Hath brought you hither into Faery land, I. ix. 6. 3
she was proud, and of too *high* intent, . . . I. ix. 27. 8
High heaped up with huge iniquitee . . . I. ix. 46. 4
vowed all Their life to service of *high* heavens King, . . . I. x. 36. 4
an hill that was both steepe and *hy,* . . . I. x. 46. 2
high heaven to attaine? . . . I. x. 50. 3
that sacred hill, whose head full *hie,* . . . I. x. 54. 1
wals and towres were builded *high* and strong . . . I. x. 55. 4
Too *high* a ditty for my simple song. . . . I. x. 55. 7
What stately building durst so *high* extend . . . I. x. 56. 7
high emongst all knights hast hong thy shield, . . . I. x. 60. 6
High reard their royall throne in Britans land, . . . I. x. 65. 4
High time now gan it wex . . . I. xi. 1. 1
High heven behold the tedious toyle . . . I. xi. 1. 9
he reared *high* afore His body monstrous, . . . I. xi. 8. 6
Himselfe up *high* he lifted . . . I. xi. 18. 2
for twelve huge labours *high* extold, . . . I. xi. 27. 3
Gan *high* advaunce his broad discoloured brest . . . I. xi. 31. 7
High brandishing his bright deaw-burning blade, . . . I. xi. 35. 6
high trees overthrew, and rocks in peeces tore. . . . I. xi. 37. 9
The same advauncing *high* above his head, . . . I. xi. 38. 1
high her burning torch set up . . . I. xi. 49. 9
From heven *high* to chace the chearelesse darke; . . . I. xi. 51. 8
Then gan triumphant Trompets sownd on *hye,* . . . I. xii. 4. 1
well arrived are, (*high* God be blest!) . . . I. xii. 17. 8
High God be witnesse that I guiltlesse ame; . . . I. xii. 30. 6
many an Angels voice . . . In their trinall triplicities on *hye:* I. xii. 39. 5
see the Redcrosse thus advaunced *hye;* . . . II. i. 23. 6
two hils, whose *high* heads overplast . . . II. i. 24. 4
With feeble hands then stretched forth on *hye,* . . . II. i. 49. 1
when him *high* corage did emmove, . . . II. i. 50. 5
high God . . . Imprinted had that token . . . II. ii. 4. 3
In chiefe degree are heaped up on *hye:* . . . II. ii. 41. 2
to be advaunced *hye:* . . . II. iii. 10. 7
Before her gate *high* God did Sweate ordaine, . . . II. iii. 41. 5
either hellish feends, or powres on *hye:* . . . II. iii. 45. 5
hurling *high* his yron braced arme, . . . II. v. 7. 5
he smote his haughty crest so *hye,* . . . II. v. 12. 4
a pleasaunt grove Was shott up *high,* . . . II. v. 31. 2
Both of them *high* attonce their handes enhaunst, . . . II. vi. 31. 1
low abase the *high* heroicke spright, . . . II. vii. 10. 6
on *hye* He over him did hold . . . II. vii. 27. 5
Arachne *high* did lifte Her cunning web, . . . II. vii. 28. 7
His harmefull club he gan to hurtle *hye,* . . . II. vii. 42. 3
where was advaunced *hye* A stately siege . . . II. vii. 44. 4
Some thought to raise themselves to *high* degree . . . II. vii. 47. 1
what she was that did so *high* aspyre? . . . II. vii. 48. 3
Worthie of heven and *hye* felicitie, . . . II. vii. 49. 5
so great grace and offred *high* estate; . . . II. vii. 50. 2
Of whom *high* Jove wont whylome feasted bee; . . . II. vii. 59. 6
unto all that live in *high* degree, . . . II. vii. 60. 3
Above the water were on *high* extent, . . . II. vii. 61. 5
his hand, . . . Uplifting *high,* . . . II. viii. 30. 6
hurling up his harmefull blade on *hy,* . . . II. viii. 33. 5
As when a windy tempest bloweth *hye,* . . . II. viii. 48. 1
Doth blesse her servaunts, and them *high* advaunce. . . . II. ix. 5. 5
And in her favor *high* bee reckoned, . . . II. ix. 6. 8
so *high* as foe might not it clime, . . . II. ix. 21. 2
lifted *high* above this earthly masse, . . . II. ix. 45. 3
With *high* renowme and great felicity: . . . II. x. 36. 3
wondrous wit to menage *high* affayres, . . . II. x. 37. 2
(O too *high* ditty for my simple rime!) . . . II. x. 50. 7
Semiramis, Whom antique history so *high* doth rayse, . . . II. x. 56. 3
Did *high* advaunce the crowne of Faery: . . . II. x. 75. 5
most gent, That ever brandished bright steele on *hye!* . . . II. xi. 17. 6
tombling low From the *high* mountaines, . . . II. xi. 18. 5
Joves harnesse-bearing Bird from *hye* . . . II. xi. 43. 1
craggie clift Depending from on *high,* . . . II. xii. 4. 3
lifting up his vertuous staffe on *hye,* . . . II. xii. 26. 6
On th' other side an *high* rocke toured still, . . . II. xii. 30. 5
The painted flowres, the trees upshooting *hye,* . . . II. xii. 58. 5
Presume so *high* to stretch mine humble quill? . . . III. Pr. 3. 3
'He should advaunced bee to *high* regard,' . . . III. i. 27. 8
high Jove Doth light the lower world, . . . III. i. 57. 6
High time it seemed then for everie wight . . . III. i. 58. 1

High—*Continued.*
When in so *high* an object they do lyte, . . . III. ii. 3. 7
Onely for honour and for *high* regard, . . . III. ii. 7. 4
bright ventayle, lifted up on *hye,* . . . III. ii. 24. 3
stirredst up th' Heroes *high* intents, . . . III. iii. 2. 8
standing *high* aloft low lay thine eare, . . . III. iii. 9. 1
Al holding crosses in their hands on *hye,* . . . III. iii. 38. 6
caused to be hanged *hy* In his chiefe Church, . . . III. iii. 59. 2
all the conquests which them *high* did reare, . . . III. iv. 1. 5
Is this thine *high* advauncement? . . . III. iv. 36. 3
her whilome upon *high* Pindus hill He loved, . . . III. iv. 41. 4
her bowre Is built of hollow billowes heaped *hye,* . . . III. iv. 43. 2
Was mounted *high* in top of heaven sheene, . . . III. iv. 51. 7
The prayses of *high* God he faire displayes, . . . III. iv. 59. 3
to all *high* desert and honour doth aspire. . . . III. v. 1. 9
a gentle Lady of great sway And *high* accompt . . . III. v. 4. 6
by no meanes the *high* banke he could sease, . . . III. v. 19. 8
Of Gods *high* praise, and of their loves sweet teene, . . . III. v. 40. 4
so disloyally Deeme of her *high* desert, . . . III. v. 45. 7
A Faerie was, yborne of *high* degree. . . . III. vi. 4. 3
With which *high* God his workmanship hath deckt; . . . III. vi. 12. 5
having hong upon a bough on *high* Her bow . . . III. vi. 18. 1
set his triumphes *hye,* . . . III. vi. 49. 7
Through the tops of the *high* trees . . . III. vii. 5. 1
His caytive thought durst not so *high* aspire: . . . III. vii. 16. 5
(*high* God did so ordaine) . . . III. vii. 27. 1
with blasphemous bannes *high* God in peeces tare. . . . III. vii. 39. 9
Bad that same boaster, as he mote, on *high,* . . . III. viii. 16. 3
So much *high* God doth innocence embrace. . . . III. viii. 29. 5
From top of Hemus by him heaped *hye;)* . . . III. ix. 22. 6
Troynovant . . . which stands so *hy,* . . . III. ix. 45. 6
High over hilles and over dales he fledd, . . . III. x. 55. 1
'O soverayne Lord! that sit'st on *hye* . . . III. xi. 9. 2
submit you to *high* providence; . . . III. xi. 14. 4
High heven beholdes sad lovers nightly theeveryes. . . . III. xi. 45. 9
him selfe up rearing *hye* . . . III. xii. 23. 1
clapt on *hye* his coulourd winges twaine, . . . III. xii. 23. 7
she did extend Her sword *high* over him, . . . III. xii. 36. 9
From her *high* spirit chase imperious feare, . . . IV. Pr. 5. 3
on *high* there hong The golden Apple, . . . IV. i. 22. 4
his mightie hand He heav'd on *high,* . . . IV. iii. 33. 2
For their *high* merits and great dignitie, . . . IV. iii. 44. 4
With dreadfull force falles on some steeple *hie:* . . . IV. vi. 14. 3
At last his lucklesse hand he heav'd on *hie,* . . . IV. vi. 18. 6
had done outrage in so *high* degree: . . . IV. vi. 22. 7
Daughter unto a Lord of *high* degree; . . . IV. vii. 15. 2
to wreake on worthlesse wight Your *high* displesure, . . . IV. viii. 17. 3
Ryding upon a Dromedare on *hie,* . . . IV. viii. 38. 7
right hand In full avengement heaved up on *hie,* . . . IV. viii. 43. 2
lov'd a Ladie of *high* parentage; . . . IV. viii. 50. 2
might not aspire To match so *high;* . . . IV. viii. 50. 4
hangd on *high* with golden ribbands laced; . . . IV. x. 8. 5
The roofe up *high* was reared from the ground, . . . IV. x. 37. 5
when thou spredst thy mantle forth on *hie,* . . . IV. x. 44. 7
Wayting when as the Antheme should be sung on *hye.* . . . IV. x. 48. 9
Faire Ister, flowing from the mountaines *hie;* . . . IV. xi. 20. 5
Bearing his sixe deformed heads on *hye,* . . . IV. xi. 32. 2
High Swale, unquiet Nide, and troublous Skell; . . . IV. xi. 37. 7
To tell the sands, or count the starres on *hye,* . . . IV. xi. 53. 2
much more eath to tell the starres on *hy,* . . . IV. xii. 1. 5
yours the waift by *high* prerogative. . . . IV. xii. 31. 6
high ador'd with solemne feasts, . . . V. Pr. 9. 8
For his great justice, held in *high* regard, . . . V. i. 30. 2
place deserved with the Gods on *hy.* . . . V. ii. 1. 7
Which she with wrongs hath heaped up so *hy* . . . V. ii. 9. 5
as if he band *High* God, . . . V. ii. 18. 8
He pitcht upon a pole, on *high* ordayned; . . . V. ii. 19. 4
made them stoupe that looked earst so *hie.* . . . V. ii. 21. 5
Still holding up her suppliant hands on *hye,* . . . V. ii. 26. 4
nayld on *high* that all might them behold. . . . V. ii. 26. 9
holding forth on *hie* An huge great paire of ballance . . . V. ii. 30. 2
'Therefore I will throw downe these mountaines *hie,* . . . V. ii. 38. 1
All creatures must obey the voice of the Most *Hie.* . . . V. ii. 40. 9
He pulleth downe, he setteth up on *hy;* . . . V. ii. 41. 7
she causd his warlike armes Be hang'd on *high,* . . . V. v. 21. 7
lampe of lightsome day Up-lifted in the porch of heaven *hie:* V. vii. 17. 4
For *high* disdaine of such indignity, . . . V. vii. 28. 6
a mayden Queene of *high* renowne, . . . V. viii. 17. 2
mounting straight uppon a charret *hye,* . . . V. viii. 28. 4
he was mounted in his seat so *high,* . . . V. viii. 33. 3
High over hilles, and lowly over dales, . . . V. viii. 39. 2
by heavens *high* decree, . . . V. viii. 44. 6
With many towres, and tarras mounted *hye,* . . . V. ix. 21. 6
high over his head There written was . . . V. ix. 26. 1
sate on *high,* that she might all men see . . . V. ix. 27. 3
a thousand more of such as sings Hymns to *high* God, . . . V. ix. 29. 5
With which *high* God had blest her happie land, . . . V. ix. 30. 4
All lovely daughters of *high* Jove, . . . V. ix. 31. 4
So sitting *high* in dreaded soverayntie, . . . V. ix. 34. 1
through *high* heavens grace, . . . V. ix. 42. 1
many *high* regards and reasons gainst her red. . . . V. ix. 43. 9
Next gan Religion gainst her to impute *High* Gods beheast, . V. ix. 44. 6
high alliance unto forren powre; . . . V. ix. 45. 6
wretched ruine of so *high* estate; . . . V. ix. 46. 5
meriteth to have as *high* a place, . . . V. x. 1. 6
Eftsoones againe his axe he raught on *hie,* . . . V. xi. 10. 1
The which this Gyant reared first on *hie,* . . . V. xi. 19. 3
To him assynd her *high* beheast to doo, . . . V. xii. 3. 7
No shame to stoupe, ones head more *high* to reare; . . . V. xii. 19. 3
the cursed felon *high* did reare His cruell hand . . . V. xii. 20. 2

High—*Continued.*
from low to *high* uplifted is your fame. . . . VI. Pr. 6. 9
through *high* disdaine And proud despight . . . VI. i. 15. 1
both their hands on *hie* At once did heave . . . VI. i. 38. 1
placed *high* above Or low beneath, . . . VI. ii. 1. 5
Upon him tooke the roiall *high* degree, . . . VI. ii. 28. 8
Whether *high* towring or accoasting low, . . . VI. ii. 32. 2
yet past a boy, And being now *high* time . . . VI. ii. 32. 9
the *high* desire . . . which in you doth aspire, . . . VI. ii. 34. 4
in atchievement of her *high* behest . . . VI. ii. 37. 7
That made them grow so *high* t' all honorable hap.' . . . VI. iv. 36. 9
To happie blisse he was full *high* uprear'd, . . . VI. v. 12. 4
did stryde At every step uppon the tiptoes *hie:* . . . VI. vii. 42. 6
from the *high* degree of happy state Fell . . . VI. viii. 2. 8
They prayd *high* God them farre from them to send. . . . VI. ix. 6. 5
Unmyndfull of his vow, and *high* beheast . . . VI. x. 1. 3
From so *high* step to stoupe unto so low; . . . VI. x. 3. 2
to low, to *hie,* To friends, to foes; . . . VI. x. 23. 8
With ragged weedes, and lockes upstaring *hye,* . . . VI. xi. 27. 4
The same is yonder Lady, whom *high* God did save.' . . . VI. xii. 17. 9
Of good and bad alike, of low and *hie,* . . . VI. xii. 28. 6
Whom though *high* Jove of kingdome did deprive, . . . VII. vi. 2. 8
obtain'd Great power of Jove, and *high* authority: . . . VII. vi. 3. 2
doth sound on *hie* Warres and allarums . . . VII. vi. 3. 7
come before *high* Jove her dooings to discharge. . . . VII. vi. 17. 9
To thrust . . . eke our selves from heavens *high* Empire, . . . VII. vi. 21. 4
To Joves *high* Palace straight cast to ascend, . . . VII. vi. 23. 8
Or from *high* hilles or from the dales belowe, . . . VII. vi. 39. 5
dooth oft refuse This too *high* flight, . . . VII. vii. 1. 4
Then any of the gods or Powers on *hie:* . . . VII. vii. 5. 4
his *high* head, that seemeth alwayes hore . . . VII. vii. 11. 3
Whether those same on *high,* or these belowe; . . . VII. vii. 20. 2
daughters of *high* Jove And timely Night; . . . VII. vii. 45. 1
that *high* look, with which she doth comptroll . . . *Am.* x. 10
ye *high* hevens, that all this sorowe see, . . . *Am.* xlvi. 9
Not earth, for her *high* thoghts more heavenly are: . . . *Am.* lv. 5
And eke her mind is pure immortall *hye.* . . . *Am.* lv. 12
High time it is this warre now ended were . . . *Am.* lvii. 2
high worths surpassing paragon . . . *Am.* lxvi. 5
Shall lift you up unto an *high* degree. . . . *Am.* lxxxii. 14
Garnisht with heavenly guifts of *high* degree, . . . *Epith.* 187
Bring her up to th' *high* altar, . . . *Epith.* 215
walkes about *high* heaven al the night? . . . *Epith.* 375
ye *high* heavens, the temple of the gods, . . . *Epith.* 409
ayry Towers upraised much more *high.* . . . *Com. Son.* iv. 4
forme, which now doth dwell In his *high* thought, . . . *H.L.* 194
Advance the banner of thy conquest *hie,* . . . *H.B.* 268
Unto the God of Love, *high* heavens king. . . . *H.H.L.* 7
That *High* Eternall Powre, which now doth move . . . *H.H.L.* 27
where those Idees on *hie* Enraunged be, . . . *H.H.B.* 82
Which in their *high* protections doe containe . . . *H.H.B.* 87
That sits upon the righteous throne on *hy,* . . . *H.H.B.* 151
With which she rules the house of God on *hy,* . . . *H.H.B.* 193
Through observation of her *high* beheast, . . . *H.H.B.* 202
Of Gods *high* praise, that filles the brasen sky; . . . *H.H.B.* 263
cropt full feateously The tender stalkes on *hye.* . . . *Proth.* 28
From those *high* Towers this noble Lord issuing, . . . *Proth.* 163
High-adored. *See* **Adored, High.**
High-advanced. *high advaunced* crests downe meekely feld; . . . II. xii. 40. 5
High-aspiring. she beholds, with *high aspiring* thought, . . . *Col.* 612
So was the *high-aspyring* with huge ruine humbled. . . . V. ii. 50. 9
High-blowing. Nor th' horrible uprore of windes *high blowing,* *Ro.* xiii. 9
High-conceited. Do kindle love in *high conceipted* sprights; *H.H.B.* 5
Higher. honor Pan with hymnes of *higher* vaine. . . . *S.C.* N. 8
The kindelye dewe drops from the *higher* tree, . . . *S.C.* N. 31
if ought *higher* were than that, did it desyre. . . . I. iv. 11. 9
thother rather *higher* did arise, . . . II. xii. 66. 5
yet love can *higher* stye Then reasons reach, . . . III. ii. 36. 5
The *higher* place in her Heroick mynd: . . . III. v. 55. 5
eke in stature *higher* by a span; . . . IV. vii. 5. 3
He shouldered him from off the *higher* ground, . . . V. ii. 49. 8
meriteth indeede an *higher* name: . . . VI. Pr. 6. 8
Higher then all the rest, . . . Vi. ix. 8. 2
Though meane her lot, yet *higher* did her mind ascend. . . . VI. ix. 10. 9
From pitch of *higher* place unto this low degree.' . . . VI. ix. 28. 9
My spirit to an *higher* pitch will rayse, . . . *Am.* lxxx. 12
he gan to mount up *hyre,* . . . *H.L.* 68
His dunghill thoughts . . . no *higher* dare aspyre, . . . *H.L.* 184
Thereof he fashions in his *higher* skill . . . *H.B.* 221
How ever here on *higher* steps we stand, . . . *H.H.L.* 201
The hearts of men, . . . may lift themselves up *hyer,* . . . *H.H.B.* 19
How much lesse those, much *higher* in degree, . . . *H.H.B.* 61
Highest. the toppes even of the *hiest* hilles . . . *Bel.*[1] vi. 6
Proud of his *highest* service, . . . *Van.* iv. 3
they bene daughters of the *hyghest* Jove, . . . *S.C.* Jun. 67
honor now of *highest* gods she is, . . . *S.C.* N. 197
Into the *highest* top of heaven gan clime, . . . *Gn.* 157
downe on them to fall from *highest* towres: . . . *Gn.* 580
Abides in *highest* place above the best, . . . *Gn.* 614
in *highest* place, t' approach him nigh, . . . *Hub.* 470
the *highest* now in grace Be the wilde beasts, . . . *Hub.* 619
From *highest* staire to lowest step me drave, . . . *Ti.* 25
I doo dailie see things *highest* placed, . . . *Ti.* 180
That him to *highest* honour shall advaunce. . . . *Ti.* 271
raised they the puissant brood . . . To *highest* heaven, . . . *Ti.* 383
sits in *highest* seate Of this worlds glorie, . . . *Ti.* 463
out of sight to *highest* heaven mounted, . . . *Ti.* 600
To raine in th' aire from th' earth to *highest* skie, . . . *Mui.* 212
in the *highest* place, Urania, sister unto Astrofell, . . . *Col.* 486
th' youngest is the *highest* in degree. . . . *Col.* 543

Highest—*Continued.*
all harts that hornes the *highest* beares; . . . *Col.* 714
highest lookes have not the *highest* mynd, . . . *Col.* 715
Nor haughtie words most full of *highest* thoughts: . . . *Col.* 716
purchace *highest* rowmes in bowre and hall: . . . *Col.* 726
Whose girland now is set in *highest* place, . . . *Ded. Son.* xiii. 2
thou, most dreaded impe of *highest* Jove, . . . I. Pr. 3. 1
highest God, the Lord of life and light: . . . I. i. 37. 6
faire Hesperus in *highest* skie Had spent his lampe, . . . I. ii. 6. 6
Through *highest* heaven with weaker hand to rayne: . . . I. iv. 9. 4
to the *highest* she did still aspyre, . . . I. iv. 11. 8
'O lightsome day! the lampe of *highest* Jove, . . . I. vii. 23. 1
Both loftie towres and *highest* trees hath rent, . . . I. viii. 9. 7
that all this doth behold From *highest* heven, . . . I. ix. 47. 2
he leads him to the *highest* Mount, . . . I. x. 53. 1
descend From *highest* heven . . . I. x. 56. 3
gan to *highest* God entirely pray . . . I. xi. 32. 4
Till it the pitch of *highest* praise exceeds: . . . II. ii. 31. 4
That warlike feats doest *highest* glorifie. . . . II. iii. 38. 3
set in *highest* seat of dignitee, . . . II. iv. 19. 4
As if the *highest* God defy he would: . . . II. vii. 40. 5
upper end to *highest* heven was knitt, . . . II. vii. 46. 3
Accusing *highest* Jove and gods ingrate; . . . II. vii. 60. 7
highest God that loves his creatures so, . . . II. viii. 1. 6
forth looked from the *highest* spire The watch, . . . II. ix. 11. 6
Like *highest* heaven compassed around, . . . II. ix. 45. 2
lift it selfe unto the *highest* skyes? . . . II. x. 1. 5
To pricke of *highest* prayse forth to advaunce, . . . II. xii. 1. 3
Imperious Love hath *highest* set his throne, . . . III. ii. 23. 2
to the *highest* and the worthiest . . . III. v. 2. 5
in her hart finde *highest* rowme . . . III. v. 11. 3
doth not *highest* God vouchsafe to take The love . . . III. v. 47. 6
Forthy she standeth on the *highest* stayre . . . III. v. 54. 7
Goddesse, that doest *highest* sit . . . V. Pr. 11. 1
Though vertue then were held in *highest* price, . . . V. i. 1. 1
whylome rebelled Gainst *highest* heaven: . . . V. i. 9. 7
are rul'd by righteous lore Of *highest* Jove, . . . V. vii. 1. 6
heavenly honours in the *highest* place; . . . V. vii. 2. 4
till she the *highest* stage had scand, . . . VII. vi. 8. 8
that soveraigne seat By *highest* Jove assign'd, . . . VII. vi. 12. 2
in th' *highest* sky, Was placed . . . VII. vi. 19. 3
even the *highest* Powers of heaven to check) . . . VII. vi. 22. 4
to the *highest* him, that is behight . . . VII. vi. 35. 4
upon the *highest* hights Of Arlo-hill . . . VII. vi. 36. 5
That is the *highest* head (in all mens sights) . . . VII. vi. 36. 7
standeth on the *hyghest* stayre, . . . *Am.* lviii. 11
striving . . . To be advanced *highest* in degree. . . . *Com. Son.* ii. 8
As to the *Highest* they approch more neare, . . . *H.H.B.* 100
Yet is that *Highest* farre beyond all telling, . . . *H.H.B.* 101
crowne . . . in signe of *highest* soveraignty; . . . *H.H.B.* 191
High-flying. To impe the wings of thy *high flying* mynd, *H.H.B.* 135
Highgate. *Hygate* made the meare thereof by West, . . . III. ix. 46. 2
Highly. them for ever *highly* to advaunce, . . . *Hub.* 961
they him *highly* prayse. . . . *T.M.* 414
all the brood of Greece so *highly* praised, . . . *Col.* 413
highly honourd in his haughtie eye: . . . I. vii. 16. 2
Whom *highly* he did reverence and adore, . . . I. x. 49. 5
Was never king more *highly* magnifide, . . . II. x. 52. 1
for Apolloes temple *highly* herried.' . . . II. xii. 13. 9
To heare her Love so *highly* magnifyde; . . . III. ii. 11. 2
in all His famous conquests *highly* magnifide: . . . III. vii. 31. 7
Gan *highly* to commend the happie life . . . VI. ix. 18. 8
High-minded. *High minded* Cleopatra . . . I. v. 50. 7
High-mounted. *See* **High, Mounted.**
On which a grove of Oakes *high-mounted* growes, . . . VII. vi. 41. 2
High-reared. *High reared* mounts, the lands about to vew; . . . IV. x. 24. 5
High-soaring. As a faire stoupe of her *high soaring* thought, . . . V. ix. 34. 7
Hight. *See* **Height, Hote.**
Say it out, Diggon, whatever it *hight,* . . . *S.C.* S. 172
The gentle shepheard . . . That Colin *hight,* . . . *S.C.* D. 3
th' halfe-horsy people, Centaures *hight,* . . . *Gn.* 41
a good old woman was, *Hight* Mother Hubberd, . . . *Hub.* 34
all that in this world is worthie *hight* . . . *T.M.* 105
So hee his sonnes both Syre and brother *hight.* . . . *T.M.* 264
Therefore the nurse of vertue I am *hight,* . . . *T.M.* 457
a gentle Nymph was found, *Hight* Astery, . . . *Mui.* 119
Aragnoll (so his foe was *hight*) . . . *Mui.* 385
Ne let the sacred Sisters here be *hight,* . . . *D.* 11
Astrophel he *hight.* . . . *As.* 6
first his sister that Clorinda *hight,* . . . *As.* 211
another swaine . . . *Hight* Thestylis, . . . *As.* Interl. 221
(a jolly groome . . . *Hight* Hobbinol;) . . . *Col.* 15
when I asked . . . how he *hight,* . . . *Col.* 65
a bonie swaine, That Cuddy *hight,* . . . *Col.* 81
(Mole *hight* that mountain gray . . . *Col.* 104
Mulla . . . so *hight* The Nimph, . . . *Col.* 108
her owne brother river, Bregog *hight,* . . . *Col.* 117
So *hight* because of this deceitfull traine, . . . *Col.* 118
Allo *hight,* Broad-water called farre; . . . *Col.* 123
a gentle bonylasse . . . That Marin *hight;* . . . *Col.* 173
a great shepheardesse, that Cynthia *hight,* . . . *Col.* 234
a lovely lasse, *hight* Lucida: . . . *Col.* 456
The false Duessa, now Fidessa *hight,* . . . I. ii. 44. 1
charge of them was to a Porter *hight,* . . . I. iv. 6. 3
That noble order *hight* of maidenhed, . . . I. vii. 46. 4
at her parting said, She Queene of Faeries *hight.* . . . I. ix. 14. 9
Sir Terwin *hight,* that well himselfe advaunst . . . I. ix. 27. 3
'I, that *hight* Trevisan,' (quoth he) . . . I. ix. 32. 5
He was an aged syre, . . . *Hight* Humilta. . . . I. x. 5. 8
them receives a gentle Squyre, . . . *Hight* Reverence. . . . I. x. 7. 6

Hight—*Continued.*
the eldest, that Fidelia *hight*, . . . I. x. 12. 6
Her younger sister, that Speranza *hight*, . . . I. x. 14. 1
The Citty of the greate king *hight* it well, . . . I. x. 55. 8
this false woman that Fidessa *hight*, . . . I. xii. 32. 2
Fidessa *hight* the falsest Dame on grownd, . . . I. xii. 32. 3
'I wote not how he *hight*, . . . II. i. 18. 5
it *hight* the *Bowre of blis*. . . . II. i. 51. 9
Was *hight* Sir Huddibras, . . . II. ii. 17. 2
Elissa (so the eldest *hight*) . . . II. ii. 35. 1
that same Hag, his aged mother, *hight* Occasion; . . . II. iv. 10. 8
'My friend, *hight* Philemon, . . . II. iv. 20. 1
Pryene, (so she *hight*,) . . . II. iv. 25. 6
'Phaon I *hight*,' (quoth he) . . . II. iv. 36. 7
'How *hight* he then,' (sayd Guyon) . . . II. iv. 41. 1
Herebus sonne of Aeternitie is *hight*. . . . II. iv. 41. 9
rash Pyrochles varlett, Atin *hight*, . . . II. v. 25. 4
hight by name The Idle lake, . . . II. vi. 10. 1
fayre Philotime she rightly *hight*, . . . II. vii. 49. 1
The Gardin of Proserpina this *hight*; . . . II. vii. 53. 1
Wherefore *Mordddure* it rightfully is *hight*. . . . II. viii. 21. 6
He Steward was, *hight* Diet; . . . II. ix. 27. 8
The kitchin clerke, that *hight* Digestion, . . . II. ix. 31. 3
hight Phantastes by his nature trew, . . . II. ix. 52. 2
An auncient booke, *hight Briton moniments*, . . . II. ix. 59. 6
booke, That *hight Antiquitee of Faery lond*: . . . II. ix. 60. 2
River that whylome was *hight* The ancient Abus, . . . II. x. 16. 2
germans did subdew all Germany, Of whom it *hight*; . . . II. x. 22. 8
woody hilles . . . *hight* of him Glamorgan, . . . II. x. 33. 8
Most mercilesse of women, Wyden *hight*, . . . II. x. 35. 7
built that gate which of his name is *hight*, . . . II. x. 46. 6
most famous *hight* For skil in Musicke . . . II. x. 59. 7
their Capitayns, which *hight* Hengist and Horsus, . . . II. x. 65. 1
Uther, which Pendragon *hight*, . . . II. x. 68. 1
Therefore a Fay he her according *hight*, . . . II. x. 71. 8
Forthy this *hight* The Rocke of vile Reproch, . . . II. xii. 8. 1
therefore are they *hight* The Wandring Islands. . . . II. xii. 11. 6
Verdant (so he *hight*) he soone untyde, . . . II. xii. 82. 8
hight Grylle by name, . . . II. xii. 86. 7
she th' Errant Damzell *hight*; . . . III. i. 24. 7
(For so that Castle *hight* by commun name) . . . III. i. 31. 3
The first of them by name Gardante *hight*, . . . III. i. 45. 1
one of those sixe knights, Gardante *hight*, . . . III. i. 65. 1
The which I seeke to wreake, and Arthegall he *hight*.' . . . III. ii. 8. 9
In Deheubarth, that now South-wales is *hight*, . . . III. ii. 18. 4
Her aged Nourse, whose name was Glauce *hight*, . . . III. ii. 30. 2
a faire Lady Nonne, that whilome *hight* Matilda, . . . III. iii. 13. 5
'His sonne, *hight* Vortipore, shall him succeede . . . III. iii. 31. 1
the king of Louthiane, *Hight* Adin, . . . III. iii. 37. 6
the Paynim brethren, *hight* Octa and Oza, . . . III. iii. 52. 6
'how is she *hight*?' . . . III. iii. 56. 1
Tryphon of sea gods the soveraine leach is *hight*. . . . III. iv. 43. 9
Yet she loves none but one, that Marinell is *hight*. . . . III. v. 8. 9
'A Sea-nymphes sonne, that Marinell is *hight*, . . . III. v. 9. 1
sith love is franticke *hight*. . . . III. vii. 20. 9
She Palladine is *hight*. . . . III. vii. 52. 6
the more to seeme such as she *hight*, . . . III. viii. 10. 4
one old Nymph, *hight* Panope, . . . III. viii. 37. 9
Sometimes he boasted that a God he *hight*, . . . III. viii. 39. 6
'Malbecco he, and Hellenore she *hight*; . . . III. ix. 6. 1
Whiles yet on Ida he a shepeheard *hight*, . . . III. ix. 36. 3
by him cald Paros, which before *Hight* Nausa: . . . III. ix. 37. 2
'It Troynovant is *hight*, . . . III. ix. 45. 1
he . . . Forgot he was a man, and Gelosy is *hight*. . . . III. x. 60. 9
Aeolus faire daughter, Arne *hight*, . . . III. xi. 42. 2
The one of them the false Duessa *hight*, . . . IV. i. 18. 1
It was to weete the bold Sir Ferraugh *hight*, . . . IV. ii. 4. 5
the first *hight* Priamond, . . . IV. ii. 41. 8
Hight Bruncheval the bold, who fiersly forth did ride. . . . IV. iv. 17. 9
knowne to few, that Arthegall he *hight*, . . . IV. iv. 42. 8
That goodly belt was Cestus *hight* by name, . . . IV. v. 6. 1
sith ye my name have *hight*, . . . IV. vi. 4. 4
a privy place, betwixt us *hight*, . . . IV. vii. 17. 7
it woxe warre old, (Whereof it *hight*) . . . IV. viii. 31. 7
one daughter that is *hight* The faire Poeana, . . . IV. viii. 49. 3
so much favour she to him hath *hight* . . . IV. viii. 54. 1
hight The Queene of beautie, . . . IV. x. 29. 5
The one of them *hight* Love, . . . IV. x. 32. 6
Every of which was to a damzell *hight*; . . . IV. x. 38. 8
(This Tryphon is the seagods surgeon *hight*,) . . . IV. xi. 6. 6
Now *hight* Palemon, and is saylers frend; . . . IV. xi. 13. 6
hight The Churne and Charwell, . . . IV. xi. 25. 2
a Scythian king, that Humber *hight*, . . . IV. xi. 37. 8
she that *hight* of many heastes Polynome; . . . IV. xi. 50. 9
that which vice was *hight*, Is now *hight* vertue, . . . V. Pr. 4. 2, 3
the Lady, which Irena *hight*, . . . V. i. 4. 1
Chrysaor it was *hight*; . . . V. i. 9. 7
'His name is *hight* Pollente, . . . V. ii. 7. 1
The first of them was *hight* Sir Orimont, . . . V. iii. 5. 1
called Brigadore, (so was he *hight*,) . . . V. iii. 34. 3
For powre is the right hand of Justice truely *hight*. . . . V. iv. 1. 9
That further mayd, *hight* Philtera the faire, . . . V. iv. 8. 7
What better dowre can to a dame be *hight*? . . . V. iv. 9. 5
So, Amidas, the land was yours first *hight*; . . . V. iv. 19. 8
'How *hight* that Amazon?' . . . V. iv. 33. 1
The goodman of this house was Dolon *hight*; . . . V. vi. 32. 1
stird up . . . By his bad wife that *hight* Adicia; . . . V. viii. 20. 3
So said this Damzell, that *hight* Samient; . . . V. viii. 23. 7
His name *hight* Order; . . . V. ix. 23. 8
All lovely daughters of high Jove, that *hight* Litae, . . . V. ix. 31. 4

Hight—*Continued.*
First gan he tell how this . . . Duessa *hight*; . . . V. ix. 40. 2
Kept by a cowheard, *hight* Eurytion, . . . V. x. 10. 2
With his two-headed dogge that Orthrus *hight*; . . . V. x. 10. 6
His sonne was this Geryoneo *hight*; . . . V. x. 11. 1
the sad steele seizd not, where it was *hight*, . . . V. xi. 8. 7
'My name is Burbon *hight*, . . . V. xi. 49. 1
that faire Lady . . . Flourdelis *hight*, . . . V. xi. 49. 6
a Tyrant, which Grandtorto *hight*, . . . V. xi. 50. 3
Her name was *hight* Detraction, . . . V. xii. 35. 5
by name Briana *hight*, . . . VI. i. 14. 6
my mother, which then *hight* Faire Emiline, . . . VI. ii. 29. 1
The which the fertile Lionesse is *hight*, . . . VI. ii. 30. 4
But faire Priscilla (so that Lady *hight*) . . . VI. iii. 10. 1
The faire Serena (so his Lady *hight*) . . . VI. iii. 23. 2
Sir Calepine (so *hight*) Came to the place . . . VI. iii. 27. 1
aread to me, how *hight* thy Lord, . . . VI. iii. 39. 8
'His name . . . Is *hight* Sir Turpine, . . . VI. iii. 40. 2
Albe his Lady, that Blandina *hight*, . . . VI. iii. 42. 6
This hellish Dog, that *hight* the Blatant Beast; . . . VI. vi. 12. 2
She could or save or spill whom she would *hight*: . . . VI. vii. 31. 8
The fayrest Pastorella her by name did *hight*. . . . VI. ix. 9. 9
Meliboee (so *hight* that good old man) . . . VI. ix. 16. 1
The first of them *hight* mylde Euphrosyne, . . . VI. x. 22. 7
A lawlesse people, Brigants *hight* of yore, . . . VI. x. 39. 3
whose father *hight* The Lord of Many Ilands, . . . VI. xii. 4. 1
her owne handmayd, that Melissa *hight*, . . . VI. xii. 14. 8
Old aged Sire, with hower-glasse in hand, *Hight* Time,) . . . VII. vi. 8. 7
by her side there ran her Page, that *hight* Vesper, . . . VII. vi. 9. 5
there was a Nymph that *hight* Molanna; . . . VII. vi. 40. 1
Phoebus selfe, that god of Poets *hight*, . . . VII. vii. 12. 6
The seed of Saturne and faire Nais, Chiron *hight*. . . . VII. vii. 40. 9
With Him that is the God of Sabaoth *hight*: . . . VII. viii. 2. 8

Highway. they con to heaven the *high-way*, . . . *S.C.* S. 90
towards it a broad *high way* that led, . . . I. iv. 2. 8
All keepe the broad *high way*, . . . I. x. 10. 5
Through which a beaten broad *high way* did trace, . . . II. vii. 21. 3
he freed the Travellers *high-way*, . . . II. x. 39. 3

Hild. *See* **Held.**

Hilding. Thinking to take them from that *hylding* hound; . . . VI. v. 25. 7

Hill. *See* **Arlo.**
On *hill*, a frame . . . I sawe . . . *Bel.*[1] ii. 1
sodein earthquake loe, Shaking the *hill* . . . *Bel.*[1] ii. 13
Upon a *hill* I saw a kindled flame, . . . *Bel.*[1] ix. 1
An earthquake shooke the *hill* . . . *Bel.*[2] ii. 13
Upon an *hill* a bright flame I did see . . . *Bel.*[2] xi. 1
High on a *hill* a goodly Cedar grewe, . . . *Van.* vii. 1
Tho to a *hill* his faynting flocke he ledde, . . . *S.C.* Ja. 11
I never lyst presume to Parnasse *hyll*, . . . *S.C.* Jun. 70
Come up the *hyll* to me; . . . *S.C.* Jul. 6
they dwell (As goteheards wont) upon a *hill*, . . . *S.C.* Jul. 47
Suffice this *hill* of our. . . . *S.C.* Jul. 76
Whom Ida *hyll* dyd beare, . . . *S.C.* Jul. 146
One daye he sat upon a *hyll*, . . . *S.C.* Jul. 217
sith thys *hyll* Thou hast such doubt to climbe. . . . *S.C.* Jul. 231
Sitting upon a *hill* so hye, . . . *S.C.* Au. 57
Hey, ho, the high *hyll*! . . . *S.C.* Au. 58
Sitte we downe here under the *hill*; . . . *S.C.* S. 52
with the same fill every *hill* and dale. . . . *D.* 322
did roll downe from his *hill* Huge mightie stones, . . . *Col.* 149
High on an *hill*, his flocke to vewen wide, . . . I. i. 23. 3
Phoebus fiery carre . . . was climbing up the Easterne *hill*, . . . I. ii. 1. 8
she . . . every *hil* and dale, . . . Did search, . . . I. ii. 8. 7
hee . . . turned wyde Unto an *hil*; . . . I. iii. 26. 5
on a sandie *hill*, . . . it mounted was full hie, . . . I. iv. 5. 5
Sisyphus an . . . stone did reele Against an *hill*, . . . I. v. 35. 4
they pas Forth to an *hill* that was both steepe and hy, . . . I. x. 46. 2
That *hill* they scale with all their powre and might, . . . I. x. 47. 7
that sacred *hill*, . . . Adornd with fruitfull Olives . . . I. x. 54. 1
he lay upon the sunny side Of a great *hill*, . . . I. xi. 4. 6
Dragon . . . himselfe like a great *hill*: . . . I. xi. 4. 6
to an *hill* herselfe withdraw asyde; . . . I. xi. 5. 2
Fayre marching underneath a shady *hill*, . . . II. i. 5. 7
Still he him guided over dale and *hill*, . . . II. i. 34. 5
Like as Cupido on Idaean *hill*, . . . II. viii. 6. 1
the ruines of great Ossa *hill*, . . . II. x. 3. 3
the brode shadow of an hoarie *hill*; . . . II. xii. 30. 4
the pleasaunt *hill* Of Rhodope, . . . II. xii. 52. 1
her whilome upon high Pindus *hill* He loved, . . . III. iv. 41. 4
Whether in Paphos, or Cytheron *hill*, . . . III. vi. 29. 4
he came unto a rocky *hill* . . . III. x. 56. 3
the Trojane boy so fayre He snatcht from Ida *hill*, . . . III. xi. 34. 5
Nor hedge, nor ditch, nor *hill*, nor dale she staies, . . . IV. vii. 22. 1
A gentle Faulcon sitting on an *hill*, . . . V. v. 15. 2
Like a wyld Gote, leaping from *hill* to *hill*, . . . V. ix. 15. 4
chaced them both over *hill* and dale. . . . V. xi. 59. 7
uppon yond rocky *hill*, . . . VI. i. 13. 1
out of an *hill* fresh gushing did appere. . . . VI. iii. 50. 9
It was an *hill* plaste in an open plaine, . . . VI. x. 6. 1
the *hill* . . . Did seeme to overlooke the lowly vale; . . . VI. x. 8. 7
are wont to haunt Uppon this *hill*, . . . VI. x. 15. 3
upon an *hill* not farre away, . . . VI. xi. 36. 6
highest hights Of Arlo-*hill* (Who knowes not Arlo-*hill*?) . . . VII. vi. 36. 6
(Beeing of old the best and fairest *Hill* . . . VII. vi. 37. 6
The gods assembled all on Arlo *Hill*; . . . VII. vii. 3. 2
So full they filled every *hill* and Plaine; . . . VII. vii. 4. 5
In a fayre Plaine upon an equall *Hill* . . . VII. vii. 8. 1
assembled were On Haemus *hill* . . . VII. vii. 12. 3
she was bred and nurst On Cynthus *hill*, . . . VII. vii. 50. 4

Hillock. Upon a litle *hillocke* she was placed . . . VI. ix. 8. 1

Hill's. On high *hills* top I saw a stately frame, . . . *Bel.*[2] ii. 1
affrayd To clime this *hilles* height. . . . *S.C.* Jul. 72
at length she came To an *hilles* side, . . . III. vii. 4. 7
Under a steepe *hilles* side it placed was, . . . IV. v. 33. 1
Hills. the toppes even of the hiest *hilles*, . . . *Bel.*[1] vi. 6
from nie *hilles* a naked rout of Faunes . . . *Bel.*[1] x. 11
faire Dodonian tree . . . Upon seaven *hills* (*hilles*[1]) . . . *Bel.* v. 2
from nigh *hills*, with hideous outcrie, . . . *Bel.*[2] xii. 11
Seven Romane *Hils*, the worlds Seven Wonderments. . . . *Ro.* ii. 14
Jove . . . Her whelm'd with *hills*, these seven *hils*, . . . *Ro.* iv. 7
Heapt *hils* on *hils* to scale the starrie skie, . . . *Ro.* xii. 2
heaped was On these seven Romane *hils*, . . . *Ro.* xii. 10
Keeping his sheepe on the *hils* of Kent? . . . *S.C.* F. 93
Leave me those *hilles* . . . *S.C.* Jun. 19
thou wert wont on wastfull *hylls* to singe, . . . *S.C.* Jun. 50
on *hylls*, or dales, or other where, . . . *S.C.* Jun. 107
The wastefull *hylls* . . . Is a playne overture. . . . *S.C.* Jul. 27
Thus holy *hylles* to blame, . . . *S.C.* Jul. 38
the *hills* bene nigher heven, . . . *S.C.* Jul. 89
The *hylls* where dwelled holy saints . . . *S.C.* Jul. 113
They heapen *hylles* of wrath; . . . *S.C.* Jul. 202
Where thickest grasse did cloath the open *hills*. . . . *Gn.* 74
th' hollow *hills*, from which their silver voyces . . . *T.M.* 21
do feed Your carelesse flocks on *hils* . . . *D.* 520
where may I the *hills* and pastures see, . . . *Col.* 238
'These be the *hills* (quoth he) the surges hie, . . . *Col.* 240
lie, On *hills* and downes, . . . *Col.* 317
woods, and *hills*, and valleyes . . . *Col.* 482
the high *hils* Titan discovered, . . . I. ii. 7. 4
High over *hills*, and lowe adowne the dale, . . . I. vii. 28. 8
dale that lowly lay Betwixt two *hils*, . . . II. i. 24. 4
to remove . . . Those pretious *hils* . . . II. vii. 6. 3
these rich *hils* of welth doest hide apart . . . II. vii. 7. 3
it survewd as *hils* doen lower ground; . . . II. ix. 45. 4
as he to those woody *hilles* did fly, . . . II. x. 33. 7
Through *hils* and dales he speedy way did make, . . . II. xi. 26. 4
The dales for shade, the *hilles* for breathing space, . . . II. xii. 58. 6
Emongst the woody *hilles* of Dynevowre: . . . III. iii. 8. 6
huge *hills* Of dying people, . . . III. iii. 41. 1
heaped *hils* on hight To scale the skyes . . . III. vii. 47. 4
a shady glade Of the Riphoean *hils*, . . . III. viii. 6. 4
High over *hilles* and over dales he fledd, . . . III. x. 55. 1
The *hils* doe not the lowly dales disdaine, . . . V. ii. 41. 3
The dales doe not the lofty *hils* envy. . . . V. ii. 41. 4
High over *hilles*, and lowly over dales, . . . V. viii. 39. 2
over rockes, and *hilles*, and every place . . . V. ix. 16. 4
Through woods and *hils* he follow'd him . . . VI. iii. 26. 6
Through *hils* and dales, through bushes and through breres, . VI. viii. 32. 1
Through *hils*, through dales, through forests, . . . VI. ix. 2. 6
in *hils*, in woods, in dales, . . . VI. x. 3. 6
To sing of *hilles* and woods mongst warres and Knights, . VII. vi. 37. 2
Or from high *hilles* or from the dales belowe, . . . VII. vi. 39. 5
Now like great *Hills*, and streight like sluces . . . VII. vii. 20. 9
His golden beame upon the *hils* doth spred, . . . *Epith.* 20
Hilly. There is a *hyllye* place, . . . *S.C.* Jul. 58
Hilts. *hilts* were burnisht gold, and handle strong . . . I. vii. 30. 8
Him (*partial list*).
A shepeheards boye, (no better doe *him* call,) . . . *S.C.* Ja. 1
Him rested the goodman on the lea, . . . *S.C.* F. 158
but happely I *hym* spyde, . . . *S.C.* Mar. 31
give *him* curds and clouted Creame. . . . *S.C.* N. 99
Eternally *Him* praise that hath them blest; . . . *D.* 286
A lovely Ladie rode *him* faire beside, . . . I. i. 4. 1
Him als accompanyd upon the way . . . II. i. 7. 1
With *him* went Hope . . . a handsome Mayd, . . . III. xii. 13. 1
Betwixt *him* and his hurt bene happily, . . . IV. viii. 43. 7
As one that had no life *him* left . . . VI. vi. 32. 9
highest *him*, that is behight Father of Gods . . . VII. vi. 35. 4
Him first to love that us so dearely bought, . . . *H.H.L.* 188
Himself (*partial list*).
Unto his journey did *himselfe* addresse, . . . *Mui.* 146
Like as *himselfe* us pleaseth save or spill. . . . *Col.* 814
like *himselfe* desire for to beget: . . . *Col.* 864
Whereas that Pagan proud *him selfe* did rest . . . I. vi. 40. 5
death he could not worke *himselfe* thereby, . . . I. ix. 54. 6
Himselfe to cherish, . . . I. x. 29. 5
The knight *him selfe* even trembled at his fall, . . . I. xi. 55. 1
Mournes inwardly, and makes to *him selfe* mone; . . . II. i. 42. 7
As with lamenting eyes *him selfe* did lately vew. . . . II. ii. 45. 9
Cursing his Gods, and *him selfe* damning deepe: . . . II. viii. 37. 2
In which *himselfe* was charged heavily . . . II. x. 49. 3
That powre . . . makes them like *himselfe* . . . V. Pr. 10. 7
From her unto the miscreant *him selfe*; . . . V. viii. 19. 6
the food of life, . . . Even he *himselfe*, . . . *H.H.L.* 195
Hind. At my right hand a *Hynde* (*Hinde*[1]) appear'd . . . *Pet.* i. 4
the stout *hynde* arm'd his right hand with steele: . . . *Ro.* xviii. 6
With love long time did languish, as the striken *hind*. . . . I. ii. 24. 9
slew with glauncing dart amisse A gentle *Hynd*, . . . I. vi. 17. 6
As gentle *Hynd*, . . . forth her bleeding life does raine, . . . II. i. 38. 6
The hartlesse *Hynd* and Robucke to dismay, . . . II. ii. 7. 4
As *hynd* from her, so she fled from her enimy. . . . II. ii. 7. 9
didst not thou see a bleeding *Hynde*, . . . II. iii. 32. 7
Like as an *Hynd* forth singled from the heard, . . . III. vii. 1. 1
Thrust to an *Hynd* within some covert glade, . . . IV. vi. 12. 4
Like warie *Hynd* within the weedie soyle, . . . IV. x. 55. 8
an *Hynde*, whose calfe is falne unwares . . . IV. xii. 17. 6
a sturdy ploughman with his *hynde* . . . VI. viii. 12. 1
Coridon it was, the silly shepherds *hynd*. . . . VI. xi. 27. 9
a young fawne, that late hath lost the *hynd*; . . . *Am.* lxxviii. 2
Hinder. His *hinder* heele was wrapt in a clout, . . . *S.C.* May 243

Hinder—*Continued.*
Full closely creeping by the *hinder* side, . . . *Mui.* 403
all the *hinder* partes, . . . Were ruinous and old, . . . I. iv. 5. 8
To *hinder* soule from her desired rest, . . . II. i. 48. 2
That nought mote *hinder* his quicke prejudize: . . . II. ix. 49. 7
All that did earst it *hinder* and molest, . . . II. xi. 32. 7
they agayn returne backe by the *hinder* gate. . . . III. vi. 32. 9
Till on her horses *hinder* parts it fell; . . . IV. vi. 13. 6
To *hinder* thee from the just heritage . . . V. vii. 23. 3
heavy armes . . . *hinder* him from libertie to pant; . . . VI. iv. 19. 3
her *hinder* parts did plaine expresse A monstrous Dragon, . . VI. vi. 10. 8
what should *hinder*, but that we likewise Should handle . . VII. vi. 30. 4
Now none doth *hinder* you, . . . *Epith.* 370
Hindering. *Hindering* with his shade my lovely light, . . . *S.C.* F. 173
for *hindring* of her haste, . . . III. vi. 18. 7
Hinders. That *hinders* heavenly thoughts . . . *Am.* xiii. 12
Hindmost. led to th' *hindmost* rowme of three. . . . II. ix. 54. 9
he saw the *hindmost* overtake One of those two, . . . V. viii. 5. 6
hindmost in the gate he overhent, . . . V. x. 36. 6
Hind parts. his *hindparts*, whereof heed I tooke, . . . IV. x. 20. 3
Hindrance. in Princes courts to worke great scath and *hindrance*: . . . V. ix. 22. 9
Hinds. perfect pleasures . . . grow Amongst poore *hyndes*, . VI. x. 3. 6
Hinge. To move the world from off his stedfast *henge*, . . . I. xi. 21. 8
Hippodames. Infernall Hags, Centaurs, feendes, *Hippodames*, . II. ix. 50. 8
Which foure great *Hippodames* did draw in temewise tyde. . . . III. xi. 40. 9
Hippolytus. *Hippolytus* a jolly huntsman was, . . . I. v. 37. 1
of *Hippolytus* was lefte no moniment. . . . I. v. 38. 9
Hippolytus'. For that *Hippolytus* rent corse he did redresse. . I. v. 36. 9
By Dianes meanes, who was *Hippolyts* frend, . . . I. v. 39. 7
Hipponoe. *Hyponeo* with salt-bedewed wrests; . . . IV. xi. 51. 2
Hippothoe. *Speedy* Hippothoe, and chaste Actea, . . . IV. xi. 50. 1
Hips. Though eating *hipps*, and drinking watry fome. . . . *Hub.* 948
Her dainty limbes above her tender *hips*; . . . II. v. 33. 8
Hire. The one for the *hire* which he doth take, . . . *S.C.* May 52
privily his servant thereto *hire*: . . . *Hub.* 682
here thy shield is hangd for victors *hyre*? . . . I. v. 10. 7
the measure of thy sinfull *hire* . . . I. ix. 46. 3
thankes . . . He thens departing gave for his paynes *hyre* . . I. x. 68. 5
him reave of armes, the victors *hire*, . . . II. viii. 15. 7
sufficient were that *hire* For losse of thousand lives, . . . II. ix. 5. 8
cald Canutium, for his *hyre*; . . . II. x. 12. 8
Shall give th' enchaunter his unhappy *hire*. . . . III. iii. 36. 6
To heape on him dew vengeaunce for his *hire*. . . . III. ix. 17. 5
for her loves first *hire* Give it to her, . . . IV. v. 4. 5
'Loe! there thy *hire*;' . . . V. ii. 11. 8
had receiv'd their follies worthy *hire*, . . . V. viii. 15. 3
Nor land nor fee for *hyre* of his good deede, . . . VI. i. 47. 2
unrighteous ire . . . had given him his owne due *hire*? . . . VI. ii. 13. 9
I . . . wish that some more noble *hire* . . . VI. ii. 34. 7
So hard a taske as life for *hyre* to sell; . . . VI. vii. 15. 3
Where I did sell my selfe for yearely *hire*, . . . VI. ix. 24. 7
now sought *hyre* elswhere. . . . VI. xi. 39. 9
offer made To *hyre* them well . . . VI. xi. 40. 2
To keepe their flockes for litle *hyre* and chepe, . . . VI. xi. 40. 7
they for better *hyre* did shortly looke: . . . VI. xi. 40. 8
for *hyre* She should it cause be fostred . . . VI. xii. 6. 8
bold Procrustes *hire* . . . Would have suffiz'd . . . VII. vi. 29. 5
Her to discover for some secret *hire*: . . . VII. vi. 43. 3
for his *hire* to so foole-hardy dew, . . . VII. vi. 45. 4
Well worthy thou to have found better *hyre*, . . . *Am.* xlviii. 5
Upon thee fall for thine accursed *hyre* . . . *Am.* lxxxv. 6
That He for him might pay sinnes deadly *hyre*, . . . *H.H.L.* 138
Hired. *See* **Outhired.**
they bene *hyred* for little pay . . . *S.C.* May 47
Keeping their fleecy flockes as they were *hyr'd*, . . . III. vi. 15. 7
(Both two her paramours, both by her *hyred*, . . . V. ix. 41. 4
The wretch that *hyr'd* you to this wicked deed.' . . . VI. vii. 13. 5
His (*partial list*).
rather made by *his* owne skilfull hande . . . *Bel.*[1] iv. 10
all were it Jove *his* sire, . . . *Ro.* xi. 13
Hys pleasaunt Pipe, whych made us meriment, . . . *S.C.* Ap. 14
let the Lambe be Willye *his* owne: . . . *S.C.* Au. 132
Dido! the greate shepehearde *his* daughter sheene. . . . *S.C.* N. 38
To Pan *his* owne selfe pype I neede not yield: . . . *S.C.* D. 46
to match thy pipe with Tityrus *his* (*hys) style. . . . *S.C.* Env. 9
Great Nereus *his* daughter and *his* joy. . . . *Gn.* 492
And left his sonne t' ensue those steps of *his*. . . . *Ti.* 266
There now the joy is *his*, here sorrow mine. . . . *Ti.* 602
Not mine, but *His*, which mine awhile her made; . . . *D.* 235
Mine to be *His*, with him to live for ay. . . . *D.* 236
sweetly tempred is that Muse of *his*, . . . *Col.* 430
for servitors of *his*.' . . . *Col.* 770
on a tree Sansfoy *his* shield is hangd . . . I. v. 5. 8
his foe thy shield with *his* doth beare.' . . . I. v. 13. 4
a fole of Pegasus *his* kynd. . . . I. ix. 21. 9
His am I Atin, *his* in wrong and right, . . . II. iv. 42. 5
others it to use according to *his* kynd. . . . II. ix. 31. 9
Where you him lately lefte, in Mars *his* bed: . . . III. vi. 24. 3
Satyrane *his* chaunce Was her before, . . . III. ix. 27. 1
Then was she judged Triamond *his* one; . . . IV. v. 21. 8
garnisht all with gold . . . whereof it tooke *his* name, . . V. i. 10. 4
it was Talus, Artegall *his* groome: . . . V. vi. 8. 6
those sterne behests and cruell doomes of *his*. . . . V. vii. 22. 9
Or other *his* old foes . . . VII. vii. 15. 9
be partakers of those joyes of *his*. . . . *H.H.L.* 63
Hisseth. Fellie he *hisseth*, and doth fiercely stare, . . . *Gn.* 277
Hissing. her he hated as the *hissing* snake; . . . I. ii. 9. 8
Orion, flying fast from *hissing* snake, . . . II. ii. 46. 2

History. th' whole *history* Is but a jest, ... *Gn.* 5
That I may tell this haplesse *history?'* . . . . I. ix. 26. 4
all this famous antique *history* . . . . II. Pr. 1. 2
Semiramis, Whom antique *history* so high doth rayse, . . . II. x. 56. 3
the famous *history* Of Jason and Medaea . . . . II. xii. 44. 3
As ye may elswhere reade that ruefull *history*. . . . . . . III. vi. 53. 9
So oft as I this *history* record, ... III. viii. 1. 1
A famous *history* to bee enrold . . . . III. ix. 50. 7
Hit. he . . . *hit* me running in the heele: . . . . *S.C.* Mar. 97
Furthest fro the marke, weening it to *hit*. . . . . *S.C.* May 307
Another arrow hath your lovers hart to *hit.'* . . . . III. ii. 35. 9
where I thereon may *hit* In all this forrest . . . . VI. ii. 9. 5
Hither (*partial list*).
Forsake your watry bowres, and *hether* looke, ... *S.C.* Ap. 39
'Bring *hether* the Pincke . . . . *S.C.* Ap. 136
if you come *hether* . . . . *S.C.* Ap. 151
'*Hether* . . . me Archimago sent, ... I. i. 43. 6
hath thee *hether* brought . . . . I. iii. 39. 3
thy foes thee *hither* sent . . . . I. vi. 42. 2
brought you *hither* into Faery land, ... I. ix. 6. 4
Me *hither* brought . . . . I. ix. 7. 6
What grace hath thee now *hither* brought this way? . . . . I. x. 9. 8
Or doen thy feeble feet unweeting *hither* stray? . . . . . . I. x. 9. 9
through which ye *hither* came, ... I. x. 17. 3
shall *hither* backe retourne . . . . I. xii. 19. 8
that me *hither* led. . . . . II. i. 30. 2
'Come *hither!* [*come] *hither!* O, come hastily!' . . . . . II. viii. 3. 8
Caesar, . . . (O hideous hunger of dominion!) *hither* came. . II. x. 47. 9
hither hastly sent Vespasian, ... II. x. 52. 6
Hither came Joseph of Arimathy, ... II. x. 53. 7
having fate obayd, Hath *hither* brought . . . . III. iii. 19. 8
Hither great Venus brought . . . . III. vi. 51. 1
Me *hether* brought with him . . . . IV. vii. 18. 7
have perforce him *hether* brought away.' . . . . IV. viii. 62. 5
doth thee *hither* drive, ... V. xi. 38. 5
How ever by hard hap he *hether* came, ... VI. v. 2. 8
to me thou *hether* bring . . . . VI. vii. 13. 4
Hither those Brigants brought their . . . . VI. x. 43. 1
Hitherto. More ample spirit then *hitherto* was wount . . . . II. x. 1. 6
the thing that *hethertoo* Hath troubled . . . . IV. vi. 30. 6
hethertoo Had it forslackt: . . . . V. xii. 3. 5
all that *hetherto* hath long delayd . . . . VI. xii. 2. 1
Hitherward. over the pousse *hetheward* (**hetherward*) doth post. *S.C.* Au. 46
as *hitherward* I lately traveild, ... I. xii. 31. 6
turne thy rudder *hitherward* awhile . . . . II. xii. 32. 6
Hits. where he *hits* nought knowes, ... II. iv. 7. 9
Hive. honny . . . which doth softly trickle from the *hive,* . . . *Col.* 597
In bitter *hyve* to grope for honny: . . . . *Epig.* i. 4
Hives. After their *hives* with honny do abound. . . . . . . II. ix. 51. 5
creeping close amongst the *hives* . . . . III. x. 53. 5
Ho. *See* **Hey-ho, What ho.**
Hoar. *See* **Frory-hoar, Mossy-hoar.**
Under the foote of Mole, that mountaine *hore,* . . . . *Col.* 57
Under the steepe foot of a mountaine *hore:* . . . . I. iii. 10. 6
Through wisedome of a matrone grave and *hore;* . . . . . . I. x. 3. 5
fast her hent By the *hoare* lockes . . . . II. iv. 12. 3
Mamon in a delve Sunning his threasure *hore;* . . . . II. vii. Arg.
the *hoare* waters from his frigot ran, ... II. xii. 10. 3
having vewd awhile the surges *hore* . . . . III. iv. 7. 4
An aged sire with head all frory *hore,* . . . . III. viii. 30. 3
his *hore* beard Was fowly dight, ... III. x. 52. 4
the *hore* Congealed litle drops . . . . IV. xi. 46. 8
Doth frie with fome above the surges *hore*. . . . . V. ii. 15. 8
his high head, that seemeth alwayes *hore* . . . . VII. vii. 11. 3
Hoard. Ne car'd to *hoord* for those whom he did breede: . . I. x. 38. 5
To *hoord* up heapes of evill gotten masse, ... III. ix. 4. 2
Barow which doth *hoord* Great heapes of salmons . . . . . . IV. xi. 43. 5
'Sith then ye needs will know the griefe I *hoord,* . . . . . IV. vi. 29. 2
Hoarded. An heape of earth he *hoorded* up on hie, ... *Gn.* 657
he found great store of *hoorded* threasure, ... IV. ix. 12. 2
Hoarse. My Muse is *hoarse* and wearie of thys stounde: . . . *S.C.* D. 140
Horrible, hideous, roaring with *hoarse* crie.' . . . . *Col.* 199
sung so long untill quite *hoarse* he grew. . . . . *Col.* 399
Seagulles *hoars* and bace, ... II. xii. 8. 4
The *hoars* Night-raven, trump of dolefull drere; . . . . . . II. xii. 36. 5
Hoary. Lifting to heaven her aged *hoarie* head, ... *Ro.* xxviii. 3
now are clothd with mosse and *hoary* frost, ... *S.C.* Ja. 33
Clothed with cold, and *hoary* wyth frost, ... *S.C* F. 79
oft his *hoarie* locks downe doth cast, ... *S.C.* F. 181
draweth newe delightes with *hoary* heares. . . . . *S.C.* Jun. 40
My head besprent with *hoary* frost I fynd, ... *S.C.* D. 135
She compast with a wreathe of Olyves *hoarie*. . . . . *Mui.* 328
With *hoary* head and deawy dropping beard, ... *Col.* 250
His feete all bare, his beard all *hoarie* gray, ... I. i. 29. 3
when he sees his age, And *hoarie* head of Archimago old, . . I. iii. 38. 4
He was an aged syre, all *hory* gray, ... I. x. 5. 5
As *hoary* frost with spangles doth attire . . . . I. x. 48. 3
he hath lefte his plumes all *hory* gray, ... I. xi. 34. 4
that *hoarie* king, with all his traine, ... I. xii. 12. 2
Of rypest yeares, and heares all *hoarie* gray, ... II. i. 7. 3
loathly were and *hoarie* gray, ... II. iv. 4. 5
Whose *hoary* locks great gravitie did crowne, ... II. vi. 47. 5
With *hoary* lockes all loose, ... II. xi. 23. 3
the brode shadow of an *hoarie* hill; . . . . II. xii. 30. 4
his *hoarie* hed Dropped with brackish deaw: . . . . III. xi. 40. 3
With rugged beard, and *hoarie* shagged heare, ... IV. v. 34. 8
sad Asopus, comely with his *hoarie* head. . . . . IV. xi. 14. 9
With head all *hoary,* and his beard all gray, ... IV. xi. 25. 8
many scarres and many *hoary* heares, ... V. vii. 39. 8
the hope that to my *hoary* heare Thou brings? . . . . VI. iii. 4. 7

Hoary—*Continued.*
the bare ground with *hoarie* mosse bestrowed . . . . VI. iv. 14. 4
there sate an *hory* Old aged Sire, ... VII. vi. 8. 5
on his *hoary* beard his breath did freese, ... VII. vii. 31. 3
on the *hoary* mountayne use to towre; . . . . *Epith.* 68
Hobbin. *Hobbin,* ah *Hobbin!* I curse the stounde . . . . . *S.C.* S. 56
I wote ne, *Hobbin,* how I was bewitcht . . . . *S.C.* S. 74
'*Hobbin,* thou temptest me to that I covet: . . . . *Col.* 37
Hobbin desires, thou maist it not forsake;— . . . . *Col.* 50
Hobbinol. 'It is not *Hobbinol* wherefore I plaine, ... *S.C.* Ja. 55
Ah, foolish *Hobbinol!* thy gyfts bene vayne; . . . . *S.C.* Ja. 59
Tell me, good *Hobbinoll,* what garres thee greete? . . . . . *S.C.* Ap. 1
I pray thee, *Hobbinoll,* recorde some one, ... *S.C.* Ap. 30
O happy *Hobbinoll!* I blesse thy state, ... *S.C.* Jun. 9
Of Muses, *Hobbinol,* I conne no skill, ... *S.C.* Jun. 65
Hobbinol, I pray thee, gall not my old griefe: . . . . . . *S.C.* S. 12
Hobbinoll, all this long tale Nought easeth the care . . . . *S.C.* S. 242
good *Hobbinoll,* mought I thee praye Of ayde . . . . *S.C.* S. 246
were *Hobbinoll* as God mought please, ... *S.C.* S. 252
Ah, *Hobbinoll!* God mought it thee requite; . . . . *S.C.* S. 258
if that *Hobbinol* right judgement bare, ... *S.C.* D. 45
Adieu, good *Hobbinoll,* (**Hobbinol*) that was so true, . . . *S.C.* D. 155
(a jolly groome . . . Hight *Hobbinol;*) . . . . *Col.* 15
'Ah! Colin, (then said *Hobbinol*) . . . . *Col.* 731
'That ill (said *Hobbinol*) they him requite, ... *Col.* 903
Hobgoblins. *hob Goblins,* names whose sence we see not, . . *Epith.* 343
Hog. one . . . That had an *hog* beene late, ... II. xii. 86. 7
Hoggish. had from *hoggish* forme him brought to naturall. . II. xii. 86. 9
Let Gryll be Gryll, and have his *hoggish* minde; . . . . . . II. xii. 87. 8
Hogh. The westerne *Hogh,* besprincled with the gore . . . . II. x. 10. 7
Hogs. he had been a fatting *hogs* of late, ... VII. vii. 40. 3
Hold. *See* **Ground-hold.**
this world doth nought but grievance *hold!* . . . . *Bel.*[2] iii. 12
Whose foote in ground hath left but feeble *holde,* . . . . . *Ro.* xxviii. 4
Nought aske I, but onely to *hold* my right; . . . . *S.C.* F. 186
Sicker I *hold* him for a greater fon, ... *S.C.* Ap. 158
with her hard *hold,* and straight embracing, ... *S.C.* May 99
I *hold* it best for us home to hye. . . . . *S.C.* May 317
hold theyr peace, for shame . . . . *S.C.* Jun. 56
holden scorne of homely shepheards quill: . . . . *S.C.* Jun. 68
to *holden* chat With seely shepherds swayne, ... *S.C.* Jul. 29
they *holden* shame of theyr cote: . . . . *S.C.* S. 111
hold up thy heavye head, ... *S.C.* O. 1
That did her buried body *hould.* . . . . *S.C.* N. 159
Knitting his wanton armes with grasping *hold,* . . . . . . *Gn.* 218
with proud vaunt his head aloft doth *holde;* . . . . *Gn.* 259
catching hastie *holde* Of a yong alder . . . . *Gn.* 298
hold in hugger mugger in their hand, ... *Hub.* 139
at the length he published to *holde* A Visitation, ... *Hub.* 568
weake was my remembrance it to *hold,* . . . . *Hub.* 1387
hold by wrong that wee should have by right. . . . . *T.M.* 318
some bride, her joyous night to *hold:* . . . . *Ti.* 635
Which th' ashes seem'd of some great Prince to *hold,* . . . . *Ti.* 661
Nymphs, which she doth *hold* In her retinew, ... *Col.* 459
great Cynthia her in chiefest grace Doth *hold,* . . . . . . *Col.* 501
Thrise happie do I *hold* thee, noble swaine, ... *Col.* 552
to *hold* eternally Their bounteous deeds . . . . *Col.* 581
So long as life my limbs doth *hold* together; . . . . *Col.* 629
'Happie indeed (said Colin) I him *hold,* . . . . *Col.* 660
it forst him slacke His grasping *hold,* . . . . I. i. 20. 5
I . . . *hold* me to you bound: . . . . I. i. 54. 3
The Fort, that Ladies *hold* in soveraigne dread. . . . . . . I. ii. 25. 4
suddeine catching *hold,* did her dismay . . . . I. iii. 12. 5
Una cride, 'O! *hold* that heavie hand, ... I. iii. 37. 2
His hasty hand he doth amased *hold,* . . . . I. iii. 38. 5
by her cleanly garment catching *hold,* . . . . I. iii. 40. 8
did usurpe . . . Upon the scepter which she now did *hold:* . . I. iv. 12. 6
coffers . . . With precious metall full as they might *hold;* . . I. iv. 27. 4
forgett the raines to *hold* Of reasons rule, ... I. iv. 41. 3
In vaine he seekes that having cannot *hold.* . . . . I. vi. 33. 7
O! *hold* thy mortall hand for Ladies sake; . . . . I. vii. 14. 6
Hold for my sake, and doe him not to dye, ... I. vii. 14. 7
The combat which he with Sansjoy did *hould;* . . . . I. vii. 26. 7
Remedilesse for aie he doth him *hold.* . . . . I. vii. 51. 8
You to have helpt I *hold* my selfe yet blest.' . . . . I. ix. 7. 7
she fast did *hold* A booke, ... I. x. 13. 7
take assured *hold* Upon her silver anchor, ... I. x. 22. 2
Much was the man encombred with his *hold,* . . . . I. xi. 41. 1
Thrise happy man the knight himselfe did *hold,* . . . . . . I. xii. 40. 6
heven thee deignes to *hold* in living state, ... II. i. 37. 3
hold sad life in long captivitee; . . . . II. i. 48. 3
An yearely solemne feast she wontes to *hold,* . . . . II. ii. 42. 6
Ne ever shall I rest in house nor *hold,* . . . . II. ii. 44. 5
'*Hold,* O deare Lord! *hold* your dead-doing hand,' . . . . . II. iii. 8. 1
cleeped him his liege, to *hold* of him in fee, ... II. iii. 8. 9
none thereof could ever taken *hold;* . . . . II. iv. 4. 8
gan soone unbrace His grasping *hold:* . . . . II. iv. 9. 8
catching *hold* of her ungratious tonge, ... II. iv. 12. 8
catching *hold* him strongly stayd From drowning. . . . . . . II. vi. 46. 3
'What secret place . . . can safely *hold* . . . . II. vii. 20. 1
He over him did *hold* his cruell clawes, ... II. vii. 27. 6
To catchen *hold* of that long chaine, ... II. vii. 46. 6
neither mayle could *hold,* Ne shield defend . . . . II. viii. 41. 2
with long siege us in the castle *hould.* . . . . II. ix. 12. 7
in her hand a Poplar braunch did *hold:* . . . . II. ix. 37. 3
What wight she was that Poplar braunch did *hold?* . . . . . II. ix. 39. 7
hold of him, as subject to Britayne. . . . . II. x. 41. 9
catching *hold* of him, as downe he lent, ... II. xi. 29. 1
the Briton Prince him rouzd Out of his *holde,* . . . . II. xi. 33. 2
all that here on earth we dreadfull *hold,* . . . . II. xii. 25. 7

Hold—*Continued.*
those unruly beasts to *hold* without; . . . II. xii. 43. 3
fledd so fast that nothing mote him *hold,* . . . III. i. 15. 8
her knights service ought, to *hold* of her in fee. . . . III. i. 44. 9
hold them backe that would in error fall: . . . III. i. 46. 5
infixed faster *hold* Within my bleeding bowells, . . . III. ii. 39. 1
Enough to *hold* a foole in vaine delight. . . . III. viii. 10. 7
all that could not from affright her *hold,* . . . III. viii. 34. 5
sure a foole I doe him firmely *hold,* . . . III. ix. 8. 4
often to him calling to take surer *hould.* . . . III. xi. 34. 9
A mortall bow and arrowes keene did *hold,* . . . III. xi. 48. 2
in her hand did *hold* An holy-water-sprinckle, . . . III. xii. 13. 5
Shame burning brond-yrons in her hand did *hold:* . . . III. xii. 24. 8
unawares upon her laying *hold,* . . . IV. ii. 45. 6
Therefore this Fay I *hold* but fond and vaine, . . . IV. iii. 2. 1
Whether shall have the Hag, or *hold* the Lady still.' . . . IV. iv. 12. 9
would no longer *hold* The wrathfull weapon . . . IV. vi. 27. 4
To whom his faith he firmely ment to *hold,* . . . IV. viii. 53. 2
she him still detaines in captive *hold,* . . . IV. viii. 53. 7
greedy *hold* of that his blouddy feast: . . . IV. ix. 31. 8
sith all by lot we *hold.* . . . IV. x. 4. 9
Delay . . . Caught *hold* on me, . . . IV. x. 14. 6
Were cowards knowne, and litle count did *hold,* . . . IV. x. 18. 7
Upon a recluse Virgin to lay *hold,* . . . IV. x. 54. 4
Cupids man with Venus mayd to *hold,* . . . IV. x. 54. 7
warlike people which the Britaine Islands *hold:* . . . IV. xi. 15. 9
from all men so rich a kingdome *hold!* . . . IV. xi. 22. 2
One prison fittest is to *hold* us two. . . . IV. xii. 10. 7
in his hand an yron flale did *hould,* . . . V. i. 12. 8
on him catching *hold* gan loud to crie, . . . V. i. 18. 2
Else he doth *hold* him backe or beat away. . . . V. ii. 6. 5
Eftsoones him selfe he from his *hold* unbownd, . . . V. ii. 16. 4
catching *hold* of this Sea-beaten chest, . . . V. iv. 11. 6
I *hold* mine owne, and so will *hold* it still. . . . V. iv. 14. 5
All the brave Knights that *hold* of Maidenhead, . . . V. iv. 29. 6
apply His mightie hands the distaffe vile to *hold* . . . V. v. 24. 4
Yet doubting least his *hold* was but unsound . . . V. v. 42. 7
Devize how to enlarge him out of *hould.* . . . V. v. 55. 3
from thy tongue thy hearts intent doth *hold.'* . . . V. vi. 10. 3
she bad them forth to *hold.* So there without . . . V. vii. 25. 9
Nor *hold* from suite of his avowed quest, . . . V. viii. 3. 2
Eftsoones they gan their wrothfull hands to *hold,* . . . V. viii. 12. 4
Fit to catch *hold* of all that he could weld, . . . V. ix. 11. 3
Warning him *hold* it fast for feare of slights: . . . V. ix. 18. 3
on his shield tooke *hold* with all her might, . . . V. xi. 27. 3
dearer then them both your faith once plighted *hold.'* . . . V. xi. 63. 9
still the way did *hold* To Faerie Court; . . . V. xii. 43. 8
'I *hold* it no indignity; . . . VI. i. 28. 2
through strong powre had now her self in *hould,* . . . VI. i. 29. 7
Of which occasion Aldine taking *hold* . . . VI. iii. 15. 1
Tho on his shield he griple *hold* did lay, . . . VI. iv. 6. 7
and laying mightie *hold* Upon his throte, . . . VI. iv. 22. 3
And quietly doth *hold* it in his hand, . . . VI. iv. 30. 3
plucke the pray oftimes out of their greedy *hould.* . . . VI. v. 15. 9
the steele-head no stedfast *hold* could fynd, . . . VI. vii. 10. 8
his well-learned speare Tooke surer *hould,* . . . VI. vii. 11. 2
They downe him *hold,* . . . VI. viii. 12. 3
now have prov'd what happinesse ye *hold* . . . VI. ix. 28. 3
that all contented rest With that they *hold:* . . . VI. ix. 29. 9
In his strong hand their rugged teats to *hold,* . . . VI. ix. 37. 8
The rest take if they would; he her to him would *hold.* . . . VI. xi. 14. 9
whilest one sought her to *hold,* . . . VI. xi. 30. 8
Which to our selves we *hold,* . . . VII. vi. 33. 8
couldst not *hold* thy selfe so hidden blest, . . . VII. vi. 46. 7
Ne Poole so small, that can his smoothnesse *holde* . . . VII. vii. 20. 6
which doe the world in being *hold;* . . . VII. vii. 27. 3
in his hand a sickle he did *holde,* . . . VII. vii. 30. 8
those lilly hands, Which *hold* my life . . . *Am.* i. 2
Shall handle you, and *hold* in loves soft bands, . . . *Am.* i. 3
all your tempests cannot *hold* me backe, . . . *Am.* xlvi. 10
catching *hold* on thine owne wicked hed, . . . *Am.* lxxxv. 10
the same doth *hold* A beauteous soule, . . . *H.B.* 136
He gave as their inheritance to *hold,* . . . *H.H.L.* 61
in her hand a scepter she doth *hold,* . . . *H.H.B.* 192
But who so may, thrise happie man him *hold,* . . . *H.H.B.* 239
Holdeth. of my rurall musicke *holdeth* scorne. . . . *S.C.* Ja. 64
Holding. Wicked for *holding* guilefully away Ulysses men, . . *Gn.* 194
holding idely The broken reliques of their former cruelty. . . . I. ii. 16. 8
Holding in hand a goodly arming sword, . . . II. vi. 47. 6
Holding a staffe in hand for mere formalitee. . . . II. xii. 48. 9
Al *holding* crosses in their hands on hye, . . . III. iii. 38. 6
Holding a lattis still before his face, . . . III. xii. 15. 7
Stood still amaz'd, *holding* his idle sweard; . . . IV. iii. 31. 7
Holding her hand upon her gentle hart; . . . IV. x. 51. 2
Still *holding* up her suppliant hands on hye, . . . V. ii. 26. 4
holding forth on hie An huge great paire of ballance . . . V. ii. 30. 2
Holding a Scepter in her royall hand, . . . V. ix. 30. 2
Crying, and *holding* up her wretched hands . . . V. xi. 44. 8
holding up his hands, with silence mercie prayd. . . . VI. vii. 25. 9
holding fast twixt both his armes extended Fayre Pastorell, . VI. xi. 19. 7
numbd with *holding* all the day An hatchet . . . VII. vii. 42. 5
Holds. Rome, that *holds* the world in sovereigntie, . . . *Gn.* 597
necessitie, That *holds* the world . . . I. ix. 42. 7
she *holds* them with her blessed hands. . . . IV. x. 35. 7
By which he stil them *holds,* . . . V. ii. 5. 9
Hands that *houlds* my life in her deaddoing might . . . *Am.*[1] i. 2
Hole. *See* **Whole.**
could make a jolly *hole* in theyr furre: . . . *S.C.* S. 165
Into the *hole,* the which the Badger swept. . . . *Ti.* 217
forth unto the darksom *hole* he went, . . . I. i. 14. 3

Hole—*Continued.*
yawning gulfe of deepe Avernus *hole.* . . . I. v. 31. 3
By that same *hole* an entraunce, darke and bace, . . . I. v. 31. 4
downe them poured through an *hole* full wide . . . II. vii. 6. 4
that darke dreadfull *hole* of Tartare steepe . . . II. xii. 6. 4
Holes. all worm-eaten and full of canker *holes.* . . . II. ix. 57. 9
hid themselves in *holes* and bushes from his vew. . . . V. ii. 53. 9
Holiday. It was upon a *holiday,* . . . *S.C.* Mar. 61
At the Kerke, when it is *holliday;* . . . *S.C.* May 310
Hey, ho, *hollidaye!* . . . *S.C.* Au. 54
Hey, ho, *holidaye!* . . . *S.C.* Au. 122
to morrow is an *holy day.* . . . III. xii. 47. *or.* 9
Holidays. To read Homelies upon *holidayes;* . . . *Hub.* 393
was the Lady of your *holy-dayes?* . . . *D.* 319
Holiness. The Patrone of true *Holinesse.* . . . I. i. Arg.
knight faire Una brings To house of *Holinesse;* . . . I. x. Arg.
Holland. drowne all *Holland* with his excrement, . . . IV. xi. 35. 3
Hollow. kindling fire within the *hollow* tree, . . . *Van.* iv. 7
The *hollow* Echo of my carefull cryes: . . . *S.C.* Au. 160
called Lowder, with a *hollow* throte, . . . *S.C.* S. 217
clambring through the *hollow* cliffes on hy . . . *Gn.* 79
On everie bush, and everie *hollow* rocke, . . . *Gn.* 235
th' *hollow* hills, from which their silver voyces . . . *T.M.* 21
With *hollow* browes and greisly countenaunce, . . . *T.M.* 185
he saide, with *hollow* sound, . . . *D.* 61
those *hollow* eyes and deadly view, . . . *D.* 304
To which him needs a guilefull *hollow* hart, . . . *Col.* 699
a *hollowe* cave Amid the thickest woods. . . . I. i. 11. 6
they gan loudly bray, With *hollow* houling, . . . I. iii. 23. 2
with his breath . . . Her *hollow* womb did secretly inspyre, . . I. vii. 9. 4
The neighbor woods arownd with *hollow* murmur ring. . . . I. viii. 11. 9
an *hollow,* dreary, murmuring voyce . . . I. viii. 38. 1
His sad dull eies, deepe sunck in *hollow* pits, . . . I. viii. 41. 1
staring wyde With stony eyes and hartlesse *hollow* hew, . . . I. ix. 24. 3
His dwelling has, low in an *hollow* cave, . . . I. ix. 33. 2
his *hollow* eyne Lookt deadly dull, . . . I. ix. 35. 6
sayles, in which the *hollow* wynd Is gathered full, . . . I. xi. 10. 2
as in a *hollow* glade, Those glaring lampes were sett . . . I. xi. 14. 8
deepe emperst his darksom *hollow* maw, . . . I. xi. 53. 8
remaynd Some lingring life within his *hollow* brest, . . . I. xii. 10. 4
downe them poured . . . Into the *hollow* earth, . . . II. vii. 6. 5
in the *hollow* earth have their eternall brood. . . . II. vii. 8. 9
deep descended through the *hollow* grownd, . . . II. vii. 20. 8
Staring with *hollow* eies, and stiffe upstanding heares. . . . II. ix. 13. 9
Bent *hollow* beetle browes, . . . II. ix. 52. 6
fire, the which in *hollow* cave Hath long bene underkept . . . II. xi. 32. 1
mightily doth drive The *hollow* vessell . . . II. xii. 5. 6
dreadfull noise and *hollow* rombling rore . . . II. xii. 25. 3
it round and *hollow* shaped was, . . . III. ii. 19. 8
Sorrow is heaped in thy *hollow* chest, . . . III. ii. 32. 7
Certein sad words with *hollow* voice and bace, . . . III. ii. 50. 5
It is an hideous *hollow* cave . . . III. iii. 8. 3
housed is within her *hollow* brest, . . . III. iii. 18. 7
Out of their *hollow* bosome forth to throw . . . III. iv. 22. 4
her bowre Is built of *hollow* billowes heaped hye, . . . III. iv. 43. 2
There in a gloomy *hollow* glen . . . III. vii. 6. 1
with fell looke and *hollow* deadly gaze . . . III. vii. 7. 6
trampling feete upon the *hollow* lay . . . III. viii. 15. 4
Therein is eaten out an *hollow* cave, . . . III. viii. 37. 5
in th' earthes *hollow* caves hath long ben hid . . . III. ix. 15. 3
fast closed in some *hollow* greave, . . . III. x. 42. 3
under it hidde hate and *hollow* guyle. . . . IV. ii. 29. 5
With *hollow* eyes and rawbone cheekes forspent, . . . IV. v. 34. 4
His cheeke-bones raw, and eie-pits *hollow* grew, . . . IV. xii. 20. 3
The cry whereof entring the *hollow* cave . . . V. ix. 10. 1
with *hollow* eyes deepe pent, . . . V. ix. 10. 5
his shield, . . . like to an *hollow* beare; . . . VI. ii. 48. 2
Farre in the forrest, by a *hollow* glade . . . VI. iv. 13. 5
many feete fast thumping th' *hollow* ground, . . . VI. x. 10. 4
their way was made Through *hollow* caves, . . . VI. x. 42. 2
with *hollow* throates, The Choristers . . . sing, . . . *Epith.* 220
Hollowness. Nought is there under heav'ns wide *hollownesse,* . I. iii. 1. 1
Holly-bush. Nor *holly-bush,* nor brere, . . . *S.C.* Jun. 20
Holm. the blacke *Holme* that loves the watrie vale; . . . *Gn.* 215
The carver *Holme;* . . . I. i. 9. 9
Holpen. *See* **Helped.**
by his foolish feare Was *holpen* up, . . . VI. viii. 25. 9
Holy. *See* **Holiday.**
The *holy* Citie of the Lorde, from hye . . . *Rev.* iv. 3
to wrong *holy* eld did forbeare; . . . *S.C.* F. 206
Such merimake *holy* Saints doth queme, . . . *S.C.* May 15
Thus *holy* hylles to blame, . . . *S.C.* Jul. 38
as *holy* fathers sayne, . . . *S.C.* Jul. 57
Here han the *holy* Faunes recourse, . . . *S.C.* Jul. 77
The hylls where dwelled *holy* saints . . . *S.C.* Jul. 113
'It fell upon a *holy* (*holly) eve, . . . *S.C.* Au. 53
When *holy* fathers wont to shrieve; . . . *S.C.* Au. 55
So learnd I love on a *holye* (*hollye) eve, . . . *S.C.* Au. 121
thou *holie* Pales, . . . *Gn.* 28
Their service and their *holie* things to say, . . . *Hub.* 450
speach Against Gods *holie* Ministers . . . *Hub.* 840
treadeth under foote hir *holie* things, . . . *T.M.* 569
made The *holie* brethren falslie to have praid. . . . *Ti.* 497
O *holy* virgin! chiefe of nyne, . . . I. Pr. 2. 1
With *holy* father sits not with such thinges to mell. . . . I. i. 30. 9
a litle wyde There was an *holy* chappell edifyde, . . . I. i. 34. 5
wont to say His *holy* thinges each morne and eventyde: . . . I. i. 34. 7
The *holy* Saints of their rich vestiments He did disrobe, . . I. iii. 17. 5
none the *holy* things in safety kept, . . . I. iii. 17. 8
Arayd in habit blacke, . . . Like to an *holy* Monck, . . . I. iv. 18. 9

Holy—*Continued.*
The sacred thinges, and *holy* heastes foretaught. . . . I. vii. 18. 7
His reverend heares and *holy* gravitee . . . I. viii. 32. 1
holy Martyres often doen to dye With cruell malice . . . I. viii. 36. 4
unto an *holy* Hospitall . . . I. x. 36. 1
frame In *holy* righteousnesse, without rebuke or blame. . . . I. x. 45. 9
Wherein an aged *holy* man did lie, . . . I. x. 46. 5
'Most trew,' then said the *holy* aged man; . . . I. x. 59. 1
'O *holy* Sire!' (quoth he) . . . I. x. 67. 1
thy daughter linck, in *holy* band Of wedlocke, . . . I. xii. 26. 6
His owne two hands the *holy* knotts did knitt, . . . I. xii. 37. 1
brought with him the *holy* grayle, . . . II. x. 53. 8
from the *holy* herse Her love-sicke hart . . . did steale; . . . III. ii. 48. 6
holy Church with faithlesse handes deface, . . . III. iii. 34. 2
Distaines the pillours and the *holy* grownd, . . . III. iv. 17. 7
'The second was an *holy* Nunne to chose, . . . III. vii. 58. 6
Altars defyld, and *holy* things defast; . . . IV. i. 21. 5
Weening therein some *holy* Hermit lay, . . . IV. vii. 42. 7
from the Altar all about did blow The *holy* fire, . . . V. vii. 14. 5
full busily About their *holy* things . . . V. vii. 17. 8
by the *holy* vow which me doth bind, . . . V. vii. 19. 7
High Gods beheast, and powre of *holy* lawes; . . . V. ix. 44. 6
Was wont his howres and *holy* things to bed; . . . VI. v. 35. 7
His bloudy vessels wash, and *holy* fire prepare. . . . VI. viii. 39. 9
Regarding nought religion, nor their *holy* heast. . . . VI. xii. 24. 9
fairest Hill That was in all this *holy* Islands hights) . . . VII. vi. 37. 7
This *holy* season, fit to fast and pray, . . . *Am.* xxii. 1
on so *holy* day, . . . *Am.* xxii. 3
When so ye come into those *holy* places, . . . *Epith.* 213
Hearing the *holy* priest that to her speakes, . . . *Epith.* 224
This day for ever to me *holy* is. . . . *Epith.* 249
This day is *holy;* . . . *Epith.* 263
Most wise, most *holy,* most almightie Spright! . . . *H.H.L.* 39
Such mercy he by his most *holy* reede . . . *H.H.L.* 211
Holy water. *See* **Holy, Water.**
often halowed with *holy-water* dewe: . . . *S.C.* F. 210
With *holy water* they doen hem all drench. . . . *S.C.* S. 89
that *holy water* dew Wherein he fell, . . . I. xi. 36. 2
holy water thereon sprinckled wide; . . . I. xii. 37. 5
Holy-water sprinkle. did hold An *holy-water-sprinckle,* . . . III. xii. 13. 6
Holy Writ. renownd For tongues confusion in *Holie Writ,* . . . *Ti.* 510
Homage. with *homage* due Themselves to humble . . . *Hub.* 1082
running Heralds humble *homage* made, . . . I. v. 15. 7
'To her I *homage* and my service owe, . . . II. ii. 42. 1
kisse my stirrup; that thy *homage* bee.' . . . II. iii. 8. 6
Such *homage* till that instant never learned hee. . . . II. v. 11. 9
to her *homage* made with humble grace: . . . II. ix. 36. 3
call Their sondry kings to do their *homage* severall. . . . III. iii. 32. 9
humble *homage* did unto him make, . . . IV. vii. 44. 8
Those two strange knights such *homage* to her make, . . . V. ix. 35. 6
to bow their bloosming heads full lowe For *homage* unto her, VII. vii. 8. 9
Home. *home* him hasted with furious heate, . . . *S.C.* F. 193
Hye thee *home,* shepheard, . . . *S.C.* F. 246
For als at *home* I have a syre, . . . *S.C.* Mar. 40
home they hasten the postes to dight, . . . *S.C.* May 11
To fetchen *home* May with their musicall: . . . *S.C.* May 28
home they bringen in a royall throne, . . . *S.C.* May 29
Home when the doubtfull Damme had her hyde, . . . *S.C.* May 294
I hold it best for us *home* to hye. . . . *S.C.* May 317
ryse, ye blessed Flocks, and *home* apace, . . . *S.C.* Jun. 118
till safe and sound 'She *home* returne, . . . *S.C.* Au. 181
shepheards, til you be at *home;* . . . *S.C.* Au. 197
Driven for neede to come *home* agayne. . . . *S.C.* S. 67
she would call him often *heame,* (**heme*) . . . *S.C.* N. 98
To cut the ships from turning *home* againe To Argos; . . . *Gn.* 522
'Th' Argolicke power returning *home* againe, . . . *Gn.* 561
to wexe olde at *home* in idlenesse Is disadventrous, . . . *Hub.* 99
home him leading, lent to him the charge . . . *Hub.* 299
Who ever leaves sweete *home,* . . . *Hub.* 909
leave the sweetnes of contented *home,* . . . *Hub.* 947
Departed to his *home* in dreadfull awe, . . . *Hub.* 1109
My thought returned greeved *home* againe, . . . *Ti.* 478
Abandon quiet *home* to seeke for it, . . . *Col.* 686
Doth to his *home* entreate . . . I. i. Arg.
with that godly father to his *home* they went. . . . I. i. 33. 9
home she came, whereas her mother blynd Sate . . . I. iii. 12. 3
marcheth *home,* and by her takes the knight, . . . I. v. 16. 6
Home is he brought, and layd in sumptuous bed, . . . I. v. 17. 1
home he suffred her for to retyre, . . . I. vi. 23. 5
To come unto his wished *home* in haste, . . . I. ix. 39. 2
home ye may report thrise happy newes; . . . II. i. 33. 8
Abroad in armes, at *home* in studious kynd, . . . II. iii. 40. 8
'I *home* retourning, fraught with fowle despight, . . . II. iv. 29. 1
wouldest be reckoned A straunger in thy *home,* . . . II. vi. 9. 6
life ere long shall to her *home* retire, . . . II. viii. 7. 8
he it knew at *home* before he hard Tydings thereof, . . . III. ii. 21. 4
Returned *home,* the royall Infant fell . . . III. ii. 49. 1
With lighter hearts unto their *home* retird; . . . III. iii. 51. 4
He, comming *home* at undertime, . . . III. vii. 13. 1
with them *home* her ledd, . . . III. x. 36. 6
home he marcht emongst the horned heard, . . . III. x. 47. 8
home returne, where all should be renewd . . . III. x. 51. 3
comming *home,* in warlike fresh aray Them found . . . IV. ii. 53. 3
flie Unto her native *home* from mortall miserie. . . . IV. iii. 30. 9
Unto her Coch remounting, *home* did ride, . . . IV. iii. 51. 8
Whom when the watch . . . Saw comming *home,* . . . IV. ix. 5. 7
seem'd unlike unto his earthly *home:* . . . IV. xii. 4. 7
So *home* with her she streight the virgin lad, . . . IV. xii. 33. 8
sent them *home* to tell a piteous tale . . . V. iv. 24. 8
yet so fast they could not *home* retrate, . . . V. vii. 35. 1

Home—*Continued.*
Come *home* to her in piteous wretchednesse, . . . V. vii. 39. 5
brought the pillage *home,* whence none could get it out. . . . V. ix. 4. 9
Calidore brings Priscilla *home;* . . . VI. iii. Arg.
brought *home* upon a beare . . . VI. iii. 4. 2
Him oft desired *home* with her to wend, . . . VI. iv. 39. 6
brought *home* and noursed well As his owne chyld; . . . VI. ix. 14. 7
To helpe faire Pastorella *home* to drive Her fleecie flocke; . . . VI. ix. 15. 8
began Him to invite unto his simple *home;* . . . VI. ix. 16. 4
home with him did go. . . . VI. ix. 16. 9
home came the fayrest Pastorell, . . . VI. ix. 17. 5
leaving *home,* to roiall court I sought, . . . VI. ix. 24. 6
ten yeares my selfe excluded From native *home,* . . . VI. ix. 25. 4
To call the soule backe to her *home* againe; . . . VI. xi. 22. 4
So *home* unto his honest wife it bore, . . . VI. xii. 9. 8
bring *home* the bride againe; . . . *Epith.* 242
Bring *home* the triumph of our victory: . . . *Epith.* 243
Bring *home* with you the glory of her gaine . . . *Epith.* 244
Hast thee, O fayrest Planet, to thy *home,* . . . *Epith.* 282
Home-bred. if of . . . *homebredd* evil ye desire to heare, . . . I. i. 31. 2
Homely. The *homely* shepheard, nor the ruder clowne; . . . *Pet.* iv. 4
holden scorne of *homely* shepheards quill: . . . *S.C.* Jun. 68
Who taught me *homely,* as I can, to make; . . . *S.C.* Jun. 82
built of stickes and reedes In *homely* wize, . . . III. vii. 6. 3
Nor s'deignfull of so *homely* fashion, . . . III. vii. 10. 6
Enur'd to hardnesse and to *homely* fare, . . . IV. viii. 27. 6
shall see Stamford, though now *homely* hid, . . . IV. xi. 35. 4
in his *homely* wize began to assay T'amend what was amisse, . . . VI. v. 10. 8
Yet was their fare but *homely,* . . . VI. v. 39. 1
Ere long to him a *homely* groome there came, . . . VI. vi. 20. 1
Such *homely* what as serves the simple clowne, . . . VI. ix. 7. 4
There he was welcom'd . . . *homely* well; . . . VI. ix. 17. 2
this *homely* verse, of many meanest, . . . VI. xii. 41. 1
Home-made. Yclad in *home-made* greene that her owne hands had dyde. . . . VI. ix. 7. 9
Homer. To heare the warlike feates which *Homere* spake . . . III. iv. 2. 4
Homes. Them reconcyld againe, and to their *homes* did drive. . . IV. ii. 2. 9
warn'd the shepheards to their *homes* to hast . . . VI. ix. 13. 3
Homeward. Arose, and *homeward* drove his sonned sheepe, . . . *S.C.* Ja. 77
time to hast us *homeward.* . . . *S.C.* Mar. 117
let us *homeward,* for night draweth on, . . . *S.C.* Ap. 160
now is time, I gesse, *homeward* to goe: . . . *S.C.* Jun. 117
hye we *homeward* fast. . . . *S.C.* N. 208
Gathered together, and them *homeward* bare: . . . VI. ix. 15. 5
both together chose *Homeward* to march, . . . IV. iii. 51. 5
every one gan *homeward* to resort: . . . IV. xii. 18. 2
backe againe they *homeward* turnd their feete; . . . V. iv. 51. 7
Gathered together, and them *homeward* bare: . . . VI. ix. 15. 5
So oft as *homeward* I from her depart, . . . *Am.* lii. 1
Homilies. To read *Homelies* upon holidayes; . . . *Hub.* 393
Honest. Pales, To whome the *honest* care of husbandrie . . . *Gn.* 29
honest mirth, that seem'd her well: . . . *Hub.* 35
A good yeoman he was of *honest* place, . . . *Hub.* 230
The *honest* man, that heard him thus complaine, . . . *Hub.* 259
we are as *honest* as we seeme, . . . *Hub.* 376
How manie *honest* men see ye arize . . . *Hub.* 419
Being some *honest* Curate, . . . *Hub.* 429
Were it by *honest* wayes, or otherwise, . . . *Hub.* 848
Nor *honest* mynd might there be found at all. . . . *Col.* 734
Her *honest* merth and pleasaunce to partake; . . . II. vi. 21. 6
treading under foote her *honest* name: . . . III. i. 50. 4
ply himselfe to any *honest* trade, . . . III. vii. 12. 6
his faire wife, whom *honest* long he kept uneath. . . . III. x. 2. 9
Ne ever Lady of so *honest* name, . . . VI. vi. 12. 8
There he was welcom'd of that *honest* syre . . . VI. ix. 17. 1
So home unto his *honest* wife it bore, . . . VI. xii. 9. 8
Honesty. sure his *honestie* Got him small gaines, . . . *Hub.* 849
single Truth and simple *Honestie* . . . *Col.* 727
for report of spotlesse *honestie,* . . . *Col.* 753
loved simple truth and stedfast *honesty.* . . . VI. i. 3. 9
Honey. Of *Hony* and of Gaule in love . . . *S.C.*Mar.Emb.3
The *Honye* is much, but the Gaule is more. . . . *S.C.*Mar.Emb.4
Butter enough, *honye,* milke, and whay, . . . *S.C.* May 115
Large streames of *honnie* and sweete Nectar flowe, . . . *T.M.* 218
Sweet without sowre, and *honny* without gall: . . . *As.* 26
Her words were like a streame of *honny* fleeting, . . . *Col.* 596
With fowle words tempring faire, soure gall with *hony* sweet. . I. vii. 3. 9
His subtile tong like dropping *honny* mealt'h Into the heart, . I. ix. 31. 5
Sweete wordes like dropping *honny* she did shed; . . . II. iii. 24. 7
After their hives with *honny* do abound. . . . II. ix. 51. 5
love with gall and *hony* doth abound; . . . IV. x. 1. 2
For every dram of *hony* therein found . . . IV. x. 1. 4
In bitter hyve to grope for *honny:* . . . *Epig.* i. 4
Honey-bee. I was wont to seeke the *honey Bee,* . . . *S.C.* D. 67
Honeycomb. amongst the hives to reare An *hony-combe,* . . . III. x. 53. 6
Honey-crock. Like foolish flies about an *hony-crocke;* . . . V. ii. 33. 3
Honey-dew. sweet wordes, dropping like *honny dew;* . . . II. v. 33. 4
Did raine into her lap an *hony dew;* . . . III. xi. 31. 4
Honey-laden. Th' other in hers an *hony-laden* Bee. . . . III. xii. 18. 8
Honey-lady. *Th' other in hers an *hony-lady* Bee; . . . III. xii. 18. 8
Hong. *See* **Hanged, Hung.**
His carelesse locks . . . *Hong* long adowne, . . . *D.* 44
Two iron coffers *hong* on either side, . . . I. iv. 27. 3
his brothers shield, which *hong* thereby: . . . I. v. 10. 3
then downe his taile he *hong,* . . . I. v. 34. 7
There thristy Tantalus *hong* by the chin; . . . I. v. 35. 5
He snatcht the vele that *hong* her face before: . . . I. vi. 4. 7
Thereby his mortall blade full comely *hong* In yvory sheath, I. vii. 30. 6
an horne . . . Which *hong* adowne his side . . . I. viii. 3. 6
Her dried dugs, lyke bladders lacking wind, *Hong* downe, . . I. viii. 47. 7

Hong—*Continued.*
Disordred *hong* about his shoulders round, . . . I. ix. 35. 5
with it *hong* him selfe, unbid, unblest. . . . I. ix. 54. 5
A multitude of babes about her *hong*, . . . I. x. 31. 1
high emongst all knights hast *hong* thy shield, . . . I. x. 60. 6
The paw . . . *hong* still on the shield, . . . I. xi. 43. 9
His credit now in doubtfull ballaunce *hong:* . . . II. i. 3. 8
Grew all afore, and loosely *hong* unrold; . . . II. iv. 4. 6
the hoare lockes that *hong* before her eyes, . . . II. iv. 12. 3
hong their conquerd armes . . . On gallow trees, . . . II. v. 26. 8
where hath he *hong* up his mortall blade, . . . II. v. 35. 7
the ragged breaches *hong* Embost with massy gold . . . II. vii. 28. 3
over it a fayre Portcullis *hong*, . . . II. ix. 24. 6
weary of that wretched life her selfe she *hong*. . . . II. x. 32. 9
right over him she *hong* . . . II. xii. 73. 1
His warlike Armes, . . . were *hong* upon a tree; . . . II. xii. 80. 2
Both speare she tooke and shield which *hong* by it; . . . III. iii. 60. 8
having *hong* upon a bough on high Her bow . . . III. vi. 18. 1
Now loose about her shoulders *hong* undight, . . . III. vi. 18. 8
Upon his lips *hong* faire Dame Hellenore . . . III. ix. 52. 2
hong adowne his head as he did dreame; . . . III. xi. 41. 7
walles were *hong* With warlike spoiles . . . III. xi. 52. 1
on high there *hong* The golden Apple, . . . IV. i. 22. 4
Whilst thus the case in doubtfull ballance *hong*, . . . IV. iii. 37. 1
still upon him *hong*. . . . V. ii. 14. 9
Hong still upon his melting mouth attent; . . . VI. ix. 26. 2

Honor. the mettall that we *honour* most. . . . *Bel.*[1] iii. 6
all worldes hap [and *honour*] . . . *Bel.*[1] viii. 7
The *honour* of these noble boughs . . . *Bel.* v. 11
the mettall, which we most do *honour;* . . . *Bel.*[2] iii. 6
Gods and men my *honour* up did raise? . . . *Bel.*[2] x. 8
The *honour* yet in ashes doo maintaine; . . . *Ro.* vii. 4
Should not her name and endles *honour* keep. . . . *Ro.* viii. 14
that brave *honour* of the Latine name, . . . *Ro.* xxii. 1
such this Cities *honour* was of yore, . . . *Ro.* xxviii. 13
Th' olde *honour* of the people gowned long. . . . *Ro.* xxxii. 14
Live, happie spirits, th' *honour* of your name, . . . *Ro.* Env. 13
when his *honor* has thee redde, . . . *To his Booke* 11
His *honor* decayed, his braunches sere. . . . *S.C.* F. 114
That bene the *honor* of your Coronall: . . . *S.C.* F. 178
O! what an *honor* is it, . . . *S.C.* O. 21
sonne-bright *honour* pend in shamefull coupe. . . . *S.C.* O. 72
honor Pan with hymnes of higher vaine. . . . *S.C.* N. 8
honor now of highest gods she is, . . . *S.C.* N. 197
loftie type of *honour*, . . . is downe in dust . . . *Gn.* 557
Equall in *honour* to the former crue, . . . *Gn.* 594
Regard of *honour* harbours more than ought, . . . *Hub.* 718
all his minde on *honour* fixed is, . . . *Hub.* 771
Desire of *honor* or brave thought of armes . . . *Hub.* 825
into whose brest Never crept thought of *honor,* . . . *Hub.* 978
such as hate the *honour* of our name, . . . *T.M.* 63
Didst to the type of *honour* earst advaunce: . . . *T.M.* 70
Hunt after *honour* and advauncement vaine, . . . *Ti.* 51
Whom England high in count of *honour* held, . . . *Ti.* 185
That him to highest *honour* shall advaunce. . . . *Ti.* 271
The sacred brood of learning and all *honour;* . . . *Ti.* 279
ye, faire Ladie, th' *honour* of your daies, . . . *Ti.* 680
If ought against thine *honour* I have tolde; . . . *Mui.* 103
gathered more store Of the fields *honour* . . . *Mui.* 123
Will *honour* heaven, or heavenlie powers adore, . . . *D.* 198
Her he did love, her he alone did *honor,* . . . *As.* 59
serve and *honour* her with faithfull mind. . . . *Col.* 255
There learned arts do florish in great *honor,* . . . *Col.* 320
they cannot her *honour* worthylie?' . . . *Col.* 375
favour thee, and *honour* Cynthia: . . . *Col.* 458
The *honor* of the noble familie: . . . *Col.* 537
with chaste heart to *honor* him alway: . . . *Col.* 888
Yet that I may her *honour* paravant, . . . *Col.* 941
All goodly bountie and true *honour* sits. . . . *Ded. Son.* v. 12
In which trew *honor* yee may fashioned see, . . . *Ded. Son.* x. 10
To like desire of *honor* may ye raise, . . . *Ded. Son.* x. 11
For *honor* of your name and high descent. . . . *Ded. Son.* x. 14
That all posteritie thy *honor* may reherse. . . . *Ded. Son.* xi. 14
Moste noble Lord, the *honor* of this age, . . . *Ded. Son.* xiv. 6
Come, see where your false Lady doth her *honor* staine.' . . . I. ii. 4. 9
turnament With greatest *honour* he atchieven might: . . . I. v. 1. 8
all for praise and *honour* he did fight. . . . I. v. 7. 6
one that with his prowesse may Defend thine *honour,* . . . I. ix. 16. 8
even dead we *honour* should. . . . I. x. 42. 8
more mindfull of his *honour* deare . . . I. xi. 39. 1
Thy life and *honor* late adventurest, . . . I. xii. 29. 8
Of chastity and *honour* virginall: . . . II. i. 10. 8
that false Traytour did my *honour* reave?' . . . II. i. 17. 5
with reprochfull shame mine *honour* shent, . . . II. i. 27. 4
he *honour* still away did beare, . . . II. i. 35. 3
Ne thought of *honour* ever did assay His baser brest, . . . II. iii. 4. 3
honour . . . Doth beare the fayrest flowre . . . II. iii. 10. 8
mote him *honour* win to wreak so foule despight. . . . II. iii. 13. 9
All good and *honour* might therein be red, . . . II. iii. 24. 5
honour in their festivall resort; . . . II. iii. 28. 4
all the like, which *honor* have pursewd . . . II. iii. 37. 7
Who seekes with painfull toile shall *honor* soonest fynd: . . . II. iii. 40. 9
to rayse our house to *honour* did begin.' . . . II. iv. 36. 9
So hast thou oft with guile thine *honor* blent; . . . II. v. 5. 7
in *honour* of his dearest Dame. . . . II. v. 26. 9
Honour, estate, and all this worldes good, . . . II. vii. 8. 6
Honour and dignitie from her alone Derived are, . . . II. vii. 48. 7
Thus for to blott the *honor* of the dead, . . . II. viii. 13. 3
Ne blame your *honor* with so shamefull vaunt . . . II. viii. 16. 3
ought that els your *honour* might maintaine; . . . II. viii. 19. 7

Honor—*Continued.*
Honour is least where oddes appeareth most. . . . II. viii. 26. 5
His *honour* staines with rancour and despight, . . . II. viii. 29. 8
dye with *honour* and desert of fame; . . . II. viii. 44. 5
by well doing sought to *honour* to aspyre. . . . II. ix. 39. 9
Ne for them ne for *honour* cared hee, . . . II. xii. 80. 5
they *honour* ever wonne, . . . III. i. 3. 7
To loose long gotten *honour* with one evill hond. . . . III. i. 10. 9
To let not others *honour* be defaste . . . III. i. 12. 4
Then *honour* was the meed of victory, . . . III. i. 13. 6
To crowne his golden lockes with *honour* dew; . . . III. i. 35. 5
meet respect of *honor* putt to flight: . . . III. i. 48. 8
in each gentle hart desire of *honor* breeds. . . . III. i. 49. 9
Onely for *honour* and for high regard, . . . III. ii. 7. 4
both I wish welfare, And *honour* both; . . . III. ii. 10. 9
So is his soveraine *honour* raisde to hevens hight.' . . . III. ii. 14. 9
with great *honour* many batteills try; . . . III. iii. 31. 4
Proud of his dying *honor* and deare bandes, . . . III. iv. 17. 3
Now lyest thou of life and *honor* refte; . . . III. iv. 36. 6
to all high desert and *honour* doth aspire. . . . III. v. 1. 9
honour of trew Ladies, . . . III. v. 10. 6
honor which thou didst atchive. . . . III. v. 26. 9
To blott her *honour,* and her heavenly light. . . . III. v. 45. 5
The girlond of her *honour* did adorne: . . . III. v. 51. 3
beareth fruit of *honour* and all chast desyre. . . . III. v. 52. 9
used her so hard To reave her *honor,* . . . III. viii. 14. 9
To save her *honor* from that villaine vilde, . . . III. viii. 27. 4
shame of all that doe for *honor* strive, . . . III. x. 27. 4
proude of that new *honour* which they redd, . . . III. x. 44. 7
Of her dew *honour* was despoyled quight; . . . III. xii. 20. 4
it of *honor* and all vertue is The roote, . . . IV. Pr. 2. 6
Lest she with blame her *honor* should attaint, . . . IV. i. 5. 5
her *honor,* dearer then her life, . . . IV. i. 6. 6
attended duly on her, . . . and did to her all *honor*. . . . IV. i. 8. 9
noble knights Which hunt for *honor,* . . . IV. i. 19. 7
So hast thou to thy selfe false *honour* often wonne.' . . . IV. i. 44. 9
Bidding them fight for *honour* of their love, . . . IV. ii. 19. 6
save her *honour* with your ventrous paines: . . . IV. ii. 27. 8
turne both him and her to *honour,* . . . IV. ii. 37. 9
Assembled for to get the *honour* of that game. . . . IV. iv. 13. 9
purchase *honour* in his friends behalve, . . . IV. iv. 27. 3
Yet evermore his *honour* he recured, . . . IV. iv. 37. 8
eke of *honour* she did him forestall. . . . IV. v. 9. 3
Fro me the *honour* of that game did reare; . . . IV. vi. 6. 7
Thine *honor* sav'd, though into thraldome throwne?' . . . IV. vii. 19. 5
Wherein the *honor* both of Armes ye shame, . . . IV. ix. 37. 4
To winne me *honour* by some noble gest, . . . IV. x. 4. 4
In *honour* of the spousalls . . . IV. xi. 8. 3
He would be there, and *honor* to her spousall ad. . . . V. ii. 3. 9
whose The *honour* of the prize should be adjudg'd . . . V. iii. 13. 9
this dayes *honour* sav'd to Marinell: . . . V. iii. 21. 2
Adorn'd with *honor* and all comely grace: . . . V. iii. 23. 2
make paragone And triall, whether should the *honor* get. . . . V. iii. 24. 4
after fame and *honour* for to hunt, . . . V. iv. 29. 3
such blot his *honour* blemish should. . . . V. vi. 2. 9
all his other *honour* overthrew. . . . V. vi. 12. 4
How to revenge that blot of *honour* blent, . . . V. vi. 13. 2
so great *honour* with so fowle reproch had blent. . . . V. vi. 18. 9
much lesse *honour* by that warlike kinde Of life; . . . V. vi. 32. 5
his *honor,* which she tendred chiefe, . . . V. vii. 44. 4
the brave Prince for *honour* and for right, . . . did fight: . . . V. viii. 30. 6
all her other *honour* did obscure, . . . V. ix. 38. 6
What heavenly Muse shall thy great *honour* rayse . . . V. x. 3. 3
yeelding the last *honour* to her wretched corse. . . . V. x. 4. 9
the *honour* that is dew To God, . . . V. x. 27. 8
Is ought on earth so pretious or deare As prayse and *honour?* . . . V. xi. 62. 7
honour with indignitie debased! . . . V. xi. 63. 7
Saying that he had . . . his *honour* blent, . . . V. xii. 40. 4
it to ripenesse grew, and forth to *honour* burst. . . . VI. Pr. 3. 9
And flame forth *honour* in thy noble brest; . . . VI. ii. 37. 4
the badge of *honour* and of fame, . . . VI. iii. 35. 3
ne was there shepheards swayne, But her did *honour;* . . . VI. ix. 10. 2
In which all trees of *honour* stately stood, . . . VI. x. 6. 4
differing in *honour* and degree: . . . VI. x. 21. 5
Have for more *honour* brought her to this place, . . . VI. x. 26. 8
to *honour* her the more, . . . VII. vii. 11. 1
Such pride is praise; such portlinesse is *honor;* . . . *Am.* v. 9
Such life should be the *honor* of your light, . . . *Am.* vii. 13
all, which did Loves *honor* rayse, . . . *Am.* xix. 9
I *honor* and admire the Makers art. . . . *Am.* xxiv. 4
Mote have your life in *honour* long maintayned. . . . *Am.* xxxvi. 12
Adorn'd with *honour,* love, and chastity! . . . *Am.* lxix. 8
That *honour* and large richesse to me lent: . . . *Am.* lxxiv. 8
If ever I did *honour* thee aright, . . . *Epith.* 122
Regard of *honour,* and mild modesty; . . . *Epith.* 193
For to receyve this Saynt with *honour* dew, . . . *Epith.* 208
Made in the *honor* of your Soveraigne king. . . . *H.L.* 42
Why then do I this *honor* unto thee, . . . *H.L.* 148
in *honour* of thy Mother deare, . . . *H.B.* 9
Singing this Hymne in *honour* of thy name, . . . *H.B.* 272
Whom he therefore with equall *honour* crownd. . . . *H.H.L.* 35
pompe to which proud minds aspyre By name of *honor,* . . . *H.H.B.* 278
Great store of Flowers, the *honour* of the field, . . . *Proth.* 74
Faire branch of *Honor,* . . . *Proth.* 150

Honorable. beside the *honourable* band Of great Heroes . . . *Gn.* 479
He stands on tearmes of *honourable* minde, . . . *Hub.* 721
the *honorable* race Of mightie Peeres . . . *T.M.* 79
Well worthie of so *honourable* place, . . . *Col.* 502
best of all that *honourable* crew, . . . *Col.* 517
Adorned with all *honourable* parts: . . . *Col.* 529

Hope—*Continued.*
the rare *hope* which in his yeares appear'd, ... VI. ii. 34. 3
In *hope* he sure would prove a doughtie knight: . . . . . . VI. ii. 36. 8
Is this the *hope* that to my hoary heare Thou brings? . . . . VI. iii. 4. 7
'Such is the weakenesse of all mortall *hope*, ... VI. iii. 5. 7
In *hope* there for his love some succour to provyde. . . . . VI. iii. 29. 9
Twixt darkenesse dread and *hope* of living light, ... VI. iii. 45. 4
implore To send her succour, being of all *hope* forlore. . . . VI. iv. 10. 9
no *hope* of his retourne She saw now left, ... VI. v. 7. 1
In vaine of me ye *hope* for remedie, ... VI. vi. 6. 8
'What *hope* of helpe doth then for us remaine, ... VI. vi. 13. 6
Ne powre had to withstand, ne *hope* of any ayd. . . . . . VI. vii. 48. 9
To *hope* for to release or mollify, ... VI. viii. 3. 7
gave his foe good *hope* of victory: . . . . VI. viii. 9. 6
better tearmes . . . Which gave him *hope*, ... VI. xi. 7. 3
In *hope* there newes to learne, ... VI. xi. 36. 9
Hope to escape his venemous despite, ... VI. xii. 41. 2
fild her wombe with fruitfull *hope* of nourishment. . . . . VII. vii. 32. 9
New yeare, . . . Doth seeme to promise *hope* . . . . . . *Am.* iv. 2
Twixt feare and *hope* depending doubtfully! . . . . *Am.* xxv. 4
Gives me great *hope* of your relenting mynd: . . . . *Am.* xxviii. 2
Yet *hope* I well . . . . *Am.* xxxiv. 9
Without *hope* of aswagement or release? . . . . *Am.* xxxvi. 4
So doe I *hope* her stubborne hart to bend, ... *Am.* li. 11
the happy shore, In which I *hope* . . . to arryve: . . . . . *Am.* lxiii. 6
when I *hope* to see theyr trew object, ... *Am.* lxxviii. 11
So let us rest, sweet love, in *hope* of this, ... *Epith.* 424
His care, his joy, his *hope*, is all on this, ... *H.L.* 206
that ever I might *hope*, ... *H.L.* 294
verse With equall words can *hope* it to reherse. . . . . . *H.H.L.* 42
Fell from the *hope* of promist heavenly place, ... *H.H.L.* 122
How then can mortall tongue *hope* to expresse . . . . . . *H.H.B.* 104
Or *hope* t' expresse her least perfection part, ... *H.H.B.* 227

Hoped. Might well have *hop'd* to have obtained it. . . . . *Ro.* xxxii. 8
all my *hoped* gaine is turnd to scathe: . . . . *S.C.* D. 100
still I *hoped* to be up advaunced, ... *Hub.* 63
there to hunt after the *hoped* pray, ... *Hub.* 503
Lyes in ambushment of his *hoped* pray, ... *Mui.* 404
For *hoped* love to winne me certaine hate? . . . . I. i. 51. 5
ere my *hoped* day of spousall shone, ... I. ii. 23. 6
To muse on meanes of *hoped* victory. . . . . I. iv. 44. 5
hop'd to reape the crop of all my care, ... I. iv. 47. 2
She fownd not in that perilous hous . . . Her *hoped* pray, . . I. vii. 2. 4
'Well *hoped* I, and faire beginnings had, ... I. vii. 49. 1
he *hoped* faire To call backe life . . . . II. i. 43. 6
Well *hoped* hee, ere long that hardy guest, ... II. vii. 27. 1
Far from the *hoped* haven of reliefe, ... III. iv. 8. 3
Well *hoped* shee the beast engor'd had beene, ... III. v. 28. 7
hayle The greedy villein from his *hoped* pray, ... III. viii. 31. 6
well they *hoped* to have got great good, ... V. ii. 51. 6
'Well *hop't* he then, when this was propheside, ... VI. iv. 33. 1
Long time had lov'd, and *hop'd* her love to gaine, ... VI. ix. 38. 2

Hopeful. Till which we cease our *hopefull* hap to sing; . . . *Epith.* 388

Hopeless. In gage for his gay Masters *hopelesse* dett: . . . . *Hub.* 865
shortly brought to *hopelesse* wretchednesse. . . . . *Hub.* 934
Who haplesse, and eke *hopelesse*, . . . Did to him pace . . . . I. vii. 11. 4
hopelesse, hartlesse, gan the cunning thiefe Perswade us dye, . I. ix. 29. 7
From whence descend all *hopelesse* remedies: . . . . III. v. 34. 5
hopelesse ever to attaine My Ladies love . . . . III. vii. 60. 6
in which ye her all *hopelesse* left, ... IV. vi. 35. 5
like one that *hopelesse* was depryv'd . . . . V. iv. 35. 1
'Unhappie Knight! upon whose *hopelesse* state . . . . . . V. v. 36. 1
I will it graunt, your *hopelesse* life to save, ... VI. i. 42. 5

Hopes. long deluded With idle *hopes* . . . . VI. ix. 25. 2
On which he safety *hopes* that earst feard to be lost. . . . . VI. xi. 44. 9
by proffers vaine Of idle *hopes* . . . . VII. vi. 34. 8
idle *hopes*, which still doe fly away, ... *Proth.* 8

Hoping. *hoping* griefe may lessen being told, ... IV. xii. 6. 3
hoping that the change of aire and place Would change her paine, . . . V. vii. 45. 3
Hoping thereby to have my love obtayned; . . . . V. xi. 54. 6
Hoping unto some refuge to withdraw: . . . . VI. vi. 29. 3

Horatii. *Horatii* that in vertue did excell. . . . . *Gn.* 600

Hore. *See* **Hoar.**

Horld. *See* **Hurled.**

Horn. Triton, blowing loud his wreathed *horne:* . . . . *Col.* 245
An high headland, . . . Like to an *horne*, ... *Col.* 282
Then tooke that Squire an *horne* of bugle small, ... I. viii. 3. 5
At last they heard a *horne* . . . . II. iii. 20. 7
When first I heard her *horn* sound . . . . II. iii. 44. 9
when earst that *horne* I heard, ... II. iii. 45. 6
His precious *horne*, sought of his enimyes, ... II. v. 10. 7
wind his *horne* under the castle wall, ... II. ix. 11. 4
On her they poured forth of plenteous *horne:* . . . . III. vi. 2. 6
the Bull hath with his bow-bent *horne* . . . . V. Pr. 6. 1
And by his side his hunters *horne* . . . . VI. ii. 5. 9
wanton as a Kid whose *horne* new buds: . . . . VII. vii. 33. 2
The Fly . . . Hath hurt me with his little *horne.*' . . . . . . *Epig.* iv. 30

Horned. Their *horned* fronts so fierce on either side Doe meete, I. ii. 16. 3
with their *horned* feet doe weare the ground, ... I. vi. 14. 3
with their *horned* feet the greene gras wore, ... III. x. 45. 7
home he marcht emongst the *horned* heard, ... III. x. 47. 8
till the *horned* moone three courses did expire. . . . . . . IV. vi. 43. 9
Bending her *horned* browes, did put her back; . . . . VII. vi. 12. 6
Now *hornd*, now round, now bright, ... VII. vii. 50. 8

Hornpipe. to the many a *Horne-pype* playd, ... *S.C.* May 23

Horn's. Wyde wonders . . . Of that same *hornes* great vertues . I. viii. 3. 8

Horns. seven heads, ten crounes, ten *hornes* did beare, ... *Rev.* i. 2
Ten *hornes* also the stately beast did beare. . . . . *Rev.* ii. 5
With gilden *hornes* embowed like the Moone, ... *Van.* ii. 3

Horns—*Continued.*
His *hornes* bene as broade as Rainebowe bent, ... *S.C.* F. 73
his wreathed *hornes* gan newly sprout: . . . . *S.C.* May 186
so his hauty *hornes* did he weld.' . . . . *S.C.* May 206
with theyr *hornes* butten the more stoute; . . . . *S.C.* S. 125
his broad forhead like two *hornes* divide, ... *Gn.* 22
So did this flie outstretch his fearefull *hornes*, ... *Mui.* 87
manie Tritons which their *hornes* did sound. . . . . *Mui.* 296
His broad outstretched *hornes*, his hayrie thies, ... *Mui.* 335
measured by his weed, As harts by *hornes*, ... *Col.* 712
all harts that *hornes* the highest beares; . . . . *Col.* 714
frowning forheades, with rough *hornes* yclad, ... I. vi. 11. 5
thrise three tymes had fild her crooked *hornes*, ... II. i. 53. 3
with his dreadfull *hornes* them drives afore, ... II. viii. 42. 4
With gilden *hornes* and flowry girlonds crownd, ... III. iv. 17. 2
through the helpe of his faire *hornes* on hight, ... III. x. 47. 4
butted him with *hornes* on every syde, ... III. x. 52. 3
threats his *horns*, and bellowes like the thonder: . . . . . VI. v. 19. 8
Bull, whose cruell *hornes* doe threat Desperate daunger, . . . VI. vii. 47. 2
Then gan the bagpypes and the *hornes* to shrill . . . . . . VI. viii. 46. 1
Thence forth they drew him by the *hornes*, ... VII. vi. 47. 7
His *hornes* were gilden all with golden studs, ... VII. vii. 33. 5

Horoscope. In th' *Horoscope* of her nativitee, ... III. vi. 2. 4

Horrible. Nor th' *horrible* uprore of windes high blowing, . . *Ro.* xiii. 9
for to shunne the *horrible* mischiefe, ... *Ti.* 143
all that him so *horrible* did see . . . . *Mui.* 70
Horrible, hideous, roaring with hoarse crie.' . . . . *Col.* 199
Upon his foe, a Dragon *horrible* and stearne. . . . . I. i. 3. 9
A floud of poyson *horrible* and blacke, ... I. i. 20. 2
choosing out few words most *horrible*, ... I. i. 37. 1
An hideous Geaunt, *horrible* and hye, ... I. vii. 8. 4
An huge great Dragon, *horrible* in sight, ... I. vii. 44. 2
that fire-mouthed Dragon, *horrible* and bright? . . . . . . I. ix. 52. 9
His body monstrous, *horrible*, and vaste; . . . . I. xi. 8. 7
So huge and *horrible* a masse it seemd; . . . . I. xi. 55. 2
With *horrible* assault, and fury fell, ... II. ii. 20. 4
with *horrible* affright And hellish fury . . . . II. iv. 30. 1
Deformed creatures, *horrible* in sight; . . . . II. vii. 35. 7
the fift troupe, most *horrible* of hew . . . . II. xi. 13. 1
seemd more *horrible* then hell to bee, ... II. xii. 6. 3
Most ugly shapes and *horrible* aspects, ... II. xii. 23. 1
The *horrible* Sea-satyre, ... II. xii. 24. 5
O *horrible* enchantment, that him so did blend! . . . . . . II. xii. 80. 9
Yet did possesse their *horrible* intent; . . . . III. ii. 43. 7
An hideous beast of *horrible* aspect, ... III. vii. 22. 2
With showre and hayle so *horrible* and dred, ... III. ix. 11. 6
Of stature huge, and *horrible* of hew, ... IV. viii. 38. 8
drives Upon a rocke with *horrible* dismay, ... V. ii. 50. 2
Seem'd to awake in *horrible* dismay, ... V. vii. 15. 3
Of *horrible* aspect and dreadfull mood, ... V. x. 8. 7
Horrible, hideous, and of hellish race, ... V. xi. 23. 4
bitter curses, *horrible* to tell; . . . . V. xi. 28. 3
Gan cry aloud with *horrible* affright, ... VI. iv. 8. 8
fared like a feend right *horrible* in hew: . . . . VI. xii. 31. 9

Horribly. Thou then adowne might'st fall more *horriblie*. . . *Ro.* xxxi. 14
snakes . . . hang in heapes, that *horribly* affray . . . . . . *Gn.* 349
like a serpent *horribly* displaide, ... I. i. 14. 7
horribly misshapes with ugly sightes, ... II. v. 27. 7
Horribly then he gan to rage and rayle, ... II. viii. 37. 1
Whose carcases on ground were *horribly* prostrate. . . . . . II. viii. 54. 9
From under that deepe Rock most *horribly* rebowndes. . . . . III. iii. 9. 9
on them layd so huge and *horribly*, ... VI. vi. 23. 4
He gaz'd about and stared *horriblie*, ... VI. vii. 42. 8
roring *horribly*, did him compell To see the hatefull sunne, . . VI. xii. 35. 4

Horrid. Being the Judge of all that *horrid* hous: . . . . . . *Gn.* 485
With *horrid* sound though having little sence, ... *T.M.* 554
horrid house of sad Proserpina, ... *Ti.* 373
his own syre, . . . Did often tremble at his *horrid* vew; . . . I. vi. 25. 3
His haughtie Helmet, *horrid* all with gold, ... I. vii. 31. 1
Privily moystening his *horrid* cheeke: . . . . III. xi. 44. 7
all the plagues, and *horrid* paines, of hell . . . . *Am.* lxxxv. 5

Horror. *Horrour* and dreadfull name of blasphemie . . . . . . *Rev.* ii. 3
with black *horror* did the ayre appall: . . . . *Bel.*^{2} viii. 4
The whiles that I with sacred *horror* sing . . . . *Ro.* i. 13
That antique *horror*, which made heaven adredd. . . . . . . *Ro.* xvii. 8
rustie *horrour* and fowle fashion; . . . . *Gn.* 443
Image of hellish *horrour*, Ignorance, ... *T.M.* 259
Let him behold the *horror* of my fall, ... *Ti.* 466
frosen *horror* ran through everie part. . . . . *Ti.* 483
none durst vewe the *horror* of his face, ... *Ti.* 535
drery *horror* dim the chearfull light, ... *D.* 328
with that suddein *horror* could no member move. . . . . . . I. ii. 31. 9
With hideous *horror* both together smight, ... I. v. 8. 6
forheades, with rough hornes yclad, And rustick *horror*, . . . I. vi. 11. 6
stony *horrour* all her sences fild . . . . I. vi. 37. 3
suddeine *horrour* to faint hartes did show; . . . . I. vii. 31. 8
what suddein stowre Had wrought that *horror* strange, ... I. viii. 5. 9
That to have heard great *horror* would have bred; . . . . . I. viii. 17. 2
trembling *horrour* ran through every joynt, ... I. viii. 39. 3
trembling *horror* did his conscience daunt, ... I. ix. 49. 3
a Serpent . . . *horrour* made to all . . . . I. x. 13. 5
Which sinfull *horror* workes in wounded hart, ... I. x. 23. 3
scared nations doest with *horror* sterne astownd. . . . . . . I. xi. 6. 9
with their *horror* heven and earth did ring; . . . . I. xi. 7. 5
So shaked he, that *horror* was to heare: . . . . I. xi. 9. 7
al the land with stench and heven with *horror* choke. . . . . I. xi. 44. 9
what *horrour* and tormenting griefe . . . . II. iv. 28. 6
Deadly dismayd with *horror* of that dint . . . . II. v. 8. 1
with dread and *horror* compassed arownd. . . . . II. vii. 20. 9
over them sad *horror* with grim hew . . . . II. vii. 23. 1

Horror—*Continued.*
her light Doth dim with *horror* and deformity; . . . II. vii. 49. 4
suddeine *horrour* and confused cry . . . II. xi. 20. 1
carries into smoake with rage and *horror* great. . . . II. xi. 32. 9
Halfe in amaze with *horror* hideous, . . . II. xi. 38. 4
Unweeting what such *horrour* straunge did reare. . . . II. xii. 22. 7
all that els does *horror* breed, . . . II. xii. 37. 1
Through ghastly *horror* and eternall shade: . . . II. xii. 41. 5
hideous *horror* and sad trembling sownd, . . . III. i. 14. 6
every daintie limbe with *horrour* shake; . . . III. ii. 5. 5
Halfe of thy dayes doest lead in *horrour* hideous. . . . III. iv. 55. 9
Fowle *horror*, and eke hellish dreriment: . . . III. iv. 58. 5
Trembling with *horror*, as that did foresee . . . III. v. 24. 3
with sterne *horror* backward gan to starte; . . . III. v. 30. 6
In hatefull darknes and in deepe *horrore*, . . . III. vi. 36. 7
all the forest did with *horrour* fill. . . . III. x. 43. 4
through privy griefe and *horrour* vaine, . . . III. x. 60. 7
with griesly hate And dreadfull *horror* . . . III. xi. 21. 8
Straunge *horrour* to deforme his griesly shade: . . . III. xii. 11. 4
in that *horror* shewd a seemely grace, . . . III. xii. 19. 8
That *horrour* gan the virgins hart to perse, . . . III. xii. 36. 5
Whilest trembling *horrour* did his sense assayle, . . . IV. vi. 22. 8
darknesse and dread *horrour* where she dwelt, . . . IV. vii. 9. 7
For *horrour* of his shamefull villany: . . . IV. vii. 21. 5
Lay hid in *horrour* of eternall night? . . . IV. vii. 33. 6
in the midst thereof did *horror* dwell, . . . IV. xi. 4. 1
bide the *horror* of his wreakfull hand, . . . V. i. 8. 8
their faint harts with senselesse *horrour* queld, . . . V. iii. 26. 3
horrour of fowle death for Knight unfit, . . . V. iv. 25. 4
aggravate the *horror* of her blame: . . . V. ix. 43. 4
for more *horror* and more crueltie, . . . V. x. 29. 1
hell unto him selfe with *horrour* great. . . . V. xi. 12. 5
for endlesse *horrour* of his shame, . . . V. xi. 19. 5
To hide the *horrour* which did lurke behinde, . . . V. xi. 23. 8
Who with the *horrour* of her haplesse care . . . VI. iii. 24. 7
doth lie In hideous *horrour* and obscurity, . . . VI. vi. 11. 5
in the *horror* of the griesly night, . . . VI. xi. 16. 6
As well for *horror* of their count'naunce ill, . . . VII. vii. 3. 7
From feare of perrill and foule *horror* free. . . . *Epith.* 322
Where they in darknesse and dread *horror* dwell, . . . *H.H.L.* 90
In that deepe *horror* of despeyred hell, . . . *H.H.L.* 130
Horsa. their Capitayns, which hight Hengist and *Horsus*, . . . II. x. 65. 2
Horse. *See* **Horse's.**
upon a white *horse* set The faithfull man . . . *Rev.* iii. 1
bent his speare, and spurd his *horse* with yron heele. . . . I. iii. 34. 9
horse and man to ground did rush. . . . I. xi. 16. 9
Both *horse* and man up lightly rose againe, . . . I. xi. 17. 1
Snatcht up both *horse* and man, . . . I. xi. 18. 9
Vaine Braggadocchio, getting Guyons *horse*, . . . II. iii. Arg.
Both *horse* and man nigh able for to choke; . . . II. v. 3. 5
horse and man it made to reele asyde: . . . II. viii. 31. 2
With stedfast hand upon his *horse* did stay, . . . II. xi. 48. 8
Lightly she leaped . . . From her dull *horse*, . . . III. vii. 25. 8
the *horse* whereon faire Florimell was wont to ride, . . . III. vii. 31. 1
Lying athwart her *horse* in great distresse, . . . III. vii. 37. 7
laying thwart her *horse*, In loathly wise . . . III. vii. 43. 4
Hard is to teach an old *horse* amble trew: . . . III. viii. 26. 3
They rudely drove to ground both man and *horse*, . . . III. ix. 16. 4
like a winged *horse* he tooke his flight . . . III. xi. 42. 7
Each other *horse* and man to ground did send; . . . IV. ii. 15. 7
horse and foote knew Diamond to wield: . . . IV. ii. 42. 6
on an heape were tumbled *horse* and man: . . . IV. iv. 19. 7
horse and man to ground he quite did beare, . . . IV. iv. 20. 8
to the ground she smote both *horse* and man; . . . IV. vi. 10. 7
The Ladies both on *horse*, together fast embraced. . . . IV. viii. 34. 9
horse and man he equally dismaies, . . . V. ii. 8. 8
great hurly-burly moved was . . . for that same warlike *horse*; . . . V. iii. 30. 2
His *horse* purloyned was by subtill traine, . . . V. iii. 31. 5
one did take The *horse* in hand . . . V. iii. 33. 2
areed That unto him the *horse* belong'd, . . . V. iii. 35. 2
till he an *horse* have gayned.' . . . V. iii. 35. 6
It had himselfe transfixed or his *horse*, . . . V. viii. 32. 8
he them overthrew both man and *horse*, . . . V. xii. 7. 7
both man and *horse*, . . . VI. i. 33. 8
And offred him . . . Both *horse* and armes . . . VI. iv. 39. 8
with cursed hands uncleane Whipping her *horse*, . . . VI. vii. 39. 8
led that Ladies *horse* Through thick and thin, . . . VI. vii. 44. 1
Horse-back. They reared him on *horsebacke* and upstayd, . . . IV. i. 37. 4
On *horsebacke* used Triamond to fight, . . . IV. ii. 42. 4
To prove if better foote then *horsebacke* would ensew. . . . VI. i. 35. 9
an armed knight that did on *horsebacke* ryde. . . . VI. ii. 3. 9
'The knight, . . . on *horsebacke* was, . . . VI. ii. 10. 1
Horse-feet. rudely tumbling downe under his *horse-feete* fell. . . . IV. iv. 30. 9
Horse-foot. The sacred springs of *horsefoot* Helicon, . . . *T.M.* 271
Horse's. glauncing fell On his *horse* necke . . . II. v. 4. 5
Over his *horses* taile above a stryde; . . . IV. iv. 44. 5
Till on her *horses* hinder parts it fell; . . . IV. vi. 13. 6
Ran fierce at me that fire glaunst from his *horses* hoofe, . . . IV. x. 9. 9
him forst forsake His *horses* backe . . . V. ii. 16. 2
blacke spot doth appeare, Shapt like a *horses* shoe, . . . V. iii. 32. 9
yet neither has forgon His *horses* backe, . . . V. viii. 9. 8
Gave way unto his *horses* speedie flying, . . . V. viii. 32. 3
lighting his *horses* head him quite did mall. . . . V. xi. 8. 9
this his Ladie . . . by his *horse* side did pas . . . VI. ii. 10. 3
from his *horses* backe . . . him forth did beare, . . . VI. vii. 11. 2
Horses. *See* **Sea-horses.**
on *horses* white, A puissant armie come . . . *Rev.* iii. 6
Unto his *horses* gave his guests for meat, . . . V. viii. 31. 2
Horses'. Hellespont trampled with *horses* feete, . . . *Gn.* 49
either bare The other downe under their *horses* feete, . . . IV. i. 41. 8

Horses'—*Continued.*
under his fierce *horses* feet have borne, . . . V. viii. 31. 8
comming full before his *horses* vew, . . . V. viii. 37. 8
Horsus. *See* **Horsa.**
Horsy. *See* **Half-horsy.**
Hose. his *hose* broken high above the heeling, . . . *Hub.* 213
Hospitage's. vile ungentlenesse, or *hospitages* breach. . . . III. x. 6. 9
Hospital. unto an holy *Hospitall* . . . I. x. 36. 1
Which choosing for that evenings *hospitale*, . . . II. ix. 10. 5
Host. stoope-gallaunt Age, the *hoste* of Greevaunce. . . . *S.C.* F. 90
Taking to *hoste*, it quite from him did stay; . . . *Gn.* 196
Her mightie *hoast* against my bulwarkes brought, . . . *Ti.* 107
With railing tearmes defied the Jewish *hoast*, . . . *Ti.* 538
reatch his hand into his enemies *hoast*. . . . *Ti.* 542
Withouten sword or shield, an *hoste* to quayle? . . . II. iii. 16. 7
her *Host* she did renew, . . . II. x. 55. 6
Her *Host* two hundred thousand numbred is; . . . II. x. 56. 5
an hideous *hoast* arrayd Of huge Sea monsters, . . . II. xii. 22. 8
an huge *hoste* into Northumber lead, . . . III. iii. 39. 2
Malbecco will no straunge knights *host*, . . . III. ix. Arg.
secretly their *hoste* did on them lowre, . . . III. ix. 19. 3
Maulgre his *host*, who grudged . . . To house a guest . . . III. x. 2. 2
his ungentle *host* n'ote him appeach . . . III. x. 6. 8
Three such as able were to match a puissant *host*? . . . IV. iii. 24. 9
that Hag, unmeet to *host* such guests, . . . IV. viii. 27. 1
For he, their *host*, them goodly well did cheare, . . . V. vi. 22. 8
Which when their *Host* perceiv'd, . . . V. vi. 24. 1
none can there arrive without an *hoste*: . . . V. xi. 42. 8
Ne would I gladly combate with mine *host*, . . . VI. iii. 39. 5
Whom when her *Host* saw readie to depart, . . . VI. v. 8. 1
Gan greatly thanke his *host* and his good wife; . . . VI. ix. 18. 6
all the *host* of heaven in rankes doost lead, . . . *Epith.* 289
Prepare your selves to march amongst his *host*, . . . *H.L.* 40
Hostages. *hostages* doe offer for my truth; . . . *Am.* xi. 2
Hostess. that accursed Hag, her *hostesse* late, . . . III. viii. 2. 1
Hostless. Forth ryding from Malbeccoes *hostlesse* hous, . . . III. xi. 3. 2
Hostry. Yeeld me an *hostry* mongst the croking frogs, . . . V. x. 23. 8
Hosts. famous light of all the Greekish *hosts*; . . . *Gn.* 547
he that serves the Lord of *hoasts* most high, . . . *Hub.* 469
great *hostes* of men she could dismay; . . . I. x. 20. 4
Huge *hostes* of men he could alone dismay, . . . III. iii. 12. 5
hostes of men of meanest thinges could frame, . . . III. iii. 12. 6
Ne *hostes* of men with banners brode dispred, . . . IV. viii. 47. 7
great *hoastes* to subdew? . . . V. vi. 40. 5
Great *hostes* of men in order martiall, . . . V. xii. 4. 8
Calidore *hostes* with Meliboe, . . . VI. ix. Arg.
Hot. *See* **Fiery-hot, Hote, Red-hot.**
Into the Gothicke colde *hot* rage instil'd. . . . *Ro.* xi. 8
A stepdame eke, as *whott* as fyre, . . . *S.C.* Mar. 41
(*whote* cole on her tongue!) . . . *S.C.* S. 112
Hyperion, throwing foorth his beames full *hott*, . . . *Gn.* 156
the *hot* Syrian Dog on him awayting, . . . *Hub.* 5
Spurring so *hote* with rage dispiteous, . . . I. ii. 15. 2
Hurled his beame so scorching cruell *hot*, . . . I. ii. 29. 5
when corage *hott* The fire of love, . . . First kindled . . . I. ii. 35. 1
his *hot* ryder spurd his chauffed side: . . . I. iii. 33. 6
to melt in pleasures *whott* desyre, . . . II. i. 58. 3
He soone approched, panting, breathlesse, *whot*, . . . II. iv. 37. 6
his *whott* fyre burnes in mine entralles bright, . . . II. vi. 50. 4
From their *whot* work they did themselves withdraw . . . II. vii. 37. 3
Coles of contention and *whot* vengeaunce tind. . . . II. viii. 11. 5
a mightie fornace, burning *whott*, . . . II. ix. 29. 6
More *whott* then Aetn', or flaming Mongiball, . . . II. ix. 29. 7
Now seeming flaming *whott*, . . . II. ix. 39. 5
Of his sharpe dartes and *whot* artilleree: . . . III. vi. 14. 5
So *whot* she burned in that lustfull fyre; . . . III. vii. 49. 8
cruell blades, yet steeming with *whot* bloud, . . . IV. ix. 29. 4
One day, as she to shunne the season *whot* . . . IV. xi. 42. 4
Ne ought the water cooled their *whot* bloud, . . . V. ii. 13. 3
But he was fierce and *whot*, . . . VI. ii. 19. 6
inly burnt with flames most raging *whot*, . . . VI. xi. 4. 2
What course were best to take in this *hot* bold emprize. . . . VII. vi. 22. 9
Now boyling *hot*, streight friezing deadly cold; . . . VII. vii. 23. 3
hot July boyling like to fire, . . . VII. vii. 36. 1
dissolv'd through my so *hot* desyre, . . . *Am.* xxx. 3
did delay *Hot* Titans beames, . . . *Proth.* 4
Hot-burning. fell Erynnis, with *hot burning* tongs, . . . *Ro.* xxiv. 5
Hot-emboiling. now quench thy *whott emboyling* wrath: . . . II. v. 18. 5
Hote. not so true As he that earst I *hote*. . . . *S.C.* Jul. 164
(for so his dog *hote*) . . . *S.C.* S. 194
it rightly *hot* The well of life, . . . I. xi. 29. 8
another Knight, that *hote* Sir Brianor, . . . IV. iv. 40. 8
Hotspur. The *hot-spurre* youth so scorning to be crost, . . . IV. i. 35. 5
Hottest. many flyes, in *whottest* sommers day, . . . VI. xi. 48. 1
Hound. *See* **Lyam-hound.**
His musicks might the hellish *hound* did tame. . . . *S.C.* O. 30
scorching flames of fierce Orions *hound*; . . . I. iii. 31. 6
no'te without an *hound* fine footing trace. . . . II. Pr. 4. 5
as sure as *hound* The stricken Deare doth chalenge . . . II. i. 12. 8
His crest was covered with a couchant *Hownd*, . . . III. ii. 25. 1
'as doth an eger *hound* Thrust to an Hynd . . . IV. vi. 12. 3
like *hound* full greedy of his pray, . . . V. viii. 7. 1
like to an hungry *hound* . . . V. viii. 36. 4
the Pagan *hound* . . . Torne all to rags, . . . V. viii. 42. 5
scarse an *hound* by smell Can follow out . . . V. ix. 6. 7
creeping like a fawning *hound*, . . . VI. iv. 11. 2
Is bayted of a mastiffe and a *hound* . . . VI. v. 19. 2
Thinking to take them from that hylding *hound*; . . . VI. v. 25. 7
for chace of beasts with *hound* or boawe, . . . VII. vi. 39. 2
Hounds. Some like to *houndes*, . . . II. xi. 11. 4

Hounds—*Continued.*
vew Of hunter swifte and sent of *howndes* trew. . . . . . . III. iv. 46. 5
Was of his *hounds* devour'd in Hunters hew. . . . . VII. vi. 45. 5
in that plight To hunt him with their *hounds,* . . . . VII. vi. 50. 9
chast With all their *hounds* . . . . VII. vi. 52. 3
panting *hounds* beguiled of their pray: . . . . *Am.* lxvii. 4
Hour. yet aggreeves my hart even to this *howre.* . . . . . . *Pet.* iv. 12
'A thousand sithes I curse that carefull *hower* . . . . *S.C.* Ja. 49
In evill *houre* thou hentest in hond . . . . *S.C.* Jul. 37
Vesper in his timely *howre* From golden Oeta . . . . *Gn.* 315
One joyous *howre* in blisfull happines, ... *Hub.* 983
Taste no one *hower* of happines or merth; . . . . *Ti.* 46
(O sad hap, and *howre* unfortunate!) . . . . *Mui.* 421
from that *houre* . . . was not like mourning seen. . . . . . *As.* 209
her dwarfe, that wont to wait each *howre:* . . . . I. ii. 7. 8
whom unhappy *howre* Hath now made thrall . . . . I. ii. 22. 2
one loving *howre* For many yeares of sorrow can dispence; . I. iii. 30. 2
I never joyed *howre,* . . . . I. iv. 46. 6
In evill *houre* thy foes thee hither sent . . . . I. vi. 42. 2
When *houre* of death is come, ... I. ix. 42. 9
God to us forgiveth every *howre* . . . . I. x. 40. 6
They wist their *houre* was spent; . . . . II. ii. 46. 9
withhold this deadly *howre.* . . . . II. iii. 34. 9
He promised to bring me at that *howre,* . . . . II. iv. 24. 7
by this Cymochles *howre* was spent, ... II. vi. 27. 1
now arrived is his fatall *howre,* . . . . II. viii. 43. 8
Nath'lesse the same enjoyed but short happy *howre:* . . . . . II. x. 57. 9
Fairer and nobler liveth none this *howre,* . . . . II. x. 76. 6
from the *howre* I taken was from nourses tender pap, ... III. ii. 6. 1
better fortune thine, and better *howre,* . . . . III. ii. 45. 5
would not stay For . . . pretious stones, an *howre,* . . . . . III. iv. 18. 8
the *howre* that first he did them lett The same behold, ... III. x. 34. 8
From the fourth *howre* of night untill the sixt; . . . . III. xii. 2. 7
every *houre* they knocke at deathes gate? . . . . IV. iii. 1. 7
with his axe him smote in evill *hower,* . . . . IV. iii. 20. 5
The which Rinaldo drunck in happie *howre,* . . . . IV. iii. 45. 3
where many an *howre* She . . . wont to play. . . . . IV. v. 5. 5
Upon them fell, before her timely *howre;* . . . . IV. v. 32. 4
unhappy *houre* me thither brought, ... IV. vii. 18. 1
'The morrow next, about the wonted *howre,* . . . . IV. viii. 59. 1
Whose like they never saw till that same *houre* . . . . IV. ix. 22. 5
this *houre,* this present lucklesse *howre,* . . . . IV. ix. 39. 2
I never joyed *howre,* . . . . IV. x. 1. 9
never tasted blis Nor happie *howre,* . . . . IV. x. 28. 2
Terpine, borne to' a more unhappy *howre,* . . . . V. v. 18. 4
Brought in untimely *houre,* ere it was sought: . . . . V. vi. 3. 5
Each *hour* did seeme a moneth, and every moneth a yeare. . . V. vi. 5. 9
so soone as dawning *houre* Discovered had the light . . . . . V. vi. 35. 1
ne ever *howre* did cease Till he redeemed had . . . . V. vi. 45. 7
he gan forth from that *howre* To stirre up strife . . . . . . V. x. 13. 4
Weening her lifes last *howre* then neare to bee, ... V. xii. 11. 8
The salvage man, that never till this *houre* . . . . VI. iv. 3. 1
'Perdie,' (said he) 'in evill *houre* it fell, ... VI. vii. 15. 1
farre From malicing, or grudging his good *houre,* . . . . . . VI. ix. 39. 7
Looking each *houre* into deathes mouth to fall, ... VI. xi. 44. 7
in evill *hower* He from his Jove such message to her brought, VII. vi. 18. 5
Which every *howre* is chang'd and altred cleane . . . . . . VII. vii. 22. 7
For lusty Spring now in his timely *howre* . . . . *Am.* iv. 9
In one short *houre* I find by her undonne. . . . . *Am.* xxiii. 8
whom this happie *hower* Doth leade . . . . *Proth.* 92
Hour-glass. an hory Old aged Sire, with *hower-glasse* in hand, VII. vi. 8. 6
Hours. They cast in course to waste the wearie *howres.* . . . . *Hub.* 27
houres in ease to wast, ... *Mui.* 36
wandring spirits walke untimely *howres.* . . . . *D.* 336
it desir'd at timely *houres* to heare, ... *Col.* 362
on the top a Diall told the timely *howres.* . . . . I. iv. 4. 9
Consumed had their goods and thriftlesse *howres,* . . . . . . I. v. 51. 8
waste thy joyous *howres* in needelesse paine, ... II. vi. 17. 4
in Amours the passing *howres* to spend, ... II. vi. 35. 4
choose my flitting *houres* to spend, ... II. vii. 33. 7
by the *houres* he measured, ... III. ix. 53. 8
thought it all one night that did no *houres* divide. . . . . . IV. xi. 4. 9
Some blisfull *houres* at last must needes appeare; . . . . . . V. iii. 1. 4
For *houres,* but dayes; for weekes . . . She told but moneths, . V. vi. 5. 6
the *Howres,* faire daughters of high Jove . . . . VII. vii. 45. 1
Was wont his *howres* and holy things to bed; . . . . VI. v. 35. 7
joyous *houres* doe fly away too fast. . . . . *Am.* lxxxvi. 14
first come ye fayre *houres,* . . . . *Epith.* 98
How slowly do the *houres* theyr numbers spend? . . . . *Epith.* 280
mightie bound which . . . parts their *houres* by space, ... *H.H.L.* 26
House. *See* **Dairy-house, Store-house.**
The firie sunnes bid them one and other *hous:* . . . . *Ro.* x. 8
I hate the *house,* since thence my love did part, ... *S.C.* Au. 161
love then in the Lyons *house* did dwell) . . . . *S.C.* D. 57
Being the Judge of all that horrid *hous:* . . . . *Gn.* 485
Ne suffer it to *house* there halfe a day. . . . . *Hub.* 828
Ah, wretched world! the *house* of heavinesse, ... *T.M.* 123
Of former being in this mortall *hous,* . . . . *Ti.* 354
horrid *house* of sad Proserpina, ... *Ti.* 373
Arrived there, the litle *house* they fill, ... I. i. 35. 1
To Morpheus *house* doth hastily repaire; . . . . I. i. 39. 3
how long time,' . . . 'Are you in this misformed *hous* to dwell?' I. ii. 43. 2
all . . . Unto this *house* he brought, ... I. iii. 18. 2
To sinfull *hous* of Pryde Duessa Guydes . . . . I. iv. Arg.
The *house* of mightie Prince it seemd to be, ... I. iv. 2. 7
when she does ride To Joves high *hous* . . . . I. iv. 17. 7
shyning lampes in Joves high *house* were light; . . . . I. v. 19. 2
that great *house* of Gods caelestiall, ... I. v. 22. 4
downe to Plutoes *house* are come bilive: . . . . I. v. 32. 3
The *house* of endlesse paine is built thereby, ... I. v. 33. 7

House—*Continued.*
The dreadfull spectacle of that sad *house* of Pryde. . . . . . I. v. 53. 9
She fownd not in that perilous *hous* of Pryde, ... I. vii. 2. 2
to the *hous* of hevenly gods it raught: . . . . I. vii. 18. 2
The *house* of Pryde, and perilles round about; . . . . I. vii. 26. 6
Then gan he lowdly through the *house* to call; . . . . I. viii. 29. 6
knight faire Una brings To *house* of Holinesse; . . . . I. x. Arg.
There was an auncient *house* not far away, ... I. x. 3. 1
In that sad *house* of Penaunce, ... I. x. 32. 8
Of all the *house* had charge and governement, ... I. x. 37. 2
that most glorious *house,* that glistreth bright . . . . I. x. 50. 5
all the *house* did sweat with great aray: . . . . I. xii. 38. 5
The *house* was raysd, ... II. ii. 20. 7
Ne ever shall I rest in *house* nor hold, ... II. ii. 44. 5
to rayse our *house* to honour did begin.' . . . . II. iv. 36. 9
did the *house* of Richesse from hell-mouth divide. . . . . . . II. vii. 24. 9
his *house* is unto his annext: . . . . II. vii. 25. 8
Did never in that *house* it selfe display, ... II. vii. 29. 5
the while that Guyon did abide In Mamons *house,* . . . . . . II. viii. 3. 2
The *house* of Temperance, . . . Besiegd of many foes, ... II. ix. Arg.
When oblique Saturne sate in th' *house* of agonyes. . . . . . II. ix. 52. 9
Did shrieke alowd, that through the *hous* it rong, ... III. i. 62. 6
the *house* that beares the stile Of roiall majesty . . . . . . III. iii. 48. 7
To heare so often, in that royall *hous,* . . . . III. iii. 54. 2
To light their blessed lamps in Joves eternall *hous.* . . . . . III. iv. 51. 9
Thy dwelling is in Herebus black *hous,* . . . . III. iv. 55. 6
Into the balefull *house* of endlesse night, ... III. v. 22. 3
Him for to seeke, she left her heavenly *hous,* . . . . III. vi. 12. 1
The *house* of goodly formes and faire aspect, ... III. vi. 12. 2
To *house* a guest that would be needes obayd, ... III. x. 2. 3
Assayes the *house* of Busyrane, ... III. xi. Arg.
Brought thee from balefull *house* of Proserpine, ... III. xi. 1. 2
Forth ryding from Malbeccoes hostlesse *hous,* . . . . III. xi. 3. 2
all the people in that ample *hous* . . . . III. xi. 49. 3
a stormy whirlwind blew Throughout the *house,* . . . . III. xii. 3. 2
Anon she gan perceive the *house* to quake, ... III. xii. 37. 1
Such was her *house* within; . . . . IV. i. 25. 1
To the three fatall sisters *house* she went. . . . . IV. ii. 47. 4
Scudamour, comming to Cares *House,* . . . . IV. v. Arg.
the dogs did barke and howle About the *house,* . . . . IV. v. 41. 7
having left that restlesse *house* of Care, ... IV. vi. 2. 1
Like to the balefull *house* of lowest hell, ... IV. xi. 4. 3
for the Gods in Proteus *house* be made: . . . . IV. xi. 9. 2
Proteus *house* they fild even to the dore; . . . . IV. xii. 3. 3
where it was kept in store In Joves eternall *house,* . . . . . . V. i. 9. 4
filled all the *house* with feare and great uprore. . . . . V. ii. 21. 9
The goodman of this *house* was Dolon hight; . . . . V. vi. 32. 1
joyous light the *house* of Jove forsooke; . . . . V. vii. 8. 7
And foule Echidna in the *house* of night: . . . . V. x. 10. 8
bore Downe to the *house* of dole, ... V. xi. 14. 9
Now comest thou to rob my *house* unmand, ... VI. i. 25. 4
till to her fathers *house* he had her brought. . . . . VI. iii. 15. 9
Till to that Ladies fathers *house* he came; . . . . VI. iii. 17. 8
Withouten . . . *house* to hide his head from heavens spight, . . VI. iv. 39. 4
Small was his *house,* and like a little cage, ... VI. v. 38. 3
The people of the *house* rose forth in great uprore. . . . . . . VI. vi. 22. 9
he was descended of the *hous* Of those old Gyants, ... VI. vii. 41. 5
frames her *house,* in which she will be placed, ... *H.B.* 117
The *house* of blessed God, which men call Skye, ... *H.H.B.* 52
With which she rules the *house* of God on hy, ... *H.H.B.* 193
An *house* of auncient fame: . . . . *Proth.* 131
Housed. to weet if living wight Were *housed* therewithin, . . . I. viii. 37. 9
housed is within her hollow brest, ... III. iii. 18. 7
House-fires. *house-fyres,* nor lightnings helpelesse harmes, . . *Epith.* 340
Houseling. The *housling* fire did kindle and provide, ... I. xii. 37. 4
House-room. an errant Knight, That *house-rome* craves; . . . VI. iii. 41. 3
House's. That *houses* forme within was rude and strong, . . . II. vii. 28. 1
Houses. *See* **Banquet-houses.**
The *houses* golde, the pavement precious stone. . . . . *Rev.* iv. 11
Were forst their auncient *houses* to let lie, ... *Hub.* 1178
Large streetes, brave *houses,* sacred sepulchers, ... *Ti.* 94
spoyld their *houses,* and them selves did murder, ... VI. x. 39. 8
Housewife. With them as *housewife* ever to abide, ... III. x. 36. 7
Like as an *huswife,* that with busie care . . . . VII. vi. 48. 1
Hove. Astond he stood, and up his heare did *hove;* . . . . . . I. ii. 31. 8
ought that under heaven doth *hove* . . . . *Am.* lxxxviii. 9
Hoved. The which in Court continually *hooved,* . . . . *Col.* 666
A couple, . . . Which *hoved* close under a forest side, ... III. x. 20. 8
Hover. darkenesse dred and daily night did *hover* . . . . . . VI. x. 42. 5
Hovered. with his servant Trompart *hoverd* there, ... III. x. 23. 2
Hovers. Like to a storme which *hovers* under skie, ... IV. ix. 33. 4
Hoving. A little bote lay *hoving* her before, ... III. vii. 27. 4
How (*partial list*).
O, *how* great ruth, ... *Pet.*[2] ii. 11
how that she . . . Tam'd all the world, ... *Ro.* iii. 6
He well foresaw *how* that the Romane courage, ... *Ro.* xxiii. 5
also marke *how* Rome . . . Renewes herselfe . . . . *Ro.* xxvii. 9
'Lo! *how* the least the greatest may reprove,' . . . . *Van.* iv. 14
O! *how* great vainnesse is it . . . . *Van.* vi. 13
Seest *howe* brag yond Bullocke beares, ... *S.C.* F. 71
See *howe* he venteth into the wynd; . . . . *S.C.* F. 75
Seest *how* fresh my flowers . . . . *S.C.* F. 129
How falls it then . . . . *S.C.* F. 169
Seest not . . . *How* bragly . . . . *S.C.* Mar. 14
How kenst thou that he is awoke? . . . . *S.C.* Mar. 28
Ne wote I *how* to cease it. . . . . *S.C.* Mar. 102
how art thou dasht! . . . . *S.C.* Ap. 85
how broade her beames did spredde, ... *S.C.* Ap. 75
how finely the Graces can it foote . . . . *S.C.* Ap. 109
How falles it, then, we no merrier bene, ... *S.C.* May 3

How—*Continued.*
How great sport they gaynen *S.C.* May 36
How shoulden shepheardes live, *S.C.* May 148
'Thy father, . . . *How* would he have joyed *S.C.* May 197
How can Bagpipe or joynts be well apayd? *S.C.* Au. 6
How I admire ech turning of thy verse! *S.C.* Au. 194
how truely I note, *S.C.* S. 110
howe done the flocks creepe? *S.C.* S. 140
How mought we, Diggon, hem be-hold? *S.C.* S. 229
How, but, with heede *S.C.* S. 230
How I could reare the Muse *S.C.* O. 112
And *howe* my rimes bene rugged *S.C.* N. 51
to ken, *How* Phoebe fayles, where Venus sittes, *S.C.* D. 84
Nor *how* th' halfe-horsy people, Centaures hight, *Gn.* 41
If Hell . . . Knew *how* to pardon, *Gn.* 476
They sought my troubled sense *how* to deceave *Hub.* 23
how t' acquite themselves . . . They were in doubt, *Hub.* 323
How manie honest men see ye arize *Hub.* 419
end of all, *How* to obtaine a Beneficiall. *Hub.* 486
How saist thou (friend) have I not *Hub.* 541
'*How* els (said he) but with a good bold face, *Hub.* 645
complaine; *How* that the Wolfe, *Hub.* 1209
Lord! *how* he fum'd, and sweld, *Hub.* 1340
How in his cradle first he fostred was; *T.M.* 500
'*How* manie great ones *Ti.* 358
how can mortall immortalitie give? *Ti.* 413
Lord! *how* he gan for to bestirre him *Mui.* 252
Arachne figur'd *how* Jove did abuse Europa *Mui.* 277
How happie was I *D.* 308, 309
how great a losse *Col.* 16
when I asked . . . *how* he hight, *Col.* 65
how bold and swift the monster was, *Col.* 220
How to begin, then know *how* to have donne. *Col.* 591
make religion *how* we rashly go To serve that God, *Col.* 797
'*how* should, alas! Silly old man, I. i. 30. 5
meanes doth make, *How* he may worke I. ii. 9. 7
Was afterward, I know not *how,* convaid, I. ii. 24. 2
how long time' . . . 'Are you in this I. ii. 43. 1
Heard *how* in vaine Fradubio did lament, I. ii. 44. 2
How fayre he was, . . . And *how* he slew I. vi. 17. 4, 5
'*how* might that bee, I. vi. 39. 1
'*How* may a man,' (said he) I. ix. 31. 1
taught him *how* to take assured hold I. x. 22. 2
How dare I thinke such glory to attaine?' I. x. 62. 2
'O holy Sire!' (quoth he) '*how* shall I quight I. x. 67. 1
'*How* can I tell, I. xii. 11. 5
what course he takes, and *how* he fares, II. i. 4. 4
'*How* may it be,' sayd then the knight II. i. 11. 1
'I wote not *how* he hight, II. i. 18. 5
Enchaunteresse perceiv'd, *How* . . . I would reprive, II. i. 55. 2
but *how,* or where, here fits not tell. II. ii. 11. 9
ne thinks *how* erst she did her hide. II. iii. 36. 9
read *how* art thou nam'd, and of what kin?' II. iv. 36. 6
'*How* hight he then,' (sayd Guyon) II. iv. 41. 1
Ne care, ne feare I *how* the wind do blow, II. vi. 10. 4
How they them selves doe thine ensample make, II. vi. 15. 3
how no man knowes, They spring, II. vi. 15. 5
how brave she decks her bounteous boure, II. vi. 16. 5
avize, *howe* ill did him beseme II. vi. 27. 4
how the fowles in aire Doe flocke, II. vi. 28. 7
how can Your cruell eyes endure II. vi. 32. 5
How without stop or stay he fiersly lept, II. vi. 42. 2
'O! *how* I burne with implacable fyre; II. vi. 44. 2
I read, *How* that thou art partaker II. viii. 30. 3
'*How* is it that this mood in me ye blame, II. ix. 38. 2
How shall fraile pen, with feare disparaged, II. x. 2. 8
whence they sprong, or *how* they were begott, II. x. 8. 1
O! *how* dearely deare II. x. 69. 3
How brutish is it not to understand *How* much II. x. 69. 7, 8
how the time was fled they quite forgate; II. x. 77. 4
Where now on earth, or *how,* he may be fownd; III. ii. 14. 2
yet wist she nether *how,* nor why. III. ii. 27. 6
can ye read, Sir, *how* I may her finde, III. v. 6. 9
how and what Her sonne had to them doen; III. vi. 15. 8
How soone would yee assemble many a fleete, III. viii. 28. 3
how mote it ever bee, III. viii. 48. 7
Ne wist he *how* to turne, nor to what place: III. x. 14. 8
With purpose *how* they might it best betray; III. x. 34. 7
Ah! *how* the fearefull Ladies tender hart III. xi. 30. 7
How oft for Venus, and *how* often eek III. xi. 44. 4
(Ah man! beware *how* thou those dartes behold.) III. xi. 48. 5
Wayting *how* Fortune would resolve V. v. 5. 9
newes . . . *How* that the Lady Belge V. xi. 2. 2
His studie was true Justice *how* to deale, V. xii. 26. 2
how to enter in, Or *how* to issue forth VI. i. 6. 3, 4
know I not or *how,* or in what place VI. i. 7. 4
Lying in waite *how* him he damadge might; VI. i. 20. 7
How can he mercy ever hope to have? VI. i. 42. 2
these Knights arriv'd, they wist not where nor *how.* VI. v. 35. 9
'*How* now, Sir knight, What meaneth this VI. vii. 14. 6
How many of their friends were slaine, *how* many fone. VI. xi. 20. 9
Hark! *how* the cheerefull birds do chaunt *Epith.* 78
how the Minstrils gin to shrill aloud *Epith.* 129
How the red roses flush up in her cheekes, *Epith.* 226
How slowly do the houres theyr numbers spend? *Epith.* 280
How slowly does sad Time his feathers move? *Epith.* 281
How chearefully thou lookest from above, *Epith.* 291
Behold *how* goodly my faire love does ly, *Epith.* 305
O *how* doth it torment His troubled mynd *H.L.* 252
In which *how* many wonders doe they reede *H.B.* 246

How—*Continued.*
in what rags, and in *how* base aray, *H.H.L.* 228
How be. *How be* I am but rude and borrell, Yet *S.C.* Jul. 95
Howbe that carefull Hermite did his best, VI. vi. 2. 6
Howell. *Howell* Dha shall goodly well indew III. iii. 45. 4
Hower, -s. *See* **Hour, -s.**
However. *how ever* base thou bee, *Ro.* xxxii. 12
How ever yet they mee despise *T.M.* 523
deeds doe die, *how ever* noblie donne, *Ti.* 400
how ever sweete they beene, *Mui.* 157
'*how ever* now, in garments gilt . . . I to thee came, I. v. 26. 7
How ever now accompted Elfins sonne, I. x. 60. 2
fairely fare on foot, *how ever* loth: II. ii. 12. 3
How ever, sure I rew his pitteous plight.' II. viii. 24. 5
How ever may Thy cursed hand II. viii. 46. 6
How ever finely she it faind to hyde. III. ii. 11. 5
'*How ever,* Sir, ye fyle Your courteous tongue III. ii. 12. 4
However list her now her knowledge fayne, III. ii. 17. 2
For they, *how ever* shamefull and unkinde, III. ii. 43. 6
However gay and goodly be the style, IV. ii. 29. 7
How ever she her paynd . . . To hide IV. vi. 40. 7
how ever malcontent She inly were IV. vi. 44. 2
how ever loth to rest; IV. ix. 32. 7
How ever gay their blossome or their blade Doe flourish V. ii. 40. 4
How ever it his noble heart did gall V. v. 26. 3
However loth he were his way to slake, V. viii. 5. 8
And forced them, *how ever* strong and stout V. xi. 47. 4
However strong and fortunate in fight, VI. i. 41. 3
He up arose, *however* liefe or loth, VI. i. 44. 3
(*how ever* thorough fate . . . I my countrie have forlorne, VI. ii. 27. 7
Calepine, *however* inly wroth, VI. iii. 45. 6
how ever it be wrapt In sad misfortunes foule deformity VI. v. 1. 2
How ever by hard hap he hether came, VI. v. 2. 8
How ever they through treason doe trespasse. VI. vii. 27. 6
Ne ought would buy, *how ever* prisd with measure, VI. xi. 14. 4
how ever it him greeves, VI. xi. 15. 3
How-ever faire it flourish for a time, VII. vii. 18. 2
How-ever these, . . . do claime the rule VII. vii. 26. 2
However now thereof ye little weene! *Am.* xxvii. 4
all the rest, *how ever* fayre it be, *Am.* lxxix. 5
How ever fleshes fault it filthy make; *H.B.* 160
How ever here on higher steps we stand, *H.H.L.* 201
with selfe-same price redeemed . . . *how ever* of us light esteemed. *H.H.L.* 203
Howl. hungry wolves continually did *howle* I. v. 30. 8
all about it wandring ghostes did wayle and *howle.* I. ix. 33. 9
the dogs did barke and *howle* About the house, IV. v. 41. 6
Howled. Some fearing shriekt, some being harmed *hould,* IV. iii. 41. 7
howld aloud to see his Lord there slaine, IV. viii. 46. 4
Howling. With fearfull *howling* do all places fill; *T.M.* 284
they gan loudly bray, With hollow *houling,* I. iii. 23. 2
Howls. feeble Eccho now lamentes and *howles* *T.M.* 285
How so. Then is she mortall borne, *how-so* ye crake: VII. vii. 50. 5
Howsoever. *howsoever* base and meane it were, VI. iv. 15. 1
howsoever it may grow mis-shapt, VI. v. 1. 5
Hoys. arrived here three *hoyes* Of Saxons, II. x. 64. 8
Hubbard. a good old woman was, Hight Mother *Hubberd,* *Hub.* 34
So Mother *Hubberd* her discourse did end, *Hub.* 1385
Hubbubs. shrieking *Hububs* them approching nere, III. x. 43. 3
Huckster-man. his *huckster man,* That wont provide his necessaries, *Hub.* 925
Hudibras. Was hight Sir *Huddibras,* II. ii. 17. 2
Huddibras, more like a Malecontent, II. ii. 37. 6
Next *Huddibras* his realme did not encrease, II. x. 25. 4
Hue. a Woman . . . of Orenge colour *hew:* *Rev.* ii. 2
crest of golden *hewe* (*hew*[1]); *Pet.* v. 2
In hundred formes to change his fearefull *hew;* *Bel.*[2] viii. 10
all the waves were stain'd with filthie *hewe.* *Van.* v. 12
in whose transformed *hew* *Gn.* 197
whatso other hearb of lovely *hew,* *Gn.* 682
that Ambrosiall *hew,* Which wonts to decke the Gods *Hub.* 1267
There stood a snowie Swan of heavenly *hiew,* *Ti.* 590
In curteous usage and unstained *hewe;* *Mui.* 120
her faire face to fowle and loathsome *hewe,* *Mui.* 351
those pallid cheekes and ashy *hew,* *D.* 302
No nightly bordrags, nor no *hue* and cries; *Col.* 315
of divine regard and heavenly *hew,* *Col.* 933
portraict Venus in her perfect *hew,* *Ded. Son.* xvii. 2
semblance she did carrie under feigned *hew.* I. i. 46. 9
I chaunst to see her in her proper *hew,* I. ii. 40. 6
with pale and deadly *hew,* At last she up gan lift: I. ii. 45. 5
that dredd Lyons looke her cast in deadly *hew.* I. iii. 11. 9
As ashes pale of *hew,* and seeming ded; I. iv. 33. 7
his shield is hangd with bloody *hew;* I. v. 5. 8
she all day did hide her hated *hew.* I. v. 20. 5
Both breathing vengeaunce, both of wrathfull *hew.* I. vi. 38. 5
He would them gazing blind, or turne to other *hew.* I. vii. 35. 9
three Moones have changed thrice their *hew,* I. viii. 38. 6
this misseeming *hew* your manly looks doth marre? I. viii. 42. 9
chaunge of *hew* great passion did bewray; I. ix. 16. 2
he recovered had his former *hew;* I. ix. 20. 8
staring wyde With stony eyes and hartlesse hollow *hew,* I. ix. 24. 3
hevenly portraict of bright Angels *hew,* II. iii. 22. 2
no man can Discerne the *hew* thereof. II. vi. 41. 8
griesly *hew* and fowle ill favour'd sight; II. vii. 3. 5
over them sad horror with grim *hew* II. vii. 23. 1
none could behold The *hew* thereof; II. vii. 29. 4
was not that same her owne native *hew,* II. vii. 45. 4
with sorrowfull demayne And deadly *hew,* II. viii. 23. 8
With so fresh *hew* uprysing him to see, II. viii. 54. 3

Hue—*Continued.*
Thousand times fairer than her mortall *hew,* . . . . II. ix. 3. 7
too oft she chaung'd her native *hew.* . . . . II. ix. 40. 4
Of swarth complexion, and of crabbed *hew,* . . . . II. ix. 52. 4
the fift troupe, most horrible of *hew* . . . . II. xi. 13. 1
grassy greene of delectable *hew;* . . . . II. xii. 12. 3
like him lookes in dreadfull *hew;* . . . . II. xii. 24. 2
th' upper halfe their *hew* retayned still, ... II. xii. 31. 6
A trayle of yvie in his native *hew;* . . . . II. xii. 61. 2
in living colours, and right *hew,* . . . . III. Pr. 4. 1
staynes his snowy skin with hatefull *hew:* . . . . III. i. 38. 6
So soone as Night had with her pallid *hew* . . . . III. ii. 28. 1
to former *hew* Hee turnd againe, ... III. iii. 50. 8
All suddeinly abasht shee chaunged *hew,* . . . . III. v. 30. 5
Her soveraine bountie and celestiall *hew,* . . . . III. v. 44. 5
She, hevenly borne and of celestiall *hew.* . . . . III. v. 47. 4
soyle, which did deforme their lively *hew;* . . . . III. vi. 17. 7
then of him are clad with other *hew,* . . . . III. vi. 33. 6
all the fruitfull spawne of fishes *hew* . . . . III. vi. 35. 7
To chaunge her *hew,* and sondry formes to don, ... III. vi. 38. 4
She was astonisht at her heavenly *hew,* . . . . III. vii. 11. 5
his *hew* Gan greatly chaunge . . . . III. viii. 48. 1
Her goodly personage and glorious *hew,* . . . . III. ix. 23. 6
Whenas the God to golden *hew* him selfe transfard. . . . . III. xi. 31. 9
As ashes pale of *hew,* . . . . III. xii. 12. 6
now had chang'd her former wonted *hew;* . . . . IV. i. 18. 2
two Ladies of most goodly *hew,* . . . . IV. ii. 30. 6
Made her to change her *hew,* and hidden love t' appeare. . . . IV. iii. 46. 9
most perfect *hew* And passing beautie . . . . IV. v. 10. 3
The heavenly pourtraict of bright Angels *hew.* . . . . IV. v. 13. 4
a Ruby of right perfect *hew,* . . . . IV. viii. 6. 7
Before misfortune did his *hew* deface; . . . . IV. viii. 14. 5
Of stature huge, and horrible of *hew,* . . . . IV. viii. 38. 8
through the likenesse of my outward *hew,* . . . . IV. viii. 56. 2
With nimble wings of gold and purple *hew;* . . . . IV. x. 42. 3
All decked in a robe of watchet *hew,* . . . . IV. xi. 27. 2
his wonted chearefull *hew* Gan fade, ... IV. xii. 20. 1
Withouten pitty of her goodly *hew,* . . . . V. ii. 25. 8
Ne of that goodly *hew* remayned ought, ... V. iii. 24. 8
As to have robde you of that manly *hew?* . . . . V. vii. 40. 7
He much admired both his heart and *hew,* . . . . V. viii. 12. 8
Being returned to his former *hew;* . . . . V. ix. 18. 8
He brought forth that old hag of hellish *hew,* . . . . . . V. ix. 47. 3
they were all, they say, of purple *hew,* . . . . V. x. 10. 1
her *hew* Was wan and leane, ... V. xii. 29. 4
and brode displayes his smyling *hew.* . . . . VI. ii. 35. 9
nought regarding her so goodly *hew,* . . . . VI. vii. 32. 3
Wasting her goodly *hew* in heavie teares, ... VI. vii. 38. 3
deadly pallied *hew* Benumbes her cheekes: . . . . VI. viii. 40. 6
some miracle of heavenly *hew* . . . . VI. ix. 8. 8
twixt his pleasing tongue, and her faire *hew,* . . . . VI. ix. 26. 8
(Save onely Glorianaes heavenly *hew,* . . . . VI. x. 4. 7
her sad plight, so chang'd from pleasaunt *hew.* . . . . . . VI. xi. 2. 9
Faire Pastorella, whose sad mournefull *hew* . . . . VI. xi. 3. 8
askt againe, what ment that rufull *hew:* . . . . VI. xi. 28. 8
The *hue* and cry was raysed all about; . . . . VI. xi. 46. 2
her countenaunce and her likely *hew,* . . . . VI. xii. 18. 7
th' Images, for all their goodly *hew,* Did cast to ground, . . VI. xii. 25. 4
fared like a feend right horrible in *hew:* . . . . VI. xii. 31. 9
Was of his hounds devour'd in Hunters *hew.* . . . . VII. vi. 45. 5
To hide the terror of her uncouth *hew* . . . . VII. vii. 6. 2
Tenne thousand mores of sundry sent and *hew,* . . . . . . VII. vii. 10. 4
though he lesse appeare To change his *hew,* . . . . VII. vii. 51. 2
At wondrous sight of so celestiall *hew.* . . . . *Am.* iii. 8
when ye mildly looke with lovely *hew,* . . . . *Am.* vii. 5
sweet allurement of her lovely *hew;* . . . . *Am.* xxxi. 10
The fayre Idea of your celestiall *hew* . . . remaines . . . . *Am.* xlv. 7
with the goodly semblant of her *hew,* . . . . *Am.* liii. 6
turne to nought and loose that glorious *hew;* . . . . *Am.* lxxix. 6
The contemplation of whose heavenly *hew,* . . . . *Am.* lxxx. 11
arayd with much more orient *hew,* . . . . *H.B.* 79
that same goodly *hew* of white and red, ... *H.B.* 92
That goodly beautie . . . and that celestiall *hew,* . . . . . *H.B.* 150
adde more brightnesse to your goodly *hew,* . . . . *H.B.* 178
The pourtraict of so heavenly *hew* to paint. . . . . *H.H.B.* 231
two Swannes of goodly *hewe* . . . . *Proth.* 37

Hues. Whom then she does transforme to monstrous *hewes,* . . II. v. 27. 6

Huge. Under deep ruines, with *huge* walls opprest, ... *Ro.* i. 2
Tossing *huge* tempests through the troubled skie, ... *Ro.* xvi. 6
as ye see *huge* flames spred diverslie, ... *Ro.* xvi. 9
destinie this *huge* Chaos turmoyling, ... *Ro.* xix. 9
The *huge* Leviathan, dame Natures wonder, ... *Van.* v. 6
by their *huge* Navy cast, ... *Gn.* 47
An *huge* great Serpent, all with speckles pide, ... *Gn.* 250
there *huge* Othos sits in sad distresse, ... *Gn.* 373
thwarting his *huge* shield, Them battell bad, ... *Gn.* 514
Heapes of *huge* wordes uphoorded hideously, ... *T.M.* 553
huge Colosses built with costlie paine, ... *Ti.* 409
the *huge* anguish, which dooth multiplye My dying paines, . . . *D.* 73
the *huge* burden of my cares unlade. . . . . *D.* 489
so *huge* streames of blood thereout did flow, ... *As.* 122
did roll downe . . . *Huge* mightie stones, ... *Col.* 150
Behold! an *huge* great vessell to us came, ... *Col.* 213
huge castles . . . ye did before you chace; . . . . *Ded. Son.* vi. 7
Her *huge* long taile her den all overspred, ... I. i. 15. 2
her *huge* traine All suddenly about his body wound, ... I. i. 18. 6
Huge heapes of mudd he leaves, ... I. i. 21. 6
Huge routs of people did about them band, ... I. iv. 36. 5
Sisyphus an *huge* round stone did reele . . . . I. v. 35. 3
in a dungeon deepe *huge* nombers lay . . . . I. v. 45. 8

Huge—*Continued.*
Una, with *huge* heavinesse opprest, Could not . . . follow . . I. vi. 40. 2
With *huge* force and insupportable mayne, ... I. vii. 11. 2
whenas monsters *huge* he would dismay, ... I. vii. 34. 2
hart . . . heaped with so *huge* misfortunes, ... I. vii. 39. 3
An *huge* great Dragon, horrible in sight, ... I. vii. 44. 2
his foe, a Gyaunt *huge* and tall; . . . . I. vii. 51. 2
He . . . soft withdrew His weapon *huge,* . . . . I. viii. 19. 8
That *huge* great body, which the Gyaunt bore, ... I. viii. 24. 7
sparkes . . . troubled once, into *huge* flames will grow; . . . I. ix. 8. 2
High heaped up with *huge* iniquitee, ... I. ix. 46. 4
huge mountaines . . . She would commaund themselves to beare away, ... I. x. 20. 6
For dread of that *huge* feend . . . . I. xi. 3. 3
made wide shadow under his *huge* waste, ... I. xi. 8. 4
His *huge* long tayle, wownd up in hundred foldes, ... I. xi. 11. 1
for twelve *huge* labours high extold, ... I. xi. 27. 3
his *huge* taile he quite a sonder clefte; . . . . I. xi. 39. 8
Huge flames that dimmed all the hevens light, ... I. xi. 44. 3
huge rocky clift, Whose false foundacion waves have washt away, I. xi. 54. 5
So *huge* and horrible a masse it seemd; . . . . I. xi. 55. 2
The Amazon *huge* river, now found trew? . . . . II. Pr. 2. 8
Hath with so *huge* misfortune you opprest; . . . . II. i. 48. 7
More *huge* in strength then wise in workes he was, ... II. ii. 17. 6
They heapt *huge* strokes the scorned life to quell, ... II. ii. 20. 5
both attonce their *huge* blowes down did sway. . . . . II. vi. 31. 2
feede his eye And covetous desire with his *huge* threasury. . . II. vii. 4. 9
the matter of his *huge* desire And pompous pride . . . . . . II. vii. 17. 6
'can safely hold So *huge* a masse, ... II. vii. 20. 2
Lyke an *huge* cave hewne out of rocky clifte, ... II. vii. 28. 2
huge great yron chests, and coffers strong, ... II. vii. 30. 2
Like an *huge* Gyant of the Titans race; . . . . II. vii. 41. 6
upbeare The massy roofe, and riches *huge* sustayne; . . . . II. vii. 43. 6
in *huge* perplexity The Prince now stood, ... II. viii. 39. 5
An *huge* great payre of bellowes, ... II. ix. 30. 4
A labor *huge,* exceeding far my might. . . . . II. x. 2. 7
Of stature *huge,* and eke of corage bold, ... II. x. 7. 8
that *huge* sonne of hideous Albion, ... II. x. 11. 6
So *huge* and infinite their numbers were, ... II. xi. 5. 6
planted there their *huge* artillery, ... II. xi. 7. 8
two then all more *huge* and violent, ... II. xi. 9. 8
An *huge* great stone, which stood upon one end, ... II. xi. 35. 7
the Carle as fast Gan heap *Huge* strokes on him, ... II. xi. 43. 9
In th' *huge* abysse of his engulfing grave, ... II. xii. 5. 8
huge Sea monsters, such as living sence dismayd: . . . . . II. xii. 22. 9
Huge Ziffius, whom Mariners eschew . . . . II. xii. 24. 7
the moist daughters of *huge* Atlas . . . . III. i. 57. 8
Like an *huge* Aetn' of deepe engulfed gryefe, ... III. ii. 32. 6
When too *huge* toile and labour them constraines, ... III. iii. 9. 7
Huge hostes of men he could alone dismay, ... III. iii. 12. 5
having with *huge* mightinesse Ireland subdewd, ... III. iii. 33. 5
an *huge* hoste into Northumber lead, ... III. iii. 39. 2
huge hills Of dying people, ... III. iii. 41. 1
Nor vengeaunce *huge* relent it selfe at last? . . . . III. iii. 43. 6
how Camill' hath slaine The *huge* Orsilochus, ... III. iv. 2. 9
'*Huge* sea of sorrow and tempestuous griefe, ... III. iv. 8. 1
forth to throw All the *huge* threasure, ... III. iv. 22. 5
To sorrow *huge* she turnd her former play, ... III. iv. 30. 3
An *huge* eternall Chaos, ... III. vi. 36. 8
with *huge* strokes and cruell battery . . . . III. vii. 32. 3
She caught in hand an *huge* great yron mace, ... III. vii. 40. 1
Makes the *huge* element, . . . To move . . . . III. ix. 15. 5
So *huge* a scope at first him seemed best, ... III. ix. 46. 5
So *huge* a mind could not in lesser rest, ... III. ix. 46. 7
Save an *huge* nation of the Geaunts broode . . . . III. ix. 49. 8
Into *huge* waves of griefe and gealosye . . . . III. x. 17. 4
that wastefull wildernesse *Huge* monsters haunt, ... III. x. 40. 4
Threates with *huge* ruine him to fall upon, ... III. x. 58. 5
fled From an *huge* Geaunt, ... III. xi. 3. 4
an *huge* heape of singultes did oppresse His strugling soule, . III. xi. 12. 1
'What *huge* heroicke magnanimity . . . . III. xi. 19. 2
With *huge* impatience he inly swelt, ... III. xi. 27. 1
Besides the *huge* massacres, which he wrought . . . . III. xi. 29. 8
when she saw The *huge* seas under her . . . . III. xi. 30. 9
huge mischiefe and vile villany . . . . III. xii. 35. 2
overcommen quight Of *huge* affection, ... III. xii. 45. *or.*6
Nations captived, and *huge* armies slaine: . . . . IV. i. 21. 8
An *huge* great speare, such as he wont to wield, ... IV. iv. 17. 2
All which at once *huge* strokes on him did pound, ... IV. iv. 31. 8
With *huge* great hammers, that did never rest . . . . IV. v. 36. 3
So *huge* his hammer, and so fierce his heat, ... IV. v. 37. 7
Heaping *huge* strokes as thicke as showre of hayle, ... IV. vi. 16. 5
huge great teeth, like to a tusked Bore: . . . . IV. vii. 5. 6
over it his *huge* great nose did grow, ... IV. vii. 6. 5
The hideous noise of their *huge* strokes did heare, ... IV. vii. 29. 3
Of stature *huge,* and horrible of hew, ... IV. viii. 38. 8
Of an *huge* Geauntesse whylome was bred, ... IV. viii. 47. 2
Deepe in the bottome of an *huge* great rocke . . . . IV. xi. 3. 1
huge Orion, that doth tempests still portend; . . . . IV. xi. 13. 9
that *huge* River, which doth beare his name . . . . IV. xi. 21. 8
So *huge* their numbers, ... IV. xii. 1. 9
layd on load with his *huge* yron flaile, ... V. ii. 24. 2
holding forth on hie An *huge* great paire of ballance . . . . V. ii. 30. 3
So was the high-aspyring with *huge* ruine humbled. . . . . . V. ii. 50. 9
he raught her Such an *huge* stroke, ... V. iv. 41. 5
With *huge* redoubled strokes she on him layd; . . . . V. v. 14. 6
his *huge* club, which had subdew'd of old So many monsters . V. v. 24. 5
in his hand an *huge* long staffe he held, ... V. ix. 11. 1
Gan drive at him with so *huge* might and maine, ... V. ix. 19. 3
An *huge* great Lyon lay, ... V. ix. 33. 4

Huge—*Continued.*
For his *huge* powre and great oppression, V. x. 9. 4
in her necke a Castle *huge* had made, V. x. 25. 8
with so *huge* might and maine V. x. 32. 3
Rebutting him . . . With so *huge* rigour, V. x. 35. 6
with *huge* terrour, to be more ydrad, V. xi. 3. 5
with his *huge* great yron axe gan hew V. xi. 5. 3
Ere that *huge* stroke arrived on him neare, V. xi. 10. 5
An *huge* great Beast it was, V. xi. 23. 1
Tho with her *huge* long taile she at him strooke, V. xi. 28. 6
stound with stroke of her *huge* taile; V. xi. 29. 6
With his *huge* flaile began to lay about; V. xi. 47. 7
in his hand an *huge* Polaxe did beare, V. xii. 14. 7
Of stature *huge* and hideous he was, V. xii. 15. 1
their *huge* strokes full daungerously bestow, V. xii. 17. 3
the *huge* stroke, which he before intended, V. xii. 21. 1
heaped strokes did round about him haile With so *huge* force, VI. v. 18. 4
So hideous is her shape, so *huge* her hed, VI. vi. 10. 3
on them layd so *huge* and horribly, VI. vi. 23. 4
joyning close *huge* lode at him did lay; VI. vi. 28. 8
eeke of person *huge* and hideous, VI. vii. 41. 2
so well enured was With such *huge* strokes, VI. viii. 14. 2
unable to support So *huge* a burden VI. viii. 16. 7
That *huge* great foole oppressing th' other Knight, VI. viii. 28. 2
doth mongst them stalke, And makes *huge* havocke, VI. xi. 16. 8
with *huge* resistlesse might The dores assayled, VI. xi. 43. 2
With thousand Crystall pillors of *huge* hight, VII. vi. 10. 4
Upon an *huge* great Earth-pot steane he stood, VII. vii. 42. 8
being now with her *huge* brightnesse dazed, *Am.* iii. 5
The *huge* massacres which her eyes do make; *Am.* x. 6
huge Pyramids, which do heaven threat. *Com. Son.* iii. 8
gan to raunge them selves in *huge* array, *H.L.* 79
O *huge* and most unspeakable impression *H.H.L.* 155
being thus with her *huge* love possest, *H.H.B.* 237

Hugely. So *hugely* stroke, that it the steele did rive, I. ii. 19. 4
With heaped strokes more *hugely* then before; I. vi. 45. 4
Strooke him so *hugely,* II. v. 11. 5
Smote him so *hugely* on his haughtie crest, II. viii. 33. 6
He stroke so *hugely* with his borrowd blade, II. viii. 45. 2
Strooke him so *hugely* that in swowne he lay, IV. iii. 34. 3

Hugeness. by her heaps her *hugenesse* testifies. *Ti.* 77
with this mightie one in *hugenes* boast; *Ti.* 539

Hugger-mugger. a few Now hold in *hugger mugger* in their hand, *Hub.* 139

Hulk. the Mast of some well-timbred *hulke* V. xi. 29. 1

Human. The image of the heavens in shape *humane.*' *Col.* 351
cride to heven, from *humane* helpe exild. III. viii. 27. 5
deem'st of things divine As of *humane,* IV. ii. 51. 6
The worke of heavens will surpasseth *humaine* thought.' V. iv. 27. 9
Such chaunces oft exceed all *humaine* thought! VI. iii. 51. 8
With heavenly thoughts farre above *humane* skil, *H.H.L.* 282
That it doth farre exceed all *humane* thought, *H.H.B.* 209

Humanity. wonderfull to fynd So milde *humanity* VI. v. 29. 9

Humber. (Their Chiefetain *Humber* named was aright,) II. x. 16. 7
Ne storming *Humber,* though he looked stout; IV. xi. 30. 7
a Scythian king, that *Humber* hight, IV. xi. 37. 8
Which the proud *Humber* unto them had donne, IV. xi. 38. 3

Humble. all that *humble* is, and meane debaced, *Van.* i. 6
Thou placer of plants both *humble* and tall, *S.C.* F. 164
In *humble* dales is footing fast, *S.C.* Jul. 13
Humble, and like in eche degree The flocke *S.C.* Jul. 131
content us in thys *humble* shade, *S.C.* O. 116
to well I wote my *humble* vaine, *S.C.* N. 50
Themselves to *humble* to the Ape prostrate, Hub. 1083
with *humble* minde and high insight, *T.M.* 511
Thereto doo thou my *humble* spirite raise, *Ti.* 313
t' adore, with *humble* mind, *Col.* 350
With *humble* hearts to heaven uplifted hie, *Col.* 816
To you this *humble* present I prepare, *Ded. Son.* x. 5
But to make *humble* present of good will: *Ded.Son.*xvi.12
raise my thoughtes, too *humble* and too vile, I. Pr. 4. 6
mightie proud to *humble* weake does yield, I. iii. 7. 3
With *humble* service to her will prepard: I. iii. 9. 7
they, on *humble* knee Making obeysaunce, I. iv. 13. 6
running Heralds *humble* homage made, I. v. 15. 7
Their harts she ghesseth by their *humble* guise, I. vi. 13. 1
She to her Syre made *humble* reverence, I. xii. 24. 2
Vouchsafe to stay your steed for *humble* misers sake.' II. i. 8. 9
He stayd his steed for *humble* misers sake, II. i. 9. 1
'I am your *humble* thrall.' II. iii. 8. 2
The Porter eke to her did lout with *humble* gestes. II. ix. 26. 9
to her homage made with *humble* grace: II. ix. 36. 3
Presume so high to stretch mine *humble* quill? III. Pr. 3. 3
thought her to adore with *humble* spright: III. vii. 11. 8
with *humble* pride and pleasing guile: III. x. 9. 3
In lofty looks to hide an *humble* minde, III. x. 30. 2
Did to that image bowe their *humble* knee, III. xi. 49. 4
humble homage did unto him make, IV. vii. 44. 8
by faire and *humble* wise IV. xii. 14. 3
Made *humble* suit unto his Majestie IV. xii. 29. 6
with right *humble* hart . . . her silent prayers did impart. V. vii. 7. 8
With *humble* prayers and intreatfull teares; V. x. 6. 5
Then taking *humble* leave of that great Queene, V. x. 17. 1
with right *humble* thankes him goodly greeting V. x. 39. 1
falling downe with *humble* awe, VI. vii. 36. 8
With *humble* service, and with daily sute, VI. x. 38. 2
An *humble* suppliant loe! I lowely fly, VII. vii. 14. 2
With trembling steps, and *humble* reverence, *Epith.* 210
To *humble* your proud faces: *Epith.* 214
Betweene the toylefull Oxe and *humble* Asse, *H.H.L.* 227

Humble—*Continued.*
His *humble* carriage, his unfaulty wayes, *H.H.L.* 233
And learne to love, with zealous *humble* dewty, *H.H.B.* 20

Humbled. To make men heavenly wise through *humbled* will. *T.M.* 522
So was the high-aspyring with huge ruine *humbled.* V. ii. 50. 9
as he lay upon the *humbled* gras, VI. vii. 26. 3
humbled harts brings captive unto thee, *Am.* x. 7
And doe myne *humbled* hart before her poure; *Am.* xx. 2
To be so cruell to an *humbled* foe? *Am.* xli. 2
him, that at your footstoole *humbled* lies, *Am.* xlix. 11
spirit Is inly toucht, and *humbled* with meeke zeale *H.H.L.* 254
Humbled with feare and awfull reverence, *H.H.B.* 141

Humbleness. her adored with due *humblenesse* V. xii. 24. 7

Humblesse. Her *humblesse* low, In so ritch weedes, I. ii. 21. 4
with faire fearefull *humblesse* towards him shee came: I. iii. 26. 9
Themselves to ground with gracious *humblesse* bent, I. xii. 8. 3
falling flat great *humblesse* he did make, I. xii. 25. 6
Tho turning all his pride to *humblesse* meeke, V. vii. 16. 1
with meeke *humblesse* and afflicted mood, *Am.* ii. 11
Myld *humblesse,* mixt with awfull majesty. *Am.* xiii. 5

Humblest. With *humblest* suit that he imagine mot, IV. ii. 8. 7

Humbly. of love I alwayes *humbly* deemed, *Col.* 828
Their backward bent knees teach her *humbly* to obay. I. vi. 11. 9
He *humbly* louted in meeke lowlinesse, I. x. 44. 6
Who, well them greeting, *humbly* did requight, I. x. 49. 8
at their feet her selfe most *humbly* feld, II. vi. 32. 3
Do one or other good, I you most *humbly* pray. III. v. 10. 9
Besought them *humbly* him to beare withall, III. ix. 18. 5
humbly thanked him a thousand sith III. x. 33. 3
those Knights he *humbly* did beseech IV. ii. 21. 1
She then began them *humbly* to intreate IV. ii. 51. 1
At last fell *humbly* downe upon his knee, IV. vi. 22. 2
I *humbly* crave your Majestie It to replevie, IV. xii. 31. 7
To whom their sute they *humbly* did present V. x. 14. 8
humbly gan that mightie Queene entreat V. x. 15. 8
She *humbly* thankt him for that wondrous grace, V. xi. 18. 1
humbly praid to let them in VI. iii. 38. 6
So *humbly* taking leave she turnd aside; VI. viii. 30. 6
little Cupid *humbly* came, *Epig.* iii. 2

Humid. A litle noursling of the *humid* ayre; *Gn.* 282
through his *humid* eyes did sucke his spright, II. xii. 73. 7
humid evening ill for sicke folkes cace; III. ix. 26. 4
now the *humid* night was farforth spent, III. ix. 53. 4
gan the *humid* vapour shed the grownd With perly deaw, III. x. 46. 5
Nights *humid* curtaine from the heavens withdrew, V. v. 1. 2

Humility. Streight at his foot in base *humilitee,* II. iii. 8. 8
they were borne to base *humilitie,* V. v. 25. 8
shee with great *humility* Did enter in, V. vii. 3. 7
made him stoupe to ground with meeke *humilitie:* VI. i. 38. 9
With meek obaysance and *humilitie,* VII. vii. 13. 8
mine eies, with meek *humility,* *Am.* xliii. 11
my faire love does ly, In proud *humility!* *Epith.* 306

Humilta. He was an aged syre, . . . Hight *Humilta.* I. x. 5. 8

Humor. their faire faces with salt *humour* steep. *T.M.* 112
the sad *humor* loading their eyeliddes, I. i. 36. 2
for her *humor* fitting purpose faine, I. vii. 38. 7
every sence the *humour* sweet embayd, I. ix. 13. 5
to uphold His ydle *humour* with fine flattery, II. iii. 9. 8
To feede her foolish *humour* and vaine jolliment. II. vi. 3. 9
their yellow heare Christalline *humor* dropped downe apace. II. xii. 65. 6
To feed her *humor* with his pleasing style, III. ii. 12. 2
The Christall *humor* stood congealed rownd; III. v. 29. 4
tempred right With heate and *humour,* III. vi. 9. 5
Trompart, that his maistres *humor* knew III. x. 30. 1
A filthy blood, or *humour* rancorous, III. x. 59. 4
The drowzie *humour* of the dampish night, IV. viii. 34. 4
the deawy *humour* shed Did tricle downe IV. xi. 46. 7
To feede the *humour* of her maladie, V. v. 55. 7
no need Of dreaded daunger might his doubtfull *humor* feed. VI. ii. 29. 9
The poysnous *humour* which did most infest VI. vi. 2. 8
Her deawy *humour* gan on th' earth to shed, VI. ix. 13. 2

Humor's. Soone growes through *humours* superfluitie. *Ro.* xxiii. 12

Humors. their vaine *humours* fed With fruitles follies *Hub.* 822
In ashes . . . array His daintie corse, proud *humors* to abate; I. x. 26. 2
deckt with smyles that all sad *humors* chaced, IV. x. 50. 8

Hundred. *See* **Four hundred, Nine hundred, Seven hundred, Three hundred, Two hundred, Two hundred thousand.**
I sawe, an *hundred* pillers eke about, *Bel.*[1] ii. 2
an *hundred* steps of purest golde *Bel.*[1] ii. 8
an *hundred* such as Hercules, *Bel.*[1] viii. 12
frame, An *hundred* cubits high *Bel.* ii. 2
Of *hundred* Hercules to be assaide, *Bel.* x. 11
hundred Nymphes sate side by side *Bel.* xii. 10
An *hundred* vanquisht Kings *Bel.* xv. 9
With *hundreth* pillours fronting faire *Bel.*[2] ii. 3
hundred steps of Afrike golds enchase: *Bel.*[2] ii. 8
with an *hundred* speares her flank wide rended. *Bel.*[2] vi. 11
monsters kinde In *hundred* formes to change *Bel.*[2] viii. 10
an *hundred* Nymphs all heavenly borne, *Col.* 256
His huge long tayle, wownd up in *hundred* foldes, I. xi. 11. 1
As *hundred* ramping Lions seemd to rore, I. xi. 37. 3
With *hundred* yron chaines he did him bind, II. iv. 15. 1
hundred knots, that did him sore constraine; II. iv. 15. 2
Therein an *hundred* raunges weren pight, II. vii. 35. 4
hundred fournaces all burning bright: II. vii. 35. 5
An *hundred* knights of honorable name III. iv. 21. 1
It is not yron bandes, nor *hundred* eyes, III. ix. 7. 4
An *hundred* knights had him enclosed round, IV. iv. 31. 6
an *hundred* Ladies moe Appear'd in place, IV. v. 11. 8

Hundred—*Continued.*
Upon an *hundred* marble pillors round . . . IV. x. 37. 4
'An *hundred* Altars round about were set, . . . IV. x. 38. 1
eke an *hundred* brasen caudrons bright, . . . IV. x. 38. 6
not if an *hundred* tongues to tell, . . . IV. xi. 9. 6
hundred mouthes, and voice of brasse I had, . . . IV. xi. 9. 7
a Diademe embattild wide With *hundred* turrets, . . . IV. xi. 28. 6
An *hundred* times about the pit side fares . . . IV. xii. 17. 8
They were an *hundred* knights of that array, . . . V. iii. 11. 5
All were they nigh an *hundred* knights of name, . . . V. viii. 50. 6
So dreadfully his *hundred* tongues did bray: . . . V. xii. 41. 7
An *hundred* naked maidens lilly white . . . VI. x. 11. 8
wont the shepheards . . . feed an *hundred* flocks, . . . VI. xi. 26. 9
he gan his *hundred* tongues apply, . . . VI. xii. 33. 2
sweetly doe appeare An *hundred* Graces . . . *Am.* xl. 4
an *hundred* little winged loves, . . . *Epith.* 357
Hung. *See* **Hanged, Hong.**
costly trappings that to ground downe *hung* . . . *Hub.* 584
hung With ragged monuments of times forepast, . . . IV. i. 21. 1
The same aloft he *hung* in open vew, . . . IV. iv. 16. 1
twixt doubtfull feare And feeble hope *hung* . . . IV. vi. 34. 2
on her shoulder *hung* her shield, . . . V. v. 3. 6
He caused them be *hung* in all mens sight, . . . V. viii. 45. 2
nigh withered was, And *hung* the head, . . . V. xii. 13. 3
her foule heare *Hung* loose and loathsomely: . . . V. xii. 29. 4
He by the heeles him *hung* upon a tree, . . . VI. vii. 27. 2
Hunger. Having his *hunger* throughly satisfide . . . *Van.* x. 2
to keep sheepe, with *hunger* and with toyle? . . . *Col.* 658
a greedy Wolfe, through *honger* fell, . . . I. vi. 10. 3
Payne, *hunger*, cold that makes the hart to quake, . . . I. ix. 44. 7
Lions . . . ravenous *hunger* did thereto constraine: . . . I. xi. 37. 4
he sterv'd with *hunger*, . . . II. vii. 58. 8
satisfy The greedy *hunger* of revenging yre, . . . II. viii. 15. 4
(O hideous *hunger* of dominion!) . . . II. x. 47. 9
Through *hunger* long that hart to him doth lend, . . . IV. iii. 19. 2
(welcommed with cold And chearelesse *hunger*) . . . IV. viii. 28. 2
O sacred *hunger* of ambitious mindes, . . . V. xii. 1. 1
when they had their *hunger* slaked well, . . . VI. ix. 18. 1
full glad That he had banisht *hunger*, . . . VII. vii. 30. 4
Hungered. Both *hongred* after death; . . . I. vi. 43. 9
Hunger's. *hungers* poynt or Venus sting . . . II. xii. 39. 3
two Tygers prickt with *hungers* rage . . . IV. iii. 16. 1
Hungrily. On which he fed and gnawed *hungrily*, . . . V. xii. 30. 6
though she *hungrily* Earst chawd thereon, . . . V. xii. 39. 5
Hungry. With *hungrie* eares to heare his harmonie: . . . *Col.* 53
the *hungry* t' eat, . . . *Col.* 849
the *hungry* rage, which late Him prickt, . . . I. iii. 7. 4
who with gratious bread the *hungry* feeds, . . . I. iv. 32. 3
hungry wolves continually did howle . . . I. v. 30. 8
His office was the *hungry* for to feed, . . . I. x. 38. 2
bare to ready spoyle Of *hungry* eies, . . . II. xii. 78. 2
with a crew Of *hungry* whelpes, . . . III. iii. 47. 4
the *hungry* Spaniells she does spye . . . III. viii. 33. 6
With wonder of her beauty fed their *hongry* vew. . . . III. ix. 23. 9
note their *hongry* vew be satisfide, . . . III. ix. 24. 1
More hard for *hungry* steed t' abstaine from pleasant lare. . . IV. viii. 29. 9
henceforth he oft shall *hungry* sit.' . . . V. iv. 49. 9
at spoyling of some *hungry* pray, . . . V. vii. 30. 2
like to an *hungry* hound . . . V. viii. 36. 4
if he *hungry* were, him offred eke to eat. . . . VI. ix. 6. 9
On which his *hungry* eye was alwayes bent; . . . VI. ix. 26. 7
Like a sort of *hungry* dogs, . . . VI. xi. 17. 1
My *hungry* eyes, through greedy covetize . . . *Am.* xxxv. 1
He thereon feeds his *hungrie* fantasy, . . . *H.L.* 198
in his deare sacrament, To feede our *hungry* soules, . . . *H.H.L.* 196
Ah, then, my *hungry* soule! which long hast fed . . . *H.H.B.* 288
Huns. gan the *Hunnes* and Picts invade this land, . . . II. x. 61. 6
Hunt. For feare of raungers and the great *hunt*, . . . *S.C.* S. 159
hunt the hartlesse hare til shee were tame. . . . *S.C.* D. 28
hurtful beastes to *hont?* . . . *S.C.* D. 82
there to *hunt* after the hoped pray, . . . *Hub.* 503
Hunt after honour and advauncement vaine, . . . *Ti.* 51
Then *hunt* the steps of pure unspotted Maid: . . . I. vi. 46. 8
To *hunt* for glory and renowmed prayse. . . . III. i. 3. 3
To *hunt* the salvage beast in forrest wyde, . . . III. i. 37. 4
To *hunt* out perilles and adventures hard, . . . III. ii. 7. 2
noble knights Which *hunt* for honor, . . . IV. i. 19. 7
Doe *hunt* for shade, where shrowded they may lie, . . . IV. iv. 47. 4
after fame and honour for to *hunt*, . . . V. iv. 29. 3
to *hunt* him out Amongst loose Ladies . . . V. vi. 6. 7
she to *hunt* the beast first tooke in hond; . . . V. vii. 30. 8
all about the fields like Squirrels *hunt;* . . . V. xi. 59. 3
my most delight . . . To *hunt* the salvage chace, . . . VI. ii. 31. 7
'Sometimes I *hunt* the Fox, . . . VI. ix. 23. 1
hunt still after shadowes vaine Of courtly favour, . . . VI. x. 2. 7
by such trafficke after gaines to *hunt*, . . . VI. xi. 9. 4
in that plight To *hunt* him with their hounds, . . . VII. vi. 50. 9
Hunted. Which when by tract they *hunted* had throughout, . I. i. 11. 5
he him *hunted* like a Foxe full fast: . . . V. ix. 17. 2
Had *hunted* late the Libbard or the Bore, . . . VII. vii. 29. 8
As Diane *hunted* on a day, . . . *Epig.* ii. 1
Hunter. vew Of *hunter* swifte and sent of howndes trew. . . . III. iv. 46. 5
Hunter's. A goodly Ladie clad in *hunters* weed, . . . II. iii. 21. 7
by chaunce doth fall Into the *hunters* toile, . . . IV. iv. 32. 6
And by his side his *hunters* horne . . . VI. ii. 5. 9
Was of his hounds devour'd in *Hunters* hew. . . . VII. vi. 45. 5
Huntest. Young knight whatever, that . . . through long
labours *huntest* after fame, . . . I. iv. 1. 2
Hunting. in *hunting* such felicitie, . . . he found, . . . *As.* 79
Hunting full greedy after salvage blood. . . . I. iii. 5. 3

Hunting—*Continued.*
By *hunting* and by spoiling liveden; . . . II. x. 7. 7
like a Lyon *hunting* after spoile; . . . III. xi. 39. 7
hunting then the Libbards and the Beares . . . IV. vii. 23. 7
hound That *hunting* after game hath carrion found, . . . V. viii. 36. 5
one day, when Calidore Was *hunting* in the woods, . . . VI. x. 39. 2
Huntingdon. Thence doth by *Huntingdon* and Cambridge flit, . IV. xi. 34. 6
Huntress. How that a noble *hunteresse* did wonne, . . . III. v. 27. 6
Hunts. The rampant Lyon *hunts* he fast, . . . *S.C.* Jul. 21
a Tygre, that with greedinesse *Hunts* after bloud; . . . *Am.* lvi. 3
Huntsman. Hippolytus a jolly *huntsman* was, . . . I. v. 37. 1
his chacing steedes aghast Both charett swifte and *huntsman*
overcast: . . . I. v. 38. 5
Lyke as a *huntsman* after weary chace, . . . *Am.* lxvii. 1
Huntsman's. being wounded of the *huntsmans* hand . . . V. viii. 35. 6
Huntsmen. a thousand *huntsmen*, which descended . . . *Bel.*[2] vi. 9
Huon's. knighthood tooke of good Sir *Huons* hand, . . . II. i. 6. 8
Hurl. His eies did *hurle* forth sparcles fiery red, . . . I. iv. 33. 5
How can ye . . . *hurle* not flashing flames . . . I. vi. 5. 9
Hurled. In raine, or snowe, or haile, he forth is *horld;* . . . *Ro.* xx. 8
From fiery wheeles of his faire chariot *Hurled* his beame . . I. ii. 29. 5
Phoebus . . . *hurld* his glistring beams through gloomy ayre. I. v. 2. 5
His hideous tayle then *hurled* he about, . . . I. xi. 23. 1
Hurling. *hurling* her hideous taile About her cursed head; . . I. i. 16. 2
hurling high his yron braced arme, . . . II. v. 7. 5
hurling up his harmefull blade on hy, . . . II. viii. 33. 5
Hurling his sword away he lightly lept Upon the beast, . . . III. vii. 33. 6
Hurls. He *hurles* out vowes, and Neptune oft doth blesse. . . I. iii. 32. 5
almightie Jove, . . . *Hurles* forth his thundring dart . . . I. viii. 9. 3
Hurly-burly. Thereof great *hurly-burly* moved was . . . V. iii. 30. 1
Hurt. being downe, is . . . brouzed, and sorely *hurt*. . . . *S.C.* F. 236
Ewe, Whose clouted legge her *hurt* doth shewe, . . . *S.C.* Mar. 50
herbs, both which can *hurt* and ease, . . . *S.C.* D. 88
Eternall *hurte* left unto many one: . . . *Gn.* 203
being *hurt*, seeke to be medicynd Of her . . . *Col.* 877
him encombred sore, but could not *hurt* at all. . . . I. i. 22. 9
Making . . . eke her *hurt* their good. . . . I. i. 25. 9
fearest not that more thee *hurten* might, . . . I. v. 43. 4
oft, for dread of *hurt*, would him advise . . . I. vi. 25. 4
He hath no powre to *hurt*, nor to defend, . . . I. viii. 21. 7
hardly could bee *hurt* who was already stong. . . . II. i. 3. 9
oft himselfe he chaunst to *hurt* unwares, . . . II. iv. 7. 6
*Of whom sore *hurt*, for his revenge . . . II. v. Arg.
he his foe has *hurt* and wounded sore, . . . II. v. 22. 3
Nought could he *hurt*, but still at warde did ly; . . . II. viii. 39. 7
As *hurt* he had not beene. . . . II. xi. 35. 6
Wounds without *hurt*, a body without might, . . . II. xi. 40. 5
Hart that is inly *hurt* is greatly eased With hope . . . III. ii. 15. 3
Of *hurt* unwist most daunger doth redound; . . . III. ii. 26. 6
did the best His grievous *hurt* to guarish, . . . III. v. 41. 6
She his *hurt* thigh to him recurd againe, . . . III. v. 42. 3
hurt his hart, the which before was sound, . . . III. v. 42. 4
hurt far off unknowne whom ever she envide. . . . III. vi. 6. 9
he thereby receiv'd no *hurt* at all; . . . III. x. 57. 6
As she were never *hurt*, . . . III. xii. 38. 7
To *hurt* good knights, . . . IV. i. 31. 3
he her must *hurt*, or hazard neare: . . . IV. vii. 27. 4
Betwixt him and his *hurt* bene happily, . . . IV. viii. 43. 7
his old *hurt*, which was not throughly cured. . . . IV. xii. 23. 6
Yet nought they could him *hurt*, . . . V. ii. 53. 4
Yet would he not him *hurt* although he might; . . . VI. i. 34. 3
that same Ladies *hurt* no herbe he found . . . VI. iv. 16. 8
passing by doth *hurt* no more. . . . VI. vii. 9. 9
Whence he assayd to rise, but could not for his *hurt*. . . . VI. viii. 16. 9
The Fly . . . Hath *hurt* me . . . *Epig.* iv. 30
Hurtful. *hurtful* beastes to hont? . . . *S.C.* D. 82
Hurtle. All *hurtlen* forth; and she, with princely pace, . . I. iv. 16. 3
Therewith they gan to *hurtlen* greedily, . . . I. iv. 40. 1
hurtle rownd in warlike gyre, . . . II. v. 8. 7
His harmefull club he gan to *hurtle* hye, . . . II. vii. 42. 3
Hurtless. My *hurtlesse* pleasaunce did me ill upbraide; . . *S.C.* D. 51
On gentle Dame, so *hurtlesse* and so trew: . . . I. vi. 31. 7
they doe play Their *hurtlesse* sports, . . . *H.L.* 288
Hurtling. the Gyaunt . . . Came *hurtling* in full fiers, . . . I. vii. 17. 9
Now *hurtling* round advantage for to take: . . . IV. iv. 29. 7
Hurts. his *hurts*, that yet still freshly bled. . . . I. v. 17. 3
Found never help who never would his *hurts* impart.' . . . I. vii. 40. 9
All healed of his *hurts* and woundes wide, . . . I. xi. 52. 2
whom he *hurts* nought cares. . . . II. iv. 7. 9
all your *hurts* may soone through temperance be easd.' . . II. iv. 33. 9
ryde he could not, till his *hurts* he did amend. . . . III. x. 1. 9
The *hurts* whereof me now from battell stay, . . . IV. i. 40. 4
handling soft the *hurts* which she did get; . . . IV. vii. 35. 7
Through her late *hurts*, and through that haplesse wound . . IV. viii. 19. 8
in short space his *hurts* he had redrest, . . . IV. xi. 7. 3
*that same Ladies *hurts* no herbe . . . Which could redresse, . VI. iv. 16. 8
Can remedy such *hurts:* such *hurts* are hellish paine. . . . VI. vi. 1. 9
Husband. as in season due the *husband* mowes . . . *Ro.* xxx. 5
mochell mast to the *husband* did yielde, . . . *S.C.* F. 109
wholesome Statutes to her *husband* brought. . . . II. x. 42. 6
Whom fortune for her *husband* would allot: . . . III. ii. 23. 6
(Black Herebus, thy *husband*, is the foe Of all the Gods,) . III. iv. 55. 7
care of credite, or of *husband* old, . . . III. x. 11. 4
her *husband* ran with sory haste To quench the flames . . III. x. 13. 2
an heard, farre from the *husband* farme, . . . IV. iv. 35. 7
Her *husband* Vulcan whylome for her sake, . . . IV. v. 4. 1
To bring it to her *husband* new ordained, . . . V. iv. 13. 7
with her *husband* under hand so wrought, . . . VI. iv. 38. 4
Husbandman. Which th' *husbandman* behind him chanst to
scater. . . . *Ro.* xxx. 14

Husbandman—*Continued.*
The *Hus-bandman* selfe to come that way, . . . *S.C.* F. 144
A simple *husbandman* in garments gray; . . . *Hub.* 228
With that the *husbandman* gan him avize, . . . *Hub.* 281
The *Husbandman* was meanly well content . . . *Hub.* 297
So was the *husbandman* left to his losse, . . . *Hub.* 341
The wofull *husbandman* doth lowd complaine . . . III. vii. 34. 7
Husbandman's. the sad *husbandmans* long hope . . . II. xi. 18. 7
Husbandry. Pales, To whome the honest care of *husbandrie* . . . *Gn.* 29
Askt if in *husbandrie* he ought did knowe, . . . *Hub.* 262
care of thrift, and *husbandry,* . . . *Hub.* 1170
Husband's. her *husbands* daies She did prolong . . . *Gn.* 426
husbands life is labourous and hard? . . . *Hub.* 266
'Ne may I let thy *husbands* sister die, . . . *Ti.* 274
through *husbands* toyle, Is often seene full freshly to have florisht, . . . IV. iii. 29. 6
She threw her *husbands* murdred infant out; . . . V. viii. 47. 2
After her Noble *husbands* late decesse; . . . V. x. 11. 8
wrought her *husbands* peace: . . . VI. vi. 43. 6
Hush. at these straungers presence every one did *hush.* . . . II. ix. 35. 9
Husher. *See* **Usher.**
Hyacinth. *See* **Hyacinthus.**
The purple *Hyacinthe,* and fresh Costmarie; . . . *Gn.* 670
Some deepe empurpled as the *Hyacine* (**Hyacint*), . . . II. xii. 54. 7
Hyacinthus. Fresh *Hyacinthus,* Phoebus paramoure . . . III. vi. 45. 3
So lovedst thou the lusty *Hyacinct;* . . . III. xi. 37. 1
Hyde. *See* **Hide, Hied.**
Hydra. this new *Hydra* mete to be assailde . . . *Bel.*[1] viii. 11
hydra new, Of hundred Hercules to be assaide, . . . *Bel.* x. 10
An *Hydra* was of warriours glorious, . . . *Ro.* x. 6
like the hell-borne *Hydra,* . . . VI. xii. 32. 1
Hydras. Spring-headed *Hydres* (**Hydraes*); and sea-shoulding Whales; . . . II. xii. 23. 6
Hyena. likest it to an *Hyena* was, . . . III. vii. 22. 8
finding not th' *Hyena* to be slayne, . . . III. viii. 44. 4
Hyer, Hygate. *See* **Higher, Highgate.**

Hylas. the Nymphes eke *Hylas* cryde. . . . III. xii. 7. 9
great Hercules and *Hyllus* (**Hylas*) deare . . . IV. x. 27. 1
Hylas'. He filld with *Hylas* name; . . . III. xii. 7. 9
Hylding. *See* **Hilding.**
Hyllus. *See* **Hylas.**
Hymen. *Hymen,* at your Spousalls sad, . . . *Gn.* 395
the Graces seemed all to sing, *Hymen Io Hymen!* . . . I. i. 48. 8
Bid her awake; for *Hymen* is awake, . . . *Epith.* 25
Hymen, io *Hymen, Hymen,* they do shout; . . . *Epith.* 140
evermore they *Hymen, Hymen* sing, . . . *Epith.* 146
Hymen also crowne with wreathes of vine; . . . *Epith.* 256
And thou, fayre Hebe! and thou, *Hymen* free! . . . *Epith.* 405
Hymn. some *hymne,* or morall laie, . . . *Col.* 86
did sing the spousall *hymne* full cleere, . . . VII. vii. 12. 7
all the way this sacred *hymne* do sing, . . . *H.L.* 41
An heavenly *Hymne,* such as the Angels sing, . . . *H.L.* 302
An honourable *Hymne* I eke should frame, . . . *H.B.* 10
beautifie this sacred *hymne* of thyne: . . . *H.B.* 21
Singing this *Hymne* in honour of thy name, . . . *H.B.* 272
That I thereof an heavenly *Hymne* may sing . . . *H.H.L.* 6
Hymns. hery with *hymnes* thy lasses glove; . . . *S.C.* F. 62
honor Pan with *hymnes* of higher vaine. . . . *S.C.* N. 8
her with heavenly *hymnes* doth deifie, . . . *D.* 230
For her he made *hymnes* of immortall praise, . . . *As.* 63
most sweet *hymnes* of this thy famous deed . . . III. viii. 42. 8
a thousand more of such as sings *Hymns* to high God, . . . V. ix. 29. 5
Renowmed hath with *hymnes* fit for a rurall skill. . . . VII. vi. 36. 9
And caroll *Hymnes* of love both day and night. . . . *H.H.L.* 70
Hyperion. *Hyperion,* throwing foorth his beames full hott, . . . *Gn.* 156
Hyperion's. *Hyperions* fierie childe Ascending . . . *Mui.* 51
Hypocrisy. *Hypocrisie,* him to entrappe, . . . I. i. Arg.
Hyponeo. *See* **Hipponoe.**
Hypsiphyle. to *Hypsiphil',* or to Thomiris. . . . II. x. 56. 4
Hyre. *See* **Higher.**
Hyssop. Sharpe *Isope,* good for greene wounds remedies, . . . *Mui.* 190

I

I (*partial list*).
Picturing that which *I* in minde embraced, . . . *Van.* i. 11
I saw a Bull as white as driven snowe, . . . *Van.* ii. 2
I saw a little Bird cal'd Tedula, . . . *Van.* iii. 7
I saw the fish (if fish *I* may it cleepe) . . . *Van.* v. 2
Hereby *I* learned have not to despise . . . *Van.* v. 13
I, . . . was much dismayed . . . *Van.* vii. 13
Soone after this *I* saw an Elephant, . . . *Van.* viii. 1
I saw a wasp, . . . *Van.* x. 7
Thenceforth *I* gan in my engrieved brest . . . *Van.* xii. 5
And *I* will send more after thee. . . . *To his Booke* 18
I have made a Calender for every yeare, . . . *S.C.* Env. 1
if *I* marked well the starres revolution, . . . *S.C.* Env. 3
I aske no more. . . . *S.C.* Env. 12
the happy above happiest men *I* read; . . . *Com. Son.* i. 2
I did behold A Woman sitting, . . . *Ti.* 8
Much was *I* mooved at her piteous plaint, . . . *Ti.* 29
That, shedding teares a while, *I* still did rest, . . . *Ti.* 32
That *I,* through inward sorrowe wexen faint, . . . *Ti.* 472
Looking still, if *I* might of her have sight. . . . *Ti.* 476
Which when *I* missed, . . . My thought returned . . . *Ti.* 477
I felt such anguish wound my feeble heart, . . . *Ti.* 482
Whose meaning much *I* labored foorth to wreste, . . . *Ti.* 486
I saw an Image, all of massie gold, . . . *Ti.* 491
That *I,* it seeing, dearelie did lament. . . . *Ti.* 504
I saw this Towre fall sodainelie to dust, . . . *Ti.* 517
Then did *I* see a pleasant Paradize, . . . *Ti.* 519
Since that *I* sawe this gardine wasted quite, . . . *Ti.* 529
That *I,* . . . Could not from teares . . . *Ti.* 531
Then did *I* see a Bridge, . . . *Ti.* 547
I saw two Beares, as white as anie milke, . . . *Ti.* 561
Henceforth all worlds felicitie *I* hate. . . . *Ti.* 574
Much was *I* troubled in my heavie spright, . . . *Ti.* 575
And *I* in minde remained sore agast, . . . *Ti.* 578
I heard a voyce, which loudly to me called, . . . *Ti.* 580
That with the suddein shrill *I* was appalled. . . . *Ti.* 581
To cast mine eye, where other sights *I* spide. . . . *Ti.* 588
Whilest thus *I* looked, loe! . . . *Ti.* 603
I sawe an Harpe stroong all with silver twyne, . . . *Ti.* 604
Soone after this *I* saw, . . . A curious Coffer . . . *Ti.* 617
Looking aside *I* saw a stately Bed, . . . *Ti.* 631
I heard a voyce that called farre away, . . . *Ti.* 638
And *I* in languor left there all alone. . . . *Ti.* 644
Still as *I* gazed, *I* beheld where stood A Knight . . . *Ti.* 645
Lastly *I* saw an Arke of purest golde . . . *Ti.* 659
And *I* for dole was almost like to die. . . . *Ti.* 672
I walkt abroade to breath the freshing ayre . . . *D.* 26
So as *I* muzed on the miserie In which men live, . . . *D.* 36
and *I* of many most Most miserable man; . . . *D.* 37
I did espie Where . . . a sory wight did cost, . . . *D.* 38
Approaching nigh, his face *I* vewed nere, . . . *D.* 50
Me seemd *I* had his person seene elsewhere, . . . *D.* 52
I softlie sayd, Alcyon! . . . *D.* 58
Yet stayed not, till *I* againe did call: . . . *D.* 60
The heaviest plaint that ever *I* heard sound, . . . *D.* 541
Which when *I* saw, *I* (stepping to him light) . . . *D.* 544
That in his traunce *I* would not let him lie, . . . *D.* 550
That *I* sore griev'd to see his wretched case. . . . *D.* 553
I him desirde sith daie was overcast, . . . *D.* 556
But by no meanes *I* could him win thereto, . . . *D.* 561
But what of him became *I* cannot weene. . . . *D.* 567

I—*Continued.*
To you alone *I* sing this mournfull verse, . . . *As.* Pr. 7
To you *I* sing and to none other wight, . . . *As.* Pr. 11
For well *I* wot my rymes bene rudely dight. . . . *As.* Pr. 12
least *I* marre the sweetnesse of the vearse, . . . *As.* 215
In sort as she it sung *I* will rehearse. . . . *As.* 216
To thee, . . . *I* send This present . . . *Ded. Son.* iv. 13
I now doe live, bound yours by vassalage; . . . *Ded. Son.* vii. 5
Which in your noble hands for pledge *I* leave . . . *Ded. Son.* vii. 9
Of all the rest that *I* am tyde t' account: . . . *Ded. Son.* vii.10
Why doe *I* send this rusticke Madrigale, . . . *Ded. Son.* viii. 3
My rimes *I* know unsavory and sowre, . . . *Ded. Son.* viii. 8
Unfitly *I* these ydle rimes present, . . . *Ded. Son.* ix. 7
To you this humble present *I* prepare, . . . *Ded. Son.* x. 5
In vain *I* thinke, . . . to memorize thy name, . . . *Ded. Son.* xii. 1
Ne may *I,* without blot of endlesse blame, . . . *Ded. Son.* xvi. 1
If all the world to seeke *I* overwent, . . . *Ded.Son.*xvii.9
A fairer crew yet no where could *I* see . . . *Ded.Son.*xvii.10
Of each a part *I* stole by cunning thefte: . . . *Ded.Son.*xvii.13
Lo! *I,* the man whose Muse . . . I. Pr. i. 1
That *I* must rue his undeserved wrong: . . . I. Pr. 2. 8
'*I,* that do seeme not *I,* Duessa ame,' . . . I. v. 26. 6
Till *I* of warres and bloody Mars doe sing, . . . I. xi. 7. 2
I this man of God his godly armes may blaze. . . . I. xi. 7. 9
Behold! *I* see the haven nigh at hand . . . I. xii. 1. 1
To which *I* meane my wearie course to bend; . . . I. xii. 1. 2
Which *I* so much doe vaunt, . . . II. Pr. 1. 8
How then shall *I,* . . . Presume . . . III. Pr. 3. 1
That *I* in colourd showes may shadow itt, . . . III. Pr. 3. 8
Here have *I* cause in men just blame to find, . . . III. ii. 1. 1
by record of antique times *I* finde . . . III. ii. 2. 1
whose prayse *I* would endyte, . . . III. ii. 3. 4
Endite *I* would as dewtie doth excyte; . . . III. ii. 3. 5
For all too long *I* burne with envy sore . . . III. iv. 2. 3
But when *I* reade, how stout Debora strake . . . III. iv. 2. 7
I swell with great disdaine. . . . III. iv. 2. 9
Whose lignage from this Lady *I* derive along. . . . III. iv. 3. 9
So oft as *I* this history record, . . . III. viii. 1. 1
To whom *I* levell all my labours end, . . . III. ix. 1. 2
Whiles of a wanton Lady *I* doe write, . . . III. ix. 1. 6
If shee were thine, and thou as now am *I?* . . . III. xi. 19. 4
whilest here *I* doe respire. . . . III. xii. 45. 9
To such therefore *I* do not sing at all; . . . IV. Pr. 4. 1
To her *I* sing of love, . . . IV. Pr. 4. 6
spirit! That *I* thy labours lost may thus revive, . . . IV. ii. 34. 2
Ne dare *I* like; but, through infusion sweete . . . IV. ii. 34. 6
I follow here the footing of thy feete, . . . IV. ii. 34. 8
That with thy meaning so *I* may the rather meete . . . IV. ii. 34. 9
The which, for length, *I* will not here pursew, . . . IV. ii. 54. 8
Therefore this Fay *I* hold but fond and vaine, . . . IV. iii. 2. 1
Where *I* . . . will also rest a whyle. . . . IV. iv. 48. 9
I here will stay . . . that *I* it finish may. . . . IV. vi. 47. 8, 9
So doest thou now to her of whom *I* tell, . . . IV. vii. 2. 3
I will deferre the end untill another tide. . . . IV. vii. 47. 9
those daungers . . . *I* will them in another tell. . . . IV. ix. 41. 9
So ended he his tale, where *I* this Canto end. . . . IV. x. 58. 9
that *I* have thus long Left a fayre Ladie . . . IV. xi. 1. 1
that *I* have doen such wrong, . . . IV. xi. 1. 3
Unto an other Canto *I* will overpas. . . . IV. xi. 53. 9
What an endlesse worke have *I* in hand, . . . IV. xii. 1. 1
blame me not if *I* have err'd in count . . . IV. xii. 2. 6

I—*Continued.*
Which to another place *I* leave to be perfected. . . . . . . IV. xii. 35. 9
So oft as *I* . . . compare, ... V. Pr. 1. 1
Such oddes *I* finde twixt those, ... V. Pr. 1. 5
if in discipline Of vertue . . . *I* doe not forme . . . . V. Pr. 3. 3
In those old times of which *I* doe entreat, ... V. i. 1. 2
such was he of whom *I* have to tell, ... V. i. 3. 1
Whereof *I* have to treat here presently: . . . . V. vii. 3. 5
Whether this heavenly thing whereof *I* treat, ... V. x. 1. 2
This well *I* wote, that sure she is as great, ... V. x. 1. 5
through which my weary steps *I* guyde . . . . VI. Pr. 1. 1
That *I*, nigh ravisht with rare thoughts . . . . VI. Pr. 1. 6
when *I* gin to feele decay of might, ... VI. Pr. 1. 8
where shall *I* . . . So faire a patterne finde, ... VI. Pr. 6. 1
That from your selfe *I* doe this vertue bring, ... VI. Pr. 7. 2
I must awhile forbeare to you to tell; . . . . VI. vi. 17. 3
Till that, as comes by course, *I* doe recite What . . . . VI. vi. 17. 4
The coward Turpine, whereof now *I* treat; . . . . VI. vii. 2. 2
Till Mirabellaes fortunes *I* doe further say. . . . . VI. vii. 50. 9
Backe to the furrow which *I* lately left. . . . . VI. ix. 1. 2
I lately left a furrow, one or twayne, ... VI. ix. 1. 3
seem'd the soyle both fayre . . . As *I* it past: . . . . VI. ix. 1. 6
sith *I* left him last Sewing the Blatant Beaste; . . . . VI. ix. 2. 2
now *I* come into my course againe, ... VI. xii. 2. 6
I will rehearse that whylome *I* heard say, ... VII. vi. 1. 7
As *I* have found it registred of old . . . . VII. vi. 2. 3
I would abate the sternenesse of my stile, ... VII. vi. 37. 3
sith *I* needs must follow thy behest, ... VII. vii. 2. 1
When *I* bethinke me on that speech . . . . VII. viii. 1. 1
Then gin *I* thinke on that which Nature sayd, ... VII. viii. 2. 1
Whom if ye please, *I* care for other none! . . . . *Am.* i. 14
Unquiet thought! whom at the first *I* bred . . . . *Am.* ii. 1
I with thee will perish. . . . . *Am.* ii. 14
Base thing *I* can no more endure to view: . . . . *Am.* iii. 6
But, looking still on her, *I* stand amazed . . . . *Am.* iii. 7
Yet in may hart *I* then both speake and write . . . . *Am.* iii. 13
The thing which *I* doo most in her admire, ... *Am.* v. 3
Then doe *I* die, ... *Am.* vii. 8
I sought to what *I* might compare . . . . *Am.* ix. 1
Yet find *I* nought on earth, to which *I* dare Resemble . . . . *Am.* ix. 3
That *I* may laugh at her in equall sort, ... *Am.* x. 13
Dayly when *I* do seeke and sew for peace, ... *Am.* xi. 1
One day *I* sought . . . To make a truce, ... *Am.* xii. 1
as *I* then disarmed did remaine, ... *Am.* xii. 5
Too feeble *I* t' abide the brunt so strong, ... *Am.* xii. 9
So, Ladie, now to you *I* doo complaine, ... *Am.* xii. 13
that justice *I* may gaine. . . . . *Am.* xii. 14
as *I* unwarily did gaze On those fayre eyes, ... *Am.* xvi. 1
One of those archers closely *I* did spy, ... *Am.* xvi. 9
Had she not so doon, sure *I* had bene slayne; . . . . *Am.* xvi. 13
Yet as it was, *I* hardly scap't with paine. . . . . *Am.* xvi. 14
Yet cannot *I*, . . . soften her hard hart; . . . . *Am.* xviii. 5
But, when *I* pleade, she bids me play my part; . . . . *Am.* xviii. 9
when *I* weep, she sayes, ... *Am.* xviii. 10
when *I* sigh, she sayes, ... *Am.* xviii. 11
when *I* waile, she turnes hir selfe . . . . *Am.* xviii. 12
So do *I* weepe, and wayle, and pleade . . . . *Am.* xviii. 13
In vaine *I* seeke and sew to her for grace, ... *Am.* xx. 1
Such art of eyes *I* never read in bookes! . . . . *Am.* xxi. 14
Therefore, *I* lykewise, . . . service fit will find. . . . . . . *Am.* xxii. 3
There *I* to her, . . . Will builde an altar . . . . *Am.* xxii. 9
For all that *I* in many dayes doo weave, ... *Am.* xxiii. 7
In one short houre *I* find by her undonne. . . . . *Am.* xxiii. 8
when *I* thinke to end that *I* begonne, ... *Am.* xxiii. 9
I must begin and never bring to end: . . . . *Am.* xxiii. 10
with one looke she spils that long *I* sponne; . . . . *Am.* xxiii. 11
When *I* behold that beauties wonderment, ... *Am.* xxiv. 1
I honor and admire the Makers art. . . . . *Am.* xxiv. 4
But when *I* feele the bitter balefull smart, ... *Am.* xxiv. 5
I thinke that *I* a new Pandora see, ... *Am.* xxiv. 8
Then all the woes and wrecks which *I* abide, ... *Am.* xxv. 11
As meanes of blisse *I* gladly wil embrace; . . . . *Am.* xxv. 12
My love is lyke to yse, and *I* to fyre; . . . . *Am.* xxx. 1
But harder growes the more *I* her intreat! . . . . *Am.* xxx. 4
But that *I* burne much more in boyling sweat, ... *Am.* xxx. 7
Yet cannot all these flames, in which *I* fry, ... *Am.* xxxii. 5
prayers, with which *I* Doe beat on th' andvile . . . . *Am.* xxxii. 7
What then remaines but *I* to ashes burne, ... *Am.* xxxii. 13
Great wrong *I* doe, *I* can it not deny, ... *Am.* xxxiii. 1
How then should *I* . . . Thinck ever to endure . . . . *Am.* xxxiii. 9
Seemd every bit which thenceforth *I* did eat. . . . . *Am.* xxxix. 14
The more *I* love and doe embrace my bane. . . . . *Am.* xlii. 4
Ne doe *I* wish . . . To be acquit . . . . *Am.* xlii. 5
Shall *I* then silent be, ... *Am.* xliii. 1
if *I* speake, her wrath renew *I* shall; . . . . *Am.* xliii. 2
if *I* silent be, my hart will breake, ... *Am.* xliii. 3
That nether *I* may speake nor thinke at all, ... *Am.* xliii. 7
Yet *I* my hart with silence . . . Will teach . . . . *Am.* xliii. 9
when in hand my tunelesse harp *I* take, ... *Am.* xliv. 9
Then doe *I* more augment my foes despight; . . . . *Am.* xliv. 10
the more *I* seeke to settle peace, ... *Am.* xliv. 13
The more *I* fynd their malice to increase. . . . . *Am.* xliv. 14
Whom then shall *I*, or heaven or her, obay? . . . . *Am.* xlvi. 5
Doe *I* not see that fayrest ymages . . . . *Am.* li. 1
Why then doe *I*, . . . Her hardnes blame, ... *Am.* li. 5
which *I* should more commend? . . . . *Am.* li. 6
So doe *I* hope her stubborne hart to bend, ... *Am.* li. 11
So oft as homeward *I* from her depart, ... *Am.* lii. 1
I goe lyke one that, . . . Is prisoner led away . . . . *Am.* lii. 2
So doe *I* now my selfe a prisoner yceld . . . . *Am.* lii. 5

I—*Continued.*
So *I* her absens will my penaunce make, ... *Am.* lii. 13
That of her presens *I* my meed may take. . . . . *Am.* lii. 14
Sometimes *I* joy when glad occasion fits, ... *Am.* liv. 5
I waile, and make my woes a Tragedy. . . . . *Am.* liv. 8
when *I* laugh, she mocks; and, when *I* cry, She laughes, . . . *Am.* liv. 11
So oft as *I* her beauty doe behold, ... *Am.* lv. 1
I marvaile of what substance was the mould, ... *Am.* lv. 3
that same beast, am *I*, Whom ye doe . . . destroy. . . . . . . *Am.* lvi. 13
when shall *I* have peace with you? . . . . *Am.* lvii. 1
Which *I* no lenger can endure to sue, ... *Am.* lvii. 3
That wonder is how *I* should live a jot, ... *Am.* lvii. 6
Which *I* have wasted in long languishment, ... *Am.* lx. 11
Which hardly *I* endured heretofore, ... *Am.* lxiii. 2
I doe at length descry the happy shore, ... *Am.* lxiii. 5
In which *I* hope ere long for to arryve: . . . . *Am.* lxiii. 6
Comming to kisse her lyps, (such grace *I* found,) . . . . *Am.* lxiv. 1
Me seemd, *I* smelt a gardin of sweet flowres, ... *Am.* lxiv. 2
When *I* all weary had the chace forsooke, ... *Am.* lxvii. 6
Till *I* in hand her yet halfe trembling tooke, ... *Am.* lxvii. 11
What trophee then shall *I* most fit devize, ... *Am.* lxix. 5
In which *I* may record the memory . . . . *Am.* lxix. 6
I joy to see how, . . . Your selfe unto the Bee . . . . *Am.* lxxi. 1
One day *I* wrote her name upon the strand; . . . . *Am.* lxxv. 1
Agayne, *I* wrote it with a second hand; . . . . *Am.* lxxv. 3
For *I* my selve shall lyke to this decay, ... *Am.* lxxv. 7
How was *I* ravisht with your lovely sight, ... *Am.* lxxvi. 5
Sweet thoughts! *I* envy your so happy rest, ... *Am.* lxxvi. 13
Which oft *I* wisht, yet never was so blest. . . . . *Am.* lxxvi. 14
Was it a dreame, or did *I* see it playne; . . . . *Am.* lxxvii. 1
Lackyng my love, *I* go from place to place, ... *Am.* lxxviii. 1
And seeke . . . where last *I* sawe her face, ... *Am.* lxxviii. 3
Whose ymage yet *I* carry fresh in mynd. . . . . *Am.* lxxviii. 4
I seeke the fields with her late footing synd; . . . . *Am.* lxxviii. 5
I seeke her bowre . . . . *Am.* lxxviii. 6
Yet nor in field nor bowre *I* her can fynd; . . . . *Am.* lxxviii. 7
But, when myne eyes *I* thereunto direct, ... *Am.* lxxviii. 9
And, when *I* hope to see theyr trew object, ... *Am.* lxxviii. 11
I fynd my selfe but fed with fancies vayne. . . . . *Am.* lxxviii. 12
After so long a race as *I* have run . . . . *Am.* lxxx. 1
Out of my prison *I* will breake anew; . . . . *Am.* lxxx. 6
I blesse my lot, that was so lucky placed: . . . . *Am.* lxxxii. 2
But then the more your owne mishap *I* rew, ... *Am.* lxxxii. 3
That little, that *I* am, shall all be spent . . . . *Am.* lxxxii. 11
When *I* doe praise her, say *I* doe but flatter: . . . . *Am.* lxxxiv. 2
Since *I* did leave the presence of my love, ... *Am.* lxxxvi. 1
Many long weary dayes *I* have outworne; . . . . *Am.* lxxxvi. 2
I wish that night the noyous day would end: . . . . *Am.* lxxxvi. 6
I wish that day would shortly reascend. . . . . *Am.* lxxxvi. 8
Thus *I* the time with expectation spend, ... *Am.* lxxxvi. 9
Since *I* have lackt the comfort of that light, ... *Am.* lxxxvii. 1
I wander as in darkenesse of the night, ... *Am.* lxxxvii. 3
Ne ought *I* see, though in the clearest day, ... *Am.* lxxxvii. 5
With light thereof *I* doe my selfe sustayne, ... *Am.* lxxxvii. 11
whylest *I* fill my mind, ... *Am.* lxxxvii. 13
I starve my body, ... *Am.* lxxxvii. 14
So *I* alone, now left disconsolate, ... *Am.* lxxxviii. 5
So *I* unto my selfe alone will sing; . . . . *Epith.* 17
If ever *I* did honour thee aright, ... *Epith.* 122
Then *I* thy soverayne prayses loud wil sing, ... *Epith.* 127
Faine would *I* seeke to ease my bitter smart . . . . *H.L.* 5
By any service *I* might do to thee, ... *H.L.* 6
I meane to sing the praises of thy name, ... *H.L.* 10
Onely *I* feare my wits enfeebled late. . . . . *H.L.* 15
I should enabled be thy actes to sing. . . . . *H.L.* 21
Why then do *I* this honor unto thee, ... *H.L.* 148
Ay me! deare Lord! that ever *I* might hope, ... *H.L.* 294
For all the paines and woes that *I* endure, ... *H.L.* 295
Then would *I* thinke these paines no paines . . . . *H.L.* 299
Then would *I* sing of thine immortall praise . . . . *H.L.* 301
And thy triumphant name then would *I* raise . . . . *H.L.* 303
That as *I* earst, in praise of thine owne name, ... *H.B.* 8
An honourable Hymne *I* eke should frame, ... *H.B.* 10
That both to thee, to whom *I* meane it most, ... *H.B.* 22
May owe to her, of whom *I* it receaved. . . . . *H.B.* 280
Where *I* may see those admirable things . . . . *H.H.L.* 3
That *I* thereof an heavenly Hymne may sing . . . . *H.H.L.* 6
I have in th' heat of youth made heretofore, ... *H.H.L.* 10
But all those follies now *I* do reprove, ... *H.H.L.* 12
I faine to tell the things that *I* behold, ... *H.H.B.* 6
that *I* may show Some litle beames . . . . *H.H.B.* 11
Which in my weake distraughted mynd *I* see; . . . . *H.H.B.* 14
Of the soare faulcon so *I* learne to fly, ... *H.H.B.* 26
When *I* . . . Walkt forth to ease my payne . . . . *Proth.* 5
Sweete Themmes! runne softly, till *I* end my Song . . . . *Proth.* 18
With that *I* saw two Swannes of goodly hewe . . . . *Proth.* 37
Two fairer Birds *I* yet did never see; . . . . *Proth.* 39
Though from another place *I* take my name, ... *Proth.* 130
Where oft *I* gayned giftes and goodly grace . . . . *Proth.* 138

Ice. My love is lyke to *yse*, and I to fyre; . . . . *Am.* xxx. 1
That fire . . . should harden *yse;* And *yse* . . . should kindle fyre . . . . *Am.* xxx. 10, 11

Icicles. Whose drops in drery *ysicles* remaine. . . . . *S.C.* Ja. 36
on your boughes the *ysicles* depend. . . . . *S.C.* Ja. 42
the cold *ysickles* from his rough beard . . . . III. viii. 35. 3

Ida. Whom *Ida* hyll dyd beare, ... *S.C.* Jul. 146
The shepheard of *Ida* that judged beauties Queene. . . . . *S.C.* Au. 138
Ida selfe, in ayde of that fierce fight, ... *Gn.* 505
Ida, where the Gods lov'd to repayre, ... II. xii. 52. 6
Whiles yet on *Ida* he a shepheard hight, ... III. ix. 36. 3

Ida—*Continued.*
the Trojane boy so fayre He snatcht from *Ida* hill, . . . III. xi. 34. 5
Idaean. th' *Idaean* Ladies disagreed, . . . II. vii. 55. 6
Like as Cupido on *Idaean* hill, . . . II. viii. 6. 1
nourisht by th' *Idaean* mayd; . . . VII. vii. 41. 7
Idea. The fayre *Idea* of your celestiall hew . . . remaines . . . *Am.* xlv. 7
beholding the *Idaea* playne, . . . *Am.* lxxxvii. 9
plainely see Th' *Idee* of his pure glorie . . . *H.H.L.* 284
Ideas. where those *Idees* on hie Enraunged be, . . . *H.H.B.* 82
Idle. the shepeheards bene *ydle* and still, . . . *S.C.* S. 80
lighter seeme than this Gnats *idle* name. . . . *Gn.* 8
his limbs, resolv'd through *idle* leisour, . . . *Gn.* 141
pleasant tales (fit for that *idle* stound) . . . *Hub.* 26
Each *idle* wit at will presumes to make, . . . *T.M.* 215
Doth rather choose to sit in *idle* Cell, . . . *T.M.* 221
Care now his *idle* bagpipe up to raise, . . . *Ti.* 226
provoke them might To *idle* pleasance; . . . *D.* 327
Ne her with *ydle* words alone he wowed, . . . *As.* 67
Counted but toyes to busie *ydle* braines; . . . *Col.* 704
use his *ydle* name to other needs, . . . *Col.* 789
And to these *ydle* rymes lend litle space, . . . *Ded. Son.* i. 13
Unfitly I these *ydle* rimes present, . . . *Ded. Son.* ix. 7
when that *ydle* dreame was to him brought, . . . I. i. 46. 1
Through widest ayre making his *ydle* way, . . . I. v. 8. 4
in *ydle* pomp, or wanton play, . . . I. v. 51. 7
His silver shield, now *idle*, maisterlesse; . . . I. vii. 19. 6
The *ydle* stroke, . . . Did fall to ground, . . . I. viii. 8. 2
'That *ydle* name of love . . . I ever scornd, . . . I. ix. 10. 1
'How may a man . . . with *idle* speach Be wonne . . . I. ix. 31. 1
th' *ydle* stroke yet backe recoyld in vaine, . . . I. xi. 17. 3
The sight with *ydle* feare did them dismay, . . . I. xii. 9. 8
'What meane these bloody vowes and *idle* threats, . . . I. xii. 30. 1
With *ydle* force did faine them to withstand, . . . I. xii. 35. 8
th' aboundance of an *ydle* braine Will judged be, . . . II. Pr. 1. 3
One sitting *ydle* on a sunny banck, . . . II. iii. 6. 2
to uphold His *ydle* humour with fine flattery, . . . II. iii. 9. 8
the man that moulds in *ydle* cell . . . II. iii. 41. 3
It's eath his *ydle* fury to aswage, . . . II. iv. 11. 7
though he scornd his *ydle* vanitee, . . . II. iv. 39. 7
ydle pleasures in her Bowre of Blisse, . . . II. v. 27. 3
pourd out his *ydle* mynd In daintie delices, . . . II. v. 28. 5
hight by name The *Idle* lake, . . . II. vi. 10. 2
he awoke out of his *ydle* dreme; . . . II. vi. 27. 2
bent his hastie course towardes the *ydle* flood. . . . II. vi. 41. 9
Whiles thus they strugled in that *ydle* wave, . . . II. vi. 47. 1
guyde, Late left beyond that *Ydle* lake, . . . II. vii. 2. 2
idle offers of thy golden fee; . . . II. vii. 9. 7
all thine *ydle* offers I refuse. . . . II. vii. 39. 2
So lost his labour vaine and *ydle* industry. . . . II. vii. 61. 9
Archimago slie Foreby that *idle* strond, . . . II. viii. 10. 8
suffred rash Pyrochles waste his *ydle* might. . . . II. viii. 48. 9
Hewing and slashing at their *idle* shades; . . . II. ix. 15. 8
never *idle* was, ne once would rest a whit. . . . II. ix. 49. 9
Such as in *idle* fantasies do flit; . . . II. ix. 50. 7
All those were *idle* thoughtes and fantasies, . . . II. ix. 51. 6
Vaine feastes, and *ydle* superfluity: . . . II. xi. 12. 8
to the ground the *idle* quarrell fell: . . . II. xi. 24. 8
th' *ydle* breath all utterly exprest. . . . II. xi. 42. 4
Did ferry him over the *Idle* lake: . . . II. xii. 17. 2
he his *ydle* curtesie defide, . . . II. xii. 49. 7
the *ydle* instruments Of sleeping praise, . . . II. xii. 80. 1
wishing it far off his *ydle* wish doth lose. . . . III. i. 46. 9
'Sir knight, these *ydle* termes forbeare; . . . III. ii. 16. 1
'These *idle* wordes' (said she) 'doe nought aswage . . . III. ii. 37. 1
Was of him selfe the *ydle* Paramoure, . . . III. ii. 45. 2
that old Dame said many an *idle* verse, . . . III. ii. 48. 8
No *ydle* charmes so lightly may remove: . . . III. ii. 51. 8
thousand Fancies bett his *ydle* brayne . . . III. iv. 54. 4
ydle thoughts . . . cleave unto the lowly clay, . . . III. v. 1. 4
Ne lend we leisure to his *idle* toy: . . . III. vi. 24. 5
from Prince Arthure fled with wings of *idle* feare. . . . III. vi. 54. 9
tell the *idle* tidings to his Dame: . . . III. vii. 28. 6
to God he made so many an *idle* boone: . . . III. vii. 34. 9
Her to disport and *idle* time to pas . . . III. viii. 11. 3
in her lap did shed her *idle* draught, . . . III. ix. 31. 3
'Troy, that art now nought but an *idle* name, . . . III. ix. 33. 1
in the *ydle* ayre he mov'd still here and theare. . . . III. xii. 8. 9
Nether of *ydle* showes, nor of false charmes aghast. . . . III. xii. 29. 9
Stood still amaz'd, holding his *idle* sweard; . . . IV. iii. 31. 7
in their hands their *idle* troncheons held, . . . IV. iv. 18. 8
feare His *ydle* braine gan busily molest, . . . IV. v. 43. 7
Hath troubled both your mindes with *idle* thought, . . . IV. vi. 30. 7
fild his ballaunce full of *idle* toys: . . . V. ii. 30. 8
With many *idle* stoups her troubling still: . . . V. v. 15. 7
with bold vaunts and *ydle* threatning, . . . V. xi. 3. 7
Who scornes thy *ydle* scoffe, and bids thee be defyde.' . . . VI. i. 27. 9
long deluded With *idle* hopes . . . VI. ix. 25. 2
What *idle* errand hast thou earths mansion to forsake?' . . . VII. vi. 25. 9
'Then ceasse thy *idle* claime, thou foolish gerle; . . . VII. vi. 34. 1
by proffers vaine Of *idle* hopes . . . VII. vi. 34. 8
by their *idle* skill Are wont . . . to fashion; . . . VII. vii. 8. 3
And doth his *ydle* message set at nought. . . . *Am.* xix. 12
that same glorious beauties *ydle* boast . . . *Am.* xli. 9
He gan to move out of his *idle* seate; . . . *H.L.* 66
To breake his sleepe, and waste his *ydle* braine: . . . *H.L.* 256
How vainely then doe *ydle* wits invent, . . . *H.B.* 64
Or *idle* thought of earthly things, remaine; . . . *H.H.B.* 268
fed On *idle* fancies of thy foolish thought, . . . *H.H.B.* 289
idle hopes, which still doe fly away, . . . *Proth.* 8
Idleness. Through *idlenes* would turne to civill rage, . . . *Ro.* xxiii. 7

Idleness—*Continued.*
to wexe olde at home in *idlenesse* Is disadventrous, . . . *Hub.* 99
lothefull *idlenes* he doth detest, . . . *Hub.* 735
Clerks they to loathly *idlenes* entice, . . . *T.M.* 335
they their dayes to *ydlenesse* divide, . . . *Col.* 761
the first, . . . Was sluggish *Idlenesse*, the nourse of sin; . . . I. iv. 18. 6
Such one was *Idlenesse*, first of this company. . . . I. iv. 20. 9
uncomely *idlenesse* . . . to build her sluggish nest, . . . III. v. 2. 1
stretched forth in *ydlenesse* alwayes, . . . III. vii. 12. 4
Idlesse. spilt the blossome of my tender yeares In *ydlesse*; . . . VI. ii. 31. 3
Idly. all his yongthly forces *idly* spent, . . . *Mui.* 431
holding *idely* The broken reliques of their former cruelty. . . I. ii. 16. 8
some *ydly* satt at ease; . . . II. ix. 35. 3
Ne day nor night did ever *idly* rest; . . . V. viii. 3. 7
My love, lyke the Spectator, *ydly* sits; . . . *Am.* liv. 2
They *ydly* back returne to me agayne: . . . *Am.* lxxviii. 10
Idol. Doo make her *Idole* through the world appeare. . . . *Ro.* v. 14
Not that great *Idoll* might with this compaire, . . . *Ti.* 495
As th' *Idole* of her makers great magnificence. . . . II. ii. 41. 9
To walke the woodes with that his *Idole* faire, . . . III. viii. 11. 2
So hard this *Idole* was to be ared, . . . IV. v. 15. 7
Thence forth unto the *Idoll* they her brought; . . . V. vii. 6. 1
the *Idoll*, as it were inclining, . . . V. vii. 8. 1
setting up an *Idole* of his owne, . . . V. x. 13. 8
to doe unto his *Idole* most untrew. . . . V. x. 27. 9
that cursed *Idole*, farre proclamed, . . . V. x. 28. 4
in this Church hereby There stands an *Idole* . . . V. xi. 19. 2
underneath this *Idoll* there doth lie An hideous monster . . . V. xi. 20. 1
There he that *Idoll* saw of massy gold . . . V. xi. 21. 8
eke that *Idoll* deem'd so costly dere, . . . V. xi. 33. 7
That goodly *Idoll*, now so gay beseene, . . . *Am.* xxvii. 5
My soverayne saynt, the *Idoll* of my thought, . . . *Am.* lxi. 2
Above that *Idole* of his fayning thought, . . . *H.H.B.* 223
Idolatries. worshipt her in vaine, And made her th' Image of *Idolatryes*; . . . I. vi. 19. 7
Idolatry. oft committed fowle *Idolatree*. . . . III. xi. 49. 5
Idol's. saw the wicked fire . . . scorch his *Idoles* face, . . . III. x. 14. 6
at the *Idoles* feet apart . . . IV. x. 48. 7
lay Under the *Idols* feete in fearelesse bowre, . . . V. vii. 15. 2
Under that cursed *Idols* altar-stone . . . V. x. 29. 2
Idols. All other *Idoles* which the heathen adore, . . . IV. x. 40. 2
makes his God of his ungodly pelfe, And *Idols* serves: . . . V. viii. 19. 9
so let his *Idols* serve the Elfe! . . . V. viii. 19. 9
to his *Idols* sacrifice their blood, . . . V. x. 8. 4
If (*partial list*). *See* **And if, As if, But if.**
(*If* ought here worthie) of immortall dayes, . . . *Bel.*[2] xiv. 7
if things nam'd their names doo equalize, . . . *Ro.* xxvi. 10
if that time doo let thy glorie live, . . . *Ro.* xxxii. 11
If then a Goose great Rome from ruine stayde, . . . *Van.* xi. 9
if that fortune chaunce you up to call . . . *Van.* xii. 11
(*If* any gods the paine of lovers pitie) . . . *S.C.* Ja. 14
Listening *if* any thing did rushe, . . . *S.C.* Mar. 71
if hys ditties bene so trimly dight, . . . *S.C.* Ap. 29
Let him, *if* he dare, . . . *S.C.* Ap. 79
if you come hether . . . I will part them . . . *S.C.* Ap. 151
Or prive or pert *yf* any bene, . . . *S.C.* S. 162
if that Hobbinol right judgement bare, . . . *S.C.* D. 45
if the flocking Nymphes did folow Pan, . . . *S.C.* D. 47
One *if* I please, . . . *S.C.* D. 120
if that any Oedipus unware Shall chaunce, . . . *Gn. Ded.* 5
Ne cares he *if* the fleece, . . . Be not twice steeped . . . *Gn.* 97
if that anie other place you have, . . . *Hub.* 277
if he could willing bee To keep his sheep, . . . *Hub.* 284
if thee list unto the Court to throng, . . . *Hub.* 502
if fortune thee in Court to live, . . . *Hub.* 631
(*if* ever they would hope) . . . *Hub.* 959
if he be spide, . . . *Hub.* 975
if that wrong on eyther side there were, . . . *Hub.* 1097
Let God, . . . *if* please, care for the manie, . . . *Hub.* 1195
yf chaunce him fall into calamitie, . . . *T.M.* 305
if good were not praised more than ill, . . . *T.M.* 455
If in Bed, . . . *If* at Boorde, . . . *If* at hir Virginals, tell hir, *U.V.* 7, 8, 9
if I might of her have sight. . . . *Ti.* 476
If ought against thine honour I have tolde; . . . *Mui.* 103
flowers *if* it were prime, Or mellow fruit *if* it were harvest . *As.* 47, 48
'But *if* that land be there . . . *Col.* 304
danger great, *if* not assurd decay, . . . I. ii. 41. 8
if dwelling place were nigh at hand; . . . I. iii. 11. 2
Or *if* that any else did Jove excell; . . . I. iv. 11. 7
prove, *If* from their loyall loves he might them move: . . . I. iv. 26. 5
to weet *if* living wight . . . I. viii. 37. 8
Yf living man mote worthie be to be her liefe.' . . . I. ix. 17. 9
If not well ended at our dying day. . . . I. x. 41. 7
if knight thou bee, . . . II. iv. 39. 2
'*If* ever love of Lady did empierce . . . II. vi. 33. 1
'Fly . . . *If* that your lives ye love, . . . II. ix. 12. 2
if please you it discure, . . . II. ix. 42. 8
if that he were depriv'd Of native strength . . . II. ix. 57. 4
Ne wonder, *if* these did the knight appall; . . . II. xii. 25. 6
be not displeasd *if* disobayd: . . . II. xii. 28. 5
more white, *if* more might bee: . . . II. xii. 77. 6
'But *if* he have a Lady or a Love, . . . III. i. 27. 1
'Therefore aread, Sir, *if* thou have a love.' . . . III. i. 28. 1
She softely felt *if* any member moov'd, . . . III. i. 60. 7
If any puffe of breath . . . shee fond. . . . III. i. 60. 9
If chaunce I him encounter paravaunt; . . . III. ii. 16. 4
My crime, (*if* crime it be) . . . III. ii. 37. 7
to sleepe, *if* that she might; . . . III. ii. 47. 3
'*Yf* any leaches skill, . . . could have redrest . . . III. iii. 18. 1
If ay more goodly creature thou didst see? . . . III. iii. 32. 2

If—*Continued.*
to weete *if* life . . . did remaine; III. v. 31. 1
if that ye my sonne have heard III. vi. 23. 1
and worse, *if* worse ought were. III. xi. 3. 9
'*If* good find grace, III. xi. 10. 1
or *if* that ought doe death exceed; III. xii. 35. 3
if ought he did offend. III. xii. 36. 9
if he thereto list strive. IV. v. 37. 9
if one did rightly deeme; IV. x. 39. 8
not *if* an hundred tongues to tell . . . I had, IV. xi. 9. 6
blame me not *if* I have err'd IV. xii. 2. 6
'Ye Gods of seas, *if* any Gods at all IV. xii. 9. 1
listening *if* he mote her heare againe, IV. xii. 17. 4
If ought lay hidden in his grieved thought, IV. xii. 24. 8
And *if* then those may any worse be red, V. Pr. 2. 8
What time, *if* naught me let, I will be there. V. ii. 4. 3
If ought he had the same to counterpoys; V. ii. 30. 6
nothing lost, that may be found *if* sought. V. ii. 39. 9
'Now tell me, Amidas, *if* that ye may, V. iv. 17. 2
try *if* thou . . . can Move Radigund? V. v. 40. 3
if two met, the one mote needes fall over V. vi. 36. 9
If not, we will it force, V. x. 24. 3
And *if* all fayle, yet farewell open field; V. x. 24. 5
asked him, *if* that he were the same, V. xi. 4. 4
if shipping readie he mote there descry. V. xii. 3. 9
'Now tell, *if* please you, VI. i. 5. 1
Ne stayd to aske *if* it were he VI. i. 33. 3
if please her make the priefe; VI. iv. 34. 5
'*If* that the cause of this your languishment VI. iv. 35. 1
To seeke *if* he perchance asleep were layd, VI. v. 3. 7
If therefore health ye seeke, VI. vi. 7. 5
Wayting *if* he unwares him murther might; VI. vi. 26. 8
he sought *If* yet he were alive, VI. vi. 37. 9
if he hungry were, him offred eke to eat. VI. ix. 6. 9
'*If* happie, then it is in this intent, VI. ix. 20. 2
The joyes of love, *if* they should ever last VI. xi. 1. 1
Threatned to strike her *if* she did with-stand: VII. vi. 13. 5
if that any were on earth belowe VII. vi. 16. 5
If ever I did honour thee aright, *Epith.* 122
if thou be indeede, . . . The worlds great Parent, *H.L.* 155
if . . . He may but purchase lyking *H.L.* 238
If so be. *If so be* . . . voyce of wight alive May reach *Ro.* i. 5
bad them, *if so be* they were not bound, To come IV. vii. 33. 7
to depart them, *if so be* he may: VI. ii. 4. 5
Ignaro. His name *Ignaro* did his nature right aread. I. viii. 31. 9
Ignorance. The sonnes of darknes and of *ignoraunce,* *T.M.* 68
ugly Barbarisme, And brutish *Ignorance,* *T.M.* 188
Image of hellish horrour, *Ignorance,* *T.M.* 259
Whilest *Ignorance* the Muses doth oppresse. *T.M.* 288
Sith *ignorance* our kingdome did confound, *T.M.* 311
love of blindnesse and of *ignorance,* *T.M.* 485
Is *ignorance,* the enemy of grace, *T.M.* 497
sencelesse speach, and doted *ignorance,* I. viii. 34. 2
of your *ignorance* great merveill make, II. ii. 5. 4
Britomart dissembled it with *ignorance.* III. i. 50. 9
Ignorant. *ignoraunt* Of Phaedria, (for so my name is red) II. vi. 9. 6
Unmindfull of his wound, of his fate *ignoraunt.* II. viii. 34. 9
All *ignorant* of her contrary sex, III. i. 47. 2
brought Unto your dwelling, *ignorant* and loth, III. vii. 8. 8
ignorant of servants bad abuse III. ix. 18. 6
Ne was she *ignoraunt* of that leud lore, III. ix. 28. 5
Ile. *See* **Isle.**
Iliac. The Dorick flames consum'd the *Iliack* posts. *Gn.* 549
Ilion. stately towres of *Ilion* III. ix. 34. 3
Of sacred Salem; and sad *Ilion,* IV. i. 22. 3
Ilk. *ylke* can I you rehearse. *S.C.* Au. 142
Ill. Mayst witnesse well, by thy *ill* governement, *S.C.* Ja. 45
I play to please myselfe, all be it *ill.* *S.C.* Jun. 72
he was proude, that *ill* was payd, *S.C.* Jul. 149
Tway things doen *ill* agree. *S.C.* Jul. 152
I am taught, by Algrinds *ill,* *S.C.* Jul. 219
Ah! good Algrind! his hap was *ill,* *S.C.* Jul. 229
ill may they thrive! *S.C.* Au. 19
Their *ill* haviour garres men missay *S.C.* S. 106
Such *ill,* as is forced, mought nedes be endured. *S.C.* S. 139
he should so *ill* have thrive, *S.C.* S. 226
with love so *ill* bedight, *S.C.* O. 89
to weete whats good or *ill,* S.C. N. 183
We deeme of Death as doome of *ill* desert; *S.C.* N. 184
such pryde at length was *ill* repayde *S.C.* D. 49
My hurtlesse pleasaunce did me *ill* upbraide; *S.C.* D. 51
With minde that *ill* use doth before deprave, *Gn.* 91
inconstant fortune, bent to *ill,* *Gn.* 247
To be the author of her *ill* unwares, *Gn.* 631
In this *ill* plight there came to visite mee *Hub.* 17
They shall him make an *ill* accompt of thrift. *Hub.* 307
For a full complement of all their *ill,* *Hub.* 338
they so *ill* Did order their affaires, *Hub.* 559
At everie thing which they heare spoken *ill,* *Hub.* 715
the best speaches with *ill* meaning spill, *Hub.* 716
each practise *ill* Of coosinage *Hub.* 856
had not power to doo him good or *ill.* *Hub.* 890
Ill might it prosper that ill gotten was; *Hub.* 1149
did he good to none, to manie *ill,* *Hub.* 1197
Sweete Love devoyd of villanie or *ill,* *T.M.* 387
As heretofore of good, so now of *ill.* *T.M.* 408
if good were not praised more than *ill,* *T.M.* 455
whatso else of vertue good or *ill* *Mui.* 201
what thee dooth so *ill* apay.' *D.* 70
grieve my ghost, that *ill* mote him behove, *D.* 265

Ill—*Continued.*
Found ought in him, that she could say was *ill.* *As.* 24
Ill mynd so much to mynd anothers *ill,* *As.* 111
with hope of good, and hate of *ill,* *Col.* 192
I of gentle Mayds should *ill* deserve! *Col.* 465
To quite them *ill,* that me demeand so well: *Col.* 681
selfe-regard of private good or *ill* *Col.* 682
'That *ill* (said Hobbinol) they him requite, *Col.* 903
Briton Prince . . . suffered so much *ill,* I. Pr. 2. 7
the Ash for nothing *ill;* I. i. 9. 7
seeming to mistrust Some secret *ill,* or hidden foe I. i. 49. 4
Craving of you, in pitty of my state, To doe none *ill,* I. ii. 26. 4
nor in word nor deede *ill* meriting, I. iii. 2. 7
To follow her that was the causer of their *ill.* I. iii. 22. 9
damned sprights sent forth to make *ill* men aghast. I. v. 31. 9
Yet *ill* thou blamest me I. vi. 42. 4
How *ill* it sits with that same silver hed, I. viii. 33. 5
with his glistring armes does *ill* agree; I. ix. 22. 8
Th' *ill* to prevent, that life ensewen may; I. ix. 44. 3
If any strength we have, it is to *ill,* I. x. 1. 8
the cause and root of all his *ill,* I. x. 25. 1
bitter sence of his deepe rooted *ill,* I. xi. 22. 8
eftsoones did know Both good and *ill,* I. xi. 47. 8
to my foe betrayd when least I feared *ill.'* I. xii. 32. 9
He chaungd his mynd from one to other *ill;* II. i. 5. 4
'Fayre Lady, through fowle sorrow *ill* bedight, II. i. 14. 2
what bootes it to weepe . . . When *ill* is chaunst, II. i. 16. 6
but doth the *ill* increase, II. i. 16. 6
me he knew not, nether his owne *ill;* II. i. 54. 5
Ill by ensample good doth often gayne.' II. ii. 45. 5
The *ill* . . . he now to Guyon ment. II. iii. 11. 9
(and sure I feare it *ill*) II. iii. 44. 3
That *ill* beseemes thee, such as I thee see, II. v. 17. 6
would not seeme so rude, and thewed *ill,* II. vi. 26. 3
howe *ill* did him beseme II. vi. 27. 4
His head and beard with sout were *ill* bedight, II. vii. 3. 7
'Me *ill* besits, II. vii. 10. 1
To proove he lived *il* that did thus fowly dye. II. viii. 12. 9
Lives any that you hath thus *ill* apayd? II. ix. 37. 7
What ever bee the cause, it sure beseemes you *ill.'* II. ix. 37. 9
Him *ill* beseemes anothers fault to name, II. ix. 38. 4
other *ill* to feare II. ix. 42. 3
To ease you of that *ill,* II. ix. 42. 9
these rent reliques, speaking their *ill* plightes? II. xii. 9. 7
ill it were to hearken to her cry, II. xii. 28. 6
Which ever after they abusd to *ill,* II. xii. 31. 8
ofte of secret *ill* bids us beware: II. xii. 47. 7
to the *ill* purveyaunce of his page, III. i. 11. 7
Her wanton eyes, *ill* signes of womanhed, III. i. 41. 7
It *ill* beseemes a knight of gentle sort, III. ii. 12. 6
my deare daughters deepe engraffed *ill,* III. iii. 18. 3
Ne is thy fate, ne is thy fortune *ill,* III. iii. 24. 6
pittying his peoples *ill,* III. iii. 35. 8
First *ill,* and after ruled wickedly; III. iii. 46. 3
of a woman he should have much *ill;* III. iv. 25. 8
'Sir, *ill* mote I stay To tell the same: III. v. 4. 2
Ill weares he armes, that nill them use for Ladies sake.' III. v. 11. 9
A cruell shaft, headed with deadly *ill,* III. v. 20. 4
To yield himselfe unto the mightie *ill,* III. v. 48. 3
ill mote ye bene apayd.' III. vi. 21. 5
ill beseemes it to upbrayd A dolefull heart III. vi. 21. 7
ill becomes you, . . . To scorne the joy III. vi. 22. 5
least ought did *ill* betide To that faire Maide, III. vii. 31. 4
ill they seemed sure avizd to bee, III. vii. 57. 8
Where *ill* became him rashly would have thrust; III. viii. 25. 7
what men say of him, *ill* or well; III. ix. 3. 7
why doe wee devise of others *ill,* III. ix. 8. 6
humid evening *ill* for sicke folkes cace; III. ix. 26. 4
So readie rype to *ill ill* wemens counsels bee! III. x. 11. 9
Ne ever looked back for good or *ill;* III. x. 43. 7
Fury was full *ill* appareiled In rags, III. xii. 17. 1
did her *ill* become, III. xii. 30. 7
Such ones *ill* judge of love that cannot love, IV. Pr. 2. 1
the Ladie, *ill* of friends bestedded, IV. i. 3. 7
That doth *ill* cause or evill end enure; IV. ii. 29. 8
life it selfe seemd loathsome, and long safetie *ill.* IV. iii. 36. 9
For enmitie, that of no *ill* proceeds IV. iv. 1. 6
lay musing long on that him *ill* apayd. IV. v. 42. 9
wiping out remembrance of all *ill,* IV. vi. 32. 4
some *ill* whose cause did not appeare. IV. x. 12. 9
As every one had cause of good or *ill.* IV. x. 43. 6
ill your goddesse services are drest By virgins, IV. x. 54. 8
For his deare sake, that *ill* deserv'd that plight: IV. xii. 19. 5
ill perhaps mote fall to either side; V. i. 25. 4
Ill can he rule the great that cannot reach the small.' V. ii. 43. 9
whylest they were thus *ill* beset, V. iii. 10. 1
what so good or *ill* . . . I hold mine owne, V. iv. 14. 2
he was soone aware of their *ill* minde, V. iv. 24. 1
all the *ill* which chaunst to me of late, V. iv. 28. 7
to doe all the *ill* Which she could doe V. iv. 30. 8
Was lately broken by some fortune *ill;* V. v. 15. 4
for such good him recompence with *ill?* V. v. 32. 6
report of him much *ill,* V. vi. 1. 2
since she no *ill* did heare, V. vi. 4. 8
To thinke of him so *ill;* V. vi. 4. 9
with conscience Of his *ill* newes, V. vi. 9. 6
(for she ful *ill* Could sleepe all night, V. vii. 27. 3
'Ne him sufficeth all the wrong and *ill,* V. viii. 19. 1
never did her *ill,* ne once deserved blame. V. viii. 22. 9
where footing was so *ill;* V. ix. 15. 7

Ill—*Continued.*
better to reforme then to cut off the *ill.* . . . V. x. 2. 9
Yet him nought terrified that feared nothing *ill.* . . . V. xi. 22. 9
if she heard of *ill* that any did, . . . V. xii. 32. 5
turne to *ill* the thing that well was ment; . . . V. xii. 34. 5
if that any *ill* she heard of any, . . . V. xii. 35. 1
speake so *ill* of him that well deserved, . . . V. xii. 43. 2
doth observe a custome lewd and *ill,* . . . VI. i. 13. 3
feeling *ill* Of his late fall, . . . VI. i. 35. 4
this his Ladie (that him *ill* became) . . . VI. ii. 10. 2
he, that hath your Knight so *ill* bestad, . . . VI. ii. 45. 5
his sonne so *ill* bedight With bleeding wounds, . . . VI. iii. 4. 1
To thinke of this *ill* state in which she stood; . . . VI. iii. 11. 6
Without suspect of *ill* or daungers . . . VI. iii. 23. 9
'*Ill* seemes,' (sayd he) 'if he so valiaunt be, . . . VI. iii. 40. 6
And like in time to further *ill* to grow, . . . VI. iv. 30. 8
from those outward sences, *ill* affected, . . . VI. vi. 8. 1
to avoide the occasion of the *ill:* . . . VI. vi. 14. 2
With which he had those two so *ill* bestad: . . . VI. vi. 18. 5
prayd to pitty his *ill* plight. . . . VI. vi. 20. 9
With her unworthy knight, who *ill* him entertayned. . . . VI. vi. 39. 9
how to please the minds of good and *ill,* . . . VI. vi. 41. 8
Least unto me betide a greater *ill;* . . . VI. viii. 30. 4
he For *ill* rewards him well. . . . VI. ix. Arg.
'It is the mynd that maketh good or *ill,* . . . VI. ix. 30. 1
to whom ye *ill* display That mucky masse, . . . VI. ix. 33. 4
'That my *ill* fortune did them hence displace; . . . VI. x. 20. 7
Was made the most unpleasant and most *ill:* . . . VII. vi. 37. 8
As well for horror of their count'naunce *ill,* . . . VII. vii. 3. 7
sweet is Moly, but his root is *ill.* . . . *Am.* xxvi. 8
did she know how *ill* these two accord . . . *Am.* xxxi. 13
And speake her good, though she requite it *ill.* . . . *Am.* xlviii. 14
not on him that never thought you *ill,* . . . *Am.* xlix. 7
Good shames to be to *ill* an instrument! . . . *Am.* liii. 12
Without constraynt, or dread of any *ill:* . . . *Am.* lxv. 6
to tempt her mind to *ill.* . . . *Epith.* 199
for this time it *ill* ordained was, . . . *Epith.* 270
what ye do, albe it good or *ill.* . . . *Epith.* 367
Whatever *ill* before he did aby: . . . *H.L.* 242
theirs that do abuse it unto *ill:* . . . *H.B.* 156
(for pride and love may *ill* agree) . . . *H.H.L.* 95
I'll (*partial list*).
Ile write in termes as she . . . *Hub.* 41
Her name *Ile* teach . . . *Ile* teach to call for Cynthia . . . *Col.* 637, 639
The end whereof *Ile* keepe untill another cast. . . . VI. viii. 51. 9
Ill-advised. thou *ill advized* man, . . . V. v. 40. 1
Ill-apaid. she is inly nothing *ill apayd;* . . . II. xii. 28. 7
rudenes be no breach . . . ne be *ill ypaid;* . . . III. x. 25. 4
Or *ill apayd* or much dismayd ye be; . . . V. vii. 18. 8
So bore her quite away, nor well nor *ill apayd.* . . . V. xi. 64. 9
To leave his love he should be *ill apayd,* . . . VI. ii. 18. 8
Ill-assayed. the hart is *ill assayde,* . . . *S.C.* Au. 5
Ill-bested. Thus *ill bestedd,* and fearefull more of shame . . . I. i. 24. 1
that seemed *ill* bested, . . . II. i. 30. 4
Whom when I heard to beene so *ill bestad,* . . . II. i. 52. 7
He found him selfe unwist so *ill bestad,* . . . V. i. 22. 4
whiles he him saw so *ill bested,* . . . V. xii. 23. 5
Ill-disposed. of him selfe to treason *ill disposd,* . . . II. iv. 22. 3
borne with *ill-disposed* skyes, . . . II. ix. 52. 8
Ill-faced. The *ill-faste* Owle, deaths dreadfull messengere; . . . II. xii. 36. 4
Ill-favored. each one Of sundrie shapes, yet all *ill-favored:* . . . I. i. 15. 7
A loathly, wrinckled hag, *ill favoured,* old, . . . I. viii. 46. 8
eke her face *ill-favourd,* full of wrinckles old. . . . II. iv. 4. 9
griesly hew and fowle *ill favour'd* sight; . . . II. vii. 3. 5
A foule *ill-favoured* foster, . . . III. v. 6. 3
he was fowle, *ill-favoured,* and grim, . . . III. xii. 15. 1
Shame most *ill-favourd,* bestiall, and blinde: . . . III. xii. 24. 5
two old *ill favour'd* Hags he met, . . . V. xii. 28. 4
Ill-fitting. were it not *ill fitting* for this file . . . VII. vi. 37. 1
Ill-gotten. Ill might it prosper that *ill gotten* was; . . . *Hub.* 1149
Ill-grounded. dyes like *ill grounded* seeds. . . . IV. iv. 1. 9
Ill-headed. every man, Surcharg'd with wine, were heedlesse and *ill-hedded,* . . . IV. i. 3. 4
Illimitable. To them the heavens *illimitable* hight . . . *H.H.L.* 57
Ill luck. as signes of *ill luck,* . . . *S.C.* May 232
Ill-pleasing. His witlesse pleasance, and *ill pleasing* vaine. . . . *Hub.* 799
Ills. not yielding to his *ills,* . . . III. iii. 41. 3
Ill-succeeding. bootelesse paines, and *ill succeeding* night: . . . I. ii. 2. 4
Illude. falsed oft his blowes t' *illude* him with such bayt. . . . II. v. 9. 9
Illuminate. T' *illuminate* my dim and dulled eyne, . . . *H.B.* 20
That need no Sunne t' *illuminate* their spheres, . . . *H.H.B.* 69
Illumine. more *illumine* your resplendent ray, . . . *H.B.* 177
Illusion. through so false *illusion,* Doth turne the name . . . *Hub.* 219
with such vaine *illusion* Hath so wise men bewitcht, . . . *Ti.* 456
Through vaine *illusion* of their lust unclene, . . . II. x. 8. 7
magicall *Illusion* that did beguile his sense, . . . II. xi. 39. 6
By false *illusion* of a guilefull Spright . . . III. iii. 13. 4
Through sweet *illusion* of her lookes delight; . . . *Am.* xvi. 4
Illusions. doe that sence besiege with light *illusions.* . . . II. xi. 11. 9
Image. in setting of hir *image* up. . . . *Rev.* i. 14
the storie Of Joves great *Image* . . . *Ro.* ii. 6
Her owne like *image* in a christall brooke. . . . *Gn.* 88
The *Image* of that Gnat appeard to him, . . . *Gn.* 324
mans life in his likest *image* Was limned forth, . . . *T.M.* 201
Image of hellish horrour, Ignorance, . . . *T.M.* 259
I saw an *Image,* all of massie gold, . . . *Ti.* 491
th' Altare, on the which this *Image* staid, . . . *Ti.* 498
To make the *image* of true heavinesse: . . . *D.* 329
The *image* of the heavens in shape humane.' . . . *Col.* 351
Bids me, . . . to adore His goodly *image,* . . . *Ded. Son.* xv. 9

Image—*Continued.*
Joyous to see his *ymage* in mine eye, . . . I. iv. 45. 6
worshipt her in vaine, And made her th' *Image* of Idolatryes; . . . I. vi. 19. 7
in this antique *ymage* thy great auncestry. . . . II. Pr. 4. 9
On that fayre *ymage* of that heavenly Mayd, . . . II. i. 28. 7
deare Lady, which the *ymage* art Of ruefull pitty . . . II. i. 44. 4
Behold the *ymage* of mortalitie, . . . II. i. 57. 2
In springing flowre the *image* of thy day. . . . II. xii. 74. 3
Whose *image* shee had seene in Venus looking glas. . . . III. i. 8. 9
The *image* of superfluous riotize, . . . III. i. 33. 6
'With thee yet shall he leave . . . his *ymage* dead, . . . III. iii. 29. 2
'Deare *image* of my selfe, (she sayd) . . . III. iv. 36. 1
The dreary *image* of sad death appeares: . . . III. iv. 57. 7
there stood an *Image* all alone . . . III. xi. 47. 4
Did to that *image* bowe their humble knee, . . . III. xi. 49. 4
She, . . . Had Deathes owne *ymage* figurd in her face, . . . III. xii. 19. 6
heavenly *image* of perfection, . . . IV. vi. 24. 6
present time The *image* of the antique world compare, . . . V. Pr. 1. 2
Like the true saint beside the *image* set, . . . V. iii. 24. 2
The *image* of his monstrous parent Geryone. . . . V. x. 13. 9
Upon the *Image* with his naked blade . . . he strooke; . . . V. xi. 22. 1
So fresh the *image* of her former dread, . . . VI. viii. 31. 6
Ne could be seene but like an *image* in a glass. . . . VII. vii. 6. 9
to which I dare Resemble th' *ymage* . . . *Am.* ix. 4
In which her glorious *ymage* placed is; . . . *Am.* xxii. 6
The goodly *ymage* . . . would therein appere. . . . *Am.* xlv. 11
The glorious *image* of the Makers beautie, . . . *Am.* lxi. 1
Whose *ymage* yet I carry fresh in mynd. . . . *Am.* lxxviii. 4
th' onely *image* of that heavenly ray, . . . *Am.* lxxxvii. 7
Fresh burning in the *image* of their eye, . . . *H.L.* 132
Whose *image* printing in his deepest wit, . . . *H.L.* 197
Most lively *image* of thy Fathers face, . . . *H.H.L.* 171
to love . . . our brethren, to his *image* wrought. . . . *H.H.L.* 189
in thy brest his blessed *image* beare. . . . *H.H.L.* 259
The *image* of such endlesse perfectnesse? . . . *H.H.B.* 105
And shew himselfe in th' *image* of his grace, . . . *H.H.B.* 114
Imageries. Wrought with faire pillours and fine *imageries;* . . . *Ti.* 96
Imagery. *Imagery* Of Baetus or of Alcons vanity. . . . *Gn.* 103
An Altare, carv'd with cunning *ymagery,* . . . I. viii. 36. 2
Woven with antickes and wyld *ymagery;* . . . II. vii. 4. 6
Most goodly it with curious *ymageree* Was overwrought, . . . II. xii. 60. 5
Princes bowres adorne with painted *imagery.* . . . VII. vii. 10. 9
Images. Doo not restraine your *images* still mourning) . . . *Ro.* xv. 8
The *images* of God in earthly clay; . . . I. x. 39. 7
th' *Images* . . . Did cast to ground, . . . VI. xii. 25. 4
ymages Of hardest marble are of purpose made, . . . *Am.* li. 1
lively *images* of heavens light, . . . *H.B.* 163
And glorious *images* in heaven wrought, . . . *H.H.B.* 3
Imagine. With humblest suit that he *imagine* mot, . . . IV. ii. 8. 7
Who had him seene *imagine* mote thereby . . . V. v. 24. 1
meekest boone that they *imagine* mought: . . . V. ix. 34. 5
The which for him she could *imagine* best: . . . VI. vi. 41. 5
Imbrace, Imbrast. *See* **Embrace, -d.**
Imbrue. T' *embrew* her teeth and clawes . . . *Bel.*[2] vi. 7
To see their blades so greedily *imbrew,* . . . I. vi. 38. 7
never could the force of fleshly arme . . . in his blood *embrew;* . . . I. xi. 36. 7
in her streaming blood he did . . . tender joints *embrew:* . . . II. i. 40. 8
did soft *embrew* The sugred licour . . . II. v. 33. 5
A murdrous knife . . . In her tormented bodie to *embrew:* . . . III. xii. 32. 7
his hand in Ladies bloud *embrew,* . . . V. i. 16. 4
loth he was his noble hands t' *embrew* In the base blood . . . V. ii. 52. 4
the which ye wont t' *embrew* In bloud of Kings, . . . V. vii. 40. 4
with their bloud did all the flore *imbrew,* . . . VI. v. 5. 3
rends her golden locks, and snowy brests *embrew.* . . . VII. viii. 40. 9
in bloody bath . . . her cruell hands *embrew.* . . . *Am.* xxxi. 12
To make the bayte her gazers to *embrew:* . . . *Am.* liii. 11
That may my rymes with sweet infuse *embrew,* . . . *H.H.L.* 47
Imbrued. His precious robe I saw *embrued* with bloud. . . . *Rev.* iii. 5
Your blades in your owne bowels you *embrew'd?* . . . *Ro.* xxiv. 8
all *embrewd* in blood his eyes did shine as glas. . . . I. vii. 17. 9
manly hands *imbrewd* in guilty blood Had never beene, . . . I. vii. 47. 3
Thy litle hands *embrewd* in bleeding brest . . . II. i. 37. 8
Shall him defeate withouten blood *imbrewd:* . . . III. iii. 38. 7
After late chace of their *embrewed* game, . . . III. vi. 17. 3
avenge on Sanglier His Ladies bloud *embrewed.* . . . V. i. Arg.
thy hand too bold it selfe *embrewed* In blood . . . VI. ii. 7. 3
Great shame in lieges blood to be *embrew'd!* . . . VI. vii. 23. 6
many harts to bleed . . . with wyde wounds *embrewed,* . . . *H.L.* 13
Imbued. grype your hearts with noysome rage *imbew'd,* . . . *Ro.* xxiv. 6
Imitate. To mock her selfe, and Truth to *imitate,* . . . *T.M.* 206
with usage sly He taught to *imitate* that Lady trew, . . . I. i. 46. 8
best alyve, That natures worke by art can *imitate:* . . . II. xii. 42. 4
It was her selfe whom it did *imitate,* . . . III. viii. 9. 4
they thy vertuous deedes may *imitate,* . . . III. viii. 43. 6
Immaculate. whie be they themselves *immaculate,* . . . *D.* 206
Swift Rhene, and Alpheus still *immaculate* . . . IV. xi. 21. 4
Immeasured. far exceeded men in their *immeasurd* mights. . . . II. x. 8. 9
Mighty Monoceroses with *immeasured* tayles. . . . II. xii. 23. 9
Immerito. who will saye: *this was Immerito?* . . . *U.V.* 21
Imminent. Shamefull deceipt, and daunger *imminent,* . . . III. iv. 58. 4
Their counsell crav'd in daunger *imminent.* . . . III. x. 41. 3
Immixing. Amongst her teares *immixing* prayers meeke, . . . IV. iii. 47. 6
Immodest. Guyon is of *immodest* Merth Led into loose desyre; . . . II. vi. Arg.
A foe of folly and *immodest* toy, . . . II. vi. 37. 4
Immodestly. Now throwing forth lewd wordes *immodestly;* . . . II. xii. 16. 4
Immortal. right worthie sure . . . of *immortall* dayes, . . . *Bel.*[2] xiv. 7
Such *immortall* mirrhor, as he doth admire, . . . *S.C.* O. 93
the *immortal* praise of womankinde, . . . *Gn.* 428
wonts to decke the Gods *immortall* crew . . . *Hub.* 1268
pierce *immortall* breasts with mortall smarts? . . . *T.M.* 48

Immortal—*Continued.*
To sing with Angels her *immortall* praize. . . . *T.M.* 588
So thou both here and there *immortall* art, . . . *Ti.* 342
them *immortall* make, which els would die . . . *Ti.* 377
that blinde bard did him *immortall* make . . . *Ti.* 430
Immortall spirite of Philisides, . . . *Ti.* 673
For her he made hymnes of *immortall* praise, . . . *As.* 63
heavenly borne, And of *immortall* race, . . . *Col.* 257
do their Cynthia *immortall* make: . . . *Col.* 453
And crownes their ashes with *immortall* baies. . . . *Ded. Son.* iv. 12
In golden verse, worthy *immortal* fame: . . . *Ded. Son.* xii. 4
Which now triumpheth, through *immortall* merit . . . *Ded. Son.* xv. 3
in th' *immortall* booke of fame To be eternized, . . . I. x. 59. 5
fame, That warlike handes ennoblest with *immortall* name; . . I. xi. 5. 9
'So from *immortall* race he does proceede, . . . II. iv. 42. 1
Unworthy match for such *immortall* mate . . . II. vii. 50. 4
Th' other *immortall,* perfect, masculine; . . . II. ix. 22. 5
laid them up in his *immortall* scrine, . . . II. ix. 56. 6
Immortall fame for ever hath enrold; . . . II. x. 4. 8
A woman worthy of *immortall* praise, . . . II. x. 42. 4
ennoble with *immortall* name The warlike Worthies, . . . III. iii. 4. 3
from the sacred mould Of her *immortall* womb, . . . III. iv. 11. 9
O! is this Th' *immortall* name, . . . III. iv. 36. 4
of *immortall* seed To beene ybredd . . . III. iv. 38. 1
Should happy bee, and have *immortall* blis: . . . III. vi. 41. 3
As an *immortall* mote a mortall wight, . . . III. viii. 38. 4
Even *immortal* prayse and glory wyde, . . . III. xii. 39. 6
crowne true lovers with *immortall* blis, . . . IV. Pr. 2. 8
that which is th' *immortall* spright Lives still, . . . IV. xi. 16. 8
Great Ganges, and *immortall* Euphrates, . . . IV. xi. 21. 1
Loose so *immortall* glory, and so endlesse gaines. . . . IV. xi. 22. 9
Of mortall sire, though of *immortall* wombe, . . . IV. xii. 4. 2
He might not with *immortall* food be fed, . . . IV. xii. 4. 3
Can from th' *immortall* Gods ought hidden bee? . . . V. vii. 21. 6
May you in heaven *immortall* guerdon gaine . . . V. x. 21. 4
Crowned with girlonds of *immortall* baies; . . . V. xi. 34. 6
that *immortall* spright Of Podalyrius . . . VI. vi. 1. 7
Wasting the strength of her *immortall* age: . . . VI. vi. 11. 6
Which should befall to Calidores *immortall* name. . . . VI. ix. 1. 9
Kindle fresh sparks of that *immortall* fire . . . VII. vii. 2. 4
their minds (which they *immortall* call) . . . VII. vii. 19. 8
yee make *Immortall* and unchangeable to be: . . . VII. vii. 54. 3
those fayre eyes, my loves *immortall* light; . . . *Am.* xvi. 2
that, which shall you make *immortall,* cherish. . . . *Am.* xxvii. 14
And eke her mind is pure *immortall* hye. . . . *Am.* lv. 12
this verse . . . Shall be thereof *immortall* moniment; . . . *Am.* lxix. 10
setting your *immortall* prayses forth: . . . *Am.* lxxxii. 12
man that breathes a more *immortall* mynd, . . . *H.L.* 103
th' *immortall* flame Of heavenly light, . . . *H.L.* 115
Then would I sing of thine *immortall* praise . . . *H.L.* 302
faire *immortall* beame Hath darted fyre . . . *H.B.* 23
out of that great *immortall* Spright, . . . *H.B.* 107
things *immortall* no corruption take. . . . *H.B.* 161
In endlesse glorie and *immortall* might, . . . *H.H.L.* 37
resemble . . . as mortall thing *immortall* could; . . . *H.H.L.* 114
beames . . . Of that *immortall* beautie, there with thee, . . . *H.H.B.* 13
To contemplation of th' *immortall* sky; . . . *H.H.B.* 25
But that *immortall* light, which there doth shine, . . . *H.H.B.* 169
Immortality. *immortalitie* So meane Harpes worke may challenge . . . *Ro.* xxxii. 3
Well worthie thou of *immortalitie,* . . . *Ro.* Env. 3
how can mortall *immortalitie* give? . . . *Ti.* 413
Immortalize. will henceforth *immortalize* no more; . . . *T.M.* 464
That their brave deeds she might *immortalize* . . . *Ded. Son.* xiv. 3
A mortall thing so to *immortalize;* . . . *Am.* lxxv. 6
Immortalized. living handes *immortalizd* his name. . . . II. viii. 13. 5
Immortally. every part remaines *immortally:* . . . *Am.* xlv. 8
Immovable. *Immoveable,* resistlesse, without end; . . . V. i. 12. 7
In which it doth *immoveable* abide, . . . V. ii. 35. 6
like a lifelesse corse *immoveable* he stood. . . . V. iii. 26. 9
Imp. Brave *Impe* of Bedford! grow apace in bountie, . . . *Ti.* 272
thou, most dreaded *impe* of highest Jove, . . . I. Pr. 3. 1
he taught the tender *ymp* . . . To banish cowardize . . . I. vi. 24. 1
'Well worthy *impe,*' said then the Lady gent, . . . I. ix. 6. 1
faire *ymp,* sprong out from English race, . . . I. x. 60. 1
Fayre *ympe* of Phoebus and his aged bryde, . . . I. xi. 5. 7
Matchable ether to that *ympe* of Troy, . . . III. xii. 7. 3
O! thou sacred *imp* of Jove . . . IV. xi. 10. 1
The noble *ympe,* . . . It gladly did accept, . . . VI. ii. 38. 6
To *impe* the wings of thy high flying mynd, . . . *H.H.B.* 135
Impacable. freed from bands of *impacable* fate, . . . *Ti.* 395
wondred at their *impacable* stoure, . . . IV. ix. 22. 4
Impair. *See* **Pair.**
Enaunter their heritage doe *impaire.* . . . *S.C.* May 78
'Flesh may *empaire,*' . . . 'but reason can repaire.' . . . I. vii. 41. 9
nothing may my present hope *empare.*' . . . I. x. 63. 5
Ne poysnous Envy justly can *empayre* The prayse . . . III. v. 54. 5
So all the rest did others parts *empaire,* . . . V. ii. 32. 5
So his encreased, but mine did *empaire.* . . . V. iv. 8. 5
knights of Maidenhead, whose praise she would *empaire.*' . . . V. iv. 34. 9
sought his life for to *empaire:* . . . V. xi. 48. 5
mote *empaire* my peace with daungers dread; . . . VI. ix. 33. 6
The faire doth it prolong; the fowle doth it *impaire.* . . . VII. vii. 22. 9
Impaired. Whose praise hereby no whit *impaired* is, . . . *Col.* 755
their powres, *empayrd* through labor long, . . . I. ix. 2. 1
Her bountie she abated, and his cheare *empayrd.* . . . II. x. 30. 9
Impale. her worke she did *empale* With a faire border . . . *Mui.* 297
Impaneled. Therefore a Jurie was *impaneld* streight . . . VI. vii. 34. 4
Imparlance. To speake to them, and some *emparlance* move; . IV. ix. 31. 2
with his Lord she would *emparlaunce* make. . . . V. iv. 50. 9
Impart. Found never help who never would his hurts *impart.*' . . . I. vii. 40. 9
He oft finds present helpe who does his griefe *impart.*' . . . II. i. 46. 9
unto him she would *impart* the same. . . . II. iv. 20. 8
That gentle Lady did to him *impart:* . . . II. vi. 26. 5
To whom no share in armes and chevalree They doe *impart,* . III. ii. 1. 5
will to none her maladie *impart?* . . . IV. vi. 1. 7
The penance which ye shall to him *empart:* . . . IV. vi. 32. 6
to my wound her gratious help *impart.* . . . IV. x. 48. 5
Unto her selfe her silent prayers did *impart.* . . . V. vii. 7. 9
I am adjur'd best counsell to *impart* . . . V. vii. 19. 8
She thankt him . . . for that newes he did to her *impart,* . . VI. ii. 46. 7
all thy blessings unto us *impart.* . . . *Epith.* 397
Imparted. Eche thing *imparted* is more eath to beare: . . . *S.C.* S. 17
Imparts. He oft finds med'cine who his griefe *imparts,* . . . I. ii. 34. 4
Impassion. yet those sights *empassion* me full nere. . . . *Van.* i. 12
yet my soule it deepely doth *empassion.* . . . *D.* 35
Impassionate. he thereby was more *empassionate;* . . . *D.* 193
The Briton Prince was sore *empassionate,* . . . V. ix. 46. 2
Impassioned. Yet pittie me in your *empassiond* spright, . . . *D.* 515
now it is *empassioned* so deepe, . . . I. iii. 2. 1
The Damzell was full deepe *empassioned* . . . III. iii. 43. 1
She was *empassiond* at that piteous act, . . . III. ix. 38. 4
The warlike Damzell was *empassiond* sore, . . . III. xi. 18. 2
Was much *empassiond* in her gentle sprite, . . . III. xii. 46. *or.* 7
Impatience. Through great *impatience* of his grieved hed, . . I. viii. 17. 4
Direfull *impatience,* and hart-murdring love: . . . II. v. 16. 4
Yet nothing could him to *impatience* entise. . . . II. v. 21. 9
th' other was *Impatience,* . . . II. xi. 23. 9
Eftsoones she grew to great *impatience,* . . . III. i. 48. 1
With huge *impatience* he inly swelt, . . . III. xi. 27. 1
did to great *impatience* move her: . . . V. v. 51. 7
did him selfe from fraile *impatience* refraine. . . . VI. i. 30. 9
Impatient. *Impatient* of pleasures faint desires, . . . *Ro.* xxiii. 6
With bitter torture, and *impatient* paines, . . . *Gn.* 628
Might be the cause of so *impatient* plight? . . . *T.M.* 44
The rest of her *impatient* regret, . . . *As.* 169
impatient of unwonted payne, He loudly brayd . . . I. viii. 11. 2
The beast, *impatient* of his smarting wound . . . I. xi. 25. 6
Throwne out from womanish *impatient* mynd? . . . I. xii. 30. 2
Of ruefull pitty and *impatient* smart, . . . II. i. 44. 5
him affronted with *impatient* might: . . . II. v. 20. 7
*The one she slew in that *impatient* stoure, . . . II. x. 19. 5
Of whose fowle outrage they *impatient,* . . . III. iv. 45. 7
With other signes of sorrow and *impatient* teene. . . . III. xi. 37. 9
Being *impatient* of impediment, . . . V. viii. 7. 2
Nor cease her sorrow and *impatient* stound, . . . VI. v. 6. 7
Sorrow, and anguish, and *impatient* paine, . . . VI. vi. 8. 6
Impatient of any paramoure: . . . VI. ix. 39. 5
But pride, *impatient* of long resting peace, . . . *H.H.L.* 78
Impeach. th' heavens striving them for to *impeach.* . . . *Gn.* 576
There was no barre to stop, nor foe him to *empeach.* . . . I. viii. 34. 9
Which with sad cares *empeach* our native joyes. . . . II. vii. 15. 6
secret pleasure did offence *empeach,* . . . II. x. 68. 8
without fowle *empeach,* . . . II. xii. 56. 5
nought our passage may *empeach,* . . . III. iii. 53. 1
swelling throbs *empeach* His foltring toung . . . III. xi. 12. 2
th' other eke his malice did *empeach,* . . . IV. x. 36. 8
To lodge with him that night, unles good cause *empeach.* . . V. vi. 21. 9
Like to an hideous storme, which nothing may *empeach.* . . V. vii. 35. 9
The vaile, which did his powrefull light *empeach,* . . . V. viii. 37. 7
let not your griefe *empeach* To tell . . . VI. ii. 42. 2
T' expresse his passions, which his reason did *empeach.* . . VI. iv. 11. 9
armes . . . Whose burden mote *empeach* his needfull speed, . . VI. iv. 19. 2
Imped. having *ympt* the head to it agayne, . . . IV. ix. 4. 7
Impediment. forth without *impediment* I past, . . . IV. x. 11. 1
Being impatient of *impediment,* . . . V. viii. 7. 2
Imperfect. All that's *imperfect,* borne belowe the Moone; . . *Ro.* xix. 2
The one *imperfect,* mortall, foeminine, . . . II. ix. 22. 4
Imperfection. deform'd with some foule *imperfection.* . . . *H.B.* 147
Imperial. thence th' *Imperiall* Eagle rooting tooke, . . . *Ro.* xviii. 10
Subject unto that powre *imperiall.*' . . . *Hub.* 972
By his great lookes and power *Imperiall.* . . . *Mui.* 312
imperiall Majestie to frame In lofty numbers . . . *Ded. Son.* xii. 7
Like as a Lyon, whose *imperiall* powre . . . II. v. 10. 1
That is, her bounty, and *imperiall* powre, . . . II. ix. 3. 6
he parted his *imperiall* state, . . . II. x. 13. 6
brave ensample, . . . to kinges and states *imperiall.* . . . II. x. 74. 9
Under his Diademe *imperiall:* . . . IV. xi. 11. 4
wandring on his seas *imperiall* . . . IV. xii. 32. 4
Resembling God in his *imperiall* might; . . . V. Pr. 10. 2
He may dispose by his *imperiall* might, . . . V. iv. 19. 6
Yet tempred with some majestie *imperiall.* . . . V. ix. 34. 9
Jove confirm'd in his *imperiall* see. . . . VII. vii. 59. 7
All mortall Princes and *imperiall* States; . . . *H.H.B.* 88
lower creatures all Subjected to her powre *imperiall.* . . . *H.H.B.* 196
Imperil. His person to *emperill* so in fight; . . . IV. iv. 10. 6
Imperious. *imperious* love her hart did vexe, . . . III. i. 54. 4
Imperious Love hath highest set his throne, . . . III. ii. 23. 2
The wretched man at his *imperious* speach . . . III. x. 25. 1
with *imperious* sway Him forst, . . . III. xi. 26. 7
man and beast with powre *imperious* Subdeweth . . . III. xii. 22. 4
From her high spirit chase *imperious* feare, . . . IV. Pr. 5. 3
To shew the powre of your *imperious* eyes; . . . *Am.* xlix. 6
that *imperious* boy Doth therwith tip his . . . darts, . . . *H.L.* 120
Impetuous. finally the storme *impetuous* . . . *Bel.*[2] xiii. 9
adding more *impetuous* forse, . . . II. iv. 6. 3
That thee against me drew with so *impetuous* dread. . . . II. v. 16. 9
with such puissance and *impetuous* maine . . . II. ix. 14. 5
met Together with *impetuous* rage and forse, . . . III. ix. 16. 2

Impetuous—*Continued.*
threw A shivering dart with so *impetuous* force, ... V. viii. 32. 6
did him smite Full in the shield with so *impetuous* powre, . . VI. vii. 8. 2
Rencountred him with so *impetuous* might, ... VI. xii. 29. 2
Impetuously. round about him flocke *impetuously,* . . . . II. xi. 18. 3
Impictured. His palled face, *impictured* with death, ... *As.* 163
Impierceable. never felt his *imperceable* brest So wondrous force . . . . I. xi. 17. 7
Impiety. lewd *Impietie,* that her accused sore. . . . . V. ix. 48. 9
guilty be of thine *impietie?* . . . . I. ix. 47. 4
Implacable. Displeasure too *implacable* was it, ... *Gn.* 379
'O! how I burne with *implacable* fyre; . . . . II. vi. 44. 2
to avenge the *implacable* wrong . . . . III. vii. 35. 5
Implements. Of all those goodly *implements* of prayse, . . . VI. ii. 39. 2
Implied. in those lofty lookes is close *implide,* . . . . *Am.* v. 5
Implies. An hatefull Snake, the which his . . . mortall sting *implyes.* . . . . I. iv. 31. 5
Phoebus, . . . His blushing face in foggy cloud *implyes,* . . . I. vi. 6. 7
Himselfe in streighter bandes too rash *implyes,* . . . . . . I. xi. 23. 5
Implore. With percing wordes and pittifull *implore,* . . . . II. v. 37. 5
ne her need *implore* Lucinaes aide: . . . . III. vi. 27. 3
nothing so much pitty doth *implore* . . . . III. xi. 18. 5
whence mortal men *implore* Right in their wrongs, ... V. vii. 1. 4
whom she did oft *implore* To send her succour, ... VI. iv. 10. 8
Imploy. *See* **Employ.**
Implunged. Into huge waves of griefe . . . Full deepe *emplonged* was, ... III. x. 17. 5
Imply. in themselves eternall moisture they *imply.* . . . . . III. vi. 34. 9
did close *implie* The course of all her fortune . . . . V. vii. 12. 8
Importable. With hideous strokes and *importable* powre, . . . II. viii. 35. 2
Importune. with *importune* might Warre against us, ... *Mui.* 230
Th' *importune* fates, which vengeance on me seeke, ... *D.* 387
Ran through his mouth with so *importune* might, ... I. xi. 53. 7
often blame the too *importune* fate . . . . I. xii. 16. 5
with *importune* outrage him assayld; . . . . II. vi. 29. 2
The which dividing with *importune* sway, ... II. viii. 38. 8
with their *importune* sway, ... II. x. 15. 5
with greedie malice and *importune* toyle, ... II. xi. 7. 7
their *importune* fates all satisfide: . . . . III. iii. 44. 7
Britomart did him *importune* hard . . . . IV. ix. 41. 2
Importune care of their owne publicke cause; . . . . V. ix. 44. 8
smote at him with so *importune* might, ... V. xi. 11. 6
with most *importune* might, ... VI. i. 20. 2
him pursewed with *importune* speed, ... VI. iv. 8. 2
At last, when him she so *importune* saw, ... VI. xi. 6. 1
Th' *importune* suit of my desire to shonne: . . . . *Am.* xxiii. 6
Importuned. ever her *importund* not to feare . . . . III. ii. 34. 8
the wide sea *importuned* long space With shrilling shriekes, . III. viii. 29. 7
Importunely. To weet who called so *importunely:* . . . . . II. viii. 4. 2
Importunes. it *importunes* death and dolefull dreryhedd. . . III. i. 16. 9
Importuneth. With loud plaintes *importuneth* the skyes, . . . I. vi. 6. 4
Importuning. With praiers lowd *importuning* the skie, ... *Col.* 880
Importunity. to th' *importunity* Of froward fortune . . . . . III. iii. 31. 5
Impose. He unto her a penance did *impose,* . . . . VI. vii. 37. 6
Ne ever any durst till then *impose;* . . . . VI. xii. 36. 3
Imposed. To prove her surname true, that she *imposed* has. . . V. viii. 49. 9
now he hath new lawes and orders new *Imposd* on it . . . . V. x. 27. 7
Impossible. 'Things ofte *impossible* . . . seeme, ere begonne. . III. ii. 36. 9
Impotence. *Impotence* her name. . . . . II. xi. 23. 8
Impotence with her owne wilfull hands . . . . II. xi. 47. 7
Impotent. *impotent* desire of men to raine! . . . . V. xii. 1. 2
Impregnable. also it *impregnable* did make; . . . . III. ii. 20. 8
Impress. Which Venus blood did in her leaves *impresse,* . . . *D.* 109
they do *impresse* Deepe dinted furrowes . . . . I. v. 6. 7
word so deepe did in their harts *impresse,* . . . . II. viii. 18. 7
nothing may *impresse* so deare constraint . . . . III. ix. 40. 3
least passions doe *impresse,* . . . . *H.L.* 170
Through every part she doth the same *impresse,* . . . . . . *H.B.* 115
Impressed. that Gnats death, which deeply was *imprest,* . . . *Gn.* 645
'One, whome like wofulnesse, *impressed* deepe, ... *D.* 64
exceeding feare Their visages *imprest* . . . . II. xi. 5. 9
feare . . . Was earst *impressed* in her gentle spright. . . . . III. iv. 49. 3
Albe the wound were nothing deepe *imprest,* . . . . III. xii. 33. 7
in his head an hideous wound *imprest:* . . . . IV. iii. 34. 4
Where byting deepe so deadly it *imprest,* . . . . IV. vi. 13. 7
Impression. ravished with rare *impression* in his sprite. . . . I. xii. 39. 9
Through deepe *impression* of thy secret might, ... III. iii. 2. 7
through *impression* Of the sunbeames . . . . III. vi. 8. 4
More eath was new *impression* to receive; . . . . IV. vi. 40. 6
no new loves *impression* ever could Bereave it thence: . . . . V. vi. 2. 8
Worke like *impression* in the lookers vew? . . . . *H.B.* 81
Doe both expresse the faces first *impression.* . . . . *H.B.* 182
O huge and most unspeakable *impression* . . . . *H.H.L.* 155
Imprinted. *Imprinted* had that token of his wrath, ... II. ii. 4. 4
Imprisoned. sad Aesculapius far apart *Emprisond* was . . . . I. v. 36. 8
my parents deare For dread of that huge feend *emprisond* be; . I. xi. 3. 3
had them . . . fast *imprisoned* in seiged fort. . . . . I. xii. 4. 5
She firmely hath *emprisoned* for ay, ... III. vi. 48. 6
He is by her *imprisoned,* . . . . V. v. Arg.
her *imprisond* hath, and her life often sought. . . . . V. xi. 39. 9
Imprisonment. freed from wretched long *imprisonment!* . . . *D.* 273
his sinewes woxen weake and raw, Through long *enprisonment,* I. x. 2. 4
Improvided. To worke new woe and *improvided* scath, ... I. xii. 34. 3
Imps. learned *Impes* that wont to shoote up still, ... *T.M.* 75
one of those three fatall *Impes* . . . . *Ti.* 17
the love which thou doest beare To th' Heliconian *ymps,* . . . *Ded. Son.* iii. 11
th' unkindly *Impes,* of heaven accurst, ... I. i. 26. 2
Fayre *ympes* of beautie, ... III. v. 53. 1
when strife was growen Amongst those famous *ympes* of Greece, IV. ii. 1. 8
chaung'd at pleasure for those *impes* of thine! . . . . IV. ii. 51. 7

Imps—*Continued.*
So many learned *impes,* that shoote abrode, ... IV. xi. 26. 5
these weake *impes* replanted by thy might, ... V. xi. 16. 7
Ye sacred *imps,* that on Parnasso dwell, ... VI. Pr. 2. 2
thought that those brave *imps* were sowen Here by the Gods, . VI. iv. 36. 7
Impudence. All were she fraught with pride and *impudence,* . VII. vi. 25. 2
Impudent. his *impudent* lewde speach . . . . *Hub.* 839
With wanton Bardes, and Rymers *impudent,* . . . . III. xii. 5. 5
Impugn. proudly did *impugne* her sentence just: . . . . . . V. iv. 2. 5
Impugneth. By thee no knight; which armes *impugneth* plaine?' . . . . VI. ii. 7. 5
Impure. allure Chast Ladies eares to fantasies *impure.* . . . . *Hub.* 820
To waile the wretchednes of world *impure?* . . . . *T.M.* 120
Faire Ladies loves they spot with thoughts *impure,* . . . . . *T.M.* 333
Yet was by them as thing *impure* rejected; . . . . *D.* 209
with hands *impure* To spoyle so goodly workmanship . . . . . IV. vi. 17. 3
he with his tooth *impure* Him heedlesse bit, ... VI. v. 16. 8
All dewfull service, voide of thoughts *impure;* . . . . VI. x. 32. 6
looser lookes that stir up lustes *impure;* . . . . *Am.* xxi. 8
Sith purest Angels fell to be *impure?* . . . . *H.H.L.* 98
Impute. gan Religion gainst her to *impute* High Gods beheast, V. ix. 44. 5
Imputed. fairely quit him of th' *imputed* blame; . . . . . . II. i. 20. 2
she . . . cleard that stripling of th' *imputed* blame, ... VI. ii. 14. 2
Imputest. the blame Which thou *imputest,* . . . . *Col.* 732
In (*partial list*). *See* **Infixed, Inn, Wherein.**
In God alone do stay my confidence. . . . . *Bel.*[1] i. 14
And gird *in* your waste, ... *S.C.* Ap. 134
There crept *in* Wolves, ... *S.C.* May 127
in came The false Foxe, ... *S.C.* May 278
He popt him *in,* . . . . *S.C.* May 291
they *in* thee, and thou *in* sleepe art dead. . . . . *S.C.* O. 6
Let powre *in* lavish cups . . . . *S.C.* O. 105
deep Charybdis gulphing *in* and out: . . . . *Gn.* 542
how shall we first come *in,* . . . . *Hub.* 643
Or sell fee-simples *in* his Masters name, ... *Hub.* 869
a Broker, and draw *in* Both wares and money, ... *Hub.* 869
Nor anie one doth care to call us *in,* . . . . *T.M.* 343
the danger hee is *in,* . . . . *T.M.* 491
Mars sleeping with his wife to compasse *in,* . . . . *Mui.* 371
that none them *in* doth call.' . . . . *Col.* 730
some end they finde, or *in* or out, That path . . . . I. i. 11. 2
unto the darksom hole he went, And looked *in:* . . . . I. i. 14. 4
By them the Sprite doth passe *in* quietly, ... I. i. 40. 7
Retourning to his bed *in* torment great, ... I. ii. 6. 1
yeelding soft, *in* that she nought gainsaid, ... I. ii. 27. 7
the wicket open rent, And let her *in;* . . . . I. iii. 13. 3
One knocked at the dore, and *in* would fare: . . . . I. iii. 16. 4
in at the window crept. . . . . I. iii. 17. 9
him *in* to lett. . . . . I. iii. 19. 3
they passed *in* forth right; . . . . I. iv. 6. 1
So deepely dinted *in* the driven clay, ... I. viii. 8. 5
Came hurtling *in* full fiers, ... I. viii. 17. 9
Then asked he, which way he *in* might pas? . . . . I. viii. 33. 1
Where entred *in,* his foot could find no flore, ... I. viii. 39. 7
They passe *in,* stouping low; . . . . I. x. 5. 8
entred *in,* a spatious court they see, ... I. x. 6. 2
Both plaine and pleasaunt to be walked *in;* . . . . I. x. 6. 3
Downe *in* a darksome lowly place far *in,* . . . . I. x. 25. 7
To call *in* commers-by . . . . I. x. 36. 9
And comfort those *in* point of death which lay; . . . . I. x. 41. 2
For those to dwell *in* . . . . I. x. 57. 3
Came running *in,* . . . A Messenger . . . . I. xii. 24. 8
and all that *in* did dwell. . . . . II. ii. 20. 7
rushed *in* on foot to ayd her . . . . II. iii. 3. 9
that same warlike Lord She *in* receiv'd; . . . . II. vi. 4. 8
He brought him *in.* . . . . II. vii. 43. 3
Therein two gates . . . by which all *in* did pas, ... II. ix. 23. 2
when ever *in* they came, ... II. ix. 28. 4
at them gan fly, As *in* their mistresse reskew . . . . II. xii. 84. 7
To enter *in* . . . ; and then *in* they all together far'd. . . . III. i. 30. 8, 9
When *in* so high an object they do lyte, ... III. ii. 3. 7
Ne durst adventure rashly *in* to wend, ... III. iii. 14. 2
they him laide *in* easy couch . . . . III. iv. 43. 6
to lett him *in* Into the balefull house. . . . . III. v. 22. 2
And girt *in* with two walls . . . . III. vi. 31. 2
By which both *in* and out men moten pas: . . . . III. vi. 31. 6
He letteth *in,* he letteth out to wend . . . . III. vi. 32. 1
The Damzell there arriving entred *in;* . . . . III. vii. 7. 1
entreat The man . . . to let us *in,* . . . . III. ix. 9. 2
But none to issue forth when one is *in;* . . . . IV. i. 20. 8
that shone as Phebes light . . . *in* evening cleare. . . . . . IV. v. 14. 4
There entring *in,* they found . . . . IV. v. 34. 1
And there he threw her *in,* . . . . IV. vii. 8. 9
wisht it were *in* her to do him any grace . . . . IV. viii. 12. 9
in together far'd. IV. ix. 5. 9
That warded all which *in* or out did wend, ... IV. x. 7. 3
So *in* I past, and streight he closd the gate: . . . . IV. x. 14. 4
But being *in,* Delay . . . Caught hold on me, ... IV. x. 14. 5
Crept *in* by stouping low, ... IV. x. 18. 9
Or creepe betweene his legs, so *in* to goe, ... IV. x. 19. 3
And either beat him *in,* or drive him out. . . . . IV. x. 19. 5
he found no way To enter *in,* . . . . IV. xii. 15. 4
Hemd *in* with waters like a wall . . . . V. ii. 35. 7
Did beat uppon the gates to enter *in;* . . . . V. iv. 37. 2
Made them all enter *in* before her sight; . . . . V. iv. 45. 7
And all the wounded, . . . To be convayed *in,* . . . . V. iv. 45. 9
There entred *in* he round about him saw . . . . V. v. 22. 1
That *in* and out thou mayst have passage free. . . . . V. v. 34. 5
shee with great humility Did enter *in,* . . . . V. vii. 3. 8
Pelmell with them attonce did enter *in.* . . . . V. vii. 35. 4

In—*Continued.*
Her selfe came *in,* her glory to partake; . . . V. vii. 36. 2
were Directed *in,* and shewed all the sight; . . . V. ix. 22. 2
by whom they passing *in* Went up the hall, . . . V. ix. 23. 1
Mal was now put *in:* . . . V. ix. 26. 5
as he pressed *in,* him there did slay: . . . V. x. 36. 7
hard preased *in* betweene, And entraunce wonne: . . . V. x. 37. 6
Then *in* he brought her, . . . V. xi. 33. 5
Or good direction how to enter *in,* . . . VI. i. 6. 3
The gate soone opened to receive him *in;* . . . VI. i. 23. 2
whilest Calidore Did enter *in,* . . . VI. i. 23. 9
but streightway *in* did pas: . . . VI. v. 36. 1
He found the gate wyde ope, and *in* he rode, . . . VI. vi. 19. 2
With that the foole, . . . Came running *in;* . . . VI. viii. 11. 2
That all which I put *in* fals out anon, . . . VI. viii. 24. 7
no way Appeard for people *in* nor out to pas, . . . VI. x. 41. 8
But when as Calidore was comen *in,* . . . VI. xi. 44. 1
Shee there arriving boldly *in* did pass; . . . VII. vi. 24. 1
Thus sitting *in* her throne, . . . VII. vii. 13. 5
her foot she *in* my necke doth place, . . . *Am.* xx. 3
tread my life downe *in* the lowly floure. . . . *Am.* xx. 4
Open them wide that she may enter *in,* . . . *Epith.* 205
to receyve this Saynt . . . That commeth *in* to you. . . . *Epith.* 209
She commeth *in,* before th' Almighties view; . . . *Epith.* 211
Which may let *in* a little thought unsownd. . . . *Epith.* 237
lewd layes . . . *In* praise of that mad fit . . . *H.H.L.* 8
grone *in* grieved thought. . . . *H.H.L.* 252
Inachus. What oddes twixt Irus and old *Inachus,* . . . *T.M.* 447
old Assaracus, and *Inachus* divine. . . . II. ix. 56. 9
Inachus, renowmd above the rest; . . . IV. xi. 15. 5
Inburning. The outward sparkes of her *inburning* fire; . . . III. i. 53. 3
her *inburning* wrath she gan abate, . . . IV. viii. 17. 8
Incarnate. The one a feend, the other an *incarnate* devill. . . . IV. ii. 3. 9
Incense. *incense* of precious Cedar tree, . . . *Bel.* xi. 3
She through her wicked working did *incense* . . . IV. v. 23. 2
Incensed. what fury mad Hath thee *incenst* . . . I. vi. 47. 2
Whose sharpe provokement them *incenst* so sore, . . . IV. iv. 4. 6
Much was the knight *incenst* with his lewd word . . . V. iii. 36. 1
Incessant. poure forth fountaines of *incessant* teares? . . . *D.* 247
Our life afflicted with *incessant* paine, . . . *D.* 275
with *incessaunt* force and endlesse hate . . . II. xi. 6. 8
pursew The fearefull damzell with *incessant* payns; . . . III. iv. 46. 3
having through *incessant* traveill spent His force, . . . III. vii. 3. 6
with *incessaunt* paine To wander through the world . . . III. vii. 54. 3
In wretched anguishe and *incessant* woe, . . . IV. ix. 39. 6
And lay *incessant* battery to her heart; . . . *Am.* xiv. 10
your *incessant* battry more to beare: . . . *Am.* lvii. 4
Incessantly. I mourne and waile *incessantly,* . . . *T.M.* 293
with that old Dragon fights Two days *incessantly:* . . . I. xi. Arg.
For which men swinck and sweat *incessantly,* . . . II. vii. 8. 7
faynd to wash themselves *incessantly,* . . . II. vii. 61. 6
All those this sences Fort assayle *incessantly.* . . . II. xi. 12. 9
through the world *incessantly* doe chase, . . . VI. i. 7. 2
A salvage man, . . . *incessantly* did ronne . . . VI. iv. 2. 4
Incest. Through *incest* her of his owne mother Earth . . . III. vii. 47. 8
did shame Himselfe with *incest* of his kin unkend; . . . IV. xi. 13. 8
Incited. The Beast, with their pursuit *incited* more, . . . VI. iii. 25. 1
Inclination. of the trees owne *inclination* made, . . . III. vi. 44. 3
Calidore, of courteous *inclination,* . . . VI. ix. 42. 1
Incline. To other delights they would *encline:* . . . *S.C.* F. 60
doo not doubt but duly to *encline* My wits theretoo, . . . *Hub.* 548
Thou doest . . . his avenging wrath to clemency *incline.* . . . I. x. 51. 9
loyall truth to treason doest *incline:* . . . II. vii. 13. 3
to the gate directly did *incline* . . . II. ix. 24. 7
did them selves into their *hands* incline, . . . II. xii. 54. 5
made him low *incline* his lofty crest, . . . III. vii. 42. 4
Unsure to whether side it would *incline,* . . . IV. iii. 37. 2
And loved all that did to armes *incline;* . . . VI. iii. 3. 6
made him downe unto the earth *encline;* . . . VI. v. 26. 4
to his prayer nought he would *incline,* . . . VI. vii. 26. 2
Encline thy will t' effect our wishfull vow, . . . *Epith.* 385
Inclined. hope of heaven, and heart to God *inclinde;* . . . *Ti.* 585
to mine oaten pipe *enclin'd* her eare, . . . *Col.* 360
To which though nobly ye *inclined* are, . . . *Ded. Son.* x. 7
Gave him great ayd, and made him more *inclynd:* . . . II. iii. 4. 7
if he *inclyned* had at all, . . . II. vii. 64. 3
when she your courage hath *inclind* . . . II. xii. 29. 1
this was not to love, but lust, *inclind;* . . . III. i. 49. 7
to all great exploites them selves *inclind,* . . . III. ii. 2. 3
Trompart, lowly to the grownd *inclinde,* . . . III. x. 30. 7
of princely grace to be *inclyn'd* thereto. . . . V. v. 41. 9
woxe *inclined* much unto her part, . . . V. ix. 46. 3
everie thing to which one is *inclin'd* . . . VI. ii. 2. 7
Unto her prayers piteously *enclynd,* . . . VI. vii. 37. 3
Men to devotion ought to be *inclynd* . . . *Am.* xxii. 2
Ye . . . doe seeme to me *inclind:* . . . *Am.* xxviii. 4
Inclining. he knew His errour; and, himselfe *inclyning,* sayd; . . . I. ii. 28. 2
himselfe *inclyning* on his knee . . . II. ii. 3. 1
oft *inclining* downe, with kisses light . . . II. xii. 73. 5
the Idoll, as it were *inclining,* . . . V. vii. 8. 1
To whom she eke *inclyning* her withall, . . . V. ix. 34. 6
Therefore *inclyning* to his goodly reason, . . . VI. iv. 37. 4
Inclose. *See* **Enclose.**
Incomber. *See* **Encumber.**
Incoming. He, at his first *incomming,* charg'd his spere . . . IV. iv. 40. 1
Incompared. That Mantuane Poetes *incompared* spirit, . . . *Ded. Son.* xiii. 1
Inconstance. to see th' *inconstance* of the heavens: . . . *Bel.*[1] xi. 3
Inconstancies. I, that know this worlds *inconstancies,* . . . *Bel.*[2] i. 12
Inconstancy. O worlds *inconstancie!* . . . *Ro.* iii. 12
there is no greater shame Then . . . *inconstancie* in love: . . . I. iv. 1. 8

Inconstancy—*Continued.*
His fickle mind full of *inconstancie:* . . . IV. i. 32. 5
Inconstant. *inconstant* fortune, bent to ill, . . . *Gn.* 247
the common winde Of Courts *inconstant* mutabilitie, . . . *Hub.* 723
Inconstant man, that loved all he saw, . . . I. iv. 26. 1
Inconstant Chaunge, and false Disloyalty; . . . III. xii. 25. 6
Incontinence. Delightes in filth and fowle *incontinence:* . . . II. xii. 87. 7
That plaine discovered her *incontinence;* . . . III. i. 48. 3
with her loose *incontinence* doth blend The shyning glory . . . III. ix. 1. 7
Then brought he forth *Incontinence* of lyfe, . . . V. ix. 48. 7
Incontinent. Unto the place they come *incontinent:* . . . I. vi. 8. 5
That any wownd could heale *incontinent.* . . . I. ix. 19. 5
incontinent Doth loose his dignity and native grace: . . . II. ix. 1. 7
stinted all the strife *incontinent:* . . . IV. iii. 18. 4
Dispersed all their troupe *incontinent,* . . . V. iv. 24. 7
Then ganne it runne away *incontinent,* . . . V. ix. 18. 7
Shall to your eyes appeare *incontinent.* . . . VII. vii. 17. 5
Incorrupted. As *incorrupted* Nature did them sow, . . . I. xi. 47. 4
Where they for ever *incorrupted* dweld: . . . II. ix. 56. 7
Increase. as my cryes . . . *Increase,* . . . *S.C.* Au. 178
Giving accompt of th' annuall *increce* . . . *Hub.* 301
For to *encrease* the common treasures store; . . . *Hub.* 1171
Did more *increase* the sharpnes of her showre. . . . *T.M.* 478
with my mourning plaints your *plaint* increase. . . . *Ti.* 238
Fit matter for his cares *increase* would finde, . . . *D.* 3
So will I wilfully *increase* my paine. . . . *D.* 378
to *increase* his feares, . . . an hempen rope he weares, . . . I. ix. 22. 5
thankt be God, and her *encrease* so evermore!' . . . I. x. 16. 9
to *increase* his wondrous greatnes more, . . . I. xi. 8. 8
to *increase,* and all atonce to kill, . . . I. xi. 13. 6
but doth the ill *increase,* . . . II. i. 16. 6
more affection to *increase,* . . . II. i. 60. 8
strong thing does *increace,* . . . II. ii. 31. 3
Abusd her plenty and fat swolne *encreace* . . . II. vii. 16. 7
Next Huddibras his realme did not *encrease,* . . . II. x. 25. 4
Their wanton meriments they did *encreace,* . . . II. xii. 68. 7
Their direfull rancour rather did *encreasse;* . . . III. i. 23. 4
t' *increase* thy lover's pray. . . . III. iii. 28. 4
So evermore he did *increase* his speed, . . . III. iv. 48. 4
bad them to *increase* and multiply: . . . III. vi. 34. 6
gan *encrease* his speed as she encreast her flight. . . . III. vii. 43. 9
Bring foorth an infinite *increase,* . . . IV. i. 25. 7
They did much more their cruelty *encrease;* . . . IV. ii. 19. 5
t' *increase* affection naturall, . . . IV. ii. 54. 4
Whereto her bashful shamefastnesse ywrought A great *increase* . . . V. iii. 23. 4
through his want her woe did more *increase:* . . . V. vii. 45. 2
to *increase* his shame, . . . Would thumpe her forward . . . VI. ii. 10. 5
made him evermore *increase* his speedie pace. . . . VI. vi. 29. 9
My lambes doe every yeare *increase* their score, . . . VI. ix. 21. 7
their cruelty doth still *increace,* . . . *Am.* xxxvi. 7
take delight t' *encrease* a wretches woe; . . . *Am.* xli. 7
The more I fynd their malice to *increase.* . . . *Am.* xliv. 14
Of blessed Saints for to *increase* the count. . . . *Epith.* 423
An infinite *increase* of Angels bright, . . . *H.H.L.* 55
to *increase* Above the fortune of their first condition, . . . *H.H.L.* 80
Increased. soone it sore *encreased;* . . . *S.C.* Mar. 99
his owne treasure he *encreased* more, . . . *Hub.* 1172
Right glad with him to have *increast* their crew; . . . I. iv. 15. 2
hath *encreast* the world with one sonne more, . . . I. x. 16. 6
Which she *increased* with her bleeding hart, . . . II. i. 40. 3
Their fell contention still *increased* more, . . . II. v. 22. 1
more thereby *increased* Furors might, . . . II. v. 22. 2
His prowd presumed force *increased* more, . . . II. vi. 30. 3
much *increast* Through his Heroicke grace . . . III. ii. 24. 8
his bad deedes, which daily he *increast,* . . . III. v. 14. 7
So still his Malady the more *increast,* . . . III. v. 43. 6
both *encreast* the prayse of woman kynde, . . . III. v. 55. 7
both *encreast* her beautie excellent: . . . III. v. 55. 8
still *increast* till she her terme had full outgone. . . . III. vi. 9. 9
her terror hath *encreast;* . . . III. vii. 1. 5
gan encrease his speed as she *encreast* her flight. . . . III. vii. 43. 9
that more suspicion *encreast,* . . . III. viii. 49. 7
still the smart thereof *increased* more, . . . III. x. 18. 4
evermore *encreased* her consuming paine. . . . III. xii. 21. 9
all the more, the more his praise *increst:* . . . IV. iv. 21. 7
th' earth it selfe how daily its *increast* . . . V. ii. 37. 6
threats the more *increast* their mood. . . . V. iv. 4. 9
So his *encreased,* but mine did empaire. . . . V. iv. 8. 5
Yet still her crueltie *increased* more, . . . V. v. 7. 3
more *increast* her outrage mercilesse, . . . V. v. 14. 7
The one of them, which most her wrath *increast,* . . . V. vi. 39. 4
having force *increast* through furious paine, . . . V. vii. 33. 6
cruell enemies *increased* more, . . . V. xi. 54. 2
as he still decayd so he *encreased* more. . . . VI. i. 21. 9
as it still *encreast,* so still *increast* Their cruell strokes . . . VI. i. 36. 6
whose griefe through suffraunce sore *increast.* . . . VI. v. 39. 9
were now much more *increast* . . . VI. vi. 2. 3
that same foole, which most *increast* her paines, . . . VI. vii. 44. 5
more *increast* the anguish of his paine: . . . VI. xi. 26. 3
the more he rag'd, the more his powre *increast.* . . . VI. xii. 32. 9
With my reflex yours shall *encreased* be. . . . *Am.* lxvi. 14
Their being have, and dayly are *increast* . . . *H.L.* 96
By which they first were made, and still *increast.* . . . *H.H.B.* 203
beautie . . . more *increast* by her owne goodly grace, . . . *H.H.B.* 208
Increaseth. dayly he his wrongs *encreaseth* more; . . . V. ii. 6. 1
Increasing. *Encreasing* his wrath with many a threate: . . . *S.C.* F. 194
increasing more Their puissant force, . . . I. vi. 45. 2
Ind. pearles of *Ynde,* or gold of Opher, . . . *Col.* 490
daintie spices fetch from furthest *Ynd,* . . . I. v. 4. 6
She wandred had from one to other *Ynd,* . . . I. vi. 2. 7

Ind—*Continued.*
Through boyling sands of Arabie and *Ynde*, ... I. vi. 35. 6
Indecent. none then it more fowle and *indecent*, ... II. ix. 1. 5
Indeed. *Indeede*, thy Ball is a bold bigge curre, ... *S.C.* S. 164
Indeede the Romish Tityrus, I heare, ... *S.C.* O. 55
there (said the Priest) is arte *indeed:* . . . . *Hub.* 483
Thinking *indeed* that it the Lyon was. . . . . *Hub.* 1093
King *indeed* himselfe he shortly thought, ... *Hub.* 1105
'Happie *indeed* (said Colin) I him hold, ... *Col.* 660
Indeed . . . passeth reasons reach, ... *Col.* 837
Indeed (said Lucid) I have often heard . . . . *Col.* 907
There, *in deede*, dwel faire Graces many one, ... *Ded. Son.* v. 9
Th' one seeming such, the other such *indeede*, ... I. ii. 37. 2
Being *in deed* old Archimage, did stay. . . . . I. vi. 48. 2
'*Indeed*,' (quoth she) 'that should her trouble sore; . . . I. x. 16. 8
Dead was it sure, as sure as death *in deed*, ... I. xi. 12. 3
to weet if trew *indeed* Those tydinges were, ... I. xii. 3. 3
he saw him move his eyes *indeed*. . . . . I. xii. 10. 9
'*Indeede*,' . . . Frayle men are oft captiv'd . . . . II. vii. 15. 1
'*Indeed*,' . . . the evill donne Dyes not, ... II. viii. 29. 1
these same Monsters are not these *in deed*, ... II. xii. 26. 2
'These seeming beasts are men *indeed*, ... II. xii. 85. 1
'*Indeede* the fates are firme, ... III. iii. 25. 6
Indeed, in sleepe The slouthfull body . . . . III. iv. 56. 4
sheweth each thing as it is *in deed:* . . . . III. iv. 59. 2
'*Indeed*, Sir knight,' (said he) 'one word may tell . . . . III. vii. 57. 1
seeing them resolvd *indeed* To flame the gates, ... III. ix. 18. 1
Indeed he said, . . . there grew Another plant, ... III. ix. 47. 5
it was *indeed* Her old Malbecco, ... III. x. 50. 2
well she wist, as true it was *indeed*, ... IV. i. 6. 1
a man, such as *indeed* he seemed; . . . . IV. i. 8. 2
was *indeed* a man of mickle might; . . . . IV. i. 32. 3
whom Paridell Seeing so faire *indeede*, ... IV. ii. 7. 7
shew'd themselves to her such as *indeed* they were. . . . . IV. vi. 25. 9
Feebly she shriekt, but so feebly *indeed* . . . . IV. vii. 4. 7
'That shield, which thou doest beare, was it *indeed* . . . . V. iii. 21. 1
whether it *indeede* be so or no, ... V. iv. 14. 1
it was one sent from her love *indeede;* . . . . V. vi. 8. 4
it *indeed* is nought but forgerie. . . . . VI. Pr. 5. 3
meriteth *indeede* an higher name: . . . . VI. Pr. 6. 8
The Squire, for that he courteous was *indeed*, ... VI. vi. 16. 4
He weened well that he *in deed* was dead, ... VI. vii. 20. 2
A foolish Faune *indeed*, ... VII. vi. 46. 6
That can expresse the life of things *indeed*. . . . . *Am.* xvii. 14
if thou be *indeede*, as men thee call, ... *H.L.* 155
is *indeede* the bondslave of defame; . . . . *H.B.* 173
they, which love *indeede*, looke otherwise, ... *H.B.* 211
Counting it fairer then it is *indeede*, ... *H.B.* 230
yet *indeede* her fairenesse doth exceede. . . . . *H.B.* 231
Indevour. *See* **Endeavour.**
Indew, -ed. *See* **Endue, -d.**
India. him all *India* obayd, ... II. x. 72. 5
Indian. from *Indian* seas brought far away; . . . . *Gn.* 106
Who ever heard of th' *Indian* Peru? . . . . II. Pr. 2. 6
beyond the Africk Ismael Or th' *Indian* Peru . . . . III. iii. 6. 8
pearles which th' *Indian* seas for her prepaire. . . . . . . IV. xi. 11. 9
Yet dropping fresh out of the *Indian* fount, ... V. x. 16. 6
Indians. Such as the *Indians* in their quivers hide: . . . . II. xi. 21. 5
the sunburnt *Indians* do aray Their tawney bodies . . . . III. xii. 8. 3
Indias. both the *Indias* of their treasure spoile; . . . . . *Am.* xv. 3
Indict. *See* **Indite.**
never so deserved to *endite*. . . . . VI. xii. 41. 7
Indicted. Of all those crymes she there *indited* was: . . . . VI. vii. 35. 2
Indicting. So thy renowme lives ever by *endighting*. . . . . *Com. Son.* i. 14
Indifferent. not *indifferent* to woman kind, ... III. ii. 1. 3
Dealing with Justice with *indifferent* grace, ... V. ix. 36. 4
Indifferently. made judge of my life or death *indifferently*. . I. i. 51. 9
Right to all dost deale *indifferently*, ... VII. vii. 14. 4
Indign. Sith she her selfe was of his grace *indigne;* . . . . IV. i. 30. 5
Indignance. With great *indignaunce* he that sight forsooke, . III. xi. 13. 5
Indignant. with proud envy and *indignant* yre . . . . III. iv. 47. 3
Full of fiers fury and *indignant* hate . . . . III. v. 23. 3
with sterne countenance and *indignant* pride . . . . V. i. 23. 5
Which breaking open with *indignant* ire, ... V. vii. 37. 4
Much was I moved in *indignant* mind, ... VI. ii. 11. 2
Indignation. With furious force and *indignation* fell; . . . . I. viii. 39. 6
all with suddein *indignation* fraight, ... I. xii. 35. 2
him move to wrath, and *indignation* reare. . . . . II. iv. 5. 9
Deepe *indignation* and compassion frayle . . . . III. viii. 31. 4
His mightie *indignation* did forbeare; . . . . IV. i. 45. 2
His mighty heart with *indignation* sweld, ... IV. ix. 32. 3
to swell With *indignation* at her vaunting vaine, ... V. v. 10. 6
he so full of *indignation* was, ... VI. vii. 26. 1
His gentle heart with *indignation* sweld, ... VI. vii. 45. 3
Diana, full of *indignation*, ... VII. vi. 54. 1
Indignified. fowle entreaty him *indignifyde*, ... VI. i. 30. 5
Indignify. then by discourse them to *indignifie*.' . . . . . . *Col.* 583
Indignities. grieve the noble spright . . . with great *indignities*, *Ti.* 444
Indignity. chafte at that *indignitie* right sore: . . . . *Hub.* 1338
his late fall and fowle *indignity*, ... III. ix. 25. 2
cast t' avenge his friends *indignity*. . . . . IV. iv. 28. 5
deepe disdaine and great *indignity*, ... IV. vii. 36. 3
For high disdaine of such *indignity*, ... V. vii. 28. 6
honour with *indignitie* debased! . . . . V. xi. 63. 7
'I hold it no *indignity;* . . . . VI. i. 28. 2
Indite. *See* **Indict.**
And dainty love learnd sweetly to *endite*. . . . . *Ded. Son.* viii. 7
O soveraine Queene! whose prayse I would *endyte*, ... III. ii. 3. 4
Endite I would as dewtie doth excyte; . . . . III. ii. 3. 5
The wonder that my wit cannot *endite*. . . . . *Am.* iii. 14
Indited. *See* **Indicted.**
Induced. The Foxe was well *induc'd* to be a Parson, ... *Hub.* 480
Inducement. Through some vaine errour, or *inducement* light, VII. vi. 32. 2
Indued, Indure. *See* **Endued, Endure.**
Indus. More great then th' eares of Elephants by *Indus* flood. . IV. vii. 6. 9
Deepe *Indus*, and Maeander intricate, ... IV. xi. 21. 2
Industrious. nimbler joynted than the rest, And more *industrious*, ... *Mui.* 122
Industry. wrought by his owne *industry*, ... *Bel.*[2] iv. 10
Shee him instructed with great *industree*. . . . . I. x. 45. 5
So lost his labour vaine and ydle *industry*. . . . . II. vii. 61. 9
was taught By faire Astraea with great *industrie*, ... V. i. 5. 4
through long and perfect *industry*, ... VI. ix. 43. 7
In-dwellers. Which too-too true that lands *in-dwellers* since have found. . . . . VII. vi. 55. 9
Infamies. Ebranck salved both their *infamies* . . . . II. x. 21. 6
slaunderous reproches, and fowle *infamies*. . . . . II. xi. 10. 6
Infamous. False erraunt knight, *infamous*, ... I. xii. 27. 4
A false *infamous* faitour . . . . II. i. 30. 3
with fowle *infamous* blot, ... III. vi. 13. 4
her from so *infamous* fact assoyld, ... III. viii. 32. 7
forced me to so *infamous* deed, ... V. xi. 57. 4
Infamy. Brings to reproach and common *infamie!* . . . . . . *Hub.* 222
anie Should of his race be voyd of *infamie;* . . . . *Hub.* 1242
By him begotten of fowle *infamy;* . . . . *T.M.* 316
Unles they mentiond be with *infamie*. . . . . *Ti.* 350
Doe breede repentaunce late, and lasting *infamy*.' . . . . . II. v. 13. 9
All losse is lesse, and lesse the *infamy*, ... III. i. 25. 5
Vile Poverty; and, lastly, Death with *infamy*. . . . . III. xii. 25. 9
Let ugly shame and endlesse *infamy* Colour thy name . . . . IV. i. 53. 6
all his face deform'd with *infamie*, ... V. iii. 38. 4
the poysnous sting, which *infamy* Infixeth . . . . VI. vi. 1. 3
for greater *infamie*, ... VI. vii. 27. 1
foule *Infamie* and fell Despight Gave evidence, ... VI. vii. 34. 7
blotted them with *infamie*, ... VI. xii. 28. 8
With bitter termes of shamefull *infamy;* . . . . VI. xii. 33. 4
Infancies. He remembred both their *infancis:* . . . . II. ix. 57. 3
Infancy. for sustenaunce Of his weake *infancie*, ... *T.M.* 262
from her *infancy* Her nourced had in trew Nobility: . . . . III. v. 32. 4
antique age, yet in the *infancie* Of time, ... IV. viii. 30. 1
Even from the cradle of his *infancie*, ... V. i. 5. 2
The wondrous cradle of thine *infancie*, ... *H.L.* 51
Infant. Her long borne *Infant*, fruit of heavinesse, ... *D.* 32
To whom the *Infant* thus; . . . . II. viii. 56. 1
Whom to poursue the *Infant* after hide . . . . II. xi. 25. 7
the royall *Infant* fell Into her former fitt; . . . . III. ii. 49. 1
Whyles yet in *infant* cradle he did crall; . . . . III. iii. 26. 7
faire *Infant*, her ensample make Unto thy selfe, ... III. iii. 56. 8
Hither great Venus brought this *infant* fayre, ... III. vi. 51. 1
dred *infant*, Venus dearling dove, ... IV. Pr. 5. 2
doeth deceive The *infant*, so for want of nourture spoyld; . . V. v. 53. 4
She threw her husbands murdred *infant* out; . . . . V. viii. 47. 2
his brother, seeing mee An *infant*, ... VI. ii. 28. 7
whylest an *Infant* from a Beare He saves, ... VI. iv. Arg.
A cruell Beare, the which an *infant* bore . . . . VI. iv. 17. 8
he ran with zealous haste To rescue th' *infant*, ... VI. iv. 18. 7
when that *infant* unto him she brought, ... VI. iv. 38. 5
The *Infant* hearkned wisely to her tale, ... VI. viii. 25. 1
In th' open fields an *Infant* left alone; . . . . VI. ix. 14. 6
The rosie marke . . . That litle *Infant* had, ... VI. xii. 15. 7
this faire Mayd Was that same *infant*, ... VI. xii. 16. 3
Is her owne daughter, her owne *infant* deare. . . . . VI. xii. 20. 6
Infant's. Soone as the *infants* sunlike shield they saw, ... V. viii. 41. 2
Would for the wretched *infants* helpe provyde; . . . . . . VI. xii. 8. 8
Led with the *infants* cry that loud did weepe, ... VI. xii. 9. 3
Infants. faire Chrysogone Conceiv'd these *infants*, ... III. vi. 5. 3
Infants.' th' *Infants* tutors gathering to feare, ... II. x. 64. 4
Infect. pestilence, That mortall mindes doth inwardly *infect* . *T.M.* 484
Infected. Inward corruption and *infected* sin, ... I. x. 25. 2
Those that with sicknesse were *infected* sore . . . . I. xi. 30. 3
Their blood with secret filth *infected* hath, ... II. ii. 4. 7
at the first, before it had *infected*, ... VI. vi. 8. 3
And clense the guilt of that *infected* cryme . . . . *H.H.L.* 167
Infection. free from fleshes frayle *infection*. . . . . *H.B.* 217
Infectious. by the powre of his *infectious* sight, ... IV. viii. 47. 8
Infelicity. in hunting such felicitie, Or rather *infelicitie*, . . *As.* 80
Inferior. No whit *inferiour* to thy Fanchins praise, ... *Col.* 301
whence, to none *inferior*, ye came, ... III. iii. 54. 3
doth true justice deale To his *inferiour* Gods, ... V. vii. 1. 7
Infernal. to awake out of th' *infernall* shade . . . . *Ro.* xxv. 2
Till that *infernall* feend . . . Forwasted all their land, . . . I. i. 5. 7
mourning altars . . . The black *infernall* Furies doen aslake: I. iii. 36. 8
th' *infernall* powres . . . Have borne him hence . . . . . I. v. 14. 6
all the hellish brood Of feends *infernall* . . . . I. v. 32. 8
Infernall furies with their chaines untyde. . . . . I. ix. 24. 5
that *infernall* Monster . . . . I. xi. 31. 5
From his *infernall* fournace forth he threw Huge flames . . . I. xi. 44. 2
Kindled through his *infernall* brond of spight, ... II. vi. 50. 5
*there sate *infernall* Payne, ... II. vii. 21. 5
to th' *infernall* shade Fast flying, ... II. viii. 45. 7
Infernall Hags, Centaurs, feendes, Hippodames, ... II. ix. 50. 8
Th' *infernall* feends with it he can asswage, ... II. xii. 41. 6
by *infernall* furies nourished; . . . . IV. i. 26. 8
other like *infernall* furies kinde; . . . . V. xi. 23. 6
powred out of her *infernall* sinke Most ugly filth; . . . . . V. xi. 31. 6
sacrifizeth to th' *infernall* feends: . . . . VI. viii. 49. 4
to th' *infernall* Powers her need give lone Of her faire light VII. vi. 11. 7
Onely th' *infernall* Powers might not appeare; . . . . VII. vii. 3. 6
Inferred. afeard Of villany to be to her *inferd:* . . . . VI. viii. 31. 5
Infest. gathering also filth him to *infest*, ... *Van.* iv. 11

Infest—*Continued.*
do my soule with inward griefe *infest:* . . . *Ti.* 460
rage, Wherewith the martiall troupes thou doest *infest,* . . . I. xi. 6. 3
The bitter pangs that doth your heart *infest.* . . . I. i. 48. 5
Then doth this wicked evill thee *infest,* . . . III. ii. 32. 4
this sad evill, which doth her *infest,* . . . III. iii. 18. 5
with fierce fury and with force *infest* . . . VI. iv. 5. 3
humour which did most *infest* Their ranckling wounds, . . . VI. vi. 2. 8
to *infest* The noblest wights with notable defame: . . . VI. vi. 12. 5
Of every wight, that were not too *infest;* . . . VI. vi. 41. 7
Infested. mindfull of that olde *Enfested* grudge, . . . *Mui.* 354
Infestered. scarsely suffring her *infestred* wound . . . to be drest. . . . VI. xi. 24. 6
Infidels. The scourge of Turkes, and plague of *infidels,* . . . *Com.Son.*iii.13
Infinite. Besides the *infinite* extortions, . . . *Hub.* 1311
Infinite sortes of people did abide There waiting long, . . . I. iv. 6. 7
Infinite mischiefes of them doe arize, . . . II. vii. 12. 6
Infinite moe tormented in like paine He there beheld, . . . II. vii. 63. 1
infinite desire into your spirite poure. . . . II. ix. 3. 9
Infinite shapes of thinges dispersed thin; . . . II. ix. 50. 3
This man of *infinite* remembraunce was, . . . II. ix. 56. 1
were too long their *infinite* contents Here to record, . . . II. x. 74. 5
So huge and *infinite* their numbers were, . . . II. xi. 5. 6
Infinit streames continually did well . . . II. xii. 62. 1
worthy worke of *infinite* reward, . . . III. ii. 21. 7
Him forth through *infinite* endevour to have sought. . . . III. iii. 6. 9
Infinite shapes of creatures men doe fynd . . . III. vi. 8. 8
Infinite shapes of creatures there are bred, . . . III. vi. 35. 1
Bring foorth an *infinite* increase, . . . IV. i. 25. 7
Of Lords and Ladies *infinite* great store; . . . V. iii. 2. 8
seem'd to be of *infinite* great strength: . . . V. xi. 23. 3
All overcome with *infinite* affect . . . VI. i. 45. 2
'Therein the changes *infinite* beholde, . . . VII. vii. 23. 1
nought may quench his *infinite* desyre, . . . *H.L.* 202
An *infinite* increase of Angels bright, . . . *H.H.L.* 55
heavens . . . *infinite* in largenesse and in hight, . . . *H.H.B.* 67
bereave Their soule of sense, through *infinite* delight, . . . *H.H.B.* 258
Infirmities. Fainting at last through long *infirmities,* . . . *Ti.* 656
her strength recur'd from fraile *infirmitis.'* . . . I. x. 52. 9
Clear'd from grosse mists of fraile *infirmities.* . . . *H.H.B.* 140
Infirmity. like *infirmity* like chaunce may beare; . . . I. ix. 30. 8
The strong it weakens with *infirmitie,* . . . II. i. 57. 7
through *infirmity* Of the fraile flesh, . . . II. xi. 1. 5
most strong in most *infirmitee;* . . . II. xi. 40. 8
To comfort him in his *infirmity.* . . . II. xi. 49. 5
Your stubborne hart t' affect with fraile *infirmity.* . . . II. xii. 28. 9
him selfe weaker through *infirmity.* . . . III. vii. 33. 4
faint *Infirmity;* Vile Poverty; . . . III. xii. 25. 8
Infix. All striving to *infixe* their feeble stinges, . . . I. i. 23. 6
Infixed. *See* **Far-infixed.**
at the point two stinges *in fixed* (**in-fixed*) arre, . . . I. xi. 11. 8
Which his sad speach *infixed* in my brest, . . . II. iv. 23. 2
infixed faster hold Within my bleeding bowells, . . . III. ii. 39. 1
Infixt such secrete sting of greedy lust, . . . III. viii. 25. 2
Where fast *infixed,* . . . the staffe asunder brake, . . . IV. iii. 10. 5
bitter thoughts, which deepe therein *infixed* lay. . . . IV. viii. 1. 9
Infixeth. the poysnous sting, which infamy *Infixeth* . . . VI. vi. 1. 4
Infixing. His little needle there *infixing* deep, . . . *Gn.* 287
Inflame. might *Inflame* the Navie of their enemies, . . . *Gn.* 510
For her that did his heart with love *inflame.* . . . *As.* 40
lust did now *inflame* His corage more, . . . I. iii. 41. 7
Fitt to *inflame* faire Lady with loves rage, . . . II. i. 41. 8
seemd him to *enflame* on every side: . . . II. v. 2. 7
with forst wind the fewell did *inflame;* . . . II. vii. 36. 2
face The flashing blood with blushing did *inflame,* . . . II. ix. 43. 3
affections move In brutish mindes, and filthy lust *inflame,* . . . III. iii. 1. 6
it ought your corage much *inflame* . . . III. iii. 54. 1
That warre was kindled which did Troy *inflame,* . . . III. ix. 34. 2
doth *inflame* The eyes of all . . . VI. Pr. 6. 6
that shall thy feeble brest *Inflame* with love, . . . *H.H.L.* 270
lampe, which useth to *inflame* (**enflame*) The hearts of men . . . *H.H.B.* 274
Inflamed. with *enflamed* breath . . . hot rage instil'd. . . . *Ro.* xi. 7
when choler is *inflamed* with rage, . . . *S.C.* May 136
Enflam'd with fury and fiers hardy hed, . . . I. iv. 38. 7
Inflamd with scornefull wrath and high disdaine, . . . I. viii. 7. 2
Exceeding rage *enflam'd* the furious Beast, . . . I. xi. 17. 5
Inflam'd with wrath, his raging blade he hefte, . . . I. xi. 39. 6
So they him left *inflam'd* with wrathfulnesse, . . . II. i. 25. 8
Inflamed was to follow beauties pray, . . . II. ii. 7. 7
when the frantick fitt *inflamd* his spright, . . . II. iv. 7. 3
It was not long ere she *inflam'd* him so, . . . II. v. 20. 1
Ne would with vaine occasions be *inflam'd;* . . . II. v. 21. 7
He then uprose, *inflamd* with fell despight, . . . II. v. 37. 8
inflam'd with rage That sire he fowl bespake: . . . II. viii. 12. 1
secrete powre t' appease *inflamed* rage: . . . II. viii. 26. 8
All sodainely *enflam'd* with furious fit . . . V. iv. 39. 5
Her burning tongue with rage *inflamed* hath, . . . V. viii. 49. 2
Both *inflam'd* with furious despight; . . . VI. i. 36. 5
Inflames. with whirling wheeles, *inflames* the skyen With fire . . . I. iv. 9. 8
Inflameth. learned minds *inflameth* with desire Of heavenly things: . . . VII. vii. 2. 5
Inflaming. *Inflaming* feeble eyes that her do view. . . . *Col.* 519
Inflict. Upon him did *inflict* this punishment: . . . V. iii. 37. 4
On whom he did *inflict* most grievous punishment. . . . V. xii. 26. 9
Which I to others did *inflict* afore, . . . VI. viii. 22. 4
Inflicting. *Inflicting* on her selfe his punishment. . . . V. vi. 13. 5
Inflicts. No wound, which warlike hand of enemy *Inflicts* . . . VI. vi. 1. 2
Influence. th' heavenly gift of wisdomes *influence,* . . . *T.M.* 86
wicked *influence* Of Starres conspiring . . . *T.M.* 481
Are thereby fild with happie *influence;* . . . *T.M.* 586

Influence—*Continued.*
influence of all celestiall grace, . . . *Ti.* 289
what evill starre On you hath . . . pourd his *influence* bad, . . . I. viii. 42. 7
Seemes to be borne by native *influence;* . . . II. iv. 1. 5
Through *influence* of th' hevens fruitfull ray . . . III. vi. 6. 2
The wicked engine through false *influence* . . . III. ix. 29. 3
From thence pour'd down on men by *influence* of grace. . . . V. x. 1. 9
with subtill *influence* Of his thin spirit . . . VII. vii. 22. 3
happy *influence* upon us raine, . . . *Epith.* 416
Or more or lesse, by *influence* divine, . . . *H.B.* 44
Inforce, -d, -ment. *See* **Enforce,** *etc.*
Inform. then *informe* his Master hastely, . . . *Hub.* 880
(as travellers *informe*) . . . II. xii. 24. 8
that young Squyre Gan them *informe* the cause, . . . III. viii. 52. 7
Which with sage counsell . . . He could *enforme,* . . . VI. vi. 3. 8
the chast wombe *informe* with timely seed, . . . *Epith.* 386
Informed. in each point her selfe *informd* aright, . . . III. iv. 4. 3
Informed in the mud on which the Sunne hath shynd. . . . III. vi. 8. 9
still preserve your first *informed* grace, . . . *H.B.* 167
Infuse. goodly fury into them *infuse,* . . . VI. Pr. 2. 6
That may my rymes with sweet *infuse* embrew, . . . *H.H.L.* 47
Infused. From thence *infused* into mortall brests. . . . *T.M.* 390
secret vertues are *infusd* In every fountaine, . . . II. ii. 5. 6
Through secret sparks of his *infused* fyre, . . . *H.L.* 97
Infusion. Through the divine *infusion* of their skill, . . . *T.M.* 38
through *infusion* sweete Of thine owne spirit . . . IV. ii. 34. 6
your gentle brest inspire With sweet *infusion,* . . . *Am.* xxviii. 7
through *infusion* of celestiall powre, . . . *H.B.* 50
Ingate. like as at the *ingate* of their berth . . . *Ti.* 47
Which hath in charge the *ingate* of the yeare: . . . IV. x. 12. 6
Ingenerate. That is *ingenerate* in fleshly slime. . . . III. vi. 3. 5
Inglorious. dwell in dust *inglorious* and bace, . . . *Hub.* 981
sleepes in dust, dead and *inglorious,* . . . *Ti.* 355
Loe! where he now *inglorious* doth lye, . . . II. viii. 12. 8
left *inglorious* on the vanquisht playne, . . . II. x. 58. 2
Inglorious now lies in sencelesse swownd, . . . III. iv. 29. 3
'Daunger without discretion to attempt *Inglorious,* [*and] beastlike is: . . . III. xi. 23. 2
Ingots. distent Into great *Ingowes* (**Ingoes*) and to wedges square; . . . II. vii. 5. 6
Ingrate. Accusing highest Jove and gods *ingrate;* . . . II. vii. 60. 7
in his mind, malitious and *ingrate,* . . . VI. vii. 2. 5
Ingrateful. Or art *ingratefull* to each gentle mayd, . . . *Col.* 462
Ingrave. So both agree their bodies to *engrave:* . . . II. i. 60. 1
Inhabitants. With Thames *inhabitants* of noble fame, . . . *Ro.* xxii. 3
Inherit. where now he doth *inherite* All happinesse . . . *Ti.* 383
Ne mongst true lovers they shall place *inherit,* . . . *Col.* 893
This lowly quiet life which I *inherite* here.' . . . VI. ix. 25. 9
May heavenly tabernacles there *inherit,* . . . *Epith.* 422
Inheritance. That his father left by *inheritaunce;* . . . *S.C.* May 89
When shepeheards had none *inheritaunce,* . . . *S.C.* May 105
Pan himselfe was their *inheritaunce,* . . . *S.C.* May 111
To you th' *inheritance* belonges by right . . . I. iv. 48. 5
He gave as their *inheritance* to hold, . . . *H.H.L.* 61
Inholders. every parts *inholders* to convent, . . . VII. vii. 17. 4
Inhumanity. No greater shame to man then *inhumanitie.* . . . VI. i. 26. 9
Iniquity. Deformd with filth and fowle *iniquitie;* . . . *T.M.* 122
High heaped up with huge *iniquitee,* . . . I. ix. 46. 4
my soule was soyld with fowle *iniquity.'* . . . II. vii. 62. 9
fell Into all filth and foule *iniquitie,* . . . V. i. 5. 7
Injuries. Each place abounding with fowle *injuries,* . . . *Hub.* 1305
their sharpe wounds and noyous *injuries,* . . . II. ix. 16. 7
Injurious. The which *injurious* time hath quite outworne, . . . *Ro.* xxvii. 6
reft That piteous spoile by so *injurious* theft; . . . VI. i. 18. 5
Injuriously. thou, Jove, *injuriously* hast held The Heavens rule . . . VII. vi. 27. 6
Injury. maugre fortunes *injurie,* And times decay, . . . *Ti.* 166
them conjure t' avenge this shamefull *injury.* . . . I. xii. 27. 9
wreake on him her will for so great *injurie.* . . . IV. vi. 23. 9
Boldly him bad such *injurie* forbeare; . . . VI. xi. 15. 2
bit them with his banefull teeth of *injury.* . . . VI. xii. 28. 9
Damning all wrong and tortious *Injurie,* . . . VII. vii. 14. 5
Injustice. Justice he solde *injustice* for to buy, . . . *Hub.* 1147
Ink. Deformed monsters, fowle, and blacke as *inke,* . . . I. i. 22. 7
Inland. 'In this wide *Inland* sea, . . . II. vi. 10. 1
far *in land* a salvage nation dwelt . . . II. x. 7. 1
th' *inland* folke, which sought him backe to drive, . . . III. ix. 42. 3
Inly. their fondnesse *inly* I pitie: . . . *S.C.* May 38
Enaunter they mought be *inly* knowe. . . . *S.C.* S. 161
for which intent He *inly* burns, . . . *Gn.* 275
His *inly* grieved minde full sore opprest; . . . *Gn.* 643
at the Lyons skin he *inly* quooke; . . . *Hub.* 1060
inlie greeving in my groning brest, . . . *Ti.* 484
Yet did she *inly* fret and felly burne, . . . *Mui.* 343
His heart with vengefull malice *inly* swelt; . . . *Mui.* 356
He sighed soft, and *inly* deepe did grone, . . . *D.* 48
Yet if their deeper sence be *inly* wayd, . . . *Ded. Son.* ix. 9
As one that *inly* mournd, so was she sad, . . . I. i. 4. 6
trembling every joynt, did *inly* quake, . . . I. ix. 24. 8
Her heart with joy unwonted *inly* sweld, . . . I. x. 8. 8
she was *inly* glad her purpose so to gaine. . . . II. i. 20. 9
grutch And *inly* grieve, . . . II. ii. 34. 7
inly did him selfe torment. . . . II. ii. 37. 9
inly bate Deepe in his flesh, . . . II. v. 7. 8
Eftsoones he gan to rage, and *inly* frett, . . . II. vi. 28. 3
Yet nought can quench mine *inly* flaming syde, . . . II. vi. 44. 3
with the hidden fire too *inly* warmd. . . . II. vi. 51. 5
The Prince was *inly* moved at her speach, . . . II. ix. 39. 1
inly tremble at the memory Of Brennus . . . II. x. 40. 8
recure their wounds; so *inly* they did tine. . . . II. xi. 21. 9

Inly—*Continued.*
With murmurous disdayne doth *inly* rave, ... II. xi. 32. 3
she is *inly* nothing ill apayd; . . . . II. xii. 28. 7
shee *inly* deemd Her love too light, ... III. i. 55. 6
ne word she spake, But *inly* sigh'd. . . . . III. i. 61. 7
The royall Maid woxe *inly* wondrous glad, ... III. ii. 11. 1
Hart that is *inly* hurt is greatly eased With hope . . . . . III. ii. 15. 3
weeting *inly* well That she to him dissembled . . . . III. iii. 17. 2
sighing softly sore, and *inly* deepe, ... III. iv. 11. 1
groning *inly* deepe, ... III. v. 34. 2
Least that his wound were *inly* well not heald, ... III. v. 49. 2
Shee *inly* sory was, and gan relent . . . . III. vi. 25. 2
with terrour and with aw So *inly* smot, ... III. vii. 13. 6
with the frosen cold Benumbd so *inly*, ... III. viii. 34. 8
inly tickled with that golden vew. . . . . III. x. 30. 3
With huge impatience he *inly* swelt, ... III. xi. 27. 1
inly being more then seeming sad: . . . . III. xii. 16. 4
The warlike virgine . . . wexed *inlie* wroth; . . . . IV. i. 10. 6
inly grudge at him that he had sped so well. . . . . IV. ii. 7. 9
Whereat full *inly* wroth was Triamond, ... IV. iv. 45. 1
inly thought of that despightfull deede . . . . IV. v. 9. 5
inly feeds it selfe with thoughts unkind, ... IV. vi. 1. 3
Scudamour, now woxen *inly* glad . . . . IV. vi. 28. 1
Thereat full *inly* blushed Britomart, ... IV. vi. 32. 8
how ever malcontent She *inly* were . . . . IV. vi. 44. 3
sighing *inly* deepe, her thus bespake: . . . . IV. viii. 16. 3
Full *inly* sorie, for the fervent zeale . . . . IV. viii. 55. 2
Through jealous passion weeping *inly* wroth, ... IV. ix. 9. 8
my heart did *inly* earne, ... IV. x. 9. 1
inly groning deepe and sighing oft, ... IV. x. 48. 3
even to thinke thereof it *inly* pitties mee. . . . . IV. xi. 1. 9
inly wish that in his powre it weare . . . . IV. xii. 12. 7
all the way did *inly* mourne, like one astray. . . . . IV. xii. 18. 9
inly troubled was the truth to learne. . . . . IV. xii. 24. 5
feeble spirit *inly* felt refection: . . . . IV. xii. 34. 5
he was full *inly* glad, ... V. ii. 3. 6
She *inly* yet conceived great disgrace: . . . . V. iii. 23. 7
inly did to great impatience move her: . . . . V. v. 51. 7
The yron man, . . . did *inly* chill and quake, ... V. vi. 9. 6
inly burning To be avenged . . . . V. vi. 31. 1
Then would she *inly* fret, and grieve, ... V. xii. 32. 3
his hart was *inly* child With great amazement, ... VI. ii. 4. 8
He *inly* gan her lover to envy, ... VI. ii. 17. 2
inly touched with compassion deare, ... VI. iii. 4. 4
inly did afflict her pensive thought . . . . VI. iii. 6. 8
yet, *inly* wroth Against her Knight, ... VI. iii. 33. 1
his heart did *inly* flame With wrathfull fury . . . . VI. iii. 43. 4
Calepine, however *inly* wroth, ... VI. iii. 45. 6
Which when he heard, he *inly* touched was . . . . VI. iv. 34. 1
for exceeding griefe which *inly* grew . . . . VI. iv. 40. 1
yet *inly* neate and clene, ... VI. v. 38. 4
To cloke the mischiefe which he *inly* ment, ... VI. vii. 4. 2
inly burnt with flames most raging whot, ... VI. xi. 4. 2
chauffed *inly*, seeing now no more Him liberty was left . . VI. xii. 36. 4
inly quaking, seem'd as reft of sense . . . . VII. vi. 25. 4
in his spright Did *inly* grudge, ... VII. vi. 35. 8
Whether she man or woman *inly* were, ... VII. vii. 5. 6
with like beauties parts be *inly* deckt; . . . . *H.B.* 193
Which seeing now so *inly* faire to be, ... *H.B.* 225
whilest so thy softened spirit Is *inly* toucht, ... *H.H.L.* 254

Inmost. Shortly within her *inmost* pith there bred . . . . *Van.* vii. 6
Fashiond above within their *inmost* part, ... III. vi. 44. 7
'Into the *inmost* Temple thus I came, ... IV. x. 37. 1
in her *inmost* brest He may embosomd bee . . . . *H.L.* 248
wounds the life, and wastes the *inmost* marrow. . . . . . . *H.B.* 63
to their eyes that *inmost* faire display, ... *H.B.* 237

Immove. Did much *emmove* his stout heroicke heart; . . . . I. ii. 21. 6
when him high corage did *emmove*, ... II. i. 50. 5
With deare compassion deeply did *emmove*, ... IV. viii. 3. 7

Inmoved. Wherewith *enmovd*, these bleeding words she gan to say. . . . . I. vii. 38. 9
The knight was much *enmoved* with his speach, ... I. ix. 48. 1
Mammon *emmoved* was with inward wrath; . . . . II. vii. 51. 1
She was *emmoved* in her noble minde, ... III. xi. 4. 7
Though much *emmov'd*, but stedfast . . . . III. xii. 2. 9
Was much *emmoved* at his perils vew, ... VI. iv. 3. 4
His manly mynde was much *emmoved* therewithall; . . . . . . VI. viii. 5. 9

Inn. Whose way is wildernesse, whose *ynne* Penaunce, ... *S.C.* F. 89
taken up his *ynne* in Fishes haske. . . . . *S.C.* N. 16
The ghastlie Owle her grievous *ynne* doth keepe. . . . . . . *S.C.* D. 72
will I take up my *Inne*. . . . . *D.* 469
with me ye may take up your *In* . . . . I. i. 33. 7
the common *In* of rest; . . . . II. i. 59. 2
The worldes sweet *In* from paine and wearisome turmoyle.' . II. xii. 32. 9
He shall his dayes with peace bring to his earthly *In*. . . . III. iii. 30. 9
Phoebus . . . Unto his *Inne* began to draw apace; . . . . . . VI. iii. 29. 2

Inner. came rushing forth from *inner* bowre, ... I. viii. 5. 6
sup, . . . secret poyson through their *inner* Partes, ... I. viii. 14. 4
Those were the keyes of every *inner* dore; . . . . I. viii. 30. 8
as doth an hidden moth The *inner* garment frett, ... II. ii. 34. 8
in a darkesome *inner* bowre Her oft to meete: . . . . II. iv. 24. 5
fild his *inner* thought. . . . . II. vii. 24. 4
forth were led Into an *inner* rowme, ... III. i. 33. 2
the *inner* part Of every thing consumes, ... III. v. 48. 8
many wide woundes launched through his *inner* partes. . . . III. xi. 44. 9
the *inner* rowme from whence they first did rise. . . . . . III. xii. 26. 9
As one whose *inner* parts had bene ythrild . . . . IV. iii. 22. 4
Tho gan he swell in every *inner* part . . . . IV. vi. 7. 4
Her spightfull words did pricke and wound the *inner* part. . IV. viii. 26. 9
The *inner* parts now gan to putrify, ... VI. vi. 5. 4

Inner—*Continued.*
anguish, and impatient paine, In th' *inner* parts; . . . . . VI. vi. 8. 7
daily night did hover Through all the *inner* parts, ... VI. x. 42. 6
Breake forth at length out of the *inner* part, ... *Am.* ii. 5
And kindled flame in all their *inner* parts, ... *H.L.* 124
sharply launching every *inner* part, ... *H.H.L.* 158

Innocence. he her wronged *innocence* did weet. . . . . I. iii. 6. 3
In death avowing th' *innocence* of her sonne. . . . . I. v. 39. 3
in lieu of *innocence*, Imprinted had that token . . . . II. ii. 4. 3
they his mothers *innocence* may tell, ... II. ii. 10. 5
So much high God doth *innocence* embrace. . . . . III. viii. 29. 5
of his *innocence* to make her pray. . . . . V. v. 52. 4
That boldned *innocence* beares in hir eies; . . . . *Am.* v. 10
Throw thy selfe downe, with trembling *innocence*, ... *H.H.B.* 143

Innocent. To save the *innocent* from the beastes pawes, . . . *S.C.* Au. 33
to afflict so sore The *innocent*, ... *D.* 201
His sports were faire, his joyance *innocent*, ... *As.* 25
So pure and (*an) *innocent*, as that same lambe, ... I. i. 5. 1
of whose most *innocent* death When tidings came to mee, . . I. ii. 24. 3
That from the blood he might be *innocent*, ... I. ii. 44. 7
The *innocent* pray in hast he does forsake; . . . . I. vi. 10. 7
happy earth, Whereon thy *innocent* feet doe ever tread! . . . I. x. 9. 2
with *innocent* blood Defyld those sacred waves, ... I. xi. 29. 7
innocent Of that was doen; . . . . II. ii. 1. 7
With wrathfull hand I slew her *innocent*, ... II. iv. 29. 4
To wreake it selfe on beast all *innocent*, ... II. v. 5. 4
the sad virgin, *innocent* of all, ... II. x. 19. 6
did live then like an *innocent*, ... IV. viii. 30. 2
In guiltlesse blood of many an *innocent*: . . . . V. xii. 40. 7
and guiltlesse *innocent* Of blame, ... VI. iii. 18. 3
Innocent paper; . . . matter to avenge her yre: . . . . . . *Am.* xlviii. 1

Innocents. *innocents* trew, Which there were slaine as sheepe out of the fold, ... I. viii. 35. 6

Innovation. to have got great good . . . by his *innovation*. . . V. ii. 51. 7

Innumerable. an *innumerable* flight Of harmefull fowles . . . II. xii. 35. 6

Ino. Like raging *Ino*, when with knife in hand . . . . V. viii. 47. 1
neither *Ino*, nor Medea stout, ... V. viii. 47. 7

Inogene. Borne of fayre *Inogene* of Italy; . . . . II. x. 13. 5

Ino's. tragicke *Inoes* sonne, ... IV. xi. 13. 4

Inquest. what *inquest* Made her dissemble her disguised kind? III. ii. 4. 6
He now went with him in this new *inquest*, ... V. i. 13. 1
by diligent *inquest* Provided him a sword . . . . VI. xi. 42. 5

Inquire. T' *enquire* of custome, what and whence they were? *Hub.* 245
of the Priest eftsoones gan to *enquire*, ... *Hub.* 481
By secrete meanes gan of his state *enquire*, ... *Hub.* 681
He gan *enquire* of some in secret wize, ... *Hub.* 1272
each part t' *inquire* Of the wide rule . . . . *Mui.* 39
'Of such,' (saide he,) 'I chiefly doe *inquere*, ... I. i. 31. 5
after for that Lady did *inquere*; . . . . I. iii. 25. 7
good hap hath brought You to *inquere* the secrets . . . . . . I. vii. 42. 6
Whereat he wondred much, and gan *enquere*, ... I. x. 56. 6
Of faery lond yet if he more *inquyre*, ... II. Pr. 4. 1
coming close to Trompart gan *inquere* . . . . II. iii. 12. 1
he gan *inquyre* What hard mishap . . . . II. iv. 16. 7
Ne staied for his Damsell to *inquire*, ... II. vi. 27. 8
he gan *inquire*, What meant that preace . . . . II. vii. 48. 1
he did *inquyre* What wight she was . . . . II. ix. 39. 6
Cantium, which Kent we comenly *inquyre*. . . . . II. x. 12. 9
Tho gan she myldly of them to *inquyre* . . . . III. i. 23. 8
after gan *inquire* his parentage, ... III. vii. 46. 7
'*inquire* of thee what were those three, ... III. vii. 57. 6
Gan first *inquire* of tydinges farre abrode, ... III. viii. 45. 8
of each one he mett he tidings did *inquere*. . . . . III. x. 19. 9
Thence to depart for further aide t' *enquire*: . . . . III. xii. 45. 8
each of other gan *inquire* his name. . . . . IV. iv. 42. 3
Of whom she gan *enquire* of her estate, ... IV. vii. 34. 8
He gan of them *inquire*, ... IV. viii. 21. 2
oft of them did earnestly *inquire*, ... IV. viii. 22. 3
he gan *enquire* his cause of dread: . . . . IV. viii. 41. 4
to *inquire* Of all the accident there hapned plaine, ... IV. viii. 46. 6
to *enquire* What thing so many nations met did there desire. V. ii. 29. 8
t' *inquire* The cause of their array, ... V. ii. 52. 8
gan *inquire* how was that steed bereaved, ... V. iii. 30. 8
gan *enquire* of him with mylder mood . . . . V. vi. 15. 6
She for that yron prison did *enquire*, ... V. vii. 37. 2
Then Artegall gan of the Prince *enquire*, ... V. viii. 15. 1
Of whom Sir Artegall gan then *enquire* . . . . V. xi. 48. 6
Both man and beast doe fly, and succour doe *inquyre*. . . . V. xi. 58. 9
Sir Calidore . . . further gan *inquire* . . . . VI. ii. 13. 6
did *inquire* After adventures, ... VI. v. 11. 5
T' *enquire* of them, whether by force . . . they were away convayd? . . . . VI. vii. 34. 5
still suppressing, gan of her *inquire*, ... VI. viii. 18. 3
For further fortune then I would *inquire*; . . . . VI. ix. 24. 5
Arrived in this Isle . . . T' *inquire* for slaves; . . . . . . VI. xi. 9. 6
Gan to *inquire* for that faire shepherdesse, ... VI. xi. 11. 6
Ne wight he found of whom he might *inquire*, ... VI. xi. 26. 2
The matrone stayd no lenger to *enquire*, ... VI. xii. 19. 1
Ne any then shall after it *inquire*, ... *Am.* xxvii. 9
another Element *inquire* Whereof she mote be made; . . . . . *Am.* lv. 9

Inquired. of him *inquerd* Tidings of warre, ... I. vi. 36. 1
with speeches sage *Inquyrd*, ... II. x. 27. 9
Of all that needed them to be *inquird*, ... III. iii. 51. 2
she *inquir'd* One day of Proteus . . . . III. iv. 25. 1
in the rurall cottages *inquir'd*; . . . . III. vi. 15. 2
having long beheld, at last *enquired* The cause . . . . IV. v. 38. 3
inquired Where they might tydings get of her estate; . . . . IV. vi. 47. 3

Inquireth. *Inquireth* of our states, and of our knightly deedes. I. ix. 28. 9

Inquiring. there *enquiring* privily, to learne What did of late . *Hub.* 1249

Inquiry. Ne by *inquirie* learne, nor ghesse by ayme; . . . . VI. iv. 24. 7

Intent—*Continued.*
with felonous despight And fell *intent*, . . . III. i. 65. 4
For such *intent* into these partes I came, . . . III. ii. 7. 6
Yet did possesse their horrible *intent;* . . . III. ii. 43. 7
of their first *intent* gan make new dout, . . . III. iii. 14. 3
Shal be by vision staide from his *intent:* . . . III. iii. 41. 6
Unto the gladsome port of her *intent*. . . . III. iv. 10. 5
To bring to passe his mischievous *intent*, . . . III. iv. 45. 2
Carried her forward with her first *intent:* . . . III. iv. 50. 5
Light-shonning thefte, and traiterous *intent*, . . . III. iv. 58. 2
His steed eke seemd t' apply his steps to his *intent*. . . III. iv. 61. 9
He knockt his brest with desperate *intent*, . . . III. vii. 20. 3
to reward my trusty true *intent*, . . . III. vii. 55. 8
prosecuting of her first *intent*, . . . III. xi. 50. 8
To shew the victors might and mercilesse *intent*. . . . III. xi. 52. 9
turning to herselfe, his fell *intent*, . . . III. xii. 33. 3
met With dreadfull force and furious *intent*, . . . IV. iii. 6. 6
so gave way unto his fell *intent;* . . . IV. iii. 18. 7
his felonous *intent* Returning disappointed his desire, . . IV. vi. 11. 6
With fell *intent* on him to bene ywroke; . . . IV. vi. 23. 3
To hide th' *intent* which in my heart did lurke, . . . IV. vii. 17. 3
messengers of his true meaning and *intent*. . . . IV. viii. 13. 9
void of vile and treacherous *intent*, . . . IV. viii. 30. 5
The more did she pursue her lewd *intent*, . . . IV. viii. 35. 8
firmely following her first *intent*, . . . IV. viii. 50. 8
Upon the sea to wreake his fell *intent;* . . . IV. ix. 23. 4
loved not as these for like *intent*, . . . IV. x. 26. 5
To follow his adventures first *intent*, . . . V. iv. 3. 6
To joyne the combate with cruell *intent*, . . . V. iv. 6. 6
drawing backe deceived their *intent:* . . . V. iv. 24. 2
with fell *intent* And countenaunce fierce, . . . V. v. 5. 3
The trustie Mayd, conceiving her *intent*, . . . V. v. 35. 1
Which speaches she applying to the scope Of her *intent*, . . . V. v. 39. 9
from thy tongue thy hearts *intent* doth hold.' . . . V. vi. 10. 3
Of armed men comming with close *intent* . . . V. vi. 28. 7
With full *intent* t' avenge that villany . . . V. vi. 35. 4
rode him selfe uppon his first *intent*, . . . V. viii. 3. 6
'Then let not that' (said they) 'stay your *intent;* . . . V. ix. 7. 8
his false *intent* to shade, . . . V. ix. 12. 7
To turne her eyes from his *intent* away; . . . V. ix. 13. 7
with constant firme *intent* For zeale of Justice, . . . V. ix. 49. 4
With dreadfull terror and with fell *intent;* . . . V. xii. 17. 2
to misconstrue of a mans *intent*, . . . V. xii. 34. 4
with vile tongue and venemous *intent* . . . VI. i. 8. 8
With full *intent* him cruelly to kill, . . . VI. iii. 49. 2
He to him turnd with furious *intent*, . . . VI. vi. 27. 2
Willing to worke his villenous *intent* . . . VI. vi 44. 4
ere his stroke attayned his *intent*, . . . VI. viii. 15. 6
'If happie, then it is in this *intent*, . . . VI. ix. 20. 2
usde him friendly for further *intent*, . . . VI. x. 37. 7
But greedily her fell *intent* poursewth, . . . *Am.* xi. 7
A close *intent* at last to shew me grace: . . . *Am.* xxv. 10
With pure regard and spotlesse true *intent*, . . . *H.B.* 212
Intentive. whilest she lent her *intentive* mind, . . . V. ix. 14. 1
Intents. reliefe, Which given was to them for good *intents:* I. iii. 17. 4
Her nathelesse Th' enchaunter finding fit for his *intents* . . . II. i. 22. 8
stirredst up th' Heroes high *intents*, . . . III. iii. 2. 8
Interchanged. *interchanged* life unto them lent, . . . *Ti.* 387
strokes, . . . The whiles were *enterchaunged* twixt them two; IV. iii. 17. 2
Interdeal. To learne the *enterdeale* of Princes strange, . . . *Hub.* 785
To treat with her, by way of *enterdeale*, . . . V. viii. 21. 7
Interess. May challenge ought in Heavens *interesse;* . . . VII. vi. 33. 3
Interest. all is now repayd with *interest* againe. . . . VI. viii. 21. 9
Interlace. As roses did with lilies *interlace;* . . . V. iii. 23. 5
Interlacing. Oft *interlacing* many a forged lie, . . . VI. xii. 33. 5
Internal. there sate *internall* (*infernall) Payne, . . . II. vii. 21. 5
Cros-cuts the liver with *internall* smart, . . . III. x. 59. 8
Interrupted. *interrupted* all her other speache . . . *S.C.* May 209
Interrupting. There *interrupting* him, a bonie swaine, . . . *Col.* 80
Intimate. to her he sought to *intimate* His inward griefe, . . III. ix. 30. 1
gan to *intimate* Each others griefe with zeale affectionate, . VI. iii. 12. 4
Into (*partial list*).
Sweetely sliding *into* the eyes of men, . . . *Bel.*[1] i. 2
beating downe . . . *Into* her mothers bosome, . . . *Ro.* xi. 12
See howe he venteth *into* the wynd; . . . *S.C.* F. 75
many han *into* mischiefe fall, . . . *S.C.* S. 147
Dido nis dead, but *into* heaven hent. . . . *S.C.* N. 169
high shoote up their heads *into* the skyes. . . . *Gn.* 192
Maide, . . . *Into* her silver bowre the Sunne received; . . . *Hub.* 4
Transformed them, . . . *Into* one flowre . . . *As.* 184
drawne together *into* one . . . *Col.* 845
soone him brought *into* a secret part, . . . I. ii. 5. 3
every way did seeke *into* his life; . . . II. v. 9. 2
him that raignd *into* his rowme thrust downe, . . . II. vii. 11. 8
it fell *into* that Fairies mind To aske . . . III. ii. 4. 4
lett him in *Into* the balefull house . . . III. v. 22. 3
shortly grew *into* outrageous fire; . . . III. vii. 16. 2
Mote not be entertaynd . . . *Into* that Castle, . . . III. ix. 3. 4
Into the Martian field adowne descended . . . IV. v. 6. 8
allure such fondlings . . . *Into* her trap . . . VI. vi. 42. 4
golden haire *Into* their comely tresses dewly drest, . . . VI. xii. 15. 4
Intolerable. careles hear'st my *intollerable* cares. . . . *Gn.* 632
to avoyde th' *intollerable* stowre, . . . III. ix. 13. 1
Intrapped, Intreat. *See* **Entrapped, Entreat.**
Intricate. dilate Their clasping armes in wanton wreathings *intricate:* . . . II. xii. 53. 9
Deepe Indus, and Maeander *intricate*, . . . IV. xi. 21. 2
Introld. *In which her royall presence is *introld;* . . . II. ii. 44. 4
Intuse. after having searcht the *intuse* deepe, . . . III. v. 33. 8
Inundation. after Nilus *inundation*, Infinite shapes of creatures III. vi. 8. 7

Inure. Ne to strong labour can it selfe *enure:* . . . *Hub.* 276
That doth ill cause or evill end *enure;* . . . IV. ii. 29. 8
T' *enure* them selves to sufferaunce thereby, . . . V. vii. 9. 4
her eyes she doth *inure*, . . . *Am.* xxi. 9
His dunghill thoughts . . . themselves *enure* To dirtie drosse, *H.L.* 183
Inured. *Enur'd* to hardnesse and to homely fare, . . . IV. viii. 27. 6
Their hardned hearts, *enur'd* to bloud and cruelty. . . . V. viii. 1. 9
Of many haynous crymes by her *enured;* . . . V. ix. 39. 6
But yet the Prince so well *enured* was . . . VI. viii. 14. 1
Such haughty mynds, *enur'd* to hardy fight, . . . *Am.* xiv. 7
againe *enured* His former cruelty. . . . *Epig.* iv. 53
Invade. he whose heart like sorrow did *invade*. . . . *As.* 172
With fire and sword the region to *invade:* . . . I. xi. 14. 6
he it oft adventur'd to *invade*. . . . I. xi. 49. 4
Now forst to yield, now forcing to *invade;* . . . II. ii. 25. 7
The shame and death, which will thee soone *invade?* . . . II. vi. 39. 7
did deepe *invade* Into his head, . . . II. viii. 45. 4
Gan more the same frequent, and further to *invade*. . . . II. x. 6. 9
gan the Hunnes and Picts *invade* this land, . . . II. x. 61. 6
Least that his Lord they should behinde *invade;* . . . II. xi. 31. 5
he wonts the Stygian realmes *invade* . . . II. xii. 41. 4
That never foes his kingdome might *invade*, . . . III. ii. 21. 3
forreine Paynims which *invade* thy land. . . . III. iii. 27. 9
feare did all *invade*, . . . III. iv. 21. 4
invade The state of life out of the griesly shade. . . . III. vi. 37. 4
whiles sleepe their sences did *invade*. . . . III. x. 46. 9
seeme too suddeinly him to *invade*. . . . III. xi. 8. 5
Foolhardy . . . so we a God *invade*. . . . III. xi. 32. 9
the proud Bird . . . did her *invade:* . . . III. xi. 32. 7
With th' one his foes he threatned to *invade*, . . . III. xii. 11. 7
Those be unquiet thoughts that carefull minds *invade*. . . . IV. v. 35. 9
Whom without perill he cannot *invade*. . . . IV. vi. 12. 5
With which in case thou canst him not *invade*, . . . V. v. 49. 7
The gentle Aladine did earst *invade*, . . . VI. iii. 8. 4
Out of their ambush broke, and gan him to *invade*. . . . VI. v. 17. 9
The dwelling of these shepheards did *invade*, . . . VI. x. 39. 7
to *invade* Now all unwares, . . . VI. xi. 38. 5
Invaded. This land *invaded* with like violence, . . . II. x. 15. 6
By a strong Tyrant, who *invaded* has Her land, . . . V. x. 6. 8
Invader's. wall'd by nature gainst *invaders* wrong, . . . IV. x. 6. 3
Invades. Fast bound with serpents that him oft *invades;* . . . *Gn.* 374
Invasion. Upon his fleshly corpse to make *invasion:* . . . *Hub.* 1090
Inveigle. easy was t' *inveigle* weaker sight: . . . I. xii. 32. 5
Inveigled. *Inveigled* him to follow her desires unmeete. . . I. vii. 50. 9
Invent. Bacchus merry fruit they did *invent*, . . . I. vi. 15. 2
thousand waies *invent* To feede her foolish humour . . . II. vi. 3. 8
Till him alive or dead she did *invent*. . . . III. v. 10. 4
Fie on the man that did it first *invent* . . . IV. v. 18. 6
At last, when as no meanes he could *invent*, . . . IV. xii. 16. 1
to *invent* Which way he enter might . . . V. ii. 20. 8
Well therefore did the antique world *invent* . . . V. vii. 2. 1
she would streightwayes *invent* How to deprave . . . V. xii. 34. 2
fouly rayle with all she could *invent;* . . . V. xii. 40. 2
By all the courteous meanes he could *invent;* . . . VI. v. 32. 6
The villaine stayd not aunswer to *invent*, . . . VI. viii. 8. 1
With all kind courtesies he could *invent;* . . . VI. ix. 34. 6
by that count, which lovers books *invent*, . . . *Am.* lx. 9
ye mote *invent* Som hevenly wit, . . . *Am.* lxxxii. 6
How vainely then doe ydle wits *invent*, . . . *H.B.* 64
Invented. Such mournfull tunes were never since *invented*. . . *T.M.* 12
Such as that prudent Romane well *invented*, . . . IV. ii. 2. 7
the antique wisards well *invented* . . . IV. xii. 2. 1
Ay me, that ever guyle in wemen was *invented!* . . . V. xi. 50. 9
Invention. Muse, full of high thoughts *invention*, . . . *Col.* 446
Invest. Cannot find one this girdle to *invest*. . . . IV. v. 18. 5
Inviolable. bound them with *inviolable* bands; . . . IV. x. 35. 4
Inviolate. 'There chast Alceste lives *inviolate*, . . . *Gn.* 425
Inviolated. to preserve *inviolated* right . . . V. x. 2. 3
Invisible. hat . . . Which maketh him *invisible* in sight, . . *Hub.* 1280
Invite. began Him to *invite* unto his simple home; . . . VI. ix. 16. 4
Invulnerable. He was *invulnerable* made by Magicke leare. . VI. iv. 4. 9
Inward. breathing furie from his *inward* gall . . . *Bel.*[2] xiv. 11
With *inward* ruth and deare affection, . . . *Van.* xii. 3
Heare, then, my paine and *inward* agonie. . . . *Hub.* 58
tell the anguish of my *inward* smart, . . . *T.M.* 422
do my soule with *inward* griefe infest: . . . *Ti.* 460
through *inward* sorrowe wexen faint, . . . *Ti.* 472
With *inward* anguish and great griefe opprest: . . . *As.* 206
t' expresse their *inward* woe, . . . *As.* Interl. 225
full of *inward* feare, . . . *Col.* 228
alleies wide, With footing worne, and leading *inward* farr. . I. i. 7. 8
the Maple seeldom *inward* sound. . . . I. i. 9. 9
And wast his *inward* gall with deepe despight, . . . I. ii. 6. 4
still he strove to cloke his *inward* bale, . . . I. ix. 16. 3
Inward corruption and infected sin, . . . I. x. 25. 2
With heat, toyle, wounds, armes, smart, and *inward* fire, . . I. xi. 28. 2
to quake Through *inward* feare, . . . II. i. 9. 4
His stout courage to stoupe, and shew his *inward* paine. . . II. i. 42. 9
Mammon emmoved was with *inward* wrath; . . . II. vii. 51. 1
prickt with guiltie shame And *inward* griefe, . . . II. viii. 44. 3
And stared ghastly; some for *inward* shame, . . . II. xii. 86. 4
by long triall of the *inward* griefe . . . III. i. 54. 3
from like *inward* fire that outward smoke had steemd. . . III. i. 55. 9
her wound still *inward* freshly bledd, . . . III. i. 56. 3
gan ransack fast His *inward* partes, . . . III. v. 48. 5
The *inward* smoke, that did before but steeme, . . . III. viii. 26. 4
to her he sought to intimate His *inward* griefe, . . . III. ix. 30. 2
Shewing desire her *inward* flame to slake. . . . III. ix. 31. 4
Twixt *inward* doole and felonous despight: . . . III. x. 17. 6
Long thus he chawd the cud of *inward* griefe, . . . III. x. 18. 1

Inward—*Continued.*
inward wounds of dolours dart. III. xii. 16. 9
his heart Was thrild with *inward* griefe: IV. i. 49. 7
through *inward* griefe or wilfull scorne IV. viii. 15. 5
T' expresse the meaning of the *inward* mind, IV. viii. 26. 2
poysnous spirit sent From *inward* parts, IV. viii. 26. 4
inward grudge fild his heroicke brest: IV. ix. 32. 4
That none mote have accesse, nor *inward* fare, IV. x. 6. 4
In generation seeke to quench their *inward* fire. IV. x. 46. 9
languish of some *inward* thought, IV. xii. 25. 7
reading it with *inward* loathfulnesse, IV. xii. 32. 8
her private fire, which boyld Her *inward* brest, V. v. 53. 8
Chawing the cud of griefe and *inward* paine, V. vi. 19. 2
By outward shew her *inward* sence desining: V. vii. 8. 3
With *inward* griefe and malice did against them swell. V. vii. 10. 9
teare Her flesh for felnesse, which she *inward* hid: V. xii. 32. 4
not in outward shows, but *inward* thoughts defynd. VI. Pr. 5. 9
hearts dismay and *inward* dolour queld, VI. i. 18. 3
pearst Her stubborne hart with *inward* deepe effect, VI. i. 45. 4
Burning with *inward* rancour and despight, VI. v. 18. 2
he sighed deepe for *inward* tyne: VI. v. 24. 1
ranckling *inward* with unruly stounds, VI. vi. 5. 3
For all that shame, which kindled *inward* hate: VI. vii. 2. 7
inward shame of her uncomely case She did conceive, VI. viii. 51. 1
bred Of th' *inward* bale of my love-pined hart; *Am.* ii. 2
in my selfe, my *inward* selfe, I meane, *Am.* xlv. 3
The *inward* languor of my wounded hart, *Am.* l. 10
The *inward* beauty of her lively spright, *Epith.* 186
Move such affection in the *inward* mynd, *H.B.* 76
Which they have written in their *inward* ey; *H.H.B.* 285
Inwardly. *inwardly* it festreth sore, *S.C.* Mar. 101
pestilence, That mortall mindes doth *inwardly* infect *T.M.* 484
Did tickle *inwardly* in everie vaine; *Mui.* 394
inwardly he chawed his owne maw I. iv. 30. 5
Disarmd, disgraste, and *inwardly* dismayde; I. vii. 11. 6
As Lion, . . . Mournes *inwardly,* II. i. 42. 7
Ranckled so sore, and festred *inwardly,* II. iv. 23. 3
Whereof she seemes ashamed *inwardly:* III. iii. 20. 7
flam'd with zeale of vengeance *inwardly,* V. i. 14. 7
Griev'd to the soule, and groning *inwardly,* V. iv. 22. 8
his great hart gan *inwardly* to swell V. v. 10. 5
With great admiraunce *inwardly* was moved, V. x. 39. 4
and groaned *inwardly,* To thinke of this ill state VI. iii. 11. 5
His heart with vengeaunce *inwardly* did swell, VI. iii. 34. 8
that same Ladies hurt . . . was *inwardly* unsound. VI. iv. 16. 9
And feele such joy and pleasure *inwardly,* *H.H.B.* 264
Inwoven. *Enwoven* with an Yvie-winding trayle: *Mui.* 299
in thy colours bright Wast there *enwoven,* III. xi. 36. 2
all her gowne *Enwoven* was with gold, IV. x. 31. 9
So cunningly *enwoven* were, IV. xi. 27. 4
Io. the Graces seemed all to sing, *Hymen Io Hymen!* I. i. 48. 8
Hymen, *io* Hymen, Hymen, they do shout; *Epith.* 140
Then *Io,* tryumph! *H.B.* 267
Iola's. How for *Iolas* sake he did apply His mightie hands V. v. 24. 3
Ionic. After th' *Ionicke,* Atticke, Doricke guise; *Ro.* xxix. 3
Iphimedia. He loved eke *Iphimedia* deare, III. xi. 42. 1
Ire. his proude heart is fild with fretting *ire:* *Van.* x. 10
kindle coales of conteck and *yre,* *S.C.* S. 86
with sterne lookes to threaten kindled *yre.* *Gn.* 264
feare and *yre* Had blent so much his sense, *Gn.* 310
from th' Argolick ships with furious *yre* *Gn.* 495
he . . . would have slaine them in his furious *ire,* I. ii. 5. 8
hath thee hither brought to taste mine *yre?* I. iii. 39. 3
All these, and many evils moe haunt *ire,* I. iv. 35. 6
Therewith redoubled was his raging *yre,* I. v. 10. 4
fild her hidden caves with stormie *yre,* I. vii. 9. 5
the Gyaunt . . . all enrag'd with smart and frantick *yre,* I. viii. 17. 8
death was dew to him that had provokt Gods *ire.* I. ix. 50. 9
So flam'd his eyne with rage and rancorous *yre;* I. xi. 14. 7
fraught with rancour and engorged *yre,* I. xi. 40. 5
with fierce *yre* And zealous haste II. i. 13. 1
By which she triumphes over *yre* and pride, II. ii. 31. 6
with dredd Majestie and awfull *yre,* II. iii. 23. 8
bitt his tawny beard to shew his raging *yre.* II. iv. 15. 9
I, breathing *yre,* Sore chauffed at my stay II. iv. 32. 6
Headed with *yre* and vengeable despight. II. iv. 46. 2
His steed was bloody red, and fomed *yre,* II. v. 2. 8
wel nigh molt his hart in raging *yre:* II. v. 8. 5
quench the brond of his conceived *yre:* II. vi. 27. 6
satisfy The greedy hunger of revenging *yre,* II. viii. 15. 4
The cause of their dissention and outrageous *yre.* III. i. 23. 9
on their Paynim foes avenge their ranckled *ire.* III. iii. 36. 9
with proud envy and indignant *yre* III. iv. 47. 3
So them with bitter words he stird to bloodie *yre.* III. v. 15. 9
with faire treaty pacifide their *yre.* III. ix. 17. 2
To stirre up strife twixt love and spight and *ire,* IV. ii. 11. 8
Against her rode, full of despiteous *ire,* IV. vi. 11. 4
Gnawing her nayles for felnesse and for *yre,* IV. viii. 23. 8
With curses vaine in his avengefull *ire;* IV. viii. 40. 3
They from them selves gan turne their furious *ire,* IV. ix. 29. 3
Beare off the burden of her raging *yre:* V. v. 16. 4
Which breaking open with indignant *ire,* V. vii. 37. 4
Nought may abide the tempest of his *yre;* V. xi. 58. 8
backstarting with disdainefull *yre* V. xi. 61. 5
th' unrighteous *ire* . . . had given him his owne due hire? VI. ii. 13. 8
Tell me what worlds despight, or heavens *yre,* VI. v. 23. 7
with his dreadfull instrument of *yre* VI. viii. 15. 2
Fearelesse of foes, or fortunes wrackfull *yre* VI. ix. 27. 7
all the stormes of fortunes former *yre* Were turnd, VI. xii. 10. 4
great Prometheus tasting of our *ire,* VII. vi. 29. 7

Ire—*Continued.*
With hardned frosts of former winters *ire,* VII. vii. 11. 4
Upon a Lyon raging yet with *ire* VII. vii. 36. 3
Will builde an altar to appease her *yre;* *Am.* xxii. 10
the gods, in theyr revengefull *yre,* *Am.* xxviii. 11
make the matter to avenge her *yre:* *Am.* xlviii. 2
In my true love did stirre up coles of *yre;* *Am.* lxxxv. 8
Love relented their rebellious *yre.* *H.L.* 84
to provoke the *yre* Of damned fiends, *H.L.* 234
Kindled the flame of His consuming *yre,* *H.H.L.* 86
The instruments of his avenging *yre.* *H.H.B.* 182
Ireland. In Fraunce and *Ireland* left a famous gage; *Ded.Son.*xiv.11
Jett or Marble far from *Ireland* brought; II. ix. 24. 3
A seate in *Ireland* safely to remayne, II. x. 41. 8
having with huge mightinesse *Ireland* subdewd, III. iii. 33. 6
when *Ireland* florished in fame Of wealths VII. vi. 38. 1
Irena. the Lady, which *Irena* hight, V. i. 4. 1
opprest The faire *Irena* with his foule misdeede, V. i. 13. 4
whilome did attend On faire *Irene* V. xi. 37. 7
For faire *Irena,* whom they loved deare: V. xii. 10. 6
running all with greedie joyfulnesse To faire *Irena,* V. xii. 24. 6
having freed *Irena* from distresse, V. xii. 27. 8
For freeing from their snares *Irena* thrall: V. xii. 37. 5
Irena's. Artegall trayn'd in Justice lore *Irenaes* quest pursewed; V. i. Arg.
to worke *Irenaes* franchisement, V. xi. 36. 4
to trie the right Of fayre *Irenaes* cause V. xii. 8. 9
the dismall day Appointed for *Irenas* death V. xii. 11. 2
Such was *Irenas* countenance, such her case, V. xii. 13. 7
Ires. By all meanes seeking to asswage their *ires;* V. iv. 4. 7
Iris. the proud Pavone . . . or *Iris* bright, III. xi. 47. 8
Iris'. so manie sundrie colours arre In *Iris* bowe; *Mui.* 93
Irish. As when two billowes in the *Irish* sowndes, IV. i. 42. 1
Ne thence the *Irishe* Rivers absent were, IV. xi. 40. 1
Irketh. 'Now sure it *yrketh* mee, VI. x. 29. 2
Irks. despite, That *yrkes* each gentle heart *Col.* 906
Yt *yrkes* me leave thee in this wofull state, III. viii. 43. 8
what I was it *irkes* me to reherse; IV. vii. 15. 1
Irksome. so let your *yrksome* yells augment. *S.C.* Au. 178
dull wearines . . . Having yrockt asleepe his *irkesome* spright, I. i. 55. 5
Yrkesome of life, and too long lingring night. I. ii. 6. 5
One day, nigh wearie of the *yrkesome* way, I. iii. 4. 1
faint through *yrkesome* wearines, III. vi. 7. 1
He therein saw that *yrkesome* sight, III. viii. 31. 3
At last with *irkesom* trouble she abrayd; III. x. 50. 1
what filth and ordure . . . Were *yrkesome* to report; VI. xii. 24. 6
Iron. Semed, the sencelesse *yron* dyd feare, *S.C.* F. 205
yron bands abord The Pontick sea *Gn.* 46
Girt with long snakes, and thousand *yron* chaynes, *Gn.* 626
This *yron* world (that same he weeping sayes) *Hub.* 254
yron sides that sighing may endure, *T.M.* 119
'The sevenfold *yron* gates of grislie Hell, *Ti.* 372
his life from *yron* death assure, *Mui.* 59
through their *iron* sides . . . Does seeke to perce; I. ii. 17. 5
a courser . . . the sharpe *yron* did for anger eat, I. iii. 33. 5
bent his speare, and spurd his horse with *yron* heele. I. iii. 34. 9
he perced . . . With thrilling point of deadly *yron* brand, I. iii. 42. 7
Two *iron* coffers hong on either side, I. iv. 27. 3
The *yron* walles to ward their blowes are weak and fraile. I. v. 6. 9
The Sarazin . . . heaped blowes like *yron* hammers great; I. v. 7. 2
Before the dore her *yron* charet stood, I. v. 20. 6
to her *yron* wagon she betakes, I. v. 28. 1
With which her *yron* wheeles did them affray, I. v. 30. 4
The trembling ghosts . . . Chattring their *iron* teeth, I. v. 32. 6
Wyld beastes in *yron* yokes he would compell; I. vi. 26. 2
that divelish *yron* Engin, wrought In deepest Hell, I. vii. 13. 1
An *yron* brest, and back of scaly bras, I. viii. 17. 8
The *yron* rowels into frothy fome he bitt. I. vii. 37. 9
in my heart his *yron* arrow steep, I. vii. 39. 5
At last he came unto an *yron* doore, I. viii. 37. 3
Which shaking off, he rent that *yron* dore I. viii. 39. 5
this lesson deare Deepe written in my heart with *yron* pen, I. viii. 44. 8
bitter Penaunce, with an *yron* whip, I. x. 27. 1
Three ranckes of *yron* teeth enraunged were, I. xi. 13. 2
Upon his crest the hardned *yron* fell, I. xi. 24. 4
clapt his *yron* wings as victor he did dwell. I. xi. 31. 9
glauncing fire out of the *yron* plaid, I. xi. 42. 5
bound him hand and foote with *yron* chains; I. xii. 36. 2
on his shield like *yron* sledges bet: II. ii. 22. 4
Thereon an *yron* lock did fasten II. iv. 12. 9
both his feet in fetters to an *yron* racke. II. iv. 14. 9
With hundred *yron* chaines he did him bind, II. iv. 15. 1
his great *yron* teeth he still did grind II. iv. 15. 3
Captiv'd eternally in *yron* mewes II. v. 27. 8
Deepe in their flesh, quite through the *yron* walles, II. vi. 29. 8
'If ever love of Lady did empierce Your *yron* brestes, II. vi. 33. 2
His *yron* cote, all overgrowne with rust, II. vii. 4. 1
The one in hand an *yron* whip did strayne, II. vii. 21. 7
Did alwaies sore, beating his *yron* wings; II. vii. 23. 2
huge great *yron* chests, and coffers strong, II. vii. 30. 2
they came unto an *yron* dore, II. vii. 31. 2
the dying bronds repayre With *yron* tongs, II. vii. 36. 4
In his right hand an *yron* club he held, II. vii. 40. 6
him so sore smott with his *yron* mace, II. xi. 34. 8
such ghastly noyse of *yron* chaines III. iii. 9. 2
The one of *yron,* the other of bright gold, III. vi. 31. 3
She caught in hand an huge great *yron* mace, III. vii. 40. 1
He reard him up and loosd his *yron* bands, III. vii. 46. 6
It is not *yron* bandes, nor hundred eyes, III. ix. 7. 4
kept th' *yron* dore fast bard, III. xi. 31. 6

Iron—*Continued.*
Another *yron* dore, on which was writ, ... III. xi. 54. 7
that *yron* wicket open flew, ... III. xii. 3. 3
her small waste girt rownd with *yron* bands . . . . . III. xii. 30. 8
did his *yron* brond so fast applie, ... IV. iii. 25. 7
they heard the sound Of many *yron* hammers . . . . . IV. v. 33. 7
to small purpose *yron* wedges made; . . . . . IV. v. 35. 8
rap Upon his headpeece with his *yron* mall; . . . . . IV. v. 42. 4
A paire of red-whot *yron* tongs did take . . . . . IV. v. 44. 2
What *yron* courage ever could endure . . . . . IV. vi. 17. 1
his massie *yron* mace Betwixt him and his hurt . . . . . IV. viii. 43. 6
gnasht his *yron* tuskes at that displeasing sight. . . . . . IV. x. 33. 9
neither *yron* barres, nor brasen locke, ... IV. xi. 3. 3
In her great *iron* charet wonts to ride, ... IV. xi. 28. 2
tameth stubborne youth With *iron* bit, ... IV. xii. 13. 4
she left her groome An *yron* man, ... V. i. 12. 2
His name was Talus, made of *yron* mould, ... V. i. 12. 6
in his hand an *yron* flale did hould, ... V. i. 12. 8
streight he after sent His *yron* page, ... V. i. 20. 2
Him in his *iron* paw he seized had; . . . . . V. i. 22. 2
Uppon his *iron* coller griped fast, ... V. ii. 14. 4
with his *iron* flale at it let flie, ... V. ii. 21. 2
entreat that *iron* man below To cease his outrage, ... V. ii. 22. 5
layd on load with his huge *yron* flaile, ... V. ii. 24. 2
that great *yron* groome, his gard and government. . . . . . V. iv. 3. 9
Fast bound on every side with *iron* bands, ... V. iv. 5. 2
with few sowces of his *yron* flale . . . . . V. iv. 24. 6
Those *yron* fetters wherewith he was gyv'd, ... V. iv. 35. 3
that mighty *yron* man . . . Them sorely vext, ... V. iv. 44. 1
With his great *yron* sledge doth strongly on it beat. . . . . . V. v. 7. 9
As if she had an *yron* andvile beene, ... V. v. 8. 2
He with his *yron* flaile amongst them thondred, ... V. v. 19. 2
Cold *yron* chaines with which let him be tide; . . . . . V. v. 50. 8
many *yron* bands on him to lade: . . . . . V. v. 54. 7
The *yron* man . . . did inly chill and quake, ... V. vi. 9. 4
(sayd then the *yron* man) . . . . . V. vi. 16. 1
to lay about With his rude *yron* flaile, ... V. vi. 30. 2
chiefly by that *yron* page he ghest, ... V. vi. 34. 3
when they of that *yron* man had told, ... V. vii. 25. 8
He with his *yron* flale did thresh so thin, ... V. vii. 35. 7
She for that *yron* prison did enquire, ... V. vii. 37. 2
(With *yron* wheeles and hookes arm'd dreadfully, ... V. viii. 28. 5
they did draw The *yron* charet, ... V. viii. 41. 6
Amongst the *yron* hookes and graples keene . . . . . V. viii. 42. 6
Whose top was arm'd with many an *yron* hooke, ... V. ix. 11. 2
his *yron* man he sent To follow him; . . . . . V. ix. 16. 1
he with his *yron* flayle Gan drive at him . . . . . V. ix. 19. 2
With a strong *yron* chaine and coller bound, ... V. ix. 33. 6
any *yron* eyes to see it would agrize. . . . . . V. x. 28. 9
with his huge great *yron* axe gan hew . . . . . V. xi. 5. 3
that *yron* man With his huge flaile . . . . . V. xi. 47. 6
chiefly Talus with his *yron* flayle, ... V. xi. 59. 4
Nathlesse the *yron* man did still pursew . . . . . V. xi. 65. 1
All armed in a cote of *yron* plate . . . . . V. xii. 14. 3
through the *yron* walles their way they rent, ... V. xii. 17. 7
did his *yron* axe so nimbly wield, ... V. xii. 19. 7
that same *yron* man, which could reveale All hidden crimes, . V. xii. 26. 5
Would her have chastiz'd with his *yron* flaile, ... V. xii. 43. 3
That *yron* heart it hardly could sustaine: . . . . . VI. i. 30. 6
Made all of rusty *yron* ranckling sore, ... VI. vi. 9. 3
in his hand a mighty *yron* club he bore. . . . . . VI. vii. 43. 9
with his *yron* batton which he bore . . . . . VI. vii. 46. 3
with his *yron* club to ground him strooke; . . . . . VI. vii. 48. 4
In *yron* chaines of liberty bereft, ... VI. viii. 1. 4
with his *yron* club preparing way, ... VI. viii. 8. 2
All set with *yron* teeth in raunges twaine, ... VI. xii. 26. 7
he tooke a muzzel strong Of surest *yron*, ... VI. xii. 34. 3
Against his will fast bound in *yron* chaine, ... VI. xii. 35. 3
he broke his *yron* chaine, ... VI. xii. 38. 8
The hardest *yron* soone doth mollify; . . . . . *Am.* xxxii. 2
Her hart more harde then *yron* . . . . . *Am.* xxxii. 6
Iron-braced. hurling high his *yron braced* arme, ... II. v. 7. 5
Iron-coated. Disarmed all of *yron-coted* Plate; . . . . . I. vii. 2. 8
Iron-headed. His *yron-headed* spade tho making cleene, . . . *Gn.* 653
Iron-rust. preserv'd from *yron* rust Of rude oblivion . . . . . V. iv. 2. 7
Titans beames . . . in darkenesse, duld with *yron* rust, . . . VI. iii. 13. 7
Irons. *See* **Plough-irons.**
Iron-studded. Whose steale was *yron-studded,* but not long, . . V. xii. 14. 8
Irrenowned. end their daies with *irrenowmed* shame, ... II. i. 23. 4
Irrevocable. Ne can thy *irrevocable* desteny bee wefte. . . . III. iv. 36. 9
sith that he is gone *irrevocable,* . . . . . VI. ii. 15. 1
Irus. What oddes twixt *Irus* and old Inachus, ... *T.M.* 447
Is (*partial list*). *See* **It's, What's, Where's.**
Loe all *is* nought but flying vanitie. . . . . . *Bel.*[1] i. 11
Ys love such pinching payne to them . . . . . *S.C.* Ap. 18
The wastefull hylls . . . *Is* a playne overture. . . . . . *S.C.* Jul. 28
shrieking sound *Ys* signe of dreery death, ... *S.C.* Au. 174
Most wretched he, that *is* and cannot tell.' . . . . . *Col.* 659
'Where *is*,' (said Satyrane) 'that Paynims sonne, ... I. vi. 39. 5
For she it *is*, that did my Lord bethrall, ... I. viii. 28. 6
Such *is* the face of falshood: . . . . . I. viii. 49. 4
nothing *is* but that which he hath seene? . . . . . II. Pr. 3. 5
all the wealth which *is*, or was of yore, ... II. vii. 31. 7
Hard by the gates of hell her dwelling *is;* . . . . . IV. i. 20. 1
Ne any *is* that may him now restraine, ... VI. xii. 40. 3
I-same. in a bag all sorts of seeds *ysame,* . . . . . VII. vii. 32. 7
Ishmael. though beyond the Africk *Ismael* . . . he were, . . . III. iii. 6. 7
Isis. The Ouze, whom men doe *Isis* rightly name; . . . . . IV. xi. 24. 7
Britomart comes to *Isis* Church, ... V. vii. Arg.
His wife was *Isis;* . . . . . V. vii. 3. 1

Isis—*Continued.*
To shew that *Isis* doth the Moone portend; . . . . . V. vii. 4. 7
Under the wings of *Isis* all that night; . . . . . V. vii. 12. 2
as she was doing sacrifize To *Isis,* . . . . . V. vii. 13. 2
Isis'. under *Isis* feete doth sleepe for ever; . . . . . V. vii. 22. 7
Island. An *island,* which the first to west was showne. . . . . *Col.* 271
Within a wandring *Island* . . . her dwelling is. . . . . . II. i. 51. 5
come unto an *Island* waste and voyd, ... II. vi. 11. 3
Soone shee that *Island* far behind her lefte, ... II. vi. 18. 8
Ne was it *Island* then, ... II. x. 5. 5
this sweet *Island* never conquered, ... II. x. 47. 7
they in an *Island* did espy . . . . . II. xii. 27. 5
they driven were Into an *Island* spatious and brode, ... III. ix. 49. 2
it was seated in an *Island* strong, ... IV. x. 6. 1
like an *Island* fayre, ... IV. xi. 44. 3
since the salvage *Island* I did leave,' . . . . . VI. i. 9. 1
Their dwelling in a little *Island* was, ... VI. x. 41. 6
Island's. Within the compasse of that *Islands* space; . . . . . IV. x. 21. 2
To meete her at the salvage *Ilands* syde, ... V. xi. 39. 3
fairest Hill That was in all this holy *Islands* hights) . . . . VII. vi. 37. 7
Islands. far off they many *Islandes* spy . . . . . II. xii. 10. 6
those same *Islands,* seeming now and than, ... II. xii. 11. 3
are they hight The Wandring *Islands.* . . . . . II. xii. 11. 7
Islands, which doe fleet In the wide sea, ... II. xii. 14. 3
the six *Islands,* comprovinciall . . . unto great Britainee, . . III. iii. 32. 6
warlike people which the Britaine *Islands* hold: . . . . . IV. xi. 15. 9
Two *Ilands,* which ye there before you see . . . . . V. iv. 7. 5
whose father hight The Lord of Many *Ilands,* . . . . . VI. xii. 4. 2
Islands'. Of all that beare the British *Islands* name, ... VII. vi. 38. 3
Isle. Great Ladie of the greatest *Isle,* . . . . . I. Pr. 4. 3
Till they arrived in that pleasaunt *Ile,* . . . . . II. vi. 22. 3
'As th' *Isle* of Delos whylome, ... II. xii. 13. 1
Bee freshly kindled in the fruitfull *Ile* Of Mona, ... III. iii. 48. 4
She with her bringes into a secret *Ile,* . . . . . III. vii. 50. 6
sayling thence to th' *isle* of Paros came. . . . . . III. ix. 36. 9
Phidias did make in Paphos *Isle* of yore, ... IV. x. 40. 4
that same other *Isle,* that greater bredth now beares. . . . . V. iv. 7. 9
Her weary barke at last uppon mine *Isle* did rest. . . . . . V. iv. 11. 9
Arrived in this *Isle,* though bare and blunt, ... VI. xi. 9. 5
Ismael. *See* **Ishmael.**
Isope. *See* **Hyssop.**
Issa. *See* **Isse.**
Isse. He loved *Isse* for his dearest Dame, ... III. xi. 39. 1
Issue. That none might enter but with *issue* hard: . . . . . *Hub.* 1116
it must needs to *issue* come? . . . . . *Mui.* 227
had no *issue* male him to succeed, ... II. x. 27. 2
This good king shortly without *issew* dide, ... II. x. 54. 1
wanting *yssew* male, ... II. x. 61. 1
th' utmost *yssew* of his owne decay. . . . . . II. xi. 41. 5
Then shall he *issew* forth with dreadfull might . . . . . III. iii. 29. 8
'Whereat Cadwallin wroth shall forth *issew,* . . . . . III. iii. 39. 1
To finde some *issue* thence; . . . . . III. v. 3. 2
Untill that it an *issew* forth may finde: . . . . . III. ix. 15. 7
watcht that none should enter nor *issew:* . . . . . III. xi. 31. 7
More easie *issew* now then entrance late She found; . . . . . III. xii. 43. 1
none to *issue* forth when one is in; . . . . . IV. i. 20. 8
a tryall Of the bad *issue* of his counsell vaine, ... IV. ii. 6. 2
that none Might *issue* forth, ... IV. vii. 20. 6
after them the royall *issue* came, ... IV. xi. 12. 6
all the world have with their *issue* fild? . . . . . IV. xi. 17. 2
To enter in, or *issue* forth below; . . . . . IV. xii. 15. 4
Did forth *issue* all ready for the fight: . . . . . V. vii. 27. 8
Did *issue* forth gainst all that warlike rout . . . . . V. viii. 50. 2
when as the caytive carle Should *issue* forth, ... V. ix. 9. 2
Latonaes childrens wrath that all her *issue* wasted. . . . . . V. x. 7. 9
for her entrailes made an open way To *issue* forth; . . . . . V. xi. 31. 4
Talus into the sea did forth *issew* . . . . . V. xii. 5. 4
how to *issue* forth in waies untryde, ... VI. i. 6. 4
Did *issue* forth to meete his foe afore; . . . . . VI. i. 32. 7
To weet what *issue* would thereof betyde: . . . . . VI. iii. 47. 2
a Capias Should *issue* forth . . . . . VI. vii. 35. 5
That fruitfull *issue* may to you afford, ... *Proth.* 104
Issued. *issewd* forth on shore; . . . . . II. vi. 24. 2
Shee forth *issewed* with a goodly traine . . . . . II. ix. 17. 7
She forth *issewed,* and on her journey went: . . . . . III. vii. 19. 2
remounting to his steed He forth *issew'd:* . . . . . III. ix. 15. 2
forth *yssewd,* . . . a grave personage . . . . . III. xi. 3. 5
a joyous fellowship *issewed* Of Minstrales . . . . . III. xii. 5. 3
the brave Maid . . . *Issewed* forth, ... III. xii. 27. 6
lightly *issewd* forth to take his lot. . . . . . IV. iv. 33. 7
forth *issewed* To have rencountred him . . . . . IV. vi. 3. 1
forth the sad Aemylia *issewed,* . . . . . IV. vii. 34. 1
Streight forth *issewed* a Knight all arm'd to proofe, ... IV. x. 9. 6
first of all *issu'd* Sir Marinell, ... V. iii. 4. 6
forth *issewed,* And unto all himselfe there open shewed, . . . V. iii. 20. 4
She forth *yssew'd* out of her loathed bowre, ... V. vi. 35. 3
he forth *issued* Unto that Lady, ... V. x. 38. 6
forth *issewd* from under th' Altars smooke A dreadfull feend V. xi. 22. 4
The Salvage forth out of the wood *issew'd* . . . . . VI. vii. 23. 8
Then forth *issewed* (great goddesse) great dame Nature . . . VII. vii. 5. 1
forth *issew'd* the Seasons of the *yeare.* . . . . . VII. vii. 28. 1
heavens gate (whence all the gods *issued*) . . . . . VII. vii. 45. 7
Issues. Whenceforth *issues* a warlike steed in sight, ... *Mui.* 316
No bloodie *issues* nor no leprosies, ... *Col.* 313
Issuing. that gay payre, *issewing* on the shore, ... II. vi. 11. 6
With his gay Squyre *issewing* did espye, ... II. xi. 17. 8
Thence streames of purple bloud *issuing* rife . . . . . IV. iii. 12. 8
Then Talus forth *issuing* from the tent . . . . . V. iv. 50. 5
All arm'd to point, *issuing* forth apace, ... V. x. 34. 2
forth *issuing* with his scouts afore, ... V. xii. 6. 8

Issuing—*Continued.*
From those high Towers this noble Lord *issuing,* . . . . *Proth.* 163
Ister. Faire *Ister,* flowing from the mountaines hie: . . . . IV. xi. 20. 5
It (*partial list*). *See* **Be it, Itself.**
I saw the fish (if fish I may *it* cleepe) . . . . *Van.* v. 2
alas! *yt* is already donne. . . . . *S.C.* Ja. 30
Ill might *it* prosper that ill gotten was; . . . . *Hub.* 1149
it seemes that some celestiall rage . . . . *Col.* 823
that charme from thee forwarned *itt:* . . . . I. ii. 18. 4
every breath of heaven shaked *itt:* . . . . I. iv. 5. 7
'*Yt* was my chaunce . . . There for to find . . . . I. vii. 47. 1
It lov'd it selfe, because it selfe was faire; . . . . *H.H.L.* 29
Italian. Along the bankes of the *Italian* streame. . . . . *Bel.*[1] v. 4
Italy. Borne of fayre Inogene of *Italy;* . . . . II. x. 13. 5
Itched. although it *itched* naught: . . . . V. xii. 30. 4
Itis. Calling on *Itis, Itis!* evermore, ... *Gn.* 402
It's (*partial list*).
It's like a corse . . . . *Ro.* v. 7
Yts time to hast us homeward. . . . . *S.C.* Mar. 117
With mery thing *its* good to medle sadde. . . . . *S.C.* Au. 144
yts time to be gone. . . . . *S.C.* Au. 198
Its hard to read: . . . . *Gn.* 303
Its an hard case, ... *Hub.* 369
For not so great, . . . *It's* now a dayes, ... *Hub.* 448
Such helplesse harmes *yts* better hidden keep, ... I. vii. 39. 7
Where ease abownds *yt's* eath to doe amis: . . . . II. iii. 40. 5
Its now so farre from that which then it was, ... VI. Pr. 5. 2
Itself (*partial list*).
Her power *it selfe* against *it selfe* did arme; . . . . *Ro.* xxi. 10
To tempt the cause *it selfe* for to bewray, ... I. vii. 38. 8
Ecchoes three aunswer'd *it selfe* againe: . . . . I. viii. 4. 4
Shamefastnes *it selfe* is shee.' . . . . II. ix. 43. 9
When good was onely for *it selfe* desyred, ... V. Pr. 3. 6
thy hand too bold *it selfe* embrewed In blood . . . . VI. ii. 7. 3
even *itselfe* is mov'd, as wizards saine: . . . . VII. vii. 55. 7
It lov'd *it selfe,* because *it selfe* was faire; . . . . *H.H.L.* 29
of *it selfe* begot, Like to *it selfe* his eldest sonne . . . . *H.H.L.* 30, 31
Iulus. His sonne *Iulus* did from thence depart . . . . III. ix. 43. 5
Ivory. raisde up on pillers of *Ivorie,* . . . . *Bel.*[1] iv. 1
seates and benches shone as *yvorie* (*ivorie*[1]), ... *Bel.* xii. 9
raysde upon *yvorie* pillours [*text,* pillowes] tall, ... *Bel.*[2] iv. 1
Made all of Heben and white *Yvorie* (*Ivorie*[1]); . . . . *Pet.* ii. 2
Theyr *yvory* Luyts and Tamburins forgoe, ... *S.C.* Jun. 59
Playing on *yvorie* harp with silver strong. . . . . *Gn.* 16
Made of golde and costlie *yvorie,* . . . . *Ti.* 605
The one faire fram'd of burnisht *Yvory,* . . . . I. i. 40. 2
backe returning by the *Yvorie* dore, ... I. i. 44. 6
yvory sheath, ycarv'd with curious slights, ... I. vii. 30. 7
she sitting in an *yvory* chayre. . . . . I. x. 31. 9

Ivory—*Continued.*
princely gifts of *yvory* and gold, ... I. xii. 12. 6
Her *yvorie* forhead, full of bountie brave, ... II. iii. 24. 1
her became, as polisht *yvory* . . . . II. ix. 41. 5
Yt framed was of precious *yvory,* . . . . II. xii. 44. 1
seemd the waves were into *yvory* . . . sent; . . . . II. xii. 45. 3
yvory into the waves were sent; . . . . II. xii. 45. 4
th' *yvorie* in golden mantle gownd: . . . . II. xii. 67. 5
her pure *yvory* Into a cleare Carnation suddeine dyde; . . . . III. iii. 20. 2
Gold, amber, *yvorie,* perles, owches, rings, ... III. iv. 23. 5
Dropped adowne upon her *yvory* brest: . . . . III. viii. 35. 4
naked, as nett *yvory* . . . . III. xii. 20. 1
all the others pavement were with *yvory* spilt. . . . . IV. x. 5. 9
Whose *yvorie* shoulders weren covered all, ... IV. xi. 11. 7
an Altar framed Of costly *Ivory* . . . . V. x. 28. 3
when her face Like the faire *yvory* shining they did see, ... VI. viii. 37. 3
Her *yvorie* neck; her alablaster brest; . . . . VI. viii. 42. 1
the crowne, which Ariadne wore Upon her *yvory* forehead, ... VI. x. 13. 2
Chaunst to espy upon her *yvory* chest The rosie marke, ... VI. xii. 15. 5
Her sitting on an *Ivory* throne shee found, ... VII. vi. 9. 1
let her selfe into that *Ivory* throne; . . . . VII. vi. 11. 2
If *Yvorie,* her forehead *Yvory* weene; . . . . *Am.* xv. 10
A goodly table of pure *yvory,* . . . . *Am.* lxxvii. 2
lie like Gods in *yvorie* beds arayd, ... *H.L.* 285
Ivory-white. Her forehead *yvory white,* . . . . *Epith.* 172
Ivy. Emongst the rest the clambring *Yvie* grew, ... *Gn.* 217
pallid *Yvie,* building his owne bowre; . . . . *Gn.* 675
Framed of wanton *Yvie,* flouring fayre, ... II. v. 29. 3
A trayle of *yvie* in his native hew; . . . . II. xii. 61. 2
surely deeme it to bee *yvie* trew: . . . . II. xii. 61. 5
His wast was with a wreath of *yvie* greene Engirt about, ... IV. vii. 7. 1
being all with *Yvy* overspred . . . . VI. v. 35. 2
Ivy-garland. freshest Flora her with *Yvie girlond* crownd. . . . . I. i. 48. 9
he . . . on his head an *yvie girland* had, ... I. iv. 22. 3
Ivy-tod. At length within an *Yvie todde,* . . . . *S.C.* Mar. 67
Ivy-twine. Entrailed with a wanton *Yvie twine.* . . . . *S.C.* Au. 30
girt in girlonds of wild *Yvie twine,* . . . . *S.C.* O. 111
with an *yvie twyne* his waste is girt about. . . . . I. vi. 14. 9
Enchaced with a wanton *yvie twine;* . . . . II. ix. 24. 5
With wanton *yvie twine* entrayld athwart, ... III. vi. 44. 5
Ivy-winding. Enwoven with an *Yvie-winding* trayle: . . . . *Mui.* 299
Iwis. *See* **Wist.**
Well *ywis* was it with shepheards thoe: . . . . *S.C.* May 109
A right good knight, and trew of word *ywis:* . . . . II. i. 19. 5
Not this the worke of womans hand *ywis,* . . . . III. iv. 37. 3
'That shall I you recount' (quoth he) '*ywis,* . . . . III. vii. 53. 4
Ixion. There was *Ixion* turned on a wheele . . . . I. v. 35. 1
Ixione. The faire *Ixione* captiv'd from Troy; . . . . *Gn.* 490
Ixion's. Typhons fall, or proud *Ixions* paine, ... VII. vi. 29. 6

J

Jacket. In a blew *jacket* with a crosse of redd . . . . *Hub.* 205
All in a woodmans *jacket* he was clad . . . . VI. ii. 5. 6
in a *Jacket,* quilted richly rare . . . . VI. vii. 43. 3
Jacob's staff. *Jaakob staffe* in hand devoutlie crost, ... *D.* 41
in his hand a *Jacobs staffe,* . . . . I. vi. 35. 7
Jade. Snatcht first the one, and then the other *Jade,* . . . . II. xi. 31. 2
His tyreling *Jade* he fiersly forth did push . . . . III. i. 17. 4
Upon a mangy *jade* unmeetely set, ... VI. vi. 16. 8
the former villaine, which did lead Her tyreling *jade,* . . . . VI. vii. 40. 7
Jagged. underneath, his breech was all to-torne and *jagged.* . V. ix. 10. 9
Jail. to heaven went Out of this fleshlie *gaole,* (**goale*) . . . . *Ti.* 296
Jambeux. a large purple streame adowne their *giambeux* falles. II. vi. 29. 9
Jane. Because I could not give her many a *Jane.*' . . . . III. vii. 58. 4
January. Then came old *January,* . . . . VII. vii. 42. 1
Janus. Therein resembling *Janus* auncient . . . . IV. x. 12. 5
Janus'. New yeare, forth looking out of *Janus* gate, ... *Am.* iv. 1
Jar. we will appease our *jarre;* . . . . *Hub.* 1048
from small *jarre* . . . broke into open warre. . . . . *Mui.* 7
his peace is but continual *jarre:* . . . . II. ii. 26. 8
fowle revenging rage, and base contentious *jarre.* . . . . II. ii. 30. 9
Acrates, sonne of Phlegeton and *Jarre;* . . . . II. iv. 41. 7
Outrageous anger, and woe-working *jarre,* . . . . II. v. 16. 3
Troubled with terrour and unquiet *jarre,* . . . . II. vi. 37. 8
making vantage of their civile *jarre,* . . . . II. x. 65. 4
Till universall peace compound all civill *jarre.* . . . . III. iii. 23. 9
breedes Tumultuous trouble, and contentious *jarre,* . . . . IV. i. 25. 8
Ne private *jarre,* ne spite of enemis, ... IV. ix. 16. 3
Ne ever shewed signe of rancour or of *jarre.* . . . . VI. ix. 39. 9
Thrugh stubborn pride, amongst themselves did *jar,* . . . . *Am.* xliv. 2
well agree withouten breach or *jar.* . . . . *Epith.* 132
unlike parts amongst themselves do *jarre.* . . . . *H.B.* 196
Jarring. frogs . . . their *jarring* voyces bent, ... *Gn.* 230
Jason. the famous history Of *Jason* and Medaea . . . . II. xii. 44. 4
Jasp. The floore of *Jasp* and Emeraude was dight. . . . . *Bel.*[2] ii. 11
Jasper. All pav'd beneath with *Jaspar* shining bright, ... II. xii. 62. 8
Jaspis. The floor was *Jaspis,* and of Emeraude. . . . . *Bel.*[1] ii. 11
Javel. To heare the *Javell* so good men to nip; . . . . *Hub.* 712
Javelin. her *Javelin* bright Against him bent, ... II. iii. 42. 7
ever when the Squire his *javelin* shooke, ... IV. vii. 26. 2
in his hand a *javelin* he did beare, ... VII. vii. 28. 6
Javels. these two *javels* Should render up a reckning . . . . *Hub.* 309
Jaw. all the poison ran about his *chaw;* . . . . I. iv. 30. 4
in either *jaw* Three ranckes of yron teeth . . . . I. xi. 13. 1
from Cerberus greedy *jaw* To plucke a bone, ... I. xi. 41. 4
Taking advantage of his open *jaw,* . . . . I. xi. 53. 6
Jaws. *jawes,* that with blacke venime swell. . . . . *Van.* iii. 12
bad him battaile even to his *jawes:* . . . . *Van.* x. 8

Jaws—*Continued.*
Thereby is a Lambe in the Wolves *jawes:* . . . . *S.C.* Au. 31
hath his *jawes* with angrie spirits rent, ... *Gn.* 278
With gaping *jawes* full greedy at him came, ... I. iii. 41. 4
for feare into his *jawes* to fall, ... I. vii. 44. 6
His raw-bone cheekes . . . Were shronke into his *jawes,* . . . . I. ix. 35. 9
his deepe devouring *jawes* Wyde gaped, ... I. xi. 12. 7
whiles they fly that Gulfes devouring *jawes,* . . . . II. xii. 4. 8
With greedy *jawes* her ready for to teare: . . . . III. viii. 33. 7
round about her *jawes* one might descry . . . . V. xii. 30. 8
Betwixt his bloodie *jawes,* besprinckled all with gore. . . . . VI. iv. 17. 9
fomed all about his bloody *jawes:* . . . . VI. xii. 29. 6
Jays. Decked with diverse plumes, like painted *Jayes,* . . . . II. viii. 5. 8
Jealous. Whereof the Goddesse gathering *jealous* feare, ... *Mui.* 129
from far observ'd, with *jealous* eie, ... *Col.* 134
he burnt with *gealous* fire; . . . . I. ii. 5. 6
Still flying from his thoughts and *gealous* feare: . . . . I. ii. 12. 3
with her *gealous* termes his open eares abusd: . . . . I. v. 37. 9
without *gealous* feares Or faultie thoughts, ... II. iv. 18. 7
Then wounde of *gealous* worme, ... II. iv. 29. 8
to be free from hard restraynt and *gealous* feares. . . . . III. ix. 4. 9
Empoisned was with privy lust and *gealous* dredd. . . . . III. ix. 28. 9
Deceivd of *gealous* Juno, ... III. xi. 33. 2
That stryfull hag with *gealous* discontent Had fild, ... IV. v. 30. 8
like thornes did pricke his *gealous* hart, ... IV. v. 31. 3
ghesse the man to be dismayd with *gealous* dread. . . . . IV. v. 45. 9
gnaw his *gealous* hart, ... IV. vi. 7. 5
all his *gealous* feare he false had found, ... IV. vi. 28. 2
Through *jealous* passion weeping inly wroth, ... IV. ix. 9. 8
Scarse so conceived in her *jealous* thought, ... V. vi. 3. 2
secretly afflict with *jealous* feare, ... V. vi. 4. 6
Did closely harbour such a *jealous* guest) . . . . V. vii. 27. 5
Jealous suspect as true untruely drad: . . . . V. vii. 38. 7
Sate with a knight . . . free from all *gealous* spyes. . . . . VI. ii. 16. 6
Whose *gealous* dread induring not a peare . . . . VI. ii. 29. 5
many *gealous* thoughts conceiv'd in vaine, ... VI. ix. 38. 4
Jealousy. whally eies (the signe of *gelosy,*) . . . . I. iv. 24. 3
Ne wicked envy, ne vile *gealosy,* . . . . I. xii. 41. 3
'The gnawing anguish, and sharp *gelosy,* . . . . II. iv. 23. 1
Wrath, *gelosy,* griefe, love, this Squyre have laide thus low. II. iv. 34. 9
'Wrath, *gealosie,* griefe, love, do thus expell: . . . . II. iv. 35. 1
Wrath is a fire; and *gealosie* a weede; . . . . II. iv. 35. 2
So shall wrath, *gealosy,* griefe, love, die and decay.' . . . . II. iv. 35. 9
gnawing *Gealosy,* . . . his bitter lips did bight; . . . . II. vii. 22. 4
Full of great envy and fell *gealosy* . . . . III. i. 18. 2
Without fell rancor or fond *gealosy.* . . . . III. vi. 41. 6
Malbecco will no straunge knights host, For peevish *gealosy.* . III. ix. Arg.

Jealousy—*Continued.*
Into huge waves of griefe and *gealosye* . . . III. x. 17. 4
the father of fowle *gealosy,* . . . III. x. 22. 5
all his hart with *gealousy* did swell; . . . III. x. 48. 6
Griefe, and despight, and *gealosy,* and scorne, . . . III. x. 55. 5
he . . . Forgot he was a man, and *Gelosy* is hight. . . . III. x. 60. 9
Fowle *Gealosy!* that turnest love divine To joylesse dread, . . . III. xi. 1. 5
being free from feare and *gealosye* . . . IV. x. 28. 5
for *gealousie* Was readie oft his owne heart to devoure, . . . VI. ix. 39. 3
the Shepheard streight with *jealousie* did frize. . . . VI. x. 33. 9
That cancker-worme, that monster, *Gelosie,* . . . *H.L.* 267
Jeer. when he saw her toy, and gibe, and *geare,* . . . II. vi. 21. 7
Jelly-blood. They softly wipt away the *gelly blood* . . . III. iv. 40. 6
Jeopardy. when thou art past *jeopardee,* . . . *To his Booke* 16
In this adventures chauncefull *jeopardie:* . . . *Hub.* 98
sith I For it did put my life in *jeopardie:* . . . *Hub.* 1028
Feareles of foes and hidden *jeopardie,* . . . *Mui.* 251
Floting amid the sea in *jeopardie,* . . . *Col.* 273
To tell from whence he came through *jeopardy,* . . . II. ii. 39. 5
Or bide the chaunce at thine owne *jeopardee.'* . . . II. iv. 39. 5
Hard is his hap that first fals in his *jeopardee.'* . . . II. iv. 43. 9
shortly he forgot the *jeopardy,* . . . II. x. 17. 3
a whirlepoole of hidden *jeopardy;* . . . II. xii. 18. 2
In such distresse and doubtfull *jeopardy* . . . III. i. 22. 6
thy great grace and my great *jeopardee,* . . . III. iv. 10. 8
carried her beyond all *jeopardy;* . . . III. vii. 3. 4
seeing nigh him *jeopardy* extreme, . . . III. viii. 16. 8
they had past with mickle *jeopardy,* . . . III. ix. 53. 3
buried in the ground from *jeopardy,* . . . III. x. 42. 4
till safe him selfe he see from *jeopardy.* . . . III. x. 53. 9
through paines and perlous *jeopardie,* . . . IV. x. 28. 7
in times of *jeopardy,* To keepe a nightly watch . . . V. iv. 46. 8
all the Temple put in *jeopardy* Of flaming, . . . V. vii. 14. 8
his life . . . was certes in great *jeopardy,* . . . VI. iii. 51. 5
Ne skilfull of the uncouth *jeopardy;* . . . VI. v. 16. 4
to save his friend from *jeopardy.* . . . VI. viii. 12. 9
Jerusalem. *'Hierusalem* that is,. The new *Hierusalem,* . . . I. x. 57. 1, 2
pilgrimage To yonder same *Hierusalem* doe bend, . . . I. x. 61. 4
Jessamines. Her nipples, lyke yong blossomed *Jessemynes:* . . . *Am.* lxiv. 12
Jesses. freed From bels and *jesses* which did let her flight, . . . VI. iv. 19. 8
Jest. th' whole history Is but a *jest,* . . . *Gn.* 6
did her earnest end in *jest.* . . . II. vi. 23. 9
Cambell thus did shut up all in *jest:* . . . IV. iv. 12. 1
He lowdly gan to laugh, and thus to *jest;* . . . IV. v. 18. 2
All gan to *jest* and jibe full merilie . . . V. iii. 39. 4
of her shame to make a gamesome *jest;* . . . VII. vi. 51. 3
Jesting. Was tickled with delight, and *jesting* sayd; . . . IV. i. 33. 6
Jesus. *'Jesus* blesse that sweete face I espye, . . . *S.C.* May 256
That same hath *Jesus* Christ now to him raught, . . . *Hub.* 441
Jet. fowle smoke and clouds more black then *Jett.* . . . II. vii. 28. 9
Jett or Marble far from Ireland brought; . . . II. ix. 24. 3
Jewel. nought he deemed deare for the *jewell:* . . . *S.C.* May 277
they fastned were . . . In a rich *jewell,* . . . II. iii. 27. 7
Amongst the rest a *jewell* rich he found, . . . IV. viii. 6. 6
his *juell* he had lost so light, . . . IV. viii. 8. 5
about her purple brest That precious *juell,* . . . IV. viii. 10. 3
Then know that mercy is the Mighties *jewell:* . . . *Am.* xlix. 3
Jewels. Adornd with gold and *jewels* shining cleare, . . . I. v. 21. 2
Her selfe adorn'd with gems and *jewels* manifold. . . . V. vii. 13. 9
richly clad In roiall robes, and many *jewels* dight; . . . V. xi. 60. 7
first they spoile her of her *jewels* deare, . . . VI. viii. 41. 2
all with gemmes and *jewels* gorgeously Adornd, . . . *H.H.B.* 187
Jewish. With railing tearmes defied the *Jewish* hoast, . . . *Ti.* 538
So whylome learnd that mighty *Jewish* swaine, . . . V. viii. 2. 1
Jewry. that which that wise King of *Jurie* framed . . . IV. x. 30. 6
Jews. with the budding rod Did rule the *Jewes,* . . . *Hub.* 440
to *Jewes* despiteous Delivered up the Lord . . . II. vii. 62. 5
Joan. Sometimes she laught, as merry as Pope *Jone;* . . . II. vi. 3. 4
Jocante. next to him *Jocante* did ensew; . . . III. i. 45. 4
John. new Earth, new Heaven, sayde Saint *John.* . . . *Rev.* iv. 1
For our Sir *John,* to say to morrowe . . . *S.C.* May 309
Join. arte and nature strived to *joyne* . . . all pleasures . . . *Bel.*[1] x. 5
three valiaunt knights to see Three combates *joine* in one, . . . II. ii. 26. 2
mortal vengeaunce *joyne* to crime abhord? . . . II. ii. 30. 4
in friendship for her sake To *joyne* your force, . . . IV. ii. 24. 7
Like faithfull friends thenceforth to *joyne* in one . . . IV. ii. 28. 6
she them forced hand to *joyne* in hand, . . . IV. x. 33. 2
joyne in neighbourhood of kingdome nere, . . . IV. xi. 40. 3
accord To *joyne* in one, . . . IV. xi. 43. 8
To *joyne* the combate with cruell intent, . . . V. iv. 6. 6
ere she could *joyne* hand with him to fight, . . . V. iv. 43. 5
joyne in equall portion of thy realme; . . . V. vii. 23. 6
I should no creature *joyne* unto mine ayde: . . . VI. ii. 37. 8
To *joyne* with him and vengeance to devize, . . . VI. vii. 22. 8
Least they should *joyne* against the weaker side, . . . VI. xi. 18. 2
joyne together in sweete sympathie, . . . *H.B.* 199
Joined. The lowest earth join'd to the heaven hie; . . . *Ro.* viii. 8
At last againe with him in travell *joynd,* . . . *Hub.* 941
Both male and female through commixture *joynd:* . . . *Col.* 802
Aesculape . . . *joyned* every part. . . . I. v. 39. 9
knights . . . as pledges firme, right hands together *joynd.* . . . I. ix. 18. 9
cruell combat *joynd* in middle space: . . . II. ii. 20. 3
In love of Canacee they *joyned* all: . . . IV. ii. 54. 5
The prize of beautie still hath *joyned* beene; . . . IV. v. 1. 3
They both together *joyned* might and maine, . . . V. iii. 12. 3
should have *joyned* bene to her in wedlocks knot. . . . V. iv. 8. 9
with her *joyn'd* Regard of womanhead; . . . V. ix. 45. 4
cruell fate Hath *joyn'd* one evill, . . . VI. iv. 30. 6
Though all their beauties *joynd* together were; . . . *H.H.B.* 103
Joining. beast and Kings also *Joinyng* their force . . . *Rev.* iii. 12

Joining—*Continued.*
Ay *joyning* foot to foot, and syde to syde; . . . III. i. 66. 8
joyning close huge lode at him did lay; . . . VI. vi. 28. 8
joyning joy with her in one accord, . . . VI. xii. 22. 3
Joint. full large of limbe and every *joint* He was, . . . I. ii. 12. 8
Ne word to speake, ne *joynt* to move, she had; . . . I. vi. 11. 2
so faint in every *joynt* and vayne, . . . I. vii. 11. 7
trembling horrour ran through every *joynt,* . . . I. viii. 39. 3
trembling every *joynt,* did inly quake, . . . I. ix. 24. 8
Upon the *joint* the lucky steele did light, . . . I. xi. 43. 6
panting softe, and trembling every *joynt,* . . . III. i. 60. 1
every trembling *joynt* and every vaine . . . III. ii. 34. 3
Both *joynt* partakers of their fatall payne: . . . III. iii. 37. 7
trembling every *joynt* through former feare . . . IV. vii. 34. 2
every *joynt* for dread of death did quake, . . . VI. vi. 29. 7
His dearest *joynt* he sure had broken quight. . . . VI. ix. 44. 5
Jointed. Mought her necke bene *joynted* attones, . . . *S.C.* Mar. 53
beeing nimbler *joynted* than the rest, . . . *Mui.* 121
with his sword it strooke, that without faile He *jointed* it, . . . V. xi. 29. 9
Joints. The stonie *joynts* of these old walls now rent, . . . *Ro.* xxv. 7
hath the Crampe thy *joynts* benomd . . . *S.C.* Au. 4
How can Bagpipe or *joynts* be well apayd? . . . *S.C.* Au. 6
unto rest his wearie *joynts* prepare. . . . *Gn.* 320
through kindly aptnes of his *joynts.* . . . *Hub.* 695
Typhoeus *joynts* were stretched on a gin; . . . I. v. 35. 7
Five *joints* thereof he hewd, . . . I. xi. 39. 9
in her streaming blood he did . . . tender *joints* embrew: . . . II. i. 40. 8
Her feeble *joynts* layd eke adowne to rest; . . . IV. v. 39. 7
With trembling *joynts,* as he for terrour shooke; . . . V. xi. 28. 8
now high time these strong *joynts* to imploy. . . . VI. ii. 32. 9
Jolliment. To feede her foolish humour and vaine *jolliment.* . . . II. vi. 3. 9
For goodly triumph and great *jollyment,* . . . IV. xi. 12. 4
in joyous *jolliment* Of their franke loves, . . . VI. ii. 16. 5
Jollities. Mart, In loves and gentle *jollities* arraid, . . . I. Pr. 3. 8
Jollity. send thee joy of thy *jollitee.* . . . *S.C.* May 192
A thousand Nymphes, with mirthfull *jollitee,* . . . *Ti.* 137
That night they pas in joy and *jollity,* . . . I. iv. 43. 5
heares . . . Did shake, and seemd to daunce for *jollity,* . . . I. vii. 32. 4
prickt forth with *jollitee* Of looser life . . . I. ix. 12. 5
one sung a song of love and *jollity,* . . . I. xii. 38. 9
Now gan his hart all swell in *jollity,* . . . II. iii. 5. 1
did of joy and *jollity* devize, . . . II. vi. 21. 3
some seemd with lively *jollitee* To fly about, . . . II. xii. 60. 7
Ay caroling of love and *jollity,* . . . III. i. 40. 5
That much Malbecco joyed in his *jollity.* . . . III. x. 33. 9
Triumphing in great joy and *jolity,* . . . IV. iv. 28. 2
With joyance bring her and with *jollity.* . . . *Epith.* 245
Jolly. With singing, and shouting, and *jolly* chere: . . . *S.C.* May 21
What, ho! thou *jollye* shepheards swayne, . . . *S.C.* Jul. 5
wont to make the *jolly* shepeheards gladde, . . . *S.C.* Au. 9
ye *jolly* shepheards twayne: . . . *S.C.* Au. 51
The *jolly* shepheard that was of yore . . . *S.C.* S. 26
Is nowe nor *jollye,* nor shepeheard more. . . . *S.C.* S. 27
could make a *jolly* hole in theyr furre: . . . *S.C.* S. 165
Then up, I say, thou *jolly* shepeheard swayne, . . . *S.C.* N. 47
All *jolly* Prelates, worthie rule to beare, . . . *Hub.* 423
all joy and *jolly* meriment Is also deaded, . . . *T.M.* 209
Alcyon he, the *jollie* Shepheard swaine . . . *D.* 54
(a *jolly* groome was he, . . . *Col.* 12
Harke then, ye *jolly* shepheards, to my song.' . . . *Col.* 51
Full *jolly* knight he seemd, . . . I. i. 1. 8
Full *jolly* knight he seemde, and wel addrest; . . . I. ii. 11. 7
Hippolytus a *jolly* huntsman was, . . . I. v. 37. 1
strike your sailes, yee *jolly* Mariners, . . . I. xii. 42. 1
A *jolly* yeoman, Marshall of the same, . . . II. ix. 28. 2
Courted of many a *jolly* Paramoure, . . . II. ix. 34. 3
A *jolly* person, and of comely vew; . . . III. i. 45. 2
hee too simple ever to surprise The *jolly* Paridell, . . . III. x. 20. 4
The *jolly* Satyres, full of fresh delight, . . . III. x. 44. 3
chose emongst the *jolly* Satyres still to wonne. . . . III. x. 51. 9
After whom marcht a *jolly* company, . . . III. xii. 5. 8
Amongst the rest there was a *jolly* knight, . . . IV. i. 10. 1
Her mate, he was a *jollie* youthfull knight . . . IV. i. 32. 1
left him now as sad, as whilome *jollie,* . . . IV. i. 36. 8
he their sonne full fresh and *jolly* was, . . . IV. xi. 27. 1
to come whereas a *jolly* Knight . . . did safely rest, . . . VI. iii. 20. 2
Now turne againe my teme, thou *jolly* swayne, . . . VI. ix. 1. 1
She was, to weete, that *jolly* Shepheards lasse, . . . VI. x. 16. 1
That *jolly* shepheard, which there piped, . . . VI. x. 16. 3
Pype, *jolly* shepheard, pype thou now apace . . . VI. x. 16. 6
'Haile, *jolly* shepheard, . . . VI. x. 19. 2
Then came the *jolly* Sommer, . . . VII. vii. 29. 1
after her came *jolly* June, . . . VII. vii. 35. 1
Jollyhead. Despoyled of those joyes and *jolly-head,* . . . VI. xi. 32. 8
Jonathan. Trew *Jonathan* and David trustie tryde . . . IV. x. 27. 2
Jone. *See* **Joan.**
Jones. thanks . . . to *Jones,* that truely it translated. . . . *Com. Son.* ii. 14
Jordan. Both Silo this, and *Jordan,* did excell, . . . I. xi. 30. 6
Joseph. Hither came *Joseph* of Arimathy, . . . II. x. 53. 7
Jot. soone in him was lefte no one corrupted *jott.* . . . I. x. 26. 9
wonder is how I should live a *jot,* . . . *Am.* lvii. 6
in whom no *jot* Of loves dislike or pride was to be found, . . . *H.H.L.* 33
Jouisance. To see those folkes make such *jovysaunce,* . . . *S.C.* May 25
songs of some *jouisaunce?* . . . *S.C.* N. 2
Journal. from their *journall* labours they did rest; . . . I. xi. 31. 4
All woxen weary of their *journall* toyle: . . . III. xii. 47. *or.*4
Journey. On their intended *journey* to proceede; . . . *Hub.* 105
Unto his *journey* did himselfe addresse, . . . *Mui.* 146
on their former *journey* forward pas, . . . I. iii. 21. 3
he . . . told her all that fell, in *journey* as she went. . . . I. iii. 32. 9

Journey—*Continued.*
Already harnessed for *journey* new, ... I. v. 20. 7
on her wearie *journey* she did ride; . . . . I. xii. 22. 5
So parted we, and on our *journey* drive; . . . . II. i. 55. 7
him addrest Unto the *journey* . . . . II. iii. 1. 7
to his purposd *journey* him prepar'd: . . . . II. xi. 3. 6
draw from on this *journey* to proceed.' . . . . II. xii. 26. 5
As lay her *journey*, through that perlous Pace, ... III. i. 19. 7
forth upon their *journey* went. . . . . III. i. 67. 9
T' abridg their *journey* long, and lingring day; . . . . . III. ii. 4. 3
he forth on his *journey* did proceede, ... III. iv. 4. 6
She forth issewed, and on her *journey* went: . . . . III. vii. 19. 2
forth on their *journey* for to wend: . . . . III. x. 1. 6
One may his *journey* bring too soone to evill end.' . . . . III. x. 40. 9
did themselves unto their *journey* dight. . . . . IV. viii. 34. 5
leaving him forth on his *journey* far'd: . . . . V. i. 30. 7
unto his former *journey* he retourned: . . . . V. ii. 28. 9
Himselfe unto his *journey* gan prepare, ... V. x. 16. 2
to his former *journey* him addrest; . . . . V. xi. 35. 8
That she her selfe had to the *journey* dight, ... VI. iii. 16. 3
forth on his *journey* goth. . . . . VI. iii. 45. 9
gan them selves to dight Unto their *journey;* . . . . VI. v. 40. 6
Journey's. now at her *journeyes* end; . . . . I. xii. 1. 7
Yet nought the nearer to his *journeys* end, ... VI. iv. 25. 6
Joust, -ed, -s. *See* **Giust,** *etc.*
Jove. thunder-dartes for *Jove* his syre . . . . *Bel.* iv. 11
Jove fearing . . . The Giants old should once again uprise, . *Ro.* iv. 5
all were it *Jove* his sire, ... *Ro.* xi. 13
Whiles *Jove* at them his thunderbolts let flie, ... *Ro.* xii. 4
said *Jove,* 'Lo! how the least the greatest may reprove.' . . *Van.* iv. 13
Jove himselfe, the patron of the place, ... *Van.* xi. 10
they bene daughters of the hyghest *Jove,* . . . . *S.C.* Jun. 66
high *Jove,* in whose almightie hand . . . . *Hub.* 1225
whom thou, great *Jove,* by doome unjust . . . . *T.M.* 69
Jove, the father of eternitie, ... *Ti.* 369
Arachne figur'd how *Jove* did abuse Europa . . . . *Mui.* 277
Jove in midst with awfull Majestie, ... *Mui.* 308
but *Jove* above them all, ... *Mui.* 311
Jove himselfe his powre began to dread, ... *Col.* 809
thou, most dreaded impe of highest *Jove,* . . . . I. Pr. 3. 1
angry *Jove* an hideous storme of raine Did poure . . . . . . I. i. 6. 6
thundring *Jove,* . . . she claymed for her syre, ... I. iv. 11. 5
if that any else did *Jove* excell; . . . . I. iv. 11. 7
More old then *Jove,* whom thou at first didst breede, ... I. v. 22. 3
ghosts . . . Cursing high *Jove,* . . . . I. v. 33. 6
Such wondrous science . . . When *Jove* avizd, ... I. v. 40. 2
thundering *Jove,* that rules both night and day?' . . . . . I. v. 42. 9
'O lightsome day! the lampe of highest *Jove,* . . . . I. vii. 23. 1
almightie *Jove,* . . . Hurles forth his thundring dart . . . I. viii. 9. 1
dedicated is t' Olympick *Jove,* . . . . II. v. 31. 3
Ne swelling Neptune ne lowd thundring *Jove* . . . . II. vi. 10. 7
Of whom high *Jove* wont whylome feasted bee; . . . . II. vii. 59. 6
Accusing highest *Jove* and gods ingrate; . . . . II. vii. 60. 7
triumphes of Phlegraean *Jove,* . . . . II. x. 3. 4
he was by *Jove* depryv'd Of life . . . . II. x. 70. 8
high *Jove* Doth light the lower world, ... III. i. 57. 6
Jove laught on Venus from his soverayne see, ... III. vi. 2. 7
To scorne the joy that *Jove* is glad to seeke: . . . . III. vi. 22. 6
To scale the skyes and put *Jove* from his right: . . . . . . III. vii. 47. 5
often thondring *Jove* Had felt the point . . . . III. xi. 30. 1
Whyles thus on earth great *Jove* these pageaunts playd, . . . III. xi. 35. 5
take me for their *Jove,* whiles *Jove* to earth is gone.' . . . III. xi. 35. 9
that ympe of Troy, Whom *Jove* did love . . . . III. xii. 7. 4
Well worthie thou to be of *Jove* accurst, ... IV. ii. 49. 8
Not all the gods can chaunge, nor *Jove* him self can free!' . IV. ii. 51. 9
As *Jove* will have advaunced to the skie, ... IV. iii. 44. 2
Throwne out by angry *Jove* in his vengeance, ... IV. vi. 14. 2
O! thou sacred imp of *Jove* . . . . IV. xi. 10. 1
those two twinnes of *Jove,* . . . . V. Pr. 6. 2
in that same day when *Jove* those Gyants quelled: . . . . . V. i. 9. 9
With which thou canst even *Jove* himselfe to love entise.' . . V. v. 34. 9
are rul'd by righteous lore Of highest *Jove,* . . . . V. vii. 1. 6
joyous light the house of *Jove* forsooke; . . . . V. vii. 8. 7
slaine By thundring Jove in the Phlegrean plaine: . . . . . V. vii. 10. 5
All lovely daughters of high *Jove,* . . . . V. ix. 31. 4
'They are the daughters of sky-ruling *Jove,* . . . . VI. x. 22. 1
Whom though high *Jove* of kingdome did deprive, ... VII. vi. 2. 8
obtain'd Great power of *Jove,* and high authority: . . . . . VII. vi. 3. 2
Jove himselfe to shoulder from his right. . . . . VII. vi. 7. 5
had to her that soveraigne seat By highest *Jove* assign'd, . . VII. vi. 12. 2
come before high *Jove* her dooings to discharge. . . . . . . VII. vi. 17. 9
He from his *Jove* such message to her brought, ... VII. vi. 18. 6
Sith shee his *Jove* and him esteemed nought, ... VII. vi. 18. 8
It did them all exceedingly amate, Save *Jove;* . . . . VII. vi. 19. 8
Jove, all fearlesse, forc't them to aby; . . . . VII. vi. 24. 6
Until that *Jove* himselfe her selfe bespake: . . . . VII. vi. 25. 6
thou, *Jove,* injuriously hast held The Heavens rule . . . . . VII. vi. 27. 6
having pauz'd awhile, *Jove* thus bespake: . . . . VII. vi. 29. 1
if *Jove* should do still what he can. . . . . VII. vi. 31. 9
Have *Jove* thy gracious Lord and Soveraine.' . . . . VII. vi. 34. 5
thee, O *Jove!* no equall Judge I deeme . . . . VII. vi. 35. 1
There-at *Jove* wexed wroth, ... VII. vi. 35. 7
She bath'd her lovely limbes, for *Jove* a likely pray. . . . VII. vi. 45. 9
Pealing from *Jove* to Nature's bar, ... VII. vii. Arg.
'To thee therefore of this same *Jove* I plaine, ... VII. vii. 15. 1
the gods owne principality, Which *Jove* usurpes unjustly, . . VII. vii. 16. 6
mauger *Jove,* and all his gods beside, ... VII. vii. 17. 1
The same wherewith Dan *Jove* . . . was nourisht . . . . . . VII. vii. 41. 6
daughters of high *Jove* And timely Night, ... VII. vii. 45. 5
the charge to them foreshewed By mighty *Jove;* . . . . VII. vii. 45. 6

Jove—*Continued.*
Then thus gan *Jove:* . . . . VII. vii. 48. 1
you, Dan *Jove,* that only constant are, ... VII. vii. 53. 1
Jove confirm'd in his imperiall see. . . . . VII. vii. 59. 7
she wants to temper angry *Jove,* . . . . *Am.* xxxix. 3
Like unto Maia, when as *Jove* her took . . . . *Epith.* 307
Lyke as when *Jove* with fayre Alcmena lay, ... *Epith.* 328
Nor *Jove* himselfe, . . . whiter did appeare; . . . . *Proth.* 42
like the twins of *Jove* they seem'd . . . . *Proth.* 173
Jove's. the storie Of *Joves* great Image . . . . *Ro.* ii. 6
So long as *Joves* great Bird did make his flight, ... *Ro.* xvii. 1
The kingly Bird, that beares *Joves* thunder-clap, ... *Van.* iv. 1
drove in *Joves* owne lap his egs to lay; . . . . *Van.* iv. 10
ornament of great *Joves* progenie, ... *Gn.* 14
through *Joves* avengefull wrath, ... *T.M.* 8
The goodly off-spring of *Joves* progenie, ... *T.M.* 429
woven even now Of *Joves* owne hand, ... *Mui.* 236
when she does ride To *Joves* high hous . . . . I. iv. 17. 7
shyning lampes in *Joves* high house were light; . . . . . . I. v. 19. 2
Which fast is tyde to *Joves* eternall seat? . . . . I. v. 25. 6
Joves dreaded thunder light Does scorch not halfe so sore, . . II. vi. 50. 7
Joves harnesse-bearing Bird from hye . . . . II. xi. 43. 1
To light their blessed lamps in *Joves* eternall hous. . . . . III. iv. 51. 9
Frame thunderbolts for *Joves* avengefull threate. . . . . . . IV. v. 37. 4
When to *Joves* pallace she doth take her way, ... IV. xi. 28. 3
Joves and Phoebus kinde; . . . . IV. xi. 52. 7
where it was kept in store In *Joves* eternall house, ... V. i. 9. 4
those, they say, Upon *Joves* judgement-seat wayt . . . . . . V. ix. 31. 7
To *Joves* faire palace fixt in heavens hight; . . . . VII. vi. 15. 2
To *Joves* high Palace straight cast to ascend, ... VII. vi. 23. 8
that to be My heritage *Jove's* selfe cannot denie, ... VII. vii. 16. 7
whom so much ye make *Joves* dearest darling, ... VII. vii. 50. 3
In *Joves* sweet paradice of Day and Night; . . . . *Epith.* 99
Jovial. the Heavens alwayes *joviall* Lookte on them lovely, . II. xii. 51. 1
Jovysaunce. *See* **Jouisance.**
Joy. *See* **Sans Joy.**
she mounted up to *joy.* . . . . *Pet.* vi. 10
Ah, God! that love should breede both *joy* and payne! . . . *S.C.* Ja. 54
Some in much *joy,* many in many teares, ... *S.C.* F. 18
on him was all my care and *joye,* . . . . *S.C.* Ap. 23
send thee *joy* of thy jollitee. . . . . *S.C.* May 192
false Fortune such *joy* did him spight, ... *S.C.* May 198
In such delights did *joy* . . . . *S.C.* Jun. 35
O Colin, Colin! the shepheards *joye,* . . . . *S.C.* Au. 193
(Ah, for Colin, he whilome my *joye!*) . . . . *S.C.* S. 177
Great Nereus his daughter and his *joy.* . . . . *Gn.* 492
So wilde a beast so tame ytaught . . . is *joy* to see; . . . . *Hub.* 626
Ladies gentle sports, The *joy* of youth, ... *Hub.* 758
Her loved Twinnes, the dearlings of her *joy,* . . . . *T.M.* 14
Of wretched life the onely *joy* shee is, ... *T.M.* 131
all *joy* and jolly meriment Is also deaded, ... *T.M.* 209
I, whose *joy* was earst with Spirit full . . . . *T.M.* 289
That which I eate did I *joy,* and that which I greedily gorged, *Ex Tempore* 1
The worlds late wonder and the heavens new *joy;* . . . . . *Ti.* 303
Robbed of sense, and ravished with *joy:* . . . . *Ti.* 321
O sad *joy,* made of mourning and anoy! . . . . *Ti.* 322
joy in pleasures vaine, ... *Ti.* 528
There now the *joy* is his, ... *Ti.* 602
wrought both *joy* and sorrow in my mind: . . . . *Ti.* 614
(small *joy* to him, alas!) . . . . *Ti.* 652
with secret *joy* therefore Did tickle inwardly . . . . *Mui.* 393
all my *joy* was on my gentle sheepe, ... *D.* 104
well did hope my *joy* would have no end, ... *D.* 149
her faire brest, the threasury of *joy,* . . . . *As.* 161
The blossome of sweet *joy* and perfect love, ... *Col.* 470
Bathed in wanton blis and wicked *joy.* . . . . I. i. 47. 6
Them both together laid to *joy* in vaine delight. . . . . . I. ii. 3. 9
when corage hott The . . . *joy* of chevalree, First kindled . I. ii. 35. 2
Such *joy* made Una, when her knight she found; . . . . I. iii. 32. 1
Huge routs of people . . . Showting for *joy;* . . . . I. iv. 36. 6
That night they pas in *joy* and jollity, ... I. iv. 43. 5
Cause of my new griefe, cause of my new *joy;* . . . . I. iv. 45. 5
in doubt ne dares To *joy* at his foolhappie oversight: . . . I. vi. 1. 6
doubly is distrest twixt *joy* and cares . . . . I. vi. 1. 7
For griefe whereof the lad n'ould after *joy,* . . . . I. vi. 17. 8
Therion, . . . Who had more *joy* to raunge the forrest wyde, I. vi. 21. 7
Such *joy* he had their stubborne harts to quell, ... I. vi. 26. 7
'Ah Satyrane, my dearling and my *joy,* . . . . I. vi. 28. 6
That him of life, and us of *joy,* hath refte?' . . . . I. vi. 39. 6
'What worlds delight, or *joy* of living speach, ... I. vii. 39. 1
to him she ran With hasty *joy:* . . . . I. viii. 42. 2
'Ensample make of him your haplesse *joy,* . . . . I. ix. 12. 1
Whose onely *joy* was to relieve the needes . . . . I. x. 3. 6
Her heart with *joy* unwonted inly sweld, ... I. x. 8. 8
greatly *joy* each other for to see: . . . . I. x. 15. 4
The knight and Una . . . bid her *joy* . . . . I. x. 32. 2
with great *joy* into that Citty wend, ... I. x. 56. 4
Fayre Una to the Redcrosse Knight Betrouthed is with *joy:* . I. xii. Arg.
Uprose with hasty *joy,* and feeble speed, ... I. xii. 3. 1
Proclaymed *joy* and peace through all his state; . . . . . . I. xii. 3. 8
Of their new *joy,* and happie victory . . . . I. xii. 4. 3
Great *joy* was made that day of young and old, ... I. xii. 40. 1
swimming in that sea of blisfull *joy,* . . . . I. xii. 41. 5
'*Joy* may you have, and everlasting fame, ... II. i. 32. 1
Is this the *joy* of armes? . . . . II. ii. 29. 5
in her loosenesse tooke exceeding *joy.* . . . . II. ii. 37. 3
Did shew her selfe in great triumphant *joy,* . . . . II. iii. 31. 8
did of *joy* and jollity devize, ... II. vi. 21. 3
of her *joy* And vaine delight . . . . II. vi. 37. 2
I *joy* thy face to vew: . . . . II. viii. 53. 8

Joy—*Continued.*
some laught for *joy;* . . . . II. ix. 35. 2
Joy thereof have thou and eternall blis!' . . . . III. ii. 42. 5
Both love and lover, without hope of *joy,* . . . . III. ii. 45. 3
He lives, but takes small *joy* of his renowne; . . . . III. v. 26. 1
left her blisfull bowre of *joy* above: . . . . III. vi. 11. 5
To scorne the *joy* that Jove is glad to seeke: . . . . III. vi. 22. 6
we scorne his foolish *joy,* . . . . III. vi. 24. 4
There now he lives in everlasting *joy,* . . . . III. vi. 49. 1
she does *joy* to play emongst her peares, ... III. ix. 4. 8
Depriv'd of kindly *joy* and naturall delight. . . . . III. ix. 5. 9
for remembrance of her passed *joy,* . . . . III. ix. 36. 5
his liefest pelfe . . . the *joy* of misers blinde. . . . . III. x. 15. 9
passing *joy,* which so great marvaile brings, ... IV. iii. 49. 8
Triumphing in great *joy* and jolity, ... IV. iv. 28. 2
I *joy* to see you lout so low on ground, ... IV. vi. 28. 7
For sudden *joy* and secret feare withall; . . . . IV. vi. 29. 3
as was her wonted *joy,* . . . . IV. vii. 23. 8
no *joy* In all his life, which afterwards he lad, ... IV. viii. 2. 3
For all his *joy,* he said, in that distresse . . . . IV. viii. 57. 6
for more *joy,* that captive Lady faire, ... IV. ix. 13. 1
To bath in *joy* and amorous desire, ... IV. x. 38. 7
The *joy* of Gods and men, ... IV. x. 44. 2
nathlesse he takes great *joy* . . . . IV. xi. 19. 8
Joy on those warlike women, ... IV. xi. 22. 1
all the raging seas for *joy* forgot to rore. . . . . IV. xi. 23. 9
Joy to you both, ... IV. xi. 26. 8
joy likewise this solemne day to see? . . . . IV. xi. 40. 5
joy that for his sake I suffer prisonment. . . . . IV. xii. 7. 9
To tast of *joy,* and to wont pleasures to retourne. . . . . V. iii. 1. 9
for *joy* he brake His bands, ... V. iii. 34. 7
Timely to *joy* and carrie comely cheare: . . . . V. v. 38. 5
They shouted all for *joy* of his successe, ... V. xii. 24. 2
take great *joy* to publish it to many, ... V. xii. 35. 3
the use of armes, which most I *joy,* . . . . VI. ii. 32. 6
is this the timely *joy,* Which I expected long, ... VI. iii. 4. 8
For *joy* of such good hap by heavenly grace. . . . . VI. viii. 37. 5
last forth brought The fruite of *joy* and blisse, ... VI. ix. 45. 9
wondrous *joy* felt in her spirits thrall: . . . . VI. xi. 44. 5
full of *joy,* streight forth she ran in hast . . . . VI. xii. 16. 6
this mothers *joy* descrive; . . . . VI. xii. 21. 4
nigh she swelt For passing *joy,* . . . . VI. xii. 21. 9
joyning *joy* with her in one accord, ... VI. xii. 22. 3
There leave we them in *joy,* . . . . VI. xii. 22. 5
joy to weary wandring travailers did lend: . . . . VII. vi. 9. 9
for great *joy* of some-what he did spy, ... VII. vi. 46. 3
Full of delightfull health and lively *joy,* . . . . VII. vii. 46. 8
how the Tyrannesse doth *joy* to see . . . . *Am.* x. 5
rapt with *joy* resembling heavenly madnes, ... *Am.* xxxix. 9
joy, her thrall for ever to remayne, ... *Am.* xlii. 7
having her, my *joy* will be the greater. . . . . *Am.* li. 14
There let no thought of *joy,* . . . Dare to approch, ... *Am.* lii. 9
Sometimes I *joy* when glad occasion fits, ... *Am.* liv. 5
Soone after, when my *joy* to sorrow flits, I waile, ... *Am.* liv. 7
The bud of *joy,* the blossome of the morne, ... *Am.* lxi. 9
Then shall the new yeares *joy* forth freshly send, ... *Am.* lxii. 9
This joyous day . . . with *joy* begin; . . . . *Am.* lxviii. 5
I *joy* to see how, in your drawen work, ... *Am.* lxxi. 1
Joy of my life! . . . . *Am.* lxxxii. 1
Ne *joy* of ought that under heaven doth hove . . . . *Am.* lxxxviii. 9
Doe ye to her of *joy* and solace sing, ... *Epith.* 35
they of *joy* and pleasance to you sing, ... *Epith.* 90
these glad many, which for *joy* doe sing, ... *Epith.* 294
annoy The safety of our *joy;* . . . . *Epith.* 325
His care, his *joy,* his hope, is all on this, ... *H.L.* 206
What heavens of *joy* then to himselfe he faynes! . . . . *H.L.* 240
To worke ech others *joy* and true content, ... *H.B.* 200
voide of sinfull blot, The firstling of his *joy,* . . . . *H.H.L.* 33
All *joy,* all blisse, all happinesse, have place; . . . . *H.H.B.* 243
And feele such *joy* and pleasure inwardly, ... *H.H.B.* 264
Their *joy,* their comfort, their desire, their gaine, ... *H.H.B.* 271
All happie *joy* and full contentment fynd. . . . . *H.H.B.* 287
Joy may you have, ... *Proth.* 94
Joy have thou of thy noble victorie, ... *Proth.* 152

Joyance. wee that earst in *joyance* did abound, ... *T.M.* 307
all his gladfulnes, and kingly *joyaunce.* . . . . *Mui.* 208
His sports were faire, his *joyance* innocent, ... *As.* 25
Him selfe estraunging from their *joyaunce* vaine, ... I. iv. 37. 8
As for great *joyance* of his newcome guest. . . . . I. xi. 15. 4
She chearfull, fresh, and full of *joyaunce* glad, ... III. xii. 18. 4
made full goodly *joyance* to her new-found mate. . . . . IV. i. 31. 9
with great *joyance* and with gladsome glee . . . . IV. viii. 59. 6
in this joyous place they mote have *joyance* free. . . . . IV. x. 23. 9
So blesse thee God, and give thee *joyance* of thy dreame!' . . . . V. vii. 23. 9
he in time her *joyance* should obtaine: . . . . VI. xi. 7. 4
Had never *joyance* felt nor chearefull thought, ... VI. xi. 45. 2
such *joyance* hath thee well beseene. . . . . VII. vii. 11. 9
Was never such great *joyance* . . . . VII. vii. 12. 1
With *joyance* bring her and with jollity. . . . . *Epith.* 245
After full *joyance* of their gentle game; . . . . *H.L.* 291

Joyed. How would he have *joyed* at this sweete sight! . . . . *S.C.* May 197
joyed oft to chace the trembling Pricket, ... *S.C.* D. 27
But th' other *joy'd,* that . . . He compast Troy . . . . *Gn.* 526
with sharp quips *joy'd* others to deface, ... *Hub.* 707
joy'd to range abroad in fresh attire, ... *Mui.* 37
'Long thus I *joyed* in my happinesse, ... *D.* 148
joyd that country shepheard ought could fynd . . . . *Col.* 366
in the witch unweeting *joyd* long time, ... I. ii. 40. 2
his looser life . . . *joyd* weake wemens hearts to tempt, ... I. iv. 26. 4
I never *joyed* howre, ... I. iv. 46. 6

Joyed—*Continued.*
joyd to make proofe of her cruelty . . . . I. vi. 31. 6
joyd to stirre up strife, ... I. ix. 10. 3
I sorrowed all so much as earst I *joyd,* . . . . I. ix. 15. 3
joyd to see her lover languish and lament: . . . . I. ix. 27. 9
babes . . . Playing their sportes, that *joyd* her to behold; . . . . I. x. 31. 2
Una, who him *joyd* to see; . . . . I. x. 68. 6
In sumptuous tire she *joyd* her selfe to pranck, ... II. ii. 36. 8
Th' enchaunter greatly *joyed* in the vaunt, ... II. iii. 13. 1
greatly *joyed* merry tales to faine, ... II. vi. 6. 4
joyd his dayes in great tranquillity. . . . . II. x. 53. 2
joyd his love in secret unespyde: . . . . III. i. 37. 2
joyd that ever she affixed had Her hart . . . . III. ii. 11. 3
rather *joyd* to bee then seemen sich, ... III. vii. 29. 8
Extremely *joyed* in so happy sight, ... III. viii. 10. 2
As Hellene, . . . *joyed* at that dolefull sight. . . . . III. x. 12. 9
That much Malbecco *joyed* in his jollity. . . . . III. x. 33. 9
that most on earth him *joyd,* . . . . III. xii. 44. *or.* 1
from the time . . . she never *joyed* day; . . . . IV. i. 2. 2
none alive but *joy'd* in Florimell, ... IV. ii. 23. 2
Artegall close smyling *joy'd* in secret hart. . . . . IV. vi. 32. 9
joyd in happy peace, till fates perverse . . . . IV. vii. 15. 3
I never *joyed* happinesse nor rest; . . . . IV. ix. 39. 3
I never *joyed* howre, but still with care was moved. . . . . IV. x. 1. 9
he onely *joyed* In combats of sweet love, ... V. v. 24. 8
joyed to behold Her selfe adorn'd with gems . . . . V. vii. 13. 8
joyd much in his semblance glad. . . . . V. vii. 41. 9
Whereat Sir Calidore . . . greatly *joy'd* . . . . VI. ii. 36. 7
joyed long in close felicity, ... VI. x. 38. 6
Thenceforth they *joy'd* in happinesse together, ... VI. xii. 10. 6
As though he *joyed* in his plentious store, ... VII. vii. 30. 2
joyed in theyr praise; . . . . *Epith.* 6

Joyest. fond, that *joyest* in the woe thou hast! . . . . I. ix. 39. 7

Joyeth. (In which shee *joyeth* in eternall blis) . . . . *D.* 381

Joyful. O *joyfull* verse! . . . . *S.C.* N.172, 182, 192, 202
when flowrd my *joyfull* spring, ... *S.C.* D. 19
leads as *joyfull* life; . . . . *Gn.* 150
Most *joyfull* man her sire was her to see, ... VI. iii. 19. 1
With many a *joyfull* kisse . . . . VI. xii. 20. 9
Fit for so *joyfull* day: . . . . *Epith.* 115
Never had man more *joyfull* day then this, ... *Epith.* 246

Joyfulest. The *joyfulst* day that ever sunne did see. . . . . *Epith.* 116

Joyfully. with him brought a present *joyfully* . . . . IV. xi. 33. 7
She gan take hart and looke up *joyfully;* . . . . V. x. 19. 8
Most *joyfully* she them did entertaine; . . . . VI. i. 46. 2

Joyfulness. So my delight is all in *joyfulnesse,* . . . . III. vi. 22. 3
When she with Mars was meynt in *joyfulnesse:* . . . . III. xi. 36. 5
running all with greedie *joyfulnesse* To faire Irena, ... V. xii. 24. 5

Joying. *joying* in the brightnes of your day, ... *Ro.* xv. 2
Joying to heare the birdes sweete harmony, ... I. i. 8. 2
Joying his goddesse, and of her enjoyd; . . . . III. vi. 48. 2
Joying his love in likenes more entire: . . . . III. xi. 33. 7
Joying together in unblam'd delight; . . . . VI. ii. 43. 3
As *joying* in the sight Of these glad many, ... *Epith.* 293

Joyless. turnest love divine To *joylesse* dread, ... III. xi. 1. 6

Joyous. The *joyous* time now nighes fast, ... *S.C.* Mar. 4
long lasting life with *joyous* glee, ... *Gn.* 59
perfect pleasure buildes her *joyous* bowre, ... *Gn.* 135
Both seeming now full glad and *joyeous* . . . . *Gn.* 483
The *joyous* Spring out of the ground brings forth, ... *Gn.* 683
One *joyous* howre in blisfull happines, ... *Hub.* 983
The *joyous* Nymphes and lightfoote Faeries . . . . *T.M.* 31
Marring my *joyous* gentle dalliaunce. . . . . *T.M.* 186
Now change the tenor of your *joyous* layes, ... *T.M.* 367
some bride, her *joyous* night to hold: . . . . *Ti.* 635
when he spide the *joyous* Butterflie . . . . *Mui.* 249
into plaints convert your *joyous* playes, ... *D.* 321
to dye must needes be *joyeous,* . . . . *D.* 451
since mine eie your *joyous* sight did mis, ... I. iii. 27. 6
th' enchaunter *joyous* seemde no lesse Then the glad marchant, ... I. iii. 32. 2
Joyous to see his ymage in mine eye, ... I. iv. 45. 6
all as glad as birdes of *joyous* Pryme, ... I. vi. 13. 5
bathe in pleasaunce of the joyous shade, ... I. vii. 4. 2
with sweet *joyous* cheare him thus bespake: . . . . I. viii. 26. 6
Una . . . *joyous* of his cured conscience, ... I. x. 29. 3
She was right *joyous* of her just request; . . . . I. x. 33. 1
Brings them to *joyous* rest and endlesse blis. . . . . I. x. 52. 6
watch the noyous night, and wait for *joyous* day. . . . . I. xi. 50. 9
The *joyous* day gan early to appeare; . . . . I. xi. 51. 1
She nigher drew, and saw that *joyous* end: . . . . I. xi. 55. 7
song In well attuned notes a *joyous* lay, ... I. xii. 7. 4
all the way the *joyous* people singes, ... I. xii. 13. 3
Her *joyous* presence and sweet company, ... I. xii. 41. 1
doest not it for *joyous* court exchaunge, ... II. iii. 39. 3
greatly *joyous* seemed for my sake, ... II. iv. 20. 3
Most *joyous* man . . . my selfe I did esteeme, ... II. iv. 21. 7
my falser friend did no less *joyous* deeme. . . . . II. iv. 21. 9
In *joyous* pleasure then in grievous paine; . . . . II. vi. 1. 2
waste thy *joyous* howres in needelesse paine, ... II. vi. 17. 4
O *joyous* memorie of happy time, ... II. x. 50. 5
They crownd the second Constantine with *joyous* teares. . . . . II. x. 62. 9
The *joyous* birdes, shrouded in chearefull shade . . . . II. xii. 71. 1
stately port of Castle *Joyeous,* . . . . III. i. 31. 2
His *joyous* face did to the world revele, ... III. ii. 48. 2
warnd his other brethren *joyeous* . . . . III. iv. 51. 8
O Titan! hast to reare thy *joyous* waine; . . . . III. iv. 60. 3
her conception of the *joyous* Prime; . . . . III. vi. 3. 2
She brought her to her *joyous* Paradize, ... III. vi. 29. 1
The whiles the *joyous* birdes make their pastyme . . . . III. vi. 42. 7

Joyous—*Continued.*
to enjoy Her deare Adonis *joyous* company, . . . III. vi. 46. 2
who that smites it mars his *joyous* play, . . . III. vii. 41. 8
bad that none their *joyous* treason should reveale. . . . III. x. 5. 9
all the night did minde his *joyous* play: . . . III. x. 48. 4
a *joyous* fellowship issewd Of Minstrales . . . III. xii. 5. 3
The morrowe next appeard with *joyous* cheare, . . . III. xii. 28. 6
to make you *joyous* meriment?' . . . IV. ii. 5. 9
Glad man was he to see that *joyous* sight, . . . IV. ii. 23. 1
making *joyous* feast theire daies they spent . . . IV. iii. 52. 1
To *joyous* feast and other gentle play, . . . IV. iv. 48. 7
Joyous to see her safe after long toyle. . . . IV. vi. 25. 5
Midst sorrow showing *joyous* semblance for his sake. . . . IV. vii. 44. 9
in her *joyous* glee, To view the thrals . . . IV. viii. 52. 2
in peace and *joyous* blis . . . IV. ix. 16. 1
in this *joyous* place they mote have joyance free. . . . IV. x. 23. 9
al the world shews *joyous* cheare. . . . IV. x. 44. 9
Thou art the root of all that *joyous* is: . . . IV. x. 47. 6
Joyous Thalia, goodly Amphitrite, . . . IV. xi. 49. 2
was right *joyous* that she gotten had . . . IV. xii. 33. 6
The sunne at length his *joyous* face doth cleare: . . . V. iii. 1. 2
Where he her spous'd, and made his *joyous* bride. . . . V. iii. 2. 4
Spending their *joyous* dayes and gladfull nights, . . . V. iii. 40. 2
joyous light the house of Jove forsooke; . . . V. vii. 8. 7
fild with courage and with *joyous* glee, . . . V. vii. 25. 4
joyous peace and quietnesse alway . . . V. ix. 24. 7
Now rise againe at this your *joyous* sight. . . . V. x. 20. 6
Came dauncing forth, and *joyous* carrols song: . . . V. xi. 34. 4
Making great feast and *joyous* merriment, . . . V. xi. 35. 2
in *joyous* jolliment Of their franke loves, . . . VI. ii. 16. 5
Full glad and *joyous* then young Tristram grew; . . . VI. ii. 35. 6
so soone as *joyous* day Did shew it selfe . . . VI. iii. 45. 1
thy *joyous* dayes Here leadest in this goodly merry-make, . . . VI. x. 19. 2
forth her bringing to the *joyous* light, . . . VI. xi. 50. 4
the *joyous* oyle, whose gentle gust Made him so frollick . . . VII. vii. 39. 4
The *joyous* safety of so sweet a rest; . . . *Am.* lxiii. 10
This *joyous* day, deare Lord, with joy begin; . . . *Am.* lxviii. 5
Tell her the *joyous* time wil not be staid, . . . *Am.* lxx. 7
fill your selfe with those most *joyous* sights, . . . *Am.* lxxxiii. 9
joyous houres doe fly away too fast. . . . *Am.* lxxxvi. 14
comfort me, but her owne *joyous* sight: . . . *Am.* lxxxviii. 10
T' awayt the comming of your *joyous* make, . . . *Epith.* 87
The Choristers the *joyous* Antheme sing, . . . *Epith.* 221
all delight and *joyous* happie rest, . . . *H.L.* 281
forth those *joyous* Birdes did passe along, . . . *Proth.* 114
Joyously. Whom when she saw so *joyously* come forth, . . . V. xi. 33. 1
Joys. Looke from above, where you in *joyes* remaine, . . . *S.C.* Ja. 15
joyes enjoyes that mortall men doe misse. . . . *S.C.* N. 196
He *joyes* in groves, . . . *Gn.* 131
chieflie *joyes* on foote them to beholde, . . . *Hub.* 623
joyes on wretched lovers to be wroken, . . . *Mui.* 99
My good to heare, and toward *joyes* to see! . . . *D.* 280
the world, whose *joyes* so fruitlesse are; . . . I. x. 63. 2
The usuall *joyes* at knitting of loves band. . . . I. xii. 40. 5
joyes Throughout the world her mercy to maintaine, . . . II. ii. 43. 6
In daintie delices, and lavish *joyes,* . . . II. v. 28. 6
Calling thy help in vaine that here in *joyes* art dround.' . . . II. v. 36. 9
The *joyes* whereof and happy fruitfulnesse, . . . II. vi. 24. 3
That *joyes* for crownes and kingdomes to contend: . . . II. vii. 10. 7
Which with sad cares empeach our native *joyes.* . . . II. vii. 15. 6
wanton *joyes* and lustes intemperate, . . . II. xii. 7. 7
others did them selves embay in liquid *joyes.* . . . II. xii. 60. 9
In secret shade after long wanton *joyes,* . . . II. xii. 72. 6
mournefel meed of *joyes* delicious! . . . II. xii. 85. 7
litle loves, and sports, and *joyes,* . . . IV. x. 42. 2
all those *joyes* that weake mankind entyse. . . . IV. xi. 5. 4
running unto them with greedy *joyes,* . . . V. x. 20. 1
Mongst *joyes* mixing some tears, . . . V. xi. 16. 3
Such be our *joyes* which in these forrests grow: . . . VI. ii. 32. 5
one evill, which doth overthrow All these our *joyes,* . . . VI. iv. 30. 7
The *joyes* of love, if they should ever last . . . VI. xi. 1. 1
Despoyled of those *joyes* and jolly-head, . . . VI. xi. 32. 8
In much delight, and many *joyes* among, . . . VI. xii. 11. 8
No eies but *joyes,* in which al powers conspire, . . . *Am.* viii. 3
Thinks more upon her paradise of *joyes,* . . . *Epith.* 366
cease till then our tymely *joyes* to sing: . . . *Epith.* 425
all his *joyes* defaced! . . . *H.L.* 272
And be partakers of those *joyes* of his. . . . *H.H.L.* 63
fruitfull issue . . . make your *joyes* redound . . . *Proth.* 106
here fits not well Olde woes, but *joyes,* to tell . . . *Proth.* 142
Judge. *Judge,* by these ample ruines vew, the rest . . . *Ro.* xxvii. 5
one would *judge,* that the Romaine Daemon . . . *Ro.* xxvii. 12
who shall *judge* the wager wonne or lost? . . . *S.C.* Au. 44
Sike a *judge* as Cuddie were for a king. . . . *S.C.* Au. 52
Should Colin make *judge* of my fooleree: . . . *S.C.* N. 28
judgement seates, whose *Judge* is deadlie dred, . . . *Gn.* 446
A *judge,* that after death doth punish sore . . . *Gn.* 447
Being the *Judge* of all that horrid hous: . . . *Gn.* 485
their cruell *Judge* compell With bitter torture, . . . *Gn.* 627
judge of Natures cunning operation, . . . *T.M.* 501
To *judge* the strife betweene them stirred late: . . . *Mui.* 309
As the Great *Judge* at first did it ordaine, . . . *D.* 363
to *judge* of things divine: . . . *Col.* 345
You, . . . destinie Hath made *judge* of my life or death . . . I. i. 51. 9
Be *judge,* ye heavens, that all things right esteeme, . . . I. vii. 49. 7
What justice can but *judge* against thee right, . . . I. ix. 37. 8
'I Pilate am, the falsest *Judge,* alas! . . . II. vii. 62. 3
So streightly God doth *judge.* . . . II. viii. 29. 6
Could *judge* what paines doe loving harts perplexe. . . . III. i. 54. 5
Such ones ill *judge* of love that cannot love, . . . IV. Pr. 2. 1

Judge—*Continued.*
judge, whether with truth or falshood they agree. . . . V. ii. 47. 9
To you that are our *judge* of equity, . . . V. iii. 36. 7
They for their *Judge* did Pastorella chose; . . . VI. ix. 43. 3
thee, O Jove! no equall *Judge* I deeme . . . VII. vi. 35. 1
judge thyselfe, by verdit of thine eye, . . . VII. vii. 27. 6
mighty mother, now be *judge,* . . . VII. vii. 47. 2
judge then, (O thou greatest goddesse trew) . . . VII. vii. 56. 6
Judged. The shepheard of Ida that *judged* beauties Queene. . . . *S.C.* Au. 138
th' aboundance of an ydle braine Will *judged* be, . . . II. Pr. 1. 4
Satyrane that day was *judg'd* to beare the bell. . . . IV. iv. 25. 9
There was it *judged,* by those worthie wights, . . . IV. v. 7. 3
It yielded was by them that *judged* it: . . . IV. v. 20. 3
Then was she *judged* Triamond his one; . . . IV. v. 21. 8
Judges. at th' one side sixe *judges* were dispos'd, . . . IV. iii. 4. 3
Judges rose, and Marshals of the field . . . IV. iii. 35. 3
The *judges,* which thereto selected were, . . . IV. v. 6. 7
the *judges* did arret her Unto the second best . . . IV. v. 21. 4
Then did the trompets sound, and *Judges* rose, . . . V. iii. 13. 6
Judges'. Ne *Judges* powre, ne reasons rule, mote them restraine. IV. v. 24. 9
Judgment. if that Hobbinol right *judgement* bare, . . . *S.C.* D. 45
forth with shame unto his *judgement* brought. . . . *Hub.* 1376
Through *judgement* of the gods to been ywroken, . . . *Col.* 921
What justice ever other *judgement* taught, . . . I. ix. 38. 3
In face of *judgement* he their right would plead, . . . I. x. 43. 4
I to them for *judgement* just doe fly, . . . I. xii. 27. 8
Els never should thy *judgement* be so frayle . . . II. iii. 16. 4
O vaine *judgement,* and conditions vaine, . . . IV. xii. 11. 1
In seate of *judgement* . . . V. Pr. 11. 2
So ye will sweare my *judgement* to abide.' . . . V. i. 25. 7
judgement so unjust against him had ordayned. . . . V. iii. 35. 9
To bide that *judgement* ye shall us afford.' . . . V. iv. 16. 5
on the threasure by that *judgement* seased, . . . V. iv. 20. 4
his contempt, that did her *judg'ment* breake. . . . V. iv. 40. 5
to their Queene for *judgement* loudly call, . . . V. ix. 49. 8
So *judgement* past, as is by law ordayned . . . VI. vii. 36. 5
wondred much at Cupids *judg'ment* wise, . . . VI. viii. 25. 2
Under the rigour of his *judgement* just; . . . *H.H.B.* 158
Judgment-hall. He which doth summon lovers to loves *judgement hall.* . . . VI. vii. 35. 9
Judgment-seat. Upon Joves *judgement-seat* wayt day and night; . . . V. ix. 31. 7
Judgment-seats. *judgement seates,* whose Judge is deadlie dred, *Gn.* 446
Judgments. their *judgments* share Mongst earthlie wightes, . . . *D.* 199
Of lawes, of *judgementes,* and of decretals, . . . II. ix. 53. 7
That they might execute her *judgements* wise, . . . V. iv. 2. 3
Dealing just *judgements,* that mote not be broken . . . V. ix. 24. 8
Juell. *See* **Jewel.**
Juggle. *juggle* finely, that became him well. . . . *Hub.* 700
Juggler. like a Gipsen, or a *Juggeler,* . . . *Hub.* 86
Juggling. he in slights and *jugling* feates did flow, . . . V. ix. 13. 8
Juice. Into his wound the *juice* thereof did scruze; . . . III. v. 33. 4
like withered tree that wanteth *juyce,* . . . IV. i. 31. 5
herbe . . . The *juyce* whereof into his wound he wrought, . . . VI. iv. 12. 8
July. hot *July* boyling like to fire, . . . VII. vii. 36. 1
Juncates. *See* **Junkets.**
June. jolly *June,* arrayd All in greene leaves, . . . VII. vii. 35. 1
Juniper. From lowest *Juniper* to Ceder tall, . . . IV. x. 22. 2
Sweet is the *Junipere,* but sharpe his bough; . . . *Am.* xxvi. 2
Junkets. beare with you both wine and *juncates* fit, . . . V. iv. 49. 8
A goodly table . . . All spred with *juncats,* . . . *Am.* lxxvii. 3
Juno. Deceived of gealous *Juno,* . . . III. xi. 33. 2
Juno, of the ayre; . . . VII. vii. 26. 6
great *Juno!* which with awful might . . . *Epith.* 390
Juno's. *Junoes* Bird in her ey-spotted traine . . . *Mui.* 95
strove to match, . . . Great *Junoes* golden chayre, . . . I. iv. 17. 5
Flying from *Junoes* wrath and hard assay, . . . II. xii. 13. 5
Jurie. *See* **Jewry.**
Jurisdiction. Through their Syres dreadfull *jurisdiction,* . . . *Gn.* 484
Jury. Therefore a *Jurie* was impaneld streight . . . VI. vii. 34. 4
Just. *See* **Giust, Joust.**
An hundred cubits high by *just* assize, . . . *Bel.*[2] ii. 2
just Minos righteous soules doth sever . . . *Gn.* 623
Cause of my death and *just* complaint to tell: . . . *Gn.* 629
Yet thy *just* labours ever shall endure. . . . *Ti.* 175
How can ye vengeance *just* so long withhold, . . . I. vi. 5. 8
a noble warlike knight By *just* occasion to that forrest came . . . I. vi. 20. 2
time in her *just* term the truth to light should bring.' . . . I. ix. 5. 9
As, when *just* time expired, should appeare. . . . I. ix. 14. 4
'Is not he *just,* that all this doth behold . . . I. ix. 47. 1
She was right joyous of her *just* request; . . . I. x. 33. 1
I to them for judgement *just* doe fly, . . . I. xii. 27. 8
forgery, Rather then matter of *just* memory; . . . II. Pr. 1. 5
'despise The doome of *just* revenge, . . . II. i. 36. 2
hevens *just* with equall brow Vouchsafed . . . II. i. 50. 3
to her *just* conditions of faire peace to heare. . . . II. ii. 27. 9
not regard dew right and *just* desarts? . . . II. ii. 29. 7
she may thee advance for works and merits *just.'* . . . II. vii. 49. 9
just wronges to vengeaunce doe provoke, . . . II. viii. 27. 3
Here have I cause in men *just* blame to find, . . . III. ii. 1. 1
the *just* revolution measured . . . III. iii. 44. 3
indew . . . with skill of *just* and trew: . . . III. iii. 45. 5
did ye see *Just* cause of dread, . . . III. viii. 48. 6
Lesse she thee lov'd then was thy *just* desart, . . . III. xi. 36. 8
Cymo, Eupompe, and Themiste *just;* . . . IV. xi. 51. 6
alwaies doe their powre within *just* compasse pen. . . . V. ii. 19. 9
so much is more then *just* to trow. . . . V. ii. 34. 9
proudly did impugne her sentence *just:* . . . V. iv. 2. 5
thought it *just* t' obay. . . . V. v. 19. 9
Like to Osyris in all *just* endever: . . . V. vii. 22. 5

Just—*Continued.*
To hinder thee from the *just* heritage . . . . . . V. vii. 23. 3
To messengers that come for causes *just:* . . . . . . V. viii. 22. 2
Dealing *just* judgements, that mote not be broken . . . . V. ix. 24. 8
Just Dice, wise Eunomie, myld Eirene; . . . . . . V. ix. 32. 6
Yet would not let *just* vengeance on her light; . . . . . . V. ix. 50. 5
from *just* verdict will for nothing start, ... V. x. 2. 2
refused To take me up . . . for no *just* cause accused, ... VI. ii. 22. 4
and to his dealing *just.* . . . . . . VI. iii. 13. 4
slaine The day before by *just* avengement . . . . . . VI. iii. 17. 3
'Certes,' (sayd then the Prince) 'the God is *just,* . . VI. viii. 23. 1
Yet could he not their *just* demaund deny, ... VI. xi. 10. 7
my *just* cause to plead; . . . . . . *Am.* xliii. 10
And slew the *Just* by most unjust decree. . . . . . . *H.H.L.* 154
From the *just* wrath of his avengefull threate . . . . . . *H.H.B.* 150
Under the rigour of his judgement *just;* . . . . . . *H.H.B.* 158
Juster. sith thy *juster* merit Might else have with felicitie bene crowned: . . . . . . V. v. 36. 6
Justest. The *justest* man and trewest in his daies, ... II. x. 42. 2
The *justest* man alive and truest did appeare. . . . . . V. vii. 2. 9
Justice. th' antique faith of *Justice* long agone . . . . . . *Gn.* 359
No care of *justice,* nor no rule of reason, ... *Hub.* 1131
Justice he solde injustice for to buy, ... *Hub.* 1147
What *justice* can but judge against thee right . . . . . . I. ix. 37. 8
What *justice* ever other judgement taught, ... I. ix. 38. 3
Where *justice* growes, there grows eke greater grace, ... I. ix. 53. 6
Of God; of grace; of *justice;* of free-will; . . . . . . I. x. 19. 6
doth thy *justice* sleepe and silent ly? . . . . . . III. xi. 9. 7
if that hevenly *justice* may withstand . . . . . . III. xi. 10. 5
When *Justice* was not for most meed out-hyred, ... V. Pr. 3. 8
Justice sate high ador'd with solemne feasts, ... V. Pr. 9. 8
all his workes with *Justice* hath bedight. . . . . . V. Pr. 10. 5
so divine a read As thy great *justice,* . . . . . . V. Pr. 11. 8
There *Justice* first her princely rule begonne. . . . . . V. i. 2. 5
The club of *Justice* dread with kingly powre endewed. . . . V. i. 2. 9
The Champion of true *Justice,* Artegall: . . . . . . V. i. 3. 2
Artegall in *justice* was upbrought . . . . . . V. i. 5. 1
in the rules of *justice* them instructed well. . . . . . V. i. 5. 9
all the discipline of *justice* there him taught. . . . . . V. i. 6. 9
For his great *justice,* held in high regard, ... V. i. 30. 2
Yet for no pitty would he change the course Of *Justice,* . . . V. ii. 26. 2
sought unrighteousnesse, and *justice* sold, ... V. ii. 26. 8
Such heavenly *justice* doth among them raine, ... V. ii. 36. 1
True *Justice* unto people to divide, ... V. iv. 1. 2
makes wrong doers *justice* to deride, ... V. iv. 1. 7
For *powre* is the right hand of *Justice* truely hight. . . . V. iv. 1. 9
The charge of *Justice* given was in trust, ... V. iv. 2. 2
doth true *justice* deale To his inferiour Gods, ... V. vii. 1. 6

Justice—*Continued.*
Justice was a God of soveraine grace, ... V. vii. 2. 2
That part of *Justice* which is Equity, ... V. vii. 3. 4
they both like race in equall *justice* runne. . . . . . V. vii. 4. 9
did true *Justice* deale, ... V. vii. 42. 7
she her selfe professeth mortall foe To *Justice,* . . . . . . V. viii. 20. 7
Justice that day of wrong her selfe had wroken; . . . . . . V. viii. 44. 7
Dealing with *Justice* with indifferent grace, ... V. ix. 36. 4
lastly *Justice* charged her with breach of lawes. . . . . . V. ix. 44. 9
with constant firme intent For zeale of *Justice,* . . . . . . V. ix. 49. 5
call, Unto Mercilla myld, for *Justice* gainst the thrall. . . V. ix. 49. 9
Whether this heavenly thing . . . be of *Justice* part, . . . V. x. 1. 3
Those Nations farre thy *justice* doe adore; . . . . . . V. x. 3. 8
Justice, though her dome she doe prolong, ... V. xi. 1. 5
His studie was true *Justice* how to deale, ... V. xii. 26. 2
of necessity His course of *Justice* he was forst to stay, . . . V. xii. 27. 4
that bright sword, the sword of *Justice* lent, ... V. xii. 40. 5
eke of *Justice,* and of Policie; . . . . . . VII. vi. 6. 2
after Wrong was lov'd, and *Justice* solde, ... VII. vii. 37. 8
equall gave to each as *Justice* duly scann'd. . . . . . VII. vii. 38. 9
I doo complaine, . . . that *justice* I may gaine. . . . . . *Am.* xii. 14
Justice'. such as sate in *justice* seate, ... *Hub.* 921
Artegall trayn'd in *Justice* lore . . . . . . V. i. Arg.
to perils great for *justice* sake proceedes. . . . . . V. ii. 1. 9
Justified. he his title *justifide* by might, ... II. x. 60. 6
To him that hath it better *justifyde,* . . . . . . VI. i. 18. 8
Justify. To weene your wrong by force to *justify;* . . . . . . III. i. 25. 2
offred that to *justifie* alowd. . . . . . IV. i. 10. 4
justifie my cause on yonder knight.' . . . . . . IV. i. 40. 6
His life he then would spend to *justifie* his right. . . . . . IV. iv. 10. 9
But what to them Fortune would *justify:* . . . . . . V. iv. 6. 4
would his doings *justifie* with his owne hand. . . . . . V. xi. 4. 9
her cause in battailous array Against him *justifie,* . . . . V. xi. 40. 4
With which he wont to fight to *justifie* his wrong: . . . . V. xii. 14. 9
Her to defend, or his to *justifie,* . . . . . . VI. ii. 19. 2
To *justifie* thy fault gainst me in equall fight.' . . . . . . VI. iii. 35. 9
Justly. *Justly* proportion'd up unto his hight, ... *Bel.* iii. 3
who with blame can *justly* her upbrayd . . . . . . *Col.* 913
heaven may *justly* vaunt . . . . . . I. x. 59. 9
Ne I against the same can *justly* preace: . . . . . . I. xii. 19. 4
Scoffing at him that did her *justly* wite, ... II. xii. 16. 8
Ne poysnous Envy *justly* can empayre The prayse . . . . III. v. 54. 5
All is his *justly* that all freely dealth. . . . . . IV. i. 6. 5
He as a Knight might *justly* be admitted; . . . . . . IV. i. 12. 8
he could *justly* weigh the wrong or right. . . . . . V. ii. 45. 3
'Most haplesse well ye may Me *justly* terme, ... V. iv. 27. 6
Yet was he *justly* damned by the doome Of his owne mouth, . V. v. 17. 3

K

Kaies. *See* **Keys.**
Kaisers. the care of *Kesars* and of Kings. . . . . . *T.M.* 570
The antique shapes of kings and *kesars* straunge and rare. . . II. vii. 5. 9
mighty kings and *kesars* into thraldome brought. . . . . . III. xi. 29. 9
Kings and *Keasars* to thy service bound; . . . . . . IV. vii. 1. 4
Whylest kings and *kesars* at her feet did them prostrate. . . V. ix. 29. 9
This is the state of *Keasars* and of Kings! . . . . . . VI. iii. 5. 7
Ne *Kesars* spared he a whit, ... VI. xii. 28. 7
Keasars. *See* **Kaisers.**
Keel. there clove unto her *keele* A little fish, ... *Van.* ix. 9
with her crooked *keele* the land she strooke: . . . . . . II. xii. 38. 3
Keels. their crooked *keeles* the surges clave. . . . . . *Gn.* 568
Keen. The *kene* cold blowes through my beaten hyde, ... *S.C.* F. 3
Never had shepheard so *kene* a kurre, ... *S.C.* S. 182
Hewen out of Adamant rocke with engines *keene,* . . . . . . I. vii. 33. 7
Whose hartstrings with *keene* steele nigh hewen be; . . . . I. viii. 22. 7
He to him raught a dagger sharpe and *keene,* . . . . . . I. ix. 51. 2
clothes meet to keepe *keene* cold away, ... I. x. 39. 4
prickt with courage *kene,* did cruell battell breath. . . . . . II. i. 27. 9
Wandreth alone with bow and arrowes *keene,* . . . . . . II. iii. 31. 4
backe rebownding left the forckhead *keene:* . . . . . . II. iv. 46. 8
All deadly daungerous, all cruell *keene,* . . . . . . II. xi. 21. 3
The secrete vertue of that weapon *keene,* . . . . . . III. i. 10. 5
fierce Bacchante seemd too fell and *keene;* . . . . . . III. i. 45. 6
Drew out a deadly bow and arrow *keene,* . . . . . . III. i. 65. 2
Yet he her followd still with corage *keene* . . . . . . III. iv. 51. 5
which with her arrowes *keene* She wounded had, ... III. v. 28. 2
rough Masons hand with engines *keene* . . . . . . III. viii. 37. 6
therewith their *keene* desires were whett. . . . . . III. x. 34. 9
A mortall bow and arrowes *keene* did hold, ... III. xi. 48. 2
Entrenched deep with knyfe accursed *keene,* . . . . . . III. xii. 20. 6
try the edges *keene.* . . . . . . IV. vii. 45. 9
From the dread daunger of his weapon *keene,* . . . . . . V. v. 8. 7
Amongst the yron hookes and graples *keene* . . . . . . V. viii. 42. 6
Are so exceeding venemous and *keene,* . . . . . . VI. vi. 9. 2
An hatchet *keene,* with which he felled wood . . . . . . VII. vii. 42. 6
can the sight that is most sharpe and *keene* . . . . . . *H.H.B.* 59
Keep. *See* **Underkeep.**
Should not her name and endles honour *keep.* . . . . . . *Ro.* viii. 14
which they did *keepe.* . . . . . . *S.C.* May 108
the shepheards that did hem *keepe:* . . . . . . *S.C.* May 129
keepe both our flockes from straying. . . . . . *S.C.* May 173
keepe your corpse from the carefull stounds . . . . . . *S.C.* May 257
mery tales to *keepe* us wake, ... *S.C.* Jun. 87
The flocke which he did *keepe,* . . . . . . *S.C.* Jul. 132
used of hys *keepe* A sacrifice to bring, ... *S.C.* Jul. 133
Their fasting flockes to *keepe.* . . . . . . *S.C.* Jul. 200
They *keepen* all the path. . . . . . *S.C.* Jul. 204
Woode as he that did them *keepe.* . . . . . . *S.C.* Au. 76

Keep—*Continued.*
sorrow close shrouded in hart, . . . to *kepe* . . . . . . *S.C.* S. 16
I whilome usd to *keepe,* . . . . . . *S.C.* S. 63
Now she is gone that safely did hem *keepe:* . . . . . . *S.C.* N. 137
of our tender Lambkins takest *keepe,* . . . . . . *S.C.* D. 8
The ghastlie Owle her grievous ynne doth *keepe.* . . . . . . *S.C.* D. 72
from the falsers fraude his folded flock to *keepe.* . . . . . . *S.C.* Env. 6
Of trecherie or traines nought tooke he *keep,* . . . . . . *Gn.* 241
Warnd him awake, from death himselfe to *keep.* . . . . . . *Gn.* 288
Cattell to *keep,* or grounds to oversee; . . . . . . *Hub.* 283
if he could willing bee To *keep* his sheep, ... *Hub.* 285
of your fleecie sheepe . . . would take on me the *keep.* . . . *Hub.* 290
but *keepe* this as a lawe: . . . . . . *Hub.* 1054
My little flocke on westerne downes to *keepe,* . . . . . . *D.* 100
She of my flock would take full warie *keepe.* . . . . . . *D.* 133
Did *keepe* his sheep, ... *As.* 4
Where be the flockes and heards, which she doth *keep?* . . . *Col.* 237
Here to *keep* sheepe, ... *Col.* 658
of nothing he takes *keepe.* . . . . . . I. i. 40. 9
at her feete the Lyon watch doth *keepe:* . . . . . . I. iii. 15. 4
left to *keepe* the forlorne maid From raging spoile . . . . . . I. iii. 43. 1
Such helplesse harmes yts better hidden *keep,* . . . . . . I. vii. 39. 7
he gave . . . That scarlot whore to *keepen* carefully; . . . . I. viii. 29. 2
With a fayre knight to *keepen* companee, ... I. ix. 27. 2
All *keepe* the broad high way, ... I. x. 10. 5
clothes meet to *keepe* keene cold away, ... I. x. 39. 4
pyn'd his flesh to *keepe* his body low and chast. . . . . . I. x. 48. 9
they him . . . with continual watch did warely *keepe.* . . . I. xii. 36. 3
yet shall it not thee *keepe* From the third brunt . . . . . . II. viii. 37. 7
constant *keepe* the way in which ye stand; . . . . . . II. ix. 8. 6
The third things past could *keep* in memoree: . . . . . . II. ix. 49. 3
keepe his standing, and his shaftes eschew, ... II. xi. 27. 7
stere aright, And *keepe* an even course; . . . . . . II. xii. 3. 2
Sir Palmer, *keepe* an even hand, ... II. xii. 18. 3
their entred guestes to *keep* within, ... II. xii. 43. 2
nothing else might *keepe* her safe and sound: . . . . . . II. xii. 82. 7
their wealth, which he from them did *keepe.* . . . . . . III. iv. 22. 9
Bad her from womankind to *keepe* him well, ... III. iv. 25. 7
The world in his continuall course to *keepe,* . . . . . . III. iv. 56. 2
Now God thee *keepe,* thou gentlest squire alive, ... III. v. 26. 6
did bind the wound from cold to *keepe.* . . . . . . III. v. 33. 9
To lurke emongst your Nimphes . . . Or *keepe* their cabins: III. vi. 23. 3
vow . . . I plighted have, and yet *keepe* stedfastly. . . . . . III. vii. 51. 7
all his windes Dan Aeolus did *keepe* . . . . . . III. viii. 21. 6
one old Nymph, hight Panope, to *keepe* it cleane. . . . . . III. viii. 37. 9
keepe continuall spy Upon her . . . . . . III. ix. 5. 4
ne *keepe* her company, ... III. ix. 5. 7
dotard old To *keepe* us out in scorne, ... III. ix. 8. 8
'I take no *keepe* of her,' (sayd Paridell) . . . . . . III. x. 38. 2

Keep—*Continued.*
to possesse . . . ne them *keepe* with carefulnesse. . . . . . III. xi. 53. 9
pledges pawnd the same to *keepe* aright: . . . . IV. iii. 3. 4
To *keepe* a nightly watch for dread of treachery. . . . . . V. iv. 46. 9
To thinke of your nights want, that should yee waking *keepe*.' V. vi. 25. 9
Uppon their wall good watch and ward did *keepe*. . . . . . V. vii. 26. 6
There let her ever *keepe* her damned den, ... V. ix. 2. 3
That they the whiles may take lesse heedie *keepe* . . . . . . V. ix. 13. 3
To *keepe* out guyle, and malice, and despight, ... V. ix. 22. 7
Can *keepe* from outrage and from doing wrong, ... V. xii. 1. 6
seem'd of them to take no *keepe*. . . . . V. xii. 42. 9
keepe your body from the daunger drad, ... VI. i. 10. 7
wary watch about her . . . *keepe*. . . . . VI. iii. 44. 9
to *keepe* him selfe so safely as he may. . . . . VI. iii. 47. 9
The end whereof Ile *keepe* untill another cast. . . . . . . VI. viii. 51. 9
in it She used most to *keepe* her royall court, ... VI. x. 9. 7
Fit to *keepe* sheepe, unfit for loves content: . . . . VI. x. 37. 4
Albe with all their might those Brigants her did *keepe*. . . . VI. xi. 23. 9
when he saw the theeves which did them *keepe*, ... VI. xi. 37. 8
To hyre them well if they their flockes would *keepe;* . . . . VI. xi. 40. 2
To *keepe* their flockes for litle hyre and chepe, ... VI. xi. 40. 7
Yet did so streightly them asunder *keepe*, ... VI. xii. 5. 8
there by did *keepe* His fleecie flock . . . . VI. xii. 9. 1
Therefore do you, my rimes, *keep* better measure, ... VI. xii. 41. 8
wrapped well . . . to *keep* the cold away; . . . . VII. vii. 42. 2
still compell To *keepe* his course? . . . . VII. vii. 48. 6
ye likewise, which *keepe* the rushy lake, ... *Epith.* 60
ye lightfoot mayds, which *keepe* the dore, ... *Epith.* 67
let stil Silence trew night-watches *keepe*, ... *Epith.* 353
To *keepe* them selves within their sundrie raines, ... *H.L.* 88
Keeper. Whether should of those ashes *keeper* bee. . . . . . *Ti.* 665
This was the auncient *keeper* of that place, ... I. viii. 31. 7
Having a *keeper* still with him in place; . . . . IV. viii. 54. 4
Which *keeper* is this Dwarfe, ... IV. viii. 54. 5
Keepers. Whom now her *keepers* had forsaken quight . . . V. xi. 60. 2
so with his *keepers* wrought, ... VI. xii. 6. 2
Keeping. *Keeping* your beastes in the budded broomes: . . . *S.C.* F. 36
Keeping his sheepe on the hils of Kent? . . . . *S.C.* F. 93
Keeping my sheepe amongst the cooly shade . . . . *Col.* 58
Whiles he had *keeping* of his grasing steed, ... I. vii. 19. 2
bee at your *keeping* well, ... I. xi. 2. 4
keeping wary watch and ward, ... II. vii. 25. 2
Keeping that slombred corse to him assind: . . . . II. viii. 11. 7
Day and night duely *keeping* watch and ward; . . . . II. ix. 25. 2
Keeping their fleecy flockes as they were hyr'd, ... III. vi. 15. 7
Keeping there close with him . . . his false Ladie, ... V. iii. 13. 4
Whom Trompart had in *keeping* there beside, ... V. iii. 17. 2
the *keeping* have of learnings threasures . . . . VI. Pr. 2. 3
weary now with carefull *keeping* ward, ... VI. v. 21. 2
Whereas the Heardes were *keeping* of their neat, ... VI. ix. 4. 2
Keeping all noysome things away from it, ... VI. x. 7. 8
as they sate *Keeping* their sheepe, ... VI. x. 33. 6
Keeps. 'Curse on that Cross,' . . . 'That *keepes* thy body . . I. ii. 18. 2
keepes in coverts close from living wight, ... II. ix. 40. 8
one eye Still ope he *keepes* . . . . III. x. 58. 7
Demogorgon, . . . The hideous Chaos *keepes*, ... IV. ii. 47. 9
ne *keepes* his course more right, ... V. Pr. 7. 3
keepes a Bridges passage by strong hond, ... V. ii. 4. 7
he stil them holds, and *keepes* with strong effort. . . . . . V. ii. 5. 9
part The raging waves, and *keepes* her course . . . . . . *Am.* lix. 6
Keight. *See* **Caught.**
Kempt. with long locks comely *kemd*, ... V. vii. 4. 5
Ken. Palinode (if thou him *ken*) . . . . *S.C.* Jul. 181
The shepheardes swayne you cannot wel *ken*, ... *S.C.* S. 42
I learned als the signes of heaven to *ken*, ... *S.C.* D. 83
who so list the like assayes to *ken*, ... *H.B.* 88
Kend, Kenet. *See* **Kenned, Kennet.**
Kenned. Not as a Foxe, for then he had be *kend*, ... *S.C.* May 237
From thence another world of land we *kend*, ... *Col.* 272
the land . . . afore is fayrly to be *kend*, ... I. xii. 1. 4
well he *kend* His credit now in doubtfull ballaunce hong: . . II. i. 3. 7
Well *kend* him so far space . . . . II. viii. 17. 7
this weapons powre I well have *kend* . . . . II. viii. 19. 8
well they *kent* That their fayre guest was gone, ... III. vii. 19. 7
whom when he passed *kend*, ... III. x. 38. 8
He *kend* it streight, ... IV. x. 14. 3
Whose ugly shape none ever saw, nor *kend*, ... V. xi. 20. 5
A rout of people they before them *kend*, ... V. xi. 43. 7
(as none they *kend*) . . . . VI. ix. 6. 4
Kennel. As if he did a dogge in *kenell* rate . . . . III. ix. 14. 7
Kennest. *See* **Kenst.**
Kennet. The chaulky *Kenet*, and the Thetis gray, ... IV. xi. 29. 5
Kenst. Cuddie, I wote thou *kenst* little good, ... *S.C.* F. 85
How *kenst* thou that he is awoke? . . . . *S.C.* Mar. 28
Colin thou *kenst*, the Southerne shepheardes boye; . . . . . *S.C.* Ap. 21
thou *kenst* the great care . . . . *S.C.* May 215
Thou *kenst* not, Percie, howe the ryme should rage, ... *S.C.* O. 109
Kent. *See* **Kenned.**
His dewelap as lythe as lasse of *Kent:* . . . . *S.C.* F. 74
Keeping his sheepe on the hils of *Kent?* . . . . *S.C.* F. 93
All *Kent* can rightly boaste: . . . . *S.C.* Jul. 44
stremis Adowne the dales of *Kent* . . . . *S.C.* Jul. 82
Nor in all *Kent*, nor in Christendome; . . . . *S.C.* S. 153
Cantium, which *Kent* we comenly inquyre. . . . . II. x. 12. 9
Kentish. by your flocks on *Kentish* downes abyde, ... *S.C.* N. 63
Kept. *kept* yfere The flockes of mighty Pan. . . . . *S.C.* Jul. 143
whatso he likte he *kept*. . . . . *Hub.* 1146
kept them lowe, and streigned verie hard. . . . . *Hub.* 1190
Without regard, or due Decorum *kept*; . . . . *T.M.* 214
kept from looking on the lightsome day: . . . . *T.M.* 593

Kept—*Continued.*
Full carefully he *kept* them day and night, ... *As.* 5
since first on grassie greene Shepheards *kept* sheep, ... *As.* 210
her boldly *kept* From turning backe, ... I. i. 17. 3
That path he *kept* which beaten was most plaine, ... I. i. 28. 3
when she slept, he *kept* both watch and ward; . . . . I. iii. 9. 5
none the holy things in safety *kept*, ... I. iii. 17. 8
Me, . . . ever since hath *kept* in darksom cave, ... I. iv. 47. 8
Thenceforth he *kept* her goodly company, ... I. vi. 31. 8
beast . . . which he had *kept* long time in darksom den. . . . I. vii. 16. 9
he could not them use, but *kept* them still in store. . . . . . I. viii. 30. 9
So *kept* she them in order, ... II. ii. 38. 9
Ne of his safetie seemed care he *kept;* . . . . II. vi. 42. 5
safe I have them *kept* in secret mew . . . . II. vii. 19. 8
ever as he went dew watch upon him *kept*. . . . . II. vii. 26. 9
Those that were up themselves *kept* others low; . . . . . . II. vii. 47. 6
Whiles it is *kept* in sober government; . . . . II. ix. 1. 4
In her owne hand the crowne she *kept* in store, ... II. x. 20. 3
overcommen *kept* in prison long, ... II. x. 32. 8
cumming to his Squyre that *kept* his steed, ... II. xi. 48. 2
nathemore Would they once turne, *kept* on as afore: . . . . II. xii. 15. 5
Whom nought regarding they *kept* on their gate, ... II. xii. 17. 3
Quit from that danger forth their course they *kept;* . . . . II. xii. 27. 1
Yet swarved not, but *kept* their forward way . . . . II. xii. 76. 5
his faire wife, whom honest long he *kept* uneath. . . . . . III. x. 2. 9
Paridell *kept* better watch then hee, ... III. x. 4. 1
Kept watch and ward about her warily, ... III. ii. 28. 7
Britomart *kept* on her former course, ... III. iv. 5. 1
kept her ready way Along the strond; . . . . III. iv. 18. 2
of each turning still *kept* wary heed: . . . . III. iv. 48. 5
Him *kept* from landing at his wished will. . . . . III. v. 20. 2
garde, . . . *kept* th' yron dore fast bard, ... III. xi. 31. 6
Seven moneths he so her *kept* in bitter smart, ... IV. i. 4. 1
that both the custome showne Were *kept*, ... IV. i. 11. 8
Stood still awhile, and his fast footing *kept*, ... IV. iii. 20. 8
Yet still that direfull stroke *kept* on his way, ... IV. iii. 34. 1
evermore from villenie her *kept:* . . . . IV. vi. 35. 7
He durst not nigh approch, but *kept* aloofe, ... IV. vii. 37. 4
Which he in store about him *kept* alway, ... IV. viii. 20. 7
They passing forth *kept* on their readie way, ... IV. viii. 37. 1
the watch, that *kept* continuall ward, ... IV. ix. 5. 6
tooke, and sithence *kept* as thrall. . . . . IV. xii. 32. 5
where it was *kept* in store In Joves eternall house, ... V. i. 9. 3
kept the crowne in which she should succeed: . . . . V. i. 13. 5
kept her place with courage confident, ... V. vi. 28. 4
Kept himselfe still in his straunge armour dight: . . . . . . V. viii. 27. 5
Whom she had causd be *kept* as prisonere . . . . V. viii. 46. 5
The whiles the Prince there *kept* the entrance still. . . . . V. ix. 15. 2
Kept by a cowheard, hight Eurytion, ... V. x. 10. 2
kept from complishing the faith which I did owe. . . . . . V. xi. 41. 9
Kept on his course, as he did it direct, ... V. xii. 21. 2
the rest the which the Castle *kept* . . . . VI. i. 24. 1
She bore it thence, and ever as her owne it *kept*. . . . . . VI. iv. 37. 9
sternely with strong hand it from his handling *kept*. . . . . VI. v. 25. 9
Kept and delivered me from deadly dread. . . . . VI. v. 29. 5
kept so well his wise commaundements, ... VI. vi. 15. 3
kept aloofe for dread to be descryde, ... VI. vii. 3. 3
on a day, when Cupid *kept* his court, ... VI. vii. 32. 6
ded, Or *kept* in bands, or from their loves exyled, ... VI. vii. 33. 4
downe he *kept* him with his scornefull sway, ... VI. viii. 11. 4
kept her sheepe with diligent attent, ... VI. ix. 37. 3
kept them with continuall watch and ward; . . . . VI. x. 43. 2
Merchants, which them *kept* in bondage hard, ... VI. x. 43. 5
kept with gard Of griesly theeves, ... VI. x. 43. 7
for want of heards, themselves then *kept*. . . . . VI. xi. 37. 5
Is forcibly *kept* downe, till he be throughly queld. . . . . . VI. xii. 30. 9
Have ever since me *kept* in cruell bands. . . . . *Am.* xii. 12
Amongst thy deerest relicks to be *kept*. . . . . *Am.* xxii. 14
in deepe darknesse *kept*, ... *H.L.* 60
Kerke. *See* **Kirk.**
Kerns. They han fatte *kernes*, ... *S.C.* Jul. 199
Kerve. *See* **Carve.**
Kesars. *See* **Kaisers.**
Kest. *See* **Cast.**
Kestrel. in his *kestrell* kynd A pleasing vaine of glory . . . . II. iii. 4. 4
Ketch. *See* **Catch.**
Key. *key* found not at all Emongst that bounch . . . . I. viii. 37. 4
Had bene the *keye* of all that kingdomes crowne; . . . . . . V. x. 26. 4
Keys. on his arme a bounch of *keyes* he bore, ... I. viii. 30. 6
Those were the *keyes* of every inner dore; . . . . I. viii. 30. 8
from his arme did reach Those *keyes*, ... I. viii. 34. 7
the *keies* are to thy hand behight . . . . I. x. 50. 7
all the *keyes* convayd Unto their maister, ... III. ix. 10. 4
the *keyes* of every prison dore . . . . IV. viii. 54. 6
stealing of the *kaies*. . . . . IV. x. 18. 9
Kicked. smott, and bitt, and *kickt*, and scratcht, and rent . II. iv. 6. 8
Kicks. *kicks*, and squals, and shriekes for fell despight; . . . V. vi. 14. 5
Kid. Will doe as did the Foxe by the *Kidde*. . . . . *S.C.* May 171
Thilke same *Kidde* . . . Was too very foolish . . . . *S.C.* May 174
full of favour as *kidde* mought be. . . . . *S.C.* May 184
The *Kidd*, pittying hys heavinesse, ... *S.C.* May 259
the *Kidde* made him good glee, ... *S.C.* May 282
for the *Kidde* to fynd: . . . . *S.C.* May 289
when the *Kidde* stooped downe to catch, ... *S.C.* May 290
lowdly she gan to call Her *Kidde;* . . . . *S.C.* May 297
her *Kidde* shee knewe well was gone: . . . . *S.C.* May 300
Such end had the *Kidde*, ... *S.C.* May 302
Nowe with a *Kidde*, now with a sheepe, ... *S.C.* Jul. 135
A Lambe, or a *Kidde*, or a weanell wast; . . . . *S.C.* S. 198
Cuddie shall have a *Kidde* to store his farme. . . . . *S.C.* O. 120

Kid—*Continued.*
Much greater gyfts . . . Then *Kidde* or Cosset . . . . . . *S.C.* N. 46
from the Goat her *kidde*, how to convay: . . . . . . VI. ix. 23. 4
wanton as a *Kid* whose horne new buds: . . . . . . VII. vii. 33. 2
Kiddie. '*Kiddie*, (quoth shee) thou kenst the great care . . . *S.C.* May 215
For-thy, my *Kiddie*, be ruld by mee, ... *S.C.* May 221
Kiddie the dore sperred after her fast. . . . . . . *S.C.* May 234
Well heard *Kiddie* al this sore constraint, ... *S.C.* May 249
while *Kiddie* unwares did looke, ... *S.C.* May 275
Kids. His *kiddes*, his cracknelles, and his early fruit. . . . *S.C.* Ja. 58
The one my madding *kiddes* to smere, ... *S.C.* Jul. 87
Leaping like wanton *kids* in pleasant Spring. . . . . . . I. vi. 14. 4
Kilkenny. By faire *Kilkenny* and Rosseponte boord; . . . . IV. xi. 43. 4
Kill. No beast so salvage but he could it *kill;* . . . . . . *As.* 83
His care was all how he them all might *kill*, ... *As.* 109
Cleopatra . . . with stroke Of Aspes sting her selfe did stoutly *kill;* . . . . . . I. v. 50. 8
Engin, . . . ramd with bollet rownd, ordaind to *kill*, ... I. vii. 13. 4
to *kill*, And rayse againe to life the hart . . . . . . I. x. 19. 8
all atonce to *kill*, ... I. xi. 13. 6
Still cald upon to *kill* him in the place. . . . . . . II. iv. 9. 4
traveillers, whom gotten they did *kill*. . . . . . . II. xii. 31. 9
herselfe for griefe did *kill;* . . . . . . II. xii. 52. 3
Shall stoutly him defeat, and thousand Saxons *kill*. . . . . III. iii. 35. 9
A virgin straunge and stout him should dismay or *kill*. . . . III. iv. 25. 9
rather do not ransack all, and him selfe *kill?'* . . . . . III. ix. 8. 9
whom he could not *kill* he practizd to entrap. . . . . . . III. xii. 11. 9
thrise his hand to *kill* her did upreare, ... IV. i. 54. 8
like the stings of aspes that *kill* with smart, ... IV. viii. 26. 8
Made *kill* her selfe for very hearts despight . . . . . . V. xii. 25. 4
With full intent him cruelly to *kill*, ... VI. iii. 49. 2
To rescue th' infant, ere he did him *kill;* . . . . . . VI. iv. 18. 7
first of all their captives they doe *kill*, ... VI. xi. 18. 1
Is it because your eyes have powre to *kill?* . . . . . . *Am.* xlix. 2
kill with looks as Cockatrices doo: . . . . . . *Am.* xlix. 10
Killed. Eftsoones I . . . would have *kild* her; . . . . . . I. ii. 39. 7
what art thou, that telst of Nephews *kilt?'* . . . . . . I. v. 26. 5
for the sinnes of al the world was *kilt:* . . . . . . I. x. 57. 7
who-so *kild* that monster most deforme, ... I. xii. 20. 3
For thirst of single kingdom him he *kild*. . . . . . . II. x. 21. 5
Elfar, who two brethren gyauntes *kild*, ... II. x. 73. 5
As if he could have *kild* him with his looke, ... III. x. 24. 2
that selfe arrow which the Carle had *kild;* . . . . . . IV. vii. 36. 5
With which he *killed* all that came within his might. . . . IV. viii. 47. 9
he it was not which that Lady *kild*, ... V. i. 24. 7
that youth had *kild* That armed knight, ... VI. ii. 4. 6
Their Captaine there they cruelly found *kild*, ... VI. xi. 21. 1
Killeth. convay Into the lookers hart, *killeth* farre away. . . IV. viii. 39. 9
Killing. with his *killing* bow And cruell shafts, ... IV. x. 55. 3
Kills. Appear'd like Aspis sting that closely *kils*, ... V. xii. 36. 4
Whome, . . . she *kills* with cruell pryde, ... *Am.* xlvii. 7
Kilnamulla. Cittie, Which *Kilnemullah* cleped is of old; . . . *Col.* 113
Kilt. *See* **Killed.**
Kimarus. then *Kimarus;* and then Danius: . . . . . . II. x. 43. 2
Kimbeline. Tenantius raignd; then *Kimbeline*, ... II. x. 50. 1
Kin. Nor prince, nor peere, nor *kin*, they would abide. . . . *Ro.* xxiii. 14
some one perhaps of gentle *kin*, ... *T.M.* 345
read how art thou nam'd, and of what *kin?'* . . . . . . II. iv. 36. 6
From whom I Paridell by *kin* descend: . . . . . . III. ix. 37. 6
I greet you well Your countrey *kin;* . . . . . . III. ix. 51. 7
did shame Himselfe with incest of his *kin* unkend; . . . . IV. xi. 13. 8
Kind. *See* **Womankind.**
monsters *kinde* In hundred formes to change . . . . . . *Bel.*[2] viii. 9
Be it by fortune, or by course of *kinde*, ... *Ro.* ix. 3
where Byrds of every *kynde* . . . their tunes attemper . . . . *S.C.* Jun. 7
never was abhord The simple shepheards *kynd*. . . . . . . *S.C.* Jul. 140
Such is the rightfull Courtier in his *kinde*, ... *Hub.* 793
he was school'd by *kinde* in all the skill . . . . . . *Hub.* 855
crueltie, the signe of currish *kinde*, ... *Hub.* 1134
To be bemoned with compassion *kinde*, ... *Ti.* 160
gentle *kinde* as ever Fowle afore; . . . . . . *Ti.* 591
though fairest thou Of all thy *kinde*, ... *Mui.* 234
though by *kind* shee stout and salvage were, ... *D.* 121
She fell away against all course of *kinde*. . . . . . . *D.* 242
All these do florish in their sundry *kynd*, ... *Col.* 452
Borne without Syre or couples of one *kynd;* . . . . . . *Col.* 800
Doth man allure for to enlarge his *kynd;* . . . . . . *Col.* 872
Hast Cupid selfe depainted in his *kynd*, ... *Col.* 898
Doth promise fruite worthy the noble *kind* . . . . . . *Ded. Son.* x. 3
'Time and suffised fates to former *kynd* Shall us restore; . . I. ii. 43. 8
More mild in beastly *kind* then that her beastly foe. . . . . I. iii. 44. 9
all the Satyres scorne their woody *kind*, ... I. vi. 18. 8
A Satyre . . . made her person thrall unto his beastly *kind*. . I. vi. 22. 9
comforted with curteous *kind* reliefe: . . . . . . I. vi. 37. 6
chearefull birds of sundry *kynd* . . . . . . I. vii. 3. 4
Her neather parts, the shame of all her *kind*, ... I. viii. 48. 1
As he had beene a fole of Pegasus his *kynd*. . . . . . . I. ix. 21. 9
Many *kind* speeches they betweene them spend, ... I. x. 15. 3
meates and drinkes of every *kinde* . . . . . . I. xii. 15. 1
quite contrary to her sisters *kynd;* . . . . . . II. ii. 36. 3
in his kestrell *kynd* A pleasing vaine of glory . . . . . . II. iii. 4. 4
In his owne *kind* he gan him selfe unfold; . . . . . . II. iii. 9. 4
Abroad in armes, at home in studious *kynd*, ... II. iii. 40. 8
he by *kynd* Was given all to lust . . . . . . II. v. 28. 2
Not this rude *kynd* of battaill, ... II. vi. 34. 2
others it to use according to his *kynd*. . . . . . . II. ix. 31. 9
the first author of all Elfin *kynd;* . . . . . . II. x. 71. 2
a straunge *kinde* of harmony, ... II. xii. 33. 6
'The donghill *kinde* Delightes in filth . . . . . . II. xii. 87. 6
what inquest Made her dissemble her disguised *kind?* . . . . III. ii. 4. 7

Kind—*Continued.*
Of filthy lust, contrary unto *kinde;* . . . . . . III. ii. 40. 4
lov'd their native flesh against al *kynd*, ... III. ii. 41. 3
Wise, warlike, personable, courteous, and *kind*. . . . . . III. iv. 5. 9
great Dame Natures handmaide chearing every *kind*. . . . III. iv. 56. 9
she was so courteous and *kynde*, ... III. v. 55. 2
Doe life conceive and quickned are by *kynd:* . . . . . . III. vi. 8. 6
By course of *kinde* and by occasion; . . . . . . III. vi. 38. 7
through her so *kind* And curteise use, ... III. vii. 15. 6
many *kinde* remembraunces. . . . . . . III. vii. 16. 9
the huge element, against her *kinde*, ... III. ix. 15. 5
his proud spoile . . . he might behold in perfect *kinde;* . . . III. xii. 22. 8
all three according to their *kynd:* . . . . . . IV. ii. 53. 4
in this Ladie wrought Against the course of *kind*, ... IV. vi. 30. 5
Her second care, though in another *kind:* . . . . . . IV. vi. 46. 7
Of this accursed Carle of hellish *kind*, ... IV. vii. 18. 4
Latonaes daughter, cruell *kynde*, ... IV. vii. 30. 5
No service lothsome to a gentle *kind*, ... IV. viii. 22. 7
noble *kind* at first was sure of heavenly seed. . . . . . IV. viii. 33. 9
with *kind* words accoyd, ... IV. viii. 59. 9
neither gifts nor graces *kind* . . . . . . IV. xi. 2. 7
Lovely Pasithee, *kinde* Eulimene, ... IV. xi. 49. 3
Joves and Phoebus *kinde;* . . . . . . IV. xi. 52. 7
love . . . that leads each living *kind*. . . . . . . IV. xii. 25. 9
With wrongfull powre oppressing others of their *kind*. . . V. i. 7. 9
With daily shew of courteous *kind* behaviour, ... V. v. 35. 7
For such your *kind* regard I can but rest your detter. . . . V. v. 37. 9
a Queene, and come of Princely *kynd*, ... V. v. 41. 5
much lesse honour by that warlike *kinde* Of life; . . . . V. vi. 32. 5
The fayrest kyne alive, but of the fiercest *kynd:* . . . . . V. x. 9. 9
other like infernall furies *kinde;* . . . . . . V. xi. 23. 6
Agreeing in bad will and cancred *kynd;* . . . . . . V. xii. 33. 2
some so goodly gratious are by *kind*, ... VI. ii. 2. 2
with usage *kind* He rather should have taken up . . . . . . VI. ii. 11. 4
at the last breake forth in his owne proper *kynd*. . . . . . VI. v. 1. 9
In such a salvage wight, of brutish *kynd*, ... VI. v. 29. 6
with medicine To goe about to salve such *kynd* of sore, . . VI. vi. 13. 2
Whether such grace were given her by *kynd*, ... VI. vi. 43. 1
By such discourteous deeds discovering his base *kind*. . . . VI. vii. 1. 9
Did counterfeit *kind* pittie where was none: . . . . . . VI. vii. 18. 4
The sonne of Venus, who is myld by *kynd* . . . . . . VI. vii. 37. 1
as ye soft and tender are by *kynde*, ... VI. viii. 2. 1
A monstrous cruelty gainst course of *kynde!* . . . . . . VI. viii. 36. 5
clothes to cover what they ought by *kind*, ... VI. viii. 50. 4
afterwards to cheare with speaches *kind;* . . . . . . VI. viii. 50. 7
With all *kind* courtesies he could invent; . . . . . . VI. ix. 34. 6
comely carriage, entertainement *kynde*, ... VI. x. 23. 4
to each degree and *kynde* We should our selves demeane, . . VI. x. 23. 7
Had in his *Plaint of kinde* describ'd it well: . . . . . . VII. vii. 9. 7
Such love, not lyke to lusts of baser *kynd*, ... *Am.* vi. 3
it can alter all the course of *kynd*. . . . . . . *Am.* xxx. 14
The first my being to me gave by *kind*, ... *Am.* lxxiv. 5
my sovereigne Queene most *kind*, ... *Am.* lxxiv. 7
vile adders sting, Of that selfe *kynd* . . . . . . *Am.* lxxxv. 2
To multiply the likenesse of their *kynd*, ... *H.L.* 100
the most *kind* preserver Of living wights, ... *H.L.* 156
by chaunce, against the course of *kynd*, ... *H.B.* 143
like the native brood of Eagles *kynd*, ... *H.H.B.* 138
Kinded. She yet forgets that she of men was *kynded:* . . . . V. v. 40. 8
Kindle. *kindle* coales of conteck and yre, ... *S.C.* S. 86
kindle wise desire, ... *Hub.* 830
lustfull yongth began to *kindle* fast, ... *Mui.* 34
spices . . . To *kindle* heat of corage privily; . . . . . . I. v. 4. 7
To *kindle* love in every living brest: . . . . . . I. ix. 9. 4
The housling fire did *kindle* and provide, ... I. xii. 37. 4
his lustfull fyre To *kindle* oft assayd, ... II. iii. 23. 7
she sought To *kindle* his quencht fyre, ... II. v. 19. 9
as a cole to *kindle* fleshly flame, ... III. i. 50. 2
The beames whereof did *kindle* lovely fire . . . . . . VI. vii. 28. 8
in my feeble brest *Kindle* fresh sparks . . . . . . VII. vii. 2. 4
wondrous beauty fit to *kindle* love; . . . . . . VII. vii. 45. 3
So hard it is to *kindle* new desire . . . . . . *Am.* vi. 9
May *kindle* living fire within my brest. . . . . . . *Am.* vii. 12
kindle fyre by wonderfull devyse! . . . . . . *Am.* xxx. 12
The sparkes whereof let *kindle* thine own fyre, ... *Am.* lxxxv. 9
Do *kindle* love in high conceipted sprights; . . . . . . *H.H.B.* 5
Kindled. a *kindled* flame, Mounting like waves . . . . . . *Bel.*[1] ix. 1
Cooling againe his former *kindled* heate, ... *Ro.* xi. 5
his enemie Had *kindled* such coles of displeasure, ... *S.C.* F. 191
The raging fyre that *kindled* at his ray. . . . . . . *S.C.* D. 58
with sterne lookes to threaten *kindled* yre. . . . . . . *Gn.* 264
With beawtie *kindled*, and with pleasure fed, ... *T.M.* 364
glorious fire it *kindled* in his hart; . . . . . . I. Pr. 3. 4
when corage hott The fire of love, . . . First *kindled* . . . . I. ii. 35. 3
nought their *kindled* corage may aswage: . . . . . . I. xi. 6. 5
Her hellish brond hath *kindled* with despight, ... II. ii. 29. 3
Kindled above at th' hevenly makers light, ... II. iii. 23. 2
with my heat *kindled* his cruell fyre; . . . . . . II. iv. 32. 8
Which *kindled* once, his mother did more rage inspyre. . . . II. iv. 32. 9
in Stygian lake, ay burning bright, Had *kindled:* . . . . . II. v. 22. 8
The wrath which Atin *kindled* in his mind, ... II. vi. 2. 3
With wrathfull fire his corage *kindled* bright, ... II. vi. 30. 7
Kindled through his infernall brond of spight, ... II. vi. 50. 5
kindled life-devouring fire.' . . . . . . II. vii. 17. 9
The secrete signes of *kindled* lust appeare, ... II. xii. 68. 6
Cupid still emongest them *kindled* lustfull fyres. . . . . . III. i. 39. 9
ykindled first above Emongst th' eternall spheres . . . . . . III. iii. 1. 2
Bee freshly *kindled* in the fruitfull Ile Of Mona, ... III. iii. 48. 4
Love and despight attonce her courage *kindled* hath. . . . . III. iv. 12. 9
kindled heat that soone in flame forth brust: . . . . . . III. viii. 25. 4

Kindled—*Continued.*
That warre was *kindled* which did Troy inflame, ... III. ix. 34. 2
sparks . . . Which still he blew and *kindled* busily, ... III. xii. 9. 8
The crime which cursed Ate *kindled* earst, ... IV. v. 31. 2
rather in them *kindled* choler new: . . . . V. ii. 13. 4
Together strove, and *kindled* wrathfull fires: . . . . V. iv. 4. 5
kindled privily, Into outragious flames unwares did grow, . . V. vii. 14. 6
That mote thy *kindled* courage set on fire, ... VI. ii. 37. 3
For all that shame, which *kindled* inward hate: . . . . . . VI. vii. 2. 7
Had in him *kindled* youthfull fresh desire, ... VII. vii. 11. 7
The light whereof hath *kindled* heavenly fyre . . . . *Am.* iii. 3
fire, *Kindled* above unto the Maker neere; . . . . *Am.* viii. 2
gentle furie, *kindled* of thy fire. . . . . *H.L.* 28
Kindled at first from heavens life-giving fyre, ... *H.L.* 65
And *kindled* flame in all their inner parts, ... *H.L.* 124
Once *kindled* through that first conceived fyre. . . . . *H.L.* 203
by like way *Kindled* of yours, ... *H.B.* 180
Kindled the flame of His consuming yre, ... *H.H.L.* 86
love, *Kindled* through sight of those faire things above. . . . *H.H.L.* 287
Kindles. enrage Her frantick sonne, and *kindles* his corage; . II. iv. 11. 5
when Rancor rife *Kindles* Revenge, ... II. iv. 44. 5
in brave sprite it *kindles* goodly fire, ... III. v. 1. 8
Kindlest. Thou in me *kindlest* much more great desyre, . . . *H.B.* 5
Kindleth. he *kindleth* his ambitious sprights. . . . . *Hub.* 768
fyre Which *kindleth* love in generous desyre, ... *H.L.* 187
the thing . . . that kindleth lively *fyre,* . . . . *H.B.* 58
light proceedes, which *kindleth* lovers fire, ... *H.B.* 100
That *kindleth* love in every godly spright . . . . *H.H.B.* 297
Kindling. *See* **Love-kindling.**
kindling fire within the hollow tree, ... *Van.* iv. 7
kindling rage her selfe she gathered round, ... I. i. 18. 2
A Satyre . . . *kindling* coles of lust in brutish eye, ... I. vi. 22. 7
kindling fire at her faire-burning eye, ... II. ii. 7. 6
kindling new his corage seeming queint, ... II. v. 11. 4
kindling coles of cruell enmity, ... II. x. 33. 5
in their spirits *kindling* zealous fire, ... IV. x. 26. 8
courage chill *Kindling* afresh, gan battell to renew, ... VI. i. 35. 8
Is long ere it conceive the *kindling* fyre; . . . . *Am.* vi. 6
Kindly. The *kindelye* (*kindlye) dewe drops from the higher tree, ... *S.C.* N. 31
can undoe Dame Natures *kindly* course; . . . . *S.C.* N. 124
Ida selfe . . . like a *kindly* nourse, ... *Gn.* 507
seeing *kindly* sleep refuse to doe His office, ... *Hub.* 21
To doo their *kindly* services as needeth. . . . . *Hub.* 273
through *kindly* aptnes of his joynts. . . . . *Hub.* 695
the false Foxe most *kindly* plaid his part; . . . . *Hub.* 1137
Whom not their *kindly* Sovereigne did welde, ... *Hub.* 1232
With *kindly* counter under Mimick shade, ... *T.M.* 207
Am put from practice of my *kindlie* skill, ... *T.M.* 383
I nightly waste, wanting my *kindely* reste: . . . . *U.V.* 16
the *kindly* fire Of lustfull yongth . . . . *Mui.* 33
Her youthfull sports and *kindlie* wantonnesse, ... *D.* 111
cease henceforth things *kindly* forth to bring, ... *D.* 339
powred *kindly* heat and formall feature, ... *Col.* 862
her *kindly* skil To bring forth fruit, ... I. iii. 28. 7
An heard of Bulles, whom *kindly* rage doth sting, ... I. viii. 11. 6
Then first the cole of *kindly* heat appeares . . . . I. ix. 9. 3
when their wearie limbes with *kindly* rest, ... I. x. 18. 1
eien . . . through great age had lost their *kindly* sight, . . . I. x. 47. 4
did beguyle their eyes Of *kindly* sleepe . . . . II. ii. 46. 7
Them to betake unto their *kindly* rest: . . . . III. i. 58. 2
Depriv'd of *kindly* joy and naturall delight . . . . III. ix. 5. 9
a *kindly* pride Of gratious speach . . . . III. ix. 32. 6
Ne in their frosen hearts feele *kindly* flame; . . . . IV. Pr. 2. 2
Drives backe the current of his *kindly* course, ... IV. iii. 27. 4
gave place to *kindly* rest, ... IV. v. 43. 4
mother call to coole their *kindly* rages. . . . . IV. x. 45. 9
Towards all womenkind them *kindly* to behave. . . . . VI. ii. 14. 9
Would to no bed, nor take no *kindely* sleepe, ... VI. iii. 10. 2
his *kyndly* courtesie to prove, ... VI. iii. 15. 5
The cruell worker of your *kindly* smarts, ... *H.L.* 32
They . . . shew their *kindly* might. . . . . *H.L.* 91
whose soverayne grace and *kindly* dewty . . . . *H.B.* 17
mery London, my most *kyndly* Nurse, ... *Proth.* 128
Kindness. each one himselfe did payne All *kindnesse* . . . to shew, ... I. iv. 15. 4
Of *kindnesse* and of courteous aggrace; . . . . II. viii. 56. 8
as they two of *kindnes* treated long, ... III. viii. 15. 1
all his fained *kindnes* did detest, ... III. viii. 39. 4
rather then she *kindnesse* would despize, ... V. vi. 20. 5
That curt'sie with like *kindnesse* to repay, ... V. xi. 11. 5
For so great *kindnesse* as he found that day . . . . VI. ix. 18. 5
From that day forth he *kyndnesse* to her showed, ... VI. xi. 4. 6
Kindred. The base *kinred* of so simple swaine. . . . . *S.C.* May 271
knight . . . to that forrest came To seeke his *kindred,* . . . . I. vi. 20. 3
knowes no *kinred,* nor regardes no right, ... II. x. 35. 2
every one his *kindred* and his name. . . . . III. ix. 32. 5
The deare affection unto *kindred* sweet, ... IV. ix. 1. 5
Though of meane parentage and *kindred* base, ... VI. vii. 28. 4
Kinds. kydst the hidden *kinds* of many a wede, ... *S.C.* D. 92
monstrous beasts . . . Bred of two *kindes,* . . . . *Hub.* 1123
they brought forth other *kynds* . . . . *Col.* 853
Ten thousand *kindes* of creatures, partly male And partly femall, ... I. i. 21. 7
amiddes His magick bookes, and artes of sundrie *kindes,* . . I. i. 36. 8
With like conditions to their *kindes* applyde: . . . . I. iv. 18. 4
whose *kinds* mote not be redd: . . . . II. vii. 51. 5
shewes his powre in variable *kindes:* . . . . III. v. 1. 3
According to their *kynds.* . . . . III. vi. 30. 6
When all three *kinds* of love together meet . . . . IV. ix. 1. 2

Kinds—*Continued.*
she hath both *kinds* in one, ... IV. x. 41. 6
all their sundry *kinds,* and all their hid abodes. . . . . . . IV. xi. 10. 9
With many *kindes* of medicines meete, ... VI. vi. 2. 7
Of sundry *kindes* and sundry quality; . . . . VI. xii. 27. 2
According to their sundry *kinds* of features, ... VII. vii. 4. 3
therein reed The endlesse *kinds* of creatures . . . . *H.H.B.* 32
Kine. take his charge of *kyne?* . . . . *Hub.* 286
to his *kyne* for food assynd; . . . . V. x. 9. 8
The fayrest *kyne* alive, but of the fiercest kynd: . . . . . . V. x. 9. 9
King. *See* **Mock-king.**
Whilome had bene the *King* of the field, ... *S.C.* F. 108
Crowned as *king:* . . . . *S.C.* May 30
Sike a judge as Cuddie were for a *king.* . . . . *S.C.* Au. 52
sith the Saxon *king* Never was Woolfe seene, ... *S.C.* S. 151
flying vengeance sore Of *king* Nictileus . . . . *Gn.* 173
For whome the Thracian *king,* lamenting sore, ... *Gn.* 404
Who will not venture life a *King* to be, ... *Hub.* 979
the *King* did favour to them beare; . . . . *Hub.* 1076
In the mean-time upon the *King* t' attend. . . . . *Hub.* 1100
King indeed himselfe he shortly thought, ... *Hub.* 1105
therefore crav'd to come unto the *King,* . . . . *Hub.* 1211
Unto the *King* so rash ye may not goe; . . . . *Hub.* 1214
of the *King,* and of his government, ... *Hub.* 1273
Such one *King* Edmond, but was rent for gaine. . . . . *Ti.* 418
that great Towre, . . . *King* Ninus worke, ... *Ti.* 511
those huge castles of Castilian *King,* . . . . *Ded. Son.* vi. 7
The builder Oake, sole *king* of forrests all; . . . . I. i. 8. 8
the daughter of a *king,* Now a loose Leman . . . . I. i. 48. 5
the onely haire Of a most mighty *king,* . . . . I. ii. 23. 3
she . . . Though true as touch, though daughter of a *king,* . . I. iii. 2. 5
he was . . . Not meet to be of counsell to a *king,* . . . . . . I. iv. 23. 3
heavens *king* From hope of heaven hath thee excluded quight, I. v. 43. 1
There was that great proud *king* of Babylon, ... I. v. 47. 1
There also was *king* Croesus, ... I. v. 47. 6
th' onely daughter of a *King* and Queene, ... I. vii. 43. 3
That I was sonne and heire unto a *king,* . . . . I. ix. 5. 8
vowed all Their life to service of high heavens *King,* . . . . I. x. 36. 4
The Citty of the greate *king* hight it well, ... I. x. 55. 8
Twixt that great faery Queene and Paynim *king,* . . . . I. xi. 7. 4
that hoarie *king,* with all his traine, ... I. xii. 12. 2
That godly *King* and Queene did passionate, ... I. xii. 16. 2
that proud Paynim *king* that works her teene: . . . . I. xii. 18. 8
fast before the *king* he did alight; . . . . I. xii. 25. 5
most mighty *king* of Eden fayre, ... I. xii. 26. 1
'My Lord, my *king,* be nought hereat dismayd, ... I. xii. 31. 2
The *king* was greatly moved at her speach; . . . . I. xii. 35. 1
with *king* Oberon he came to Faery land. . . . . II. i. 6. 9
king Nine whilome built Babell towre. . . . . II. ix. 21. 6
The warres he well remembred of *king* Nine, ... II. ix. 56. 8
The *king* retourned proud of victory, ... II. x. 17. 1
His sonne, *king* Leill, ... II. x. 25. 1
Next him *king* Leyr in happie peace long raynd, ... II. x. 27. 1
wedded th' one to Maglan *king* of Scottes, ... II. x. 29. 1
wedded . . . thother to the *king* of Cambria, ... II. x. 29. 2
As for her Syre and *king* her seemed best; . . . . II. x. 31. 7
him streight did choose Their *king,* . . . . II. x. 37. 9
that of Cambry *king* confirmed late, ... II. x. 38. 5
the *king* was by a Treachetour Disguised slaine, ... II. x. 51. 3
Was never *king* more highly magnifide, ... II. x. 52. 1
This good *king* shortly without issew dide, ... II. x. 54. 1
With whome *king* Coyll made an agreement, ... II. x. 59. 3
What time *king* Ryence raign'd and dealed right, ... III. ii. 18. 5
gave unto *king* Ryence for his gard, ... III. ii. 21. 2
coosen unto *king* Ambrosius; . . . . III. iii. 13. 8
brother unto Cador, Cornish *king;* . . . . III. iii. 27. 2
a straunger *king,* from unknowne soyle Arriving, ... III. iii. 33. 3
Together with the *king* of Louthiane, ... III. iii. 37. 5
the *king* of Orkeny, ... III. iii. 37. 6
Against the good *king* Oswald, ... III. iii. 38. 4
Late *king,* now captive; late lord, now forlorne; . . . . III. iii. 42. 4
good *king* Uther now doth make Strong warre . . . . III. iii. 52. 5
King Ryence caused to be hanged hy . . . . III. iii. 59. 2
like a *king* he was to her exprest, ... III. viii. 40. 3
To sitt in second seat of soveraine *king* . . . . III. ix. 44. 4
that which that wise *King* of Jurie framed . . . . IV. x. 30. 6
a Scythian *king,* that Humber hight, ... IV. xi. 37. 8
thence Apollo, *King* of Leaches, brought. . . . . IV. xii. 25. 4
unto great *king* Neptune selfe did goe, ... IV. xii. 29. 4
tribute backe repay as to their *King:* . . . . VI. Pr. 7. 5
I am a Briton borne, Sonne of a *King,* . . . . VI. ii. 27. 7
Tristram . . . the onely heire Of good *king* Meliogras . . . . VI. ii. 28. 2
Sitting like *King* of fowles in majesty and powre: . . . . . . VI. x. 6. 9
Ran forth in haste unto the *king* of Gods to plaine. . . . . . VII. vi. 14. 9
to tell of heavens *King* . . . his fortunate successe; . . . . . VII. vii. 1. 5
King of all the rest, as ye doe clame, ... VII. vii. 53. 2
That warnes al lovers wayt upon their *king,* . . . . *Am.* xix. 3
Spring, the herald of loves mighty *king,* . . . . *Am.* lxx. 1
Made in the honor of your Soveraigne *king.* . . . . *H.L.* 42
My guide, my God, my victor, and my *king:* . . . . *H.L.* 305
Unto the God of Love, high heavens *king.* . . . . *H.H.L.* 7
Eternall *King* of Glorie, Lord of Might, ... *H.H.L.* 172
As *King* and Queene, the heavens Empire sway; . . . . *H.H.B.* 56
that faire love of mightie heavens *King;* . . . . *H.H.B.* 235
Kingcups. Cowslips, and *Kingcups,* and loved Lillies: . . . . *S.C.* Ap. 141
Kingdom. ever thinke a *Kingdome* is your part.' . . . . *Hub.* 1004
The title of the *Kingdome* to possesse. . . . . *Hub.* 1046
did he all the *kingdome* rob and pill, ... *Hub.* 1198
What time the Ape the *kingdome* first did gaine, ... *Hub.* 1207
troubled *kingdome* of wilde beasts behelde, ... *Hub.* 1231

Kingdom—*Continued.*
thy *kingdome* from thy head is rent, . . . *Hub.* 1329
Sith ignorance our *kingdome* did confound, . . . *T.M.* 311
thy *Kingdome* is defaced quight, . . . *T.M.* 399
sway The burdeine of this *kingdom* mightily, . . . *Ded. Son.* i. 10
forst me . . . to leave My fathers *kingdom*'— . . . I. i. 52. 2
rightfull *kingdome* she had none at all, . . . I. iv. 12. 3
six wisards . . . with their counsels bad, her *kingdome* did uphold. . . . I. iv. 12. 9
Their *kingdome* spoild, and countrey wasted quight: . . . I. vii. 44. 5
their forwasted *kingdom* to repayre: . . . I. xi. 1. 3
of my *kingdome* heyre apparaunt bee: . . . I. xii. 20. 6
Both daughter and eke *kingdome* lo! I yield to thee.' . . . I. xii. 20. 9
did earst restore To native crowne and *kingdom* . . . II. i. 2. 7
For thirst of single *kingdom* him he kild. . . . II. x. 21. 5
twixt the other twain his *kingdom* whole did shayre. . . . II. x. 28. 9
great trouble in the *kingdome* grew, . . . II. x. 54. 2
So settled he his *kingdome*, . . . II. x. 60. 9
him with her made of his *kingdome* heyre, . . . II. x. 61. 3
Vortiger have forst the *kingdome* to aband. . . . II. x. 65. 9
That never foes his *kingdome* might invade, . . . III. ii. 21. 3
shall him succeede In *kingdome*, . . . III. iii. 31. 2
With price of silver shall his *kingdome* buy; . . . III. iii. 39. 6
the *kingdom* he from them should beare. . . . III. iii. 45. 9
with Latinus did the *kingdom* part; . . . III. ix. 43. 2
a third *kingdom* yet is to arise . . . III. ix. 44. 6
Jove . . . leaving heavens *kingdome*, . . . III. xi. 30. 3
Subdeweth to his *kingdome* tyrannous. . . . III. xii. 22. 5
setst thy *kingdome* in the captive harts Of Kings . . . IV. vii. 1. 3
enjoyes The wide *kingdome* of love . . . IV. x. 42. 8
from all men so rich a *kingdome* hold! . . . IV. xi. 22. 2
joyne in neighbourhood of *kingdome* nere, . . . IV. xi. 40. 3
Where they may hope a *kingdome* to obtaine: . . . V. xii. 1. 7
An infant, weake a *kingdome* to sustaine, . . . VI. ii. 28. 7
Love hath the glory of his *kingdome* left, . . . VI. viii. 1. 2
His *kingdome* would continue but a while. . . . VI. viii. 23. 5
Whom though high Jove of *kingdome* did deprive, . . . VII. vi. 2. 8
to her selfe to have gained The *kingdome* of the Night, . . . VII. vi. 10. 9
Unlesse the *kingdome* of the sky yee make Immortall . . . VII. vii. 54. 2
spred thy lovely *kingdome* over-all. . . . *H.B.* 266
Kingdom's. reckned him the *kingdomes* corner stone. . . . *Hub.* 1166
founded for the *Kingdomes* ornament, . . . *Hub.* 1181
grow to height of *kingdomes* government, . . . *T.M.* 76
For their usurped *kingdomes* maintenaunce, . . . *T.M.* 338
The burdein of this *kingdomes* governement, . . . *Ded. Son.* ix. 4
Whose *kingdomes* seat Cleopolis is red; . . . I. vii. 46. 7
To be the compasse of his *kingdomes* seat: . . . III. ix. 46. 6
In which her *kingdomes* throne is chiefly resiant. . . . IV. xi. 28. 9
Unto the type of *kingdomes* title clymes! . . . V. ix. 42. 7
had to name The *Kingdomes* Care, . . . V. ix. 43. 8
Had bene the keye of all that *kingdomes* crowne; . . . V. x. 26. 4
to her *kingdomes* seat restore agayne: . . . V. xii. 25. 4
Whose *kingdomes* throne no thought of earthly wight Can comprehend, . . . *H.H.L.* 40
Kingdoms. those same mournfull *kingdomes*, . . . *Gn.* 442
left his whelps their *kingdomes* to devoure? . . . *Ti.* 70
That vainly threatned *kingdomes* to displace, . . . *Ded. Son.* vi. 8
That joyes for crownes and *kingdomes* to contend: . . . II. vii. 10. 7
crownes and *kingdomes* to thee multiply. . . . II. vii. 11. 5
'Ne thine be *kingdomes*, ne the scepters thine; . . . II. vii. 13. 1
In constant peace their *kingdomes* did contayne. . . . II. x. 34. 4
their decayed *kingdomes* shall amend: . . . III. iii. 23. 5
Towres, citties, *kingdomes*, ye would ruinate . . . III. viii. 28. 5
offred *kingdoms* unto her in vew, . . . III. viii. 40. 4
your *kingdomes* make In th' harts of men, . . . III. xi. 2. 6
mightie *kingdomes* of his force adred: . . . IV. viii. 47. 5
When those gainst states and *kingdomes* to conjure, . . . V. x. 26. 8
all their *kingdoms* sought. . . . VII. vi. 18. 9
To bandie Crownes, and *Kingdoms* to bestowe: . . . VII. vi. 32. 8
Kingdoms'. Of *kingdomes* change, of divers gouvernment, . . . *Hub.* 766
Welds *kingdomes* causes and affaires of state, . . . IV. Pr. 1. 2
Kingly. Then tooke the shepheards *Kingly* ornaments, . . . *Ro.* xviii. 5
The *kingly* Bird, that beares Joves thunder-clap, . . . *Van.* iv. 1
borne to be a *Kingly* soveraigne.' . . . *Hub.* 1032
all his gladfulnes, and *kingly* joyaunce. . . . *Mui.* 208
A goodly worke, full fit for *kingly* bowres; . . . *Mui.* 300
The *kingly* beast upon her gazing stood: . . . I. iii. 8. 4
her fiers servant, full of *kingly* aw And high disdaine, . . . I. iii. 41. 1
Begotten by her *kingly* Paramoure, . . . II. x. 19. 2
all that seemed fitt for *kingly* seed: . . . II. x. 27. 4
The club of Justice dread with *kingly* powre endewed. . . . V. i. 2. 9
in his *kingly* pride Soring through his wide Empire . . . V. iv. 42. 1
the might Of him that did the *kingly* Scepter beare, . . . VI. ii. 29. 4
King's. in the *Kings* name bad them both to stay, . . . *Hub.* 1071
Kings. Should warre upon the *kings*, and eate their flesh. . . . *Rev.* iii. 10
Then did I see the beast and *Kings* also . . . *Rev.* iii. 11
An hundred vanquisht *Kings* . . . *Bel.* xv. 9
Kings of Beasts, and Lords of forests all . . . *Hub.* 971
The care of *Kings* and power of Empires stand, . . . *Hub.* 1226
the care of Kesars and of *Kings*. . . . *T.M.* 570
Royall lynage . . . Of ancient *Kinges* and Queenes, . . . I. i. 5. 4
thou springst from ancient race Of Saxon *kinges*, . . . I. x. 65. 2
The antique shapes of *kings* and kesars straunge and rare. . II. vii. 5. 9
Do not I *kings* create, . . . II. vii. 11. 6
So mak'st thou *kings*, and gaynest wrongfull government. . . II. vii. 13. 9
A chronicle of Briton *kings*, . . . II. x. Arg.
mighty *kings* and conquerours in warre, . . . II. x. 4. 5
Brennus and Belinus, *kinges* of Britany. . . . II. x. 40. 9
oft the Briton *kings* against them strongly swayd. . . . II. x. 49. 9
puissant *kinges* which all the world warrayd, . . . II. x. 72. 2

Kings—*Continued.*
brave ensample, . . . to *kinges* and states imperiall. . . . II. x. 74. 9
'Renowmed *kings*, and sacred Emperours, . . . III. iii. 23. 1
call Their sondry *kings* to do their homage severall. . . . III. iii. 32. 9
Saxon *kinges* his friendship shall intreat; . . . III. iii. 45. 3
The wealth of th' East, and pompe of Persian *kings*: . . . III. iv. 23. 4
mighty *kings* and kesars into thraldome brought. . . . III. xi. 29. 9
Kings, Queenes, Lords, Ladies, . . . III. xi. 46. 1
Kings and Keasars to thy service bound; . . . IV. vii. 1. 4
He maketh *Kings* to sit in soverainty; . . . V. ii. 41. 5
Of th' old Aegyptian *Kings* that whylome were, . . . V. vii. 2. 6
the which ye wont t' embrew In bloud of *Kings*, . . . V. vii. 40. 5
the heyre of ancient *kings* And mightie Conquerors, . . . V. ix. 29. 7
Whylest *kings* and kesars at her feet did them prostrate. . . V. ix. 29. 9
Unto the pallace where their *kings* did rayne, . . . V. xii. 25. 2
This is the state of Keasars and of *Kings*! . . . VI. iii. 5. 7
With such queint usage, fit for Queenes and *Kings*, . . . VI. ix. 35. 2
Ne Kesars spared he a whit, nor *Kings*; . . . VI. xii. 28. 7
Ye may attribute to your selves as *Kings*, . . . VII. vii. 49. 3
Kinmark. Lago, and *Kinmarke* did rayne, . . . II. x. 34. 5
Kinred. *See* **Kindred.**
Kinsman. childe ne *kinsman* living had he none . . . I. iv. 28. 6
Kirk. the postes to dight, And all the *Kirke* pillours . . . *S.C.* May 12
to say to morrowe At the *Kerke*, . . . *S.C.* May 310
To *Kerke* the narre, from God more farre, . . . *S.C.* Jul. 97
Kirkrapine. finding *Kirkrapine* there slayne, . . . I. iii. 22. 3
Kirtle. in a *Kirtle* of greene saye, . . . *S.C.* Au. 67
All in a *kirtle* of discolourd say He clothed was, . . . I. iv. 31. 1
Kiss. to *kisse* their christall faces, . . . *S.C.* Jun. 30
Seeking to *kisse* her, brok'st the Gods decree, . . . *Gn.* 471
kisse thy lips like faded leaves of rose. . . . *As.* 138
as halfe blushing offred him to *kis*, . . . I. i. 49. 7
With bloudy mouth his mother earth did *kis*, . . . I. ii. 19. 6
They, . . . Doe *kisse* her feete, . . . I. vi. 12. 9
prostrated fall, And *kisse* my stirrup; . . . II. iii. 8. 6
Her alablaster brest she soft did *kis*, . . . III. ii. 42. 7
I *kisse* thy blessed feete.' . . . III. v. 35. 9
I saw him *kisse*; I saw him her embrace; . . . IV. i. 49. 2
With many a joyfull *kisse* and many a melting teare. . . . VI. xii. 20. 9
Comming to *kisse* her lyps, . . . *Am.* lxiv. 1
Bathing thy wings in her ambrosiall *kisse*, . . . *H.L.* 25
Kissed. not with *kissed* hand belowe the knee, . . . *Hub.* 730
Her up he tooke, . . . And oft her *kist*. . . . I. ii. 45. 8
In stead thereof he *kist* her wearie feet, . . . I. iii. 6. 1
bowing downe her aged backe, she *kist* The wicked witch, . . I. v. 27. 1
Una . . . Him dearely *kist*, . . . I. x. 29. 4
kist the ground whereon his foot was pight; . . . I. xii. 25. 7
with his frory lips full softly *kist*, . . . III. viii. 35. 2
Instead of strokes, each other *kissed* glad, . . . IV. iii. 49. 3
how the ground he *kist* Wherein it written was, . . . IV. vii. 46. 8
kist the ground on which her sole did tread, . . . IV. viii. 13. 2
A thousand times embrast, and *kist* a thousand more. . . . VI. xi. 45. 9
Kisses. with sweet *kisses* suckt the wasting breath . . . *As.* 165
Some bathed *kisses*, . . . II. v. 33. 5
with *kisses* light For feare of waking him, . . . II. xii. 73. 5
with ambrosiall *kisses* bathe his eyes; . . . III. i. 36. 4
with *kisses* deare Shee ofte did bathe, . . . III. ii. 34. 6
She promist *kisses* sweet, and sweeter things, . . . III. vi. 12. 8
Deawd with ambrosiall *kisses*, . . . IV. Pr. 5. 6
Kisseth. Her dearely doth imbrace, and *kisseth* manifold. . . . I. xii. 12. 9
Kissing. *kissing* them atweene, . . . IV. vii. 35. 6
kissing oft his visage pale and wan: . . . IV. ix. 9. 5
Came to her . . . *Kissing* his hands, . . . VI. iv. 11. 5
Kitchen-clerk. The *kitchin clerke*, that hight Digestion, . . II. ix. 31. 3
Kitchen-room. ledd her guestes anone Into the *kitchin rowme*, II. ix. 28. 9
Kite. be entombed in the raven or the *kight*?' . . . II. viii. 16. 9
The foolish *Kyte*, led with licentious will, . . . V. v. 15. 5
He flew upon him like a greedy *kight* . . . VI. viii. 28. 4
Knack. he could shewe many a fine *knack*: . . . *S.C.* May 286
Knavery. coosinage and cleanly *knaverie*, . . . *Hub.* 857
In cunning sleightes and practick *knavery*. . . . II. iii. 9. 6
At the remembrance of their *knaverie*: . . . V. iii. 39. 5
Knaves. They han fatte kernes, and leany *knaves*, . . . *S.C.* Jul. 199
Knee. Shee set her youngling before her *knee*, . . . *S.C.* May 182
not with kissed hand belowe the *knee*, . . . *Hub.* 730
they, on humble *knee* Making obeysaunce, . . . I. iv. 13. 6
he . . . forced him to stoupe upon his *knee*: . . . I. v. 12. 8
falling her before on lowly *knee*, . . . I. v. 16. 2
But misseth . . . buskins to her *knee*. . . . I. vi. 16. 9
smote off quite his right leg by the *knee*, . . . I. viii. 22. 4
himselfe inclyning on his *knee* . . . II. ii. 3. 1
they fastned were under her *knee* . . . II. iii. 27. 6
He made him stoup perforce unto his *knee*, . . . II. v. 11. 6
Did to that image bowe their humble *knee*, . . . III. xi. 49. 4
At last fell humbly downe upon his *knee*, . . . IV. vi. 22. 2
on her *knee* before him falling lowe, . . . IV. xii. 29. 5
friskt, and flong aloft, and louted low on *knee*. . . . V. iii. 34. 9
her bowd Upon her *knee*, intreating him for grace, . . . VI. vi. 31. 6
smote him on the *knee* that never yet was bent. . . . VI. viii. 15. 9
Whom greatest Princes sought on lowest *knee*. . . . *H.H.L.* 231
Kneel. Fell straight about their neckes as they did *kneele*, . . V. x. 20. 2
There him he causd to *kneele*, . . . VI. ii. 35. 1
Kneeling. *kneeling* at his feete submissively: . . . V. ii. 26. 5
Knees. flocke . . . Whose *knees* are weake through fast . . . *S.C.* Ja. 44
Their backward bent *knees* teach her humbly to obay. . . I. vi. 11. 9
stubs of trees . . . Did hang upon the ragged rocky *knees*; . I. ix. 34. 3
With folded hands, and *knees* full lowly bent, . . . I. xi. 32. 6
Knells. th' ayre be filled with noyse of dolefull *knells*, . . . *D.* 335
Knew. Whereby by chaunce I him *knewe*. . . . *S.C.* Mar. 36
her Kidde shee *knewe* well was gone: . . . *S.C.* May 300

Knew—*Continued.*
(his name I *knewe*) . . . *S.C.* Jul. 161
Never *knew* I lovers sheepe in good plight: . . . *S.C.* Au. 20
knewe we, fooles, what it us bringes until, . . . *S.C.* N. 185
If Hell at least . . . *Knew* how to pardon, . . . *Gn.* 476
As whome he *knew* to him both fast and true. . . . *Hub.* 1081
of all wisedome *knew* the perfect somme? . . . *Ti.* 60
yet since no' untruth he *knew,* . . . I. i. 53. 6
The false Duessa, . . . *knew* well all was true. . . . I. ii. 44. 3
As all unweeting of that well she *knew;* . . . I. ii. 45. 2
Saying, that harlott she too lately *knew,* . . . I. iii. 25. 3
the old man well *knew* he, though untold, . . . I. iii. 38. 7
In living Princes court none ever *knew* Such endlesse richesse, I. iv. 7. 4
in that court whylome her well they *knew:* . . . I. iv. 15. 5
such an one . . . *knew* not whether right he went, . . . I. iv. 19. 9
from his frend he seeldome *knew* his fo. . . . I. iv. 23. 5
Whose like in womens witt he never *knew;* . . . I. vi. 31. 2
Una gan to aske, if ought he *knew,* . . . I. vi. 36. 4
he *knew* Some secret sorrow did her heart distraine; . . . I. vii. 38. 3
him to be yet weake and wearie well she *knew.* . . . I. ix. 20. 9
when he *knew,* and felt our feeble harts Embost with bale, . I. ix. 29. 1
knew his good to all of each degree, . . . I. x. 7. 5
Whom well she *knew* to spring from hevenly race, . . . I. x. 8. 7
streight way he *knew* His errour; . . . II. i. 28. 1
me he *knew* not, nether his owne ill; . . . II. i. 54. 5
when I other *knew,* my self I boldly reard. . . . II. iii. 45. 9
The quivering steele his aymed end wel *knew,* . . . II. iv. 46. 3
Him Atin spying *knew* right well of yore, . . . II. vi. 48. 1
Furious ever I thee *knew* to bee, . . . II. vi. 49. 3
his griefe He *knew* right well, . . . II. vi. 51. 2
Well *knew* they both his person, . . . II. viii. 11. 8
Well *knew* The Prince, . . . II. viii. 47. 6
yf the beauty of her mind ye *knew,* . . . II. ix. 3. 5
knew them how to order without blame, . . . II. ix. 28. 5
Then did he raigne alone, when he none equall *knew.* . . . II. x. 33. 9
as well that art she *knew,* . . . III. i. 35. 2
Yet him in everie part before she *knew,* . . . III. ii. 17. 1
he it *knew* at home before he hard Tydings thereof, . . . III. ii. 21. 4
shee *knew* there staied still Some litle life . . . III. iv. 41. 7
they *knew* that Squyre unknowne Mote algates passe: . . . III. v. 17. 5
uncouth formes, which none yet ever *knew:* . . . III. vi. 35. 2
she *knew,* she said, I would disclose Her counsell, . . . III. vii. 58. 8
all the wyles of wemens wits *knew* passing well. . . . III. viii. 8. 9
he, that never good nor maners *knew,* . . . III. viii. 26. 1
Into the utmost Angle of the world he *knew.* . . . III. ix. 47. 9
Trompart, that his maistres humor *knew* . . . III. x. 30. 1
foolish garde, that litle *knew* Of such deceipt, . . . III. xi. 31. 5
horse and foote *knew* Diamond to wield: . . . IV. ii. 42. 6
Seeking adventures where they anie *knew.* . . . IV. ii. 46. 5
Yet he him *knew* not, ne aviz'd at all, . . . IV. vii. 43. 6
She *knew* him not, but pittied much his case, . . . IV. viii. 12. 8
unto every person *knew* her part; . . . IV. x. 51. 4
that use well *knew* To fight in water, . . . V. ii. 13. 5
never there the like resort they *knew.* . . . V. ii. 29. 7
Whom soone as he beheld he *knew,* . . . V. iv. 25. 9
Dismayd so with the stroke that he no colours *knew.* . . . V. iv. 39. 9
brave Knights, whose names right well he *knew,* . . . V. v. 22. 2
Whose life and manners straunge she never *knew;* . . . V. vi. 12. 7
she *knew* not his favours likelynesse, . . . V. vii. 39. 7
as well he *knew:* . . . V. viii. 38. 6
snatching her soone up, ere well she *knew,* . . . V. ix. 14. 4
he *knew* anone That it was he . . . V. xi. 37. 5
They *knew* them selves, and both their persons rad; . . . VI. i. 4. 7
I, that *knew* my selfe from perill free, . . . VI. i. 9. 7
his own thought he *knew* most cleare from wite: . . . VI. iii. 16. 6
man, that . . . neither gentlesse *knew,* . . . VI. iv. 3. 2
Ne *knew* the use of warlike instruments, . . . VI. iv. 4. 2
him well he *knew* To be his Timias, . . . VI. v. 23. 1
He *knew* the diverse went of mortall wayes, . . . VI. vi. 3. 5
As he the art of words *knew* wondrous well, . . . VI. vi. 6. 3
well she *knew* the wayes to win good will . . . VI. vi. 41. 6
Of whom what was becomen no man *knew.* . . . VI. vii. 34. 3
cleane were gone, which way he never *knew;* . . . VI. x. 18. 3
sith he well *knew* The readie way . . . VI. xi. 35. 1
Right well *knew* Coridon his owne late sheepe, . . . VI. xi. 37. 6
For Bellamour *knew* Calidore right well, . . . VI. xii. 11. 2
gan to question streight, how she it *knew?* . . . VI. xii. 18. 2
nothing *knew* Of all that chaunced heere, . . . VII. vi. 14. 1
As if they *knew* the meaning of their layes. . . . *Am.* xix. 8

Knewest. 'Daphne thou *knewest,* quoth he, . . . *D.* 183
(Lobbin well thou *knewest,*) . . . *Col.* 736

Knife. Ne runs in perill of foes cruell *knife,* . . . *Gn.* 125
him that slew Sansfoy with bloody *knife:* . . . I. iii. 36. 4
Bitter despight, with rancours rusty *knife,* . . . I. iv. 35. 4
Her wicked daies with wretched *knife* did end, . . . I. v. 39. 2
The Redcrosse knight was slain with Paynim *knife.'* . . . I. vi. 38. 9
To me he lent this rope, to him a rusty *knife.* . . . I. ix. 29. 9
In which a rusty *knife* fast fixed stood, . . . I. ix. 36. 8
Out of his hand she snatcht the cursed *knife,* . . . I. ix. 52. 4
did stick A cruell *knife* . . . II. i. 39. 6
threats his rusty *knife.* . . . II. iv. 44. 5
yeilded passage to his cruell *knife.* . . . II. v. 9. 4
The other brandished a bloody *knife;* . . . II. vii. 21. 8
after all his warre to rest his wearie *knife.* . . . III. iv. 24. 9
Entrenched deep with *knyfe* accursed keene, . . . III. xii. 20. 6
A murdrous *knife* out of his pocket drew, . . . III. xii. 32. 5
Through cruell *knife* that her deare heart did kerve: . . . IV. i. 4. 5
Die had she lever with Enchanters *knife* . . . IV. i. 6. 8
With cursed *knife* cutting the twist in twaine. . . . IV. ii. 48. 8
when ye shred with fatall *knife* His line, . . . IV. ii. 52. 3

Knife—*Continued.*
With *knife* in hand, . . . V. viii. 46. 3
with *knife* in hand She threw . . . V. viii. 47. 1
with bloudie *knyfe* Yet dropping . . . V. ix. 48. 2
new launcht with murdrous *knife,* . . . VI. v. 5. 4
murdrous *knife* well whet, . . . VI. viii. 45. 5
Eftsoones he saw one with a naked *knife* . . . VI. viii. 48. 8

Knife-hook. for harvests toyle, He held a *knife-hook;* . . . VII. vii. 38. 6

Knight. *See* **Mock-knight.**
A *Knight* all arm'd, upon a winged steed; . . . *Ti.* 646
Full mortally this *Knight* ywounded was, . . . *Ti.* 650
At that good *knight* so cunningly didst rove, . . . I. Pr. 3. 3
A gentle *Knight* was pricking on the plaine, . . . I. i. 1. 1
Full jolly *knight* he seemd, . . . I. i. 1. 8
Whom to avenge she had this *Knight* from far compeld. . . . I. i. 5. 9
your stroke, Sir *Knight,* with-hold, . . . I. i. 12. 6
The youthfull *Knight* could not . . . be staide; . . . I. i. 14. 2
Sir *knight,* shew what ye bee; . . . I. i. 19. 2
same so sore annoyed has the *knight,* . . . I. i. 22. 1
'Faire *knight,* borne under happie starre, . . . I .i. 27. 3
He faire the *knight* saluted, louting low, . . . I. i. 30. 1
'Right well, Sir *knight,* ye have advised bin.' . . . I. i. 33. 4
The *knight* was well content; . . . I. i. 33. 8
Unto that Elfin *knight* he bad him fly, . . . I. i. 46. 2
comming where the *knight* in slomber lay, . . . I. i. 47. 2
like that virgin true which for her *knight* him took. . . . I. i. 49. 9
words made that redoubted *knight* Suspect her truth: . . . I. i. 53. 5
Enchaunter parts The Redcrosse *Knight* from Truth: . . . I. ii. Arg.
The royall virgin . . . Lookt for her *knight,* . . . I. ii. 7. 7
seemde best the person to put on Of that good *knight,* . . . I. ii. 11. 2
Full jolly *knight* he seemde, and wel addrest; . . . I. ii. 11. 7
the *knight* whose semblaunt he did beare, . . . I. ii. 12. 1
she saw the *knight* his speare advaunce, . . . I. ii. 14. 3
She . . . bad her *knight* addresse him to the fray, . . . I. ii. 14. 5
The *knight* of the Redcrosse, . . . Gan fairely couch his speare, I. ii. 15. 1
this good *knight,* . . . him thither hastly got: . . . I. ii. 29. 1
'Say on, Fradubio, . . . Quoth then the *Knight;* . . . I. ii. 34. 2
Me chaunced of a *knight* encountred bee, . . . I. ii. 35. 7
'But how long time,' said then the Elfin *knight,* . . . I. ii. 43. 1
the good *knight,* . . . The bleeding bough did thrust . . . I. ii. 44. 3
she . . . Is from her *knight* divorced in despayre, . . . I. iii. 2. 8
In wildernesse . . . strayd, To seeke her *knight;* . . . I. iii. 3. 5
the late losse of her deare loved *knight,* . . . I. iii. 15. 6
By which she thought her wandring *knight* shold pas, . . . I. iii. 10. 2
pas, In waies unknowne, her wandring *knight* to seeke, . . I. iii. 21. 4
A *knight* her mett in mighty armes embost, . . . I. iii. 24. 4
knight was not for all his bragging bost; . . . I. iii. 24. 5
her *knight* by name She weend it was, . . . I. iii. 26. 6
a felon strong To many *knights* did daily worke disgrace; I. iii. 29. 4
knight he now shall never more deface: . . . I. iii. 29. 5
Before her stands her *knight,* for whom she toyld so sore . I. iii. 30. 9
Such joy made Una, when her *knight* she found; . . . I. iii. 32. 1
he . . . saw the Red-crosse which the *knight* did beare, . . I. iii. 34. 2
he is one the truest *knight* alive, . . . I. iii. 37. 6
so misfeigning her true *knight* to bee: . . . I. iii. 40. 4
Duessa Guydes the faithfull *knight;* . . . I. iv. Arg.
Young *knight* whatever, that dost armes professe, . . . I. iv. 1. 1
unto *knight* there is no greater shame . . . I. iv. 1. 7
Soone as the Elfin *knight* in presence came, . . . I. iv. 13. 1
Goodly they all that *knight* doe entertayne, . . . I. iv. 15. 1
That to strange *knight* no better countenance allowd. . . . I. iv. 15. 9
that good *knight* would not so nigh repaire, . . . I. iv. 37. 7
an errant *knight* in armes ycled, . . . I. iv. 38. 4
th' Elfin *knight,* . . . Disdaind to loose the meed . . . I. iv. 39. 7
to see this recreaunt *knight,* No *knight,* but treachour . . I. iv. 41. 4, 5
The prowest *knight* that ever field did fight, . . . I. iv. 41. 7
Him litle answerd th' angry Elfin *knight;* . . . I. iv. 42. 8
The faithfull *knight* . . . Subdewes his faithlesse foe; . . . I. v. Arg.
torment The flaming corage of that Faery *knight,* . . . I. v. 1. 6
To weet what end to straunger *knights* may fall. . . . I. v. 3. 3
The *knight* was fiers, and full of youthly heat, . . . I. v. 7. 4
prowest *knight,* That ever Ladie to her love did chose, . . . I. v. 14. 2
marcheth home, and by her takes the *knight,* . . . I. v. 16. 6
the place where th' Hethen *knight* . . . Lay . . . I. v. 19. 4
To Aesculapius brought the wounded *knight:* . . . I. v. 41. 3
she found the Faery *knight* Departed thence; . . . I. v. 45. 3
The dreadlesse corage of this Elfin *knight,* . . . I. vi. 1. 8
a noble warlike *knight* . . . to that forrest came . . . I. vi. 20. 1
she, all vowd unto the Redcrosse *Knight,* . . . I. vi. 32. 1
tidings of her *knight* of the Redcrosse; . . . I. vi. 34. 6
The *knight,* approching nigh, of him inquerd . . . I. vi. 36. 1
These eies did see that *knight* . . . I. vi. 36. 9
The *knight* her lightly reared up againe, . . . I. vi. 37. 5
The Redcrosse *knight* was slain with Paynim knife.' . . . I. vi. 38. 9
he the stoutest *knight* that ever wonne?' . . . I. vi. 39. 2
Therewith the *knight* thence marched forth in hast, . . . I. vi. 40. 1
That good *knight* of the Redcrosse to have slain: . . . I. vi. 41. 4
That Redcrosse *knight,* perdie, I never slew; . . . I. vi. 42. 6
The Redcrosse *knight* is captive made . . . I. vii. Arg.
Where she had left the noble Redcrosse *knight,* . . . I. vii. 2. 3
Hereof this gentle *knight* unweeting was; . . . I. vii. 6. 1
when the *knight* he spyde, he gan advaunce . . . I. vii. 11. 1
So daunted when the Geaunt saw the *knight,* . . . I. vii. 14. 1
valiant *knight* become a caytive thrall, . . . I. vii. 19. 3
she did love the *knight* of the Redcrosse, . . . I. vii. 27. 8
A goodly *knight,* faire marching by the way, . . . I. vii. 29. 2
Whenas this *knight* nigh to the Lady drew, . . . I. vii. 38. 1
'Ah Lady deare,' quoth then the gentle *knight,* . . . I. vii. 40. 1
There to obtaine some such redoubted *knight,* . . . I. vii. 46. 8
There for to find a fresh unproved *knight;* . . . I. vii. 47. 2

Knight—*Continued.*
Ne was there *Knight* ne was there Lady . . . . VI. i. 3. 1
'Haile, noblest *Knight* Of all . . . . VI. i. 4. 8
may no *Knight* nor Lady passe along That way, ... VI. i. 13. 5
She long time hath deare lov'd a doughty *Knight*, ... VI. i. 14. 8
'False traytor *Knight!*' . . . 'no *Knight* at all, ... VI. i. 25. 1
some better *Knight* Then thou, ... VI. i. 25. 6
Much was the *Knight* abashed at that word . . . . . . VI. i. 26. 1
Vouchsafe to reskue her against a *Knight*, ... VI. i. 29. 6
The comming of that so much threatned *Knight;* . . . . VI. i. 30. 3
The Dwarfe, which bore that message to her *knight*, ... VI. i. 31. 3
a *Knight* He spide come pricking on . . . . VI. i. 32. 8
nothing is more blamefull to a *knight*, ... VI. i. 41. 1
slay A proud discourteous *knight:* . . . . VI. ii. Arg.
What vertue is so fitting for a *knight*, ... VI. ii. 1. 1
a Ladie whom a *knight* should love, ... VI. ii. 1. 2
Fighting on foot, . . . Against an armed *knight* . . . . . VI. ii. 3. 9
that youth had kild That armed *knight*, ... VI. ii. 4. 7
thy hand too bold it selfe embrewed In blood of *knight* . . . VI. ii. 7. 4
the which by thee is slaine, By thee no *knight;* . . . . . VI. ii. 7. 5
great blame' . . . For armed *knight* a wight unarm'd to wrong: VI. ii. 8. 7
I chaunst to meete this *knight*, who there lyes slaine, ... VI. ii. 9. 8
'The *knight*, . . . on horsebacke was, ... VI. ii. 10. 1
th' unrighteous ire Of her owne *knight* . . . . VI. ii. 13. 9
Against both which that *knight* wrought knightlesse shame; . VI. ii. 14. 7
'Certes, Sir *Knight*' (sayd she) 'full loth I were . . . . . VI. ii. 15. 6
a Ladie gent Sate with a *knight* . . . . VI. ii. 16. 5
'Whom when my *knight* did see so lovely faire, ... VI. ii. 17. 1
with presumpteous powre against that *knight* streight go'th. . VI. ii. 17. 9
'Unarm'd all was the *knight*, ... VI. ii. 18. 1
He him requested, as he was a *knight*, ... VI. ii. 19. 3
My *knight* hers . . . to daunger drove, ... VI. ii. 20. 5
'May be, Sir *knight*, . . . Harme may arise . . . . VI. ii. 27. 2
fortune hath . . . Given to me the spoile of this dead *knight*, . VI. ii. 33. 8
Faith to his *knight*, and truth to Ladies all, ... VI. ii. 35. 2
In hope he sure would prove a doughtie *knight:* . . . . . VI. ii. 36. 8
Tristram, then despoyling that dead *knight* . . . . VI. ii. 39. 1
Upon the steed of her owne late dead *knight;* . . . . . . VI. ii. 39. 8
This *knight*, whom Tristram slew, ... VI. ii. 40. 5
This knight, . . . had wounded sore Another *knight* . . . . VI. ii. 40. 6
There he that *knight* found lying on the flore . . . . . . VI. ii. 40. 7
what cruell hand hath thus arayd This *knight* unarm'd . . . . VI. ii. 42. 4
that discourteous *knight*, (Whom Tristram slew) . . . . . . VI. ii. 43. 1
he, that hath your *Knight* so ill bestad, ... VI. ii. 45. 5
Which to your selfe he wrought and to your loved *knight*. . . VI. ii. 45. 9
In which a worthy auncient *Knight* did wonne: . . . . VI. ii. 48. 8
that courteous deed Done to that wounded *Knight* . . . . . VI. iii. 2. 5
the *Knight*, the which that Castle ought, ... VI. iii. 2. 8
And was the Father of that wounded *Knight*, ... VI. iii. 3. 7
By a faire Lady and a straunger *Knight*, ... VI. iii. 4. 3
did that good old *Knight* Temper his griefe, ... VI. iii. 6. 1
But lov'd this fresh young *Knight* who dwelt her ny, ... VI. iii. 7. 5
that proud *Knight* in his presumption . . . . VI. iii. 8. 3
that old *Knight* by all meanes did assay . . . . VI. iii. 9. 4
A courteous *Knight* and full of faithfull trust; . . . . . . VI. iii. 13. 2
him seemed fit that wounded *Knight* To visite, ... VI. iii. 14. 1
to the carkasse of that *Knight* he went, ... VI. iii. 17. 1
a discourteous *Knight*, who had her reft . . . . VI. iii. 18. 6
to come whereas a jolly *Knight* . . . did safely rest, ... VI. iii. 20. 2
knowing that her *Knight* now neare did draw, ... VI. iii. 26. 3
he nigh espyde An armed *Knight* approaching . . . . . . VI. iii. 30. 7
thou peasant *Knight* mightst rightly reed . . . . VI. iii. 31. 7
inly wroth Against her *Knight*, ... VI. iii. 33. 2
fowle discourtesie, unfit for *Knight*, ... VI. iii. 33. 6
that same discourteous *Knight* . . . laught, and mockt . . . VI. iii. 34. 1
'Unknightly *Knight*, the blemish of that name, ... VI. iii. 35. 1
And be for ever held a recreant *Knight*, ... VI. iii. 35. 6
Nathelesse the *Knight*, now in so needy case, ... VI. iii. 38. 4
no place Of lodging fit for any errant *Knight*, ... VI. iii. 38. 8
stearne In all assaies to every errant *Knight*, ... VI. iii. 40. 4
an errant *Knight*, That house-rome craves; . . . . VI. iii. 41. 2
Declar'd the message which that *Knight* did move; . . . . VI. iii. 42. 2
an armed *Knight*, . . . Pursuing him . . . . VI. iii. 46. 6
To spare her *Knight*, and rest with reason pacifyde: . . . . VI. iii. 49. 9
Such was the state of this most courteous *knight* . . . . . VI. iv. 1. 6
And shrieked out, a thing uncomely for a *knight*. . . . . . VI. iv. 8. 9
There he that *knight* full sorely bleeding found, ... VI. iv. 9. 6
By reason that her *knight* was wounded sore: . . . . . . VI. iv. 10. 6
comming likewise to the wounded *knight*, ... VI. iv. 12. 1
the bold *knight* no whit thereat dismayd, ... VI. iv. 21. 1
That it became a famous *knight* well knowne, ... VI. iv. 38. 8
a *knight*, together with his squire, ... VI. v. 11. 2
Eftsoones he spide a *Knight* approching nye; . . . . . . VI. v. 22. 1
cryde Unto the *Knight*, them to dispart in twaine; . . . . . VI. v. 27. 2
trayterously did wound her weary *Knight*. . . . . VI. v. 33. 9
avenge th' abuses of that proud And shamefull *Knight* . . . VI. v. 34. 4
he had bene a doughty *Knight*, ... VI. vi. 4. 1
Ne ever *Knight* that bore so lofty creast, ... VI. vi. 12. 7
Pursuing that proud *Knight*, ... VI. vi. 17. 6
he was an errant *Knight*, ... VI. vi. 20. 6
that same *Knight* and Salvage standing by, ... VI. vi. 23. 2
that same *Knight* And salvage . . . . VI. vi. 24. 6
that craven cowherd *Knight* Was at his backe . . . . . . VI. vi. 26. 6
So likewise turnde the Prince upon the *Knight*, ... VI. vi. 27. 8
Atwene that Lady myld and recreant *knight*, ... VI. vi. 37. 2
where that Dame remayned With her unworthy *knight*, . . . VI. vi. 39. 9
That well appears in this discourteous *knight*, ... VI. vii. 2. 1
a straunge *knight*, that neare afore him went, ... VI. vii. 4. 4
Bidding him turne againe, false traytour *knight*, ... VI. vii. 7. 2
'There is a straunger *knight*, ... VI. vii. 12. 6

Knight—*Continued.*
'How now, Sir *knight*, What meaneth this . . . . VI. vii. 14. 6
That recreant *knight*, whose hated life I sought? . . . . . VI. vii. 16. 4
Slayne of that errant *knight* with whom he fought; . . . . VI. vii. 16. 7
Like as that other *knight* to him had sayd; . . . . VI. vii. 20. 3
much griev'd against that straunger *knight*, ... VI. vii. 20. 6
that same *knight* would not once let him start, ... VI. vii. 21. 1
the gentle *knight* Would not be tempted . . . . VI. vii. 23. 1
The traytour Turpin with that other *knight*, ... VI. vii. 25. 2
kindle lovely fire In th' harts of many a *knight*, ... VI. vii. 28. 9
noblest she that served is of noblest *knight*. . . . . . . VI. vii. 29. 9
By Arthure, when as Unas *Knight* he did maintaine. . . . . VI. vii. 41. 9
(That was that courteous *Knight*, ... VI. viii. 4. 4
'See you, Sir *Knight*, The greatest shame . . . . VI. viii. 6. 1
Ne list the *Knight* the powre thereof assay, ... VI. viii. 8. 7
So did these two this *Knight* oft tug and teare. . . . . . VI. viii. 12. 5
'Stay, stay, Sir *Knight!* for love of God abstaine . . . . . VI. viii. 17. 5
I was belov'd of many a gentle *Knight*, ... VI. viii. 20. 5
That huge great foole oppressing th' other *Knight*, ... VI. viii. 28. 2
'Ah! nay, Sir *Knight*,' (said she) 'it may not be, ... VI. viii. 30. 1
The good Sir Calepine, her owne true *Knight*, ... VI. viii. 33. 2
The *knight* was nothing nice, where was no need, ... VI. ix. 7. 1
The *knight* full gladly soone agreed thereto, ... VI. ix. 16. 8
The gentle *knight*, as he that did excell In courtesie . . . . VI. ix. 18. 3
the *knight* . . . Hong still upon his melting mouth attent; . . VI. ix. 26. 1
'Sir *knight*, your bounteous proffer Be farre fro me, ... VI. ix. 33. 3
Thus did the gentle *knight* himselfe abeare . . . . VI. ix. 45. 1
Unto this place when as the Elfin *Knight* Approcht, ... VI. x. 10. 1
Thus did the courteous *Knight* excuse his blame, ... VI. x. 29. 8
With which the *Knight* him selfe did much content, ... VI. x. 30. 3
was the conquest of the gentlest *Knight* . . . . VI. x. 40. 8
Whereat the *knight* amaz'd yet did not rest, ... VI. xi. 28. 7
the bold *knight* Encountring him with small resistence slew, . VI. xi. 43. 5
delayd This gentle *knight* . . . . VI. xii. 2. 2
A lustie *knight* as ever wielded speare, ... VI. xii. 3. 6
The Elfin *Knight* . . . into a Monastere did light, ... VI. xii. 23. 6
the more the *Knight* Did him suppresse, ... VI. xii. 31. 5
For never more defaming gentle *Knight*, ... VI. xii. 34. 6
So led this *Knight* his captyve with like conquest wonne. . . VI. xii. 35. 9
much admyr'd the Beast, but more admyr'd the *Knight*. . . VI. xii. 37. 9

Knighthood. to all *knighthood* it is foule disgrace, ... I. i. 31. 8
To thinke that *knighthood* I so much should shame, ... I. iii. 28. 3
Miscreaunt, That hast . . . Faire *knighthood* fowly shamed, . I. vi. 41. 3
All other powres and *knighthood* he did scorne. . . . . . . I. vii. 10. 4
knighthood tooke of good Sir Huons hand, ... II. i. 6. 8
'That knight should *knighthood* ever so have shent?' . . . . II. i. 11. 2
by the *knighthood* which they sure had sworn, ... II. ii. 27. 7
be these the parts Of glorious *knighthood*, ... II. ii. 29. 6
Braggadocchio, . . . is made the scorne Of *knighthood* trew; . II. iii. Arg.
The scorne of *knighthood* and trew chevalrye, ... II. iii. 10. 5
unto *knighthood* workes much shame and woe; . . . . . . II. iv. 10. 7
That knights and *knighthood* doest with shame upbray, . . . II. iv. 45. 3
For suffering such abuse as *knighthood* sham'd, ... II. v. 21. 5
The famous name of *knighthood* fowly shend; . . . . II. vi. 35. 2
Ne canst of prowesse ne of *knighthood* deeme, ... II. viii. 14. 2
when he *knighthood* swore, ... II. viii. 20. 3
First prayse of *knighthood* is fowle outrage to deface.' . . . II. viii. 25. 9
sith I armes and *knighthood* first did plight, ... II. ix. 7. 2
worke so hainous tort, In shame of *knighthood*, ... III. ii. 12. 9
Advent'rous *knighthood* on her selfe to don; . . . . III. iii. 57. 6
for love of *knighthood* gent, ... III. v. 10. 5
knighthood fowle defaced by a faithlesse knight. . . . . . III. ix. 1. 9
hath thy lady reft and *knighthood* shent, ... III. x. 32. 4
Whereby the name of *knight-hood* thou dost shend, ... IV. i. 51. 3
They loved armes, and *knighthood* did ensew, ... IV. ii. 46. 4
In shame of *knighthood* and fidelitie; . . . . IV. vi. 8. 4
love, That is the crowne of *knighthood*, ... IV. vi. 31. 7
So ought all faytours that true *knighthood* shame, ... V. iii. 38. 6
made the scorne of *Knighthod* . . . . V. iv. 27. 7
by the faith that I To Maydenhead and noble *knighthood* owe, V. iv. 34. 2
with lone Of armes hast *knighthood* stolne, ... V. vi. 37. 5
as he did on his *Knighthood* sweare, ... VI. iii. 18. 4
The name of *knighthood* he did disavow; . . . . VI. v. 37. 7
ne ever *knighthood* dare Hence to professe; . . . . VI. vi. 36. 3

Knighthood's. In fowle reproch of *knighthoodes* fayre degree, . I. ix. 22. 6
'For *knighthoods* love doe not so fowle a deed, ... II. viii. 16. 2

Knightless. hast with *knightlesse* guile, . . . Faire knighthood fowly shamed, ... I. vi. 41. 2
that knight wrought *knightlesse* shame; . . . . VI. ii. 14. 7
all knights hast shamed with this *knightlesse* part. . . . . VI. vi. 33. 9

Knightliness. Traind up in feats of armes and *knightlinesse;* VI. vii. 45. 7

Knightly. with faire exercise Of *knightly* feates, ... *Hub.* 738
As one for *knightly* giusts and fierce encounters fitt. . . . . I. i. 1. 9
Thought all their glorie vaine in *knightly* vew, ... I. iv. 15. 7
Inquireth of our states, and of our *knightly* deedes, ... I. ix. 28. 9
Might not revive desire of *knightly* exercize. . . . . II. vi. 25. 9
crownd his coward crest with *knightly* stile; . . . . II. viii. 12. 7
knightly worth which he too late did try, ... III. ix. 25. 5
The battell, offred in so *knightly* wize: . . . . IV. iv. 11. 5
Into the thickest of that *knightly* preasse . . . . IV. iv. 34. 1
Of all the ornaments of *knightly* name, ... V. v. 20. 4
They should accomplish both a *knightly* deed, ... VI. vii. 4. 8
lastly to despoyle of *knightly* bannerall. . . . . VI. vii. 26. 9
Ne ever had such *knightly* service seene, ... VI. ix. 35. 3

Knight's. this Redcrosse *knights* ensample plainly prove. . . I. iv. 1. 9
The dead *knights* sword out of his sheath he drew, ... II. i. 61. 1
ruth emperced deepe In that *knightes* hart, ... II. ii. 1. 9
that same *knights* owne sword this is, ... II. viii. 20. 1
leave unto me thy *knights* last patronage.' . . . . II. viii. 26. 9
her *knights* service ought, to hold of her in fee. . . . . . . III. i. 44. 9

Knights—*Continued.*
Those *knights* began afresh them to assayle, . . . V. xi. 59. 2
the two *knights* themselves their captains did subdew. . . . V. xi. 59. 9
Whom when those *knights* so froward and forlore Beheld, . . . V. xi. 61. 8
So stoutest *knights* doen oftentimes in field. . . . V. xii. 19. 5
Where curteous *Knights* and Ladies most did won . . . VI. i. 1. 8
Good *Knights* and Ladies true, . . . VI. i. 7. 9
With beards of *Knights* and locks of Ladies lynd: . . . VI. i. 15. 5
all errant *knights,* whereso on ground; . . . VI. i. 42. 8
For *knights* and all men this by nature have, . . . VI. ii. 14. 8
Crying aloud . . . Unto the *Knights,* . . . VI. iii. 24. 6
More brave and noble *knights* have raysed beene. . . . VI. iv. 36. 3
To be two errant *knights,* . . . VI. v. 11. 5
Whenas these *Knights* arriv'd, . . . VI. v. 35. 9
his Lord of old Did hate all errant *Knights* . . . VI. vi. 21. 4
all *knights* hast shamed with this knightlesse part. . . . VI. vi. 33. 9
Gainst errant *Knights* and Ladies . . . VI. vi. 34. 5
valiant *Knights* doe rashly enterprize . . . VI. vi. 35. 4
his two *knights* Doe gaine their treasons meed: . . . VI. vii. Arg.
At last he met two *knights* to him unknowne, . . . VI. vii. 3. 6
The *knights* beleev'd that all he sayd was trew; . . . VI. vii. 5. 1
no might in man, nor heart in *Knights,* . . . VI. viii. 18. 6
To sing of hilles and woods mongst warres and *Knights,* . . . VII. vi. 37. 2
There whylome wont the Templer *Knights* to byde, . . . *Proth.* 135
Two gentle *Knights* of lovely face and feature, . . . *Proth.* 169
Knights'. And sing of *Knights* and Ladies gentle deeds; . . . I. Pr. 1. 5
in all those *knights* and ladies sight . . . IV. i. 52. 3
sield With moniments of many *Knights* decay, . . . V. v. 21. 4
Knit. being *knit,* they brought forth other kynds . . . *Col.* 853
wicked wights Have *knit* themselves in Venus shameful chaine: I. ii. 4. 8
The knights *knitt* friendly bands: . . . I. ix. Arg.
His owne two hands the holy knotts did *knitt,* . . . I. xii. 37. 1
with Guyon *knitt* in one consent, . . . II. iii. 11. 8
Knit with a golden bauldricke, . . . II. iii. 29. 5
Knitt all his forces, . . . II. iv. 9. 7
Our selves in league of vowed love wee *knitt,* . . . II. iv. 18. 6
upper end to highest heven was *knitt,* . . . II. vii. 46. 3
Thus reconcilement was betweene them *knitt,* . . . III. i. 12. 1
a wanton payre Of lovers loosely *knit,* . . . III. x. 16. 9
About their tender loynes to *knit* the same; . . . IV. v. 17. 7
being *knit* with vertue, never will remove. . . . IV. vi. 31. 9
About their middles that faire belt to *knit;* . . . V. iii. 28. 2
To *knit* the knot, that ever shall remaine. . . . *Am.* vi. 14
Knittest. *knittest* each to each, as brother unto brother. . . . VII. vii. 14. 9
Knitting. *Knitting* his wanton armes with grasping hold, . . . *Gn.* 218
In skilfull *knitting* of soft silken twyne, . . . *Mui.* 362
knitting all his force, got one hand free, . . . I. i. 19. 7
Withhold . . . your hasty hond From *knitting* league with him, I. xii. 28. 4
The usuall joyes at *knitting* of loves band. . . . I. xii. 40. 5
knitting their rancke braunches, part to part, . . . III. vi. 44. 4
Knives. Some rusty *knifes,* some staves in fier warmd: . . . II. ix. 13. 7
Some whet their *knives,* and strip their elboes bare: . . . VI. viii. 39. 6
Knock. every houre they *knocke* at deathes gate? . . . IV. iii. 1. 7
knocke his head, and rend his rugged heares, . . . IV. viii. 4. 8
I persever'd still to *knocke* and call, . . . IV. x. 11. 6
to him leaping lent him such a *knocke,* . . . V. i. 21. 8
Knocked. *knockt* his brest, as one that did repent. . . . I. i. 29. 9
One *knocked* at the dore, and in would fare: . . . I. iii. 16. 4
He *knocked* fast, and often curst, and sware, . . . I. iii. 16. 5
when they *knockt,* The Porter opened unto them . . . I. x. 5. 3
He *knockt* his brest with desperate intent, . . . III. vii. 20. 3
I *knockt,* but no man aunswred me by name; . . . IV. x. 11. 4
Knocking. soft *knocking* entrance he desyrd. . . . III. ix. 10. 1
Knocks. does beat her brest and forhead *knockes.* . . . V. xii. 38. 9
Knot. Striving to loose the *knott* that fast him tyes, . . . I. xi. 23. 4
formerly were bownd Up in one *knott,* . . . II. xii. 67. 3
her life at last must lincke in that same *knot.* . . . III. ii. 23. 9
her golden lockes, that were upbound Still in a *knot,* . . . IV. i. 13. 3
should have joyned bene to her in wedlocks *knot.* . . . V. iv. 8. 9
To knit the *knot,* that ever shall remaine. . . . *Am.* vi. 14
Knots. taile . . . in *knots* and many boughtes upwound, . . . I. i. 15. 3
thick entangled *knots* adown does slack, . . . I. xi. 11. 4
His owne two hands the holy *knotts* did knitt, . . . I. xii. 37. 1
therein entrayld The ends of all the (*their) *knots,* . . . II. iii. 27. 8
hundred *knots,* that did him sore constraine; . . . II. iv. 15. 2
Knotted. The *knotted* rush-ringes, and gilte Rosemaree? . . . *S.C.* N. 116
His sandy lockes, . . . *Knotted* in blood and dust, . . . II. v. 14. 5
Knotted with blood in bounches rudely ran; . . . III. v. 29. 6
Knotty. All armd with ragged snubbes and *knottie* graine, . . I. viii. 7. 4
the *knotty* string Of his huge taile . . . I. xi. 39. 7
knottie snags were sharpned all afore, . . . IV. vii. 7. 5
Know. I, that *know* this worlds inconstancies, . . . *Bel.*[2] i. 12
I *know* him by a token; . . . *S.C.* Mar. 105
lengd to *know* the cause of his complaint: . . . *S.C.* May 250
Much needeth all shepheards him to *knowe.* . . . *S.C.* May 313
St. Michels Mount who does not *know,* . . . *S.C.* Jul. 41
nearer wayes I *knowe.* . . . *S.C.* Jul. 96
I *know,* to kepe is a burdenous smart: . . . *S.C.* S. 16
Enaunter they mought be inly *knowe.* . . . *S.C.* S. 161
what my selfe *knowe* Chaunced to Roffynn . . . *S.C.* S. 170
know the purporte of my evill plight, . . . *Gn.* Ded. 8
Askt if in husbandrie he ought did *knowe,* . . . *Hub.* 262
To let him *knowe* the order of the thing. . . . *Hub.* 1212
know their names, or speak their praises dew, . . . *T.M.* 442
By knowledge wee do learne our selves to *knowe* . . . *T.M.* 503
(as thou right well doest *know*) . . . *D.* 99
I *know* not right: . . . *Col.* 63
hablest wit of most I *know* this day. . . . *Col.* 383
then *know* how to have donne. . . . *Col.* 591
fill with stones, that all men may it *know.* . . . *Col.* 635

Know—*Continued.*
My rimes I *know* unsavory and sowre, . . . *Ded. Son.* viii. 8
asked him, if he did *know* Of straunge adventures . . . I. i. 30. 3
Was afterward, I *know* not how, convaid, . . . I. ii. 24. 2
Abessa, . . . With whom he whoredome usd, that few did *know,* I. iii. 18. 5
O! who does *know* the bent of womens fantasy? . . . I. iv. 24. 9
eftsoones did *know* Both good and ill, . . . I. xi. 47. 7
treasons, which of late I *know* To have bene wrought . . . I. xii. 33. 5
does *know* Where is that happy land of Faery, . . . II. Pr. 1. 6
vouch antiquities, which no body can *know.* . . . II. Pr. 1. 9
all these were, when no man did them *know,* . . . II. Pr. 3. 1
I *know* your goodly governaunce, . . . II. i. 29. 8
know it by the name: it hight the *Bowre of blis* . . . II. i. 51. 9
know, that secret vertues are infusd . . . II. ii. 5. 6
Such ye may her *know:* . . . II. ii. 9. 5
th' equall die of warre he well did *know:* . . . II. v. 13. 4
I *know* it well be gott; . . . II. vii. 19. 2
That he might *know* and ease her sorrow sad; . . . II. xii. 28. 3
Britomart would not such guilfull message *know.* . . . III. i. 51. 9
(For what doest thou not *knowe?*) . . . III. iii. 21. 2
How shall she *know,* how shall she finde the man? . . . III. iii. 25. 3
The surest signe, whereby ye may her *know,* . . . III. v. 5. 8
That much they faynd to *know* who she mote bee; . . . III. ix. 24. 7
know that your loving Make . . . III. xii. 40. 8
Her false Duessa, who full well did *know* . . . IV. i. 19. 5
desirous th' end of all their dayes To *know,* . . . IV. ii. 47. 2
know the measure of their utmost date . . . IV. ii. 50. 4
seekes to *know* anothers griefe in vaine, . . . IV. vii. 10. 7
To *know* what Virgin did them thence unbind, . . . IV. viii. 22. 2
He ment to make them *know* their follies prise, . . . IV. ix. 35. 2
'The cause . . . Was hard to *know,* . . . IV. x. 41. 2
know the moniments of passed age: . . . IV. xi. 17. 6
Know, Marinell, that all this is for thee.' . . . IV. xii. 11. 7
with him beare where none of her might *know:* . . . IV. xii. 15. 2
By which it's easie him to *know* againe, . . . V. i. 19. 7
thou oughtest first to *know* . . . V. ii. 34. 6
every one doe *know* their certaine bound, . . . V. ii. 36. 2
Thou doest not *know* the causes, nor their courses dew. . . . V. ii. 42. 9
how canst thou those greater secrets *know,* . . . V. ii. 43. 7
doest not *know* the least thing of them all? . . . V. ii. 43. 8
'Then sith ye needs' (quoth he) 'will *know* my shame, . . . V. iv. 28. 6
wend with me, that ye may see and *know* . . . V. iv. 34. 7
ran to meete him forth to *know* his tidings somme. . . . V. vi. 8. 9
Now mote ye *know* . . . whence all this did proceede; . . . V. vi. 31. 6
Of whom we may at will the whole occasion *know.'* . . . V. viii. 15. 9
of legierdemayne the mysteries did *know.* . . . V. ix. 13. 9
know How cleare I am from blame of this upbraide; . . . V. xi. 41. 6
as they approcht the cause to *know,* . . . V. xi. 44. 1
know I not or how, or in what place . . . VI. i. 7. 4
know that I doe much disdaine . . . VI. i. 27. 7
ought they well to *know* Their good; . . . VI. ii. 1. 6
I . . . all her pray and all her diet *know.* . . . VI. ii. 32. 4
And fitteth most for noble swayne to *know,* . . . VI. ii. 32. 7
'Sith then ye needs will *know* the griefe I hoord, . . . VI. iv. 29. 2
As ye may *know* when time shall be to tell the same. . . . VI. v. 2. 9
hardly one could *know* . . . VI. viii. 13. 8
Sith they *know* best what is the best for them; . . . VI. ix. 29. 3
As they doe *know* each can most aptly use: . . . VI. ix. 29. 5
resolving what it was to *know,* . . . VI. x. 17. 8
some, which did the sundry prisoners *knowe,* . . . VI. xi. 11. 5
if her syre Should *know* thereof . . . VI. xii. 6. 7
'ye *know* that long ygo . . . ye to me gave A little mayde, . VI. xii. 17. 5
To *know* what meant that suddaine lacke of light. . . . VII. vi. 15. 5
to *knowe* The cause of this so strange astonishment, . . . VII. vi. 16. 2
how we then defeated all their deed, Yee all do *knowe,* . . VII. vi. 20. 6
when I sigh, she sayes, I *know* the art; . . . *Am.* xviii. 11
know no end of her owne mysery, . . . *Am.* xxv. 2
did she *know* how ill these two accord . . . *Am.* xxxi. 13
The heavens *know* best what is the best for me. . . . *Am.* xlvi. 6
Then *know* that mercy is the Mighties jewell: . . . *Am.* xlix. 3
All that they *know* not envy or admyre; . . . *Am.* lxxxiv. 6
I, that have often prov'd, too well it *know,* . . . *H.B.* 87
Know this for certaine, . . . *H.B.* 136
That is a signe to *know* the gentle blood. . . . *H.B.* 140
they did see And *know* ech other . . . *H.B.* 203
Knowest. Full little *knowest* thou, that hast not tride, . . . *Hub.* 895
'Sith then thou *knowest* all our griefe, . . . III. iii. 21. 1
Well *know'st* thou, when we friendship first did sweare, . . IV. ii. 13. 3
Knoweth. Alebius, that *know'th* The waters depth, . . . IV. xi. 14. 7
Knowing. I *knowing* the worldes unstedfastnesse, . . . *Bel.*[1] i. 12
well *knowing* trew all that he did reherse, . . . I. ix. 48. 4
both of old well *knowing* by their names, . . . IV. ii. 20. 5
Knowing the miserie of their estate, . . . IV. iii. 1. 4
Well *knowing* her to be his deaths sole instrument. . . . IV. vii. 29. 9
Not *knowing* natures worke, . . . V. iii. 19. 6
he me . . . Assayld, not *knowing* what to armes doth long.' VI. ii. 8. 5
Twixt life and death, not *knowing* what was donne. . . . VI. ii. 48. 6
Yet *knowing* that her Knight now neare did draw, . . . VI. iii. 26. 3
Knowing his voice, although not heard long sin, . . . VI. xi. 44. 3
Yet *knowing* not what meant that sodaine thro, . . . VI. xii. 17. 2
Knowing his fatall hand by former feare; . . . VI. xii. 25. 8
The Panther, *knowing* that his spotted hyde Doth please . *Am.* liii. 1
Not *knowing* Venus from the other. . . . *Epig.* iii. 6
Knowing that, whatsoere to them we give, . . . *H.H.L.* 209
Knowledge. Ne other *knowledge* ever did attaine, . . . *Hub.* 837
When th' heavenlie light of *knowledge* is put out, . . . *T.M.* 488
Through *knowledge* we behold the worlds creation, . . . *T.M.* 499
By *knowledge* wee do learne our selves to knowe . . . *T.M.* 503
raced Out of the *knowledge* of posteritie, . . . *Ti.* 178
much more that does from mens *knowledge* lurke. . . . *Col.* 295

Knowledge—*Continued.*
Shall he thy sins up in his *knowledge* fold, . . . I. ix. 47. 3
However list her now her *knowledge* fayne, . . . III. ii. 17. 2
knowledge of those woods where he did dwell, . . . III. v. 14. 3
The lines of life, from living *knowledge* hid. . . . IV. ii. 48. 4
out of all mens *knowledge* he was worne at last. . . . IV. vii. 41. 9
From peoples *knowledge* labour'd to concele: . . . IV. x. 41. 3
For feare her mistresse shold have *knowledge* gayned; . . . V. v. 44. 4
From whom all guifts of wit and *knowledge* flow, . . . *H.H.B.* 9

Known. *See* **Well-known.**
be *knowne* for such thy villanee. . . . *S.C.* Jun. 104
Well is *knowne* that sith the Saxon king . . . *S.C.* S. 151
May by this Gnatts complaint be easily *knowen.* . . . *Gn.* Ded. 14
before That Ceres seede of mortall men were *knowne,* . . . *Gn.* 207
that which common is, and *knowne* to all, . . . *Hub.* 613
by his like visnomie Eathe to be *knowen;* . . . *Mui.* 311
The shepheards boy (best *knowen* by that name) . . . *Col.* 1
As if the way she perfectly had *knowne.* . . . *Col.* 269
skill, though *knowen* yet to few; . . . *Col.* 401
were he *knowne* to Cynthia as he ought, . . . *Col.* 402
Best *knowne* by bearing up great Cynthiaes traine: . . . *Col.* 509
Her name Ile teach in *knowen* terms to frame: . . . *Col.* 637
is Love then . . . once *knowne* In Court, . . . *Col.* 771
Yet, till that thou thy Poeme wilt make *knowne,* . . . *Ded. Son.* viii. 13
danger . . . I saw before mine eyes, if I were *knowne* to stray. . I. ii. 41. 9
Desyrd of forreine foemen to be *knowne,* . . . I. vi. 29. 6
They both, deformed, scarsely could bee *known.* . . . I. vi. 45. 6
he that made the same was *knowne* right well . . . I. vii. 36. 2
borrowed light Is laid away, and counterfesaunce *knowne.'* . . . I. viii. 49. 6
Which *knowne,* . . . eftsoones he gan apply relief . . . I. x. 24. 3
well *knowne* over-all To be both gratious and eke liberall: . . I. x. 34. 4
Some daily seene and *knowen* by their names, . . . II. ix. 50. 6
thy prayses tell, and make them *knowen* farre. . . . III. ii. 3. 9
By *knowen* signes and passions which I see, . . . III. ii. 33. 3
Ne other to himselfe is *knowne* this day, . . . III. iii. 26. 8
with sharpe speare the rest made dearly *knowne.* . . . III. iv. 15. 6
Foreby a narrow foord, to them well *knowne,* . . . III. v. 17. 2
by meanes to him well *knowne:* . . . III. ix. 30. 2
full easie to be *knowne,* . . . III. xi. 7. 8
whose voices *knowen* sound . . . III. xii. 43. *or.*8
By way of sport, as oft in maskes is *knowen,* . . . IV. i. 3. 8
a girdle . . . Well *knowne* to appertaine to Florimell, . . . IV. ii. 25. 8
Well was that rings great vertue *knowen* to all; . . . IV. ii. 40. 1
well *knowne* to be the same Which Triamond had worne, . . . IV. iv. 27. 5
his utmost prowesse there made *knowen;* . . . IV. iv. 38. 2

Known—*Continued.*
well was *knowen* to be a valiant Knight, . . . IV. iv. 40. 4
knowne to few, that Arthegall he hight, . . . IV. iv. 42. 8
That rather seemes, sith *knowen* armes ye shonne.' . . . IV. vi. 5. 5
knowne by fame, and by an Hebene speare, . . . IV. vi. 6. 4
'of all that ever hath bene *knowen!* . . . IV. vii. 14. 2
formerly Had *knowne* right well, . . . IV. viii. 10. 4
in hard assaies Were cowards *knowne,* . . . IV. x. 18. 7
Rich Oranochy, though but *knowen* late; . . . IV. xi. 21. 7
brawney armes had lost their *knowen* might, . . . IV. xii. 20. 4
No warre was *knowne,* . . . V. Pr. 9. 5
So did the Ladies both, as may be *knowne:* . . . V. i. 17. 4
by what markes may he be *knowne* againe?' . . . V. i. 19. 2
Known by good markes and perfect good espiall: . . . V. iv. 15. 8
Being the dowry of his wife well *knowne,* . . . V. iv. 18. 4
For her great bounty *knowen* over all . . . V. viii. 17. 3
Well *knowen* by his feates, . . . V. ix. 5. 9
Her name was Envie, *knowen* well thereby, . . . V. xii. 31. 1
tell, if thou have it *knowne.'* . . . VI. i. 14. 4
The gentle minde by gentle deeds is *knowne:* . . . VI. iii. 1. 2
Unwilling to be *knowne* or seene at all, . . . VI. viii. 27. 3
made her *knowen* to him at last: . . . VI. viii. 51. 8
by all meanes the daunger *knowne* did shonne: . . . VI. xi. 35. 7
closely did her wed, but *knowne* to few: . . . VI. xii. 5. 4
So farre past memory of man that may be *knowne?* . . . VII. vii. 2. 9
as is well *knowen* to thee. . . . VII. vii. 16. 9
Despoyld of warlike armes and *knowen* shield. . . . *Am.* lii. 4

Knows. (who *knowes* not Rosalend?) . . . *S.C.* Au. 141
No greedy riches *knowes* nor bloudie strife, . . . *Gn.* 123
When as he *knowes* his meede, . . . To be . . . *Hub.* 975
'*knowes* best the termes established; . . . I. ix. 41. 7
where he hits nought *knowes,* . . . II. iv. 7. 9
knowes her port, and thither sayles by ayme, . . . II. vi. 10. 3
how no man *knowes,* They spring, . . . II. vi. 15. 5
knowes no kinred, nor regardes no right, . . . II. x. 35. 2
The bird that *knowes* not the false fowlers call, . . . III. i. 54. 8
fortune, Boteswaine, no assurance *knowes;* . . . III. iv. 9. 7
Franckly each Paramor his leman *knowes,* . . . III. vi. 41. 7
(who *knowes* not Colin Clout?) . . . VI. x. 16. 4
(Who *knowes* not Arlo-hill?) . . . VII. vi. 36. 6

Kon, -d. *See* **Con, Conned.**

Kurre. *See* **Cur.**

Kydst. *kydst* the hidden kinds of many a wede, . . . *S.C.* D. 92
kydst not ene to cure thy sore hart-roote, . . . *S.C.* D. 93

L

Labor. The ploughmans hope and shepheards *labour* vaine: . *Ro.* xiv. 4
Ere Roffy could for his *laboure* him thanck. . . . *S.C.* S. 201
Nor chaunge of *labour* may intreated bee; . . . *Gn.* 418
to what *labour* els he was prepar'd, . . . *Hub.* 265
talke Of *labour,* that did from his liking balke, . . . *Hub.* 268
Ne to strong *labour* can it selfe enure: . . . *Hub.* 276
loose thy *labour* and thy fruitles cost. . . . *Hub.* 636
With so great *labour* and long lasting paine, . . . *Ti.* 53
Were but lost *labour,* . . . *Ti.* 90
After his dayes long *labour* drew to rest, . . . *D.* 23
these ydle rimes . . . The *labor* of lost time, . . . *Ded. Son.* ix. 8
Now needeth him no lenger *labour* spend, . . . I. i. 26. 8
when he saw his *labour* all was vaine, . . . I. i. 55. 8
Shee backe retourned with some *labour* lost; . . . I. iii. 24. 2
ne might from *labour* lin; . . . I. v. 35. 4
many heades . . . Did breed him endlesse *labor* to subdew. . . I. vii. 17. 5
their powres, empayrd through *labor* long, . . . I. ix. 2. 1
To seek her out with *labor* and long tyne, . . . I. ix. 15. 7
Feare, sicknesse, age, losse, *labour,* sorrow, strife, . . . I. ix. 44. 6
Did *labour* lively to expresse the same, . . . I. x. 6. 8
A worke of *labour* long, and endlesse prayse: . . . I. xi. 7. 6
The knight, him seeing *labour* so in vaine, . . . II. vii. 59. 1
So lost his *labour* vaine and ydle industry. . . . II. vii. 61. 9
sure yt would deceive thy *labor* and thy might.' . . . II. viii. 21. 9
I *labour* would to guide you through al Faery land.' . . . II. ix. 8. 9
A *labor* huge, exceeding far my might. . . . II. x. 2. 7
by fathers *labour* long, . . . II. x. 25. 1
labour lost it was to weene approch him neare. . . . II. xi. 25. 9
all his *labor* brought to happy end; . . . II. xi. 35. 2
thought his *labor* lost, and travell vayne, . . . II. xi. 44. 2
to tell the sumptuous aray . . . should be *labour* lost; . . . III. i. 32. 2
When too huge toile and *labour* them constraines, . . . III. iii. 9. 7
their *labor* not to slake. . . . III. iii. 10. 9
lose the hope Of his long *labour,* . . . III. iv. 52. 7
seeme to *labour* under their fruites lode: . . . III. vi. 42. 6
both to be and seeme to him was *labor* lich. . . . III. vii. 29. 9
To see his whole yeares *labor* lost so soone, . . . III. vii. 34. 8
with like *labour* walke the world arownd, . . . III. vii. 56. 2
Great *labour* fondly hast thou hent in hand, . . . III. vii. 61. 2
'Thy *labour* all is lost, I greatly dread, . . . III. viii. 47. 2
But to the rest, . . . My *labour* adde, . . . III. viii. 50. 9
Laught at his foolish *labour* spent in waste, . . . III. x. 13. 4
life and *labour* both in vaine to spend. . . . IV. iii. 32. 5
Through toylesome heate and *labour* of her weary fight. . . IV. vi. 19. 9
yet did he *labour* long, . . . V. ii. 46. 7
By any skill or *labour* it would sit, . . . V. iii. 28. 7
she thenceforth did *labour* . . . to curry favour . . . V. v. 35. 4
Give him more *labour,* . . . V. v. 50. 3
by them long with carefull *labour* nurst, . . . VI. Pr. 3. 8
when the Salvage saw his *labour* vaine . . . VI. iv. 9. 1
of all his *labour* and long paine . . . VI. ix. 38. 5

Labor—*Continued.*
with *labour* and long paine, . . . VI. xi. 22. 5
his limbes with *labor* heated sore. . . . VII. vii. 29. 9
Such *labour* like the Spyders web I fynd, . . . *Am.* xxiii. 13
glorious spoile, Gotton at last with *labour* . . . *Am.* lxix. 14
That long daies *labour* doest at last defray, . . . *Epith.* 316

Labored. *laboured* lands to yield the timely eare, . . . *S.C.* O. 58
Whose meaning much I *labored* foorth to wreste, . . . *Ti.* 486
Labour'd in vaine to have recur'd their prize, . . . II. xii. 19. 7
labour'd long in that deepe ford with vaine disease. . . . III. v. 19. 9
long while *laboured* it to engrave: . . . III. viii. 37. 7
From peoples knowledge *labour'd* to concele: . . . IV. x. 41. 3
by the lilly hand her *labour'd* up to reare. . . . IV. x. 53. 9
laboured fast To sperre the gate; . . . V. x. 37. 1
Him selfe thereof he *labour'd* to acquite, . . . VI. iii. 21. 7
After that he had *labourd* long in vaine . . . VI. xii. 32. 3

Laboring. Each *labouring* t' advance the others gest, . . . IV. iv. 36. 7

Laborous. husbands life is *labourous* and hard? . . . *Hub.* 266

Labor's. To whom I levell all my *labours* end, . . . III. ix. 1. 2
my lives and *labors* end.' . . . III. ix. 37. 9
litle prays'd his *labours* evill speed, . . . IV. v. 22. 4

Labors. Yet thy just *labours* ever shall endure. . . . *Ti.* 175
O vaine *labours* of terrestriall wit, . . . *Ti.* 512
them requitest with thy thankfull *labours.* . . . *Col.* 587
Such were the *labours* of this Lady meeke, . . . I. iii. 21. 7
Young knight whatever, that . . . through long *labours* huntest after fame, . . . I. iv. 1. 2
After long *labours* and adventures spent, . . . I. vi. 30. 2
After long paines and *labours* manifold, . . . I. viii. 40. 5
of youre toyle And *labors* long . . . Ye both forwearied be: . I. x. 17. 3
after *labors* long and sad delay, . . . I. x. 52. 5
for twelve huge *labours* high extold, . . . I. xi. 27. 3
from their journall *labours* they did rest; . . . I. xi. 31. 4
travell long and *labours* manifold. . . . II. i. 24. 9
who his limbs with *labours,* . . . II. iii. 40. 6
Bid thee to them thy fruitlesse *labors* yield, . . . II. vi. 16. 3
may emongst Alcides *labours* stand.' . . . III. vii. 61. 4
through wearie wars and *labours* long, . . . III. ix. 50. 1
Not caring his long *labours* to deface; . . . III. xii. 32. 3
For many *labours* more then I have found, . . . III. xii. 40. 3
That I thy *labours* lost may thus revive, . . . IV. ii. 34. 2
bad them leave their *labours* and long toyle . . . IV. iv. 48. 6
In perils strange, in *labours* long and wide; . . . VI. i. 6. 5
earely light To guide mens *labours,* . . . VI. v. 40. 3
on the *labours* of poore men to feed, . . . VI. viii. 35. 8
did their *labours* share, . . . VI. ix. 15. 7
to present her with their *labours* late; . . . VI. x. 33. 7
leave your wonted *labors* for this day: . . . *Epith.* 262
sith of wemens *labours* thou hast charge, . . . *Epith.* 383

Labors'. To these first *labours* needed furtheraunce. . . . *Ded. Son.* ii. 14

Labryde. Fayre Thyamis, the daughter of *Labryde,* . . . I. vi. 21. 4

Labyrinth. Crete will boast the *Labyrinth;* . . . . *Ro.* ii. 8
like to lead the *labyrinth* about; . . . . I. i. 11. 4
within the utmost bound Of his wide *Labyrinth,* . . . . II. xii. 20. 9
Labyrinths. False *Labyrinthes,* fond runners eyes to daze; . . IV. x. 24. 8
Lace. gird in your waste . . . with a tawdrie *lace.* . . . . . . *S.C.* Ap. 135
trebly breaded in a threefold *lace,* . . . . III. ii. 50. 2
jacket . . . Of Lincolne greene, belayd with silver *lace;* . . . VI. ii. 5. 7
Laced. hangd on high with golden ribbands *laced;* . . . . . IV. x. 8. 5
painted buskins . . . *laced* close afore; . . . . V. v. 3. 3
having her snowy brest As yet not *laced,* . . . . VI. xii. 15. 3
Lacedaemon. From *Lacedaemon* fetcht the fayrest Dame . . III. ix. 34. 7
Laces. the more in *laces* strong Himselfe he tide, ... *Mui.* 427
Lachesis. the thrid By griesly *Lachesis* was spun . . . . . IV. ii. 48. 6
Lachesis thereat gan to repine, ... IV. ii. 51. 4
Lack. little *lack* of dead, ... *S.C.* May 264
good matter Lost for *lacke* of telling: . . . . *S.C.* Jul. 206
Theyr rootes bene dryed up for *lacke* of dewe, ... *S.C.* D. 111
my late maymed limbs *lack* wonted might . . . . *Hub.* 272
be thou sure one not to *lacke* or long. . . . . *Hub.* 501
To growe into great *lacke,* . . . . *Hub.* 927
by *lacke* of thee to heaven hent, ... *Ti.* 677
with her *lacke* I might tormented be. . . . . *D.* 368
how great a losse . . . by thy *lacke:* . . . . *Col.* 17
loathly frogs and toades, which eyes did *lacke,* . . . . I. i. 20. 7
Whose greedy lust did *lacke* in greatest store; . . . . I. iv. 29. 2
The forlorne mayd . . . could not *lacke* her lovers company; . I. vi. 22. 2
of three furlongs does but litle *lacke;* . . . . I. xi. 11. 7
griev'd so long to *lacke* his greedie pray; . . . . II. vii. 34. 2
doen you *lack* your will? . . . . II. ix. 37. 8
To be a beast, and *lacke* intelligence!' . . . . II. xii. 87. 5
lacke of reskewes, will to parley drive; . . . . III. x. 10. 4
felt some ruth or sence his hand did *lacke,* . . . . IV. vi. 21. 7
for *lacke* Of breath, ... IV. ix. 25. 7
to curse and ban, for *lacke* Of that faire bootie, ... VI. ii. 21. 4
Be *lacke* of children to supply your place, ... VI. iv. 35. 2
for *lacke* of heed Now gan to faint, ... VI. v. 31. 7
thy love, for *lacke* of hardiment, . . . hast shamed . . . . VI. vi. 33. 7
fearing death, and next to death the *lacke* Of clothes . . . VI. viii. 50. 3
this sweet peace, whose *lacke* did then appeare: . . . . . . VI. ix. 25. 6
what were they all, whose *lacke* thee grieves so sore?' . . . VI. x. 20. 9
To know what meant that suddaine *lacke* of light. . . . . . VII. vi. 15. 5
Lacked. *See* **Long-lacked.**
my Lord . . . Whose presence I have *lackt* too long a day: . . I. viii. 43. 2
'Long *lackt,* alas! Hath bene thy faithfull aide . . . . . . II. viii. 7. 3
his shield he *lakt* And sword saw not, ... II. viii. 53. 3
whom wandring to and fro I long have *lackt,* . . . . II. viii. 53. 8
long time he *lacked* had The good Sir Calepine, ... VI. v. 3. 1
whilest love *lackt* place, ... VI. vii. 38. 7
Whereof she long had *lackt* the wishfull sight, ... VI. xi. 50. 5
Since I have *lackt* the comfort of that light, ... *Am.* lxxxvii. 1
would speake, but that he *lackt* a tong, ... *Proth.* 116
Lackest. thou *lackest* somedele their delight. . . . . . . *S.C.* May 56
Lacketh. Little *lacketh* Perigot of the best, ... *S.C.* Au. 126
Whatever thing *lacketh* chaungeable rest, ... *S.C.* S. 240
Lackey. unfit to tread And *lackey* by him, ... VI. ii. 15. 5
Lacking. Her dried dugs, lyke bladders *lacking* wind, Hong I. viii. 47. 6
fiers Pyrochles, *lacking* his owne sword, ... II. viii. 19. 1
lacking it, they cannot lyfe sustayne; . . . . *Am.* xxxv. 5
Lackyng my love, I go from place to place, ... *Am.* lxxviii. 1
Lacks. The earth now *lacks* her wonted light, ... *S.C.* N. 68
Lad. *See* **Led.**
Lewdly complainest thou, laesie *ladde,* . . . . *S.C.* F. 9
sayd, he was a winged *lad,* . . . . *S.C.* Mar. 112
the *ladde,* whome long I lovd so deare, ... *S.C.* Ap. 10
What is he for a *Ladde* you so lament? . . . . *S.C.* Ap. 17
the *Ladde* can keepe both our flockes from straying. . . . . *S.C.* May 173
Now say it, Cuddie, as thou art a *ladde:* . . . . *S.C.* Au. 143
a milkewhite lambe she *lad.* . . . . I. i. 4. 9
For griefe whereof the *lad* n'ould after joy, ... I. vi. 17. 8
in their mistresse reskew whom they *lad;* . . . . II. xii. 84. 7
therewith shott an arrow at the *lad;* . . . . III. v. 24. 7
that same daintie *lad,* which was so deare . . . . III. xii. 7. 5
from thenceforth a wretched life they *ladd,* . . . . III. xii. 16. 7
all his life, which afterwards he *lad,* . . . . IV. viii. 2. 4
So home with her she streight the virgin *lad,* . . . . IV. xii. 33. 8
Thence he him *lad,* . . . . V. i. 22. 5
by slights allur'd, and to their purpose *lad.* . . . . V. xii. 37. 9
this lucklesse mayd away was *lad,* . . . . VI. x. 40. 4
Lade. *See* **Overlade.**
many yron bands on him to *lade:* . . . . V. v. 54. 7
Laden. *See* **Heavy-laden, Honey-laden, Loaden, Rich-laden.**
his broad braunches, *laden* with rich fee, ... II. vii. 56. 3
Laden from far with precious merchandize, ... II. xii. 19. 2
Laden with fruits that made him laugh, ... VII. vii. 30. 3
Ladies. whither rennes this bevie of *Ladies* bright, ... *S.C.* Ap. 118
They bene all *Ladyes* of the lake behight, ... *S.C.* Ap. 120
To helpen the *Ladyes* their Maybush beare!) . . . . *S.C.* May 34
Some tolde of *Ladies,* and their Paramoures; . . . . *Hub.* 28
he mongst *Ladies* could their fortunes read . . . . *Hub.* 698
Sweete Ladie Muses, *Ladies* of delight, ... *Hub.* 761
The Fort, that *Ladies* hold in soveraigne dread. . . . . . . I. ii. 25. 4
'So doubly lov'd of *ladies,* unlike faire, ... I. ii. 37. 1
a noble crew Of Lords and *Ladies* stood on every side, . . . I. iv. 7. 8
Her Lordes and *Ladies* . . . devise Themselves to setten forth I. iv. 14. 5
he of *Ladies* oft was loved deare, ... I. iv. 24. 7
warres for *Ladies* doen by many a Lord. . . . . I. v. 3. 9
the thrise three learned *Ladies* play Their hevenly notes, . . I. x. 54. 8
to these *Ladies* love did countenaunce, ... II. ii. 16. 8
Both knightes and *Ladies* forth right angry far'd, ... II. ii. 19. 8
Mingled emongst loose *Ladies* and lascivious boyes. . . . . . II. v. 28. 9

Ladies—*Continued.*
th' Idaean *Ladies* disagreed, ... II. vii. 55. 6
The whiles the other *Ladies* mind theyr mery glee. . . . . . II. viii. 6. 9
a goodly traine Of Squires and *Ladies* equipaged well, ... II. ix. 17. 8
A lovely bevy of faire *Ladies* sate, ... II. ix. 34. 2
They were faire *Ladies,* . . . . II. xii. 31. 1
Many faire *Ladies* and lascivious boyes, ... II. xii. 72. 8
all *Ladies,* which have it profest, ... III. Pr. 1. 7
glee of many gratious Faire *Ladies,* . . . . III. i. 31. 6
Faire *Ladies,* that to love captived arre, ... III. i. 49. 1
Was usd of knightes and *Ladies* seeming gent: . . . . III. i. 67. 6
I loathed have my life to lead, As *Ladies* wont, ... III. ii. 6. 7
Doe many famous knightes and *Ladies* wonne, ... III. ii. 8. 2
Yet many *Ladies* fayre did oft complaine, ... III. iv. 26. 7
honour of trew *Ladies,* . . . . III. v. 10. 6
Of all good *Ladies* through the worlde so wide, ... III. v. 11. 2
That *Ladies* all may follow her ensample dead. . . . . III. v. 54. 9
Well may I weene, faire *Ladies,* . . . . III. vi. 1. 1
Ladies and Lordes she everywhere mote heare Complayning, . III. vi. 13. 6
all fayre *Ladies* that doe live on grownd. . . . . III. vi. 52. 6
The which himselfe then *Ladies* more defames, ... III. viii. 44. 3
all faire *Ladies* may for ever sory bee.' . . . . III. viii. 47. 9
madest many *Ladies* deare lament . . . . III. ix. 35. 3
Of knights and *ladies* any meetings were; . . . . III. x. 19. 8
all faire *Ladies* magnify your might, ... III. x. 28. 7
ye, faire *Ladies,* . . . ensample take. . . . . III. xi. 2. 6
Ladies, knights, and Damsels gent, ... III. xi. 46. 1
Such when those Knights and *Ladies* all about Beheld her, . . IV. i. 14. 1
Ladies none they were, ... IV. i. 17. 5
Loathed of *ladies* all, and of all knights defyde!' . . . . . . IV. i. 51. 9
that which is for *Ladies* most besitting, ... IV. ii. 19. 1
first laide on those *Ladies* thousand blames, ... IV. ii. 20. 7
all knights with them their *Ladies* are to bring: . . . . . . IV. ii. 26. 9
two *Ladies* of most goodly hew, ... IV. ii. 30. 6
those two *Ladies* their two lovers deare; . . . . IV. ii. 31. 7
eke those masked *Ladies* riding them beside. . . . . IV. iv. 2. 9
those two *Ladies* late, Aemylia and Amoret, abode, ... IV. viii. 19. 2
'Brave Knights and *Ladies,* certes, ye doe wrong . . . . . . IV. iv. 12. 2
The knights in couples marcht with *ladies* linckt attone. . . . IV. iv. 14. 9
The *Ladies* for the girdle strive Of famous Florimell: . . . . IV. v. Arg.
Which *Ladies* ought to love, and seeke for to obtaine. . . . . IV. v. 2. 9
to winne the same So many *Ladies* sought, ... IV. v. 6. 4
an hundred *Ladies* moe Appear'd in place, ... IV. v. 11. 8
many other *Ladies* likewise tride . . . . IV. v. 17. 6
Thereat all Knights gan laugh, and *Ladies* lowre: . . . . . . IV. v. 19. 1
In feeble *Ladies* tyranning so sore, ... IV. vii. 1. 6
those two *Ladies* late, Aemylia and Amoret, abode, ... IV. viii. 19. 2
The evill case in which those *Ladies* lay; . . . . IV. viii. 20. 2
These gentle *Ladies* will misdeeme too light . . . . IV. viii. 29. 4
The *Ladies* both on horse, together fast embraced. . . . . . IV. viii. 34. 9
those two *Ladies* much asham'd did wexe: . . . . IV. viii. 35. 7
the Prince tooke downe those *Ladies* twaine . . . . IV. viii. 41. 1
nigh at hand Those *Ladies* two, ... IV. viii. 62. 7
solace in soft pleasure Those weaker *Ladies* . . . . IV. ix. 12. 8
eke the love of *Ladies* foule defame; . . . . IV. ix. 37. 5
hearke, ye gentle knights and *Ladies* free, ... IV. x. 3. 6
So did the *Ladies* both, as may be knowne: . . . . V. i. 17. 4
Of Lords and *Ladies* infinite great store; . . . . V. iii. 2. 8
The pride of *Ladies,* and the worth of knights, ... V. iii. 3. 4
Full many *Ladies* often had assayd . . . . V. iii. 28. 1
Ladies can laugh at *Ladies,* Knights at Knights, ... V. iii. 39. 6
Fit for such *Ladies* and such lovely knights; . . . . V. iii. 40. 5
Amongst loose *Ladies* lapped in delight: . . . . V. vi. 6. 8
both Knights envide, and *Ladies* eke did spight. . . . . . . V. vi. 6. 9
In th' hearing of full many Knights and *Ladies* gent. . . . . V. x. 14. 9
Faire Lords and *Ladies* which about you dwell, ... VI. Pr. 7. 8
Where curteous Knights and *Ladies* most did won . . . . . . VI. i. 1. 8
Good Knights and *Ladies* true, ... VI. i. 7. 9
With beards of Knights and locks of *Ladies* lynd: . . . . . VI. i. 15. 5
Ladies ayde in every stead and stound.' . . . . VI. i. 42. 9
Faith to his knight, and truth to *Ladies* all, ... VI. ii. 35. 2
Gainst errant Knights and *Ladies* . . . . VI. vi. 34. 5
Ye gentle *Ladies,* in whose soveraine powre . . . . VI. viii. 1. 1
There he a troupe of *Ladies* dauncing found . . . . VI. x. 10. 7
Three other *Ladies* did both daunce and sing, ... VI. x. 12. 3
all those *Ladies,* which thou sawest late, ... VI. x. 21. 3
Ladies'. with Loves, and *Ladies* gentle sports, ... *Hub.* 757
allure Chast *Ladies* eares to fantasies impure. . . . . *Hub.* 820
some good *Ladies* gifts: . . . . *Hub.* 852
Faire *Ladies* loves they spot with thoughts impure, ... *T.M.* 333
Hath farre exiled from your *Ladies* grace, ... *D.* 506
to . . . sing of Knights and *Ladies* gentle deeds; . . . . . . I. Pr. 1. 5
with bowres, and beds, and *ladies* deare delight: . . . . . . I. i. 55. 7
Fell from high Princes courtes, or *Ladies* bowres, ... I. v. 51. 6
All for their *Ladies* froward love to gaine, ... II. ii. 26. 4
Ne *Ladies* loves, ne sweete entreaties, ... II. v. 38. 3
ever from fayre *Ladies* love did fly; . . . . III. iv. 26. 6
Ladies love his mother long ygoe Did him, they say, forwarne . III. v. 9. 6
'So well I to faire *Ladies* service did, ... III. vii. 55. 1
Seeking to match the chaste with th' unchaste *Ladies* traine.' . III. vii. 60. 9
in all those knights and *ladies* sight . . . . IV. i. 52. 3
so weening way to make To *Ladies* love, ... IV. iv. 4. 4
Braggadochio is uncas'd In all the *Ladies* sights. . . . . . . V. iii. Arg.
Ladles. Some stird the molten owre with *ladles* great; . . . II. vii. 36. 8
many Cookes accoyld With hookes and *ladles,* . . . . II. ix. 30. 7
Lads. *See* **Love-lads.**
the shepheards *laddes* to leade In rymes, ... *S.C.* O. 4
Lady. *See* **Honey-lady, May-lady.**
so faire a *Ladie* did I spie, ... *Pet.* vi. 1
ye, faire *Ladie,* in whose bounteous brest . . . . *Pet.*[2] vii. 9

Lady—*Continued.*

Such as they were (faire *Ladie!*) take in worth,	*Van.* i. 13
Let that rowme to my *Lady* be yeven:	*S.C.* Ap. 114
his Queene attone Was *Lady* Flora,	*S.C.* May 31
'She, (*Ladie*) having well before approoved	*Gn.* 465
Sweete *Ladie* Muses, Ladies of delight,	*Hub.* 761
thy husbands sister die, That goodly *Ladie,*	*Ti.* 275
thine owne sister, peerles *Ladie* bright,	*Ti.* 317
ye, faire *Ladie,* th' honour of your daies,	*Ti.* 680
Full many a *Ladie* faire, in Court	*Mui.* 105
That was the *Lady* of your holy-dayes?	*D.* 319
Of Cynthia the *Ladie* of the Sea,	*Col.* 166
His liege, his *Ladie,* and his lifes Regent.—	*Col.* 235
With the sweet *Lady* Muses for to play:	*Ded. Son.* i. 6
Remembraunce . . . Bids me, most noble *Lady,* to adore	*Ded. Son.* xv. 8
Ne may I, . . . You, fairest *Lady,* leave out.	*Ded. Son.* xvi. 2
Great *Ladie* of the greatest Isle,	I. Pr. 4. 3
A lovely *Ladie* rode him faire beside,	I. i. 4. 1
'Be well aware,' quoth then that *Ladie* milde,	I. i. 12. 1
'Ah *Ladie,*' (sayd he)	I. i. 12. 7
His *Lady,* sad to see his sore constraint,	I. i. 19. 1
His *Lady,* seeing all that chaunst from farre,	I. i. 27. 1
with the *Lady* backward sought to wend.	I. i. 28. 2
'Now,' (saide the *Ladie,*) 'draweth toward night,	I. i. 32. 4
made a *Lady* of that other Spright,	I. i. 45. 2
with usage sly He taught to imitate that *Lady* trew,	I. i. 46. 8
Then seemed him his *Lady* by him lay,	I. i. 47. 7
there before his face his *Ladie* is,	I. i. 49. 5
Come, see where your false *Lady* doth her honor staine.'	I. ii. 4. 9
A goodly *Lady* clad in scarlot red,	I. ii. 13. 2
The *Lady,* . . . Staid not to waile his woefull funerall,	I. ii. 20. 1
'faire *lady,* hart of flint would rew The undeserved woes	I. ii. 26. 8
And his new *Lady* it endured not.	I. ii. 29. 7
that happened to me heare, And to this wretched *Lady,*	I. ii. 31. 6
it was my lott To love this gentle *Lady,*	I. ii. 35. 4
whome ye see Now not a *Lady,* but a seeming tree;	I. ii. 35. 5
That had a like faire *Lady* by his syde;	I. ii. 35. 8
Lyke a faire *Lady,* but did fowle Duessa hyde.	I. ii. 35. 9
His *Lady,* . . . Did yield her comely person to be at my call.	I. ii. 36. 8
turning to his *Lady,* dead with feare her fownd.	I. ii. 44. 9
most faithfull *Ladie,* all this while Forsaken,	I. iii. 3. 1
never . . . Face of fayre *Lady* she before did vew,	I. iii. 11. 8
Such were the labours of this *Lady* meeke,	I. iii. 21. 7
If that of such a *Lady* shee could tellen ought.	I. iii. 24. 9
after for that *Lady* did inquere;	I. iii. 25. 7
his *Lady* did so well him cheare,	I. iii. 34. 7
Of her, that was the *Lady* of that Pallace bright.	I. iv. 6. 9
false Duessa, seeming *Lady* fayre,	I. iv. 13. 2
Emongst the rest rode that false *Lady* faire,	I. iv. 37. 4
Soone as the Faerie heard his *Ladie* speake,	I. v. 12. 1
prowest knight, That ever *Ladie* to her love did chose,	I. v. 14. 3
A wondrous way it for this *Lady* wrought,	I. vi. 7. 3
there begotten of a *Lady* myld,	I. vi. 21. 3
Straunge *Lady* in so straunge habiliment,	I. vi. 30. 7
Were it not better I that *Lady* had	I. vi. 47. 3
on the way He wofull *Lady,* wofull Una, met,	I. vii. 20. 2
Was never *Lady* loved dearer day	I. vii. 27. 7
Whenas this knight nigh to the *Lady* drew,	I. vii. 38. 1
'Ah *Lady* deare,' quoth then the gentle knight,	I. vii. 40. 1
woefull *Lady,* let me you intrete,	I. vii. 40. 5
The noble knight . . . badd the *Ladie* stay,	I. viii. 2. 8
Whome when his *Lady* saw, to him she ran	I. viii. 42. 1
'Faire *Lady,*' then said that victorious knight,	I. viii. 44. 1
'Well worthy impe,' said then the *Lady* gent,	I. ix. 6. 1
He lov'd, as was his lot, a *Lady* gent,	I. ix. 27. 6
to this *Lady* mild Thou falsed hast thy faith	I. ix. 46. 6
That aged Dame, the *Lady* of the place,	I. x. 8. 2
Then badd the knight his *Lady* yede aloof,	I. xi. 5. 1
which when his pensive *Lady* saw from farre,	I. xi. 32. 1
his deare *Lady,* that beheld it all,	I. xi. 55. 3
to his Lord and *Lady* lowd gan call,	I. xii. 2. 8
So faire and fresh that *Lady* shewd herselfe in sight.	I. xii. 21. 9
'Deare *Lady!* how shall I declare thy cace,	II. i. 9. 6
Where sate a gentle *Lady* all alone,	II. i. 13. 5
'Fayre *Lady,* through fowle sorrow ill bedight,	II. i. 14. 2
the man, that ever would deceave A gentle *Lady,*	II. i. 17. 8
fayre *Lady,* comfort to you make,	II. i. 18. 1
Lady, rise out of your paine,	II. i. 20. 6
A knight had wrought against a *Ladie* gent;	II. i. 30. 6
Fitt to inflame faire *Lady* with loves rage,	II. i. 41. 8
deare *Lady,* which the ymage art Of ruefull pitty	II. i. 44. 4
Speake, O dear *Lady,* speake! help never comes too late.'	II. i. 44. 9
Tell then, O *Lady!* tell what fatall priefe	II. i. 48. 6
Which plonged had faire *Lady* in so wretched state.	II. i. 56. 9
thy demaund, O *Lady!* doth revive Fresh memory	II. ii. 40. 1
He lately heard that dying *Lady* grone,	II. iii. 3. 7
Had slayne Sir Mordant and his *Lady* bright:	II. iii. 13. 8
A goodly *Ladie* clad in hunters weed,	II. iii. 21. 7
'But what art thou, O *Lady!*	II. iii. 39. 1
that *Lady* should agayne Depart to woods untoucht,	II. iii. 43. 8
To love a *Lady* fayre of great degree,	II. iv. 19. 2
gratious to that *Lady* as to mee;	II. iv. 20. 4
I that *Lady* to my spouse had wonne;	II. iv. 21. 2
That *Lady,* whom I had to me assynd,	II. iv. 22. 6
Did court the handmayd of my *Lady* deare,	II. iv. 25. 2
Tho' she thy *Lady* be,	II. iv. 26. 6
therein sate a *Lady* fresh and fayre,	II. vi. 3. 1
'The lilly, *Lady* of the flowring field,	II. vi. 16. 1
That gentle *Lady* did to him impart:	II. vi. 26. 5

Lady—*Continued.*

Crying; 'Let be that *Lady* debonaire,	II. vi. 28. 4
'If ever love of *Lady* did empierce Your yron brestes,	II. vi. 33. 1
love avowd to other *Lady* late,	II. vii. 50. 7
Did dewty to their *Lady,* as became;	II. ix. 28. 7
each one sought his *Lady* to aggrate:	II. ix. 34. 5
The Prince by chaunce did on a *Lady* light,	II. ix. 36. 6
that great *Lady* thence away them sought	II. ix. 44. 6
lov'd faire *Ladie* Estrild,	II. x. 17. 6
The noble Virgin, *Ladie* of the Place,	II. xi. 16. 1
many a *lady,*' and many a Paramowre.	II. xii. 75. 5
That wanton *Lady* with her lover lose,	II. xii. 76. 8
A goodly *Lady* did foreby them rush,	III. i. 15. 3
For knight to leave his *Lady* were great shame	III. i. 25. 3
Within this castle wall a *Lady* fayre,	III. i. 26. 2
In case he have no *Lady* nor no love,	III. i. 26. 8
'But if he have a *Lady* or a Love,	III. i. 27. 1
'Love have I sure,' (quoth she) 'but *Lady* none;	III. i. 28. 2
Ne to your *Lady* will I service done,	III. i. 28. 4
of them cleeped was the *Lady* of Delight.	III. i. 31. 9
Now were they liegmen to this *Ladie* free,	III. i. 44. 8
when the *Lady* saw so faire a wight,	III. i. 47. 1
The *Lady* did faire Britomart entreat	III. i. 52. 3
fownd Their *lady* lying on the sencelesse grownd:	III. i. 63. 5
About their *Ladye* first they flockt arownd;	III. i. 64. 1
Faire *Lady* she him seemd, like *Lady* drest.	III. ii. 4. 8
the *Lady* of the Lake, Whom long he lov'd,	III. iii. 10. 6
a faire *Lady* Nonne, that whilome hight Matilda,	III. iii. 13. 5
Whose lignage from this *Lady* I derive along.	III. iv. 3. 9
That fearefull *Ladie* fledd from him,	III. iv. 50. 2
wish that *Lady* faire mote bee His Faery Queene,	III. iv. 54. 6
Served a gentle *Lady* of great sway	III. v. 4. 5
Dwarfe, aread what is that *Lady* bright	III. v. 7. 7
'That *Ladie* is,' . . . The bountiest virgin	III. v. 8. 1
To seeke his *Lady* where he mote her finde;	III. v. 12. 2
that *Lady* bright, Besides all hope,	III. v. 30. 3
where their *Lady* was arrived at the last.	III. v. 37. 9
their *Lady* dresse his wownd.	III. v. 38. 2
How him in deadly case theyr *Lady* fownd,	III. v. 38. 4
love so fayre a *Lady* that his life releast?	III. v. 43. 9
She, gracious *Lady,* yet no paines did spare	III. v. 50. 1
The *Lady* gent Thereat was suddein strook	III. vii. 3. 8
That gentle *Lady* whom I love and serve,	III. vii. 53. 6
The Witch creates a snowy *Lady*	III. viii. Arg.
the *Lady* selfe whom he so long had sought.	III. viii. 9. 9
'this *Lady* is my deare;	III. viii. 12. 8
faynd to cheare his *lady* in dismay,	III. viii. 15. 7
To leave to him that *lady* for excheat,	III. viii. 16. 4
had no regard Him to poursew, but to the *lady* rode;	III. viii. 19. 2
The whiles the pitteous *Lady* up did ryse,	III. viii. 32. 1
To be his Leman and his *Lady* trew:	III. viii. 40. 5
Whiles of a wanton *Lady* I doe write,	III. ix. 1. 6
of his *lady* they might have the sight	III. ix. 25. 8
fairest *Lady* knight,' . . . 'Pardon, I pray,	III. ix. 47. 1
He did resemble to his *lady* bright;	III. x. 21. 8
A silly Pilgrim . . . That seeke a *Lady*'	III. x. 25. 7
'What *Lady,* man?' (said Trompart)	III. x. 26. 1
for a *Lady* gainst a faithlesse knight:	III. x. 28. 6
hath thy *lady* reft and knighthood shent,	III. x. 32. 4
The gentle *Lady,* loose at randon lefte,	III. x. 36. 1
My *lady* and my love so cruelly to pen!	III. xi. 10. 9
'My *lady* and my love is cruelly pend	III. xi. 11. 1
For whom so faire a *Lady* feeles so sore a wound!'	III. xi. 11. 9
She, dolefull *Lady,* like a dreary Spright	III. xii. 19. 4
Save that same woefull *Lady,*	III. xii. 30. 6
fiercely running to that *Lady* trew,	III. xii. 32. 4
the *Lady,* which by him stood bound,	III. xii. 34. 3
wretched *Lady,* quitt from wofull state,	III. xii. 39. 3
faire *Lady,* comfort to you take,	III. xii. 40. 6
He bound that pitteous *Lady* prisoner,	III. xii. 41. 7
she, faire *Lady,* did in pleasure melt,	III. xii. 45. *or.*5
eke the *Ladie* selfe he brought away,	IV. i. 2. 7
the *Ladie,* ill of friends bestedded,	IV. i. 3. 7
ech of them had ryding by his side A *Ladie,*	IV. i. 17. 4
Knight That had a goodly *Ladie* by his side,	IV. ii. 4. 3
Where is my part then of this *Ladie* bright,	IV. ii. 13. 6
'Seest not the *Ladie* there before thy face?'	IV. ii. 22. 6
for this *Ladie,* present in your vew,	IV. ii. 24. 3
Shall to that fairest *Ladie* be prefard.	IV. ii. 27. 4
That was the learnedst *Ladie* in her dayes,	IV. ii. 35. 2
therein sate a *Ladie,* passing faire	IV. iii. 39. 6
In lovely wise she gan that *Lady* greet,	IV. iii. 50. 6
Sith each of them his *Ladie* had him by,	IV. iv. 6. 2
His roving eie did on the *Lady* glaunce	IV. iv. 7. 7
sith ye this *Lady* clame,	IV. iv. 9. 1
(For so to lose a *Lady* were great shame)	IV. iv. 9. 3
to match that *Lady* they had sought Another like,	IV. iv. 10. 7
Whether shall have the Hag, or hold the *Lady* still.'	IV. iv. 12. 9
Thrise happie *Ladie,* and thrise happie knight,	IV. iv. 16. 7
To her therefore The fayrest *Ladie* was adjudgd	IV. v. 8. 9
Let never *Ladie* to his love assent,	IV. v. 18. 8
The fayrest *Ladie* reft, and ever since withheld.'	IV. vi. 6. 9
Which secret fate hath in this *Ladie* wrought	IV. vi. 30. 4
faire *Ladie* knight, my dearest Dame,	IV. vi. 32. 1
she, deare *Ladie,* all the way was dead,	IV. vii. 9. 1
Pursuing that faire *Lady* full of feare:	IV. vii. 24. 5
He held the *Lady* forth before him right,	IV. vii. 26. 3
lov'd a *Ladie* of high parentage;	IV. viii. 50. 2
love of fairest *Ladie* could constraine;	IV. ix. 3. 5
that captive *Lady* faire, The faire Poeana,	IV. ix. 13. 1

Lady's—*Continued.*
which did maintaine That *Ladies* part, . . . V. viii. 50. 4
behight Unto that Damzell in her *Ladies* right, . . . V. ix. 3. 5
it should let your pace Towards my *Ladies* presence, . . . V. ix. 7. 6
To seeke for succour of this *Ladies* gieft; . . . V. x. 14. 7
The which whylome that *Ladies* owne had bene; . . . V. x. 25. 2
Well tride in all thy *Ladies* troubles . . . V. xi. 38. 3
they that *Ladies* lockes doe shave away, . . . VI. i. 13. 8
'To take defiaunce at a *Ladies* word . . . VI. i. 28. 1
is the boast of that proud *Ladies* threat, . . . VI. i. 40. 4
'Unarm'd . . . as then more meete For *Ladies* service, . . . VI. ii. 18. 2
To give faire colour to that *Ladies* cause in sight. . . . VI. iii. 16. 9
Till to that *Ladies* fathers house he came; . . . VI. iii. 17. 8
dare, for thy deare *Ladies* sake . . . VI. iii. 35. 7
Yet for the feeble *Ladies* sake, . . . VI. iii. 45. 8
refuge was still Behind his *Ladies* back; . . . VI. iii. 49. 6
But chaste him still for all his *Ladies* cry; . . . VI. iii. 51. 2
Drawne with that *Ladies* loud and piteous shright, . . . VI. iv. 2. 3
that same *Ladies* hurt no herbe he found . . . VI. iv. 16. 8
Till that his *Ladies* sight he mote attaine, . . . VI. iv. 40. 8
Such were this *Ladies* pangs and dolorous assay. . . . VI. v. 5. 9
led that *Ladies* horse Through thick and thin, . . . VI. vii. 44. 1
had not the *Ladies* cry Procur'd the Prince . . . VI. viii. 29. 1

Laertes'. from him *Laertes* sonne his vewe Doth turne aside, . *Gn.* 533

Laesie. *See* **Lazy.**

Laestrygones. blacke *Laestrigones,* a people stout: . . . *Gn.* 538

Lag. Behind her farre away a Dwarfe did *lag,* . . . I. i. 6. 1

Lagged. When so she *lagged,* . . . Would thumpe her forward . VI. ii. 10. 6

Lago. *Lago,* and Kinmarke did rayne, . . . II. x. 34. 5

Laid. *See* **Overlaid.**
Upon her stomache *laid* Mount Quirinal, . . . *Ro.* iv. 11
bound in sheaves, and *layd* in comely rowes, . . . *Ro.* xxx. 7
layd him downe, and groned, . . . *S.C.* May 246
the cave where Phoebe *layed* The shepheard . . . *S.C.* Jul. 63
makes the Grashopper . . . ligge so *layd,* when Winter . . . *S.C.* O. 12
when my Gates shall han their bellies *layd,* . . . *S.C.* O. 119
Delight is *layd* abedde; . . . *S.C.* D. 137
On this side them there is a yongman *layd,* . . . *Gn.* 493
all those needlesse works are *laid* away; . . . *Hub.* 455
he at last *laid* forth on balefull beare. . . . *T.M.* 162
Is *layd* abed, and no where now to see; . . . *T.M.* 183
He *laid* the brutish nation to enwrap: . . . *As.* 98
And the dim vele . . . aside lie *layd,* . . . *Ded. Son.* ix. 11
Them both together *laid* to joy in vaine delight. . . . I. ii. 3. 9
she . . . *layd* her stole aside. . . . I. iii. 4. 6
squared bricke, Which cunningly was without morter *laid,* . I. iv. 4. 2
goodly galleries far over *laid,* Full of faire windowes . . . I. iv. 4. 7
The warlike youthes, on dayntie couches *layd,* . . . I. iv. 44. 3
Home is he brought, and *layd* in sumptuous bed, . . . I. v. 17. 1
Nor wayld of friends, nor *layd* on groning beare, . . . I. v. 23. 4
that mightie Monarch *layd* Low under all, . . . I. v. 48. 5
he askt, where that same knight was *layd,* . . . I. viii. 32. 6
such the sight . . . when her borrowed light Is *laid* away, . . I. viii. 49. 6
downe to sleepe me *layd,* . . . I. ix. 13. 2
ever burning wrath before him *laid,* . . . I. ix. 50. 3
a Groome, that forth him ledd . . . and *laid* in easie bedd. . . I. x. 17. 8
he *laid* him privily Downe . . . I. x. 25. 6
The grace of God he *layd* up still in store, . . . I. x. 38. 6
why they in bands were *layd;* . . . I. x. 40. 7
three mens strength unto the stroake he *layd,* . . . I. xi. 20. 4
double blowes about him stoutly *laid,* . . . I. xi. 42. 4
she had *layd* her mournefull stole aside, . . . I. xii. 22. 2
they him *layd* full low in dungeon deepe, . . . I. xii. 36. 1
Laid first his filthie hands on virgin cleene, . . . II. i. 10. 4
slyding soft, as downe to sleepe her *layd,* . . . II. i. 56. 3
Me leading, in a secret corner *layd,* . . . II. iv. 27. 5
this Squyre have *laide* thus low. . . . II. iv. 34. 9
thus low me *laid* in dust.' . . . II. v. 12. 9
On a sweet bed of lillies softly *laid,* . . . II. v. 32. 3
laid forth for ensample of the best: . . . II. vi. 12. 5
layd him downe upon a grassy playn; . . . II. vi. 14. 4
lips he *layd* on thing that likte him best, . . . II. vii. 27. 3
Such grace now to be happy is before thee *laid.'* . . . II. vii. 32. 9
Sir Guyon, *layd* in swowne, . . . II. viii. Arg.
having *laid* his cruell bow away . . . II. viii. 6. 2
rude hand upon his shield he *laid,* . . . II. viii. 17. 1
Whom fortune hath already *laid* in lowest seat.' . . . II. viii. 27. 9
So fierce he *laid* about him, . . . II. viii. 41. 1
so soone as his outrageous powre Is *layd,* . . . II. viii. 48. 5
having from him *layd* His cruel bow, . . . II. ix. 34. 8
laid them up in his immortall scrine, . . . II. ix. 56. 6
when thinges were lost, or *laid* amis, . . . II. ix. 58. 6
Elfinan, who *laid* Cleopolis foundation first of all: . . . II. x. 72. 7
Upon him fell, and lode upon him *layd:* . . . II. xi. 29. 5
In sumptuous bed shee made him be *layd;* . . . II. xi. 49. 8
There she had him now *laid* aslombering . . . II. xii. 72. 5
Upon a bed of Roses she was *layd,* . . . II. xii. 77. 1
That speare enchaunted was which *layd* thee on the greene. . . III. i. 7. 9
laid the blame, not to his carriage, . . . III. i. 11. 5
Mainely they all attonce upon him *laid,* . . . III. i. 21. 1
Ne did she stay till three on ground she *layd* . . . III. i. 29. 1
by her side her selfe she softly *layd,* . . . III. i. 61. 4
Whom having *laid* in comfortable couch, . . . III. i. 64. 2
with her flaming sword about her *layd,* . . . III. i. 66. 2
sith they warlike armes have *laide* away, . . . III. ii. 2. 7
her downe she *layd* In her warme bed . . . III. ii. 47. 2
Beene they all dead, and *laide* in dolefull herse, . . . III. iv. 1. 8
There they him *laide* in easy couch well dight, . . . III. iv. 43. 6
Downe himselfe he *layd* Upon the grassy ground . . . III. iv. 53. 7
load upon him *layd* his life for to have had. . . . III. v. 22. 9

Laid—*Continued.*
To commun accidents stil open *layd,* . . . III. v. 36. 7
layd In easie couch his feeble limbes to rest. . . . III. v. 41. 1
Whiles dayly playsters to his wownd she *layd,* . . . III. v. 43. 5
Upon the grassy ground her selfe she *layd* . . . III. vi. 7. 2
their maister, who in bed was *layd,* . . . III. ix. 10. 5
overthrowne and *laide* on th' earth full cold, . . . III. ix. 50. 5
none espyde His . . . drift, till he her *layd* abord. . . . III. x. 6. 4
her trembling hart . . . in a silver basin *layd,* . . . III. xii. 21. 2
laid the noble Championesse strong hond Upon th' enchaunter . III. xii. 41. 3
first *laide* on those Ladies thousand blames, . . . IV. ii. 20. 7
with his brondiron round about him *layd;* . . . IV. iv. 32. 3
layd aside when so she usd her looser sport. . . . IV. v. 3. 9
in his armour *layd* him down to rest: . . . IV. v. 39. 2
To rest he *layd* him downe upon the flore, . . . IV. v. 39. 3
Her feeble joynts *layd* eke adowne to rest; . . . IV. v. 39. 7
oft in wrath he *layd* him downe againe. . . . IV. v. 40. 6
layd Before the ryder, as he captive were, . . . IV. ix. 5. 1
laid on load with all their might and powre, . . . IV. ix. 22. 7
Paridell and Druon fiercely *laid* At Scudamour, . . . IV. ix. 30. 3
layd at them so sharpely and so sore, . . . IV. ix. 34. 7
those rolles, *layd* up in heaven above, . . . IV. xi. 10. 3
layd above, Like ruefull ghost, . . . IV. xii. 20. 8
In which his life unluckily was *layd,* . . . IV. xii. 28. 2
on the ground he *layd* him like a sencelesse blocke. . . . V. i. 21. 9
layd on load with his huge yron flaile, . . . V. ii. 24. 2
the least word that ever could be *layd* Within his ballaunce . V. ii. 44. 3
then the false he *layd* In th' other scale; . . . V. ii. 45. 6
So each of them *layd* downe his sword . . . V. iv. 16. 9
Your brothers land the which the sea hath *layd* Unto your part, V. iv. 17. 3
Then all that rout uppon them rudely *laid,* . . . V. iv. 38. 7
She hewd, she foynd, she lasht, she *laid* on every side. . . . V. v. 6. 9
With huge redoubled strokes she on him *layd;* . . . V. v. 14. 6
Full fiercely *layde* the Amazon about, . . . V. vii. 31. 1
Where being *layd,* the wrothfull Britonesse Stayd not . . . V. vii. 34. 1
In which her wretched love was captive *layd:* . . . V. vii. 37. 3
What were those knights which there on ground were *layd,* . V. viii. 15. 2
at her feet her sword was likewise *layde,* . . . V. ix. 30. 6
laid his Seneschall low on the ground, . . . V. xi. 2. 4
That bloudie scutchin, being battered sore, I *layd* aside, . . . V. xi. 54. 5
still the tyrant sternely at him *layd,* . . . V. xii. 19. 6
layd On hideous strokes . . . VI. i. 20. 1
and downeward *layd* Upon the ground, . . . VI. ii. 48. 1
layd her underneath a bush to sleepe, . . . VI. iii. 44. 6
To seeke if he perchance asleepe were *layd,* . . . VI. v. 3. 7
it perceiving hand upon him *layd,* . . . VI. v. 26. 8
on them *layd* so huge and horribly, . . . VI. vi. 23. 4
layd at him amaine with all his will and might. . . . VI. vi. 27. 9
he *layd* about, and made them fast to flie. . . . VI. vi. 38. 9
downe his weapons *layd,* . . . VI. vi. 39. 5
He there in shade himselfe had *layd* to rest, . . . VI. vii. 19. 2
Whom when as Turpin saw so loosely *layd,* . . . VI. vii. 20. 1
his left hand upon his collar *layd.* . . . VI. vii. 25. 6
Till heavy hand the Carle upon him *layd,* . . . VI. vii. 48. 6
Laide heavy hands on him and held so strayte, . . . VI. viii. 11. 3
Sometimes aloft he *layd,* sometimes alow, . . . VI. viii. 13. 6
The which the God of love hath on me *layd,* . . . VI. viii. 19. 7
Upon the grasse her selfe adowne she *layd;* . . . VI. viii. 34. 3
by the Faery Queene was on him *layd,* . . . VI. x. 1. 4
in dreadfull darknesse *layd* Amongst those theeves, . . . VI. xi. 2. 3
He at the length was slaine and *layd* on ground, . . . VI. xi. 19. 6
Seeme much more lovely in that darknesse *layd,* . . . VI. xi. 21. 7
She in the open fields had loosely *layd* . . . VI. xii. 16. 4
Rent up her brest, and bosome open *layd,* . . . VI. xii. 19. 4
on her shoulder *laid* His snaky-wreathed Mace, . . . VII. vi. 18. 1
Then all attonce their hands upon Molanna *laid.* . . . VII. vi. 51. 9
Goe to my love, where she is carelesse *layd,* . . . *Am.* lxx. 5
Whether in earth *layd* up in secret store, . . . *H.B.* 37

Lain. *See* **Lien.**
underneath her scornefull feete was *layne* A dreadfull Dragon . I. iv. 10. 4
By any Ladies side for Leman to have *laine,* . . . IV. vii. 15. 9

Lair. More hard for hungry steed t' abstaine from pleasant *lare.* . . . IV. viii. 29. 9
lies there on the *laire* An headlesse heape, . . . IV. viii. 51. 5

Laisure. *See* **Leisure.**

Lake. That nowe sleepeth in Lethe *lake,* . . . *S.C.* Mar. 23
They bene all Ladyes of the *lake* behight, . . . *S.C.* Ap. 120
In that wide *lake* looking for plenteous praie . . . *Ti.* 151
Is now no *lake,* nor anie fishers store, . . . *Ti.* 153
not to have been dipt in Lethe *lake,* . . . *Ti.* 428
Sometime a fowle, sometime a fish in *lake,* . . . I. ii. 10. 5
'What voice of damned Ghost from Limbo *lake,* . . . I. ii. 32. 5
his ghost . . . In peace may passen over Lethe *lake;* . . . I. iii. 36. 6
Doest thou sit wayling by blacke Stygian *lake,* . . . I. v. 10. 6
Snake . . . Long fostred in the filth of Lerna *lake:* . . . I. vii. 17. 3
In every fountaine, and in everie *lake,* . . . II. ii. 5. 7
in Stygian *lake,* ay burning bright, Had kindled: . . . II. v. 22. 7
hight by name The Idle *lake,* . . . II. vi. 10. 2
floted in the midst of that great *lake;* . . . II. vi. 11. 4
The slouthfull wave of that great griesy *lake:* . . . II. vi. 18. 7
in the *lake* his loftie crest was stept, . . . II. vi. 42. 4
Nor sea of licour cold, nor *lake* of myre: . . . II. vi. 44. 4
Into the *lake* he lept his Lord to ayd, . . . II. vi. 46. 1
guyde, Late left beyond that Ydle *lake,* . . . II. vii. 2. 2
(As wonts the Tartar by the Caspian *lake,* . . . II. xi. 26. 7
Until he came unto a standing *lake;* . . . II. xi. 46. 6
Hedlong her selfe did cast into that *lake;* . . . II. xi. 47. 6
Did ferry him over the Idle *lake:* . . . II. xii. 17. 2
like a litle *lake* it seemd to bee; . . . II. xii. 62. 5
the Lady of the *Lake,* Whom long he lov'd, . . . III. iii. 10. 6

Lake—*Continued.*
made a *lake* Of Greekish blood . . . III. iv. 2. 5
By Stygian *lake* I vow, . . . III. vi. 24. 7
From Limbo *lake* him late escaped sure would say. . . . III. x. 54. 9
He is declyned . . . to the Southerne *lake;* . . . V. Pr. 7. 8
More loathed then Lerna, or then Stygian *lake,* . . . V. xi. 32. 4
like to a purple *lake* Of bloudy gore . . . VI. i. 37. 7
Witnesse the wounds, and this wyde bloudie *lake,* . . . VI. vii. 15. 5
Ne any *Lake,* that seems most still and slowe, . . . VII. vii. 20. 5
ye likewise, which keepe the rushy *lake,* . . . *Epith.* 60
To deepest hell, and *lake* of damned fyre, . . . *H.H.L.* 89
Lakes. Lastly the squalid *lakes* of Tartarie, . . . *Gn.* 543
the sad *lakes* that Phoebus sunnie rayes Doo never see, . . . *Gn.* 619
Dragon . . . Bred in the loathly *lakes* of Tartary, . . . I. vii. 44. 3
Lamb. To her will I offer a milkwhite *Lamb:* . . . *S.C.* Ap. 96
what peace has the Lion with the *Lambe?* . . . *S.C.* May 169
Thereby is a *Lambe* in the Wolves jawes: . . . *S.C.* Au. 31
Thereto will I pawne yonder spotted *Lambe,* . . . *S.C.* Au. 37
let the *Lambe* be Willye his owne: . . . *S.C.* Au. 132
with many a *Lambe* had glutted his gulfe, . . . *S.C.* S. 185
A *Lambe,* or a Kidde, or a weanell wast; . . . *S.C.* S. 198
not a *lambe* of all their flockes supply . . . *Hub.* 316
slaine her *Lambe* most cruellie, . . . *Hub.* 1210
He is with greater matter busied Than a *Lambe,* . . . *Hub.* 1216
As the least *lamb* in all my flock that went: . . . *D.* 126
a milkewhite *lamb* she lad . . . I. i. 4. 9
So pure and innocent, as that same *lambe,* . . . I. i. 5. 1
Wolfe, . . . A seely *Lamb* . . . does take, . . . I. vi. 10. 4
unspotted *lam,* that for the sinnes of al the world was kilt: I. x. 57. 6
trembled like a *lambe* fled from the pray; . . . III. vii. 36. 6
The Lyon there did with the *Lambe* consort, . . . IV. viii. 31. 1
disdeigneth to devoure The silly *lambe* . . . *Am.* xx. 8
Meeke *Lambe* of God, before all worlds behight, . . . *H.H.L.* 173
Lambkin. twixt them both they not a *lambkin* left, . . . *Hub.* 321
Lambkins. of our tender *Lambkins* takest keepe, . . . *S.C.* D. 8
Lamb's. the *Lambes* owne mothers hed. . . . *Hub.* 1216
mercie seate, Close covered with the *Lambes* integrity . . . *H.H.B.* 149
Lambs. The rather *Lambes* bene starved with cold, . . . *S.C.* F. 83
hath some Wolfe thy tender *Lambes* ytorne? . . . *S.C.* Ap. 2
your tender *Lambes* that by you trace. . . . *S.C.* Jun. 120
Adieu, my little *Lambes* and loved sheepe; . . . *S.C.* D. 153
of their *lambes,* and of their woolly fleece. . . . *Hub.* 302
when *lambes* fail'd the old sheepes lives they reft; . . . *Hub.* 322
shepheards leave their *lambs* unto mischaunce, . . . *Ti.* 327
Where on a sunnie banke the *Lambes* doo play, . . . *Mui.* 402
Him forth did bring, and taught her *lambs* to feed; . . . *As.* 14
my *lambs,* when for their dams they call, . . . *Col.* 638
leave their *lambes* to losse, misled amisse. . . . *Col.* 687
My *lambes* doe every yeare increase their score, . . . VI. ix. 21. 7
the Fox, the vowed foe Unto my *Lambes,* . . . VI. ix. 23. 2
Lame. as he were starke *lame:* . . . *S.C.* May 279
Her other leg was *lame,* . . . II. iv. 4. 3
the one her other legge had *lame,* . . . II. xi. 23. 6
that *lame* Hag, . . . II. xi. 28. 1
was bescracht and both his feet nigh *lame.* . . . III. v. 3. 9
He sett upon her Palfrey tired *lame,* . . . III. vii. 28. 8
Repentaunce feeble, sorrowfull, and *lame;* . . . III. xii. 24. 3
their sides were sore; their feete were *lame.* . . . VI. v. 40. 9
Lament. What is he for a Ladde you so *lament?* . . . *S.C.* Ap. 17
I *lament* thy case; . . . *S.C.* Jun. 113
I *lament* The haplesse mischiefe . . . *S.C.* S. 248
O Lobb! thy losse no longer *lament;* . . . *S.C.* N. 168
with sweete teares did *lament.* . . . *Gn.* 200
almost sterv'd did much *lament* and mourne. . . . *Hub.* 580
hearing them so heavily *lament,* . . . *T.M.* 35
Therewith she lowdly did *lament* and shrike, . . . *T.M.* 229
did the losse of some dere love *lament,* . . . *Ti.* 16
'O Rome! thy ruine I *lament* and rue, . . . *Ti.* 78
to *lament* My long decay, . . . *Ti.* 156
I, it seeing, dearelie did *lament.* . . . *Ti.* 504
to *lament* His losse, . . . *Ti.* 676
Then gan she greatly to *lament* and weepe. . . . *Mui.* 288
seeking misse, and missing doe *lament.*' . . . *D.* 168
Well may the shepheard lasses now *lament;* . . . *D.* 222
Why should Alcyon then so sore *lament* That I . . . *D.* 271
Lament my lot, and tell your fellow-swaines . . . *D.* 524
all their fish with languor did *lament:* . . . *Col.* 28
Melting in teares, then gan shee thus *lament.* . . . I. ii. 22. 1
Heard how in vaine Fradubio did *lament,* . . . I. ii. 44. 2
In stead of rest she does *lament* and weepe, . . . I. iii. 15. 5
To weet what wight so loudly did *lament.* . . . I. vi. 8. 4
His wandring perill closely did *lament,* . . . I. vi. 32. 2
Then gins her grieved ghost to *lament* and mourne: . . . I. vii. 21. 9
joyd to see her lover languish and *lament:* . . . I. ix. 27. 9
praying still did wake, and waking did *lament.* . . . I. xi. 32. 9
oft they did *lament* his lucklesse state, . . . I. xii. 16. 4
Had with dew rites and dolorous *lament* . . . II. ii. 1. 2
after soone I dearely did *lament;* . . . II. iv. 29. 5
to *lament* and mourne The royall seed, . . . III. iii. 42. 7
The martiall Mayd stayd not him to *lament,* . . . III. iv. 18. 1
Whiles all her sisters did for her *lament* . . . III. iv. 30. 7
their great mother Venus did *lament* . . . III. vi. 40. 3
did the most *lament* For her depart, . . . III. vii. 20. 1
That madest many Ladies deare *lament* . . . III. ix. 35. 3
threw Her selfe uppon her bed, and did *lament:* . . . V. vi. 13. 7
Yet did she not *lament* with loude alew, . . . V. vi. 13. 8
for his sake Diana did *lament,* . . . V. viii. 43. 6
'What be you, wofull Dame, which thus *lament,* . . . VI. iv. 27. 8
ruth it was to see him so *lament:* . . . VI. v. 4. 6
To see her sore *lament* . . . VI. vii. 44. 9

Lament—*Continued.*
Did laugh at those that did *lament* and plaine; . . . VI. viii. 21. 8
she nought did but *lament* Her wretched life . . . VI. x. 44. 3
These eyes saw die, and dearely did *lament;* . . . VI. xi. 31. 7
teach the woods and waters to *lament* . . . *Epith.* 10
Lamentable. leave this *lamentable* plaint behinde: . . . *Gn.* 635
wring Her wretched hands in *lamentable* wise; . . . *T.M.* 170
launch your hearts with *lamentable* wounds . . . *T.M.* 375
Ne sheddeth teares from *lamentable* eie; . . . *Ti.* 163
where shall I finde *lamentable* cryes, . . . *Mui.* 411
a *lamentable* lay Of great unkindnesse, . . . *Col.* 164
to tell her *lamentable* cace, . . . I. vi. 48. 8
strowe with flowres the *lamentable* beare. . . . III. iv. 42. 5
'O *lamentable* fall of famous towne! . . . III. ix. 39. 2
thereof made a *lamentable* lay, . . . IV. viii. 4. 3
the *lamentable* voice of one, That piteously complaind . . . IV. xii. 5. 2
He gan record the *lamentable* stowre, . . . IV. xii. 19. 3
tell with all the *lamentable* plight . . . VI. iii. 41. 7
Then thus began the *lamentable* Dame: . . . VI. iv. 29. 1
Which she beheld with *lamentable* eye, . . . VI. viii. 3. 2
My life will by his death have *lamentable* end. . . . VI. viii. 17. 9
Lamentation. pitious *lamentation* did make; . . . *T.M.* 296
Lamented. By his disloyalty *lamented* sore, . . . *Gn.* 202
Of you, his mournfull Sisters, was *lamented,* . . . *T.M.* 11
much *lamented* his calamity, . . . VI. viii. 3. 4
Lamenting. *See* **Great-lamenting.**
For whome the Thracian king, *lamenting* sore, . . . *Gn.* 404
heavily *lamenting* from them went. . . . *T.M.* 36
lamenting Love marreth the Musicall. . . . *U.V.* 12
Lamenting lowde my Daphnes Elegie, . . . *D.* 509
With hollow houling, and *lamenting* cry; . . . I. iii. 23. 2
As with *lamenting* eyes him selfe did lately vew. . . . II. ii. 45. 9
Lamenting Sorrow did in darknes lye, . . . II. vii. 22. 8
Lamenting his mishap and heavy plight; . . . III. iv. 44. 2
Lamenting sore his sorrowfull sad tyne, . . . V. i. 13. 8
thy sire *lamenting* sore for thee, . . . V. vii. 21. 8
Which to her selfe *lamenting* loudly cryde, . . . VI. iv. 26. 8
lamenting her unluckie strife, . . . VI. viii. 48. 6
She tooke him streight full pitiously *lamenting,* . . . *Epig.* iv. 41
Let no *lamenting* cryes . . . Be heard . . . *Epith.* 334
Laments. *Laments* the wound that death did launch. . . . *S.C.* N. 139
feeble Eccho now *laments* . . . *T.M.* 285
With lowd *laments* her answered . . . *T.M.* 418
He wept, and wayld, false *laments* belyde, . . . III. x. 7. 7
piteously complayning With loud *laments* . . . VI. ii. 41. 3
Lamorack. after him Sir *Lamoracke* of yore, . . . VI. xii. 39. 7
Lamp. Beautie, the burning *lamp* of heavens light, . . . *Col.* 873
Like Phoebus *lampe* throughout the world doth shine, . . . I. Pr. 4. 4
faire Hesperus . . . Had spent his *lampe,* . . . I. ii. 6. 7
my light, and shining *lampe* of blis!' . . . I. iii. 27. 9
'O lightsome day! the *lampe* of highest Jove, . . . I. vii. 23. 1
sacred *lamp* in secret chamber hide, . . . I. xii. 37. 7
The faithfull light of that faire *lampe* . . . II. vii. 1. 4
a *lamp,* whose life does fade away, . . . II. vii. 29. 7
The dronken *lamp* down in the oyl did steepe, . . . III. ii. 47. 8
Phoebus *Lamp* Bewrayed had the world . . . III. x. 1. 1
that same great glorious *lampe* of light, . . . V. Pr. 7. 1
Untill she spide the *lampe* of lightsome day . . . V. vii. 17. 3
leading th' ever-burning *lampe* astray, . . . V. viii. 40. 7
light then Phoebus *lampe* doth shine more cleare? . . . V. xi. 62. 9
the *lampe* of light Above the earth upreard . . . VI. i. 31. 1
therein to beare Nights burning *lamp,* . . . VII. vi. 12. 3
the worlds light-giving *lampe* . . . *Epith.* 19
glorious *lampe* of love! . . . *Epith.* 288
lampe doth yet remaine Fresh burning . . . *H.L.* 131
Light of thy *lampe;* . . . *H.B.* 59
that faire *lampe,* from whose celestiall ray . . . *H.B.* 99
O most blessed Spirit! pure *lampe* of light, . . . *H.H.L.* 43
O glorious Morning-Starre! O *Lampe* of Light! . . . *H.H.L.* 170
And that faire *lampe,* which useth to inflame . . . *H.H.B.* 274
Lamp-burning. the Sunne, with his *lamp-burning* light, . . . II. ix. 7. 5
Lamping. Emongst th' eternall spheres and *lamping* sky, . . . III. iii. 1. 3
with starry light, Those *lamping* eyes will . . . look, . . . *Am.* i. 6
Lamps. Lightned with deadly *lamps* on everie post? . . . *Gn.* 341
shyning *lampes* in Joves high house were light; . . . I. v. 19. 2
The everburning *lamps* from thence it braught, . . . I. vii. 18. 4
Those glaring *lampes* were sett that made a dreadfull shade. I. xi. 14. 9
In her faire eyes two living *lamps* did flame, . . . II. iii. 23. 1
th' eternall *lampes* . . . were halfe yspent, . . . III. i. 57. 6
To light their blessed *lamps* in Joves eternall hous. . . . III. iv. 51. 9
whose faire eyes, like *lamps* of quenched fire, . . . III. v. 29. 3
two burning *lampes* she set In silver sockets, . . . III. viii. 7. 1
hevenly *lampes* were halfendeale ybrent: . . . III. ix. 53. 5
both adorn'd with *lampes* of flaming light; . . . V. iii. 19. 4
Few perling drops from her faire *lampes* of light; . . . V. ix. 50. 7
all the rest like lesser *lamps* did dim: . . . VI. ix. 9. 5
baseborne mynds such *lamps* regard the lesse, . . . *H.L.* 173
Adornd with thousand *lamps* of burning light, . . . *H.H.L.* 59
Lancaster. to old *Loncaster* his name doth lend; . . . IV. xi. 39. 2
Lance. he forward gan advaunce . . . his charmed *launce.* . . . I. iii. 25. 9
with stiffe force shaking his mortall *launce,* . . . II. iii. 14. 4
she lefte her percing *launce,* . . . II. iii. 34. 4
bore after him an heben *launce* And coverd shield. . . . II. viii. 17. 6
within his flesh Did breake the *launce,* . . . II. viii. 36. 7
the length of all her *launce;* . . . III. iv. 16. 7
fortune all in equall *launce* doth sway, . . . III. vii. 4. 4
Braggadochio, with his bloody *launce,* . . . III. viii. 18. 7
that same knight, whom by his *launce* I read, . . . IV. vi. 7. 8
eft aventring his steele-headed *launce,* . . . IV. vi. 11. 3
casting from her that enchaunted *launce,* . . . IV. vi. 14. 7

Lance—*Continued.*
all his *launce* in peeces shivered quite, ... VI. vii. 8. 3
Lanced. *See* **Out-lanced, Through-lanced.**
Lance's. Above a *launces* length him forth did beare, ... VI. vii. 11. 3
Lances. dart at them their litle fierie *launces;* . . . . *H.B.* 241
Land. *See* **Faery-land, Inland, Mainland, Upland.**
bottome yellow like the shining *land,* . . . . *Bel.*[1] x. 3
Both *land* and sea in roundnes had survew'd, ... *Ro.* viii. 3
Atcheived the golden Fleece in Colchid *land,* . . . . *Ro.* x. 2
Queene of *land* and sea her selfe she made. . . . . *Ro.* xx. 11
When *land* and sea ye name, ... *Ro.* xxvi. 11
naming Rome, ye *land* and sea comprize: . . . . *Ro.* xxvi. 12
To be the primrose of all thy *land;* . . . . *S.C.* F. 166
Long wandring up and downe the *land,* . . . . *S.C.* Mar. 64
Ne of *land,* nor fee in sufferaunce, ... *S.C.* May 106
Out of the *land* is fled away and gone. . . . . *Gn.* 360
To follow Orpheus musicke through the *land:* . . . . *Gn.* 452
all the rest doo rob of good and *land.* . . . . *Hub.* 140
like a Lawyer, when he *land* would lett, ... *Hub.* 866
part by *land* and part by water fed; . . . . *Hub.* 1120
She seem'd still backe unto the *lond* to looke, ... *Mui.* 281
When as the *land* she saw no more appeare, ... *Mui.* 286
Dauncing upon the waters back to *lond,* . . . . *Col.* 214
land, our mother, us did leave, ... *Col.* 226
beside a thousand moe at *land:* . . . . *Col.* 261
land and sea my Cynthia doth deserve . . . . *Col.* 262
at length we *land* far off descryde: . . . . *Col.* 265
I feard, least *land* we never should have eyde: . . . . *Col.* 267
From thence another world of *land* we kend, ... *Col.* 272
put us all ashore on Cynthias *land.* . . . . *Col.* 289
'What *land* is that thou meant, ... *Col.* 290
that same *land* much larger is then this, ... *Col.* 296
if that *land* be there . . . as here, ... *Col.* 304
much more . . . abound in that same *land* then this: . . . . *Col.* 309
'Foorth on our voyage we by *land* did passe, ... *Col.* 330
And, in so faire a *land* as may be redd, ... *Ded. Son.* v. 5
Till that infernall feend . . . Forwasted all their *land,* . . I. i. 5. 8
and ech to other yealdeth *land.* . . . . I. ii. 15. 9
never in that *land* Face of fayre Lady she . . . did vew, . . I. iii. 11. 7
plenty, which in all the *land* did grow: . . . . I. iii. 18. 7
the thirsty *land* Dronke up his life; . . . . I. iii. 20. 4
that by *land* and seas Have vowd you to defend. . . . . . . I. iii. 29. 8
conquered now he lye on lowly *land;* . . . . I. iii. 37. 7
A foggy mist had covered all the *land;* . . . . I. iv. 36. 7
High reard their royall throne in Britans *land,* . . . . . . I. x. 65. 4
with his largenesse measured much *land,* . . . . I. xi. 8. 3
It sweepeth all the *land* behind him farre, ... I. xi. 11. 6
drowned all the *land* whereon he stood; . . . . I. xi. 22. 5
before that cursed Dragon got That happy *land,* . . . . . . I. xi. 29. 7
That al the *land* with stench and heven with horror choke. . . I. xi. 44. 9
Vere the maine shete, and beare up with the *land,* . . . . . I. xii. 1. 3
That aged Syre, the Lord of all that *land,* . . . . I. xii. 3. 2
Glad signe of victory and peace in all their *land.* . . . . . I. xii. 5. 9
To prove how many acres he did spred of *land.* . . . . . . I. xii. 11. 9
he already plighted his right hand . . . to another *land.* . . . I. xii. 26. 9
solemne feast proclaymd throughout the *land,* . . . . I. xii. 40. 2
rode, Where we must *land* some of our passengers, ... I. xii. 42. 3
happy *land* of Faery, Which I so much doe vaunt, ... II. Pr. 1. 7
thine owne realmes in *lond* of Faery, ... II. Pr. 4. 8
mickle worship in his native *land;* . . . . II. i. 6. 6
The cursed *land* where many wend amis, ... II. i. 51. 8
Into the *land* that lay them faire before, ... II. vi. 11. 8
It was a chosen plott of fertile *land,* . . . . II. vi. 12. 1
whenas Guyon of that *land* had sight, ... II. vi. 22. 5
Where gladsome Guyon salied forth to *land,* . . . . II. vi. 38. 5
The *land* which warlike Britons now possesse, ... II. x. 5. 1
Into this *land* by chaunce have driven bene; . . . . II. x. 8. 5
They held this *land,* . . . . II. x. 9. 1
This *land* invaded with like violence, ... II. x. 15. 6
in his *land* he lately did appease, ... II. x. 17. 4
monuments remaine, which yet that *land* envies. . . . . . . II. x. 21. 9
taught the *land* from wearie wars to cease: . . . . II. x. 25. 5
Nought els but treason from the first this *land* did foyle. . . II. x. 48. 9
this *land* was tributarie made T' ambitious Rome, ... II. x. 49. 6
gan the Hunnes and Picts invade this *land,* . . . . II. x. 61. 6
got large portions of *land,* . . . . II. x. 65. 6
The royall Ofspring of his native *land,* . . . . II. x. 69. 2
fast the *land* behynd them fled away. . . . . II. xi. 4. 6
all the *land* they under them did hyde; . . . . II. xi. 5. 7
noblest borne of all in Britayne *land;* . . . . II. xi. 30. 7
Ne ever *land* beheld, ne living wight, ... II. xii. 2. 2
'Lo! I the *land* descry; . . . . II. xii. 10. 8
not firme *land,* nor any certein wonne, ... II. xii. 11. 4
From the departing *land* it launched light, ... II. xii. 15. 8
The *land* to which their course they leveled; . . . . II. xii. 34. 4
the faire *land* it selfe did playnly sheow. . . . . II. xii. 37. 6
with her crooked keele the *land* she strooke: . . . . II. xii. 38. 3
with the liquor stained all the *lond:* . . . . II. xii. 57. 5
By sea, by *land,* where so they may be mett, ... III. ii. 7. 3
The *Land* to sea, and sea to maineland dry, ... III. iii. 12. 3
He wonneth in the *land* of Fayeree, ... III. iii. 26. 3
forreine Paynims which invade thy *land.* . . . . III. iii. 27. 9
As was in all the *lond* of Faery, or else wheare. . . . . . . III. iv. 23. 9
high accompt through out all Elfin *land,* . . . . III. v. 4. 6
safety fownd at sea which she fownd not at *land.* . . . . . . III. vii. 27. 9
backe returning to the former *land,* . . . . III. vii. 61. 5
to chaunge The *land* for sea, ... III. viii. 20. 5
Least worse on sea then us on *land* befell.' . . . . III. viii. 24. 5
To fetch from sea that ye at *land* lost late! . . . . III. viii. 28. 4
Confounds both *land* and seas, ... III. ix. 15. 9

Land—*Continued.*
that is the bownd Toward the *land;* . . . . III. ix. 46. 4
To seeke her endlong both by sea and *lond.* . . . . III. x. 19. 5
upon the face of living *land?* . . . . III. xi. 10. 4
fly Unto her rest in Plutoes griesly *land;* . . . . IV. iii. 13. 3
they were left uppon the *land,* . . . . IV. iv. 21. 8
whylome they have conquerd sea and *land,* . . . . IV. vi. 31. 4
he was full light and nimble on the *land.* . . . . IV. vii. 25. 9
all which there had hapned on the *land.* . . . . IV. viii. 62. 9
of Lordship with both *land* and fee: . . . . IV. ix. 13. 7
chiefe Of all her *land* and lordship during life. . . . . . . IV. ix. 15. 8
afterward both sea and *land* possest; . . . . IV. xi. 18. 4
quaile in conquest of that *land* of gold. . . . . IV. xi. 22. 5
the plenteous Ouse came far from *land,* . . . . IV. xi. 34. 1
betwixt Logris *land* And Albany: . . . . IV. xi. 36. 6
fruitfull seede farre passeth those in *land,* . . . . IV. xii. 1. 3
from the water to the *land* betooke his flight. . . . . . . V. ii. 17. 9
to tread upon the *land,* . . . . V. ii. 18. 4
Encroch uppon the *land* there under thee? . . . . V. ii. 37. 5
part of my *land* hath washt away, ... V. iv. 8. 3
though my *land* he first did winne away, ... V. iv. 14. 6
what so about our *land* My brother here declared hath . . . V. iv. 15. 2
Your brothers *land* the which the sea . . . . V. iv. 17. 3
So, Amidas, the *land* was yours first hight; . . . . V. iv. 19. 8
her selfe uppon the *land* She did prostrate, ... V. vii. 7. 7
Unto the *land* of Amazons, as she was bent. . . . . V. vii. 24. 9
like a stone it fell upon the *land;* . . . . V. ix. 17. 8
With which high God had blest her happie *land,* . . . . . . V. ix. 30. 4
witnesse forth aright in forrain *land,* . . . . V. ix. 37. 5
from forrein *land* where they did dwell, ... V. x. 6. 3
By a strong Tyrant, who invaded has Her *land,* . . . . . . V. x. 6. 9
brought that *land* to his subjection, ... V. x. 9. 5
streight tooke his flight From that sad *land* . . . . V. x. 11. 4
Within the *land* where dwelt that Ladie sad; . . . . V. x. 18. 2
from her native *land* Exiled her, ... V. xi. 4. 6
ever, ere he saw the stroke to *land,* . . . . V. xi. 7. 4
all the people, both of towne and *land,* . . . . V. xi. 15. 5
them forbad to *land,* and footing did forstall. . . . . V. xii. 4. 9
nathemore would they from *land* refraine: . . . . V. xii. 5. 1
they lay scattred over all the *land,* . . . . V. xii. 7. 8
as he backe returned from that *land,* . . . . V. xii. 28. 1
In this delightfull *land* of Faery, ... VI. Pr. 1. 2
Nor *land* nor fee for hyre of his good deede, ... VI. i. 47. 2
away me to remove . . . Into some forrein *land,* . . . . . . VI. ii. 29. 8
adviz'd to send me . . . Into the *land* of Faerie, ... VI. ii. 30. 5
she . . . sent me streight Into this *land,* . . . . VI. ii. 30. 8
bold Sir Bruin, who is Lord Of all this *land,* . . . . VI. iv. 29. 5
'So is my Lord now seiz'd of all the *land,* . . . . VI. iv. 30. 1
all this *land* with endlesse losse to overflow. . . . . VI. iv. 30. 9
all this *land* unto his foe shall fall, ... VI. iv. 32. 3
Famous through all the *land* of Faerie: . . . . VI. vii. 28. 3
to forray the *land,* or scoure the deepe. . . . . VI. xi. 40. 5
like a fearefull dog him followed through the *land.* . . . . . VI. xii. 36. 9
all his brethren borne in Britaine *land;* . . . . VI. xii. 39. 8
rule both sea and *land* unto their will: . . . . VII. vii. 3. 5
Where they shall have like heritage of *land,* . . . . *H.H.L.* 200
As these are fairer then the *land* and seas? . . . . *H.H.B.* 63
Landed. this fayre virgin wearie of her way Must *landed* bee, I. xii. 1. 7
Land-herds. the fields In which dame Cynthia her *landheards* fed; *Col.* 277
Landing. Him kept from *landing* at his wished will. . . . III. v. 20. 2
Landmark. Some *land-marke* seemd to bee, ... II. xi. 35. 9
Land's. of this *lands* first conquest did devize, ... II. ix. 59. 7
Which too-too true that *lands* in-dwellers since have found. . VII. vi. 55. 9
Lands. laboured *lands* to yield the timely eare, ... *S.C.* O. 58
Of forreine *lands,* of people different, ... *Hub.* 765
He had . . . fild far *landes* with glorie of his might: . . . . I. vi. 20. 6
knight he understands To beene departed out of Eden *landes,* II. i. 1. 5
Like two mad dogs they ran about the *lands,* . . . . II. xi. 47. 2
shall their conquests through all *lands* extend, ... III. iii. 23. 4
Searching all *lands* and each remotest part, ... III. iv. 6. 7
who that was which chaced her along the *lands.* . . . . . . III. vii. 46. 9
many perilles past in forreine *landes,* . . . . III. ix. 41. 8
it a wonder of the world is song In forreine *landes;* . . . . III. ix. 45. 8
High reared mounts, the *lands* about to vew; . . . . IV. x. 24. 5
Else would the waters overflow the *lands,* . . . . IV. x. 35. 5
The waters play, and pleasant *lands* appeare, ... IV. x. 44. 8
being carried farre from forraine *lands.* . . . . V. iv. 5. 5
Did equally bequeath his *lands* in fee, ... V. iv. 7. 4
when Philtra saw my *lands* decay . . . . V. iv. 9. 6
the love of Lordship and of *lands* . . . . V. xii. 2. 3
Language. For other *language* had he none, nor speach, . . VI. iv. 11. 6
Languages. The ledden of straunge *languages* in charge: . . . *Col.* 744
Languish. mourne for me that *languish* out my dayes. . . . . *D.* 538
whose deepe wounded mind With love . . . did *languish,* . . . I. ii. 24. 9
joyd to see her lover *languish* and lament: . . . . I. ix. 27. 9
languish, as the leafe faln from the tree, ... III. ii. 39. 8
with entire Affection I doe *languish* and expire. . . . . . . III. ii. 44. 5
With hatefull thoughts to *languish* and to pine, ... III. xi. 1. 7
As blasted bloosme through heat doth *languish* . . . . IV. viii. 2. 9
did *languish* of some inward thought, ... IV. xii. 25. 7
Did *languish* long in life-consuming smart, ... VI. vii. 31. 3
For her did *languish,* and his deare life spend; . . . . . . VI. ix. 10. 6
I *languish,* till he please My pining anguish to appease. . . *Epig.* iv. 59
Languished. she *languisht* as the gathered floure; . . . . . *Pet.* vi. 9
pyn'd, and mourn'd, and *languisht,* . . . . IV. xii. 19. 9
Languisheth. plight In which this Lady *languisheth* forlorne, VI. iii. 41. 8
Languishing. Lo! where beyond he lyeth *languishing,* . . . . III. i. 38. 1
had left them *languishing* twixt hope and feare. . . . . . . III. vi. 13. 9
leave me to my former *languishing?* . . . . III. xi. 24. 2
Long *languishing* there in unpittied paine, ... IV. x. 13. 8

Languishing—*Continued.*
Left a fayre Ladie *languishing* in payne: . . . IV. xi. 1. 2
Long *languishing* in double malady . . . *Am.* l. 1
they lye *languishing* like thrals forlorne, . . . *H.L.* 136
Languishment. secret sorrow and sad *languishment,* . . . *T.M.* 376
Yet it is comfort in great *languishment,* . . . *Ti.* 159
But rather riddance from long *languishment.* . . . *D.* 364
heaven, first author of my *languishment,* . . . IV. viii. 16. 5
new *languishment* Of his old hurt, . . . IV. xii. 23. 5
'If that the cause of this your *languishment* . . . VI. iv. 35. 1
Which I have wasted in long *languishment,* . . . *Am.* lx. 11
Languor. I in *languor* left there all alone. . . . *Ti.* 644
th' heavens with long *languor* pacifide, . . . *D.* 388
all their fish with *languor* (**languour*) did lament: . . . *Col.* 28
Let me not die in *languor* and long teares.' . . . I. i. 52. 7
That he my captive *languor* (**langour*) should redeeme: . . . I. vii. 49. 2
through *languour* of her late sweet toyle, . . . II. xii. 78. 3
through long *languour* and hart-burning brame, . . . III. ii. 52. 4
'Whiles thus thy Britons doe in *languour* pine, . . . III. iii. 35. 1
In wilfull *languor* and consuming smart, . . . III. xii. 16. 8
He left him there in *languor* to remaine, . . . IV. vii. 47. 5
Whereas that wofull man in *languor* did abide. . . . IV. viii. 11. 9
of the wound he yet in *languor* lyes, . . . IV. xi. 5. 7
In *languor* wastes his life: . . . IV. xii. Arg.
left his love . . . Faire Britomart in *languor* and unrest, . . V. viii. 3. 5
here thus long now lie In piteous *languor* . . . VI. vi. 6. 7
al my dayes in pining *langour* (**languor*) spend, . . . *Am.* xxxvi. 3
The inward *languor* (**languour*) of my wounded hart, . . . *Am.* l. 10
Long-while alone in *langour* (**languor*) to remaine. . . . *Am.* lii. 8
Languorous. Whom late I left in *languorous* (**langourous*) constraynt? . . . II. i. 9. 7
Languors. heare the *languors* (**languours*) of my too long dying, . . . *Col.* 948
Lank. her *lanck* loynes ungirt, and brests unbraste, . . . III. vi. 18. 4
flowd from her *lanck* syde . . . III. ix. 21. 5
Lansack. The sixt was *Lansack,* a redoubted Knight; . . . V. iii. 5. 8
Lantern. *lanterne* unto late succeeding age, . . . *Ti.* 170
Laomedia. *Laomedia* like the christall sheene; . . . IV. xi. 51. 3
Laomedon. Such as *Laomedon* of Phoebus race did breed. . . II. xi. 19. 9
Lap. drove in Joves owne *lap* his egs to lay; . . . *Van.* iv. 10
in the *lap* of soft delight Beene long time luld, . . . *T.M.* 301
in gathering Into her *lap* the children of the spring. . . . *Mui.* 128
so plenteouslie Her *lap* she filled had, . . . *Mui.* 141
Did poure into his Lemans *lap* so fast, . . . I. i. 6. 7
in his *lap* an heap of coine he told; . . . I. iv. 27. 5
in her *lap* a lovely babe did play His cruell sport, . . . II. i. 40. 5
filles with flowres fayre Floraes painted *lap:* . . . II. ii. 6. 5
In her rude heares sweet flowres themselves did *lap,* . . . II. iii. 30. 8
entrap The man most wary in her whelming *lap:* . . . II. iv. 17. 5
That here in Ladies *lap* entombed art, . . . II. v. 36. 3
laying his head disarmd In her loose *lap,* . . . II. vi. 14. 7
nature them forth throwes Out of her fruitfull *lap;* . . . II. vi. 15. 5
in his *lap* a masse of coyne he told, . . . II. vii. 4. 7
Whose sleepie head she in her *lap* did soft dispose. . . . II. xii. 76. 9
As Ladies wont, in pleasures wanton *lap,* . . . III. ii. 6. 7
She bore before her *lap* a dolefull Squire, . . . III. vii. 37. 6
Downe in her *lap* she hid her face, . . . III. viii. 32. 9
in her *lap* did shed her idle draught, . . . III. ix. 31. 3
Did raine into her *lap* an hony dew; . . . III. xi. 31. 4
Out of her fruitfull *lap* aboundant flowres; . . . IV. x. 45. 2
Even in the *lap* of Womanhood there sate, . . . IV. x. 52. 3
put before his *lap* a napron white, . . . V. v. 20. 8
on their mother Earths deare *lap* did lie, . . . V. vii. 9. 2
Then those which have bene dandled in the *lap:* . . . VI. iv. 36. 6
That other swayne . . . Lay in the *lap* of death, . . . VI. vii. 17. 9
throwing flowres out of her *lap* around: . . . VII. vii. 34. 3
Love lay sweetly slumbring All in his mothers *lap;* . . . *Epig.* iv. 2
Where thou doest sit in Venus *lap* above, . . . *H.L.* 24
Love, that had . . . securely slept In Venus *lap,* . . . *H.L.* 62
Lapithae. Fought with the bloudie *Lapithaes* at bord: . . . *Gn.* 42
the drunken fray, The which amongst the *Lapithees* befell; . IV. i. 23. 2
With the fierce *Lapithes* which did them dismay, . . . VI. x. 13. 5
Lapped. *lapped* up her silken leaves most chayre, . . . III. v. 51. 6
Lapped in flowres and pretious spycery, . . . III. vi. 46. 5
Amongst loose Ladies *lapped* in delight: . . . V. vi. 6. 8
Lapwing. Turn'd to a *Lapwing,* fowlie them upbraydes, . . . *Gn.* 405
Lard. full grosse and fat As fed with *lard,* . . . VII. vii. 40. 2
Larded. with his nuts *larded* many swine: . . . *S.C.* F. 110
Lare. *See* **Lair.**
Large. letting their sheepe runne at *large,* . . . *S.C.* May 40
stretch her selfe at *large* from East to West; . . . *S.C.* O. 44
make so *large* a flight; . . . *S.C.* O. 86
with libertie full *large,* . . . *Hub.* 300
(*large* breath in armes most needfull) . . . *Hub.* 745
Large streames of honnie and sweete Nectar flowe, . . . *T.M.* 218
Large streetes, brave houses, sacred sepulchers, . . . *Ti.* 94
spreading forth at *large,* . . . *Col.* 111
gives to their professors stipends *large.* . . . *Col.* 746
Noble Lord, . . . Through whose *large* bountie, . . . *Ded. Son.* vii. 3
full *large* of limbe and every joint He was, . . . I. ii. 12. 8
a *large* share it hewd out of the rest, . . . I. ii. 18. 8
Large floods of blood adowne their sides did raile; . . . I. vi. 43. 7
Large streames of blood . . . Forth gushed, . . . I. viii. 10. 8
flames of fire he threw forth from his *large* nosethril. . . . I. xi. 22. 9
Stretcht on the ground in monstrous *large* extent, . . . I. xii. 9. 7
The *large* discourse of roiall Princes state. . . . I. xii. 14. 6
made a *large* And open gash therein: . . . II. v. 6. 4
that wofull theame For to dilate at *large,* . . . II. v. 37. 4
a *large* purple streame adowne their giambeux falles. . . . II. vi. 29. 9
The rowme was *large* and wyde, . . . II. vii. 43. 3
Large—*Continued.*
a *large* lukewarme flood, Red as the Rose, . . . II. viii. 39. 1
the *large* leape which Debon did compell . . . II. x. 11. 2
got *large* portions of land, . . . II. x. 65. 6
Full *large* he was of limbe, . . . II. xi. 20. 7
A *large* and spacious plaine, . . . II. xii. 50. 2
Large were his limbes, and terrible his looke, . . . III. i. 17. 8
for ye beene tall, And *large* of limbe . . . III. iii. 53. 7
his *large* bountie rightly doth areed: . . . III. iv. 59. 4
a *large* streame of blood out of the wound did flow. . . . III. v. 21. 9
to stay to rest, or breath at *large,* . . . III. vii. 23. 3
has full *large* to live and spend at libertie. . . . III. ix. 3. 9
Of which he dealt *large* almes, as did befall: . . . IV. iv. 32. 4
Who all to her at *large,* as hapned, did relate. . . . IV. vii. 34. 9
promist *large* amends to make. . . . IV. viii. 60. 6
graunt more scope to me to walke at *large.* . . . IV. viii. 61. 4
told at *large* how that same errant Knight, . . . IV. ix. 36. 1
Large Lisianassa, and Pronaea sage, . . . IV. xi. 50. 2
Into a long *large* chamber, . . . V. v. 21. 3
he gan at *large* to her dilate The whole discourse . . . V. vi. 17. 1
gave to them great living and *large* fee: . . . V. vii. 43. 4
Went up the hall, that was a *large* wyde roome, . . . V. ix. 23. 2
dreadfull blowes with *large* dispence, . . . V. xi. 45. 4
Him thus describ'd; to be of stature *large,* . . . VI. ii. 44. 6
Of his *large* paines in her deliveraunce . . . VI. iii. 19. 4
making way for death at *large* to walke; . . . VI. xi. 16. 5
Ceasse to molest the Moone to walke at *large,* . . . VII. vi. 17. 8
Bold Alteration pleades *Large* Evidence: . . . VII. vii. Arg.
That honour and *large* richesse to me lent: . . . *Am.* lxxiv. 8
That we may raise a *large* posterity, . . . *Epith.* 417
Largely. With armes full strong and *largely* displayd, . . . *S.C.* F. 104
to give *largely* to the boxe refused. . . . *Hub.* 1224
yong toward yeares . . . Did *largely* promise, . . . *Mui.* 29
as I *largely* can report. . . . III. ii. 12. 9
largely overflow the fruitfull plaine, . . . III. vii. 34. 4
Largeness. Beast . . . with his *largenesse* measured much land, I. xi. 8. 3
heavens . . . infinite in *largenesse* and in hight, . . . *H.H.B.* 67
Larger. rise, and with a *larger* flight . . . *Bel.* vii. 5
that same land much *larger* is then this, . . . *Col.* 296
when she list poure out her *larger* spright, . . . I. x. 20. 1
At length they came into a *larger* space, . . . II. vii. 21. 1
Lark. I more delight then *larke* in Sommer dayes: . . . *S.C.* Jun. 51
our pypes, that shrild as lowde as *Larke;* . . . *S.C.* N. 71
As Somers *larke* that with her song doth greet . . . *As.* 33
Remounted up as light as chearefull *Larke;* . . . I. i. 44. 7
her lowd salutes the mounting *larke.* . . . I. xi. 51. 9
Sometimes she song as lowd as *larke* in ayre, . . . II. vi. 3. 3
Like darred *Larke,* not daring up to looke . . . VII. vi. 47. 5
The merry *Larke* hir mattins sings aloft; . . . *Epith.* 80
Larum-bell. His *larumbell* might lowd and wyde be hard . . . II. ix. 25. 7
Lascivious. Mingled emongst loose Ladies and *lascivious* boyes. II. v. 28. 9
Low his *lascivious* armes adown did creepe, . . . II. xii. 61. 6
Many faire Ladies and *lascivious* boyes, . . . II. xii. 72. 8
They sdeigned such *lascivious* disport, . . . III. i. 40. 8
Therewith to bind *lascivious* desire, . . . IV. v. 4. 7
Those villeins view'd with loose *lascivious* sight, . . . VI. viii. 43. 3
Lashed. whip . . . With which he forward *lasht* the laesy teme, I. iv. 36. 3
He hewd, and *lasht,* and foynd, . . . II. v. 9. 1
strooke, and foynd, and *lasht* outrageously, . . . II. viii. 47. 5
He stroke, he soust, he foynd, he hewd, he *lasht,* . . . IV. iii. 25. 6
She hewd, she foynd, she *lasht,* she laid on every side. . . . V. v. 6. 9
Lashing. *lashing* dreadfully at every part, . . . IV. vi. 16. 6
Lass. *See* **Bonnilass.**
'I love thilke *lasse,* (alas! why doe I love?) . . . *S.C.* Ja. 61
His dewelap as lythe as *lasse* of Kent: . . . *S.C.* F. 74
art thou of thy loved *lasse* forlorne? . . . *S.C.* Ap. 4
Nowe loves a *lasse* that all his love doth scorne. . . . *S.C.* Ap. 11
Didst underfong my *lasse* to wexe so light, . . . *S.C.* Jun. 103
tell the *lasse,* whose flowre is woxe a weede, . . . *S.C.* Jun. 109
left hys flocke to fetch a *lasse,* . . . *S.C.* Jul. 147
Yet should thilk *lasse* not from my thought, . . . *S.C.* Au. 107
Whether thee list thy loved *lasse* advaunce, . . . *S.C.* N. 7
The loser *Lasse* I cast to please no more; . . . *S.C.* D. 119
unto his loved *lasse* . . . him dolefully did beare. . . . *As.* 147
carol made to praise thy loved *lasse,'* . . . *Col.* 87
'Nor of my love, nor of my *lasse* . . . *Col.* 88
late he sung unto a scornfull *lasse.* . . . *Col.* 419
a lovely *lasse,* hight Lucida: . . . *Col.* 456
is he lincked to a lovely *lasse,* . . . III. ix. 4. 4
To have efforst the love of that faire *lasse,* . . . III. xii. 43. 8
The faire Tindarid *lasse,* . . . IV. xi. 19. 4
And eke that Lady, his faire lovely *lasse.* . . . VI. iii. 14. 4
issue forth t' attach that scornefull *lasse.* . . . VI. vii. 35. 5
She was, to weete, that jolly Shepheards *lasse,* . . . VI. x. 16. 1
Yet was she certes but a countrey *lasse;* . . . VI. x. 25. 8
Litle for him to have one silly *lasse;* . . . VI. xi. 12. 6
Lasses. *See* **Shepherd-lasses.**
Our lovely *Lasses,* or bright shining Brides: . . . *Hub.* 476
their *lasses,* which my luck envide, . . . *D.* 142
Environ'd with a girland . . . Of lovely *lasses;* . . . VI. ix. 8. 4
all other countrey *lasses* farre did passe: . . . VI. x. 25. 9
Above all other *lasses* beare the bell; . . . VI. x. 26. 4
Lasses'. Young Astrophel, the rusticke *lasses* love: . . . *As.* 8
Lass's. hery with hymnes thy *lasses* glove; . . . *S.C.* F. 62
to breed Compassion in a countrey *lasses* hart . . . *As.* Pr. 4
Last. *See* **At last.**
at the *last,* and in short time, I spide, . . . *Pet.* i. 10
At *last* so faire a Ladie did I spie, . . . *Pet.* vi. 1
each thing at *last* . . . Doth passe away: . . . *Pet.*[2] v. 7
hath tam'd herselfe at *last;* . . . *Ro.* iii. 7

Last—*Continued.*

your *last* reliques marre.	*Ro.* vii. 11
at *last,* there being then not living An Hercules	*Ro.* x. 9
Till at the *last* . . . he forth is horld;	*Ro.* xx. 7
At *last,* not able to beare so great weight,	*Ro.* xx. 12
brought forth in her *last* declining season,	*Van.* i. 7
At *last* her solein silence she broke,	*S.C.* May 213
he has voued thy *last* confusion.	*S.C.* May 220
till my *last* sleepe Doe close mine eyes:	*S.C.* Au. 170
sithence I saw thy head *last,*	*S.C.* S. 19
Tho deemed I my spring would ever *laste.*	*S.C.* D. 30
when as at *last* he spide,	*Gn.* 266
so long as it did *last?*	*Gn.* 332
At *last* they chaunst to meet	*Hub.* 227
at the *last* they gan to be descryed	*Hub.* 345
At *last* they chaunst to meete upon the way	*Hub.* 581
At *last* againe with him in travell joynd,	*Hub.* 941
Yet at the *last,* (so well he him applyde)	*Hub.* 1014
(for what thing can ever *last?*)	*Hub.* 1176
At *last* he found, where sleeping he did ly.	*Hub.* 1320
At *last* he came unto his mansion,	*Hub.* 1349
him at *last* the Lyon spide,	*Hub.* 1375
he at *last* laid forth on balefull beare.	*T.M.* 162
though at *last* by force I conquered were	*Ti.* 113
at *last* I heard a voyce,	*Ti.* 579
At *last,* when all his mourning melodie He ended	*Ti.* 596
Fainting at *last* through long infirmities,	*Ti.* 656
At *last* me seem'd wing-footed Mercurie,	*Ti.* 666
with *last* duties of this broken verse,	*Ti.* 678
Vouchsafe this moniment of his *last* praise	*Ti.* 682
sad Clarion did at *last* decline	*Mui.* 14
breaking foorth at *last,* thus dearnelie plained:	*D.* 196
so shall our love for ever *last.*	*D.* 291
those *last* deadly accents, which like swords Did wound	*D.* 297
life I hate, because it will not *last;*	*D.* 425
At *last,* when paine his vitall powres had spent,	*As.* 173
At *last,* when as he piped had his fill,	*Col.* 10
last not least, is Aetion,	*Col.* 444
Till Thestylis at *last* their silence brake,	*Col.* 651
To the *last* praises of this Faery Queene;	*Ded. Son.* ii. 10
lasie seemd, in being ever *last,*	I. i. 6. 2
At *last* resolving forward still to fare,	I. i. 11. 1
The which at *last* out of the wood them brought.	I. i. 28. 6
At *last,* dull wearines of former fight	I. i. 55. 4
At *last* faire Hesperus . . . Had spent his lampe,	I. ii. 6. 6
At *last* him chaunst to meete . . . A faithlesse Sarazin,	I. ii. 12. 5
at *last* it flitted is,	I. ii. 19. 8
'At *last* it chaunced this proud Sarazin	I. ii. 25. 1
they came at *last* Where grew two goodly trees,	I. ii. 28. 2
At *last* whenas the dreadfull passion Was overpast,	I. ii. 32. 1
with pale and deadly hew, At *last* she up gan lift:	I. ii. 45. 6
At *last,* . . . Arose the virgin,	I. iii. 8. 6
till at *last* she has A damzel spyde,	I. iii. 10. 7
till at *last* they see A goodly building bravely garnished;	I. iv. 2. 5
Such one was Wrath, the *last* of this ungodly tire.	I. iv. 35. 9
'At *last,* when perils all I weened past,	I. iv. 47. 1
He lives that shall him pay his dewties *last,*	I. iv. 49. 8
At *last,* the golden Orientall gate . . . gan to open	I. v. 2. 1
At *last* forth comes that far renowmed Queene:	I. v. 5. 1
At *last* the Paynim . . . cast his eye,	I. v. 10. 1
At *last* the trumpets Triumph sound on hie;	I. v. 15. 6
cryes, The *last* vaine helpe of wemens great distresse,	I. vi. 6. 3
At *last* in privy wise	I. vi. 32. 6
In hope to bring her to her *last* decay.	I. vi. 48. 7
Till at the *last* he heard a dreadfull sownd,	I. vii. 7. 4
At *last* . . . he does begin To rubb her temples,	I. vii. 21. 4
At *last* when life recover'd had the raine,	I. vii. 24. 5
At *last* when fervent sorrow slaked was,	I. vii. 28. 1
At *last* she chaunced . . . to meet A goodly knight,	I. vii. 29. 1
'At *last,* yled with far reported praise,	I. vii. 46. 1
'At *last,* . . . she him betraid Unto his foe,	I. vii. 51. 1
as a Castle . . . At *last* downe falles;	I. viii. 23. 5
At *last,* . . . forth came An old old man,	I. viii. 30. 1
At *last* he came unto an yron doore,	I. viii. 37. 3
will at *last* be wonne with battrie long,	I. ix. 11. 3
at *last,* these words seemd forth to shake;	I. ix. 24. 9
forst, at *last* he made through silence suddein breach.	I. ix. 25. 9
draw thy dayes forth to their *last* degree?	I. ix. 46. 2
At *last,* resolv'd to work his finall smart,	I. ix. 51. 8
Till he should die his *last,* that is, eternally.	I. ix. 54. 9
have mind of that *last* bitter throw;	I. x. 41. 8
from the first unto the *last* degree,	I. x. 45. 7
by her helpe the top at *last* he wonne.	I. x. 47. 9
deeds of armes must I at *last* be faine . . . to leave,	I. x. 62. 5
streightway on that *last* long voiage fare,	I. x. 63. 4
At *last,* whenas himselfe he gan to fynd,	I. x. 68. 1
At *last,* low stouping with unweldy sway,	I. xi. 18. 8
struggling strong did him at *last* constraine	I. xi. 19. 3
At *last* she saw where he upstarted brave	I. xi. 34. 1
His trusty sword he cald to his *last* aid,	I. xi. 42. 2
at *last* he forst him to unty One of his . . . feete,	I. xi. 42. 8
at *last,* whenas the direfull feend	I. xi. 55. 5
the *last* deadly smoke aloft did steeme,	I. xii. 2. 4
That signe of *last* outbreathed life	I. xii. 2. 5
From first to *last* in your late enterprise,	I. xii. 17. 3
At *last* his solemn silence thus he brake,	I. xii. 29. 5
they came at *last* Into a pleasant dale	II. i. 24. 2
At *last,* . . . They heard a ruefull voice,	II. i. 35. 5
At *last* his mighty ghost gan deepe to grone,	II. i. 42. 5
at the *last* shee gan to breath out living aire.	II. i. 43. 9
'Him so I sought; and so at *last* I fownd,	II. i. 54. 1
'At *last,* when fayling breath began to faint,	II. ii. 8. 1
As she bequeathd in her *last* testament;	II. ii. 10. 6
at *last* they to a Castle came,	II. ii. 12. 6
at the *last* . . . They gan abstaine	II. ii. 28. 7
At *last,* when lust of meat and drinke was ceast,	II. ii. 39. 3
Sith *last* I left that honorable place,	II. ii. 44. 3
At *last,* when they had markt the chaunged skyes,	II. ii. 46. 8
At *last* they heard a horne	II. iii. 20. 7
she at *last* him spying thus bespake:	II. iii. 32. 6
Seeing at *last* her selfe from daunger rid,	II. iii. 36. 5
beckned him, the *last* help she had left;	II. iv. 13. 3
Being at *last* recured, he gan inquyre	II. iv. 16. 7
'At *last* such grace I found,	II. iv. 21. 1
She *last* should smart:	II. iv. 31. 6
at the *last* all breathlesse, weary, faint,	II. v. 11. 2
At *last* he was compeld to cry perforse,	II. v. 23. 7
O Atin! helpe to me *last* death to give.'	II. vi. 45. 5
At *last* he came unto a gloomy glade,	II. vii. 3. 1
At *last* him to a litle dore he brought,	II. vii. 24. 5
his life and . . . *last* Philosophy To the fayre Critias,	II. vii. 52. 8
to that shady delve him brought at *last,*	II. viii. 4. 6
At *last,* him turning to his charge behight,	II. viii. 9. 5
At *last* he spide where towards him did pace	II. viii. 10. 1
leave unto me thy knights *last* patronage.'	II. viii. 26. 9
at *last,* when he advantage spyde,	II. viii. 36. 2
at the *last* them fond	II. viii. 40. 8
at *last* thus sayd; 'Traytour, what hast thou doen?	II. viii. 46. 5
At *last,* when as the Sarazin perceiv'd	II. viii. 49. 1
Those two the first and *last* proportions are;	II. ix. 22. 3
At *last* ripe age bad him surrender	II. x. 13. 8
Yet he at *last,*	II. x. 26. 8
At *last,* resolv'd likewise to prove the rest,	II. x. 31. 4
Ne had they footing found at *last,*	II. x. 48. 5
At *last,* quite ravisht with delight	II. x. 69. 1
Him to succeede therein, by his *last* will:	II. x. 76. 5
At *last* breakes forth with furious unrest,	II. xi. 32. 5
At *last* them driven hath	II. xii. 8. 9
At *last* far off they many Islandes spy	II. xii. 10. 6
At *last* they in an Island did espy	II. xii. 27. 5
for your ruine at the *last* awayt.'	II. xii. 29. 4
at *last* the weather gan to cleare,	II. xii. 37. 5
at *last* display That wanton Lady	II. xii. 76. 7
At *last,* as through an open plaine they yode,	III. i. 4. 1
At *last,* as nigh out of the wood she came,	III. i. 20. 1
at *last* she told her briefe,	III. i. 53. 4
At *last* the royall Mayd . . . did awake,	III. i. 61. 7
by ensample of the *last* dayes losse,	III. i. 64. 6
At *last,* the passion past, she thus him answered.	III. ii. 5. 9
yield the pray of love to lothsome death at *last.*	III. ii. 17. 9
her life at *last* must lincke in that same knot.	III. ii. 23. 9
at *last* she thus bespake.	III. ii. 42. 9
at *last* a litle creeping sleepe Surprisd her sence:	III. ii. 47. 6
At *last* she her avisde,	III. iii. 6. 1
his *last* fate him from thee take away;	III. iii. 28. 7
at the *last* . . . shall be forst to yield:	III. iii. 31. 5
Nor vengeaunce huge relent it selfe at *last?*	III. iii. 43. 6
At *last,* . . . to former hew Hee turnd	III. iii. 50. 8
At *last* the Nourse . . . Conceiv'd a bold devise,	III. iii. 52. 1
In the *last* field before Menevia,	III. iii. 55. 3
At *last* their wayes so fell,	III. iii. 62. 6
At *last* blow up some gentle gale of ease,	III. iv. 10. 3
at *last* The watry Southwinde,	III. iv. 13. 3
To bring her sonne unto his *last* decay.	III. iv. 28. 5
at *last* her wombe did fill With hevenly seed,	III. iv. 41. 5
At *last* they came unto a double way;	III. iv. 46. 6
At *last* of her far off he gained vew.	III. iv. 48. 1
at *last* He met a Dwarfe	III. v. 3. 2
At *last,* through wrath and vengeaunce	III. v. 21. 1
the only *last* of three	III. v. 24. 1
at *last* his eies . . . He up gan lifte	III. v. 34. 2
where their Lady was arrived at the *last.*	III. v. 37. 9
he was forst at *last* To yield	III. v. 48. 2
At *last* she her bethought	III. vi. 16. 3
At *last* they both agreed her . . . not to awake	III. vi. 27. 7
at *last* perforce adowne did ly,	III. vii. 3. 7
came at *last* in weary wretched plight	III. vii. 5. 7
At *last,* turning her feare to foolish wrath,	III. vii. 8. 1
Softly at *last* he gan his mother aske,	III. vii. 14. 1
dismayd At that same *last* extremity	III. vii. 25. 2
At *last* in vaine was forst to turne his flight,	III. vii. 28. 5
at the *last* his fiercenes gan abate,	III. vii. 35. 3
was as far at *last,* as when I first begon.	III. vii. 59. 9
At *last* when droncke with drowsinesse he woke,	III. viii. 22. 1
compeld at *last* To fly for succour	III. ix. 11. 7
At *last,* avizing right Her goodly personage	III. ix. 23. 5
at *last* she thus: 'O lamentable fall	III. ix. 39. 1
'At *last* in Latium he did arryve,	III. ix. 42. 1
'At *last* by fatall course they driven were	III. ix. 49. 1
At *last* when sorrow he saw booted nought,	III. x. 18. 6
At *last* resolving, like a Pilgrim pore,	III. x. 19. 1
At *last* he thus; 'Thou clod of vilest clay,	III. x. 31. 2
At *last* with irkesom trouble she abrayd;	III. x. 50. 1
at the *last* he found a cave with entrance small.	III. x. 57. 9
she at *last* came to a fountaine sheare,	III. xi. 7. 2
At *last* forth breaking into bitter plaintes	III. xi. 9. 1
As if his dayes were come to their *last* reach:	III. xi. 12. 5
with proofe of *last* extremity,	III. xi. 18. 8
At *last* she spyde at that rowmes upper end	III. xi. 54. 6

Last—*Continued.*
saw both first and *last*, . . . III. xii. 27. 5
At *last* that mightie chaine, . . . III. xii. 37. 7
At *last* she came unto the place, . . . III. xii. 43. *or.*1
at the *last* they spide Two armed Knights . . . IV. i. 17. 1
Unto his *last* confusion to bring, . . . IV. i. 30. 7
at the *last* they brake His slomber, . . . IV. i. 43. 8
so did at *last* forbeare. . . . IV. i. 54. 9
'*Last* turne was mine, well proved to my paine; . . . IV. ii. 6. 4
both resolv'd the *last* extremities to prove. . . . IV. ii. 19. 9
they at *last* their wrothfull hands let fall, . . . IV. ii. 21. 8
when at *last* she had beheld her fill, . . . IV. ii. 49. 3
Sir Triamond at *last* full faint and feeble stood. . . . IV. iii. 28. 9
At *last* arriving by the listes side, . . . IV. iii. 46. 1
It chaunst Sir Satyrane his steed at *last* . . . To stumble, . . . IV. iv. 30. 2
The *last* day came, . . . IV. iv. 37. 1
from the first he to the *last* endured: . . . IV. iv. 37. 6
For he *last* ended, having first begonne. . . . IV. v. 7. 5
to the *last* unconquer'd did appeare; . . . IV. v. 8. 7
For *last* is deemed best. . . . IV. v. 8. 8
At *last*, the most redoubted Britonesse . . . IV. v. 13. 1
at *last* the gentle Amoret Likewise assayd . . . IV. v. 19. 2
At *last* to Braggadochio selfe alone She came . . . IV. v. 26. 8
he which was the *last* the first did farre exceede. . . . IV. v. 36. 9
at *last* enquired The cause and end thereof, . . . IV. v. 38. 3
at the *last* his wearie sprite, opprest . . . IV. v. 43. 2
at *last* his lucklesse hand he heav'd on hie, . . . IV. vi. 18. 6
At *last* fell humbly downe upon his knee, . . . IV. vi. 22. 2
At *last*, through many vowes which forth he pour'd, . . . IV. vi. 41. 6
At *last*, when all her speeches she had spent, . . . IV. vi. 46. 1
at the *last* he did himselfe attaine, . . . IV. vii. 27. 6
At *last*, when long he follow'd had . . . IV. vii. 38. 1
out of all mens knowledge he was worne at *last*. . . . IV. vii. 41. 9
at the *last*, of all his woe . . . Companion she became, . . . IV. viii. 5. 8
At *last*, when they were passed out of sight, . . . IV. viii. 36. 1
for his love him promist libertie at *last*. . . . IV. viii. 52. 9
over-ruld at *last*, he did to me agree. . . . IV. viii. 58. 9
at the *last* I spide within the same . . . IV. x. 11. 7
graunt that of my love at *last* I may not misse!" . . . IV. x. 47. 9
At *last* to Tryphon she for helpe did hie, . . . IV. xi. 6. 5
at *last* relenting, she to him was wed. . . . IV. xi. 8. 9
All which, long sundred, doe at *last* accord . . . IV. xi. 43. 7
all one at *last* become. . . . IV. xi. 43. 9
At *last*, when as no meanes he could invent, . . . IV. xii. 16. 1
Till they arrive at their *last* ruinous decay. . . . V. Pr. 6. 9
Some blisfull houres at *last* must needes appeare; . . . V. iii. 1. 4
at the *last* the trompets did proclame . . . V. iii. 7. 7
Her weary barke at *last* uppon mine Isle did rest. . . . V. iv. 11. 9
when she saw at *last* that he ne would . . . V. iv. 30. 5
mongst the rest the fight did untill evening *last*. . . . V. iv. 43. 9
mindefull to pursew The *last* daies purpose . . . V. v. 1. 6
Weening at *last* to win advantage new; . . . V. v. 7. 2
At *last*, when long she struggled had in vaine, . . . V. v. 28. 6
my *last* bale to breed.' . . . V. v. 29. 9
Looke up at *last*, and wake thy dulled spirit . . . V. v. 36. 8
though (unlike) they should for ever *last*, . . . V. v. 38. 8
His resolution was, both first and *last*, . . . V. v. 46. 8
he, at first or *last*, was trapt . . . V. vi. 1. 9
at *last* she spide One comming towards her . . . V. vi. 8. 1
To fight with him, and goodly die her *last*. . . . V. vi. 13. 3
Into the river, where he drunke his deadly *last*. . . . V. vi. 39. 9
thorough evill rest of this *last* night, . . . V. vii. 18. 7
At *last* proud Radigund . . . Let drive at her . . . V. vii. 32. 1
At *last* when as to her owne Love she came, . . . V. vii. 38. 1
In hope to have her overhent at *last*: . . . V. viii. 4. 5
So long as in his steedes the flaming breath did *last*. . . . V. viii. 33. 9
At *last* from his victorious shield he drew The vaile, . . . V. viii. 37. 6
At *last* they have all overthrowne to ground . . . V. viii. 42. 4
till that at *last* Into a bird it chaung'd, . . . V. ix. 17. 4
yeelding the *last* honour to her wretched corse. . . . V. x. 4. 9
she did at *last* commit All to his hands, . . . V. x. 13. 1
Yet glad at *last* to make most base submission, . . . V. x. 27. 4
Yet at the *last* she will her owne cause right: . . . V. xi. 1. 6
till that he came at *last* Unto the Castle . . . V. xi. 3. 3
At *last* they came whereas that Ladie bode, . . . V. xi. 60. 1
Weening her lifes *last* howre then neare to bee, . . . V. xii. 11. 8
at the *last* He stroke him with Chrysaor . . . V. xii. 23. 1
at the *last* like to a purple lake . . . VI. i. 37. 7
the onely helpe now left them *last* . . . VI. iii. 12. 8
forth at *last* did breake . . . VI. iii. 34. 9
At *last* some fisher-barke doth neare behold, . . . VI. iv. 1. 4
the place, whereas he *last* Had left that couple . . . VI. iv. 9. 4
At *last*, about the setting of the Sunne, . . . VI. iv. 26. 1
at the *last* breake forth in his owne proper kynd. . . . VI. v. 1. 9
At *last* he up into the chamber came . . . VI. vi. 30. 1
rising up at *last* in ghastly wize, . . . VI. vi. 32. 7
At *last* he met two knights to him unknowne, . . . VI. vii. 3. 6
at the *last* through dreary dolour die: . . . VI. vii. 31. 4
which when at *last* she saw, . . . VI. vii. 36. 6
at advantage him at *last* he tooke, . . . VI. vii. 48. 2
At *last* the caytive, after long discourse, . . . VI. viii. 14. 6
at *last* she thought Her selfe now past the perill . . . VI. viii. 32. 2
made her knowen to him at *last*: . . . VI. viii. 51. 8
sith I left him *last* Sewing the Blatant Beast; . . . VI. ix. 2. 2
last forth brought The fruite of joy and blisse, . . . VI. ix. 45. 8
Next faire Aglaia, *last* Thalia merry; . . . VI. x. 22. 8
at the *last* unto his will he brought her; . . . VI. x. 38. 3
The joyes of love, if they should ever *last* . . . VI. xi. 1. 1
At *last*, when him she so importune saw, . . . VI. xi. 6. 1
At *last* when all the rest them offred were, . . . VI. xi. 14. 1

Last—*Continued.*
they to life recovered her at *last*: . . . VI. xi. 22. 6
At *last*, as there he romed up and downe, . . . VI. xi. 27. 1
needs mote she die at *last*. . . . VI. xi. 32. 2
he at *last* Began to mitigate his swelling sourse, . . . VI. xi. 34. 2
How he might save her life, if life did *last*; . . . VI. xi. 34. 5
faire bespoke with words, that he at *last* agreed. . . . VI. xi. 35. 9
So her uneath at *last* he did revive . . . VI. xi. 50. 8
She found at *last*, by very certaine signes . . . VI. xii. 20. 3
to the Clergy now was come at *last*; . . . VI. xii. 23. 3
At *last*, when as he found his force to shrincke . . . VI. xii. 34. 1
At *last* he bade her (with bold stedfastnesse) . . . VII. vi. 17. 7
'*Last* is the fire; . . . VII. vii. 24. 1
shew the *last* ensample of your pride; . . . *Am.* xxv. 6
A close intent at *last* to shew me grace: . . . *Am.* xxv. 10
That greater meede at *last* may turne to mee. . . . *Am.* xxv. 14
shine again, and looke on me at *last*, . . . *Am.* xxxiv. 11
She meanes at *last* to make her pitious spoyle. . . . *Am.* xli. 12
at *last* atchyve . . . so sweet a rest; . . . *Am.* lxiii. 9
glorious spoile, Gotten at *last* with labour . . . *Am.* lxix. 14
The third, my love, my lifes *last* ornament, . . . *Am.* lxxiv. 9
seeke each where, where *last* I saw her face, . . . *Am.* lxxviii. 3
So sorrow still doth seeme too long to *last*; . . . *Am.* lxxxvi. 13
For lo! the wished day is come at *last*, . . . *Epith.* 31
at *last* I see it gloome, . . . *Epith.* 285
That long daies labour doest at *last* defray, . . . *Epith.* 316
Fayre Venice, flower of the *last* worlds delight; . . . *Com. Son.* iv. 10
And *last*, the food of life, which now we have, . . . *H.H.L.* 194
Which in his *last* bequest he to us spake, . . . *H.H.L.* 207
And looke at *last*, how . . . He taken was, . . . *H.H.L.* 239
And, *last*, that mightie shining christall wall, . . . *H.H.B.* 41
till to his perfect end Of purest beautie it at *last* ascend; . . . *H.H.B.* 47
till they at *last* arive To the most faire, . . . *H.H.B.* 76
And looke at *last* up to that Soveraine Light, . . . *H.H.B.* 295

Lasted. For wonder of the world, long in me *lasted*, . . . *Ti.* 118
In friendly sort that *lasted* but a while; . . . IV. ii. 29. 2

Lasting. *See* **Long-Lasting.**
'Live they for ever through their *lasting* praise! . . . *Gn.* 617
O short pleasure, bought with *lasting* paine! . . . *Ti.* 526
Till I have told her praises *lasting* long: . . . *Col.* 49
Live, Lord, for ever in this *lasting* verse, . . . *Ded. Son.* xi. 13
crownd with *lasting* baies Of hevenlie blis . . . *Ded. Son.* xv. 4
Doe breede repentaunce late, and *lasting* infamy.' . . . II. v. 13. 9
Enjoyd an heritage of *lasting* peace, . . . II. x. 25. 2
live in *lasting* blesse, . . . IV. x. 23. 5
No love so *lasting* then, that may enduren long. . . . V. xii. 1. 9
which they may long possesse With *lasting* happinesse, . . . *Epith.* 419
Seekes to enlarge his *lasting* progenie; . . . *H.L.* 105

Last-left. My *last left* comfort is my woes to weepe . . . I. vii. 39. 9
he that *last left* helpe away did take, . . . II. iv. 13. 4

Lastly. *Lastly* the squalid lakes of Tartarie, . . . *Gn.* 543
lastly, when the bodie list to pause, . . . *Hub.* 759
Lastly I saw an Arke of purest golde . . . *Ti.* 659
Lastly his shinie wings . . . *Mui.* 89
And *lastly* thrown themselves into these heavy stowres. . . . I. v. 51. 9
Thou have it *lastly* brought unto her Excellence. . . . III. iii. 4. 9
Vile Poverty; and, *lastly*, Death with infamy. . . . III. xii. 25. 9
lastly all that Castle quite he raced, . . . V. ii. 28. 1
lastly, to make proofe of utmost shame, . . . V. viii. 22. 6
lastly, that no shame might wanting be, . . . V. viii. 23. 1
lastly Justice charged her with breach of lawes. . . . V. ix. 44. 9
lastly Griefe did plead, . . . V. ix. 45. 9
lastly, scattering Contagious poyson . . . VI. vi. 8. 7
lastly, in approvance of thy wrong, . . . VI. vi. 35. 1
lastly to despoyle of knightly bannerall. . . . VI. vii. 26. 9
Lastly, came Winter . . . VII. vii. 31. 1
lastly came cold February, . . . VII. vii. 43. 1
after all came Life, and *lastly* Death; . . . VII. vii. 46. 1
And *lastly*, how twixt robbers crucifyde, . . . *H.H.L.* 244

Latch. his basket did *latch*: . . . *S.C.* May 291

Latched. oft the pumies *latched*. . . . *S.C.* Mar. 93

Late. to the spring, that *late* devoured was. . . . *Pet.* v. 6
Thy mantle mard, wherein thou maskedst *late*. . . . *S.C.* Ja. 24
gan he repent his pryde to *late*; . . . *S.C.* F. 229
wander may thy flocke, early or *late*, . . . *S.C.* Jun. 11
Yode *late* on Pilgrimage . . . *S.C.* Jul. 182
the wrong which he had done of *late*, . . . *Gn.* 327
late in warres have spent my deerest blood, . . . *Hub.* 247
That art so leane and meagre waxen *late*, . . . *Hub.* 599
his *late* chayne his Liege unmeete esteemeth; . . . *Hub.* 628
Full of the feared sight which *late* they sawe. . . . *Hub.* 1110
What did of *late* chaunce happen to the Lyon stearne, . . . *Hub.* 1250
As one *late* in a traunce, . . . *Hub.* 1325
Which *late* ye powred forth . . . *T.M.* 4
I *late* was wont to raine as Queene, . . . *T.M.* 179
ycrept of *late* Out of dredd darknes . . . *T.M.* 188
Our pleasant Willy, ah! is dead of *late*: . . . *T.M.* 208
The sweete companions of the Muses *late*, . . . *T.M.* 404
that *late* posteritie Should know their names, . . . *T.M.* 441
no man . . . that *late* him loved deare: . . . *Ti.* 193
The worlds *late* wonder, and the heavens new joy; . . . *Ti.* 303
rich spoyles, which *late* he did purchas . . . *Ti.* 654
morning faire may bring fowle evening *late*, . . . *Mui.* 219
the strife betweene them stirred *late*: . . . *Mui.* 309
griefe of folly *late* repented: . . . *Mui.* 348
the *late* love the which betwixt us past, . . . *D.* 289
They stopt his wound, (too *late* to stop it was!) . . . *As.* 145
That us, *late* dead, has made againe alive: . . . *Col.* 31
fortunes, which to thee befell In thy *late* voyage, . . . *Col.* 34
there is a new shepheard *late* up sprong, . . . *Col.* 416

Late—*Continued.*
Having *late* slaine her Seneschall in fight, . . . VI. i. 29. 8
feeling ill Of his *late* fall, . . . VI. i. 35. 5
comming forth yet full of *late* affray . . . VI. i. 44. 7
sith ye so courteous seemed *late,* . . . VI. ii. 27. 4
Upon the steed of her owne *late* dead knight; . . . VI. ii. 39. 8
By *late* ensample of that courteous deed . . . VI. iii. 2. 4
th' adventure of her *late* mischaunce; . . . VI. iii. 19. 2
adventures, which had . . . to him befallen *late.* . . . VI. iii. 22. 6
that vile lozell which her *late* offended; . . . VI. iv. 10. 2
this land, *late* conquer'd by his sword . . . VI. iv. 29. 5
'In salvage forrest I him lost of *late,* . . . VI. v. 29. 1
wounded was Of that same Monster *late* . . . VI. v. 31. 7
Which Turpine had unto her shewed *late,* . . . VI. v. 33. 3
her excluded *late* at night, . . . VI. v. 33. 8
for grievous paine Of their *late* woundes, . . . VI. v. 39. 8
shame For his *late* villanies. . . . VI. vi. Arg.
He of the Prince his life received *late,* . . . VI. vii. 2. 4
Backe to the place where Turpine *late* he lore; . . . VI. vii. 14. 2
Of all his mischiefe and *late* lucklesse smart; . . . VI. vii. 21. 3
Had for his food *late* gathered from the tree, . . . VI. vii. 24. 5
Whom *late* we left ryding upon an Asse, . . . VI. vii. 27. 8
Fell into wretched woes, which she repented *late.* . . . VI. viii. 2. 9
through his *late* luckelesse prise, . . . VI. viii. 25. 7
hath bene beaten *late* With stormes of fortune . . . VI. ix. 31. 4
all those Ladies, which thou sawest *late,* . . . VI. x. 21. 3
to present her with her labours *late;* . . . VI. x. 33. 7
Gan cry to them aloud to helpe her all too *late.* . . . VI. x. 34. 9
As if he did from some *late* daunger fly, . . . VI. xi. 27. 5
whose hart through feare was *late* fordonne, . . . VI. xi. 35. 5
Right well knew Coridon his owne *late* sheepe, . . . VI. xi. 37. 6
when all the theeves did rest, After a *late* forray, . . . VI. xi. 42. 3
Having of *late* . . . Provided him a sword . . . VI. xi. 42. 5
with noyse of *late* uprore, . . . VI. xi. 46. 1
He growen is so great and strong of *late,* . . . VI. xii. 40. 4
the love of some new Nymph, *late* seene, . . . VII. vii. 11. 6
Had hunted *late* the Libbard or the Bore, . . . VII. vii. 29. 8
he had been a fatting hogs of *late,* . . . VII. vii. 40. 3
is of *late* far out of order gone. . . . VII. vii. 51. 4
Retourne agayne, my forces *late* dismayd, . . . *Am.* xiv. 1
on me thou shinedst *late* in sadnesse, . . . *Am.* xxxix. 6
Comes forth afresh out of their *late* dismay, . . . *Am.* xl. 11
a young fawne, that *late* hath lost the hynd; . . . *Am.* lxxviii. 2
I seeke the fields with her *late* footing synd; . . . *Am.* lxxviii. 5
her bowre with her *late* presence deckt; . . . *Am.* lxxviii. 6
his returne that seemes to linger *late:* . . . *Am.* lxxxviii. 4
Yet never day so long, but *late* would passe. . . . *Epith.* 273
I feare my wits enfeebled *late,* . . . *H.L.* 15
have left thee nought But *late* repentance . . . *H.H.B.* 293
late through all Spaine did thunder, . . . *Proth.* 147
Late-attempted. his leud lusts, and *late attempted* sin, . . . I. vi. 46. 3
Late-beguiled. that good knight, his *late beguiled* guest: . . . I. ii. 11. 2
Late-betrothed. loth to leave her *late betrothed* make, . . . IV. vi. 42. 8
Late-born. For ransome leaving him the *late-borne* childe; . . . I. vi. 23. 6
Late-decayed. Till he recovered had his *late decayed* plight. . . . I. x. 2. 9
Late-devoured. gobbets raw, Of *late devoured* bodies . . . I. xi. 13. 4
Late-forbidden. He gan renew the *late forbidden* bains, . . . I. xii. 36. 7
Lately. He *lately* slue his dreadfull foe . . . *Gn.* 648
Us to advise, which forth but *lately* moved, . . . *Hub.* 410
the Priests holesome counsell *lately* tought, . . . *Hub.* 553
'From royall Court I *lately* came . . . *Hub.* 607
woods, which he did *lately* fell, . . . *Hub.* 872
The beautie of the world hath *lately* wasted, . . . *T.M.* 248
our royall thrones, which *lately* stood . . . *T.M.* 313
Had *lately* built his hatefull mansion; . . . *Mui.* 246
verse of noblest shepheard *lately* dead . . . *Col.* 534
And *lately* shakt the Lusitanian soile. . . . *Ded.Son.*xiv.12
I, whether *lately* through her brightnes blynd, . . . I. iii. 1. 5
that harlott she too *lately* knew, . . . I. iii. 25. 3
'I *lately* chaunst . . . I. ix. 27. 1
By that which *lately* hapned Una saw . . . I. x. 2. 1
as hitherward I *lately* traveild, . . . I. xii. 31. 7
with lamenting eyes him selfe did *lately* vew. . . . II. ii. 45. 9
his good steed is *lately* from him gone; . . . II. iii. 3. 2
He *lately* heard that dying Lady grone, . . . II. iii. 3. 7
in his land he *lately* did appease, . . . II. x. 17. 4
by Maximian *lately* ledd away, . . . II. x. 62. 2
where they *lately* had Charm'd those wild-beasts . . . II. xii. 84. 4
those six, which *lately* with her fought, . . . III. i. 44. 1
whome hee *lately* brake . . . in victorious fight, . . . III. iii. 52. 7
he asked, whence he *lately* came, . . . III. v. 3. 6
I *lately* did depart From Faery court, . . . III. v. 4. 3
lately left the same, and tooke this way. . . . III. v. 4. 7
Where you him *lately* lefte, in Mars his bed: . . . III. vi. 24. 3
Fayre Psyche to him *lately* reconcyld, . . . III. vi. 50. 2
a ghost, that *lately* is reviv'd . . . III. vii. 14. 7
upon thy selfe hast *lately* ta'ne?' . . . III. vii. 53. 3
lately did dispart Her bleeding brest, . . . III. xii. 38. 3
much the more by that he *lately* wrought, . . . IV. i. 8. 3
It *lately* so befell, . . . IV. ii. 25. 6
Hath *lately* caus'd to be proclaim'd each where . . . IV. ii. 26. 7
It was the same which *lately* Florimel had lost. . . . IV. iv. 15. 9
those Knights That *lately* turneyd . . . IV. v. 7. 2
in an open Turney *lately* held, . . . IV. vi. 6. 6
'For *lately* he my love hath fro me reft, . . . IV. vi. 8. 1
By Braggadochio *lately* was redeemed; . . . IV. ix. 20. 7
Which he had *lately* seene, . . . IV. xii. 26. 9
He *lately* tooke, and sithence kept as thrall. . . . IV. xii. 32. 5
(as ye *lately* mote remember well) . . . V. i. 3. 3
With Braggadochio, whom he *lately* met . . . V. iii. 10. 3

Lately—*Continued.*
having *lately* left that lovely payre, . . . V. iv. 3. 1
From deathes dore at which he *lately* lay, . . . V. iv. 35. 2
Was *lately* broken by some fortune ill; . . . V. v. 15. 4
From which he *lately* had through reskew fled: . . . V. v. 18. 8
Whom from her Seneschall he *lately* freed, . . . VI. i. 47. 4
Since I him *lately* lost, . . . VI. v. 28. 9
So lewdly had abusde, as ye did *lately* heare. . . . VI. vi. 17. 9
Through many wounds, which *lately* he in fight Received had, VI. vi. 20. 8
lately sought his Lord for to displease: . . . VI. vi. 40. 4
an oaken plant which *lately* hee Rent by the root; . . . VI. vii. 24. 7
Backe to the furrow which I *lately* left. . . . VI. ix. 1. 2
I *lately* left a furrow, one or twayne, Unplough'd, . . . VI. ix. 1. 3
like that which *lately* she did vew. . . . VI. xi. 43. 9
Lately-bruised. their *lately bruzed* parts to bring in plight. III. ix. 19. 9
Lately-wrought. weetlesse eke of *lately wrought* despight, . . . II. v. 36. 5
Late-maimed. my *late maymed* limbs lack wonted might . . . *Hub.* 272
Late-miswandred. His *late miswandred* wayes now to re-measure right. . . . III. vii. 18. 9
Later. Their names shall of the *later* age be heard, . . . *Ti.* 348
Ne bene so much admir'd of *later* age. . . . *Ded. Son.* xiii. 6
when his *later* spring gins to avale, . . . I. i. 21. 5
of your *later* fight Ye all forwearied be; . . . I. i. 32. 5
later times thinges more unknowne shall show. . . . II. Pr. 3. 3
But other some, by guifte of *later* grace, . . . II. ii. 6. 6
Least worse betide thee by some *later* chaunce. . . . II. iv. 36. 5
later ages pride, like corn-fed steed, . . . II. vii. 16. 6
Thou, that doest live in *later* times, . . . II. vii. 18. 4
But *later* day, Finding in it fit ports . . . II. x. 6. 7
Let *later* age that noble use envy, . . . III. i. 13. 8
Their ofspring hath . . . *later* glory shent? . . . III. ix. 33. 9
The glory of the *later* world to spring, . . . III. ix. 44. 2
Our love shall live, and *later* life renew. . . . *Am.* lxxv. 14
Lo! one, whom *later* age hath brought to light, . . . *Com. Son.* iii. 9
Late-received. Through grievaunce of his *late received* wound, IV. iv. 26. 8
Late-renewed. to prove his *late-renewed* might, . . . I. xi. 35. 5
Latest. "Alcyon! ah, my first and *latest* love! . . . *D.* 263
Braies out her *latest* breath, and up her eies doth seele. . . . II. i. 38. 9
Late-succeeding. lanterne unto *late succeeding* age, . . . *Ti.* 170
Late-wounded. his *late wounded* wing unserviceable found. . . . I. xi. 25. 9
Latin. I chaunst to see Upon the *Latine* Coast . . . *Bel.*[2] xiii. 4
that brave honour of the *Latine* name, . . . *Ro.* xxii. 1
Ne yet of *Latine,* ne of Greeke, . . . *Hub.* 386
Latinus. he with old *Latinus* was constraind To contract wedlock, . . . III. ix. 42. 4
with *Latinus* did the kingdom part; . . . III. ix. 43. 2
Latium. 'At last in *Latium* he did arryve, . . . III. ix. 42. 1
Latmian. The *Latmian* shepherd once unto thee brought, . . . *Epith.* 380
Latona. The golden ofspring of *Latona* pure, . . . *Gn.* 13
thy displeasure, O *Latona* faire! . . . *Gn.* 378
Latona traveiling that way, . . . II. xii. 13. 4
Latona's. I will not match her with *Latonaes* seede, . . . *S.C.* Ap. 86
Latonaes daughter, cruell kynde, In vengement . . . IV. vii. 30. 5
Latonaes childrens wrath that all her issue wasted. . . . V. x. 7. 9
repayre, . . . unto *Latonaes* sonne After his chace . . . VI. ii. 25. 4
Latter. my yeare drawes to his *latter* terme, . . . *S.C.* D. 127
Lattice. Holding a *lattis* still before his face, . . . III. xii. 15. 8
Laud. loud advaunce her *laud;* . . . *Epith.* 145
Lauding. *Lauding* and praysing his renowmed worth . . . V. xi. 33. 3
Laugh. there thou needs must learne to *laugh,* to lie, . . . *Hub.* 505
Yet would he *laugh* it out, . . . *Hub.* 703
pleased, And made to *laugh,* . . . *Hub.* 710
Might *laugh* at them, and scorne their shamefull sin, . . . *Mui.* 373
Ay wont to *laugh* when them I heard to cry, . . . I. ix. 10. 5
The fields . . . Did seeme to *laugh* on me, . . . I. ix. 12. 9
to do him *laugh,* . . . II. vi. 7. 6
To *laugh* at shaking of the leaves light . . . II. vi. 7. 7
The fields did *laugh,* the flowres did freshly spring, . . . II. vi. 24. 6
'Both foolish knights! I can but *laugh* at both, . . . IV. i. 47. 2
At which they all gan *laugh* full merrily: . . . IV. iv. 10. 3
He lowdly gan to *laugh,* and thus to jest; . . . IV. v. 18. 2
Thereat all Knights gan *laugh,* and Ladies lowre: . . . IV. v. 19. 1
Then would he *laugh* aloud, and gather great delight. . . . IV. vii. 26. 9
heavens *laugh,* and al the world shews joyous cheare. . . . IV. x. 44. 9
To *laugh* at me, and favour my pretence, . . . IV. x. 56. 4
Ladies can *laugh* at Ladies, Knights at Knights, . . . V. iii. 39. 6
Did *laugh* at her that many did deride, . . . VI. vii. 32. 4
Did *laugh* at those that did lament and plaine; . . . VI. viii. 21. 8
Laden with fruits that made him *laugh,* . . . VII. vii. 30. 3
That I may *laugh* at her in equall sort, . . . *Am.* x. 13
laugh at her . . . As she doth *laugh* at me, . . . *Am.* x. 14
when I *laugh,* she mocks; . . . *Am.* liv. 11
when he saw me *laugh,* for shame His face . . . did flame, . . . *Epig.* iii. 4
could not chose but *laugh* at his fond game, . . . *Epig.* iv. 33
seemst to *laugh* atweene thy twinkling light, . . . *Epith.* 292
Love doest *laugh* and scorne At their complaints, . . . *H.L.* 134
Laughed. Sometimes she *laught,* as merry as Pope Jone; . . . II. vi. 3. 4
Therewith she *laught,* . . . II. vi. 23. 9
some *laught* for joy; . . . II. ix. 35. 2
therewith lowdly *laught:* . . . II. xii. 15. 4
Withall she *laughed,* and she blusht withall, . . . II. xii. 68. 1
Jove *laught* on Venus from his soverayne see, . . . III. vi. 2. 7
(Thereat full hartely *laughed* Satyrane.) . . . III. vii. 58. 5
Laught at his foolish labour spent in waste, . . . III. x. 13. 4
as Dissemblaunce *laught* on him, . . . III. xii. 15. 3
Some *laught* for sport, some did for wonder shout, . . . IV. iii. 41. 8
Ne ever *laught,* ne once shew'd countenance glad, . . . IV. viii. 2. 7
laught so loud, that all his teeth wide bare . . . V. xi. 9. 7
At whose calamity, . . . He *laught,* . . . VI. iii. 34. 4
But *laught* them out, . . . VI. iii. 36. 3

Laughed—*Continued.*
how all creatures *laught* when her they spide . . . VII. vii. 34. 7
Laugheth. when the shining sunne *laugheth* once, . . . *S.C.* F. 37
Laughing. *laughing* lope to a tree; . . . *S.C.* Mar. 81
Full of disport, still *laughing*, loosely light, . . . II. ii. 36. 2
Some as the Rubine *laughing* sweetely red, . . . II. xii. 54. 8
the boughes doe *laughing* blossoms beare, . . . III. vi. 42. 3
(then *laughing* sayd The knight) . . . III. vii. 57. 5
with Sardonian smyle *Laughing* on her, . . . V. ix. 12. 7
Laughing-game. Are now despizd, and made a *laughing game*. *T.M.* 204
Laughing-stock. *laughing stocke* of all that list to scorne; . *T.M.* 224
forlorne Maiden . . . The *laughing stocke* of fortunes mockeries, I. vii. 43. 2
Laughs. *laughes* the songs that Colin Clout doth make. . . . *S.C.* Ja. 66
goes loose, and *laughes* at me. . . . IV. xii. 11. 4
when she complaines, The more he *laughes*, . . . VI. vii. 44. 8
mocketh all my paine, and *laughs* the more I mourn.' . . . VI. viii. 24. 9
She *laughes*, and hardens evermore her hart. . . . *Am.* liv. 12
Laughter. Delight, and *Laughter*, deckt in seemly sort. . . . *T.M.* 198
all her wordes she drownd with *laughter* vaine, . . . II. vi. 6. 7
blushing to her *laughter* gave more grace, And *laughter* to her blushing, . . . II. xii. 68. 2, 3
brusting forth in *laughter*, . . . III. iii. 19. 2
by his grenning *laughter* mote farre off be rad. . . . IV. vii. 24. 9
Mother of *laughter*, and welspring of blisse, . . . IV. x. 47. 8
breaking forth in *laughter*, . . . VII. vi. 46. 5
when I waile, she turnes hir selfe to *laughter*. . . . *Am.* xviii. 12
Launch. Laments the wound that death did *launch*. . . . *S.C.* N. 139
launch your hearts with lamentable wounds . . . *T.M.* 375
he eftsoones gan *launch* his barke forthright. . . . II. xi. 4. 4
With which he wont to *launch* the salvage hart . . . VI. ii. 6. 7
with a naked knife Readie to *launch* her brest, . . . VI. viii. 48. 9
What hart can feele least touch of so sore *launch*, . . . *H.H.L.* 162
Launched. *See* **Through-launched.**
Launched his thigh with so mischievous might, . . . *As.* 119
he . . . *launcht* his Lordly hart: . . . I. iii. 42. 8
since my brest was *launcht* with lovely dart . . . I. iv. 46. 5
wound That *launched* hath my brest with bleeding smart. . . . I. vii. 25. 7
griefe, Which love had *launched* with his deadly darts, . . . I. ix. 29. 3
whose sides with cruell steele Through *launched*, . . . II. i. 38. 7
Forth *launched* quickly as she did desire, . . . II. vi. 20. 4
From the departing land it *launched* light, . . . II. xii. 15. 8
launched this wound wyde. . . . III. ii. 37. 9
His feeble hart wide *launched* with loves cruel wownd. . . . III. vi. 52. 9
many wide woundes *launched* through his inner partes. . . . III. xi. 44. 9
being whylome *launcht* with lovely dart, . . . IV. vi. 40. 5
with deadly wound My heart was *launcht*, . . . IV. x. 1. 8
new *launcht* with murdrous knife, . . . VI. v. 5. 4
with the selfe same wound *Launcht* through the arme, . . . VI. xi. 19. 9
Launchedst. their lives thou *lanchedst* long afore, . . . IV. vii. 1. 8
Launching. sharply *launching* every inner part, . . . *H.H.L.* 158
Laurel. faire greene *Laurel* witherd up and dide. . . . *Bel.*[1] vii. 14
head with *Lawrell* garnisht was about. . . . *Bel.*[2] ix. 12
While on this *Lawrell* fixed was mine eie, . . . *Pet.* iii. 8
Lawrell, th' ornament of Phoebus toyle. . . . *Gn.* 672
The *Laurell*, meed of mightie Conquerours . . . I. i. 9. 1
her face did with a *Lawrell* shade. . . . III. x. 44. 9
in his hand a braunch of *laurell* bore, . . . III. xii. 3. 7
Laurel-bough. His head was garnisht with the *Laurel bow*. . *Bel.*[1] vii. 12
Laurel-boughs. at his feet their *lawrell boughes* did throw. . I. xii. 6. 4
Laurel-branch. faire greene *Lawrell branch* did quite decay. *Bel.*[2] ix. 14
Laurel-branches. now they *laurell braunches* bore in hand, . I. xii. 5. 8
Laurel-garland. with *laurell girlond* cround. . . . II. iii. 38. 9
Laurel-garlands. Like virgin Queenes, with *laurell garlands* cround . . . *T.M.* 309
Both those the *lawrell girlonds* to the victor dew. . . . I. v. 5. 9
Laurel-leaf. The *laurel-leafe*, which you this day doe weare, . *Am.* xxviii. 1
Laurels. Planted with mirtle trees and *laurells* greene, . . . III. v. 40. 2
Laurel-tree. the fresh and lustie *Lawrell* (*Laurell*[1]) *tree*, . . . *Pet.* iii. 2
Did her transforme into a *laurell-tree*. . . . *Am.* xxviii. 12
Laurel-trees. sett With shady *Laurell trees*, . . . II. xii. 63. 2
Lavender. The wholesome Saulge, and *Lavender* still gray, . . *Mui.* 187
Laver. The which into an ample *laver* fell, . . . II. xii. 62. 3
Lavish. *See* **Love-lavish.**
Let powre in *lavish* cups . . . *S.C.* O. 105
lavish Nature, in her best attire, . . . *Mui.* 163
which her *lavish* lovers to her gave. . . . I. ii. 13. 6
Accourting each her frend with *lavish* fest: . . . II. ii. 16. 5
of her love too *lavish*: . . . II. ii. 36. 9
In daintie delices, and *lavish* joyes, . . . II. v. 28. 6
made there to abound with *lavish* affluence. . . . II. xii. 42. 9
Lavishly. like a pompous bride . . . too *lavishly* adorne, . . . II. xii. 50. 8
So *lavishly* enricht with Natures threasure, . . . IV. x. 23. 3
Lavishness. spent with pride and *lavishnesse*, . . . II. vii. 12. 4
Law. ne by the *law* of Nature, . . . *Hub.* 145
keepe this as a *lawe*: . . . *Hub.* 1054
Ne would his looser life be tide to *law*, . . . I. iv. 26. 3
Theseus condemned to endlesse slouth by *law*; . . . I. v. 35. 8
by *law* of that proud Tyrannesse, . . . I. v. 46. 6
his beheast they feared as a tyrans *law*. . . . I. vi. 26. 9
Is not his *lawe*, Let every sinner die; . . . I. ix. 47. 5
By righteous sentence of th' Almighties *law*. . . . I. ix. 50. 4
as a *law* for ever should endure; . . . II. ii. 32. 8
thou broken hast The *law* of armes . . . II. viii. 31. 7
feele the *law* the which thou hast defast.' . . . II. viii. 31. 9
he, now subject to the victours *law*, . . . II. viii. 50. 5
She hath ordaind this *law*, which we approve, . . . III. i. 26. 6
by her owne *law* to your lot doth light, . . . III. i. 30. 4
Hath me subjected to loves cruell *law*: . . . III. ii. 38. 5
all that lives is subject to that *law*; . . . III. vi. 40. 8
Gainst natures *law* and good behaveoure; . . . III. vii. 49. 2

Law—*Continued.*
in martiall *law* And deedes of armes . . . III. vii. 52. 3
t' obay her servaunts *law*. . . . III. xi. 30. 9
eke unto her lookes a *law* she made, . . . IV. ii. 36. 6
each unto his lust did make a *lawe*, . . . IV. viii. 30. 8
to his *law* compels all creatures to obay. . . . IV. x. 42. 9
According to the custome of their *law*: . . . V. ii. 11. 7
Tyrants, that make men subject to their *law*, . . . V. ii. 38. 6
By *law* of armes there neede ones right to trie, . . . V. iii. 32. 2
if I vanquishe him, he shall obay My *law*, . . . V. iv. 49. 3
There bound t' obay that Amazons proud *law*, . . . V. v. 22. 3
Chiefely by him whose life her *law* doth bynd, . . . V. v. 41. 7
Give him more labour, and with streighter *law*, . . . V. v. 50. 3
To breake all bonds of *law* and rules of right: . . . V. viii. 20. 5
scornd all former *law*: . . . V. viii. 41. 4
adjudged so by *law*; . . . V. ix. 25. 3
then the *Law* of Nations gainst her rose, . . . V. ix. 44. 3
'loth were I to have broken The *law* of armes: . . . VI. ii. 7. 7
So judgement past, as is by *law* ordayned . . . VI. vii. 36. 5
Cryde mercie, to abate the extremitie of *law*. . . . VI. vii. 36. 9
against all reason and all *law*, . . . VI. viii. 6. 4
were no *law* in love, . . . His kingdome would continue but a while. . . . VI. viii. 23. 3
Unto his lust, and make his will his *law*, . . . VI. xi. 6. 3
Unrighteous Lord of Love, what *law* is this, . . . *Am.* x. 1
Lawful. looser thoughts to *lawfull* bounds withdraw; . . . IV. vi. 33. 7
Unlesse the heavens them lift to *lawfull* soveraintie. . . . V. v. 25. 9
did rebell gainst *lawfull* government; . . . V. xii. 26. 8
Lawless. to restraine The lust of *lawlesse* youth . . . *S.C.* O. 22
raging spoile of *lawlesse* victors will? . . . I. iii. 43. 2
otherwise His life he led in *lawlesse* riotise, . . . I. iv. 20. 5
From *lawlesse* lust . . . Fayre Una is releast: . . . I. vi. Arg.
all to *lawlesse* lust encouraged . . . II. ii. 18. 5
lawlesse lustes, corrupt envyes, . . . II. xi. 8. 8
Unto abuse of *lawlesse* lust was lent, . . . IV. viii. 32. 3
lawlesse lust to rule with reasons lore; . . . IV. ix. 19. 4
Which *lawlesse* men had formerly fordonne: . . . V. i. 2. 4
Fro me reft mine away by *lawlesse* might, . . . V. i. 17. 8
Which *lawlesse* multitude him comming too . . . V. ii. 52. 1
Gainst tortious powre and *lawlesse* regiment, . . . V. viii. 30. 7
Purchast through *lawlesse* powre and tortious wrong . . . V. viii. 51. 6
sought with *lawlesse* powre him to oppresse, . . . V. xi. 44. 4
In execution of her *lawlesse* doome . . . VI. i. 16. 3
A *lawlesse* people, Brigants hight of yore, . . . VI. x. 39. 3
made unfit to serve his *lawlesse* mindes behest. . . . VI. xi. 7. 9
Lawlessness. *lawlesnes* raigning with riotize; . . . *Hub.* 1310
Lawns. Faire *lawnds*, to take the sunne in season dew; . . . IV. x. 24. 2
Laws. breach of *lawes* to privie ferme did let: . . . *Hub.* 1160
The sacred *lawes* therein they wont expresse, . . . *T.M.* 561
Ne ruld her Realme with *lawes*, but pollicie, . . . I. iv. 12. 7
T' observe the sacred *lawes* of armes . . . I. v. 4. 9
Emongst wild beastes and woods, from *lawes* of men exilde. I. vi. 23. 9
If ever he transgrest the fatall Stygian *lawes*. . . . II. vii. 27. 9
Of *lawes*, of judgementes, and of decretals, . . . II. ix. 53. 7
Then made he sacred *lawes*, . . . II. x. 39. 1
Those yet of her be Mertian *lawes* both nam'd and thought. II. x. 42. 9
Gan coyne streight *lawes* to curb their liberty: . . . III. ii. 2. 6
what prescribed were by *lawes* of chevalrie. . . . V. vii. 28. 9
High Gods beheast, and powre of holy *lawes*; . . . V. ix. 44. 6
lastly Justice charged her with breach of *lawes*. . . . V. ix. 44. 9
now he hath new *lawes* and orders new Imposd on it . . . V. x. 27. 6
lawes of men, that common-weales containe, . . . V. xii. 1. 4
Ne shee the *lawes* of Nature onely brake, . . . VII. vi. 6. 1
vertue . . . giveth *lawes* alone, . . . *Epith.* 195
The *lawes* of wedlock still dost patronize; . . . *Epith.* 391
Lawyer. like a *Lawyer*, when he land would lett, . . . *Hub.* 866
Lawyers. studious *Lawyers* have their bowers, . . . *Proth.* 134
Lay. *See* **Lea, Love-lay, Overlay.**
there *lay* . . . foure great Lions of golde. . . . *Bel.*[1] iii. 9
Strake on a rock, that under water *lay*, . . . *Pet.* ii. 9
An hundred vanquisht Kings under her *lay*, . . . *Bel.*[2] xv. 9
outstretched *lay*, In monstrous length, . . . *Van.* iii. 2
drove in Joves owne lap his egs to *lay*; . . . *Van.* iv. 10
fiercely the good man at him did *laye*. . . . *S.C.* F. 214
will I singe his *laye* Of fayre Elisa, . . . *S.C.* Ap. 33
Which once he made as by a spring he *laye*, . . . *S.C.* Ap. 35
live ylike as men of the *laye*. . . . *S.C.* May 76
layen her faults the world beforne, . . . *S.C.* May 160
Then listneth ech unto my heavy *laye*, . . . *S.C.* Au. 149
layen baytes to beguile her brother; . . . *S.C.* S. 39
To take his owne where ever it *laye*? . . . *S.C.* S. 209
Ystabled hath his steedes in lowlye *laye*, . . . *S.C.* N. 15
Into thick shadowes, there themselves to *lay*. . . . *Gn.* 168
this Shepheards flocke *Lay* everie where, . . . *Gn.* 234
murdred troupes upon great heapes to *lay*. . . . *Gn.* 400
with like lovely *lay* The Queene of hell to move . . . *Gn.* 461
Where *lay* the ships which they did seeke to burne. . . . *Gn.* 512
We are but charg'd to *lay* the meate before: . . . *Hub.* 435
The Lyon sleeping *lay* in secret shade, . . . *Hub.* 952
when his Syre with Alcumena *lay*. . . . *Hub.* 1299
The wicked weed, which there the Foxe did *lay*, . . . *Hub.* 1321
Can rightfully aread so dolefull *lay*. . . . *T.M.* 52
upon his lips to *laie* The sacred sod, . . . *Ti.* 195
low in ashes *lay*, . . . *Ti.* 502
these Beares *lay* sleeping sound, . . . *Ti.* 570
Therein a goodly Virgine sleeping *lay*; . . . *Ti.* 636
lurking closely, in awayte now *lay*, . . . *Mui.* 247
Lay lurking covertly him to surprise; . . . *Mui.* 386
So *lay* she downe, as if to sleepe she went, . . . *D.* 256
Where as the lucklesse boy yet bleeding *lay*; . . . *As.* 142

Lay—*Continued.*
Yet bleeding *lay*, and yet would still have bled, . . . *As.* 143
Clorinda . . . began this dolefull *lay*. . . . *As.* 214
after Tityrus first sung his *lay*, . . . *Col.* 2
some hymne, or morall *laie*, . . . *Col.* 86
Record to us that lovely *lay* againe: . . . *Col.* 97
'Now by my life this was a mery *lay*, . . . *Col.* 157
a lamentable *lay* Of great unkindnesse, . . . *Col.* 164
Religion hath *lay* powre to rest upon her, . . . *Col.* 322
Lay forth . . . The antique rolles, which there lye hidden . I. Pr. 2. 3
Lay now thy deadly Heben bowe apart, . . . I. Pr. 3. 5
as she *lay* upon the durtie ground, . . . I. i. 15. 1
downe did *lay* His heavie head, . . . I. i. 44. 3
comming where the knight in slomber *lay*, . . . I. i. 47. 2
Then seemed him his Lady by him *lay*, . . . I. i. 47. 7
Long after *lay* he musing at her mood, . . . I. i. 55. 1
on the grasse her dainty limbs did *lay* . . . I. iii. 4. 3
As if her life upon the wager *lay;* . . . I. iii. 12. 2
He answered nought, but in a traunce still *lay*, . . . I. iii. 39. 6
Like loathsome lazars, by the hedges *lay*. . . . I. iv. 3. 6
in his bosome secretly there *lay* An hatefull Snake, . . . I. iv. 31. 3
underneath their feet, all scattered *lay* Dead sculls . . . I. iv. 36. 8
Who all that while *lay* hid in secret shade. . . . I. v. 15. 4
knight . . . *Lay* cover'd with inchaunted cloud . . . I. v. 19. 6
Unto the place whereas the Paynim *lay*, . . . I. v. 29. 2
So *lay* him in her charett, . . . I. v. 29. 9
dreadfull Cerberus His three deformed heads did *lay* along, I. v. 34. 2
His cunning hand gan to his wounds to *lay*, . . . I. v. 44. 2
in a dungeon deepe huge nombers *lay* . . . I. v. 45. 8
most of all, which in that dongeon *lay*, . . . I. v. 51. 5
many corses . . . *lay* Without remorse . . . I. v. 53. 3
rocke . . . That *lay* in waite her wrack for to bewaile, . . . I. vi. 1. 3
Their frowning forheads, . . . all asyde doe *lay;* . . . I. vi. 11. 6
all his sences stound that still he *lay* full low. . . . I. vii. 12. 9
love fresh coles unto her fire did *lay;* . . . I. vii. 27. 5
headlesse his unweldy bodie *lay*, . . . I. viii. 24. 3
she it is, that did my Lord . . . deepe in dongeon *lay*, . . . I. viii. 28. 7
Love! *lay* down thy bow, the whiles I may respyre. . . . I. ix. 8. 9
Her daintie limbes full softly down did *lay:* . . . I. ix. 13. 8
there *lay* upon the gras A dreary corse, . . . I. ix. 36. 4
Upon her arme a silver anchor *lay*, . . . I. x. 14. 6
The man that . . . *lay* at deathes dore. . . . I. x. 27. 9
those in point of death which *lay;* . . . I. x. 41. 2
forst him *lay* his hevenly thoughts aside; . . . I. x. 49. 3
learned Ladies . . . make full many a lovely *lay*. . . . I. x. 54. 9
he *lay* upon the sunny side Of a great hill, . . . I. xi. 4. 5
Fayre Goddesse, *lay* that furious fitt asyde, . . . I. xi. 7. 1
ne once adowne would *lay* Her dainty limbs . . . I. xi. 32. 7
the well, wherein he drenched *lay:* . . . I. xi. 34. 2
lay, as in a dreame of deepe delight, . . . I. xi. 50. 4
like an heaped mountaine *lay*. . . . I. xi. 54. 9
song In well attuned notes a *joyous* lay. . . . I. xii. 7. 4
they came where that dead Dragon *lay*, . . . I. xii. 9. 6
Still as he went he craftie stales did *lay*, . . . II. i. 4. 1
Into a pleasant dale that lowly *lay* . . . II. i. 24. 3
With percing shriekes and many a dolefull *lay;* . . . II. i. 35. 8
where that sad pourtraict Of death and dolour *lay*, . . . II. i. 39. 4
Beside a bubling fountaine low she *lay*, . . . II. i. 40. 2
They *lay* therein their corses tenderly, . . . II. i. 60. 5
this misseeming discord meekely *lay* aside.' . . . II. ii. 31. 9
in the bush he *lay*, . . . II. iii. 43. 5
His mighty hands did on the madman *lay*, . . . II. iv. 6. 4
overthrew him selfe unwares, and lower *lay:* . . . II. iv. 8. 9
To lull him soft asleepe that by it *lay:* . . . II. v. 30. 4
Into the land that *lay* them faire before, . . . II. vi. 11. 8
*with a loud *lay* she thus him sweetly charm'd. . . . II. vi. 14. 9
Such as he saw she gan him *lay* before, . . . II. vi. 24. 4
round about him *lay* on every side . . . II. vii. 5. 1
All these before the gates of Pluto *lay*, . . . II. vii. 24. 1
drenched *lay* full deepe under the Garden side. . . . II. vii. 57. 9
Where Guyon *lay* in traunce; . . . II. viii. 3. 6
some relish of that hevenly *lay* . . . II. x. 3. 6
all along the Southerne sea-coast *lay* . . . II. x. 6. 4
lay strong siege about it far and wyde. . . . II. xi. 5. 5
Did *lay* strong siege . . . II. xi. 9. 2
Against that Castle restlesse siege did *lay*, . . . II. xi. 14. 2
Thereby there *lay* An huge great stone, . . . II. xi. 35. 6
He soone in vomit up againe doth *lay*, . . . II. xii. 3. 7
some one did chaunt this lovely *lay:* . . . II. xii. 74. 1
Their diverse notes t' attune unto his *lay*, . . . II. xii. 76. 2
As *lay* her journey, through that perlous Pace, . . . III. i. 19. 7
her soft arme *lay* underneath his hed, . . . III. i. 36. 3
doth the charmed Snake in slomber *lay*. . . . III. ii. 15. 6
dischord ofte in Musick makes the sweeter *lay:*— . . . III. ii. 15. 9
Lay hidden in the bottome of the pot. . . . III. ii. 26. 5
mortall men their weary cares Do *lay* away, . . . III. ii. 32. 2
standing high aloft low *lay* thine eare, . . . III. iii. 9. 1
Whiles thus he *lay* in deadly stonishment, . . . III. iv. 19. 1
Was taken with her love, and by her closely *lay*. . . . III. iv. 19. 9
lay as in a swowne, . . . III. iv. 30. 6
he *lay* wallowd all in his owne gore. . . . III. v. 26. 5
Comfort to him that comfortlesse now *lay*. . . . III. v. 27. 4
With blood deformed, *lay* in deadly swownd; . . . III. v. 29. 2
lay bleding out his hart-blood neare. . . . III. v. 32. 9
whiles that he *lay* in swownd, . . . III. v. 38. 7
Beside the same a dainty place there *lay*, . . . III. v. 40. 1
the birds song many a lovely *lay* . . . III. v. 40. 3
Others *lay* shaded from the scorching heat, . . . III. vi. 17. 8
whereas *lay* Faire Crysogone in slombry traunce . . . III. vi. 26. 6
A little bote *lay* hoving her before, . . . III. vii. 27. 4

Lay—*Continued.*
her sonne that *lay* in feeble state; . . . III. viii. 9. 7
lay tombled in the myre, Unable to arise, . . . III. vii. 45. 8
each awhile *lay* like a sencelesse corse. . . . III. ix. 16. 5
What fortune and his fate on him will *lay;* . . . III. x. 3. 2
where all his wealth *Lay* hid; . . . III. x. 12. 4
As if they *lay* in wait, . . . III. x. 20. 9
lay still in the winde, Waiting advauntage . . . III. x. 30. 5
The silly man that in the thickett *lay* . . . III. x. 45. 1
Whereas his lovely wife emongst them *lay*, . . . III. x. 48. 2
a fountaine sheare, By which there *lay* a knight . . . III. xi. 7. 3
A *lay* of loves delight with sweet concent: . . . III. xii. 5. 7
nycely trode, as thornes *lay* in his way, . . . III. xii. 10. 6
shrunck when hard thereon he *lay*. . . . III. xii. 10. 9
foe . . . rolled on an heape, *lay* still in swound . . . IV. i. 43. 1
Upon the ground awhile in slomber *lay;* . . . IV. ii. 7. 2
Strooke him so hugely that in swowne he *lay*, . . . IV. iii. 34. 3
Out of the swowne, in which too long he *lay;* . . . IV. iv. 22. 2
His weapons which *lay* scattered all abrode, . . . IV. iv. 23. 2
many swords that lode on him did *lay*. . . . IV. iv. 31. 5
There as he *lay*, his wound he soone forgot, . . . IV. iv. 33. 2
There *lay* Sir Scudamour long while . . . IV. v. 40. 1
lay musing long on that him ill apayd. . . . IV. v. 42. 9
So long he muzed, and so long he *lay*, . . . IV. v. 43. 1
Where fearelesse I to sleepe me downe did *lay:* . . . IV. vi. 36. 4
lay Continuall siege unto her gentle hart; . . . IV. vi. 40. 3
through weary travel she *lay* sleeping sound. . . . IV. vii. 4. 9
will not he the lovely spoile downe *lay;* . . . IV. vii. 25. 5
Lay hid in horrour of eternall night? . . . IV. vii. 33. 6
Who *lay* the whiles in swoune, full sadly set, . . . IV. vii. 35. 4
Weening therein some holy Hermit *lay*, . . . IV. vii. 42. 7
bitter thoughts, which deepe therein infixed *lay*. . . . IV. viii. 1. 9
Shee sitting by him, as on ground he *lay*, . . . IV. viii. 4. 1
thereof made a lamentable *lay*, . . . IV. viii. 4. 3
The evill case in which those Ladies *lay;* . . . IV. viii. 20. 2
lay long while in senselesse swowne. . . . IV. viii. 42. 9
the thrals which there in bondage *lay:* . . . IV. viii. 52. 3
lay on load, as they him downe would beare; . . . IV. ix. 33. 3
With all my might I gan to *lay* about: . . . IV. x. 19. 7
lay in ambushment there, . . . IV. x. 20. 7
all about her altar scattered *lay* . . . IV. x. 43. 1
Upon a recluse Virgin to *lay* hold, . . . IV. x. 54. 4
to *lay* hand on her not one of all them daring. . . . IV. x. 56. 9
old Styx her aged bones alway . . . doth *lay*. . . . IV. xi. 4. 5
his wretched love *lay* day and night . . . IV. xii. 19. 4
which in his hart *lay* unrevealed. . . . IV. xii. 22. 9
If ought *lay* hidden in his grieved thought, . . . IV. xii. 24. 8
At length found out whereas she hidden *lay* . . . V. ii. 25. 5
all the wrongs that he therein could *lay* . . . V. ii. 46. 6
His battred ballances in peeces *lay*, . . . V. ii. 50. 7
when at him he with his flaile gan *lay*, . . . V. ii. 53. 5
thrise did *lay* his hand upon his sword; . . . V. iii. 36. 3
let each *lay* downe his sword; . . . V. iv. 16. 7
the sea it to my share did *lay?'* . . . V. iv. 17. 7
Meaning on him their cruell hands to *lay*, . . . V. iv. 23. 8
lay on heaven the guilt of their owne crimes. . . . V. iv. 28. 3
From deathes dore at which he lately *lay*, . . . V. iv. 35. 2
She mote revenge that blot which on her *lay*. . . . V. iv. 47. 5
So did Sir Artegall upon her *lay*, . . . V. v. 8. 1
when they thought on Talus hands to *lay*, . . . V. v. 19. 1
if in his owne powre occasion *lay*, . . . V. v. 39. 2
lay upon him . . . Cold yron chaines . . . V. v. 50. 7
there where on ground he *lay*, . . . V. vi. 29. 6
soone as he began to *lay* about . . . V. vi. 30. 1
here and there like scattred sheepe they *lay:* . . . V. vi. 30. 6
the Crocodile, which sleeping *lay* . . . V. vii. 15. 1
So thereuppon long while she musing *lay*, . . . V. vii. 17. 1
first the Tygre clawes thereon did *lay*, . . . V. vii. 30. 4
To *lay* his spoiles before his lemans traine: . . . V. viii. 2. 3
those two Knights which dead there *lay;* . . . V. viii. 25. 5
Forth of her window as she looking *lay*, . . . V. viii. 26. 6
Onely his shield and armour, which there *lay*, . . . V. viii. 44. 1
roiall pompe, which there long hidden *lay*, . . . V. viii. 51. 5
A straunge adventure, which not farre thence *lay;* . . . V. ix. 4. 5
Gan forth to *lay* his bayte . . . V. ix. 12. 8
Charmes to the birds full many a pleasant *lay*, . . . V. ix. 13. 2
How he his nets doth for their ruine *lay:* . . . V. ix. 13. 4
An huge great Lyon *lay*, . . . V. ix. 33. 4
and all her treasons forth did *lay*. . . . V. ix. 47. 9
Right in the middest of the threshold *lay*, . . . V. x. 37. 4
The Monster underneath the Altar *lay:* . . . V. xi. 21. 7
With his huge flaile began to *lay* about; . . . V. xi. 47. 7
they *lay* scattred over all the land, . . . V. xii. 7. 8
hard at him did *lay;* . . . VI. i. 24. 2
his foe *lay* fast in sencelesse swound; . . . VI. i. 34. 2
save my life, which lot before your foot doth *lay*.' . . . VI. i. 39. 9
low on ground he *lay:* . . . VI. ii. 4. 7
And him unarm'd, as now he *lay* on ground, . . . VI. ii. 43. 4
'Therefore, faire Lady, *lay* aside this griefe, . . . VI. ii. 46. 1
steeped *lay* All night in darkenesse, . . . VI. iii. 13. 6
Uprear'd her from the ground whereon she *lay*, . . . VI. iii. 27. 8
Tho on his shield he griple hold did *lay*, . . . VI. iv. 6. 7
Compeld him soone the spoyle adowne to *lay*. . . . VI. iv. 20. 4
ragged stone Which *lay* thereby . . . VI. iv. 21. 3
And every part that under sweath-bands *lay*, . . . VI. iv. 23. 7
There she long groveling and deepe groning *lay*, . . . VI. v. 5. 6
streight his cumbrous armes aside did *lay* . . . VI. v. 10. 6
By which a little Hermitage there *lay*, . . . VI. v. 34. 8
rude hand on him did *lay*, To thrust him out . . . VI. vi. 21. 8
joyning close huge lode at him did *lay;* . . . VI. vi. 28. 8

Lay—*Continued.*
he bathed *lay* in his owne bloody gore. . . . VI. vii. 8. 9
That other swayne . . . *Lay* in the lap of death, . . . VI. vii. 17. 9
Whereas the Prince himselfe *lay* all alone, . . . VI. vii. 18. 7
The whiles his Lord in silver slomber *lay,* . . . VI. vii. 19. 8
as he *lay* upon the humbled gras, . . . VI. vii. 26. 3
he *lay,* ne out of swoune awooke, . . . VI. vii. 48. 5
from them *lay* your loathly hands, . . . VI. viii. 7. 8
whilest on ground he *lay,* . . . VI. viii. 11. 2
whilest in Morpheus bosome safe she *lay,* . . . VI. viii. 34. 6
in the depth of sleepe all fearelesse *lay.* . . . VI. viii. 36. 9
all bootes not; they hands upon her *lay:* . . . VI. viii. 41. 1
I downe doe *lay* My limbes . . . VI. ix. 23. 7
Nor draw unto the lure of his lewd *lay,* . . . VI. xi. 5. 3
who so hardie hand on her doth *lay,* . . . VI. xi. 15. 8
There *lay* she covered with confused preasse . . . VI. xi. 20. 1
Lay sleeping soundly in the bushes shade, . . . VI. xi. 38. 4
Gan all upon him *lay:* . . . VI. xi. 47. 9
gan *lay* unto the open light The litle babe, . . . VI. xii. 7. 4
on the . . . grasse her dainty limbes to *lay* . . . VII. vi. 42. 4
There-on an heavy haplesse curse did *lay;* . . . VII. vi. 55. 3
A wicked ambush which *lay* hidden long . . . *Am.* xii. 6
And *lay* incessant battery to her heart; . . . *Am.* xiv. 10
With pretious merchandize she forth doth *lay;* . . . *Am.* lxxxi. 6
She chaunst to come where Cupid *lay,* . . . *Epig.* ii. 2
Love *lay* sweetly slumbring . . . *Epig.* iv. 1
on it he hasty hand did *lay,* . . . *Epig.* iv. 25
Now *lay* those sorrowfull complaints aside; . . . *Epith.* 12
Whiles ye forget your former *lay* to sing, . . . *Epith.* 183
in her bed her *lay;* . . . *Epith.* 301
Lay her in lillies and in violets, . . . *Epith.* 302
leave likewise your former *lay* to sing: . . . *Epith.* 313
when Jove with fayre Alcmena *lay,* . . . *Epith.* 328
in her snowy bosome boldly *lay* Their quiet heads, . . . *H.L.* 289
forth to *lay* That heavenly riches . . . *H.B.* 184
The glory of our heavenly riches *lay,* . . . *H.H.L.* 229
one did sing this *Lay,* . . . *Proth.* 87

Laybourne. Both slaine in battaile upon *Layburne* playne, . III. iii. 37. 4

Laying. *laying* his head disarmd In her loose lap, . . . II. vi. 14. 6
laying his sad dartes Asyde, . . . III. vi. 49. 8
on his collar *laying* puissaunt hand, . . . III. vii. 43. 1
laying thwart her horse, In loathly wise . . . III. vii. 43. 4
unawares upon her *laying* hold, . . . IV. ii. 45. 6
Chasing, and *laying* on them heavy lode, . . . IV. iv. 23. 7
laying both his hands upon his glave, . . . IV. vii. 28. 2
and, *laying* mightie hold Upon his throte, . . . VI. iv. 22. 3
laying hand upon his wrathfull blade . . . VI. v. 26. 6
laying yet afresh . . . Upon the rest . . . VI. vi. 38. 3
laying feare aside to doe his charge, . . . VII. vi. 17. 6

Lays. *See* **Loving-lays.**
Thy lovely *layes* . . . freely boste. . . . *S.C.* Jun. 13
for shame of thy swete *layes.* . . . *S.C.* Jun. 56
into weeping turne your wanton *layes.* . . . *S.C.* N. 79
Fayre fieldes and pleasaunt *layes* there bene; . . . *S.C.* N. 188
So oft bedeawed with our learned *layes,* . . . *T.M.* 272
change the tenor of your joyous *layes,* . . . *T.M.* 367
doost heare their heavenlie *layes,* . . . *Ti.* 335
layes forth her threatfull pikes . . . *Mui.* 85
ye read these wofull *layes,* On my grave written, . . . *D.* 536
with your piteous *layes* have learnd to breed Compassion . . . *As.* Pr. 3
layes of love he also could compose: . . . *As.* 35
expresse their inward woe, With dolefull *layes* . . . *As.* Interl. 226
Laies of sweet love, without rebuke or blame, . . . *Col.* 3
tourn Sweet *layes* of love to endlesse plaints . . . *Col.* 387
raise His tunes from *laies* to matter of more skill. . . . *Col.* 395
In loves soft *laies* and looser thoughts delight. . . . *Col.* 423
My *layes* made of her shall not be forgotten, . . . *Col.* 642
To sing his sweet delights in lowlie *laies;* . . . *Ded. Son.* xv. 7
Sad Una downe her *laies* in weary plight, . . . I. iii. 15. 3
layes the soule to sleepe in quiet grave? . . . I. ix. 40. 7
Before, behind, and round about him *laies;* . . . II. ii. 25. 8
for this Realme found many goodly *layes,* . . . II. x. 42. 5
As well in curious instruments as cunning *laies.* . . . II. x. 59. 9
Their daintie *layes* and dulcet melody, . . . III. i. 40. 4
making *layes* of love and lovers paine, . . . III. x. 8. 4
Straight he upstarted from the loathed *layes,* . . . III. xii. 44. *or.*5
The fift Armeddan, skild in lovely *layes;* . . . V. iii. 5. 7
He him preventing *layes* on earth along, . . . VI. viii. 49. 3
Layes of sweete love and youthes delightfull heat: . . . VI. ix. 4. 4
His *layes,* . . . she did them all despize. . . . VI. ix. 35. 9
to thee flocke to heare thy lovely *layes!* . . . VI. x. 19. 5
mongst so many *layes* As he hath sung . . . VI. x. 28. 4
As if they knew the meaning of their *layes.* . . . *Am.* xix. 8
To heare theyr names sung in your simple *layes,* . . . *Epith.* 5
how the cheerefull birds do chaunt theyr *laies* . . . *Epith.* 78
Many lewd *layes* (ah! woe is me the more!) . . . *H.H.L.* 8

Laystall. many corses, like a great *Lay-stall,* . . . I. v. 53. 2

Lazars. Like loathsome *lazars,* by the hedges lay. . . . I. iv. 3. 6

Laziness. Such *laesinesse* both lewd and poore attonce him made. . . . III. vii. 12. 9

Lazy. Lewdly complainest thou, *laesie* ladde, . . . *S.C.* F. 9
thous but a *laesie* loord, . . . *S.C.* Jul. 33
laesie Vesper in his timely howre . . . *Gn.* 315
be the shepheards which do serve her *laesie,* . . . *Col.* 372
Vaine votaries of *laesie* Love professe, . . . *Col.* 766
a Dwarfe did lag, That *lasie* seemd, . . . I. i. 6. 2
whip . . . With which he forward lasht the *laesy* teme, . . . I. iv. 36. 3
A *laesy* loord, for nothing good to donne, . . . III. vii. 12. 3

Lea. Him rested the goodman on the *lea,* . . . *S.C.* F. 158
With sundrie colours paints the sprinckled *lay:* . . . *Gn.* 110

Lea—*Continued.*
In silver channell, downe along the *Lee,* . . . *Ti.* 135
adowne the *Lee* I sawe an Harpe . . . Swimming, . . . *Ti.* 603
seemed to be a goodly pleasant *lea:* . . . *Col.* 283
trampling feete upon the hollow *lay* Seemed to thunder, . . . III. viii. 15. 4
comming him before low louted on the *lay.* . . . III. x. 23. 9
Do meete together on the watry *lea,* . . . IV. ii. 16. 3
There was the Liffy rolling downe the *lea,* . . . IV. xi. 41. 1
His corps was carried downe along the *Lee,* . . . V. ii. 19. 1
swimming downe along the *Lee;* . . . *Proth.* 38
Birdes did passe along, Adowne the *Lee,* . . . *Proth.* 115

Leach, Leachour. *See* **Leech, Lecher.**

Lead. line, or *lead,* or rule, or squaire, to measure . . . *Ro.* xxvi. 3
pray him *leaden* our daunce. . . . *S.C.* Mar. 24
dead he is, and lyeth wrapt in *lead,* . . . *S.C.* Jun. 89
shepeheards (sayd he) there doen *leade,* . . . *S.C.* Jul. 185
the fayre flocke thou was wont to *leade?* . . . *S.C.* S. 9
the shepheards laddes to *leade* In rymes, . . . *S.C.* O. 4
leade the Myllers rownde, . . . *S.C.* O. 52
all the worthies liggen wrapt in *leade,* . . . *S.C.* O. 63
Dead, and lyeth wrapt in *lead.* . . . *S.C.* N. 59
where death doth *leade* the daunce, . . . *S.C.* N. 105
Woulde *leade* me forth on Fancies bitte to playe: . . . *S.C.* D. 64
who can *lead,* then, a more happie life . . . *Gn.* 121
Wylde beasts and forrests after him to *lead,* . . . *Ti.* 608
leade The Shepheards daughters dauncing in a rownd! . . . *D.* 309
who shall *lead* Your wandring troupes, . . . *D.* 316
life, For shepheard fit to *lead* . . . *Col.* 689
bow and shafts of gold and *lead,* . . . *Col.* 807
like to *lead* the labyrinth about; . . . I. i. 11. 4
Thence *lead* her forth, about her dauncing round, . . . I. vi. 13. 6
wander where wilde fortune would me *lead,* . . . I. vii. 50. 2
Both feet and face one way are wont to *lead.* . . . I. viii. 31. 6
ceassest not thy weary soles to *lead;* . . . I. x. 9. 7
To *leade* aright, that he should never fall . . . I. x. 34. 7
staggering steps thy steady hand doth *lead,* . . . I. x. 51. 2
with slow pace the knight did *lead,* . . . II. i. 7. 8
death did sitt as sad As lump of *lead,* . . . II. i. 45. 3
day that first doth *lead* the yeare around, . . . II. ii. 42. 7
thee to endlesse bale captived *lead.* . . . II. v. 16. 6
streight did *lead* to Plutoes griesly rayne. . . . II. vii. 21. 4
his hand, more sad then lomp of *lead,* . . . II. viii. 30. 5
life *ledd* in Albania With Gonorill, . . . II. x. 29. 7
Sithence I loathed have my life to *lead,* . . . III. ii. 6. 6
an huge hoste into Northumber *lead,* . . . III. iii. 39. 2
Halfe of thy dayes doest *lead* in horrour hideous. . . . III. iv. 55. 9
arrowes . . . Some headed with sad *lead,* . . . III. xi. 48. 4
they, which *lead* him, soone enforced beene . . . IV. iv. 34. 7
up he rose, like heavie lumpe of *lead,* . . . IV. v. 45. 6
His dayes in dole doth *lead.* . . . IV. vii. Arg.
Death is to him, that wretched life doth *lead,* . . . IV. vii. 11. 7
afterwards did *lead* An happie life . . . IV. viii. 18. 1
That glorious spoyle of beautie with me *lead,* . . . IV. x. 58. 3
Therefore me thither *lead.'* . . . V. ii. 10. 8
now they *lead* him thence, of all forsaken, . . . V. iii. 9. 8
to *lead* your selfe unto your owne decay?' . . . V. iv. 26. 9
lead that shamefull life, . . . V. iv. 32. 9
villaine, which did *lead* Her tyreling jade, . . . VI. vii. 40. 6
the happie life Which Shepheards *lead,* . . . VI. ix. 18. 9
life, which here in lowlinesse ye *lead,* . . . VI. ix. 27. 6
simple sort of life that shepheards *lead,* . . . VI. ix. 33. 8
Calidore should *lead* the ring, . . . VI. ix. 41. 7
should *lead* the daunce, as was his fashion; . . . VI. ix. 42. 3
Which with those gentle shepherds here I wont to *lead.'* . . . VI. xi. 32. 9
To see him *leade* that Beast in bondage . . . VI. xii. 37. 5
But Angels come to *lead* fraile mindes to rest . . . *Am.* viii. 7
was wont to *lead* my thoughts astray; . . . *Am.* lxxxvii. 2
all the host of heaven in rankes doost *lead,* . . . *Epith.* 289
happie hower Doth *leade* unto your lovers blisfull bower, . . . *Proth.* 93

Leaden. with *leaden* mace Arrested all that courtly company, . I. iv. 44. 6
Forthy he thrild thee with a *leaden* dart . . . III. xi. 36. 6

Leadest. joyous dayes Here *leadest* in this goodly merry-make, VI. x. 19. 3

Leadeth. the way, that *leadeth* right To that most glorious house, . . . I. x. 50. 4

Leading. home him *leading,* lent to him the charge . . . *Hub.* 299
waies unknowne, waies *leading* down to hell. . . . *Col.* 211
alleies wide, . . . *leading* inward farr. . . . I. i. 7. 8
Me *leading,* in a secret corner layd, . . . II. iv. 27. 5
them *leading* forth, the same did shew. . . . II. ix. 20. 9
Now *leading* him into a secret shade . . . III. i. 35. 6
She hath the *leading* of a Martiall And mightie people, . . . III. iii. 56. 4
Leading his friend away, . . . IV. iv. 33. 9
Where they were *leading* Marinell away; . . . V. iii. 11. 2
leading th' ever-burning lampe astray, . . . V. viii. 40. 7
streight her *leading* with meete majestie . . . V. xii. 25. 1
a lewd foole her *leading* thorough dry and wet. . . . VI. vi. 16. 9
Leading a life so free and fortunate . . . VI. ix. 19. 3

Leads. *leades* in lowly dales, . . . *S.C.* Jul. 102
leads as joyfull life; . . . *Gn.* 150
afterwardes them to his Dame he *leades,* . . . I. x. 8. 1
That never *leads* the traveiler astray, . . . I. x. 52. 4
he *leads* him to the highest Mount, . . . I. x. 53. 1
love . . . that *leads* each living kind. . . . IV. xii. 25. 9

Leaf. *See* **Laurel-leaf.**
'All so my lustfull *leafe* is drye and sere, . . . *S.C.* Ja. 37
Beating the withered *leafe* from the tree, . . . *S.C.* S. 51
waketh and if but a *leafe* sturre. . . . *S.C.* S. 183
turne the next *leafe* of the booke: . . . *Hub.* 68
Afraid of everie *leafe* that stir'd him by, . . . *Hub.* 1007
Whil'st yet her *leafe* was greene, . . . *D.* 240

Leafe—*Continued.*
trees, Whereon nor fruit nor *leafe* was ever seene, . . . I. ix. 34. 2
like a *leafe* of Aspin greene, . . . I. ix. 51. 4
Each trembling *leafe* and whistling wind they heare, . . . II. iii. 20. 4
direfull deadly black, both *leafe* and bloom, . . . II. vii. 51. 8
Of mortall life the *leafe,* the bud, the flowre; . . . II. xii. 75. 2
Both *leafe* and fruite, both too untimely shed, . . . III. ii. 31. 8
languish, as the *leafe* faln from the tree, . . . III. ii. 39. 8
every *leafe,* that shaketh . . . III. vii. 1. 4
gins to spread his *leafe* before the faire sunshine. . . . IV. xii. 34. 9
in your brest his *leafe* and love embrace. . . . *Am.* xxviii. 14
Leafy. Chirpe loud to thee out of their *leavy* cages, . . . IV. x. 45. 8
League. Withhold . . . your hasty hond From knitting *league* with him, . . . I. xii. 28. 4
fast to bind their *league,* . . . II. ii. 33. 1
Our selves in *league* of vowed love wee knitt, . . . II. iv. 18. 6
A friendly *league* of love perpetuall . . . III. iv. 4. 4
The *league* twixt them, that loyal love hath bound: . . . *Am.* lxv. 10
Leak. fifty sisters water in *leke* vessels draw. . . . I. v. 35. 9
Yet is the bottle *leake,* and bag so torne, . . . VI. viii. 24. 6
Leams. Threw forth abrode a thousand shining *leames,* . . . *Bel.*[1] ix. 10
Lean. Thou weake, I wanne; thou *leane,* I quite forlorne: . . . *S.C.* Ja. 47
Upon whose toppe . . . all the skie doth *leane;* . . . *S.C.* Jul. 62
the *leane* soules treaden under foote, . . . *S.C.* S. 126
so *leane* and meagre waxen late, . . . *Hub.* 599
His body *leane* and meagre as a rake, . . . II. xi. 22. 2
her hew Was wan and *leane,* . . . V. xii. 29. 5
O weake life! that does *leane* On thing so tickle . . . VII. vii. 22. 5
Leander. Witnesse *Leander* in the Euxine waves, . . . *H.L.* 231
Leaned. On which he *leaned,* as one farre in elde. . . . *Hub.* 218
a silver anchor . . . Whereon she *leaned* ever, . . . I. x. 14. 7
Leaning. *leaning* on (against[1]) the belly of a pot, . . . *Bel.* ix. 5
leaning on his elbowe, these few words lett fly. . . . III. xi. 15. 9
Leans. So on thy corbe shoulder it *leanes* amisse. . . . *S.C.* F. 56
Leant. as downe he *lent,* . . . II. xi. 29. 1
his backe for best safegard He *lent* against a tree, . . . VI. v. 18. 9
Leany. They han fatte kernes, and *leany* knaves, . . . *S.C.* Jul. 199
Leap. flockes to *leap* and daunce, . . . *Ti.* 326
Well made to strike, to throw, to *leape,* to lift, . . . *As.* 75
out of the path Did lightly *leape,* . . . II. v. 18. 8
the large *leape* which Debon did compell Coulin to make, . . . II. x. 11. 2
Feeling her *leape* out of her loathed nest, . . . III. ii. 30. 3
In minde to *leape* into the mighty maine, . . . III. vii. 27. 3
Did *leape* to her, as doth an eger hound . . . IV. vi. 12. 3
Her hart did *leape,* and all her hart-strings tremble, . . . IV. vi. 29. 2
To *leape* into the same after our lives end. . . . VI. iv. 31. 9
Leaped. *See* **Leapt.**
he to him *leaped* furiously, . . . II. viii. 33. 2
Lightly she *leaped,* as a wight forlore, . . . III. vii. 25. 7
Like a fell Lyon *leaped* to him light, . . . VI. vii. 25. 5
Leaping. *Leaping* like wanton kids in pleasant Spring. . . . I. vi. 14. 4
lightly *leaping* from so monstrous maine, . . . I. viii. 7. 7
The knight, then lightly *leaping* to the pray, . . . I. viii. 24. 1
leaping light, Thought . . . her to embrace. . . . II. iii. 42. 5
Guyon, lightly to him *leaping,* . . . II. vii. 6. 6
Upon him lightly *leaping* without heed . . . II. viii. 49. 5
the stout Damzell, to him *leaping* light, . . . III. xii. 32. 8
to him *leaping* lent him such a knocke, . . . V. i. 21. 8
Like a wyld Gote, *leaping* from hill to hill, . . . V. ix. 15. 4
leaping to him light would have unlast His Helme, . . . VI. i. 39. 5
to him *leaping* vengeance thought to take . . . VI. vii. 11. 7
Leaps. *See* **Overleaps.**
Leapes forth into the floud, . . . V. ii. 8. 6
Leapt. *See* **Leaped, Lope.**
From bough to bough he *lepped* light, . . . *S.C.* Mar. 92
All offices, all leases by him *lept,* . . . *Hub.* 1145
he *lept* As Lyon fierce upon the flying pray, . . . I. i. 17. 1
she . . . *Lept* fierce upon his shield, . . . I. i. 18. 6
He to him *lept,* in minde to reave his life, . . . I. iii. 36. 2
burning all with rage, He to him *lept,* . . . I. iv. 39. 5
he . . . lightly *lept* from underneath the blow: . . . I. vii. 12. 6
How without stop or stay he fiersly *lept,* . . . II. vi. 42. 2
Into the lake he *lept* his Lord to ayd, . . . II. vi. 46. 1
forth there *lept* An ugly feend, . . . II. vii. 26. 6
Octavius here *lept* into his roome, . . . II. x. 60. 4
grownd he gave, and lightly *lept* areare: . . . II. xi. 36. 5
She lightly *lept* out of her filed bedd, . . . III. i. 62. 2
Into the same shee *lept,* and with the ore Did thrust . . . III. vii. 27. 7
he lightly *lept* Upon the beast, . . . III. vii. 33. 6
Rudely to her he *lept,* . . . III. viii. 25. 6
He lightly *lept* out of his place of rest, . . . IV. iii. 22. 6
Lightly Cambello *leapt* downe from his steed . . . IV. iv. 31. 1
streight *leapt* the Carle unblest, . . . V. ii. 12. 7
But he was well aware, and *leapt* before his fall. . . . V. ii. 12. 9
She lightly to him *leapt;* . . . V. iv. 40. 2
He to her *lept* with deadly dreadfull looke, . . . V. v. 11. 7
he it seeing lightly to him *lept,* . . . VI. v. 25. 8
leapt and daunc't as they had ravisht beene! . . . VII. vii. 34. 8
Lear. had well ycond his *lere,* . . . *S.C.* May 262
he of Tityrus his songs did *lere:* . . . *S.C.* D. 4
they of love, and of his sacred *lere,* . . . *Col.* 783
Next him king *Leyr* in happie peace long raynd, . . . II. x. 27. 1
By strong enchauntments and blacke Magicke *leare,* . . . III. xi. 16. 7
Thereto she learned was in Magicke *leare,* . . . IV. iii. 40. 1
He was invulnerable made by Magicke *leare.* . . . VI. iv. 4. 9
Learn. *See* **Outlearn.**
Learne by their losse to love the low degree; . . . *Van.* xii. 10
Tho wouldest thou *learne* to caroll of Love, . . . *S.C.* F. 61
learne with Lettice to wexe light, . . . *S.C.* Mar. 20
learne to ligge soft: . . . *S.C.* May 125

Learn—*Continued.*
learne these woods to wayle my woe, . . . *S.C.* Jun. 95
learne to looke alofte; . . . *S.C.* Jul. 10
learne the little what, . . . *S.C.* Jul. 31
better *learne* of hem that learned bee, . . . *S.C.* N. 29
as they would *learne* to weepe; . . . *S.C.* N. 134
there thou needs must *learne* to laugh, to lie, . . . *Hub.* 505
Needes anie more to *learne* to get a living?' . . . *Hub.* 544
To *learne* the enterdeale of Princes strange, . . . *Hub.* 785
he would *learne* their busines secretly, . . . *Hub.* 879
to *learne* What did of late chaunce happen . . . *Hub.* 1249
Did *learne* to move their nimble-shifting feete, . . . *T.M.* 34
By knowledge wee do *learne* our selves to knowe . . . *T.M.* 503
gan by litle *learne* to love each other: . . . *Col.* 852
Doe yet but flagg, and lowly *learne* to fly, . . . *Ded. Son.* 2. 8
his new force to *learne,* . . . I. i. 3. 8
subdewd to *learne* Dame Pleasures toy. . . . I. i. 47. 9
'I *learne* that litle sweet Oft tempred is,' . . . I. iv. 46. 3
he would *learne* The Lyon stoup to him in lowly wise, . . . I. vi. 25. 6
learne from pleasures poyson to abstaine: . . . II. ii. 45. 4
A harder lesson to *learne* Continence . . . II. vi. 1. 1
persuade The warlike minds to *learne* her goodly lore, . . . III. iii. 49. 4
it shall make him shake, and shortly *learn* to fall. . . . III. iii. 49. 9
till thou tidings *learne* what her betide, . . . III. v. 11. 7
to *learne* What end unto that fearefull Damozell . . . befell: . . . III. vi. 54. 1
to *learne* his wanton playes; . . . III. xi. 44. 3
that I the man may *learne,* . . . IV. ii. 25. 3
when they could not *learne* it by no wize, . . . IV. iv. 42. 4
My hard mishaps that ye may *learne* to shonne; . . . IV. x. 3. 7
Ne stayed further newes thereof to *learne,* . . . IV. x. 9. 3
They all doe *learne* to play the Paramours; . . . IV. x. 45. 5
to *learne* and see The manner of the Gods . . . IV. xii. 3. 8
learne to love by learning lovers paines to rew. . . . IV. xii. 13. 9
inly troubled was the truth to *learne.* . . . IV. xii. 24. 5
to *lerne* So fond a lesson as to love againe: . . . V. v. 46. 3
greatly it desir'd of her to *learne,* . . . V. ix. 7. 3
prayd the place of her abode to *learne;* . . . V. xi. 21. 3
learne Strangers no more so rudely to entreat, . . . VI. i. 40. 6
I may beare armes, and *learne* to use them right; . . . VI. ii. 33. 6
'if that thou list to *learne,* . . . VI. iii. 40. 1
Ne by inquirie *learne,* nor ghesse by ayme; . . . VI. iv. 24. 7
First *learne* your outward senses to refraine . . . VI. vi. 7. 6
that he the truth of all by him mote *learne.* . . . VI. x. 18. 9
In hope there newes to *learne,* . . . VI. xi. 36. 9
Wil soon conceive, and *learne* to construe well. . . . *Am.* xliii. 14
he there may *learne,* with rare delight, . . . *Am.* lxxiii. 11
Of her ye virgins *learne* obedience, . . . *Epith.* 212
Learne him to love that loved thee so deare, . . . *H.H.L.* 258
And *learne* to love, with zealous humble dewty, . . . *H.H.B.* 20
Of the soare faulcon so I *learne* to fly, . . . *H.H.B.* 26
Learned. *See* **Greater-learned, Love-learned, Well-learned.**
Some greater *learned* wit will magnifie: . . . *Ro.* ii. 12
long hast traveld, by thy *learned* writs, . . . *Ro.* Env. 4
Hereby I *learned* have not to despise . . . *Van.* v. 13
Whence floweth Helicon, the *learned* well, . . . *S.C.* Ap. 42
the spring was in his *learned* hedde, . . . *S.C.* Jun. 94
upon a hill, Beside a *learned* well. . . . *S.C.* Jul. 48
now I have *learnd* a newe daunce; . . . *S.C.* Au. 11
So *learnd* I love on a holye eve, . . . *S.C.* Au. 121
he had eft *learned* a curres call,) . . . *S.C.* S. 191
To put in preace emong the *learned* troupe: . . . *S.C.* O. 70
better learne of hem that *learned* bee, . . . *S.C.* N. 29
Now have I *learnd* (a lesson derely bought) . . . *S.C.* N. 156
learnd of lighter timber cotes to frame, . . . *S.C.* D. 77
I *learned* als the signes of heaven to ken, . . . *S.C.* D. 83
To *learned* wits givest courage worthily, . . . *Gn.* 36
learned Impes that wont to shoote up still, . . . *T.M.* 75
to grace The *learned* forheads, . . . *T.M.* 82
learnd themselves behoves to bee, . . . *T.M.* 83
to be *learned* it a base thing deeme: . . . *T.M.* 87
So oft bedeawed with our *learned* layes, . . . *T.M.* 272
The faithfull service of my *learned* skill, . . . *T.M.* 428
For prize of value, or for *learned* lore: . . . *T.M.* 466
all their *learned* instruments did breake: . . . *T.M.* 599
Where be those *learned* wits and antique Sages, . . . *Ti.* 59
In *learned* artes, and goodlie governaunce, . . . *Ti.* 270
with your piteous layes have *learnd* to breed Compassion . . . *As.* Pr. 3
There *learned* arts do florish in great honor, . . . *Col.* 320
emongst the *learned* throng.' . . . *Col.* 367
having *learnd* repentance late, . . . *Col.* 674
for profession of all *learned* arts, . . . *Col.* 754
dwel . . . gentle Nymphes, delights of *learned* wits; . . . *Ded. Son.* v. 10
And dainty love *learnd* sweetly to endite. . . . *Ded. Son.* viii. 7
Whose *learned* Muse hath writ her owne record . . . *Ded. Son.* xii. 3
To blazon broade emongst her *learned* throng: . . . I. Pr. 1. 8
learned had to love with secret lookes; . . . I. iv. 25. 6
the *learned* leach His cunning hand . . . I. v. 44. 1
he *learned* had . . . The hidden cause . . . I. v. 46. 2
Late *learnd* what harme to hasty trust ensu'th. . . . I. vi. 12. 4
learnd her discipline of faith and verity. . . . I. vi. 31. 9
mortall life he *learned* had to frame . . . I. x. 45. 8
the thrise three *learned* Ladies play Their hevenly notes, . . . I. x. 54. 8
O thou sacred Muse! most *learned* Dame, . . . I. xi. 5. 6
Such homage till that instant never *learned* hee. . . . II. v. 11. 9
well of yore he *learned* had to ryde, . . . II. viii. 31. 4
His *learned* daughters would to me report . . . II. x. 3. 7
Exceld at Athens all the *learned* preace, . . . II. x. 25. 7
Ne like in grace, ne like in *learned* skill; . . . II. x. 76. 7
lov'd a Bul, and *learnd* a beast to bee. . . . III. ii. 41. 6
May *learned* be by cyphers, or by Magicke might. . . . III. ii. 45. 9

Learned—*Continued.*
the *learned* Merlin, well could tell . . . III. iii. 6. 4
any leaches skill, Or other *learned* meanes, . . . III. iii. 18. 2
by fatall lore Hast *learn'd* to love, . . . III. iii. 21. 7
She *learned* had th' estate of Arthegall, . . . III. iv. 4. 2
had *learned* skill In leaches craft, . . . III. iv. 41. 2
As he had long bene *learned* to obay; . . . III. vii. 36. 8
never *learned* he such service till that day. . . . III. vii. 36. 9
For all that art he *learned* had of yore; . . . III. ix. 28. 4
well she redd out of the *learned* line: . . . III. ix. 30. 8
The *learned* lover lost no time nor tyde . . . III. x. 6. 1
powre of hand, nor skill of *learned* brest, . . . III. xi. 16. 3
Thereto she *learned* was in Magicke leare, . . . IV. iii. 40. 1
As she had *learned* readily by rote; . . . IV. ix. 6. 5
goodly *learned* had of yore . . . IV. ix. 19. 2
learned to have loved, . . . IV. x. 1. 8
So many *learned* impes, that shoote abrode, . . . IV. xi. 26. 5
many a gentle Muse and many a *learned* wit. . . . IV. xi. 34. 9
Nemertea *learned* well to rule her lust. . . . IV. xi. 51. 9
learned Ptolomaee his hight did take, . . . V. Pr. 7. 6
So whylome *learnd* that mighty Jewish swaine, . . . V. viii. 2. 1
Who hath not *learnd* him selfe first to subdew: . . . VI. i. 41. 6
Or noursle up in lore of *learn'd* Philosophy. . . . VI. iv. 35. 9
Ne ever saw faire guize, ne *learned* good, . . . VI. v. 2. 4
Or *learn'd* the art to please, . . . VI. vi. 43. 3
To love my selfe I *learned* had in schoole. . . . VI. viii. 21. 5
have *learn'd* to love more deare This lowly quiet life . . . VI. ix. 25. 8
Had ever *learn'd* to love the lowly things, . . . VI. ix. 35. 5
As if he *learned* had obedience long, . . . VI. xii. 37. 2
Ne spareth he most *learned* wits to rate, . . . VI. xii. 40. 7
all living wights have *learn'd* to die, . . . VII. vi. 6. 5
learned minds inflameth with desire Of heavenly things: . . . VII. vii. 2. 5
And eke his *learned* hand at pleasure guide, . . . *Am.* xvii. 6
Ye *learned* sisters, which have oftentimes Beene . . . *Epith.* 1
Learned's. doth the *Learneds* taske upon him take. . . . *T.M.* 216
accounted heretofore The *learneds* meed . . . *T.M.* 412
Learnedst. That was the *learnedst* Ladie in her dayes, . . . IV. ii. 35. 2
Learning. Of such deep *learning* little had he neede, . . . *Hub.* 385
Much good deep *learning* one thereout may reed; . . . *Hub.* 484
Ne let thy *learning* question'd be of anie. . . . *Hub.* 524
For *learning* sake to living them to raise; . . . *Hub.* 538
he would scoffe at *learning,* . . . *Hub.* 832
men of *learning* little he esteemed; . . . *Hub.* 1191
His wisdome he above their *learning* deemed. . . . *Hub.* 1192
The foes of *learning* and each gentle thought; . . . *T.M.* 64
us, that patronize The name of *learning?* . . . *T.M.* 148
tell their Prince that *learning* is but vaine: . . . *T.M.* 332
name of *learning* utterly doo scorne. . . . *T.M.* 438
nought to *learning* they may spare; . . . *T.M.* 470
The sacred brood of *learning* and all honour; . . . *Ti.* 279
Since whose decease, *learning* lies unregarded, . . . *Ti.* 440
of her heavenly *learning* he might taste, . . . I. x. 18. 5
Learning his ship from those white rocks to save, . . . II. x. 6. 3
see Stamford . . . Then shine in *learning,* . . . IV. xi. 35. 5
learne to love by *learning* lovers paines to rew. . . . IV. xii. 13. 9
Learning's. Where be the sweete delights of *learnings* treasure *T.M.* 175
the keeping have of *learnings* threasures . . . VI. Pr. 2. 3
Learns. who of you it *learnes,* . . . *T.M.* 51
This lowly Muse, that *learns* like steps to trace, . . . *Ded. Son.* xiii. 7
salvage nation . . . *learnes* her wise beheast. . . . I. vi. Arg.
of him *learnes* His state and present plight. . . . VI. ii. Arg.
Lears. She turnd her selfe backe to her wicked *leares;* . . . III. vii. 21. 7
In gentle thewes and such like seemly *leres:* . . . VI. ii. 31. 5
Leas. lived in lowly *leas:* . . . *S.C.* Jul. 122
Leases. All offices, all *leases* by him lept, . . . *Hub.* 1145
Leasing. Fye on thee, Diggon, and all thy foule *leasing!* . . . *S.C.* S. 150
No *leasing* new, nor Grandams fable stale, . . . *Col.* 102
with evil deed or *leasing* vaine Blaspheme . . . *Col.* 821
that false Pilgrim, which that *leasing* told, . . . I. vi. 48. 1
he loathd *leasing* and base flattery, . . . VI. i. 3. 8
Leasings. tell many *lesinges* of this and that, . . . *S.C.* May 285
merie *leasings* tell, . . . *Hub.* 699
He hates fowle *leasings,* and vile flatterie, . . . *Hub.* 733
Through *leasings* lewd, and fained forgerie; . . . *Col.* 696
leasings, tales, and lies. . . . II. ix. 51. 9
Leasinges, backbytinges, and vain-glorious crakes, . . . II. xi. 10. 7
Whom she with *leasings* lewdly did miscall . . . IV. viii. 24. 8
cluster thicke unto his *leasings* vaine, . . . V. ii. 33. 2
others worth with *leasings* doest deface, . . . V. iii. 20. 8
faynes to weave false tales and *leasings* bad, . . . V. xii. 36. 8
Least. that at *least* I could . . . Fashion the pourtraicts . . . *Ro.* xxv. 9
The *least* of thousands which on earth abide, . . . *Van.* iii. 8
greatest things the *least* disdaine, . . . *Van.* iii. 13
'Lo! how the *least* the greatest may reprove.' . . . *Van.* iv. 14
of my woe cannot bewray *least* part) . . . *S.C.* Au. 176
If Hell at *least* . . . Knew how to pardon, . . . *Gn.* 475
for the rascall Commons *least* he cared, . . . *Hub.* 1193
least mishap the most blisse alter may? . . . *Mui.* 220
As the *least* lamb in all my flock that went: . . . *D.* 126
neither most nor *least* I found miscaried . . . *D.* 139
I among the rest, of many *least,* . . . *Col.* 252
hast not seene *least* part of natures worke: . . . *Col.* 293
last not *least,* is Aetion, . . . *Col.* 444
him againe lov'd in the *least* degree; . . . I. ix. 27. 7
when *least* I feared ill.' . . . I. xii. 32. 9
of the world *least* part to us is red; . . . II. Pr. 2. 2
if she had her *least* helpe to thee lent, . . . II. iv. 26. 1
staynd their prayses with thy *least* good part; . . . II. iv. 26. 4
Honour is *least* where oddes appeareth most. . . . II. viii. 26. 5
The *least* of which was match for any knight. . . . II. viii. 34. 5

Least—*Continued.*
th' Author selfe could not at *least* attend To finish it: . . . II. x. 68. 5
living art may not *least* part expresse, . . . III. Pr. 2. 1
At *least* eternall meede shall you abide.' . . . III. v. 11. 5
out of sight escaped at the *least:* . . . III. v. 14. 5
Ah God! what other could he do at *least,* . . . III. v. 43. 8
shaketh with the *least* Murmure of winde, . . . III. vii. 1. 4
speaking token sheweth at the *least* . . . III. viii. 49. 5
That *least* avantage mote to him afford, . . . III. x. 6. 2
At *least* it faire endevour will apply.' . . . III. xi. 15. 6
he that happie seemes, and *least* in payne, . . . IV. iii. 1. 8
To which they all repayr'd, both most and *least,* . . . IV. xi. 9. 3
with her *least* word can asswage The surging seas, . . . IV. xi. 50. 4
Least did she thinke, . . . IV. xii. 22. 8
from the most that some were given to the *least?* . . . V. ii. 37. 9
doest not know the *least* thing of them all? . . . V. ii. 43. 8
the *least* word that ever could be layd Within his ballaunce . V. ii. 44. 3
Whose life did lie in her *least* eye-lids fall; . . . V. v. 47. 5
the *least* twinckling sleepe to start Into her eye, . . . V. vi. 24. 7
if the *least* appear'd, her eyes she streight reprieved: . . . V. vi. 24. 9
Gainst all, both good and bad, both most and *least,* . . . VI. vi. 12. 4
Even unto the lowest and the *least.* . . . VI. xii. 2. 5
ransacke all their dennes from most to *least,* . . . VI. xii. 24. 8
The *least* of which this little pleasure should excell. . . . VII. vi. 44. 9
fruitlesse worke is broken with *least* wynd. . . . *Am.* xxiii. 14
a rest; Whose *least* delight sufficeth . . . *Am.* lxiii. 11
Affrayd of every dangers *least* dismay. . . . *Am.* lxxxvii. 4
things . . . both most and *least,* . . . *H.L.* 95
Least part of th' evils which poore lovers greeve. . . . *H.L.* 258
What hart can feele *least* touch of so sore launch, . . . *H.H.L.* 162
Then life were *least,* that us so litle cost. . . . *H.H.L.* 182
Compared to his *least* resplendent sparke? . . . *H.H.B.* 126
Or hope t' expresse her *least* perfections part, . . . *H.H.B.* 227
Leasure. *See* **Leisure.**
Leather. Her lips were, like raw *lether,* pale and blew: . . . V. xii. 29. 7
Leather-winged. The *lether-winged* Batt, dayes enimy; . . . II. xii. 36. 6
Leave. When shepheardes groomes han *leave* to playe, . . . *S.C.* Mar. 62
To *leave* enriched with that he hath spard? . . . *S.C.* May 84
leave to live hard, . . . *S.C.* May 125
Leave me those hilles . . . *S.C.* Jun. 19
My sheepe did *leave* theyr wonted food, . . . *S.C.* Au. 73
I was so fonde To *leave* the good, . . . *S.C.* S. 59
better *leave* of with a little losse, . . . *S.C.* S. 134
From Plutoes balefull bowre withouten *leave,* . . . *S.C.* O. 29
'Now *leave,* ye shepheards boyes, your merry glee; . . . *S.C.* D. 139
(with Phoebus friendly *leave*) . . . *Gn.* 52
leave this lamentable plaint behinde: . . . *Gn.* 635
his credite he did often *leave* In gage . . . *Hub.* 864
he cast to *leave* The Court, . . . *Hub.* 935
to leave The Court, not asking any passe or *leave;* . . . *Hub.* 936
leave the sweetnes of contented home, . . . *Hub.* 947
leave me here distressed With mortall cares . . . *Ti.* 304
shepheards *leave* their lambs unto mischaunce, . . . *Ti.* 327
Give *leave* to him . . . to lament His losse, . . . *Ti.* 676
Ne did he *leave* the mountaines bare unseene, . . . *Mui.* 155
a pledge I *leave* with thee . . . *D.* 288
Is it so uneath To *leave* this life, . . . *D.* 448
without taking *leave* he foorth did goe . . . *D.* 563
The which to *leave,* thenceforth he counseld mee, . . . *Col.* 184
land, our mother, us did *leave,* . . . *Col.* 226
Her name recorded I will *leave* for ever. . . . *Col.* 631
Why didst thou ever *leave* that happie place, . . . *Col.* 654
And *leave* their lambes to losse, misled amisse. . . . *Col.* 687
Which in your noble hands for pledge I *leave* . . . *Ded. Son.* vii. 9
But, sith thou maist not so, give *leave* a while . . . *Ded. Son.* xii. 9
Ne may I, . . . You, fairest Lady, *leave* out . . . *Ded. Son.* xvi. 2
forst me . . . to *leave* My fathers kingdom'— . . . I. i. 52. 1
'O! *leave* her soone, or let her soone be slaine." . . . I. ii. 39. 4
The Lyon would not *leave* her desolate, . . . I. iii. 9. 1
you to *leave* that have me loved stil, . . . I. iii. 28. 4
shall sooner *leave* her kindly skil . . . Then I *leave* you, . . . I. iii. 28. 7
Her servile beast yet would not *leave* her so, . . . I. iii. 44. 6
kinsman living had he none To *leave* them to; . . . I. iv. 28. 7
They all . . . *Leave* off their worke, . . . I. v. 36. 2
speed The fayre Duess' had forst him *leave* behind; . . . I. vi. 2. 2
make the Libbard sterne *Leave* roaring, . . . I. vi. 25. 9
For love of me *leave* off this dreadfull play; . . . I. vi. 28. 7
The souldier may not . . . *leave* his stand . . . I. ix. 41. 5
arise, and *leave* this cursed place.' . . . I. ix. 53. 9
Disdeining life, desiring *leave* to dye, . . . I. x. 22. 8
Ladies love to *leave,* so dearely bought? . . . I. x. 62. 6
leave they take of Caelia . . . I. x. 68. 9
thought his armes to *leave,* and helmet to unlace. . . . I. xi. 26. 9
To see faire heavens face, and life not *leave,* . . . II. i. 17. 4
So give me *leave* to rest.' . . . II. i. 37. 9
Thy litle hands . . . I for pledges *leave.* . . . II. i. 37. 9
'*Leave,* ah! *leave* off, . . . II. i. 47. 6
Depart to woods untoucht, and *leave* so proud disdayne.' . . . II. iii. 43. 9
soone *leave* off this toylsome weary stoure: . . . II. vi. 16. 4
Guyon was loath to *leave* his guide behind, . . . II. vi. 20. 1
Ne gave him *leave* to bid that aged sire Adieu; . . . II. vi. 20. 5
leave the rudenesse of that antique age . . . II. vii. 18. 2
If thee list not, *leave* have thou to refuse: . . . II. vii. 18. 8
give me *leave* to follow mine emprise.' . . . II. vii. 39. 6
How oft do they their silver bowers *leave,* . . . II. viii. 2. 1
leave these relicks of his living might . . . II. viii. 16. 6
leave unto me thy knights last patronage.' . . . II. viii. 26. 9
when breath the body first doth *leave;* . . . II. viii. 29. 2
Crav'd *leave* of Alma and that aged sire . . . II. ix. 60. 8
lend A little *leave* unto a rusticke Muse . . . III. Pr. 5. 2

Leave—*Continued.*
For knight to *leave* his Lady were great shame . . . III. i. 25. 3
shall he *leave* . . . his ymage dead, . . . III. iii. 29. 1
To *leave* that desert mansion, . . . III. vii. 18. 2
Him forst to *leave* his pray, . . . III. vii. 32. 4
To *leave* to him that lady for excheat, . . . III. viii. 16. 4
Yt yrkes me *leave* thee in this wofull state, . . . III. viii. 43. 8
Both were full loth to *leave* that needfull tent, . . . III. ix. 14. 1
take to his new love, *leave* her old despysd. . . . III. x. 8. 9
loth to *leave* his liefest pelfe behinde; . . . III. x. 15. 6
'that ye doe *leave* Your treasure here . . . III. x. 42. 1
to *leave* that lewd And loathsom life, . . . III. x. 51. 1
leave me to my former languishing? . . . III. xi. 24. 2
gave her *leave* at pleasure forth to passe. . . . III. xii. 43. 6
being forst his saddle soone to *leave,* . . . IV. i. 36. 4
she passed forth, not taking *leave,* . . . IV. i. 36. 7
Yet *leave* unto his sorrow did not yeeld, . . . IV. iii. 14. 3
forced him to *leave* his loftie sell, . . . IV. iv. 30. 8
bad them *leave* their labours and long toyle . . . IV. iv. 48. 6
I vow you dead or living not to *leave,* . . . IV. vi. 38. 8
loth to *leave* her late betrothed make, . . . IV. vi. 42. 8
she for the present was appeased, And yeelded *leave,* . . . IV. vi. 44. 2
Full oftentimes she *leave* of him did take; . . . IV. vi. 45. 6
her shortly *leave,* and former love forget. . . . IV. viii. 53. 9
taking *leave* of all, with him did beare . . . IV. ix. 17. 6
folly seem'd to *leave* the thing undonne . . . IV. x. 53. 4
leave his love in that sea-walled fort. . . . IV. xii. 18. 5
Which to another place I *leave* to be perfected. . . . IV. xii. 35. 9
Not so to *leave* her, nor away to cast, . . . V. i. 18. 3
ye would for little *leave* the same, . . . V. i. 28. 6
Therefore *leave* off to weigh them all againe, . . . V. ii. 36. 8
None was debard, but all had *leave* that lust. . . . V. iii. 6. 3
There *leave* we them in pleasure and repast, . . . V. iii. 40. 1
Leave nought unpromist that may him perswade, . . . V. v. 49. 2
Yet taking *leave* of her he did depart. . . . V. vi. 24. 4
Then taking *leave* of them, she forward went . . . V. vii. 24. 6
where late We did him *leave,* . . . V. ix. 2. 7
resolving now to *leave* the place, . . . V. ix. 3. 3
soone did make To *leave* his proper forme, . . . V. ix. 16. 9
Then taking humble *leave* of that great Queene, . . . V. x. 17. 1
Gave *leave* unto his ghost . . . To wander . . . V. x. 33. 5
did the Prince him *leave* in deadly swound, . . . V. x. 33. 7
yet taking *leave* thence forth he went, . . . V. xi. 35. 7
from the day that he thus did it *leave,* . . . V. xi. 46. 7
To *leave* the love that ye before embraced, . . . V. xi. 63. 4
lends unto it *leave* the emptie ayre to beat. . . . V. xii. 18. 9
He tooke his *leave* of her there left . . . V. xii. 27. 9
since the salvage Island I did *leave,'* . . . VI. i. 9. 1
both tooke goodly *leave,* and parted severall. . . . VI. i. 10. 9
'*Leave,* faytor, quickely that misgotten weft . . . VI. i. 18. 7
'then liberty I *leave* to you . . . VI. i. 28. 8
when as I was loth My loves owne part to *leave,* . . . VI. ii. 17. 7
To *leave* his love he should be ill apayd, . . . VI. ii. 18. 8
So taking courteous *leave* they parted twayne, . . . VI. ii. 38. 8
There to their fortune *leave* we them awhile, . . . VI. ii. 40. 1
both them thus nigh dead did *leave.* . . . VI. ii. 43. 9
safe-conduct his love, and not for ought To *leave* . . . VI. iii. 15. 9
if he needes will fight, crave *leave* till morne, . . . VI. iii. 41. 6
force to . . . *leave* his enterprize. . . . VI. iv. 6. 9
she cast to *leave* the place, . . . VI. v. 7. 2
Was forced there to *leave* them both behynd . . . VI. v. 41. 3
Of that good Hermite both they tooke their *leave,* . . . VI. vi. 15. 8
ne ech would other *leave:* . . . VI. vi. 15. 9
Would not her *leave* alone in her great need. . . . VI. vi. 16. 5
if ye please to lend me *leave* awhile, . . . VI. viii. 6. 8
Ne list me *leave* my loved libertie . . . VI. viii. 21. 3
Unto your selfe I freely *leave* to chose, . . . VI. viii. 29. 8
Whether I shall you *leave,* or from these villaines lose.' . . . VI. viii. 29. 9
So humbly taking *leave* she turnd aside; . . . VI. viii. 30. 6
As her to *leave* in such a piteous plight: . . . VI. viii. 33. 5
'To them that list the worlds gay showes I *leave,* . . . VI. ix. 22. 1
Give *leave* awhyle, good father, . . . VI. ix. 31. 3
he should never *leave,* nor be delayd . . . VI. x. 1. 5
taking *leave* of that same gentle Swaine, . . . VI. x. 32. 1
Ne stayeth *leave* to take . . . VI. xi. 18. 9
So *leave* we her in wretched thraldome bound, . . . VI. xi. 24. 8
he bethought To *leave* his love, . . . VI. xii. 13. 3
taking *leave* of his faire Pastorell, . . . VI. xii. 13. 6
There *leave* we them in joy, . . . VI. xii. 22. 5
bid her *leave* faire Cynthias silver bower; . . . VII. vi. 18. 7
Great shame it is to *leave,* like one afrayd, . . . *Am.* xiv. 3
Leave, lady! in your glasse of cristall clene, . . . *Am.* xlv. 1
Give *leave* to rest me being halfe fordonne, . . . *Am.* lxxx. 3
give *leave* to me . . . To sport my muse, . . . *Am.* lxxx. 9
Since I did *leave* the presence of my love, . . . *Am.* lxxxvi. 1
change thy cruelty, Or give like *leave* unto the fly.' . . . *Epig.* iv. 20
leave your wonted labors for this day: . . . *Epith.* 262
lende me *leave* to come unto my love? . . . *Epith.* 279
leave my love alone, . . . *Epith.* 312
leave likewise your former lay to sing: . . . *Epith.* 313
lend unto my mynd *Leave* to bethinke . . . *H.H.B.* 107

Leaved. after all an army strong she *leav'd,* . . . II. x. 31. 8

Leaves. *See* **Bay-leaves, Bramble-leaves, Vine-leaves.**
Conquerors bedecked with his *leaves* . . . *Bel.*[1] v. 3
'You naked trees, whose shady *leaves* are lost, . . . *S.C.* Ja. 31
of their *leaves* they were disarayde: . . . *S.C.* F. 105
With *Leaves* engrained in lusty greene; . . . *S.C.* F. 131
the Woods With greene *leaves,* . . . *S.C.* May 8
shroude in shady *leaves* . . . *S.C.* Jun. 54
Oft lives by losse, and *leaves* with payne. . . . *S.C.* S. 73

Leaves—*Continued.*
groves, with green *leaves* dight. . . . *Gn.* 32
not these *leaves* do sing that dreadfull stound, . . . *Gn.* 39
Who ever *leaves* sweete home, . . . *Hub.* 909
Now without fruite or *leaves* are to be found. . . . *T.M.* 252
Ne with his feete their silken *leaves* deface, . . . *Mui.* 175
Emongst these *leaves* she made a Butterflie, . . . *Mui.* 329
Which Venus blood did in her *leaves* impresse, . . . *D.* 109
kisse thy lips like faded *leaves* of rose. . . . *As.* 138
Faire spreading forth her *leaves* with fresh delight, . . . *Col.* 545
doth need a golden quill, And silver *leaves,* . . . *Ded.Son.*xvi.11
Huge heapes of mudd he *leaves,* . . . I. i. 21. 6
their greene *leaves,* . . . Made a calme shadowe . . . I. ii. 28. 5
He *leaves* the welkin way most beaten playne, . . . I. iv. 9. 7
through the trembling *leaves* full gently playes, . . . I. vii. 3. 3
morning deaw upon their *leaves* doth light; . . . I. xii. 6. 8
narrow *leaves* cannot in them contayne . . . I. xii. 14. 5
flourishing fresh *leaves* and blossomes did enwrap. . . . II. iii. 30. 9
To laugh at shaking of the *leaves* light . . . II. vi. 7. 7
Clothed with *leaves,* that none the wood mote see, . . . II. vii. 53. 8
so long *leaves* here to repeat: . . . II. x. 70. 4
As withered *leaves* drop from their dryed stockes, . . . II. xi. 19. 4
the tall trees with *leaves* appareled . . . II. xii. 12. 4
Their tender buds or *leaves* to violate; . . . II. xii. 51. 4
did themselves emongst the *leaves* enfold, . . . II. xii. 55. 3
His locks, like faded *leaves* fallen to grownd, . . . III. v. 29. 5
lapped up her silken *leaves* most chayre, . . . III. v. 51. 6
Beates downe both *leaves* and buds without regard, . . . III. vi. 39. 8
Emongst the shady *leaves,* their sweet abode, . . . III. vi. 42. 8
The rest he *leaves* in ground: . . . III. x. 19. 4
gan streight to over-looke Those cursed *leaves,* . . . III. xii. 36. 2
all his steed With oaken *leaves* attrapt, . . . IV. iv. 39. 6
Dispreds the glorie of her *leaves* gay; . . . V. xii. 13. 6
a flowre, whose silken *leaves* small . . . VI. ii. 35. 7
his Squyre, With th' Hermit *leaves* behynd. . . . VI. v. Arg.
may her feeble *leaves* with comfort glade— . . . VI. x. 44. 7
leaves no skill nor difference of wight. . . . VI. xi. 16. 9
like a rose her silken *leaves* did faire unfold. . . . VI. xii. 7. 9
leaves of flowres That freshly budded . . . VII. vii. 28. 2
jolly June, arrayd All in greene *leaves,* . . . VII. vii. 35. 2
Happy, ye *leaves!* when as those lilly hands, . . . *Am.* i. 1
Leaves, lines, and rymes, seeke her to please alone, . . . *Am.* i. 13
proud mayd, whom now those *leaves* attyre: . . . *Am.* xxviii. 8
Lillyes, ere theyr *leaves* be shed; . . . *Am.* lxiv. 11
The deawy *leaves* among! . . . *Epith.* 89
those sweete rosy *leaves,* so fairely spred . . . *H.B.* 94

Leaving. for *leaving* his Lords taske, . . . *S.C.* May 53
Leaving behind them nought but griefe of minde, . . . *D.* 398
The false Duessa, *leaving* noyous Night, . . . I. v. 45. 1
For ransome *leaving* him the late-borne childe; . . . I. vi. 23. 6
Upbrayd, for *leaving* her in place unmeet, . . . I. vii. 3. 8
leaving all behind her fled away: . . . I. viii. 25. 6
Leaving behind them griefe and heavinesse: . . . II. vii. 12. 5
Jove . . . *leaving* heavens kingdome, . . . III. xi. 30. 3
leaving watry gods, as booting nought, . . . IV. xii. 25. 2
leaving him forth on his journey far'd: . . . V. i. 30. 7
Whom *leaving* there in that dispiteous plight, . . . V. viii. 8. 7
leaving Artegall to his owne care, . . . V. x. 17. 4
leaving there this Ladie all dismayd, . . . VI. v. 3. 5
The villaine, *leaving* him unto his mate . . . VI. viii. 13. 1
leaving home, to roiall court I sought, . . . VI. ix. 24. 6
Not sparing wight, ne *leaving* any balke, . . . VI. xi. 16. 4
Nought *leaving* but their barren ashes . . . VII. vii. 24. 9

Leawd. *See* **Lewd.**

Lebanon. Mongst all the daughters of proud *Libanon,* . . . *Van.* vii. 4

Lecher. Truth . . . fals in hand of *leachour* . . . I. iii. Arg.
in minde to gride The loathed *leachour.* . . . III. i. 62. 4
that old *leachour,* which with bold assault . . . III. viii. 36. 1

Lechers. The heavie plague that for such *leachours* is prepard. . . . III. v. 14. 9

Lechery. next to him rode lustfull *Lechery* Upon a bearded Gote, . . . I. iv. 24. 1
Such one was *Lechery,* the third of all this traine. . . . I. iv. 26. 9

Led. *See* **Lad, Misled.**
Led forth his flock, that had bene long ypent: . . . *S.C.* Ja. 4
Tho to a hill his faynting flocke he *ledde,* . . . *S.C.* Ja. 11
ledde of theyr sheepe what way they wyll, . . . *S.C.* S. 81
'Forth was I *ledde,* . . . *S.C.* D. 61
So parted they, as eithers way them *led.* . . . *Hub.* 551
To such delights the noble wits he *led* . . . *Hub.* 821
with base thoughts are into blindnesse *led,* . . . *T.M.* 592
his sweete waters away with him *led.* . . . *Ti.* 147
her owne people *led* with warlike rage: . . . *Ti.* 173
Was *led* away of them that did abuse her. . . . *Mui.* 136
Had not good hap those shepheards thether *led.* . . . *As.* 144
thither *led* by chaunce, . . . *Col.* 63
love will not be drawne, but must be *ledde;* . . . *Col.* 129
through our rudenesse into errour *led,* . . . *Col.* 796
foorth they passe, with pleasure forward *led,* . . . I. i. 8. 1
Led with delight, they thus beguile the way, . . . I. i. 10. 1
His wanton daies that ever loosely *led,* . . . I. ii. 3. 5
Will was his guide, and griefe *led* him astray. . . . I. ii. 12. 4
who perforce me *led* With him away, . . . I. ii. 25. 2
towards it a broad high way that *led,* . . . I. iv. 2. 8
May seeme the wayne was very evill *ledd,* . . . I. iv. 19. 7
otherwise His life he *led* in lawlesse riotise, . . . I. iv. 20. 5
He *led* a wretched life, unto himselfe unknowne. . . . I. iv. 28. 9
Upon a Lion, loth for to be *led;* . . . I. iv. 33. 2
Led her away into a forest wilde; . . . I. vi. 3. 2
The gentle virgin, left behinde alone, He *led* away . . . I. vi. 33. 4

Led—*Continued.*
Led with their noise . . . I. vi. 45. 8
yled with far reported praise, . . . I. vii. 46. 1
knight his way with me addrest, *Ledd* with thy prayses, . . . I. x. 11. 4
Then called she a Groome, that forth him *ledd* . . . I. x. 17. 6
Mercie, that his steps upbare And alwaies *led*, . . . I. x. 44. 5
A little path . . . to a goodly Citty *led* his vew, . . . I. x. 55. 3
The fond encheason that me hither *led*. . . . II. i. 30. 2
Which to avenge he to this place me *led*, . . . II. i. 30. 7
She *led* him up into a goodly bowre, . . . II. ii. 15. 1
Guyon is of immodest Merth *Led* into loose desyre; . . . II. vi. Arg.
Into a shady dale she soft him *led*, . . . II. vi. 14. 3
ledd with the troublous sowne: . . . II. vi. 47. 7
Guyon . . . Is by him tempted, and *led* downe . . . II. vii. Arg.
Through that thick covert he him *led*, . . . II. vii. 20. 6
Thence forward he him *ledd*, . . . II. vii. 35. 1
thence him forward *ledd* him further to entise. . . . II. vii. 39. 9
forcing it to fayne, him forth thence *ledd*, . . . II. vii. 51. 2
she them *led* up to the Castle wall, . . . II. ix. 21. 1
forth *ledd* her guestes anone . . . II. ix. 28. 8
backe againe faire Alma *led* them right, . . . II. ix. 33. 5
Alma thence them *led* . . . II. ix. 54. 9
by Maximian lately *ledd* away, . . . II. x. 62. 2
led him to the Castle by the beaten way. . . . II. xi. 48. 9
Then *led* they her away, . . . II. xii. 84. 1
eke that knight They with them *led*, . . . II. xii. 84. 2
forth were *led* Into an inner rowme, . . . III. i. 33. 1
be *led* in courteous wize Into a bowre, . . . III. i. 42. 3
one day, as me misfortune *led*, . . . III. ii. 38. 6
Led with eternall providence, . . . III. iii. 24. 4
old Glauce thither *led* Faire Britomart, . . . III. iii. 59. 6
Into that forest farre they thence him *led*, . . . III. v. 39. 1
Thus as he *led* the Beast along the way, . . . III. vii. 37. 1
without reskew *led* her quite away. . . . III. viii. 13. 5
he through fatal errour long was *led* . . . III. ix. 41. 4
with him *ledd* to sea an youthly trayne; . . . III. ix. 48. 6
with them home her *ledd*, . . . III. x. 36. 6
with them nimbly *ledd* Faire Helenore . . . III. x. 44. 4
a most faire Dame, *Led* of two grysie Villeins, . . . III. xii. 19. 2
captive with her *led* to wretchednesse and wo. . . . III. xii. 41. 9
By which fraile youth is oft to follie *led*, . . . IV. Pr. 1. 6
the vulgar sort, That still are *led* with every light report: . . . IV. i. 28. 5
Love is free, and *led* with selfe delight, . . . IV. i. 46. 8
With whom he *ledd* a long and happie life; . . . IV. iii. 52. 5
Led with that wofull Ladies piteous crying, . . . IV. vii. 25. 3
She drew her far, and *led* with slow delay. . . . IV. viii. 11. 7
many Nations into thraldome *led*, . . . IV. viii. 47. 4
forth *led* her thence . . . IV. x. 56. 7
forth I *led* her through the Temple gate, . . . IV. x. 57. 6
to his love be *led*; . . . IV. xi. 8. 8
The foolish Kyte, *led* with licentious will, . . . V. v. 15. 5
forthwith *led* Unto the crooke, . . . V. v. 18. 6
Was thence by them into the Temple *led*; . . . V. vii. 5. 2
led her to the Souldans right: . . . V. viii. 26. 4
Thenceforth into that Castle he her *led* . . . V. x. 39. 6
So him they *led* through all their streetes along . . . V. xi. 34. 5
as liking *led* Her wavering lust . . . VI. iii. 23. 6
Therein the Hermite, which his life here *led* . . . VI. v. 35. 5
He thence them *led* into his Hermitage, . . . VI. v. 38. 1
Led by a Carle and foole . . . VI. vii. 27. 9
led that Ladies horse Through thick and thin, . . . VI. vii. 44. 1
Led in a rope which both his hands did bynd; . . . VI. vii. 49. 2
He like a dog was *led* in captive case, . . . VI. viii. 5. 4
The whiles his Pastorell is *led* Into captivity. . . . VI. x. Arg.
as fit occasion forth them *led*; . . . VI. x. 30. 2
all his people captive *led* away; . . . VI. x. 40. 3
Led with the infants cry that loud did weepe, . . . VI. xi. 9. 3
So *led* this Knight his captyve with like conquest wonne. . . . VI. xii. 35. 9
led Europa floting through th' Argolick fluds: . . . VII. vii. 33. 3
led a lovely Mayd Forth by the lilly hand, . . . VII. vii. 37. 3
prisoner *led* away with heavy hart, . . . *Am.* iii. 3
my frayle thoughts too rashly *led* astray! . . . *Am.* lxxvi. 6
Leda. To win faire *Leda* to his lovely trade: . . . III. xi. 32. 2
The twinnes of *Leda*; . . . VII. vii. 34. 5
when he a Swan would be, For love of *Leda*, . . . *Proth.* 43
Yet *Leda* was (they say) as white as he, . . . *Proth.* 44
Leda's. 'So raisde they eke faire *Ledaes* warlick twinnes, . . . *Ti.* 386
Ledden. *See* **Leden.**
Leden. The *ledden* of straunge languages in charge: . . . *Col.* 744
could the *ledden* of the gods unfold; . . . IV. xi. 19. 2
Ledge. if two met, the one mote needes fall over the *lidge*. . . . V. vi. 36. 9
Lee. *See* **Lea.**
The wanton *Lee*, that oft doth loose his way; . . . IV. xi. 29. 7
The spreading *Lee* that, like an Island fayre, . . . IV. xi. 44. 3
Leech. the learned *leach* His cunning hand . . . I. v. 44. 1
sent with carefull diligence, To fetch a *Leach*, . . . I. x. 23. 7
Tryphon of sea gods the soveraine *leach* is hight. . . . III. iv. 43. 9
So well that *Leach* did hearke to her request, . . . IV. xi. 7. 1
he no worke at all left for the *leach*: . . . V. vii. 35. 8
a *leach*, that would apply Fit medicines . . . *Am.* l. 3
my lyfes *Leach!* doe your skill reveale; . . . *Am.* l. 13
Leechcraft. More neede of *leach-crafte* hath your Damozell, . . . III. iii. 17. 5
Leeches. it to *Leaches* seemed strange and geason. . . . *Hub.* 12
many skilfull *leaches* him abide To salve his hurts, . . . I. v. 17. 2
thence Apollo, King of *Leaches*, brought. . . . IV. xii. 25. 4
Leech's. let stay Aveugles sonne there in the *leaches* cure; . . . I. v. 44. 6
any *leaches* skill, Or other learned meanes, . . . III. iii. 18. 1
had learned skill In *leaches* craft, . . . III. iv. 41. 3
What medicine can any *Leaches* art Yeeld such a sore, . . . IV. vi. 1. 5
by no art, nor any *leaches* might, . . . VI. vi. 1. 5

Leech's—*Continued.*
he right well in *Leaches* craft was seene; . . . VI. vi. 3. 1
no skill of *Leaches* art Mote him availe, . . . VI. x. 31. 5
Leese. *See* **Lose.**
by much wrestling to *leese* the gresse. . . . *S.C.* S. 135
Left. *See* **Last-left.**
he bare . . . in *left* the conquering Palme, . . . *Bel.*[1] vii. 11
His *left* the palme tree stout, . . . *Bel.*[2] ix. 10
this nothing, which they have thee *left*, . . . *Ro.* xiii. 13
Whose foote in ground hath *left* but feeble holde, . . . *Ro.* xxviii. 4
left of it but these olde markes to see, . . . *Ro.* xxx. 11
naked *left* and disconsolate, . . . *S.C.* F. 230
what they *left* behind them is lost. . . . *S.C.* May 70
That his father *left* by inheritaunce; . . . *S.C.* May 89
a bell, which he *left* behind . . . *S.C.* May 288
That *left* hys flocke to fetch a lasse, . . . *S.C.* Jul. 147
I *left* the head in my hart-roote, . . . *S.C.* Au. 99
the Romish Tityrus . . . *left* his Oaten reede, . . . *S.C.* O. 56
Her like shee has not *left* behinde . . . *S.C.* N. 40
My freedome lorne, my life he *lefte* to mone. . . . *S.C.* D. 52
Are *left* both bare and barrein . . . *S.C.* D. 105
Eternall hurte *left* unto many one: . . . *Gn.* 203
left mine owne his safetie to tender; . . . *Gn.* 362
the slothfull fit . . . Had *left* the heavie Shepheard, . . . *Gn.* 642
twixt them both they not a lambkin *left*, . . . *Hub.* 321
So was the husbandman *left* to his losse, . . . *Hub.* 341
all within were dead and hartles *left*: . . . *Hub.* 1355
all Apes but halfe their eares have *left*, . . . *Hub.* 1383
left Withouten helme or Pilot her to sway: . . . *T.M.* 141
none is *left* to remedie my paine, . . . *T.M.* 423
What difference twixt man and beast is *left*, . . . *T.M.* 487
As for those many goodly matters *leaft* I for others. . . . *Ex Tempore* 2
left his whelps their kingdomes to devoure? . . . *Ti.* 70
no man *left* to mone His dolefull fate, . . . *Ti.* 192
Scarse anie *left* to close his eylids neare; . . . *Ti.* 194
Scarse anie *left* upon his lips to laie . . . *Ti.* 195
left his sonne t' ensue those steps of his. . . . *Ti.* 266
all the rest must needs be *left* behinde: . . . *Ti.* 586
I in langour *left* there all alone. . . . *Ti.* 644
left me here his losse for to deplore. . . . *Ti.* 658
Under the *left* wing stroke his weapon . . . *Mui.* 437
His bodie *left* the spectacle of care. . . . *Mui.* 440
(since fayre Astraea *left* The sinfull world) . . . *D.* 218
no sweet on earth is *left*; . . . *D.* 418
Having his Amaryllis *left* to mone. . . . *Col.* 435
soyl . . . being through long wars *left* almost waste, . . . *Ded. Son.* v. 3
nor one Helicone, *Left* for sweete Muses . . . *Ded. Son.* v. 7
Which of their praises have *left* you the haire; . . . *Ded. Son.* x. 4
In Fraunce and Ireland *left* a famous gage; . . . *Ded. Son.* xiv. 11
Forgive it me, faire Dames, sith lesse ye have not *lefte*. . . . *Ded. Son.* xvii. 14
his Lord, where he him *left* afore. . . . I. i. 44. 9
He so ungently *left* her, whome she loved best. . . . I. ii. 8. 9
She soone *left* off her mirth and wanton play, . . . I. ii. 14. 4
His Lady, *left* as a prise martiall, Did yield . . . I. ii. 36. 8
So *left* her, where she now is turnd to treen mould. . . . I. ii. 39. 9
his corse *left* on the strand. . . . I. iii. 20. 5
sooth to say, why I *lefte* you so long, . . . I. iii. 29. 1
He *left* him lying so, ne would no lenger stay: . . . I. iii. 39. 9
Left in the hand of that same Paynim bold, . . . I. iii. 40. 6
Who now is *left* to keepe the forlorne maid . . . I. iii. 43. 1
Whom when she found, as she him *left* in plight, . . . I. v. 19. 7
of Hippolytus was *lefte* no moniment. . . . I. v. 38. 9
As her outrageous foe had *left* her . . . I. vi. 9. 4
The gentle virgin, *left* behinde alone, . . . I. vi. 33. 3
where I late him *lefte* . . . I. vi. 39. 8
lefte the doubtfull battell hastily, . . . I. vi. 46. 4
He *left* his stond, and her pursewd apace, . . . I. vi. 48. 6
Where she had *left* the noble Redcrosse knight, . . . I. vii. 2. 3
this man forlorne, And *left* to losse; . . . I. vii. 10. 6
now he hath *left* you heare . . . I. vii. 48. 5
Where have yee *left* your lord . . . I. vii. 48. 9
He smott off his *left* arme, . . . I. viii. 10. 6
He lightly *left* the foe with whom he fought, . . . I. viii. 15. 6
of that monstrous mas Was nothing *left*, . . . I. viii. 24. 9
in him was *lefte* no one corrupted jott. . . . I. x. 26. 9
Charissa, . . . *left* her fruitfull nest: . . . I. x. 29. 8
as a stocke he *left* unto his seede. . . . I. x. 38. 7
her base Elfin brood there for thee *left*: . . . I. x. 65. 8
did glyde Close under his *left* wing, . . . I. xi. 20. 7
left not any marke where it did light, . . . I. xi. 25. 4
he hath *lefte* his plumes all hory gray, . . . I. xi. 34. 4
Five joints thereof he hewd, and but the stump him *lefte*. . . . I. xi. 39. 9
he shortly did, and Una *left* to mourne. . . . I. xii. 41. 9
Whom Princes late displeasure *left* in bands, . . . II. i. 1. 2
His shackles emptie *lefte*, himselfe escaped cleene. . . . II. i. 1. 9
Whom late I *left* in languorous constraynt? . . . II. i. 9. 7
So they *left* inflam'd with wrathfulnesse, . . . II. i. 25. 8
where ye have *left* your marke, . . . II. i. 32. 6
Me then he *left* enwombed of this childe, . . . II. i. 50. 8
weenest thou what sorrowes are *Left* thee . . . II. ii. 2. 4
He *left* his loftie steed . . . II. ii. 11. 6
Sith last I *left* that honorable place, . . . II. ii. 44. 3
He *left* his steed without, . . . II. iii. 3. 8
that weake eld hath *left* thee nothing wise; . . . II. iii. 16. 3
she *lefte* her percing launce, . . . II. iii. 34. 4
Sir Guyon *left* his first emprise, . . . II. iv. 12. 1
beckned him, the last helpe she had *left*; . . . II. iv. 13. 3
Where *left*, he went, and his owne false part playd, . . . II. iv. 27. 7
backe rebownding *left* the forckhead keene: . . . II. iv. 46. 8
all his *left* side it did quite disarme; . . . II. v. 7. 7

Left—*Continued.*
So she him *lefte*, and did her selfe betake . . . II. vi. 18. 5
shee that Island far behind her *lefte*, . . . II. vi. 18. 8
Where sleeping late she *lefte* her other knight . . . II. vi. 22. 4
There by his maister *left*, . . . II. vi. 38. 8
guyde, Late *left* beyond that Ydle lake, . . . II. vii. 2. 2
their vile carcases now *left* unburied . . . II. vii. 30. 9
The Palmer seeing his *lefte* empty place, . . . II. viii. 9. 1
no way is *lefte* to wreake my spight, . . . II. viii. 15. 6
left his headlesse body bleeding all the place . . . II. viii. 52. 9
many Giaunts *left* on groning flore: . . . II. x. 10. 5
He *left* three sonnes, . . . II. x. 13. 4
Locrine *left* chiefe Lord of Britany . . . II. x. 13. 7
Locrine was *left* the soveraine Lord of all: . . . II. x. 14. 1
was *left* no moniment Of Brutus, . . . II. x. 36. 8
left two sonnes, of pearelesse prowesse both, . . . II. x. 40. 2
Five sonnes he *left*, . . . II. x. 44. 1
Left of his life most famous memory, . . . II. x. 46. 2
He *left* two sonnes, too young to rule . . . II. x. 46. 8
left inglorious on the vanquisht playne, . . . II. x. 58. 2
dying *left* none heire them to withstand, . . . II. x. 61. 8
Three sonnes he dying *left*, . . . II. x. 64. 1
He *left* three sonnes, . . . II. x. 74. 1
He *left* two sonnes, . . . II. x. 75. 6
He dying *left* the fairest Tanaquill, . . . II. x. 76. 4
What now is *left* of miserable wightes, . . . II. xii. 9. 4
she *left* her lockes undight, . . . II. xii. 15. 6
Nought but her lovely face she for his looking *left* . . . II. xii. 67. 9
The wicked steel through his *left* side did glaunce . . . III. iv. 16. 5
Ne of thy late life memory is *lefte*, . . . III. iv. 36. 8
who that lives is *lefte* to waile . . . III. iv. 38. 6
in chace of beauty excellent Shee *lefte*, . . . III. iv. 45. 6
lately *left* the same, and tooke this way . . . III. v. 4. 7
The want of his good Squire late *lefte* behinde, . . . III. v. 12. 4
stayd not till it did light In his *left* thigh, . . . III. v. 20. 7
neither blood in face nor life in hart It *left*, . . . III. v. 48. 7
left her blisfull bowre of joy above: . . . III. vi. 11. 5
Him for to seeke, she *left* her heavenly hous, . . . III. vi. 12. 1
had *left* them languishing . . . III. vi. 13. 9
Where you him lately *lefte*, in Mars his bed: . . . III. vi. 24. 3
He *lefte* his captive Beast at liberty, . . . III. vii. 38. 2
Where late he *left* the Beast he overcame, . . . III. vii. 61. 6
garments gay, Which Florimell had *left* behind . . . III. viii. 9. 2
lefte his love to losse, and fled him selfe apace . . . III. viii. 18. 9
To tell of Satyrane where I him *left* of late . . . III. viii. 43. 9
shield gins to untye From her *left* arme, . . . III. ix. 22. 9
The which he dying *lefte* next in remaine . . . III. ix. 37. 4
for . . . glories gaine, My native soile have *lefte*, . . . III. ix. 37. 8
of his owne him *lefte* not liberty: . . . III. x. 2. 4
he turnd, And *left* the fire; . . . III. x. 15. 2
He *left* his wife; money did love disclame: . . . III. x. 15. 4
The gentle Lady, loose at randon *lefte*, . . . III. x. 36. 1
dearest Dame, . . . *left* in yonder forest wyld; . . . III. x. 39. 6
seemd no help for him was *left* in living sight . . . III. x. 56. 9
nothing *left* but like an aery Spright, . . . III. x. 57. 4
hideous tayle his *lefte* foot did enfold, . . . III. xi. 48. 7
She *left* Sir Scudamour in great distresse, . . . III. xii. 43. *or.*2
Where late she *left* the pensife Scudamore . . . III. xii. 44. 2
left him now as sad, as whilome jollie, . . . IV. i. 36. 8
More for the love which he had *left* behynd, . . . IV. i. 37. 8
left the head behinde: . . . IV. iii. 10. 7
in his hand nought but the troncheon *left*; . . . IV. iii. 12. 2
finding no fit seat, the lifelesse corse it *left* . . . IV. iii. 21. 9
It *left*; but that same soule which therein dwelt . . . IV. iii. 22. 1
they were *left* uppon the land, . . . IV. iv. 21. 8
left behind her in her secret bowre . . . IV. v. 5. 4
having *left* that restlesse house of Care, . . . IV. vi. 2. 1
The sacred pledge which in his faith was *left*, . . . IV. vi. 8. 3
That where ye *left* I may her seeke, . . . IV. vi. 34. 9
in which ye her all hopelesse *left*, . . . IV. vi. 35. 5
I found her not where I her *left* whyleare, . . . IV. vi. 36. 6
She *left* him to his fortunes government, . . . IV. vi. 46. 3
To Scudamour, whom she had *left* behind: . . . IV. vi. 46. 5
left that Turneyment for beauties prise, . . . IV. vii. 3. 2
therein *left* the pike-head of his speare: . . . IV. vii. 27. 7
Having his carrion corse quite sencelesse *left* . . . IV. vii. 32. 4
She *left* the gentle Squire with Amoret: . . . IV. vii. 35. 2
He *left* him there in languor to remaine, . . . IV. vii. 47. 5
hath he *left* one daughter . . . IV. viii. 49. 3
left in his protection whileare, . . . IV. ix. 17. 8
Left in the victors powre, like vassall bond, . . . IV. ix. 18. 7
her had to her liking *left* . . . IV. ix. 36. 9
left them groning there upon the plaine: . . . IV. x. 10. 6
Left a fayre Ladie languishing in payne: . . . IV. xi. 1. 2
The dongeon was, in which her bound he *left*, . . . IV. xi. 3. 2
So *left* he her withouten remedie . . . IV. xii. 24. 3
she *left* her groome An yron man, . . . V. i. 12. 1
left me here . . . to morne.' . . . V. i. 18. 9
So were they *left* Lords of the field alone: . . . V. iii. 12. 8
The which of all her spoyle was onely *left*; . . . V. iii. 27. 2
having lately *left* that lovely payre, . . . V. iv. 3. 1
she *left* me quight, And to my brother did ellope . . . V. iv. 9. 7
his owne love *left* astray . . . V. iv. 9. 9
As thing at randon *left*, . . . V. iv. 19. 7
that same wretched man, . . . They *left* behind them, . . . V. iv. 25. 2
he *left* the bloudy slaughter In which he swam, . . . V. iv. 41. 2
Left to her will by his owne wilfull blame, . . . V. v. 20. 2
'What now is *left*, Clarinda? . . . V. v. 48. 1
to their sire their carcasses *left* to bestow . . . V. vi. 40. 9
her sole victor *left* . . . V. vii. 34. 9

Leisure—*Continued.*
he no worke at all *left* for the leach: . . . V. vii. 35. 8
else he sure had *left* not one alive, . . . V. vii. 36. 8
left his love, albe her strong request, . . . V. viii. 3. 4
his necke asunder broke, And *left* there dead . . . V. viii. 8. 4
left their scorched path yet in the firmament . . . V. viii. 40. 9
his faire limbs *left* in the woods forlorne; . . . V. viii. 43. 5
There they him *left* a carrion outcast . . . V. ix. 19. 8
Had *left* her now but five of all that brood: . . . V. x. 8. 2
The woefull widow had no meanes now *left*, . . . V. x. 14. 2
'What is there else' (sayd he) '*left* of their rout? . . . V. xi. 18. 8
left so in the loathely soyle . . . V. xi. 33. 9
having *left* Mercilla, streight way went . . . V. xi. 36. 2
Whiles she alone is *left*, and thou here found? . . . V. xi. 38. 6
They spide a Lady *left* all succourlesse, . . . V. xi. 44. 7
encountred ere they *left* the shore: . . . V. xii. 6. 9
on the ground he *left* full many a corse; . . . V. xii. 7. 5
Not one was *left* that durst her once have disobayd . . . V. xii. 25. 9
He tooke his leave of her there *left* in heavinesse . . . V. xii. 27. 9
him *left* With hearts dismay . . . VI. i. 18. 2
And in his *left* he held a sharpe bore-speare, . . . VI. ii. 6. 6
hers . . . to daunger drove, And *left* sore wounded: . . . VI. ii. 20. 6
he turned backe Unto the place where me he *left* behind: . . . VI. ii. 21. 3
the onely helpe now *left* them . . . VI. iii. 12. 8
he shew'd his head there *left*, . . . VI. iii. 18. 8
when he the Lady saw There *left* on ground, . . . VI. iii. 26. 2
And his sad Ladie *left* in pitifull affright: . . . VI. iv. 1. 9
the place, whereas he last Had *left* that couple . . . VI. iv. 9. 5
shield and speare, Which earst he *left*, . . . VI. iv. 13. 2
But Calepine, now being *left* alone . . . VI. iv. 39. 1
no hope of his retourne She saw now *left*, . . . VI. v. 7. 2
armes which Calepine whyleare Had *left* behind . . . VI. v. 8. 5
Why have ye me alone thus long *yleft?* . . . VI. v. 23. 6
Now *left* alone in great extremity; . . . VI. vi. 16. 3
few of them he *left* alive, . . . VI. vi. 24. 2
no life him *left* through former feare . . . VI. vi. 32. 9
left that salvage wight Amongst so many foes, . . . VI. vi. 37. 5
He had not *left* one limbe of him unrent: . . . VI. vi. 40. 8
seeing him so lie, he *left* his steed, . . . VI. vii. 11. 6
Whom late we *left* ryding upon an Asse, . . . VI. vii. 27. 8
Love hath the glory of his kingdome *left*, . . . VI. viii. 1. 2
He *left* his lofty steede . . . VI. viii. 12. 7
Backe to the furrow which I lately *left* . . . VI. ix. 1. 2
I lately *left* a furrow . . . Unplough'd, . . . VI. ix. 1. 3
sith I *left* him last Sewing the Blatant Beast; . . . VI. ix. 2. 2
In th' open fields an Infant *left* alone; . . . VI. ix. 14. 6
Now seeing Calidore *left* all alone, . . . VI. ix. 16. 2
poysnous point deepe fixed in his hart Had *left*, . . . VI. x. 31. 3
Her selfe sole *left* a second spoyle to bee . . . VI. xi. 23. 3
What now is *left* her but to wayle and weepe, . . . VI. xi. 23. 6
They *left* her so, in charge of one, . . . VI. xi. 24. 2
certaine of the theeves there by them *left*, . . . VI. xi. 37. 4
Ne any *left* that victorie to him envide . . . VI. xi. 49. 9
Bedeaw'd with teares there *left* it in the place: . . . VI. xii. 8. 4
Yet *left* not quite, but drew a little space . . . VI. xii. 8. 5
Departed life, and *left* unto them all: . . . VI. xii. 10. 3
left in heavy care Through daily mourning . . . VI. xii. 14. 4
In which he many massacres had *left*, . . . VI. xii. 23. 2
now no place besides unsought had *left*, . . . VI. xii. 23. 7
no more Him liberty was *left* aloud to rore: . . . VI. xii. 36. 5
they *left* him nought; . . . VII. vi. 47. 8
all that . . . Thence-forth she *left*; . . . VII. vi. 55. 2
She *left* th' unrighteous world, . . . VII. vii. 37. 9
I alone, now *left* disconsolate, . . . *Am.* lxxxviii. 5
The Rosy Morne long since *left* Tithones bed, . . . *Epith.* 75
Now seeing *left* a waste and emptie place . . . *H.H.L.* 101
But he our life hath *left* unto us free, . . . *H.H.L.* 183
all are fled, and now have *left* thee nought . . . *H.H.B.* 292

Left hand. On her *left hand* the noysome Esquiline, . . . *Ro.* iv. 12
The force, . . . In one alone *left* hand he now unites, . . . I. viii. 18. 2
In her *left hand* a Cup of gold she held, . . . II. xii. 56. 1
the *left hand* rubs the right.' . . . IV. i. 40. 9
his *left hand* upon his collar layd . . . VI. vii. 25. 6

Leg. Ewe, Whose clouted *legge* her hurt doth shewe, . . . *S.C.* Mar. 50
smote off quite his right *leg* by the knee, . . . I. viii. 22. 4
Her other *leg* was lame, . . . II. iv. 4. 3
her staffe, though it her one *leg* were, . . . II. iv. 5. 6
the one her other *legge* had lame, . . . II. xi. 23. 6
that *leg*, which did his body beare, . . . VI. viii. 16. 4
his *leg* . . . Was crackt in twaine, . . . VI. viii. 25. 7

Legerdemain. he so light was at *legierdemaine*, . . . *Hub.* 701
of *legierdemayne* the mysteries did know . . . V. ix. 13. 9

Legion. having overcome The Romane *legion* . . . II. x. 60. 8
a whole *legione* Of wicked Sprightes . . . III. ix. 2. 7

Legions. forth he cald . . . *Legions* of Sprights, . . . I. i. 38. 2
Legions of loves with little wings did fly; . . . *Am.* xvi. 6

Legs. His tayle he clapt betwixt his *legs* . . . *S.C.* May 280
scarse thy *legs* uphold thy feeble gate.' . . . *Hub.* 600
manly *legs*, still passing too and fro, . . . *Hub.* 748
her white streight *legs* were altered . . . *Mui.* 349
swarming all about his *legs* did crall, . . . I. i. 22. 8
her streight *legs* most bravely were embayld . . . II. iii. 27. 2
his long *legs* nigh raught unto the ground . . . II. xi. 20. 6
creepe betweene his *legs*, . . . IV. x. 19. 3
both her feete and *legs* together twyned . . . IV. x. 40. 8
on her *legs* she painted buskins wore, . . . V. v. 3. 1
th' armes and *legs* of three to succour him in fight . . . V. x. 8. 9

Leill. His sonne, king *Leill*, . . . II. x. 25. 1

Leisure. should With cancring *laisure* not be overworne: . . . *Ro.* xxiii. 4
the good man noulde stay his *leasure*, . . . *S.C.* F. 192

Leisure—*Continued.*
here liven at ease and *leasure?* . . . *S.C.* May 66
to theyr foldes yeed at their owne *leasure*. . . . *S.C.* S. 145
his limbs, resolv'd through idle *leisour,* . . . *Gn.* 141
Now at thy *leisure* them to us to tell.' . . . *Col.* 35
Thou much more fit (were *leasure* to the same) . . . *Ded. Son.* xii. 5
Them list no lenger there at *leasure* dwell, . . . I. ix. 2. 4
volume, that doth far excead My *leasure* . . . II. x. 70. 4
scarse them *leasure* gave her passing to behold. . . . III. i. 15. 9
Ne lend we *leisure* to his idle toy: . . . III. vi. 24. 5
finding litle *leasure* her to wooe . . . III. viii. 13. 3
leasure had and liberty to frame Their purpost flight, . . . III. x. 16. 4
the fresh Swayne would not his *leasure* dwell, . . . III. x. 38. 7
gan the Prince at *leasure* to inquire . . . IV. viii. 46. 6
unto Ladies love would lend no *leasure:* . . . IV. ix. 21. 2
drew him on with hope fit *leasure* to awayt. . . . V. v. 42. 9
they mote treat of things abrode at *leasure,* . . . VI. iii. 22. 4

Leke. *See* **Leak.**

Leman. a loose *Leman* to vile service bound: . . . I. i. 48. 6
me, thy worthy meed, unto thy *Leman* take.' . . . I. vii. 14. 9
his faire *Leman* flying through a brooke She overhent, . . . II. x. 18. 8
Franckly each Paramor his *leman* knowes, . . . III. vi. 41. 7
To be his *Leman* and his Lady trew: . . . III. viii. 40. 5
had no love nor *lemman* there in store, . . . IV. i. 9. 8
By any Ladies side for *Leman* to have laine, . . . IV. vii. 15. 9
A *leman* fit for such a lover deare: . . . IV. vii. 34. 5
recoure His *Leman* from the Stygian Princes boure: . . . IV. x. 58. 5

Leman's. Did poure into his *Lemans* lap so fast, . . . I. i. 6. 7
To serve his *Lemans* love: . . . II. v. 28. 2
Great Ptolomaee it for his *lemans* sake Ybuilded . . . III. ii. 20. 6
To lay his spoiles before his *lemans* traine: . . . V. viii. 2. 3

Lemans. change his liking, and new *Lemans* prove; . . . IV. ix. 21. 6

Lemnian. The which the *Lemnian* God framde craftily, . . . *Mui.* 370

Lemnos. wrought in *Lemno* with unquenched fire: . . . IV. v. 4. 4

Lend. Unto sweete sleepe he may securely *lend* . . . *Gn.* 142
Cupide . . . Did *lend* her secret aide, . . . *Mui.* 127
And to these ydle rymes *lend* litle space, . . . *Ded. Son.* i. 13
to affections does the bridle *lend!* . . . II. iv. 34. 2
To them that list these base regardes I *lend;* . . . II. vii. 33. 5
should I *lend* The same to thee, . . . II. viii. 21. 7
them sought and unto him did *lend:* . . . II. ix. 58. 7
who shall *lend* me wings, . . . II. x. 1. 3
lend A little leave unto a rusticke Muse . . . III. Pr. 5. 1
to her cry they list not *lenden* eare, . . . III. i. 23. 1
she did *lend* her short reliefe And doe her comfort, . . . III. i. 53. 5
Ne *lend* we leisure to his idle toy: . . . III. vi. 24. 5
she thereto would *lend* but light regard, . . . III. viii. 14. 6
Through hunger long that hart to him doth *lend,* . . . IV. iii. 19. 2
To *lend* an eare, and softly to relent. . . . IV. vi. 41. 5
unto Ladies love would *lend* no leasure: . . . IV. ix. 21. 2
Ne *lend* an eare to ought that might behove. . . . IV. ix. 31. 4
to old Loncaster his name doth *lend;* . . . IV. xi. 39. 2
To see an helplesse evill double griefe doth *lend.* . . . IV. xii. 21. 9
That powre he also doth to Princes *lend,* . . . V. Pr. 10. 6
due tryall *lend* Of all the rest; . . . V. iii. 8. 3
great helpe dame Nature selfe doth *lend;* . . . VI. ii. 2. 1
He him requested, . . . To *lend* him day . . . VI. ii. 19. 4
Both horse and armes and what so else to *lend,* . . . VI. iv. 39. 8
if ye please to *lend* me leave awhile, . . . VI. viii. 6. 8
Did care a whit, ne any liking *lend:* . . . VI. ix. 10. 8
at length the raines would *lend* Unto his lust, . . . VI. xi. 6. 2
joy to weary wandring travailers did *lend:* . . . VII. vi. 9. 9
take what fortune, time, and place would *lend.* . . . VII. vi. 23. 6
O Clio! *lend* Calliope thy quill. . . . VII. vi. 37. 9
lend you me another living brest. . . . *Am.* xxxiii. 14
lende me leave to come unto my love? . . . *Epith.* 279
In dreadful darknesse *lend* desired light; . . . *Epith.* 412
lend him light from her owne goodly ray; . . . *H.L.* 73
heavens such happie grace did to him *lend,* . . . *H.L.* 213
Cease then, my tongue! and *lend* unto my mynd . . . *H.H.B.* 106
their best service *lend* . . . *Proth.* 124

Lendest. Instead of rest thou *lendest* rayling teares; . . . III. iv. 57. 4

Lendeth. 'I hate the day, because it *lendeth* light . . . *D.* 407

Lending. thraldome find For *lending* life to me, . . . V. v. 32. 5

Lends. strength and wealth and happinesse she *lends,* . . . IV. x. 34. 6
heaven, that unto all *lends* equall eare, . . . IV. xii. 6. 5
The earth to all her creatures lodging *lends.'* . . . V. x. 24. 6
lends unto it leave the emptie ayre to beat. . . . V. xii. 18. 9
how sweete musicke that unto them *lends!* . . . *H.B.* 252
By which he *lends* us of himselfe a sight! . . . *H.H.B.* 112

Lenged. *See* **Longed.**
lengd to know the cause of his complaint: . . . *S.C.* May 250

Lenger. *See* **Longer.**
this morrowe, no *lenger* agoe, . . . *S.C.* May 19
no *lenger* hope I see, . . . *Hub.* 65
his rule might *lenger* have endurance. . . . *Hub.* 1114
His forces faile, ne can no *lenger* fight: . . . I. i. 22. 3
Now needeth him no *lenger* labour spend, . . . I. i. 26. 8
He would no *lenger* stay him to advize, . . . I. iii. 19. 4
He left him lying so, ne would no *lenger* stay: . . . I. iii. 39. 9
Then forth she rose, ne *lenger* would abide, . . . I. v. 19. 3
he no *lenger* would There dwell . . . I. v. 52. 3
she would no *lenger* byde, . . . I. vii. 2. 4
Why doe ye *lenger* feed on loathed light, . . . I. vii. 22. 3
list no *lenger* there at leasure dwell, . . . I. ix. 2. 4
That wofull lover, loathing *lenger* light, . . . I. ix. 30. 2
'The *lenger* life, I wote, the greater sin; . . . I. ix. 43. 1
He stayd not *lenger* talke, . . . II. i. 13. 1
Why livest thou, dead dog, a *lenger* day, . . . II. iii. 7. 6
lenger time then that no living wight . . . II. vii. 66. 2

Lenger—*Continued.*
After so wicked deede why liv'st thou *lenger* day?' . . . II. viii. 46. 9
no *lenger* time . . . workemanship should not endure: . . . II. ix. 21. 7
ne her selfe would *lenger* vex. . . . II. x. 20. 9
To make there *lenger* sojourne and abode; . . . III. i. 1. 6
For nothing would she *lenger* there be stayd, . . . III. i. 67. 4
The wisard could no *lenger* beare her bord, . . . III. iii. 19. 1
Whose empire *lenger* here then ever any stood?' . . . III. iii. 42. 9
Ne *lenger* stayd for th' other to reply, . . . III. iv. 15. 5
for want of *lenger* light, . . . III. iv. 52. 5
her pleasures *lenger* to partake. . . . III. xi. 33. 9
She *lenger* yet is like captiv'd to bee; . . . IV. xi. 1. 8
lenger he note stand upright, . . . IV. xii. 20. 7
Astraea loathing *lenger* here to space . . . V. i. 11. 2
He list no *lenger* to use lothfull speach, . . . V. vi. 21. 6
She saw it vaine to make there *lenger* stay, . . . V. vi. 36. 1
would no *lenger* treat, but bad them sound; . . . V. vii. 28. 7
full loth To make there *lenger* stay, . . . VI. iii. 45. 9
Would not permit to make there *lenger* stay, . . . VI. v. 41. 2
could no *lenger* beare so great abuse . . . VI. vii. 45. 4
The matrone stayd no *lenger* to enquire, . . . VI. xii. 19. 1
be no *lenger* proud of that shall perish; . . . *Am.* xxvii. 13
no *lenger* can endure to sue, . . . *Am.* lvii. 3
Him, wretch, in doole would let no *lenger* dwell, . . . *H.H.L.* 131

Length. Eche thing at *length* we see Doth passe . . . *Pet.*[1] v. 7
At *length,* even at the time, when Morpheus . . . *Bel.* xv. 1
When as at *length* I saw the wrathfull winde, . . . *Bel.*[2] viii. 11
To be the measure of her bredth and *length:* . . . *Ro.* viii. 4
to measure Her *length,* her breadth, . . . *Ro.* xxvi. 4
outstretched lay, In monstrous *length,* . . . *Van.* iii. 3
Of wondrous *length,* and streight proportion, . . . *Van.* vii. 2
At *length* within an Yvie todde, . . . *S.C.* Mar. 67
such pryde at *length* was ill repayde: . . . *S.C.* D. 49
all his foldes are now in *length* outstrained. . . . *Gn.* 280
At *length* chaunst with a formall Priest to meete, . . . *Hub.* 361
Gan at the *length* them to rebuke againe, . . . *Hub.* 397
at the *length* he published to holde A Visitation, . . . *Hub.* 568
they were descride At *length* . . . *Hub.* 921
Wake, shepheards boy, at *length* awake for shame! . . . *Ti.* 231
At *length,* by demonstration me to teach, . . . *Ti.* 488
At *length* out of the River it was reard . . . *Ti.* 610
At *length,* when most in perill it was brought, . . . *Ti.* 624
Their wraths at *length* broke into open warre. . . . *Mui.* 8
At *length,* the foolish Flie, without foresight, . . . *Mui.* 389
at *length* we land far off descryde: . . . *Col.* 265
At *length* it brought them to a hollowe cave . . . I. i. 11. 6
whose folds . . . Were stretcht now forth at *length* . . . I. i. 16. 4
At *length* they chaunst to meet . . . I. i. 29. 1
At *length,* . . . He set her on her steede, . . . I. ii. 45. 8
at *length* she found the troden gras, . . . I. iii. 10. 4
hardly doen, at *length* she gan them pray, . . . I. iii. 14. 8
they be come at *length* Unto the place . . . I. v. 29. 1
His tayle was stretched out in wondrous *length,* . . . I. vii. 18. 1
Loe! where your foe lies strecht in monstrous *length;* . . . I. viii. 45. 3
at *length* with Archimage they meet: . . . II. iii. 11. 2
At *length* they came into a larger space, . . . II. vii. 21. 1
Nigh a speares *length* behind his crouper fell; . . . III. i. 6. 7
At *length* they came into a forest wyde, . . . III. i. 14. 5
at *length* him thus bespake: . . . III. iii. 43. 4
to the sea-coast at *length* she her addrest. . . . III. iv. 6. 9
spightfull wrong At *length* allay, . . . III. iv. 8. 5
the *length* of all her launce; . . . III. iv. 16. 7
at *length* she came To an hilles side, . . . III. vii. 4. 6
At *length* he spyde . . . that wofull Squyre, . . . III. vii. 45. 6
shee at *length* persuaded him to rise, . . . III. xi. 20. 1
At *length* they both upstarted in amaze, . . . IV. ii. 17. 1
The which, for *length,* I will not here pursew, . . . IV. ii. 54. 8
at *length,* upon th' appointed day . . . IV. iv. 13. 5
At *length,* when as he saw her hastie heat Abate, . . . IV. vi. 16. 1
at the *length* unto a bay he brought her, . . . IV. vi. 41. 3
At *length* did marke about her purple brest . . . IV. viii. 10. 2
at *length* into that forrest wide She drew her . . . IV. viii. 11. 6
At *length* they spide where towards them . . . IV. viii. 38. 1
At *length* they came whereas a troupe of Knights . . . IV. ix. 20. 1
At *length* breakes downe in raine, . . . IV. ix. 33. 6
of my love at *length* I rest assured, . . . IV. x. 2. 8
So Artegall at *length* him forst forsake . . . V. ii. 16. 1
at the *length* he has yrent the dore, . . . V. ii. 24. 3
At *length* found out whereas she hidden lay . . . V. ii. 25. 5
Till that at *length* nigh to the sea they drew; . . . V. ii. 29. 2
The sunne at *length* his joyous face doth cleare: . . . V. iii. 1. 2
To whom he thus at *length:* . . . V. vi. 10. 4
At *length* he saw the hindmost overtake One . . . V. viii. 5. 6
at *length* she did before her spie Sir Artegall; . . . V. viii. 6. 4
bore him . . . longer Then two speares *length:* . . . V. viii. 7. 9
yet at *length* she did requight, . . . V. xi. 1. 8
when it in *length* Was stretched forth, . . . V. xi. 23. 1
Till nigh unto the place at *length* approcht . . . V. xi. 36. 9
Who came at *length* with proud presumpteous gate . . . V. xii. 14. 1
Nathlesse at *length* him selfe he did upreare . . . VI. i. 35. 1
At *length* it chaunst that both . . . VI. i. 38. 1
Whom Calidore . . . At *length* bespake; . . . VI. ii. 7. 2
Like as a flowre, . . . At *length* breakes forth, . . . VI. ii. 35. 9
the deadly swound . . . she at the *length* dispacht him, . . . VI. iii. 10. 8
at *length,* in his extreamest neede, . . . VI. iii. 46. 5
at *length,* after long weary chace, . . . VI. iii. 50. 3
At *length* he heard under the forrests syde . . . VI. iv. 26. 6
At *length,* when as no hope of his retourne . . . VI. v. 7. 1
at *length* unto a woody glade He came, . . . VI. v. 17. 6
at *length,* nigh tyrd with former chace, . . . VI. v. 21. 1

Length—*Continued.*
Above a launces *length* him forth did beare, . . . VI. vii. 11. 3
Yet thus at *length* he said: . . . VI. vii. 14. 6
Fearing least he at *length* the raines would lend . . . VI. xi. 6. 2
He at the *length* was slaine . . . VI. xi. 19. 6
At *length,* when they occasion fittest found, . . . VI. xi. 42. 1
At *length* espyes at hand the happie cost, . . . VI. xi. 44. 8
At *length* a Shepheard . . . Came to the place; . . . VI. xii. 9. 1
At *length* into a Monastere did light, . . . VI. xii. 23. 8
Did unto them at *length* these speeches wise unfold; . . . VII. vi. 19. 9
At *length,* when they had flouted him . . . VII. vi. 50. 1
At *length* she, looking up with chearefull view, . . . VII. vii. 57. 8
turning to themselves at *length* againe, . . . VII. vii. 58. 6
Breake forth at *length* out of the inner part, . . . *Am.* ii. 5
she to stones at *length* all frosen turne! . . . *Am.* xxxii. 14
I doe at *length* descry the happy shore, . . . *Am.* lxiii. 5
To come at *length* unto the wished scope . . . *H.L.* 296
she at *length* will streame Some deaw of grace . . . *H.B.* 26
One drop of grace at *length* will to me give, . . . *H.B.* 277
At *length* him nayled on a gallow-tree, . . . *H.H.L.* 153
At *length* they all to mery London came, . . . *Proth.* 127
Lengthen. Agape Doth *lengthen* her sonnes lives. . . . IV. ii. Arg.
Lent. *See* **Leant, Long-lent.**
All that is *lent* to love wyll be lost. . . . *S.C.* F. 70
Theyr sample onely to us *lent,* . . . *S.C.* Jul. 119
The weapons, which Nature to him hath *lent:* . . . *Gn.* 276
the two pearles which sight unto him *lent,* . . . *Gn.* 285
what ever power his aged yeares Him *lent,* . . . *Gn.* 647
lent to him the charge Of all his flocke, . . . *Hub.* 299
unto such the Ape *lent* not his minde: . . . *Hub.* 794
his eare he *lent* To everie sound . . . *Hub.* 1010
is now *lent* to the foole: . . . *T.M.* 412
interchanged life unto them *lent,* . . . *Ti.* 387
Him to the mercy of th' avenger *lent.* . . . *Mui.* 432
had he beene where earst his armes were *lent,* . . . I. vi. 42. 7
To me he *lent* this rope, to him a rusty knife. . . . I. ix. 29. 9
when yeares More rype us reason *lent* . . . II. iv. 18. 5
if she had her least helpe to thee *lent,* . . . II. iv. 26. 1
Nathelesse so sore a buff to him it *lent,* . . . II. v. 6. 8
'What dismall day hath *lent* this cursed light, . . . II. vi. 43. 7
The Palmer *lent* his eare unto the noyce, . . . II. viii. 4. 1
lent her wary eare to understand . . . III. i. 60. 8
both full liefe him lodging to have *lent,* . . . III. ix. 14. 3
Yet she to none of them her liking *lent,* . . . IV. ii. 36. 2
his sisters skill unto him *lent* Most confidence . . . IV. ii. 39. 5
unto rest themselves all onely *lent,* . . . IV. viii. 28. 7
Unto abuse of lawlesse lust was *lent,* . . . IV. viii. 32. 3
she, whose hart to love was wholly *lent,* . . . IV. viii. 50. 6
Unto whose trust the charge thereof was *lent:* . . . IV. x. 12. 2
To cure her sonne, as he his faith had *lent,* . . . IV. xii. 23. 4
to him leaping *lent* him such a knocke, . . . V. i. 21. 8
So courage *lent* a cloke to cowardise. . . . V. iii. 15. 5
altars unto him and temples *lent,* . . . V. vii. 2. 3
whilest she *lent* her intentive mind, . . . V. ix. 14. 1
to his Lord Sir Artegall it *lent,* . . . V. ix. 18. 2
to his first emprize his mind he *lent,* . . . V. xi. 35. 5
how long space . . . *lent* a Champion to provide?' . . . V. xi. 42. 2
new life to her *lent* in midst of deadly feare. . . . V. xii. 12. 9
that bright sword, the sword of Justice *lent,* . . . V. xii. 40. 5
So soone as passage is unto him *lent,* . . . VI. i. 21. 4
such as sudden rage him *lent* to smite; . . . VI. iv. 4. 3
That ever I this life unto thee *lent,* . . . VI. vi. 33. 5
in lieu of life him *lent,* . . . VI. vii. 21. 6
such a stroke him *lent,* . . . VI. vii. 45. 6
A little well is *lent* that gaineth more withall. . . . VI. xi. 6. 9
ye your love *lent* to so meane a one. . . . *Am.* lxvi. 4
Him lodging in your bosome to have *lent.* . . . *Am.* lxxiii. 14
That honour and large richesse to me *lent:* . . . *Am.* lxxiv. 8
himselfe, . . . To feede our hungry soules, unto us *lent.* . . . *H.H.L.* 196
The meanes, therefore, which unto us is *lent* . . . *H.H.B.* 127
Lentulus. Proud Tarquin, and too lordly *Lentulus;* . . . I. v. 49. 6
Leopard. The cruell *Leopard* she resembled much: . . . *Rev.* i. 4
Who of the Grecian *Libbard* now ought heares, . . . *Ti.* 68
he would . . . make the *Libbard* sterne Leave roaring, . . . I. vi. 25. 8
when the flying *Libbard* she did chace, . . . II. iii. 28. 8
Had hunted late the *Libbard* or the Bore, . . . VII. vii. 29. 8
Leopards. hunting then the *Libbards* and the Beares . . . IV. vii. 23. 7
Lepped. *See* **Leaped, Leapt.**
Leprosies. No bloodie issues nor no *leprosies,* . . . *Col.* 313
Leprous. spightfull poison spues From *leprous* mouth on all that ever writt. . . . I. iv. 32. 8
Lere, -s. *See* **Lear, -s.**
Lerna. Snake . . . Long fostred in the filth of *Lerna* lake: . . . I. vii. 17. 3
More loathd then *Lerna,* or then Stygian lake, . . . V. xi. 32. 4
Lesinges. *See* **Leasings.**
Less. *See* **No less.**
Thought all things *lesse* than his disdainful pride. . . . *Van.* iii. 6
(Were it more or *lesse*) . . . *S.C.* May 108
little good hath got, and much *lesse* gayne. . . . *S.C.* O. 10
will he had . . . that made him *lesse* adrad. . . . *Gn.* 304
blent so much his sense, that *lesse* he feard) . . . *Gn.* 311
Ne *lesse* praise-worthie I Theana read, . . . *Col.* 492
Ne *lesse* praise-worthie is her sister deare, . . . *Col.* 504
Ne *lesse* praise-worthie is Mansilia, . . . *Col.* 508
Ne *lesse* praise-worthie Galathea seemes, . . . *Col.* 516
Ne *lesse* praise-worthie faire Neaera is, . . . *Col.* 524
Ne *lesse* praise-worthie Stella do I read, . . . *Col.* 532
Ne *lesse* praisworthie are the sisters three, . . . *Col.* 536
Ne thee *lesse* worthie, gentle Flavia, . . . *Col.* 572
Ne thee *lesse* worthie, curteous Candida, . . . *Col.* 574

Less—*Continued.*
Forgive it me, faire Dames, sith *lesse* ye have not lefte. . . . *Ded.Son.*xvii. 14
If *lesse* then that I feare, more favour I have found.' . . . I. vii. 25. 9
had he *lesse,* yet some he would give to the pore. . . . I. x. 38. 9
Losse is no shame, nor to bee *lesse* then foe; . . . II. v. 15. 6
That fairer seemes the *lesse* ye see her may. . . . II. xii. 74. 6
All losse is *lesse,* and *lesse* the infamy, . . . III. i. 25. 5
No whit *lesse* fayre then terrible in fight: . . . III. iii. 56. 3
What can I *lesse* doe then her love therefore, . . . III. v. 46. 4
all the sorrow . . . is *lesse* Then vertues might . . . III. xi. 14. 6
your cause is nothing *lesse* Then is your sorrow certes, . . . III. xi. 18. 3
To love faire Daphne, which thee loved *lesse;* . . . III. xi. 36. 7
Lesse she thee lov'd then was thy just desart, . . . III. xi. 36. 8
Ne *lesse* approved was Cambelloes might, . . . IV. iii. 7. 3
Ne *lesse* his skill in weapons did appeare; . . . IV. iii. 7. 4
whose beauties wonderment She *lesse* esteem'd . . . IV. v. 20. 9
Ne *lesse* thereat did Paridell complaine, . . . IV. v. 22. 6
dread Untride is *lesse* then when thou shalt it try: . . . IV. vii. 11. 6
'Then *lesse,'* (said she) 'by all the woe I pas, . . . IV. viii. 63. 7
in thoughts *lesse* hard and bold, . . . IV. xi. 22. 4
lesse she feared that same fatall read, . . . IV. xii. 27. 1
Ne *lesse* was she in secret hart affected, . . . IV. xii. 35. 6
much *lesse* him match in fight, . . . V. i. 8. 7
ere thou limit what is *lesse* or more . . . V. ii. 34. 5
Ne is the earth the *lesse,* or loseth ought, . . . V. ii. 39. 6
Ne *lesse* did Talus suffer sleepe to seaze His eye-lids sad, . . . V. vi. 26. 5
much *lesse* honour by that warlike kinde Of life; . . . V. vi. 32. 5
of all other weapons *lesse* or more, . . . V. viii. 34. 4
That they the whiles may take *lesse* heedie keepe . . . V. ix. 13. 3
All perill ought be *lesse,* and *lesse* all paine . . . V. xi. 55. 7
thought more the *lesse* she sed. . . . V. xii. 29. 9
of *lesse* livelood and hability, . . . VI. iii. 7. 7
Ne *lesse* the Lady did advaunce. . . . VI. iii. 19. 5
Ne she *lesse* glad; for she so wisely did, . . . VI. iv. 38. 3
Ne *lesse* in vertue . . . Doth she exceede . . . VI. x. 26. 5
Ne *lesse* in hart rejoyced Calidore, . . . VI. xi. 45. 6
Claribell Ne *lesse* did tender the faire Pastorell, . . . VI. xii. 11. 5
Much *lesse* the Title of old Titans Right: . . . VII. vi. 33. 4
waights, with which he did assoyle Both more and *lesse,* . . . VII. vii. 38. 8
in all thy creatures more or *lesse* . . . VII. vii. 47. 3
though he *lesse* appeare To change his hew, . . . VII. vii. 51. 1
baseborne mynds such lamps regard the *lesse,* . . . *H.L.* 173
Or more or *lesse,* by influence divine, . . . *H.B.* 44
Which powre retayning still or more or *lesse,* . . . *H.B.* 113
much *lesse* my trembling verse . . . can hope it to reherse. . . . *H.H.L.* 41
what can us *lesse* then that behove? . . . *H.H.L.* 178
Thou canst not count, much *lesse* their natures aime; . . . *H.H.B.* 33
How much *lesse* those, much higher in degree, . . . *H.H.B.* 61
Lessen. nought on earth may *lessen* or appease; . . . *D.* 276
hoping griefe may *lessen* being told, . . . IV. xii. 6. 3
Lessened. Yet is the stocke not *lessened* nor spent, . . . III. vi. 36. 3
mans life For nought may *lessened* nor enlarged bee, . . . IV. ii. 52. 2
his worke *lessened,* that his love mote grow: . . . V. v. 57. 3
Lesseneth. sithens silence *lesseneth* not my fire, . . . I. ix. 8. 6
Lesser. The *lesser* pangs can beare who hath endur'd the chief. I. vi. 37. 9
shone, Like Hesperus emongst the *lesser* lights, . . . I. vii. 30. 4
That it should not deface all others *lesser* light? . . . II. iv. 25. 9
to bee *lesser* then himselfe . . . II. v. 15. 7
in thy selfe thy *lesser* partes do move; . . . II. v. 16. 2
So huge a mind could not in *lesser* rest, . . . III. ix. 46. 7
shone as Phebes light Amongst the *lesser* starres . . . IV. v. 14. 4
They soone would loath their *lesser* happinesse, . . . IV. x. 23. 7
light, That doth enlumine all these *lesser* fyres, . . . V. Pr. 7. 2
all the rest like *lesser* lamps did dim: . . . VI. ix. 9. 5
All other *lesser* lights in light excell; . . . VI. x. 26. 2
Cynthia doth shend The *lesser* starres. . . . *Proth.* 122
Lesson. (a *lesson* derely bought) . . . *S.C.* N. 156
learne The Lyon stoup to him . . . (A *lesson* hard) . . . I. vi. 25. 8
hath this *lesson* deare Deepe written . . . I. viii. 44. 7
A harder *lesson* to learne Continence . . . II. vi. 1. 1
A *lesson* too too hard for living clay . . . III. iv. 26. 3
Need teacheth her this *lesson* hard and rare, . . . III. vii. 4. 3
That she may . . . reade this *lesson* often. . . . IV. Pr. 5. 9
to lerne So fond a *lesson* as to love againe: . . . V. v. 46. 4
Love is the *lesson* which the Lord us taught. . . . *Am.* lxviii. 14
Lessoned. her *lessoned* In all the lore of love, . . . III. vi. 51. 8
Lessons. Of love full manie *lessons* did apply, . . . IV. Pr. 3. 8
Lest (*partial list*). *See* **List.**
Jove fearing, *least* if she should greater growe, . . . *Ro.* iv. 5
Least thou the price of my displeasure prove.' . . . *S.C.* F. 138
Lest he should be descried . . . *S.C.* May 281
Then ryse, . . . *Least* night with stealing steppes . . . *S.C.* Jun. 119
Least that the Poplar happely should rew . . . *Gn.* 219
least he my Loove happely chaunce to beholde. . . . *Tetrasticon* 4
Least that the world thee dead accuse of guilt, . . . *D.* 82
Least that his toyle should . . . be brust. . . . *As.* 106
least I marre the sweetnesse of the vearse, . . . *As.* 215
I feard, *least* land we never should have eyde: . . . *Col.* 267
aware' . . . '*Least* suddaine mischiefe . . . I. i. 12. 2
fly, . . . *Least* to you hap . . . I. ii. 31. 5
least to themselves the like mishappen might. . . . I. iii. 20. 9
Beware . . . *Least* thou of her believe too lightly blame, . . . I. iv. 1. 5
Least so great good . . . Should die . . . I. ix. 2. 8
ayd, *least* they should be undone; . . . I. x. 43. 3
Least his long way his aged limbes should tire: . . . II. i. 7. 5
feared *least* his boldnesse should offend, . . . II. iii. 17. 5
Least by her presence daunger mote befall; . . . II. iii. 44. 2
guyde thy waies . . . *Least* worse betide thee . . . II. iv. 36. 5
fly . . . *Least* thy foolhardize worke thy sad confusion.' . . . II. iv. 42. 9
feare *least* Force or Fraud should unaware . . . II. vii. 25. 3

Lest—*Continued.*
Avise thee well, . . . *Least* thou perhaps . . . . II. vii. 38. 9
least by mischaunce It might breake out . . . . II. ix. 30. 1
Least that his Lord they should behinde invade; . . . . II. xi. 31. 5
doubted *least* it were some magicall Illusion . . . . II. xi. 39. 5
'*Least* wee unweeting hap to be fordonne; . . . . II. xii. 11. 2
aware, *Least* that too farre . . . . III. ii. 10. 7
I feare *least* love it bee! . . . . III. ii. 33. 1
for feare *least* blame . . . should in her be fond, ... III. ii. 52. 7
care she tooke, . . . *Least* that it should . . . . III. iii. 5. 7
feare, *Least* back againe the kingdom he . . . . III. iii. 45. 9
Least afterwards it be too late . . . . III. iv. 14. 9
Least they their finnes should bruze, ... III. iv. 34. 5
affeard *Least* he like one of them . . . . III. vi. 23. 4
feare *Least* his fraile senses . . . . III. vii. 20. 8
feared he *least* ought did ill betide . . . . III. vii. 31. 4
Have care, . . . *Least* worse on sea . . . befell,' . . . . III. viii. 24. 5
great doubt . . . *Least* salvage beastes her person . . . . III. x. 39. 8
least doubt of us ye have, . . . we will . . . . III. x. 42. 6
Fearing *least* . . . the wearie soule would flit. . . . . III. xi. 12. 9
through feare *least* down he fallen should, ... III. xi. 34. 8
fearefull was . . . *Lest* she with blame . . . . IV. i. 5. 5
dout Their safetie; *least* by searching daungers . . . . IV. ii. 46. 7
Fearing *least* she . . . should woo: . . . . IV. vi. 30. 8
Fearing, *least* if she should him freely set, ... IV. viii. 53. 8
fear'd *least* they with shame would him pursew: . . . . V. ii. 52. 7
doubt *least* she him sought t' appeach Of treason, ... V. v. 37. 3
doubting *least* his hold was but unsound . . . . V. v. 42. 7
she feared *least* some hard mishap Had him misfalne . . . . V. vi. 4. 1
Spaniell wayting carefully *Least* any should betray . . . . V. vi. 26. 9
heede, *Least* any more such practise should proceede. . . . . V. vi. 31. 5
to watch . . . *Least* by such slight he were unwares . . . . V. xi. 7. 3
To save her selfe, *least* that he did her slay; . . . . V. xi. 26. 8
'bewray, *Least* ye therefore mote happily me . . . . V. xi. 52. 8
misdoubting *least* he should misguyde . . . . VI. iii. 47. 7
Least that the beasts sharpe teeth had . . . . VI. iv. 23. 8
aware . . . *Least*, if men you of cruelty accuse, ... VI. viii. 1. 8
least he should recover foote againe, ... VI. viii. 17. 2
Least unto me betide a greater ill; . . . . VI. viii. 30. 4
Least they should joyne . . . . VI. xi. 18. 2
misdoubting *least* of-new Some uprore were . . . . VI. xi. 43. 8
(for dread *least* if her syre Should know . . . . VI. xii. 6. 6
Doubting *least* Typhon were againe uprear'd, ... VII. vi. 15. 8
Least, trembling, it his workmanship should spill; . . . . *Am.* xvii. 7
enfyred . . . *least* passions doe impresse, ... *H.L.* 170
For feare, *lest* if he chaunce to looke . . . . *H.H.B.* 146
least they might Soyle their fayre plumes . . . . *Proth.* 49

Let. *Let* me no more see faire thing . . . . *Bel.* iv. 12
O *let* mine eyes no more see such a sight! . . . . *Pet.*² v. 14
Then *let* those deep Abysses open rive, ... *Ro.* i. 7
O Rome! thee *let* him see, ... *Ro.* v. 2
Whiles Jove at them his thunderbolts *let* flie, ... *Ro.* xii. 4
let him record That such this Cities honour was . . . . *Ro.* xxviii. 12
if that time doo *let* thy glorie live, ... *Ro.* xxxii. 11
let him feede, as Nature did provide, ... *Van.* iii. 11
Let therefore nought, that great is, therein glorie, ... *Van.* viii. 13
Anger nould *let* him speake to the tree, ... *S.C.* F. 199
Let be, as may be, that is past: . . . . *S.C.* Mar. 58
That is to come, *let* be forecast: . . . . *S.C.* Mar. 59
Let him, if he dare, His brightnesse compare . . . . *S.C.* Ap. 79
Let that rowme to my Lady be yeven: . . . . *S.C.* Ap. 114
Let none come there but that Virgins bene, ... *S.C.* Ap. 129
Let dame Elisa thanke you for her song: . . . . *S.C.* Ap. 150
let us homeward, for night draweth on, ... *S.C.* Ap. 160
letten them runne at randon alone: . . . . *S.C.* May 46
Let none mislike of that may not be mended: . . . . *S.C.* May 162
lette me thy tale borrowe . . . . *S.C.* May 308
Did *let* me walke withouten lincks of love, ... *S.C.* Jun. 34
The corne is theyrs, *let* other thresh, ... *S.C.* Jul. 191
A shell-fish downe *let* flye: . . . . *S.C.* Jul. 224
Let thy follye be the priefe. . . . . *S.C.* Au. 116
let the Lambe be Willye his owne: . . . . *S.C.* Au. 132
'*Let* stremes of teares supply the place of sleepe; . . . . *S.C.* Au. 163
Let all, that sweete is, voyd: . . . . *S.C.* Au. 164
so *let* your yrksome yells augment. . . . . *S.C.* Au. 178
Let breake your sounder sleepe, ... *S.C.* Au. 191
let hem gange alone a Gods name; . . . . *S.C.* S. 100
As they han brewed, so *let* hem beare blame. . . . . *S.C.* S. 101
let out the sheepes bloud at his throte. . . . . *S.C.* S. 207
let us cast with what delight to chace, ... *S.C.* O. 2
Let powre in lavish cups . . . . *S.C.* O. 105
Let not my small demaund be so contempt. . . . . *S.C.* N. 48
Let streaming teares be poured out in store; . . . . *S.C.* N. 61
Let me, ah! *lette* me in your foldes ye lock, ... *S.C.* D. 147
Let everlasting lightsome glory strive, ... *Gn.* 55
let an happie roome remaine for thee . . . . *Gn.* 57
let long lasting life . . . remembered be . . . . *Gn.* 59
let us turne to our first businesse. . . . . *Gn.* 64
let destruction be the punishment, ... *Gn.* 367
let the flitting aire my vaine words sever.' . . . . *Gn.* 638
Let us all servile base subjection scorne; . . . . *Hub.* 134
Let us our fathers heritage divide, ... *Hub.* 136
Let such vile vassals . . . Drudge . . . . *Hub.* 156
Ne *let* thy learning question'd be of anie. . . . . *Hub.* 524
Let not sweete Poets praise, ... *Hub.* 811
Ne *let* such verses Poetrie be named! . . . . *Hub.* 814
like a Lawyer, when he land would *lett*, ... *Hub.* 866
that ye *let* none other ever drawe Your minde . . . . *Hub.* 1053
breach of lawes to privie ferme did *let*: . . . . *Hub.* 1160
Were forst their auncient houses to *let* lie, ... *Hub.* 1178

Let—*Continued.*
Ne would he anie *let* to have accesse . . . . *Hub.* 1201
He did uncase, and then away *let* flie: . . . . *Hub.* 1380
let the rest in order thee ensew. . . . . *T.M.* 54
Now being *let* to runne at libertie . . . . *T.M.* 550
'Ne may I *let* thy husbands sister die, ... *Ti.* 274
O *let* the man, of whom the Muse is scorned, ... *Ti.* 454
Let them behold the piteous fall of mee, ... *Ti.* 461
Let him behold the horror of my fall, ... *Ti.* 466
unto heaven *let* your high minde aspire, ... *Ti.* 685
Let reade the rufull plaint herein exprest, ... *D.* 4
Let him be banisht farre away from hence; . . . . *D.* 10
Ne *let* the sacred Sisters here be hight, ... *D.* 11
Let those three fatall Sisters . . . Approach hereto; . . . . *D.* 16
let the dreadfull Queene Of Darkenes deepe come . . . . *D.* 19
'Ne *let* Elisa, royall Shepheardesse, . . . envy, ... *D.* 225
let compassion creepe Into his brest, ... *D.* 248
Let now your blisse be turned into bale, ... *D.* 320
'*Let* Bagpipe never more be heard to shrill, ... *D.* 323
let ghastlinesse And drery horror dim the chearfull light, . . *D.* 327
'*Let* birds be silent on the naked spray, ... *D.* 330
Let streaming floods their hastie courses stay, ... *D.* 332
Let th' earth be barren, ... *D.* 334
Let rest her selfe from her long wearinesse, ... *D.* 338
in his traunce I would not *let* him lie, ... *D.* 550
Let him be moov'd to pity such a case. . . . . *As.* Pr. 18
having none to *let*, to wood did wend. . . . . *As.* 126
Let him to sea, and he shall see it there. . . . . *Col.* 207
let us heare what grace she shewed thee, ... *Col.* 356
To *let* thy fame lie so in hidden shade: . . . . *Col.* 407
so much grace *let* her vouchsafe to grant . . . . *Col.* 939
doe not sdeigne to *let* thy name be writt . . . . *Ded. Son.* ii. 4
Let thy faire Cinthias praises be thus rudely showne. . . . . *Ded. Son.* viii. 14
words most horrible, (*Let* none them read) . . . . I. i. 37. 2
Let me not die in languor . . . . I. i. 52. 7
Ne *let* vaine feares procure your needlesse smart, ... I. i. 54. 4
the seeming simple maid *Let* fal her eien, ... I. ii. 27. 6
'O! leave her soone, or *let* her soone be slaine." . . . . I. ii. 39. 4
her unruly Page . . . *let* her in; . . . . I. iii. 13. 3
The Lyon frayed them, him in to *lett*. . . . . I. iii. 19. 3
Let not his love, *let* not his restlesse spright, Be unreveng'd, I. iv. 48. 7
Let now abate the terrour of your might, ... I. v. 14. 4
let be seene That dreaded Night . . . . I. v. 24. 3
let stay Aveugles sonne there . . . . I. v. 44. 5
fainting, each themselves to breathen *lett*, ... I. vi. 44. 2
Satyrane him from pursuit did *let*. . . . . I. vii. 20. 4
let the stony dart . . . Perce to my hart, ... I. vii. 22. 7
let eternall night so sad sight fro me hyde. . . . . I. vii. 22. 9
Ne *let* it seeme that credence this exceedes; . . . . I. vii. 36. 1
woefull Lady, *let* me you intrete, ... I. vii. 40. 5
Scorning the *let* of so unequall foe: . . . . I. viii. 13. 5
He downe *let* fall his arme, ... I. viii. 19. 7
Ne *let* that wicked woman scape away; . . . . I. viii. 28. 5
Now in your powre, to *let* her live, or die.' . . . . I. viii. 45. 6
spoile her of her scarlot robe, and *let* her fly.' . . . . I. viii. 45. 9
They *let* her goe at will, and wander waies unknowne. . . . . I. viii. 49. 9
A wyde way made to *let* forth living breath: . . . . I. ix. 30. 3
God you never *let* his charmed speaches heare!' . . . . I. ix. 30. 9
let him dye, that loatheth living breath, ... I. ix. 38. 8
let him die at ease, that liveth here uneath? . . . . I. ix. 38. 9
Why wilt not *let* him passe, ... I. ix. 39. 8
let none aske whence, nor why. . . . . I. ix. 42. 9
his lawe, *Let* every sinner die; . . . . I. ix. 47. 5
Ne *let* vaine words bewitch thy manly hart, ... I. ix. 53. 2
Ne *let* the man ascribe it to his skill, ... I. x. 1. 6
'O! *let* me not,' (quoth he) 'then turne againe . . . . I. x. 63. 1
But *let* me heare for aie in peace remaine, ... I. x. 63. 3
lett downe that haughtie string, ... I. xi. 7. 7
To *let* them downe before his flightes end: . . . . I. xi. 19. 4
Let nought be hid . . . . I. xii. 29. 9
let that man with better sence advize, ... II. Pr. 2. 1
Let one word fall that may your grief unfold, ... II. i. 46. 7
To *lett* a weary wretch from her dew rest, ... II. i. 47. 7
Her deare besought to *let* her die a mayd. . . . . II. ii. 8. 5
let them still be bloody, ... II. ii. 10. 4
downe they *lett* their cruell weapons fall, ... II. ii. 32. 3
To *let* him weet his doughtie valiaunce, ... II. iii. 14. 5
'*let* be thy deepe advise: . . . . II. iii. 16. 1
'*lett* her pas at will, ... II. iii. 44. 1
Let us soone hence depart.' . . . . II. iii. 46. 2
the truth to *let* me understand. . . . . II. iv. 23. 9
'*let* that message to thy Lord be brought.' . . . . II. iv. 44. 9
So up he *let* him rise; . . . . II. v. 14. 1
Ne *let* thy stout hart melt in pitty vayne: . . . . II. v. 24. 6
Crying; '*Let* be that Lady debonaire, ... II. vi. 28. 4
'*lett* be thy bitter scorne, ... II. vii. 18. 1
As author of unjustice, there to *let* him dye. . . . . II. vii. 60. 9
Ne Mammon would there *let* him long remayne, ... II. vii. 63. 3
who shall *let* me now . . . . II. viii. 28. 3
Let Scaldis tell, and *let* tell Hania, And *let* the marsh . . . . II. x. 24. 1
their tribute he refusd to *let* be payd. . . . . II. x. 50. 9
land behynd them fled away. But *let* them pas, ... II. xi. 4. 7
at him *let* fly Their fluttring arrowes, ... II. xi. 18. 1
Let all that live hereby be counselled . . . . II. xii. 9. 8
bad . . . *let* him heare some part . . . . II. xii. 33. 9
straunge phantomes doth *lett* us ofte foresee, ... II. xii. 47. 6
Let them returned be unto their former state.' . . . . II. xii. 85. 9
Let Gryll be Gryll, and have his hoggish minde; . . . . II. xii. 87. 8
let us hence depart whilest wether serves and winde.' . . . . II. xii. 87. 9
let that same delitious Poet lend A little leave . . . . III. Pr. 5. 1

Let—*Continued.*

let him mend, If ought amis . . . III. Pr. 5. 3
Ne *let* his fayrest Cynthia refuse . . . III. Pr. 5. 5
either Gloriana *let* her chuse, . . . III. Pr. 5. 7
besought The Prince of grace to *let* him ronne that turne. . . III. i. 5. 2
Let not thee grieve dismounted to have beene, . . . III. i. 7. 6
To *let* not others honour be defaste . . . III. i. 12. 4
Let later age that noble use envy, . . . III. i. 13. 8
so did *let* her goodly visage to appere. . . . III. i. 42. 9
Let not her fault your sweete affections marre, . . . III. i. 49. 3
'Faire Sir, I *let* you weete, . . . III. ii. 6. 1
'*Let* bee therefore my vengeaunce to disswade, . . . III. ii. 13. 1
To *let* the secret of her hart to her appeare. . . . III. ii. 34. 9
'*Let* not it thee offend, . . . III. iii. 15. 6
was loth to *let* her purpose plaine appeare; . . . III. iii. 17. 9
let no whit thee dismay . . . III. iii. 21. 7
Let us in feigned armes our selves disguize, . . . III. iii. 53. 2
O *let* them soone awake! . . . III. iv. 2. 2
her great courage would not *let* her weepe, . . . III. iv. 11. 3
let their temed fishes softly swim . . . III. iv. 34. 3
oft *let* fall Many meeke wordes . . . III. iv. 48. 8
Did *let* him forage. . . . III. iv. 53. 7
There *let* her with the damned spirits dwell, . . . III. iv. 60. 8
his passage through the ford to *let*. . . . III. v. 17. 9
did bite The bitter earth, and bad to *lett* him in . . . III. v. 22. 2
She did it fayre dispred and *let* to florish fayre. . . . III. v. 51. 9
(*let* not it be envide.') . . . III. vi. 23. 8
Ne did she *let* dull sleepe once to relent, . . . III. vii. 2. 3
trickling teares she softly forth *let* fall, . . . III. vii. 9. 2
would not *let* me be her Chappellane, . . . III. vii. 58. 7
Downe in a Dongeon deepe he *let* her fall, . . . III. viii. 41. 8
The which to *let* you weet will further time requyre. . . . III. viii. 52. 9
never *let* th' ensample of the bad Offend the good; . . . III. ix. 2. 1
Nay, *let* us first' (sayd Satyrane) 'entreat . . . III. ix. 9. 1
'entreat The man by gentle meanes to *let* us in, . . . III. ix. 9. 2
So as he was not *let* to enter there: . . . III. ix. 13. 5
her well-plighted frock, . . . Shee low *let* fall, . . . III. ix. 21. 5
therein write to *lett* his love be showne; . . . III. ix. 30. 7
In speaking many false belgardes at her *let* fly. . . . III. ix. 52. 9
let not my rudenes be no breach . . . III. x. 25. 3
the howre that first he did them *lett* The same behold, . . . III. x. 34. 8
and *lett* her fly alone: . . . III. x. 35. 8
But *let* him passe as lightly as he came: . . . III. x. 39. 2
let us goe to seeke my dearest Dame, . . . III. x. 39. 5
ne *let* him be descryde, . . . III. x. 50. 8
let him far be banished away, . . . III. xi. 2. 1
in his stead *let* Love for ever dwell; . . . III. xi. 2. 2
these few words *lett* fly. . . . III. xi. 15. 9
let me die that ought: . . . III. xi. 19. 6
Rather *let* try extremities of chaunce, . . . III. xi. 24. 8
ne *let* sleepe oppresse Her heavy eyes . . . III. xi. 55. 6
Where *let* them wend at will, . . . III. xii. 45. 9
she wisht, that fate n'ould *let* her yet possesse. . . . III. xii. 46. *or.*9
Which straight to her was yeelded without *let*. . . . IV. i. 12. 5
of friendship *let* me now you pray, . . . IV. i. 40. 2
Let ugly shame and endlesse infamy . . . IV. i. 53. 6
Yet would not *let* their battell so be broken, . . . IV. ii. 21. 4
they at last their wrothfull hands *let* fall, . . . IV. ii. 21. 8
Have I thus long thy life unto thee *let*: . . . IV. iii. 11. 4
streames of purple bloud . . . *Let* forth his wearie ghost, . . . IV. iii. 12. 9
warded, or avoyded and *let* goe, . . . IV. iii. 17. 4
He can *let* drive at him with all his power, . . . IV. iii. 20. 4
did not from him *let* One drop of bloud to fall, . . . IV. iii. 24. 2
With heapes of strokes, which he at him *let* flie . . . IV. iii. 25. 4
To *let* them passe at will, for dread of shame. . . . IV. iv. 3. 5
soone enforced beene To *let* him loose . . . IV. iv. 34. 8
Let never Ladie to his love assent, . . . IV. v. 18. 8
Did find it fit withouten breach or *let*. . . . IV. v. 19. 5
Ne *let* his speeches come unto their eare. . . . IV. v. 38. 6
'Sir Salvage knight, *Let* me this crave, . . . IV. vi. 9. 7
With dreadfull strokes *let* drive at him so sore, . . . IV. vii. 28. 3
He *let* to grow and griesly to concrew, . . . IV. vii. 40. 5
thinking to *let* her weet The great tormenting griefe . . . IV. viii. 9. 7
Against those two *let* drive, . . . IV. ix. 29. 5
twixt her selfe and Love did *let* me pas; . . . IV. x. 36. 3
her sacrifices *let* to rest." . . . IV. x. 54. 9
often me besought . . . to *let* her goe, . . . IV. x. 57. 2
To *let* faire Florimell in bands remayne, . . . IV. xi. 1. 4
Let them record them that are better skild, . . . IV. xi. 17. 5
And *let* their swelling waters low before him fall. . . . IV. xi. 30. 9
to *let* men plainely wot . . . IV. xi. 45. 8
But *let* me waste in woe my wretched yeares, . . . IV. xii. 7. 7
Let then this plaint unto his eares be borne, . . . IV. xii. 8. 3
To *let* her die whom he might have redrest.' . . . IV. xii. 8. 5
let me die and end my daies attone, . . . IV. xii. 9. 8
let him live unlov'd, or love him selfe alone. . . . IV. xii. 9. 9
Then *let* mee live as lovers ought to do, . . . IV. xii. 10. 2
Such thraldome or such freedome *let* it surely be. . . . IV. xii. 10. 9
Let none then blame me, . . . V. Pr. 3. 1
Let both the dead and living equally Devided be . . . V. i. 26. 3
if naught me *let*, I will be there . . . V. ii. 4. 3
a trap was *letten* downe to fall . . . V. ii. 12. 6
with his iron flale at it *let* flie, . . . V. ii. 21. 2
'Well then,' sayd Artegall, '*let* it be tride: . . . V. ii. 45. 4
let it tell What strokes . . . it stird this day; . . . V. ii. 21. 5
Braggadochio would not *let* him pas, . . . V. iii. 30. 3
let that losell . . . Hence fare on foot, . . . V. iii. 35. 5
Under my foote *let* each lay downe his sword; . . . V. iv. 16. 7
'Now, Bracidas, *let* this likewise be showne; . . . V. iv. 18. 2
ne *let* you amate Your misery, . . . V. iv. 28. 4

Let—*Continued.*

ne *let* him once respyre, . . . V. v. 16. 7
they were fayne to *let* him scape away, . . . V. v. 19. 3
want of meanes hath bene mine onely *let* . . . V. v. 42. 1
Let him feele hardnesse of thy heavie arme: . . . V. v. 49. 8
Let him lodge hard, and lie in strawen bed, . . . V. v. 50. 5
Cold yron chaines with which *let* him be tide; . . . V. v. 50. 8
let what ever he desires be him denide. . . . V. v. 50. 9
By a false trap was *let* adowne to fall . . . V. vi. 27. 7
They seeing that *let* drive at him streightway, . . . V. vi. 29. 8
Let drive at her with all her dreadfull might, . . . V. vii. 32. 3
him from force to *let*. . . . V. viii. 6. 9
so *let* his Idols serve the Elfe! . . . V. viii. 19. 9
refusing him to *let* unlace, . . . V. viii. 27. 3
There *let* her wonne, . . . V. ix. 2. 1
There *let* her ever keepe her damned den, . . . V. ix. 2. 3
it should *let* your pace Towards my Ladies presence, . . . V. ix. 7. 5
'Then *let* not that' (said they) 'stay your intent; . . . V. ix. 7. 8
A chearefull countenance on them *let* fall, . . . V. ix. 34. 8
would not *let* just vengeance on her light; . . . V. ix. 50. 5
let, instead thereof, to fall Few perling drops . . . V. ix. 50. 6
can *let* drive at him so dreadfullie, . . . V. xi. 10. 3
'Yet *let* me you of courtesie request' . . . V. xi. 57. 1
let your fame with falshood be defaced? . . . V. xi. 63. 5
He gan at him *let* drive . . . V. xii. 22. 9
Rather then *let* my selfe of wight be stroken, . . . VI. ii. 7. 8
when as my presence he did spy To be a *let*, . . . VI. ii. 17. 5
sith now occasion fit Doth fall, . . . *Let* me this crave, . . . VI. ii. 33. 3
let not your griefe empeach To tell . . . VI. ii. 42. 2
let it not you seeme disgrace To beare this burden . . . VI. ii. 47. 7
Let none therefore . . . Too greatly grieve . . . VI. iii. 5. 8
follow'd him so fast, That he nould *let* him breath, . . . VI. iii. 26. 7
And *let* thy Lady likewise doe the same, . . . VI. iii. 32. 3
humbly praid to *let* them in that night; . . . VI. iii. 38. 6
freed From bels and jesses which did *let* her flight, . . . VI. iv. 19. 8
Or loth to *let* her sorrowes be bewrayd: . . . VI. iv. 27. 4
'*Let* me therefore this favour for him finde, . . . VI. v. 30. 1
so boldly, without *let* or shame, . . . VI. vi. 20. 3
Let drive at him with so malitious mynd, . . . VI. vii. 10. 6
that same knight would not once *let* him start, . . . VI. vii. 21. 1
Let them that list their lucklesse lot deplore, . . . VI. vii. 30. 7
Yet would not *let* her lite, nor rest a little stead: . . . VI. vii. 40. 9
Let drive at him so dreadfully amaine, . . . VI. vii. 46. 4
let them love that list, . . . VI. viii. 21. 1
let him rise. . . . VI. viii. 29. 5
to *let* her Sleepe out her fill . . . VI. viii. 38. 1
Readie to launch her brest, and *let* out loved life. . . . VI. viii. 48. 9
let men weet That here on earth . . . VI. xi. 1. 6
With which her winged speed is *let* and crost, . . . VI. xii. 1. 4
Let her . . . this mothers joy descrive; . . . VI. xii. 21. 3
let us tell Of Calidore; . . . VI. xii. 22. 5
let her selfe into that Ivory throne; . . . VII. vi. 11. 2
let me aske you this withouten blame; . . . VII. vii. 53. 4
What then should *let*, but I aloft should reare My Trophee, . . . VII. vii. 56. 4
To force me live, and will not *let* me dy. . . . *Am.* xi. 12
Ere Cuckow end, *let* her a rebell be! . . . *Am.* xix. 14
let none ever say, That ye were blooded . . . *Am.* xx. 13
better were attonce to *let* me die, . . . *Am.* xxv. 5
Let it lykewise your gentle brest inspire . . . *Am.* xxviii. 6
Let her accept me as her faithfull thrall; . . . *Am.* xxix. 10
O fayrest fayre! *let* never it be named, . . . *Am.* xli. 13
Let her, yf please her, bynd with adamant chayne: . . . *Am.* xlii. 10
Onely *let* her abstaine from cruelty. . . . *Am.* xlii. 13
Let them feele the utmost of your crueltyes; . . . *Am.* xlix. 9
Ne *let* theyr famous moniments to fade? . . . *Am.* li. 4
There *let* no thought of joy, . . . Dare to approch, . . . *Am.* lii. 9
To *let* them gaze, whylest he on them may pray: . . . *Am.* liii. 4
let my loves fayre Planet short her wayes, . . . *Am.* lx. 13
So *let* us, which this chaunge of weather vew, . . . *Am.* lxii. 5
The old yeares sinnes forepast *let* us eschew, . . . *Am.* lxii. 7
let us love . . . lyke as we ought: . . . *Am.* lxviii. 13
let baser things devize To dy in dust, . . . *Am.* lxxv. 9
let my thoughts behold her selfe in mee. . . . *Am.* lxxviii. 14
let her prayses yet be low and meane, . . . *Am.* lxxx. 13
Let not one sparke of filthy lustfull fyre Breake out, . . . *Am.* lxxxiii. 1
Rather then envy, *let* them wonder at her, . . . *Am.* lxxxiv. 7
Let the world chose to envy or to wonder. . . . *Am.* lxxxiv. 14
Let all the plagues, and horrid paines, of hell . . . fall . . . *Am.* lxxxv. 5
The sparkes whereof *let* kindle thine own fyre, . . . *Am.* lxxxv. 9
Ne *let* the same of any be envide: . . . *Epith.* 15
let them also with them bring in hand . . . *Epith.* 41
let them make great store of bridale poses, . . . *Epith.* 45
let them eeke bring store of other flowers, . . . *Epith.* 46
let the ground . . . Be strewed with fragrant flowers . . . *Epith.* 48
Let all the virgins therefore well awayt: . . . *Epith.* 111
let thy lifull heat not fervent be . . . *Epith.* 118
let this day, *let* this one day, be myne; . . . *Epith.* 125
Let all the rest be thine. . . . *Epith.* 126
let the roring Organs loudly play . . . *Epith.* 218
Which may *let* in a little thought unsownd. . . . *Epith.* 237
let the Graces daunce unto the rest, . . . *Epith.* 257
Let no false treason seeke us to entrap, . . . *Epith.* 323
let the night be calme, and quietsome, . . . *Epith.* 326
let the mayds and yongmen cease to sing; . . . *Epith.* 332
Ne *let* the woods them answer . . . *Epith.* 333
Let no lamenting cryes . . . Be heard . . . *Epith.* 334
Ne *let* false whispers . . . Breake gentle sleepe . . . *Epith.* 336
Let no deluding dreames, nor dreadfull sights, . . . *Epith.* 338
Ne *let* house-fyres, nor lightnings . . . *Epith.* 340
Ne *let* the Pouke, nor other evill sprights, . . . *Epith.* 341

Let—*Continued.*
Ne *let* mischivous witches with theyr charmes, ... *Epith.* 342
Ne *let* hob Goblins, names whose sence we see not, ... *Epith.* 343
Let not the shriech Oule nor the Storke be heard, ... *Epith.* 345
Ne *let* th' unpleasant Quyre of Frogs still croking . . . . . . *Epith.* 349
Let none of these theyr drery accents sing; . . . . *Epith.* 351
Ne *let* the woods them answer, ... *Epith.* 352
let stil Silence trew night-watches keepe, ... *Epith.* 353
Ne *let* the woods us answere, ... *Epith.* 389
So *let* us rest, sweet love, in hope of this, ... *Epith.* 424
To *let* her live thus free, and me to dy. . . . . *H.L.* 154
Deigne to *let* fall one drop of dew reliefe, ... *H.B.* 284
Him, wretch, in doole would *let* no lenger dwell, ... *H.H.L.* 131
Then *let* thy flinty hart, that feeles no paine, ... *H.H.L.* 246
And *let* thy bowels bleede in every vaine, ... *H.H.L.* 248
And *let* thy soule . . . Melt into teares, ... *H.H.L.* 251
Let Angels, . . . her soveraigne praises sing, ... *H.H.B.* 232
And *let* faire Venus, that is Queene of love, ... *Proth.* 96
Let endlesse Peace your steadfast hearts accord, ... *Proth.* 101
let your bed with pleasures chast abound, ... *Proth.* 103

Lethe. That nowe sleepeth in *Lethe* lake, ... *S.C.* Mar. 23
not to have been dipt in *Lethe* lake, ... *Ti.* 428
his ghost . . . In peace may passen over *Lethe* lake; . . . . . I. iii. 36. 6

Lethe's. forst to ferrie over *Lethes* river, ... *Gn.* 338

Lets. oft he *lets* his cancker-wormes light . . . . *S.C.* F. 179
Lets none shoot up that nigh him planted bee: . . . . *Ti.* 453
Ne *lets* it rest untill it forth have brought . . . . *D.* 31
'Love of your selfe,' . . . *Lets* me not sleepe, ... I. i. 53. 2
Ne *lets* her waves with any filth be dyde; . . . . II. ii. 9. 8
to her mother Nature all her care she *letts.* . . . . II. vi. 16. 9
His chiefest *letts* and authors of his harmes, ... II. xi. 31. 3
thy faithful zele *lets* me not hyde My crime, ... III. ii. 37. 6
It *lettes* not fall, it *lettes* it not to rest; . . . . III. v. 2. 7
It *lettes* not scarse this Prince to breath at all, ... III. v. 2. 8
Whiles neither *lets* the other touch the soyle, ... IV. iii. 16. 7
never wight he *lets* to passe that way . . . . V. ii. 6. 2
whom God . . . *lets* his owne Beloved to behold; . . . . . . *H.H.B.* 241

Letter. Ne tell a written word, ne write a *letter*, ... *Hub.* 383

Letters. whenso love of *letters* did inspire Their gentle wits, . *Hub.* 829
In whose great shield was writ with *letters* gay . . . . I. ii. 12. 7
heathnish shield, wherein with *letters* red, Was writt *Sansjoy*, I. iv. 38. 5
writt with golden *letters* rich and brave: . . . . I. ix. 19. 8
writt in stone With bloody *letters* . . . . I. x. 53. 7
A Messenger with *letters*, which his message sayd. . . . . . I. xii. 24. 9
suborned hath This crafty messenger with *letters* vaine, . . . I. xii. 34. 2
For falsed *letters*, and suborned wyle, ... II. i. 1. 3
Ease, on his robe in golden *letters* cyphered. . . . . III. xii. 4. 9
With golden *letters* goodly well enchaced; . . . . IV. x. 8. 7
Love-learned *letters* to her eyes to read; . . . . *Am.* xliii. 12
Most happy *letters!* fram'd by skilfull trade, ... *Am.* lxxiv. 1

Lettest. ne *lettest* see The beautie of his worke? . . . . . . III. iv. 56. 3
Thou, being blind, *letst* him not see his feares, ... *H.L.* 226

Letteth. *letteth* her that ought the scepter weeld, ... II. xi. 2. 3
He *letteth* in, he *letteth* out to wend . . . . III. vi. 32. 1
And *letteth* them her lovely face to see, ... *H.H.B.* 255

Lettice. learne with *Lettice* to wexe light, ... *S.C.* Mar. 20

Letting. *letting* their sheepe runne at large, ... *S.C.* May 40
Letting their steedes to graze upon the greene. . . . . VI. v. 38. 2
letting him arise like abject thrall, ... VI. vii. 26. 6

Lettuce. Colde *Lettuce*, and refreshing Rosmarine. . . . . . *Mui.* 200

Leud, *etc. See* **Lewd,** *etc.*

Level. far as Archer might his *level* see: . . . . *Bel.*[2] iii. 4
To builde, with *levell* of my loftie style, ... *Ro.* xxv. 13
To whom I *levell* all my labours end, ... III. ix. 1. 2
make them *levell* with the lowly plaine; . . . . V. ii. 38. 2
at his head did *levell*, ... V. iv. 40. 3

Leveled. That seeing, I *levelde* againe . . . . *S.C.* Mar. 85
The land to which their course they *leveled;* . . . . II. xii. 34. 4
leveld all against one certaine place, ... V. x. 34. 7

Levels. To which he *levels* all his purposis, ... *Hub.* 772

Lever. *See* **Liefer.**

Levers. As it with mighty *levers* had bene tore; . . . . III. xii. 3. 4

Leviathan. The huge *Leviathan*, dame Natures wonder, ... *Van.* v. 6

Levin. As well can prove the piercing *levin*, ... *S.C.* Jul. 91
Wherein the lightsome *levin* shroudes, ... *S.C.* Au. 87
As percing *levin*, which . . . every thing consumes, ... III. v. 48. 8
As when the flashing *Levin* haps to light . . . . V. vi. 40. 1

Levin-brand. his burning *levin-brond* in hand he tooke. . . . . VII. vi. 30. 9

Lewd. But little ease of thy *lewd* tale I tasted: . . . . *S.C.* F. 245
thou speakes lyke a *lewde* lorrell, ... *S.C.* Jul. 93
with *lewde* lust was overlayd: . . . . *S.C.* Jul. 151
Such would descrie his *lewd* conditions; . . . . *Hub.* 796
his impudent *lewde* speach . . . . *Hub.* 839
gentle mindes with *lewd* delights distaine; . . . . *T.M.* 334
Through leasings *lewd*, and fained forgerie; . . . . *Col.* 696
with *lewd* speeches, and licentious deeds, ... *Col.* 787
wanton lust and *leud* enbracement: . . . . I. ii. 5. 5
revive the memory Of his *leud* lusts, ... I. vi. 46. 3
lewd rybauld, with vyle lust advaunst, ... II. i. 10. 3
In chaines of lust and *lewde* desyres ybownd, ... II. i. 54. 3
Of her *leawd* parts to make companion: . . . . II. ii. 37. 5
all the sinnes wherewith his *lewd* life did abound. . . . . . II. viii. 45. 9
spent their looser daies in *leud* delightes, ... II. xii. 9. 5
Now throwing forth *lewd* wordes immodestly; . . . . II. xii. 16. 4
Quite molten into lust and pleasure *lewd;* . . . . II. xii. 73. 8
in *lewd* loves, and wastfull luxuree, ... II. xii. 80. 7
Love, my *lewd* Pilott, hath a restlesse minde; . . . . III. iv. 9. 6
in *lewd* slouth to wast his carelesse day; . . . . III. v. 1. 7
Such laesinesse both *lewd* and poore attonce him made. . . . III. vii. 12. 9
that *lewd* lover did the most lament . . . . III. vii. 20. 1

Lewd—*Continued.*
Ne was she ignoraunt of that *leud* lore, ... III. ix. 28. 5
to leave that *lewd* And loathsom life, ... III. x. 51. 1
Lewd Losse of Time, ... III. xii. 25. 5
with *lewd* termes their lovers to deface. . . . . IV. iv. 4. 5
The more did she pursue her *lewd* intent, ... IV. viii. 35. 8
with *lewd* loves and lust intemperate . . . . IV. ix. 16. 7
sterne Druon, and *lewd* Claribell, ... IV. ix. 20. 8
through *lewd* upbraide Of Ate and Duessa, ... IV. ix. 24. 5
Much was the knight incenst with his *lewd* word . . . . . . V. iii. 36. 1
Where none may be with her *lewd* parts defyled, ... V. ix. 2. 4
with *lewd* poems which he did compyle; . . . . V. ix. 25. 7
lewd Impietie, that her accused sore. . . . . V. ix. 48. 9
doth observe a custome *lewd* and ill, ... VI. i. 13. 3
to make avoure Of the *lewd* words and deedes . . . . VI. iii. 48. 6
a *lewd* foole her leading thorough dry and wet. . . . . . . VI. vi. 16. 9
With these two *lewd* companions, ... VI. viii. 22. 7
Nor draw unto the lure of his *lewd* lay, ... VI. xi. 5. 3
Many *lewd* layes (ah! woe is me the more!) . . . . *H.H.L.* 8

Lewdly. *Lewdly* complainest thou, laesie ladde, ... *S.C.* F. 9
For naught caren that bene so *lewdly* bent. . . . . *S.C.* Ap. 157
He lov'd faire Ladie Estrild, *leudly* lov'd, ... II. x. 17. 6
though my love be not so *lewdly* bent . . . . III. ii. 43. 2
Whom she with leasings *lewdly* did miscall . . . . IV. viii. 24. 8
Whom when so *lewdly* minded Talus found, ... V. ii. 49. 6
'*Lewdly* thou my love depravest, ... V. vii. 32. 8
Talus, hearing her so *lewdly* raile, ... V. xii. 43. 1
my daies I have not *lewdly* spent, ... VI. ii. 31. 1
So *lewdly* had abusde, as ye did lately heare. . . . . VI. vi. 17. 9

Lewdness. if he mislive in *leudnes* and lust, ... *S.C.* May 87
those that Love with *leawdnes* fill. . . . . *T.M.* 384
lewdnes fild him with reprochfull pain Of that foule evill, . . I. iv. 26. 6
Sweete love such *lewdnes* bands from his faire companee. . . III. ii. 41. 9
all that *lewdnesse* love doe hate the light to see. . . . . . . III. iv. 58. 9
With termes of love and *lewdnesse* dissolute; . . . . III. viii. 14. 3
oft their *lewdnes* blotteth good deserts with blame. . . . . . V. iii. 38. 9

Lewkenor's. *Lewkenors* stile that hath her beautie told. . . . *Com. Son.* iv.14

Liagore. the lilly handed *Liagore* . . . . III. iv. 41. 1
(This *Liagore* whilome had learned skill . . . . III. iv. 41. 2
Liagore much praisd for wise behests; . . . . IV. xi. 51. 4

Libanon. *See* **Lebanon.**

Libbard, -s. *See* **Leopard, -s.**

Liberal. To be both gratious and eke *liberall:* . . . . I. x. 34. 5
Shewing her selfe both wise and *liberall.* . . . . II. ix. 20. 5

Liberties. loosing one, two *liberties* ye gayne, ... *Am.* lxv. 3

Liberty. ylike to me was *libertee* and lyfe. . . . . *S.C.* D. 36
why should he that is at *libertie* Make himselfe bond? . . . . *Hub.* 132
with *libertie* full large, ... *Hub.* 300
have the Gospell of free *libertie.*' . . . . *Hub.* 478
Free *libertie* to chaunt our charmes at will, ... *T.M.* 244
Now being let to runne at *libertie* . . . . *T.M.* 550
Like a great Lord of peerelesse *liberty;* . . . . *Com. Son.* i. 10
to enjoy delight with *libertie*, ... *Mui.* 210
round about them feed at *libertie*. . . . . *Col.* 55
Their God himselfe, grievd at my *libertie*, ... I. ix. 10. 7
that proud avenging boy . . . curbd my *libertee*. . . . . . . I. ix. 12. 4
To him that gives thee life and *liberty;* . . . . II. v. 13. 6
to her captive sonne yield his first *libertee*. . . . . II. v. 17. 9
Gan coyne streight lawes to curb their *liberty:* . . . . III. ii. 2. 6
He lefte his captive Beast at *liberty*, ... III. vii. 38. 2
has full large to live and spend at *libertie*. . . . . III. ix. 3. 9
of his owne him lefte not *liberty:* . . . . III. x. 2. 4
liberty to frame Their purpost flight, ... III. x. 16. 4
for his love him promist *libertie* at last. . . . . IV. viii. 52. 9
To win her grace his *libertie* to get: . . . . IV. viii. 53. 6
mine and his Aemylias *libertie*. . . . . IV. viii. 57. 7
For whose sole *libertie* I love and life did stake. . . . . . . IV. viii. 60. 9
unto former *liberty* restore. . . . . IV. ix. 8. 7
How she that Ladies *libertie* might enterprize. . . . . IV. xii. 28. 9
To purchase a licentious *libertie:* . . . . V. v. 25. 6
Make meanes to win thy *libertie* forlorne, ... V. v. 40. 2
The Fayrie, glad to gaine his *libertie*, ... V. v. 55. 4
The *liberty* of women did repeale, ... V. vii. 42. 5
'then *liberty* I leave to you . . . . VI. i. 28. 7
heavy armes . . . hinder him from *libertie* to pant; . . . . . VI. iv. 19. 3
she, the Ladie of her *libertie*, ... VI. vii. 31. 5
In yron chaines of *liberty* bereft, ... VI. viii. 1. 4
Ne list me leave my loved *libertie* . . . . VI. viii. 21. 3
if ye list have *liberty* ye may; . . . . VI. viii. 29. 7
no more Him *liberty* was left aloud to rore: . . . . VI. xii. 36. 5
got into the world at *liberty* againe. . . . . VI. xii. 38. 9
fondly feare to loose your *liberty;* . . . . *Am.* lxv. 2

Library. as they gan his *Library* to vew, ... II. ix. 59. 3

Libyan. under him he saw his *Lybian* steed to praunce; . . . . II. viii. 17. 9

License. wot what *license*, or what Pas they had? . . . . . . *Hub.* 367
Doth *license* him depart at sound of morning droome.' . . . . I. ix. 41. 9

Licentious. with lewd speeches, and *licentious* deeds, ... *Col.* 787
Abusd her plenty . . . To all *licentious* lust, ... II. vii. 16. 8
ever mixt their song with light *licentious* toyes. . . . . . . II. xii. 72. 9
with their might beat downe *licentious* lust, ... V. iv. 2. 4
The foolish Kyte, led with *licentious* will, ... V. v. 15. 5
To purchase a *licentious* libertie: . . . . V. v. 25. 6
spake *licentious* words and hatefull things . . . . VI. xii. 28. 5
lordeth in *licentious* blisse Of her freewill, ... *Am.* x. 3

Lich. *See* **Like.**

Lick. the fat from their beards doen *lick:* . . . . *S.C.* S. 123

Licked. he . . . *lickt* her lilly hands with fawning tong, . . I. iii. 6. 2

Lid. *See* **Eyelid.**

Lidded. *See* **Black-lidded.**

Lidge. *See* **Ledge.**

Lids. *See* **Eyelids.**
through their *lids* his wanton eies do peepe . . . II. v. 34. 5
Cover'd with *lids* deviz'd of substance sly, . . . II. ix. 46. 7

Lie. on the plaine outstretched *lie,* . . . *Bel.*[2] vi. 12
spirites, whose ashie cinders *lie* Under deep ruines, . . . *Ro.* i. 1
So broke his oaten pype, and downe dyd *lye.* . . . *S.C.* Ja. 72
learne to *ligge* soft: . . . *S.C.* May 125
many wyld beastes *liggen* in waite . . . *S.C.* May 217
The fatte Oxe, that wont *ligge* in the stal, . . . *S.C.* S. 118
ever *liggen* in watch and ward, . . . *S.C.* S. 234
There mayst thou *ligge* in a vetchy bed, . . . *S.C.* S. 256
ligge so layd, when Winter doth her straine. . . . *S.C.* O. 12
all the worthies *liggen* wrapt in leade, . . . *S.C.* O. 63
All slaine with darts, *lie* wallowed in their blood. . . . *Gn.* 432
there thou needs must learne to laugh, to *lie,* . . . *Hub.* 505
everie stick that underneath did *ly,* . . . *Hub.* 1008
Were forst their auncient houses to let *lie,* . . . *Hub.* 1178
he found, where sleeping he did *ly.* . . . *Hub.* 1320
Shall die in darknesse, and *lie* hid in slime: . . . *T.M.* 106
lie drowned in deep wretchednes, . . . *T.M.* 149
like brute beasts doo *lie* in loathsome den . . . *T.M.* 531
lye in mine owne ashes, . . . *Ti.* 40
shall in rustie darknes ever *lie,* . . . *Ti.* 349
die In foule forgetfulnesse, and nameles *lie.* . . . *Ti.* 378
the deaw which yet on them does *lie,* . . . *Mui.* 181
thousand perills *lie* in close awaite . . . *Mui.* 221
The velvet nap which on his wings doth *lie,* . . . *Mui.* 333
as one toyld with travaile downe doth *lye,* . . . *D.* 255
in his traunce I would not let him *lie,* . . . *D.* 550
all dead in dole did *lie:* . . . *Col.* 22
The shepheards there abroad may safely *lie,* . . . *Col.* 316
To let thy fame *lie* so in hidden shade: . . . *Col.* 407
drownded *lie* in pleasures wastefull well, . . . *Col.* 762
The antique rolles, which there *lye* hidden still, . . . I. Pr. 2. 4
your vanquisht foes before you *lye,* . . . I. i. 27. 4
wakeful dogges before them farre doe *lye,* . . . I. i. 40. 4
all in deadly sleepe did drowned *lye* . . . I. iii. 16. 3
Though conquered now he *lye* on lowly land; . . . I. iii. 37. 7
my liege, doth lucklesse *ly* . . . I. viii. 2. 4
to have slain the man, that on the ground did *lye.* . . . I. viii. 19. 9
me . . . that here *lye* dying every stound, . . . I. viii. 38. 4
wasted life doe *lye* in ashes low: . . . I. ix. 8. 5
here *ly* downe, and to thy rest betake, . . . I. ix. 44. 2
Hermitage . . . Wherein an aged holy man did *lie,* . . . I. x. 46. 5
streight on grownd made him full low to *lye;* . . . II. v. 12. 5
him that low in dust doth *ly,* . . . II. vii. 11. 7
Lamenting Sorrow did in darknes *lye,* . . . II. vii. 22. 8
Lo! Tantalus, I here tormented *lye:* . . . II. vii. 59. 5
Loe! where he now inglorious doth *lye,* . . . II. viii. 12. 8
at his feet . . . an armed corse did *lye,* . . . II. viii. 23. 8
Nought could he hurt, but still at warde did *ly:* . . . II. viii. 39. 7
passe on forward: so their way does *ly,* . . . II. xi. 14. 2
twixt them both the narrow way doth *ly.'* . . . II. xii. 18. 4
Into great Tethys bosome, where they hidden *lye.* . . . II. xii. 26. 9
what meant those beastes which there did *ly?* . . . II. xii. 84. 9
She with her Nourse adowne to sleepe did *lye;* . . . III. ii. 28. 4
she did *lye* All night in old Tithonus frozen bed, . . . III. iii. 20. 5
there hidden *lye* Light-shonning thefte, . . . III. iv. 58. 1
Mongst whom might be that he did closely *lye,* . . . III. vi. 16. 6
There yet, some say, in secret he does *ly,* . . . III. vi. 46. 4
at last perforce adowne did *ly,* . . . III. vii. 3. 7
After she long in waite for me did *lye,* . . . III. vii. 51. 2
rather had he dy Then, . . . in coward corner *ly.* . . . III. ix. 14. 9
in thine ashes buried low dost *lie,* . . . III. ix. 33. 2
Malbecco, seeing how his losse did *lye,* . . . III. x. 17. 2
tell thy griefe, if any hidden *lye:* . . . III. x. 26. 2
Hence farre away we will blyndfolded *ly,* . . . III. x. 42. 7
His face upon the grownd did groveling *ly,* . . . III. xi. 8. 1
doth thy justice sleepe and silent *ly?* . . . III. xi. 9. 7
A wounded Dragon under him did *ly,* . . . III. xi. 48. 6
either winne him one, or *lye* without the dore. . . . IV. i. 9. 9
the rest him seeing *lie* on ground Ran hastily, . . . IV. i. 43. 3
'Vile hag!' (sayd Scudamour) why dost thou *lye,* . . . IV. i. 48. 1
shade, where shrowded thy may *lie,* . . . IV. iv. 47. 4
he in hell doth *lie,* That lives a loathed life, . . . IV. vii. 11. 8
He bowed low, and so a while did *lie:* . . . IV. viii. 43. 5
namelesse there his bodie now doth *lie;* . . . IV. viii. 49. 2
miserie In which so long he mercilesse did *lie.* . . . IV. viii. 64. 5
did *ly* Long languishing there . . . IV. x. 13. 7
For feare of harme that might *lie* hidden there; . . . IV. x. 20. 2
A bevie of fayre damzels close did *lye,* . . . IV. x. 48. 8
lowest hell, to which I *lie* most neare, . . . IV. xii. 6. 7
This lucklesse Ladie which now here doth headlesse *lie.* . . . V. i. 16. 9
In that same place whereas it now doth *lie.* . . . V. i. 18. 7
Of Justice, which in Talus hand did *lye;* . . . V. ii. 26. 2
All in the powre of their great Maker *lie:* . . . V. ii. 40. 8
Doth not your handmayds life at your foot *lie?'* . . . V. v. 31. 6
Whose life did *lie* in her least eye-lids fall; . . . V. v. 47. 5
Let him lodge hard, and *lie* in strawen bed, . . . V. v. 50. 5
by hard mishap doth *lie* In wretched bondage, . . . V. vi. 10. 6
the bed, where she should *lie,* . . . V. vi. 27. 6
backe returning where his Dame did *lie,* . . . V. vi. 30. 7
on their mother Earths deare lap did *lie,* . . . V. vii. 9. 2
her earthly parts . . . did deeply drowned *lie,* . . . V. vii. 12. 6
An hideous monster doth in darknesse *lie,* . . . V. x. 29. 3
underneath this Idoll there doth *lie* . . . V. xi. 20. 1
it in silver bowre does hidden *ly* . . . VI. Pr. 3. 3
never . . . His limbes would rest, ne *lig* in ease embost, . . . VI. iv. 40. 7
here thus long now *lie* In piteous languor . . . VI. vi. 6. 6
in your selfe your onely helpe doth *lie* . . . VI. vi. 7. 1

Lie—*Continued.*
Mongst rocks and caves, where she enrold doth *lie* . . . VI. vi. 11. 4
still did *lie* as dead, and quake, and quiver, . . . VI. vi. 32. 3
their weapons which thereby did *lie,* . . . VI. vi. 38. 8
when he saw his fellow lifelesse *ly,* . . . VI. vii. 10. 3
Where seeing him so *lie,* he left his steed, . . . VI. vii. 11. 6
to the litle cots, where shepherds *lie* . . . VI. ix. 4. 8
that she thus sicke did *lie,* . . . VI. xi. 9. 1
Oft interlacing many a forged *lie,* . . . VI. xii. 33. 5
in a silver dish did *ly* Twoo golden apples . . . *Am.* lxxvii. 5
when you come whereas my love doth *lie,* . . . *Epith.* 65
Behold how goodly my faire love does *ly,* . . . *Epith.* 305
lyke as when he with thy selfe did *lie* . . . *Epith.* 330
fallen . . . And buried now in their own ashes *ly;* . . . *Com. Son.* iv. 7
they *lye* languishing like thrals forlorne, . . . *H.L.* 136
like a moldwarpe in the earth doth *ly.* . . . *H.L.* 182
Like Tantale, that in store doth sterved *ly,* . . . *H.L.* 200
lie like Gods in yvorie beds arayd, . . . *H.L.* 285
Seeing him *lie* like creature long accurst . . . *H.H.L.* 129
Even heavenly riches, which there hidden *ly* . . . *H.H.B.* 248

Lief. all these were lowe and *lief,* . . . *S.C.* Jul. 165
for love of that is to thee moste *leefe,* . . . *S.C.* S. 11
My little flock, that was to me so *liefe;* . . . *S.C.* D. 146
'I cannot, my *lief* brother, like but well . . . *Hub.* 177
'Colin, my *liefe,* my life, . . . *Col.* 16
you, my *liefe,* yborn of hevenly berth. . . . I. iii. 28. 9
living man mote worthie be to be her *liefe.'* . . . I. ix. 17. 9
'Madame, my *liefe,* For Gods deare love . . . II. i. 16. 1
My *liefe,* my liege, my Soveraine, my deare, . . . II. ix. 4. 5
To chaunge my *liefe,* and love another Dame; . . . III. i. 24. 3
tell me therefore, my liefest *liefe!'* . . . III. ii. 33. 9
more *liefe* Then losse of chastitie, . . . III. viii. 42. 1
them dislodge, all were they *liefe* or loth; . . . III. ix. 13. 8
both full *liefe* him lodging to have lent, . . . III. ix. 14. 3
both full *liefe* his boasting to abate: . . . III. ix. 14. 4
as life were to each other *liefe.* . . . IV. iii. 52. 7
Not to despise that dame which lov'd him *liefe,* . . . IV. ix. 15. 4
He up arose, however *liefe* or loth, . . . VI. i. 44. 3
'My *liefe,* my lifes desire, . . . VI. v. 23. 5
'My *liefe,'* (sayd she) 'ye know that long ygo, . . . VI. xii. 17. 5
she entred, were he *liefe* or sory; . . . VII. vi. 8. 7

Liefer. Had *lever* my foe then my freend he be; . . . *S.C.* May 167
lever had I die then see his deadly face.' . . . I. ix. 32. 9
Me *liefer* were ten thousand deathes priefe . . . II. iv. 28. 8
That death me *liefer* were then such despight, . . . III. i. 24. 4
Me *lever* were with point of foemans speare be dead. . . . III. ii. 6. 9
'Perdy, me *lever* were to weeten that,' . . . III. v. 7. 1
thousand deathes me *lever* were to dye . . . III. vii. 51. 5
Die had she *lever* with Enchanters knife . . . IV. i. 6. 8

Liefest. Cuddie, fresh Cuddie, the *liefest* boye, . . . *S.C.* Au. 195
My *liefest* Lord she thus beguiled had; . . . II. i. 52. 5
fly, O my *liefest* Lord! . . . II. ii. 30. 5
tell me therefore, my *liefest* liefe!' . . . III. ii. 33. 9
loth to leave his *liefest* pelfe behinde; . . . III. x. 15. 6
likly was his *liefest* love to be, . . . IV. vii. 46. 3

Liege. 'O, my *liege* Lord! the God of my life! . . . *S.C.* F. 150
his late chayne his *Liege* unmeete esteemeth; . . . *Hub.* 628
Ah, my *liege* Lord! forgive it unto mee, . . . *Mui.* 102
His *liege,* his Ladie, and his lifes Regent.— . . . *Col.* 235
my dread Lord, that doest *liege* hearts possesse, . . . *Col.* 793
'Ah Sir, my *liege* Lord, and my love, . . . I. i. 51. 1
my *liege,* doth lucklesse ly . . . I. viii. 2. 4
cleeped him his *liege,* to hold of him in fee. . . . II. iii. 8. 9
my *liege,* whose warlike name Is far renowmd . . . II. iii. 35. 3
thus sayd; 'My Lord, my *liege,* . . . II. viii. 55. 5
My liefe, my *liege,* my Soveraine, my deare, . . . II. ix. 4. 5
'Which my *liege* Lady seeing, . . . V. viii. 21. 1
As their true *Liege* and Princesse naturall; . . . V. xii. 24. 8

Liege man. Eftsoones this *liegeman* gan to wexe more bold, . . . II. iii. 9. 2
my trew *liegeman* yield thy selfe for ay, . . . II. viii. 51. 7
Shall yield him selfe his *liegeman,* and sweare fealty. . . . III. iii. 37. 9
Compyld by me, which thy poore *liegeman* am! . . . *H.B.* 273

Liege men. we your *liegemen* faith unto you plight.' . . . III. i. 30. 5
Now were they *liegmen* to this Ladie free, . . . III. i. 44. 8

Liege's. Great shame in *lieges* blood to be embrew'd! . . . VI. vii. 23. 6

Lien. *See* **Lain.**
spirit, . . . Might long perhaps have *lien* in silence . . . *Ded. Son.* xiii. 5
nought but pressed gras where she had *lyen,* . . . I. ix. 15. 2
Who now long time had *lyen* in prison sad; . . . IV. ix. 4. 3
stretcht it selfe as it had long *lyen* still; . . . V. xi. 22. 6
long had *lyen* dead, . . . VI. xi. 50. 9
The which before had *lyen* confused ever. . . . *H.L.* 77

Lies. halfe disbowel'd *lies* above the ground, . . . *Ro.* xxviii. 5
He *lyes* in lingring payne. . . . *S.C.* Jul. 228
With her owne weight down pressed now shee *lies,* . . . *Ti.* 76
Since whose decease, learning *lies* unregarded, . . . *Ti.* 440
Lyes in ambushment of his hoped pray, . . . *Mui.* 404
Amyntas quite is gone, and *lies* full low, . . . *Col.* 434
two, . . . fittest for to forge true-seeming *lyes:* . . . I. i. 38. 7
carelesse Quiet *lyes* Wrapt in eternall silence . . . I. i. 41. 8
There *lies* he now with foule dishonor dead, . . . I. ii. 25. 5
now the pray of fowles in field he *lyes,* . . . I. v. 23. 3
Loe! where your foe *lies* strecht in monstrous length; . . . I. viii. 45. 3
as the tree does fall, so *lyes* it ever low. . . . I. x. 41. 9
this dead corpse, that *lies* here underneath, . . . II. i. 49. 7
now in shade he shrowded yonder *lies.'* . . . II. iii. 35. 5
hidden *lyes* unwares him to surpryse? . . . II. iv. 17. 3
Whiles sad Pyrochles *lies* on sencelesse ground, . . . II. v. 36. 6
Bad therefore I him deeme that thus *lies* dead on field.' . . . II. viii. 14. 9
in the secret of your hart close *lyes,* . . . II. ix. 42. 4

Lies—*Continued.*
leasings, tales, and *lies*. . . . . II. ix. 51. 9
By which he *lyes* entombed solemnly. . . . . II. x. 46. 7
now entombed *lies* at Stoneheng by the heath. . . . . II. x. 67. 9
here before a perlous passage *lyes*, ... II. xii. 17. 8
Rock that *lyes* a litle space From the swift Barry, ... III. iii. 8. 4
Inglorious now *lies* in sencelesse swownd, ... III. iv. 29. 3
there *lyes* . . . An huge eternall Chaos, ... III. vi. 36. 6
lies there on the laire An headlesse heape, ... IV. viii. 51. 5
of the wound he yet in languor *lyes*, ... IV. xi. 5. 7
lies in wretched thraldome, weake and wan, ... V. vi. 16. 3
I chaunst to meete this knight, who there *lyes* slaine, . . . VI. ii. 9. 8
At an Herneshaw, that *lyes* aloft on wing, ... VI. vii. 9. 2
'He *lyes*' (said he) 'upon the cold bare ground, ... VI. vii. 16. 6
in that villaines health her safety *lies*; . . . . . VI. viii. 18. 5
him, that at your footstoole humbled *lies*, ... *Am.* xlix. 11
false forged *lyes*, which thou didst tel, ... *Am.* lxxxv. 7
Liest. beast, That here *liest* senseles, like the corpse deceast, . *Hub.* 1328
Now *lyest* thou of life and honor refte; . . . . . III. iv. 36. 6
Now *lyest* thou a lumpe of earth forlorne; . . . . . III. iv. 36. 7
Lieth. There *lyeth* the Oake, pitied of none! . . . . . *S.C.* F. 221
dead he is, and *lyeth* wrapt in lead, ... *S.C.* Jun. 89
Dead, and *lyeth* wrapt in lead. . . . . . *S.C.* N. 59
lyeth buryed long in Winters bale; . . . . . *S.C.* N. 84
Lo! where beyond he *lyeth* languishing, ... III. i. 38. 1
Lieu. in *lieu* of paines so gracious, ... *Gn.* 333
To thee, small Gnat, in lieu of his *life* saved, ... *Gn.* 687
in *lieu* of mee, Love her; . . . . . *D.* 290
in *lieu* of innocence, Imprinted had that token . . . . . II. ii. 4. 3
Yield you in *lieu* of this your gracious deed? . . . . . III. xii. 39. 4
And me in *lieu* thereof revil'd againe, ... VI. ii. 11. 8
In *lieu* whereof he would to him descrie Great treason . . . VI. vii. 12. 3
in *lieu* of life him lent, ... VI. vii. 21. 6
Song! made in *lieu* of many ornaments, ... *Epith.* 427
In *lieu* whereof graunt, ... *H.B.* 274
nought thou ask'st in *lieu* of all this love, ... *H.H.L.* 176
Life. Which make this *life* wretched and miserable, ... *Pet.*² vi. 13
I wish I might this wearie *life* forgoe, ... *Pet.*² vii. 5
give a second *life* to dead decayes! . . . . . *Ro.* Env. 6
'O, my liege Lord! the God of my *life!* . . . . . *S.C.* F. 150
shepheardes so witen ech others *life*, ... *S.C.* May 159
her, whose love as *lyfe* I wayd, ... *S.C.* Jun. 47
ylike to me was libertee and *lyfe*. . . . . . *S.C.* D. 36
My freedome lorne, my *life* he lefte to mone. . . . . . *S.C.* D. 52
long lasting *life* with joyous glee, ... *Gn.* 59
who can lead, then, a more happie *life* . . . . . *Gn.* 121
leads as joyfull *life*; . . . . . *Gn.* 150
His dearest *life* did trust to careles sleep; . . . . . *Gn.* 243
life out of his members did depart: . . . . . *Gn.* 293
thy *life* more deare and precious Was than mine owne, . . . *Gn.* 331
For that I thee restor'd to *life* againe, ... *Gn.* 354
sad Eurydice . . . no more Must turne to *life*, ... *Gn.* 434
The faults which *life* hath trespassed before. . . . . . *Gn.* 448
his vowed *life* to spill For Countreyes health, ... *Gn.* 603
To thee, small Gnat, in *lieu* of his life saved, ... *Gn.* 687
As well of worldly livelode as of *life*, ... *Hub.* 147
Beggers *life* is best; . . . . . *Hub.* 180
husbands *life* is labourous and hard? . . . . . *Hub.* 266
An easie *life*, and fit high God to please. . . . . . *Hub.* 395
no good trade of *life* did entertaine, ... *Hub.* 398
on us taken anie state of *life*, ... *Hub.* 407
The bread of *life* powr'd downe from heavenly place. . . . *Hub.* 438
Delights of *life*, and ornaments of light! . . . . . *Hub.* 762
doth his *life* in so long tendance spend! . . . . . *Hub.* 908
Who will not venture *life* a King to be, ... *Hub.* 979
I chose before a *life* of wretchednes. . . . . . *Hub.* 984
sith I For it did put my *life* in jeopardie: . . . . . *Hub.* 1028
Of wretched *life* the onely joy shee is, ... *T.M.* 131
all mans *life* me seemes a Tragedy, ... *T.M.* 157
mans *life* in his likest image Was limned forth, ... *T.M.* 201
the troublous state Of Lovers *life* . . . . . *T.M.* 382
Life, and Death, is in thy doomefull writing! . . . . . *Com. Son.* i. 13
So *life* exchanging for his countries good. . . . . . *Ti.* 301
interchanged *life* unto them lent, ... *Ti.* 387
Her back againe to *life* sent for his sake. . . . . . *Ti.* 392
to those ashes gave a second *life*, ... *Ti.* 669
his *life* from yron death assure, ... *Mui.* 59
to sheild Achilles *life* from fate of Troyan field. . . . . *Mui.* 64
in this wretched *life* dooth take delight, ... *D.* 9
'Who *life* dooes loath, and longs to bee unbound . . . . . *D.* 85
harts deep sorrow hates both *life* and light. . . . . . *D.* 91
reft fro me my love, my *life*, my hart: . . . . . *D.* 160
Revoked *life*, that would have fled away, ... *D.* 188
ere that *life* her lodging did forsake, ... *D.* 260
Our *life* afflicted with incessant paine, ... *D.* 275
life I hate, because it will not last; . . . . . *D.* 425
death I hate, because it *life* doth marre; . . . . . *D.* 426
Is it so uneath To leave this *life*, ... *D.* 448
life drawes care, and care continuall woe; . . . . . *D.* 450
wishfull thing this sad *life* to forgoe: . . . . . *D.* 452
when *life* parts vouchsafe to close mine eye. . . . . . *D.* 511
His wasted *life* her wearie lodge forwent. . . . . . *As.* 174
'Colin, my liefe, my *life*, ... *Col.* 16
'Now by my *life* this was a mery lay, ... *Col.* 157
goddesse of my *life*, ... *Col.* 170
Who *life* doth loath, and longs death to behold, ... *Col.* 204
Bold men, presuming *life* for gaine to sell, ... *Col.* 209
life to move it selfe upon the water. . . . . . *Col.* 219
To her my *life* I wholly sacrifice: . . . . . *Col.* 475
My thought, my heart, my love, my *life* is shee, ... *Col.* 476

Life—*Continued.*
thy chaste *life* and vertue I esteeme: . . . . . *Col.* 573
So long as *life* my limbs doth hold together; . . . . . *Col.* 629
sooth to say, it is no sort of *life*, ... *Col.* 688
praise, Which gives them *life*, ... *Ded. Son.* iv. 11
Most Noble Lord, the pillor of my *life*, ... *Ded. Son.* vii. 1
So pure . . . She was in *life* and every vertuous lore; . . . . I. i. 5. 2
Making her death their *life*, ... I. i. 25. 9
such as drunke her *life* the which them nurst! . . . . . I. i. 26. 7
highest God, the Lord of *life* and light: . . . . . I. i. 37. 6
You, . . . destinie Hath made judge of my *life* or death . . . I. i. 51. 9
all so deare as *life* is to my hart, I deeme your love, ... I. i. 54. 2
Yrkesome of *life*, and too long lingring night. . . . . . I. ii. 6. 5
ever most adord As the God of my *life?* . . . . . I. iii. 7. 9
As if her *life* upon the wager lay; . . . . . I. iii. 12. 2
the thirsty land Dronke up his *life*; . . . . . I. iii. 20. 5
He to him lept, in minde to reave his *life*, ... I. iii. 36. 2
mourning altars, purgd with enimies *life*, ... I. iii. 36. 7
Life from Sansfoy thou tookst, Sansloy shall from thee take.' . I. iii. 36. 9
therefore, of *life* him not deprive.' . . . . . I. iii. 37. 9
life forsooke his stubborne brest. . . . . . I. iii. 42. 9
otherwise His *life* he led in lawlesse riotise, ... I. iv. 20. 5
In shape and *life* more like a monster then a man. . . . . . I. iv. 22. 9
Ne would his looser *life* be tide to law, ... I. iv. 26. 3
His *life* was nigh unto deaths dore yplaste; . . . . . I. iv. 28. 1
hee . . . scarse good morsell all his *life* did taste, ... I. iv. 28. 3
He led a wretched *life*, unto himselfe unknowne. . . . . . I. iv. 28. 9
fretting griefe, the enemy of *life*: . . . . . I. iv. 35. 5
Dead sculls and bones of men whose *life* had gone astray. . . I. iv. 36. 9
to my loathed *life* now shewes some light, ... I. iv. 48. 2
Of endlesse *life* he might him not deprive, ... I. v. 40. 4
which the lovely boy Did love as *life*, ... I. vi. 17. 7
Whom, . . . He nousled up in *life* and manners wilde, ... I. vi. 23. 8
dronke with blood, yet thristed after *life*: . . . . . I. vi. 38. 8
That him of *life*, and us of joy, hath refte?' . . . . . I. vi. 39. 6
hardly he the flitted *life* does win . . . . . I. vii. 21. 7
threds . . . The which my *life* and love together tyde? . . . I. vii. 22. 6
life recover'd had the raine, And over-wrestled his strong enimy, ... I. vii. 24. 5
captiv'd, of *life* or death he stood in doubt. . . . . . I. vii. 26. 9
That *life* nigh crusht out of his panting brest: . . . . . I. viii. 15. 3
so soone as *life* did me admitt Into this world, ... I. ix. 3. 5
wasted *life* doe lye in ashes low: . . . . . I. ix. 8. 5
lovers *life*, As losse of time . . . I ever scornd, ... I. ix. 10. 1
prickt forth with jollitee Of looser *life* . . . . . I. ix. 12. 6
you, my Lord, the Patrone of my *life*, ... I. ix. 17. 6
Nor . . . blood in all his face appeares, Nor *life* in limbe; . . I. ix. 22. 5
hope . . . That earst us held in love of lingring *life*; . . . . I. ix. 29. 6
Ne yet assur'd of *life* by you, Sir knight, ... I. ix. 30. 7
A dreary corse, whose *life* away did pas, ... I. ix. 36. 5
death after *life*, does greatly please.' . . . . . I. ix. 40. 9
'The terme of *life* is limited, ... I. ix. 41. 2
'Who *life* did limit by almightie doome,' . . . . . I. ix. 41. 6
'The lenger *life*, I wote, the greater sin; . . . . . I. ix. 43. 1
life must *life*, and blood must blood, repay. . . . . . I. ix. 43. 6
Is not enough thy evill *life* forespent? . . . . . I. ix. 43. 7
Th' ill to prevent, that *life* ensewen may; . . . . . I. ix. 44. 3
what hath *life* that may it loved make, ... I. ix. 44. 4
All which, and thousands mo, do make a loathsome *life*. . . I. ix. 44. 9
Thy *life* shutt up for death so oft did call; . . . . . I. ix. 45. 6
The crudled cold ran to her well of *life*, ... I. ix. 52. 2
sacred lore And pure unspotted *life*: . . . . . I. x. 3. 3
to kill, And rayse againe to *life* . . . . . I. x. 19. 9
mortall *life* gan loath as thing forlore, ... I. x. 21. 5
Disdeining *life*, desiring leave to dye, ... I. x. 22. 8
vowed all Their *life* to service of high heavens King, ... I. x. 36. 4
His mortall *life* he learned had to frame . . . . . I. x. 45. 8
it rightly hot The well of *life*, ... I. xi. 29. 9
unto *life* the dead it could restore, ... I. xi. 30. 1
Ne living wight would have him *life* behott: . . . . . I. xi. 38. 4
happy *life* to all which thereon fedd, ... I. xi. 46. 5
life eke everlasting did befall: . . . . . I. xi. 46. 6
The tree of *life*, the crime of our first fathers fall. . . . . I. xi. 46. 9
Life and long health that gracious ointment gave, ... I. xi. 48. 6
al that *life* preserved did detest; . . . . . I. xi. 49. 3
downe he fell, and forth his *life* did breath, ... I. xi. 54. 1
That signe of last outbreathed *life* . . . . . I. xii. 2. 5
remaynd Some lingring *life* within his hollow brest, ... I. xii. 10. 4
Thy *life* and honor late adventurest, ... I. xii. 29. 8
To see faire heavens face, and *life* not leave, ... II. i. 17. 4
forth her bleeding *life* does raine, ... II. i. 38. 7
he hoped faire To call backe *life* . . . . . II. i. 43. 7
as hating *life* and light. . . . . . II. i. 45. 9
hold sad *life* in long captivitee; . . . . . II. i. 48. 3
Thus enter we Into this *life* with woe, ... II. ii. 2. 9
They heapt huge strokes the scorned *life* to quell, ... II. ii. 20. 5
I give thee *life*: . . . . . II. iii. 8. 5
her silly *life* to save, ... II. iii. 36. 3
Whom that mad man of *life* nigh late deprivd, ... II. iv. 16. 3
during *life* will never be appeasd!' . . . . . II. iv. 33. 6
rash Occasion makes unquiet *life!'* . . . . . II. iv. 44. 7
Who ever doth to temperaunce apply His stedfast *life*, ... II. v. 1. 2
every way did seeke into his *life*; . . . . . II. v. 9. 2
To him that gives thee *life* and liberty: . . . . . II. v. 13. 6
her enemies And foes of *life*, ... II. vi. 1. 7
make the *life* unsweet: . . . . . II. vii. 14. 2
Like Angels *life* was then mens happy cace; . . . . . II. vii. 16. 5
life for gold engage. . . . . . II. vii. 18. 5
both did gnash their teeth, and both did threten *life*. . . . II. vii. 21. 9
a lamp, whose *life* does fade away, ... II. vii. 29. 7

Life—*Continued.*
had both *life* and sence, II. vii. 40. 8
Socrates; . . . Pourd out his *life* II. vii. 52. 8
Delivered up the Lord of *life* to dye, II. vii. 62. 6
this frayle *life* of man, II. vii. 65. 4
The *life* did flit away out of her nest, II. vii. 66. 8
life ere long shall to her home retire, II. viii. 7. 8
finding *life* not yet dislodged quight, II. viii. 9. 7
did his *life* her fatall date expyre, II. viii. 24. 3
His *life* for dew revenge should deare abye? II. viii. 28. 8
his Lordes *life* did assure. II. viii. 30. 9
His cursed *life* out of her lodge have rent; II. viii. 32. 3
cleft his head in twaine, and *life* thence dispossest. II. viii. 33. 9
all the sinnes wherewith his lewd *life* did abound. II. viii. 45. 9
Ne thenceforth *life* ne corage did appeare; II. viii. 46. 3
As one that loathed *life,* and yet despysd to dye. II. viii. 50. 9
More glory thought to give *life* then decay, II. viii. 51. 4
Life will I graunt thee for thy valiaunce, II. viii. 51. 8
in despight of *life* for death doe call.' II. viii. 52. 4
Life having maystered her sencelesse foe, II. viii. 53. 2
with reverence dew As to the patrone of his *life,* II. viii. 55. 4
'if in that picture dead Such *life* ye read, II. ix. 3. 2
did them meditate all his *life* long, II. ix. 54. 3
Whence all that lives does borrow *life* and light, II. x. 2. 2
His *life,* and long good fortune, II. x. 13. 9
he an end of batteill and of *life* did make. II. x. 16. 9
she much more than her owne *life* him lov'd; II. x. 28. 2
A private *life* ledd in Albania With Gonorill, II. x. 29. 7
weary of that wretched *life* her selfe she hong. II. x. 32. 9
First Gorboman, a man of vertuous *life,* II. x. 44. 3
Till he surrendered Realme and *life* to fate. II. x. 45. 5
Left of his *life* most famous memory, II. x. 46. 2
he was by Jove depryv'd Of *life* II. x. 70. 9
his dearest *life* For her defence II. xi. 16. 6
She him remercied as the Patrone of her *life.* II. xi. 16. 9
So feeble is mans state, and *life* unsound, II. xi. 30. 3
Yet *life* he saw, and felt his mighty mayne, II. xi. 44. 4
How to take *life* from that dead-living swayne, II. xi. 44. 7
so often as his *life* decayd, II. xi. 45. 3
Did *life* with usury to him restore, II. xi. 45. 4
The lothfull *life,* now loosd from sinfull bands, II. xi. 46. 3
Ne stird, till hope of *life* did him forsake: II. xi. 46. 8
he began to faint, and *life* decay: II. xi. 48. 6
Both of their *life* and fame, II. xii. 7. 9
powre, to whom the care Of *life,* . . . perteines II. xii. 47. 3
The foe of *life,* that good envyes to all, II. xii. 48. 4
Of mortall *life* the leafe, the bud, the flowre; II. xii. 75. 2
'Sad end,' (quoth he) 'of *life* intemperate, II. xii. 85. 6
excellence Of his creation, when he *life* began, II. xii. 87. 3
mischievous mischaunce his *life* and limbs did spare. III. i. 6. 9
so loose *life,* and so ungentle trade, III. i. 67. 5
Sithence I loathed have my *life* to lead, III. ii. 6. 6
her *life* at last must lincke in that same knot. III. ii. 23. 9
which on my *life* doth feed, III. ii. 37. 4
Threatning to swallow up my fearefull *lyfe?* III. iv. 8. 6
Some hard mishap in hazard of his *life.* III. iv. 24. 6
soone as *life* recovered had the raine, III. iv. 35. 5
Now lyest thou of *life* and honor refte; III. iv. 36. 6
Ne of thy late *life* memory is lefte, III. iv. 36. 8
So *life* is losse, and death felicity: III. iv. 38. 7
Sad *life* worse then glad death; III. iv. 38. 8
Some litle *life* his feeble sprites emong; III. iv. 41. 8
Our *life* is day, but death with darknesse doth begin. III. iv. 59. 9
fro me reft both *life* and light attone. III. v. 7. 6
load upon him layd his *life* for to have had. III. v. 22. 9
made more haste the *life* to have bereav'd; III. v. 28. 8
if *life* Yett in his frosen members did remaine; III. v. 31. 1
By this he had sweet *life* recur'd agayne, III. v. 34. 1
deemd the beast had bene depriv'd Of *life,* III. v. 37. 5
love so fayre a Lady that his *life* releast? III. v. 43. 9
Thy *life* she saved by her gratious deed; III. v. 45. 3
Thy *life* she gave, thy *life* she doth deserve: III. v. 46. 8
neither blood in face nor *life* in hart It left, III. v. 48. 6
More deare then *life* she tendered, III. v. 51. 2
Doe *life* conceive and quickned are by kynd: III. vi. 8. 6
th' authour of *life* and light; III. vi. 9. 2
Was the disturber of all civill *life,* III. vi. 14. 8
The state of *life* out of the griesly shade. III. vi. 37. 5
when the *life* decayes and forme does fade, III. vi. 37. 7
He wist not how him to despoile of *life,* III. vii. 33. 1
Wherewith she many had of *life* depriv'd; III. vii. 40. 2
Badd her command my *life* to save or spill. III. vii. 54. 2
in the stead Of *life,* she put a Spright. III. viii. 7. 9
her honor, which she more then *life* prefard. III. viii. 14. 9
Him bett so sore, that *life* and sence did much dismay III. viii. 31. 9
had from death to *life* him newly wonne. III. x. 33. 4
he her prayd, . . . To save his *life,* III. x. 50. 8
to leave that lewd And loathsom *life,* III. x. 51. 2
hardly he with *life* away does fly, III. x. 53. 8
death and *life* attonce unto him gives, III. x. 60. 3
Threatning into his *life* to make a breach, III. xi. 12. 7
life is wretchednesse. III. xi. 14. 9
'*Life* is not lost,' (said she) III. xi. 19. 8
soone they *life* conceiv'd, III. xii. 9. 9
from thenceforth a wretched *life* they ladd, III. xii. 16. 7
life she him envyde, and long'd revenge to see: III. xii. 34. 9
He, glad of *life,* that lookt for death III. xii. 35. 8
wearied his *life* with dull delayes. III. xii. 44. *or.* 4
her honor, dearer then her *life,* IV. i. 6. 6
each of *life* sought others to deprive, IV. i. 23. 8

Life—*Continued.*
life it is to her, when others sterve IV. i. 26. 3
That she may sucke their *life,* IV. i. 26. 5
'Unworthy *life,* that love with guile hast gotten; IV. i. 51. 7
as if their springs of *life* were spent; IV. ii. 18. 4
wondrous chaste of *life,* yet lov'd of Knights and Lords. IV. ii. 35. 9
life to hazard for faire Ladies looke; IV. ii. 40. 6
like that roote that doth her *life* divide, IV. ii. 43. 7
with unwearied fingers drawing out The lines of *life,* IV. ii. 48. 4
Beholding how the thrids of *life* they span: IV. ii. 49. 2
durst Come see the secret of the *life* of man, IV. ii. 49. 7
'the terme of each mans *life* IV. ii. 52. 1
Eftsoones his *life* may passe into the next: IV. ii. 52. 6
in seeking for her children three Long *life,* IV. iii. 2. 3
As if that *life* to losse they had forelent, IV. iii. 6. 8
Have I thus long thy *life* unto thee let: IV. iii. 11. 4
making way unto his dearest *life,* IV. iii. 12. 6
In whom he liv'd anew, of former *life* deprived. IV. iii. 13. 9
still the *life* stood fearelesse of her foe; IV. iii. 17. 5
feeling *life* to fayle, it fell, IV. iii. 20. 9
him fild With double *life* and griefe; IV. iii. 22. 3
Into his throate and *life* it pierced quight, IV. iii. 30. 4
life and labour both in vaine to spend. IV. iii. 32. 5
Ne either cared *life* to save or spill, IV. iii. 36. 6
life it selfe seemd loathsome, and long safetie ill. IV. iii. 36. 9
With whom he ledd a long and happie *life;* IV. iii. 52. 5
as *life* were to each other liefe. IV. iii. 52. 7
His *life* he then would spend to justifie his right. IV. iv. 10. 9
so sore that none him *life* behote. IV. iv. 40. 9
as her *life* by her esteemed deare. IV. v. 6. 2
Ne in his face or bloud or *life* appeard; IV. vi. 37. 3
Death is to him, that wretched *life* doth lead, IV. vii. 11. 7
lives a loathed *life,* and wishing cannot die. IV. vii. 11. 9
She ran in hast his *life* to have bereft; IV. vii. 32. 2
all his *life,* which afterwards he lad, IV. viii. 2. 4
selfe-disliked *life,* doth thee thus wretched make? IV. viii. 14. 9
inward griefe or wilfull scorne Of *life* IV. viii. 15. 6
make me loath this *life,* still longing for to die. IV. viii. 16. 9
An happie *life* with grace and good accord, IV. viii. 18. 2
The whiles his *life* ran foorth in bloudie streame, IV. viii. 45. 8
eke too loose of *life,* and eke of love too light. IV. viii. 49. 9
For whose sole libertie I love and *life* did stake. IV. viii. 60. 9
chiefe Of all her land and lordship during *life.* IV. ix. 15. 8
Druons delight was all in single *life,* IV. ix. 21. 1
I wast my *life,* and doe my daies devowre. IV. ix. 39. 5
I neither can my love ne yet my *life* forgo.' IV. ix. 39. 9
Venus Temple is describ'd; And lovers *life* forth set. IV. x. Arg.
wish to *life* return'd againe to bee. IV. x. 23. 8
that wretched Greeke, that *life* forlore, IV. x. 40. 5
In languor wastes his *life:* IV. xii. Arg.
greedy seas doe in the spoile of *life* delight. IV. xii. 6. 9
if that *life* ye unto me decree, IV. xii. 10. 1
deeme unworthy or of love or *life,* IV. xii. 16. 6
In which his *life* unluckily was layd, IV. xii. 28. 2
love forbid him, that is *life* denayd; IV. xii. 28. 7
To graunt to her her sonnes *life,* IV. xii. 29. 7
True love despiseth shame, when *life* is cald in dread. V. i. 27. 9
The fortune of her *life* long time did feare: V. ii. 3. 4
'Now by my *life,*' (sayd he) 'and God to guide, V. ii. 10. 5
Twixt *life* and death long to and fro she weaved, V. iv. 10. 7
Which to her in that daunger hope of *life* did offer. V. iv. 10. 9
For any death to chaunge *life,* though most bad: V. iv. 11. 5
more then losse of *life* ydreaded it; V. iv. 25. 5
lead that shamefull *life,* unworthy of a Knight.' V. iv. 32. 9
all that while her *life* she safely garded; V. v. 8. 8
as if her *life* forsooke, V. v. 11. 4
might have had of *life* or death election: V. v. 26. 5
have agreed To thrall my looser *life,* V. v. 29. 9
Doth not your handmayds *life* at your foot lie?' V. v. 31. 6
thraldome find For lending *life* to me, V. v. 32. 5
she might his wretched *life* bereave. V. v. 37. 5
Chiefely by him whose *life* her law doth bynd, V. v. 41. 7
Whose *life* did lie in her least eye-lids fall; V. v. 47. 5
Life, freedome, grace, and gifts of great availe, V. v. 49. 3
Whose *life* and manners straunge she never knew; V. vi. 12. 7
will ye betray My *life* now too, V. vi. 25. 3
much lesse honour by that warlike kinde Of *life:* V. vi. 32. 6
They tied were to stedfast chastity And continence of *life,* V. vii. 9. 8
for his sake thy *life* thou gavest.' V. vii. 32. 6
Then brought he forth Incontinence of *lyfe,* V. ix. 48. 7
'yet now I gin new *life* to feele; V. x. 20. 4
nought else but bare *life* doth remaine; V. x. 21. 7
Is liker lingring death then loathed *life* to bee.' V. x. 21. 9
life enjoy for any composition: V. x. 27. 5
powred forth his wretched *life* in deadly dreare. V. x. 35. 9
It often fals, in course of common *life,* V. xi. 1. 1
earst was dead, restor'd to *life* againe, V. xi. 16. 6
her imprisond hath, and her *life* often sought. V. xi. 39. 9
'Now sure and by my *life,* V. xi. 41. 1
Though I this dearest *life* for her doe spend.' V. xi. 43. 4
Fro dangers dread his doubtfull *life* to save; V. xi. 46. 4
sought his *life* for to empaire: V. xi. 48. 5
Dearer is love then *life,* and fame then gold; V. xi. 63. 8
new *life* to her lent in midst of deadly feare. V. xii. 12. 9
never washt In all her *life,* V. xii. 30. 2
some *life* remayned secretly; V. xii. 39. 7
Into the *life* of his malignant foe: VI. i. 37. 3
save my *life,* which lot before your foot doth lay.' VI. i. 39. 9
I will it graunt, your hopelesse *life* to save, VI. i. 42. 5
By which he had to her both *life* and love restord. VI. i. 45. 9

Life—*Continued.*
Twixt *life* and death, not knowing what was donne. . . . . . VI. ii. 48. 6
For first, next after *life,* he tendered her good. . . . . . . VI. iii. 11. 9
wretched *life* forlorne for vengement of his theft. . . . . VI. iii. 18. 9
ran at him, as he would devoure His *life* . . . . VI. iii. 48. 8
He saw his *life* powrd forth despiteously; . . . . VI. iii. 51. 4
Would streight dislodge the wretched wearie *life*. . . . . . VI. v. 5. 5
Therein the Hermite, which his *life* here led . . . . . . VI. v. 35. 5
As one that had no *life* him left through former feare. . . . VI. vi. 32. 9
That ever I this *life* unto thee lent, ... VI. vi. 33. 5
thy *life* unto this Ladie fayre I given have, ... VI. vi. 36. 1
onely suffred him this wretched *life* to live. . . . . . . VI. vi. 36. 9
To whom his *life* he graunted for her love, ... VI. vi. 37. 3
He of the Prince his *life* received late, ... VI. vii. 2. 4
Great treason to him meant, his *life* to reave. . . . . . . VI. vii. 12. 4
The Prince soone hearkned, and his *life* forgave. . . . . . VI. vii. 12. 5
glad of *life,* and willing eke to wreake The guilt on him . VI. vii. 13. 6
So hard a taske as *life* for hyre to sell; . . . . VI. vii. 15. 3
life so dearely did redeeme.' . . . . VI. vii. 15. 9
That recreant knight, whose hated *life* I sought? . . . . . VI. vii. 16. 4
for his sake his deare *life* had forgone; . . . . VI. vii. 18. 2
Plaine signes in him of *life* and livelihead: . . . . . . VI. vii. 20. 5
in lieu of *life* him lent, ... VI. vii. 21. 6
Having subdew'd yet did to *life* restore;) . . . . VI. viii. 4. 5
My *life* will by his death have lamentable end. . . . . . VI. viii. 17. 9
endured for her sake Great perill of his *life,* . . . . . . VI. viii. 33. 9
Readie to launch her brest, and let out loved *life*. . . . . VI. viii. 48. 9
For her did languish, and his deare *life* spend; . . . . . VI. ix. 10. 6
to commend the happie *life* Which Shepheards lead, ... VI. ix. 18. 8
Leading a *life* so free and fortunate . . . . VI. ix. 19. 3
learn'd to love more deare This lowly quiet *life* . . . . . VI. ix. 25. 9
Of *life,* which here in lowlinesse ye lead, ... VI. ix. 27. 6
Sith each unto himselfe his *life* may fortunize.' . . . . . VI. ix. 30. 9
This simple sort of *life* that shepheards lead, ... VI. ix. 33. 8
His *life* he steemed dearer then his frend: . . . . VI. x. 35. 5
she nought did but lament Her wretched *life* . . . . . . VI. x. 44. 4
They found that *life* did yet in her remaine: . . . . . . VI. xi. 22. 2
they to *life* recovered her at last: . . . . VI. xi. 22. 6
How he might save her *life,* if *life* did last; . . . . . . VI. xi. 34. 5
life to feele that long for death had sought. . . . . . . VI. xi. 45. 5
till that her syre Departed *life,* . . . . VI. xii. 10. 3
death for *life* exchanged foolishlie: . . . . VII. vi. 6. 4
death, instead of *life,* have sucked from our Nurse! . . . . . VII. vi. 6. 9
all other creatures, What-ever *life* or motion do retaine, . . VII. vii. 4. 2
all creatures to maintaine In state of *life?* . . . . VII. vii. 22. 5
O weake *life!* that does leane On thing so tickle . . . . . VII. vii. 22. 5
with their death his cruell *life* dooth feed; . . . . . . VII. vii. 24. 8
after all came *Life,* and lastly Death; . . . . VII. vii. 46. 1
Life was like a faire young lusty boy, ... VII. vii. 46. 6
loath this state of *life* so tickle, ... VII. viii. 1. 6
those lilly hands, Which hold my *life* . . . . *Am.* i. 2
both *lyfe* and death forth from you dart, ... *Am.* vii. 3
Then is my soule with *life* and love inspired: . . . . . . *Am.* vii. 6
since that *lyfe* is more then death desyred, ... *Am.* vii. 9
Such *life* should be the honor of your light, ... *Am.* vii. 13
Of my poore *life* to make unpittied spoile. . . . . *Am.* xi. 8
Yet my poore *life,* . . . I would her yield, ... *Am.* xi. 9
That can expresse the *life* of things indeed. . . . . . . *Am.* xvii. 14
And tread my *life* downe in the lowly floure. . . . . . . *Am.* xx. 4
with one looke, she doth my *life* dismay; . . . . *Am.* xxi. 10
How long shall this lyke dying *lyfe* endure, ... *Am.* xxv. 1
My Helice, the lodestar of my *lyfe,* . . . . *Am.* xxxiv. 10
lacking it, they cannot *lyfe* sustayne; . . . . *Am.* xxxv. 5
him, whose *life,* though ye despyse, ... *Am.* xxxvi. 11
Mote have your *life* in honour long maintayned. . . . . . *Am.* xxxvi. 12
All carelesse how my *life* for her decayes: . . . . *Am.* xxxviii. 10
as she will, whose will my *life* doth sway, ... *Am.* xlvi. 7
So shall you live, by giving *life* to me. . . . . *Am.* xlix. 14
al those fourty which my *life* out-went. . . . . *Am.* lx. 8
Lord of *lyfe!* that . . . Didst make thy triumph over death . *Am.* lxviii. 1
Our love shall live, and later *life* renew. . . . . *Am.* lxxv. 14
Joy of my *life!* . . . . *Am.* lxxxii. 1
dead my *life* that wants such lively blis. . . . . *Am.* lxxxviii. 14
suckes the blood, and drinketh up the *lyfe,* . . . . *H.L.* 125
her Whose love before their *life* they doe prefer. . . . . . *H.L.* 140
make a lovers *life* a wretches hell. . . . . *H.L.* 265
wounds the *life,* and wastes the inmost marrow. . . . . . *H.B.* 63
life, which first fro me she reaved, ... *H.B.* 279
great Goddesse of my *life,* . . . . *H.B.* 282
Had he required *life* of us againe, ... *H.H.L.* 179
He gave us *life,* he it restored lost; . . . . *H.H.L.* 181
Then *life* were least, that us so litle cost. . . . . *H.H.L.* 182
But he our *life* hath left unto us free, ... *H.H.L.* 183
Who first to us our *life* and being gave, ... *H.H.L.* 191
And last, the food of *life,* which now we have, ... *H.H.L.* 194
From thence reade on the storie of his *life,* . . . . . . *H.H.L.* 232

Life-blood. My *life-bloud* friesing with unkindly cold; . . . . *S.C.* Ja. 26
his *life blood* forth with all did draw. . . . . I. xi. 53. 9

Life-consuming. Did languish long in *life-consuming* smart, . VI. vii. 31. 3

Life-devouring. kindled *life-devouring* fire.' . . . . II. vii. 17. 9

Lifeful. Like *lyfull* heat to nummed senses brought, ... VI. xi. 45. 4
let thy *lifull* heat not fervent be, ... *Epith.* 118
life-full spirits privily doth powre . . . . *H.B.* 52

Life-giving. on them the Suns *life-giving* light Had powred . *Col.* 861
Kindled at first from heavens *life-giving* fyre, ... *H.L.* 65

Lifeless. Against this *lifelesse* shadow so to fight: . . . . . II. xi. 44. 3
finding no fit seat, the *lifelesse* corse it left. . . . . . . IV. iii. 21. 9
like a *lifelesse* corse immoveable he stood. . . . . V. iii. 26. 9
when he saw his fellow *lifelesse* ly, ... VI. vii. 10. 3

Life-resembling. Nor *life-resembling* pencill it can paynt: . . III. Pr. 2. 2

Life's. There growes *lifes* fruite . . . . *Rev.* iv. 14
despise The noble Lion after his *lives* end, ... *Ro.* xiv. 6
the sloathfull fit of *lifes* sweete rest . . . . *Gn.* 641
this worlds vainnesse and *lifes* wretchednesse, ... *D.* 34
'Why doo I longer live in *lifes* despight, ... *D.* 442
sad Alcyon dyde in *lifes* disdaine. . . . . *D.* 525
His *lifes* desire, and his deare loves delight. . . . . . . *As.* 54
My *lifes* sole blisse, my hearts eternall threasure. . . . . . *Col.* 47
His liege, his Ladie, and his *lifes* Regent.— . . . . *Col.* 235
through report of that *lives* painted blisse, ... *Col.* 685
bownd by them to live in *lives* despight; . . . . II. i. 36. 4
my *lives* and labors end.' . . . . III. ix. 37. 9
her *lives* Lord and patrone of her health . . . . IV. i. 6. 2
That could her purchase with his *lives* adventur'd gage. . . IV. iii. 4. 9
For *lifes* succession in those brethren three. . . . . . . IV. iii. 21. 5
forst to seeke my *lifes* deare patronnesse: . . . . IV. x. 28. 8
of my *lifes* deare love beloved be: . . . . IV. xii. 10. 3
I rather chose to die in *lives* despight, ... V. iv. 32. 8
Weening her *lifes* last howre then neare to bee, ... V. xii. 11. 8
him adoring as her *lives* deare Lord, ... VI. i. 45. 6
he through *lives* despeire Untimely dyde, ... VI. ii. 28. 3
'My liefe, my *lifes* desire, ... VI. v. 23. 5
Of forreine helpes to *lifes* due nourishment: . . . . . . VI. ix. 20. 7
to fashion his owne *lyfes* estate, ... VI. ix. 31. 2
his *lives* threed to breake. . . . . VI. xi. 34. 9
my *lyfes* Leach! doe your skill reveale; . . . . *Am.* l. 13
The third, my love, my *lifes* (*lives) last ornament, ... *Am.* lxxiv. 9
That to me gave this *Lifes* first native sourse, ... *Proth.* 129

Liffar. the *Liffar* deep, ... IV. xi. 41. 6

Liffey. There was the *Liffy* rolling downe the lea, ... IV. xi. 41. 1

Lift. *lift* her loftie face Against the heaven, ... *Ro.* xii. 11
Lyft up thy selfe out of the lowly dust, ... *S.C.* O. 38
lowly thoughts *lift* up to heavens hight. . . . . *T.M.* 459
Well made to strike, to throw, to leape, to *lift,* . . . . . . *As.* 75
Lift up thy notes unto their wonted height, ... *Col.* 390
Who first my Muse did *lift* out of the flore, ... *Ded. Son.* xv. 6
with pale and deadly hew, At last she up gan *lift:* . . . . . I. ii. 45. 6
Did grone, as feeble so great load to *lift;* . . . . I. xi. 54. 4
Arachne high did *lifte* Her cunning web, ... II. vii. 28. 7
lift it selfe unto the highest skyes? . . . . II. x. 1. 5
Over the waves his rugged armes doth *lift,* . . . . II. xii. 4. 4
Sometimes the one would *lift* the other . . . . II. xii. 64. 1
Th' embroder'd quilt she lightly up did *lifte,* . . . . . . III. i. 61. 3
He up gan *lifte* toward the azure skies, ... III. v. 34. 4
When so he list in wrath *lift* up his steely brand, ... V. i. 8. 9
Unlesse the heavens them *lift* to lawfull soveraintie. . . . . V. v. 25. 9
quite smit off his arme as he it up did *lift.* . . . . . . V. xi. 7. 9
That pride doe not to tyranny you *lift;* . . . . VI. viii. 1. 7
my fraile spirit . . . *Lift* up aloft, ... VII. vii. 1. 5
to the light *lift* up theyr drouping hed. . . . . *Am.* xl. 12
Shall *lift* you up unto an high degree. . . . . *Am.* lxxxii. 14
Ne dare *lift* up her countenance too bold, ... *Epith.* 162
Love, *lift* me up upon thy golden wings, ... *H.H.L.* 1
Lift up to him thy heavie clouded eyne, ... *H.H.L.* 222
Lift up thy mind to th' Author of thy weale, ... *H.H.L.* 256
The hearts of men, . . . may *lift* themselves up hyer, ... *H.H.B.* 19

Lifted. *See* **Uplifted.**
Professing thee I *lifted* am aloft . . . . *Gn.* 33
losels *lifted* up on high, ... *Hub.* 67
lifted up his loftie towres thereby, ... *Hub.* 1173
lifted up above the worldes gaze, ... *T.M.* 587
High *lifted* up were many loftie towres, ... I. iv. 4. 6
He *lifted* up his hand, that backe againe did start. . . . . I. ix. 51. 9
Himselfe up high he *lifted* from the ground, ... I. xi. 18. 2
Vaine-glorious man . . . is *lifted* up to skye; . . . . . . II. iii. 10. 4
lifted high above this earthly masse, ... II. ix. 45. 3
bright ventayle, *lifted* up on hye, ... III. ii. 24. 3
lifted up to honorable place, ... VI. vii. 28. 2
with desyre *Lifted* aloft, ... *H.L.* 68

Lifteth. His glittering breast he *lifteth* up on hie, ... *Gn.* 258
Lifteth it up that els would lowly fall: . . . . III. v. 2. 6

Lifting. *See* **Fore-lifting.**
Lifting to heaven her aged hoarie head, ... *Ro.* xxviii. 3
Lifting the Good up to high Honours seat, ... *Com. Son.* i. 11
lifting up her brave heroick thought . . . . *Ti.* 109
lifting up his lompish head, ... I. i. 43. 4
lifting up his dreadfull club on hight, ... I. viii. 7. 3
Lifting to heven her everlasting fame: . . . . I. xii. 8. 5
lifting up his head, him answerd thus; . . . . II. vii. 62. 2
lifting up his vertuous staffe on hye. . . . . II. xii. 26. 6
lifting up her golden wand, ... VII. vi. 13. 4
Lifting himselfe out of the lowly dust . . . . *H.L.* 177

Lifts. *lyftes* him up out of the loathsome myre: . . . . . . *S.C.* O. 92
excellence *Lifts* me above the measure of my might: . . . . *Col.* 621
Liftes up his head that did before decline, ... IV. xii. 34. 8

Lig(ge), Liggen. *See* **Lie.**

Light. *See* **Candle-light, Daylight, Thunder-light.**
the foule that shunnes the cherefull *light* . . . . *Bel.*[1] vi. 13
the foule, that doth the *light* dispise, ... *Bel.*[2] vii. 13
Proud that so manie Gods she brought to *light;* . . . . . *Ro.* vi. 3
th' Ausonian *light* might be restor'd! . . . . *Ro.* xxv. 8
Hindering with his shade my lovely *light,* . . . . *S.C.* F. 173
lets his cancker-wormes *light* Upon my braunches, ... *S.C.* F. 179
learne with Lettice to wexe *light,* . . . . *S.C.* Mar. 20
From bough to bough he lepped *light,* . . . . *S.C.* Mar. 92
what concord han *light* and darke sam? . . . . *S.C.* May 168
Didst underfong my lasse to wexe so *light,* . . . . *S.C.* Jun. 103
Mischiefe *light* on him, ... *S.C.* S. 212
Diggon on fewe such freends did ever *lite.* . . . . *S.C.* S. 259
if thou algate lust *light* virelayes, ... *S.C.* N. 21

Light—*Continued.*
The earth now lacks her wonted *light*, . . . *S.C.* N. 68
was the saynt of shepheards *light*, . . . *S.C.* N. 176
Have care for to pursue his footing *light* . . . *Gn.* 31
Out of his golden Charet glistering *light;* . . . *Gn.* 67
famous *light* of all the Greekish hosts; . . . *Gn.* 547
see *Light* out of heavens windowes forth to looke, . . . *Hub.* 109
Light not on some that may our state amend; . . . *Hub.* 171
Shame *light* on him, . . . *Hub.* 219
a composition . . . for *light* condition, . . . *Hub.* 572
he so *light* was at legierdemaine, . . . *Hub.* 701
what he toucht came not to *light* againe; . . . *Hub.* 702
Delights of life, and ornaments of *light!* . . . *Hub.* 762
The Ape was glad to end the strife so *light*, . . . *Hub.* 1056
succeeding ages have no *light* Of things forepast, . . . *T.M.* 103
he *light* and heaven does hate: . . . *T.M.* 190
hath our fayre *light* defaced; . . . *T.M.* 266
ye three Twins, to *light* by Venus brought, . . . *T.M.* 403
When th' heavenlie *light* of knowledge is put out, . . . *T.M.* 488
It is their *light*, their loadstarre, and their day; . . . *T.M.* 495
The Starres pure *light*, the Spheres swift movement, . . . *T.M.* 508
the *light* of simple veritie Buried in ruines, . . . *Ti.* 171
with pineons *light* To mount aloft . . . *Mui.* 43
all the champain o're he soared *light;* . . . *Mui.* 149
Love, . . . *light* fluttering Upon the waves, . . . *Mui.* 290
his heavie eyes were throwne, As loathing *light;* . . . *D.* 47
harts deep sorrow hates both life and *light*. . . . *D.* 91
dubble losse by her hath on them *light*, . . . *D.* 223
drery horror dim the chearfull *light*, . . . *D.* 328
'I hate the day, because it lendeth *light* . . . *D.* 407
Why doo I longer see this loathsome *light* . . . *D.* 444
to give them *light* Which dwell in darknes, . . . *D.* 478
(stepping to him *light*) . . . *D.* 544
her heavens fairest *light*, . . . *Col.* 41
Excelling most in glorie and great *light:* . . . *Col.* 497
Though blame do *light* on those that faultie bee; . . . *Col.* 756
the *light* to mount on hie, And th' heavie downe to peize; . . . *Col.* 848
on them the Suns life-giving *light* Had powred . . . *Col.* 861
Beautie, the burning lamp of heavens *light*, . . . *Col.* 873
Great Ladie . . . whose *light* Like Phoebus lampe . . . I. Pr. 4. 3
Did spred so broad, that heavens *light* did hide, . . . I. i. 7. 5
light through darknesse for to wade.' . . . I. i. 12. 9
A litle glooming *light*, much like a shade; . . . I. i. 14. 5
Soone as that uncouth *light* upon them shone, . . . I. i. 15. 8
light she hated as the deadly bale, . . . I. i. 16. 7
highest God, the Lord of life and *light:* . . . I. i. 37. 6
He, . . . Remounted up as *light* as chearefull Larke; . . . I. i. 44. 7
Much griev'd to thinke that gentle Dame so *light*, . . . I. i. 55. 2
firme is fixt, and sendeth *light* from farre . . . I. ii. 1. 4
faire Hesperus . . . brought forth dawning *light;* . . . I. ii. 6. 7
night she thinks too long, and often lookes for *light*. . . . I. iii. 15. 9
ought . . . That should as death unto my deare heart *light:* . . . I. iii. 27. 5
welcome now, my *light*, and shining lampe of blis!' . . . I. iii. 27. 9
He, . . . Remounted up as *light* as chearefull Larke; . . . I. i. 44. 7
he had faire Una lorne, Through *light* misdeeming of her loialtie; . . . I. iv. 2. 2
Her glorious glitterand *light* doth all mens eies amaze. . . . I. iv. 16. 9
to my loathed life now shewes some *light*, . . . I. iv. 48. 2
Still did he wake, and still did watch for dawning *light*. . . . I. v. 1. 9
from their shields forth flyeth firie *light*, . . . I. v. 7. 8
shyning lampes in Joves high house were *light;* . . . I. v. 19. 2
She . . . th' unacquainted *light* began to feare, . . . I. v. 21. 4
Night . . . can the children of fayre *light* deface.' . . . I. v. 24. 5
dawning *light* Discovered had the world to heaven wyde, . . . I. v. 52. 5
Why doe ye lenger feed on loathed *light*, . . . I. vii. 22. 3
armour . . . Like glauncing *light* of Phoebus brightest ray; . . . I. vii. 29. 5
He could not rearen up againe so *light*, . . . I. viii. 10. 2
The *light* whereof, that hevens *light* did pas, . . . I. viii. 19. 3
As where th' Almighties lightning brond does *light*, . . . I. viii. 21. 8
Whose feeble thighes, . . . him scarse to *light* could beare; . . . I. viii. 40. 8
such the sight . . . when her borrowed *light* Is laid away, . . . I. viii. 49. 5
so soone as life . . . shewed hevens *light*, . . . I. ix. 3. 6
time in her just term the truth to *light* should bring.' . . . I. ix. 5. 9
O fayrest virgin! full of heavenly *light*, . . . I. ix. 17. 3
That wofull lover, loathing lenger *light*, . . . I. ix. 30. 2
beames . . . did shine like hevens *light*. . . . I. x. 12. 9
opened his dull eyes, that *light* mote in them shine. . . . I. x. 18. 9
he his paine endur'd, as seeming now more *light*. . . . I. x. 24. 9
Those glistring armes that heven with *light* did fill, . . . I. xi. 4. 8
beast about him turned *light*, . . . I. xi. 16. 7
steele . . . left not any marke where it did *light*, . . . I. xi. 25. 4
Upon the joint the lucky steele did *light*, . . . I. xi. 43. 6
Huge flames that dimmed all the hevens *light*, . . . I. xi. 44. 3
morning deaw upon their leaves doth *light;* . . . I. xii. 6. 8
to the world does bring long-wished *light:* . . . I. xii. 21. 8
glorious *light* of her sunshyny face, . . . I. xii. 23. 2
the bushy Teade a groome did *light*, . . . I. xii. 37. 6
light this weary vessell of her lode: . . . I. xii. 42. 4
enfold In covert vele, and wrap in shadowes *light*, . . . II. Pr. 5. 2
would bee dazled with exceeding *light*. . . . II. Pr. 5. 5
That short revenge . . . soone upon him *light*.' . . . II. i. 18. 4
take away this long lent loathed *light:* . . . II. i. 36. 7
as hating life and *light*. . . . II. i. 45. 9
The gentle knight her . . . Uplifted *light*, . . . II. i. 46. 2
Full of disport, still laughing, loosely *light*, . . . II. ii. 36. 2
Gan cleare the deawy ayre with springing *light*, . . . II. iii. 1. 4
ran away full *light*. . . . II. iii. 4. 9
when fluttring wind does blow In his *light* winges, . . . II. iii. 10. 4
The Northerne wind . . . reared him up *light* . . . II. iii. 19. 4
Kindled above at th' hevenly makers *light*, . . . II. iii. 23. 2

Light—*Continued.*
leaping *light*, . . . II. iii. 42. 5
Where this same wicked villein did me *light* upon. . . . II. iv. 17. 9
That it should not deface all others lesser *light?* . . . II. iv. 25. 9
carries thee so swifte and *light*.' . . . II. iv. 43. 4
Their wanton follies and *light* meriments: . . . II. v. 32. 6
To laugh at shaking of the leaves *light* . . . II. vi. 7. 7
Her *light* behaviour and loose dalliaunce . . . II. vi. 8. 1
of her joy . . . she saw he *light* did pas, . . . II. vi. 37. 3
'What dismall day hath lent this cursed *light*, . . . II. vi. 43. 7
The faithfull *light* of that faire lampe . . . II. vii. 1. 4
Cover'd with boughes and shrubs from heavens *light*, . . . II. vii. 3. 2
a faint shadow of uncertein *light:* . . . II. vii. 29. 6
More *light* then Culver in the Faulcons fist. . . . II. vii. 34. 6
with their brightnesse made that darknes *light*, . . . II. vii. 42. 2
neather world her *light* Doth dim . . . II. vii. 49. 3
backe againe him brought to living *light*. . . . II. vii. 66. 4
on his hacqueton did *lyte*, . . . II. viii. 38. 7
all desperate, as loathing *light*, . . . II. viii. 47. 1
with her *light* the earth enlumines cleare: . . . II. ix. 4. 7
the Sunne, with his lamp-burning *light*, . . . II. ix. 7. 5
The Prince by chaunce did on a Lady *light*, . . . II. ix. 36. 6
gave *light*, and flamd continually; . . . II. ix. 46. 4
Whence all that lives does borrow life and *light*, . . . II. x. 2. 2
when the oyle is spent, The *light* goes out, . . . II. x. 30. 2
soone againe as he his *light* withhault, . . . II. xi. 9. 5
doe that sence besiege with *light* illusions. . . . II. xi. 11. 9
Upon his head he wore an Helmet *light*, . . . II. xi. 22. 8
Upon the waves to spred her trembling *light*, . . . II. xii. 2. 5
the *light* bubles daunced all along, . . . II. xii. 10. 4
From the departing land it launched *light*, . . . II. xii. 15. 8
Her to rebuke for being loose and *light:* . . . II. xii. 16. 6
the gate was wrought of substaunce *light*, . . . II. xii. 43. 8
ever mixt their song with *light* licentious toyes. . . . II. xii. 72. 9
with kisses *light* For feare of waking him, . . . II. xii. 73. 5
like starry *light*, Which, sparckling . . . II. xii. 78. 8
His Cynthia, his heavens fayrest *light?* . . . III. Pr. 4. 6
by her owne law to your lot doth *light*, . . . III. i. 30. 4
Did sparckle forth great *light*, . . . III. i. 32. 9
Where she may finde the substance thin and *light*, . . . III. i. 43. 3
With which fayre Britomart gave *light* unto the day. . . . III. i. 43. 9
to faire semblaunce doth *light* faith annexe: . . . III. i. 54. 7
shee inly deemd Her love too *light*, . . . III. i. 55. 7
wherewith high Jove Doth *light* the lower world, . . . III. i. 57. 7
Eftesoones long waxen torches weren *light* . . . III. i. 58. 3
When in so high an object they do *lyte*, . . . III. ii. 3. 7
That body, wheresoever that it *light*, . . . III. ii. 45. 8
three Moones with borrowd brothers *light* . . . III. iii. 16. 2
Tho to their ready Steedes they clombe full *light*, . . . III. iii. 61. 6
to her Courser mounting *light:* . . . III. iv. 12. 5
To *light* their blessed lamps in Joves eternall hous. . . . III. iv. 51. 9
for want of lenger *light*, . . . III. iv. 52. 5
Fancies bett his ydle brayne With their *light* wings, . . . III. iv. 54. 5
light doe shonne for feare of being shent; . . . III. iv. 58. 7
light ylike is loth'd of them and thee; . . . III. iv. 58. 8
all that lewdnesse love doe hate the *light* to see. . . . III. iv. 58. 9
bring with him his long expected *light?* . . . III. iv. 60. 2
fro me reft both life and *light* attone. . . . III. v. 7. 6
stayd not till it did *light* In his left thigh, . . . III. v. 20. 6
from his head his heavy burganet did *light*. . . . III. v. 31. 9
That hast from darkenes me returnd to *light*, . . . III. v. 35. 7
To blott her honour, and her heavenly *light*. . . . III. v. 45. 5
disloyally Deeme of her high desert, or seeme so *light;* . . . III. v. 45. 7
Adorne the world with like to heavenly *light*, . . . III. v. 53. 2
th' authour of life and *light;* . . . III. vi. 9. 2
some *light* displeasure which him crost, . . . III. vi. 11. 3
were with sweet Ambrosia all besprinckled *light*. . . . III. vi. 18. 9
A litle smoke, whose vapour thin and *light* . . . III. vii. 5. 2
made her selfe more *light* away to fly: . . . III. vii. 44. 4
Coyly rebutted his embracement *light;* . . . III. viii. 10. 5
she thereto would lend but *light* regard, . . . III. viii. 14. 6
He it dissembled well, and *light* seemd to esteeme . . . III. viii. 16. 9
with rare *light* his bote did beautifye, . . . III. viii. 22. 6
Both *light* of heven and strength of men relate: . . . III. viii. 51. 8
doth blend The shyning glory of your soveraine *light;* . . . III. ix. 1. 8
To dry them selves by Vulcanes flaming *light*, . . . III. ix. 19. 8
in a cloud their *light* did long time stay, . . . III. ix. 20. 7
'Pardon, I pray, . . . for my wits beene *light*. . . . III. ix. 47. 4
Bewrayed had the world with early *light*, . . . III. x. 1. 2
all the passions that in man may *light* . . . III. x. 17. 8
al yclad in garments *light* . . . III. x. 21. 6
He up remounted *light*, . . . III. x. 38. 9
Upon his handes and feete he crept full *light*, . . . III. x. 47. 2
before the heavens fairest *light* . . . was fully reard, . . . III. x. 52. 6
on the rockes he fell so flit and *light*, . . . III. x. 57. 5
chaunced on a craggy cliff to *light*, . . . III. x. 57. 7
stouping downe she him amoved *light;* . . . III. xi. 13. 1
with his owne *light* shone; . . . III. xi. 47. 5
As those same plumes so seemd he vaine and *light*, . . . III. xii. 8. 5
In silken samite she was *light* arayd, . . . III. xii. 13. 3
the stout Damzell, to him leaping *light*, . . . III. xii. 32. 8
himself he reared *light* from ground. . . . III. xii. 43. *or.* 9
Is creasted all with lines of firie *light*, . . . IV. i. 13. 8
still are led with every *light* report: . . . IV. i. 28. 5
Ne for *light* Ladies love that soone is lost.' . . . IV. i. 35. 4
mounting *light*, his foe for lying long upbrayes: . . . IV. i. 42. 9
whose fancie *light* Was alwaies flitting . . . IV. ii. 5. 1
Sometimes him blessing with a *light* eyeglance, . . . IV. ii. 9. 4
So soone as heavens window shewed *light*, . . . IV. iii. 3. 7
The warie fowle, . . . avoydes it, shunning *light*, . . . IV. iii. 19. 6

Light 493 Lighting

Light—*Continued.*
suddenly they both upstarted *light,* . . . . IV. iii. 35. 6
Whom he that hath were loth to lose so *light,* . . . . IV. iv. 9. 2
Till by mishap he in his foemens hand did *light.* . . . . . . IV. v. 7. 9
daz'd the eyes of all as with exceeding *light.* . . . . IV. v. 10. 9
shone as Phebes *light* Amongst the lesser starres . . . . . . IV. v. 14. 3
Ne her owne Amoret forgoe so *light* . . . . IV. v. 20. 7
he their words as wind esteemed *light.* . . . . IV. v. 27. 7
by this heavens *light,* I vow you dead or living not to leave, . IV. vi. 38. 7
overleapes them all, like Robucke *light,* . . . . IV. vii. 22. 2
he was full *light* and nimble on the land. . . . . IV. vii. 25. 9
That any little blow on her did *light,* . . . . IV. vii. 26. 8
To come and shew themselves before the *light,* . . . . IV. vii. 33. 8
He seeing her depart arose up *light,* . . . . IV. vii. 37. 1
his juell he had lost so *light,* . . . . IV. viii. 8. 5
Ye may redresse, and me restore to *light!* . . . . IV. viii. 17. 5
These gentle Ladies will misdeeme too *light* . . . . IV. viii. 29. 4
Did shun the proofe thereof, and it avoyded *light.* . . . . . IV. viii. 44. 9
eke too loose of life, and eke of love too *light.* . . . . . . IV. viii. 49. 9
By fortune in that place did chance to *light:* . . . . IV. ix. 28. 3
Shyning with beauties *light* and heavenly vertues grace. . . . IV. x. 52. 9
Light Doto, wanton Glauce, and Galene glad: . . . . IV. xi. 48. 9
Euagore, and *light* Pontoporea, ... IV. xi. 50. 3
great glorious lampe of *light,* . . . . V. Pr. 7. 1
wheresoever it did *light,* it throughly shard. . . . . V. i. 10. 9
His yron page, who him pursew'd so *light,* . . . . V. i. 20. 2
you, Sir Knight, that love so *light* esteeme, ... V. i. 28. 5
weigh the *light* that in the East doth rise; . . . . V. ii. 43. 3
he of little things made reckoning *light;* . . . . V. ii. 44. 2
sayd that words were *light,* . . . . V. ii. 45. 1
so soone as morrow *light* Appear'd in heaven, ... V. iii. 7. 1
both adorn'd with lampes of flaming *light;* . . . . V. iii. 19. 4
She chaunst unwares to *light* uppon this coffer, ... V. iv. 10. 8
him restoring unto living *light,* . . . . V. iv. 25. 6
All in a Camis *light* of purple silke . . . . V. v. 2. 1
short tucked for *light* motion Up to her ham; . . . . V. v. 2. 6
though darkned be her *light.* . . . . V. v. 12. 9
For yeelding to a straungers love so *light,* . . . . V. vi. 12. 6
Now seeking darkenesse, and now seeking *light,* . . . . . . V. vi. 14. 7
as next to hand did *light,* . . . . V. vi. 20. 8
many things demaund, to which she answer'd *light.* . . . . . V. vi. 20. 9
so soone as dawning houre Discovered had the *light* . . . . V. vi. 35. 2
tooke her steede; and thereon mounting *light* . . . . V. vi. 36. 2
from her eies did flash out fiery *light,* . . . . V. vi. 38. 8
haps to *light* Uppon two stubborne oakes, ... V. vi. 40. 1
joyous *light* the house of Jove forsooke; . . . . V. vii. 8. 7
The morrow next, so soone as dawning *light* . . . . V. vii. 26. 7
did his powrefull *light* empeach, ... V. viii. 37. 7
So *light* of hand, and nymble of his pace, ... V. ix. 5. 5
to follow him that was so swift and *light.* . . . . V. ix. 15. 9
Yet would not let just vengeance on her *light;* . . . . V. ix. 50. 5
Few perling drops from her faire lampes of *light;* . . . . . V. ix. 50. 7
bringing *light* into the heavens fayre, ... V. x. 16. 7
he car'd no more which way he strooke, Nor where it *light;* . V. xi. 12. 7
Untill late mischiefe did uppon me *light,* . . . . V. xi. 49. 3
(for nought so hard may *light* . . . . V. xi. 55. 3
goodly *light* then Phoebus lampe doth shine more cleare? . . . V. xi. 62. 9
light to men restore, ... V. xii. 11. 4
the lampe of *light* Above the earth upreard . . . . VI. i. 31. 1
Calidore uprose againe full *light,* . . . . VI. i. 34. 1
Prevented him before his stroke could *light,* . . . . VI. i. 38. 7
leaping to him *light* would have unlast His Helme, ... VI. i. 39. 5
The Ladie, . . . Gan reare her eyes as to the chearefull *light,* . VI. ii. 42. 8
abasht, . . . That he so rudely did uppon them *light,* . . . . VI. iii. 21. 4
Calidore, Who was more *light* of foote . . . . VI. iii. 25. 4
and hope of living *light,* . . . . VI. iii. 45. 4
Now wanting them he felt himselfe so *light,* . . . . VI. iv. 19. 6
the morning, bringing earely *light* . . . . VI. v. 40. 2
No wound . . . so sore doth *light* . . . . VI. vi. 1. 2
What fortune to the Briton Prince did *lite,* . . . . VI. vi. 17. 5
whether thwart or flatly it did *lyte,* . . . . VI. vi. 30. 8
him too *light* of credence did mislead, ... VI. vii. 20. 7
Like a fell Lyon leaped to him *light,* . . . . VI. vii. 25. 5
Yet would not let her *lite,* nor rest a little stead: . . . . . VI. vii. 40. 9
Dismounting *light,* his shield about him threw, ... VI. viii. 7. 2
wayt advantage when they downe did *light.* . . . . VI. viii. 14. 5
For being of his love to her so *light,* . . . . VI. viii. 33. 4
had he not upon him fallen *light,* . . . . VI. ix. 44. 4
fed with *light* report Of every blaste, ... VI. x. 2. 8
to course about their bases *light;* . . . . VI. x. 8. 4
All other lesser lights in *light* excell; . . . . VI. x. 26. 2
Her lovely *light* was dimmed and decayd . . . . VI. xi. 21. 4
make even that dimmed *light* Seeme much more lovely . . . VI. xi. 21. 6
till *light* the sky forsooke. . . . . VI. xi. 40. 9
the theefe awaking *light* Unto the entrance ran; . . . . . . VI. xi. 43. 4
he forth went into th' open *light,* . . . . VI. xi. 47. 6
forth her bringing to the joyous *light,* . . . . VI. xi. 50. 4
She forth gan lay unto the open *light* The litle babe, ... VI. xii. 7. 4
At length into a Monastere did *light,* . . . . VI. xii. 23. 8
her need give lone Of her faire *light* . . . . VII. vi. 11. 8
Of happy wights, now unpurvaid of *light,* . . . . VII. vi. 14. 4
To know what meant that suddaine lacke of *light.* . . . . . VII. vi. 15. 5
Through some vaine errour, or inducement *light,* . . . . . . VII. vi. 32. 2
then into the open *light* they forth him brought. . . . . . VII. vi. 47. 9
that seem'd penaunce *light:* . . . . VII. vi. 50. 6
That was unlyned all, to be more *light;* . . . . VII. vii. 29. 3
with starry *light,* Those lamping eyes will . . . look, ... *Am.* i. 5
The *light* whereof hath kindled heavenly fyre . . . . *Am.* iii. 3
Such life should be the honor of your *light,* . . . . *Am.* vii. 13
Dark is the world, where your *light* shined never; . . . . . *Am.* viii. 13

Light—*Continued.*
th' ymage of their goodly *light.* . . . . *Am.* ix. 4
Whose *light* doth lighten all that here we see. . . . . *Am.* ix. 14
to leave, . . . for one repulse so *light.* . . . . *Am.* xiv. 4
those fayre eyes, my loves immortall *light;* . . . . *Am.* xvi. 2
lovely *light* to cleare my cloudy grief, ... *Am.* xxxiv. 12
to the *light* lift up theyr drouping hed. . . . . *Am.* xl. 12
Not ayre; for she is not so *light* or rare: . . . . *Am.* lv. 7
The beame of *light,* whom mortal eyes admyre; . . . . *Am.* lxi. 10
now your *light* doth more itselfe dilate, ... *Am.* lxvi. 11
your *light* hath once enlumind me, ... *Am.* lxvi. 13
Resembling heavens glory in her *light,* . . . . *Am.* lxxii. 6
cloud of pryde, that oft doth dark Her goodly *light,* . . . . *Am.* lxxxi. 8
Ne one *light* glance of sensuall desyre . . . . *Am.* lxxxiii. 3
when as night hath us of *light* forlorne, ... *Am.* lxxxvi. 7
Since I have lackt the comfort of that *light,* . . . . *Am.* lxxxvii. 1
With *light* thereof I doe my selfe sustayne, ... *Am.* lxxxvii. 11
Dark is my day, whyles her fayre *light* I mis, ... *Am.* lxxxviii. 13
Bynd up the locks the which hang scatterd *light,* . . . . . *Epith.* 62
He somewhat loseth of his heat and *light,* . . . . *Epith.* 268
seemst to laugh atweene thy twinkling *light,* . . . . *Epith.* 292
In dreadful darknesse lend desired *light;* . . . . *Epith.* 412
Lo! one, whom later age hath brought to *light,* . . . . . . *Com. Son.* iii. 9
Through all that great wide wast, yet wanting *light.* . . . . *H.L.* 70
Yet wanting *light* to guide his wandring way, ... *H.L.* 71
lend him *light* from her owne goodly ray; . . . . *H.L.* 73
He is enlumind with that goodly *light,* . . . . *H.L.* 108
th' immortall flame Of heavenly *light,* . . . . *H.L.* 116
Their lives they loath, and heavens *light* disdaine; . . . . . *H.L.* 130
No *light* but that, ... *H.L.* 131
The flaming *light* of that celestiall fyre . . . . *H.L.* 186
Admires the mirrour of so heavenly *light.* . . . . *H.L.* 196
admiration of that heavenly *light,* . . . . *H.B.* 13
vouchsafe with thy love-kindling *light* . . . . *H.B.* 19
the *light* Of that faire beame . . . . *H.B.* 48
Light of thy lampe; . . . . *H.B.* 59
Shall turne to dust, and loose their goodly *light.* . . . . . *H.B.* 98
light proceedes, which kindleth lovers fire, ... *H.B.* 100
it then tooke *light* And lively spirits . . . . *H.B.* 110
The most resemblance of that heavenly *light,* . . . . *H.B.* 121
hath in it the more of heavenly *light,* . . . . *H.B.* 128
lively images of heavens *light,* . . . . *H.B.* 163
the *light* of your bright shyning starre. . . . . *H.B.* 175
From *light* of his pure fire; . . . . *H.B.* 179
Love is not so *light* As streight to burne . . . . *H.B.* 209
conforming it unto the *light,* . . . . *H.B.* 218
As plaine as *light* discovers dawning day. . . . . *H.B.* 238
That in *light* wits did loose affection move; . . . . *H.H.L.* 11
O most blessed Spirit! pure lampe of *light,* . . . . *H.H.L.* 43
All glistring glorious in their Makers *light.* . . . . *H.H.L.* 56
Adornd with thousand lamps of burning *light,* . . . . *H.H.L.* 59
Where they behold the glorie of his *light,* . . . . *H.H.L.* 69
The brightest Angell, even the Child of *Light,* . . . . *H.H.L.* 83
Hating the happie *light* from which they fell. . . . . *H.H.L.* 91
O glorious Morning-Starre! O Lampe of *Light!* . . . . *H.H.L.* 170
with selfe-same price redeemed . . . how ever of us *light* esteemed. . . . . *H.H.L.* 203
With admiration of their passing *light,* . . . . *H.H.L.* 279
some sparkling *light* Of thine eternall Truth, ... *H.H.B.* 10
others farre exceeding these in *light,* . . . . *H.H.B.* 65
their owne native *light* farre passing theirs. . . . . *H.H.B.* 70
Which from their faces dart out fierie *light;* . . . . *H.H.B.* 95
all about him sheddeth glorious *light:* . . . . *H.H.B.* 161
Light, farre exceeding that bright blazing sparke . . . . . *H.H.B.* 162
But that immortall *light,* which there doth shine, ... *H.H.B.* 169
With the great glorie of that wondrous *light* . . . . *H.H.B.* 176
Whose beautie filles the heavens with her *light,* . . . . . . *H.H.B.* 228
And looke at last up to that Soveraine *Light,* . . . . *H.H.B.* 295
beauties bright, That shone as heavens *light,* . . . . *Proth.* 52
Lighted. *See* **Light.**
Then it had *lighted* on an aged Oke, ... III. vii. 41. 3
She from her palfrey *lighted* on the plaine; . . . . VI. viii. 32. 6
Lighten. She bad to *lighten* my too heavie band, ... IV. viii. 61. 3
all the earth doest *lighten* with thy rayes, ... VI. x. 28. 2
Those powrefull eies, which *lighten* my dark . . . . *Am.* ix. 2
Whose light doth *lighten* all that here we see. . . . . *Am.* ix. 14
Lightened. *Lightned* with deadly lamps on everie post? . . . *Gn.* 341
being *lightned* with her beawties beme, ... *T.M.* 585
she of late is *lightned* of her wombe, ... I. x. 16. 5
Ne *lightned* was with window, nor with lover, ... VI. x. 42. 7
Her *lightened* all the way where she should wend, ... VII. vi. 9. 8
Lighter. learnd of *lighter* timber cotes to frame, ... *S.C.* D. 77
lighter seeme than this Gnats idle name. . . . . *Gn.* 8
so soone as *lighter* sleepe Was entered, ... *Gn.* 321
With *lighter* hearts unto their home retird; . . . . III. iii. 51. 4
Light-fluttering. *See* **Fluttering, Light.**
Lightfoot. *lightfoote* Nymphes, can chace the lingring Night . *S.C.* Jun. 26
The joyous Nymphes and *lightfoote* Faeries . . . . *T.M.* 31
For him so far had borne his *light-foot* steede, ... I. ii. 8. 3
all the troupe of *light-foot* Naiades . . . . I. vi. 18. 3
The *light-foot* Squyre her quickly turnd around, ... I. viii. 25. 7
far before a *light-foote* Page did flie, ... II. viii. 10. 4
turning quicke aside His *light-foot* beast, ... II. xi. 25. 6
alighted from her *light-foot* beast, ... III. iv. 7. 1
from them fled, as *light-foot* hare from vew . . . . III. iv. 46. 4
Lightfoote Cymothoe, and sweete Melite, ... IV. xi. 49. 4
ye *lightfoot* mayds, which keepe the dore, ... *Epith.* 67
Light-giving. the worlds *light-giving* lampe . . . . *Epith.* 19
Lighting. *lighting* on his horses head him quite did mall. . . V. xi. 8. 9
lighting candles new, gan search anone, ... VI. xi. 20. 8

Lightly. bowe . . . Which *lightly* he bent at me: *S.C.* Mar. 84
lightly slake The flames which love *S.C.* Jun. 85
things *lightly* done amis *Gn.* 475
Out of the swelling streame it *lightly* caught, *Ti.* 626
I . . . *lightlie* him uprearing, Revoked life, *D.* 187
Dismounting *lightly* from his loftie steed, I. iii. 36. 1
Least thou of her believe too *lightly* blame, I. iv. 1. 5
The knight her *lightly* reared up againe, I. vi. 37. 5
Th' Elfe, therewith astownd, Upstarted *lightly* I. vii. 7. 8
lightly lept from underneath the blow: I. vii. 12. 6
lightly leaping from so monstrous maine, I. viii. 7. 7
She *lightly* sprinkled on his weaker partes: I. viii. 14. 7
He *lightly* left the foe with whom he fought, I. viii. 15. 6
The knight, then *lightly* leaping to the pray, I. viii. 24. 1
Both horse and man up *lightly* rose againe, I. xi. 17. 1
From loathed soil he can him *lightly* reare, I. xi. 39. 3
the cruell steel He *lightly* snatcht, II. i. 43. 2
An heavie load, himselfe did *lightly* reare; II. ii. 11. 4
lightly did upstart, II. iv. 9. 8
lightly shunned it; and, passing by, II. v. 4. 1
out of the path Did *lightly* leape, II. v. 18. 8
lightly mounted passeth on his way; II. v. 38. 2
on the dull waves did *lightly* flote, II. vi. 38. 3
Guyon, *lightly* to him leaping, II. vii. 6. 6
Sir Guyons sword he *lightly* to him raught, II. viii. 40. 2
devoyd of dreed, Upon him *lightly* leaping II. viii. 49. 5
grownd he gave, and *lightly* lept areare: II. xi. 36. 5
Mordure . . . he *lightly* threw away, II. xi. 41. 7
His falsed fayth, and love too *lightly* flitt; II. xii. 44. 7
do not in th' ayre more *lightly* flee. II. xii. 77. 9
Would not so *lightly* follow beauties chace, III. i. 19. 2
Did roll too *lightly*, and too often glaunce, III. i. 41. 8
Lightly arose out of her wearie bed, III. i. 59. 6
Th' embroder'd quilt she *lightly* up did lifte, III. i. 61. 3
She *lightly* lept out of her filed bedd, III. i. 62. 2
lightly rased her soft silken skin, III. i. 65. 7
No ydle charmes so *lightly* may remove: III. ii. 51. 8
Timias him *lightly* overhent, III. v. 25. 2
Lightly upstarted from the dustie ground, III. vii. 7. 5
Lightly she leaped, as a wight forlore, III. vii. 25. 7
he *lightly* lept Upon the beast, III. vii. 33. 6
She *lightly* unto him adjoyned syde to syde; III. vii. 42. 9
having her from Trompart *lightly* reard, III. viii. 19. 3
loosenes, that she *lightly* did remove. III. viii. 42. 5
let him passe as *lightly* as he came: III. x. 39. 2
Lightly he clipt her twixt his armes twaine, III. xii. 45. *or.*1
By meanes whereof he hath him *lightly* overborne. IV. ii. 6. 9
She litle answer'd him, but *lightly* did aggrate. IV. ii. 23. 9
Full *lightly*, ere himselfe he could recower IV. iii. 20. 2
He *lightly* lept out of his place of rest, IV. iii. 22. 6
They *lightly* her requit, IV. iii. 47. 1
Shee smote them *lightly* with her powrefull wand. IV. iii. 48. 2
They up againe them selves can *lightly* reare, IV. iv. 29. 1
Lightly Cambello leapt downe from his steed IV. iv. 31. 1
lightly issewd forth to take his lot. IV. iv. 33. 7
lightly started up as one affrayd, IV. v. 42. 6
her selfe she *lightly* gan To dight, IV. vi. 10. 4
Lightly he started up out of that stound, IV. vi. 12. 1
after her full *lightly* he uprose, IV. vii. 21. 6
flew away as *lightly* as the wind: IV. viii. 7. 7
looser thought will *lightly* be misled, IV. viii. 29. 3
shield, which *lightly* he did throw IV. viii. 42. 3
To whom she did her liking *lightly* cast, IV. viii. 52. 6
I *lightly* snatcht him up and with me bore away. IV. viii. 61. 9
rocke Is *lightly* stricken with some stones throw; V. i. 21. 7
from you *lightly* throw This squalid weede, V. iv. 34. 5
She *lightly* to him leapt; V. iv. 40. 2
he him selfe full *lightly* from him freed, V. xi. 9. 3
Unto a strangers love, so *lightly* placed, V. xi. 63. 2
He *lightly* reft his head to ease him of his paine. V. xii. 23. 9
he them all from him full *lightly* swept, VI. i. 24. 3
Or stay till he his armes, . . . Might *lightly* fetch: VI. ii. 19. 6
he it seeing *lightly* to him lept, VI. v. 25. 8
therefore *lightly* bad him packe away, VI. vi. 21. 6
lightly slipping by, Unwares defrauded his intended destiny: VI. viii. 8. 8
He *lightly* started up like one aghast, VI. viii. 47. 8
lightly did delay Hot Titans beames, *Proth.* 3

Lightness. there is no greater shame Then *lightnesse* and inconstancie in love: I. iv. 1. 8
Was *lightnesse* seene or looser vanitie, II. ii. 15. 4
For feare she should of *lightnesse* be detected: IV. xii. 35. 8

Lightning. All suddenly with *lightning* overthrowne, *Ro.* xii. 5
the foule, that serves to beare the *lightning*, *Ro.* xvii. 13
limbs, with *lightening* rent, *Gn.* 199
The skie . . . Throwes *lightning* forth, *Gn.* 582
as it had beene a flake Of *lightning* III. ii. 5. 8
With dreadfull thunder and *lightning* atwixt, III. xii. 2. 2
fire did flash, like *lightning* after thunder, IV. iii. 15. 8
through her eyes like sudden *lightning* flashed, V. v. 30. 3
No more then *lightening* from the lofty sky: VI. viii. 8. 6
Then doe I die, as one with *lightning* fyred. *Am.* vii. 8
Nor to the *Lightning*; for they still persever; *Am.* ix. 9
Thunder, and *lightning*, and tempestuous fyre, *H.H.B.* 181

Lightning-brand. As where th' Almighties *lightning brond* does light, I. viii. 21. 8
Like as the *lightning brond* from riven skie, IV. vi. 14. 1

Lightning-fire. Armd with his thunderbolts and *lightning fire*, III. xi. 33. 4

Lightning-flash. Like *lightening flash* that hath the gazer burned, V. viii. 38. 1

Lightning's. house-fyres, nor *lightnings* helpelesse harmes, *Epith.* 340

Lights. shone, Like Hesperus emongst the lesser *lights*, I. vii. 30. 4
The stroke upon his shield so heavie *lites*, I. viii. 18. 7
faire lookes, glancing like evening *lights*; II. v. 33. 3
for so much as to my lot here *lights*, V. iii. 3. 7
As if his lungs and *lites* were nigh asunder brast. VI. iii. 26. 9
glyding through the ayre *lights* all the heavens darke. VI. vii. 7. 9
All other lesser *lights* in light excell; VI. x. 26. 2
dreadfull thunder-claps . . . With flames and flashing *lights* VII. vii. 23. 9
that fayrest starre Which *lights* the world *H.B.* 112

Light-shunning. *Light-shonning* thefte, and traiterous intent, III. iv. 58. 2

Lightsome. Wherein the *lightsome* levin shroudes, *S.C.* Au. 87
Let everlasting *lightsome* glory strive, *Gn.* 55
kept from looking on the *lightsome* day: *T.M.* 593
'O *lightsome* day! the lampe of highest Jove, I. vii. 23. 1
Ere they into the *lightsom* world were brought, III. vii. 48. 7
Untill she spide the lampe of *lightsome* day V. vii. 17. 3
Phoebus selfe, who *lightsome* is alone, VII. vii. 51. 7

Lignage. *See* **Lineage.**

Like. *See* **Angel-like, Balm-like, Beam-like, Beastlike, Fiendlike, Giantlike, Lion-like, Moon-like, Saintlike, Saturn-like, Shepherd-like, Soldier-like, Sun-like, Victor-like, Widow-like, Woman-like.**
Mounting *like* waves with triple point to heaven, *Bel.*[1] ix. 2
What one is *like* . . . This honoured Dragon, *Rev.* i. 9
yeallow, *like* the golden grayle *Bel.* xii. 3
Clad *like* a Nimph, *Bel.*[2] iv. 6
Out of her dust *like* to a worm arise. *Bel.*[2] vii. 14
like incense of precious Cedar tree, *Bel.*[2] xi. 3
I saw a Citie *like* unto that same, *Bel.*[2] xiv. 2
So great riches as *like* (*lyke*[1]) cannot be found! *Pet.* ii. 14
what els in the world is of *like* worth, *Ro.* ii. 11
It's *like* a corse drawne forth out of the tombe *Ro.* v. 7
Like as whilome the children of the earth *Ro.* xii. 1
Like as ye see the wrathfull Sea from farre *Ro.* xvi. 1
Like as ye see fell Boreas with sharpe blast *Ro.* xvi. 5
Like a Pandora, locked long in store. *Ro.* xix. 8
Like as the seeded field greene grasse first showes, *Ro.* xxx. 1
With gilden hornes embowed *like* the Moone, *Van.* ii. 3
the sea did roare *like* heavens thunder. *Van.* v. 11
shields of brasse that shone *like* burnisht golde, *Van.* vi. 3
So semest thou *like* Good Fryday to frowne: *S.C.* F. 30
Thy Ewes, . . . *Like* wailefull widdowes *S.C.* F. 82
Am *like* for desperate doole to dye, *S.C.* F. 155
Now stands the Brere *like* a lord alone, *S.C.* F. 222
spotted winges, *like* Peacocks trayne, *S.C.* Mar. 80
Like April shoure so stremes the trickling teares *S.C.* Ap. 7
Yclad in Scarlot, *like* a mayden Queene, *S.C.* Ap. 57
her angelick face, *Like* Phoebe fayre? *S.C.* Ap. 65
Where have you seene the *like* but there? *S.C.* Ap. 72
thou speakes *lyke* a lewde lorrell, *S.C.* Jul. 93
My seely sheepe *like* well belowe, *S.C.* Jul. 105
they . . . *liken* theyr abode; *S.C.* Jul. 108
like not of the frowie fede, *S.C.* Jul. 111
like in eche degree The flocke *S.C.* Jul. 131
make *like* account of his brother. *S.C.* Au. 43
they bene *like* foule wagmoires overgrast, *S.C.* S. 130
Her *like* shee has not left behinde *S.C.* N. 40
Like Swallow swift I wandred here and there; *S.C.* D. 20
like a cobweb weaving slenderly, *Gn.* 3
his broad forhead *like* two hornes divide, *Gn.* 22
Her owne *like* image in a christall brooke. *Gn.* 88
Did shrowd her selfe *like* punishment to shonne. *Gn.* 176
On everie side did shine *like* scalie golde; *Gn.* 261
The same was able with *like* lovely lay *Gn.* 461
like a kindly nourse, did yeeld *Gn.* 507
'Here manie other *like* Heroes bee. *Gn.* 593
Like as he had conceiv'd it *Gn.* 656
lyeke with his *lyeke*, *Hub.* 48
Or *like* a Pilgrim, or a Lymiter, *Hub.* 85
like a Gipsen, or a Juggeler, *Hub.* 86
if this device Doth *like* you, or may you to *like* entice.' *Hub.* 94
she gave *like* blessing to each creture, *Hub.* 146
Like two free men, *Hub.* 160
live *like* Lords of that which they doo gather, *Hub.* 164
Well seemd the Ape to *like* this ordinaunce; *Hub.* 173
like but well The purpose *Hub.* 177
we shall ronne Into great daunger, *like* to be undone, *Hub.* 184
For feare least we *like* rogues should be reputed, *Hub.* 187
loose *like* an emptie gut; *Hub.* 212
like a handsome swaine it him became. *Hub.* 242
what ever such *like* paine Ye put on me, *Hub.* 287
Much *like* to begging, but much better named, *Hub.* 351
the Ape anon Himselfe had cloathed *like* a Gentleman, *Hub.* 660
the slie Foxe, as *like* to be his groome, *Hub.* 661
here arriv'd, to see if *like* he found. *Hub.* 688
whilst that other *like* vaine wits he pleased, *Hub.* 709
like desire and praise of noble fame, *Hub.* 769
Now *like* a Merchant, Merchants to deceave, *Hub.* 863
like a Lawyer, when he land would lett, *Hub.* 866
nor ought *like* the same. *Hub.* 868
Like as a Puppit placed in a play, *Hub.* 931
in person and in stature Most *like* a Man, *Hub.* 1030
for outward shape Most *like* a man, Man is not *like* an Ape *Hub.* 1042
I therein most *like* to him doo merite, *Hub.* 1044
Like as the Foxe did guide his graceles skill; *Hub.* 1128
stouping, *like* an arrowe from a bowe, *Hub.* 1262
senseles, *like* the corpse deceast, *Hub.* 1328
Like heavily lamenting from them went. *T.M.* 36
Is *like* a ship in midst of tempest left *T.M.* 141
all his dayes, *like* dolorous Trophees, *T.M.* 160

Like—*Continued.*
those sweete wits, which wont the *like* to frame, *T.M.* 203
all her Sisters, with compassion *like,* *T.M.* 231
Like as the dearling of the Summers pryde, *T.M.* 235
Like wofull Culvers, doo sit wayling now, *T.M.* 246
like to troubled puddles have them made. *T.M.* 276
Like virgin Queenes, with laurell garlands cround *T.M.* 309
prune his plumes *like* ruffed Dove. *T.M.* 402
all her sisters, with compassion *like,* *T.M.* 477
like brute beasts doo lie in loathsome den *T.M.* 531
like a Looker-on Of this worldes Stage, *Com. Son.* i. 2
Like a great Lord of peerelesse liberty; *Com. Son.* i. 10
her yeolow locks, *like* wyrie gold *Ti.* 10
like as at the ingate of their berth *Ti.* 47
Like beast whose breath but in his nostrels is, *Ti.* 356
broad spreading *like* an aged tree, *Ti.* 452
That of *like* ruine he may warned bee, *Ti.* 468
Like tragicke Pageants seeming to appeare. *Ti.* 490
like the coloured Rainbowe arched wide: *Ti.* 550
I for dole was almost *like* to die. *Ti.* 672
Like two sharpe speares *Mui.* 83
Like as a warlike Brigandine, *Mui.* 84
how Jove did abuse Europa *like* a Bull, *Mui.* 278
by his *like* visnomie Eathe to be knowen; *Mui.* 310
seem'd to live, so *like* it was in sight: *Mui.* 332
Was *like* to this. *Mui.* 374
Like as a wily Foxe, *Mui.* 401
Like a grimme Lyon rushing *Mui.* 434
Like to some Pilgrim come from farre away. *D.* 42
Most *like* Alcyon seeming at a glaunce; *D.* 53
'One, whome *like* wofulnesse, impressed deepe, *D.* 64
given *like* cause with thee to waile *D.* 66
Griefe findes some ease by him that *like* does beare. *D.* 67
Whose *like* before mine eye had seldome seene, *D.* 114
Living on earth *like* Angell new divinde, *D.* 214
Powr'd upon her, *like* showers of Castaly, *D.* 228
She fel away *like* fruit blowne downe with winde. *D.* 244
deadly accents, which *like* swords Did wound *D.* 297
Like a Mill-wheele in midst of miserie, *D.* 432
like her that did him breed, *As.* 16
kisse thy lips *like* faded leaves of rose. *As.* 138
She likewise did deforme, *like* him to bee. *As.* 156
Out of his lips *like* lilies pale and soft: *As.* 166
he whose heart *like* sorrow did invade. *As.* 172
followed her make *like* turtle chaste, *As.* 178
Like Astrophel, which thereinto was made. *As.* 186
was not *like* mourning seen. *As.* 210
Like hartlesse deare, dismayd with thunders sound. *Col.* 9
banisht had my selfe, *like* wight forlore, *Col.* 182
Rolling *like* mountaines in wide wildernesse, *Col.* 198
An high headland . . . *Like* to an horne, *Col.* 282
if *like* heaven, be heavenly graces there, *Col.* 306
Like as in this same world where we do wone?' *Col.* 307
if I her *like* ought on earth might read, *Col.* 336
like the circlet of a Turtle true, *Col.* 340
like faire Phebes garlond shining new, *Col.* 342
Doth *like* himselfe Heroically sound. *Col.* 447
like a goodly beacon high addrest, *Col.* 562
Her words were *like* a streame of honny fleeting, *Col.* 596
Her deeds were *like* great clusters of ripe grapes, *Col.* 600
Her lookes were *like* beames of the morning Sun, *Col.* 604
Her thoughts are *like* the fume of Franckincence, *Col.* 608
Much *like* an Angell in all forme and fashion. *Col.* 615
I feele my selfe *like* one yrapt in spright. *Col.* 623
like bladders blowen up with wynd, *Col.* 717
like Moldwarps nousling still they lurke, *Col.* 763
Like as himselfe us pleaseth save or spill. *Col.* 814
like wormes out of her slimie nature. *Col.* 860
Thenceforth they gan each one his *like* to love, *Col.* 863
like himselfe desire for to beget: *Col.* 864
Like as himselfe was fairest by creation: *Col.* 870
she is not *like* as the other crew *Col.* 931
With *like* delightes . . . delay The rugged brow *Ded. Son.* i. 11
Then, by *like* right the noble Progeny, *Ded. Son.* iv. 5
Like flying doves ye did before you chace; *Ded. Son.* vi. 9
To tast the streames that, *like* a golden showre, *Ded. Son.* viii. 9
To *like* desire of honor may ye raise, *Ded. Son.* x. 11
And for your owne high merit in *like* cace: *Ded. Son.* xi. 7
This lowly Muse, that learns *like* steps to trace, *Ded. Son.* xiii. 7
This lowly Muse, . . . Flies for *like* aide *Ded. Son.* xiii. 8
whose light *Like* Phoebus lampe I. Pr. 4. 4
Upon his shield the *like* was also scor'd, I. i. 2. 5
like to lead the labyrinth about; I. i. 11. 4
A litle glooming light, much *like* a shade; I. i. 14. 5
Halfe *like* a serpent horribly displaide, I. i. 14. 7
henceforth ever wish that *like* succeed it may!' I. i. 27. 9
and other spelles *like* terrible, I. i. 37. 3
Legions of Sprights, the which, *like* litle flyes I. i. 38. 2
winde, much *like* the sowne Of swarming Bees, I. i. 41. 4
partes, So lively and so *like* in all mens sight, I. i. 45. 4
a black stole, most *like* to seeme for Una fit. I. i. 45. 9
like that virgin true which for her knight him took. I. i. 49. 9
he spred A seeming body . . . *Like* a young Squire, I. ii. 3. 4
Now *like* a foxe, now *like* a dragon fell; I. ii. 10. 6
And *like* a Persian mitre on her hed Shee wore, I. ii. 13. 4
tinsell trappings, woven *like* a wave, I. ii. 13. 8
her champion fall *Like* the old ruines of a broken towre, I. ii. 20. 2
That had a *like* faire Lady by his syde; I. ii. 35. 8
Lyke a faire Lady, but did fowle Duessa hyde. I. ii. 35. 9
Affraid least to themselves the *like* mishappen might. I. iii. 20. 9

Like—*Continued.*
forth they ran, *like* two amazed deare, I. iii. 22. 7
Much *like,* as when the beaten marinere, I. iii. 31. 1
Like loathsome lazars, by the hedges lay. I. iv. 3. 6
Ne Persia selfe, the nourse of Pompous pride, *Like* ever saw. I. iv. 7. 7
Exceeding shone, *like* Phoebus fayrest childe, I. iv. 9. 1
With *like* conditions to their kindes applyde: I. iv. 18. 4
Like to an holy Monck, I. iv. 18. 9
like a Crane his necke was long and fyne I. iv. 21. 5
most *like* a brutish beast, I. iv. 21. 8
more *like* a monster then a man. I. iv. 22. 9
Was *like* the person selfe whom he did beare: I. iv. 24. 4
He hated . . . him no lesse, that any *like* did use; I. iv. 32. 2
ne you the *like* need to reherce. I. iv. 50. 9
heaped blowes *like* yron hammers great; I. v. 7. 2
doubled strokes, *like* dreaded thunders threat; I. v. 7. 5
With *like* attempt to *like* end to renew. I. v. 42. 4
Like carkases of beastes in butchers stall. I. v. 49. 2
thousands moe the *like* that did that dongeon fill. I. v. 50. 9
dwell in perill of *like* painefull plight, I. v. 52. 4
many corses, *like* a great Lay-stall, I. v. 53. 2
molten starres doe drop *like* weeping eyes; I. vi. 6. 5
monstrous rablement, Whose *like* he never saw, I. vi. 8. 8
Leaping *like* wanton kids in pleasant Spring. I. vi. 14. 4
In these and *like* delightes of bloody game I. vi. 29. 1
now he thither came for *like* intent; I. vi. 30. 5
Whose *like* in womens witt he never knew; I. vi. 31. 2
with *like* treason now maintain Thy guilty wrong, I. vi. 41. 5
cast her coulours . . . To seeme *like* truth, I. vii. 1. 5
greene boughes . . . About the fountaine *like* a girlond made; I. vii. 4. 5
Which *like* a fever fit through all his bodie swelt. I. vii. 6. 9
His living *like* saw never living eye, I. vii. 8. 7
Like glauncing light of Phoebus brightest ray: I. vii. 29. 5
shind, *like* twinkling stars, with stones I. vii. 29. 9
one pretious stone . . . Shapt *like* a Ladies head, I. vii. 30. 3
shone, *Like* Hesperus emongst the lesser lights, I. vii. 30. 4
Like to an almond tree ymounted hye I. vii. 32. 5
earth, . . . did *like* an erthquake show. I. viii. 8. 9
his left arme, which *like* a block Did fall I. viii. 10. 6
blood . . . Forth gushed, *like* fresh water streame I. viii. 10. 9
threatned all his heades *like* flaming brandes. I. viii. 12. 6
twixt him and his Lord did *like* a bulwarke stand. I. viii. 12. 9
like an emptie blader was. I. viii. 24. 9
his flesh shronk up *like* withered flowres. I. viii. 41. 9
Is to be wise, and ware of *like* agein. I. viii. 44. 6
dried dugs, *lyke* bladders lacking wind, I. viii. 47. 6
one of them was *like* an Eagles claw, I. viii. 48. 6
The other *like* a beares uneven paw, I. viii. 48. 8
Ne living man *like* wordes did ever heare, I. ix. 14. 7
like infirmity *like* chaunce may beare; I. ix. 30. 8
That *like* would not for all this worldes wealth. I. ix. 31. 4
His subtile tong *like* dropping honny mealt'h I. ix. 31. 5
Darke, dolefull, dreary, *like* a greedy grave, I. ix. 33. 4
death then would the *like* mishaps forestall, I. ix. 45. 8
his hand did quake And tremble *like* a leafe I. ix. 51. 4
Like sunny beames threw from her Christall face I. x. 12. 7
beames . . . did shine *like* hevens light. I. x. 12. 9
them encounters with *like* courtesee; I. x. 15. 2
drops of blood thence *like* a well did play: I. x. 27. 4
like a Lyon he would cry and rore, I. x. 28. 2
blood-red billowes *like* a walled front, I. x. 53. 3
like that sacred hill, whose head full hie, I. x. 54. 1
like that pleasaunt Mount, I. x. 54. 6
'These, that have it attaynd, were in *like* cace, I. x. 62. 3
As wretched men, and lived in *like* paine.' I. x. 62. 4
himselfe *like* a great hill: I. xi. 4. 6
Like plated cote of steele, I. xi. 9. 2
His flaggy winges, . . . Were *like* two sayles, I. xi. 10. 2
Were *like* mayne-yardes with flying canvas lynd; I. xi. 10. 5
Wyde gaped, *like* the griesly mouth of hell, I. xi. 12. 8
blazing eyes, *like* two bright shining shieldes, I. xi. 14. 1
from thenceforth he shund the *like* to take, I. xi. 24. 8
He lowdly brayd, that *like* was never heard; I. xi. 26. 2
Like Eyas hauke up mounts I. xi. 34. 6
In all the world *like* was not to be fownd, I. xi. 47. 1
Another *like* faire tree eke grew thereby, I. xi. 47. 6
like an heaped mountaine lay. I. xi. 54. 9
That seemd *like* silke and silver woven neare; I. xii. 22. 8
much *like* a man dismayd, I. xii. 24. 8
Like as it had bene many an Angels voice I. xii. 39. 3
vertues *like* mote unto him allye. II. i. 23. 9
Must now anew begin *like* race to ronne. II. i. 32. 7
her semblance seemes to show, Shapt *like* a maide, II. ii. 9. 5
ever, *like* herselfe, unstayned II. ii. 9. 9
on his shield *like* yron sledges bet: II. ii. 22. 4
he, not *like* a weary traveilere, II. ii. 23. 1
Huddibras, more *like* a Malecontent, II. ii. 37. 6
a sword that flames *like* burning brond. II. iii. 18. 5
red did shew *Like* roses in a bed of lillies shed, II. iii. 22. 6
forhead . . . *Like* a broad table II. iii. 24. 2
Sweete wordes *like* dropping honny II. iii. 24. 7
glistred bright *Like* twinckling starres; II. iii. 26. 8
Like two faire marble pillours II. iii. 28. 1
paps; which, *like* young fruit in May, II. iii. 29. 7
yellow lockes, crisped *like* golden wyre, II. iii. 30. 1
lockes . . . waved *like* a penon II. iii. 30. 4
well may thee befall, As all the *like,* II. iii. 37. 7
his long locks colourd *like* copper-wyre, II. iv. 15. 8
'Ere long with *like* againe he boorded mee, II. iv. 24. 1
Disguised *like* that groome of base degree, II. iv. 27. 8

Like—*Continued.*

looking round about, *like* one dismaid, . . . IV. iv. 22. 3
Like sparke of fire that from the andvile glode, . . . IV. iv. 23. 5
Like as a Lion . . . doth rage and rore, . . . IV. iv. 32. 5
Like captive thral two other Knights atweene: . . . IV. iv. 34. 5
like salvage weed With woody mosse bedight, . . . IV. iv. 39. 4
Far'd *like* a lyon in his bloodie game, . . . IV. iv. 41. 5
Like as in sommers day, . . . IV. iv. 47. 1
Which else was *like* to have bene lost, . . . IV. iv. 48. 3
As *like* can not be seene from East to West, . . . IV. v. 18. 4
like thornes did pricke his gealous hart, . . . IV. v. 31. 3
through his soule *like* poysned arrow perst, . . . IV. v. 31. 4
a little cottage, *like* some poore mans nest. . . . IV. v. 32. 9
Of muddie water, that *like* puddle stanke, . . . IV. v. 33. 4
Like belles in greatnesse orderly succeed, . . . IV. v. 36. 8
He *like* a monstrous Gyant seem'd in sight, . . . IV. v. 37. 1
Like to the Northren winde, . . . IV. v. 38. 8
up he rose, *like* heavie lumpe of lead, . . . IV. v. 45. 6
Like as the lightning brond from riven skie, . . . IV. vi. 14. 1
Like to the ruddie morne appeard in sight, . . . IV. vi. 19. 6
Like to a golden border did appeare, . . . IV. vi. 20. 3
it did glister *like* the golden sand, . . . IV. vi. 20. 7
Like to a stubborne steede . . . IV. vi. 33. 9
senselesse stood, *like* to a mazed steare . . . IV. vi. 37. 4
Yet was no man, but onely *like* in shape, . . . IV. vii. 5. 2
huge great teeth, *like* to a tusked Bore: . . . IV. vii. 5. 6
His neather lip was not *like* man nor beast, . . . IV. vii. 6. 1
like a wide deepe poke, . . . IV. vii. 6. 2
all his haire was *like* a garment seene; . . . IV. vii. 7. 3
Unweeting of thine owne *like* haplesse plight: . . . IV. vii. 10. 8
like unlucky lot Hath linckt with me . . . IV. vii. 14. 6
like a ghastly Gelt whose wits are reaved, . . . IV. vii. 21. 3
overleapes them all, *like* Robucke light, . . . IV. vii. 22. 2
seemd *like* a sodaine flood. . . . IV. vii. 32. 9
like a pined ghost he soone appeares: . . . IV. vii. 41. 4
like strange wight, whom he had seene no where, . . . IV. vii. 43. 7
liv'd *like* outcast thrall. . . . IV. vii. 43. 9
Like as it fell to this unhappy boy, . . . IV. viii. 2. 1
Which losse her made *like* passion also prove: . . . IV. viii. 3. 5
Shap'd *like* a heart yet bleeding of the wound, . . . IV. viii. 6. 8
Like ghost late risen from his grave agryz'd, . . . IV. viii. 12. 7
From his moist eies, and *like* two streames procead; . . . IV. viii. 13. 4
like the stings of aspes that kill with smart, . . . IV. viii. 26. 8
did live then *like* an innocent, . . . IV. viii. 30. 2
Like as a curre doth felly bite . . . IV. viii. 36. 5
Like as the Basiliske, of serpents seede, . . . IV. viii. 39. 7
were her vertue *like* her beautie bright, . . . IV. viii. 49. 6
never two so *like* did living creature see. . . . IV. viii. 55. 9
error and misthought Of our *like* persons, . . . IV. viii. 58. 3
weake and wan, not *like* him selfe to bee. . . . IV. ix. 8. 9
they so *like* in person did appeare, . . . IV. ix. 10. 8
Their *like* resemblaunce much admired there, . . . IV. ix. 11. 2
Left in the victors powre, *like* vassall bond, . . . IV. ix. 18. 7
Whose *like* they never saw till that same houre . . . IV. ix. 22. 5
Like to a storme which hovers under skie, . . . IV. ix. 33. 4
like on earth no where I recken may: . . . IV. x. 15. 7
through gifts, or guile, or such *like* waies, . . . IV. x. 18. 8
loved not as these for *like* intent, . . . IV. x. 26. 5
like to this be clamed. . . . IV. x. 30. 9
much *like* unto a Danisk hood, . . . IV. x. 31. 7
like to christall glasse, . . . IV. x. 39. 7
shapes seem'd not *like* to terrestriall boyes, . . . IV. x. 42. 4
like to Angels playing heavenly toyes, . . . IV. x. 42. 5
eyes, *like* twinkling stars in evening cleare, . . . IV. x. 50. 7
Like to the Morne, . . . IV. x. 52. 6
Like warie Hynd within the weedie soyle, . . . IV. x. 55. 8
All looking on, and *like* astonisht staring, . . . IV. x. 56. 8
She lenger yet is *like* captiv'd to bee; . . . IV. xi. 1. 8
Like to the balefull house of lowest hell, . . . IV. xi. 4. 3
like her thrall: . . . IV. xi. 7. 6
the waves, glittering *like* Christall glas, . . . IV. xi. 27. 3
like to a Coronet . . . IV. xi. 27. 6
Like as the mother of the Gods, . . . IV. xi. 28. 1
hundred turrets, *like* a Turribant; . . . IV. xi. 28. 6
like a nousling Mole doth make His way . . . IV. xi. 32. 8
decked all with woods *Like* a wood God, . . . IV. xi. 33. 2
Whose *like* none else could shew, . . . IV. xi. 33. 9
those sixe sad brethren, *like* forlorne, . . . IV. xi. 37. 1
The spacious Shenan spreading *like* a sea, . . . IV. xi. 41. 3
like an Island fayre, . . . IV. xi. 44. 3
seem'd *like* silver, sprinckled here and theare . . . IV. xi. 45. 4
glittering spangs that did *like* starres appeare, . . . IV. xi. 45. 5
wav'd upon, *like* water Chamelot, . . . IV. xi. 45. 6
like to the hore Congealed litle drops . . . IV. xi. 46. 8
Both clad in colours *like*, and *like* array, . . . IV. xi. 47. 8
Laomedia *like* the christall sheene; . . . IV. xi. 51. 3
Till *like* a victor on his backe he ride, . . . IV. xii. 13. 5
Like as an Hynde, whose calfe is falne unwares . . . IV. xii. 17. 6
did inly mourne, *like* one astray. . . . IV. xii. 18. 9
nothing *like* himselfe he seem'd in sight. . . . IV. xii. 20. 5
Like ruefull ghost, . . . IV. xii. 20. 9
makes them *like* himselfe in glorious sight . . . V. Pr. 10. 7
Next Hercules his *like* ensample shewed, . . . V. i. 2. 6
Bursting forth teares *like* springs . . . V. i. 15. 2
on the ground he layd him *like* a sencelesse blocke. . . . V. i. 21. 9
Bound *like* a beast appointed to the stall: . . . V. i. 22. 6
Could swim *like* to a fish, . . . V. ii. 13. 9
Talus, that could *like* a lime-hound winde her, . . . V. ii. 25. 3
never there the *like* resort they knew. . . . V. ii. 29. 7
Like as the sea . . . Had worne the earth; . . . V. ii. 32. 3

Like—*Continued.*

Like foolish flies about an hony-crocke; . . . V. ii. 33. 3
Hemd in with waters *like* a wall in sight, . . . V. ii. 35. 7
'They live, they die, *like* as he doth ordaine, . . . V. ii. 41. 1
Like as a ship, whom cruell tempest . . . V. ii. 50. 1
He *like* a swarme of flyes them overthrew; . . . V. ii. 53. 6
through the thickest *like* a Lyon flew, . . . V. iii. 8. 5
like as one whom feends had made affrayd, . . . V. iii. 18. 4
Like the true saint beside the image set, . . . V. iii. 24. 2
like a lifelesse corse immoveable he stood. . . . V. iii. 26. 9
While she was flying, *like* a weary weft, . . . V. iii. 27. 5
Shapt *like* a horses shoe, . . . V. iii. 32. 9
like a little Mount of small degree, . . . V. iv. 7. 7
like tyrants mercilesse, the more Rejoyced . . . V. iv. 23. 1
bread and water or *like* feeble thing, . . . V. iv. 31. 8
like one that hopelesse was depryv'd . . . V. iv. 35. 1
like a sort of Bees in clusters swarmed: . . . V. iv. 36. 7
their Queene her selfe, halfe *like* a man, . . . V. iv. 36. 8
Like a fell Lionesse at him she flew, . . . V. iv. 39. 6
Like to an Eagle, in his kingly pride . . . V. iv. 42. 1
like a sort of sheepe dispersed farre . . . V. iv. 44. 7
What ever he shall *like* to doe or say. . . . V. iv. 49. 5
Like as the workeman had their courses taught; . . . V. v. 2. 5
to the Moone it mote be *like* in each respect. . . . V. v. 3. 9
he, that had *like* tempests often tride, . . . V. v. 6. 6
Like as a Smith . . . V. v. 7. 6
like a greedie Beare unto her pray, . . . V. v. 9. 7
Like as the Moone in foggie winters night . . . V. v. 12. 8
Like one that from his dreame is waked suddenlye. . . . V. v. 13. 9
Like as a Puttocke having spyde in sight A gentle Faulcon . . . V. v. 15. 1
through her eyes *like* sudden lightning flashed, . . . V. v. 30. 3
not *like* a lover, But *like* a rebell stout, I will him use; . . . V. v. 51. 2, 3
to her chamber went *like* solitary cell. . . . V. vi. 11. 9
Like as a wayward childe, . . . V. vi. 14. 1
Like to a Spaniell wayting carefully . . . V. vi. 26. 8
here and there *like* scattred sheepe they lay: . . . V. vi. 30. 6
He had three sonnes, all three *like* fathers sonnes, . . . V. vi. 33. 1
Like treacherous, *like* full of fraud and guile, . . . V. vi. 33. 2
Streight was the passage, *like* a ploughed ridge, . . . V. vi. 36. 8
Like coles that through a silver Censer sparkle bright. . . . V. vi. 38. 9
They wore rich Mitres shaped *like* the Moone, . . . V. vii. 4. 6
Like as Osyris signifies the Sunne: . . . V. vii. 4. 8
they both *like* race in equall justice runne. . . . V. vii. 4. 9
Whose *like* before she never saw nor red; . . . V. vii. 5. 7
Like to a weake faint-hearted man he fared . . . V. vii. 20. 5
Like one adawed with some dreadfull spright: . . . V. vii. 20. 8
Like to Osyris in all just endever: . . . V. vii. 22. 5
on the ground their lives did strow, *Like* fruitles seede, . . . V. vii. 31. 9
Like to an hideous storme, which nothing may empeach. . . . V. vii. 35. 9
Whom *like* disguize no lesse deformed had, . . . V. vii. 38. 2
Carried with wings of feare, *like* fowle aghast, . . . V. viii. 4. 7
like hound full greedy of his pray, . . . V. viii. 7. 1
So both together, ylike felly bent, *Like* fiercely met. . . . V. viii. 7. 6
tottred, *like* two towres which through a tempest quooke. . . . V. viii. 9. 9
Me *like* a dog she out of dores did thrust, . . . V. viii. 22. 7
Like one of those two Knights which dead there lay; . . . V. viii. 25. 5
With *like* fierce minds, but meanings different; . . . V. viii. 30. 2
Like to the Thracian Tyrant, . . . V. viii. 31. 1
made him rave, *like* to a Lyon wood, . . . V. viii. 35. 5
like to an hungry hound . . . V. viii. 36. 4
Like lightening flash that hath the gazer burned, . . . V. viii. 38. 1
like mazed deare dismayfully they flew. . . . V. viii. 38. 9
Like as the cursed son of Theseus, . . . V. viii. 43. 1
By *like* ensample mote for ever warned bee. . . . V. viii. 44. 9
Streight downe she ranne, *like* an enraged cow . . . V. viii. 46. 1
Like raging Ino, when with knife in hand . . . V. viii. 47. 1
like one enfelon'd or distraught, . . . V. viii. 48. 5
like wyld Goates them chaced all about, . . . V. viii. 50. 7
Like as the fouler on his guilefull pype . . . V. ix. 13. 1
oversprad her *like* a puffe wind; . . . V. ix. 14. 3
thereon flew *Like* a wyld Gote, . . . V. ix. 15. 4
he him hunted *like* a Foxe full fast: . . . V. ix. 17. 2
like a stone it fell upon the land; . . . V. ix. 17. 8
never saw they there the *like* array; . . . V. ix. 24. 5
like a cloud, as likest may be told, . . . V. ix. 28. 4
Glistring *like* gold amongst the plights enrold, . . . V. ix. 28. 7
appall An hardie courage, *like* captived thrall . . . V. ix. 33. 5
like a bulwarke firmely did abyde, . . . V. x. 35. 4
Like to a rancke of piles that pitched are awry. . . . V. xi. 9. 9
That curt'sie with *like* kindnesse to repay, . . . V. xi. 11. 5
two more of his armes did fall away, *Like* fruitlesse braunches, V. xi. 11. 8
Like a fell mastiffe through enraging heat, . . . V. xi. 12. 2
other *like* infernall furies kinde; . . . V. xi. 23. 6
like in foulnesse and deformity Unto that Monster, . . . V. xi. 25. 1
So also did this Monster use *like* slight . . . V. xi. 25. 7
Whom she did put to death, deceived *like* a foole. . . . V. xi. 25. 9
She flew at him *like* to an hellish feend, . . . V. xi. 27. 2
Like to a great Mill-damb forth fiercely gusht, . . . V. xi. 31. 5
For ye into *like* thraldome me did throw, . . . V. xi. 41. 8
like a Lion wood amongst them fares, . . . V. xi. 45. 3
Like scattred chaffe the which the wind away doth fan. . . . V. xi. 47. 9
all about the fields *like* Squirrels hunt; . . . V. xi. 59. 3
for *like* cause faire Belge did oppresse, . . . V. xii. 2. 6
to fly *like* doves whom the Eagle doth affray. . . . V. xii. 5. 9
Like as a tender Rose in open plaine, . . . V. xii. 13. 1
Like to a Giant for his monstrous hight, . . . V. xii. 15. 2
gaped *like* a gulfe when he did gerne; . . . V. xii. 15. 8
oft had seene *like* sight, . . . V. xii. 16. 6
Did underneath him *like* a pond appeare, . . . V. xii. 20. 7
Her lips were, *like* raw lether, pale and blew: . . . V. xii. 29. 7

Like—*Continued.*
her lookes, which *like* to Cordials bee; . . . *H.B.* 250
seeme *like* twinckling starres in frostie night; . . . *H.B.* 257
lips, *like* rosy buds in May, . . . *H.B.* 258
begot, *Like* to it selfe his eldest sonne and heire, . . . *H.H.L.* 31
loves to get Things *like* himselfe, and to enlarge his race, . . . *H.H.L.* 52
He made by love out of His owne *like* mould, . . . *H.H.L.* 116
That *like* itselfe in lovely shape may bee. . . . *H.H.L.* 119
Seeing him lie *like* creature long accurst . . . *H.H.L.* 129
like a most demisse And abject thrall, . . . *H.H.L.* 136
Where they shall have *like* heritage of land, . . . *H.H.L.* 200
That we the *like* should to the wretches shew, . . . *H.H.L.* 215
soyle, In which thou wallowest *like* to filthy swyne, . . . *H.H.L.* 219
like the native brood of Eagles kynd, . . . *H.H.B.* 138
Clad *like* a Queene in royall robes, . . . *H.H.B.* 185
doe fly away, *Like* empty shaddowes, . . . *Proth.* 9
like old Peneus Waters they did seeme, . . . *Proth.* 78
they appeare . . . *Like* a Brydes Chamber flore. . . . *Proth.* 82
this noble Lord issuing, *Like* Radiant Hesper, . . . *Proth.* 164
like the twins of Jove they seem'd in sight, . . . *Proth.* 173

Liked. whatso he *likte* he kept. . . . *Hub.* 1146
lips he layd on thing that *likte* him best, . . . II. vii. 27. 3
did vew his Personage And *liked* well, . . . III. ii. 26. 2
every one her *likte,* and every one her lov'd. . . . III. ix. 24. 9
th' Amazon, as best it *likt* her selfe to dight. . . . V. v. 1. 9
To be his Love, and of him *liked* well: . . . VII. vi. 44. 6
at first Made of meere love, and after *liked* well, . . . *H.H.L.* 128

Likeliness. she knew not his favours *likelynesse,* . . . V. vii. 39. 7

Likely. *likly* was his liefest love to be, . . . IV. vii. 46. 3
th' other two well *likely* to have harmed. . . . V. iv. 36. 5
Ne surely thus unarm'd I *likely* were; . . . VI. ii. 8. 3
a ship . . . Now farre from harbour *likely* to be lost, . . . VI. iv. 1. 3
her countenaunce and her *likely* hew, . . . VI. xii. 18. 7
She bath'd her lovely limbes, for Jove a *likely* pray. . . . VII. vi. 45. 9
likely harts composd of starres concent, . . . *H.B.* 198

Liken. *See* **Like.**
I would her *lyken* to a crowne of lillies, . . . *Col.* 337
tell me whereto can ye *lyken* it; . . . *Am.* xl. 2

Likened. he *likened* was to a welhed Of evill words, . . . V. ix. 26. 8
sith so heaven ye *lykened* are the best, . . . *Am.* lv. 13

Likeness. through *likenesse* of his gotish beard, . . . III. x. 47. 6
Joying his love in *likenes* more entire: . . . III. xi. 33. 7
through the *likenesse* of my outward hew, . . . IV. viii. 56. 2
Deceived through great *likenesse* of their face: . . . IV. ix. 10. 7
The flesh of men, to Gods owne *likenesse* framed, . . . V. x. 28. 7
To multiply the *likenese* of their kynd, . . . *H.L.* 100
your *likenesse* doth display; . . . *H.B.* 180

Liker. *liker* bene they to pluck away more, . . . *S.C.* S. 128
But was secure; the *liker* he to fall. . . . *Mui.* 382
Is *liker* lingring death then loathed life to bee.' . . . V. x. 21. 9
Liker to heaven then mortall wretchednesse: . . . VI. xi. 1. 5

Likes. it *likes* me wondrous well; . . . *Hub.* 95
Foolish Narcisse, that *likes* the watry shore; . . . III. vi. 45. 5

Like-seeming. By his *like seeming* shield her knight by name
She weend . . . I. iii. 26. 6

Likest. Souldier, for you *likest* are For manly semblance, . . . *Hub.* 199
mans life in his *likest* image Was limned forth, . . . *T.M.* 201
paint in rimes the troublous state . . . in *likest* fashion, . . . *T.M.* 382
He *likest* is to fall into mischaunce, . . . *Mui.* 383
likest is unto that heavenly towre . . . II. ix. 47. 4
likest it to an Hyena was, . . . III. vii. 22. 8
Him selfe to fashion *likest* Florimell, . . . III. viii. 8. 6
likest glasse did seeme. . . . IV. x. 39. 9
like a cloud, as *likest* may be told, . . . V. ix. 28. 4
Then to the Maker selfe they *likest* be, . . . *Am.* ix. 13
Lykest . . . Unto the fayre sunshine . . . *Am.* xl. 5
likest to your selves ye them select, . . . *H.B.* 191

Likewise. Rhodian will *likewise* set forth The great Colosse, . . . *Ro.* ii. 9
I *likewise* have wasted much good time, . . . *Hub.* 75
ye *likewise* Might unto some of those . . . arise? . . . *Hub.* 425
Her selfe *likewise* unto her worke to dight. . . . *Mui.* 304
She *likewise* did deforme, like him to bee. . . . *As.* 156
is theyr heaven *likewise* there all one? . . . *Col.* 305
I in defence of mine did *likewise* stand, . . . I. ii. 36. 3
His answere *likewise* was, . . . I. viii. 34. 1
Who *likewise* gan himselfe to batteill dight, . . . II. vii. 42. 5
resolv'd *likewise* to prove the rest, . . . II. x. 31. 4
Likewise that same third Fort, . . . II. xi. 11. 1
the other *likewise* up arose, . . . II. xii. 67. 1
What wonder then, if she were *likewise* carried? . . . III. x. 9. 9
he *likewise* gan assay . . . III. xi. 26. 2
over that same dore was *likewise* writ, . . . III. xi. 54. 2
Likewise unequall were her handes twaine; . . . IV. i. 29. 1
when the next shall *likewise* ended bee, . . . IV. ii. 52. 7
both their lives may *likewise* be annext Unto the third, . . . IV. ii. 52. 8
th' end of both *likewise* of both their ends: . . . IV. iv. 1. 5
him *likewise* with that same speare he eke did quell. . . . IV. iv. 19. 9
him *likewise* he quickly downe did smight, . . . IV. iv. 21. 3
shortly was *likewise* seene lying on the plaine. . . . IV. iv. 44. 9
Full many others at him *likewise* ran, . . . IV. iv. 46. 1
all of them *likewise* dismounted were; . . . IV. iv. 46. 2
many other Ladies *likewise* tride . . . IV. v. 17. 6
Likewise assayd to prove that girdles powre; . . . IV. v. 19. 3
likewise sought her lover long miswent, . . . IV. v. 30. 6
So *likewise* did the hammers which they bore, . . . IV. v. 36. 7
likewise late had lost her dearest love, . . . IV. viii. 3. 4
Being *likewise* beguiled in her thought, . . . IV. viii. 56. 3
being doubly smitten *likewise* doubly smit. . . . IV. ix. 29. 9
till that *likewise* fleet; . . . IV. ix. 33. 8
So gan the rest him *likewise* to require, . . . IV. ix. 41. 1

Likewise—*Continued.*
all the twenty I *likewise* entreated, . . . IV. x. 10. 5
she her selfe *likewise* divinely grew; . . . IV. x. 34. 4
Why should they not *likewise* in love agree, . . . IV. xi. 40. 4
joy *likewise* this solemne day to see? . . . IV. xi. 40. 5
likewise on her hed A Chapelet . . . IV. xi. 46. 5
likewise the wicked seede of vice Began to spring; . . . V. i. 1. 3
'*Likewise* the earth is not augmented more . . . V. ii. 40. 1
'Now take the right *likewise,*' . . . V. ii. 46. 1
so *likewise* of words, the which be spoken, . . . V. ii. 47. 7
Which when as Marinell beheld *likewise,* . . . V. iii. 18. 1
Yet my good lucke he shall not *likewise* pray, . . . V. iv. 14. 8
'Now, Bracidas, let this *likewise* be showne; . . . V. iv. 18. 2
whom they *likewise* made A Goddesse . . . V. vii. 3. 1
He gan to threaten her *likewise* to eat, . . . V. vii. 15. 8
All night *likewise* they of the towne . . . V. vii. 26. 5
did enterprise Both to redresse, and both redrest *likewise:* . . . V. viii. 11. 5
followed was of him *likewise* full fast, . . . V. viii. 33. 8
at her feet her sword was *likewise* layde, . . . V. ix. 30. 6
that those knights *likewise* mote understand, . . . V. ix. 37. 4
praise *likewise* deserve good thewes . . . VI. ii. 2. 9
let thy Lady *likewise* doe the same, . . . VI. iii. 32. 3
the other came in place *likewise,* . . . VI. iii. 48. 1
comming *likewise* to the wounded knight, . . . VI. iv. 12. 1
this Squire, who *likewise* wounded was . . . VI. v. 31. 6
therein he *likewise* was praying now, . . . VI. v. 35. 8
I *likewise* in vaine doe salves to you applie: . . . VI. vi. 6. 9
So *likewise* turnde the Prince upon the Knight, . . . VI. vi. 27. 8
Whom he *likewise* right sorely did constraine, . . . VI. vi. 38. 5
Sith he *likewise* did wrong by him sustaine, . . . VI. vii. 22. 7
Then all the rest about her rose *likewise,* . . . VI. ix. 15. 3
who her *likewise* Long time had lov'd, . . . VI. ix. 38. 1
That we *likewise* should mylde and gentle be; . . . VI. x. 24. 2
So *likewise* did this Titanesse aspire . . . VII. vi. 4. 1
likewise Should handle as the rest of her allies, . . . VII. vi. 30. 4
'So *likewise* are all watry living wights Still tost . . . VII. vii. 21. 1
likewise chang'd and subject unto mee? . . . VII. vii. 49. 9
So *likewise* grim Sir Saturne oft doth spare . . . VII. vii. 52. 7
I *lykewise* . . . some service fit will find. . . . *Am.* xxii. 3
Let it *lykewise* your gentle brest inspire . . . *Am.* xxviii. 6
So my storme-beaten hart *likewise* is cheared . . . *Am.* xl. 13
So, *likewise,* Love! cheare you your heavy spright, . . . *Am.* lxii. 13
thy love we weighing worthily, May *likewise* love thee . . . *Am.* lxviii. 10
eek my name bee wyped out *lykewize.* . . . *Am.* lxxv. 8
thou thyselfe *likewise* art lyttle made, . . . *Epig.* iv. 13
ye *likewise,* which keepe the rushy lake, . . . *Epith.* 60
leave *likewise* your former lay to sing: . . . *Epith.* 313
For thou *likewise* didst love, . . . *Epith.* 378
So those *likewise* doe by degrees redound, . . . *H.H.B.* 75

Liking. labour, that did from his *liking* balke, . . . *Hub.* 268
in his *liking* to winne worthie place, . . . *Hub.* 776
raigne in *liking* of the multitude; . . . *T.M.* 326
the Nymph her former *liking* held; . . . *Col.* 128
He gan to cast great *lyking* to my lore, . . . *Col.* 180
found I *lyking* in her royall mynd, . . . *Col.* 454
Why doe ye . . . *liking* find to gaze . . . I. vii. 22. 4
will ryde Against my *liking* backe to doe you grace: . . . I. ix. 32. 6
If ought amis her *liking* may abuse: . . . III. Pr. 5. 4
greatest Princes *liking* it mote well delight. . . . III. v. 40. 9
To winne her *liking* unto his delight: . . . III. viii. 38. 5
great *liking* sheowe, Great *liking* unto many, . . . III. xii. 13. 8, 9
her love prepare, and *liking* win theretoo. . . . IV. ii. 8. 9
Yet she to none of them her *liking* lent, . . . IV. ii. 36. 2
Whether she would them love, or in her *liking* brooke. . . . IV. ii. 40. 9
From all forbidden things his *liking* to withdraw. . . . IV. viii. 30. 9
To whom she did her *liking* lightly cast, . . . IV. viii. 52. 6
change his *liking,* and new Lemans prove; . . . IV. ix. 21. 6
her had to her *liking* left. . . . IV. ix. 36. 9
Gan cast a secret *liking* to this captive straunge. . . . V. v. 26. 9
his foes love or *liking* entertaine. . . . V. v. 46. 7
Yet found no place that could her *liking* please, . . . V. vi. 7. 3
The which in all mens *liking* gayned place, . . . VI. i. 3. 4
And in the eyes of men great *liking* find, . . . VI. ii. 2. 4
Ne could her *liking* to his love apply, . . . VI. iii. 7. 4
Wandred about the fields, as *liking* led . . . VI. iii. 23. 6
When ought he did, that did their *lyking* gaine. . . . VI. iv. 16. 5
in her soveraine *lyking* he dwelt evermore. . . . VI. v. 12. 9
Did care a whit, ne any *liking* lend: . . . VI. ix. 10. 8
liking in her yet untamed heart procure. . . . VI. x. 32. 9
He may but purchase *lyking* in her eye, . . . *H.L.* 239

Lilies. Cowslips, and Kingcups, and loved *Lillies:* . . . *S.C.* Ap. 141
Out of his lips like *lilies* (*lillies) pale and soft: . . . *As.* 166
I would her lyken to a crowne of *lillies,* . . . *Col.* 337
Like roses in a bed of *lillies* shed, . . . II. iii. 22. 6
On a sweet bed of *lillies* softly laid, . . . II. v. 32. 3
As roses did with *lilies* interlace; . . . V. iii. 23. 5
brest, lyke *Lillyes,* ere theyr leaves be shed; . . . *Am.* lxiv. 11
Another gay girland . . . of *lillyes* and of roses, . . . *Epith.* 43
Her paps lyke *lyllies* budded, . . . *Epith.* 176
Lay her in *lillies* and in violets, . . . *Epith.* 302
With rose and *lillies* over them displayd. . . . *H.L.* 286

Lilies'. through *Lillies* plenteous store, . . . *Proth.* 81

Lilled. Cerberus . . . *lilled* forth his bloody flaming tong: . . . I. v. 34. 4

Lily. The *Lilly* fresh, and Violet belowe; . . . *Gn.* 667
he . . . lickt her *lilly* hands with fawning tong, . . . I. iii. 6. 2
'The *lilly,* Lady of the flowring field, . . . II. vi. 16. 1
her two *lilly* paps aloft displayd, . . . II. xii. 66. 6
did her *lilly* smock with staines of vermeil steep. . . . III. i. 65. 9
atweene her *lilly* handes twaine . . . III. v. 33. 3
As doth the *lilly* fresh before the sunny ray. . . . III. vi. 38. 9

Lily—*Continued.*
by the *lilly* hand her labour'd up to reare. . . . IV. x. 53. 9
Whom she receiving by the *lilly* hand, . . . IV. xii. 33. 3
He tooke her up forby the *lilly* hand, . . . V. xi. 17. 1
led a lovely Mayd Forth by the *lilly* hand, . . . VII. vii. 37. 4
Happy, ye leaves! when as those *lilly* hands, . . . *Am.* i. 1
The virgin *Lillie,* and the Primrose trew, . . . *Proth.* 32
Lily-handed. the *lilly handed* Liagore . . . III. iv. 41. 1
Lily-white. Dyed in *Lilly white* and Cremsin redde, . . . *S.C.* F. 130
She was araied all in *lilly white,* . . . I. x. 13. 1
a garment she did weare All *lilly white,* . . . I. xii. 22. 7
in a silken Camus *lilly* whight, . . . II. iii. 26. 4
In robe of *lilly white* she was arayd, . . . II. ix. 19. 1
The which was all in *lilly white* arayd, . . . IV. x. 52. 4
Fairest Pherusa, Phao *lilly white,* . . . IV. xi. 49. 5
An hundred naked maidens *lilly white* . . . VI. x. 11. 8
Limb. sleep . . . seized everie *lim.* . . . *Gn.* 240
now loosing everie *lim,* . . . *Gn.* 322
Ne stirreth *limbe;* . . . *Mui.* 405
full large of *limbe* and every joint He was, . . . I. ii. 12. 8
Which, quitt from death, yet quakes in every *lim* . . . I. vi. 10. 8
Nor . . . blood in all his face appeares, Nor life in *limbe;* . . . I. ix. 22. 5
feigning then in every *limb* to quake . . . II. i. 9. 3
Full large he was of *limbe,* . . . II. xi. 20. 7
She secretly would search each daintie *lim,* . . . III. i. 36. 6
every daintie *limbe* with horrour shake; . . . III. ii. 5. 5
for ye beene tall, and large of *limbe* . . . III. iii. 53. 7
seemd for feare to quake in every *lim,* . . . III. viii. 15. 8
everie *limbe* that touched her did quake; . . . IV. i. 5. 8
so weake of *limbe,* and sicke of love He woxe, . . . IV. xii. 20. 6
That *lim* he could not wag: . . . V. i. 22. 5
And every litle *limbe* he searcht around, . . . VI. iv. 23. 6
He had not left one *limbe* of him unrent: . . . VI. vi. 40. 8
Began to tremble every *limbe* and vaine; . . . VI. vii. 22. 2
perfectly well shapt in every *lim,* . . . VI. ix. 9. 2
Limbeck. As from a *limbeck* did adown distill. . . . VII. vii. 31. 5
Limbo. 'What voice of damned Ghost from *Limbo* lake, . . . I. ii. 32. 5
From *Limbo* lake him late escaped sure would say. . . . III. x. 54. 9
Limbs. On the soft grasse his *limbs* doth oft display, . . . *Gn.* 108
his *limbs,* resolv'd through idle leisour, . . . *Gn.* 141
To rest their *limbs* with wearines redounding. . . . *Gn.* 189
limbs, with lightening rent, . . . *Gn.* 199
their wearie *limbs* to rest, . . . *Gn.* 234
Thy careles *limbs* in loose sleep dost display. . . . *Gn.* 336
in long service lost both *limbs* and good; . . . *Hub.* 248
my late maymed *limbs* lack wonted might . . . *Hub.* 272
Ne will I rest my *limmes* for frailtie, . . . *D.* 461
So long as life my *limbs* doth hold together; . . . *Col.* 629
she her weary *limbes* would never rest; . . . I. ii. 8. 6
rest their weary *limbs* a tide. . . . I. ii. 29. 9
on the grasse her dainty *limbs* did lay . . . I. iii. 4. 3
in his lustlesse *limbs,* . . . A shaking fever raignd . . . I. iv. 20. 7
governing . . . aged *limbs* on cypresse stadle stout, . . . I. vi. 14. 8
staffe, to stay His weary *limbs* upon; . . . I. vi. 35. 8
Her daintie *limbes* . . . down did lay: . . . I. ix. 13. 8
tyred *limbes* to rest, . . . 'I hither came; . . . I. x. 11. 1
when their wearie *limbes* with kindly rest, . . . I. x. 18. 1
ne once adowne would lay Her dainty *limbs* . . . I. xi. 32. 8
Least his long way his aged *limbes* should tire: . . . II. i. 7. 5
who his *limbs* with labours, . . . II. iii. 40. 6
then by it his wearie *limbes* display, . . . II. v. 30. 7
does yield to vew Her dainty *limbes* . . . II. v. 33. 8
their snowy *limbes,* as through a vele, . . . II. xii. 64. 6
Having their weary *limbes* to perfect plight Restord, . . . III. i. 1. 3
mischievous mischaunce his life and *limbs* did spare. . . . III. i. 6. 9
Large were his *limbes,* and terrible his looke, . . . III. i. 17. 8
with delightfull sport To loose her warlike *limbs* . . . III. i. 52. 5
doth love to steepe His lustlesse *limbes,* . . . III. iv. 56. 6
In easie couch his feeble *limbes* to rest. . . . III. v. 41. 2
From off their dainty *limbs* the dusty sweat . . . III. vi. 17. 6
to rest her faint And wearie *limbes* awhile. . . . III. vii. 10. 5
the faire feature of her *limbs* did hyde; . . . III. ix. 21. 2
From scorching heat her daintie *limbes* to shade; . . . III. xi. 32. 5
thought his wearie *limbs* to have redrest. . . . IV. v. 39. 5
wearie *limmes* recur'd after late usage bad. . . . IV. vi. 39. 9
T' alight, and rest their wearie *limbs* awhile. . . . IV. vii. 3. 6
admir'd his monstrous shape, and oft His mighty *limbs,* . . . IV. vii. 32. 8
manly *limbs* endur'd with litle care . . . IV. viii. 27. 8
though his *limbs* could not his bodie beare, . . . IV. xii. 35. 3
his faire *limbs* left in the woods forlorne; . . . V. viii. 43. 5
gan to stretch his *limbs;* . . . VI. i. 35. 4
never . . . His *limbes* would rest, ne lig in ease embost, . . . VI. iv. 40. 7
Through feeblenesse, which all his *limbes* oppressed has. . . . VI. v. 31. 9
I downe doe lay My *limbes* . . . VI. ix. 23. 8
on the . . . grasse her dainty *limbes* to lay . . . VII. vi. 42. 4
doffing her array, She bath'd her lovely *limbes,* . . . VII. vi. 45. 9
So much delight to bathe her *limbes* she tooke: . . . VII. vi. 54. 4
now would bathe his *limbes* with labor heated sore. . . . VII. vii. 29. 9
scarse his loosed *limbes* he hable was to weld. . . . VII. vii. 31. 9
May poure his *limbs* forth on your pleasant playne; . . . *Epith.* 356
Lime. There now is but an heap of *lyme* and sand, . . . *Ti.* 129
Not built of bricke, ne yet of stone and *lime,* . . . II. ix. 21. 4
He of his name Coylchester built of stone and *lime.* . . . II. x. 58. 9
Lime-hound. *See* **Lyam-hound.**
Limit. 'Who life did *limit* by almightie doome,' . . . I. ix. 41. 6
Twede, the *limit* betwixt Logris land And Albany: . . . IV. xi. 36. 6
ere thou *limit* what is lesse or more . . . V. ii. 34. 5
Limited. 'The terme of life is *limited,* . . . I. ix. 41. 2
'Nay but the terme' (sayd he) 'is *limited,* . . . III. iii. 44. 1
Limiter. Or like a Pilgrim, or a *Lymiter,* . . . *Hub.* 85
Limned. mans life in his likest image Was *limned* forth, . . . *T.M.* 202
Limning. in perfect *limming* every part? . . . *H.B.* 84
Limy. wrapt his winges twaine In *lymie* snares . . . *Mui.* 429
Lin. Ne will I lodge, ne will I ever *lin,* . . . *D.* 467
soone to lose, before he once would *lin;* . . . I. i. 24. 5
ne might from labour *lin;* . . . I. v. 35. 4
shall not *lin* Till they to hevens hight . . . III. iii. 22. 3
if he then with victorie can *lin,* . . . III. iii. 30. 8
his deceiptfull eyes did never *lin* To looke . . . III. viii. 24. 8
Lincoln. his worke is eke Faire *Lincolne,* . . . III. ix. 51. 2
Of which the auncient *Lincolne* men doe call: . . . IV. xi. 39. 8
Lincoln green. in a woodmans jacket . . . Of *Lincolne greene,* VI. ii. 5. 7
Lindus. *Lindus* that his pikes doth most commend, . . . IV. xi. 39. 7
Line. *line,* or lead, or rule, or squaire, to measure Her length, . . . *Ro.* xxvi. 3
In dieper, in damaske, or in *lyne,* . . . *Mui.* 364
in a *line,* a milkewhite lambe she lad. . . . I. i. 4. 9
roiall stocke of old Assaracs *line,* . . . II. x. 9. 7
from wretched Adams *line* To purge away . . . II. x. 50. 3
Those could he well direct and streight as *line,* . . . II. xi. 21. 6
well she redd out of the learned *line:* . . . III. ix. 30. 8
when ye shred with fatall knife His *line,* . . . IV. ii. 52. 4
I doe not forme them to the common *line* . . . V. Pr. 3. 3
According to the *line* of conscience, . . . V. i. 7. 4
clothed all in garments made of *line,* . . . V. vii. 6. 4
Lineage. Descended all from Rome by *linage* due; . . . *Gn.* 596
by descent from Royall *lynage* came . . . I. i. 5. 3
the *lignage* right From whence he tooke his weldeserved name: I. vi. 20. 3
His loves and *lignage* Arthure tells: . . . I. ix. Arg.
the *lignage,* and the certein Sire . . . from mee are hidden . . . I. ix. 3. 3
Of what loines and what *lignage* I did spring; . . . I. ix. 5. 6
Lives ought that to her *linage* may compaire; . . . II. x. 2. 3
Of whom all Faeryes spring, and fetch their *lignage* right. . . . II. x. 71. 9
Whose *lignage* from this Lady I derive along. . . . III. iv. 3. 9
'From him my *linage* I derive aright, . . . III. ix. 36. 1
thy *linage,* and thy Lordly brood, . . . V. vii. 21. 7
That of the like, whose *linage* was unknowne, . . . VI. iv. 36. 2
Her antique race and *linage* ancient, . . . VII. vi. 2. 2
Lineal. of them sprung by *lineall* descent: . . . IV. xi. 12. 7
Lineally. She heard that she was *lineally* extract; . . . III. ix. 38. 7
Lineaments. The old *lineaments* of his fathers grace. . . . *S.C.* May 212
Her heavenly *lineaments* for to enchace. . . . I. xii. 23. 5
Lined. like mayne-yardes with flying canvas *lynd;* . . . I. xi. 10. 5
From inward parts, with cancred malice *lind,* . . . IV. viii. 26. 4
With beards of Knights and locks of Ladies *lynd:* . . . VI. i. 15. 5
Linen. all the Priests were damzels in soft *linnen* dight. . . . IV. x. 38. 9
With silver streames amongst the *linnen* stray'd; . . . IV. x. 52. 5
what their hands could earne by twisting *linnen* twyne. . . . V. v. 22. 9
All clad in *linnen* robes with silver hemd; . . . V. vii. 4. 4
linnen stole after those Priestes guize, . . . V. vii. 13. 3
All sodainely she saw transfigured Her *linnen* stole . . . V. vii. 13. 5
on his head a roll of *linnen* plight, . . . VI. vii. 43. 5
Lines. Not that these few *lines* can in them comprise . . . *Ded. Son.* xvi. 6
my frayle eies these *lines* with teares do steepe, . . . I. iii. 2. 3
on his shield *Sansloy* in bloody *lines* was dyde. . . . I. iii. 33. 9
Her greeting sends in these sad *lines* addrest . . . I. xii. 26. 2
Hearing him those same bloody *lynes* reherse; . . . III. xii. 36. 7
Is creasted all with *lines* of firie light, . . . IV. i. 13. 8
with unwearied fingers drawing out The *lines* of life, . . . IV. ii. 48. 4
happy *lines!* on which, with starry light, . . . *Am.* i. 5
Leaves, *lines,* and rymes, seeke her to please alone, . . . *Am.* i. 13
When your faire eyes these fearefull *lines* shal read, . . . *H.B.* 283
Linger. *linger* till the glas be all out ronne? . . . I. ix. 47. 8
his returne that seemes to *linger* late: . . . *Am.* lxxxviii. 4
Lingering. *See* **Long-lingering.**
chace the *lingring* Night With Heydeguyes, . . . *S.C.* Jun. 26
He lyes in *lingring* payne. . . . *S.C.* Jul. 228
nigh consumed is the *lingring* day. . . . I. iv. 3. 9
The better part now of the *lingring* day . . . I. vi. 34. 1
That earst us held in love of *lingring* life; . . . I. ix. 29. 6
remaynd Some *lingring* life within his hollow brest, . . . I. xii. 10. 4
T' abridg their journey long, and *lingring* day; . . . III. ii. 4. 3
Touching her loves successe, her *lingring* smart. . . . V. v. 45. 3
Is liker *lingring* death then loathed life to bee.' . . . V. x. 21. 9
As each thought best to spend the *lingring* space: . . . VI. viii. 39. 3
Link. thy daughter *linck,* in holy band Of wedlocke, . . . I. xii. 26. 6
"So soone as Bacchus with the Nymphe does *lincke!*" . . . II. i. 55. 6
every *linck* thereof a step of dignity. . . . II. vii. 46. 9
sought with her to *lincke* in marriage: . . . II. ix. 18. 5
her life at last must *lincke* in that same knot. . . . III. ii. 23. 9
muzzel strong . . . made with many a *lincke:* . . . VI. xii. 34. 3
Linked. *lincked* chaunst with thee to bee, . . . *Ti.* 248
yfere The vertues *linked* are in lovely wize; . . . I. ix. 1. 2
faire Charissa to a lovely fere was *lincked,* . . . I. x. 4. 9
Ylinked arme in arme in lovely wise: . . . I. x. 12. 3
She held a great gold chaine *ylincked* well, . . . II. vii. 46. 2
quite disparted all the *linked* frame, . . . II. viii. 44. 7
through the *linked* mayles empierced quite, . . . III. v. 19. 4
To whom her loving hart she *linked* fast . . . III. vi. 53. 3
is he *lincked* to a lovely lasse, . . . III. ix. 4. 4
Two knights that *lincked* rode in lovely wise, . . . IV. ii. 30. 3
With Canacee and Cambine *linckt* in lovely bond. . . . IV. ii. 31. 9
The knights in couples marcht with ladies *linckt* attone. . . . IV. iv. 14. 9
linckt with me in the same chaine attone?' . . . IV. vii. 14. 7
lovers *lincked* in true harts consent, . . . IV. x. 26. 4
Both *linckt* together never to dispart; . . . IV. x. 51. 7
linckt together gainst Sir Artegall; . . . V. xii. 37. 2
With a faire Lady *lincked* by his syde, . . . VI. iii. 30. 8
Together *linkt* with Adamantine chaines; . . . *H.L.* 89
Links. walke withouten *lincks* of love, . . . *S.C.* Jun. 34

Links—*Continued.*	
The loyall *linkes* of wedlocke did unbinde,	I. vi. 22. 8
Linus. With Orpheus, and with *Linus*, and the choice	*Ti.* 333
Lion. despise The noble *Lion* after his lives end,	*Ro.* xiv. 6
A mighty *Lyon*, Lord of all the wood,	*Van.* x. 1
what peace has the *Lion* with the Lambe?	*S.C.* May 169
The rampant *Lyon* hunts he fast,	*S.C.* Jul. 21
The *Lyon* now doth take the most delight;	*Hub.* 622
The *Lyon* sleeping lay in secret shade,	*Hub.* 952
whiles the *Lyon* sleepeth sound,	*Hub.* 967
Thinking indeed that it the *Lyon* was.	*Hub.* 1093
What did of late chaunce happen to the *Lyon* stearne,	*Hub.* 1250
he bad the *Lyon* be remitted Into his seate,	*Hub.* 1254
cast to seeke the *Lion* where he may,	*Hub.* 1316
The *Lion* looking up gan him avize,	*Hub.* 1324
the false Foxe, when he the *Lion* heard,	*Hub.* 1359
to the *Lion* came, full lowly creeping,	*Hub.* 1361
him at last the *Lyon* spide,	*Hub.* 1375
Like a grimme *Lyon* rushing	*Mui.* 434
the *Lyon*, which with toyle Alcides slew,	*D.* 165
The *Lyon* chose his mate,	*Col.* 865
lept As *Lyon* fierce upon the flying pray,	I. i. 17. 2
Forsaken Truth . . . makes the *Lyon* mylde;	I. iii. Arg.
out of the thickest wood A ramping *Lyon* rushed	I. iii. 5. 2
'The *Lyon*, Lord of everie beast in field,'	I. iii. 7. 1
he, my *Lyon*, and my noble Lord,	I. iii. 7. 6
The *Lyon* would not leave her desolate,	I. iii. 9. 1
seeing by her side the *Lyon* stand,	I. iii. 11. 5
at her feete the *Lyon* watch doth keepe:	I. iii. 15. 4
The *Lyon* frayed them, him in to lett.	I. iii. 19. 3
Up Una rose, up rose the *lyon* eke;	I. iii. 21. 2
he askt her, what the *Lyon* ment;	I. iii. 32. 8
him beside rides fierce revenging Wrath, Upon a *Lion*,	I. iv. 33. 2
a greedy Wolfe, . . . A *Lyon* spyes	I. vi. 10. 6
yet quakes . . . to see the *Lyon* looke so grim.	I. vi. 10. 9
His trembling hand he would him force to put Upon the *Lyon*	I. vi. 24. 4
he would learne The *Lyon* stoup to him in lowly wise,	I. vi. 25. 7
like a *Lyon* he would cry and rore,	I. x. 28. 2
As *Lion*, grudging in his great disdaine,	II. i. 42. 6
Like as a *Lyon*, whose imperiall powre	II. v. 10. 1
Lyon, which hath long time saught His robbed whelpes,	II. viii. 40. 7
A *Lyon* and a Tigre doth espye,	II. ix. 14. 8
a *Lion* passant in a golden field.	III. i. 4. 9
a *Lyon* that in drowsie cave Hath long time slept,	III. iii. 30. 1
a *Lion* from the sea-bord wood Of Neustria	III. iii. 47. 2
like a *Lyon* hunting after spoile;	III. xi. 39. 7
riding on a *Lion* ravenous,	III. xii. 22. 2
Like as a *Lion* . . . doth rage and rore,	IV. iv. 32. 5
Far'd like a *lyon* in his bloodie game,	IV. iv. 41. 5
The *Lyon* there did with the Lambe consort,	IV. viii. 31. 1
strong as *Lyon* in his lordly might.	V. i. 20. 5
through the thickest like a *Lyon* flew,	V. iii. 8. 5
forth did bring a *Lion* of great might,	V. vii. 16. 6
To which the *Lion* strongly doth gainesay,	V. vii. 30. 7
made him rave, like to a *Lyon* wood,	V. viii. 35. 5
An huge great *Lyon* lay,	V. ix. 33. 4
like a *Lion* wood amongst them fares,	V. xi. 45. 3
to launch the salvage hart Of many a *Lyon*	VI. ii. 6. 8
Like a fell *Lyon* at him fiercely flew,	VI. vi. 22. 4
Like a fell *Lion* leaped to him light,	VI. vii. 25. 5
Like as a *Lion* mongst an heard of dere,	VI. xi. 49. 1
her face did like a *Lion* shew,	VII. vii. 6. 4
Upon a *Lyon* raging yet with ire	VII. vii. 36. 3
And yet the *Lyon* that is Lord of power,	*Am.* xx. 5
Then either *Lyon* or the Lyonesse;	*Am.* xx. 10
Lioness. 'What nowe is of th' Assyrian *Lyonesse*,	*Ti.* 64
a faire young *Lionesse*, White as the native Rose	*D.* 107
My lovelie *Lionesse* . . . So carefull was	*D.* 137
To see my *Lyonesse*, whose praises wide	*D.* 144
My *Lyonesse* (ah, woe is mee!) is gon!	*D.* 161
The riddle of thy loved *Lionesse*;	*D.* 177
When after him a *Lyonesse* did runne,	I. vi. 27. 5
Like a fell *Lionesse* at him she flew,	V. iv. 39. 6
As when a Tygre and a *Lionesse* Are met	V. vii. 30. 1
Then either Lyon or the *Lyonesse;*	*Am.* xx. 10
Lion-like. *Lion-like* shall shew his powre extreame.	V. vii. 23. 8
Lion's. Feete of a beare, a *Lions* throte she had.	*Rev.* i. 5
love then in the *Lyons* house did dwell)	*S.C.* D. 57
After the chafed *Lyons* cruell bayting,	*Hub.* 6
at the *Lyons* skin he inly quooke;	*Hub.* 1060
Thinke him Alcides with the *Lyons* skin,	*Mui.* 71
For being borne an auncient *Lions* haire,	*D.* 122
that dredd *Lyons* looke her cast in deadly hew.	I. iii. 11. 9
From *Lyons* clawes to pluck the gryped pray.	I. vi. 7. 4
Into the great Nemaean *lions* grove.	V. Pr. 6. 4
His *Lyons* skin chaungd to a pall of gold,	V. v. 24. 7
For his loves sake his *Lions* skin undight;	V. viii. 2. 5
A *Lions* clawes, with powre and rigour clad,	V. xi. 24. 3
Her *Lions* clawes he from her feete away did wipe.	V. xi. 27. 9
Lions. foure great *Lyons* (*Lions*[1]) of gold;	*Bel.* iii. 10
hundred ramping *Lions* seemd to rore,	I. xi. 37. 3
Apes, *Lyons*, Aegles, Owles,	II. ix. 50. 9
Beares, *Lyons*, and Buls, which romed them arownd.	III. i. 14. 9
Of two grim *lyons*, taken from the wood,	IV. iii. 39. 2
The *Lyons* rore; the Tygres loudly bray;	IV. x. 46. 3
all embost with *Lyons* and with Flourdelice.	V. ix. 27. 9
doest the *Lions* and fell Tigers tame,	*H.L.* 46
Lion-whelps. The *Lyon whelpes* she saw how he did beare,	I. vi. 27. 8
Lip. the right gentle minde would bite his *lip*,	*Hub.* 711
His neather *lip* was not like man nor beast,	IV. vii. 6. 1
Lip—*Continued.*	
bit his *lip* for felonous despight,	IV. x. 33. 8
sore lament and bite her tender *lip*.	VI. vii. 44. 9
he would loure And byte his *lip*,	VI. ix. 39. 3
Thereat frown'd Coridon, and his *lip* closely bit.	VI. ix. 41. 9
Lipari. in *Lipari* doe day and night Frame thunderbolts	IV. v. 37. 3
Lips. Ne car'd with them his daintie *lips* to sweeten:	*Van.* ii. 9
upon his *lips* to laie The sacred sod,	*Ti.* 195
kisse thy *lips* like faded leaves of rose.	*As.* 138
suckt the wasting breath Out of his *lips*	*As.* 166
Trew sacred lore, which from her sweet *lips* did redound.	I. vi. 30. 9
His ruddy *lips* did smyle,	II. i. 41. 4
With *lips* full pale and foltring tong opprest,	II. i. 47. 4
The sugred licour through his melting *lips:*	II. v. 33. 6
gnawing Gealosy . . . his bitter *lips* did bight;	II. vii. 22. 5
lips he layd on thing that likte him best,	II. vii. 27. 3
with kisses light . . . his *lips* bedewd,	II. xii. 73. 6
on his tender *lips* the downy heare	II. xii. 79. 8
his sweete *lips*, on which before that stownd	III. v. 29. 7
as a fountaine from her sweete *lips* went.	III. vi. 25. 5
with his frory *lips* full softly kist,	III. viii. 35. 2
Upon his *lips* hong faire Dame Hellenore	III. ix. 52. 2
The signe whereof yet stain'd his bloudy *lips* afore.	IV. vii. 5. 9
Weigh but one word which from thy *lips* doth fall:	V. ii. 43. 6
shame my doubtfull *lips* doth still restraine.'	V. v. 30. 9
Her *lips* were, like raw lether, pale and blew:	V. xii. 29. 7
Some praise her paps; some praise her *lips* and nose;	VI. viii. 39. 5
If Rubies, loe, hir *lips* be Rubies sound;	*Am.* xv. 8
Comming to kisse her *lyps*,	*Am.* lxiv. 1
Her *lips* did smell lyke unto Gillyflowers;	*Am.* lxiv. 5
Her *lips* lyke cherryes charming men to byte,	*Epith.* 174
rosy leaves, so fairely spred Upon the *lips*,	*H.B.* 95
lips, like rosy buds in May,	*H.B.* 258
Liquid. With *liquid* foote doth slide downe easily.	*Gn.* 24
The *liquid* clowdes, and lucid firmament;	*Hub.* 1259
In *liquid* waves to cut their fomie waie,	*Ti.* 149
fram'd of *liquid* ayre her tender partes,	I. i. 45. 3
Himselfe refreshing with the *liquid* cold,	II. i. 24. 8
feedes each living plant with *liquid* sap,	II. ii. 6. 4
More swift then swallow sheres the *liquid* skye,	II. vi. 5. 2
sprinckled ofte the same With *liquid* waves,	II. vii. 36. 5
others did them selves embay in *liquid* joyes.	II. xii. 60. 9
with her pineons cleaves the *liquid* firmament.	III. iv. 49. 9
Some of them washing with the *liquid* dew	III. vi. 17. 5
Her goodly bow, which paints the *liquid* ayre,	V. iii. 25. 3
Liquor. flowrie bancks with silver *liquor* steepe;	*D.* 102
Wherein were closd few drops of *liquor* pure,	I. ix. 19. 3
The sugred *licour* through his melting lips:	II. v. 33. 6
Nor sea of *licour* cold, nor lake of myre:	II. vi. 44. 4
the cold *liquor* which he waded in;	II. vii. 58. 3
all the *liquour*, which was fowle and waste,	II. ix. 32. 1
sappy *liquor*, that with fulnesse sweld,	II. xii. 56. 3
with the *liquor* stained all the lond:	II. xii. 57. 5
of the fruitfull *liquor* over flowne;	III. ix. 30. 5
Eftsoones that pretious *liquour* forth he drew,	IV. viii. 20. 6
The fruitfull vine; whose *liquor* blouddy red,	V. vii. 11. 3
Liquors. Then she with *liquors* strong his eies did steepe,	II. vi. 18. 3
Lisianassa. *See* **Lysianassa.**	
Lisippus. *See* **Lysippus.**	
List. Who *list* the Romane greatnes forth to figure,	*Ro.* xxvi. 1
I *list* none accordaunce make	*S.C.* May 164
if by me thou *list* advised be,	*S.C.* Jun. 17
I never *lyst* presume to Parnasse hyll,	*S.C.* Jun. 70
lord it as they *list:*	*S.C.* Jul. 176
Gynne when ye *lyst*,	*S.C.* Au. 51
Whereto thou *list* their trayned willes entice.	*S.C.* O. 24
Whither thou *list* in fayre Elisa rest,	*S.C.* O. 45
Whether thee *list* thy loved lasse advaunce,	*S.C.* N. 7
The mornefull Muse in myrth now *list* ne maske,	*S.C.* N. 19
list at will them to revile or snib:	*Hub.* 372
Eate they that *list*,	*Hub.* 436
Ne are we tyde to fast, but when we *list;*	*Hub.* 459
if thee *list* unto the Court to throng,	*Hub.* 502
when the bodie *list* to pause,	*Hub.* 759
none, but whom he *list*,	*Hub.* 1188
What shape he *list* in apparition.	*Hub.* 1290
when him *list*,	*Hub.* 1297
laughing stocke of all that *list* to scorne;	*T.M.* 224
freely doest, of what thee *list*, entreat,	*Com. Son.* i. 9
'Looke backe, who *list*, unto the former ages,	*Ti.* 57
Praise who so *list*, yet I will him dispraise,	*Ti.* 229
when she *list* advance her heavenly voyce,	*D.* 313
which way he *list*, and whether.	*Col.* 251
they *list* not their mery pipes applie?	*Col.* 373
when they *list* to blow Their pipes aloud,	*Col.* 378
when he *list* shew grace,	*Col.* 881
When so thee *list* thy lofty Muse to raise:	*Ded. Son.* viii. 12
Before that angry heavens *list* to lowre,	I. ii. 22. 4
when him *list* the raskall routes appall,	I. vii. 35. 5
when him *list* the prouder lookes subdew,	I. vii. 35. 8
Them *list* no lenger there at leasure dwell,	I. ix. 2. 4
when she *list* poure out her larger spright,	I. x. 20. 1
whenas him *list* the ayre to beat,	I. xi. 10. 6
She *list* not heare, but her disports poursewd,	II. vi. 26. 8
If then thee *list* my offred grace to use,	II. vii. 18. 6
If thee *list* not, leave have thou to refuse:	II. vii. 18. 8
'Me *list* not' . . . receave Thing offred,	II. vii. 19. 1
To them that *list* these base regardes I lend;	II. vii. 33. 5
Behold, who *list*, both one and other in this place.	II. ix. 1. 9
Whose dolefull moniments who *list* to rew,	II. x. 66. 8

List—*Continued.*
to her cry they *list* not lenden eare, III. i. 23. 1
Ne *list* me chaunge; III. i. 24. 7
Her *list* in stryfull termes with him to balke, III. ii. 12. 3
Yet *list* the same efforce with faind gainesay; III. ii. 15. 8
However *list* her now her knowledge fayne, III. ii. 17. 2
When so him *list* his enimies to fray; III. iii. 12. 7
Yet *list* them bid their businesse to unfold, III. iii. 15. 3
Dy, who so *list* for him, he was loves enimy. III. iv. 26. 9
Such as him *list*, such as eternall fate Ordained hath, III. vi. 32. 6
she *list* not the batteill to abide, III. vii. 44. 3
if thee *list* to see thy Courser ronne, III. viii. 17. 4
if ye *list* to weet The cause III. ix. 3. 1
when she *list* misdonne? III. ix. 7. 3
they gone yfere, . . . where *list* them to repayre. III. x. 16. 9
he shot at randon, when him *list*, III. xi. 48. 3
she sprinckled favours manifold On whom she *list*, III. xii. 13. 8
who so *list* looke backe to former ages, IV. Pr. 3. 1
Ne *list* I for revenge provoke new fight, IV. i. 35. 3
That she, your love, *list* love another knight, IV. i. 46. 6
List not to hearke, but made this faire denyall: IV. ii. 6. 3
whenso her face She *list* discover, IV. ii. 44. 7
Then entred Cambell first into the *list*, IV. iii. 5. 1
When who so *list* to fight may fight his fill: IV. iv. 12. 6
Her *list* no longer in that place abide; IV. v. 29. 2
if he thereto *list* strive. IV. v. 37. 9
at his will may whom he *list* restore, IV. viii. 54. 8
whom he *list* reserve to be afflicted more. IV. viii. 54. 9
All which who *list* by tryall to assay IV. ix. 3. 1
as *list* them to devise; IV. ix. 35. 7
though he never *list* to me relent, IV. xii. 7. 6
He where he *list* goes loose, IV. xii. 11. 4
For who so *list* into the heavens looke, V. Pr. 5. 1
When so he *list* in wrath lift up his steely brand, V. i. 8. 9
what he *list* doe, he may. V. ii. 41. 9
them against came all that *list* to giust, V. iii. 6. 1
who *list* to seeke it there.' V. iii. 32. 9
dispose . . . to whom he *list*. V. iv. 19. 7
when she *list*, it raught Downe to her lowest heele; V. v. 2. 7
He *list* no lenger to use lothfull speach, V. vi. 21. 6
go which way they *list*, V. viii. 39. 9
Till that th' offended heavens *list* to lowre V. x. 26. 6
Behinde, beside, before, as he it *list* apply. V. xi. 6. 9
Whereto she ever *list* to make her hardy flight. V. xi. 24. 9
To passe them over where them *list* to tell. V. xii. 4. 4
looking up unto the cry to *lest*, VI. i. 17. 4
He . . . sought her so long as him *list*. VI. ii. 20. 9
And sent me, where him *list*, instructed for to bee. VI. ii. 28. 9
'His name,' (quoth he) 'if that thou *list* to learne, VI. iii. 40. 1
Whatever formes ye *list* thereto apply, VI. iv. 35. 6
Whether ye *list* him traine in chevalry, VI. iv. 35. 8
if ye *list* to haste a litle more, VI. vii. 6. 3
Let them that *list* their lucklesse lot deplore, VI. vii. 30. 7
Ne *list* the Knight the powre thereof assay, VI. viii. 8. 7
To be captiv'd and handled as he *list*, VI. viii. 13. 2
let them love that *list*, VI. viii. 21. 1
Me *list* not die for any lovers doole; VI. viii. 21. 2
Ne *list* me leave my loved libertie VI. viii. 21. 3
To pitty him that *list* to play the foole; VI. viii. 21. 4
if ye *list* have liberty ye may; VI. viii. 29. 7
'To them that *list* the worlds gay showes I leave, VI. ix. 22. 1
all the day to what I *list* I doe attend. VI. ix. 22. 9
whilest him *list* remaine, VI. ix. 34. 2
But whom they of them selves *list* so to grace.' VI. xi. 5. 6
The same againe if now ye *list* to have, VI. xii. 17. 8
as she them *list* divide; VII. vi. 3. 6
fashion to what he it *list* apply. *Am.* xxxii. 4
when ye *list* your owne mishaps to mourne, *Epith.* 7
who so *list* the like assayes to ken, *H.B.* 88
Then looke, who *list* thy gazefull eyes to feed *H.H.B.* 29
Listed. when her *listed* she could fawne and flatter; VI. vi. 42. 6
Listen. Now *listen* a while and hearken the end. *S.C.* F. 101
they nill *listen* to the shepheards voyce, *S.C.* S. 142
Then *listen*, Lordings, III. ix. 3. 1
if please ye *listen* to my lore, III. xi. 18. 7
Came to the open hall to *listen* V. iii. 13. 8
Listened. So longe have I *listened* to thy speche, *S.C.* F. 241
Listeners'. with pleasure The *listners* eyes and eares with melodie; *T.M.* 178
Listeneth. Then *listneth* ech unto my heavy laye, *S.C.* Au. 149
Listening. *Listening* if any thing did rushe, *S.C.* Mar. 71
Ne tell his sorrow to the *listning* rout *Ti.* 227
Which she long *listning*, softly askt againe IV. vii. 10. 4
Oft *listening* if he mote her heare againe, IV. xii. 17. 4
Listeth. wander free Where so us *listeth*, *Hub.* 169
Listful. with greedie *listfull* eares, *Col.* 7
to his doome with *listfull* eares did both attend. V. i. 25. 9
Lists. Who *lists* to see what ever nature, *Ro.* v. 1
Ne ever wont in field, ne in round *lists*, to fight: I. iii. 38. 9
In equall *lists* they should the morrow next it fight. I. iv. 40. 9
Well could he tourney, and in *lists* debate, II. i. 6. 7
The field with *listes* was all about enclos'd, IV. iii. 4. 1
Marshals of the field Broke up the *listes*, IV. iii. 35. 4
first the *Lists* did enter: V. v. 5. 2
The *Lists* were closed fast, V. v. 5. 6
Soone as he did within the *listes* appeare, V. xii. 16. 1
Lists'. At last arriving by the *listes* side, IV. iii. 46. 1
Litae. All lovely daughters of high Jove, that hight *Litae*, V. ix. 31. 5
Lite, -s. *See* **Light, -s.**
Lithe. His dewelap as *lythe* as lasse of Kent: *S.C.* F. 74

Lithe—*Continued.*
enfold With her *lythe* twigs, *Gn.* 221
Little. I saw her *litle* ones *Bel.*[2] vi. 2
Alas! by *little* ye to nothing flie, *Ro.* vii. 7
a Brize, a scorned *little* creature, *Van.* ii. 10
I saw a *little* Bird cal'd Tedula, *Van.* iii. 7
there bred A *litle* wicked worme, *Van.* vii. 7
a *little* Ant, a silly worme, *Van.* viii. 9
A *little* fish, that men called Remora, *Van.* ix. 10
Goe, *little* booke! *To his Booke* 1
So loytring live you *little* heardgroomes, *S.C.* F. 35
Cuddie, I wote thou kenst *little* good, *S.C.* F. 85
Little him aunswered the Oake againe, *S.C.* F. 140
(Ay *little* helpe to harme there needeth!) *S.C.* F. 198
Here is a long tale, and *little* worth. *S.C.* F. 240
But *little* ease of thy lewd tale I tasted: *S.C.* F. 245
Tho will we *little* Love awake, *S.C.* Mar. 22
(There shrouded was the *little* God) *S.C.* Mar. 68
For then I *little* smart did feele, *S.C.* Mar. 98
Yet hath so *little* skill to brydle love? *S.C.* Ap. 20
How great sport they gaynen with *little* swinck? *S.C.* May 36
Those faytours *little* regarden their charge, *S.C.* May 39
they bene hyred for *little* pay *S.C.* May 47
caren as *little* as they *S.C.* May 48
Little bootes all the welth and the trust, *S.C.* May 88
little them served for their mayntenaunce. *S.C.* May 112
sicke, alas! and *little* lack of dead, *S.C.* May 264
well he meanes, but *little* can say. *S.C.* May 311
if on me some *little* drops would flowe *S.C.* Jun. 93
learne the *little* what, *S.C.* Jul. 31
little needes to strow my store, *S.C.* Jul. 75
lived with *little* gayne: *S.C.* Jul. 128
Little lacketh Perigot of the best, *S.C.* Au. 126
to seeke redresse mought *little* boote; *S.C.* S. 127
better leave of with a *little* losse, *S.C.* S. 134
Better it were a *little* to feyne, *S.C.* S. 137
had his wesand bene a *little* widder, *S.C.* S. 210
little good hath got, *S.C.* O. 10
wets the *little* plants that lowly dwell. *S.C.* N. 32
'Gather together ye my *little* flocke, *S.C.* D. 145
My *little* flock, that was to me so liefe; *S.C.* D. 146
'Adieu, my *little* Lambes and loved sheepe; *S.C.* D. 153
Goe, *lyttle* Calender! *S.C.* Env. 7
His *little* Goats gan drive out of their stalls, *Gn.* 71
A *litle* nourslíng of the humid ayre, *Gn.* 282
His *little* needle there infixing deep, *Gn.* 287
A *little* mount, of greene turffs edifide; *Gn.* 660
little thrift for him he did it too: *Hub.* 240
little els (God wote) could thereof skill; *Hub.* 381
Of such deep learning *little* had he neede, *Hub.* 385
Content with *little* in condition sicker. *Hub.* 430
Full *little* knowest thou, that hast not tride, *Hub.* 895
so he got it, *little* did he pas. *Hub.* 1150
men of learning *little* he esteemed; *Hub.* 1191
little wote what doth thereto behove. *T.M.* 396
With horrid sound though having *little* sence, *T.M.* 554
Nor anie *little* moniment to see, *Ti.* 5
Litle wist he his fatall future woe, *Mui.* 381
snatcheth quite away One of the *litle* yonglings *Mui.* 407
My *little* flocke on westerne downes to keepe, *D.* 100
'My *little* flocke, whom earst I lov'd so well, *D.* 344
Did keepe his sheep, his *litle* stock and store: *As.* 4
the rest but *litle* he esteemed. *As.* 66
Full *litle* faileth but thou shalt be dead, *As.* 135
those *little* streames so broken *Col.* 141
by that which *little* while I prooved, *Col.* 664
gan by *little* learne to love each other: *Col.* 852
And to these ydle rymes lend *litle* space, *Ded. Son.* i. 13
A *litle* glooming light, much like a shade; I. i. 14. 5
A *little* lowly Hermitage it was, I. i. 34. 1
a *litle* wide There was an holy chappell edifyde, I. i. 34. 4
Arrived there, the *litle* house they fill, I. i. 35. 1
Legions of Sprights, . . . like *litle* flyes I. i. 38. 2
on his *litle* winges the dreame he bore I. i. 44. 8
That much was worne, but therein *little* redd; I. iv. 19. 2
of devotion he had *little* care, I. iv. 19. 3
Him *litle* answerd th' angry Elfin knight; I. iv. 42. 8
litle sweet Oft tempred is,' . . . 'with muchell smart: I. iv. 46. 3
in vaine glorious frayes he *litle* did delight. I. vi. 20. 9
His loving mother came . . . to see her *little* sonne; I. vi. 27. 2
Yet outwardly some *little* comfort shewes. I. vii. 21. 3
everie *little* breath that under heaven is blowne. I. vii. 32. 9
in the same a *little* grate was pight, I. viii. 37. 6
What if some *little* payne the passage have, I. ix. 40. 4
knight now grew in *litle* space, . . . To such perfection I. x. 21. 1
eke a *litle* Hermitage thereby, I. x. 46. 4
A *little* path that was both steepe and long, I. x. 55. 2
after *litle* rest, I. x. 68. 7
turnd a *little* wyde.— I. xi. 5. 5
of three furlongs does but *litle* lacke; I. xi. 11. 7
forst him to retire A *little* backeward I. xi. 45. 3
her *litle* babe revyld, I. xii. 11. 3
Death were too *litle* paine for such a fowle despight. II. i. 17. 9
Through midst thereof a *little* river rold, II. i. 24. 6
Thy *litle* hands embrewd in bleeding brest II. i. 37. 8
in her streaming blood he did embay His *litle* hands, II. i. 40. 8
The *litle* babe up in his armes he hent; II. ii. 1. 4
Full *little* weenest thou what sorrowes are Left thee II. ii. 2. 3
still the *litle* hands were bloody seene: II. ii. 3. 7
So long they traveiled with *litle* ease, II. ii. 12. 5

Little—*Continued.*
One thought her cheare too *litle*, . . . II. ii. 34. 9
(*litle* have she thanck!) . . . II. ii. 36. 9
Thou *little* wotest what this right-hand can: . . . II. iii. 16. 8
Now *little* gan to swell, . . . II. iii. 29. 8
The fire of sparkes, the weede of *little* seede, . . . II. iv. 35. 4
litle may such guile thee now avayl, . . . II. v. 5. 8
Though otherwise it did him *little* harme: . . . II. v. 7. 4
A *litle* Gondelay, bedecked trim . . . II. vi. 2. 7
like a *litle* forrest seemed outwardly. . . . II. vi. 2. 9
The *little* barke unto the shore to draw, . . . II. vi. 4. 3
worke and play About her *little* frigot, . . . II. vi. 7. 9
My *little* boat can safely passe this perilous bourne.' . . . II. vi. 10. 9
Emongst wide waves sett, like a *little* nest, . . . II. vi. 12. 2
Me *litle* needed from my right way to have straid.' . . . II. vi. 22. 9
At last him to a *litle* dore he brought, . . . II. vii. 24. 5
Betwixt them both was but a *little* stride, . . . II. vii. 24. 8
He lookt a *litle* further, . . . II. vii. 61. 1
litle Cupid playd His wanton sportes, . . . II. ix. 34. 6
A *little* boy did on him still attend To reach, . . . II. ix. 58. 4
with a staffe, all full of *litle* snags, . . . II. xi. 23. 7
Full *little* wanted but he had him slaine, . . . II. xi. 29. 6
By whom a *little* skippet floting did appeare. . . . II. xii. 14. 9
like a *litle* lake it seemd to bee; . . . II. xii. 62. 5
lend A *little* leave unto a rusticke Muse . . . III. Pr. 5. 2
He bore a crowned *little* Ermelin, . . . III. ii. 25. 8
'Beldame, your words doe worke me *litle* ease; . . . III. ii. 43. 1
a *litle* creeping sleepe Surprisd her sence: . . . III. ii. 47. 6
With great devotion, and with *little* zele: . . . III. ii. 48. 5
lyes a *litle* space From the swift Barry, . . . III. iii. 8. 4
A *litle* whyle Before that Merlin dyde, . . . III. iii. 10. 1
Some *little* life his feeble sprites emong; . . . III. iv. 41. 8
in the midst a *little* river plaide . . . III. v. 39. 7
Little shee weend that love he close conceald. . . . III. v. 49. 4
faire Venus having lost Her *little* sonne, . . . III. vi. 11. 2
in her *litle* loves stead, which was strayd, . . . III. vi. 28. 8
A *little* valley subject to the same, . . . III. vii. 4. 8
she did descry A *little* smoke, . . . III. vii. 5. 2
A *little* cottage, built of stickes and reedes . . . III. vii. 6. 2
A *little* bote lay hoving her before, . . . III. vii. 27. 4
Full *little* weened I that chastitee Had lodging . . . III. vii. 59. 3
finding *litle* leasure her to wooe . . . III. viii. 13. 3
Her sharpe rebuke full *little* did esteeme; . . . III. viii. 26. 2
Of which he now did very *little* fayle, . . . III. viii. 31. 7
To fly for succour to a *little* shed, . . . III. ix. 11. 8
litle good of him is to be got, . . . III. x. 39. 3
A *little* off his shield was rudely throwne, . . . III. xi. 7. 6
foolish garde, that *litle* knew Of such deceipt, . . . III. xi. 31. 5
litle drops empurpled her faire brest. . . . III. xii. 33. 5
Now growen great, at first of *little* seedes, . . . IV. i. 25. 4
He *little* answer'd, but . . . did forbeare; . . . IV. i. 45. 1
lookt a *little* up at that his speech, . . . IV. ii. 21. 3
She *little* answer'd him, but lightly did aggrate. . . . IV. ii. 23. 9
brought to nought by *little* bits? . . . IV. ii. 33. 9
Adowne their sides like *litle* rivers stremed, . . . IV. iii. 28. 7
Whence *litle* lust he had to rise againe: . . . IV. iv. 44. 6
litle prays'd his labours evill speed, . . . IV. v. 22. 4
They spide a *little* cottage, . . . IV. v. 32. 9
fast beside a *little* brooke did pas . . . IV. v. 33. 3
any *litle* nap Upon his heavie eye-lids chaunst to fall, . . . IV. v. 42. 1
That any *little* blow on her did light, . . . IV. vii. 26. 8
Some *little* whispering, and soft groning sound. . . . IV. vii. 33. 4
with a *litle* golden chaine about it bound. . . . IV. viii. 6. 9
the Dove Would flit a *litle* forward, . . . IV. viii. 11. 2
A *little* cotage farre away they spide, . . . IV. viii. 23. 2
manly limbs endur'd with *litle* care . . . IV. viii. 27. 8
Bearing a *litle* Dwarfe before his steed, . . . IV. viii. 38. 3
th' other *litle* gained by the lone, . . . IV. ix. 30. 7
So *litle* did they hearken to her sweet beheast. . . . IV. ix. 31. 9
little count did hold, . . . IV. x. 18. 7
Of *litle* much, of foes she maketh friends, . . . IV. x. 34. 8
A flocke of *litle* loves, . . . IV. x. 42. 2
for sparing *litle* cost or paines, . . . IV. xi. 22. 8
All *little* Rivers which owe vassallage To him, . . . IV. xi. 29. 3
Congealed *litle* drops which doe the morne adore. . . . IV. xi. 46. 9
Yet *litle* losse it were, and mickle thanke, . . . V. i. 15. 5
ye would for *little* leave the same, . . . V. i. 28. 6
in my way, a *little* here beyond, . . . V. ii. 4. 5
as his head he gan a *litle* reare . . . V. ii. 18. 3
he of *little* things made reckoning light; . . . V. ii. 44. 2
Yet all the wrongs could not a *litle* right downe way. . . . V. ii. 46. 9
yet *little* lost or wonne: . . . V. iii. 6. 7
words did *little* good, . . . V. iv. 4. 8
like a *little* Mount of small degree, . . . V. iv. 7. 7
To whom but *little* dowre allotted was: . . . V. iv. 9. 3
(though now it *little* skill) . . . V. iv. 14. 7
little had for his excuse to say, . . . V. iv. 27. 4
Of both beloved well, but *litle* frended, . . . V. v. 57. 7
little lust had she to talke of ought, . . . V. vi. 21. 1
Not farre away, but *little* wide by West, . . . V. vi. 22. 4
for which a *little* whyle Ye will not watch? . . . V. vi. 25. 3
little good could finde, And much lesse honour . . . V. vi. 32. 4
of his shape appear'd no *litle* moniment. . . . V. viii. 43. 9
passing *litle* further, . . . V. ix. 21. 3
Mongst which crept *little* Angels . . . V. ix. 28. 9
Seemed those *litle* Angels did uphold The cloth of state, . . . V. ix. 29. 1
much to gaine, a *litle* for to yield: . . . V. xii. 19. 4
A distaffe . . . Upon the which she *litle* spinnes, . . . V. xii. 36. 7
little bootes against him hand to reare. . . . VI. i. 16. 5
Wilt give thy beard, though it but *little* bee? . . . VI. i. 19. 8

Little—*Continued.*
so after *little* stay, . . . VI. iii. 16. 2
The *litle* babe did loudly scrike and squall, . . . VI. iv. 18. 1
The *little* babe, sweet relickes of his pray; . . . VI. iv. 23. 2
And every *little* limbe he searcht around, . . . VI. iv. 23. 6
his lovely *litle* spoile Crying for food . . . VI. iv. 25. 7
This *little* babe, of sweete and lovely face, . . . VI. iv. 35. 4
having over it a *litle* wept, . . . VI. iv. 37. 8
By which a *little* Hermitage there lay, . . . VI. v. 34. 8
nigh thereto a *little* Chappell stoode, . . . VI. v. 35. 1
Small was his house, and like a *little* cage, . . . VI. v. 38. 3
Mote easie be supprest with *little* thing; . . . VI. vi. 8. 4
if ye list to haste a *litle* more, . . . VI. vii. 6. 3
ere that *little* while they ridden had, . . . VI. vii. 6. 6
Yet would not let her lite, nor rest a *little* stead: . . . VI. vii. 40. 9
Unto a *litle* grove not farre asyde, . . . VI. viii. 44. 2
He mote perceive a *little* dawning sight . . . VI. viii. 48. 3
to the *litle* cots, where shepherds lie . . . VI. ix. 4. 8
Upon a *litle* hillocke she was placed . . . VI. ix. 8. 1
streight unto her *little* flocke did fare: . . . VI. ix. 15. 2
doth *litle* crave contented to abyde. . . . VI. ix. 17. 9
nature, which doth *litle* need Of forreine helpes . . . VI. ix. 20. 6
The *litle* that I have growes dayly more . . . VI. ix. 21. 5
other, that hath *litle,* askes no more, . . . VI. ix. 30. 5
in that *litle* is both rich and wise; . . . VI. ix. 30. 6
Did *little* whit regard his courteous guize, . . . VI. ix. 35. 6
litle sparrowes stolen from their nest, . . . VI. ix. 40. 2
Old love is *litle* worth when new is more prefard. . . . VI. ix. 40. 9
Their dwelling in a *little* Island was, . . . VI. x. 41. 6
A *little* well is lent that gaineth more withall. . . . VI. xi. 6. 9
Litle for him to have one silly lasse; . . . VI. xi. 12. 6
To sparke out *litle* beames, . . . VI. xi. 21. 9
To keepe their flockes for *litle* hyre and chepe, . . . VI. xi. 40. 7
with their *litle* stings right felly fare; . . . VI. xi. 48. 4
gan lay unto the open light The *litle* babe, . . . VI. xii. 7. 5
Upon the *litle* brest, like christall bright, . . . VI. xii. 7. 7
She mote perceive a *litle* purple mold, . . . VI. xii. 7. 8
drew a *litle* space Behind the bushes, . . . VI. xii. 8. 5
The rosie marke . . . That *litle* Infant had, . . . VI. xii. 15. 7
ye to me gave A *little* mayde, . . . VI. xii. 17. 7
I with these eyes did view The *litle* purple rose . . . VI. xii. 18. 5
this *little* pleasure should excell. . . . VII. vi. 44. 9
taking *litle* paine To knit the knot, . . . *Am.* vi. 13
But her proud hart doe thou a *little* shake, . . . *Am.* x. 9
Legions of loves with *little* wings did fly; . . . *Am.* xvi. 6
Most sorts of men doe set but *little* store. . . . *Am.* xxvi. 12
Why then should I accoumpt of *little* paine, . . . *Am.* xxvi. 13
However now thereof ye *little* weene! . . . *Am.* xxvii. 4
how *litle* glory ye have gayned . . . *Am.* xxxvi. 10
little priefe In deep discovery of the mynds disease; . . . *Am.* l. 5
wounds wil heale in *little* space. . . . *Am.* lvii. 14
your thrall, in whom is *little* worth; . . . *Am.* lxxxii. 10
That *little,* that I am, shall all be spent . . . *Am.* lxxxii. 11
to my Dame How *little* Cupid humbly came, . . . *Epig.* iii. 2
thou thyselfe likewise art *lyttle* made, . . . *Epig.* iv. 13
The Fly . . . Hath hurt me with his *little* horne.' . . . *Epig.* iv. 30
Which may let in a *little* thought unsownd. . . . *Epith.* 237
an hundred *little* winged loves, . . . *Epith.* 357
whole remaines scarse any *little* part; . . . *H.L.* 144
dart at them their *litle* fierie launces; . . . *H.B.* 241
Some *little* drop of thy celestiall dew, . . . *H.H.L.* 46
Then life were least, that us so *little* cost. . . . *H.H.L.* 182
show Some *litle* beames to mortall eyes below . . . *H.H.B.* 12
each one had a *little* wicker basket, . . . *Proth.* 24
The *little* Dazie, that at evening closes, . . . *Proth.* 31

Live. if that time doo let thy glorie *live,* . . . *Ro.* xxxii. 11
Live, happie spirits, th' honour of your name, . . . *Ro.* Env. 13
Where will he *live* tyll the lusty prime? . . . *S.C.* F. 16
So loytring *live* you little heardgroomes, . . . *S.C.* F. 35
here *liven* at ease and leasure? . . . *S.C.* May 66
Mought not *live* ylike as men of the laye. . . . *S.C.* May 76
leave to *live* hard, . . . *S.C.* May 125
How shoulden shepheardes *live,* . . . *S.C.* May 148
If I may rest, I nill *live* in sorrowe. . . . *S.C.* May 151
'Why doe we longer *live,* . . . *S.C.* N. 73
why *live* we so long?) . . . *S.C.* N. 73
Live thou for ever in all happinesse! . . . *Gn.* 63
here the antique fame of stout Camill Doth ever *live;* . . . *Gn.* 602
'*Live* they for ever through their lasting praise! . . . *Gn.* 617
to *live* in blisse for ever. . . . *Gn.* 624
have no wit to *live* withouten toyle; . . . *Hub.* 158
live like Lords of that which they doo gather, . . . *Hub.* 164
I driven am to seeke some meanes to *live:* . . . *Hub.* 250
wayes enough for all therein to *live;* . . . *Hub.* 401
In the meane-time to *live* in good estate, . . . *Hub.* 427
Seemes that in fruitfull pastures ye doo *live,* . . . *Hub.* 593
if fortune thee in Court to *live,* . . . *Hub.* 631
Live she for ever, . . . *T.M.* 580
whilst that thou, faire flower of chastitie, Dost *live,* . . . *Ti.* 252
whiles this verse Shall *live,* and surely it shall *live* for ever: *Ti.* 254
For ever it shall *live,* and shall rehearse . . . *Ti.* 255
thou thy selfe herein shalt also *live:* . . . *Ti.* 258
'O noble spirite! *live* there ever blessed, . . . *Ti.* 302
Live ever there, and leave me here . . . *Ti.* 304
Provide therefore (ye Princes) whilst ye *live,* . . . *Ti.* 365
they *live* for aye above, . . . *Ti.* 396
wise wordes . . . *live* for ay; . . . *Ti.* 403
To make their memories for ever *live;* . . . *Ti.* 412
To *live* in heaven where happines is rife: . . . *Ti.* 670
seem'd to *live,* so like it was in sight: . . . *Mui.* 332

Live—*Continued.*
the miserie In which men *live*, . . . *D.* 37
they, that *live* on ground, . . . *D.* 87
Mine to be His, with him to *live* for ay. . . . *D.* 236
'So doo I *live*, so doo I daylie die, . . . *D.* 435
'Why doo I longer *live* in lifes despight, . . . *D.* 442
'To *live* I finde it deadly dolorous, . . . *D.* 449
yet would *live* with heart halfe stonie cold, . . . *Col.* 206
Where I will *live* or die at her beheast, . . . *Col.* 254
while as Astrofell did *live* and raine, . . . *Col.* 450
engraven . . . That it may *live* to all posterity. . . . *Ded. Son.* vi. 14
Through whose large bountie, . . . I now doe *live*, . . . *Ded. Son.* vii. 5
Live, Lord, for ever in this lasting verse, . . . *Ded. Son.* xi. 13
Whither the soules doe fly of men that *live* amis. . . . I. ii. 19. 9
they should *live* in wo, and dye in wretchednesse. . . . I. v. 46. 9
Yet *live* perforce in balefull darkenesse bound? . . . I. viii. 38. 5
Now in your powre, to let her *live*, or die.' . . . I. viii. 45. 6
he should dye who merites not to *live*? . . . I. ix. 38. 4
to health restore The man that would not *live*, . . . I. x. 27. 9
if he *live* that hath you doen despight, . . . II. i. 14. 7
bownd by them to *live* in lives despight; . . . II. i. 36. 4
Long maist thou *live*, and better thrive withall . . . II. i. 37. 4
Live thou; and to thy mother dead attest . . . II. i. 37. 6
losse of love to her that loves to *live*, . . . II. i. 55. 5
'*Live*, and alleagaunce owe To him . . . II. v. 13. 5
Thou, that doest *live* in later times, . . . II. vii. 18. 4
unto all that *live* in high degree, . . . II. vii. 60. 3
The trespass still doth *live*, albee the person dye.' . . . II. viii. 28. 9
by whose most gratious ayd I *live* this day, . . . II. viii. 55. 6
Donwallo dyde, (for what may *live* for ay?) . . . II. x. 40. 1
Long mayst thou, Glorian, *live* in glory and great powre! . . . II. x. 76. 9
Let all that *live* hereby be counselled . . . II. xii. 9. 8
To *live* in thraldome of his fathers foe! . . . III. iii. 42. 3
I feared love; but they that love doe *live*, . . . III. iv. 37. 5
Of all things that are borne to *live* and dye, . . . III. vi. 30. 5
sendeth forth to *live* in mortall state, . . . III. vi. 32. 8
Therfore needs mote he *live*, that living gives to all. . . . III. vi. 47. 9
all fayre Ladies that doe *live* on grownd. . . . III. vi. 52. 6
has full large to *live* and spend at libertie. . . . III. ix. 3. 9
againe he him bethought to *live*, . . . III. x. 7. 6
Must not here thinke to *live*; . . . III. xi. 14. 9
both in flowres doe *live*, . . . III. xi. 37. 4
This doe, and *live*, els dye undoubtedly.' . . . III. xii. 35. 7
them that love, and do not *live* amisse. . . . IV. Pr. 2. 9
Long may you *live* in health and happie state!' . . . IV. ii. 23. 8
What time she usd to *live* in wively sort, . . . IV. v. 3. 8
die or *live*, for nought he would upstand, . . . IV. vi. 23. 7
now become to *live* a Ladies thrall, . . . IV. vi. 28. 8
on the spoile of women he doth *live*, . . . IV. vii. 12. 5
did *live* then like an innocent, . . . IV. viii. 30. 2
live in lasting blesse, . . . IV. x. 23. 5
there did *live* for ever; . . . IV. x. 27. 8
let him *live* unlov'd, or love him selfe alone. . . . IV. xii. 9. 9
let mee *live* as lovers ought to do, . . . IV. xii. 10. 2
'They *live*, they die, like as he doth ordaine, . . . V. ii. 41. 1
if I *live* till those ten daies have end, . . . V. xi. 43. 2
live in reproch and scorne, . . . VI. vi. 36. 2
onely suffred him this wretched life to *live*. . . . VI. vi. 36. 9
so would ever *live*, and love her owne delight. . . . VI. vii. 30. 9
let them love that list, or *live* or die, . . . VI. viii. 21. 1
a salvage nation, which did *live* Of stealth and spoile, . . . VI. viii. 35. 2
that might contented *live*. . . . VI. ix. 22. 5
As graunt me *live* in like condition; . . . VI. ix. 28. 7
in this quiet make you safer *live*.' . . . VI. ix. 32. 8
never usde to *live* by plough nor spade, . . . VI. x. 39. 4
'That ever I did *live* this day to see, . . . VI. xi. 29. 2
your daughter sure, which yet doth *live*.' . . . VI. xii. 18. 9
The Wood-gods breed, which must for ever *live*: . . . VII. vi. 50. 4
though it *live* for ever, . . . VII. vii. 24. 1
Which if she graunt, then *live*, and my love cherish: . . . *Am.* ii. 13
To force me *live*, and will not let me dy. . . . *Am.* xi. 12
So dying *live*, and living do adore her. . . . *Am.* xiv. 14
thinck they dy with pleasure, *live* with payne. . . . *Am.* xlvii. 14
Yet *live* for ever, though against her will, . . . *Am.* xlviii. 13
So shall you *live*, by giving life to me. . . . *Am.* xlix. 14
wonder is how I should *live* a jot, . . . *Am.* lvii. 6
slaying him that would *live* gladly yours! . . . *Am.* lvii. 12
grant that we . . . May *live* for ever in felicity! . . . *Am.* lxviii. 8
Ye three Elizabeths! for ever *live*, . . . *Am.* lxxiv. 13
you shall *live* by fame: . . . *Am.* lxxv. 10
Our love shall *live*, and later life renew. . . . *Am.* lxxv. 14
Thereby they all do *live*, and moved are . . . *H.L.* 99
To let her *live* thus free, and me to dy. . . . *H.L.* 154
To *live* thus happie as her grace to gaine. . . . *H.L.* 244
immortall Spright, By whom all *live* to love, . . . *H.B.* 108
That I her bounden thrall by her may *live*, . . . *H.B.* 278
We give to him by whom we all doe *live*. . . . *H.H.L.* 210
Lived. *See* **Longest-lived.**
'Thy father, had he *lived* this day, . . . *S.C.* May 195
whilst he *lived*, . . . *S.C.* Jun. 83
lived in lowlye leas: . . . *S.C.* Jul. 122
lived with little gayne: . . . *S.C.* Jul. 128
whilste he *lived* was of none envyde, . . . *Ti.* 241
'He, whilest he *lived*, happie was through thee, . . . *Ti.* 246
Whilest here he *liv'd*, . . . *As.* Interl. 220
He whilest he *lived* was the noblest swaine, . . . *Col.* 440
Who, whiles he *livde*, was called proud Sans foy, . . . I. ii. 25. 6
he her takes To be the fairest wight that *lived* yit; . . . I. ii. 30. 4
wretched men, and *lived* in like paine.' . . . I. x. 62. 4
best shall bee to them that *lived* best; . . . II. i. 59. 4

Lived—*Continued.*
them that *liv'd* therin in state forlorne: . . . II. vii. 18. 3
To proove he *lived* il that did thus fowly dye. . . . II. viii. 12. 9
if he *lived* had thus long, . . . II. viii. 28. 7
The wisest men, I weene, that *lived* in their ages. . . . II. ix. 47. 9
By hunting and by spoiling *liveden*; (**lived* then) . . . II. x. 7. 7
where long in wretched cace He *liv'd*, . . . III. iii. 41. 5
'So *liv'd* they ever after in like sin, . . . III. vii. 49. 1
whilest they *lived* none did ever see More happie creatures . . . IV. iii. 2. 4
In whom he *liv'd* anew, of former life deprived. . . . IV. iii. 13. 9
It would have *lived*, and revived eft; . . . IV. iii. 21. 8
The doughtiest knight that *liv'd* that day, . . . IV. iv. 42. 9
he *liv'd* all on ravin and on rape . . . IV. vii. 5. 7
pitty much his plight, that *liv'd* like outcast thrall. . . . IV. vii. 43. 9
ne ever Dame So chast and loyall *liv'd*, . . . IV. viii. 25. 6
They *liv'd* together long without debate; . . . IV. ix. 16. 2
Whilest here on earth she *lived* mortallie: . . . V. i. 5. 5
Ne any *liv'd* on ground that durst withstand . . . V. i. 8. 6
Osyris, whilest he *lived* here, The justest man . . . V. vii. 2. 8
As any one that *lived* in his daies, . . . VI. vi. 4. 2
In which he *liv'd* alone, like carelesse bird in cage. . . . VI. vi. 4. 9
the conquest of the gentlest Knight That ever *liv'd*, . . . VI. x. 40. 9
There did they find . . . That Pastorell yet *liv'd*; . . . VI. xi. 41. 6
lived long in peace and love entyre, . . . VI. xii. 10. 7
Liv'd here on earth, and plenty made abound; . . . VII. vii. 37. 7
Ne could that Painter (had he *lived* yet) . . . *H.H.B.* 211
Liveden. *See* **Lived.**
Livedst. whilest thou *livedst*, madest the forrests ring, . . . *Ti.* 325
Livelihead. sorrowes are Left thee for porcion of thy *livelyhed*; II. ii. 2. 4
the trew *lively-head* Of that most glorious visage . . . II. ix. 3. 3
Plaine signes in him of life and *livelihead*: . . . VI. vii. 20. 5
Livelihood. As well of worldly *livelode* as of life, . . . *Hub.* 147
saw my lands decay And former *livelod* fayle, . . . V. iv. 9. 7
of lesse *livelood* and hability, . . . VI. iii. 7. 7
Livelode. *See* **Livelihood.**
Livelong. Make feast therefore now all this *live-long* day; . . *Epith.* 248
Lively. A *lively* streame, more cleere than Christall . . . *Rev.* iv. 12
In either cheeke depeincten *lively* chere: . . . *S.C.* Ap. 69
livelie spirits of each living wight, . . . *T.M.* 254
starve, wanting my *lively* foode: . . . *U.V.* 17
'He, noble bud, his Grandsires *livelie* hayre, . . . *Ti.* 267
so *lively* seene, That it true Sea . . . ye would weene. . . . *Mui.* 279
partes, So *lively* and so like in all mens sight, . . . I. i. 45. 4
'His blessed body, spoild of *lively* breath, . . . I. ii. 24. 1
lively breath her sad brest did forsake; . . . I. vii. 20. 8
labour *lively* to expresse the same, . . . I. x. 6. 8
Full *lively* is the semblaunt, . . . II. ix. 2. 9
lively vigour rested in his mind, . . . II. ix. 55. 7
some seemd with *lively* jollitee To fly about, . . . II. xii. 60. 7
formd so *lively* in each perfect part, . . . III. Pr. 1. 6
Who can it doe more *lively*, or more trew, . . . III. Pr. 4. 3
in that cloth was wrought as if it *lively* grew. . . . III. i. 38. 9
Chaunged thy *lively* cheare, and living made thee dead? . . . III. ii. 30. 9
soyle, which did deforme their *lively* hew; . . . III. vi. 17. 7
in shape and looke So *lively* and so like, . . . III. viii. 5. 9
like a *lively* sanguine it seemd to the eye. . . . III. viii. 6. 9
She, . . . full glade, Daunst *lively*, . . . III. x. 44. 9
hart Did *lively* seeme to tremble, . . . III. xi. 30. 8
ye mote have *lively* seene The God . . . III. xi. 37. 6
All which in that faire arras was most *lively* writ. . . . III. xi. 39. 9
So *lively* and so like that living sence it fayld. . . . III. xi. 46. 9
By *lively* actions he gan bewray Some argument . . . III. xii. 4. 5
lively spirits deaded quight: . . . IV. xii. 20. 2
Full of delightfull health and *lively* joy, . . . VII. vii. 46. 8
Most *lively* lyke behold your semblant trew. . . . *Am.* xlv. 4
dead my life that wants such *lively* blis. . . . *Am.* lxxxviii. 14
The inward beauty of her *lively* spright, . . . *Epith.* 186
The praises of the Lord in *lively* notes; . . . *Epith.* 219
the thing . . . that kindleth *lively* fyre, . . . *H.B.* 58
it then tooke light And *lively* spirits . . . *H.B.* 111
lively images of heavens light, . . . *H.B.* 163
Most *lively* image of thy Fathers face, . . . *H.H.L.* 171
Liver. His deadly woundes within my *liver* swell, . . . II. vi. 50. 3
Cros-cuts the *liver* with internall smart, . . . III. x. 59. 8
Liveries. Our bloncket *liveryes* bene all to sadde . . . *S.C.* May 5
Livers. *His deadly woundes within my *livers* swell, . . . II. vi. 50. 3
ghosts doen often creepe . . . bad *livers* to torment: . . . II. xii. 6. 6
Livery. As of her owne by *liverey* and seisin; . . . VI. iv. 37. 7
Lives. *lyves* on earth, and loved her most dere. . . . *S.C.* Jun. 112
Content who *lives* with tryed state . . . *S.C.* S. 70
Oft *lives* by losse, and leaves with payne. . . . *S.C.* S. 73
There *lives* shee with the blessed Gods . . . *S.C.* N. 194
'There chast Alceste *lives* inviolate, . . . *Gn.* 425
there *lives* also the immortall praise Of womankinde, . . . *Gn.* 428
here wise Curius . . . *lives* in endles rest; . . . *Gn.* 610
when lambes fail'd the old sheepes *lives* they reft; . . . *Hub.* 322
One onelie *lives*, her ages ornament, . . . *T.M.* 571
So thy renowme *lives* ever by endighting. . . . *Com. Son.* i. 14
all that *lives* on face of sinfull earth! . . . *Ti.* 44
Nor anie *lives* that mentioneth my name . . . *Ti.* 164
dying *lives*, and living still does dye. . . . *D.* 434
The gentlest shepheardesse that *lives* this day, . . . *As.* 212
Who *lives* that can match that heroick song, . . . *Col.* 404
Silly old man, that *lives* in hidden cell, . . . I. i. 30. 6
such a cursed creature *lives* so long a space.' . . . I. i. 31. 9
He *lives* that shall him pay his dewties last, . . . I. iv. 49. 8
mortgaging their *lives* to Covetise, . . . I. v. 46. 4
'And *lives* he yet, . . . II. i. 12. 2
'He *lives*,' (quoth he) 'and boasteth of the fact, . . . II. i. 12. 4
As if their *lives* had in his hand beene gagd; . . . II. iii. 14. 3

Lives—*Continued.*
To shed your *lives* on ground? . . . II. vi. 32. 7
lives, it seemed, whilome there were shed, . . . II. vii. 30. 8
sufficient were that hire For losse of thousand *lives,* . . . II. ix. 5. 9
If that your *lives* ye love, . . . II. ix. 12. 2
Lives any that you hath thus ill apayd? . . . II. ix. 37. 7
Whence all that *lives* does borrow life and light, . . . II. x. 2. 2
Lives ought that to her linage may compaire; . . . II. x. 2. 3
Yet *lives* his memorie, though carcas sleepe . . . II. x. 43. 9
generation of all That *lives,* . . . II. xii. 47. 4
who that *lives* is lefte to waile his losse: . . . III. iv. 38. 6
Lives none this day that may with her compare . . . III. v. 8. 4
the Squire *lives* with renowne. . . . III. v. 25. 9
He *lives,* but takes small joy of his renowne; . . . III. v. 26. 1
whose *lives* and fortunes bee . . . stil open layd, . . . III. v. 36. 6
all that *lives* is subject to that law; . . . III. vi. 40. 8
There now he *lives* in everlasting joy, . . . III. vi. 49. 1
in stedfast love and happy state She with him *lives,* . . . III. vi. 50. 7
fruitlesse *lives* were under furrow sowne, . . . III. ix. 35. 8
Yet can he never dye, but dying *lives,* . . . III. x. 60. 1
Agape Doth lengthen her sonnes *lives.* . . . IV. ii. Arg.
The perilous present stownd in which their *lives* were set. . . IV. ii. 15. 9
That so their *lives* might be prolonged late: . . . IV. ii. 51. 3
both their *lives* may likewise be annext Unto the third, . . . IV. ii. 52. 8
how their *lives* were eekt, she did not tell; . . . IV. ii. 53. 6
their *lives* thou lanchedst long afore, . . . IV. vii. 1. 8
lives a loathed life, and wishing cannot die. . . . IV. vii. 11. 9
'And *lives* yet Amyas?' . . . IV. viii. 63. 5
'He *lives,*' (quoth he) 'and his Aemylia loves.' . . . IV. viii. 63. 6
Out of their wretched corses, and their *lives* deprive. . . . IV. ix. 22. 9
lives although decay'd, yet loves decayed never. . . . IV. x. 27. 9
that which is th' immortall spright *Lives* still, . . . IV. xi. 16. 9
on the ground their *lives* did strow, . . . V. vii. 31. 8
was never seene of none That *lives* on earth; . . . V. x. 29. 5
The wretchedest Dame that *lives* this day on ground; . . . VI. v. 28. 2
Chaunge eke our mynds, and former *lives* amend; . . . *Am.* lxii. 6
Their *lives* they loath, and heavens light disdaine; . . . *H.L.* 130
Lives'. Thereby to make their loves beginning their *lives* end. IV. vi. 17. 9
To leape into the same after our *lives* end. . . . VI. iv. 31. 9
Livest. Why *livest* thou stil, . . . *S.C.* D. 95
'So *livest* thou; but my poore wretched ghost . . . *Gn.* 337
'So there thou *livest,* singing evermore, . . . *Ti.* 337
here thou *livest,* being ever song Of us, . . . *Ti.* 338
Why *livest* thou, dead dog, . . . II. iii. 7. 6
After so wicked deede why *liv'st* thou lenger day?' . . . II. viii. 46. 9
'And *livest* thou, my daughter, now againe? . . . VI. xii. 19. 8
Liveth. Where he now *liveth* in eternall blis, . . . *Ti.* 265
let him die at ease, that *liveth* here uneath? . . . I. ix. 38. 9
Fairer and nobler *liveth* none this howre, . . . II. x. 76. 6
There now he *liveth* in eternall blis, . . . III. vi. 48. 1
'She *liveth* sure and sound, . . . V. xi. 38. 8
Then which a prouder Lady *liveth* none: . . . VI. i. 14. 7
Living. *See* **Dead-living, Ever-living, Long-living.**
there being then not *living* An Hercules . . . *Ro.* x. 9
Rome, *living,* was the worlds sole ornament, . . . *Ro.* xxix. 13
pray of beasts and spoyle of *living* blood, . . . *Van.* x. 3
for our selves we may a *living* make. . . . *Hub.* 116
Drudge in the world, and for their *living* droyle, . . . *Hub.* 157
To take what paines may anie *living* wight; . . . *Hub.* 271
would they take no paines to get their *living,* . . . *Hub.* 349
Is not that name enough to make a *living* . . . *Hub.* 417
Doo not thou therefore seeke a *living* there, . . . *Hub.* 521
if the *living* yerely doo arise To fortie pound, . . . *Hub.* 528
way for one that is unlern'd *Living* to get, . . . *Hub.* 536
For learning sake to *living* them to raise; . . . *Hub.* 538
Needes anie more to learne to get a *living?'* . . . *Hub.* 544
their *living* they resigned quight . . . *Hub.* 573
livelie spirits of each *living* wight, . . . *T.M.* 254
none *living* pittieth our paine. . . . *T.M.* 354
Whose *living* praises in heroick style, . . . *T.M.* 431
The rest untold no *living* tongue can speake. . . . *T.M.* 600
Living, on God and on thy selfe relie; . . . *Ti.* 209
Spite bites the dead, that *living* never baid. . . . *Ti.* 215
dead is now, as *living,* counted deare, . . . *Ti.* 242
Living, that lincked chaunst with thee to bee, . . . *Ti.* 248
him dead thou dost adore As *living,* . . . *Ti.* 250
living loved thee afore, . . . *Ti.* 339
they *living* cared not to cherishe No gentle wits, . . . *Ti.* 362
To sing his *living* praises being dead, . . . *Ti.* 437
Above the reach of anie *living* sight: . . . *Ti.* 628
my reliefe exceedeth *living* thought;) . . . *D.* 95
Living on earth like Angell new divinde, . . . *D.* 214
Nature, nurse of every *living* thing, . . . *D.* 337
By *living* long to multiplie their paine; . . . *D.* 361
pitie me that *living* thus doo die; . . . *D.* 383
dying lives, and *living* still does dye. . . . *D.* 434
Made not to please the *living* but the dead. . . . *As.* Pr. 16
(A fairer star saw never *living* eie,) . . . *As.* 57
living were in love so firmly tide. . . . *As.* 180
world . . . In which I saw no *living* people dwell. . . . *Col.* 231
all things else that *living* creatures need. . . . *Col.* 299
everie *living* wight Crept forth . . . *Col.* 859
To be thy *living* praises instrument, . . . *Ded. Son.* ii. 3
In bigger tunes to sound your *living* prayse. . . . *Ded.Son.*xiii. 14
image, *living* evermore In the divine resemblaunce . . . *Ded. Son.* xv. 9
dead, as *living,* ever him ador'd: . . . I. i. 2. 4
'this is no place for *living* men.' . . . I. i. 13. 9
by which no *living* wight May ever passe, . . . I. i. 32. 2
hot, That *living* creature mote it not abide; . . . I. ii. 29. 6
Banish from *living* wights, our wearie daies we waste.' . . . I. ii. 42. 9

Living—*Continued.*
Till we be bathed in a *living* well: . . . I. ii. 43. 4
When all this speech the *living* tree had spent, . . . I. ii. 44. 5
faire as ever *living* wight was fayre, . . . I. iii. 2. 6
never shew of *living* wight espyde; . . . I. iii. 10. 3
In *living* Princes court none ever knew . . . I. iv. 7. 4
she was wondrous faire, as any *living* wight. . . . I. iv. 10. 9
childe ne kinsman *living* had he none To leave them to; . . . I. iv. 28. 6
not a pin Does care for looke of *living* creatures eye. . . . I. v. 4. 4
see that knight both *living* and eke ded.' . . . I. vi. 36. 9
it would pitty any *living* eie. . . . I. vi. 43. 6
His *living* like saw never *living* eye, . . . I. vii. 8. 7
excell All *living* wightes in might of magicke spell: . . . I. vii. 36. 5
'What worlds delight, or joy of *living* speach, . . . I. vii. 39. 1
Where never foote of *living* wight did tread, . . . I. vii. 50. 4
ne *living* wight To warde the same, . . . I. viii. 3. 3
living creature none he did espye. . . . I. viii. 29. 5
to weet if *living* wight Were housed therewithin, . . . I. viii. 37. 8
More ugly shape yet never *living* creature saw. . . . I. viii. 48. 9
From *living* eies her open shame to hide, . . . I. viii. 50. 4
rules the thoughts of *living* wight. . . . I. ix. 6. 9
Till *living* moysture into smoke do flow, . . . I. ix. 8. 4
To kindle love in every *living* brest: . . . I. ix. 9. 4
Ne *living* man like wordes did ever heare, . . . I. ix. 14. 7
living man mote worthie be to be her liefe.' . . . I. ix. 17. 9
A wyde way made to let forth *living* breath: . . . I. ix. 30. 3
let him dye, that loatheth *living* breath, . . . I. ix. 38. 8
All is but lost, that *living* we bestow, . . . I. x. 41. 6
end, which every *living* wight Should make his marke . . . I. x. 50. 2
Did burne with wrath, and sparkled *living* fyre: . . . I. xi. 14. 2
So wondrous force from hand of *living* wight; . . . I. xi. 17. 8
kest His wearie foe into that *living* well, . . . I. xi. 31. 6
Ne *living* wight would have him life behott: . . . I. xi. 38. 4
The face of earth and wayes of *living* wight, . . . I. xi. 49. 8
never *living* man . . . was distrest: . . . I. xii. 17. 5
Or false or trew, or *living* or else dead, . . . I. xii. 28. 2
none that breatheth *living* aire does know . . . II. Pr. 1. 6
With *living* eye more fayre was never seene . . . II. i. 10. 7
heven thee deignes to hold in *living* state, . . . II. i. 37. 3
if any drop Of *living* blood . . . II. i. 43. 5
shee gan to breath out *living* aire. . . . II. i. 43. 9
feedes each *living* plant with liquid sap, . . . II. ii. 6. 4
In her faire eyes two *living* lamps did flame, . . . II. iii. 23. 1
that stroke of *living* arme Should him dismay, . . . II. v. 7. 2
Was given all to lust and loose *living,* . . . II. v. 28. 3
In his owne flesh, and make way to the *living* spright! . . . II. vi. 32. 9
shame his ugly face did hide from *living* eye. . . . II. vii. 22. 9
That *living* eye before did never see. . . . II. vii. 38. 2
ne *living* wight Like ever saw, . . . II. vii. 54. 3
no *living* wight Below the earth . . . II. vii. 66. 2
backe againe him brought to *living* light. . . . II. vii. 66. 4
living handes immortalizd his name. . . . II. viii. 13. 5
leave these relicks of his *living* might . . . II. viii. 16. 6
keepes in coverts close from *living* wight, . . . II. ix. 40. 8
they of *living* fire most subtilly Were made, . . . II. ix. 46. 5
Fayre Helena, the fairest *living* wight; . . . II. x. 59. 5
Ne ever land beheld, ne *living* wight, . . . II. xii. 2. 2
huge Sea monsters, such as *living* sence dismayd: . . . II. xii. 22. 9
sweete and pleasing unto *living* sense, . . . II. xii. 42. 6
Such as attonce might not on *living* ground, . . . II. xii. 70. 3
all that pleasing is to *living* eare . . . II. xii. 70. 7
If pourtrayd it might bee by any *living* art. . . . III. Pr. 1. 9
living art may not least part expresse, . . . III. Pr. 2. 1
in *living* colours, and right hew, . . . III. Pr. 4. 1
tract of *living* creature none they fownd, . . . III. i. 14. 8
Whose soveraine beautie hath no *living* pere; . . . III. i. 26. 3
living wit, I weene, cannot display . . . III. i. 32. 3
Whose prowesse paragone saw never *living* wight. . . . III. ii. 13. 9
Chaunged thy lively cheare, and *living* made thee dead? . . III. ii. 30. 9
'Nor man it is, nor other *living* wight, . . . III. ii. 38. 1
burnest mightily In *living* brests, . . . III. iii. 1. 2
through the earth have spredd their *living* prayse, . . . III. iii. 3. 8
That of no *living* wight he mote be found, . . . III. iii. 7. 8
Then ever him before, or after, *living* wight: . . . III. iii. 11. 9
Of mortall Syre or other *living* wight, . . . III. iii. 13. 2
living him in all activity To thee shall represent. . . . III. iii. 29. 3
Nor so fowle outrage doen by *living* men; . . . III. iii. 34. 6
A lesson too too hard for *living* clay . . . III. iv. 26. 3
That ever *living* eye, I weene, did see. . . . III. v. 8. 3
Providence hevenly passeth *living* thought, . . . III. v. 27. 1
Saw never *living* eie more heavy sight, . . . III. v. 30. 1
Dying her serve, and *living* her adore; . . . III. v. 46. 7
none *living* may compayre: . . . III. v. 54. 4
the fruitfull seades Of all things *living,* . . . III. vi. 8. 4
breedes the *living* wight. . . . III. vi. 9. 5
Therfore needs mote he live, that *living* gives to all. . . . III. vi. 47. 9
in the same did wonne some *living* wight. . . . III. vii. 5. 5
Like never yet did *living* eie detect; . . . III. vii. 22. 7
No *living* creature could his cruelty asswage. . . . III. viii. 28. 9
ne *living* wight was seene . . . III. viii. 37. 8
Ne suffreth he resort of *living* wight Approch to her, . . . III. ix. 5. 6
Fruitfull of all thinges fitt for *living* foode, . . . III. ix. 49. 6
the Geaunts broode That fed on *living* flesh, . . . III. ix. 49. 9
His money, which he lov'd as *living* breath; . . . III. x. 2. 8
living creature it would terrify To looke adowne, . . . III. x. 56. 5
seemd no help for him was left in *living* sight. . . . III. x. 56. 9
upon the face of *living* land? . . . III. xi. 10. 4
Whereas no *living* creature he mistooke, . . . III. xi. 13. 4
Ne may by *living* meanes be thence relest: . . . III. xi. 17. 8
so like that *living* sence it fayld. . . . III. xi. 46. 9

Living—*Continued.*
playd In the rich metall as they *living* were. . . . III. xi. 51. 6
living creature none she saw appeare. . . . III. xi. 55. 2
fearfull to *living* sight; . . . . III. xii. 19. 7
Ne *living* wight she saw in all that roome, ... III. xii. 30. 5
With *living* blood he those characters wrate, ... III. xii. 31. 3
Whom of all *living* wightes she loved best. . . . . III. xii. 41. 2
Conveyed quite away to *living* wight unknowen. . . . . IV. i. 3. 9
cursed seedes . . . yeeld her *living* food: . . . . IV. i. 26. 2
to her service bind each *living* creature, ... IV. ii. 44. 4
Farre under ground from tract of *living* went, ... IV. ii. 47. 5
The lines of life, from *living* knowledge hid. . . . . IV. ii. 48. 4
dreddest day that *living* wight Did ever see . . . . IV. iii. 3. 5
As all men do, that lose the *living* spright. . . . . IV. iii. 30. 7
dreadfull seem'd to every *living* wight, ... IV. v. 32. 3
I vow you dead or *living* not to leave, ... IV. vi. 38. 8
Emong the *living*, or emong the dead? . . . . IV. vii. 11. 2
Ne *living* aide for her on earth appeares, ... IV. vii. 23. 2
So faire as ever yet saw *living* eie; . . . . IV. viii. 49. 5
never two so like did *living* creature see. . . . . IV. viii. 55. 9
living thus a wretch, ... IV. ix. 39. 8
Should happen this with *living* eye to see, ... IV. x. 23. 6
There worshipped of every *living* wight; . . . . IV. x. 29. 7
all *living* wights, soone as they see . . . . IV. x. 45. 3
love . . . that leads each *living* kind. . . . . IV. xii. 25. 9
she all *living* creatures did excell; . . . . IV. xii. 33. 5
And both the *living* Lady claime your right, ... V. i. 26. 2
Let both the dead and *living* equally Devided be . . . . V. i. 26. 3
thine I deeme The *living* Lady, ... V. i. 28. 3
him restoring unto *living* light, ... V. iv. 25. 6
Discovered had the light to *living* eye, ... V. vi. 35. 2
gave to them great *living* and large fee: . . . . V. vii. 43. 4
As that I did mistake the *living* for the ded. . . . . V. viii. 13. 9
till this day mongst many *living* are, ... V. x. 5. 8
All solitarie without *living* wight; . . . . V. x. 19. 2
Of all this day on ground that breathen *living* spright! . . . . VI. i. 4. 9
To rayse a *lyving* blame against the dead; . . . . VI. ii. 15. 7
Ere they were well aware of *living* wight, ... VI. iii. 21. 2
seldome yet did *living* creature see . . . . VI. iii. 40. 8
and hope of *living* light, ... VI. iii. 45. 4
Where foot of *living* creature never trode, ... VI. iv. 13. 8
Cannot redressed be by *living* wight!' . . . . VI. iv. 28. 5
As no whit dreading any *living* wight; . . . . VI. vii. 43. 2
gifts, that pleasde each *living* sight, ... VI. viii. 20. 4
shade From view of *living* wight . . . . VI. x. 42. 4
The fayrest Ladie then of all that *living* were: . . . . VI. xii. 3. 9
where *living* wight Mote not bewray . . . . VI. xii. 7. 2
all *living* wights have learn'd to die, ... VII. vi. 6. 5
not the worth of any *living* wight . . . . VII. vi. 33. 2
much she hated sight of *living* eye. . . . . VII. vi. 42. 6
So hard it is for any *living* wight . . . . VII. vii. 9. 1
are all watry *living* wights Still tost . . . . VII. vii. 21. 1
Ne any *living* creatures doth he breed, ... VII. vii. 24. 6
Of all the world and of all *living* wights) . . . . VII. vii. 25. 2
May kindle *living* fire within my brest. . . . . *Am.* vii. 12
full of the *living* fire, Kindled above . . . . *Am.* viii. 1
So dying live, and *living* do adore her. . . . . *Am.* xiv. 14
mote enlarge her *living* prayses, dead. . . . . *Am.* xxxiii. 4
lend you me another *living* brest. . . . . *Am.* xxxiii. 14
in every *living* wight They mixe themselves, ... *H.L.* 90
the most kind preserver Of *living* wights, ... *H.L.* 157
and breathd a *living* spright Into his face . . . . *H.H.L.* 110
Him to be Lord of every *living* wight He made . . . . *H.H.L.* 115

Livings. without reward *Livings* in Court be gotten, ... *Hub.* 514

Lo (*partial list*).
And *loe*, the sea (quod he) is now no more. . . . . *Rev.* iv. 2
A sodein earthquake *loe*, Shaking the hill . . . . *Bel.*[1] ii. 12
crying lowd, *Loe!* now beholde . . . . *Bel.* i. 9
'*Lo!* how the least the greatest may reprove.' . . . . *Van.* iv. 14
'*Lo!* how finely the Graces can it foote . . . . *S.C.* Ap. 109
Lo! Collin, here the place . . . . *S.C.* Jun. 1
Then *loe*, Perigot, the Pledge . . . . *S.C.* Au. 25
Loe! I have made a Calender . . . . *S.C.* Env. 1
Lo! there lives also the immortall praise . . . . *Gn.* 428
for *loe!* he was in sight . . . . *Hub.* 234
Lo! where they spide, ... *Hub.* 951
For *lo!* thy Kingdome is defaced quight, ... *T.M.* 399
Whilest thus I looked, *loe!* adowne the Lee . . . . *Ti.* 603
For *lo!* her Bridegrome was in readie ray . . . . *Ti.* 640
For *loe!* the drerie stownd is now arrived, ... *Mui.* 415
Lo! I, the man . . . . I. Pr. 1. 1
Lo! there before his face his Ladie is, ... I. i. 49. 5
'*Lo!* there the worthie meed Of him that slew . . . . I. iii. 36. 3
Lo! underneath her scornefull feete was layne . . . . I. iv. 10. 4
the faire Fidessa, *loe!* . . . . I. iv. 42. 2
Lo! his Fidessa, to thy secret faith I flye.' . . . . I. iv. 45. 9
when *lo!* a darkesome clowd Upon him fell: . . . . I. v. 13. 6
lo! th' infernall powres, Covering your foe . . . . I. v. 14. 6
Lo! where the stout Sansjoy doth sleepe . . . . I. v. 22. 9
Lo! now I goe with thee.' . . . . I. v. 27. 9
Lo! then, for thine ayd, Here take thy . . . . I. vi. 47. 6
'*Lo!* yonder is the same, ... I. viii. 2. 3
Loe! where your foe lies strecht . . . And *loe!* that wicked woman . . . . I. viii. 45. 3, 4
lo! they gan espy An armed knight . . . . I. ix. 21. 1
For *loe!* he comes, ... I. ix. 25. 2
Loe! two most goodly virgins came in place, ... I. x. 12. 2
'*Lo!* yonder is,' . . . 'The brasen towre, ... I. xi. 3. 1
Both daughter and eke kingdome *lo!* I yield . . . . I. xii. 20. 9
'*Lo!* yonder he,' . . . 'That wrought . . . . II. i. 25. 1

Lo—*Continued.*
Thy litle hands . . . *Loe!* I for pledges leave. . . . . II. i. 37. 9
Loe! this dead corpse, ... II. i. 49. 7
'*Lo!* now she is that stone; . . . . II. ii. 9. 1
But *loe!* my Lord, my liege, ... II. iii. 35. 3
lo! far away they spyde A varlet . . . . II. iv. 37. 1
'Then *loe!* wher bound she sits, ... II. iv. 44. 8
Loe! there they bee; . . . . II. v. 18. 6
Loe, loe! how brave she decks her bounteous boure, ... II. vi. 16. 5
Loe, loe! already how the fowles in aire Doe flocke, ... II. vi. 28. 7
Lo! to that shore one . . . By fortune came, ... II. vi. 47. 4
At thy commaund *lo!* all these mountaines bee: . . . . II. vii. 9. 2
'*Loe!* here the worldes blis: *loe!* here the end, ... II. vii. 32. 7
The thing, . . . *lo!* now is reveald to thee. . . . . II. vii. 38. 5
Lo! Tantalus, I here tormented lye: . . . . II. vii. 59. 5
Lo! here I now for want of food doe dye: . . . . II. vii. 59. 7
Loe! where he now inglorious doth lye, ... II. viii. 12. 8
Lo! where the dreadfull Death . . . doth stond.' . . . . II. viii. 37. 9
loe! . . . A thousand villeins rownd about them swarmd . . . . II. ix. 13. 1
'*Lo!* I the land descry; . . . . II. xii. 10. 8
'*Lo!* where does appeare The sacred soile . . . . II. xii. 37. 7
'*Lo!* see soone after how more bold and free . . . . II. xii. 74. 7
Lo! see . . . how she fades and falls away. . . . . II. xii. 74. 9
Lo! where a griesly foster forth did rush, ... III. i. 17. 2
Lo! where beyond he lyeth languishing, ... III. i. 38. 1
For *loe!* great grace . . . brought Comfort to him. . . . . III. v. 27. 3
For *lo!* . . . a whole legione Of wicked Sprightes did fall . . . . III. ix. 2. 6
For *lo!* that Guest did beare her forcibly, ... III. x. 13. 8
'*Lo!* now the hevens obey to me alone, ... III. xi. 35. 8
But *lo!* they streight were vanisht . . . . III. xii. 30. 4
Lo! thus they rode, ... IV. i. 17. 1
'*Lo!* there, Sir Paridel, ... IV. i. 33. 7
'*Lo!* recreant,' . . . 'the fruitlesse end Of thy vaine boast, ... IV. i. 51. 1
'*Lo!* sluggish Knight, the victors happie pray! . . . . IV. ii. 7. 5
'*Lo!* faitour, there thy meede unto thee take, ... IV. iii. 11. 1
Lo! where they spyde . . . One in a charet . . . . IV. iii. 38. 3
And *lo!* shee shall be placed here in sight, ... IV. iv. 9. 5
lo! farre away A Knight . . . they spyde, ... IV. vi. 9. 1
Loe! hard behind his backe his foe was prest, ... IV. viii. 41. 6
loe! . . . Those Ladies two, . . . In presence came, ... IV. viii. 62. 6
And *loe!* his hindparts, . . . ugly were, ... IV. x. 20. 3
'Yet *loe!* the seas, I see, ... IV. xii. 7. 1
loe! here thy Artegall. . . . . V. Pr. 11. 9
'*Loe!* there thy hire;' . . . . V. ii. 11. 8
'*Lo* there! Sir Guyon, take to you the steed, ... V. iii. 35. 3
Loe! here this ring, ... V. v. 34. 2
And *lo!* the Damzell selfe, ... V. viii. 15. 8
'*Loe!* now, right noble knights, arriv'd ye bee . . . . V. ix. 20. 4
Loe! I defie thee; and here challenge make, ... VI. iii. 35. 4
Lo! this my cause of griefe to you appeares; . . . . VI. iv. 33. 8
Lo! how good fortune doth to you present . . . . VI. iv. 35. 3
Lo! where a knight, . . . came ryding thetherward; . . . . VI. v. 11. 2
But *loe!* the Gods, that mortall follies vew, ... VI. vii. 32. 1
'For *loe!* the winged God . . . . VI. viii. 22. 1
'To thee, . . . *loe!* I lowely fly, ... VII. vii. 14. 2
'*Lo!* mighty mother, now be judge, ... VII. vii. 47. 2
For *loe*, my love doth in her selfe. . . . . *Am.* xv. 5
If Saphyres, *loe*, her eies be Saphyres plaine; . . . . *Am.* xv. 7
If Rubies, *loe*, hir lips be Rubies sound; . . . . *Am.* xv. 8
For *lo!* the wished day is come at last, ... *Epith.* 31
Loe! where she comes along with portly pace, ... *Epith.* 148
Lo! one, whom later age hath brought to light, ... *Com. Son.* iii. 9

Load. *load* the braunches of the fruitfull vine; . . . . *Col.* 601
on his backe a heavy *load* he bare . . . . I. iii. 16. 7
Did grone, as feeble so great *load* to lift; . . . . I. xi. 54. 4
light this weary vessell of her *lode:* . . . . I. xii. 42. 4
An heavie *load*, himselfe did lightly reare; . . . . II. ii. 11. 4
With heavie *load* on him they freshly gan to smight. . . . . II. ii. 23. 9
as the winde ran underneath his *lode,* . . . . II. xi. 20. 5
Upon him fell, and *lode* upon him layd: . . . . II. xi. 29. 5
the weake boughes, with so rich *load* opprest . . . . II. xii. 55. 5
load upon him layd his life for to have had. . . . . III. v. 22. 9
seeme to labour under their fruites *lode:* . . . . III. vi. 42. 6
Her selfe to fight addrest, and threw her *lode* aside. . . . . III. vii. 38. 9
Upon his Courser sett the lovely *lode,* . . . . III. viii. 19. 4
laying on them heavy *lode,* . . . . IV. iv. 23. 7
many swords that *lode* on him did lay. . . . . IV. iv. 31. 5
laid on *load* with all their might and powre, ... IV. ix. 22. 7
lay on *load*, as they him downe would beare; . . . . IV. ix. 33. 3
by reason of the *lode* . . . . IV. xi. 26. 2
layd on *load* with his huge yron flaile, ... V. ii. 24. 2
soft dismounting, like a weary *lode,* . . . . VI. vi. 19. 4
joyning close huge *lode* at him did lay; . . . . VI. vi. 28. 8
throwing downe his *load* out of his hand, ... VI. vii. 24. 3
Mote not bewray the secret of her *lode,* . . . . VI. xii. 7. 3
nathemore his heavy *load* releast, ... VI. xii. 32. 8

Loaded. *loded* them with lordships and with might, ... *Hub.* 1156
with rich metall *loaded* every rifte, ... II. vii. 28. 5

Loaden. *See* Laden.
Avarice . . . did ride, Uppon a Camell *loaden* all with gold; . . . . I. iv. 27. 2
Loaden with fruit and apples rosy redd, ... I. xi. 46. 2
loaden all with fruit as thick as it might bee. . . . . II. vii. 53. 9

Loading. the sad humor *loading* their eyeliddes, ... I. i. 36. 2

Loam. though it were a cottage clad with *lome,* . . . . VI. ix. 16. 5

Loan. th' other litle gained by the *lone,* . . . . IV. ix. 30. 7
with *lone* Of armes hast knighthood stolne, ... V. vi. 37. 4
her need give *lone* Of her faire light . . . . VII. vi. 11. 7

Loast. *See* Loosed.

Loath. *See* Loathe.
Loath was the Ape, though praised, to adventer, ... *Hub.* 1005

Loath—*Continued.*
up rose eke all the rest: All *loth* to part, ... *Col.* 954
Loth was that other, and did faint through feare, ... I. iii. 34. 5
With loftie eyes, halfe *loth* to looke so lowe, ... I. iv. 14. 1
Upon a Lion, *loth* for to be led; . . . . I. iv. 33. 2
when he heard her answers *loth*, ... I. vii. 38. 3
Full *loth* she seemd thereto, ... II. i. 20. 8
fairely fare on foot, how ever *loth:* . . . . II. ii. 12. 3
all were they wondrous *loth*, ... II. ii. 34. 2
Guyon was *loath* to leave his guide behind, ... II. vi. 20. 1
The God, though *loth*, yet was constraynd t' obay; . . . . . II. vii. 66. 1
yet their praises speake, all be they *loth*, ... II. x. 40. 7
suffered him to passe, all were she *loth;* . . . . II. xii. 57. 8
was *loth* to let her purpose plaine appeare; . . . . III. iii. 17. 9
Certes I should be *loth* thee to molest; . . . . III. iii. 18. 4
brought Unto your dwelling, ignorant and *loth*, ... III. vii. 8. 8
them dislodge, all were they liefe or *loth;* . . . . III. ix. 13. 8
Both were full *loth* to leave that needfull tent, ... III. ix. 14. 1
both full *loth* in darkenesse to debate; . . . . III. ix. 14. 2
was he *loth* to loose his loved Dame, ... III. x. 15. 5
loth to leave his liefest pelfe behinde; . . . . III. x. 15. 6
That was him *loth*, yet durst he not gainesay, ... III. x. 23. 8
stayd her hand, *loth* stayd to bee; . . . . III. xii. 34. 8
her love to lose she was full *loth*, ... IV. i. 10. 8
Whom he that hath were *loth* to lose so light, ... IV. iv. 9. 2
loth to leave her late betrothed make, ... IV. vi. 42. 8
Her dearest love full *loth* so shortly to forsake. . . . . . IV. vi. 42. 9
So *loth* she was his companie for to forsake. . . . . IV. vi. 45. 9
full *loth* was he, ne would for ought Consent . . . . IV. viii. 58. 5
see the sight perforce that both her eyes were *loth*. . . . IV. ix. 9. 9
how ever *loth* to rest; . . . . IV. ix. 32. 7
Albe that Hatred was thereto full *loth*, ... IV. x. 33. 3
Loth was the Dwarfe, yet did he stay perforse, ... V. ii. 2. 5
loth he was his noble hands t' embrew . . . . V. ii. 52. 4
Yet *loth* she was . . . To thinke of him so ill; . . . . V. vi. 4. 8
loth to loose her right away, ... V. vii. 30. 5
However *loth* he were his way to slake, ... V. viii. 5. 8
Full *loath* to Belgae and to all the rest; . . . . V. xi. 35. 6
He up arose, however liefe or *loth*, ... VI. i. 44. 3
'*loth* were I to have broken The law of armes: . . . . . . VI. ii. 7. 6
'full *loth* I were To rayse a lyving blame . . . . VI. ii. 15. 6
when as I was *loth* My loves owne part to leave . . . . . VI. ii. 17. 6
'Full *loth* am I,' (quoth he) . . . . VI. iii. 39. 1
loth t' assay The proofe of battell now . . . . VI. iii. 41. 3
full *loth* To make there lenger stay, ... VI. iii. 45. 8
Or *loth* to let her sorrowes be bewrayd: . . . . VI. iv. 27. 4
As *loth* to see or to be seene at all: . . . . VI. viii. 5. 6
Loathe. *Loath* this base world, ... *Pet.*² vii. 12
lofty love doth *loath* a lowly eye. . . . . *S.C.* O. 96
Doth *loath* such base condition, ... *Hub.* 719
loath this drosse of sinfull worlds desire! . . . . *Ti.* 686
'Who life dooes *loath*, and longs to bee unbound . . . . . *D.* 85
Who life doth *loath*, and longs death to behold, ... *Col.* 204
loath each lowly thing with loftie eie. . . . . *Col.* 938
mortall life gan *loath* as thing forlore, ... I. x. 21. 5
(So love does *loath* disdainefull nicitee) . . . . II. ii. 3. 3
'Thy offers base I greatly *loth*, ... III. x. 29. 6
that golden pray, . . . I *loath* as doung, ... III. x. 31. 6
For her, that each of you alike doth *loth*, ... IV. i. 47. 4
make me *loath* this life, still longing for to die. . . . . . IV. viii. 16. 9
They soone would *loath* their lesser happinesse, ... IV. x. 23. 7
loath their wonted food: . . . . IV. x. 46. 2
He now t' abhorre and *loath* her person had procured. . . . V. ix. 39. 9
Now *loath* great Lordship and ambition; . . . . VI. ix. 28. 5
loath this state of life so tickle, ... VII. viii. 1. 6
lothe the things which they did like before, ... *Am.* xxxv. 11
Their lives they *loath*, and heavens light disdaine; . . . . *H.L.* 130
Loath that foule blot, ... *H.B.* 169
Loathed. *loathed* Paddocks lording on the same: . . . . . *S.C.* D. 70
loath'd of losels as a thing forlorne: . . . . *T.M.* 226
to my *loathed* life now shewes some light, ... I. iv. 48. 2
Why doe ye lenger feed on *loathed* light, ... I. vii. 22. 3
skin, . . . So scabby was that would have *loathd* all woman-kind. . . . . I. viii. 47. 9
From *loathed* soile he can him lightly reare, ... I. xi. 39. 3
take away this long lent *loathed* light: . . . . II. i. 36. 7
Soone as my *loathed* love appeard in sight, ... II. iv. 29. 3
As one that *loathed* life, and yet despysd to dye. . . . . . II. viii. 50. 9
their owne mother *loathd* their beastlinesse, ... II. x. 9. 3
loath'd the loose demeanure of that wanton sort. . . . . . III. i. 40. 9
in minde to gride The *loathed* leachour. . . . . III. i. 62. 4
Sithence I *loathed* have my life to lead, ... III. ii. 6. 6
Feeling her leape out of her *loathed* nest, ... III. ii. 30. 3
light ylike is *loth'd* of them and thee; . . . . III. iv. 58. 8
he himselfe himselfe *loath'd* so forlorne, ... III. x. 55. 7
Straight he upstarted from the *loathed* layes, ... III. xii. 44. *or.*5
Be thou, . . . *Loathed* of ladies all, ... IV. i. 51. 9
lives a *loathed* life, and wishing cannot die. . . . . IV. vii. 11. 9
in conditions to be *loath'd* no lesse; . . . . IV. viii. 24. 2
his big hart *loth'd* so uncomely vew: . . . . V. v. 22. 5
She forth yssew'd out of her *loathed* bowre, ... V. vi. 35. 3
Is liker lingring death then *loathed* life to bee.' . . . . . V. x. 21. 9
More *loathd* then Lerna, or then Stygian lake, ... V. xi. 32. 4
he *loathd* leasing and base flattery, ... VI. i. 3. 8
Loathes. Who so *loathes* not too much the poore estate, . . *Gn.* 90
Such shamefull lustes who *loaths* not, ... III. ii. 41. 7
Loatheth. *loatheth* sike delightes as thou doest prayse: . . . *S.C.* N. 18
let him dye, that *loatheth* living breath, ... I. ix. 38. 8
Loathful. *lothefull* idlenes he doth detest, ... *Hub.* 735
Which when he did with *lothfull* eyes beholde, ... *Hub.* 1314

Loathful—*Continued.*
The *lothfull* life, now loosd from sinfull bands, ... II. xi. 46. 3
Which when the Prince beheld, a *lothfull* sight, ... III. iv. 52. 4
He list no lenger to use *lothfull* speach, ... V. vi. 21. 6
Loathfulness. reading it with inward *loathfulnesse*, ... IV. xii. 32. 8
Loathing. Gay without good is good hearts greatest *loathing*. *Hub.* 232
loathing earth, I looke up to the sky, ... *T.M.* 527
Loathing this sinfull earth and earthlie slime . . . . *Ti.* 290
his heavie eyes were throwne, As *loathing* light; . . . . . . *D.* 47
Best musicke breeds delight in *loathing* eare; . . . . I. viii. 44. 4
That wofull lover, *loathing* lenger light, ... I. ix. 30. 2
all desperate, as *loathing* light, ... II. viii. 47. 1
Astraea *loathing* lenger here to space . . . . V. i. 11. 2
which *loathing* brings Of this vile world . . . . *H.H.B.* 298
Loathly. Clerks they to *loathly* idlenes entice, ... *T.M.* 335
loathly frogs and toades, which eyes did lacke, ... I. i. 20. 7
Her *loathly* visage viewing with disdaine, ... I. ii. 39. 5
Dragon . . . Bred in the *loathly* lakes of Tartary, ... I. vii. 44. 3
A *loathly*, wrinckled hag, ill favoured, old, ... I. viii. 46. 8
To hide her shame and *loathly* filthinesse, ... II. i. 22. 5
loathly were and hoarie gray, ... II. iv. 4. 5
Guyon much disdeigned so *loathly* sight. . . . . II. v. 23. 6
Resolv'd to put away that *loathly* blame, ... II. viii. 44. 4
some faste Like *loathly* Toades; . . . . II. xi. 12. 5
So shamelesse beauty soone becomes a *loathly* sight. . . . . III. i. 48. 9
Pure and unspotted from all *loathly* crime . . . . III. vi. 3. 4
in *loathly* weedes And wilfull want, ... III. vii. 6. 4
In *loathly* wise like to a carrion corse, ... III. vii. 43. 5
loosenesse of her love and *loathly* deed, ... III. x. 50. 4
loathly mouth, unmeete a mouth to bee, ... IV. i. 27. 3
A foule and *loathly* creature sure in sight, ... IV. viii. 24. 1
when she saw that *lothly* uncouth sight . . . . V. vii. 37. 6
Such *loathly* matter were small lust to speake or thinke. . . V. xi. 31. 9
left so in the *loathely* soyle. . . . . V. xi. 33. 9
Abide, and from them lay your *loathly* hands, ... VI. viii. 7. 8
Above the reach of *loathly* sinfull lust, ... *H.L.* 179
Loathsome. lyftes him up out of the *loathsome* myre: . . . . *S.C.* O. 92
in *loathsome* den Of ghostly darkenes, ... *T.M.* 531
to subject his desire To *loathsome* sloth, ... *Mui.* 36
her faire face to fowle and *loathsome* hewe, ... *Mui.* 351
Why doo I longer see this *loathsome* light . . . . *D.* 444
Most *lothsom*, filthie, foule, and full of vile disdaine. . . . I. i. 14. 9
Like *lothsome* lazars, by the hedges lay. . . . . I. iv. 3. 6
by his side rode *loathsome* Gluttony, ... I. iv. 21. 1
All which, and thousands mo, do make a *loathsome* life. . . I. ix. 44. 9
wild like beastes lurking in *loathsome* den, ... II. x. 7. 4
yield the pray of love to *lothsome* death at last. . . . . . III. ii. 17. 9
Her *lothsom* pleasure there to satisfye; . . . . III. vii. 51. 4
to leave that lewd And *loathsom* life, ... III. x. 51. 2
life it selfe seemd *loathsome*, ... IV. iii. 36. 9
A foule and *lothsome* creature, did appeare, ... IV. vii. 34. 4
No service *lothsome* to a gentle kind, ... IV. viii. 22. 7
Treading downe earth as *lothsome* . . . . *Am.* xiii. 11
Loathsomely. her foule heare Hung loose and *loathsomely:* . . V. xii. 29. 4
The bloudie gore and poyson dropping *lothsomely*. . . . . . V. xii. 30. 9
Lobb. O *Lobb!* thy losse no longer lament; . . . . *S.C.* N. 168
Lobbin. 'O thou greate shepheard, *Lobbin*, ... *S.C.* N. 113
Why then weepes *Lobbin* so without remorse? . . . . *S.C.* N. 167
To wait on *Lobbin*, (*Lobbin* well thou knewest,) . . . . . . *Col.* 736
Lock. *See* **Snaky-lock.**
Fast in theyr folds he did them *locke*, ... *S.C.* S. 205
lette me in your foldes ye *lock*, ... *S.C.* D. 147
no *locke* so firme and fast, But . . . flew open . . . . . . I. viii. 4. 8
he cutt a *lock* of all their heare, ... II. i. 61. 2
Thereon an yron *lock* did fasten . . . . II. iv. 12. 9
Doubly disparted, it did *locke* and close, ... II. ix. 23. 6
neither yron barres, nor brasen *locke*, ... IV. xi. 3. 3
Locked. Like a Pandora, *locked* long in store. . . . . *Ro.* xix. 8
all the gates he found fast *lockt* anon, ... *Hub.* 1350
In which all heavenly treasures *locked* are. . . . . *Ti.* 630
All heavenly gifts and riches *locked* are; . . . . *Col.* 489
double gates he findeth *locked* fast, ... I. i. 40. 1
he came unto an yron doore, That fast was *lockt*, ... I. viii. 37. 4
Arrived there, the dore they find fast *lockt*, ... I. x. 5. 1
every loup fast *lockt*, as fearing foes despight. . . . . . . II. ix. 10. 9
when it *locked* none might thorough pas, ... II. ix. 23. 7
the dore streightway Fast *locked*, ... III. xii. 27. 2
fownd it *locked* fast: . . . . III. xii. 27. 7
and yet that Knight not *locked* out; . . . . IV. i. 11. 8
The which I found sure *lockt* and chained fast. . . . . . . IV. x. 11. 3
Locks. With side-long beard, and *locks* down hanging . . . *Bel.*² ix. 3
mowes The waving *lockes* of those faire yeallow heares, . . . *Ro.* xxx. 6
her faire *lockes* fell from her loftie head, ... *Van.* vii. 11
oft his hoarie *locks* downe doth cast, ... *S.C.* F. 181
He, plongd in payne, his tressed *locks* dooth teare. . . . . *S.C.* Ap. 12
To crowne her golden *locks:* . . . . *S.C.* Jun. 46
The faded *lockes* fall from the loftie oke, ... *S.C.* N. 125
His looser *locks* doth wrap in wreath of vine: . . . . *Gn.* 114
lockes uncombed cruell adders be. . . . . *Gn.* 344
Rending her yeolow *locks*, like wyrie gold . . . . *Ti.* 10
His carelesse *locks* uncombed and unshore, ... *D.* 43
Her yellow *locks* that shone so bright and long, ... *As.* 157
tree . . . Whose tender *locks* do tremble every one . . . . . I. vii. 32. 8
His griesie *lockes*, long growen and unbound, ... I. ix. 35. 4
With snowy *lockes* adowne his shoulders shed; . . . . I. x. 48. 2
Her golden *locks* for hast were loosely shed . . . . I. xi. 51. 5
the morning starre . . . with flaming *lockes* bedight, ... I. xii. 21. 6
Her looser golden *lockes* he rudely rent, ... II. i. 11. 5
Her golden *lockes* most cruelly she rent, ... II. i. 15. 4
Her golden *lockes* she roundly did uptye . . . . II. ii. 15. 7

Locks—*Continued.*
Her yellow *lockes,* crisped like golden wyre, . . . II. iii. 30. 1
Her *lockes,* that loathly were and hoarie gray, . . . II. iv. 4. 5
fast her hent By the hoare *lockes* . . . II. iv. 12. 3
Shakt his long *locks* colourd like copper-wyre, . . . II. iv. 15. 8
shooke His sandy *lockes,* . . . II. v. 14. 4
Whose hoary *locks* great gravitie did crowne, . . . II. vi. 47. 5
When the wroth Western wind does reave their *locks:* . . . II. xi. 19. 5
With hoary *lockes* all loose, . . . II. xi. 23. 3
she left her *lockes* undight, . . . II. xii. 15. 6
her faire *lockes,* which formerly were bownd . . . II. xii. 67. 2
So hidd in *lockes* and waves from lookers theft, . . . II. xii. 67. 8
her faire yellow *locks* behind her flew, . . . III. i. 16. 3
a blazing starre doth . . . flaming *lockes* dispredd, . . . III. i. 16. 6
To crowne his golden *lockes* with honour dew; . . . III. i. 35. 5
in her snow-white smocke, with *locks* unbownd, . . . III. i. 63. 7
her faire deawy *lockes* yrent; . . . III. iv. 30. 2
Her faire *lockes* in rich circlet be enrold, . . . III. v. 5. 4
His *locks,* like faded leaves fallen to grownd, . . . III. v. 29. 5
Her golden *lockes,* that late in tresses bright Embreaded were III. vi. 18. 6
her loose *lockes* to dight in order dew . . . III. vii. 11. 2
Instead of yellow *locks* she did devyze With golden wyre . III. viii. 7. 5
Her golden *locks,* that were in trammells gay Upbounden, . . III. ix. 20. 4
her fayre *lockes* were woven up in gold: . . . III. xii. 13. 4
her faire *locks* up stared stiffe on end, . . . III. xii. 36. 6
her golden *lockes,* that were upbound . . . IV. i. 13. 2
Combing her golden *lockes,* as seemd her good; . . . IV. ii. 45. 5
his faire *lockes,* that wont with ointment sweet . . . IV. vii. 40. 3
With filthy *lockes* about her scattered wide, . . . IV. viii. 23. 7
His dewy *lockes* did drop with brine apace . . . IV. xi. 11. 3
Her goodly *lockes* adowne her backe did flow . . . IV. xi. 46. 1
Thence he her drew By the faire *lockes,* . . . V. ii. 25. 7
Now scratching her, and her loose *locks* misusing, . . . V. vi. 14. 6
with long *locks* comely kemd, . . . V. vii. 4. 5
with long *locks* up-standing, stifly stared . . . V. vii. 20. 7
Each of whose *lockes* did match a man in might, . . . V. viii. 2. 2
With *locks* all loose, and rayment all to-rent; . . . V. viii. 4. 8
long curld *locks* that downe his shoulders shagged; . . . V. ix. 10. 6
bynding up her *locks* and weeds, . . . V. x. 24. 9
with rude flaring *lockes* About her eares, . . . V. xii. 38. 8
they that Ladies *lockes* doe shave away, . . . VI. i. 13. 8
With beards of Knights and *locks* of Ladies lynd: . . . VI. i. 15. 5
from her head her *lockes* he nigh did teare, . . . VI. i. 17. 8
shall it not her *lockes* for raunsome fro me free.' . . . VI. i. 19. 9
his *locks,* as blacke as pitchy night, . . . VI. vii. 43. 7
rends her golden *locks,* and snowy brests embrew. . . . VI. viii. 40. 9
Whose silver *lockes* bedeckt his beard and hed, . . . VI. ix. 13. 7
With ragged weedes, and *lockes* upstaring hye, . . . VI. xi. 27. 4
The dores assayled, and the *locks* upbrast: . . . VI. xi. 43. 3
he shooke His Nectar-deawed *locks,* . . . VII. vi. 30. 7
to deck the *locks* Of som faire Bride, . . . VII. vi. 41. 3
her *locks* are finest Gold on ground; . . . *Am.* xv. 11
Bynd up the *locks* the which hang scatterd light, . . . *Epith.* 62
Her long loose yellow *locks* lyke golden wyre, . . . *Epith.* 154
Flocke of Nymphes . . . With goodly greenish *locks,* . . . *Proth.* 22
Locrinus. *Locrine* left chiefe Lord of Britany. . . . II. x. 13. 7
Locrine was left the soveraine Lord of all: . . . II. x. 14. 1
Locrine . . . Did head against them make . . . II. x. 15. 8
her sonne, which she to *Locrin* bore, . . . II. x. 20. 1
Brutus warlicke sonne, *Locrinus,* . . . IV. xi. 38. 2
Lode, -d. *See* **Load, -ed.**
Lodestar. now the Pylote can no *loadstarre* see, . . . *Gn.* 573
It is their light, their *loadstarre,* and their day; . . . *T.M.* 495
a ship, whose *Lodestar* suddeinly Covered with cloudes . . . III. iv. 53. 3
Lodestarre of all chaste affection . . . III. vi. 52. 5
My Helice, the *lodestar* of my lyfe, . . . *Am.* xxxiv. 10
Lodge. Here no night-ravenes *lodge,* . . . *S.C.* Jun. 23
Ne will I *lodge,* ne will I ever lin, . . . *D.* 467
Shall ever *lodge* upon mine ey-lids more; . . . *D.* 471
His wasted life her wearie *lodge* forwent. . . . *As.* 174
forth him ledd Into a goodly *lodge,* . . . I. x. 17. 7
His cursed life out of her *lodge* have rent; . . . II. viii. 32. 3
To *lodge* the warlike maide, unwisely loov'd; . . . III. i. 60. 4
swore that he would *lodge* with them yfere, . . . III. ix. 13. 7
Her body, . . . the sweet *lodge* of love and deare delight: . . III. xii. 45. *or.*4
Let him *lodge* hard, and lie in strawen bed, . . . V. v. 50. 5
To *lodge* with him that night, . . . V. vi. 21. 9
yet better so To *lodge* then in the salvage fields to rome. . . VI. ix. 16. 7
therein now doth *lodge* a noble Peer, . . . *Proth.* 145
Lodged. they came Unto a Castell, *lodged* there to bee, . . . IV. i. 9. 2
my love was *lodged* day and night, . . . IV. x. 29. 4
that they might Finde favour to be *lodged* there . . . VI. iii. 42. 9
Lodging. ere that life her *lodging* did forsake, . . . *D.* 260
And to the Paynims *lodging* comes . . . I. iv. 44. 9
lodging unto all that came and went; . . . I. x. 37. 5
Into her *lodging* to repaire awhile, . . . II. ii. 33. 4
Had *lodging* in so meane a maintenaunce; . . . III. vii. 59. 4
dore Was shut to all which *lodging* did desyre: . . . III. viii. 52. 8
both full liefe him *lodging* to have lent, . . . III. ix. 14. 3
lodging there without her owne consent: . . . IV. viii. 28. 5
The earth to all her creatures *lodging* lends.' . . . V. x. 24. 6
And myld entreaty *lodging* did for her beseeke. . . . VI. iii. 37. 9
there was no place Of *lodging* . . . VI. iii. 38. 8
Ne *lodging* would to any of them graunt; . . . VI. vi. 21. 5
Him *lodging* in your bosome to have lent. . . . *Am.* lxxiii. 14
The neast of love, the *lodging* of delight, . . . *Am.* lxxvi. 2
Lodgings. Unto their *lodgings* then his guestes he riddes: . . I. i. 36. 5
Lodovic. *Lodwick,* this of grace to me aread; . . . *Am.* xxxiii. 5
Loft. ever-drizling raine upon the *loft,* . . . I. i. 41. 3
The *loft* was raysd againe, that no man could it spie. . . . V. vi. 27. 9

Loftily. My lowly verse may *loftily* arise, . . . II. x. 1. 4
Lofty. lift her *loftie* face Against the heaven, . . . *Ro.* xii. 11
To builde, with levell of my *loftie* style, . . . *Ro.* xxv. 13
her faire lockes fell from her *loftie* head, . . . *Van.* vii. 11
The *loftie* verse of hem was loved aye. . . . *S.C.* O. 66
lofty love doth loath a lowly eye. . . . *S.C.* O. 96
The faded lockes fall from the *loftie* oke, . . . *S.C.* N. 125
loftie type of honour, . . . is downe in dust . . . *Gn.* 557
his lookes *loftie,* as if he aspyr'd To dignitie, . . . *Hub.* 678
lifted up his *loftie* towres thereby, . . . *Hub.* 1173
aspire Unto so *loftie* pitch of perfectnesse, . . . *T.M.* 394
With *loftie* flight above the earth he bounded, . . . *Ti.* 599
There did a *loftie* mount at first us greet, . . . *Col.* 284
Such *loftie* flight base shepheard seemeth not, . . . *Col.* 618
loath each lowly thing with *loftie* eie. . . . *Col.* 938
When so thee list thy *lofty* Muse to raise: . . . *Ded.Son.*viii.12
In *loftie* numbers and heroicke stile. . . . *Ded. Son.* xii. 8
loftie trees, yclad with sommers pride, . . . I. i. 7. 4
Dismounting lightly from his *loftie* steed, . . . I. iii. 36. 1
High lifted up were many *loftie* towres, . . . I. iv. 4. 6
With *loftie* eyes, . . . She thancked them . . . I. iv. 14. 1
Upon the top of all his *loftie* crest, . . . I. vii. 32. 1
The noble knight alighted . . . From *loftie* steed, . . . I. viii. 2. 8
Both *loftie* towres and highest trees hath rent, . . . I. viii. 9. 7
His gorgeous ryder from her *loftie* sted . . . I. viii. 17. 5
I did alight From *loftie* steed, . . . I. ix. 13. 2
extend Her *lofty* towres unto the starry sphere, . . . I. x. 56. 8
He left his *loftie* steed . . . II. ii. 11. 6
lowly did abase their *lofty* crests . . . II. ii. 32. 4
From *lofty* siege began these words aloud to sownd. . . . II. ii. 39. 9
he from his *loftie* steed Downe fell . . . II. iii. 21. 2
For Love his *loftie* triumphes to engrave, . . . II. iii. 24. 3
his *lofty* crest Did fiercely shake, . . . II. iii. 35. 8
in the lake his *loftie* crest was stept, . . . II. vi. 42. 4
all the Gods admird his *lofty* note. . . . II. x. 3. 5
the fether in her *lofty* crest, . . . III. ii. 27. 1
Badd her old Squyre unlace her *lofty* creast: . . . III. iv. 7. 3
from his *loftie* steed dismounting low . . . III. iv. 53. 6
ill becomes you, with your *lofty* creasts, . . . III. vi. 22. 5
made him low incline his *lofty* crest, . . . III. vii. 42. 4
whenas vailed was her *lofty* crest, . . . III. ix. 20. 3
loosd her helmet from her *lofty* hedd, . . . III. ix. 22. 7
In *lofty* looks to hide an humble minde, . . . III. x. 30. 2
the Boaster from his *loftie* sell Faynd to alight, . . . III. x. 38. 5
In hast she from her *lofty* chaire descended, . . . IV. iii. 50. 2
forced him to leave his *loftie* sell, . . . IV. iv. 30. 8
Unto his *lofty* steede he clombe anone, . . . IV. v. 46. 1
tooke downe those Ladies twaine From *loftie* steede, . . . IV. viii. 41. 2
From my *lofty* steede dismounting low . . . IV. x. 15. 3
The dales doe not the *lofty* hils envy. . . . V. ii. 41. 4
low dismounting from his *loftie* steede . . . V. x. 22. 2
Ne ever Knight that bore so *lofty* creast, . . . VI. vi. 12. 7
No more then lightening from the *lofty* sky: . . . VI. viii. 8. 6
He left his *lofty* steede to aide him neare; . . . VI. viii. 12. 7
To chaunge the manner of his *loftie* looke; . . . VI. ix. 36. 2
in those *lofty* lookes is close implide, . . . *Am.* v. 5
that same *lofty* countenance seemes to scorne . . . *Am.* xiii. 9
Such lowlinesse shall make you *lofty* be. . . . *Am.* xiii. 14
The lovely pleasance; and the *lofty* pride; . . . *Am.* xvii. 11
Whose *lofty* argument, uplifting me, . . . *Am.* lxxxii. 13
Logris. quart, Which Severne now from *Logris* doth depart: . . II. x. 14. 5
Ymner slew of *Logris* miscreate; . . . II. x. 38. 2
Twede, the limit betwixt *Logris* land And Albany; . . . IV. xi. 36. 6
Loins. The sonne of his *loines* why should he regard . . . *S.C.* May 83
Of what *loines* and what lignage I did spring; . . . I. ix. 5. 6
From whose two *loynes* thou afterwardes did rayse . . . III. iii. 3. 6
her lanck *loynes* ungirt, and brests unbraste, . . . III. vi. 18. 4
About their tender *loynes* to knit the same; . . . IV. v. 17. 7
Yet it to none of all their *loynes* would fit, . . . V. iii. 28. 4
Loitering. So *loytring* live you little heardgroomes, . . . *S.C.* F. 35
Lombardy. mountaines bordring *Lombardie,* . . . *Bel.*[2] vi. 10
Lomp, -ish. *See* **Lump, -ish.**
Loncaster, Lond. *See* **Lancaster, Land.**
London. they all to mery *London* came, . . . *Proth.* 127
To mery *London,* my most kyndly Nurse, . . . *Proth.* 128
Lone. *See* **Loan.**
These after came the stony shallow *Lone,* . . . IV. xi. 39. 1
Long. *See* **Erelong, Livelong, Longwhile, Sidelong.**
Long was his beard, . . . *Bel.*[1] vii. 3
Ere it be *long* within the earth to rest. . . . *Pet.*[1] vii. 4
All pleasure . . . for which mans hart could *long;* . . . *Bel.*[2] xii. 6
Long having deeply gron'd these Visions . . . *Bel.*[2] xiv. 1
Why have your hands *long* sithence traveiled . . . *Ro.* ix. 5
frame this world that doth endure so *long?* . . . *Ro.* ix. 6
So *long* as Joves great Bird did make his flight, . . . *Ro.* xvii. 1
Like a Pandora, locked *long* in store. . . . *Ro.* xix. 8
Long as her ship, tost with so manie freakes, . . . *Ro.* xxi. 5
As he that having *long* in tempest sailed, . . . *Ro.* xxi. 11
Those antique Caesars, sleeping *long* in darke, . . . *Ro.* xxv. 3
All that the Ocean graspes in his *long* armes; . . . *Ro.* xxvi. 6
To greatnes growne, through *long* prosperitie, . . . *Ro.* xxxi. 13
Th' olde honour of the people gowned *long.* . . . *Ro.* xxxii. 14
long hast traveld, by thy learned writs, . . . *Ro.* Env. 4
Sith nought on earth can chalenge *long* endurance? . . . *Van.* xi. 14
his flock, that had bene *long* ypent: . . . *S.C.* Ja. 4
Here is a *long* tale, and little worth. . . . *S.C.* F. 240
longe have I listened . . . *S.C.* F. 241
Long wandring up and downe the land, . . . *S.C.* Mar. 64
So *long* I shott, that al was spent; . . . *S.C.* Mar. 88
ladde, whome *long* I lovd . . . *S.C.* Ap. 10

Long—*Continued.*
may shee florish *long* . . . *S.C.* Ap. 48
I have troubled your troupes to *longe:* . . . *S.C.* Ap. 149
tract of time, and *long* prosperitie, . . . *S.C.* May 117
It was not *long*, after shee was gone, . . . *S.C.* May 235
with *long* traveile I am brent in the sonne: . . . *S.C.* May 267
long to dreame. . . . *S.C.* Jul. 64
hath bene *long* ypent. . . . *S.C.* Jul. 216
long agoe, . . . *S.C.* S. 98
not *long* ygoe? . . . *S.C.* S. 171
Long time he used this slippery pranck, . . . *S.C.* S. 200
sleepe, as some doen, all the *long* day; . . . *S.C.* S. 233
this *long* tale Nought easeth the care . . . *S.C.* S. 242
I have pyped erst so *long* with payne, . . . *S.C.* O. 7
great Augustus *long* ygoe is dead, . . . *S.C.* O. 62
Thy Muse to *long* slombreth . . . *S.C.* N. 3
Relieve thy Oaten pypes that sleepen *long*. . . . *S.C.* N. 24
(ah! why live we so *long?*) . . . *S.C.* N. 73
Nay, time was *long* ygoe: . . . *S.C.* N. 81
lyeth buryed *long* in Winters bale; . . . *S.C.* N. 84
withered, as they had bene gathered *long;* . . . *S.C.* D. 110
so *long* since past. . . . *Gn.* 48
Thus wise *long* time he did himselfe dispace . . . *Gn.* 265
So *long* as thankfull will may it relent. . . . *Gn.* 368
th' antique faith of Justice *long* agone . . . *Gn.* 359
so *long* as thankfull will may it relent. . . . *Gn.* 368
Girt with *long* snakes, . . . *Gn.* 626
Long they thus travailed, . . . *Hub.* 223
in *long* service lost both limbs and good; . . . *Hub.* 248
be thou sure one not to lacke or *long*. . . . *Hub.* 501
Better a short tale than a bad *long* shriving: . . . *Hub.* 543
ere *long* time had passed, . . . *Hub.* 559
So *long* persisted obstinate and bolde, . . . *Hub.* 567
long straied here and there, . . . *Hub.* 577
through the world had with *long* travel far'd, . . . *Hub.* 686
What hell it is in suing *long* to bide: . . . *Hub.* 896
To wast *long* nights in pensive discontent; . . . *Hub.* 898
doth his life in so *long* tendance spend! . . . *Hub.* 908
in the world *long* time they wandered, . . . *Hub.* 943
long experience the platforme was: . . . *Hub.* 1168
for their memories *long* moniment: . . . *Hub.* 1182
what had of *long* Become of him; . . . *Hub.* 1325
th' Apes *long* taile . . . he quight Cut off, . . . *Hub.* 1381
Whom all the Muses did bewaile *long* space, . . . *T.M.* 17
in the lap of soft delight Beene *long* time luld, . . . *T.M.* 302
long ere this, Bunduca, Britonnesse, . . . *Ti.* 106
For wonder of the world, *long* in me lasted, . . . *Ti.* 118
to lament My *long* decay, . . . *Ti.* 157
'It is not *long*, since these two eyes beheld . . . *Ti.* 183
long agoe did grieve . . . Salomon . . . *Ti.* 443
sate *long* time in sencelesse sad affright, . . . *Ti.* 475
when I missed, having looked *long*, . . . *Ti.* 477
what can *long* abide above this ground . . . *Ti.* 568
Fainting at last through *long* infirmities, . . . *Ti.* 656
not *long* agoe Her sonne to Psyche . . . *Mui.* 130
love did beare, And *long* it close conceal'd, . . . *Mui.* 132
what on earth can *long* abide in state, . . . *Mui.* 217
She stood astonied *long*, ne ought gainesaid; . . . *Mui.* 339
the fond Flie, entangled, strugled *long*, . . . *Mui.* 425
After his dayes *long* labour drew to rest, . . . *D.* 23
His carelesse locks . . . Hong *long* adowne, . . . *D.* 44
'*Long* thus I joyed in my happinesse, . . . *D.* 148
freed from wretched *long* imprisonment! . . . *D.* 273
' "I goe, and *long* desired have to goe; . . . *D.* 281
Let rest her selfe from her *long* wearinesse, . . . *D.* 338
By living *long* to multiplie their paine; . . . *D.* 361
But rather riddance from *long* languishment. . . . *D.* 364
th' heavens with *long* languor pacifide, . . . *D.* 388
She . . . Will send for me; for which I daylie *long;* . . . *D.* 390
mocking such as thinke they *long* will stay. . . . *D.* 399
There will I sigh, and sorrow all day *long*, . . . *D.* 488
Be sure that they shall have no *long* endurance, . . . *D.* 501
The which, I, wretch, endured have thus *long*. . . . *D.* 532
Her yellow locks that shone so bright and *long*, . . . *As.* 157
Till I have told her praises lasting *long:* . . . *Col.* 49
so *long* As water doth within his bancks appeare.' . . . *Col.* 94
sung so *long* untill quite hoarse he grew. . . . *Col.* 399
So *long* as life my limbs doth hold together; . . . *Col.* 629
long before the world he was ybore, . . . *Col.* 839
long affliction which I have endured: . . . *Col.* 944
heare the languors of my too *long* dying, . . . *Col.* 948
soyl . . . being through *long* wars left almost waste, . . . *Ded. Son.* v. 3
spirit, . . . Might *long* perhaps have lien in silence . . . *Ded. Son.* xiii. 5
deeds; Whose praises having slept in silence *long*, . . . I. Pr. 1. 6
Whom that most noble Briton Prince so *long* Sought . . . I. Pr. 2. 6
Her huge *long* taile her den all overspred, . . . I. i. 15. 2
Long way he traveiled before he heard of ought. . . . I. i. 28. 9
An aged Sire, in *long* blacke weedes yclad, . . . I. i. 29. 2
such a cursed creature lives so *long* a space.' . . . I. i. 31. 9
The Sunne, that measures heaven all day *long*, . . . I. i. 32. 8
Let me not die in languor and *long* teares.' . . . I. i. 52. 7
Long after lay he musing . . . I. i. 55. 1
Full envious that night so *long* his roome did fill: . . . I. ii. 1. 9
Dead *long* ygoe, I wote, thou haddest bin, . . . I. ii. 18. 3
whose deepe wounded mind . . . *long* time did languish, . . . I. ii. 24. 9
Long time they thus together traveiled; . . . I. ii. 28. 1
in the witch unweeting joyd *long* time, . . . I. ii. 40. 2
how *long* time,' . . . 'Are you in this misformed hous to dwell?' . . . I. ii. 43. 1
Forsaken Truth *long* seekes her love, . . . I. iii. Arg.

Long—*Continued.*
when she had marked *long*, Her hart gan melt . . . I. iii. 6. 7
Long she thus traveiled . . . I. iii. 10. 1
All night she thinks too *long*, and often lookes for light. . . . I. iii. 15. 9
long the dore with rage and threats he bett, . . . I. iii. 19. 1
plagues, and mischiefes, and *long* misery, Might fall on her, . I. iii. 23. 7
Where have ye bene thus *long* . . . I. iii. 27. 2
why I lefte you so *long*, . . . I. iii. 29. 1
long hath wandred in the Ocean wide, . . . I. iii. 31. 2
long time having tand his tawney hide . . . I. iii. 31. 4
Young knight . . . through *long* labours huntest after fame, I. iv. 1. 2
Long with her traveild; . . . I. iv. 2. 5
waiting *long*, to win the wished sight . . . I. iv. 6. 8
like a Crane his necke was *long* and fyne . . . I. iv. 21. 5
after blood and vengeance he did *long:* . . . I. v. 7. 3
Alone, he, wandring, thee too *long* doth want: . . . I. v. 13. 3
Where, *long* remaining, he did alwaies strive . . . I. v. 40. 7
them *long* time before, great Nimrod was, . . . I. v. 48. 1
How can ye vengeance just so *long* withhold, . . . I. vi. 5. 8
The God himselfe, . . . Stood *long* amazd, . . . I. vi. 15. 7
long time with that salvage people stayd, . . . I. vi. 19. 3
So *long* . . . there he held Her captive . . . I. vi. 23. 1
After *long* labours and adventures spent, . . . I. vi. 30. 2
soild with dust of the *long* dried way; . . . I. vi. 35. 2
So *long* they fight, . . . I. vi. 44. 1
beast . . . which he had kept *long* time in darksom den. . . I. vii. 16. 9
Snake . . . *Long* fostred in the filth of Lerna lake: . . . I. vii. 17. 3
He had not travaild *long*, when . . . I. vii. 20. 1
late repentance which shall *long* abyde: . . . I. vii. 23. 7
Long tost with stormes, . . . I. vii. 28. 7
scourging th' emptie ayre with his *long* trayne, . . . I. viii. 17. 3
his eye sight him fayled *long* ygo; . . . I. viii. 30. 5
After *long* paines and labors manifold, He found the meanes . I. viii. 40. 5
my Lord . . . Whose presence I have lackt too *long* a day: . . I. viii. 43. 2
lurkt in rocks and caves, *long* unespide. . . . I. viii. 50. 5
their powres, empayrd through labor *long*, . . . I. ix. 2. 1
will at last be wonne with battrie *long*, . . . I. ix. 11. 3
To seek her out with labor and *long* tyne, . . . I. ix. 15. 7
that *long* hath stood Upon the bancke, . . . I. ix. 39. 8
Is not short payne well borne, that bringes *long* ease . . . I. ix. 40. 6
woxen weake and raw, Through *long* emprisonment, . . . I. x. 2. 4
Hast wandred through the world now *long* a day, . . . I. x. 9. 6
of youre toyle And labors *long*, . . . Ye both forwearied be: . I. x. 17. 3
every sinew seene, through his *long* fast: . . . I. x. 48. 6
nought he car'd his carcas *long* unfed; . . . I. x. 48. 7
after labors *long* and sad delay, . . . I. x. 52. 5
A little path that was both steepe and *long*, . . . I. x. 55. 2
streightway on that last *long* voiage fare, . . . I. x. 63. 4
A worke of labour *long*, and endlesse prayse: . . . I. xi. 7. 6
His huge *long* tayle, wownd up in hundred foldes, . . . I. xi. 11. 1
Does overspred his *long* bras-scaly back, . . . I. xi. 11. 2
passing by, did brush With his *long* tayle, . . . I. xi. 16. 9
Long he them bore above the subject plaine, . . . I. xi. 19. 1
aged *long* decay Renew, . . . I. xi. 30. 4
Life and *long* health that gracious ointment gave, . . . I. xi. 48. 6
her deare knight, who weary of *long* fight . . . I. xi. 50. 2
gate, Which *long* time had beene shut, . . . I. xii. 3. 7
victory Gainst him, that had them *long* opprest . . . I. xii. 4. 4
Discourst his voyage *long*, according his request. . . . I. xii. 15. 9
He was affyaunced *long* time before, . . . I. xii. 27. 2
still he sate *long* time astonished, . . . I. xii. 29. 3
he there did *long* enjoy; . . . I. xii. 41. 2
On the *long* voiage whereto she is bent: . . . I. xii. 42. 8
when he *long* awaited had in vayne, . . . II. i. 5. 3
Least his *long* way his aged limbes should tire: . . . II. i. 7. 5
Himselfe refreshing . . . After his travell *long* . . . II. i. 24. 9
In this faire wize they traveild *long* yfere, . . . II. i. 35. 1
That *long* captived soules from weary thraldome free. . . . II. i. 36. 9
Long maist thou live, . . . II. i. 37. 4
hold sad life in *long* captivitee; . . . II. i. 48. 3
So *long* as hevens just . . . Vouchsafed to behold us . . . II. i. 50. 3
So *long* they traveiled . . . II. ii. 12. 5
fearfull fowle, that *long* . . . her selfe hath hid, . . . II. iii. 36. 1
Shakt his *long* locks colourd like copper-wyre, . . . II. iv. 15. 8
In which we *long* time . . . contynewd as was fitt; . . . II. iv. 18. 7
Long I her serv'd, . . . II. iv. 19. 6
Through woods and plaines so *long* I did her chace, . . . II. iv. 32. 2
After that varlets flight, it was not *long* . . . II. v. 2. 1
His sandy lockes, *long* hanging downe behind, . . . II. v. 14. 4
It was not *long* ere she inflam'd him so, . . . II. v. 20. 1
(That day it selfe him seemed all too *long*) . . . II. v. 38. 6
Him needed not *long* call; . . . II. vi. 19. 4
Disdeigning to bee held so *long* in fight. . . . II. vi. 30. 4
The maysters of his *long* experiment, . . . II. vii. 1. 7
long he yode, . . . II. vii. 2. 6
'*Long* were to tell the troublous stormes . . . II. vii. 14. 1
griev'd so *long* to lacke his greedie pray; . . . II. vii. 34. 2
To catchen hold of that *long* chaine, . . . II. vii. 46. 6
lover trew, Whom he had *long* time sought . . . II. vii. 55. 3
too *long* here to be told: . . . II. vii. 63. 2
Ne Mammon would there let him *long* remayne, . . . II. vii. 63. 3
now he has so *long* remained theare, . . . II. vii. 65. 1
'*Long* lackt, alas! Hath bene thy faithfull aide . . . II. viii. 7. 3
if he lived had thus *long*, . . . II. viii. 28. 7
Lyon, which hath *long* time saught His robbed whelpes, . . . II. viii. 40. 7
Long trembling still he stoode: . . . II. viii. 46. 5
the Palmer, whom he *long* ygoe Had lost, . . . II. viii. 53. 5
whom wandring to and fro I *long* have lackt, . . . II. viii. 53. 8
the gates fast barred *long* ere night . . . II. ix. 10. 8
with *long* siege us in the castle hould. . . . II. ix. 12. 7

Long—*Continued.*
when *long* he follow'd had in vaine, IV. vii. 38. 1
through *long* fasting woxen pale and wan, IV. vii. 43. 3
when he *long* had marked his demeanor, IV. vii. 47. 1
it is too *long* here to abide, IV. vii. 47. 8
long this gentle bird to him did use IV. viii. 5. 1
Companion she became, and so continued *long*. IV. viii. 5. 9
long did mark which way she straid. IV. viii. 7. 9
long he looked had in vaine, IV. viii. 8. 1
His sodaine silence which he *long* had pent, IV. viii. 16. 2
he *long* time afterwards did lead An happie life IV. viii. 18. 1
it did astonish him *long* space. IV. viii. 43. 9
where I did *long* conceale My selfe, IV. viii. 55. 4
my friend that had her *long* refus'd, IV. viii. 60. 2
what mishap thus *long* him fro my selfe removes?' IV. viii. 63. 9
In which so *long* he mercilesse did lie. IV. viii. 64. 5
Who now *long* time had lyen in prison sad; IV. ix. 4. 3
Thus gazing *long* at them IV. ix. 11. 8
They liv'd together *long* without debate; IV. ix. 16. 2
seeking *long* to weet which way she straid, IV. ix. 24. 4
Long here and there and round about doth stie, IV. ix. 33. 5
them *long* forbore: IV. ix. 34. 4
'*Long* were to tell the travell and *long* toile IV. x. 3. 1
both *long* since this same, IV. x. 5. 7
All twenty tride in warres experience *long;* IV. x. 7. 7
Long languishing there in unpittied paine, IV. x. 13. 8
long here to relate. IV. x. 16. 3
I have thus *long* Left a fayre Ladie IV. xi. 1. 1
In which he *long* time after did remaine IV. xi. 7. 5
Long had the Thames . . . her wooed IV. xi. 8. 5
The rich Cteatus; and Eurytus *long;* IV. xi. 14. 1
Long Rhodanus, whose sourse springs from the skie; IV. xi. 20. 4
so *long* Can . . . so rich a kingdome hold! IV. xi. 22. 1
past not *long* ere Brutus warlicke sonne, IV. xi. 38. 1
Dee, which Britons *long* ygone Did call divine, IV. xi. 39. 3
All which, *long* sundred, doe at last accord IV. xi. 43. 7
damzels, deckt with *long* greene haire, IV. xi. 48. 2
Whose names and nations were too *long* to tell, IV. xii. 3. 2
In which I daily dying am too *long:* IV. xii. 9. 5
long given him in vaine: IV. xii. 14. 6
daunger well he wist *long* to continue there. IV. xii. 15. 9
him had sought through trouble and *long* strife, IV. xii. 16. 8
through *long* continuance of his course, . . . the world V. Pr. 1. 6
'him soone to overtake That hence so *long* departed, V. i. 19. 4
It was not *long* before he overtooke Sir Sanglier, V. i. 20. 6
The fortune of her life *long* time did feare: V. ii. 3. 4
is but narrow, but exceeding *long;* V. ii. 7. 7
There they together strove and struggled *long* V. ii. 14. 6
Long they her sought, V. ii. 25. 1
We are not sure they would so *long* remaine: V. ii. 36. 6
yet did he labour *long,* V. ii. 46. 7
the people, which had there about *Long* wayted, V. ii. 51. 2
After *long* stormes and tempests overblowne V. iii. 1. 1
After *long* sorrowes suffered whyleare, V. iii. 1. 7
He *long* astonisht stood, ne ought he sayd, V. iii. 18. 5
Of rude oblivion and *long* times decay, V. iv. 2. 8
Which *long* agoe he taken had in hond: V. iv. 3. 7
Twixt life and death *long* to and fro she weaved, V. iv. 10. 7
After *long* tossing in the seas distrest, V. iv. 11. 8
Into a *long* large chamber, which was sield With moniments V. v. 21. 3
Which *long* concealing in her covert brest, V. v. 27. 1
At last, when *long* she struggled had in vaine, V. v. 28. 6
To thinke how this *long* death thou mightest disinherit.' V. v. 36. 9
Great shame to lose so *long* employed paines, V. v. 48. 3
she *long* had sought for ease In every place, V. vi. 7. 1
There as she looked *long,* at last she spide One V. vi. 8. 1
Her selfe there close afflicted *long* in vaine, V. vi. 15. 2
It was not *long* before she heard the sound V. vi. 28. 6
with *long* locks comely kemd, V. vii. 4. 5
She stretched forth a *long* white sclender wand. V. vii. 7. 5
whom when Britomart Had *long* beheld, V. vii. 7. 7
After that *long* daies toile and weary plight: V. vii. 12. 4
Through great astonishment . . . with *long* locks upstanding, V. vii. 20. 7
'The end whereof, and all the *long* event, V. vii. 22. 1
the which now she Had *long* surceast, V. vii. 25. 6
Who, *long* before awoke, . . . Was to the battell V. vii. 27. 3
So *long* they fought, that all the grassie flore V. vii. 31. 5
dead *long* since in dolorous distresse, V. vii. 39. 4
After *long* travell of full twenty yeares, V. vii. 39. 6
stood *long* staring on him mongst uncertaine feares. V. vii. 39. 9
liberty of women did repeale, Which they had *long* usurpt; V. vii. 42. 6
long in captive shade Had shrowded bene, V. vii. 43. 1
yet to and fro *long* shooke And tottred, V. viii. 9. 8
So *long* as in his steedes the flaming breath did last. V. viii. 33. 9
Thus *long* they trast and traverst to and fro, V. viii. 37. 1
roiall pompe, which there *long* hidden lay, V. viii. 51. 5
there having stayd not *long,* V. viii. 51. 8
long courld locks that downe his shoulders shagged; V. ix. 10. 6
in his hand an huge *long* staffe he held, V. ix. 11. 1
he then stones at it so *long* did cast, V. ix. 17. 7
Whose *long* rest rusted the bright steely brand; V. ix. 30. 7
Which *long* he usd with carefull diligence, V. x. 12. 8
It was not *long* till that the Prince arrived V. x. 18. 1
Stryving *long* time in vaine it to withstond; V. x. 27. 3
Long sought the Prince; V. x. 38. 5
right *long* time is overborne of wrong V. xi. 1. 2
whose wrongs though *long* She suffred, V. xi. 1. 7
all that wrong unto that wofull Dame So *long* had done, V. xi. 4. 6
stretcht it selfe as it had *long* lyen still; V. xi. 22. 6
her *long* taile and fethers strongly shooke, V. xi. 22. 7

Long—*Continued.*
Tho with her huge *long* taile she at him strooke, V. xi. 28. 6
On which *long* way he rode, V. xi. 35. 9
long since aside had set The use of armes, V. xi. 37. 3
how *long* space Hath he her lent a Champion to provide?' V. xi. 42. 1
who *long* in vaine their rage withstands. V. xi. 44. 9
Gainst whom my selfe I *long* in vaine have bent V. xi. 51. 3
Stood *long* amaz'd as she amated weare: V. xi. 64. 5
No love so lasting then, that may enduren *long*. V. xii. 1. 9
long having since Taken in hand th' exploit, V. xii. 3. 1
Whose steale was yron-studded, but not *long,* V. xii. 14. 8
with strong powre did them *long* time oppresse; V. xii. 24. 4
with *long* nayles over-raught, V. xii. 30. 2
As if that *long* she had not eaten ought; V. xii. 30. 7
long the marke was to be read. V. xii. 39. 9
by them *long* with carefull labour nurst, VI. Pr. 3. 8
In perils strange, in labours *long* and wide; VI. i. 6. 5
he was fostred *long* in Stygian fen, VI. i. 8. 4
Sir Calidore thence travelled not *long,* VI. i. 11. 1
it hath *long* mayntaind with mighty wrong: VI. i. 13. 4
She *long* time hath deare lov'd a doughty Knight, VI. i. 14. 8
Him *long* forbore, and still his spirite spar'd, VI. i. 20. 6
long restrayned of his ready course, VI. i. 21. 3
With his *long* taile the bryzes brush away. VI. i. 24. 5
Where *long* he stayed not, VI. i. 32. 8
Thus *long* they trac'd and traverst to and fro, VI. i. 37. 1
So *long* as these two armes were able to be wroken. VI. ii. 7. 9
he me . . . Assayld, not knowing what to armes doth *long*.' VI. ii. 8. 5
He . . . sought her so *long* as him list. VI. ii. 20. 9
After *long* search and chauff he turned backe VI. ii. 21. 2
I . . . perswaded *long;* VI. ii. 21. 8
And when he *long* had him beholding stood, VI. ii. 24. 8
this land, where I have wond thus *long* VI. ii. 30. 8
whose silken leaves small *Long* shut up in the bud VI. ii. 35. 8
when they *long* had treated to and fro, VI. ii. 36. 1
Tristram, . . . *Long* fed his greedie eyes VI. ii. 39. 3
And powring balme, which he had *long* purvayd, VI. ii. 48. 3
the timely joy, Which I expected *long,* VI. iii. 4. 9
in his measure Of so *long* waies VI. iii. 22. 6
His *long* adventures gan to him relate, VI. iii. 22. 8
In travelling on foote so *long* a space, VI. iii. 29. 4
at length, after *long* weary chace, VI. iii. 50. 3
having *long* eschew'd His violence in vaine; VI. iii. 50. 5
Like as a ship with dreadfull storme *long* tost, VI. iv. 1. 1
Long did he wrest and wring it to and fro, VI. iv. 7. 1
having now no use of his *long* speare VI. iv. 7. 6
For having *long* time, as his daily weed, VI. iv. 19. 4
For which he *long* in vaine did sweate and swinke, VI. iv. 32. 4
long time he lacked had The good Sir Calepine, VI. v. 3. 1
she *long* groveling and deepe groning lay, VI. v. 5. 6
now strong through rest so *long* a space, VI. v. 7. 5
Why have ye me alone thus *long* yleft? VI. v. 23. 6
Hath you thus *long* away from me bereft? VI. v. 23. 8
Where I had surely *long* ere this bene dead, VI. v. 29. 2
So *long* as age enabled him thereto, VI. v. 37. 2
through the *long* experience of his dayes, VI. vi. 3. 2
here thus *long* now lie In piteous languor VI. vi. 6. 6
long in darksome Stygian den upbrought, VI. vi. 9. 8
As if he *long* had to his heasts bene trayned. VI. vi. 39. 6
Did languish *long* in life-consuming smart, VI. vii. 31. 3
which *long* time she sought, VI. vii. 50. 5
At last the caytive, after *long* discourse, VI. viii. 14. 6
Thus I triumphed *long* in lovers paine, VI. viii. 21. 6
Long thus she fled, VI. viii. 32. 2
awhile bethought Of her *long* travell VI. viii. 32. 8
Long had he sought her, VI. viii. 47. 1
So stood he still *long* gazing thereupon, VI. ix. 12. 1
long deluded With idle hopes VI. ix. 25. 1
Long time had lov'd, and hop'd her love to gaine, VI. ix. 38. 2
of all his labour and *long* paine VI. ix. 38. 5
through *long* and perfect industry, VI. ix. 43. 7
though *long* time dearely bought. VI. ix. 45. 9
Thus Calidore continu'd there *long* time VI. ix. 46. 1
Whose sundry parts were here too *long* to tell; VI. x. 14. 2
standing *long* astonished in spright, VI. x. 17. 3
In such discourses they together spent *Long* time, VI. x. 30. 2
joyed *long* in close felicity, VI. x. 38. 6
envies lovers *long* prosperity, VI. x. 38. 8
with the rest they tooke not *long* agoe; VI. xi. 11. 7
with labour and *long* paine, VI. xi. 22. 5
Their Captaine *long* withstood, and did her death forstall. VI. xi. 31. 9
Knowing his voice, although not heard *long* sin, VI. xi. 44. 3
being *long* in tempest tost, VI. xi. 44. 6
now *long* season past Had never joyance felt VI. xi. 45. 1
long for death had sought. VI. xi. 45. 5
So *long* till all the entry was with bodies mand. VI. xi. 46. 9
Whereof she *long* had lackt the wishfull sight, VI. xi. 50. 5
long had lyen dead, VI. xi. 50. 9
Which they from many *long* had robd and rent, VI. xi. 51. 3
Right so it fares with me in this *long* way, VI. xii. 1. 8
all that hetherto hath *long* delayd This gentle knight VI. xii. 2. 1
Thus *long* continu'd Claribell a thrall, VI. xii. 10. 1
lived *long* in peace and love entyre, VI. xii. 10. 7
sith they twaine *Long* since had fought in field: VI. xii. 11. 4
Seeing her weake and wan through durance *long*. VI. xii. 11. 6
Of his first quest, which he had *long* forlore, VI. xii. 12. 2
The which the Faery Queene had *long* afore Bequeath'd to him, VI. xii. 12. 4
long sith past She in the open fields had loosely layd VI. xii. 16. 3
long ygo, Whilest ye in durance dwelt, VI. xii. 17. 5
She *long* so held, and softly weeping sayd; VI. xii. 19. 7

Long—*Continued.*
art thou yet alive, whom dead I *long* did faine?' . . . . . . VI. xii. 19. 9
wondring *long* at those so straunge events, ... VI. xii. 20. 7
having thought *long* dead she fyndes alive, ... VI. xii. 21. 2
After that he had laboured *long* in vaine . . . . VI. xii. 32. 3
thereunto a great *long* chaine he tight, ... VI. xii. 34. 8
As if he learned had obedience *long,* . . . . VI. xii. 37. 2
So did he eeke *long* after this remaine, ... VI. xii. 38. 6
long time after Calidore, ... VI. xii. 39. 5
Yet many of their stemme *long* after did survive: . . . . . . VII. vi. 2. 9
shee had out of measure *Long* lov'd the Fanchin, ... VII. vi. 44. 4
Can tell things doen in heaven so *long* ygone, ... VII. vii. 2. 8
So nothing heere *long* standeth in one stay: . . . . VII. vii. 47. 7
So having ended, silence *long* ensewed; . . . . VII. vii. 57. 1
Did hang in *long* suspence what would ensew, ... VII. vii. 57. 6
that *long* hath slept in cheerlesse bower, ... *Am.* iv. 6
Oake . . . Is *long* ere it conceive the kindling fyre; . . . . . *Am.* vi. 6
thinke not *long* in taking litle paine . . . . *Am.* vi. 13
A wicked ambush which lay hidden *long* . . . . *Am.* xii. 6
with many a dropping teare And *long* intreaty, ... *Am.* xviii. 6
with one looke she spils that *long* I sponne; . . . . *Am.* xxiii. 11
How *long* shall this lyke dying lyfe endure, ... *Am.* xxv. 1
Mote have your life in honour *long* maintayned. . . . . *Am.* xxxvi. 12
being *long* in her loves tempest tost, ... *Am.* xli. 11
Long languishing in double malady . . . . *Am.* l. 1
wasted in *long* languishment, ... *Am.* lx. 11
long stormes and tempests sad assay, ... *Am.* lxiii. 1
after *long* pursuit . . . The gentle deare returnd . . . . . . *Am.* lxvii. 5
Gotten at last with labour and *long* toyle. . . . . *Am.* lxix. 14
After so *long* a race as I have run . . . . *Am.* lxxx. 1
Many *long* weary dayes I have outworne; . . . . *Am.* lxxxvi. 2
So sorrow still doth seeme too *long* to last; . . . . *Am.* lxxxvi. 13
long since ready forth his maske to move, ... *Epith.* 26
Pay to her usury of *long* delight: . . . . *Epith.* 33
The Rosy Morne *long* since left Tithones bed, ... *Epith.* 75
why doe ye sleepe thus *long,* . . . . *Epith.* 85
Her *long* loose yellow locks lyke golden wyre, ... *Epith.* 154
Yet never day so *long,* but late would passe. . . . . *Epith.* 273
when will this *long* weary day have end, ... *Epith.* 278
Thy tyred steedes *long* since have need of rest. . . . . *Epith.* 284
Long though it be, at last I see it gloome, ... *Epith.* 285
Now welcome, night! thou night so *long* expected, ... *Epith.* 315
That *long* daies labour doest at last defray, ... *Epith.* 316
from the earth, which they may *long* possesse . . . . *Epith.* 418
Love, that *long* since hast to thy mighty powre . . . . *H.L.* 1
his goodly face *long* hidden was . . . . *H.L.* 59
Love, that had now *long* time securely slept . . . . *H.L.* 61
After *long* sorrow and consuming smart. . . . . *H.B.* 28
Seeing him lie like creature *long* accurst . . . . *H.H.L.* 129
hungry soule! which *long* hast fed On idle fancies . . . . . *H.H.B.* 288
Through discontent of my *long* fruitlesse stay . . . . *Proth.* 6
the Brydale day, which is not *long:* . . . . *Proth.* 17
Against the Brydale day, which was not *long:* . . . . *Proth.* 35
their Brydale day, which was not *long:* . . . . *Proth.* 53, 71, 89
Upon your Brydale day, which is not *long:* . . . . *Proth.* 107
their brydale daye should not be *long:* . . . . *Proth.* 111
their wedding day, which was not *long:* . . . . *Proth.* 125
Against the bridale daye, which is not *long:* . . . . *Proth.* 143
the Brydale day, which is not *long:* . . . . *Proth.* 161
Against their Brydale day, which is not *long:* . . . . *Proth.* 179
Long-borne. forth have brought Her *long borne* Infant, . . . *D.* 32
Longed. *See* **Lenged.**
I *longd* the neighbour towne to see, ... *S.C.* Ja. 50
O welcome, child! whom I have *longd* to see, ... I. v. 27. 8
Which *long'd* to Angela, the Saxon Queene, ... III. iii. 58. 8
long'd revenge to see: . . . . III. xii. 34. 9
longed foolishly To see her naked . . . . VII. vi. 42. 8
Long-endured. His *long endured* famine needed more reliefe. I. viii. 43. 9
Long-enduring. his spright Had past the paines of . . . *long-enduring* night. . . . . I. x. 32. 9
thousand sprights with *long enduring* paines Doe tosse, . . . III. iii. 9. 4
Longer. *See* **Lenger.**
'Why doe we *longer* live, ... *S.C.* N. 73
thy losse no *longer* lament; . . . . *S.C.* N. 168
That balefull sorrow he no *longer* beares . . . . *Gn.* 644
'Why doo I *longer* live in lifes despight, ... *D.* 442
Why doo I *longer* see this loathsome light . . . . *D.* 444
Ne *longer* him intreate with me to staie, ... *D.* 562
To draw them *longer* out, ... IV. ii. 51. 2
Her list no *longer* in that place abide; . . . . IV. v. 29. 2
would no *longer* hold The wrathfull weapon . . . . IV. vi. 27. 4
No *longer* space thereto he did desire, ... IV. vi. 43. 8
his faint foe no *longer* could abide His puissance, ... V. ii. 17. 7
He could no *longer* beare, ... V. iii. 20. 4
bore him . . . *longer* Then two speares length: . . . . V. viii. 7. 8
ne gave him *longer* day: . . . . V. xii. 9. 8
Whenas the Carle no *longer* could sustaine, ... VI. i. 22. 2
'Dame, be no *longer* sad; . . . . VI. ii. 45. 4
Some in short space, and some in *longer* yeares, ... VII. vii. 55. 3
doth *longer* unto me appeare, ... *Am.* lx. 7
seemd the *longer* for my greater paines. . . . . *Am.* lx. 12
Longest. To chose the *longest* day in all the yeare, ... *Epith.* 271
shortest night, when *longest* fitter weare: . . . . *Epith.* 272
Longest-lived. Ne yet Mathusalem, though *longest liv'd;* . . II. ix. 57. 2
Long-expected. bring with him his *long expected* light? . . . III. iv. 60. 2
Long-gotten. To loose *long gotten* honour with one evill hond. III. i. 10. 9
Long-grown. His griesie lockes, *long growen* and unbound, . . I. ix. 35. 4
Long-lacked. weeping said, 'Ah, my *long lacked* Lord, ... I. iii. 27. 1
My soules *long-lacked* foode, my heavens blis; . . . . *Am.* i. 12
Long-lent. take away this *long lent* loathed light: . . . . . II. i. 36. 7
Longing. Wemen, that of Loves *longing* once lust, ... *S.C.* May 134
The forlorne mayd did with loves *longing* burne, ... I. vi. 22. 1
make me loath this life, still *longing* for to die. . . . . . . IV. viii. 16. 9
Long-lasting. *long lasting* life with joyous glee, ... *Gn.* 59
With so great labour and *long lasting* paine, ... *Ti.* 53
Long-lingering. weary thys *long lingring* Phoebus race. . . . *S.C.* O. 3
Yrkesome of life, and too *long lingring* night. . . . . I. ii. 6. 5
chace away this too *long lingring* night; . . . . III. iv. 60. 5
Long-living. And eke thine owne *long living* memory, ... *Ded. Son.* iii. 8
Long-passed. Yet brave ensample of *long passed* daies, . . . *Ded. Son.* x. 9
Long-pining. That may recure my harts *long pyning* griefe, . *H.B.* 285
Long-resting. But pride, impatient of *long resting* peace, . . *H.H.L.* 78
Longs. *longs* to bee unbound From the strong shackles . . . . *D.* 85
and *longs* death to behold, ... *Col.* 204
to you eke *longes* his love. . . . . I. iv. 48. 6
Long-slumbering. As one awakte out of *long slombring* shade, II. xi. 31. 7
Long-wandering. that *long wandring* Greeke, ... I. iii. 21. 5
soone redeeme from his *long-wandring* woe: . . . . I. v. 11. 2
Long while. After which sort they wandered *long while,* . . . *Hub.* 343
long while after I am dead and rotten, ... *Col.* 640
so remaynd *long while,* . . . . *Col.* 922
longwhile Bene in his ashes raked up and hid, ... III. iii. 48. 2
Long while he strove in his corageous brest . . . . III. v. 44. 1
So stared he on her, and stood *long while* amaz'd. . . . . . III. vii. 13. 9
long while laboured it to engrave: . . . . III. viii. 37. 7
Long while they then continued in that wize, ... IV. iii. 36. 1
There lay Sir Scudamour *long while* . . . . IV. v. 40. 1
lay *long while* in senselesse swowne. . . . . IV. viii. 42. 9
they *long* while continued in fight; . . . . IV. ix. 28. 1
Thus there *long while* continu'd Artegall, ... V. v. 26. 1
Thus he *long while* in thraldome there remayned, ... V. v. 57. 6
thereuppon *long while* stood gazing still, ... V. vii. 5. 8
So thereuppon *long while* she musing lay, ... V. vii. 17. 1
long while did contend; . . . . V. xi. 27. 7
The same *long while* I bore, ... V. xi. 53. 6
Long while he tug'd and strove to get it out, ... V. xii. 22. 1
that night Sir Calidore did dwell, And *long while* after, . . VI. ix. 34. 2
Long-while I sought to what I might compare . . . . *Am.* ix. 1
Long-while alone in langour to remaine. . . . . *Am.* lii. 8
Long-wished. to the world does bring *long-wished* light: . . I. xii. 21. 8
Look. *See* **Overlook.**
He bade me upwarde unto heaven *looke.* . . . . *Bel.*[1] i. 8
All as the Sheepe, such was the shepeheards *looke,* . . . . . *S.C.* Ja. 7
Looke from above, where you in joyes remaine, ... *S.C.* Ja. 15
hether *looke,* At my request: . . . . *S.C.* Ap. 39
Tho gan shepheards swaines to *looke* aloft, ... *S.C.* May 124
while Kiddie unwares did *looke,* . . . . *S.C.* May 275
learne to *looke* alofte; . . . . *S.C.* Jul. 10
Theyr boyes can *looke* to those. . . . . *S.C.* Jul. 196
They *looken* bigge as Bulls that bene bate, ... *S.C.* S. 44
on high, where I did *looke,* . . . . *Hub.* 67
Light out of heavens windowes forth to *looke,* . . . . *Hub.* 109
Unto my fathers sheepe I usde to *looke,* . . . . *Hub.* 292
looke lowly on the ground, ... *Hub.* 498
laugh it out, and proudly *looke,* . . . . *Hub.* 703
looke into the Christall firmament: . . . . *T.M.* 506
loathing earth, I *looke* up to the sky, ... *T.M.* 527
'*Looke* backe, who list, unto the former ages, ... *Ti.* 57
She seem'd still backe unto the land to *looke,* . . . . *Mui.* 281
Ne *looke* for entertainement where none was; . . . . I. i. 35. 2
With gentle blandishment and lovely *looke,* . . . . I. i. 49. 8
that dredd Lyons *looke* her cast in deadly hew. . . . . I. iii. 11. 9
true love hath no powre To *looken* backe; . . . . I. iii. 30. 8
His *looke* was sterne, and seemed still to threat . . . . I. iii. 33. 7
With loftie eyes, halfe loth to *looke* so lowe, ... I. iv. 14. 1
To *looken* whether it were night or day. . . . . I. iv. 19. 6
not a pin Does care for *looke* of living creatures eye. . . . . I. v. 4. 4
her darke griesly *looke* them much dismay: . . . . I. v. 30. 5
yet quakes . . . to see the Lyon *looke* so grim. . . . . I. vi. 10. 9
casting up a deadly *looke,* . . . . II. i. 47. 1
with grim *looke* And count'naunce sterne, ... II. v. 14. 1
Sterne was his *looke,* and full of stomacke vayne; . . . . . . II. vii. 41. 3
Sterne was their *looke;* like wild amazed steares, ... II. ix. 13. 8
In which whenas he greedily did *looke,* . . . . II. ix. 60. 3
nought moved with her piteous *looke;* . . . . II. x. 18. 9
into the world the dawning day Might *looke,* . . . . II. xi. 3. 4
As pale and wan as ashes was his *looke,* . . . . II. xi. 22. 1
being men they did unmanly *looke,* . . . . II. xii. 86. 3
Large were his limbes, and terrible his *looke,* . . . . III. i. 17. 8
With heavy *look* and lumpish pace, ... III. iv. 61. 7
with fell *looke* and hollow deadly gaze . . . . III. vii. 7. 6
in shape and *looke* So lively and so like, ... III. viii. 5. 8
To *looke* on her faire face and marke her snowy skin. . . . . III. viii. 24. 9
As if he could have kild him with his *looke,* . . . . III. x. 24. 2
terrify To *looke* adowne, or upward . . . . III. x. 56. 6
up gan *looke,* And seeing . . . a stranger knight, ... III. xi. 13. 2
Hope . . . Of chearefull *looke* and lovely to behold: . . . . . III. xii. 13. 2
who so list *looke* backe to former ages, ... IV. Pr. 3. 1
everie *looke* was coy and wondrous quaint, ... IV. i. 5. 7
life to hazard for faire Ladies *looke;* . . . . IV. ii. 40. 6
looke to whom she voluntarie came, ... IV. v. 25. 7
had With one sterne *looke* so daunted, ... IV. viii. 2. 3
Bad them not *looke* for better entertayne; . . . . IV. viii. 27. 4
Durst not the sternnesse of his *looke* abide; . . . . IV. ix. 18. 3
I did backeward *looke,* . . . . IV. x. 20. 1
thy smyling *looke* doest pacifie The raging seas, ... IV. x. 44. 4
Ne ever once did *looke* up from her desse, ... IV. x. 50. 3
For who so list into the heavens *looke,* . . . . V. Pr. 5. 1
Whom at the first he ghessed by his *looke,* . . . . V. i. 20. 8
looke, who does dissent from this my read, ... V. i. 26. 6

Look—*Continued.*
looke what surplus did of each remaine, . . . V. ii. 31. 8
looke then how much it doth overflow . . . V. ii. 34. 8
Doe hide themselves from her astonying *looke* . . . V. ii. 54. 5
All suddenly, ere one can *looke* aside, . . . V. iii. 25. 5
within his mouth to *looke:* . . . V. iii. 33. 2
He to her lept with deadly dreadfull *looke,* . . . V. v. 11. 7
Looke up at last, and wake thy dulled spirit . . . V. v. 36. 8
Her wand did move with amiable *looke,* . . . V. vii. 8. 2
by the change of her unchearefull *looke,* . . . V. vii. 18. 1
Where is that dreadfull manly *looke?* . . . V. vii. 40. 3
ever round about he cast his *looke:* . . . V. ix. 11. 5
She gan take hart and *looke* up joyfully; . . . V. x. 19. 8
sternely him beheld with grim and ghastly *looke.* . . . V. xi. 12. 9
A dreadfull feend with fowle deformed *looke,* . . . V. xi. 22. 5
Like as a tender Rose . . . Gins to *looke* up, . . . V. xii. 13. 5
With dreadfull *looke* he Artegall beheld, . . . V. xii. 16. 2
With her dull eyes did seeme to *looke* askew, . . . V. xii. 29. 2
put away proud *looke* and usage sterne, . . . VI. i. 40. 8
Gnashing his grinded teeth with griesly *looke,* . . . VI. v. 26. 1
when he up did *looke* And saw him selfe captiv'd, . . . VI. vii. 48. 7
To chaunge the manner of his loftie *looke;* . . . VI. ix. 36. 2
that sunne-shine that makes them *looke* askew: . . . VI. x. 4. 5
Looke! how the crowne, which Ariadne wore . . . VI. x. 13. 1
they for better hyre did shortly *looke:* . . . VI. xi. 40. 8
on her . . . sterne *looke* still gazed. . . . VII. vi. 13. 9
Like darred Larke, not daring up to *looke* . . . VII. vi. 47. 5
Those lamping eyes will deigne sometimes to *look,* . . . *Am.* i. 6
When ye behold that Angels blessed *looke,* . . . *Am.* i. 11
loosely they ne dare to *looke* upon her. . . . *Am.* v. 8
when ye mildly *looke* with lovely hew, . . . *Am.* vii. 5
when ye lowre, or *looke* on me askew, . . . *Am.* vii. 7
Looke ever lovely, as becomes you best; . . . *Am.* vii. 10
that high *look,* with which she doth comptroll . . . *Am.* x. 10
Yet lowly still vouchsafe to *looke* on me; . . . *Am.* xiii. 13
Or *looke* with pitty on my payneful smart; . . . *Am.* xviii. 8
with one *looke,* she doth my life dismay; . . . *Am.* xxi. 10
with one *looke* she spils that long I sponne; . . . *Am.* xxiii. 11
shine again, and *looke* on me at last, . . . *Am.* xxxiv. 11
can no more endure on them to *looke.* . . . *Am.* xxxv. 12
Her eyes *looke* lovely, and upon them smyle; . . . *Am.* xlvii. 10
beholding me with mylder *looke,* . . . *Am.* lxvii. 9
suffers not one *looke* to glaunce awry, . . . *Epith.* 236
they, which love indeede, *looke* otherwise, . . . *H.B.* 211
And *looke* at last, how . . . He taken was, . . . *H.H.L.* 239
Then *looke,* who list thy gazefull eyes to feed . . . *H.H.B.* 29
looke on the frame Of this wyde universe, . . . *H.H.B.* 30
Looke thou no further, but affixe thine eye . . . *H.H.B.* 50
Him to behold, is on his workes to *looke,* . . . *H.H.B.* 128
Ne dare *looke* up with corruptible eye . . . *H.H.B.* 144
For feare, lest if he chaunce to *looke* on thee, . . . *H.H.B.* 146
Of all that *looke* thereon with eyes unsound; . . . *H.H.B.* 179
And *looke* at last up to that Soveraine Light, . . . *H.H.B.* 295

Looked. *See* **Overlooked.**
th' heavens *looked* lovely all the while, . . . *Van.* ix. 6
having *looked* long, . . . *Ti.* 477
Whilest thus I *looked,* . . . *Ti.* 603
He *lookt* aside as in disdainefull wise, . . . *D.* 59
to my selfe the blame that *lookt* so hie: . . . *Col.* 936
forth . . . he went, And *looked* in: . . . I. i. 14. 4
She *lookt* about, and seeing one in mayle, . . . I. i. 16. 5
The royall virgin . . . *Lookt* for her knight, . . . I. ii. 7. 7
Full fast she fled, ne ever *lookt* behynd, . . . I. iii. 12. 1
his hollow eyne *Lookt* deadly dull, . . . I. ix. 35. 7
adowne he *looked* to the grownd . . . I. x. 67. 5
the gentle virgin . . . *looked* all about, . . . I. xi. 33. 6
looked forth, to weet if trew indeed Those tydinges were, . . . I. xii. 3. 3
They *lookt* about, . . . II. iii. 19. 6
He *lookt* a litle further, and espyde . . . II. vii. 61. 1
forth *looked* from the highest spire The watch, . . . II. ix. 11. 6
he *looked* evermore When the hart blood should gush . . . II. xi. 37. 6
the Heavens . . . *Lookte* on them lovely, . . . II. xii. 51. 2
lookt still forward right, . . . II. xii. 53. 4
Lookt foorth, as Phoebus face out of the east . . . III. ii. 24. 6
looked grim, And faynd to cheare his lady . . . III. viii. 15. 6
when she *looked* up, to weet what wight . . . III. viii. 32. 6
he on it *lookt* scornefully askew, . . . III. x. 29. 3
Ne ever *looked* back for good or ill; . . . III. x. 43. 7
never *looked* who behind him was, . . . III. x. 53. 3
as she *lookt* about, she did behold . . . III. xi. 54. 1
He *lookt* askew with his mistrustfull eyes, . . . III. xii. 10. 5
He *looked* round about with sterne disdayne, . . . III. xii. 23. 2
He, glad of life, that *lookt* for death but late, . . . III. xii. 35. 8
lookt on Glauce grim; . . . IV. i. 50. 3
lookt a little up at that his speech, . . . IV. ii. 21. 3
He *looked* backe, and, her avizing well, . . . IV. ii. 22. 7
when she long had *lookt* upon each one, . . . IV. v. 26. 6
when she *lookt* about, and nothing found . . . IV. vii. 9. 6
long he *looked* had in vaine, . . . IV. viii. 8. 1
all that on him *lookt* without good heed, . . . IV. viii. 39. 5
Ne storming Humber, though he *looked* stout; . . . IV. xi. 30. 7
made them stoupe that *looked* earst so hie. . . . V. ii. 21. 5
There as she *looked* long, at last she spide One . . . V. vi. 8. 1
ne ever *lookt* aside, But still right downe; . . . V. vi. 18. 4
they *lookt* about To weete if it were true . . . V. viii. 12. 1
Lookt up with eyes full sad and hart full sore, . . . V. xii. 11. 7
when he *lookt* about on every syde, . . . VI. iv. 24. 3
being up he *lookt* againe aloft, . . . VI. viii. 26. 1
With drearie drouping eyne *lookt* up like one aghast. . . . VI. xi. 22. 9
when he *looked* on her lovely face, . . . VII. vi. 31. 1

Looker. So that it to the *looker* appertaynd: . . . III. ii. 19. 4

Looker-on. like a *Looker-on* Of this worldes Stage, . . . *Com. Son.* i. 2

Looker's. So hidd in lockes and waves from *lookers* theft, . . . II. xii. 67. 8
close venim doth convay Into the *lookers* hart, . . . IV. viii. 39. 9
to the *lookers* sight They seeme to please; . . . *H.B.* 53
Worke like impression in the *lookers* vew? . . . *H.B.* 81

Lookers'. She to her love doth *lookers* eyes allure; . . . *Am.* xxi. 6

Lookers on. mocketh th' eyes of all the *lookers on,* . . . *Hub.* 1281
End of the doubtfull battaile deemed tho The *lookers on;* . . . I. v. 11. 8
fild the *lookers on* attonce with ruth and wonder. . . . IV. iii. 15. 9
whilst all the *lookers-on* Him dead behight, . . . IV. iii. 31. 1
Which when as all the *lookers-on* beheld, . . . IV. iii. 35. 1

Lookest. How chearefully thou *lookest* from above, . . . *Epith.* 291

Looking. *See* **Low-looking.**
Looking far foorth into the Ocean wide, . . . *Van.* ix. 1
there detained bee For *looking* back, . . . *Gn.* 435
The Lion *looking* up gan him avize, . . . *Hub.* 1324
kept from *looking* on the lightsome day: . . . *T.M.* 593
In that wide lake *looking* for plenteous praie . . . *Ti.* 151
Looking still, if I might of her have sight. . . . *Ti.* 476
Looking aside I saw a stately Bed, . . . *Ti.* 631
Forth *looking* through the windowes of the East, . . . *Col.* 605
Looking to heaven, for earth she did disdayne, . . . I. iv. 10. 2
looking lovely and oft sighing sore, . . . I. vi. 4. 2
Eft *looking* back would faine have runne away; . . . I. ix. 25. 3
looking downe saw many damned wightes . . . II. vii. 57. 2
looking up, whenas his shield he lakt . . . II. viii. 53. 3
Nought but her lovely face she for his *looking* left. . . . II. xii. 67. 9
oft *looking* backward, well she vewde . . . III. iv. 50. 6
Looking with myld aspect upon the earth . . . III. vi. 2. 3
looking still askaunce Gainst Britomart, . . . III. ix. 27. 3
Big *looking* like a doughty Doucepere, . . . III. x. 31. 1
Still fled he forward, *looking* backward still; . . . III. x. 56. 1
Under his eiebrowes *looking* still askaunce; . . . III. xii. 15. 2
He *looking* lompish and full sullein sad, . . . III. xii. 18. 2
Trembling in heart, and *looking* pale and wan, . . . IV. ii. 49. 4
looking round about, like one dismaid, . . . IV. iv. 22. 3
looking round about him, none could see, . . . IV. v. 44. 8
looking sterne, still over him did stand, . . . IV. vi. 23. 4
She *looking* backe espies that griesly wight . . . IV. vii. 22. 5
looking after long did mark which way . . . IV. viii. 7. 9
Th' one forward *looking,* th' other backeward . . . IV. x. 12. 4
All *looking* on, and like astonisht staring, . . . IV. x. 56. 8
There *looking* forth, shee in her heart did find . . . V. vi. 7. 6
Forth of her window as she *looking* lay, . . . V. viii. 26. 6
could deceive one *looking* in his face: . . . V. ix. 5. 7
Where she with her two sonnes did *looking* stand, . . . V. xi. 15. 2
looking up unto the cry to lest, . . . VI. i. 17. 4
Looking at that same Carle with count'nance grim, . . . VI. iii. 34. 7
looking all about where he mote fynd . . . VI. iv. 26. 4
Still *looking* after him that did him chace, . . . VI. vi. 29. 8
Then *looking* round about, . . . VI. viii. 32. 4
Looking each houre into deathes mouth to fall, . . . VI. xi. 44. 7
all creatures, *looking* in her face, . . . VII. vii. 57. 4
looking up with chearefull view, . . . VII. vii. 57. 8
But, *looking* still on her, I stand amazed . . . *Am.* iii. 7
New yeare, forth *looking* out of Janus gate, . . . *Am.* iv. 1
looking on the earth whence she was borne, . . . *Am.* xiii. 6

Looking-glass. Whose image shee had seene in Venus *looking glas.* . . . III. i. 8. 9
A *looking glasse,* right wondrously aguiz'd, . . . III. ii. 18. 8
Glauncing unwares in charmed *looking glas,* . . . III. iii. 24. 2
in his face, as in a *looking glasse,* . . . IV. v. 45. 7
And shew himselfe . . . As in a *looking-glasse,* . . . *H.H.B.* 115

Look's. With staggring pace and dismall *lookes* dismay, . . . *D.* 564
Through sweet illusion of her *lookes* delight; . . . *Am.* xvi. 4

Looks. to reare My *lookes* to heaven . . . *Bel.*[2] i. 8
as the lowring Wether *lookes* downe, . . . *S.C.* F. 29
scornefully *lookes* askaunce; . . . *S.C.* Mar. 21
From cheerefull *lookes* great mirth and gladsome glee. . . . *Gn.* 184
with sterne *lookes* to threaten kindled yre. . . . *Gn.* 264
These *lookes* (nought saying) doo a benefice seeke, . . . *Hub.* 500
stare . . . with big *lookes* basen wide, . . . *Hub.* 670
his *lookes* loftie, as if he aspyr'd To dignitie, . . . *Hub.* 678
By his great *lookes* and power Imperiall. . . . *Mui.* 312
onely by his *lookes* did tell his thought. . . . *As.* 168
Her *lookes* were like beames of the morning Sun, . . . *Col.* 604
highest *lookes* have not the highest mynd, . . . *Col.* 715
he feining seemely merth, And shee coy *lookes:* . . . I. ii. 27. 9
ever by her *lookes* conceived her intent. . . . I. iii. 9. 9
night she thinks too long, and often *lookes* for light. . . . I. iii. 15. 9
he . . . learned had to love with secret *lookes;* . . . I. iv. 25. 6
the cruell Sarazin . . . sternly *lookes* at him, . . . I. v. 4. 3
wordes, and *lookes,* and sighes she did abhore; . . . I. vi. 4. 4
when him list the prouder *lookes* subdew, . . . I. vii. 35. 8
this misseeming hew your manly *looks* doth marre? . . . I. viii. 42. 9
With *lookes* full lowly cast, . . . I. x. 5. 6
sober *lookes* her wisedome well descryde: . . . I. x. 34. 3
if by *lookes* one may the mind aread, . . . II. i. 7. 6
bashed not For Guyons *lookes,* . . . II. iv. 37. 9
Some framd faire *lookes,* . . . II. v. 33. 3
with sterne *lookes,* and stomachous disdaine, . . . II. viii. 23. 4
like him *lookes* in dreadfull hew; . . . II. xii. 24. 2
chearfull *looks* as earst did shew. . . . III. iii. 50. 9
With nought but ghastly *lookes* him answered; . . . III. vii. 14. 6
With speaking *lookes,* that close embassage bore, . . . III. ix. 28. 2
In lofty *looks* to hide an humble minde, . . . III. x. 30. 2
With ghastly *looks* and dreadfull drerihed; . . . III. xii. 17. 3
coy *lookes* tempring with loose dalliance; . . . IV. ii. 9. 5
eke unto her *lookes* a law she made, . . . IV. ii. 36. 6

Looks—*Continued.*
Onely few ruefull *lookes* unto her sent, IV. viii. 13. 8
Armies of lovely *lookes,* and speeches wise, V. v. 34. 8
Nought fear'd the childe his *lookes,* V. xi. 13. 1
Nymphs . . . Which daily may to thy sweete *lookes* repayre, VI. ii. 25. 3
By signes, by *lookes,* and all his other gests; VI. iv. 14. 3
Through tempering of her words and *lookes* VI. vi. 41. 9
Yet were her words and *lookes* but false VI. vi. 42. 1
such proud *looks* would make her praysed more; VI. vii. 30. 2
His *lookes* were dreadfull, and his fiery eies, VI. vii. 42. 1
As if he with his *lookes* would all men terrifie. VI. vii. 42. 9
he his *lookes* despised, and his boast dispraized. VI. viii. 26. 9
His layes, his loves, his *lookes,* she did them all despize. VI. ix. 35. 9
With *looks,* with words, with gifts he oft her wowed, VI. xi. 4. 8
Saturne oft doth . . . calme his crabbed *lookes.* VII. vii. 52. 8
in those lofty *lookes* in close implide, *Am.* v. 5
Their looser *lookes* that stir up lustes impure; *Am.* xxi. 8
traine and teach me with her *lookes;* *Am.* xxi. 13
sunshine, when cloudy *looks* are cleared. *Am.* xl. 14
Trust not the treason of those smyling *lookes,* *Am.* xlvii. 1
kill with *looks* as Cockatrices doo: *Am.* xlix. 10
but that his *looks* them fray; *Am.* liii. 2
to the heaven her haughty *lookes* aspire: *Am.* lv. 11
her *lookes,* which like to Cordials bee; *H.B.* 250
Loom. workes with *loome,* with needle, and with quill. *Mui.* 272
And roughly wrought in an unlearned *Loome:* *Ded. Son.* vii.13
not with arras made in painefull *loome,* III. xi. 51. 3
Loop. every *loop* fast lockt, as fearing foes despight. II. ix. 10. 9
Loops. Nor anie skil'd in *loupes* of fingring fine, *Mui.* 366
In lymie snares the subtill *loupes* among; *Mui.* 429
Loord. *See* **Lourd.**
Loos. *See* **Lose.**
Loose. Thy careles limbs in *loose* sleep dost display. *Gn.* 336
Al Portugese, loose like an emptie gut; *Hub.* 212
lost their time in wandring *loose* abroad; *Hub.* 399
Titan draweth neere To *loose* his teeme, *D.* 469
soone to *loose* her wicked bands did her constraine. I. i. 19. 9
a *loose* Leman to vile service bound: I. i. 48. 6
Therion, a *loose* unruly swayne, I. vi. 21. 6
As for *loose* loves, they'are vaine, I. x. 62. 9
Striving to *loose* the knott that fast him tyes, I. xi. 23. 4
strove to *loose* the far infixed sting: I. xi. 39. 4
nor stroks mote him constraine To *loose,* I. xi. 43. 3
Was given all to lust and *loose* living, II. v. 28. 3
Mingled emongst *loose* Ladies and lascivious boyes. II. v. 28. 9
Guyon is of immodest Merth Led into *loose* desyre; II. vi. Arg.
Her light behaviour and *loose* dalliaunce II. vi. 8. 1
laying his head disarmd In her *loose* lap, II. vi. 14. 7
The traine whereof *loose* far behind her strayd, II. ix. 19. 3
Gathered the Princes of the people *loose* II. x. 37. 6
With hoary lockes all *loose,* II. xi. 23. 3
Her to rebuke for being *loose* and light: II. xii. 16. 6
garments *loose* that seemd unmeet for womanhed. II. xii. 55. 9
she low adowne did *lose,* II. xii. 67. 3
That wanton Lady with her lover *lose,* II. xii. 76. 8
loath'd the *loose* demeanure of that wanton sort. III. i. 40. 9
with delightfull sport To *loose* her warlike limbs III. i. 52. 5
so *loose* life, and so ungentle trade, III. i. 67. 5
Now *loose* about her shoulders hong undight, III. vi. 18. 8
She was asham'd to be so *loose* surpriz'd; III. vi. 19. 2
her garments *loose* Upgath'ring, III. vi. 19. 6
that none him *losen* may. III. vi. 48. 9
her *loose* lockes to dight in order dew III. vii. 11. 2
lose the teme out of his weary wayne, III. viii. 51. 5
with her *loose* incontinence doth blend III. ix. 1. 7
The gentle Lady, *loose* at randon lefte, III. x. 36. 1
streight would *lose* The worlds foundations III. xii. 2. 3
coy lookes tempring with *loose* dalliance) IV. ii. 9. 5
soone enforced beene To let him *loose* IV. iv. 34. 8
There might ye see *loose* steeds at randon ronne, IV. iv. 38. 6
it would *loose,* or else asunder teare. IV. v. 3. 5
loose affections streightly to restraine; IV. v. 4. 8
eke too *loose* of life, and eke of love too light. IV. viii. 49. 9
The course of *loose* affection to forstall, IV. ix. 19. 3
He where he list goes *loose,* IV. xii. 11. 4
So ever *loose,* so ever happy be! IV. xii. 11. 5
where so *loose* or happy that thou art, IV. xii. 11. 6
Ne *loose* that he hath bound with stedfast band, V. ii. 42. 4
it would *lose* or breake, V. iii. 28. 9
Amongst *loose* Ladies lapped in delight: V. vi. 6. 8
Now scratching her, and her *loose* locks misusing, V. vi. 14. 6
With locks all *loose,* and rayment all to-rent; V. viii. 4. 8
he had red her Riddle, which no wight Could ever *loose* V. xi. 25. 6
out of her greedy gripe To *loose* his shield, V. xi. 27. 7
To *loose* the badge that should his deedes display.' V. xi. 52. 5
her foule heare Hung *loose* and loathsomely: V. xii. 29. 4
by no wize He could him force to *loose,* VI. iv. 6. 9
the beast enrag'd to *loose* his pray VI. iv. 20. 5
Subdue desire, and bridle *loose* delight; VI. vi. 14. 6
forst him th' halter from his hand to *loose,* VI. vii. 45. 7
Whether I shall you leave, or from these villaines *lose.'* VI. viii. 29. 9
Those villeins view'd with *loose* lascivious sight, VI. viii. 43. 3
heares With the *loose* wynd ye waving chance to marke; *Am.* lxxxi. 2
Her long *loose* yellow locks lyke golden wyre, *Epith.* 154
Such fancies feele no love, but *loose* desyre. *H.L.* 175
That in light wits did *loose* affection move; *H.H.L.* 11
goodly greenish locks, all *loose* untyde, *Proth.* 22
Loosed. side-long beard, and locks down hanging *loast,* *Bel.*[2] ix. 3
Caried to heaven, from sinfull bondage *losed;* *Ro.* xix. 12
The lothfull life, now *loosd* from sinfull bands, II. xi. 46. 3

Loosed—*Continued.*
doth disperse the vapour *lo'ste,* III. iv. 13. 5
He reard him up and *loosd* his yron bands, III. vii. 46. 6
loosd her helmet from her lofty hedd, III. ix. 22. 7
The heardes out of their foldes were *loosed* quight, III. x. 52. 8
she from her middle *loosd,* And left behind her IV. v. 5. 3
ever as they fastned it, it *loos'd* IV. v. 16. 6
Having through stirring *loosd* their wonted band, IV. vi. 20. 2
first him *losde,* and afterwards thus to him saide. VI. i. 11. 9
Eftsoones he *loosd* that Squire, VI. i. 18. 2
scarse his *loosed* limbes he hable was to weld. VII. vii. 31. 9
Loosely. *looslie* on the grassie greene dispredd, *Gn.* 242
Seeing them wander *loosly,* *Hub.* 244
His wanton daies that ever *locsely* led, I. ii. 3. 5
Her golden locks for hast were *loosely* shed I. xi. 51. 5
Full of disport, still laughing, *loosely* light, II. ii. 36. 2
About her shoulders weren *loosely* shed, II. iii. 30. 2
Her lockes, . . . *loosely* hong unrold; II. iv. 4. 6
did *loosely* disaray Her upper partes II. v. 32. 7
Loosely disperst with puff of every blast: III. i. 16. 4
a wanton payre Of lovers *loosely* knit, III. x. 16. 9
Caught her, thus *loosely* wandring here and there, VI. iii. 24. 3
Loosely displayd upon the grassie ground, VI. vii. 18. 8
Whom when as Turpin saw so *loosely* layd, VI. vii. 20. 1
She in the open fields had *loosely* layd VI. xii. 16. 4
That *loosely* they ne dare to looke upon her. *Am.* v. 8
They *loosely* did theyr wanton winges display, *Am.* lxxvi. 11
if you *loosely* love without respect, *H.B.* 194
Looseness. Pourd out in *loosnesse* on the grassy grownd, I. vii. 7. 2
in her *loosenesse* tooke exceding joy: II. ii. 37. 3
loosenes, that she lightly did remove. III. viii. 42. 5
loosenesse of her love and loathly deed, III. x. 50. 4
Looser. *looser* songs of love to underfong, *S.C.* N. 22
in thilke same *looser* yeares, *S.C.* D. 37
The *loser* Lasse I cast to please no more; *S.C.* D. 119
His *looser* locks doth wrap in wreath of vine: *Gn.* 114
In loves soft laies and *looser* thoughts delight. *Col.* 423
Ne would his *looser* life be tide to law, I. iv. 26. 3
Upstarted lightly from his *looser* make, I. vii. 7. 8
prickt forth with jollitee Of *looser* life I. ix. 12. 5
Her *looser* golden lockes he rudely rent, II. i. 11. 5
Was lightnesse seene or *looser* vanitie, II. ii. 15. 4
that no *looser* heares Did out of order stray II. ii. 15. 8
spent their *looser* daies in leud delightes, II. xii. 9. 5
His *looser* garment to the ground did fall, II. xii. 46. 7
did divide Her *looser* notes with Lydian harmony; III. i. 40. 2
Nought so of love this *looser* Dame did skill, III. i. 50. 1
My *looser* rimes (I wote) doth sharply wite IV. Pr. 1. 3
layd aside when so she usd her *looser* sport. IV. v. 3. 9
looser thoughts to lawfull bounds withdraw; IV. vi. 33. 7
looser thought will lightly be misled, IV. viii. 29. 3
have agreed To thrall my *looser* life, V. v. 29. 9
Their *looser* lookes that stir up lustes impure; *Am.* xxi. 8
Loosers. *See* **Loser's.**
Loosing. *See* **Losing.**
now *loosing* everie lim, *Gn.* 322
loosing soone his shield did it forgoe; V. xii. 22. 7
Lop. Now thy selfe hast lost both *lopp* and topp, *S.C.* F. 57
with sharpe teeth the bramble leaves doth *lop,* *Gn.* 85
Whose shady boughes sharp steele did never *lop,* III. vi. 43. 4
from the trees did *lop* the needlesse spray: VII. vii. 42. 7
Lope. *See* **Leaped, Leapt.**
laughing *lope* to a tree; *S.C.* Mar. 81
Lord. The holy Citie of the *Lorde,* from hye *Rev.* iv. 3
yelde unto thy *lorde* a sweete request, *Pet.*[1] vii. 3
is in Winter *lord* of all the plaine, *Ro.* xiv. 2
A mighty Lyon, *Lord* of all the wood, *Van.* x. 1
lowdly cryed Unto his *lord,* *S.C.* F. 149
'O, my liege *Lord!* the God of my life! *S.C.* F. 150
'Ah, my soveraigne! *Lord* of creatures all, *S.C.* F. 163
Now stands the Brere like a *lord* alone, *S.C.* F. 222
Ah, deare *Lord!* and sweete Saint Charitee! *S.C.* May 247
So lowted he unto hys *Lord,* *S.C.* Jul. 137
lord it as they list: *S.C.* Jul. 176
you (great *Lord*) the causer of my care, *Gn.* Ded. 2
Lord of himselfe, with palme bedight, *Gn.* 113
how t' acquite themselves unto their *Lord* *Hub.* 323
he that serves the *Lord* of hoasts most high, *Hub.* 469
Whether of them should be the *Lord* of Lords: *Hub.* 1020
Man, the *Lord* of everie creature, *Hub.* 1030
Lord! how he fum'd, and sweld, and rag'd, and panted; *Hub.* 1340
O soveraigne *Lord!* O soveraigne happinesse, *T.M.* 515
Like a great *Lord* of peerelesse liberty; *Com. Son.* i. 10
by thee thy *Lord* shall never die. *Ti.* 252
'Thy *Lord* shall never die, *Ti.* 253
Ah, my liege *Lord!* forgive it unto mee, *Mui.* 102
to be *Lord* of all the workes of Nature, *Mui.* 211
Lord, how he gan for to bestirre him tho, *Mui.* 252
(*Lord!*) how she in everie member shooke, *Mui.* 285
unto the bridale feast Of his great *Lord,* *D.* 269
dread *Lord,* that doest liege hearts possesse, *Col.* 793
love is *Lord* of all the world by right, *Col.* 883
Thus ought all lovers of their *lord* to deeme, *Col.* 887
So you, great *Lord,* that with your counsell sway *Ded. Son.* i. 9
Magnificke *Lord,* whose vertues excellent, *Ded. Son.* ii. 1
Receive, most Noble *Lord,* in gentle gree, *Ded. Son.* iii. 1
right noble *Lord,* I send This present *Ded. Son.* iv. 13
Receive, most noble *Lord,* a simple taste *Ded. Son.* v. 1
Receive, dear *Lord,* in worth, the fruit of barren field. *Ded. Son.* v. 14
And ye, brave *Lord,* whose goodly personage *Ded. Son.* vi. 1

Lord—*Continued.*
Most Noble *Lord,* the pillor of my life, ... *Ded. Son.* vii. 1
The which vouchsafe, dear *Lord,* your favorable doome. . . . *Ded. Son.* vii.14
To you, right noble *Lord,* whose carefull brest . . . . . . *Ded. Son.* ix. 1
Redoubted *Lord,* in whose corageous mind . . . . *Ded. Son.* x. 1
Receive it, *Lord,* therefore, as it was ment, ... *Ded. Son.* x. 13
Renowmed *Lord,* that, for your worthinesse . . . . . . *Ded. Son.* xi. 1
Live, *Lord,* for ever in this lasting verse, ... *Ded. Son.* xi. 13
In vain I thinke, right honourable *Lord,* . . . . *Ded. Son.* xii. 1
Most noble *Lord,* the honor of this age, ... *Ded. Son.* xiv. 6
The deare remembrance of his dying *Lord,* . . . . I. i. 2. 2
highest God, the *Lord* of life and light: . . . . I. i. 37. 6
the dreame he bore In hast unto his *Lord,* . . . . I. i. 44. 9
'Ah Sir, my liege *Lord,* and my love, ... I. i. 51. 1
My dearest *Lord* fell from high honors staire . . . . I. ii. 23. 7
'The Lyon, *Lord* of everie beast in field,' . . . . I. iii. 7. 1
he, my Lyon, and my noble *Lord,* . . . . I. iii. 7. 6
weeping said, 'Ah my long lacked *Lord,* . . . . I. iii. 27. 1
He now, *Lord* of the field, ... I. iii. 43. 5
warres for Ladies doen by many a *Lord.* . . . . I. v. 3. 9
'Ah! dearest *Lord,*' (quoth she) 'how might that bee, ... I. vi. 39. 1
your *lord* that could so well you tosse? . . . . I. vii. 48. 9
my *Lord,* . . . doth lucklesse ly . . . . I. viii. 2. 4
twixt him and his *Lord* did like a bulwarke stand. . . . . . I. viii. 12. 9
To her yeeld passage gainst his *Lord* to goe, ... I. viii. 13. 7
So brought unto his *Lord* as his deserved pray. . . . . I. viii. 25. 9
For she it is, that did my *Lord* bethrall, My dearest *Lord,* . I. viii. 28. 6, 7
'Ah dearest *Lord!* what evill starre On you hath frownd, . . . I. viii. 42. 6
welcome now, my *Lord* in wele or woe, ... I. viii. 43. 1
you, my *Lord,* the Patrone of my life, ... I. ix. 17. 6
that deare *Lord* who oft thereon was fownd, ... I. x. 54. 4
to his *Lord* and Lady lowd gan call, ... I. xii. 2. 8
That aged Syre, the *Lord* of all that land, ... I. xii. 3. 2
Forth came that auncient *Lord,* and aged Queene, ... I. xii. 5. 1
Their *Lord* and Patrone loud did him proclame, ... I. xii. 6. 3
That auncient *Lord* gan fit occasion finde, ... I. xii. 15. 3
'Ah dearest *Lord!*' said then that doughty knight, ... I. xii. 18. 1
'My *Lord,* my king, be nought hereat dismayd, ... I. xii. 31. 2
'O! pardon me, my soveraine *Lord,* . . . . I. xii. 33. 4
cryde, 'Mercie, Sir knight! and mercie, *Lord,* . . . . II. i. 27. 1
My *Lord,* my love, my deare *Lord,* my deare love! . . . . . . II. i. 50. 2
My liefest *Lord* she thus beguiled had; . . . . II. i. 52. 5
my *Lord* from her I would reprive, ... II. i. 55. 2
'Ye bene right hard amated, gratious *Lord,* . . . . II. ii. 5. 3
fly, O my liefest *Lord!* . . . . II. ii. 30. 5
O deare *Lord!* hold your dead-doing hand,' . . . . II. iii. 8. 1
when he felt the folly of his *Lord,* . . . . II. iii. 9. 3
'Certes, my *Lord,*' (said he) . . . . II. iii. 15. 1
my *Lord,* my liege, whose warlike name Is far renowmd . . . II. iii. 35. 3
'My *Lord,*' (quoth he) 'me sent, ... II. iv. 43. 5
'let that message to thy *Lord* be brought.' . . . . II. iv. 44. 9
When late he saw his *Lord* in heavie plight . . . . II. v. 25. 5
where that same warlike *Lord* She in receiv'd; . . . . II. vi. 4. 7
O man! that of them all Art *Lord,* . . . . II. vi. 17. 2
should he but his owne deare *Lord* there see, ... II. vi. 43. 3
His owne deare *Lord* Pyrochles in sad plight, ... II. vi. 43. 4
To see my *Lord* so deadly damnifyde? . . . . II. vi. 43. 8
Into the lake he lept his *Lord* to ayd, ... II. vi. 46. 1
The carefull servaunt stryving with his raging *Lord.* . . . . II. vi. 47. 9
To save my *Lord* in wretched plight forlore; . . . . II. vi. 48. 3
to be *Lord* of those that riches have, ... II. vii. 33. 8
him thus bespake their soveraine *Lord* and syre; . . . . . . II. vii. 37. 9
Delivered up the *Lord* of life to dye, ... II. vii. 62. 6
lend The same to thee, against his *lord* to fight; . . . . . . II. viii. 21. 8
thus sayd; 'My *Lord,* my liege, ... II. viii. 55. 5
'Noble *Lord,* what meed so great, ... II. ix. 6. 1
many a *Lord* of noble parentage, ... II. ix. 18. 4
Locrine left chiefe *Lord* of Britany. . . . . II. x. 13. 7
Locrine was left the soveraine *Lord* of all; . . . . II. x. 14. 1
th' eternall *Lord* in fleshly slime Enwombed was, ... II. x. 50. 2
Persuaded him to ceasse, and her *lord* to relent. . . . . . . II. x. 52. 9
Least that his *Lord* they should behinde invade; . . . . . . II. xi. 31. 5
Who was the *lord* of Mathraval by right, ... III. iii. 13. 7
with guifts his *Lord* Cadwallin pacify. . . . . III. iii. 39. 9
Late king, now captive; late *lord,* now forlorne; . . . . . . III. iii. 42. 4
shortly he a great *Lord* did appeare, ... III. iv. 23. 8
Ladies love unto his *Lord* forlent, ... III. iv. 47. 2
whiles his *Lord* pursewd that noble Mayd, ... III. v. 13. 3
Els shall thy loving *Lord* thee see no more; . . . . III. v. 26. 7
'Mercy, deare *Lord!*' (said he) 'what grace is this . . . . . III. v. 35. 1
first was spoken by th' Almighty *Lord,* . . . . III. vi. 34. 5
Against that Castles *Lord* they gan conspire, ... III. ix. 17. 4
bad before his soveraine *Lord* appere. . . . . III. x. 23. 7
you, most noble *Lord,* that can and dare . . . . III. x. 28. 1
My *Lord* and I will search the wide forest.' . . . . III. x. 41. 7
'O soverayne *Lord!* that sit'st on hye . . . . III. xi. 9. 2
hast thou, *Lord,* of good mens cause no heed? . . . . III. xi. 9. 6
her lives *Lord* and patrone of her health . . . . IV. i. 6. 2
Whose *Lord* hath done my love this foule despight? . . . . . IV. i. 52. 8
when the wicked feend his *Lord* tormented, ... IV. ii. 2. 2
There Satyrane *Lord* of the field he found, ... IV. iv. 28. 1
To be his love, and take him for her *Lord,* . . . . IV. vi. 41. 8
Daughter unto a *Lord* of high degree; . . . . IV. vii. 15. 2
His owne deare *Lord* Prince Arthure came that way, ... IV. vii. 42. 2
his owne deare *Lord* The noble Prince, ... IV. viii. 18. 4
howld aloud to see his *Lord* there slaine, ... IV. viii. 46. 4
as to their *Lord,* . . . . IV. xi. 29. 4
So brought unto his *Lord,* . . . . V. iv. 25. 7
with his *Lord* she would emparlaunce make. . . . . V. iv. 50. 9
So he them streight conducted to his *Lord;* . . . . V. iv. 51. 1

Lord—*Continued.*
To reskew his owne *Lord,* . . . . V. v. 19. 9
of her servant make her soverayne *Lord:* . . . . V. v. 27. 8
'And where is he thy *Lord,* and how far hence? . . . . . . V. vi. 9. 2
My *Lord,* your love, by hard mishap doth lie . . . . V. vi. 10. 6
Which had her *Lord* in her base prison pent, ... V. vi. 18. 8
To see her *Lord,* that was reported drent . . . . V. vii. 39. 3
'Ah, my deare *Lord!* what sight is this?' . . . . V. vii. 40. 1
her noble *Lord,* sir Artegall, ... V. vii. 45. 6
as he had beene Before directed by his *Lord;* . . . . V. viii. 29. 8
to his *Lord* Sir Artegall it lent, ... V. ix. 18. 2
To be my love, and take me for her *Lord;* . . . . V. xi. 50. 2
him adoring as her lives deare *Lord,* . . . . VI. i. 45. 6
she was daughter to a noble *Lord* . . . . VI. iii. 7. 1
Unlesse that with his *Lord* he formerly did fight. . . . . . VI. iii. 38. 9
aread to me, how hight thy *Lord,* . . . . VI. iii. 39. 8
and to his *Lord* Declar'd the message . . . . VI. iii. 42. 1
bold Sir Bruin, who is *Lord* Of all this land, ... VI. iv. 29. 4
'So is my *Lord* now seiz'd of all the land, ... VI. iv. 30. 1
'But most my *Lord* is grieved herewithall, ... VI. iv. 32. 1
his *Lord* of old Did hate all errant Knights . . . . VI. vi. 21. 3
Those evill tidings to their *Lord* to shew: . . . . VI. vi. 24. 3
streight to him obayd, As to his *Lord,* . . . . VI. vi. 39. 5
lately sought his *Lord* for to displease: . . . . VI. vi. 40. 4
The whyles his *Lord* in silver slomber lay, ... VI. vii. 19. 8
whereas his *Lord* he sleeping vew'd. . . . . VI. vii. 23. 9
his *Lord* The witnesse of his wretchednesse in place, ... VI. viii. 5. 1
Lord! what gladfull glee They made . . . . VI. viii. 37. 1
Whereof was *Lord* the good Sir Bellamoure; . . . . VI. xii. 3. 4
whose father hight The *Lord* of Many Ilands, ... VI. xii. 4. 2
Thence running forth unto her loved *Lord,* . . . . VI. xii. 22. 1
his doings to relate Unto his *Lord;* . . . . VII. vi. 19. 3
Have Jove thy gracious *Lord* and Soveraine.' . . . . VII. vi. 34. 5
their glorious *Lord* in strange disguise Transfigur'd sawe; . . VII. vii. 7. 8
Lord! how all creatures laught . . . . VII. vii. 34. 7
Unrighteous *Lord* of Love, what law is this, ... *Am.* x. 1
And yet the Lyon that is *Lord* of power, ... *Am.* xx. 5
Most glorious *Lord* of lyfe! . . . . *Am.* lxviii. 1
This joyous day, deare *Lord,* with joy begin; . . . . *Am.* lxviii. 5
Love is the lesson which the *Lord* us taught. . . . . *Am.* lxviii. 14
The praises of the *Lord* in lively notes; . . . . *Epith.* 219
the soveraine *Lord* of all, ... *H.L.* 157
love is *Lord* of truth and loialtie, ... *H.L.* 176
Ay me! deare *Lord!* . . . . *H.L.* 294
Till then, dread *Lord!* vouchsafe . . . . *H.L.* 306
Lord, how sweete musicke that unto them lends! . . . . . . *H.B.* 252
Had not they dar'd their *Lord* to disobay. . . . . *H.H.L.* 77
Him to be *Lord* of every living wight He made . . . . *H.H.L.* 115
Till that great *Lord* of Love, which him at first . . . . . . *H.H.L.* 127
pierst the piteous hart Of that deare *Lord* . . . . *H.H.L.* 157
Eternall King of Glorie, *Lord* of Might, ... *H.H.L.* 172
since that loving *Lord* Commaunded us to love them . . . . *H.H.L.* 204
Unmindfull of that dearest *Lord* of thyne; . . . . *H.H.L.* 221
goodly grace Of that great *Lord,* . . . . *Proth.* 139
this noble *Lord* issuing, ... *Proth.* 163

Lordeth. The whiles she *lordeth* in licentious blisse . . . . . *Am.* x. 3

Lording. loathed Paddocks *lording* on the same: . . . . . . *S.C.* D. 70

Lordings. Then listen, *Lordings,* . . . . III. ix. 3. 1
Lordings curbe that commons over-aw, ... V. ii. 38. 8

Lordly. *lordly* love is such a Tyranne fell, ... *S.C.* O. 98
On which the *lordly* Faulcon wont to towre . . . . *Ti.* 128
Under his *Lordly* foot him proudly hath supprest. . . . . . . I. iii. 19. 9
he . . . launcht his *Lordly* hart: . . . . I. iii. 42. 8
Proud Tarquin, and too *lordly* Lentulus; . . . . I. v. 49. 6
enjoyes The wide kingdome . . . with *lordly* sway, ... IV. x. 42. 8
strong as Lyon in his *lordly* might. . . . . V. i. 20. 5
thy linage, and thy *Lordly* brood, ... V. vii. 21. 7

Lord's. for leaving his *Lords* taske, ... *S.C.* May 53
I can carve . . . His *Lords* owne flesh.' . . . . II. viii. 22. 5
his *Lordes* life did assure. . . . . II. viii. 30. 9
Into his *Lords* forbidden hall to passe? . . . . VI. vi. 20. 4

Lords. auncient glorie of the Romane *lordes.* . . . . *Bel.*[1] iv. 8
You thinken to be *Lords* of the yeare; . . . . *S.C.* F. 41
As *Lordes* done other where; . . . . *S.C.* Jul. 186
live like *Lords* of that which they doo gather, ... *Hub.* 164
fashion both our selves to bee, *Lords* of the world; . . . . . *Hub.* 168
To *Lords,* to Principalls, to Prebendaries? . . . . *Hub.* 422
Kings of Beasts, and *Lords* of forests all . . . . *Hub.* 971
Whether of them should be the Lord of *Lords.* . . . . *Hub.* 1020
either (algates) would be *Lords* alone; . . . . *Hub.* 1025
a noble crew Of *Lords* and Ladies stood on every side, . . . I. iv. 7. 8
Her *Lordes* and Ladies . . . devise Themselves to setten forth I. iv. 14. 5
'Ah, puissaunt *Lords!* what cursed evil Spright, ... II. ii. 29. 1
Be, therefore, O my deare *Lords!* pacifide, ... II. ii. 31. 8
'Ah, well away! most noble *Lords,* . . . . II. vi. 32. 5
three hundred *Lords* he slew Of British blood, ... II. x. 66. 6
Ladies and *Lordes* she everywhere mote heare Complayning, . III. vi. 13. 6
Kings, Queenes, *Lords,* Ladies, ... III. xi. 46. 1
yet lov'd of Knights and *Lords.* . . . . IV. ii. 35. 9
Full many *Lords* and many Knights her loved, ... IV. ii. 36. 1
squiers make hast to helpe their *Lords* fordonne. . . . . . . IV. iv. 38. 8
many *Lords* have her to wife desired, ... V. ii. 10. 3
Of *Lords* and Ladies infinite great store; . . . . V. iii. 2. 8
So were they left *Lords* of the field alone: . . . . V. iii. 12. 8
Faire *Lords* and Ladies which about you dwell, ... VI. Pr. 7. 8

Lordship. Lovers of *Lordship,* and troublers of states. . . . *S.C.* May 123
Love and *Lordship* bide no paragone. . . . . *Hub.* 1026
of *Lordship* with both land and fee: . . . . IV. ix. 13. 7
chiefe Of all her land and *lordship* during life. . . . . . . IV. ix. 15. 8
the love of *Lordship* and of lands . . . . V. xii. 2. 3

Lordship—*Continued.*
Now loath great *Lordship* and ambition; . . . VI. ix. 28. 5
Lordships. loded them with *lordships* and with might, . . . *Hub.* 1156
Having great *Lordships* got and goodly farmes, . . . V. ii. 5. 7
Lore. *See* **Lorn.**
luck and loves unbridled *lore* . . . *S.C.* D. 63
For prize of value, or for learned *lore:* . . . *T.M.* 466
He gan to cast great lyking to my *lore,* . . . *Col.* 180
his sweet *lore* professed there? . . . *Col.* 772
Are outlawes, and his *lore* do disobay. . . . *Col.* 890
So pure . . . She was in life and every vertuous *lore;* . . . I. i. 5. 2
Teaching the Satyres, . . . Trew sacred *lore,* . . . I. vi. 30. 9
all my daies he trained mee up in vertuous *lore.* . . . I. ix. 4. 9
Renowmd throughout the world for sacred *lore* . . . I. x. 3. 2
By hearing her, and by her sisters *lore,* . . . I. x. 21. 2
In vertuous *lore* to traine his tender youth, . . . II. iii. 2. 4
by fatall *lore* Hast learn'd to love, . . . III. iii. 21. 6
persuade The warlike minds to learne her goodly *lore,* . . . III. iii. 49. 4
Yet he his mothers *lore* did well retaine, . . . III. iv. 26. 5
skill In leaches craft, by great Apolloes *lore,* . . . III. iv. 41. 3
all the *lore* of love, and goodly womanhead. . . . III. vi. 51. 9
Ne was she ignoraunt of that leud *lore,* . . . III. ix. 28. 5
hearken to his *lore,* and all his counsell hyde. . . . III. x. 50. 9
if please ye listen to my *lore,* . . . III. xi. 18. 7
Neither of them she found where she them *lore:* . . . III. xii. 44. 4
Entrayled mutually in lovely *lore,* . . . IV. iii. 42. 3
lawlesse lust to rule with reasons *lore;* . . . IV. ix. 19. 4
Stood still by him astonisht at his *lore,* . . . IV. xi. 23. 8
of civill uses *lore,* . . . V. Pr. 3. 2
Artegall trayn'd in Justice *lore* . . . V. i. Arg.
to her he seem'd best skild in righteous *lore.* . . . V. i. 4. 9
ever to my *lore* be bound; . . . V. iv. 49. 3
are rul'd by righteous *lore* Of highest Jove, . . . V. vii. 1. 5
They heare him not, they have forgot his *lore,* . . . V. viii. 39. 8
where he her had *lore,* . . . V. x. 38. 7
ne would unto his *lore* Allured be . . . V. xi. 61. 6
Thy courteous *lore,* that doest my love deride, . . . VI. i. 27. 8
Or noursle up in *lore* of learn'd Philosophy. . . . VI. iv. 35. 9
Backe to the place where Turpine late he *lore;* . . . VI. vii. 14. 2
Lorel. thou speakes lyke a lewde *lorrell,* . . . *S.C.* Jul. 93
Loring. Her wisedome did admire, and hearkned to her *loring.* V. vii. 42. 9
Lorn. *See* **Lore.**
And am forlorne, (alas! why am I *lorne?*) . . . *S.C.* Ja. 62
I cast to have *lorne* this grounde: . . . *S.C.* S. 57
My freedome *lorne,* my life he lefte to mone. . . . *S.C.* D. 52
after that he had faire Una *lorne,* . . . I. iv. 2. 1
Lorrel. *See* **Lorel.**
Lose. *See* **Loose.**
loose thy labour and thy fruitles cost. . . . *Hub.* 636
To *loose* good dayes, that might be better spent; . . . *Hub.* 897
faire Calliope did *lose* Her loved Twinnes, . . . *T.M.* 13
To *loose* both her and bounties ornament. . . . *D.* 224
in a moment *loose* their grace and glorie. . . . *D.* 497
Did *lose* his name: . . . *Col.* 155
Resolvd . . . to win, Or soone to *lose,* . . . I. i. 24. 5
daily care To get, and nightly feare to *lose* his owne, . . . I. iv. 28. 8
th' Elfin knight, . . . Disdaind to *loose* the meed . . . I. iv. 39. 8
his shield, that covered was, Did *loose* his vele . . . I. viii. 19. 2
In feare to *lose* his weapon in his paw, . . . I. xi. 41. 2
incontinent Doth *loose* his dignity and native grace: . . . II. ix. 1. 8
swore him fealty to win or *loose.* . . . II. x. 37. 9
To *loose* long gotten honour with one evill hond. . . . III. i. 10. 9
wishing it far off his ydle wish doth *lose.* . . . III. i. 46. 9
lose Both leafe and fruite, . . . III. ii. 31. 7
lose the hope Of his long labour, . . . III. iv. 52. 6
Madnesse to save a part, and *lose* the whole! . . . III. v. 43. 3
was he loth to *loose* his loved Dame, . . . III. x. 15. 5
her love to *lose* she was full loth, . . . IV. i. 10. 8
As all men do, that *lose* the living spright. . . . IV. iii. 30. 7
Whom he that hath were loth to *lose* so light, . . . IV. iv. 9. 2
(For so to *lose* a Lady were great shame) . . . IV. iv. 9. 3
For glorie vaine, their fellowship to *lose,* . . . IV. iv. 14. 5
Loose so immortall glory, and so endlesse gaines. . . . IV. xi. 22. 9
The wanton Lee, that oft doth *loose* his way; . . . IV. xi. 29. 7
rather had to *lose* then trie in armes his right. . . . V. iii. 31. 9
Great shame to *lose* so long employed paines, . . . V. v. 48. 3
loth to *loose* her right away, . . . V. vii. 30. 5
Till she had sav'd so many loves as she did *lose.* . . . VI. vii. 37. 9
They, that have much, feare much to *loose* thereby, . . . VI. ix. 21. 3
Besides the losse of so much *loos* and fame, . . . VI. xii. 12. 8
To *lose* their heat and shortly to decay; . . . VII. vii. 24. 4
lose their native mights; . . . VII. vii. 25. 5
fondly feare to *loose* your liberty; . . . *Am.* lxv. 2
turne to nought and *loose* that glorious hew; . . . *Am.* lxxix. 6
Shall turne to dust, and *loose* their goodly light. . . . *H.B.* 98
Losel. a *losell* wandring by the way, . . . II. iii. 4. 1
'Thou *losell* base, That hast with borrowed plumes . . . V. iii. 20. 6
that *losell,* plainely now displayd, . . . V. iii. 35. 5
that vile *lozell* which her late offended; . . . VI. iv. 10. 2
Losel's. Be with the worke of *losels* wit defamed, . . . *Hub.* 813
Losels. *losels* lifted up on high, . . . *Hub.* 67
loath'd of *losels* as a thing forlorne: . . . *T.M.* 226
good men blame, and *losels* magnify. . . . *T.M.* 324
those two *losels* scared; . . . V. vi. 38. 5
Losen. *See* **Loose.**
Loser. *See* **Looser.**
Loser's. Both *loosers* lott, and victours prayse alsoe; . . . II. v. 15. 8
Loseth. Ne is the earth the lesse, or *loseth* ought, . . . V. ii. 39. 6
He somewhat *loseth* of his heat and light, . . . *Epith.* 268
Losing. *loosing* one, two liberties ye gayne, . . . *Am.* lxv. 3

Losing—*Continued.*
Through feare of *loosing* his felicitie. . . . *H.L.* 270
Loss. Learne by their *losse* to love the low degree; . . . *Van.* xii. 10
losse of her, whose love as lyfe I wayd, . . . *S.C.* Jun. 47
now by thy *losse* art taught, . . . *S.C.* S. 68
Oft lives by *losse,* and leaves with payne. . . . *S.C.* S. 73
better leave of with a little *losse,* . . . *S.C.* S. 134
My piteous plight and *losse* to amend? . . . *S.C.* S. 245
O Lobb! thy *losse* no longer lament; . . . *S.C.* N. 168
So was the husbandman left to his *losse,* . . . *Hub.* 341
did the *losse* of some dere love lament, . . . *Ti.* 16
left me here his *losse* for to deplore. . . . *Ti.* 658
to lament His *losse,* . . . *Ti.* 677
dubble *losse* by her hath on them light, . . . *D.* 223
how great a *losse* Had all the shepheards . . . *Col.* 16
*Nor of my love, nor of my *losse* (quoth he). . . . *Col.* 88
Helpe Amaryllis this her *losse* to mourne: . . . *Col.* 437
Her *losse* is yours, your *losse* Amyntas is, . . . *Col.* 438
leave their lambes to *losse,* misled amisse. . . . *Col.* 687
the late *losse* of her deare loved knight, . . . I. iii. 15. 6
To make one great by others *losse* is bad excheat. . . . I. v. 25. 9
Ladies love as *losse* of time forbore: . . . I. v. 37. 4
For feare, as seemd, or for some feigned *losse:* . . . I. vi. 34. 8
this man forlorne, And left to *losse;* . . . I. vii. 10. 6
greater love, the greater is the *losse.* . . . I. vii. 27. 6
the record of his ruefull *losse,* . . . I. vii. 48. 6
lovers life, As *losse* of time, . . . I ever scornd, . . . I. ix. 10. 2
Feare, sicknesse, age, *losse,* labour, sorrow, strife, . . . I. ix. 44. 6
faint through *losse* of blood, . . . I. xi. 50. 3
losse of love to her that loves to live, . . . II. i. 55. 5
To *losse* of love adjoyning *losse* of frend, . . . II. iv. 31. 2
shortly gaynd that *losse* exceeded farre. . . . II. v. 15. 5
Losse is no shame, nor to bee lesse then foe; . . . II. v. 15. 6
sufficient were that hire For *losse* of thousand lives, . . . II. ix. 5. 9
Through *losse* of blood which from his wounds did bleed, . . . II. xi. 48. 5
All *losse* is lesse, and lesse the infamy, . . . III. i. 25. 5
losse of love to him that loves but one: . . . III. i. 25. 6
by ensample of the last dayes *losse,* . . . III. i. 64. 6
Avenge his fathers *losse* with speare and shield, . . . III. iii. 31. 8
who that lives is lefte to waile his *losse:* . . . III. iv. 38. 6
So life is *losse,* and death felicity: . . . III. iv. 38. 7
did lament The *losse* of her deare brood, . . . III. vi. 40. 4
lefte his love to *losse,* and fled him selfe apace. . . . III. viii. 18. 9
losse of chastitie, or chaunge of love: . . . III. viii. 42. 2
sheweth at the least Her certeine *losse,* . . . III. viii. 49. 6
lament The heavie *losse* of their brave Paramours, . . . III. ix. 35. 4
Subdewd with *losse* of many Britons bold: . . . III. ix. 50. 2
Malbecco, seeing how his *losse* did lye, . . . III. x. 17. 2
More is more *losse;* one is enough to dy.' . . . III. xi. 19. 7
Lewd *Losse* of Time, . . . III. xii. 25. 5
her deare nourslings *losse* no lesse did mourne, . . . III. xii. 45. 7
As if that life to *losse* they had forelent, . . . IV. iii. 6. 8
Which *losse* her made like passion also prove: . . . IV. viii. 3. 5
grieved was for *losse* both of her sire, . . . IV. ix. 13. 6
griefe entire For *losse* of her new love, . . . IV. ix. 13. 9
For *losse* of his deare love by Neptune hent, . . . IV. ix. 23. 2
her *losse* ought me to sorrow most, . . . IV. ix. 38. 7
Some of their *losse,* some of their loves delay, . . . IV. x. 43. 3
mourn'd to see her *losse* before her eyne, . . . IV. xii. 21. 7
Yet litle *losse* it were, and mickle thanke, . . . V. i. 15. 5
With a fayre love, whose *losse* I now do rew, . . . V. i. 16. 7
For certaine *losse* of so great expectation: . . . V. ii. 51. 5
more then *losse* of life ydreaded it; . . . V. iv. 25. 5
watch both night and day Unto your *losse;* . . . V. vi. 25. 6
Fought many battels without wound or *losse;* . . . V. xi. 53. 7
losse of fame in disaventrous field: . . . V. xi. 55. 8
in anothers *losse* great pleasure take, . . . V. xii. 32. 8
And all this land with endlesse *losse* to overflow. . . . VI. iv. 30. 9
Besides the *losse* of so much loos and fame, . . . VI. xii. 12. 8
And all mirth sadnesse, and all lucre *losse.* . . . *H.H.B.* 280
Lost. There was she *lost;* . . . *Bel.* vii. 9
to see *lost* and drown'd, So great riches . . . *Pet.* ii. 13
'You naked trees, whose shady leaves are *lost,* . . . *S.C.* Ja. 31
Now thy selfe hast *lost* both lopp and topp, . . . *S.C.* F. 57
All that is lent to love wyll be *lost.* . . . *S.C.* F. 70
Thy flocks father his corage hath *lost.* . . . *S.C.* F. 80
what they left behind them is *lost.* . . . *S.C.* May 70
That Paradise hast found whych Adam *lost:* . . . *S.C.* Jun. 10
good matter *Lost* for lacke of telling: . . . *S.C.* Jul. 206
who shall judge the wager wonne or *lost?* . . . *S.C.* Au. 44
So *lost* the Dogge the flesh in his mouth. . . . *S.C.* S. 61
manie *lost,* of whom no moniment Remaines, . . . *Gn.* 589
in long service *lost* both limbs and good; . . . *Hub.* 248
yet the skill thereof I have not *loste:* . . . *Hub.* 293
lost their time in wandring loose abroad; . . . *Hub.* 399
Have now quite *lost* their naturall delight, . . . *T.M.* 552
Were but *lost* labour, . . . *Ti.* 90
thy *lost* deare love deplore. . . . *Ti.* 250
had *lost* their beautie faire. . . . *D.* 28
And, *lost* emong those rocks into him rold, . . . *Col.* 154
one, that fairest Helene did revile, . . . *Lost* both his eyes . . . *Col.* 922
these ydle rimes . . . The labor of *lost* Time, . . . *Ded. Son.* ix. 8
Having . . . *lost* an old foe that did you molest; . . . I. ii. 27. 3
Shee backe retourned with some labour *lost;* . . . I. iii. 24. 2
All is but *lost,* that living we bestow, . . . I. x. 41. 6
eien . . . through great age had *lost* their kindly sight, . . . I. x. 47. 4
sometimes had the worse, and *lost* by warre, . . . II. v. 15. 4
Guyon having *lost* his trustie guyde, . . . II. vii. 2. 1
So *lost* his labour vaine and ydle industry. . . . II. vii. 61. 9
the Palmer, whom he long ygoe Had *lost,* . . . II. viii. 53. 6

Lost—*Continued.*
Prince recov'ring his stolne sword, And Guyon his *lost* shield, . II. ix. 2. 3
when thinges were *lost,* or laid amis, ... II. ix. 58. 6
lost his sword, yet to be seene this day. . . . . II. x. 49. 5
labour *lost* it was to weene approch him neare. . . . . . . II. xi. 25. 9
thought his labor *lost,* and travell vayne. . . . . II. xi. 44. 2
After *lost* credit and consumed thrift, ... II. xii. 8. 8
lost much blood through many a wownd, ... III. i. 21. 5
to tell the sumptuous aray . . . should be labour *lost;* . . . III. i. 32. 2
faire Venus having *lost* Her little sonne, ... III. vi. 11. 1
called is by her *lost* lovers name, ... III. vi. 29. 8
To see his whole yeares labor *lost* so soone, ... III. vii. 34. 8
To fetch from sea that ye at land *lost* late! . . . . III. viii. 28. 4
'Thy labour all is *lost,* I greatly dread, ... III. viii. 47. 2
The learned lover *lost* no time nor tyde . . . . III. x. 6. 1
Then all the world is *lost,* . . . . III. x. 39. 9
'Life is not *lost,*' (said she) . . . . III. xi. 19. 8
a dismayed Deare . . . hath his right way *lost.* . . . . . . III. xii. 17. 9
Ne for light Ladies love that soone is *lost.*' . . . . IV. i. 35. 4
Misdoubted *lost* through mischiefe that befell. . . . . . . IV. ii. 23. 7
when as she her selfe was *lost* and gone, ... IV. ii. 26. 1
That *lost* faire Ladies ornament should weare, ... IV. ii. 26. 4
That I thy labours *lost* may thus revive, ... IV. ii. 34. 2
He soone her *lost:* . . . . IV. iv. 8. 5
It was the same which lately Florimel had *lost.* . . . . . . IV. iv. 15. 9
Which else was like to have bene *lost,* . . . . IV. iv. 48. 3
for to winne the saddle *lost* the steed. . . . . IV. v. 22. 5
Where sorie Britomart had *lost* her late; . . . . IV. vi. 47. 2
likewise late had *lost* her dearest love, ... IV. viii. 3. 4
his juell he had *lost* so light, ... IV. viii. 8. 5
Whom they had *lost* in Turneyment of late; . . . . IV. ix. 24. 3
I thereby my former love have *lost;* . . . . IV. ix. 38. 2
some *lost* great hope unheedily, ... IV. x. 13. 5
Whose smallest minute *lost* no riches render may. . . . . . IV. x. 14. 9
As he had *lost* him selfe he wist not where; . . . . IV. xii. 17. 3
brawney armes had *lost* their knowen might, ... IV. xii. 20. 4
Whom having *lost,* (as ye have heard whyleare) . . . . . . V. ii. 3. 2
For there is nothing *lost,* that may be found if sought. . . . V. ii. 39. 9
yet little *lost* or wonne: . . . . V. iii. 6. 7
have you *lost* your selfe and your discretion, ... V. iv. 26. 2
He wilfull *lost* that he before attayned: . . . . V. v. 17. 8
hath he *lost* or wun?' . . . . V. vi. 9. 3
And *lost* the crowne . . . . VI. ii. 27. 9
a ship . . . Now farre from harbour likely to be *lost,* . . . . VI. iv. 1. 3
That he his love so lucklesse now had *lost,* . . . . VI. iv. 40. 2
Since I him lately *lost,* . . . . VI. v. 28. 9
'In salvage forrest I him *lost* of late, ... VI. v. 29. 1
the wretched stormes, In which his love was *lost,* . . . . . VI. viii. 47. 6
He *lost* himselfe, and like one halfe entraunced grew. . . . . VI. ix. 26. 9
On which he safety hopes that earst feard to be *lost.* . . . . . VI. xi. 44. 9
ne hath her compasse *lost:* . . . . VI. xii. 1. 7
he his way doth seem quite to have *lost,* . . . . VII. vii. 52. 3
all her natures goodly guifts are *lost:* . . . . *Am.* xli. 8
I goe lyke one that, having *lost* the field, ... *Am.* lii. 2
a young fawne, that late hath *lost* the hynd; . . . . *Am.* lxxviii. 2
He gave us life, he it restored *lost;* . . . . *H.H.L.* 181

Lot. ever was her *lot* To beare such an one. . . . . *S.C.* Ap. 93
the world parting by an equall *lott,* . . . . *Gn.* 158
Lament my *lot,* and tell your fellow-swaines . . . . *D.* 524
great dislyking to my lucklesse *lot,* . . . . *Col.* 181
it was my *lott* To love this gentle Lady, ... I. ii. 35. 3
He lov'd, as was his *lot,* a Lady gent, ... I. ix. 27. 6
Both lossers *lott,* and victours prayse alsoe; . . . . II. v. 15. 8
thou didst these goods bereave . . . by unrighteous *lott,* . . . II. vii. 19. 4
'Whom gracious *lott* and thy great valiaunce . . . . II. ix. 5. 2
assigned for his worthy *lott,* . . . . II. x. 12. 3
my lucklesse *lott* doth me constrayne Hereto perforce. . . . III. Pr. 3. 4
by her owne law to your *lot* doth light, ... III. i. 30. 4
her unlucky *lot* Lay hidden in the bottome of the pot. . . . . III. ii. 26. 4
needs love or death must bee thy *lott,* . . . . III. ii. 46. 7
of his lucklesse *lott* and cruell love thus playnd: . . . . . . III. v. 44. 9
Emongst the rest my *lott* (unworthy') is to be one.' . . . . . III. viii. 46. 9
from her went to seeke another *lott,* . . . . III. x. 37. 3
To him was fallen for his happie *lot,* . . . . IV. ii. 8. 4
lightly issewd forth to take his *lot.* . . . . IV. iv. 33. 7
like unlucky *lot* Hath linckt with me . . . . IV. vii. 14. 6
It was my *lot* to love a gentle swaine, ... IV. vii. 15. 6
Might be my lucky *lot;* sith all by *lot* we hold. . . . . . . IV. x. 4. 9
for so much as to my *lot* here lights, ... V. iii. 3. 7
I lov'd, as was my *lot,* That further mayd, ... V. iv. 8. 6
save my life, which *lot* before your foot doth lay.' . . . . . VI. i. 39. 9
Let them that list their lucklesse *lot* deplore, ... VI. vii. 30. 7
Though meane her *lot,* yet higher did her mind ascend. . . . . VI. ix. 10. 9
wish my *lot* were plast in such felicitie.' . . . . VI. ix. 19. 9
when the *lot* to Pastorell did fall, ... VI. xi. 31. 8
full oft for loving you I blesse my *lot,* . . . . *Am.* lxxxii. 2

Loth, *etc. See* **Loath, Loathe,** *etc.*

Lothian. Together with the king of *Louthiane,* . . . . III. iii. 37. 5

Lotos. them amongst the wicked *Lotos* grew, ... *Gn.* 193

Lots. twixt them shayrd his realme by equall *lottes;* . . . . . II. x. 29. 3

Loud. crying *lowd,* Loe! now beholde . . . . *Bel.*[2] i. 9
Thrice unto you with *lowd* voyce I appeale, ... *Ro.* i. 11
The sweete Nightingale singing so *lowde;* . . . . *S.C.* F. 123
carroll *lowde,* and leade the Myllers rownde, ... *S.C.* O. 52
our pypes, that shrild as *lowde* as Larke; . . . . *S.C.* N. 71
sound their praises *lowd.* . . . . *Gn.* 616
lowd shrieks and drerie dolefull cries. . . . . *T.M.* 172
With *lowd* laments her answered . . . . *T.M.* 418
lowd plaints have duld mine eares; . . . . *D.* 415
Lamenting *lowde* my Daphnes Elegie, ... *D.* 509

Loud—*Continued.*
Triton, blowing *loud* his wreathed horne: . . . . *Col.* 245
With praiers *lowd* importuning the skie, ... *Col.* 880
lowd to him gan call . . . . I. v. 11. 8
with *loud* plaintes importuneth the skyes, ... I. vi. 6. 4
Her shrill outcryes and shrieks so *loud* did bray, ... I. vi. 7. 5
a Lyonesse . . . did *lowd* requere Her children deare, ... I. vi. 27. 6
sownd, Which through the wood *loud* bellowing did rebownd, . I. vii. 7. 5
Duessa *loud* to him gan crye, ... I. vii. 14. 4
lowd did call With all his powre, ... I. viii. 37. 7
loud he yelled for exceeding paine; . . . . I. xi. 37. 2
her *lowd* salutes the mounting larke. . . . . I. xi. 51. 9
to his Lord and Lady *lowd* gan call, ... I. xii. 2. 8
Their Lord and Patrone *loud* did him proclame, ... I. xii. 6. 3
to Diana calling *lowd* for ayde, ... II. ii. 8. 4
lowde thunder . . . Did rend the ratling skyes . . . . II. ii. 20. 8
her two other sisters, . . . Her *lowd* gainsaid, ... II. ii. 28. 2
crying, 'Mercy!' *loud,* . . . . II. iii. 6. 9
with big thundring voice revyld him *lowd:* . . . . II. iii. 7. 3
loud he cryde; . . . . II. iii. 8. 2
Sometimes she song as *lowd* as larke in ayre, ... II. vi. 3. 3
*with a *loud* lay she thus him sweetly charm'd. . . . . . . II. vi. 14. 9
'I burne, I burne, I burne!' then *lowd* he cryde, ... II. vi. 44. 1
a voyce that called *lowd* and cleare, ... II. viii. 3. 7
For very felnesse *lowd* he gan to weepe, ... II. viii. 37. 5
lowd unto the knights did call, ... II. ix. 11. 7
His larumbell might *lowd* and wyde be hard . . . . II. ix. 25. 7
loud to them can call, ... II. xii. 15. 1
lowd to them for succour called evermore. . . . . II. xii. 27. 9
sweet Zephyrus *lowd* whisteled His treble, ... II. xii. 33. 5
Now soft, now *loud,* unto the wind did call; . . . . II. xii. 71. 8
oftentimes *loud* strokes and ringing sowndes . . . . III. iii. 9. 8
The wofull husbandman doth *lowd* complaine . . . . III. vii. 34. 7
the beast, that *lowd* did rore . . . . III. vii. 36. 3
he stampt, he *lowd* did cry, ... III. x. 17. 7
shrill trompets *lowd* did bray, ... III. xii. 6. 6
shril trompets and *loud* clarions sweetly playd. . . . . . . IV. iii. 5. 9
now the Owle *Lowde* shriking, ... IV. v. 41. 9
I cal'd her *loud,* I sought her farre and neare, ... IV. vi. 36. 8
all the way full *loud* for aide did crie, ... IV. viii. 38. 4
Chirpe *loud* to thee out of their leavy cages, ... IV. x. 45. 8
on him catching hold gan *loud* to crie, ... V. i. 18. 2
In vaine *loud* crying, ... V. ii. 27. 2
To Marinell, whose name the Heralds *loud* resounded. . . . . V. iii. 6. 9
Then for that stranger knight they *loud* did call, ... V. iii. 14. 5
They shouted *loud,* and signes of gladnesse all did shew. . . . V. iii. 23. 9
sounding *loud* a Trumpet from the wall, ... V. iv. 50. 3
Yet did she not lament with *loude* alew, ... V. vi. 13. 8
caused streight a Trumpet *loud* to shrill . . . . V. vii. 27. 1
laught so *loud,* that all his teeth wide bare . . . . V. xi. 9. 7
Thereat he brayed *loud,* and yelled dreadfully. . . . . V. xii. 20. 9
a ruefull shrieke Of one *loud* crying, ... VI. i. 17. 2
loude to him he cryde: . . . . VI. i. 18. 6
he for dread of death gan *loude* to crie . . . . VI. i. 22. 8
piteously complayning With *loud* laments . . . . VI. i. 41. 3
And called oft with prayers *loud* and shrill, ... VI. iii. 49. 7
Drawne with that Ladies *loud* and piteous shright, ... VI. iv. 2. 3
shouted all, and made a *loud* alarme. . . . . VI. viii. 45. 9
being waked with these *loud* alarmes, ... VI. viii. 47. 7
Wringing her hands, and ruefully *loud* crying? . . . . VI. xi. 23. 7
Led with the infants cry that *loud* did weepe, ... VI. xii. 9. 3
loud profest His foolish thought: . . . . VII. vi. 46. 5
Did ring againe, and *loud* re-eccho to the skie. . . . . VII. vi. 52. 9
A gentle Bee, with hir *loud* trumpet murm'ring, ... *Epig.* iv. 3
Then I thy soverayne prayses *loud* wil sing, ... *Epith.* 127
loud advaunce her laud; . . . . *Epith.* 145
But blush to heare her prayses sung so *loud,* . . . . *Epith.* 163
Nathlesse doe ye still *loud* her prayses sing, ... *Epith.* 165

Louder. Roaring yet *lowder* that all harts it daunted, ... *Hub.* 1368
Then gan she cry much *louder* then afore, ... V. xi. 30. 1

Loudly. Causelesse complained, and *lowdly* cryed . . . . . . *S.C.* F. 148
lowdly she gan to call . . . . *S.C.* May 296
bells and bosses that full *lowdly* rung, ... *Hub.* 583
she *lowdly* did lament and shrike, ... *T.M.* 229
she *lowdly* gan to waile and shrike, ... *T.M.* 475
a voyce, which *loudly* to me called, ... *Ti.* 580
enrag'd she *loudly* gan to bray, ... I. i. 17. 5
they gan *loudly* bray, With hollow houling, ... I. iii. 23. 1
To weet what wight so *loudly* did lament. . . . . I. vi. 8. 4
impatient of unwonted payne, He *loudly* brayd . . . . I. viii. 11. 3
Unto the Gyaunt *lowdly* she gan call; . . . . I. viii. 20. 8
Then gan he *lowdly* through the house to call; . . . . I. viii. 29. 6
with the uncouth smart the Monster *lowdly* cryde. . . . . . . I. xi. 20. 9
He *lowdly* brayd, ... I. xi. 26. 2
when the Palmer saw, he *loudly* cryde, ... II. iv. 10. 1
all enraged thus him *loudly* shent; . . . . II. v. 5. 2
Fiercely approching to him *lowdly* cryde, ... II. v. 35. 3
He *lowdly* cald to such as were abord . . . . II. vi. 4. 2
lowdly cald; 'Help, helpe! O Archimage! . . . . II. vi. 48. 2
therewith *lowdly* laught: . . . . II. xii. 15. 4
gainst the craggy clifts did *loudly* rore, ... III. iv. 7. 5
she hid her face, and *lowdly* shright. . . . . III. viii. 32. 9
shrilling trompets *loudly* gan to bray, ... IV. iv. 48. 5
He *lowdly* gan to laugh, ... IV. v. 18. 2
Then gan she *loudly* cry, ... IV. ix. 7. 6
The Lyons rore; the Tygres *loudly* bray; . . . . IV. x. 46. 3
Where that same Damzell *lowdly* him bespake, ... V. iv. 50. 8
to their Queene for judgment *loudly* call, ... V. ix. 49. 8
They both arose, and at him *loudly* cryde, ... V. xii. 38. 4
he bayd and *loudly* barkt at mee, ... VI. i. 9. 5

Loudly—*Continued.*
The litle babe did *loudly* scrike and squall, . . . VI. iv. 18. 1
woman kynd, Which to her selfe lamenting *loudly* cryde, . . . VI. iv. 26. 8
with the noise, whilest he did *loudly* rore, . . . VI. vi. 22. 8
the beast doth rage and *loudly* rore; . . . VI. vii. 47. 6
For which it *loudly* cald, and pittifully cryde. . . . VI. xii. 8. 9
let the roring Organs *loudly* play . . . *Epith.* 218
Loud-thundering. swelling Neptune ne *lowd thundring* Jove . II. vi. 10. 7
Loup, -es. *See* **Loop, -s.**
Lour. Before that angry heavens list to *lowre,* . . . I. ii. 22. 4
When so the froward skye began to *lowre;* . . . III. v. 51. 7
secretly their hoste did on them *lowre,* . . . III. ix. 19. 3
Thereat all Knights gan laugh, and Ladies *lowre:* . . . IV. v. 19. 1
at them both Sir Paridell did *loure.* . . . IV. v. 24. 4
As he on whom the lucklesse stars did *lowre,* . . . V. v. 18. 5
th' offended heavens list to *lowre* Upon their blisse, . . . V. x. 26. 6
he would *loure* And byte his lip, . . . VI. ix. 39. 2
Where-at the Titanesse did sternly *lower,* . . . VII. vi. 18. 4
when ye *lowre,* or looke on me askew, . . . *Am.* vii. 7
Lourd. thous but a laesie *loord,* . . . *S.C.* Jul. 33
A laesy *loord,* for nothing good to donne, . . . III. vii. 12. 3
Loure. *See* **Lower.**
Loured. He *lowrd* on her with daungerous eyeglaunce, . . . III. xii. 15. 4
Shame *lowrd,* Repentaunce sighd, Reproch did scould; . . . III. xii. 24. 6
Louring. as the *lowring* Wether lookes downe, . . . *S.C.* F. 29
since faire Sunne hath sperst that *lowring* clowd, . . . I. iv. 48. 1
with bent *lowring* browes, . . . II. ii. 35. 7
Lout. The Porter eke to her did *lout* with humble gestes. . . . II. ix. 26. 9
I joy to see you *lout* so low on ground, . . . IV. vi. 28. 7
much disdaining unto him to *lout,* . . . IV. x. 19. 2
none disdained low to him to *lout:* . . . IV. xi. 30. 5
maintaine The Ladies part, and to the Souldan *lout:* . . . V. viii. 50. 4
Unto thy love that made thee low to *lout:* . . . VI. x. 16. 7
Louted. So *lowted* he unto hys Lord, . . . *S.C.* Jul. 137
He humbly *louted* in meeke lowlinesse, . . . I. x. 44. 6
comming him before low *louted* on the lay. . . . III. x. 23. 9
to him *louted* low, and greeted . . . III. x. 37. 9
Thrise *lowted* lowly to the noble Mayd, . . . IV. iii. 5. 8
He *louted* lowly, as did him becum, . . . IV. vii. 44. 7
friskt, and flong aloft, and *louted* low on knee. . . . V. iii. 34. 9
Louteth. when the courting masker *louteth* lowe, . . . *Ti.* 202
Louthiane. *See* **Lothian.**
Louting. He faire the knight saluted, *louting* low, . . . I. i. 30. 1
louting lowly did begin To plaine of wronges, . . . II. iii. 13. 4
lowly to her *lowting* thus behight: . . . IV. ii. 23. 3
Louver. Ne lightned was with window, nor with *lover,* . . . VI. x. 42. 7
Love. *See* **Truelove.**
For pitie and *love* my heart yet burnes . . . *Pet.*[1] v. 12
yet *Love* she proudly did forsake: . . . *Pet.* vi. 4
Learne by their losse to *love* the low degree; . . . *Van.* xii. 10
'Ye Gods of *love,* that pitie lovers payne, . . . *S.C.* Ja. 13
Pan, thou shepheards God that once didst *love,* . . . *S.C.* Ja. 17
Ah, God! that *love* should breede both joy and payne! . . . *S.C.* Ja. 54
Albee my *love* he seeke with dayly suit; . . . *S.C.* Ja. 56
'I *love* thilke lasse, (alas! why doe I *love?*) . . . *S.C.* Ja. 61
Tho wouldest thou learne to caroll of *Love,* . . . *S.C.* F. 61
Thou art a fon of thy *love* to boste; . . . *S.C.* F. 69
All that is lent to *love* wyll be lost. . . . *S.C.* F. 70
Weenest of *love* is not his mynd? . . . *S.C.* F. 76
And some of *love,* and some of chevalrie? . . . *S.C.* F. 99
Tho will we little *Love* awake, . . . *S.C.* Mar. 22
lustie *Love* still sleepeth not, . . . *S.C.* Mar. 26
Perdie with *Love* thou diddest fight: . . . *S.C.* Mar. 104
To be wise, and eke to *love,* . . . *S.C.* Mar. Emb. 1
Of Hony and of Gaule in *love* . . . *S.C.* Mar. Emb. 3
Nowe loves a lasse that all his *love* doth scorne. . . . *S.C.* Ap. 11
Ys *love* such pinching payne to them that prove? . . . *S.C.* Ap. 18
Yet hath so little skill to brydle *love?* . . . *S.C.* Ap. 20
Him *Love* hath wounded with a deadly darte: . . . *S.C.* Ap. 22
Ah, foolish Boy! that is with *love* yblent: . . . *S.C.* Ap. 155
for the *love* of the glasse he did see. . . . *S.C.* May 283
walke withouten lincks of *love,* . . . *S.C.* Jun. 34
Tho couth I sing of *love,* . . . *S.C.* Jun. 41
her, whose *love* as lyfe I wayd, . . . *S.C.* Jun. 47
shepheards all that bene with *love* ytake: . . . *S.C.* Jun. 84
which *love* within his heart had bredd, . . . *S.C.* Jun. 86
should my plaints . . . Flye to my *love,* . . . *S.C.* Jun. 99
Whose *love* he bought to deare; . . . *S.C.* Jul. 148
To *love* the lowe degree); . . . *S.C.* Jul. 220
Love hath misled both my younglings and mee: . . . *S.C.* Au. 17
So *love* into thy hart did streame: . . . *S.C.* Au. 84
Love is a curelesse sorrowe. . . . *S.C.* Au. 104
whether in paynefull *love* I pyne, . . . *S.C.* Au. 109
So learnd I *love* on a holye eve, . . . *S.C.* Au. 121
since thence my *love* did part, . . . *S.C.* Au. 161
for *love* of that is to thee moste leefe, . . . *S.C.* S. 11
Of *love* and lustihead tho mayst thou sing, . . . *S.C.* O. 51
were he not with *love* so ill bedight, . . . *S.C.* O. 89
love does teach him climbe so hie, . . . *S.C.* O. 91
lofty *love* doth loath a lowly eye. . . . *S.C.* O. 96
lordly *love* is such a Tyranne fell, . . . *S.C.* O. 98
Nor Pan to herye, nor with *love* to playe; . . . *S.C.* N. 10
looser songs of *love* to underfong, . . . *S.C.* N. 22
Thus gan he make of *love* his piteous mone. . . . *S.C.* D. 6
Love they him called . . . *S.C.* D. 53
love then in the Lyons house did dwell) . . . *S.C.* D. 57
'Adieu, my deare, whose *love* I bought so deare, . . . *S.C.* D. 152
sweete *love* of pardon worthie is, . . . *Gn.* 473
th' other was with Thetis *love* assaid, . . . *Gn.* 491
Seeing his beautie, in *love* with it fell. . . . *Gn.* 680

Love—*Continued.*
askt an almes for Gods deare *love.* . . . *Hub.* 363
Loving that *love,* and hating those that hate; . . . *Hub.* 428
common Courtiers *love* to gybe and fleare . . . *Hub.* 714
whenso *love* of letters did inspire Their gentle wits, . . . *Hub.* 829
Love and Lordship bide no paragone. . . . *Hub.* 1026
Thoughts halfe devine, full of the fire of *love,* . . . *T.M.* 363
those bitter stounds Of raging *love* . . . *T.M.* 374
those that *Love* with leawdnes fill. . . . *T.M.* 384
Love wont to be schoolmaster of my skill, . . . *T.M.* 385
Sweete *Love* devoyd of villanie or ill, . . . *T.M.* 387
rime at riot, and doo rage in *love;* . . . *T.M.* 395
thy gay Sonne, that winged God of *Love,* . . . *T.M.* 401
He sings of *love,* and maketh loving layes, . . . *T.M.* 413
love of blindnesse and of ignorance, . . . *T.M.* 485
His *love,* his truth, his glorie, and his might, . . . *T.M.* 513
least he my *Loove* happely chaunce to beholde. . . . *Tetrasticon* 4
fly forth unto my *Love* whersoever she be: . . . *U.V.* 3
Waking *Love* suffereth no sleepe: . . . *U.V.* 10
raging *Love* dothe appall the weake stomacke: . . . *U.V.* 11
lamenting *Love* marreth the Musicall. . . . *U.V.* 12
did the losse of some dere *love* lament, . . . *Ti.* 16
thy lost deare *love* deplore. . . . *Ti.* 250
In whom all bountie and all vertuous *love* Appeared . . . *Ti.* 283
Too soone for all that did his *love* embrace, . . . *Ti.* 292
Whom the Pierian sacred sisters *love,* . . . *Ti.* 394
her *Love* would her provide; . . . *Mui.* 108
Her sonne to Psyche secrete *love* did beare, . . . *Mui.* 131
Before the Bull she pictur'd winged *Love,* . . . *Mui.* 289
As in their Syres new *love* both triumphing: . . . *Mui.* 294
(Signe of thy *love,* though nought for my reliefe, . . . *D.* 94
reft fro me my *love,* my life, my hart: . . . *D.* 160
The praises of my parted *love* envy, . . . *D.* 226
"Alcyon! ah, my first and latest *love!* . . . *D.* 263
the late *love* the which betwixt us past, . . . *D.* 289
in lieu of mee, *Love* her; . . . *D.* 291
so shall our *love* for ever last. . . . *D.* 291
she, my *love* that was, my Saint that is . . . *D.* 379
Me from my *love,* and eke my *love* from me; . . . *D.* 401
To see all things, and not my *love* to see; . . . *D.* 408
because I doo not finde My *love* with them, . . . *D.* 424
Young Astrophel, the rusticke lasses *love:* . . . *As.* 8
layes of *love* he also could compose: . . . *As.* 35
For her that did his heart with *love* inflame. . . . *As.* 40
Her he did *love,* her he alone did honor, . . . *As.* 59
Her, and but her, of *love* he worthie deemed; . . . *As.* 65
unto . . . His dearest *love,* him dolefully did beare. . . . *As.* 148
when she saw her *love* in such a plight, . . . *As.* 151
were in *love* so firmly tide. . . . *As.* 180
Laies of sweet *love,* without rebuke or blame, . . . *Col.* 3
'Nor of my *love,* nor of my lasse . . . *Col.* 88
love had me forlorne, forlorne of me, . . . *Col.* 90
of my river Bregogs *love* I soong, . . . *Col.* 92
love will not be drawne, but must be ledde; . . . *Col.* 129
So secretly did he his *love* enjoy . . . *Col.* 145
so deare his *love* he bought.' . . . *Col.* 155
tourn Sweet layes of *love* to endlesse plaints of pittie. . . . *Col.* 387
The blossome of sweet joy and perfect *love,* . . . *Col.* 470
To her my *love* I lowly do prostrate, . . . *Col.* 474
My thought, my heart, my *love,* my life is shee, . . . *Col.* 476
thy true *love* and loyaltie I deeme. . . . *Col.* 575
Vaine votaries of laesie *Love* professe, . . . *Col.* 766
is *Love* then . . . once knowne In Court, . . . *Col.* 771
Love most aboundeth there. . . . *Col.* 775
All full of *love,* and *love,* and *love* my deare, . . . *Col.* 777
Unlesse he swim in *love* up to the eares. . . . *Col.* 782
they of *love,* and of his sacred lere, . . . *Col.* 783
some celestiall rage Of *Love* . . . is breath'd into thy brest, . *Col.* 824
Albe of *love* I alwayes humbly deemed, . . . *Col.* 828
gan by litle learne to *love* each other: . . . *Col.* 852
Thenceforth they gan each one his like to *love,* . . . *Col.* 863
Chose for his *love* the fairest in his sight. . . . *Col.* 869
Then do they cry and call to *love* apace, . . . *Col.* 879
love is Lord of all the world by right, . . . *Col.* 883
doth not merit The name of *love,* . . . *Col.* 892
thou now full deeply hast divynd Of *Love* and beautie; . . . *Col.* 897
who can *love* compell? . . . *Col.* 914
sith her I may not *love:* . . . *Col.* 940
for the *love* which thou doest beare . . . *Ded. Son.* iii. 10
so *love* That loves and honours thee, . . . *Ded. Son.* iii. 13
And dainty *love* learnd sweetly to endite. . . . *Ded. Son.* viii. 7
For *love* of vertue and of Martiall praise; . . . *Ded. Son.* x. 6
Love him that hath eternized your name. . . . *Ded. Son.* xiv. 14
'Ah Sir, my liege Lord, and my *love,* . . . I. i. 51. 1
For hoped *love* to winne me certaine hate? . . . I. i. 51. 5
'*Love* of your selfe' . . . Lets me not sleepe, . . . I. i. 53. 1
Her fawning *love* . . . He would not shend; . . . I. i. 53. 7
all so deare as life is to my hart, I deeme your *love,* . . . I. i. 54. 3
whose deepe wounded mind With *love* . . . did languish, . . . I. ii. 24. 9
that happened . . . to this wretched Lady, my deare *love;* . . . I. ii. 31. 6
O, too deare *love, love* bought with death too deare!' . . . I. ii. 31. 7
when corage hott The fire of *love,* . . . First kindled . . . I. ii. 35. 2
it was my lott To *love* this gentle Lady, . . . I. ii. 35. 4
Forsaken Truth long seekes her *love,* . . . I. iii. Arg.
that . . . Greeke, That for his *love* refused deitye. . . . I. iii. 21. 6
true *love* hath no powre To looken backe; . . . I. iii. 30. 7
there is no greater shame Then . . . inconstancie in *love:* . . . I. iv. 1. 8
he . . . learned had to *love* with secret lookes; . . . I. iv. 25. 6
Inconstant man, that . . . lusted after all that he did *love;* . . . I. iv. 26. 2
His dearest *love,* . . . Is there possessed of the traytour vile; . . . I. iv. 42. 2

Love—*Continued.*

to you eke longes his *love*. . . . . I. iv. 48. 6
Let not his *love*, . . . Be unreveng'd, ... I. iv. 48. 7
prowest knight, That ever Ladie to her *love* did chose, ... I. v. 14. 3
Ladies *love* as losse of time forbore: . . . . I. v. 37. 4
Her *love* she turnd to hate, ... I. v. 37. 7
for his *love*, . . . She wandred had from one to other Ynd, . . I. vi. 2. 6
greater conquest of hard *love* he gaynes, ... I. vi. 3. 8
By vew of her he ginneth to revive His ancient *love*, ... I. vi. 17. 2
which the lovely boy Did *love* as life, ... I. vi. 17. 7
Then serve his Ladies *love*, and waste in pleasures vayne. . . I. vi. 21. 9
with *love* revokt from vaine affright, ... I. vi. 28. 3
For *love* of me leave off this dreadfull play; . . . . I. vi. 28. 7
himselfe doth hate, To *love* another: . . . . I. vi. 47. 6
threds . . . The which my life and *love* together tyde? . . . . I. vii. 22. 6
love fresh coles unto her fire did lay; . . . . I. vii. 27. 5
greater *love*, the greater is the losse. . . . . I. vii. 27. 6
she did *love* the knight of the Redcrosse, ... I. vii. 27. 8
the breach Which *love* and fortune in her heart had wrought; I. vii. 42. 4
I him lov'd, and *love* with all my might. . . . . I. vii. 49. 8
Her *love* is firme, her care continuall, ... I. viii. 1. 5
Love! lay down thy bow, the whiles I may respyre. . . . . . I. ix. 8. 9
To kindle *love* in every living brest: . . . . I. ix. 9. 4
'That ydle name of *love* . . . I ever scornd, ... I. ix. 10. 1
She . . . badd me *love* her deare; . . . . I. ix. 14. 2
dearely sure her *love* was to me bent, ... I. ix. 14. 3
Next to that Ladies *love*, shalbe the place, ... I. ix. 17. 2
love establish each to other trew, ... I. ix. 18. 7
Arthur on his way To seeke his *love*, ... I. ix. 20. 2
'For Gods deare *love*, Sir knight, doe me not stay; . . . . . I. ix. 25. 1
griefe, Which *love* had launched with his deadly darts, ... I. ix. 29. 3
hope . . . That earst us held in *love* of lingring life; . . . . I. ix. 29. 6
a woman . . . Full of great *love*, ... I. x. 30. 5
Of *love*, and righteousness, and well to donne; . . . . I. x. 33. 4
Ladies *love* to leave, so dearely bought? . . . . I. x. 62. 6
he already plighted his right hand Unto another *love*, ... I. xii. 26. 9
Here heaped up with termes of *love* unkynd, ... I. xii. 30. 4
breach of *love* and loialty betrayd. . . . . I. xii. 31. 5
one sung a song of *love* and jollity. . . . . I. xii. 38. 9
For Gods deare *love* be not so wilfull bent, ... II. i. 16. 2
My Lord, my *love*, my deare Lord, my deare *love!* . . . . . II. i. 50. 2
losse of *love* to her that loves to live, ... II. i. 55. 5
(So *love* does loath disdainefull nicitee) . . . . II. ii. 3. 3
to these Ladies *love* did countenaunce, ... II. ii. 16. 8
made *love* unto the eldest Dame, ... II. ii. 17. 1
chose for *love* to fight. . . . . II. ii. 18. 9
All for their Ladies froward *love* to gaine, ... II. ii. 26. 4
So *love* does raine In stoutest minds, ... II. ii. 26. 5
of her *love* too lavish: . . . . II. ii. 36. 9
For *Love* his loftie triumphes to engrave, ... II. iii. 24. 3
thou maist *love*, and dearly loved be, ... II. iii. 39. 6
As feates of armes, and *love* to entertaine: . . . . II. iv. 1. 6
Our sleves in league of vowed *love* wee knitt, ... II. iv. 18. 6
To *love* a Lady fayre of great degree, ... II. iv. 19. 2
seemd no lesse to *love* then lov'd to bee: . . . . II. iv. 19. 5
Love, that two harts makes one, ... II. iv. 19. 8
Of all my *love* and all my privitie; . . . . II. iv. 20. 2
of my *love* was partener Paramoure: . . . . II. iv. 24. 4
drive me to withdraw my blind abused *love*. . . . . II. iv. 24. 9
proud through praise and mad through *love*, ... II. iv. 27. 1
Whom he had feignd th' abuser of my *love* to bee. . . . . . . II. iv. 27. 9
weend it was my *love* with whom he playd. . . . . II. iv. 28. 5
Soone as my loathed *love* appeard in sight, ... II. iv. 29. 3
To losse of *love* adjoyning losse of frend, ... II. iv. 31. 2
Wrath, gelosy, griefe, *love*, this Squyre have laide thus low. II. iv. 34. 9
'Wrath, gealosie, griefe, *love*, do thus expell: . . . . II. iv. 35. 1
Griefe is a flood; and *love* a monster fell: . . . . II. iv. 35. 3
So shall wrath, gealosy, griefe, *love*, die and decay.' . . . . II. iv. 35. 9
Direfull impatience, and hart-murdring *love*: . . . . II. v. 16. 4
To serve his Lemans *love*: . . . . II. v. 28. 2
if thou meane her *love* to gayn. . . . . II. vi. 28. 6
'If ever *love* of Lady did empierce Your yron brestes, ... II. vi. 33. 1
Another warre, and other weapons, I Doe *love*, ... II. vi. 34. 7
where *love* does give his sweet Alarmes Without bloodshed, . . II. vi. 34. 7
Of *love* they ever greater glory bore . . . . II. vi. 35. 6
(So *Love* the dread of daunger doth despise) . . . . II. vi. 46. 2
love avowd to other Lady late, ... II. vii. 50. 7
To chaunge *love* causelesse is reproch to warlike knight.' . . II. vii. 50. 9
And is there *love* In heavenly spirits . . . . II. viii. 1. 2
all for *love*, and nothing for reward. . . . . II. viii. 2. 8
'For knighthoods *love* doe not so fowle a deed, ... II. viii. 16. 2
If that your lives ye *love*, ... II. ix. 12. 2
Or doen you *love?* or doen you lack your will? . . . . II. ix. 37. 8
Such was the end that to disloyall *love* did fall. . . . . . . II. x. 19. 9
which of them most did *love* her parentage? . . . . II. x. 27. 9
Regan greater *love* to him profest Then all the world, ... II. x. 28. 3
love is not where most it is profest; . . . . II. x. 31. 2
His falsed fayth, and *love* too lightly flitt; . . . . II. xii. 44. 7
Fayre Daphne Phoebus hart with *love* did gore; . . . . II. xii. 52. 5
Gather the Rose of *love* whilest yet is time, ... II. xii. 75. 8
(*love* far sought alas!) . . . . III. i. 8. 8
Ne reckt of Ladies *Love*, ... III. i. 19. 3
To chaunge my liefe, and *love* another Dame; . . . . III. i. 24. 3
For I *love* one, the truest one on grownd, ... III. i. 24. 6
losse of *love* to him that loves but one: . . . . III. i. 25. 6
Ne may *love* be compeld by maistery; . . . . III. i. 25. 7
sweet *Love* anone Taketh his nimble winges, ... III. i. 25. 8
In case he have no Lady nor no *love*, ... III. i. 26. 8
'But if he have a Lady or a *Love*, ... III. i. 27. 1
have our Ladies *love* for his reward. . . . . III. i. 27. 9

Love—*Continued.*

'Therefore aread, Sir, if thou have a *love*.' . . . . III. i. 28. 1
'*Love* have I sure,' (quoth she) 'but Lady none; . . . . . . III. i. 28. 2
Yet will I not fro mine own *love* remove, ... III. i. 28. 3
trew *love* most of might, ... III. i. 29. 8
The *love* of Venus and her Paramoure, ... III. i. 34. 4
joyd his *love* in secret unespyde: . . . . III. i. 37. 2
Ay caroling of *love* and jollity, ... III. i. 40. 5
Faire Ladies, that to *love* captived arre, ... III. i. 49. 1
this was not to *love*, but lust, inclind; . . . . III. i. 49. 7
love does alwaies bring forth bounteous deeds, ... III. i. 49. 8
Nought so of *love* this looser Dame did skill, ... III. i. 50. 1
Such *love* is hate, and such desire is shame. . . . . III. i. 50. 5
she did prepare Way to her *love*, ... III. i. 51. 8
imperious *love* her hart did vexe, ... III. i. 54. 4
great rebuke it is *love* to despise, ... III. i. 55. 3
shee inly deemd Her *love* too light, ... III. i. 55. 7
Some to make *love*, some to make meryment, ... III. i. 57. 2
she In *love* with him did fall. . . . . III. ii. Arg.
To heare her *Love* so highly magnifyde; . . . . III. ii. 11. 2
yield the pray of *love* to lothsome death at last. . . . . . . III. ii. 17. 9
much more straungely gan to *love* his sight, ... III. ii. 18. 2
when his *love* was false he with a peaze it brake. . . . . . . III. ii. 20. 9
Imperious *Love* hath highest set his throne, ... III. ii. 23. 2
the fether in her lofty crest, Ruffed of *love*, ... III. ii. 27. 2
thought it was not *love*, but some melancholy. . . . . III. ii. 27. 9
how much I feare least *love* it bee! . . . . III. ii. 33. 1
if that *love* it be, as sure I read . . . . III. ii. 33. 2
yet *love* can higher stye Then reasons reach, ... III. ii. 36. 5
neither God of *love* nor God of skye . . . . III. ii. 36. 7
love hath gryde My feeble brest of late, ... III. ii. 37. 8
To *love* the semblaunt pleasing most your minde, ... III. ii. 40. 7
No guilt in you, but in the tyranny of *love*. . . . . III. ii. 40. 9
Sweete *love* such lewdnes bands from his faire companee. . . III. ii. 41. 9
though my *love* be not so lewdly bent . . . . III. ii. 43. 2
was with the *love* thereof beguyld; . . . . III. ii. 44. 8
I, fonder, *love* a shade, the body far exyld.' . . . . III. ii. 44. 9
Both *love* and lover, without hope of joy, ... III. ii. 45. 3
needs *love* or death must bee thy lott, ... III. ii. 46. 7
So thought she to undoe her daughters *love*; . . . . III. ii. 51. 6
love, that is in gentle brest begonne, ... III. ii. 51. 7
thence pourd into men, which men call *Love!* . . . . III. iii. 1. 4
that sweete fit that doth true beautie *love*, ... III. iii. 1. 7
by what means his *love* might best be wrought: . . . . III. iii. 6. 6
the hardy Mayd (with *love* to frend) . . . . III. iii. 14. 5
by fatall lore Hast learn'd to *love*, ... III. iii. 21. 7
To *love* the prowest knight that ever was. . . . . III. iii. 24. 7
for her sake And *love*, ... III. iii. 56. 7
A friendly league of *love* perpetuall . . . . III. iv. 4. 4
such as fittest she for *love* could find, ... III. iv. 5. 8
love it steres, and fortune rowes: . . . . III. iv. 9. 5
Love, my lewd Pilott, hath a restlesse minde; . . . . III. iv. 9. 6
Love and despight attonce her courage kindled hath. . . . . III. iv. 12. 9
Was taken with her *love*, and by her closely lay. . . . . . . III. iv. 19. 9
The *love* of women not to entertaine; . . . . III. iv. 26. 2
From *love* in course of nature to refraine. . . . . III. iv. 26. 4
ever from fayre Ladies *love* did fly; . . . . III. iv. 26. 6
they for *love* of him would algates dy: . . . . III. iv. 26. 8
His mother bad him wemens *love* to hate, ... III. iv. 27. 7
vainely did expownd To be hart-wownding *love*, ... III. iv. 28. 4
I feared *love*; but they that *love* doe live, ... III. iv. 37. 5
they that dye doe nether *love* nor hate: . . . . III. iv. 37. 6
Ladies *love* unto his Lord forlent, ... III. iv. 47. 2
doth *love* to steepe His lustlesse limbes, ... III. iv. 56. 5
all that lewdnesse *love* doe hate the light to see. . . . . . . III. iv. 58. 9
How diversly *love* doth his pageaunts play, ... III. v. 1. 2
Ladies *love* his mother long ygoe Did him, they say, forwarne III. v. 9. 6
for *love* of knighthood gent, ... III. v. 10. 5
love so fayre a Lady that his life releast? . . . . III. v. 43. 9
love for to dislodge out of his nest: . . . . III. v. 44. 3
The same to *love* he strongly was constraynd; . . . . III. v. 44. 6
of his lucklesse lott and cruell *love* thus playnd: . . . . . . III. v. 44. 9
Dye rather, dy, then ever *love* disloyally. . . . . III. v. 45. 9
if to *love* disloyalty it bee, ... III. v. 46. 1
What can I lesse doe then her *love* therefore, ... III. v. 46. 4
of all *love* taketh equall vew; . . . . III. v. 47. 5
The *love* and service of the basest crew? . . . . III. v. 47. 7
Dye rather, dye, then ever so faire *love* forsake!' . . . . . . III. v. 47. 9
Litle shee weend that *love* he close conceald. . . . . III. v. 49. 4
in perfect *love* and spotlesse fame Of chastitie, ... III. v. 54. 3
Her little sonne, the winged god of *love*, ... III. vi. 11. 2
How he their heedelesse harts with *love* had fir'd, ... III. vi. 15. 4
the *love* of some of them him tyde: . . . . III. vi. 16. 7
To search the God of *love* her Nimphes she sent . . . . III. vi. 26. 1
sweete *love* gentle fitts emongst them throwes, ... III. vi. 41. 5
Phoebus paramoure And dearest *love*; . . . . III. vi. 45. 4
Stygian Gods, which doe her *love* envy; . . . . III. vi. 46. 7
That her sweet *love* his malice mote avoyd, ... III. vi. 48. 7
his trew *love* faire Psyche with him playes, ... III. vi. 50. 1
in stedfast *love* and happy state . . . . III. vi. 50. 6
all the lore of *love*, and goodly womanhead. . . . . III. vi. 51. 9
To be th' ensample of true *love* alone, ... III. vi. 52. 4
she to none of them her *love* did cast, ... III. vi. 53. 1
her loving hart she linked fast In faithfull *love*, ... III. vi. 53. 4
Her former *love* and stedfast loialty, ... III. vi. 53. 8
cast to *love* her in his brutish mind: . . . . III. vii. 15. 8
No *love*, but brutish lust, that was so beastly tind. . . . . . III. vii. 15. 9
love to frenzy turnd, sith *love* is franticke hight. . . . . . III. vii. 20. 9
That gentle Lady whom I *love* and serve, ... III. vii. 53. 6
Did aske me, how I could her *love* deserve, ... III. vii. 53. 8

Love—*Continued.*

the fairer *love* to gaine, . . . V. i. 24. 8
rather then his *love* should suffer paine, . . . V. i. 27. 7
True *love* despiseth shame, . . . V. i. 27. 9
you, Sir Knight, that *love* so light esteeme, . . . V. i. 28. 5
Love that same other Damzell, . . . V. iv. 9. 2
his owne *love* left astray. . . . V. iv. 9. 9
my land he first did winne away, And then my *love,* . . . V. iv. 14. 7
To whom she bore most fervent *love* of late, . . . V. iv. 30. 3
She turn'd her *love* to hatred manifold, . . . V. iv. 30. 7
he onely joyed In combats of sweet *love,* . . . V. v. 24. 9
with sweet *love* and sure benevolence, . . . V. v. 33. 4
With which thou canst even Jove himselfe to *love* entise.' . . . V. v. 34. 9
albe all *love* of men she scorne, . . . V. v. 40. 7
proudest harts base *love* hath blynded.' . . . V. v. 40. 9
all the wayes she sought his *love* for to have wonne: . . . V. v. 45. 9
to lerne So fond a lesson as to *love* againe: . . . V. v. 46. 4
his foes *love* or liking entertaine. . . . V. v. 46. 7
All which nathlesse she for his *love* forbore; . . . V. v. 54. 8
To his owne absent *love* to be untrew: . . . V. v. 56. 3
She daily told her *love* he did defye; . . . V. v. 56. 8
his worke lessened, that his *love* mote grow: . . . V. v. 57. 3
Untill his owne true *love* his freedome gayned: . . . V. v. 57. 8
With which those Amazons his *love* still craved, . . . V. vi. 2. 4
To his owne *love* his loialtie he saved: . . . V. vi. 2. 5
his owne *love,* the noble Britomart, . . . V. vi. 3. 1
Least some new *love* had him from her possest: . . . V. vi. 4. 7
Towards which coast her *love* his way addrest: . . . V. vi. 7. 5
To beare unto her *love* the message of her mind. . . . V. vi. 7. 9
it was one sent from her *love* indeede; . . . V. vi. 8. 4
your *love,* by hard mishap doth lie In wretched bondage, . . . V. vi. 10. 6
For yeelding to a straungers *love* so light, . . . V. vi. 12. 6
gan for grace and *love* of her to seeke; . . . V. vii. 16. 3
They doe thy *love* forlorne in womens thraldome see. . . . V. vii. 21. 9
she forward went To seeke her *love,* . . . V. vii. 24. 7
Unto the man whom thou doest *love* so deare; . . . V. vii. 32. 5
Thus answer'd: 'Lewdly thou my *love* depravest, . . . V. vii. 32. 8
In which her wretched *love* was captive layd: . . . V. vii. 37. 3
when as to her owne *Love* she came, . . . V. vii. 38. 1
left his *love,* albe her strong request, . . . V. viii. 3. 4
Working to all that *love* her deadly woe, . . . V. viii. 20. 8
Is mine owne *love,* though me she have forlore, . . . V. xi. 49. 7
To be my *love,* and take me for her Lord; . . . V. xi. 50. 2
Hoping thereby to have my *love* obtayned; . . . V. xi. 54. 6
Yet can I not my *love* have nathemore, . . . V. xi. 54. 7
That yet my *love* may from their hands be freed.' . . . V. xi. 57. 5
change of *love* for any worlds delight! . . . V. xi. 62. 5
Unto a strangers *love,* so lightly placed, . . . V. xi. 63. 2
To leave the *love* that ye before embraced, . . . V. xi. 63. 4
Dearer is *love* then life, and fame then gold; . . . V. xi. 63. 8
No *love* so lasting then, that may enduren long. . . . V. xii. 1. 9
the *love* of Lordship and of lands . . . V. xii. 2. 3
sought to win his *love* by all the meanes she might. . . . VI. i. 14. 9
Refused hath to yeeld her *love* againe, . . . VI. i. 15. 3
his *love,* which thus ye seeke t' obtaine.' . . . VI. i. 27. 5
Thy courteous lore, that doest my *love* deride, . . . VI. i. 27. 8
By which he had to her both life and *love* restord. . . . VI. i. 45. 9
a Ladie whom a knight should *love,* . . . VI. ii. 1. 2
bids him . . . to yeeld his *Love,* or else to fight: . . . VI. ii. 18. 5
To leave his *love* he should be ill apayd, . . . VI. ii. 18. 8
For *love* amongst the woodie Gods to dwell) . . . VI. ii. 26. 3
the high desire To *love* of armes, . . . VI. ii. 34. 5
which he did beare Both to her *love* and to her selfe . . . VI. ii. 46. 9
Ne could her liking to his *love* apply, . . . VI. iii. 7. 4
But by her wounded *love* did watch all night, . . . VI. iii. 10. 3
Gan breake to him the fortunes of his *love,* . . . VI. iii. 15. 2
He him by all the bands of *love* besought, . . . VI. iii. 15. 6
To safe-conduct his *love,* . . . VI. iii. 15. 8
In hope there for his *love* some succour to provyde. . . . VI. iii. 29. 9
But both himselfe revil'd and eke his *love;* . . . VI. iii. 42. 5
Calepine . . . his *love* doth misse. . . . VI. iv. Arg.
That he his *love* so lucklesse now had lost, . . . VI. iv. 40. 2
I was erewhile the *love* of Calepine; . . . VI. v. 28. 6
Was greatly growne in *love* of that brave pere,) . . . VI. v. 41. 8
Whereas his *love* was sitting all alone, . . . VI. vi. 30. 2
thy *love,* for lacke of hardiment, . . . hast shamed . . . VI. vi. 33. 7
To whom his life he graunted for her *love,* . . . VI. vi. 37. 3
Devizing of his *love* more then of daunger drad. . . . VI. vii. 6. 9
scornd them all that *love* unto her ment: . . . VI. vii. 29. 3
the more she did all *love* despize, . . . VI. vii. 30. 3
so would ever live, and *love* her owne delight. . . . VI. vii. 30. 9
Her stubborne hart, which *love* before disdayned, . . . VI. vii. 36. 7
whilest *love* lackt place, . . . VI. vii. 38. 7
how could her *love* make half amends therefore? . . . VI. vii. 38. 9
Love hath the glory of his kingdome left, . . . VI. viii. 1. 2
from you turne the *love* of men to hate: . . . VI. viii. 2. 6
'Stay, stay, Sir Knight! for *love* of God abstaine . . . VI. viii. 17. 5
The which the God of *love* hath on me layd, . . . VI. viii. 19. 7
let them *love* that list, . . . VI. viii. 21. 1
To *love* my selfe I learned had in schoole. . . . VI. viii. 21. 5
were no law in *love,* . . . His kingdome would continue but a while. . . . VI. viii. 23. 3
often did of *love,* and oft of lucke complaine. . . . VI. viii. 32. 9
For being of his *love* to her so light, . . . VI. viii. 33. 4
For *love* in soft delight thereon to rest; . . . VI. viii. 42. 3
the wretched stormes, In which his *love* was lost, . . . VI. viii. 47. 6
Layes of sweete *love* and youthes delightfull heat: . . . VI. ix. 4. 4
eke many a one Burnt in her *love,* . . . VI. ix. 10. 3
have learn'd to *love* more deare This lowly quiet life . . . VI. ix. 25. 8
Had ever learn'd to *love* the lowly things, . . . VI. ix. 35. 5

Love—*Continued.*

When he the *love* of fayre Oenone sought, . . . VI. ix. 36. 8
love so much could. . . . VI. ix. 37. 9
Long time had lov'd, and hop'd her *love* to gaine, . . . VI. ix. 38. 2
she did *love* a stranger swayne then him more dere. . . . VI. ix. 38. 9
Old *love* is litle worth when new is more prefard. . . . VI. ix. 40. 9
in her mynde the seeds Of perfect *love* did sow, . . . VI. ix. 45. 8
To winne the *love* of the faire Pastorell, . . . VI. ix. 46. 2
entrapt of *love,* which him betrayd, . . . VI. x. 1. 7
whose *love* his heart hath sore engrieved. . . . VI. x. 1. 9
the guerdon of his *love* to gaine; . . . VI. x. 2. 4
Unto thy *love* that made thee low to lout: . . . VI. x. 16. 7
Thy *love* is present there with thee in place; . . . VI. x. 16. 8
Thy *love* is there advaunst to be another Grace. . . . VI. x. 16. 9
her to his *love* allure, . . . VI. x. 32. 8
he colour might Both his estate and *love* . . . VI. x. 37. 9
of his *love* he reapt the timely frute, . . . VI. x. 38. 5
The joyes of *love,* if they should ever last . . . VI. xi. 1. 1
sought her *love* by all the meanes he mote; . . . VI. xi. 4. 7
To graunt him favour or afford him *love:* . . . VI. xi. 5. 4
when *love* he to her made, . . . VI. xi. 7. 1
his *love* should not be sold; . . . VI. xi. 14. 8
his *love* reft away, . . . VI. xi. 25. 3
Of which the best he did his *love* betake; . . . VI. xi. 51. 5
drove them all away, and his *love* with him bore. . . . VI. xi. 51. 9
with secret wound Of *love* to Bellamoure empierced were, . . . VI. xii. 4. 8
of her *love* he was entyrely seized, . . . VI. xii. 5. 3
to his *love* sometimes he came in place; . . . VI. xii. 6. 3
lived long in peace and *love* entyre, . . . VI. xii. 10. 7
he bethought To leave his *love,* . . . VI. xii. 13. 3
with the Nymphes the Satyres *love* to play and sport. . . . VII. vi. 39. 9
To be his *Love,* and of him liked well: . . . VII. vi. 44. 6
the *love* of some new Nymph, late seene, . . . VII. vii. 11. 6
That as some did him *love,* so others did him feare. . . . VII. vii. 28. 8
wondrous beauty fit to kindle *love;* . . . VII. vii. 45. 3
they were virgins all, and *love* eschewed . . . VII. vii. 45. 4
all that moveth doth mutation *love;* . . . VII. vii. 55. 8
love of things so vaine to cast away; . . . VII. viii. 1. 7
Which if she graunt, then live, and my *love* cherish: . . . *Am.* ii. 13
Fresh *Love,* that long hath slept . . . *Am.* iv. 6
Prepare your selfe new *love* to entertaine. . . . *Am.* iv. 14
Such *love,* not lyke to lusts of baser kynd, . . . *Am.* vi. 3
Then is my soule with life and *love* inspired: . . . *Am.* vii. 6
Unrighteous Lord of *Love,* what law is this, . . . *Am.* x. 1
Those engins can the proudest *love* convert: . . . *Am.* xiv. 12
my *love* doth in her selfe containe . . . *Am.* xv. 5
Therefore, O *Love,* unlesse she turne to thee . . . *Am.* xix. 13
She to her *love* doth lookers eyes allure; . . . *Am.* xxi. 6
fly no more, fayre *Love,* from Phebus chace, . . . *Am.* xxviii. 13
in your brest his leafe and *love* embrace. . . . *Am.* xxviii. 14
My *love* is lyke to yse, and I to fyre; . . . *Am.* xxx. 1
Such is the powre of *love* in gentle mind, . . . *Am.* xxx. 13
a proud *love,* that doth my spirite spoyle. . . . *Am.* xxxiii. 12
the daughter of the Queene of *Love,* . . . *Am.* xxxix. 1
The *love* which me so cruelly tormenteth, . . . *Am.* xlii. 1
The more I *love* and doe embrace my bane. . . . *Am.* xlii. 4
doth guyde Unto her *love,* and tempte to theyr decay; . . . *Am.* xlvii. 6
O mighty charm! which makes men *love* theyr bane, . . . *Am.* xlvii. 13
My *love,* lyke the Spectator, ydly sits; . . . *Am.* liv. 2
Not water; for her *love* doth burne like fyre: . . . *Am.* lv. 6
Base things, that to her *love* too bold aspire! . . . *Am.* lxi. 12
So, likewise, *Love!* cheare you your heavy spright, . . . *Am.* lxii. 13
The doubt which ye misdeeme, fayre *love,* is vaine, . . . *Am.* lxv. 1
true *love* doth tye . . . *Am.* lxv. 5
The league twixt them, that loyal *love* hath bound: . . . *Am.* lxv. 10
ye your *love* lent to so meane a one. . . . *Am.* lxvi. 4
thy *love* we weighing worthily, May likewise *love* thee for the same againe: . . . *Am.* lxviii. 9, 10
With *love* may one another entertayne! . . . *Am.* lxviii. 12
let us *love,* deare *love,* lyke as we ought: . . . *Am.* lxviii. 13
Love is the lesson which the Lord us taught. . . . *Am.* lxviii. 14
Adorn'd with honour, *love,* and chastity! . . . *Am.* lxix. 8
Goe to my *love,* where she is carelesse layd, . . . *Am.* lxx. 5
To wayt on *Love* amongst his lovely crew; . . . *Am.* lxx. 10
Make hast, therefore, sweet *love,* . . . *Am.* lxx. 13
thralled to his *love;* . . . *Am.* lxxi. 6
The third, my *love,* my lifes last ornament, . . . *Am.* lxxiv. 9
Our *love* shall live, and later life renew. . . . *Am.* lxxv. 14
The neast of *love,* the lodging of delight, . . . *Am.* lxxvi. 2
brought from Paradice By *Love* himselfe, . . . *Am.* lxxvii. 12
Lackyng my *love,* I go from place to place, . . . *Am.* lxxviii. 1
Fayre is my *love,* . . . *Am.* lxxxi. 1
in her eyes the fyre of *love* does sparke. . . . *Am.* lxxxi. 4
That are so much by so meane *love* embased. . . . *Am.* lxxxii. 4
In my true *love* did stirre up coles of yre; . . . *Am.* lxxxv. 8
Since I did leave the presence of my *love,* . . . *Am.* lxxxvi. 1
Mourne to my selfe the absence of my *love;* . . . *Am.* lxxxviii. 6
With that *Love* wounded my Loves hart, . . . *Epig.* ii. 7
Love lay sweetly slumbring . . . *Epig.* iv. 1
With his sharpe dart of *love:* . . . *Epig.* iv. 56
Which death, or *love,* or fortunes wreck did rayse, . . . *Epith.* 8
Go to the bowre of my beloved *love,* . . . *Epith.* 23
Another gay girland, For my fayre *love,* . . . *Epith.* 43
when you come whereas my *love* doth lie, . . . *Epith.* 65
Wake now, my *love,* awake! . . . *Epith.* 74
Ah! my deere *love,* why doe ye sleepe thus long, . . . *Epith.* 85
My *love* is now awake out of her dreames, . . . *Epith.* 92
Now is my *love* all ready forth to come: . . . *Epith.* 110
There dwels sweet *love,* and constant chastity, . . . *Epith.* 191
Open the temple gates unto my *love,* . . . *Epith.* 204

Love—*Continued.*
Why blush ye, *love,* to give to me your hand, . . . *Epith.* 238
lende me leave to come unto my *love?* . . . *Epith.* 279
glorious lampe of *love!* . . . *Epith.* 288
Behold how goodly my faire *love* does ly, . . . *Epith.* 305
leave my *love* alone, . . . *Epith.* 312
all my cares, which cruell *Love* collected, . . . *Epith.* 317
Spread thy broad wing over my *love* and me, . . . *Epith.* 319
do thou not envy My *love* with me to spy: . . . *Epith.* 377
For thou likewise didst *love,* . . . *Epith.* 378
So let us rest, sweet *love,* in hope of this, . . . *Epith.* 424
With which my *love* should duly have been dect, . . . *Epith.* 428
Love, that long since hast . . . subdude . . . *H.L.* 1
Come, then, O come, thou mightie God of *Love,* . . . *H.L.* 22
Love, that had now long time securely slept . . . *H.L.* 61
Love relented their rebellious yre. . . . *H.L.* 84
Therefore in choice of *love* he doth desyre . . . *H.L.* 110
Love doest laugh and scorne At their complaints, . . . *H.L.* 134
her Whose *love* before their life they doe prefer. . . . *H.L.* 140
Such fancies feele no *love,* but loose desyre. . . . *H.L.* 175
love is Lord of truth and loialtie, . . . *H.L.* 176
fyre Which kindleth *love* in generous desyre, . . . *H.L.* 187
to get his *love* retyre; . . . *H.L.* 235
love can not endure a Paragone. . . . *H.L.* 251
that monster placed In gentle *love,* . . . *H.L.* 272
O *Love!* thou doest thy entrance make . . . *H.L.* 273
whither, *Love!* wilt thou now carrie mee? . . . *H.B.* 1
Mother of *love,* and of all worlds delight, . . . *H.B.* 16
immortall Spright, By whom all live to *love,* . . . *H.B.* 108
gentle *Love,* that loiall is and trew, . . . *H.B.* 176
It you behoves to *love,* . . . *H.B.* 184
if you loosely *love* without respect, . . . *H.B.* 194
It is no *love,* but a discordant warre, . . . *H.B.* 195
Love is a celestiall harmonie . . . *H.B.* 197
all, that like the beautie . . . Streight do not *love;* . . . *H.B.* 209
for *Love* is not so light As streight to burne . . . *H.B.* 209
they, which *love* indeede, looke otherwise, . . . *H.B.* 211
Love, lift me up upon thy golden wings, . . . *H.H.L.* 1
Unto the God of *Love,* high heavens king. . . . *H.H.L.* 7
In praise of that mad fit which fooles call *love,* . . . *H.H.L.* 9
The heavenly prayses of true *love* to sing. . . . *H.H.L.* 14
That High Eternal Powre, . . . mov'd in it selfe by *love.* . . . *H.H.L.* 28
Yet being . . . full of fruitfull *love,* . . . *H.H.L.* 51
And caroll Hymnes of *love* both day and night. . . . *H.H.L.* 70
So that next off-spring of the Makers *love,* . . . *H.H.L.* 92
(for pride and *love* may ill agree) . . . *H.H.L.* 95
But that Eternall Fount of *love* and grace, . . . *H.H.L.* 99
He made by *love* out of His owne like mould, . . . *H.H.L.* 116
For *Love* doth *love* the thing belov'd to see, . . . *H.H.L.* 118
Till that great Lord of *Love,* which him at first . . . *H.H.L.* 127
which him at first Made of meere *love,* . . . *H.H.L.* 128
O blessed Well of *Love!* O Floure of Grace! . . . *H.H.L.* 169
Yet nought thou ask'st in lieu of all this *love,* . . . *H.H.L.* 176
Yet nought thou ask'st . . . But *love* of us, . . . *H.H.L.* 177
Him first to *love* that us so dearely bought, . . . *H.H.L.* 188
Him first to *love* great right and reason is, . . . *H.H.L.* 190
Then next, to *love* our brethren, . . . *H.H.L.* 197
Commaunded us to *love* them for his sake, . . . *H.H.L.* 205
We should them *love,* and with their needs partake; . . . *H.H.L.* 208
And *love* our brethren; thereby to approve . . . *H.H.L.* 216
to approve How much, himselfe that loved us, we *love.* . . . *H.H.L.* 217
read, through *love,* his mercies manifold. . . . *H.H.L.* 224
Learne him to *love* that loved thee so deare, . . . *H.H.L.* 258
Thou must him *love,* and his beheasts embrace; . . . *H.H.L.* 261
that shall thy feeble brest Inflame with *love,* . . . *H.H.L.* 270
With sweete enragement of celestiall *love,* . . . *H.H.L.* 286
Do kindle *love* in high conceipted sprights; . . . *H.H.B.* 5
And learne to *love,* with zealous humble dewty, . . . *H.H.B.* 20
His truth, his *love,* his wisedome, and his blis, . . . *H.H.B.* 110
that faire *love* of mightie heavens King; . . . *H.H.B.* 235
being thus with her huge *love* possest, . . . *H.H.B.* 237
That kindleth *love* in every godly spright . . . *H.H.B.* 297
That kindleth *love* . . . Even the *love* of God; . . . *H.H.B.* 298
when he a Swan would be, For *love* of Leda, . . . *Proth.* 43
faire Venus, that is Queene of *love,* . . . *Proth.* 96

Love-affamished. thereon feed my *love-affamisht* hart. . . . *Am.* lxxxvii. 12

Loved. *See* **Dear-loved, Self-loved.**
garnisht as a *loved* spouse. . . . *Rev.* iv. 4
May seeme he *lovd,* or els some care he tooke; . . . *S.C.* Ja. 9
Or art thou of thy *loved* lasse forlorne? . . . *S.C.* Ap. 4
the ladde, whome long I *lovd* so deare, . . . *S.C.* Ap. 10
Cowslips, and Kingcups, and *loved* Lillies: . . . *S.C.* Ap. 141
loved her most dere. . . . *S.C.* Jun. 112
loved their flocks to feede; . . . *S.C.* Jul. 166
The loftie verse of hem was *loved* aye. . . . *S.C.* O. 66
Whether thee list thy *loved* lasse advaunce, . . . *S.C.* N. 7
Adieu, my little Lambes and *loved* sheepe; . . . *S.C.* D. 153
that disguised Dog *lov'd* blood to spill, . . . *Hub.* 319
Her *loved* Twinnes, the dearlings of her joy, . . . *T.M.* 14
late him *loved* deare: . . . *Ti.* 193
living *loved* thee afore, . . . *Ti.* 339
Give leave to him that *lov'de* thee to lament . . . *Ti.* 676
The riddle of thy *loved* Lionesse; . . . *D.* 177
'My little flocke, whom earst I *lov'd* so well, . . . *D.* 344
unto his *loved* lasse . . . him dolefully did beare. . . . *As.* 147
The shepheards all which *loved* him full deare, . . . *As.* 200
sure full deare of all he *loved* was, . . . *As.* 201
As everie one in order *lov'd* him best, . . . *As.* Interl. 224
lov'd this shepheard dearest in degree, . . . *Col.* 14
carol made to praise thy *loved* lasse.' . . . *Col.* 87

Loved—*Continued.*
Full faine she *lov'd,* and was belov'd full faine . . . *Col.* 116
For having *loved* ever one most deare: . . . *Col.* 904
He so ungently left her, whome she *loved* best. . . . I. ii. 8. 9
'So doubly *lov'd* of ladies, unlike faire, . . . I. ii. 37. 1
to hate Her, that him *lov'd,* . . . I. iii. 7. 8
you to leave that have me *loved* stil, . . . I. iii. 28. 4
he of Ladies oft was *loved* deare, . . . I. iv. 24. 7
Inconstant man, that *loved* all he saw, . . . I. iv. 26. 1
evermore she hated, never *lov'd:* . . . I. v. 24. 9
His wanton stepdame *loved* him the more; . . . I. v. 37. 5
ever *lov'd* to fight for Ladies right; . . . I. vi. 20. 8
Was never Lady *loved* dearer day . . . I. vii. 27. 7
A gentle youth, his dearely *loved* Squire, . . . I. vii. 37. 1
How I him *lov'd,* . . . I. vii. 49. 8
To see his *loved* Squyre into such thraldom brought: . . . I. viii. 15. 9
From that day forth I *lov'd* that face divyne; . . . I. ix. 15. 5
He *lov'd,* as was his lot, a Lady gent, . . . I. ix. 27. 6
him againe *lov'd* in the least degree; . . . I. ix. 27. 7
what hath life that may it *loved* make . . . I. ix. 44. 4
she might spy Her *loved* knight . . . I. xi. 33. 7
he that *lov'd* the youngest was Sansloy; . . . II. ii. 18. 1
thou maist love, and dearly *loved* be, . . . II. iii. 39. 6
seemd no lesse to love then *lov'd* to bee: . . . II. iv. 19. 5
Lov'd of his freends, and of his foes eschewd: . . . II. x. 13. 3
He *lov'd* faire Ladie Estrild, leudly *lov'd,* . . . II. x. 17. 6
she much more than her owne life him *lov'd;* . . . II. x. 28. 2
Cordeill said she *lov'd* him as behoov'd: . . . II. x. 28. 5
Ida, where the Gods *lov'd* to repayre, . . . II. xii. 52. 6
Whilest loving thou mayst *loved* be with equall crime. . . . II. xii. 75. 9
To lodge the warlike maide, unwisely *loov'd;* . . . III. i. 60. 4
lov'd their native flesh against al kynd, . . . III. ii. 41. 3
lov'd a Bul, and learnd a beast to bee. . . . III. ii. 41. 6
To compas thy desire, and find that *loved* knight.' . . . III. ii. 46. 9
the Lady of the Lake, Whom long he *lov'd,* . . . III. iii. 10. 7
her whilome upon high Pindus hill He *loved,* . . . III. iv. 41. 5
Of my deare Dame is *loved* dearely well: . . . III. v. 9. 2
For him he *loved* above all mankinde, . . . III. v. 12. 7
her he dearely *loved,* and . . . highly magnifide: . . . III. vii. 31. 6
she a mortall creature *loved* best: . . . III. viii. 39. 7
she *lov'd* none, but a Faery knight. . . . III. viii. 39. 9
every one her likte, and every one her *lov'd.* . . . III. ix. 24. 9
lov'd so oft in vaine, . . . III. ix. 29. 8
His money which he *lov'd* as living breath; . . . III. x. 2. 8
was he loth to loose his *loved* Dame, . . . III. x. 15. 5
not for nought his wife them *loved* so well, . . . III. x. 48. 8
To love faire Daphne, which thee *loved* lesse; . . . III. xi. 36. 7
Lesse she thee *lov'd* then was thy just desart, . . . III. xi. 36. 8
He *loved* Isse for his dearest Dame, . . . III. xi. 39. 1
He *loved* eke Iphimedia deare, . . . III. xi. 42. 1
Whom of all living wightes she *loved* best. . . . III. xii. 41. 2
best is *lov'd* of all alive, I weene, . . . IV. Pr. 4. 7
Full many knights, that *loved* her like deare, . . . IV. ii. 26. 2
yet *lov'd* of Knights and Lords. . . . IV. ii. 35. 9
Full many Lords and many Knights her *loved,* . . . IV. ii. 36. 1
So much the more she *loved* was and sought, . . . IV. ii. 37. 2
lov'd in forests wyld to space. . . . IV. ii. 44. 9
They *loved* armes, and knighthood did ensew, . . . IV. ii. 46. 4
courtesie, That made them dearely *lov'd* . . . IV. iii. 2. 7
First to her brother, whom she *loved* deare, . . . IV. iii. 46. 6
So all alike did love, and *loved* were, . . . IV. iii. 52. 8
When first he *loved* her with heart entire, . . . IV. v. 4. 2
Unto the second best that *lov'd* her better; . . . IV. v. 21. 5
But Triamond *lov'd* Canacee, and other none. . . . IV. v. 21. 9
To seeke her *lov'd,* making blind love her guide. . . . IV. v. 29. 5
lov'd a Ladie of high parentage; . . . IV. viii. 50. 2
lov'd me deare, as dearest thing alive. . . . IV. viii. 56. 6
Aemylia well he *lov'd,* . . . IV. viii. 57. 8
the captive Squire she *lov'd* so deare, . . . IV. ix. 10. 6
Not to despise that dame which *lov'd* him liefe, . . . IV. ix. 15. 4
loved out of measure So eke *lov'd* Blandamour, . . . IV. ix. 21. 4, 5
learned to have *loved,* . . . IV. x. 1. 8
loved not as these for like intent, . . . IV. x. 26. 5
All *loved* vertue, . . . V. Pr. 9. 3
I *lov'd,* as was my lot, That further mayd, . . . V. iv. 8. 6
Then shalt thou take him to thy *loved* fere, . . . V. vii. 23. 5
For faire Irena, whom they *loved* deare: . . . V. xii. 10. 6
loved simple truth and stedfast honesty. . . . VI. i. 3. 9
She long time hath deare *lov'd* a doughty Knight, . . . VI. i. 14. 8
Which to your selfe he wrought and to your *loved* knight. . . . VI. ii. 45. 9
And *loved* all that did to armes incline; . . . VI. iii. 3. 6
But *lov'd* this fresh young Knight who dwelt her ny, . . . VI. iii. 7. 5
Yet was she *lov'd* of many a worthy pere: . . . VI. vii. 29. 4
Ne list me leave my *loved* libertie . . . VI. viii. 21. 3
Readie to launch her brest, and let out *loved* life. . . . VI. viii. 48. 9
Long time had *lov'd,* and hop'd her love to gaine, . . . VI. ix. 38. 2
knew Calidore right well, And *loved* for his prowesse, . . . VI. xii. 11. 3
Thence running forth unto her *loved* Lord, . . . VI. xii. 22. 1
shee had out of measure Long *lov'd* the Fanchin, . . . VII. vi. 44. 4
after Wrong was *lov'd,* and Justice solde, . . . VII. vii. 37. 8
heavenly formes ought rather worship be, Then dare be *lov'd* *Am.* lxi. 14
ye, faire Nimphs! which oftentimes have *loved* . . . *H.L.* 31
tempering . . . Their contrary dislikes with *loved* meanes, . . . *H.L.* 86
He may embosomd bee and *loved* best; . . . *H.L.* 249
yet not best, but to be *lov'd* alone; . . . *H.L.* 250
Thou that hast never *lov'd* canst not beleeve . . . *H.L.* 257
It *lov'd* it selfe, because it selfe was faire; . . . *H.H.L.* 29
It *lov'd* it selfe, . . . (For faire is *lov'd;*) . . . *H.H.L.* 30
As he himselfe hath *lov'd* us afore-hand, . . . *H.H.L.* 186
to approve How much, himselfe that *loved* us, we love. . . . *H.H.L.* 217

Loved—*Continued.*
Learne him to love that *loved* thee so deare, . . . *H.H.L.* 258
Lovedst. So *lovedst* thou the lusty Hyacinct; . . . III. xi. 37. 1
So *lovedst* thou the faire Coronis deare; . . . III. xi. 37. 2
Love-kindling. vouchsafe with thy *love-kindling* light . . . *H.B.* 19
Love-lads. When *love-lads* masken in fresh aray? . . . *S.C.* May 2
Love-lavish. *Love-lavish* Blandamour, and lustfull Paridell. . . . IV. ix. 20. 9
Love-lay. with a *love lay* she thus him sweetly charmd. . . . II. vi. 14. 9
Love-learned. *Love-learned* letters to her eyes to read; . . . *Am.* xliii. 12
the birds *love-learned* song, The deawy leaves among! . . . *Epith.* 88
Lovely. th' heavens looked *lovely* all the while, . . . *Van.* ix. 6
Hindering with his shade my *lovely* light, . . . *S.C.* F. 173
a fresh bend Of *lovely* Nymphs. . . . *S.C.* May 33
both fresh and *lovely* to see, . . . *S.C.* May 183
Thy *lovely* layes . . . freely boste. . . . *S.C.* Jun. 13
'Tho gan my *lovely* Spring bid me farewel, . . . *S.C.* D. 55
The same was able with like *lovely* lay . . . *Gn.* 461
whatso other hearb of *lovely* hew, . . . *Gn.* 682
Our *lovely* Lasses, or bright shining Brides: . . . *Hub.* 476
My *lovelie* Lionesse . . . So carefull was . . . *D.* 137
Record to us that *lovely* lay againe: . . . *Col.* 97
a *lovely* lasse, hight Lucida: . . . *Col.* 456
A *lovely* Ladie rode him faire beside, . . . I. i. 4. 1
With gentle blandishment and *lovely* looke, . . . I. i. 49. 8
His *lovely* words her seemd due recompence . . . I. iii. 30. 1
since my brest was launcht with *lovely* dart . . . I. iv. 46. 5
looking *lovely* and oft sighing sore, . . . I. vi. 4. 2
which the *lovely* boy Did love as life, . . . I. vi. 17. 6
Flocke all about to see her *lovely* face; . . . I. vi. 18. 4
With *lovely* court he gan her entertaine; . . . I. vii. 38. 2
yfere The vertues linked are in *lovely* wize; . . . I. ix. 1. 2
lovely blandishment She to me made, . . . I. ix. 14. 1
faire Charissa to a *lovely* fere Was lincked. . . . I. x. 4. 8
Ylinked arme in arme in *lovely* wise: . . . I. x. 12. 3
learned Ladies . . . make full many a *lovely* lay. . . . I. x. 54. 9
in her lap a *lovely* babe did play . . . II. i. 40. 5
lovely concord, and most sacred peace, . . . II. ii. 31. 1
No song but did containe a *lovely* ditt. . . . II. vi. 13. 4
The flowre-deluce, her *lovely* Paramoure, . . . II. vi. 16. 2
lovely peace, and gentle amity, . . . II. vi. 35. 3
A *lovely* bevy of faire Ladies sate, . . . II. ix. 34. 2
her *lovely* face The flashing blood with blushing did inflame, . II. ix. 43. 2
the Heavens . . . Lookte on them *lovely*, . . . II. xii. 51. 2
Nought but her *lovely* face she for his looking left. . . . II. xii. 67. 9
some one did chaunt this *lovely* lay: . . . II. xii. 74. 1
the birds song many a *lovely* lay . . . III. v. 40. 3
In which full many *lovely* Nymphes abyde; . . . III. vi. 16. 5
with soft sighes and *lovely* semblaunces . . . III. vii. 16. 6
a comely personage And *lovely* face, . . . III. vii. 46. 3
Upon his Courser sett the *lovely* lode, . . . III. viii. 19. 4
is he lincked to a *lovely* lasse, . . . III. ix. 4. 4
On faire Oenone got a *lovely* boy, . . . III. ix. 36. 4
of their *lovely* fellowship full glade, . . . III. x. 44. 8
Whereas his *lovely* wife emongst them lay, . . . III. x. 48. 2
To win faire Leda to his *lovely* trade: . . . III. xi. 32. 2
Long were to tell each other *lovely* fitt; . . . III. xi. 39. 6
Fansy, like a *lovely* Boy Of rare aspect, . . . III. xii. 7. 1
Hope . . . Of chearefull looke and *lovely* to behold: . . . III. xii. 13. 2
Marching in *lovely* wise, . . . IV. i. 4. 7
many a knight, and many a *lovely* Dame, . . . IV. i. 9. 3
Good lucke presents you with yond *lovely* mayd, . . . IV. i. 33. 8
the *lovely* paire drew nigh to hond: . . . IV. i. 34. 1
with whom now she goth In *lovely* wise, . . . IV. i. 47. 6
Two knights that lincked rode in *lovely* wise, . . . IV. ii. 30. 3
With Canacee and Cambine linckt in *lovely* bond. . . . IV. ii. 31. 9
Got these three *lovely* babes, . . . IV. ii. 45. 9
Entrayled mutually in *lovely* lore, . . . IV. iii. 42. 3
lovely haulst, from feare of treason free, . . . IV. iii. 49. 4
In *lovely* wise she gan that Lady greet, . . . IV. iii. 50. 6
Her *lovely* Amoret did open shew; . . . IV. v. 13. 2
taking with her *lovely* Amoret, . . . IV. v. 29. 3
Beheld the *lovely* face of Artegall . . . IV. vi. 26. 2
being whylome launcht with *lovely* dart, . . . IV. vi. 40. 5
The *lovely* Amoret, whose gentle hart Thou martyrest . . . IV. vii. 2. 4
with that *lovely* boy, . . . IV. vii. 23. 6
will not he the *lovely* spoile downe lay, . . . IV. vii. 25. 5
There she him found by that new *lovely* mate, . . . IV. vii. 35. 3
she chaunced there to see This *lovely* swaine, . . . IV. viii. 52. 5
Unwilling to behold that *lovely* band. . . . IV. x. 33. 5
Ne ought on earth that *lovely* is and fayre, . . . IV. x. 47. 4
Neleus and Pelias, *lovely* brethren both; . . . IV. xi. 14. 2
Soone after whom the *lovely* Bridegroome came, . . . IV. xi. 24. 2
the *lovely* Medua came, . . . IV. xi. 45. 1
Lovely Pasithee, kinde Eulimene, . . . IV. xi. 49. 3
The fift Armeddan, skild in *lovely* layes; . . . V. iii. 5. 7
Fit for such Ladies and such *lovely* knights; . . . V. iii. 40. 5
having lately left that *lovely* payre, . . . V. iv. 3. 1
Armies of *lovely* lookes, and speeches wise, . . . V. v. 34. 8
allure . . . As beauties *lovely* baite, . . . V. viii. 1. 3
All *lovely* daughters of high Jove, . . . V. ix. 31. 4
And unto him did shew all *lovely* courtesyes. . . . VI. ii. 16. 9
'Whom when my knight did see so *lovely* faire, . . . VI. ii. 17. 1
Seeing his face so *lovely* sterne and coy, . . . VI. ii. 24. 3
And eke that Lady, his faire *lovely* lasse. . . . VI. iii. 14. 4
And evermore his *lovely* litle spoile Crying . . . VI. iv. 25. 7
This litle babe, of sweete and *lovely* face, . . . VI. iv. 35. 4
The beames whereof did kindle *lovely* fire In th' harts . . . VI. vii. 28. 8
Environ'd with a girland . . . Of *lovely* lasses; . . . VI. ix. 8. 4
to thee flocke to heare thy *lovely* layes! . . . VI. x. 19. 5
To make them *lovely* or well-favoured show; . . . VI. x. 23. 3

Lovely—*Continued.*
with *lovely* dart Dinting his brest . . . VI. x. 31. 7
With lustfull eyes beheld that *lovely* guest, . . . VI. xi. 3. 7
Her *lovely* light was dimmed and decayd . . . VI. xi. 21. 4
make even that dimmed light Seeme much more *lovely* . . . VI. xi. 21. 7
With gladfull speaches and with *lovely* cheare; . . . VI. xi. 50. 3
unto *lovely* Lady doing wrong; . . . VI. xii. 34. 7
when he looked on her *lovely* face, . . . VII. vi. 31. 1
doffing her array, She bath'd her *lovely* limbes, . . . VII. vi. 45. 9
led a *lovely* Mayd Forth by the lilly hand, . . . VII. vii. 37. 3
when ye mildly looke with *lovely* hew, . . . *Am.* vii. 5
Looke ever *lovely*, as becomes you best; . . . *Am.* vii. 10
The *lovely* pleasance; and the lofty pride; . . . *Am.* xvii. 11
Proud Daphne, scorning Phoebus *lovely* fyre, . . . *Am.* xxviii. 9
sweet allurement of her *lovely* hew; . . . *Am.* xxxi. 10
lovely light to cleare my cloudy grief, . . . *Am.* xxxiv. 12
Her eyes looke *lovely*, and upon them smyle; . . . *Am.* xlvii. 10
Her *lovely* eyes, lyke Pincks but newly spred; . . . *Am.* lxiv. 8
To wayt on Love amongst his *lovely* crew; . . . *Am.* lxx. 10
How was I ravisht with your *lovely* sight, . . . *Am.* lxxvi. 5
So sweet, so *lovely*, and so mild as she, . . . *Epith.* 169
Eternally bind thou this *lovely* band, . . . *Epith.* 396
him that doeth thy *lovely* heasts despize, . . . *H.L.* 160
Carrying compassion to their *lovely* foe; . . . *H.B.* 243
spred thy *lovely* kingdome over-all. . . . *H.B.* 266
That like itselfe in *lovely* shape may bee. . . . *H.H.L.* 119
And letteth them her *lovely* face to see, . . . *H.H.B.* 255
lovely Daughters of the Flood . . . *Proth.* 21
Fowles, so *lovely*, . . . did deeme Them heavenly borne, . . . *Proth.* 61
Two gentle Knights of *lovely* face and feature, . . . *Proth.* 169
Love-pined. th' inward bale of my *love-pined* hart; . . . *Am.* ii. 2
Lover. *See* **Louver.**
The wily *lover* did devise this slight: . . . *Col.* 137
She intertainde her *lover* all the way; . . . I. ii. 14. 2
joyd to see her *lover* languish and lament: . . . I. ix. 27. 9
That wofull *lover*, loathing lenger light, . . . I. ix. 30. 2
fruit, With which Acontius got his *lover* trew, . . . II. vii. 55. 2
her selfe now solacing With a new *Lover*, . . . II. xii. 72. 3
That wanton Lady with her *lover* lose, . . . II. xii. 76. 8
eke her *lover* strove, but all in vaine; . . . II. xii. 82. 1
To seeke her *lover* . . . III. i. 8. 8
Both love and *lover*, without hope of joy, . . . III. ii. 45. 3
wandring for to seeke her *lover* deare, . . . III. vi. 54. 6
Her *lover* deare, her dearest Marinell, . . . III. vi. 54. 7
that lewd *lover* did the most lament . . . III. vii. 20. 1
The learned *lover* lost no time nor tyde . . . III. x. 6. 1
time and place, . . . to her *lover* told. . . . III. x. 11. 7
likewise sought her *lover* long miswent, . . . IV. v. 30. 6
A leman fit for such a *lover* deare: . . . IV. vii. 34. 5
not like a *lover*, But like a rebell stout, . . . V. v. 51. 2
The righteous Knight that is thy faithfull *lover*, . . . V. vii. 22. 4
He inly gan her *lover* to envy, . . . VI. ii. 17. 2
But sigh'd and sorrow'd for her *lover* deare, . . . VI. iii. 6. 7
Lover's. Never knew I *lovers* sheepe in good plight: . . . *S.C.* Au. 20
the troublous state Of *Lovers* life . . . *T.M.* 382
by my wretched *lovers* side me pight; . . . I. ii. 42. 7
The forlorne mayd . . . could not lacke her *lovers* company; I. vi. 22. 2
Here take thy *lovers* token on thy pate.' . . . I. vi. 47. 7
lovers life, As losse of time . . . I ever scornd, . . . I. ix. 10. 1
Another arrow hath your *lovers* hart to hit.' . . . III. ii. 35. 9
So straungely vewed her straunge *lovers* shade, . . . III. iii. 6. 3
t' increase thy *lover's* pray. . . . III. iii. 28. 4
Her *lovers* shape and chevalrous aray: . . . III. iv. 5. 5
called is by her lost *lovers* name, . . . III. vi. 29. 8
making layes of love and *lovers* paine, . . . III. x. 8. 4
ran into her *lovers* armes right fast; . . . III. x. 13. 5
Her captive *lovers* friend, young Placidas, . . . IV. viii. 63. 2
Venus Temple is describ'd; And *lovers* life forth set. . . . IV. x. Arg.
She chaw'd the cud of *lover's* carefull plight; . . . V. v. 27. 2
what reliefe . . . for this your *lovers* smart; . . . VI. ii. 46. 4
Me list not die for any *lovers* doole; . . . VI. viii. 21. 2
Why then doe I, untrainde in *lovers* trade, Her hardnes blame, *Am.* li. 5
make a *lovers* life a wretches hell. . . . *H.L.* 265
light proceedes, which kindleth *lovers* fire, . . . *H.B.* 100
Lovers. (If any gods the paine of *lovers* pitie) . . . *S.C.* Ja. 14
Lovers of Lordship, and troublers of states. . . . *S.C.* May 123
to comfort wakefull *Lovers*, . . . *Ti.* 132
joyes on wretched *lovers* to be wroken, . . . *Mui.* 99
true *Lovers!* whom desastrous chaunce Hath farre exiled . . . *D.* 505
'And ye, more happie *Lovers!* which enjoy . . . *D.* 512
pittying this paire of *lovers* trew, . . . *As.* 182
Thus ought all *lovers* of their lord to deeme, . . . *Col.* 887
Ne mongst true *lovers* they shall place inherit, . . . *Col.* 893
To thee are all true *lovers* greatly bound. . . . *Col.* 899
which her lavish *lovers* to her gave. . . . I. ii. 13. 6
As miserable *lovers* use to rew, . . . I. ix. 9. 8
she makes her *lovers* dronken mad; . . . II. i. 52. 2
Does charme her *lovers*, . . . II. v. 27. 4
Thereby more *lovers* unto her to call: . . . II. vii. 45. 6
fooles, *lovers*, children, Dames. . . . II. ix. 50. 9
her *lovers*, which her lustes did feed, . . . II. xii. 85. 3
To which sad *lovers* were transformde of yore; . . . III. vi. 45. 2
Two eies him needeth, . . . Who *lovers* will deceive. . . . III. ix. 31. 8
a wanton payre Of *lovers* loosely knit, . . . III. x. 16. 9
those *lovers*, with sweet countervayle, . . . III. xii. 47. *or.* 1
crowne true *lovers* with immortall blis, . . . IV. Pr. 2. 8
Some, of deare *lovers* foes perpetuall: . . . IV. i. 24. 5
all true *lovers* with dishonor blotten: . . . IV. i. 51. 4
those two Ladies their two *lovers* deare; . . . IV. ii. 31. 7
oftentimes unquiet strife did move Amongst her *lovers*, . . IV. ii. 37. 4

Loving—*Continued.*
To whom her *loving* hart she linked fast . . . III. vi. 53. 3
found such favour in their *loving* hartes, . . . III. vii. 55. 2
The *loving* couple neede no reskew feare, . . . III. x. 16. 3
mak'st the *loving* hart . . . to languish . . . III. xi. 1. 6
your *loving* Make Hath no lesse griefe endured . . . III. xii. 40. 8
living thus a wretch, and *loving* so, . . . IV. ix. 39. 8
for *loving* one That loves not me, . . . IV. xii. 9. 6
To take Briana for his *loving* fere . . . VI. i. 43. 7
full oft for *loving* you I blesse my lot, . . . *Am.* lxxxii. 1
of *loving* eyes be vewed never? . . . *H.B.* 189
Ne ought demaunds but that we *loving* bee, . . . *H.H.L.* 185
since that *loving* Lord Commaunded us to love them . . . *H.H.L.* 204
Loving-books. fortunes tell, and read in *loving bookes,* . . . I. iv. 25. 8
Loving-lays. He sings of love, and maketh *loving layes,* . . . *T.M.* 413
Lovingly. sacred Peace shall *lovingly* persuade . . . III. iii. 49. 3
Either embracing other *lovingly,* . . . V. viii. 14. 6
Loving-verses. Thereto he could fine *loving verses* frame, . . . *Hub.* 809
Low. *See* **Low-looking.**
no time should so *low* embase their hight, . . . *Ro.* viii. 12
In a fresh flowring meadow lying *lowe:* . . . *Van.* ii. 4
Learne by their losse to love the *low* degree; . . . *Van.* xii. 10
pyping *lowe* in shade of lowly grove, . . . *S.C.* Jun. 71
all these were *lowe* and lief, . . . *S.C.* Jul. 165
To love the *lowe* degree); . . . *S.C.* Jul. 220
Seeing the doubled shadowes *low* to fall, . . . *Gn.* 318
sdeign'd the *low* degree; . . . *Hub.* 679
kept them *lowe,* and streigned verie hard. . . . *Hub.* 1190
when the courting masker louteth *lowe,* . . . *Ti.* 202
downe it fell, and *low* in ashes lay, . . . *Ti.* 502
Amyntas quite is gone, and lies full *low,* . . . *Col.* 434
Belov'd of high and *low* with faithfull harts. . . . *Col.* 531
a vele, that wimpled was full *low;* . . . I. i. 4. 4
He faire the knight saluted, louting *low,* . . . I. i. 30. 1
the bowels of the earth full . . . *low,* . . . I. i. 39. 5
Her humblesse *low,* In so ritch weedes, . . . I. ii. 21. 4
With loftie eyes, halfe loth to looke so *lowe,* . . . I. iv. 14. 1
that mightie Monarch layd *Low* under all, . . . I. v. 48. 6
his sences stound that still he lay full *low.* . . . I. vii. 12. 9
High over hills, and *lowe* adowne the dale, . . . I. vii. 28. 8
tayle was stretcht adowne his back full *low.* . . . I. vii. 31. 9
to the ground it doubleth him full *low:* . . . I. viii. 18. 8
His dwelling is *low* in a valley greene, . . . I. ix. 4. 5
wasted life doe lye in ashes *low:* . . . I. ix. 8. 5
His dwelling has, *low* in an hollow cave, . . . I. ix. 33. 2
That cursed man, *low* sitting on the ground, . . . I. ix. 35. 2
They passe in, stouping *low:* . . . I. x. 5. 8
as the tree does fall, so lyes it ever *low.* . . . I. x. 41. 9
pyn'd his flesh to keepe his body *low* and chast. . . . I. x. 48. 9
low stouping with unweldy sway, . . . I. xi. 18. 8
him before themselves prostrating *low,* . . . I. xii. 6. 2
bowed *low,* that her right well became, . . . I. xii. 24. 3
on the ground herselfe prostrating *low,* . . . I. xii. 33. 2
they him layd full *low* in dungeon deepe, . . . I. xii. 36. 1
after gave a grone so deepe and *low* . . . II. i. 38. 3
Beside a bubling fountaine *low* she lay, . . . II. i. 40. 2
full *low* Shee sight . . . II. i. 47. 1
low behinde her backe were scattered: . . . II. iii. 30. 5
this Squyre have laide thus *low.* . . . II. iv. 34. 9
him dismounted *low* he did compell . . . II. v. 4. 7
make him stoup so *low,* . . . II. v. 7. 3
streight on grownd made him full *low* to lye; . . . II. v. 12. 5
thus *low* me laid in dust.' . . . II. v. 12. 9
low abase the high heroicke spright, . . . II. vii. 10. 6
to him that *low* in dust doth ly, . . . II. vii. 11. 7
Those that were up themselves kept others *low;* . . . II. vii. 47. 6
Those that were *low* themselves held others hard, . . . II. vii. 47. 7
tombling *low* From the high mountaines, . . . II. xi. 18. 4
Low his lascivious armes adown did creepe, . . . II. xii. 61. 6
th' one her selfe *low* ducked in the flood, . . . II. xii. 66. 3
she *low* adowne did lose, . . . II. xii. 67. 3
flowing *low* and thick her cloth'd arownd, . . . II. xii. 67. 4
The gentle warbling wind *low* answered to all. . . . II. xii. 71. 9
low underneath the ground, In a deepe delve, . . . III. iii. 7. 6
standing high aloft *low* lay thine eare, . . . III. iii. 9. 1
from his loftie steed dismounting *low* . . . III. iv. 53. 6
made him *low* incline his lofty crest, . . . III. vii. 42. 4
'The third a Damzell was of *low* degree, . . . III. vii. 59. 1
her well-plighted frock . . . Shee *low* let fall, . . . III. ix. 21. 5
in thine ashes buried *low* dost lie, . . . III. ix. 33. 2
comming him before *low* louted on the lay. . . . III. x. 23. 9
The wretched man . . . *low* prostrating said: . . . III. x. 25. 2
to him louted *low,* and greeted . . . III. x. 37. 9
I joy to see you lout so *low* on ground, . . . IV. vi. 28. 7
like a wide deepe poke, downe hanging *low,* . . . IV. vii. 6. 2
Yet was he but a Squire of *low* degree; . . . IV. vii. 15. 7
to his saddle-bow thereby He bowed *low,* . . . IV. viii. 43. 5
the Squire of *low* degree; . . . IV. viii. 52. 5
her Squire of *low* degree . . . IV. viii. 55. 6
The Squire of *low* degree, releast, . . . IV. ix. Arg.
that Squire of *low* degree . . . IV. ix. 8. 8
from my lofty steede dismounting *low* . . . IV. x. 15. 3
Crept in by stouping *low,* . . . IV. x. 18. 9
raught full *low* adowne. . . . IV. x. 31. 9
none disdained *low* to him to lout: . . . IV. xi. 30. 5
let their swelling waters *low* before him fall. . . . IV. xi. 30. 9
on her knee before him falling *lowe,* . . . IV. xii. 29. 5
friskt, and flong aloft, and louted *low* on knee. . . . V. iii. 34. 9
Amongst them all she placed him most *low,* . . . V. v. 23. 1
her proud person *low* prostrated on the plaine. . . . V. vii. 33. 9

Low—*Continued.*
bowing *low* before her Majestie, . . . V. ix. 34. 3
low dismounting from his loftie steede . . . V. x. 22. 2
laid his Seneschall *low* on the ground, . . . V. xi. 2. 4
Belge, with her sonnes, prostrated *low* . . . V. xi. 16. 1
from *low* to high uplifted is your fame. . . . VI. Pr. 6. 9
placed high above Or *low* beneath, . . . VI. ii. 1. 6
low on ground he lay: . . . VI. ii. 4. 7
Whether high towring or accoasting *low* . . . VI. ii. 32. 2
From pitch of higher place unto this *low* degree.' . . . VI. ix. 28. 9
From so high step to stoupe unto so *low;* . . . VI. x. 3. 2
Unto thy love that made thee *low* to lout: . . . VI. x. 16. 7
to *low,* to hie, To friends, to foes; . . . VI. x. 23. 8
Of good and bad alike, of *low* and hie, . . . VI. xii. 28. 6
Did seeme to bow their bloosming heads full *lowe* . . . VII. vii. 8. 8
being *lowe* before her presence feld . . . VII. vii. 13. 7
to the ground her eie-lids *low* embaseth, . . . *Am.* xiii. 3
let her prayses yet be *low* and meane, . . . *Am.* lxxx. 13
to them murmurde *low,* . . . *Proth.* 115
Lowder. send out *Lowder* (for so his dog hote) . . . *S.C.* S. 194
when as *Lowder* was farre awaye, . . . *S.C.* S. 196
called *Lowder,* with a hollow throte, . . . *S.C.* S. 217
by the hyde the Wolfe *Lowder* caught; . . . *S.C.* S. 223
Lowder had be slaine thilke same even. . . . *S.C.* S. 225
Lower. *See* **Lour.**
in the *lower* spring Did shroude . . . *S.C.* Jun. 53
from this *lower* tract he dared to stie . . . *Mui.* 42
all the heavens on *lower* creatures smilde, . . . *Mui.* 53
overthrew him selfe unwares, and *lower* lay: . . . II. iv. 8. 9
lower part did reach to lowest Hell; . . . II. vii. 46. 4
it survewd as hils doen *lower* ground; . . . II. ix. 45. 4
high Jove Doth light the *lower* world, . . . III. i. 57. 7
Of all this *lower* world, . . . V. Pr. 4. 9
was let adowne to fall Into a *lower* roome, . . . V. vi. 27. 8
forth into the *lower* parts did pas, . . . V. vii. 17. 6
This *lower* world nigh all to ashes brent, . . . V. viii. 40. 8
in their *lower* braunches sung aloud; . . . VI. x. 6. 7
Mean-while the *lower* World . . . was darkned quite; . . . VII. vi. 14. 1
this *lower* world who can deny But to be subject . . . VII. vii. 47. 8
But as she will, . . . My *lower* heaven, . . . *Am.* xlvi. 8
in the same these *lower* creatures all Subjected to her powre . . . *H.H.B.* 195
Lowest. Threwe downe this building to the *lowest* stone. . . . *Bel.*[1] ii. 14
shooke the hill from *lowest* seat, . . . *Bel.*[2] ii. 13
The *lowest* earth join'd to the heaven hie; . . . *Ro.* viii. 8
durst those *lowest* shadowes goe to see, . . . *Gn.* 438
Brings downe the stowtest hearts to *lowest* state; . . . *Hub.* 255
From highest staire to *lowest* step me drave, . . . *Ti.* 25
fall on *lowest* staire. . . . *Ti.* 494
did at last decline To *lowest* wretchednes: . . . *Mui.* 15
So goodly brought them to the *lowest* stayre . . . I. iv. 13. 5
Castle, . . . Is undermined from the *lowest* ground, . . . I. viii. 23. 3
lower part did reach to *lowest* Hell; . . . II. vii. 46. 4
Whom fortune hath already laid in *lowest* seat.' . . . II. viii. 27. 9
Betwixt the *lowest* earth and hevens hight, . . . III. ii. 19. 3
From *lowest* Juniper to Ceder tall, . . . IV. x. 22. 2
Like to the balefull house of *lowest* hell, . . . IV. xi. 4. 3
lowest hell, to which I lie most neare, . . . IV. xii. 6. 7
it raught Downe to her *lowest* heele; . . . V. v. 2. 8
Even unto the *lowest* and the least. . . . VI. xii. 2. 5
he, that standeth on the hyghest stayre, Fals *lowest;* . . . *Am.* lviii. 12
Whom greatest Princes sought on *lowest* knee. . . . *H.H.L.* 231
Lowliness. He humbly louted in meeke *lowlinesse,* . . . I. x. 44. 6
Of life, which here in *lowlinesse* ye lead, . . . VI. ix. 27. 6
Such *lowlinesse* shall make you lofty be. . . . *Am.* xiii. 14
Low-looking. *Low looking* dales, disloignd from common gaze; . . . IV. x. 24. 6
Lowly. pyping lowe in shade of *lowly* grove, . . . *S.C.* Jun. 71
Better is then the *lowly* playne, . . . *S.C.* Jul. 7
leades in *lowly* dales, . . . *S.C.* Jul. 102
lived in *lowlye* leas: . . . *S.C.* Jul. 122
thou seest my *lowly* saile, . . . *S.C.* S. 250
Lyft up thy selfe out of the *lowly* dust, . . . *S.C.* O. 38
lofty love doth loath a *lowly* eye. . . . *S.C.* O. 96
Ystabled hath his steedes in *lowlye* laye, . . . *S.C.* N. 15
the little plants that *lowly* dwell. . . . *S.C.* N. 32
Goe but a *lowly* gate . . . *S.C.* Env. 8
Out of the *lowly* vallies did arise, . . . *Gn.* 191
pray oft, looke *lowly* on the ground, . . . *Hub.* 498
Lowly they him saluted in meeke wise; . . . *Hub.* 585
to the Lion came, full *lowly* creeping, . . . *Hub.* 1361
they that dwell in *lowly* dust, . . . *T.M.* 67
lowly thoughts lift up to heavens hight, . . . *T.M.* 459
mine the Primrose in the *lowly* shade: . . . *D.* 233
doth his trembling Muse but *lowly* flie, . . . *Col.* 420
To her my love I *lowly* do prostrate, . . . *Col.* 474
loath each *lowly* thing with loftie eie. . . . *Col.* 938
Doe yet but flagg, and *lowly* learne to fly, . . . *Ded. Son.* ii. 8
This *lowly* Muse, . . . Flies for like aide . . . *Ded. Son.* xiii. 7
To sing his sweet delights in *lowlie* laies; . . . *Ded. Son.* xv. 7
Muse whylome did maske . . . in *lowly* Shephards weeds, . . . I. Pr. 1. 2
A lovely Ladie . . . Upon a *lowly* Asse . . . I. i. 4. 2
His fattie waves . . . overflow each plaine and *lowly* dale: . . . I. i. 21. 4
to the ground his eyes were *lowly* bent, . . . I. i. 29. 6
A litle *lowly* Hermitage it was, . . . I. i. 34. 1
conquered now he lye on *lowly* land; . . . I. iii. 37. 7
sitting high, for *lowly* she did hate: . . . I. iv. 10. 3
falling her before on *lowly* knee, . . . I. v. 16. 2
They, . . . all prostrate upon the *lowly* playne, . . . I. vi. 12. 8
he would learne The Lyon stoup to him in *lowly* wise, . . . I. vi. 25. 7
hory gray, with lookes full *lowly* cast, . . . I. x. 5. 6
he laid him privily Downe in a darksome *lowly* place . . . I. x. 25. 7

Lowly—*Continued.*
With folded hands, and knees full *lowly* bent, ... I. xi. 32. 6
On which they *lowly* sitt, ... I. xii. 13. 9
a pleasant dale that *lowly* lay . . . . II. i. 24. 3
lowly did abase their lofty crests . . . . II. ii. 32. 4
Tho to him louting *lowly* . . . . II. iii. 13. 4
Thus *lowly* to abase thy beautie bright, ... II. iv. 25. 8
My *lowly* verse may loftily arise, ... II. x. 1. 4
yt rebownds against the *lowly* playne, ... II. xi. 43. 4
Ruffed of love, gan *lowly* to availe; . . . . III. ii. 27. 2
Are wont to cleave unto the *lowly* clay, ... III. v. 1. 5
Lifteth it up that els would *lowly* fall: . . . . III. v. 2. 6
Thou, a meane Squyre of meeke and *lowly* place; . . . . . . III. v. 47. 3
Trompart, *lowly* to the grownd inclinde, ... III. x. 30. 7
lowly to her lowting thus behight: . . . . IV. ii. 23. 3
Thrise lowted *lowly* to the noble Mayd, ... IV. iii. 5. 8
He louted *lowly*, as did him becum, ... IV. vii. 44. 7
make them levell with the *lowly* plaine; . . . . V. ii. 38. 2
The hils doe not the *lowly* dales disdaine, ... V. ii. 41. 3
To serve the *lowly* vassall of her might, ... V. v. 27. 7
Him selfe before her feete he *lowly* threw, ... V. vii. 16. 2
High over hilles, and *lowly* over dales, ... V. viii. 39. 2
though it on a *lowly* stalke doe bowre, ... VI. Pr. 4. 3
falling *lowly* at his feet . . . . VI. vi. 31. 5
have learn'd to love more deare This *lowly* quiet life . . . VI. ix. 25. 9
Had ever learn'd to love the *lowly* things, ... VI. ix. 35. 5
Did seeme to overlooke the *lowly* vale: . . . . VI. x. 8. 8
An humble suppliant loe! I *lowely* fly, ... VII. vii. 14. 2
fall *lowly* at her feet; And, with meeke . . . . *Am.* ii. 10
Yet *lowly* still vouchsafe to looke on me; . . . . *Am.* xiii. 13
And tread my life downe in the *lowly* floure. . . . . *Am.* xx. 4
Why did ye stoup unto so *lowly* state? . . . . *Am.* lxvi. 8
Upon the *lowly* ground affixed are; . . . . *Epith.* 161
Lifting himselfe out of the *lowly* dust . . . . *H.L.* 177
But *lowly* fall before his mercie seate, ... *H.H.B.* 148
Lowre. *See* **Lour.**
Loy. *See* **Sans Loy.**
Loyal. not content with *loyall* obeysaunce, ... *S.C.* May 120
Right and loyall did his word maintaine. . . . . *Ti.* 189
If from their *loyall* loves he might them move: . . . . . . I. iv. 26. 5
A Satyre . . . The *loyall* linkes of wedlocke did unbinde, . . . I. vi. 22. 8
loyall truth to treason doest incline: . . . . II. vii. 13. 3
ne ever Dame So chast and *loyall* liv'd, ... IV. viii. 25. 6
Then *loyall* love had royall regiment, ... IV. viii. 30. 7
Enlincked fast in wedlockes *loyall* bond, ... V. iv. 3. 2
trayterous desynes Gainst *loiall* Princes, ... V. ix. 42. 3
The league twixt them, that *loyal* love hath bound: . . . . *Am.* lxv. 10
gentle Love, that *loiall* is and trew, ... *H.B.* 176
Loyalty. thy true love and *loyaltie* I deeme. . . . . *Col.* 575
he had faire Una lorne, Through light misdeeming of her *loialtie;* . . . . I. iv. 2. 2
made him to misdeeme My *loyalty*, ... I. vii. 49. 5
breach of love and *loialty* betrayd. . . . . I. xii. 31. 5
Her former love and stedfast *loialty*, ... III. vi. 53. 8
With breach of faith and *loyaltie* unsound, ... IV. vi. 28. 4
To his owne love his *loialtie* he saved: . . . . V. vi. 2. 5
love is Lord of truth and *loialtie*, ... *H.L.* 176
Lozell. *See* **Losel.**
Lucid. The liquid clowdes, and *lucid* firmament; . . . . . . *Hub.* 1259
Lucida. a lovely lasse, hight *Lucida:* . . . . *Col.* 456
'Indeed (said *Lucid*) . . . . *Col.* 907
His *Lucida*, that was full faire and sheene: . . . . IV. v. 11. 7
Lucies. *See* **Lucius'.**
Lucifera. proud *Lucifera* men did her call, ... I. iv. 12. 1
grudged at the great felicitee Of proud *Lucifera*, ... I. iv. 31. 9
The foule Duessa, next unto the chaire Of proud *Lucifer'*, (**Lucifera*) . . . . I. iv. 37. 6
Lucina. bad me call *Lucina* to me neare. . . . . II. i. 53. 5
Lucina came; a manchild forth I brought. . . . . II. i. 53. 6
Lucina's. ne her need implore *Lucinaes* aide: . . . . III. vi. 27. 4
Lucius. Then Coyll; and after him good *Lucius*, ... II. x. 53. 3
Lucius'. since *Lucies* tyme, Was of the Britons first crownd . II. x. 58. 6
Luck. *See* **Ill luck.**
luck and loves unbridled lore . . . . *S.C.* D. 63
their lasses, which my *luck* envide, ... *D.* 142
Glad of such *lucke*, the . . . mayd Did her content . . . . . I. vi. 19. 1
good *lucke* prolonged hath thy date, ... I. ix. 45. 7
Good *lucke* presents you with yong lovely mayd, ... IV. i. 33. 8
Yet my good *lucke* he shall not likewise pray, ... V. iv. 14. 8
often did of love, and of *lucke* complaine. . . . . VI. viii. 32. 9
Luckless. to shroude my *lucklesse* pate. . . . . *S.C.* Jun. 16
Red Amaranthus, *lucklesse* Paramour; . . . . *Gn.* 677
The *luckles* Clarion, whether cruell Fate . . . . *Mui.* 417
Where as the *lucklesse* boy yet bleeding lay; . . . . *As.* 142
great dislyking to my *lucklesse* lot, ... *Col.* 181
'Why Archimago, *lucklesse* syre, What doe I see? . . . . . . I. iii. 39. 1
the Paynim lay, . . . since his late *luckelesse* fray. . . . . I. v. 29. 5
the *luckelesse* lucky mayd Did her content . . . . I. vi. 19. 1
The *lucklesse* conflict with the Gyaunt stout, ... I. vii. 26. 8
my liege, doth *lucklesse* ly . . . . I. viii. 2. 4
never knight . . . More *luckless* dissaventures did amate: . . I. ix. 45. 4
oft they did lament his *lucklesse* state, ... I. xii. 16. 4
Then to thy *lucklesse* parents did befall. . . . . II. i. 37. 5
This *luckles* childe, whom thus ye see with blood defild. . . II. i. 50. 9
'Ah! *lucklesse* babe, borne under cruell starre, ... II. ii. 2. 1
in *lucklesse* warre His forlorne steed from him the victour wan: II. vi. 41. 3
my *luckelesse* lott doth me constrayne Hereto perforce. . . . III. Pr. 3. 4
they fownd The *lucklesse* Marinell . . . . III. iv. 34. 9
of his *lucklesse* lott and cruell love thus playnd: . . . . . III. v. 44. 9
Whom having slain through *luckles* arrowes glaunce, ... III. ix. 48. 3

Luckless—*Continued.*
he yet was sore of his late *lucklesse* fight. . . . . IV. iv. 3. 9
Whose *lucklesse* riders late were overthrowen; . . . . IV. iv. 38. 7
At last his *lucklesse* hand he heav'd on hie, ... IV. vi. 18. 6
this present *lucklesse* howre, ... IV. ix. 39. 2
There did this *lucklesse* mayd seven months abide, ... IV. xi. 4. 6
the mother was Of *luckelesse* Marinell, Cymodoce; . . . . . IV. xi. 53. 7
having in companie This *lucklesse* Ladie . . . . V. i. 16. 9
As he on whom the *lucklesse* stars did lowre, ... V. v. 18. 5
They met together in that *lucklesse* glade; . . . . VI. iii. 8. 2
That he his love so *lucklesse* now had lost, ... VI. iv. 40. 2
Of all his mischiefe and late *lucklesse* smart; . . . . . . VI. vii. 21. 3
Let them that list their *lucklesse* lot deplore, ... VI. vii. 30. 7
through his late *luckelesse* prise, ... VI. viii. 25. 7
to thy blisse I made this *luckelesse* breach, ... VI. x. 29. 3
this *lucklesse* mayd away was lad, ... VI. xi. 40. 4
made her *lucklesse* loves well knowne to be: . . . . VII. vi. 40. 6
Lucky. never might his *luckie* scape forget. . . . . *Gn.* 664
the luckelesse *lucky* mayd Did her content . . . . I. vi. 19. 1
I, more fearefull or more *lucky* wight, ... I. ix. 30. 4
Upon the joint the *lucky* steele did light, ... I. xi. 43. 6
Might be my *lucky* lot; . . . . IV. x. 4. 9
(The *lucky* Pylot of her passage sad,) . . . . V. iv. 11. 7
I blesse my lot, that was so *lucky* placed: . . . . *Am.* lxxxii. 2
Lucre. And all mirth sadnesse, and all *lucre* losse. . . . . *H.H.B.* 280
Lucy. that same other Damzell, *Lucy* bright, ... V. iv. 9. 2
Bracidas and *Lucy* were right glad, ... V. iv. 20. 3
Lud. two sonnes, whose eldest, called *Lud*, ... II. x. 46. 1
Lugs. being eight *lugs* of grownd, ... II. x. 11. 3
Lukewarm. embrew her teeth and clawes with *lukewarm* blood *Bel.*[2] vi. 7
All wallowd in his own yet *luke-warme* blood, ... I. ix. 36. 6
a large *lukewarme* flood, Red as the Rose, ... II. viii. 39. 1
Lull. hir pleasures were wonte to *lull* me asleepe: . . . . . *U.V.* 13
more to *lulle* him in his slumber soft, ... I. i. 41. 1
how he did . . . *lull* in rugged armes . . . . I. vi. 27. 9
made a sowne, To *lull* him soft asleepe . . . . II. v. 30. 4
Lulled. *Lulled* the shepheards in such securitie, ... *S.C.* May 119
Thou, pleasaunt spring, hast *luld* me oft asleepe, ... *S.C.* Au. 155
Lulled a sleepe through loves misgovernaunce. . . . . *S.C.* N. 4
where the chaunting birds *luld* me asleepe, ... *S.C.* D. 71
'Adieu, delightes, that *lulled* me asleepe; . . . . *S.C.* D. 151
in the lap of soft delight Beene long time *luld*, ... *T.M.* 302
By this she had him *lulled* fast asleepe, ... II. vi. 18. 1
My sences *lulled* are in slomber of delight. . . . . III. Pr. 4. 9
Possessed of sweete sleepe that *luld* him soft in swound. . . VI. vii. 18. 9
Lumining. Blinding the eyes, and *lumining* the spright. . . . *H.H.L.* 280
Lump. tombling through the aire in *lompe* of fire, ... *Bel.*[1] vi. 10
death did sitt as sad As *lump* of lead, ... II. i. 45. 3
his hand, more sad then *lomp* of lead, ... II. viii. 30. 5
Now lyest thou a *lumpe* of earth forlorne; . . . . III. iv. 36. 7
up he rose, like heavie *lumpe* of lead, ... IV. v. 45. 6
that same *lumpe* of clay, ... V. x. 37. 2
So now all three one sencelesse *lumpe* remaine, ... V. xi. 14. 5
Did choke the entraunce with a *lumpe* of sin, ... VI. i. 23. 7
fell to ground, like to a *lumpe* of durt; . . . . VI. viii. 16. 8
Lumpish. lifting up his *lompish* head, ... I. i. 43. 4
adowne he kest The *lumpish* corse . . . . II. xi. 42. 6
With heavy look and *lumpish* pace, ... III. iv. 61. 7
He looking *lompish* and full sullein sad, ... III. xii. 18. 2
Lumps. Full of great *lumps* of flesh . . . . I. i. 20. 3
Lundy. We *Lunday* passe; . . . . *Col.* 270
Lungs. As if his *lungs* and lites were nigh asunder brast. . . VI. iii. 26. 9
Lure. Nor draw unto the *lure* of his lewd lay, ... VI. xi. 5. 3
Luring. *luring* baytes oftimes doe heedlesse harts entyse. . . IV. x. 49. 9
Lurk. much more that does from mens knowledge *lurke*. . . . *Col.* 295
like Moldwarps nousling still they *lurke*, ... *Col.* 763
The false resemblaunce of Deceipt . . . Did closely *lurke;* . I. v. 27. 4
in his wombe might *lurke* some hidden nest . . . . I. xii. 10. 5
for feare of dew vengeaunce Doe *lurke*, ... II. iii. 14. 8
Wherein the Aegyptian Phao long did *lurke* . . . . III. ii. 20. 3
To *lurke* emongst your Nimphes in secret wize, ... III. vi. 23. 2
To hide th' intent which in my heart did *lurke*, ... IV. vii. 17. 3
To hide the horrour which did *lurke* behinde, ... V. xi. 23. 8
the Spyder, that doth *lurke* In close awayt, ... *Am.* lxxi. 3
Lurked. *lurkt* in rocks and caves, long unespide. . . . . . I. viii. 50. 5
under simple shew, and semblant plaine *Lurkt* false Duessa . II. i. 21. 4
Mona, where it *lurked* in exile; . . . . III. iii. 48. 5
as a Snake, still *lurked* in his wounded mynd. . . . . III. x. 55. 9
the rich metall *lurked* privily, ... III. xi. 28. 4
Lurkest. In which thou *lurkest* lyke to vipers brood; . . . . *Am.* ii. 6
Lurking. By that same River *lurking* under greene, ... *Gn.* 649
lurking closely, in awayte now lay, ... *Mui.* 247
the cave in which he *lurking* dwelt, ... *Mui.* 358
Lay *lurking* covertly him to surprise; . . . . *Mui.* 386
Lurking in rockes and caves far under ground, ... II. i. 22. 3
like an Adder *lurking* in the weedes, ... II. v. 34. 1
wild like beastes *lurking* in loathsome den, ... II. x. 7. 4
lurking from the vew of covetous guest, ... II. xii. 55. 4
Luscious. to taste their *lushious* wine, ... II. xii. 54. 4
Lusitanian. Whose warlike prowesse . . . shakt the *Lusitanian* soile. *Ded.Son.*xiv.12
Luskishness. He shooke off *luskishnesse;* . . . . VI. i. 35. 7
Lust. if he mislive in leudnes and *lust*, ... *S.C.* May 87
Wemen, that of Loves longing once *lust*, ... *S.C.* May 134
The blossomes of *lust* to bud did beginne, ... *S.C.* May 187
if thee *lust* to holden chat . . . . *S.C.* Jul. 29
with lewde *lust* was overlayd: . . . . *S.C.* Jul. 151
to restraine The *lust* of lawlesse youth . . . . *S.C.* O. 22
if thou algate *lust* light virelayes, ... *S.C.* N. 21
heate of heedlesse *lust* me so did sting, ... *S.C.* D. 21

Lust—*Continued.*
not merit The name of love, but of disloyall *lust:* . . . *Col.* 892
this great passion of unwonted *lust,* . . . I. i. 49. 1
wanton *lust* and leud embracement: . . . I. ii. 5. 5
lust did now inflame His corage more, . . . I. iii. 41. 7
Whose greedy *lust* did lacke in greatest store; . . . I. iv. 29. 2
From lawlesse *lust* . . . Fayre Una is releast: . . . I. vi. Arg.
A Satyre . . . kindling coles of *lust* in brutish eye, . . . I. vi. 22. 7
lewd rybauld, with vyle *lust* advaunst, . . . II. i. 10. 3
In chaines of *lust* and lewde desyres ybownd, . . . II. i. 54. 3
all to lawlesse *lust* encouraged . . . II. ii. 18. 5
when *lust* of meat and drinke was ceast, . . . II. ii. 39. 3
Gan burne in filthy *lust;* . . . II. iii. 42. 5
Was given all to *lust* and loose living, . . . II. v. 28. 3
whom I *lust* do heape with glory and renowne?' . . . II. vii. 11. 9
Abusd her plenty . . . To all licentious *lust,* . . . II. vii. 16. 8
Thy spouse I will her make, if that thou *lust,* . . . II. vii. 49. 8
Ne suffred *lust* his safety to betray. . . . II. vii. 64. 8
Through vaine illusion of their *lust* unclene, . . . II. x. 8. 7
With stinges of carnall *lust,* . . . II. xi. 13. 7
The secrete signes of kindled *lust* appeare, . . . II. xii. 68. 6
Quite molten into *lust* and pleasure lewd; . . . II. xii. 73. 8
Breathing out beastly *lust* her to defyle: . . . III. i. 17. 3
she was given all to fleshly *lust,* . . . III. i. 48. 5
this was not to love, but *lust,* inclind; . . . III. i. 49. 7
Of filthly *lust,* contrary unto kinde; . . . III. ii. 40. 4
affections move In brutish mindes, and filthy *lust* inflame. . . . III. iii. 1. 6
brutish *lust,* that was so beastly tind. . . . III. vii. 15. 9
In fleshly *lust* were mingled both yfere, . . . III. vii. 48. 8
Whom so she fittest findes to serve her *lust,* . . . III. vii. 50. 4
Infixt such secrete sting of greedy *lust,* . . . III. viii. 25. 2
Empoisned was with privy *lust* and gealous dredd. . . . III. ix. 28. 9
in feminine And filthy *lust* exceede all womankinde, . . . III. xi. 4. 2
Because his sinfull *lust* she would not serve, . . . IV. i. 4. 2
He had smalll *lust* to buy his love so deare, . . . IV. i. 34. 6
with shamefull spot of sinfull *lust* . . . IV. i. 53. 4
it prickt his wanton mind With sting of *lust* . . . IV. ii. 5. 5
So blind is *lust* false colours to descry. . . . IV. ii. 11. 5
litle *lust* he had to rise againe: . . . IV. iv. 44. 6
Amoret rapt by greedie *lust* Belphebe saves . . . IV. vii. Arg.
He with his shamefull *lust* doth first deflowre, . . . IV. vii. 12. 8
each unto his *lust* did make a lawe . . . IV. viii. 30. 8
Unto abuse of lawlesse *lust* was lent, . . . IV. viii. 32. 3
with lewd loves and *lust* intemperate . . . IV. ix. 16. 7
In case his burning *lust* should breake into excesse, . . . IV. ix. 18. 9
lawlesse *lust* to rule with reasons lore; . . . IV. ix. 19. 4
Nemertea learned well to rule her *lust.* . . . IV. xi. 51. 9
None was debard, but all had leave that *lust.* . . . V. iii. 6. 3
with their might beat downe licentious *lust,* . . . V. iv. 2. 4
Whose wandring fancie after *lust* did raunge, . . . V. v. 26. 8
little *lust* had she to talke of ought, . . . V. vi. 21. 1
Reviling me and rayling as she *lust,* . . . V. viii. 22. 5
Such loathly matter were small *lust* to speake or thinke. . . . V. xi. 31. 9
led Her wavering *lust* after her wandring sight, . . . VI. iii. 23. 7
all that *lust* Might them oppresse, . . . VI. viii. 23. 3
the raines would lend Unto his *lust,* . . . VI. xi. 6. 3
Made him so frollick and so full of *lust:* . . . VII. vii. 39. 5
Above the reach of loathly sinfull *lust,* . . . *H.L.* 179
Disloiall *lust* faire beauties foulest blame, . . . *H.B.* 170
Lusted. man, that . . . *lusted* after all that he did love; . . . I. iv. 26. 2
Not that she *lusted* after any one, . . . III. ii. 23. 7
had rashly *lusted* For thing unlawfull, . . . IV. i. 11. 3
lusted after all that him did move: . . . IV. ix. 21. 8
Lustful. 'All so my *lustfull* leafe is drye and sere, . . . *S.C.* Ja. 37
the kindly fire Of *lustfull* yongth . . . *Mui.* 34
made him dreame of loves and *lustfull* play, . . . I. i. 47. 4
next to him rode *lustfull* Lechery Upon a bearded Gote, . . . I. iv. 24. 1
turning wrathfull fyre to *lustfull* heat, . . . I. vi. 3. 3
to feed his fyrie *lustfull* eye, He snatcht the vele, . . . I. vi. 4. 6
his *lustfull* fyre To kindle oft assayd, . . . II. iii. 23. 6
If ever covetous hand, or *lustfull* eye, . . . II. vii. 27. 2
lustfull luxurie and thriftlesse wast. . . . II. xii. 9. 3
minding nought but *lustfull* game, . . . II. xii. 81. 2
Cupid still emongest them kindled *lustfull* fyres. . . . III. i. 39. 9
So whot she burned in that *lustfull* fyre; . . . III. vii. 49. 8
Ever when he burnt in *lustfull* fire, . . . IV. vii. 19. 8
secret flakes of *lustfull* fire . . . IV. viii. 48. 8
Love-lavish Blandamour, and *lustfull* Paridell. . . . IV. ix. 20. 9
Privily pricked with thy *lustfull* powres, . . . IV. x. 45. 7
Which as they view with *lustfull* fantasyes, . . . VI. viii. 41. 8
With *lustfull* eyes beheld that lovely guest, . . . VI. xi. 3. 7
Let not one sparke of filthy *lustfull* fyre Breake out, . . . *Am.* lxxxiii. 1
Lustfulness. Of love, and other-whiles of *lustfulnesse,* . . . IV. i. 7. 8
Lustihead. In *lustihede* and wanton meryment. . . . *S.C.* May 42
florish in flowres of *lusty-head:* . . . *S.C.* May 204
Of love and *lustihead* tho mayst thou sing, . . . *S.C.* O. 51
Yong Clarion, with vauntfull *lustie-head,* . . . *Mui.* 54
in loves and *lusty-hed* His wanton daies . . . led, . . . I. ii. 3. 4
Now in his freshest flowre of *lusty-hed,* . . . II. i. 41. 7

Lustihead—*Continued.*
All day they daunced with great *lusty-hedd,* . . . III. x. 45. 6
all of love, and al of *lusty-hed,* . . . III. xi. 29. 3
fresh Aprill, full of *lustyhed,* . . . VII. vii. 33. 1
with fresh *lusty-hed,* Go to the bowre . . . *Epith.* 22
Lustiness. Over the fields, in his franke *lustinesse,* . . . *Mui.* 148
Lustless. So *lustlesse* bene they, so weake, so wan; . . . *S.C.* F. 78
All for their Maister is *lustlesse* and old. . . . *S.C.* F. 84
in his *lustlesse* limbes, . . . A shaking fever raignd continually. I. iv. 20. 7
doth love to steepe His *lustlesse* limbes, . . . III. iv. 56. 6
he did upreare In *lustlesse* wise; . . . VI. i. 35. 2
Lustre. With bils and glayves making a dreadfull *luster,* . . . V. xi. 58. 5
Lust's. Not for *lusts* sake, but for eternitie, . . . *H.L.* 104
Lusts. revive the memory of his leud *lusts,* . . . I. vi. 46. 3
lawlesse *lustes,* corrupt envyes, . . . II. xi. 8. 8
wanton joyes and *lustes* intemperate, . . . II. xii. 7. 7
her lovers, which her *lustes* did feed, . . . II. xii. 85. 3
Such shamefull *lustes* who loaths not, . . . III. ii. 41. 7
Such love, not lyke to *lusts* of baser kynd, . . . *Am.* vi. 3
looser lookes that stir up *lustes* impure; . . . *Am.* xxi. 8
Lusty. the fresh and *lustie* (*lusty*[1]) Lawrell tree, . . . *Pet.* iii. 2
Where will he live tyll the *lusty* prime? . . . *S.C.* F. 16
With Leaves engrained in *lusty* greene; . . . *S.C.* F. 131
lustie Love still sleepeth not, . . . *S.C.* Mar. 26
Before them yode a *lusty* Tabrere, . . . *S.C.* May 22
All were they *lustye* . . . *S.C.* S. 64
the yong *lustie* gallants he did chose To follow, . . . *Hub.* 797
(For shee her weend a fresh and *lusty* knight,) . . . III. i. 47. 3
So lovedst thou the *lusty* Hyacinct; . . . III. xi. 37. 1
They were encountred of a *lustie* Knight . . . IV. ii. 4. 2
breake forth out of his *lusty* bowres, . . . IV. x. 45. 4
The *lusty* Aladine, though meaner borne . . . VI. iii. 7. 6
The *lustie* shepheard swaynes sate in a rout, . . . VI. ix. 8. 5
A *lustie* knight as ever wielded speare, . . . VI. xii. 3. 6
lusty spring, all dight in leaves of flowres . . . VII. vii. 28. 2
Life was like a faire young *lusty* boy, . . . VII. vii. 46. 6
For *lusty* Spring now in his timely howre . . . *Am.* iv. 9
Lute. my *Lute,* whom Phoebus deignd to give, . . . *Ro.* xxxii. 9
Lutes. Theyr yvory *Luyts* and Tamburins forgoe, . . . *S.C.* Jun. 59
Luxurious. Such proud *luxurious* pompe is swollen up but late. I. xii. 14. 9
'In such *luxurious* plentie of all pleasure, . . . IV. x. 23. 1
Luxury. His belly was upblowne with *luxury,* . . . I. iv. 21. 3
So deformd is *luxury,* . . . II. xi. 12. 6
lustfull *luxurie* and thriftlesse wast. . . . II. xii. 9. 3
in lewd loves, and wastfull *luxuree,* . . . II. xii. 80. 7
Luyts. *See* **Lutes.**
Lyaeus. fruitfull Ceres and *Lyaeus* fatt . . . III. i. 51. 3
Lyam-hound. Talus, that could like a *lime-hound* winde her, . V. ii. 25. 3
Lybic. In cruell fight on *Lybicke* Ocean wide, . . . II. ii. 22. 6
From shore to shore emongst the *Lybick* sandes, . . . III. ix. 41. 6
Lydian. did divide Her looser notes with *Lydian* harmony; . III. i. 40. 2
Lyeke, Lyen, Lyfull. *See* **Like, Lien, Lifeful.**
Lying. In a fresh flowring meadow *lying* lowe: . . . *Van.* ii. 4
lying all at ease from guile or spight, . . . *Gn.* 111
Lying along before him in that place, . . . *Gn.* 267
lying by our sides Our lovely Lasses, . . . *Hub.* 475
His Crowne and Scepter *lying* him beside, . . . *Hub.* 953
lying reastlesse in heavy bedde, . . . *U.V.* 4
Lying together in a mightie cave, . . . *Ti.* 562
there *lying* on the field, . . . *As.* 183
He left him *lying* so, ne would no lenger stay: . . . I. iii. 39. 9
lying downe upon the sandie graile, . . . I. vii. 6. 2
Lying on ground, all soild with blood and myre: . . . II. iv. 16. 4
To seize upon his foe flatt *lying* on the marle. . . . II. xi. 33. 9
fownd Their lady *lying* on the sencelesse grownd: . . . III. i. 63. 5
The lucklesse Marinell *lying* in deadly swownd, . . . III. iv. 34. 9
Her bow and gilden quiver *lying* him beside. . . . III. v. 34. 9
Lying athwart her horse in great distresse, . . . III. vii. 37. 7
Her *lying* tongue was in two parts divided, . . . IV. i. 27. 6
his foe for *lying* long upbrayes: . . . IV. i. 42. 9
lying still awhile, both did forget . . . IV. ii. 15. 8
shortly was likewise seene *lying* on the plaine. . . . IV. iv. 44. 9
An headlesse Ladie *lying* him beside . . . V. i. 14. 3
purchast all the countrey *lying* ny . . . V. ii. 9. 7
Lying without her dore in great disease: . . . V. vi. 26. 7
These two false Knights, whom there ye *lying* see, . . . V. viii. 23. 3
Lying in waite how him he damadge might; . . . VI. i. 20. 7
There he that knight found *lying* on the flore . . . VI. ii. 40. 7
With those brave armours *lying* on the ground, . . . VI. v. 25. 4
Her father and her friends about her *lying,* . . . VI. xi. 23. 2
stonisht are . . . and damne their *lying* bookes: . . . VII. vii. 52. 6
lying on the flowry gras, . . . *Epith.* 308
Lynx's. every one of them had *Lynces* eyes; . . . II. xi. 8. 6
Lyonnesse. the countrie wherein I was bred, . . . fertile *Lionesse* . . . VI. ii. 30. 4
Lysianassa. Large *Lisianassa,* and Pronaea sage, . . . IV. xi. 50. 2
Lysippus. Such one *Lisippus,* but is worne with raine: . . . *Ti.* 417
Lysippus'. All that *Lysippus* practike arte could forme, . . . *Ro.* xxix. 5

M

Maa. Now made of *Maa,* the Nymph delitious. . . . *Col.* 523
Mace. May we his Crowne and *Mace* take from the ground, . . *Hub.* 968
strikes the rockes with his three-forked *mace;* . . . *Mui.* 315
Morpheus had with leaden *mace* Arrested all that courtly company, . . . I. iv. 44. 6
His mortall *mace,* wherewith his foemen he dismayde. . . . I. vii. 10. 9
that royall *mace* Which now thou bear'st, . . . II. x. 4. 3

Mace—*Continued.*
him so sore smott with his yron *mace,* . . . II. xi. 34. 8
She caught in hand an huge great yron *mace,* . . . III. vii. 40. 1
his massie yron *mace* Betwixt him and his hurt . . . IV. viii. 43. 6
his murdrous *mace* he up did reare, . . . IV. viii. 44. 4
great Neptune, with his threeforkt *mace,* . . . IV. xi. 11. 1
on her shoulder laid His snaky-wreathed *Mace,* . . . VII. vi. 18. 2

Mace—*Continued.*
a *mace,* On top whereof the moon and stars were pight; VII. vii. 44. 5
Macerate. *macerate* And rend the greedie mindes Gn. 94
Macht. *See* **Matched.**
Mad. Halfe *mad* through malice and revenging will, I. iii. 22. 8
Cybeles franticke rites have made them *mad:* I. vi. 15. 3
what fury *mad* Hath thee incenst I. vi. 47. 1
she makes her lovers dronken *mad;* II. i. 52. 2
suppressing fury *mad,* They gan abstaine II. ii. 28. 7
A mad man, or that feigned *mad* to bee, II. iv. 3. 5
proud through praise and *mad* through love, II. iv. 27. 1
With hellish feends, or Furies *mad* uprore, II. v. 37. 7
Cold Coloquintida, and Tetra *mad;* II. vii. 52. 4
eyes, That *mad* or foolish seemd: II. ix. 52. 7
Like two *mad* dogs they ran about the lands, II. xi. 47. 2
those wild-beasts that rag'd with furie *mad;* II. xii. 84. 5
mad through merth, And dronke with blood of men III. vii. 47. 6
With thought whereof exceeding *mad* he grew, III. viii. 4. 1
'Extremely *mad* the man I surely deeme, III. ix. 6. 7
'Then is he not more *mad,'* III. ix. 8. 1
With extreme fury he became quite *mad,* III. x. 54. 5
Like two *mad* mastiffes, each on other flew, IV. ii. 17. 8
woxe nigh *mad* for very harts despight, IV. v. 27. 2
through his *mad* mothers blame, IV. xi. 13. 5
Gan to repent that she had beene so *mad* V. iv. 11. 4
Through vengeful wrath and sdeignfull pride half *mad;* V. iv. 43. 3
As a *mad* bytch, when as the franticke fit V. viii. 49. 1
With that all *mad* and furious he grew, V. xi. 12. 1
when her he mist, He woxe halfe *mad;* VI. ii. 20. 7
And with *mad* moode againe upon him flew, VI. iv. 6. 3
He woxe nigh *mad* with wrath and fell despight, VI. vi. 24. 8
the *mad* steele about doth fiercely fly, VI. xi. 16. 3
made him almost *mad* for fell despight: VI. xii. 31. 7
In praise of that *mad* fit which fooles call love, H.H.L. 9
Madam. 'Certes, *Madame,* ye have great cause of plaint; I. vii. 52. 3
'*Madame,* my liefe, For Gods deare love II. i. 16. 1
'Gentle *Madame,* why beene ye thus dismayd, II. ix. 37. 5
Madan. *Madan* was young, unmeet the rule to sway, II. x. 20. 2
Tho *Madan* raignd, unworthie of his race, II. x. 21. 1
Madding. now from me hys *madding* mynd is starte, S.C. Ap. 25
The one my *madding* kiddes to smere, S.C. Jul. 87
Ne within reasons rule her *madding* mood containe. V. vii. 11. 9
as that *madding* mother . . . her owne deare flesh did teare: V. viii. 47. 5
Made. *See* **Home-made, Maked.**
rather *made* by his owne skilfull hande Bel.[1] iv. 10
Made me the spoile and bootie of the world, Bel.[1] viii. 10
The worde of God *made* him a noble name. Rev. iii. 4
a pot . . . *Made* of the mettall Bel. iii. 6
Made all of Heben and white Yvorie; Pet. ii. 2
civill warres me *made* The whole worlds spoile, Bel.[2] x. 9
Made of some matter no less firme and strong? Ro. ix. 8
so oft thee, (Rome) their conquest *made;* Ro. xiii. 4
That antique horror, which *made* heaven adredd, Ro. xvii. 8
Which, *made* perpetuall, rose to so great might, Ro. xviii. 9
Queene of land and sea her selfe she *made.* Ro. xx. 11
The which this auncient Citie whilome *made!* Ro. xxv. 4
made all other Foules his thralls to bee: Van. iv. 4
Made him to swell, that nigh his bowells brust, Van. vi. 10
Art *made* a myrrhour to behold my plight: S.C. Ja. 20
crowing in pypes *made* of greene corne, S.C. F. 40
made this foolish Brere wexe so bold, S.C. F. 124
made many wounds in the wast Oake. S.C. F. 202
His wonderous weight *made* the ground to quake, S.C. F. 219
Or *made* previe to the same? S.C. Mar. 30
Hys pleasaunt Pipe, whych *made* us meriment, S.C. Ap. 14
Which once he *made* as by a spring he laye, S.C. Ap. 35
Made my heart after the pype to daunce: S.C. May 26
some old sorowe that *made* a newe breache: S.C. May 210
the Kidde *made* him good glee, S.C. May 282
made great mone. S.C. May 301
plaintive pleas in verses *made:* S.C. Jun. 42
Echo *made* the neyghbour groves to ring, S.C. Jun. 52
she the truest shepheards hart *made* bleede, S.C. Jun. 111
to heare a doolefull verse . . . That *Colin* made? S.C. Au. 142
such eeking hath *made* my hart sore. S.C. S. 31
I thought the soyle would have *made* me rich, S.C. S. 78
matter *made* for Poets on to play: S.C. O. 64
dead shee is, that myrth thee *made* of yore. S.C. N. 57
The songs that Colin *made* you in her praise, S.C. N. 78
Made me by arte more cunning in the same. S.C. D. 42
I have *made* a Calender for every yeare, S.C. Env. 1
whether God or Fortune *made* him bold Gn. 302
hardie will he had . . . that *made* him lesse adrad. Gn. 304
made him meat for wild foules of the ayre. Gn. 380
valiant fortune *made* Dan Orpheus bolde; Gn. 449
His breeches were *made* after the new cut, Hub. 211
Then *made* they revell route and goodly glee; Hub. 558
made a composition With their next neighbor Hub. 571
pleased, And *made* to laugh, Hub. 710
He *made* small choyce; Hub. 849
it seemeth I was *made* to raigne, Hub. 1031
all wylde beasts *made* vassals of his pleasures, Hub. 1129
he no count *made* of Nobilitie, Hub. 1183
made them dwell in darknes of disgrace; Hub. 1187
So *made* by nature for to serve their will, T.M. 40
could have *made* a stonie heart to weep; T.M. 110
Are now despizd, and *made* a laughing game. T.M. 204
the man whom Nature selfe had *made* T.M. 205
So am I *made* the servant of the manie, T.M. 223
like to troubled puddles have them *made.* T.M. 276

Made—*Continued.*
made exceeding mone; T.M. 416
made a monster of their fantasie. T.M. 558
made the nourslingof Nobilitie. T.M. 564
made exceeding mone, T.M. 598
have in mine owne bowels *made* my grave, Ti. 26
made one meare of th' earth and of their raine? Ti. 63
made all nations vassals of her pride, Ti. 72
all the rest, that me so honord *made* Ti. 121
O sad joy, *made* of mourning and anoy! Ti. 322
Shrines *made* of the mettall most desired, Ti. 411
'Such one Mausolus *made,* Ti. 414
made the Easterne Conquerour to crie, Ti. 432
made The holie brethren falslie to have praid. Ti. 496
Made for the gentle Squire, Ti. 524
Then did I see a Bridge, *made* all of golde, Ti. 547
Made of golde and costlie yvorie, Ti. 605
A curious Coffer *made* of Heben wood, Ti. 618
now art *made* the heavens ornament, Ti. 674
No lesse than that which Vulcane *made* Mui. 63
Made all that him so horrible did see Thinke him Alcides Mui. 70
T' excell the naturall with *made* delights; Mui. 166
She *made* the storie of the olde debate Mui. 305
Emongst these leaves she *made* a Butterflie, Mui. 329
Ne anie noyse, ne anie motion *made.* Mui. 400
Hath *made* fit mate thy wretched case to heare, D. 65
Than question *made* of his calamitie, D. 90
Not mine, but His, which mine awhile her *made;* D. 235
Both Nymphes and Muses nigh she *made* astownd, D. 314
'Hencefoorth I hate what ever Nature *made,* D. 393
Made not to please the living but the dead. As. Pr. 16
he himselfe seemed *made* for meriment, As. 27
For her he *made* hymnes of immortall praise, As. 63
Well *made* to strike, to throw, to leape, to lift, As. 75
Wide wounds emongst them many one he *made,* As. 107
piteous mone the which she for him *made,* As. 170
Like Astrophel, which thereinto was *made.* As. 186
made the Muses in his song to mourne. As. Interl. 222
Hast *made* us all so blessed and so blythe. Col. 21
That us, late dead, has *made* againe alive: Col. 31
when he heard the musicke which I *made,* Col. 70
carol *made* to praise thy loved lasse.' Col. 87
That *made* me in that desart chose to dwell. Col. 91
He none was *made,* but scattred all to nought; Col. 153
each an end of singing *made* Col. 179
she *made* them roare againe. Col. 223
fold them up, when they have *made* an end. Col. 259
song, Which he hath of that mightie Princesse *made?* Col. 405
valleyes thou hast *made* Her name to eccho Col. 482
Now *made* of Maa, the Nymph delitious. Col. 523
Made by the Maker selfe to be admired; Col. 561
My layes *made* of her shall not be forgotten, Col. 642
by his powre the world was *made* of yore, Col. 841
All being *made* the vassalls of his might, Col. 885
made amends to her with treble praise. Col. 924
The sacred Muses have *made* alwaies clame Ded. Son. iv. 1
with-hold, till further tryall *made.'* I. i. 12. 6
his glistring armor *made* A litle glooming light, I. i. 14. 4
Had *made* a Lady of that other Spright, I. i. 45. 2
made him dreame of loves and lustfull play, I. i. 47. 4
You, whom my hard avenging destinie Hath *made* judge I. i. 51. 9
doubtfull words *made* that redoubted knight Suspect her truth: I. i. 53. 5
whom unhappy howre Hath now *made* thrall I. i. 22. 3
their greene leaves, . . . *Made* a calme shadowe I. ii. 28. 6
Her angels face . . . *made* a sunshine in the shady place; I. iii. 4. 8
Such joy *made* Una, when her knight she found; I. iii. 32. 1
inflames the skyen With fire not *made* to burne, I. iv. 9. 9
That *made* her selfe a Queene, and crownd to be; I. iv. 12. 2
A gentle Husher, Vanitie by name, *Made* rowme, I. iv. 13. 4
of his wicked pelfe his God he *made,* I. iv. 27. 6
Whose welth was want, whose plenty *made* him pore; I. iv. 29. 4
neighbours welth, that *made* him ever sad, I. iv. 30. 6
Whome great griefe *made* forgett the raines to hold I. iv. 41. 3
running Heralds humble homage *made,* I. v. 15. 7
he the man that *made* Sansfoy to fall, I. v. 26. 3
made ensample of their mournfull sight I. v. 52. 2
to have . . . *made* the vassall of his pleasures vilde. I. vi. 3. 5
Cybeles franticke rites have *made* them mad: I. vi. 15. 3
truth, which . . . *made* her th' Image of Idolatryes; I. vi. 19. 7
A Satyre . . . *made* her person thrall I. vi. 22. 9
ryde their backes, not *made* to beare; I. vi. 24. 7
made wide furrowes in their fleshes fraile, I. vi. 43. 5
The Redcrosse knight is captive *made* I. vii. Arg.
greene boughes . . . like a girlond *made;* I. vii. 4. 5
goodly court he *made* still to his Dame, I. vii. 7. 1
a snaggy Oke, . . . it *made* His mortall mace, I. vii. 10. 8
that fraile fountain which him feeble *made,* I. vii. 11. 8
His poynant speare that many *made* to bleed, I. vii. 19. 7
First *made* by him mens wandring wayes to guyde, I. vii. 23. 2
shield . . . Not *made* of steele, I. vii. 33. 3
he that *made* the same was knowne right well I. vii. 36. 2
of his prowesse proofe he since hath *made* I. vii. 47. 6
made him to misdeeme My loyalty, I. vii. 49. 4
with mighty mall The monster mercilesse him *made* to fall, I. vii. 51. 5
he, . . . is to sinfull bands *made* thrall: I. viii. 1. 7
him the Squire *made* quickly to retrate, I. viii. 12. 7
of his puissaunce proud ensample *made;* I. viii. 16. 3
the heavens, . . . Have *made* you master of the field I. viii. 28. 2
Orgoglio . . . Had *made* his caytive thrall: I. viii. 32. 8

Made—*Continued.*

ne ever other answere *made*.	I. viii. 32. 9
the noble Prince . . . *made* himselfe free enterance.	I. viii. 34. 7
to see him *made* her glad,	I. viii. 42. 2
lovely blandishment She to me *made,*	I. ix. 14. 2
forst, at last he *made* through silence suddein breach.	I. ix. 25. 9
A wyde way *made* to let forth living breath:	I. ix. 30. 3
made an open passage for the gushing flood.	I. ix. 36. 9
in his conscience *made* a secrete breach,	I. ix. 48. 3
a Serpent . . . horrour *made* to all	I. x. 13. 5
Els had his sinnes, . . . *Made* him forget all	I. x. 22. 5
made him pray both earely and eke late:	I. x. 26. 5
face he *made* all beastes to feare,	I. x. 42. 7
made wide shadow under his huge waste,	I. xi. 8. 4
Those glaring lampes were sett that *made* a dreadfull shade.	I. xi. 14. 9
That *made* the Redcrosse knight nigh quake for feare,	I. xi. 15. 8
Him all amazd, and almost *made* afeard:	I. xi. 26. 5
to the scull a yawning wound it *made:*	I. xi. 35. 8
made such way that hewd it quite in twaine;	I. xi. 43. 7
he was deadly *made,*	I. xi. 49. 2
made delightfull musick all the way,	I. xii. 7. 5
She to her Syre *made* humble reverence,	I. xii. 24. 2
often semblaunce *made* to scape out of their hand.	I. xii. 35. 9
made great feast to solemnize that day:	I. xii. 38. 2
Great joy was *made* that day of young and old,	I. xii. 40. 1
Where you he *made* the marke of his intent,	II. i. 30. 8
Who *made* my hand the organ of his might:	II. i. 33. 3
fate Hath *made* sad witnesse	II. i. 37. 2
A cruell knife that *made* a griesly wownd,	II. i. 39. 6
drery death . . . *made* darke clouds appeare:	II. i. 45. 3
each *made* others foe:	II. ii. 13. 6
made love unto the eldest Dame,	II. ii. 17. 1
rare ensample *made,*	II. ii. 25. 4
made to spoile Themselves of soiled armes,	II. ii. 33. 7
Braggadocchio, . . . is *made* the scorne Of knighthood	II. iii. Arg.
Gave him great ayd, and *made* him more inclynd:	II. iii. 4. 7
So happy peace they *made* and faire accord.	II. iii. 9. 1
made the forrest ring,	II. iii. 20. 9
What hard mishap him . . . *made* that caytives thrall,	II. iv. 16. 9
Affyaunce *made,* my happinesse begonne,	II. iv. 21. 4
I *made* plaine and evident,	II. iv. 29. 7
made a large And open gash therein:	II. v. 6. 4
made him reele, and to his brest his bever bent.	II. v. 6. 9
He *made* him stoup perforce unto his knee,	II. v. 11. 6
streight on grownd *made* him full low to lye;	II. v. 12. 5
Of fowles and beastes he *made* the piteous prayes,	II. v. 26. 7
made a sowne, To lull him soft asleepe	II. v. 30. 3
made him to forget His former payne	II. v. 30. 8
made emongst them selves a sweete consort,	II. v. 31. 8
Made dronke with drugs of deare voluptuous receipt.	II. v. 34. 9
all, though pleasaunt, yet she *made* much more:	II. vi. 24. 5
naked *made* each others manly spalles;	II. vi. 29. 6
He with Pyrochles sharp debatement *made:*	II. vi. 39. 2
made a priefe Of every place	II. vi. 51. 3
al men doe ayme, rich to be *made:*	II. vii. 32. 8
Ne to be *made* so happy doe intend:	II. vii. 33. 2
made him scorne all creatures great and small,	II. vii. 41. 7
with their brightnesse *made* that darknes light,	II. vii. 42. 2
With which th' unjust Atheniens *made* to dy Wise Socrates;	II. vii. 52. 6
many noble Greekes and Trojans *made* to bleed.	II. vii. 55. 9
They *made* the further shore resounden wide.	II. vii. 57. 6
Did fly abacke, and *made* him vainely swincke;	II. vii. 58. 7
Made it selfe famous through false trechery,	II. viii. 12. 6
of his puissaunce tryall *made* extreeme:	II. viii. 14. 4
Merlin *made* by his almightie art	II. viii. 20. 2
horse and man it *made* to reele asyde:	II. viii. 31. 2
underneath his feet soone *made* a purple plesh.	II. viii. 36. 9
further way It *made,*	II. viii. 38. 7
made him twise to reele, that never moov'd afore.	II. viii. 44. 9
cruell passage *made* Quite through his brayne.	II. viii. 45. 5
Have *made* thee soldier of that Princesse bright,	II. ix. 5. 3
gentle court and gracious delight Shee to them *made,*	II. ix. 20. 4
All which compacted *made* a goodly Diapase.	II. ix. 22. 9
to her homage *made* with humble grace:	II. ix. 36. 3
they of living fire most subtilly Were *made,*	II. ix. 46. 6
buzzed all about, and *made* such sound	II. ix. 51. 2
old records . . . Some *made* in books,	II. ix. 57. 8
For safety that same his sea-marke *made,*	II. x. 6. 6
he dyde, *made* ripe for death by eld,	II. x. 32. 2
Made warre on him,	II. x. 35. 5
made he head against his enimies,	II. x. 38. 1
one, which earst were many *made* through variaunce.	II. x. 38. 9
Then *made* he sacred lawes,	II. x. 39. 1
this land was tributarie *made* T' ambitious Rome,	II. x. 49. 6
made them victors whome he did subdew.	II. x. 57. 4
With whome king Coyll *made* an agreement,	II. x. 59. 3
him with her *made* of his kingdome heyre,	II. x. 61. 3
Were to those Pagans *made* an open pray,	II. x. 62. 4
That man so *made* he called Elfe,	II. x. 71. 1
they dayly *made* most dreadfull battery.	II. xi. 7. 9
an Helmet light, *Made* of a dead mans skull,	II. xi. 22. 9
of the battell balefull end had *made,*	II. xi. 29. 7
he *made* An open passage	II. xi. 37. 3
made his sprighte to grone full piteous;	II. xi. 38. 7
In sumptuous bed shee *made* him to be layd;	II. xi. 49. 8
them of drowning *made* affeard.	II. xii. 2. 9
Ne *made* for shipping any certeine port,	II. xii. 13. 3
twixt them both a pleasaunt port they *made,*	II. xii. 30. 6
Of which Caduceus whilome was *made,*	II. xii. 41. 2
made there to abound with lavish affluence.	II. xii. 42. 9
So *made* by art to beautify the rest,	II. xii. 55. 2
so faire winepresse *made* the wine more sweet:	II. xii. 56. 6
The rest hidd underneath him more desirous *made.*	II. xii. 66. 9
voyces *made* To th' instruments divine respondence meet;	II. xii. 71. 3
of the fayrest late, now *made* the fowlest place.	II. xii. 83. 9
made him stagger, as he were not well:	III. i. 6. 5
Made them recoile, and fly from dredd decay,	III. i. 21. 8
Ne any noise she *made,* ne word she spake,	III. i. 61. 6
what inquest *Made* her dissemble her disguised kind?	III. ii. 4. 7
Such was the glassy globe that Merlin *made,*	III. ii. 21. 1
Chaunged thy lively cheare, and living *made* thee dead?	III. ii. 30. 9
he which *made* That mirrhour,	III. iii. 6. 1
vauntage *made* of that which Merlin had ared;	III. iii. 20. 9
'Thenceforth eternall union shall be *made*	III. iii. 49. 1
victorious Exployts *made* Rome to quake;	III. iii. 54. 8
Which Bladud *made* by Magick art of yore,	III. iii. 60. 2
matter *made* for famous Poets verse,	III. iv. 1. 6
made a lake Of Greekish blood	III. iv. 2. 5
Which alwaies of his paines he *made* the chiefest meed.	III. iv. 4. 9
with sharpe speare the rest *made* dearly knowne.	III. iv. 15. 6
made her downe Decline her head,	III. iv. 15. 8
He had subdew'd, and them his vassals *made*	III. iv. 21. 2
sweete daffadillyes, to have *made* Gay girlonds	III. iv. 29. 8
Shee *made* so piteous mone and deare wayment,	III. iv. 35. 6
Till he had *made* amends, and full restore	III. v. 18. 8
made more haste the life to have bereav'd;	III. v. 28. 8
could have *made* a rocke of stone to rew,	III. v. 30. 2
She *made* those Damzels search;	III. v. 38. 8
like a stately Theatre it *made,*	III. v. 39. 5
Some *made* for beasts, some *made* for birds to weare;	III. vi. 35. 6
borrow matter whereof they are *made;*	III. vi. 37. 2
of the trees owne inclination *made,*	III. vi. 44. 3
Sad Amaranthus, *made* a flowre but late,	III. vi. 45. 6
by succession *made* perpetuall,	III. vi. 47. 6
daughter Pleasure, to whom shee *Made* her companion,	III. vi. 51. 8
Such laesinesse both lewd and poore attonce him *made.*	III. vii. 12. 9
many resemblaunces To her he *made,*	III. vii. 16. 9
to God he *made* so many an idle boone:	III. vii. 34. 9
made him low incline his lofty crest,	III. vii. 42. 4
made her selfe more light away to fly:	III. vii. 44. 4
made fit for to deceive Fraile Ladies hart	III. vii. 46. 3
The substance, whereof she the body *made,*	III. viii. 6. 1
So *made* him thinke him selfe in heven that was in hell.	III. viii. 19. 9
of his bowels *made* his bloody feast:	III. viii. 49. 4
He from that deadly throw *made* no defence,	III. ix. 29. 1
Hygate *made* the meare thereof by West,	III. ix. 46. 2
will be *made* The vassall of the victors will bylive:	III. x. 10. 6
to the ground him meekely *made* to bowe,	III. x. 24. 3
Helenore . . . their May-lady they had newly *made:*	III. x. 44. 6
every bird and beast awarned *made* To shrowd themselves,	III. x. 46. 8
now *made* better speed t' escape his feared foe.	III. xi. 5. 9
as if his hart were peeces *made,*	III. xi. 8. 7
the which *made* Batteill against the Gods,	III. xi. 22. 8
her in daffadillies sleeping *made*	III. xi. 32. 4
The raging billowes, . . . *made* a long broad dyke,	III. xi. 40. 7
made the sparckling waves to smoke agayne,	III. xi. 41. 3
into her faire bosome *made* his grapes decline.	III. xi. 43. 9
not with arras *made* in painefull loome,	III. xi. 51. 3
A thousand monstrous formes therein were *made,*	III. xi. 51. 7
weed *Made* of Beares skin, that him more dreadfull *made;*	III. xii. 11. 2
all *made* in one mould.	III. xii. 24. 9
demeanure daint, That each to other *made,*	IV. i. 5. 3
Thereto her feare was *made* so much the greater	IV. i. 7. 1
other-whiles to her she purpos *made* Of love,	IV. i. 7. 7
dread . . . *Made* her not yeeld	IV. i. 8. 7
made repent that he had rashly lusted	IV. i. 11. 3
All mindlesse of the Golden fleece, which *made* them strive.	IV. i. 23. 9
made full goodly joyance to her new-found mate.	IV. i. 31. 9
made him selfe then sample of his follie.	IV. i. 36. 6
made good semblance to his companie,	IV. i. 38. 2
To whom he *made* great dalliance and delight:	IV. ii. 4. 4
whose beautie bright *Made* him seeme happie	IV. ii. 4. 8
But Paridell, . . . *made* this faire denyall:	IV. ii. 6. 3
former breaches *Made* in their friendship,	IV. ii. 12. 5
He *made* him open chalenge,	IV. ii. 12. 9
of all old dislikes they *made* faire weather;	IV. ii. 29. 3
battell *made* the dreddest daungerous	IV. ii. 32. 3
eke unto her lookes a law she *made,*	IV. ii. 36. 6
courtesie, That *made* them dearely lov'd	IV. iii. 2. 7
chevalrie, That *made* them dreaded much	IV. iii. 2. 9
made an end of strife.	IV. iii. 12. 9
Now *made* forget their former cruell mood,	IV. iii. 39. 4
there *made* gods, though borne of mortall berth,	IV. iii. 44. 3
so to see him *made* her heart to quaile:	IV. iii. 46. 7
Made her to change her hew, and hidden love t' appeare.	IV. iii. 46. 9
proffer *made* by force her to reprize:	IV. iv. 8. 8
therein *made* a very griesly wound,	IV. iv. 24. 6
his utmost prowesse there *made* knowen;	IV. iv. 38. 2
first was question *made,* which of those Knights	IV. v. 7. 1
Some proffer *made* with him for her to fight.	IV. v. 27. 5
to small purpose yron wedges *made;*	IV. v. 35. 8
made him dreame those two disloyall were:	IV. v. 43. 8
yet he her *made* To give him ground,	IV. vi. 12. 7
of his wonder *made* religion,	IV. vi. 22. 3
made ech member quake, and manly hart to quayle.	IV. vi. 22. 9
so sore a breach That sudden newes had *made*	IV. vi. 38. 4
Where goodly solace was unto them *made,*	IV. vi. 39. 6
made way Unto the love of noble Britomart,	IV. vi. 40. 1
'This dismall day hath thee a caytive *made,*	IV. vii. 12. 1

Made—*Continued.*
made him oft, when he would strike, forbeare; . . . IV. vii. 27. 2
there he his cabin *made*. . . . IV. vii. 38. 9
as in his wonted wise His doole he *made*, . . . IV. viii. 3. 2
Which losse her *made* like passion also prove: . . . IV. viii. 3. 5
thereof *made* a lamentable lay, . . . IV. viii. 4. 3
she would have *made* her (*him) understand . . . IV. viii. 12. 3
Ne then of guile had *made* experiment; . . . IV. viii. 30. 4
made to represent The great Creatours owne resemblance . . . IV. viii. 32. 1
made the baite of bestiall delight: . . . IV. viii. 32. 4
made the vassall of the victors might; . . . IV. viii. 32. 7
her deare hart full deepely *made* to rew, . . . IV. viii. 64. 3
made it so to ride as it alive was found. . . . IV. ix. 4. 9
made his Dwarfe . . . To guide the beast . . . IV. ix. 5. 3
She had them *made* a paragone to be, . . . IV. ix. 11. 6
Upon all which the Briton Prince *made* seasure, . . . IV. ix. 12. 5
made refraine from meat, . . . IV. ix. 14. 5
Till he had *made* of her some better priefe; . . . IV. ix. 15. 5
All which by nature *made* did nature selfe amaze. . . . IV. x. 24. 9
all the world by thee at first was *made*, . . . IV. x. 47. 1
in her cheekes *made* roses oft appeare: . . . IV. x. 50. 5
for the Gods in Proteus house be *made:* . . . IV. xi. 9. 2
made the rockes to roare as they were rent. . . . IV. xi. 12. 5
made it seeme to feele her grievous paine, . . . IV. xii. 5. 8
made him stoupe, till he did him bestride: . . . IV. xii. 13. 7
chyde at him that *made* her misbelieve: . . . IV. xii. 26. 4
Made humble suit unto his Majestie . . . IV. xii. 29. 6
streight his warrant *made*, . . . IV. xii. 32. 1
of most perfect metall it was *made*, . . . V. i. 10. 1
His name was Talus, *made* of yron mould, . . . V. i. 12. 6
made them stoupe that looked earst so hie. . . . V. ii. 21. 5
made way for his maister to assaile; . . . V. ii. 24. 4
They turne to that whereof they first were *made?* . . . V. ii. 40. 7
he of little things *made* reckoning light; . . . V. ii. 44. 2
Where he her spous'd, and *made* his joyous bride. . . . V. iii. 2. 4
like as one whom feends had *made* affrayd, . . . V. iii. 18. 4
what a glorious shew he *made* in all their sights. . . . V. iii. 39. 9
made the scorne of Knighthod . . . V. iv. 27. 7
made her famous, more then is believed; . . . V. iv. 33. 8
They pressed forward, entraunce to have *made;* . . . V. iv. 38. 2
It *made* her stagger oft, . . . V. iv. 41. 9
Made them all enter in before her sight; . . . V. iv. 45. 7
other wing, now *made* unmeete for flight, . . . V. v. 15. 3
she *made* him to be dight In womans weedes, . . . V. v. 20. 6
wyder *made* the wound of th' *hidden* dart. . . . V. v. 28. 5
With which the Gods themselves are mylder *made:* . . . V. v. 49. 4
Who will not stoupe with good shall be *made* stoupe with harme . . . V. v. 49. 9
How earnest suit she earst for him had *made* . . . V. v. 54. 2
Ne would abide, till she had aunswere *made*, . . . V. vi. 17. 7
Now ye have *made* my heart to wake alway, . . . V. vi. 25. 7
whom they likewise *made* A Goddesse . . . V. vii. 3. 1
clothed all in garments *made* of line, . . . V. vii. 6. 4
it bit Unto the bone, and *made* a griesly wound, . . . V. vii. 33. 3
'What May-game hath misfortune *made* of you? . . . V. vii. 40. 2
magistrates of all that city *made*, . . . V. vii. 43. 3
Made them sweare fealty to Artegall; . . . V. vii. 43. 6
Against him *made* againe. . . . V. viii. 9. 5
Amends may for the trespasse soone be *made*, . . . V. viii. 14. 2
Till he himselfe was *made* their greedie pray, . . . V. viii. 31. 3
made them both one masse withouten more remorse. . . . V. viii. 32. 9
made a griesly wound in his enriven side. . . . V. viii. 34. 9
made him rave, like to a Lyon wood, . . . V. viii. 35. 5
made him backe againe as fast to fly; . . . V. viii. 36. 3
an uncouth vestiment *Made* of staunge stuffe, . . . V. ix. 10. 8
With peremptorie powre, that *made* all mute; . . . V. ix. 44. 2
Being then new *made* widow . . . V. x. 11. 7
made smooth fields now full of flowres? . . . V. x. 23. 5
in her necke a Castle huge had *made*, . . . V. x. 25. 8
made it beare the yoke of Inquisition, . . . V. x. 27. 2
made him stagger with uncertaine sway, . . . V. xi. 11. 2
of massy gold Most richly *made*, . . . V. xi. 21. 9
Made kill her selfe for very hearts despight . . . V. xi. 25. 4
made him stagger and stand halfe agast, . . . V. xi. 28. 7
for her entrailes *made* an open way To issue forth; . . . V. xi. 31. 3
made him oftentimes in field before me fall. . . . V. xi. 53. 9
Made cruell havocke of the baser crew, . . . V. xi. 59. 6
Made him become most faithless and unsound: . . . V. xii. 2. 4
made to fly like doves whom the Eagle doth affray. . . . V. xii. 5. 9
many wounds into his flesh it *made*, . . . V. xii. 19. 8
made most ugly cases. . . . V. xii. 28. 9
made a matchlesse paragon. . . . VI. i. 1. 9
oft he *made* him stagger as unstayd, . . . VI. i. 20. 3
made such piteous mourning therewithall, . . . VI. i. 34. 8
made him stoupe to ground with meeke humilitie: . . . VI. i. 38. 9
he *made* him sweare By his owne sword, . . . VI. i. 43. 5
goodly glee and feast to them she *made*, . . . VI. i. 46. 3
the stroke That through the mayles had *made* . . . a breach . VI. ii. 13. 3
There him he . . . *made* to sweare . . . VI. ii. 35. 1
a hazard she at earst had *made* . . . VI. iii. 8. 7
He was invulnerable *made* by Magicke leare. . . . VI. iv. 4. 9
Yet in his bodie *made* no wound nor bloud appeare. . . . VI. iv. 5. 9
by rude tokens *made* to her appeare His deepe compassion . VI. iv. 11. 3
He *made* great mone after his salvage mood; . . . VI. iv. 12. 4
he signes unto them *made* . . . VI. iv. 13. 2
Recured well, and *made* him whole againe; . . . VI. iv. 16. 7
that *made* him grone And gaspe for breath, . . . VI. iv. 21. 5
wound *Made* in his tender flesh; . . . VI. iv. 23. 9
That *made* them grow so high t' all honorable hap.' . . . VI. iv. 36. 9
She *made* him think it surely was his owne; . . . VI. iv. 38. 6

Made—*Continued.*
Yet he them all withstood, and often *made* relent. . . . VI. v. 20. 9
made him downe unto the earth encline; . . . VI. v. 26. 4
Made in the bodies of that Squire and Dame; . . . VI. vi. 2. 2
Made all of rusty yron ranckling sore, . . . VI. vi. 9. 3
To whom the Prince . . . Mylde answer *made*, . . . VI. vi. 20. 6
made him evermore increase his speedie pace. . . . VI. vi. 29. 9
he layd about, and *made* them fast to flie. . . . VI. vi. 38. 9
The warrant straight was *made*, . . . VI. vii. 35. 6
Then up he *made* him rise, . . . VI. vii. 49. 1
slaine he was, or *made* a wretched thrall, . . . VI. vii. 50. 3
Lord! what gladfull glee They *made* . . . VI. viii. 37. 2
they shouted all, and *made* a loud alarme. . . . VI. viii. 45. 9
made the wood to tremble at the noyce: . . . VI. viii. 46. 4
made her knowen to him at last: . . . VI. viii. 51. 8
made him scoule, and pout, . . . VI. ix. 38. 7
When the bold Centaures *made* that bloudy fray . . . VI. x. 13. 4
That *made* him pipe so merrily, as never none. . . . VI. x. 15. 9
Unto thy love that *made* thee low to lout: . . . VI. x. 16. 7
made great mone for that unhappy turne: . . . VI. x. 18. 6
She *made* me often pipe, and now to pipe apace. . . . VI. x. 27. 9
of her this mention may be *made!'* . . . VI. x. 28. 9
to thy blisse I *made* this luckelesse breach, . . . VI. x. 29. 3
spoile and booty, which they *made* Upon their neighbours . VI. x. 39. 5
Now *made* the spoile of theeves and Brigants bad, . . . VI. x. 40. 7
their way was *made* Through hollow caves, . . . VI. x. 42. 1
pittifull complaints which there she *made*, . . . VI. x. 44. 2
when love he to her *made*, . . . VI. xi. 7. 1
made unfit to serve his lawlesse mindes behest. . . . VI. xi. 7. 9
the Captaine in full angry wize *Made* answere, . . . VI. xi. 12. 2
in his mind had closely *made* A further purpose, . . . VI. xi. 38. 7
offer *made* To hyre them well . . . VI. xi. 40. 1
Through the dead carcases he *made* his way, . . . VI. xi. 47. 4
he did revive, . . . and *made* again alive. . . . VI. xi. 50. 9
made him almost mad for fell despight: . . . VI. xii. 31. 7
muzzel strong . . . *made* with many a lincke: . . . VI. xii. 34. 3
made them all accurst That God had blest, . . . VII. vi. 5. 7
Made no resistance, ne could her contraire, . . . VII. vi. 7. 8
Made of the heavens substance, . . . VII. vi. 10. 3
Made signe to them in their degrees to speake, . . . VII. vi. 22. 5
Was *made* the most unpleasant and most ill: . . . VII. vi. 37. 8
made her lucklesse loves well knowne to be: . . . VII. vi. 40. 6
made his hart to tickle in his brest, . . . VII. vi. 46. 2
made to growe Most dainty trees, . . . VII. vii. 8. 6
made him change his gray attire to greene: . . . VII. vii. 11. 8
Laden with fruits that *made* him laugh, . . . VII. vii. 30. 3
made him to obay: . . . VII. vii. 36. 4
Liv'd here on earth, and plenty *made* abound; . . . VII. vii. 37. 7
harvests riches, which he *made* his boot, . . . VII. vii. 38. 3
Made him so frollick and so full of lust: . . . VII. vii. 39. 5
merry feasting which he *made* And great bonfires, . . . VII. vii. 41. 2
say, they by your secret powre are *made:* . . . VII. vii. 49. 4
face, *Made* to amaze weake mens confused skil, . . . *Am.* xvii. 2
ymages Of hardest marble are of purpose *made*, . . . *Am.* li. 2
Made for to be the worlds most ornament, . . . *Am.* liii. 10
The which her *made* attonce so cruell faire. . . . *Am.* lv. 4
another Element . . . Whereof she mote be *made*, . . . *Am.* lv. 10
which three times thrise happy hath me *made*, . . . *Am.* lxxiv. 3
came the tyde, and *made* my paynes his pray, . . . *Am.* lxxv. 4
He onely fayre, and what he fayre hath *made;* . . . *Am.* lxxix. 13
want of cunning *made* me bold, . . . *Epig.* i. 3
thou thyselfe likewise art lyttle *made*, . . . *Epig.* iv. 13
Song! *made* in lieu of many ornaments, . . . *Epith.* 427
made you merie oft when ye were sorie. . . . *H.L.* 35
Made in the honor of your Soveraigne king. . . . *H.L.* 42
mixture *made* Of colours faire, . . . *H.B.* 65
that celestiall hew, . . . *Made* but the bait of sinne, . . . *H.B.* 152
made out of one mould the more t' agree; . . . *H.B.* 207
I have in th' heat of youth *made* heretofore, . . . *H.H.L.* 10
Such He him *made*, that he resemble might Himselfe, . . . *H.H.L.* 113
He *made* by love out of His owne like mould, . . . *H.H.L.* 116
which him at first *Made* of meere love, . . . *H.H.L.* 128
our brethren, that were *made* Of that selfe mould, . . . *H.H.L.* 197
All which are *made* with wondrous wise respect, . . . *H.H.B.* 34
Which he hath *made* in beauty excellent, . . . *H.H.B.* 129
By which they first were *made*, and still increast. . . . *H.H.B.* 203
wicker basket, *Made* of fine twigs, . . . *Proth.* 25

Madest. thereby *mad'st* her ever damn'd to be. . . . *Gn.* 472
whilest thou livedst, *madest* the forrests ring, . . . *Ti.* 325
Helene, . . . That *madest* many Ladies deare lament . . . III. ix. 35. 3
thou *madest* many harts to bleed . . . *H.L.* 12

Madman. A *mad man*, or that feigned mad to bee, . . . II. iv. 3. 5
His mighty hands did on the *madman* lay, . . . II. iv. 6. 4
Whom that *mad man* of life nigh late deprivd, . . . II. iv. 16. 3
this *mad man*, whom your victorious might . . . II. iv. 32. 3
'*Mad man*, . . . that does seeke Occasion to wrath, . . . II. iv. 44. 1

Madness. *Madnesse* to save a part, and lose the whole! . . . III. v. 43. 3
in his *madnesse* thinke . . . To spoyle so goodly workmanship IV. vi. 17. 3
rapt with joy resembling heavenly *madnes*, . . . *Am.* xxxix. 9

Madrigal. Why doe I send this rusticke *Madrigale*, . . . *Ded. Son.* viii. 3

Maeander. Deepe Indus, and *Maeander* intricate, . . . IV. xi. 21. 2

Maecenas. Through his *Mecaenas* left his Oaten reede, . . . *S.C.* O. 56
Mecaenas is yclad in claye, . . . *S.C.* O. 61
Had not *Mecaenas*, (**Mecenas*) . . . It first advaunst . . . *Ded. Son.* xiii. 3
That are the great *Mecaenas* of this age, . . . *Ded. Son.* xiii. 9

Maenads. Nor all the *Moenades* so furious were, . . . V. viii. 47. 8

Maeonian. Argument worthy of *Maeonian* quill; . . . II. x. 3. 1

Mage. the dreadfull *Mage* there fownd Deepe busied . . . III. iii. 14. 6

Magic. By *Magicke* skill out of eternall night. . . . *Ro.* v. 8
that, which Merlin by his *magicke* slights Made . . . *Ti.* 523

Magic—*Continued.*
amiddes His *magick* bookes, and artes of sundrie kindes, . . . I. i. 36. 8
who can tell The . . . might of *Magick* spel? . . . . I. ii. 10. 9
besmeare My body all, through charmes and *magicke* might, . I. ii. 42. 4
In charmes and *magick* to have wondrous might, ... I. iii. 38. 8
when her face is staynd with *magicke* arts constraint. . . . . I. vii. 34. 9
No *magicke* arts hereof had any might, ... I. vii. 35. 1
excell All living wightes in might of *magicke* spell: . . . . I. vii. 36. 5
golden cup, . . . replete with *magick* artes; . . . . I. viii. 14. 2
Elfinor, who was in *magick* skild; . . . . II. x. 73. 7
Mongst thousand dangers, and ten thousand *Magick* mights. . II. xii. 1. 9
pleasing wordes are like to *Magick* art, ... III. ii. 15. 5
Ybuilded all of glasse, by *Magicke* powre, ... III. ii. 20. 7
May learned be by cyphers, or by *Magicke* might. . . . . . . III. ii. 45. 9
For Merlin had in *Magick* more insight . . . . III. iii. 11. 8
In vaine seekes wonders out of *Magick* spell.' . . . . III. iii. 17. 7
Which Bladud made by *Magick* art of yore, ... III. iii. 60. 2
By strong enchauntments and blacke *Magicke* leare, ... III. xi. 16. 7
Thereto she learned was in *Magicke* leare, ... IV. iii. 40. 1
He was invulnerable made by *Magicke* leare. . . . . VI. iv. 4. 9
did with charmes or *Magick* her molest, ... VII. vi. 16. 6
Magical. *magicall* Illusion that did beguile his sense, ... II. xi. 39. 5
Magician. 'Thither the great *magicien* Merlin came, ... I. ix. 5. 1
The great *Magitien* Merlin had deviz'd, ... III. ii. 18. 6
'But read,' (saide Glauce) 'thou *Magitian,* . . . . III. iii. 25. 1
Magistrates. picturals Of *Magistrates,* of courts, of tribunals, . II. ix. 53. 5
magistrates of all that city made, ... V. vii. 43. 3
Magitien. *See* **Magician.**
Maglan. wedded th' one to *Maglan* king of Scottes, ... II. x. 29. 1
Magnanimity. And fill your mind with *magnanimitee.* . . . . *Ded. Son.* x. 12
In whose dead face he redd great *magnanimity.* . . . . . . II. viii. 23. 9
'What huge heroicke *magnanimity* . . . . III. xi. 19. 2
Magnes-stone. hideous Rocke is pight Of mightie *Magnes stone,* II. xii. 4. 2
Magnific. *Magnificke* Lord, whose vertues excellent, ... *Ded. Son.* ii. 1
with *magnificke* might and wondrous wit Doest . . . . V. Pr. 11. 3
'*Magnificke* Virgin, that . . . doest maske thy royall blood, . . V. vii. 21. 1
Whose porch, that most *magnificke* did appeare, ... V. ix. 22. 3
Magnificence. As th' Idole of her makers great *magnificence.* . II. ii. 41. 9
With stately port and proud *magnificence,* . . . . V. v. 4. 2
Magnifico. As if he were some great *Magnifico,* . . . . *Hub.* 665
Magnified. would as Ammons sonne be *magnifide,* . . . . . . I. v. 48. 8
Was never king more highly *magnifide,* . . . . II. x. 52. 1
art in mightie armes most *magnifyde* . . . . II. xii. 32. 4
To heare her Love so highly *magnifyde;* . . . . III. ii. 11. 2
Of whom ye seeke to be most *magnifide;* . . . . III. v. 11. 4
in all His famous conquests highly *magnifide:* . . . . III. vii. 31. 7
The which through fame should farre be *magnifide,* . . . . . VI. iv. 33. 3
her that is Grand-mother *magnifide* Of all the Gods, ... VII. vi. 26. 5
Magnify. Some greater learned wit will *magnifie:* . . . . . *Ro.* ii. 12
good men blame, and losels *magnify.* . . . . *T.M.* 324
th' others pleasing service to abate, To *magnifie* his owne. . . II. ii. 19. 6
all faire Ladies *magnify* your might, ... III. x. 28. 7
Yet she her selfe the more doth *magnify,* . . . . V. viii. 17. 8
much did *magnifie* his noble name: . . . . V. xi. 46. 6
Magnifying. *magnifying* lovers deare debate; . . . . IV. Pr. 1. 5
Mahound. 'By *Mahoune,* cursed thiefe, ... II. viii. 33. 3
vow by *Mahoune* that he should be slaine. . . . . IV. viii. 44. 3
oftentimes by Turmagant and *Mahound* swore. . . . . VI. vii. 47. 9
Maia. The Sonne of *Maia,* . . . . *Hub.* 1257
Eftsoones the sonne of *Maia* forth he sent . . . . VII. vi. 16. 1
Like unto *Maia,* when as Jove her took . . . . *Epith.* 307
Maia's. bids make readie *Maias* bowre, ... *S.C.* Mar. 17
Like to the rod which *Maias* sonne doth wield, ... IV. iii. 42. 6
Maid. *See* **Bondmaid.**
the Galles were, by corrupting of a *mayde,* . . . . *Van.* xi. 6
they dauncen, eche one with his *mayd.* . . . . *S.C.* May 24
the month in which the righteous *Maide,* . . . . *Hub.* 1
ingratefull to each gentle *mayd,* . . . . *Col.* 462
'Thrise happie *Mayd,* . . . . *Col.* 480
who can tell what cause had that faire *Mayd* . . . . *Col.* 911
When tidings came to mee, unhappy *maid,* . . . . I. ii. 24. 4
the seeming simple *maid* Let fal her eien, ... I. ii. 27. 5
she, . . . all this while Forsaken, wofull, solitarie *mayd,* . . . I. iii. 3. 2
Who now is left to keepe the forlorne *maid* . . . . I. iii. 43. 1
Me, silly *maid,* away with him he bare, ... I. iv. 47. 7
the luckelesse lucky *mayd* Did her content . . . . I. vi. 19. 1
The forlorne *mayd* did with loves longing burne, ... I. vi. 22. 1
How with that pensive *Maid* he best might thence arise. . . I. vi. 32. 9
Then hunt the steps of pure unspotted *Maid:* . . . . I. vi. 46. 8
the whiles the royall *Mayd* Fledd farre away, ... I. vi. 47. 8
a royall *Mayd* Her daintie limbes . . . down did lay: . . . . I. ix. 13. 7
me, sad *mayd,* or rather widow sad, ... I. xii. 27. 1
Then stepped forth the goodly royall *Mayd,* . . . . I. xii. 33. 1
How shamefully that *Mayd* he did torment: . . . . II. i. 11. 4
that fayre ymage of that heavenly *Mayd,* . . . . II. i. 28. 7
Her deare besought to let her die a *mayd.* . . . . II. ii. 8. 5
Shapt like a *maide,* . . . . II. ii. 9. 5
Cymochles with that wanton *mayd* . . . . II. vi. 40. 8
That wanton *Mayd* of passage had denide, ... II. viii. 3. 3
to see the *mayd* So straungely passioned, ... II. ix. 41. 8
To stere the bote towards that dolefull *Mayd,* . . . . II. xii. 28. 2
the brave *Mayd* would not disarmed bee, ... III. i. 42. 7
To lodge the warlike *maide,* unwisely loov'd; . . . . III. i. 60. 4
At last the royall *Mayd* . . . did awake, ... III. i. 61. 7
On thother side they saw the warlike *Mayd* . . . . III. i. 63. 6
To aske this Briton *Maid,* what uncouth wind . . . . III. ii. 4. 5
'Faire martiall *Mayd,* Certes ye misavised beene, ... III. ii. 9. 4
The royall *Maid* woxe inly wondrous glad, ... III. ii. 11. 1
to beguyle A simple *maide,* . . . . III. ii. 12. 8
So thought this *Mayd* (as maydens use to done) . . . . III. ii. 23. 5

Maid—*Continued.*
She wist not, silly *Mayd,* what she did aile, ... III. ii. 27. 7
Ne ought it mote the noble *Mayd* avayle, ... III. ii. 52. 1
in this royall *Maid* of yore, ... III. iii. 3. 3
the hardy *Mayd* (with love to frend) . . . . III. iii. 14. 5
The doubtfull *Mayd,* seeing her selfe descryde, ... III. iii. 20. 1
shortly make you a *mayd* Martiall. . . . . III. iii. 53. 9
the yong *Mayd* She might in equall armes accompany, . . . III. iii. 61. 3
The martiall *Mayd* stayd not him to lament, ... III. iv. 18. 1
The warlike *Maide,* th' ensample of that might; . . . . . . III. iv. 44. 7
As meetest may beseeme a noble *mayd:* . . . . III. v. 5. 3
whiles his Lord pursewd that noble *Mayd,* . . . . III. v. 13. 3
The goodly *Maide,* ful of divinities . . . . III. v. 34. 7
the *Mayd* And daughter of a woody Nymphe, ... III. v. 36. 2
the *Mayd* His readie wound with better salves new drest: . . III. v. 41. 3
whenas he beheld the heavenly *Mayd,* . . . . III. v. 43. 4
that faire *Maide,* the flowre of wemens pride; . . . . III. vii. 31. 5
the brave *Mayd* would not for courtesy . . . him abrade, . . . III. xi. 8. 3
like a Serpent to the Thracian *mayd.* . . . . III. xi. 35. 4
The warlike *Mayd,* beholding earnestly . . . . III. xi. 53. 1
The noble *Mayd* still standing all this vewd, ... III. xii. 5. 1
Hope in ranke, a handsome *Mayd,* . . . . III. xii. 13. 1
the brave *Maid,* which al this while was plast . . . . III. xii. 27. 4
Through fine abusion of that Briton *mayd;* . . . . IV. i. 7. 2
Good lucke presents you with yond lovely *mayd,* . . . . . . IV. i. 33. 8
Thrise lowted lowly to the noble *Mayd,* . . . . IV. iii. 5. 8
that snowy *Mayd* Was in the middest plast . . . . IV. v. 26. 1
Unluckie *Mayd,* to seeke her enimie! . . . . IV. v. 29. 6
Unluckie *Mayd,* to seeke him farre and wide, ... IV. v. 29. 7
What shall of me, unhappy *maid,* become? . . . . IV. vii. 11. 3
'Unhappy *mayd'* . . . 'whose dread Untride is lesse . . . . . IV. vii. 11. 5
A wofull wretched *maid,* of God and man forgot! . . . . . . IV. vii. 14. 9
the love of that same snowy *maid,* . . . . IV. ix. 24. 2
Scudamour and that same Briton *maide* . . . . IV. ix. 28. 2
In that late Turney for the snowy *maide;* . . . . IV. ix. 28. 7
to see that gentle *maide* so tost!' . . . . IV. ix. 38. 5
in the midst of them a goodly *mayd* . . . . IV. x. 52. 2
Cupids man with Venus *mayd* to hold, ... IV. x. 54. 7
There did this lucklesse *mayd* seven months abide, ... IV. xi. 4. 6
That his decay should happen by a *mayd.* . . . . IV. xii. 28. 5
Commaunding Proteus straight t' enlarge the *mayd,* . . . . IV. xii. 32. 3
He gazed still upon that snowy *mayd;* . . . . V. iii. 18. 7
many a one suppos'd to be a *mayd:* . . . . V. iii. 28. 3
That further *mayd,* hight Philtera the faire, ... V. iv. 8. 7
'The wretched *mayd,* that earst desir'd to die, ... V. iv. 11. 1
She called forth to her a trusty *mayd,* . . . . V. iv. 48. 1
(said then the faithfull *Mayd*) . . . . V. v. 31. 1
The trustie *Mayd,* conceiving her intent, ... V. v. 35. 1
foolish *Mayd!* whyles heedlesse of the hooke . . . . V. v. 43. 1
There did the warlike *Maide* her selfe repose, ... V. vii. 12. 1
th' other still pursu'd the fearefull *Mayd;* . . . . V. viii. 6. 1
for what cause they chased so that *Mayd?* . . . . V. viii. 15. 4
the which that *mayd* complained To have bene done . . . . V. viii. 24. 2
Marcht with that *mayd;* . . . . V. viii. 51. 9
So both agreed to send that *mayd* afore, ... V. ix. 8. 6
Thence forth they passed with that gentle *Mayd* . . . . . . V. ix. 20. 1
of a *Mayd* she had the outward face, ... V. xi. 23. 7
Too much am I too blame for that faire *Maide,* . . . . . . V. xi. 41. 2
The heavy *Mayd,* to whom none tydings bore . . . . V. xii. 11. 5
this *Mayd,* whose party thou doest take, ... VI. i. 19. 7
Ran after fast to reskue the distressed *mayde.* . . . . VI. iii. 24. 9
murdred cruelly by a rebellious *Mayd.* . . . . VI. vii. 34. 9
can me, most wretched *mayd,* Deliver . . . . VI. viii. 19. 5
(sayd the sory *Mayd*) . . . . VI. viii. 24. 1
the fayre *mayd* the table ta'ne away, ... VI. ix. 18. 2
So it surely wrought With this faire *Mayd,* . . . . VI. ix. 45. 7
Whilest Calidore does follow that faire *Mayd,* . . . . VI. x. 1. 2
that fourth *Mayd,* which there amidst them traced, ... VI. x. 25. 2
this lucklesse *mayd* away was lad, ... VI. x. 40. 4
Like as is now befalne to this faire *Mayd,* . . . . VI. xi. 2. 1
the *mayd* of whom they spake Was his owne purchase, . . . VI. xi. 12. 2
that same *mayd* . . . Should with the rest be sold . . . . . . VI. xi. 15. 3
in his armes the dreary dying *mayd,* . . . . VI. xi. 21. 2
this faire *Mayd* Was that same infant . . . . VI. xii. 16. 2
ye to me gave A little *mayde,* . . . . VI. xii. 17. 7
forth in hast ran to the straunger *Mayd;* . . . . VI. xii. 19. 2
this young *Mayd,* whom chance to her presents, ... VI. xii. 20. 5
to corrupt Molanna, this her *maid,* . . . . VII. vi. 43. 2
The simple *mayd* did yield to him anone; . . . . VII. vi. 45. 1
faire May, the fayrest *mayd* on ground, ... VII. vii. 34. 1
led a lovely *Mayd* Forth by the lilly hand, ... VII. vii. 37. 3
nourisht by th' Idaean *mayd;* . . . . VII. vii. 41. 7
proud *mayd,* whom now those leaves attyre: . . . . *Am.* xxviii. 8
Maiden. Colours meete to clothe a *mayden* Queene? . . . . . *S.C.* F. 132
Yclad in Scarlot, like a *mayden* Queene, ... *S.C.* Ap. 57
A *mayden* Queene that shone as Titans ray, ... I. iv. 8. 5
The pitteous *mayden,* . . . Does throw out thrilling shriekes, I. vi. 6. 1
'The forlorne *Maiden,* whom your eies have seene . . . . . . I. vii. 43. 1
such as she was, a goodly *maiden* Queene. . . . . I. xii. 8. 9
'The *Mayden,* proud through praise . . . . II. iv. 27. 1
A seemely *Maiden* sitting by the shore, ... II. xii. 27. 6
greatest shame was to that *maiden* twin, ... III. vi. 49. 3
the false *mayden* shortly turn'd againe Unto the prison, . . . V. v. 51. 8
a *mayden* Queene of high renowne, ... V. viii. 17. 2
To wreake her on that *mayden* messengere, ... V. viii. 46. 4
Hayling that *mayden* by the yellow heare, ... VI. i. 17. 6
A faire young *Mayden,* full of comely glee; . . . . VI. vi. 10. 7
a faire *Mayden* clad in mourning weed, ... VI. vi. 16. 7
when this *Maiden* faire Was dighting her, ... VI. xii. 15. 1
Seeme lyke some *mayden* Queene. . . . . *Epith.* 158

Maiden-child. in dew time a *mayden child* forth brought: . . VI. xii. 6. 5
Maidenhead. That noble order hight of *maidenhed,* . . . . I. vii. 46. 4
on me she deigned to bestowe Order of *Maydenhead,* . . . . II. ii. 42. 4
numbred be mongst knights of *Maydenhed,* . . . . II. ix. 6. 6
The prayse of her fresh flowring *Maydenhead;* . . . . III. v. 54. 6
To be upbrought in perfect *Maydenhed,* . . . . III. vi. 28. 4
Nor halfe so fast to save her *maydenhed* . . . . III. vii. 26. 3
all the noble knights of *Maydenhead,* . . . . III. viii. 47. 7
Unto the noble Knights of *Maidenhead,* . . . . IV. iv. 22. 6
still the Knights of *Maydenhead* the better wonne; . . . . IV. iv. 38. 9
restore The prize to knights of *Maydenhead* . . . . IV. iv. 48. 2
All the brave Knights that hold of *Maidenhead,* . . . . V. iv. 29. 6
by the faith that I To *Maydenhead* and noble knighthood owe, V. iv. 34. 2
knights of *Maidenhead,* whose praise she would empaire.' . . V. iv. 34. 9
Maiden-headed. addrest his *maiden-headed* shield, ... IV. iv. 17. 4
Maiden's. Did worthily revenge this *maydens* pride; . . . . VI. vii. 32. 2
Maidens. The greene is for *maydens* meete. . . . . *S.C.* Au. 68
Full many *Maydens* often did him woo, ... *As.* 37
to the *Maydens* sownding tymbrels song . . . . I. xii. 7. 3
The wanton *Maidens,* him espying, ... II. xii. 66. 1
(as *maydens* use to done) . . . . III. ii. 23. 5
An hundred naked *maidens* lilly white . . . . VI. x. 11. 8
So did Diana and her *maydens* all . . . . VII. vi. 49. 1
The whiles the *maydens* doe theyr carroll sing, ... *Epith.* 259
Maidens'. she beheld those *maydens* meriment . . . . I. xii. 8. 1
gemmes Fit to decke *maydens* bowres, ... *Proth.* 15
Maid's. Forgoe that royal *maides* bequeathed care, ... I. x. 63. 7
her *Maides* attyre To turne into a massy habergeon, ... III. iii. 57. 7
this *maides* with whom I fastned hand, ... V. iv. 15. 7
Maids. 'There also those two Pandionian *maides,* . . . . *Gn.* 401
we silly *Maides,* whom they dispize . . . . *T.M.* 339
ye fayre *Mayds,* the matches of his yeares, ... *As.* 129
I of gentle *Mayds* should ill deserve! . . . . *Col.* 465
desird Of all the fairest *Maides* to have the vew. *Ded.Son.*xvii.4
striv'd With th' Heliconian *maides* for maystery; . . . . II. xii. 31. 2
So cruell doale amongst her *maides* divide . . . . V. iv. 39. 3
Her warlike *maides* about her flockt so fast, ... V. iv. 43. 6
ye lightfoot *mayds,* which keepe the dore, ... *Epith.* 67
let the *mayds* and yongmen cease to sing; . . . . *Epith.* 332
Mail. She lookt about, and seeing one in *mayle,* . . . . I. i. 16. 5
cruell Sarazin, In woven *maile* all armed warily; . . . . I. v. 4. 2
impresse Deepe dinted furrowes in the battred *mayle:* . . . . I. v. 6. 8
with their force they perst both plate and *maile,* . . . . I. vi. 43. 4
To measure manhood by the sword or *mayle.* . . . . II. iii. 16. 5
Ne plate, ne *male,* could ward so mighty throwes, ... II. v. 9. 3
neither *mayle* could hold, Ne shield defend . . . . II. viii. 41. 2
doft his helmet, and undid his *mayle:* . . . . IV. i. 43. 7
Through shield and *mayle* and haberjeon did wend, ... IV. ii. 15. 4
neither plate nor *mayle* . . . could once sustaine . . . . IV. iii. 15. 4
all his *mayle* yriv'd, and plates yrent, ... IV. vi. 15. 8
Mailed. through his *mayled* hauberque, ... III. iv. 16. 4
His *mayled* haberjeon she did undight, ... III. v. 31. 8
She wore for her defence a *mayled* habergeon. . . . . V. v. 2. 9
Mails. through the linked *mayles* empierced quite, ... III. v. 19. 4
shields did share, and *mailes* did rash, ... IV. ii. 17. 9
through the *mayles* into his thigh it entred, ... IV. iii. 9. 3
mailes betweene, and laced close afore; . . . . V. v. 3. 3
the stroke That through the *mayles* had made . . . a breach . VI. ii. 13. 3
Maimed. *See* **Late-maimed.**
he him *maymed* quite, and all his shoulder split. . . . . V. iii. 33. 9
Main. all that treasure, drowned in the *maine:* . . . . *Bel.*[2] xiii. 13
shott at him with might and *maine,* . . . . *S.C.* Mar. 86
Where Titan ryseth from the *mayne* . . . . *S.C.* Jul. 59
defend . . . with his might and *maine.* . . . . *Gn.* 524
with conquest of their might and *maine,* . . . . *Ti.* 62
With huge force and insupportable *mayne,* . . . . I. vii. 11. 2
lightly leaping from so monstrous *maine,* . . . . I. viii. 7. 7
He smott thereat with all his might and *maine,* . . . . I. xi. 43. 4
swimming in the *maine* Will die for thrist, ... II. vi. 17. 7
with such puissaunce and impetuous *maine* . . . . II. ix. 14. 5
defend The walles so stoutly with their sturdie *mayne,* . . . II. xi. 15. 7
Yet life he saw, and felt his mighty *mayne,* . . . . II. xi. 44. 4
they see from midst of all the *Maine* The surging waters . II. xii. 21. 5
Fiers battaill against one with cruell might and *mayne.* . . . III. i. 20. 9
upreare His deawy head out of the Ocean *maine,* . . . . III. iv. 61. 4
drove at him with all his might and *mayne* . . . . III. v. 21. 4
In minde to leape into the mighty *maine,* . . . . III. vii. 27. 3
all the countrey seemes to be a *Maine,* . . . . III. vii. 34. 5
her *maine* strength, in which she most doth trust, ... III. vii. 50. 5
Long so she on the mighty *maine* did flote, ... III. viii. 21. 3
His bowre is in the bottom of the *maine,* . . . . III. viii. 37. 1
In deawy vapours of the westerne *mayne,* . . . . III. viii. 51. 4
many fortunes prov'd in th' Ocean *mayne,* . . . . III. ix. 48. 8
Tossing them like a boate amid the *mayne,* . . . . IV. iii. 1. 6
Like as the tide, that comes fro th' Ocean *mayne,* . . . . IV. iii. 27. 1
meete with so hideous *maine,* . . . . IV. iv. 18. 4
ran at him with all his might and *maine;* . . . . IV. iv. 44. 8
day out of the Ocean *mayne* Began to peepe . . . . IV. v. 45. 3
He smote at him with all his might and *maine,* . . . . IV. viii. 45. 3
billowes beating from the *maine:* . . . . IV. xii. 5. 9
I will thrust downe into the deepest *maine,* . . . . V. ii. 38. 4
They both together joyned might and *maine,* . . . . V. iii. 12. 3
Gan drive at him with so huge might and *maine,* . . . . V. ix. 19. 3
with so huge might and *maine* . . . . V. x. 32. 3
for all his *maine* It would no passage yeeld . . . . V. xi. 10. 8
He did him smite with all his might and *maine,* . . . . V. xii. 23. 6
His stroke redoubled with such might and *maine,* . . . . VI. i. 39. 3
But hayld and puld with all his might and *maine* . . . . VI. iv. 7. 4
Upon them two they fell with might and *maine,* . . . . VI. vi. 23. 3
Like as the wounded Whale to shore flies from the *maine.* . . VI. x. 31. 9

Main—*Continued.*
despoyling all with *maine* and might. . . . . VI. xii. 23. 9
Mainland. With dreadfull poyse is from the *mayneland* rift, . I. xi. 54. 7
By sea to have bene from the Celticke *maynland* brought. . . II. x. 5. 9
The Land to sea, and sea to *maineland* dry, ... III. iii. 12. 3
no more we can the *mayn-land* see, ... III. viii. 24. 3
Mainly. strooke so *maynly* mercilesse, ... I. vii. 12. 1
Mainely they all attonce upon him laid, ... III. i. 21. 1
Main sea. Through the *maine sea* making her merry flight. . . *Van.* ix. 4
he came far from the *main-sea* deepe, ... *Col.* 67
Main-sheet. Vere the *maine shete,* and beare up with the land, ... I. xii. 1. 3
strikes his sayles, and vereth his *mainsheat,* . . . . V. xii. 18. 8
Maintain. The honour yet in ashes doo *maintaine;* . . . . *Ro.* vii. 4
wisely did *maintaine* With gallant showe, ... *Hub.* 690
with their gownes their gravitie *maintaine.* . . . . *Hub.* 838
now nor Prince nor Priest doth her *maintayne,* . . . . *T.M.* 565
Right and loyall did his word *maintaine.* . . . . *Ti.* 189
feeble spirits in their force *maintaine,* . . . . *D.* 438
Both did he other, which could pipe, *maintaine,* . . . . *Col.* 442
it to *maintaine* Against vile Zoilus backbitings . . . . *Ded. Son.* xii.13
with like treason now *maintain* Thy guilty wrong, ... I. vi. 41. 5
his wrong with greater puissance *maintaine.'* . . . . II. i. 14. 9
Throughout the world her mercy to *maintaine,* . . . . II. ii. 43. 7
drew his deadly weapon to *maintaine* his part. . . . . II. iv. 9. 9
ought that els your honour might *maintaine;* . . . . II. viii. 19. 7
Their stedfast stonds did mightily *maintaine,* . . . . II. xi. 15. 2
His glory did repose, and credit did *maintaine.* . . . . III. viii. 11. 9
none against them battell durst *maintaine:* . . . . IV. iv. 25. 5
new discord to *maintaine.* . . . . IV. v. 22. 9
vow'd with speare and shield it to *maintaine;* . . . . IV. v. 24. 8
By all meanes to *maintaine* that castels ancient rights. . . . IV. x. 7. 9
to *maintaine* that she all others did excell. . . . . V. iii. 4. 9
either others cause to *maintaine* mutually. . . . . V. viii. 14. 9
armed men, which did *maintaine* That Ladies part, ... V. viii. 50. 3
maintayne That Tyrants part with close or open ayde, . . . V. xii. 25. 5
This evill manner which ye here *maintaine,* . . . . VI. i. 27. 2
tooke in hand her quarrell to *maintaine;* . . . . VI. i. 33. 2
Ripe yeares of reason my right to *maintaine:* . . . . VI. ii. 28. 5
Maintaine this evill use, thy foes thereby to foile. . . . . VI. vi. 34. 9
A wrongfull quarrell to *maintaine* by fight; . . . . VI. vi. 35. 6
greater force there needs to *maintaine* wrong then right. . . VI. vi. 35. 9
By Arthure, when as Unas Knight he did *maintaine.* . . . . VI. vii. 41. 9
all creatures to *maintaine* In state of life? . . . . VII. vii. 22. 4
raigne over Change, and do their states *maintaine.* . . . . VII. vii. 58. 9
Maintained. therein thou maist *maintained* bee. . . . . *Hub.* 534
oft *maintain'd* his masters braverie. . . . . *Hub.* 858
when thou of none shalt be *maintained,* . . . . *D.* 83
Because he had not well *mainteind* his right, ... II. v. 20. 4
maintaynd With mightie deedes their sondry governments; . . II. x. 74. 3
whence so sumptuous guize Might be *maintaynd,* . . . . III. i. 33. 9
Uppon the Souldan selfe, which it *mayntained,* . . . . V. viii. 24. 7
it hath long *mayntaind* with mighty wrong: . . . . VI. i. 13. 4
Mote have your life in honour long *maintayned.* . . . . *Am.* xxxvi. 12
Maintenance. provide for meanes of *maintenaunce,* . . . . *S.C.* May 79
little them served for their *mayntenaunce.* . . . . *S.C.* May 112
They bene so grave and full of *mayntenaunce.* . . . . *S.C.* S. 169
For their usurped kingdomes *maintenaunce,* . . . . *T.M.* 338
there professours find small *maintenance,* . . . . *Col.* 705
lodging in so meane a *maintenaunce;* . . . . III. vii. 59. 4
Main-yards. the pennes . . . Were like *mayne-yardes* with flying canvas lynd; . . . . I. xi. 10. 5
Maire. There also was the wide embayed *Mayre;* . . . . IV. xi. 44. 1
Maist. *See* **Mayest.**
Maister, *etc. See* **Master,** *etc.*
Majesty. In *majestie* she seemde to matche the Gods. . . . . *Bel.*[1] xi. 6
Did seeme to match the Gods in *Majestie.* . . . . *Bel.*[2] xv. 6
Her *Majestie,* Where have you seene the like . . . . *S.C.* Ap. 71
with vile cloaths approach Gods *majestie,* . . . . *Hub.* 465
ne would his *majestye* Use them but well, ... *Hub.* 1079
Th' eternall Makers *majestie* wee viewe, ... *T.M.* 512
myrrour of her Makers *majestie,* . . . . *T.M.* 572
Jove in midst with awfull *Majestie,* . . . . *Mui.* 308
imperiall *Majestie* to frame In loftie numbers . . . . *Ded. Son.* xii. 7
Mirrour of grace and *Majestie* divine, ... I. Pr. 4. 2
To prove the wide report of her great *Majestee.* . . . . I. iv. 13. 9
With royall pomp and princely *majestie* She is ybrought . . . I. v. 5. 2
He . . . her endowd with royall *majestye.* . . . . I. vii. 16. 5
Present before the *majesty* divine, ... I. x. 51. 8
an Angels voice Singing before th' eternall *majesty,* . . . . I. xii. 39. 4
Adornes the person of her *Majestye;* . . . . II. ii. 41. 5
with dredd *Majestie* and awfull yre, ... II. iii. 23. 8
A stately siege of soveraine *majestye;* . . . . II. vi. 44. 5
The wise Elficleos, in great *Majestie,* . . . . II. x. 75. 2
Beares he himselfe in portly *majestee,* . . . . III. iii. 32. 4
Of roiall *majesty* and soveraine name: . . . . III. iii. 48. 8
goodly arras of great *majesty,* . . . . III. xi. 28. 2
To see him in his soverayne *majestee* . . . . III. xi. 33. 3
use of awfull *Majestie* remove. . . . . IV. Pr. 5. 4
Tempred with sternesse and stout *majestie,* . . . . IV. vi. 26. 3
Made humble suit unto his *Majestie* . . . . IV. xii. 29. 6
I humbly crave your *Majestie* It to replevie, ... IV. xii. 31. 7
A Princesse of great powre and *majestie,* . . . . V. viii. 16. 8
Thus she did sit in soverayne *Majestie,* . . . . V. ix. 30. 1
bowing low before her *Majestie,* . . . . V. ix. 34. 3
Yet tempred with some *majestie* imperiall. . . . . V. ix. 34. 9
Bate somewhat of that *Majestie* and awe . . . . V. ix. 35. 7
her leading with meete *majestie* . . . . V. xii. 25. 1
like King of fowles in *majesty* and powre: . . . . VI. x. 6. 9
in her soveraine *Majesty* to sit, ... VI. x. 9. 8

Majesty—*Continued.*
Great Gloriana, greatest *Majesty!* . . . . VI. x. 28. 3
full of grace and *Majestie,* . . . . VII. vi. 24. 8
With goodly port and gracious *Majesty,* . . . . VII. vii. 5. 2
Bade Order call them all before her *Majesty.* . . . . . . VII. vii. 27. 9
Myld humblesse, mixt with awfull *majesty.* . . . . *Am.* xiii. 5
with thy selfe did lie And begot *Majesty.* . . . . *Epith.* 331
Adore the powre of thy great *Majestie,* . . . . *H.B.* 271
face Of the Divine Eternall *Majestie;* . . . . *H.H.B.* 81
The glory of that *Majestie* Divine, ... *H.H.B.* 124
Before the footestoole of his *Majestie* . . . . *H.H.B.* 142
most fit For so great powre and peerelesse *majesty,* . . . . *H.H.B.* 186

Make. *See* **Maked, Merry-make.**
signes to *make* all wights adore The beast, ... *Rev.* i. 13
The sight wherof dyd *make* my heart rejoyce. . . . . *Pet.*[1] iv. 8
Which *make* this life wretched and miserable, ... *Pet.*[2] vi. 13
Doo *make* her Idole through the world appeare. . . . . . . *Ro.* v. 14
onely Rome could *make* great Rome to tremble: . . . . . . *Ro.* vi. 10
for a time *make* warre Gainst time, ... *Ro.* vii. 9
if that time *make* ende of things so sure, ... *Ro.* vii. 13
So long as Joves great Bird did *make* his flight, ... *Ro.* xvii. 1
laughes the songs that Colin Clout doth *make.* . . . . . . *S.C.* Ja. 66
Such an one shepeheards would *make* full faine: . . . . . . *S.C.* F. 67
Such an one would *make* thee younge againe. . . . . *S.C.* F. 68
Many meete tales of youth did he *make,* . . . . *S.C.* F. 98
bids *make* readie Maias bowre, ... *S.C.* Mar. 17
Nor thys, nor that, so muche doeth *make* me mourne, ... *S.C.* Ap. 9
hath he skill to *make* so excellent, ... *S.C.* Ap. 19
a fourth Grace, to *make* the daunce even? . . . . *S.C.* Ap. 113
To see those folkes *make* such jovysaunce, ... *S.C.* May 25
what account both these will *make;* . . . . *S.C.* May 51
They *maken* many a wrong chevisaunce, ... *S.C.* May 92
I list none accordaunce *make* . . . . *S.C.* May 164
the dore to *make* fast, ... *S.C.* May 292
Doe *make* them musick . . . . *S.C.* Jun. 29
taught me homely, as I can, to *make;* . . . . *S.C.* Jun. 82
Thy teares would *make* the hardest flint to flowe! . . . . . *S.C.* Jun. 114
wont to *make* the jolly shepeheards gladde, ... *S.C.* Au. 9
Beres and Tygres, that *maken* fiers warre; . . . . *S.C.* Au. 28
make like account of his brother. . . . . *S.C.* Au. 43
in your songs were wont to *make* a part: . . . . *S.C.* Au. 154
for such, as of guile *maken* gayne, ... *S.C.* S. 34
maken a Mart of theyr good name: . . . . *S.C.* S. 37
make a mocke at the blustring blast. . . . . *S.C.* S. 54
could *make* a jolly hole in theyr furre: . . . . *S.C.* S. 165
Then *make* thee winges of thine aspyring wit, ... *S.C.* O. 83
So high to sore and *make* so large a flight; . . . . *S.C.* O. 86
Sike myrth in May is meetest for to *make,* . . . . *S.C.* N. 11
Should Colin *make* judge of my fooleree: . . . . *S.C.* N. 28
Make hast, ye shepheards, thether to revert: . . . . *S.C.* N. 191
Thus gan he *make* of love his piteous mone. . . . . *S.C.* D. 6
gather nuttes to *make* me Christmas game, ... *S.C.* D. 26
'To *make* fine cages for the Nightingale, ... *S.C.* D. 79
Whom golden Fleece did *make* an heavenly signe; . . . . . . *Gn.* 211
To *make* the mountaines touch the starres divine, ... *Gn.* 213
skies and seas doo *make* most dreadfull warre; . . . . *Gn.* 574
I meane my Gossip privie first to *make.*' . . . . *Hub.* 70
for our selves we may a living *make.* . . . . *Hub.* 116
why should he that is at libertie *Make* himselfe bond? . . . *Hub.* 133
and *make* our ease our treasure. . . . . *Hub.* 160
make them seeke for that they wont to scorne, ... *Hub.* 257
Triall to *make* of his endevourment; . . . . *Hub.* 298
They shall him *make* an ill accompt of thrift. . . . . *Hub.* 307
Ne *make* one title worse, ne *make* one better: . . . . *Hub.* 384
readie are of anie to *make* preife. . . . . *Hub.* 408
Ye shall for ever us your bondmen *make.*' . . . . *Hub.* 412
Is not that name enough to *make* a living . . . . *Hub.* 417
it *make* A servant to the vile affection . . . . *Hub.* 816
we may our selves . . . *Make* Kings of Beasts, ... *Hub.* 971
Upon his fleshly corpse to *make* invasion: . . . . *Hub.* 1090
Doo seeke to *make* us of the world forlorne, ... *T.M.* 66
When he is sad, shee seeks to *make* him merie, ... *T.M.* 137
Each idle wit at will presumes to *make,* . . . . *T.M.* 215
pitious lamentation did *make;* . . . . *T.M.* 296
make them merrie with their fooleries; . . . . *T.M.* 320
If none of neither mention should *make,* . . . . *T.M.* 449
Therefore I mourne, and endlesse sorrow *make,* . . . . . . *T.M.* 473
To *make* men heavenly wise . . . . *T.M.* 522
make a tunefull Diapase of pleasures, ... *T.M.* 549
Make thy selfe fluttring wings . . . . *U.V.* 2
hir sweete Tongue was wonte to *make* me mirth. . . . . . . *U.V.* 15
them immortall *make,* which els would die . . . . *Ti.* 377
Which Orpheus for Eurydice did *make,* . . . . *Ti.* 391
To *make* their memories for ever live; . . . . *Ti.* 412
that blinde bard did him immortall *make* . . . . *Ti.* 430
In the wide aire to *make* her wandring flight; . . . . *Mui.* 139
deign'd with her the paragon to *make:* . . . . *Mui.* 274
To *make* new matter fit for Tragedies; . . . . *D.* 154
Weepe, Shepheard! weepe, to *make* my undersong. . . . . . *D.* 245
Weep, Shepheard! weep, to *make* mine undersong. . . . . . *D.* 294
To *make* the image of true heavinesse: . . . . *D.* 329
Weepe, Shepheard! weepe, to *make* my undersong. . . . . . *D.* 343, 392, 441, 490
make for them as he was wont to doo . . . . *As.* 39
Since round about us it doth *make* aboad! . . . . *As.* 90
after him did *make* untimely haste: . . . . *As.* 176
followed her *make* like turtle chaste, ... *As.* 178
every one did *make* exceeding mone, ... *As.* 205
Worthie of Colin selfe, that did it *make.* . . . . *Col.* 158
He cryed out, to *make* his undersong; . . . . *Col.* 169

Make—*Continued.*
Conspire in one to *make* contented blisse. . . . . *Col.* 311
carefull pipe may *make* the hearer rew: . . . . *Col.* 397
do their Cynthia immortall *make:* . . . . *Col.* 453
thee, that so of them doest *make,* . . . . *Col.* 586
eke to *make* the dead againe alive. . . . . *Col.* 599
Upon the perled grasse to *make* their feast. . . . . *Col.* 607
make him serve to them for sordid uses: . . . . *Col.* 792
Do *make* religion how we rashly go . . . . *Col.* 797
To *make* so bold a doome, ... *Col.* 929
shall it *make* more famous memory Of thine Heroicke parts, . *Ded. Son.* ii. 11
Make you ensample to the present age . . . . *Ded. Son.* vi. 3
Yet, till that thou thy Poeme wilt *make* knowne, ... *Ded.Son.*viii.13
But to *make* humble present of good will: *Ded.Son.*xvi.12
To *make* his worke more absolute, desird . . the vew. . . *Ded.Son.* xvii. 3
with so much speede As her slowe beast could *make;* . . . . I. ii. 8. 2
rests not so, but other meanes doth *make,* . . . . I. ii. 9. 6
As many formes . . . As ever Proteus to himselfe could *make:* I. ii. 10. 4
The earth shall sooner . . . *make* eternal derth, ... I. iii. 28. 8
There many Minstrales *maken* melody, ... I. v. 3. 4
Goe, guiltie ghost, to him my message *make,* . . . . I. v. 11. 3
by my ruines thinkes to *make* them great: . . . . I. v. 25. 8
To *make* one great by others losse is bad excheat. . . . . . I. v. 25. 9
damned sprights sent forth to *make* ill men aghast. . . . . I. v. 31. 9
Where none appeares can *make* her selfe a way, ... I. vi. 7. 2
Of whom he meanes his bloody feast to *make,* . . . . I. vi. 10. 5
wyld roring Buls he would him *make* To tame, ... I. vi. 24. 6
he would . . . *make* the Libbard sterne Leave roaring, ... I. vi. 25. 8
for to *make* his powre approved more, ... I. vi. 26. 1
joyd to *make* proofe of her cruelty . . . . I. vi. 31. 6
Th' Elfe, . . . Upstarted lightly from his looser *make,* . . . . I. vii. 7. 8
vanquisht thine eternall bondslave *make,* . . . . I. vii. 14. 8
Who . . . was possessed of his newfound *make.* . . . . I. vii. 15. 5
for to *make* her dreaded more of men, ... I. vii. 16. 6
He has them now fowr years besiegd to *make* them thrall. . . I. vii. 44. 9
perils doe enfold The righteous man, to *make* him daily fall, . I. viii. 1. 2
Her hastie ruine does more heavie *make,* . . . . I. viii. 23. 6
with your worth the world amazed *make,* . . . . I. viii. 26. 8
Could *make* a stony hart his hap to rew; . . . . I. viii. 41. 5
'Ensample *make* of him your haplesse joy, ... I. ix. 12. 1
from whom *make* ye this hasty flight? . . . . I. ix. 23. 8
what hath life that may it loved *make,* . . . . I. ix. 44. 4
All which, and thousands mo, do *make* a loathsome life. . . . I. ix. 44. 9
end, which every living wight Should *make* his marke . . . . I. x. 50. 3
learned Ladies . . . *make* full many a lovely lay. . . . . . I. x. 54. 9
shall ye evermore renowmed *make* . . . . I. xi. 2. 8
boystrous battaile *make,* each other to avenge. . . . . . . I. xi. 21. 9
deeper dint therein it would not *make;* . . . . I. xi. 24. 6
falling flat great humblesse he did *make,* . . . . I. xii. 25. 6
The tydings straunge did him abashed *make,* . . . . I. xii. 29. 2
Here she a while may *make* her safe abode, ... I. xii. 42. 5
that seeke . . . great your selfe to *make,* . . . . II. i. 8. 8
fayre Lady, comfort to you *make,* . . . . II. i. 18. 1
make you good amendment for the same: . . . . II. i. 20. 4
Then Guyon forward gan his voyage *make* . . . . II. i. 34. 3
of your ignorance great merveill *make,* . . . . II. ii. 5. 4
threatning to *make* the pray Of the rough rockes, ... II. ii. 24. 2
scorning both their spights, does *make* wide way, ... II. ii. 24. 7
Of her leawd parts to *make* companion: . . . . II. ii. 37. 5
*An yearely solemne feast she wontes to *make* . . . . II. ii. 42. 6
of his pitteous tale he end did *make:* . . . . II. ii. 46. 4
Of his revenge to *make* the instrument; . . . . II. iii. 11. 6
what mote that Monster *make.* . . . . II. iii. 18. 9
heavenly musicke seemd to *make.* . . . . II. iii. 24. 9
With her two crooked handes she signes did *make,* . . . . . II. iv. 13. 2
few rites to be donne, Which mariage *make:* . . . . II. iv. 21. 6
Strong warres they *make,* . . . . II. iv. 34. 7
matter *make* for him to worke upon, ... II. iv. 42. 6
make him stoup so low, ... II. v. 7. 3
So matter did she *make* of nought, ... II. v. 19. 6
Can chaunge my cheare, or *make* me ever mourne: . . . . . II. vi. 10. 8
There her small Gondelay her port did *make,* . . . . II. vi. 11. 5
How they them selves doe thine ensample *make,* . . . . . . II. vi. 15. 3
Wilfully *make* thyselfe a wretched thrall, ... II. vi. 17. 3
make way to the living spright! . . . . II. vi. 32. 9
make the life unsweet: . . . . II. vii. 14. 2
Thy spouse I will her *make,* . . . . II. vii. 49. 8
make his carkas as the outcast dong? . . . . II. viii. 28. 5
the large leape which Debon did compell Coulin to *make,* . . II. x. 11. 3
Did head against them *make* . . . . II. x. 15. 9
he an end of batteill and of life did *make.* . . . . II. x. 16. 9
all his vowes *make* vayne; . . . . II. xi. 18. 8
Through hils and dales he speedy way did *make,* . . . . . . II. xi. 26. 4
end of that Carles dayes and his owne paynes did *make.* . . . II. xi. 46. 9
ryv'd her trembling hart, and wicked end did *make.* . . . . . II. xi. 47. 9
Did afterwards *make* shipwrack violent . . . . II. xii. 7. 8
Great whirlpooles which all fishes *make* to flee; . . . . . . II. xii. 23. 7
a God him sage Antiquity Did wisely *make,* . . . . II. xii. 48. 2
To *make* there lenger sojourne and abode; . . . . III. i. 1. 6
To *make* more triall of his hardiment, ... III. i. 2. 8
With whom he ment to *make* his sport and courtly play. . . . III. i. 56. 9
Some to *make* love, some to *make* meryment, ... III. i. 57. 2
ne *maken* memoree Of their brave gestes . . . . III. ii. 1. 5
striving fit to *make,* I feare, doe marre: . . . . III. ii. 3. 8
thy prayses tell, and *make* them knowen farre. . . . . III. ii. 3. 9
ne ready answere *make,* . . . . III. ii. 5. 2
also it impregnable did *make;* . . . . III. ii. 20. 8
Till death *make* one end of my daies and miseree!' . . . . . III. ii. 39. 9
why *make* ye such Monster of your minde? . . . . III. ii. 40. 2
To *make* his wonne, low underneath the ground, ... III. iii. 7. 6

Make—*Continued.*

make them him obay;	III. iii. 12. 2
of their first intent gan *make* new dout,	III. iii. 14. 3
sith fates can *make* Way for themselves	III. iii. 25. 4
proofe of thy prow valiaunce Thou then shalt *make,*	III. iii. 28. 4
foes, that him shall *make* in mischiefe fall.	III. iii. 28. 9
make The warlike Mertians for feare to quake:	III. iii. 30. 4
the third time shall fayre accordaunce *make:*	III. iii. 30. 7
'Him shall he *make* his fatall Instrument	III. iii. 38. 1
Will not long misery late mercy *make,*	III. iii. 43. 7
it shall *make* him shake, and shortly learn to fall.	III. iii. 49. 9
make Strong warre upon the Paynim brethren,	III. iii. 52. 5
shortly *make* you a mayd Martiall.	III. iii. 53. 9
her ensample *make* Unto thy selfe,	III. iii. 56. 8
voyage rashly *make* By this forbidden way	III. iv. 14. 5
for wretched mens reliefe *make* way;	III. v. 27. 2
make him fast out of the forest ronne,	III. v. 27. 8
To *make* ensample of his heavenly grace,	III. v. 52. 2
So all did *make* in her a perfect complement.	III. v. 55. 9
make their pastyme Emongst the shady leaves,	III. vi. 42. 7
mortall miseries doth *make* her play.	III. vii. 4. 5
Would *make* to melt, or pitteously appall;	III. vii. 9. 7
make exceeding mone, as they had been undonne.	III. vii. 19. 9
Whom she did meane to *make* the thrall of her desire.	III. vii. 37. 9
semblaunce of faire fight did *make,*	III. vii. 44. 8
he gan to *make* Exceeding mone,	III. vii. 45. 3
the Titans which did *make* Warre against heven,	III. vii. 47. 3
To *make* another like the former Dame,	III. viii. 5. 7
He gan *make* gentle purpose to his Dame	III. viii. 14. 2
Then he would *make* him selfe a mortall wight;	III. viii. 39. 8
thinking for to *make* her stubborne corage quayle.	III. viii. 40. 9
threatned there to *make* her his eternall thrall.	III. viii. 41. 9
they secret way did *make* Unto their wils,	III. ix. 31. 5
make them cheese and bredd;	III. x. 36. 8
your kingdomes *make* In th' harts of men,	III. xi. 2. 6
as trew in love as Turtle to her *make.*	III. xi. 2. 9
Threatning into his life to *make* a breach,	III. xi. 12. 7
thrald your gentle *make.*	III. xi. 15. 3
forth they both yfere *make* their progresse,	III. xi. 20. 7
fought . . . to *make* his empire great;	III. xi. 29. 7
faire Alcmena better match did *make,*	III. xi. 33. 6
Ne ought but deare Bisaltis ay could *make* him glad.	III. xi. 41. 9
all his many it affraide did *make:*	III. xii. 23. 8
all perforce to *make* her him to love.	III. xii. 31. 6
all that did not her dismaied *make,*	III. xii. 37. 3
through the world *make* to be notifyde,	III. xii. 39. 8
your loving *Make* Hath no lesse griefe endured	III. xii. 40. 8
could she not but curteous countenance to her *make.*	IV. i. 5. 9
That one did *make* the other mard againe,	IV. i. 29. 3
shortly friends them *make:*	IV. ii. 1. 9
So fayre a spoyle, to *make* you joyous meriment?'	IV. ii. 5. 9
gan this bitter answere to him *make:*	IV. ii. 14. 2
of your gotten spoyle their owne triumph to *make.'*	IV. ii. 24. 9
each not farre behinde him had his *make,*	IV. ii. 30. 5
twixt themselves did gentle purpose *make,*	IV. ii. 30. 7
(The harder it to *make* them well agree)	IV. ii. 38. 4
of them all which love to her did *make,*	IV. ii. 38. 6
More wise they weend to *make* of love delight	IV. ii. 40. 5
cruell battell twixt themselves doe *make,*	IV. iii. 16. 6
To *make* an end of all that did withstand:	IV. iii. 33. 3
this doth hatred *make* in love to brenne,	IV. iii. 45. 7
so weening way to *make* To Ladies love,	IV. iv. 4. 3
all the rest it did amazed *make,*	IV. iv. 29. 4
make his praise before his owne preferd:	IV. iv. 36. 8
squiers *make* hast to helpe their Lords fordonne.	IV. iv. 38. 8
This pretious ornament, they say, did *make,*	IV. v. 4. 3
Thereby to *make* their loves beginning their lives end.	IV. vi. 17. 9
Yet durst he not *make* love so suddenly,	IV. vi. 33. 1
loth to leave her late betrothed *make,*	IV. vi. 42. 8
she forgot, whereby excuse to *make;*	IV. vi. 45. 8
humble homage did unto him *make,*	IV. vii. 44. 8
Ne ought mote *make* him change his wonted tenor,	IV. vii. 47. 3
saw her forward still to *make* her flight,	IV. viii. 8. 2
gan to her her mournfull plaint to *make,*	IV. viii. 9. 6
self-disliked life, doth thee thus wretched *make?*	IV. viii. 14. 9
make me loath this life, still longing for to die.	IV. viii. 16. 9
each unto his lust did *make* a lawe,	IV. viii. 30. 8
spoyle to *make,* and wast them unto nought,	IV. viii. 48. 7
promist large amends to *make.*	IV. viii. 60. 6
Thereto he offred for to *make* him chiefe	IV. ix. 15. 7
Paridell of love did *make* no threasure,	IV. ix. 21. 7
He ment to *make* them know their follies prise,	IV. ix. 35. 2
Phidias did *make* in Paphos Isle of yore,	IV. x. 40. 4
wherein *make* abode So many learned impes,	IV. xi. 26. 4
doth *make* His way still under ground,	IV. xi. 32. 8
gan he *make* him tread his steps anew,	IV. xii. 13. 8
And so doe *make* contrarie constitution	V. Pr. 4. 8
to *make* experience Upon wyld beasts,	V. i. 7. 7
to *make* him dreaded more,	V. i. 9. 1
'which way then did he *make?*	V. i. 19. 1
thitherward forthright his ready way did *make.*	V. ii. 10. 9
make him cease for ought.	V. ii. 22. 9
So would he of the fire one ballaunce *make,*	V. ii. 31. 3
make them levell with the lowly plaine;	V. ii. 38. 2
Tyrants, that *make* men subject to their law,	V. ii. 38. 6
Does *make* her selfe misfortunes piteous pray.	V. ii. 50. 5
Together met of all to *make* an end.	V. iii. 8. 3
With proud disdaine did scornefull answere *make,*	V. iii. 16. 2
Of both their beauties to *make* paragone	V. iii. 24. 3
Whereof to *make* due tryall,	V. iii. 33. 1
'Sir Turpine, haplesse man, what *make* you here?	V. iv. 26. 1
to them way to *make* with weapons well prepard.	V. iv. 37. 9
with his Lord she would emparlaunce *make.*	V. iv. 50. 9
of her servant *make* her soverayne Lord:	V. v. 27. 8
Thereof *make* tryall in my greatest need.	V. v. 29. 6
to his fortunes helpe *make* readie way?'	V. v. 39. 4
Make meanes to win thy libertie forlorne,	V. v. 40. 2
of his innocence to *make* her pray.	V. v. 52. 4
to *make* them seeme more few;	V. vi. 5. 7
he would *make* Her rather reade his meaning	V. vi. 9. 8
There she began to *make* her monefull plaint	V. vi. 12. 1
She saw it vaine to *make* there lenger stay,	V. vi. 36. 1
Thorough the midst of them she way did *make.*	V. vi. 39. 3
To *make* new warre against the Gods againe.	V. vii. 11. 6
the heapes which he did *make* Of slaughtred carkasses,	V. vii. 36. 4
To captive men, and *make* them all the world reject.	V. viii. 2. 9
Yet mote he algates now abide, and answere *make.*	V. viii. 5. 9
They drew their swords, in mind to *make* amends	V. viii. 10. 2
to *make* proofe of utmost shame,	V. viii. 22. 6
To their deseigne to *make* the easier way,	V. viii. 25. 2
Seeking by every way to *make* some breach;	V. viii. 37. 2
soone did *make* To leave his proper forme,	V. ix. 16. 8
Those two strange knights such homage to her *make,*	V. ix. 35. 6
with him, to *make* part against her, came	V. ix. 43. 5
Yet glad at last to *make* most base submission,	V. x. 27. 4
Whereto she ever list to *make* her hardy flight.	V. xi. 24. 9
any man would nigh awhaped *make:*	V. xi. 32. 5
signe of truce did *make:*	V. xii. 8. 2
then would she *make* Great cheare,	V. xii. 32. 6
make much worse by telling,	V. xii. 35. 2
How they might *make* him into mischiefe fall,	V. xii. 37. 4
would *make* Forget his patience,	V. xii. 42. 3
to *make* them pierce and wound more deepe,	V. xii. 42. 6
Calidore . . . doth *make* Briana wexe more mylde.	VI. i. Arg.
shall you most renowmed *make* for evermore.	VI. i. 5. 9
seeing him so fiercely towardes *make,*	VI. i. 19. 2
breake bands of civilitie, And wicked customes *make,*	VI. i. 26. 7
tryde all waies how each mote entrance *make*	VI. i. 37. 2
to *make* unto his vengeance way:	VI. i. 39. 6
What cause could *make* him so dishonourable	VI. ii. 15. 3
Let me this crave, . . . That ye will *make* me Squire	VI. ii. 33. 4
To *make* abode that night he greatly was besought.	VI. iii. 2. 9
And *make* their welcome to them well appeare.	VI. iii. 6. 4
and *make* her th' others riches scorne.	VI. iii. 7. 9
did assay To *make* them both as merry	VI. iii. 9. 5
some small continuance He there did *make,*	VI. iii. 19. 8
To *make* a garland to adorne her hed,	VI. iii. 23. 8
I defie thee; and here challenge *make,*	VI. iii. 35. 4
full loth To *make* there lenger stay,	VI. iii. 45. 9
to *make* advantage of his misery.	VI. iii. 46. 9
to *make* avoure Of the lewd words	VI. iii. 48. 5
Did underneath them *make* a gloomy shade,	VI. iv. 13. 7
if please her *make* the priefe;	VI. iv. 34. 5
To *make* them to endure the pains did them torment.	VI. v. 32. 9
Would not permit to *make* there lenger stay,	VI. v. 41. 2
unable . . . To move one foote, but there must *make* abode:	VI. vi. 19. 7
but after him did *make.*	VI. vi. 29. 5
To some hid end to *make* more easie way,	VI. vi. 42. 2
each to *make* his owne.	VI. vii. 3. 9
they mote *make* triall of their might	VI. vii. 5. 4
when a cast of Faulcons *make* their flight	VI. vii. 9. 1
as ye did promise *make,*	VI. vii. 15. 7
such proud looks would *make* her praysed more;	VI. vii. 30. 2
of their loves successe they there may *make* report;	VI. vii. 32. 9
how could her love *make* half amends therefore?	VI. vii. 38. 9
all the evill termes . . . That he could *make:*	VI. vii. 39. 6
make one end of him without ruth or remorse.	VI. viii. 14. 9
could so meekly *make* proud hearts avale,	VI. viii. 25. 3
Yet never Turtle truer to his *make,*	VI. viii. 33. 6
her eate attonce, or many meales to *make.*	VI. viii. 37. 9
sleepe, they sayd, would *make* her battill better:	VI. viii. 38. 3
To *make* a common feast, and feed with gurmandize.	VI. viii. 38. 9
in this quiet *make* you safer live.'	VI. ix. 32. 8
He would commend his guift, and *make* the best;	VI. ix. 40. 5
Were met to *make* their sports and merrie glee,	VI. ix. 41. 2
Which here with thee doe *make* their pleasant playes?	VI. x. 19. 7
To *make* them lovely or well-favoured show;	VI. x. 23. 3
To *make* one minime of thy poore handmayd,	VI. x. 28. 6
To *make* it seeme more deare and dainty,	VI. xi. 1. 9
Unto his lust, and *make* his will his law,	VI. xi. 6. 3
he himselfe which did that conquest *make:*	VI. xi. 12. 5
To *make* the prises of the rest more deare	VI. xi. 15. 5
make even that dimmed light Seeme much more lovely	VI. xi. 21. 6
fortune now the victors need did *make:*	VI. xi. 51. 4
Had reft from Meliboe and from his *make,*	VI. xi. 51. 7
wrong of right, and bad of good did *make*	VII. vi. 6. 3
Doth *make* both Gods and hellish fiends affraid:	VII. vi. 18. 3
Whence art thou, and what doost thou here now *make?*	VII. vi. 25. 8
In this bold sort to Heaven claime to *make,*	VII. vi. 29. 3
Thinks of her Dairy to *make* wondrous gaine,	VII. vi. 48. 2
of her shame to *make* a gamesome jest;	VII. vi. 51. 3
dreadfull thunder-claps (that *make* them quake)	VII. vii. 23. 8
flashing lights that thousand changes *make.*	VII. vii. 23. 9
hasting Prime did *make* them burgein round.	VII. vii. 43. 8
did them porters *make* Of heavens gate	VII. vii. 45. 6
whom so much ye *make* Joves dearest darling,	VII. vii. 50. 2
yee *make* Immortall and unchangeable to be:	VII. vii. 54. 2
That vertue have or this, or that to *make,*	VII. vii. 54. 7
The huge massacres which her eyes do *make;*	*Am.* x. 6

Make—*Continued.*
that high look, . . . bow to a baser *make,* . . . *Am.* x. 11
Of my poore life to *make* unpittied spoile. . . . *Am.* xi. 8
with her hart-thrilling eies To *make* a truce, . . . *Am.* xii. 2
Such lowlinesse shall *make* you lofty be. . . . *Am.* xiii. 14
seeke most pretious things to *make* your gain; . . . *Am.* xv. 2
the worke that she all day did *make,* . . . *Am.* xxiii. 3
that, which shall you *make* immortall, cherish. . . . *Am.* xxvii. 14
By conduct of some star, doth *make* her way; . . . *Am.* xxxiv. 2
make agreement with her thrilling eyes; . . . *Am.* xxxvi. 6
the sweet musick, which his harp did *make,* . . . *Am.* xxxviii. 3
She meanes at last to *make* her pitious spoyle. . . . *Am.* xli. 12
The which my selfe against my selfe doe *make;* . . . *Am.* xliv. 6
make the matter to avenge her yre: . . . *Am.* xlviii. 2
Such mercy shall you *make* admyr'd to be; . . . *Am.* xlix. 13
So I her absens will my penaunce *make,* . . . *Am.* lii. 13
shame it is, . . . To *make* the bayte her gazers to embrew: . . . *Am.* liii. 11
I waile, and *make* my woes a Tragedy. . . . *Am.* liv. 8
glory thinke to *make* these cruell stoures. . . . *Am.* lvii. 10
Make peace therefore, and graunt me timely grace, . . . *Am.* lvii. 13
make him bond that bondage earst dyd fly. . . . *Am.* lxv. 4
make thy triumph over death and sin; . . . *Am.* lxviii. 2
her selfe soone ready *make,* To wayt on Love . . . *Am.* lxx. 9
every one, that misseth then her *make,* . . . *Am.* lxx. 11
Make hast, therefore, sweet love, whilest it is prime; . . . *Am.* lxx. 13
Lyke as a byrd . . . to it doth *make* his flight: . . . *Am.* lxxiii. 6
her words so wise do *make* their way . . . *Am.* lxxxi. 11
thou doest spoyle of lovers *make.'* . . . *Epig.* iv. 40
let them *make* great store of bridale poses, . . . *Epith.* 45
in his waters, which your mirror *make,* . . . *Epith.* 63
T' awayt the comming of your joyous *make,* . . . *Epith.* 87
Doe *make* and still repayre: . . . *Epith.* 102
The which do endlesse matrimony *make,* . . . *Epith.* 217
Make feast therefore now all this live-long day; . . . *Epith.* 248
Ring ye the bels, to *make* it weare away, . . . *Epith.* 274
bonefiers *make* all day; . . . *Epith.* 275
Make sudden sad affrights; . . . *Epith.* 339
griesly vultures, *make* us once affeard: . . . *Epith.* 348
Make us to wish theyr choking. . . . *Epith.* 350
make thee more propitious in my need, . . . *H.L.* 9
like fresh Eagle, *make* his hardie flight . . . *H.L.* 69
The world, that was not till he did it *make,* . . . *H.L.* 75
they playne, and *make* ful piteous mone . . . *H.L.* 127
mayest them *make* it better to deserve, . . . *H.L.* 166
Doe *make* a lovers life a wretches hell. . . . *H.L.* 265
thou doest thy entrance *make* Unto thy heaven, . . . *H.L.* 273
To *make* al things such as we now behold, . . . *H.B.* 30
soule is forme, and doth the bodie *make,* . . . *H.B.* 133
How ever fleshes fault it filthy *make;* . . . *H.B.* 160
to *make* your beautie more appeare, . . . *H.B.* 183
make it more admyr'd of foe and frend; . . . *H.B.* 264
Therefore of clay . . . He man did *make,* . . . *H.H.L.* 110
Could *make* amends to God for mans misguyde, . . . *H.H.L.* 144
And *make* her native brightnes seem more cleare. . . . *H.H.B.* 189
fruitfull issue . . . *make* your joyes redound . . . *Proth.* 106
Hercules two pillors . . . Did *make* to quake and feare: . . . *Proth.* 149
at th' appointed tyde, Each one did *make* his Bryde . . . *Proth.* 178

Maked. *See* **Made.**
with which he *maked* meeke The mightie Mars, . . . III. xi. 44. 2

Maker. Unto his heavenlie *maker* to present His bodie, . . . *Ti.* 297
Made by the *Maker* selfe to be admired; . . . *Col.* 561
The *maker* selfe, . . . Was nigh beguiled . . . I. i. 45. 6
'What had th' eternall *Maker* need of thee . . . III. iv. 56. 1
His *maker* with her charmes had framed him so well. . . . III. vii. 35. 9
Such as the *maker* selfe could best by art devize. . . . IV. iii. 38. 9
The *maker* selfe resembling in her feature! . . . IV. vi. 17. 5
As their Almightie *maker* first ordained, . . . IV. x. 35. 3
All in the powre of their great *Maker* lie: . . . V. ii. 40. 8
fire, Kindled above unto the *Maker* neere; . . . *Am.* viii. 2
Then to the *Maker* selfe they likest be, . . . *Am.* ix. 13
in theyr *Maker* ye them best may see. . . . *Am.* liii. 14
As their great *Maker* did at first ordaine, . . . *H.H.B.* 201

Maker's. Moses . . . sawe hys *makers* face, . . . *S.C.* Jul. 158
Th' eternall *Makers* majestie wee viewe, . . . *T.M.* 512
myrrour of her *Makers* majestie, . . . *T.M.* 572
Out of the bosome of the *makers* blis, . . . *Ti.* 282
creature . . . Full of the *makers* guyle, . . . I. i. 46. 7
As th' Idole of her *makers* great magnificence. . . . II. ii. 41. 9
Kindled above at th' hevenly *makers* light, . . . II. iii. 23. 2
who can tell the prayses of that *makers* might? . . . II. ix. 46. 9
In goodly measure by their *Makers* might; . . . V. ii. 35. 2
I honor and admire the *Makers* art. . . . *Am.* xxiv. 4
The glorious image of the *Makers* beautie, . . . *Am.* lxi. 1
All glistring glorious in their *Makers* light. . . . *H.H.L.* 56
So that next off-spring of the *Makers* love, . . . *H.H.L.* 92
man, forgetfull of his *Makers* grace . . . *H.H.L.* 120
made Of that selfe mould, and that selfe *Makers* hand, . . . *H.H.L.* 198

Makes. Oft *makes* me wayle so hard a destenie. . . . *Pet.* i. 14
makes me much and ever to complaine; . . . *Pet.* iii. 13
Makes the world wonder what they from thee reft. . . . *Ro.* xiii. 14
fish . . . That *makes* the sea before his face to flye, . . . *Van.* v. 3
Making his sport, that manie *makes* to weep: . . . *Van.* v. 7
Now she is a stone, And *makes* dayly mone, . . . *S.C.* Ap. 89
Such pleasaunce *makes* the Grashopper so poore, . . . *S.C.* O. 11
Tom Piper *makes* us better melodie. . . . *S.C.* O. 78
makes himselfe full blythe . . . *Gn.* 131
makes the scorne of other beasts to bee: . . . *Hub.* 603
an universall night . . . he *makes* on everie wight; . . . *Hub.* 1298
(despeyre *makes* cowards stout,) . . . *As.* 117
Who all that Colin *makes* do covet faine.' . . . *Col.* 99

Makes—*Continued.*
makes them doubt their wits be not their owne: . . . I. i. 10. 7
Faire seemely pleasaunce each to other *makes,* . . . I. ii. 30. 1
Forsaken Truth . . . *makes* the Lyon mylde; . . . I. iii. Arg.
To her *makes* present of his service seene: . . . I. v. 16. 3
to the Easterne coast of heaven *makes* speedy way: . . . I. v. 19. 9
Through mirkesome aire her ready way she *makes;* . . . I. v. 28. 3
Far off he wonders what them *makes* so glad; . . . I. vi. 15. 1
That *makes* frayle flesh to feare the bitter wave, . . . I. ix. 40. 5
cold that *makes* the hart to quake, . . . I. ix. 44. 7
object of his spight And deadly food he *makes:* . . . II. i. 3. 2
Mournes inwardly, and *makes* to him selfe mone; . . . II. i. 42. 7
she *makes* her lovers dronken mad; . . . II. i. 52. 2
makes it servaunt to her basest part, . . . II. i. 57. 6
Weake she *makes* strong, and strong thing does increace; . . . II. ii. 31. 3
Love, that two harts *makes* one, *makes* eke one will; . . . II. iv. 19. 8
rash Occasion *makes* unquiet life!' . . . II. iv. 44. 7
great disparagment *makes* to his former might.' . . . II. viii. 29. 9
Gainst which the second troupe assignment *makes;* . . . II. xi. 10. 2
makes his game The flying ships with swiftnes to pursew: . . . II. xii. 24. 3
Through guilefull semblants which he *makes* us see: . . . II. xii. 48. 6
Makes for him endlesse mone, . . . III. i. 38. 4
So dischord ofte in Musick *makes* the sweeter lay:— . . . III. ii. 15. 9
(need *makes* good schollers) . . . III. iii. 53. 3
heales up one, and *makes* another wound! . . . III. v. 42. 2
cause of dread, that *makes* ye doubt so sore? . . . III. viii. 48. 6
makes him alway Suspect her truth, . . . III. ix. 5. 3
winde, . . . *Makes* the huge element, . . . To move . . . III. ix. 15. 5
makes ensample of mans wretched state, . . . III. ix. 39. 8
daunts not mighty harts, but *makes* them more to swell. . . . IV. iii. 8. 9
the tide, . . . *makes* it seeme to have some other sourse; . . . IV. iii. 27. 5
Satyrane *makes* a Turneyment For love of Florimell: . . . IV. iv. Arg.
he amongst them cruell havocke *makes,* . . . IV. iv. 34. 6
that many *makes* him dread: . . . IV. vi. 7. 9
through the thickest *makes* her nighest waies; . . . IV. vii. 22. 3
makes her feare a spur to hast her flight: . . . IV. vii. 22. 7
rules the Seas and *makes* them rise or fall; . . . IV. xi. 11. 2
That *makes* me feare . . . he will us quite forsake. . . . V. Pr. 7. 9
That powre . . . *makes* them like himselfe . . . V. Pr. 10. 7
makes all men for feare that passage for to shonne.' . . . V. ii. 4. 9
he him *makes* his passage-penny pay: . . . V. ii. 6. 4
makes them subject to his mighty wrong; . . . V. ii. 7. 4
makes wrong doers justice to deride, . . . V. iv. 1. 7
makes his God of his ungodly pelfe, . . . V. viii. 19. 8
makes the wals to stagger with astonishment: . . . V. x. 34. 9
weakens her, and *makes* her party strong; . . . V. xi. 1. 4
makes her ribs to cracke as they were torne; . . . V. xi. 29. 4
vexeth so that *makes* her eat her gall; . . . V. xii. 31. 5
of her owne foule entrayles *makes* her meat; . . . V. xii. 31. 8
makes his way more violent; . . . VI. i. 21. 5
He *makes* him Squire, . . . VI. ii. Arg.
And *makes* exceeding mone, when he does thinke . . . VI. iv. 32. 2
whose tempestuous rage *Makes* th' heavens tremble . . . VI. vi. 11. 9
Of whom he *makes* such havocke and such hew, . . . VI. viii. 49. 6
that sunne-shine that *makes* them looke askew: . . . VI. x. 4. 5
makes huge havocke; . . . VI. xi. 16. 8
That *makes* both heaven and earth to tremble at her pride. . . . VII. vi. 3. 9
faire sun-shine, that *makes* all skip and daunce; . . . VII. vii. 23. 4
That *makes* them all to shiver and to shake: . . . VII. vii. 23. 6
So *makes* himself his owne consuming pray: . . . VII. vii. 24. 5
moves them all, and *makes* them changed be? . . . VII. vii. 48. 8
makes me loath this state of life . . . VII. viii. 1. 6
and *makes* his flames to heaven aspire. . . . *Am.* vi. 8
doth laugh at me, and *makes* my paine her sport. . . . *Am.* x. 14
so plenty *makes* me poore. . . . *Am.* xxxv. 8
O mighty charm! which *makes* men love theyr bane, . . . *Am.* xlvii. 13
makes him mount above the native might . . . *H.L.* 188
it more faire accordingly it *makes,* . . . *H.B.* 45

Makest. thy selfe thou *mak'st* us more to wonder, . . . *Col.* 354
So *mak'st* thou kings, and gaynest wrongfull government. . . . II. vii. 13. 9
thou, That *mak'st* thy selfe his dayes-man, . . . II. viii. 28. 2
mak'st the loving hart With hatefull thoughts to languish . . . III. xi. 1. 6
makst the stormes to flie; . . . IV. x. 44. 5
That me thou *makest* thus tormented be, . . . *Am.* x. 2
through heaven and hell thou *makest* way . . . *H.L.* 236

Maketh. hat . . . Which *maketh* him invisible in sight, . . . *Hub.* 1280
He sings of love, and *maketh* loving layes, . . . *T.M.* 413
Of Lovers Miseries which *maketh* his bloodie game? . . . *Tetrasticon* 2
so dainty, they say, *maketh* derth. . . . I. ii. 27. 9
love . . . *maketh* monstrous warre; . . . II. ii. 26. 6
He *maketh* warre, he *maketh* peace againe, . . . II. ii. 26. 7
maketh every creature glad, . . . II. xi. 3. 4
The warie fowle, . . . *maketh* him his wing in vaine to spend; . . . IV. iii. 19. 7
Of litle much, of foes she *maketh* friends, . . . IV. x. 34. 8
maketh him abide Till . . . on his backe he ride, . . . IV. xii. 13. 4
He *maketh* Kings to sit in soverainty; . . . V. ii. 41. 5
He *maketh* subjects to their powre obay; . . . V. ii. 41. 6
'It is the mynd that *maketh* good or ill, . . . VI. ix. 30. 1
maketh wretch or happie, rich or poore; . . . VI. ix. 30. 2
That *maketh* it be coveted the more: . . . *Am.* xxvi. 10
maketh every minute seeme a myle. . . . *Am.* lxxxvi. 12
That *maketh* them all worldly cares forget, . . . *H.H.B.* 265

Making. *Making* his sport, that manie makes to weep: . . . *Van.* v. 7
Through the maine sea *making* her merry flight. . . . *Van.* ix. 4
Of Winters wracke for *making* thee sadde. . . . *S.C.* F. 10
was thilk same song of Colins owne *making?* . . . *S.C.* Ap. 154
Making his way . . . *S.C.* Jul. 19
His yron-headed spade tho *making* cleene, . . . *Gn.* 653
For *making* noyse, . . . *Hub.* 1010
Making them thinke it but a vision. . . . *Hub.* 1282

Making—*Continued.*
Making your musick of hart-breaking mone. . . . T.M. 6
By chaunge of turnes, each *making* other mery; . . . *Col.* 77
Besides her peerlesse skill in *making* well, . . . *Col.* 188
Making her death their life, . . . I. i. 25. 9
He, *making* speedy way through spersed ayre, . . . I. i. 39. 1
at his haughty helmet *making* mark, . . . I. ii. 19. 3
they, . . . *Making* obeysaunce, did the cause declare, . . . I. iv. 13. 7
Through widest ayre *making* his ydle way, . . . I. v. 8. 4
engin, *making* way, . . . highest trees hath rent, . . . I. viii. 9. 6
Wringing her handes, and *making* piteous mone: . . . II. i. 13. 7
Making sweet solace to herselfe alone: . . . II. vi. 3. 2
therein *making* way. . . . II. vi. 7. 9
making advauntage, to revenge their spight, . . . II. viii. 25. 2
making vantage of their civile jarre, . . . II. x. 65. 4
Where many Mermayds haunt *making* false melodies: . . . II. xii. 17. 9
Now *making* girlonds of each flowre that grew, . . . III. i. 35. 4
Making her seeke an unknowne Paramoure, . . . III. iii. 3. 4
through wrath and vengeaunce *making* way, . . . III. v. 21. 1
making layes of love and lovers paine, . . . III. x. 8. 4
Minstrales *making* goodly meriment, . . . III. xii. 5. 4
making way unto his dearest life, . . . IV. iii. 12. 6
Where *making* joyous feast theire daies they spent . . . IV. iii. 52. 1
To seeke her lov'd, *making* blind love her guide. . . . IV. v. 29. 5
drew thereto, *making* her eare her guide: . . . IV. vii. 29. 4
making way By sweet Clonmell, . . . IV. xi. 43. 1
making all her Knights and people to doe so. . . . V. viii. 20. 9
Oft *making* offer him to smite, . . . V. viii. 42. 2
All full of people *making* troublous din . . . V. ix. 23. 3
Making great feast and joyous merriment, . . . V. xi. 35. 2
With bils and glayves *making* a dreadfull luster, . . . V. xi. 58. 5
Weeping to him in vaine and *making* piteous woe. . . . VI. ii. 10. 9
sought by *making* signes him to asswage; . . . VI. vi. 39. 3
making nightly rode Into their neighbours borders; . . . VI. viii. 35. 3
making gladfull glee, . . . VI. x. 10. 8
making way for death at large to walke; . . . VI. xi. 16. 5
making many a borde and many a bay, . . . VI. xii. 1. 6
Making their cruell rage thy scornefull game, . . . *H.L.* 47
making their paine thy play, . . . *H.L.* 135
Making his streame run slow. . . . *Proth.* 118
Mal. *Mal* was now put in: . . . V. ix. 26. 5
Malabar. Like to the Mores of *Malaber,* . . . VI. vii. 43. 6
Maladies. There were full many moe like *maladies,* . . . III. xii. 26. 1
heales both Squire and dame Of their sore *maladies:* . . . VI. vi. Arg.
Malady. a wicked *maladie* Raign'd emongst men, . . . *Hub.* 9
lawlesse riotise, By which he grew to grievous *malady;* . . . I. iv. 20. 5
with streight diet tame his stubborne *malady.* . . . I. x. 25. 9
So still his *Malady* the more increast, . . . III. v. 43. 6
To mitigate his stubborne *malady:* . . . III. v. 50. 5
all hope wherewith he long had fedd His foolish *malady,* . . . III. viii. 3. 9
will to none her *maladie* impart? . . . IV. vi. 1. 7
could ease his rankling *maladie,* . . . IV. xi. 6. 4
Ne weene what mister *maladie* it is, . . . IV. xii. 22. 2
it was some other *maladie,* . . . IV. xii. 24. 1
she gan unfold The cause of her conceived *maladie,* . . . V. v. 31. 8
To feede the humour of her *maladie,* . . . V. v. 55. 7
From your owne will to cure your *maladie.* . . . VI. vi. 7. 3
in short space their *malady* was ceast, . . . VI. vi. 15. 4
Mourning the rigour of her *malady,* . . . VI. xi. 8. 4
double *malady* Of my harts wound, and of my bodies griefe; . *Am.* l. 1
was shortly wel recured Of that his *malady:* . . . *Epig.* iv. 52
Malbecco. *Malbecco* will no straunge knights host, . . . III. ix. Arg.
'*Malbecco* he, and Hellenore she hight; . . . III. ix. 6. 1
Malbecco, seeing them resolvd . . . III. ix. 18. 1
Then they *Malbecco* prayd of courtesy, . . . III. ix. 25. 7
Paridell rapeth Hellenore; *Malbecco* her poursewes; . . . III. x. Arg.
chaunst *Malbecco* busie be elsewhere, . . . III. x. 12. 2
Malbecco, seeing how his losse did lye, . . . III. x. 17. 2
Whom such whenas *Malbecco* spyed clere, . . . III. x. 23. 4
That much *Malbecco* joyed in his jollity. . . . III. x. 33. 9
shortly she *Malbecco* has forgott, . . . III. x. 37. 1
Where those two guilers with *Malbecco* were. . . . III. x. 37. 5
'Perdy, nay,' (said *Malbecco*) . . . III. x. 39. 1
Malbecco stopt in great astonishment, . . . III. x. 41. 1
Which when *Malbecco* saw, out of the bush . . . he crept . . . III. x. 47. 1
it was indeed Her old *Malbecco,* . . . III. x. 50. 3
Malbecco's. Thus was the ape . . . put into *Malbeccoes* cape. III. ix. 31. 9
he *Malbeccoes* halfen eye did wyle; . . . III. x. 5. 2
That counsell pleased not *Malbeccoes* mynd, . . . III. x. 41. 8
Forth ryding from *Malbeccoes* hostlesse hous, . . . III. xi. 3. 2
Malcontent. Huddibras, more like a *Malecontent,* . . . II. ii. 37. 6
how ever *malcontent* She inly were . . . IV. vi. 44. 2
Male. *See* **Mail.**
Both *male* and female through commixture joynd: . . . *Col.* 802
creatures, partly *male* And partly femall, . . . I. i. 21. 7
had no issue *male* him to succeed, . . . II. x. 27. 2
wanting yssew *male,* . . . II. x. 61. 1
Both *male* and female, both under one name: . . . IV. x. 41. 7
Malecasta. faire *Malecasta* bent Her crafty engins . . . III. i. 57. 4
Faire *Malecasta,* whose engrieved spright . . . III. i. 59. 4
Malecasta's. *Malecastaes* champions are defaced. . . . III. i. Arg.
Maleffort. Calidore saves from *Maleffort* A Damzell . . . VI. i. Arg.
Maleffort, a man of mickle might, . . . VI. i. 15. 8
Malefices. fild their mouthes with meeds of *malefices:* . . . *Hub.* 1154
Maleger. fowle *Maleger* doth deface. . . . II. xi. Arg.
Maleger was his name; . . . II. xi. 23. 1
Maleger's. One of *Malegers* cursed darts did take, . . . II. xi. 47. 8
Malengin. Of such *malengine* and fine forgerye. . . . III. i. 53. 3
Therefore by name *Malengin* they him call, . . . V. ix. 5. 8
Malfont. So now *Malfont* was plainely to be red, . . . V. ix. 26. 6

Malgo. *Malgo* shall full mightily Avenge his fathers losse . . III. iii. 31. 7
Malice. Gluttonie, *malice,* pride, and covetize, . . . *Hub.* 1309
His heart with vengefull *malice* inly swelt; . . . *Mui.* 356
each one seeks with *malice,* and with strife, . . . *Col.* 690
Simple in shew, and voide of *malice* bad; . . . I. i. 29. 7
Halfe mad through *malice* and revenging will, . . . I. iii. 22. 8
two Bores, with rancling *malice* mett, . . . I. vi. 44. 4
With cruell *malice* and strong tyranny: . . . I. viii. 36. 5
In poyson and in blood of *malice* and despight. . . . II. iv. 38. 9
t' appease the stormy winde Of *malice* . . . II. vi. 8. 9
all attonce their *malice* forth do poure: . . . II. viii. 48. 7
with greedie *malice* and importune toyle, . . . II. xi. 7. 7
not for *malice* and contentious crymes, . . . III. i. 13. 3
all the while their *malice* they did whet . . . III. v. 17. 8
Ne ever pitty may relent his *malice* hard. . . . III. vi. 39. 9
That her sweet love his *malice* mote avoyd, . . . III. vi. 48. 7
was soone wonne his *malice* to relent, . . . III. ix. 25. 3
So much her *malice* did her might surpas, . . . IV. i. 30. 1
So mortall was their *malice,* and so sore Become, . . . IV. ii. 18. 8
The furious flames of *malice* to asswage. . . . IV. ii. 28. 4
From inward parts, with cancred *malice* lind, . . . IV. viii. 26. 4
evermore their *malice* did augment; . . . IV. ix. 25. 6
Such mortall *malice* wonder was to see . . . IV. ix. 27. 6
th' other eke his *malice* did empeach, . . . IV. x. 36. 8
With inward griefe and *malice* did against them swell. . . V. vii. 10. 9
strongly beateth downe The *malice* of her foes, . . . V. viii. 17. 6
To keepe out guyle, and *malice,* and despight, . . . V. ix. 22. 7
with mortall *malice* him pursu'd so nere. . . . V. xi. 48. 9
all in spight and *malice* did agree; . . . VI. i. 9. 4
Did nought regard his *malice* nor his powre; . . . VI. i. 9. 8
His former *malice* to some new assay, . . . VI. iii. 47. 8
he of *malice,* without her desarts, . . . her excluded . . . VI. v. 33. 7
In cancred *malice* and revengefull spight: . . . VI. vii. 1. 4
Simple and true, from covert *malice* free; . . . VI. x. 24. 5
fortune, fraught with *malice,* . . . VI. x. 38. 7
The more I fynd their *malice* to increase. . . . *Am.* xliv. 14
Maliced. why he this Flie so *maliced* . . . *Mui.* 257
Yet being *malist* both of great and small. . . . *H.H.L.* 238
Malicing. did seeme so farre From *malicing,* . . . VI. ix. 39. 7
Malicious. *malicious* Envy rode Upon a ravenous wolfe, . . . I. iv. 30. 1
They envy her in their *malitious* mind, . . . I. vi. 18. 6
Castle, . . . By subtile engins and *malitious* slight Is undermined . . . I. viii. 23. 2
Forth he fares, full of *malicious* mynd, . . . II. i. 2. 1
Had so enranckled her *malitious* hart, . . . III. viii. 2. 2
serving her in her *malitious* use . . . IV. i. 31. 2
in their *malicious* mood . . . IV. ix. 29. 2
all the villany That she could forge in her *malicious* head, . . V. iv. 29. 8
Voide of *malitious* mind or foule offence: . . . V. v. 33. 5
As bent to some *malicious* enterprise, . . . VI. iii. 48. 3
in his mind, *malitious* and ingrate, . . . VI. vii. 2. 5
Let drive at him with so *malitious* mynd, . . . VI. vii. 10. 6
So torne and mangled with *malicious* forse; . . . *H.H.L.* 250
Malign. my short blis *maligne,* . . . III. iv. 39. 2
even th' Almightie selfe she did *maligne,* . . . IV. i. 30. 2
'Mongst many which *maligne* her happy state, . . . V. viii. 18. 1
Though many foes did him *maligne* therefore, . . . VI. v. 12. 6
to *maligne,* t' envie, t' use shifting slight, . . . VI. vii. 1. 5
Could not *maligne* him, but commend him needs; . . . VI. ix. 45. 4
unto Gods, whose state she did *maligne,* . . . VII. vi. 11. 6
Malignant. Into the life of his *malignant* foe: . . . VI. i. 37. 3
Malim. *See* **Manild.**
Malist. *See* **Maliced.**
Mall. *See* **Maul.**
Maltalent. In him bewraid great grudge and *maltalent:* . . . III. iv. 61. 8
Malvenu. a Porter . . . Cald *Malvenu,* who entrance none denide: . . . I. iv. 6. 4
Mammon. Guyon findes *Mamon* in a delve . . . II. vii. Arg.
Great *Mammon,* greatest god below the skye, . . . II. vii. 8. 2
'*Mammon,*' (said he) 'thy godheads vaunt is vaine, . . . II. vii. 9. 6
Mammon wexing wroth; . . . II. vii. 14. 6
So soon as *Mammon* there arrivd, . . . II. vii. 26. 1
Mammon, turning to that warriour, said; . . . II. vii. 32. 6
whenas *Mammon* saw his purpose mist, . . . II. vii. 34. 8
Mammon was much displeasd, . . . II. vii. 39. 7
Mammon did his hasty hand withhold, . . . II. vii. 42. 6
Him *Mammon* answered; 'That goodly one, . . . II. vii. 48. 4
'Gramercy, *Mammon,*' (said the gentle knight) . . . II. vii. 50. 1
Mammon emmoved was with inward wrath; . . . II. vii. 51. 1
Ne *Mammon* would there let him long remayne, . . . II. vii. 63. 3
great *Mammon* fayrely he besought . . . II. vii. 65. 8
Where *Mammon* earst did sunne his threasury; . . . II. viii. 4. 7
Mammon's. the while that Guyon did abide In *Mamons* house, II. viii. 3. 2
Man. *See* **Craftsman, Daysman, Englishman, Huckster-man, Huntsman, Liege man, Madman, News-man, Nobleman, No man, Old man, Ploughman, Wise man, Young man.**
The worke did shew it selfe not wrought by *man.* . . . *Bel.*[1] iv. 9
erst of Gods and *man* I worshipt was? . . . *Bel.*[1] viii. 8
The faithfull *man* with flaming countenaunce, . . . *Rev.* iii. 2
Joinyng their force to slea the faithfull *man.* . . . *Rev.* iii. 12
O! warie wisedome of the *man,* . . . *Ro.* xxiii. 1
the good *man* noulde stay his leasure, . . . *S.C.* F. 192
fiercely the good *man* at him did laye. . . . *S.C.* F. 214
all burdens, that a *man* can beare, . . . *S.C.* May 140
I, unhappy *man!* . . . *S.C.* Jun. 14
God shield, *man,* that I should clime, . . . *S.C.* Jul. 9
God shield, *man,* he should so ill have thrive, . . . *S.C.* S. 226
Nor anie *man,* we should our selves applie; . . . *Hub.* 131
that good *man,* Seeing them . . . *Hub.* 243

Man—*Continued.*
The honest *man,* that heard him thus complaine, ... *Hub.* 259
The *man* straightway his choler up did move, ... *Hub.* 364
'To feede mens soules . . . is not in *man;* . . . . *Hub.* 433
his *man* Reynold, with fine counterfesaunce, ... *Hub.* 667
his *man* Raynolds purchase which he gain'd. . . . . *Hub.* 854
So would he worke the silly *man* by treason . . . . *Hub.* 888
Most miserable *man,* whom wicked fate Hath brought to Court, *Hub.* 892
such as hath a Reynold to his *man,* . . . . *Hub.* 917
in person and in stature Most like a *Man,* . . . . *Hub.* 1030
for outward shape Most like a *man,* . . . . *Hub.* 1042
Man is not like an Ape In his chiefe parts, ... *Hub.* 1042
Man without understanding doth appeare; . . . . *T.M.* 128
So is the *man* that wants intendiment. . . . . *T.M.* 144
the *man* whom Nature selfe had made . . . . *T.M.* 205
What difference twixt *man* and beast is left, ... *T.M.* 487
what to *man,* and what to God, wee owe. . . . . *T.M.* 504
what ever *man* bearst worldlie sway, ... *Ti.* 208
the *man,* of whom the Muse is scorned, ... *Ti.* 454
Such as on earth *man* could not more devize, ... *Ti.* 521
What-ever *man* be he whose heavie minde, ... *D.* 1
(I weene), the wofulst *man* alive, ... *D.* 5
I of many most Most miserable *man;* . . . . *D.* 38
The wretchedst *man* that treades this day on ground?' . . . *D.* 63
'Cease, foolish *man!*' . . . . *D.* 71
fond *man!* that in worlds ficklenesse Reposedst hope, ... *D.* 150
That *man,* who doth the whole worlds rule possesse, ... *D.* 179
'What *man* henceforth that breatheth vitall ayre . . . . . . *D.* 197
The mournfulst verse that ever *man* heard tell: . . . . *As.* Pr. 8
Full happie *man* (misweening much) was hee, ... *As.* 101
The dolefulst beare that ever *man* did see, ... *As.* 149
that waste . . . Unmeet for *man,* . . . . *Col.* 185
I, silly *man,* . . . . *Col.* 668
man, that had the sparke of reasons might . . . . *Col.* 867
bayt which with delight Doth *man* allure . . . . *Col.* 872
nor God nor *man* can fynd Defence, ... *Col.* 875
I, the *man* whose Muse whylome did maske, ... I. Pr. 1. 1
A monster vile, whom God and *man* does hate: . . . . I. i. 13. 7
the *man* so wrapt in Errours endlesse traine! . . . . I. i. 18. 9
Of a straunge *man* I can you tidings tell, ... I. i. 31. 3
Quoth then that aged *man:* . . . . I. i. 33. 5
A bold bad *man,* that dar'd to call . . . Gorgon, ... I. i. 37. 7
He . . . cared not for God or *man* a point. . . . . I. ii. 12. 9
once a *man,* Fradubio, now a tree; . . . . I. ii. 33. 3
Wretched *man,* wretched tree, whose nature weake . . . . . I. ii. 33. 4
'Say on, Fradubio, then, or *man* or tree,' . . . . I. ii. 34. 1
more foule . . . Then womans shape *man* would beleeve to bee. I. ii. 41. 4
In shape and life more like a monster then a *man.* . . . . . I. iv. 22. 9
Unseemely *man* to please faire Ladies eye; . . . . I. iv. 24. 6
Inconstant *man,* that loved all he saw, ... I. iv. 26. 1
Yet, wilfull *man,* he never would forecast . . . . I. iv. 34. 8
none can wound the *man* that does them wield.' . . . . . . I. iv. 50. 7
The foolish *man,* that pities . . . His mournefull plight, . . . I. v. 18. 7
he the *man* that made Sansfoy to fall, ... I. v. 26. 3
scornd of God and *man,* a shamefull death he dide. . . . . . I. v. 48. 9
A silly *man,* in simple weeds forworne, ... I. vi. 35. 1
Most sencelesse *man* he, that himselfe doth hate, ... I. vi. 47. 5
What *man* so wise, what earthly witt so ware, ... I. vii. 1. 1
The guiltlesse *man* with guile to entertaine? . . . . I. vii. 1. 7
this *man* forlorne, And left to losse; . . . . I. vii. 10. 5
how many perils doe enfold The righteous *man,* . . . . . . I. viii. 1. 2
heaved was on hye For to have slain the *man,* . . . . I. viii. 19. 9
forth came An old old *man,* . . . . I. viii. 30. 2
The chearelesse *man,* whom sorrow did dismay, ... I. viii. 43. 7
Old Timon, . . . In warlike feates th' expertest *man* alive, . . I. ix. 4. 3
Ne living *man* like wordes did ever heare, ... I. ix. 14. 7
living *man* mote worthie be to be her liefe.' . . . . I. ix. 17. 9
A *man* of hell that calls himselfe Despayre: . . . . I. ix. 28. 5
'How may a *man,*' . . . 'with idle speach Be wonne . . . . . I. ix. 31. 1
That cursed *man,* low sitting on the ground, ... I. ix. 35. 2
'hath thus distraught Thee, foolish *man,* . . . . I. ix. 38. 2
None els to death this *man* despayring drive . . . . I. ix. 38. 5
Most envious *man,* that grieves at neighbours good; . . . . . I. ix. 39. 6
Ne may a *man* prolong, nor shorten, it; . . . . I. ix. 41. 3
'Thou, wretched *man,* of death hast greatest need, ... I. ix. 45. 1
'Why then, doest thou, O *man* of sin! desire . . . . I. ix. 46. 1
What *man* is he, that boasts of fleshly might . . . . I. x. 1. 1
Ne let the *man* ascribe it to his skill, ... I. x. 1. 6
documents . . . That weaker witt of *man* could never reach; . . I. x. 19. 5
they did to health restore The *man* . . . . I. x. 27. 9
O *man!* have mind of that last bitter throw; . . . . I. x. 41. 8
Hermitage . . . Wherein an aged holy *man* did lie, ... I. x. 46. 5
'Thrise happy *man,*' said then the father grave, ... I. x. 51. 1
come, thou *man* of earth, and see the way, ... I. x. 52. 2
Such one as that same mighty *man* of God, ... I. x. 53. 2
nor wit of *man* can tell; . . . . I. x. 55. 6
'Most trew,' then said the holy aged *man;* . . . . I. x. 59. 1
I this *man* of God his godly armes may blaze. . . . . I. xi. 7. 9
horse and *man* to ground did rush. . . . . I. xi. 16. 9
Both horse and *man* up lightly rose againe, ... I. xi. 17. 1
Snatcht up both horse and *man,* . . . . I. xi. 18. 9
never *man* such mischiefes did torment: . . . . I. xi. 28. 3
Much was the *man* encombred with his hold, ... I. xi. 41. 1
To see the face of that victorious *man,* . . . . I. xii. 9. 3
never living *man* . . . was distrest: . . . . I. xii. 17. 5
Came running in, much like a *man* dismayd, ... I. xii. 24. 8
Archimago . . . , The falsest *man* alive: . . . . I. xii. 34. 9
Thrise happy *man* the knight himselfe did hold, ... I. xii. 40. 6
let that *man* with better sence advize, ... II. Pr. 2. 1
Why then should witlesse *man* so much misweene, ... II. Pr. 3. 4

Man—*Continued.*
'False traytour certes' . . . 'I read the *man,* . . . . II. i. 17. 7
That short revenge the *man* may overtake, ... II. i. 18. 3
'Heare then, O *man!* the sorrowes . . . . II. i. 49. 5
Thrise happy *man,* who fares them both atweene! . . . . . . II. i. 58. 5
Was hight Sir Huddibras, an hardy *man;* . . . . II. ii. 17. 2
The seely *man,* seeing him ryde so ranck, ... II. iii. 6. 7
Trompart, fitt *man* for Braggadochio, ... II. iii. 10. 1
Vaine-glorious *man* . . . is lifted up to skye; . . . . II. iii. 10. 3
Is not enough fowre quarters of a *man,* . . . . II. iii. 16. 6
The *man* was much abashed at his boast; . . . . II. iii. 17. 1
the *man* that moulds in ydle cell . . . . II. iii. 41. 3
the foolish *man,* fild with delight . . . . II. iii. 42. 2
he was a *man* of mickle might, ... II. iv. 7. 1
'what *man* can shun the hap, ... II. iv. 17. 2
to entrap The *man* most wary . . . . II. iv. 17. 5
O wretched *man,* that would abuse so gentle Dame! . . . . II. iv. 20. 9
Most joyous *man* . . . my selfe I did esteeme, ... II. iv. 21. 7
'This gracelesse *man,* for furtherance of his guile, ... II. iv. 25. 1
'Most wretched *man,* That to affections does the bridle lend! . II. iv. 34. 1
Both horse and *man* nigh able for to choke; . . . . II. v. 3. 5
Was never *man,* who most conquestes atchiev'd, ... II. v. 15. 3
To ridd a wretched *man* from handes of hellish wight!' . . . II. v. 23. 9
He was a *man* of rare redoubted might, ... II. v. 26. 1
out of his delightfull dreame The *man* awoke, ... II. v. 37. 2
'Vaine *man,*' (saide she) . . . . II. vi. 9. 5
Carelesse the *man* soone woxe, ... II. vi. 13. 7
'Behold, O *man!* that toilesome paines doest take, ... II. vi. 15. 1
O *man!* that of them all Art Lord, ... II. vi. 17. 1
Wo worth the *man,* That first did teach . . . . II. vi. 32. 7
'That am, I weene, most wretched *man* alive; . . . . II. vi. 45. 2
'That cursed *man,* that cruel feend of hell, ... II. vi. 50. 1
'What art thou, *man,* (if *man* at all thou art) . . . . II. vii. 7. 1
As eie of *man* did never see before, ... II. vii. 31. 5
ugly shapes did nigh the *man* dismay, ... II. vii. 37. 7
this frayle life of *man,* . . . . II. vii. 65. 4
To serve to wicked *man,* . . . . II. viii. 1. 9
horse and *man* it made to reele asyde: . . . . II. viii. 31. 2
as a *man* whom hellish feendes have frayd, ... II. viii. 46. 4
'Thrise happy *man,*' (said then the Briton knight) . . . . . . II. ix. 5. 1
Ne *man* nor beast may rest, ... II. ix. 16. 6
A carefull *man,* and full of comely guyse. . . . . II. ix. 31. 2
A *man* of yeares yet fresh, as mote appere, ... II. ix. 52. 3
There sate a *man* of ripe and perfect age, ... II. ix. 54. 2
therein sat an old old *man,* halfe blind, ... II. ix. 55. 5
This *man* of infinite remembraunce was, ... II. ix. 56. 1
An happy *man* in his first dayes he was, ... II. x. 22. 1
The wretched *man* gan then avise too late, ... II. x. 31. 1
up arose a *man* of matchlesse might, ... II. x. 37. 1
The justest *man* and trewest in his daies, ... II. x. 42. 2
First Gorboman, a *man* of vertuous life, ... II. x. 44. 3
Constantius, a *man* of mickle might, ... II. x. 59. 2
A *man,* of many parts from beasts deryv'd, ... II. x. 70. 6
That *man* so made he called Elfe, ... II. x. 71. 1
Proofe be thou, Prince, the prowest *man* alyve, ... II. xi. 30. 6
it would tempt a *man* to touchen there; . . . . II. xii. 14. 6
'See the mind of beastly *man,* . . . . II. xii. 87. 1
That *man* to hard conditions to bind, ... III. ii. 13. 7
'Nor *man* it is, nor other living wight, ... III. ii. 38. 1
Under what coast of heaven the *man* did dwell, ... III. iii. 6. 5
how shall she finde the *man?* . . . . III. iii. 25. 3
'The *man,* whom heavens have ordaynd . . . . III. iii. 26. 1
'Behold the *man!* and tell me, Britomart, ... III. iii. 32. 1
till he became A mighty *man* at armes, ... III. iv. 20. 5
never *man* he suffred by that same Rich strond to travell, . . III. iv. 20. 7
the *man* that of him tydings to her brings. . . . . III. vi. 12. 9
most lament For her depart, that ever *man* did heare: . . . III. vii. 20. 2
As ever *man* that bloody field did fight; . . . . III. vii. 29. 5
Proud *man* himselfe then Braggadochio deem'd, ... III. viii. 13. 6
good *man,* sith far in sea we bee, ... III. viii. 24. 1
'Extremely mad the *man* I surely deeme, ... III. ix. 6. 7
'entreat The *man* by gentle meanes . . . . III. ix. 9. 2
The good *man* selfe, which then the Porter playd, ... III. ix. 10. 2
They rudely drove to ground both *man* and horse, ... III. ix. 16. 4
The wretched *man* hearing her call for ayd, ... III. x. 14. 1
Was never wretched *man* in such a wofull cace. . . . . III. x. 14. 9
all the passions that in *man* may light . . . . III. x. 17. 8
'Thou *man* of nought, what doest thou here . . . . III. x. 24. 6
The wretched *man* at his imperious speach . . . . III. x. 25. 1
'What Lady, *man?*' (said Trompart) . . . . III. x. 26. 1
pardon simple *man* that rash did him displease. . . . . III. x. 30. 9
The foolish *man* thereat woxe wondrous blith, ... III. x. 33. 1
The silly *man* that in the thickett lay . . . . III. x. 45. 1
loathsom life, of God and *man* abhord, ... III. x. 51. 2
he has quight Forgot he was a *man,* . . . . III. x. 60. 9
thou, vile *man,* vile Scudamore, art sound, ... III. xi. 11. 6
sweet wit of the *man,* . . . . III. xi. 32. 3
(Ah *man!* beware how thou those dartes behold.) . . . . . . III. xi. 48. 5
man and beast with powre imperious Subdeweth . . . . III. xii. 22. 4
'Thou wicked *man,* whose meed . . . Is death, ... III. xii. 35. 1
he, sad *man,* when he had long . . . Awayted . . . . III. xii. 45. 1
every *man,* Surcharg'd with wine, ... IV. i. 3. 3
him she surely thought To be a *man,* . . . . IV. i. 8. 2
wicked wordes that God and *man* offended. . . . . IV. i. 27. 5
Because to *man* so mercifull he was, ... IV. i. 30. 3
was indeed a *man* of mickle might; . . . . IV. i. 32. 3
Untrue to God, and unto *man* unjust! . . . . IV. i. 53. 2
None but a God or godlike *man* can slake; . . . . IV. ii. 1. 6
Nathlesse proud *man* himselfe the other deemed, ... IV. ii. 8. 1
Each other horse and *man* to ground did send; . . . . IV. ii. 15. 7

Man 538 Manly

Man—*Continued.*
Glad *man* was he to see that joyous sight, ... IV. ii. 23. 1
that I the *man* may learne, ... IV. ii. 25. 3
durst Come see the secret of the life of *man,* . . . . IV. ii. 49. 7
on an heape were tumbled horse and *man:* . . . . IV. iv. 19. 7
horse and *man* to ground he quite did beare, ... IV. iv. 20. 8
no powre of *man* Could bide the force . . . . IV. iv. 46. 3
Fie on the *man* that did it first invent . . . . IV. v. 18. 6
ghesse the *man* to be dismayd with gealous dread. . . . . IV. v. 45. 9
to the ground she smote both horse and *man;* . . . . IV. vi. 10. 7
It was to weet a wilde and salvage *man;* . . . . IV. vii. 5. 1
His neather lip was not like *man* nor beast, ... IV. vii. 6. 1
A wofull wretched maid, of God and *man* forgot! . . . . . IV. vii. 14. 9
he found this wretched *man* . . . . IV. vii. 43. 1
Whereas that wofull *man* in languor did abide. . . . . . IV. viii. 11. 9
Well weend that he had beene some *man* of place, ... IV. viii. 14. 4
wofull *man,* what heavens hard disgrace, ... IV. viii. 14. 7
wont to vanquish God and *man,* . . . . IV. viii. 32. 6
Whom after did a mightie *man* pursew, ... IV. viii. 38. 6
would have maz'd a *man* his dreadfull face to vew; . . . . IV. viii. 38. 9
'This mightie *man,*' (quoth he) 'whom you have slaine, . . IV. viii. 47. 1
Ne was there *man* so strong, but he downe bore; . . . . . IV. viii. 48. 3
what ever *man* it sayd, ... IV. x. 1. 1
Blessed the man that well can use his blis: . . . . IV. x. 8. 8
meanest *man* of many moe, ... IV. x. 19. 1
sense of *man* so coy and curious nice, ... IV. x. 22. 6
Cupids *man* with Venus mayd to hold, ... IV. x. 54. 7
To which no wit of *man* may comen neare; . . . . IV. xi. 10. 5
she left her groome An yron *man,* . . . . V. i. 12. 2
'He is' (said he) 'a *man* of great defence, ... V. ii. 5. 3
horse and *man* he equally dismaies, ... V. ii. 8. 8
entreat that iron *man* below To cease his outrage, ... V. ii. 22. 5
not that arme, nor thou the *man,* I reed, ... V. iii. 21. 3
Would ye remit it to some righteous *man.*' . . . . V. iv. 16. 3
what cause brought that *man* to decay, ... V. iv. 23. 6
that same wretched *man,* ordayned to die, ... V. iv. 25. 1
'Sir Turpine! haplesse *man,* what make you here? . . . . V. iv. 26. 1
Much was the *man* confounded in his mind, ... V. iv. 27. 1
their Queene her selfe, halfe like a *man,* . . . . V. iv. 36. 8
that mighty yron *man* . . . Them sorely vext, ... V. iv. 44. 1
Warn'd *man* and beast in quiet rest be shrowded, ... V. iv. 45. 3
Earely calling forth both *man* and beast . . . . V. v. 1. 3
thou ill advized *man,* . . . . V. v. 40. 1
the *man,* that say or doe so dare, ... V. vi. 1. 6
The yron *man* . . . did inly chill and quake, ... V. vi. 9. 4
(sayd then the yron *man*) . . . . V. vi. 16. 1
A *man* of subtill wit and wicked minde, ... V. vi. 32. 2
On that vilde *man* and all his family; . . . . V. vi. 35. 5
The justest *man* alive and truest did appeare. . . . . . . V. vii. 2. 9
Like to a weake faint-hearted *man* he fared . . . . V. vii. 20. 5
when they of that yron *man* had told, ... V. vii. 25. 8
Unto the *man* whom thou doest love so deare; . . . . . . V. vii. 32. 5
so strongly doth allure The sence of *man,* . . . . V. viii. 1. 2
Each of whose lockes did match a *man* in might, ... V. viii. 2. 2
There is a mighty *man,* which wonnes hereby, ... V. viii. 18. 2
doth wreake her wrath On *man* and beast . . . . V. viii. 49. 5
his yron *man* he sent To follow him; . . . . V. ix. 16. 1
of a *man,* they say, It has the voice, ... V. xi. 20. 6
any *man* would nigh awhaped make: . . . . V. xi. 32. 5
did about them throng To see the *man,* . . . . V. xi. 34. 8
that yron *man* With his huge flaile . . . . V. xi. 47. 6
Both *man* and beast doe fly, and succour doe inquyre. . . . V. xi. 58. 9
Nathlesse the yron *man* did still pursew . . . . V. xi. 65. 1
foot of *man* might sound the bottome plaine, ... V. xii. 5. 3
he them overthrew both *man* and horse, ... V. xii. 7. 7
whether *man* or monster one could scarse discerne. . . . . V. xii. 15. 9
that same yron *man,* which could reveale All hidden crimes, V. xii. 26. 5
they the mildest *man* alive would make Forget his patience, V. xii. 42. 3
happy *man,*' (sayd then Sir Calidore) . . . . VI. i. 5. 6
Maleffort, a *man* of mickle might, ... VI. i. 15. 8
No greater shame to *man* then inhumanitie. . . . . VI. i. 26. 9
both *man* and horse, ... VI. i. 33. 8
The wretched *man,* that all this while . . . . VI. i. 43. 1
a *man* by nothing is so well bewrayd As by his manners; . VI. iii. 1. 3
He was to weete a *man* of full ripe yeares, ... VI. iii. 3. 1
Most pensive *man,* through feare what of his childe became. VI. iii. 17. 9
Most joyfull *man* her sire was her to see, ... VI. iii. 19. 1
him descryde To be the *man* . . . . VI. iii. 47. 5
Calepine by a salvage *man* . . . . reskewed is; . . . . . VI. iv. Arg.
A salvage *man,* which in those woods did wonne, ... VI. iv. 2. 2
The salvage *man* . . . Was much emmoved . . . . VI. iv. 3. 1
With that the wyld *man* more enraged grew, ... VI. iv. 6. 1
after him the wyld *man* ran apace, ... VI. iv. 8. 1
perill, by this salvage *man* pretended, ... VI. iv. 10. 4
the wyld *man,* . . . Came to her creeping . . . . VI. iv. 11. 1
that wyld *man* did apply His best endevour . . . . VI. iv. 16. 1
Like this wyld *man* being undisciplynd, ... VI. v. 1. 6
That plainely may in this wyld *man* be red, ... VI. v. 2. 1
A salvage *man* matcht with a Ladie fayre, ... VI. v. 9. 3
So now they be arrived both in sight Of this wyld *man,* . . . VI. v. 25. 2
Albe the wyld-*man* hardly would refraine. . . . . VI. v. 27. 5
Had not this wylde *man* . . . Kept and delivered me . . . . VI. v. 29. 4
he had bene a *man* of mickle name, ... VI. v. 37. 3
Ne wight with him . . . went, But that wylde *man;* . . . . VI. vi. 18. 7
The whiles the salvage *man* did take his steede, ... VI. vi. 19. 8
With a wyld *man* soft footing by his syde; . . . . VI. vii. 6. 2
The whiles that mighty *man* did her demeane . . . . VI. vii. 39. 4
no might in *man,* nor heart in Knights, ... VI. viii. 18. 6
Meane-while the Salvage *man,* when he beheld . . . . . . VI. viii. 28. 1
the good *man* . . . did thrust it farre away, ... VI. ix. 33. 1

Man—*Continued.*
What *man* that sees the ever-whirling wheele, Of Change, . . . VII. vi. 1. 1
Then shortly should the progeny of *man* Be rooted out, . . . VII. vi. 31. 8
So farre past memory of *man* that may be knowne? . . . . . VII. vii. 2. 9
Whether she *man* or woman inly were, ... VII. vii. 5. 6
As for her tenants, that is, *man* and beasts, ... VII. vii. 19. 1
Mars, that valiant *man,* . . . . VII. vii. 52. 1
she will plague the *man* that loves her most, ... *Am.* xli. 6
Enough it is for one *man* to sustaine The stormes, ... *Am.* xlvi. 13
Vayne *man,* quod I, that hast but little priefe . . . . *Am.* l. 5
Vayne *man,* sayd she, that doest in vaine assay . . . . . . *Am.* lxxv. 5
sweet aspect both God and *man* can move, ... *Am.* lxxxviii. 11
Never had *man* more joyfull day then this, ... *Epith.* 246
man that breathes a more immortall mynd, ... *H.L.* 103
Thrise happie *man!* . . . . *H.L.* 209
Therefore of clay . . . He *man* did make, ... *H.H.L.* 110
man, forgetfull of his Makers grace . . . . *H.H.L.* 120
Nor spirit, nor Angell, though they *man* surpas, ... *H.H.L.* 143
onely *man* himselfe, who selfe did slyde: . . . . *H.H.L.* 145
For mans deare sake he did a *man* become. . . . . *H.H.L.* 147
But who so may, thrise happie *man* him hold, ... *H.H.B.* 239
Manage. To *menage* of most grave affaires is bent; . . . . *Ded. Son.* ix. 2
A goodly person, and could *menage* faire His stubborne steed I. vii. 37. 5
some others faine To *menage* steeds, ... II. iv. 1. 9
well could *menage* and subdew his pride, ... II. iv. 2. 2
wondrous wit to *menage* high affayres, ... II. x. 37. 2
Taught to obay the *menage* of that Elfe . . . . III. xii. 22. 3
Managed. the boldest boy That ever warlike weapons *menaged,* II. ii. 18. 4
in his hand a white rod *menaged:* . . . . II. ix. 27. 7
menaged so well, ... VI. ix. 46. 4
Manageth. And *menageth* the ever-moving sky, ... *H.H.B.* 194
Managing. *menaging* the mouthes of stubborne steedes, . . . *Hub.* 739
fayre defence and goodly *menaging* Of armes . . . . II. iv. 8. 3
Man-child. a *manchild* forth I brought . . . . II. i. 53. 6
Manfully. And *manfully* thereat shotte. . . . . *S.C.* Mar. 78
Mangled. bleeding hart . . . thou *mangled* hast so sore, . . . *H.L.* 143
sacred heavenly corse, So torne and *mangled* . . . . *H.H.L.* 250
Mangy. Upon a *mangy* jade unmeetely set, ... VI. vi. 16. 8
Manhood. mightie *manhode* brought a bedde of ease, ... *S.C.* O. 68
the dreadfull passion Was overpast, and *manhood* well awake, I. ii. 32. 2
To measure *manhood* by the sword or mayle. . . . . II. iii. 16. 5
thine armes seem strong, but *manhood* frayl: . . . . II. v. 5. 6
trust unto his strength and *manhood* meare, ... II. xi. 34. 3
too late his *manhood* and his might I did assay, ... IV. i. 35. 1
By his sole *manhood* and atchievement stout Dismay'd, . . . IV. iv. 43. 2
Resolv'd him to assault with *manhood* stout, ... IV. x. 19. 4
dight In womans weedes, that is to *manhood* shame, ... V. v. 20. 7
deedes ought not be scand By th' authors *manhood,* . . . . V. xi. 17. 4
prove thy *manhood* on the billowes vayne.' . . . . VI. iii. 32. 5
one of mickle might And *manhood* rare, ... VI. iii. 40. 3
That curtesie and *manhood* ever disagree. . . . . VI. iii. 40. 9
not with *manhood,* but with guile, Maintaine this evil use, . VI. vi. 34. 8
Manifold. Yet sure those wings were fairer *manifolde.* . . . . *Mui.* 104
Which had approved bene in uses *manifold.* . . . . I. viii. 3. 9
After long paines and labors *manifold,* He found the meanes I. viii. 40. 5
his sinnes, so great and *manifold,* . . . . I. x. 22. 4
doth imbrace, and kisseth *manifold.* . . . . I. xii. 12. 9
His heart did seeme to melt in pleasures *manifold.* . . . . . I. xii. 40. 9
After his travell long and labours *manifold.* . . . . II. i. 24. 9
For terrour of the tortures *manifold,* . . . . II. vii. 63. 4
Yet she her selfe is whiter *manifold.* . . . . III. v. 5. 7
fraught With pleasures *manifold.* . . . . III. vi. Arg.
she sprinckled favours *manifold* On whom she list, ... III. xii. 13. 7
Approved oft in perils *manifold,* . . . . IV. ii. 39. 3
She turn'd her love to hatred *manifold,* . . . . V. iv. 30. 7
Her selfe adorn'd with gems and jewels *manifold.* . . . . . . V. vii. 13. 9
The prayses of that Prince so *manifold;* . . . . V. ix. 21. 2
Her mind adornd with vertues *manifold.* . . . . *Am.* xv. 14
feele my flames augmented *manifold!* . . . . *Am.* xxx. 8
read, through love, his mercies *manifold.* . . . . *H.H.L.* 224
Manild. Memprise . . . being consorted with *Manild,* . . . . . II. x. 21. 4
Mankind. For him he loved above all *mankinde,* . . . . III. v. 12. 7
all those joyes that weake *mankind* entyse. . . . . IV. xi. 5. 4
all *mankinde* do nourish with their waters clere. . . . . . . IV. xi. 52. 9
for want there of *mankind,* . . . . V. i. 7. 6
Victor of gods, subduer of *mankynd,* . . . . *H.L.* 45
Manliness. Unmindfull of chiefe parts of *manlinesse;* . . . . *Col.* 764
by secret signes of *manlinesse* . . . . IV. vii. 45. 4
mighty hands forget their *manlinesse;* . . . . V. viii. 1. 5
Manlius. *See* **Manild.**
Manly. you likest are For *manly* semblance, ... *Hub.* 200
manly legs, still passing too and fro, ... *Hub.* 748
With shuttelcocks, misseeming *manlie* wit, ... *Hub.* 804
Whose warlike prowesse and *manly* courage, ... *Ded. Son.* xiv. 8
stroke at her with more then *manly* force, ... I. i. 24. 6
nigh his *manly* hart did melt away, ... I. i. 47. 5
he . . . greatly shunned *manly* exercise; . . . . I. iv. 20. 2
Eftsoones his *manly* forces gan to fayle, ... I. vii. 6. 4
manly hands imbrewd in guilty blood Had never beene, . . . I. vii. 47. 3
his mightie shild Upon his *manly* arme . . . . I. viii. 6. 7
this misseeming hew your *manly* looks doth marre? . . . . . I. viii. 42. 9
When corage first does creepe in *manly* chest, ... I. ix. 9. 2
all his *manly* powres it did disperse, ... I. ix. 48. 7
Ne let vaine words bewitch thy *manly* hart, ... I. ix. 53. 2
spy Her loved knight to move his *manly* pace: . . . . I. xi. 33. 7
bruze with clownish fistes his *manly* face; . . . . II. iv. 9. 2
He smote so *manly* on his shoulder plate, ... II. v. 7. 6
In which that *manly* person late did fade. . . . . II. v. 35. 5
naked made each others *manly* spalles; . . . . II. vi. 29. 6
downe to his *manly* brest Have cleft his head . . . . II. viii. 33. 8

Manly—*Continued.*
Not fitt for speedy pace, or *manly* exercize. . . . . II. xii. 46. 9
amiable grace, Mixed with *manly* sternesse, ... II. xii. 79. 6
for prayse, and proofe of *manly* might, ... III. i. 13. 4
manly terror mixed therewithall; . . . . III. i. 46. 2
His *manly* face, that did his foes agrize, ... III. ii. 24. 4
How like a Gyaunt in each *manly* part . . . . III. iii. 32. 3
in his port appeared *manly* hardiment. . . . . III. viii. 44. 9
in *manly* heart His mightie indignation did forbeare; . . . . IV. i. 45. 1
made ech member quake, and *manly* hart to quayle. . . . . . IV. vi. 22. 9
manly limbs endur'd with litle care . . . . IV. viii. 27. 8
through stout disdaine of *manly* mind . . . . V. iv. 32. 1
Where is that dreadfull *manly* looke? . . . . V. vii. 40. 3
As to have robde you of that *manly* hew? . . . . V. vii. 40. 7
for want of *manly* hart, . . . hast shamed . . . . VI. vi. 33. 8
His *manly* mynde was much emmoved therewithall; . . . . . VI. viii. 5. 9
Manned. till all the entry was with bodies *mand*. . . . . . . VI. xi. 46. 9
Manner. Whom they in civill *manner* first did greete, ... *Hub.* 362
Yet evermore it was his *maner* faire, ... I. vi. 30. 1
in her modest *maner* thus bespake: . . . . I. xi. 1. 6
was their *manner* then but bare and playne; . . . . I. xii. 14. 7
All threatning death, all in straunge *manner* armd; . . . . . II. ix. 13. 5
the Prince in courteous *maner* sayd; . . . . II. ix. 37. 4
when his uncouth *manner* he did vew, ... II. xi. 27. 5
To read what *manner* musicke that mote bee; . . . . II. xii. 70. 6
Which stately *manner* whenas they did see, ... III. i. 33. 5
Him seemed more their *maner* did agree; . . . . III. x. 21. 3
marcht . . . In *manner* of a maske, enranged orderly. . . . . III. xii. 5. 9
The *manner* of their worke and wearie paine; . . . . IV. v. 38. 2
against all *manner* wights . . . to maintaine that castels ancient
rights. . . . . IV. x. 7. 8
Whose *manner* was all passengers to stay . . . . IV. x. 13. 3
The *manner* of the Gods when they at banquet be. . . . . . IV. xii. 3. 9
So forth he fared, as his *manner* was, ... V. xi. 36. 6
in bad *maner* they did disagree, ... V. xii. 33. 3
This evill *manner* which ye here maintaine, ... VI. i. 27. 2
What *manner* wight he was, and how yclad, ... VI. ii. 44. 3
Hast slaine my men in this unmanly *maner*, ... VI. vi. 25. 2
To chaunge the *manner* of his loftie looke; . . . . VI. ix. 36. 2
All quite unarm'd, as then their *manner* was. . . . . VII. vi. 24. 3
as her *manner* was on sunny day, ... VII. vi. 45. 6
Manners. seene the *manners* of all beasts on ground; . . . . *Hub.* 687
Whom, . . . He nousled up in life and *manners* wilde, ... I. vi. 23. 8
Whose secret filth good *manners* biddeth not be told. . . . . I. viii. 46. 9
he, that never good nor *manners* knew, ... III. viii. 26. 1
Whose life and *manners* straunge she never knew; . . . . . V. vi. 12. 7
of all goodly *manners* is the ground, ... VI. i. 1. 5
gentlenesse of spright And *manners* mylde . . . . VI. i. 2. 4
a man by nothing is so well bewrayd As by his *manners*; . . VI. iii. 1. 4
noble courage shew with curteous *manners* met. . . . . . . VI. iii. 1. 9
gentle bloud will gentle *manners* breed; . . . . VI. iii. 2. 2
the rude Porter that no *manners* had . . . . VI. iii. 38. 1
Man's. *See* **Old man's, Ploughman's.**
All pleasure . . . for which *mans* hart could long; . . . . . *Bel.*[2] xii. 6
all *mans* life me seemes a Tragedy, ... *T.M.* 157
mans life in his likest image Was limned forth, ... *T.M.* 201
sad ensample of *mans* suddein end: . . . . *As.* 134
No ravenous wolves the good *mans* hope destroy . . . . . . *Col.* 318
each *mans* worth is measured by his weed, ... *Col.* 711
Such wondrous science in *mans* witt to rain . . . . I. v. 40. 1
That tree through one *mans* fault hath doen us all to dy. . . I. xi. 47. 9
more faire and excellent Then is *mans* body, ... II. ix. 1. 3
Till it reduced was to one *mans* governments. . . . . II. ix. 59. 9
when her sonne to *mans* estate did wex, ... II. x. 20. 8
an Helmet light, Made of a dead *mans* skull, ... II. xi. 22. 9
So feeble is *mans* state, ... II. xi. 30. 3
makes ensample of *mans* wretched state, ... III. ix. 39. 8
Till that to ripenesse of *mans* state they grew: . . . . IV. ii. 46. 2
'the terme of each *mans* life, ... IV. ii. 52. 1
like some poore *mans* nest. . . . . IV. v. 32. 9
time to steale, the threasure of *mans* day, ... IV. x. 14. 8
When as *mans* age was in his freshest prime, ... V. Pr. 1. 3
Untill the ripenesse of *mans* yeares he raught; . . . . V. i. 8. 3
weigh the thought that from *mans* mind doth flow: . . . . . V. ii. 43. 4
Both darting forth faire beames to each *mans* eye, ... V. iii. 19. 3
T' obay the heasts of *mans* well-ruling hand. . . . . V. v. 25. 4
to misconstrue of a *mans* intent, ... V. xii. 34. 4
Exceeding much the measure of *mans* stature, ... VI. vii. 41. 3
in each *mans* self' (said Calidore) 'It is . . . . VI. ix. 31. 1
Sufficient worke for one *mans* simple head, ... *Am.* xxxiii. 7
Could make amends to God for *mans* misguyde, ... *H.H.L.* 144
For *mans* deare sake he did a man become. . . . . *H.H.L.* 147
Mansilia. Ne lesse praise-worthie is *Mansilia*, ... *Col.* 508
Mansion. At last he came unto his *mansion*, ... *Hub.* 1349
Had lately built his hatefull *mansion*; . . . . *Mui.* 246
But where thy selfe hast thy brave *mansione*: . . . . *Ded. Son.* v. 8
Unto her happy *mansion* attaine: . . . . II. iii. 41. 4
To leave that desert *mansion*, ... III. vii. 18. 2
Resolv'd to build his balefull *mansion* . . . . III. x. 58. 2
To her fraile *mansion* of mortality: . . . . VI. iii. 28. 3
What idle errand hast thou earths *mansion* to forsake?' . . . VII. vi. 25. 9
Mansions. she raught the Gods owne *mansions*: . . . . *Bel.*[2] vii. 8
Mantle. Thy *mantle* mard, wherein thou maskedst late. . . . *S.C.* Ja. 24
Her *mantle* black through heaven gan overhaile: . . . . . . *S.C.* Ja. 75
soone as spring his *mantle* hath displayde, ... *S.C.* N. 85
sad Night over him her *mantle* black doth spred. . . . . . I. i. 39. 9
Night, . . . in a foule blacke pitchy *mantle* clad, ... I. v. 20. 3
night Who with her sable *mantle* . . . . I. xi. 49. 7
th' yvorie in golden *mantle* gownd: . . . . II. xii. 67. 5
Her *mantle*, colour'd like the starry skyes, ... III. i. 36. 2

Mantle—*Continued.*
Her with a scarlott *mantle* covered . . . . III. i. 59. 8
'Under thy *mantle* black there hidden lye . . . . III. iv. 58. 1
when thou spredst thy *mantle* forth on hie, ... IV. x. 44. 7
Untill a *Mantle* she for him doe fynd . . . . VI. i. 15. 4
He tooke it up and in his *mantle* wound; . . . . VI. xii. 9. 7
To decke hir selfe, and her faire *mantle* weave. . . . . . . *Am.* iv. 12
Doe lyke a golden *mantle* her attyre; . . . . *Epith.* 156
in thy sable *mantle* us enwrap, ... *Epith.* 321
Mantled. The *mantled* medowes mourne, ... *S.C.* N. 128
fayre grassy grownd *Mantled* with greene, ... II. xii. 50. 4
a spatious playne, *Mantled* with greene, ... III. i. 20. 7
Mantles. Their watchet *mantles* frindgd with silver rownd, . III. iv. 40. 5
Mantleth. 'Ne is there hauke which *mentleth* her on pearch, . VI. ii. 32. 1
There my fraile fancy . . . *mantleth* most at ease; . . . . *Am.* lxxii. 10
Mantuan. That *Mantuane* Poetes incompared spirit, ... *Ded. Son.* xiii. 1
Many (*partial list*).
many an auncient Trophee . . . And *many* a spoyle, and *many*
a goodly show, ... *Bel.* v. 5. 6
So *many* Neroes and Caligulaes . . . . *Bel.* x. 13
And there a noyse . . . Of *manie* accords . . . . *Bel.* xii. 8
So *manie* strange things happened . . . . *Pet.* i. 2
Wherto approched . . . *manie* Muses, ... *Pet.* iv. 5
Proud that so *manie* Gods she brought to light; . . . . . . *Ro.* vi. 3
her ship, tost with so *manie* freakes, ... *Ro.* xxi. 5
And *manie* yong plants spring . . . . *Ro.* xxviii. 11
Making his sport, that *manie* makes to weep: . . . . *Van.* v. 7
Some in much joy, *many* in *many* teares, ... *S.C.* F. 18
Phyllis is myne for *many* dayes. . . . . *S.C.* F. 64
Many meete tales of youth did he make, ... *S.C.* F. 98
with his nuts larded *many* swine: . . . . *S.C.* F. 110
For this, and *many* more such outrage, ... *S.C.* F. 183
Encreasing his wrath with *many* a threate: . . . . *S.C.* F. 194
made *many* wounds in the wast Oake. . . . . *S.C.* F. 202
Sacred with *many* a mysteree, ... *S.C.* F. 208
to the *many* a Horne-pype playd, ... *S.C.* May 23
They maken *many* a wrong chevisaunce, ... *S.C.* May 92
many wyld beastes liggen in waite . . . . *S.C.* May 217
medled his talke with *many* a teare: . . . . *S.C.* May 263
tell *many* lesinges of this and that, ... *S.C.* May 285
he could shewe *many* a fine knack: . . . . *S.C.* May 286
frendly Faeries, met with *many* Graces, ... *S.C.* Jun. 25
Wherein is enchased *many* a fayre sight . . . . *S.C.* Au. 27
And mone with *many* a mocke. . . . . *S.C.* Au. 120
For one, opened, mote unfolde *many* moe. . . . . *S.C.* S. 14
So as thou can *many* thinges relate; . . . . *S.C.* S. 23
to compasse *many* wrong emprise: . . . . *S.C.* S. 83
woulden drawe with hem *many* moe. . . . . *S.C.* S. 99
Ylike as a Monster of *many* heads; . . . . *S.C.* S. 121
For *many* han into mischiefe fall, ... *S.C.* S. 147
Never was Woolfe seene, *many* nor some, ... *S.C.* S. 152
Shepheards sich, God mought us *many* send, ... *S.C.* S. 178
with *many* a Lambe had glutted his gulfe, ... *S.C.* S. 185
I wearied with *many* a stroke . . . . *S.C.* D. 33
witnesse *many* a wofull stowre. . . . . *S.C.* D. 66
That kydst the hidden kinds of *many* a wede, ... *S.C.* D. 92
he stormes with *many* a sturdy stoure; . . . . *S.C.* D. 131
Hereafter *many* yeares remembred be . . . . *Gn.* 61
swift Dryades, With *many* Fairies . . . . *Gn.* 179
Eternall hurte left unto *many* one: . . . . *Gn.* 203
Cerberus, whose *many* mouthes doo bay . . . . *Gn.* 345
there bay *Manie* great bandogs . . . . *Gn.* 540
manie lost, of whom no moniment Remaines, ... *Gn.* 589
'Here *manie* other like Heroes bee, ... *Gn.* 593
that *manie* did to die, ... *Hub.* 10
My fortune was, mongst *manie* others moe, ... *Hub.* 13
Thus *manie* yeares I now have spent . . . . *Hub.* 59
if we (emongst so *manie*) Light not . . . . *Hub.* 170
a blew jacket with . . . *manie* slits, ... *Hub.* 206
Much blood throgh *many* wounds . . . . *Hub.* 207
Yet *manie* waies they sought, and *manie* tryed, ... *Hub.* 225
Abusing *manie* through their cloaked guile, ... *Hub.* 344
For *manie* beg which are thereof ashamed. . . . . *Hub.* 352
their adventures fell, Through *manie* haps, ... *Hub.* 360
How *manie* honest men see ye arize . . . . *Hub.* 419
Yet *manie* eke of them . . . are driven . . . . *Hub.* 539
he could doo *manie* other poynts, ... *Hub.* 696
manie one hath mist! . . . . *Hub.* 894
To have thy asking, yet waite *manie* yeeres; . . . . *Hub.* 902
Let God, (said he) if please, care for the *manie*, ... *Hub.* 1195
So did he good to none, to *manie* ill, ... *Hub.* 1197
So *many* moe, so everie one was used, ... *Hub.* 1223
manie warders round about them stood: . . . . *Hub.* 1351
So am I made the servant of the *manie*, ... *T.M.* 223
manie often did abie full sore; . . . . *Ti.* 101
Yet *manie* Poets honourd him alive. . . . . *Ti.* 224
(For *manie* did, which doo it now denie,) . . . . *Ti.* 235
'How *manie* great ones may remembred be, ... *Ti.* 358
was he deckt . . . With *manie* garlands . . . . *Ti.* 653
Not halfe so *manie* sundrie colours arre . . . . *Mui.* 92
Distinguished with *manie* a twinckling starre. . . . . *Mui.* 94
So *many* goodly colours doth containe. . . . . *Mui.* 96
in his wings so *manie* a changefull token, ... *Mui.* 101
Full *many* a Ladie faire, ... *Mui.* 105
mickle woe . . . and *manie* a rufull teare, ... *Mui.* 133
Ne may thee help the *manie* hartie vow, ... *Mui.* 237
manie Nymphes about them . . . And *manie* Tritons . . . . *Mui.* 295, 296
weaving straight a net with *manie* a fold . . . . *Mui.* 357
I of *many* most Most miserable man; . . . . *D.* 37
sound his Oaten quill Unto the *many* . . . . *D.* 326

Many—*Continued.*

Full *many* Maydens often did him woo,	*As.* 37
And *many* a Nymph . . . forsooke,	*As.* 43
Wide wounds emongst them *many* one he made,	*As.* 107
I, poore swaine, of *many*, greatest crosse!	*Col.* 18
woods were heard to waile full *many* a sythe,	*Col.* 23
My pipe, before that aemuled of *many*,	*Col.* 73
into *many* parts his streame he shar'd,	*Col.* 138
I among the rest, of *many* least,	*Col.* 252
hath so *many* shepheards in her fee,	*Col.* 370
All these, and *many* others moe remaine,	*Col.* 448
of so *many* Nymphs, which she doth hold.	*Col.* 459
yet *many* mo that Cynthia serve,	*Col.* 576
Full *many* worthie ones then waiting were,	*Col.* 737
Of which among you *many* yet remaine,	*Col.* 739
Full *many* persons of right worthie parts,	*Col.* 752
There, in deede, dwel faire Graces *many* one,	*Ded. Son.* v. 9
woxen insolent Through *many* victories,	*Ded. Son.* vi. 11
So *man* pathes, so *many* turnings seene,	I. i. 10. 8
taile . . . in knots and *many* boughtes upwound,	I. i. 15. 3
Your first adventure: *many* such I pray,	I. i. 27. 8
in her *many* troubles did most pleasure take.	I. ii. 9. 9
he could take As *many* formes and shapes	I. ii. 10. 3
many yeares throughout the world I straid,	I. ii. 24. 7
That *many* errant knights hath broght to wretchednesse.	I. ii. 34. 9
That causd her shed so *many* a bitter teare;	I. iii. 25. 4
felon strong To *many* knights did daily worke disgrace;	I. iii. 29. 4
one loving howre For *many* yeares of sorrow can dispence;	I. iii. 30. 3
Shee has forgott how *many* a woeful stowre	I. iii. 30. 5
High lifted up were *many* loftie towres,	I. iv. 4. 6
Snake, the which his taile uptyes In *many* folds,	I. iv. 31. 5
How *many* mischieves should ensue his heedlesse hast.	I. iv. 34. 9
Full *many* mischiefes follow cruell Wrath:	I. iv. 35. 1
All these, and *many* evils moe haunt ire,	I. iv. 35. 6
have felt full *many* an heavie stowre.	I. iv. 46. 9
earely waite him *many* a gazing eye,	I. v. 3. 2
There *many* Minstrales maken melody,	I. v. 3. 4
many Bardes, that . . . Can tune their timely voices	I. v. 3. 6
many Chroniclers, that can record Old loves,	I. v. 3. 8
warres for Ladies doen by *many* a Lord.	I. v. 3. 9
many skilfull leaches him abide To salve his hurts,	I. v. 17. 2
Acheron, Where *many* soules sit wailing woefully,	I. v. 33. 2
many corses . . . Of murdred men,	I. v. 53. 2
stayd, To gather breath in *many* miseryes.	I. vi. 19. 4
As he had traveild *many* a sommers day	I. vi. 35. 5
Whose *many* heades . . . breed him endlesse labor to subdew.	I. vii. 17. 4
His poynant speare that *many* made to bleed,	I. vii. 19. 7
For whose deare sake so *many* troubles her did tosse.	I. vii. 27. 9
She wandred *many* a wood, and measurd *many* a vale.	I. vii. 28. 9
Had riven *many* a brest with pikehead square:	I. vii. 37. 4
'Full *many* knights, adventurous and stout,	I. vii. 45. 1
proofe he since hath made . . . in *many* a cruell fight;	I. vii. 47. 7
The groning ghosts of *many* one dismaide	I. vii. 47. 8
Which have endured *many* a dreadfull stowre,	I. vii. 48. 3
how *many* perils doe enfold The righteous man,	I. viii. 1. 1
Death and despeyre did *many* thereof sup,	I. viii. 14. 3
Their God . . . Shott *many* a dart	I. ix. 10. 8
Queene . . . hast fownd, Mongst *many*, one	I. ix. 16. 7
On which had *many* wretches hanged beene,	I. ix. 34. 4
His garment, nought but *many* ragged clouts,	I. ix. 36. 1
by him had *many* pledges dere.	I. x. 4. 9
watched night and day, For feare of *many* foes;	I. x. 5. 3
take delight With *many* rather for to goe astray,	I. x. 10. 6
Many kind speeches they betweene them spend,	I. x. 15. 3
goodly gan discourse of *many* a noble gest.	I. x. 15. 9
many soules in dolours had fordonne:	I. x. 33. 7
learned Ladies . . . make full *many* a lovely lay.	I. x. 54. 9
many bloody battailes fought in face,	I. x. 65. 3
The *many* favours I with thee have fownd,	I. x. 67. 2
prov'd the powre of *many* a puissant knight.	I. xi. 17. 9
So *many* furies and sharpe fits did haunt,	I. xi. 27. 4
after all the raskall *many* ran,	I. xii. 9. 1
nest Of *many* Dragonettes, his fruitfull seede:	I. xii. 10. 6
prove how *many* acres he did spred of land.	I. xii. 11. 9
fate That heaped on him so *many* wrathfull wreakes;	I. xii. 16. 6
Like as it had bene *many* an Angels voice	I. xii. 39. 3
through hardy enterprize *Many* great Regions are discovered,	II. Pr. 2. 4
he . . . threatned death with *many* a bloodie word:	II. i. 11. 8
Through *many* hard assayes which did betide;	II. i. 35. 2
With percing shriekes and *many* a dolefull lay;	II. i. 35. 8
many bitter throbs did throw,	II. i. 47. 3
many errant knightes hath fowle fordonne;	II. i. 51. 4
The cursed land where *many* wend amis,	II. i. 51. 8
shedding *many* teares they closd the earth agayne.	II. i. 61. 9
he by *many* rash adventures wan,	II. ii. 17. 4
many whelmd in deadly paine;	II. ii. 43. 4
oft approv'd in *many* hard assay;	II. iii. 15. 7
through *many* yeares thy wits thee faile,	II. iii. 16. 2
Upon her eyelids *many* Graces sate,	II. iii. 25. 1
Purfled upon with *many* a folded plight,	II. iii. 26. 5
far renowmd through *many* bold emprize;	II. iii. 35. 4
many battailes fought and *many* fraies	II. iii. 38. 5
gor'd with *many* a wownd,	II. iv. 3. 8
the Hag, with *many* a bitter threat,	II. iv. 9. 3
weake wretch, of *many* weakest one,	II. iv. 17. 6
Full oft approvd in *many* a cruell warre;	II. iv. 41. 4
Full *many* doughtie knightes	II. v. 26. 4
naked, deckt with *many* ornaments.	II. v. 32. 9
That hath so *many* haughty conquests wonne?	II. v. 35. 8
many a stroke and *many* a streaming wound,	II. v. 36. 8
purple robe gored with *many* a wound,	II. vii. 13. 7
Doth not, I weene, so *many* evils meet.'	II. vii. 14. 5
By every fournace *many* feendes did byde,	II. vii. 35. 6
Many great golden pillours did upbeare	II. vii. 43. 5
blis . . . few gett, but *many* mis:	II. vii. 48. 9
many noble Greekes and Trojans made to bleed.	II. vii. 55. 9
full *many* soules do endlesse wayle and weepe.	II. vii. 56. 9
many damned wightes In those sad waves,	II. vii. 57. 2
to Pyrochles *many* strokes he told;	II. viii. 41. 4
Eft to Cymochles twise so *many* fold;	II. viii. 41. 5
many foes, whom straunger knightes	II. ix. Arg.
wasted had much way, and measurd *many* miles.	II. ix. 9. 9
many good knights slaine	II. ix. 12. 9
was shee woo'd of *many* a gentle knight,	II. ix. 18. 3
many a Lord of noble parentage,	II. ix. 18. 4
Wherein were *many* tables fayre dispred,	II. ix. 27. 2
With *many* raunges reard along the wall,	II. ix. 29. 2
About the Caudron *many* Cookes accoyld	II. ix. 30. 6
Courted of *many* a jolly Paramoure,	II. ix. 34. 3
her garment . . . tuckt with *many* a plight:	II. ix. 40. 6
compar'd to these by *many* parts:	II. ix. 48. 3
Like *many* swarmes of Bees assembled round,	II. ix. 51. 4
things foregone through *many* ages	II. ix. 56. 2
many Giaunts left on groning flore:	II. x. 10. 5
so *many* weekes as the yeare has, So *many* children he did multiply:	II. x. 22. 3, 4
Now one, which earst were *many* made	II. x. 38. 9
for this Realme found *many* goodly layes,	II. x. 42. 5
Her *many* deemd to have beene of the Fayes,	II. x. 42. 7
great bloodshed and *many* a sad assay,	II. x. 49. 2
A man, of *many* parts from beasts deryv'd,	II. x. 70. 6
many bold repulse and *many* hard Atchievement	II. xi. 15. 3
many arrowes under his right side,	II. xi. 21. 2
had not bene removed *many* a day;	II. xi. 35. 8
Where *many* Groomes and Squyres ready were	II. xi. 49. 1
far off they *many* Islandes spy	II. xii. 10. 6
drawne *many* a wandring wight	II. xii. 11. 8
Where *many* Mermayds haunt	II. xii. 17. 9
In which full *many* had . . . Beene suncke,	II. xii. 20. 3
these, and thousands thousands *many* more,	II. xii. 25. 1
an hideous bellowing Of *many* beasts,	II. xii. 39. 2
And shewd him *many* sights	II. xii. 68. 9
Many faire Ladies and lascivious boyes,	II. xii. 72. 8
Of *many* a lady', and *many* a Paramowre.	II. xii. 75. 5
Through *many* covert groves and thickets close,	II. xii. 76. 6
Full *many* Countreyes they did overronne,	III. i. 3. 4
many hard adventures did atchieve;	III. i. 3. 6
lost much blood through *many* a wownd,	III. i. 21. 5
many a bitter stownd . . . endurd, and tasted *many* a bloody wownd.'	III. i. 24. 8, 9
glee of *many* gratious Faire Ladies, and of *many* a gentle knight,	III. i. 31. 5, 6
Which her essayd with *many* a fervent fit,	III. i. 34. 8
rownd about it *many* beds were dight,	III. i. 39. 2
many famous knightes and Ladies wonne, And *many* straunge adventures	III. ii. 8. 2, 3
old Dame said *many* an idle verse,	III. ii. 48. 8
And *many* drops of milk and blood	III. ii. 49. 9
through *many* a bitter stowre:	III. iii. 3. 5
Full *many* wayes within her troubled mind	III. iii. 5. 1
Full *many* waies she sought,	III. iii. 5. 3
with great honour *many* batteils try;	III. iii. 31. 4
with *many* one Of his Norveyses,	III. iii. 33. 8
Bards tell of *many* wemen valorous,	III. iii. 54. 4
full *many* feats adventurous Performd,	III. iii. 54. 5
wreckes of *many* wretches,	III. iv. 22. 8
Tryde often to the scath of *many* Deare,	III. iv. 24. 2
many Ladies fayre did oft complaine,	III. iv. 26. 7
Many meeke wordes to stay and comfort	III. iv. 48. 9
where I have *many* a day Served	III. v. 4. 4
Faire Florimell belov'd of *many* a knight,	III. v. 8. 8
the birds song *many* a lovely lay.	III. v. 40. 3
Many Restoratives of vertues rare,	III. v. 50. 3
But *many* there she found	III. vi. 13. 3
many plaintes to her were brought,	III. vi. 15. 3
In which full *many* lovely Nymphes abyde;	III. vi. 16. 5
With *many* of the Gods in company	III. vi. 49. 2
in the wofull harts Of *many* wretches	III. vi. 49. 7
where *many* one Admyrd her goodly haveour,	III. vi. 52. 7
nor *many* wakefull spyes, That can withhold	III. ix. 7. 5
That this faire *many* were compeld	III. ix. 11. 7
That madest *many* Ladies deare lament	III. ix. 35. 3
there he *many* yeares did raine,	III. ix. 37. 2
Which raignd so *many* yeares victorious,	III. ix. 39. 3
through fatall errour long was led Full *many* yeares,	III. ix. 41. 5
many perilles past in forreine landes,	III. ix. 41. 8
that *many* deare complaind:	III. ix. 42. 7
many fortunes prov'd in th' Ocean mayne,	III. ix. 48. 8
Subdewed with losse of *many* Britons bold:	III. ix. 50. 2
many false belgardes at her let fly.	III. ix. 52. 9
many weake harts had subdewed . . . and *many* had ylike misled:	III. x. 9. 7, 8
blood hath of so *many* thousands shedd,	III. x. 32. 6
many a wood and *many* an uncouth way,	III. x. 34. 2
So had he served *many* one.	III. x. 35. 9
many dangers dwell;	III. x. 40. 4
many wilde woodmen which robbe and rend	III. x. 40. 6
a noyse of *many* bagpipes shrill,	III. x. 43. 2
many dreadfull feends hath pointed to her gard.	III. xi. 16. 9

Many—*Continued.*

Many faire pourtraicts, and *many* a faire feate; . . . III. xi. 29. 2
For *many* other Nymphes, he sore did shreek, . . . III. xi. 44. 5
many wide woundes launched . . . III. xi. 44. 9
wrought to *many* others moe, . . . III. xi. 45. 5
with how *many* eyes High heven beholdes . . . III. xi. 45. 8
richlier by *many* partes arayd; . . . III. xi. 51. 2
He wailed womanlike with *many* a teare, . . . III. xii. 7. 7
great liking sheowe, Great liking unto *many*, . . . III. xii. 13. 9
all his *many* it affraide did make: . . . III. xii. 23. 8
There were full *many* moe like maladies, . . . III. xii. 26. 1
So *many* moe, as there be phantasies . . . III. xii. 26. 3
measur'd *many* a sad verse, . . . III. xii. 36. 4
reward enough I weene, For *many* labours . . . III. xii. 40. 3
many a knight, and *many* a lovely Dame, . . . IV. i. 9. 3
she could d'on so *manie* shapes in sight, . . . IV. i. 18. 3
great riches, gathered *manie* a day, . . . IV. i. 29. 5
all *manie* nights; and *manie* . . . present were . . . IV. i. 49. 4
one, of *many*, was so strongly bent . . . IV. iii. 8. 1
hath this day so *many* so unmanly shent.' . . . IV. v. 18. 9
Full *many* great calamities and rare . . . IV. vii. 14. 3
after him full *many* threatnings threw, . . . IV. viii. 40. 2
after *many* teares and sorrowes spent, . . . IV. viii. 64. 6
many miles they two together wore, . . . IV. ix. 19. 7
Through *many* perils wonne, and *many* fortunes waide. . . . IV. ix. 38. 9
this shield, of *many* sought in vaine, . . . IV. x. 8. 3
Feigning full *many* a fond excuse to prate, . . . IV. x. 14. 7
Full *many* did affray, . . . IV. x. 16. 9
many doughty warriours, . . . IV. x. 18. 1
'But I, though meanest man of *many* moe, . . . IV. x. 19. 1
With *many* moe lay in ambushment . . . IV. x. 20. 7
Might match with this by *many* a degree: . . . IV. x. 30. 5
worth *many* a pound, . . . IV. x. 37. 7
many salves did to his sore applie, . . . IV. xi. 6. 2
many herbes did use. . . . IV. xi. 6. 3
with *many* a champion bold . . . IV. xi. 19. 5
So *many* learned impes, that shoote abrode, . . . IV. xi. 26. 5
In which were *many* towres and castels set, . . . IV. xi. 27. 8
And round about him *many* a pretty Page . . . IV. xi. 29. 1
By *many* a city and by *many* a towne And *many* rivers . . . IV. xi. 34. 2, 3
many a gentle Muse and *many* a learned wit. . . . IV. xi. 34. 9
many a band Of Scots and English both, . . . IV. xi. 36. 8
many countreis scowrd. . . . IV. xi. 42. 9
The pleasaunt Bandon crownd with *many* a wood; . . . IV. xi. 44. 2
With *many* more whose names no tongue can tell: . . . IV. xi. 44. 6
she that hight of *many* heastes Polynome; . . . IV. xi. 50. 9
All those were there, and *many* other more, . . . IV. xii. 3. 1
Did march amongst the *many* . . . IV. xii. 18. 8
With *many* bitter teares shed . . . V. i. 13. 9
many errant Knights hath there fordonne; . . . V. ii. 4. 8
in the same are *many* trapfals pight, . . . V. ii. 7. 8
many Princes she in wealth exceedes, . . . V. ii. 9. 6
many Lords have her to wife desired, . . . V. ii. 10. 3
Where *many* years it afterwards remayned, . . . V. ii. 19. 5
Paynims daughter . . . Guarded of *many* . . . V. ii. 20. 3
They saw before them . . . Full *many* people . . . V. ii. 29. 5
so *many* nations . . . desire. . . . V. ii. 29. 9
they doe these *many* yeares remaine, . . . V. ii. 36. 3
Where turney *many* knights: . . . V. iii. Arg.
she *many* moneths did mourne, . . . V. iii. 1. 8
prov'd in *many* a fight. . . . V. iii. 5. 9
many deeds of armes that day were donne, . . . V. iii. 6. 5
many knights unhorst, and *many* wounded, . . . V. iii. 6. 6
battell, that so *many* did dismay. . . . V. iii. 21. 9
as *many* it mistooke, . . . V. iii. 27. 3
Full *many* Ladies often had assayd . . . V. iii. 28. 1
And *many* a one suppos'd to be a mayd: . . . V. iii. 28. 3
that *many* had disgrast. . . . V. iii. 28. 9
ere *many* yeares, . . . V. iv. 7. 8
A rout of *many* people farre away; . . . V. iv. 21. 3
and *many* done be dead. . . . V. iv. 29. 9
the Knights, . . . Threw *many* threats, . . . V. iv. 37. 4
none of all the *many* once did darre . . . V. iv. 44. 5
she came . . . Guarded with *many* Damzels . . . V. v. 4. 3
With *many* idle stoups her troubling . . . V. v. 15. 7
he had bene trayned *many* a day, . . . V. v. 21. 2
With moniments of *many* Knights decay, . . . V. v. 21. 4
round about him saw *Many* brave knights, . . . V. v. 22. 2
subdew'd of old So *many* monsters . . . V. v. 24. 6
That *many* hath with dread of death dismayd, . . . V. v. 31. 3
she vow'd, with *many* a cursed threat, . . . V. v. 47. 6
many yron bands on him to lade: . . . V. v. 54. 7
in heart did find *Many* vaine fancies . . . V. vi. 7. 7
gan the other . . . *many* things demaund, . . . V. vi. 20. 9
after them full *many* other more, . . . V. vi. 29. 3
many brought to shame . . . V. vi. 32. 9
many treasons vile His father Dolon had deviz'd . . . V. vi. 33. 7
he weend . . . by *many* tokens plaine; . . . V. vi. 34. 2
she received was . . . Of *many* Priests . . . V. vii. 4. 2
that *many* foes shall reare . . . V. vii. 23. 2
many scarres and *many* hoary heares, . . . V. vii. 39. 8
reft from *many* a noble Knight, . . . V. vii. 41. 5
'Mongst *many* which maligne . . . V. viii. 18. 1
Miscalling me by *many* a bitter name, . . . V. viii. 22. 8
fenst himselfe about with *many* a flaming brand. . . . V. viii. 35. 9
rent with *many* a wound; . . . V. viii. 42. 7
he *many* doth confound: . . . V. ix. 6. 1
top was arm'd with *many* an yron hooke, . . . V. ix. 11. 2
Charmes to the birds full *many* a pleasant lay, . . . V. ix. 13. 2
the villaine . . . *many* pleasant trickes . . . show, . . . V. ix. 13. 6

Many—*Continued.*

a stately pallace . . . With *many* towres, . . . V. ix. 21. 6
Maugre so *many* foes . . . V. ix. 30. 5
she . . . Admyr'd of *many*, . . . V. ix. 33. 2
That whylome wont to doe so *many* quake, . . . V. ix. 35. 8
strongly to appele Of *many* haynous crymes . . . V. ix. 39. 6
wrought . . . mischiefe unto *many* a knight, . . . V. ix. 40. 4
many other crimes . . . Against her brought, . . . V. ix. 43. 2
with him, . . . came *Many* grave persons . . . V. ix. 43. 6
That *many* high regards . . . gainst her red. . . . V. ix. 43. 9
for her, . . . Rose *many* advocates . . . V. ix. 45. 2
many teares forth powre. . . . V. ix. 45. 9
many fearefull objects to them to present. . . . V. ix. 46. 9
Which till this day mongst *many* living are, . . . V. x. 5. 8
stirre up strife and *many* a tragicke stowre; . . . V. x. 13. 5
In th' hearing of full *many* Knights . . . V. x. 14. 9
Imposd on it with *many* a hard condition, . . . V. x. 27. 7
so *many* knights had fouly bene fordonne. . . . V. x. 30. 9
forth he far'd with all his *many* bad, . . . V. xi. 3. 2
many a one which came . . . V. xi. 25. 8
So forth he fared, . . . Through *many* perils; . . . V. xi. 36. 8
approv'd in *many* a doubt, . . . V. xi. 47. 5
With . . . *many* a guilefull word . . . V. xi. 50. 4
and therewithall Fought *many* battels . . . V. xi. 53. 7
'But for that *many* did that shield envie, . . . V. xi. 54. 1
The raskall *manie* soone they overthrew; . . . V. xi. 59. 8
In roiall robes, and *many* jewels dight; . . . V. xi. 60. 7
the yron man did still pursew That raskall *many* . . . V. xi. 65. 2
he left full *many* a corse; . . . V. xii. 7. 5
though *many* would right faine . . . V. xii. 10. 5
That *many* wounds into his flesh it made, . . . V. xii. 19. 8
And take great joy to publish it to *many*. . . . V. xii. 35. 3
In guiltlesse blood of *many* an innocent: . . . V. xii. 40. 7
Good Knights and Ladies true, and *many* else destroyd. . . . VI. i. 7. 9
Though *many* foes did him maligne therefore, . . . VI. v. 12. 6
in so great daunger set Mongst *many* foes, . . . VI. v. 22. 3
With *many* kindes of medicines . . . VI. vi. 2. 7
had in *many* fortunes tossed beene . . . VI. vi. 3. 3
past through *many* perillous assayes, . . . VI. vi. 3. 4
proved oft in *many* perillous fight, . . . VI. vi. 4. 3
fall'n into this feeble case Through *many* wounds, . . . VI. vi. 20. 8
whilest *many* underneath him fell. . . . VI. vi. 23. 9
To fight with *many* foes about him ment, . . . VI. vi. 27. 5
left that salvage wight Amongst so *many* foes, . . . VI. vi. 37. 6
my selfe with *many* a wound Did slay againe, . . . VI. vii. 16. 8
In th' harts of *many* a knight, and *many* a gentle squire. . . . VI. vii. 28. 9
Yet was she lov'd of *many* a worthy pere: . . . VI. vii. 29. 4
The more it is admir'd of *many* a wight, . . . VI. vii. 29. 8
Many a wretch . . . Did languish . . . VI. vii. 31. 2
at her that *many* did deride, . . . VI. vii. 32. 4
many there were missing; . . . VI. vii. 33. 3
Then found he *many* missing of his crew, . . . VI. vii. 34. 1
Till she had sav'd so *many* loves as she did lose. . . . VI. vii. 37. 9
past through *many* perils . . . VI. vii. 50. 6
Like *many* water streames, . . . VI. viii. 19. 2
It was belov'd of *many* a gentle Knight, . . . VI. viii. 20. 5
Full *many* a one for me deepe groand . . . VI. viii. 20. 7
Till I have sav'd so *many* as I earst did slay.' . . . VI. viii. 22. 9
her eate attonce, or *many* meales to make. . . . VI. viii. 37. 9
round about her flocke, like *many* flies, . . . VI. viii. 40. 2
through *many* a soyle Had traveld . . . VI. viii. 47. 1
Full *many* pathes and perils he hath past, . . . VI. ix. 2. 5
and eke *many* a one Burnt in her love, . . . VI. ix. 10. 2
Full *many* a night for her did sigh and grone: . . . VI. ix. 10. 4
And *many* gealous thoughts conceiv'd . . . VI. ix. 38. 4
And *many* feete fast thumping . . . VI. x. 10. 4
In whom so *many* Graces gathered are, . . . VI. x. 27. 2
mongst so *many* layes As he hath sung . . . VI. x. 28. 4
And Coridon with *many* other moe, . . . VI. xi. 11. 2
His aged wife, with *many* others wide; . . . VI. xi. 18. 5
How *many* of their friends were slaine, how *many* fone. . . . VI. xi. 20. 9
the best Of *many* worst, . . . VI. xi. 24. 3
How *many* flyes, in whottest sommers day, . . . VI. xi. 48. 1
So *many* theeves about him swarming are, . . . VI. xi. 48. 5
from *many* long had robd . . . VI. xi. 51. 3
a ship . . . Is met of *many* a counter winde . . . VI. xii. 1. 3
making *many* a borde and *many* a bay, . . . VI. xii. 1. 6
had endured *many* a dreadfull stoure . . . VI. xii. 3. 7
whose father hight The Lord of *Many* Ilands, . . . VI. xii. 4. 2
In much delight, and *many* joyes among, . . . VI. xii. 11. 8
With *many* a joyfull kisse and *many* a melting teare. . . . VI. xii. 20. 9
he *many* massacres had left, . . . VI. xii. 23. 2
Oft interlacing *many* a forged lie, . . . VI. xii. 33. 5
a muzzel strong . . . made with *many* a lincke: . . . VI. xii. 34. 3
vile tongue, which *many* had defamed, . . . VI. xii. 38. 4
And *many* causelesse caused to be blamed. . . . VI. xii. 38. 5
this homely verse, of *many* meanest, . . . VI. xii. 41. 1
play Her cruell sports to *many* mens decay? . . . VII. vi. 1. 5
many of their stemme long after did survive: . . . VII. vi. 2. 9
many of them afterwards obtain'd . . . VII. vi. 3. 1
to *many* ones great paine, . . . VII. vi. 4. 7
bowre, that *many* flowers strowes: . . . VII. vi. 41. 5
Through *many* woods and shady coverts flowes, . . . VII. vi. 41. 7
though full *many* a day He saw her clad, . . . VII. vi. 42. 7
her debter For *many* moe good turnes . . . VII. vi. 44. 8
That *many* now much worship and admire! . . . *Am.* xxvii. 8
apples . . . That *many* sought, yet none could ever taste; . . . *Am.* lxxvii. 10
Full *many* thou hast pricked to the hart, . . . *Epig.* iv. 37
bright Tead that flames with *many* a flake, And *many* a bachelor to waite on him, . . . *Epith.* 27, 28

Many—*Continued.*
So *many* gazers as on her do stare, ... *Epith.* 160
Ascending up, with *many* a stately stayre, ... *Epith.* 179
joying in the sight Of these glad *many,* . . . . . *Epith.* 294
Song! made in lieu of *many* ornaments, ... *Epith.* 427
thou madest *many* harts to bleed . . . . . *H.L.* 12
many a gentle mynd Dwels in deformed tabernacle . . . . . *H.B.* 141
In which how *many* wonders doe they reede . . . . . *H.B.* 246
So *many* millions of chaste pleasures play. . . . . . *H.B.* 259
Many lewd layes (ah! woe is me the more!) . . . . . *H.H.L.* 8
Many-folded. *many-folded* shield he bound about his wrest. II. iii. 1. 9
Many-headed. Duessa came, High mounted on her *many headed* beast, ... I. viii. 6. 2
Map. The *map* of all the wide world doth containe. . . . . . *Ro.* xxvi. 14
Maple. A mazer ywrought of the *Maple* warre, ... *S.C.* Au. 27
the *Maple* seeldom inward sound. . . . . . I. i. 9. 9
Her wrizled skin, as rough as *maple* rind, So scabby was . . I. viii. 47. 8
Mar. your last reliques *marre*. . . . . . *Ro.* vii. 11
all did *marre;* . . . . . *Ro.* xi. 12
death I hate, because it life doth *marre;* . . . . . *D.* 426
least I *marre* the sweetnesse of the vearse, ... *As.* 215
He . . . oft doth *mar* their murmurings. . . . . . I. i. 23. 9
this misseeming hew your manly looks doth *marre?* . . . . . I. viii. 42. 9
marre the blossom of your beauty bright: . . . . . II. i. 14. 4
Ne ought the praise of prowesse more doth *marre* . . . . . II. ii. 30. 8
doth *marre* Both loosers lott, and victours prayse alsoe; . . . II. v. 15. 7
that ought those puissant hands may *marre:* . . . . . II. vi. 44. 8
through want of words, her excellence to *marre.* . . . . . III. Pr. 2. 9
Let not her fault your sweete affections *marre,* . . . . . III. i. 49. 3
striving fit to make, I feare, doe *marre,* . . . . . III. ii. 3. 8
she it all did *mar* with cruelty and pride. . . . . . IV. ix. 14. 9
broke their bowes, and did their shooting *marre,* . . . . . V. iv. 44. 4
she it with foule abuse did *marre;* . . . . . V. ix. 38. 3
the garland of your glorie *marre,* . . . . . *H.B.* 174
marre their beauties bright, ... *Proth.* 51
Marble. Of bricke, ne yet of *marble* was the wall, ... *Bel.*[1] ii. 5
Nor brick nor *marble* was the wall . . . . . *Bel.*[2] ii. 5
in Porphyre and *Marble* doo appeare, ... *Ro.* xxxii. 7
Like two faire *marble* pillours they were seene, ... II. iii. 28. 1
Jett or *Marble* far from Ireland brought; . . . . . II. ix. 24. 3
the *marble* Pillour that is pight . . . . . III. vii. 41. 4
that rich Romane of white *marble* wrought, ... III. xii. 46. *or.* 3
Upon an hundred *marble* pillors round . . . . . IV. x. 37. 4
hardest *marble* weares: . . . . . IV. xii. 7. 2
seem'd a *marble* rocke asunder could have rive. . . . . . V. xi. 5. 9
seem'd a *marble* pillour it could bow; . . . . . VI. viii. 16. 3
she springs out of two *marble* Rocks, ... VII. vi. 41. 1
ymages Of hardest *marble* are of purpose made, ... *Am.* li. 2
Her snowie necke lyke to a *marble* towre; . . . . . *Epith.* 177
Marbles. betwixt two *marbles* plaine Shee pownded small, . . III. v. 33. 1
Marble-stone. Of smoothest *marble stone* in order set, ... *Gn.* 663
there beside of *marble stone* was built An Altare, ... I. viii. 36. 1
His hart gan wexe as starke as *marble stone,* . . . . . II. i. 42. 2
in the *marble stone* was written this, ... IV. x. 8. 6
Marcellus. Such one *Marcellus,* but was torne with thunder: . *Ti.* 416
March. So forth they *marchen* in this goodly sort, ... I. iv. 37. 1
before did *march* a goodly band Of tall young men, ... I. xii. 5. 6
Then they *march* forward brave. . . . . . III. x. 42. 9
march not past the mountenaunce of a shott, ... III. xi. 20. 8
Nathelesse he forth did *march,* well as he might, ... IV. i. 38. 1
both together chose Homeward to *march,* . . . . . IV. iii. 51. 5
Did *march* amongst the many all the way, ... IV. xii. 18. 8
sturdy *March,* with brows full sternly bent . . . . . VII. vii. 32. 3
Prepare your selves to *march* amongst his host, ... *H.L.* 40
Marched. Therewith the knight thence *marched* forth in hast, . I. vi. 40. 1
So with his Squire, . . . He *marched* forth . . . . . I. viii. 3. 2
marched to the Strond there passage to require. . . . . . II. vi. 27. 9
choosing for that evenings hospitale, They thither *marcht:* . II. ix. 10. 6
she *marched* streight against her foes, ... II. x. 54. 8
They *marched* fayrly forth, of nought ydred. . . . . . II. xii. 38. 7
Forth *marched* to a Castle them before; . . . . . III. viii. 52. 2
home he *marcht* emongst the horned heard, ... III. x. 47. 8
After whom *marcht* a jolly company, ... III. xii. 5. 8
the maskers *marched* forth in trim aray. . . . . . III. xii. 6. 9
him beside *marcht* amorous Desyre, ... III. xii. 9. 1
Dissemblaunce and Suspect *Marcht* in one rancke, ... III. xii. 14. 2
Thus *marched* these six couples forth in faire degree. . . . III. xii. 18. 9
After all these there *marcht* a most faire Dame, ... III. xii. 19. 1
All which disguized *marcht* in masking wise . . . . . III. xii. 26. 6
then returned, having *marched* thrise, ... III. xii. 26. 8
marched all in close disguise Of fayned love, ... IV. ii. 30. 1
The knights in couples *marcht* with ladies . . . . . IV. iv. 14. 9
These *marched* farre afore the other crew: . . . . . IV. xi. 12. 1
Avon *marched* in more stately path, ... IV. xi. 31. 6
together *marched* toward Proteus hall. . . . . . IV. xi. 39. 9
after these the Sea Nymphs *marched* all, ... IV. xi. 48. 1
So forth into the field she *marched* thence, ... V. v. 4. 7
Marcht with that mayd; . . . . . V. viii. 51. 9
thence unto the Castle *marched* right, ... V. x. 33. 8
He sternely *marcht* before the Castle gate, ... V. xi. 3. 6
forward *marched* to a towne in sight. . . . . . V. xii. 6. 3
ere he *marched* farre he with them met, ... V. xii. 7. 1
So with her *marched* forth, ... VI. ii. 39. 9
Next him September *marched,* eeke on foote, ... VII. vii. 38. 1
Marcheth. *marcheth* home, and by her takes the knight, . . . I. v. 16. 6
Such now he *marcheth* to this man forlorne, ... I. vii. 10. 5
Marching. A goodly knight, faire *marching* by the way, . . . I. vii. 29. 2
Fayre *marching* underneath a shady hill, ... II. i. 5. 7
Fayre *marching* forth in honorable wize, ... II. ii. 14. 8
marching forth with fury insolent . . . . . III. iii. 38. 3

Marching—*Continued.*
forth the Boaster *marching* brave . . . . . III. x. 33. 5
now she is with her . . . *Marching* in lovely wise, ... IV. i. 4. 7
marching thrise in warlike ordinance, ... IV. iii. 5. 7
those two other Knights espide *Marching* afore, ... IV. iv. 2. 7
These, *marching* softly, thus in order went; . . . . . VII. vii. 32. 1
Mares. watch his *mares,* or take his charge of kyne? . . . . *Hub.* 286
Marge. the upper *marge* Of his sevenfolded shield . . . . . II. v. 6. 2
by the flowrie *marge* Of a fresh streame . . . . . IV. viii. 61. 5
Margent. all the *margent* round about . . . . . II. xii. 63. 1
Along the *margent* of the fomy shore, ... III. iv. 34. 4
Unto the *margent* of the Molucas? . . . . . V. x. 3. 7
Marian. Faire *Marian,* the Muses onely darling: . . . . . *Col.* 505
Maridunum. To *Maridunum* . . . they tooke their way: . . . III. iii. 7. 3
Marie. *See* **Marry.**
Marigold. The *Marigolde,* and cherefull Rosemarie; . . . . . *Gn.* 668
Marigolds. Faire *Marigoldes,* and Bees-alluring Thime . . . . *Mui.* 191
Marin. a gentle bonylasse . . . That *Marin* hight; . . . . . *Col.* 173
Marin for love of Florimell In languor wastes . . . . . IV. xii. Arg.
Marinell. *See* **Marin.**
Bold *Marinell* of Britomart Is throwne . . . . . III. iv. Arg.
So fell proud *Marinell* upon the pretious shore. . . . . . III. iv. 17. 9
She, of his father, *Marinell* did name; . . . . . III. iv. 20. 2
the sad end of her sweet *Marinell:* . . . . . III. iv. 25. 5
Too trew the famous *Marinell* it fownd, ... III. iv. 29. 1
The lucklesse *Marinell* lying in deadly swownd, ... III. iv. 34. 9
the dim eies of my deare *Marinell* . . . . . III. iv. 39. 4
Yet she loves none but one, that *Marinell* is hight. . . . . . III. v. 8. 9
'A Sea-nymphes sonne, that *Marinell* is hight, ... III. v. 9. 1
all her delight is set on *Marinell,* . . . . . III. v. 9. 4
Her lover deare, her dearest *Marinell,* . . . . . III. vi. 54. 7
the late ruine of proud *Marinell,* . . . . . III. viii. 46. 4
all this was for love of *Marinell,* . . . . . IV. xi. 5. 1
the mother was Of lucklesse *Marinell,* Cymodoce; . . . . . IV. xi. 53. 7
The mother of unlucky *Marinell,* . . . . . IV. xii. 3. 7
Know, *Marinell,* that all this is for thee.' . . . . . IV. xii. 11. 7
All which complaint when *Marinell* had heard, ... IV. xii. 12. 1
Marinell was sore offended . . . . . IV. xii. 18. 3
So faire a wife for her sonne *Marinell.* . . . . . IV. xii. 33. 7
Right so himselfe did *Marinell* upreare, ... IV. xii. 35. 1
How she was found againe, and spousde to *Marinell.* . . . . . V. ii. 2. 9
being freed from Proteus cruell band By *Marinell* . . . . . V. iii. 2. 2
first of all issu'd Sir *Marinell,* . . . . . V. iii. 4. 6
To *Marinell,* whose name the Heralds loud resounded. . . . . V. iii. 6. 9
Marinell that day deserved best. . . . . . V. iii. 7. 8
There *Marinell* great deeds of armes did shew, ... V. iii. 8. 4
What evil hap to *Marinell* betid, ... V. iii. 10. 6
Where they were leading *Marinell* away; . . . . . V. iii. 11. 2
So backe he brought Sir *Marinell* againe; . . . . . V. iii. 12. 1
So *Marinell* by him was rescu'd from his fone. . . . . . V. iii. 12. 9
Which when as *Marinell* beheld likewise, ... V. iii. 18. 1
So stood Sir *Marinell,* . . . . . V. iii. 19. 8
this dayes honour sav'd to *Marinell:* . . . . . V. iii. 21. 2
Bold *Marinell* with Florimell the fayre, ... V. iv. 3. 3
Marinell's. *Marinells* former wound is heald, ... IV. xi. Arg.
Mariner. the beaten *marinere,* That long hath wandred . . . I. iii. 31. 1
The *Marriner* yet halfe amazed stares At perill past, ... I. vi. 1. 4
The merry *mariner* unto his word Soone hearkned, ... II. vi. 4. 5
the venturous *Mariner* that way Learning . . . . . II. x. 6. 2
taught the carefull *Mariner* to play, ... III. viii. 20. 3
As when a skilfull *Marriner* doth reed A storme approching . V. xii. 18. 5
Mariners. both ship and *mariners* each one, ... *Bel.*[2] xiii. 12
strike your sailes, yee jolly *Mariners,* . . . . . I. xii. 42. 1
mariners and merchants with much toyle . . . . . II. xii. 19. 6
Ziffius, whom *Mariners* eschew No lesse then rockes, ... II. xii. 24. 7
Marishes. Onely these *marishes* and myrie bogs, ... V. x. 23. 6
Marius. Ambitious Sylla, and sterne *Marius;* . . . . . I. v. 49. 8
He dide, and him succeeded *Marius,* . . . . . II. x. 53. 1
Marjoram. *See* **Sweet marjoram.**
Mark. *See* **Landmark, Sea-mark.**
marke how Rome . . . Renewes herselfe . . . . . *Ro.* xxvii. 9
Furthest fro the *marke,* . . . . . *S.C.* May 307
Thilk same shepheard mought I well *marke,* . . . . . *S.C.* S. 180
To *marke* th' intent of Counsells, ... *Hub.* 786
at his haughty helmet making *mark,* . . . . . I. ii. 19. 3
Missing the *marke* of his misaymed sight, ... I. viii. 8. 3
end, which every living wight Should make his *marke* . . . . I. x. 50. 3
steele . . . left not any *marke* where it did light, ... I. xi. 25. 4
Una her did *marke* Clymbe to her charet, ... I. xi. 51. 6
Where you he made the *marke* of his intent, ... II. i. 30. 8
where ye have left your *marke,* . . . . . II. i. 32. 6
In mind to *marke* the beast. . . . . . II. iii. 34. 6
the aymed *marke* which he had eyde: . . . . . II. iv. 7. 5
ere it empight In the meant *marke,* . . . . . II. iv. 46. 6
shund the *marke* at which it should be ment; . . . . . II. v. 5. 5
swarving from the *marke,* . . . . . II. viii. 30. 9
bid them strike the *marke* which he had eyde; . . . . . II. xi. 21. 7
looke on her faire face and *marke* her snowy skin. . . . . . III. viii. 24. 9
missing of the *marke* which he had eyde, ... IV. iii. 18. 8
He open shewd, that all men it mote *marke:* . . . . . IV. iv. 15. 5
With pearle and precious stone, worth many a *marke;* . . . . IV. iv. 15. 7
The arrow to his deadly *marke* desynde. . . . . . IV. vii. 30. 4
long did *mark* which way she straid. . . . . . IV. viii. 7. 9
did *marke* about her purple brest . . . . . IV. viii. 10. 2
declyned from that *marke* . . . Nigh thirtie minutes . . . . . V. Pr. 7. 7
suffred all his secret *marke* to see: . . . . . V. iii. 34. 6
long the *marke* was to be read. . . . . . V. xii. 39. 9
th' one did misse his *marke,* . . . . . VI. vii. 7. 6
espy upon her yvory chest The rosie *marke,* . . . . . VI. xii. 15. 6
Mark when she smiles with amiable cheare, ... *Am.* xl. 1

Mark—*Continued.*
ye waving chance to *marke;* . . . *Am.* lxxxi. 2
Marked. *See* **Ear-marked.**
doe misse the *marked* scope; . . . *S.C.* N. 155
if I *marked* well the starres revolution, . . . *S.C.* Env. 3
when she had *marked* long, Her hart gan melt . . . I. iii. 6. 7
doted ignorance, Whenas the noble Prince had *marked* well, . I. viii. 34. 3
when they had *markt* the chaunged skyes, . . . II. ii. 46. 8
Whom still he *marked* freshly to arize . . . II. xi. 44. 8
when he *marked* how his money burnd, . . . III. x. 15. 3
when he long had *marked* his demeanor, . . . IV. vii. 47. 1
as I *marked,* bore upon his shield . . . A broken sword . . . V. i. 19. 6
Him stedfastly he *markt,* . . . VI. ii. 5. 1
markt her rare demeanure, . . . VI. ix. 11. 2
Well she it *markt,* and pittied the more, . . . VI. xii. 8. 1
marked well her grace, . . . VII. vi. 28. 2
Market. This new-come shepheard had his *market* mard. . . . VI. ix. 40. 8
Marking. *marking* him with melting eyes, . . . *S.C.* May 207
marking where his ey-lids . . . Shewd the two pearles . . . *Gn.* 284
Which Guyon *marking* said; 'Be nought agriev'd, . . . II. v. 15. 1
Marks. left of it but these olde *markes* to see, . . . *Ro.* xxx. 11
The previe *marks* I would bewray, . . . *S.C.* Mar. 35
The cruell *markes* of many' a bloody fielde; . . . I. i. 1. 4
Markes which doe byte their hasty supper best; . . . I. i. 23. 4
hewen helmets deepe shew *marks* of eithers might. . . . I. v. 7. 9
Th' eternall *marks* of treason may at Stonheng vew. . . . II. x. 66. 9
Tell me some *markes* by which he may appeare, . . . III. ii. 16. 3
by what *markes* may he be knowne againe?' . . . V. i. 19. 2
by the other *markes* which of his shield he tooke. . . . V. i. 20. 9
Known by good *markes* and perfect good espiall: . . . V. iv. 15. 8
'Most certaine *markes'* (sayd she) 'do me it teach; . . . VI. xii. 18. 3
speaking *markes* of passed monuments, . . . VI. xii. 20. 4
Mark-white. Even at the *marke-white* of his hart she roved, . V. v. 35. 8
Marl. To seize upon his foe flatt lying on the *marle.* . . . II. xi. 33. 9
Maro. So *Maro* oft did Caesars cares allay. . . . *Ded. Son.* i. 8
Marred. Thy mantle *mard,* wherein thou maskedst late. . . . *S.C.* Ja. 24
now the gray mosse *marred* his rine; . . . *S.C.* F. 111
My old musick *mard* by a newe mischaunce. . . . *S.C.* Au. 12
Hath *marred* quite, and all their blossoms blasted; . . . *T.M.* 250
Hath *mard* the face of all that semed fayre. . . . *T.M.* 258
cut downe, and all their pleasaunce *mard,* . . . *T.M.* 281
Have *mard* the face of goodly Poesie, . . . *T.M.* 557
the strong passion *mard* her modest grace, . . . II. ix. 43. 4
So underneath her feet their swords they *mard,* . . . III. i. 30. 6
Where they do wither, and are fowly *mard:* . . . III. vi. 39. 6
To see so faire thinges *mard* and spoiled quight; . . . III. vi. 40. 2
minds of mortall men are muchell *mard* . . . III. x. 31. 8
That one did make the other *mard* againe, . . . IV. i. 29. 3
Cursing his hand that had that visage *mard:* . . . V. v. 13. 4
Shut up her haven, *mard* her marchants trade, . . . V. x. 25. 6
mard the swinging of her flaile. . . . V. xi. 29. 9
This new-come shepheard had his market *mard.* . . . VI. ix. 40. 8
The sight of whom, though now decayd and *mard,* . . . VI. xi. 13. 1
Marreth. lamenting Love *marreth* the Musicall. . . . *U.V.* 12
Marriage. Renown'd in choyce of happie *marriage* . . . *Gn.* 487
The *marriage* to accomplish vowd betwixt you twayn. . . . I. xii. 19. 9
few rites to be donne, Which *mariage* make: . . . II. iv. 21. 6
sought with her to lincke in *marriage:* . . . II. ix. 18. 5
to him allide His daughter Genuiss' in *marriage:* . . . II. x. 52. 4
Till they with *mariage* meet might finish that accord. . . . IV. vi. 41. 9
Marring. *Marring* my joyous gentle dalliaunce. . . . *T.M.* 186
Marrow. crooked crawling shankes, of *marrowe* empted; . . . *Mui.* 350
that foule evill, . . . That rotts the *marrow,* . . . I. iv. 26. 8
Close creeping twixt the *marow* and the skin: . . . I. x. 25. 5
wounds the life, and wastes the inmost *marrow.* . . . *H.B.* 63
Marry. *Marrie!* that great Pan bought with deare borrow, . *S.C.* S. 96
Marry, Diggon, what should him affraye . . . *S.C.* S. 208
'*Marie,* there (said the Priest) is arte indeed: . . . *Hub.* 483
'*Marie,* (said he) the highest now in grace . . . *Hub.* 619
'*Marie,* that shall your selfe, . . . *Hub.* 999
Mars. *See* **Mart.**
Mars, shaming to have given so great head . . . *Ro.* xi. 1
sing of bloody *Mars,* of wars, of giusts; . . . *S.C.* O. 39
Mars sleeping with his wife to compasse in, . . . *Mui.* 371
Truth . . . *Marres* blind Devotions mart, . . . I. iii. Arg.
I of warres and bloody *Mars* doe sing, . . . I. xi. 7. 2
'Fayre sonne of *Mars,* that seeke with warlike spoyle, . . . I. i. 8. 7
Mars is Cupidoes frend, . . . II. vi. 35. 7
Where you him lately lefte, in *Mars* his bed: . . . III. vi. 24. 3
who that smites it *mars* his joyous play, . . . III. vii. 41. 8
When she with *Mars* was meynt in joyfulnesse: . . . III. xi. 36. 5
with which he maked meeke The mightie *Mars,* . . . III. xi. 44. 3
most is *Mars* amisse . . . V. Pr. 8. 8
Mars, that valiant man, is changed most; . . . VII. vii. 52. 1
Mars in three-score yeares doth run his spheare. . . . *Am.* lx. 4
Marsh. let the *marsh* of Esthambruges tell, . . . II. x. 24. 2
Marshal. A jolly yeoman, *Marshall* of the same, . . . II. ix. 28. 2
The *marshall* of the hall to them did come, . . . V. ix. 23. 7
Marshalling. *marshalling* the evill-ordered trayne, . . . III. xii. 23. 4
Marshals. *Marshals* of the field Broke up the listes, . . . IV. iii. 35. 3
Marshes. moorish fennes, and *marshes* ever greene. . . . *Ti.* 140
into moores and *marshes* banishit had, . . . V. x. 18. 4
Mart. *See* **Mars.**
maken a *Mart* of theyr good name: . . . *S.C.* S. 37
with you bring triumphant *Mart,* . . . I. Pr. 3. 7
Truth . . . Marres blind Devotions *mart,* . . . I. iii. Arg.
Martelled. on his helmet *martelled* so hard . . . III. vii. 42. 3
Martia. *See* **Mertia.**
Renowmed *Martia;* and redoubted Emmilen. . . . III. iii. 54. 9
Martial. Fitter, perhaps, to thonder *Martiall* stowre, . . . *Ded.Son.*viii.11
Martial—*Continued.*
For love of vertue and of *Martiall* praise; . . . *Ded. Son.* x. 6
As those that are inspir'd with *Martial* rage, . . . *Ded.Son.*xiii.11
more honourable prize . . . then did the *Martiall* crew, . . *Ded. Son.* xiv. 2
His Lady, left as a prise *martiall,* Did yield . . . I. ii. 36. 8
Have thither come the noble *Martial* crew . . . I. vii. 45. 4
upbrought in gentle thewes and *martiall* might. . . . I. ix. 3. 9
Prince Arthure, crowne of *Martiall* band?' . . . I. ix. 6. 5
the *martiall* troupes thou doest infest, . . . I. xi. 6. 3
Through deeds of armes and prowesse *martiall.* . . . II. iii. 37. 8
to weake wench did yield his *martiall* might: . . . II. vi. 8. 5
noise of armes, or vew of *martiall* guize, . . . II. vi. 25. 8
The mightie *martiall* handes doe most commend: . . . II. vi. 35. 5
brave ensample, both of *martiall* And civil rule, . . . II. x. 74. 8
The *martiall* brood accustomed to fight: . . . III. i. 13. 5
Of their brave gestes and prowesse *martiall:* . . . III. ii. 1. 6
'Faire *martiall* Mayd, Certes ye misavised beene . . . III. ii. 9. 4
shortly make you a mayd *Martiall.* . . . III. iii. 53. 9
She hath the leading of a *Martiall* And mightie people, . . III. iii. 56. 4
The *martiall* Mayd stayd not him to lament, . . . III. iv. 18. 1
in *martiall* law And deedes of armes . . . III. vii. 52. 3
Great hostes of men in order *martiall,* . . . V. xii. 4. 8
Martian. *See* **Mertian.**
Into the *Martian* field adowne descended . . . IV. v. 6. 8
Martyrdom. crowne with *martiredome* his sacred head: . . . III. iii. 39. 4
bosting in their *martyrdome* unmeet. . . . IV. x. 2. 5
Martyrest. whose gentle hart Thou *martyrest* . . . IV. vii. 2. 5
Martyrize. To her my heart I nightly *martyrize:* . . . *Col.* 473
Martyrs. The bloud of *Martyrs* dere . . . *Rev.* ii. 10
holy *Martyres* often doen to dye With cruell malice . . . I. viii. 36. 4
Bangor with massacred *Martyrs* fill, . . . III. iii. 35. 6
Marvel. No *marveile,* Thenot, if thou can beare . . . *S.C.* F. 25
of your ignorance great *merveill* make, . . . II. ii. 5. 4
For *marveill* of that accident extreame: . . . III. viii. 22. 4
passing joy, which so great *marvaile* brings, . . . IV. iii. 49. 8
ne *mervaile* nought, Ne thenceforth feare . . . IV. vi. 30. 5
Much did he *marvell* at her uncouth speach, . . . V. v. 37. 1
ne *marvaile* ought, For that same beast was bred . . . VI. vi. 9. 6
I *marvaile* of what substance was the mould, . . . *Am.* lv. 3
Marvelled. Guyon *mervayld* at her uncouth cace; . . . II. ix. 43. 5
whiles he *marveild* still, did still him payne; . . . II. xi. 44. 5
Much *merveiled* thereat, as well he might, . . . III. viii. 12. 3
He *marveild* more, and thought he yet did dreame . . . III. viii. 22. 7
most they *mervaild* at her chevalree . . . III. ix. 24. 5
she *mervaild* that no footings trace Nor wight appeard, . . III. xi. 53. 5
marveild at his straunge intendiment. . . . III. xii. 5. 2
Whose nature yet so much is *marvelled* Of mortall wits, . . *H.H.B.* 166
Marvellous. O *mervelous* great change! . . . *Ro.* xxix. 12
Whence he indued was with skill so *merveilous.* . . . III. iii. 13. 9
Marvels. *marveiles* at himselfe stil as he flies: . . . I. xi. 34. 8
With which they wrought such wondrous *marvels* there, . . IV. iv. 29. 3
To tell the *marveiles* by thy mercie wrought. . . . *H.H.L.* 49
Mary. *See* **Ave Mary.**
Masculine. Th' other immortall, perfect, *masculine;* . . . II. ix. 22. 5
So he surpassed his sex *masculine,* . . . III. xi. 4. 3
Mask. When love-lads *masken* in fresh aray? . . . *S.C.* May 2
The mornefull Muse in myrth now list ne *maske,* . . . *S.C.* N. 19
maske in mirth with Graces well beseene? . . . *T.M.* 180
whylome did *maske,* . . . in lowly Shephards weeds, . . . I. Pr. 1. 1
deceipt doth *maske* in visour faire, . . . I. vii. 1. 3
diverse plots did frame to *maske* in strange disguise. . . . III. iii. 51. 9
in so straunge disguizement there did *maske,* . . . III. vii. 14. 3
The *maske* of Cupid, and th' enchanted Chamber . . . III. xii. Arg.
In manner of a *maske,* enranged orderly. . . . III. xii. 5. 9
When that same *Maske* againe should forth arize. . . . III. xii. 28. 5
Brought in that *mask* of love which late was showen; . . . IV. i. 3. 6
to hide her fained sex . . . And *maske* her wounded mind, . IV. i. 7. 4
Some thought . . . it was a *maske* of strange disguise: . . . IV. i. 14. 8
under *maske* of beautie and good grace Vile treason . . . IV. i. 17. 7
queint disguise . . . doest *maske* thy royall blood, . . . V. vii. 21. 2
Of so unmanly *maske* in misery misdight. . . . V. vii. 37. 9
And *mask* in myrth lyke to a Comedy: . . . *Am.* liv. 6
long since ready forth his *maske* to move, . . . *Epith.* 26
Masked. *Masked* with faire dissembling curtesie, . . . *Col.* 700
eke those *masked* Ladies riding them beside. . . . IV. iv. 2. 9
That *masked* Mock-knight was their sport and play. . . . IV. iv. 13. 4
she *masked* it with modestie, . . . IV. xii. 35. 7
Maskedst. Thy mantle mard, wherein thou *maskedst* late. . . . *S.C.* Ja. 24
Masker. when the courting *masker* louteth lowe, . . . *Ti.* 202
Maskers. the *maskers* marched forth in trim aray. . . . III. xii. 6. 9
Masking. With mumming and with *masking* all around, . . . *Hub.* 802
Merily *masking* both in bowre and hall. . . . *As.* 28
All which disguized marcht in *masking* wise . . . III. xii. 26. 6
A thousand Graces *masking* in delight; . . . *H.B.* 254
Masks. By way of sport, as oft in *maskes* is knowen, . . . IV. i. 3. 8
Mason's. rough *Masons* hand with engines keene . . . III. viii. 37. 6
Mass. rejoyned to the spirite Of this great *masse,* . . . *Ro.* v. 11
How things she formed of a formelesse *mas:* . . . *T.M.* 502
All such vaine moniments of earthlie *masse,* . . . *Ti.* 419
She . . . Brought forth this monstrous *masse* of earthly slyme, I. vii. 9. 8
of that monstrous *mas,* Was nothing left, . . . I. viii. 24. 8
So huge and horrible a *masse* it seemd; . . . I. xi. 55. 2
in his lap a *masse* of coyne he told, . . . II. vii. 4. 7
'can safely hold So huge a *masse,* . . . II. vii. 20. 2
lifted high above this earthly *masse,* . . . II. ix. 45. 3
this great Universe seemd one confused *mas.* . . . II. xii. 34. 9
To hoord up heapes of evill gotten *masse,* . . . III. ix. 4. 2
quaked under their so hideous *masse;* . . . III. ix. 50. 6
Began to peepe above this earthly *masse,* . . . IV. v. 45. 4
as the soule doth rule the earthly *masse,* . . . IV. ix. 2. 6

Mass—*Continued.*
an altar of some costly *masse*, . . . IV. x. 39. 2
About their holy things for morrow *Mas;* . . . V. vii. 17. 8
made them both one *masse* withouten more remorse. . . . V. viii. 32. 9
Then downe to ground fell that deformed *Masse*, . . . V. xi. 32. 1
Ne could he brooke the coldnesse of the stony *masse*. . . . VI. iv. 21. 9
to whom ye ill display That mucky *masse*, . . . VI. ix. 33. 5
this worlds still moving mightie *masse* . . . *H.L.* 57
On that bright shynie round still moving *Masse*, . . . *H.H.B.* 51
Massacre. Tydings of death and *massacre* unkinde: . . . *Gn.* 396
Massacred. Bangor with *massacred* Martyrs fill, . . . III. iii. 35. 6
The beasts we daily see *massacred* dy . . . VII. vii. 19. 2
Massacres. Besides the huge *massacres*, which he wrought . III. xi. 29. 8
In which he many *massacres* had left, . . . VI. xii. 23. 2
The huge *massacres* which her eyes do make; . . . *Am.* x. 6
Masses. Their penie *Masses*, and their Complynes meete, . . . *Hub.* 452
Massy. out of her *massie* wombe forth sent That antique horror, . . . *Ro.* xvii. 7
I saw an Image, all of *massie* gold, . . . *Ti.* 491
one *massy* entire mould, Hewen out of Adamant rocke . . . I. vii. 33. 6
massy gold of glorious guifte, . . . II. vii. 28. 4
Many great golden pillours did upbeare The *massy* roofe, . . II. vii. 43. 6
wondrous *massy* and assured sownd, . . . III. ii. 25. 3
her Maides attyre To turne into a *massy* habergeon, . . . III. iii. 57. 8
purest snow in *massy* mould congeald, . . . III. viii. 6. 2
mov'd amisse with *massy* mucks unmeet regard. . . . III. x. 31. 9
there stood an Image all alone Of *massy* gold, . . . III. xi. 47. 5
his *massie* yron mace Betwixt him and his hurt . . . IV. viii. 43. 6
There he that Idoll saw of *massy* gold . . . V. xi. 21. 8
Mast. mochell *mast* to the husband did yielde, . . . *S.C.* F. 109
All were the beame in bignes like a *mast*, . . . III. vii. 40. 6
the *Mast* of some well-timbered hulke . . . V. xi. 29. 1
Master. All for their *Maister* is lustlesse and old. . . . *S.C.* F. 84
the Foxe, *maister* of collusion: . . . *S.C.* May 219
'Ah, good young *maister!'* . . . *S.C.* May 255
render up a reckning . . . Unto their *master*, . . . *Hub.* 311
all men, which anie *master* serve, . . . *Hub.* 467
Ye a great *master* are in your degree: . . . *Hub.* 546
then informe his *Master* hastely, . . . *Hub.* 880
wish him to chuse His *Master*, . . . *Hub.* 885
by his shifts his *Master* furnish can. . . . *Hub.* 918
messengers of hell, . . . Came to their wicked *maister*, . . . I. ii. 2. 3
O, how can beautie *maister* the most strong, . . . I. iii. 6. 4
made ensample of their mournfull sight Unto his *Maister*, . . I. v. 52. 3
the *maister* of his guise, Did often tremble at his horrid vew; I. vi. 25. 2
She . . . strove to *maister* sorrowfull assay, . . . I. vii. 27. 2
the heavens, . . . Have made you *master* of the field . . . I. viii. 28. 2
Your fortune *maister* eke with governing, . . . I. viii. 28. 3
maister these mishaps with patient might. . . . I. viii. 45. 2
There by his *maister* left, . . . II. vi. 38. 8
The *maister* Cooke was cald Concoction; . . . II. ix. 31. 1
if the passion *mayster* thy fraile might, . . . III. ii. 46. 6
all the keyes convayd Unto their *maister*, . . . III. ix. 10. 5
purloyned for his *maister* bad) . . . III. x. 54. 4
the wicked carle, the *maister* Smith, . . . IV. v. 44. 1
To guide the beast that did his *maister* beare, . . . IV. ix. 5. 4
made way for his *maister* to assaile; . . . V. ii. 24. 4
for to *maister* wrong and puissant pride: . . . V. iv. 1. 5
Masterdom. Ne will enforced be with *maisterdome* or might.' IV. i. 46. 9
The *maysterdome* of each by force to gaine, . . . V. ii. 15. 4
Mastered. *See* **Overmastered.**
these brave Pallaces, which *maystred* bee Of time, . . . *Ro.* xviii. 3
mastered with workmanship so rare, . . . *Mui.* 338
Mishaps are *maistred* by advice discrete, . . . I. vii. 40. 7
That Monster can be *maistred* or destroyd: . . . II. iv. 10. 3
That him so noble knight had *maystered;* . . . II. v. 14. 8
with strong reason *maistred* passion fraile, . . . II. vi. 40. 4
Life having *maystered* her sencelesse foe, . . . II. viii. 53. 2
the stout Damzell, . . . *maistered* his might. . . . III. xii. 32. 9
him *maystred* still in all debate. . . . IV. x. 32. 9
To be downe held, and *maystred* so with might, . . . VI. xii. 31. 2
brought Into like bands, ne *maystred* any more: . . . VI. xii. 39. 4
Masteries. Guyon in them all shewes goodly *maysteries*. . . II. vi. 1. 9
To practise games and *maisteries* to try, . . . VI. ix. 43. 2
Mastering. When with the *maistring* spur he did him roughly stire. . . . II. v. 2. 9
maistring might on enimy dismayd; . . . II. v. 13. 3
maystring them, renewd his former heat: . . . II. vii. 36. 6
Brydling his will and *maystering* his might, . . . II. xii. 53. 5
having conquered The *maistring* raines out of her weary wrest, III. vii. 2. 8
them with *maystring* discipline doth tame, . . . IV. ix. 2. 4
Into his mouth his *maystring* bridle threw, . . . IV. xii. 13. 6
by the *maystring* might Of doughty Calidore, . . . VI. xii. 38. 1
Ne could that Painter . . . Have purtrayd this, for all his *maistring* skill; . . . *H.H.B.* 214
Masterless. His silver shield, now idle, *maisterlesse;* . . . I. vii. 19. 6
Master's. Thy *maysters* mind is overcome with care: . . . *S.C.* Ja. 46
The dog his *maisters* voice did it wene, . . . *S.C.* S. 219
to be a beetle-stock Of thy great *Masters* will, . . . *Hub.* 508
oft maintain'd his *masters* braverie. . . . *Hub.* 858
In gage for his gay *Masters* hopelesse dett: . . . *Hub.* 865
sell fee-simples in his *Masters* name, . . . *Hub.* 867
To buy his *Masters* frivolous good will, . . . *Hub.* 889
The wofull Dwarfe, which saw his *maisters* fall . . . I. vii. 19. 1
Trompart, that his *maistres* humor knew . . . III. x. 30. 1
badly doest thou hide Thy *maisters* shame, . . . V. vi. 11. 5
plead thy *maisters* cause, unjustly payned. . . . *Am.* xlviii. 8
Masters. of their *maisters* hast no lesse regarde . . . *S.C.* D. 11
The *maysters* of his long experiment, . . . II. vii. 1. 7
her Sprighters to entertaine, The *maisters* of her art: . . . III. viii. 4. 5

Masters—*Continued.*
Had from their *maisters* fled, . . . VI. xi. 39. 9
Mastery. striv'd With th' Heliconian maides for *maystery;* . . II. xii. 31. 2
Ne may love be compeld by *maistery;* . . . III. i. 25. 7
soone as *maistery* comes . . . III. i. 25. 8
feared, . . . That fiers youngmans unruly *maystery;* . . . III. x. 2. 7
fray Betwixt them two for *maystery* of might; . . . VI. i. 36. 2
Mastiff. an eager *mastiffe* once doth prove The tast of bloud . IV. ix. 31. 5
Like a fell *mastiffe* through enraging heat, . . . V. xi. 12. 2
Is bayted of a *mastiffe* and a hound . . . VI. v. 19. 2
Like as a *Mastiffe* having at a bay A salvage Bull, . . . VI. vii. 47. 1
Mastiffs. salvage Bull, whom two fierce *mastives* bayt, . . . II. viii. 42. 1
Like two mad *mastiffes*, each on other flew, . . . IV. ii. 17. 8
Masts. spent all her *mastes* and her ground-hold, . . . VI. iv. 1. 2
Match. In majestie she seemde to *matche* the Gods. . . . *Bel.*[1] xi. 6
Did seeme to *match* the Gods in Majestie. . . . *Bel.*[2] xv. 6
her equall *match* could see. . . . *Ro.* vi. 8
Her that did *match* the whole earths puissaunce, . . . *Ro.* vi. 13
Her *match* in beautie was not anie one. . . . *Van.* vii. 5
I will not *match* her with Latonaes seede, . . . *S.C.* Ap. 86
Shall *match* with the fayre flowre Delice. . . . *S.C.* Ap. 144
match them selfe with mighty potentates, . . . *S.C.* May 122
Wherefore with myne thou dare thy musick *matche?* . . . *S.C.* Au. 2
to *match* thy pype with Tityrus his style. . . . *S.C.* Env. 9
Their *match* in glorie, mightie, fierce, and coy; . . . *Gn.* 494
In Britannie was none to *match* with mee, . . . *Ti.* 100
I *match* with that sweet smile . . . *D.* 306
to *match* her with the neighbour flood, . . . *Col.* 122
Who lives that can *match* that heroick song, . . . *Col.* 404
Can *match* that Muse when it with bayes is crowned, . . . *Col.* 414
strove to *match*, . . . Great Junoes golden chayre, . . . I. iv. 17. 4
Ne can Cephise, nor Hebrus, *match* this well: . . . I. xi. 30. 8
On foot with him to *matchen* equall fight: . . . II. v. 4. 8
Unworthy *match* for such immortall mate . . . II. vii. 50. 4
match his brother proud in battailous aray. . . . II. viii. 22. 9
The least of which was *match* for any knight. . . . II. viii. 34. 5
ever hope to *match* in equall fight, . . . III. ii. 13. 8
none in equall armes him *matchen* might: . . . III. iv. 24. 3
Ne any may that Monster *match* in fight, . . . III. vii. 52. 8
Seeking to *match* the chaste with th' unchaste Ladies traine.' . III. vii. 60. 9
thought that *match* a fowle disparagement: . . . III. viii. 12. 4
faire Alcmena better *match* did make, . . . III. xi. 33. 6
Once thinke to *match* three such on equall cost, . . . IV. iii. 24. 8
Three such as able were to *match* a puissant host? . . . IV. iii. 24. 9
to *match* that Lady they had sought Another like, . . . IV. iv. 10. 7
might not aspire To *match* so high, . . . IV. viii. 50. 4
That she mote *match* the fairest of her daies, . . . IV. ix. 16. 6
With ods of so unequall *match* opprest, . . . IV. ix. 32. 2
Might *match* with this by many a degree: . . . IV. x. 30. 5
much lesse him *match* in fight, . . . V. i. 8. 7
Each of whose lockes did *match* a man in might, . . . V. viii. 2. 2
Ne ever any found his *match* in might; . . . V. xii. 15. 4
Did strive to *match* with strong contention, . . . VI. x. 33. 3
By all meanes shund to *match* with any forrein fere. . . . VI. xii. 4. 9
If that her might were *match* to her desire. . . . VII. vi. 21. 5
Seek with my playnts to *match* that mournful dove. . . . *Am.* lxxxviii. 8
Matchable. To tell my forces, *matchable* to none, . . . *Ti.* 89
Matchable either to Semiramis, . . . II. x. 56. 2
Was *matchable* to this in equall vewing. . . . *Ti.* 553
Matchable ether to that ympe of Troy, . . . III. xi. 7. 3
high worths . . . Ne but in heaven *matchable* to none, . . . *Am.* lxvi. 7
Lo! one . . . *Matchable* to the greatest of those great; . . . *Com. Son.* iii.10
Matched. *See* **Evil-matched, Overmatched.**
skill, *matcht* with such courage as he had, . . . *As.* 85
should *matched* have the best: . . . II. x. 43. 6
white seemes fayrer *macht* with blacke attone; . . . III. ix. 2. 4
Griefe and Fury, *matcht* yfere; . . . III. xii. 16. 1
being *matcht* with plaine Antiquitie, . . . VI. Pr. 4. 7
A salvage man *matcht* with a Ladie fayre, . . . VI. v. 9. 3
Matched with equall years, . . . VI. xii. 18. 8
Matches. ye fayre Mayds, the *matches* of his yeares, . . . *As.* 129
Matcheth. their musicke *matcheth* Phoebus quill. . . . *T.M.* 330
Matching. *Matching* the wealth of th' auncient Frankincence; *Gn.* 674
Machless. How he may flow in quiets *matchles* treasour, . . . *Gn.* 139
through presumption of his *matchlesse* might, . . . I. vii. 10. 3
Through strong opinion of his *matchlesse* might; . . . II. ii. 18. 6
up arose a man of *matchlesse* might, . . . II. x. 37. 1
Our faulty weakenes, and your *matchlesse* might: . . . III. i. 30. 2
The whiles her *matchlesse* beautie him dismayd. . . . III. v. 43. 7
With *matchlesse* eares deformed and distort, . . . IV. i. 28. 2
To vanquish all the world with *matchlesse* might; . . . IV. xi. 16. 6
soothly he was one of *matchlesse* might, . . . V. x. 8. 6
made a *matchlesse* paragon, . . . VI. i. 1. 9
was bordered with a wood Of *matchlesse* hight, . . . VI. x. 6. 3
Mate. *See* **Copemate.**
womankinde, most faithfull to her *mate*, . . . *Gn.* 429
Hath made fit *mate* thy wretched case to heare, . . . *D.* 65
The Lyon chose his *mate*, . . . *Col.* 865
a faythfull *mate* Of her sad troubles and misfortunes hard: I. iii. 9. 3
Phoebus, fresh as brydegrome to his *mate*, . . . I. v. 2. 3
With stony feare of that rude rustick *mate*, . . . II. ii. 8. 8
In hope to win more favour with his *mate*, . . . II. ii. 19. 4
Fitt *mate* for such a mincing mineon, . . . II. ii. 37. 2
Unworthy match for such immortall *mate* . . . II. vii. 50. 4
each Paramor his leman knowes, Each bird his *mate;* . . . III. vi. 41. 8
made full goodly joyance to her new-found *mate*. . . . IV. i. 31. 9
Her *mate*, he was a jollie youthfull knight . . . IV. i. 32. 1
stolne away from her beloved *mate*, . . . IV. vi. 47. 7
There she him found by that new lovely *mate*, . . . IV. vii. 35. 3
Which sory words her mightie hart did *mate* . . . IV. viii. 17. 6

Mate—*Continued.*
The villaine, leaving him unto his *mate* . . . VI. viii. 13. 1
Could not on earth have found one fit for *mate*, . . . *Am.* lxvi. 6
Sits mourning for the absence of her *mate;* . . . *Am.* lxxxviii. 2
Mated. 'Ensample make . . . of my selfe now *mated*, . . . I. ix. 12. 2
Material. too long . . . Here to record, ne much *materiall:* . II. x. 74. 6
Mates. That may thy Muse and *mates* to mirth allure. . . *Col.* 391
Nereus crownes with cups; his *mates* him pledg around. . . I. iii. 31. 9
Mathraval. Who was the lord of *Mathraval* by right, . . . III. iii. 13. 7
Mathusalem. *See* **Methuselah.**
Matilda. *Matilda,* daughter to Pubidius, . . . III. iii. 13. 6
I am th' unfortunate *Matilde* by name, . . . VI. iv. 29. 3
Matins. When one so oft a night did ring his *matins* bell. . . III. x. 48. 9
The merry Larke hir *mattins* sings aloft; . . . *Epith.* 80
Matrimonial. Most famous fruites of *matrimoniall* bowre, . . III. iii. 3. 7
Matrimony. The which do endlesse *matrimony* make, . . . *Epith.* 217
Matron. Through wisedome of a *matrone* grave . . . I. x. 3. 5
tyred limbes to rest, O *matrone* sage,' (quoth she) . . . I. x. 11. 2
An auncient *matrone* she to her does call, . . . I. x. 34. 2
The godly *Matrone* by the hand him beares Forth . . . I. x. 35. 1
that formost *matrone* me did blame, . . . IV. x. 54. 1
Yet did that auncient *matrone* all she might, . . . VI. xii. 14. 6
The *matrone* stayd no lenger to enquire, . . . VI. xii. 19. 1
Matronly. toward them full *matronely* did pace. . . . I. x. 8. 5
Matter. Made of some *matter* no less firme and strong? . . . *Ro.* ix. 8
be her selfe the *matter* of her fires; . . . *Ro.* xxiii. 8
Here is a great deale of good *matter* Lost . . . *S.C.* Jul. 205
him to heare, or *matter* of his deede. . . . *S.C.* Au. 148
matter made for Poets on to play: . . . *S.C.* O. 64
Matter of myrth now shalt thou have no more; . . . *S.C.* N. 56
Base is the style, and *matter* meane withall. . . . *Hub.* 44
Ye have this *matter* motioned in season; . . . *Hub.* 125
may be *matter* meete to gaine him praise: . . . *Hub.* 779
He is with greater *matter* busied Than a Lambe, . . . *Hub.* 1215
none more tragick *matter* I can finde . . . *T.M.* 155
Because that mourning *matter* I have none. . . . *T.M.* 168
the devicefull *matter* of my song; . . . *T.M.* 386
Fit *matter* for his cares increase would finde, . . . *D.* 3
To make new *matter* fit for Tragedies; . . . *D.* 154
Glewed togither with some subtile *matter*. . . . *Col.* 217
raise His tunes from laies to *matter* of more skill. . . . *Col.* 395
filthy *matter* from them weld; . . . I. viii. 47. 7
forgery, Rather then *matter* of just memory; . . . II. Pr. 1. 5
matter make for him to worke upon, . . . II. iv. 42. 6
So *matter* did she make of nought, . . . II. v. 19. 6
new *matter* fram'd Upon the old, . . . II. v. 21. 2
Matter of merth enough, though there were none, . . . II. vi. 3. 7
the *matter* of his huge desire And pompous pride . . . II. vii. 17. 6
matter made for famous Poets verse, . . . III. iv. 1. 6
thee, O Queene! the *matter* of my song, . . . III. iv. 3. 8
his faire sister for creation Ministreth *matter* fit, . . . III. vi. 9. 4
borrow *matter* whereof they are made; . . . III. vi. 37. 2
Matter of doubt and dread suspitious, . . . III. x. 59. 5
Some argument of *matter* passioned: . . . III. xii. 4. 6
Great *matter* growing of beginning small, . . . IV. ii. 54. 7
New *matter* added to his former fire; . . . IV. vi. 11. 2
fit *matter* for another song. . . . V. viii. 51. 9
Where they mote heare the *matter* throughly scand . . . V. ix. 37. 7
Such loathly *matter* were small lust to speake or thinke. . . . V. xi. 31. 9
every *matter* worse was for her melling: . . . V. xii. 35. 4
Now glooming sadly, so to cloke her *matter;* . . . VI. vi. 42. 8
what the *matter* was that mov'd her so? . . . VI. xii. 17. 4
make the *matter* to avenge her yre: . . . *Am.* xlviii. 2
they that skill not of so heavenly *matter*, . . . *Am.* lxxxiv. 5
The wondrous *matter* of my fyre to prayse. . . . *H.B.* 7
the grosse *matter* of this earthly myne . . . *H.B.* 46
grosse *matter* by a soveraine might Tempers . . . *H.B.* 124
ceasse to gaze on *matter* of thy grief: . . . *H.H.B.* 294
Matters. Muttred of *matters* as their bookes them shewd, . . *Hub.* 836
As for those many goodly *matters* leaft I for others. . . . *Ex Tempore* 2
rare in-sight hard *matters* to revele; . . . V. ix. 39. 2
Maugre. *maugre* death, and dreaded sisters deadly spight, . . *S.C.* N. 163
Maugre the sacred Muses, . . . *Hub.* 816
maugre Fortunes injurie, And times decay, . . . *Ti.* 166
hath (*maugre* her spight) thus low me laid in dust.' . . . II. v. 12. 9
maugre thee will passe or dy.' . . . III. iv. 15. 4
Such happinesse did, *maulgre*, to me spight, . . . III. v. 7. 5
Maulgre his host, who grudged . . . To house a guest . . . III. x. 2. 2
Him forst, (*maulgre*) his fiercenes to relent, . . . III. xi. 26. 8
Tell what thou saw'st, *maulgre* who so it heares.' . . . IV. i. 48. 6
maugre all his powre, . . . IV. x. 58. 2
forced him, *maulgre*, it up to reare. . . . V. i. 29. 6
they disparted them, *maugre* their might, . . . V. iv. 43. 7
Maugre so many foes which did withstand: . . . V. ix. 30. 5
If not, we will it force, *maugre* your foe, . . . V. x. 24. 3
Maugre the might of all those troupes in vew, . . . V. xii. 5. 7
On the cold ground *maugre* himselfe he threw . . . VI. iv. 40. 3
maugre all their might, he did repell And beat them back, . VI. vi. 23. 8
maugre all his might backe to relent: . . . VI. vii. 45. 8
'Yet *mauger* Jove, and all his gods beside, . . . VII. vii. 17. 1
Maul. with mighty *mall* The monster mercilesse him made to fall, . . . I. vii. 51. 4
rap Upon his headpeece with his yron *mall;* . . . IV. v. 42. 4
lighting on his horses head him quite did *mall*. . . . V. xi. 8. 9
Maulgre. *See* **Maugre.**
Mausolus. 'Such one *Mausolus* made, . . . *Ti.* 414
Mausolus'. *Mausolus* worke will be the Carians glorie; . . . *Ro.* ii. 7
Mavis. So does the Cuckow, when the *Mavis* sings, . . . *Am.* lxxxiv. 3
the *Mavis* descant playes: . . . *Epith.* 81
Maw. she spewd out of her filthie *maw* . . . I. i. 20. 1

Maw—*Continued.*
inwardly he chawed his owne *maw* At neighbours welth, . . . I. iv. 30. 5
Tityus fed a vultur on his *maw;* . . . I. v. 35. 6
deepe emperst his darksom hollow *maw*, . . . I. xi. 53. 8
She feedes on her owne *maw* unnaturall, . . . V. xii. 31. 7
Maws. when your *mawes* are with those weeds corrupted, . . *D.* 348
Maximian. his daughter deare He gave in wedlocke to *Maximian*, . . . II. x. 61. 2
by *Maximian* lately ledd away, . . . II. x. 62. 2
Maximinian. During the raigne of *Maximinian;* . . . II. x. 61. 7
May (*partial list of auxiliary*).
immortalitie So meane Harpes worke *may* chalenge . . . *Ro.* xxxii. 4
when time serves *may* bring things better forth. . . . *Van.* i. 14
Let be, as *may* be, that is past: . . . *S.C.* Mar. 58
Is not thilke the mery moneth of *May*, . . . *S.C.* May 1
To gather *May* bus-kets and smelling brere: . . . *S.C.* May 10
To fetchen home *May* with their musicall: . . . *S.C.* May 28
Sike myrth in *May* is meetest for to make, . . . *S.C.* N. 11
The fayrest *May* she was that ever went, . . . *S.C.* N. 39
We *may* seeke favour of the best of all?' . . . *Hub.* 618
cast to seeke the Lion where he *may*, . . . *Hub.* 1316
I waile and weepe all that I *may*. . . . *T.M.* 594
That happie there I *maie* thee alwaies see. . . . *Ti.* 308
The Roses raigning in the pride of *May*, . . . *Mui.* 189
He had a daughter fresh as floure of *May*, . . . *Col.* 106
May seeme the wayne was very evill ledd, . . . I. iv. 19. 7
Deare dame,' (quoth he) 'well *may* I rew . . . I. vi. 36. 7
trample th' earth, the whiles they *may* respire, . . . I. vi. 44. 8
blisse *may* not abide in state of mortall men. . . . I. viii. 44. 9
lay down thy bow, the whiles I *may* respyre. . . . I. ix. 8. 9
'How *may* a man' . . . Be wonne to spoyle . . . I. ix. 31. 1
Ne *may* a man prolong, nor shorten, it: . . . I. ix. 41. 3
The souldier *may* not move from watchfull sted, . . . I. ix. 41. 4
Th' ill to prevent, that life ensewen *may*. . . . I. ix. 44. 3
'Ah! no,' said they, 'but forth she *may* not come; . . . I. x. 16. 4
So far as ewghen bow a shaft *may* send, . . . I. xi. 19. 2
So faire and fresh, as freshest flowre in *May;* . . . I. xii. 22. 1
like young fruit in *May*, . . . II. iii. 29. 7
so wisely as I *may*.' . . . II. ix. 42. 9
him assailes with all the might he *may;* . . . IV. vii. 25. 4
flowres as fresh as *May*. . . . IV. x. 37. 9
I will it defend whilst ever that I *may*. . . . V. iv. 14. 9
'*May* be, Sir knight, that, . . . VI. ii. 27. 1
make them both as merry as he *may*. . . . VI. iii. 9. 5
faire *May*, the fayrest mayd on ground, . . . VII. vii. 34. 1
blowe his nayles to warme them if he *may;* . . . VII. vii. 42. 4
twixt her paps, (like early fruit in *May*, . . . *Am.* lxxvi. 9
lips, like rosy buds in *May*, . . . *H.B.* 258
May-bush. To helpen the Ladyes their *Maybush* beare!) . . *S.C.* May 34
Mayest. Well *maist* thou boast, . . . *Ro.* xxxii. 12
Of love and lustihead tho *mayst* thou sing, . . . *S.C.* O. 51
To sadder times thou *mayst* attune thy quill, . . . *S.C.* N. 35
So *maist* thou chaunce mock out a Benefice, . . . *Hub.* 509
queene of beautie, now thou *maist* go pack; . . . *T.M.* 398
Hobbin desires, thou *maist* it not forsake;— . . . *Col.* 50
But, sith thou *maist* not so, give leave a while . . . *Ded. Son.* xii. 9
Into the which heareafter thou *maist* happen fall. . . . I. ix. 45. 9
'ne *maist* thou yitt Forgoe . . . I. x. 63. 6
happy thou that *mayst* them freely see! . . . VI. x. 19. 8
in thine owne behalfe *maist* partiall seeme: . . . VII. vi. 35. 3
in mens harts thou *mayst* thy throne enstall, . . . *H.B.* 265
May-game. 'What *May-game* hath misfortune made of you? . V. vii. 40. 2
May-lady. Helenore . . . their *May-lady* they had newly made: III. x. 44. 6
Mayre. *See* **Maire.**
Mayster, *etc.* *See* **Master,** *etc.*
Maze. Where in a *maze* they both did long remaine, . . . IV. iv. 18. 7
Mazed. Much was I *mazde*, to see this monsters kinde . . . *Bel.*[2] viii. 9
I thus *mazed* was with great affray, . . . *Bel.*[2] xv. 11
yet so *mazed* that he nothing spake. . . . IV. i. 43. 9
senselesse stood, like to a *mazed* steare . . . IV. vi. 37. 4
would have *maz'd* a man his dreadfull face to vew: . . . IV. viii. 38. 9
mazd how nature had so well disguized Her worke, . . . IV. ix. 11. 3
like *mazed* deare dismayfully they flew. . . . V. viii. 38. 9
Fayre eyes! the myrrour of my *mazed* hart, . . . *Am.* vii. 1
Mazeful. lyke to those which red Medusaes *mazeful* hed. . . *Epith.* 190
Mazer. A *mazer* ywrought of the Maple warre, . . . *S.C.* Au. 26
To him be the wroughten *mazer* alone. . . . *S.C.* Au. 134
A mighty *Mazer* bowle of wine was sett, . . . II. xii. 49. 3
Mazy. 'I wont to raunge amydde the *mazie* thickette, . . . *S.C.* D. 25
Me (*partial list*). *See* **Ay me.**
calling *me* then by my propre name, . . . *Bel.*[1] i. 7
Then cried a shining Angell as *me* thought, . . . *Rev.* iii. 8
So manie strange things happened *me* to see, . . . *Pet.* i. 2
Ten feete each way in square appeare to *mee*, . . . *Bel.*[2] iii. 2
Strowe *me* the ground with Daffadowndillies, . . . *S.C.* Ap. 140
at the dore he cast *me* downe hys pack, . . . *S.C.* May 245
Enough is *me* to paint out my unrest, . . . *S.C.* Jun. 79
But say *me*, what is Algrind, . . . *S.C.* Jul. 213
No Muses aide *me* needes heretoo to call; . . . *Hub.* 43
Rehearse to *me*, ye Sacred Sisters nine, . . . *T.M.* 1
It chaunced *me* on day beside the shore . . . *Ti.* 1
Let them behold the piteous fall of *mee*, . . . *Ti.* 461
At length, by demonstration *me* to teach, . . . *Ti.* 488
I heard a voyce, which loudly to *me* called, . . . *Ti.* 580
left *me* here his losse for to deplore. . . . *Ti.* 658
My Lyonesse (ah, woe is *mee!*) is gon! . . . *D.* 161
she it is that hath *me* done this wrong, . . . *D.* 341
And staie with *me*, . . . *D.* 559
It falls *me* here to write of Chastity, . . . III. Pr. 1. 1
death *me* liefer were then such despight, . . . III. i. 24. 4

Me—*Continued.*
Me lever were . . . be dead . . . . III. ii. 6. 9
first it falleth *me* by course to tell . . . . VI. viii. 31. 1
(woe is *me!*) . . . . VI. xi. 31. 1
me needeth to declare What did betide . . . . VI. xii. 14. 2
But when ye lowre, or looke on *me* askew, ... *Am.* vii. 7
That *me* thou makest thus tormented be, ... *Am.* x. 2
Of her freewill, scorning both thee and *me?* . . . . *Am.* x. 4
As she doth laugh at *me,* . . . . *Am.* x. 14
To force *me* live, and will not let *me* dy. . . . . *Am.* xi. 12
did thick about *me* throng. . . . . *Am.* xii. 8
Who, *me* captiving streight . . . . *Am.* xii. 11
Have ever since *me* kept in cruell bands. . . . . *Am.* xii. 12
which have oftentimes Beene to *me* ayding, ... *Epith.* 2
Helpe *me* mine owne loves prayses to resound; . . . . *Epith.* 14
Why blush ye, love, to give to *me* your hand, ... *Epith.* 238
This day for ever to *me* holy is. . . . . *Epith.* 249
words should faile *me* to relate . . . . *H.L.* 17
to overspred *Me* with the shadow . . . . *H.L.* 20
vouchsafe to take of *me* This simple song, ... *H.L.* 306
Ah! whither, Love! wilt thou now carrie *mee?* . . . . *H.B.* 1
Thou in *me* kindlest much more great desyre, ... *H.B.* 5
Love, lift *me* up upon thy golden wings, ... *H.H.L.* 1
Mead. diapred lyke the discolored *mead*. . . . . *Epith.* 51
freshest Flowres which in that *Mead* they found, ... *Proth.* 84
Meadow. In a fresh flowring *meadow* lying lowe: . . . . *Van.* ii. 4
As fresh as flowres in *medow* greene doe grow . . . . I. xii. 6. 7
in a *Meadow,* by the Rivers side, ... *Proth.* 19
Of every sort, which in that *Meadow* grew, ... *Proth.* 29
Meadows. The mantled *medowes* mourne, ... *S.C.* N. 128
The woods, the rivers, and the *medowes* green, ... *Mui.* 153
Meads. washeth Winborne *meades* in season drye. . . . . IV. xi. 32. 4
meades adornd with daintie gemmes . . . . *Proth.* 14
Meadwort. The metall first he mixt with *Medaewart,* . . . . II. viii. 20. 5
Meagre. so leane and *meagre* waxen late, ... *Hub.* 599
His body leane and *meagre* as a rake, ... II. xi. 22. 2
with heary glib deform'd and *meiger* face, ... IV. viii. 12. 6
Meals. her eate attonce, or many *meales* to make. . . . . VI. viii. 37. 9
Mean. *See* **Mien.**
So *meane* Harpes worke may chalenge for her meed? . . . . *Ro.* xxxii. 4
all that humble is, and *meane* debaced, ... *Van.* i. 6
Why do vaine men *mean* things so much deface, ... *Van.* xi. 12
No being for those that truely *mene;* . . . . *S.C.* S. 33
Base is the style, and matter *meane* withall. . . . . *Hub.* 44
meane regard, and basest fortunes scorne, ... *Hub.* 60
I *meane* to turne the next leafe of the booke: . . . . *Hub.* 68
I *meane* my Gossip privie first to make.' . . . . *Hub.* 70
meane for better winde about to throwe. . . . . *Hub.* 80
I *meane* me to disguize In some straunge habit, ... *Hub.* 83
though his vesture were but *meane* and bace, ... *Hub.* 229
meane estate In safe assurance, ... *Hub.* 909
I saw him die, as one Of the *meane* people, ... *Ti.* 191
Me, all too *meane,* the sacred Muse areeds . . . . I. Pr. 1. 7
To which I *meane* my wearie course to bend; . . . . I. xii. 1. 2
'What *meane* these bloody vowes and idle threats . . . . I. xii. 30. 1
Betwixt them both can measure out a *meane;* . . . . II. i. 58. 2
in the *meane,* vouchsafe her honorable toombe.' . . . . II. i. 58. 9
The face of golden *Meane:* Her sisters, two Extremities, ... II. ii. Arg.
if thou *meane* her love to gayn. . . . . II. vi. 28. 6
The measure of her *meane* and naturall first need. . . . . II. vii. 16. 9
A solemne *Meane* unto them measured; . . . . II. xii. 33. 4
Exceeding much the state of *meane* degree, ... III. i. 33. 7
I *meane* not thee entreat To passe, ... III. iv. 15. 3
when his *meane* estate he did revew, ... III. v. 44. 7
Thou, a *meane* Squyre of meeke and lowly place; . . . . III. v. 47. 3
Whom she did *meane* to make the thrall of her desire. . . . . III. vii. 37. 9
lodging in so *meane* a maintenaunce; . . . . III. vii. 59. 4
meane of your deliverance have beene. . . . . III. xii. 40. 5
for his *meane* degree . . . . IV. viii. 50. 3
by no *meane* could in the weight be stayd; . . . . V. ii. 45. 8
of the *meane* he greatly did misleeke. . . . . V. ii. 49. 5
'Ah gentle Knights! what *meane* ye thus . . . . V. viii. 11. 2
hearing pleas of people *meane* and base: . . . . V. ix. 36. 5
by such *mene* Unto the type of kingdomes title clymes! . . . . V. ix. 42. 6
howsoever base and *meane* it were, ... VI. iv. 15. 1
As if his cry did *meane* for helpe to call . . . . VI. iv. 18. 3
Yet, as I well it *meane,* vouchsafe it without blame. . . . . VI. iv. 34. 9
With salve, or antidote, or other *mene,* . . . . VI. vi. 9. 5
Though of *meane* parentage and kindred base, ... VI. vii. 28. 4
Though *meane* her lot, yet higher did her mind ascend. . . . . VI. ix. 10. 9
all things therein *meane,* . . . . VI. ix. 16. 6
your *meane* food shall be my daily feast, ... VI. ix. 32. 3
Excelling much the *meane* of her degree; . . . . VI. x. 27. 3
(For of all sense it is the middle *meane*) . . . . VII. vii. 22. 2
in my selfe, my inward selfe, I *meane,* . . . . *Am.* xlv. 3
Then dare be lov'd by men of *meane* degree. . . . . *Am.* lxi. 14
ye your love lent to so *meane* a one. . . . . *Am.* lxvi. 4
let her prayses yet be low and *meane,* . . . . *Am.* lxxx. 13
That are so much by so *meane* love embased. . . . . *Am.* lxxxii. 4
I *meane* to sing the praises of thy name, ... *H.L.* 10
thee, to whom I *meane* it most, ... *H.B.* 22
Mean-debased. *See* **Debased, Mean.**
Meaner. Goe . . . emongste the *meaner* sorte: . . . . *S.C.* Env. 8
Nor unto any *meaner* to complaine; . . . . IV. xii. 29. 3
Let none therefore, that is in *meaner* place, ... VI. iii. 5. 8
The lusty Aladine, though *meaner* borne . . . . VI. iii. 7. 6
Meaner's. mischief fel upon the *meaners* crowne. . . . . III. v. 25. 8
Meanest. 'What land is that thou *meanst,* . . . . *Col.* 290
Of which I *meanest* boast my selfe to be, ... *Col.* 538
What *meanest* thou by this reprochfull strife? . . . . I. ix. 52. 7

Meanest—*Continued.*
hostes of men of *meanest* thinges could frame, ... III. iii. 12. 6
perfect gold surmounts the *meanest* brasse. . . . . IV. ix. 2. 9
meanest man of many moe, ... IV. x. 19. 1
Provided him a sword of *meanest* sort; . . . . VI. xi. 42. 6
this homely verse, of many *meanest,* . . . . VI. xii. 41. 1
Meaneth. 'Shame be his meede,' (quoth he) 'that *meaneth* shame! . . . . IV. vi. 6. 1
What *meaneth* this which here I see before? . . . . VI. vii. 14. 7
Meaning. *See* **True-meaning.**
deceitfull *meaning* is double eyed. . . . . *S.C.* May 254
this Curdog, by my coste, (*Meaning* the Foxe) . . . . *Hub.* 295
they more subtill *meaning* had than he; . . . . *Hub.* 330
the best speaches with ill *meaning* spill, ... *Hub.* 716
Whose *meaning* much I labored foorth to wreste, ... *Ti.* 486
meaning her much better to preferre, ... *Col.* 121
The secret *meaning* of th' eternall might, ... I. ix. 6. 8
Ne reckt shee who her *meaning* did mistrust, ... III. i. 48. 4
told her *meaning* in her countenaunce; . . . . III. i. 50. 8
in his eye his *meaning* wisely redd, ... III. ix. 28. 6
That with thy *meaning* so I may the rather meete. . . . . IV. ii. 34. 9
messengers of his true *meaning* and intent. . . . . IV. viii. 13. 9
nathemore his *meaning* she ared, ... IV. viii. 14. 1
T' expresse the *meaning* of the inward mind, ... IV. viii. 26. 2
Meaning on him their cruell hands to lay, ... V. iv. 23. 8
Her rather reade his *meaning* then him selfe it spake. . . . . V. vi. 9. 9
meaning to suppress both forged guile And open force: . . . . V. vii. 7. 3
To show her thankefull mind and *meaning* faine, ... VI. i. 46. 4
He doubted much what mote their *meaning* bee; . . . . VI. vii. 24. 2
What *meaning* mote those uncouth words comprize, ... VI. viii. 18. 4
Meaning . . . For slaves to sell them . . . . VI. x. 43. 3
As if they knew the *meaning* of their layes. . . . . *Am.* xix. 8
doth deprave My simple *meaning* . . . . *Am.* xxix. 2
Meanings. With like fierce minds, but *meanings* different; . . . . V. viii. 30. 2
Meanly. The Husbandman was *meanly* well content . . . . *Hub.* 297
there is Corydon though *meanly* waged, ... *Col.* 382
Meanness. he through pride and fatnes gan despise Their *meanesse;* . . . . *Hub.* 587
for his *meannesse* and disparagement, ... IV. vii. 16. 1
valour the which did adorne His *meanesse* much, ... VI. iii. 7. 9
Means. provide for *meanes* of maintenaunce, ... *S.C.* May 79
well he *meanes,* but little can say. . . . . *S.C.* May 311
And *meanes* of gladsome solace to devise: . . . . *Hub.* 20
come by readie *meanes* unto his end, ... *Hub.* 127
I driven am to seeke some *meanes* to live: . . . . *Hub.* 250
By secrete *meanes* gan of his state enquire, ... *Hub.* 681
all the cunning *meanes* he could devise: . . . . *Hub.* 847
he by *meanes* might cast them to prevent, ... *Hub.* 881
Reveale to me, and all the *meanes* detect, ... *Mui.* 13
Arachne, by his *means* was vanquished . . . . *Mui.* 261
by no *meanes* I could him win thereto, ... *D.* 561
meanes deviz'd to shew his sorrow best. . . . . *As.* 208
whenas timely *meanes* it purchase may, ... *Ded.Son.*xvi.13
rests not so, but other *meanes* doth make, ... I. ii. 9. 6
To muse on *meanes* of hoped victory. . . . . I. iv. 44. 5
By Dianes *meanes,* who was Hippolyts frend, ... I. v. 39. 7
Of whom he *meanes* his bloody feast to make, ... I. vi. 10. 5
by hard *meanes* enforcing her to stay, ... I. viii. 25. 8
He found the *meanes* that Prisoner up to reare; . . . . I. viii. 40. 6
Himselfe he frees by secret *meanes* unseene; . . . . II. i. 1. 8
by what *meanes* may I his footing tract?' . . . . II. i. 12. 7
Then *meanes* I gan devise for his deliveraunce. . . . . II. i. 54. 9
saw no *meanes* to scape, ... II. ii. 8. 2
them began With goodly *meanes* to pacifie, ... II. ii. 21. 9
Ne any evill *meanes* she did forbeare, ... II. iv. 5. 8
restraine from her reprochfull blame And evill *meanes,* . . . . II. iv. 11. 4
such grace I found, and *meanes* I wrought, ... II. iv. 21. 1
soone by *meanes* thereof the Empire wan, ... II. x. 61. 4
all under age; By *meanes* whereof . . . . II. x. 64. 2
th' utmost *meanes* of victory assay, ... II. xi. 41. 4
By such good *meanes* he him discounselled . . . . III. i. 11. 1
Who *meanes* no guile be guiled soonest shall, ... III. i. 54. 6
by what *means* his love might best be wrought: . . . . III. iii. 6. 6
any leaches skill, Or other learned *meanes,* . . . . III. iii. 18. 2
doe by all dew *meanes* thy destiny fulfill.' . . . . III. iii. 24. 9
What *meanes* shall she out seeke, or what waies take? . . . . III. iii. 25. 2
by no *meanes* the high banke he could sease, ... III. v. 19. 8
Sought by all *meanes* his dolor to prolong, ... III. vii. 35. 7
glad by any *meanes* her grace to gaine, ... III. vii. 54. 1
With harder *meanes* he cast her to subdew, ... III. viii. 40. 7
'entreat The man by gentle *meanes* . . . . III. ix. 9. 2
by *meanes* to him well knowne: . . . . III. ix. 30. 2
by no *meanes* would to his will be wonne, ... III. x. 51. 8
by any *meanes* remov'd away; . . . . III. xi. 23. 8
By *meanes* whereof he hath him lightly overborne. . . . . IV. ii. 6. 9
By sundry *meanes* thereto she prickt him forth; . . . . IV. ii. 12. 1
by no *meanes* they could it thereto frame; . . . . IV. v. 16. 5
to accord them all this *meanes* deviz'd: . . . . IV. v. 25. 3
He by no *meanes* could wished ease obtaine: . . . . IV. v. 40. 8
in vaine, sith *meanes,* ye see, there wants theretoo. . . . . IV. vi. 30. 9
Unto my choise by no *meanes* would assent, ... IV. vii. 16. 3
I sought by secret *meanes* to worke Time to my will, ... IV. vii. 17. 1
Finding no *meanes* how I might us enlarge, ... IV. viii. 61. 7
By all *meanes* to maintaine that castels ancient rights. . . . . IV. x. 7. 9
by no *meanes* my way I would forslow . . . . IV. x. 15. 1
since he *meanes* found none, ... IV. xii. 12. 8
At last, when as no *meanes* he could invent, ... IV. xii. 16. 1
Ne could by search nor any *meanes* out find . . . . IV. xii. 21. 3
Whereby to seeke some *meanes* it to appease. . . . . IV. xii. 22. 3
he thereto would by no *meanes* consent, ... V. i. 30. 6

Means—*Continued.*
by no *meanes* the false will with the truth be wayd V. ii. 45. 9
As by no *meanes* he can himselfe outwind: V. iii. 9. 5
By all *meanes* seeking to asswage their ires; V. iv. 4. 7
she thenceforth did labour By all the *meanes* she might V. v. 35. 5
Make *meanes* to win thy libertie forlorne, V. v. 40. 2
want of *meanes* hath bene my onely let V. v. 42. 1
by no *meanes* could her thereto perswade; V. v. 54. 4
He wold, by all good *means* he might, deserve such grace. V. v. 55. 9
found No easie *meanes* according to his mind: V. viii. 42. 3
she them woo'd, by all the *meanes* she might, V. ix. 3. 7
By *meanes* whereof she did at last commit V. x. 13. 1
The woefull widow had no *meanes* now left, V. x. 14. 2
I long in vaine have bent . . . and daily *meanes* assay; V. xi. 51. 4
Yet rescue her thence by no *meanes* I may, V. xi. 51. 5
by no *meanes* it backe againe he forth could wrast V. xii. 21. 9
by what *meanes* did they at first it reare, VI. i. 14. 3
sought to win his love by all the *meanes* she might VI. i. 14. 9
By all the *meanes* she mote it best explaine: VI. i. 46. 5
'What *meanes* this, gentle Swaine, VI. ii. 7. 2
when as her he by no *meanes* could find, VI. ii. 21. 1
that old Knight by all *meanes* did assay VI. iii. 9. 4
Yet had no *meanes* to comfort, VI. iii. 43. 9
she saw no *meanes* to be defended, VI. iv. 10. 5
Albe that Dame, by all the *meanes* she might, VI. iv. 39. 5
sought by all the *meanes* that he could VI. v. 6. 3
The Blatant Beast the fittest *meanes* they found VI. v. 14. 8
By all the courteous *meanes* he could invent; VI. v. 32. 6
by what *meanes* that shame to her befell, VI. vi. 17. 1
Whylest time did offer *meanes* him sleeping to surprize VI. vii. 22. 9
By *meanes* his leg . . . Was crackt in twaine, VI. viii. 25. 7
I needes must by all *meanes* fulfill This penaunce, VI. viii. 30. 2
to occasion *meanes* to worke his mind, VI. ix. 27. 1
he *meanes* no more to sew His former quest, VI. x. 2. 1
Whom by no *meanes* thou canst recall againe; VI. x. 20. 3
to recomfort him all comely *meanes* did frame VI. x. 29. 9
sought her love by all the *meanes* he mote VI. xi. 4. 7
She found no *meanes* to barre him, VI. xi. 7. 7
By *meanes* whereof she would not him permit VI. xi. 8. 1
By *meanes* whereof . . . was slaine and layd on ground, VI. xi. 19. 5
by all *meanes* the daunger knowne did shonne: VI. xi. 35. 7
Deviz'd all goodly *meanes* from her to drive VI. xi. 50. 6
By all *meanes* shund to match with any forrein fere VI. xii. 4. 9
Whom to recomfort all the *meanes* he wrought, VI. xii. 13. 7
by unjust And guilefull *meanes*, VII. vi. 27. 4
As *meanes* of blisse I gladly wil embrace; *Am.* xxv. 12
Is there no *meanes* for me to purchace peace, *Am.* xxxvi. 5
Out of her bands ye by no *meanes* shall get *Am.* xxxvii. 12
She *meanes* at last to make her pitious spoyle *Am.* xli. 12
to conspyre . . . by all *meanes* they may, *H.L.* 81
tempering . . . Their contrary dislikes with loved *meanes*, *H.L.* 86
The *meanes*, therefore, which unto us is lent *H.H.B.* 127

Meanst. *See* **Meanest.**

Meant. when as good is *meant*, *S.C.* May 101
morrowes meed they closely *ment*, . . . for to prevent: *Hub.* 331
they their occupation *meant* to change, *Hub.* 355
thither they themselves *meant* to addresse, *Hub.* 657
beg the sute the which the other *ment*, *Hub.* 882
yet to prove more true he *meant* to see, *Hub.* 1277
Lunday . . . by that same name is *ment* An island, *Col.* 270
Receive it, Lord, therefore, as it was *ment*, *Ded. Son.* x. 13
he askt her, what the Lyon *ment*; I. iii. 32. 8
He never *meant* with words, but swords, to plead his right: I. iv. 42. 9
he *meant* his corrosives to apply, I. x. 25. 8
both against the middest *meant* to worken woe II. ii. 13. 9
The ill . . . he now to Guyon *ment* II. iii. 11. 9
I *meant* to purge both with a third mischiefe, II. iv. 31. 3
ere it empight In the *meant* marke, II. iv. 46. 6
shund the marke at which it should be *ment*; II. v. 5. 5
what that usage *ment*, II. vi. 9. 3
What *meant* that preace about that Ladies throne, II. vii. 48. 2
Askt who he was, and what he *ment* thereby? II. vii. 59. 2
To shonne the engin of his *meant* decay; II. xi. 36. 3
what *meant* those beastes which there did ly? II. xii. 84. 9
ne evill thing she *ment* III. i. 19. 9
With whom he *ment* to make his sport and courtly play III. i. 56. 9
Yet wist not what their wailing *ment*; III. iv. 32. 4
ment To her no evill thought nor evill deed; III. iv. 50. 2
meant unto her prison to have brought, III. vii. 51. 3
The which she *meant* away with her to beare; III. x. 12. 5
meant to ravish her, that rather had to dy III. x. 13. 9
what so were therein or writ or *ment*, III. xi. 50. 6
With th' other he his friends *ment* to enwrap; III. xii. 11. 8
From her, to whom his fury first he *ment*, III. xii. 33. 1
met, As if that each *ment* other to devoure; IV. iii. 15. 2
Full many strokes, that mortally were *ment*, IV. iii. 17. 1
arrived Where it was *ment*, (so deadly it was *ment*) IV. iii. 18. 2
To weeten what that sudden clamour *ment*: IV. iii. 38. 2
As if he naught but peace and pleasure *ment*, IV. iv. 7. 3
What mister wight he was, or what he *ment*; IV. viii. 13. 6
Her words were not, as common words are *ment*, IV. viii. 26. 1
False crimes and facts, such as they never *ment*, IV. viii. 35. 6
To whom his faith he firmely *ment* to hold, IV. viii. 53. 2
He *ment* to make them know their follies prise, IV. ix. 35. 2
being *ment* of mortall creatures sead, IV. xii. 27. 3
She *ment* him to corrupt with goodly meede; V. ii. 23. 3
He *ment* the thiefe there deadly to have smit: V. iii. 29. 8
To weeten what that trumpets sounding *ment*: V. iv. 50. 7
In which she *meant* him warelesse to enfold, V. v. 52. 3
to receive In her owne mouth the food *ment* for her chyld, V. v. 53. 2

Meant—*Continued.*
never *meant* . . . To his owne absent love to be untrew: V. v. 56. 2
by his modest semblant that no evill *ment* V. vi. 19. 9
He should his purpose misse, which close he *ment*: V. vi. 24. 3
Perceiving well the treason which was *ment*; V. vi. 28. 2
for what cause so great mischievous smart Was *ment* V. vi. 31. 9
to her that never evill *ment* in hart V. vi. 31. 9
therefore *ment* him surely to have slaine: V. vi. 34. 5
Towards my Ladies presence, by you *ment*, V. ix. 7. 6
Eftsoones brought forth the villaine, as they *ment*, V. ix. 10. 2
Meant them to have encountred ere they left the shore: V. xii. 6. 9
To doe most dammage where as most they *ment*: V. xii. 17. 4
turne to ill the thing that well was *ment*; V. xii. 34. 5
To which he *meant* his weary steps to guyde, VI. iii. 29. 8
That *meant* to make advantage of his misery VI. iii. 46. 9
From whom he *meant* to free him, if he might, VI. iv. 3. 8
the Prince . . . did rest not weeting what was *ment*, VI. vi. 44. 2
To cloke the mischiefe which he inly *ment*, VI. vii. 4. 2
Great treason to him *meant*, his life to reave VI. vii. 12. 4
scornd them all that love unto her *ment*: VI. vii. 29. 3
His head *meant* from his shoulders to have swept VI. viii. 17. 3
meant them to the damzels fantazy VI. ix. 12. 9
askt againe, what *meant* that rufull hew: VI. xi. 28. 8
Yet knowing not what *meant* that sodaine thro, VI. xii. 17. 2
To know what *meant* that suddaine lacke of light VII. vi. 15. 5

Mean time. In the *meane-time* to live in good estate, *Hub.* 427
In the *mean-time* upon the King 't attend *Hub.* 1100
In the *meane time* . . . He was surprisd, III. iii. 11. 1

Mean while. *Mean-while* her noble Lord, sir Artegall, V. vii. 45. 6
Meane-while the other Knight Defeated had the other faytour V. viii. 8. 4
'*Mean while* his Ladie, . . . did her selfe withdraw, VI. ii. 20. 1
Meane-while the Salvage man, when he beheld VI. viii. 28. 1
Mean-while the lower World . . . was darkned quite; VII. vi. 14. 1
Mean-while th' Earths daughter . . . gan now advise VII. vi. 22. 7
Meane-while, O Clio! lend Calliope thy quill VII. vi. 37. 9
Meane-while all creatures, looking in her face, VII. vii. 57. 4
those Nymphes, *meane while*, two Garlands bound *Proth.* 83

Mear, -ed, -s. *See* **Mere, -d, -s.**

Measure. *measure* the most haughtie mountaines hight, *Bel.*[2] vii. 7
To be the *measure* of her bredth and length: *Ro.* viii. 4
to *measure* Her length, her breadth, her deepnes, *Ro.* xxvi. 3
abound in riches above *measure* *Gn.* 128
to the *measure* of their melodies *T.M.* 33
I that rule in *measure* moderate *T.M.* 379
not by *measure* of her owne great mynd, *Col.* 364
excellence Lifts me above the *measure* of my might: *Col.* 621
the *measure* of thy sinfull hire I. ix. 46. 3
some more bold to *measure* him nigh stand, I. xii. 11. 8
Betwixt them both can *measure* out a meane; II. i. 58. 2
No *measure* in her mood, no rule of right, II. ii. 36. 4
With equall *measure* she did moderate II. ii. 38. 3
To *measure* manhood by the sword or mayle II. iii. 16. 5
The *measure* of her meane and naturall first need II. vii. 16. 9
To swell above the *measure* of his guise, II. xii. 21. 8
Might wanting *measure* moveth surquedry III. x. 2. 5
know the *measure* of their utmost date IV. ii. 50. 4
by wrong And tortious powre, without respect or *measure*: IV. ix. 12. 4
loved out of *measure* IV. ix. 21. 4
Passing the *measure* of my feeble powre; IV. ix. 39. 7
equitie to *measure* out along V. i. 7. 3
In goodly *measure* by their Makers might; V. ii. 35. 2
I the *measure* of her flight doe search, VI. ii. 32. 3
adventures, which had in his *measure* VI. iii. 22. 5
Exceeding much the *measure* of mans stature, VI. vii. 41. 3
religion held even theeves in *measure* VI. viii. 43. 9
Ne ought would buy, how ever prised with *measure*, VI. xi. 14. 4
Therefore do you, my rimes, keep better *measure*, VI. xii. 41. 8
shee had out of *measure* Long lov'd the Fanchin, VII. vi. 44. 3

Measured. *See* **Well-measured.**
thou hast *measured* much grownd, *S.C.* S. 21
plotteth out a tombe by *measured* space: *Gn.* 652
With his aire-cutting wings he *measured* wide, *Mui.* 154
each mans worth is *measured* by his weed, *Col.* 711
She wandred many a wood, and *measurd* many a vale I. vii. 28. 9
with his largenesse *measured* much land, I. xi. 8. 3
who in venturous vessell *measured* The Amazon II. Pr. 2. 7
Full *measured* three quarters of her yeare, II. i. 53. 2
They wasted had much way, and *measurd* many miles II. ix. 9. 9
A solemne Meane unto them *measured*; II. xii. 33. 4
the just revolution *measured* III. iii. 44. 3
Every discourse, . . . by the houres he *measured*, III. ix. 53. 8
measur'd many a sad verse, III. xii. 36. 4
In which they *measur'd* mickle weary way, V. ii. 29. 1
Of parts well *measurd* with meet disposition! *H.B.* 70

Measureless. To see thee, and thy mercie *measurelesse*! *T.M.* 516

Measures. Ne *measures* all things by the costly rate *Gn.* 92
the sweet numbers and melodious *measures*, *T.M.* 547
The Sunne, that *measures* heaven all day long, I. i. 32. 8

Meat. Onely supports herselfe for *meate* of wormes; *Ro.* xxviii. 8
lavish cups and thriftie bitts of *meate*, *S.C.* O. 105
made him *meat* for wild foules of the ayre *Gn.* 380
We are but charg'd to lay the *meate* before: *Hub.* 435
tell hir, that my mouth can eate no *meate*: *U.V.* 8
Whose mind in *meat* and drinke was drowned so, I. vi. 23. 4
discontent for want of merth or *meat*: II. ii. 35. 4
when lust of *meat* and drinke was ceast, II. ii. 39. 3
he did bestow Both guestes and *meate*, II. ix. 28. 4
the sight And company at *meat*, III. ix. 25. 9
They sate to *meat*; III. ix. 27. 1

Meat—*Continued.*
brute beasts, forst to refraine fro *meat*, IV. iv. 47. 3
made refraine from *meat*, IV. ix. 14. 5
to earne their *meat*, V. iv. 31. 5
Unto his horses gave his guests for *meat*, V. viii. 31. 2
of her owne foule entrayles makes her *meat;* V. xii. 31. 8
Meat fit for such a monsters monsterous dyeat: V. xii. 31. 9
More sweet than Nectar, or Ambrosiall *meat*, *Am.* xxxix. 13
Meats. *meates* and drinkes of every kinde I. xii. 15. 1
In wine and *meats* she flowd above the banck, II. ii. 36. 6
with *meates* of every sort, III. i. 52. 2
when of *meats* and drinks they had their fill, III. ix. 32. 1
with full satietie Of *meates* and drinkes V. iii. 4. 2
Mecaenas. *See* **Maecenas.**
Medaewart. *See* **Meadwort.**
Meddle. With mery thing its good to *medle* sadde. *S.C.* Au. 144
Meddled. The Redde rose *medled* with the White yfere, *S.C.* Ap. 68
medled his talke with many a teare: *S.C.* May 263
Ne *medled* with their controversies vaine; *Hub.* 391
Meddlest. Thou *medlest* more then shall have thanke. *S.C.* Jul. 209
Meddling. *medling* with their blood and earth II. i. 61. 3
Medea. the famous history Of Jason and *Medaea* II. xii. 44. 4
fell *Medea*, when on Colchicke strand V. viii. 47. 3
neither Ino, nor *Medea* stout, V. viii. 47. 7
Medicine. those that skill of *medicine* professe, *Col.* 742
He oft finds *med'cine* who his griefe imparts, I. ii. 34. 4
shew thy famous might In *medicine*, I. v. 43. 8
Full of great vertues, and for *med'cine* good: I. xi. 29. 5
goodly counsell, that for wounded hart Is meetest *med'cine*, II. i. 44. 3
Ne was there salve, ne was there *medicine*, II. xi. 21. 8
seeking *medicine* whence she was stong, II. xii. 73. 3
choicest *med'cine* for sick harts reliefe: III. iii. 5. 5
Good both for erthly *med'cine* and for hevenly food. III. iv. 40. 9
gan apply Fit *medicine* to his griefe, III. xi. 13. 9
What *medicine* can any Leaches art Yeeld such a sore, IV. vi. 1. 5
Whereby she might apply some *medicine;* IV. xii. 21. 5
with *medicine* To goe about to salve such kynd of sore, VI. vi. 13. 1
Medicined. be *medicynd* Of her that first did stir that mortall stownd. *Col.* 877
Medicines. he gan apply relief Of salves and *med'cines*, I. x. 24. 5
Sharpe be thy wounds, but sweete the *medicines* be, II. i. 36. 8
Salves to his wounds, and *medicines* of might; III. iv. 43. 8
with thy hevenly salves and *med'cines* sweete III. v. 35. 8
With many kindes of *medicines* meete, VI. vi. 2. 7
Fit *medicines* for my bodies best reliefe. *Am.* l. 4
Medina. *Medina* was her name, II. ii. 14. 4
The faire *Medina*, with her tresses torne II. ii. 27. 2
Betwixt them both the faire *Medina* sate II. ii. 38. 1
Meditate. did them *meditate* all his life long, II. ix. 54. 3
Meditation. to enter into *meditation* deepe *Van.* i. 3
through *meditation* Of this worlds vainnesse *D.* 33
Of God and goodnes was his *meditation*. I. x. 46. 9
Through *meditation* of his endlesse merit, *H.H.L.* 255
Medua. *See* **Medway.**
Medusa. To snaky-locke *Medusa* to repayre, III. xi. 42. 8
Medusa's. bred was of *Medusaes* blood, *Ti.* 647
lyke to those which red *Medusaes* mazeful hed. *Epith.* 190
Medway. Here has the salt *Medway* his sourse, *S.C.* Jul. 79
The salt *Medway*, that trickling stremis *S.C.* Jul. 81
Where Thames doth the *Medway* wedd, IV. xi. Arg.
Betwixt the *Medway* and the Thames agreed. IV. xi. 8. 4
the lovely *Medua* came, IV. xi. 45. 1
Meed. So meane Harpes worke may chalenge for her *meed?* *Ro.* xxxii. 4
thy due *meede* that thou deservest best, *Gn.* 60
that thankes so much should faile of *meed;* *Gn.* 353
the next morrowes *meed* they closely ment, *Hub.* 331
he knowes his *meede*, . . . To be a thousand deathes, *Hub.* 975
driven downe to hell, his dewest *meed:* *Hub.* 1237
For vertues *meed* and ornament of wit, *T.M.* 310
accounted heretofore The learneds *meed* *T.M.* 412
If none should yeeld him his deserved *meed*, *T.M.* 453
for former vertues *meede*, *Ti.* 398
everie gift, and everie goodly *meed*, *Col.* 592
The Laurell, *meed* of mightie Conquerours I. i. 9. 1
A Rosy girlond was the victors *meede*. I. ii. 37. 5
the worthie *meed* Of him that slew Sansfoy I. iii. 36. 3
th' Elfin knight, . . . Disdaind to loose the *meed* I. iv. 39. 8
me, thy worthy *meed*, unto thy Leman take.' I. vii. 14. 9
eyes . . . seeled up with death shall have their deadly *meed*.' I. vii. 23. 9
Great thankes, and goodly *meed*, I. x. 68. 4
honour, vertues *meed*, Doth beare the fayrest flowre II. iii. 10. 8
great sure shal be thy *meed*, II. iii. 14. 6
had of her fayre Helen for his *meed*, II. vii. 55. 8
What may suffice to be for *meede* repayd II. viii. 55. 7
To bind their dooers to receive their *meed?* II. viii. 56. 3
'Noble Lord, what *meed* so great, II. ix. 6. 1
In *meed* of these great conquests by them gott, II. x. 12. 1
mourneful *meed* of joyes delicious! II. xii. 85. 7
Then honour was the *meed* of victory, III. i. 13. 6
in hope to win thereby Most goodly *meede*, III. i. 18. 8
Which alwaies of his paines he made the chiefest *meed*. III. iv. 4. 9
At least eternall *meede* shall you abide.' III. v. 11. 5
'Unthankfull wretch,' (said he) 'is this the *meed*, III. v. 45. 1
Most vertuous virgin! glory be thy *meed*, III. viii. 42. 6
Whom Venus to him gave for *meed* of worthinesse; III. ix. 34. 9
Fame is my *meed*, and glory vertues pay: III. x. 31. 7
for mercy or for *meed*, To save his life, III. x. 50. 7
If goodnesse find no grace, nor righteousnes no *meed?* III. xi. 9. 9
meed For so huge mischiefe III. xii. 35. 1
what worthy *meede* Can wretched Lady . . . Yield you III. xii. 39. 2

Meed—*Continued.*
The *meed* of them that love, IV. Pr. 2. 9
Right well deserved, as his duefull *meed*, IV. i. 6. 3
Ten thousand thankes did yeeld her for her *meed*, IV. i. 15. 3
steale from thee the *meede* of thy due merit, IV. ii. 34. 3
there thy *meede* unto thee take, IV. iii. 11. 1
The *meede* of thy mischalenge and abet. IV. iii. 11. 2
whylome wont to be the victors *meed;* IV. iv. 31. 3
of victors *meede* And eke of honour IV. v. 9. 2
Who was right glad to gaine so goodly *meed:* IV. v. 22. 2
From wight unworthie of so noble *meed*. IV. v. 28. 4
'Shame be his *meede*,' (quoth he) 'that meaneth shame! IV. vi. 6. 1
for no worldly *meed*, Nor no entreatie, IV. xi. 8. 7
When Justice was not for most *meed* out-hyred, V. Pr. 3. 8
She ment him to corrupt with goodly *meede;* V. ii. 23. 3
goodly *meede* of him it purchase may, V. v. 33. 8
th' actours won the *meede* meet for their crymes. V. ix. 42. 5
Such be the *meede* of all that by such mene V. ix. 42. 6
For other *meede* may hope for none of mee, V. x. 21. 6
What other *meed*, then, need me to requight, V. xi. 17. 7
that which yeeldeth vertues *meed* alway? V. xi. 17. 8
for prayer nor for *meed:* V. xi. 61. 7
to his damzell, as their rightfull *meed* VI. i. 47. 5
The *meede* of his desert for that despight, VI. ii. 45. 8
The *meede* whereof shall shortly be thy shame, VI. vi. 25. 6
his two knights Doe gaine their treasons *meed:* VI. vii. Arg.
for their paines obtaine of him a goodly *meed*. VI. vii. 4. 9
desirous of the offred *meed:* VI. vii. 5. 6
for all his former follies *meed*, VI. vii. 11. 8
for promise of great *meed*, VI. vii. 12. 7
'Now sure ye well have earn'd your *meed;* VI. vii. 13. 2
for *meed* did undertake So hard a taske VI. vii. 15. 2
A garland was the *meed* of victory: VI. ix. 43. 4
Yet Calidore so well him wrought with *meed*, VI. xi. 35. 8
fortune now the victors *meed* did make: VI. xi. 51. 4
Babblers unworthy been of so divine a *meed*. VII. vi. 46. 9
That greater *meede* at last may turne to mee. *Am.* xxv. 14
That of her presens I my *meed* may take. *Am.* lii. 14
Shame be thy *meed*, and mischiefe thy reward, *Am.* lxxxv. 13
Meeds. fild their mouthes with *meeds* of malefices: *Hub.* 1154
winnes an Olive girlond for her *meeds*. II. ii. 31. 7
With the revenue of her plenteous *meedes:* V. ii. 9. 8
Yielded them by the vanquisht as theyr *meeds*, *Am.* xxix. 6
Meek. *meeke* he was, as *meeke* mought be, *S.C.* Jul. 129
shepheard mought be *meeke* and mylde, *S.C.* Jul. 153
He is so *meeke*, wise, and merciable, *S.C.* S. 174
unto everie one doo curtesie *meeke:* *Hub.* 499
Lowly they him saluted in *meeke* wise, *Hub.* 585
all things needfull for contentment *meeke*, *Hub.* 911
milde of speach, and *meeke* of nature: *Ti.* 536
shee became so *meeke* and milde of cheare, *D.* 125
for pure pitie of my sufferaunce *meeke*, *D.* 389
Was never Prince so *meeke* and debonaire, I. ii. 23. 5
Such were the labours of this Lady *meeke*, I. iii. 21. 7
They turne themselves, at Unaes *meeke* request, I. x. 15. 6
His name was *meeke* Obedience, rightfully aredd. I. x. 17. 9
He humbly louted in *meeke* lowlinesse, I. x. 44. 6
Many *meeke* wordes to stay and comfort her withall. III. iv. 48. 9
Thou, a meane Squyre of *meeke* and lowly place; III. v. 47. 3
tend our charges with obeisaunce *meeke*. III. vi. 22. 8
the fayre Virgin was so *meeke* and myld, III. vii. 15. 1
all which she of him tooke with countenance *meeke* and mild. III. vii. 17. 9
with which he maked *meeke* The mightie Mars, III. xi. 44. 2
Amongst her teares immixing prayers *meeke*, IV. iii. 47. 6
with *meeke* service and much suit, IV. vi. 40. 3
The more that he with *meeke* intreatie prayd V. v. 14. 8
To *meeke* obeysance of loves mightie raine, V. v. 28. 8
Tho turning all his pride to humblesse *meeke*, V. vii. 16. 1
made him stoupe to ground with *meeke* humilitie: VI. i. 38. 9
with prayers *meeke* . . . lodging did for her beseeke. VI. iii. 37. 8
With *meek* obaysance and humilitie, VII. vii. 13. 8
with *meeke* humblesse and afflicted mood, *Am.* ii. 11
mine eies, with *meek* humility, *Am.* xliii. 11
Meeke Lambe of God, before all worlds behight, *H.H.L.* 173
spirit Is inly toucht, and humbled with *meeke* zeale *H.H.L.* 254
Meekest. *meekest* boone that they imagine mought: V. ix. 34. 5
Meekly. this misseeming discord *meekely* lay aside.' II. ii. 31. 9
high advaunced crests downe *meekely* feld; II. xii. 40. 5
Meekely shee bowed downe, III. v. 31. 1
dye *meekly* for her sake: III. v. 47. 8
meekely stoup unto the victor strong III. vii. 35. 4
her to save from outrage *meekely* prayed him. III. viii. 15. 9
to the ground him *meekely* made to bowe, III. x. 24. 3
haughtie spirits *meekely* to adaw, IV. vi. 26. 8
could so *meekly* make proud hearts avale, VI. viii. 25. 3
She at his bidding *meekely* did arise, VI. ix. 15. 1
Meekness. everie one with *meekenesse* to her bowes. II. iii. 25. 5
pride and *meeknesse*, mixt by equall part, *Am.* xxi. 3
Meet. this new Hydra *mete* to be assailde *Bel.*[1] viii. 11
Mount Viminall and Aventine doo *meete*. *Ro.* iv. 14
Many *meete* tales of youth did he make, *S.C.* F. 98
Colours *meete* to clothe a mayden Queene? *S.C.* F. 132
The greene is for maydens *meete*. *S.C.* Au. 68
More *meete* to wayle my woe *S.C.* Au. 165
as for her power more *meete*, *Gn.* 51
worse than that I have I cannot *meete*. *Hub.* 89
they chaunst to *meet* upon the way *Hub.* 227
chaunst with a formall Priest to *meete*, *Hub.* 361
Their penie Masses, and their Complynes *meete*, *Hub.* 452
At last they chaunst to *meete* upon the way *Hub.* 581

Meet—*Continued.*
may be matter *meete* to gaine him praise: . . . . *Hub.* 779
meete to whom he might disclose His witlesse pleasance, . . *Hub.* 798
I with reason *meete* will rest content, ... *Hub.* 1049
Now sucking of the sap of herbe most *meete,* . . . . *Mui.* 180
Passe unespide to *meete* her by the way; . . . . *Col.* 140
they chaunst to *meet* upon the way An aged Sire, ... I. i. 29. 1
him chaunst to *meete* . . . A faithlesse Sarazin, ... I. ii. 12. 5
Soone *meete* they both, both fell and furious, ... I. ii. 15. 4
Their horned *fronts* so fierce on either side Doe *meete,* . . I. ii. 16. 4
it chaunced this proud Sarazin To *meete* me wandring, . . . I. ii. 25. 2
he was . . . Not *meet* to be of counsell to a king, ... I. iv. 23. 3
traveiler . . . Doth *meete* a cruell craftie Crocodile, ... I. v. 18. 4
His loving mother . . . chaunst unwares to *meet* him . . . . I. vi. 27. 3
she chaunced by good hap to *meet* A goodly knight, ... I. vii. 29. 1
Together with his Squyre, arayed *meet:* . . . . I. vii. 29. 3
him chaunced false Duessa *meete,* . . . . I. vii. 50. 6
Where them does *meete* a francklin faire and free, ... I. x. 6. 4
He them with speaches *meet* Does faire entreat; . . . . . . I. x. 7. 6
take assured hold Upon her silver anchor, as was *meet;* . . . I. x. 22. 3
them requites with court'sies seeming *meet,* . . . . I. x. 32. 3
clothes *meet* to keepe keene cold away, ... I. x. 39. 4
mounting up, they fynd purveyaunce *meet* . . . . I. xii. 13. 5
refte of His sences *meet,* . . . . I. xii. 39. 8
him fortuned to *meete* . . . A goodly knight, ... II. i. 5. 6
A goodly knight, all armd in harnesse *meete,* . . . . II. i. 5. 8
entertaine themselves with court'sies *meet.* . . . . II. i. 29. 4
with . . . fell intent, ye did at earst me *meet;* . . . . . . II. i. 29. 7
late befell Me for to *meet,* . . . . II. i. 30. 4
Dan Faunus chaunst to *meet* her by the way, ... II. ii. 7. 5
comely courted with *meet* modestie; . . . . II. ii. 15. 2
pleasd them all with *meete* satiety. . . . . II. ii. 39. 2
at length with Archimage they *meet:* . . . . II. iii. 11. 2
supposed him a person *meet* Of his revenge to make . . . . II. iii. 11. 5
in a darkesome inner bowre Her oft to *meete:* . . . . II. iv. 24. 6
disaray Her upper partes of *meet* habiliments, ... II. v. 32. 8
nor these armes Are *meet,* . . . . II. vi. 34. 3
Sheilds, steeds, and armes, and all things for thee *meet,* . . II. vii. 11. 3
Doth not, I weene, so many evils *meet.'* . . . . II. vii. 14. 5
By faithfull service and *meete* amenaunce, ... II. ix. 5. 7
my succour or advizement *meete* . . . . II. ix. 9. 3
your lives ye love, as *meete* ye should; . . . . II. ix. 12. 2
They to him hearken, as beseemeth *meete,* . . . . II. xii. 14. 1
Whom passing by she happened to *meet:* . . . . II. xii. 56. 8
voyces made To th' instruments divine respondence *meet;* . . II. xii. 71. 4
meet With the base murmure of the waters fall; . . . . . . II. xii. 71. 5
meet respect of honor putt to flight: . . . . III. i. 48. 8
Pitty our playnt, and yield us *meet* reliefe.' . . . . III. iii. 21. 3
other offices for mother *meet* . . . . III. iv. 39. 6
Farewell, my sweetest sonne, sith we no more shall *meet!'* . . III. iv. 39. 9
What service may I doe unto thee *meete,* . . . . III. v. 35. 6
Meet for her temper and complexion: . . . . III. vi. 38. 5
both in equall tilt May *meete* againe, ... III. viii. 18. 4
entertaynd, as seemed *meet,* . . . . III. ix. 3. 3
timely service to her pleasures *meet,* . . . . III. ix. 7. 8
in open place . . . He fortun'd her to *meet,* . . . . III. x. 6. 6
Him to receive with entertainment *meete.* . . . . IV. i. 41. 6
As when two billowes . . . Do *meete* together, ... IV. i. 42. 3
Brigandines . . . Do *meete* together on the watry lea, ... IV. ii. 16. 3
That with thy meaning so I may the rather *meete.* . . . . . IV. ii. 34. 9
entertaining her with curt'sies *meet,* . . . . IV. iii. 50. 8
meete with so hideous maine, ... IV. iv. 18. 4
not *meet* for any guest, ... IV. v. 32. 8
Till they with mariage *meet* might finish that accord. . . . . IV. vi. 41. 9
Yet was he *meet,* unless mine eye did faine, ... IV. vii. 15. 8
Within a grove appointed him to *meete;* . . . . IV. vii. 17. 8
his garment, to be thereto *meet,* . . . . IV. vii. 40. 1
to rest as seem'd her *meet.* . . . . IV. viii. 9. 4
When all three kinds of love together *meet* . . . . IV. ix. 1. 2
zeale of friends combynd with vertues *meet:* . . . . IV. ix. 1. 7
all the cares and evill which they *meet* . . . . IV. x. 2. 2
with *meet* service waited him about, ... IV. xi. 30. 4
Which she receiving with *meete* thankefulnesse, ... IV. xii. 32. 6
for want of other *meete* reward, ... V. i. 30. 4
He chaunst to *meet* a Dwarfe in hasty course, ... V. ii. 2. 2
whereas they brest to brest Should *meete,* . . . . V. ii. 12. 6
Them fairely entertayned with curt'sies *meete,* . . . . V. iv. 51. 5
ran to *meete* him forth to know his tidings somme. . . . . V. vi. 8. 9
She chaunst to *meete,* toward the even-tide, A Knight . . . . V. vi. 19. 3
th' actours won the meede *meet* for their crymes. . . . . . V. ix. 42. 5
He would it *meete* and warily withstand. . . . . V. xi. 7. 5
To *meete* her at the salvage Ilands syde, ... V. xi. 39. 3
her leading with *meete* majestie . . . . V. xii. 25. 1
Did issue forth to *meete* his foe afore; . . . . VI. i. 32. 7
I chaunst to *meete* this knight, ... VI. ii. 9. 8
'Unarm'd . . . as then more *meete* For Ladies service, ... VI. ii. 18. 1
fearing any foeman there to *meete:* . . . . VI. ii. 18. 3
this young man . . . Spake, as was *meet,* . . . . VI. ii. 23. 3
To clad his corpse with *meete* habiliments, ... VI. iv. 4. 5
With many kindes of medicines *meete,* . . . . VI. vi. 2. 7
To make it seeme more deare and dainty, as is *meet.* . . . . VI. xi. 1. 9
seeking all things *meete* for remedy; . . . . VI. xi. 8. 5
nothing *meet* in merchandise to passe: . . . . VI. xi. 12. 8
In good estate, and in *meet* order ranged, ... VII. vi. 5. 3
parts well measurd, with *meet* disposition! . . . . *H.B.* 70
Meeter. When *meeter* were that ye should now awake, ... *Epith.* 86
Meetest. Sike myrth in May is *meetest* for to make, ... *S.C.* N. 11
goodly counsell, that for wounded hart Is *meetest* med'cine, . II. i. 44. 3
As every one seem'd *meetest* in that cace. . . . . II. xi. 6. 5
As *meetest* may beseeme a noble mayd: . . . . III. v. 5. 3

Meeting. He thereto *meeting* said, 'My dearest Dame, ... I. iii. 28. 1
meeting earst with Archimago slie . . . . II. viii. 10. 7
meeting with this Redcrosse Knight, ... III. iii. 62. 3
both *meeting* at one tyme; . . . . III. vi. 42. 2
meeting Plim, to Plimmouth thence declines: . . . . IV. xi. 31. 4
Even in the dore him *meeting,* . . . . V. vi. 9. 1
meeting him right in the middle race . . . . V. x. 34. 4
Meetings. Of knights and ladies any *meetings* were; . . . . III. x. 19. 8
Meets. Prince Arthure *meets* with Una . . . . I. vii. Arg.
meetes a flood that doth his passage stay, ... I. ix. 39. 3
Meetes two contrarie billowes . . . . II. ii. 24. 4
The hard beginne that *meetes* thee in the dore, ... III. iii. 21. 8
She goes to seeke him, Dolon *meetes,* . . . . V. vi. Arg.
Megaera. Fit for *Megera* or Persephone; . . . . *T.M.* 164
Meiger. *See* **Meager.**
Meinie. *See* **Many** (III. ix. 11. 7; xii. 23. 8; V. xi. 3. 2).
Meint. *See* **Menged.**
Melampod. Here growes *Melampode* every where, ... *S.C.* Jul. 85
They neede not *Melampode:* . . . . *S.C.* Jul. 106
Melancholic. as she thus *melancholicke* did ride, ... V. vi. 19. 1
Melancholy. melody, To drive away the dull *melancholy;* . . I. v. 3. 5
To drive away the dull *Melancholy;* . . . . I. xii. 38. 8
Sterne *melancholy* did his courage pas, ... II. ii. 17. 8
gnaw His hart in twaine with sad *melancholy;* . . . . II. viii. 50. 8
him full of *melancholy* did shew; . . . . II. ix. 52. 5
thought it was not love, but some *melancholy.* . . . . III. ii. 27. 9
Full of *melancholie* and sad misfare . . . . IV. vi. 2. 3
covered all with shade And sad *melancholy:* . . . . IV. vii. 38. 9
Then up she rose fraught with *melancholy,* . . . . V. vii. 17. 5
The pensive fit of her *melancholie;* . . . . VI. iii. 9. 3
Meliboe. in this halfe happie I doo read Good *Melibae,* . . . . *Ti.* 436
Calidore hostes with *Meliboe,* . . . . VI. ix. Arg.
Meliboee (so hight that good old man) . . . . VI. ix. 16. 1
(said then old *Meliboe*) . . . . VI. ix. 29. 1
They spoyld old *Melibee* of all he had, ... VI. x. 40. 2
Theeves fall out for Pastorell, Whilest *Melibee* is slaine: . . VI. xi. Arg.
Then forth the good old *Meliboe* was brought, ... VI. xi. 11. 1
Old *Meliboe* is slaine; . . . . VI. xi. 18. 4
Old *Meliboe* and his good wife withall These eyes saw die, . . VI. xi. 31. 6
From *Meliboe* and from themselves whyleare; . . . . VI. xi. 37. 3
Had reft from *Meliboe* and from his make, ... VI. xi. 51. 7
Meliogras. Tristram . . . the onely heire Of good king *Meliogras* . . . . VI. ii. 28. 2
Melissa. Then thus *Melissa* said; . . . . *Col.* 480
So having said, *Melissa* spake at will; . . . . *Col.* 895
her owne handmayd, that *Melissa* hight, ... VI. xii. 14. 8
Melite. Lightfoote Cymothoe, and sweete *Melite,* . . . . . . IV. xi. 49. 4
Mell. *See* **Pell-mell.**
With holy father sits not with such thinges to *mell.* . . . . I. i. 30. 9
Not fit mongst men that doe with reason *mell,* . . . . V. ix. 1. 4
In his *Foules parley* durst not with it *mel,* . . . . VII. vii. 9. 5
Melling. Harme may come of *melling.* . . . . *S.C.* Jul. 208
every matter worse was for her *melling:* . . . . V. xii. 35. 4
Mellow. Or *mellow* fruit if it were harvest time. . . . . . . *As.* 48
Mellow-ripe. rotted ere they were halfe *mellow ripe;* . . . . *S.C.* D. 107
Melodies. to the measure of their *melodies* . . . . *T.M.* 33
Where many Mermayds haunt making false *melodies:* . . . . II. xii. 17. 9
Melodious. the sweet numbers and *melodious* measures, . . . *T.M.* 547
Eftsoones they heard a most *melodious* sound, ... II. xii. 70. 1
Melody. singing with most plesant *melodie* . . . . *Bel.*[1] ix. 7
Chaunting in shade their sundrie *melodie,* . . . . *Pet.* iii. 6
Tom Piper makes us better *melodie.* . . . . *S.C.* O. 78
delay Thy nightly course, to heare his *melodie?* . . . . . . *Gn.* 460
with pleasure The listners eyes and eares with *melodie;* . . . *T.M.* 178
when all his mourning *melodie* He ended had, ... *Ti.* 596
As base, or blunt, unmeet for *melodie.* . . . . *Col.* 710
There many Minstrales maken *melody,* . . . . I. v. 3. 4
most heavenly *melody* . . . sweet musicke did divide, ... I. v. 17. 6
their sweet skill in wonted *melody;* . . . . II. xii. 31. 7
let him heare some part of their rare *melody.* . . . . II. xii. 33. 9
Their daintie layes and dulcet *melody,* . . . . III. i. 40. 4
the rare sweetnesse of the *melody* . . . . III. xii. 6. 3
the Graces daunce To Colins *melody;* . . . . VI. x. Arg.
Melpomene. 'Up, then, *Melpomene!* the mournefulst Muse . *S.C.* N. 53
Melt. The heavens doe *melt* in teares without remorse; . . . *S.C.* N. 131
(Whilst oft his heart did *melt* in tender teares) . . . . . . *Mui.* 30
Hable to *melt* the hearers heart unweeting, ... *Col.* 598
nigh his manly hart did *melt* away, ... I. i. 47. 5
Her hart gan *melt* in great compassion; . . . . I. iii. 6. 8
cheareful blood in fayntnes chill did *melt,* . . . . I. vii. 6. 8
His heart did seeme to *melt* in pleasures manifold. . . . . . I. xii. 40. 9
to *melt* in pleasures whott desyre, ... II. i. 58. 3
Ne let thy stout hart *melt* in pitty vayne: . . . . II. v. 24. 6
his busy paines applyde To *melt* the golden metall, ... II. vii. 35. 9
Would make to *melt,* or pitteously appall; . . . . III. vii. 9. 7
My heart doth *melt* with meere compassion, ... III. viii. 1. 2
she, faire Lady, did in pleasure *melt,* . . . . III. xii. 45. *or.*6
eft gan into tender teares to *melt.* . . . . IV. vii. 9. 5
For passing joy, which did all into pitty *melt.* . . . . VI. xii. 21. 9
And let thy soule . . . *Melt* into teares, ... *H.H.L.* 252
Melted. *See* **Molt, Molten.**
Her snowy substance *melted* as with heat, ... V. iii. 24. 7
Melteth. His subtile tong . . . *mealt'h* Into the heart, ... I. ix. 31. 5
Melting. marking him with *melting* eyes, ... *S.C.* May 207
Could not from teares my *melting* eyes withholde. . . . . . *Ti.* 532
Melting in teares, then gan shee thus lament. . . . . I. ii. 22. 1
The sugred licour through his *melting* lips: . . . . II. v. 33. 6
all that might his *melting* hart entyse . . . . II. xii. 66. 7
with his *melting* sweetnes ravished, ... III. Pr. 4. 7
with *melting* eies did vew, ... III. v. 30. 4

Melting—*Continued.*
with drops of *melting* love . . . Sprinckle her heart, ... IV. Pr. 5. 5
with *melting* pleasaunce mollifye Their hardned hearts, ... V. viii. 1. 8
Hong still upon his *melting* mouth attent; . . . . VI. ix. 26. 2
With many a joyfull kisse and many a *melting* teare. . . . . VI. xii. 20. 9
A *melting* pleasance ran through every part, ... *Am.* xxxix. 7
Melts. fire, which all things *melts,* . . . . *Am.* xxx. 10
Member. (Lord!) how she in everie *member* shooke, ... *Mui.* 285
with that suddein horror could no *member* move. . . . . I. ii. 31. 9
eger greedinesse through every *member* thrild. . . . . I. viii. 6. 9
She softely felt if any *member* moov'd, ... III. i. 60. 7
every *member* of his body quooke. . . . . III. x. 24. 5
made ech *member* quake, and manly hart to quayle. . . . . IV. vi. 22. 9
Members. life out of his *members* did depart: . . . . *Gn.* 293
his *members* chast Scattered on every mountaine . . . . I. v. 38. 7
so deepe wound through these deare *members* drive. . . . . III. iv. 37. 4
if life Yett in his frosen *members* did remaine; . . . . III. v. 31. 2
hart . . . rules the *members* as it selfe doth please? . . . . *Am.* l. 8
Memorable. *memorable* gestes Of famous Wisards, ... II. ix. 53. 3
of his name and *memorable* gest . . . . II. x. 12. 4
to enroll thy *memorable* name . . . . III. viii. 43. 4
Memorial. yet remaines his wide *memoriall.* . . . . II. x. 76. 3
Memories. Their *memories,* their singings, and their gifts. . . *Hub.* 454
out of dust their *memories* awake? . . . . *T.M.* 450
To make their *memories* for ever live; . . . . *Ti.* 412
Memories'. for their *memories* long moniment: . . . . *Hub.* 1182
Memorize. might their names for ever *memorize.* . . . . *Ti.* 364
In vain I thinke . . . to *memorize* thy name, ... *Ded. Son.* xii. 2
Memorized. the auncestrie Of th' old Heroes *memorizde* anew; . . . . *T.M.* 440
Memory. wounds my soule with rufull *memorie,* . . . . *Pet.*[2] iv. 13
The great Colosse, erect to *Memorie;* . . . . *Ro.* ii. 10
the more taugment The *memory* of hys misdeede . . . . *S.C.* Au. 186
Thereof nought remaynes but the *memoree;* . . . . *S.C.* N. 121
nor *memorie* is to be showne: . . . . *Gn.* 590
Of which there now remaines no *memorie,* . . . . *Ti.* 4
Whose *memorie* is quite worne out with yeares, ... *Ti.* 67
they be daughters of Dame *Memorie* . . . . *Ti.* 368
Enclosde therein for endles *memorie* Of him, ... *Ti.* 662
for *memorie* Of her pretended crime, ... *Mui.* 142
When as ye heare her *memory* renewed, ... *Col.* 645
make more famous *memory* Of thine Heroike parts, ... *Ded. Son.* ii. 1
And eke thine owne long living *memory,* . . . . *Ded. Son.* iii. 8
The record of enduring *memory.* . . . . *Ded. Son.* xi. 12
he gan revive the *memory* Of his leud lusts, ... I. vi. 46. 2
he of rope or armes has now no *memoree.* . . . . I. ix. 22. 9
for endlesse *memory* Of that deare Lord . . . . I. x. 54. 3
O mournfull *memory!* . . . . I. xi. 47. 8
forgery, Rather then matter of just *memory;* . . . . II. Pr. 1. 5
revive Fresh *memory* in me of that great Queene, ... II. ii. 40. 2
for *memory* of that dayes ruth, ... II. iii. 2. 7
The third things past could keep in *memoree:* . . . . II. ix. 49. 3
inly tremble at the *memory* Of Brennus . . . . II. x. 40. 8
Yet lives his *memorie,* though carcas sleepe . . . . II. x. 43. 9
Left of his life most famous *memory,* . . . . II. x. 46. 2
O joyous *memorie* of happy time, ... II. x. 50. 5
of whom no *memorie* did stay: . . . . II. xii. 20. 4
ne maken *memoree* Of their brave gestes . . . . III. ii. 1. 5
Daughter of Phoebus and of *Memorye,* . . . . III. iii. 4. 2
the sleeping *memoree* Of those same antique Peres, ... III. iii. 22. 7
for *memory* Of his late puissaunce, ... III. iii. 29. 1
that field, for endlesse *memory,* Shall Hevenfield be cald . . III. iii. 38. 8
quite from off the earth their *memory* be raste?' . . . . III. iii. 43. 9
Ne of thy late life *memory* is lefte, ... III. iv. 36. 8
For *memorie* of which on high there hong The golden Apple, IV. i. 22. 4
Are washt away quite from their *memorie.* . . . . IV. iii. 44. 7
endlesse *memorie* that mote excell, ... IV. xi. 9. 8
The noursling of Dame *Memorie* his deare, ... IV. xi. 10. 2
As to his *memory* they had recourse; . . . . V. ii. 2. 7
Nor *memory* thereof to any nation. . . . . V. ii. 28. 5
So farre past *memory* of man that may be knowne? . . . . VII. vii. 2. 9
record the *memory* Of my loves conquest, ... *Am.* lxix. 6
Eftsoones he wypes quite out of *memory* . . . . *H.L.* 241
Mempricius. *See* **Memprise.**
Memprise. Next *Memprise,* as unworthy of that place; . . . . II. x. 21. 3
Men. *See* **Beadsmen, Craftsmen, Liegemen, Wise men, Young men.**
Sweetely sliding into the eyes of *men,* . . . . *Bel.*[1] i. 2
the bright abode Of God and *men.* . . . . *Rev.* iv. 6
Gods and *men* my honour up did raise? . . . . *Bel.*[2] x. 8
mortall *men* tossed by troublous fate . . . . *Pet.*[2] vii. 3
that which Rome *men* call. . . . . *Ro.* iii. 4
Out of the earth engendred *men* of armes . . . . *Ro.* x. 3
Nor wrath of Gods, nor spight of *men* unstable, ... *Ro.* xiii. 7
As *men* in Summer fearles passe the foord . . . . *Ro.* xiv. 1
A little fish, that *men* called Remora, ... *Van.* ix. 10
Why do vaine *men* mean things so much deface, ... *Van.* xi. 12
we tway bene *men* of elder witt. . . . . *S.C.* May 18
live ylike as *men* of the laye. . . . . *S.C.* May 76
Sike mister *men* bene all misgone, ... *S.C.* Jul. 201
In forrein costes *men* sayd was plentye; . . . . *S.C.* S. 28
cannot wel ken . . . from other *men:* . . . . *S.C.* S. 43
Their ill haviour garres *men* missay . . . . *S.C.* S. 106
We bene of fleshe, *men* as other bee, ... *S.C.* S. 238
mortal *men,* that swincke and sweate for nought, ... *S.C.* N. 154
'Unwise and wretched *men,* . . . . *S.C.* N. 183
joyes enjoyes that mortall *men* doe misse. . . . . *S.C.* N. 196
reigned (as *men* sayd) in Venus seate. . . . . *S.C.* D. 60
good *men,* of whom thou oft are blest; . . . . *Gn.* 62
rend the greedie mindes of covetous *men,* . . . . *Gn.* 95

Men—*Continued.*
fond *men* doe all their dayes turmoyle. . . . . *Gn.* 152
Wicked for holding guilefully away Ulysses *men,* . . . . *Gn.* 195
before That Ceres seede of mortall *men* were knowne, ... *Gn.* 207
a wicked maladie Raign'd emongst *men,* . . . . *Hub.* 10
the condition of mortall *men.* . . . . *Hub.* 150
Like two free *men,* . . . . *Hub.* 160
Free *men* some beggers call, but they be free, ... *Hub.* 161
all *men* would them wyte: . . . . *Hub.* 348
when *men* of good deserving . . . . *Hub.* 369
How manie honest *men* see ye arize . . . . *Hub.* 419
all *men,* which anie master serve, ... *Hub.* 467
That *men* may thinke of you in generall, ... *Hub.* 647
To heare the Javell so good *men* to nip; . . . . *Hub.* 712
eke of private *men* somewhile, ... *Hub.* 787
simple *men,* which never came in place Of worlds affaires, *Hub.* 834
Thereby to coosin *men* not well aware: . . . . *Hub.* 874
all *men* him uncased gan deride, ... *Hub.* 930
Whose part once past all *men* bid take away: . . . . *Hub.* 932
Of *men* of armes he had but small regard, ... *Hub.* 1189
men of learning little he esteemed; . . . . *Hub.* 1191
men to God thereby are nighest raised. . . . . *T.M.* 90
Whie then doo foolish *men* so much despize . . . . *T.M.* 145
men depriv'd of sense and minde. . . . . *T.M.* 156
They in the mindes of *men* now tyrannize, ... *T.M.* 191
Scorning the boldnes of such base-borne *men,* . . . . *T.M.* 219
In th' hearts of *men* to rule them carefully, ... *T.M.* 314
good *men* blame, and losels magnify. . . . . *T.M.* 324
mortall *men* have powre to deifie: . . . . *T.M.* 460
Starres conspiring wretched *men* t' afflict, ... *T.M.* 482
ignorance . . . mindes of *men* borne heavenlie doth debace. *T.M.* 498
mercie more than mortall *men* can vew. . . . . *T.M.* 514
To make *men* heavenly wise . . . . *T.M.* 522
Thence I behold the miserie of *men,* . . . . *T.M.* 529
Harvey, the happy above happiest *men* . . . . *Com. Son.* i. 1
faulty *men,* which daunger to thee threat: . . . . *Com. Son.* i. 8
draw the dayes of *men* forth in extent; . . . . *Ti.* 18
'O! trustlesse state of miserable *men,* . . . . *Ti.* 197
evill *men,* now dead, his deeds upbraid: . . . . *Ti.* 214
Muses . . .unto *men* eternitie do give; . . . . *Ti.* 367
do those *men* in golden thrones repose, ... *Ti.* 370
thoughts of *men* do as themselves decay; . . . . *Ti.* 401
Admir'd of base-borne *men* from farre away: . . . . *Ti.* 424
men of armes doo wander unrewarded. . . . . *Ti.* 441
Such rancour in the harts of mightie *men?* . . . . *Mui.* 16
the miserie In which *men* live, ... *D.* 37
grace, That *men* admire in goodlie womankinde, ... *D.* 212
heavenly spirits have compassion On mortall *men,* . . . . *D.* 385
'I hate all *men,* and shun all womankinde; . . . . *D.* 421
calls foorth *men* unto their toylsome trade, ... *D.* 485
'And ye fond *men!* on fortunes wheele that ride, ... *D.* 498
As *men* use most to covet forreine thing.' . . . . *Col.* 162
Bold *men,* presuming life for gaine to sell, ... *Col.* 209
other *men* and beasts and birds doth feed: . . . . *Col.* 297
gracelesse *men* them greatly do abuse.' . . . . *Col.* 327
fill with stones, that all *men* may it know . . . . *Col.* 635
mustring all his *men* in Venus vew, ... *Col.* 769
us fraile *men,* his wretched vassals here, ... *Col.* 813
'this is no place for living *men.*' . . . . I. i. 13. 9
Whither the soules doe fly of *men* that live amis. . . . . I. ii. 19. 9
Both which fraile *men* doe oftentimes mistake, ... I. ii. 32. 7
Saints . . . He did disrobe, when all *men* carelesse slept, . . I. iii. 17. 6
proud Lucifera *men* did her call, ... I. iv. 12. 1
pain Of that foule evill, which all *men* reprove, ... I. iv. 26. 7
underneath their feet, all scattered lay . . . bones of *men* . I. iv. 36. 9
Coverd with charmed cloud from . . . sight of *men,* . . . . I. v. 29. 5
damned sprights sent forth to make ill *men* aghast. . . . . I. v. 31. 9
Amongst these mightie *men* were wemen mixt, ... I. v. 50. 1
many corses . . . Of murdred *men,* . . . . I. v. 53. 3
Emongst wild beastes and woods, from lawes of *men* exilde. I. vi. 23. 9
for to make her dreaded more of *men,* . . . . I. vii. 16. 6
Men into stones therewith he could transmew, ... I. vii. 35. 6
Unlike to *men,* who ever as they trace, ... I. viii. 31. 5
blisse may not abide in state of mortall *men.* . . . . I. viii. 44. 9
Dame Caelia *men* did her call, ... I. x. 4. 1
O foolish *men!* why hast ye to your own decay?' . . . . I. x. 10. 9
great hostes of *men* she could dismay; . . . . I. x. 20. 4
wrath . . . That drew on *men* Gods hatred . . . . I. x. 33. 6
Ne ought the powre of mighty *men* did dread . . . . I. x. 43. 5
wretched *men,* and lived in like paine.' . . . . I. x. 62. 4
Such, *men* do Chaungelings call, ... I. x. 65. 9
Such is the state of *men:* . . . . II. ii. 2. 8
O miserable *men* that to him subject arre! . . . . II. ii. 26. 9
men, beholding so great excellence . . . . II. ii. 41. 6
He gan to hope of *men* to be receiv'd . . . . II. iii. 5. 5
whom Cymochles *men* did call. . . . . II. v. 25. 9
doe *men* in bale to sterve, ... II. vi. 34. 3
For which *men* swinck and sweat incessantly, ... II. vii. 8. 7
charmes, With which weake *men* thou witchest, ... II. vii. 10. 4
'Are mortall *men* so fond and undiscreet . . . . II. vii. 14. 7
Frayle *men* are oft captiv'd to covetise; . . . . II. vii. 15. 2
the end, To which al *men* doe ayme, ... II. vii. 32. 8
Far passing th' hight of *men* terrestriall, ... II. vii. 41. 5
More fitt emongst black fiendes then *men* to have his place. II. vii. 41. 9
that all *men* might it see: . . . . II. vii. 45. 3
blis, For which ye *men* doe strive; . . . . II. vii. 48. 9
earth out of her fruitfull woomb Throwes forth to *men,* . . II. vii. 51. 7
three dayes of *men* were full outwrought, ... II. vii. 65. 6
more wretched were the cace Of *men* then beasts. . . . . II. viii. 1. 5
why should hevenly God to *men* have such regard? . . . . II. viii. 2. 9

Men—*Continued.*
all earthes glorie, on which *men* do gaze, ... *H.H.L.* 275
The hearts of *men*, . . . may lift themselves up hyer, . . . *H.H.B.* 16
The house of blessed God, which *men* call Skye, ... *H.H.B.* 52
to God . . . even the thoughts of *men*, do plaine appeare; . . *H.H.B.* 173
inflame The hearts of *men* with selfe-consuming fyre . . . . *H.H.B.* 275
Menace. fiercely did *menace:* . . . . II. iii. 42. 8
With whose reproch, and odious *menace*, ... II. iv. 9. 5
Menaced. The antique pride which *menaced* the skie, ... *Ro.* xxvii. 2
menaced me from the field to beat, ... VI. i. 40. 5
Unto a straunge mischaunce that *menac'd* her decay. . . . . VI. viii. 34. 9
Menage, *etc. See* **Manage,** *etc.*
Menalcas. *Menalcas,* that by trecheree Didst underfong my lasse . . . . *S.C.* Jun. 102
Mend. To seeke my fortune, where I may it *mend:* . . . . . *Hub.* 88
let him *mend,* If ought amis . . . . III. Pr. 5. 3
His speares default to *mend* with cruell blade; . . . . III. i. 10. 3
Faynd to alight, something amisse to *mend;* . . . . III. x. 38. 6
she gins to *mend* her pace, ... IV. vii. 22. 6
on her waited things amisse to *mend,* . . . . IV. xi. 47. 3
griev'd her more that she it could not *mend:* . . . . IV. xii. 21. 8
Sith otherwise he could not *mend* thing past; . . . . VI. xi. 34. 7
she may it *mend* with skill: . . . . *Am.* xli. 3
Mended. Let none mislike of that may not be *mended:* . . . *S.C.* May 162
Mends. All wrongs have *mendes*, but no amendes of shame. . II. i. 20. 5
Menevia. In the last field before *Menevia,* . . . . III. iii. 55. 3
Menged. His brackish waves be *meynt.* . . . . *S.C.* Jul. 84
how bene thy verses *meint* With doleful pleasaunce, ... *S.C.* N. 203
They now amongst the woods and thickets *ment,* . . . . . . *Gn.* 75
Where that false couple were full closely *ment* . . . . . . I. ii. 5. 4
When she with Mars was *meynt* in joyfulnesse: . . . . III. xi. 36. 5
bath'd in bloud and sweat together *ment;* . . . . V. v. 12. 5
To fight with many foes about him *ment,* . . . . VI. vi. 27. 5
Menippe. *Menippe* true in trust, ... IV. xi. 51. 8
Men's. *See* **Wise men's, Young men's.**
From heavens hight into *mens* heavy eyes, ... *Bel.*² i. 2
Sike *mens* follie I cannot compare . . . . *S.C.* May 95
it *mens* follies mote be forst to fayne, ... *S.C.* O. 75
sad cares that rich *mens* hearts devowre. . . . . *Gn.* 136
The chaungfull turning of *mens* slipperie state, ... *Gn.* 554
the charge is wondrous great, To feede *mens* soules . . . . *Hub.* 432
'To feede *mens* soules . . . is not in man; . . . . *Hub.* 433
all *mens* states alike unstedfast be. . . . . *D.* 518
all *mens* hearts . . . He stole away, ... *As.* 21
much more that does from *mens* knowledge lurke. . . . . . . *Col.* 295
partes, So lively and so like in all *mens* sight, ... I. i. 45. 4
'To have before bewitched all *mens* sight: . . . . I. ii. 39. 3
In secrete shadow, far from all *mens* sight: . . . . I. iii. 4. 4
Wont to robbe . . . poor *mens* boxes of their due reliefe, . . I. iii. 17. 3
Her glorious glitterand light doth all *mens* eies amaze. . . . I. iv. 16. 9
in all *mens* open vew Duessa placed is, ... I. v. 5. 6
First made by him *mens* wandring wayes to guyde, ... I. vii. 23. 2
th' eternall might, That rules *mens* waies, ... I. ix. 6. 9
three *mens* strength unto the stroake he layd; . . . . I. xi. 20. 4
To see sad pageaunts of *mens* miseries, ... II. i. 36. 3
Like Angels life was then *mens* happy cace; . . . . II. vii. 16. 5
dead *mens* bones, which round about were flong; . . . . . . II. vii. 30. 7
they encombred all *mens* eares and eyes; . . . . II. ix. 51. 3
all *mens* harts in dew obedience held; . . . . II. x. 32. 5
So th' other did *mens* rash desires apall, ... III. i. 46. 4
From all *mens* vew, that none might her discoure, ... III. ii. 20. 4
Yet ought *mens* good endevours them confirme, ... III. iii. 25. 8
for wretched *mens* reliefe make way; . . . . III. v. 27. 2
In a fresh fountaine, far from all *mens* vew, ... III. vi. 6. 6
in close bowre her mewes from all *mens* sight, ... III. ix. 5. 8
the Geaunts broode . . . dronck *mens* vitall blood. . . . . III. ix. 49. 9
free from all *mens* reclame; . . . . III. x. 16. 5
hast thou, Lord, of good *mens* cause no heed? . . . . III. xi. 9. 6
downe he fell as dead in all *mens* sight; . . . . IV. iii. 30. 5
all *mens* eyes and hearts . . . filled were . . . . IV. iii. 37. 3
His wondrous worth declared in all *mens* view, ... IV. iv. 37. 5
Cambell victour was in all *mens* sight, ... IV. v. 7. 8
Florimell her selfe in all *mens* vew She seem'd to passe: . . IV. v. 15. 8
out of all *mens* knowledge he was worne at last. . . . . . . IV. vii. 41. 9
all *mens* eares possest, ... IV. x. 4. 2
womens powre, that boast of *mens* subjection? . . . . V. iv. 26. 5
them restoring To *mens* subjection, ... V. vii. 42. 7
He caused them to be hung in all *mens* sight, ... V. viii. 45. 2
deadly daunger seem'd in all *mens* sight To tempt . . . . . V. ix. 15. 6
all she sought was *mens* good name to have bereaved. . . . V. xii. 33. 9
did steale *mens* hearts away: . . . . VI. i. 2. 6
The which in all *mens* liking gayned place, ... VI. i. 3. 4
earely light To guide *mens* labours, ... VI. v. 40. 3
That mucky masse, the cause of *mens* decay, ... VI. ix. 33. 5
doth play Her cruell sports to many *mens* decay? . . . . . VII. vi. 1. 5
That is the highest head (in all *mens* sights) . . . . VII. vi. 36. 7
dy As thralls and vassals unto *mens* beheasts; . . . . VII. vii. 19. 3
to amaze weak *mens* confused skil, ... *Am.* xvii. 2
mens frayle eyes, which gaze too bold, ... *Am.* xxxvii. 5
more sharply sighted bee Then other *mens,* . . . . *H.B.* 233
in *mens* harts thou mayst thy throne enstall, ... *H.B.* 265
Ment. *See* **Menged.**
Mention. If none of neither *mention* should make, ... *T.M.* 449
When Scudamour heard *mention* of that speare, ... IV. vi. 7. 1
of her this *mention* may be made!' . . . . VI. x. 28. 9
Ne any *mention* shall thereof remaine, ... *Am.* xxvii. 10
Mentioned. Unles they *mentiond* be with infamie. . . . . . *Ti.* 350
Regions . . . Which to late age were never *mentioned.* . . . . II. Pr. 2. 5
As it in antique bookes is *mentioned.* . . . . III. vi. 6. 3
She much was cheard to heare him *mentiond,* . . . . III. xii. 41. 1
Mentioneth. Nor anie lives that *mentioneth* my name . . . . *Ti.* 164
Merchandise. she saw the *merchaundise* . . . . *S.C.* May 298
Laden from far with precious *merchandize,* . . . . II. xii. 19. 2
by adventrous *marchandize* to thrive, ... VI. viii. 35. 7
nothing meet in *merchandize* to passe: . . . . VI. xi. 12. 8
With pretious *merchandize* she forth doth lay; . . . . *Am.* lxxxi. 6
Merchant. Now like a *Merchant,* Merchants to deceave, . . . *Hub.* 863
the glad *marchant,* that does vew from ground His ship . . . I. iii. 32. 3
Merchants. Now like a Merchant, *Merchants* to deceave, . . . *Hub.* 863
sought Of *merchants* farre . . . . II. x. 5. 7
mariners and *merchants* with much toyle . . . . II. xii. 19. 6
For slaves to sell them for no small reward To *Merchants,* . . VI. x. 43. 5
a sort of *merchants* . . . Arrived in this Isle, ... VI. xi. 9. 2
how those *marchants* were Arriv'd in place . . . . VI. xi. 10. 1
how faire Pastorell should have bene sold To *marchants,* . . . VI. xi. 30. 7
Ye tradefull *Merchants,* that, with weary toyle, ... *Am.* xv. 1
Merchants'. Shut up her haven, mard her *marchants* trade, . V. x. 25. 6
All which he to the *marchants* sale did showe: . . . . VI. xi. 11. 4
These *marchants* fixed eyes did so amaze, ... VI. xi. 13. 6
Tell me, ye *merchants* daughters, ... *Epith.* 167
Merciable. He is so meeke, wise, and *merciable,* . . . . . . *S.C.* S. 174
Mercian, -s. *See* **Mertian, -s.**
Mercies. In heavenly *mercies* hast thou not a part? . . . . . I. ix. 53. 4
Far reach her *mercies,* and her praises farre, ... II. ix. 4. 8
even to her foes her *mercies* multiply. . . . . V. viii. 17. 9
Royall examples of her *mercies* rare . . . . V. x. 5. 6
read, through love, his *mercies* manifold. . . . . *H.H.L.* 224
Mercified. Whilest she did weepe, of no man *mercifide:* . . . VI. vii. 32. 5
Merciful. Because to man so *mercifull* he was, ... IV. i. 30. 3
him, . . . With *mercifull* regard give mercy too. . . . . . . *Am.* xlix. 12
Merciless. Mow'd downe themselves with slaughter *mercilesse;* *Ro.* x. 12
No nurse, but Stepdame, cruell, *mercilesse.* . . . . *D.* 342
They were . . . Condemned to that Dongeon *mercilesse,* . . . I. v. 46. 8
strooke so maynly *mercilesse,* . . . . I. vii. 12. 1
with mighty mall The monster *mercilesse* him made to fall, . I. vii. 51. 5
his mother *mercilesse,* Most *mercilesse* of women, ... II. x. 35. 6, 7
To shew the victors might and *mercilesse* intent. . . . . . . III. xi. 52. 9
When as he saw the *mercilesse* affray . . . . IV. iv. 22. 4
all dismayd through *mercilesse* despaire . . . . IV. viii. 51. 7
In which so long he *mercilesse* did lie. . . . . IV. viii. 64. 5
like tyrants *mercilesse,* the more Rejoyced . . . . V. iv. 23. 1
more increast her outrage *mercilesse,* . . . . V. v. 14. 7
Mercilla. 'Her name *Mercilla* most men use to call . . . . . V. viii. 17. 1
Which she against the dred *Mercilla* oft did frame. . . . . . V. ix. 40. 9
how for to depryve *Mercilla* of her crowne, ... V. ix. 41. 7
Unto *Mercilla* myld, for Justice gainst the thrall. . . . . . . V. ix. 49. 9
Who then can thee, *Mercilla,* throughly prayse, ... V. x. 3. 1
unto gratious great *Mercilla* call For ayde . . . . V. x. 14. 3
having left *Mercilla,* streight way went . . . . V. xi. 36. 2
Mercilla's. Those did upon *Mercillaes* throne attend, ... V. ix. 32. 5
Mercury. he *Mercurie* unto him cal'd, ... *Hub.* 1246
'Arise, (said *Mercurie*) . . . . *Hub.* 1327
At last me seem'd wing-footed *Mercurie,* . . . . *Ti.* 666
Caduceus, the rod of *Mercury,* . . . . II. xii. 41. 3
The same she tempred with fine *Mercury* . . . . III. viii. 6. 6
chiefely *Mercury,* that next doth raigne, ... VII. vi. 14. 8
Mercury; who though he lesse appeare To change . . . . . . VII. vii. 51. 1
Mercy. Of *mercye* and favour, then, I you pray . . . . . . *S.C.* May 272
mercie more than mortall men can vew. . . . . *T.M.* 514
To see thee, and thy *mercie* measurelesse! . . . . *T.M.* 516
Him to the *mercy* of th' avenger lent. . . . . *Mui.* 432
Her power, her *mercy,* her wisdome, ... *Col.* 346
'Mercy, mercy, Sir, vouchsafe to show On silly Dame, ... I. ii. 21. 2
doth vanquisht stand Now at thy *mercy: Mercy* not withstand; . . . . I. iii. 37. 5
Her name was *Mercy;* . . . . I. x. 34. 4
Mercy in the end his righteous soule might save. . . . . . . I. x. 34. 9
Mercie, that his steps upbare And alwaies led, ... I. x. 44. 4
cryde, *'Mercie,* Sir Knight! and *mercie,* Lord, ... II. i. 27. 1
in her face faire peace and *mercy* doth appeare. . . . . II. ii. 40. 9
Throughout the world her *mercy* to maintaine, ... II. ii. 43. 7
crying, *'Mercy!'* loud, ... II. iii. 6. 9
doe for *mercy* call. II. iii. 8. 4
he cryde; *'Mercy!* doe me not dye, ... II. v. 12. 7
sith in might thou didst my *mercie* prove, ... II. v. 16. 7
Great *mercy,* sure, for to enlarge a thrall, ... II. v. 18. 3
all his workes with *mercy* doth embrace, ... II. viii. 1. 7
Will not long misery late *mercy* make, ... III. iii. 43. 7
'Mercy, deare Lord!' (said he) 'what grace is this . . . . . III. v. 35. 1
With which her soverain *mercy* thou dost quight? . . . . . . III. v. 45. 2
misery craves rather *mercy* then repriefe. . . . . III. viii. 1. 9
but if she *Mercie* would him give, ... III. x. 7. 8
for *mercy* or for meed, To save his life, ... III. x. 50. 7
to her *mercie* him submitted in plaine field. . . . . V. v. 16. 9
more my gratious *mercie* by this wise, ... V. v. 48. 7
this heavenly thing whereof I treat, To weeten *Mercie,* . . . V. x. 1. 3
thine owne people do thy *mercy* prayse much more. . . . . . . V. x. 3. 9
'Ah *mercie,* Sir! doe me not slay, ... VI. i. 39. 8
'Who will not *mercie* unto others shew, ... VI. i. 42. 1
How can he *mercy* ever hope to have? . . . . VI. i. 42. 2
since ye *mercie* now doe need to crave, ... VI. i. 42. 4
Cryde out aloud for *mercie,* . . . . VI. vii. 12. 2
with silence *mercie* prayd. . . . . VI. vii. 25. 9
Cryde *mercie,* to abate the extremitie of law. . . . . VI. vii. 36. 9
Then know that *mercy* is the Mighties jewell: . . . . *Am.* xlix. 3
him, . . . With mercifull regard give *mercy* too. . . . . . . *Am.* xlix. 12
Such *mercy* shall you make admyr'd to be; . . . . *Am.* xlix. 13
then no *mercy* will unto me shew. . . . . *Am.* liii. 8
But *mercy* doth with beautie best agree, ... *Am.* liii. 13
Be lyke in *mercy* as in all the rest. . . . . *Am.* lv. 14

Mercy—*Continued.*
To tell the marveiles by thy *mercie* wrought. . . . . *H.H.L.* 49
Such *mercy* he by his most holy reede . . . . *H.H.L.* 211
Shewing us *mercie* (miserable crew!) . . . . *H.H.L.* 214
And to his soveraine *mercie* doe appeale; . . . . *H.H.L.* 257
His grace, his doome, his *mercy*, and his might, ... *H.H.B.* 111
Mercy-seat. But lowly fall before his *mercie seate*, ... *H.H.B.* 148
Merdin. *See* **Cairmardin.**
Mere. made one *meare* of th' earth and of their raine? . . . *Ti.* 63
chose in Faery court, of *meere* goodwil, ... I. iii. 28. 5
trust unto his strength and manhood *meare*, ... II. xi. 34. 3
Holding a staffe in hand for *mere* formalitee. . . . . II. xii. 48. 9
My heart doth melt with *meere* compassion, ... III. viii. 1. 2
Hygate made the *meare* thereof by West, ... III. ix. 46. 2
meriting a *meere* triumphant seate. *Com.Son.*iii.12
which him at first Made of *meere* love, ... *H.H.L.* 128
Mered. Which *mear'd* her rule with Africa, and Byze. . . . . *Ro.* xxii. 2
Meres. Ne in small *meares* containe his glory great, ... III. ix. 46. 8
Meriflure. In thy sweete Eglantine of *Meriflure;* . . . . *Col.* 389
Merit. which her famous *merite* . . . out of the dust doth reare, *Ro.* v. 12
I therein most like to him doo *merite*, ... *Hub.* 1044
raised they the puissant brood . . . for great *merite*, ... *Ti.* 380
doth not *merit* The name of love, ... *Col.* 891
whose vertues . . . *merit* a most famous Poets witt . . . . *Ded. Son.* ii. 2
And for your owne high *merit* in like cace: . . . . *Ded. Son.* xi. 7
Had not Mecaenas, for his worthy *merit*, ... *Ded. Son.* xiii. 3
Which now triumpheth, through immortall *merit* . . . . *Ded. Son.* xv. 3
steale from thee the meede of thy due *merit*, ... IV. ii. 34. 3
thy juster *merit* Might else have with felicitie bene crowned: V. v. 36. 6
for the guerdon of theyr glorious *merit*, ... *Epith.* 421
Through meditation of his endlesse *merit*, ... *H.H.L.* 255
Meriteth. *meriteth* to have as high a place, ... V. x. 1. 6
meriteth indeede an higher name: . . . . VI. Pr. 6. 8
Meriting. she . . . nor in word nor deede ill *meriting*, ... I. iii. 2. 7
meriting a meere triumphant seate *Com.Son.*iii.12
Merits. Whose *merits* they to glorifie do chose. . . . . *Ti.* 371
all things see With equall eye, their *merites* to restore, . . . I. viii. 27. 7
he should dye who *merites* not to live? . . . . I. ix. 38. 4
All vertue *merits* praise, ... II. iii. 37. 9
she may thee advance for works and *merits* just.' . . . . II. vii. 49. 9
all the antique Worthies *merits* far did passe. . . . . III. ix. 50. 9
For their high *merits* and great dignitie, ... IV. iii. 44. 4
Merlin. that, which *Merlin* by his magicke slights Made . . . *Ti.* 523
It *Merlin* was, which whylome did excell All living wightes . I. vii. 36. 4
'Thither the great magicien *Merlin* came, ... I. ix. 5. 1
Merlin made by his almightie art . . . . II. viii. 20. 2
The great Magitien *Merlin* had deviz'd, ... III. ii. 18. 6
Such was the glassy globe that *Merlin* made, ... III. ii. 21. 1
Merlin bewrayes to Britomart The state of Arthegall; . . . III. iii. Arg.
the learned *Merlin*, well could tell . . . . III. iii. 6. 4
There the wise *Merlin* whylome wont . . . To make his wonne, III. iii. 7. 5
A litle whyle Before that *Merlin* dyde, ... III. iii. 10. 2
For *Merlin* had in Magick more insight . . . . III. iii. 11. 8
vauntage made of that which *Merlin* had ared; . . . . III. iii. 20. 9
Then *Merlin* thus: 'Indeede the fates are firme, ... III. iii. 25. 6
There *Merlin* stayd, As overcomen . . . . III. iii. 50. 1
as *Merlin* them directed late: . . . . III. iii. 62. 2
Through hope of those, which *Merlin* had her told . . . . III. iv. 11. 6
Mermaid's. accords more sweete than *Mermaids* song: . . . . *Bel.* xii. 8
Mermaids. Where many *Mermayds* haunt . . . . II. xii. 17. 9
the sted Whereas those *Mermayds* dwelt: . . . . II. xii. 30. 2
Merrier. How falles it, then, we no *merrier* bene, ... *S.C.* May 3
Merrily. full *merrilie* to pipe and daunce, ... *D.* 55
Merily masking both in bowre and hall. . . . . *As.* 28
His chearfull whistle *merily* doth sound, ... I. iii. 31. 8
At which they all gan laugh full *merrily:* . . . . IV. iv. 10. 3
All gan to jest and jibe full *merilie* . . . . V. iii. 39. 4
There he a troupe of Ladies dauncing found Full *merrily*, . VI. x. 10. 8
That made him pipe so *merrily*, as never none. . . . . VI. x. 15. 9
Merriment. Hys pleasaunt Pipe, whych made us *meriment*, . . *S.C.* Ap. 14
singen soote, In their *meriment*. . . . . *S.C.* Ap. 112
In lustihede and wanton *meryment*. . . . . *S.C.* May 42
so hath raft us of our *meriment*. . . . . *S.C.* Au. 14
Accorde not with thy Muses *meriment*, ... *S.C.* N. 34
all joy and jolly *meriment* Is also deaded, ... *T.M.* 209
he himselfe seemed made for *meriment*, ... *As.* 27
their cause of *meriment*, ... *Col.* 30
In haste forsooke their rurall *meriment*, ... I. vi. 8. 2
she beheld those maydens *meriment* . . . . I. xii. 8. 1
*Their wanton follies, and light *meriment;* . . . . II. v. 32. 6
That to her might move cause of *meriment:* . . . . II. vi. 3. 6
Some to make love, some to make *meryment*, ... III. i. 57. 2
Their goodly *meriment* and gay felicity. . . . . III. vi. 41. 9
Minstrales making goodly *meriment*, ... III. xii. 5. 4
to make you joyous *meriment?'* . . . . IV. ii. 5. 9
Making great feast and joyous *merriment*, ... V. xi. 35. 2
So goodly all agree . . . To this dayes *merriment*. . . . . *Epith.* 84
Merriments. Their wanton follies and light *meriments:* . . . II. v. 32. 6
Their wanton *meriments* they did encreace, ... II. xii. 68. 7
Merry. Through the maine sea making her *merry* flight . . . *Van.* ix. 4
Is not thilke the *mery* moneth of May, ... *S.C.* May 1
tell us *mery* tales to keepe us wake, ... *S.C.* Jun. 87
With *mery* thing its good to medle sadde. . . . . *S.C.* Au. 144
'Now leave, ye shepheards boyes, your *merry* glee; . . . . *S.C.* D. 139
As *merrie* notes upon his rusticke Fife, ... *Gn.* 148
to follow any *merrie* motion. . . . . *Hub.* 458
merie leasings tell, ... *Hub.* 699
When he is sad, shee seeks to make him *merie*, ... *T.M.* 137
make them *merrie* with their fooleries; . . . . *T.M.* 320
each making other *mery;* . . . . *Col.* 77

Merry—*Continued.*
'Now by my life this was a *mery* lay, ... *Col.* 157
they list not their *mery* pipes applie? . . . . *Col.* 373
ne wont there sound His *mery* oaten pipe, ... I. ii. 28. 9
all the way their *merry* pipes they sound. . . . . I. vi. 14. 1
Bacchus *merry* fruit they did invent, ... I. vi. 15. 2
Saint George of *mery England*, the signe of victoree.' . . . . I. x. 61. 9
With *mery* note her lowd salutes the mounting larke. . . . . I. xi. 51. 9
mery wynd and weather call her thence away. . . . . I. xii. 1. 9
Therein the *mery* birdes of every sorte . . . . II. v. 31. 6
Sometimes she laught, as *merry* as Pope Jone; . . . . II. vi. 3. 4
The *merry* mariner unto his word Soone hearkned, ... II. vi. 4. 5
greatly joyed *merry* tales to faine, ... II. vi. 6. 4
Her *mery* fitt shee freshly gan to reare, ... II. vi. 21. 2
The whiles the other Ladies mind theyr *mery* glee. . . . . II. viii. 6. 9
she in *merry* sort Them gan to bord, ... II. xii. 16. 1
up they gan their *mery* pypes to trusse, ... III. x. 46. 1
the *merry* birds, thy prety pages, ... IV. x. 45. 6
Ne ought on earth that *merry* is and glad, ... IV. x. 47. 3
To make them both as *merry* as he may. . . . . VI. iii. 9. 5
Somewhile with *merry* purpose, fit to please, ... VI. v. 32. 7
Were met to make their sports and *merrie* glee, ... VI. ix. 41. 2
the *merry* sound Of a shrill pipe he playing heard . . . . VI. x. 10. 2
piped there unto that *merry* rout; . . . . VI. x. 16. 2
Next faire Aglaia, last Thalia *merry;* . . . . VI. x. 22. 8
Then came October full of *merry* glee; . . . . VII. vii. 39. 1
merry feasting which he made . . . . VII. vii. 41. 2
The *merry* Cuckow, messenger of Spring, ... *Am.* xix. 1
The *merry* Larke hir mattins sings aloft; . . . . *Epith.* 80
Their *merry* Musick that resounds from far, ... *Epith.* 130
All night therefore attend your *merry* play, ... *Epith.* 368
made you *merie* oft when ye were sorie. . . . . *H.L.* 35
they all to *mery* London came, ... *Proth.* 127
To *mery* London, my most kyndly Nurse, ... *Proth.* 128
Merry-make. Such *merimake* holy Saints doth queme, ... *S.C.* May 15
now nis the time of *merimake*, ... *S.C.* N. 9
passe the bonds of modest *merimake*, ... II. vi. 21. 8
thy joyous dayes Here leadest in this goodly *merry-make*, . . . VI. x. 19. 3
Mertia. had to wife Dame *Mertia* the fayre, ... II. x. 42. 3
Mertian. Those yet of her be *Mertian* lawes both nam'd and thought. . . . . II. x. 42. 9
Mertians. make The warlike *Mertians* for feare to quake: . . III. iii. 30. 5
Merveil, -ed. *See* **Marvel, -led.**
Meseemed. At last *me seem'd* wing-footed Mercurie, ... *Ti.* 666
Me seemd I had his person seene elsewhere, ... *D.* 52
Me seemed, by my side a royall Mayd . . . . I. ix. 13. 7
sacrilege *me seem'd* the Church to rob, ... IV. x. 53. 3
Me seemd, I smelt a gardin . . . . *Am.* lxiv. 2
Strange thing, *me seemd*, to see a beast so wyld, ... *Am.* lxvii. 13
Meseemeth. Straunge thing, *me seemeth*, ... *Van.* ix. 13
Such myster saying *me seemeth* to mirke. . . . . *S.C.* S. 103
Meseems. all mans life *me seemes* a Tragedy, ... *T.M.* 157
most, *me seemes*, thy accent will excell . . . . *Col.* 426
thou hast forgot Thy selfe, *me seemes*, ... *Col.* 617
Me seemes I see Amintas wretched fate, ... III. vi. 45. 8
Certes, *me seemes*, bene not advised well; . . . . IV. ii. 24. 5
That well (*me seemes*) appeares, ... IV. iv. 2. 1
he, *me seemes*, most fit the faire to serve, ... IV. v. 1. 6
the band of vertuous mind, *Me seemes*, ... IV. ix. 1. 9
me seemes, this war ye wrongfully have wielded.' . . . . IV. ix. 37. 9
me seemes of double wrong ye plaine, ... IV. xii. 30. 2
Me seemes the world is runne quite out of square . . . . V. Pr. 1. 7
Instead of right *me seemes* great wrong dost shew, ... V. ii. 34. 3
'and right, *Me seemes*, that him befell . . . . VI. ii. 23. 6
Me seemes, that though she all unworthy were . . . . VII. viii. 1. 3
Mesprise. *See* **Misprize.**
Message. The subtile Foxe so well his *message* sayd, ... *Hub.* 1101
The one of them he gave a *message* . . . . I. i. 38. 8
Goe, guiltie ghost, to him my *message* make, ... I. v. 11. 3
Thyselfe thy *message* do to german deare; . . . . I. v. 13. 2
Abyde, till I have told the *message* which I have.' . . . . I. v. 21. 9
A Messenger with letters, which his *message* sayd. . . . . I. xii. 24. 9
'let that *message* to thy Lord be brought.' . . . . II. iv. 44. 9
Britomart would not such guilfull *message* know. . . . . III. i. 51. 9
To doe the *message* which I shall expresse. . . . . V. iv. 48. 5
Till they had told their *message* word by word: . . . . V. iv. 51. 3
To beare unto her love the *message* of her mind. . . . . V. vi. 7. 9
So me in *message* unto her she sent, ... V. viii. 21. 6
Which *message* when Grantorto heard, ... V. xii. 9. 5
The Dwarfe, which bore that *message* to her knight, ... VI. i. 31. 3
Declar'd the *message* which that Knight did move; . . . . VI. iii. 42. 2
His mindes sad *message* backe unto him sent; . . . . VI. viii. 8. 3
He from his Jove such *message* to her brought, ... VII. vi. 18. 6
To whom when Hermes had his *message* told, ... VII. vi. 19. 6
thogh she nought did reck Of Hermes *message*, ... VII. vi. 22. 8
And doth his ydle *message* set at nought. . . . . *Am.* xix. 12
To beare the *message* of her gentle spright. . . . . *Am.* lxxxi. 12
carrie privie *message* to the spright, ... *H.B.* 236
Messages. sent close *messages* of love to her at will. . . . . III. ix. 27. 9
When he them on his *messages* doth send, ... *H.H.L.* 67
Messenger. Which saw the *messenger* of tidings glad; . . . . *Bel.*² xiv. 3
since the *messenger* is come for mee, ... *D.* 267
When as her *messenger* doth come for me; . . . . *D.* 459
the sad humor . . . As *messenger* of Morpheus, ... I. i. 36. 3
The *Messenger* approching to him spake; . . . . I. i. 42. 1
The *messenger* of death, the ghastly owle, ... I. v. 30. 6
The *messenger* of so unhappie newes Would faine have dyde: I. vii. 21. 1
As it a ronning *messenger* had beene. . . . . I. ix. 51. 7
A *Messenger* with letters, which his message sayd. . . . . I. xii. 24. 9
she suborned hath This crafty *messenger* . . . . I. xii. 34. 2

Midst—*Continued.*
Right in the *middest* of the threshold lay, . . . V. x. 37. 4
new life to her lent in *midst* of deadly feare. . . . V. xii. 12. 9
They bene ymett in *middest* of the plaine . . . VI. i. 33. 5
Him overtooke in *middest* of his race; . . . VI. iii. 25. 5
in the *midst* a Shepheard piping he did see . . . VI. x. 10. 9
in the *midst* of them Three other Ladies . . . VI. x. 12. 2
in the *middest* of those same three . . . VI. x. 12. 6
she that in the *midst* of them did stand . . . VI. x. 14. 3
that faire one, That in the *midst* was placed paravaunt, . . . VI. x. 15. 7
those three in the *midst* doe chiefe on her attend. . . . VI. x. 21. 9
Midway. Met him *mid-way* with equall hardiment, . . . IV. iv. 28. 8
Midwives. The woods, the nymphes, my bowres, my *midwives,*
weare: . . . II. i. 53. 7
Mien. With all the evill termes and cruell *meane* . . . VI. vii. 39. 5
So farre the *meane* of shepheards to excell, . . . VI. ix. 11. 3
Mieve. *See* **Move.**
Might (*partial list of auxiliary*).
Then *might* I see upon a white horse . . . *Rev.* iii. 1
Heaven had not feare of that presumptuous *might,* . . . *Ro.* xvii. 3
rose to so great *might,* . . . *Ro.* xviii. 9
th' heaven it selfe, opposing gainst her *might,* . . . *Ro.* xviii. 11
So weakest may anoy the most of *might!* . . . *Van.* x. 14
the Romaine Empire . . . florisht most in *might,* . . . *Van.* xi. 2
in their *might* repose their most assurance, . . . *Van.* xi. 13
to aswage The ranckorous rigour of his *might,* . . . *S.C.* F. 185
shott at him with *might* and maine, . . . *S.C.* Mar. 86
They soone *myght* be corrupted, . . . *S.C.* Jul. 110
His musicks *might* the hellish hound did tame. . . . *S.C.* O. 30
Might I once come to thee, (O that I *might!*) . . . *S.C.* N. 181
mount Athos through exceeding *might* Was digged downe, . . *Gn.* 45
What God or Fortune would assist his *might.* . . . *Gn.* 301
defend . . . with his *might* and maine. . . . *Gn.* 524
through their *might* He lately slue his dreadfull foe . . . *Gn.* 647
Dooing my countrey service as I *might,* . . . *Hub.* 61
my late maymed limbs lack wonted *might* . . . *Hub.* 272
(*Might* it you please) would take on me . . . *Hub.* 290
Therefore *might* please you, . . . *Hub.* 409
loded them with lordships and with *might,* . . . *Hub.* 1156
His love, his truth, his glorie, and his *might,* . . . *T.M.* 513
with conquest of their *might* and maine, . . . *Ti.* 62
neither could the others greater *might* . . . endure; . . . *Mui.* 6
by her heavenly *might,* . . . *Mui.* 137
all the Gods, which saw his wondrous *might,* . . . *Mui.* 318
rushing with fierce *might* Out of his den, . . . *Mui.* 434
Launched his thigh with so mischievous *might,* . . . *As.* 119
me recomforting all that he *might,* . . . *Col.* 232
excellence Lifts me above the measure of my *might:* . . . *Col.* 621
So well thou wot'st the mysterie of his *might,* . . . *Col.* 833
man, that had the sparke of reasons *might* . . . *Col.* 867
All being made the vassalls of his *might,* . . . *Col.* 885
what . . . wanting rest, will also want of *might?* . . . I. i. 32. 7
all in rage to see his skilfull *might* Deluded so, . . . I. ii. 2. 5
he praisd his divelish arts, That had such *might* . . . I. ii. 9. 5
who can tell The . . . *might* of Magick spel? . . . I. ii. 10. 9
did besmeare My body all, through charmes and magicke *might,* I. ii. 42. 4
In charmes and magick to have wondrous *might,* . . . I. iii. 38. 8
his rage is more of *might* . . . I. iii. 43. 9
If from their loyall loves he *might* them move: . . . I. iv. 26. 5
coffers . . . With precious metall full as they *might* hold; . . . I. iv. 27. 4
Most wretched wight, whom nothing *might* suffise; . . . I. iv. 29. 1
upon eternall paine Of high displeasure that ensewen *might,* . I. iv. 40. 6
Fore-casting how his foe he *might* annoy; . . . I. iv. 45. 2
With greatest honour he atchieven *might:* . . . I. v. 1. 8
hewen helmets deepe shew marks of eithers *might.* . . . I. v. 7. 9
Let non abate the terrour of your *might,* . . . I. v. 14. 4
shew thy famous *might* In medicine, . . . I. v. 43. 7
He had . . . fild far landes with glorie of his *might:* . . . I. vi. 20. 6
In which his *might* was never overthrowne; . . . I. vi. 29. 8
How with that pensive Maid he best *might* thence arise. . . . I. vi. 32. 9
'Ah! dearest Lord,' (quoth she) 'how *might* that bee, . . . I. vi. 39. 1
'how *might* I see The thing . . . I. vi. 39. 3
The thing that *might* not be, and yet was donne?' . . . I. vi. 39. 4
through presumption of his matchlesse *might,* . . . I. vii. 10. 3
Yet *might* her pitteous hart be seene to pant . . . I. vii. 20. 9
all closely cover'd was, Ne *might* . . . be ever seene; . . . I. vii. 33. 2
No magicke arts hereof had any *might,* . . . I. vii. 35. 1
excell All living wightes in *might* of magicke spell: . . . I. vii. 36. 5
will to *might* gives greatest aid.' . . . I. vii. 41. 4
Dragon . . . With murdrous ravine, and devouring *might,* . . I. vii. 44. 4
ne ever by his *might* Had throwne to ground . . . I. vii. 47. 4
I him lov'd, and love with all my *might.* . . . I. vii. 49. 8
with his Squire, th' admirer of his *might,* . . . I. viii. 3. 1
Three miles it *might* be easy heard arownd, . . . I. viii. 4. 3
No . . . deceiptfull traine, *Might* once abide . . . I. viii. 4. 6
Ne shame he thought to shonne so hideous *might:* . . . I. viii. 8. 1
all that *might* his angry passage stay; . . . I. viii. 9. 8
Did fall to ground, depriv'd of native *might:* . . . I. viii. 10. 7
Enforst her purple beast with all her *might,* . . . I. viii. 13. 3
That strongest Oake *might* seeme to overthrow. . . . I. viii. 18. 6
yields it selfe unto the victours *might.* . . . I. viii. 23. 7
Then asked he, which way he in *might* pas? . . . I. viii. 33. 1
That greatest Princes presence *might* behold. . . . I. viii. 35. 4
wight Were housed therewithin, whom he enlargen *might.* . . I. viii. 37. 9
maister these mishaps with patient *might* . . . I. viii. 45. 2
Such as she was their eies *might* her behold, . . . I. viii. 46. 6
upbrought in gentle thewes and martiall *might.* . . . I. ix. 3. 9
The secret meaning of th' eternall *might,* . . . I. ix. 6. 8
who most trustes in arme of fleshly *might,* . . . I. ix. 11. 6
Nigh as he drew, they *might* perceive . . . I. ix. 22. 1

Might—*Continued.*
Till he these words to him deliver *might:* . . . I. ix. 23. 6
all that *might* him to perdition draw; . . . I. ix. 50. 7
What man is he, that boasts of fleshly *might* . . . I. x. 1. 1
She cast to bring him where he chearen *might,* . . . I. x. 2. 8
As *might* become a Squyre so great persons to greet. . . . I. x. 7. 9
of her heavenly learning he *might* taste, . . . I. x. 18. 5
Her wisely comforted all that she *might,* . . . I. x. 23. 4
added wordes of wondrous *might.* . . . I. x. 24. 6
ay thereof her babes *might* sucke their fill; . . . I. x. 30. 8
That hill they scale with all their powre and *might,* . . . I. x. 47. 7
As he thereon stood gazing, he *might* see . . . I. x. 56. 1
That . . . *might* I happily Unto you bring, . . . I. xi. 3. 8
fiersely ran at him with rigorous *might:* . . . I. xi. 16. 2
hardy fowle above his hable *might,* . . . I. xi. 19. 6
smot againe with more outrageous *might;* . . . I. xi. 25. 2
to prove his late-renewed *might,* . . . I. xi. 35. 5
By subtilty, nor slight, nor *might,* nor mighty charme. . . . I. xi. 36. 9
He smott thereat with all his *might* and maine, . . . I. xi. 43. 4
The paw yett missed not his minisht *might,* . . . I. xi. 43. 8
Balme, whose vertuous *might* Did heale his woundes, . . . I. xi. 50. 5
Ran through his mouth with so importune *might,* . . . I. xi. 53. 7
atchievde so great a conquest by his *might,* . . . I. xi. 55. 9
Too false and strong for earthly skill or *might,* . . . I. xii. 32. 7
deceave A gentle Lady, or her wrong through *might:* . . . II. i. 17. 8
Who made my hand the organ of his *might:* . . . II. i. 33. 3
with words, and weedes, of wondrous *might,* . . . II. i. 52. 3
Through strong opinion of his matchlesse *might;* . . . II. ii. 18. 6
in excesse exceeded her owne *might;* . . . II. ii. 36. 7
Might not be found a franker franion, . . . II. ii. 37. 4
To kindle oft assayd, but had no *might;* . . . II. iii. 23. 7
he was a man of mickle *might,* . . . II. iv. 7. 1
whom your victorious *might* Hath now fast bound, . . . II. iv. 32. 3
mortall hands may not withstand his *might,* . . . II. iv. 42. 2
shewest th' ensample of thy childishe *might,* . . . II. iv. 45. 4
maistring *might* on enimy dismayd; . . . II. v. 13. 3
Whose bounty more then *might,* yet both, he wondered. . . . II. v. 14. 9
sith in *might* thou didst my mercy prove, . . . II. v. 16. 7
him affronted with impatient *might:* . . . II. v. 20. 7
more thereby increased Furors *might,* . . . II. v. 22. 2
He was a man of rare redoubted *might,* . . . II. v. 26. 1
Unmindfull of thy praise and prowest *might,* . . . II. v. 36. 4
to weake wench did yield his martiall *might:* . . . II. vi. 8. 5
Sir Guyon, grudging not so much his *might* . . . II. vi. 30. 5
such is the *might* Of courteous clemency . . . II. vi. 36. 5
to remove the same I have no *might:* . . . II. vii. 50. 8
As overcome with too exceeding *might,* . . . II. vii. 66. 7
leave these relicks of his living *might* . . . II. viii. 16. 6
sure yt would deceive thy labor and thy *might.'* . . . II. viii. 21. 9
'Ye warlike payre, whose valorous great *might* . . . II. viii. 27. 2
great disparagment makes to his former *might.'* . . . II. viii. 29. 9
two foes of so exceeding *might,* . . . II. viii. 34. 4
nothing seemd mote beare so monstrous *might:* . . . II. viii. 38. 2
Assembling all his force and utmost *might,* . . . II. viii. 47. 3
suffred rash Pyrochles waste his ydle *might.* . . . II. viii. 48. 9
To serve that Queene with al my powre and *might.* . . . II. ix. 7. 4
Tall yeomen seemed they and of great *might,* . . . II. ix. 26. 4
readily they shut and open *might.* . . . II. ix. 46. 8
who can tell the prayses of that makers *might?* . . . II. ix. 46. 9
A labor huge, exceeding far my *might.* . . . II. x. 2. 7
unto him assembling forreigne *might,* . . . II. x. 35. 4
up arose a man of matchlesse *might,* . . . II. x. 37. 1
Androgeus and Tenantius, pictures of his *might.* . . . II. x. 46. 9
whiles good fortune favoured her *might,* . . . II. x. 56. 6
Constantius, a man of mickle *might,* . . . II. x. 59. 2
he his title justifide by *might,* . . . II. x. 60. 6
men of renowmed *might;* . . . II. x. 65. 3
Wounds without hurt, a body without *might,* . . . II. xi. 40. 5
after them did drive with all her power and *might.* . . . II. xii. 15. 9
wisedomes powre, and temperaunces *might,* . . . II. xii. 43. 6
Brydling his will and maystering his *might,* . . . II. xii. 53. 5
as over-maystered by *might,* . . . II. xii. 64. 3
for prayse, and proofe of manly *might,* . . . III. i. 13. 4
Fiers battaill against one with cruell *might* and mayne. . . . III. i. 20. 9
me enforce by oddes of *might* To chaunge my liefe, . . . III. i. 24. 2
trew love most of *might,* . . . III. i. 29. 8
Our faulty weakenes, and your matchlesse *might:* . . . III. i. 30. 2
by *might* That man to hard conditions to bind, . . . III. ii. 13. 6
comfortlesse through tyranny or *might:* . . . III. ii. 14. 8
By his deepe science and hell-dreaded *might,* . . . III. ii. 18. 7
May learned be by cyphers, or by Magicke *might.* . . . III. ii. 45. 9
if the passion mayster thy fraile *might,* . . . III. ii. 46. 6
over mortall mindes hast so great *might,* . . . III. iii. 2. 2
Through deepe impression of thy secret *might,* . . . III. iii. 2. 7
Then shall he issew forth with dreadfull *might* . . . III. iii. 29. 8
I read thee soone retyre, whiles thou hast *might,* . . . III. iv. 14. 8
Salves to his wounds, and medicines of *might;* . . . III. iv. 43. 8
The warlike Maide, th' ensample of that *might;* . . . III. iv. 44. 7
Out of that forest should escape their *might:* . . . III. v. 16. 8
drove at him with all his *might* and mayne . . . III. v. 21. 4
through conquest of your wondrous *might,* . . . III. v. 53. 4
a goodly Swaine, and of great *might,* . . . III. vii. 29. 4
him he held, and did through *might* amate. . . . III. vii. 35. 1
stouping with all his *might,* . . . III. vii. 39. 4
she no more was moved with that *might* . . . III. vii. 41. 2
dronke with blood of men slaine by his *might,* . . . III. vii. 47. 7
entertained her the best he *might,* . . . III. viii. 38. 2
Might wanting measure moveth surquedry. . . . III. x. 2. 5
all faire Ladies magnify your *might,* . . . III. x. 28. 7
vertues *might* and values confidence: . . . III. xi. 14. 7

Might—*Continued.*
neither may This fire be quencht by any witt or *might*, ... III. xi. 23. 7
resolv'd to prove her utmost *might*, ... III. xi. 25. 1
To shew the victors *might* and mercilesse intent. . . . . . . III. xi. 52. 9
the stout Damzell, . . . maistered his *might*. . . . . III. xii. 32. 9
So much her malice did her *might* surpas, ... IV. i. 30. 1
was indeed a man of mickle *might;* . . . . IV. i. 32. 3
too late his manhood and his *might* I did assay, ... IV. i. 35. 1
Ne will enforced be with maisterdome or *might*.' . . . . . . IV. i. 46. 9
Why do I not it wreake on thee, now in my *might?* . . . . IV. i. 52. 9
with the shocke of their owne heedlesse *might* . . . . IV. ii. 16. 5
dread thereof and his redoubted *might* Did . . . appall, . . . IV. ii. 40. 2
Ne lesse approved was Cambelloes *might*, ... IV. iii. 7. 3
Againe he drove at him with double *might*, ... IV. iii. 10. 2
with the weight of his owne weedlesse *might* He falleth . . . IV. iii. 19. 8
now feeling sommers *might*, ... IV. iii. 23. 8
one of equall *might* with most, ... IV. iii. 24. 6
smote the other with so wondrous *might*, ... IV. iii. 30. 2
For that had *might* to change the hearts of men . . . . . . IV. iii. 45. 5
Upon them gladly would have prov'd his *might*, ... IV. iv. 3. 8
To be the prize of beautie and of *might;* . . . . IV. iv. 16. 2
thereto all his power and *might* applide: . . . . IV. iv. 24. 2
With that he drives at them with dreadfull *might*, ... IV. iv. 35. 1
The doughtiest knight that liv'd that day, and most of *might*. IV. iv. 42. 9
ran at him with all his *might* and maine; . . . . IV. iv. 44. 8
Some thought from him her to have reft by *might;* . . . . . IV. v. 27. 4
him assailes with all the *might* he may; . . . . IV. vii. 25. 4
made the vassall of the victors *might;* . . . . IV. viii. 32. 7
rescue him, through succour of his *might*, ... IV. viii. 40. 8
smote at him with all his *might;* . . . . IV. viii. 44. 6
He smote at him with all his *might* and maine, ... IV. viii. 45. 3
With which he killed all that came within his *might*. . . . . IV. viii. 47. 9
He her unwares attacht, and captive held by *might*. . . . . IV. ix. 6. 9
laid on load with all their *might* and powre, ... IV. ix. 22. 7
With all my *might* I gan to lay about: . . . . IV. x. 19. 7
she was of such grace and vertuous *might*, ... IV. x. 33. 6
To vanquish all the world with matchlesse *might;* . . . . . IV. xi. 16. 6
Oze the most of *might*, ... IV. xi. 37. 6
brawney armes had lost their knowen *might*, ... IV. xii. 20. 4
Resembling God in his imperiall *might;* . . . . V. Pr. 10. 2
with magnificke *might* and wondrous wit . . . . V. Pr. 11. 3
with furious *might* All th' East . . . did over-ronne, ... V. i. 2. 1
men admyr'd his over-ruling *might;* . . . . V. i. 8. 5
Fro me reft mine away by lawlesse *might*, ... V. i. 17. 8
strong as Lyon in his lordly *might*. . . . . V. i. 20. 5
towards th' end grew greater in his *might*, ... V. ii. 17. 6
In goodly measure by their Makers *might;* . . . . V. ii. 35. 2
The fourth Ecastor, of exceeding *might;* . . . . V. iii. 5. 6
all men stood amaz'd, and at his *might* did wonder. . . . . . V. iii. 8. 9
They both together joyned *might* and maine, ... V. iii. 12. 3
Whether by *might* extort, or else by slight deceaved? . . . . V. iii. 30. 9
Unlesse it be perform'd with dreadlesse *might;* . . . . . . V. iv. 1. 8
with their *might* beat downe licentious lust, ... V. iv. 2. 4
He may dispose by his imperiall *might*, ... V. iv. 19. 6
I will not rest till I her *might* doe trie, ... V. iv. 34. 3
they disparted them, maugre their *might*, ... V. iv. 43. 7
try in equall field whether hath greater *might*. . . . . V. iv. 48. 9
To serve the lowly vassall of her *might*, ... V. v. 27. 7
Subjected hath to my unequall *might*. . . . . V. v. 32. 3
Ne can be stild for all his nurses *might*, ... V. vi. 14. 4
forth did bring a Lion of great *might*, ... V. vii. 16. 6
Let drive at her with all her dreadfull *might*, ... V. vii. 32. 3
Each of whose lockes did match a man in *might*, ... V. viii. 2. 2
he saw another Knight, That . . . prickt with all his *might:* . V. viii. 5. 3
counsels him, through confidence of *might*, ... V. viii. 20. 4
More in his causes truth he trusted then in *might*. . . . . . V. viii. 30. 9
She at her ran with all her force and *might*, ... V. viii. 46. 8
when it hath arm'd it selfe with *might?* . . . . V. ix. 1. 3
Gan drive at him with so huge *might* and maine, ... V. ix. 19. 3
Yet warded well by one of mickle *might* . . . . V. ix. 22. 5
if that Vertue be of so great *might* . . . . V. x. 2. 1
soothly he was one of matchlesse *might*, ... V. x. 8. 6
set a Seneschall of dreaded *might*, ... V. x. 30. 2
Eftsoones forth pricked proudly in his *might*, ... V. x. 31. 8
with so huge *might* and maine . . . . V. x. 32. 3
assemble all the *might* Of all his hands, ... V. xi. 8. 4
smote at him with so importune *might*, ... V. xi. 11. 6
these weake impes replanted by thy *might*, ... V. xi. 16. 7
her recomforted the best he *might*, ... V. xi. 17. 2
By th' authors manhood, nor the doers *might*, ... V. xi. 17. 4
That nothing may escape her reaching *might*, ... V. xi. 24. 8
on his shield tooke hold with all her *might*, ... V. xi. 27. 3
withheld from me by wrongfull *might*, ... V. xi. 49. 8
with unequall *might* doe overlay, ... V. xi. 51. 7
set upon those troupes with all his powre and *might*. . . . . V. xi. 57. 9
Maugre the *might* of all those troupes in vew, ... V. xii. 5. 7
Ne ever any found his match in *might;* . . . . V. xii. 15. 4
He did him smite with all his *might* and maine, ... V. xii. 23. 6
when I gin to feele decay of *might*, ... VI. Pr. 1. 8
win his love by all the meanes she *might*. . . . . VI. i. 14. 9
Maleffort, a man of mickle *might*, ... VI. i. 15. 8
with most importune *might*, ... VI. i. 20. 2
The heavy burden of whose dreadfull *might* . . . . VI. i. 22. 1
all her people murdred with outragious *might:* . . . . VI. i. 29. 9
with all his powre and *might*. . . . . VI. i. 32. 9
Yet would he not him hurt although he *might;* . . . . VI. i. 34. 3
fray Betwixt them two for maystery of *might;* . . . . VI. i. 36. 2
with all their powre and *might*, ... VI. i. 38. 2
His stroke redoubled with such *might* and maine, ... VI. i. 39. 3
thinkes through confidence of *might*, . . . To wrong the weaker, VI. ii. 23. 7

Might—*Continued.*
my fraile safetie, resting in the *might* Of him . . . . VI. ii. 29. 3
That in his youth had beene of mickle *might*, ... VI. iii. 3. 2
fiercely charging him with all his *might*, ... VI. iii. 25. 6
staide his Lady up with steddy *might*. . . . . VI. iii. 33. 9
Sir Turpine, one of mickle *might* . . . . VI. iii. 40. 2
But hayld and puld with all his *might* and maine, ... VI. iv. 7. 4
her to defend from bold oppressors *might*. . . . . VI. v. 7. 9
rather seem'd the conquest of his *might*, ... VI. v. 9. 4
sought by open *might* To overthrow, ... VI. v. 13. 4
by no art, nor any leaches *might*, ... VI. vi. 1. 5
Upon them two they fell with *might* and maine, ... VI. vi. 23. 3
maugre all their *might*, he did repell And beat them back, . . VI. vi. 23. 8
layd at him amaine with all his will and *might*. . . . . . . VI. vi. 27. 9
what it dare not doe by open *might*, ... VI. vii. 1. 7
they mote make triall of their *might*, ... VI. vii. 5. 4
both with equall *might* Against him ran; . . . . VI. vii. 7. 5
The whyles they strike at him with heedlesse *might*, ... VI. vii. 9. 3
himself thereto did want sufficient *might*.' . . . . VI. vii. 12. 9
His trustie sword, the servant of his *might*, ... VI. vii. 25. 4
Did boast her beautie had such soveraine *might*, ... VI. vii. 31. 6
wont doe suit and service to his *might*, ... VI. vii. 34. 2
maugre all his *might* backe to relent: . . . . VI. vii. 45. 8
with his owne hands *might*, ... VI. viii. 10. 5
Ne would endure the daunger of their *might*, ... VI. viii. 14. 4
no *might* in man, nor heart in Knights, ... VI. viii. 18. 6
th' onely glory of his *might*. . . . . VI. x. 40. 9
Albe with all their *might* those Brigants her did keepe. . . . VI. xi. 23. 9
with huge resistlesse *might* The dores assayled, ... VI. xi. 43. 2
with all their *might* Gan all upon him lay: . . . . VI. xi. 47. 8
He her gan to recomfort all he *might* . . . . VI. xi. 50. 2
For his great riches and his greater *might:* . . . . VI. xii. 4. 3
despoyling all with maine and *might*. . . . . VI. xii. 23. 9
Rencountred him with so impetuous *might*, ... VI. xii. 29. 2
To be downe held, and maystred so with *might*, ... VI. xii. 31. 2
by the maystring *might* Of doughty Calidore, ... VI. xii. 38. 1
thralled to her *might*, ... VII. vi. 7. 2
she cast by force and tortious *might* Her to displace, ... VII. vi. 10. 7
Gan call to him aloud with all their *might* . . . . VII. vi. 15. 4
If that her *might* were match to her desire. . . . . VII. vi. 21. 5
hast held The Heavens rule . . . by *might*, ... VII. vi. 27. 7
through ensample of thy sisters *might*, ... VII. vi. 32. 4
by conquest, of our soveraine *might*, ... VII. vi. 33. 5
behight Father of Gods and men by equall *might*, ... VII. vi. 35. 5
delight Of his celestiall song, and Musicks wondrous *might*. . VII. vii. 12. 9
that is onely dew unto thy *might* . . . . VII. vii. 16. 3
Mov'd by your *might* and ordered by your ayde, ... VII. vii. 49. 7
Which hold my life in their dead-doing *might*, ... *Am.* i. 2
Such death the sad ensample of your *might*. . . . . *Am.* vii. 14
needeth greater *might* Then those small forts . . . . *Am.* xiv. 5
The silly lambe that to his *might* doth yield. . . . . *Am.* xx. 8
in the stay of her owne stedfast *might*, ... *Am.* lix. 11
salve of soveraigne *might:* . . . . *Epig.* iv. 46
with awful *might* The lawes of wedlock still dost patronize; . *Epith.* 390
Great both by name, and great in power and *might*, ... *Com. Son.* iii.11
Great God of *Might*, that reignest in the mynd, ... *H.L.* 43
Who can expresse the glorie of thy *might?* . . . . *H.L.* 49
They . . . shew their kindly *might*. . . . . *H.L.* 91
the native *might* Of heavie earth, ... *H.L.* 188
proceeds such soule-enchaunting *might*. . . . . *H.B.* 14
That is thy soveraine *might*, ... *H.B.* 54
by a soveraine *might* Tempers so trim, ... *H.B.* 124
Which there thou workest by thy soveraine *might*, ... *H.H.L.* 4
In endlesse glorie and immortall *might*, ... *H.H.L.* 37
Yet form'd by wondrous skill, and by His *might*, ... *H.H.L.* 107
Eternall King of Glorie, Lord of *Might*, ... *H.H.L.* 172
His grace, his doome, his mercy, and his *might*, ... *H.H.B.* 111

Mightest (*partial list*).
adowne *might'st* fall more horriblie. . . . . *Ro.* xxxi. 14
thinke how this long death thou *mightest* disinherit.' . . . . V. v. 36. 9
thou peasant Knight *mightst* rightly reed . . . . VI. iii. 31. 7

Mightier. mighty spirites bound with *mightier* band, ... IV. iii. 48. 7

Mightiest. the *mightiest* things efforced bin: . . . . II. xii. 43. 7

Mightily. The bodie bigge, and *mightely* pight, ... *S.C.* F. 106
With those himselfe he strengthned *mightelie*, ... *Hub.* 1125
That doest their cause so *mightily* defend: . . . . *Col.* 900
sway The burdeine of this kingdom *mightily*, ... *Ded. Son.* i. 10
mightily upheld that royall mace . . . . II. x. 4. 3
mightily that scepter did sustayne, ... II. x. 75. 3
Their stedfast stonds did *mightily* maintaine, ... II. xi. 15. 2
So *mightely* the Briton Prince him rouzd . . . . II. xi. 33. 1
mightily doth drive The hollow vessell . . . . II. xii. 5. 5
her mortall speare She *mightily* aventred . . . . III. i. 28. 7
burnest *mightily* In living brests, ... III. iii. 1. 1
mightily defend Against their forren foe . . . . III. iii. 23. 7
Malgo shall full *mightily* Avenge his fathers losse . . . . . III. iii. 31. 7
Cadwallin *mightily* . . . all those wrongs shall wreake; . . . III. iii. 36. 1
So *mightily* she smote him, . . . He fell halfe dead: . . . . . III. xii. 34. 1
Did him assayle, and *mightily* amate, ... IV. iii. 26. 8
their assault withstood so *mightily*, ... VI. vi. 23. 7
he was strong and *mightily* stiffe pight, ... VI. ix. 44. 2

Mightiness. having with huge *mightinesse* Ireland subdewd, . III. iii. 33. 5

Mights. stone Of wondrous worth, and eke of wondrous *mights*, I. vii. 30. 2
far exceeded men in their immeasurd *mights*. . . . . II. x. 8. 9
Mongst thousand dangers, and ten thousand Magick *mights*. . . III. xii. 1. 9
lose their native *mights;* . . . . VII. vii. 25. 5

Mighty. The *mightie* Dragon gave to hir his power. . . . . *Rev.* i. 6
The ashes of a *mightie* Emperour: . . . . *Bel.* iii. 8
all astonied with this *mighty* ghoast, ... *Bel.*[2] ix. 1
with her *mightie* powre Tam'd all the world, ... *Ro.* iii. 6

Mild. *Milde* was the winde, calme seem'd the sea . . . *Pet.* ii. 4
Milde, but yet Love she proudly did forsake: . . . *Pet.* vi. 4
shepheard mought be meeke and *mylde,* . . . *S.C.* Jul. 153
milde of speach, and meeke of nature: . . . *Ti.* 536
Of *milde* aspect, and haire as soft as silke, . . . *Ti.* 563
season *milde* With gentle calme the world had quieted, . . . *Mui.* 49
shee became so meeke and *milde* of cheare, . . . *D.* 125
with *milde* counsaile strove to mitigate . . . *D.* 191
With gentle usage and demeanure *myld:* . . . *As.* 20
Through the *myld* temperance of her goodly raies. . . . *Col.* 551
with thy mother *mylde* come to mine ayde; . . . I. Pr. 3. 6
'Be well aware,' quoth then that Ladie *milde,* . . . I. i. 12. 1
Forsaken Truth . . . makes the Lyon *mylde;* . . . I. iii. Arg.
More *mild* in beastly kind then that her beastly foe. . . . I. iii. 44. 9
there begotten of a Lady *myld,* . . . I. vi. 21. 3
With sober gladnesse and *myld* modestie; . . . I. viii. 26. 5
to this Lady *mild* Thou falsed hast thy faith . . . I. ix. 46. 6
them receives a gentle Squyre, Of *myld* demeanure, . . . I. x. 7. 2
when *myld* Zephyrus emongst them blew, . . . II. v. 29. 8
the *milde* ayre with season moderate . . . II. xii. 51. 7
Full *myld* to her he spake, . . . III. iv. 48. 8
Looking with *myld* aspect upon the earth . . . III. vi. 2. 3
the fayre Virgin was so meeke and *myld,* . . . III. vii. 15. 1
All which she of him tooke with countenance meeke and *mild.* III. vii. 17. 9
th' ayre was *milde* and cleared was the skie, . . . III. viii. 21. 5
he endevored with speaches *milde* . . . III. viii. 34. 1
Vouchsafe with *mild* regard a wretches cace to heare.' . . . III. x. 26. 9
she was gentle and of *milde* aspect, . . . III. xii. 14. 3
with perswasions *myld* Did mitigate the fiercenesse . . . IV. iv. 5. 1
brought forth speeches *myld* when she would have missayd. . . . IV. vi. 27. 9
We did alight, and sate in shadow *myld,* . . . IV. vi. 36. 3
With *mild* regard to see his ruefull plight, . . . IV. viii. 17. 7
they endured all with patience *milde,* . . . IV. viii. 28. 6
them with speaches *milde* gan first disswade . . . IV. ix. 34. 3
Myld Titus and Gesippus without pryde; . . . IV. x. 27. 5
Swift Proto, *milde* Eucrate, Thetis faire, . . . IV. xi. 48. 7
She did allure with gifts and speaches *milde* . . . V. i. 6. 5
Just Dice, wise Eunomie, *myld* Eirene; . . . V. ix. 32. 6
Did to her *myld* obeysance, as they ought, . . . V. ix. 34. 4
with more *myld* aspect those two to entertake. . . . V. ix. 35. 9
Unto Mercilla *myld,* for Justice gainst the thrall. . . . V. ix. 49. 9
Calidore . . . doth make Briana wexe more *mylde.* . . . VI. i. Arg.
gentlenesse of spright And manners *mylde* . . . VI. i. 2. 4
doe instead thereof *mild* curt'sie showe . . . VI. i. 27. 3
with prayers meeke And *myld* entreaty . . . VI. iii. 37. 9
wonderfull to fynd So *milde* humanity . . . VI. v. 29. 9
To whom the Prince . . . *Mylde* answer made, . . . VI. vi. 20. 6
Atwene that Ladie *myld* and recreant knight, . . . VI. vi. 37. 2
The sonne of Venus, who is *myld* by kynd . . . VI. vii. 37. 1
The first of them hight *mylde* Euphrosyne, . . . VI. x. 22. 7
That we likewise should *mylde* and gentle be; . . . VI. x. 24. 2
Myld humblesse, mixt with awful majesty. . . . *Am.* xiii. 5
mild pleasance, which doth pride displace, . . . *Am.* xxi. 5
With shew of morning *mylde* he hath begun, . . . *Am.* lxii. 3
So sweet, so lovely, and so *mild* as she, . . . *Epith.* 169
Regard of honour, and *mild* modesty; . . . *Epith.* 193
Milder. both *milder* beasts and fiercer foes . . . *Bel.*[2] viii. 7
of a truce to treat In *milder* tearmes, . . . IV. ix. 35. 7
With which the Gods themselves are *mylder* made: . . . V. v. 49. 4
gan enquire of him with *mylder* mood . . . V. vi. 15. 6
He thus againe in *milder* wise began: . . . VII. vi. 31. 6
beholding me with *mylder* looke, . . . *Am.* lxvii. 9
Mildest. they the *mildest* man alive would make Forget his patience, . . . V. xii. 42. 3
Mildly. A spring of water, *mildly* rumbling downe, . . . *Pet.* iv. 2
Yet *mildly* him to purpose answered; . . . II. iv. 39. 8
Tho gan she *myldly* of them to inquyre . . . III. i. 23. 8
Her *mildly* answer'd: . . . III. vii. 8. 6
She chang'd that threatfull mood, and *mildly* gan entreat: . . . V. v. 47. 9
when ye *mildly* looke with lovely hew, . . . *Am.* vii. 5
Mildness. So well I wrought with *mildnes* and with paine, . . . *D.* 117
delight Shee to them made, with *mildnesse* virginall, . . . II. ix. 20. 4
To better termes of *myldnesse* did entreat . . . IV. ix. 14. 2
Allur'd with *myldnesse* of the gentle wether . . . VI. iii. 23. 3
Mile. from thence not past a *mile* or tway, . . . V. iv. 35. 7
ere he thence had traveild many a *mile,* . . . VI. ii. 40. 3
So up and downe he wandred many a *mile* . . . VI. iv. 25. 4
maketh every minute seeme a *myle.* . . . *Am.* lxxxvi. 12
Miles. Three *miles* it might be easy heard arownd, . . . I. viii. 4. 3
They wasted had much way, and measurd many *miles.* . . . II. ix. 9. 9
many *miles* they two together wore, . . . IV. ix. 19. 7
Milesio. our sire, *Milesio* by name, . . . V. iv. 7. 3
Militant. Against fowle feendes to ayd us *militant!* . . . II. viii. 2. 5
Milk. Butter enough, honye, *milke,* and whay, . . . *S.C.* May 115
fed with Furies *milke* for sustenaunce . . . *T.M.* 261
I saw two Beares, as white as anie *milke,* . . . *Ti.* 561
many drops of *milk* and blood through it did spill. . . . III. ii. 49. 9
as housewife . . . To *milk* their gotes . . . III. x. 36. 8
fostred up with bitter *milke* of tine, . . . III. xi. 1. 4
certes was with *milke* of Wolves and Tygres fed. . . . IV. vii. 7. 9
quilted uppon sattin white as *milke;* . . . V. v. 2. 3
out of them to presse the *milke:* . . . VI. ix. 37. 9
Milk-dropping. There his *milk-dropping* Goats be his delight, *Gn.* 115
Milk-white. To her will I offer a *milkwhite* Lamb: . . . *S.C.* Ap. 96
a *milkewhite* lambe she lad. . . . I. i. 4. 9
Upon a *milkwhite* Palfrey all alone, . . . III. i. 15. 2
Upon that *milke-white* Palfreyes carcas fedd, . . . III. vii. 30. 8
snowy neckd Doris, and *milkewhite* Galathaea: . . . IV. xi. 49. 9
Milky. Bulles, . . . Doe for the *milky* mothers want complaine, I. viii. 11. 7
Mill. *See* **Water-mill.**

Mill—*Continued.*
the Sallow for the *mill;* . . . I. i. 9. 5
whose swelling sourse Shall drive a *Mill,* . . . VI. i. 21. 2
Mill-dam. Like to a great *Mill-damb* forth fiercely gusht, . . . V. xi. 31. 5
Miller's. leade the *Myllers* rownde, . . . *S.C.* O. 52
Millions. So many *millions* of chaste pleasures play. . . . *H.B.* 259
Drew *millions* more against their God to fight. . . . *H.H.L.* 84
Mill-wheel. Like a *Mill-wheele* in midst of miserie, . . . *D.* 432
Mimic. With kindly counter under *Mimick* shade, . . . *T.M.* 207
Mincing. Fitt mate for such a *mincing* mineon, . . . II. ii. 37. 2
Mind. Picturing that which I in *minde* embraced, . . . *Van.* i. 11
Thy maysters *mind* is overcome with care: . . . *S.C.* Ja. 46
unlucky Muse, that wontst to ease My musing *mynd,* . . . *S.C.* Ja. 70
Weenest of love is not his *mynd?* . . . *S.C.* F. 76
To nought more, Thenot, my *mind* is bent . . . *S.C.* F. 94
now from me hys madding *mynd* is starte, . . . *S.C.* Ap. 25
hath weand my wandring *mynde:* . . . *S.C.* Jun. 2
Would rayse ones *mynd* above the starry skie, . . . *S.C.* O. 94
With *minde* that ill use doth before deprave, . . . *Gn.* 91
with cleane *minde,* and heart sincere, . . . *Gn.* 122
To this his minde and senses he doth bend, . . . *Gn.* 138
The which conceiv'd in her revengefull *minde* . . . *Gn.* 398
Whilst Hector raged with outragious *minde,* . . . *Gn.* 503
wilde greene woods and fruitful pastures *minde;* . . . *Gn.* 637
His inly grieved *minde* full sore opprest; . . . *Gn.* 643
the right gentle *minde* woulde bite his lip, . . . *Hub.* 711
He stands on tearmes of honourable *minde,* . . . *Hub.* 721
His *minde* unto the Muses he withdrawes: . . . *Hub.* 760
all his *minde* on honour fixed is, . . . *Hub.* 771
unto such the Ape lent not his *minde:* . . . *Hub.* 794
chieflie doth each noble *minde* adorne, . . . *Hub.* 831
let none other ever drawe Your *minde* from me, . . . *Hub.* 1054
ever enter in his *minde;* . . . *Hub.* 1133
men depriv'd of sense and *minde.* . . . *T.M.* 156
with humble *minde* and high insight, . . . *T.M.* 511
mitigates the anguish of the *minde.* . . . *Ti.* 161
who so els his bounteous *minde* did trie, . . . *Ti.* 233
I in *minde* remained sore agast, . . . *Ti.* 578
all is vanitie and griefe of *minde,* . . . *Ti.* 583
wrought both joy and sorrow in my *mind:* . . . *Ti.* 614
unto heaven let your high *minde* aspire, . . . *Ti.* 685
What-ever man be he whose heavie *minde,* . . . *D.* 1
There came unto my *minde* a troublous thought, . . . *D.* 29
all the dowries of a noble *mind,* . . . *D.* 216
My bread shall be the anguish of my *mind,* . . . *D.* 375
Leaving behind them nought but griefe of *minde,* . . . *D.* 398
I to *minde* will call How my fair Starre . . . *D.* 479
doubly faire wox both in *mynd* and face. . . . *As.* 18
Ill *mynd* so much to *mynd* anothers ill, . . . *As.* 111
My *mind,* full of my thoughts satietie, . . . *Col.* 42
serve and honour her with faithfull *mind.* . . . *Col.* 255
t' adore, with humble *mind,* . . . *Col.* 350
not by measure of her owne great *mynd,* . . . *Col.* 364
found I lyking in her royall *mynd,* . . . *Col.* 454
In whose brave *mind,* as in a golden cofer, . . . *Col.* 488
She is the well of bountie and brave *mynd,* . . . *Col.* 496
in closure of a thankfull *mynd,* . . . *Col.* 580
highest lookes have not the highest *mynd,* . . . *Col.* 715
Nor honest *mynd* might there be found at all. . . . *Col.* 734
Darting her beames into each feeble *mynd:* . . . *Col.* 874
Redoubted Lord, in whose corageous *mind* . . . *Ded. Son.* x. 1
And fill your *mind* with magnanimitee. . . . *Ded. Son.* x. 12
Resolvd in *minde* all suddenly to win, . . . I. i. 24. 4
The noblest *mind* the best contentment has. . . . I. i. 35. 4
A virgin widow, whose deepe wounded *mind* . . . did languish, I. ii. 24. 8
in *minde* to slipp away, Soone as appeard safe opportunitie: I. ii. 41. 6
Nought . . . That moves more deare compassion of *mind.* . . I. iii. 1. 2
He to him lept, in *minde* to reave his life, . . . I. iii. 36. 2
Whose *mind* in meat and drinke was drowned so, . . . I. iv. 23. 4
nourish bloody vengeaunce in his bitter *mind.* . . . I. iv. 38. 9
calles to *mind* his pourtraiture alive, . . . I. vi. 17. 3
They envy her in their malitious *mind,* . . . I. vi. 18. 6
chaunt sweet musick to delight his *mynd.* . . . I. vii. 3. 5
in constant carefull *mind,* She fedd her wound . . . I. vii. 28. 5
From that day forth I cast in carefull *mynd,* . . . I. ix. 15. 6
goodly gifts, the signes of gratefull *mynd,* . . . I. ix. 18. 8
Musing full sadly in his sullein *mind:* . . . I. ix. 35. 3
his owne guiltie *mind,* deserving death. . . . I. ix. 38. 6
have *mind* of that last bitter throw; . . . I. x. 41. 8
His *mind* was full of spiritual repast, . . . I. x. 48. 8
him awaited still with pensive *mynd.* . . . I. x. 68. 3
Throwne out from womanish impatient *mynd?* . . . I. xii. 30. 2
Forth he fares, full of malicious *mynd,* . . . II. i. 2. 1
He chaungd his *mynd* from one to other ill; . . . II. i. 5. 4
if by lookes one may the *mind* aread, . . . II. i. 7. 6
the weake *minde* with double woe torment?' . . . II. i. 16. 7
dwell In her sonnes flesh, to *mind* revengement, . . . II. ii. 10. 8
stryfull *mind* and diverse qualitee . . . II. ii. 13. 5
young Perissa was of other *mynd,* . . . II. ii. 36. 1
One that to bountie never cast his *mynd,* . . . II. iii. 4. 2
wondred in his *minde* what mote that Monster make. . . . II. iii. 18. 9
He was dismayed in his coward *minde,* . . . II. iii. 32. 2
In *mind* to marke the beast. . . . II. iii. 34. 6
his *mynd* Behaves with cares, . . . II. iii. 40. 6
my engreeved *mind* could find no rest, . . . II. iv. 23. 4
for grief of *mind* That he in ods of armes was conquered: . . . II. v. 14. 5
pourd out his ydle *mynd* In daintie delices, . . . II. v. 28. 5
The wrath which Atin kindled in his *mind,* . . . II. vi. 2. 3
So easie was to quench his flamed *minde* . . . II. vi. 8. 6
For to allure fraile *mind* to carelesse ease: . . . II. vi. 13. 6

Mind—*Continued.*
the flitt barke, obaying to her *mind*, ... II. vi. 20. 3
if to thy great *mind*, or greedy vew, ... II. vii. 9. 3
Ensample be of *mind* intemperate, ... II. vii. 60. 4
The whiles the other Ladies *mind* theyr mery glee. . . . . . II. viii. 6. 9
stryful Atin in their stubborne *mind* . . . . II. viii. 11. 4
full of princely bounty and great *mind*, ... II. viii. 51. 1
yf the beauty of her *mind* ye knew, ... II. ix. 3. 5
Others to beare the same away did *mynd;* . . . . II. ix. 31. 8
Pensive I yeeld I am, and sad in *mind*, ... II. ix. 38. 6
lively vigour rested in his *mind*, ... II. ix. 55. 7
To which whiles absent he his *mind* did sett, ... II. x. 60. 3
deemd in *mynd* To be no earthly wight, ... II. x. 71. 5
guilefull bayt She will embosome deeper in your *mind*, . . . II. xii. 29. 3
To sincke into his sence, nor *mind* affect, ... II. xii. 53. 3
'See the *mind* of beastly man, ... II. xii. 87. 1
Let Gryll be Gryll, and have his hoggish *minde;* . . . . . . II. xii. 87. 8
constant *mind* Would not so lightly follow beauties chace, . . III. i. 19. 1
chaste desires doe nourish in your *mind*, ... III. i. 49. 2
in *minde* to gride The loathed leachour. . . . . III. i. 62. 3
it fell into that Fairies *mind* . . . . III. ii. 4. 4
To slake your wrath, and mollify your *mind*' . . . . III. ii. 13. 4
why make ye such Monster of your *minde?* . . . . III. ii. 40. 2
To love the semblaunt pleasing most your *minde*, ... III. ii. 40. 7
Not so th' Arabian Myrrhe did set her *mynd*, ... III. ii. 41. 1
So was their fortune good, though wicked were their *minde*. . III. ii. 43. 9
wicked fortune mine, though *minde* be good, ... III. ii. 44. 1
within her troubled *mind* Old Glauce cast . . . . III. iii. 5. 1
into the *mynd* Of the yong Damzell sunke, ... III. iii. 57. 1
A thousand thoughts she fashiond in her *mind*, ... III. iv. 5. 6
Love, my lewd Pilott, hath a restlesse *minde;* . . . . III. iv. 9. 6
drowne his baser *mind*, ... III. iv. 56. 6
he wondrous pensive grew in *minde*, ... III. v. 12. 5
The higher place in her Heroick *mynd:* . . . . III. v. 55. 5
Ne ever cast his *mind* to covet prayse, ... III. vii. 12. 5
cast to love her in his brutish *mind:* . . . . III. vii. 15. 8
In *minde* to leape into the mighty maine, ... III. vii. 27. 3
all his *minde* is set on mucky pelfe, ... III. ix. 4. 1
So huge a *mind* could not in lesser rest, ... III. ix. 46. 7
seest every secret of the *minde;* . . . . III. x. 4. 7
In his disquiet *mind* was much dismayd: . . . . III. x. 14. 3
the dearest to his dounghill *minde*, ... III. x. 15. 8
In lofty looks to hide an humble *minde*, ... III. x. 30. 2
That counsell pleased not Malbeccoes *mynd*, ... III. x. 41. 8
all the night did *minde* his joyous play: . . . . III. x. 48. 4
as a Snake, still lurked in his wounded *mynd*. . . . . III. x. 55. 9
Of all the passions in the *mind* thou vilest art! . . . . . . III. xi. 1. 9
She was emmoved in her noble *minde*, ... III. xi. 4. 7
though she did bend Her earnest *minde*, ... III. xi. 54. 9
As if in *minde* he somewhat had to say; . . . . III. xii. 4. 2
he much rejoyced in his cruell *minde*. . . . . III. xii. 22. 9
to hide her fained sex . . . And maske her wounded *mind*, . . IV. i. 7. 4
much she feard his *mind* would grow to some excesse. . . . . IV. i. 7. 9
His fickle *mind* full of inconstancie: . . . . IV. i. 32. 5
with wondrous griefe of *mynd* And shame, ... IV. i. 37. 6
it prickt his wanton *mind* With sting of lust . . . . IV. ii. 5. 4
Departed thence with full contented *mynd;* . . . . IV. ii. 53. 2
in *mind* with that same blow To make an end . . . . IV. iii. 33. 2
quiet-age It doth establish in the troubled *mynd*. . . . . . IV. iii. 43. 6
in base *mind* nor friendship dwels nor enmity. . . . . IV. iv. 11. 9
thought in *mind* it shortly to amend: . . . . IV. iv. 45. 7
in *mind* her to have reav'd From wight unworthie . . . . . . IV. v. 28. 3
What equall torment to the griefe of *mind* . . . . IV. vi. 1. 1
She gan eftsoones it to her *mind* to call . . . . IV. vi. 26. 4
whylome in your *minde* wont to despise them all.' . . . . . . IV. vi. 28. 9
in her *mind* displeased. IV. vi. 44. 3
backe returned with right heavie *mind* . . . . IV. vi. 46. 4
Selfe to forget to *mind* another is over-sight.' . . . . IV. vii. 10. 9
nothing could my fixed *mind* remove, ... IV. vii. 16. 5
Did greatly solace his engrieved *mind*. . . . . IV. viii. 7. 4
nought according to his *mind* He could out-learne, ... IV. viii. 22. 5
T' expresse the meaning of the inward *mind*, ... IV. viii. 26. 2
the band of vertuous *mind*, ... IV. ix. 1. 8
minde did travell as with chylde . . . . IV. ix. 17. 3
missing to his *mind* That Virgins love to win . . . . IV. xi. 2. 2
Her constant *mind* could move . . . . IV. xi. 2. 8
even for griefe of *minde* he oft did grone, ... IV. xii. 12. 6
Now gan he in his grieved *minde* devise, ... IV. xii. 14. 1
she in her *mind* Was troubled sore, ... IV. xii. 21. 1
The which afflicted his engrieved *mind;* . . . . IV. xii. 25. 8
rather gan in troubled *mind* devize . . . . IV. xii. 28. 8
weigh the thought that from mans *mind* doth flow: . . . . . V. ii. 43. 4
in the *mind* the doome of right must bee: . . . . V. ii. 47. 6
he was soone aware of their ill *minde*, ... V. iv. 24. 1
Much was the man confounded in his *mind*, ... V. iv. 27. 1
through stout disdaine of manly *mind* . . . . V. iv. 32. 1
tossed in her troublous *minde* . . . . V. iv. 47. 4
A sordid office for a *mind* so brave: . . . . V. v. 23. 4
her proud *mind* convert To meeke obeysance . . . . V. v. 28. 7
his owne brave *mind* Subjected hath . . . . V. v. 32. 2
Voide of malitious *minde* or foule offence: . . . . V. v. 33. 5
'But what so stonie *minde*,' (she then replyde) . . . . V. v. 39. 1
not of cancred will,' (Sayd he) 'nor obstinate disdainefull *mind*, V. v. 41. 2
never meant he in his noble *mind* . . . to be untrew: . . . . V. v. 56. 2
She gan to cast in her misdoubtfull *mynde* A thousand feares, V. vi. 3. 8
she did her troubled *mynd* molest, ... V. vi. 4. 5
To beare unto her love the message of her *mind*. . . . . . . V. vi. 7. 9
Her *minde* was whole possessed of one thought, ... V. vi. 21. 3
right discontent In *minde* he grew, ... V. vi. 24. 2
A man of subtill wit and wicked *minde*, ... V. vi. 32. 2

Mind—*Continued.*
The troublous passion of my pensive *mind*, ... V. vii. 19. 2
As well as to her *minde* it had recourse. . . . . V. vii. 20. 3
doth allure The sence of man, and all his *minde* possesse, . . V. viii. 1. 2
They drew their swords, in *mind* to make amends . . . . . . V. viii. 10. 2
found No easie meanes according to his *mind:* . . . . V. viii. 42. 3
whilest she lent her intentive *mind*, ... V. ix. 14. 1
As tokens of her thankefull *mind* besecne, ... V. x. 17. 3
he doth wield Her *mind* so well, ... V. x. 24. 8
from her balefull *minde* all care he banished. . . . . V. x. 39. 9
Then to his first emprize his *mind* he lent, ... V. xi. 35. 5
albe he earst did wyte His wavering *mind*, ... V. xi. 57. 7
Much was the Ladie in her gentle *mind* Abasht . . . . V. xi. 64. 1
She did conceale, and murder her owne *mynd;* . . . . V. xii. 33. 5
vertues seat is deepe within the *mynd*, ... VI. Pr. 5. 8
In whose pure *minde*, as in mirrour sheene, ... VI. Pr. 6. 5
proud despight of his selfe-pleasing *mynd*, ... V. i. 15. 2
To show her thankefull *mind* . . . . VI. i. 46. 4
others that have greater skill in *mind*, ... VI. ii. 2. 5
Much was I moved in indignant *mind*, ... VI. ii. 11. 2
The gentle *minde* by gentle deeds is knowne: . . . . VI. iii. 1. 2
Forgetfull of her owne to *minde* his feares: . . . . VI. iii. 12. 3
Some place of succour to content his *mynd*, ... VI. iv. 26. 5
haps that sorrowes of the *mynd* Find remedie . . . . VI. iv. 28. 8
He gan in *mind* conceive a fit reliefe . . . . VI. iv. 34. 4
Yet will it shew some sparkes of gentle *mynd*, ... VI. v. 1. 8
in *minde*, the which most grieveth me, ... VI. v. 28. 3
So milde humanity and perfect gentle *mynd*. . . . . VI. v. 29. 9
Sith he cannot expresse his simple *minde*, ... VI. v. 30. 3
great affaires in *mynd* Would not permit . . . . VI. v. 41. 1
Give salves to every sore, but counsell to the *minde*. . . . . VI. vi. 5. 9
in *mynd* to bene ywroken Of all the vile demeane . . . . . . VI. vi. 18. 3
Even so the baser *mind* it selfe displayes . . . . VI. vii. 1. 3
Be arguments of a vile donghill *mind*, ... VI. vii. 1. 6
in his *mind*, malitious and ingrate, ... VI. vii. 2. 5
Let drive at him with so malitious *mynd*, ... VI. vii. 10. 6
fume in his disdainefull *mynd* the more, ... VI. vii. 47. 8
to his gentle *mynd* Was much more grievous . . . . VI. vii. 49. 7
So be ye soft and tender eeke in *mynde;* . . . . VI. viii. 2. 3
His manly *mynde* was much emmoved therewithall; . . . . . VI. viii. 5. 9
Though meane her lot, yet higher did her *mind* ascend. . . . VI. ix. 10. 9
he in his *mind* her worthy deemed . . . . VI. ix. 11. 4
to occasion meanes to worke his *mind*, ... VI. ix. 27. 1
'It is the *mynd* that maketh good or ill, ... VI. ix. 30. 1
in her *mynde* the seeds Of perfect love did sow, ... VI. ix. 45. 7
decke the body or adorne the *mynde*, ... VI. x. 23. 2
her in *mynde* did to him selfe allot. . . . . VI. xi. 4. 5
Her constant *mynd* could not a whit remove, ... VI. xi. 5. 2
Her sickenesse was not of the body, but the *mynde*. . . . . VI. xi. 8. 9
in his *mind* with better reason cast . . . . VI. xi. 34. 4
in his *mind* had closely made A further purpose, ... VI. xi. 38. 7
she gan to cast In her conceiptfull *mynd* . . . . VI. xii. 16. 2
thousand deathes deviseth in her vengefull *mind*. . . . . . . VII. vi. 48. 9
His Saviour's birth his *mind* so much did glad. . . . . VII. vii. 41. 4
her unmoved *mind* Doth still persist . . . . *Am.* vi. 1
Her *minde* remembreth her mortalitie, ... *Am.* xiii. 7
Her *mind* adornd with vertues manifold. . . . . *Am.* xv. 14
Her temple fayre is built within my *mind*, ... *Am.* xxii. 5
Gives me great hope of your relenting *mynd:* . . . . *Am.* xxviii. 2
put you in *mind* Of that proud mayd, ... *Am.* xxviii. 7
Such is the powre of love in gentle *mind*, ... *Am.* xxx. 13
And eke her *mind* is pure immortall hye. . . . . *Am.* lv. 12
In *mind* to mount up to the purest sky; . . . . *Am.* lxxii. 2
With guifts of body, fortune, and of *mind*. . . . . *Am.* lxxiv. 4
Whose ymage yet I carry fresh in *mynd*. . . . . *Am.* lxxviii. 4
the gentle wit, And vertuous *mind*, ... *Am.* lxxix. 4
with such brightnesse whylest I fill my *mind*, ... *Am.* lxxxvii. 13
sing the thing that mote thy *mind* delight, ... *Epith.* 123
to tempt her *mind* to ill. *Epith.* 199
Great God of Might, that reignest in the *mynd*, ... *H.L.* 43
man that breathes a more immortall *mynd*, ... *H.L.* 103
the refyned *mynd* doth newly fashion . . . . *H.L.* 192
Thereon his *mynd* affixed wholly is, ... *H.L.* 204
O how doth it torment His troubled *mynd* . . . . *H.L.* 253
Move such affection in the inward *mynd*, ... *H.B.* 76
many a gentle *mynd* Dwels in deformed tabernacle . . . . . . *H.B.* 141
forme, which they present Unto their *mind*, ... *H.B.* 215
it embracing in his *mind* entyre, ... *H.B.* 223
And doest thy *mynd* in durty pleasures moyle, ... *H.H.L.* 220
Lift up thy *mind* to th' Author of thy weale, ... *H.H.L.* 256
With all thy hart, with all thy soule and *mind*, ... *H.H.L.* 260
Which in my weake distraughted *mynd* I see; . . . . *H.H.B.* 14
Cease then, my tongue! and lend unto my *mynd* . . . . *H.H.B.* 106
To impe the wings of thy high flying *mynd*, ... *H.H.B.* 135
in their fastened *mynd* All happie joy . . . . *H.H.B.* 286

Minded. *See* **Base-minded, Cruel-minded, High-minded, Savage-minded.**
Whom when so lewdly *minded* Talus found, ... V. ii. 49. 6

Mindeth. He *mindeth* more how he may be relieved With grace from her, ... VI. x. 1. 8

Mindful. Tityus, *mindefull* yet Of thy displeasure, ... *Gn.* 377
Box, yet *mindfull* of his olde offence; . . . . *Gn.* 676
mindfull of that olde Enfested grudge, ... *Mui.* 353
Of her adventure *myndfull* for to bee. . . . . I. x. 68. 8
more *mindfull* of his honour deare . . . . I. xi. 39. 1
Sir Guyon, *mindfull* of his vow yplight, ... II. iii. 1. 5
Yet *mindfull* how he late by one was feld. . . . . IV. i. 34. 4
mindefull to pursew The last daies purpose . . . . V. v. 1. 5
mindfull still of your first countries sight, ... *H.B.* 166

Minding. *minding* nought but lustfull game, ... II. xii. 81. 2

Minding—*Continued.*
minding more her safety then himselfe, . . . VI. xi. 19. 3
Mindless. All *mindlesse* of the Golden fleece, which made them strive. . . . IV. i. 23. 9
All *mindlesse* of his owne deare Lord . . . IV. viii. 18. 4
All *mindlesse* of her wonted modestie . . . IV. viii. 63. 3
Mind's. Weake body wel is chang'd for *minds* redoubled forse. II. ix. 55. 9
His *mindes* sad message backe unto him sent; . . . VI. viii. 8. 3
Ne once my *minds* unmoved quiet grieve; . . . VI. ix. 22. 7
made unfit to serve his lawlesse *mindes* behest. . . . VI. xi. 7. 9
In deep discovery of the *mynds* disease; . . . *Am.* l. 6
Attempt to work her gentle *mindes* unrest: . . . *Am.* lxxxiii. 4
Minds. Griefe of good *mindes,* to see goodnesse disgraced! . . *Van.* i. 8
rend the greedie *mindes* of covetous men, . . . *Gn.* 95
miserie doth bravest *mindes* abate, . . . *Hub.* 256
The gentle *minds,* in midst of worldlie smarts: . . . *T.M.* 136
They in the *mindes* of men now tyrannize, . . . *T.M.* 191
gentle *mindes* with lewd delights distaine; . . . *T.M.* 334
pestilence, That mortall *mindes* doth inwardly infect . . . *T.M.* 484
ignorance . . . *mindes* of men borne heavenlie doth debace. . . *T.M.* 498
mighty charmes to trouble sleepy *minds.* . . . I. i. 36. 9
Forgetfull of his owne that *mindes* an others cares. . . . I. v. 18. 9
noble *mindes* of yore allyed were, . . . I. ix. 1. 3
grieved *mindes,* which choler did englut, . . . II. ii. 23. 5
So love does raine In stoutest *minds,* . . . II. ii. 26. 6
to prepare Their *minds* to pleasure, . . . II. ii. 33. 9
to him that *mindes* his chaunce t' abye?' . . . II. iv. 40. 4
it the goodly peace of staied *mindes* Does overthrow, . . . II. v. 1. 6
gazing wonder they their *mindes* did fill; . . . II. ix. 33. 3
did apply Their *mindes* to prayse . . . II. x. 22. 6
According to their *mindes* like monstruous.' . . . II. xii. 85. 5
doth base affections move In brutish *mindes,* . . . III. iii. 1. 6
over mortall *mindes* hast so great might, . . . III. iii. 2. 2
indew The salvage *minds* with skill of just and trew: . . . III. iii. 45. 5
persuade The warlike *minds* to learne her goodly lore, . . . III. iii. 49. 4
Wonder it is to see in diverse *mindes* . . . III. v. 1. 1
minds of mortall men are muchell mard . . . III. x. 31. 8
To moderate stiffe *mindes* disposd to strive: . . . IV. ii. 2. 6
Thus whilest their *minds* were doubtfully distraught, . . . IV. iii. 48. 6
The cause of both, of both their *minds* depends, . . . IV. iv. 1. 4
Those be unquiet thoughts that carefull *minds* invade. . . . IV. v. 35. 9
The things, that day most *minds,* . . . IV. v. 43. 9
Hath troubled both your *mindes* . . . IV. vi. 30. 7
the band Of noble *minds* derived from above, . . . IV. vi. 31. 8
sloth that oft doth noble *mindes* annoy. . . . IV. vii. 23. 9
May nought at all their setled *mindes* remove, . . . IV. x. 2. 3
to afflicted *minds* sweet rest and quiet sends. . . . IV. x. 34. 9
should their *mindes* up to devotion call, . . . V. vi. 27. 4
Having the *mindes* of men with fury fraught, . . . V. vii. 11. 4
With like fierce *minds,* but meanings different; . . . V. viii. 30. 2
O sacred hunger of ambitious *mindes,* . . . V. xii. 1. 1
Into the *mindes* of mortall men doe well, . . . VI. Pr. 2. 5
in the *mindes* of men had great insight; . . . VI. vi. 3. 6
how to please the *minds* of good and ill, . . . VI. vi. 41. 8
With whom he *myndes* for ever to remaine, . . . VI. x. 2. 5
learned *minds* inflameth with desire . . . VII. vii. 2. 5
their *minds* (which they immortall call) . . . VII. vii. 19. 8
to lead fraile *mindes* to rest In chast desires, . . . *Am.* viii. 7
Such haughty *mynds,* . . . Disdayne to yield . . . *Am.* xiv. 7
Chaunge eke our *mynds,* and former lives amend; . . . *Am.* lxii. 6
The more of stedfast *mynds* to be admyred, . . . *H.L.* 171
baseborne *mynds* such lamps regard the lesse, . . . *H.L.* 173
That workes such wonders in the *minds* of men; . . . *H.B.* 86
And all that pompe to which proud *minds* aspyre . . . *H.H.B.* 277
Mine (*partial list of pronoun*).
a ghost appeare before *mine* eyes . . . *Bel.*[1] i. 5
were thy yeares greene, as now bene *myne,* . . . *S.C.* F. 59
Phyllis is *myne* for many dayes. . . . *S.C.* F. 64
Or thrive in welth, she shalbe *mine,* . . . *S.C.* Au. 111
Nor ought cald *mine* or thine: . . . *Hub.* 149
To cast *mine* eye, where other sights I spide. . . . *Ti.* 588
There now the joy is his, here sorrow *mine.* . . . *Ti.* 602
Mine, ah! not *mine;* amisse I *mine* did say: . . . *D.* 234
Not *mine,* but His, which *mine* awhile her made; . . . *D.* 235
Mine to be His, with him to live for ay. . . . *D.* 236
see his ymage in *mine* eye, . . . I. iv. 45. 6
harbour in *mine* hart: . . . I. vii. 25. 4
Mine onely foe, *mine* onely deadly dread; . . . I. vii. 50. 7
since *mine* he is, or free or bond, . . . I. xii. 28. 1
Last turne was *mine,* . . . IV. ii. 6. 4
Mulla *mine,* whose waves I whilom taught to weep. . . . IV. xi. 41. 9
All paine hath end, . . . But *mine,* . . . *Am.* xi. 14
Helpe me *mine* owne loves prayses to resound; . . . *Epith.* 14
the grosse matter of this earthly *myne* . . . *H.B.* 46
with the rage of *mine* own ravisht thought, . . . *H.H.B.* 1
Minerva. *Minerva* did the chalenge not refuse, . . . *Mui.* 273
*Like as *Minerva,* being late returnd From slaughter . . . III. ix. 22. 1
Mines. Dart, nigh chockt with sands of tinny *mines.* . . . IV. xi. 31. 5
Mingle. Mongst these sterne stounds to *mingle* soft delights; . VII. vi. 37. 4
Mingled. they *mingled* were in furious armes, . . . II. ii. 27. 1
mingled all with sweate, . . . II. iv. 37. 5
Mingled emongst loose Ladies and lascivious boyes. . . . II. v. 28. 9
the rude And scorned partes were *mingled* with the fine) . . . II. xii. 59. 2
As smoke and sulphure *mingled* with confused stryfe. . . . III. ii. 32. 9
In fleshly lust were *mingled* both yfere, . . . III. vii. 48. 8
mingled them with perfect vermily; . . . III. viii. 6. 8
mingled with the raskall rablement, . . . III. xi. 46. 3
mingled here and there The tongues of Serpents, . . . VI. xii. 28. 1
Minim. To make one *minime* of thy poore handmayd, . . . VI. x. 28. 6
Miniments. *See* **Muniments.**

Minion. Fitt mate for such a mincing *mineon,* . . . II. ii. 37. 2
Minished. The paw yett missed not his *minisht* might, . . . I. xi. 43. 8
Ministered. Out of her mountaines *ministred* supplies; . . . *Gn.* 506
Against the viaundes should be *ministred.* . . . II. ix. 27. 4
Ministers. speach Against Gods holie *Ministers* . . . *Hub.* 840
Ministreth. his faire sister for creation *Ministreth* matter fit, III. vi. 9. 4
Minos. just *Minos* righteous soules doth sever . . . *Gn.* 623
Minotaurs. as Griffons, *Minotaures,* Crocodiles, . . . *Hub.* 1123
Dragons, and *Minotaures,* and feendes of hell, . . . III. x. 40. 5
Minstrels. There many *Minstrales* maken melody, . . . I. v. 3. 4
Minstrales making goodly meriment, . . . III. xii. 5. 4
how the *Minstrils* gin to shrill aloud . . . *Epith.* 129
Minute. Whose smallest *minute* lost no riches render may. . . IV. x. 14. 9
to her creatures every *minute* chaunce; . . . VII. vii. 23. 2
maketh every *minute* seeme a myle. . . . *Am.* lxxxvi. 12
Minutes. declyned . . . nigh thirtie *minutes* . . . V. Pr. 7. 8
Mirabella. Fayre *Mirabella* was her name, . . . VI. vii. 35. 1
Prince Arthure . . . Quites *Mirabell* from dreed: . . . VI. viii. Arg.
Mirabella's. Fayre *Mirabellaes* punishment For loves disdaine VI. vii. Arg.
Till *Mirabellaes* fortunes I doe further say. . . . VI. vii. 50. 9
Ensample take of *Mirabellaes* case, . . . VI. viii. 2. 7
Miracle. By *miracle,* not yet appearing playne, . . . IV. xi. 1. 7
He saw, . . . A *Miracle* of natures goodly grace . . . V. v. 12. 3
some *miracle* of heavenly hew . . . VI. ix. 8. 8
Miraculous. *Miraculous* may seeme to him that reades . . . III. vi. 8. 1
What more *miraculous* thing may be told, . . . *Am.* xxx. 9
Mire. *See* **Wag-mire.**
lyftes him up out of the loathsome *myre:* . . . *S.C.* O. 92
So oft as Slowth still in the *mire* did stand. . . . I. iv. 36. 4
Would have cast downe, and trodd in durty *myre,* . . . I. viii. 17. 6
free his feet that in the *myre* sticke fast? . . . I. ix. 39. 5
gathering up himselfe out of the *mire* . . . I. xi. 40. 7
in the *mire* His nigh forewearied feeble feet did slide, . . . I. xi. 45. 7
all soild with blood and *myre:* . . . II. iv. 16. 4
Drew him through durt and *myre* . . . II. v. 23. 4
dull billowes thicke as troubled *mire,* . . . II. vi. 20. 7
Nor sea of licour cold, nor lake of *myre:* . . . II. vi. 44. 4
he clothes with sinfull *mire,* . . . III. vi. 32. 7
lay tombled in the *myre,* Unable to arise, . . . III. vii. 45. 8
Did wallow in all other fleshly *myre,* . . . III. vii. 49. 6
touch celestiall seats with earthly *mire?* . . . VII. vi. 29. 4
Mirke, Mirkesome. *See* **Murk, Murksome.**
Mirror. Art made a *myrrhour* to behold my plight: . . . *S.C.* Ja. 20
Such immortal *mirrhor,* as he doth admire, . . . *S.C.* O. 93
myrrour of her Makers majestie, . . . *T.M.* 572
onely *mirrhor* of feminitie: . . . *Col.* 513
Mirrour of grace and Majestie divine, . . . I. Pr. 4. 2
in her hand she held a *mirrhour* bright, . . . I. iv. 10. 6
The God himselfe, vewing that *mirrhour* rare, . . . I. vi. 15. 6
In this fayre *mirrhour* maist behold thy face, . . . II. Pr. 4. 7
So glorious *mirrhour* of celestiall grace, . . . II. iii. 25. 6
wondrous *myrrhour,* by which she In love with him did fall. . III. ii. Arg.
To her revealed in a *mirrhour* playne; . . . III. ii. 17. 4
when she had espyde that *mirrhour* fayre, . . . III. ii. 22. 5
I in my fathers wondrous *mirrhour* saw, . . . III. ii. 38. 7
he which made That *mirrhour,* . . . III. iii. 6. 2
To be a *mirrour* to all mighty men, . . . V. ii. 19. 6
as in a *mirrour* sheene, . . . VI. Pr. 6. 5
Fayre eyes! the *myrrour* of my mazed hart, . . . *Am.* vii. 1
in his waters, which your *mirror* make, . . . *Epith.* 63
Admires the *mirrour* of so heavenly light. . . . *H.L.* 196
The *mirrour* of his owne thought doth admyre. . . . *H.B.* 224
Mirrors. In *mirrours* more then one her selfe to see; . . . III. Pr. 5. 6
two *mirrours,* by opposd reflexion, . . . *H.B.* 181
Mirth. Sike *myrth* in May is meetest for to make, . . . *S.C.* N. 11
The mornefull Muse in *myrth* now list ne maske, . . . *S.C.* N. 19
Matter of *myrth* now shalt thou have no more; . . . *S.C.* N. 56
dead shee is, that *myrth* thee made of yore. . . . *S.C.* N. 57
ybent to song and musicks *mirth,* . . . *S.C.* D. 40
great *mirth* and gladsome glee. . . . *Gn.* 184
honest *mirth,* that seem'd her well: . . . *Hub.* 35
maske in *mirth* with Graces well beseene? . . . *T.M.* 180
tell hir, I can heare no *mirth.* . . . *U.V.* 9
hir sweete Tongue was wonte to make me *mirth.* . . . *U.V.* 15
dye, wanting thy timely *mirth.* . . . *U.V.* 18
Taste no one hower of happines or *merth;* . . . *Ti.* 46
That may thy Muse and mates to *mirth* allure. . . . *Col.* 391
She soone left off her *mirth* and wanton play, . . . I. ii. 14. 4
So forth they rode, he feining seemely *merth,* . . . I. ii. 27. 8
Their wanton sportes and childish *mirth* did play, . . . I. xii. 7. 2
their exceeding *merth* may not be told: . . . I. xii. 40. 3
discontent for want of *merth* or meat: . . . II. ii. 35. 4
Guyon is of immodest *Merth* Led into loose desyre; . . . II. vi. Arg.
Matter of *merth* enough, though there were none, . . . II. vi. 3. 7
New *merth* her passenger to entertaine; . . . II. vi. 6. 2
Her honest *merth* and pleasaunce to partake; . . . II. vi. 21. 6
gamesom *merth* to grievous dreriment: . . . III. iv. 30. 4
mad through *merth,* And dronke with blood of men . . . III. vii. 47. 6
turned hath great *mirth* to mourning sad, . . . III. viii. 46. 3
All bent to *mirth* before the bride was bedded, . . . IV. i. 3. 5
me in *mirth* do cherry! . . . VI. x. 22. 9
mask in *myrth* lyke to a Comedy: . . . *Am.* liv. 6
Delights not in my *merth,* nor rues my smart: . . . *Am.* liv. 10
What then can move her? if nor *merth* nor mone, . . . *Am.* liv. 13
And all *mirth* sadnesse, and all lucre losse. . . . *H.H.B.* 280
Mirthful. A thousand Nymphes, with *mirthfull* jollitee, . . . *Ti.* 137
Miry. Onely these marishes and *myrie* bogs, . . . V. x. 23. 6
Misadvised. Certes ye *misavised* beene . . . III. ii. 9. 5
Misaimed. Missing the marke of his *misaymed* sight, . . . I. viii. 8. 3
Misavised. *See* **Misadvised.**

Misbelieve. chyde at him that made her *misbelieve:* . . . . IV. xii. 26. 4
Misborn. drawing nigh him, said; 'Ah! *misborn* Elfe, ... I. vi. 42. 1
Miscall. did him *miscall* That had from hoggish forme him brought . . . . II. xii. 86. 8
Whom she with leasings lewdly did *miscall* . . . . IV. viii. 24. 8
They mocke and scorne him, and him foule *miscall;* . . . . VII. vi. 49. 3
Miscalling. *Miscalling* me by many a bitter name, ... V. viii. 22. 8
Miscarriage. blame Of her *miscarriage* should in her be fond, . III. ii. 52. 8
Miscarried. *miscaried* or in plaine or wood. . . . . D. 140
lampe of light . . . is *miscaried* with the other Spheres: . . V. Pr. 7. 4
Mischallenge. The meede of thy *mischalenge* and abet. . . . IV. iii. 11. 2
Mischance. with stout courage arm'd against *mischaunce,* . . *Ro.* xxi. 3
My old musick mard by a newe *mischaunce.* . . . . *S.C.* Au. 12
Mischiefe mought to that *mischaunce* befall, ... *S.C.* Au. 13
when our flocks into *mischaunce* mought fall, ... *S.C.* D. 9
Bid strange *mischance* his quietnes to spill. . . . . *Gn.* 248
'Well may appeare by proofe of their *mischaunce,* . . . . . . *Gn.* 553
shepheards leave their lambes unto *mischaunce,* . . . . . . *Ti.* 327
He likest is to fall into *mischaunce,* . . . . *Mui.* 383
In Tragick plaints and passionate *mischance.* . . . . *Col.* 427
On silly Dame, subject to hard *mischaunce,* . . . . I. ii. 21. 3
in her way throwes mischiefe and *mischaunce,* . . . . II. ix. 8. 3
by *mischaunce* It might breake out . . . . II. ix. 30. 1
mischievous *mischaunce* his life and limbs did spare. . . . . III. i. 6. 9
by *mischaunce* The wicked steele through his left side did glaunce. . . . . III. iv. 16. 4
late *mischaunce* had her compeld to chaunge The land for sea, . III. viii. 20. 4
walkte each where for feare of hid *mischaunce,* . . . . III. xii. 15. 7
Artegall, beholding his *mischaunce,* . . . . IV. vi. 11. 1
the which it fairely blest From foule *mischance;* . . . . . IV. vi. 13. 5
teares it all with terrible *mischance.* . . . . IV. vi. 14. 5
his mortall part by great *mischance* Was slaine; . . . . . . IV. xi. 16. 7
th' adventure of her late *mischaunce;* . . . . VI. iii. 19. 2
Unto a straunge *mischaunce* that menac'd her decay. . . . . VI. viii. 34. 9
Mischanced. but still it has *mischaunced.* . . . . *Hub.* 64
Mischief. fall into some *mischiefe:* . . . . *S.C.* Mar. 45
Mischiefe mought to that mischaunce befall, ... *S.C.* Au. 13
bene they chaffred, or at *mischiefe* dead? . . . . *S.C.* S. 10
sike *mischiefe* graseth hem emong, ... *S.C.* S. 113
many han into *mischiefe* fall, ... *S.C.* S. 147
Mischiefe light on him, ... *S.C.* S. 212
The haplesse *mischiefe* that has thee hent; . . . . *S.C.* S. 249
Doest save from *mischiefe* the unwary sheepe, ... *S.C.* D. 10
How to prevent this *mischiefe* ere it fall, ... *Hub.* 190
for to shunne the horrible *mischiefe,* . . . . *Ti.* 143
Greedie of *mischiefe,* ranging all about, ... *D.* 157
'Least suddaine *mischiefe* ye too rash provoke: . . . . I. i. 12. 2
full of malicious mynd, To worken *mischiefe,* . . . . II. i. 2. 2
She brought to *mischiefe* through Occasion, ... II. iv. 17. 8
I meant to purge both with a third *mischiefe,* . . . . II. iv. 31. 3
Falne into *mischiefe* through intemperaunce, ... II. iv. 36. 2
in her way throwes *mischiefe* and mischaunce, ... II. ix. 8. 3
through flight into fond *mischief* fell. . . . . II. x. 26. 9
tombling into *mischiefe* unespide: . . . . II. xii. 35. 4
none of them foule *mischiefe* could eschew, ... III. i. 66. 3
him shall make in *mischiefe* fall. . . . . III. iii. 28. 9
mischief fel upon the meaners crowne. . . . . III. v. 25. 8
Still when he mused on his late *mischiefe,* . . . . III. x. 18. 3
all were her whole delight In *mischiefe,* . . . . III. vii. 9. 9
A net . . . this *Mischiefe,* that Mishap: . . . . III. xii. 11. 6
For feare of *mischiefe,* which she did forecast . . . . III. vii. 18. 4
huge *mischiefe* and vile villany . . . . III. xii. 35. 2
A new unknowen *mischiefe* did from him remove. . . . . . . IV. i. 2. 9
Misdoubted lost through *mischiefe* that befell. . . . . . . IV. ii. 23. 7
Cambell . . . Perceiv'd would breede great *mischiefe,* . . . . IV. ii. 37. 7
The wicked steele, for *mischiefe* first ordained, ... IV. iv. 24. 3
This *mischiefe* framd for their first loves defeature, ... IV. vi. 17. 7
So *mischiefe* overmatcht the wronger. . . . . V. viii. 7. 9
By some bad spirit that it to *mischiefe* bore, ... V. viii. 34. 7
mickle *mischiefe* unto many a knight, ... V. ix. 40. 4
Untill late *mischiefe* did uppon me light, ... V. xi. 49. 3
A wicked hag, and Envy selfe excelling In *mischiefe;* . . . . V. xii. 35. 8
How they might make him into *mischiefe* fall, ... V. xii. 37. 4
the present *mischiefe* to redresse, ... VI. iii. 44. 2
To cloke the *mischiefe* which he inly ment, ... VI. vii. 4. 2
on him which did this *mischiefe* breed, ... VI. vii. 13. 7
Of all his *mischiefe* and late lucklesse smart; . . . . VI. vii. 21. 3
greater *mischiefe* on her threw, ... VI. xi. 2. 6
Thenceforth more *mischiefe* and more scath he wrought . . . VI. xii. 39. 1
Shame be thy meed, and *mischiefe* thy reward, ... *Am.* lxxxv. 13
Mischiefs. plagues, and *mischiefes,* and long misery, Might fall on her, ... I. iii. 23. 7
How many *mischieves* should ensue his heedlesse hast. . . . I. iv. 34. 9
Full many *mischiefes* follow cruell Wrath: . . . . I. iv. 35. 1
never man such *mischiefes* did torment: . . . . I. xi. 28. 3
did complaine Of grievous *mischiefes* . . . . II. ii. 43. 3
Infinite *mischiefes* of them doe arize, ... II. vii. 12. 6
Mischievous. Hath stirred up so *mischievous* despight? . . . *T.M.* 46
Launched his thigh with so *mischievous* might, ... *As.* 119
'by whose *mischievous* arts Art thou misshaped thus, ... I. ii. 34. 2
his *mischievous* bow full readie bent, ... II. xi. 24. 4
mischievous mischaunce his life and limbs did spare. . . . . III. i. 6. 9
To bring to passe his *mischievous* intent, ... III. iv. 45. 2
reproches rife Of his *mischievous* deedes, ... III. vi. 14. 7
Through *mischievous* debate and deadly feood, ... IV. i. 26. 4
he was full bent to some *mischievous* deede. . . . . IV. vi. 2. 9
for what cause so great *mischievous* smart Was ment . . . . V. vi. 31. 8
mischivous witches with theyr charmes, ... *Epith.* 342
Misconceit. Full of melancholie and sad misfare Through *misconceipt,* . . . . IV. vi. 2. 4
Misconceived. Breake gentle sleepe with *misconceived* dout. . . *Epith.* 337
Misconceiving. misty dampe of *misconceyving* night, ... III. x. 47. 5
Misconstrue. to *misconstrue* of a mans intent, ... V. xii. 34. 4
Misconstruing. Which she *misconstruing,* . . . . III. i. 55. 8
Miscounselled. things *miscounselled* must needs miswend. . . *Hub.* 128
Miscreance. through this, and other their *miscreaunce* . . . *S.C.* May 91
if thou wilt renounce thy *miscreaunce,* . . . . II. viii. 51. 6
Miscreant. 'Goe now, proud *Miscreant,* . . . . I. v. 13. 1
'Arise, thou cursed *Miscreaunt,* . . . . I. vi. 41. 1
when the *Miscreaunt* Perceived him to waver, ... I. ix. 49. 1
'Vile *Miscreaunt,'* (said he) wither dost thou flye . . . . . II. vi. 39. 6
'False traitour! *miscreaunt!* . . . . II. viii. 31. 6
turne away From her unto the *miscreant* him selfe; . . . . . V. viii. 19. 6
Miscreate. Ymner slew of Logris *miscreate;* . . . . II. x. 38. 2
Miscreated. Eftsoones he tooke that *miscreated* faire, ... I. ii. 3. 1
Ne mortall steele emperce his *miscreated* mould. . . . . . . II. vii. 42. 9
Misdeed. the more taugment The memory of hys *misdeede* . *S.C.* Au. 186
oppress The faire Irena with his foule *misdeede,* . . . . . V. i. 13. 4
Misdeem. because you shall not us *misdeeme,* . . . . *Hub.* 375
made him to *misdeeme* My loyalty, ... I. vii. 49. 4
Such as no doubt of him he neede *misdeeme,'* . . . . III. ix. 6. 5
These gentle Ladies will *misdeeme* too light . . . . IV. viii. 29. 4
carry colours faire that feeble eies *misdeeme.* . . . . VI. Pr. 4. 9
Why then doe ye, proud fayre, *misdeeme* so farre, ... *Am.* lviii. 13
The doubt which ye *misdeeme,* fayre love, is vaine, ... *Am.* lxv. 1
not, as fond men *misdeeme,* An outward shew . . . . *H.B.* 90
Misdeemed. *See* **Misdempt.**
Durst not approch for dread which she *misdeemd;* . . . . . I. xi. 55. 4
Misdeemest. 'Sith thou *misdeem'st* so much of things in sight? V. ii. 39. 3
Misdeeming. Covered with darkenes and *misdeeming* night, . I. ii. 3. 8
Una lorne, Through light *misdeeming* of her loialtie; . . . I. iv. 2. 2
Misdeeming sure that her those flames did burne; . . . . . III. xii. 45. 5
Your high displeasure, through *misdeeming* bred: . . . . . . IV. viii. 17. 3
Misdempt. *See* **Misdeemed.**
much disdeigning to be so *misdempt,* . . . . III. x. 29. 4
Misdesert. not occasiond through my *misdesert,* . . . . . . VI. i. 12. 6
Misdid. for doubt of blame If he *misdid,* . . . . IV. iv. 27. 8
Misdiet. dropsie . . . Which by *misdiet* daily greater grew. . I. iv. 23. 8
Surfeat, *misdiet,* and unthriftie waste, ... II. xi. 12. 7
Misdight. Of so unmanly maske in misery *misdight.* . . . . V. vii. 37. 9
Misdo. when she list *misdonne?* . . . . III. ix. 7. 3
Misdone. *See* **Misdo.**
He fled for feare of that he had *misdonne,* . . . . III. ix. 48. 4
Misdoubt. did *misdoubt* some ill whose cause did not appeare. IV. x. 12. 9
Misdoubted. *Misdoubted* lost through mischiefe that befell. . IV. ii. 23. 7
Misdoubtful. She gan to cast in her *misdoubtfull* mynde A thousand feares, ... V. vi. 3. 8
Misdoubting. *misdoubting* least he should misguyde . . . . VI. iii. 47. 7
misdoubting least of—new Some uprore were . . . . VI. xi. 43. 8
Miser. The *Miser* threw him selfe, as an Offall, ... II. iii. 8. 7
Miserable. Which make this life wretched and *miserable,* . . *Pet.*[2] vi. 13
Most *miserable* man, whom wicked fate . . . . *Hub.* 892
Heare, and beholde the *miserable* state Of us, ... *T.M.* 59
Most *miserable* creature under sky . . . . *T.M.* 127
'O! trustlesse state of *miserable* men, ... *Ti.* 197
I of many most Most *miserable* man; . . . . *D.* 38
Help me to wayle my *miserable* case, ... *D.* 510
friendlesse, unfortunate, Now *miserable* I, Fidessa, dwell, . I. ii. 26. 2
As *miserable* lovers use to rew, ... I. ix. 9. 8
O *miserable* men that to him subject arre! . . . . II. ii. 26. 9
What now is left of *miserable* wightes, ... II. xii. 9. 4
Redresse the wrong of *miserable* wight, ... III. x. 28. 2
There dwels he ever, *miserable* swaine, ... III. x. 60. 5
all the gods did mone her *miserable* case. . . . . IV. vii. 30. 9
the more Rejoyced at his *miserable* case, ... V. iv. 23. 2
As now in *miserable* state he stands; . . . . V. v. 33. 3
For wretched woman, *miserable* wight, ... V. x. 21. 3
Shewing us mercie (*miserable* crew!) . . . . *H.H.L.* 214
Through which he past his *miserable* dayes, ... *H.H.L.* 236
Miserably. So *miserably* him all helpelesse slew, ... VI. vi. 22. 7
Miseries. The carefull thoughts of mortall *miseries;* . . . . *Bel.*[2] i. 4
Of Lovers *Miseries* which maketh his bloodie game? . . . . *Tetrasticon* 2
glories most in mortall *miseries,* . . . . *D.* 152
stayd, To gather breath in many *miseryes.* . . . . I. vi. 19. 4
To see sad pageaunts of mens *miseries,* . . . . II. i. 36. 3
with wretched *miseryes* and woefull ruth, ... II. x. 62. 3
mortall *miseries* doth make her play. . . . . III. vii. 4. 5
dayly more augment my *miseryes?* . . . . *Am.* xxxvi. 8
Miser's. Vouchsafe to stay your steed for humble *misers* sake.' II. i. 8. 9
He stayd his steed for humble *misers* sake, ... II. i. 9. 1
Misers. his liefest pelfe . . . the joy of *misers* blinde. . . . III. x. 15. 9
Misery. With weeping, and wayling, and *misery.* . . . . . . *S.C.* F. 50
broughten this Oake to this *miserye;* . . . . *S.C.* F. 212
so there is, but all of *miserye:* . . . . *S.C.* S. 29
Why should we be bound to such *miseree?* . . . . *S.C.* S. 239
miserie doth bravest mindes abate, ... *Hub.* 256
My wealth, compar'd to thine owne *miserie,* . . . . *Hub.* 598
To come so farre to seeke for *misery,* . . . . *Hub.* 946
Fild with the wreaks of mortall *miserie;* . . . . *T.M.* 124
Doo mone my *miserie* with silence soft: . . . . *T.M.* 292
Findes greater burthen of his *miserie.* . . . . *T.M.* 306
Thence I behold the *miserie* of men, ... *T.M.* 529
to worke thy *miserie.* . . . . *Mui.* 236
as I muzed on the *miserie* In which men live, ... *D.* 36
That I from *miserie* shall be releast, ... *D.* 272
mortall men, and rue their *miserie.* . . . . *D.* 385
Like a Mill-wheele in midst of *miserie,* . . . . *D.* 432
plagues, and mischiefes, and long *misery,* Might fall on her, I. iii. 23. 7
to ease you of your *misery!'* . . . . I. xi. 3. 9
Thus enter we . . . with woe, and end with *miseree!'* . . . II. ii. 2. 9

Misery—*Continued.*
Till death make one end of my daies and *miseree!'* . . . . III. ii. 39. 9
Will not long *misery* late mercy make, ... III. iii. 43. 7
waste in woe and waylfull *miserye:* . . . . III. iv. 38. 4
misery craves rather mercy then repriefe. . . . . III. viii. 1. 9
I graunt to thy great *misery* Gratious respect; . . . . . . III. x. 32. 1
gentle Ladyes helplesse *misery:* . . . . III. xi. 18. 6
Knowing the *miserie* of their estate, ... IV. iii. 1. 4
flie Unto her native home from mortall *miserie.* . . . . . IV. iii. 30. 9
To cloud my daies in dolefull *misery,* . . . . IV. viii. 16. 8
miserie In which so long he mercilesse did lie. . . . . . IV. viii. 64. 4
He could no more but her great *misery* bemone. . . . . . IV. xii. 12. 9
ne let you amate Your *misery,* . . . . V. iv. 28. 5
she sternely bade His *miserie* to be augmented more, . . . V. v. 54. 6
Of so unmanly maske in *misery* misdight. . . . . V. vii. 37. 9
meant to make advantage of his *misery.* . . . . VI. iii. 46. 9
for her sake fell into *misery;* . . . . VI. viii. 3. 5
Nor better cheare to shew in *misery,* . . . . VI. xi. 8. 7
know no end of her owne *mysery,* . . . . *Am.* xxv. 2
Turning all loves delight to *miserie,* . . . . *H.L.* 269
Misfallen. she feared least some hard mishap Had him *misfalne* V. vi. 4. 2
Misfare. great comfort in her sad *misfare* Was Amoret, . . IV. v. 30. 4
Full of melancholie and sad *misfare* . . . . IV. vi. 2. 3
That much did ease his mourning and *misfare:* . . . . . IV. viii. 5. 5
Against all hard mishaps and fortunelesse *misfare.* . . . . IV. viii. 27. 9
His stubborne heart, that never felt *misfare,* . . . . . . IV. xii. 12. 4
The whole occasion of his late *misfare,* . . . . V. xi. 48. 7
Crying aloud to shew her sad *misfare* . . . . VI. iii. 24. 5
Through daily mourning and nightly *misfare:* . . . . . . VI. xii. 14. 5
Are you not subject eeke to this *misfare?* . . . . VII. vii. 53. 3
Misfaring. their owne *misfaring* will not see: . . . . . *Col.* 758
Misfeigning. so *misfeigning* her true knight to bee: . . . . I. iii. 40. 4
Misfell. to upbrayd that chaunce which him *misfell,* . . . V. v. 10. 2
Misformed. With that *misformed* spright he backe returnd . . I. i. 55. 9
how long time,' . . . 'Are you in this *misformed* hous to dwell?' I. ii. 43. 2
that *misformed* shape misshaped more. . . . . I. viii. 16. 5
Misfortune. O great *misfortune,* O great griefe, ... *Pet.*[1] ii. 10
wretched persons to *misfortune* borne; . . . . *T.M.* 154
Hath with so huge *misfortune* you opprest; . . . . II. i. 48. 7
Misfortune waites advantage to entrap The man . . . . . II. iv. 17. 4
What great *misfortune* hath betidd this knight? . . . . . . II. viii. 24. 2
Seemed some great *misfortune* to deplore, ... II. xii. 27. 8
gan fayre perswade Not to provoke *misfortune,* . . . . . . III. i. 10. 2
one day, as me *misfortune* led, ... III. ii. 38. 6
Should of his dearest daughters hard *misfortune* heare. . . . III. iii. 5. 9
Into *misfortune* fell, as ye did heare, ... III. vi. 54. 8
What hard *misfortune* brought me to this same; . . . . . . III. viii. 23. 8
having now *misfortune* got for guide. . . . . IV. iv. 24. 4
by what haplesse fate Or hard *misfortune* . . . . IV. vi. 47. 6
Before *misfortune* did his hew deface; . . . . IV. viii. 14. 5
To tell through what *misfortune* he had far'd . . . . . . IV. ix. 41. 5
by *misfortune* in his hand did fall.' . . . . V. iii. 22. 8
In hope ye will not turne *misfortune* to my blame. . . . . . V. iv. 28. 9
'What May-game hath *misfortune* made of you? . . . . . . V. vii. 40. 2
in his fall *misfortune* him mistooke; . . . . V. viii. 8. 1
misfortune, which did me abase Unto this shame, ... VI. i. 12. 7
As he of some *misfortune* were afrayd; . . . . VI. v. 3. 4
He dreads no danger, nor *misfortune* feares, ... *H.L.* 223
Misfortune's. Does make her selfe *misfortunes* piteous pray. V. ii. 50. 5
Great ruth through her *misfortunes* tragicke stowre; . . . . V. ix. 45. 8
wrapt In sad *misfortunes* foule deformity . . . . VI. v. 1. 3
To save her chylde, which in *misfortunes* mouth was plaste. VI. xii. 16. 9
Misfortunes. her sad troubles and *misfortunes* hard: . . . . I. iii. 9. 4
hart . . . heaped with so huge *misfortunes,* . . . . I. vii. 39. 3
She sought with ruth to salve his sad *misfortunes* sore. . . . V. vii. 38. 9
Misgone. Sike mister men bene all *misgone,* . . . . . . *S.C.* Jul. 201
Misgotten. spoile of love *misgotten,* . . . . IV. i. 51. 2
'Leave, faytor, quickely that *misgotten* weft . . . . VI. i. 18. 7
Misgovernance. All will be soone wasted with *misgovernaunce;* *S.C.* May 90
Lulled a sleepe through loves *misgovernaunce.* . . . . . . *S.C.* N. 4
Misguide. *misguyde* His former malice to some new assay, . . VI. iii. 47. 7
(which none yet durst . . . to alter or *misguide*) . . . . . VII. vi. 5. 6
Could make amends to God for mans *misguyde,* . . . . . *H.H.L.* 144
Misguided. the Foxe and th' Ape by him *misguided;* . . . . *Hub.* 38
Mishap. All the *mishap* the which our daies outweares, . . . *Ro.* xix. 5
pittied is *mishappe* that nas remedie, ... *S.C.* May 61
Into the same *mishap* I now am cast, ... *Gn.* 363
least *mishap* the most blisse alter may? . . . . *Mui.* 220
With griefe of mournefull great *mishap* opprest, ... *D.* 2
that any should bemone My hard *mishap,* . . . . *D.* 76
such *mishap,* as chaunst to me, ... *D.* 516
what hard *mishap* is this, That hath thee hether brought . . I. iii. 39. 2
as if some new *mishap* Had him betide, ... II. i. 26. 8
What hard *mishap* him brought to such distresse, ... II. iv. 16. 8
Unweeting and unware of such *mishap,* . . . . II. iv. 17. 7
affrap The warlike ryder to his most *mishap:* . . . . . . III. ii. 6. 5
Some hard *mishap* in hazard of his life. . . . . III. iv. 24. 6
Lamenting his *mishap* and heavy plight; . . . . III. iv. 44. 2
a rusty blade . . . this Mischiefe, that *Mishap:* . . . . . . III. xii. 11. 6
Till by *mishap* he in his foemens hand did light. . . . . . IV. v. 7. 9
His hard *mishap* in dolor to deplore, ... IV. vii. 39. 7
An hard *mishap* and disaventrous case . . . . IV. viii. 51. 3
what *mishap* thus long him fro my selfe removes?' . . . . . IV. viii. 63. 9
bravely mounted to his most *mishap* . . . . IV. x. 9. 7
Talus brings newes . . . Of Artegals *mishap:* . . . . V. vi. Arg.
she feared least some hard *mishap* Had him misfalne . . . . V. vi. 4. 1
by hard *mishap* doth lie In wretched bondage, ... V. vi. 10. 6
what hard *mishap* thee brought . . . . VI. i. 12. 1
discourse Of former daies *mishap,* . . . . VI. iii. 14. 9
though no lesse sory wight For that *mishap,* . . . . VI. x. 18. 8

Mishap—*Continued.*
then the more your owne *mishap* I rew, ... *Am.* lxxxii. 3
Mishappen. Affraid least to themselves the like *mishappen* might. . . . . I. iii. 20. 9
Mishaps. my *mishaps,* which oft I to him plained, ... *Ti.* 142
Mishaps are maistred by advice discrete, ... I. vii. 40. 7
maister these *mishaps* with patient might. . . . . I. viii. 45. 2
death then would the like *mishaps* forestall, ... I. ix. 45. 8
in my *mishaps,* as hitherward I lately traveild, ... I. xii. 31. 6
Against all hard *mishaps* and fortunelesse misfare. . . . . IV. viii. 27. 9
My hard *mishaps* that ye may learne to shonne; . . . . . . IV. x. 3. 7
with ruth (as I perceave) Of my *mishaps* . . . . V. v. 37. 8
when ye list your owne *mishaps* to mourne, ... *Epith.* 7
Misintended. The Damzell broke his *misintended* dart. . . . . *Am.* xvi. 12
Mislead. Thus to *mislead* mee, whiles I you obaid: . . . . II. vi. 22. 8
him too light of credence did *mislead,* . . . . IV. vii. 20. 7
Misled. Love hath *misled* both my younglings and mee: . . . *S.C.* Au. 17
wicked Fortune faultles him *misled,* . . . . *Mui.* 418
leave their lambes to losse, *misled* amisse. . . . . *Col.* 687
fedd His foolish malady, and long time had *misledd.* . . . . III. viii. 3. 9
nets dispred, With which he . . . many had ylike *misled:* . . . III. x. 9. 8
looser thought will lightly be *misled,* . . . . IV. viii. 29. 3
How he *mis-led* the simple peoples traine, ... V. ii. 33. 7
whom errour so *misled,* . . . . V. viii. 13. 8
with false beauties flattring bait *misled,* . . . . *H.H.B.* 290
Misleeke. *See* **Mislike.**
Mislike. Let none *mislike* of that may not be mended: . . . . *S.C.* May 162
Mote not *mislike* you also to abate Your zealous hast, . . . III. viii. 51. 6
of the meane he greatly did *misleeke.* . . . . V. ii. 49. 5
Mislikedst. that which thou *mislikedst* in a few.' . . . . . . *Col.* 748
Mislive. if he *mislive* in leudnes and lust, ... *S.C.* May 87
Misplaced. th' one long, the other short, And both *misplast;* . IV. i. 28. 8
Misprize. beare the rigour of his bold *mesprise;* . . . . . . II. vii. 39. 8
through great disaventure, or *mesprize,* . . . . II. xii. 19. 4
reward the wretch for his *mesprise,* . . . . III. ix. 9. 6
With love of her, and shame of such *mesprize.* . . . . . . IV. iv. 11. 7
pardon their *mesprise:* . . . . IV. ix. 35. 4
greater shame t' abide so great *misprize,* . . . . V. v. 48. 4
Misregard. when as these rimes be red With *misregard,* . . IV. viii. 29. 2
Misrule. Distempred through *misrule* and passions bace; . . . II. ix. 1. 6
Miss. Yet is his *misse* not mickle. . . . . *S.C.* Jul. 16
doe *misse* the marked scope; . . . . *S.C.* N. 155
joyes enjoyes that mortall men doe *misse.* . . . . *S.C.* N. 196
seeking *misse,* and missing doe lament.' . . . . *D.* 168
since mine eie your joyous sight did *mis,* . . . . I. iii. 27. 6
swim in pleasure, which thou here doest *mis:* . . . . . . II. iii. 39. 7
cannot so easy *mis.* . . . . II. iii. 40. 7
blis . . . few gett, but many *mis:* . . . . II. vii. 48. 9
What wonder then if one, of women all, did *mis?* . . . . III. ix. 2. 9
O graunt that of my love at last I may not *misse!"* . . . . IV. x. 47. 9
Of all whose weight he would not *misse* a fether: . . . . . V. ii. 31. 7
least by that art He should his purpose *misse,* . . . . . . V. vi. 24. 3
Calepine . . . his love doth *misse.* . . . . VI. iv. Arg.
th' one did *misse* his marke, ... VI. vii. 7. 6
Dark is my day, whyles her fayre light I *mis,* . . . . . . *Am.* lxxxviii. 13
Missaid. As her repenting so to have *missayd,* . . . . . . III. ii. 9. 2
brought forth speeches myld when she would have *missayd.* . IV. vi. 27. 9
Though out of course, yet hath not bene *missayd,* . . . . VI. xii. 2. 3
Missay. Or Diggon her is, or I *missaye.* . . . . *S.C.* S. 2
missay Both of their doctrine, and of theyr faye. . . . . . *S.C.* S. 106
Missed. few have found, and manie one hath *mist!* . . . . . *Hub.* 894
Which when I *missed,* having looked long, ... *Ti.* 477
he that once hath *missed* the right way, ... I. ix. 43. 8
The paw yett *missed* not his minisht might, ... I. xi. 43. 8
whenas Mammon saw his purpose *mist,* . . . . II. vii. 34. 8
when her he *mist,* He woxe halfe mad; . . . . VI. ii. 20. 6
Like to a Tygre that hath *mist* his pray, ... VI. iv. 6. 2
Now here, now there, and oft him neare he *mist;* . . . . . VI. viii. 13. 7
Misseem. that same warlike wize, I weene, would you *misseeme;* III. iii. 53. 6
Forcyng to doe that did him fowle *misseeme.* . . . . III. viii. 26. 7
Misseeming. With shuttelcocks, *misseeming* manlie wit, . . . *Hub.* 804
with her witchcraft, and *misseeming* sweete, ... I. vii. 50. 8
this *misseeming* hew your manly looks doth marre? . . . . . I. viii. 42. 9
never knight I saw in such *misseeming* plight.' . . . . . . I. ix. 23. 9
this *misseeming* discord meekely lay aside.' . . . . II. ii. 31. 9
Met her in such *misseeming* foule array; . . . . VI. vii. 39. 3
Misseth. Diana he her takes to be, But *misseth* bow . . . . I. vi. 16. 9
every one, that *misseth* then her make, ... *Am.* lxx. 11
Misshape. her *mis-shape* much helpt; . . . . V. xii. 29. 3
Misshaped. *See* **Misshapen.**
'by whose mischievous arts Art thou *misshaped* thus, ... I. ii. 34. 3
it . . . that misformed shape *misshaped* more. . . . . I. viii. 16. 5
her *misshaped* parts did them appall: . . . . I. viii. 46. 7
Monstrous, *mishapt,* and all his backe was spect . . . . . . III. vii. 22. 4
howsoever it may grow *mis-shapt,* . . . . VI. v. 1. 5
Misshapen. *See* **Misshaped.**
'Her neather partes *misshapen,* monstruous, Were hidd in water, I. ii. 41. 1
A rude, *mishapen,* monstrous rablement, ... I. vi. 8. 7
a monstrous rablement Of fowle *misshapen* wightes, ... II. xi. 8. 2
Misshapes. horribly *misshapes* with ugly sightes, ... II. v. 27. 7
Missing. seeking misse, and *missing* doe lament.' . . . . . . *D.* 168
His mightie Armour, *missing* most at need; . . . . I. vii. 19. 5
Missing the marke of his misaymed sight, ... I. viii. 8. 3
missing of the marke which he had eyde, ... IV. iii. 18. 8
missing it, faine from themselves to flie; . . . . IV. iv. 47. 5
missing to his mind That Virgins love to win . . . . IV. xi. 2. 2
not a dram was *missing* of their right: . . . . V. ii. 35. 4
many there were *missing;* which were ded, ... VI. vii. 33. 3
Then found he many *missing* of his crew, ... VI. vii. 34. 1
Mist. *See* **Missed.**

Mist—*Continued.*
by her hellish science raisd . . . A foggy *mist* . . . I. ii. 38. 5
A foggy *mist* had covered all the land; . . . I. iv. 36. 7
feard to wander in that fastefull *mist,* . . . II. xii. 35. 3
a foggy *mist* hath overcast The face of heven, . . . III. iv. 13. 1
The *mist* of griefe dissolv'd did into vengeance powre. . . . III. iv. 13. 9
Mistake. Both which fraile men doe oftentimes *mistake,* . . . I. ii. 32. 7
cause not well conceived ye *mistake:* . . . II. ii. 5. 5
The guilty cup she fained to *mistake,* . . . III. ix. 31. 2
For me he did *mistake* that Squire to bee, . . . IV. viii. 55. 8
As that I did *mistake* the living for the ded. . . . V. viii. 13. 9
Calidore he greatly did *mistake,* . . . VI. ix. 44. 1
Mister. Sike *mister* men bene all misgone, . . . *S.C.* Jul. 201
Such *myster* saying me seemeth to mirke. . . . *S.C.* S. 103
Wondring what *mister* wight he was, . . . *Hub.* 671
To weet what *mister* wight was so dismayd. . . . I. ix. 23. 2
'What *mister* wight,' (saide he) 'and how arayd?' . . . III. v. 5. 1
What *mister* wight that was, and whence deriv'd, . . . III. vii. 14. 2
What *mister* wight it was that so did plaine? . . . IV. vii. 10. 5
What *mister* wight he was, or what he ment; . . . IV. viii. 13. 6
Ne weene what *mister* maladie it is, . . . IV. xii. 22. 2
'What *mister* wight . . . Is he, . . . V. ii. 5. 1
What *mister* men, and eke from whence they were: . . . VI. xi. 39. 6
Mistereth. As for my name, it *mistreth* not to tell: . . . III. vii. 51. 8
Misthought. through error and *misthought* Of our like persons, IV. viii. 58. 2
Mistook. tell them that they greatly him *mistooke.* . . . *Hub.* 704
So lively and so like, that many it *mistooke.* . . . III. viii. 5. 9
Which they so much *mistooke,* . . . III. ix. 23. 7
Whereas no living creature he *mistooke,* . . . III. xi. 13. 4
Which was not hers, as many it *mistooke,* . . . V. iii. 27. 3
in his fall misfortune him *mistooke;* . . . V. viii. 8. 1
Mistrained. with corruptfull brybes is to untruth *mis-trayned.'* V. xi. 54. 9
Mistress. Great *maistresse* of her art was that false Dame, . . . I. vii. 1. 8
Whom when his *maistresse* proud perceiv'd to fall, . . . I. viii. 20. 6
to his *mistresse* each himselfe strove to advaunce. . . . II. ii. 16. 9
So great a *mistresse* of her art she was, . . . IV. ii. 10. 1
with his *mistresse* toyed. . . . V. v. 24. 9
For feare her *mistresse* shold have knowledge gayned; . . . V. v. 44. 4
unto her *mistresse* most unkind She daily told . . . V. v. 56. 7
streight forth she ran in hast Unto her *mistresse,* . . . VI. xii. 16. 7
Mistress'. His *mistresse* name, and his owne fame to raise. . *As.* 88
Unlesse that some gay *Mistresse* badge he beares: . . . *Col.* 780
in their *mistresse* reskew whom they lad; . . . II. xii. 84. 7
To sing his *mistresse* prayse; . . . III. Pr. 5. 3
His *maistresse* praises sweetly caroled: . . . III. vii. 17. 4
Mistreth. *See* **Mistereth.**
Mistrust. seeming to *mistrust* Some secret ill, or hidden foe . I. i. 49. 3
Ne reckt shee who her meaning did *mistrust,* . . . III. i. 48. 4
Mistrustful. He lookt askew with his *mistrustfull* eyes, . . . III. xii. 10. 5
Mists. When foggy *mistes* or cloudy tempests . . . II. vii. 1. 3
Clear'd from grosse *mists* of fraile infirmities. . . . *H.H.B.* 140
Misty. Disperst the shadowes of the *misty* night, . . . II. iii. 1. 2
misty dampe of misconceyving night, . . . III. x. 47. 5
Like the faire Morning clad in *misty* fog . . . VI. xi. 3. 9
Misusage. He saw thilke *misusage;* . . . *S.C.* Jul. 184
Misused. forst to trot on foot, and foule *misused,* . . . VI. ii. 22. 5
The more they him *misust,* and cruelly did beat. . . . VI. viii. 3. 9
Misusing. Now scratching her, and her loose locks *misusing,* . V. vi. 14. 6
Miswandered. *See* **Late-miswandered.**
Misween. Why then should witlesse man so much *misweene,* . II. Pr. 3. 4
Misweened. *misween'd* for her owne Knight, . . . V. viii. 46. 6
Misweening. Full happie man (*misweening* much) was hee, . *As.* 101
Least . . . rash *misweening* doe thy hart remove: . . . I. iv. 1. 6
Miswend. things miscounselled must needs *miswend.* . . . *Hub.* 128
Miswent. bene thy younglings *miswent?* . . . *S.C.* Au. 16
likewise sought her lover long *miswent,* . . . IV.v. 30. 6
Mitigate. strove to *mitigate* The stormie passion . . . *D.* 191
The swelling of his woundes to *mitigate;* . . . I. x. 26. 4
'Ne shall he yet his wrath so *mitigate,* . . . III. iii. 37. 1
To *mitigate* his stubborne malady: . . . III. v. 50. 5
Did *mitigate* the fierceness of their mode, . . . IV. iv. 5. 2
Ne ought mote ease or *mitigate* his paine, . . . IV. vii. 47. 4
naught the same may calme ne *mitigate,* . . . IV. viii. 1. 5
So did he *mitigate* Sir Artegall; . . . V. iii. 37. 1
Began to *mitigate* his swelling sourse, . . . VI. xi. 34. 3
Mitigates. *mitigates* the anguish of the minde. . . . *Ti.* 161
counsell *mitigates* the greatest smart: . . . I. vii. 40. 8
Mitre. like a Persian *mitre* on her hed Shee wore, . . . I. ii. 13. 4
she . . . crowned *mitre* rudely threw asyde: . . . I. viii. 25. 3
deckt with *Mitre* on her hed . . . V. vii. 13. 2
Moone-like *Mitre* to a Crowne of gold; . . . V. vii. 13. 6
Mitres. They wore rich *Mitres* shaped like the Moone, . . . V. vii. 4. 6
Mix. They *mixe* themselves, and shew their kindly might. . *H.L.* 91
Mixed. There drincks she Nectar with Ambrosia *mixt,* . . . *S.C.* N. 195
raine . . . *Mixt* with a murmuring winde, . . . I. i. 41. 4
Amongst these mightie men were wemen *mixt,* . . . I. v. 50. 1
Great pleasure, *mixt* with pittiful regard, . . . I. xii. 16. 1
The metall first he *mixt* with Medaewart, . . . II. viii. 20. 5
ever *mixt* their song with light licentious toyes. . . . II. xii. 72. 9
amiable grace, *Mixed* with manly sternesse, . . . II. xii. 79. 6
manly terror *mixed* therewithall; . . . III. i. 46. 2
all the gravell *mixt* with golden owre: . . . III. iv. 18. 6
A flaming fire, *ymixt* with smouldry smoke . . . III. xi. 21. 6
A direfull stench of smoke and sulphure *mixt* Ensewd, . . . III. xii. 2. 5
mixed threats among, and much unto her vowed. . . . VI. xi. 4. 9
Myld humblesse, *mixt* with awfull majesty. . . . *Am.* xiii. 5
pride and meeknesse, *mixt* by equall part, . . . *Am.* xxi. 3
Mixing. Mongst joyes *mixing* some tears, . . . V. xi. 16. 3
Mixture. Through goodly *mixture* of complexions dew; . . . II. iii. 22. 4
mixture made Of colours faire, . . . *H.B.* 65

Mizzle. Now gynnes to *mizzle,* . . . *S.C.* N. 208
Mnemon. forgot that whylome I heard tell From aged *Mnemon;* III. ix. 47. 4
so heard I say Old *Mnemon.* . . . III. ix. 51. 6
Mnemosyne. A shepeheard, when *Mnemosyne* he catcht; . . . III. xi. 35. 3
Mo. free spirite might not anie *mo* Be vext . . . *Pet.*[2] vii. 7
They sleepen in rest, well as other *moe:* . . . *S.C.* May 68
I sawe Calliope wyth Muses *moe,* . . . *S.C.* Jun. 57
one, opened, mote unfolde many *moe.* . . . *S.C.* S. 14
woulden drawe with hem many *moe.* . . . *S.C.* S. 99
sing no *moe* The songs that Colin made . . . *S.C.* N. 77
mongst manie others *moe,* To be partaker . . . *Hub.* 13
ye may better thrive than thousands *moe.'* . . . *Hub.* 642
So many *moe,* so everie one was used, . . . *Hub.* 1223
beside a thousand *moe* at land: . . . *Col.* 261
many others *mo* remaine, . . . *Col.* 448
Besides yet many *mo* that Cynthia serve, . . . *Col.* 576
All these, and many evils *moe* haunt ire, . . . I. iv. 35. 6
thousands *moe* the like . . . I. v. 50. 9
All which, and thousands *mo,* do make a loathsome life. . . I. ix. 44. 9
Infinite *moe* tormented in like paine He there beheld, . . . II. vii. 63. 1
Which he had wrought to many others *moe.* . . . III. xi. 45. 5
There were full many *moe* like maladies, . . . III. xii. 26. 1
So many *moe,* as there be phantasies . . . III. xii. 26. 3
eke of private persons many *moe,* . . . IV. i. 24. 1
an hundred Ladies *moe* Appear'd in place, . . . IV. v. 11. 8
meanest man of many *moe,* . . . IV. x. 19. 1
With many *moe* lay in ambushment . . . IV. x. 20. 7
Coridon with many other *moe,* . . . VI. xi. 11. 2
he vow'd to be her debter For many *moe* good turnes . . . VII. vi. 44. 8
Moan. Now she is a stone, And makes dayly *mone,* . . . *S.C.* Ap. 89
made great *mone.* . . . *S.C.* May 301
mone with many a mocke. . . . *S.C.* Au. 120
Thus gan he make of love his piteous *mone.* . . . *S.C.* D. 6
my life he lefte to *mone.* . . . *S.C.* D. 52
Making your musick of hart-breaking *mone.* . . . *T.M.* 6
I mourne, and pitifully *mone,* . . . *T.M.* 167
Doo *mone* my miserie with silence soft: . . . *T.M.* 292
made exceeding *mone;* . . . *T.M.* 416
made exceeding *mone,* . . . *T.M.* 598
My long decay, which no man els doth *mone,* . . . *Ti.* 157
no man left to *mone* His dolefull fate, . . . *Ti.* 192
piteous *mone* the which she for him made, . . . *As.* 170
every one did make exceeding *mone,* . . . *As.* 205
every one did weep and waile, and *mone,* . . . *As.* 207
Having his Amaryllis left to *mone.* . . . *Col.* 435
My dearest Lord . . . was slaine; that shall I ever *mone.* . . . I. ii. 23. 9
Much seemed he to *mone* her haplesse chaunce, . . . I. iii. 25. 6
helplesse hap it booteth not to *mone.* . . . I. iv. 49. 5
hardest heart would bleede to hear their piteous *mone.* . . I. viii. 36. 9
bitter doome of death and balefull *mone* . . . I. x. 53. 8
With piteous *mone* his percing speach gan paynt: . . . II. i. 9. 5
Wringing her handes, and making piteous *mone:* . . . II. i. 13. 7
Mournes inwardly, and makes to him selfe *mone;* . . . II. i. 42. 7
To frett for anger, or for griefe to *mone?* . . . II. iii. 3. 4
Makes for him endlesse *mone,* . . . III. i. 38. 4
Shee made so piteous *mone* and deare wayment, . . . III. iv. 35. 6
of her errour straunge I have great ruth and *mone.'* . . . III. v. 7. 9
To make exceeding *mone,* as they had been undonne. . . . III. vii. 19. 9
he gan to make Exceeding *mone,* . . . III. vii. 45. 4
with earnest *mone* . . . late entrance deare besought: . . . III. ix. 12. 3
Till thou cam'st hither to augment our *mone;* . . . IV. vii. 13. 8
each did other much bewaile and *mone,* . . . IV. vii. 20. 2
all the gods did *mone* her miserable case. . . . IV. vii. 30. 9
she gan *mone* his undeserved smart, . . . IV. viii. 3. 8
He made great *mone* after his salvage mood; . . . VI. iv. 12. 4
And makes exceeding *mone,* when he does thinke . . . VI. iv. 32. 2
shewed semblant of exceeding *mone* . . . VI. v. 4. 2
Much did the Craven seeme to *mone* his case, . . . VI. vii. 18. 1
wheres no courage, theres no ruth nor *mone.* . . . VI. vii. 18. 5
made great *mone* for that unhappy turne: . . . VI. x. 18. 6
his death, which some perhaps will *mone,* . . . *Am.* xxxvi. 13
What then can move her? if nor merth nor *mone,* . . . *Am.* liv. 13
they playne, and make ful piteous *mone* . . . *H.L.* 127
Moanful. There she began to make her *monefull* plaint . . . V. vi. 12. 1
Mochell. *See* **Mickle.**
Mock. mone with many a *mocke.* . . . *S.C.* Au. 120
make a *mocke* at the blustring blast. . . . *S.C.* S. 54
Of thy great Masters will, to scorne, or *mock.* . . . *Hub.* 508
So maist thou chaunce *mock* out a Benefice, . . . *Hub.* 509
mocke Divines and their profession. . . . *Hub.* 841
mocke high God himselfe, . . . *Hub.* 843
To *mock* her selfe, and Truth to imitate, . . . *T.M.* 206
In vaine to *mocke,* or mockt in vaine to bee: . . . I. viii. 33. 6
They *mocke* and scorne him, and him foule miscall; . . . VII. vi. 49. 3
he the fly did *mock.* . . . *Epig.* iv. 44
Mocked. her selfe so *mockt* to see By him, . . . I. iii. 40. 2
In vaine to mocke, or *mockt* in vaine to bee: . . . I. viii. 33. 6
At whose calamity, . . . He laught, and *mockt* . . . VI. iii. 34. 4
Mockeries. The laughing stocke of fortunes *mockeries,* . . . I. vii. 43. 2
Mockery. So would he scoffe them out with *mockerie,* . . . *Hub.* 705
so himselfe to *mockerie* to sell. . . . *T.M.* 222
Gods with common *mockerie* Might laugh at them, . . . *Mui.* 372
Mocketh. *mocketh* th' eyes of all the lookers on, . . . *Hub.* 1281
mocketh all my paine, and laughs the more I mourn.' . . . VI. viii. 24. 9
Mocking. *mocking* such as thinke they long will stay. . . . *D.* 399
Mock-king. soone as they this *mock-King* did espy, . . . *Hub.* 1091
Mock-knight. That masked *Mock-knight* was their sport and play. . . . IV. iv. 13. 4
Mocks. with bitter *mockes* and mowes . . . VI. vii. 49. 6
when I laugh, she *mocks;* and, when I cry, She laughes, . . *Am.* liv. 11

Mode. Did mitigate the fiercenesse of their *mode,* . . . IV. iv. 5. 2
Moderate. My sad desires, rest therefore *moderate;* . . . *Ro.* vii. 12
I that rule in measure *moderate* . . . *T.M.* 379
she did *moderate* The strong extremities of their outrage. . . II. ii. 38. 3
the milde ayre with season *moderate* . . . attempred, . . . II. xii. 51. 7
To *moderate* stiffe mindes disposd to strive: . . . IV. ii. 2. 6
Modest. Her *modest* eye, Her Majestie, . . . *S.C.* Ap. 70
Him goodly greeted in her *modest* guyse, . . . I. x. 11. 6
Which she did more augment with *modest* grace . . . VI. ix. 9. 3
in her *modest* maner thus bespake: . . . I. xi. 1. 6
rich arayd, and yet in *modest* guize, . . . II. ii. 14. 6
passe the bonds of *modest* merimake, . . . II. vi. 21. 8
The which them did in *modest* wise amate, . . . II. ix. 34. 4
was right fayre and *modest* of demayne, . . . II. ix. 40. 3
Unto the grownd she cast her *modest* eye, . . . II. ix. 41. 2
the strong passion mard her *modest* grace, . . . II. ix. 43. 4
She *modest* was in all her deedes and words, . . . IV. ii. 35. 8
her *modest* countenance he saw So goodly grave, . . . IV. vi. 33. 4
by his *modest* semblant that no evill ment. . . . V. vii. 19. 9
Which she did more augment with *modest* grace . . . VI. ix. 9. 3
modest thoughts breathd from weltempred sprites, . . . *Am.* lxxxiii. 6
Her *modest* eyes, abashed to behold So many gazers . . . *Epith.* 159
Modesty. The pearle of peerlesse grace and *modestie:* . . . *Col.* 471
With sober gladnesse and myld *modestie;* . . . I. viii. 26. 5
In word and deede that shewd great *modestee,* . . . I. x. 7. 4
to the knight with shamefast *modestie* They turne themselves, I. x. 15. 5
comely courted with meet *modestie;* . . . II. ii. 15. 2
full of grace and goodly *modestee,* . . . II. ix. 18. 8
She is the fountaine of your *modestee:* . . . II. ix. 43. 8
peepe foorth with bashfull *modestee,* . . . II. xii. 74. 5
From course of nature and of *modestee?* . . . III. ii. 41. 8
Tempred with grace and goodly *modesty,* . . . III. v. 55. 3
Downe to her foot with carelesse *modestee.* . . . III. ix. 21. 6
All mindlesse of her wonted *modestie* . . . IV. viii. 63. 3
next to her sate sober *Modestie,* . . . IV. x. 51. 1
she masked it with *modestie,* . . . IV. xii. 35. 7
Regard of honour, and mild *modesty;* . . . *Epith.* 193
Are governed with goodly *modesty,* . . . *Epith.* 235
Moenads. *See* **Maenads.**
Moiety. th' one *moyity* Transformd to fish . . . II. xii. 31. 4
Moil. And doest thy mynd in durty pleasures *moyle,* . . . *H.H.L.* 220
Moist. dissolving his *moist* frame, . . . *Ro.* xx. 7
the slimie scowring Of the *moist* moores, . . . *Gn.* 230
his *moyst* wings to dry. . . . *Mui.* 184
the *moist* daughters of huge Atlas . . . III. i. 57. 8
thy *moyst* mountaines each on others throng, . . . III. iv. 8. 5
through impression Of the sunbeames in *moyst* complexion, . III. vi. 8. 5
water which did well From his *moist* eies, . . . IV. viii. 13. 4
Moisten. *moysten* their roots dry; . . . III. vi. 34. 8
Moistened. her faire eyes, . . . *Moystened* their fierie beames, II. xii. 78. 7
Moistening. Privily *moystening* his horrid cheeke: . . . III. xi. 44. 7
Moisture. on her sap and vitall *moysture* fed: . . . *Van.* vii. 8
Till living *moysture* into smoke do flow, . . . I. ix. 8. 4
Their welheads spring, and are with *moisture* deawd; . . . II. ii. 6. 3
in themselves eternall *moisture* they imply. . . . III. vi. 34. 9
Moisty. the *moystie* night approching fast . . . VI. ix. 13. 1
Molanna. there was a Nymph that hight *Molanna;* . . . VII. vi. 40. 2
this *Molanna,* were she not so shole, . . . VII. vi. 40. 7
to corrupt *Molanna,* this her maid, . . . VII. vi. 43. 2
'twas *Molanna* which her so bewraid. . . . VII. vi. 51. 8
Then all attonce their hands upon *Molanna* laid. . . . VII. vi. 51. 9
back returning to *Molann'* againe, . . . VII. vi. 53. 2
Mold. *See* **Mole.**
what might be in earthlie *mould,* . . . *S.C.* N. 158
th' Okes, deep grounded in the earthly *molde,* . . . *Gn.* 453
the *mold* Of fleshly slime and fraile mortalitie; . . . *D.* 402
Of ought that framed is of mortall *moulde,* . . . *D.* 493
So left her, where she now is turnd to treen *mould.* . . . I. ii. 39. 9
so faire a *mould* Did on so weake foundation ever sitt: . . . I. iv. 5. 3
Why doe ye . . . liking find to gaze on earthly *mould,* . . . I. vii. 22. 4
The wretched payre transformed to treen *mould;* . . . I. vii. 26. 5
one massy entire *mould,* Hewen out of Adamant rocke . . . I. vii. 33. 6
The wondrous workmanship of Gods owne *mould,* . . . I. x. 42. 6
A worke of rich entayle and curious *mould,* . . . II. vii. 4. 5
he himselfe was all of golden *mould,* . . . II. vii. 40. 7
Ne mortall steele emperce his miscreated *mould.* . . . II. vii. 42. 9
all his armour seemd of antique *mould,* . . . III. ii. 25. 2
Now ranckleth in this same fraile fleshly *mould,* . . . III. ii. 39. 3
from the sacred *mould* Of her immortall womb, . . . III. iv. 11. 8
purest snow in massy *mould* congeald, . . . III. viii. 6. 2
all made in one *mould.* . . . III. xii. 24. 9
Borne of one mother in one happie *mold,* . . . IV. ii. 41. 3
Eftsoones outsprung two more of equall *mould;* . . . IV. x. 10. 3
And men . . . at first were framed Of earthly *mould,* . . . V. Pr. 2. 4
His name was Talus, made of yron *mould,* . . . V. i. 12. 6
in th' Adamantine *mould* Of his true hart . . . V. vi. 2. 6
nought tempted with the offer Of his rich *mould,* . . . VI. ix. 33. 2
I marvaile of what substance was the *mould,* . . . *Am.* lv. 3
to whose perfect *mould* He fashiond them . . . *H.B.* 32
made out of one *mould* the more t' agree; . . . *H.B.* 207
He made by love out of His owne like *mould,* . . . *H.H.L.* 116
our brethren, that were made Of that selfe *mould,* . . . *H.H.L.* 198
Moldered. There where the *mouldred* earth had cav'd the banke; . . . IV. v. 33. 2
Moldering. nor shining gold, nor *mouldring* clay it was; . . . IV. x. 39. 5
Molds. the man that *moulds* in ydle cell . . . II. iii. 41. 3
Moldwarp. like a *moldwarpe* in the earth doth ly. . . . *H.L.* 182
Moldwarps. like *Moldwarps* nousling still they lurke, . . . *Col.* 763
Moldy. The *mouldie* mosse, which thee accloieth, . . . *S.C.* F. 135
Mole. Under the foote of *Mole,* that mountaine hore, . . . *Col.* 57
Mole—*Continued.*
'Old father *Mole,* (*Mole* hight that mountain gray . . . *Col.* 104
Mulla, the daughter of old *Mole,* . . . *Col.* 108
springing out of *Mole,* doth run downe . . . *Col.* 110
Mole, that like a nousling *Mole* . . . IV. xi. 32. 8
She mote perceive a litle purple *mold,* . . . VI. xii. 7. 8
my old father *Mole,* whom Shepheards quill Renowmed hath . VII. vi. 36. 8
daughter of old Father *Mole,* . . . VII. vi. 40. 2
Mole . . . Did deck himselfe in freshest faire attire; . . . VII. vii. 11. 1
Ah, gentle *Mole!* such joyance hath thee well beseene. . . . VII. vii. 11. 9
Molest. sights, that doo her peace *molest.* . . . *Pet.*[2] vii. 8
May come their happie quiet to *molest;* . . . *D.* 284
A cloud of cumbrous gnattes doe him *molest,* . . . I. i. 23. 5
Having . . . lost an old foe that did you *molest;* . . . I. ii. 27. 3
this wise You to *molest,* . . . II. ix. 42. 3
All that did earst it hinder and *molest,* . . . II. xi. 32. 7
Certes I should be loth thee to *molest;* . . . III. iii. 18. 4
hammers sound his senses did *molest,* . . . IV. v. 41. 2
feare His ydle braine gan busily *molest,* . . . IV. v. 43. 7
she did her troubled mynd *molest,* . . . V. vi. 4. 5
Fearelesse of foes that mote his peace *molest;* . . . VI. vii. 19. 4
Fearelesse of ought that mote her peace *molest,* . . . VI. viii. 34. 7
her all night did watch, and all the day *molest.* . . . VI. xi. 5. 9
her did much *molest;* . . . VI. xi. 24. 4
did with charmes or Magick her *molest,* . . . VII. vi. 16. 6
Ceasse to *molest* the Moone to walke at large, . . . VII. vi. 17. 8
that may her sacred peace *molest;* . . . *Am.* lxxxiii. 2
Theyr sleepe thou doost *molest.* . . . *Epig.* iv. 18
Mollified. with sweet science *mollifide* their stubborne harts. II. x. 25. 9
Being through former bathing *mollifide,* . . . III. vi. 7. 6
mighty courage *mollifide,* . . . IV. xi. 13. 2
Soone as he feeles it *mollifide* with heat, . . . V. v. 7. 8
Mollify. To slake your wrath, and *mollify* your mind' . . . III. ii. 13. 4
mollifie, and calme her raging heat: . . . IV. ix. 14. 7
ruth of beautie will it *mollifie.* . . . V. v. 13. 6
with melting pleasaunce *mollifye* Their hardned hearts, . . . V. viii. 1. 8
To hope for to release or *mollify,* . . . VI. viii. 3. 7
The hardest yron soone doth *mollify;* . . . *Am.* xxxii. 2
Molt. *See* **Melted, Molten.**
wel nigh *molt* his hart in raging yre: . . . II. v. 8. 5
The soring clouds into sad showres *ymolt;* . . . III. xi. 25. 8
Molten. *See* **Melted, Molt.**
In quiet rest his *molten* heart did steep, . . . *Gn.* 245
molten starres doe drop like weeping eyes; . . . I. vi. 6. 5
Through riven cloudes and *molten* firmament; . . . I. viii. 9. 5
Ne *molten* mettall, in his blood embrew; . . . I. xi. 36. 7
ragged ribs of mountaines *molten* new, . . . I. xi. 44. 7
In slouthfull sleepe his *molten* hart to steme, . . . II. vi. 27. 5
Some stird the *molten* owre with ladles great; . . . II. vii. 36. 8
Quite *molten* into lust and pleasure lewd; . . . II. xii. 73. 8
softly sunck into her *molten* hart: . . . III. ii. 15. 2
Moluccas. Unto the margent of the *Molucas?* . . . V. x. 3. 7
Moly. sweet is *Moly,* but his root is ill. . . . *Am.* xxvi. 8
Mome. hanging downe his head, did like a *Mome* appeare. . . VII. vi. 49. 9
Moment. Thus in a (one[1]) *moment* to see lost and drown'd, . . *Pet.* ii. 13
in a *moment* loose their grace and glorie. . . . *D.* 497
Mona. Bee freshly kindled in the fruitfull Ile Of *Mona,* . . . III. iii. 48. 5
Monarch. That mightie *Monarch* layd Low under all, . . . I. v. 48. 5
That Romaine *Monarch* built a brasen wall, . . . IV. xi. 36. 2
Monarch's. After the Persian *Monarks* antique guize, . . . IV. iii. 38. 8
Monarchy. So whilom did this *Monarchie* aspyre, . . . *Ro.* xvi. 12
Monastery. At length into a *Monastere* did light, . . . VI. xii. 23. 8
Money. *See* **Passage-money.**
draw in Both wares and *money,* . . . *Hub.* 870
unto hell him selfe for *money* sold: . . . I. iv. 27. 7
money can thy wantes at will supply? . . . II. vii. 11. 2
Beautie and *Money,* they that Bulwarke sorely rent. . . . II. xi. 9. 9
His *money,* which he lov'd as living breath; . . . III. x. 2. 8
when to him she cryde, . . . love *money* overcame: . . . III. x. 15. 2
when he marked how his *money* burnd, . . . III. x. 15. 3
He left his wife; *money* did love disclame: . . . III. x. 15. 4
I tread in dust thee and thy *money* both, . . . III. x. 29. 8
Money-god. 'Suffise it then, thou *Money God,*' . . . II. vii. 39. 1
Monger. *See* **War-monger.**
Mongiball. More whott then Aetn', or flaming *Mongiball* . . II. ix. 29. 7
Mongst (*partial list*). *See* **Amongst.**
mongst all Cities flourished much more, . . . *Ro.* xxviii. 14
Mongst all the daughters of proud Libanon, . . . *Van.* vii. 4
Mongst heavenly ranks, where blessed soules . . . *Gn.* 58
My fortune was, *mongst* manie others moe, . . . *Hub.* 13
that breede Doubts *mongst* Divines, . . . *Hub.* 387
he *mongst* Ladies could their fortunes read . . . *Hub.* 698
Mongst simple shepheards they do boast . . . *T.M.* 329
thee worship *mongst* that blessed throng . . . *Ti.* 340
their judgments share *Mongst* earthlie wightes, . . . *D.* 200
Ne *mongst* true lovers they shall place inherit, . . . *Col.* 893
Yet the stout Faery *mongst* the middest crowd . . . I. iv. 15. 6
Mongst many, one that with his prowesse . . . I. ix. 16. 7
Mongst whom on me she deigned to bestowe . . . II. ii. 42. 3
Mongst which Cymochles of her questioned . . . II. vi. 9. 2
numbred be *mongst* knights of Maydenhed, . . . II. ix. 6. 6
Mongst whom he parted his imperiall state, . . . II. x. 13. 6
'*Mongst* thousands good one wanton Dame to find: . . . III. i. 49. 5
Mongst which it fell into that Fairies mind To aske . . . III. ii. 4. 4
Mongst whom might be that he did closely lye, . . . III. vi. 16. 6
Mongst gentle Knights to nourish evermore? . . . IV. i. 46. 4
Mongst the manie vertues which we reed, . . . IV. ii. 39. 8
Mongst men of worth, . . . IV. x. 53. 8
mongst men and beasts, . . . V. Pr. 9. 6
Yeeld me an hostry *mongst* the croking frogs, . . . V. x. 23. 8

Mongst—*Continued.*
Mongst joyes mixing some tears, *mongst* wele some wo, . . . V. xi. 16. 3
Mongst which my most delight hath alwaies been . . . . VI. ii. 31. 6
Mongst which he namely did to him discourse . . . . . . VI. iii. 14. 8
Mongst salvage beasts both rudely borne . . . . VI. v. 2. 3
in so great daunger set *Mongst* many foes, ... VI. v. 22. 3
appointed have her place *Mongst* rocks and caves, ... VI. vi. 11. 4
mongst so many layes As he hath sung . . . . VI. x. 28. 4
Mongst which he found a sword . . . . VI. xi. 47. 5
Like as a Lion *mongst* an heard of dere, ... VI. xi. 49. 1
In Faery Land *mongst* records permanent. . . . . VII. vi. 2. 4
Mongst wretched men (dismaide with her affright) . . . VII. vi. 32. 7
sing of hilles and woods *mongst* warres . . . . VII. vi. 37. 2
Mongst these sterne stounds to mingle . . . . VII. vi. 37. 4
To see her naked *mongst* her Nymphes . . . . VII. vi. 42. 9
But *mongst* them all, which did Loves honor rayse, ... *Am.* xix. 9
Mongst whome the more I seeke to settle peace, ... *Am.* xliv. 13
Mongst which, there in a silver dish did ly . . . . *Am.* lxxvii. 5
Moniment, -s. *See* **Monument, -s.**
Monk. Arayd in habit blacke, . . . Like to an holy *Monck,* . . I. iv. 18. 9
Monks. Through which the *Monckes* he chaced here and there, VI. xii. 24. 2
Monoceroses. Mighty *Monoceroses* with immeasured tayles. . . II. xii. 23. 9
Monster. Ylike as a *Monster* of many heads; . . . . *S.C.* S. 121
made a *monster* of their fantasie. . . . . *T.M.* 558
how bold and swift the *monster* was, ... *Col.* 220
A *monster* vile, whom God and man does hate: . . . . . . I. i. 13. 7
he saw the ugly *monster* plaine, ... I. i. 14. 6
In shape and life more like a *monster* then a man. . . . . . I. iv. 22. 9
this same *Monster* much more ugly was, ... I. vii. 17. 6
many knights . . . Have enterpriz'd that *Monster* to subdew. . I. vii. 45. 2
with mighty mall The *Monster* mercilesse him made to fall, . I. vii. 51. 5
with the uncouth smart the *Monster* lowdly cryde. . . . . . I. xi. 20. 9
that infernall *Monster,* having kest His wearie foe into that
living well, ... I. xi. 31. 5
who-so kild that *monster* most deforme, ... I. xii. 20. 3
what mote that *Monster* make. . . . . II. iii. 18. 9
That *Monster* can be maistred or destroyd: . . . . II. iv. 10. 3
Griefe is a flood; and love a *monster* fell; . . . . II. iv. 35. 3
the *Monster* filth did breede: . . . . II. iv. 35. 5
It growes a *Monster,* and incontinent . . . . II. ix. 1. 7
why make ye such *Monster* of your minde? . . . . III. ii. 40. 2
The *Monster,* swifte as word that from her went, ... III. vii. 23. 6
Florimell fled from that *Monster* yond, ... III. vii. 26. 5
The *Monster,* ready on the pray to sease, ... III. vii. 28. 1
the *Monster* vilde Upon that milke-white Palfreyes carcas fedd, III. vii. 30. 7
Ne any may that *Monster* match in fight, ... III. vii. 52. 8
While she was flying . . . From that foule *monster* . . . . . V. iii. 27. 6
Unto a dreadfull *Monster* to devoure, ... V. x. 13. 7
An hideous *monster* doth in darknesse lie, ... V. x. 29. 3
Prince Arthure . . . Doth slay the *Monster,* . . . . V. xi. Arg.
An hideous *monster* that doth it defend, ... V. xi. 20. 2
For great desire that *Monster* to assay, ... V. xi. 21. 2
The *Monster* underneath the Altar lay: . . . . V. xi. 21. 7
there no *Monster* did behold. . . . . V. xi. 21. 9
Monster, whom the Theban Knight . . . Made kill her selfe . V. xi. 25. 2
So also did the *Monster* use like slight . . . . V. xi. 25. 7
whether man or *monster* one could scarse discerne. . . . . . V. xii. 15. 9
A *monster,* which the Blatant Beast men call, ... V. xii. 37. 7
'It is a *Monster* bred of hellishe race,' . . . . VI. i. 7. 7
But follow'd fast the *Monster* in his flight: . . . . VI. iii. 26. 5
Seeing the ugly *Monster* passing by, ... VI. v. 16. 2
wounded was Of that same *Monster* late, ... VI. v. 31. 7
'Echidna is a *Monster* direfull dred, ... VI. vi. 10. 1
A wicked *Monster,* that his tongue doth whet Gainst all, . . VI. vi. 12. 3
So sharply he the *Monster* did pursew, ... VI. ix. 3. 1
so sternely he the *monster* strooke, ... VI. x. 36. 3
whylest he that *monster* sought Throughout the world, . . . VI. xii. 13. 4
Thus was this *Monster* . . . supprest and tamed, ... VI. xii. 38. 1
That cancker-worme, that *monster,* Gelosie, ... *H.L.* 267
that *monster* placed In gentle love, ... *H.L.* 271
Monster's. *monsters* kinde In hundred formes to change . . . *Bel.*[2] viii. 9
refuge from the *Monsters* cruelty, ... III. viii. 21. 2
The present of his paines, that *Monsters* spoyle, ... V. xi. 33. 6
Meat fit for such a *monsters* monsterous dyeat: . . . . . . V. xii. 31. 9
Monsters. *See* **Sea-monsters.**
hideous *monsters* full of uglinesse; . . . . *D.* 340
Deformed *monsters,* fowle, and blacke as inke, ... I. i. 22. 7
From surging gulf two *Monsters* streight were brought, . . . I. v. 38. 3
whenas *monsters* huge he would dismay, ... I. vii. 34. 2
more deformed *Monsters* thousand fold, ... II. xii. 25. 2
these same *Monsters* are not these in deed, ... II. xii. 26. 2
All *monsters* to subdew to him that did it beare. . . . . . . II. xii. 40. 9
griesly *Monsters* of the See Stood gaping . . . . III. iv. 32. 8
that wastefull wildernesse Huge *monsters* haunt, ... III. x. 40. 4
ten thousand *monsters* foule abhor'd . . . . IV. xi. 3. 8
had subdew'd of old So many *monsters* . . . . V. v. 24. 6
Monstrous. seven springing heds of *monstrous* crimes, ... *Bel.*[1] viii. 13
seven heads, budding *monstrous* crimes . . . . *Bel.*[2] x. 12
outstretched lay, In *monstrous* length, ... *Van.* iii. 3
unto him all *monstrous* beasts resorted . . . . *Hub.* 1122
monstrous error, flying in the ayre, ... *T.M.* 257
Such ugly *monstrous* shapes . . . . I. i. 21. 9
'Her neather partes misshapen, *monstruous,* . . . . I. ii. 41. 1
A rude, mishapen, *monstrous* rablement, ... I. vi. 8. 7
monstrous enimy With sturdie steps came stalking . . . . . I. vii. 8. 2
she . . . Brought forth this *monstrous* masse of earthly slyme, I. vii. 9. 8
A *monstrous* beast ybredd in filthy fen He chose, ... I. vii. 16. 8
lightly leaping from so *monstrous* maine, ... I. viii. 7. 7
His *monstrous* scalpe downe to his teeth it tore, ... I. viii. 16. 4
What mortall wight could ever beare so *monstrous* blow? . . . I. viii. 18. 9

Monstrous—*Continued.*
of that *monstrous* mas Was nothing left, ... I. viii. 24. 8
Loe! where your foe lies strecht in *monstrous* length; . . . I. viii. 45. 3
her feete most *monstrous* were in sight; . . . . I. viii. 48. 5
His body *monstrous,* horrible, and vaste; . . . . I. xi. 8. 7
Stretcht on the ground in *monstrous* large extent, ... I. xii. 9. 7
In case he could that *monstrous* beast destroy, ... I. xii. 41. 7
love . . . maketh *monstrous* warre; . . . . II. ii. 26. 6
Whom then she does transforme to *monstrous* hewes, ... II. v. 27. 6
The which with *monstrous* stalke behind him stept, ... II. vii. 26. 8
nothing seemd mote beare so *monstrous* might: . . . . II. viii. 38. 2
uneath to wene That *monstrous* error, ... II. x. 8. 3
those three *monstrous* stones doe most excell, ... II. x. 11. 5
a *monstrous* rablement Of fowle misshapen wightes, ... II. xi. 8. 1
Sith now he is far from his *monstrous* swarme, ... II. xi. 34. 4
According to their mindes like *monstruous.'* . . . . II. xii. 85. 5
Yet playd Pasiphae a more *monstrous* part, ... III. ii. 41. 5
Monstrous, mishapt, and all his backe was spect . . . . . . III. vii. 22. 4
in that *monstrous* wise did to the world appere. . . . . . . III. vii. 48. 9
a *monstrous* beast The Palfrey whereon she did travell slew, . III. viii. 49. 2
'What *monstrous* enmity provoke we heare? . . . . III. xi. 22. 7
A thousand *monstrous* formes therein were made, ... III. xi. 51. 7
love in thousand *monstrous* formes doth oft appeare. . . . . III. xi. 51. 9
That by her *monstrous* shape might easily be red. . . . . . IV. i. 26. 9
He like a *monstrous* Gyant seem'd in sight, ... IV. v. 37. 1
oft admir'd his *monstrous* shape, ... IV. vii. 32. 7
monstrous tyrants with his club subdewed: . . . . V. i. 2. 8
Soone as they did the *monstrous* Scorpion vew . . . . V. viii. 40. 3
after that his *monstrous* father fell Under Alcides club, . . . V. x. 11. 2
The image of his *monstrous* parent Geryone. . . . . V. x. 13. 9
Like to a Giant for his *monstrous* hight, ... V. xii. 15. 2
with such *monstrous* poise adowne descended, ... V. xii. 21. 3
Meat fit for such a monsters *monsterous* dyeat: . . . . . . V. xii. 31. 9
A *monstrous* Dragon, full of fearefull uglinesse. . . . . . . VI. vi. 10. 9
rather like a Gyant *monstruous:* . . . . VI. vii. 41. 4
A *monstrous* cruelty gainst course of kynde! . . . . VI. viii. 36. 5
That *monstrous* Beast by finall force to quell, ... VI. xii. 22. 7
Month. Is not thilke the mery *moneth* of May, ... *S.C.* May 1
the *month* in which the righteous Maide, ... *Hub.* 1
Each hour did seeme a *moneth,* and every *moneth* a yeare. . . V. vi. 5. 9
Monthly. (O *monthly* Virgin!) thou delay Thy nightly course, *Gn.* 459
Month's. *See* **Twelvemonth's.**
Months. sixe *months* greater a great deele; . . . . *Ro.* xviii. 8
Nyne *monethes* I seek in vain, ... I. ix. 15. 9
*That have twelve *moneths* sought one, ... II. ix. 38. 9
The loving mother, that nine *monethes* did beare . . . . . . III. ii. 11. 6
After she had nine *moneths* fulfild and gone: . . . . III. vi. 5. 5
Seven *moneths* he so her kept in bitter smart, ... IV. i. 4. 1
There did this lucklesse mayd seven *months* abide, ... IV. xi. 4. 6
she many *moneths* did mourne, ... V. iii. 1. 8
for weekes that passed were, She told but *moneths,* . . . . V. vi. 5. 7
after them the *Monthes* all riding came. . . . . VII. vii. 32. 2
So past the twelve *Months* forth, ... VII. vii. 43. 9
Months'. these seven *monethes* day, ... III. xi. 10. 8
Monument. stroke downe this noble *monument.* . . . . *Bel.*[1] iii. 14
this brave *monument* with flash did rend. . . . . *Bel.*[2] iii. 14
Rome, . . . dead, is now the worlds sole *moniment.* . . . . . *Ro.* xxix. 14
manie lost, of whom no *moniment* Remaines, ... *Gn.* 589
for their memories long *moniment:* . . . . *Hub.* 1182
Nor anie little *moniment* to see, ... *Ti.* 5
The *moniment* of whose sad funerall, ... *Ti.* 117
Vouchsafe this *moniment* of his last praise . . . . *Ti.* 682
Thy praises everlasting *monument* Is in this verse . . . . . *Ded. Son.* vi. 12
of Hippolytus was lefte no *moniment.* . . . . I. v. 38. 9
be for all chaste Dames an endlesse *moniment.'* . . . . . . II. ii. 10. 9
soveraine *moniment* of mortall vowes, ... II. iii. 25. 7
Some in round plates withouten *moniment;* . . . . II. vii. 5. 7
no *moniment* Of Brutus, nor of Britons glorie auncient. . . . II. x. 36. 8
O famous *moniment* of womens prayse! . . . . II. x. 56. 1
for eternall *moniment* Of thy great grace . . . . III. iv. 10. 7
Time . . . That famous *moniment* hath quite defaste, ... IV. ii. 33. 3
of his shape appear'd no litle *moniment.* . . . . V. viii. 43. 9
To be a *moniment* for evermore. . . . . V. viii. 45. 3
this verse . . . Shall be thereof immortall *moniment;* . . . . *Am.* lxix. 10
enchased Your glorious name in golden *moniment.* . . . . . *Am.* lxxxii. 8
for short time an endlesse *moniment.* . . . . *Epith.* 433
Monuments. above all *moniments* Seven Romane Hils, ... *Ro.* ii. 13
Olde *moniments,* which of so famous sprights . . . . *Ro.* vii. 3
These *moniments,* which not in paper writ, ... *Ro.* xxxii. 6
Of things forepast, nor *moniments* of time; . . . . *T.M.* 104
though Time all *moniments* obscure, ... *Ti.* 174
all my antique *moniments* defaced? . . . . *Ti.* 179
All such vaine *moniments* of earthlie masse, ... *Ti.* 419
The rueful *moniments* of heavinesse; . . . . I. vii. 19. 8
An auncient booke, hight Briton *moniments,* . . . . II. ix. 59. 6
of his victories Brave *moniments* remaine, ... II. x. 21. 9
endlesse *moniments* of his great good: . . . . II. x. 46. 3
Whose dolefull *moniments* who list to rew, ... II. x. 66. 8
should they be most famous *moniments,* . . . . II. x. 74. 7
his brave shield, full of old *moniments,* . . . . II. xii. 80. 3
Which the late world admyres for wondrous *moniments.* . . . III. iii. 2. 9
for endlesse *moniments* Of his successe . . . . III. iii. 59. 3
to bee enrold In everlasting *moniments* of brasse, ... III. ix. 50. 8
hung With ragged *monuments* of times forepast, ... IV. i. 21. 2
The *moniments* whereof there byding beene, ... IV. i. 24. 8
know the *moniments* of passed age: . . . . IV. xi. 17. 6
sield With *moniments* of many Knights decay, ... V. v. 21. 4
speaking markes of passed *monuments,* . . . . VI. xii. 20. 4
Ne let theyr famous *moniments* to fade? . . . . *Am.* li. 4
vaine antiquitie so vaunt Her ancient *monuments* . . . . . . *Com. Son.* iii. 2

Mood. beating downe these walls with furious *mood* . . . . *Ro.* xi. 11
with gentle *mood* Of Poets Prince, ... *Gn.* 17
seeing her sad *mood,* . . . . *T.M.* 417
Long after lay he musing at her *mood,* . . . . I. i. 55. 1
With pittie calmd downe fell his angry *mood.* . . . . I. iii. 8. 5
The trembling ghosts with sad amazed *mood,* . . . . I. v. 32. 5
Venus never had so sober *mood:* . . . . I. vi. 16. 7
Jove, in wrathfull *mood,* . . . Hurles forth his thundring dart I. viii. 9. 1
she no whitt did chaunge her constant *mood:* . . . . I. x. 13. 6
entertaynes with friendly chearefull *mood.* . . . . I. xi. 32. 4
Trebly augmented was his furious *mood* . . . . I. xi. 22. 7
wondred at his breathlesse hasty *mood:* . . . . I. xii. 25. 3
Therewith amoved from his sober *mood,* . . . . II. i. 12. 1
No measure in her *mood,* no rule of right, ... II. ii. 36. 4
One day unto me came in friendly *mood,* . . . . II. iv. 22. 4
Avise thee well, and chaunge thy wilfull *mood,* . . . . II. vii. 38. 8
'How is it that this *mood* in me ye blame, ... II. ix. 38. 2
Forceth it swell above his wonted *mood,* . . . . III. vii. 34. 3
Now made forget their former cruell *mood,* . . . . IV. iii. 39. 4
fayned still her former angry *mood,* . . . . IV. vi. 29. 8
all the while beheld their wrathfull *moode,* . . . . IV. ix. 22. 3
in their malicious *mood* . . . . IV. ix. 29. 2
seem'd to be of very sober *mood,* . . . . IV. x. 31. 4
So daunted was in his despeyring *mood,* . . . . V. iii. 26. 8
threats the more increast their *mood.* . . . . V. iv. 4. 9
Therewith she gan at first to change her *mood,* . . . . V. v. 45. 4
She chang'd that threatfull *mood,* . . . . V. v. 47. 9
gan enquire of him with mylder *mood* . . . . V. vi. 15. 6
Ne within reasons rule her madding *mood* containe. . . . . V. vii. 11. 9
He mote not come to wreake his wrathfull *mood:* . . . . V. viii. 35. 4
Of horrible aspect and dreadfull *mood,* . . . . V. x. 8. 7
And with mad *moode* againe upon him flew, ... VI. iv. 6. 3
He made great mone after his salvage *mood;* . . . . VI. iv. 12. 4
in so unwomanly a *mood* . . . . VI. viii. 51. 4
The sober mother seeing such her *mood,* . . . . VI. xii. 17. 1
with meeke humblesse and afflicted *mood,* . . . . *Am.* ii. 11
Moon. all things which beneath the *Moone* have being . . . . *Ro.* ix. 10
All that's imperfect, borne belowe the *Moone;* . . . . *Ro.* xix. 2
With gilden hornes embowed like the *Moone,* . . . . *Van.* ii. 3
eke the *Moone* her hastie steedes did stay, ... *Gn.* 457
my dreaded name to raise Above the *Moone,* . . . . II. iii. 38. 8
the *Moone,* cloathed with clowdy night, ... II. vii. 29. 8
could call out of the sky Both Sunne and *Moone,* . . . . III. iii. 12. 2
till the horned *moone* three courses did expire. . . . . IV. vi. 43. 9
As the faire *Moone* in her most full aspect . . . . V. v. 3. 8
to the *Moone* it mote be like in each respect. . . . . V. v. 3. 9
Like as the *Moone* in foggie winters night . . . . V. v. 12. 8
They wore rich Mitres shaped like the *Moone,* . . . . V. vii. 4. 6
To shew that Isis doth the *Moone* portend; . . . . V. vii. 4. 7
in mortall things Beneath the *Moone* to raigne) . . . . VII. vi. Arg.
Thence to the Circle of the *Moone* she clambe, ... VII. vi. 8. 1
forth he sent Downe to the Circle of the *Moone,* . . . . VII. vi. 16. 2
Ceasse to molest the *Moone* to walke at large, ... VII. vi. 17. 8
On top whereof the *moon* and stars were pight; . . . . VII. vii. 44. 6
'as changefull as the *Moone'* men use to say. . . . . VII. vii. 50. 9
Nor to the *Moone;* for they are changed never; . . . . *Am.* ix. 6
In sight of whom both Sun and *Moone* are darke, ... *H.H.B.* 125
Moonlight. Hey, ho, the *Moonelight!* . . . . *S.C.* Au. 90
Moon-like. *Moone-like* Mitre to a Crowne of gold; . . . . V. vii. 13. 6
Moon's. within the *Moones* fayre shining spheare, ... II. Pr. 3. 6
the *Moones* bright wagon still did stand, ... VII. vi. 13. 7
Moons. Thrise three *Moones* bene fully spent . . . . *S.C.* S. 20
three *Moones* have changed thrice their hew, ... I. viii. 38. 6
three *Moones* with borrowd brothers light . . . . III. iii. 16. 2
Moor. One hand on Scythia, th' other on the *More,* . . . . *Ro.* iv. 3
all the *moore* twixt Elversham and Dell, ... II. x. 24. 4
Moorish. To drench himselfe in *moorish* slime did trace, . . *Gn.* 251
moorish fennes, and marshes ever greene. . . . . *Ti.* 140
The *morish* Cole, and the soft sliding Breane, ... IV. xi. 29. 6
Moors. the slimie scowring Of the moist *moores,* . . . . *Gn.* 230
into *moores* and marshes vanisht had, ... V. x. 18. 4
Like to the *Mores* of Malaber, ... VI. vii. 43. 6
Moot. *See* **Folkmoot.**
Moral. some hymne, or *morall* laie, ... *Col.* 86
Moralize. Fierce warres and faithful loves shall *moralize* my song. . . . . I. Pr. 1. 9
Morands. Against the forreine *Morands* he exprest; . . . . II. x. 43. 8
Mordant. Guyon . . . Fyndes *Mordant* and Amavia slaine . . II. i. Arg.
this dead corpse . . . the good Sir *Mortdant* was: . . . . II. i. 49. 9
Mordant and Amavia did rew, ... II. ii. 45. 8
Had slayne Sir *Mordant* and his Lady bright: . . . . II. iii. 13. 8
Morddure. Wherefore *Morddure* it rightfully is hight. . . . . II. viii. 21. 6
with *Morddure,* His owne good sword *Morddure,* . . . . II. viii. 30. 6, 7
His owne good sword *Mordure,* . . . . II. xi. 41. 6
More (*partial list*). *See* **Moor, More and More, Nevermore, No more.**
A lively streame, *more* cleere than Christall is, ... *Rev.* iv. 12
By *more* and *more* she gan her wings t' assure . . . . *Bel.* vii. 3
more sweete than Mermaids song: . . . . *Bel.* xii. 8
What say I *more?* . . . . *Pet.* v. 7
Citie, *more* than that great Phrygian mother Renowm'd . . *Ro.* vi. 5
mongst all Cities flourished much *more.* . . . . *Ro.* xxviii. 14
Thou . . . might'st fall *more* horriblie. . . . . *Ro.* xxxi. 14
I will send *more* after thee. . . . . *To his Booke* 18
To nought *more,* Thenot, my mind is bent . . . . *S.C.* F. 94
to worke me *more* spight; . . . . *S.C.* F. 180
For this, and many *more* such outrage, ... *S.C.* F. 183
She shoulde have neede no *more* spell; . . . . *S.C.* Mar. 54
now it ranckleth *more* and *more,* . . . . *S.C.* Mar. 100
The Honye is much, but the Gaule is *more.* . . . . *S.C.* Mar. Emb. 4

More—*Continued.*
For *more* finenesse, with a tawdrie lace. . . . . *S.C.* Ap. 135
(Were it *more* or lesse) . . . . *S.C.* May 108
Of their falshode *more* could I recount, ... *S.C.* May 314
night-ravenes . . . *more* black then pitche, ... *S.C.* Jun. 23
musick for their *more* delight: . . . . *S.C.* Jun. 29
but yeeres *more* rype, ... *S.C.* Jun. 46
I *more* delight then larke in Sommer dayes: . . . . *S.C.* Jun. 51
can I tell thee *more,* . . . . *S.C.* Jul. 73
To Kerke the narre, from God *more* farre, ... *S.C.* Jul. 97
His face, *more* cleare then Christall glasse. . . . . *S.C.* Jul. 159
Thou medlest *more* then shall have thanke, ... *S.C.* Jul. 209
it ranckleth, ay *more* and *more,* . . . . *S.C.* Au. 101
Never dempt *more* right of beautye, ... *S.C.* Au. 137
More meete to wayle my woe . . . . *S.C.* Au. 165
the *more* taugment The memory of hys misdeede . . . . *S.C.* Au. 185
Eche thing imparted is *more* eath to beare: . . . . *S.C.* S. 17
Is nowe nor jollye, nor shepeheard *more.* . . . . *S.C.* S. 27
That uneth may I stand any *more:* . . . . *S.C.* S. 48
the *more* bene fraight with fraud and spight, ... *S.C.* S. 84
That with theyr hornes butten the *more* stoute; . . . . *S.C.* S. 125
For liker bene they to pluck away *more,* . . . . *S.C.* S. 128
The *more* to wind it out thou doest swinck, ... *S.C.* S. 132
The *more* bene the Foxes that here remaine. . . . . *S.C.* S. 155
but they gang in *more* secrete wise, ... *S.C.* S. 156
But who rewards him ere the *more* for-thy, ... *S.C.* O. 33
Made me by arte *more* cunning in the same. . . . . *S.C.* D. 42
the worse despise; I aske no *more.* . . . . *S.C.* Env. 12
when as season *more* secure Shall bring forth . . . . *Gn.* 9
But my soft Muse, as for her power *more* meete, ... *Gn.* 51
O, who can lead, then, a *more* happie life . . . . *Gn.* 121
more and *more* having himselfe enrolde, ... *Gn.* 257
Eftsoones *more* fierce in visage, ... *Gn.* 269
thy life *more* deare and precious thus Was . . . . *Gn.* 331
but the Greekes themselves, *more* dolorous, ... *Gn.* 550
That death . . . to worke *more* ghastly feares. . . . . *Gn.* 584
To whom may I *more* trustely complaine . . . . *Hub.* 55
they which call them so *more* beggers bee; . . . . *Hub.* 162
more for thrift did care than for . . . . *Hub.* 231
But they *more* subtill meaning had than he; . . . . *Hub.* 330
That before God we may appeare *more* gay, ... *Hub.* 462
For each thing fained ought *more* warie bee. . . . . *Hub.* 495
But of *more* private persons seeke elswhere, ... *Hub.* 522
Needes anie *more* to learne to get a living?' . . . . *Hub.* 544
Alla Turchesca, much the *more* admyr'd: . . . . *Hub.* 677
With gallant showe, and daylie *more* augment . . . . *Hub.* 691
Regard of honour harbours *more* than ought, ... *Hub.* 718
For which also I claime my selfe *more* fit . . . . *Hub.* 1038
But his owne treasure he encreased *more,* . . . . *Hub.* 1172
Which yet to prove *more* true he meant to see, ... *Hub.* 1277
But none *more* tragick matter I can finde . . . . *T.M.* 155
far *more* bitter storme than winters . . . . *T.M.* 247
Darknesse *more* than Cymerians daylie night: . . . . *T.M.* 256
shall anie *more* Find entertainment . . . . *T.M.* 409
if good were not praised *more* than ill, ... *T.M.* 455
Did *more* increase the sharpnes of her showre. . . . . *T.M.* 478
mercie *more* than mortall men can vew. . . . . *T.M.* 514
with rehearsing would me *more* agreeve. . . . . *Ti.* 91
Nor ever ship shall saile there anie *more.* . . . . *Ti.* 154
And, being dead, is happie now much *more;* . . . . *Ti.* 247
count of wisedome *more* than of thy Countie. . . . . *Ti.* 273
But now, *more* happie thou, ... *Ti.* 330
Such as on earth man could not *more* devize, ... *Ti.* 521
Was none *more* favourable, nor *more* faire, ... *Mui.* 20
Yet so as him their terrour *more* adornes. . . . . *Mui.* 88
And *more* industrious, gathered *more* store . . . . *Mui.* 122
What *more* felicitie can fall to creature . . . . *Mui.* 209
Himselfe he close upgathered *more* and *more* . . . . *Mui.* 397
For striving *more,* the *more* in laces strong . . . . *Mui.* 427
never didst thou heare *more* haplesse fate. . . . . *D.* 98
more plaine aread this doubtfull case.' . . . . *D.* 182
'She now is dead;' ne *more* endured to say, ... *D.* 184
he thereby was *more* empassionate; . . . . *D.* 193
Becomes *more* fierce and fervent in his gate; . . . . *D.* 195
do not spare the best or fayrest, *more* than . . . . *D.* 202
Which did her beautie much *more* beautifie. . . . . *D.* 217
'No age hath bred . . . *more* vertue in a wight; . . . . *D.* 219
'Ne sleepe . . . Shall ever lodge upon mine ey-lids *more;* . *D.* 471
'And ye, *more* happie Lovers! . . . . *D.* 512
Which daily *more* and *more* he did augment, ... *As.* 19
her old sire *more* carefull of her good, ... *Col.* 120
'Fearful much *more* . . . . *Col.* 201
wondring *more* And *more,* . . . . *Col.* 264, 265
None fairer, nor *more* fruitfull to be red: . . . . *Col.* 279
Much *more* there is unkend . . . . *Col.* 294
much *more* that does from mens knowledge lurke. . . . . *Col.* 295
heaven and heavenly graces do much *more* . . . abound . . *Col.* 308
More fit it is t' adore, ... *Col.* 350
thy selfe thou mak'st us *more* to wonder, ... *Col.* 354
raise His tunes from laies to matter of *more* skill. . . . . *Col.* 395
he himselfe may rewed be *more* right, ... *Col.* 398
More rich then pearles of Ynde, . . . And in her sex *more* wonderfull . . . . *Col.* 490, 491
'*More* eath (quoth he) . . . . *Col.* 590
'Blame is . . . *more* blamelesse . . . . *Col.* 749
But man, . . . might *More* then the rest . . . . *Col.* 868
rymes . . . for their titles sake may find *more* grace. . *Ded. Son.* i. 14
Who ever gave *more* honourable prize . . . . *Ded. Son.* xiv. 1
Who then ought *more* to favour her then you, ... *Ded. Son.* xiv. 5
Which with your vertues ye embellish *more,* . . . . *Ded. Son.* xv. 11

More—*Continued.*

Much *more* me needs,	*Ded. Son.* xvii. 5
a lowly Asse *more* white then snow,	I. i. 4. 2
fearefull *more* of shame Then of the certeine perill	I. i. 24. 1
stroke at her with *more* then manly force,	I. i. 24. 6
And *more* to lulle him in his slumber soft,	I. i. 41. 1
The Sprite then gan *more* boldly him to wake,	I. i. 43. 1
guest, . . . gan now to take *more* sound repast;	I. ii. 4. 3
More busying his quicke eies her face to view,	I. ii. 26. 6
they did seeme *more* foule and hideous,	I. ii. 41. 3
Nought . . . That moves *more* deare compassion	I. iii. 1. 2
But to the pray when as he drew *more* ny,	I. iii. 5. 7
to augment her painefull penaunce *more,*	I. iii. 14. 1
Yet is she now in *more* perplexitie,	I. iii. 40. 5
lust did now inflame His corage *more,*	I. iii. 41. 8
his rage is *more* of might.	I. iii. 43. 9
More mild in beastly kind then that her	I. iii. 44. 9
In shape and life *more* like a monster	I. iv. 22. 9
Who had enough, yett wished ever *more;*	I. iv. 29. 5
he beares renverst, the *more* to heap disdayn.	I. iv. 41. 9
Grandmother of all. *More* old then Jove,	I. v. 22. 3
His wanton stepdame loved him the *more;*	I. v. 37. 5
fearest not that *more* thee hurten might,	I. v. 43. 4
And yet *more* sad, that Una, his deare dreed,	I. vi. 2. 3
She, *more* amazd, in double dread	I. vi. 10. 1
Who had *more* joy to raunge the forrest wyde,	I. vi. 21. 7
for to make his powre approved *more,*	I. vi. 26. 1
More greedy they of newes	I. vi. 34. 9
What *more?* The Redcrosse knight was slain	I. vi. 38. 9
increasing *more* Their puissant force,	I. vi. 45. 2
fight . . . With heaped strokes *more* hugely then before;	I. vi. 45. 4
Then, for to make her dreaded *more* of men,	I. vii. 16. 6
this same Monster much *more* ugly was,	I. vii. 17. 6
for *more* aw and dread.	I. vii. 18. 9
Thy sad tong cannot tell *more* heavy plight	I. vii. 25. 3
If lesse then that I feare, *more* favour I have found.'	I. vii. 25. 9
Which greater grew the *more* she did contend,	I. vii. 27. 3
much *more* admirable deedes.	I. vii. 36. 3
can *more* easily be thought then said.'	I. vii. 41. 2
cause of griefe, *more* great then may be told.'	I. vii. 51. 9
that misformed shape misshaped *more.*	I. viii. 16. 5
Which is through rage *more* strong	I. viii. 18. 3
Her hastie ruine does *more* heavie make,	I. viii. 23. 6
His long endured famine needed *more* reliefe.	I. viii. 43. 9
More ugly shape yet never living creature saw.	I. viii. 48. 9
more fearefull or *more* lucky wight,	I. ix. 30. 4
For never knight, . . . *More* luckless dissaventures	I. ix. 45. 4
hath encreast the world with one sonne *more,*	I. x. 16. 6
paine endur'd, as seeming now *more* light.	I. x. 24. 9
what need him care for *more?*	I. x. 38. 8
God to us forgiveth . . . Much *more* then that	I. x. 40. 7
to the rest *more* hable he might bee;	I. x. 45. 2
had he not that Dame respected *more,*	I. x. 49. 4
Saints . . . *More* dear unto their God then	I. x. 57. 9
to increase his wondrous greatnes *more,*	I. xi. 8. 8
And, that *more* wondrous was,	I. xi. 13. 1
his *more* hardned crest was armd so well,	I. xi. 24. 5
smot againe with *more* outrageous might;	I. xi. 25. 2
He cast to suffer him no *more* respire,	I. xi. 28. 7
more mindfull of his honour deare	I. xi. 39. 1
Whiles some *more* bold to measure him	I. xii. 11. 8
That I note whether praise or pitty *more;*	I. xii. 17. 4
later times thinges *more* unknowne shall show.	II. Pr. 3. 3
He wonder would much *more;*	II. Pr. 3. 9
Of faery lond yet if he *more* inquyre,	II. Pr. 4. 1
With living eye *more* fayre was never seene	II. i. 10. 7
More then goodwill to me attribute nought;	II. i. 33. 4
Not one word *more* she sayd,	II. i. 56. 1
more affection to increace,	II. i. 60. 8
More huge in strength then wise in workes	II. ii. 17. 6
was, for terrour *more,* all armd in shyning bras.	II. ii. 17. 9
In hope to win *more* favour with his mate,	II. ii. 19. 4
more to mighty hands then rightfull cause	II. ii. 29. 9
the praise of prowesse *more* doth marre	II. ii. 30. 8
Huddibras, *more* like a Malecontent,	II. ii. 37. 6
His Palmer now shall foot no *more* alone.	II. iii. 3. 5
and made him *more* inclynd:	II. iii. 4. 7
this liegeman gan to wexe *more* bold,	II. iii. 9. 2
He stayd not for *more* bidding,	II. iii. 19. 1
and thousand thousand times *more* faire,	II. iii. 26. 1
delight does raigne, much *more* then this?	II. iii. 39. 5
heape *more* vengeance on that wretched wight:	II. iv. 5. 4
adding *more* impetuous forse,	II. iv. 6. 3
strooke *more* often wyde, Then at	II. iv. 7. 4
But *more* enfierced through his currish play,	II. iv. 8. 6
more for ranck despight then for great paine,	II. iv. 15. 7
when yeares *More* rype us reason lent	II. iv. 18. 5
wisht me stay till I *more* truth should fynd.	II. iv. 22. 9
Did all she might *more* pleasing to appeare.	II. iv. 25. 4
One day, to worke her to his will *more* neare,	II. iv. 25. 5
That I may *more* delight in thy embracement	II. iv. 26. 9
his mother did *more* rage inspyre.	II. iv. 32. 9
Whose bounty *more* then might, yet both, he wondered.	II. v. 14. 9
Yet others she *more* urgent did devise;	II. v. 21. 8
Their fell contention still increased *more,*	II. v. 22. 1
more thereby increased Furors might,	II. v. 22. 2
more to augment his spight,	II. v. 22. 5
armd with fire *more* hardly he mote him withstond.	II. v. 22. 9
hong their conquerd armes, for *more* defame,	II. v. 26. 8
would have questiond *more;*	II. v. 37. 2

More—*Continued.*

More swift then swallow sheres the liquid skye,	II. vi. 5. 2
all, though pleasaunt, yet she made much *more:*	II. vi. 24. 5
she, *more* sweete then any bird on bough,	II. vi. 25. 1
His prowd presumed force increased *more,*	II. vi. 30. 3
Mars . . . is for Venus loves renowmed *more*	II. vi. 35. 8
more happy he then wise,	II. vi. 46. 4
helpe, he saw, he needed *more* Then pitty,	II. vi. 48. 8
An ugly feend, *more* fowle then dismall day,	II. vii. 26. 7
clouds *more* black then Jett.	II. vii. 28. 9
More light then Culver in the Faulcons fist,	II. vii. 34. 6
To covet *more* then I have cause to use?	II. vii. 39. 4
More fitt emongst black fiendes then men	II. vii. 41. 9
Thereby *more* lovers unto her to call:	II. vii. 45. 6
else much *more* wretched were the cace	II. viii. 1. 4
Againe he heard a *more* efforced voyce,	II. viii. 4. 3
that shield, *more* worthy of good knight;	II. viii. 15. 8
his hand, *more* sad then lomp of lead,	II. viii. 30. 5
Three times *more* furious and *more* puissaunt,	II. viii. 34. 8
More glory thought to give life then decay,	II. viii. 51. 4
There is no one *more* faire and excellent	II. ix. 1. 2
none then it *more* fowle and indecent,	II. ix. 1. 5
of *more* worthy substance fram'd it was:	II. ix. 23. 5
Stone *more* of valew, and more smooth and fine,	II. ix. 24. 2
burning whott, *More* whott then Aetn',	II. ix. 29. 7
more abasht for shame	II. ix. 43. 1
More ample spirit then hitherto was wount	II. x. 1. 6
Gan *more* the same frequent,	II. x. 6. 9
she much *more* than her owne life him lov'd;	II. x. 28. 2
Was never king *more* highly magnifide,	II. x. 52. 1
fowr hundred yeares And *more* had wasted,	II. x. 62. 7
two then all *more* huge and violent,	II. xi. 9. 8
him his foe *more* fiercely should poursew:	II. xi. 27. 4
then assayle him fresh, ere he could shift for *more.*	II. xi. 27. 9
Becomes *more* fell, and all . . . Treads down	II. xi. 33. 5
streame *more* violent and greedy growes:	II. xii. 5. 3
seemd *more* horrible then hell to bee,	II. xii. 6. 3
more scornfully Scoffing at him	II. xii. 16. 7
All these, and thousand thousands many *more,*	II. xii. 25. 1
more deformed Monsters thousand fold,	II. xii. 25. 2
more might in that goodly gate Be red,	II. xii. 46. 1
semblaunce pleasing, *more* then naturall,	II. xii. 46. 5
More sweet and holesome then the pleasaunt hill	II. xii. 52. 1
so faire winepresse made the wine *more* sweet:	II. xii. 56. 6
Each did the others worke *more* beautify;	II. xii. 59. 6
The rest hidd underneath him *more* desirous made.	II. xii. 66. 9
blushing to her laughter gave *more* grace,	II. xii. 68. 2
to him beckned to approch *more* neare,	II. xii. 68. 8
how *more* bold and free	II. xii. 74. 7
Ne *more* doth florish after first decay,	II. xii. 75. 3
rather shewd *more* white, if *more* might be:	II. xii. 77. 6
do not in th' ayre *more* lightly flee.	II. xii. 77. 9
Few drops, *more* cleare then Nectar,	II. xii. 78. 4
starry light . . . does seeme *more* bright.	II. xii. 78. 9
In mirrours *more* then one her selfe to see;	III. Pr. 5. 6
To make *more* triall of his hardiment,	III. i. 2. 8
Ne ought the *more* their mightie strokes surceasse.	III. i. 23. 2
gathering him rownd about *more* neare,	III. i. 23. 3
the fruit *more* sweetnes did contayne,	III. ii. 17. 7
much *more* straungely gan to love his sight,	III. ii. 18. 2
but *more* annoiaunce breed:	III. ii. 37. 2
th' ulcer groweth daily *more* and *more;*	III. ii. 39. 5
Of much *more* uncouth thing I was affrayd,	III. ii. 40. 3
Yet playd Pasiphae a *more* monstrous part,	III. ii. 41. 5
thy dredd dartes in none doe triumph *more,*	III. iii. 3. 1
For Merlin had in Magick *more* insight	III. iii. 11. 8
More neede of leach-crafte hath your Damozell,	III. iii. 17. 5
ye . . . thus arayd, *More* hidden are then Sunne	III. iii. 19. 6
If ay *more* goodly creature thou didst see?	III. iii. 32. 2
more then all the rest may sway,	III. iii. 55. 1
dreaded *more* then all The other Saxons,	III. iii. 56. 5
so her smart was much *more* grievous bredd,	III. iv. 6. 3
the deepe wound *more* deep engord her hart,	III. iv. 6. 4
to advaunce his name and glory *more,*	III. iv. 21. 6
for his *more* assuraunce,	III. iv. 25. 1
they *more* fond that credit to thee give!	III. iv. 37. 2
that they might him handle *more* at will,	III. iv. 40. 3
each to assay Whether *more* happy were	III. iv. 46. 9
on a Palfrey rydes *more* white then snow,	III. v. 5. 6
more that him he could not come to smite;	III. v. 19. 7
more that with his foes he could not come to fight.	III. v. 20. 9
made *more* haste the life to have bereav'd;	III. v. 28. 8
Saw never living eie *more* heavy sight,	III. v. 30. 1
So still his Malady the *more* increast,	III. v. 43. 6
Fayre death it is, to shonne *more* shame, to dy:	III. v. 45. 8
More deare then life she tendered,	III. v. 51. 2
shall embellish *more* your beautie bright,	III. v. 53. 7
So striving each did other *more* augment,	III. v. 55. 6
she was *more* engrieved, and replide;	III. vi. 21. 6
it to replenish *more;*	III. vi. 36. 2
more fresh And fierce he still appeard,	III. vii. 32. 8
the *more* he did him thresh.	III. vii. 32. 9
made her selfe *more* light away to fly:	III. vii. 44. 4
more bent to eke my smartes	III. vii. 55. 7
furie fresh reviv'd Much *more* then earst,	III. viii. 3. 5
the *more* to seeme such as she hight,	III. viii. 10. 4
her honor, which she *more* then life prefard.	III. viii. 14. 9
He marveild *more,* and thought he yet did dreame	III. viii. 22. 7
For shame, but *more* for feare of his grim sight,	III. viii. 32. 8
Eternal thraldome was to her *more* liefe	III. viii. 42. 1

More—*Continued.*
The which himselfe then Ladies *more* defames, . . . III. viii. 44. 3
that *more* suspicion encreast, . . . III. viii. 49. 7
Till triall doe *more* certeine truth bewray.' . . . III. viii. 50. 5
good . . . may *more* notably be rad, . . . III. ix. 2. 3
'Then is he not *more* mad,' . . . III. ix. 8. 1
welcomde *more* for feare then charitee; . . . III. ix. 19. 4
seeing still the *more* desir'd to see, . . . III. ix. 24. 2
to doe them *more* delight . . . III. ix. 25. 9
still the smart thereof increased *more*, . . . III. x. 18. 4
seemd *more* grievous then it was before, . . . III. x. 18. 5
Him seemed *more* their maner did agree; . . . III. x. 21. 3
'And *more:* I graunt to thy great misery . . . III. x. 32. 1
her for to awake he did the *more* constraine . . . III. x. 49. 9
more bounteous creature never far'd On foot . . . III. xi. 10. 3
cause . . . lesse Then is your sorrow certes, if not *more;* . . . III. xi. 18. 4
what couldst thou *more*, If shee were thine, . . . III. xi. 19. 3
More is *more* losse; one is enough to dy.' . . . III. xi. 19. 7
renowm, that, *more* then death, is to be sought.' . . . III. xi. 19. 9
did the *more* augment His mighty rage, . . . III. xi. 26. 6
More for great sorrow that he could not pas . . . III. xi. 27. 2
Joying his love in likenes *more* entire: . . . III. xi. 33. 7
More eath to number with how many eyes . . . III. xi. 45. 8
More sondry colours then the proud Pavone Beares . . . III. xi. 47. 7
ever *more* and *more* upon it gazd, . . . III. xi. 49. 8
more she mervaild that no . . . wight appeard, . . . III. xi. 53. 5
Beares skin, that him *more* dreadfull made; . . . III. xii. 11. 2
inly being *more* then seeming sad: . . . III. xii. 16. 4
For many labours *more* then I have found, . . . III. xii. 40. 3
more worthy to be so, . . . III. xii. 41. 8
More easie issew now . . . She found; . . . III. xii. 43. 1
much the *more* by that he lately wrought, . . . IV. i. 8. 3
Whom when as Paridel *more* plaine beheld, . . . IV. i. 34. 2
dismayd *More* for the love which he had left behynd, . . . IV. i. 37. 8
Ne do your selfe dislike a whit the *more;* . . . IV. i. 46. 7
he the *more* with furious rage was fyred, . . . IV. i. 54. 7
Yet he to her did dayly service *more*, . . . IV. ii. 11. 1
dayly *more* deceived was thereby; . . . IV. ii. 11. 2
with opinion of his owne *more* worth, . . . IV. ii. 12. 3
did much *more* their cruelty encrease; . . . IV. ii. 19. 5
So much the *more* as she refusd to love, . . . IV. ii. 37. 1
So much the *more* she loved was and sought, . . . IV. ii. 37. 2
More wise they weend to make of love delight . . . IV. ii. 40. 5
Priamond on foote had *more* delight; . . . IV. ii. 42. 5
thereby did *more* prolong their paine: . . . IV. iii. 2. 3
did the *more* enhaunce His haughtie courage . . . IV. iii. 8. 7
Smart daunts not mighty harts, but makes them *more* to swell. IV. iii. 8. 9
Much *more* of price and of *more* gratious powre, . . . IV. iii. 45. 1
That men on him the *more* might gaze alone . . . IV. iv. 14. 6
the *more* strong and stiffely that he ran, . . . IV. iv. 19. 5
all the *more*, the *more* his praise increst: . . . IV. iv. 21. 7
all in vaine: for what might one do *more?* . . . IV. iv. 32. 8
He much *more* goodly glosse thereon doth shed . . . IV. v. 15. 5
So much the *more* her griefe, the *more* her toyle; . . . IV. v. 30. 1
aye the *more* that she the same reherst, . . . IV. v. 31. 7
The *more* it gauld and griev'd him . . . IV. v. 31. 8
All sixe strong groomes, but one then other *more;* . . . IV. v. 36. 5
through long sufferance growing now *more* great, . . . IV. vi. 16. 3
renewed His strength still *more*, but she still *more* decrewed. . IV. vi. 18. 5
ne harm'd her any *more* . . . IV. vi. 19. 4
ne unto whom I *more* true love did beare: . . . IV. vi. 35. 9
new occasion fayld her *more* to find, . . . IV. vi. 46. 2
heaping stormes of trouble on them daily *more?* . . . IV. vii. 1. 9
'Is this the faith?' she said—and said no *more*, . . . IV. vii. 36. 8
Ne ever word to speake to woman *more;* . . . IV. vii. 39. 4
The *more* his weakened body so to wast, . . . IV. vii. 41. 8
The *more* did she pursue her lewd intent, . . . IV. viii. 35. 8
toyle the *more*, the *more* that was his care . . . IV. viii. 37. 9
More sharpe then points of needles, . . . IV. viii. 39. 2
whom he list to be afflicted *more* . . . IV. viii. 54. 9
him the *more* agreev'd I found thereby: . . . IV. viii. 57. 5
To my friends good *more* then for mine owne sake, . . . IV. viii. 60. 8
'Thenceforth I found *more* favour at her hand, . . . IV. viii. 61. 1
graunt *more* scope to me to walke at large . . . IV. viii. 61. 4
these Squires true friendship *more* did sway . . . IV. ix. 3. 3
for *more* joy, that captive Lady faire, . . . IV. ix. 13. 1
now in feare of shame she *more* did stond, . . . IV. ix. 18. 5
The *more* was Claribell enraged rife . . . IV. ix. 21. 3
they much *more* furiously gan fare, . . . IV. ix. 27. 1
through suffrance hartned *more*, . . . IV. ix. 34. 5
Much *more* then that which was in Paphos built, . . . IV. x. 5. 6
Eftsoones outsprung two *more* of equall mould; . . . IV. x. 10. 3
Much *more* deformed fearefull, ugly were, . . . IV. x. 20. 4
much *more* rare and pretious to esteeme, . . . IV. x. 39. 6
I was emboldned with *more* confidence; . . . IV. x. 56. 5
then which none *more* upright, . . . IV. xi. 18. 6
Ne *more* sincere in word and deed profest; . . . IV. xi. 18. 7
much *more* aged was his wife then he, . . . IV. xi. 24. 6
Avon marched in *more* stately path, . . . IV. xi. 31. 6
more then ever did Cambridge or Oxford, . . . IV. xi. 35. 5
With many *more* whose names no tongue can tell: . . . IV. xi. 44. 6
three thousand *more* there were Of th' Oceans seede, . . . IV. xi. 52. 6
more eath it were for mortall wight . . . IV. xi. 53. 1
count the starres on hye, Or ought *more* hard, . . . IV. xi. 53. 3
much *more* eath to tell the starres on hy, . . . IV. xii. 1. 5
though their numbers do much *more* surmount, . . . IV. xii. 2. 8
All those were there, and many other *more*, . . . IV. xii. 3. 1
hardned *more* with my abundant teares: . . . IV. xii. 7. 5
griev'd her *more* that she it could not mend: . . . IV. xii. 21. 8
to make him dreaded *more*, . . . V. i. 9. 1

More—*Continued.*
that same Squire, to whom she was *more* dere, . . . V. i. 27. 3
Nought is *more* honorable to a knight, . . . V. ii. 1. 1
more emboldned by the wicked charmes, . . . V. ii. 5. 5
dayly he his wrongs encreaseth *more;* . . . V. ii. 6. 1
still continu'd his assault the *more*, . . . V. ii. 24. 1
ere thou limit what is lesse or *more* . . . V. ii. 34. 5
so much is *more* then just to trow . . . V. ii. 34. 9
'Likewise the earth is not augmented *more* . . . V. ii. 40. 1
'Which is' (sayd he) '*more* heavy then in weight, . . . V. ii. 44. 5
with him sixe knights *more*, . . . V. iii. 4. 7
Whom ever as he did the *more* avize, . . . V. iii. 18. 8
The *more* to be true Florimell he did surmize . . . V. iii. 18. 9
Another, that would seeme to have *more* wit, . . . V. iii. 33. 6
threats the *more* increast their mood . . . V. iv. 4. 9
the *more* Rejoyced at his miserable case, . . . V. iv. 23. 1
Who *more* then losse of life ydreaded it; . . . V. iv. 25. 5
made her famous, *more* then is believed; . . . V. iv. 33. 8
The *more* she rag'd, the *more* he did abide; . . . V. v. 6. 8
Yet still her crueltie increased *more*, . . . V. v. 7. 3
more increast her outrage mercilesse, . . . V. v. 14. 7
The *more* that he with meeke intreatie prayd . . . V. v. 14. 8
Terpine, borne to' a *more* unhappy howre, . . . V. v. 18. 4
still the *more* she strove it to subdew . . . V. v. 28. 3
The *more* she still augmented her owne smart, . . . V. v. 28. 4
The *more* thereby her tender hart was payned; . . . V. v. 44. 7
more my gratious mercie by this wize, . . . V. v. 48. 7
tride againe, and tempted him *more* neare . . . V. v. 48. 9
Give him *more* labour, . . . V. v. 50. 3
The *more* that she it sought to cover . . . V. v. 53. 9
sternely bade His miserie to be augmented *more*, . . . V. v. 54. 6
more then that, she promist that she would, . . . V. v. 55. 1
That she with him mote be the *more* offended . . . V. v. 57. 5
to make them seeme *more* few; . . . V. vi. 5. 7
her winged thoughts, *more* swift then wind, . . . V. vi. 7. 8
with him went without gaine-saying *more* . . . V. vi. 22. 3
Yet stirred not at all for doubt of *more*, . . . V. vi. 28. 3
after them full many other *more*, . . . V. vi. 29. 3
Least any *more* such practise should proceede . . . V. vi. 31. 5
Nought is on earth *more* sacred or divine, . . . V. vii. 1. 1
them repaide againe with double *more* . . . V. vii. 31. 4
through his want her woe did *more* increase: . . . V. vii. 45. 2
That for another Canto will *more* fitly fall . . . V. vii. 45. 9
For her beginning a *more* fearefull fray, . . . V. viii. 10. 6
What doe ye then devise Of *more* revenge? . . . V. viii. 11. 8
if *more*, then I am shee Which was the roote of all: . . . V. viii. 11. 8
'Certes me needeth *more* To crave the same; . . . V. viii. 13. 7
Yet she her selfe the *more* doth magnify, . . . V. viii. 17. 8
More in his causes truth he trusted then in might . . . V. viii. 30. 9
made them both one masse withouten *more* remorse . . . V. viii. 32. 9
of all other weapons lesse or *more*, . . . V. viii. 34. 4
much the *more*, that . . . He mote not come . . . V. viii. 35. 3
much *more* then she had told; . . . V. ix. 21. 5
a thousand *more* of such as sings Hymns . . . V. ix. 29. 4
with *more* myld aspect those two to entertake . . . V. ix. 35. 9
Did her appeach; and, to her *more* disgrace, . . . V. ix. 47. 7
So much *more*, then, is that of powre and art . . . V. x. 2. 5
thine owne people do thy mercy prayse much *more* . . . V. x. 3. 9
Much *more* it praysed was . . . V. x. 4. 1
With *more* then needfull naturall remorse, . . . V. x. 4. 8
More happie mother would her surely weene . . . V. x. 7. 7
sunne to shine *more* bright Then it was wont, . . . V. x. 20. 8
for *more* horror and *more* crueltie, . . . V. x. 29. 1
with huge terrour, to be *more* ydrad, . . . V. xi. 3. 5
two *more* of his armes did fall away, . . . V. xi. 11. 7
onely wexed now the *more* aware . . . V. xi. 13. 2
The *more* t' aggrate his God . . . V. xi. 19. 9
more fiercely reard Uppon her wide great wings, . . . V. xi. 30. 5
More loathd then Lerna, or then Stygian lake, . . . V. xi. 32. 4
cruell enemies increased *more*, . . . V. xi. 54. 2
light then Phoebus lampe doth shine *more* cleare? . . . V. xi. 62. 9
No shame to stoupe, ones head *more* high to reare; . . . V. xii. 19. 3
let drive *more* fiercely then afore . . . V. xii. 22. 9
their disgraces Did much the *more* augment, . . . V. xii. 28. 9
thought *more* the lesse she sed . . . V. xii. 29. 9
And *more*, to make them pierce and wound *more* deepe, . V. xii. 42. 6
So much the *more* at him still did she scold, . . . V. xii. 43. 6
Calidore . . . doth make Briana wexe *more* mylde . . . VI. i. Arg.
none *more* courteous Knight Then Calidore, . . . VI. i. 2. 1
he the *more* his wicked poyson forth did poure.' . . . VI. i. 9. 9
That thorough some *more* mighty enemies wrong . . . VI. i. 11. 3
rather *more* enrag'd for those words sake; . . . VI. i. 19. 4
gan to drive at him *more* hard . . . VI. i. 20. 9
makes his way *more* violent; . . . VI. i. 21. 5
as he still decayd so he encreased *more* . . . VI. i. 21. 9
That shall you glory gaine *More* then his love, . . . VI. i. 27. 5
gan t' augment her bitternesse much *more;* . . . VI. i. 32. 2
no whit *more* appalled for the same, . . . VI. i. 32. 3
rather did *more* chearefull seeme therefore: . . . VI. i. 32. 5
Calidore, that was *more* quicke of sight . . . VI. i. 38. 5
nothing is *more* blamefull to a knight, . . . VI. i. 41. 1
Whereof she now *more* glad then sory earst, . . . VI. i. 45. 1
more to increase his shame, . . . Would thumpe her forward VI. ii. 10. 5
Sir Calidore . . . *more* admyr'd the stroke . . . VI. ii. 13. 2
But *more* enforst my paine, the *more* my plaints to heare. VI. ii. 22. 9
Him much *more* now then earst he gan admire . . . VI. ii. 34. 2
His care *more* then her owne . . . VI. iii. 12. 2
So much the *more* was Calepine offended, . . . VI. iii. 36. 6
But he the *more* thereby enraged was, . . . VI. iii. 50. 1
Ne sparing him the *more* for all his grievous wound . . . VI. iv. 2. 9

More—*Continued.*
More brave and noble knights have raysed beene . . . VI. iv. 36. 3
ever *more* and *more* her owne affliction wrought. . . . VI. v. 6. 9
To weary him the *more* and waste his spight, . . . VI. v. 17. 4
were now much *more* increast . . . VI. vi. 2. 3
outward salves that may augment it *more.'* . . . VI. vi. 13. 4
the *more* outrageous and bold, . . . VI. vi. 21. 1
To some hid end to make *more* easie way, . . . VI. vi. 42. 2
if ye list to haste a litle *more,* . . . VI. vii. 6. 3
Devizing of his love *more* then of daunger drad. . . . VI. vii. 6. 9
with much *more* steddy stowre, . . . VI. vii. 8. 5
passing by doth hurt no *more.* . . . VI. vii. 9. 9
With flaming sword in hand his terror *more* to breed. . . . VI. vii. 11. 9
Regarding *more* his faith which he did plight, . . . VI. vii. 23. 3
beautie is *more* glorious bright and clere, . . . VI. vii. 29. 7
The *more* it is admir'd of many a wight, . . . VI. vii. 29. 8
such proud looks would make her praysed *more;* . . . VI. vii. 30. 2
the *more* she did all love despize, . . . VI. vii. 30. 3
The *more* would wretched lovers her adore. . . . VI. vii. 30. 4
What could the Gods doe *more,* but doe it *more* aright? . . . VI. vii. 31. 9
She had destroyed two and twenty *more.* . . . VI. vii. 38. 8
did the *more* her beate and bruse: . . . VI. vii. 40. 5
when she complaines, The *more* he laughes, . . . VI. vii. 44. 8
fume in his disdainefull mynd the *more,* . . . VI. vii. 47. 8
Was much *more* grievous then the others blowes: . . . VI. vii. 49. 8
For aye the *more* that she did them entreat, . . . VI. viii. 3. 8
The *more* they him misust, and cruelly did beat. . . . VI. viii. 3. 9
augment Their cruelty, and him to punish *more,* . . . VI. viii. 4. 7
Scourging and haling him *more* vehement; . . . VI. viii. 4. 8
Whether *more* wary were to give or ward the blow. . . . VI. viii. 13. 9
more on him doth then him selfe depend: . . . VI. viii. 17. 8
for these Carles to carry much *more* comely were?' . . . VI. viii. 23. 9
mocketh all my paine, and laughs the *more* I mourn.' . . . VI. viii. 24. 9
The whyles she wayld, the *more* they did rejoyce. . . . VI. viii. 46. 5
by chaunce *more* then by choyce, . . . VI. viii. 46. 7
Which she did *more* augment . . . VI. ix. 9. 3
'How much' (sayd he) '*more* happie is the state . . . VI. ix. 19. 1
ne wish for *more* it to augment, . . . VI. ix. 20. 4
The litle that I have growes dayly *more* . . . VI. ix. 21. 5
love *more* deare This lowly quiet life . . . VI. ix. 25. 8
to quench his fire he did it *more* augment. . . . VI. ix. 34. 9
cared *more* for Colins carolings . . . VI. ix. 35. 7
she did love a stranger swayne then him *more* dere. . . . VI. ix. 38. 9
Old love is litle worth when new is *more* prefard. . . . VI. ix. 40. 9
Shall *more* conveniently in other place be ended. . . . VI. ix. 46. 9
mindeth *more* how he may be relieved . . . VI. x. 1. 8
Besides a thousand *more* which ready bee . . . VI. x. 21. 7
Have for *more* honor brought her to this place, . . . VI. x. 26. 8
daily *more* her favour to augment; . . . VI. x. 37. 2
make it seeme *more* deare . . . VI. xi. 1. 9
at *more* ease continue there his thrall: . . . VI. xi. 6. 8
A little well is lent that gaineth *more* withall. . . . VI. xi. 6. 9
The *more* t' augment her price . . . VI. xi. 11. 9
then the Captaine, fraught with *more* displeasure, . . . VI. xi. 14. 7
To make the prises of the rest *more* deare. . . . VI. xi. 15. 5
minding *more* her safety then himselfe, . . . VI. xi. 19. 3
make . . . Seeme much *more* lovely . . . VI. xi. 21. 7
more increast the anguish of his paine: . . . VI. xi. 26. 3
A thousand times embrast, and kist a thousand *more.* . . . VI. xi. 45. 9
Well she it markt, and pittied the *more,* . . . VI. xii. 8. 1
Damzell gan to wex *more* sound and strong. . . . VI. xii. 11. 9
Nought sparing them, the *more* did tosse and teare, . . . VI. xii. 24. 7
the *more* he strove, the *more* the Knight Did him suppresse, . . . VI. xii. 31. 5
the *more* he rag'd, the *more* his powre increast. . . . VI. xii. 32. 9
much admyr'd the Beast, but *more* admyr'd the Knight. . . . VI. xii. 37. 9
Thenceforth *more* mischiefe and *more* scath he wrought . . . VI. xii. 39. 1
Ne ever could, by any, *more* be brought . . . VI. xii. 39. 3
brought Into like bands, ne maystred any *more:* . . . VI. xii. 39. 4
More then my former writs, . . . VI. xii. 41. 3
she her selfe *more* worthy thereof wend, . . . VII. vi. 11. 3
more full of grace and Majestie, . . . VII. vi. 24. 8
none of all there-in *more* pleasure found Then Cynthia, . . . VII. vi. 38. 6
Sprinkled with wholsom waters *more* then most on ground: . . . VII. vi. 38. 9
Cynthia's selfe, *more* angry then the rest, . . . VII. vi. 51. 1
more speedy, from them fled *more* fast . . . VII. vi. 52. 4
Being far greater and *more* tall . . . VII. vii. 5. 3
to honour her the *more,* . . . VII. vii. 11. 1
'Ne is the water in *more* constant case, . . . VII. vii. 20. 1
waights, with which he did assoyle Both *more* and lesse, . . . VII. vii. 38. 8
in all thy creatures *more* or lesse . . . VII. vii. 47. 3
since that lyfe is *more* then death desyred, . . . *Am.* vii. 9
More then most faire, full of the living fire, . . . *Am.* viii. 1
wish that *more* and greater they might be, . . . *Am.* xxv. 13
That maketh it be coveted the *more:* . . . *Am.* xxvi. 10
harder growes the *more* I her intreat! . . . *Am.* xxx. 4
I burne much *more* in boyling sweat, . . . *Am.* xxx. 7
the *more* she fervent sees my fit, The *more* she frieseth . . . *Am.* xxxii. 9, 10
having it, they gaze on it the *more;* . . . *Am.* xxxv. 6
dayly *more* augment my miseryes? . . . *Am.* xxxvi. 8
all the *more* my sorrow it augmenteth, . . . *Am.* xlii. 3
The *more* I love and doe embrace my bane. . . . *Am.* xlii. 4
Then doe I *more* augment my foes despight; . . . *Am.* xliv. 10
the *more* I seeke to settle peace, The *more* I fynd their malice to increase. . . . *Am.* xliv. 13, 14
Onely my paines wil be the *more* to get her; . . . *Am.* li. 13
Ne your incessant battry *more* to beare: . . . *Am.* lvii. 4
the trew fayre . . . is much *more* praysd of me: . . . *Am.* lxxix. 4
then the *more* your owne mishap I rew, . . . *Am.* lxxxii. 3
More bright then Hesperus . . . *Epith.* 95
Much *more* then would ye wonder . . . *Epith.* 188

More—*Continued.*
seemes *more* fayre, The *more* they on it stare. . . . *Epith.* 232, 233
Never had man *more* joyfull day then this, . . . *Epith.* 246
Thinks *more* upon her paradise of joyes, . . . *Epith.* 366
More then we men can fayne! . . . *Epith.* 414
But man that breathes a *more* immortall mynd, . . . *H.L.* 103
nought *more* divine doth seeme, Or that resembleth *more* th' immortall flame . . . *H.L.* 114, 115
So hast thou often done (ay me, the *more!*) . . . *H.L.* 141
Yet herein eke thy glory seemeth *more,* . . . *H.L.* 162
may it *more* esteeme; For things hard gotten men *more* dearely deeme. . . . *H.L.* 167, 168
The *more* . . . to be admyred, The *more* they stayed be on stedfastnesse; . . . *H.L.* 171, 172
striveth still T' approch *more* neare, . . . *H.L.* 248
torment . . . with *more* then hellish paine! . . . *H.L.* 253
thousands *more* then any tongue can tell, . . . *H.L.* 264
is there one *more* cursed then they all, . . . *H.L.* 266
and doest the *more* endeere Thy pleasures . . . *H.L.* 274
The Sunne *more* bright and glorious . . . *H.L.* 277
Thou in me kindlest much *more* great desyre, . . . *H.B.* 5
Or *more* or lesse, by influence divine, . . . *H.B.* 44
So it *more* faire accordingly it makes, . . . *H.B.* 45
blossomes . . . arayd with much *more* orient hew, . . . *H.B.* 79
beleeve me there is *more* then so, . . . *H.B.* 85
Which powre retayning still or *more* or lesse, . . . *H.B.* 113
hath in it the *more* of heavenly light, . . . *H.B.* 128
it *more* fairely dight With chearefull grace . . . *H.B.* 130
And oft it falles, (aye me, the *more* to rew!) . . . *H.B.* 148
gentle Love, . . . Will *more* illumine . . . *H.B.* 177
adde *more* brightnesse to your goodly hew, . . . *H.B.* 178
Therefore, to make your beautie *more* appeare, . . . *H.B.* 183
That men the *more* admyre their fountaine may; . . . *H.B.* 186
made out of one mould the *more* t' agree; . . . *H.B.* 207
Drawing out . . . A *more* refyned forme, . . . *H.B.* 214
lovers eyes *more* sharply sighted bee . . . *H.B.* 232
See *more* then any other eyes can see, . . . *H.B.* 234
and thousands *more* Thy handmaides be, . . . *H.B.* 260
That may it *more* to mortall eyes commend, And make it *more* admyr'd of foe and frend; . . . *H.B.* 263, 264
Many lewd layes (ah! woe is me the *more!*) . . . *H.H.L.* 8
Drew millions *more* against their God to fight. . . . *H.H.L.* 84
Ayre *more* then water, fire much *more* then ayre, . . . *H.H.B.* 48
And so much fairer, and much *more* than these, . . . *H.H.B.* 62
How much *more* those essentiall parts. . . . *H.H.B.* 109

Mores. Tenne thousand *mores* of sundry sent and hew, . . . VII. vii. 10. 4

Morgan. fierce Cundah gan shortly to envy His brother *Morgan,* . . . II. x. 33. 3

Moriani. *See* **Morands.**

Morindus. Next whom *Morindus* did the crowne sustayne; . . . II. x. 43. 3

Morini. *See* **Morands.**

Morion. head full bravely with a *morian* armed, . . . *Bel.*[1] xi. 5
head, full bravely with a *morion* hidd, . . . *Bel.*[2] xv. 5
steelhed speare, and *morion* on her hedd, . . . *Mui.* 322
A guilt engraven *morion* he did weare: . . . VII. vii. 28. 8

Morish. *See* **Moorish.**

Morn. At *morne* and even, besides their Anthemes sweet, . . . *Hub.* 451
Wend too and fro at evening and at *morne.* . . . *Col.* 247
wont to say His holy thinges each *morne* and eventyde: . . . I. i. 34. 7
before the *Morne* with cremosin ray . . . II. xi. 3. 1
forth from virgin bowre she comes in th' early *morne.* . . . II. xii. 50. 9
that faire Starre, the messenger of *morne,* . . . II. xii. 65. 1
That daintie Rose, the daughter of her *Morne,* . . . III. v. 51. 1
floures so fresh at *morne,* . . . III. ix. 39. 9
Nor ward to waite at *morne* and evening late; . . . III. xi. 21. 4
Borne at one burden in one happie *morne;* . . . IV. ii. 41. 4
Thrise happie mother, and thrise happie *morne,* . . . IV. ii. 41. 5
Like to the ruddie *morne* appeard in sight, . . . IV. vi. 19. 6
though Poeana were as faire as *morne,* . . . IV. ix. 3. 6
the *Morne,* when first her shyning face . . . IV. x. 52. 6
Congealed litle drops which doe the *morne* adore. . . . IV. xi. 46. 9
following his chace in dewy *morne,* . . . V. viii. 43. 2
if he needes will fight, crave leave till *morne,* . . . VI. iii. 41. 6
The bud of joy, the blossome of the *morne,* . . . *Am.* lxi. 9
move Theyr sad protract from evening untill *morne.* . . . *Am.* lxxxvi. 4
The Rosy *Morne* long since left Tithones bed, . . . *Epith.* 75

Morning. One foote on Thetis, th' other on the *Morning,* . . . *Ro.* iv. 2
Sith *morning* faire may bring fowle evening late, . . . *Mui.* 219
beautie shyneth as the *morning* cleare, . . . *Col.* 506
Her lookes were like beames of the *morning* Sun, . . . *Col.* 604
rosy fingred *Morning* faire, . . . Had spred her purple robe . . . I. ii. 7. 1
Doth license him depart at sound of *morning* droome.' . . . I. ix. 41. 9
morning deaw upon their leaves doth light; . . . I. xii. 6. 8
As *morning* Sunne her beames dispredden cleare, . . . II. ii. 40. 8
right faire and fresh as *morning* rose, . . . II. ix. 36. 7
Her berth was of the wombe of *Morning* dew, . . . III. vi. 3. 1
Faire Canacee, as fresh as *morning* rose, . . . IV. iii. 51. 7
With pearly dew sprinkling the *morning* grasse: . . . V. v. 45. 5
the *morning,* bringing early light . . . VI. v. 40. 2
Like the faire *Morning* clad in misty fog . . . VI. xi. 3. 9
in a *morning,* when this Maiden faire Was dighting her, . . . VI. xii. 15. 1
With shew of *morning* mylde he hath begun, . . . *Am.* lxii. 3

Morning's. Ne ever evening saw, ne *mornings* ray, . . . IV. xi. 4. 7

Morning star. Mine, that did then shine as the *Morning starre.* I. ii. 36. 4
As bright as doth the *morning starre* appeare . . . I. xii. 21. 5
Whose glory shineth as the *morning starre,* . . . II. ix. 4. 6
O glorious *Morning-Starre!* O Lampe of Light! . . . *H.H.L.* 170

Morpheus. the time, when *Morpheus* Most trulie doth appeare, *Bel.* xv. 1
the sad humor . . . As messenger of *Morpheus,* . . . I. i. 36. 3
the Sprite . . . unto *Morpheus* comes, . . . I. i. 40. 8

Morpheus—*Continued.*
whenas *Morpheus* had . . . Arrested all that courtly company, I. iv. 44. 6
Morpheus'. To *Morpheus* house doth hastily repaire. . . . . . I. i. 39. 3
whilest in *Morpheus* bosome safe she lay, ... VI. viii. 34. 6
Morrow. *See* **To-morrow.**
why sytten we soe . . . Upon so fayre a *morow?* . . . . . *S.C.* Mar. 3
sithens is but the third *morowe* . . . . *S.C.* Mar. 46
Sicker this *morrowe,* no lenger agoe, ... *S.C.* May 19
the *morrow* next ensuing, ... *Hub.* 103
The *morrow* next, so soone as one might see . . . . . *Hub.* 108
to require Respite till *morrow* . . . . *Hub.* 326
to appeare The *morrow* next at Court, ... *Hub.* 1099
In equall lists they should the *morrow* next it fight. . . . . I. iv. 40. 9
Returne . . . Till *morrow* next that I the Elfe subdew, . . . I. iv. 51. 4
The *morrow* next gan earely to appeare, ... I. xi. 33. 1
earely, ere the *morrow* . . . . I. xi. 33. 3
the *morrow* fayre with purple beames . . . . II. iii. 1. 1
when appeared the third *Morrow* bright . . . . II. xii. 2. 4
Earely, the *morrow* next, before that day . . . . . . III. ii. 48. 1
ere the *morrow* did upreare His deawy head . . . . . . III. iv. 61. 3
till *morrow* next againe . . . . III. viii. 51. 7
The *morow* next, . . . that same Faery knight Uprose, . . . III. x. 1. 1
Till *morrow* next shee did her selfe avize, ... III. xii. 28. 4
The *morrowe* next appeard with joyous cheare, ... III. xii. 28. 6
she, as *morrow* fresh, her selfe did reare . . . . III. xii. 28. 8
The *morow* next, so soone as Titan shone, ... IV. i. 16. 5
The *morrow* next the Turney gan anew: . . . . IV. iv. 26. 1
early in the *morrow* next, he went . . . . IV. vi. 44. 4
'The *morrow* next, about the wonted howre, ... IV. viii. 59. 1
so soone as *morrow* light Appear'd in heaven, ... V. iii. 7. 1
The *morrow* next, so soone as dawning houre . . . . . . V. vi. 35. 1
About their holy things for *morrow* Mas; . . . . V. vii. 17. 8
The *morrow* next, so soone as dawning light . . . . . . V. vii. 26. 7
That nought the *morrow* next mote stay his fare. . . . . . V. x. 16. 4
The *morrow* next appear'd with purple hayre . . . . . . V. x. 16. 5
pointed for the combat twixt them twayne The *morrow* next, V. xii. 9. 8
The *morrow* next, that was the dismall day . . . . . . VI. xii. 11. 1
The *morrow* next, before the lampe of light . . . . . . VI. i. 31. 1
The *morrow* next, when day gan to uplooke, ... VI. iii. 11. 1
The *morrow* next, so soone as joyous day . . . . VI. iii. 45. 1
The *morrow* next the Prince did early rize, ... VI. vi. 44. 8
Morrow's. the next *morrowes* meed they closely ment, . . . *Hub.* 331
Morsel. hee . . . scarse good *morsell* all his life did taste, . I. iv. 28. 3
Morsels. Some with their eyes the daintest *morsels* chose; . . VI. viii. 39. 4
Mortal. The carefull thoughts of *mortall* miseries; . . . . *Bel.*² i. 4
mortall men tossed by troublous fate . . . . *Pet.*² vii. 3
that *mortall* puissaunce, Puft up with pride . . . . *Ro.* xi. 2
No *mortall* blemishe may her blotte. . . . . *S.C.* Ap. 54
that dreerie Death should strike so *mortall* stroke, ... *S.C.* N. 123
mortal men, that swincke and sweate for nought, ... *S.C.* N. 154
joyes enjoyes that *mortall* men doe misse. . . . . *S.C.* N. 196
before That Ceres seede of *mortall* men were knowne, . . . *Gn.* 207
yet they both doe *mortall* foes remaine, ... *Gn.* 415
the condition of *mortall* men. . . . . *Hub.* 150
the Wolfe, her *mortall* enemie, ... *Hub.* 1209
pierce immortall breasts with *mortall* smarts? . . . . . *T.M.* 48
Fild with the wreaks of *mortall* miserie; . . . . *T.M.* 124
From thence infused into *mortall* brests. . . . . *T.M.* 390
mortall men have powre to deifie: . . . . *T.M.* 460
pestilence, That *mortall* mindes doth inwardly infect . . . *T.M.* 484
mercie more than *mortall* men can vew. . . . . *T.M.* 514
leave me here distressed With *mortall* cares . . . . . . *Ti.* 305
Of former being in this *mortall* hous, ... *Ti.* 354
Where *mortall* wreakes their blis may not remove; . . . . *Ti.* 397
how can *mortall* immortalitie give? . . . . *Ti.* 413
Drawne into armes, and proofe of *mortall* fight, ... *Mui.* 4
glories most in *mortall* miseries, ... *D.* 152
heavenly spirits have compassion On *mortall* men, ... *D.* 385
Of ought that framed is of *mortall* moulde, ... *D.* 493
her that first did stir that *mortall* stownd. . . . . . . *Col.* 878
Her huge long taile . . . Pointed with *mortall* sting. . . . . I. i. 15. 4
Did never *mortall* eye behold such heavenly grace. . . . . . I. iii. 4. 9
An hatefull Snake, the which his . . . *mortall* sting implyes. . I. iv. 31. 5
The wise Southsayer . . . telles of warres and *mortall* fight. . I. v. 8. 9
What witt of *mortal* wight Can now devise . . . . I. vi. 6. 8
The hight of three the tallest sonnes of *mortall* seed. . . . I. vii. 8. 9
His *mortall* mace, wherewith his foemen he dismayde. . . . . I. vii. 10. 9
O! hold thy *mortall* hand for Ladies sake; . . . . I. vii. 14. 6
Thereby his *mortall* blade full comely hong In yvory sheath, . I. vii. 30. 6
Ne might of *mortall* eye be ever seene; . . . . I. vii. 33. 2
Jove, . . . To wreake the guilt of *mortall* sins is bent, . . . I. viii. 9. 2
What *mortall* wight could ever beare so monstrous blow? . . I. viii. 18. 9
With *mortall* steele him smot againe so sore, ... I. viii. 24. 2
blisse may not abide in state of *mortall* men. . . . . . . I. viii. 44. 9
mortall life gan loath as thing forlore, ... I. x. 21. 5
His *mortall* life he learned had to frame . . . . I. x. 45. 8
The *mortall* sting his angry needle shott . . . . I. xi. 38. 5
tell the secrete of your *mortall* smart: . . . . II. i. 46. 8
him beset With strokes of *mortall* steele . . . . II. ii. 22. 3
mortal vengeaunce joyne to crime abhord? . . . . II. ii. 30. 4
great or glorious in *mortall* eye, ... II. ii. 41. 4
told the story of the *mortall* payne, ... II. ii. 45. 7
with stiffe force shaking his *mortall* launce, ... II. iii. 14. 4
soveraine moniment of *mortall* vowes, ... II. iii. 25. 7
Nor voyce sound *mortall;* . . . . II. iii. 33. 4
to stay the *mortall* chaunce, ... II. iii. 34. 7
in me yet stickes the *mortall* sting, ... II. iv. 33. 5
mortall hands may not withstand his might, ... II. iv. 42. 2
where hath he hong up his *mortall* blade, ... II. v. 35. 7
The *mortall* steele despiteously entayld . . . . II. vi. 29. 7

Mortal—*Continued.*
'Are *mortall* men so fond and undiscreet . . . . II. vii. 14. 7
'Behold, thou Faeries sonne, with *mortall* eye, ... II. vii. 38. 1
Ne *mortall* steele emperce his miscreated mould. . . . . . . II. vii. 42. 9
titles vaine, Which *mortall* Princes wore . . . . II. vii. 43. 9
Mortall Samnitis, and Cicuta bad, ... II. vii. 52. 5
mortall arrowes, wherewith he doth fill The world . . . . . II. viii. 6. 3
through his thigh the *mortall* steele did gryde: . . . . . . II. viii. 36. 5
Thousand times fairer than her *mortall* hew, ... II. ix. 3. 7
The one imperfect, *mortall,* foeminine, ... II. ix. 22. 4
Three ages, such as *mortall* men contrive, ... II. ix. 48. 5
Ne can devized be of *mortall* wit; . . . . II. ix. 50. 5
the Prince his *mortall* speare Soone to him raught, ... II. xi. 25. 1
could not die, yet seemd a *mortall* wight, ... II. xi. 40. 7
Of *mortall* life the leafe, the bud, the flowre; . . . . . . II. xii. 75. 2
That *mortall* puissaunce mote not withstond. . . . . III. i. 10. 6
her *mortall* speare She mightily aventred . . . . III. i. 28. 6
every *mortall* wight Was drowned . . . . III. i. 59. 2
The *mortall* steele stayd not . . . . III. i. 65. 5
mortall men their weary cares Do lay away, ... III. ii. 32. 1
over *mortall* mindes hast so great might, ... III. iii. 2. 2
Of *mortall* Syre or other living wight, ... III. iii. 13. 2
That *mortall* speare she in her hand did take, ... III. iv. 14. 2
with *mortall* stroke astownd, ... III. iv. 17. 5
So ticle be the termes of *mortall* state, ... III. iv. 28. 6
Had she not beene devoide of *mortall* slime, ... III. iv. 35. 3
Wee *mortall* wights, whose lives and fortunes bee . . . . . III. v. 36. 6
That *mortall* men her glory should admyre. . . . . III. v. 52. 6
sendeth forth to live in *mortall* state, ... III. vi. 32. 8
Fleshly corruption, nor *mortall* payne. . . . . III. vi. 33. 4
mortall miseries doth make her play. . . . . III. vii. 4. 5
As an immortall mote a *mortall* wight, ... III. viii. 38. 4
she a *mortall* creature loved best: . . . . III. viii. 39. 7
Then he would make him selfe a *mortall* wight; . . . . . . III. viii. 39. 8
minds of *mortall* men are muchell mard . . . . III. x. 31. 8
day and night afflicts with *mortall* paine, ... III. xi. 17. 2
A *mortall* bow and arrowes keene did hold, ... III. xi. 48. 2
gan the world to hyde From *mortall* vew, ... III. xi. 55. 4
fiercely forth her *mortall* blade she drew, ... III. xii. 33. 8
So *mortall* was their malice, and so sore Become, ... IV. ii. 18. 8
in his side The *mortall* point most cruelly empight; . . . . IV. iii. 10. 4
Unto her native home from *mortall* miserie. . . . . IV. iii. 30. 9
there made gods, though borne of *mortall* berth, ... IV. iii. 44. 3
So *mortall* foes so friendly to agree, ... IV. iii. 49. 7
mortall foes doe turne to faithfull frends, ... IV. iv. 1. 2
weend no *mortall* creature she should bee, ... IV. v. 14. 6
of *mortall* stroke the stound doth beare, ... IV. vi. 37. 5
Her *mortall* arrowes she at him did threat, ... IV. vii. 37. 8
Such *mortall* malice wonder was to see . . . . IV. ix. 27. 6
his *mortall* part by great mischance Was slaine; . . . . . IV. xi. 16. 7
It was no *mortall* worke, ... IV. xi. 45. 9
for *mortall* wight To tell the sands, ... IV. xi. 53. 1
he was halfe *mortall,* being bred Of *mortall* sire, ... IV. xii. 4. 1, 2
being ment of *mortall* creatures sead, ... IV. xii. 27. 3
till she revenge had wrought . . . uppon a *mortall* foe; . . . V. vi. 23. 8
whence *mortal* men implore Right in their wrongs, ... V. vii. 1. 4
she her selfe professeth *mortall* foe To Justice, ... V. viii. 20. 6
Upon the thrones of *mortall* Princes tend, ... V. ix. 32. 2
his *mortall* speare Past through his shield . . . . V. x. 35. 6
with his *mortal* steel quite through the body strooke. . . . . V. xi. 13. 9
with *mortall* malice him pursu'd so nere. . . . . V. xi. 48. 9
For whom they wayted as his *mortall* fone, ... V. xii. 37. 3
Into the mindes of *mortall* men doe well, ... VI. Pr. 2. 5
his *mortall* hand a while he stayd; . . . . VI. i. 40. 1
'Such is the weaknesse of all *mortall* hope, ... VI. iii. 5. 1
both in minde, . . . And body have receiv'd a *mortall* wound, VI. v. 28. 4
He knew the diverse went of *mortall* wayes, ... VI. vi. 3. 5
All were it to his *mortall* enemie, ... VI. vii. 23. 4
the Gods, that *mortall* follies vew, ... VI. vii. 32. 1
Liker to heaven then *mortall* wretchednesse: . . . . VI. xi. 1. 5
what *mortall* hand or heavens grace . . . . VI. xii. 8. 7
most of them were tongues of *mortall* men, ... VI. xii. 27. 8
more scath he wrought To *mortall* men . . . . VI. xii. 39. 2
Proud Change (not pleasd in *mortall* things . . . to raigne) VII. vi. Arg.
Of Change, the which all *mortall* things doth sway, ... VII. vi. 1. 2
'Will never *mortall* thoughts ceasse to aspire . . . . VII. vi. 29. 2
To see that *mortall* eyes have never seene; . . . . VII. vi. 32. 3
To hide the terror of her uncouth hew From *mortall* eyes . . VII. vii. 6. 3
out of their decay and *mortall* crime, ... VII. vii. 18. 5
Then is she *mortall* borne, how-so ye crake: . . . . VII. vii. 50. 5
'Then are ye *mortall* borne, and thrall to me . . . . . . VII. vii. 54. 1
The beame of light, whom *mortal* eyes admyre; . . . . . . *Am.* lxi. 10
A *mortall* thing so to immortalize; . . . . *Am.* lxxv. 6
all that in this *mortall* frame Contained is, ... *H.L.* 113
doth so much excell All *mortall* sence, ... *H.B.* 42
may it more to *mortall* eyes commend, ... *H.B.* 263
resemble . . . as *mortall* thing immortall could; . . . . . *H.H.L.* 114
show Some litle beames to *mortall* eyes below . . . . . . *H.H.B.* 12
th' Aire . . . Never consum'd, nor quencht with *mortall* hands; *H.H.B.* 40
All *mortall* Princes and imperiall States; . . . . *H.H.B.* 88
How then can *mortall* tongue hope to expresse . . . . . . *H.H.B.* 104
Whose nature yet so much is marvelled Of *mortall* wits, . . . *H.H.B.* 167
to God all *mortall* actions here, . . . do plaine appeare; . . *H.H.B.* 172
Mortality. Of fleshlie slime and fraile *mortalitie;* . . . . . . *D.* 403
boasts of . . . vaine assuraunce of *mortality,* . . . . I. x. 1. 2
Behold the ymage of *mortalitie,* . . . . II. i. 57. 2
rare perfection in *mortalitye,* . . . . II. ii. 41. 7
All be he subject to *mortalitie,* . . . . III. vi. 47. 4
To her fraile mansion of *mortality:* . . . . VI. iii. 28. 3
Her minde remembreth her *mortalitie,* . . . . *Am.* xiii. 7

Mortality—*Continued.*
clogd with burden of *mortality;* . . . Am. lxxii. 4
Mortally. Full *mortally* this Knight ywounded was, . . . *Ti.* 650
Whom *mortally* he hated evermore, . . . IV. i. 39. 4
Had power to staunch al wounds that *mortally* did bleed. . . IV. ii. 39. 9
Full many strokes, that *mortally* were ment, . . . IV. iii. 17. 1
Whilest here on earth she lived *mortallie:* . . . V. i. 5. 5
high did reare His cruell hand to smite him *mortally,* . . . V. xii. 20. 3
And him unarm'd, . . . *mortally* did wound, . . . VI. ii. 43. 5
drove away the stound which *mortally* attacht him. . . . VI. iii. 10. 9
Mortar. squared bricke, Which cunningly was without *morter* laid, . . . I. iv. 4. 2
Mortgaging. *mortgaging* their lives to Covetise, . . . I. v. 46. 4
Mortify. proud rebellious flesh to *mortify:* . . . V. vii. 9. 5
Moses. Sike one (sayd Algrind) *Moses* was, . . . *S.C.* Jul. 157
Moss. now are clothd with *mosse* and hoary frost, . . . *S.C.* Ja. 33
now the gray *mosse* marred his rine; . . . *S.C.* F. 111
The mouldie *mosse,* which thee accloieth, . . . *S.C.* F. 135
mosse as greene as any goord, . . . *Gn.* 164
Where grew two goodly trees, . . . with gray *mosse* overcast; I. ii. 28. 4
with greene *moss* cov'ring her nakednesse . . . II. i. 22. 4
like salvage weed With woody *mosse* bedight, . . . IV. iv. 39. 5
the bare ground with hoarie *mosse* bestrowed . . . VI. iv. 14. 4
Unmard with ragged *mosse* or filthy mud; . . . VI. x. 7. 3
Mossy. The *mossy* braunches of an Oke halfe ded. . . . I. x. 48. 4
mossy trees, which covered all with shade . . . IV. vii. 38. 8
a hollow glade Covered with *mossie* shrubs, . . . VI. iv. 13. 6
Mossy-hoar. His dwelling . . . Under the foot of Rauran *mossy hore,* . . . I. ix. 4. 6
Most (*partial list of adv.*).
when Morpheus *Most* trulie doth . . . appeare . . . *Bel.* xv. 2
measure the *most* haughtie mountaines . . . *Bel.*[2] vii. 7
as at Troy *most* dastards of the Greekes . . . *Ro.* xiv. 9
So weakest may anoy the *most* of might! . . . *Van.* x. 14
florisht *most* in might, . . . *Van.* xi. 2
in their might repose their *most* assurance, . . . *Van.* xi. 13
of himselfe is *most* secure, Shall finde his state *most* fickle . *Van.* xii. 13, 14
Yet for thou pleasest not where *most* I would: . . . *S.C.* Ja. 68
(As *most* usen Ambitious folke:) . . . *S.C.* F. 161
Most is, a fooles talke to beare . . . *S.C.* May 141
But *most* the Foxe, maister of collusion: . . . *S.C.* May 219
yet is Princes pallace the *most* fitt,) . . . *S.C.* O. 81
thing on earth that is of *most* availe, . . . *S.C.* N. 87
And thou, *most* dread (Octavius), . . . *Gn.* 35
most faithfull to her mate, Penelope; . . . *Gn.* 429
Under whose conduct *most* victorious, . . . *Gn.* 548
how we may, with *most* securitie, . . . *Hub.* 191
he that serves the Lord of hoasts *most* high, . . . *Hub.* 469
The Lyon now doth take the *most* delight; . . . *Hub.* 622
(large breath in armes *most* needfull) . . . *Hub.* 745
thereto doth his Courting *most* applie: . . . *Hub.* 784
Of such, as he depended *most* upon; . . . *Hub.* 818
Most miserable man, whom wicked fate . . . *Hub.* 892
And the Foxe guilefull, and *most* covetous, . . . *Hub.* 1022
Most like a Man, the Lord of everie creature, . . . *Hub.* 1030
for outward shape *Most* like a man, . . . *Hub.* 1042
But I therein *most* like to him doo merite, . . . *Hub.* 1044
great Father . . . That *most* art dreaded . . . *T.M.* 56
It *most* behoves the honorable race . . . *T.M.* 79
For God himselfe for wisedome *most* is praised, . . . *T.M.* 89
Most miserable creature under sky . . . *T.M.* 127
Most unhappie wretches! . . . *T.M.* 148
become *most* wretched wightes on ground. . . . *T.M.* 312
Most peereles Prince, *most* peereles Poetresse, . . . *T.M.* 577
A mightie Prince, of *most* renowmed race, . . . *Ti.* 184
unto thee *most* deare, O dearest Dame! . . . *Ti.* 244
'*Most* gentle spirite, breathed from above . . . *Ti.* 281
Which in their daies *most* famouslie did florish; . . . *Ti.* 359
Shrines made of the metall *most* desired, . . . *Ti.* 411
At length, when *most* in perill it was brought, . . . *Ti.* 624
with *most* varietie And change of sweetnesse, . . . *Mui.* 177
the sap of herbe *most* meete, . . . *Mui.* 180
least mishap the *most* blisse alter may? . . . *Mui.* 220
The *most* fine-fingred workwoman on ground, . . . *Mui.* 260
which her vaunteth *most* In skilfull knitting . . . *Mui.* 361
I of many *most* *Most* miserable man; . . . *D.* 37, 38
Most like Alcyon seeming at a glaunce; . . . *D.* 53
neither *most* nor least I found miscaried . . . *D.* 139
glories *most* in mortall miseries, . . . *D.* 152
most faire, *most* pure shee was, . . . *D.* 208
graunt his boone that *most* desires to dye. . . . *D.* 357
May happen unto the *most* happiest wight; . . . *D.* 517
that such are for such ones *most* fit, . . . *As.* Pr. 15
where salvage beasts do *most* abound, . . . *As.* 82
A cruell beast of *most* accursed brood . . . *As.* 116
in his grace did boast you *most* to bee! . . . *As.* 130
most resembling both in shape and spright Her brother deare, *As.* 213
I do covet *most* the same to heare, . . . *Col.* 161
As men use *most* to covet forreine thing.' . . . *Col.* 162
grace was great, and bounty *most* rewardfull. . . . *Col.* 187
most goodly rivers there appeare, . . . *Col.* 300
hablest wit of *most* I know this day. . . . *Col.* 383
most, me seemes, thy accent will excell . . . *Col.* 426
Excelling *most* in glorie and great light: . . . *Col.* 497
boast my selfe . . . *most* that unto them I am so nie; . . . *Col.* 539
Most wretched he, that is and cannot tell.' . . . *Col.* 659
still are wont *most* happie states t' annoy: . . . *Col.* 663
Nor haughtie words *most* full of highest thoughts: . . . *Col.* 716
greatest, when their garments are *most* gay. . . . *Col.* 722
'Not so, (quoth he) Love *most* aboundeth there. . . . *Col.* 775

Most—*Continued.*
But *most,* all wemen are thy debtors found, . . . *Col.* 901
having loved ever one *most* deare: . . . *Col.* 904
most doth rest The burdein . . . *Ded. Son.* ix. 3
Wherewith that courtly garlond *most* ye grace . . . *Ded. Son.* xvi. 4
thou, *most* dreaded impe of highest Jove, . . . I. Pr. 3. 1
her grace . . . Which of all earthly thinges he *most* did crave: I. i. 3. 5
path . . . that beaten seemd *most* bare, . . . I. i. 11. 3
Most lothsom, filthie, foule, . . . I. i. 14. 9
path he kept which beaten was *most* plaine, . . . I. i. 28. 3
in her many troubles did *most* pleasure take. . . . I. ii. 9. 9
haire Of a *most* mighty king, *most* rich and sage: . . . I. ii. 23. 3
O, how can beautie maister the *most* strong, . . . I. iii. 6. 4
ever *most* adord As the God of my life? . . . I. iii. 7. 8
furthest . . . when *most* she weened nye. . . . I. iii. 21. 9
He leaves the welkin way *most* beaten playne, . . . I. iv. 9. 7
Still drownd in sleepe, and *most* of his daies dedd: . . . I. iv. 19. 4
most like a brutish beast, He spued up . . . I. iv. 21. 8
all the while *most* heavenly melody . . . I. v. 17. 6
'O! thou *most* auncient Grandmother of all, . . . I. v. 22. 2
most of all . . . Fell from high Princes courtes, . . . I. v. 51. 5
Phoebus, flying so *most* shamefull sight, . . . I. vi. 6. 6
His mightie Armour, missing *most* at need; . . . I. vii. 19. 5
stones *most* pretious rare. . . . I. vii. 29. 9
feete *most* monstrous were . . . I. viii. 48. 5
who *most* trustes in arme of fleshly might, . . . I. ix. 11. 6
yeeldes his caytive neck to victours *most* despight. . . . I. ix. 11. 9
Most envious man, that grieves at neighbours . . . I. ix. 39. 6
from the fielde *most* cowardly doth fly! . . . I. x. 1. 5
The eldest two, *most* sober, chast, and wise, . . . I. x. 4. 5
For them *most* needeth comfort in the end, . . . I. x. 41. 3
When sin, and hell, and death, doe *most* dismay . . . I. x. 41. 4
when they stood in *most* necessitee, . . . I. x. 43. 8
'*Most* trew,' then said the holy aged man; . . . I. x. 59. 1
now *most* of all him harmd. . . . I. xi. 27. 9
A trickling streame of Balme, *most* soveraine . . . I. xi. 48. 2
who-so kild that monster *most* deforme, . . . I. xii. 20. 3
'To thee, *most* mighty king of Eden fayre, . . . I. xii. 26. 1
His owne two hands, for such a turne *most* fitt, . . . I. xii. 37. 3
Right well I wote, *most* mighty Soveraine, . . . II. Pr. 1. 1
the loves which were to them *most* deare, . . . II. ii. 27. 6
'But lovely concord, and *most* sacred peace, . . . II. ii. 31. 1
Great and *most* glorious virgin Queene alive, . . . II. ii. 40. 3
Order of Maydenhead, the *most* renownd . . . II. ii. 42. 4
such the *most* of all.' . . . II. iii. 37. 9
to entrap The man *most* wary . . . II. iv. 17. 5
Most joyous man . . . my selfe I did esteeme, . . . II. iv. 21. 7
Aray thyselfe in her *most* gorgeous geare, . . . II. iv. 26. 8
'*Most* wretched man, That to affections does the bridle lend! II. iv. 34. 1
'Varlet, this place *most* dew to me I deeme, . . . II. iv. 40. 1
'His be that care, whom *most* it doth concerne,' . . . II. iv. 43. 1
whilest his foe did rage *most* rife: . . . II. v. 9. 7
Was never man, who *most* conquestes atchiev'd, . . . II. v. 15. 3
helpe, *most* noble knight, . . . II. v. 23. 8
strove with *most* delights Him to aggrate, . . . II. v. 33. 1
As her fantasticke wit did *most* delight: . . . II. vi. 7. 2
at their feet her selfe *most* humbly feld, . . . II. vi. 32. 3
'Ah, well away! *most* noble Lords, . . . II. vi. 32. 5
'*Most* wretched woman and of wicked race, . . . II. vi. 33. 7
The mighty martiall handes doe *most* commend: . . . II. vi. 35. 5
'That am, I weene, *most* wretched man alive; . . . II. vi. 45. 2
counsell is *most* strong in age.' . . . II. vi. 48. 5
most were stampt, . . . II. vii. 5. 8
'*Most* cursed of all creatures under skye, . . . II. vii. 59. 4
Honour is least where oddes appeareth *most*. . . . II. viii. 26. 5
That Turrets frame *most* admirable was, . . . II. ix. 45. 1
they of living fire *most* subtilly Were made, . . . II. ix. 46. 5
auncestryes Of my *most* dreaded Soveraigne I recount, . . . II. x. 1. 8
those three monstrous stones doe *most* excell, . . . II. x. 11. 5
which of them *most* did love her parentage? . . . II. x. 27. 9
love is not where *most* it is profest; . . . II. x. 31. 2
Most mercilesse of women, . . . II. x. 35. 7
with *most* cruell hand him murdred pittilesse. . . . II. x. 35. 9
Left of his life *most* famous memory, . . . II. x. 46. 2
most famous hight For skil in Musicke . . . II. x. 59. 7
Elfant was of *most* renowmed fame, . . . II. x. 73. 3
should they be *most* famous moniments, . . . II. x. 74. 7
exercise *most* bitter tyranny . . . II. xi. 1. 7
Alma, like a virgin Queene *most* bright, . . . II. xi. 2. 6
his contrary object *most* deface, . . . II. xi. 6. 4
they dayly made *most* dreadfull battery. . . . II. xi. 7. 9
most horrible of hew And ferce of force, . . . II. xi. 13. 1
the prowest and *most* gent, . . . II. xi. 17. 5
They reard a *most* outrageous dreadfull yelling cry: . . . II. xi. 17. 9
greatest and *most* glorious thing on ground . . . II. xi. 30. 1
most strong in *most* infirmitee; . . . II. xi. 40. 8
most deadly daunger and distressed plight. . . . II. xii. 11. 9
Most ugly shapes and horrible aspects, . . . II. xii. 23. 1
From her *most* cunning hand . . . II. xii. 23. 4
art in mightie armes *most* magnifyde . . . II. xii. 32. 4
rule the Furyes when they *most* doe rage. . . . II. xii. 41. 8
the *most* daintie Paradise on ground . . . II. xii. 58. 1
which all faire workes doth *most* aggrace, . . . II. xii. 58. 8
Most goodly it with curious ymageree Was overwrought, . . . II. xii. 60. 5
Eftsoones they heard a *most* melodious sound, . . . II. xii. 70. 1
Where daungers dwelt, and perils *most* did wonne, . . . III. i. 3. 2
in hope to win thereby *Most* goodly meede, . . . III. i. 18. 8
That Castle was *most* goodly edifyde, . . . III. i. 20. 4
trew love *most* of might, . . . III. i. 29. 8
Basciante did him selfe *most* courteous shew; . . . III. i. 45. 5

Most—*Continued.*
wemen wont in warres to beare *most* sway, ... III. ii. 2. 2
affrap The warlike ryder to his *most* mishap: . . . . . III. ii. 6. 5
what so else his person *most* may vaunt?' . . . . . III. ii. 16. 7
Of hurt unwist *most* daunger doth redound; . . . . . III. ii. 26. 6
Then I avow, by this *most* sacred head . . . . . III. ii. 33. 5
To love the semblaunt pleasing *most* your minde, ... III. ii. 40. 7
Th' uneven nomber for this busines is *most* fitt.' . . . . . III. ii. 50. 9
Most sacred fyre, that burnest mightily . . . . . III. iii. 1. 1
Most famous fruites of matrimoniall bowre, ... III. iii. 3. 7
From under that deepe Rock *most* horribly rebowndes. . . . . . III. iii. 9. 9
'*Most* noble Virgin, that by fatall lore . . . . . III. iii. 21. 6
Brave Captaines, and *most* mighty warriours, ... III. iii. 23. 3
during this their *most* obscuritee, ... III. iii. 44. 8
I deeme that counsel aye *most* fit, ... III. iii. 52. 3
most of Arthegall and his estate. . . . . . III. iii. 62. 5
when he sleepes in *most* security . . . . . III. iv. 27. 3
Most sacred virgin without spot of sinne. . . . . . III. iv. 59. 8
The bountiest virgin and *most* debonaire . . . . . III. v. 8. 2
Do one or other good, I you *most* humbly pray. . . . . . III. v. 10. 9
Of whom ye seeke to be *most* magnifide; . . . . . III. v. 11. 4
was al within *most* richly dight, ... III. v. 40. 8
lapped up her silken leaves *most* chayre, ... III. v. 51. 6
where *most* he us'd Whylome to haunt, ... III. vi. 13. 1
Wher *most* she wonnes when she on earth does dwell; . . . . . III. vi. 29. 2
Threw forth *most* dainty odours and *most* sweet delight. . . . . III. vi. 43. 9
that lewd lover did the *most* lament . . . . . III. vii. 20. 1
her maine strength, in which she *most* doth trust, ... III. vii. 50. 5
The fairest wight on ground, and *most* of men esteem'd. . . . . . III. viii. 13. 9
Of falsehood or of slouth, when *most* it may behove. . . . . III. viii. 27. 9
Most vertuous virgin! . . . . . III. viii. 42. 6
most they mervaild at her chevalree . . . . . III. ix. 24. 5
'*Most* famous Worthy of the world, ... III. ix. 34. 1
bold he sayd; O *most* redoubted Pere! . . . . . III. x. 26. 8
you, *most* noble Lord, that can and dare . . . . . III. x. 28. 1
Cannot employ your *most* victorious speare . . . . . III. x. 28. 3
'You, that are the *most* opprest . . . . . III. x. 41. 4
with *most* painefull pangs to sigh and sob, ... III. xi. 8. 8
'There he tormenteth her *most* terribly . . . . . III. xi. 17. 1
All which in that faire arras was *most* lively writ. . . . . . III. xi. 39. 9
The whiles a *most* delitious harmony . . . was sweetly heard . III. xii. 6. 1
there marcht a *most* faire Dame, ... III. xii. 19. 1
Shame *most* ill-favourd, bestiall, and blinde: . . . . . III. xii. 24. 5
was stonisht sore; But *most* faire Amoret, ... III. xii. 44. 6
that *most* on earth him joyd, ... III. xii. 44. *or.* 1
prov'd himselfe *most* foole in what he seem'd *most* wise. . . . IV. ii. 9. 9
vertue is the band that bindeth harts *most* sure. . . . . . IV. ii. 29. 9
two Ladies of *most* goodly hew, ... IV. ii. 30. 6
his sisters skill unto him lent *Most* confidence . . . . . IV. ii. 39. 6
Most wretched men, whose dayes depend on thrids so vaine! IV. ii. 48. 9
Yet is as nigh his end as he that *most* doth playne. . . . . . IV. iii. 1. 9
one of equall might with *most,* . . . . . IV. iii. 24. 6
The prize of her which did in beautie *most* excell. . . . . . IV. iv. 5. 9
when *most* us needeth rest, ... IV. iv. 12. 3
The doughtiest knight . . . and *most* of might. . . . . . IV. iv. 42. 9
to her that doth the *most* excell, ... IV. v. 2. 4
when he was unto her selfe *most* nie, ... IV. v. 29. 8
The things, that day *most* minds, at night doe *most* appeare. . IV. vi. 34. 9
most was moved at the piteous vew, ... IV. viii. 20. 3
most of strength and beautie . . . . . IV. viii. 48. 6
the gentle hart should *most* assured bind. . . . . . IV. ix. 1. 9
most she touched was with griefe entire . . . . . IV. ix. 13. 8
Faint friends when they fall out *most* cruell fomen bee. . . . IV. ix. 27. 9
her losse ought me to sorrow *most,* . . . . . IV. ix. 38. 7
seeme . . . to them *most* sweet; . . . . . IV. x. 2. 4
Abounding all with delices *most* rare, ... IV. x. 6. 2
bravely mounted to his *most* mishap: . . . . . IV. x. 9. 7
most adorne thy place; . . . . . IV. x. 44. 3
To which they all repayr'd, both *most* and least, ... IV. xi. 9. 3
Faire Amphitrite, *most* divinely faire, ... IV. xi. 11. 6
There also some *most* famous founders were . . . . . IV. xi. 15. 1
Most voide of guile, *most* free from fowle despight, ... IV. xi. 18. 8
this to you, O Britons! *most* pertaines, ... IV. xi. 22. 6
a *most* celestiall sound Of dainty musicke, ... IV. xi. 23. 1
Oxford, thine doth Thame *most* glorify. . . . . . IV. xi. 26. 9
Oze the *most* of might, ... IV. xi. 37. 6
Lindus that his pikes doth *most* commend, ... IV. xi. 39. 7
the seas by her are *most* augmented: . . . . . IV. xii. 2. 3
lowest hell, to which I lie *most* neare, ... IV. xii. 6. 7
Most did she thinke, but *most* she thought amis, ... IV. xii. 22. 4
that which he *most* concealed, ... IV. xii. 22. 8
of *most* perfect metall it was made, ... V. i. 10. 1
from the *most* that some were given to the least? . . . . . V. ii. 37. 9
All creatures must obey the voice of the *Most* Hie. . . . . V. ii. 40. 9
The bridegromes state, the brides *most* rich aray, ... V. iii. 3. 3
The *most* part of my land hath washt away, ... V. iv. 8. 3
For any death to chaunge life, though *most* bad: . . . . . V. iv. 11. 5
'*Most* haplesse well ye may Me justly terme, ... V. iv. 27. 5
To whom she bore *most* fervent love of late, ... V. iv. 30. 3
As the faire Moone in her *most* full aspect . . . . . V. v. 3. 8
Amongst them all she placed him *most* low, ... V. v. 23. 1
Her nearest handmayd, whom she *most* did trust, ... V. v. 29. 2
dare even deathes *most* dreadfull face behold? . . . . . V. v. 31. 4
most the knight, whom she with guilefull call . . . . . V. v. 52. 8
unto her mistresse *most* unkind She daily told . . . . . V. v. 56. 7
most she did her troubled mynd molest, ... V. vi. 4. 5
gan gently her salute . . . in the *most* comely wize; . . . . . V. vi. 20. 2
The one of them, which *most* her wrath increast, ... V. vi. 39. 4
Did the *most* chast Penelope possesse . . . . . V. vii. 39. 2
'Her name Mercilla *most* men use to call . . . . . V. viii. 17. 1

Most—*Continued.*
with *most* fell despight and deadly hate . . . . . V. viii. 18. 3
Her selfe *most* gratefull shew'd, ... V. viii. 23. 9
Swearing and banning *most* blasphemously, ... V. viii. 28. 2
they that *most* in boldnesse doe excell . . . . . V. ix. 1. 7
they that most in boldnesse doe excell Are dreadded *most,* . V. ix. 1. 8
Most sacred wight, *most* debonayre and free, ... V. ix. 20. 7
Whose porch, that *most* magnificke did appeare, ... V. ix. 22. 3
to doe unto his Idole *most* untrew. . . . . . V. x. 27. 9
me, of all *most* wretched wight, ... V. xi. 16. 5
of massy gold *Most* richly made, ... V. xi. 21. 9
Albe that it *most* safety to him gave, ... V. xi. 46. 5
did in strength *most* sorts of men surpas, ... V. xii. 15. 3
To doe *most* dammage where as *most* they ment: . . . . . V. xii. 17. 4
Most shamefull, *most* unrighteous, *most* untrew, ... V. xii. 42. 2
pardon me, *most* dreaded Soveraine, ... VI. Pr. 7. 1
it there *most* useth to abound; . . . . . VI. i. 1. 2
Where curteous Knights and Ladies *most* did won . . . . . VI. i. 1. 8
shall you *most* renowmed make for evermore. . . . . . VI. i. 5. 9
with *most* importune might, ... VI. i. 20. 2
Mongst which my *most* delight hath alwaies been . . . . . VI. ii. 31. 6
the use of armes, which *most* I joy, ... VI. ii. 32. 6
the use of armes, which . . . fitteth *most* . . . . . VI. ii. 32. 7
When day is spent, and rest us needeth *most,* . . . . . VI. iii. 39. 2
But *most* for pitty of his dearest Dame, ... VI. iii. 43. 7
Three mightie enemies did him *most* despight, ... VI. v. 13. 2
most that curre, barking with bitter sownd, ... VI. v. 19. 5
most of all Defetto him annoyde, ... VI. v. 20. 4
in minde, the which *most* grieveth me, ... VI. v. 28. 3
humour which did *most* infest Their ranckling wounds, . . . VI. vi. 2. 8
your talk restraine From that they *most* affect, ... VI. vi. 7. 9
Gainst all, . . . both *most* and least, ... VI. vi. 12. 4
most the former villaine, ... VI. vii. 40. 6
that same foole, which *most* increast her paines, ... VI. vii. 44. 5
Thereto they usde one *most* accursed order, ... VI. viii. 36. 1
most of all the shepheard Coridon For her did languish, . . VI. ix. 10. 5
Coridon *most* helpe did give. . . . . . VI. ix. 15. 9
As they doe know each can *most* aptly use: . . . . . VI. ix. 29. 5
not that which men covet *most* is best, ... VI. ix. 29. 6
Nor that thing worst which men do *most* refuse; . . . . . VI. ix. 29. 7
wisedome is *most* riches: . . . . . VI. ix. 30. 7
Colin Clout should pipe, as one *most* fit; . . . . . VI. ix. 41. 6
most in Pastorellaes grace did sit: . . . . . VI. ix. 41. 8
in it She used *most* to keepe her royall court, ... VI. x. 9. 7
most of all those three did her with gifts endew. . . . . . VI. x. 14. 9
Most sorrowfull, *most* sad, that ever sight, ... VI. x. 40. 6
inly burnt with flames *most* raging whot, ... VI. xi. 4. 2
for their *most* commodity Be sold, ... VI. xi. 10. 4
sold for *most* advantage, ... VI. xi. 10. 9
chiefly Calidore, whom griefe had *most* possest. . . . . . VI. xi. 41. 9
'*Most* certaine markes' (sayd she) 'do me it teach; . . . . . VI. xii. 18. 3
ransacke all their dennes from *most* to least, ... VI. xii. 24. 8
most of them were tongues of mortall men, ... VI. xii. 27. 8
Ne spareth he *most* learned wits to rate, ... VI. xii. 40. 7
Of her faire light and bounty *most* benigne, ... VII. vi. 11. 8
of all that rule she deemed *most* condigne. . . . . . VII. vi. 11. 9
Was made the *most* unpleasant and *most* ill: . . . . . VII. vi. 37. 8
Sprinkled with wholsom waters more then *most* on ground: . VII. vi. 38. 9
most agreed, and did this sentence give, ... VII. vi. 50. 7
those three sacred Saints, though else *most* wise, ... VII. vii. 7. 6
made to growe *Most* dainty trees, ... VII. vii. 8. 7
I do possesse the worlds *most* regiment; . . . . . VII. vii. 17. 2
Ne any Lake, that seems *most* still . . . . . VII. vii. 20. 5
The thing which I doo *most* in her admire, ... *Am.* v. 3
Is of the world unworthy *most* envide; . . . . . *Am.* v. 4
No word was heard of her that *most* it ought; . . . . . *Am.* xix. 10
Most sorts of men doe set but little store. . . . . . *Am.* xxvi. 12
she will plague the man that loves her *most,* . . . . . *Am.* xli. 6
Made for to be the worlds *most* ornament, ... *Am.* liii. 10
when as she *most* supposeth Her selfe assurd, ... *Am.* lviii. 3
There my fraile fancy . . . mantleth *most* at ease; . . . . . *Am.* lxxii. 10
Her harts desire with *most* contentment please. . . . . . *Am.* lxxii. 12
most of all, the Damzels doe delite . . . . . *Epith.* 133
sterve their harts that needeth nourture *most,* . . . . . *H.L.* 39
things . . . both *most* and least, ... *H.L.* 95
seemes on earth *most* heavenly to embrace, ... *H.L.* 111
on thy subjects *most* doest tyrannize? . . . . . *H.L.* 161
So doth he pine in *most* satiety; . . . . . *H.L.* 201
thee, to whom I meane it *most,* . . . . . *H.B.* 22
The *most* resemblance of that heavenly light, ... *H.B.* 121
most beautifull and brave Their fleshly bowre, ... *H.B.* 122
So every spirit, as it is *most* pure, ... *H.B.* 127
And slew the Just by *most* unjust decree. . . . . . *H.H.L.* 154
O huge and *most* unspeakable impression . . . . . *H.H.L.* 155
But those two *most* which, ruling night and day, ... *H.H.B.* 55
mery London, my *most* kyndly Nurse, ... *Proth.* 128

Mostwhat. They that con . . . Sayne *most-what,* . . . . . *S.C.* Jul. 46
playnely to speake of shepheards *most what,* . . . . . *S.C.* S. 104
all the rest do *most-what* fare amis, ... *Col.* 757

Mote (*partial list*). *See* **Not.**
faire as *mote* (mought[1]) the greatest god delite; . . . . . *Pet.* i. 5
For one, opened, *mote* unfolde many moe. . . . . . *S.C.* S. 14
Or it mens follies *mote* be forst to fayne, ... *S.C.* O. 75
breathe on them the whistling wind *mote* best; . . . . . *Gn.* 236
But none of these, . . . *Mote* please his fancie, ... *Mui.* 158
that ill *mote* him behove, ... *D.* 265
Her face, the fairest face that eye *mote* see, ... *As.* 155
so . . . hot That living creature *mote* it not abide; . . . . . I. ii. 29. 6
Fraelissa was as faire as faire *mote* bee, ... I. ii. 37. 8
'O! how,' sayd he, '*mote* I that well out find, ... I. ii. 43. 6

Mote—*Continued.*
Good cause of mine excuse, that *mote* ye please . . . . . . I. iii. 29. 6
A fordonne wight from dore of death *mote* raise, ... I. v. 41. 8
That of no envious eyes he *mote* be spyde; . . . . I. v. 52. 8
eye *mote* not the same endure to vew. . . . . I. viii. 19. 5
Yf living man *mote* worthie be to be her liefe.' . . . . . I. ix. 17. 9
not so happy as *mote* happy bee: . . . . I. ix. 27. 5
you, Sir knight, whose name *mote* I request, ... I. ix. 32. 3
opened his dull eyes, that light *mote* in them shine. . . . I. x. 18. 9
cote of steele, . . . That nought *mote* perce; . . . . . . I. xi. 9. 3
no strength nor stroks *mote* him constraine . . . . I. xi. 43. 2
Yet algates *mote* he soft himselfe appease, ... II. ii. 12. 2
mote nathelesse Himselfe appease, ... II. vi. 24. 1
if ought else that I *mote* not devyse, ... II. ix. 42. 7
not on ground *mote* like to this be found: . . . . II. ix. 45. 5
Fayre *mote* he thee, ... II. xi. 17. 5
That never any *mote* with her compayre; . . . . III. i. 26. 5
Mote Princes place be seeme so deckt to bee. . . . . . . III. i. 33. 4
Dreadfull of daunger that *mote* him betyde, ... III. i. 37. 5
Mote breede him scath unwares: . . . . III. i. 37. 8
By which both in and out men *moten* pas; . . . . III. vi. 31. 6
With humblest suit that he imagine *mot,* . . . . IV. ii. 8. 7
Which *mote* the feebled Britons strongly flancke . . . . . IV. xi. 36. 3
Admyr'd her beautie much, as she *mote* well, ... IV. xii. 33. 4
if two met, the one *mote* needes fall over the lidge. . . . V. vi. 36. 9
'Ah! Sir, but *mote* ye please, ... V. xi. 18. 3
Dye, rather then doe ought that *mote* dishonour yield.' . . . V. xi. 55. 9
sought her love by all the meanes he *mote;* . . . . VI. xi. 4. 7
Moth. as doth an hidden *moth* The inner garment frett, . . . II. ii. 34. 7
Mother. *See* **Grandmother.**
more than that great Phrygian *mother* . . . . *Ro.* vi. 5
answerd his *mother,* all should be done. . . . . *S.C.* May 228
With them that cruell Colchid *mother* dwells, ... *Gn.* 397
a good old woman was, Hight *Mother* Hubberd, ... *Hub.* 34
So *Mother* Hubberd her discourse did end, ... *Hub.* 1385
By yawning Sloth on his owne *mother* Night; . . . . . . *T.M.* 263
Faire Cytheree, the *Mother* of delight, ... *T.M.* 397
his *Moother* with a Veale hath coovered his Face?' . . . . *Tetrasticon* 3
his *mother,* which him bore and bred, ... *Mui.* 259
Enfested grudge, the which his *mother* felt, ... *Mui.* 354
as the *mother* of the Gods, that sought For faire Eurydice, . . *D.* 463
the Nymph his *mother* Him forth did bring, ... *As.* 13
land, our *mother,* us did leave, ... *Col.* 226
out of the fruitfull wombe of their great *mother.* . . . . *Col.* 854
with thy *mother* mylde come to mine ayde; . . . . I. Pr. 3. 6
her *mother* blynd Sate in eternall night: . . . . I. iii. 12. 3
I the *mother* bee Of falshood, ... I. v. 27. 6
arose away The *mother* of dredd darknesse, ... I. v. 44. 5
His loving *mother* came . . . to see her little sonne; . . . I. vi. 27. 1
The greatest Earth his uncouth *mother* was, ... I. vii. 9. 1
The *mother* of three daughters, well upbrought . . . . . . I. x. 4. 3
One *mother* . . . her litle babe revyld, ... I. xii. 11. 1
the earth, great *mother* of us all, ... II. i. 10. 6
to thy *mother* dead attest That cleare she dide . . . . . II. i. 37. 6
that same Hag, his aged *mother,* hight Occasion; . . . . . II. iv. 10. 8
his *mother* did more rage inspyre. . . . . II. iv. 32. 9
His *mother* eke, more to augment his spight, ... II. v. 22. 5
to her *mother* Nature all her care she letts. . . . . . . II. vi. 16. 9
With his faire *mother* he him dights to play, ... II. viii. 6. 5
their owne *mother* loathd their beastlinesse, ... II. x. 9. 3
his *mother* mercilesse, Most mercilesse of women, ... II. x. 35. 6
th' Earth his *mother* was, ... II. xi. 45. 2
her *mother* Art, as halfe in scorne . . . . II. xii. 50. 6
The loving *mother,* that nine monethes did beare . . . . . III. ii. 11. 6
His *mother* was the blacke-browd Cymoent, ... III. iv. 19. 3
The which his *mother* seeing gan to feare . . . . III. iv. 24. 4
His *mother* bad him womens love to hate, ... III. iv. 27. 7
his *mother* vainely did expownd . . . . III. iv. 28. 3
Which when his *mother* deare did understond, ... III. iv. 29. 5
His *mother* swowned thrise, ... III. iv. 35. 1
The wretched sonne of wretched *mother* borne, ... III. iv. 36. 2
other offices for *mother* meet . . . . III. iv. 39. 6
Which to his *mother* told, despeyre she from her flong. . . . III. iv. 41. 9
ofte his *mother,* vewing his wide wownd, ... III. iv. 44. 3
'Night! thou foule *Mother* of annoyaunce sad, ... III. iv. 55. 1
his *mother* long ygoe Did him, they say, forwarne . . . . . III. v. 9. 6
Her *mother* was the faire Chrysogenee, ... III. vi. 4. 1
their great *mother* Venus did lament . . . . III. vi. 40. 3
With which his *mother* Venus her revyld, ... III. vi. 50. 4
Sitting beside his *mother* on the ground; . . . . III. vii. 13. 3
Softly at last he gan his *mother* aske, ... III. vii. 14. 1
his sad *mother,* seeing his sore plight, ... III. vii. 20. 6
in his rage his *mother* would have slaine, ... III. viii. 4. 2
scoffing thus unto his *mother* sayd: . . . . III. xi. 35. 7
Ne did he spare . . . His owne deare *mother,* . . . . . . III. xi. 45. 2
thy sweete smyling *mother* from above, ... IV. Pr. 5. 7
mother of debate And all dissention . . . . IV. i. 19. 1
Borne of one *mother* in one happie mold, ... IV. ii. 41. 3
Thrise happie *mother,* and thrise happie morne, ... IV. ii. 41. 5
like that roote that doth her life divide, Their *mother* was; . IV. ii. 43. 8
Their *mother* was a Fay, ... IV. ii. 44. 1
Which when their *mother* saw, she gan to dout Their safetie; IV. ii. 46. 6
Like as his *mother* prayd the Destinie, ... IV. iii. 13. 7
well instructed by the Fay her *mother,* . . . . IV. iii. 40. 4
of great *mother* Venus bare the name, ... IV. x. 5. 4
The Queene of beautie, and of love the *mother,* . . . . . IV. x. 29. 6
Begotten by two fathers of one *mother,* . . . . IV. x. 32. 4
Mother of blessed Peace and Friendship trew; . . . . . . IV. x. 34. 2
She syre and *mother* is her selfe alone, ... IV. x. 41. 8
thee their *mother* call to coole their kindly rages. . . . . IV. x. 45. 9

Mother—*Continued.*
Mother of laughter, and welspring of blisse, ... IV. x. 47. 8
farre and neare the Nymph his *mother* sought, ... IV. xi. 6. 1
There with the Nymph his *mother,* . . . . IV. xi. 7. 6
Like as the *mother* of the Gods, ... IV. xi. 28. 1
My *mother* Cambridge, whom as with a Crowne He doth adorne, IV. xi. 34. 7
the *mother* was Of lucklesse Marinell, Cymodoce; . . . . . IV. xi. 53. 6
The Nymph his *mother,* getteth her . . . . IV. xii. Arg.
The *mother* of unlucky Marinell, ... IV. xii. 3. 7
durst he not his *mother* disobay, ... IV. xii. 18. 6
Which when his *mother* saw, ... IV. xii. 21. 1
Which when he had unto his *mother* told, ... V. xii. 26. 1
It had depriv'd her *mother* of a daughter: . . . . V. iv. 41. 7
as that madding *mother* . . . her owne deare flesh did teare: . V. viii. 47. 5
Sent by their *mother,* who, a widow, was . . . . V. x. 6. 6
mother of a frutefull heritage, ... V. x. 7. 3
More happie *mother* would her surely weene . . . . V. x. 7. 7
downe he fell uppon his *mother* deare, ... V. x. 35. 8
'The widow Queene my *mother,* . . . conceiving then great feare VI. ii. 29. 1
The sober *mother* seeing such her mood, ... VI. xii. 17. 1
Who ever is the *mother* of one chylde, ... VI. xii. 21. 1
Sith of them all thou art the equall *mother,* . . . . VII. vii. 14. 8
the Earth (great *mother* of us all) . . . . VII. vii. 17. 6
mighty *mother,* now be judge, ... VII. vii. 47. 2
Cupid humbly came, And sayd to her; 'All hayle, my *mother!'* . *Epig.* iii. 3
his *mother* closely smiling sayd, ... *Epig.* iv. 11
Unto his *mother* straight he weeping came. . . . . *Epig.* iv. 31
When thy great *mother* Venus first thee bare, ... *H.L.* 52
His owne faire *mother,* for all creatures sake, ... *H.L.* 72
in honour of thy *Mother* deare, ... *H.B.* 9
Mother of love, and of all worlds delight, ... *H.B.* 16
Mother earth. With bloudy mouth his *mother earth* did kis, . I. ii. 19. 6
gave against his *mother earth* a gronefull sownd. . . . . . II. xi. 42. 9
her of his owne *mother Earth* Whylome begot, ... III. vii. 47. 8
falling on his *mother earth* he fed: . . . . V. xii. 23. 7
Mother earth's. on their *mother Earths* deare lap did lie, . . V. vii. 9. 2
Motherly. a *motherly* care Of her young sonne, ... *S.C.* May 180
Mother of pearl. hilts were burnisht gold, and handle strong Of *mother perle;* . . . . I. vii. 30. 9
Mother's. th' ensample of her *mothers* sight: . . . . *Bel.*[2] vii. 4
beating downe these walls . . . Into her *mothers* bosome, . . . *Ro.* xi. 12
the Lambes owne *mothers* hed. . . . . *Hub.* 1216
They crying creep out of their *mothers* woomb, ... *Ti.* 48
They . . . sucked up their dying *mothers* bloud, ... I. i. 25. 8
chaunge in that great *mothers* face: . . . . I. v. 24. 7
Oke, which he had torne Out of his *mothers* bowelles, ... I. vii. 10. 8
From *mothers* pap I taken was unfitt, ... I. ix. 3. 7
they his *mothers* innocence may tell, ... II. ii. 10. 5
from my *mothers* wombe this grace I have . . . . II. iii. 45. 1
Tydings hereof came to his *mothers* eare: . . . . III. iv. 19. 2
Yet he his *mothers* lore did well retaine, ... III. iv. 26. 5
While in their *mothers* wombe enclosd they were, ... III. vii. 48. 6
That thou bewray'dst his *mothers* wantonnesse, ... III. xi. 36. 4
In vengement of her *mothers* great disgrace, ... IV. vii. 30. 6
through his mad *mothers* blame, ... IV. xi. 13. 5
his *mothers* former charge Gainst womens love, ... IV. xii. 14. 5
Being returned to his *mothers* bowre, ... IV. xii. 19. 1
from his *mothers* wombe, . . . He was invulnerable . . . . VI. iv. 4. 8
this *mothers* joy descrive; . . . . VI. xii. 21. 4
'I am a daughter, by the *mothers* side, Of . . . great Earth, . VII. vi. 26. 4
Expressing all thy *mothers* powrefull art. . . . . *Am.* xxxix. 2
From *mothers* womb deriv'd by dew descent: . . . . *Am.* lxxiv. 6
Love lay sweetly slumbring All in his *mothers* lap; . . . . . *Epig.* iv. 2
forgets . . . His *mothers* heast to prove. . . . . *Epig.* iv. 58
Mothers. The children of one syre by *mothers* three, ... II. ii. 13. 2
Mothers'. Bulles, . . . Doe for the milky *mothers* want complaine, ... I. viii. 11. 7
Mother-wit. whatsoever *mother-wit* or arte Could worke, . . . *Hub.* 1138
all that nature by her *mother-wit* Could frame . . . . . . IV. x. 21. 6
Motion. to follow any merrie *motion.* . . . . *Hub.* 458
Ne anie noyse, ne anie *motion* made. . . . . *Mui.* 400
with *motion* nimble To succour it, ... IV. vi. 29. 4
short tucked for light *motion* Up to her ham; . . . . . . V. v. 2. 6
all other creatures, What-ever life or *motion* do retaine, . . . VII. vii. 4. 2
th' Earth herselfe, of her owne *motion,* . . . . VII. vii. 8. 5
Motioned. Ye have this matter *motioned* in season; . . . . *Hub.* 125
Motions. the sundry *motions* of your Spheares, ... VII. vii. 55. 1
Mott. by measure . . . she *mott* my simple song, ... *Col.* 365
Mought (*partial list*).
So hie as *mought* an Archer reache with sight. . . . . *Bel.*[1] iii. 4
faire as *mought* (mote[2]) the greatest god delite; . . . . . . *Pet.*[1] i. 5
Winter or Sommer they *mought* well fare. . . . . *S.C.* F. 24
Enaunter his rage *mought* cooled bee; . . . . *S.C.* F. 200
For nought *mought* they quitten him . . . . *S.C.* F. 213
Mought her necke bene joynted attones, ... *S.C.* Mar. 53
She *mought* ne gang on the greene. . . . . *S.C.* Mar. 57
Who touches Pitch, *mought* needes be defilde; . . . . *S.C.* May 74
Mought not live ylike as men of the laye. . . . . *S.C.* May 76
We *mought* with our shoulders beare . . . . *S.C.* May 157
So conteck soone by concord *mought* be ended. . . . . . . *S.C.* May 163
And full of favour as kidde *mought* be. . . . . *S.C.* May 184
'God blesse thee, . . . as he *mought* me, ... *S.C.* May 191
She *mought* see the dore stand open wyde. . . . . *S.C.* May 295
That als we *mought* doe soe. . . . . *S.C.* Jul. 120
meeke he was, as meeke *mought* be . . . . *S.C.* Jul. 129
(No such *mought* shepheards bee) . . . . *S.C.* Jul. 150
But shepheard *mought* be meeke and mylde, ... *S.C.* Jul. 153
Such simplesse *mought* them shend: . . . . *S.C.* Jul. 172
(*Mought* they good sheepeheards bene?) . . . . *S.C.* Jul. 178
Mischiefe *mought* to that mischaunce befall, ... *S.C.* Au. 13

Mought—*Continued.*
Well *mought* it beseme any harvest Queene. . . . *S.C.* Au. 36
to seeke redresse *mought* little boote; . . . *S.C.* S. 127
Thou *mought* ay deeper and deeper sinck. . . . *S.C.* S. 133
Such ill, as is forced, *mought* nedes be endured. . . . *S.C.* S. 139
Enaunter they *mought* be inly knowne, . . . *S.C.* S. 161
For not but well *mought* him betight: . . . *S.C.* S. 173
Shepheards sich, God *mought* us many send, . . . *S.C.* S. 178
Thilk same shepheard *mought* I well marke, . . . *S.C.* S. 180
How *mought* we, Diggon, hem be-hold? . . . *S.C.* S. 229
Mought needes decay, when it is at best. . . . *S.C.* S. 241
good Hobbinoll, *mought* I thee praye . . . *S.C.* S. 246
were Hobbinoll as God *mought* please, . . . *S.C.* S. 252
God *mought* it thee requite; . . . *S.C.* S. 258
So *mought* our Cuddies name to heaven sownde. . . . *S.C.* O. 54
when our flocks into mischaunce *mought* fall, . . . *S.C.* D. 9
As it with pleasaunce *mought* thy fancie feede) . . . *S.C.* D. 16
better *mought* they have behote him Hate. . . . *S.C.* D. 54
Tode-stoole growne there *mought* I se, . . . *S.C.* D. 69
That *mought* his life from yron death assure, . . . *Mui.* 59
that nought *mought* him awake. . . . I. i. 42. 3
He gan devise how her he reskew *mought:* . . . III. x. 18. 8
meekest boone that they imagine *mought:* . . . V. ix. 34. 5
fled away with all the speed she *mought,* . . . VI. vii. 50. 4
Which doubt of daunger to her offer *mought,* . . . VI. viii. 32. 5
such basenesse *mought* offend her, . . . *Am.* ix. 12
Mould, Mouldred, *etc. See* **Mold, Moldered,** *etc.*
Mound. this great gardin, compast with a *mound;* . . . II. vii. 56. 5
From sea to sea he heapt a mighty *mound,* . . . II. x. 63. 8
Mount. With feeble wings assay to *mount* on hight; . . . *Bel.*[2] vii. 2
With feeble flight venture to *mount* to heaven, . . . *Bel.*[1] vi. 2
Upon her head he heapt *Mount* Saturnal, . . . *Ro.* iv. 9
Upon her stomacke laid *Mount* Quirinal, . . . *Ro.* iv. 11
Mount Viminall and Aventine doo meete. . . . *Ro.* iv. 14
St. Michels *Mount* who does not know, . . . *S.C.* Jul. 41
wonned not the great God Pan Upon *Mount* Olivet, . . . *S.C.* Jul. 50
Would *mount* as high, . . . *S.C.* O. 90
mount Parnasse, the Muses brood, . . . *Gn.* 21
how *mount* Athos . . . Was digged downe, . . . *Gn.* 45
A little *mount,* of greene turffs edifide; . . . *Gn.* 660
He planted there, and reard a *mount* of earth, . . . *Gn.* 685
that raignst in Castalie And *mount* Parnasse, . . . *T.M.* 58
From hence wee *mount* aloft unto the skie, . . . *T.M.* 505
assay To *mount* to heaven, . . . *Ti.* 426
To *mount* aloft unto the Cristall skie, . . . *Mui.* 44
There did a loftie *mount* at first us greet, . . . *Col.* 284
daring not too rashly *mount* on hight, . . . *Col.* 421
thou hast forgot Thy selfe . . . to *mount* so hie: . . . *Col.* 617
the light to *mount* on hie, And th' heavie downe . . . *Col.* 848
In savadge soyle, far from Parnasso *Mount,* . . . *Ded.Son.*vii.12
By them they passe, . . . And to the Presence *mount;* . . . I. iv. 7. 2
castes up a *mount* of clay. . . . I. viii. 9. 9
he leads him to the highest *Mount,* . . . I. x. 53. 1
Mount, . . . Through famous Poets verse each where renownd, . I. x. 54. 6
strives to *mount* unto his native seat; . . . II. xi. 32. 6
There stood a stately *Mount,* . . . III. vi. 43. 2
Hewen underneath that *Mount,* . . . III. vi. 48. 9
Upon the top of *Mount* Olympus hight, . . . III. vii. 41. 5
in her secret bowre On Acidalian *mount,* . . . IV. v. 5. 5
like a little *Mount* of small degree, . . . V. iv. 7. 7
When he was readie to his steede to *mount* . . . V. x. 16. 8
Therefore it rightly cleeped was *mount* Acidale. . . . VI. x. 8. 9
Yet on *mount* Thabor quite their wits forgat, . . . VII. vii. 7. 7
In mind to *mount* up to the purest sky; . . . *Am.* lxxii. 2
Up to your haughty pallaces may *mount;* . . . *Epith.* 420
he gan to *mount* up hyre, . . . *H.L.* 68
makes him *mount* above the native might . . . *H.L.* 188
From thence to *mount* aloft, by order dew, . . . *H.H.B.* 24
Mount up aloft through heavenly contemplation, . . . *H.H.B.* 136
Mountain. In a great *mountaine* heap't with hideous noyse, . *Ro.* xvi. 2
sitting hye, Upon the *Mountaine* sayles. . . . *S.C.* Jul. 104
Against a *mountaine* rolls a mightie stone, . . . *Gn.* 391
Under the foote of Mole, that *mountaine* hore, . . . *Col.* 57
(Mole hight that *mountain* gray . . . *Col.* 104
Under the steepe foot of a *mountaine* hore: . . . I. iii. 10. 6
his members chast Scattered on every *mountaine* . . . I. v. 38. 8
As *mountaine* doth the valley overcaste. . . . I. xi. 8. 5
like an heaped *mountaine* lay. . . . I. xi. 54. 9
The surging waters like a *mountaine* rise, . . . I. xii. 21. 6
all that *Mountaine,* which doth over-looke The richest champian VII. vi. 54. 7
on the hoary *mountayne* use to towre; . . . *Epith.* 68
Mountain's. To an high *mountaines* top he with them went, . *Gn.* 73
Mountains. the *mountaines* bordring Lombardie, . . . *Bel.*[2] vi. 10
to arise Out of these *mountaines,* . . . *Ro.* xvii. 12
To make the *mountaines* touch the starres divine, . . . *Gn.* 213
Out of her *mountaines* ministred supplies; . . . *Gn.* 506
Ne did he leave the *mountaines* bare unseene, . . . *Mui.* 155
Rolling like *mountaines* in wide wildernesse, . . . *Col.* 198
huge *mountaines* . . . She would commaund themselves to beare away, . . . I. x. 20. 6
ragged ribs of *mountaines* molten new, . . . I. xi. 44. 7
Through woods and *mountaines,* till they came at last . . . II. i. 24. 2
At thy commaund lo! all these *mountaines* bee: . . . II. vii. 9. 2
tombling low From the high *mountaines,* . . . II. xi. 18. 5
Betwixt two shady *mountaynes* doth arize: . . . III. ii. 24. 7
Shall to the utmost *mountaines* fly apace. . . . III. iii. 34. 4
thy moyst *mountaines* each on others throng, . . . III. iv. 8. 5
through *mountains* and through playns, . . . III. iv. 46. 1
With *mountaines* rownd about environed, . . . III. v. 39. 3
Faire Ister, flowing from the *mountaines* hie: . . . IV. xi. 20. 5

Mountains—*Continued.*
'Therefore I will throw downe these *mountaines* hie, . . . V. ii. 38. 1
Through woods, and rocks, and *mountaines* . . . V. viii. 41. 5
through *mountains* and through plains, . . . VI. viii. 44. 2
Mountains'. the most haughtie *mountaines* hight, . . . *Bel.*[2] vii. 7
Mounted. *See* **High-mounted.**
she *mounted* up to joy. . . . *Pet.* vi. 10
The fiery Sun was *mounted* now on hight . . . *Gn.* 65
out of sight to highest heaven *mounted,* . . . *Ti.* 600
Then *mounted* he upon his Steede againe, . . . I. i. 28. 1
golden Phoebus, now *ymounted* hie, . . . Hurled his beame . I. ii. 29. 3
when Aldeboran was *mounted* hye . . . I. iii. 16. 1
on a sandie hill, . . . it *mounted* was full hie, . . . I. iv. 5. 6
an almond tree *ymounted* hye On top of greene Selinis . . . I. vii. 32. 5
Duessa came, High *mounted* on her many headed beast, . . . I. viii. 6. 2
lightly *mounted* passeth on his way; . . . II. v. 38. 2
Thought to have *mounted;* but his feeble vaines . . . II. xi. 48. 3
Was *mounted* high in top of heaven sheene, . . . III. iv. 51. 7
On Tromparts steed her *mounted* without stay, . . . III. viii. 13. 4
though she *mounted* were, . . . IV. vi. 12. 7
bravely *mounted* to his most mishap: . . . IV. x. 9. 7
Mounted in Phoebus charet fierie bright, . . . V. iii. 19. 2
he was *mounted* in his seat so high, . . . V. viii. 33. 3
With many towres, and tarras *mounted* hye, . . . V. ix. 21. 6
Full nobly *mounted* in right warlike wize; . . . V. xi. 4. 3
being thereon *mounted* forth did pace . . . VI. v. 7. 7
Mountenance. they both a furlongs *mountenaunce* Retird their steeds, . . . III. viii. 18. 5
march not past the *mountenaunce* of a shott, . . . III. xi. 20. 8
She had not rid the *mountenance* of a flight, . . . V. vi. 36. 4
Mounting. flame, *Mounting* like waves with triple point . . *Bel.*[1] ix. 2
mounting up againe from whence he came, . . . *Ro.* xx. 5
her lowd salutes the *mounting* larke. . . . I. xi. 51. 9
mounting up, they fynd purveyaunce meet . . . I. xii. 13. 5
to her Courser *mounting* light: . . . III. iv. 12. 5
mounting light, his foe for lying long upbrayes: . . . IV. i. 42. 9
mounting in their stead Came to that Squire, . . . IV. viii. 41. 2
mounting to her steede bad Talus guide her on. . . . V. vi. 17. 9
tooke her steede; and thereon *mounting* light . . . V. vi. 36. 2
mounting straight upon a charret hye, . . . V. viii. 28. 4
Mounts. throwing forth sweet odours *mounts* fro thence . . *Col.* 610
Like Eyas hauke up *mounts* unto the skies, . . . I. xi. 34. 6
High reared *mounts,* the lands about to vew; . . . IV. x. 24. 5
Mourn. With mourning pyne I; you with pyning *mourne.* . . *S.C.* Ja. 48
Nor thys, nor that, so muche doeth make me *mourne,* . . . *S.C.* Ap. 9
Morne nowe, my Muse, now *morne* with teares . . . *S.C.* N. 111
The mantled medowes *mourne,* . . . *S.C.* N. 128
Morne now, my Muse, now *morne* . . . *S.C.* N. 151
where soules doo alwaies *mourne;* . . . *Gn.* 620
almost sterv'd did much lament and *mourne.* . . . *Hub.* 580
Therefore I *mourne* with deep harts sorrowing, . . . *T.M.* 107
I *mourne,* and pitifully mone, . . . *T.M.* 167
Therefore I *mourne* and sorrow with the rest, . . . *T.M.* 227
Therefore I *mourne* and waile incessantly, . . . *T.M.* 293
Therefore we *mourne* and pittilesse complaine, . . . *T.M.* 353
Therefore I *mourne,* and endlesse sorrow make, . . . *T.M.* 473
For whom I *mourne,* and for my selfe complaine, . . . *T.M.* 533
mourne my fall with dolefull dreriment. . . . *Ti.* 158
the whilest you *mourne* for his decease, . . . *Ti.* 237
Ah! why does my Alcyon weepe and *mourne,* . . . *D.* 264
To *mourne* in sorrow and sad sufferaunce, . . . *D.* 507
mourne for me that languish out my dayes. . . . *D.* 538
made the Muses in his song to *mourne.* . . . *As.* Interl. 222
The fields with faded flowers did seem to *mourne,* . . . *Col.* 25
there is sad Alcyon bent to *mourne,* . . . *Col.* 384
Helpe Amaryllis this her losse to *mourne:* . . . *Col.* 437
to *mourne* Emongst those wretches . . . *Col.* 674
Then gins her grieved ghost thus to lament and *mourne:* . . I. vii. 21. 9
he shortly did, and Una left to *mourne.* . . . I. xii. 41. 9
Can chaunge my cheare, or make me ever *mourne:* . . . II. vi. 10. 8
to lament and *mourne* The royall seed, . . . III. iii. 42. 7
her deare nourslings losse no lesse did *mourne,* . . . III. xii. 45. 7
all the way did inly *mourne,* like one astray. . . . IV. xi. 18. 9
left me here both his and mine owne love to *morne.'* . . . V. i. 18. 9
she many moneths did *mourne,* . . . V. iii. 1. 8
all the wooddy Nymphes did wayle and *mourne;* . . . V. viii. 43. 7
For which I thus doe *mourne,* and poure forth ceaselesse teares.' . . . VI. iv. 33. 9
mocketh all my paine, and laughs the more I *mourn.'* . . . VI. viii. 24. 9
seeing him to *mourne,* Drew neare, . . . VI. x. 18. 8
Mourne to my selfe the absence of my love; . . . *Am.* lxxxviii. 6
when ye list your owne mishaps to *mourne,* . . . *Epith.* 7
Mourned. ynough thou *morned* hast; . . . *S.C.* N. 207
As one that inly *mournd,* so was she sad, . . . I. i. 4. 6
eke him selfe *mournd* at their mournful plight, . . . III. iv. 32. 3
pyn'd, and *mourn'd,* and languisht, . . . IV. xii. 19. 9
mourn'd to see her losse before her eyne, . . . IV. xii. 21. 7
Mournful. The *morneful* Muse in myrth now list ne maske, . *S.C.* N. 19
there is *mournfull* Tityus, mindefull yet . . . *Gn.* 377
those same *mournfull* kingdomes, . . . *Gn.* 442
Of you, his *mournfull* Sisters, was lamented, . . . *T.M.* 11
Such *mournfull* tunes were never since invented. . . . *T.M.* 12
Began her *mournfull* plaint, as doth ensew. . . . *T.M.* 540
mournfull tunes enough my griefe to show? . . . *Mui.* 412
With griefe of *mournfull* great mishap opprest, . . . *D.* 2
To you alone I sing this *mournfull* verse, . . . *As.* Pr. 7
began his *mournfull* tourne: . . . *As.* Interl. 221
As fittest flowres to deck his *mournfull* hearse. . . . *As.* Interl. 228
seemd she to appease Her *mournefull* plaintes, beguiled of her art, . . . I. i. 54. 7

Mournful—*Continued.*
pities all this while His *mournefull* plight, ... I. v. 18. 8
Their *mournefull* charett, fild with rusty blood, ... I. v. 32. 2
made ensample of their *mournfull* sight Unto his Maister, . . I. v. 52. 2
In middest of their *mournfull* Tragedy; . . . . I. ix. 10. 4
O *mournfull* memory! . . . . I. xi. 47. 8
she had layd her *mournefull* stole aside, ... I. xii. 22. 2
There *mournfull* Cypresse grew in greatest store, ... II. vii. 52. 1
mourneful meed of joyes delicious! . . . . II. xii. 85. 7
eke him selfe mournd at their *mournful* plight, ... III. iv. 32. 3
to declare the *mournfull* Tragedyes . . . . III. xi. 45. 6
Her *mournefull* notes full piteously did frame, ... IV. viii. 4. 2
with her *mournefull* muse . . . . IV. viii. 5. 3
gan to her her *mournfull* plaint to make, ... IV. viii. 9. 6
His mightie hart their *mournefull* case gan rew, ... VI. ii. 41. 8
Faire Pastorella, whose sad *mournefull* hew . . . . VI. xi. 3. 8
Seek with my playnts to match that *mournful* dove. . . . *Am.* lxxxviii. 8
Mournfulest. Melpomene! the *mournefulst* Muse of nyne, . . *S.C.* N. 53
O thou the *mournfulst* Muse of nyne! . . . . *Mui.* 10
The *mournfulst* verse that ever man heard tell: . . . . . *As.* Pr. 8
Mourning. Doo not restraine your images still *mourning*) . *Ro.* xv. 8
With *mourning* pyne I; you with pyning mourne. . . . . . *S.C.* Ja. 48
Such cause of *mourning* never hadst afore; . . . . *S.C.* N. 54
Because that *mourning* matter I have none. . . . . *T.M.* 168
with my *mourning* plaints your plaint increase. . . . . . . *Ti.* 238
O sad joy, made of *mourning* and anoy! . . . . *Ti.* 322
when all his *mourning* melodie He ended had, ... *Ti.* 596
Clad all in black, that *mourning* did bewray, ... *D.* 40
was not like *mourning* seen. . . . . *As.* 210
mourning stole of carefull wydowhead, ... *Col.* 494
mourning altars, purgd with enimies life, ... I. iii. 36. 7
turned hath great mirth to *mourning* sad, ... III. viii. 46. 3
That much did ease his *mourning* and misfare: . . . . . . IV. viii. 5. 5
Right sorrowfully *mourning* her bereaved cares. . . . . . . IV. xii. 17. 9
made such piteous *mourning* therewithall, ... VI. i. 34. 8
a faire Mayden clad in *mourning* weed, ... VI. vi. 16. 7
Mourning the rigour of her malady, ... VI. xi. 8. 4
grief . . . spent it selfe in *mourning*, ... VI. xi. 34. 2
Through daily *mourning* and nightly misfare: . . . . VI. xii. 14. 5
Sits *mourning* for the absence of her mate: . . . . *Am.* lxxxviii. 2
Mourns. grudging in his great disdaine, *Mournes* inwardly, . . II. i. 42. 7
Mouth. *See* **Hell-mouth.**
So lost the Dogge the flesh in his *mouth*. . . . . *S.C.* S. 61
Scarce this right hand the *mouth* with diet feedeth, ... *Hub.* 274
tell hir, that my *mouth* can eate no meate: . . . . *U.V.* 8
Offring to fall into each *mouth* that gapes, ... *Col.* 602
Into her *mouth* thy crept, ... I. i. 15. 9
their wonted entrance . . . At her wide *mouth;* . . . . . . I. i. 25. 6
With bloudy *mouth* his mother earth did kis, ... I. ii. 19. 6
With gaping *mouth* at her ran greedily, ... I. iii. 5. 5
spightfull poison spues From leprous *mouth* on all that ever writt. . . . . I. iv. 32. 8
From flaming *mouth* bright sparckles fiery redd, ... I. vii. 31. 7
like the griesly *mouth* of hell, ... I. xi. 12. 8
Ran through his *mouth* with so importune might, ... I. xi. 53. 7
flood from *mouth,* Did fly abacke, ... II. vii. 58. 6
that grisely *mouth* did see Sucking the seas . . . . II. xii. 6. 1
round about the Pots *mouth* bound the thread; . . . . III. ii. 50. 3
loathly *mouth,* unmeete a *mouth* to bee, ... IV. i. 27. 3
his wide *mouth* did gape With huge great teeth, ... IV. vii. 5. 5
stop the *mouth* thereof, that none Might issue forth, ... IV. vii. 20. 5
Into his *mouth* his maystring bridle threw, ... IV. xii. 13. 6
Within his *mouth* a blacke spot doth appeare, ... V. iii. 32. 8
take The horse in hand within his *mouth* to looke: . . . . . V. iii. 33. 2
Ne he his *mouth* would open unto wight, ... V. iii. 34. 1
From dreadfull *mouth* of death, ... V. iv. 12. 3
justly damned by the doome Of his owne *mouth,* . . . . . . V. v. 17. 4
fayning to receive In her owne *mouth* the food . . . . . . V. v. 53. 2
Her face was ugly, and her *mouth* distort, ... V. xii. 36. 1
Then from her *mouth* the gobbet she does take, ... V. xii. 39. 1
in his wide great *mouth* away her bare . . . . VI. iii. 24. 4
Hong still upon his melting *mouth* attent; . . . . VI. ix. 26. 2
greedy *mouth* wide gaping like hell-gate, ... VI. x. 34. 6
Looking each houre into deathes *mouth* to fall, ... VI. xi. 44. 7
To save her chylde, which in misfortunes *mouth* was plaste. . VI. xii. 16. 9
ran at him amaine With open *mouth,* . . . . VI. xii. 26. 5
Appearing like the *mouth* of Orcus griesly grim: . . . . . . VI. xii. 26. 9
Therewith he mured up his *mouth* along, ... VI. xii. 34. 4
From whose wide *mouth* there flowed forth the Romane Flood. . . . . VII. vii. 42. 9
my glad *mouth* with her sweet prayses fill. . . . . *Am.* lxxxiv. 12
Fell . . . Into the *mouth* of death, ... *H.H.L.* 123
Mouthed. *See* **Bloody-mouthed, Fiery-mouthed, Fire-mouthed, Seven-mouthed.**
Some *mouth'd* like greedy Oystriges; . . . . II. xi. 12. 4
Mouths. Cerberus, whose many *mouthes* doo bay . . . . . . *Gn.* 345
menaging the *mouthes* of stubborne steedes, ... *Hub.* 739
fild their *mouthes* with meeds of malefices: . . . . *Hub.* 1154
beguile Their greedie *mouthes* of the expected spoyle; . . . . *Hub.* 1286
beasts with deep *mouthes* gaping direfull . . . . *Col.* 202
flaming *mouthes* of steedes, unwonted wilde, . . . to rayne: . I. iv. 9. 3
she chaunst their stubborne *mouths* to twitch; . . . . I. v. 28. 7
Their minds to pleasure, and their *mouths* to dainty fare. . . II. ii. 33. 9
hundred *mouthes,* and voice of brasse I had, ... IV. xi. 9. 7
Move. winde nor tide could *move* her thence away. . . . . . *Van.* ix. 12
My fancye eke from former follies *move* . . . . *S.C.* Jun. 37
th' Okes . . . Did *move,* as if they could him understand; . . *Gn.* 454
The Queene of hell to *move* as easily, ... *Gn.* 462
The man straightway his choler up did *move,* . . . . *Hub.* 364
Did learne to *move* their nimble-shifting feete, ... *T.M.* 34

Move—*Continued.*
A burning Teade about his head did *move,* . . . . *Mui.* 293
move to take him to her grace againe. . . . . *Col.* 175
life to *move* it selfe upon the water. . . . . *Col.* 219
with that suddein horror could no member *move*. . . . . . . I. ii. 31. 9
If from their loyall loves he might them *move:* . . . . . . I. iv. 26. 5
From wandring Stygian shores, where it doth endlesse *move.'* I. iv. 48. 9
Ne word to speak, ne joynt to *move,* she had; . . . . I. vi. 11. 2
The souldier may not *move* from watchfull sted, ... I. ix. 41. 4
To *move* the world from off his stedfast henge, ... I. xi. 21. 8
spy Her loved knight to *move* his manly pace: . . . . I. xi. 33. 7
Another said, he saw him *move* his eyes indeed. . . . . . . I. xii. 10. 9
Which when he felt to *move,* he hoped faire . . . . II. i. 43. 6
She could them nimbly *move,* . . . . II. iii. 28. 9
That might him *move* to wrath, and indignation reare. . . . II. iv. 5. 9
I should see that would me nearer *move,* . . . . II. iv. 24. 8
in thy selfe thy lesser partes do *move;* . . . . II. v. 16. 2
That to her might *move* cause of meriment: . . . . II. vi. 3. 6
may compassion of their evilles *move?* . . . . II. viii. 1. 3
Did not once *move,* nor upward cast his eye, ... II. viii. 50. 6
doth base affections *move* In brutish mindes, ... III. iii. 1. 5
Ne foot could further *move*. . . . . III. vii. 3. 8
To *move* and tremble as it were aghast, ... III. ix. 15. 6
with her feeble feete did *move* a comely pace. . . . . . . III. xii. 19. 9
With which vaine termes so much they did them *move,* . . . IV. ii. 19. 8
oftentimes unquiet strife did *move* Amongst her lovers, . . . IV. ii. 37. 3
Those Pensifenesse did *move;* and Sighes the bellows weare. . IV. v. 38. 9
That trusty Squire he wisely well did *move* . . . . IV. ix. 15. 3
lusted after all that him did *move:* . . . . IV. ix. 21. 8
To speake to them, and some emparlance *move;* . . . . . . IV. ix. 31. 2
Her constant mind could *move* . . . . IV. xi. 2. 8
unable once to stirre or *move*. . . . . IV. xii. 20. 9
Which of the Nymphes his heart so sore did *mieve;* . . . . . IV. xii. 26. 7
this world with them amisse doe *move*. . . . . V. Pr. 6. 7
try if thou by faire entreatie can *Move* Radigund? . . . . . V. v. 40. 4
did to great impatience *move* her: . . . . V. v. 51. 7
Her wand did *move* with amiable looke, ... V. vii. 8. 2
That once he could not *move,* nor quich at all; . . . . . . V. ix. 33. 7
That Calidore it dearly deepe did *move:* . . . . VI. iii. 15. 4
Declar'd the message which that Knight did *move;* . . . . . VI. iii. 42. 2
As he unable were for very neede To *move* one foote, ... VI. vi. 19. 7
Ne any will had thence to *move* away, ... VI. ix. 12. 2
round about her *move* in order excellent. . . . . VI. x. 13. 9
Times do change and *move* continually: . . . . VII. vii. 47. 6
who is it . . . That Time himselfe doth *move,* . . . . VII. vii. 48. 5
Yet do the Starres and Signes therein still *move,* . . . . . VII. vii. 55. 6
move the Dolphin from her stubborn will, ... *Am.* xxxviii. 8
What then can *move* her? if nor merth nor mone, ... *Am.* liv. 13
his planet cleare Began in me to *move,* . . . . *Am.* lx. 6
slowly seemd to *move* Theyr sad protract . . . . *Am.* lxxxvi. 3
sweet aspect both God and man can *move,* . . . . *Am.* lxxxviii. 11
long since ready forth his maske to *move,* . . . . *Epith.* 26
How slowly does sad Time his feathers *move?* . . . . *Epith.* 281
He gan to *move* out of his idle seat; . . . . *H.L.* 66
Ne once *move* ruth in that rebellious Dame, ... *H.L.* 151
Move such affection in the inward mynd, ... *H.B.* 76
That in light wits did loose affection *move;* . . . . *H.H.L.* 11
Powre, which now doth *move* In all these things, ... *H.H.L.* 27
Moved. My spright was greatly *moved* in her rest, ... *Van.* xii. 2
Ne ever spake, ne cause of speaking *mooved;* . . . . *Gn.* 469
ye will (I hope) well *mooved* bee.' . . . . *Hub.* 378
Us to advise, which forth but lately *moved,* . . . . *Hub.* 410
Much was I *mooved* at her piteous plaint, ... *Ti.* 29
in himselfe be *moov'd* to pittie mee.' . . . . *Ti.* 469
'Much was I *moved* at so goodly sight,' . . . . *D.* 113
Let him be *moov'd* to pity such a case. . . . . *As.* Pr. 18
the whole assembly of those heards *Moov'd* at his speech, . . *Col.* 649
mov'd with wrath, and shame, and Ladies sake, ... I. v. 12. 5
Her feeling speaches some compassion *mov'd* . . . . I. v. 24. 6
as he forward *moovd* his footing old, ... I. viii. 31. 3
He would not once have *moved* for the knight. . . . . I. x. 49. 6
faint through losse of blood, *moov'd* not at all, ... I. xi. 50. 3
The king was greatly *moved* at her speach; . . . . I. xii. 35. 1
The noble Guyon, *mov'd* with great remorse, ... II. iv. 6. 1
The knight was greatly *moved* at his playnt, ... II. v. 24. 1
Though somewhat *moved* in his mightie hart, ... II. vi. 40. 3
made him twise to reele, that never *moov'd* afore. . . . . . II. viii. 44. 9
The Prince was inly *moved* at her speach, ... II. ix. 39. 1
nought *moved* with her piteous looke; . . . . II. x. 18. 9
him to displeasaunce *moov'd,* . . . . II. x. 28. 7
Her fearfull feete towards the bowre she *mov'd,* . . . . . . III. i. 60. 2
She softely felt if any member *moov'd,* . . . . III. i. 60. 7
He nought was *moved* at their entraunce bold, ... III. iii. 15. 1
much *moved* at so pitteous sight; . . . . III. vii. 9. 9
she no more was *moved* with that might . . . . III. vii. 41. 2
Purpose was *moved* by that gentle Dame . . . . III. ix. 32. 2
mov'd amisse with massy mucks unmeet regard. . . . . III. x. 31. 9
in the ydle ayre he *mov'd* still here and theare. . . . . . . III. xii. 8. 9
many of them *mov'd* to eye her sore. . . . . IV. i. 9. 6
Ne ever was with fond affection *moved,* . . . . IV. ii. 36. 3
Moved with pity of her plenteous teares. . . . . IV. vii. 23. 4
mov'd Belphebe her no lesse to hate, ... IV. vii. 34. 6
being *mov'd* with ruth she thus bespake: . . . . IV. viii. 14. 6
most was *moved* at the piteous vew, ... IV. viii. 20. 3
I never joyed howre, but still with care was *moved*. . . . . IV. x. 1. 9
ruth it *moved* in the rocky stone, ... IV. xii. 5. 7
Much was he *moved* at that ruefull sight; . . . . V. i. 14. 6
Who *mov'd* no more therewith, ... V. i. 21. 6
he was nothing *mov'd* nor tempted therewithall: . . . . V. ii. 23. 9
He much was *mov'd* at so unworthie shame, ... V. iii. 10. 7

Moved—*Continued.*
Thereof great hurly-burly *moved* was . . . V. iii. 30. 1
Much was she *moved* with the mightie sway . . . V. v. 9. 5
art *mov'd* to wish me better, . . . V. v. 37. 8
Were *moved* much thereat; . . . V. viii. 24. 5
Much was he *moved* with her piteous plight, . . . V. x. 22. 1
With great admiraunce inwardly was *moved,* . . . V. x. 39. 4
Which when I saw, . . . Much was I *moved* . . . VI. ii. 11. 2
this young man . . . being *moov'd* with pittie . . . VI. ii. 23. 2
And *moved* speach to him of things of course, . . . VI. iii. 14. 6
as *moved* with the sight, He made great mone . . . VI. iv. 12. 3
Wherewith the Prince sore *moved* there avoud . . . VI. v. 34. 1
when they *mov'd* the carcases aside, . . . VI. xi. 22. 1
Askt her, what the matter was that *mov'd* her so? . . . VI. xii. 17. 4
we see not how they are *mov'd* and swayd . . . VII. vii. 49. 2
Mov'd by your might and ordered by your ayde, . . . VII. vii. 49. 7
even itselfe is *mov'd,* as wizards saine: . . . VII. vii. 55. 7
Ne wilbe *moov'd* with reason, or with rewth, . . . *Am.* xi. 5
live, and *moved* are To multiply the likenesse . . . *H.L.* 99
That High Eternall Powre, . . . *mov'd* in it selfe by love. . . *H.H.L.* 28
Movement. The Starres pure light, the Spheres swift *movement,* *T.M.* 508
Mover's. Untill they come to their first *Movers* bound, . . . *H.H.B.* 72
Moves. selfe-regard . . . *Moves* me of each, so as I found, to tell . . . *Col.* 683
Nought . . . That *moves* more deare compassion of mind. . . I. iii. 1. 2
His artes he *moves,* and . . . Himselfe he frees . . . II. i. 1. 7
daily warre against his foeman *moves,* . . . II. ii. 19. 3
moves them all, and makes them changed be? . . . VII. vii. 48. 8
Mowed. *Mow'd* downe themselves with slaughter mercilesse; *Ro.* x. 12
th' Ocean *moveth* still from place to place, . . . VII. vii. 20. 3
all that *moveth* doth mutation love; . . . VII. vii. 55. 8
all that *moveth* doth in Change delight: . . . VII. viii. 2. 6
Moving. *See* **Ever-moving, Quick-moving, Still-moving.**
Might see the *moving* of some quicke . . . *S.C.* Mar. 74
feard each shadow *moving* too or froe; . . . III. xii. 12. 3
Still *mooving,* yet unmoved from her sted; . . . VII. vii. 13. 3
Mow. To hedge, to ditch, to thrash, to thetch, to *mowe?* . . . *Hub.* 264
Does *mow* the flowring herbes and goodly things, . . . III. vi. 39. 4
Mowed. *Mow'd* downe themselves with slaughter mercilesse; *Ro.* x. 12
Mown. brakes and brambles to be *mowne.* . . . *S.C.* D. 102
Mows. As in season due the husband *mowes* . . . *Ro.* xxx. 5
with bitter mockes and *mowes* . . . VI. vii. 49. 6
Much (*partial list*). *See* **So much as.**
Much was I mazde, to see this monsters kinde . . . *Bel.*[2] viii. 9
As *much* it grieveth me to thinke thereon. . . . *Pet.* i. 3
Which makes me *much* and ever to complaine; . . . *Pet.* iii. 13
Why do vaine men mean things so *much* deface, . . . *Van.* xi. 12
Some in *much* joy, many in many teares, . . . *S.C.* F. 18
My Sinamon smell to *much* annoieth: . . . *S.C.* F. 136
The Honye is *much,* but the Gaule is more. . . . *S.C.*Mar.Emb.4
so *muche* doeth make me mourne, . . . *S.C.* Ap. 9
And blamest hem *much* for small encheason. . . . *S.C.* May 147
him to *much* rebuke and Daunger drove, . . . *S.C.* Jun. 69
And rekes *much* of thy swinck, . . . *S.C.* Jul. 34
thou hast measured *much* grownd, . . . *S.C.* S. 21
I dempt there *much* to have eeked my store, . . . *S.C.* S. 30
All for thy casten too *much* of worlds care, . . . *S.C.* S. 114
by *much* wrestling to leese the grosse. . . . *S.C.* S. 135
The dapper ditties, . . . Delighten *much;* . . . *S.C.* O. 15
let thus *much* then excuse . . . *Gn.* 4
Who so loathes not too *much* the poore estate, . . . *Gn.* 90
Not so *much* did Dan Orpheus represse . . . *Gn.* 180
Much he disdaines that anie one should dare . . . *Gn.* 273
(for feare and yre Had blent so *much* his sense, . . . *Gn.* 311
that thankes so *much* should faile of meed; . . . *Gn.* 353
Much do I feare among such fiends to sit; . . . *Gn.* 381
Much do I feare back to them to repayre, . . . *Gn.* 382
I likewise have wasted *much* good time, . . . *Hub.* 75
Much blood throgh many wounds . . . *Hub.* 207
Whenas the Ape him hard so *much* to talke . . . *Hub.* 267
Much good deep learning one thereout may reed; . . . *Hub.* 484
Fast *much,* pray oft, . . . *Hub.* 498
Not so *much* for to gaine, . . . *Hub.* 774
Much was I mooved at her piteous plaint, . . . *Ti.* 29
being dead, is happie now *much* more; . . . *Ti.* 247
Whose meaning *much* I labored foorth to wreste, . . . *Ti.* 486
'*Much* was I moved at so goodly sight; . . . *D.* 113
Which did her beautie *much* more beautifie. . . . *D.* 217
Full happie man (misweening *much*) was hee, . . . *As.* 101
Ill mynd so *much* to mynd anothers ill, . . . *As.* 111
meaning her *much* better to preferre, . . . *Col.* 121
'Fearful *much* more . . . *Col.* 201
Thereat I wondred *much,* . . . *Col.* 264
Which sight *much* gladed me; for *much* afore I feard, . . . *Col.* 266
Much more there is unkend . . . *Col.* 294
much more that does from mens knowledge lurke. . . . *Col.* 295
heaven and heavenly graces do *much* more . . . abound . . . *Col.* 308
Nor Po nor Tyburs swans so *much* renowned, . . . *Col.* 412
Much like an Angell in all forme and fashion.' . . . *Col.* 615
thou hast forgot Thy selfe . . . too *much,* . . . *Col.* 617
Much was the whole assembly of those heards Moov'd . . . *Col.* 648
so *much* grace let her vouchsafe to grant . . . *Col.* 939
Thou *much* more fit . . . praises to compile, . . . *Ded. Son.* xii. 5
Briton Prince . . . suffered so *much* ill, . . . I. Pr. 2. 7
As *much* disdayning to the curbe to yield: . . . I. i. 1. 7
Much can they praise the trees . . . I. i. 8. 5
That detestable sight him *much* amazde, . . . I. i. 26. 1
much like the sowne Of swarming Bees, . . . I. i. 41. 4
with so *much* speede As her slowe beast could make; . . . I. ii. 8. 1
Much seemed he to mone her haplesse chaunce, . . . I. iii. 25. 6

Much—*Continued.*
That *much* was worne, but therein little redd; . . . I. iv. 19. 2
not rashly to despise, Nor too *much* to provoke; . . . I. vi. 25. 6
much rejoyced in their bloody fray: . . . I. vi. 48. 4
this same Monster *much* more ugly was, . . . I. vii. 17. 6
To have done *much* more admirable deedes. . . . I. vii. 36. 3
I sorrowed all so *much* as earst I joyd, . . . I. ix. 15. 3
So *much* the dart . . . the soule dismayes. . . . I. x. 21. 9
much aswag'd the passion of his plight, . . . I. x. 24. 8
Much more then that why they in bands . . . I. x. 40. 7
with his largenesse measured *much* land, . . . I. xi. 8. 3
Much was the man encombred . . . I. xi. 41. 1
Came running in, *much* like a man dismayd, . . . I. xii. 24. 8
Which I so *much* doe vaunt, . . . II. Pr. 1. 8
should witlesse man so *much* misweene, . . . II. Pr. 3. 4
He wonder would *much* more; . . . II. Pr. 3. 9
Her swollen eyes were *much* disfigured, . . . II. i. 13. 8
'Now by my head,' . . . '*much* I muse, . . . II. i. 19. 1
Which whoso wants, wants so *much* of his rest: . . . II. i. 59. 7
as knight of so *much* worth became, . . . II. ii. 14. 2
th' other thought too *mutch.* . . . II. ii. 34. 9
The man was *much* abashed at his boast; . . . II. iii. 17. 1
delight does raigne, *much* more then this? . . . II. iii. 39. 5
unto knighthood workes *much* shame and woe; . . . II. iv. 10. 7
If wonted force and fortune doe me not *much* fayl.' . . . II. v. 5. 9
much ashamd that stroke of living arme Should him dismay, II. v. 7. 2
Guyon *much* disdeigned so loathly sight. . . . II. v. 23. 6
albe the knight her *much* did pray. . . . II. vi. 4. 9
all, though pleasaunt, yet she made *much* more: . . . II. vi. 24. 5
Sir Guyon, grudging not so *much* his might . . . II. vi. 30. 5
much he wondred at that uncouth sight: . . . II. vi. 43. 2
so *much* be nombred francke and free.' . . . II. vii. 9. 5
so *much* gold Thou canst preserve . . . II. vii. 20. 3
Mammon was *much* displeasd, . . . II. vii. 39. 7
else *much* more wretched were the cace . . . II. viii. 1. 4
Mote stead you *much* your purpose to subdew.' . . . II. ix. 9. 4
They wasted had *much* way, and measurd many miles. . . II. ix. 9. 9
that which ye so *much* embrace? . . . II. ix. 43. 7
wanton pleasures him too *much* did please, . . . II. x. 17. 7
she *much* more than her owne life him lov'd; . . . II. x. 28. 2
How *much* to her we owe, . . . II. x. 69. 8
too long . . . Here to record, ne *much* materiall: . . . II. x. 74. 6
much dismayed with that dreadful sight, . . . II. xi. 16. 2
with *much* toyle Labour'd in vaine . . . II. xii. 19. 6
all the three thereat woxe *much* afrayd, . . . II. xii. 22. 6
He *much* rebukt those wandring eyes of his, . . . II. xii. 69. 2
lost *much* blood through many a wownd, . . . III. i. 21. 5
Exceeding *much* the state of meane degree, . . . III. i. 33. 7
Doth not so *much* rejoyce as she rejoyced theare. . . . III. ii. 11. 9
His feeling wordes her feeble sence *much* pleased, . . . III. ii. 15. 1
much more straungely gan to love his sight, . . . III. ii. 18. 2
much increast Through his Heroicke grace . . . III. ii. 24. 8
how *much* I feare least love it bee! . . . III. ii. 33. 1
Of *much* more uncouth thing I was affrayd, . . . III. ii. 40. 3
much cheard the feeble spright Of the sicke virgin, . . . III. ii. 47. 1
it ought your corage *much* inflame . . . III. iii. 54. 1
so her smart was *much* more grievous bredd, . . . III. iv. 6. 3
Whereat she wondred *much,* . . . III. iv. 18. 7
of a woman he should have *much* ill; . . . III. iv. 25. 8
mote they well Thus *much* afford me, . . . III. iv. 39. 3
They wondred *much;* and shortly understood . . . III. v. 38. 3
much I am affeard Least he . . . him selfe disguize, . . . III. vi. 23. 3
so *much* as doth need must needs be counted here. . . . III. vi. 30. 9
much moved at so pitteous sight; . . . III. vii. 9. 9
with too *much* brightnes daz'd, . . . III. vii. 13. 8
Much feared he least ought did ill betide . . . III. vii. 31. 4
Thought with that sight him *much* to have reliv'd . . . III. viii. 3. 2
furie fresh reviv'd *Much* more then earst, . . . III. viii. 3. 5
Much merveiled thereat, as well he might, . . . III. viii. 12. 3
So *much* high God doth innocence embrace. . . . III. viii. 29. 5
life and sence did *much* dismay . . . III. viii. 31. 9
Which they so *much* mistooke, . . . III. ix. 23. 7
That *much* they faynd to know who she mote bee; . . . III. ix. 24. 7
far *much* greater then thy fame, . . . III. ix. 33. 3
emongst the Lybick sandes, . . . *Much* there he suffered, . . III. ix. 41. 7
much he did advaunce In all his speach, . . . III. ix. 48. 1
In his disquiet mind was *much* dismayd: . . . III. x. 14. 3
ever his faint hart *much* earned at the sight: . . . III. x. 21. 9
That cheerful word his weak heart *much* did cheare, . . . III. x. 26. 6
So shall your glory bee advaunced *much,* . . . III. x. 28. 5
much disdeigning to be so misdempt, . . . III. x. 29. 4
That *much* Malbecco joyed in his jollity. . . . III. x. 33. 9
he was *much* afraid him selfe alone to fynd. . . . III. x. 41. 9
nothing so *much* pitty doth implore . . . III. xi. 18. 5
Be bold; That *much* she muz'd, . . . III. xi. 54. 4
nought ydred, Though *much* emmov'd, . . . III. xii. 2. 9
he *much* rejoyced in his cruell minde. . . . III. xii. 22. 9
She *much* was cheard to heare him mentiond, . . . III. xii. 41. 1
sight of such a chaunge her *much* dismayd . . . III. xii. 42. 5
Was *much* empassiond in her gentle sprite, . . . III. xii. 46. *or.*7
Thereto her feare was made so *much* the greater . . . IV. i. 7. 1
much she feard his mind would grow to some excesse. . . . IV. i. 7. 9
much the more by that he lately wrought, . . . IV. i. 8. 3
For which no service she too *much* esteemed: . . . IV. i. 8. 5
Made her not yeeld so *much* as due she deemed. . . . IV. i. 8. 7
Yet otherwise *much* worse, if worse might bee, . . . IV. i. 18. 8
her feet were odde, And *much* unlike; . . . IV. i. 28. 7
So *much* her malice did her might surpas, . . . IV. i. 30. 1
So *much* they did, that at the last . . . IV. i. 43. 8
They did *much* more their cruelty encrease; . . . IV. ii. 19. 5

Much—*Continued.*

so *much* they did them move, . . . IV. ii. 19. 8
So *much* the more as she refusd to love, . . . IV. ii. 37. 1
So *much* the more she loved was . . . IV. ii. 37. 2
Did all that youthly rout so *much* appall, . . . IV. ii. 40. 3
when she saw, it did her *much* amate . . . IV. ii. 50. 7
much augmented all their other praise; . . . IV. ii. 54. 3
O! why doe wretched men so *much* desire . . . IV. iii. 1. 1
That made them dreaded *much* of all men . . . IV. iii. 2. 9
Much was he grieved with that gracelesse chaunce; . . . IV. iii. 8. 5
Were *much* amaz'd the headlesse tronke to see . . . IV. iii. 21. 2
Much was Cambello daunted with his blowes: . . . IV. iii. 26. 1
Much more of price and of more gratious powre, . . . IV. iii. 45. 1
Admir'd of all the people and *much* glorifide. . . . IV. iii. 51. 9
So *much* more sorely to the ground he fell, . . . IV. iv. 19. 6
Much was he daunted with that direfull stound, . . . IV. iv. 24. 8
much he gan his glorie to envy, . . . IV. iv. 28. 4
Much wondred all men what or whence he came, . . . IV. iv. 42. 1
Which Cambell seeing *much* the same envyde, . . . IV. iv. 44. 7
either doth on other *much* relie. . . . IV. v. 1. 5
much repynd, that . . . she did him forestall. . . . IV. v. 9. 2
He *much* more goodly glosse thereon doth shed . . . IV. v. 15. 5
So *much* the more her griefe, the more her toyle; . . . IV. v. 30. 1
much admired The manner of their worke . . . IV. v. 38. 1
That needed *much* her weake age to desire, . . . IV. v. 39. 8
at which so suddain case He wondred *much*. . . . IV. vi. 3. 6
(so *much* his force prevayled) . . . IV. vi. 12. 8
with meeke service and *much* suit . . . IV. vi. 40. 3
The feare whereof seem'd *much* her to affray; . . . IV. vi. 45. 4
each did other *much* bewaile and mone, . . . IV. vii. 20. 2
Which subtill sleight did him encumber *much*, . . . IV. vii. 27. 1
pitty *much* his plight, . . . IV. vii. 43. 9
The Prince did wonder *much*, . . . IV. vii. 45. 2
That *much* did ease his mourning and misfare: . . . IV. viii. 5. 5
Which sodaine accident him *much* dismaid, . . . IV. viii. 7. 8
pittied *much* his case, . . . IV. viii. 12. 8
wondred *much* at his so selcouth case; . . . IV. viii. 14. 2
her great daunger did him *much* dismay. . . . IV. viii. 20. 5
At which he wondred *much* when all those signes he fond. . . IV. viii. 21. 9
that *much* did vexe His noble hart: . . . IV. viii. 35. 4
those two Ladies *much* asham'd did wexe: . . . IV. viii. 35. 7
so *much* favour she to him hath hight . . . IV. viii. 54. 1
Gan blame me *much* for being so untrew . . . IV. viii. 56. 4
Their like resemblaunce *much* admired there, . . . IV. ix. 11. 2
gazing long at them *much* wondred he: . . . IV. ix. 11. 8
all *men* much admyrde her change, . . . IV. ix. 16. 9
they *much* more furiously gan fare, . . . IV. ix. 27. 1
Who wondring *much* at that so sodaine fit, . . . IV. ix. 29. 6
ye seemen *much* to blame . . . IV. ix. 37. 2
Hath me *much* sorrow and *much* travell cost: . . . IV. ix. 38. 4
is the paine thereof *much* greater then the fee. . . . IV. x. 3. 9
Much more then that which was in Paphos built, . . . IV. x. 5. 6
much disdaining unto him to lout, . . . IV. x. 19. 2
Much more deformed fearefull, ugly were, . . . IV. x. 20. 4
much admyring that so goodly frame, . . . IV. x. 31. 1
Of litle *much*, of foes she maketh friends, . . . IV. x. 34. 8
much more rare and pretious to esteeme, . . . IV. x. 39. 6
By which I hardly past with *much* adoe: . . . IV. x. 57. 7
much more aged was his wife then he, . . . IV. xi. 24. 6
Liagore *much* praisd for wise behests; . . . IV. xi. 51. 4
much more eath to tell the starres on hy, . . . IV. xii. 1. 5
though their numbers do *much* more surmount, . . . IV. xii. 2. 8
Admyr'd her beautie *much*, . . . IV. xii. 33. 4
They all are wandred *much;* . . . V. Pr. 5. 5
much lesse him match in fight, . . . V. i. 8. 7
Much was he moved at that ruefull sight; . . . V. i. 14. 6
Sangliere disdained *much* his doome, . . . V. i. 29. 1
Much did that Squire Sir Artegall adore . . . V. i. 30. 1
Whose great assembly they did *much* admire, . . . V. ii. 29. 6
Yet was admired *much* of fooles, women, and boys. . . . V. ii. 30. 9
looke then how *much* it doth overflow . . . V. ii. 34. 8
so *much* is more then just to trow. . . . V. ii. 34. 9
'Sith thou misdeem'st so *much* of things in sight? . . . V. ii. 39. 3
Therewith the Gyant *much* abashed sayd, . . . V. ii. 44. 1
counterpeise the same with so *much* wrong.' . . . V. ii. 46. 2
To fill the other scale with so *much* wrong; . . . V. ii. 46. 5
He *much* was troubled, ne wist what to doo: . . . V. ii. 52. 3
for so *much* as to my lot here lights, . . . V. iii. 3. 7
He *much* was mov'd at so unworthie shame, . . . V. iii. 10. 7
Much did his words the gentle Ladie quell, . . . V. iii. 16. 8
Much was the knight incenst with his lewd word . . . V. iii. 36. 1
see how *much* her purpose was deceaved! . . . V. iv. 10. 5
Much was the man confounded in his mind, . . . V. iv. 27. 1
Much was she moved with the mightie sway . . . V. v. 9. 5
Whose presence all their troups so *much* encombred, . . . V. v. 19. 5
So great her pride that she such basenesse *much* abhord. . . . V. v. 27. 9
So *much* the greater still her anguish grew, . . . V. v. 28. 1
Therewith *much* comforted she gan unfold The cause . . . V. v. 31. 7
Much did he marvell at her uncouth speach, . . . V. v. 37. 1
Yet thus *much* friendship she to him did show, . . . V. v. 57. 1
report of him *much* ill, . . . V. vi. 1. 2
Ne doffe her armes, though he her *much* besought: . . . V. vi. 23. 5
much lesse honour by that warlike kinde Of life; . . . V. vi. 32. 5
even she her selfe *much* wondered At such a chaunge, . . . V. vii. 13. 7
Or ill apayd or *much* dismayd ye be; . . . V. vii. 18. 8
She *much* was eased in her troublous thought, . . . V. vii. 24. 2
joyd *much* in his semblance glad. . . . V. vii. 41. 9
Consisted *much* in that adventures priefe: . . . V. vii. 44. 5
He *much* admired both his heart and hew, . . . V. viii. 12. 8
Since neither is endamadg'd *much* thereby.' . . . V. viii. 14. 3

Much—*Continued.*

By that proud dame which her so *much* disdained, . . . V. viii. 24. 4
Were moved *much* thereat; . . . V. viii. 24. 5
Much was he grieved with that haplesse throe, . . . V. viii. 35. 1
much the more, that . . . He mote not come . . . V. viii. 35. 3
much renound For noble courage . . . V. viii. 36. 7
it *much* appald her troubled spright: . . . V. viii. 45. 5
The gentle knights rejoyced *much* to heare The prayses . . . V. ix. 21. 1
much more then she had told; . . . V. ix. 21. 5
Straunge there to see, it did them *much* amaze, . . . V. ix. 24. 3
woxe inclined *much* unto her part, . . . V. ix. 46. 3
So *much* more, then, is that of powre and art . . . V. x. 2. 5
thine owne people do thy mercy prayse *much* more. . . . V. x. 3. 9
Much more it praysed was of those two knights, . . . V. x. 4. 1
Much was he moved with her piteous plight, . . . V. x. 22. 1
Good hart in evils doth the evils *much* amend. . . . V. x. 22. 9
Much like in foulnesse and deformity Unto that Monster, . . V. xi. 25. 1
much dismayd with that dismayfull sight, . . . V. xi. 26. 4
forth he fared . . . and *much* way did pas, . . . V. xi. 36. 8
tidings sad Did *much* abash Sir Artegall . . . V. xi. 40. 7
Too *much* am I too blame for that faire Maide, . . . V. xi. 41. 2
much did magnifie his noble name: . . . V. xi. 46. 6
Much was the Ladie . . . Abasht at his rebuke, . . . V. xi. 64. 1
much to gaine, a litle for to yield: . . . V. xii. 19. 4
their disgraces Did *much* the more augment, . . . V. xii. 28. 9
her mis-shape *much* helpt; . . . V. xii. 29. 3
So *much* the more at him still did she scold, . . . V. xii. 43. 6
him did *much* renowme, and far his fame display. . . . VI. i. 2. 9
ye have *much* adoe to deale withall.' . . . VI. i. 10. 8
Much was the Knight abashed at that word . . . VI. i. 26. 1
I doe *much* disdaine Thy courteous lore, . . . VI. i. 27. 7
The comming of that so *much* threatned Knight; . . . VI. i. 30. 3
gan t' augment her bitternesse *much* more; . . . VI. i. 32. 2
every action doth them *much* commend, . . . VI. ii. 2. 3
'Which when I saw, . . . *Much* was I moved . . . VI. ii. 11. 2
Much did Sir Calidore admyre his speach . . . VI. ii. 13. 1
He praysd it *much*, and *much* admyred it; . . . VI. ii. 24. 5
Him *much* more now then earst he gan admire . . . VI. ii. 34. 2
Whereat Sir Calidore did *much* delight, . . . VI. ii. 36. 6
Is now himselfe in *much* more wretched plight: . . . VI. ii. 45. 6
valour the which did adorne His meanesse *much*, . . . VI. iii. 7. 9
approaching nye, . . . Them *much* abasht, . . . VI. iii. 21. 3
With which rude speach his Lady *much* displeased . . . VI. iii. 32. 6
So *much* the more was Calepine offended, . . . VI. iii. 36. 6
so *much* her wounds did bleede; . . . VI. iii. 46. 4
Was *much* emmoved at his perils vew, . . . VI. iv. 3. 4
his fierce steed that mote him *much* dismay: . . . VI. iv. 6. 5
Much was he then encombred, . . . VI. iv. 25. 1
So *much* more wofull, as my wofull plight . . . VI. iv. 28. 4
Whence soone upstarting *much* he gan repine, . . . VI. v. 26. 5
Renowmed *much* in armes and derring doe; . . . VI. v. 37. 4
were now *much* more increast . . . VI. vi. 2. 3
The Lady, for that she was *much* in dred, . . . VI. vi. 16. 2
now doe I *much* repent, . . . VI. vi. 33. 4
the stout Prince, with *much* more steddy stowre, . . . VI. vii. 8. 5
He *much* was daunted with so dismall sight; . . . VI. vii. 10. 4
The Prince *much* mused at such villenie, . . . VI. vii. 13. 1
Much did the Craven seeme to mone his case, . . . VI. vii. 18. 1
much griev'd against that straunger knight, . . . VI. vii. 20. 6
therewith *much* abashed and affrayd, . . . VI. vii. 22. 1
He doubted *much* what mote their meaning bee; . . . VI. vii. 24. 2
all men did her person *much* admire, . . . VI. vii. 28. 6
much augment her doole. . . . VI. vii. 39. 9
Exceeding *much* the measure of mans stature, . . . VI. vii. 41. 3
Was *much* more grievous then the others blowes: . . . VI. vii. 49. 8
much lamented his calamity, . . . VI. viii. 3. 4
The Squire him selfe . . . Was *much* asham'd . . . VI. viii. 5. 3
His manly mynde was *much* emmoved therewithall; . . . VI. viii. 5. 9
for these Carles to carry *much* more comely were?' . . . VI. viii. 23. 9
wondred *much* at Cupids judg'ment wise, . . . VI. viii. 25. 2
'How *much*' (sayd he) 'more happie is the state . . . VI. ix. 19. 1
They, that have *much*, feare *much* to loose thereby, . . . VI. ix. 21. 3
wish th' heavens so *much* had graced mee, . . . VI. ix. 28. 6
may perhaps you better *much* withall, . . . VI. ix. 32. 7
forth he drew *much* gold, and toward him it drive. . . . VI. ix. 32. 9
love so *much* could. . . . VI. ix. 37. 9
He *much* was troubled at that straungers guize, . . . VI. ix. 38. 3
There he did see that pleased *much* his sight, . . . VI. x. 11. 6
with her goodly presence all the rest *much* graced. . . . VI. x. 12. 9
Much wondred Calidore at this straunge sight, . . . VI. x. 17. 1
graced her so *much* to be another Grace. . . . VI. x. 26. 9
Excelling *much* the meane of her degree; . . . VI. x. 27. 3
With which the Knight him selfe did *much* content, . . . VI. x. 30. 3
with other *much* disorder. . . . VI. x. 39. 9
mixed threats among, and *much* unto her vowed. . . . VI. xi. 4. 9
This their request the Captaine *much* appalled, . . . VI. xi. 10. 6
They fall to strokes, the frute of too *much* talke, . . . VI. xi. 16. 2
make even that dimmed light Seeme *much* more lovely . . . VI. xi. 21. 7
her did *much* molest; . . . VI. xi. 24. 4
In *much* delight, and many joyes among, . . . VI. xii. 11. 8
much he feared least reprochfull blame . . . VI. xii. 12. 6
Besides the losse of so *much* loos and fame, . . . VI. xii. 12. 8
Much was the Lady troubled at that speach, . . . VI. xii. 18. 1
seeing it *much* wondred at the sight: . . . VI. xii. 37. 6
Rejoyced *much* to see his captive plight, . . . VI. xii. 37. 8
much admyr'd the Beast, but more admyr'd the Knight. . . . VI. xii. 37. 9
Were *much* afraid, and wondred at that sight; . . . VII. vi. 14. 5
Was troubled *much* at their so strange affright, . . . VII. vi. 15. 7
He wondred *much*, and feared her no lesse: . . . VII. vi. 17. 5
Much lesse the Title of old Titans Right: . . . VII. vi. 33. 4

Much—*Continued.*
much she hated sight of living eye. . . . VII. vi. 42. 6
Faunus saw that pleased *much* his eye, . . . VII. vi. 46. 1
On her whose sight before so *much* he sought. . . . VII. vi. 47. 6
He, *much* affeard, to her confessed short . . . VII. vi. 51. 7
So *much* delight to bathe her limbes she tooke: . . . VII. vi. 54. 4
They would have caused *much* confusion and disorder. . . . VII. vii. 4. 9
His Saviour's birth his mind so *much* did glad. . . . VII. vii. 41. 4
whom so *much* ye make Joves dearest darling, . . . VII. vii. 50. 2
many now *much* worship and admire! . . . *Am.* xxvii. 8
I burne *much* more in boyling sweat, . . . *Am.* xxx. 7
the trew fayre . . . is *much* more praysd of me: . . . *Am.* lxxix. 4
That are so *much* by so meane love embased. . . . *Am.* lxxxii. 4
had the equall hevens so *much* you graced . . . *Am.* lxxxii. 5
The Fly, that I so *much* did scorne, Hath hurt me . . . *Epig.* iv. 29
Much more then would ye wonder at that sight, . . . *Epith.* 188
Her ayry Towers upraised *much* more high. . . . *Com. Son.* iv. 4
At sight thereof so *much* enravisht bee? . . . *H.L.* 119
Thou in me kindlest *much* more great desyre, . . . *H.B.* 5
much lesse my trembling verse . . . can hope it to reherse. *H.H.L.* 41
to approve How *much,* himselfe that loved us, we love. . . . *H.H.L.* 217
Thou canst not count, *much* lesse their natures aime; . . . *H.H.B.* 33
fire *much* more then ayre . . . appeares more pure and fayre. *H.H.B.* 48
How *much* lesse those, *much* higher in degree, . . . *H.H.B.* 61
And so *much* fairer, and *much* more then these, . . . *H.H.B.* 62
Yet fairer then they both, and *much* more bright, . . . *H.H.B.* 96
How *much* more those essentiall parts of his, . . . *H.H.B.* 109
Whose nature yet so *much* is marvelled Of mortall wits, . . . *H.H.B.* 166
it doth *much* amaze The greatest wisards . . . *H.H.B.* 167
Of all on earth whom God so *much* doth grace, . . . *H.H.B.* 240
pompe to which proud minds aspyre . . . and so *much* desyre, *H.H.B.* 278
Muchall, -ell. *See* **Mickle.**
Mucius. prudent *Mutius,* Who in his flesh endur'd the scorching flame, . . . *Gn.* 606
Muck. Regard of worldly *mucke* doth fowly blend . . . II. vii. 10. 5
Muck's. mov'd amisse with massy *mucks* unmeet regard. . . . III. x. 31. 9
Mucky. *mucky* filth his braunching armes annoyes, . . . II. vii. 15. 8
all his minde is set on *mucky* pelfe, . . . III. ix. 4. 1
Thereafter all that *mucky* pelfe he tooke, . . . V. ii. 27. 6
to whom ye ill display That *mucky* masse, . . . VI. ix. 33. 5
Mud. Huge heapes of *mudd* he leaves, . . . I. i. 21. 6
Engrost with *mud* which did them fowle agrise, . . . II. vi. 46. 7
Informed in the *mud* on which the Sunne hath shynd. . . . III. vi. 8. 9
there her drowned in the durty *mud;* . . . V. ii. 27. 4
Unmard with ragged mosse or filthy *mud;* . . . VI. x. 7. 3
Muddy. Beside the fruitfull shore of *muddie* Nile, . . . *Van.* iii. 1
muddy shore of broad seven-mouthed Nile, . . . I. v. 18. 2
muddie water, that like puddle stanke, . . . IV. v. 33. 4
Mugger. *See* **Hugger-mugger.**
Mulciber. cruell *Mulciber* would not obay His threatfull pride, III. xi. 26. 5
Mulciber's. owre, not purifide Of *Mulcibers* devouring element; II. vii. 5. 4
Mule. The *Mule* all deckt in goodly rich aray, . . . *Hub.* 582
'Ah! sir *Mule,* now blessed be the day, . . . *Hub.* 589
'Foolish Foxe (said the *Mule*) . . . *Hub.* 595
Mulla. to the shiny *Mulla* he did beare, . . . *Col.* 93
Mulla, the daughter of old Mole, . . . *Col.* 108
traine, Which he with *Mulla* wrought . . . *Col.* 119
Or unto Allo, or to *Mulla* cleare: . . . *Col.* 302
Mulla mine, whose waves I whilom taught to weep. . . . IV. xi. 41. 9
sister unto *Mulla* faire and bright, . . . VII. vi. 40. 3
Ye Nymphes of *Mulla,* which . . . trouts doe tend . . . *Epith.* 56
Mulla's. greene alders by the *Mullaes* shore; . . . *Col.* 59
Till they into the *Mullaes* water slide. . . . *Col.* 144
Multiplied. Through his three double hands thrise *multiplyde,* V. xi. 6. 2
Multiply. anguish . . . dooth *multiplye* My dying paines, . . . *D.* 73
By living long to *multiplie* their paine; . . . *D.* 361
crownes and kingdomes to thee *multiply.* . . . II. vii. 11. 5
So many children he did *multiply:* . . . II. x. 22. 4
bad them to increase and *multiply:* . . . III. vi. 34. 6
even to her foes her mercies *multiply.* . . . V. viii. 17. 9
as they words amongst them *multiply,* . . . VI. xi. 16. 1
To *multiply* the likenesse of their kynd, . . . *H.L.* 100
Multitude. raigne in liking of the *multitude;* . . . *T.M.* 326
A *multitude* of babes about her hong, . . . I. x. 31. 1
him with *multitude* oppresse; . . . III. iii. 33. 4
He with their *multitude* was nought dismayd, . . . IV. iv. 32. 1
Which lawlesse *multitude* him comming too . . . V. ii. 52. 1
they doe me with *multitude* oppresse, . . . V. xi. 51. 6
Mum. unto every thing did aunswere *mum:* . . . IV. vii. 44. 5
Mumbled. As one then in a dreame, . . . He *mumbled* soft, . . . I. i. 42. 9
Mumming. With *mumming* and with masking all around, . . . *Hub.* 802
Munera. Artegall . . . drownes Lady *Munera,* . . . V. ii. Arg.
Her name is *Munera,* agreeing with her deedes. . . . V. ii. 9. 9
Munificence. Did head against them make and strong *munificence.* . . . II. x. 15. 9
Muniments. By chance he certaine *miniments* forth drew, . . . IV. viii. 6. 2
Murder. many mischiefes follow cruell Wrath: . . . Unmanly *murder,* . . . I. iv. 35. 3
with their sad instruments Of spoyle and *murder* . . . III. v. 16. 2
hatred, *murther,* treason, and despight, . . . IV. x. 20. 6
brought he forth with griesly grim aspect Abhorred *Murder,* V. ix. 48. 2
She did conceale, and *murder* her owne mynd; . . . V. xii. 33. 5
Wayting if he unwares him *murther* might; . . . VI. vi. 26. 8
spoyld their houses, and them selves did *murder,* . . . VI. x. 39. 8
Murdered. *murdred* troupes upon great heapes to lay. . . . *Gn.* 400
many corses . . . Of *murdred* men, . . . I. v. 53. 3
with most cruell hand him *murdred* pittilesse. . . . II. x. 35. 9
murdred by the freends of Gratian. . . . II. x. 61. 5
by thee slaine, and *murdred* by thy slight.' . . . V. vi. 37. 9
She threw her husbands *murdred* infant out; . . . V. viii. 47. 2

Murdered—*Continued.*
Murdred my men, and slaine my Seneschall, . . . VI. i. 25. 3
all her people *murdred* with outragious might: . . . VI. i. 29. 9
they were all betrayd And *murdred* cruelly . . . VI. vii. 34. 9
Murderer. did acquite a *murdrer* felonous; . . . II. vii. 62. 7
Murdering. *See* **Heart-murdering. Self-murdering.**
Murderous. A cruell Satyre with his *murdrous* dart, . . . *D.* 156
After his *murdrous* spoyles and bloudie rage allayd. . . . I. Pr. 3. 9
Dragon . . . With *murdrous* ravine, and devouring might, . . . I. vii. 44. 4
When I at her my *murdrous* blade did bend, . . . II. iv. 31. 7
murdrous spoiles and bloody pray, . . . II. viii. 6. 4
A *murdrous* knife out of his pocket drew, . . . III. xii. 32. 5
With *murdrous* weapons arm'd to cruell fight, . . . IV. ii. 16. 2
heav'd his *murdrous* axe at him . . . IV. iii. 17. 9
his *murdrous* mace he up did reare, . . . IV. viii. 44. 4
new launcht with *murdrous* knife, . . . VI. v. 5. 4
murdrous knife well whet, . . . VI. viii. 45. 5
Mured. Therewith he *mured* up his mouth along, . . . VI. xii. 34. 4
Murk. Such myster saying me seemeth to *mirke.* . . . *S.C.* S. 103
Murksome. Through *mirkesome* aire her ready way she makes; I. v. 28. 3
Murmur. With gentle *murmure* of the breathing ayre, . . . *Gn.* 186
a gentle *murmure* sent; . . . *Gn.* 228
To romble gently downe with *murmur* soft, . . . *T.M.* 26
The neighbor woods arownd with hollow *murmur* ring. . . . I. viii. 11. 9
the base *murmure* of the waters fall; . . . II. xii. 71. 6
seemd to plaine With gentle *murmure* . . . III. v. 39. 9
shaketh with the least *Murmure* of winde, . . . III. vii. 1. 5
the river rolling still With *murmure* soft, . . . IV. x. 15. 9
I with *murmure* soft, . . . IV. x. 48. 1
Yet did he *murmure* with rebellious sound, . . . V. ix. 33. 8
a soft *murmure* and confused sound . . . VI. iv. 11. 7
Murmured. the Lee, that to them *murmurde* low, . . . *Proth.* 115
Murmuring. The speaking woods, and *murmuring* waters fall, . *Col.* 636
raine . . . Mixt with a *murmuring* winde, . . . I. i. 41. 4
an hollow, dreary, *murmuring* voyce . . . I. viii. 38. 1
whose *murmuring* wave did play Emongst the pumy stones, . II. v. 30. 2
Their *murmuring* small trompetts sownden wide, . . . II. ix. 16. 3
A gentle Bee, with his loud trumpet *murm'ring,* . . . *Epig.* iv. 3
Murmurings. He . . . oft doth mar their *murmurings.* . . . I. i. 23. 9
Murmurous. With *murmurous* disdayne did inly rave, . . . II. xi. 32. 3
Murrains. with plagues and *murrins* pestilent Consume, . . . III. iii. 40. 8
Muscaroll. Clarion, the eldest sonne and haire Of *Muscaroll;* *Mui.* 23
Muscles. it both bone and *muscles* ryved quight. . . . *As.* 120
Muse. gins Bartas hie to rayse His heavenly *Muse,* . . . *Ro.* Env. 12
unlucky *Muse,* that wontst to ease My musing mynd, . . . *S.C.* Ja. 69
Both pype and *Muse* shall sore the while abye.' . . . *S.C.* Ja. 71
I *muse,* what account both these will make; . . . *S.C.* May 51
my poore *Muse* hath spent her spared store, . . . *S.C.* O. 9
There may thy *Muse* display her fluttryng wing, . . . *S.C.* O. 43
How I could reare the *Muse* on stately stage, . . . *S.C.* O. 112
Thy *Muse* to long slombreth in sorrowing, . . . *S.C.* N. 3
The mornefull *Muse* in myrth now list ne maske, . . . *S.C.* N. 19
Melpomene! the mournefulst *Muse* of nyne, . . . *S.C.* N. 53
Morne nowe, my *Muse,* . . . *S.C.* N. 111
my *Muse,* now morne with heavy cheare, . . . *S.C.* N. 151
my *Muse,* now cease thy sorrowes sourse; . . . *S.C.* N. 171
Tuning our song unto a tender *Muse,* . . . *Gn.* 2
this *Muse* shall speak to thee In bigger notes, . . . *Gn.* 10
my soft *Muse,* as for her power more meete, . . . *Gn.* 51
the man, of whom the *Muse* is scorned, . . . *Ti.* 454
Nor alive nor dead be of the *Muse* adorned! . . . *Ti.* 455
O thou the mournfulst *Muse* of nyne! . . . *Mui.* 10
Helpe, O thou Tragick *Muse!* . . . *Mui.* 413
the *Muse* so wrought me from my byrth, . . . *S.C.* D. 38
My *Muse* is hoarse and wearie of thys stounde: . . . *S.C.* D. 140
Of rustick *muse* full hardly to be betterd. . . . *D.* 231
sith thy *Muse* first since thy turning backe Was heard . . . *Col.* 19
my sleepie *Muse,* awake; . . . *Col.* 48
That may thy *Muse* and mates to mirth allure. . . . *Col.* 391
match that *Muse* when it with bayes is crowned, . . . *Col.* 414
doth his trembling *Muse* but lowly flie, . . . *Col.* 420
Full sweetly tempred is that *Muse* of his, . . . *Col.* 430
Muse, full of high thoughts invention, . . . *Col.* 446
my *Muse,* whose fethers . . . yet but flagg, . . . *Ded. Son.* ii. 7
Rude rymes, the which a rustick *Muse* did weave . . . *Ded. Son.* vii. 11
When so thee list thy lofty *Muse* to raise: . . . *Ded. Son.* viii. 12
Whose learned *Muse* hath writ her owne record . . . *Ded. Son.* xii. 3
This lowly *Muse,* . . . Flies for like aide . . . *Ded. Son.* xiii. 7
gave more honourable prize To the sweet *Muse* . . . *Ded. Son.* xiv. 2
Who first my *Muse* did lift out of the flore, . . . *Ded. Son.* xv. 6
I, the man whose *Muse* whylome did maske, . . . I. Pr. 1. 1
Me, . . . the sacred *Muse* areeds To blazon broade . . . I. Pr. 1. 7
To *muse* on meanes of hoped victory. . . . I. iv. 44. 5
My chaster *Muse* for shame doth blush to write; . . . I. viii. 48. 2
O thou sacred *Muse!* most learned Dame, . . . I. xi. 5. 6
still he sate . . . As in great *muse,* . . . I. xii. 29. 4
I *muse,* How that same knight should doe . . . II. i. 19. 1
lend A little leave unto a rusticke *Muse* . . . III. Pr. 5. 2
whatso my feeble *Muse* can frame . . . III. viii. 43. 2
Yet at her choice they all did greatly *muse.* . . . IV. v. 21. 3
with her mournefull *muse* Him to recomfort . . . IV. viii. 5. 3
many a gentle *Muse* and many a learned wit. . . . IV. xi. 34. 9
my *Muse* her selfe now tyred has, . . . IV. xi. 53. 8
What heavenly *Muse* shall thy great honour rayse . . . V. x. 3. 3
Ne none can find but who was taught them by the *Muse.* . . . VI. Pr. 2. 9
whither doost thou now, thou greater *Muse,* Me . . . bring, . . . VII. vii. 1. 1
sport my *muse,* and sing my loves sweet praise; . . . *Am.* lxxx. 10
O fayrest Phoebus! father of the *Muse!* . . . *Epith.* 121
Ah! gentle *Muse!* thou art too weake and faint . . . *H.H.B.* 230
some brave *muse* may sing . . . *Proth.* 159

Mused. as I *muzed* on the miserie In which men live, . . . *D.* 36
Still when he *mused* on his late mischiefe, . . . III. x. 18. 3
That much she *muz'd,* yet could not construe it . . . III. xi. 54. 4
So long he *muzed,* and so long he lay, . . . IV. v. 43. 1
The Prince much *mused* at such villenie, . . . VI. vii. 13. 1
Muse's. Accorde not with thy *Muses* meriment, . . . *S.C.* N. 34
No *Muses* aide me needes heretoo to call; . . . *Hub.* 43
And Patrone of my *Muses* pupillage; . . . *Ded. Son.* vii. 2
Muses. manie *Muses,* and the Nymphes withall, . . . *Pet.* iv. 5
after her the other *Muses* trace, . . . *S.C.* Ap. 102
I sawe Calliope wyth *Muses* moe, . . . *S.C.* Jun. 57
Of *Muses,* Hobbinol, I conne no skill, . . . *S.C.* Jun. 66
Ne wont with crabbed care the *Muses* dwell: . . . *S.C.* O. 101
The *Muses,* that were wont greene bayes to weare, . . . *S.C.* N. 146
The wiser *Muses* after Colin ranne. . . . *S.C.* D. 48
His minde unto the *Muses* he withdrawes: . . . *Hub.* 760
Sweete Ladie *Muses,* Ladies of delight, . . . *Hub.* 761
Maugre the sacred *Muses,* . . . *Hub.* 816
Whom all the *Muses* did bewaile long space, . . . *T.M.* 17
Whilest Ignorance the *Muses* doth oppresse. . . . *T.M.* 288
The sweete companions of the *Muses* late, . . . *T.M.* 404
of the *Muses* ye may friended bee, . . . *Ti.* 366
Recorded by the *Muses,* . . . *Ti.* 403
Both Nymphes and *Muses* nigh she made astownd, . . . *D.* 314
made the *Muses* in his song to mourne. . . . *As.* Interl. 222
With the sweet Lady *Muses* for to play: . . . *Ded. Son.* i. 6
The sacred *Muses* have made alwaies clame . . . *Ded. Son.* iv. 1
Nor one Helicone, Left for sweete *Muses* . . . *Ded. Son.* v. 7
sweet Parnasse, the haunt of *Muses* fayre; . . . II. xii. 52. 8
ye, sweet *Muses!* which have often proved . . . *H.L.* 29
Muses'. they that con of *Muses* skill . . . *S.C.* Jul. 45
han be watered at the *Muses* well; . . . *S.C.* N. 30
mount Parnasse, the *Muses* brood, . . . *Gn.* 21
Faire Marian, the *Muses* onely darling: . . . *Col.* 505
Music. of my rurall *musicke* holdeth scorne. . . . *S.C.* Ja. 64
Doe make them *musick* . . . *S.C.* Jun. 29
Wherefore with myne thou dare thy *musick* matche? . . . *S.C.* Au. 2
My old *musick* mard by a newe mischaunce. . . . *S.C.* Au. 12
All *musick* sleepes, . . . *S.C.* N. 105
To follow Orpheus *musicke* through the land: . . . *Gn.* 452
Making your *musick* of hart-breaking mone. . . . *T.M.* 6
thether came to heare their *musick* sweet, . . . *T.M.* 32
with our *musick* wont so oft to ring, . . . *T.M.* 278
their *musicke* matcheth Phoebus quill. . . . *T.M.* 330
when he heard the *musicke* which I made, . . . *Col.* 70
most heavenly melody . . . sweet *musicke* did divide, . . . I. v. 17. 7
birds . . . Doe chaunt sweet *musick* to delight his mynd. . . . I. vii. 3. 5
Best *musicke* breeds delight in loathing eare; . . . I. viii. 44. 4
made delightfull *musick* all the way, . . . I. xii. 7. 5
sweete *Musicke* did apply Her curious skill . . . I. xii. 38. 6
heavenly *musicke* seemd to make. . . . II. iii. 24. 9
strive to passe . . . Their native *musicke* . . . II. vi. 25. 4
most famous hight For skil in *Musicke* . . . II. x. 59. 8
To read what manner *musicke* that mote bee; . . . II. xii. 70. 6
whence that *Musick* seemed heard to bee, . . . II. xii. 72. 1
sweet *Musicke* did divide Her looser notes . . . III. i. 40. 1
So dischord ofte in *Musick* makes the sweeter lay:— . . . III. ii. 15. 9
Such *Musicke* is wise words, . . . IV. ii. 2. 5
a most celestiall sound Of dainty *musicke,* . . . IV. xi. 23. 2
the sweet *musick,* which his harp did make, . . . *Am.* xxxviii. 3
my rude *musick,* which was wont to please . . . *Am.* xxxviii. 5
Their merry *Musick* that resounds from far, . . . *Epith.* 130
how sweete *musicke* that unto them lends! . . . *H.B.* 252
Musical. lamenting Love marreth the *Musicall.* . . . *U.V.* 12
To fetchen home May with their *musicall:* . . . *S.C.* May 28
quickned the dull spright with *musicall* comfort. . . . II. v. 31. 9
Music's. His *musicks* might the hellish hound did tame. . . . *S.C.* O. 30
ybent to song and *musicks* mirth, . . . *S.C.* D. 40
with sweete delight Of *Musicks* skill . . . *Hub.* 756
delight Of his celestiall song, and *Musicks* wondrous might. . . . VII. vii. 12. 9
Musing. unlucky Muse, that wontst to ease My *musing* mynd, . . . *S.C.* Ja. 70
deepelie *muzing* at her doubtfull speach, . . . *Ti.* 485
Long after lay he *musing* at her mood, . . . I. i. 55. 1
musing at the straunge occasion, . . . he thus bespake: . . . I. ii. 32. 3
Musing full sadly in his sullein mind: . . . I. ix. 35. 3
lay *musing* long on that him ill apayd. . . . IV. v. 42. 9
So thereuppon long while she *musing* lay, . . . V. vii. 17. 1
Must (*partial list of auxiliary*).
the budde eke needes *must* quaile; . . . *S.C.* N. 91
must passe over to th' Elisian plaine: . . . *Gn.* 421
sad Eurydice . . . no more *Must* turne to life, . . . *Gn.* 434
There *must* thou fashion eke a godly zeale, . . . *Hub.* 493
it *must* needs to issue come? . . . *Mui.* 227
life *must* life, and blood *must* blood, repay. . . . I. ix. 43. 6
Thou . . . *must* wage Thy workes for wealth, . . . II. vii. 18. 4
Where in eternall bondage dye he *must,* . . . III. vii. 50. 7
the bare ground . . . *Must* be their bed; . . . VI. iv. 14. 5
'For Titan (as ye all acknowledge *must*) . . . VII. vi. 27. 1
For yet his noule was totty of the *must,* . . . VII. vii. 39. 2
Muster. over all the fields themselves did *muster,* . . . V. xi. 58. 4
That he might see his men, and *muster* them by oth. . . . VI. vii. 33. 9
Mustering. *mustring* all his men in Venus vew, . . . *Col.* 769
Mutability. fall through fortunes *mutabilitie.* . . . *Gn.* 560
the common winde Of Courts inconstant *mutabilitie,* . . . *Hub.* 723
Yet is eterne in *mutabilitie,* . . . III. vi. 47. 5
How *Mutability* in them doth play Her cruell sports . . . VII. vi. 1. 4
O pittious worke of *Mutability,* . . . VII. vi. 6. 7
Before her came dame *Mutability;* . . . VII. vii. 13. 6
unto *Mutabilitie* not thrall, . . . VII. vii. 17. 8
'So in them all raignes *Mutabilitie;* . . . VII. vii. 26. 1

Mutability—*Continued.*
subject still to *Mutability?* . . . VII. vii. 47. 9
To whom thus *Mutability:* . . . VII. vii. 49. 1
that speech whyleare Of *Mutabilitie,* . . . VII. viii. 1. 2
That is contrayr to *Mutabilitie;* . . . VII. viii. 2. 5
Mutation. all that moveth doth *mutation* love; . . . VII. vii. 55. 8
Mute. stood still *mute,* as if he had beene dum, . . . IV. vii. 44. 2
stood still *mute,* as one in great suspence; . . . V. vi. 9. 7
desirous rather to rest *mute,* . . . V. vi. 20. 3
With peremptorie powre, that made all *mute;* . . . V. ix. 44. 2
Mutining. *mutining* to stirre up civill faction . . . V. ii. 51. 4
Mutinous. Her nourslings did with *mutinous* uprore . . . *Ro.* xxii. 5
In troublous wits, and *mutinous* uprore: . . . V. ix. 48. 6
Mutius. *See* **Mucius.**
Mutter. Gan *mutter* close a certaine secret charme, . . . VI. viii. 45. 6
Muttered. *Muttred* of matters as their bookes them shewd, . . . *Hub.* 836
Mutual. Allide with bands of *mutuall* couplement; . . . IV. iii. 52. 3
Which might concluded be by *mutuall* consent. . . . V. viii. 21. 9
simple truth, and *mutuall* good-will, . . . *Am.* lxv. 11
Through *mutuall* receipt of beames bright, . . . *H.B.* 235
Mutually. Entrayled *mutually* in lovely lore, . . . IV. iii. 42. 3
either others cause to maintaine *mutually.* . . . V. viii. 14. 9
Muzzle. he tooke a *muzzel* strong Of surest yron, . . . VI. xii. 34. 2
My (*partial list*).
whiles that *my* daylie cares did sleepe, . . . *Van.* i. 1
My spirit shaking off her earthly prison, . . . *Van.* i. 2
On which when as *my* thought was throghly placed, . . . *Van.* i. 9
yet those sights empassion *me* full nere . . . *Van.* i. 12
My spright was greatly moved in her rest, . . . *Van.* xii. 2
And felt *my* heart nigh riven in *my* brest . . . *Ti.* 30
My thought returned greeved home againe, . . . *Ti.* 478
Whose wordes recording in *my* troubled braine, . . . *Ti.* 481
I felt such anguish wound *my* feeble heart, . . . *Ti.* 482
So inlie greeving in *my* groning brest, . . . *Ti.* 484
Much was I troubled in *my* heavie spright, . . . *Ti.* 575
That all *my* senses were bereaved quight, . . . *Ti.* 577
There came unto *my* minde a troublous thought, . . . *D.* 29
Which dayly dooth *my* weaker wit possesse, . . . *D.* 30
That yet *my* soule it deepely doth empassion. . . . *D.* 35
place *my* dolefull plaint your plaints emong. . . . *As.* Pr. 6
well I wot *my* rymes bene rudely dight. . . . *As.* Pr. 12
But when *my* Muse, . . . Doe yet but flagg, . . . *Ded. Son.* ii. 7
Most Noble Lord, the pillor of *my* life, . . . *Ded. Son.* vii. 1
And Patrone of *my* Muses pupillage; . . . *Ded. Son.* vii. 2
My rimes I know unsavory and sowre, . . . *Ded. Son.* viii. 8
To sharpe *my* sence with sundry beauties vew, . . . *Ded. Son.* xvii. 7
Fierce warres . . . shall moralize *my* song. . . . I. Pr. 1. 9
O, helpe thou *my* weake wit, and sharpen *my* dull tong! . . . I. Pr. 2. 9
Shed thy faire beames into *my* feeble eyne, . . . I. Pr. 4. 5
raise *my* thoughtes, too humble . . . I. Pr. 4. 6
O! gently come into *my* feeble brest; . . . I. xi. 6. 1
And to *my* tunes thy second tenor rayse, . . . I. xi. 7. 8
To which I meane *my* wearie course to bend; . . . I. xii. 1. 2
Yet now *my* luckelesse lott doth me constrayne . . . III. Pr. 3. 4
But ah! *my* rymes too rude and rugged arre, . . . III. ii. 3. 6
all *my* (*mine) entrailes flow with poisnous gore, . . . III. ii. 39. 4
My heart doth melt with meere compassion, . . . III. viii. 1. 2
My looser rimes (I wote) doth sharply wite . . . IV. Pr. 1. 3
But here *my* wearie teeme, . . . Shall breath . . . IV. v. 46. 8
through which *my* weary steps I guyde . . . VI. Pr. 1. 1
and chears *my* dulled spright. . . . VI. Pr. 1. 9
Guyed ye *my* footing, . . . VI. Pr. 2. 7
Now turne againe *my* teme, thou jolly swayne, . . . VI. ix. 1. 1
the which *my* coulter hath not cleft; . . . VI. ix. 1. 4
Faire Pastorell, of whom is now *my* song: . . . VI. xi. 2. 2
But now I come into *my* course againe, . . . VI. xii. 2. 6
Hope to escape . . . More then *my* former writs, . . . VI. xii. 41. 3
do you, *my* rimes, keep better measure, . . . VI. xii. 41. 8
in *my* feeble brest Kindle fresh sparks . . . VII. vii. 2. 3
Which hold *my* life in their dead-doing might, . . . *Am.* i. 2
My soules long-lacked foode, *my* heavens blis; . . . *Am.* i. 12
Which if she graunt, . . . *my* love cherish: . . . *Am.* ii. 13
And, when *my* pen would write her titles true, . . . *Am.* iii. 11
Rudely thou wrongest *my* deare harts desire, . . . *Am.* v. 1
Fayre eyes! the myrrour of *my* mazed hart, . . . *Am.* vii. 1
Then is *my* soule with life and love inspired: . . . *Am.* vii. 6
your bright beams, of *my* weak eies admyred, . . . *Am.* vii. 11
she doth laugh at me, and makes *my* pain her sport. . . . *Am.* x. 14
To graunt small respit to *my* restlesse toile; . . . *Am.* xi. 6
Retourne agayne, *my* forces late dismayd, . . . *Am.* xiv. 1
my love doth in her selfe containe . . . *Am.* xv. 5
The whiles *my* stonisht hart stood in amaze, . . . *Am.* xvi. 3
Ayming his arrow at *my* very hart: . . . *Am.* xvi. 10
Or looke with pitty on *my* payneful smart; . . . *Am.* xviii. 8
The whiles her foot she in *my* necke doth place, . . . *Am.* xx. 3
And tread *my* life downe in the lowly floure. . . . *Am.* xx. 4
On which *my* thoughts doo . . . attend, . . . *Am.* xxii. 7
And on the same *my* hart will sacrifise, . . . *Am.* xxii. 11
That for *my* faults ye will me gently beat. . . . *Am.* xxiv. 14
doth deprave *My* simple meaning . . . *Am.* xxix. 2
triumph, which *my* skill exceeds, . . . *Am.* xxix. 11
My love is lyke to yse, and I to fyre; . . . *Am.* xxx. 1
Is not dissolv'd through *my* so hot desyre, . . . *Am.* xxx. 3
Or how comes it that *my* exceeding heat . . . *Am.* xxx. 5
And feele *my* flames augmented manifold! . . . *Am.* xxx. 8
the more she fervent sees *my* fit, The more . . . *Am.* xxxii. 9
Of a proud love, that doth *my* spirite spoyle. . . . *Am.* xxxiii. 12
My Helice, the lodestar of *my* lyfe, . . . *Am.* xxxiv. 10
With lovely light to cleare *my* cloudy grief, . . . *Am.* xxxiv. 12
But al *my* dayes in pining languor spend, . . . *Am.* xxxvi. 3

My—*Continued.*
But *my* rude musick, which was wont to please . . . *Am.* xxxviii. 5
All carelesse how *my* life for her decayes: . . . *Am.* xxxviii. 10
My soule was ravisht quite as in a traunce; . . . *Am.* xxxix. 10
Lykest it seemeth, in *my* simple wit, . . . *Am.* xl. 5
So *my* storme-beaten hart likewise is cheared . . . *Am.* xl. 13
So pleasing is in *my* extreamest paine, . . . *Am.* xlii. 2
That, all the more *my* sorrow it augmenteth, . . . *Am.* xlii. 3
To be acquit fro *my* continual smart; . . . *Am.* xlii. 6
And doe me not before *my* time to dy. . . . *Am.* xlii. 14
if I silent be, *my* hart will breake, . . . *Am.* xliii. 3
What tyranny is this, both *my* hart to thrall, . . . *Am.* xliii. 5
And eke *my* toung with proud restraint to tie; . . . *Am.* xliii. 6
Yet I *my* hart with silence . . . Will teach . . . *Am.* xliii. 9
my just cause to plead; . . . *Am.* xliii. 10
When *my* abodes prefixed time is spent, . . . *Am.* xlvi. 1
My cruell fayre streight bids me wend *my* way: . . . *Am.* xlvi. 2
But as she will, whose will *my* life doth sway, . . . *Am.* xlvi. 7
My lower heaven, so it perforce must bee. . . . *Am.* xlvi. 8
Of *my* harts wound, and of *my* bodies griefe; . . . *Am.* l. 2
Fit medicines for *my* bodies best reliefe. . . . *Am.* l. 4
The inward languor of *my* wounded hart, . . . *Am.* l. 10
Then, *my* lyfes Leach! doe your skill reveale; . . . *Am.* l. 13
But, having her, *my* joy wil be the greater. . . . *Am.* li. 14
From presence of *my* dearest deare exylde, . . . *Am.* lii. 7
that may *my* solace breed; . . . *Am.* lii. 10
So I her absens will *my* penaunce make, . . . *Am.* lii. 13
Right so *my* cruell fayre with me doth play; . . . *Am.* liii. 5
Disguysing diversly *my* troubled wits. . . . *Am.* liv. 4
I waile, and make *my* woes a Tragedy. . . . *Am.* liv. 8
Delights not in *my* merth, nor rues *my* smart: . . . *Am.* liv. 10
So weake *my* powres, so sore *my* wounds, appeare, . . . *Am.* lvii. 5
Seeing *my* hart through-launced every where . . . *Am.* lvii. 7
That al *my* wounds wil heale in little space. . . . *Am.* lvii. 14
Then al those fourty which *my* life out-went. . . . *Am.* lx. 8
That seemd the longer for *my* greater paines. . . . *Am.* lx. 12
let *my* loves fayre Planet short her wayes, . . . *Am.* lx. 13
short her wayes, . . . or else short *my* dayes. . . . *Am.* lx. 14
My soverayne saynt, the Idoll of *my* thought, . . . *Am.* lxi. 2
light . . . in *my* darknesse, greater doth appeare, . . . *Am.* lxvi. 12
Oft, when *my* spirit doth spred . . . *Am.* lxxii. 1
There *my* fraile fancy . . . Doth bath in blisse, . . . *Am.* lxxii. 9
My hart, . . . Breaking his prison, . . . *Am.* lxxiii. 2
Even so *my hart,* . . . flyes backe unto your sight. . . . *Am.* lxxiii. 7
The first *my* being to me gave by kind, . . . *Am.* lxxiv. 5
The second is *my* sovereigne Queene . . . *Am.* lxxiv. 7
The third, *my* love, *my* lifes last ornament, . . . *Am.* lxxiv. 9
By whom *my* spirit out of dust was raysed: . . . *Am.* lxxiv. 10
came the tyde, and made *my* paynes his pray. . . . *Am.* lxxv. 4
And eek *my* name bee wyped out lykewize. . . . *Am.* lxxv. 8
My verse your vertues rare shall eternize, . . . *Am.* lxxv. 11
My thoughts the guests, . . . *Am.* lxxvii. 14
And let *my* thoughts behold her selfe in mee. . . . *Am.* lxxviii. 14
To sport *my* muse, and sing *my* loves sweet praise; . . . *Am.* lxxx. 10
My spirit to an higher pitch will rayse, . . . *Am.* lxxx. 12
Fayre is *my* love, . . . *Am.* lxxxi. 1
Joy of *my* life! . . . *Am.* lxxxii. 1
Deepe, in the closet of *my* parts entyre, . . . *Am.* lxxxiv. 9
my glad mouth with her sweet prayses fill. . . . *Am.* lxxxiv. 12
In *my* true love did stirre up coles of yre; . . . *Am.* lxxxv. 8
was wont to lead *my* thoughts astray; . . . *Am.* lxxxvii. 2
thereon feed *my* love-affamisht hart. . . . *Am.* lxxxvii. 12
Mourne to my selfe the absence of *my* love; . . . *Am.* lxxxviii. 6
Seek with *my* playnts to match that . . . *Am.* lxxxviii. 8
Dark is *my* day, whyles her fayre light I mis, . . . *Am.* lxxxviii. 13

My—*Continued.*
dead *my* life that wants such lively blis. . . . *Am.* lxxxviii. 14
Go to the bowre of *my* beloved love, . . . *Epith.* 23
My truest turtle dove; . . . *Epith.* 24
That when you come whereas *my* love doth lie, . . . *Epith.* 65
Wake now, *my* love, awake! . . . *Epith.* 74
Ah! *my* deere love, why doe ye sleepe . . . *Epith.* 85
My love is now awake out of her dreames, . . . *Epith.* 92
Now is *my* love all ready forth to come: . . . *Epith.* 110
Open the temple gates unto *my* love, . . . *Epith.* 204
Behold how goodly *my* faire love does ly, . . . *Epith.* 305
And leave *my* love alone, . . . *Epith.* 312
Who is the same, which at *my* window peepes? . . . *Epith.* 372
With which *my* love should duly have been dect, . . . *Epith.* 428
Perforce subdue *my* poore captived hart, . . . *H.L.* 2
unto the wished scope Of *my* desire, . . . *H.L.* 297
My guide, *my* God, *my* victor, and *my* king: . . . *H.L.* 305
dost thou now inspire Into *my* feeble breast, . . . *H.B.* 3
And up aloft above *my* strength doest rayse . . . *H.B.* 6
The wondrous matter of *my* fyre to prayse. . . . *H.B.* 7
T' illuminate *my* dim and dulled eyne, . . . *H.B.* 20
And you, faire Venus dearling, *my* deare dread! . . . *H.B.* 281
great Goddesse of *my* life, . . . *H.B.* 282
To reade *my* fault, and, wondring at *my* flame, . . . *H.H.L.* 16
at *my* wide sparkling fire, . . . *H.H.L.* 17
now that heat is quenched, quench *my* blame, . . . *H.H.L.* 18
in her ashes shrowd *my* dying shame; . . . *H.H.L.* 19
For who *my* passed follies now pursewes, . . . *H.H.L.* 20
But feele *my* wits to faile, . . . *H.H.B.* 7
To shed into *my* breast some sparkling light . . . *H.H.B.* 10
Ah, then, *my* hungry soule! . . . *H.H.B.* 288
Walkt forth to ease *my* payne . . . *Proth.* 10

Myrrh. The *Mirrhe* sweete-bleeding in the bitter wound; . . . I. i. 9. 6
'Not so th' Arabian *Myrrhe* did set her mynd, . . . III. ii. 41. 1

Myrrha. Not halfe so fast the wicked *Myrrha* fled . . . III. vii. 26. 1
More swift then *Myrrh'* or Daphne in her race, . . . IV. vii. 22. 8

Myrrhour. *See* **Mirror.**

Myrtle. The Spartan *Mirtle,* whence sweet gumb does flowe; . . . *Gn.* 669

Myrtle-tree. Next did the *Myrtle* tree to her approach, . . . *Gn.* 223

Myrtle-trees. Planted with *mirtle trees* and laurells greene, . . . III. v. 40. 2
A gloomy grove of *mirtle trees* did rise, . . . III. vi. 43. 3

Myself (*partial list*).
shall I tell thee what *my selfe* knowe . . . *S.C.* S. 170
eke because *my selfe* am touched neare; . . . *Hub.* 74
My selfe would offer you t' accompanie . . . *Hub.* 97
You to have helpt I hold *my selfe* yet blest.' . . . I. ix. 7. 7
my self I boldly reard. . . . II. iii. 45. 9
Most joyous man . . . *my selfe* I did esteeme, . . . II. iv. 21. 8
My selfe well wote, and mine unequall fate: . . . II. vii. 50. 5
my selfe will for you fight, As ye have done for me: . . . IV. i. 40. 8
Was forst to yeeld *my selfe* into their hands; . . . *Am.* xii. 10
I *my selve* shall lyke to this decay, . . . *Am.* lxxv. 7
So I unto *my selfe* alone will sing; . . . *Epith.* 17
or might *myselfe* assure That happie port . . . *H.L.* 297

Myster. *See* **Mister.**

Mysteries. His mightie *mysteries* they do prophane, . . . *Col.* 788
of legierdemayne the *mysteries* did know. . . . V. ix. 13. 9
And those most sacred *mysteries* unfold . . . *H.H.B.* 234

Mystery. The name of *Mysterie* writ in hir face; . . . *Rev.* ii. 9
Sacred with many a *mysteree,* . . . *S.C.* F. 208
the name of Souldiers . . . the noblest *mysterie,* . . . *Hub.* 221
Dares to pollute hir hidden *mysterie;* . . . *T.M.* 568
So well thou wot'st the *mysterie* of his might, . . . *Col.* 833
A sacrament prophane in *mistery* of wine. . . . III. ix. 30. 9

N

Naiad. *See* **Nais.**

Naiads. fayre *Naiades,* Go too, . . . *Gn.* 26
all the troupe of light-foot *Naiades* . . . I. vi. 18. 3

Nailed. *nayld* on high that all might them behold. . . . V. ii. 26. 9
whose tongue was for his trespasse vyle *Nayld* to a post, . . . V. ix. 25. 3
At length him *nayled* on a gallow-tree, . . . *H.H.L.* 153

Nails. *nayles* like clawes appeard. . . . II. vii. 3. 9
fingers filthie with long *nayles* unpared, . . . IV. v. 35. 4
Gnawing her *nayles* for felnesse and for yre, . . . IV. viii. 23. 8
with long *nayles* over-raught, . . . V. xii. 30. 2
with his teeth and *nailes* . . . Him rudely rent . . . VI. vi. 22. 5
with his *nayles* and teeth Gan him to hale, . . . VI. viii. 28. 6
blowe his *nayles* to warme them if he may; . . . VII. vii. 42. 4

Nais. The seed of Saturne and faire *Nais,* . . . VII. vii. 40. 9

Naked. a *naked* rout of Faunes . . . *Bel.*[1] x. 11
Shewing her wreathed rootes, and *naked* armes, . . . *Ro.* xxviii. 6
Upon the *naked* fields in stackes he reares: . . . *Ro.* xxx. 8
'You *naked* trees, whose shady leaves are lost, . . . *S.C.* Ja. 31
Whose *naked* Armes stretch unto the fyre, . . . *S.C.* F. 171
naked left and disconsolate, . . . *S.C.* F. 230
With that sprong forth a *naked* swayne . . . *S.C.* Mar. 79
'Let birds be silent on the *naked* spray, . . . *D.* 330
Next gan the earth to shew her *naked* head, . . . *Col.* 857
they gan to . . . beat their brests, and *naked* flesh to teare: . . . I. iii. 22. 5
Ne spared they to strip her *naked* all. . . . I. viii. 46. 4
The which his *naked* sides he wrapt abouts; . . . I. ix. 36. 3
naked nature seemely to aray; . . . I. x. 39. 5
Her, late forlorne and *naked,* he had found . . . II. i. 22. 1
with her tresses torne And *naked* brest, . . . II. ii. 27. 3
shewd them *naked,* deckt with many ornaments. . . . II. v. 32. 9
naked made each others manly spalles; . . . II. vi. 29. 6

Naked—*Continued.*
All *naked* without shame or care of cold, . . . II. x. 7. 6
with his *naked* hands him forcibly assayld. . . . II. xi. 41. 9
with curious ymageree . . . and shapes of *naked* boyes, . . . II. xii. 60. 6
Two *naked* Damzelles he therein espyde, . . . II. xii. 63. 6
all *naked* bare displayd. . . . III. vi. 7. 4
A thousand thousand *naked* babes attend About him . . . III. vi. 32. 3
naked nigh she did appeare, . . . III. xii. 17. 2
Her brest all *naked,* as nett yvory . . . III. xii. 20. 1
From daungers dread to ward his *naked* side, . . . IV. iii. 20. 3
To weld his *naked* sword, . . . IV. vii. 45. 9
halfe her side it selfe did *naked* show, . . . V. v. 9. 3
His side all bare and *naked* overtooke, . . . V. xi. 13. 8
Upon the Image with his *naked* blade . . . he strooke; . . . V. xi. 22. 1
naked, without needfull vestiments . . . VI. iv. 4. 4
being *naked,* . . . The goodly threasures of nature appeare: . . . VI. viii. 41. 6
the Priest with *naked* armes full net Approching nigh, . . . VI. viii. 45. 4
Eftsoones he saw one with a *naked* knife . . . VI. viii. 48. 8
An hundred *naked* maidens lilly white . . . VI. x. 11. 8
naked are, that . . . all them plaine may see, . . . VI. x. 24. 3
longed foolishly To see her *naked,* . . . VII. vi. 42. 9
Love, . . . unarmed then and *naked,* . . . *H.L.* 62

Nakedness. with greene mosse cov'ring her *nakednesse* . . . II. i. 22. 4

Name. calling me then by my propre *name,* . . . *Bel.*[1] i. 7
the vile blaspheming *name.* . . . *Rev.* i. 3
dreadfull *name* of blasphemie . . . *Rev.* ii. 3
The *name* of Mysterie writ in hir face; . . . *Rev.* ii. 9
The worde of God made him a noble *name.* . . . *Rev.* iii. 4
Which, calling me by *name,* . . . *Bel.*[2] i. 7
doo the *name* of Rome retaine, . . . *Ro.* vii. 2
Should not her *name* and endles honour keep. . . . *Ro.* viii. 14

Name—*Continued.*

that brave honour of the Latine *name*, . . . *Ro.* xxii. 1
When land and sea ye *name*, then *name* ye Rome; . . . *Ro.* xxvi. 11
Live, happie spirits, th' honour of your *name*, . . . *Ro.* Env. 13
if that any aske thy *name*, . . . *To his Booke* 13
of them han theyr *name*. . . . *S.C.* Jul. 40
(his *name* I knewe) . . . *S.C.* Jul. 161
maken a Mart of theyr good *name:* . . . *S.C.* S. 37
let hem gange alone a Gods *name;* . . . *S.C.* S. 100
So mought our Cuddies *name* to heaven sownde. . . . *S.C.* O. 54
Wrenock was his *name*, . . . *S.C.* D. 41
lighter seeme than this Gnats idle *name*. . . . *Gn.* 8
put themselves (a Gods *name*) on their way; . . . *Hub.* 111
turne the *name* of Souldiers to abusion, . . . *Hub.* 220
Is not that *name* enough to make a living . . . *Hub.* 417
backbite Anies good *name* for envie or despite: . . . *Hub.* 720
he the *name* on him would rashly take, . . . *Hub.* 815
sell fee-simples in his Masters *name*, . . . *Hub.* 867
none shall *name* the number of his place? . . . *Hub.* 982
in the Kings *name* bad them both to stay, . . . *Hub.* 1071
seeke with slaunder his good *name* to blot; . . . *Hub.* 1219
blot his brutish *name* Unto the world, . . . *Hub.* 1240
such as hate the honour of our *name*, . . . *T.M.* 63
us, that patronize The *name* of learning? . . . *T.M.* 148
name of learning utterly doo scorne. . . . *T.M.* 438
did her *name* of her request. . . . *Ti.* 33
'*Name* have I none (quoth she) . . . *Ti.* 34
Nor anie lives that mentioneth my *name* . . . *Ti.* 164
His *name* is worne alreadie out of thought, . . . *Ti.* 222
'Who is it that dooth *name* me, . . . *D.* 62
Them to vouchsafe emongst his rimes to *name*, . . . *As.* 38
His mistresse *name*, and his owne fame to raise. . . . *As.* 88
That hearbe of some Starlight is cald by *name*, . . . *As.* 193
The shepheards boy (best knowen by that *name*) . . . *Col.* 1
The Shepheard of the Ocean by *name*, . . . *Col.* 66
gave that *name* unto that pleasant vale; . . . *Col.* 107
It gievth *name* unto that auncient Cittie, . . . *Col.* 112
Did lose his *name:* . . . *Col.* 155
Lunday . . . by that same *name* is ment An island, . . . *Col.* 270
Like to an horne, whereof the *name* it has, . . . *Col.* 282
her *name* to glorifie, . . . *Col.* 379
Her *name* to eccho unto heaven hie. . . . *Col.* 483
Her *name* recorded I will leave for ever. . . . *Col.* 631
Her *name* in every tree I will endosse, . . . *Col.* 632
as the trees do grow, her *name* may grow: . . . *Col.* 633
Her *name* Ile teach in knowen terms to frame: . . . *Col.* 637
lambs . . . Ile teach to call for Cynthia by *name*. . . . *Col.* 639
by slaundring his well-deemed *name*, . . . *Col.* 695
any gentle wit of *name* Nor honest mynd . . . *Col.* 733
use his ydle *name* to other needs, . . . *Col.* 789
doth not merit The *name* of love, . . . *Col.* 892
Yet doe not sdeigne to let thy *name* be writt . . . *Ded. Son.* ii. 4
For honor of your *name* and high descent. . . . *Ded. Son.* x. 14
In vain I thinke . . . to memorize thy *name*, . . . *Ded. Son.* xii. 2
Love him that hath eternized your *name*. . . . *Ded.Son.*xiv.14
But with remembraunce of your gracious *name*, . . . *Ded. Son.* xvi. 3
A . . . man, that dar'd to call by *name* Great Gorgon, . . . I. i. 37. 7
The Sprite . . . threatned . . . the dreaded *name* Of Hecate: . I. i. 43. 2
her knight by *name* She weend it was, . . . I. iii. 26. 6
A gentle Husher, Vanitie by *name*, Made rowme, . . . I. iv. 13. 3
name of native syre did fowle upbrayd, . . . I. v. 48. 7
the lignage right From whence he tooke his weldeserved *name:* . . . I. vi. 20. 4
whylst any beast of *name* Walkt in that forrest, . . . I. vi. 29. 3
having blent My *name* with guile and traiterous intent: . . I. vi. 42. 5
The false Duessa, cloked with Fidessaes *name*. . . . I. vii. 1. 9
His *name* Ignaro did his nature right aread. . . . I. viii. 31. 9
Una faire besought That straunger knight his *name* . . . tell; I. ix. 2. 7
'That ydle *name* of love . . . I ever scornd, . . . I. ix. 10. 1
you, Sir knight, whose *name* mote I request, . . . I. ix. 32. 3
His *name* was Zele, that him right well became: . . . I. x. 6. 6
His *name* was meeke Obedience, rightfully aredd. . . . I. x. 17. 9
His *name* was Patience. . . . I. x. 23. 9
Her *name* was Mercy; . . . I. x. 34. 4
His *name* was hevenly Contemplation; . . . I. x. 46. 8
wel beseemes all knights of noble *name*, . . . I. x. 59. 4
Georgos he thee gave to *name;* . . . I. x. 66. 6
That hast my *name* and nation redd aright, . . . I. x. 67. 3
fame, That warlike handes ennoblest with immortall *name;* I. xi. 5. 9
her ador'd by honorable *name*, . . . I. xii. 8. 4
costly scarlott of great *name*, . . . I. xii. 13. 8
see the salving of your blotted *name*.' . . . II. i. 20. 7
enrolled is your glorious *name* In heavenly Regesters . . . II. i. 32. 3
know it by the *name:* it hight the *Bowre of blis*. . . . II. i. 51. 9
Medina was her *name*, . . . II. ii. 14. 4
not so good of deedes as great of *name*, . . . II. ii. 17. 3
To weete which of the gods I shall thee *name*, . . . II. iii. 33. 8
my liege, whose warlike *name* Is far renowmd . . . II. iii. 35. 3
my dreaded *name* to raise Above the Moone, . . . II. iii. 38. 7
'Pyrochles is his *name*, . . . II. iv. 41. 2
To which right wel the wise doe give that *name*, . . . II. v. 1. 5
for terrour of his *name*, . . . II. v. 26. 6
Of Phaedria, (for so my *name* is red) . . . II. vi. 9. 7
hight by *name* The Idle lake, . . . II. vi. 10. 1
The famous *name* of knighthood fowly shend; . . . II. vi. 35. 2
living handes immortalizd his *name*. . . . II. viii. 13. 5
A jolly yeoman . . . Whose *name* was Appetite: . . . II. ix. 28. 3
Him ill beseemes anothers fault to *name*, . . . II. ix. 38. 4
her *name* was Prays-desire, . . . II. ix. 39. 8
I would assay Thy *name*, O soveraine Queene! . . . II. x. 3. 9

Name—*Continued.*

Thy *name*, O soveraine Queene! . . . II. x. 4. 1
Ne did it then deserve a *name* to have, . . . II. x. 6. 1
of his *name* and memorable gest . . . II. x. 12. 4
of her *name* now Severne men do call; . . . II. x. 19. 8
second both in *name* And eke in semblaunce . . . II. x. 23. 2
built that gate which of his *name* is hight, . . . II. x. 46. 6
tempted with the *name* Of this sweet Island . . . II. x. 47. 6
He of his *name* Coylchester built of stone and lime. . . . II. x. 58. 9
Maleger was his *name;* . . . II. xi. 23. 1
Impotence her *name:* . . . II. xi. 23. 8
The dreadful Fish that hath deserv'd the *name* Of Death, . II. xii. 24. 1
hight Grylle by *name*, . . . II. xii. 86. 7
(For so that Castle hight by commun *name*) . . . III. i. 31. 3
The first of them by *name* Gardante hight, . . . III. i. 45. 1
treading under foote her honest *name:* . . . III. i. 50. 4
is by *name* The greater Brytayne, . . . III. ii. 7. 8
The noble Arthegall hath ever borne the *name*. . . . III. ii. 9. 9
Her aged Nourse, whose *name* was Glauce hight, . . . III. ii. 30. 2
ennoble with immortall *name* The warlike Worthies, . . . III. iii. 4. 3
is now by chaunge Of *name* Cayr-Merdin cald, . . . III. iii. 7. 4
The feends do quake when any him to them does *name*. . . III. iii. 12. 9
his mighty puissaunce And dreaded *name* . . . III. iii. 28. 2
shall their *name* for ever be defaste, . . . III. iii. 43. 8
Of roiall majesty and soveraine *name:* . . . III. iii. 48. 8
themselves of her *name* *Angles* call. . . . III. iii. 56. 7
of her *name* and nation be chiefe, . . . III. iv. 11. 7
She, of his father, Marinell did *name;* . . . III. iv. 20. 2
An hundred knights of honorable *name* . . . III. iv. 21. 1
to advaunce his *name* and glory more, . . . III. iv. 21. 6
O! is this Th' immortall *name*, . . . III. iv. 36. 4
Belphoebe was her *name*, as faire as Phoebus sunne. . . . III. v. 27. 9
of her selfe, her *name* Belphoebe red: . . . III. vi. 28. 5
called is by her lost lovers *name*, . . . III. vi. 29. 8
As for my *name*, it mistreth not to tell: . . . III. vii. 51. 8
to enroll thy memorable *name* In th' heart . . . III. viii. 43. 4
every one his kindred and his *name*. . . . III. ix. 32. 5
'Troy, that art now nought but an idle *name*, . . . III. ix. 33. 1
by *name* Sir Paris far renowmd . . . III. ix. 34. 4
Whom . . . She, of his Father, Parius did *name;* . . . III. ix. 36. 6
passing by, his *name* discovered, Ease, . . . III. xii. 4. 8
every valley wyde He filld with Hylas *name;* . . . III. xii. 7. 9
The other cleped Cruelty by *name:* . . . III. xii. 19. 3
Her *name* was Ate, mother of debate . . . IV. i. 19. 1
There also was the *name* of Nimrod strong; . . . IV. i. 22. 7
His *name* was Blandamour, . . . IV. i. 32. 4
whose *name* I wote not well, . . . IV. i. 48. 7
Whereby the *name* of knight-hood thou dost shend, . . . IV. i. 51. 3
Colour thy *name* with foule reproaches rust! . . . IV. i. 53. 7
Her *name* was Agape, . . . IV. ii. 41. 7
they were doughtie knights of dreaded *name*, . . . IV. iv. 3. 2
for to salve his *name* And purchase honour . . . IV. iv. 27. 2
each of other gan inquire his *name*. . . . IV. iv. 42. 3
certes his right *name* was otherwize, . . . IV. iv. 42. 7
That goodly belt was Cestus hight by *name*, . . . IV. v. 6. 1
His *name* was Care; a blacksmith by his trade, . . . IV. v. 35. 6
sith ye my *name* have hight, . . . IV. vi. 4. 4
excuse Me from discovering you my *name* aright, . . . IV. vi. 4. 7
'A stranger knight,' sayd he, 'unknowne by *name*, . . . IV. vi. 6. 3
Soone as she heard the *name* of Artegall, . . . IV. vi. 29. 1
How he the *name* of one engraven had . . . IV. vii. 46. 2
Him seemed oft he heard his owne right *name*. . . . IV. viii. 4. 5
Her *name* men Sclaunder call. . . . IV. viii. 24. 9
steale away the crowne of their good *name:* . . . IV. viii. 25. 4
of great mother Venus bare the *name*, . . . IV. x. 5. 4
no man aunswred me by *name;* . . . IV. x. 11. 4
His *name* was Doubt, . . . IV. x. 12. 3
'His *name* was Daunger, . . . IV. x. 17. 1
both under one *name:* . . . IV. x. 41. 7
Her *name* was Womanhood; . . . IV. x. 49. 5
River, which doth beare his *name* Of warlike Amazons, . . IV. xi. 21. 8
The Ouze, whom men doe Isis rightly *name;* . . . IV. xi. 24. 7
of his wylinesse his *name* doth take, . . . IV. xi. 32. 6
of him selfe doth *name* the shire thereby: . . . IV. xi. 32. 7
to old Loncaster his *name* doth lend; . . . IV. xi. 39. 2
To damne him selfe by every evil *name*, . . . IV. xii. 16. 5
'Then, it is by *name* Proteus, . . . IV. xii. 31. 1
Grantorto was his *name*. . . . V. i. 3. 9
whereof it tooke his *name*, . . . V. i. 10. 4
His *name* was Talus, made of yron mould, . . . V. i. 12. 6
'His *name* is hight Pollente, . . . V. ii. 7. 1
Her *name* is Munera, agreeing with her deedes. . . . V. ii. 9. 9
The second had to *name* Sir Bellisont, . . . V. iii. 5. 3
To Marinell, whose *name* the Heralds loud resounded. . . . V. iii. 6. 9
Don Braggadochios *name* resounded thrise: . . . V. iii. 15. 4
our sire, Milesio by *name*, . . . V. iv. 7. 3
'Her *name*' (quoth he) 'they Radigund doe call, . . . V. iv. 33. 3
How Fortune will your ruin'd *name* repaire . . . V. iv. 34. 8
A goodly citty . . . of her owne *name*, she called Radegone. . V. iv. 35. 9
Her *name* was Clarin, . . . V. iv. 48. 3
Of all the ornaments of knightly *name*, . . . V. v. 20. 4
His *name* was Guizor; . . . V. vi. 33. 6
'Her *name* Mercilla most men use to call, . . . V. viii. 17. 1
Miscalling me by many a bitter *name*, . . . V. viii. 22. 8
All were they nigh an hundred knights of *name*, . . . V. viii. 50. 6
Therefore by *name* Malengin they him call, . . . V. ix. 5. 8
His *name* was Awe; . . . V. ix. 23. 1
His *name* hight Order; . . . V. ix. 23. 8
Ne ever was the *name* of warre there spoken, . . . V. ix. 24. 6
his *name* was called Zele. . . . V. ix. 39. 4

Name—*Continued.*
had to *name* The Kingdomes Care, ... V. ix. 43. 7
Her *name* was Belgae; . . . . V. x. 7. 1
There stands an Idole of great note and *name,* . . . . V. xi. 19. 2
Whom by his *name* saluting, thus he gan: . . . . V. xi. 38. 1
much did magnifie his noble *name:* . . . . V. xi. 46. 6
'My *name* is Burbon hight, ... V. xi. 49. 1
Fie on the pelfe for which good *name* is sold, ... V. xi. 63. 6
Her *name* was Envie, knowen well thereby, ... V. xii. 31. 1
all she sought was mens good *name* to have bereaved. . . . . V. xii. 33. 9
Her *name* was hight Detraction, ... V. xii. 35. 5
meriteth indeede an higher *name:* . . . . VI. Pr. 6. 8
*Yet so from low to high uplifted is your *name.* . . . . VI. Pr. 6. 9
by *name* Briana hight, ... VI. i. 14. 6
'His *name* is Crudor; . . . . VI. i. 15. 1
Ne stayd to aske if it were he by *name,* . . . . VI. i. 33. 3
'And Tristram is my *name,* . . . . VI. ii. 28. 1
And Aldus was his *name;* . . . . VI. iii. 3. 9
to what case her *name* should now be brought: . . . . VI. iii. 6. 9
'Unknightly Knight, the blemish of that *name,* . . . . VI. iii. 35. 1
'His *name,*' (quoth he) . . . Is hight Sir Turpine, ... VI. iii. 40. 1
I am th' unfortunate Matilde by *name,* . . . . VI. iv. 29. 3
The first of them by *name* was cald Despetto, ... VI. v. 13. 6
he had bene a man of mickle *name,* . . . . VI. v. 37. 3
The *name* of knighthood he did disavow; . . . . VI. v. 37. 7
infamy Infixeth in the *name* of noble wight: . . . . VI. vi. 1. 4
Ne ever Lady of so honest *name,* . . . . VI. vi. 12. 8
Fayre Mirabella was her *name,* . . . . VI. vii. 35. 1
Whom they by *name* there Portamore did call; . . . . VI. vii. 35. 8
Which should befall to Calidores immortall *name.* . . . . VI. ix. 1. 9
caroling her *name* both day and night, ... VI. ix. 9. 8
The fayrest Pastorella her by *name* did hight. . . . . VI. ix. 9. 9
To her, whose *name* he often did repeat; . . . . VI. xi. 33. 7
Her *name* was Claribell; . . . . VI. xii. 4. 1
through the world thereby should glorifie his *name.* . . . . VI. xii. 12. 9
Whereof her *name* ye then to her did give. . . . . VI. xii. 18. 6
Of all that beare the British Islands *name,* . . . . VII. vi. 38. 3
Cynthus hill, whence she her *name* did take; . . . . VII. vii. 50. 4
Some say in Crete by *name,* . . . . VII. vii. 53. 5
To sing your *name* and prayses over-all: . . . . *Am.* lxiii. 12
letters! . . . With which that happy *name* was first desynd, ... *Am.* lxxiv. 2
One day I wrote her *name* upon the strand; . . . . *Am.* lxxv. 1
eek my *name* bee wyped out lykewize. . . . . *Am.* lxxv. 8
in the hevens wryte your glorious *name.* . . . . *Am.* lxxv. 12
enchased Your glorious *name* in golden moniment. . . . . *Am.* lxxxii. 8
Great both by *name,* and great in power and might, ... *Com.Son.*iii.11
I meane to sing the praises of thy *name,* . . . . *H.L.* 10
Thus to ennoble thy victorious *name,* . . . . *H.L.* 149
thy triumphant *name* then would I raise . . . . *H.L.* 303
in praise of thine owne *name,* . . . . *H.B.* 8
Commend to you by loves abused *name,* . . . . *H.B.* 172
Singing this Hymne in honour of thy *name,* . . . . *H.B.* 272
creatures which by *name* Thou canst not count, ... *H.H.B.* 32
pompe to which proud minds aspyre By *name* of honor, ... *H.H.B.* 278
from another place I take my *name,* . . . . *Proth.* 130
Whose dreadfull *name* . . . did thunder, ... *Proth.* 147
great Elisaes glorious *name* may ring . . . . *Proth.* 157
have thou . . . endlesse happinesse of thine owne *name* . . . . *Proth.* 153
Named. if things *nam'd* their names doo equalize, ... *Ro.* xxvi. 10
Much like to begging, but much better *named,* . . . . *Hub.* 351
Ne let such verses Poetrie be *named!* . . . . *Hub.* 814
read how art thou *nam'd,* and of what kin?' . . . . II. iv. 36. 6
namd it ALBION: . . . . II. x. 6. 7
(Their Chiefetain Humber *named* was aright,) . . . . II. x. 16. 7
Those yet of her be Mertian lawes both *nam'd* and thought. . . . . II. x. 42. 9
Of her fond favorites so *nam'd* amis, ... II. xii. 69. 5
all, that else through all the world is *named* . . . . IV. x. 30. 8
nam'd the river of his wretched fate . . . . IV. xi. 38. 7
from the golden age, that first was *named,* . . . . V. Pr. 2. 1
when as he him *nam'd,* . . . . V. iii. 34. 7
him his God hath *named;* . . . . V. x. 28. 5
Who as her owne it nurst (and *named*) evermore. . . . . VI. xii. 9. 9
Of fayrest fayre! let never it be *named,* . . . . *Am.* xli. 13
Nameless. die In foule forgetfulnesse, and *nameles* lie. . . . . *Ti.* 378
namelesse there his bodie now doth lie; . . . . IV. viii. 49. 2
Namely. His auncient parents, *namely* th' auncient Thame. . . . . IV. xi. 24. 5
Mongst which he *namely* did to him discourse . . . . VI. iii. 14. 8
Is not that *namely* wee . . . . VII. vii. 48. 6
Names. shall ruinate Your workes and *names,* . . . . *Ro.* vii. 11
if things nam'd their *names* doo equalize, ... *Ro.* xxvi. 10
by the *names* of Souldiers us protect: . . . . *Hub.* 197
better farre it were to hide their *names,* . . . . *T.M.* 101
know their *names,* or speak their praises dew, ... *T.M.* 442
Their *names* shall of the later age be heard, ... *Ti.* 348
might their *names* for ever memorize. . . . . *Ti.* 364
names I cannot readily now ghesse: . . . . *Col.* 740
Some daily seene and knowen by their *names,* . . . . II. ix. 50. 6
should bring their *names* And pledges, ... III. vii. 54. 8
Into their *names* the title to convart, ... III. ix. 43. 4
rout Of persons . . . whose *names* is hard to read: . . . . III. xii. 25. 2
maladies, Whose *names* and natures I note readen well; . . . . III. xii. 26. 2
both of old well knowing by their *names,* . . . . IV. ii. 20. 5
Helpe me to tell the *names* of all those floods . . . . IV. xi. 10. 6
what doe I their *names* seeke to reherse, ... IV. xi. 17. 1
by their *names* were hight The Churne and Charwell, ... IV. xi. 25. 2
With many more whose *names* no tongue can tell: . . . . IV. xi. 44. 6
Whose *names* and nations were too long to tell, ... IV. xii. 3. 2
Many brave knights, whose *names* right well he knew, ... V. v. 22. 2
By all the *names* that honorable were. . . . . V. xi. 33. 4
In which the *names* of all loves folke were fyled, ... VI. vii. 33. 2

Names—*Continued.*
To heare theyr *names* sung in your simple layes, ... *Epith.* 5
hob Goblins, *names* whose sence we see not, ... *Epith.* 343
Naming. *naming* Rome, ye land and sea comprize: . . . . *Ro.* xxvi. 12
Nap. The velvet *nap* which on his wings doth lie, ... *Mui.* 333
any litle *nap* Upon his heavie eye-lids chaunst to fall, ... IV. v. 42. 1
Nape. in his *nape* arriving, through it thrild . . . . IV. vii. 31. 6
Napron. *See* **Apron.**
Nar. *See* **Nearer.**
To Kerke the *narre,* from God more farre, ... *S.C.* Jul. 97
Eftsoones of thousand billowes shoulderd *narre,* . . . . *Ro.* xvi. 3
Narcissus. Ne wants there pale *Narcisse,* . . . . *Gn.* 679
Foolish *Narcisse,* that likes the watry shore; . . . . III. vi. 45. 5
lyke *Narcissus* vaine, Whose eyes him starv'd: . . . . *Am.* xxxv. 7
Narrow. streight and *narrow* was the way which he did show. I. x. 5. 9
So few there bee, That chose the *narrow* path, ... I. x. 10. 4
a *narrow* way, Scattred with bushy thornes . . . . I. x. 35. 2
narrow leaves cannot in them contayne The large discourse I. xii. 14. 5
through a darksom *narrow* strayt, ... II. vii. 40. 1
twixt them both the *narrow* way doth ly.' . . . . II. xii. 18. 4
a covert glade, Foreby a *narrow* foord, ... III. v. 17. 2
Great heapes of them, like sheepe in *narrow* fold, ... IV. iii. 41. 4
in this so *narrow* verse . . . . IV. xi. 17. 3
is but *narrow,* but exceeding long; . . . . V. ii. 7. 7
Him in a *narrow* place he overtooke, ... VI. xii. 26. 1
Narrowly. every Nimph full *narrowly* shee eide. . . . . III. vi. 23. 9
Nas. pittied is mishappe that *nas* remedie, ... *S.C.* May 61
Natheless. *Nath'les* my Lute, whom Phoebus . . . . *Ro.* xxxii. 9
Natheles, because you shall not us misdeeme, ... *Hub.* 375
Nath'les perhaps ye things may . . . . *Hub.* 641
Nath'les . . . since we passed are . . . . *Hub.* 1047
Hardly, *naythles,* were they restrayned so, ... *Hub.* 1073
Nath'les the royall Beast forbore beleeving, ... *Hub.* 1365
Nath-lesse the Nymph her former liking held; . . . . *Col.* 128
Yet *nathelesse* it could not doe him die, ... I. ix. 54. 8
Nathlesse with wonted rage he him advaunced neare. . . . . I. xi. 52. 9
Nath'lesse th' Enchaunter would not spare his payne, ... II. i. 5. 1
'*Nathlesse* he shortly shall againe be tryde, ... II. i. 20. 1
Her *nathelesse* Th' enchaunter . . . Did thus revest, ... II. i. 22. 7
nathelesse he did her still torment, ... II. iv. 12. 7
Nathelesse so sore a buff to him it lent, ... II. v. 6. 8
Nath'lesse now quench thy whott emboyling wrath: . . . . II. v. 18. 5
halfe discontent, mote *nathelesse* Himselfe appease, ... II. vi. 24. 1
Nath'lesse most hevenly faire . . . She by creation was, ... II. vi. 45. 7
Nath'lesse the Prince would not forsake his sell, ... II. viii. 31. 3
Nath'lesse the same enjoyed but short happy howre: . . . . II. x. 57. 9
Nathelesse it bore his foe not from his sell, ... III. i. 6. 4
nath'lesse shee inly deemd Her love too light, ... III. i. 55. 6
Nath'lesse those feends may not their work forbeare, ... III. iii. 11. 4
Nath'lesse to thee thy folly I forgive; . . . . III. iv. 37. 7
Nathlesse the villein sped himselfe so well, ... III. v. 14. 1
Nathelesse she was so courteous and kynde, ... III. v. 55. 2
Nathlesse her honor . . . She sought to save, ... IV. i. 6. 6
Nathlesse he forth did march, ... IV. i. 38. 1
nathlesse, as neede required, ... IV. i. 54. 2
Nathlesse proud man himselfe the other deemed, ... IV. ii. 8. 1
nathelesse, whilst all the lookers-on Him dead behight, ... IV. iii. 31. 1
Yet *nathelesse* to her . . . It yielded was . . . . IV. v. 20. 2
Nathelesse she, full of wrath for that late stroke, ... IV. vi. 23. 1
Nathlesse her tongue not to her will obayd, ... IV. vi. 27. 8
Nathlesse he hardly of her chearefull speech Did comfort take, IV. vi. 38. 1
Nathlesse it fell with so despiteous dreare . . . . IV. viii. 42. 5
'*Nathlesse* that Dame so well them tempred both, ... IV. x. 33. 1
Nathlesse his pride full dearely he did pryse; . . . . IV. xi. 5. 5
nathlesse he takes great joy . . . . IV. xi. 19. 8
Nathlesse she rested not so satisfide; . . . . IV. xii. 25. 1
Nathlesse for all the powre she did apply . . . . V. iv. 41. 8
yet *nathelesse* With huge redoubled strokes she on him layd; . . . . V. v. 14. 5
Nathlesse . . . She chang'd that threatfull mood, ... V. v. 47. 8
All which *nathlesse* she for his love forbore; . . . . V. v. 54. 8
Nath'lesse that stroke so cruell passage found, ... V. vii. 33. 1
'*Nathlesse,*' (said he) 'deare Ladie, with me goe; . . . . V. x. 24. 1
Nathelesse him selfe he armed all in hast, ... V. xi. 3. 1
Nathlesse the yron man did still pursew . . . . V. xi. 65. 1
Nathlesse, for all that ever he could doe, ... V. xii. 22. 4
Nathlesse thereto he was full stout and tall, ... VI. i. 2. 7
Nathlesse at length him selfe he did upreare . . . . VI. i. 35. 1
Nathelesse, . . . I will not feare it to relate. . . . . VI. ii. 27. 4
Who *nathelesse,* when he the Lady saw . . . . VI. iii. 26. 1
Nathelesse the Knight, . . . Gan him entreat . . . . VI. iii. 38. 1
'*Nathlesse,*' (quoth he) 'if need doe not you bynd, ... VI. iv. 28. 6
nathelesse, not therewith satisfyde, ... VI. vi. 43. 7
Nathelesse, for all his speach the gentle knight . . . . VI. vii. 23. 1
nathelesse He unto her a penance did impose, ... VI. vii. 37. 5
Nathelesse so sharpely still he him pursewd, ... VI. vii. 48. 1
Nathlesse Sir Bellamour . . . so with his keepers wrought, ... VI. xii. 6. 1
Nath'lesse Diana, full of indignation, ... VII. vi. 54. 1
Nathelesse, the cruell boy . . . Would needs the fly pursue; . . . . *Epig.* iv. 21
Nathelesse doe ye still loud her prayses sing, ... *Epith.* 165
Nathelesse the soule is faire and beauteous still, ... *H.B.* 159
Nathemore. *nathemore* would that corageous swayne . . . . I. viii. 13. 6
nathemore . . . Could his blood frosen hart emboldened bee, I. ix. 25. 6
yet *nathemoe* Was he abashed now, ... II. iv. 8. 4
Yet *nathemore* did it his fury stint, ... II. v. 8. 3
his dead corse upon the flore fell *nathemore.* . . . . II. xi. 37. 9
nathemore forth fled his groning spright, ... II. xi. 38. 8
nathemore Would they once turne, ... II. xi. 15. 4
nathemore for that spectacle bad . . . . III. v. 22. 6
she the way shund *nathemore* forthy, ... III. vii. 38. 5
nathemore the steele asonder riv'd, ... III. vii. 40. 5

Nathemore—*Continued.*
Yet *nathemore* would it her bodie fit; . . . IV. v. 20. 1
nathemore his meaning she ared, . . . IV. viii. 14. 1
nathemore would I Forgoe the purchase . . . IV. viii. 62. 3
nathemore would she Shew gladsome countenaunce . . . IV. ix. 13. 4
Yet can I not my love have *nathemore*, . . . V. xi. 54. 7
nathemore would they from land refraine: . . . V. xii. 5. 1
Yet *nathemore* him suffred to arize; . . . VI. viii. 18. 2
nathemore his heavy load releast, . . . VI. xii. 32. 8
Yet *nathemore* the Giantesse forbare, . . . VII. vi. 13. 1
He *nathemore* can so contented rest, . . . *H.L.* 246
Yet *nathemore* is that faire beauties blame, . . . *H.B.* 155
Nation. that *Nation*, th' earths new Giant brood, . . . *Ro.* xi. 9
thou art first, which of thy *Nation* song . . . *Ro.* xxxii. 13
the brutish *nation* to enwrap: . . . *As.* 98
how great a losse Had all the shepheards *nation* . . . *Col.* 17
Una . . . Whom salvage *nation* does adore, . . . I. vi. Arg.
The salvage *nation* feele her secret smart, . . . I. vi. 11. 3
besought That straunger knight his . . . *nation* tell; . . . I. ix. 2. 7
what unknowen *nation* there empeopled were? . . . I. x. 56. 9
That hast my name and *nation* redd aright, . . . I. x. 67. 3
Of every sort and *nation* under skye, . . . II. vii. 44. 2
far in land a salvage *nation* dwelt . . . II. x. 7. 1
a *nation* straunge, with visage swart, . . . II. x. 15. 1
health to every forreyne *nation:* . . . II. x. 26. 7
all the *nation* of unfortunate And fatall birds . . . II. xii. 36. 1
of her name and *nation* be chiefe, . . . III. iv. 11. 7
Greekes cruell fact Against that *nation*, . . . III. ix. 38. 6
an huge *nation* of the Geaunts broode . . . III. ix. 49. 8
so numberlesse their *nation*. . . . IV. xii. 1. 9
Nor memory thereof to any *nation*. . . . V. ii. 28. 5
The salvage *nation* doth all dread despize, . . . VI. iv. 6. 6
There dwelt a salvage *nation*, . . . VI. viii. 35. 2
Nation's. thine owne *nations* frend And Patrone: . . . I. x. 61. 7
Nations. The *nations* gan their soveraigntie disdaine, . . . *Van.* xi. 3
doth all *Nations* unto her subdue: . . . *Gn.* 598
of all *Nations* now I am forlorne, . . . *Ti.* 27
made all *nations* vassals of her pride, . . . *Ti.* 72
That would compell all *nations* to adore, . . . I. v. 47. 2
scared *nations* doest with horror sterne astownd. . . . I. xi. 6. 9
to them selves all *Nations* did subdew. . . . II. x. 72. 3
Betweene the *nations* different afore, . . . III. iii. 49. 2
when both *nations* gan to strive . . . III. ix. 43. 3
Nations captived, and huge armies slaine: . . . IV. i. 21. 8
many *Nations* into thraldome led, . . . IV. viii. 47. 4
Of puissant *Nations* which the world possest, . . . IV. xi. 15. 2
Whose names and *nations* were too long to tell, . . . IV. xii. 3. 2
furthest *Nations* filles with awful dread, . . . V. Pr. 11. 5
to enquire What thing so many *nations* met did there desire. V. ii. 29. 9
so were realmes and *nations* run awry. . . . V. ii. 32. 6
then the Law of *Nations* gainst her rose, . . . V. ix. 44. 3
Those *Nations* farre thy justice doe adore; . . . V. x. 3. 8
Being with fame through many *Nations* blowen,) . . . VI. iv. 36. 5
Warres and allarums unto *Nations* wide, . . . VII. vi. 3. 8
Native. Both borrowed pride, and *native* beautie stained. . . . *Van.* viii. 12
From our owne *native* heritage exilde, . . . *T.M.* 341
Appeared in their *native* propertis, . . . *Ti.* 284
Fled back too soone unto his *native* place; . . . *Ti.* 291
White as the *native* Rose before the chaunge . . . *D.* 108
And *native* beauty deck with hevenlie grace: . . . *Ded. Son.* xv. 12
the sleeping spark Of *native* vertue gan eftsoones revive; . . . I. ii. 19. 2
she had none . . . Ne heritage of *native* soveraintie; . . . I. iv. 12. 4
the Paynim lay, Devoid of . . . *native* strength, . . . I. v. 29. 3
name of *native* syre did fowle upbrayd, . . . I. v. 48. 7
Unto those *native* woods for to repaire, . . . I. vi. 30. 3
life does win Unto her *native* prison to retourne; . . . I. vii. 21. 8
Did fall to ground, depriv'd of *native* might: . . . I. viii. 10. 7
huge mountaines from their *native* seat . . . to beare away, I. x. 20. 6
'Now are we come unto my *native* soyle, . . . I. xi. 2. 1
his victorious handes did earst restore To *native* crowne . . . II. i. 2. 7
mickle worship in his *native* land; . . . II. i. 6. 6
As budding braunch rent from the *native* tree, . . . II. ii. 2. 6
soone renews her *native* pride: . . . II. iii. 36. 6
Seemes to be borne by *native* influence; . . . II. iv. 1. 5
strive to passe . . . Their *native* musicke . . . II. vi. 25. 4
Which with sad cares empeach our *native* joyes. . . . II. vii. 15. 6
was not that same her owne *native* hew, . . . II. vii. 45. 4
incontinent Doth loose his dignity and *native* grace: . . . II. ix. 1. 8
too oft she chaung'd her *native* hew. . . . II. ix. 40. 4
depriv'd Of *native* strength . . . II. ix. 57. 5
All were they borne of her owne *native* slime: . . . II. x. 9. 5
Androgeus, false to *native* soyle, . . . II. x. 48. 6
The royall Ofspring of his *native* land, . . . II. x. 69. 2
strives to mount unto his *native* seat; . . . II. xi. 32. 6
A trayle of yvie in his *native* hew; . . . II. xii. 61. 2
Far fro my *native* soyle, . . . III. ii. 7. 8
lov'd their *native* flesh against al kynd, . . . III. ii. 41. 3
To this his *native* soyle thou backe shalt bring, . . . III. iii. 27. 7
retourning to his *native* place, . . . III. iii. 41. 5
the old sparkes renew Of *native* corage, . . . III. iii. 45. 8
Whence he it fetcht out of her *native* place, . . . III. v. 52. 4
native corage unto him supply, . . . III. vii. 3. 2
so fowly to devoure Her *native* flesh . . . III. vii. 49. 5
for . . . glories gaine, My *native* soile have lefte, . . . III. ix. 37. 8
flie Unto her *native* home from mortall miserie. . . . IV. iii. 30. 9
the *native* Belman of the night, . . . V. vi. 27. 1
from her *native* land Exiled her, . . . V. xi. 4. 6
Hath pruned from the *native* tree, . . . V. xi. 11. 9
ten yeares my selfe excluded From *native* home, . . . VI. ix. 25. 4
lose their *native* mights; . . . VII. vii. 25. 5

Native—*Continued.*
the *native* might Of heavie earth, . . . *H.L.* 188
Unto her *native* planet shall retyre; . . . *H.B.* 103
their owne *native* light farre passing theirs. . . . *H.H.B.* 70
like the *native* brood of Eagles kynd, . . . *H.H.B.* 138
And make her *native* brightnes seem more cleare. . . . *H.H.B.* 189
gave this Lifes first *native* sourse, . . . *Proth.* 129
Nativity. In th' Horoscope of her *nativitee*, . . . III. vi. 2. 4
elder then thine owne *nativitie*, . . . *H.L.* 54
Natural. rob'd of rest and *naturall* reliefe. . . . *Hub.* 16
Have now quite lost their *naturall* delight, . . . *T.M.* 552
T' excell the *naturall* with made delights; . . . *Mui.* 166
The measure of her meane and *naturall* first need. . . . II. vii. 16. 9
naturall desire of countryes state, . . . II. x. 77. 2
semblaunce pleasing, more then *naturall*, . . . II. xii. 46. 5
had from hoggish forme him brought to *naturall*. . . . II. xii. 86. 9
All night afflict thy *naturall* repose; . . . III. ii. 31. 2
Doth course of *naturall* cause farre exceed, . . . III. iii. 18. 6
Depriv'd of kindly joy and *naturall* delight . . . III. ix. 5. 9
Ne *naturall* affection faultlesse blame . . . IV. Pr. 2. 4
all bountie *naturall* And treasures of true love . . . IV. Pr. 4. 3
t' increase affection *naturall*, . . . IV. ii. 54. 4
naturall affection soone doth cesse, . . . IV. ix. 2. 1
there was planted, or grew *naturall:* . . . IV. x. 22. 5
With more then needfull *naturall* remorse, . . . V. x. 4. 8
As their true Liege and Princesse *naturall;* . . . V. xii. 24. 8
In whom . . . manners mylde were planted *naturall;* . . . VI. i. 2. 4
Nature. arte and *nature* strived to joyne . . . *Bel.*[1] x. 5
Art and *Nature* had assembled . . . *Bel.*[2] xii. 5
what ever *nature*, arte, And heaven could doo, . . . *Ro.* v. 1
Heaven envious, and bitter stepdame *Nature!* . . . *Ro.* ix. 2
let him feede, as *Nature* did provide, . . . *Van.* iii. 11
when *nature* craveth sleepe, . . . *S.C.* Au. 177
The verie *nature* of the place, . . . *Gn.* 185
The weapons, which *Nature* to him hath lent: . . . *Gn.* 276
ne by the law of *Nature*, . . . *Hub.* 145
as their due by *Nature* doo it clame. . . . *Hub.* 166
So made by *nature* for to serve their will, . . . *T.M.* 40
the man whom *Nature* selfe had made . . . *T.M.* 205
milde of speach, and meeke of *nature:* . . . *Ti.* 536
salvage *nature* seemed not to have, . . . *Ti.* 564
lavish *Nature*, in her best attire, . . . *Mui.* 163
to be Lord of all the workes of *Nature*, . . . *Mui.* 211
The shame of *Nature*, the bondslave of spight, . . . *Mui.* 245
Nature, nurse of every living thing, . . . *D.* 337
'Hencefoorth I hate what ever *Nature* made, . . . *D.* 393
of his *nature* rightly to define, . . . *Col.* 836
like wormes out of her slimie *nature*. . . . *Col.* 860
whose *nature* weake A cruell witch, . . . Hath thus transformd, I. ii. 33. 4
His name Ignaro did his *nature* right aread. . . . I. viii. 31. 9
He ghest his *nature* by his countenance, . . . I. viii. 34. 4
naked *nature* seemely to aray; . . . I. x. 39. 5
As incorrupted *Nature* did them sow, . . . I. xi. 47. 4
feeble *nature* cloth'd with fleshly tyre. . . . II. i. 57. 3
from their sourse indewd By great Dame *Nature*, . . . II. ii. 6. 2
wondrous strong by *nature*, . . . II. ii. 12. 9
art, stryving to compayre With *nature*, . . . II. v. 29. 2
From that which feeble *nature* covets faine: . . . II. vi. 1. 5
Whiles nothing envious *nature* them forth throwes . . . II. vi. 15. 4
to her mother *Nature* all her care she letts. . . . II. vi. 16. 9
eke of *nature* Soveraine, . . . II. vi. 17. 2
Of that seas *nature* did him not avise: . . . II. vi. 46. 5
Untroubled *Nature* doth her selfe suffise, . . . II. vii. 15. 4
hight Phantastes by his *nature* trew, . . . II. ix. 52. 2
Such as Dame *Nature* selfe mote feare to see, . . . II. xii. 23. 2
Such as by *nature* men abhorre and hate; . . . II. xii. 36. 3
Art, as halfe in scorne Of niggard *Nature*, . . . II. xii. 50. 7
nature had for wantonesse ensude Art, . . . II. xii. 59. 3
Art at *nature* did repine; . . . II. xii. 59. 4
When feeble *nature* felt her selfe opprest, . . . III. ii. 29. 3
From course of *nature* and of modestee? . . . III. ii. 41. 8
From love in course of *nature* to refraine. . . . III. iv. 26. 4
So faire a place as *Nature* can devize: . . . III. vi. 29. 3
Wherewith dame *Nature* doth her beautify, . . . III. vi. 30. 2
Old Genius, the which a double *nature* has. . . . III. vi. 31. 9
even *Nature* selfe envide the same, . . . III. viii. 5. 4
Shewing his *nature* in his countenaunce: . . . III. xii. 15. 5
all the powres of *nature*, . . . IV. ii. 44. 2
To spoyle so goodly workmanship of *nature*, . . . IV. vi. 17. 4
Her *nature* is all goodnesse to abuse, . . . IV. viii. 25. 1
nature had so well disguized Her worke, . . . IV. ix. 11. 3
she, whom *Nature* did so faire create . . . IV. ix. 16. 5
wall'd by *nature* gainst invaders wrong, . . . IV. x. 6. 3
all that *nature* by her mother-wit Could frame . . . IV. x. 21. 6
all that *nature* did omit, . . . IV. x. 21. 8
All which by *nature* made did *nature* selfe amaze. . . . IV. x. 24. 9
The secret cause and *nature* of his teene, . . . IV. xii. 21. 4
Expressing well his *nature* . . . V. i. 19. 9
With which wise *Nature* did them strongly bynd . . . V. v. 25. 3
Their dainty parts, which *nature* had created So faire . . . V. vii. 29. 6
bands of *nature*, that wilde beastes restraine, . . . V. xii. 1. 5
Whose *nature* is to grieve and grudge at all . . . V. xii. 31. 2
great helpe dame *Nature* selfe doth lend; . . . VI. ii. 2. 1
For knights and all men this by *nature* have, . . . VI. ii. 14. 8
senselesse words, which *nature* did him teach . . . VI. iv. 11. 8
For he was sterne and terrible by *nature*, . . . VI. vii. 41. 1
Nature me endu'd with plenteous dowre Of all her gifts, . . . VI. viii. 20. 3
being naked . . . The goodly threasures of *nature* appeare: . . . VI. viii. 41. 7
they to it fell With small adoe, and *nature* satisfyde, . . . VI. ix. 17. 8
So taught of *nature*, . . . VI. ix. 20. 6

Nature—*Continued.*
all which *Nature* had establisht first In good estate, ... VII. vi. 5. 2
Ne shee the lawes of *Nature* onely brake, ... VII. vi. 6. 1
To weet, the God of *Nature*, ... VII. vi. 35. 6
Nature soone Her righteous Doome areads. . . . . VII. vii. Arg.
Then forth issewed (great goddesse) great dame *Nature* . . . VII. vii. 5. 1
Great *Nature*, ever young, yet full of eld; . . . . VII. vii. 13. 2
Nature did yeeld thereto; . . . . VII. vii. 27. 8
Is checkt and changed from his *nature* trew, ... VII. vii. 54. 8
Ne *Nature* to or fro spake for a space, ... VII. vii. 57. 2
Then gin I thinke on that which *Nature* sayd, ... VII. viii. 2. 1
the worke of *Nature* or of Art, ... *Am.* xxi. 1
why hath *nature* . . . Given so goodly giftes . . . . *Am.* xxxi. 1
Is it her *nature*, or is it her will, ... *Am.* xli. 1
If *nature;* then she may it mend with skill: . . . . *Am.* xli. 3
if her *nature* and her wil be so, ... *Am.* xli. 5
we *nature* see of art Exceld, ... *H.B.* 83
all that faire is, is by *nature* good; . . . . *H.B.* 139
Whose *nature* yet so much is marvelled Of mortall wits, . . *H.H.B.* 166
With gifts of wit, and ornaments of *nature*, ... *Proth.* 171
Nature's. The huge Leviathan, dame *Natures* wonder, ... *Van.* v. 6
Waile ye this wofull waste of *Natures* warke; . . . . *S.C.* N. 64
can undoe Dame *Natures* kindly course; . . . . *S.C.* N. 124
To him that hath a whit of *Natures* giving? . . . . *Hub.* 418
Of *Natures* workes, of heavens continuall course, ... *Hub.* 764
judge of *Natures* cunning operation, ... *T.M.* 501
hast not seene least part of *natures* worke: . . . . *Col.* 293
if thou be, as thou art pourtrahed With *natures* pen, ... I. viii. 33. 8
by *Natures* cunning hand Bene choycely picked out . . . . . II. vi. 12. 3
best alyve, That *natures* worke by art can imitate: . . . . . II. xii. 42. 4
great Dame *Natures* handmaide chearing every kind. . . . . III. iv. 56. 9
The substaunces of *natures* fruitfull progenyes. . . . . . . III. vi. 36. 9
Gainst *natures* law and good behaveoure; . . . . III. vii. 49. 2
heavy eyes with *natures* burdein deare, ... III. xi. 55. 7
every secret worke of *natures* wayes; . . . . IV. ii. 35. 4
That peerelesse paterne of Dame *Natures* pride . . . . . . IV. vi. 24. 5
Art, playing second *natures* part, supplyed it. . . . . IV. x. 21. 9
So lavishly enricht with *Natures* threasure, ... IV. x. 23. 3
Not knowing *natures* worke, ... V. iii. 19. 6
He saw, . . . A miracle of *natures* goodly grace . . . . . . V. v. 12. 3
obaying *natures* first beheast. . . . . VI. iv. 14. 9
deckt with wondrous giftes of *natures* grace, ... VI. vii. 28. 5
Ne rested he himselfe, but *natures* dew, ... VI. ix. 3. 3
by *natures* skill Devized to worke delight . . . . VI. x. 5. 6
Yet gathering spirit of her *natures* pride, ... VII. vi. 26. 2
Before great *Natures* presence should appeare, ... VII. vi. 36. 3
Pealing from Jove to *Nature's* bar, ... VII. vii. Arg.
had not *Natures* Sergeant . . . Them well disposed . . . . VII. vii. 4. 6
Natur's selfe did vanish, ... VII. vii. 59. 9
Of *natures* skill the onely complement; . . . . *Am.* xxiv. 3
all her *natures* goodly guifts are lost: . . . . *Am.* xli. 8
The rest be works of *natures* wonderment: . . . . *Am.* lxxxi. 13
Natures. their *natures* bad appeard in both; . . . . II. ii. 34. 5
maladies, Whose names and *natures* I note readen well; . . . III. xii. 26. 2
of contrarie *natures* each to other: . . . . IV. x. 32. 5
your owne *natures* change; . . . . VII. vii. 54. 6
Thou canst not count, much lesse their *natures* aime; . . . . *H.H.B.* 33
Naught. *See* **Nought.**
Yet all for *naught:* such sight hath bred my bane. . . . . . *S.C.* Ja. 53
For *naught* caren that bene so lewdly bent. . . . . *S.C.* Ap. 157
naught on earth her griefe might pacifie; . . . . *T.M.* 356
prowdly threw to ground, as things of *naught;* . . . . I. vii. 18. 5
glauncing fel to ground, but him annoyed *naught.* . . . . . III. v. 24. 9
As if he *naught* but peace and pleasure ment, ... IV. iv. 7. 3
naught the same may calme ne mitigate, ... IV. viii. 1. 5
I count as *naught*, ... IV. x. 2. 7
if *naught* me let, I will be there . . . . V. ii. 4. 3
Sea, that *naught* doth spare, ... V. iv. 8. 2
naught may boot to banishe them . . . . V. xi. 45. 7
although it itched *naught:* . . . . V. xii. 30. 4
With chast affects that *naught* but death can sever; . . . . *Am.* vi. 12
That to the world *naught* else be counted deare; . . . . . . *Am.* viii. 4
Nausa. cald Paros, which before Hight *Nausa:* . . . . III. ix. 37. 2
Nausicle. built *Nausicle* by the Pontick shore; . . . . III. ix. 37. 3
Navy. by their huge *Navy* cast, ... *Gn.* 47
that they might Inflame the *Navie* of their enemies, ... *Gn.* 510
Nay. *Nay*, but thy seeing will not serve, ... *S.C.* Mar. 43
Nay, say I thereto, ... *S.C.* May 150
Nay, but sorrow close shrouded in hart, ... *S.C.* S. 15
Nay, better learne of hem that learned bee, ... *S.C.* N. 29
Nowe is time to dye: *Nay*, time was long ygoe: . . . . . . *S.C.* N. 81
'*Nay* . . . Sir Ape, you are astray: . . . . *Hub.* 1033
If cause requir'd, or els in sleepe, if *nay*, ... *D.* 130
'Ah! *nay* (said Colin) neither so, nor so: . . . . *Col.* 376
Nay, nay, thou greedy Tantalus,' . . . . II. vii. 60. 1
'*Nay* but the terme' (sayd he) 'is limited, ... III. iii. 44. 1
'*Nay*, let us first' (sayd Satyrane) . . . . III. ix. 9. 1
'Perdy, *nay*,' (said Malbecco) . . . . III. x. 39. 1
"*Nay*, but it fitteth best . . . . IV. x. 54. 6
'Ah! *nay*, Sir Knight,' (said she) 'it may not be, ... VI. viii. 30. 1
Ne (*partial list*). *See* **Not.**
ne yet of marble was the wall, ... *Bel.*[1] ii. 5
ne in ashes rest; . . . . *Ro.* i. 4
Ne ought save Tyber hastning to his fall . . . . *Ro.* iii. 11
Ne stroke on stroke . . . *Ne* rust . . . Nor wrath . . . . . *Ro.* xiii. 5, 6
Ne Afrike thereof guiltie is, nor Spaine, ... *Ro.* xxxi. 5
Ne ever was to Fortune foeman, ... *S.C.* F. 21
She mought *ne* gang on the greene. . . . . *S.C.* Mar. 57
Ne wote I how to cease it. . . . . *S.C.* Mar. 102
Ne durst againe his fyrye face out showe; . . . . *S.C.* Ap. 78

Ne—*Continued.*
Sorrowe *ne* neede be hastened on, ... *S.C.* May 152
Ne for all his worst, nor for his best, ... *S.C.* May 225
Ne strive to winne renowne, or passe . . . . *S.C.* Jun. 74
I wote *ne*, Hobbin, how I was bewitcht . . . . *S.C.* S. 74
Ne in good nor goodnes taken delight, ... *S.C.* S. 85
in myrth now list *ne* maske, ... *S.C.* N. 19
Ne would she scorne the simple shepheards . . . . *S.C.* N. 97
so as I *ne* wotte Whether rejoyce . . . . *S.C.* N. 204
Ne pictures beautie, ... *Gn.* 101
Ne ought the whelky pearles esteemeth hee, ... *Gn.* 105
Ne ever did her ey-sight turne arere, *Ne* ever spake, *ne* . . *Gn.* 468, 469
Ne was it so by institution . . . *ne* by the law of . . . . *Hub.* 144, 145
Ne tell a written word, *ne* write a letter, ... *Hub.* 383
Ne make one title worse, *ne* make one better: . . . . . . *Hub.* 384
Ne yet of Latine, *ne* of Greeke, ... *Hub.* 386
he would it drive away, *Ne* suffer it . . . . *Hub.* 828
Ne new ones could he easily provide, ... *Hub.* 929
Ne ever stayd in place, *ne* spake to wight, ... *Hub.* 938
ne none durst of him plaine, ... *Hub.* 1199
Ne would he anie let to have accesse . . . . *Hub.* 1201
Ne onely they that dwell in lowly dust, ... *T.M.* 67
Ne ever dare their dunghill thoughts aspire . . . . *T.M.* 393
Ne anie Poet seekes him to revive, ... *Ti.* 223
Which never was, *ne* ever with regard . . . . *Ti.* 347
ne ought gainesaid; . . . . *Mui.* 339
Ne anie noyse, *ne* anie motion made. . . . . *Mui.* 400
Ne fear'd the Wolfe, *ne* fear'd the wildest beast, ... *D.* 135
Ne will I lodge, *ne* will I ever lin, *Ne*, ... *D.* 467, 468
Ne is there place for any gentle wit, ... *Col.* 707
His forces faile, *ne* can no lenger fight: . . . . I. i. 22. 3
Ne dare to weepe, ... I. iii. 20. 7
ne would no lenger stay: . . . . I. iii. 39. 9
ne ought he feares To be partaker . . . . I. iii. 44. 7
Ne Persia selfe, . . . Like ever saw. . . . . I. iv. 7. 6
Ne scarse good morsell all his life did taste, ... I. iv. 28. 3
childe *ne* kinsman living had he none . . . . I. iv. 28. 6
forth she rose, *ne* lenger would abide, ... I. v. 19. 3
ne dares To joy at his foolhappie oversight: . . . . I. vi. 1. 5
Ne let vaine words . . . *Ne* divelish thoughts . . . . I. ix. 53. 2, 3
Ne in her speach, *ne* in her haviour, Was lightnesse seene . II. ii. 15. 3
fled attonce, *ne* ever backe retourned eye; . . . . II. iii. 19. 9
Ne Ladies loves, *ne* sweete entreaties, might Appease . . . . II. v. 38. 3
Ne care, *ne* feare I how the wind do blow, ... II. vi. 10. 4
nether spinnes nor cards, *ne* cares nor fretts, ... II. vi. 16. 8
Ne tong did tell, *ne* hand these handled not; . . . . II. vii. 19. 7
Ne darkenesse him, *ne* daunger might dismay. . . . . . . II. vii. 26. 4
Ne Mammon would there let him long remayne, ... II. vii. 63. 3
Ne had they footing found at last, ... II. x. 48. 5
Ne like in grace, *ne* like in learned skill; . . . . II. x. 76. 7
Ne was there salve, *ne* was there medicine, ... II. xi. 21. 8
Ne hedge *ne* ditch his readie passage brake; . . . . II. xi. 26. 5
Ne ever shroncke, *ne* ever sought to bayt . . . . II. xi. 29. 7
Yet no'te the same amend, *ne* yet withstond, ... II. xii. 57. 7
Ne wonder; for the heavens . . . . V. Pr. 4. 6
Ne is the earth the lesse, ... V. ii. 39. 6
ne ought he sayd, *Ne* ought he did, ... V. iii. 18. 5, 6
Yet nould she hearke, *ne* let him once respyre, ... V. v. 16. 7
Ne either sought the others strokes to shun, ... V. vii. 29. 3
Ne day nor night did ever idly rest; . . . . V. viii. 3. 7
Ne none can backe returne . . . . V. ix. 6. 9
Ne day nor night did sleepe t' attend them on, ... V. x. 10. 4
Ne none can find . . . . VI. Pr. 2. 9
Ne ever shewed signe of foule disloyalty. . . . . VI. v. 9. 9
Ne ever Knight . . . *Ne* ever Lady . . . . VI. vi. 12. 7, 8
Ne ever armes *ne* ever knighthood dare . . . professe; . . . VI. vi. 36. 3
wore no armour, *ne* for none did care, ... VI. vii. 43. 1
ne ought partake, But he himselfe . . . . VI. xi. 12. 4
Neaera. Ne lesse praise-worthie faire *Neaera* is, ... *Col.* 524
Neaera ours, not theirs, ... *Col.* 525
Near. Typhoeus sister comming *neare;* . . . . *Bel.*[2] xv. 4
with their sweetnes I was ravish't *nere.* . . . . *Pet.*[2] iii. 7
those sights empassion me full *nere* . . . . *Van.* i. 12
The subtill vermin, creeping closely *neare*, ... *Van.* vi. 7
sighed to see his *neare* overthrow. . . . . *S.C.* F. 216
For nowe no succoure was seene him *nere.* . . . . *S.C.* F. 228
With your ayd to fore-stall my *neere* decay.' . . . . *S.C.* May 273
all that may augment My doole, draw *neare!* . . . . *S.C.* Au. 165
my selfe am touched *neare:* . . . . *Hub.* 74
Which when the Priest beheld, he vew'd it *nere*, ... *Hub.* 379
spite bites *neare.* . . . . *Hub.* 424
everie field and forrest farre and *nere*, ... *Hub.* 578
Scarse anie left to close his eylids *neare;* . . . . *Ti.* 194
garments gathered *neare;* . . . . *Mui.* 284
Approaching nigh, his face I vewed *nere*, ... *D.* 50
Daylie resort to me from farre and *neare*, ... *D.* 143
when as drouping Titan draweth *neere* . . . . *D.* 468
they all gan throng about him *neare*, ... *Col.* 52
all this countrie, farre and *neare.*' . . . . I. i. 31. 4
Did fayre avoide the violence him *nere:* . . . . I. viii. 7. 8
ne durst approchen *neare;* . . . . I. ix. 34. 8
whenas they now approched *neare*, ... I. xi. 1. 4
couched *neare* That nought mote perce; . . . . I. xi. 9. 2
bidding bold defyaunce to his foeman *neare.* . . . . I. xi. 15. 9
he him advaunced *neare.* . . . . I. xi. 52. 9
her foolehardy chyld Did come too *neare*, ... I. xii. 11. 2
To tell that dawning day is drawing *neare*, ... I. xii. 21. 7
That seemd like silke and silver woven *neare;* . . . . I. xii. 22. 8
bad me call Lucina to me *neare.* . . . . II. i. 53. 5
suffred not their blowes to byte him *nere*, ... II. ii. 23. 3

Near—*Continued.*
to worke her to his will more *neare*, . . . II. iv. 25. 5
Ne should faire Claribell . . . approch thee *neare:* . . . II. iv. 26. 6
It booted nought Sir Guyon, comming *neare*, . . . II. v. 3. 8
preaced to draw *nere* To th' upper part, . . . II. vii. 44. 3
approched *neare* Where Guyon lay in traunce; . . . II. viii. 3. 5
Throughout the world, renowmed far and *neare*, . . . II. ix. 4. 4
save your selves from *neare* decay; . . . II. ix. 12. 3
Their visages imprest when they approched *neare*. . . . II. xi. 5. 9
now it gan to threaten *neare* decay: . . . II. xi. 14. 5
labour lost it was to weene approch him *neare*. . . . II. xi. 25. 9
once hath failed of her souse full *neare*, . . . II. xi. 36. 7
he drew him *neare*, . . . II. xii. 65. 7
to him beckned to approch more *neare*, . . . II. xii. 68. 8
gathering him rownd about more *neare*, . . . III. i. 23. 3
sent out of the thicket *neare* A cruell shaft, . . . III. v. 20. 3
lay bleding out his hart-blood *neare*. . . . III. v. 32. 9
To seeke the fugitive both farre and *neare*. . . . III. vi. 26. 4
He *nere* was touched in his noble spright, . . . III. vii. 43. 8
the sharpe hauke which her attached *neare*, . . . III. viii. 33. 4
He was compeld to seeke some refuge *neare*, . . . III. ix. 13. 2
he sought her far and *nere*, . . . III. x. 19. 6
shrieking Hububs them approching *nere*, . . . III. x. 43. 3
he has gotten to a forrest *neare*, . . . III. xi. 6. 6
by him *neare* His haberjeon, . . . III. xi. 7. 4
Those feeling words so *neare* the quicke did goe, . . . III. xi. 15. 7
Ne none can suffer to approchen *neare:* . . . III. xi. 22. 5
Woven with gold and silke, so close and *nere* . . . III. xi. 28. 3
having once escaped perill *neare*, . . . IV. i. 34. 8
that Squire . . . viewing them more *neare*, . . . IV. ii. 31. 4
overthrew what ever came her *neare*, . . . IV. iv. 46. 7
soone as she him saw approching *neare* . . . IV. vi. 10. 3
Throwes forth upon the rivage round about him *nere*. . . . IV. vi. 20. 9
to them drew *nere*, . . . IV. vi. 25. 3
I cal'd her loud, I sought her farre and *neare*, . . . IV. vi. 36. 8
he her must hurt, or hazard *neare:* . . . IV. vii. 27. 4
stay Till she drew *neare*, . . . IV. viii. 11. 3
Amoret, so *neare* unto decay, . . . IV. viii. 20. 4
before the harme came *neare:* . . . IV. viii. 42. 4
ere that it to him approched *neare*, . . . IV. viii. 44. 7
to his castle they approched *neare;* . . . IV. ix. 5. 5
counterfet her selfe so *nere*, . . . IV. ix. 11. 4
I to her stepped *neare*, . . . IV. x. 53. 8
farre and *neare* the Nymph his mother sought, . . . IV. xi. 6. 1
To which no wit of man may comen *neare;* . . . IV. xi. 10. 5
joyne in neighbourhood of kingdome *nere*, . . . IV. xi. 40. 3
I will them tell though unto no man *neare:* . . . IV. xii. 6. 4
lowest hell, to which I lie most *neare*, . . . IV. xii. 6. 7
Artegall pursewd him still so *neare* . . . V. ii. 18. 1
she feared The sad effect of her *neare* overthrow; . . . V. ii. 22. 4
In sdeignfull wize he drew unto him *neare*, . . . V. ii. 33. 8
weighed out in ballaunces so *nere*, . . . V. ii. 35. 3
To whom when he approched *neare* in sight, . . . V. iv. 21. 6
now the Knights, being arrived *neare*, . . . V. iv. 37. 1
Till thou have tride againe, and tempted him more *neare*. . . V. v. 48. 9
when she reckned them, still drawing *neare*, . . . V. vi. 5. 8
He comming *neare* gan gently her salute . . . V. vi. 20. 1
Uppon two stubborne oakes, which stand so *neare* . . . V. vi. 40. 2
he so *neare* her drew . . . V. vii. 16. 4
Having by chaunce espide advantage *neare*, . . . V. vii. 32. 2
In hope some stroke to fasten on him *neare*, . . . V. viii. 33. 2
Cannot come *neare* him in the covert wood, . . . V. viii. 35. 7
Which when the Damzell *neare* at hand did spy, . . . V. ix. 8. 3
The other on the other side, and *neare* them none. . . . V. ix. 37. 9
With the *neare* touch whereof in tender hart . . . V. ix. 46. 1
brest was touched *nere* With piteous ruth . . . V. ix. 50. 1
Ere that huge stroke arrived on him *neare*, . . . V. xi. 10. 5
He drawing *neare* began to greete them faire, . . . V. xi. 48. 2
with mortall malice him pursu'd so *nere*. . . . V. xi. 48. 9
Abasht at his rebuke, that bit her *neare*, . . . V. xi. 64. 2
Weening her lifes last howre then *neare* to bee, . . . V. xii. 11. 8
Under his stroke he to him stepping *neare* . . . V. xii. 20. 4
her dwelling Was *neare* to Envie, . . . V. xii. 35. 6
Then th' other comming *neare* gan him revile, . . . V. xii. 40. 1
unto his hand in chase did happen *neare*. . . . VI. ii. 6. 9
Thence they him carried to a Castle *neare*, . . . VI. ii. 48. 7
All sodainely out of the forrest *nere* . . . VI. iii. 24. 1
knowing that her Knight now *neare* did draw, . . . VI. iii. 26. 3
At last some fisher-barke doth *neare* behold, . . . VI. iv. 1. 4
left that couple *nere* their utmost cast: . . . VI. iv. 9. 5
With him to wend unto his wonning *neare;* . . . VI. iv. 13. 3
without weapon him assayling *neare*, . . . VI. iv. 20. 3
He sought him farre and *neare*, . . . VI. v. 3. 9
in some stable *neare* did set him up to feede. . . . VI. vi. 19. 9
Approching to him *neare*, his hand he stayd, . . . VI. vi. 39. 2
Yet would not *neare* approch in daungers eye, . . . VI. vii. 3. 2
a straunge knight, that *neare* afore him went, . . . VI. vii. 4. 4
when he saw those two so *neare* him stand, . . . VI. vii. 24. 1
snatching *neare* his syde His trustie sword, . . . VI. vii. 25. 3
He left his lofty steede to aide him *neare;* . . . VI. viii. 12. 7
Now here, now there, and oft him *neare* he mist; . . . VI. viii. 13. 7
him supported standing *neare*. . . . VI. viii. 25. 9
approaching *neare* he plainely found . . . VI. viii. 27. 5
Whose sensefull words empierst his hart so *neare*, . . . VI. ix. 26. 3
seeing him to mourne, Drew *neare*, . . . VI. x. 18. 9
had bene to her succour *nere*. . . . VI. xi. 33. 9
And all that *nere* him came did hew and slay, . . . VI. xi. 49. 4
Unto the Prince of Picteland, bordering *nere;* . . . VI. xii. 4. 6
A thousand times she her embraced *nere*, . . . VI. xii. 20. 8
searched all their cels and secrets *neare:* . . . VI. xii. 24. 4

Near—*Continued.*
he him fast pursuing soone approched *neare*. . . . VI. xii. 25. 9
strained him so streightly that he chokt him *neare*. . . . VI. xii. 33. 9
Water fights With Fire, . . . approaching *neere:* . . . VII. vii. 25. 8
fire, Kindled above unto the Maker *neere;* . . . *Am.* viii. 2
Sweet is the Eglantine, but pricketh *nere;* . . . *Am.* xxvi. 3
of the sea that neighbours to her *neare:* . . . *Epith.* 39
With your steele darts doo chace from comming *neer;* . . . *Epith.* 70
Venice, . . . next to them in beauty draweth *neare*, . . . *Com. Son.* iv. 11
striveth still T' approch more *neare*, . . . *H.L.* 248
As to the Highest they approch more *neare*, . . . *H.H.B.* 100
Could once come *neare* this beauty soverayne. . . . *H.H.B.* 217
not so white as these, nor nothing *neare;* . . . *Proth.* 45
Hercules two pillors standing *neere* . . . *Proth.* 148

Nearer. *See* **Nar.**
nearer wayes I knowe. . . . *S.C.* Jul. 96
they, that are great Clerkes, have *nearer* wayes, . . . *Hub.* 537
I should see that would me *nearer* move, . . . II. iv. 24. 8
He closely *nearer* crept the truth to weet: . . . III. x. 22. 6
he stayd, till that he *nearer* drew, . . . VI. iii. 47. 1
Yet nought the *nearer* to his journeys end, . . . VI. iv. 25. 6

Nearest. they that shooten *neerest* the pricke . . . *S.C.* S. 122
Furthest from end then, when they *neerest* weene, . . . I. i. 10. 6
crost the *nearest* way, . . . III. vii. 38. 3
hast to crosse him by the *nearest* way, . . . IV. vii. 25. 2
she did call Her *nearest* handmayd, . . . V. v. 29. 2

Nearly. thee fierce Fortune did so *nearely* drive, . . . II. xi. 30. 8

Nearness. Both for your *nearnes* to that Faerie Queene . . . *Ded. Son.* xi. 6

Neast. *See* **Nest.**

Neat. fresh springing wells, as christall *neate*, . . . *Gn.* 119
yet inly *neate* and clene, . . . VI. v. 38. 4
Whereas the Heardes were keeping of their *neat*, . . . VI. ix. 4. 2

Necessaries. huckster man, That wont provide his *necessaries*, *Hub.* 926

Necessities. serve their owne *necessities* with others need. . . VI. viii. 35. 9

Necessity. who can . . . breake the chayne of strong *necessitee*, I. v. 25. 5
Who then can strive with strong *necessitie*, . . . I. ix. 42. 6
when they stood in most *necessitee*, . . . I. x. 43. 8
'Unhappy falls that hard *necessity*,' . . . I. xii. 19. 1
When as *necessitie* doth it constraine.' . . . V. xi. 56. 5
of *necessity* His course of Justice he was forst to stay, . . . V. xii. 27. 3

Neck. she her *neck* wreath'd from them . . . *Bel.*[2] vi. 4
Mought her *necke* bene joynted attones, . . . *S.C.* Mar. 53
Adowne whose *necke*, in terrible array, . . . *Gn.* 347
in the *necke* of all the world did ride? . . . *Ti.* 74
And in the *neck* of all the world to rayne; . . . *Ded. Son.* i. 4
like a Crane his *necke* was long and fyne . . . I. iv. 21. 5
beast, Who on his *neck* his bloody clawes did seize, . . . I. viii. 15. 2
yeeldes his caytive *neck* to victours most despight. . . . I. ix. 11. 9
About his *neck* an hempen rope he weares, . . . I. ix. 22. 7
Her *necke* and brests were ever open bare, . . . I. x. 30. 7
glauncing from his scaly *necke* . . . I. xi. 20. 6
glauncing fell On his horse *necke* . . . II. v. 4. 5
fresh flowrets dight About her *necke*, . . . II. vi. 7. 5
Upon great Neptunes *necke* they softly swim, . . . III. iv. 42. 8
His double folded *necke* she reard upright, . . . III. v. 31. 6
Upon whose stubborne *neck*, . . . She fastned hath her foot; III. ix. 45. 3
did bind About the turtles *necke*, . . . IV. viii. 7. 3
all about her *necke* and shoulders . . . IV. x. 42. 1
round about his *necke* an halter tight, . . . V. iv. 22. 3
in his *necke* Her proud foote setting, . . . V. iv. 40. 2
his owne waight his *necke* asunder broke, . . . V. viii. 8. 3
in her *necke* a Castle huge had made, . . . V. x. 25. 8
There he the *necke* thereof did cut in twaine, . . . VI. iii. 17. 5
His foot he set on his vile *necke*, . . . VI. vii. 26. 4
He in his *necke* had set his foote with fell disdaine. . . . VI. viii. 10. 9
Her yvorie *neck;* her alablaster brest; . . . VI. viii. 42. 1
with one fall his *necke* he almost brake; . . . VI. ix. 44. 3
The whiles her foot she in my *necke* doth place, . . . *Am.* xx. 3
Her *neck*, lyke to a bounch of Cullambynes; . . . *Am.* lxiv. 10
Her snowie *necke* lyke to a marble towre; . . . *Epith.* 177

Necked. *See* **Snowy-necked.**

Necks. Fell straight about their *neckes* as they did kneele, . V. x. 20. 2

Nectar. There drincks she *Nectar* with Ambrosia mixt, . . . *S.C.* N. 195
Large streames of honnie and sweete *Nectar* flowe, . . . *T.M.* 218
On *Nectar* and Ambrosia do feede. . . . *Ti.* 399
Few drops, more cleare then *Nectar*, . . . II. xii. 78. 4
that sweete verse, with *Nectar* sprinckeled, . . . III. Pr. 4. 4
with sweet *Nectar* she did sprinkle him. . . . III. i. 36. 9
They pourd in soveraine balme and *Nectar* good, . . . III. iv. 40. 8
In blessed *Nectar* and pure Pleasures well, . . . III. xi. 2. 4
More sweet than *Nectar*, or Ambrosiall meat, . . . *Am.* xxxix. 13
kisse, That sweeter farre then any *Nectar* is; . . . *H.L.* 26
Where they doe feede on *Nectar* heavenly-wize, . . . *H.L.* 282
Like Gods with *Nectar* in their bankets free; . . . *H.B.* 249

Nectar-dewed. he shooke His *Nectar-deawed* locks, . . . VII. vi. 30. 7

Need. She shoulde have *neede* no more spell; . . . *S.C.* Mar. 54
if *neede* were, pitied would be, . . . *S.C.* May 59
Sorrowe ne *neede* be hastened on, . . . *S.C.* May 152
They *neede* not Melampode: . . . *S.C.* Jul. 106
What *neede* hem caren for their flocks, . . . *S.C.* Jul. 195
Driven for *neede* to come home agayne. . . . *S.C.* S. 67
Neede feare no chaunge of frowning fate; . . . *S.C.* S. 71
To Pan his owne selfe pype I *neede* not yield: . . . *S.C.* D. 46
whatso theretoo did *neede* Each did prepare, . . . *Hub.* 106
Of such deep learning little had he *neede*, . . . *Hub.* 385
we *need* to doo no more. . . . *Hub.* 436
thy wretched *need* Praiseth the thing . . . *Hub.* 595
feare he *neede* no force of enemie. . . . *Hub.* 1126
where were ye, when he of you had *need*, . . . *As.* 131
Small needments else *need* shepheard to prepare. . . . *Col.* 195

Need—*Continued.*
all things else that living creatures *need*. . . . *Col.* 299
For thereunto doth *need* a golden quill, . . . *Ded.Son.*xvi.10
Whose *need* had end, but no end covetise; . . . I. iv. 29. 3
ne you the like *need* to reherce. . . . I. iv. 50. 9
to tell her lamentable cace, . . . will *need* another place. I. vi. 48. 9
His mightie Armour, missing most at *need;* . . . I. vii. 19. 5
none did . . . aid envy to him in *need* that stands; . . . I. ix. 1. 6
'Thou, wretched man, of death hast greatest *need,* . . . I. ix. 45. 1
He feard not once himselfe to be in *need,* . . . I. x. 38. 4
what *need* him care for more? . . . I. x. 38. 8
'What *need* of armes, where peace doth ay remaine,' . . . I. x. 62. 7
shall finde friends, if *need* requireth soe. . . . I. xii. 28. 8
Hard help at *need!* So deare thee, babe, I bought; . . . II. i. 53. 8
of her plenty adde unto their *need:* . . . II. ii. 38. 8
Should *neede* of all his armes him to defend, . . . II. iii. 17. 4
The measure of her meane and naturall first *need*. . . . II. vii. 16. 9
All that I *need* I have: . . . II. vii. 39. 3
that straunge sword refusd to serve his *neede,* . . . II. viii. 49. 2
With hookes and ladles, as *need* did requyre; . . . II. ix. 30. 7
May often *need* the helpe of weaker hand; . . . II. xi. 30. 2
never fayld At *need* till now, . . . II. xi. 41. 7
his feeble vaines . . . served not his *need,* . . . II. xi. 48. 4
Need but behold the pourtraict of her hart; . . . III. Pr. 1. 8
'what *need* ye be dismayd? . . . III. ii. 40. 1
More *neede* of leach-crafte hath your Damozell, . . . III. iii. 17. 5
(*need* makes good schollers) . . . III. iii. 53. 3
*our weake hands (whom *need* new strength shall teach) . . . III. iii. 53. 3
'Fly they, that *need* to fly; . . . III. iv. 15. 2
'What had th' eternall Maker *need* of thee . . . III. iv. 56. 1
ne her *need* implore Lucinaes aide: . . . III. vi. 27. 3
so much as doth *need* must needs be counted here. . . . III. vi. 30. 9
Ne doe they *need* with water of the ford, . . . III. vi. 34. 7
Need teacheth her this lesson hard and rare, . . . III. vii. 4. 3
No *need* to bid her fast away to flie: . . . III. vii. 24. 2
fear gave her wings, and *need* her corage taught. . . . III. vii. 26. 9
Such as no doubt of him he *neede* misdeeme.' . . . III. ix. 6. 5
Was for like *need* enforst to disaray: . . . III. ix. 20. 2
The loving couple *neede* no reskew feare, . . . III. x. 16. 3
ne did *need* Straunge horrour to deforme . . . III. xii. 11. 3
as *neede* required, . . . sought to have assuaged . . . IV. i. 54. 2
In no lesse *neede* of helpe then him he weend. . . . IV. iv. 45. 4
it here doth *neede* The hard adventures . . . to tell, . . . IV. v. 28. 7
It shall not fayle when so ye shall it *need*.' . . . IV. vi. 8. 8
Walkt through the wood, for pleasure or for *need;* . . . IV. vii. 4. 2
neede, that answers not to all requests, . . . IV. viii. 27. 3
to the present *neede* it wisely usd. . . . IV. viii. 60. 4
Here *neede* you to remember, . . . IV. xi. 2. 1
nor brasen locke, Did *neede* to gard from force, . . . IV. xi. 3. 4
For love of Nymphes she thought she *need* not care, . . . IV. xii. 27. 4
Him for to aide, if aide he chaunst to *neede,* . . . V. i. 13. 2
By law of armes there *neede* ones right to trie, . . . V. iii. 32. 2
Had *neede* have mightie hands . . . V. iv. 1. 3
Thereof make tryall in my greatest *need*. . . . V. v. 29. 6
With hope of helpe in that her greatest *neede*. . . . V. x. 22. 5
What other meed, then, *need* me to requight, . . . V. xi. 17. 7
'to assist me now at *need* . . . V. xi. 57. 2
if *need* constraine, His hope of refuge used to remaine: . . . VI. i. 22. 4
since ye mercie now doe *need* to crave, . . . VI. i. 42. 4
some forrein land, where as no *need* Of dreaded daunger . . . VI. ii. 29. 8
that wounded Knight in his great *need,* . . . VI. iii. 2. 5
Besought of courtesie, in that his *neede,* . . . VI. iii. 31. 2
in his extreamest *neede,* . . . VI. iii. 46. 5
had he not in his extreamest *need* Bene helped . . . VI. iv. 8. 4
wont to . . . wend on foot for *need,* . . . VI. iv. 19. 5
To whom she thus: 'What *need* me, Sir, to tell . . . VI. iv. 28. 1
'Nathlesse,' (quoth he) 'if *need* doe not you bynd, . . . VI. iv. 28. 6
she did th' assistance *need* Of this her groome; . . . VI. v. 10. 4
Finde harbour fit to comfort her great *neede;* . . . VI. v. 31. 4
sith we *need* good counsell,' . . . VI. vi. 13. 8
Would not her leave alone in her great *need*. . . . VI. vi. 16. 5
As he unable were for very *neede* To move one foote, . . . VI. vi. 19. 6
if they would afford him ayde at *need* . . . VI. vii. 4. 6
serve their owne necessities with others *need*. . . . VI. viii. 35. 9
The knight was nothing nice, where was no *need,* . . . VI. ix. 7. 1
nature, which doth litle *need* Of forreine helpes . . . VI. ix. 20. 6
for *need,* he did assay . . . their rugged teats to hold, . . . VI. ix. 37. 7
her *need* give lone Of her faire light . . . VII. vi. 11. 7
A greater craftesmans hand thereto doth *neede,* . . . *Am.* xvii. 13
Such selfe-assurance *need* not feare . . . *Am.* lix. 9
Hart *need* not wish none other happinesse, . . . *Am.* lxxii. 13
Thy tyred steedes long since have *need* of rest. . . . *Epith.* 284
make thee more propitious in my *need,* . . . *H.L.* 9
That *need* no Sunne t' illuminate their spheres, . . . *H.H.B.* 69
Needed. nought my praises of her *needed* arre, . . . *Col.* 533
To these first labours *needed* furtheraunce. . . . *Ded. Son.* ii. 14
His long endured famine *needed* more reliefe. . . . I. viii. 43. 9
Him *needed* not long call; . . . II. vi. 19. 4
Me litle *needed* from my right way to have straid.' . . . II. vi. 22. 9
helpe, he saw, he *needed* more Then pitty, . . . II. vi. 48. 8
Of all that *needed* them to be inquird, . . . III. iii. 51. 2
Th' old woman nought that *needed* did omit, . . . III. iii. 58. 1
Him *needed* not instruct which way were best . . . III. viii. 8. 5
That *needed* much her weake age to desire, . . . IV. v. 39. 8
thrise have *needed* for the nonce Them to have stricken, . . . V. xi. 14. 3
rather *needed* to be disciplinde . . . VI. vi. 5. 6
Thereto, when *needed,* she could weepe and pray, . . . VI. vi. 42. 5
Needeth. Him *needeth* not to seeke for usage right Of line, . . . *Ro.* xxvi. 2
(Ay little helpe to harme there *needeth!*) . . . *S.C.* F. 198
Much *needeth* all shepheards hem to knowe. . . . *S.C.* May 313

Needeth—*Continued.*
not good Dogges hem *needeth* to chace, . . . *S.C.* S. 166
To doo their kindly services as *needeth*. . . . *Hub.* 273
What *needeth* perill to be sought abroad, . . . *As.* 89
what *needeth* shee . . . To heare thee sing, . . . *Col.* 368
Now *needeth* him no lenger labour spend, . . . I. i. 26. 8
them most *needeth* comfort in the end, . . . I. x. 41. 3
what *needeth* mee To covet more . . . II. vii. 39. 3
what *needeth* thee to eke my payne? . . . III. ii. 35. 2
Two eies him *needeth,* for to watch and wake, . . . III. ix. 31. 7
when most us *needeth* rest, . . . IV. iv. 12. 3
Him *needeth* sure a golden pen, I weene, . . . IV. v. 12. 2
ne *needeth* other none. . . . IV. x. 41. 9
Onely what *needeth* shall be here fulfild, . . . IV. xi. 17. 7
'Certes me *needeth* more To crave the same; . . . V. viii. 13. 7
since this Ladie . . . *needeth* safegard . . . VI. ii. 38. 2
When day is spent, and rest us *needeth* most, . . . VI. iii. 39. 2
me *needeth* to declare What did betide . . . VI. xii. 14. 2
Gaynst such strong castles *needeth* greater might . . . *Am.* xiv. 5
What *needeth* you to seeke so farre . . . *Am.* xv. 4
sterve their harts that *needeth* nourture most, . . . *H.L.* 39
Needful. (large breath in armes most *needfull*) . . . *Hub.* 745
Findes all things *needfull* for contentment meeke, . . . *Hub.* 911
Nor ordinaunce so *needfull,* but that hee Would violate, . . . *Hub.* 1162
Voide of all succour and *needfull* comfort; . . . II. v. 17. 5
Both were full loth to leave that *needfull* tent, . . . III. ix. 14. 1
servd of all things that mote *needfull* bee; . . . III. ix. 19. 2
With more then *needfull* naturall remorse, . . . V. x. 4. 8
He all things did purvay which for them *needfull* weare. . . V. xii. 10. 9
in this her *needfull* state, To succour her . . . VI. ii. 38. 3
naked, without *needfull* vestiments . . . VI. iv. 4. 4
armes . . . Whose burden mote empeach his *needfull* speed, . VI. iv. 19. 2
Needing. now *needing* strong defence, . . . V. x. 12. 6
The which did her command without *needing* perswade. . . V. x. 25. 9
Needle. His little *needle* there infixing deep, . . . *Gn.* 287
workes with loome, with *needle,* and with quill. . . . *Mui.* 272
his angry *needle* shott Quite through his shield, . . . I. xi. 38. 5
To finger the fine *needle* and nyce thread, . . . III. ii. 6. 8
Needles. More sharpe then points of *needles,* . . . IV. viii. 39. 2
Needless. all those *needlesse* works are laid away; . . . *Hub.* 455
disswaded them from *needlesse* feare, . . . *Hub.* 1075
to the Dwarfe a while his *needlesse* spere he gave. . . . I. i. 11. 9
Ne let vaine feares procure your *needlesse* smart, . . . I. i. 54. 4
needlesse dread for to remove away, . . . I. iii. 14. 6
needlesse feare did never vantage none; . . . I. iv. 49. 4
From *needlesse* trouble of renewing fight . . . II. v. 25. 2
waste thy joyous howres in *needelesse* paine, . . . II. vi. 17. 4
Long worke it were, and *needlesse,* . . . III. i. 42. 1
To doe away vaine doubt and *needlesse* dreed: . . . III. iv. 48. 7
'Faire Sir, be nought dismayd With *needlesse* dread, . . . IV. vi. 37. 7
rather bent To peace then *needlesse* trouble to constraine, . V. vi. 19. 7
speare and shield, as things that *needlesse* were, . . . VI. iv. 7. 8
from the trees did lop the *needlesse* spray: . . . VII. vii. 42. 7
Needments. Small *needments* else need shepheard to prepare. *Col.* 195
her bag Of *needments* at his backe. . . . I. i. 6. 4
in which his *needments* he did bind. . . . I. vi. 35. 9
Needs. *Needes* must he all eternitie survive, . . . *Ro.* Env. 7
Who touches Pitch, mought *needes* be defilde; . . . *S.C.* May 74
little *needes* to strow my store, . . . *S.C.* Jul. 75
Such ill, as is forced, mought *nedes* be endured. . . . *S.C.* S. 139
Mought *needes* decay, when it is at best. . . . *S.C.* S. 241
the budde eke *needes* must quaile; . . . *S.C.* N. 91
No Muses aide me *needes* heretoo to call; . . . *Hub.* 43
things miscounselled must *needs* miswend. . . . *Hub.* 128
Through manie haps, which *needs* not here to tell, . . . *Hub.* 360
there thou *needs* must learne to laugh, to lie, . . . *Hub.* 505
The Courtier *needes* must recompenced bee . . . *Hub.* 516
Needes anie more to learne to get a living?' . . . *Hub.* 544
all the rest must *needs* be left behinde: . . . *Ti.* 586
it must *needs* to issue come? . . . *Mui.* 227
' "I . . . must *needes* depart from thee, . . . *D.* 269
to dye must *needes* be joyeous, . . . *D.* 451
To which him *needs* a guilefull hollow hart, . . . *Col.* 699
use his ydle name to other *needs,* . . . *Col.* 789
And *needs* his priest t' expresse his powre divine. . . . *Col.* 838
Much more me *needs* . . . To sharpe my sence . . . *Ded. Son.* xvii. 5
What then must *needs* be donne, . . . I. ix. 47. 6
to relieve the *needes* Of wretched soules, . . . I. x. 3. 6
death will never come when *needes* require. . . . I. xi. 28. 5
What *needes* me tell their feast and goodly guize, . . . I. xii. 14. 1
What *needes* of dainty dishes to devize, . . . I. xii. 14. 3
Els mote it *needes* . . . Have cleft his head in twaine, . . . II. viii. 33. 8
More ample spirit . . . Here *needes* me, . . . II. x. 1. 7
yonder way We *needes* must pas . . . II. xii. 3. 3
they *needes* must passen by, . . . II. xii. 14. 4
what *needes* me fetch from Faery . . . III. Pr. 1. 3
needs love or death must bee thy lott, . . . III. ii. 46. 7
'Glauce, what *needes* this colourable word . . . III. iii. 19. 3
what *needes* her to toyle, . . . III. iii. 25. 4
needes it must be wrackt On the rough rocks, . . . III. iv. 9. 3
so much as doth need must *needs* be counted here. . . . III. vi. 30. 9
Ne *needs* there Gardiner to sett or sow, . . . III. vi. 34. 1
Therfore *needs* mote he live, that living gives to all. . . . III. vi. 47. 9
all carelesse of her *needes;* . . . III. vii. 6. 5
'*needes* thou wilt Thy daies abridge . . . III. viii. 18. 1
To house a guest that would be *needes* obayd, . . . III. x. 2. 3
'To tell' (quoth she) 'that what ye see, *needs* not; . . . IV. vii. 14. 8
if it chaunst, (as *needs* it must in fight) . . . IV. vii. 26. 6
When so it *needs* with rigour to dispence: . . . V. i. 7. 5
Some blisfull houres at last must *needes* appeare; . . . V. iii. 1. 4

Needs—*Continued.*
'Then sith ye *needs*' (quoth he) 'will know my shame, . . . V. iv. 28. 6
'The tidings sad . . . will *needs,* I see, be rad. . . . . . . V. vi. 10. 5
now *neede*s will ye sleepe? . . . . V. vi. 25. 6
if two met, the one mote *needes* fall over the lidge. . . . . V. vi. 36. 9
yet they *needs* must passe that way, ... VI. i. 13. 6
When so she lagged, as she *needs* mote so, ... VI. ii. 10. 6
if he *needes* will fight, crave leave till morne, ... VI. iii. 41. 6
'Sith then ye *needs* will know the griefe I hoord, ... VI. iv. 29. 2
By straunge occasion that here *needs* forth be set. . . . . VI. v. 11. 9
with him eke the salvage, . . . Would *needes* depart; . . . . VI. v. 41. 9
needes wise read and discipline, ... VI. vi. 13. 3
greater force there *needs* to maintaine wrong then right. . . VI. vi. 35. 9
needs with him streight to the place would ryde, ... VI. vii. 17. 2
I *needes* must by all meanes fulfill This penaunce, ... VI. viii. 30. 2
Could not maligne him, but commend him *needs;* . . . . . VI. ix. 45. 4
It could not boot: *needs* mote she die at last. . . . . VI. xi. 32. 2
wouldest *needs* thine owne conceit areed! . . . . VII. vi. 46. 8
sith I *needs* must follow thy behest, ... VII. vii. 2. 1
she will the conquest challeng *needs,* . . . . *Am.* xxix. 9
needs another Element inquire Whereof she mote be made, . . *Am.* lv. 9
the cruell boy . . . Would *needs* the fly pursue; . . . . . . *Epig.* iv. 22
We should them love, and with their *needs* partake; . . . . *H.H.L.* 208
Needy. To call in commers-by that *needy* were and pore. . . I. x. 36. 9
the Knight, now in so *needy* case, ... VI. iii. 38. 4
Neglect. so did warlike Antony *neglect* The worlds whole rule V. viii. 2. 6
Neglected. they *neglected* his commaundement. . . . . *Hub.* 566
sith fairenesse is *neglected?* . . . . *D.* 205
Neighbor. I longd the *neighbour* towne to see, ... *S.C.* Ja. 50
Echo made the *neyghbour* groves to ring, ... *S.C.* Jun. 52
'*Neighbour* Ape, and my Gossip eke beside, ... *Hub.* 53
their next *neighbor* Priest, ... *Hub.* 572
they began to threat the *neighbour* sky; . . . . *Hub.* 1174
to match her with the *neighbour* flood, ... *Col.* 122
her plaint, Which softly ecchoed from the *neighbour* wood; . I. iii. 8. 2
The *neighbor* woods arownd with hollow murmur ring. . . . I. viii. 11. 9
he would eat His *neighbour* element in his revenge: . . . . I. xi. 21. 6
neighbour Scots, and forrein Scatterlings . . . . II. x. 63. 5
his *neighbour* flouds which nigh him dwell, ... IV. xi. 30. 1
her dwelling Was neare to Envie, even her *neighbour* next; . V. xii. 35. 6
gentle Eccho from the *neighbour* ground . . . . *Proth.* 112
Neighborhood. From my unhappie *neighborhood* farre fled, . . *Ti.* 146
joyne in *neighbourhood* of kingdome nere, ... IV. xi. 40. 3
Far from all *neighbourhood* the which annoy it may. . . . . VI. v. 34. 9
Neighbor's. he chawed his owne maw At *neighbours* welth, . . I. iv. 30. 6
Most envious man, that grieves at *neighbours* good; . . . . I. ix. 39. 6
Neighbors. Triumphant Arcks, spyres, *neighbours* to the skie, *Ro.* vii. 5
Far from all *neighbours,* . . . . III. vii. 6. 7
spoile and booty, which they made Upon their *neighbours* . . VI. x. 39. 6
of the sea that *neighbours* to her neare: . . . . *Epith.* 39
Neighbors'. making nightly rode Into their *neighbours* borders; . VI. viii. 35. 4
Neighing. proudlie *neighing,* from them parted hee. . . . . *Hub.* 654
with his *neighing* fast Did warne his rider . . . . VI. v. 21. 6
Neither (*partial list*).
cursed steele, of *neither* well withstood, ... *Gn.* 413
neither pleased was to have the rayne Twixt them divided . *Hub.* 1023
For *neither* you nor we shall anie more . . . . *T.M.* 409
If none of *neither* mention should make, ... *T.M.* 449
'But such as *neither* of themselves can sing, ... *Ti.* 344
neither could the others greater might . . . endure; . . . . *Mui.* 6
Neither envying other, nor envied, ... *Col.* 78
That *neither* car'd for wynd, nor haile, ... *Col.* 221
nay (said Colin) *neither* so, nor so: . . . . *Col.* 376
nether darkenesse fowle, nor filthy bands, ... I. viii. 40. 1
His harder hyde would *nether* perce nor bight, ... I. xi. 16. 4
But *neither* silke nor silver therein did appeare. . . . . . . I. xii. 22. 9
Thy *neither* friend nor foe, *Fidessa.'* . . . . I. xii. 28. 9
me he knew not, *nether* his owne ill; . . . . II. i. 54. 5
Nether to melt in pleasures whott desyre, ... II. i. 58. 3
For *nether* doth thy face terrestriall shew, ... II. iii. 33. 3
Yet *nether* spinnes nor cards, ne cares nor frets, ... II. vi. 16. 8
Whom *nether* wind out of their seat could forse . . . . . . II. vi. 20. 8
that *nether* steele nor stone . . . may defend; . . . . II. viii. 21. 1
neither mayle could hold, Ne shield defend . . . . II. viii. 41. 2
neither could his mightie puissaunce sustaine. . . . . II. viii. 42. 9
For *neither* can he fly, nor other harme, ... II. xi. 34. 2
But *neither* toyle nor traveill might . . . . II. xii. 19. 9
neither guile nor force . . . distraine . . . . II. xii. 82. 3
yet wist she *nether* how, nor why, ... III. ii. 27. 6
His garment *nether* was of silke nor say, ... III. xii. 8. 1
Nether of ydle showes, nor of false charmes aghast. . . . . III. xii. 29. 9
Neither of them she found where she them lore: . . . . . . III. xii. 44. 4
he should *neither* of them have, or both. . . . . IV. i. 10. 9
Whiles *neither* lets the other touch the soyle, ... IV. iii. 16. 7
neither could the others force sustaine; . . . . IV. iv. 18. 2
Which *neither* able were to wag, or once to weld. . . . . . IV. iv. 18. 9
neither could in hast themselves againe upreare. . . . . . . IV. iv. 20. 9
neither day nor night from working spared, ... IV. v. 35. 7
Whence *neither* greatly hasted to arise, ... IV. vi. 10. 8
Yet *neither* showed to other their hearts privity. . . . . . . IV. ix. 19. 9
Yet *neither* would their fiendlike fury slacke, ... IV. ix. 25. 5
I *neither* can my love ne yet my life forgo.' . . . . IV. ix. 39. 9
neither pretious stone, nor durefull brasse, Nor . . . . . . IV. x. 39. 4
neither he did shed that Ladies bloud, Nor tooke . . . . . V. i. 23. 8
all were fled for feare; but whether, *nether* kond. . . . . . V. vi. 35. 9
yet *neither* has forgon His horses backe, ... V. viii. 9. 7
Since *neither* is endamadg'd much thereby.' . . . . V. viii. 14. 3
That *neither* hath religion nor fay, ... V. viii. 19. 7
Yet *neither* Ino, nor Medea stout, ... V. viii. 47. 7
neither will one foot, till we that carle have hent.' . . . . . V. ix. 7. 9

Neither—*Continued.*
That *neither* could the others stroke sustaine, ... VI. i. 33. 7
Neither of other taking pitty nor remorse. . . . . VI. i. 33. 9
never . . . Did taste of pittie, *neither* gentlesse knew. . . . . VI. iv. 3. 2
now West . . . Then North, then *neither,* . . . . VI. iv. 25. 3
Nether of envy nor of chaunge afeard: . . . . VI. v. 12. 5
neither they by force could him destroy, Ne yet . . . . . . VI. v. 14. 3
neither she for him nor other none Did care . . . . VI. ix. 10. 7
neither could to company of th' other creepe. . . . . VI. xii. 5. 9
nether I may speake nor thinke . . . . *Am.* xliii. 7
neyther gods in sky, Nor men in earth, ... *Epig.* iv. 15
Neleus. *Neleus* and Pelias, lovely brethren both; . . . . . . IV. xi. 14. 2
Nemea. *Gaynd in *Nemea* goodly victoree; . . . . II. v. 31. 5
Nemean. When the *Naemean* Conquest he did win. . . . . . *Mui.* 72
Into the great *Nemaean* lions grove. . . . . V. Pr. 6. 4
whylome did forray The *Nemaean* forrest, ... VII. vii. 36. 6
Nemertea. *Nemertea* learned well to rule her lust. . . . . . IV. xi. 51. 9
Nemesis'. Stir'd up through wrathfull *Nemesis* despight, . . *Mui.* 2
Nempt. a war-monger to be basely *nempt;* . . . . III. x. 29. 5
Nemus. whenas hee In *Nemus* gayned goodly victoree: . . . . II. v. 31. 5
Nen. next to him the *Nene* downe softly slid; . . . . IV. xi. 35. 7
Nenna. thanks . . . To *Nenna* first, that first this worke created, *Com. Son.* ii. 13
Nennius. hardy *Nennius,* whom he yet did slay, ... II. x. 49. 4
Nepenthe. was with *Nepenthe* to the brim upfild. . . . . . . IV. iii. 42. 9
Nepenthe is a drinck of soverayne grace, ... IV. iii. 43. 1
Nephew. To doen his *Nephew* in all riches flow; . . . . III. iv. 22. 2
Nephew's. He would at her request prolong her *nephews* daies. I. v. 41. 9
from the grandsyre to the *Nephewes* sonne, ... II. viii. 29. 3
Nephews. so fruitfull was Of vertuous *nephewes,* . . . . . . *Ro.* viii. 6
Why suffredst thou thy *Nephewes* deare to fall, ... I. v. 22. 7
two of three her *Nephewes* are so fowle forlorne? . . . . . . I. v. 23. 9
what art thou, that telst of *Nephews* kilt?' . . . . I. v. 26. 5
all their *Nephewes* late; Even thrise eleven descents . . . . II. x. 45. 7
Neptune. Which she with *Neptune* did for Athens trie: . . . *Mui.* 306
He hurles out vowes, and *Neptune* oft doth blesse. . . . . . I. iii. 32. 5
rolling downe great *Neptune* doth dismay: . . . . I. xi. 54. 8
Ne swelling *Neptune* ne lowd thundring Jove . . . . II. vi. 10. 7
wrathfull *Neptune* did them drive before His whirling charet II. xii. 22. 3
Great *Neptune,* I avow to hallow unto thee!' . . . . III. iv. 10. 9
Great *Neptune* stoode amazed at their sight, ... III. iv. 32. 1
Next unto him was *Neptune* pictured, ... III. xi. 40. 1
For losse of his deare love by *Neptune* hent, ... IV. ix. 23. 2
great *Neptune,* with his threeforkt mace, ... IV. xi. 11. 1
sonnes of *Neptune,* now assembled here: . . . . IV. xi. 15. 3
Albion the sonne of *Neptune* was, ... IV. xi. 16. 1
from great *Neptune* do derive their parentage. . . . . IV. xi. 17. 9
unto great king *Neptune* selfe did goe, ... IV. xii. 29. 4
To whom God *Neptune,* softly smyling, thus: . . . . IV. xii. 30. 1
Neptune, of seas; . . . . VII. vii. 26. 7
Neptune's. Upon great *Neptunes* necke they softly swim, . . . III. iv. 42. 8
hath the charge of *Neptunes* mighty heard; . . . . III. viii. 30. 2
to this feast with *Neptunes* seed was dight. . . . . IV. xi. 16. 9
Nereids. Whom of their sire *Nereides* men call, ... IV. xi. 48. 3
Nereis. *Nereis* to the Seas a token gave, ... *Gn.* 567
Nereus. Within the gulfe of greedie *Nereus.* . . . . *Bel.*[2] xiii. 11
Great *Nereus* his daughter and his joy. . . . . *Gn.* 492
Nereus crownes with cups; his mates him pledg around. . . I. iii. 31. 9
blacke-browd Cymoent, The daughter of great *Nereus,* . . . III. iv. 19. 4
Thy Grandsire *Nereus* promist to adorne? . . . . III. iv. 36. 5
Nereus, th' eldest and the best, ... IV. xi. 18. 5
So wise is *Nereus* old, ... IV. xi. 19. 7
All these the daughters of old *Nereus* were, ... IV. xi. 52. 1
Neros. So many *Neroes* and Caligulaes . . . . *Bel.* x. 13
Nesaea. Wondred Agave, Poris, and *Nesaea,* . . . . IV. xi. 49. 6
Neso. *Neso,* and Eione well in age, ... IV. xi. 50. 7
Nest. where the Eagle built his towring *nest,* . . . . *Van.* iv. 6
The Swallow peepes out of her *nest,* . . . . *S.C.* Mar. 11
to dislodge the Raven of her *nest?* . . . . *S.C.* D. 32
Charissa, . . . left her fruitfull *nest:* . . . . I. x. 29. 8
some hidden *nest* Of many Dragonettes, ... I. xii. 10. 5
he crauld out of his *nest,* . . . . II. iii. 35. 6
Emongst wide waves sett, like a litle *nest,* . . . . II. vi. 12. 2
The life did flit away out of her *nest,* . . . . II. vii. 66. 8
safe committ to her soft fethered *nest,* . . . . III. i. 58. 7
Feeling her leape out of her loathed *nest,* . . . . III. ii. 30. 3
In his free thought to build her sluggish *nest,* . . . . III. v. 2. 2
love for to dislodge out of his *nest:* . . . . III. v. 44. 3
out of that same fishers filthy *nest* Removing her, ... III. viii. 35. 7
They spide a little cottage, like some poore mans *nest.* . . . IV. v. 32. 9
litle sparrowes stolen from their *nest,* . . . . VI. ix. 40. 2
he streight went to the Captaines *nest:* . . . . VI. xi. 42. 7
The *neast* of love, the lodging of delight, ... *Am.* lxxvi. 2
Nestor. The yeares of *Nestor* nothing were to his, ... II. ix. 57. 1
Nests. th' Almighties bosome, where he *nests;* . . . . *T.M.* 389
Net. *See* **Fowling-net.**
weaving straight a *net* with manie a fold . . . . *Mui.* 357
Arachne high did . . . spred her subtile *nett,* . . . . II. vii. 28. 8
on them rusht, and threw A subtile *net,* . . . . II. xii. 81. 4
that same *net* so cunningly was wound, ... II. xii. 82. 2
Into his hidden *nett* full easely doth fall. . . . . III. i. 54. 9
A *net* in th' one hand, ... III. xii. 11. 5
naked, as *nett* yvory . . . . III. xii. 20. 1
at his backe a great wyde *net* he bore, ... V. ix. 11. 6
He suddenly his *net* upon her threw, ... V. ix. 14. 2
the Priest with naked armes full *net* Approching nigh, . . . VI. viii. 45. 4
under a *net* of gold; . . . . *Am.* xxxvii. 2
stare Henceforth too rashly on that guilefull *net,* . . . . . *Am.* xxxvii. 10
Nethelesse. *Nethelesse* thou seest my lowly saile, ... *S.C.* S. 250
Nether. 'Her *neather* partes misshapen, monstruous, Were hidd
in water, ... I. ii. 41. 1

Nether—*Continued.*
Her *neather* parts, . . . Muse for shame doth blush to write; I. viii. 48. 1
Thrise seene the shadowes of the *neather* world, II. ii. 44. 2
this darksom *neather* world her light Doth dim II. vii. 49. 3
His *neather* lip was not like man nor beast, IV. vii. 6. 1
Nets. The whiles the captive heard his *nets* did rend, *As.* 125
the fine *nets,* which oft we woven see II. xii. 77. 8
The whiles his *nets* were drying on the sand. III. vii. 27. 6
Thus finely did he his false *nets* dispred, III. x. 9. 6
There all her subtill *nets* she did unfold, V. v. 52. 1
How he his *nets* doth for their ruine lay: V. ix. 13. 4
Another while I baytes and *nets* display VI. ix. 23. 5
Network. With this so curious *networke* to compare. *Mui.* 368
Neustria. a Lion from the sea-bord wood Of *Neustria* III. iii. 47. 3
Never. your praise, the which shall *never* die *Ro.* i. 3
Was *never* seene, that anie fortunes wreakes *Ro.* xxi. 7
These bitter blasts *never* ginne tasswage? *S.C.* F. 2
never complained of cold nor heate, *S.C.* F. 19
never give trust to his trecheree: *S.C.* May 222
I *never* lyst presume to Parnasse hyll, *S.C.* Jun. 70
That sithens *never* was abhord *S.C.* Jul. 139
They *never* stroven to be chiefe, *S.C.* Jul. 167
Never knew I lovers sheepe in good plight: *S.C.* Au. 20
Never shall be sayde that Perigot was dared. *S.C.* Au. 24
Sike a song *never* heardest thou but Colin *S.C.* Au. 50
sike a roundle *never* heard I none: *S.C.* Au. 125
Never dempt more right of beautye, *S.C.* Au. 137
never thing on earth so pleaseth me *S.C.* Au. 147
Never I wist thee in so poore a plight. *S.C.* S. 8
They *never* sette foote in that same troade, *S.C.* S. 92
Never was Woolfe seene, *S.C.* S. 152
Never had shepheard so kene a kurre, *S.C.* S. 182
Such cause of mourning *never* hadst afore; *S.C.* N. 54
It floureth fresh, as it should *never* fayle? *S.C.* N. 86
Was *never* pype of reede did better sounde. *S.C.* D. 142
Not unto him that *never* hath trespast, *Gn.* 365
that Phoebus sunnie rayes Doo *never* see, *Gn.* 620
I now depart, returning to thee *never,* *Gn.* 634
That *never* might his luckie scape forget. *Gn.* 664
yet doo *never* thanke them for the same, *Hub.* 165
yet *never* met Adventure *Hub.* 223
never found occasion for their tourne, *Hub.* 579
queint devises, *never* seene In Court before, *Hub.* 673
which *never* came in place Of worlds affaires, *Hub.* 834
Which he had *never,* nor ought like the same. *Hub.* 868
into whose brest *Never* crept thought of honor, *Hub.* 978
never after anie Should . . . be voyd of infamie; *Hub.* 1241
From whence he *never* should be quit, *Hub.* 1245
gard, which *never* him descride, . . . watchmen, who him *never* spide: *Hub.* 1301, 1302
Such mournfull tunes were *never* since invented. *T.M.* 12
A sea of teares that *never* may be dryde, *T.M.* 116
'Wasted it is, as if it *never* were; *Ti.* 120
Forgotten quite as they were *never* borne. *Ti.* 182
Spite bites the dead, that living *never* baid. *Ti.* 215
thy Lord shall *never* die. *Ti.* 252, 253
vertues dying *never,* *Ti.* 256
Which *never* was, ne ever with regard *Ti.* 347
brasen Pillours *never* to be fired, *Ti.* 410
Deserving *never* here to be forgot, *Ti.* 438
A fairer wight saw *never* summers day. *Ti.* 637
shame, and sorrow *never* ended. *Mui.* 264
never didst thou heare more haplesse fate. *D.* 98
bring to hand that yet had *never* beene; *D.* 116
never standeth in one certaine state, *D.* 430
(A fairer star saw *never* living eie,) *As.* 57
I feard, least land we *never* should have eyde: *Col.* 267
One ever I, and others *never* none.' *Col.* 479
A fairer Nymph yet *never* saw mine eie: *Col.* 559
never wist I till this present day, *Col.* 827
things celestiall which ye *never* saw. *Col.* 930
Yet armes till that time did he *never* wield. I. i. 1. 5
The vine-propp Elme; the Poplar *never* dry, I. i. 8. 7
where dawning day doth *never* peepe, I. i. 39. 5
was in Ocean waves yet *never* wet, I. ii. 1. 3
she her weary limbes would *never* rest; I. ii. 8. 6
Was *never* Prince so faithfull . . . Was *never* Prince so meeke I. ii. 23. 4, 5
yet could *never* win The Fort, I. ii. 25. 3
Under them *never* sat, I. ii. 28. 8
Did *never* mortall eye behold such I. iii. 4. 9
never shew of living wight espyde; I. iii. 10. 3
never in that land . . . she before did vew, I. iii. 11. 7
wilfull man, he *never* would forecast I. iv. 34. 8
He *never* meant with words, but swords, to plead I. iv. 42. 9
I *never* joyed howre, I. iv. 46. 6
needlesse feare did *never* vantage none; I. iv. 49. 4
The noble hart . . . Can *never* rest, I. v. 1. 3
Phoebus chearefull face durst *never* vew, I. v. 20. 2
never did such brightnes there appeare; I. v. 21. 5
pitty in her hart was *never* prov'd Till then, I. v. 24. 8
evermore she hated, *never* lov'd: I. v. 24. 9
The wakefull dogs did *never* cease to bay, I. v. 30. 2
Great pains, and greater praise, both *never* to be donne.' I. v. 43. 9
cryme in her could *never* creature find; I. vi. 2. 5
monstrous rablement, Whose like he *never* saw, I. vi. 8. 8
But Venus *never* had so sober mood: I. vi. 16. 7
In which his might was *never* overthrowne; I. vi. 29. 8
Whose like in womens witt he *never* knew; I. vi. 31. 2
That Redcrosse knight, perdie, I *never* slew; I. vi. 42. 6
His living like saw *never* living eye, I. vii. 8. 7

Never—*Continued.*
Was *never* Lady loved dearer day I. vii. 27. 7
point of speare it *never* percen could, I. vii. 33. 8
The same to wight he *never* wont disclose, I. vii. 34. 1
Found *never* help who *never* would his hurts impart.' I. vii. 40. 9
he that *never* would Could *never:* I. vii. 41. 3, 4
Yet *never* any could that girlond win, I. vii. 45. 6
hands imbrewd in guilty blood Had *never* beene, I. vii. 47. 4
Where *never* foote of living wight did tread, I. vii. 50. 4
Whose fall did *never* foe before behold: I. vii. 51. 6
Was *never* wight that heard I. viii. 4. 1
More ugly shape yet *never* living creature saw. I. viii. 48. 9
hither brought by wayes yet *never* found, I. ix. 7. 6
So fayre a creature yet saw *never* sunny day. I. ix. 13. 9
Was *never* hart so ravisht with delight, I. ix. 14. 6
never vowd to rest till her I fynd: I. ix. 15. 8
never knight I saw in such misseeming plight.' I. ix. 23. 9
(Would I had *never* chaunst!) I. ix. 27. 1
God you *never* let his charmed speaches heare!' I. ix. 30. 9
O! *never,* Sir, desire to try I. ix. 31. 9
'hence shall I *never* rest, Till I I. ix. 32. 1
as he did *never* dyne. I. ix. 35. 9
never knight, that dared warlike deed, I. ix. 45. 3
That weaker witt of man could *never* reach; I. x. 19. 5
his cryme could els be *never* cleare. I. x. 28. 9
To leade aright, that he should *never* fall I. x. 34. 7
That *never* yet was seene I. x. 52. 3
never leads the traveiler astray, I. x. 52. 4
awake, sleepe *never* he so sownd; I. xi. 6. 8
never felt his imperceable brest I. xi. 17. 7
like was *never* heard; I. xi. 26. 2
never man such mischiefes did torment: I. xi. 28. 3
death will *never* come when needes require. I. xi. 28. 5
never could the force of fleshly arme, I. xi. 36. 6
till that stownd could *never* wight him harme I. xi. 36. 8
never gentle knight, . . . So tossed was I. xii. 16. 7
never living man, I weene, so sore . . . was distrest: I. xii. 17. 5
Oft had he seene her faire, but *never* so faire dight. I. xii. 23. 9
Which to late age were *never* mentioned. II. Pr. 2. 5
With living eye more fayre was *never* seene II. i. 10. 7
help *never* comes too late.' II. i. 44. 9
One that to bountie *never* cast his mynd, II. iii. 4. 2
hath vowd . . . *never* to wearen none: II. iii. 12. 8
Els *never* should thy judgement be so frayle II. iii. 16. 4
in battaile *never* sword to beare, II. iii. 17. 8
never thinke that so II. iv. 10. 2
That during life will *never* be appeasd!' II. iv. 33. 6
That *never* yet encountred enemy II. iv. 40. 7
Woe *never* wants where every cause is caught; II. iv. 44. 6
he *never* staid to greete, II. v. 3. 1
homage till that instant *never* learned hee. II. v. 11. 9
Was *never* man, who most conquestes atchiev'd, II. v. 15. 3
dens, where Titan his face *never* shewes. II. v. 27. 9
The wind unstable, and doth *never* stay. II. vi. 23. 5
that had *never* mett before So puissant foe, II. vi. 30. 1
He *never* stood, But bent his hastie course II. vi. 41. 8
Yet *never* in this straunge astonishment.' II. vi. 49. 4
heapes of gold that *never* could be spent; II. vii. 5. 2
'yet *never* eie did vew, II. vii. 19. 6
Did *never* in that house it selfe display, II. vii. 29. 5
As eie of man did *never* see before, II. vii. 31. 5
never creature saw that cam that way: II. vii. 37. 5
That living eye before did *never* see. II. vii. 38. 2
That *never* earthly Prince . . . His glory did enhaunce, II. vii. 44. 8
On earth like *never* grew, II. vii. 54. 3
He daily dyde, yet *never* throughly dyen couth. II. vii. 58. 9
Was *never* wight that treason of him told: II. viii. 13. 8
yet did he *never* quaile, II. viii. 35. 6
that *never* moov'd afore. II. viii. 44. 9
whom daunger *never* fro me drew. II. viii. 53. 9
When cause requyrd, but *never* out of time; II. ix. 25. 8
never had they seene so straunge a sight. II. ix. 33. 4
working wit That *never* idle was, II. ix. 49. 9
Some such as in the world were *never* yit, II. ix. 50. 4
a salvage nation dwelt . . . That *never* tasted grace, II. x. 7. 3
Of this sweet Island *never* conquered, II. x. 47. 7
Was *never* king more highly magnifide, II. x. 52. 1
That *never* entraunce any durst pretend, II. xi. 15. 8
never was she in so evill cace, II. xi. 16. 3
That in assuraunce it may *never* stand, II. xi. 30. 4
Like did he *never* heare, like did he *never* see. II. xi. 40. 9
Mordure, that *never* fayld At need II. xi. 41. 6
may *never* it recure, II. xii. 12. 8
never yet, . . . He fownd him selfe dishonored III. i. 7. 2
brought to grownd that *never* wast before; III. i. 7. 7
That *never* any mote with her compayre: III. i. 26. 5
doe unto her service, *never* to remove: III. i. 26. 9
that had *never* priefe Of such malengine III. i. 53. 7
The noble corage *never* weeneth ought III. ii. 10. 4
prowesse paragone saw *never* living wight. III. ii. 13. 9
That *never* foes his kingdome might invade, III. ii. 21. 3
never sore but might a salve obtaine: III. ii. 35. 7
'Was *never* such, but mote the like be fownd,' III. ii. 36. 3
Whose shape or person yet I *never* saw, III. ii. 38. 4
'Was *never* such, but mote the like be fownd,' III. ii. 36. 3
but will hevens fury *never* slake, III. iii. 43. 5
never wight so fast in sell could sit, III. iii. 60. 6
never man he suffred by that same III. iv. 20. 7
never borne to dye? III. iv. 38. 2
A fayrer wight did *never* Sunne behold; III. v. 5. 5

Never—Continued.

vowed *never* to returne againe,	III. v. 10. 3
I here avow thee *never* to forsake.	III. v. 11. 8
never he alive . . . should escape	III. v. 16. 7
Saw *never* living eie more heavy sight,	III. v. 30. 1
never he his hart to her reveald;	III. v. 49. 7
as they had *never* seene Fleshly corruption,	III. vi. 33. 3
boughes sharp steele did *never* lop,	III. vi. 43. 4
Like *never* yet did living eie detect;	III. vii. 22. 7
never learned he such service till that day.	III. vii. 36. 9
I would *never* swerve?	III. vii. 53. 9
that nev'r did fashions see.'	III. vii. 57. 9
'Safe her, I *never* any woman found	III. vii. 60. 1
Whose like on earth was *never* framed yit;	III. viii. 5. 3
virgin wex that *never* yet was seald,	III. viii. 6. 7
his deceiptfull eyes did *never* lin To looke	III. viii. 24. 8
he, that *never* good nor maners knew,	III. viii. 26. 1
never suffred her to be at rest,	III. viii. 39. 2
never let th' ensample of the bad Offend	III. ix. 2. 1
the cause why *never* any knight.	III. ix. 6. 3
Was *never* wretched man in such a wofull cace.	III. x. 14. 9
Was *never* better time to shew thy smart	III. x. 26. 3
never looked who behind him was,	III. x. 53. 8
That he dare *never* sleepe,	III. x. 58. 6
Yet can he *never* dye,	III. x. 60. 1
more bounteous creature *never* far'd	III. xi. 10. 3
His rolling eies did *never* rest in place,	III. xii. 15. 6
As she were *never* hurt, was soone restord.	III. xii. 38. 7
oftentimes doe wish it *never* had bene writ.	IV. i. 1. 9
In perilous fight she *never* joyed day;	IV. i. 2. 2
never met with none . . .	IV. i. 16. 7
That *never* thoght one thing,	IV. i. 27. 9
'Sir, him wise I *never* held,	IV. i. 34. 7
Three bolder brethren *never* were yborne,	IV. ii. 41. 2
never discord did amongst them fall,	IV. ii. 54. 2
he *never* thought . . . His person to emperill	IV. iv. 10. 4
from her faith *never* swerve.	IV. v. 1. 9
Let *never* Ladie to his love assent,	IV. v. 18. 8
which he *never* wont to combe,	IV. v. 34. 9
hammers, that did *never* rest	IV. v. 36. 3
being knit with vertue, *never* will remove.	IV. vi. 31. 9
who *never* heard one word	IV. viii. 18. 5
crimes and facts, such as they *never* ment,	IV. viii. 35. 6
never two so like did living creature see.	IV. viii. 55. 9
Whose like they *never* saw	IV. ix. 22. 5
I *never* joyed happinesse nor rest;	IV. ix. 39. 3
I *never* joyed howre,	IV. x. 1. 9
Which *never* they recover might againe;	IV. x. 13. 6
yet loves decayed *never*.	IV. x. 27. 9
I, that *never* tasted blis	IV. x. 28. 1
linckt together *never* to dispart;	IV. x. 51. 7
Which Ladies love, I heard, had *never* wonne.	IV. x. 55. 3
darkenesse dredd that *never* viewed day,	IV. xi. 4. 2
Which *never* she before disclosd to none,	IV. xii. 5. 4
though he *never* list to me relent,	IV. xii. 7. 6
Yet will I *never* of my love repent,	IV. xii. 7. 8
His stubborne heart, that *never* felt misfare,	IV. xii. 12. 4
never wight so evill did	IV. xii. 30. 8
never wight he lets to passe that way	V. ii. 6. 2
never the like resort they have.	V. ii. 29. 7
never word from that day forth he spoke.	V. iii. 33. 5
rage of waves that *never* rest,	V. iv. 19. 4
never had she suffred such despight:	V. iv. 43. 4
never wont in warre, Them sorely vext,	V. iv. 44. 2
never meant he . . . to be untrew:	V. v. 56. 2
never yet was wight so well aware,	V. vi. 1. 8
life and manners straunge she *never* knew;	V. vi. 12. 7
never word did say	V. vi. 18. 3
to her that *never* evill ment in hart.	V. vi. 31. 9
Whose like before she *never* saw nor red;	V. vii. 5. 7
she thereon could *never* gaze her fill.	V. vii. 5. 9
Never thenceforth to nourish enmity,	V. viii. 14. 8
Miscalling me . . . That *never* did her ill,	V. viii. 22. 9
never saw they there the like array; Ne ever	V. ix. 24. 5
never doth from doome of right depart,	V. x. 2. 7
shape was *never* seene of none	V. x. 29. 4
Her hands were . . . *never* washt	V. xii. 30. 1
strange waies where *never* foote did use,	VI. Pr. 2. 8
I *never* saw in any greater hope appeare.'	VI. ii. 26. 9
never to be recreant for feare Of perill,	VI. ii. 35. 3
The salvage man, that *never* till this houre	VI. iv. 3. 1
Where foot of living creature *never* trode,	VI. iv. 13. 8
Vowing that *never* he in bed againe	VI. iv. 40. 6
It *never* rests till it have wrought,	VI. vi. 8. 9
Which *never* yet they had approv'd in fight,	VI. vii. 5. 5
the knee that *never* yet was bent.	VI. viii. 15. 9
It *never* yet was bent.	VI. viii. 16. 1
As if he *never* had received fall;	VI. viii. 26. 2
never Turtle truer to his make,	VI. viii. 33. 6
such vainenesse as I *never* thought.	VI. ix. 24. 9
she that *never* had acquainted beene	VI. ix. 35. 1
he should *never* leave,	VI. x. 1. 5
made him pipe so merrily, as *never* none.	VI. x. 15. 9
Whose like before his eye had *never* seene;	VI. x. 17. 2
which way he *never* knew;	VI. x. 18. 3
That *never* usde to live by plough nor spade,	VI. x. 39. 4
Had *never* joyance felt nor chearefull	VI. xi. 45. 2
Whose course is often stayd, yet *never* is astray.	VI. xi. 1. 9
Whose like he *never* once did speake,	VI. xii. 33. 6
whose like till then he *never* bore, Ne ever any	VI. xii. 36. 2

Never—Continued.

That *never* so deserved to endite.	VI. xii. 41. 7
that *never* still did stand.	VII. vi. 8. 9
'Will *never* mortall thoughts ceasse to aspire	VII. vi. 29. 2
To see that mortall eyes have *never* seene;	VII. vi. 32. 3
That *never* any saw,	VII. vi. 45. 3
Was *never* so great joyance since the day	VII. vii. 12. 1
Never abiding in their stedfast plights:	VII. vii. 21. 3
The fish, . . . *never* rest,	VII. vii. 21. 5
Was *never* in this world ought worthy tride,	Am. v. 13
Dark is the world, where your light shined *never*;	Am. viii. 13
Nor to the Moone; for they are changed *never*;	Am. ix. 6
Such art of eyes I *never* read in bookes!	Am. xxi. 14
Lyke sacred priests that *never* thinke amisse!	Am. xxii. 1
I must begin and *never* bring to end:	Am. xxiii. 10
be forgot as it had *never* beene;	Am. xxvii. 7
this verse, that *never* shall expyre,	Am. xxvii. 11
shall their ruthlesse torment *never* cease;	Am. xxxvi. 2
O fayrest fayre! let *never* it be named,	Am. xli. 13
that it from her may *never* start,	Am. xlii. 9
him that *never* thought you ill,	Am. xlix. 7
never ought was excellent assayde	Am. li. 7
So firmely, that ye *never* may remove.	Am. lxxi. 8
Which oft I wisht, yet *never* was so blest.	Am. lxxvi. 14
The which my selfe could *never* yet attayne.	Am. lxxxiii. 10
never blush, Cupid, quoth I,	Epig. iii. 7
many thou hast pricked . . . That pitty *never* found:	Epig. iv. 38
Never had man more joyfull day then this,	Epith. 246
never day so long,	Epith. 273
Is it not Cinthia, she that *never* sleepes,	Epith. 374
yet *never* satisfyde with it;	H.L. 199
represent Sights *never* seene,	H.L. 255
Thou that hast *never* lov'd canst not beleeve	H.L. 257
Shall *never* be extinguisht	H.B. 101
That it of loving eyes be vewed *never*?	H.B. 189
that others *never* see!	H.B. 247
That darkenesse there appeareth *never* none;	H.H.L. 73
Doing him die that *never* it deserved,	H.H.L. 160
Whose bleeding sourse their streames yet *never* staunch	H.H.L. 164
Never consum'd, nor quencht with mortall hands;	H.H.B. 40
Two fairer Birds I yet did *never* see;	Proth. 39
snow . . . Did *never* whiter shew,	Proth. 41
they *never* saw a sight so fayre,	Proth. 60

Never-dead. Of *never-dead* yet ever-dying paine; . . H.H.L. 126

Never-dying. fill the world with *never dying* fame! . . Ro. Env. 14
| Whence spring all noble deedes and *never dying* fame: . | III. iii. 1. 9 |

Nevermore. 'Let Bagpipe *never more* be heard to shrill, . . D. 323
mine eyes shall *never more* behold	D. 491
knight he now shall *never more* deface:	I. iii. 29. 5
Would *never more* delight in painted show	VI. x. 3. 7
That *never more* they should endure the shew	VI. x. 4. 4
For *never more* defaming gentle Knight,	VI. xii. 34. 6
That *never more* he mote endammadge wight .	VI. xii. 38. 3

Never-resting. bad him flie with *never-resting* speed . . . Hub. 1247

New. this *new* Hydra mete to be assailde . . . . Bel.² viii. 11
I saw *new* Earth, *new* Heaven,	Rev. iv. 1
hydra *new*, Of hundred Hercules to be assaide,	Bel.² x. 10
Did blowe *new* fire,	Ro. xi. 7
that Nation, th' earths *new* Giant brood,	Ro. xi. 9
That *newe* is upryst from bedde:	S.C. Mar. 18
some old sorowe that made a *newe* breache:	S.C. May 210
draweth *newe* delightes with hoary heares.	S.C. Jun. 40
now I have learnd a *newe* daunce;	S.C. Au. 11
My old musick mard by a *newe* mischaunce.	S.C. Au. 12
Sike question ripeth up cause of *newe* woe,	S.C. S. 13
rapt with sweetenes *new*,	Gn. 195
To cloath her selfe in colours fresh and *new*,	Gn. 684
Even as *new* occasion appeares?	Hub. 119
His breeches were made after the *new* cut,	Hub. 211
times delay *new* hope of helpe still breeds.	Hub. 327
Novices, *new* come abroad,	Hub. 405
Ne *new* ones could he easily provide,	Hub. 929
in his *new* glory sheene,	Hub. 1066
gan he to himselfe *new* shape to frame;	Hub. 1266
The worlds late wonder, and the heavens *new* joy;	Ti. 303
As in their Syres *new* love both triumphing:	Mui. 294
To make *new* matter fit for Tragedies;	D. 154
Living on earth like Angell *new* divine,	D. 214
No leasing *new*, nor Grandams fable stale,	Col. 102
like faire Phebes garlond shining *new*,	Col. 342
there is a *new* shepheard late up sprong,	Col. 416
she doth *new* bands adventure dread;—	Col. 567
taking up to heaven, him godded *new*.	Col. 810
his *new* force to learne,	I. i. 3. 8
He passed forth, and *new* adventure sought:	I. i. 28. 8
with *new* day *new* worke at once begin;	I. i. 33. 2
that *new* creature, borne without her dew,	I. i. 46. 6
streames of purple bloud *new* die the verdant fields.	I. ii. 17. 9
Having both found a *new* friend you to aid,	I. ii. 27. 2
Better *new* friend then an old foe is said.'	I. ii. 27. 4
And his *new* Lady it endured not.	I. ii. 29. 7
By traynes *new* troubles to have toste:	I. iii. 24. 7
hope of *new* good hap he gan to feele	I. iii. 34. 8
an errant knight . . . they *new* arrived find:	I. iv. 38. 6
Cause of my *new* griefe, cause of my *new* joy;	I. iv. 45. 5
Into *new* woes unweeting I was cast	I. iv. 47. 3
Heralds . . . Greeting him goodly with *new* victorie,	I. v. 15. 8
Already harnessed for journey *new*,	I. v. 20. 7
redoubled crime with vengeaunce *new* Thou biddest	I. v. 42. 7
Ne in this *new* acquaintaunce could delight;	I. vi. 32. 3

New—*Continued.*
Tidings of warre, and of adventures *new;* . . . . I. vi. 36. 2
warres, nor *new* adventures, none he herd. . . . . I. vi. 36. 3
two knights, . . . arraung'd in batteill *new,* . . . . I. vi. 38. 4
backe to fight againe, *new* breathed and entire. . . . . . . I. vi. 44. 9
many heades, out budding ever *new,* . . . . I. vii. 17. 4
the Prince, to batteill *new* addrest . . . . I. viii. 22. 1
sacred ashes over it was strowed *new*. . . . . I. viii. 35. 9
still wex old in woe, whiles wo stil wexeth *new*. . . . . . I. ix. 9. 9
adding *new* Feare to his first amazment, ... I. ix. 24. 1
'Hierusalem that is, The *new* Hierusalem, ... I. x. 57. 2
So *new* this new-borne knight to battell *new* did rise. . . . I. xi. 34. 9
ragged ribs of mountaines molten *new,* . . . . I. xi. 44. 7
Of their *new* joy, and happie victory . . . . I. xii. 4. 3
thy daughter linck . . . to that *new* unknowen guest: . . . . I. xii. 26. 7
To worke *new* woe and improvided scath, ... I. xii. 34. 3
The fish that once was caught *new* bait wil hardly byte. . . . II. i. 4. 9
as if some *new* mishap, Had him betide, ... II. i. 26. 8
Gan with *new* rage their shieldes to hew . . . . II. ii. 23. 7
whither now on *new* adventure bownd: . . . . II. ii. 39. 6
kindling *new* his corage seeming queint, ... II. v. 11. 4
new matter fram'd Upon the old, ... II. v. 21. 2
the wanton Damsell found *New* merth . . . . II. vi. 6. 2
Till season serve *new* passage to assay: . . . . II. vi. 23. 7
Some others were *new* driven, ... II. vii. 5. 5
Whose tender bud to blossome *new* began, ... II. viii. 5. 3
Received is to grace and *new* accord, ... II. x. 66. 4
from her womb *new* spirits to reprize. . . . . II. xi. 44. 9
her selfe now solacing With a *new* Lover, ... II. xii. 72. 3
Which by that *new* rencounter he should reare; . . . . . . III. i. 9. 8
of their first intent gan make *new* dout, ... III. iii. 14. 3
*our weake hands (whom need *new* strength shall teach) . . III. iii. 53. 3
Breeder of *new,* renewer of old smarts: . . . . III. iv. 57. 3
His readie wound with better salves *new* drest: . . . . . . III. v. 41. 4
So, like a wheele, arownd they ronne from old to *new*. . . . III. vi. 33. 9
Did heape on her *new* waves of weary wretchednesse. . . . . III. viii. 20. 9
in his old corage *new* delight To gin awake, ... III. viii. 23. 4
nothing *new* to him was that same paine, ... III. ix. 29. 6
entysd To take to his *new* love, ... III. x. 8. 9
proude of that *new* honour which they redd, ... III. x. 44. 7
doth himselfe with sorrow *new* sustaine, ... III. x. 60. 2
to see what *new* successe Mote him befall . . . . III. xi. 20. 2
successe Mote him befall upon *new* enterprise. . . . . . . III. xi. 20. 3
fild with *new* affright. . . . . III. xii. 44. 9
yokes assoyle . . . till a *new* day; . . . . III. xii. 47. *or.*6
A *new* unknowen mischiefe did from him remove. . . . . . . IV. i. 2. 9
As ever could Cameleon colours *new;* . . . . IV. i. 18. 4
Ne list I for revenge provoke *new* fight, ... IV. i. 35. 3
Him selfe he did of his *new* love deceave; . . . . IV. i. 36. 5
as bent to charge them *new:* . . . . IV. i. 38. 6
She it revives, and *new* occasion reaches; . . . . IV. ii. 12. 7
by searching daungers *new,* . . . . IV. ii. 46. 7
will reserve it for a Canto *new*. . . . . IV. ii. 54. 9
with *new* encouragement Did him assayle, ... IV. iii. 26. 7
with vigour *new* . . . him cherisht, ... IV. iii. 29. 3
now a *new* debate Stird up . . . . IV. iv. 2. 3
Unable he *new* battell to darraine, ... IV. iv. 26. 7
So both together give a *new* allarme, ... IV. iv. 35. 4
new discord to maintaine. . . . . IV. v. 22. 9
readie were *new* battell to darraine. . . . . IV. v. 24. 6
Oft chaunging sides, and oft *new* place electing, ... IV. v. 40. 3
New matter added to his former fire; . . . . IV. vi. 11. 2
More eath was *new* impression to receive; . . . . IV. vi. 40. 6
new occasion fayld her more to find, ... IV. vi. 46. 2
There she him found by that *new* lovely mate, ... IV. vii. 35. 3
a riband *new,* In which his Ladies colours were, ... IV. viii. 7. 1
there a piteous ditty *new* deviz'd, ... IV. viii. 12. 2
Thence she commaunded me to prison *new;* . . . . IV. viii. 56. 7
griefe entire For losse of her *new* love, ... IV. ix. 13. 9
change his liking, and *new* Lemans prove; . . . . IV. ix. 21. 6
new parts take; . . . . IV. ix. 26. 1
The fertile Nile, which creatures *new* doth frame; . . . . . IV. xi. 20. 3
all her shoulders spred As a *new* spring; . . . . IV. xi. 46. 5
new languishment Of his old hurt, ... IV. xii. 23. 5
it was no old sore which his *new* paine procured; . . . . . . IV. xii. 23. 9
He now went with him in this *new* inquest, ... V. i. 13. 1
rather in them kindled choler *new:* . . . . V. ii. 13. 4
if thou now shouldst weigh them *new* in pound, ... V. ii. 36. 5
To bring it to her husband *new* ordained, ... V. iv. 13. 7
Weening at last to win advantage *new;* . . . . V. v. 7. 2
no *new* loves impression ever could Bereave it thence: . . . . V. vi. 2. 8
Least some *new* love had him from her possest: . . . . V. vi. 4. 7
To make *new* warre against the Gods againe. . . . . V. vii. 11. 6
she the face of her *new* foe might see: . . . . V. vii. 25. 7
For his departure, her *new* cause of griefe: . . . . V. vii. 44. 2
new accusements to produce in place: . . . . V. ix. 47. 2
Being then *new* made widow . . . . V. x. 11. 7
'yet now I gin *new* life to feele; . . . . V. x. 20. 4
now he hath *new* lawes and orders *new* Imposd on it . . . . V. x. 27. 6
What *new* occasion doth thee hither drive, ... V. xi. 38. 5
new life to her lent in midst of deadly feare. . . . . V. xii. 12. 9
Subject to fortunes chance, still chaunging *new:* . . . . . . VI. i. 41. 8
The noble ympe, of such *new* service fayne, ... VI. ii. 38. 6
His former malice to some *new* assay, ... VI. iii. 47. 8
new launcht with murdrous knife, ... VI. v. 5. 4
Were glad to heare of that adventure *new,* . . . . VI. vii. 5. 3
Himselfe addrest unto this *new* debate, ... VI. viii. 13. 3
Old love is litle worth when *new* is more prefard. . . . . . VI. ix. 40. 9
lighting candles *new,* gan search anone, ... VI. xi. 20. 8
misdoubting least of-*new* Some uprore were . . . . VI. xi. 43. 8

New—*Continued.*
Began some smacke of comfort *new* to tast, ... VI. xi. 45. 3
ere he *new* helpe could call, ... VI. xii. 30. 5
To crop his thousand heads, the which still *new* Forth budded, VI. xii. 32. 4
Before they could *new* counsels re-allie, ... VII. vi. 23. 4
the love of some *new* Nymph, late seene, ... VII. vii. 11. 6
We daily see *new* creatures to arize, ... VII. vii. 18. 6
Still change and vary thoughts, as *new* occasions fall. . . . VII. vii. 19. 9
new bloosmes did beare, ... VII. vii. 28. 3
wanton as a Kid whose horne *new* buds: . . . . VII. vii. 33. 2
Doth seeme to promise hope of *new* delight: . . . . *Am.* iv. 2
Prepare your selfe *new* love to entertaine. . . . . *Am.* iv. 14
So hard it is to kindle *new* desire . . . . *Am.* vi. 9
I thinke that I a *new* Pandora see, ... *Am.* xxiv. 8
The *new* begins his compast course anew: . . . . *Am.* lxii. 2
chaunge old yeares annoy to *new* delight. . . . . *Am.* lxii. 14
gather to myselfe *new* breath awhile. . . . . *Am.* lxxx. 4
now t' asswage the force of this *new* flame, ... *H.L.* 8
enstall A *new* unknowen Colony therein, ... *H.H.L.* 104

New-born. this *new-borne* knight to battell new did rise. . I. xi. 34. 9
Some *newborne* wight ye would him surely weene; . . . . . IV. iii. 23. 5

New-budded. gan his *newe-budded* beard to stroke. . . . . *S.C.* May 214

New-come. As for great joyance of his *newcome* guest. . . I. xi. 15. 4
to entertaine her *new-come* guest, ... II. ii. 16. 2
all *new-come* guests he gratyfide: . . . . II. xi. 49. 5
This *new-come* shepheard had his market mard. . . . . . . VI. ix. 40. 8

Newel. He was so enamored with the *newell,* . . . . *S.C.* May 276

Newfangleness. he them in *newfanglenesse* did pas. . . . . *Hub.* 675
The schooles they fill with fond *new fanglenesse,* . . . . . *T.M.* 327
a burning hart he bare, Full of . . . *new fanglenesse:* . . . I. iv. 25. 4

New-found. Who . . . was possessed of his *newfound* make. . I. vii. 15. 5
made full goodly joyance to her *new-found* mate. . . . . . IV. i. 31. 9

New-grown. some soft Willow, or *new growen* stud; . . . . *Gn.* 84

Newly. his wreathed hornes gan *newly* sprout: . . . . *S.C.* May 186
of good passed *newly* to discus, ... *Col.* 38
To catch her, *newly* offred to his eie; . . . . I. vi. 46. 5
As chicken *newly* hatcht, ... II. viii. 9. 9
This of Albany *newly* nominate, ... II. x. 38. 4
newly borne Of th' Ocean's fruitfull froth, ... II. xii. 65. 3
Whose clawes were *newly* dipt in cruddy blood, ... III. iii. 47. 5
had from death to life him *newly* wonne. . . . . III. x. 33. 4
Helenore . . . their May-lady they had *newly* made: . . . . III. x. 44. 6
old despight . . . forth *newly* brake Gainst Blandamour, . . . IV. ix. 26. 3
lyke Pincks but *newly* spred; . . . . *Am.* lxiv. 8
the refyned mynd doth *newly* fashion . . . . *H.L.* 192

Newly-budded. His *newly-budded* pineons to assay, ... I. xi. 34. 7

Newre. *See* **Nore.**

News. *Newes* may perhaps some good unweeting beare.' . . . *Hub.* 606
To weete of *newes* that did abroad betide, ... I. vi. 34. 5
More greedy they of *newes* fast towards him do crosse. . . . I. vi. 34. 9
Una greatly with those *newes* distrest. . . . . I. vii. Arg.
The messenger of so unhappie *newes* Would faine have dyde: . I. vii. 21. 1
home ye may report thrise happy *newes;* . . . . II. i. 33. 8
Newes hereof to her other sisters came, ... II. ii. 16. 3
readie *newes,* that those same weare Two of the prowest . . IV. ii. 31. 5
Whereof when *newes* to Triamond was brought . . . . IV. iv. 33. 1
Some gladfull *newes* and sure intelligence, ... IV. vi. 34. 4
so sore a breach That sudden *newes* had made . . . . IV. vi. 38. 4
Ne stayed further *newes* thereof to learne, ... IV. x. 9. 3
gan of sundry *newes* his store to tell, ... V. ii. 2. 6
then bring me *newes* Of his demeane: . . . . V. v. 51. 1
Talus brings *newes* to Britomart . . . . V. vi. Arg.
with conscience Of his ill *newes,* . . . . V. vi. 9. 6
Whereof when *newes* to Radigund was brought, ... V. vii. 25. 1
Whereof when *newes* was to that Tyrant brought, ... V. xi. 2. 1
She thankt him deare Both for that *newes* . . . . VI. ii. 46. 7
When Calidore these ruefull *newes* had raught, ... VI. xi. 33. 1
In hope there *newes* to learne, ... VI. xi. 36. 9

News-man. 'Cease, thou bad *newes-man!* . . . . V. vi. 11. 4

New-supplied. his late enimy . . . , or other *new supplied* knight. . . . . I. xi. 35. 4

New-year. *New yeare,* forth looking out of Janus gate, . . . *Am.* iv. 1

New-year's. Then shall the *new yeares* joy forth freshly send, *Am.* lxii. 9

Next. The *next* to heale theyr throtes. . . . . *S.C.* Jul. 88
(whose turne shall be the *next?*) . . . . *S.C.* N. 193
Next did the Myrtle tree to her approach, ... *Gn.* 223
'There *next* the utmost brinck . . . . *Gn.* 385
I meane to turne the *next* leafe of the booke: . . . . *Hub.* 68
the morrow *next* ensuing, ... *Hub.* 103
The morrow *next,* so soone as one might see . . . . *Hub.* 108
bad *next* day that all should readie be: . . . . *Hub.* 329
the *next* morrowes meed they closely ment, ... *Hub.* 331
their *next* neighbor Priest, ... *Hub.* 572
if he awake, yet is not death the *next,* . . . . *Hub.* 987
to appeare The morrow *next* at Court, ... *Hub.* 1099
then the *next* anew, Began her grievous plaint . . . . . . *T.M.* 113
then the *next* in rew Began her grievous plaint, ... *T.M.* 173, 233, 299, 419
then the *next* in rew Began her piteous plaint, ... *T.M.* 359
then the *next* in rew Began her plaint, ... *T.M.* 479
the *next* in rew Began her mournfull plaint, ... *T.M.* 539
Next unto this a statelie Towre appeared, ... *Ti.* 505
and *next* unto her selfe advance, ... *Col.* 501
Worthie *next* after Cynthia to tread, ... *Col.* 514
she is *next* her in nobilitie. . . . . *Col.* 515
The *next* to her is bountifull Charillis: . . . . *Col.* 542
Next gan the earth to shew her naked head, ... *Col.* 857
And *next* her wrinkled skin rough sackecloth . . . . I. iii. 14. 3
next to him rode lustfull Lechery Upon a bearded Gote, . . . I. iv. 24. 1
next to him malicious Envy rode Upon a ravenous wolfe, . . I. iv. 30. 1

Next—*Continued.*
The foule Duessa, *next* unto the chaire Of proud Lucifer,' . . I. iv. 37. 5
In equall lists they should the morrow *next* it fight. . . . . I. iv. 40. 9
as a sacred pledge His cause . . . the *next* day to try: . . . I. iv. 43. 2
'Ah deare Sansjoy, *next* dearest to Sansfoy, ... I. iv. 45. 4
Returne . . . Till morrow *next* that I the Elfe subdew, . . . I. iv. 51. 4
'Thine, . . . *Next* to that Ladies love, shalbe the place, . . . I. ix. 17. 2
The morrow *next* gan earely to appeare, ... I. xi. 33. 1
ere the morrow *next* gan reare Out of the sea . . . . I. xi. 33. 3
you, faire Sir, whose pageant *next* ensewes, ... II. i. 33. 6
What coward hand shall doe thee *next* to dye, ... II. vi. 39. 8
to the gate of Hell, . . . Was *next* adjoyning, ... II. vii. 24. 7
albe his drowsy den were *next;* . . . . II. vii. 25. 6
Next thereunto did grow a goodly tree, ... II. vii. 53. 6
The *next* could of thinges present best advize; . . . . II. ix. 49. 2
Next Memprise, as unworthy of that place; . . . . II. x. 21. 3
Next Huddibras his realme did not encrease, ... II. x. 25. 4
Next him king Leyr in happie peace long raynd, ... II. x. 27. 1
Next great Gurgustus, then faire Caecily, ... II. x. 34. 3
Next them did Gurgiunt . . . In rule succeede, ... II. x. 41. 1
Next whom Morindus did the crowne sustayne; . . . . II. x. 43. 3
Next Archigald, who for his proud disdayne . . . . II. x. 44. 4
Next him Tenantius raignd; . . . . II. x. 50. 1
Good Claudius, that *next* was Emperour, ... II. x. 51. 1
Next him was noble Elfinan, ... II. x. 72. 7
Then to the *next* she rode, and downe the *next* did beare. . . III. i. 28. 9
next to him Jocante did ensew; . . . . III. i. 45. 4
Earely, the morrow *next,* before that day . . . . III. ii. 48. 1
next to none after that happy day, ... III. viii. 13. 7
till morrow *next* againe . . . . III. viii. 51. 7
lefte *next* in remaine To Paridas his sonne, ... III. ix. 37. 4
The morow *next,* . . . Paridell complayned, ... III. x. 1. 1
Next unto him was Neptune pictured, ... III. xi. 40. 1
Next Saturne was, ... III. xi. 43. 1
forward with bold steps into the *next* roome went. . . . . . III. xi. 50. 9
Next after him went Doubt, ... III. xii. 10. 1
Next him was Feare, all arm'd . . . . III. xii. 12. 1
Next him went Griefe and Fury, ... III. xii. 16. 1
Next after her, the winged God . . . . III. xii. 22. 1
Reproch the first, Shame *next,* Repent behinde: . . . . III. xii. 24. 2
Till morrow *next* shee did her selfe avize, ... III. xii. 28. 4
The morrowe *next* appeard with joyous cheare, ... III. xii. 28. 6
next stroke him should have slaine, ... III. xii. 34. 2
The morow *next,* so soone as Titan shone, ... IV. i. 16. 5
Eftsoones his life may passe into the *next:* . . . . IV. ii. 52. 6
when the *next* shall likewise ended bee, ... IV. ii. 52. 7
Whom when on ground his brother *next* beheld, ... IV. iii. 14. 1
First to her brother, . . . And *next* to Cambell, ... IV. iii. 46. 8
Albee his turne were *next;* . . . . IV. iv. 20. 3
The morrow *next* the Turney gan anew: . . . . IV. iv. 26. 1
So fitly now here commeth *next* in place, ... IV. v. 2. 1
next ensew'd the Paragon to see . . . . IV. v. 9. 8
Next did Sir Triamond unto their sight . . . . IV. v. 10. 6
The *next* day, as he on his way did ride, ... IV. vi. 2. 2
early in the morrow *next,* he went . . . . IV. vi. 44. 4
'The morrow *next,* about the wonted howre, ... IV. viii. 59. 1
next to her sate goodly Shamefastnesse, ... IV. x. 50. 1
next to her sate sober Modestie, ... IV. x. 51. 1
Next came the aged Ocean and his Dame . . . . IV. xi. 18. 1
musicke, which did *next* ensew Before the spouse: . . . . . . IV. xi. 23. 2
Next him went Wylibourne . . . . IV. xi. 32. 5
Next these the plenteous Ouse came . . . . IV. xi. 34. 1
next to him the Nene downe softly slid; . . . . IV. xi. 35. 7
Next these came Tyne, ... IV. xi. 36. 1
The *next,* the stubborne Newre . . . . IV. xi. 43. 3
next to him old Saturne, ... V. Pr. 8. 9
Next Hercules his like ensample shewed, ... V. i. 2. 6
next her selfe her righteous ballance hanging bee. . . . . . V. i. 11. 9
That he mote fresher be against the *next* daies fight. . . . V. iv. 51. 9
at the *next* blow Halfe of her shield he shared quite away, . . V. v. 9. 1
as *next* to hand did light, ... V. vi. 20. 8
The morrow *next,* so soone as dawning light . . . . V. vii. 26. 7
Next gan Religion gainst her to impute High Gods beheast, . V. ix. 44. 5
That nought the morrow *next* mote stay his fare. . . . . . . V. x. 16. 4
The morrow *next* appear'd with purple hayre . . . . V. x. 16. 5
pointed for the combat twixt them twayne The morrow *next,* V. xii. 9. 8
The morrow *next,* that was the dismall day . . . . V. xii. 11. 1
her dwelling Was neare to Envie, even her neighbour *next;* . V. xii. 35. 6
The morrow *next,* before the lampe of light . . . . VI. i. 31. 1
Next, that ye Ladies ayde . . . . VI. i. 42. 9
what ensu'd shall in *next* Canto be begonne. . . . . VI. ii. 48. 9
The morrow *next,* when day gan to uplooke, ... VI. iii. 11. 1
For first, *next* after life, he tendered her good. . . . . . VI. iii. 11. 9
The morrow *next,* so soone as joyous day . . . . VI. iii. 45. 1
all the water which doth ronne In the *next* brooke, ... VI. iv. 32. 9
The morrow *next* the Prince did early rize, ... VI. vi. 44. 8
fearing death, and *next* to death the lacke Of clothes . . . VI. viii. 50. 3
Next faire Aglaia, last Thalia merry; . . . . VI. x. 22. 8
chiefely Mercury, that *next* doth raigne, ... VII. vi. 14. 8
'*Next* is the Ayre; . . . . VII. vii. 22. 1
Next came fresh Aprill, ... VII. vii. 33. 1
Next him September marched, ... VII. vii. 38. 1
Next was November; he full grosse and fat . . . . VII. vii. 40. 1
after him came *next* the chill December: . . . . VII. vii. 41. 1
'*Next* Mercury; . . . . VII. vii. 51. 1
Thinking to quench her thirst at the *next* brooke: . . . . . *Am.* lxvii. 8
thanks . . . *next* to Jones, that truely it translated. . . . *Com. Son.* ii. 14
Fayre Venice . . . *next* to them in beauty draweth neare, . . *Com. Son.* iv. 11
next he did beget . . . Angels bright, ... *H.H.L.* 54
So that *next* off-spring of the Makers love, ... *H.H.L.* 92

Next—*Continued.*
Next to Himselfe in glorious degree, ... *H.H.L.* 93
Therefore of clay, base, vile, and *next* to nought, ... *H.H.L.* 106
Him first to love . . . And *next* our brethren, ... *H.H.L.* 189
Then *next,* to love our brethren, ... *H.H.L.* 197
Next whereunto there standes a stately place, ... *Proth.* 137
Nibble. *Nibble* the bushie shrubs . . . . *Gn.* 80
Nice. To finger the fine needle and *nyce* thread, ... III. ii. 6. 8
sense of man so coy and curious *nice,* . . . . IV. x. 22. 6
The knight was nothing *nice,* where was no need, ... VI. ix. 7. 1
Nicely. Upon his tiptoes *nicely* he up went, ... *Hub.* 1009
He . . . *nycely* trode, as thornes lay in his way, ... III. xii. 10. 6
Niceness. ne spard for *nicenesse* none. . . . . II. ix. 28. 9
eke that age despysed *nicenesse* vaine, ... IV. viii. 27. 5
nought for *nicenesse* nor for envy sparing, ... IV. x. 56. 6
Nicer. if any *nycer* wit Shall hap to heare, ... *As.* Pr. 13
(Entire affection hateth *nicer* hands) . . . . I. viii. 40. 3
Nicety. no courting *nicetee,* But simple, trew, ... I. x. 7. 7
(So love does loath disdainefull *nicitee*) . . . . II. ii. 3. 3
Nictileus. *See* **Nyctelius.**
Nidd. High Swale, unquiet *Nide,* and troublous Skell; . . . . IV. xi. 37. 7
Nie. *See* **Nigh.**
Niece's. she to whom Daphnaida Upon her *neeces* death I did complaine: . . . . *Col.* 511
Niggard. Art, as halfe in scorne Of *niggard* Nature, ... II. xii. 50. 7
Niggardise. will not use his gifts for thanklesse *nigardise.'* . IV. viii. 15. 9
Nigh. *See* **Well-nigh.**
from *nie* hilles a naked rout of Faunes . . . . *Bel.*[1] x. 11
odours fil'd th' ayre farre and *nie.* . . . . *Bel.*[2] xi. 4
from *nigh* hills, with hideous outcrie, ... *Bel.*[2] xii. 11
to swell, that *nigh* his bowells brust, ... *Van.* vi. 10
Possest *nigh* of the Capitol through slight, ... *Van.* xi. 7
Age and Winter accord full *nie,* . . . . *S.C.* F. 27
the day is *nigh* wasted. . . . . *S.C.* F. 246
a sigh had *nigh* rent her heart in twaine) . . . . *S.C.* May 194
the deawie night now doth *nye,* . . . . *S.C.* May 316
if you goe *nye,* . . . . *S.C.* S. 116
throat through thirst to nought *nigh* being dride . . . . . . *Gn.* 387
In th' Hellespont being *nigh* drowned all. . . . . *Gn.* 552
When as they *nigh* approached, ... *Hub.* 243
Whom no uncleannes may approachen *nie;* . . . . *Hub.* 466
in highest place, t' approach him *nigh,* . . . . *Hub.* 470
with the weight their backs *nigh* broken were: . . . . *Hub.* 1158
unto the Pallace *nigh* he came. . . . . *Hub.* 1265
Nigh where the goodly Verlame stood . . . . *Ti.* 3
felt my heart *nigh* riven . . . . *Ti.* 30
none shoot up that *nigh* him planted bee: . . . . *Ti.* 453
nigh unto the Heavens in height upreared, ... *Ti.* 507
nigh with griefe thereof my heart was brust. . . . . *Ti.* 518
Approaching *nigh,* his face I vewed nere, ... *D.* 50
Both Nymphes and Muses *nigh* she made astownd, ... *D.* 314
suffer solace to approach him *nie,* . . . . *D.* 548
the outragious passion *nigh* appeased, ... *D.* 555
none is *nigh,* thine eylids up to close, ... *As.* 137
The first, to which we *nigh* approched, ... *Col.* 280
most that unto them I am so *nie;* . . . . *Col.* 539
Enforst to seeke some covert *nigh* at hand, ... I. i. 7. 1
The maker . . . Was *nigh* beguiled . . . . I. i. 45. 7
nigh his manly hart did melt away, ... I. i. 47. 5
His foe was *nigh* at hand. . . . . I. ii. 14. 6
nigh wearie of the yrkesome way, ... I. iii. 4. 1
to the pray when as he drew more *ny,* . . . . I. iii. 5. 7
To weet if dwelling place were *nigh* at hand; . . . . I. iii. 11. 2
Nigh dead with feare, ... I. iii. 13. 4
furthest from her hope, when most she weened *nye.* . . . . . I. iii. 21. 9
too *nigh* at hand, ... I. iii. 26. 4
Approaching *nigh* she wist . . . . I. iii. 26. 8
nigh he drew unto this gentle payre, ... I. iii. 34. 1
nigh consumed is the lingring day. . . . . I. iv. 3. 9
His life was *nigh* unto deaths dore yplaste; . . . . I. iv. 28. 1
that good knight would not so *nigh* repaire, ... I. iv. 37. 7
In slombring swownd, *nigh* voyd of vitall spright, ... I. v. 19. 5
her *nigh* weary wayne, ... I. v. 41. 2
They, drawing *nigh,* . . . present That flowre of fayth . . . I. vi. 15. 4
The knight, approching *nigh,* . . . . I. vi. 36. 1
And, drawing *nigh* him, said; . . . . I. vi. 42. 1
this knight *nigh* to the Lady drew, ... I. vii. 38. 1
untill they came *Nigh* to a castle . . . . I. viii. 2. 2
life *nigh* crusht out of his panting brest: . . . . I. viii. 15. 3
Whose hartstrings with keene steele *nigh* hewen be; . . . . . I. viii. 22. 7
you, . . . these sad eyes saw *nigh* unto deaths dore, ... I. viii. 27. 2
Nigh as he drew, ... I. ix. 22. 1
'no daunger now is *nye.'* . . . . I. ix. 26. 5
his fraile thighes, *nigh* weary and fordonne, ... I. x. 47. 8
the dreadful Beast drew *nigh* to hand, ... I. xi. 8. 1
Approching *nigh,* . . . . I. xi. 8. 6
made the Redcrosse knight *nigh* quake . . . . I. xi. 15. 8
ayre, which *nigh* too feeble found . . . . I. xi. 18. 4
nigh thereto the . . . Beast Durst not approch, ... I. xi. 49. 1
Behold! I see the haven *nigh* at hand . . . . I. xii. 1. 1
Ne durst approch him *nigh* to touch, ... I. xii. 9. 9
some more bold to measure him *nigh* stand, ... I. xii. 11. 8
The knight, approching *nigh,* thus to her said: . . . . II. i. 14. 1
dead through great affright They both *nigh* were, ... II. iii. 19. 8
Whom that mad man of life *nigh* late deprivd, ... II. iv. 16. 3
Approching *nigh,* he never staid to greete, ... II. v. 3. 1
Both horse and man *nigh* able for to choke; . . . . II. v. 3. 5
*Sometimes she laught, that *nigh* her breth was gone, ... II. vi. 3. 4
thereof *nigh* one quarter sheard away; . . . . II. vi. 31. 4
Atin drew *nigh* to weet what it mote bee, ... II. vi. 43. 1

Nigh—*Continued.*
ugly shapes did *nigh* the man dismay, ... II. vii. 37. 7
Out of the rockes and caves adjoyning *nye;* . . . . II. ix. 13. 3
forth rushing from the forest *nye*. . . . . II. ix. 14. 9
feeble age *Nigh* to his utmost date . . . . II. x. 27. 7
his long legs *nigh* raught unto the ground. . . . . II. xi. 20. 6
Still as the greedy knight *nigh* to him drew; . . . . . . II. xi. 27. 2
Nigh his wits end then woxe th' amazed knight, ... II. xi. 44. 1
whoso cometh *nigh; yet nigh* it drawes All passengers, . . . II. xii. 4. 6
Untill they *nigh* unto that Gulfe arryve, ... II. xii. 5. 2
Ne that approcheth *nigh* the wyde descent, ... II. xii. 6. 8
That quicksand *nigh* with water covered; . . . . II. xii. 18. 6
they *nigh* approched to the sted . . . . II. xii. 30. 1
Now are they come *nigh* to the Bowre of blis, ... II. xii. 69. 4
drew So *nigh* them, ... II. xii. 81. 2
Nigh a speares length behind his crouper fell; . . . . . . III. i. 6. 7
as *nigh* out of the wood she came, ... III. i. 20. 1
plaste for pleasure *nigh* that forrest syde: . . . . III. i. 20. 5
nigh he breathlesse grew, ... III. i. 21. 3
was bescracht and both his feet *nigh* lame. . . . . III. v. 3. 9
They were through wonder *nigh* of sence berev'd, ... III. vi. 27. 5
as one *nigh* of her wits depriv'd, ... III. vii. 14. 5
Whom when the fearefull Damzell *nigh* espide, ... III. vii. 24. 1
With burning charet wheeles it *nigh* to smite; . . . . . . III. vii. 41. 7
Whom when as *nigh* approching she espyde, ... III. vii. 44. 1
her the hardy knight pursewd so *nye* . . . . III. vii. 44. 5
did *nigh* affray That Capons corage: . . . . III. viii. 15. 5
nigh Approching, with bold words and bitter threat . . . III. viii. 16. 1
seeing *nigh* him jeopardy extreme, ... III. viii. 16. 8
when she is *nigh* defild Of filthy wretch? . . . . III. viii. 27. 7
sith that none of all her knights is *nye*, ... III. viii. 29. 1
Her heart *nigh* broken was with weary toyle, ... III. viii. 32. 4
her wits *nigh* fayld, ... III. viii. 34. 8
comming *nigh*, eftsoones he gan to gesse, ... III. viii. 45. 3
Full deepe emplonged was, and drowned *nye* . . . . III. x. 17. 5
durst not for dread approchen *nie*, ... III. x. 22. 2
Signe of *nigh* battaill, or got victory: . . . . III. xii. 1. 6
the frayle soule in deepe delight *nigh* drownd: . . . . . III. xii. 6. 5
naked *nigh* she did appeare, ... III. xii. 17. 2
Like as a Deare, . . . now *nigh* breathlesse. . . . . . . III. xii. 44. *or*. 9
Approching *nigh*, eftsoones his wanton hart Was tickled . . . IV. i. 33. 5
the lovely paire drew *nigh* to hond: . . . . IV. i. 34. 1
when as Blandamour approching *nie* . . . . IV. i. 38. 7
Their wooden ribs are shaken *nigh* asonder. . . . . IV. ii. 16. 6
Drew *nigh*, to weete the cause of their debate: . . . . . . IV. ii. 20. 6
as they now approched *nigh* at hand, ... IV. ii. 31. 1
Yet is as *nigh* his end as he that most doth playne. . . . IV. iii. 1. 9
made them dreaded much of all men farre and *nie*. . . . . IV. iii. 2. 9
Was with the force *nigh* feld, ... IV. iii. 18. 9
He falleth *nigh* to ground, ... IV. iii. 19. 9
Yet *nigh* approching he them fowle bespake, ... IV. iv. 4. 1
Him weening, ere he *nigh* approcht, to have represt. . . . IV. iv. 6. 9
To stumble, that his rider *nigh* he cast; . . . . IV. iv. 30. 4
beating downe what ever *nigh* him came, ... IV. iv. 41. 7
woxe *nigh* mad for very harts despight, ... IV. v. 27. 2
when he was unto her selfe most *nie*, ... IV. v. 29. 8
Whereto approaching *nigh* they heard the sound . . . . . . IV. v. 33. 6
Besmeard with smoke that *nigh* his eye-sight blent; . . . . IV. v. 34. 7
my wearie teeme, *nigh* over spent, ... IV. v. 46. 8
as th' other *nigh* approaching vewed The armes . . . . . IV. vi. 3. 3
Whom, when they *nigh* approcht, they plaine descryde . . IV. vi. 9. 4
drawing *nigh*, when as he plaine descride . . . . IV. vi. 24. 4
griefe, that her deare hart *nigh* swelt, ... IV. vii. 9. 4
espies that griesly wight Approching *nigh*, ... IV. vii. 22. 6
when that theefe approching *nigh* espide . . . . IV. vii. 29. 5
drawing *nigh*, ere he her well beheld, ... IV. vii. 36. 7
He durst not *nigh* approch, but kept aloofe, ... IV. vii. 37. 4
ever, when she *nigh* approcht, ... IV. viii. 11. 1
nigh at hand Those Ladies two, ... IV. viii. 62. 6
his neighbour floods which *nigh* him dwell, ... IV. xi. 30. 1
Dart, *nigh* chockt with sands of tinny mines. . . . . . . IV. xi. 31. 5
The Easterne Saxons from the Southerne *ny*, ... IV. xi. 33. 4
count my cares when none is *nigh* to heare, ... IV. xii. 6. 2
Nigh thirtie minutes . . . . V. Pr. 7. 8
purchast all the countrey lying *ny* . . . . V. ii. 9. 7
oftentimes him *nigh* he overthrew: . . . . V. ii. 13. 7
with the straint his wesand *nigh* he brast. . . . . V. ii. 14. 5
Till that at length *nigh* to the sea they drew; . . . . . . V. ii. 29. 2
Approching *nigh* unto him, cheeke by cheeke, ... V. ii. 49. 7
soone as they him *nigh* approching spide, ... V. ii. 53. 1
He *nigh* them drew . . . . V. iii. 30. 7
nor once approach him *nie;* . . . . V. iv. 44. 6
when he *nigh* approcht, shee mote arede That it was Talus, . V. vi. 8. 5
as she *nigh* unto them drew, ... V. vi. 37. 2
touched with intire affection *nigh* him drew; . . . . . . V. viii. 12. 9
Then they that Damzell called to them *nie*, ... V. viii. 16. 1
Famous through all the world, and honor'd far and *nie*. . . . V. viii. 16. 9
Oft drew the Prince unto his charret *nigh*, ... V. viii. 33. 1
Still when he sought t' approch unto him *ny* . . . . V. viii. 36. 1
Yet could the Prince not *nigh* unto him goe, ... V. viii. 37. 3
This lower world *nigh* all to ashes brent, ... V. viii. 40. 8
All were they *nigh* an hundred knights of name, ... V. viii. 50. 6
till they approched *ny* Unto the rocke . . . . V. ix. 8. 1
Where she might sit *nigh* to the den alone, ... V. ix. 8. 7
she was *nigh* dismayd, ... V. ix. 12. 2
when as *ny* He came unto his cave, ... V. ix. 14. 6
Nigh to the place which ye desir'd to see: . . . . V. ix. 20. 5
nigh fild all the place, ... V. xi. 23. 2
Did quake to heare, and *nigh* asunder brast: . . . . V. xi. 28. 5
him *nigh* choked with the deadly stinke. . . . . V. xi. 31. 8

Nigh—*Continued.*
any man would *nigh* awhaped make: . . . . V. xi. 32. 5
Till *nigh* unto the place at length approcht he has. . . . . V. xi. 36. 9
now time drawing *ny* . . . . V. xii. 3. 6
when as *nigh* unto the shore they drew . . . . V. xii. 5. 2
Sith no redemption *nigh* she did nor heare nor see. . . . . V. xii. 11. 9
with untimely drought *nigh* withered was, ... V. xii. 13. 2
when they *nigh* approching had espyde Sir Artegall, ... V. xii. 38. 2
all the woods and rockes *nigh* to that way Began to quake . V. xii. 41. 4
nigh ravisht with rare thoughts delight, ... VI. Pr. 1. 6
from her head her lockes he *nigh* did teare, ... VI. i. 17. 8
if I yet him *nigh* may reach, I may avenge him . . . . . . VI. ii. 42. 5
He, her not finding, both them thus *nigh* dead did leave. . . VI. ii. 43. 9
young Knight who dwelt her *ny*, ... VI. iii. 7. 5
Sir Calidore approaching *nye*, ... VI. iii. 21. 1
As if his lungs and lites were *nigh* asunder brast. . . . . VI. iii. 26. 9
he *nigh* espyde An armed Knight . . . . VI. iii. 30. 6
whenas he approched *nigh* in vew, ... VI. iii. 47. 3
from his steed him *nigh* he drew againe: . . . . VI. iv. 7. 5
his long speare So *nigh* at hand, ... VI. iv. 7. 7
ever as he saw him *nigh* succeed, ... VI. iv. 8. 7
In seeking all the woods both farre and *nye* . . . . VI. iv. 16. 3
he *nigh* choked was, ... VI. iv. 21. 6
Stryving in vaine that *nigh* his bowels brast, ... VI. iv. 22. 2
For nought but woods and forrests farre and *nye*, ... VI. iv. 24. 8
at length, *nigh* tyrd with former chace, ... VI. v. 21. 1
the Squire, now *nigh* aghast, Revived was, ... VI. v. 21. 8
Eftsoones he spide a Knight approching *nye;* . . . . VI. v. 22. 1
nigh thereto a little Chappell stoode, ... VI. v. 35. 1
He woxe *nigh* mad with wrath and fell despight, ... VI. vi. 24. 8
all his bones in peeces *nigh* he brake. . . . . VI. vii. 11. 5
The fearfull swayne beholding death so *nie*, ... VI. vii. 12. 1
when he *nigh* approcht, ... VI. vii. 20. 4
though she were with wearinesse *nigh* dead, ... VI. vii. 40. 8
Where none is *nigh* to heare that will her rew, ... VI. viii. 40. 8
the Priest with naked armes full net Approching *nigh*, . . . VI. viii. 45. 5
He followed fast, and chaced him so *nie*, ... VI. ix. 4. 6
Upon their neighbours which did *nigh* them border, ... VI. x. 39. 6
as he unto him approched *nye*, ... VI. xi. 27. 7
all his wits with doole were *nigh* distraught, ... VI. xi. 33. 3
to the place when they approched *nye*, ... VI. xi. 36. 5
when no more could *nigh* to him approch, ... VI. xi. 47. 1
nigh she swelt For passing joy, ... VI. xii. 21. 8
shooke *Nigh* all to peeces, ... VII. vi. 47. 8
Nigh-aimed. Now the *nigh aymed* ring away to beare. . . . . *Hub.* 742
Nigher. the hills bene *nigher* heven, ... *S.C.* Jul. 89
off-shaking vaine affright She *nigher* drew, ... I. xi. 55. 7
the Squire gan *nigher* to approch, ... II. ix. 11. 3
Bidding them *nigher* draw unto the shore, ... II. xii. 15. 2
Acrasia he sent . . . a *nigher* way, ... III. i. 2. 2
ever as he *nigher* to her drew, ... III. iv. 48. 3
as he *nigher* drew, he easily Might scerne . . . . III. x. 22. 7
as he *nigher* drew, three knights he spyde, ... V. x. 34. 1
And for their better comfort to them *nigher* drew. . . . . VI. ii. 41. 9
He *nigher* drew to weete what mote it be: . . . . VI. x. 10. 6
Nighest. men to God thereby are *nighest* raised. . . . . . . *T.M.* 90
through the thickest makes her *nighest* waies; . . . . . . IV. vii. 22. 3
Nigheth. *The joyous time now *nigheth* fast, ... *S.C.* Mar. 4
The night *nigheth* fast, ... *S.C.* Au. 198
Nigh-forwearied. His *nigh forweried* feeble feet did slide, . I. xi. 45. 8
Nigh hand. with flowres which they *nigh hand* obtayned. . . VI. viii. 44. 9
Nighing. Now day is doen, and night is *nighing* fast, ... *Epith.* 298
Nighly. Their weedes bene not so *nighly* wore; . . . . *S.C.* Jul. 171
Nighs. The joyous time now *nighes* fast, ... *S.C.* Mar. 4
Night. By Magicke skill out of eternall *night*. . . . . *Ro.* v. 8
when all shrouded were in silent *night*, ... *Van.* xi. 5
the frosty *Night* Her mantle black . . . gan overhaile: . . . *S.C.* Ja. 74
let us homeward, for *night* draweth on, ... *S.C.* Ap. 160
the deawie *night* now doth nye, ... *S.C.* May 316
chace the lingring *Night* With Heydeguyes, ... *S.C.* Jun. 26
night with stealing steppes doe you forsloe, ... *S.C.* Jun. 119
my cryes . . . You heare all *night*, ... *S.C.* Au. 177
Thus all the *night* in plaints, ... *S.C.* Au. 179
The *night* nigheth fast, ... *S.C.* Au. 198
now at earst the dirke *night* doth hast. . . . . *S.C.* S. 6
at *night* wont to repayre Unto the flocke, ... *S.C.* S. 186
oft in the *night* came to the shepe-cote, ... *S.C.* S. 216
all we dwell in deadly *night*. . . . . *S.C.* N. 69
She hath the bonds broke of eternall *night*, ... *S.C.* N. 165
the *Night* forth from the darksome bowre . . . . *Gn.* 313
With bloodie *night*, and darke confusion; . . . . *Gn.* 445
over *night* whatso theretoo did neede . . . . *Hub.* 106
Carried in clowdes of all-concealing *night*. . . . . *Hub.* 340
ran away by *night*. *Hub.* 574
ran away in his rent rags by *night*, ... *Hub.* 937
an universall *night* Throughout the world he makes . . . . *Hub.* 1297
Darknesse more than Cymerians daylie *night*: . . . . *T.M.* 256
By yawning Sloth on his owne mother *Night;* . . . . *T.M.* 263
some bride, her joyous *night* to hold: . . . . *Ti.* 635
The sea, the aire, the fire, the day, the *night*, ... *Mui.* 228
all the *night* that I in watch did spend, ... *D.* 129
Shee would all *night* by mee or watch or sleepe . . . . . . *D.* 131
On which the clowde of ghastly *night* did sit, ... *D.* 305
I hate the darknesse and the drery *night*, ... *D.* 409
I will wake and sorrow all the *night* . . . . *D.* 474
day is turnd to *night*, ... *D.* 482
night without a Venus starre is found. . . . . *D.* 483
darke *night* fast approched, ... *D.* 557
Full carefully he kept them day and *night*, ... *As.* 5
'Now,' . . . 'draweth toward *night*, ... I. i. 32. 4

Night—*Continued.*
The Sunne, . . . At *night* doth baite his steedes . . . . . . I. i. 32. 9
Untroubled *night*, . . . gives counsell best.' . . . . I. i. 33. 3
take up your In For this same *night*.' . . . . I. i. 33. 8
The drouping *night* thus creepeth on them fast; . . . . . . I. i. 36. 1
Great Gorgon, prince of darknes and dead *night;* . . . . . I. i. 37. 8
sad *Night* over him her mantle black doth spred. . . . . . . I. i. 39. 9
waste the wearie *night* In secret anguish . . . . I. i. 53. 2
Full envious that *night* so long his roome did fill: . . . . . I. ii. 1. 9
Their bootelesse paines, and ill succeeding *night:* . . . . . . I. ii. 2. 4
Covered with darkenes and misdeeming *night*, ... I. ii. 3. 8
Yrkesome of life, and too long lingring *night*. . . . . I. ii. 6. 5
drownd in sleepie *night*, . . . did besmeare My body . . . . I. ii. 42. 2
her mother blynd Sate in eternall *night:* . . . . I. iii. 12. 4
that old woman day and *night* did pray . . . . I. iii. 13. 6
in their cotage small that *night* she rest her may. . . . . . I. iii. 14. 9
The day is spent; and commeth drowsie *night*, ... I. iii. 15. 1
does steepe Her tender brest in bitter teares all *night;* . . . I. iii. 15. 8
All *night* she thinks too long, ... I. iii. 15. 9
fearefull freends weare out the wofull *night*, ... I. iii. 20. 6
My chearefull day is turnd to chearelesse *night*, ... I. iii. 27. 7
eke my *night* of death the shadow is; . . . . I. iii. 27. 8
people traveild thetherward Both day and *night*, ... I. iv. 3. 2
To looken whether it were *night* or day. . . . . I. iv. 19. 6
That *night* they pas in joy and jollity, ... I. iv. 43. 5
darkesome *night* had all displayd Her coleblacke curtein . . I. iv. 44. 1
Such restlesse passion did all *night* torment . . . . I. v. 1. 5
Covering your foe with cloud of deadly *night*, ... I. v. 14. 7
griesly *Night*, with visage deadly sad, ... I. v. 20. 1
dreaded *Night* in brightest day hath place, ... I. v. 24. 4
So lay him in her charett, close in *night* conceald. . . . . . I. v. 29. 9
erthly wight that with the *Night* durst ride. . . . . I. v. 32. 9
auncient *Night* arriving did alight . . . . I. v. 41. 1
Can *Night* defray The wrath of thundring Jove, ... I. v. 42. 8
thundring Jove, that rules both *night* and day?' . . . . . . I. v. 42. 9
Now in the powre of everlasting *Night?* . . . . I. v. 43. 5
The false Duessa, leaving noyous *Night*, ... I. v. 45. 1
caytive wretched thralls, that wayled *night* and day: . . . . I. v. 45. 9
returning from the drery *Night*, ... I. vii. 2. 1
let eternall *night* so sad sight fro me hyde. . . . . I. vii. 22. 9
wound . . . day and *night* Whilome doth rancle . . . . I. ix. 7. 3
As she to me delivered all that *night;* . . . . I. ix. 14. 8
All *night* she spent in bidding of her bedes, ... I. x. 3. 8
it was warely watched *night* and day, ... I. x. 5. 2
his spright Had past the paines of . . . long-enduring *night*. I. x. 32. 9
day and *night* said his devotion, ... I. x. 46. 6
All *night* shee watcht, ... I. xi. 32. 7
yield his rowme to sad succeeding *night*, ... I. xi. 49. 6
watch the noyous *night*, and wait for joyous day. . . . . . . I. xi. 50. 9
it should not be quenched day nor *night*, ... I. xii. 37. 8
Night was far spent; . . . . II. ii. 46. 1
Disperst the shadowes of the misty *night*, ... II. iii. 1. 2
day and *night* her dores to all stand open wide. . . . . . . II. iii. 41. 9
Phlegeton is sonne of Herebus and *Night;* . . . . II. iv. 41. 8
Day and *night* keeping wary watch and ward, ... II. vii. 25. 2
the Moone, cloathed with clowdy *night*, ... II. vii. 29. 8
warily awaited day and *night*, ... II. vii. 32. 3
cloudes of deadly *night* . . . his heavy eylids cover'd have, . II. viii. 24. 7
They found the gates fast barred long ere *night*, ... II. ix. 10. 8
Day and *night* duely keeping watch and ward; . . . . II. ix. 25. 2
day and *night* it brent, ... II. ix. 29. 8
They battred day and *night*, and entraunce did awate. . . . II. xi. 6. 9
Ne once did yield it respitt day nor *night;* . . . . II. xi. 9. 3
day and *night* . . . they continued fight. . . . . II. xi. 13. 8
afterwards did rule the *night* and day: . . . . II. xii. 13. 7
sore annoyed, groping in that griesly *night*. . . . . II. xii. 35. 9
Dauncing and reveling both day and *night*, ... III. i. 39. 7
in darkesome *night*, Is in a noyous cloud enveloped, ... III. i. 43. 1
under the blacke vele of guilty *Night*, ... III. i. 59. 7
So soone as *Night* had with her pallid hew . . . . III. ii. 28. 1
One *night*, when she was tost with such unrest, ... III. ii. 30. 1
All *night* afflict thy naturall repose; . . . . III. ii. 31. 2
there doe toyle and traveile day and *night*, ... III. iii. 11. 6
darksom *night* he eke could turne to day: . . . . III. iii. 12. 4
she did lye All *night* in old Tithonus frozen bed, ... III. iii. 20. 6
Covered with secret cloud of silent *night*, ... III. iii. 61. 8
cursed *night* that reft from him so goodly scope. . . . . . . III. iv. 52. 9
ever hasty *Night* he blamed bitterlie. . . . . III. iv. 54. 9
'*Night!* thou foule Mother of annoyaunce sad, ... III. iv. 55. 1
chace away this too long lingring *night;* . . . . III. iv. 60. 5
Thus did the Prince that wearie *night* outweare . . . . . . III. iv. 61. 1
froward fortune, and too forward *Night*, ... III. v. 7. 4
Into the balefull house of endlesse *night*, ... III. v. 22. 3
attend About him day and *night*, ... III. vi. 32. 4
In balefull *night* where all thinges are forgot: . . . . III. vi. 47. 3
all that *night* her course continewed, ... III. vii. 2. 2
the *night* was forward spent, ... III. ix. 11. 3
In one sad *night* consumd and throwen downe: . . . . III. ix. 39. 5
now the humid *night* was farforth spent, ... III. ix. 53. 4
suffer her, nor *night* nor day, Out of his sight . . . . III. x. 3. 7
Night, the patronesse of love-stealth fayre, ... III. x. 16. 6
misty dampe of misconceyving *night*, ... III. x. 47. 5
At *night*, when all they went to sleepe, ... III. x. 48. 1
all the *night* did minde his joyous play: . . . . III. x. 48. 4
When one so oft a *night* did ring his matins bell. . . . . . III. x. 48. 9
day and *night* afflicts with mortall paine, ... III. xi. 17. 2
whenas chearelesse *Night* ycovered had Fayre heaven . . . . III. xii. 1. 1
From the fourth howre of *night* untill the sixt; . . . . . . III. xii. 2. 7
Cald by strong charmes out of eternall *night*, ... III. xii. 19. 5
Like as the shining skie in summers *night*, ... IV. i. 13. 6

Night—*Continued.*
all that *night* they of their loves did treat, ... IV. i. 16. 1
I saw him sleepe with her all *night* his fill; . . . . IV. i. 49. 3
secretly from thence that *night* her bore away. . . . . . . IV. v. 27. 9
The more it gauld and griev'd him *night* and day, ... IV. v. 31. 8
the drouping *night*, Covered with cloudie storme . . . . . . IV. v. 32. 1
neither day nor *night* from working spared, ... IV. v. 35. 7
in Lipari doe day and *night* Frame thunderbolts . . . . . . IV. v. 37. 3
all the *night* the dogs did barke and howle . . . . IV. v. 41. 6
The things, that day most minds, at *night* doe most appeare. IV. v. 43. 9
He all that *night*, that too long *night*, did passe . . . . . IV. v. 45. 2
When ever he this way shall passe by day or *night*.' . . . . IV. vi. 5. 9
hid in horrour of eternall *night?* . . . . IV. vii. 33. 6
alwaies wept and wailed *night* and day, ... IV. viii. 2. 8
To which they drew ere *night* upon them fell; . . . . IV. viii. 23. 3
The drowzie humour of the dampish *night*, ... IV. viii. 34. 4
day and *night* did watch and duely ward . . . . IV. x. 17. 2
my love was lodged day and *night*, ... IV. x. 29. 4
Ne ever from the day the *night* descride, ... IV. xi. 4. 8
thought it all one *night* that did no houres divide. . . . . . IV. xi. 4. 9
In which his wretched love lay day and *night* . . . . IV. xii. 19. 4
weeping day and *night* did him attend, ... IV. xii. 21. 6
yclowded With fearefull shadowes of deformed *night*, ... V. iv. 45. 2
Together with Sir Terpin all that *night:* . . . . V. iv. 46. 7
Like as the Moone in foggie winters *night* . . . . V. v. 12. 8
it tormented her both day and *night:* . . . . V. v. 27. 5
To lodge with him that *night*, ... V. vi. 21. 9
now seeing *night* at dore, ... V. vi. 22. 1
talk't of pleasant things the *night* away to weare. . . . . . V. vi. 22. 9
There all that *night* remained Britomart, ... V. vi. 24. 5
I wote when ye did watch both *night* and day . . . . V. vi. 25. 5
weare the weary *night* In waylfull plaints . . . . V. vi. 26. 1
the native Belman of the *night*, ... V. vi. 27. 1
Whom soone as Talus spide by glims of *night*, ... V. vi. 29. 5
Thus she all *night* wore out in watchfulnesse, ... V. vi. 34. 8
No more shall now the darkenesse of the *night* Defend thee . V. vi. 37. 6
Did enter in, ne would that *night* depart; . . . . V. vii. 3. 8
Under the wings of Isis all that *night;* . . . . V. vii. 12. 2
thorough evill rest of this last *night*, ... V. vii. 18. 7
Whiles Talus watched at the dore all *night*. . . . . V. vii. 26. 4
All *night* likewise they of the towne . . . . V. vii. 26. 5
(for she ful ill Could sleepe all *night*, ... V. vii. 27. 4
Ne day nor *night* did ever idly rest; . . . . V. viii. 3. 7
stird up day and *night* . . . . V. viii. 20. 2
Stood open wyde to all men day and *night;* . . . . V. ix. 22. 4
Upon Joves judgement-seat wayt day and *night;* . . . . . . V. ix. 31. 7
Ne day nor *night* did sleepe t' attend them on, ... V. x. 10. 4
And foule Echidna in the house of *night:* . . . . V. x. 10. 8
To wander in the griesly shades of *night*. . . . . V. x. 33. 6
Where all that *night* them selves they cherished, ... V. x. 39. 8
with a cloud of *night* him covering, ... V. xi. 14. 8
He day and *night* doth ward both farre and wide, ... V. xi. 42. 7
That *night* Sir Artegall did cause his tent There to be pitched V. xii. 10. 1
day and *night* employ'd his busie paine . . . . V. xii. 26. 3
his way did hast, and went all *night;* . . . . VI. i. 30. 1
To make abode that *night* he greatly was besought. . . . . . VI. iii. 2. 9
his guests whom he had stayd that *night*, ... VI. iii. 6. 3
Did sleepe all *night* through weary travell . . . . VI. iii. 9. 9
by her wounded love did watch all *night*, ... VI. iii. 10. 3
And all the *night* for bitter anguish weepe, ... VI. iii. 10. 4
lay All *night* in darkenesse, ... VI. iii. 13. 7
humbly praid to let them in that *night;* . . . . VI. iii. 38. 6
loth t' assay . . . now in doubtfull *night*, ... VI. iii. 41. 4
to be lodged there for that same *night*. . . . . VI. iii. 42. 9
all *night* did nought but weepe, ... VI. iii. 44. 8
And there all *night* himselfe in anguish tost, ... VI. iv. 40. 5
day and *night* did vexe her carefull thought, ... VI. v. 6. 8
faithfully did serve both day and *night* . . . . VI. v. 9. 7
her excluded late at *night*, ... VI. v. 33. 8
towards *night* they came unto a plaine, ... VI. v. 34. 7
faire Serene all *night* could take no rest, ... VI. v. 39. 6
So all that *night* they past in great disease, ... VI. v. 40. 1
The Prince himselfe there all that *night* did rest; . . . . . VI. vi. 41. 2
all that *night*, the whyles the Prince did rest . . . . VI. vi. 44. 1
whylest all the *night* was spent. . . . . VI. vi. 44. 7
who did wayle or watch the wearie *night?* . . . . VI. vii. 30. 6
his locks, as blacke as pitchy *night*, ... VI. vii. 43. 7
by th' uncertaine glims of starry *night*, ... VI. viii. 48. 1
though the *night* did cover her disgrace, ... VI. viii. 51. 3
all that *night* to him unknowen she past; . . . . VI. viii. 51. 6
day nor *night* he suffred him to rest, ... VI. ix. 3. 2
to the folds, where sheepe at *night* doe seat, ... VI. ix. 4. 7
caroling her name both day and *night*, ... VI. ix. 9. 8
Full many a *night* for her did sigh and grone: . . . . VI. ix. 10. 4
the moystie *night* approching fast . . . . VI. ix. 13. 1
night arrived hard at hand, ... VI. ix. 16. 3
all the *night* in silver sleepe I spend, ... VI. ix. 22. 8
So there that *night* Sir Calidore did dwell, ... VI. ix. 34. 1
daunce there day and *night:* . . . . VI. x. 15. 3
in the covert of the *night*, ... VI. x. 41. 3
darkenesse dred and daily *night* did hover . . . . VI. x. 42. 5
day and *night* she nought did but lament . . . . VI. x. 44. 3
Ne day nor *night* he suffred her to rest, ... VI. xi. 5. 8
her all *night* did watch, and all the day molest. . . . . . . VI. xi. 5. 9
In doubtfull shadow of the darkesome *night* . . . . VI. xi. 13. 4
in the horror of the griesly *night*, ... VI. xi. 16. 6
like starres in foggie *night*. . . . . VI. xi. 21. 9
when as towards darksome *night* it drew, ... VI. xi. 41. 1
In dead of *night*, when all the theeves did rest, ... VI. xi. 42. 2
Appointed to attend her dewly day and *night*. . . . . VI. xii. 14. 9

Night—*Continued.*
Some were of dogs, that barked day and *night;* . . . VI. xii. 27. 3
duly her attended day and *night;* . . . VII. vi. 9. 4
to her selfe to have gained The kingdome of the *Night,* . . . VII. vi. 10. 9
brought againe on them eternall *night;* . . . VII. vi. 14. 7
after these there came the Day and *Night,* . . . VII. vii. 44. 1
Night had covered her uncomely face . . . VII. vii. 44. 4
daughters of high Jove And timely *Night;* . . . VII. vii. 45. 2
Though faire all *night,* yet is she darke all day: . . . VII. vii. 51. 6
calling forth out of sad Winters *night* . . . *Am.* iv. 5
Not to the Sun; for they doo shine by *night;* . . . *Am.* ix. 5
my thoughts doo day and *night* attend, . . . *Am.* xxii. 7
The same at *night* she did againe unreave: . . . *Am.* xxiii. 4
I wish that *night* the noyous day would end: . . . *Am.* lxxxvi. 6
when as *night* hath us of light forlorne, . . . *Am.* lxxxvi. 7
I wander as in darkenesse of the *night,* . . . *Am.* lxxxvii. 3
In Joves sweet paradice of Day and *Night;* . . . *Epith.* 99
shortest *night,* when longest fitter weare: . . . *Epith.* 272
Now day is doen, and *night* is nighing fast, . . . *Epith.* 298
The *night* is come, now soon her disaray, . . . *Epith.* 300
Now it is *night,* ye damsels may be gon, . . . *Epith.* 311
Now welcome, *night!* thou *night* so long expected, . . . *Epith.* 315
let the *night* be calme, and quietsome, . . . *Epith.* 326
Be heard all *night* within, nor yet without: . . . *Epith.* 335
Conceald through covert *night.* . . . *Epith.* 363
All *night* therefore attend your merry play, . . . *Epith.* 368
walkes about high heaven al the *night?* . . . *Epith.* 375
Send us the timely fruit of this same *night.* . . . *Epith.* 404
twinckling starres in frostie *night;* . . . *H.B.* 257
And caroll Hymnes of love both day and *night.* . . . *H.H.L.* 70
Both day, and *night,* is unto them all one; . . . *H.H.L.* 71
But those two most, which, ruling *night* and day, . . . *H.H.B.* 55

Nightingale. The sweete *Nightingale* singing so lowde; . . . *S.C.* F. 123
with the *Nightingale* will I take part, . . . *S.C.* Au. 183
The *Nightingale* is sovereigne of song, . . . *S.C.* N. 25
'To make fine cages for the *Nightingale,* . . . *S.C.* D. 79
the *Nightingale* wont forth to powre Her restles plaints, . . . *Ti.* 131
To thee, that art the sommers *Nightingale,* . . . *Ded. Son.* viii. 1

Nightly. all astonned with this *nightly* ghost, . . . *Bel.*[1] vii. 1
the sound Of these my *nightly* cryes . . . *S.C.* Au. 189
delay Thy *nightly* course, to heare his melodie? . . . *Gn.* 460
I *nightly* waste, wanting my kindely reste: . . . *U.V.* 16
No *nightly* bordrags, nor no hue and cries; . . . *Col.* 315
To her my heart I *nightly* martyrize: . . . *Col.* 473
load . . . Of *nightly* stelths, and pillage severall, . . . I. iii. 16. 8
daily care To get, and *nightly* feare to lose . . . I. iv. 28. 8
High heven beholdes sad lovers *nightly* theeveryes. . . . III. xi. 45. 9
Ne dayly food did take, ne *nightly* sleepe, . . . IV. xii. 19. 8
Mongst those twelve signes, which *nightly* we doe see . . . V. i. 11. 6
To keepe a *nightly* watch for dread of treachery. . . . V. iv. 46. 9
making *nightly* rode Into their neighbours borders; . . . VI. viii. 35. 3
Through daily mourning and *nightly* misfare: . . . VI. xii. 14. 5
Which they did daily watch, and *nightly* wake . . . VII. vii. 45. 8

Night-raven. The hoars *Night-raven,* trump of dolefull drere; II. xii. 36. 5
the *night Raven,* that still deadly yels; . . . *Epith.* 346

Night-ravens. Here no *night-ravenes* lodge, . . . *S.C.* Jun. 23
after him Owles and *Night-ravens* flew, . . . II. vii. 23. 3

Night's. who shall not great *Nightes* children scorne, . . . I. v. 23. 8
that *nights* ensample did bewray . . . III. x. 48. 7
Nights humid curtaine from the heavens withdrew, . . . V. v. 1. 2
weepe To thinke of your *nights* want, . . . V. vi. 25. 9
To visite, after this *nights* perillous passe, . . . VI. iii. 14. 2
Which that *nights* fortune . . . VI. iii. 44. 4
therein to beare *Nights* burning lamp, . . . VII. vi. 12. 3
Having disperst the *nights* unchearefull dampe, . . . *Epith.* 21
guydest lovers through the *nights* sad dread, . . . *Epith.* 290
*guydest lovers through the *nightes* dread, . . . *Epith.* 290

Nights. To wast long *nights* in pensive discontent; . . . *Hub.* 898
Three *nights* in one, . . . He then did put, . . . III. xi. 33. 8
Where she in darknes wastes her cursed daies and *nights.* . . . IV. i. 19. 9
I saw him sleepe with her all night his fill; All manie *nights;* IV. i. 49. 4
Spending their joyous dayes and gladfull *nights,* . . . V. iii. 40. 2
many *nights,* that slowly seemd to move . . . *Am.* lxxxvi. 3
the *nights* they grieve and grone, . . . *H.L.* 129

Night-watches. let stil Silence trew *night-watches* keepe, . . . *Epith.* 353

Nile. By *Nyle,* or Gange, or Tygre, or Euphrate; . . . *Ro.* xxxi. 4
Beside the fruitfull shore of muddie *Nile,* . . . *Van.* iii. 1
As when old father *Nilus* gins to swell . . . I. i. 21. 1
muddy shore of broad seven-mouthed *Nile,* . . . I. v. 18. 2
The fertile *Nile,* which creatures new doth frame; . . . IV. xi. 20. 3

Nile's. *Nylus* nurslings their Pyramides faire; . . . *Ro.* ii. 4
after *Nilus* inundation, Infinite shapes of creatures men doe fynd . . . III. vi. 8. 7

Nill. sorowe, That now *nill* be quitt . . . *S.C.* May 131
If I may rest, I *nill* live in sorrowe. . . . *S.C.* May 151
they *nill* listen to the shepheards voyce, . . . *S.C.* S. 142
will or *nill,* Beares her away upon his courser light: . . . I. iii. 43. 7
Nyne monethes I seek in vain, yet *ni'll* that vow unbynd.' . . . I. ix. 15. 9
'Certes,' (sayd he) 'I *n'ill* thine offred grace, . . . II. vii. 33. 1
Ill weares he armes, that *nill* them use for Ladies sake.' . . . III. v. 11. 9
who *nill* bide the burden of distresse, . . . III. xi. 14. 8

Nilled. whether willed or *nilled* friend or foe, . . . IV. vii. 16. 6

Nimble. in their speedie course and *nimble* flight . . . *Hub.* 621
ye be fine and *nimble* it to doo; . . . *Hub.* 1000
the worke of your *nimble* hand, . . . *Hub.* 1035
he so swift and *nimble* was of flight, . . . *Mui.* 41
In wrestling *nimble,* and in renning swift, . . . *As.* 73
enwrapt the *nimble* thyes Of his froth-fomy steed, . . . I. xi. 23. 2
he gan display His painted *nimble* wings, . . . II. viii. 8. 9
through his *nimble* sleight did under him down cast. . . . II. viii. 49. 9

Nimble—*Continued.*
the *nimble* bote so well her sped, . . . II. xii. 38. 2
Taketh his *nimble* winges, and soone away is gone.' . . . III. i. 25. 9
after her his *nimble* winges doth straine, . . . III. iv. 49. 7
unlaste Her silver buskins from her *nimble* thigh, . . . III. vi. 18. 3
apply His *nimble* feet to her conceived feare, . . . III. vii. 24. 6
when he spedd His *nimble* feet, . . . III. x. 55. 4
with motion *nimble* To succour it, . . . IV. vi. 29. 4
he was full light and *nimble* on the land. . . . IV. vii. 25. 9
winged feete as *nimble* as the winde, . . . IV. vii. 30. 2
her *nimble* wings displaid, . . . IV. viii. 7. 6
With *nimble* wings of gold and purple hew; . . . IV. x. 42. 3
with *nimble* flight Flowne at a flush of Ducks . . . V. ii. 54. 1
So light of hand, and *nymble* of his pace, . . . V. ix. 5. 5
Either with *nimble* wings to cut the skies, . . . *H.H.L.* 66

Nimbler-handed. *nimbler handed* then his enemie, . . . VI. i. 38. 6

Nimbler-jointed. beeing *nimbler joynted* than the rest, . . . *Mui.* 121

Nimble-shifting. Did learne to move their *nimble-shifting* feete, . . . *T.M.* 34
Did beare the pendants through their *nimblesse* bold: . . . V. ix. 29. 3

Nimbless. with such *nimblesse* sly Could wield about, . . . V. xi. 6. 6

Nimbly. She could them *nimbly* move, . . . II. iii. 28. 9
nimbly ran her wonted course . . . II. vi. 20. 6
with them *nimbly* ledd Faire Helenore . . . III. x. 44. 4
nimbly did him dight to guide the way . . . V. iv. 35. 5
did his yron axe so *nimbly* wield, . . . V. xii. 19. 7
Eftsoones the Prince to him full *nimbly* stept, . . . VI. viii. 17. 1

Nimrod. them long time before, great *Nimrod* was, . . . I. v. 48. 1
There also was the name of *Nimrod* strong; . . . IV. i. 22. 7

Nine. *See* **Ninus.**
systers *nyne,* which dwell on Parnasse hight, . . . *S.C.* Jun. 28
Melpomene! the mournefulst Muse of *nyne,* . . . *S.C.* N. 53
Rehearse to me, ye sacred Sisters *nine,* . . . *T.M.* 1
O thou the mournfulst Muse of *nyne!* . . . *Mui.* 10
O holy virgin! chiefe of *nyne,* . . . I. Pr. 2. 1
Nyne monethes I seek in vain, . . . I. ix. 15. 9
Proportiond equally by seven and *nine;* . . . II. ix. 22. 7
Nine was the circle sett in heavens place: . . . II. ix. 22. 8
The loving mother, that *nine* monethes did beare . . . III. ii. 11. 6
After she had *nine* moneths fulfild and gone: . . . III. vi. 5. 5
Nine times he heard him come aloft ere day, . . . III. x. 48. 5

Nine hundred. *Nine hundred Pater nosters* every day, . . . I. iii. 13. 8
thrise *nine hundred Aves* she was wont to say. . . . I. iii. 13. 9

Ninus. old *Ninus* far did pas In princely pomp, . . . I. v. 48. 3
king *Nine* whilome built Babell towre. . . . II. ix. 21. 6
The warres he well remembred of king *Nine,* . . . II. ix. 56. 8

Ninus'. that great Towre, . . . King *Ninus* worke, . . . *Ti.* 511

Niobe. Such follie great sorow to *Niobe* did breede: . . . *S.C.* Ap. 87
More happie mother would her surely weene Then famous *Niobe,* . . . V. x. 7. 8

Niobe's. Gainst wofull *Niobes* unhappy race, . . . IV. vii. 30. 8

Nip. To heare the Javell so good men to *nip;* . . . *Hub.* 712
sharp Remorse his hart did prick and *nip,* . . . I. x. 27. 3

Nipped. The byting frost *nipt* his stalke dead, . . . *S.C.* F. 231
'The carefull cold hath *nypt* my rugged rynde, . . . *S.C.* D. 133
therewith Under his side him *nipt;* . . . IV. v. 44. 4
fed, and *nipt* the tender bloomes; . . . VI. ix. 5. 5

Nipples. Her *nipples,* lyke yong blossomed Jessemynes: . . . *Am.* lxiv. 12

Nis (*partial list*).
Thou findest faulte where *nys* to be found, . . . *S.C.* May 144
those hilles where harbrough *nis* to see, . . . *S.C.* Jun. 19
Of all my flocke there *nis* sike another, . . . *S.C.* Au. 38
now *nis* the time of merimake, . . . *S.C.* N. 9
That *nys* on earth assuraunce to be sought; . . . *S.C.* N. 157
Dido *nis* dead, but into heaven hent. . . . *S.C.* N. 169

Nitre. With windy *Nitre* and quick Sulphur fraught, . . . I. vii. 13. 3

No (*partial list*). *See* **Nobody, No less, No man, No more, Noway.**
No worke it seem'd of earthly craftsmans wit, . . . *Bel.*[2] iv. 9
For *no* such shadow shalbe had againe. . . . *Pet.* iii. 14
Yet *no* time should so low embase their hight, . . . *Ro.* viii. 12
No otherwise than raynie cloud, . . . *Ro.* xx. 1
That which *no* hands can evermore compyle. . . . *Ro.* xxv. 14
No blame to thee, . . . *Ro.* xxxi. 3
The silly Flie, that *no* redresse did see, . . . *Van.* iv. 5
A shepeheards boye, (*no* better doe him call,) . . . *S.C.* Ja. 1
No marveile, Thenot, if thou can beare . . . *S.C.* F. 25
But all this glee had *no* continuaunce: . . . *S.C.* F. 224
For nowe *no* succoure was seene him nere. . . . *S.C.* F. 228
No: but happely I hym spyde, . . . *S.C.* Mar. 31
Thomalin, have *no* care for-thy; . . . *S.C.* Mar. 37
No mortall blemishe may her blotte. . . . *S.C.* Ap. 54
How falles it, then, we *no* merrier bene, . . . *S.C.* May 3
this morrowe, *no* (*ne) lenger agoe, . . . *S.C.* May 19
Good is *no* good, but if it be spend; . . . *S.C.* May 71
Here *no* night-ravenes lodge, . . . *S.C.* Jun. 23
Of Muses, Hobbinol, I conne *no* skill, . . . *S.C.* Jun. 65
(*No* such mought shepheards bee) . . . *S.C.* Jul. 150
and fynd *no* part 'Of pleasure past. . . . *S.C.* Au. 168
And you that feele *no* woe, . . . *S.C.* Au. 187
No being for those that truely mene; . . . *S.C.* S. 33
No such countrye as there to remaine; . . . *S.C.* S. 35
Neede feare *no* chaunge of frowning fate; . . . *S.C.* S. 71
No sooner was out, but, swifter then thought, . . . *S.C.* S. 222
Where *no* such troublous tydes han us assayde; . . . *S.C.* O. 117
sing *no* moe The songs that Colin . . . *S.C.* N. 77
For beauties prayse and plesaunce had *no* peere; . . . *S.C.* N. 94
O Lobb! thy losse *no* longer lament; . . . *S.C.* N. 168
No daunger there the shepheard can astert; . . . *S.C.* N. 187
I of doubted daunger had *no* feare: . . . *S.C.* D. 22

No—*Continued.*

The learned lover lost *no* time nor tyde . . . III. x. 6. 1
No fort so fensible, *no* wals so strong, . . . III. x. 10. 1
The loving couple neede *no* reskew feare, . . . III. x. 16. 3
let not my rudenes be *no* breach . . . III. x. 25. 3
a knight, *no* knight at all perdee, . . . III. x. 27. 3
'I take *no* keepe of her,' (sayd Paridell) . . . III. x. 38. 2
As if *no* trespas ever had beene donne: . . . III. x. 51. 6
And by *no* meanes would to his will be wonne, . . . III. x. 51. 8
That seemd *no* help for him was left . . . III. x. 56. 9
Or hast thou, Lord, of good mens cause *no* heed? . . . III. xi. 9. 6
If goodnesse find *no* grace, nor righteousnes *no* meed? . . . III. xi. 9. 9
Whereas *no* living creature he mistooke, . . . III. xi. 13. 4
glad, As if *no* sorrow she ne felt ne drad; . . . III. xii. 18. 5
No word they spake, nor earthly thing they . . . III. xii. 45. *or.*8
when they could not learne it by *no* wize, . . . IV. iv. 42. 4
No words may rate, nor rigour him remove . . . IV. ix. 31. 7
minute lost *no* riches render may. . . . IV. x. 14. 9
'*No* tree, that is of count, . . . IV. x. 22. 1
No flowre in field, that daintie odour throwes, . . . IV. x. 22. 3
would for *no* worldly meed, Nor *no* entreatie, . . . IV. xi. 8. 7, 8
To which *no* wit of man may comen neare; . . . IV. xi. 10. 5
Ne none disdained low to him to lout: *No,* not the . . . IV. xi. 30. 6
many more whose names *no* tongue can tell: . . . IV. xi. 44. 6
men plainely wot It was *no* mortall worke, . . . IV. xi. 45. 9
hard rocky hart for *no* entreating Will yeeld, . . . IV. xii. 7. 3
for-why he found *no* way To enter in, . . . IV. xii. 15. 3
of *no* worldly thing he tooke delight; . . . IV. xii. 19. 7
was *no* old sore which his new paine procured; . . . IV. xii. 23. 9
It was *no* time to scan the prophecie, . . . IV. xii. 28. 3
there *no* substance was so firme and hard, . . . V. i. 10. 6
No sooner sayd, but streight he . . . V. i. 20. 1
Yet for *no* pitty would he change . . . V. ii. 26. 1
That there mote be *no* hope of reparation, . . . V. ii. 28. 4
mongst them al *no* change hath yet beene found; . . . V. ii. 36. 4
And by *no* meane could in the weight be stayd; For by *no* meanes the false . . . V. ii. 45. 8, 9
to *no* womans wast . . . it would sit, . . . V. iii. 28. 6
Whereof *no* braver president this day Remaines . . . V. iv. 2. 6
whether it be so or *no,* I can not say. . . . V. iv. 13. 9
whether it indeede be so or *no,* . . . V. iv. 14. 1
Dismayd so . . . that he *no* colours knew. . . . V. iv. 39. 9
But Radigund . . . Could take *no* rest, . . . V. iv. 47. 3
No hand so cruell, nor *no* hart so hard, . . . V. v. 13. 5
No fayrer conquest then that with goodwill . . . V. v. 17. 9
no new loves impression ever could Bereave . . . V. vi. 2. 8
so thin, That he *no* worke at all left for the leach: . . . V. vii. 35. 8
'And lastly, that *no* shame might wanting be, . . . V. viii. 23. 1
That *no* whole peece of him was to be seene, . . . V. viii. 42. 8
his owne . . . To which they had *no* right, . . . V. xi. 3. 9
yron flayle, Gainst which *no* flight nor rescue . . . V. xi. 59. 5
No faith so firme, *no* trust can be so strong, *No* love so lasting then, . . . V. xii. 1. 8, 9
Sith *no* redemption nigh she did nor heare . . . V. xii. 11. 9
No shame to stoupe, ones head more high . . . V. xii. 19. 3
(said she) '*no* Knight at all, . . . VI. i. 25. 1
Bloud is *no* blemish, for it is *no* blame . . . VI. i. 26. 4
No greater shame to man then inhumanitie. . . . VI. i. 26. 9
(Quoth he) 'I hold it *no* indignity; . . . VI. i. 28. 2
For by *no* art, nor any leaches might, . . . VI. vi. 1. 5
Yet for *no* bidding . . . Would he restrayned be . . . VI. vi. 18. 8
As one that had *no* life him left . . . VI. vi. 32. 9
wheres *no* courage, theres *no* ruth nor mone. . . . VI. vii. 18. 5
He wore *no* armour, ne for none did care, . . . VI. vii. 43. 1
were *no* might in man, . . . VI. viii. 18. 6
For were *no* law in love, . . . VI. viii. 23. 3
nothing nice, where was *no* need, . . . VI. ix. 7. 1
No better doe I weare, *no* better doe I feed. . . . VI. ix. 20. 9
Me *no* such cares . . . offend, . . . VI. ix. 22. 6
to recure *no* skill of Leaches art Mote him availe, . . . VI. x. 31. 5
Like to a flowre that feeles *no* heate of sunne, . . . VI. x. 44. 6
here on earth is *no* sure happinesse, . . . VI. xi. 1. 7
'But thee, O Jove! *no* equall Judge I deeme . . . VII. vi. 35. 1
none *no* more change shal see.' . . . VII. vii. 59. 5
But if ye saw that which *no* eyes can see, . . . *Epith.* 185
Let *no* lamenting cryes, nor dolefull teares, . . . *Epith.* 334
Let *no* deluding dreames, nor dreadfull sights, . . . *Epith.* 338
No light but that, whose lampe doth yet remaine . . . *H.L.* 131
That *no* one drop of pitie there doth rest. . . . *H.L.* 147
Such fancies feele *no* love, but loose desyre. . . . *H.L.* 175
For things immortall *no* corruption take. . . . *H.B.* 161
It is *no* love, but a discordant warre, . . . *H.B.* 195

Noah's. Like *Noyes* great flood, . . . II. x. 15. 5

Nobility. he no count made of *Nobilitie,* . . . *Hub.* 1183
That is the girlond of *Nobilitie.* . . . *T.M.* 84
made the noursling of *Nobilitie.* . . . *T.M.* 564
Robd of all right and true *nobilitie.* . . . *Ti.* 294
she is next her in *nobilitie.* . . . *Col.* 515
She is the braunch of true *nobilitie,* . . . *Col.* 530
Succeeding them in true *nobility:* . . . *Ded. Son.* iii. 9
made alwaies clame To be the Nourses of *nobility,* . . . *Ded. Son.* iv. 2
to see Him his *nobility* so fowle deface: . . . II. xii. 79. 4
Her nourced had in trew *Nobility:* . . . III. v. 32. 5
all her other honour did obscure, And titles of *nobilitie* deface: . . . V. ix. 38. 7
Then came *Nobilitie* of birth, . . . V. ix. 45. 7
brancheth forth in brave *nobilitie,* . . . VI. Pr. 4. 4
t' attaine, Unto the type of true *Nobility;* . . . *Com. Son.* ii. 2

Noble. stroke downe this *noble* monument. . . . *Bel.*[1] iii. 14
The worde of God made him a *noble* name. . . . *Rev.* iii. 4
The honour of these *noble* boughs . . . *Bel.* v. 11

Noble—*Continued.*

Cruell death vanquishing so *noble* beautie, . . . *Pet.* i. 13
of Paradise Some *noble* plant I thought . . . *Pet.* iii. 4
despise The *noble* Lion after his lives end, . . . *Ro.* xiv. 6
With Thames inhabitants of *noble* fame, . . . *Ro.* xxii. 3
'Gainst which the *noble* sonne of Telamon Oppos'd himselfe, *Gn.* 513
wise Curius, companion Of *noble* vertues, . . . *Gn.* 610
A *noble* Gentleman of high regard, . . . *Hub.* 685
Two filthie blots in *noble* gentrie; . . . *Hub.* 734
like desire and praise of *noble* fame, . . . *Hub.* 769
To such delights the *noble* wits he led . . . *Hub.* 821
into their *noble* sprights Desire of honor . . . *Hub.* 824
chieflie doth each *noble* minde adorne, . . . *Hub.* 831
with their *noble* countenaunce to grace . . . *T.M.* 81
all *noble* feates professe To register, . . . *T.M.* 97
Because I nothing *noble* have to sing. . . . *T.M.* 108
The *noble* hearts to pleasures they allure, . . . *T.M.* 331
doth degenerate the *noble* race, . . . *T.M.* 436
noble Peeres, whom I was wont to raise, . . . *T.M.* 467
Supports the praise of *noble* Poesie; . . . *T.M.* 574
His brother Prince, his brother *noble* Peere, . . . *Ti.* 240
His *noble* Spouse, and Paragon of fame. . . . *Ti.* 245
And *noble* Patrone of weake povertie; . . . *Ti.* 262
'He, *noble* bud, his Grandsires livelie hayre, . . . *Ti.* 267
did enrich that *noble* breast of his . . . *Ti.* 285
'O *noble* spirite! live there ever blessed, . . . *Ti.* 302
So brave a Trompe, thy *noble* acts to sound! . . . *Ti.* 434
did grieve the *noble* spright Of Salomon . . . *Ti.* 443
Before his *noble* heart he firmely bound, . . . *Mui.* 58
to a beast his *noble* hart embase, . . . *D.* 180
all the dowries of a *noble* mind, . . . *D.* 216
For her great worth and *noble* governance; . . . *Col.* 503
The honor of the *noble* familie: . . . *Col.* 537
Thrise happie do I hold thee, *noble* swaine, . . . *Col.* 552
Right *noble* Nymphs, and high to be commended: . . . *Col.* 577
Their bounteous deeds and *noble* favours shrynd, . . . *Col.* 582
With Cynthia and all her *noble* crew; . . . *Col.* 653
vouchsafe thy *noble* countenaunce . . . *Ded. Son.* ii. 13
Receive, most *noble* Lord, in gentle gree, . . . *Ded. Son.* iii. 1
Then, by like right the *noble* Progeny, . . . *Ded. Son.* iv. 5
right *noble* Lord, I send This present . . . *Ded. Son.* iv. 13
Receive, most *Noble* Lord, a simple taste . . . *Ded. Son.* v. 1
brave Lord, whose goodly personage And *noble* deeds, . . . *Ded. Son.* vi. 2
Most *Noble* Lord, the pillor of my life, . . . *Ded. Son.* vii. 1
Which in your *noble* hands for pledge I leave . . . *Ded. Son.* vii. 9
To you, right *noble* Lord, whose carefull brest . . . *Ded. Son.* ix. 1
Doth promise fruite worthy the *noble* kind . . . *Ded. Son.* x. 3
for your . . . *noble* deeds, have your deserved place . . . *Ded. Son.* xi. 2
Moste *noble* Lord, the honor of this age, . . . *Ded. Son.* xiv. 6
Remembraunce . . . Bids me, most *noble* Lady, to adore . . . *Ded. Son.* xv. 8
Tanaquill, Whom that most *noble* Briton Prince . . . Sought I. Pr. 2. 6
ruth . . . for her *noble* blood, and for her tender youth. . . . I. i. 50. 9
he, my Lyon, and my *noble* Lord, . . . I. iii. 7. 6
a *noble* crew Of Lords and Ladies stood on every side, . . . I. iv. 7. 7
him rencountring fierce, reskewd the *noble* pray. . . . I. iv. 39. 9
The *noble* hart that harbours vertuous thought, . . . I. v. 1. 1
a *noble* warlike knight . . . to that forrest came . . . I. vi. 20. 1
Where she had left the *noble* Redcrosse knight, . . . I. vii. 2. 3
Have thither come the *noble* Martial crew . . . I. vii. 45. 4
That *noble* order hight of maidenhed, . . . I. vii. 46. 4
The *noble* knight alighted . . . From loftie steed, . . . I. viii. 2. 7
wise and wary was that *noble* Pere; . . . I. viii. 7. 6
the *noble* Prince had marked well, . . . I. viii. 34. 3
noble mindes of yore allyed were, . . . I. ix. 1. 3
goodly gan discourse of many a *noble* gest. . . . I. x. 15. 9
well beseemes all knights of *noble* name? . . . I. x. 59. 4
The sparke of *noble* corage now awake, . . . I. xi. 2. 6
A *noble* crew about them waited rownd . . . I. xii. 5. 4
By dew desert of *noble* chevalree, . . . I. xii. 20. 8
He was an Elfin borne of *noble* state . . . II. i. 6. 5
chaunst, That you, most *noble* Sir, had present beene . . . II. i. 10. 2
in your *noble* harts Her hellish brond hath kindled . . . II. ii. 29. 2
His puissant armes about his *noble* brest, . . . II. iii. 1. 8
without desert of gentle deed And *noble* worth, . . . II. iii. 10. 7
difference Betweene the vulgar and the *noble* seed, . . . II. iv. 1. 3
The *noble* Guyon, mov'd with great remorse, . . . II. iv. 6. 1
was borne of *noble* parentage, . . . II. iv. 19. 3
That him so *noble* knight had maystered; . . . II. v. 14. 8
helpe, most *noble* knight, . . . II. v. 23. 8
'Ah, well away! most *noble* Lords, . . . II. vi. 32. 5
That *noble* heart as great dishonour doth despize. . . . II. vii. 12. 9
many *noble* Greekes and Trojans made to bleed. . . . II. vii. 55. 9
Ne was there ever *noble* corage seene, . . . II. viii. 26. 3
'*Noble* Lord, what meed so great, . . . II. ix. 6. 1
many a Lord of *noble* parentage, . . . II. ix. 18. 4
Goodly shee entertaind those *noble* knights, . . . II. ix. 20. 1
noble deeds above the Northern starre . . . II. x. 4. 7
The *noble* daughter of Corineus . . . II. x. 18. 1
salved both their infamies With *noble* deedes, . . . II. x. 21. 7
The *noble* braunch from th' antique stocke was torne . . . II. x. 36. 4
Next him was *noble* Elfinan, . . . II. x. 72. 7
fayrely feasted as so *noble* knightes she ought. . . . II. x. 77. 9
The *noble* Virgin, Ladie of the Place, . . . II. xi. 16. 1
forth the *noble* Guyon sallied, . . . II. xii. 38. 4
The *noble* Elfe and carefull Palmer . . . II. xii. 81. 1
Let later age that *noble* use envy, . . . III. i. 13. 8
The *noble* Britomartis her arayd, . . . III. i. 67. 2
The *noble* Arthegall hath ever borne the name. . . . III. ii. 9. 9
The *noble* corage never weeneth ought . . . III. ii. 10. 4
Ne ought it mote the *noble* Mayd avayle, . . . III. ii. 52. 1

Noble—*Continued.*
Whence spring all *noble* deedes and never dying fame: . . . III. iii. 1. 9
'Most *noble* Virgin, that by fatall lore . . . III. iii. 21. 6
Cannot with *noble* Britomart compare, . . . III. iv. 3. 2
through all Faerie lond his *noble* fame Now blazed was, . . III. iv. 21. 3
well did brooke Her *noble* deeds, . . . III. iv. 44. 9
did vexe his *noble* brest, . . . III. iv. 54. 3
Ever to creepe into his *noble* brest; . . . III. v. 2. 4
As meetest may beseeme a *noble* mayd: . . . III. v. 5. 3
whiles his Lord pursewd that *noble* Mayd, . . . III. v. 13. 3
How that a *noble* hunteresse did wonne, . . . III. v. 27. 6
Ye wonder how this *noble* Damozell . . . III. vi. 1. 2
Of grace and beautie *noble* Paragone, . . . III. vi. 52. 2
the *noble* knight Sir Scudamore, . . . III. vi. 53. 2
He nere was touched in his *noble* spright, . . . III. vii. 43. 8
all the *noble* knights of Maydenhead, . . . III. viii. 47. 7
hand should dare for to engore Her *noble* blood? . . . III. viii. 48. 9
'Ye *noble* knights,' . . . 'Well may yee speede . . . III. viii. 51. 1
they mervaild at her chevalree And *noble* prowesse, . . . III. ix. 24. 6
Sir Paris far renowmd through *noble* fame; . . . III. ix. 34. 5
carcases of *noble* warrioures . . . III. ix. 35. 7
the *noble* Britomart heard tell . . . III. ix. 38. 1
noble Britons sprong from Trojans bold, . . . III. ix. 38. 8
straunge affaires, and *noble* hardiment, . . . III. ix. 53. 2
now that *noble* succor is thee by, . . . III. x. 26. 4
you, most *noble* Lord, that can and dare . . . III. x. 28. 1
She was emmoved in her *noble* minde, . . . III. xi. 4. 7
ever in your *noble* hart prepense, . . . III. xi. 14. 5
shameful . . . t' abandon *noble* chevisaunce . . . III. xi. 24. 6
The *noble* Mayd still standing all this vewd, . . . III. xii. 5. 1
'Ah *noble* knight! . . . III. xii. 39. 2
laid the *noble* Championesse strong hond Upon th' enchaunter III. xii. 41. 3
Thereat her *noble* hart was stonisht sore; . . . III. xii. 44. 5
Untill such time as *noble* Britomart Released her, . . . IV. i. 4. 3
noble knights Which hunt for honor, . . . IV. i. 19. 6
did drive The *noble* Argonauts to outrage fell; . . . IV. i. 23. 7
These three so *noble* babes to bring forth at one clap. . . . IV. ii. 41. 3
a *noble* youthly knight, Seeking adventures . . . IV. ii. 45. 1
Thrise lowted lowly to the *noble* Mayd, . . . IV. iii. 5. 8
how that *noble* Knight . . . Could stand on foot . . . IV. iii. 23. 1
Which when the *noble* Ferramont espide, . . . IV. iv. 19. 1
Unto the *noble* Knights of Maidenhead, . . . IV. iv. 22. 6
Appear'd in place, with all his *noble* crew: . . . IV. iv. 26. 3
From wight unworthie of so *noble* meed. . . . IV. v. 28. 4
Hath doen to *noble* knights, . . . IV. vi. 7. 9
the band Of *noble* minds derived from above, . . . IV. vi. 31. 8
made way Unto the love of *noble* Britomart, . . . IV. vi. 40. 2
so and so to *noble* Britomart: . . . IV. vii. 2. 2
sloth that oft doth *noble* mindes annoy. . . . IV. vii. 23. 9
Her *noble* heart with sight thereof was fild . . . IV. vii. 36. 2
his owne deare Lord The *noble* Prince, . . . IV. viii. 18. 5
thus conversing with this *noble* Knight; . . . IV. viii. 29. 5
noble kind at first was sure of heavenly seed. . . . IV. viii. 33. 9
that much did vexe His *noble* hart: . . . IV. viii. 35. 5
Had not the *noble* Prince his readie stroke represt: . . . IV. viii. 41. 9
To winne me honour by some *noble* gest, . . . IV. x. 4. 4
Brave thoughts and *noble* deedes did evermore aspire. . . . IV. x. 26. 9
The *noble* Thamis, with all his goodly traine; . . . IV. xi. 24. 3
did in *noble* deedes of armes excell, . . . IV. xi. 37. 4
loth he was his *noble* hands t' embrew . . . V. ii. 52. 4
A *noble* Knight, and tride in hard assayes; . . . V. iii. 5. 2
So forth the *noble* Ladie was ybrought, . . . V. iii. 23. 1
by the faith that I To Maydenhead and *noble* knighthood owe, V. iv. 34. 2
These *noble* warriors . . . Them selves thereto preparde . . . V. v. 1. 5
with bootlesse paine Annoy this *noble* Knight, . . . V. v. 15. 9
Then tooke the Amazon this *noble* knight, . . . V. v. 20. 1
How ever it his *noble* heart did gall . . . V. v. 26. 3
never meant he in his *noble* mind . . . to be untrew: . . . V. v. 56. 2
his owne love, the *noble* Britomart, . . . V. vi. 3. 1
All *noble* Knights, which were adventurous, . . . V. vi. 32. 8
the *noble* Conqueresse Her selfe came in, . . . V. vii. 36. 1
Which had bene reft from many a *noble* Knight, . . . V. vii. 41. 5
her *noble* Lord, sir Artegall, . . . V. vii. 45. 6
for their so *noble* ayd . . . V. viii. 23. 8
much renound For *noble* courage . . . V. viii. 36. 8
turne we to the *noble* Prince, . . . V. ix. 2. 6
'Loe! now, right *noble* knights, arriv'd ye bee . . . V. ix. 20. 4
The *noble* Prince and righteous Artegall, . . . V. x. 4. 2
Approving dayly to their *noble* eyes . . . V. x. 5. 5
After her *Noble* husbands late decesse; . . . V. x. 11. 8
The *noble* Briton Prince with his brave Peare; . . . V. x. 15. 2
through comfort of this *noble* knight.' . . . V. x. 20. 9
turne we now to *noble* Artegall; . . . V. xi. 36. 1
much did magnifie his *noble* name: . . . V. xi. 46. 6
Both *noble* armes and gentle curtesie. . . . VI. i. 26. 8
he deem'd him borne of *noble* race: . . . VI. ii. 5. 5
sure he weend him borne of *noble* blood, . . . VI. ii. 24. 6
zeale Which to thy *noble* personage I beare, . . . VI. ii. 26. 6
To whom then thus the *noble* Youth: . . . VI. ii. 27. 1
I . . . Have trayned bene with many *noble* feres . . . VI. ii. 31. 4
And fitteth most for *noble* swayne to know, . . . VI. ii. 32. 7
I . . . wish that some more *noble* hire . . . VI. ii. 34. 7
none more *noble* then is chevalrie) . . . VI. ii. 34. 8
And greatly joy'd at his so *noble* hart, . . . VI. ii. 36. 7
And flame forth honour in thy *noble* brest; . . . VI. ii. 37. 4
The *noble* ympe, . . . It gladly did accept, . . . VI. ii. 38. 6
Doth *noble* courage shew with curteous manners met. . . . VI. iii. 1. 9
she was daughter to a *noble* Lord . . . VI. iii. 7. 1
and blam'd her *noble* blood: . . . VI. iii. 11. 8
by just avengement Of *noble* Tristram, . . . VI. iii. 17. 4

Noble—*Continued.*
That from his sides some *noble* chyld should rize, . . . VI. iv. 33. 2
More brave and *noble* knights have raysed beene . . . VI. iv. 36. 3
And did right *noble* deedes; the which els where are showne. VI. iv. 38. 9
certes he was borne of *noble* blood, . . . VI. v. 2. 7
infamy Infixeth in the name of *noble* wight: . . . VI. vi. 1. 4
The *noble* childe, preventing his desire, . . . VI. viii. 15. 7
The proved powre of *noble* Calidore, . . . VI. xii. 36. 7
those renoumed *noble* Peres of Greece, . . . *Am.* xliv. 1
therein now doth lodge a *noble* Peer, . . . *Proth.* 145
Joy have thou of thy *noble* victorie, . . . *Proth.* 152
this *noble* Lord issuing, . . . *Proth.* 163
Nobleman. Then to some *Noble-man* your selfe applye, . . . *Hub.* 489
Nobler. Fairer and *nobler* liveth none this howre, . . . II. x. 76. 6
in signe Of servile yoke, that *nobler* harts repine: . . . VI. vii. 26. 5
Noblesse. the president Of *Noblesse* and of chevalree: . . . *To his Booke* 4
'Fayre braunch of *noblesse*, flowre of chevalrie, . . . I. viii. 26. 7
Prince Arthur, flowre of grace and *nobilesse*, . . . II. viii. 18. 4
Herein the *noblesse* of this knight exceedes, . . . V. ii. 1. 8
Noblest. the name of Souldiers . . . the *noblest* mysterie, . . *Hub.* 221
He whilest he lived was the *noblest* swaine, . . . *Col.* 440
verse of *noblest* shepheard lately dead . . . *Col.* 534
The *noblest* mind the best contentment has. . . . I. i. 35. 4
Faery court . . . Where *noblest* knights were to be found . . I. iii. 28. 6
In number of the *noblest* knightes on ground; . . . II. ii. 42. 2
that which *noblest* knight on earth doth weare.' . . . II. iii. 17. 9
the best and *noblest* knight alive Prince Arthur is, . . . II. iii. 18. 3
noblest borne of all in Britayne land; . . . II. xi. 30. 7
workes of *noblest* wits to nought outweare, . . . IV. ii. 33. 2
'Haile, *noblest* Knight Of all . . . VI. i. 4. 8
to infest The *noblest* wights with notable defame: . . . VI. vi. 12. 6
noblest she that served is of *noblest* knight. . . . VI. vii. 29. 9
Nobly. *nobly* bredd? . . . *T.M.* 446
deeds doe die, how ever *noblie* donne, . . . *Ti.* 400
To which though *nobly* ye inclined are, . . . *Ded. Son.* x. 7
Full *nobly* mounted in right warlike wize; . . . V. xi. 4. 3
Nobody. vouch antiquities, which *no body* can know. . . . II. Pr. 1. 9
Noctante. yett in armes *Noctante* greater grew: . . . III. i. 45. 7
Noise. With so great *noyse* I start . . . *Bel.*[1] xi. 14
a *noyse* (*noise*[1]) alluring sleepe . . . *Bel.* xii. 7
with great *noyse* I wakte . . . *Bel.*[2] xv. 14
In a great mountaine heap't with hideous *noyse*, . . . *Ro.* xvi. 2
Upon his tiptoes nicely . . . For making *noyse*, . . . *Hub.* 1010
With troublous *noyse* did dull their daintie eares. . . . *T.M.* 30
all the way most heavenly *noyse* was heard . . . *Ti.* 612
Ne anie *noyse*, ne anie motion made. . . . *Mui.* 400
th' ayre be filled with *noyse* of dolefull knells, . . . *D.* 335
No other *noyse*, . . . Might there be heard; . . . I. i. 41. 6
ran towardes the far rebownded *noyce*, . . . I. vi. 8. 3
Who, with the *noyse* awaked, commeth out . . . I. vi. 14. 6
Led with their *noise* . . . I. vi. 45. 8
the heavens it doth fill With thundring *noyse*, . . . I. vii. 13. 6
No gate . . . But with that percing *noise* flew open . . . I. viii. 4. 9
As great a *noyse*, as when . . . complaine, . . . I. viii. 11. 5
Such *noyse* his rouzed scales did send unto the knight. . . . I. xi. 9. 9
there was an heavenly *noise* Heard sownd . . . I. xii. 39. 1
The *noyse* thereof cald forth that straunger knight, . . . II. ii. 21. 1
With *noyse* whereof he from his loftie steed Downe fell . II. iii. 21. 2
noise of armes, or vew of martiall guize, . . . II. vi. 25. 8
The Palmer lent his eare unto the *noyce*, . . . II. viii. 4. 1
with the *noise* it shooke as it would fall. . . . II. ix. 11. 5
dreadfull *noise* and hollow rombling rore . . . II. xii. 25. 3
Ne any *noise* she made, ne word she spake, . . . III. i. 61. 6
such ghastly *noyse* of yron chaines . . . III. iii. 9. 2
Each shade she saw, and each *noyse* she did heare, . . . III. vii. 1. 8
She went in perill, of each *noyse* affeard, . . . III. vii. 19. 3
They heard a *noyse* of many bagpipes shrill, . . . III. x. 43. 2
All suddenly they heard a troublous *noyes*, . . . IV. iii. 37. 6
The bellowes *noyse* disturb'd his quiet rest, . . . IV. v. 41. 4
The hideous *noise* of their huge strokes did heare, . . . IV. vii. 29. 3
With *noise* whereof the Lady forth appeared . . . V. ii. 22. 1
She heard a wondrous *noise* below the hall: . . . V. vi. 27. 5
With *noyse* whereof when as the caytive carle Should issue . V. ix. 9. 1
making troublous din And wondrous *noyse*, . . . V. ix. 23. 4
With *noise* whereof the Squire . . . Revived was, . . . VI. v. 21. 8
with the *noise*, whilest he did loudly rore, . . . VI. vi. 22. 8
made the wood to tremble at the *noyce*: . . . VI. viii. 46. 4
streight to the *noise* forth past. . . . VI. viii. 47. 9
With *noyse* whereof the theefe awaking . . . VI. xi. 43. 4
with *noyse* of late uprore, . . . VI. xi. 46. 1
The Goddesse, all abashed with that *noise*, . . . VII. vi. 47. 1
With *noyse* whereof the quyre of Byrds resounded, . . . *Am.* xix. 5
he was wakened with the *noyse*, . . . *Epig.* iv. 5
Crying aloud with strong confused *noyce*, . . . *Epith.* 138
Noises. the heavenly *noyses* Of their sweete instruments . . . *T.M.* 19
Noisome. On her left hand the *noysome* Esquiline, . . . *Ro.* iv. 12
grype your hearts with *noysome* rage imbew'd, . . . *Ro.* xxiv. 6
With dogges of *noysome* breath, . . . *S.C.* Jul. 22
Corrupted had th' ayre with his *noysome* breath, . . . *Hub.* 7
But *noysome* breath, and poysnous spirit sent . . . IV. viii. 26. 3
Keeping all *noysome* things away from it, . . . VI. x. 7. 8
No less. *no lesse* rich than faire, right worthie sure . . . *Bel.*[2] xiv. 6
some matter *no less* firme and strong? . . . *Ro.* ix. 8
of their maisters hast *no lesse* regarde . . . *S.C.* D. 11
No lesse, I dare saie, than the prowdest wight; . . . *Hub.* 62
No lesse than that which Vulcane made . . . *Mui.* 63
joyous seemde *no lesse* Then the glad marchant, . . . I. iii. 32. 2
He hated all . . . And him *no lesse*, . . . I. iv. 32. 2
who tries, shall find *no lesse*.' . . . I. xii. 34. 9
I,' (said Braggadocchio) 'thought *no lesse*, . . . II. iii. 44. 8

No less—*Continued.*
seemd *no lesse* to love then lov'd to bee: . . . . II. iv. 19. 5
my falser friend did *no less* joyous deeme. . . . . II. iv. 21. 9
She *no lesse* glad then he desirous was . . . . II. vi. 37. 1
Hath walkte about the world, and I *no lesse,* . . . . II. ix. 7. 6
Ziffius, whom Mariners eschew *No lesse* then rockes, ... II. xii. 24. 8
that which reft it *no lesse* faire was fownd. . . . . II. xii. 67. 7
With *no lesse* hast, and eke with *no lesse* dreed, ... III. iv. 50. 1
she *no lesse* the knight feard then that villein rude. . . . . III. iv. 50. 9
no lesse afrayd Then of wilde beastes . . . . III. iv. 51. 3
no lesse carefully her tendered Then her owne daughter . . . III. vi. 51. 6
it she shund *no lesse* then dread to die; . . . . III. vii. 24. 4
no lesse griefe endured . . . . III. xii. 40. 9
her deare nourslings losse *no lesse* did mourne, ... III. xii. 45. 7
She, that *no lesse* was courteous then stout, ... IV. i. 11. 6
Against so many *no lesse* mightie met, ... IV. iii. 24. 7
gan shun his dreadfull sight, *No lesse* then death . . . . . IV. iv. 41. 9
In *no lesse* neede of helpe then him he weend. . . . . IV. iv. 45. 4
mov'd Belphebe her *no lesse* to hate, ... IV. vii. 34. 6
in conditions to be loath'd *no lesse;* . . . . IV. viii. 24. 2
No lesse then perfect gold surmounts the meanest brasse. . . IV. ix. 2. 9
'*No lesse* did Daunger threaten me with dread, ... IV. x. 58. 1
No lesse then do her elder sisters broode. . . . . IV. xi. 26. 7
no lesse famous then the rest they bee, ... IV. xi. 40. 2
was of *no lesse* vertue then of fame; . . . . V. i. 10. 5
to a courage great It is *no lesse* beseeming . . . . V. v. 38. 2
Whom like disguize *no lesse* deformed had, ... V. vii. 38. 2
no lesse Then all the rest burst out to all outragiousnesse. . V. xii. 2. 8
I *no lesse* disdayning, backe returned His . . . taunts . . . . VI. ii. 12. 1
no lesse encombrance she did see, ... VI. iv. 10. 3
Yet *no lesse* thankes to you for your good will.' . . . . . . VI. viii. 30. 5
though *no lesse* sory wight For that mishap, ... VI. x. 18. 7
He wondred much, and feared her *no lesse:* . . . . VII. vi. 17. 5
sure thy worth *no lesse* then hers . . . . VII. vi. 32. 9
no lesse faire and beautifull then shee; . . . . VII. vi. 40. 8
No lesse then Angels whom he did ensew, ... *H.H.L.* 121
Noll. For yet his *noule* was totty of the must, ... VII. vii. 39. 2
No man. My long decay, which *no man* els doth mone, ... *Ti.* 157
me *no man* bewaileth, but in game, ... *Ti.* 162
no man left to mone His dolefull fate, ... *Ti.* 192
A fairer one . . . might *no man* view: . . . . *Ti.* 593
Such . . . shapes elswher may *no man* reed. . . . . I. i. 21. 9
no man car'd to answere to his crye: . . . . I. viii. 29. 7
all these were, when *no man* did them know, ... II. Pr. 3. 1
how *no man* knowes, They spring, ... II. vi. 15. 5
Yet *no man* for them taketh paines or care, ... II. vi. 15. 8
Yet *no man* to them can his carefull paines compare. . . . . II. vi. 15. 9
no man can Discerne the hew thereof. . . . . II. vi. 41. 7
A darkesome way, which *no man* could descry, ... II. vii. 20. 7
when it opened, *no man* might it close, ... II. ix. 23. 8
That *no man* forth might draw, ne *no man* remedye. . . . . III. xi. 48. 9
A straunger knight, from whence *no man* could reed, ... IV. iv. 39. 2
no man, but onely like in shape, ... IV. vii. 5. 2
no man aunswred me by name; . . . . IV. x. 11. 4
no man answred to my clame: . . . . IV. x. 11. 5
I will them tell though unto *no man* neare: . . . . IV. xii. 6. 4
no man was affrayd Of force, ... V. Pr. 9. 3
The loft was raysd againe, that *no man* could it spie. . . . V. vi. 27. 9
how deepe *no man* can tell, ... V. ix. 6. 4
reasons brought that *no man* could refute: . . . . V. ix. 44. 4
Whilest she did weepe, of *no man* mercifide: . . . . VI. vii. 32. 5
Of whom what was becomen *no man* knew. . . . . VI. vii. 34. 3
which *no man* can appease; . . . . VI. ix. 19. 7
Through hollow caves, that *no man* mote discover . . . . . VI. x. 42. 2
He sought the woods, but *no man* could see there; . . . . . VI. xi. 26. 4
a fayrer flood may *no man* see. . . . . VII. vi. 40. 9
whither *no man* wist. . . . . VII. vii. 59. 9
That *no man* may us see; . . . . *Epith.* 320
no man may it see With sinfull eyes, ... *H.B.* 38
Nominate. Whom all a Faeries sonne doen *nominate?*' . . . . I. x. 64. 7
This of Albany newly *nominate,* . . . . II. x. 38. 4
No more. And loe, the sea . . . is now *no more.* . . . . . . *Rev.* iv. 2
Let me *no more* see faire thing under sky, ... *Bel.* iv. 12
O let mine eyes *no more* see such a sight! . . . . *Pet.*[2] v. 14
Rome is *no more:* . . . . *Ro.* v. 5
In which the foule, . . . Is now *no more* seen . . . . *Ro.* xvii. 14
That nowe upright he can stand *no more;* . . . . *S.C.* F. 234
She shoulde have neede *no more* spell; . . . . *S.C.* Mar. 54
But then heard *no more* rustling: . . . . *S.C.* Mar. 72
Matter of myrth now shalt thou have *no more;* . . . . . . *S.C.* N. 56
The loser Lasse I cast to please *no more;* . . . . *S.C.* D. 119
I aske *no more.* . . . . *S.C.* Env. 12
Eurydice thence now *no more* Must turne to life, ... *Gn.* 433
we need to doo *no more.* . . . . *Hub.* 436
He would *no more* endure, but came his way, ... *Hub.* 1315
will henceforth immortalize *no more;* . . . . *T.M.* 464
Sith I *no more* finde worthie to commend . . . . *T.M.* 465
When as the land she saw *no more* appeare, ... *Mui.* 286
she speakes *no more* Of past: . . . . I. iii. 30. 6
Mine eyes *no more* on vanitie shall feed, ... I. vii. 23. 8
His Palmer now shall foot *no more* alone. . . . . II. iii. 3. 5
his owne health remembring now *no more,* . . . . II. vi. 45. 8
him henceforth the same can save *no more;* . . . . II. viii. 43. 7
pierced to the skin, but bit *no more;* . . . . II. viii. 44. 8
He gan avize to follow him *no more,* . . . . II. xi. 27. 6
Therefore to grownd he would him cast *no more,* . . . . . . II. xi. 45. 7
civile armes to exercise *no more:* . . . . III. iii. 49. 5
sith we *no more* shall meet!' . . . . III. iv. 39. 9
when her wayes he could *no more* descry, ... III. iv. 53. 1
Els shall thy loving Lord thee see *no more;* . . . . III. v. 26. 7

No more—*Continued.*
Ile clip his wanton wings, that he *no more* shall flye.' . . . III. vi. 24. 9
As it befell, that she could flie *no more,* . . . . III. vii. 25. 5
she *no more* was moved with that might . . . . III. vii. 41. 2
no more returnd his face, ... III. viii. 18. 8
no more we can the mayn-land see, ... III. viii. 24. 3
Bidding her feare *no more* her foeman vilde, ... III. viii. 34. 3
Which when that warriour saw, he said *no more,* . . . . . IV. v. 39. 1
now *no more* for him but I alone, ... IV. vii. 13. 6
'Is this the faith?' she said—and said *no more,* . . . . . IV. vii. 36. 8
threw away, with vow to use *no more,* . . . . IV. vii. 39. 2
said *no more:* . . . . IV. x. 55. 6
He could *no more* but her great misery bemone. . . . . . . IV. xii. 12. 9
all men sought their owne, and none *no more;* . . . . . . V. Pr. 3. 7
mov'd *no more* therewith, ... V. i. 21. 6
No more he spake, ... V. ii. 10. 8
that they *no more* may raine; . . . . V. ii. 38. 7
it is *no more* at all; . . . . V. ii. 39. 5
(though *no more* By law of armes there neede . . . . V. iii. 32. 1
No more shall now the darkenesse of the night Defend thee . V. vi. 37. 6
Which vaine conceipt now nourishing *no more,* . . . . . . V. vii. 38. 8
The resty raynes, regarded now *no more:* . . . . V. viii. 39. 6
when he found *no more* T' oppose against his powre . . . . V. x. 38. 5
Thenceforth he car'd *no more* which way he strooke, ... V. xi. 12. 6
Which Artegall perceiving strooke *no more,* . . . . V. xii. 22. 6
learne Strangers *no more* so rudely to entreat, ... VI. i. 40. 7
No more then for the stroke of strawes or bents: . . . . . VI. iv. 4. 7
and passing by doth hurt *no more.* . . . . VI. vii. 9. 9
No more then lightening from the lofty sky: . . . . VI. viii. 8. 6
With these two lewd companions, and *no more,* . . . . . . VI. viii. 22. 7
other, that hath litle, askes *no more,* . . . . VI. ix. 30. 5
he meanes *no more* to sew His former quest, ... VI. x. 2. 1
when *no more* could nigh to him approch, ... VI. xi. 47. 1
seeing now *no more* Him liberty was left . . . . VI. xii. 36. 4
him esteemed nought, *No more* then Cynthia's selfe; . . . . VII. vi. 18. 9
gods *no more* then men thou doest esteeme; . . . . VII. vii. 15. 8
from thenceforth none *no more* change shal see.' . . . . . VII. vii. 59. 5
that same time when *no more* Change shall be, ... VII. viii. 2. 2
Base thing I can *no more* endure to view: . . . . *Am.* iii. 6
fly *no more,* fayre Love, ... *Am.* xxviii. 13
can *no more* endure on them to looke. . . . . *Am.* xxxv. 12
feeling thence, *no more* her sorowes sadnesse, ... *Am.* xxxix. 11
The woods *no more* shall answere, ... *Epith.* 314
The woods *no more* us answer, ... *Epith.* 426
Nonce. she her neck wreath'd from them for the *nones:* . . *Bel.*[2] vi. 4
thrise have needed for the *nonce* Them to have stricken, . V. xi. 14. 3
None. This ship to which *none* other might compare: . . . *Bel.*[2] xiii. 8
Sunke up these riches, second unto *none,* . . . . *Bel.*[2] xiii. 10
by the greatnes of *none* other, But by her selfe, ... *Ro.* vi. 7
none, all were it Jove his sire, ... *Ro.* xi. 13
A litle wicked worme, perceiv'd of *none,* . . . . *Van.* vii. 7
But *none* fitter then this to applie. . . . . *S.C.* F. 100
There lyeth the Oake, pitied of *none!* . . . . *S.C.* F. 221
But bowe and shafts as then *none* had, ... *S.C.* Mar. 113
Let *none* come there but that Virgins bene, ... *S.C.* Ap. 129
God giveth good for *none* other end. . . . . *S.C.* May 72
(And yet, God wote, such cause hath she *none*) . . . . . . *S.C.* May 98
When shepeheards had *none* inheritaunce, ... *S.C.* May 105
Let *none* mislike of that may not be mended: . . . . *S.C.* May 162
I list *none* accordaunce make . . . . *S.C.* May 164
Sike syrlye shepheards han we *none,* . . . . *S.C.* Jul. 203
and *none* other, Which over the pousse . . . . *S.C.* Au. 45
sike a roundle never heard I *none:* . . . . *S.C.* Au. 125
(perdie God was he *none*) . . . . *S.C.* D. 50
Calling in vaine for rest, and can have *none.* . . . . *Gn.* 392
That *none* whom fortune freely doth advaunce . . . . *Gn.* 555
Yet for their purposes *none* fit espyed. . . . . *Hub.* 226
For *none* would give, ... *Hub.* 348
where *none* might them surprize; . . . . *Hub.* 576
But tidings there is *none,* . . . . *Hub.* 612
For *none* but such as this bold Ape, ... *Hub.* 915
Where *none* shall name the number of his place? . . . . . *Hub.* 982
let *none* other ever drawe Your minde . . . . *Hub.* 1053
That *none* might enter but with issue hard: . . . . *Hub.* 1116
For *none,* but whom he list, might come . . . . *Hub.* 1188
So did he good to *none,* to manie ill, ... *Hub.* 1197
none durst speake, ne *none* durst of him plaine, ... *Hub.* 1199
Yet would he further *none* but for availe; . . . . *Hub.* 1204
that *none* the same espies; . . . . *Hub.* 1288
none but you, or who of you it learnes, ... *T.M.* 51
none more tragick matter I can finde . . . . *T.M.* 155
Because that mourning matter I have *none.* . . . . *T.M.* 168
Yet *none* doth care to comfort us at all; . . . . *T.M.* 350
Yet *none* vouchsafes to answere to our call; . . . . *T.M.* 352
Because *none* living pittieth our paine. . . . . *T.M.* 354
Sith *none* is left to remedie my paine, ... *T.M.* 423
If *none* of neither mention should make, ... *T.M.* 449
If *none* should yeeld him his deserved meed, ... *T.M.* 453
None would choose goodnes . . . . *T.M.* 456
Whilom in ages past *none* might professe . . . . *T.M.* 559
'Name have I *none* (quoth she) nor anie being, ... *Ti.* 34
To tell my forces, matchable to *none,* . . . . *Ti.* 89
In Britannie was *none* to match with mee, ... *Ti.* 100
That whilste he lived was of *none* envyde, ... *Ti.* 241
Lets *none* shoot up that nigh him planted bee: . . . . . . *Ti.* 453
That *none* durst vewe the horror of his face, ... *Ti.* 535
Was *none* more favourable . . . Then Clarion, ... *Mui.* 20
though crime *none* were: . . . . *Mui.* 143
none gainsaid, nor *none* did him envie. . . . . *Mui.* 152
none of these, how ever sweete they beene, ... *Mui.* 157

None—*Continued.*

Yet *none* of them he rudely doth disorder, ... *Mui.* 174
That *none,* except a God, or God him guide, ... *Mui.* 223
when thou of *none* shalt be maintained, ... *D.* 83
Of a small time, which *none* ascertaine may. . . . . . *D.* 504
To you I sing and to *none* other wight, ... *As.* Pr. 11
But he for *none* of them did care a whit, ... *As.* 49
He vanquisht all, and vanquisht was of *none.* . . . . . *As.* 78
That *none* might scape, (so partiall unto *none:*) . . . . . *As.* 110
having *none* to let, to wood did wend. . . . . . *As.* 126
Whilest *none* is nigh, thine eylids up to close, ... *As.* 137
He *none* was made, but scattred all to nought; . . . . . *Col.* 153
None fairer, nor more fruitfull to be red: . . . . . *Col.* 279
her wisdome, *none* Can deeme, ... *Col.* 346
Amongst all these was *none* his paragone. . . . . . *Col.* 451
with *none* of them thou favor foundest, ... *Col.* 461
That *none* of all their due deserts resoundest.' . . . . . *Col.* 463
One ever I, and others never *none.'* . . . . . *Col.* 479
Admyr'd of all, yet envied of *none,* . . . . . *Col.* 550
'Cause have I *none* . . . . . *Col.* 680
that *none* them in doth call.' . . . . . *Col.* 730
Where plain *none* might her see, ... I. i. 16. 9
Ne looke for entertainement where *none* was; . . . . . I. i. 35. 2
words most horrible (Let *none* them read) . . . . . I. i. 37. 2
smart Where cause is *none;* . . . . . I. i. 54. 5
For present cause was *none* of dread her to dismay. . . . . . I. ii. 20. 9
Craving of you, in pitty of my state, To doe *none* ill, ... I. ii. 26. 4
Then was she fayre alone, when *none* was faire in place. . . . . . I. ii. 38. 9
none else from hence may us unbynd.' . . . . . I. ii. 43. 9
wished tydinges *none* of him unto her brought. . . . . . I. iii. 3. 9
when *none* yielded, her unruly Page . . . the wicket open rent, I. iii. 13. 1
none the holy things in safety kept, ... I. iii. 17. 8
of those fearfull women *none* durst rize, ... I. iii. 19. 2
blustring breath of Heaven, that *none* can bide, ... I. iii. 31. 5
Cald Malvenu, who entrance *none* denide: . . . . . I. iv. 6. 4
In living Princes court *none* ever knew Such endlesse richesse, . I. iv. 7. 4
rightfull kingdome she had *none* at all, ... I. iv. 12. 3
childe ne kinsman living had he *none* To leave them to; . . . . . I. iv. 28. 6
wept, that cause of weeping *none* he had; . . . . . I. iv. 30. 8
needlesse feare did never vantage *none;* . . . . . I. iv. 49. 4
enchaunted armes, that *none* can perce; . . . . . I. iv. 50. 6
none can wound the man that does them wield.' . . . . . I. iv. 50. 7
The Elfe him calls alowd, But answer *none* receives; . . . . . I. v. 13. 9
Where *none* appeares can make her selfe a way. . . . . . I. vi. 7. 2
warres, nor new adventures, *none* he herd. . . . . . I. vi. 36. 3
none can breath, nor see, nor heare at will, ... I. vii. 13. 7
living creature *none* he did espye. . . . . . I. viii. 29. 5
none did others safety despize, ... I. ix. 1. 5
None els to death this man despayring drive . . . . . I. ix. 38. 5
When houre of death is come, let *none* aske whence, nor why. . I. ix. 42. 9
whenas *none* of them he saw him take, ... I. ix. 51. 1
That *none* could reade except she did them teach, ... I. x. 19. 2
*(Said he) and battailes *none* are to be fought? . . . . . I. x. 62. 8
none but death for ever can divide; . . . . . I. xii. 37. 2
none that breatheth living aire does know . . . . . II. Pr. 1. 6
'*None* but that saw,' (quoth he) 'would weene . . . . . II. i. 11. 3
Take not away, now got, which *none* would give to me.' . . . II. i. 47. 9
Bynempt a sacred vow, which *none* should ay releace. . . . II. i. 60. 9
hath vowd . . . never to wearen *none:* . . . . . II. iii. 12. 8
none might see How they . . . enwrapped bee: . . . . . II. iii. 27. 8
none thereof could ever taken hold; . . . . . II. iv. 4. 8
And all so soyld that *none* could him descry: . . . . . II. iv. 37. 7
though there were *none,* She could devise; . . . . . II. vi. 3. 7
of *none* accompanyde, ... II. vii. 2. 3
unto *none* my graces do envye: . . . . . II. vii. 8. 4
none could behold The hew thereof; . . . . . II. vii. 29. 3
none could weene Them to efforce . . . . . II. vii. 30. 3
Clothed with leaves, that *none* the wood mote see, ... II. vii. 53. 8
none without the same enduren can: . . . . . II. vii. 65. 5
none then it more fowle and indecent, ... II. ix. 1. 5
when it locked *none* might thorough pas, ... II. ix. 23. 7
ne spard for nicenesse *none.* . . . . . II. ix. 28. 9
By secret wayes, that *none* might it espy, ... II. ix. 32. 6
when he *none* equall knew. . . . . . II. x. 33. 9
dying left *none* heire them to withstand, ... II. x. 61. 8
Fairer and nobler liveth *none* this howre, ... II. x. 76. 6
that *none* from it can shift: . . . . . II. xii. 4. 7
none does others happinesse envye; . . . . . II. xii. 58. 4
ras't, that *none* the signes might see: . . . . . II. xii. 80. 4
tract of living creature *none* they fownd, ... III. i. 14. 8
That *none* of all the six before him . . . . . III. i. 21. 9
'Love have I sure,' (quoth she) 'but Lady *none;* . . . . . III. i. 28. 2
That *none* of them himselfe could reare againe: . . . . . III. i. 29. 2
Which whenas *none* she fond, ... III. i. 61. 1
None of them rashly durst to her approch, ... III. i. 64. 7
That *none* of them foule mischiefe could eschew, ... III. i. 66. 3
Her wrathfull steele, that *none* mote it abyde; . . . . . III. i. 66. 6
that *none* might her discoure, ... III. ii. 20. 4
dartes in *none* doe triumph more, ... III. iii. 3. 1
Full many waies she sought, but *none* could find, ... III. iii. 5. 3
And base atyre, that *none* might them bewray, ... III. iii. 7. 2
From whence, to *none* inferior, ye came, ... III. iii. 54. 3
that *none* might them espy, ... III. iii. 61. 7
That *none* durst passen through . . . . . III. iv. 21. 5
That *none* in equall armes him matchen might: . . . . . III. iv. 24. 3
But *none* of all those curses overtooke . . . . . III. iv. 44. 6
Lives *none* this day that may with her compare . . . . . III. v. 8. 4
Yet she loves *none* but one, ... III. v. 8. 9
In other *none,* but him, she sets delight; . . . . . III. v. 9. 3
none living may compayre: . . . . . III. v. 54. 4

None—*Continued.*

Disguiz'd . . . that *none* might him bewray.) . . . . . III. vi. 11. 9
But when in *none* of all these she him got, ... III. vi. 16. 1
That *none* might thorough breake, ... III. vi. 31. 4
formes, which *none* yet ever knew: . . . . . III. vi. 35. 2
that *none* him losen may. . . . . . III. vi. 48. 9
But she to *none* of them her love did cast, ... III. vi. 53. 1
seeing *none* in place, he gan to make . . . . . III. vii. 45. 3
next to *none* after that happy day, ... III. viii. 13. 7
she said she lov'd *none,* but a Faery knight. . . . . . III. viii. 39. 9
none him durst awake out of his dreme; . . . . . III. ix. 10. 6
none of all them her thereof amov'd . . . . . III. ix. 24. 8
none of those excuses could take place, ... III. ix. 26. 5
ever and anone, when *none* was ware, ... III. ix. 28. 1
Thou seest all, yet *none* at all sees thee: . . . . . III. x. 4. 8
that *none* their joyous treason should reveale. . . . . . III. x. 5. 9
that *none* espyde His secret drift, ... III. x. 6. 3
that *none* but she it vewd, ... III. x. 9. 4
none of all the Satyres him espyde or heard. . . . . . III. x. 47. 9
Ne *none* can suffer to approchen neare: . . . . . III. xi. 22. 5
watcht that *none* should enter nor issew: . . . . . III. xi. 31. 7
that *none* was to possesse So rich purveyaunce, ... III. xi. 53. 8
Yet living creature *none* she saw appeare. . . . . . III. xi. 55. 2
that *none* can tell, ... III. xii. 26. 4
sith *none* but hee Which wrought it . . . . . III. xii. 34. 6
yet never met with *none* That to their . . . . . IV. i. 16. 7
That *none* durst ever whilest thou wast alive, ... IV. ii. 34. 4
Yet she to *none* of them her liking lent, ... IV. ii. 36. 2
That *none* of them once out of order went, ... IV. ii. 36. 7
That *none* of them durst undertake the fight; . . . . . IV. ii. 40. 4
none against them battell durst maintaine: . . . . . IV. iv. 25. 5
But it would not on *none* of them abide, ... IV. v. 17. 8
But Triamond lov'd Canacee, and other *none.* . . . . . IV. v. 21. 9
the Northren winde, that *none* could heare: . . . . . IV. v. 38. 8
And will to *none* her maladie impart? . . . . . IV. vi. 1. 7
hide her wound, that *none* might it perceive: . . . . . IV. vi. 40. 8
Yet found they *none.* . . . . . IV. vi. 47. 5
that *none* Might issue forth, ... IV. vii. 20. 5
'If heaven, then *none* may it redresse or blame, ... IV. viii. 15. 1
Though there were *none* her hatefull words to heare. . . . . IV. viii. 36. 4
Ne *none* there was to reskue her, ne *none* to baile. . . . . IV. ix. 7. 9
cause of feare, sure, had she *none* at all . . . . . IV. ix. 19. 1
And wall'd . . . That *none* mote have accesse, ... IV. x. 6. 4
Behinde the gate that *none* her might espy; . . . . . IV. x. 13. 2
I thought there was *none* other heaven then this; . . . . . IV. x. 28. 3
Begets and eke conceives, ne needeth other *none.* . . . . . IV. x. 41. 9
That *none* might heare the sorrow of my hart, ... IV. x. 48. 2
then which *none* more upright, ... IV. xi. 18. 6
whose streames of *none* may be withstood; . . . . . IV. xi. 20. 9
Ne *none* disdained low to him to lout: . . . . . IV. xi. 30. 5
Whose like *none* else could shew, ... IV. xi. 33. 9
wondrous sholes which may of *none* be red. . . . . . IV. xii. 2. 5
Which never she before disclosd to *none,* . . . . . IV. xii. 5. 4
count my cares when *none* is nigh to heare, ... IV. xii. 6. 2
but since he meanes found *none,* . . . . . IV. xii. 12. 8
where *none* of her might know: . . . . . IV. xii. 15. 2
To *none* but to the seas sole Soveraine. . . . . . IV. xii. 30. 5
None other way will I this day betake, ... V. ii. 10. 6
That *none* of them the feeble over-ren, ... V. ii. 19. 8
And *none* appear'd of all that raskall rout, ... V. ii. 54. 8
second unto *none* in prowesse prayse; . . . . . V. iii. 5. 4
None was debard, ... V. iii. 6. 3
none Against them durst his head to perill shew. . . . . V. iii. 12. 6
what of it became *none* understood: . . . . . V. iii. 26. 6
it to *none* of all their loynes would fit, ... V. iii. 28. 4
his souce, which *none* enduren dare, ... V. iv. 42. 7
That *none* of all the many once did darre . . . . . V. iv. 44. 5
But *none* she found so fit to serve . . . . . V. vi. 6. 3
his owne doome, that *none* can now undoo.' . . . . . V. vi. 16. 5
possessed of one thought, That gave *none* other place. . . . . V. vi. 21. 4
waylfull plaints that *none* was to appease; . . . . . V. vi. 26. 2
yet Knight art *none,* . . . . . V. vi. 37. 5
That way betwixt them *none* appeares in sight; . . . . . V. vi. 40. 3
other beds the Priests there used *none,* . . . . . V. vii. 9. 1
Where *none* may be with her . . . . . V. ix. 2. 4
Nor *none* but beasts may be of her despoyled; . . . . . V. ix. 2. 5
whence *none* could get it out. . . . . . V. ix. 4. 9
Ne *none* can backe returne . . . . . V. ix. 6. 9
and neare them *none.* . . . . . V. ix. 37. 9
Whylest he of *none* was stopped . . . . . V. x. 8. 5
Who when he *none* of all . . . did see . . . . . V. x. 15. 3
For other meede may hope for *none* of mee, ... V. x. 21. 6
dreadfull shape was never seene of *none* . . . . . V. x. 29. 4
Whose ugly shape *none* ever saw, ... V. xi. 20. 5
None can have tidings to assist her side: . . . . . V. xi. 42. 5
That *none* can there arrive without an hoste: . . . . . V. xi. 42. 8
there being *none* them neare, ... V. xii. 6. 2
That *none* should dare him once to entertaine; . . . . . V. xii. 10. 4
Which *none* durst breake, ... V. xii. 10. 5
to whom *none* tydings bore . . . . . V. xii. 11. 5
Ne *none* can find but who was taught them by the Muse. . . . VI. Pr. 2. 9
mongst them all was *none* more courteous . . . . . VI. i. 2. 1
Yet shall it not by *none* be testifyde.' . . . . . VI. i. 6. 7
tidings, which of *none* afore . . . I have had; . . . . . VI. i. 10. 3
Then which a prouder Lady liveth *none:* . . . . . VI. i. 14. 7
if *none* do, yet shame shal thee . . . . . VI. i. 25. 9
none them rightly may reprove . . . . . VI. ii. 1. 7
Let *none* therefore . . . Too greatly grieve . . . . . VI. iii. 5. 8
For other language had he *none,* . . . . . VI. iv. 11. 6
That *none* of them in his soft flesh did bite; . . . . . VI. v. 18. 7

None—*Continued.*
Who can him cure that will be cur'd of *none?* . . . . VI. vi. 7. 4
Did counterfeit kind pittie where was *none:* . . . . VI. vii. 18. 4
That *none* she worthie thought to be . . . . VI. vii. 29. 2
He wore no armour, ne for *none* did care, ... VI. vii. 43. 1
Where *none* is nigh to heare . . . . VI. viii. 40. 8
if that such there were (as *none* they kend) . . . . . . VI. ix. 6. 4
for him nor other *none* Did care a whit, ... VI. ix. 10. 7
As his owne chyld; for other he had *none;* . . . . VI. ix. 14. 8
made him pipe so merrily, as never *none.* . . . . VI. x. 15. 9
being gone, *none* can them bring in place, ... VI. x. 20. 4
since things passed *none* may now restore, ... VI. x. 20. 8
in the covert . . . that *none* Mote them descry, ... VI. x. 41. 3
With which *none* had to doe, ... VI. xi. 12. 4
That *none* his daunger daring to abide . . . . VI. xi. 49. 6
Whilst *none* was him to stop, nor *none* him to restraine. . . . VI. xii. 2. 9
For other *none* such passion can contrive . . . . VI. xii. 21. 5
whilest *none* was them to rew; . . . . VI. xii. 25. 5
Yet *none* of them could ever bring him . . . . VI. xii. 39. 9
(which *none* yet durst . . . to alter . . . . VII. vi. 5. 5
none of all there-in more pleasure found . . . . VII. vi. 38. 6
In covert shade, where *none* behold her may, ... VII. vi. 42. 5
Her head . . . was hid that mote to *none* appeare. . . . . . VII. vii. 5. 9
from thenceforth *none* no more change shal see.' . . . . . VII. vii. 59. 5
Whom if ye please, I care for other *none!* . . . . *Am.* i. 14
let *none* ever say, That ye were blooded . . . . *Am.* xx. 13
high worths . . . Ne but in heaven matchable to *none,* . . . . *Am.* lxvi. 7
For *none* can call againe the passed time. . . . . *Am.* lxx. 14
Hart need not wish *none* other happinesse, ... *Am.* lxxii. 13
Where *none* doo fishes take; . . . . *Epith.* 61
Let *none* of these theyr drery accents sing; . . . . *Epith.* 351
in the secret darke, that *none* reproves, ... *Epith.* 360
Now *none* doth hinder you, ... *Epith.* 370
that *none* the same may tell. . . . . *H.B.* 42
That darknesse there appeareth never *none;* . . . . *H.H.L.* 73
Offending *none,* and doing good to all, ... *H.H.L.* 237
Nones. *See* **Nonce.**
Nonne. *See* **Nun.**
Nook. To reade enregistred in every *nooke* His goodnesse, . . *H.H.B.* 131
Nor (*partial list*).
Nor brick *nor* marble was the wall in view, ... *Bel.*[2] ii. 5
Is nowe *nor* jollye, *nor* shepeheard more. . . . . *S.C.* S. 27
Nor in all Kent, *nor* in Christendome; . . . . *S.C.* S. 153
If *nor* in Princes pallace thou doe sitt, ... *S.C.* O. 80
Nor yet are sung of others . . . . *Ti.* 345
So wide a forest . . . *Nor* famous Ardeyn, *nor* fowle Arlo, is. . *As.* 96
'Ah! nay (said Colin) neither so, *nor* so: . . . . *Col.* 376
Nor Po *nor* Tyburs swans so much renowned, *Nor* all the brood *Col.* 412, 413
nor God *nor* man can fynd Defence, ... *Col.* 875
plain none might her see, *nor* she see any . . . . I. i. 16. 9
Though *nor* in word *nor* deede ill meriting, ... I. iii. 2. 7
Nor wayld of friends, *nor* layd on groning beare, ... I. v. 23. 4
Nor voice was heard, *nor* wight was seene . . . . I. viii. 29. 9
nether darkenesse fowle, *nor* filthy bands, ... I. viii. 40. 1
nor for gold *nor* glee . . . . I. ix. 32. 7
Losse is no shame, *nor* to bee lesse than foe; . . . . II. v. 15. 6
nether spinnes *nor* cards, ne cares *nor* fretts, ... II. vi. 16. 8
Nor sea of licour cold, *nor* lake of myre: . . . . II. vi. 44. 4
Nor bounds *nor* banks his headlong ruine may sustayne. . . . II. xi. 18. 9
none could find, *Nor* herbes, *nor* charmes, *nor* counsel, ... III. iii. 5. 4
no redemption nigh she did *nor* heare *nor* see. . . . . . . V. xii. 11. 9
Nore. The next, the stubborne *Newre* . . . . IV. xi. 43. 3
Noriture. *See* **Nouriture.**
North. did themselves through all the *North* display: . . . . II. x. 15. 7
Proud Etheldred shall from the *North* arise, ... III. iii. 35. 2
Hygate . . . by West, And Overt gate by *North:* . . . . . III. ix. 46. 3
The furthest *North* that did to them appeare: . . . . III. ix. 49. 3
now West he went awhile, Then *North,* . . . . VI. iv. 25. 3
Northern. from the *Northerne* coast a storme arose, ... *Bel.*[2] xiv. 10
So I of this small *Northerne* world was Princesse. . . . . . *Ti.* 84
The Harpe well knowne beside the *Northern* Beare. . . . . . *Ti.* 616
So soone as on them blowes the *Northern* winde, ... *D.* 396
that tumultuous rage . . . Of *Northerne* rebels . . . . . . *Ded. Son.* xi. 10
the *Northerne* wagoner had set His sevenfold teme . . . . . I. ii. 1. 1
The *Northerne* winde his wings did broad display . . . . . II. iii. 19. 3
the fierce *Northerne* wind with blustring blast . . . . . . II. ix. 16. 8
Albanact had all the *Northerne* (**Northrene*) part, ... II. x. 14. 2
Ne the sharp *Northerne* wind thereon to showre; . . . . . . III. v. 51. 5
by the *Northerne* blast Quite overblowne, ... IV. i. 45. 6
Like to the *Northern* (**Northren*) winde, that none could
heare: . . . . IV. v. 38. 8
Northern star. noble deeds above the *Northern starre* . . . . II. x. 4. 7
North-side. the *Northside* of Armulla dale) . . . . *Col.* 105
Northumber. an huge hoste into *Northumber* lead, ... III. iii. 39. 2
Norways. with many one Of his *Norveyses,* . . . . III. iii. 33. 9
Norwich. Yar, soft washing *Norwitch* wall, ... IV. xi. 33. 6
Nose. over it his huge great *nose* did grow, ... IV. vii. 6. 5
Some praise her paps; some praise her lips and *nose;* . . . . VI. viii. 39. 5
Some by the *nose* him pluckt, some by the taile, ... VII. vi. 49. 4
Nosegays. Where bene the *nosegayes* that she dight for thee? . *S.C.* N. 114
Nose-thirl. fire he threw forth from his large *nosethril* . . . I. xi. 22. 9
Nose-thirls. *See* **Nostrils.**
wide *nosethrils* burnd With breathed flames, ... III. ix. 22. 3
from their *nosethrilles* blow the brynie streame, ... III. xi. 41. 2
Nosters. *See* **Paternosters.**
Nostrils. *See* **Nose-thirl, -s.**
Into his *nosthrils* creeping, so him pained, ... *Van.* viii. 10
Like beast whose breath but in his *nostrels* is, ... *Ti.* 356
Not (*partial list of adv.*). *See* **Cannot, If not.**
worke did shew it selfe *not* wrought by man, ... *Bel.*[1] iv. 9

Not—*Continued.*
Other sayne, but how truely I *note,* . . . . *S.C.* S. 110
His chaunged powres at first them selves *not* felt; . . . . . I. vii. 6. 7
I *note* whether praise or pitty more; . . . . I. xii. 17. 4
no'te without an hound fine footing trace. . . . . II. Pr. 4. 5
durst he *nott* Pursew her steps . . . . II. iii. 43. 2
Her other leg was lame, that she *no'te* walke, ... II. iv. 4. 3
her handes fast bownd . . . That she *note* stirre. . . . . . . II. iv. 13. 6
no'te he chuse But beare the rigour . . . . II. vii. 39. 7
no'te avoyded be by earthly skill or powre. . . . . II. viii. 43. 9
Yet *no'te* the same amend, ... II. xii. 57. 7
hungry eies, which *n'ote* therewith be fild; . . . . II. xii. 78. 2
yield thee *nott* Til thou . . . . III. ii. 46. 4
secretly he saw, yet *note* discoure: . . . . III. iii. 50. 4
Yet *no'te* she find redresse for such despight: . . . . III. iv. 40. 7
he was so stund that he *n'ote* ryde, ... III. vii. 42. 6
'father, I *note* read aright . . . . III. viii. 23. 7
note their hongry vew be satisfide, ... III. ix. 24. 1
host *n'ote* him appeach Of vile ungentlenesse, ... III. x. 6. 8
sith he *n'ote* save both, he saved that . . . dearest . . . . III. x. 15. 7
let *not* my rudenes be no breach . . . . III. x. 25. 3
not for nought his wife them loved . . . . III. x. 48. 8
names and natures I *note* readen well; . . . . III. xii. 26. 2
he for paine himselfe *n'ote* right upreare, ... IV. iii. 9. 6
would *not* on none of them abide, ... IV. v. 17. 8
lenger he *note* stand upright, ... IV. xii. 20. 7
Yet whether side was victor *note* be ghest: . . . . V. iii. 7. 6
Notable. to infest The noblest wights with *notable* defame: . . VI. vi. 12. 6
Notably. good . . . may more *notably* be rad, ... III. ix. 2. 3
Not-deserver. Thou doest afflict as well the *not-deserver,* . . *H.L.* 159
Note. *See* **Not.**
doest *note* with critique pen . . . . *Com. Son.* i. 3
chearefull Chaunticlere with his *note* shrill . . . . I. ii. 1. 6
the ghastly Owle, Shrieking his balefull *note,* . . . . I. ix. 33. 7
With mery *note* her lowd salutes the mounting larke. . . . . I. xi. 51. 9
all the Gods admird his lofty *note.* . . . . II. x. 3. 5
singing all her sorrow to the *note,* . . . . IV. ix. 6. 4
There stands an Idole of great *note* and name, ... V. xi. 19. 2
Begin his witlesse *note* apace to clatter. . . . . *Am.* lxxxiv. 4
N'ote, No'te. *See* **Not.**
Notes. most pleasant *notes* did sing, ... *Bel.*[2] xi. 7
Soone as thou gynst to sette thy *notes* in frame, ... *S.C.* O. 25
if thee please in bigger *notes* to sing, ... *S.C.* O. 46
speak to thee In bigger *notes,* . . . . *Gn.* 11
As merrie *notes* upon his rusticke Fife, ... *Gn.* 148
All places with our pleasant *notes* to fill, ... *T.M.* 242
Notes sad enough t'expresse this bitter throw: . . . . *Mui.* 414
All were my *notes* but rude and roughly dight; . . . . *Col.* 363
Lift up thy *notes* unto their wonted height, ... *Col.* 390
the thrise three learned Ladies play Their hevenly *notes,* . . . I. x. 54. 9
song In well attuned *notes* a joyous lay, ... I. xii. 7. 4
apply Her curious skill the warbling *notes* to play, ... I. xii. 38. 7
No bird but did her shrill *notes* sweetely sing; . . . . . . II. vi. 13. 3
Their *notes* unto the voice attempred sweet; . . . . II. xii. 71. 2
Their diverse *notes* t' attune unto his lay, ... II. xii. 76. 2
Musicke did divide Her looser *notes with* Lydian harmony; . . . III. i. 40. 2
harmony In full straunge *notes* . . . . III. xii. 6. 2
With heavenly *notes,* that did all other pas . . . . IV. ii. 2. 3
Her mournefull *notes* full piteously did frame, ... IV. viii. 4. 2
victory in bigger *notes* to sing . . . . VII. vii. 1. 7
The praises of the Lord in lively *notes;* . . . . *Epith.* 219
And heare such heavenly *notes* and carolings, ... *H.H.B.* 262
Notes'. with his vitall *notes* accord, ... *Ro.* xxv. 6
Nothing. Alas, on earth so *nothing* doth endure, ... *Pet.* vi. 11
Of *nothing* now but noyous sulphure smeld. . . . . *Bel.*[2] xi. 14
Alas! by little ye to *nothing* flie, ... *Ro.* vii. 7
this *nothing,* which they have thee left, ... *Ro.* xiii. 13
nothing such thilk shepehearde was . . . . *S.C.* Jul. 145
nowe I wote it is *nothing* sich; . . . . *S.C.* S. 79
shee deemed *nothing* too deere for thee. . . . . *S.C.* N. 117
without golde now *nothing* wilbe got, ... *Hub.* 153
nothing there is done without a fee: . . . . *Hub.* 515
he *nothing* can admire, ... *Hub.* 610
Finde *nothing* worthie to be writ, ... *T.M.* 100
Because I *nothing* noble have to sing. . . . . *T.M.* 108
Is turnd to smoake, that doth to *nothing* fade; . . . . *Ti.* 123
thou hast *nothing* sayd; . . . . *Col.* 460
whose fethers, *nothing* flitt, Doe yet but flagg, ... *Ded. Son.* ii. 7
Sith *nothing* ever may redeeme, nor reave . . . . *Ded. Son.* vii. 6
nothing did he dread, but ever was ydrad. . . . . I. i. 2. 9
the Ash for *nothing* ill; . . . . I. i. 9. 7
of *nothing* he takes keepe. . . . . I. i. 40. 9
he, enrag'd with rancor, *nothing* heares. . . . . I. iii. 44. 5
Whose wals were high, but *nothing* strong nor thick, ... I. iv. 4. 3
Most wretched wight, whom *nothing* might suffise; . . . . . . I. iv. 29. 1
henceforth *nothing* faire but her on earth they find. . . . . . I. vi. 18. 9
of that monstrous mas Was *nothing* left, ... I. viii. 24. 9
Nothing is sure that growes on earthly grownd; . . . . I. ix. 11. 5
nothing might his ready passage stay: . . . . I. x. 35. 5
nothing may my present hope empare.' . . . . I. x. 63. 5
nothing seemd the puissaunce could withstand: . . . . I. xi. 24. 3
In which was *nothing* riotous nor vaine? . . . . I. xii. 14. 2
nothing is but that which he hath seene? . . . . II. Pr. 3. 5
She weakely started, yet she *nothing* drad: . . . . II. i. 45. 7
that weake eld hath left thee *nothing* wise; . . . . II. iii. 16. 3
Yet *nothing* could him to impatience entise. . . . . II. v. 21. 9
nothing might sustaine his furious forse: . . . . II. v. 23. 2
nothing well they her became; . . . . II. vi. 6. 6
Whiles *nothing* envious nature them forth throwes . . . . . . II. vi. 15. 4
What bootes it al to have, and *nothing* use? . . . . II. vi. 17. 6

Nothing—*Continued.*
That *nothing* should him hastily awake. . . . II. vi. 18. 4
Nothing but death can doe me to respyre.' . . . II. vi. 44. 5
nothing to be seene But . . . chests, . . . II. vii. 30. 1
nothing might abash the villein bold, . . . II. vii. 42. 8
nothing cleaner were for such intent, . . . II. vii. 61. 7
all for love, and *nothing* for reward. . . . II. viii. 2. 8
nothing seemd mote beare so monstrous might: . . . II. viii. 38. 2
nothing may withstand his stormy stowre, . . . II. viii. 48. 2
In which was *nothing* pourtrahed nor wrought; . . . II. ix. 33. 8
The yeares of Nestor *nothing* were to his, . . . II. ix. 57. 1
she is inly *nothing* ill apayd; . . . II. xii. 28. 7
all things one, and one as *nothing* was, . . . II. xii. 34. 8
Orcus tame, whome *nothing* can persuade, . . . II. xii. 41. 7
nothing else might keepe her safe and sound: . . . II. xii. 82. 7
Nothing on earth mote alwaies happy beene: . . . III. i. 10. 7
fledd so fast that *nothing* mote him hold, . . . III. i. 15. 8
For *nothing* would she lenger there be stayd, . . . III. i. 67. 4
nothing he from her reserv'd apart, . . . III. ii. 22. 3
this affection *nothing* straunge I finde; . . . III. ii. 40. 5
nothing might relent her hasty flight, . . . III. iv. 49. 1
Doth it consume and into *nothing* goe, . . . III. vi. 37. 8
She, *nothing* quaint Nor 'sdeignfull of so homely fashion, . . III. vii. 10. 5
A laesy loord, for *nothing* good to donne, . . . III. vii. 12. 3
when all this he *nothing* saw prevaile, . . . III. viii. 40. 6
nothing new to him was that same paine, . . . III. ix. 29. 6
nothing may impresse so deare constraint . . . III. ix. 40. 3
nothing left but like an aery Spright, . . . III. x. 57. 4
your cause is *nothing* lesse Then is your sorrow certes, . . III. xi. 18. 3
nothing so much pitty doth implore . . . III. xi. 18. 5
Albe the wound were *nothing* deepe imprest, . . . III. xii. 33. 7
yet so mazed that he *nothing* spake. . . . IV. i. 43. 9
was *nothing* slow Him selfe to save . . . IV. iii. 33. 4
nothing found But darknesse . . . IV. vii. 9. 6
nothing could my fixed mind remove, . . . IV. vii. 16. 5
nothing like himselfe he seem'd in sight. . . . IV. xi. 20. 5
he was *nothing* mov'd nor tempted therewithall: . . . V. ii. 23. 9
For there is *nothing* lost, that may be found if sought. . . . V. ii. 39. 9
So did this Ladies goodly forme decay, And into *nothing* goe, V. iii. 25. 9
he was *nothing* valorous, . . . V. vi. 32. 6
Like to an hideous storme, which *nothing* may empeach. . . V. vii. 35. 9
as *nothing* glad To have beheld a spectacle so bad; . . . V. vii. 38. 4
Though *nothing* whole, but all to-brusd and broken, . . . V. viii. 44. 2
from just verdict will for *nothing* start, . . . V. x. 2. 2
Yet him nought terrified that feared *nothing* ill. . . . V. xi. 22. 9
That *nothing* may escape her reaching might, . . . V. xi. 24. 8
Was with his ghastly count'nance *nothing* queld; . . . V. xii. 16. 7
The other *nothing* better was then shee, . . . V. xii. 33. 1
nothing is more blamefull to a knight, . . . VI. i. 41. 1
a man by *nothing* is so well bewrayd As by his manners; . . VI. iii. 1. 3
Found *nothing* that he said unmeet nor geason, . . . VI. iv. 37. 2
seemed *nothing* might Beare off their blowes . . . VI. v. 18. 4
The knight was *nothing* nice, where was no need, . . . VI. ix. 7. 1
nothing meet in merchandise to passe: . . . VI. xi. 12. 8
nothing knew Of all that chaunced heere, . . . VII. vi. 14. 1
So *nothing* heere long standeth in one stay: . . . VII. vii. 47. 7
Nothing doth firme and permanent appeare, . . . VII. vii. 56. 2
nothing else they brooke, . . . *Am.* xxxv. 10
All paines are *nothing* in respect of this; . . . *Am.* lxiii. 13
Nothing on earth seemes fayre to fleshly sight, . . . *H.B.* 18
Nothing so good, but that . . . May be corrupt, . . . *H.B.* 157
not so white as these, nor *nothing* neare; . . . *Proth.* 45
Notified. they as Straungers shal be *notifide:* . . . III. iii. 44. 4
I . . . Shall through the world make to be *notifyde,* . . . III. xii. 39. 8
Notwithstanding. For *notwithstanding* that one soule was reft, IV. iii. 21. 6
notwithstanding all the subtill bait . . . V. vi. 2. 3
notwithstanding that in former fight He . . . life received . . VI. vii. 2. 3
Nought. *See* **Naught.**
all is *nought* but flying vanitee! . . . *Bel.* i. 11
this world doth *nought* but grievance hold! . . . *Bel.* iii. 12
This dreadfull shape was vanished to *nought.* . . . *Bel.*[2] viii. 14
nought of Rome in Rome perceiv'st at all, . . . *Ro.* iii. 2
Nought from the Romane Empire might be quight; . . . *Ro.* viii. 10
all this whole shall one day come to *nought.* . . . *Ro.* ix. 14
Now to become *nought* els but heaped sands? . . . *Ro.* xv. 14
To shew that all in th' end to *nought* shall fade. . . . *Ro.* xx. 14
That same is now *nought* but a champian wide, . . . *Ro.* xxxi. 1
all his plenteous pasture *nought* him pleased: . . . *Van.* ii. 13
nought, that great is, . . . *Van.* viii. 13
nought on earth can chalenge long endurance? . . . *Van.* xi. 14
To *nought* more, Thenot, my mind is bent . . . *S.C.* F. 94
Nought aske I, but onely to hold my right; . . . *S.C.* F. 186
For *nought* mought they quitten him from decay, . . . *S.C.* F. 213
pumie stones I . . . threwe; but *nought* availed: . . . *S.C.* Mar. 90
Nought having, *nought* feared they to forgoe; . . . *S.C.* May 110
of *nought* they were unprovided; . . . *S.C.* May 114
nought seemeth sike strife, . . . *S.C.* May 158
nought he deemed deare for the jewell: . . . *S.C.* May 277
Nought weigh I who my song doth prayse . . . *S.C.* Jun. 73
Nought easeth the care that doth me forhaile; . . . *S.C.* S. 243
The vaunting Poets found *nought* worth a pease . . . *S.C.* O. 69
Thereof *nought* remaynes but the memoree; . . . *S.C.* N. 121
that swincke and sweate for *nought,* . . . *S.C.* N. 154
Was *nought* but brakes and brambles . . . *S.C.* D .102
Nought reaped but a weedye crop of care; . . . *S.C.* D. 122
Of trecherie or traines *nought* tooke he keep, . . . *Gn.* 241
throat through thirst to *nought* nigh being dride . . . *Gn.* 387
a few have all, and all have *nought,* . . . *Hub.* 141
doubting *nought* their deeds, . . . *Hub.* 328
These lookes (*nought* saying) doo a benefice seeke, . . . *Hub.* 500

Nought—*Continued.*
Where *nought* but dread and death do seeme in show? . . . *Hub.* 966
The Ape, that earst did *nought* but chill and quake, . . . *Hub.* 993
Nought suffered he the Ape to give or graunt, . . . *Hub.* 1143
Did now rebound with *nought* but rufull cries, . . . *T.M.* 23
finde *nought* to busie me: . . . *T.M.* 166
onely seeke for pleasure, *nought* for praise. . . . *T.M.* 468
nought to learning they may spare; . . . *T.M.* 470
nought at all but ruines now I bee, . . . *Ti.* 39
now to *nought* through spoyle of time is wasted. . . . *Ti.* 119
all his greatnes vapoured to *nought,* . . . *Ti.* 219
in time to *nought* doo passe. . . . *Ti.* 420
It almost drowned was, and done to *nought,* . . . *Ti.* 622
Nought may thee save from heavens avengement. . . . *Mui.* 240
'*Nought* cares at all what they, that live on ground, . . . *D.* 87
carest for one that for himselfe cares *nought,* . . . *D.* 93
(Signe of thy love, though *nought* for my reliefe, . . . *D.* 94
Nought carde I then for worldly change or chaunce, . . . *D.* 103
paine, That *nought* on earth may lessen . . . *D.* 276
nought but griefe of minde, . . . *D.* 398
the fire, because to *nought* it flyes; . . . *D.* 404
nought of them is yours, . . . *D.* 503
of daunger *nought* ydrad, . . . *As.* 87
alive was *nought* so deare as hee: . . . *As.* 128
who answerd *nought,* . . . *As.* 167
Since that same day in *nought* I take delight, . . . *Col.* 44
The staie whereof shall *nought* these eares annoy, . . . *Col.* 98
scattred all to *nought;* . . . *Col.* 153
Nought tooke I with me, but mine oaten quill: . . . *Col.* 194
nought but sea and heaven to us appeare. . . . *Col.* 227
Nought hast thou, foolish boy, seene in thy daies.' . . . *Col.* 303
nought my praises of her needed arre, . . . *Col.* 533
Nought else but smoke, . . . *Col.* 720
I die, *nought* to the world denying, . . . *Col.* 950
Nought is thy worth disparaged thereby; . . . *Ded. Son.* ii. 6
nought aghast, his mightie hand enhaunst: . . . I. i. 17. 8
So sound he slept, that *nought* mought him awake. . . . I. i. 42. 3
yeelding soft, in that she *nought* gainsaid, . . . I. ii. 27. 7
Nought is there under heav'ns wide hollownesse, . . . I. iii. 1. 1
She, of *nought* affrayd, . . . him daily sought; . . . I. iii. 3. 7
the rude wench her answerd *nought* at all: . . . I. iii. 11. 3
nought could she say; . . . I. iii. 12. 4
she saw her prayers *nought* prevaile, . . . I. iii. 24. 1
He answered *nought,* but in a traunce still lay, . . . I. iii. 39. 6
Her prayers *nought* prevaile, . . . I. iii. 43. 9
'Faire Dame, be *nought* dismaid . . . I. iv. 49. 1
earthly sight can *nought* but sorrow breed, . . . I. vii. 23. 6
transmew . . . stones to dust, and dust to *nought* at all; . . . I. vii. 35. 7
It booted *nought* to thinke such thunderbolts to beare. . . . I. viii. 7. 9
nought but pressed gras where she had lyen, . . . I. ix. 15. 2
He answerd *nought* at all; . . . I. ix. 24. 1
nought to him replyde; . . . I. ix. 24. 7
'Fear *nought,*' (quoth he) . . . I. ix. 26. 5
His garment, *nought* but many ragged clouts, . . . I. ix. 36. 1
nought but death before his eies he saw, . . . I. ix. 50. 2
For *nought* he car'd his carcas long unfed; . . . I. x. 48. 7
blood can *nought* but sin, . . . yield. . . . I. x. 60. 9
they 'are vaine, and vanish into *nought.*' . . . I. x. 62. 9
nought their kindled corage may aswage: . . . I. xi. 6. 5
cote of steele, so couched neare That *nought* mote perce; . . . I. xi. 9. 3
It booted *nought* to thinke to robbe him of his pray. . . . I. xi. 41. 9
nought so wondrous puissaunce might sustaine: . . . I. xi. 43. 5
As if late fight had *nought* him damnifyde, . . . I. xi. 52. 7
he for *nought* would stay his passage right, . . . I. xii. 25. 4
Let *nought* be hid from me that ought to be exprest. . . . I. xii. 29. 9
be *nought* hereat dismayd, . . . I. xii. 31. 2
He *nought* forgott how he whilome had sworne, . . . I. xii. 41. 6
More then goodwill to me attribute *nought;* . . . II. i. 33. 4
nought too dear I deemd, . . . II. i. 53. 9
nought they beene For all his washing cleaner. . . . II. ii. 3. 5
reason, blent through passion, *nought* descryde; . . . II. iv. 7. 7
where he hits *nought* knowes, and whom he hurts *nought* cares. II. iv. 7. 9
him gainstriving *nought* at all prevaild; . . . II. iv. 14. 2
There wanted *nought* but few rites to be donne, . . . II. iv. 21. 5
For not to grow of *nought* he it conjectured. . . . II. iv. 39. 9
It booted *nought* Sir Guyon, . . . To thincke . . . II. v. 3. 8
said; 'Be *nought* agriev'd, Sir knight, . . . II. v. 15. 1
matter did she make of *nought,* . . . II. v. 19. 6
nought can quench mine inly flaming syde, . . . II. vi. 44. 3
nought but desert wildernesse shewed all around. . . . II. vii. 2. 9
they passing spake unto them *nought;* . . . II. vii. 24. 2
he *nought* could say, Till him the childe bespoke; . . . II. viii. 7. 2
who *nought* againe Him answered, as courtesie became; . . II. viii. 23. 2
bids them *nought* availe. . . . II. viii. 35. 9
Nought could he hurt, but still at warde did ly: . . . II. viii. 39. 7
Nought booted it the Paynim then to strive; . . . II. viii. 50. 1
The Conquerour *nought* cared him to slay; . . . II. viii. 51. 2
all the rest, that noyous was and *nought,* . . . II. ix. 32. 5
She answerd *nought,* but more abasht . . . II. ix. 43. 1
That *nought* mote hinder his quicke prejudize: . . . II. ix. 49. 7
nought moved with her piteous looke; . . . II. x. 18. 9
nought him griev'd to beene from rule deposed downe. . . . II. x. 29. 9
Nought els but treason from the first this land did foyle. . . II. x. 48. 9
his bright shield that *nought* him now avayld, . . . II. xi. 41. 8
nought that falles into this direfull deepe . . . II. xii. 6. 7
Whom *nought* regarding they kept on their gate, . . . II. xii. 17. 3
'Feare *nought,*' then saide the Palmer . . . II. xii. 26. 1
They marched fayrly forth, of *nought* ydred. . . . II. xii. 38. 7
nought they feard, but past on . . . II. xii. 39. 5
Nought feard theyr force that fortilage to win, . . . II. xii. 43. 5

Nouriture—*Continued.*
from thy hand Did commun breath and *nouriture* receave. . . II. x. 69. 6
Noursle, *etc. See* **Nursle,** *etc.*
Nourtred. *See* **Nurtured.**
Nousled, Nousling. *See* **Nuzzled, Nuzzling.**
Novels. to heare *novells* of his devise; . . . *S.C.* F. 95
Novelties. Beguyld thus with delight of *novelties,* . . . II. x. 77. 1
November. Next was *November;* he full grosse and fat . . . VII. vii. 40. 1
Novice. Helpe . . . Thy weaker *Novice* to performe thy will; . I. Pr. 2. 2
How dare I then, the *novice* of his Art, . . . *H.H.B.* 225
Novices. We are but *Novices,* new come abroad, . . . *Hub.* 405
Now (*partial list*).
Now for a truth great Babylon is fallen. . . . *Rev.* ii. 14
Of nothing *now* but noyous sulphure smeld. . . . *Bel.*[2] xi. 14
Rome *now* of Rome is th' onely funerall, . . . *Ro.* iii. 9
these seven hils, which be *nowe* Tombes . . . *Ro.* iv. 7
Now to become nought els but . . . *Ro.* xv. 14
the foule, . . . Is *now* no more seen . . . *Ro.* xvii. 14
now unnethes their feete could them uphold. . . . *S.C.* Ja. 6
but *now* my spring begonne, . . . *S.C.* Ja. 29
nowe the frosty Night . . . gan overhaile: . . . *S.C.* Ja. 74
nowe no succoure was seene him nere. . . . *S.C.* F. 228
nowe upright he can stand no more; . . . *S.C.* F. 234
Now I pray thee, . . . *S.C.* F. 239
The joyous time *now* nighes fast, . . . *S.C.* Mar. 4
Now tell us what thou hast seene. . . . *S.C.* Mar. 60
Now she is a stone, . . . *S.C.* Ap. 88
'*Now* ryse up, Elisa, decked as thou art . . . *S.C.* Ap. 145
now ye daintie Damsells may depart . . . *S.C.* Ap. 147
now nill be quitt with baile . . . *S.C.* May 131
the deawie night *now* doth nye. . . . *S.C.* May 316
Nowe with a Kidde, *now* with a sheepe, The Altars hallowing. *S.C.* Jul. 135
now I have learnd a newe daunce; . . . *S.C.* Au. 11
now at earst the dirke night doth hast. . . . *S.C.* S. 6
Now, by my soule, Diggon, I lament . . . *S.C.* S. 248
now nis the time of merimake, . . . *S.C.* N. 9
Sing *now,* ye shepheards daughters, . . . *S.C.* N. 77
Nowe is time to dye: . . . *S.C.* N. 81
Morne *nowe,* my Muse, *now* morne . . . *S.C.* N. 111
Morne *now,* my Muse, *now* morne . . . *S.C.* N. 151
Cease *now,* my Muse, *now* cease thy sorrowes . . . *S.C.* N. 171
is enstalled *nowe* in heavens hight. . . . *S.C.* N. 177
Ceasse *now,* my song, my woe *now* wasted is; . . . *S.C.* N. 201
Are left both bare and barrein *now* at erst; . . . *S.C.* D. 105
Where then is *now* the guerdon of my paine? . . . *Gn.* 356
sad Eurydice thence *now* no more . . . *Gn.* 433
I *now* depart, . . . *Gn.* 634
For *now* a few have all, . . . *Hub.* 141
For without golde *now* nothing wilbe got, . . . *Hub.* 153
'*Now* sure, . . . Ye a great master are . . . *Hub.* 545
'Marie, (said he) the highest *now* in grace . . . *Hub.* 619
Did *now* rebound with nought but rufull cries, . . . *T.M.* 23
Was turned *now* to dismall heavinesse, Was turned *now* to dreadfull uglinesse. . . . *T.M.* 41, 42
no where *now* to see; . . . *T.M.* 183
Like wofull Culvers, doo sit wayling *now,* . . . *T.M.* 246
That *now* no pastorall is to bee hard. . . . *T.M.* 282
Those *now* renew, . . . *T.M.* 378
As heretofore of good, so *now* of ill. . . . *T.M.* 408
Now only seeke for pleasure, nought for praise. . . . *T.M.* 468
Have *now* quite lost their naturall delight, . . . *T.M.* 552
Nowe doe I nightly waste, . . . *Nowe* doe I dayly starve, . . . *Nowe* doe I alwayes dye, . . . *U.V.* 16, 17, 18
Of which there *now* remaines no memorie, . . . *Ti.* 4
of all Nations *nowe* I am forlorne, . . . *Ti.* 27
nought at all but ruines *now* I bee, . . . *Ti.* 39
But *now* to nought . . . *Ti.* 119
of that brightnes *now* appeares no shade, . . . *Ti.* 124
dead is *now,* as living, counted deare, . . . *Ti.* 242
being dead, is happie *now* much more; . . . *Ti.* 247
no word we heare, nor signe *now* see, . . . *Ti.* 360
Where *now* he is become an heavenly signe, There *now* the joy is his, . . . *Ti.* 601, 602
Now this, *now* that, he tasteth tenderly, . . . *Mui.* 173
Whose cruell fate is woven even *now* . . . *Mui.* 235
'She *now* is dead; 'ne more endured to say, . . . *D.* 184
'But *now,* . . . who shall lead . . . *D.* 316
he made, *Now* with his sharp bore-spear, *now* with his blade. *As.* 108
'*Now* by my life this was a mery lay, . . . *Col.* 157
(ah no, he is not *now!*) . . . *Col.* 432
Now made of Maa, the Nymph delitious. . . . *Col.* 523
Whose girland *now* is set in highest place, . . . *Ded. Son.* xiii. 2
'*Now,* now, Sir knight, shew what ye bee; . . . I. i. 19. 2
Now needeth him no lenger labour spend, . . . I. i. 26. 8
'*Now,*' . . . 'draweth toward night, . . . I. i. 32. 4
now day is spent: . . . I. i. 33. 6
Now, when that ydle dreame was to him . . . I. i. 46. 1
Now when . . . Morning faire, . . . Had spred . . . I. ii. 7. 1
Now like a foxe, *now* like a dragon fell; . . . I. ii. 10. 6
now Fidessa hight, Heard how . . . Fradubio did lament, . . . I. ii. 44. 1
Now when Aldeboran was mounted hye . . . I. iii. 16. 1
Now then, your plaint appease.' . . . I. iii. 29. 9
Now whenas darkesome night had all displayd . . . I. iv. 44. 1
Now in the powre of everlasting Night? . . . I. v. 43. 5
he of rope or armes has *now* no memoree. . . . I. ix. 22. 9
'Fear nought,' (quoth he) 'no daunger *now* is nye.' . . . I. ix. 26. 5
'He there does *now* enjoy eternall rest . . . I. ix. 40. 1
those great battels, . . . *Now* praysed, . . . I. ix. 43. 5
Hast wandred . . . *now* long a day, . . . I. x. 9. 6
The seventh, *now* after death and buriall done, . . . I. x. 43. 1

Now—*Continued.*
'Till *now,*' . . . 'I weened well, . . . I. x. 58. 1
But *now* aread, old father, . . . I. x. 64. 5
High time *now* gan it wex for Una fayre . . . I. xi. 1. 1
The sparke of noble corage *now* awake, . . . I. xi. 2. 6
Now, strike your sailes, . . . I. xii. 42. 1
The Amazon huge river, *now* found trew? . . . II. Pr. 2. 8
now so wise and wary was the knight . . . II. i. 4. 6
Must *now* anew begin like race to ronne. . . . II. i. 32. 7
Take not away, *now* got, which none . . . II. i. 47. 9
'Was, (ay the while, that he is not so *now!*) . . . II. i. 50. 1
'Lo! *now* she is that stone; . . . II. ii. 9. 1
He, *now* this Ladies Champion, . . . II. ii. 18. 9
Now forst to yield, *now* forcing to invade; . . . II. ii. 25. 7
wither *now* on new adventure bownd: . . . II. ii. 39. 6
His Palmer *now* shall foot no more alone. . . . II. iii. 3. 5
now the best and noblest knight alive . . . II. iii. 18. 3
yet nathemoe Was he abashed *now,* . . . II. iv. 8. 5
Now after all was ceast, . . . II. vi. 36. 7
'Harrow *now* out, and well away!' . . . II. vi. 43. 6
his owne health remembring *now* no more, . . . II. vi. 45. 8
all the wealth . . . *now* is reveald to thee. . . . II. vii. 38. 5
Now, therefore, if thou wilt enriched bee, . . . II. vii. 38. 7
now On this vile body from to wreak . . . II. viii. 28. 3
Now seeming flaming whott, *now* stony cold: . . . II. ix. 39. 5
Which Severne *now* from Logris doth depart: . . . II. x. 14. 5
all that *now* America men call: . . . II. x. 72. 6
now it gan to threaten neare decay: . . . II. xi. 14. 5
that never fayld At need till *now,* . . . II. xi. 41. 7
shield that nought him *now* avayld; . . . II. xi. 41. 8
Now faining dalliaunce and wanton sport, *Now* throwing forth lewd wordes . . . II. xii. 16. 3, 4
now they nigh approched to the sted . . . II. xii. 30. 1
Now when they spyde the knight . . . II. xii. 68. 4
Now are they come nigh to the Bowre of blis, . . . II. xii. 69. 4
waters fall . . . *Now* soft, *now* loud, unto the wind did call; II. xii. 71. 8
Where *now* on earth, or how, he may be fownd; . . . III. ii. 14. 2
her prowd portaunce . . . *now* did quaile: . . . III. ii. 27. 4
Late king, *now* captive; late lord, *now* forlorne; . . . III. iii. 42. 4
Now this, *now* that, twixt them they did devize, . . . III. iii. 51. 8
Where is the Antique glory *now* become, . . . III. iv. 1. 1
his noble fame *Now* blazed was, . . . III. iv. 21. 4
Now lyest thou of life and honor refte; *Now* lyest thou a lumpe III. iv. 36, 6, 7
Now God thee keepe, . . . III. v. 26. 6
There *now* he liveth in eternall blis, . . . III. vi. 48. 1
There *now* he lives in everlasting joy, . . . III. vi. 49. 1
'Troy, that art *now* nought but an idle name, . . . III. ix. 33. 1
now the humid night was farforth spent, . . . III. ix. 53. 4
Was never better time . . . Then *now* that . . . III. x. 26. 4
now the hevens obey to me alone, . . . III. xi. 35. 8
Now, like a Lyon . . . *Now,* like a stag; *now,* like a faulcon III. xi. 39. 7, 8
Now the sweet lodge of love and deare delight: . . . III. xii. 45. *or.*4
Now cease your worke, . . . III. xii. 47. *or.* 8, 9
For old despight which *now* forth newly brake . . . IV. ix. 26. 3
Now well-away! . . . IV. xi. 1. 3
Till *now,* at last relenting, . . . IV. xi. 8. 9
Where she hath *now* an everlasting place . . . V. i. 11. 5
He *now* went with him in this new inquest, . . . V. i. 13. 1
'*Now* by my life,' . . . V. ii. 10. 5
if thou *now* shouldst weigh them . . . V. ii. 36. 5
now they doe with captive bands him bind; And *now* they lead him thence, . . . V. iii. 9. 7, 8
Now with faire words, . . . *Now* with sharpe threats, . . . V. iv. 4. 8, 9
In which condition I right *now* did stand: . . . V. iv. 32. 5
now the Knights, being arrived neare, . . . V. iv. 37. 1
Now is the time that I untimely must . . . V. v. 29. 5
Now seeking darkenesse, and *now* seeking light, . . . V. vi. 14. 7
that none can *now* undoo.' . . . V. vi. 16. 5
now seeing night at dore, . . . V. vi. 22. 1
Now walking soft, *now* sitting still upright, . . . V. vi. 26. 3
No more shall *now* the darkenesse . . . Defend thee . . . V. vi. 37. 6
now by this the noble Conqueresse Her selfe came . . . V. vii. 36. 1
Which vaine conceipt *now* nourishing no more, . . . V. vii. 38. 8
The resty raynes, regarded *now* no more: . . . V. viii. 39. 6
now, right noble knights, arriv'd ye bee . . . V. ix. 20. 4
Now at that instant, as occasion fell, . . . V. ix. 36. 1
He *now* t' abhorre and loath her person . . . V. ix. 39. 9
But not for those she *now* in question came, . . . V. ix. 40. 6
now needing strong defence, . . . V. x. 12. 6
The woefull widow had no meanes *now* left, . . . V. x. 14. 2
'yet *now* I gin new life to feele; . . . V. x. 20. 4
So *now* he hath new lawes . . . V. x. 27. 6
turne we *now* to noble Artegall; . . . V. xi. 36. 1
'*Now* sure and by my life, . . . V. xi. 41. 1
'to assist me *now* at need . . . V. xi. 57. 2
now time drawing ny . . . V. xii. 3. 6
Its *now* so farre from that which then it was, . . . VI. Pr. 5. 2
Yet since ye mercie *now* doe need to crave, . . . VI. i. 42. 4
Whereof she *now* more glad then sory earst, . . . VI. i. 45. 1
Now wringing both his wretched hands in one, *Now* beating his hard head . . . VI. v. 4. 4, 5
now nigh aghast, Revived was, . . . VI. v. 21. 8
therein he likewise was praying *now,* . . . VI. v. 35. 8
Now smyling smoothly, . . . *Now* glooming sadly, . . . VI. vi. 42. 7, 8
'How *now,* Sir knight, What meaneth this . . . VI. vii. 14. 6
Now here, *now* there, . . . VI. viii. 13. 7
It never yet was bent, ne bent it *now,* . . . VI. viii. 16. 1
Now being naked, to their sordid eyes . . . VI. viii. 41. 6
Pype, jolly shepheard, pype thou *now* apace . . . VI. x. 16. 6
since things passed none may *now* restore, . . . VI. x. 20. 8

Now—*Continued.*
She made me often pipe, and *now* to pipe apace. . . . VI. x. 27. 9
now by this, with noyse of late uprore, . . . VI. xi. 46. 1
To leave his love, *now* perill being past, . . . VI. xii. 13. 3
livest thou, my daughter, *now* againe? . . . VI. xii. 19. 8
what doost thou here *now* make? . . . VII. vi. 25. 8
Now hornd, *now* round, *now* bright, *now* browne . . . VII. vii. 50. 8
My love is *now* awake out of her dreames, . . . *Epith.* 92
Now welcome, night! . . . *Epith.* 315
now t' asswage the force . . . *H.L.* 8
Now-a-days. It's *now a dayes,* ne halfe so streight and sore. . *Hub.* 448
now of dayes such temperance is rare . . . IV. viii. 29. 6
Now and then. Islands, seeming *now and than,* Are not firme land, II. xii. 11. 3
(hearkned *now and then* Some litle whispering, . . . IV. vii. 23. 3
Noway. *See* **No, Way.**
But he *no waie* recomforted would be, . . . *D.* 547
On which it seizing *no way* enter might, . . . II. iv. 46. 7
Whose will her weakenesse could *no way* represse, . . . IV. ix. 18. 8
Nowhere. so coole, as *no where* else I fynde: . . . *S.C.* Jun. 5
Can *nowhere* fynd to shroude my lucklesse pate. . . . *S.C.* Jun. 16
Two fellowes might *no where* be better fitted. . . . *Hub.* 50
but *no where* it espide. . . . *Hub.* 1336
th' Ape still flying he *no where* might get: . . . *Hub.* 1372
layd abed, and *no where* now to see; . . . *T.M.* 183
A gentler shepheard may *no where* be found: . . . *Col.* 445
A fairer crew yet *no where* could I see . . . *Ded.Son.* xvii. 10
from their noyance he *no where* can rest; . . . I. i. 23. 7
he *no where* doth appeare, But vanisht is. . . . I. v. 13. 7
no where could he find that wofull thrall: . . . I. viii. 37. 2
so much doe vaunt, yet *no where* show, . . . II. Pr. 1. 8
nowhere could espye Tract of his foot: . . . II. iii. 19. 6
Eftsoones he fled away, and might *no where* be seene. . . . II. iv. 46. 9
Yet *no where* can her find: . . . II. ix. 7. 8
yet *no where* can her find.' . . . II. ix. 38. 9
now their acts be *no where* to be found, . . . IV. ii. 32. 5
no where could her find, nor tydings of her heare.' . . . IV. vi. 36. 9
Strange wight, whom he had seene *no where,* . . . IV. vii. 43. 7
Him seeking evermore, yet *no where* him descride. . . . IV. viii. 18. 9
like on earth *no where* I recken may: . . . IV. x. 15. 7
no where could they finde her, . . . V. ii. 25. 1
yet him *no where* he spyde. . . . VI. v. 3. 9
No whit. *See* **Whit.**
Now that. *now that* he them surviv'd. . . . II. ix. 57. 5
Now that he had her singled from the crew . . . III. iv. 45. 3
Noyance. from their *noyance* he no where can rest; . . . I. i. 23. 7
stench . . . whose *noyaunce* fild the fearefull sted . . . III. xii. 2. 6
Noyce. *See* **Noise.**
Noyed. all that *noyd* his heavie spright . . . I. x. 24. 3
harmefull pestilence, So sore him *noyd,* . . . I. xi. 45. 2
Noyes. *See* **Noah's, Noise.**
Noyous. Of nothing now but *noyous* sulphure smeld. . . . *Bel.*[2] xi. 14
Hath powrd on earth this *noyous* pestilence, . . . *T.M.* 483
The false Duessa, leaving *noyous* Night, . . . I. v. 45. 1
nether darkenesse fowle, . . . Nor *noyous* smell, . . . I. viii. 40. 2
watch the *noyous* night, and wait for joyous day. . . . I. xi. 50. 9
their sharpe wounds and *noyous* injuries, . . . II. ix. 16. 7
all the rest, that *noyous* was and nought, . . . II. ix. 32. 5
Is in a *noyous* cloud enveloped, . . . III. i. 43. 2
I wish that night the *noyous* day would end: . . . *Am.* lxxxvi. 6
Numa. The gratious *Numa* of great Britany; . . . II. x. 39. 6
As was Aegerie that *Numa* tought: . . . II. x. 42. 8
Numbed. my flesh is *numbd* with feares: . . . *D.* 419
Like lyfull heat to *nummed* senses brought, . . . VI. xi. 45. 4
numbd with holding all the day An hatchet . . . VII. vii. 42. 5
Number. none shall name the *number* of his place? . . . *Hub.* 982
In *number* of the noblest knightes on ground; . . . II. ii. 42. 2
Th' uneven *nomber* for this busines is most fitt.' . . . III. ii. 50. 9
to *number* with how many eyes . . . III. xi. 45. 8
in greater *number* grew. . . . VI. xii. 32. 5
Numbered. thousand Fishers *numbred* to have been, . . . *Ti.* 150
They *numbred* even steps and equall pace; . . . I. x. 12. 5
shall to thee Ten times so much be *nombred* . . . II. vii. 9. 5
numbred be mongst knights of Maydenhed, . . . II. ix. 6. 6
Her Host two hundred thousand *numbred* is; . . . II. x. 56. 5
th' heapes of those . . . might not be *nombred:* . . . V. v. 19. 7
Numberless. so *numberlesse* their nation. . . . IV. xii. 1. 9
Numbers. The *nombers* flowe as fast as spring doth ryse. . . . *S.C.* O. 108
the sweet *numbers* and melodious measures, . . . *T.M.* 547
wise wordes, taught in *numbers* for to runne, . . . *Ti.* 402
In loftie *numbers* and heroicke stile. . . . *Ded. Son.* xii. 8
in a dungeon deepe huge *nombers* lay . . . I. v. 45. 8
So huge and infinite their *numbers* were, . . . II. xi. 5. 6
With warlike *numbers* and Heroicke sound, . . . IV. ii. 32. 7
So huge their *numbers,* . . . IV. xii. 1. 9
though their *numbers* do much more surmount, . . . IV. xii. 2. 8
their *numbers* are so great, . . . V. xi. 45. 6
How slowly do the houres theyr *numbers* spend? . . . *Epith.* 280
Nun. a faire Lady *Nonne,* that whilome hight Matilda, . . . III. iii. 13. 5
'The second was an holy *Nunne* to chose, . . . III. vii. 58. 6
Nurse. That *nource* of vice, this of insolencie, . . . *S.C.* May 118
Ida . . . like a kindly *nourse,* . . . *Gn.* 507
Therefore the *nurse* of vertue I am hight, . . . *T.M.* 457
'Cambden! the *nourice* of antiquitie, . . . *Ti.* 169
Nature, *nurse* of every living thing, . . . *D.* 337
No *nurse,* but Stepdame, cruell, mercilesse. . . . *D.* 342
Ne Persia selfe, the *nourse* of pompous pride, Like ever saw. I. iv. 7. 6
Was sluggish Idlenesse, the *nourse* of sin; . . . I. iv. 18. 6
As carefull *Nourse* her child from falling oft does reare. . I. x. 35. 9
The *Nourse* of time and everlasting fame, . . . I. xi. 5. 8
from tender dug of commune *nourse* . . . II. iv. 18. 3

Nurse—*Continued.*
Greece, the *Nourse* of all good arts, . . . II. ix. 48. 1
She with her *Nourse* adowne to sleepe did lye; . . . III. ii. 28. 4
Her aged *Nourse,* whose name was Glauce hight, . . . III. ii. 30. 2
'Ah! *Nurse,* what needeth thee to eke my payne? . . . III. ii. 35. 2
no usuall fire, no usuall rage Yt is, O *Nourse!* . . . III. ii. 37. 4
th' aged *Nourse,* her calling to her bowre, . . . III. ii. 49. 4
her olde *Nourse* was nought dishartened, . . . III. iii. 20. 8
At last the *Nourse* . . . Conceiv'd a bold devise, . . . III. iii. 52. 1
counseld with her *Nourse* . . . III. iii. 57. 7
Sister of heavie death, and *nourse* of woe, . . . III. iv. 55. 2
Thou art the roote and *nourse* of bitter cares, . . . III. iv. 57. 2
She is the *nourse* of pleasure and delight, . . . IV. x. 35. 8
As a bad *Nurse,* which, fayning to receive . . . V. v. 53. 1
death, instead of life, have sucked from our *Nurse!* . . . VII. vi. 6. 9
mery London, my most kyndly *Nurse,* . . . *Proth.* 128
Nursed. in the gardens of Adonis *nurst:* . . . *Col.* 804
such as drunke her life the which them *nurst!* . . . I. i. 26. 7
Her *nourced* had in trew Nobility: . . . III. v. 32. 5
in her bosome she thee long had *nurst,* . . . III. xi. 1. 3
by them long with carefull labour *nurst,* . . . VI. Pr. 3. 8
brought home and *noursed* well As his owne chyld; . . . VI. ix. 14. 7
Who as her owne it *nurst* (and named) evermore. . . . VI. xii. 9. 9
she was bred and *nurst* On Cynthus hill, . . . VII. vii. 50. 3
Nurseries. Store of firebronds out of her *nourseries* . . . *Gn.* 508
Nursery. ye double *noursery* Of Arts! . . . IV. xi. 26. 8
Revele to me the sacred *noursery* Of vertue, . . . VI. Pr. 3. 1
Nurse's. from the howre I taken was from *nourses* tender pap, III. ii. 6. 2
Ne can be stild for all his *nurses* might, . . . V. vi. 14. 4
Nurses. made alwaies clame To be the *Nourses* of nobility, . . *Ded. Son.* iv. 2
Nursing. a Wolfe . . . *Noursing* two whelpes; . . . *Bel.*[2] vi. 2
Nursle. Or *noursle* up in lore of learn'd Philosophy. . . . VI. iv. 35. 9
Nursled. *He *noursled* up in life and manners wilde, . . . I. vi. 23. 8
In which she *noursled* him till yeares he raught, . . . V. i. 6. 8
Nursling. A litle *noursling* of the humid ayre; . . . *Gn.* 282
made the *noursling* of Nobilitie. . . . *T.M.* 564
made by his almightie art For that his *noursling,* . . . II. viii. 20. 3
The *noursling* of Dame Memorie his deare, . . . IV. xi. 10. 2
Nursling's. her deare *nourslings* losse no lesse did mourne, . . III. xii. 45. 7
Nurslings. Nylus *nurslings* their Pyramides faire; . . . *Ro.* ii. 4
Her *nourslings* did with mutinous uprore . . . *Ro.* xxii. 5
Nurslings'. Did fill with her renowmed *nourslings* praise . . . *Ro.* x. 7
Nurture. The infant, so for want of *nourture* spoyld; . . . V. v. 53. 4
sterve their harts that needeth *nourture* most, . . . *H.L.* 39
Nurtured. both in deeds and words he *nourtred* was, . . . *As.* 71
Nut. Sweet is the *Nut,* but bitter is his pill; . . . *Am.* xxvi. 6
Nuts. with his *nuts* larded many swine: . . . *S.C.* F. 110
gather *nuttes* to make me Christmas game, . . . *S.C.* D. 26
fell all for *nuts* at strife? . . . *S.C.* D. 35
Nuzzled. Whom, . . . He *nousled* up in life and manners wilde, I. vi. 23. 8
Nuzzling. like Moldwarps *nousling* still they lurke, . . . *Col.* 763
like a *nousling* Mole doth make His way . . . IV. xi. 32. 8
Ny. *See* **Nigh.**
Nyctelius. flying vengeance sore Of king *Nictileus* . . . *Gn.* 173
Nymph. With golden wings in habite of a *Nymph.* . . . *Bel.*[1] iv. 6
Hard by a rivers side, a wailing *Nimphe,* . . . *Bel.*[1] viii. 1
like a *Nimph,* that wings of silver weares, . . . *Bel.*[2] iv. 6
Chloris, that is the chiefest *Nymph* of all, . . . *S.C.* Ap. 122
Emongst the rest a gentle *Nymph* was found, . . . *Mui.* 118
the *Nymph* his mother Him forth did bring, . . . *As.* 13
many a *Nymph* both of the wood and brooke, . . . *As.* 43
The *Nimph,* which of that water course has charge, . . . *Col.* 109
Nath-lesse the *Nymph* her former liking held; . . . *Col.* 128
Now made of Maa, the *Nymph* delitious. . . . *Col.* 523
of the famous Shure, the *Nymph* she is, . . . *Col.* 526
A fairer *Nymph* yet never saw mine eie: . . . *Col.* 559
The sacred *Nymph* . . . Was out of Dianes favor, . . . I. vii. 4. 8
This *nymph,* quite tyr'd with heat of scorching ayre, . . . I. vii. 5. 3
"So soone as Bacchus with the *Nymphe* does lincke!" . . . II. i. 55. 6
occasion straunge, Which to her *Nymph* befell. . . . II. ii. 7. 2
the *Nimphe* that bore A gyaunt babe . . . II. xii. 52. 2
Finding the *Nymph* asleepe in secret wheare, . . . III. iv. 19. 7
the *Nymphe* which from her infancy Her nourced had . . . III. v. 32. 4
the Mayd And daughter of a woody *Nymphe,* . . . III. v. 36. 3
fresh in face and guize As any *Nimphe;* . . . III. vi. 23. 8
every *Nimph* full narrowly shee eide. . . . III. vi. 23. 9
Dame Phoebe to a *Nymphe* her babe betooke . . . III. vi. 28. 3
one old *Nymph,* hight Panope, . . . III. viii. 37. 9
farre and neare the *Nymph* his mother sought, . . . IV. xi. 6. 1
There with the *Nymph* his mother, . . . IV. xi. 7. 6
the proud *Nymph* would for no worldly meed, . . . IV. xi. 8. 7
Sixe valiant Knights of one faire *Nymphe* yborne, . . . IV. xi. 37. 3
the faire *Nimph* Rheusa wandring there. . . . IV. xi. 42. 3
The *Nymph,* his mother, getteth her . . . IV. xii. Arg.
there was a *Nymph* that hight Molanna . . . VII. vi. 40. 1
the love of some new *Nymph,* late seene, . . . VII. vii. 11. 6
Nymph's. *See* **Sea-nymph's.**
Nymphs. *See* **Sea-nymphs, Water-nymphs.**
hundred *Nymphes* sate side by side . . . *Bel.* xii. 10
drove the *Nymphes* away (to flight[1]) . . . *Bel.* xii. 14
manie Muses, and the *Nymphes* withall, . . . *Pet.* iv. 5
'Ye dayntye *Nymphs,* that in this blessed brooke . . . *S.C.* Ap. 37
a fresh bend Of lovely *Nymphs.* . . . *S.C.* May 33
lightfoote *Nymphes,* can chace the lingring Night . . . *S.C.* Jun. 26
Wherein the *Nymphes* doe bathe; . . . *S.C.* Jul. 80
if the flocking *Nymphes* did folow Pan, . . . *S.C.* D. 47
where the countrey *Nymphs* are rife, . . . *Gn.* 146
The joyous *Nymphes* and lightfoote Faeries . . . *T.M.* 31
one of that Rivers *Nymphes,* . . . *Ti.* 15
A thousand *Nymphes,* with mirthfull jollitee, . . . *Ti.* 137

Nymphs—*Continued.*
Walking abroad with all her *Nymphes* to play, ... *Mui.* 115
manie *Nymphes* about them flocking round, ... *Mui.* 295
Both *Nymphes* (**Nimphs*) and Muses nigh she made astownd, *D.* 314
an hundred *Nymphs,* all heavenly borne, ... *Col.* 256
many *Nymphes,* which she doth hold In her retinew, ... *Col.* 459
Right noble *Nymphs,* and high to be commended: . . . . . *Col.* 577
dwel . . . gentle *Nymphes,* delights of learned wits; . . . . . *Ded. Son.* v. 10
The wooddy *nymphes,* . . . Her to behold do thither runne . I. vi. 18. 1
Beholdes her *nymphes* enraung'd in shady wood, ... I. xii. 7. 8
The woods, the *nymphes,* my bowres, my midwives, weare: . . II. i. 53. 7
with the woody *Nymphes* when she did play, ... II. iii. 28. 7
Where all the *Nymphes* have her unwares forlore, ... II. iii. 31. 3
all her sister *Nymphes* with one consent . . . . III. iv. 35. 8
the *Nymphes* sitt all about him rownd, ... III. iv. 44. 1
In which full many lovely *Nymphes* abyde; . . . . III. vi. 16. 5
Whiles all her *Nymphes* did like a girlond her enclose. . . . III. vi. 19. 9
To lurke emongst your *Nimphes* in secret wize, ... III. vi. 23. 2
To search the God of love her *Nimphes* she sent . . . . III. vi. 26. 1
how often eek For many other *Nymphes,* . . . . III. xi. 44. 5
the *Nymphes* eke Hylas cryde. . . . . III. xii. 7. 9
any of the Thracian *Nimphes* in salvage chase. . . . . IV. vii. 22. 9
Belphebe with her peares, The woody *Nimphs,* . . . . IV. vii. 23. 6
Sweet springs, in which a thousand *Nymphs* did play; . . . . IV. x. 24. 3

Nymphs—*Continued.*
all those *Nymphes,* which then assembled were . . . . IV. xi. 10. 7
amongst the wanton *Nymphs* to sport and toy. . . . . IV. xi. 19. 9
Of Gods, of *Nymphs,* of rivers, yet unred; . . . . IV. xii. 2. 7
Which of the *Nymphes* his heart so sore did mieve; . . . . . IV. xii. 26. 7
For love of *Nymphes* she thought she need not care, ... IV. xii. 27. 4
all the wooddy *Nymphes* did wayle and mourne; . . . . V. viii. 43. 7
That in these woods amongst the *Nymphs* dost wonne, ... VI. ii. 25. 2
Nymphes and Faeries by the bancks did sit . . . . VI. x. 7. 6
Nymphes, or Faeries, or enchaunted show, ... VI. x. 17. 6
Frequented of these gentle *Nymphes* alwayes, ... VI. x. 19. 4
where she did resort With all her *Nymphes* . . . . VII. vi. 39. 7
with the *Nymphes* the Satyres love to play and sport. . . . . VII. vi. 39. 9
To see her naked mongst her *Nymphes* in privity. . . . . . . VII. vi. 42. 9
Diana, with her *Nymphes* about her, ... VII. vi. 45. 7
Which of her *Nymphes* . . . Him thither brought, ... VII. vi. 51. 5
the *Nymphes* from all the brooks thereby . . . . VII. vii. 10. 6
Nymphes, of Rivers all: . . . . VII. vii. 26. 7
Bring with you all the *Nymphes* that you can heare . . . . . *Epith.* 37
Ye *Nymphes* of Mulla, which . . . trouts doe tend . . . . . . *Epith.* 56
ye, faire *Nimphs!* which oftentimes have loved . . . . *H.L.* 31
A Flocke of *Nymphes* I chaunced to espy, ... *Proth.* 20
the *Nymphes,* . . . Ran all in haste . . . . *Proth.* 55
Two of those *Nymphes,* meane while, two Garlands bound . . *Proth.* 83

O

O (*partial list*).
O holy virgin! chiefe of nyne, ... I. Pr. 2. 1
O! how great wonder . . . . II. ix. 3. 8
But *O* great pitty! . . . . II. ix. 21. 7
O worke divine! . . . . II. ix. 22. 2
Oak. He that hath seene a great *Oke* drie and dead, ... *Ro.* xxviii. 1
Who such an *Oke* hath seene, let him record . . . . *Ro.* xxviii. 12
A goodly *Oake* sometime had it bene, ... *S.C.* F. 103
to scold And snebbe the good *Oake,* . . . . *S.C.* F. 126
Little him aunswered the *Oake* againe, ... *S.C.* F. 140
How falls it then that this faded *Oake,* . . . . *S.C.* F. 169
To this the *Oake* cast him to replie . . . . *S.C.* F. 189
made many wounds in the wast *Oake.* . . . . *S.C.* F. 202
broughten this *Oake* to this miserye; . . . . *S.C.* F. 212
There lyeth the *Oake,* pitied of none! . . . . *S.C.* F. 221
The faded lockes fall from the loftie *oke,* . . . . *S.C.* N. 125
'How often have I scaled the craggie *Oke,* . . . . *S.C.* D. 31
Whom als accompanied the *Oke,* . . . . *Gn.* 204
The *Oke,* whose Acornes were our foode, ... *Gn.* 206
The builder *Oake,* sole king of forrests all; . . . . I. i. 8. 8
his stalking steps are stayde Upon a snaggy *Oke,* . . . . . I. vii. 10. 7
That strongest *Oake* might seeme to overthrow. . . . . I. viii. 18. 6
The mossy braunches of an *Oke* halfe ded. . . . . I. x. 48. 4
Then it had lighted on an aged *Oke,* . . . . III. vii. 41. 3
Like an old *Oke,* whose pith and sap is seare, ... IV. iii. 9. 8
in his hand a tall young *oake* he bore, ... IV. vii. 7. 4
The durefull *Oake,* whose sap is not yet dride, ... *Am.* vi. 5
Oaken. all his steed With *oaken* leaves attrapt, ... IV. iv. 39. 6
an *oaken* plant, which lately hee Rent by the root; . . . . . VI. vi. 41. 2
Then was the *oaken* crowne by Pastorell Given to Calidore . VI. ix. 44. 6
He with an *Oaken* girlond now did tire, ... VII. vii. 11. 5
Oaker. *See* **Ochre.**
Oaks. th' *Okes,* deep grounded in the earthly molde, ... *Gn.* 453
haps to light Uppon two stubborne *oakes,* . . . . V. vi. 40. 2
On which a grove of *Oakes* high-mounted growes, ... VII. vi. 41. 2
Oar. Withouten *oare* or Pilot it to guide, ... II. vi. 5. 3
running to her boat withouten *ore,* . . . . II. xii. 15. 7
with the *ore* Did thrust the shallop . . . . III. vii. 27. 7
Oars. doth stryve To strike his *oares,* . . . . II. xii. 5. 5
that Ferryman With his stiffe *oares* . . . . II. xii. 10. 2
with his *oares* did sweepe the watry wildernesse. . . . . . . II. xii. 29. 9
with their finny *oars* the swelling sea did sheare. . . . . . . III. iv. 33. 9
Oaten. So broke his *oaten* pype, and downe dyd lye. . . . . . *S.C.* Ja. 72
thy *oaten* pype began to sound, ... *S.C.* Jun. 58
all mine *Oten* reedes bene rent and wore, ... *S.C.* O. 8
the Romish Tityrus . . . left his *Oaten* reede, ... *S.C.* O. 56
Relieve thy *Oaten* pypes that sleepen long. . . . . *S.C.* N. 24
Rude ditties, tund to shepheards *Oaten* reede, ... *S.C.* D. 14
Ne ever Shepheard sound his *Oaten* quill . . . . *D.* 325
on pipes of *oaten* reed, Oft times to plaine . . . . *As.* Pr. 1
Soone as his *oaten* pipe began to shrill, ... *As.* 44
Charming his *oaten* pipe unto his peres, ... *Col.* 5
As ever piped on an *oaten* reed, ... *Col.* 13
Nought tooke I with me, but mine *oaten* quill: . . . . *Col.* 194
to mine *oaten* pipe enclin'd her eare, ... *Col.* 360
noblest swaine, That ever piped in an *oaten* quill: . . . . . . *Col.* 441
For trumpets sterne to chaunge mine *Oaten* reeds, ... I. Pr. 1. 4
ne wont there sound His mery *oaten* pipe, ... I. ii. 28. 9
Oath. hereupon an *oath* unto me plight.' . . . . *Hub.* 1055
in the wine a solemne *oth* they bynd . . . . I. v. 4. 8
with solemne *oath* and plighted hand Assurd, ... II. iv. 23. 8
Are not all knightes by *oath* bound . . . . II. viii. 56. 4
The recompence of their perjured *oth;* . . . . II. x. 40. 4
both . . . with many a cursed *oth* Sweare she is yours, . . . IV. i. 47. 7
with faithfull *oth* Bynding himselfe . . . . VI. i. 44. 1
That he might see his men, and muster them by *oth.* . . . . VI. vii. 33. 9
Oaths. through many vowes which forth he pour'd, And many *othes,* . . . . IV. vi. 41. 7
Obedience. His name was meeke *Obedience,* rightfully aredd. . I. x. 17. 9
all mens harts in dew *obedience* held; . . . . II. x. 32. 5
both of them did thinke *obedience* To doe . . . . IV. vi. 21. 8
Soft Silence, and submisse *Obedience,* . . . . IV. x. 51. 6

Obedience—*Continued.*
all *obedience* both to words and deeds They quite forgot, . . V. viii. 41. 3
As if he learned had *obedience* long, ... VI. xii. 37. 2
Of her ye virgins learne *obedience,* . . . . *Epith.* 212
Obedient. The Eugh, *obedient* to the benders will; . . . . . . I. i. 9. 4
yeeld His partes to reasons rule *obedient,* . . . . II. xi. 2. 2
The waves, *obedient* to theyr beheast, ... III. iv. 31. 8
Obeisance. not content with loyall *obeysaunce,* . . . . *S.C.* May 120
they, . . . Making *obeysaunce,* did the cause declare, ... I. iv. 13. 7
They did *obeysaunce,* as beseemed right, ... II. ix. 26. 7
tend our charges with *obeisaunce* meeke. . . . . III. vi. 22. 8
To meeke *obeysance* of loves mightie raine, ... V. v. 28. 8
Did to her myld *obeysance,* as they ought, ... V. ix. 34. 4
With meek *obaysance* and humilitie, ... VII. vii. 13. 8
Oberon. with king *Oberon* he came to Faery land. . . . . II. i. 6. 9
Whose emptie place the mightie *Oberon* Doubly supplide, . . II. x. 75. 8
Obey. straight *obay* his soveraine beheast; . . . . *D.* 270
Taught to *obay* their bestiall beheasts, ... I. iv. 18. 3
Their backward bent knees teach her humbly to *obay.* . . . . I. vi. 11. 9
The God, through loth, yet was constraynd t' *obay;* . . . . . II. vii. 66. 1
first taught men a woman to *obay:* . . . . II. x. 20. 7
did their rule *obay,* . . . . II. x. 49. 7
make them him *obay;* . . . . III. iii. 12. 2
They were all taught by Triton to *obay* . . . . III. iv. 33. 3
As he had long bene learned to *obay;* . . . . III. vii. 36. 8
cruell Mulciber would not *obay* His threatfull pride, ... III. xi. 26. 5
she saw The huge seas . . . t' *obay* her servaunts law. . . . . III. xi. 30. 9
now the hevens *obey* to me alone, ... III. xi. 35. 8
Taught to *obay* the menage of that Elfe . . . . III. xii. 22. 3
T' *obey* their riders hest, as seemed good. . . . . IV. iii. 39. 5
to his law compels all creatures to *obay.* . . . . IV. x. 42. 9
ready to *obay;* . . . . IV. xi. 29. 2
Ne would for ought *obay,* as did become, ... V. i. 29. 3
All creatures must *obey* the voice of the Most Hie. . . . . . V. ii. 40. 9
He maketh subjects to their powre *obay;* . . . . V. ii. 41. 6
if I vanquishe him, he shall *obay* My law, ... V. iv. 49. 2
thought it just t' *obay.* . . . . V. v. 19. 9
There bound t' *obay* that Amazons proud law, ... V. v. 22. 3
thereto did himselfe right well behave Her to *obay,* . . . . V. v. 23. 8
T' *obay* the heasts of mans well-ruling hand. . . . . V. v. 25. 4
T' *obay* a womans tyrannous direction, ... V. v. 26. 4
Bynding himselfe most firmely to *obay,* . . . . VI. i. 44. 2
made him to *obay:* . . . . VII. vii. 36. 4
Whom then shall I, or heaven or her, *obay?* . . . . *Am.* xlvi. 5
The which the base affections doe *obay,* . . . . *Epith.* 196
To win them worship which to thee *obay.* . . . . *H.L.* 237
Both heaven and earth *obey* unto her will, ... *H.H.B.* 197
Obeyed. the proud beasts him readily *obayd:* . . . . *Hub.* 1102
The God *obayde;* and calling forth . . . A diverse Dreame . . I. i. 44. 1
So, passing forth, she him *obaid.* . . . . I. iv. 51. 9
old Ninus . . . of all the world *obayd.* . . . . I. v. 48. 4
She him *obayd,* and turnd a little wyde.— . . . . I. xi. 5. 5
Guyon *obayd:* So him away he drew . . . . II. v. 25. 1
Thus to mislead mee, whiles I you *obaid:* . . . . II. vi. 22. 8
him all India *obayd,* . . . . II. x. 72. 5
thy good fortune, having fate *obayd,* . . . . III. iii. 19. 7
To house a guest that would be needes *obayd,* . . . . III. x. 2. 3
Nathlesse her tongue not to her will *obayd,* . . . . IV. vi. 27. 8
the swift bird *obayd* not her behest, ... IV. viii. 10. 7
unto her *obayed* all the best. . . . . IV. x. 49. 4
The Damzell streight *obayd,* . . . . V. iv. 50. 1
them perceiving streight to him *obayd,* . . . . VI. vi. 39. 4
Obeying. the flitt barke, *obaying* to her mind, ... II. vi. 20. 3
their bad Stuard . . . *obaying* Natures first beheast. . . . . VI. iv. 14. 9
Object. when the *object* of her vertue failed, ... *Ro.* xxi. 9
Him therefore now the *object* of his spight . . . . II. i. 3. 1
his contrary *object* most deface, ... II. xi. 6. 4
When in so high an *object* they do lyte, ... III. ii. 3. 7
He gan to him *object* his haynous crime, ... VI. vii. 26. 7
the *object* of his vew, ... VI. ix. 26. 6
Into the *object* of your mighty view? . . . . *Am.* vii. 4
Still to behold the *object* of their paine, ... *Am.* xxxv. 2

Odors—*Continued.*

sent forth *odours* sweet;	VII. vii. 10. 3
flowres, That dainty *odours* from them threw	Am. lxiv. 3
to the sense most daintie *odours* yield,	H.B. 80
did fragrant *odours* yeild,	Proth. 75

Oedipus. any *Oedipus* unware Shall chaunce, . . . Gn. Ded. 5

Oenone. On faire *Oenone* got a lovely boy, . . . III. ix. 36. 4

    When he the love of fayre *Oenone* sought, . . . VI. ix. 36. 8

Oeta. in his timely howre From golden *Oeta* . . . Gn. 316

Oetaean. the *Oetaean* wood Had him consum'd, . . . Ti. 381

    So also did that great *Oetean* Knight . . . V. viii. 2. 4

Of (*partial list*). *See* **Now-a-days, Whereof.**

the time when rest the gift *of* Gods	Bel.¹ i. 1
onely Rome *of* Rome hath victorie;	Ro. iii. 10
Ne ought save Tyber . . . Remaines *of* all.	Ro. iii. 12
Or like not *of* the frowie fede,	S.C. Jul. 111
Fayth *of* my soule, thou shalt	S.C. Au. 145
We deeme *of* Death as doome *of* ill desert;	S.C. N. 184
to dislodge the Raven *of* her nest?	S.C. D. 32
Of him his God is worship with his sythe,	Gn. 129
of mortall men were knowne,	Gn. 207
Lords *of* that which they doo gather,	Hub. 164
uncontrol'd *of* anie:	Hub. 169
be descryed *Of* everie one,	Hub. 345
All shalbe taught *of* God.	Hub. 440
learning question'd be *of* anie.	Hub. 524
that he might be seene *Of* the wilde beasts	Hub. 1066
both eares pared *of* their hight;	Hub. 1382
thou livest, being ever song *Of* us,	Ti. 339
neither *of* themselves can sing, Nor yet are sung *of* others .	Ti. 344, 345
worshipped *of* all,	Ti. 464
led away *of* them	Mui. 136
woven . . . *Of* Joves owne hand,	Mui. 236
was vanquished *Of* Pallas,	Mui. 262
when thou *of* none shalt be maintained,	D. 83
Of rustick muse full hardly to be betterd.	D. 231
Unpitied, unplaynd, *of* foe or frend:	As. 136
hearbe *of* some Starlight is cald . . . *Of* others Penthia, .	As. 193, 194
of all he loved was,	As. 201
my pipe, before that aemuled *of* many,	Col. 73
love had me forlorne, forlorne *of* me,	Col. 90
belov'd full faine *Of* her owne brother	Col. 117
of a River, which he was *of* old, He none was made,	Col. 152
nought my praises *of* her needed arre,	Col. 533
Admyr'd *of* all, yet envied *of* none,	Col. 550
despys'd *of* all;	Col. 729
to be medicynd *Of* her .	Col. 878
Faire Rosalind *of* divers fowly blamed	Col. 908
of his cheere did seeme too solemne sad;	I. i. 2. 8
will also want *of* might?	I. i. 32. 7
restreined *of* that aged sire.	I. ii. 5. 9
of himselfe he ofte for feare would quake,	I. ii. 10. 7
three bred *Of* one bad sire,	I. ii. 25. 8
Me chaunced *of* a knight encountred bee,	I. ii. 35. 7
lov'd *of* ladies,	I. ii. 37. 1
Drawne *of* fayre Pecocks,	I. iv. 17. 8
drawne *of* six unequall beasts,	I. iv. 18. 1
he *of* Ladies oft was loved	I. iv. 24. 7
Fidessa, loe! Is there possessed *of* the traytour vile;	I. iv. 42. 3
a Gryfon, seized *of* his pray,	I. v. 8. 2
what *of* gods then boots it to be borne,	I. v. 23. 6
of no envious eyes he mote be spyde;	I. v. 52. 8
A Satyres sonne . . . begotten *of* a Lady	I. vi. 21. 3
sorrowes rew, Blaming *of* Fortune,	I. vi. 31. 5
To weete *of* newes that did abroad betide,	I. vi. 34. 5
More greedy they *of* newes	I. vi. 34. 9
dreaded more *of* men,	I. vii. 16. 6
Ne might *of* mortall eye be ever seene;	I. vii. 33. 2
Of grace do me unto his cabin guyde.'	I. ix. 32. 4
right joyous *of* her just request;	I. x. 33. 1
well beseemes all knights *of* noble name,	I. x. 59. 4
of three furlongs does but litle lacke;	I. xi. 11. 7
Witnesse . . . heavens *of* his bold perjury;	I. xii. 27. 6
not so good *of* deedes as great *of* name,	II. ii. 17. 3
purvay Your selfe *of* sword	II. iii. 15. 4
Guyon is *of* immodest Merth Led into loose desyre;	II. vi. Arg.
Cymochles *of* her questioned	II. vi. 9. 2
did *of* joy and jollity devize,	II. vi. 21. 3
Infinite mischiefes *of* them doe arize,	II. vii. 12. 6
to drinke *Of* the cold liquor	II. vii. 58. 3
Unmindfull *of* his wound, *of* his fate ignoraunt.	II. viii. 34. 9
Which *of* himselfe Albania he did call;	II. x. 14. 3
that gate which *of* his name is hight,	II. x. 46. 6
Full large he was *of* limbe,	II. xi. 20. 7
That *of* them cleeped was.	III. i. 31. 9
he by an Elfe was gotten *of* a Fay;	III. iii. 26. 9
On her they poured forth *of* plenteous horne,	III. vi. 2. 6
not by art But *of* the trees owne inclination	III. vi. 44. 3
they restrained were *Of* ready entraunce,	III. viii. 52. 4
of his owne him lefte not liberty:	III. x. 2. 4
The cause *of* both, *of* both their minds depends,	IV. iv. 1. 4
amidst the billowes beating *of* her,	V. vi. 10. 6
Me to deceive *of* faith unto me plight,	V. vi. 16. 8
'Sir Knight, *of* pardon I you pray,	V. viii. 13. 1
Forth *of* her window as she looking lay,	V. viii. 26. 6
doing and receiving curtesies *Of* that great Ladie,	V. x. 5. 3
as he was searching *of* their wounds,	VI. vi. 5. 1
to bene ywroken *Of* all the vile demeane,	VI. vi. 18. 4
glauncing by deceiv'd him *of* that he desynd.	VI. vii. 10. 9
vengeance thought to take *Of* him .	VI. vii. 11. 8

Of—*Continued.*

a salvage nation, which did live *Of* stealth and spoile,	VI. viii. 35. 3
The best advizement was, *of* bad, to let her Sleepe	VI. viii. 38. 1
escaping craftily, Creepes forth *of* dores,	VI. xi. 18. 7
misdoubting least *of*-new Some uprore were	VI. xi. 43. 8
fayrest ymages *Of* hardest marble are *of* purpose made,	Am. li. 2
thou ask'st . . . But love *of* us, for guerdon	H.H.L. 177

Off. Casting mine eyes farre *off*, . . . Bel.² xiii. 3

My spirit shaking *off* her earthly prison,	Van. i. 2
cutte *of* hys dayes with untimely woe,	S.C. May 199
better leave *of* with a little losse,	S.C. S. 134
But followe them farre *off*,	S.C. Env. 11
he was but slowe, did slowth *off* shake	Gn. 309
Far *of* beholding Ephialtes tide,	Gn. 375
They fled farre *off*,	Hub. 576
shake *off* this vile harted cowardree,	Hub. 986
th' Apes long taile . . . he quight Cut *off*,	Hub. 1382
in their wrath breake *off* the vitall bands,	D. 18
at length we land far *off* descryde:	Col. 265
The royall virgin shooke *off* drousy-hed;	I. i. 7. 5
She soone left *off* her mirth and wanton play,	I. ii. 14. 4
But followes her far *off*,	I. iii. 44. 7
Leave *of* their worke,	I. v. 36. 2
Far *off* he wonders what them makes so glad;	I. vi. 15. 1
leave *off* this dreadfull play;	I. vi. 28. 7
He smott *off* his left arme,	I. viii. 10. 6
smote *off* quite his right leg	I. viii. 22. 4
Which shaking *off*, he rent that yron dore	I. viii. 39. 5
far *off* he unto him did shew	I. x. 55. 1
Send forth their flames far *off* to every shyre,	I. xi. 14. 4
move the world from *off* his steadfast henge,	I. xi. 21. 8
ryse From *off* the earth,	I. xi. 23. 7
we far *off* will here abide to vew.'	II. i. 25. 7
leave *off*, whatever wight thou bee,	II. i. 47. 6
breaking *off* the end for want of breath,	II. i. 56. 2
From *off* the earth to take his aerie flight.	II. iii. 19. 5
She shakes *off* shame.	II. iii. 36. 9
when far *off* Cymochles heard and saw,	II. vi. 4. 1
leave *off* this toylsome weary stoure:	II. vi. 16. 4
shaking *off* his drowsy dreriment,	II. vi. 27. 3
far *off* they many Islandes spy	II. xii. 10. 6
wishing it far *off*.	III. i. 46. 9
taking thrise three heares from *off* her head,	III. ii. 50. 1
cut *off* by practise criminall.	III. iii. 28. 8
quite from *off* (**of*) the earth their memory be raste?'	III. iii. 43. 9
of her far *off* he gained vew.	III. iv. 48. 1
farre *off* espyde a Tassell gent,	III. iv. 49. 6
From *off* their dainty limbs the dusty sweat	III. vi. 17. 6
hurt far *off* unknowne whom ever she envide.	III. vii. 6. 9
Which they far *off* beheld	III. ix. 35. 5
Far *off* aspyde a young man,	III. xi. 3. 3
A little *off* his shield was rudely throwne,	III. xi. 7. 6
Casts *off* his ragged skin.	IV. iii. 23. 9
mote farre *off* be rad.	IV. vii. 24. 9
They gan remember *of* the fowle upbraide,	IV. x. 28. 5
shaking *off* all doubt.	IV. x. 53. 6
at one stroke cropt *off* her head with scorne,	V. i. 18. 6
rather chose his challenge *off* to breake,	V. i. 24. 3
He smote it *off*,	V. ii. 18. 5
her feete, . . . Chopt *off*, and nayld	V. ii. 26. 9
leave *off* to weigh them all againe,	V. ii. 36. 8
shouldered him from *off* the higher ground,	V. ii. 49. 8
Rashing *off* helmes, and ryving plates asonder,	V. iii. 8. 6
Beare *off* the burden of her raging yre;	V. v. 16. 4
they have shaken *off* the shamefast band,	V. v. 25. 2
She thus oft times was beating *off* and on,	V. v. 43. 2
he chaunst far *off* to heed A Damzell,	V. viii. 4. 1
better to reforme then to cut *off* the ill.	V. x. 2. 9
That quite smit *off* his arme .	V. xi. 7. 9
He shooke *off* luskishnesse;	VI. i. 35. 7
off he did his shield, and downeward layd	VI. ii. 48. 1
He chaunst far *off* an armed Knight to spy	VI. iii. 46. 6
Beare *off* their blowes from percing thorough quite:	VI. v. 18. 5
Which breaking *off* he toward them did pace	VI. v. 36. 4
unwares to be descryde' For breaking *off* their daunce,	VI. x. 11. 3
hewing *off* his head,	VI. x. 36. 6
To pluck her . . . from *off* her chaire;	VII. vi. 13. 3
Which cutting *off* through hasty accidents,	Epith. 429

Offal. The Miser threw him selfe, as an *Offall*, . . . II. iii. 8. 7

Offence. Box, yet mindfull of his olde *offence*; . . . Gn. 676

mercie, Lord, For mine *offence*.	II. i. 27. 2
Your court'sie takes on you anothers dew *offence*.'	II. i. 28. 9
whether blott of fowle *offence* Might not be purgd	II. ii. 4. 1
with bloodguiltinesse to heape *offence*,	II. ii. 30. 3
secret pleasure did *offence* empeach,	II. x. 68. 8
without *offence* Mote I request you tydings of my love,	IV. vi. 34. 5
Both girlonds of his Saints against their foes *offence*.	IV. x. 51. 9
for feare of her *offence*;	IV. x. 56. 2
Voide of malitious mind or foule *offence*:	V. v. 33. 5
all that earst seemd sweet seemes now *offense*,	H.H.B. 269

Offend. hasty tong that did *offend*: . . . I. v. 39. 5

seemeth safe from storms that may *offend*;	I. xi. 1. 5
him to *offend*. . . . He seekes,	II. i. 3. 2
feared least his boldnesse should *offend*,	II. iii. 17. 5
she did first *offend*,	II. iv. 31. 5
evill is at hand him to *offend*.'	II. viii. 8. 7
Ne forst his rightfull owner to *offend*;	II. viii. 21. 4
The Prince him selfe halfe seemed to *offend*;	II. ix. 8. 7
each might best *offend* his proper part,	II. xi. 6. 3
those which therein bathed mote *offend*.	II. xii. 63. 4

Offend—*Continued.*
‘Let not it thee *offend*, ... III. iii. 15. 6
ought your goodly patience *offend*, ... III. ix. 1. 5
never let th’ ensample of the bad *Offend* the good; . . . . III. ix. 2. 2
his late fight . . . so sore did him *offend*, ... III. x. 1. 8
if ought he did *offend*. . . . . III. xii. 36. 9
As one in feare the Stygian gods t’ *offend*, ... IV. iii. 32. 2
To suppliants, through frayltie which *offend*: . . . . V. ix. 32. 4
his lovely litle spoile . . . did greatly him *offend*: . . . . VI. iv. 25. 8
feend that mote *offend* Their happie flockes, ... VI. ix. 6. 2
Me no such cares nor cumbrous thoughts *offend*, ... VI. ix. 22. 6
such basenesse mought *offend* her. . . . . *Am.* ix. 12
all their faults with which they did *offend*. . . . . *Am.* xxiv. 12
And fly the faults with which we did *offend*. . . . . *Am.* lxii. 8
Offended. wicked wordes that God and man *offended*. . . . . IV. i. 27. 5
offended That his departure thence should be so short, ... IV. xii. 18. 3
That she with him mote be the more *offended*. . . . . V. v. 57. 5
Till that th’ *offended* heavens list to lowre . . . . V. x. 26. 6
So much the more was Calepine *offended*, ... VI. iii. 36. 6
that vile lozell which her late *offended*; . . . . VI. iv. 10. 2
Offender. punishment is due to the *offender*. . . . . *Gn.* 366
Offending. *Offending* none, and doing good to all, ... *H.H.L.* 237
Offensive. dayly more *offensive* unto each degree. . . . . IV. i. 18. 9
Offer. the gay floures did *offer* to be eaten; . . . . *Van.* ii. 6
To her will I *offer* a milkwhite Lamb: . . . . *S.C.* Ap. 96
My selfe would *offer* you t’ accompanie . . . . *Hub.* 97
poursewed fast The present *offer* of faire victory, ... II. v. 12. 2
It selfe doth *offer* to his sober eye, ... II. xii. 58. 2
Scorne the faire *offer* of good will profest; . . . . III. i. 55. 2
Which scornefull *offer* Blandamour gan soone despize; . . . . IV. iv. 8. 9
That *offer* pleased all the company: . . . . IV. iv. 10. 1
Which to her in that daunger hope of life did *offer*. . . . . V. iv. 10. 9
That will not take the *offer* of good hope, ... V. v. 39. 6
Oft making *offer* him to smite, ... V. viii. 42. 2
‘For not I him, . . . did *offer* first to wrong, ... VI. ii. 8. 2
did *offer* meanes him sleeping to surprize. . . . . VI. vii. 22. 9
seeing nought Which doubt of daunger to her *offer* mought, VI. viii. 32. 5
To *offer* sacrifice divine thereon; . . . . VI. viii. 42. 6
tooke their gentle *offer*: . . . . VI. ix. 7. 2
nought tempted with the *offer* Of his rich mould, ... VI. ix. 33. 1
offer made To hyre them well . . . . VI. xi. 40. 1
hostages doe *offer* for my truth; . . . . *Am.* xi. 2
Offered. With patience to forbeare the *offred* bowle? . . . . *S.C.* May 139
their owne happie chaunce Them freely *offred*, ... *Hub.* 963
as halfe blushing *offred* him to kis, ... I. i. 49. 7
when she saw her *offred* sweets refusd, ... I. v. 37. 6
To catch her, newly *offred* to his eie; . . . . I. vi. 46. 5
offred hope of comfort did despise: . . . . II. i. 15. 3
If then thee list my *offred* grace to use, ... II. vii. 18. 6
‘Me list not . . . receave Thing *offred*, ... II. vii. 19. 2
‘Certes,’ (sayd he) ‘I n’ill thine *offred* grace, ... II. vii. 33. 1
so great grace and *offred* high estate; . . . . II. vii. 50. 2
she to Guyon *offred* it to tast, ... II. xii. 57. 1
offered faire guiftes t’ allure her sight; . . . . III. viii. 38. 7
offred kingdoms unto her in vew, ... III. viii. 40. 4
a jolly knight, . . . *offred* that to justifie alowd. . . . . IV. i. 10. 4
The battell, *offred* in so knightly wize: . . . . IV. iv. 11. 5
For his friends sake her *offred* favours scorne, ... IV. ix. 3. 8
Thereto he *offred* for to make him chiefe . . . . IV. ix. 15. 7
offred streight the Lady to be slaine; . . . . V. i. 27. 2
as his Squire him *offred* evermore To serve, ... V. i. 30. 3
Offred his service to disarme the Knight; . . . . V. viii. 27. 2
Himselfe and service to her *offered*, ... V. x. 12. 3
The which good Fortune to him *offred* faire; . . . . V. xi. 13. 5
He *offred* up for daily sacrifize My children . . . . V. xi. 19. 6
And *offred* him, his courtesie to requite, ... VI. iv. 39. 7
desirous of the *offred* meed: . . . . VI. vii. 5. 6
Unto some carrion *offered* to his sight; . . . . VI. viii. 28. 5
Offred him drinke to quench his thirstie heat, ... VI. ix. 6. 8
if he hungry were, him *offred* eke to eat. . . . . VI. ix. 6. 9
At last when all the rest them *offred* were, ... VI. xi. 14. 1
offred store of gold: . . . . VI. xi. 14. 6
Offerer. she both offers and the *offerer* Despysde, ... III. viii. 38. 8
Offerest. *offrest* sacrifice unto the dead: . . . . III. viii. 47. 4
Offering. powre forth th’ *offring* of his guiltles blood: . . . . *Ti.* 300
Offring to fall into each mouth that gapes, ... *Col.* 602
Offring his service, and his dearest life . . . . II. xi. 16. 6
As freely *offering* to be gathered; . . . . II. xii. 54. 6
Offring to him in sinfull sacrifice The flesh of men, ... V. x. 28. 6
Offerings. fed her fatt with feast of *offerings*, ... I. iii. 18. 6
Offers. idle *offers* of thy golden fee; . . . . II. vii. 9. 7
all thine ydle *offers* I refuse. . . . . II. vii. 39. 2
she both *offers* and the offerer Despysde, ... III. viii. 38. 8
‘Thy *offers* base I greatly loth, ... III. x. 29. 6
Scorning her *offers* and conditions vaine; . . . . V. v. 46. 2
With which thee dares our *offers* thus despize: . . . . V. v. 48. 5
Office. seeing kindly sleep refuse to doe His *office*, ... *Hub.* 22
His *office* was to give entertainement . . . . I. x. 37. 4
His *office* was the hungry for to feed, ... I. x. 38. 2
The fourth appointed by his *office* was . . . . I. x. 40. 1
Whose *office* was . . . to maintaine that castels ancient rights. IV. x. 7. 8
A sordid *office* for a mind so brave: . . . . V. v. 23. 4
Which if I might by your good *office* get, ... V. v. 42. 3
each sought to supply the *office* of her page. . . . . VI. v. 30. 9
Offices. How fowlie they their *offices* abus’d, ... *Hub.* 563
All *offices*, all leases by him lept, ... *Hub.* 1145
The rest had severall *offices* assynd; . . . . II. ix. 31. 6
other *offices* for mother meet . . . . III. iv. 39. 6
Sweete semblaunt, friendly *offices* that bynde, ... VI. x. 23. 5
Offric. *Offricke* and Osricke, twinnes unfortunate, ... III. iii. 37. 3

Offscum. this *off-scum* of that cursed fry . . . . VII. vi. 30. 1
Off-shaked. Having *off-shakt* them and escapt their hands, . . II. xi. 33. 4
Off-shaking. *off-shaking* vaine affright She nigher drew, . . . I. xi. 55. 6
Offspring. shaming to have given so great head To his *off-spring*, ... *Ro.* xi. 2
The golden *ofspring* (**offspring*) of Latona pure, ... *Gn.* 13
The goodly *off-spring* of Joves progenie, ... *T.M.* 429
as ye be of heavenlie *off-spring* borne, ... *Ti.* 684
Of th’ old Heroes, whose famous *ofspring* . . . . *Ded. Son.* vi. 4
To see his syre and *offspring* auncient. . . . . I. vi. 30. 4
Th’ *ofspring* of Elves and Faeryes there he fond, ... II. ix. 60. 4
The royall *Ofspring* of his native land, ... II. x. 69. 2
all their *Ofspring*, in their dew descents; . . . . II. x. 74. 2
sacred Emperours, Thy fruitfull *Ofspring*, ... III. iii. 23. 2
thy worthy prayses . . . Their *ofspring* hath embaste, ... III. ix. 33. 9
Out of the Trojans scattered *ofspring*, ... III. ix. 44. 7
there did succeed An *off-spring* of their bloud, ... VII. vi. 20. 8
So that next *off-spring* of the Makers love, ... *H.H.L.* 92
all his *off-spring* into thraldome threw, ... *H.H.L.* 124
Oft. *Oft* makes me wayle . . . . *Pet.* i. 14
which so *oft* thee, (Rome) their conquest made; . . . . *Ro.* xiii. 4
blinde furie, which warres breedeth *oft*, ... *Ro.* xxiv. 1
by the small the great is *oft* diseased. . . . . *Van.* ii. 14
The weake, that hath the strong so *oft* forlorne! . . . . *Van.* vi. 14
oft the bloud springeth from woundes . . . . *S.C.* F. 176
oft he lets his cancker-wormes light . . . . *S.C.* F. 179
oft his hoarie locks downe doth cast, ... *S.C.* F. 181
The Axes edge did *oft* turne againe, ... *S.C.* F. 203
The blocke *oft* groned . . . . *S.C.* F. 215
he . . . *oft* the pumies latched. . . . . *S.C.* Mar. 93
Oft stombles at a strawe. . . . . *S.C.* Jul. 100
Algrind, he That is so *oft* bynempt? . . . . *S.C.* Jul. 214
hast luld me *oft* asleepe, ... *S.C.* Au. 155
Whose streames my tricklinge teares did *ofte* augment. . . . *S.C.* Au. 156
who will seeke . . . *Oft* lives by losse, ... *S.C.* S. 73
oft in the night came . . . . *S.C.* S. 216
joyed *oft* to chace the trembling Pricket, ... *S.C.* D. 27
ye Woodes, that *oft* my witnesse were: . . . . *S.C.* D. 154
(Octavius), which *oft* To learned wits givest courage . . . . *Gn.* 35
good men, of whom thou *oft* are blest; . . . . *Gn.* 62
his limbs doth *oft* display, ... *Gn.* 108
oft were dauncing seene. . . . . *Gn.* 179
oft faining to retire And *oft* him to assaile, ... *Gn.* 306, 307
Fast bound with serpents that him *oft* invades; . . . . *Gn.* 374
that great warre, which Trojanes *oft* behelde? . . . . *Gn.* 498
oft beheld the warlike Greekish forces, ... *Gn.* 499
Fast much, pray *oft*, ... *Hub.* 498
And play the Poet *oft*. . . . . *Hub.* 810
speach Against Gods holie Ministers *oft* reach, ... *Hub.* 840
Which *oft* maintain’d his masters braverie. . . . . *Hub.* 858
he us’d *oft* to beguile Poore suters, ... *Hub.* 877
who would not *oft* sweare, And *oft* unsweare, ... *Hub.* 1057, 1058
beare A Bases part . . . *oft*, ... *T.M.* 28
oft bedeawed with our learned layes, ... *T.M.* 272
with our musick wont so *oft* to ring, ... *T.M.* 278
wont so *oft* their Pastoralls to sing, ... *T.M.* 280
mishaps, which *oft* I to him plained, ... *Ti.* 142
pure streames with guiltles blood *oft* stained; . . . . *Ti.* 145
oft his heart did melt in tender teares . . . . *Mui.* 30
oft would dare to tempt the troublous winde. . . . . *Mui.* 48
full *oft* Beholding them, ... *Mui.* 105
as she *oft* is seene in warlicke field: . . . . *Mui.* 323
‘*Oft* did the Shepeheards . . . And *oft* their lasses, ... *D.* 141, 142
So *oft* as I record those piercing words, ... *D.* 295
She bathed *oft* with teares, and dried *oft*: . . . . *As.* 164
oft she cald to him, ... *As.* 167
when I think of her, as *oft* I ought, ... *Col.* 624
well I wote, that *oft* I heard it spoken, ... *Col.* 919
Oft from those grave affaires were wont abstaine, ... *Ded. Son.* i. 5
So Maro *oft* did Caesars cares allay. . . . . *Ded. Son.* i. 8
Oft fire is without smoke, ... I. i. 12. 4
their tender wings He brusheth *oft*, and *oft* doth mar . . . . I. i. 23. 9
Care . . . Who *oft* is wont to trouble gentle Sleepe. . . . . I. i. 40. 6
of himselfe he *ofte* for feare would quake, ... I. ii. 10. 7
And *oft* would flie away. . . . . I. ii. 10. 8
He *oft* finds med’cine who his griefe imparts, ... I. ii. 34. 4
Her up he tooke . . . And *oft* her kist. . . . . I. ii. 45. 8
Ofte soust in swelling Tethys saltish teare; . . . . I. iii. 31. 3
He . . . Neptune *oft* doth blesse. . . . . I. iii. 32. 5
For want whereof poore people *oft* did pyne: . . . . I. iv. 21. 7
Of which he supt so *oft*, ... I. iv. 22. 7
he of Ladies *oft* was loved . . . . I. iv. 24. 7
So *oft* as Slowth still in the mire did stand. . . . . I. iv. 36. 4
sweet *Oft* tempred is,’ . . . ‘with muchell smart: . . . . I. iv. 46. 4
oft sighing sore, ... I. vi. 4. 2
And *oft*, for dread of hurt, would him advise . . . . I. vi. 25. 4
And, *ofte* refreshed, battell *oft* renue. . . . . I. vi. 44. 3
So *oft* as he, . . . is to sinfull bands made thrall: . . . . I. viii. 1. 6
oft and *oft* I askt in privity, ... I. ix. 5. 5
Thy life shutt up for death so *oft* did call; . . . . I. ix. 45. 6
Nourse her child from falling *oft* does reare. . . . . I. x. 35. 9
that deare Lord who *oft* thereon was fownd, ... I. x. 54. 4
death did he *oft* desire, ... I. xi. 28. 4
he it *oft* adventur’d to invade. . . . . I. xi. 49. 4
oft they did lament . . . . I. xii. 16. 4
Oft had he seene her faire, ... I. xii. 23. 9
he hath polluted *oft* of yore, ... I. xii. 27. 7
From fowle intemperaunce he *ofte* did stay, ... II. i. 34. 8
He *oft* finds present helpe who does his griefe impart.’ . . . II. i. 46. 9
He washt them *oft* and *oft*, ... II. ii. 3. 5

Oft—*Continued.*
oft approv'd in many hard assay; II. iii. 15. 7
his lustfull fyre To kindle *oft* assayd, II. iii. 23. 7
oft himselfe he chaunst to hurt unwares, II. iv. 7. 6
Oft he re'nforst, and *oft* his forces fayld, II. iv. 14. 5
Who used . . . Her *oft* to meete: II. iv. 24. 6
Full *oft* approvd in many a cruell warre; II. iv. 41. 4
So hast thou *oft* with guile thine honor blent; II. v. 5. 7
falsed *oft* his blowes t' illude him with such bayt. II. v. 9. 9
in which she *oft* him blam'd II. v. 21. 4
guiltlesse blood pourd *oft* on ground, II. vii. 13. 4
Frayle men are *oft* captiv'd to covetise; II. vii. 15. 2
sprinckled *ofte* the same With liquid waves, II. vii. 36. 4
How *oft* do they their silver bowers leave, II. viii. 2. 1
How *oft* do they . . . cleave The flitting skyes, II. viii. 2. 3
Which *oft* the Paynim sav'd II. viii. 43. 6
too *oft* she chaung'd her native hew. II. ix. 40. 4
oft when thinges were lost, II. ix. 58. 6
How *oft* that day did sad Brunchildis see II. x. 24. 6
Yet *oft* . . . against them strongly swayd. II. x. 49. 9
Triumphed *oft* against her enemis; II. x. 56. 7
having *oft* in batteill vanquished Those spoylefull Picts, II. x. 63. 1
oft annoyd with sondry bordragings, II. x. 63. 4
oft of error did himselfe appeach: II. xi. 40. 3
they have *ofte* drawne many a wandring wight II. xii. 11. 8
with their wicked wings them *ofte* did smight, II. xii. 35. 8
straunge phantomes doth let us *ofte* foresee, II. xii. 47. 6
ofte of secret ill bids us beware: II. xii. 47. 7
oft inclining downe, with kisses light II. xii. 73. 5
the fine nets, which *oft* we woven see II. xii. 77. 8
She *oft* and *oft* adviz'd him to refraine III. i. 37. 6
So dischord *ofte* in Musick makes the sweeter lay:— III. ii. 15. 9
oft out of her bed she did astart, III. ii. 29. 6
Shee *ofte* did bathe, and *ofte* againe did dry; III. ii. 34. 7
oft hath wonders donne.' III. ii. 36. 6
'Things *ofte* impossible' (quoth she) 'seeme, ere begonne. III. ii. 36. 9
Their beames shall *ofte* breake forth, III. iii. 44. 9
boastfull men so *oft* abasht to heare? III. iv. 1. 7
made a lake Of Greekish blood so *ofte* III. iv. 2. 6
Forthy she *oft* him counseld III. iv. 24. 7
Yet many Ladies fayre did *oft* complaine, III. iv. 26. 7
ofte his mother, vewing his wide wownd, III. iv. 44. 3
oft let fall Many meeke wordes III. iv. 48. 8
oft looking backward, III. iv. 50. 6
Oft did he wish that Lady faire mote bee His Faery Queene, III. iv. 54. 6
Doth praise thee *oft*, III. iv. 56. 7
oft from Stygian deepe Calles thee his goddesse, III. iv. 56. 7
oft him threatned death for his outrageous wrong. III. v. 13. 9
Transformed *oft*, and chaunged diverslie III. vi. 47. 7
Oft from the forrest wildings he did bring, III. vii. 17. 1
oft young birds, which he had taught to sing, III. vii. 17. 3
almost in the backe he *oft* her strake; III. vii. 44. 6
So *oft* as I this history record, III. viii. 1. 1
he so *ofte* had tryde The powre thereof, III. ix. 29. 7
lov'd so *oft* in vaine, III. ix. 29. 8
Oft purposes, *oft* riddles, he devysd, III. x. 8. 6
When one so *oft* a night did ring his matins bell. III. x. 48. 9
How *oft* for Venus . . . he sore did shreek, III. xi. 44. 4
oft committed fowle Idolatree. III. xi. 49. 5
Bee bold: she *oft* and *oft* it over-red, III. xi. 50. 4
Such as false love doth *oft* upon him weare; III. xi. 51. 8
love in thousand monstrous formes doth *oft* appeare. III. xi. 51. 9
from her head *ofte* rente her snarled heare: III. xii. 17. 5
oft wisht like happinesse: III. xii. 46. *or.* 8
By which fraile youth is *oft* to follie led, IV. Pr. 1. 6
shaded *oft* from sunne, IV. Pr. 3. 7
I with teares full *oft* doe pittie it, IV. i. 1. 8
By way of sport, as *oft* in maskes is knowen, IV. i. 3. 8
though spite did *oft* assay To blot her with dishonor IV. i. 4. 8
That each to other made, as *oft* befell: IV. i. 5. 3
many a publike state, . . . *oft* doth overthrow. IV. i. 19. 4
oft for her in bloudie armes they fought. IV. ii. 37. 5
Approved *oft* in perils manifold, IV. ii. 39. 3
had in many a battell *oft* bene tride, IV. iv. 17. 8
Approved *oft* in many a perlous fight. IV. iv. 40. 5
Full *oft* about her wast she it enclos'd, IV. v. 16. 8
it as *oft* was from about her wast disclos'd: IV. v. 16. 9
Oft chaunging sides, and *oft* new place electing, IV. v. 40. 3
oft in wrath he thence againe uprose, IV. v. 40. 5
oft in wrath he layd him downe againe. IV. v. 40. 6
when in vaine to fight she *oft* assayd, IV. vi. 27. 6
To banish sloth that *oft* doth noble mindes annoy. IV. vii. 23. 9
as *oft* it fals in chace, IV. vii. 24. 1
made him *oft*, when he would strike, forbeare; IV. vii. 27. 2
oft admir'd his monstrous shape, and *oft* His mighty limbs, IV. vii. 32. 7
Him seemed *oft* he heard his owne right name. IV. viii. 4. 5
oft of them did earnestly inquire, IV. viii. 22. 3
oft with bitternesse It forth would breake, IV. viii. 24. 4
great feeblesse, which did *oft* assay Faire Amoret IV. viii. 37. 3
oft imbrast, as if that I were hee, IV. viii. 59. 8
kissing *oft* his visage pale and wan: IV. ix. 9. 5
full *oft* she both of them had seene Asunder, IV. ix. 10. 3
inly groning deepe and sighing *oft*, IV. x. 48. 3
in her cheekes made roses *oft* appeare: IV. x. 50. 5
fayled *oft* through faint and feeble plight: IV. xi. 25. 5
The wanton Lee, that *oft* doth loose his way; IV. xi. 29. 7
Oft tossed with his stormes which therein still remaine. IV. xi. 38. 9
oft to grone with billowes beating from the maine: IV. xii. 5. 9
even for griefe of minde he *oft* did grone, IV. xii. 12. 6
Oft listening if he mote her heare againe, IV. xii. 17. 4

Oft—*Continued.*
So *oft* as I with state of present time . . . compare, V. Pr. 1. 1
oft their lewdnes blotteth good deserts with blame. V. iii. 38. 9
It made her stagger *oft*, V. iv. 41. 9
henceforth he *oft* shall hungry sit.' V. iv. 49. 9
sooth *oft* seene, that proudest harts base love hath blynded.' V. v. 40. 9
Oft did she blame her selfe, and often rew, V. vi. 12. 5
To shew that clemence *oft*, . . . Restraines those sterne behests V. vii. 22. 8
doth procure Great warriours *oft* their rigour to represse, V. viii. 1. 4
Oft drew the Prince unto his charret nigh, V. viii. 33. 1
Oft making offer him to smite, V. viii. 42. 2
Which she against the dred Mercilla *oft* did frame. V. ix. 40. 9
Oft spilles the principall to save the part; V. x. 2. 4
They turne afresh, and *oft* renew their former threat. V. xi. 45. 9
oft I driven am to great distresse, V. xi. 51. 8
oft had seene like sight, V. xii. 16. 6
stouped *oft* his head from shame to shield: V. xii. 19. 2
oft he made him stagger as unstayd, VI. i. 20. 3
oft recuile to shunne his sharpe despight: VI. i. 20. 4
Who ever thinkes . . . To wrong the weaker, *oft* falles VI. ii. 23. 9
and calling *oft* for ayde; VI. iii. 24. 6
called *oft* with prayers loud and shrill, VI. iii. 49. 7
Such chaunces *oft* exceed all humaine thought! VI. iii. 51. 8
whom she did *oft* implore To send her succour, VI. iv. 10. 8
And *oft* complayn'd of fate, and fortune *oft* defyde. VI. iv. 26. 9
Having *oft* seene it tryde as he did teach: VI. iv. 37. 3
Him *oft* desired home with her to wend, VI. iv. 39. 6
proved *oft* in many perillous fight, VI. vi. 4. 3
Makes th' heavens tremble *oft*, VI. vi. 11. 9
whom though he *oft* forbad, VI. vi. 18. 7
oft it falles, VI. vi. 35. 3
did with his smarting toole *Oft* whip her dainty selfe, VI. vii. 39. 9
So did these two this Knight *oft* tug and teare. VI. viii. 12. 5
Now here, now there, and *oft* him neare he mist; VI. viii. 13. 7
approved *oft* in fight, VI. viii. 14. 2
with sterne eye-browes stared at him *oft*, VI. viii. 26. 3
him did *oft* embrace, and *oft* admire, VI. viii. 27. 8
often did of love, and *oft* of lucke complaine. VI. viii. 32. 9
oft rejoyce, and *oft* for wonder shout, VI. ix. 8. 7
oft through pride do their owne perill weave, VI. ix. 22. 3
oft complaine Of Pastorell to all the shepheards VI. ix. 38. 7
Was readie *oft* his owne heart to devoure, VI. ix. 39. 4
oft, when Coridon unto her brought . . . litle sparrowes VI. ix. 40. 1
had tasted once (as *oft* did he) The happy peace VI. x. 3. 3
With looks, with words, with gifts he *oft* her wowed, VI. xi. 4. 8
Where wont the shepheards *oft* their pypes resound, VI. xi. 26. 8
Oft cursing th' heavens, that so cruell were To her, VI. xi. 33. 6
wishing *oft* that he were present there VI. xi. 33. 8
Oft interlacing many a forged lie, VI. xii. 33. 5
Oft to resort there-to, when seem'd them best, VII. vi. 38. 5
With whom the woody Gods did *oft* consort, VII. vi. 39. 8
In her sweet streames Diana used *oft* . . . To bathe VII. vi. 42. 1
dooth *oft* refuse This too high flight, VII. vii. 1. 3
oft him pinched sore: VII. vii. 30. 5
Yet is he *oft* eclipsed by the way, VII. vii. 51. 8
grim Sir Saturne oft doth spare His sterne aspect, VII. vii. 52. 7
The powre thereof, which *ofte* in me I find, *Am.* xxviii. 5
So *oft* as homeward I from her depart, *Am.* lii. 1
So *oft* as I her beauty doe behold, *Am.* lv. 1
Oft, when my spirit doth spred her bolder winges, *Am.* lxxii. 1
Which *oft* I wisht, yet never was so blest. *Am.* lxxvi. 14
cloud of pryde, which *oft* doth dark Her goodly light, *Am.* lxxxi. 7
full *oft* for loving you I blesse my lot, *Am.* lxxxii. 1
Who would not *oft* be stung as this, To be so bath'd *Epig.* iv. 49
Ofte peeping in her face, *Epith.* 232
made you merie *oft* *H.L.* 35
oft it falles that many a gentle mynd *H.B.* 141
oft it falles . . . That *H.B.* 148
Where *oft* I gayned giftes and goodly grace *Proth.* 138

Often. Which hath so *often* . . . Thee drenched, *Ro.* xiii. 11
the greatest *often* are opprest, *Van.* xii. 7
often crost with the priestes crewe, *S.C.* F. 209
often halowed with holy-water dewe: *S.C.* F. 210
often devoured their owne sheepe, And *often* the shepheards *S.C.* May 128, 129
I have heard Old Algrind *often* sayne) *S.C.* Jul. 126
Often he used . . . A sacrifice to bring, *S.C.* Jul. 133
she would cal him *often* heame, *S.C.* N. 98
'How *often* have I scaled the craggie Oke, *S.C.* D. 31
small oddes I *often* see Twixt them that aske, *Hub.* 373
Pursivants he *often* for them sent; *Hub.* 565
With whom his credite he did *often* leave *Hub.* 864
manie *often* did abie full sore; *Ti.* 101
Full many Maydens *often* did him woo, *As.* 37
woodgods for them *often* sighed sore: *As.* 50
I have *often* heard Faire Rosalind . . . fowly blamed *Col.* 907
often knockt his brest, as one that did repent. I. i. 29. 9
The fearefull shepheard, *often* there aghast, I. ii. 28. 7
night she thinks too long, and *often* lookes for light. I. iii. 15. 9
often curst, and sware, I. iii. 16. 5
her face she *often* vewed fayne, I. iv. 10. 7
His cruel facts he *often* would repent; I. iv. 34. 7
Did *often* tremble at his horrid vew; I. vi. 25. 3
On which trew Christians blood was *often* spilt, I. viii. 36. 3
holy Martyres *often* doen to dye I. viii. 36. 4
with great griefe were *often* heard to grone, I. viii. 36. 8
True loves are *often* sown, I. ix. 16. 9
his torment *often* was so great, I. x. 28. 1
often tore Her guiltlesse garments I. x. 28. 5
God he *often* saw from heavens hight: I. x. 47. 2

Often—*Continued.*
often bounding on the brused gras, I. xi. 15. 3
often blame the too importune fate I. xii. 16. 5
often semblaunce made to scape out of their hand. I. xii. 35. 9
To proofe of passing wonders hath full *often* usd: II. ii. 5. 9
Ill by ensample good doth often gayne.' II. ii. 45. 5
strooke more *often* wyde, II. iv. 7. 4
With such faire sleight him Guyon *often* fayld, II. v. 11. 1
Therein did *often* quench his thristy heat, II. v. 30. 6
The crowned *often* slaine, II. vii. 13. 5
thick Arber . . . In which she *often* usd II. vii. 53. 4
did *often* thinke To reach the fruit II. vii. 58. 4
all his seede the curse doth *often* cleave, II. viii. 29. 4
often need the helpe of weaker hand; II. xi. 30. 2
so *often* as his life decayd, II. xi. 45. 3
Through which the damned ghosts doen *often* creepe II. xii. 6. 5
Did roll too lightly, and too *often* glaunce, III. i. 41. 8
often steepe Her dainty couch with teares III. ii. 28. 8
To heare so *often*, in that royall hous, III. iii. 54. 2
did weepe And *often* wayle their wealth, III. iv. 22. 9
Tryde *often* to the scath of many Deare, III. iv. 24. 2
(So from her *often* he had fled away, III. vi. 11. 6
chaunged is, and *often* altred to and froe. III. vi. 37. 9
Yet pitty *often* did the gods relent, III. vi. 40. 1
There wont fayre Venus *often* to enjoy III. vi. 46. 1
with sharpe threates her *often* did assayle; III. viii. 40. 8
often thondring Jove Had felt the point III. xi. 30. 1
often to him calling to take surer hould. III. xi. 34. 9
how *often* eek For many other Nymphes, III. xi. 44. 4
That she may . . . reade this lesson *often*. IV. Pr. 5. 9
most *often* end in bloudshed and in warre. IV. i. 25. 9
She in short space did *often* bring to nought, IV. i. 29. 6
their possessours *often* did dismay: IV. i. 29. 7
So hast thou to thy selfe false honour often wonne.' IV. i. 44. 9
After he had so *often* wounded beene, IV. iii. 23. 2
Is *often* seene full freshly to have florisht, IV. iii. 29. 7
having *often* by him stricken beene, IV. iii. 31. 8
It *often* fals, (as here it earst befell) IV. iv. 1. 1
often did my folly fowle reprove: IV. vii. 16. 4
saw he *often* how he wexed glad IV. vii. 46. 7
seeking *often* entraunce IV. x. 13. 9
often tride In greater perils IV. x. 18. 1
'She *often* prayd, and *often* me besought, IV. x. 57. 1
often stainde with bloud of many a band IV. xi. 36. 8
by *often* beating Doe pearce the rockes, IV. xii. 7. 1
Full many Ladies *often* had assayd V. iii. 28. 1
he, that had like tempests *often* tride, V. v. 6. 6
Oft did she blame her selfe, and *often* rew, V. vi. 12. 5
(As *often* falles) of sundry things did commen: V. ix. 4. 3
often treat for pardon and remission To suppliants, V. ix. 32. 3
It *often* fals, in course of common life, V. xi. 1. 1
her imprisond hath, and her life *often* sought. V. xi. 39. 9
she used *often* to resort To common haunts, V. xii. 34. 6
often hath annoyd Good Knights VI. i. 7. 8
a rude churle, whom *often* he accused VI. iii. 33. 5
(As their victorious deedes have *often* showen, VI. iv. 36. 4
wretched sorrowes, which have *often* hapt! VI. v. 1. 4
Yet he them all withstood, and *often* made relent. VI. v. 20. 9
often him besought, and prayd, and vowd, VI. vi. 31. 7
Him *often* scourg'd, and forst his feete to fynd: VI. vii. 49. 5
Downe on his golden feete he *often* gazed, VI. viii. 26. 6
often did of love, and oft of lucke complaine. VI. viii. 32. 9
She made me *often* pipe, and now to pipe apace. VI. x. 27. 9
To her, whose name he *often* did repeat; VI. xi. 33. 7
Whose course is *often* stayd, yet never is astray. VI. xii. 1. 9
The rolling wheele that runneth *often* round, *Am.* xviii. 1
drizling drops, that *often* doe redound, *Am.* xviii. 3
eeke for comfort *often* called art *Epith.* 394
Muses! which have *often* proved The piercing points *H.L.* 29
So hast thou *often* done *H.L.* 141
I, that have *often* prov'd, too well it know, *H.B.* 87
Oftentime. *oftentime* Great clymbers fall unsoft. *S.C.* Jul. 11
Oftentimes. So *often times*, . . . Evil ensueth of wrong entent *S.C.* May 101
my plaints did *oftentimes* resound: *S.C.* Au. 152
He *oftentimes* me dreadfullie doth threaten *Gn.* 351
which fraile men doe *oftentimes* mistake, I. ii. 32. 7
oftentimes he quakt, and fainted *oftentimes*. I. ix. 48. 9
Would *oftentimes* emongst them beare a part, II. vi. 25. 2
oftentimes he would relent his pace, II. xi. 27. 3
oftentimes great grones, and grievous stownds, III. iii. 9. 6
oftentimes loud strokes and ringing sowndes III. iii. 9. 8
Alowd to her he *oftentimes* did call, III. iv. 48. 6
That stratageme had *oftentimes* assayd This crafty Paramoure, III. x. 10. 8
oftentimes doe wish it never had bene writ. IV. i. 1. 9
oftentimes unquiet strife did move Amongst her lovers, IV. ii. 37. 3
So *oftentimes* he out of sleepe abrayd, IV. v. 42. 8
Full *oftentimes* she leave of him did take; IV. vi. 45. 6
Full *oftentimes* did Britomart assay IV. ix. 31. 1
oftentimes faint hearts, IV. x. 17. 6
oftentimes him nigh he overthrew: V. ii. 13. 7
use *oftentimes* To attribute their folly unto fate, V. iv. 28. 1
made him *oftentimes* in field before me fall. V. xi. 53. 9
So stoutest knights doen *oftentimes* in field. V. xii. 19. 5
'And, certes, it hath *oftentimes* bene seene, VI. iv. 36. 1
oftentimes by Turmagant and Mahound swore. VI. vii. 47. 9
Ye learned sisters, which have *oftentimes* *Epith.* 1
Nimphs! which *oftentimes* have loved *H.L.* 31
Oft-times. *Oft-times* to begging are content to fall. *Hub.* 182
Oft times to plaine your loves concealed smart; *As.* Pr. 2
Merlin came . . . *offtimes* to visitt mee, I. ix. 5. 2

Oft-times—*Continued.*
Such as the troubled Theatres *oftimes* annoyes. IV. iii. 37. 9
luring baytes *oftimes* doe heedlesse harts entyse. IV. x. 49. 9
Oft-times amongst the wanton Nymphs to sport and toy. IV. xi. 19. 9
Else should afflicted wights *oftimes* despeire: V. iii. 1. 5
She thus *oft times* was beating off and on, V. v. 43. 2
under shew *oftimes* of fayned semblance V. ix. 22. 8
Oftimes it haps that sorrowes of the mynd VI. iv. 28. 8
Oftimes their sundry powres they did employ, VI. v. 14. 1
plucke the pray *oftimes* out of their greedy hould. VI. v. 15. 9
oft-times we nature see of art Exceld, *H.B.* 83
Ogyges. Ancient *Ogyges*, even th' auncientest; IV. xi. 15. 4
Oh. But *oh*, fond man! that . . . Reposedst hope, *D.* 150
Oil. In wine and *oyle* they wash his woundes wide, I. v. 17. 4
when the *oyle* is spent, The light goes out, II. x. 30. 1
The dronken lamp down in the *oyl* did steepe, III. ii. 47. 8
the joyous *oyle*, whose gentle gust Made him so frollick VII. vii. 39. 4
Oils. If either salves, or *oyles*, or herbes, or charmes, I. v. 41. 7
Ointment. Life and long health that gracious *ointment* gave, I. xi. 48. 6
wont with *ointment* sweet To be embaulm'd, IV. vii. 40. 3
Ointments. With wicked herbes and *oyntments* did besmeare My body I. ii. 42. 3
Old. the ground-work of an *old* great wall; *Bel.*^{2} viii. 2
Greece will the *olde* Ephesian buildings blaze, *Ro.* ii. 3
olde walls, *olde* arches, . . . *Olde* Palaces, *Ro.* iii. 3, 4
The Giants *old* should once again uprise, *Ro.* iv. 6
Olde moniments, which of so famous sprights *Ro.* vii. 3
the ruin'd pride Of these *old* Romane works, *Ro.* xv. 13
these *old* wals, which ye see, *Ro.* xviii. 1
Was this . . . your hard destinie, Or some *old* sinne, *Ro.* xxiv. 10
The stonie joynts of these *old* walls now rent, *Ro.* xxv. 7
These haughtie heapes, these palaces of *olde*, *Ro.* xxvii. 3
these *olde* fragments are for paternes borne: *Ro.* xxvii. 8
clad with reliques of some Trophees *olde*, *Ro.* xxviii. 2
left of it but these *olde* markes to see, *Ro.* xxx. 11
Cease not to sound these *olde* antiquities; *Ro.* xxxii. 10
Th' *olde* honour of the people gowned long. *Ro.* xxxii. 14
Olde Rome out of her ashes to revive, *Ro.* Env. 5
As if my yeare were wast and woxen *old;* *S.C.* Ja. 28
All for their Maister is lustlesse and *old*. *S.C.* F. 84
snebbe the good Oake, for he was *old*. *S.C.* F. 126
So beate his *old* boughes my tender side, *S.C.* F. 175
Of my *old* age have this one delight, *S.C.* May 202
some *old* sorowe that made a newe breache: *S.C.* May 210
The *old* lineaments of his fathers grace. *S.C.* May 212
(As garments doen, which wexen *old* above,) *S.C.* Jun. 39
(as I have heard *Old* Algrind often sayne) *S.C.* Jul. 126
My *old* musick mard by a newe mischaunce. *S.C.* Au. 12
I pray thee, gall not my *old* griefe: *S.C.* S. 12
any buddes of Poesie, Yet of the *old* stocke, *S.C.* O. 74
A good *old* shephearde, Wrenock was his name, *S.C.* D. 41
the bad daughter of *old* Cadmus brood, *Gn.* 171
Not yet unmindfull of her *olde* reproach. *Gn.* 224
Box, yet mindfull of his *olde* offence; *Gn.* 676
to wexe *olde* at home in idlenesse Is disadventrous, *Hub.* 99
That was the golden age of Saturne *old*, *Hub.* 151
Upon his head an *old* Scotch cap he wore, *Hub.* 209
when lambes fail'd the *old* sheepes lives they reft; *Hub.* 322
in those his garments *olde;* *Hub.* 928
their *olde* Castles to the ground to fall, *Hub.* 1179
the auncestrie Of th' *old* Heroes *T.M.* 440
What oddes twixt Irus and *old* Inachus, *T.M.* 447
thy *old* Sire with sacred pietie *Mui.* 238
the *olde* debate Which she with Neptune *Mui.* 305
mindfull of that *olde* Enfested grudge, *Mui.* 353
auncient truth confirm'd with credence *old*. *Col.* 103
'*Old* father Mole, *Col.* 104
Mulla, the daughter of *old* Mole, *Col.* 108
Cittie, Which Kilnemullah cleped is of *old;* *Col.* 113
her *old* sire more carefull of her good, *Col.* 120
a River, which he was of *old*, *Col.* 152
old Palemon free from spight *Col.* 396
ensample to the present age Of th' *old* Heroes, *Ded. Son.* vi. 4
Wherein *old* dints of deepe woundes did remaine, I. i. 1. 3
As when *old* father Nilus gins to swell I. i. 21. 1
unhappy Swaine, That here wex *old* in sleepe, I. ii. 4. 7
Like the *old* ruines of a broken towre, I. ii. 20. 2
Having . . . lost an *old* foe that did you molest; I. ii. 27. 3
Better new friend then an *old* foe is said.' I. ii. 27. 4
when he sees his age, And hoarie head of Archimago *old*, I. iii. 38. 4
all the hinder partes, . . . Were ruinous and *old*, I. iv. 5. 9
strong advizement of six wisards *old*, I. iv. 12. 8
Chroniclers, that can record *Old* loves, I. v. 3. 9
More *old* then Jove, whom thou at first didst breede, I. v. 22. 3
If *old* Aveugles sonnes so evill heare? I. v. 23. 7
the *old* cause of my continued paine I. v. 42. 3
old Ninus far did pas In princely pomp, I. v. 48. 3
Whiles *old* Sylvanus slept in shady arber sownd: I. vi. 7. 9
So towards *old* Sylvanus they her bring; I. vi. 14. 5
old Sylvanus selfe bethinkes not what To thinke I. vi. 16. 3
To do their service to Sylvanus *old*, I. vi. 33. 2
Being in deed *old* Archimage, did stay I. vi. 48. 2
The subtile traines of Archimago *old;* I. vii. 26. 2
forth came An *old old* man, I. viii. 30. 2
as he forward moovd his footing *old*, I. viii. 31. 3
'*Old* syre, it seemes thou hast not red I. viii. 33. 4
A loathly, wrinckled hag, ill favoured, *old*, I. viii. 46. 8
'Unto *Old* Timon he me brought bylive; I. ix. 4. 1
Old Timon, . . . In warlike feates th' expertest man alive, I. ix. 4. 2
me had warnd *old* Timons wise behest, I. ix. 9. 5

Old—*Continued.*
still wex *old* in woe, whiles wo stil wexeth new . . . . I. ix. 9. 9
all about *old* stockes and stubs of trees, ... I. ix. 34. 1
thrust them forth still as they wexed *old:* . . . . I. x. 31. 4
But now aread, *old* father, ... I. x. 64. 5
The knight with that *old* Dragon fights . . . . I. xi. Arg.
Great joy was made that day of young and *old,* . . . . I. xii. 40. 1
'*Old* syre, Behold the ymage of mortalitie, ... II. i. 57. 1
'There this *old* Palmer shewd himselfe that day, ... II. ii. 43. 1
growne *old* In cunning sleightes . . . . II. iii. 9. 5
her face ill-favourd, full of wrinckles *old.* . . . . II. iv. 4. 9
The sonnes of *old* Acrates and Despight; . . . . II. iv. 41. 6
new matter fram'd Upon the *old,* . . . . II. v. 21. 3
appeared to have beene of *old* . . . . II. vii. 4. 4
overgrowne with dust and *old* decay, ... II. vii. 29. 2
Those were the two sonnes of Acrates *old,* . . . . II. viii. 10. 6
By whose advise *old* Priams cittie fell, ... II. ix. 48. 6
That chamber seemed ruinous and *old,* . . . . II. ix. 55. 1
therein sat an *old old* man, ... II. ix. 55. 5
old Assaracus, and Inachus divine. . . . . II. ix. 56. 9
old records from auncient times derivd, ... II. ix. 57. 7
this lands . . . *old* division into Regiments, ... II. ix. 59. 8
Thy fathers and great Grandfathers of *old,* . . . . II. x. 4. 6
roiall stocke of *old* Assaracs line, ... II. x. 9. 7
old Syre, thy course doe thereunto apply.' . . . . II. xii. 10. 9
his brave shield, full of *old* moniments, ... II. xii. 80. 3
As it in bookes hath written beene of *old.* . . . . III. ii. 18. 3
In which there written was, with cyphres *old,* . . . . III. ii. 25. 5
that *old* Dame said many an idle verse, ... III. ii. 48. 8
That when *old* Glauce saw, ... III. ii. 52. 7
Old Glauce cast to cure this Ladies griefe; . . . . III. iii. 5. 2
she did lye All night in *old* Tithonus frozen bed, ... III. iii. 20. 6
her *olde* Nourse was nought dishartened, ... III. iii. 20. 8
one of th' *old* Heroes seemes to bee! . . . . III. iii. 32. 5
the *old* sparkes renew Of native corage, ... III. iii. 45. 7
old Glauce thither led Faire Britomart, ... III. iii. 59. 6
Badd her *old* Squyre unlace her lofty creast: . . . . III. iv. 7. 3
old Glauce gan with sharpe repriefe Her to restraine, ... III. iv. 11. 4
Breeder of new, renewer of *old* smarts: . . . . III. iv. 57. 3
It sited was in fruitfull soyle of *old,* . . . . III. vi. 31. 1
Th' one faire and fresh, the other *old* and dride. . . . . III. vi. 31. 7
Old Genius the porter of them was, ... III. vi. 31. 8
Old Genius, the which a double nature has. . . . . III. vi. 31. 9
So, like a wheele, arownd they ronne from *old* to new. . . . III. vi. 33. 9
In which there slept a fisher *old* and pore, ... III. vii. 27. 5
in his *old* corage new delight To gin awake, ... III. viii. 23. 4
Hard is to teach an *old* horse amble trew: . . . . III. viii. 26. 3
that *old* leachour, which with bold assault . . . . III. viii. 36. 1
one *old* Nymph, hight Panope, ... III. viii. 37. 9
he is *old,* and withered like hay, ... III. ix. 5. 1
we suffer this same dotard *old* . . . . III. ix. 8. 7
from whose race of *old* . . . she was lineally extract; . . . . III. ix. 38. 6
Troynovant was built of *old* Troyes ashes cold. . . . . III. ix. 38. 9
he with *old* Latinus was constraind To contract wedlock, . . III. ix. 42. 4
Goemagot of strong Corineus, and Coulin of Debon *old,* . . . III. ix. 50. 4
so heard I say *Old* Mnemon. . . . . III. ix. 51. 6
take to his new love, and leave her *old* despysd. . . . . III. x. 8. 9
care of credite, or of husband *old,* . . . . III. x. 11. 4
it was indeed Her *old* Malbecco, ... III. x. 50. 3
gan advize with her *old* Squire, ... III. xii. 45. 6
Of lovers sad calamities of *old* . . . . IV. i. 1. 1
like withered tree . . . She *old* and crooked were, ... IV. i. 31. 6
He now unable was to wreake his *old* despight. . . . . IV. i. 39. 9
old and crooked and not good for ought. . . . . IV. ii. 3. 5
both of *old* well knowing by their names, ... IV. ii. 20. 5
of all *old* dislikes they made faire weather; . . . . IV. ii. 29. 3
Like an *old* Oke, whose pith and sap is seare, ... IV. iii. 9. 8
So did those *olde* Heroes hereof taste, ... IV. iii. 44. 8
that *old* aged Dame, his faithfull Squire, ... IV. v. 39. 6
when the world woxe *old,* it woxe warre *old,* . . . . IV. viii. 31. 6
Of his *old* love conceav'd in secret brest, ... IV. ix. 17. 4
old despight which now forth newly brake . . . . IV. ix. 26. 3
In which *old* Styx her aged bones alway . . . doth lay. . . IV. xi. 4. 4
Old Styx the Grandame of the Gods, ... IV. xi. 4. 5
By whom those *old* Heroes wonne such fame; . . . . IV. xi. 13. 2
Phoenix, and Aon, and Pelasgus *old;* . . . . IV. xi. 15. 6
old Gall, that now is cleeped France, ... IV. xi. 16. 4
the aged Ocean and his Dame *Old* Tethys, ... IV. xi. 18. 2
So wise is Nereus *old,* . . . . IV. xi. 19. 7
Old Cybele, arayd with pompous pride, ... IV. xi. 28. 4
if *old* sawes prove true . . . . IV. xi. 35. 2
to *old* Loncaster his name doth lend; . . . . IV. xi. 39. 2
All these the daughters of *old* Nereus were, ... IV. xi. 52. 1
his *old* hurt, which was not throughly cured. . . . . IV. xii. 23. 6
it was no *old* sore which his new paine procured; . . . . IV. xii. 23. 9
Whether *old* Proteus true or false had sayd, ... IV. xii. 28. 4
Aegyptian wisards *old,* . . . . V. Pr. 8. 1
next to him *old* Saturne, ... V. Pr. 8. 9
In those *old* times of which I doe entreat, ... V. i. 1. 2
To follow his *old* quest, ... V. iv. 20. 9
had subdew'd of *old* So many monsters . . . . V. v. 24. 5
token true to *old* Eumenias, ... V. v. 34. 3
Of th' *old* Aegyptian Kings that whylome were, ... V. vii. 2. 6
Mote in them stirre up *old* rebellious thought . . . . V. vii. 11. 5
First was a sage *old* Syre, ... V. ix. 43. 7
He brought forth that *old* hag of hellish hew, ... V. ix. 47. 3
Sir Artegall with that *old* knight Did forth descend, ... V. xii. 6. 1
yet *old* Sergis did so well him paine, ... V. xii. 10. 7
two *old* ill favour'd Hags he met, ... V. xii. 28. 4
where I have wond . . . Since I was ten yeares *old,* . . . . VI. ii. 30. 9

Old—*Continued.*
did that good *old* Knight Temper his griefe, ... VI. iii. 6. 1
that *old* Knight by all meanes did assay . . . . VI. iii. 9. 4
his Lord of *old* Did hate all errant Knights . . . . VI. vi. 21. 3
he was descended of the hous Of those *old* Gyants, ... VI. vii. 41. 6
Then came to them a good *old* aged syre, ... VI. ix. 13. 6
as *old* stories tell, ... VI. ix. 14. 4
(said then *old* Meliboe) . . . . VI. ix. 29. 1
Old love is litle worth when new is more prefard. . . . . VI. ix. 40. 9
They spoyld *old* Melibee of all he had, ... VI. x. 40. 2
Then forth the good *old* Meliboe was brought, ... VI. xi. 11. 1
Old Meliboe is slaine; . . . . VI. xi. 18. 4
Old Meliboe and his good wife withall These eyes saw die, . VI. xi. 31. 6
As I have found it registred of *old* . . . . VII. vi. 2. 3
a daughter by descent Of those *old* Titans . . . . VII. vi. 2. 6
there sate an hory *Old* aged Sire, ... VII. vi. 8. 6
his *old* foes that once him sorely fear'd. . . . . VII. vi. 15. 9
Much lesse the Title of *Old* Titans Right: . . . . VII. vi. 33. 4
my *old* father Mole, whom Shepheards quill Renowmed hath VII. vi. 36. 8
(Beeing of *old* the best and fairest Hill . . . . VII. vi. 37. 6
daughter of *old* Father Mole, ... VII. vi. 40. 2
old Dan Geffrey . . . durst not with it mel, ... VII. vii. 9. 3
the righteous Virgin, which of *old* Liv'd here . . . . VII. vii. 37. 6
Then came *old* January, ... VII. vii. 42. 1
February, sitting In an *old* wagon, ... VII. vii. 43. 2
New yeare, . . . bidding th' *old* Adieu, ... *Am.* iv. 3
Bids all *old* thoughts to die in dumpish spright: . . . . *Am.* iv. 4
The *old* yeares sinnes forepast let us eschew, ... *Am.* lxii. 7
chaunge *old* yeares annoy to new delight. . . . . *Am.* lxii. 14
In youth, before I waxed *old,* . . . . *Epig.* i. 1
ancient monuments of mightie peeres, And *old* Heroes, . . . *Com. Son.* iii. 3
Beginnes his owne, and my *old* fault renewes. . . . . *H.H.L.* 21
like *old* Peneus Waters they did seeme, ... *Proth.* 78
here fits not well *Olde* woes, but joyes, to tell . . . . *Proth.* 142

Old man. *See* **Man, Old.**
Ah, foolish *old man!* I scorne thy skill, ... *S.C.* F. 51
What ever that good *old man* bespake. . . . . *S.C.* F. 97
When the good *old man* used to sleepe. . . . . *S.C.* S. 189
As if it the *old man* selfe had bene: . . . . *S.C.* S. 218
Silly *old man,* that lives in hidden cell, ... I. i. 30. 6
that *olde man* of pleasing wordes had store, ... I. i. 35. 6
he . . . with the *old man* went; . . . . I. ii. 5. 2
the *old man* well knew he, though untold, ... I. iii. 38. 7
Great grace that *old man* to him given had; . . . . I. x. 47. 1
'*Old man* great sure shal be thy meed, ... II. iii. 14. 6
To ferry that *old man* over the perlous foord. . . . . II. vi. 19. 9
Him when the *old man* saw, ... II. vi. 48. 6
'Foolish *old man,*' said then the Pagan wroth, ... II. viii. 22. 1
that *old man* Eumnestes, ... II. ix. 58. 9
Thereat th' *old man* did nought but fondly grin, ... III. viii. 24. 6
th' *old man* seeing wel, ... III. ix. 53. 6
Soone as the *old man* saw Sir Paridell, ... III. x. 37. 6
The *old man* could not fly, ... III. x. 43. 9
Meliboee (so hight that good *old man*) . . . . VI. ix. 16. 1

Old man's. As in that *old mans* booke they were in order told. . . . . II. x. 4. 9

Old-said. Has bene an *old-sayd* sawe, ... *S.C.* Jul. 98

Old woman. Amongst the rest a good *old woman* was, ... *Hub.* 33
A filthy foule *old woman* I did vew, ... I. ii. 40. 8
that *old woman* day and night did pray . . . . I. iii. 13. 6
the fearfull twayne, That blind *old woman,* and her daughter I. iii. 22. 2
Of that *old* woman tidings he besought, ... I. iii. 24. 8
With silly weake *old woman* that did fight! . . . . II. iv. 45. 5
the *old-woman* carefully displayd The clothes . . . . III. ii. 47. 4
Th' *old woman* wox half blanck those wordes to heare, . . . III. iii. 17. 8
Th' *old woman* nought that needed did omit, ... III. iii. 58. 1
this *old woman,* here remaining beene, ... IV. vii. 13. 7
'Through helpe' (quoth she) 'of this *old woman* here . . . IV. vii. 19. 6
one *old woman* sitting there beside . . . . IV. viii. 23. 5

Old-conceived. colde through feare and *old conceived* dreads; II. ii. 9. 3

Oldest. All the good hap of th' *oldest* times afore, ... *Ro.* xix. 6
th' *oldest* two of all the rest; . . . . IV. xi. 18. 2

Olive. sodenly the Palme and *Olive* fell, ... *Bel.*[1] vii. 13
right hand did the peacefull *olive* wield; . . . . *Bel.*[2] ix. 11
Sudden both Palme and *Olive* fell away, ... *Bel.*[2] ix. 13
The fruitfull *Olive;* . . . . I. i. 9. 8

Olive-branches. Chloris . . . Of *Olive braunches* beares a Coronall: . . . . *S.C.* Ap. 123
for her girlond *Olive braunches* beare, ... *S.C.* N. 144

Olive-garland. Do worship her as Queene with *olive girlond* crownd. . . . . I. vi. 13. 9
winnes an *Olive girlond* for her meeds. . . . . II. ii. 31. 7
both were with one *olive garland* crownd, ... IV. iii. 42. 5

Olives. *Olives* bene for peace, When wars doe surcease: . . . . *S.C.* Ap. 124
She compast with a wreathe of *Olyves* hoarie. . . . . *Mui.* 328
Fluttring among the *Olives* wantonly, ... *Mui.* 331
hill, . . . Adornd with fruitfull *Olives* . . . . I. x. 54. 2

Olivet. wonned not the great God Pan Upon mount *Olivet,* . . *S.C.* Jul. 50

Olive-tree. A fruitfull *Olyve tree,* with berries spredd, ... *Mui.* 326

Ollyphant. the mightie *Ollyphant,* that wrought Great wreake III. vii. 48. 2
Britomart chaceth *Ollyphant;* . . . . III. xi. Arg. 1
It was that *Ollyphant,* . . . . III. xi. 3. 6

Olympic. dedicated is t' *Olympick* Jove, ... II. v. 31. 3

Olympus. Joves great Image in *Olympus* placed; . . . . *Ro.* ii. 6
Upon the top of Mount *Olympus* hight, ... III. vii. 41. 5

Omit. Th' old woman nought that needed did *omit,* . . . . III. iii. 58. 1
all that nature did *omit,* . . . . IV. x. 21. 8

Omitted. how to pardon, when ought is *omitted;* . . . . *Gn.* 476

On (*partial list*). *See* **Don, Looker-on, Lookers-on, One, Whereon.**

On—*Continued.*

On hill, a frame . . . I sawe, — *Bel.*[1] ii. 1
a naked rout . . . assembled *on* the place, — *Bel.*[1] x. 12
One hand *on* Scythia, th' other *on* the More, — *Ro.* iv. 3
on thy corbe shoulder it leanes — *S.C.* F. 56
night draweth *on,* — *S.C.* Ap. 160
bene not thy teeth *on* edge, — *S.C.* May 35
Thou raylest *on,* right withouten reason, — *S.C.* May 146
Sorrowe ne neede be hastened *on,* — *S.C.* May 152
Now say *on,* Diggon, what ever thou hast. — *S.C.* S. 55
That matter made for Poets *on* to play: — *S.C.* O. 64
Throwing his firie eyes *on* everie side, — *Gn.* 270
He commeth *on,* and all things in his way — *Gn.* 271
gazing ghastly *on,* (for feare and yre — *Gn.* 310
bodie, set *on* fire with griefe, — *Hub.* 15
through the power of that, he putteth *on* — *Hub.* 1289
But tell *on* further, Colin, — *Col.* 176
'But say *on* further — *Col.* 328
But now seemde best the person to put *on* — I. ii. 11. 1
'Say *on,* Fradubio, then, or man or tree,' — I. ii. 34. 1
And bad say *on* the secrete of her hart: — I. iv. 46. 2
make proofe of her cruelty *On* gentle Dame, — I. vi. 31. 7
'Tell *on,*' (quoth she) — I. vii. 24. 8
all dauncing *on* a row, — I. xii. 6. 5
all *on* uprore from her settled seat, — II. ii. 20. 6
'Tell *on,* fayre Sir,' said she, — II. ii. 45. 1
So proudly pricketh *on* his courser strong, — II. v. 38. 8
thus lies dead *on* field.' — II. viii. 14. 9
tombling downe *on* ground, — II. viii. 45. 6
Champions broke *on* them, that forst them fly, — II. ix. 14. 6
Shee triumphed *on* death, in enemies despight. — II. x. 56. 9
They to him hearken, . . . And passe *on* forward: — II. xii. 14. 2
Would they once turne, but kept *on* as afore: — II. xii. 15. 5
Yet nought they feard, but past *on* hardily, — II. xii. 39. 5
He bad tell *on;* — III. iii. 16. 1
Who, rolled *on* an heape, lay still in swound — IV. i. 43. 1
Ne followd *on* so fast, but rather sought — IV. iii. 32. 3
That *on* an heape were tumbled horse and man: — IV. iv. 19. 7
Who, seeing him come *on* so furiously, — IV. iv. 28. 7
Tydings of all which there had hapned *on* the land. — IV. viii. 62. 9
All looking *on,* and like astonisht staring, — IV. x. 56. 8
Ne day nor night did sleepe t' attend them *on,* — V. x. 10. 9
Say *on,* my soverayne Ladie, and be bold: — V. v. 31. 5
But drew him *on* with hope fit leasure to awayt. — V. v. 42. 9
She thus oft times was beating off and *on,* — V. v. 43. 2
bad Talus guide her *on.* — V. vi. 17. 9
'Say *on*' (quoth he) 'the secret of your hart — V. vii. 19. 6
He ran still *on,* thinking to follow fast — V. viii. 8. 8
seeing him come still so fiercely *on,* — V. viii. 9. 4
the Blatant Beast, by them set *on,* — V. xii. 41. 1
Yet he past *on,* — V. xii. 42. 9
a Knight He spide come pricking *on* — VI. i. 32. 9
end which still attendeth *on* her.' — VI. vi. 25. 7
Complayning *out on me* that would not *on* them rew. — VI. viii. 20. 9
an altar shortly they erected To slay her *on.* — VI. viii. 44. 4
All *on* confused heapes themselves assay, — VI. xi. 17. 5
boldly preacing- *on* raught forth her hand — VII. vi. 13. 2
With all her Nymphes enranged *on* a rowe, — VII. vi. 39. 7
But forceth further *on,* — *H.L.* 247

Once. *See* **At once.**

Where *once* the Troyan Duke with Turnus fought. — *Bel.*[1] vii. 8
The Giants old should *once* again uprise, — *Ro.* iv. 6
Where all this worlds pride *once* was situate. — *Ro.* xxxi. 2
thou shepheards God that *once* didst love, — *S.C.* Ja. 17
That, *once* sea-beate, will to sea againe: — *S.C.* F. 34
when the shining sunne laugheth *once,* — *S.C.* F. 37
For *once* I heard my father say, — *S.C.* Mar. 106
his laye . . . Which *once* he made — *S.C.* Ap. 35
The time was *once,* and may againe retorne, — *S.C.* May 103
Wemen, that of Loves longing *once* lust, — *S.C.* May 134
That some good body woulde *once* pitie mee!' — *S.C.* May 248
Ne stayed he *once* the dore to make fast, — *S.C.* May 292
if thy galage *once* sticketh fast, — *S.C.* S. 131
who . . . feedes him *once* the fuller by a graine? — *S.C.* O. 34
The braunch *once* dead, the budde — *S.C.* N. 91
Als Colin Cloute she would not *once* disdayne; — *S.C.* N. 101
Might I *once* come to thee; — *S.C.* N. 181
Dye would we dayly, *once* it to expert! — *S.C.* N. 186
Which *once* assai'd to burne this world — *Gn.* 376
Of fortune and of hope at *once* forlorne.' — *Hub.* 258
Now *once* a weeke, upon the Sabbath day, — *Hub.* 456
Whose part *once* past all men bid take away: — *Hub.* 932
Or *once* vouchsafeth us to entertaine, — *T.M.* 344
'This *once* was she,' may warned be to say. — *Ti.* 7
That I, which *once* that beautie did beholde. — *Ti.* 531
is Love then . . . *once* knowne In Court, — *Col.* 771
soone to lose, before he *once* would lin; — I. i. 24. 5
with new day new worke at *once* begin: — I. i. 33. 2
chearefull Chaunticlere . . . Had warned *once,* — I. ii. 1. 7
But *once* a man, Fradubio, now a tree; — I. ii. 33. 3
With whome, as *once* I rode accompanyde, — I. ii. 35. 6
Scarse could he *once* uphold his heavie hedd, — I. iv. 19. 5
unhable *once* to stirre or go; — I. iv. 23. 2
when these knights had breathed *once,* — I. vi. 45. 1
Might *once* abide the terror of that blast, — I. viii. 4. 6
sparkes . . . troubled *once,* into huge flames will grow; — I. ix. 8. 2
he that *once* hath missed the right way, — I. ix. 43. 8
Was wont him *once* to disple every day: — I. x. 27. 2
He feard not *once* himselfe to be in need, — I. x. 38. 4
He would not *once* have moved for the knight. — I. x. 49. 6

Once—*Continued.*

All night shee watcht, ne *once* adowne would lay — I. xi. 32. 7
to touch, or *once* assay. — I. xii. 9. 9
The fish that *once* was caught — II. i. 4. 9
could her Paramour intreat Her *once* to show, — II. ii. 35. 6
'*Once* I did sweare, When with one sword — II. iii. 17. 6
Which kindled *once,* his mother did more rage inspyre. — II. iv. 32. 9
when they *once* to perfect strength do grow, — II. iv. 34. 6
Ne would for price or prayers *once* affoord — II. vi. 19. 8
once to requyre, After pursewing death — II. vi. 44. 7
suffer Sleepe *once* thither-ward Approch, — II. vii. 25. 5
When rancour doth with rage him *once* engore, — II. viii. 42. 2
So he, . . . Did not *once* move, — II. viii. 50. 6
ne *once* would rest a whit. — II. ix. 49. 9
That *once* their quiet government annoyd; — II. x. 14. 8
Ne *once* did yield it respitt day nor night; — II. xi. 9. 3
That *once* hath failed of her souse full neare, — II. xi. 36. 7
To which nor fish nor fowle did *once* approch, — II. xii. 8. 3
whosoever *once* hath fastened His foot thereon, — II. xii. 12. 7
nathemore Would they *once* turne, — II. xii. 15. 5
the which him *once* annoyd, — III. vi. 48. 5
Ne did she let dull sleepe *once* to relent, — III. vii. 2. 3
Ne *once* to stay to rest, — III. vii. 23. 3
But Braggadochio, . . . *Once* having turnd, — III. viii. 18. 8
Out of his sight her selfe *once* to absent: — III. x. 3. 8
Once to me yold, not to be yolde againe: — III. xi. 17. 4
Once, when he with Asterie did scape; — III. xi. 34. 3
having *once* escaped perill neare, — IV. i. 34. 8
finding him unable *once* to weld, — IV. i. 37. 3
whose small sparkes *once* blowen — IV. ii. 1. 5
Yet scarcely *once* to breath would they relent, — IV. ii. 18. 7
That none of them *once* out of order went, — IV. ii. 36. 7
for what the Fates do *once* decree, — IV. ii. 51. 8
could *once* sustaine the hideous stowre, — IV. iii. 15. 5
how could one . . . *Once* thinke to match three — IV. iii. 24. 8
Of which so soone *as* they *once* tasted had, — IV. iii. 49. 1
neither able were to wag, or *once* to weld. — IV. iv. 18. 9
at *once* huge strokes on him did pound, — IV. iv. 31. 8
Which, being *once* withdrawne, — IV. v. 10. 3
The sight of whom *once* seene did all the rest dismay. — IV. v. 13. 9
neither toyle nor griefe she *once* did spare, — IV. v. 30. 2
scarse the Squire his hand could *once* upreare, — IV. vii. 28. 6
Ne ever laught, ne *once* shew'd countenance glad, — IV. viii. 2. 7
ne *once* abacke did flit, — IV. ix. 29. 8
once doth prove The tast of bloud — IV. ix. 31. 5
To rip up wrong that battell *once* hath tried; — IV. ix. 37. 3
Ne ever *once* did looke up from her desse, — IV. x. 50. 3
Sad Trowis, that *once* his people over-ran, — IV. xi. 41. 7
unable *once* to stirre or move. — IV. xii. 20. 9
once amisse growes daily wourse and wourse: — V. Pr. 1. 9
For what the mighty Sea hath *once* possest, — V. iv. 19. 2
Weening at *once* her wrath on him to wreake — V. iv. 40. 4
That none of all the many *once* did darre Him to assault,
nor *once* approach him nie; — V. iv. 44. 5, 6
To be convayed in, ere she would *once* retrate. — V. iv. 45. 9
Thinking at *once* both head and helmet to have raced. — V. v. 11. 9
Yet nould she hearke, ne let him *once* respyre, — V. v. 16. 7
Yet all that while he would not *once* assay — V. v. 19. 8
Declare at *once:* and hath he lost or wun?' — V. vi. 9. 3
Ne *once* for ought her speedy passage stayd, — V. viii. 6. 3
That never did her ill, ne *once* deserved blame. — V. viii. 22. 9
none can . . . that *once* are gone amis. — V. ix. 6. 9
but Bon, that *once* had written bin, — V. ix. 26. 4
That *once* he could not move, — V. ix. 33. 7
the which, *once* being brust, Like to a — V. xi. 31. 4
so foule blame as breach of faith *once* plight, — V. xi. 62. 4
your faith *once* plighted hold.' — V. xi. 63. 9
That none should dare him *once* to entertaine; — V. xii. 10. 4
that durst her *once* have disobayd. — V. xii. 25. 9
When *once* he felt his foeman to relent, — VI. i. 21. 7
Ne *once* for ruth their rigour they releast, — VI. i. 36. 8
Ne *once* to breath awhile their angers tempest ceast. — VI. i. 36. 9
when he *once* his dreadfull strokes — VI. vi. 28. 1
the Prince had *once* him plainely eyde, — VI. vi. 28. 5
Ne would him suffer *once* to shrinke asyde, — VI. vi. 28. 7
would not *once* let him start, — VI. vii. 21. 1
Rather than *once* his burden to sustaine: — VI. vii. 46. 7
Ne *once* my minds unmoved quiet grieve; — VI. ix. 22. 7
'The time was *once,* in my first prime of yeares, — VI. ix. 24. 1
For who had tasted *once* . . . The happy peace — VI. x. 3. 3
not him permit *Once* to approch to her — VI. xi. 8. 2
Whose like he never *once* did speake, nor heare, — VI. xii. 33. 6
nor *once* withstand The proved powre — VI. xii. 36. 6
his old foes that *once* him sorely fear'd. — VII. vi. 15. 9
But, when it *once* doth burne, — *Am.* vi. 7
That she will *once* vouchsafe my plaint to heare, — *Am.* xviii. 7
your light hath *once* enlumind me, — *Am.* lxvi. 13
Had ye *once* seene these her celestial threasures, — *Epith.* 200
When *once* the Crab behind his back he sees. — *Epith.* 269
Nor any dread disquiet *once* annoy The safety — *Epith.* 324
Nor griesly vultures, make us *once* affeard: — *Epith.* 348
The Latmian shepherd *once* unto thee brought, — *Epith.* 380
Ne *once* move ruth in that rebellious Dame, — *H.L.* 151
nought may quench his . . . desyre, *Once* kindled — *H.L.* 203
Could *once* come neare this beauty soverayne. — *H.H.B.* 217

One. *See* **Any one, At one, Ene, Every one, Some one.**

joyne There in *one* place all pleasures — *Bel.*[1] x. 6
One of hir heads yet there I did espie, — *Rev.* i. 7
One cride aloude. What *one* is like (quod he) — *Rev.* i. 9
Being *one* day at my window all alone, — *Pet.* i. 1

One—*Continued.*

the *one* was blacke, the other white: . . . *Pet.* i. 7
I saw both ship and mariners each *one,* . . . *Bel.*[2] xiii. 12
One foote on Thetis, th' other on the Morning, . . . *Ro.* iv. 2
One hand on Scythia, th' other on the More . . . *Ro.* iv. 3
one would weene that *one* sole Cities strength . . . *Ro.* viii. 2
all this whole shall *one* day come to nought. . . . *Ro.* ix. 14
The firie sunnes both *one* and other hous: . . . *Ro.* x. 8
some *one* of you . . . secretly doth hide) . . . *Ro.* xv. 9
flames . . . Gathered in *one* up to the heavens to spyre, . . . *Ro.* xvi. 10
one would judge, that the Romaine Daemon . . . *Ro.* xxvii. 12
One day, whiles that my daylie cares did sleepe, . . . *Van.* i. 1
Bird . . . *One* day did scorne the simple Scarabee, . . . *Van.* iv. 2
Should able be so great an *one* to wring. . . . *Van.* ix. 14
Such an *one* shepeheards would make full faine; . . . *S.C.* F. 67
Such an *one* would make thee younge againe. . . . *S.C.* F. 68
I pray thee, Hobbinoll, recorde some *one,* . . . *S.C.* Ap. 30
her lot To beare such an *one.* . . . *S.C.* Ap. 94
may depart Eche *one* her way. . . . *S.C.* Ap. 148
they dauncen, eche *one* with his mayd. . . . *S.C.* May 24
The *one* for the hire which he doth take, . . . *S.C.* May 52
so enamoured of her young *one,* . . . *S.C.* May 97
Of my old age have this *one* delight, . . . *S.C.* May 202
though *one* fall through heedlesse hast, . . . *S.C.* Jul. 15
by his foly *one* did fall, . . . *S.C.* Jul. 67
The *one* my madding kiddes to smere, . . . *S.C.* Jul. 87
Such *one* he was . . . *S.C.* Jul. 125
Sike *one* (sayd Algrind) Moses was, . . . *S.C.* Jul. 157
One daye he sat upon a hyll, . . . *S.C.* Jul. 217
one, opened, mote unfolde many moe. . . . *S.C.* S. 14
All were Elisa *one* of thilke same ring; . . . *S.C.* O. 53
One bitter blast blewe all away. . . . *S.C.* N. 119
One if I please, enough is me therefore. . . . *S.C.* D. 120
gan the shepheard gather into *one* His stragling Goates, . . . *Gn.* 161
Eternall hurte left unto many *one:* . . . *Gn.* 203
Through fatall charmes transformd to such an *one;* . . . *Gn.* 205
th' *one* was ravisht of his owne bondmaide, . . . *Gn.* 489
th' *one* with fire and weapons did contend . . . *Gn.* 521
th' *one* Aeacide did his fame extend; . . . *Gn.* 525
all the heavenly powres Conspire in *one* to wreake . . . *Gn.* 579
two is better than *one* head.' . . . *Hub.* 82
so soone as *one* might see Light . . . *Hub.* 108
On which he leaned, as *one* farre in elde. . . . *Hub.* 218
Ne make *one* title worse, ne make *one* better: . . . *Hub.* 384
Much good deep learning *one* thereout may reed; . . . *Hub.* 484
other great *one* in the worldes eye, . . . *Hub.* 490
be thou sure *one* not to lacke or long. . . . *Hub.* 501
Unlesse thou canst *one* conjure by device, . . . *Hub.* 510
if *one* could, it were but a schoole trick. . . . *Hub.* 512
This is the way for *one* that is unlern'd . . . *Hub.* 535
being *one* of great regard In Court, . . . *Hub.* 885
few have found, and manie *one* hath mist! . . . *Hub.* 894
One joyous howre in blisfull happines, . . . *Hub.* 983
each *one* by and by Departed to his home . . . *Hub.* 1108
Sitting *one* day within his turret hye, . . . *Hub.* 1227
evermore he heard each *one* complaine . . . *Hub.* 1275
As *one* late in a traunce, . . . *Hub.* 1325
as *one* whose wits were reft, . . . *Hub.* 1356
some *one* perhaps of gentle kin, . . . *T.M.* 345
One onelie lives, her ages ornament, . . . *T.M.* 571
as *one* carelesse of suspition, . . . *Com. Son.* i. 5
It chaunced me *on* day beside the shore . . . *Ti.* 1
one of that Rivers Nymphes, . . . *Ti.* 15
one of those three fatall Impes . . . *Ti.* 17
Taste no *one* hower of happines or merth; . . . *Ti.* 46
made *one* meare of th' earth and of their raine? . . . *Ti.* 63
Save *One* that . . . Hath writ my record . . . *Ti.* 166
I saw him die, as *one* Of the meane people, . . . *Ti.* 190
when th' *one* dies, th' other then beginnes . . . *Ti.* 388
'Such *one* Mausolus made, . . . *Ti.* 414
Such *one* Marcellus, but was torne with thunder: . . . *Ti.* 416
Such *one* Lisippus, but is worne with raine: . . . *Ti.* 417
Such *one* King Edmond, but was rent for gaine. . . . *Ti.* 418
Scorns th' *one* and th' other in his deeper skill. . . . *Ti.* 448
with this mightie *one* in hugenes boast; . . . *Ti.* 539
from the *one* he could to th' other coast Stretch . . . *Ti.* 540
One of his feete unwares from him did slide, . . . *Ti.* 544
Over the Sea from *one* to other side, . . . *Ti.* 548
This goodlie bridge, *one* foote not fastned well, . . . *Ti.* 557
A fairer *one* in all the goodlie criew . . . *Ti.* 592
That he in time would sure prove such an *one,* . . . *Mui.* 31
from *one* to other border, . . . *Mui.* 170
The *one* his bowe and shafts, . . . *Mui.* 292
her silence, signe of *one* dismaid, . . . *Mui.* 341
snatcheth quite away *One* of the litle yonglings . . . *Mui.* 407
Of *one,* (I weene), the wofulst man alive, . . . *D.* 5
'*One,* whome like wofulnesse, impressed deepe, . . . *D.* 64
carest for *one* that for himselfe cares nought, . . . *D.* 93
'Yet fell she not as *one* enforst to dye, . . . *D.* 253
as *one* toyld with travaile downe doth lye, . . . *D.* 255
Throughout the world from *one* to other end, . . . *D.* 373
The *one,* because as I they wretched are; . . . *D.* 422
never standeth in *one* certaine state, . . . *D.* 430
As *one* disposed wilfullie to die, . . . *D.* 552
In *one* thing onely fayling of the best, . . . *As.* 11
For *one* alone he cared, for *one* he sigh't, . . . *As.* 53
Wide wounds emongst them many *one* he made, . . . *As.* 107
Into *one* flowre that is both red and blew; . . . *As.* 184
One of those groomes (a jolly groome was he, . . . *Col.* 12
'*One* day (quoth he) . . . *Col.* 56

One—*Continued.*

whilest the *one* was watcht, the other might . . . *Col.* 139
is theyr heaven likewise there all *one?* . . . *Col.* 305
Conspire in *one* to make contented blisse. . . . *Col.* 311
In which all pure perfection *one* may see. . . . *Col.* 343
Vassall to *one,* whom all my dayes I serve; . . . *Col.* 467
I hers ever onely, ever *one:* . . . *Col.* 477
One ever I all vowed hers to bee, . . . *Col.* 478
One ever I, and others never none.' . . . *Col.* 479
I feele my selfe like *one* yrapt in spright. . . . *Col.* 623
each *one* seeks with malice, and with strife, . . . *Col.* 690
Borne without Syre or couples of *one* kynd; . . . *Col.* 800
he was such an *one* as thou doest say, . . . *Col.* 829
drawne together into *one* . . . *Col.* 845
Thenceforth they gan each *one* his like to love, . . . *Col.* 863
For having loved ever *one* most deare: . . . *Col.* 904
one, that fairest Helene did revile, . . . *Col.* 920
Not *one* Parnassus nor *one* Helicone, . . . *Ded. Son.* v. 6
There, in deede, dwel faire Graces many *one,* . . . *Ded. Son.* v. 9
As *one* for knightly giusts and fierce encounters fitt. . . . I. i. 1. 9
As *one* that inly mournd, so was she sad, . . . I. i. 4. 6
each *one* Of sundrie shapes, yet all ill-favored: . . . I. i. 15. 6
She lookt about, and seeing *one* in mayle, . . . I. i. 16. 5
knitting all his force, got *one* hand free, . . . I. i. 19. 7
still did follow *one* unto the end, . . . I. i. 28. 5
knockt his brest, as *one* that did repent. . . . I. i. 29. 9
The *one* of them he gave a message too, . . . I. i. 38. 8
The *one* faire fram'd of burnisht Yvory, . . . I. i. 40. 2
As *one* then in a dreame, . . . He mumbled soft, . . . I. i. 42. 7
The *one* upon his hardie head him plaste, . . . I. i. 47. 3
As *one* aghast with feends or damned sprights, . . . I. ii. 4. 5
all three bred Of *one* bad sire, . . . I. ii. 25. 8
'The author then,' . . . 'of all my smarts, Is *one* Duessa, . . . I. ii. 34. 8
Th' *one* seeming such, the other such indeede, . . . I. ii. 37. 2
One day in doubt I cast for to compare . . . I. ii. 37. 3
One day, nigh wearie of the yrkesome way, . . . I. iii. 4. 1
One knocked at the dore, and in would fare: . . . I. iii. 16. 4
one loving howre For many yeares of sorrow can dispence; . . . I. iii. 30. 2
One pricking towards them with hastie heat, . . . I. iii. 33. 2
he is *one* the truest knight alive, . . . I. iii. 37. 6
each *one* himselfe did payne All kindnesse . . . to shew, . . . I. iv. 15. 3
When such an *one* had guiding of the way, . . . I. iv. 19. 8
Such *one* was Idlenesse, first of this company. . . . I. iv. 20. 9
Such *one* was Gluttony, the second of that crew. . . . I. iv. 23. 9
Such *one* was Lechery, the third of all this traine. . . . I. iv. 26. 9
Such *one* was Avarice, the fourth of this faire band. . . . I. iv. 29. 9
Such *one* vile Envy was, that fifte in row did sitt. . . . I. iv. 32. 9
Such *one* was Wrath, the last of this ungodly tire. . . . I. iv. 35. 9
foule Duessa, . . . as *one* of the traine: . . . I. iv. 37. 6
So th' *one* for wrong, the other strives for right. . . . I. v. 8. 1
So th' *one* for wrong, the other strives for right, . . . I. v. 9. 1
To make *one* great by others losse is bad excheat. . . . I. v. 25. 9
Here endlesse penaunce for *one* fault I pay, . . . I. v. 42. 6
All these together in *one* heape were throwne, . . . I. v. 49. 1
She wandred had from *one* to other Ynd, . . . I. vi. 2. 7
one day, when Phoebe fayre . . . was following the chace, . . . I. vii. 5. 1
Such *one* it was, as that renowmed Snake . . . I. vii. 17. 1
in the midst thereof *one* pretious stone . . . I. vii. 30. 1
one massy entire mould, Hewen out of Adamant rocke . . . I. vii. 33. 6
The groning ghosts of many *one* dismaide . . . I. vii. 47. 8
With staring countenance sterne, as *one* astownd, . . . I. viii. 5. 7
Stroke *one* of those deformed heades so sore, . . . I. viii. 16. 2
The force, . . . In *one* alone left hand he now unites, . . . I. viii. 18. 2
Both feet and face *one* way are wont to lead. . . . I. viii. 31. 6
one of them was like an Eagles claw, . . . I. viii. 48. 6
The fields, the floods, the heavens, with *one* consent, . . . I. ix. 12. 8
one that with his prowesse may Defend thine honour, . . . I. ix. 16. 7
Astonisht stood, as *one* that had aspyde Infernall furies . . . I. ix. 24. 4
ere *one* be aware, by secret stealth His powre is reft, . . . I. ix. 31. 7
hath encreast the world with *one* sonne more, . . . I. x. 16. 6
soone in him was lefte no *one* corrupted jott. . . . I. x. 26. 9
one sate wayting ever them before, . . . I. x. 36. 8
Such *one* as that same mighty man of God, . . . I. x. 53. 2
as *one* were borne that very day. . . . I. xi. 30. 5
he forst him to unty *One* of his grasping feete, . . . I. xi. 42. 9
That tree through *one* mans fault hath doen us all to dy. . . . I. xi. 47. 9
To him assembled with *one* full consort, . . . I. xii. 4. 7
One . . . Warnd him not touch, . . . I. xii. 10. 2
One mother . . . her litle babe revyld, . . . I. xii. 11. 1
one sung a song of love and jollity. . . . I. xii. 38. 9
each *one* felt secretly Himselfe thereby refte of his sences . . . I. xii. 39. 7
He chaunged his mynd from *one* to other ill; . . . II. i. 5. 4
if by lookes *one* may the mind aread, . . . II. i. 7. 6
As *one* out of a deadly dreame affright, . . . II. i. 45. 6
Let *one* word fall that may your grief unfold, . . . II. i. 46. 7
One day, when him high courage did emmove, . . . II. i. 50. 5
Not *one* word more she sayd, . . . II. i. 56. 1
The children of *one* syre by mothers three; . . . II. ii. 13. 2
three valiaunt knights to see Three combates joine in *one,* . . . II. ii. 26. 2
One thought her cheare too litle, . . . II. ii. 34. 9
One that to bountie never cast his mynd, . . . II. iii. 4. 2
One sitting ydle on a sunny banck, . . . II. iii. 6. 2
seeing *one,* that shone in armour fayre, . . . II. iii. 11. 3
with Guyon knitt in *one* consent, . . . II. iii. 11. 8
with *one* sword seven knightes I brought to end, . . . II. iii. 17. 7
through the thicke they heard *one* rudely rush, . . . II. iii. 21. 1
cause *one* foot to flye, . . . II. iii. 45. 4
I hid my selfe from it, as *one* affeard; . . . II. iii. 45. 8
gan to ride As *one* unfitt therefore, . . . II. iii. 46. 4
though it her *one* leg were, . . . II. iv. 5. 6

One—*Continued.*

He blest himselfe as *one* sore terrifide: . . . . IV. vi. 24. 7
From *one* to other so quite contrary: . . . . IV. vi. 33. 3
behind her backe she heard *One* rushing forth . . . . IV. vii. 4. 4
of us three to morrow he will sure eate *one*.' . . . . IV. vii. 13. 9
of his owne rash hand *one* wound was to be seene. . . . . IV. vii. 35. 9
As *one* with griefe and anguishe overcum, ... IV. vii. 44. 4
How he the name of *one* engraven had . . . . IV. vii. 46. 2
had With *one* sterne looke so daunted, ... IV. viii. 2. 3
as *one* daunted with her presence dread, ... IV. viii. 13. 7
with a cruell *one* consent To cloud my daies . . . . IV. viii. 16. 7
never heard *one* word Of tydings . . . . IV. viii. 18. 5
The *one* right feeble through the evill rate Of food . . . . IV. viii. 19. 5
one old woman sitting there beside . . . . IV. viii. 23. 5
hath he left *one* daughter . . . . IV. viii. 49. 3
not ever in *one* place, ... IV. ix. 10. 4
by *one* patterne, seene somewhere, She had them made . . . IV. ix. 11. 5
Exchanged out of *one* into another feare. . . . . IV. ix. 17. 9
each *one* taking part in others aide . . . . IV. ix. 24. 7
Foure charged two, and two surcharged *one;* . . . . IV. ix. 30. 5
First from *one* coast, ... IV. ix. 33. 7
thus turmoild from *one* to other stowre . . . . IV. ix. 39. 4
if the *one* be with the other wayd, ... IV. x. 1. 3
all the pillours of the *one* were guilt, ... IV. x. 5. 8
by *one* way that passage did prepare. . . . . IV. x. 6. 5
Where *one* stood peeping through a crevis small, ... IV. x. 11. 8
Th' *one* forward looking, ... IV. x. 12. 4
'On th' *one* side he, ... IV. x. 13. 1
one deniall Excludes . . . . IV. x. 17. 8
One of the worlds seven wonders sayd to bee, ... IV. x. 30. 4
Begotten by two fathers of *one* mother, ... IV. x. 32. 4
The *one* of them hight Love, ... IV. x. 32. 6
if *one* did rightly deeme; . . . . IV. x. 39. 8
she hath both kinds in *one,* . . . . IV. x. 41. 6
both under *one* name: . . . . IV. x. 41. 7
not *one* of all them daring. . . . . IV. x. 56. 9
thought it all *one* night that did no houres divide. . . . . IV. xi. 4. 9
With such an *one* was Thamis beautifide; . . . . IV. xi. 28. 7
Sixe valiant Knights of *one* faire Nymphe yborne, ... IV. xi. 37. 3
One day, as she to shunne the season whot . . . . IV. xi. 42. 4
accord To joyne in *one,* . . . . IV. xi. 43. 8
flowing all from *one,* all *one* at last become, ... IV. xi. 43. 9
One cald the Theise, the other cald the Crane, ... IV. xi. 47. 2
voice of *one,* That piteously complaind . . . . IV. xii. 5. 2
By *one* or other way . . . . IV. xii. 9. 3
for loving *one* That loves not me, ... IV. xii. 9. 6
One prison fittest is to hold us two. . . . . IV. xii. 10. 7
did inly mourne, like *one* astray. . . . . IV. xii. 18. 9
Gainst *one* that hath both wronged you and us; . . . . . . IV. xii. 30. 3
So shall you by *one* gift save all us three alive. . . . . . IV. xii. 31. 9
the golden age, . . . It's now at earst become a stonie *one;* . V. Pr. 2. 2
at *one* stroke cropt off her head with scorne, ... V. i. 18. 6
Each *one* did flie; their hearts began to faile, ... V. ii. 24. 7
of the fire *one* ballaunce make, And *one* of th' ayre, ... V. ii. 31. 3, 4
whatsoever from *one* place doth fall . . . . V. ii. 39. 7
Weigh but *one* word which from thy lips doth fall: . . . . V. ii. 43. 6
First in *one* ballance set the true aside.' . . . . V. ii. 45. 5
So first the right he put into *one* scale, ... V. ii. 46. 3
truth is *one,* and right is ever *one*.' . . . . V. ii. 48. 6
Th' *one* to diminish, th' other for to eeke; . . . . V. ii. 49. 4
As each *one* had his furnitures deviz'd. . . . . V. iii. 4. 5
Of which th' *one* halfe upon himselfe did set, ... V. iii. 11. 6
like as *one* whom feends had made affrayd, ... V. iii. 18. 4
Then did he set her by that snowy *one,* . . . . V. iii. 24. 1
All suddenly, ere *one* can looke aside, ... V. iii. 25. 5
ere *one* could it bewray. . . . . V. iii. 25. 9
many a *one* suppos'd to be a mayd: . . . . V. iii. 28. 3
th' *one* hand seizing on his golden bit, ... V. iii. 29. 6
one did take The horse in hand . . . . V. iii. 33. 1
Both brethren, whom *one* wombe together bore, ... V. iv. 4. 3
the *one* appeares But like a little Mount . . . . V. iv. 7. 6
each *one* had his right. . . . . V. iv. 20. 6
like *one* that hopelesse was depryv'd . . . . V. iv. 35. 1
A goodly citty and a mighty *one,* . . . . V. iv. 35. 8
the *one* him seem'd a Knight all armed, ... V. iv. 36. 4
Like *one* that from his dreame is waked suddenlye. . . . . V. v. 13. 9
As *one* that would confesse, yet faine would it denie. . . . V. v. 31. 9
one day she thus him proved, ... V. v. 35. 9
One day her Ladie, calling her apart, ... V. v. 45. 1
As *one* adaw'd, and halfe confused stood; . . . . V. v. 45. 5
One while she blam'd her selfe; . . . . V. vi. 5. 1
One day when as she long had sought for ease . . . . . . V. vi. 7. 1
at last she spide *One* comming towards her . . . . V. vi. 8. 2
it was *one* sent from her love indeede; . . . . V. vi. 8. 4
stood still mute, as *one* in great suspence; . . . . V. vi. 9. 7
Her minde was whole possessed of *one* thought, ... V. vi. 21. 3
if two met, the *one* mote needes fall over the lidge. . . . V. vi. 36. 9
the *one* These vile reproches gan unto her speake: . . . . V. vi. 37. 2
The *one* of them, which most her wrath increast, ... V. vi. 39. 4
doth teare Th' *one* from the earth, ... V. vi. 40. 5
The other it with force doth overthrow Uppon *one* side, . . . V. vi. 40. 7
One foote was set uppon the Crocodile, ... V. vii. 7. 1
one of them, who seem'd in sight To be the greatest . . . V. vii. 18. 4
Like *one* adawed with some dreadfull spright: . . . . V. vii. 20. 8
She with *one* stroke both head and helmet cleft. . . . . . V. vii. 34. 6
each *one* of sence bereft Fled fast into the towne, ... V. vii. 34. 8
else he sure had left not *one* alive, ... V. vii. 36. 8
he saw the hindmost overtake *One* of those two, ... V. viii. 5. 7
Like *one* of those two Knights which dead there lay; . . . V. viii. 25. 5
made them both *one* masse withouten more remorse. . . . . V. viii. 32. 9

One—*Continued.*

That *one* sure stroke he might unto him reach, ... V. viii. 37. 4
like *one* enfelon'd or distraught, ... V. viii. 48. 5
could deceive *one* looking in his face: . . . . V. ix. 5. 7
neither will *one* foot, till we that carle have hent.' . . . . V. ix. 7. 9
Yet warded well by *one* of mickle might . . . . V. ix. 22. 5
she placed th' *one* on th' *one,* The other on the other side, . . V. ix. 37. 8
soothly he was *one* of matchlesse might, ... V. x. 8. 6
had three bodies in *one* wast empight, ... V. x. 8. 8
Through his three bodies powre in *one* combynd; . . . . . V. x. 9. 6
Giving her dearest children *one* by *one* Unto a dreadfull Monster . . . . V. x. 13. 6
When *one* in armes she saw, ... V. x. 19. 6
And that so wretched *one,* as ye do see, ... V. x. 21. 8
no whit of them remayning *one* may see. . . . . V. x. 29. 9
leveld all against *one* certaine place, ... V. x. 34. 7
th' *one* did th' other stay, ... V. x. 36. 5
sith he heard but *one* that did apeare, ... V. xi. 2. 8
One time when he his weapon faynd to shift, ... V. xi. 7. 6
Gan into *one* assemble all the might Of all his hands, . . . V. xi. 8. 4
Thinking to pay him with that *one* for all: . . . . V. xi. 8. 6
all his teeth wide bare *One* might have seene . . . . . . V. xi. 9. 8
As if he would have tottered to *one* side: . . . . V. xi. 11. 3
So now all three *one* sencelesse lumpe remaine, ... V. xi. 14. 5
To many a *one* which came unto her schoole, ... V. xi. 25. 8
with *one* stripe Her Lions clawes he . . . away did wipe. . V. xi. 27. 8
'Under *one* hood to shadow faces twaine: . . . . V. xi. 56. 7
Knights ought be true, and truth is *one* in all: . . . . . . V. xi. 56. 8
in *one* day they with the coast did fall; . . . . V. xii. 4. 6
could have frayd *one* with the very sight, ... V. xii. 15. 7
whether man or monster *one* could scarse discerne. . . . . V. xii. 15. 9
Not *one* was left that durst her once have disobayd. . . . V. xii. 25. 9
The *one* of them, that elder did appeare, ... V. xii. 29. 1
with th' *one* of which she scracht Her cursed head, ... V. xii. 30. 3
round about her jawes *one* might descry The bloudie gore . . V. xii. 30. 8
like *one* unto a banquet bid, ... V. xii. 32. 7
These two now had themselves combynd in *one,* . . . . . . V. xii. 37. 1
a ruefull shrieke Of *one* loud crying, ... VI. i. 17. 2
everie thing to which *one* is inclin'd . . . . VI. ii. 2. 7
he . . . strooke me *one* stroke or twaine; . . . . VI. ii. 12. 4
Well may I, certes, such an *one* thee read, ... VI. ii. 25. 6
that *one* in basenesse set Doth noble courage shew . . . . VI. iii. 1. 8
Like *one* that out of deadly dreame awooke: . . . . VI. iii. 11. 3
With speare in th' *one* hand . . . . VI. iii. 33. 8
Sir Turpine, *one* of mickle might . . . . VI. iii. 40. 2
Because of *one* that wrought him fowle despight.' . . . . . VI. iii. 40. 5
cruell fate Hath joyn'd *one* evill, ... VI. iv. 30. 6
Now wringing both his wretched hands in *one,* . . . . . . VI. v. 4. 4
They did their counsels now in *one* compound: . . . . . . VI. v. 14. 6
no *one* beast in forrest, wylde or tame, ... VI. v. 15. 7
seeing *one* in so great daunger set . . . . VI. v. 22. 2
they ne might Endure to travell, nor *one* foote to frame: . . VI. v. 40. 8
One day, as he was searching of their wounds, ... VI. vi. 5. 1
If therefore health ye seeke, observe this *one:* . . . . . . VI. vi. 7. 5
As he unable were for very neede To move *one* foote, ... VI. vi. 19. 7
As *one* that had no life him left through former feare. . . VI. vi. 32. 9
to adorne With so brave badges *one* so basely borne: . . . . VI. vi. 36. 5
He had not left *one* limbe of him unrent: . . . . VI. vi. 40. 8
Said then the *one* of them; . . . . VI. vii. 5. 7
Then *one* of them aloud unto him cryde, ... VI. vii. 7. 1
th' *one* did misse his marke, ... VI. vii. 7. 6
th' *one* is dead, th' other soone shall die, ... VI. vii. 13. 3
to entreat The *one* or th' other better her to use; . . . . VI. viii. 40. 2
hardly *one* could know . . . . VI. viii. 13. 8
Resolved in *one* t' assemble all his force, ... VI. viii. 14. 8
make *one* end of him without ruth or remorse. . . . . . . VI. viii. 14. 9
Full many a *one* for me deepe groand and sight, ... VI. viii. 20. 7
Thereto they usde *one* most accursed order, ... VI. viii. 36. 1
they all gave *one* consent . . . . VI. viii. 38. 4
of the pray each *one* a part doth beare. . . . . VI. viii. 41. 5
He lightly started up like *one* aghast, ... VI. viii. 47. 8
Eftsoones he saw *one* with a naked knife . . . . VI. viii. 48. 8
she, for nought . . . *One* word durst speake, ... VI. viii. 50. 9
I lately left a furrow, *one* or twayne, Unplough'd, ... VI. ix. 1. 3
Then *one* of them, him seeing so to sweat, ... VI. ix. 6. 6
eke many a *one* Burnt in her love, ... VI. ix. 10. 2
like *one* halfe entraunced grew. . . . . VI. ix. 26. 9
One day, when as the shepheard swaynes together Were met . VI. ix. 41. 1
Colin Clout should pipe, as *one* most fit; . . . . VI. ix. 41. 6
with *one* fall his necke he almost brake; . . . . VI. ix. 44. 3
Like to *one* sight which Calidore did vew? . . . . VI. x. 4. 2
One day, as he did raunge the fields abroad, ... VI. x. 5. 1
that faire *one,* That in the midst was placed paravaunt, . . VI. x. 15. 6
one still towards shew'd her selfe afore; . . . . VI. x. 24. 8
To make *one* minime of thy poore handmayd, ... VI. x. 28. 6
One day, as they all three together went . . . . VI. x. 34. 1
one day, when Calidore Was hunting in the woods, ... VI. x. 39. 1
A thousand sowres hath tempred with *one* sweet, ... VI. xi. 1. 8
One day, as he did all his prisoners vew, ... VI. xi. 3. 6
Litle for him to have *one* silly lasse; . . . . VI. xi. 12. 6
lookt up like *one* aghast. . . . . VI. xi. 22. 9
in charge of *one,* the best Of many worst, ... VI. xi. 24. 2
there now not *one* he found. . . . . VI. xi. 26. 9
He chaunst *one* comming towards him to spy, ... VI. xi. 27. 2
whilest *one* sought her to hold, ... VI. xi. 30. 8
like to *one* distraught And robd of reason, ... VI. xi. 45. 7
Directs her course unto *one* certaine cost, ... VI. xii. 1. 2
Who ever is the mother of *one* chylde, ... VI. xii. 21. 1
joyning joy with her in *one* accord, ... VI. xii. 22. 3
Drawne of two steeds, th' *one* black, the other white, . . VII. vi. 9. 2

One—*Continued.*

That never any saw, save onely *one*, . . . VII. vi. 45. 3
(both combin'd) themselves in *one* faire river spred. . . . VII. vi. 53. 9
ne in *one* stead do tarry; . . . VII. vii. 21. 8
all are in *one* body, and as *one* appeare. . . . VII. vii. 25. 9
In his *one* hand . . . He held a knife-hook; . . . VII. vii. 38. 5
Th' *one* on a Palfrey blacke, the other white; . . . VII. vii. 44. 3
So nothing heere long standeth in *one* stay: . . . VII. vii. 47. 7
though he . . . alwayes seeme as *one*, . . . VII. vii. 51. 2
Then doe I die, as *one* with lightning fyred. . . . *Am.* vii. 8
One day I sought . . . To make a truce, . . . *Am.* xii. 1
Great shame it is to leave, like *one* afrayd, . . . *Am.* xiv. 3
to leave, . . . for *one* repulse so light. . . . *Am.* xiv. 4
One day as I unwarily did gaze . . . *Am.* xvi. 1
One of those archers closely I did spy, . . . *Am.* xvi. 9
with *one* looke, she doth my life dismay; . . . *Am.* xxi. 10
In *one* short houre I find by her undonne. . . . *Am.* xxiii. 8
with *one* looke she spils that long I sponne; . . . *Am.* xxiii. 11
with *one* word my whole years work doth rend. . . . *Am.* xxiii. 12
my proud *one* doth worke the greater scath, . . . *Am.* xxxi. 9
Sufficient worke for *one* mans simple head, . . . *Am.* xxxiii. 7
this *one* is tost with troublous fit Of a proud love, . . . *Am.* xxxiii. 11
Ye shall condemned be of many a *one*. . . . *Am.* xxxvi. 14
with *one* word she can it save or spill. . . . *Am.* xxxviii. 11
Enough it is for *one* man to sustaine The stormes, . . . *Am.* xlvi. 13
with *one* salve, both hart and body heale. . . . *Am.* l. 14
I goe lyke *one* that, . . . Is prisoner . . . *Am.* lii. 2
Ye cruell *one!* what glory can be got, . . . *Am.* lvii. 11
Nether to *one* her selfe nor other bends. . . . *Am.* lix. 12
he most happy, who such *one* loves best. . . . *Am.* lix. 14
one yeare is spent; . . . *Am.* lx. 6
loosing *one*, two liberties ye gayne, . . . *Am.* lxv. 3
one disparagement they to you gave, . . . *Am.* lxvi. 3
ye your love lent to so meane a *one*. . . . *Am.* lxvi. 4
on earth have found *one* fit for mate, . . . *Am.* lxvi. 6
One day I wrote her name upon the strand; . . . *Am.* lxxv. 1
Let not *one* sparke . . . Breake out, . . . *Am.* lxxxiii. 1
Ne *one* light glance of sensuall desyre . . . *Am.* lxxxiii. 3
One of his shafts she stole away. . . . *Epig.* ii. 4
one of hers did close convay . . . *Epig.* ii. 5
let this day, let this *one* day, be myne; . . . *Epith.* 125
As if it were *one* voyce, . . . *Epith.* 139
suffers not *one* looke to glaunce awry, . . . *Epith.* 236
Hast sumd in *one*, and cancelled for aye: . . . *Epith.* 318
Lo! *one*, whom later age hath brought to light, . . . *Com. Son.* iii. 9
no *one* drop of pitie there doth rest. . . . *H.L.* 147
is there *one* more cursed then they all, . . . *H.L.* 266
made out of *one* mould the more t' agree; . . . *H.B.* 207
Cures all their sorrowes with *one* sweete aspect. . . . *H.B.* 245
One drop of grace at length will to me give, . . . *H.B.* 277
Deigne to let fall *one* drop of dew reliefe, . . . *H.B.* 284
Both day, and night, is unto them all *one;* . . . *H.H.L.* 71
each *one* had a little wicker basket, . . . *Proth.* 24
one did sing this Lay, . . . *Proth.* 87
Which, . . . Each *one* did make his Bryde . . . *Proth.* 178

One another. The shepheards there robben *one another*, . . . *S.C.* S. 38
as fearing *one another;* . . . IV. x. 32. 2
may *one another* entertayne! . . . *Am.* lxviii. 12

One's. Would rayse *ones* mynd above the starry skie, . . . *S.C.* O. 94
By law of armes there neede *ones* right to trie, . . . V. iii. 32. 2
No shame to stoupe, *ones* head more high to reare; . . . V. xii. 19. 3
to many *ones* great paine, . . . VII. vi. 4. 7
a byrd, that in *ones* hand doth spy Desired food, . . . *Am.* lxxiii. 5

Ones. I saw her litle *ones* . . . *Bel.*[2] vi. 2
Burnt up his yong *ones*, . . . *Van.* iv. 8
righteous soules doth sever From wicked *ones*, . . . *Gn.* 624
Ne new *ones* could he easily provide, . . . *Hub.* 929
greatest *ones* did sue to gaine his grace; . . . *Ti.* 186
Of greatest *ones* he, greatest in his place, . . . *Ti.* 187
'How manie great *ones* may remembred be, . . . *Ti.* 358
Betwixt two mightie *ones* of great estate, . . . *Mui.* 3
There shall I be amongst those blessed *ones*. . . . *D.* 287
But the ungodly *ones* he doth forsake, . . . *D.* 360
such are for such *ones* most fit, . . . *As.* Pr. 15
Full many worthie *ones* then waiting were, . . . *Col.* 737
Of her there bred A thousand yong *ones*, . . . I. i. 15. 5
Emongst his young *ones* shall divide . . . III. iii. 47. 9
Such *ones* ill judge of love that cannot love, . . . IV. Pr. 2. 1
Three mightie *ones*, and cruell minded eeke, . . . VI. v. 13. 3
to great *ones* such follies doe forgive; . . . VI. ix. 22. 2
under foot doth tread The mightie *ones*, . . . VI. ix. 27. 9

Only. Sith *onely* God surmounts all times decay, . . . *Bel.* i. 13
Rome now of Rome is th' *onely* funerall, . . . *Ro.* iii. 9, 10
Rome *onely* might to Rome compared bee, And *onely* Rome could make . . . *Ro.* vi. 9, 10
Which *onely* doo the name of Rome retaine, . . . *Ro.* vii. 2
Onely supports herselfe for meate of wormes; . . . *Ro.* xxviii. 8
Thou *onely* cause, O Civill furie! art, . . . *Ro.* xxxi. 9
Nought aske I, but *onely* to hold my right; . . . *S.C.* F. 186
Theyr sample *onely* to us lent, . . . *S.C.* Jul. 119
Unto yourselfe, that *onely* privie are; . . . *Gn.* Ded. 4
like a cobweb . . . Have *onely* playde: . . . *Gn.* 4
Onely through kindly aptnes of his joynts. . . . *Hub.* 695
The *onely* upshot whereto he doth ayme: . . . *Hub.* 770
whose *onely* pride Is virtue to advaunce, . . . *Hub.* 811
Vouchsafe ye then, whom *onely* it concernes, . . . *T.M.* 49
Ne *onely* they that dwell in lowly dust, . . . *T.M.* 67
But they doo *onely* strive themselves to raise . . . *T.M.* 91
And *onely* boast of Armes and Auncestrie, . . . *T.M.* 94
Of wretched life the *onely* joy shee is, . . . *T.M.* 131

Only—*Continued.*

th' *only* comfort in calamities. . . . *T.M.* 132
Now *onely* seeke for pleasure, . . . *T.M.* 468
It is the *onelie* comfort which they have, . . . *T.M.* 494
One *onelie* lives, her ages ornament, . . . *T.M.* 571
Ne *onelie* favours them which it professe, . . . *T.M.* 575
th' *onely* usance Of a small time, . . . *D.* 503
In one thing *onely* fayling of the best, . . . *As.* 11
Of *onely* her he sung, he thought, . . . *As.* 64
onely by his lookes did tell his thought. . . . *As.* 168
I hers ever *onely*, ever one: . . . *Col.* 477
Faire Marian, the Muses *onely* darling: . . . *Col.* 505
onely mirrhor of feminitie: . . . *Col.* 513
And *only* woond in fields and forests here:' . . . *Col.* 774
Thou *onely* fit this Argument to write, . . . *Ded. Son.* viii. 5
He, . . . Betrothed me unto the *onely* haire . . . I. ii. 23. 2
him as *onely* God to call upon; . . . I. v. 47. 3
th' *only* breath him daunts, who hath escapt the stroke. . . . I. vii. 13. 9
th' *onely* daughter of a King and Queene, . . . I. vii. 43. 3
Mine *onely* foe, mine *onely* deadly dread; . . . I. vii. 50. 7
th' *only* good that growes of passed feare Is to be wise, . . . I. viii. 44. 5
For *onely* worthie you through prowes priefe, . . . I. ix. 17. 8
Whose *onely* joy was to relieve the needes . . . I. x. 3. 6
mine *onely* daughter to his Dame, . . . I. xii. 20. 5
The fairest Un,' his *onely* daughter deare, . . . I. xii. 21. 2
His *onely* daughter and his *only* hayre; . . . I. xii. 21. 3
for myne *only* sake Thy life and honor late adventurest, . . . I. xii. 29. 7
Shee, *onely* she, it is, . . . I. xii. 33. 7
His *onely* hart-sore, and his *onely* foe; . . . II. i. 2. 4
their places *only* signifide. . . . II. iii. 29. 9
Onely she turnd a pin, . . . II. vi. 5. 5
And that he victor *onely* did remayne; . . . II. xi. 43. 7
But *onely* womanish fine forgery, . . . II. xii. 28. 8
A subtile net, which *only* for that same . . . II. xii. 81. 4
But *onely* vented up her umbriere, . . . III. i. 42. 8
Onely for honour and for high regard, . . . III. ii. 7. 4
Being his *onely* daughter and his hayre; . . . III. ii. 22. 4
But th' *only* shade and semblant of a knight, . . . III. ii. 38. 3
doen they *onely* sleepe, and shall againe reverse? . . . III. iv. 1. 9
seeing, now the *only* last of three . . . III. v. 24. 1
But th' *only* forme and outward fashion; . . . III. vi. 38. 2
onely three they were disposd so well; . . . III. vii. 57. 3
The which not *onely* did not from him let . . . IV. iii. 24. 2
For vertues *onely* sake, . . . IV. vi. 46. 8
Yet was no man, but *onely* like in shape, . . . IV. vii. 5. 2
Onely few rueful lookes unto her sent, . . . IV. viii. 13. 8
unto rest themselves all *onely* lent, . . . IV. viii. 28. 7
th' *onely* remnant of that royall breed, . . . IV. viii. 33. 8
'There did I finde mine *onely* faithfull frend . . . IV. viii. 57. 1
The *onely* pleasant and delightfull place . . . IV. x. 21. 4
Onely what needeth shall be here fulfild, . . . IV. xi. 17. 7
When good was *onely* for itselfe desyred, . . . V. Pr. 3. 6
Ne wight with him but *onely* Talus . . . V. i. 30. 8
The which of all her spoyle was *onely* left; . . . V. iii. 27. 2
little had for his excuse to say, But *onely* thus: . . . V. iv. 27. 5
he *onely* joyed In combats of sweet love, . . . V. v. 24. 8
want of meanes hath bene mine *onely* let . . . V. v. 42. 1
Ne wight but *onely* Talus . . . V. viii. 3. 8
Not *onely* into bitter termes forth brust, . . . V. viii. 22. 4
Sought *onely* slaughter and avengement; . . . V. viii. 30. 5
th' *onely* feare that was before their vew, . . . V. viii. 38. 8
Onely his shield and armour, . . . V. viii. 44. 1
Onely these marishes and myrie bogs, . . . V. x. 23. 6
But *onely* wexed now the more aware . . . V. xi. 13. 2
stonied sore, As if the *onely* sound thereof she feard . . . V. xi. 30. 4
With *onely* Talus wayting diligent, . . . V. xi. 36. 7
her selfe she *onely* vext, . . . V. xii. 35. 8
Tristram . . . the *onely* heire Of good King Meliogras . . . VI. ii. 28. 1
Onely the use of armes, . . . I have not tasted yet; . . . VI. ii. 32. 6
Withouten cause, but *onely* her to reave . . . VI. ii. 43. 6
the *onely* helpe now left them . . . VI. iii. 12. 8
Not *onely* did not his demaund approve, . . . VI. iii. 42. 4
not *onely* sought by open might To overthrow, but . . . VI. v. 13. 4
Not *onely* her excluded late at night, . . . VI. v. 33. 8
in your selfe your *onely* helpe doth lie . . . VI. vi. 7. 1
But *onely* breath, sith that I did forgive.' . . . VI. vi. 36. 6
onely suffred him this wretched life to live. . . . VI. vi. 36. 9
with the *onely* twinckle of her eye She could . . . VI. vii. 31. 7
As th' *onely* author of her wofull tine; . . . VI. viii. 33. 3
growes dayly more Without my care, but *onely* to attend it; . . . VI. ix. 21. 6
(Save *onely* Glorianaes heavenly hew, . . . VI. x. 4. 7
the conquest . . . and th' *onely* glory of his might. . . . VI. x. 40. 9
But *onely* mongst the rest by her to sit, . . . VI. xi. 8. 3
Was his owne purchase and his *onely* prize; . . . VI. xi. 12. 3
I *onely* scapt through great confusione . . . VI. xi. 32. 3
not men *onely* (whom she soone subdewed) But . . . VII. vi. 4. 8
Ne shee the lawes of Nature *onely* brake, . . . VII. vi. 6. 1
That never any saw, save *onely* one, . . . VII. vi. 45. 3
Ne *onely* her, but also quite forsooke . . . VII. vi. 54. 5
Onely th' infernall Powers might not appeare; . . . VII. vii. 3. 6
'To thee, O greatest Goddesse, *onely* great! . . . VII. vii. 14. 1
And that is *onely* dew unto thy might Arrogate . . . VII. vii. 16. 3
the Earth . . . That *only* seemes unmov'd . . . VII. vii. 17. 7
Ne doe their bodies *only* flit and fly, . . . VII. vii. 19. 7
you, Dan Jove, that *only* constant are, . . . VII. vii. 53. 1
Onely the starry skie doth still remaine: . . . VII. vii. 55. 5
Of natures skill the *onely* complement; . . . *Am.* xxiv. 3
Onely let her abstaine from cruelty. . . . *Am.* xlii. 13
Onely my paines wil be the more to get her; . . . *Am.* li. 13
onely that is permanent . . . *Am.* lxxix. 7

Only—*Continued.*
He *onely* fayre, and what he fayre hath made; . . . *Am.* lxxix. 13
Onely behold her rare perfection, . . . *Am.* lxxxiii. 13
th' *onely* image of that heavenly ray, . . . *Am.* lxxxvii. 7
Onely I feare my wits enfeebled late, . . . *H.L.* 15
they seeke *onely,* . . . To quench . . . *H.L.* 101
Bove all the gods, thee *onely* honoring . . . *H.L.* 304
An outward shew of things that *onely* seeme. . . . *H.B.* 91
with His *onely* breath them blew away . . . *H.H.L.* 87
onely man himselfe, who selfe did slyde: . . . *H.H.L.* 145
In th' *only* wonder of her selfe to rest, . . . *H.H.B.* 238
And *onely* thinke on that before them set. . . . *H.H.B.* 266
Onset. with fresh *onsett* he assayld, . . . II. v. 11. 3
He lent against a tree, that backeward *onset* bard. . . . VI. v. 18. 9
Good *on-set* boads good end. . . . VII. vi. 23. 9
Onward. Arthure with the rest went *onward* still . . . VI. viii. 30. 7
Ooraxes. *Ooraxes,* feared for great Cyrus fate, . . . IV. xi. 21. 5
Ope. one eye Still *ope* he keepes . . . III. x. 58. 7
straight flew *ope,* and gave her way to ride. . . . IV. iii. 46. 3
He found the gate wyde *ope,* . . . VI. vi. 19. 2
Open. let those deep Abysses *open* rive, . . . *Ro.* i. 7
to *open* wide The griesly gates . . . *Van.* iii. 9
Open the dore at his request.' . . . *S.C.* May 226
see the dore stand *open* wyde. . . . *S.C.* May 295
To raunge the fields with wide *open* throte. . . . *S.C.* S. 195
Where thickest grasse did cloath the *open* hills. . . . *Gn.* 74
though the vulgar yeeld an *open* eare, . . . *Hub.* 713
Behold the fowle reproach and *open* shame, . . . *T.M.* 61
Their wraths at length broke into *open* warre. . . . *Mui.* 8
to breath the freshing ayre In *open* fields, . . . *D.* 27
Your carelesse flocks on hils and *open* plaines, . . . *D.* 520
in *open* plaines, Where Boreas doth blow full bitter bleake, . I. ii. 33. 6
With his rude clawes the wicket *open* rent, . . . I. iii. 13. 2
open breakes the dore in furious wize, . . . I. iii. 19. 5
still to all the gates stood *open* wide: . . . I. iv. 6. 2
forth they marchen . . . To take the solace of the *open* aire, . I. iv. 37. 2
the golden Orientall gate . . . gan to *open* fayre; . . . I. v. 2. 2
in all mens *open* vew Duessa placed is, . . . I. v. 5. 6
with her gealous termes his *open* eares abusd: . . . I. v. 37. 9
No gate . . . But with that percing noise flew *open* . . . I. viii. 4. 9
every dore of freewill *open* flew. . . . I. viii. 5. 3
his shield, that covered was, . . . *open* flew; . . . I. viii. 19. 2
key found not at all . . . to *open* it withall; . . . I. viii. 37. 5
all her filthy feature *open* showne, . . . I. viii. 49. 8
From living eies her *open* shame to hide, . . . I. viii. 50. 4
made an *open* passage for the gushing flood. . . . I. ix. 36. 9
Her necke and brests were ever *open* bare, . . . I. x. 30. 7
Their gates to all were *open* evermore, . . . I. x. 36. 6
two broad Beacons, sett in *open* fieldes, . . . I. xi. 14. 3
Taking advantage of his *open* jaw, . . . I. xi. 53. 6
He badd to *open* wyde his brasen gate, . . . I. xii. 3. 6
All in the *open* hall amazed stood . . . I. xii. 25. 1
By forged treason or by *open* fight, . . . II. i. 3. 3
The great earthes wombe they *open* to the sky, . . . II. i. 60. 2
her dores to all stand *open* wide. . . . II. iii. 41. 9
made a large And *open* gash therein: . . . II. v. 6. 5
the dore To him did *open* and affoorded way: . . . II. vii. 26. 2
dore forthright To him did *open,* . . . II. vii. 35. 3
The gate was *open;* . . . II. vii. 40. 3
from *open* heat Her selfe to shroud, . . . II. vii. 53. 4
open to their friendes, and closed to their foes. . . . II. ix. 23. 9
readily they shut and *open* might. . . . II. ix. 46. 8
Were to those Pagans made an *open* pray, . . . II. x. 62. 4
T' assayle with *open* force or hidden guyle, . . . II. xi. 7. 4
Remounts againe into the *open* ayre, . . . II. xi. 36. 8
An *open* passage through his riven brest, . . . II. xi. 37. 4
ever *open* stood to all Which thither came; . . . II. xii. 46. 2
as through an *open* plaine they yode, . . . III. i. 4. 1
into termes of *open* outrage brust, . . . III. i. 48. 2
Til thou in *open* fielde adowne be smott: . . . III. ii. 46. 5
To commun accidents stil *open* layd, . . . III. v. 36. 7
th' *open* freshnes of the gentle aire, . . . III. viii. 11. 4
Broke into *open* fire and rage extreme; . . . III. viii. 26. 5
in *open* place and commune bord . . . III. x. 6. 5
Through *open* outrage he her bore away, . . . III. x. 27. 6
that yron wicket *open* flew, . . . III. xii. 3. 3
That brasen dore flew *open,* . . . III. xii. 29. 7
He made him *open* chalenge, . . . IV. ii. 12. 9
The *open* wrongs thou doest me day by day: . . . IV. ii. 13. 2
He *open* shewd, that all men it mote marke: . . . IV. iv. 15. 5
The same aloft he hung in *open* vew, . . . IV. iv. 16. 1
Her lovely Amoret did *open* shew; . . . IV. v. 13. 2
in an *open* Turney lately held, . . . IV. vi. 6. 6
compeld To *open* unto him the prison dore, . . . IV. ix. 8. 2
them late had foyled In *open* turney, . . . IV. ix. 36. 3
'Before that Castle was an *open* plaine, . . . IV. x. 8. 1
The same to all stoode alwaies *open* wide; . . . IV. x. 16. 4
Unto the porch approcht which *open* stood; . . . IV. x. 31. 2
unto Venus grace the gate doth *open* right. . . . IV. x. 35. 9
Came to the *open* hall to listen . . . V. iii. 13. 8
thether also came in *open* sight Fayre Florimell, . . . V. iii. 14. 1
unto all himselfe there *open* shewed, . . . V. iii. 20. 5
Ne he his mouth would *open* unto wight, . . . V. iii. 34. 1
drawing him out of the *open* hall . . . V. iii. 37. 3
Soone as the gates were *open* to them set, . . . V. iv. 38. 1
Before the city gate, in *open* sight; . . . V. iv. 46. 5
Would to his hope a windowe *open* wyde, . . . V. v. 39. 3
meaning to suppresse both forged guile And *open* force: . . V. vi. 7. 4
But fild with courage . . . she bad to *open* bold, . . . V. vii. 25. 6
Which breaking *open* with indignant ire, . . . V. vii. 37. 4

Open—*Continued.*
Stood *open* wyde to all men day and night; . . . V. ix. 22. 4
if all fayle, yet farewell *open* field; . . . V. x. 24. 5
for her entrailes made an *open* way To issue forth; . . . V. xi. 31. 3
By *open* force to fetch her quite away: . . . V. xi. 51. 2
There to be pitched on the *open* plaine; . . . V. xii. 10. 2
Like as a tender Rose in *open* plaine, . . . V. xii. 13. 1
maintayne That Tyrants part with close or *open* ayde, . . . V. xii. 25. 6
Did spred abroad and throw in th' *open* wynd: . . . V. xii. 33. 7
crie Unto the ward to *open* to him hastilie. . . . VI. i. 22. 9
sought by *open* might To overthrow, . . . VI. v. 13. 4
Shun secresie, and talke in *open* sight: . . . VI. vi. 14. 8
what it dare not doe by *open* might, . . . VI. vii. 1. 7
From thence into the *open* fields he fled, . . . VI. ix. 4. 1
In th' *open* fields an Infant left alone; . . . VI. ix. 14. 6
It was an hill plaste in an *open* plaine, . . . VI. x. 6. 1
He durst not enter into th' *open* greene, . . . VI. x. 11. 1
he forth went into th' *open* light, . . . VI. xi. 47. 6
She forth gan lay unto the *open* light The litle babe, . . . VI. xii. 7. 4
She in the *open* fields had loosely layd . . . VI. xii. 16. 4
Rent up her brest, and bosome *open* layd, . . . VI. xii. 19. 4
ran at him amaine With *open* mouth, . . . VI. xii. 26. 5
Whether by *open* force, or counsell wise: . . . VII. vi. 21. 8
then into the *open* light they forth him brought. . . . VII. vi. 47. 9
Open the temple gates unto my love, . . . *Epith.* 204
Open them wide that she may enter in, . . . *Epith.* 205
Prepare your selves, and *open* wide your harts . . . *H.L.* 33
Descended to the Rivers *open* vewing, . . . *Proth.* 166
Opened. Tho *opened* he the dore, . . . *S.C.* May 278
opened his packe, . . . *S.C.* May 287
one, *opened,* mote unfolde many moe. . . . *S.C.* S. 14
he *opened* the dore, . . . *S.C.* S. 220
Each dore he *opened* without any breach, . . . I. viii. 34. 8
when they knockt, The Porter *opened* unto them . . . I. x. 5. 4
opened his dull eyes, that light mote in them shine. . . . I. x. 18. 9
opened wide a red floodgate. . . . II. v. 7. 9
dore, Which to them *opened* of his owne accord, . . . II. vii. 31. 3
when it *opened,* no man might it close, . . . II. ix. 23. 8
first *opened* The bowels of wide Fraunce, . . . II. x. 23. 6
The windowes of bright heaven *opened* had, . . . II. xi. 3. 2
double gates it had which *opened* wide, . . . III. vi. 31. 5
to the wound his weake heart *opened* wyde: . . . III. ix. 29. 2
that stormy blast Which first it *opened,* . . . III. xii. 27. 3
to me *opened* wide. . . . IV. x. 14. 3
thenceforth unto daunger *opened* way. . . . V. v. 9. 4
She to a window came that *opened* West, . . . V. vi. 7. 4
opened had the welspring of his blood; . . . V. viii. 35. 2
Then caused he the gates be *opened* wyde; . . . V. viii. 51. 1
The gate soone *opened* to receive him in; . . . VI. i. 23. 2
Opening. *opening* streight the Sparre, forth to him came, . . V. xi. 4. 2
Openly. out of court him scourged *openly.* . . . V. iii. 38. 5
openly Did chalenge Calidore to wrestling game; . . . VI. ix. 43. 5
Operation. judge of Natures cunning *operation,* . . . *T.M.* 501
Ophir. pearles of Ynde, or gold of *Opher,* . . . *Col.* 490
Opinion. Through strong *opinion* of his matchlesse might; . II. ii. 18. 6
Now with *opinion* of his owne more worth, . . . IV. ii. 12. 3
Opinions. Devices, dreames, *opinions* unsound, . . . II. ix. 51. 7
Opportunity. to slipp away, Soone as appeard safe *opportunitie:* I. ii. 41. 7
fit *opportunity* To stirre up strife . . . IV. ii. 11. 7
Oppose. all which did against his course *oppose,* . . . *Bel.*[2] xiv. 12
their powre against her right *oppose:* . . . V. x. 12. 5
when he found no more T' *oppose* against his powre . . . V. x. 38. 6
Opposed. Nor thou *oppos'd* against thine owne puissance; . . *Ro.* xiii. 8
'Gainst which the noble sonne of Telamon *Oppos'd* himselfe, . . *Gn.* 514
two mirrours, by *opposd* reflexion, . . . *H.B.* 181
Opposing. th' heaven it selfe, *opposing* gainst her might, . . . *Ro.* xviii. 11
Opposition. By others *opposition* or obliquid view. . . . VII. vii. 54. 9
Oppress. Whilest Ignorance the Muses doth *oppresse.* . . . *T.M.* 288
Upon them fell, and did unwares *oppresse;* . . . *Ti.* 572
do not spare . . . but doe both *oppresse?* . . . *D.* 203
appall My feeble corage, and my heart *oppresse,* . . . II. iii. 44. 6
Her other sonne fast sleeping did *oppresse,* . . . II. x. 35. 8
him with multitude *oppresse;* . . . III. iii. 33. 4
all the passions . . . Did him attonce *oppresse,* . . . III. x. 17. 9
an huge heape of singultes did *oppresse* His strugling soule, . III. xi. 12. 1
ne let sleepe *oppresse* Her heavy eyes, . . . III. xi. 55. 6
Ne suffred slothfull sleepe her eyelids to *oppresse.* . . . V. vi. 34. 9
To rend and teare what so she can *oppresse;* . . . V. xi. 24. 4
sought with lawlesse powre him to *oppresse,* . . . V. xi. 44. 4
they doe me with multitude *oppresse,* . . . V. xi. 51. 6
for like cause faire Belge did *oppresse,* . . . V. xii. 2. 6
with strong powre did them long time *oppresse;* . . . V. xii. 24. 4
round about with boystrous strokes *oppresse,* . . . VI. vi. 26. 2
Might them *oppresse,* and painefully turmoile, . . . VI. viii. 23. 4
do him assayle on every side, And sore *oppresse,* . . . VI. xi. 48. 7
a Tygre, . . . doth felly him *oppresse.* . . . *Am.* lvi. 4
Oppressed. she, alas, *opprest,* Fell to the ground . . . *Pet.* i. 11
Under deep ruines, with huge walls *opprest,* . . . *Ro.* i. 2
Sith that the greatest often are *opprest,* . . . *Van.* xii. 7
gentle slumbring sleep *oppressed* him . . . *Gn.* 239
His inly grieved minde full sore *opprest;* . . . *Gn.* 643
With griefe of mournefull great mishap *opprest,* . . . *D.* 2
flowring pride, *opprest* With early frosts, . . . *D.* 27
With inward anguish and great griefe *opprest:* . . . *As.* 206
with death *opprest* He ror'd aloud, . . . I. iii. 42. 8
Una, with huge heavinesse *opprest,* . . . I. vi. 40. 2
The Redcrosse knight is . . . By Gyaunt proud *opprest:* . . . I. vii. Arg.
him, that had them long *opprest* with tort, . . . I. xii. 4. 4
With lips full pale, and foltring tong *opprest,* . . . II. i. 47. 4
Hath with so huge misfortune you *opprest;* . . . II. i. 48. 7

Oppressed—*Continued.*
all his sences were with deadly fit *opprest* II. vii. 66. 9
the weake boughes, with so rich load *opprest* II. xii. 55. 5
The faire Enchauntresse, so unwares *opprest,* II. xii. 81. 8
Seeking the weake *oppressed* to relieve, III. i. 3. 8
When feeble nature felt her selfe *opprest,* III. ii. 29. 3
'what evill plight Hath thee *opprest,* III. ii. 30. 8
till him *oppressed* hard The heavie plague III. v. 14. 8
seized every sence with sorrow sore *opprest* III. vi. 10. 9
'You, that are the most *opprest* III. x. 41. 4
th' enchaunter which had her . . . with foule outrages *opprest.* III. xii. 41. 5
Oppressed her, and there . . . Got these three lovely babes, IV. ii. 45. 8
his wearie sprite, *opprest* With fleshly weaknesse, IV. v. 43. 2
With ods of so unequall match *opprest,* IV. ix. 32. 2
the passion that her heart *opprest;* IV. xii. 8. 7
opprest The faire Irena with his foule misdeede, V. i. 13. 3
did him entrap In traytrous traine, or had unwares *opprest;* V. vi. 4. 4
by his powre *oppressed* every one, V. x. 30. 3
Against these pesants which have me *opprest,* V. xi. 57. 3
whilest Calepine By Turpine is *opprest* VI. iii. Arg.
Being *oppressed* by that faytour bold, VI. iv. 1. 7
Through feeblenesse, which all his limbes *oppressed* has. VI. v. 31. 9
being tyrde with travell, and *opprest* With sorrow, VI. viii. 34. 4
A sodaine sickenesse which her sore *opprest,* VI. xi. 7. 8
was so *opprest,* That he no word could speake, VI. xi. 28. 4
paines which him *opprest* *Am.* lxiii. 12
Oppresseth. with sharpe fits thy tender hart *oppresseth* sore: III. iii. 21. 9
Oppressing. With wrongfull powre *oppressing* others V. i. 7. 9
So tyrannizing and *oppressing* all, V. x. 14. 1
then *oppressing* him with urgent paine, VI. iv. 22. 6
That huge great foole *oppressing* th' other Knight, VI. viii. 28. 2
(*Oppressing* them with power unequally,) VII. vii. 14. 7
Oppression. Through strong *oppression* of his powre extort, V. ii. 5. 8
yeelded you to proude *oppression* Of womens powre, V. iv. 26. 4
For his huge powre and great *oppression,* V. x. 9. 4
Oppressions. Done through the Foxes great *oppressions,* *Hub.* 1312
Oppressor's. withstond *Oppressours* powre by armes and puissant hond? II. viii. 56. 5
gard her to defend from bold *oppressors* might VI. v. 7. 9
Ops. *Ops,* of the earth; VII. vii. 26. 6
Or (*partial list*).
In raine, *or* snowe, *or* haile, *Ro.* xx. 8
Or Diggon her is, *or* I missaye *S.C.* S. 2
Or bene they chaffred, *or* at mischiefe dead? *S.C.* S. 10
Or it mens follies mote be forst to fayne, . . . *Or,* *S.C.* O. 75, 77
Find entertainment *or* in Court *or* Schoole; *T.M.* 410
I found miscaried *or* in plaine *or* wood *D.* 140
'Say on, Fradubio, then, *or* man *or* tree,' I. ii. 34. 1
Or thine the fault, *or* mine the error is, I. iii. 39. 4
Or Bacchus merry fruit . . . *Or* Cybeles franticke rites I. vi. 15. 2, 3
Or let him dye, . . . *Or* let him die at ease, I. ix. 38. 8, 9
since mine he is, *or* free *or* bond, I. xii. 28. 1
Or did his life her fatall date expyre, *Or* did he fall by treason, *or* by fight? II. viii. 24. 3, 4
deeme unworthy *or* of love *or* life, IV. xii. 16. 6
Oracles. with deepe *Oracles* their verses fill: *T.M.* 562
powreth forth these *oracles* so sage Of that high powre, *Col.* 825
Orange. a Woman . . . of *Orenge* colour hew: *Rev.* ii. 2
Oranochy. *See* **Orinoco.**
Orcus. *Orcus* tame, whome nothing can persuade, II. xii. 41. 7
Appearing like the mouth of *Orcus* griesly grim: VI. xii. 26. 9
Ordain. As the Great Judge at first did it *ordaine,* *D.* 363
Before her gate high God did Sweate *ordaine,* II. iii. 41. 5
who can shun the chance that dest'ny doth *ordaine?* III. i. 37. 9
(high God did so *ordaine*) III. vii. 27. 1
'They live, they die, like as he doth *ordaine,* V. ii. 41. 1
those whom heaven did at first *ordaine,* *H.B.* 206
As their great Maker did at first *ordaine,* *H.H.B.* 201
Ordained. Ne was it so by institution *Ordained* first, *Hub.* 145
We but his shepheard swaines *ordain'd* to bee *Hub.* 444
craftie Reynold was a Priest *ordained,* *Hub.* 556
in their secret doome *Ordained* have, *Mui.* 226
Engin, . . . ramd with bollet rownd, *ordaind* to kill, I. vii. 13. 4
shunnne the death *ordaynd* by destinie? I. ix. 42. 8
Where is for the *ordained* a blessed end: I. x. 61. 5
Encountred him in batteill well *ordaind,* II. x. 18. 4
She hath *ordaind* this law, which we approve, III. i. 26. 6
ordaynd to bee The spouse of Britomart, III. iii. 26. 1
such as eternall fate *Ordained* hath, III. vi. 32. 7
As her Creatresse had in charge to her *ordain'd.* III. viii. 10. 9
(so the fates *ordaind*) Wedlocke contract in blood, III. ix. 42. 5
To them *ordained* by eternall fate: IV. ii. 50. 5
The wicked steele, for mischiefe first *ordained,* IV. iv. 24. 3
As their Almightie maker first *ordained,* IV. x. 35. 3
Proteus, that hath *ordayn'd* my sonne to die; IV. xii. 31. 2
He pitcht upon a pole, on high *ordayned;* V. ii. 19. 4
solemne feasts and giusts *ordain'd* therefore: V. iii. 2. 6
judgement so unjust against him had *ordayned.* V. iii. 35. 9
To bring it to her husband new *ordained,* V. iv. 13. 7
that same wretched man, *ordayned* to die, V. iv. 25. 1
Thus having all things well in peace *ordayned,* VI. vi. 41. 1
as is by law *ordayned* In cases like; VI. vii. 36. 5
was the tyme *ordayned* For such a dismall deed, VI. viii. 44. 6
(as Fortune had *ordayned*) VI. xi. 3. 3
so bad end for hereticks *ordayned;* *Am.* xlviii. 6
for this time it ill *ordained* was, *Epith.* 270
Ordeal. by *ordele,* or by blooddy fight, V. i. 25. 3
Order. *See* **Battle-order.**
you . . . doo in *order* stand *Gn.* 480
Of smoothest marble stone in *order* set, *Gn.* 663

Order—*Continued.*
they so ill Did *order* their affaires, *Hub.* 560
To let him knowe the *order* of the thing *Hub.* 1212
let the rest in *order* thee ensew *T.M.* 54
every flowre and herbe there set in *order:* *Mui.* 172
his gins . . . Drest in good *order* as he could *Mui.* 388
As everie one in *order* lov'd him best, *As.* Interl. 224
The which I here in *order* will rehearse, *As.* Interl. 227
That noble *order* hight of maidenhed, I. vii. 46. 4
of their *order* she was Patronesse, I. x. 44. 8
that no looser heares Did out of *order* stray II. ii. 15. 9
So kept she them in *order,* II. ii. 38. 9
on me she deigned to bestowe *Order* of Maydenhead, II. ii. 42. 4
in good *order,* and with dew regard; II. ix. 25. 4
knew them how to *order* without blame, II. ix. 28. 5
Did *order* all th' Achates in seemely wise, II. ix. 31. 4
goodly *order* and great workmans skill II. ix. 33. 1
As in that old mans booke they were in *order* told. II. x. 4. 9
three sonnes, the which in *order* raynd, II. x. 74. 1
To *order* them as best to thee doth seeme, III. iii. 2. 3
her loose lockes to dight in *order* dew III. vii. 11. 2
To call them all in *order* to her ayde, III. viii. 4. 6
paynted plumes in goodly *order* dight, III. xii. 8. 2
none of them once out of *order* went, IV. ii. 36. 7
Shall else be told in *order,* as it fell IV. v. 28. 6
Ye will recount to us in *order* dew IV. ix. 40. 7
In *order* as they came could I recount them well IV. xi. 9. 9
in *order* seemly good Did on the Thamis attend, IV. xi. 44. 7
Yet were they all in *order,* IV. xii. 3. 4
each estate quite out of *order* goth? V. ii. 37. 3
Them selves thereto preparde in *order* dew; V. v. 1. 7
His name hight *Order;* V. ix. 23. 8
Great hostes of men in *order* martiall, V. xii. 4. 8
In *order* as it did to him arize VI. i. 5. 5
warres darraine Against the heaven in *order* battailous, VI. vii. 41. 7
Thereto they usde one most accursed *order,* VI. viii. 36. 1
round about her move in *order* excellent VI. x. 13. 9
In good estate, and in meet *order* ranged, VII. vi. 5. 3
Natures Sergeant (that is *Order*) VII. vii. 4. 6
Bade *Order* call them all VII. vii. 27. 9
These, marching softly, thus in *order* went; VII. vii. 32. 1
is of late far out of *order* gone VII. vii. 51. 4
Did place them all in *order,* *H.L.* 87
From thence to mount aloft, by *order* dew, *H.H.B.* 24
Ordered. *See* **Evil-ordered.**
Sith then they so have *ordred,* *D.* 369
The which beside the gate for swyne was *ordered* III. ix. 11. 9
Mov'd by your might and *ordered* by your ayde, VII. vii. 49. 7
Orderly. In manner of a maske, enranged *orderly* III. xii. 5. 9
Like belles in greatnesse *orderly* succeed, IV. v. 36. 8
Orders. Broke their rude troupes, and *orders* did confownd, II. ix. 15. 7
now he hath new lawes and *orders* new Imposd on all, V. x. 27. 6
Ordinance. Well seemd the Ape to like this *ordinaunce;* *Hub.* 173
Nor *ordinaunce* so needfull, but that hee Would violate, *Hub.* 1162
There added was by goodly *ordinaunce* II. ix. 30. 3
hideous *Ordinaunce* Upon the Bulwarkes cruelly did play, II. xi. 14. 3
The goodly *ordinaunce* of this rich Place, III. xi. 53. 2
heare the *ordenance* thonder, IV. ii. 16. 8
marching thrise in warlike *ordinance,* IV. iii. 5. 7
Ordinary. Depriv'd of sense and *ordinarie* reason, *Hub.* 11
to the *Ordinarie* of them complain'd, *Hub.* 562
Ordure. In which what filth and *ordure* did appeare, VI. xii. 24. 5
Ore. rude *owre,* not purifide II. vii. 5. 3
Some stird the molten *owre* with ladles great; II. vii. 36. 8
all the gravell mixt with golden *owre:* III. iv. 18. 6
Orestes. Pylades and *Orestes* by his syde; IV. x. 27. 4
Organ. Who made my hand the *organ* of his might: II. i. 33. 3
Organs. let the roring *Organs* loudly play *Epith.* 218
Orgoglio. 'O great *Orgoglio!* greatest under skye, I. vii. 14. 5
'O! helpe, *Orgoglio;* helpe! or els we perish all.' I. viii. 20. 9
Whom great *Orgoglio* . . . Had made his caytive thrall: I. viii. 32. 7
huge and hideous . . . And sib to great *Orgolio,* VI. vii. 41. 8
Orichalc. costly *Oricalche* from strange Phoenice, *Mui.* 78
Orient. an *orient* perfect pearle, *Rev.* iv. 10
To shew in Heaven his brightnes *orient;* *Ti.* 389
like pure *Orient* perles adowne it trild; II. xii. 78. 5
like to *orient* perles did purely shyne III. vii. 9. 3
arayd with much more *orient* hew, *H.B.* 79
Oriental. the golden *Orientall* gate Of greatest heaven I. v. 2. 1
Orifice. wipt away the gelly blood From th' *orifice;* III. iv. 40. 7
At that wide *orifice* her trembling hart Was drawne forth, III. xii. 21. 1
closely rankled under th' *orifis:* IV. xii. 22. 7
Origan. Bathing her selfe in *origane* and thyme: I. ii. 40. 7
Orimont. The first of them was hight Sir *Orimont,* V. iii. 5. 1
Orinoco. Rich *Oranochy,* thought but knowen late; IV. xi. 21. 7
Orion. *Orion,* flying fast from hissing snake, II. ii. 46. 2
huge *Orion,* that doth tempests still portend; IV. xi. 13. 9
by Dianaes doom unjust Slew great *Orion;* VII. vii. 39. 8
Orion's. scorching flames of fierce *Orions* hound; I. iii. 31. 6
Orkney. the king of *Orkeny,* III. iii. 37. 6
Ornament. Rome, living, was the worlds sole *ornament,* *Ro.* xxix. 13
ornament of great Joves progenie, *Gn.* 14
The great Argoan ships brave *ornament,* *Gn.* 210
Lawrell, th' *ornament* of Phoebus toyle *Gn.* 672
founded for the Kingdomes *ornament,* *Hub.* 1181
That wont to be the worlds chiefe *ornament,* *T.M.* 74
For vertues meed and *ornament* of wit, *T.M.* 310
One onelie lives, her ages *ornament,* *T.M.* 571
now art made the heavens *ornament,* *Ti.* 674
reft the spoyle his *ornament* to bee; *Mui.* 68

Ornament—*Continued.*
To loose both her and bounties *ornament*. . . . . *D.* 224
She is the *ornament* of womankind, ... *Col.* 498
Paragone Of peerlesse price, and *ornament* of praise, ... *Col.* 549
And steale from each some part of *ornament*. . . . . . . *Ded. Son.* xvii. 8
a boxe . . . Embowd with gold and gorgeous *ornament,* . . . I. ix. 19. 2
on your shield is set for *ornament!'* . . . . II. i. 27. 7
Glistring in armes and warlike *ornament,* . . . . II. xi. 24. 2
With golden wreath and gorgeous *ornament;* . . . . III. vii. 11. 3
Decked with many a costly *ornament,* . . . . III. viii. 12. 2
gazing on that Chambers *ornament,* . . . . III. xii. 29. 2
That lost faire Ladies *ornament* should weare, ... IV. ii. 26. 4
To you that *ornament* of hers pertaines . . . . IV. ii. 27. 6
Which he atchiev'd to his great *ornament;* . . . . IV. ii. 39. 4
With gold and many a gorgeous *ornament,* . . . . IV. iii. 38. 7
This pretious *ornament,* they say, did make, ... IV. v. 4. 3
In her faire visage voide of *ornament,* . . . . V. v. 12. 4
is unto the starres an *ornament,* . . . . VI. x. 13. 8
Made for to be the worlds most *ornament,* . . . . *Am.* liii. 10
The third, my love, my lifes last *ornament,* . . . . *Am.* lxxiv. 9
Be unto her a goodly *ornament,* . . . . *Epith.* 432
'Ye gentle Birdes! the worlds faire *ornament,* . . . . *Proth.* 91
Ornaments. Then tooke the shepheards Kingly *ornaments,* . . *Ro.* xviii. 5
Delights of life, and *ornaments* of light! . . . . *Hub.* 762
Those royall *ornaments* to steale away? . . . . *Hub.* 998
th' *ornaments* of wisdome are bereft? . . . . *T.M.* 489
Doth scorne the pride of wonted *ornaments:* . . . . *T.M.* 544
all the *ornaments* of wondrous wit, ... *Col.* 189
comprise Those glorious *ornaments* of hevenly grace, ... *Ded. Son.* xvi. 7
Wont to robbe churches of their *ornaments,* . . . . I. iii. 17. 2
that witch they disaraid, And robd of . . . *ornaments* . . . . I. viii. 46. 3
Sith her Prince Arthur of proud *ornaments* . . . spoyld. . . . II. i. 22. 6
shewd them naked, deckt with many *ornaments*. . . . . II. v. 32. 9
all the *ornaments* of Floraes pride, ... II. xii. 50. 5
The same, with all the other *ornaments,* . . . . III. iii. 59. 1
The goodly *ornaments* of beautie bright; . . . . III. v. 8. 6
Of all the *ornaments* of knightly name, ... V. v. 20. 4
all those pretious *ornaments* deface. . . . . *Am.* xxxi. 4
Song! made in lieu of many *ornaments,* . . . . *Epith.* 427
faire Dames! the worlds deare *ornaments* . . . . *H.B.* 162
With gifts of wit, and *ornaments* of nature, ... *Proth.* 171
Orphan. 'God blesse thee, poore *Orphane!* . . . . *S.C.* May 191
worse and worse, young *Orphane,* be thy payne, ... II. i. 61. 6
Poore *Orphane!* in the wild world scattered, ... II. ii. 2. 5
Orphan's. Defending Ladies cause and *Orphans* right, ... III. ii. 14. 6
Orphans. the tender *Orphans* of the dead . . . . I. x. 43. 2
Orpheus. did Dan *Orpheus* repress The streames of Hebrus . *Gn.* 180
Yet was the guilt thereof, *Orpheus,* in thee. . . . . *Gn.* 436
valiant fortune made Dan *Orpheus* bolde; . . . . *Gn.* 449
cruell *Orpheus,* thou much crueller, ... *Gn.* 470
With *Orpheus,* and with Linus, and the choice . . . . *Ti.* 333
Which *Orpheus* for Eurydice did make, ... *Ti.* 391
Dan *Orpheus* was seene Wylde beasts . . . to lead, ... *Ti.* 607
Orpheus, that . . . did take His silver Harpe in hand . . . . IV. ii. 1. 7
when *Orpheus* did recoure His Leman . . . . IV. x. 58. 4
Orpheus with his harp theyr strife did bar. . . . . *Am.* xliv. 4
So *Orpheus* did for his owne bride! . . . . *Epith.* 16
Orpheus, daring to provoke the yre Of damned fiends, ... *H.L.* 234
Orpheus'. To follow *Orpheus* musicke through the land: . . . *Gn.* 452
Orpine. Coole Violets, and *Orpine* growing still, ... *Mui.* 193
Orsilochus. how Camill' hath slaine The huge *Orsilochus,* . . III. iv. 2. 9
Orthrus. With his two-headed dogge that *Orthrus* hight; . . . V. x. 10. 6
Orthrus begotten by great Typhaon And foule Echidna . . . V. x. 10. 7
Osiris. Calling him great *Osyris,* . . . . V. vii. 2. 5
Osyris . . . The justest man alive and truest did appeare. . . V. vii. 2. 8
Like as *Osyris* signifies the Sunne: . . . . V. vii. 4. 8
Like to *Osyris* in all just endever: . . . . V. vii. 22. 5
that same Crocodile *Osyris* is, ... V. vii. 22. 6
Osric. Offricke and *Osricke,* twinnes unfortunate, ... III. iii. 37. 3
Ossa. the ruines of great *Ossa* hill, ... II. x. 3. 3
Ostriches. Some mouth'd like greedy *Oystriges;* . . . . . . II. xi. 12. 4
Oswald. Against the good king *Oswald,* . . . . III. iii. 38. 4
he godly *Oswald* shall subdew, ... III. iii. 39. 3
Oswin. Whose brother *Oswin,* daunted with like dread, . . . III. iii. 39. 5
Oten, Oth. *See* **Oaten, Oath.**
Other (*partial list*).
This ship to which none *other* might compare: . . . . *Bel.*² xiii. 8
Of which the one was blacke, the *other* white: . . . . *Pet.* i. 7
One foote on Thetis, th' *other* on the Morning, ... *Ro.* iv. 2
One hand on Scythia, th' *other* on the More, ... *Ro.* iv. 3
by the greatnes of none *other,* . . . . *Ro.* vi. 7
That *other* earthlie power should not resemble Her . . . . *Ro.* vi. 12
The firie sunnes both one and *other* hous: . . . . *Ro.* x. 8
each to *other* working cruell wrongs, ... *Ro.* xxiv. 7
That can to *other* give eternall dayes: . . . . *Ro.* Env. 8
made all *other* Foules his thralls to bee: . . . . *Van.* iv. 4
all *other* beasts to scorne. . . . . *Van.* viii. 8
To *other* delights they would encline: . . . . *S.C.* F. 60
Warning all *other* to take heede. . . . . *S.C.* Ap. 90
after her the *other* Muses trace, ... *S.C.* Ap. 102
they bene hyred for little pay Of *other,* . . . . *S.C.* May 48
And *thother* for leaving his Lords taske, ... *S.C.* May 53
Rather then *other* should scorne at me: . . . . *S.C.* May 60
shoulden shepheards *other* things tend, ... *S.C.* May 63
They sleepen in rest, well as *other* moe: . . . . *S.C.* May 68
God giveth good for none *other* end. . . . . *S.C.* May 72
through this, and *other* their miscreaunce . . . . *S.C.* May 91
interrupted all her *other* speache . . . . *S.C.* May 209
From *other* shades hath weand . . . . *S.C.* Jun. 2
The corn is theyrs, let *other* thresh, ... *S.C.* Jul. 191

Other—*Continued.*
yonder heardgrome, and none *other,* . . . . *S.C.* Au. 45
you cannot wel ken, . . . from *other* men: . . . . *S.C.* S. 43
Other sayne, but how truely I note, ... *S.C.* S. 110
other the fat from their beards doen lick: . . . . *S.C.* S. 123
We bene of fleshe, men as *other* bee, ... *S.C.* S. 238
Where *other* powers farre different I see, ... *Gn.* 420
th' *other* was with Thetis love assaid, ... *Gn.* 491
th' *other* strove for to defend The force . . . . *Gn.* 523
But th' *other* joy'd, ... *Gn.* 526
'Here manie *other* like Heroes bee. . . . . *Gn.* 593
whatsoever *other* flowre of worth, And whatso *other* hearb . . *Gn.* 681, 682
they doo swinke . . . to feed the *other,* . . . . *Hub.* 163
if that anie *other* place you have, ... *Hub.* 277
But seeke some *other* way to gaine by giving, ... *Hub.* 350
in *other* state abroad to range: . . . . *Hub.* 356
Or *other* great one in the worldes eye, ... *Hub.* 490
the scorne of *other* beasts . . . . *Hub.* 603
Besides, he could doo manie *other* poynts, ... *Hub.* 696
whilst that *other* like vaine wits he pleased, ... *Hub.* 709
At *other* times he casts to sew the chace . . . . *Hub.* 743
Ne *other* knowledge ever did attaine, ... *Hub.* 837
Or corne, or cattle, or such *other* ware, ... *Hub.* 873
beg the sute the which the *other* ment. . . . . *Hub.* 882
that ye let none *other* ever drawe . . . . *Hub.* 1053
whilest the *other* Peeres, for povertie, ... *Hub.* 1177
There, on the *other* side, I did behold . . . . *Ti.* 8
when th' one dies, th' *other* then beginnes . . . . *Ti.* 388
Scorns th' one and th' *other* in his deeper skill. . . . . . . *Ti.* 448
from the one he could to th' *other* coast . . . . *Ti.* 540
Over the Sea from one to *other* side, ... *Ti.* 548
Ne *other* comfort in this world can be, ... *Ti.* 584
to the *other* side To cast mine eye, where *other* sights . . . *Ti.* 587, 588
I saw, on th' *other* side, ... *Ti.* 617
From bed to bed, from one to *other* border, ... *Mui.* 170
The one his bowe and shafts, the *other* Spring . . . . *Mui.* 292
did all *other* Beasts in beawtie staine. . . . . *D.* 112
Throughout the world from one to *other* end, ... *D.* 373
The one, because as I . . .; The *other,* . . . . *D.* 423
To you I sing and to none *other* wight, ... *As.* Pr. 11
A sclender swaine, excelling far each *other,* . . . . *As.* 15
And after him full many *other* moe, ... *As.* Interl. 223
each making *other* mery; . . . . *Col.* 77
Neither envying *other,* . . . . *Col.* 78
whilest the one was watcht, the *other* might . . . . *Col.* 139
What dittie did that *other* shepheard sing: . . . . *Col.* 160
is there *other* then whereon we stand?' . . . . *Col.* 291
other men and beasts and birds doth feed: . . . . *Col.* 297
Both did he *other,* . . . maintaine, And eke . . . . *Col.* 442
rais'd above each *other* starre. . . . . *Col.* 535
To thrust downe *other* into foule disgrace, ... *Col.* 691
do themselves, for want of *other* worke, ... *Col.* 765
to *other* needs, But as a complement . . . . *Col.* 789
And gan by litle learne to love each *other:* . . . . *Col.* 852
she is not like as the *other* crew . . . . *Col.* 931
th' *other* halfe did womans shape retaine, ... I. i. 14. 8
other spelles like terrible, ... I. i. 37. 3
The *other* by him selfe staide, *other* worke to doo. . . . . . I. i. 38. 9
The *other* all with silver overcast; . . . . I. i. 40. 3
No *other* noyse, . . . Might there be heard; . . . . I. i. 41. 6
made a Lady of that *other* Spright, ... I. i. 45. 2
Eftsoones he tooke . . . that false *other* Spright, ... I. ii. 3. 2
rests not so, but *other* meanes doth make, ... I. ii. 9. 6
and ech to *other* yealdeth land. . . . . I. ii. 15. 9
Faire seemely pleasaunce each to *other* makes, ... I. ii. 30. 1
All *other* Dames to have exceeded farre: . . . . I. ii. 36. 2
Th' one seeming such, the *other* such indeede, ... I. ii. 37. 2
quaking hands, and *other* signes of feare: . . . . I. iii. 12. 6
Loth was that *other,* and did faint through feare, ... I. iii. 34. 5
Ne *other* grace vouchsafed them to showe . . . . I. iv. 14. 3
people, . . . Doe ride each *other* upon her to gaze: . . . . . . I. iv. 16. 8
other clothes he could not weare for heate; . . . . I. iv. 22. 2
thousand *other* waies to bait his fleshly hookes. . . . . . . I. iv. 25. 9
On th' *other* side . . . Duessa placed is, ... I. v. 5. 6
With greedy force each *other* doth assayle, ... I. v. 6. 6
So th' one for wrong, the *other* strives for right. . . . . . . I. v. 8. 1
So th' one for wrong, the *other* strives for right, ... I. v. 9. 1
She wandred had from one to *other* Ynd, ... I. vi. 2. 7
she . . . followes *other* game and venery: . . . . I. vi. 22. 5
Go, find some *other* play-fellowes, ... I. vi. 28. 9
they gan, . . . fiersly to assaile Each *other,* . . . . I. vi. 43. 3
sternely bad him *other* businesse plie . . . . I. vi. 46. 7
All *other* powres and knighthood he did scorne. . . . . . . I. vii. 10. 4
He would them gazing blind, or turne to *other* hew. . . . . . I. vii. 35. 9
other bywaies he himselfe betooke, ... I. vii. 50. 3
ne ever *other* answere made. . . . . I. viii. 32. 9
The *other* like a beares uneven paw, ... I. viii. 48. 8
love establish each to *other* trew, ... I. ix. 18. 7
th' *other* for to fight With Unaes foe, ... I. ix. 20. 2
other griesly thing that haunt him aghast. . . . . I. ix. 21. 4
drave Far from that haunt all *other* chearefull fowle, ... I. ix. 33. 8
th' *other* forst him staye, and comforted in feare. . . . . . I. ix. 34. 9
What justice ever *other* judgement taught, ... I. ix. 38. 3
any *other* wight, That hither turnes his steps. . . . . I. x. 10. 2
in her *other* hand she fast did hold . . . . I. x. 13. 7
Her stedfast eyes were bent, ne swarved *other* way. . . . . . I. x. 14. 9
greatly joy each *other* for to see: . . . . I. x. 15. 4
Ne *other* worldly busines did apply: . . . . I. x. 46. 7
boystrous battaile make, each *other* to avenge. . . . . I. xi. 21. 9
his late enimy . . . , or *other* new supplied knight. . . . . . I. xi. 35. 4

Other—*Continued.*

Whose *other* wing, now made unmeete . . . V. v. 15. 3
Ne yet to any *other* wight on ground, . . . V. v. 44. 3
That all his *other* honour overthrew. . . . V. vi. 12. 4
Then gan the *other* further to devize . . . V. vi. 20. 7
one thought, That gave none *other* place. . . . V. vi. 21. 4
after them full many *other* more, . . . V. vi. 29. 3
The *other* over side the Bridge she cast . . . V. vi. 39. 8
The *other* it with force doth overthrow . . . V. vi. 40. 6
One foote was set . . . the *other* fast did stand; . . . V. vii. 7. 2
in her *other* hand She stretched forth . . . V. vii. 7. 4
For *other* beds the Priests there used none, . . . V. vii. 9. 1
shortly did all *other* beasts subdew. . . . V. vii. 16. 7
On th' *other* side her foe appeared . . . V. vii. 27. 9
Which when the *other* heard, . . . V. vii. 28. 5
her no *other* termes should ever tie . . . V. vii. 28. 8
For *other* uses then they them translated; . . . V. vii. 29. 8
in their steede for *other* rayment sought, . . . V. vii. 41. 3
But th' *other* still pursu'd . . . V. viii. 6. 1
the *other* Knight Defeated had the *other* faytour . . . V. viii. 8. 4, 5
thinking to follow fast His *other* fellow Pagan . . . V. viii. 8. 9
Ventailes reare each *other* to behold. . . . V. viii. 12. 5
Either embracing *other* lovingly, . . . V. viii. 14. 6
of all *other* weapons lesse or more, . . . V. viii. 34. 4
what *other* salvage wight, . . . V. ix. 1. 1
leave his proper forme, and *other* shape to take. . . . V. ix. 16. 9
th' one on th' one, The *other* on the *other* side, . . . V. ix. 37. 9
all her *other* honour did obscure, . . . V. ix. 38. 6
many *other* crimes of foule defame . . . V. ix. 43. 2
all her *other* children, . . . Had hid . . . V. x. 19. 3
other meede may hope for none of mee, . . . V. x. 21. 6
when his *other* fellowes saw, . . . V. x. 36. 1
they entring th' one did th' *other* stay, . . . V. x. 36. 5
The *other* which was entred laboured fast . . . V. x. 37. 1
Streight th' *other* fled away, . . . V. x. 37. 7
What *other* meed, then, . . . V. xi. 17. 7
Borne . . . of Echidna base, Or *other* like infernall furies kinde; V. xi. 23. 6
Through *other* great adventures . . . V. xii. 3. 5
The *other* held a snake . . . V. xii. 30. 5
when she wanteth *other* thing to eat, . . . V. xii. 31. 6
The *other* nothing better was then shee, . . . V. xii. 33. 1
A distaffe in her *other* hand she had, . . . V. xii. 36. 6
Then th' *other* comming neare . . . V. xii. 40. 1
whenas each of *other* had a sight, . . . VI. i. 4. 6
Neither of *other* taking pitty nor remorse. . . . VI. i. 33. 9
To whom the *other* did this taunt returne: . . . VI. iii. 31. 6
With th' *other* staide his Lady up . . . VI. iii. 33. 9
ne did the *other* stay, . . . VI. iii. 37. 4
This wize did they each *other* entertaine . . . VI. v. 34. 5
With salve, . . . or *other* mene, . . . VI. vi. 9. 5
ne ech would *other* leave: . . . VI. vi. 15. 9
But each the *other* vow'd t' accompany: . . . VI. vi. 16. 1
But th' *other*, ayming better, . . . VI. vii. 8. 1
But th' *other*, . . . Fayles of her souse, . . . VI. vii. 9. 8
By this the *other*, . . . Himselfe recovering . . . VI. vii. 10. 1
th' one is dead, and th' *other* soone shall die, . . . VI. vii. 13. 3
That *other* swayne, like ashes . . . VI. vii. 17. 8
Like as that *other* knight to him had sayd; . . . VI. vii. 20. 3
with that *other* knight, . . . VI. vii. 25. 2
Or by some *other* violence despoyled: . . . VI. vii. 33. 5
The one or th' *other* better her to use; . . . VI. vii. 40. 2
That all your *other* praises will deface, . . . VI. viii. 2. 5
The whiles that *other* villaine went about . . . VI. viii. 11. 6
such pride the *other* could apall; . . . VI. viii. 26. 7
oppressing th' *other* Knight, . . . VI. viii. 28. 2
With *other* divelish ceremonies met: . . . VI. viii. 45. 7
I forbore To finish then, for *other* present hast, . . . VI. ix. 2. 4
For *other* worldly wealth they cared nought. . . . VI. ix. 5. 6
for him nor *other* none Did care a whit, . . . VI. ix. 10. 7
for *other* he had none; . . . VI. ix. 14. 8
other, that hath litle, asks no more, . . . VI. ix. 30. 5
Who, on the *other* side, did seeme . . . VI. ix. 39. 6
Or *other* daintie thing for her addrest, . . . VI. ix. 40. 4
more conveniently in *other* place . . . VI. ix. 46. 9
Three *other* Ladies did both daunce and sing, . . . VI. x. 12. 3
To be the fourth with those three *other* placed: . . . VI. x. 25. 7
she all *other* countrey lasses farre did passe: . . . VI. x. 25. 9
All *other* lesser lights in light excell; . . . VI. x. 26. 2
Above all *other* lasses beare the bell; . . . VI. x. 26. 4
with *other* much disorder. . . . VI. x. 39. 9
her alone he . . . desired Of all the *other* pray . . . VI. xi. 4. 4
Coridon with many *other* moe, . . . VI. xi. 11. 2
some *other* of the chiefest theeves . . . VI. xi. 15. 1
each to *other* calling . . . VI. xi. 20. 4
Where was his Pastorell? where all the *other* crew? . . . VI. xi. 28. 9
read what destiny Or *other* dyrefull hap . . . VI. xi. 29. 8
neither could to company of th' *other* creepe. . . . VI. xii. 5. 9
For *other* none such passion can contrive . . . VI. xii. 21. 5
to the *other* damned ghosts which dwell . . . VI. xii. 35. 7
all *other* creatures her bad dooings rewed. . . . VII. vi. 4. 9
two steeds, th' one black, the *other* white, . . . VII. vi. 9. 2
least Typhon were againe uprear'd, Or *other* his old foes . . . VII. vi. 15. 9
Which of her Nymphes, or *other* close consort, . . . VII. vi. 51. 5
As those that all the *other* world do fill, . . . VII. vii. 3. 4
thither also came all *other* creatures, . . . VII. vii. 4. 1
Injurie, Which any of thy creatures do to *other* . . . VII. vii. 14. 6
Whom if ye please, I care for *other* none! . . . *Am.* i. 14
All *other* fayre, lyke flowres, untymely fade. . . . *Am.* lxxix. 14
let them eeke bring store of *other* flowers, . . . *Epith.* 46
the Pouke, nor *other* evill sprights, . . . *Epith.* 341

Other—*Continued.*

Each against *other* by all meanes they may, . . . *H.L.* 81
In sight whereof all *other* blisse seemes vaine: . . . *H.L.* 208
know ech *other* here belov'd to bee. . . . *H.B.* 203
wrong it were that any *other* twaine Should . . . *H.B.* 204
more sharply sighted bee Then *other* mens, . . . *H.B.* 233
See more then any *other* eyes can see, . . . *H.B.* 234
These thus in faire each *other* farre excelling, . . . *H.H.B.* 99

Other's. *See* **Another's.**

That shepheardes so witen ech *others* life, . . . *S.C.* May 159
they all eternally complaine. Of *others* wrong, . . . *Gn.* 408
Each doth against the *others* bodie bend . . . *Gn.* 412
neither could the *others* greater might . . . *Mui.* 6
Each *others* equall puissaunce envies, . . . I. ii. 17. 4
each *others* greater pride does spight. . . . I. iv. 14. 9
To make one great by *others* losse is bad excheat. . . . I. v. 25. 9
some shall pay the price of *others* guilt; . . . I. v. 26. 2
none did *others* safety despize, . . . I. ix. 1. 5
friendly each did *others* praise devize, . . . I. ix. 1. 7
each made *others* foe: . . . II. ii. 13. 6
th' *others* pleasing service to abate, . . . II. ii. 19. 5
others pleasure to fulfill. . . . II. iv. 19. 9
naked made each *others* manly spalles; . . . II. vi. 29. 6
so fiers did play On th' *others* helmett, . . . II. vi. 31. 6
each his paynes to *others* profit still employd. . . . II. x. 14. 9
none does *others* happinesse envye; . . . II. xii. 58. 4
Each did the *others* worke more beautify; . . . II. xii. 59. 6
bent his dreadful speare against the *others* head. . . . III. i. 5. 9
To let not *others* honour be defaste . . . III. i. 12. 4
Ne armes to beare against the *others* syde: . . . III. i. 12. 6
crowne himselfe in th' *others* stead: . . . III. iii. 29. 7
why doe wee devise of *others* ill, . . . III. ix. 8. 6
Forgetfull each to have bene ever *others* frend. . . . IV. ii. 14. 9
Each labouring t' advance the *others* gest, . . . IV. iv. 36. 7
lesse esteem'd then th' *others* vertuous government. . . . IV. v. 20. 9
to rue the *others* heavy cheare; . . . IV. vii. 34. 7
each one taking part in *others* aide . . . IV. ix. 24. 7
all the *others* pavement were with yvory spilt. . . . IV. x. 5. 9
had encroched upon *others* share; . . . V. ii. 32. 2
So all the rest did *others* parts empaire, . . . V. ii. 32. 5
others worth with leasings doest deface, . . . V. iii. 20. 8
Ne either sought the *others* strokes to shun, . . . V. vii. 29. 3
either *others* cause to maintaine . . . V. viii. 14. 9
neither could the *others* stroke sustaine, . . . VI. i. 33. 7
gan to intimate Each *others* griefe . . . VI. iii. 12. 5
more grievous then the *others* blowes: . . . VI. vii. 49. 8
to salve each *others* wound: . . . *Am.* lxv. 12
Into the *others* stead: . . . *Epig.* ii. 6
To worke ech *others* joy . . . *H.B.* 200

Others. Ylike as *others*, girt in gawdy greene? . . . *S.C.* May 4
Others the utmost boughs of trees doe crop, . . . *Gn.* 81
mongst manie *others* moe, To be partaker . . . *Hub.* 13
others alwayes have before me stept, . . . *Hub.* 77
with sharp quips joy'd *others* to deface, . . . *Hub.* 707
strive in vertue *others* to excell, . . . *T.M.* 452
Nor yet are sung of *others* for reward, . . . *Ti.* 345
Of *others* Penthia, though not so well: . . . *As.* 194
many *others* mo remaine, . . . *Col.* 448
One ever I, and *others* never none.' . . . *Col.* 479
others trimly dight Their gay attyre; . . . I. iv. 14. 8
some *others* faine To menage steeds, . . . II. iv. 1. 8
Vaine *others* overthrowes who selfe doth overthrow. . . . II. v. 15. 9
Yet *others* she more urgent did devise; . . . II. v. 21. 8
Some framd faire lookes, . . . *Others* sweet wordes, . . . II. v. 33. 4
Some *others* were new driven, . . . II. vii. 5. 5
To climbe aloft, and *others* to excell: . . . II. vii. 46. 7
Others through friendes; *others* for base regard, . . . II. vii. 47. 4
Those that were up themselves kept *others* low; . . . II. vii. 47. 6
Those that were low themselves held *others* hard, . . . II. vii. 47. 7
Others to beare the same away did mynd; . . . II. ix. 31. 8
others it to use according to his kynd. . . . II. ix. 31. 9
Others like Dogs; *others* like Gryphons dreare; . . . II. xi. 8. 4
others did them selves embay . . . II. xii. 60. 9
thy moyst mountaines each on *others* throng, . . . III. iv. 8. 5
Others lay shaded from the scorching heat, . . . III. vi. 17. 8
feeds on wemens flesh as *others* feede on gras. . . . III. vii. 22. 9
For which he *others* wrongs, . . . III. ix. 4. 3
Which he had wrought to many *others* moe. . . . III. xi. 45. 5
each of life sought *others* to deprive, . . . IV. i. 23. 8
life it is to her, when *others* sterve . . . IV. i. 26. 3
Did not, as *others* wont, directly fly . . . IV. iii. 13. 2
many *others* at him likewise ran, . . . IV. iv. 46. 1
bet the *others* backe; . . . IV. ix. 25. 2
Eftsoones the *others* did the field recoure, . . . IV. ix. 25. 3
others, . . . did ly . . . IV. x. 13. 7
teaching *others* to doe right. . . . IV. xi. 18. 9
oppressing *others* of their kind. . . . V. i. 7. 9
maintaine that she all *others* did excell. . . . V. iii. 4. 9
Approv'd that day that she all *others* did excell. . . . V. iii. 15. 9
Both her and eke all *others* to excell: . . . V. iii. 16. 6
They being chased that did *others* chase, . . . V. viii. 5. 5
both her selfe and *others* eke perplext. . . . V. xii. 35. 9
the good which *others* had disprad, . . . V. xii. 36. 9
he seeketh *others* to suppresse, . . . VI. i. 41. 5
'Who will not mercie unto *others* shew, . . . VI. i. 42. 1
Which *others* . . . cannot attaine; . . . VI. ii. 2. 5
Which I to *others* did inflict afore, . . . VI. viii. 22. 4
the bird which gazing still on *others* stands. . . . VI. ix. 11. 9
To passe all *others* on the earth . . . VI. x. 5. 5
with many *others* wide; . . . VI. xi. 18. 5

Others—*Continued.*
Others would through the river him have drive . . . . . VII. vi. 50. 5
others tell that it so beautious was, ... VII. vii. 6. 6
all that are of *others* bredd doth slay; . . . . . VII. vii. 24. 7
Others in Thebes, and *others* other-where; . . . . VII. vii. 53. 6
Whome if you please I care for *others* none. . . . . *Am.*[1] i. 14
others gaze upon theyre shadowes . . . . . *Am.* lxxxvii. 6
Beene to me ayding, *others* to adorne, ... *Epith.* 2
(Those trouts and pikes all *others* doo excell;) . . . . *Epith.* 59
their conceipt, that *others* never see! . . . . . *H.B.* 247
Others'. with the sweete of *others* sweating toyle; . . . . *Hub.* 1152
gathered more store Of the fields honor than the *others* best. . *Mui.* 123
to be instruments of *others* gaines. . . . . . *Col.* 706
That it should not deface all *others* lesser light? . . . . II. iv. 25. 9
with his pride all *others* powre deface: . . . . . II. vii. 41. 8
Ne doest by *others* death ensample take, ... III. iv. 14. 7
and make her th' *others* riches scorne. . . . . . VI. iii. 7. 9
serve their owne necessities with *others* need. . . . . VI. viii. 35. 9
By *others* opposition or obliquid view. . . . . . VII. vii. 54. 9
scorneth *others* ayde; . . . . . . *Am.* lviii. 2
Otherwhere. Whether on hylls, or dales, or *other where,* . . . *S.C.* Jun. 107
As Lordes done *other where;* . . . . . . *S.C.* Jul. 186
otherwhere the snowy substaunce sprent With vermell, ... II. xii. 45. 5
Whose whelpes are stolne away, she being *otherwhere.* . . . . VI. xi. 25. 9
Some say in Crete . . . and others *other-where;* . . . . VII. vii. 53. 6
Otherwhile. *otherwhile* with good encouragement . . . . VI. v. 32. 8
Otherwhiles. *other whiles* vaine toyes she would devize, . . . II. vi. 7. 1
otherwhiles, with gold besprinkeled, ... II. xii. 45. 8
otherwhyles with amorous delights . . . entertaine; . . . . III. x. 8. 1
other-whiles to her she purpos made Of love, ... IV. i. 7. 7
Of love, and *other-whiles* of lustfulnesse, ... IV. i. 7. 8
other-whiles with bitter mockes and mowes . . . . . VI. vii. 49. 6
otherwhiles, for need, he did assay . . . . . VI. ix. 37. 7
And *otherwhyles* . . . Thou doest emmarble . . . . . *H.L.* 138
Otherwise. No *otherwise* than raynie cloud, ... *Ro.* xx. 1
All *otherwise* the state of Poet stands; . . . . . *S.C.* O. 97
by honest wayes, or *otherwise,* . . . . . . *Hub.* 848
Or *otherwise* false Reynold would abuse . . . . . *Hub.* 883
all *otherwise* they doo esteeme . . . . . . *T.M.* 85
all *otherwise* devise, Then we poore shepheards . . . . . *Col.* 784
sue and serve all *otherwise:* . . . . . . *Col.* 786
graunt them grace that *otherwise* would die. . . . . *Col.* 882
who so else doth *otherwise* esteeme, ... *Col.* 889
otherwise His life he led in lawlesse riotise, ... I. iv. 20. 4
by proofe all *otherwise* I weene, ... I. x. 58. 7
Though *otherwise* it did him litle harme: . . . . . II. v. 7. 4
'All *otherwise*' (saide he) 'I riches read, ... II. vii. 12. 1
Yet *otherwise* much worse, if worse might bee, ... IV. i. 18. 8
certes his right name was *otherwize,* . . . . . IV. iv. 42. 7
Might *otherwise* prevaile, or make him cease for ought. . . . V. ii. 22. 9
And *otherwise,* if that he should retire, ... V. ii. 52. 6
Him *otherwise* perswade all that she might, ... VI. v. 33. 6
Sith *otherwise* he could not mend thing past; . . . . . VI. xi. 34. 7
they, which love indeede, looke *otherwise,* . . . . . *H.B.* 211
Othos. there huge *Othos* sits in sad distresse, ... *Gn.* 373
Otter. Like a swift *Otter,* fell through emptinesse, ... III. iii. 33. 7
Ouches. a Persian mitre . . . with crowns and *owches* garnished, I. ii. 13. 5
Adornd with gemmes and *owches* wondrous fayre, ... I. x. 31. 6
Gold, amber, yvorie, perles, *owches,* rings, ... III. iv. 23. 5
Ought (*partial list*). *See* **Aught.**
each thing fained *ought* more warie bee. . . . . . *Hub.* 495
all the Beasts him feared as they *ought,* . . . . . *Hub.* 1106
he rul'd not the Empire, as he *ought?* . . . . . *Hub.* 1251
were he knowne to Cynthia as he *ought,* . . . . . *Col.* 402
when I think of her, as oft I *ought,* . . . . . *Col.* 624
Thus *ought* all lovers of their lord to deeme, ... *Col.* 887
Who then *ought* more to favour her then you, ... *Ded. Son.* xiv. 5
th' Elfin knight, which *ought* that warlike wage, ... I. iv. 39. 7
I *ought* crave pardon, till I there have beene.' . . . . . I. xii. 18. 9
Let nought be hid from me that *ought* to be exprest. . . . . I. xii. 29. 9
all I did, I did but as I *ought.* . . . . . . II. i. 33. 5
Gan smyle on them, that rather *ought* to weepe, ... II. ii. 1. 6
ere the point arrived where it *ought,* . . . . . II. viii. 32. 4
To use that sword so well as he it *ought!*' . . . . . II. viii. 40. 4
fayrely feasted as so noble knightes she *ought.* . . . . . II. x. 77. 9
letteth her that *ought* the scepter weeld, ... II. xi. 2. 3
her knights service *ought,* to hold of her in fee. . . . . III. i. 44. 9
Yet *ought* mens good endevours them confirme, ... III. iii. 25. 8
entraunce, which *ought* evermore . . . be commune: . . . . III. viii. 52. 4
let me die that *ought:* . . . . . . III. xi. 19. 6
ought in friendship for her sake To joyne your force, ... IV. ii. 24. 6
Which Ladies *ought* to love, and seeke for to obtaine. . . . . IV. v. 2. 9
her losse *ought* me to sorrow most, ... IV. ix. 38. 7
let mee live as lovers *ought* to do, ... IV. xii. 10. 2
So *ought* each Knight . . . In swimming be expert, ... V. ii. 16. 8
So *ought* all faytours that true knighthood shame, ... V. iii. 38. 6
it *ought* be rendred her without deniall.' . . . . . V. iv. 15. 9
therefore *ought* it have where ever she it fond. . . . . V. vii. 30. 9
Did to her myld obeysance, as they *ought,* . . . . . V. ix. 34. 4
of the Knight, the which that Castle *ought,* . . . . . VI. iii. 2. 8
where is eke your friend which halfe it *ought?*' . . . . . VI. vii. 16. 5
clothes to cover what they *ought* by kind, ... VI. viii. 50. 4
let us love . . . lyke as we *ought:* . . . . . . *Am.* lxviii. 13
truly pourtray'd, as they *ought* to be, ... *Com. Son.* ii. 6
Oughtest. thou *oughtest* first to know . . . . . V. ii. 34. 6
Our (*partial list*).
pray him leaden *our* daunce. . . . . . *S.C.* Mar. 24
Suffice this hill of *our.* . . . . . . *S.C.* Jul. 76
he *our* life hath left unto us free, ... *H.H.L.* 183
Oure. balefull *Oure,* late staind with English blood, ... IV. xi. 44. 5

Ours (*partial list*).
Neaera *ours,* not theirs, though there she be; . . . . . *Col.* 525
Ourselves (*partial list*).
Such will we fashion both *our selves* to bee, ... *Hub.* 167
Our selves in league of vowed love wee knitt: . . . . . II. iv. 18. 6
Let us in feigned armes *our selves* disguize, ... III. iii. 53. 2
Ouse. The *Ouze,* whom men doe Isis rightly name; . . . . IV. xi. 24. 7
the plenteous *Ouse* came far from land, ... IV. xi. 34. 1
Oze the most of might, ... IV. xi. 37. 6
Out (*partial list*). *See* **In and Out.**
Out of her womb a thousand rayons threw . . . . . *Bel.* ii. 7
Out of her dust like to a worm arise. . . . . . *Bel.* vii. 14
I saw a spring *out* of a rocke forth rayle, ... *Bel.* xii. 1
arise *Out* of the fresh and lustie Lawrell tree, ... *Pet.* iii. 2
cleane *out* of sight; . . . . . . *Pet.* iv. 11
drawne forth *out* of the tombe . . . *out* of eternall night . . *Ro.* v. 7, 8
Out of the earth engendred men of armes . . . . . *Ro.* x. 3
out of her massie wombe forth sent . . . . . *Ro.* xvii. 7
arise *Out* of these mountaines, ... *Ro.* xvii. 12
Olde Rome *out* of her ashes to revive, ... *Ro.* Env. 5
Selfe have I worne *out* thrise threttie yeares, ... *S.C.* F. 17
'I sawe Phoebus thrust *out* his golden hedde, ... *S.C.* Ap. 73
Ne durst againe his fyrye face *out* showe: . . . . . *S.C.* Ap. 78
His Vellet head began to shoote *out,* . . . . . *S.C.* May 185
Tho went the pensife Damme *out* of dore, ... *S.C.* May 229
to paint *out* my unrest, ... *S.C.* Jun. 79
poore my piteous plaints *out* . . . . . . *S.C.* Jun. 80
bene thy Bagpypes renne farre *out* of frame? . . . . . *S.C.* Au. 3
Hasting to raunch the arrow *out,* . . . . . *S.C.* Au. 97
buy his sheepe *out* of the cote, ... *S.C.* S. 40
The more to wind it *out* thou doest swinck, ... *S.C.* S. 132
Say it *out,* Diggon, ... *S.C.* S. 172
let *out* the sheepes bloud at his throte. . . . . . *S.C.* S. 207
he opened the dore, And ranne *out* . . . . . *S.C.* S. 221
No sooner was *out,* but, swifter . . . . . *S.C.* S. 222
to throwe *out* throndring words . . . . . *S.C.* O. 104
And cast hem *out* as rotten . . . . . . *S.C.* D. 118
shot each where *Out* of his golden Charet . . . . . *Gn.* 67
Out of the lowly vallies did arise . . . . . *Gn.* 191
the spirite *out* of his senses flew, ... *Gn.* 292
Out of the land is fled away and gone. . . . . . *Gn.* 360
Out of her mountaines ministred supplies; . . . . . *Gn.* 506
deep Charybdis gulphing in and *out:* . . . . . *Gn.* 542
There plotteth *out* a tombe . . . . . . *Gn.* 652
as occasion Falls *out,* . . . . . . *Hub.* 202
his shooes beaten *out* with traveling. . . . . . *Hub.* 214
So maist thou chaunce mock *out* a Benefice, ... *Hub.* 509
their fortunes read *Out* of their hands, ... *Hub.* 699
Yet would he laugh it *out,* . . . . . . *Hub.* 703
So would he scoffe them *out* with mockerie, ... *Hub.* 705
to blazon *out* their blames. . . . . . *T.M.* 102
ycrept of late *Out* of dredd darknes . . . . . *T.M.* 189
sprong *Out* of th' Almighties bosome, ... *T.M.* 389
out of dust their memories awake? . . . . . *T.M.* 450
th' heavenlie light of knowledge is put *out,* . . . . . *T.M.* 488
is raced *Out* of the knowledge of posteritie, ... *Ti.* 178
His name is worne alreadie *out* of thought, ... *Ti.* 222
to bring awaie *Out* of dread darkenesse . . . . . *Ti.* 376
out of sight to highest heaven mounted, ... *Ti.* 600
out of the gate Of Aeoles raine, ... *Mui.* 419
mourne for me that languish *out* my dayes. . . . . . *D.* 538
a straunge shepheard chaunst to find me *out,* . . . . . *Col.* 60
or *out* of doore quite shit, ... *Col.* 709
Lay forth *out* of thine everlasting scryne . . . . . I. Pr. 2. 3
some end they finde, or in or *out,* . . . . . I. i. 11. 2
she spewd *out* of her filthie maw . . . . . I. i. 20. 1
He seekes *out* mighty charmes . . . . . . I. i. 36. 9
Then choosing *out* few words . . . . . . I. i. 37. 1
rising forth *out* of her baser bowre, ... I. ii. 7. 6
'Then cride she *out,* . . . . . . I. ii. 39. 1
thus long *out* of my sight? . . . . . . I. iii. 27. 2
Out of the East the dawning day doth call. . . . . . I. iv. 16. 5
through celestiall doome throwne *out* of dore, ... I. v. 47. 4
commeth *out* To weet the cause, ... I. vi. 14. 6
Was *out* of Dianes favour, as it then befell. . . . . . I. vii. 4. 9
ere he could *out* of his swowne awake, ... I. vii. 15. 7
Whose many heads, *out* budding ever new, ... I. vii. 17. 4
Hewen *out* of Adamant rocke . . . . . . I. vii. 33. 7
acquite him *out* of all. . . . . . . I. viii. 1. 4
his combred clubbe to quight *Out* of the earth, ... I. viii. 10. 5
out of the way to overthroe, ... I. viii. 13. 4
as sheepe *out* of the fold, ... I. viii. 35. 7
unwares I strayd *Out* of my way, ... I. xii. 31. 8
departed *out* of Eden landes, ... II. i. 1. 5
artes he moves, and *out* of caytives handes . . . . . II. i. 1. 7
shee gan to breath *out* living aire. . . . . . II. i. 43. 9
As one *out* of a deadly dreame affright, ... II. i. 45. 6
out of order stray about her daintie eares. . . . . . II. ii. 15. 9
Out crying; 'O! what ever hevenly powre, ... II. iii. 34. 8
groneth *out* his utmost grudging spright . . . . . II. v. 36. 7
picked *out* from all the rest, ... II. vi. 12. 4
To bud *out* faire, and throwe her sweete smels . . . . . II. vi. 12. 9
'Harrow now *out,* and well away!' . . . . . II. vi. 43. 6
They all attonce *out* of their seates arose, ... II. ix. 36. 2
The light goes *out,* . . . . . . II. x. 30. 2
the salt brine *out* of the billowes sprong. . . . . . II. xii. 10. 5
did well *out* of this fountaine, ... II. xii. 62. 2
thence *out* to wrest. . . . . . . II. xii. 81. 9
Drew *out* a deadly bow and arrow . . . . . III. i. 65. 2
disperst *out* of the firmament, ... III. i. 67. 8

Out—*Continued.*
To hunt *out* perilles . . . III. ii. 7. 2
The worde gone *out* she backe againe would call, . . . III. ii. 9. 1
as Phoebus face *out* of the east . . . III. ii. 24. 6
seekes wonders *out* of Magick spell.' . . . III. iii. 17. 7
where the day *out* of the sea doth spring, . . . III. iii. 27. 4
upreare His deawy head *out* of the Ocean maine, . . . III. iv. 61. 4
almost *out* of hart, . . . III. v. 4. 1
tell *out* of hand.' . . . III. v. 4. 9
out of sight escaped at the least: . . . III. v. 14. 5
both in and *out* men moten pas: . . . III. vi. 31. 6
He letteth in, he letteth *out* to wend . . . III. vi. 32. 1
keepe us *out* in scorne, of his owne will, . . . III. ix. 8. 8
Out of the ruddy East was fully reard, . . . III. x. 52. 7
To draw them longer *out,* . . . IV. ii. 51. 2
But all she did was but to weare *out* day . . . IV. vi. 45. 5
loved *out* of measure: . . . IV. ix. 21. 4
through lewd upbraide . . . they fell *out;* . . . IV. ix. 24. 6
Faint friends when they fall *out* . . . IV. ix. 27. 9
all which in or *out* did wend, . . . IV. x. 7. 3
either beat him in, or drive him *out.* . . . IV. x. 19. 5
Me seemes the world is runne quite *out* of square . . . V. Pr. 1. 7
equitie to measure *out* along . . . V. i. 7. 3
At length found *out* whereas she hidden lay . . . V. ii. 25. 5
weighed *out* in ballaunces . . . V. ii. 35. 3
each estate quite *out* of order goth? . . . V. ii. 37. 3
She causeth them be hang'd up *out* of hand; . . . V. iv. 32. 4
flakes of fire . . . *Out* of her steely armes were . . . V. v. 8. 4
That in and *out* thou mayst have passage . . . V. v. 34. 5
to send some one to seeke him *out;* . . . V. vi. 6. 2
againe resolv'd to hunt him *out* . . . V. vi. 6. 7
from her eies did flash *out* fiery light, . . . V. vi. 38. 8
when they saw their foes dead *out* of doubt, . . . V. viii. 12. 3
Me like a dog she *out* of dores did thrust, . . . V. viii. 22. 7
threw her husbands murdred infant *out;* . . . V. viii. 47. 2
whence none could get it *out.* . . . V. ix. 4. 9
Bon, that once had written bin, Was raced *out,* . . . V. ix. 26. 5
dropping fresh *out* of the Indian fount, . . . V. x. 16. 6
rooted all the relickes *out* Of that vilde race, . . . V. xi. 18. 6
which she doth bray *Out* of her poysnous entrails . . . V. xi. 20. 9
all the rest burst *out* to all outragiousnesse . . . V. xii. 2. 9
strove to get it *out,* . . . V. xii. 22. 1
That forth *out* of an hill fresh gushing . . . VI. iii. 50. 9
Her to recure *out* of that stony swownd, . . . VI. v. 6. 4
Out of their ambush broke, . . . VI. v. 17. 9
Cryde *out* aloud for mercie, . . . VI. vii. 12. 2
throwing downe his load *out* of his hand, . . . VI. vii. 24. 3
Complayning *out* on me that would not on them rew . . . VI. viii. 20. 9
all which I put in fals *out* anon, . . . VI. viii. 24. 7
let her Sleepe *out* her fill . . . VI. viii. 38. 2
Then *out* aloud she cries, . . . VI. viii. 40. 7
to launch her brest, and let *out* loved life . . . VI. viii. 48. 9
redeemed . . . *out* of his cruell hands; . . . VI. ix. 11. 8
And *out* of them to presse the milke: . . . VI. ix. 37. 9
Out of the wood he rose, . . . VI. x. 17. 9
vanisht all away *out* of his sight, . . . VI. x. 18. 2
no way Appeard for people in nor *out* to pas, . . . VI. x. 41. 8
The Theeves fall *out* for Pastorell, . . . VI. xi. Arg.
To sparke *out* litle beames, . . . VI. xi. 21. 9
'Die? *out* alas!' then Calidore did cry, . . . VI. xi. 29. 5
Though *out* of course, . . . VI. xii. 2. 3
he gan fret and fome *out* bloudy gore . . . VI. xii. 31. 3
should the progeny of man Be rooted *out,* . . . VII. vi. 31. 9
Out of her bowre, that many flowers strowes: . . . VII. vi. 41. 5
had *out* of measure Long lov'd the Fanchin, . . . VII. vi. 44. 3
Go seek he *out* that Alane . . . VII. vii. 9. 9
grew *Out* of the ground, and sent forth odours . . . VII. vii. 10. 3
out alasse, he cryde, and wel-away! . . . *Epig.* iv. 27
Poure *out* the wine without restraint . . . *Epith.* 250
evening-star . . . Appeare *out* of the East . . . *Epith.* 287
Out of great Chaos ugly prison crept, . . . *H.L.* 58
to move *out* of his idle seate; . . . *H.L.* 66
Lifting himselfe *out* of the lowly dust . . . *H.L.* 177
At first, *out* of that great immortall Spright, . . . *H.B.* 107
And made *out* of one mould . . . *H.B.* 207
Out of the bosome of eternall blisse, . . . *H.H.L.* 134
out of their baskets drew . . . *Proth.* 73
Outbar. Which to *outbarre,* with painefull pyonings . . . II. x. 63. 7
Outboasts. Another her *out boastes,* and all for tryall strips . . . II. v. 33. 9
Outbrast. sudden flash of heavens fire *out brast,* . . . *Pet.*[2] iii. 11
Outbreathed. That signe of last *outbreathed* life . . . I. xii. 2. 5
Outcast. Into this bitter bale I am *outcast,* . . . *Gn.* 330
the caytive spoile Of that same *outcast* carcas, . . . II. viii. 12. 5
make his carkas as the *outcast* dong? . . . II. viii. 28. 5
doth farre *outcast* His hearie beames, . . . III. i. 16. 5
liv'd like *outcast* thrall . . . IV. vii. 43. 9
There they him left a carrion *outcast* . . . V. ix. 19. 8
Outcries. *outcries* shrill Of wretched persons . . . *T.M.* 153
The dreadfull accents of their *outcries* shrill . . . *T.M.* 286
Her shrill *outcryes* and shrieks so loud did bray, . . . I. vi. 7. 5
With yelling *outcries,* and with shrieking sowne; . . . III. iv. 30. 8
when those pittifull *outcries* he heard . . . III. viii. 30. 5
Outcry. with hideous *outcrie,* A troupe of Satyres . . . *Bel.*[2] xii. 11
Ran forth in hast with hideous *outcry,* . . . IV. vii. 21. 4
All ran together with a great *out-cry* . . . VII. vi. 15. 1
They after follow'd all with shrill *out-cry,* . . . VII. vi. 52. 6
Out-find. 'O! how' . . . 'mote I that well *out find,* . . . I. ii. 43. 6
Ne could . . . *outfind* The secret cause . . . IV. xi. 21. 3
soone as he had sought . . . did by and by *out find* That . . . IV. xii. 25. 6
Out-found. Which whenas trew by tryall he *out fond,* . . . I. xii. 3. 5

Outgo. I sawe a shole of shepeheardes *outgoe* . . . *S.C.* May 20
Shepheard to see them in theyr art *outgoe* . . . *S.C.* Jun. 64
each did strive the other to *outgoe:* . . . III. xi. 5. 6
the which each other did *outgoe* . . . IV. v. 11. 9
Outgone. still increast till she her terme had full *outgone* . . . III. vi. 9. 9
Outgushing. a water, whose *outgushing* streame . . . *Bel.*[1] vii. 6
a water, whose *out gushing* flood . . . *Bel.*[2] ix. 6
Out-hired. When Justice was not for most meed *out-hyred,* . . . V. Pr. 3. 8
Out-lanced. Strongly *outlaunced* towards either side, . . . *Mui.* 82
Outlaws. Nor *outlawes* fell affray the forest raunger . . . *Col.* 319
who so else doth otherwise esteeme, Are *outlawes,* . . . *Col.* 890
Outlearn. nought according to his mind He could *out-learne,* . . . IV. viii. 22. 6
Out-quenched. the candlelight *Out quenched* . . . VI. xi. 16. 9
Outrage. For this, and many more such *outrage,* . . . *S.C.* F. 183
Death on hym such *outrage* showe?) . . . *S.C.* Jun. 90
through the great *outrage* Of her owne people . . . *Ti.* 172
Hart cannot thinke what *outrage* . . . I. xi. 40. 1
To fly the vengeaunce for his *outrage* dew: . . . II. i. 25. 4
playnd of grievous *outrage,* . . . II. i. 30. 5
The strong extremities of their *outrage* . . . II. ii. 38. 4
with importune *outrage* him assayld; . . . II. vi. 29. 2
First prayse of knighthood is fowle *outrage* to deface.' . . . II. viii. 25. 9
to doen *outrage* to a sleeping ghost; . . . II. viii. 26. 2
Which *outrage* when those gentle knights did see, . . . III. i. 18. 1
into termes of open *outrage* brust, . . . III. i. 48. 2
Nor so fowle *outrage* doen by living men; . . . III. iii. 34. 6
Of whose fowle *outrage* they impatient, . . . III. iv. 45. 7
her to save from *outrage* meekely prayed him . . . III. viii. 15. 9
Through open *outrage* he her bore away, . . . III. x. 27. 6
with hideous And hatefull *outrage* long him chaced . . . III. xi. 3. 5
The wrongfull *outrage* of unrighteous men, . . . III. xi. 10. 6
To give him the reward for such vile *outrage* dew . . . III. xii. 33. 9
did drive The noble Argonauts to *outrage* fell; . . . IV. i. 23. 7
woxe afeard Of *outrage* . . . IV. i. 50. 4
The *outrage* of his furious fit relented . . . IV. ii. 2. 4
Have rays'd this cruell warre and *outrage* fell, . . . IV. ii. 24. 4
To worke such *outrage* on so faire a creature; . . . IV. vi. 17. 2
had done *outrage* in so high degree: . . . IV. vi. 22. 7
so great *outrage* donne: . . . IV. ix. 27. 7
gan first disswade From such foule *outrage,* . . . IV. ix. 34. 4
entreat that iron man below To cease his *outrage,* . . . V. ii. 22. 6
more increast her *outrage* mercilesse, . . . V. v. 14. 7
Tygres scath In crueltie and *outrage* she did pas, . . . V. viii. 49. 8
soone as he their *outrage* backe doth beat, . . . V. xi. 45. 8
Them also gan assaile with *outrage* bold, . . . V. xi. 47. 3
Can keepe from *outrage* and from doing wrong, . . . V. xii. 1. 6
Which cruell *outrage* when as Artegall Did well avize, . . . V. xii. 18. 1
his Ladie, which this *outrage* saw, . . . VI. ii. 20. 1
What manner wight he was, . . . Which had this *outrage* wrought . . . VI. ii. 44. 4
th' *outrage* of his violence he stayd, . . . VI. xii. 29. 3
Outraged. *Outraged* the honour of these noble bowes . . . *Bel.*[1] v. 11
heavens! that doe . . . heavenly virgin thus *outraged* see, . . . I. vi. 5. 7
faire Una late fowle *outraged,* . . . II. ii. 18. 2
freely read what wicked felon so Hath *outrag'd* you, . . . III. xi. 15. 3
Outrageous. the fourth to forbeare is *outragious:* . . . *S.C.* May 133
Whilst Hector raged with *outragious* minde, . . . *Gn.* 503
the *outragious* passion nigh appeased, . . . *D.* 555
with *outragious* wrong . . . the roses rent away; . . . *As.* 159
upon his crest With rigor so *outrageous* he smitt, . . . I. ii. 18. 7
As her *outrageous* foe had left her . . . I. vi. 9. 4
with *outrageous* strokes did him restraine, . . . I. viii. 13. 8
smot againe with more *outrageous* might; . . . I. xi. 25. 2
rusht upon him with *outragious* pryde; . . . I. xi. 53. 3
Provoking him, by her *outrageous* talke, . . . II. iv. 5. 3
when the cause of that *outrageous* deede Demaunded, . . . II. iv. 29. 6
Outrageous anger, and woe-working jarre, . . . II. v. 16. 3
Outrageous wrong, and hellish covetize, . . . II. vii. 12. 8
so soone as his *outrageous* powre Is layd, . . . II. viii. 48. 4
with *outragious* cry A thousand villeins rownd about them . . . II. ix. 13. 1
with wrath *outrageous* And cruell rancour . . . II. x. 43. 4
They reard a most *outrageous* dreadfull yelling cry: . . . II. xi. 17. 9
The cause of their dissention and *outrageous* yre . . . III. i. 23. 9
thy strong buffets and *outrageous* blowes, . . . III. iv. 9. 2
threatned death for his *outrageous* wrong . . . III. v. 13. 9
shortly grew into *outrageous* fire; . . . III. vii. 16. 2
To save her selfe from that *outrageous* spoyle; . . . III. viii. 32. 5
strive and storme with stirre *outrageous* For her, . . . IV. i. 47. 3
Into *outragious* flames unwares did grow, . . . V. vii. 14. 7
To fly his stepdames loves *outrageous,* . . . V. viii. 43. 3
for vyld treasons and *outrageous* shame, . . . V. ix. 40. 8
Is with the blast of some *outragious* storme Blowne downe, . . . V. xi. 29. 2
all her people murdred with *outragious* might: . . . VI. i. 29. 9
And by *outragious* force away did beare: . . . VI. iii. 18. 7
the more *outrageous* and bold, . . . VI. vi. 21. 1
Him follow'd by the tract of his *outragious* spoile . . . VI. xii. 22. 9
Outrageously. strooke, and foynd, and lasht *outrageously,* . . . II. viii. 47. 5
the billowes rore *Outragiously,* . . . II. xii. 22. 2
many beasts, that roard *outrageously,* . . . II. xii. 39. 2
Outrageousness. What of the Persian Beares *outragiousnesse,* . . . *Ti.* 66
no lesse Then all the rest burst out to all *outragiousnesse* . . . V. xii. 2. 9
Outrages. with foule *outrages* opprest . . . III. xii. 41. 5
Outraging. *outraging* her cheekes and golden haire, . . . *Bel.*[2] x. 3
Outran. when through craft he her *out ran* . . . II. vii. 54. 9
he them both *outran* a wondrous space, . . . III. xi. 5. 7
Out-reigned. Till they *outraigned* had their outmost date, . . . II. x. 45. 2
Outrun. ere the yeare have halfe his course *out-run,* . . . *Hub.* 305
linger till the glas be all *out ronne?* . . . I. ix. 47. 8
ere two hundred yeares be full *outronne,* . . . III. iii. 46. 4
Outseek. What meanes shall she *out seeke,* or what waies take? III. iii. 25. 2

Outsent. Towards them driving, like a storme *out sent*. . . . IV. iii. 38. 5
Outshine. seemed to *outshine* the dimmed skye, ... V. ix. 21. 8
Outshow. Ne durst againe his fyrye face *out showe*: . . . . . *S.C.* Ap. 78
Outshut. So none should be *out shut*, ... IV. i. 12. 9
Outsprung. Eftsoones *outsprung* two more of equall mould; . IV. x. 10. 3
Outspun. through the clifts the vermeil bloud *out sponne*, . . IV. ix. 27. 4
Outstrained. all his foldes are now in length *outstrained*. . . *Gn.* 280
Outstretch. dare his hardy hand to those *outstretch*, ... *Hub.* 974
So did this flie *outstretch* his fearefull hornes, ... *Mui.* 87
Outstretched. *See* **Broad-outstretched.**
on the plaine *outstretched* lie, ... *Bel.*[2] vi. 12
outstretched lay, In monstrous length, ... *Van.* iii. 2
Outward. riotise, and semblants *outward* brave! . . . . . . *Gn.* 93
for *outward* shape Most like a man, ... *Hub.* 1041
the Paynim lay, Devoid of *outward* sence . . . . I. v. 29. 3
Ne was there *outward* breach, nor grudge in hart, ... II. x. 14. 7
The *outward* sparkes of her inburning fire; . . . . III. i. 53. 3
from like inward fire that *outward* smoke had steemd. . . . III. i. 55. 9
th' only forme and *outward* fashion; . . . . III. vi. 38. 2
shewd by *outward* signes that dread her sence did daze. . III. vii. 7. 9
in face And *outward* shew faire semblance they did beare; IV. i. 17. 6
Like knight adventurous in *outward* vew, ... IV. i. 33. 3
by that her *outward* grace . . . . IV. ii. 22. 8
yet uncertaine by such *outward* sight, ... IV. ii. 40. 7
through the likenesse of my *outward* hew, ... IV. viii. 56. 2
seem'd full aged by his *outward* sight, ... IV. xi. 25. 7
By *outward* signes (as well he might) did see, ... V. vi. 21. 5
By *outward* shew her inward sence desining: . . . . V. vii. 8. 3
of a Mayd she had the *outward* face, ... V. xi. 23. 7
not in *outward* shows, but inward thoughts defynd. . . . . VI. Pr. 5. 9
your *outward* senses to refraine From things . . . . VI. vi. 7. 6
from those *outward* sences, ill affected, ... VI. vi. 8. 1
outward salves that may augment it more.' . . . . VI. vi. 13. 4
proportion of the *outward* part . . . . *H.B.* 75
An *outward* shew of things that onely seeme. . . . . *H.B.* 91
so inly faire to be, As *outward* it appeareth . . . . *H.B.* 226
Out-ward. Ne any armour could his dint *out-ward*; . . . . . V. i. 10. 8
Outwardly. dead was his hart within, Yet *outwardly* . . . . I. vii. 21. 3
like a litle forrest seemed *outwardly*. . . . . II. vi. 2. 9
seemes *outwardly* So faire . . . . IV. viii. 49. 4
chearefull signes he shewed *outwardly*. . . . . IV. xii. 35. 5
Outwear. and time in durance, shall *outweare*; . . . . *S.C.* Env. 2
Thus did the Prince that wearie night *outweare* . . . . . . III. iv. 61. 1
that day for to *outweare*. . . . . III. xii. 28. 9
workes of noblest wits to nought *outweare*, ... IV. ii. 33. 2
Outwears. All the mishap the which our daies *outweares*, . . *Ro.* xix. 5
Out-weed. the springing seed *outweed*, ... II. iv. 35. 7
Outwell. His fattie waves doe fertile slime *outwell*, ... I. i. 21. 3
Outwelled. Simois and Xanthus blood *outwelde*; . . . . . . *Gn.* 502
Outwent. His wonted songs, wherein he all *outwent*. . . . . *S.C.* Ap. 16
Yet fled she fast, and both them farre *outwent*, ... V. viii. 4. 6
al those fourty which my life *out-went*. . . . . *Am.* lx. 8
Out-win. none the same may easily *out-win*: . . . . IV. i. 20. 6
Outwind. As by no meanes he can himselfe *outwind*: . . . . V. iii. 9. 5
Outwore. All that day she *outwore* in wandering . . . . . . III. xii. 29. 1
Outworn. The which injurious time hath quite *outworne*, . . *Ro.* xxvii. 6
Many long weary dayes I have *outworne*; . . . . *Am.* lxxxvi. 2
my weary ghost, with griefe *outworne*, ... IV. xii. 8. 1
Outwrest. the truth thereof I did *out wrest*; . . . . II. iv. 23. 5
Outwrought. three dayes of men were full *outwrought*, . . . II. vii. 65. 6
Ouzel. The *Ouzell* shrills; the Ruddock warbles soft; . . . . *Epith.* 82
Oven. from his wide devouring *oven* sent A flake of fire, . . . I. xi. 26. 3
Over (*partial list*).
raisde a Trophee *over* all the worlde. . . . . *Bel.*[1] xi. 8
Over all the world did raise . . . . *Bel.*[2] xv. 8
must passe *over* to th' Elisian plaine: . . . . *Gn.* 421
all the champain *o're* he soared light; . . . . *Mui.* 149
Wherewith ye triumph *over* feeble eyes, ... *Ded. Son.* xvi. 8
goodly galleries far *over* laid, ... I. iv. 4. 7
sacred ashes *over* it was strowed . . . . I. viii. 35. 9
Is not great grace to helpe him *over* past, ... I. ix. 39. 4
him to ferry *over* that deepe ford. . . . . II. vi. 4. 4
would he not . . . Give *over* to effect his first intent, . . II. xi. 41. 3
Through thicke and thin, both *over* banck and bush, ... III. i. 17. 5
spred his banner brave *Over* the troubled South, ... III. iii. 30. 4
Stretch her white rod *over* the Belgicke shore, ... III. iii. 49. 7
over all the countrie she did raunge . . . . III. vii. 50. 1
High *over* hilles and *over* dales he fledd, ... III. x. 55. 1
Over the sea suspended dreadfully, ... III. x. 56. 4
Over the dore thus written she did spye, ... III. xi. 50. 3
solemne silence *over* all that place: . . . . III. xi. 53. 7
How *over* that same dore was likewise writ, ... III. xi. 54. 2
did extend Her sword high *over* him, ... III. xii. 36. 9
still *over* him did stand, ... IV. vi. 23. 4
spredding *over* all the flore alone, ... IV. vii. 20. 7
And *over* all his shoulders did dispred, ... IV. vii. 40. 8
he did throw *Over* his head . . . . IV. viii. 42. 4
A pound of gall doth *over* it redound: . . . . IV. x. 1. 5
Daunger, dreaded *over-all*, ... IV. x. 17. 1
deckes his branch with blossomes *over all*, ... IV. x. 22. 4
Proudly stands *over*, and a while doth pause . . . . V. iv. 40. 8
I resolve this siege not to give *over*, ... V. v. 51. 4
the one mote needes fall *over* the lidge. . . . . V. vi. 36. 9
High *over* hilles, and lowly *over* dales, ... V. viii. 39. 2
A ship all readie . . . To passe them *over* . . . . V. xii. 4. 4
they lay scattred *over* all the land, ... V. xii. 7. 8
shade From view of living wight and covered *over*; . . . . VI. x. 42. 4
His target alwayes *over* her pretended; . . . . VI. xi. 19. 4
Then *over* them Change doth not rule . . . . VII. vii. 58. 8
make thy triumph *over* death and sin; . . . . *Am.* lxviii. 2

Over—*Continued.*
silken courteins *over* her display, ... *Epith.* 303
Spread thy broad wing *over* my love . . . . *Epith.* 319
Overall. *See* **Over.**
Your toombs devoted compasse *over-all*, ... *Ro.* i. 10
th' heavens in glorie triumpht *over all*: . . . . *Ro.* xii. 8
their forefathers, famous *over-all*, ... *Hub.* 1180
a Dragon . . . *over all* did spredd His golden winges: . . . . I. vii. 31. 4
Wyde wonders *over all* . . . weren told, ... I. viii. 3. 7
There raignd a solemne silence *over all*; . . . . I. viii. 29. 8
well knowne *over-all* To be both gratious and eke liberall: . . I. x. 34. 4
over all with brasen scales was armd, ... I. xi. 9. 1
great vertues *over-all* were redd; . . . . I. xi. 46. 4
yet I quake and tremble *over-all*.' . . . . II. iii. 44. 7
over all . . . was spred A trayle of yvie . . . . II. xii. 61. 1
'His name was Daunger, dreaded *over-all*, ... IV. x. 17. 1
Through his too ventrous prowesse proved *over all*. . . . . IV. xi. 7. 9
the Picts that swarmed *over-all*, ... IV. xi. 36. 4
great justice, praysed *over-all*, ... V. Pr. 11. 8
For her great bounty knowen *over all* . . . . V. viii. 17. 3
Well knowen by his feates, and famous *over-all*. . . . . . . V. ix. 5. 9
eke her champions glorie sounded *over-all*. . . . . V. xii. 24. 9
Calidore, beloved *over-all*, ... VI. i. 2. 2
I may in trump of fame blaze *over-all*. . . . . *Am.* xxix. 12
To sing your name and prayses *over-all*: . . . . *Am.* lxxiii. 12
spred thy lovely kingdome *over-all*. . . . . *H.B.* 266
Overawe. Lordings curbe that commons *over-aw*, ... V. ii. 38. 8
Overbloweth. crave but rowme to rest while tempest *over-blo'th*.' . . . . III. vii. 8. 9
Overblown. Untill the blustring storme is *overblowne*; . . . I. i. 10. 2
by the Northerne blast Quite *overblowne*, ... IV. i. 45. 7
After long stormes and tempests *overblowne* . . . . V. iii. 1. 1
when as *overblowen* was that brunt, ... V. xi. 59. 1
Over-bold. sharpe rebuke for being *over bold*; . . . . IV. x. 54. 2
Overbore. *overbore* beyond his crouper quight; . . . . IV. iv. 40. 7
Overborne. By meanes whereof he hath him lightly *overborne*. IV. ii. 6. 9
right long time is *overborne* of wrong . . . . V. xi. 1. 2
Overburdened. Did bow adowne as *overburdened*. . . . . . . II. xii. 55. 6
Overcame. him in hardy battayle *overcame*, ... I. xii. 20. 4
now exceeding griefe him *overcame*, ... II. i. 23. 5
Asclepiodate him *overcame*, ... II. x. 58. 1
overcame The wicked Gobbelines in bloody field; . . . . . II. x. 73. 1
what reward had he that *overcame*?' . . . . III. i. 27. 7
All coverd with thick woodes that quite it *overcame*. . . . III. vii. 4. 9
Where late he left the Beast he *overcame*, ... III. vii. 61. 6
when to him she cryde, . . . love money *overcame*: . . . . III. x. 15. 2
with finall force them all he *overcame*. . . . . V. viii. 50. 9
Overcast. The skie gan everie where to *overcast*, ... *Pet.* iii. 9
cloudes han all *overcast*. . . . . *S.C.* D. 138
Hath so wise men bewitcht, and *overkest*, ... *Ti.* 457
daie was *overcast*, And darke night fast approched, ... *D.* 556
The day with cloudes was suddeine *overcast*, ... I. i. 6. 5
The other all with silver *overcast*; . . . . I. i. 40. 3
Where grew two goodly trees, . . . with gray mosse *overcast*; I. ii. 28. 4
raisd . . . A foggy mist that *overcast* the day, ... I. ii. 38. 5
his chacing steedes aghast Both charett swifte and huntsman *overcast*: . . . . I. v. 38. 5
As mountaine doth the valley *overcaste*. . . . . I. xi. 8. 5
The valley did with coole shade *overcast*: . . . . II. i. 24. 5
a foggy mist hath *overcast* The face of heven, ... III. iv. 13. 1
There a sad cloud of sleepe her *overkest*, ... III. vi. 10. 8
the faire welkin fowly *overcast* . . . . III. ix. 11. 4
with his furious blast . . . skyes doth *overcast*. . . . . . III. ix. 15. 9
it all the skie doth *overcast* With darknes dred, ... IV. i. 45. 8
A watry cloud doth *overcast* the skie, ... IV. iv. 47. 7
though this cloud have now me *overcast*, ... V. v. 38. 6
the day with dampe was *overcast*, ... V. vii. 8. 6
I, whose star, . . . with cloudes is *over-cast*, ... *Am.* xxxiv. 6
Overcaught. in the very dore him *overcaught*, ... IV. vii. 31. 5
Overcome. Thy maysters mind is *overcome* with care: . . . . *S.C.* Ja. 46
hardie will he had To *overcome*, ... *Gn.* 304
did *overcome* (**overcomme*) The world with conquest of their might . . . . *Ti.* 61
this wretched woman *overcome* Of anguish, ... II. i. 58. 6
Was *overcome* of thing that did him please; . . . . II. vi. 13. 8
As *overcome* with too exceeding might, ... II. vii. 66. 7
say, that I not *overcome* doe dye, ... II. viii. 52. 3
overcommen kept in prison long, ... II. x. 32. 8
though *overcome* in haplesse fight, ... II. x. 56. 8
having *overcome* The Romane legion . . . . II. x. 60. 7
they, *over-comen*, were depriv'd Of their proud beautie, . . II. xii. 31. 3
As *overcomen* of the spirites powre, ... III. iii. 50. 2
overcommen quight Of huge affection, ... III. xi. 45. *or.* 5
young Knight, . . . doubly *overcommen*, her ador'd. . . . . IV. i. 15. 4
As one with griefe and anguishe *overcum*, ... IV. vii. 44. 4
being *overcome* by her in fight, ... V. iv. 32. 6
So was he *overcome*; not *overcome*, But to her yeelded . . . V. v. 17. 1
Since that he was not forst, nor *overcome* in fight?' . . . . V. vi. 16. 9
they *overcommen* Agree to goe with her; . . . . V. ix. 4. 1
Hercules them all did *overcome* in fight. . . . . V. x. 10. 9
All *overcome* with infinite affect . . . . VI. i. 45. 2
Overcomes. Prince Arthure *overcomes* the great Gerioneo . . V. xi. Arg.
Prince Arthure *overcomes* Disdaine; . . . . VI. viii. Arg.
Overcraw. *See* **Overcrow.**
Overcrow. Then gan the villein him to *overcraw*, ... I. ix. 50. 5
Overcrowed. That of a weede he was *overcrawed*. . . . . . *S.C.* F. 142
Overdight. *overdight* With mourning stole . . . . *Col.* 493
a thick Arber goodly *over-dight*, ... II. vii. 53. 3
To sinfull men with darknes *overdight*, ... IV. viii. 34. 2
Cherubins, Which all with golden wings are *overdight*, . . . *H.H.B.* 93

Overflow. he with fatnes so did *overflowe,* . . . . *Van.* ii. 7
The floddes whereof shall them *overflowe* . . . . *S.C.* May 94
forst to *overflow* with brackish teares, ... *T.M.* 29
A well of teares, that all may *overflow?* . . . . *Mui.* 410
His fattie waves . . . *overflow* each plaine and lowly dale: I. i. 21. 4
overflow With suddein fury all the fertile playne, ... II. xi. 18. 5
aye the cups their bancks did *overflow;* . . . . III. i. 51. 6
largely *overflow* the fruitfull plaine, ... III. vii. 34. 4
Else would the waters *overflow* the lands, ... IV. x. 35. 5
looke then how much it doth *overflow* . . . . V. ii. 34. 8
And all this land with endlesse losse to *overflow.* . . . . VI. iv. 30. 9
The happy peace which there doth *overflow,* . . . . VI. x. 3. 4
Overflowed. A sea of blood . . . *overflowed* all the field arownd, I. viii. 16. 8
overflowed all the fertile plaine, ... I. xi. 48. 4
overflowd all countries far away, ... II. x. 15. 4
Overflowing. hath so often with his *overflowing* Thee drenched, *Ro.* xiii. 11
through the *overflowing* of the flood . . . . *Ti.* 621
choked be with *overflowing* gall. . . . . *Am.* xliii. 4
Overflown. The bankes are *overflowne* when stopped is the flood.' . . . . II. iv. 11. 9
now by fortune it was *overflowne.* . . . . III. v. 17. 4
of the fruitfull liquor *overflowne;* . . . . III. ix. 30. 5
Xanthus sandy bankes with blood all *overflowne.* . . . . III. ix. 35. 9
The place there *overflowne* seemd like a sodaine flood. . . . . IV. vii. 32. 9
Overgive. constrain'd that trade to *overgive,* . . . . *Hub.* 249
to the Saxons *over-give* their government. . . . . III. iii. 41. 9
Overgo. Reason with sudden rage did *overgoe;* . . . . *Mui.* 134
with his powre he all doth *overgo,* . . . . V. ii. 7. 3
Overgone. Willye is not greatly *overgone,* . . . . *S.C.* Au. 127
Now had the Sun halfe heaven *overgone,* . . . . *Gn.* 165
Overgrassed. they bene like foule wagmoires *overgrast,* . . . *S.C.* S. 130
Overgrew. in short time his face they *overgrew,* . . . . IV. vii. 40. 7
Overgrow. The which unused rust did *overgrow:* . . . . I. viii. 30. 7
Overgrown. *overgrowen* with blacke oblivions rust. . . . . *Ti.* 98
beard all *overgrowne,* . . . . *D.* 44
Her crafty head . . . Was *overgrowne* with scurfe . . . . I. viii. 47. 3
His yron cote, all *overgrowne* with rust, ... II. vii. 4. 1
overgrowne with dust and old decay, ... II. vii. 29. 2
with thicke woods *overgrowne,* . . . . III. v. 17. 7
All *overgrowne* with haire, that could awhape An hardy hart; IV. vii. 5. 4
All *overgrowen* with rude and rugged haire; . . . . IV. vii. 43. 4
Nor any footing fynde for *overgrowen* gras: . . . . VI. x. 41. 9
Overhale. Her mantle black through heaven gan *overhaile:* *S.C.* Ja. 75
Overhanging. Which *over-hanging,* they themselves did steepe II. vii. 56. 6
Overhead. The roofe hereof was arched *over head,* . . . . II. ix. 46. 1
Archt *over head* with an embracing vine, ... II. xii. 54. 2
all dispred With shining gold, and arched *over hed,* . . . . V. vii. 5. 5
Seem'd like a grove faire braunched *over-hed:* . . . . VI. v. 35. 4
Overhent. his faire Leman flying through a brooke She *overhent,* . . . . II. x. 18. 9
Timias him lightly *overhent,* . . . . III. v. 25. 2
she feared to be *overhent* Of that vile hag, ... III. vii. 19. 5
shortly he her *overhent.* . . . . III. vii. 23. 9
So forth he went, and soone them *over-hent,* . . . . V. iii. 11. 1
did speed . . . In hope to have her *overhent* at last: . . . . V. viii. 4. 5
hindmost in the gate he *overhent,* . . . . V. x. 36. 6
Overlade. with his burdenous blowes him sore did *overlade.* V. xii. 19. 9
Overlaid. with lewde lust was *overlayd:* . . . . *S.C.* Jul. 151
overlaid And mastered with workmanship so rare, ... *Mui.* 337
yvory Which cunning Craftesman hand hath *overlayd* . . . . II. ix. 41. 6
with pure gold it all was *overlayd,* . . . . III. xi. 51. 4
Overlay. As when a cloud his beames doth *over-lay;* . . . . I. vii. 34. 7
with unequall might doe *overlay,* . . . . V. xi. 51. 7
all the place with swarmes do *overlay,* . . . . VI. xi. 48. 3
Overleaps. *overleapes* them all, like Robucke light, ... IV. vii. 22. 2
Overlook. another high doth *overlooke* Her owne like image *Gn.* 87
Or care to *overlooke,* or trust to gather, ... *Hub.* 279
gan streight to *over-looke* Those cursed leaves, ... III. xii. 36. 1
Did seeme to *overlooke* the lowly vale; . . . . VI. x. 8. 8
doth *over-looke* The richest champain that may else be rid; VII. vi. 54. 7
Overlooked. having *overlookt* their pas at ease, ... *Hub.* 396
Overmastered. as *over-maystered* by might, ... II. xii. 64. 3
Overmatched. So mischiefe *overmatcht* the wronger. . . . . V. viii. 7. 9
Overpass. Unto an other Canto I will *overpas.* . . . . IV. xi. 53. 9
The anguish of his paine to *overpasse:* . . . . VI. iii. 14. 7
Overpassed. *See* **Over, Past.**
When these sad sights were *overpast* and gone, ... *Van.* xii. 1
Tho when the pang was somewhat *overpast,* . . . . *D.* 554
whenas the dreadfull passion Was *overpast,* . . . . I. ii. 32. 2
when the furious fitt was *overpast,* . . . . I. iv. 34. 6
two of them the rest far *overpast,* . . . . III. v. 37. 8
quickly she it *overpast,* . . . . V. v. 45. 6
Whom though he saw now somewhat *overpast,* . . . . VI. iv. 18. 8
the sharpe passion being *overpast,* . . . . VI. viii. 19. 3
Overplaced. two hils, whose high heads *overplast* . . . . II. i. 24. 4
Overran. *overran* the East with greedie powre, ... *Ti.* 69
reason with foole-hardize *over ran;* . . . . II. ii. 17. 7
they *overran* all parts with easy hand. . . . . II. x. 61. 9
Despisd and troden downe of all that *over-ran.* . . . . IV. viii. 32. 9
Sad Trowis, that once his people *over-ran,* . . . . IV. xi. 41. 7
Them sorely vext, and courst, and *overran,* . . . . V. iv. 44. 3
Overraught. with long nayles *over-raught,* . . . . V. xii. 30. 2
after long weary chace, . . . He *over raught* him, ... VI. iii. 50. 5
Overreach. it could *overreach* the wisest earthly wight. . . . IV. ii. 10. 9
Over-read. *Bee bold:* she oft and oft it *over-red,* . . . . III. xi. 50. 4
Overruled. *over-ruld* at last, he did to me agree. . . . . IV. viii. 58. 9
Overruling. *over-ruling* him in his owne rayne, ... IV. iii. 27. 3
men admyr'd his *over-ruling* might; . . . . V. i. 8. 5
Overrun. having *overrun* The compast skie, ... *D.* 24
overronne, to tread them to the grownd: . . . . II. ix. 15. 5

Overrun—*Continued.*
Full many Countreyes they did *overronne,* . . . . III. i. 3. 4
'He in his furie all shall *overronne,* . . . . III. iii. 34. 1
overronne The fruitfull plaines, ... III. iii. 46. 7
As if he heaven and hell would *over-ronne,* . . . . III. x. 33. 7
when any Knight Is weakned, then thou doest him *overronne:* IV. i. 44. 8
For hast did *over-runne,* in dust enrould: . . . . IV. iii. 41. 5
All th' East, before untam'd, did *over-ronne,* . . . . V. i. 2. 2
That none of them the feeble *over-ren,* . . . . V. ii. 19. 8
As if he would have *over-run* him streight; . . . . V. xi. 5. 2
shun The perill . . . or else be *over-run.* . . . . VI. iii. 48. 9
Oversee. Cattell to keep, or grounds to *oversee;* . . . . *Hub.* 283
he had charge . . . Tutors nouriture to *oversee.* . . . . I. ix. 5. 4
Dissembled faire, and faynd to *oversee.* . . . . II. ix. 44. 3
Whose hight all Ephesus did *oversee,* . . . . IV. x. 30. 2
Overset. For pitty so to see him *overset:* . . . . VI. v. 22. 5
Overside. The other *over side* the Bridge she cast Into the river, ... V. vi. 39. 8
Oversight. in doubt ne dares To joy at his foolhappie *oversight:* . . . . I. vi. 1. 6
'Pardon, I pray, my heedlesse *oversight,* . . . . III. ix. 47. 2
Selfe to forget to mind another is *over-sight.'* . . . . IV. vii. 10. 9
Through which the rider downe doth fall through *oversight.* V. ii. 7. 9
Oversights. thy daintie pen may . . . *oversights* amend. . . . *Ded. Son.* xii.12
Overspent. my wearie teeme, nigh *over spent,* . . . . IV. v. 46. 8
Overspread. His wings which wont the earth to *overspredd,* *Ro.* xvii. 6
With brutish barbarisme is *overspredd:* . . . . *Ded. Son.* v. 4
Her huge long taile her den all *overspred,* . . . . I. i. 15. 2
Her wanton palfrey all was *overspred* With tinsell trappings, I. ii. 13. 7
tayle . . . Does *overspred* his long bras-scaly back, ... I. xi. 11. 2
all the world with wonder *overspred;* . . . . II. x. 2. 6
fog *over-spred* With his dull vapour all that desert . . . . II. xii. 34. 5
With golden foyle doth finely *over-spred* Some baser metall, IV. v. 15. 2
overspred her like a puffe of wind; . . . . V. ix. 14. 3
being all with Yvy *overspred* . . . . VI. v. 35. 2
if thou wouldst vouchsafe to *overspred* Me . . . . *H.L.* 19
Overstride. Stretch his strong thighes, and th' Ocean *overstride,* . . . . *Ti.* 541
none might thorough breake, nor *overstride:* . . . . III. vi. 31. 4
Overstrook. as he in his rage him *overstrooke,* . . . . V. xi. 13. 6
Overswim. Shall *overswim* the sea, ... III. iii. 33. 8
Overt. Hygate . . . by West, And *Overt* gate by North: . . . III. ix. 46. 3
Overtake. To after-send his foe, that him may *overtake?* . . . I. v. 10. 9
'Goe, caytive Elfe, him quickly *overtake,* . . . . I. v. 11. 1
Till her unwares the fiers Sansloy did *overtake:* . . . . I. vi. 2. 9
he would him make . . . the Robuckes in flight to *overtake,* I. vi. 24 .8
That short revenge the man may *overtake,* . . . . II. i. 18. 3
kindly sleepe that did them *overtake.* . . . . II. ii. 46. 7
that I may her *overtake.'* . . . . II. iii. 32. 9
vew of eye could scarse him *overtake,* . . . . II. xi. 26. 2
they chaunst to *overtake* Two knights . . . . IV. ii. 30. 2
till Thamis he *overtake.* . . . . IV. xi. 32. 9
'him soone to *overtake* That hence so long departed, ... V. i. 19. 3
he saw the hindmost *overtake* One of those two, ... V. viii. 5. 6
Till I him *overtake,* or else subdew: . . . . VI. i. 7. 3
Thinking by speed to *overtake* his flight; . . . . VI. v. 17. 2
There did the Prince him *overtake* anone, ... VI. vi. 30. 4
Ye may him *overtake* in timely tyde.' . . . . VI. vii. 6. 4
Overtaken. suffred her so carelesly disguiz'd Be *overtaken.* . . III. vi. 19. 6
now he her quite *overtaken* had; . . . . IV. vii. 24. 6
Unlesse some succour had in time him *overtaken.* . . . . V. iii. 9. 9
He had him *overtaken* in his flight. . . . . VI. iv. 8. 6
Overtaking. Whome *overtaking,* they gan loudly bray, . . . I. iii. 23. 1
Whom *overtaking,* she in merry sort Them gan to bord, . . II. xii. 16. 1
Who *overtaking* him did disaray, ... V. iii. 38. 3
Whom *overtaking,* loude to him he cryde: . . . . VI. i. 18. 6
Overthrew. *overthrew* this frame with ruine great. . . . . *Bel.*[2] ii. 14
high trees *overthrew,* and rocks in peeces tore. . . . . I. xi. 37. 9
overthrew him selfe unwares, ... II. iv. 8. 9
Raisd warre, and him in batteill *overthrew.* . . . . II. x. 33. 6
He *overthrew* through his owne valiaunce; . . . . II. x. 38. 6
with her powre her owne selfe *overthrew,* . . . . II. x. 54. 4
Fought with Severus, and him *overthrew,* . . . . II. x. 57. 2
Him backeward *overthrew,* and downe him stayd . . . . II. xi. 29. 2
overthrew his bowle disdainfully, ... II. xii. 49. 8
weenedst thou what wight thee *overthrew,* . . . . III. i. 8. 1
His wicked bookes in hast he *overthrew,* . . . . III. xii. 32. 2
ere his hand he reard, he *overthrew* Seven Knights, ... IV. iv. 41. 1
overthrew what ever came her neare, ... IV. iv. 46. 7
oftentimes him nigh he *overthrew:* . . . . V. ii. 13. 7
He like a swarme of flyes them *overthrew;* . . . . V. ii. 53. 6
Whom with sore havocke soone they *overthrew,* . . . . V. iii. 12. 5
to the ground him quite she *overthrew,* . . . . V. iv. 39. 8
all his other honour *overthrew.* . . . . V. vi. 12. 4
The raskall manie soone they *overthrew;* . . . . V. xi. 59. 8
he them *overthrew* both man and horse, ... V. xii. 7. 7
That great Alcides whilome *overthrew,* . . . . VI. xii. 32. 2
Overthrow. sighed to see his neare *overthrow.* . . . . *S.C.* F. 216
to have the *overthrowe.* . . . . *S.C.* Ap. 81
in thy fall my fatall *overthrowe,* . . . . *Ti.* 79
Had framed for his finall *overthroe.* . . . . *Mui.* 424
'Deare dame, your suddein *overthrow* Much rueth me; . . . I. ii. 21. 7
with the winde it did him *overthrow,* . . . . I. vii. 12. 8
That stop out of the way to *overthroe,* . . . . I. viii. 13. 4
That strongest Oake might seeme to *overthrow.* . . . . I. viii. 18. 6
that dredd Dragon all did *overthrow.* . . . . I. xi. 47. 5
To *overthrow* him strongly did assay, ... II. iv. 8. 8
As steele can wound, or strength can *overthroe.* . . . . II. iv. 10. 5
Gainst fort of Reason, it to *overthrow:* . . . . II. iv. 34. 8
it the goodly peace of staied mindes Does *overthrow,* . . . . II. v. 1. 7

Own—*Continued.*
with the furie of their *owne* affret Each other . . . . IV. ii. 15. 6
of your gotten spoyle their *owne* triumph to make.' . . . . IV. ii. 24. 9
through infusion sweete Of thine *owne* spirit . . . . IV. ii. 34. 7
Not for thine *owne*, but for thy sisters sake, ... IV. iii. 11. 3
over-ruling him in his *owne* rayne, ... IV. iii. 27. 3
He sends the sea his *owne* with double gaine, ... IV. iii. 27. 8
in revengement of his *owne* despight; . . . . IV. iv. 35. 3
make his praise before his *owne* preferd: . . . . IV. iv. 36. 8
Ne her *owne* Amoret forgoe so light . . . . IV. v. 20. 7
nourisheth her *owne* consuming smart? . . . . IV. vi. 1. 4
What is your *owne*, that I mote ye requite?' . . . . . . IV. vi. 4. 5
Unweeting of thine *owne* like haplesse plight: . . . . . . IV. vii. 10. 8
'Thy ruefull plight I pitty as mine *owne*. . . . . IV. vii. 19. 2
Als of his *owne* rash hand one wound . . . . IV. vii. 35. 9
to wreake his follies *owne* despight. . . . . IV. vii. 39. 9
His *owne* deare Lord Prince Arthure came . . . . IV. vii. 42. 2
albeit his *owne* dear Squire he were, ... IV. vii. 43. 5
Him seemed oft he heard his *owne* right name. . . . . . . IV. viii. 4. 5
all mindlesse of his *owne* deare Lord . . . . IV. viii. 18. 4
For lodging there without her *owne* consent: . . . . IV. viii. 28. 5
The great Creatours *owne* resemblance bright, ... IV. viii. 32. 2
when she perceived Her *owne* deare sire, ... IV. ix. 7. 2
with their *owne* repayed duely weare, ... IV. ix. 30. 8
As with a robe, with her *owne* silver haire, ... IV. xi. 11. 8
all men sought their *owne*, ... V. Pr. 3. 7
To sit in his *own* seate, ... V. Pr. 10. 8
Or that he wexed weary of his *owne*, ... V. i. 17. 2
both his and mine *owne* love . . . . V. i. 18. 9
Nor tooke away his love, but his *owne* proper good . . . . V. i. 23. 9
Take here your *owne*, ... V. i. 28. 7
Your *owne* dead Ladies head, ... V. i. 28. 9
this was Dony, Florimels *owne* Dwarfe, ... V. ii. 3. 1
for his *owne* deare Ladies sake, ... V. iii. 16. 4
his *owne* love left astray. . . . . V. iv. 9. 9
Great threasure . . . Which as our *owne* we tooke, ... V. iv. 13. 3
I hold mine *owne*, and so will hold it still. . . . . V. iv. 14. 5
what the sea unto you sent your *own* should seeme.' . . . . V. iv. 17. 9
By what right doe you claime to be your *owne?*' . . . . . V. iv. 18. 5
what the sea unto you sent your *own* should seeme. . . . . V. iv. 18. 9
who can scape what his *owne* fate hath wrought? . . . . . . V. iv. 27. 8
lay on heaven the guilt of their *owne* crimes. . . . . V. iv. 28. 3
damned by the doome Of his *owne* mouth, ... V. v. 17. 4
he would not once assay To reskew his *owne* Lord, ... V. v. 19. 9
Left to her will by his *owne* wilfull blame, ... V. v. 20. 2
he it tooke in his *owne* selfes despight, ... V. v. 23. 6
his *owne* brave mind Subjected hath . . . . V. v. 32. 2
if in his *owne* powre occasion lay, ... V. v. 39. 2
eke of powre her *owne* doome to undo, ... V. v. 41. 8
She wounded was with her deceipts *owne* dart, ... V. v. 43. 6
Even so Clarinda her *owne* Dame beguyld, ... V. v. 53. 5
To his *owne* absent love to be untrew: . . . . V. v. 56. 3
Untill his *owne* true love his freedome gayned: . . . . . . V. v. 57. 8
To his *owne* love his loialtie he saved: . . . . V. vi. 2. 5
Yet his *owne* love, the noble Britomart, ... V. vi. 3. 1
none she found so fit . . . As her *owne* selfe, ... V. vi. 6. 4
Not by strong hand . . . But his *owne* doome, ... V. vi. 16. 5
slaine . . . through his *owne* guilty wile: . . . . V. vi. 33. 5
swolne with pride of his *owne* peerelesse powre, ... V. vii. 15. 7
when as to her *owne* Love she came, ... V. vii. 38. 1
They have the price of their *owne* folly payd.' . . . . . . V. viii. 23. 6
By Artegall, misween'd for her *owne* Knight, ... V. viii. 46. 6
her *owne* deare flesh did teare: . . . . V. viii. 47. 6
Thereto both his *owne* wylie wit, ... V. ix. 5. 1
thine *owne* people do thy mercy prayse . . . . V. x. 3. 9
setting up an Idole of his *owne*, ... V. x. 13. 8
when her *owne* two sonnes she had in sight, ... V. x. 19. 7
The which whylome that Ladies *owne* had bene; . . . . . . V. x. 25. 2
men, to Gods *owne* likenesse framed, ... V. x. 28. 7
Deliver him his *owne*, ere yet too late, ... V. xi. 3. 8
would his doings justifie with his *owne* hand. . . . . . . V. xi. 4. 9
Enwallow'd in his *owne* blacke bloudy gore, ... V. xi. 14. 6
of his *owne* vaine fancies thought did frame: . . . . V. xi. 19. 4
that faire Lady, . . . Is mine *owne* love, ... V. xi. 49. 7
withheld . . . with her *owne* good will, ... V. xi. 49. 9
why . . . 'forborne Your *owne* good shield . . . . V. xi. 52. 2
She feedes on her *owne* maw unnaturall, ... V. xii. 31. 7
and murder her *owne* mynd; . . . . V. xii. 33. 5
'The Lady, which doth *owne* This Castle, ... VI. i. 14. 5
To pay each with his *owne* is right . . . . VI. i. 42. 3
he made him sweare By his *owne* sword, ... VI. i. 43. 6
ire Of her *owne* knight had given him his *owne* due hire? . VI. ii. 13. 9
To wreake on me the guilt of his *owne* wrong: . . . . VI. ii. 21. 6

Own—*Continued.*
'and right, . . . that him befell by his *owne* fault: . . . . . VI. ii. 23. 6
To wrong the weaker, oft falles in his *owne* assault.' . . . . VI. ii. 23. 9
Upon the steed of her *owne* late dead knight; . . . . VI. ii. 39. 8
that is his proper *owne:* . . . . VI. iii. 1. 7
His care more then her *owne* . . . . VI. iii. 12. 2
Forgetfull of her *owne* to minde his feares: . . . . VI. iii. 12. 3
Sith his *own* thought he knew most cleare . . . . VI. iii. 16. 6
would on her *owne* Palfrey him have eased, ... VI. iii. 32. 8
for thine *owne* defence, on foote alight . . . . VI. iii. 35. 8
As of her *owne* by liverey and seisin; . . . . VI. iv. 37. 7
She bore it thence, and ever as her *owne* it kept. . . . . . VI. iv. 37. 9
She made him think it surely was his *owne;* . . . . VI. iv. 38. 6
breake forth in his *owne* proper kynd. . . . . VI. v. 1. 9
ever more and more her *owne* affliction wrought. . . . . . . VI. v. 6. 9
To be his Timias, his *owne* true Squire; . . . . VI. v. 23. 2
must proceed alone From your *owne* will . . . . VI. vi. 7. 3
allure . . . Into her trap unto their *owne* decay: . . . . VI. vi. 42. 4
both combynd, . . . each to make his *owne*. . . . . VI. vii. 3. 9
he bathed lay in his *owne* bloody gore. . . . . VI. vii. 8. 9
so would ever live, and love her *owne* delight. . . . . VI. vii. 30. 9
whether by . . . sleight, Or their *owne* guilt, ... VI. viii. 34. 6
It was his *owne* true groome, the gentle Squire, ... VI. viii. 27. 6
good Sir Calepine, her *owne* true Knight, ... VI. viii. 33. 2
serve their *owne* necessities with others need. . . . . . . VI. viii. 35. 9
Which he atchieved to his *owne* great gaines, ... VI. ix. 2. 8
noursed well As his *owne* chyld; . . . . VI. ix. 14. 8
she in tract of time accompted was his *owne*. . . . . VI. ix. 14. 9
(Being his harts *owne* wish,) . . . . VI. ix. 16. 9
through pride do their *owne* perill weave, ... VI. ix. 22. 3
'It is to fashion his *owne* lyfes estate, ... VI. ix. 31. 2
This simple sort of life . . . Be it your *owne:* . . . . VI. ix. 33. 9
feeding on the bayt of his *owne* bane: . . . . VI. ix. 34. 4
Was readie oft his *owne* heart to devoure, ... VI. ix. 39. 4
That even her *owne* Cytheron, ... VI. x. 9. 6
his *owne* purchase and his onely prize; . . . . VI. xi. 12. 3
Right well knew Coridon his *owne* late sheepe, ... VI. xi. 37. 6
Who as her *owne* it nurst . . . . VI. xii. 9. 9
Is her *owne* daughter, her *owne* infant . . . . VI. xii. 20. 6
Acknowledg'd for his *owne* faire Pastorell. . . . . VI. xii. 22. 4
That in thine *owne* behalfe maist partiall seeme: . . . . . . VII. vi. 35. 3
wouldest needs thine *owne* conceit areed! . . . . VII. vi. 46. 8
the gods *owne* principality, Which Jove usurpes . . . . . . VII. vii. 16. 5
So makes himself his *owne* consuming pray: . . . . VII. vii. 24. 5
Do worke their *owne* perfection so by fate: . . . . VII. vii. 58. 7
know no end of her *owne* mysery, ... *Am.* xxv. 2
She doth allure me to mine *owne* decay, ... *Am.* liii. 7
In her *owne* powre . . . . *Am.* lviii. 2
trusting on his *owne* assurance; . . . . *Am.* lviii. 10
in the stay of her *owne* stedfast might, ... *Am.* lix. 11
when ye list your *owne* mishaps to mourne, ... *Epith.* 7
Helpe me mine *owne* loves prayses to resound; . . . . *Epith.* 14
the weight of their *own* surquedry, ... *Com. Son.* iv. 5
elder then thine *owne* nativitie, ... *H.L.* 54
His *owne* faire mother, . . . Did lend him light from her *owne*
goodly ray; . . . . *H.L.* 72, 73
Threatning their *owne* confusion and decay: . . . . *H.L.* 82
The mirrour of his *owne* thought doth admyre, ... *H.B.* 224
Beginnes his *owne*, and my old fault renewes. . . . . *H.H.L.* 21
on his *owne* dread presence to attend, ... *H.H.L.* 68
And sit in Gods *owne* seat without commission; . . . . . . *H.H.L.* 82
He made by love out of His *owne* like mould, ... *H.H.L.* 116
Had it beene wrong to aske his *owne* with gaine? . . . . . *H.H.L.* 180
Archangels, which attend On Gods *owne* person, ... *H.H.B.* 98
His throne is . . . hid in his *owne* brightnesse . . . . *H.H.B.* 178
beautie . . . Sparkled on her from Gods *owne* glorious face, *H.H.B.* 207
beautie . . . more increast by her *owne* goodly grace, ... *H.H.B.* 208
whom God . . . lets his *owne* Beloved to behold; . . . . . . *H.H.B.* 241
endlesse happinesse of thine *owne* name . . . . *Proth.* 153

Owner. the rightfull *owner* of that steede, ... II. iv. 2. 1
thou didst these goods bereave From rightfull *owner* . . . . II. vii. 19. 4
Ne forst his rightful *owner* to offend; . . . . II. viii. 21. 4
glauncing downe would not his *owner* byte; . . . . II. viii. 38. 4

Owre. *See* **Ore.**

Ox. The fatte *Oxe*, that wont ligge in the stal, ... *S.C.* S. 118
Into an *Oxe* he was transformd of yore. . . . . I. v. 47. 5
Like as the sacred *Oxe* that carelesse stands, ... III. iv. 17. 1
Betweene the toylefull *Oxe* and humble Asse, ... *H.H.L.* 227

Ox-eye. *Oxeye* still greene, and bitter Patience; . . . . *Gn.* 678

Oxford. *Oxford*, thine doth Thame most glorify. . . . . IV. xi. 26. 9
Cambridge or *Oxford*, Englands goodly beames. . . . . IV. xi. 35. 6

Oza. the Paynim brethren, hight Octa and *Oza*, ... III. iii. 52. 7

Oze. *See* **Ouse.**

P

Pace. *See* **Footpace.**
passing by with rolling wreathed *pace*, ... *Gn.* 253
more fierce in visage, and in *pace*, ... *Gn.* 269
with big words, and with a stately *pace*, ... *Hub.* 646
walkes upright with comely stedfast *pace*, ... *Hub.* 728
With staggring *pace* and dismall lookes dismay, ... *D.* 564
Thether Duessa badd him bend his *pace*, ... I. iv. 3. 7
All hurtlen forth; and she, with princely *pace*, ... I. iv. 16. 3
And to the Paynims lodging comes with silent *pace*. . . . . I. iv. 44. 9
they . . . brought the heavy corse with easy *pace* . . . . . . I. v. 31. 2
them; who forth by them doe *pace*, ... I. v. 36. 3
Did to him *pace* sad battaile to darrayne, ... I. vii. 11. 5
with creeping crooked *pace* forth came An old old man, . . . I. viii. 30. 1

Pace—*Continued.*
How he did fashion his untoward *pace;* . . . . I. viii. 31. 2
toward them full matronely did *pace*. . . . . I. x. 8. 5
They numbred even steps and equall *pace;* . . . . I. x. 12. 5
spy Her loved knight to move his manly *pace:* . . . . I. xi. 33. 7
with slow *pace* the knight did lead, ... II. i. 7. 8
when as still he saw him towards *pace*, ... II. i. 26. 4
where towards him did *pace* Two Paynim knights . . . . . . II. viii. 10. 1
towards them did *pace* An armed knight, ... II. viii. 17. 4
With greedy *pace* forth rushing . . . . II. ix. 14. 9
oftentimes he would relent his *pace*, ... II. xi. 27. 3
Not fitt for speedy *pace*, or manly exercize. . . . . II. xii. 46. 9
somewhat gan relent his earnest *pace;* . . . . II. xii. 65. 8

Pain—*Continued.*
told the story of the mortall *payne*, . . . II. ii. 45. 7
found with perill and with *paine;* . . . II. iii. 41. 2
more for ranck despight then for great *paine*, . . . II. iv. 15. 7
Deserves to taste his follies fruit, repented *payne*.' . . . II. v. 24. 9
made him to forget His former *payne*, . . . II. v. 30. 9
In joyous pleasure then in grievous *paine;* . . . II. vi. 1. 2
waste thy joyous howres in needelesse *paine*, . . . II. vi. 17. 4
Thy carcas for their pray, the guerdon of thy *payn*.' . . . II. vi. 28. 9
By that wayes side there sate internall *Payne*, . . . II. vii. 21. 5
Infinite moe tormented in like *paine* He there beheld, . . . II. vii. 63. 1
report of that their perlous *paine*, . . . II. ix. 17. 4
wrought, with perill and with *payne*, . . . II. xi. 15. 4
Had not his gentle Squire beheld his *paine*, . . . II. xi. 29. 8
whiles he marveild still, did still him *payne;* . . . II. xi. 44. 5
The worldes sweet In from *paine* and wearisome turmoyle.' . II. xii. 32. 9
All were he wearie of his former *paine;* . . . III. i. 29. 4
Whereof did grow her first engraffed *payne*, . . . III. ii. 17. 5
what needeth thee to eke my *payne?* . . . III. ii. 35. 2
Both joynt partakers of their fatall *payne:* . . . III. iii. 37. 7
with *paine* Or powre, be hable it to remedy, . . . III. iii. 40. 3
Yet Carados himselfe from her escapt with *payne*.' . . . III. iii. 55. 9
Could scarce recovered bee out of her *paine:* . . . III. iv. 35. 2
In restlesse anguish and unquiet *paine;* . . . III. iv. 61. 2
He on the bancke arryvd with mickle *payne*, . . . III. v. 21. 2
Out of her fleshly ferme fled to the place of *paine*. . . . III. v. 23. 9
She cast to comfort him with busie *paine*. . . . III. v. 31. 5
O foolish physick, and unfruitfull *paine*, . . . III. v. 42. 1
The like that mine may be your *paine* another tide. . . . III. vi. 21. 9
Spare, gentle sister, with reproch my *paine* to eeke; . . . III. vi. 22. 9
She bore withouten *paine*, that she conceiv'd Withouten pleasure; . . . III. vi. 27. 2
Fleshly corruption, nor mortall *payne*. . . . III. vi. 33. 4
with incessaunt *paine* To wander through the world . . . III. vii. 54. 3
them conjure, upon eternall *paine*, To counsell her, . . . III. viii. 4. 7
soone forgot his former sickely *payne:* . . . III. viii. 10. 3
'Well may yee speede in so praiseworthy *payne!* . . . III. viii. 51. 2
nothing new to him was that same *paine*, . . . III. ix. 29. 6
Ne *paine* at all; . . . III. ix. 29. 7
Hath fownd another partner of your *payne;* . . . III. ix. 40. 2
making layes of love and lovers *paine*, . . . III. x. 8. 4
too simple ever to surprise . . . Paridell, for all his *paine*. . III. x. 20. 4
Your worthy *paine* shall wel reward with guerdon rich.' . . . III. x. 28. 9
painefull pleasure turnes to pleasing *paine*. . . . III. x. 60. 4
day and night afflicts with mortall *paine*, . . . III. xi. 17. 2
evermore encreased her consuming *paine*. . . . III. xii. 21. 9
else her *paine* Should be remedilesse; . . . III. xii. 34. 5
Her body, late the prison of sad *paine*, . . . III. xii. 45. *or.* 3
this of Florimels unworthie *paine* . . . IV. i. 1. 5
'Last turne was mine, well proved to my *paine;* . . . IV. ii. 6. 4
the thrid By griesly Lachesis was spun with *paine*, . . . IV. ii. 48. 6
he that happie seemes, and least in *payne*, . . . IV. iii. 1. 8
thereby did more prolong their *paine:* . . . IV. iii. 2. 3
wondrous *paine*, that did the more enhaunce His haughtie courage . . . IV. iii. 8. 7
he for *paine* himselfe n'ote right upreare, . . . IV. iii. 9. 6
So worthie of the perill, worthy of the *paine*. . . . IV. iv. 16. 9
All travellers tormented are with *paine:* . . . IV. iv. 47. 6
In seeking him that should her *paine* assoyle; . . . IV. v. 30. 3
The manner of their worke and wearie *paine;* . . . IV. v 38. 2
He felt his hart for very *paine* to quake, . . . IV. v. 44. 5
In such disquiet and hart-fretting *payne* . . . IV. v. 45. 1
the *paine* Her tender hart in peeces would divide: . . . IV. vii. 10. 2
Ne ought mote ease or mitigate his *paine*, . . . IV. vii. 47. 4
rent his haire and scratcht his face for *paine*. . . . IV. viii. 46. 5
Dislikefull *paine* so sad a taske to take, . . . IV. ix. 40. 3
To take on him that *paine:* . . . IV. ix. 41. 3
is the *paine* thereof much greater then the fee. . . . IV. x. 3. 9
for guerdon of my *paine*, . . . IV. x. 10. 8
Long languishing there in unpittied *paine*, . . . IV. x. 13. 8
Left a fayre Ladie languishing in *payne:* . . . IV. xi. 1. 2
did so well employ his carefull *paine*, . . . IV. xi. 7. 2
made it seeme to feele her grievous *paine*, . . . IV. xii. 5. 8
I him condemne, and deeme his *paine*, . . . IV. xii. 11. 3
still bemoning her unworthy *paine*. . . . IV. xii. 17. 5
it was no old sore which his new *paine* procured; . . . IV. xii. 23. 9
Florimell it was which wrought his *paine*, . . . IV. xii. 27. 8
when he wak't out of his warelesse *paine*, . . . V. i. 22. 3
rather then his love should suffer *paine*, . . . V. i. 27. 7
When as the *paine* of death she tasted had, . . . V. iv. 11. 2
with bootlesse *paine* Annoy this noble Knight, . . . V. v. 15. 8
him entreat for grace that had procur'd her *paine*. . . . V. v. 28. 9
Thereto compelled through hart-murdring *paine;* . . . V. v. 30. 8
Die rather would he in penurious *paine*, . . . V. v. 46. 5
By change of place seeking to ease her *paine;* . . . V. vi. 15. 5
chawing the cud of griefe and inward *paine*, . . . V. vi. 19. 2
to perpetuall *paine* Had damn'd her sonnes . . . V. vii. 10. 7
having force increast through furious *paine*, . . . V. vii. 33. 6
of her wound which sore did *paine*, . . . V. vii. 34. 5
the change of aire and place Would change her *paine*, . . . V. vii. 45. 4
taken have this toylesome *paine* For wretched woman, . . . V. x. 21. 2
What guerdon can I give thee for thy *paine*, . . . V. xi. 16. 8
lesse all *paine* Then losse of fame . . . V. xi. 55. 7
yet old Sergis did so well him *paine*, . . . V. xii. 10. 7
He lightly reft his head to ease him of his *paine*. . . . V. xii. 23. 9
He sorely punished with heavie *payne;* . . . V. xii. 25. 7
day and night employ'd his busie *paine* . . . V. xii. 26. 3
those hags them selves did *paine* To sharpen him, . . . V. xii. 41. 8
by the Gods with *paine* Planted in earth, . . . VI. Pr. 3. 5
She freely gave that Castle for his *paine*, . . . VI. i. 46. 7

Pain—*Continued.*
praise likewise deserve good thewes enforst with *paine*. . . . VI. ii. 2. 9
enforst to beare though to my *paine*, . . . VI. ii. 12. 5
But more enforst my *paine*, the more my plaints to heare. . VI. ii. 22. 9
And Calidore forth passed to his former *payne*. . . . VI. ii. 38. 9
The anguish of his *paine* to overpasse: . . . VI. iii. 14. 7
forth he passed thorough that daies *paine*, . . . VI. iii. 17. 7
Tho wexing weary of that toylesome *paine*, . . . VI. iii. 29. 3
beare her on thy backe with pleasing *payne*, . . . VI. iii. 32. 4
His best endevour and his daily *paine* . . . VI. iv. 16. 2
then oppressing him with urgent *paine*, . . . VI. iv. 22. 6
In th' heritage of our unhappie *paine:* . . . VI. iv. 31. 5
a fit reliefe For all her *paine*, . . . VI. iv. 34. 5
shut up all his plaint in privy *paine*. . . . VI. v. 24. 5
for grievous *paine* Of their late woundes, . . . VI. v. 39. 7
such hurts are hellish *paine*. . . . VI. vi. 1. 9
Sorrow, and anguish, and impatient *paine*, . . . VI. vi. 8. 6
After he gotten had with busie *paine* Some of their weapons . VI. vi. 38. 7
the Carle with *paine* Saved him selfe . . . VI. viii. 9. 3
Thus I triumphed long in lovers *paine*, . . . VI. viii. 21. 6
mocketh all my *paine*, and laughs the more I mourn.' . . . VI. viii. 24. 9
Of her long travell and turmoyling *paine;* . . . VI. viii. 32. 8
many a one Burnt in her love, and with sweet pleasing *payne* VI. ix. 10. 3
In seas of troubles and of toylesome *paine;* . . . VI. ix. 31. 6
of all his labour and long *paine* . . . VI. ix. 38. 5
His former quest, so full of toile and *paine:* . . . VI. x. 2. 2
had bred his restlesse *paine;* . . . VI. x. 31. 8
with labour and long *paine*, . . . VI. xi. 22. 5
more increast the anguish of his *paine:* . . . VI. xi. 26. 3
with restlesse *paine* and toile . . . VI. xii. 22. 8
to many ones great *paine*, . . . VII. vi. 4. 7
Typhons fall, or proud Ixions *paine*, . . . VII. vi. 29. 6
frustrate all her *paine*, . . . VII. vi. 48. 5
Faunus (for her *paine*) Of her beloved Fanchin did obtaine, . VII. vi. 53. 4
Them well disposed by his busie *paine*, . . . VII. vii. 4. 7
taking litle *paine* To knit the knot, . . . *Am.* vi. 13
and makes my *pain* her sport. . . . *Am.* x. 14
All *paine* hath end, . . . But mine, . . . *Am.* xi. 13
Yet as it was, I hardly scap't with *paine*. . . . *Am.* xvi. 14
Why then should I accoumpt of little *paine*, . . . *Am.* xxvi. 13
Shall to you purchas with her thankles *paine!* . . . *Am.* xxvii. 12
Still to behold the object of their *paine*, . . . *Am.* xxxv. 2
So pleasing is in my extreamest *paine*, . . . *Am.* xlii. 2
dying, doe themselves of *payne* beguyle. . . . *Am.* xlvii. 12
thinck they dy with pleasure, live with *payne*. . . . *Am.* xlvii. 14
yeeld To sorrow and to solitary *paine;* . . . *Am.* lii. 6
making their *paine* thy play, . . . *H.L.* 135
What puissant conquest, what adventurous *paine*, . . . *H.L.* 221
O how doth it torment . . . with more then hellish *paine!* . *H.L.* 253
Of never-dead yet ever-dying *paine;* . . . *H.H.L.* 126
But love of us, for guerdon of thy, *paine:* . . . *H.H.L.* 177
Then let thy flinty hart, that feeles no *paine*, . . . *H.H.L.* 246
all that pleased earst now seemes to *paine;* . . . *H.H.B.* 270
Walkt forth to ease my *payne* . . . *Proth.* 10

Pained. Into his nosthrils creeping, so him *pained*, . . . *Van.* viii. 10
Perigot, so well hath hym *payned*, . . . *S.C.* Au. 133
he saw my cruell foes me *pained*, . . . *Ti.* 144
griefe thereof my spirite greatly *pained*. . . . *Ti.* 560
paynd himselfe . . . to reare Her out of carelesse swowne. . I. ii. 45. 3
paynd with womanish art To hide her wound, . . . IV. vi. 40. 7
pained Them selves her footing to direct aright, . . . IV. xi. 25. 3
The more thereby her tender hart was *payned;* . . . V. v. 44. 7
her infestred wound, That sore her *payn'd*, . . . VI. xi. 24. 7
plead thy masters cause, unjustly *payned*. . . . *Am.* xlviii. 8
sad to see him *pained*. . . . *Epig.* iv. 34

Painful. carefull travailes of the *painefull* day: . . . *Bel.*[1] i. 4
messengers of this my *painfull* plight, . . . *S.C.* Jun. 98
whether in *paynefull* love I pyne, . . . *S.C.* Au. 109
With *painfull* torments to be sorely beaten. . . . *Gn.* 352
it may no *painfull* worke endure, . . . *Hub.* 275
Alcyon, *painfull* is thy plight, . . . *D.* 174
will till then my *painfull* penance eeke. . . . *D.* 391
too *painfull* to repeat The passed fortunes, . . . *Col.* 32
to augment her *painefull* penaunce more, . . . I. iii. 14. 1
dwell in perill of like *painefull* plight, . . . I. v. 52. 4
by that *painfull* way they pas . . . I. x. 46. 1
thy *painefull* pilgrimage To yonder same Hierusalem doe bend, I. x. 61. 3
Who seekes with *painfull* toile shall honor soonest fynd: . . II. iii. 40. 9
Which to outbarre, with *painefull* pyonings . . . II. x. 63. 7
In the deare closett of her *painefull* syde . . . III. ii. 11. 7
long enlargement of her *painefull* smart. . . . III. viii. 2. 4
painefull pleasure turnes to pleasing paine. . . . III. x. 60. 4
with most *painefull* pangs to sigh and sob, . . . III. xi. 8. 8
not with arras made in *painefull* loome, . . . III. xi. 51. 3
every place seem'd *painefull*, and ech changing vaine. . . . IV. v. 40. 9
in that *painefull* stound When he him saw, . . . VI. i. 11. 7
some asswagement of their *painefull* plight. . . . VI. v. 40. 4
for to drive The *painefull* plough, . . . VI. viii. 35. 6
Or looke with pitty on my *payneful* smart; . . . *Am.* xviii. 8
The *paynefull* smith, with force of fervent heat, . . . *Am.* xxxii. 1

Painfully. Might them oppresse, and *painefully* turmoile, . . VI. viii. 23. 4

Paining. To wype his wounds, and ease their bitter *payning*. VI. ii. 41. 5

Pains. Pitie the *paines* that thou thy selfe didst prove. . . . *S.C.* Ja. 18
in lieu of *paines* so gracious, . . . *Gn.* 333
endles *paines* and hideous heavinesse . . . *Gn.* 371
With bitter torture, and impatient *paines*, . . . *Gn.* 628
To take what *paines* may anie living wight; . . . *Hub.* 271
askes small *paines*, but thriftines to save, . . . *Hub.* 278
would they take no *paines* to get their living, . . . *Hub.* 349
Ne is the *paines* so great, but beare ye may, . . . *Hub.* 446

Pains 630 Pales

Pains—*Continued.*
In case his *paines* were recompenst with reason. . . . . . . *Hub.* 887
Our pleasant groves, which planted were with *paines*, ... *T.M.* 277
dooth multiplye My dying *paines*, ... *D.* 74
Remember yet my undeserved *paines*; . . . . *D.* 522
So well he wrought with practise and with *paines*, ... *As.* 99
I send This present of my *paines*, ... *Ded. Son.* iv. 14
messengers of hell, . . . gan tel Their bootelesse *paines*, . . . I. ii. 2. 4
though a tree I seme, yet cold and heat me *paines*.' . . . . I. ii. 33. 9
paines far passing that long wandring Greeke, ... I. iii. 21. 5
due recompence Of all her passed *paines*: . . . . I. iii. 30. 2
Dead is Sansfoy, his vitall *paines* are past, ... I. iv. 49. 6
Great *pains*, and greater praise, both never to be donne.' . . . I. v. 43. 9
How shall I quite the *paynes* ye suffer for my sake? . . . . . I. viii. 26. 9
After long *paines* and labors manifold, He found the meanes . I. viii. 40. 5
his spright Had past the *paines* of hell . . . . I. x. 32. 9
He could escape fowle death or deadly *pains*? . . . . I. xii. 36. 5
So double was his *paines*, so double be his praise. . . . . . . II. ii. 25. 9
that toilesome *paines* doest take, ... II. vi. 15. 1
Yet no man for them taketh *paines* or care, ... II. vi. 15. 8
Yet no man to them can his carefull *paines* compare. . . . . II. vi. 15. 9
every feend his busie *paines* applyde . . . . II. vii. 35. 8
each his *paynes* to others profit still employd. . . . . II. x. 14. 9
end of that Carles dayes and his owne *paynes* did make. . . II. xi. 46. 9
After long wayes and perilous *paines* endur'd, ... III. i. 1. 2
Could judge what *paines* doe loving harts perplexe. . . . . . III. i. 54. 5
with long enduring *paines* Doe tosse, ... III. iii. 9. 4
Which alwaies of his *paines* he made the chiefest meed. . . . III. iv. 4. 9
pursew The fearefull damzell with incessant *payns*; . . . . . III. iv. 46. 3
no *paines* did spare To doe him ease, ... III. v. 50. 1
'What is there ells but cease these fruitlesse *paines*, ... III. xi. 24. 1
paines in love, or punishments in hell: . . . . III. xii. 26. 5
yet no *paines* wouldst take: . . . . IV. ii. 14. 4
save her honour with your ventrous *paines*: . . . . IV. ii. 27. 8
Both equall *paines* and equall perill shared; . . . . IV. v. 46. 5
did her passed *paines* in quiet rest assoyle. . . . . IV. vii. 3. 9
seeking ever since with endlesse *paines* . . . . IV. ix. 38. 3
through *paines* and perlous jeopardie, ... IV. x. 28. 7
for his *paines* a whistle him behight, ... IV. xi. 6. 8
for sparing litle cost or *paines*, ... IV. xi. 22. 8
learne to love by learning lovers *paines* to rew. . . . . . . IV. xii. 13. 9
Great shame to lose so long employed *paines*, ... V. v. 48. 3
her shewed there The present of his *paines*, ... V. xi. 33. 6
And twixt them both with parted *paines* did beare, ... VI. ii. 48. 5
his large *paines* in her deliveraunce . . . . VI. iii. 19. 4
so well he did his busie *paines* apply, ... VI. iii. 28. 1
To make them to endure the *pains* did them torment. . . . . VI. v. 32. 9
for their *paines* obtaine of him a goodly meed. . . . . VI. vii. 4. 9
that same foole, which most increast her *paines*, ... VI. vii. 44. 5
restlesse *paines* did take. . . . . VI. viii. 33. 9
Reaping eternall glorie of his restlesse *paines*. . . . . VI. ix. 2. 9
Ne any *paines* ne perill did he shonne, ... VI. x. 32. 7
all his *paines* did closely emulate; . . . . VI. x. 33. 4
Onely my *paines* will be the more to get her; . . . . *Am.* li. 13
seemd the longer for my greater *paines*. . . . . *Am.* lx. 12
to deprive Remembrance of all *paines* . . . . *Am.* lxiii. 12
All *paines* are nothing in respect of this; . . . . *Am.* lxiii. 13
came the tyde, and made my *paynes* his pray. . . . . *Am.* lxxv. 4
all the plagues, and horrid *paines*, of hell . . . . *Am.* lxxxv. 5
for all the *paynes* and sorrowes past, ... *Epith.* 32
by all these perils and these *paynes*, ... *H.L.* 238
through *paines* of Purgatorie . . . . *H.L.* 278
all the *paines* and woes that I endure, ... *H.L.* 295
would I thinke these *paines* no *paines* at all, ... *H.L.* 299
His *paines*, his povertie, his sharpe assayes, ... *H.H.L.* 235
Pains'. Great thankes . . . gave for his *paynes* hyre . . . . I. x. 68. 5
Paint. To *peinct* their girlonds with his colowres; . . . . . *S.C.* F. 121
to *paint* out my unrest, ... *S.C.* Jun. 79
paint with pallid greene her buds of gold. . . . . *Gn.* 222
use to *paint* in rimes the troublous state . . . . *T.M.* 381
He . . . his percing speach gan *paynt*: . . . . II. i. 9. 5
rosy red Did *paint* his chearefull cheekes, ... II. i. 41. 5
wanting colours fayre To *paint* it forth, ... II. x. 28. 7
Nor life-resembling pencill it can *paynt*: . . . . III. Pr. 2. 2
The pourtraict of so heavenly hew to *paint*. . . . . *H.H.B.* 231
Painted. *See* **Gay-painted.**
With *painted* words tho gan this proude weede . . . . *S.C.* F. 160
with Comick sock to beautefie The *painted* Theaters, ... *T.M.* 177
When *painted* faces . . . Doo fawne on you, ... *Ti.* 200
Painted with thousand colours, ... *Mui.* 90
through report of that lives *painted* blisse, ... *Col.* 685
all the hinder partes, . . . Were ruinous and old, but *painted* cunningly. . . . . I. iv. 5. 9
a kirtle of discolourd say . . . *ypaynted* full of eies; . . . . I. iv. 31. 2
painted in a table plaine, The damned ghosts . . . . I. ix. 49. 6
aboundance of an ydle braine . . . and *painted* forgery, . . . II. Pr. 1. 4
filles with flowres fayre Floraes *painted* lap: . . . . II. ii. 6. 5
As Peacocke that his *painted* plumes doth pranck, ... II. iii. 6. 4
breath out bounteous smels, and *painted* colors shew. . . . . II. v. 29. 9
her *painted* bote streightway Turnd to the shore, ... II. vi. 4. 6
No arborett with *painted* blossomes drest . . . . II. vi. 12. 7
Decked with diverse plumes, like *painted* Jayes, ... II. viii. 5. 8
he gan display His *painted* nimble wings, ... II. viii. 8. 9
wals Were *painted* faire with memorable gestes . . . . II. ix. 53. 3
The *painted* flowres, the trees upshooting hye, ... II. xii. 58. 5
Her bow and *painted* quiver, ... III. vi. 18. 2
There was he *painted* full of burning dartes, ... III. xi. 44. 8
paynted plumes in goodly order dight, ... III. xii. 8. 2
was that all but *paynted* and pourloynd, ... III. xii. 14. 6
on her legs she *painted* buskins wore, ... V. v. 3. 1
Painted—*Continued.*
Would never more delight in *painted* show Of such false blisse, VI. x. 3. 7
Princes bowres adorne with *painted* imagery. . . . . VII. vii. 10. 9
by right deserts, t' attaine . . . And not by *painted* shewes, . *Com. Son.* ii. 3
rutty Bancke . . . Was *paynted* all with variable flowers, . . *Proth.* 13
Painter. The Chian *Peincter*, when he was requirde . . . . . *Ded. Son.* xvii. 1
Poets witt, that passeth *Painter* farre . . . . III. Pr. 2. 6
Ne could that *Painter* (had he lived yet) . . . . *H.H.B.* 211
Painters'. passing farre All *Painters* skill, ... *Mui.* 91
Painting. all their wealth for *painting* on a wall; . . . . . . *Col.* 724
Paints. With sundrie colours *paints* the sprinckled lay: . . . *Gn.* 110
Her goodly bow, which *paints* the liquid ayre, ... V. iii. 25. 3
Pair. pittying this *paire* of lovers trew, ... *As.* 182
nigh he drew unto this gentle *payre* . . . . I. iii. 34. 1
The wretched *payre* transformd to treen mould; . . . . . . I. vii. 26. 5
'No faith so fast' . . . 'but flesh does *paire*.' . . . . I. vii. 41. 8
there sate a gentle *payre*, Of turtle doves, ... I. x. 31. 8
That forward *paire* she ever would asswage, ... II. ii. 38. 5
So forth they pas, a well consorted *payre*, ... II. iii. 11. 1
that gay *payre*, issewing on the shore, ... II. vi. 11. 6
thus bespoke: 'Ye warlike *payre*, ... II. viii. 27. 2
An huge great *payre* of bellowes, ... II. ix. 30. 4
The constant *payre* heard all that he did say, ... II. xii. 76. 4
a wanton *payre* Of lovers loosely knit, ... III. x. 16. 8
Dissemblaunce and Suspect . . . yet an unequall *paire*; . . . III. xii. 14. 2
A *paire* of Pincers in his hand he had, ... III. xii. 16. 5
That evill matched *paire* they seemd to bee: . . . . III. xii. 18. 6
the lovely *paire* drew nigh to hond: . . . . IV. i. 34. 1
A *paire* of red-whot yron tongs did take . . . . IV. v. 44. 2
holding forth on hie An huge great *paire* of ballance . . . . V. ii. 30. 3
having lately left that lovely *payre*, ... V. iv. 3. 1
So forth they traveld, an uneven *payre* . . . . VI. v. 9. 1
A *paire* of waights, with which he did assoyle . . . . VII. vii. 38. 7
did deeme Them . . . to be that same *payre* . . . . *Proth.* 62
Pairs. These *paires* of friends in peace and setled rest, . . . IV. ix. 17. 2
therein thousand *payres* of lovers walkt, ... IV. x. 25. 6
Palace. in Princes *pallace* thou doe sitt, ... *S.C.* O. 80
yet is Princes *pallace* the most fitt,) . . . . *S.C.* O. 81
followed unto his *palaice* hye; . . . . *Hub.* 1107
unto the *Pallace* nigh he came. . . . . *Hub.* 1265
He toward his owne *Pallace* forth did pas; . . . . *Hub.* 1344
all the *Pallace* quaked at the stound, ... *Hub.* 1353
A stately *Pallace* built of squared bricke, ... I. iv. 4. 1
Of her, that was the Lady of that *Pallace* bright. . . . . . . I. iv. 6. 9
Duessa . . . Returnd to stately *pallace* of Dame Pryde: . . . I. v. 45. 2
after to his *Pallace* he them bringes, ... I. xii. 13. 1
noise Heard sownd through all the *Pallace* . . . . I. xii. 39. 2
passage plaine To pleasures *pallace*: . . . . II. iii. 41. 8
all those pleasaunt bowres, and *Pallace* brave, ... II. xii. 83. 1
When to Joves *pallace* she doth take her way, ... IV. xi. 28. 3
Where they a stately *pallace* did behold . . . . V. ix. 21. 4
Unto the *pallace* where their kings did rayne, ... V. xii. 25. 2
To whose bright shining *palace* straight she came, ... VII. vi. 8. 3
The goodly building of her *Palace* bright, ... VII. vi. 10. 2
To Joves faire *palace* fixt in heavens hight; . . . . VII. vi. 15. 2
To Joves high *Palace* straight cast to ascend, ... VII. vi. 23. 8
all her body like a *pallace* fayre, ... *Epith.* 178
A *pallace* fit for such a virgin Queene. . . . . *H.B.* 126
a waste and emptie place In His wyde *Pallace*, ... *H.H.L.* 102
Palaces. olde walls, olde arches, . . . Olde *Palaces*, ... *Ro.* iii. 4
Romane *palaces* Made of some matter no lesse firme . . . . *Ro.* ix. 7
these brave *Pallaces*, which maystred bee Of time, ... *Ro.* xviii. 3
Fashion the pourtraicts of these *Palacis*, ... *Ro.* xxv. 10
These haughtie heapes, these *palaces* of olde, ... *Ro.* xxvii. 3
the Princes *pallaces* fell fast To ruine . . . . *Hub.* 1175
her royall *P'laces* Be fild with praises . . . . *T.M.* 580
Strong walls, rich porches, princelie *pallaces*, ... *Ti.* 93
My *pallaces* possessed of my foe, ... V. x. 23. 3
Up to your haughty *pallaces* may mount; . . . . *Epith.* 420
Palaemon. old *Palemon* free from spight . . . . *Col.* 396
Now hight *Palemon*, and is saylers frend; . . . . IV. xi. 13. 6
Palatine. Upon her bellie th' antique *Palatine*, ... *Ro.* iv. 10
Pale. *pale* and wanne he was, (alas the while!) . . . . *S.C.* Ja. 8
Ne wants there *pale* Narcisse, ... *Gn.* 679
such as Envie *pale* . . . Could not accuse. . . . . *Mui.* 301
His cheekes wext *pale*, ... *D.* 542
Out of his lips like lilies *pale* and soft: . . . . *As.* 166
with *pale* and deadly hew, At last she up gan lift: . . . . . I. ii. 45. 5
As ashes *pale* of hew, and seeming ded; . . . . I. iv. 33. 7
silver Cynthia wexed *pale* and faynt, ... I. vii. 34. 8
made her . . . sad to view his visage *pale* and wan, ... I. viii. 42. 3
Thus as he spake, his visage wexed *pale*, ... I. ix. 16. 1
troubled blood through his *pale* face was seene . . . . I. ix. 51. 5
seeming *pale* and faynt, ... II. i. 9. 4
With lips full *pale* and foltring tong opprest, ... II. i. 47. 4
As *pale* and wan as ashes was his looke, ... II. xi. 22. 1
Spoild of their rosy red were woxen *pale* and wan. . . . . . III. v. 29. 9
with *pale* eyes fast fixed on the rest, ... III. x. 41. 2
he fast away did fly, As ashes *pale* of hew, ... III. xii. 12. 6
Trembling in heart, and looking *pale* and wan, ... IV. ii. 49. 4
through long fasting woxen *pale* and wan, ... IV. vii. 43. 3
kissing oft his visage *pale* and wan: . . . . IV. ix. 9. 5
Her lips were, like raw lether, *pale* and blew: . . . . V. xii. 29. 7
That other swayne, like ashes deadly *pale*, ... VI. vii. 17. 8
to prove how *pale* and weake she was. . . . . VI. xi. 12. 9
Paled. She is ybrought unto a *paled* greene, ... I. v. 5. 3
Pinckt upon gold, and *paled* part per part, ... VI. ii. 6. 2
Palemon. *See* **Palaemon.**
Pales. thou holie *Pales*, ... *Gn.* 28
fruitefull *Pales*, and the forrest greene, ... *Gn.* 116

Palfrey. heavie sate upon her *palfrey* slow; . . . . I. i. 4. 7
Her wanton *palfrey* all was overspred With tinsell trappings, I. ii. 13. 7
to her snowy *Palfrey* got agayne, ... I. iii. 8. 8
Her from her *Palfrey* pluckt, her visage to behold. . . . . . I. iii. 40. 9
Upon a milkwhite *Palfrey* all alone, ... III. i. 15. 2
on a *Palfrey* rydes more white then snow, ... III. v. 5. 6
her white *Palfrey*, having conquered The maistring raines . . III. vii. 2. 7
Her wearie *Palfrey*, closely as she might, ... III. vii. 18. 6
Her flitt *palfrey* did so well apply . . . . III. vii. 24. 5
He sett upon her *Palfrey* tired lame, ... III. vii. 28. 8
The *Palfrey* whereon she did travell . . . . III. viii. 49. 3
A Damzell, flying on a *palfrey* fast . . . . V. viii. 4. 2
would on her owne *Palfrey* him have eased, ... VI. iii. 32. 8
Haling her *palfrey* by the hempen raines: . . . . VI. vii. 44. 4
She from her *palfrey* lighted on the plaine; . . . . VI. viii. 32. 6
Th' one on a *Palfrey* blacke, the other white; . . . . VII. vii. 44. 3
Palfrey's. Upon that milkewhite *Palfreyes* carcas fedd, ... III. vii. 30. 8
Palici. *Palici* . . . did for spight destroy, ... *T.M.* 15
Palimord. after him Sir *Palimord* (**Paliumord*) forth prest: . IV. iv. 21. 5
Palin. There eke is *Palin* worthie of great praise, ... *Col.* 392
Palinode. For Younkers, *Palinode*, such follies fitte, ... *S.C.* May 17
Palinodie, thou art a worldes childe: . . . . *S.C.* May 73
Palinode (if thou him ken) . . . . *S.C.* Jul. 181
Pall. They bene yclad in purple and pall, ... *S.C.* Jul. 173
Aurora in her purple *pall* . . . the dawning day doth call. . . I. iv. 16. 4
He gave her gold and purple *pall* to weare, ... I. vii. 16. 3
that witch they . . . robd of roiall robes, and purple *pall*, . I. viii. 46. 2
In a long purple *pall*, ... II. ix. 37. 1
forestall Their furious encounter, and their fiercenesse *pall*. V. iv. 5. 9
His Lyons skin chaungd to a *pall* of gold, ... V. v. 24. 7
The which she covering with her purple *pall* . . . . V. ix. 50. 8
Palladine. She *Palladine* is hight. . . . . III. vii. 52. 6
Pallas. by his means was vanquished Of *Pallas*, ... *Mui.* 262
Such as Dame *Pallas* . . . Could not accuse. . . . . *Mui.* 301
Such as she was when *Pallas* she attempted, ... *Mui.* 346
Palled. *See* **Pallid.**
His *palled* face, impictured with death, ... *As.* 163
Pallid. *See* **Palled.**
with *pallid* cheekes The Romane triumphs glorie to behold, . *Ro.* xiv. 11
Ye *pallid* spirits, and ye ashie ghoasts, ... *Ro.* xv. 1
paint with *pallid* greene her buds of gold. . . . . *Gn.* 222
pallid Yvie, building his owne bowre; . . . . *Gn.* 675
those *pallid* cheekes and ashy hew, ... *D.* 302
So soone as Night had with her *pallid* hew . . . . III. ii. 28. 1
Gainst which the *pallid* death findes no defence; . . . . . . V. xi. 45. 5
deadly *pallied* hew Benumbes her cheekes: . . . . VI. viii. 40. 6
the Violet, *pallid* blew, ... *Proth.* 30
Palm. he bare . . . in left the conquering *Palme*, ... *Bel.*[1] vii. 11
sodenly the *Palme* and Olive fell, ... *Bel.*[1] vii. 13
Sudden both *Palme* and Olive fell away, ... *Bel.*[2] ix. 13
Lord of himselfe, with *palme* bedight, ... *Gn.* 113
Palmer. A comely *Palmer*, clad in black attyre, ... II. i. 7. 2
'Palmer' . . . 'His be the praise . . . . II. i. 33. 1
gan his voyage make With his blacke *Palmer*, ... II. i. 34. 4
Then turning to his *Palmer* said; . . . . II. i. 57. 1
'Palmer,' quoth he, 'death is an equall doome . . . . II. i. 59. 1
Whom thus at gaze the *Palmer* gan to bord . . . . II. ii. 5. 1
to the *Palmer* gave to beare; . . . . II. ii. 11. 2
'There this old *Palmer* shewd himselfe that day, ... II. ii. 43. 1
His *Palmer* now shall foot no more alone. . . . . II. iii. 3. 5
that blacke *Palmer*, his most trusty guide, ... II. iv. 2. 4
when the *Palmer* saw, he loudly cryde, ... II. iv. 10. 1
Then gan the *Palmer* thus; . . . . II. iv. 34. 1
'Mad man,' (said then the *Palmer*) . . . . II. iv. 44. 1
the *Palmer*, by his grave restraynt, Him stayd . . . . II. v. 24. 3
the Blacke *Palmer* suffred still to stond, ... II. vi. 19. 7
the *Palmer*, whom . . . passage had denide, ... II. viii. 3. 2
The *Palmer* lent his eare unto the noyce, ... II. viii. 4. 1
Whom when the *Palmer* saw, ... II. viii. 7. 1
The *Palmer* seeing his lefte empty place, ... II. viii. 9. 1
Now bene they come whereas the *Palmer* sate, ... II. viii. 11. 6
To whom the *Palmer* fearlesse answered: . . . . II. viii. 13. 1
'Palmer, thou doest dote, ... II. viii. 14. 1
'Fayr Sir,' said then the *Palmer* suppliaunt, ... II. viii. 16. 1
turning to the *Palmer*, ... II. viii. 23. 6
Sayd he then to the *Palmer:* . . . . II. viii. 24. 1
'Not one, nor other,' sayd the *Palmer* grave, ... II. viii. 24. 6
'Palmer, (said he) 'no knight so rude, I weene, ... II. viii. 26. 1
Whom when the *Palmer* saw in such distresse, ... II. viii. 40. 1
the *Palmer*, whom he long ygoe Had lost, ... II. viii. 53. 5
The *Palmer*, glad With so fresh hew . . . . II. viii. 54. 2
the *Palmer* him forth drew From Faery court. . . . . II. ix. 9. 7
the *Palmer* eke in habit sad . . . . II. xi. 3. 7
'Palmer, stere aright, ... II. xii. 3. 1
The *Palmer*, seeing them in safetie past, ... II. xii. 9. 1
the *Palmer* gan full bitterly Her to rebuke . . . . II. xii. 16. 5
Sir *Palmer*, keepe an even hand, ... II. xii. 18. 3
then saide the *Palmer* well aviz'd, ... II. xii. 26. 1
his *Palmer* bad To stere the bote . . . . II. xii. 28. 1
him the *Palmer* . . . discounselled, ... II. xii. 34. 1
Said then the *Palmer;* . . . . II. xii. 37. 7
his sage *Palmer* that him governed; . . . . II. xii. 38. 5
The *Palmer* over them his staffe upheld, ... II. xii. 40. 2
Such vertue in his staffe had eke this *Palmer* sage. . . . . . II. xii. 41. 9
On which when gazing him the *Palmer* saw, ... II. xii. 69. 1
thus the *Palmer:* 'Now, Sir, well avise; . . . . II. xii. 69. 6
The noble Elfe and carefull *Palmer* . . . . II. xii. 81. 1
The skilfull *Palmer* formally did frame: . . . . II. xii. 81. 5
them the *Palmer* soone did pacify. . . . . II. xii. 84. 8
Palmer, if it mote thee so aggrate, ... II. xii. 85. 8
Palmer—*Continued.*
To whom the *Palmer* thus: . . . . II. xii. 87. 6
Which when his *Palmer* saw, ... III. i. 9. 6
Palmer's. I wrapt myselfe in *Palmers* weed, ... II. i. 52. 8
by *Palmers* governaunce, passing through perilles great, . . . II. xii. Arg.
Palms. where be Those mighty *palmes*, . . . t' embrew In bloud of Kings, ... V. vii. 40. 4
Palm-tree. His left the *palme tree* stout, ... *Bel.*[2] ix. 10
Palm-trees. the high *Palme trees*, with braunches faire, . . . *Gn.* 190
Palsy. The shaking *Palsey*, and Saint Fraunces fire. . . . . . I. iv. 35. 8
Pampered. *Pampred* in pleasures deepe: . . . . *S.C.* Jul. 198
Pan. *See* **Brain-pan.**
Pan, thou shepheards God that once didst love, ... *S.C.* Ja. 17
my pype, albee rude *Pan* thou please, ... *S.C.* Ja. 67
Which *Pan*, the shepheards God, of her begot: . . . . *S.C.* Ap. 51
'Pan may be proud that ever he begot . . . . *S.C.* Ap. 91
When great *Pan* account of shepeherdes shall aske. . . . . . *S.C.* May 54
Pan himselfe was their inheritaunce, ... *S.C.* May 111
Pan himselfe, to kisse their christall faces, ... *S.C.* Jun. 30
I heard that *Pan* with Phoebus strove, ... *S.C.* Jun. 68
wonned not the great God *Pan* Upon Mount Olivet, ... *S.C.* Jul. 49
kept yfere The flockes of mighty *Pan*. . . . . *S.C.* Jul. 144
Theyr *Pan* theyr sheepe to them has sold, ... *S.C.* Jul. 179
that great *Pan* bought with deare borrow, ... *S.C.* S. 96
honor *Pan* with hymnes of higher vaine. . . . . *S.C.* N. 8
Nor *Pan* to herye, nor with love to playe; . . . . *S.C.* N. 10
'O soveraigne *Pan!* thou god of shepheards all, ... *S.C.* D. 7
To *Pan* his owne selfe pype I neede not yield: . . . . *S.C.* D. 46
if the flocking Nymphes did folow *Pan*, ... *S.C.* D. 47
as yet ashamd how rude *Pan* did her dight. . . . . II. ix. 40. 9
Panacea. whether yt divine Tobacco were, Or *Panachaea*, . . III. v. 32. 7
Panchaea. Ne frankincens he from *Panchaea* buyth: . . . . . *Gn.* 133
Pandar's. would he sometimes scorne A *Pandares* coate . . . *Hub.* 808
Pandionian. 'There also those two *Pandionian* maides, ... *Gn.* 401
Pandora. Like a *Pandora*, locked long in store. . . . . *Ro.* xix. 8
The true *Pandora* of all heavenly graces, ... *T.M.* 578
I thinke that I a new *Pandora* see, ... *Am.* xxiv. 8
Pang. Tho when the *pang* was somewhat overpast, ... *D.* 554
the sad *pang* approching shee does feele, ... II. i. 38. 8
Pangs. lesser *pangs* can beare who hath endur'd the chief. . . I. vi. 37. 9
The bitter *pangs* that doth your heart infest. . . . . II. i. 48. 5
with most painefull *pangs* to sigh and sob, ... III. xi. 8. 8
empeach His foltring toung with *pangs* of drerinesse, ... III. xi. 12. 3
gentle *pangues*, with which he maked meeke The mightie Mars, ... III. xi. 44. 2
pangs of death her spirit overtooke. . . . . V. v. 11. 5
Such were this Ladies *pangs* and dolorous assay. . . . . . . VI. v. 5. 9
Pannicle. Smote him so rudely on the *Pannikell*, ... III. v. 23. 5
Panope. one old Nymph, hight *Panope*, ... III. viii. 37. 9
Panope her entertaind eke well, ... III. viii. 38. 3
Panopae, and wise Protomedaea, ... IV. xi. 49. 8
Pans. *See* **Creaming-pans.**
Pansies. fragrant violets, and *Paunces* trim; . . . . III. i. 36. 8
Pansy. The pretie *Pawnce*, And the Chevisaunce, ... *S.C.* Ap. 142
The one a *Paunce*, the other a sweet-breare: . . . . III. xi. 37. 5
Pant. might her pitteous hart be seene to *pant* and quake. . I. vii. 20. 9
Which all that while shee felt to *pant* and quake, ... III. ii. 42. 8
pant with hope of that adventures hap: . . . . IV. x. 9. 2
heavy armes . . . hinder him from libertie to *pant;* . . . . . VI. iv. 19. 3
Panted. how he fum'd, and sweld, and rag'd, and *panted;* . . *Hub.* 1340
Panthea. that bright towre, . . . *Panthea*, seemd the brightest thing . . . . I. x. 58. 6
all of Christall did *Panthea* build: . . . . II. x. 73. 4
Panther. The spotted *Panther*, and the tusked Bore, ... I. vi. 26. 3
The *Panther*, knowing that his spotted hyde Doth please all beasts, ... *Am.* liii. 1
Panting. life nigh crusht out of his *panting* brest: . . . . . I. viii. 15. 3
He soone approched, *panting*, breathlesse, ... II. iv. 37. 6
panting softe, and trembling every joynt, ... III. i. 60. 1
Panting for breath, and almost out of hart, ... III. v. 4. 1
panting breath begin to fayle, ... IV. vi. 16. 2
With *panting* hounds beguiled of their pray: . . . . *Am.* lxvii. 4
Panwelt. from Alcluid to *Panwelt* did that border bownd. . . II. x. 63. 9
Pap. From mothers *pap* I taken was unfitt, ... I. ix. 3. 7
from whose fruitfull *pap* Their welheads spring, ... II. ii. 6. 2
from the howre I taken was from nourses tender *pap*, ... III. ii. 6. 2
Paper. These moniments, which not in *paper* writ, ... *Ro.* xxxii. 6
he disclosing read thus, as the *paper* spake: . . . . I. xii. 25. 9
Innocent *paper;* . . . matter to avenge her yre: . . . . . . *Am.* xlviii. 1
Papers. Those that poore Sutors *papers* do retaine, ... *Col.* 741
Her vomit full of bookes and *papers* was, ... I. i. 20. 6
Paphos. Whether in *Paphos*, or Cytheron hill, ... III. vi. 29. 4
Much more then that which was in *Paphos* built, ... IV. x. 5. 6
Phidias did make in *Paphos* Isle of yore, ... IV. x. 40. 4
Paps. did divide Her daintie *paps;* . . . . II. iii. 29. 7
her two lilly *paps* aloft displayd, ... II. xii. 66. 6
Some praise her *paps;* some praise her lips and nose; . . . VI. viii. 39. 5
Her *paps*, which like white silken pillowes were . . . . . . VI. viii. 42. 2
twixt her *paps*, (like early fruit in May, ... *Am.* lxxvi. 9
Her *paps* lyke lyllies budded, ... *Epith.* 176
Paradise. of *Paradise* Some noble plant I thought . . . . . . *Pet.* iii. 3
thy state, That *Paradise* hast founde . . . . *S.C.* Jun. 10
Then did I see a pleasant *Paradize*, ... *Ti.* 519
To spoyle the pleasures of that *Paradise;* . . . . *Mui.* 186
the most daintie *Paradise* on ground . . . . II. xii. 58. 1
not on living ground, Save in this *Paradise*, be heard . . . . II. xii. 70. 4
As it an earthly *Paradize* had beene: . . . . III. v. 40. 5
In *Paradize* whylome did plant this flowre; . . . . III. v. 52. 3
Shee brought her to her joyous *Paradize*, ... III. vi. 29. 1
Right in the middest of that *Paradise* . . . . III. vi. 43. 1

Paridell—*Continued.*
Paridell her scornd, and set at nought, . . . IV. ii. 3. 4
to Sir *Paridell* these words he sent: . . . IV. ii. 5. 6
Paridell . . . List not to hearke, . . . IV. ii. 6. 1
shewing her, did *Paridell* upbray; . . . IV. ii. 7. 4
whom *Paridell* Seeing so faire indeede, . . . IV. ii. 7. 6
Yet *Paridell* him envied therefore, . . . IV. ii. 11. 3
'Too foolish *Paridell!* that fayrest floure Wouldst gather faine, IV. ii. 14. 3
'Fond Squire,' full angry then sayd *Paridell,* . . . IV. ii. 22. 5
you, Sir Blandamour, and *Paridell,* . . . IV. ii. 24. 2
a new debate Stird up twixt Blandamour and *Paridell,* . . . IV. iv. 2. 4
Gainst whom Sir *Paridell* himselfe addrest, . . . IV. iv. 6. 8
Unto whose rescue forth rode *Paridell;* . . . IV. iv. 19. 8
did *Paridell* produce His false Duessa, . . . IV. v. 11. 1
Ne lesse thereat did *Paridell* complaine, . . . IV. v. 22. 6
at them both Sir *Paridell* did loure. . . . IV. v. 24. 4
Love-lavish Blandamour, and lustfull *Paridell.* . . . IV. ix. 20. 9
Paridell of love did make no threasure, . . . IV. ix. 21. 7
sometimes *Paridell* and Blandamour The better had, . . . IV. ix. 25. 1
Paridell did take to Druons side, . . . IV. ix. 26. 2
Paridell and Druon fiercely laid At Scudamour, . . . IV. ix. 30. 3
With faithlesse Blandamour and *Paridell,* . . . V. ix. 41. 3
Paris. him to death unfaithfull *Paris* sent; . . . *Gn.* 530
partiall *Paris* dempt it Venus dew, . . . II. vii. 55. 7
Sir *Paris* far renowmd through noble fame; . . . III. ix. 34. 5
when *Paris* brought his famous prise, . . . IV. xi. 19. 3
On Phrygian *Paris* by Plexippus brooke, . . . VI. ix. 36. 7
Parish. th' Ape his *Parish* Clarke procur'd to bee. . . . *Hub.* 557
Parishioners. th' evill will Of all their *Parishners* . . . *Hub.* 561
Parius. Whom . . . She, of his Father, *Parius* did name; . . . III. ix. 36. 6
Parlante. The second was *Parlante,* a bold knight; . . . III. i. 45. 3
Parley. daily siege, . . . will to *parley* drive; . . . III. x. 10. 4
Peece, that unto *parley* eare will give, . . . III. x. 10. 5
In his *Foules parley* durst not with it mel, . . . VII. vii. 9. 5
Parlor. soone into a goodly *Parlour* brought, . . . II. ix. 33. 6
Parnassus. you Virgins, that on *Parnasse* dwell, . . . *S.C.* Ap. 41
systers nyne, which dwell on *Parnasse* hight, . . . *S.C.* Jun. 28
I never lyst presume to *Parnasse* hyll, . . . *S.C.* Jun. 70
mount *Parnasse,* the Muses brood, . . . *Gn.* 21
that raignst in Castalie And mount *Parnasse,* . . . *T.M.* 58
Not one *Parnassus* nor one Helicone, . . . *Ded. Son.* v. 6
In savadge soyle, far from *Parnasso* Mount, . . . *Ded.Son.*vii.12
sweet *Parnasse,* the haunt of Muses fayre; . . . II. xii. 52. 8
Ye sacred imps, that on *Parnasso* dwell, . . . VI. Pr. 2. 2
Paros. sayling thence to th' isle of *Paros* came. . . . III. ix. 36. 9
'That was by him cald *Paros,* . . . III. ix. 37. 1
Parson. The Foxe was well induc'd to be a *Parson,* . . . *Hub.* 480
Parsonage. have in gage The Primitias of your *Parsonage:* . *Hub.* 518
Part. I will *part* them all you among.' . . . *S.C.* Ap. 153
in your songs were wont to make a *part:* . . . *S.C.* Au. 154
I hate the house, since thence my love did *part,* . . . *S.C.* Au. 161
fynd no *part* 'Of pleasure past. . . . *S.C.* Au. 168
of my woe cannot bewray least *part*) . . . *S.C.* Au. 176
with the Nightingale will I take *part,* . . . *S.C.* Au. 183
bad the Ape him dight To play his *part,* . . . *Hub.* 234
griev'd as he had felt *part* of his paine; . . . *Hub.* 260
Whose *part* once past all men bid take away: . . . *Hub.* 932
ever thinke a Kingdome is your *part.'* . . . *Hub.* 1004
part by land and *part* by water fed; . . . *Hub.* 1120
the false Foxe most kindly plaid his *part;* . . . *Hub.* 1137
may I take it well in *part,* That ye . . . *Hub.* 1217
Thenceforth he past into each secrete *part,* . . . *Hub.* 1303
taught to beare A Bases *part* . . . *T.M.* 28
My *part* it is and my professed skill . . . *T.M.* 151
Awake, and to his Song a *part* applie: . . . *Ti.* 236
frosen horror ran through everie *part.* . . . *Ti.* 483
each *part* t' inquire Of the wide rule . . . *Mui.* 39
to his wicked worke each *part* applie. . . . *Mui.* 253
hast not seene least *part* of natures worke: . . . *Col.* 293
Some *part* of those enormities did see, . . . *Col.* 665
uprose eke all the rest: All loth to *part,* . . . *Col.* 954
And steale from each some *part* of ornament. . . . *Ded. Son.* xvii. 8
Of each a *part* I stole by cunning thefte: . . . *Ded.Son.*xvii.13
Who soone him brought into a secret *part,* . . . I. ii. 5. 3
tel both who ye be, and who that tooke your *part.'* . . . I. ii. 21. 9
he to her brought *part* of his stolen things. . . . I. iii. 18. 9
they be come unto the furthest *part;* . . . I. v. 36. 4
Aesculape . . . joyned every *part.* . . . I. v. 39. 9
every tender *part* for feare does shake. . . . I. vi. 10. 2
The better *part* now of the lingring day . . . I. vi. 34. 1
everie tender *part* does tosse and turne: . . . I. vii. 21. 6
Who hath endur'd the whole can beare ech *part.* . . . I. vii. 25. 5
In heavenly mercies hast thou not a *part?* . . . I. ix. 53. 4
'Which, for my *part,* I covet to performe . . . I. xii. 20. 1
of the world least *part* to us is red; . . . II. Pr. 2. 2
cursed hand, hath plaid this cruell *part,* . . . II. i. 44. 7
makes it servaunt to her basest *part,* . . . II. i. 57. 6
when Guyon came to *part* their fight, . . . II. ii. 23. 8
drew his deadly weapon to maintaine his *part.* . . . II. iv. 9. 9
for my *part,* I vow, dissembled not a whitt. . . . II. iv. 18. 9
staynd their prayses with thy least good *part;* . . . II. iv. 26. 4
he went, and his owne false *part* playd, . . . II. iv. 27. 7
Would oftentimes emongst them beare a *part,* . . . II. vi. 25. 2
As to despise so curteous seeming *part* . . . II. vi. 26. 4
yield him ready passage to that other *part.* . . . II. vi. 36. 9
preaced to draw nere To th' upper *part,* . . . II. vii. 44. 4
lower *part* did reach to lowest Hell; . . . II. vii. 46. 4
partly circulare, And *part* triangulare; . . . II. ix. 22. 2
Albanact had all the Northerne *part,* . . . II. x. 14. 2
through the world then swarmd in every *part,* . . . II. x. 15. 3

Part—*Continued.*
To have a pere in *part* of soveraინty; . . . II. x. 33. 4
The Churches *part,* and Ploughmans portion, . . . II. x. 39. 4
each might best offend his proper *part,* . . . II. xi. 6. 3
let him heare some *part* of their rare melody. . . . II. xii. 33. 9
formd so lively in each perfect *part,* . . . III. Pr. 1. 6
living art may not least *part* expresse, . . . III. Pr. 2. 1
him in everie *part* before her fashioned. . . . III. ii. 16. 9
Yet him in everie *part* before she knew, . . . III. ii. 17. 1
Yet playd Pasiphae a more monstrous *part,* . . . III. ii. 41. 5
How like a Gyaunt in each manly *part* . . . III. iii. 32. 3
At last their wayes so fell, that they mote *part:* . . . III. iii. 62. 6
Searching all lands and each remotest *part,* . . . III. iv. 6. 7
Madnesse to save a *part,* and lose the whole! . . . III. v. 43. 3
the inner *part* Of every thing consumes, . . . III. v. 48. 8
knitting their rancke braunches, *part* to *part,* . . . III. vi. 44. 4
Fashiond above within their inmost *part,* . . . III. vi. 44. 7
it a *part* Of her rich spoyles . . . III. viii. 2. 7
with Latinus did the kingdom *part;* . . . III. ix. 43. 2
every *part* to safety full sownd, . . . III. xii. 38. 6
With his faire paragon, his conquests *part,* . . . IV. i. 33. 4
some *part* Thereof did in his frouning face appeare: . . . IV. i. 45. 3
Where is my *part* then of this Ladie bright, . . . IV. ii. 13. 6
came forth in hast to take his *part,* . . . IV. iii. 40. 8
gan the *part* of Chalengers anew To range the field, . . . IV. iv. 25. 3
Tho gan he swell in every inner *part* . . . IV. vi. 7. 4
Yet is not this the first unknightly *part,* . . . IV. vi. 7. 7
lashing dreadfully at every *part,* . . . IV. vi. 16. 6
With Beares and Tygers taking heavie *part,* . . . IV. vii. 2. 7
with her dolefull accent beare with him a *part.* . . . IV. viii. 3. 9
He *part* of his small feast to her would share; . . . IV. viii. 5. 7
Her spightfull words did pricke and wound the inner *part.* . IV. viii. 26. 9
To whom he did divide *part* of his purchast spoile. . . . IV. ix. 12. 9
each one taking *part* in others aide . . . IV. ix. 24. 7
The warlike Dame was on her *part* assaid . . . IV. ix. 30. 1
Art, playing second natures *part,* supplyed it. . . . IV. x. 21. 9
unto every person knew her *part;* . . . IV. x. 51. 4
his mortall *part* by great mischance Was slaine; . . . IV. xi. 16. 7
T' expresse some *part* of that great equipage . . . IV. xi. 17. 8
searching every *part,* . . . IV. xii. 23. 8
He would to his owne *part* restore the same againe: . . . V. ii. 31. 9
What was the poyse of every *part* of yore: . . . V. ii. 34. 7
The most *part* of my land hath washt away, . . . V. iv. 8. 3
brothers land the which the sea hath layd Unto your *part,* . V. iv. 17. 4
That *part* of Justice which is Equity, . . . V. vii. 3. 4
Talus mote not be admitted to her *part.* . . . V. vii. 3. 9
to his *part* allures, and bribeth under hand. . . . V. viii. 18. 9
Talus did attend, Playing his pages *part,* . . . V. viii. 29. 7
which did maintaine That Ladies *part,* . . . V. viii. 50. 4
heare the matter throughly scand On either *part,* . . . V. ix. 37. 8
with him, to make *part* against her, came . . . V. ix. 43. 5
for her, on the contrarie *part,* Rose many advocates . . . V. ix. 45. 1
woxe inclined much unto her *part,* . . . V. ix. 46. 3
Whether this heavenly thing . . . be of Justice *part,* . . . V. x. 1. 3
Oft spilles the principall to save the *part;* . . . V. x. 2. 4
maintayne That Tyrants *part* with close or open ayde, . . . V. xii. 25. 6
Pinckt upon gold, and paled *part* per *part,* . . . VI. ii. 6. 2
And wish that he *part* of his spoyle might share: . . . VI. ii. 17. 3
when as I was loth My loves owne *part* to leave . . . VI. ii. 17. 7
But wayt on him in every place and *part:* . . . VI. ii. 36. 5
And how ye may him hence, and to what *part,* Convay . . . VI. ii. 46. 5
My selfe will beare a *part,* . . . VI. ii. 47. 9
And every *part* that under sweath-bands lay, . . . VI. iv. 23. 7
gan himselfe addresse to take her *part.* . . . VI. v. 8. 3
To reskue him, and his weake *part* abet, . . . VI. v. 22. 4
all knights hast shamed with this knightlesse *part.* . . . VI. vi. 33. 9
Whooping and hallowing on every *part,* . . . VI. viii. 40. 3
of the pray each one a *part* doth beare. . . . VI. viii. 41. 5
her alone he for his *part* desired . . . VI. xi. 4. 3
Of which the greatest *part* is due to me, . . . VII. vii. 15. 4
Yet is she chang'd in *part,* and eeke in generall: . . . VII. vii. 17. 9
Breake forth at length out of the inner *part,* . . . *Am.* ii. 5
when I pleade, she bids me play my *part;* . . . *Am.* xviii. 9
pride and meeknesse, mixt by equall *part,* . . . *Am.* xxi. 3
rare perfection of each goodly *part;* . . . *Am.* xxiv. 2
pryde depraves each other better *part,* . . . *Am.* xxxi. 3
A melting pleasance ran through every *part,* . . . *Am.* xxxix. 7
And every *part* remaines immortally: . . . *Am.* xlv. 8
ship, doth strongly *part* The raging waves, . . . *Am.* lix. 5
Through contemplation of my purest *part,* . . . *Am.* lxxxvii. 10
Doest tyrannize in everie weaker *part:* . . . *H.L.* 4
whole remaines scarse any little *part;* . . . *H.L.* 144
Least *part* of th' evils which poore lovers greeve. . . . *H.L.* 258
proportion of the outward *part* . . . *H.B.* 75
in perfect limming every *part?* . . . *H.B.* 84
Through every *part* she doth the same impresse, . . . *H.B.* 115
sharply launching every inner *part,* . . . *H.H.L.* 158
on fire With burning zeale, through every *part* entire, . . . *H.H.L.* 271
Or hope t' expresse her least perfections *part,* . . . *H.H.B.* 227
Partake. With equall plaints her sorrowe did *partake.* . . . *T.M.* 298
die with you in sorrow, and *partake* your griefe.' . . . II. i. 48. 9
I did *partake* Of all my love . . . II. iv. 20. 1
Her honest merth and pleasaunce to *partake;* . . . II. vi. 21. 6
make Way for themselves their purpose to *pertake?'* . . . III. iii. 25. 5
her pleasures lenger to *partake.* . . . III. xi. 33. 9
'Not one,' (quoth he) 'but many doe *partake* Herein; . . . IV. ii. 25. 5
lincked rode . . . As if they secret counsels did *partake;* . IV. ii. 30. 4
either sdeignes with other to *partake:* . . . IV. iii. 16. 8
Ne any dar'd their perill to *partake:* . . . IV. iv. 29. 5
Her gentle Squire through her displeasure did *pertake.* . . . IV. viii. 9. 9

Partake—*Continued.*
her glory to *partake;* V. vii. 36. 2
went forth his gladnesse to *partake* With Belge, V. xi. 32. 7
With which none had to doe, ne ought *partake,* VI. xi. 12. 4
her face . . . We changed see and sundry formes *partake,* VII. vii. 50. 7
The sacred ceremonies there *partake,* *Epith.* 216
endeere Thy pleasures unto those which them *partake,* *H.L.* 275
We should them love, and with their needs *partake;* *H.H.L.* 208
For of her fulnesse . . . They all *partake,* *H.H.B.* 200
Partaker. To be *partaker* of their common woe; *Hub.* 14
ne ought he feares To be *partaker* of her wandring woe; I. iii. 44. 8
had bene *partaker* of the place. I. ix. 26. 9
thou art *partaker* of his cryme: II. viii. 30. 3
be *partaker* of their speed.' III. viii. 50. 9
Partakers. be *partakers* of their evill plight, I. x. 10. 7
Both joynt *partakers* of their fatall payne: III. iii. 37. 7
be *partakers* of thy endlesse fame. III. viii. 43. 7
worthy deeme *partakers* of our blisse to bee. VII. vi. 33. 9
And be *partakers* of those joyes of his. *H.H.L.* 63
Partakes. Thereof as every earthly thing *partakes* *H.B.* 43
Parted. So *parted* they, as eithers way them led. *Hub.* 551
proudlie neighing, from them *parted* hee. *Hub.* 654
when she *parted* hence, *D.* 220
The praises of my *parted* love envy, *D.* 226
Soone as she *parted* thence, I. iii. 22. 1
So been they *parted* both, with harts on edge I. iv. 43. 3
ere they *parted,* Una faire besought That . . . knight I. ix. 2. 6
Thus beene they *parted;* I. ix. 20. 1
So *parted* we, and on our journey drive; II. i. 55. 7
ne them *parted* ought: II. vii. 24. 7
he *parted* his imperiall state, II. x. 13. 6
when she *parted* hence she left her groome An yron man, V. i. 12. 1
She *parted* thence her anguish to appease. V. vii. 45. 5
both tooke goodly leave, and *parted* severall. VI. i. 10. 9
So taking courteous leave they *parted* twayne, VI. ii. 38. 8
And twixt them both with *parted* paines did beare, VI. ii. 48. 5
Parteth. Sture, that *parteth* with his pleasant floods IV. xi. 33. 3
Parthian. The *Parthian* strikes a stag with shivering dart, IV. i. 49. 8
Partial. That none might scape (so *partiall* unto none:) *As.* 110
partiall Paris dempt it Venus dew, II. vii. 55. 7
in their proper praise too *partiall* bee, III. ii. 1. 2
in thine owne behalfe maist *partiall* seeme: VII. vi. 35. 3
Particular. perteines in charge *particulare,* II. xii. 47. 4
Parting. the world *parting* by an equall lott, *Gn.* 158
at her *parting* said, She Queene of Faeries hight. I. ix. 14. 9
With cup thus charmd him *parting* she deceivd; II. i. 55. 3
from her *parting,* she thenceforth did labour V. v. 35. 4
parting from the place, VII. vi. 55. 2
Yet is he nought but *parting* of the breath; VII. vii. 46. 3
Partition. There is no right in this *partition,* *Hub.* 143
Partly. Ten thousand kindes of creatures, *partly* male And *partly* femall, I. i. 21. 7, 8
The frame thereof seemd *partly* circulare, II. ix. 22. 1
partly discontent With his late fall III. ix. 25. 1
Partly with shame, and *partly* with dismay, V. iv. 27. 2
Partner. With Philumene, the *partner* of my plight. *D.* 476
of my love was *partener* Paramoure: II. iv. 24. 4
Hath fownd another *partner* of your payne; III. ix. 40. 2
her Belamour, the *partner* of his sheet: III. x. 22. 9
Partridge. Like as a fearefull *partridge,* III. viii. 33. 3
Part's. This *parts* great workemanship and wondrous powre, II. ix. 47. 2
every *parts* inholders to convent, VII. vii. 17. 4
Parts. *See* **Hind parts.**
having all *parts* in their power, *Ro.* viii. 9
advaunced, For my good *parts;* *Hub.* 64
Man is not like an Ape In his chiefe *parts,* *Hub.* 1043
first was raisde for vertuous *parts,* *Ti.* 451
Toward those *parts* came flying carelesslie, *Mui.* 391
when life *parts* vouchsafe to close mine eye. *D.* 511
First into many *parts* his streame he shar'd, *Col.* 138
Adorned with all honourable *parts:* *Col.* 529
Full many persons of right worthie *parts,* *Col.* 752
Unmindfull of chiefe *parts* of manlinesse; *Col.* 764
make more famous memory Of thine Heroicke *parts,* *Ded. Son.* ii. 12
from commune vew Their fairer *parts* are hid, *Ded. Son.* ix. 11
fram'd of liquid ayre her tender *partes,* I. i. 45. 3
The . . . Enchaunter *parts* The Redcrosse Knight from Truth: I. ii. Arg.
his guests He saw divided into double *parts,* I. ii. 9. 2
'Her neather *partes* misshapen, monstruous, Were hidd in water, I. ii. 41. 1
all the hinder *partes,* . . . Were ruinous and old, I. iv. 5. 8
sup, . . . secret poyson through their inner *partes,* I. viii. 14. 4
golden cup, . . . She lightly sprinkled on his weaker *partes:* I. viii. 14. 7
her misshaped *parts* did them appall: I. viii. 46. 7
Her neather *parts,* . . . Muse for shame doth blush to write; I. viii. 48. 1
Dry-shod to passe she *parts* the flouds in tway; I. x. 20. 5
Her flitting *parts,* and element unsound, I. xi. 18. 5
Drew them in *partes,* and each made others foe: II. ii. 13. 6
be these the *parts* Of glorious knighthood, II. ii. 29. 5
Of her leawd *parts* to make companion: II. ii. 37. 5
in thy selfe thy lesser *partes* do move; II. v. 16. 2
did loosely disaray Her upper *partes* II. v. 32. 8
compar'd to these by many *parts:* II. ix. 48. 3
he brought them to these salvage *parts,* II. x. 25. 8
did her selfe in sondry *parts* divide, II. x. 54. 3
they overran all *parts* with easy hand. II. x. 61. 9
A man, of many *parts* from beasts deryv'd, II. x. 70. 6
the *partes* brought into their bondage: II. xi. 1. 8
yeeld His *partes* to reasons rule obedient, II. xi. 2. 2
the rude And scorned *partes* II. xii. 59. 2
ne car'd to hyde Their dainty *partes* II. xii. 63. 9

Parts—*Continued.*
picturing the *parts* of beauty daynt, III. Pr. 2. 7
what uncouth wind Brought her into those *partes,* III. ii. 4. 6
For such intent into these *partes* I came, III. ii. 7. 6
gan ransack fast His inward *partes,* III. v. 48. 5
with faire Adonis playes his wanton *partes.* III. vi. 49. 9
thrice three hundred thanks for my good *partes,* III. vii. 55. 5
their lately bruzed *parts* to bring in plight. III. ix. 19. 9
many wide woundes launched through his inner *partes.* III. xi. 44. 9
richlier by many *partes* arayd; III. xi. 51. 2
Her lying tongue was in two *parts* divided, IV. i. 27. 6
both the *parts* did speake, and both contended; IV. i. 27. 7
What time his people into *partes* did rive, IV. ii. 2. 8
Which did her powre into three *parts* divyde; IV. ii. 43. 4
As one whose inner *parts* had bene ythrild IV. iii. 22. 4
Till on her horses hinder *parts* it fell; IV. vi. 13. 6
there out sucking venime to her *parts* entyre, IV. viii. 23. 9
poysnous spirit sent From inward *parts,* IV. viii. 26. 4
into their harts and *parts* entire. IV. viii. 48. 9
From all foure *parts* of heaven doe rage full sore, IV. ix. 23. 6
new *parts* take; IV. ix. 26. 1
Then all his former *parts* did earst appere: IV. x. 20. 5
So all the rest did others *parts* empaire, V. ii. 32. 5
whilest her earthly *parts* . . . did deeply drowned lie, V. vii. 12. 5
forth into the lower *parts* did pas, V. vii. 17. 6
ne spared not Their dainty *parts,* V. vii. 29. 6
She entred into all the *partes* entire: V. vii. 37. 5
Where none may be with her lewd *parts* defyled, V. ix. 2. 4
even to the vitall *parts* they past, V. xii. 17. 8
The foule discourt'sies and unknightly *parts,* VI. v. 33. 2
The inner *parts* now gan to putrify, VI. vi. 5. 4
Sorrow, and anguish, and impatient paine, In th' inner *parts;* VI. vi. 8. 7
her face and former *parts* professe A faire young Mayden, VI. vi. 10. 6
all her hinder *parts* did plaine expresse A monstrous Dragon, VI. vi. 10. 8
Those daintie *parts,* the dearlings of delight, VI. viii. 43. 1
Whose sundry *parts* were here too long to tell; VI. x. 14. 2
daily night did hover Through all the inner *parts,* VI. x. 42. 6
As if ye please it into *parts* divide, VII. vii. 17. 3
We see his *parts,* . . . To lose their heat VII. vii. 24. 3
dints the *parts* entire With chast affects *Am.* vi. 11
Deepe, in the closet of my *parts* entyre, *Am.* lxxxiv. 9
Whose sundrie *parts* he from themselves did sever *H.L.* 76
And kindled flame in all their inner *parts,* *H.L.* 124
powre Through all the *parts,* *H.B.* 53
comely composition Of *parts* well measurd, *H.B.* 70
with like beauties *parts* he inly deckt; *H.B.* 193
unlike *parts* amongst themselves do jarre. *H.B.* 196
mightie bound which . . . *parts* their houres by space, *H.H.L.* 26
Whose utmost *parts* so beautifull I fynd; *H.H.B.* 108
How much more those essentiall *parts* of his, *H.H.B.* 109
Parture. suddein *parture* of faire Florimell To find him III. viii. 46. 5
Party. 'Againe great dole on either *partie* grewe, *Gn.* 529
with unwearied powre his *party* still assured. IV. iv. 37. 9
privie was and *partie* in the case: V. ix. 47. 5
from her *partie* eftsoones was drawen cleene: V. ix. 49. 3
weakens her, and makes her *party* strong; V. xi. 1. 4
this Mayd, whose *party* thou doest take, VI. i. 19. 7
Party's. To hasten greatly to his *parties* ayd, IV. iv. 20. 2
Pase. *See* **Pace.**
Pasiphae. Yet playd *Pasiphae* a more monstrous part, III. ii. 41. 5
Pasithee. Lovely *Pasithee,* kinde Eulimene, IV. xi. 49. 3
Pass. *See* **Overpass.**
each thing at last (length[1]) . . . Doth *passe* away: *Pet.* v. 8
Striving in power their grandfathers to *passe,* *Ro.* viii. 7
As men in Summer fearles *passe* the foord *Ro.* xiv. 1
That came to *passe,* *Ro.* xxiii. 13
Passen their time . . . In lustihede *S.C.* May 41
to winne renowne, or *passe* the rest: *S.C.* Jun. 74
With pyping and dauncing did *passe* the rest. *S.C.* Au. 10
must *passe* over to th' Elisian plaine *Gn.* 421
ere we farther *passe* *Hub.* 195
since their souldiers *pas* no better spedd, *Hub.* 357
askt what license, or what *Pas* they had? *Hub.* 367
asked for their *pas* by everie squib, *Hub.* 371
having overlookt their *pas* at ease, *Hub.* 396
he them in newfanglenesse did *pas.* *Hub.* 675
to leave The Court, not asking any *passe* or leave; *Hub.* 936
to prove whether his powre would *pas* As currant, *Hub.* 1094
through his hand must *passe* the Fiaunt. *Hub.* 1144
so he got it, little did he *pas.* *Hub.* 1150
when he ought would bring to *pas,* *Hub.* 1167
He toward his owne Pallace forth did *pas;* *Hub.* 1344
His hope is faild, and come to *passe* his dread, *Ti.* 213
in time to nought doo *passe.* *Ti.* 420
Yet shee in purenesse heaven it selfe did *pas.* *D.* 210
Hereof when tydings far abroad did *passe,* *As.* 199
might *Passe* unespide to meete her by the way; *Col.* 140
thorough them did *passe* So proudly, *Col.* 222
We Lunday *passe;* *Col.* 270
'Foorth on our voyage we by land did *passe,* *Col.* 330
foorth they *passe,* with pleasure forward led, I. i. 8. 1
straunge adventures, which abroad did *pas.* I. i. 30. 4
no . . . wight May ever *passe,* but thorough great distresse.' I. i. 32. 3
people that did *pas* In traveill to and froe: I. i. 34. 3
With faire discourse the evening so they *pas;* I. i. 35. 5
By them the Sprite doth *passe* in quietly, I. i. 40. 7
He that . . . high hath set his throne where Tiberis doth *pas.* I. ii. 22. 9
deserts wyde, By which . . . wandring knight shold *pas,* I. iii. 10. 2
on their former journey forward *pas,* I. iii. 21. 3
his ghost . . . In peace may *passen* over Lethe lake; I. iii. 36. 6

Pass—*Continued.*
By them they *passe,* . . . And to the Presence mount; . . . . I. iv. 7. 1
Yet did she thinke her pearelesse worth to *pas* That parentage, I. iv. 11. 3
That night they *pas* in joy and jollity, ... I. iv. 43. 5
They *pas* the bitter waves of Acheron, ... I. v. 33. 1
he . . . suffered them to *passen* quietly; . . . . I. v. 34. 8
old Ninus far did *pas* In princely pomp, ... I. v. 48. 3
when he saw the Damsell *passe* away, ... I. vi. 48. 5
with his breath, which through the world doth *pas,* . . . . I. vii. 9. 3
Perce to my hart, and *pas* through everie side, ... I. vii. 22. 8
She . . . forward forth doth *pas,* . . . . I. vii. 28. 3
The light whereof, that hevens light did *pas,* . . . . I. viii. 19. 3
soone as breath out of his brest did *pas,* . . . . I. viii. 24. 6
Then asked he, which way he in might *pas?* . . . . I. viii. 33. 1
A dreary corse, whose life away did *pas,* . . . . I. ix. 36. 5
Why wilt not let him *passe,* . . . . I. ix. 39. 8
They *passe* in, stouping low; . . . . I. x. 5. 8
Dry-shod to *passe* she parts the flouds in tway; . . . . I. x. 20. 5
The first . . . towardes him did *pas;* . . . . I. x. 44. 3
they *pas* Forth to an hill . . . . I. x. 46. 1
dreadfully he towardes him did *pas,* . . . . I. xi. 15. 1
as chaunst them by a forest side To *passe,* . . . . II. i. 35. 6
so far all sence they *pas.* . . . . II. i. 49. 6
Sterne melancholy did his courage *pas,* . . . . II. ii. 17. 8
So forth they *pas,* . . . . II. iii. 11. 1
'lett her *pas* at will, ... II. iii. 44. 1
by whose utmost brim Wayting to *passe,* . . . . II. vi. 2. 5
My little boat can safely *passe* this perilous bourne.' . . . . II. vi. 10. 9
passe the bonds of modest merimake, ... II. vi. 21. 8
strive to *passe* . . . Their native musicke . . . . II. vi. 25. 3
of her joy . . . she saw he light did *pas,* . . . . II. vi. 37. 3
They forward *passe;* ne Guyon yet spoke word, ... II. vii. 31. 1
The one before, by which all in did *pas,* . . . . II. ix. 23. 2
when it locked none might thorough *pas,* . . . . II. ix. 23. 7
Nor wight nor word mote *passe* out of the gate, ... II. ix. 25. 3
Which he recorded still as they did *pas,* . . . . II. ix. 56. 3
let them *pas,* whiles wind and wether right . . . . II. xi. 4. 7
Ne ought save perill still as he did *pas:* . . . . II. xii. 2. 3
yonder way We needes must *pas* . . . . II. xii. 3. 3
Forward they *passe,* and strongly he them rowes, ... II. xii. 5. 1
They to him hearken, . . . And *passe* on forward: . . . . II. xii. 14. 2
they needes must *passen* by, ... II. xii. 14. 4
suffered him to *passe,* . . . . II. xii. 57. 8
Therein discovered was, ne ought mote *pas,* . . . . III. ii. 19. 6
to bring his will to *pas:* . . . . III. iii. 24. 5
not thee entreat To *passe,* but maugre thee will *passe* or dy.' . III. iv. 15. 4
none durst *passen* through that perilous glade: . . . . III. iv. 21. 5
it did *pas* The wealth of th' East, ... III. iv. 23. 3
To bring to *passe* his mischievous intent, ... III. iv. 45. 2
that Squyre unknowne Mote algates *passe:* . . . . III. v. 17. 6
through the ford to *passen* did assay; . . . . III. v. 18. 4
By which both in and out men moten *pas:* . . . . III. vi. 31. 6
Thereto so swifte that it all beasts did *pas:* . . . . III. vii. 22. 6
it chaunst a knight To *passe* that way, ... III. vii. 29. 3
Her to disport and idle time to *pas* . . . . III. viii. 11. 3
all which *passen* by, . . . thinke it threates the skye. . . . . III. ix. 45. 8
all the antique Worthies merits far did *passe.* . . . . III. ix. 50. 9
let him *passe* as lightly as he came: . . . . III. x. 39. 2
So soone as he the Prison-dore did *pas,* . . . . III. x. 53. 1
More for great sorrow that he could not *pas* . . . . III. xi. 27. 2
gave her leave at pleasure forth to *passe.* . . . . III. xii. 43. 6
yet doth not *passe* so cleare, ... IV. i. 45. 7
With heavenly notes, that did all other *pas* . . . . IV. ii. 2. 3
though therein himselfe he thought to *pas,* . . . . IV. ii. 10. 3
Eftsoones his life may *passe* into the next: . . . . IV. ii. 52. 6
To let them *passe* at will, for dread of shame. . . . . IV. iv. 3. 5
Yet did the workmanship farre *passe* the cost: . . . . IV. iv. 15. 8
Florimell her selfe . . . She seem'd to *passe:* . . . . IV. v. 15. 9
fast beside a little brooke did *pas* . . . . IV. v. 33. 3
He all that night, that too long night, did *passe* . . . . IV. v. 45. 2
When ever he this way shall *passe* . . . . IV. vi. 5. 9
yeeld unto her weapon way to *pas:* . . . . IV. vi. 15. 4
lovers heaven must *passe* by sorrowes hell.' . . . . IV. vi. 32. 7
forward thence did *pas* Unto some resting place, ... IV. vi. 39. 3
undiscerned forth with him did *pas.* . . . . IV. viii. 59. 5
'by all the woe I *pas,* . . . . IV. viii. 63. 7
love of soule doth love of bodie *passe,* . . . . IV. ix. 2. 8
twixt her selfe and Love did let me *pas;* . . . . IV. x. 36. 3
did on dry-foot *pas* Into old Gall, ... IV. xi. 16. 3
never wight he lets to *passe* that way . . . . V. ii. 6. 2
In swimming be expert, through waters force to *pas.* . . . . V. ii. 16. 9
Florimell her selfe she then did *pas.* . . . . V. iii. 17. 8
Braggadochio would not let him *pas,* . . . . V. iii. 30. 3
as he did *passe* by the sea shore, ... V. iv. 4. 1
'Which that thou mayst the better bring to *pas,* . . . . V. v. 34. 1
forth into the lower parts did *pas,* . . . . V. vii. 17. 6
Tygres scath In crueltie and outrage she did *pas,* . . . . V. viii. 49. 8
That herein doest all earthly Princes *pas?* . . . . V. x. 3. 2
So forth he fared . . . and much way did *pas,* . . . . V. xi. 36. 8
To *passe* them over where them list to tell. . . . . V. xii. 4. 4
Fashion'd to please the eies of them that *pas,* . . . . VI. Pr. 5. 4
may no Knight nor Lady *passe* along That way, ... VI. i. 13. 5
yet they needs must *passe* that way, ... VI. i. 13. 6
mild curt'sie showe To all that *passe:* . . . . VI. i. 27. 4
this his Ladie . . . by his horse side did *pas* . . . . VI. ii. 10. 3
after this nights perillous *passe,* . . . . VI. iii. 14. 2
which way he through the foord mote *pas:* . . . . VI. iii. 30. 4
They mote the abler be to *passe* unto the rest. . . . . VI. iv. 15. 9
Ne could it upward come, nor downward *passe,* . . . . VI. iv. 21. 8
further could not *pas* Through feeblenesse, ... VI. v. 31. 8

Pass—*Continued.*
To *passe* the tedious travell of the way, ... VI. v. 34. 6
They stayd not there, but streightway in did *pas:* . . . . VI. v. 36. 1
Into his Lords forbidden hall to *passe?* . . . . VI. vi. 20. 4
Led by a Carle and foole which by her side did *passe.* . . . . VI. vii. 27. 9
A Baylieffe-errant forth in post did *passe,* . . . . VI. vii. 35. 7
as they forward on their way did *pas,* . . . . VI. viii. 4. 1
way to them he gave forth right to *pas;* . . . . VI. viii. 14. 3
whose pleasaunce did appere To *passe* all others . . . . VI. x. 5. 5
Yet she all other countrey lasses farre did *passe:* . . . . VI. x. 25. 9
no way Appeard for people in nor out to *pas,* . . . . VI. x. 41. 8
nothing meet in merchandise to *passe:* . . . . VI. xi. 12. 8
Shee there arriving boldly in did *pass;* . . . . VII. vi. 24. 1
So now her waves *passe* through a pleasant Plaine, ... VII. vi. 53. 7
it the Sunne a thousand times did *pass,* . . . . VII. vii. 6. 8
such sweet cordialls *passe* Physitions art. . . . . *Am.* l. 12
Yet never day so long, but late would *passe.* . . . . *Epith.* 273
passe away, like to a sommers shade; . . . . *H.B.* 68
did *pas* Downe from the top . . . . *H.B.* 108
stars . . . Whereof each other doth in brightnesse *passe,* . . . . *H.H.B.* 54
the hard diamond, which them both doth *passe.* . . . . *H.H.B.* 154
those joyous Birdes did *passe* along, ... *Proth.* 114

Passable. Styx, not *passable* to soules returning, ... *Ro.* xv. 6
hardly *passable* on foote it was; . . . . VI. iii. 30. 2

Passage. thence the *passage* ethe; . . . . *S.C.* Jul. 90
all things . . . that might his *passage* stay. . . . . *Gn.* 272
of their *passage* doth appeare no token, ... *Col.* 143
stones, the which encomber might His *passage,* . . . . *Col.* 151
A gentle Husher, . . . *passage* for them did prepaire: . . . . I. iv. 13. 4
all that might his angry *passage* stay; . . . . I. viii. 9. 8
nathemore would that corageous swayne To her yeeld *passage* . I. viii. 13. 7
made an open *passage* for the gushing flood. . . . . I. ix. 36. 9
meetes a flood that doth his *passage* stay, ... I. ix. 39. 3
What if some little payne the *passage* have, ... I. ix. 40. 4
nothing might his ready *passage* stay: . . . . I. x. 35. 5
by force unwonted *passage* fynd, ... I. xi. 10. 7
he for nought would stay his *passage* right, ... I. xii. 25. 4
easy is the way and *passage* plaine . . . . II. iii. 41. 7
yeilded *passage* to his cruell knife. . . . . II. v. 9. 4
Appease his heat, or hastie *passage* stay; . . . . II. v. 38. 4
They were far past the *passage* which he spake, ... II. vi. 11. 2
for *passage* sought. . . . . II. vi. 19. 3
Till season serve new *passage* to assay: . . . . II. vi. 23. 7
marched to the Strond there *passage* to require. . . . . II. vi. 27. 9
yield him ready *passage* to that other part. . . . . II. vi. 36. 9
Awaiting *passage* which him late did faile; . . . . II. vi. 40. 7
That wanton Mayd of *passage* had denide, ... II. viii. 3. 3
By further search had *passage* found elsewhere; . . . . II. viii. 3. 4
Through all those foldes the steelehead *passage* wrought, . . . II. viii. 32. 7
cruell *passage* made Quite through his brayne. . . . . II. viii. 45. 5
Whereby her course is stopt and *passage* staid: . . . . II. ix. 8. 4
Ne hedge ne ditch his readie *passage* brake; . . . . II. xi. 26. 5
An open *passage* through his riven brest, ... II. xi. 37. 4
here before a perlous *passage* lyes, ... II. xii. 17. 8
nought our *passage* may empeach, ... III. iii. 53. 1
Them yielded ready *passage,* and their rage surceast. . . . . III. iv. 31. 9
through the brackish waves their *passage* sheare; . . . . III. iv. 42. 7
his *passage* through the ford to let. . . . . III. v. 17. 9
Him boldly bad his *passage* there to stay, ... III. v. 18. 7
That his swift charet might have *passage* wyde . . . . III. xi. 40. 8
passage bard to all that thither came, ... III. xii. 43. 4
in their flesh a griesly *passage* rend, ... IV. ii. 15. 5
by one way that *passage* did prepare. . . . . IV. x. 6. 5
Next him went Wylibourne with *passage* slye, ... IV. xi. 32. 5
keepes a Bridges *passage* by strong hond, ... V. ii. 4. 7
makes all men for feare that *passage* for to shonne.' . . . . V. ii. 4. 9
When as they to the *passage* gan to draw, ... V. ii. 11. 4
(The lucky Pylot of her *passage* sad,) . . . . V. iv. 11. 7
That in and out thou mayst have *passage* free. . . . . V. v. 34. 5
Streight was the *passage,* like a ploughed ridge, ... V. vi. 36. 8
Nath'lesse that stroke so cruell *passage* found, ... V. vii. 33. 1
Ne once for ought her speedy *passage* stayd, ... V. viii. 6. 3
'All times have wont safe *passage* to afford . . . . V. viii. 22. 1
The armed knights stopping his *passage* by, ... V. ix. 14. 8
Into his shield it readie *passage* found, ... V. x. 33. 2
It would no *passage* yeeld unto his purpose vaine. . . . . V. xi. 10. 9
toll which they for *passage* pay.' . . . . VI. i. 13. 9
So soone as *passage* is unto him lent, ... VI. i. 21. 4
The covert was so thicke that did no *passage* shew. . . . . VI. v. 22. 9
ready *passage* to her pleasure did prepaire. . . . . VII. vi. 7. 9

Passage-money. *passage money* did of them require, ... V. ii. 11. 6

Passage-penny. he him makes his *passage-penny* pay: . . . . V. ii. 6. 4

Passant. a Lion *passant* in a golden field. . . . . III. i. 4. 9

Passed. *See* **Forepassed, Long-passed, Overpassed, Past.**
As the bonilasse *passed* bye, ... *S.C.* Au. 77
now *passed* youngthly pryme, ... *S.C.* D. 75
ere long time had *passed,* . . . . *Hub.* 559
since we *passed* are Unto this point, ... *Hub.* 1047
Thenceforth he *past* into each secrete part, ... *Hub.* 1303
the late love the which betwixt us *past,* . . . . *D.* 289
So having said, away she softly *past:* . . . . *D.* 293
The *passed* fortunes, which to thee befell . . . . *Col.* 33
of good *passed* newly to discus, ... *Col.* 38
Thus as they *past,* . . . . I. i. 6. 4
forward on his way . . . He *passed* forth, ... I. i. 28. 8
due recompence Of all her *passed* paines: . . . . I. iii. 30. 2
So forth they *past;* . . . . I. iii. 32. 6
Arrived there, they *passed* in forth right; . . . . I. iv. 6. 1
creature never *past,* That backe retourned . . . . I. v. 31. 6
for such perill *past* Wherewith you to reward? . . . . I. viii. 27. 3

Passed—*Continued.*
th' only good that growes of *passed* feare Is to be wise, . . . I. viii. 44. 5
his spright Had *past* the paines of hell . . . I. x. 32. 9
glauncing by, foorth *passed* forward right. . . . I. xi. 16. 5
Henceforth take heede of that thou now hast *past,* . . . II. iv. 36. 3
passed fayrely forth. . . . II. vi. 40. 5
they both yfere Forth *passed* on their way . . . II. ix. 2. 4
as Alma *passed* with her guestes, . . . II. ix. 26. 6
gan this Realme renew her *passed* prime: . . . II. x. 58. 8
The Palmer, seeing them in safetie *past,* . . . II. xii. 9. 1
as they *passed* by that way, . . . II. xii. 20. 7
to Guyon, as he *passed* by, . . . II. xii. 32. 1
they it *past,* and shortly gan descry . . . II. xii. 34. 3
past on hardily, . . . II. xii. 39. 5
passed forth, and lookt still forward right, . . . II. xii. 53. 4
Themselves they forth convaid, and *passed* forward right. . . . III. iii. 61. 9
With some late perill which he hardly *past,* . . . III. v. 3. 4
Her to encounter ere she *passed* by; . . . III. vii. 38. 4
so forth beside her *past.* . . . III. vii. 40. 9
The wicked engine . . . *Past* through his eies, . . . III. ix. 29. 4
for remembrance of her *passed* joy, . . . III. ix. 36. 5
many perilles *past* in forreine landes, . . . III. ix. 41. 8
they had *past* with mickle jeopardy, . . . III. ix. 53. 3
on adventure by the way he *past.* . . . III. x. 35. 5
whom when he *passed* kend, . . . III. x. 38. 8
did it selfe divide . . . That through she *passed,* . . . III. xi. 25. 6
the Championesse . . . *past* the foremost dore; . . . III. xi. 27. 8
when the second watch was almost *past,* . . . III. xii. 29. 6
she *passed* forth, not taking leave, . . . IV. i. 36. 7
passed through th' unruly preace Of people, . . . IV. iii. 41. 1
as they *passed* forth they did espy One in bright armes, . . . IV. iv. 6. 5
they *past* forth on their way. . . . IV. iv. 13. 2
did her *passed* paines in quiet rest assoyle. . . . IV. vii. 3. 9
twenty daies . . . have *past* through heven sheene, . . . IV. vii. 13. 2
forth she *past* into his dreadfull den, . . . IV. vii. 33. 1
when that forrest they had *passed* well, . . . IV. viii. 23. 1
when they were *passed* out of sight, . . . IV. viii. 36. 1
The stone which *passed* straunger at him threw: . . . IV. viii. 36. 6
who all that *passed* gan repeat: . . . IV. ix. 35. 9
forth without impediment I *past,* . . . IV. x. 11. 1
So in I *past,* . . . IV. x. 14. 4
Past forth on foote, . . . IV. x. 15. 4
'Thence forth I *passed* to the second gate, . . . IV. x. 16. 1
having *past* all perill, . . . IV. x. 21. 1
goodly workmanship farre *past* all other . . . IV. x. 29. 8
By which I hardly *past* with much adoe: . . . IV. x. 57. 7
know the moniments of *passed* age: . . . IV. xi. 17. 6
past not long ere Brutus warlicke sonne, . . . IV. xi. 38. 1
So farre he *past* amongst his enemies band, . . . V. iii. 9. 3
for weekes that *passed* were, She told but moneths, . . . V. vi. 5. 6
Till to the Bridges further end she *past;* . . . V. vi. 39. 6
His other fellow Pagan which before him *past.* . . . V. viii. 8. 9
as he *passed* by, . . . V. viii. 32. 5
So forth they *past,* till they approched ny . . . V. ix. 8. 1
Into a bird it chaung'd, and from him *past,* . . . V. ix. 17. 5
Thence forth they *passed* with that gentle Mayd . . . V. ix. 20. 1
Past through his shield and pierst through either syde; . . . V. x. 35. 7
Whose grudging ghost was thereout fled and *past,* . . . V. x. 37. 3
even to the vitall parts they *past,* . . . V. xii. 17. 8
He had not *passed* farre upon the strand, . . . V. xii. 28. 3
as he *past* afore withouten dread, . . . V. xii. 39. 8
Yet he *past* on, . . . V. xii. 42. 9
A privy token which betweene them *past,* . . . VI. i. 29. 3
then to his first quest he *passed* forth along. . . . VI. i. 47. 9
as they me *passed* by, Much was I moved . . . VI. ii. 11. 1
'So *passed* we till this young man us met; . . . VI. ii. 23. 1
And Calidore forth *passed* to his former payne. . . . VI. ii. 38. 9
So they the evening *past* till time of rest; . . . VI. iii. 9. 6
He *passed* forth with her in faire array, . . . VI. iii. 16. 4
So, as they *past* together on their way, . . . VI. iii. 16. 7
So forth he *passed* thorough that daies paine, . . . VI. iii. 17. 7
So all that night they *past* in great disease, . . . VI. v. 40. 1
past through many perillous assayes, . . . VI. vi. 3. 4
passed forth to follow his first enterprize. . . . VI. vi. 44. 9
the other, which was *passed* by, . . . VI. vii. 10. 1
As if he would have *passed* through him quight; . . . VI. vii. 10. 7
all which *passed* by . . . VI. vii. 27. 3
So judgement *past,* as is by law ordayned . . . VI. vii. 36. 5
past through many perils by the way, . . . VI. vii. 50. 6
streight to the noise forth *past.* . . . VI. viii. 47. 9
all that night to him unknowen she *past;* . . . VI. viii. 51. 6
As I it *past:* . . . VI. ix. 1. 6
Full many pathes and perils he hath *past,* . . . VI. ix. 2. 5
since things *passed* none may now restore, . . . VI. x. 20. 8
Of cryes and clamors which amongst them *past,* . . . VI. xi. 32. 4
speaking markes of *passed* monuments, . . . VI. xii. 20. 4
Through all estates he found that he had *past,* . . . VI. xii. 23. 1
snar at all that ever *passed* by: . . . VI. xii. 27. 7
she *past* the region of the ayre And of the fire, . . . VII. vi. 7. 6
past away, his doings to relate Unto his Lord; . . . VII. vi. 19. 2
So *past* the twelve Months forth, . . . VII. vii. 43. 9
his *passed* date Bids all old thoughts to die . . . *Am.* iv. 3
none can call againe the *passed* time. . . . *Am.* lxx. 14
Through which he *past* his miserable dayes, . . . *H.H.L.* 236

Passenger. New merth her *passenger* to entertaine; . . . II. vi. 6. 2

Passengers. Therein stil wait poore *passengers* to teare. . . . *Col.* 203
rode, Where we must land some of our *passengers,* . . . I. xii. 42. 3
nigh it drawes All *passengers,* . . . II. xii. 4. 8
mote the *passengers* thereto allure; . . . II. xii. 12. 6
Whose manner was all *passengers* to stay . . . IV. x. 13. 3

Passers-by. Of which all *passers by* doo somewhat pill: . . . *Ro.* xxx. 12
that *passers by* Might it behold, . . . *Gn.* 661
seemd to entice All *passers by* . . . II. xii. 54. 4

Passeth. he *passeth* through the herds Of ravenous wilde beasts, . . . *Hub.* 1284
as a speedie post that *passeth* by. . . . *D.* 413
passeth reasons reach, . . . *Col.* 837
lightly mounted *passeth* on his way; . . . II. v. 38. 2
So *passeth,* in the passing of a day, . . . II. xii. 75. 1
Poets witt, that *passeth* Painter farre . . . III. Pr. 2. 6
Providence hevenly *passeth* living thought, . . . III. v. 27. 1
as he *passeth* downe, . . . IV. xi. 34. 4
Whose fruitfull seede farre *passeth* those in land, . . . IV. xii. 1. 3

Passing. puffed up with *passing* surquedrie, . . . *Van.* viii. 7
time in *passing* weares, . . . *S.C.* Jun. 38
hys *passing* skil with him is fledde, . . . *S.C.* Jun. 91
passing by with rolling wreathed pace, . . . *Gn.* 253
passing foorth, as their adventures fell, . . . *Hub.* 359
passing through the Countrey in disguize, . . . *Hub.* 575
manly legs, still *passing* too and fro, . . . *Hub.* 748
With treasure *passing* all this worldes worth, . . . *Ti.* 286
The metall was of rare and *passing* price; . . . *Mui.* 76
passing farre All Painters skill, . . . *Mui.* 90
When *passing* by ye read these wofull layes, . . . *D.* 536
Far *passing* all the pastors of his daies, . . . *As.* 9
and held in *passing* price, . . . *As.* Interl. 220
could pipe himselfe with *passing* skill. . . . *Col.* 443
paines far *passing* that long wandring Greeke, . . . I. iii. 21. 5
So, *passing* forth, she him obaid. . . . I. iv. 51. 9
Which *passing* through, on every side them stood . . . ghosts . . . I. v. 32. 4
med'cines, which had *passing* prief; . . . I. x. 24. 5
owches . . . Whose *passing* price uneath was to be told: . . . I. x. 31. 7
dazed were his eyne Through *passing* brightnes, . . . I. x. 67. 7
passing by, did brush With his long tayle, . . . I. xi. 16. 8
To proofe of *passing* wonders hath full often usd: . . . II. ii. 5. 9
So *passing* persant, and so wondrous bright, . . . II. iii. 23. 4
lightly shunned it; and, *passing* by, . . . II. v. 4. 1
in Amours the *passing* howres to spend, . . . II. vi. 35. 4
they *passing* spake unto them nought; . . . II. vii. 24. 2
Far *passing* th' hight of men terrestriall, . . . II. vii. 41. 5
Who, *passing* by, forth ledd her guestes anone . . . II. ix. 28. 8
Guyon, . . . *Passing* through perilles great, . . . II. xii. Arg.
They, *passing* by, that grisely mouth did see . . . II. xii. 6. 1
They, *passing* by, a goodly Ship did see . . . II. xii. 19. 1
trembled as them *passing* they beheld: . . . II. xii. 40. 7
Thence *passing* forth, they shortly doe arryve . . . II. xii. 42. 1
So did he eke Sir Guyon *passing* by; . . . II. xii. 49. 6
Whom *passing* by she happened to meet: . . . II. xii. 56. 8
So passeth, in the *passing* of a day, . . . II. xii. 75. 1
scarse them leasure gave her *passing* to behold. . . . III. i. 15. 9
These stranger knights, through *passing,* forth were led . . . III. i. 33. 1
passing Dee, with hardy enterprise . . . III. iii. 35. 4
through his perfect sent And *passing* speede, . . . III. vii. 23. 9
(a thing far *passing* thought) . . . III. vii. 48. 5
all the wyles of wemens wits knew *passing* well. . . . III. viii. 8. 9
Of *passing* valew and of great renowme, . . . III. xi. 47. 3
The whiles the *passing* brightnes her fraile sences dazd. . . . III. xi. 49. 9
passing by, his name discovered, . . . III. xii. 4. 8
for *passing* great despight, Staid not to answer; . . . IV. i. 52. 1
weapon . . . *passing* forth with furious affret, . . . IV. iii. 11. 7
therein sate a Ladie, *passing* faire . . . IV. iii. 39. 6
passing joy, which so great marvaile brings, . . . IV. iii. 49. 8
passing beautie did eftsoones reveale, . . . IV. v. 10. 4
Farre *passing* Bronteus or Pyracmon great, . . . IV. v. 37. 2
passing through the eares would pierce the hart, . . . IV. viii. 26. 6
They *passing* forth kept on their readie way, . . . IV. viii. 37. 1
Passing the measure of my feeble powre; . . . IV. ix. 39. 7
Farre *passing* that, which . . . Phidias did make . . . IV. x. 40. 3
Thus *passing* th' evening well, . . . V. vi. 23. 1
She wondred at the workemans *passing* skill, . . . V. vii. 5. 6
passing litle further, . . . V. ix. 21. 3
they *passing* in Went up the hall, . . . V. ix. 23. 1
passing through the thickest preasse, . . . V. ix. 23. 6
They, *passing* by, were guyded by degree . . . V. ix. 27. 1
passing forth into the hall he came, . . . VI. i. 24. 6
passing well expert in single fight, . . . VI. i. 36. 4
I chaunst to meete this knight, . . . *passing* on the plaine. . . . VI. ii. 9. 9
Till that, by fortune *passing* all foresight, . . . VI. iv. 2. 1
Seeing the ugly Monster *passing* by, . . . VI. v. 16. 2
passing by doth hurt no more. . . . VI. vii. 9. 9
Thence *passing* forth, . . . VI. vii. 18. 6
nigh she swelt For *passing* joy, . . . VI. xii. 21. 9
At every rash beholder *passing* by. . . . *Am.* xvi. 8
Far *passing* those which Hercules came by, . . . *Am.* lxxvii. 7
With admiration of their *passing* light, . . . *H.H.L.* 279
their owne native light farre *passing* theirs. . . . *H.H.B.* 70

Passion. The tempest of that stormie *passion,* . . . *T.M.* 380
Renewing her complaint with *passion* strong, . . . *Ti.* 479
The stormie *passion* of his troubled brest, . . . *D.* 192
the outragious *passion* nigh appeased, . . . *D.* 555
sparke of reasons might . . . to rule his *passion,* . . . *Col.* 868
this great *passion* of unwonted lust, . . . I. i. 49. 1
He in great *passion* al this while did dwell, . . . I. ii. 26. 5
whenas the dreadfull *passion* Was overpast, . . . I. ii. 32. 2
Therewith she gan her *passion* to renew, . . . I. iii. 25. 1
Such restlesse *passion* did all night torment . . . I. v. 1. 5
chaunge of hew great *passion* did bewray; . . . I. ix. 16. 2
much aswag'd the *passion* of his plight, . . . I. x. 24. 8
raging *passion* with fierce tyranny . . . II. i. 57. 4
strong *passion,* or weake fleshlinesse, . . . II. iv. 2. 6

Passion—*Continued.*
reason, blent through *passion,* nought descryde; . . . II. iv. 7. 7
calme the tempest of his *passion* wood: . . . II. iv. 11. 8
Tempring the *passion* with advizement slow, . . . II. v. 13. 2
with strong reason maistred *passion* fraile, . . . II. vi. 40. 4
the strong *passion* mard her modest grace, . . . II. ix. 43. 4
ransackt all her veines with *passion* entyre. . . . III. i. 47. 9
At last, the *passion* past, she thus him answered. . . . III. ii. 5. 9
if the *passion* mayster thy fraile might, . . . III. ii. 46. 6
Full of soft *passion* and unwonted smart: . . . III. v. 30. 8
With reason dew the *passion* to subdew, . . . III. v. 44. 2
So strong is *passion* that no reason heares. . . . III. vii. 21. 5
with *passion* great And griefull pittie . . . IV. i. 16. 3
ever when his *passion* is allayd, . . . IV. ii. 12. 6
Whereby the *passion* grew more fierce and faine, . . . IV. vi. 33. 8
Which losse her made like *passion* also prove: . . . IV. viii. 3. 5
Through jealous *passion* weeping inly wroth, . . . IV. ix. 9. 8
the *passion* that her heart opprest; . . . IV. xii. 8. 7
The troublous *passion* of my pensive mind, . . . V. vii. 19. 2
With franticke *passion* and with furie fraught; . . . V. viii. 48. 7
Would have the *passion* hid, and up arose . . . V. ix. 50. 9
But still his *passion* grew more violent . . . VI. ii. 21. 9
To rule the stubborne rage of *passion* blinde: . . . VI. vi. 5. 8
the sharpe *passion* being overpast, . . . VI. viii. 19. 3
other none such *passion* can contrive . . . VI. xii. 21. 5
You calme the storme that *passion* did begin, . . . *Am.* viii. 11
The piteous *passion* of his dying smart. . . . *Am.* xlviii. 12
Such is the powre of that sweet *passion,* . . . *H.L.* 190
Passionate. In Tragick plaints and *passionate* mischance. . . *Col.* 427
Great pleasure . . . That godly King and Queene did *passionate,* I. xii. 16. 2
Passioned. to see the mayd So straungely *passioned,* . . . II. ix. 41. 9
Some argument of matter *passioned:* . . . III. xii. 4. 6
Passions. Distempred through misrule and *passions* bace; . . I. ix. 1. 6
By knowen signes and *passions* which I see, . . . III. ii. 33. 3
Both coosen *passions* of distroubled spright, . . . III. iv. 12. 7
all the *passions* that in man may light . . . III. x. 17. 8
Of all the *passions* in the mind thou vilest art! . . . III. xi. 1. 9
T' expresse his *passions,* which his reason did empeach. . . . VI. iv. 11. 9
all the *passions* heale which wound the weaker spright. . . . VI. vi. 3. 9
my weak powres of *passions* warreid arre; . . . *Am.* xliv. 7
griefe renew, and *passions* doe awake . . . *Am.* xliv. 11
least *passions* doe impresse, . . . *H.L.* 170
Passport. thou hast a free *passeporte;* . . . *S.C.* Env. 7
Withouten *pasport* or good warrantye, . . . *Hub.* 186
devise A *pasport* for us both in fittest wize, . . . *Hub.* 196
The *pasport* ended, both they forward went; . . . *Hub.* 203
Yee shall our *pasport* at your pleasure see, . . . *Hub.* 377
Past. *See* **Forepassed, Passed.**
when thou art *past* jeopardee, . . . *To his Booke* 16
Let be, as may be, that is *past:* . . . *S.C.* Mar. 58
fynd no part 'Of pleasure *past.* . . . *S.C.* Au. 169
day, that was, is wightly *past,* . . . *S.C.* S. 5
Thrise three Moones bene fully spent and *past;* . . . *S.C.* S. 20
Delight is layd abedde; and pleasure *past;* . . . *S.C.* D. 137
My volume shall renowne, so long since *past.* . . . *Gn.* 48
Whose part once *past* all men bid take away: . . . *Hub.* 932
in ages *past* none might professe . . . *T.M.* 559
all I hate that is to come or *past.* . . . *D.* 427
all *passed* feare, He set her on her steede, . . . I. ii. 45. 8
she speakes no more Of *past:* . . . I. iii. 30. 7
'At last, when perils all I weened *past,* . . . I. iv. 47. 1
'Faire Dame, be nought dismaid For sorrowes *past;* . . . I. iv. 49. 2
Dead is Sansfoy, his vitall paines are *past,* . . . I. iv. 49. 6
The Marriner yet halfe amazed stares At perill *past,* . . . I. vi. 1. 5
they the woods are *past* and come now to the plaine. . . . I. vi. 33. 9
Unkindnesse *past,* they gan of solace treat, . . . I. vii. 4. 1
Dwarfe, . . . When all was *past,* tooke up his forlorne weed; I. vii. 19. 4
Is not great grace to helpe him over *past,* . . . I. ix. 39. 4
They were far *past* the passage which he spake, . . . II. vi. 11. 2
The third things *past* could keep in memoree: . . . II. ix. 49. 3
Then thought the Prince all peril sure was *past,* . . . II. xi. 43. 6
At last, the passion *past,* she thus him answered. . . . III. ii. 5. 9
the fury *past,* to former hew Hee turnd againe, . . . III. iii. 50. 8
But, *past* a while, when she fit season saw To leave . . . III. vii. 18. 1
call alowd for helpe, ere helpe were *past;* . . . III. x. 13. 7
march not *past* the mountenaunce of a shott, . . . III. xi. 20. 8
Whom whenas Scudamour saw *past* the fire . . . III. xi. 26. 1
being *past,* he thus began amaine: . . . IV. i. 52. 5
them seeing *past* the reach of eare, . . . IV. viii. 36. 7
past perils well apay.' . . . IV. ix. 40. 9
Till I was throughly *past* the perill of his reach. . . . IV. x. 36. 9
from thence not *past* a mile or tway, . . . V. iv. 35. 7
he farre was gone and *past:* . . . V. viii. 33. 6
Crying in vaine for helpe, when helpe was *past:* . . . V. ix. 19. 6
yet *past* a boy, And being now high time . . . VI. ii. 32. 8
all other helpes were *past.* . . . VI. iii. 12. 9
saw his carriage *past* that perill well, . . . VI. iii. 34. 6
quite they seem'd *past* helpe of surgery; . . . VI. vi. 5. 5
repentaunce for things *past* and gon. . . . VI. viii. 24. 5
she thought Her selfe now *past* the perill of her feares: . . . VI. viii. 32. 3
Sith otherwise he could not mend thing *past;* . . . VI. xi. 34. 7
now long season *past* Had never joyance felt . . . VI. xi. 45. 1
To leave his love, now perill being *past,* . . . VI. xii. 13. 3
long sith *past* She in the open fields had loosely layd . . . VI. xii. 16. 3
So farre *past* memory of man that may be knowne? . . . VII. vii. 2. 9
When these were *past,* thus gan . . . VII. vii. 47. 1
when this storme is *past,* . . . *Am.* xxxiv. 9
for all the paynes and sorrowes *past,* . . . *Epith.* 32
For who my *passed* follies now pursewes, . . . *H.H.L.* 20
Pastime. After his sportes and cruell *pastime* donne; . . . I. vi. 27. 4

Pastime—*Continued.*
make their *pastyme* Emongst the shady leaves, . . . III. vi. 42. 7
Pastoral. now no *pastorall* is to bee hard. . . . *T.M.* 282
Pastorals. Were wont so oft their *Pastoralls* to sing, . . . *T.M.* 280
Pastorella. Calidore . . . loves fayre *Pastorell:* . . . VI. ix. Arg.
The fayrest *Pastorella* her by name did hight. . . . VI. ix. 9. 9
The father of the fayrest *Pastorell,* . . . VI. ix. 14. 2
To helpe faire *Pastorella* home to drive Her fleecie flocke; . . VI. ix. 15. 8
home came the fayrest *Pastorell,* . . . VI. ix. 17. 5
Dayly beholding the faire *Pastorell,* . . . VI. ix. 34. 3
unto his fields he went With the faire *Pastorella* . . . VI. ix. 37. 2
oft complaine Of *Pastorell* to all the shepheards . . . VI. ix. 38. 8
Pastorella, him to grace, Her flowry garland tooke . . . VI. ix. 42. 5
They for their Judge did *Pastorella* chose; . . . VI. ix. 43. 3
Then was the oaken crowne by *Pastorell* Given to Calidore VI. ix. 44. 6
To winne the love of the faire *Pastorell,* . . . VI. ix. 46. 2
The whiles his *Pastorell* is led Into captivity. . . . VI. x. Arg.
Whilest his faire *Pastorella* was elsewhere, . . . VI. x. 5. 2
Where his faire *Pastorella* did remaine: . . . VI. x. 32. 3
Did runne at *Pastorell* her to surprize; . . . VI. x. 34. 7
he it presented Before the feete of the faire *Pastorell;* . . . VI. x. 36. 7
Faire *Pastorella,* sorrowfull and sad, . . . VI. x. 40. 5
when faire *Pastorell* Into this place was brought, . . . VI. x. 43. 6
The Theeves fall out for *Pastorell,* . . . VI. xi. Arg.
Faire *Pastorell,* of whom is now my song: . . . VI. xi. 2. 2
beheld that lovely guest, Faire *Pastorella,* . . . VI. xi. 3. 8
Pastorella, woful wretched Elfe, . . . VI. xi. 19. 1
holding fast twixt both his armes extended Fayre *Pastorell,* . VI. xi. 19. 8
askt where were the rest? Where *Pastorell?* . . . VI. xi. 28. 3
Where was his *Pastorell?* where all the other crew? . . . VI. xi. 28. 9
Before I saw faire *Pastorella* dye.' . . . VI. xi. 29. 4
how faire *Pastorell* should have bene sold To marchants, . VI. xi. 30. 6
when the lot to *Pastorell* did fall, . . . VI. xi. 31. 8
might certaine tydings weene Of *Pastorell,* . . . VI. xi. 39. 4
There did they find . . . That *Pastorell* yet liv'd; . . . VI. xi. 41. 6
faire *Pastorell* through great affright Was almost dead, . . . VI. xi. 43. 7
gan aloud for *Pastorell* to call, . . . VI. xi. 44. 2
Fayre *Pastorella* by great hap Her parents understands. . . VI. xii. Arg.
had raught Faire *Pastorella* from those Brigants powre, . . . VI. xii. 3. 2
Till time that Calidore brought *Pastorella* thether. . . . VI. xii. 10. 9
Claribell Ne lesse did tender the faire *Pastorell,* . . . VI. xii. 11. 5
taking leave of his faire *Pastorell,* . . . VI. xii. 13. 6
What did betide to the faire *Pastorell* . . . VI. xii. 14. 3
so faire a daughter . . . As *Pastorella* was, . . . VI. xii. 21. 8
Acknowledg'd for his owne faire *Pastorell.* . . . VI. xii. 22. 4
Pastorella's. most in *Pastorellaes* grace did sit: . . . VI. ix. 41. 8
Pastors. Far passing all the *pastors* of his daies, . . . *As.* 9
Pasture. all his plenteous *pasture* nought him pleased: . . . *Van.* ii. 13
To feede abroad where *pasture* best befalls. . . . *Gn.* 72
todes and frogs, his *pasture* poysonous, . . . III. x. 59. 2
Unwont with heards to watch, or *pasture* sheepe, . . . VI. xi. 40. 4
Pastures. of sike *pastoures* howe done the flocks creepe? . . . *S.C.* S. 140
Where may I the hills and *pastures* see, . . . *Col.* 238
wilde greene woods and fruitful *pastures* minde; . . . *Gn.* 637
Seemes that in fruitfull *pastures* ye doo live, . . . *Hub.* 593
pastures on the pleasures of each place. . . . *Mui.* 176
Patched. With thornes together pind and *patched* was, . . . I. ix. 36. 2
Pate. to shroude my lucklesse *pate.* . . . *S.C.* Jun. 16
Here take thy lovers token on thy *pate.'* . . . I. vi. 47. 7
By equall dome repayd on his owne *pate:* . . . IV. xi. 38. 4
Paterne. *See* **Pattern.**
Paternosters. Nine hundred *Pater nosters* every day, . . . I. iii. 13. 8
Path. They keepen all the *path.* . . . *S.C.* Jul. 204
Beyond the compasse of his pointed *path,* . . . *T.M.* 10
that *path,* which first was showne, . . . I. i. 10. 4
That *path* they take that beaten seemd most bare, . . . I. i. 11. 3
That *path* he kept which beaten was most plaine, . . . I. i. 28. 3
So few there bee, That chose the narrow *path,* . . . I. x. 10. 4
to heaven she teacheth him the ready *path.* . . . I. x. 33. 9
A little *path* that was both steepe and long, . . . I. x. 55. 2
seek this *path* that I to thee presage, . . . I. x. 61. 1
out of the *path* Did lightly leape, . . . II. v. 18. 7
Through griesly shadowes by a beaten *path,* . . . II. vii. 51. 3
forth she beates the dusty *path:* . . . III. iv. 12. 8
what unwonted *path* Had guided her, . . . III. vii. 8. 3
Avon marched in more stately *path,* . . . IV. xi. 31. 6
left their scorched *path* yet in the firmament. . . . V. viii. 40. 9
On man and beast that commeth in her *path.* . . . V. viii. 49. 5
He could no *path* nor tract of foot descry, . . . VI. iv. 24. 6
Paths. all within were *pathes* and alleies wide, . . . I. i. 7. 7
So many *pathes,* so many turnings seene, . . . I. i. 10. 8
Full many *pathes* and perils he hath past, . . . VI. ix. 2. 5
Patience. With *patience* to forbeare the offred bowle? . . . *S.C.* May 139
Oxeye still greene, and bitter *Patience;* . . . *Gn.* 678
She armes the brest with constant *patience* . . . *T.M.* 133
She heard with *patience* all unto the end, . . . I. vii. 27. 1
His name was *Patience.* . . . I. x. 23. 9
all with *patience* wisely she did beare, . . . I. x. 28. 8
thus recover'd by wise *Patience* . . . I. x. 29. 1
Ne might his rancling paine with *patience* be appeasd. . . . I. xi. 38. 9
Patience perforce: . . . what may it boot To frett . . . II. iii. 3. 3
settle *patience* in so furious heat? . . . II. viii. 27. 6
with *pacience* and sufferaunce sly . . . to subdew: . . . II. viii. 47. 7
ought your goodly *patience* offend, . . . III. ix. 1. 5
them of *patience* gently prayd. . . . III. ix. 10. 7
patience perforce, he must abie . . . III. x. 3. 1
let not my rudenes be no breach Unto your *patience,* . . . III. x. 25. 4
pitty did the Virgins hart of *patience* rob. . . . III. xi. 8. 9
seemes t' exceede the powre of *patience,* . . . III. xi. 14. 2
they endured all with *patience* milde, . . . IV. viii. 28. 6

Patience—*Continued.*
With which my weaker *patience* fortune proves: . . . . IV. viii. 63. 8
they so farre from peace or *patience* were, ... IV. ix. 33. 1
Forget his *patience,* and yeeld vengeaunce dew . . . . . . V. xii. 42. 4
calm'd his wrathfull heat With goodly *patience,* . . . . . . VI. i. 40. 3
Yet he (poore soule!) with *patience* all did beare; . . . . . VII. vi. 49. 6
Patient. maister these mishaps with *patient* might. . . . . . I. viii. 45. 2
with *patient* eare The brave adventures . . . to heare; . . . . II. Pr. 5. 6
brought it to her *patient* deare, ... III. v. 32. 8
backe he came unto her *patient;* . . . . IV. xii. 23. 7
Patient's. By his faire *patients* side . . . . VI. xi. 9. 9
Patients. his sickely *patients* Did gladly hearken . . . . . . VI. vi. 15. 1
Patrimony. our portions dew Of all the *patrimonie,* . . . . . *Hub.* 138
Patron. Jove himselfe, the *patron* of the place, ... *Van.* xi. 10
And noble *Patrone* of weake povertie; . . . . *Ti.* 262
And *Patrone* of my Muses pupillage; . . . . *Ded. Son.* vii. 2
The *Patrone* of true Holinesse . . . . I. i. Arg.
you, my Lord, the *Patrone* of my life, ... I. ix. 17. 6
thine owne nations frend And *Patrone:* . . . . I. x. 61. 8
Their Lord and *Patrone* loud did him proclame, ... I. xii. 6. 3
with reverence dew As to the *patrone* of his life, ... II. viii. 55. 4
She him remercied as the *Patrone* of her life. . . . . II. xi. 16. 9
her lives Lord and *patrone* of her health . . . . IV. i. 6. 2
Patronage. Muse, . . . Flies for like aide unto your *Patronage,* *Ded. Son.* xiii. 8
leave unto me thy knights last *patronage.'* . . . . II. viii. 26. 9
Patroness. of their order she was *Patronesse,* . . . . I. x. 44. 8
Night, the *patronesse* of love-stealth fayre, ... III. x. 16. 6
forst to seeke my lifes deare *patronnesse:* . . . . IV. x. 28. 8
of weake Princes to be *Patronesse,* . . . . V. i. 4. 7
Patronize. us, that *patronize* The name of learning? . . . . . *T.M.* 147
To *patronize* the authour of their praise, ... *Ded. Son.* iv. 10
The lawes of wedlock still dost *patronize;* . . . . *Epith.* 391
Pattern. By *paterne* of great Virgils spirit divine! . . . . . *Ro.* xxv. 11
She is the *paterne* of true womanhead, ... *Col.* 512
That peerelesse *paterne* of Dame Natures pride . . . . IV. vi. 24. 5
by one *patterne,* seen somewhere, She had them made . . . . IV. ix. 11. 5
This squalid weede, the *patterne* of dispaire, ... V. iv. 34. 6
in all Antiquity So faire a *patterne* finde, ... VI. Pr. 6. 2
he before his eyes had plast A goodly *Paterne,* . . . . . . *H.B.* 32
That wondrous *Paterne,* wheresoere it bee, ... *H.B.* 36
According to an heavenly *patterne* wrought, ... *H.H.L.* 108
Patterns. these olde fragments are for *paternes* borne: . . . . *Ro.* xxvii. 8
worthie *paterns* of her clemencies; . . . . V. x. 5. 7
Paulinus. Corrupted by *Paulinus,* from her swerv'd: . . . . II. x. 55. 4
Paunce. *See* **Pansy.**
Pause. when the bodie list to *pause,* . . . . *Hub.* 759
There did she *pause,* . . . . IV. xii. 8. 6
a while doth *pause* To heare the piteous beast . . . . V. iv. 40. 8
Paused. The Damzell *pauzd:* and then thus fearfully: . . . . III. ii. 35. 1
having *pauz'd* awhile, Jove thus bespake: . . . . VII. vi. 29. 1
Pausing. As *pausing* in great doubt, awhile he staid, ... *Hub.* 175
Paved. *See* **Brass-paved.**
with their garments strowes the *paved* street; . . . . I. xii. 13. 4
All *pav'd* beneath with Jaspar shining bright, ... II. xii. 62. 8
Pavement. the *pavement* precious stone. . . . . *Rev.* iv. 11
all the others *pavement* were with yvory spilt. . . . . IV. x. 5. 9
Pavilion. A faire *Pavilion,* scarcely to bee seene, ... III. v. 40. 7
Causd his *pavilion* to be richly pight . . . . V. iv. 46. 4
Where was a rich *Pavilion* ready pight . . . . V. v. 4. 8
She caused her *Pavilion* be pight; . . . . V. vii. 26. 2
She placed was in a *pavilion;* . . . . VII. vii. 8. 2
Pavilions. Spredding *pavilions* for the birds to bowre, . . . VI. x. 6. 6
Pavone. More sondry colours then the proud *Pavone* Beares . III. xi. 47. 7
Paw. The other like a beares uneven *Paw,* . . . . I. viii. 48. 8
In feare to lose his weapon in his *paw,* . . . . I. xi. 41. 2
The *paw* yett missed not his minisht might, ... I. xi. 43. 8
Him in his iron *paw* he seized had; . . . . V. i. 22. 2
Pawn. Thereto will I *pawne* yonder spotted Lambe, ... *S.C.* Au. 37
Pawnce. *See* **Pansy.**
Pawned. aske hem therefore what they han *paund:* . . . . . . *S.C.* S. 95
pledges *pawnd* the same to keepe aright: . . . . IV. iii. 3. 4
Paws. he threats his teeth, his tayle, his *pawes,* . . . . . . *Van.* x. 11
To save the innocent from the beastes *pawes,* . . . . *S.C.* Au. 33
from his griping *pawes* He hath his shield redeemd, ... I. iii. 41. 8
all the crest a Dragon did enfold With greedie *pawes,* . . . . I. vii. 31. 4
what ever thing does touch his ravenous *pawes,* . . . . I. xi. 12. 4
rend in peeces with his ravenous *pawes,* . . . . II. vii. 27. 8
He rampt upon him with his ravenous *pawes,* . . . . VI. xii. 29. 8
Pay. Then *paye* you the price of your surquedrie, ... *S.C* F. 49
they bene hyred for little *pay* . . . . *S.C.* May 47
I will *pay* Penance to her, ... *D.* 369
He lives that shall him *pay* his dewties last, ... I. iv. 49. 8
some shall *pay* the price of others guilt; . . . . I. v. 26. 2
Here endlesse penaunce for one fault I *pay,* . . . . I. v. 42. 6
Fortune, . . . for these wronges shall treble penaunce *pay* . . I. viii. 43. 5
I cast to *pay* that I so dearely bought. . . . . II. iv. 30. 7
Fame is my meed, and glory vertues *pay:* . . . . III. x. 31. 7
The which sad lovers for their vowes did *pay;* . . . . IV. x. 37. 8
owe vassallage To him . . . and tribute *pay:* . . . . IV. xi. 29. 4
he him makes his passage-penny *pay:* . . . . V. ii. 6. 4
Thinking to *pay* him with that one for all: . . . . V. xi. 8. 6
the vertue selfe, which her reward doth *pay.'* . . . . V. xi. 17. 9
toll which they for passage *pay.'* . . . . VI. i. 13. 9
Will it avenge, and *pay* thee with thy right; . . . . VI. i. 25. 8
To *pay* each with his owne is right and dew; . . . . VI. i. 42. 3
It dearely shall aby, and death for handsell *pay.* . . . . . . VI. xi. 15. 9
Rayne, haile, and snowe do *pay* them sad penance, ... VII. vii. 23. 7
Pay to her usury of long delight: . . . . *Epith.* 33
And *pay* the price, all were his debt extreeme. . . . . *H.H.L.* 133
That He for him might *pay* sinnes deadly hyre, ... *H.H.L.* 138
Paying. *paying* but a peece. . . . . *S.C.* May 50
Paynim. proud *Paynim* forward came so ferce . . . . I. iii. 35. 1
Left in the hand of that same *Paynim* bold, ... I. iii. 40. 6
'Ah dearest Dame,' quoth then the *Paynim* bold, ... I. iv. 41. 1
the *Paynim* chaunst to cast his eye . . . . I. v. 10. 1
Unto the place whereas the *Paynim* lay, ... I. v. 29. 2
hurle not flashing flames upon that *Paynim* bold? . . . . . I. vi. 5. 9
the Redcrosse knight was slain with *Paynim* knife.' . . . . . I. vi. 38. 9
of that proud *Paynim* sore afrayd. . . . . I. vi. 47. 9
Bought with the blood of vanquisht *Paynim* bold; . . . . . . I. vii. 26. 4
Twixt that great faery Queene and *Paynim* king, ... I. xi. 7. 4
that proud *Paynim* king that works her teene: . . . . I. xii. 18. 8
Arthure soone hath reskewed, And *Paynim* brethren foyld. . . II. viii. Arg.
Two *Paynim* knights al armd as bright as skie, ... II. viii. 10. 2
hath to *Paynim* knights wrought gret distresse, ... II. viii. 18. 5
when the *Paynym* spyde the streaming blood, ... II. viii. 39. 3
oft the *Paynim* sav'd from deadly stowre: . . . . II. viii. 43. 6
Nought booted it the *Paynim* then to strive; . . . . II. viii. 50. 1
'*Paynim,* this is thy dismall day; . . . . II. viii. 51. 5
After the *Paynim* brethren conquer'd were, ... II. ix. 2. 1
on their *Paynim* foes avenge their ranckled ire. . . . . . . III. iii. 36. 9
make Strong warre upon the *Paynim* brethren, ... III. iii. 52. 6
A *Painim* knight that well in armes was skild, ... IV. iv. 17. 7
the *Paynim* . . . great advantage had, ... V. ii. 13. 5
She weened streight it was her *Paynim* Knight, ... V. viii. 26. 7
tost the *Paynim* without feare or awe; . . . . V. viii. 41. 7
Paynim's. Uprose Duessa . . . And to the *Paynims* lodging comes . . . . I. iv. 44. 9
'Where is,' (said Satyrane) 'that *Paynims* sonne, ... I. vi. 39. 5
Una, . . . Fast flying from that *Paynims* greedy pray, ... I. vii. 20. 3
In which the *Paynims* daughter did abide, ... V. ii. 20. 2
Paynims. The powre of forreine *Paynims* which invade thy land. . . . . III. iii. 27. 9
Witnesse the *Paynims* both, ... V. viii. 11. 6
Pays. he takes and *paies;* . . . . II. ii. 25. 6
Paysd. *See* **Peised.**
Peace. he bare The tree of *peace,* . . . . *Bel.*[1] vii. 11
sights, that doo her *peace* molest. . . . . *Pet.*[2] vii. 8
Olives bene for *peace,* When wars doe surcease: . . . . *S.C.* Ap. 124
what *peace* has the Lion with the Lambe? . . . . *S.C.* May 169
hold theyr *peace,* for shame . . . . *S.C.* Jun. 56
all happie *peace* and plenteous store . . . . *Col.* 310
his ghost . . . In *peace* may passen over Lethe lake; . . . . . I. iii. 36. 6
Wherein eternall *peace* and happinesse doth dwell. . . . . . . I. x. 55. 9
'What need of armes, where *peace* doth ay remaine, ... I. x. 62. 7
let me heare for aie in *peace* remaine. . . . . I. x. 63. 3
Proclaymed joy and *peace* through all his state; . . . . . . I. xii. 3. 8
Glad signe of victory and *peace* in all their land. . . . . . . I. xii. 5. 9
'the troubler of my happy *peace,* . . . . I. xii. 19. 2
Where she enjoyes sure *peace* for evermore, ... II. i. 2. 8
bid them sleepe in everlasting *peace.* . . . . II. i. 60. 6
He maketh warre, he maketh *peace* againe, ... II. ii. 26. 7
his *peace* is but continual jarre: . . . . II. ii. 26. 8
to her just conditions of faire *peace* to heare. . . . . . . II. ii. 27. 9
lovely concord, and most sacred *peace,* . . . . II. ii. 31. 1
in her face faire *peace* and mercy doth appeare. . . . . . . II. ii. 40. 9
So happy *peace* they made and faire accord. . . . . II. iii. 9. 1
it the goodly *peace* of staied mindes Does overthrow, ... II. v. 1. 6
lovely *peace,* and gentle amity, ... II. vi. 35. 3
her sweet *peace* and pleasures did annoy, ... II. vi. 37. 7
As well in state of *peace,* as puissaunce in warre.' . . . . . II. ix. 4. 9
Enjoyd an heritage of lasting *peace,* . . . . II. x. 25. 2
Next him king Leyr in happie *peace* long raynd, ... II. x. 27. 1
In constant *peace* their kingdomes did contayne. . . . . . . II. x. 34. 4
they to *peace* agreed. . . . . II. x. 51. 9
Long time in *peace* his realme established, ... II. x. 63. 3
All happy *peace* and goodly government . . . . II. xi. 2. 4
soone compeld to hearken unto *peace.* . . . . III. i. 23. 7
Till universall *peace* compound all civill jarre. . . . . III. iii. 23. 9
He shall his dayes with *peace* bring to his earthly In. . . . . III. iii. 30. 9
sacred *Peace* shall lovingly persuade . . . . III. iii. 49. 3
The enimy of *peace,* and authour of all strife. . . . . III. vi. 14. 9
Peece, that unto parley eare will give, ... III. x. 10. 5
With perfect *peace* and bandes of fresh accord, ... III. x. 51. 4
The Queene of love, and Prince of *peace* . . . . IV. Pr. 4. 9
To stint all strife and foster friendly *peace,* . . . . IV. ii. 19. 2
Her angrie teame breaking their bonds of *peace* . . . . IV. iii. 41. 3
In her right hand a rod of *peace* shee bore, ... IV. iii. 42. 1
Instead thereof sweet *peace* and quiet-age . . . . IV. iii. 43. 5
restraine From blouddy strife, and blessed *peace* to seeke, . . IV. iii. 47. 8
As if he naught but *peace* and pleasure ment, ... IV. iv. 7. 3
peace being confirm'd amongst them all, ... IV. vi. 39. 2
joyd in happy *peace,* till fates perverse . . . . IV. vii. 15. 3
in *peace* and joyous blis They liv'd together . . . . IV. ix. 16. 1
These paires of friends in *peace* and setled rest, ... IV. ix. 17. 2
With gentle words perswading them to friendly *peace.* . . . . IV. ix. 32. 9
they so farre from *peace* or patience were, ... IV. ix. 33. 1
Mother of blessed *Peace* and Friendship trew; . . . . IV. x. 34. 2
Peace universall rayn'd . . . . V. Pr. 9. 6
rather bent To *peace* then needlesse trouble to constraine, . . V. vi. 19. 7
Of finall *peace* and faire attonement . . . . V. viii. 21. 8
commaunding *peace,* Them guyded through the throng, . . . V. ix. 23. 8
joyous *peace* and quietnesse alway . . . . V. ix. 24. 7
The sacred pledge of *peace* and clemencie, ... V. ix. 30. 3
stablished my *peace.* . . . . V. xi. 18. 7
Thus having all things well in *peace* ordayned, ... VI. vi. 41. 1
wrought her husbands *peace:* . . . . VI. vi. 43. 6
Fearelesse of foes that mote his *peace* molest; . . . . VI. vii. 19. 4
Fearelesse of ought that mote her *peace* molest, ... VI. viii. 34. 7
this sweet *peace,* whose lacke did then appeare: . . . . VI. ix. 25. 6

Peace—*Continued.*
mote empaire my *peace* with daungers dread; . . . . . . VI. ix. 33. 6
The happy *peace* which there doth overflow, ... VI. x. 3. 4
lived long in *peace* and love entyre, ... VI. xii. 10. 7
Dayly when I do seeke and sew for *peace*, ... *Am.* xi. 1
All paine hath end, and every war hath *peace*; . . . . . . *Am.* xi. 13
Is there no meanes for me to purchace *peace*, ... *Am.* xxxvi. 5
Mongst whome the more I seeke to settle *peace*, ... *Am.* xliv. 13
Sweet warriour! when shall I have *peace* with you? . . . . *Am.* lvii. 1
Make *peace* therefore, and graunt me timely grace, ... *Am.* lvii. 13
Betokening *peace* and plenty to ensew. . . . . *Am.* lxii. 4
Seekes with sweet *peace*, to salve each others wound: . . . *Am.* lxv. 12
peace shall see Betweene the Spyder and the gentle Bee. . . . *Am.* lxxi. 13
that may her sacred *peace* molest; . . . . *Am.* lxxxiii. 2
In my sweet *peace* such breaches to have bred! . . . . . . *Am.* lxxxv. 12
That sacred *Peace* may in assurance rayne, ... *Epith.* 354
But pride, impatient of long resting *peace*, ... *H.H.L.* 78
Let endlesse *Peace* your steadfast hearts accord, ... *Proth.* 101
Peaceable. As in his fee, with *peaceable* estate, ... VI. iv. 30. 2
Peaceably. *peaceably* thy painefull pilgrimage . . . doe bend, . I. x. 61. 3
all Faery lond does *peaceably* sustene. . . . . II. ii. 40. 5
each his portion *peaceably* enjoyd, ... II. x. 14. 6
peaceably the same long time did weld, ... II. x. 32. 4
Thenceforth Aurelius *peaceably* did rayne, ... II. x. 67. 7
peaceably Enjoy the crowne, ... III. iii. 46. 1
Did her therein establish *peaceablie*, ... V. xii. 25. 3
Peaceful. right hand did the *peacefull* olive wield; . . . . . *Bel.*^{2} ix. 11
Peacock. Perke as a *Peacock*; . . . . *S.C.* F. 8
As *Peacocke* that his painted plumes doth pranck, ... II. iii. 6. 4
Peacock's. With spotted winges, like *Peacocks* trayne, ... *S.C.* Mar. 80
So praysen babes the *Peacoks* spotted traine, ... *S.C.* O. 31
Peacocks. Drawne of fayre *Pecocks*, that excell in pride, . . . I. iv. 17. 8
Peal. with sharp reasons rang her such a *pele*, ... V. ix. 39. 7
Pealing. *Pealing* from Jove to Nature's bar, ... VII. vii. Arg.
Peare, -s. *See* **Peer, -s.**
Pearl. *See* **Mother of pearl.**
with fine *perle* and golde puft up in heart. . . . . *Rev.* ii. 7
Eche gate was of an orient perfect *pearle*, ... *Rev.* iv. 10
The *pearle* of peerlesse grace and modestie: . . . . *Col.* 471
Purfled with gold and *pearle* of rich assay; . . . . I. ii. 13. 3
With sprincled *pearle* and gold full richly drest, ... I. vii. 32. 3
builded . . . Of *perle* and precious stone, ... I. x. 55. 5
Braunched with gold and *perle* most richly wrought, ... II. ix. 19. 4
curiously embost With *pearle* and precious stone, ... IV. iv. 15. 7
Poudred with *pearle* and stone; . . . . IV. x. 31. 8
Sprinckled with *perle*, and perling flowres atweene, ... *Epith.* 155
Pearled. Upon the *perled* grasse to make their feast. . . . . . *Col.* 607
Pearling. silver deaw upon the roses *pearling*. . . . . *Col.* 507
Few *perling* drops from her faire lampes of light; . . . . . V. ix. 50. 7
Sprinckled with perle, and *perling* flowres atweene, ... *Epith.* 155
Pearls. Ne ought the whelky *pearles* esteemeth hee, ... *Gn.* 105
the two *pearles* which sight unto him lent, ... *Gn.* 285
pearles of Ynde, or gold of Opher, ... *Col.* 490
twixt the *perles* and rubins softly brake A silver sound, . . . II. iii. 24. 8
like pure Orient *perles* adowne it trild; . . . . II. xii. 78. 5
with great *perles* and pretious stones embost; . . . . III. i. 32. 7
pearles and pretious stones of great assay, ... III. iv. 18. 5
would not stay For gold, or *perles*, or pretious stones, ... III. iv. 18. 8
Gold, amber, yvorie, *perles*, owches, rings, ... III. iv. 23. 5
like to orient *perles* did purely shyne . . . . III. vii. 9. 3
deckt with *pearles* which th' Indian seas for her prepaire. . . . IV. xi. 11. 9
Plenty of *pearles* to decke his dames withall; . . . . IV. xi. 39. 6
If *Pearles*, hir teeth be *Pearles*, ... *Am.* xv. 9
The gate with *pearles* and rubyes richly dight; . . . . *Am.* lxxxi. 10
Pearly. humid vapour shed the grownd With *perly* deaw, . . III. x. 46. 6
With *pearly* dew sprinkling the morning grasse: . . . . IV. v. 45. 5
Pear-tree. carrion Crowes . . . That in our *Peere-tree* haunted: *S.C.* Mar. 111
Peasant. when the *Pesaunt* saw, amazd he stood, ... II. iii. 43. 1
'Perdy, thou *peasant* Knight . . . . VI. iii. 31. 7
Peasants. Against these *pesants* which have me opprest, . . . V. xi. 57. 3
Pease. nought worth a *pease* To put in preace . . . . *S.C.* O. 69
Peaze. *See* **Peise.**
Pebble-stone. caerule streame, rombling in *Pible stone*, . . . *Gn.* 163
Peck. seemed to containe A full good *pecke* . . . . VI. xii. 26. 6
Pedlar. all as a poore *pedler* he did wend, ... *S.C.* May 238
After his chere the *Pedler* can chat, ... *S.C.* May 284
Peep. where dawning day doth never *peepe*, His dwelling is; . I. i. 39. 5
through their lids his wanton eies do *peepe* . . . . II. v. 34. 5
peepe foorth with bashfull modestee, ... II. xii. 74. 5
Through which he stil did *peep* as forward he did pace. . . . III. xii. 15. 9
day out of the Ocean mayne Began to *peepe* . . . . IV. v. 45. 4
The warlike Amazon out of her bowre did *peepe*. . . . . . . V. vii. 26. 9
Peeped. he *peeped* out through a chinck, ... *S.C.* May 252
Peeping. *peeping* close into the thicke, ... *S.C.* Mar. 73
Where one stood *peeping* through a crevis small, ... IV. x. 11. 8
Ofte *peeping* in her face, ... *Epith.* 232
Peeps. The Swallow *peepes* out of her nest, ... *S.C.* Mar. 11
Peepes forth, and soone renews her native pride: . . . . . . II. iii. 36. 6
Who is the same, which at my window *peepes*? . . . . *Epith.* 372
Peer. Nor prince, nor *peere*, nor kin, they would abide. . . . *Ro.* xxiii. 14
Strove with a Spider his unequall *peare*; . . . . *Van.* vi. 5
For beauties prayse and plesaunce had no *peere*; . . . . . . *S.C.* N. 94
His brother Prince, his brother noble *Peere*, ... *Ti.* 240
wise and wary was that noble *Pere*; . . . . I. viii. 7. 6
sayd that royall *Pere* in sober wise; . . . . I. xii. 17. 1
To have a *pere* in part of soverainty; . . . . II. x. 33. 4
Whose soveraine beautie hath no living *pere*; . . . . III. i. 26. 3
Nor Prince nor *pere* it is, ... III. ii. 37. 8
did beare This warlike sonne unto an earthly *peare*, ... III. iv. 19. 5
To prove some deeds of armes upon an equall *pere*?' . . . . . III. x. 24. 9

Peer—*Continued.*
O most redoubted *Pere!* Vouchsafe . . . to heare.' . . . . . III. x. 26. 8
Of rare aspect, and beautie without *peare*, ... III. xii. 7. 2
The noble Briton Prince with his brave *Peare*; . . . . V. x. 15. 2
Whose gealous dread induring not a *peare* . . . . VI. ii. 29. 5
sought her to affy To a great *pere*; . . . . VI. iii. 7. 3
Was greatly growne in love of that brave *pere*,) . . . . . VI. v. 41. 8
Yet was she lov'd of many a worthy *pere*: . . . . VI. vii. 29. 4
Then had ye sorted with a princes *pere*: . . . . *Am.* lxvi. 10
therein now doth lodge a noble *Peer*, ... *Proth.* 145
Peerless. Such *pierlesse* pleasures have we . . . . *S.C.* Jun. 32
O *pierlesse* Poesye! where is then thy place? . . . . *S.C.* O. 79
is her selfe a *peereles* Poetresse. . . . . *T.M.* 576
Most *peereles* Prince, most *peereles* Poetresse, ... *T.M.* 577
Like a great Lord of *peerelesse* liberty; . . . . *Com. Son.* i. 10
thine owne sister, *peerles* Ladie bright, ... *Ti.* 317
Besides her *peerlesse* skill in making well, ... *Col.* 188
Poets wits are had in *peerlesse* price: . . . . *Col.* 321
The pearle of *peerlesse* grace and modestie: . . . . *Col.* 471
the Paragone Of *peerlesse* price, ... *Col.* 549
In glistring gold and *perelesse* pretious stone; . . . . . . I. iv. 8. 6
Yet did she thinke her *pearelesse* worth to pas That parentage, I. iv. 11. 3
They were two knights of *perelesse* puissaunce, ... II. ii. 16. 6
two sonnes, of *pearelesse* prowesse both, ... II. x. 40. 2
Having so *peerelesse* paragon ygot: . . . . IV. ii. 8. 2
pearelesse she was thought that did it beare. . . . . IV. v. 6. 5
That *peerelesse* paterne of Dame Natures pride . . . . . . IV. vi. 24. 5
purchased this *peerelesse* beauties spoile, ... IV. x. 3. 3
swolne with pride of his owne *peerelesse* powre, ... V. vii. 15. 7
my loves conquest, *peerelesse* beauties prise, ... *Am.* lxix. 7
most fit For so great powre and *peerelesse* majesty, ... *H.H.B.* 186
Peer's. To have thy Princes grace, yet want her *Peeres*; . . . *Hub.* 901
bring into a mighty *Peres* displeasure, ... VI. xii. 41. 6
Peers. *See* **Shepherd peers.**
auncient glory of the Romaine *peares*. . . . . *Bel.*^{2} iv. 8
In such delights did joy amongst my *peeres*: . . . . *S.C.* Jun. 35
the other *Peeres*, for povertie, ... *Hub.* 1177
the honorable race Of mightie *Peeres* . . . . *T.M.* 80
noble *Peeres*, whom I was wont to raise, ... *T.M.* 467
Above th' ensample of his equall *peares*, ... *Mui.* 28
Charming his oaten pipe unto his *peres*, ... *Col.* 5
He all his *Peeres* in beauty did surpas, ... I. v. 37. 3
sage and sober *peres*, all gravely gownd; . . . . I. xii. 5. 5
Emongst thine equall *peres*, ... II. iii. 39. 4
yeares More rype us reason lent to chose our *Peares*, ... II. iv. 18. 5
florish faire above his equall *peares*: . . . . II. viii. 5. 4
by consent of Commons and of *Peares*, ... II. x. 62. 8
thine equall *peares* Their fit disports . . . doe chose, ... III. ii. 31. 3
the sleeping memoree Of those same antique *Peres*, ... III. iii. 22. 8
she does joy to play emongst her *peares*, ... III. ix. 4. 8
Belphebe with her *peares*, The woody Nimphs, ... IV. vii. 23. 5
all the rest were eke her equall *peares*, ... IV. x. 49. 3
Amongst his *peres* playing his childish sport; . . . . V. i. 6. 3
To seeke for succour of her and her *Peares*, ... V. x. 6. 4
To hunt the salvage chace, amongst my *peres*, ... VI. ii. 31. 7
And borne great sway in armes amongst his *peares*; . . . . VI. iii. 3. 3
amongst mine equall *peares* To follow sheepe . . . . VI. ix. 24. 3
all her *peres* cannot with her compare, ... VI. x. 27. 7
far straying from his *peeres*: . . . . VII. vi. 28. 8
he freely drinks an health to all his *peeres*. . . . . VII. vii. 41. 9
those renoumed noble *Peres* of Greece, ... *Am.* xliv. 1
ancient monuments of mightie *peeres*, ... *Com. Son.* iii. 2
yet the eldest of the heavenly *Peares*? . . . . *H.L.* 56
Peevish. Malbecco will no straunge knights host, For *peevish* gealosy. . . . . III. ix. Arg.
Peevishness. where he is provokt with *peevishnesse*, ... VI. vii. 37. 2
Pegasus. on *Pegasus* must ride, ... *Ti.* 426
As he had beene a fole of *Pegasus* his kynd. . . . . I. ix. 21. 9
On whom he got faire *Pegasus* that flitteth in the ayre. . . . III. xi. 42. 9
Peinct, -er. *See* **Paint, -er.**
Peise. th' heavie downe to *peize*; . . . . *Col.* 849
when his love was false he with a *peaze* it brake. . . . . . . III. ii. 20. 9
all the wrongs that he therein could lay Might not it *peise*; . V. ii. 46. 7
Peised. ne was it *paysd* Amid the ocean waves, ... II. x. 5. 5
Pelasgus. Phoenix, and Aon, and *Pelasgus* old; . . . . IV. xi. 15. 6
Peleus. Fierce *Peleus*, and the hardie Telamon, ... *Gn.* 482
the solemne bridall cheare Twixt *Peleus* and Dame Thetis . VII. vii. 12. 5
Pelf. of his wicked *pelfe* his God he made, ... I. iv. 27. 6
To trouble my still seate, and heapes of pretious *pelfe*. . . . II. vii. 7. 9
all his minde is set on mucky *pelfe*, ... III. ix. 4. 1
loth to leave his liefest *pelfe* behinde; . . . . III. x. 15. 6
Thereafter all that mucky *pelfe* he tooke, ... V. ii. 27. 6
makes his God of his ungodly *pelfe*, ... V. viii. 19. 8
Fie on the *pelfe* for which good name is sold, ... V. xi. 63. 6
Pelias. Neleus and *Pelias*, lovely brethren both; . . . . . . IV. xi. 14. 2
Pelleas. The good Sir *Pelleas* him tooke in hand, ... VI. xii. 39. 6
Pellitus. the wicked sorcery Of false *Pellite* . . . . III. iii. 36. 4
Pell-mell. *Pelmell* with them attonce did enter in. . . . . . V. vii. 35. 4
Pen. from whose *pen* . . . honnie and sweete Nectar flowe, . . *T.M.* 217
doest note with critique *pen* . . . . *Com. Son.* i. 3
Whose grosse defaults thy daintie *pen* may file, ... *Ded. Son.* xii. 11
if thou be, as thou art pourtrahed With natures *pen*, ... I. viii. 33. 8
this lesson deare Deepe written in my heart with yron *pen*, . . I. viii. 44. 8
How shall frayle *pen* descrive her heavenly face, ... II. iii. 25. 8
fraile *pen*, with feare disparaged, ... II. x. 2. 8
My Lady and my love so cruelly to *pen!* . . . . III. xi. 10. 9
Described by that famous Tuscane *penne*: . . . . IV. iii. 45. 4
Him needeth sure a golden *pen*, I weene, ... IV. v. 12. 2
alwaies doe their powre within just compasse *pen*. . . . . . V. ii. 19. 9
when my *pen* would write her titles true, ... *Am.* iii. 11

Pen—*Continued.*
What *pen*, what pencill, can expresse her fill? . . . . *Am.* xvii. 4
Penance. Whose way is wildernesse, whose ynne *Penaunce*, . . *S.C.* F. 89
To thee, O Troy! paid *penaunce* for thy fall; . . . . *Gn.* 551
I will pay *Penance* to her, ... *D.* 370
When she beholds . . . My bitter *penance*, ... *D.* 382
will till then my painful *penance* eeke. . . . . *D.* 391
When Witches wont do *penance* for their crime,) . . . . . I. ii. 40. 5
to augment her painefull *penaunce* more, ... I. iii. 14. 1
Here endlesse *penaunce* for one fault I pay, ... I. v. 42. 6
Fortune, . . . for these wronges shall treble *penaunce* pay . I. viii. 43. 5
bitter *Penaunce*, with an yron whip, ... I. x. 27. 1
In that sad house of *Penaunce*, ... I. x. 32. 8
with thy punishment his *penance* shalt supply.' . . . . . IV. i. 53. 9
The *penance* which ye shall to him empart: . . . . IV. vi. 32. 6
with *penaunce* sad And pensive sorrow . . . . IV. viii. 2. 5
Beare for his *penaunce* that same Ladies head, ... V. i. 26. 8
what so *penaunce* shall by you be red.' . . . . V. viii. 13. 6
He unto her a *penance* did impose, ... VI. vii. 37. 6
For *penaunce* of my proud and hard rebellious hart. . . . . VI. viii. 19. 9
Addeem'd me to endure this *penaunce* sore; . . . . VI. viii. 22. 5
I needes must by all meanes fulfill This *penaunce*, ... VI. viii. 30. 3
They gan to cast what *penaunce* him to give. . . . . VII. vi. 50. 2
that seem'd *penaunce* light: . . . . VII. vi. 50. 6
do pay them sad *penance*, ... VII. vii. 23. 7
So I her absens will my *penaunce* make, ... *Am.* lii. 13
Shall be by him amearst with *penance* dew. . . . . *Am.* lxx. 12
all my woes to be but *penance* small. . . . . *H.L.* 300
Pence. living they resigned quight For a few *pence*, ... *Hub.* 574
Pencil. with *pencill* fine, Fashion the pourtraicts . . . . . *Ro.* xxv. 9
Nor life-resembling *pencill* it can paynt: . . . . III. Pr. 2. 2
What pen, what *pencill*, can expresse her fill? . . . . *Am.* xvii. 4
Pend. *See* **Penned.**
Penda. *Penda*, fearefull of like desteny, ... III. iii. 37. 8
Penda, seeking him adowne to tread, ... III. iii. 39. 7
Pendants. With curious Corbes and *pendants* graven faire, . . IV. x. 6. 7
Did beare the *pendants* through their nimblesse bold: . . . . V. ix. 29. 3
Pendragon. That stout *Pendragon* to his perill felt, ... *Ti.* 104
Uther, which *Pendragon* hight, ... II. x. 68. 1
Penelope. most faithfull to her mate, *Penelope;* . . . . . . *Gn.* 430
Did the most chast *Penelope* possesse . . . . V. vii. 39. 2
Penelope, for her Ulisses sake, ... *Am.* xxiii. 1
Peneus. that faire troupe . . . Staied thee, (O *Peneus!*) . . . *Gn.* 183
Slow *Peneus*, and tempestuous Phasides, ... IV. xi. 21. 3
Peneus'. like old *Peneus* Waters they did seeme, ... *Proth.* 78
Penitent. did pray . . . devoutly *penitent:* . . . . I. iii. 13. 7
Penned. sonne-bright honour *pend* in shamefull coupe. . . . *S.C.* O. 72
Which pardon me, if I amisse have *pend;* . . . . *Hub.* 1386
'My Lady and my love is cruelly *pend* . . . . III. xi. 11. 1
Pennon. They waved like a *penon* wyde dispred, ... II. iii. 30. 4
Penny. *See* **Passage-penny.**
Their *peni* Masses, and their Complynes meete, ... *Hub.* 452
Whereas thou maist compound a better *penie*, ... *Hub.* 523
Pens. the *pennes*, that did his pineons bynd, ... I. xi. 10. 4
Pensive. the *pensife* boy, halfe in despight, Arose, ... *S.C.* Ja. 76
Tho went the *pensife* Damme out of dore, ... *S.C.* May 229
To wast long nights in *pensive* discontent; . . . . *Hub.* 898
sight thereof much griev'd my *pensive* thought. . . . . . . *Ti.* 623
pensive boy, pursue that brave conceipt . . . . *Col.* 388
How with that *pensive* Maid he best might thence arise. . . . I. vi. 32. 9
In *pensive* plight and sad perplexitie, ... I. viii. 26. 2
him awaited still with *pensive* mynd. . . . . I. x. 68. 3
Which when his *pensive* Lady saw from farre, ... I. xi. 32. 1
As if some *pensive* thought constraind her gentle spright. . . II. ix. 36. 9
Pensive I yeeld I am, ... II. ix. 38. 6
Grew *pensive* through that amarous discourse, ... III. iv. 5. 3
full of bitter griefe and *pensife* thought, ... III. iv. 31. 5
he wondrous *pensive* grew in minde, ... III. v. 12. 5
The God himselfe did *pensive* seeme and sad, ... III. xi. 41. 6
Where late she left the *pensife* Scudamore . . . . III. xii. 44. 2
with penaunce sad And *pensive* sorrow . . . . IV. viii. 2. 6
The troublous passion of my *pensive* mind, ... V. vii. 19. 2
inly did afflict her *pensive* thought . . . . VI. iii. 6. 8
The *pensive* fit of her melancholie; . . . . VI. iii. 9. 3
Most *pensive* man, through feare what of his childe became. . VI. iii. 17. 9
Pensively. On hearbs and flowres she walked *pensively*, ... *Pet.* vi. 3
Pensiveness. Those *Pensifenesse* did move; and Sighes the bellows weare. . . . . IV. v. 38. 9
some *pensivenesse* to heart she tooke: . . . . V. vii. 18. 3
In secret sorow, and sad *pensivenesse*. . . . . *Am.* xxxiv. 14
In *pensive* plight and sad perplexitie, ... I. viii. 26. 2
Pent. Led forth his flock, that had bene long *ypent:* . . . . *S.C.* Ja. 4
great in gree, But hath been long *ypent*. . . . . *S.C.* Jul. 216
Shee found them both in darksome corner *pent;* . . . . . . I. iii. 13. 5
Demogorgon, in dull darknesse *pent* . . . . IV. ii. 47. 7
As if he had in prison long bene *pent:* . . . . IV. v. 34. 5
His sodaine silence which he long had *pent*, ... IV. viii. 16. 2
Which had her Lord in her base prison *pent*, ... V. vi. 18. 8
with hollow eyes deepe *pent*, ... V. ix. 10. 5
within strong bancks is *pent*, ... VI. i. 21. 2
Penthesilea. Homere spake Of bold *Penthesilee*, ... III. iv. 2. 5
Penthia. Of others *Penthia*, though not so well: . . . . . . *As.* 194
Penurious. Die rather would he in *penurious* paine, ... V. v. 46. 5
Penury. Bene all sterved with pyne and *penuree:* . . . . . . *S.C.* S. 65
Where cold and care and *penury* do dwell, ... *Col.* 657
His raw-bone cheekes, through *penurie* and pine, ... I. ix. 35. 8
Through wilfull *penury* consumed quight, ... IV. vii. 41. 3
they were forst, through *penurie* and pyne, ... V. v. 22. 6
Begot of Plentie and of *Penurie*, ... *H.L.* 53
People. that his victorious *people* should . . . not be overworne: *Ro.* xxiii. 3

People—*Continued.*
in a *people* given all to ease, ... *Ro.* xxiii. 9
Yet of the devout *people* is ador'd, ... *Ro.* xxviii. 10
the bolde *people* by the Thamis brincks, ... *Ro.* xxxi. 6
Th' olde honour of the *people* gowned long. . . . . *Ro.* xxxii. 14
wretched *people* travailing that way, ... *Van.* iii. 5
'Resort of *people* doth my greefs augment, ... *S.C.* Au. 157
Thus chatten the *people* in theyr steads, ... *S.C.* S. 120
th' halfe-horsy *people*, Centaures hight, ... *Gn.* 41
people slew with sword, ... *Gn.* 44
blacke Laestrigones, a *people* stout: . . . . *Gn.* 538
Of forreine lands, of *people* different, ... *Hub.* 765
as *people* base And simple men, ... *Hub.* 833
In th' eyes of *people* they put all their praise, ... *T.M.* 93
her owne *people* led with warlike rage: . . . . *Ti.* 173
I saw him die, as one Of the meane *people*, ... *Ti.* 191
world . . . In which I saw no living *people* dwell. . . . . . *Col.* 231
Had *people* grace it gratefully to use: . . . . *Col.* 325
And that proud *people*, . . . didst first deface: . . . . . . *Ded. Son.* vi. 10
people that did pas In traveill to and froe: . . . . I. i. 34. 3
Great troupes of *people* traveild thetherward . . . . I. iv. 3. 1
Infinite sortes of *people* did abide There waiting long, ... I. iv. 6. 7
The heapes of *people*, . . . Doe ride each other . . . . . . I. iv. 16. 7
For want whereof poore *people* oft did pyne: . . . . I. iv. 21. 7
Huge routs of *people* did about them band, ... I. iv. 36. 5
all the *people* followe with great glee, ... I. v. 16. 7
The woodborne *people* fall before her flat, ... I. vi. 16. 1
long time with that salvage *people* stayd, ... I. vi. 19. 3
gently askt, where all the *people* bee, ... I. viii. 32. 3
His chosen *people*, purg'd from sinful guilt . . . . I. x. 57. 4
all the *people*, as in solemne feast, ... I. xii. 4. 6
all the way the joyous *people* singes, ... I. xii. 13. 3
all the *people* decke with girlands greene, ... II. iii. 28. 3
A route of *people* there assembled were, ... II. vii. 44. 1
to their *people* wealth they forth do well, ... II. x. 26. 6
Gathered the Princes of the *people* loose . . . . II. x. 37. 6
Was by the *people* chosen in their sted, ... II. x. 47. 2
Of these a mighty *people* shortly grew, ... II. x. 72. 1
At sight whereof the *people* stand aghast; . . . . III. i. 16. 7
thy sad *people*, utterly fordonne, ... III. iii. 34. 3
huge hills Of dying *people*, ... III. iii. 41. 2
mightie *people*, dreaded more then all . . . . III. iii. 56. 5
hellish arts from *people* she might hide, ... III. vii. 6. 8
To save his *people* sad from victours vengefull handes. . . . III. ix. 41. 9
all the *people* in that ample hous . . . . III. xi. 49. 3
he pinched *people* to the hart, ... III. xii. 16. 6
What time his *people* into partes did rive, ... IV. ii. 2. 8
To barre the prease of *people* farre away; . . . . IV. iii. 4. 2
passed through th' unruly preace Of *people*, ... IV. iii. 41. 2
Admir'd of all the *people* and much glorifide. . . . . IV. iii. 51. 9
did resort of sinfull *people* shonne, ... IV. vii. 42. 8
father of the bold And warlike *people* . . . . IV. xi. 15. 9
wonned there where now Yorke *people* dwell; . . . . IV. xi. 37. 5
Sad Trowis, that once his *people* over-ran, ... IV. xi. 41. 7
to all *people* did divide . . . . V. Pr. 9. 9
To sit in his own seate, . . . And rule his *people* right, ... V. Pr. 10. 9
Doest to thy *people* righteous doome aread, ... V. Pr. 11. 4
Full many *people* gathered in a crew; . . . . V. ii. 29. 5
the *people*, which had there about Long wayted, ... V. ii. 51. 1
when as all the *people* such did vew, ... V. iii. 23. 8
Forth from the thickest preasse of *people* came, ... V. iii. 29. 4
True Justice unto *people* to divide, ... V. iv. 1. 2
A rout of many *people* farre away; . . . . V. iv. 21. 3
Eftsoones the *people* all to harnesse ran, ... V. iv. 36. 6
Causd all her *people* to surcease from fight; . . . . V. iv. 45. 5
Rather then see her *people* spoiled quight, ... V. iv. 47. 8
Which he unto her *people* does each day; . . . . V. viii. 19. 2
making all her Knights and *people* to doe so. . . . . V. viii. 20. 9
All full of *people* making troublous din . . . . V. ix. 23. 3
hearing pleas of *people* meane and base: . . . . V. ix. 36. 5
thine owne *people* do thy mercy prayse much more. . . . . . V. x. 3. 9
Robbed her *people* that full rich had beene, ... V. x. 25. 7
all the *people*, both of towne and land, ... V. xi. 15. 5
My children and my *people*, burnt in flame . . . . V. xi. 19. 7
all the *people* there without it heard, ... V. xi. 30. 2
all the *people* which beheld that day Gan shout aloud, ... V. xi. 34. 1
A rout of *people* they before them kend, ... V. xi. 43. 7
to reclayme with speed His scattred *people*, ... V. xii. 9. 2
Which when the *people* round about him saw, ... V. xii. 24. 1
all her *people* murdred with outragious might: . . . . VI. i. 29. 9
The *people* of the house rose forth in great uprore. . . . . VI. vi. 22. 9
hearing how his *people* badly sped, ... VI. vi. 24. 4
A lawlesse *people*, Brigants hight of yore, ... VI. x. 39. 3
all his *people* captive led away; . . . . VI. x. 40. 3
no way Appeard for *people* in nor out to pas, ... VI. x. 41. 8
all the *people*, where so he did go, ... VI. xii. 37. 3
the *people* standing all about, ... *Epith.* 143
People's. The *peoples* fable, and the spoyle of all: . . . . . *Ro.* vii. 8
This *peoples* vertue yet so fruitfull was . . . . *Ro.* viii. 5
So soone as day appeard to *peoples* vewing, ... *Hub.* 104
all the *peoples* prayers to present . . . . *Hub.* 471
for warlike power, and *peoples* store, ... *Ti.* 99
nor *peoples* troublous cryes, . . . Might there be heard; . . I. i. 41. 6
she, . . . Farr from all *peoples* preace, as in exile, ... I. iii. 3. 3
gras, In which the tract of *peoples* footing was, ... I. iii. 10. 5
All bare through *peoples* feet which thether traveiled. . . . I. iv. 2. 9
peoples hartes with awfull terror tye, ... I. vii. 16. 7
pittying his *peoples* ill, ... III. iii. 35. 8
Both for his griefe, and for her *peoples* sake, ... III. iii. 43. 2
wholy waste and void of *peoples* trode, ... III. ix. 49. 7

People's—*Continued.*
it prodigious seemes in common *peoples* sight . . . . IV. i. 13. 9
Unto his cave farre from all *peoples* hearing, ... IV. vii. 8. 8
From *peoples* knowledge labour'd to concele: . . . . IV. x. 41. 3
The spoile of *peoples* evil gotten good, ... V. ii. 27. 7
How he mis-led the simple *peoples* traine, ... V. ii. 33. 7
Covered from *peoples* gazement with a vele: . . . . V. iii. 17. 3
The *peoples* great compassion unto her allure . . . . V. ix. 38. 9
Then gan the *Peoples* cry and Commons sute . . . . V. ix. 44. 7
in all that *peoples* sight, ... V. xi. 16. 2
taketh vengeaunce of his *peoples* spoile; . . . . VI. viii. 23. 2
with the *peoples* voyce Confused, ... VI. viii. 46. 2
far from all *peoples* troad, ... VI. x. 5. 3
Per. Pinckt upon gold, and paled part *per* part, ... VI. ii. 6. 2
Perce, *etc.* *See* **Pierce,** *etc.*
Perceant. wondrous quick and *persaunt* was his spright, . . . I. x. 47. 5
So passing *persant,* and so wondrous bright, ... II. iii. 23. 4
through the *persant* aire shoote forth their azure streames. . . III. ix. 20. 9
Perceive. they might *perceive* his head To bee unarmd, . . . I. ix. 22. 1
each doth in him selfe it well *perceive* to bee . . . . II. xii. 47. 9
well he mote *perceive* In that fowle plight . . . . III. vii. 46. 1
Anon she gan *perceive* the house to quake, ... III. xii. 37. 1
To hide her wound, that none might it *perceive:* . . . . . . IV. vi. 40. 8
Well did the Squire *perceive* him selfe too weake . . . . . . V. i. 24. 1
Whose hidden drift he could not well *perceive;* . . . . V. v. 37. 2
with ruth (as I *perceave*) Of my mishaps . . . . V. v. 37. 7
They might *perceive* she was not well in plight, ... V. vii. 18. 2
when they did *perceave* Their wounds recur'd, ... VI. vi. 15. 6
He mote *perceive* a litle dawning sight . . . . VI. viii. 48. 3
He mote *perceive* by signes which he did fynd, ... VI. xi. 27. 8
She mote *perceive* a litle purple mold, ... VI. xii. 7. 8
I mote *perceive* . . . Legions of loves . . . . *Am.* xvi. 5
Perceived. A litle wicked worme, *perceiv'd* of none, ... *Van.* vii. 7
Which when the valiant Elfe *perceiv'd,* . . . . I. i. 17. 1
Whose corage when the feend *perceivd* to shrinke, ... I. i. 22. 4
'The divelish hag . . . *Perceiv'd* my thought; . . . . I. ii. 42. 2
Which when the wakeful Elfe *perceiv'd,* . . . . I. v. 2. 6
Whom when his maistresse proud *perceiv'd* to fall, ... I. viii. 20. 6
when the Miscreaunt *Perceived* him to waver, ... I. ix. 49. 2
when the vile Enchaunteresse *perceiv'd,* . . . . II. i. 55. 1
in court gay portaunce he *perceiv'd,* . . . . II. iii. 5. 7
Whom whenas he *perceived* to respyre, ... II. iv. 16. 5
well *perceived* his deceiptfull sleight, ... II. vii. 64. 7
when as the Sarazin *perceiv'd* . . . . II. viii. 49. 1
By the great persue which she there *perceav'd,* . . . . III. v. 28. 6
which when they both *perceiv'd,* . . . . III. vi. 27. 4
Which whenas she *perceiv'd,* she was dismayd . . . . III. vii. 25. 1
There well *perceivd* he that it was the horse . . . . III. vii. 31. 1
her well avizing hee *perceiv'd* To be no vision . . . . III. viii. 23. 1
Who well *perceived* all, and all indewd . . . . III. x. 9. 5
Blandamour . . . *Perceiv'd* to be such as they seemd in vew, . IV. i. 38. 8
Cambell . . . *Perceiv'd* would breede great mischiefe, ... IV. ii. 37. 7
none *perceiv'd* it plaine; . . . . IV. iv. 25. 2
so soone as they *perceiv'd* That she was gone, ... IV. v. 28. 1
when as fearefull Amoret *perceived,* . . . . IV. vii. 21. 1
when she *perceived* Her owne deare sire, ... IV. ix. 7. 1
Whom when so willing Artegall *perceaved;* . . . . V. i. 28. 1
Which troublous stirre when Artegall *perceived,* . . . . . . V. iii. 30. 6
Which when the cruell Amazon *perceived,* . . . . V. v. 47. 1
Which when their Host *perceiv'd,* . . . . V. vi. 24. 1
Which when as Zele *perceived* to abate, ... V. ix. 46. 7
Which uncouth use when as the Prince *perceived,* . . . . . . V. xi. 7. 1
Yet this in all her words might be *perceived,* . . . . V. xii. 33. 8
Which when as he *perceiv'd* he thus bespake: . . . . VI. ii. 47. 6
when as she *perceived* A stranger wight in place, ... VI. iv. 27. 1
Perceivest. nought of Rome in Rome *perceiv'st* at all, . . . *Ro.* iii. 2
Perceiving. he *perceiving* greatly gan rejoice, ... II. i. 44. 1
he *perceiving,* ever privily, ... III. ix. 52. 8
perceiving that it was indeed Her old Malbecco, ... III. x. 50. 2
Which Triamond *perceiving* weened sure He gan to faint . . . IV. iii. 32. 6
Which Scudamour *perceiving* forth issewed . . . . IV. vi. 3. 1
by signes *perceiving* plaine . . . . V. i. 24. 6
Perceiving well the treason which was ment; . . . . V. vi. 28. 2
well *perceiving* how her wand she shooke, ... V. vii. 8. 4
Which Artegall *perceiving* strooke no more, ... V. xii. 22. 6
Whom Calidore *perceiving* fast to flie, ... VI. i. 22. 6
Which she *perceiving* did with plenteous teares . . . . VI. iii. 12. 1
well *perceiving* what was done, ... VI. v. 4. 7
it *perceiving* hand upon him layd, ... VI. v. 26. 8
them *perceiving* streight to him obayd, ... VI. vi. 39. 4
Calidore *perceiving,* thought it best To chaunge . . . . . . VI. ix. 36. 1
Which well *perceiving,* that imperious boy . . . . *H.L.* 120
Perch. 'Ne is there hauke which mantleth her on *pearch,* . . . VI. ii. 32. 1
Perchance. To seeke if he *perchance* asleepe were layd, . . . VI. v. 3. 7
Percheth. then he *pearcheth* on some braunch thereby, ... *Mui.* 183
Percy. Ah, *Percy!* it is all to weake and wanne, ... *S.C.* O. 85
Thou kenst not, *Percie,* howe the ryme should rage, ... *S.C.* O. 109
Perdie. *See* **Pardie.**
Perdition. all that might him to *perdition* draw; . . . . I. ix. 50. 7
Pere, -s. *See* **Peer, -s.**
Peregal. *See* **Paregal.**
Peremptory. That challenge did too *peremptory* seeme, . . . III. viii. 16. 6
Then gan Authority her to appose With *peremptorie* powre, . V. ix. 44. 2
Perfect. Eche gate was of an orient *perfect* pearle, ... *Rev.* iv. 10
All that is *perfect,* which th' heaven beautefies; . . . . . . *Ro.* xix. 1
perfect pleasure buildes her joyous bowre, ... *Gn.* 135
of all wisedome knew the *perfect* somme? . . . . *Ti.* 60
Which thou there breathest *perfect* and entire . . . . *Ti.* 315
The blossome of sweet joy and *perfect* love, ... *Col.* 470
when he was requirde To pourtraict Venus in her *perfect* hew, *Ded. Son.* xvii. 2

Perfect—*Continued.*
all of Diamond *perfect* pure and cleene . . . . I. vii. 33. 5
Shortly therein so *perfect* he became, ... I. x. 45. 6
Eftsoones of him had *perfect* cognizaunce, ... II. i. 31. 5
when they once to *perfect* strength do grow, ... II. iv. 34. 6
Th' other immortall, *perfect,* masculine; . . . . II. ix. 22. 5
There sate a man of ripe and *perfect* age, ... II. ix. 54. 2
formd so lively in each *perfect* part, ... III. Pr. 1. 6
Having their weary limbes to *perfect* plight Restord, ... III. i. 1. 3
It vertue had to shew in *perfect* sight . . . . III. ii. 19. 1
to bring to *perfect* end: . . . . III. iii. 10. 5
in *perfect* love and spotlesse fame Of chastitie, ... III. v. 54. 3
So all did make in her a *perfect* complement . . . . III. v. 55. 9
To be upbrought in *perfect* Maydenhed, ... III. vi. 28. 4
when she to *perfect* ripenes grew, ... III. vi. 52. 1
through his *perfect* sent And passing speede, ... III. vii. 23. 8
mingled them with *perfect* vermily; . . . . III. viii. 6. 8
So *perfect* in that art was Paridell, ... III. x. 5. 1
With *perfect* peace and bandes of fresh accord, ... III. x. 51. 4
his proud spoile . . . he might behold in *perfect* kinde; . . . III. xii. 22. 8
to be unbownd And *perfect* hole, ... III. xii. 38. 9
In *perfect* love, devoide of hatefull strife, ... IV. iii. 52. 2
most *perfect* hew And passing beautie . . . . IV. v. 10. 3
a Ruby of right *perfect* hew, ... IV. viii. 6. 7
perfect gold surmounts the meanest brasse . . . . IV. ix. 2. 9
of most *perfect* metall it was made, ... V. i. 10. 1
So feeble skill of *perfect* things the vulgar has . . . . V. iii. 17. 9
Known by good markes and *perfect* good espiall: . . . . . . V. iv. 15. 8
see not *perfect* things but in a glas: . . . . VI. Pr. 5. 5
Till he to *perfect* ripenesse grew; . . . . VI. i. 8. 5
The fearefull Lady . . . Most *perfect* pure, ... VI. iii. 18. 3
So milde humanity and *perfect* gentle mynd . . . . VI. v. 29. 9
through long and *perfect* industry, ... VI. ix. 43. 7
in her mynde the seeds Of *perfect* love did sow, ... VI. ix. 45. 8
prov'd the *perfect* pleasures which doe grow . . . . VI. x. 3. 5
other none such passion can contrive In *perfect* forme, ... VI. xii. 21. 6
from whom al true And *perfect* beauty did at first proceed: . *Am.* lxxix. 12
to whose *perfect* mould He fashiond them . . . . *H.B.* 32
perfect Beautie, which all men adore; . . . . *H.B.* 40
in *perfect* limming every part? . . . . *H.B.* 84
his *perfect* end Of purest beautie . . . . *H.H.B.* 46
Thence gathering plumes of *perfect* speculation, ... *H.H.B.* 134
From whose pure beams al *perfect* beauty springs, ... *H.H.B.* 296
Perfected. Which to another place I leave to be *perfected.* . . IV. xii. 35. 9
Perfection. In which all pure *perfection* one may see . . . . . *Col.* 343
to the pitch of her *perfection* raised . . . . *Col.* 415
Phyllis, the floure of rare *perfection,* . . . . *Col.* 544
growing he his owne *perfection* wrought, ... *Col.* 805
'Of loves *perfection* perfectly to speake, ... *Col.* 835
grew . . . To such *perfection* of all hevenly grace, ... I. x. 21. 3
rare *perfection* in mortalitye, ... II. ii. 41. 7
Till to her dew *perfection* she were ripened . . . . III. vi. 3. 9
heavenly image of *perfection,* . . . . IV. vi. 24. 6
Adorn'd with all divine *perfection,* . . . . IV. xii. 34. 2
till the world from his *perfection* fell . . . . V. i. 5. 6
Do worke their owne *perfection* so by fate: . . . . VII. vii. 58. 7
rare *perfection* of each goodly part; . . . . *Am.* xxiv. 2
Onely behold her rare *perfection,* . . . . *Am.* lxxxiii. 13
it reducing to her first *perfection,* . . . . *H.B.* 216
Perfection's. Or hope t' expresse her least *perfections* part, . . *H.H.B.* 227
Perfections. her *perfections* with his error taynt: . . . . . . III. Pr. 2. 5
So great *perfections* did in her compile, ... III. vi. 1. 3
Perfectly. As if the way she *perfectly* had knowne . . . . . . *Col.* 269
'Of loves perfection *perfectly* to speake, ... *Col.* 835
th' one of them he *perfectly* descride . . . . IV. i. 39. 1
perfectly practiz'd in womans craft, ... IV. ii. 10. 2
when the Prince had *perfectly* compylde, ... IV. ix. 17. 1
perfectly well shapt in every lim, ... VI. ix. 9. 2
who alive can *perfectly* declare . . . . *H.L.* 50
Perfectness. aspire Unto so loftie pitch of *perfectnesse,* . . . *T.M.* 394
The image of such endlesse *perfectnesse?* . . . . *H.H.B.* 105
Perforce. teares flowe in theyr stead *perforse:* . . . . *S.C.* N. 127
driven be *perforce* to sterving, ... *Hub.* 370
blast . . . *perforce* him drove on hed, ... *Mui.* 420
thus *perforce* he bids me do, or die . . . . I. i. 51. 6
who *perforce* me led With him away, ... I. ii. 25. 2
dying every stound, Yet live *perforce* . . . . I. viii. 38. 5
he is *perforce* constraynd To throw his ryder; . . . . I. xi. 23. 6
Who him rencountring fierce, . . . *Perforce* rebutted backe . I. xi. 53. 5
Patience *perforce:* . . . what may it boot To frett . . . . . II. iii. 3. 3
He made him stoup *perforce* unto his knee, ... II. v. 11. 6
At last he was compeld to cry *perforse,* . . . . II. v. 23. 7
him *perforce* restraynd, ... II. vii. 6. 9
chaunge of colour did *perforce* unfold, ... II. ix. 39. 4
Perforce their studies broke, ... II. x. 77. 6
them *perforce* withheld with threatned blade, ... II. xi. 31. 4
carried him *perforse* Above three furlongs, ... II. xi. 46. 4
my luckelesse lott doth me constrayne Hereto *perforce* . . . III. Pr. 3. 5
Perforce disparted their compacted gyre, ... III. i. 23. 6
him *perforce* unto the ground it bore . . . . III. iii. 60. 7
that *perforce,* for want of lenger light, ... III. iv. 52. 5
His wearisome pursuit *perforce* he stayd, ... III. iv. 53. 5
Perforce her carried where ever he thought best . . . . . . III. vii. 2. 9
at last *perforce* adowne did ly, ... III. vii. 3. 7
he *perforce* him held, and strokes upon him hept . . . . . . III. vii. 33. 9
him pluckt *perforse, Perforse* him pluckt, ... III. vii. 43. 2, 3
patience *perforce,* he must abie . . . . III. x. 3. 1
all *perforce* to make her him to love . . . . III. xii. 31. 6
seeke *perforce* her from you both to take, ... IV. ii. 24. 8
Till fortune did *perforce* it so decree: . . . . IV. viii. 58. 8

Perforce—*Continued.*
have *perforce* him hether brought away.' . . . IV. viii. 62. 5
To see the sight *perforce* that both her eyes were loth. . . . IV. ix. 9. 9
perforce with sword and targe Her forth to fetch, . . . IV. xii. 14. 7
Loth was the Dwarfe, yet did he stay *perforse,* . . . V. ii. 2. 5
now *perforce* they have him prisoner taken; . . . V. iii. 9. 6
Guyon would him algates have *perforse,* . . . V. iii. 30. 4
with their ryder ranne *perforce* away: . . . V. viii. 38. 4
th' utmost end *perforce* for to aby, . . . VI. iii. 44. 3
To pluck her downe *perforce* from off her chaire; . . . VII. vi. 13. 3
But as she will, . . . so it *perforce* must bee. . . . *Am.* xlvi. 8
Love, that . . . to thy mighty powre *Perforce* subdude . . . *H.L.* 2
Perform. Helpe . . . Thy weaker Novice to *performe* thy will; I. Pr. 2. 2
'Which, for my part, I covet to *performe* . . . I. xii. 20. 1
Which she would sure *performe,* betide her wele or wo. . . . V. vi. 23. 9
promist to *performe* his precept well, . . . VI. i. 43. 3
his faith thereto did plight It to *performe:* . . . VI. iii. 16. 2
Performed. have full many feats adventurous *Performd,* . . . III. iii. 54. 6
did with readie will consent, And well *perform'd;* . . . IV. viii. 64. 9
All which when Talus throughly had *perfourmed,* . . . V. ii. 28. 6
Which when he had *perform'd,* then backe againe . . . V. iii. 13. 1
Unlesse it be *perform'd* with dreadlesse might; . . . V. iv. 1. 8
*But is *perform'd* with some foule imperfection. . . . *H.B.* 147
Perfume. With Balmelike odor did *perfume* the aire. . . . *Bel.*[1] ix. 4
Perfumed. They all *perfumde* with frankincense divine, . . . I. xii. 38. 3
Perhaps. (for *perhaps* some one of you . . . doth hide) . . . *Ro.* xv. 9
Newes may *perhaps* some good unweeting beare.' . . . *Hub.* 606
perhaps ye things may handle soe, . . . *Hub.* 641
if *perhaps* into their noble sprights . . . *Hub.* 824
Unlesse some one *perhaps* of gentle kin, . . . *T.M.* 345
Fitter, *perhaps,* to thonder Martiall stowre, . . . *Ded. Son.* viii. 11
Perhaps not vaine they may appeare to you. . . . *Ded. Son.* ix. 12
spirit, . . . Might long *perhaps* have lien in silence . . . *Ded. Son.* xiii. 5
Which if ye yield, *perhaps* ye may her rayse . . . *Ded. Son.* xiii. 13
yet *perhaps* remayned Some lingring life . . . I. xii. 10. 3
Least thou *perhaps* hereafter wish, . . . II. vii. 38. 9
Perhaps my succour or advizement meete . . . II. ix. 9. 3
'*perhaps* ye should it better find: . . . III. ii. 13. 5
one that worthy may *perhaps* appeare; . . . III. ii. 42. 3
But fast goodwill, . . . May her *perhaps* containe, . . . III. ix. 7. 9
Perhaps this hand may helpe to ease your woe, . . . III. xi. 15. 4
ill *perhaps* mote fall to either side; . . . V. i. 25. 4
Perhaps I may all further quarrell end, . . . V. i. 25. 6
perhaps he mote it deare aby.' . . . VI. i. 28. 4
may *perhaps* you better much withall, . . . VI. ix. 32. 7
maist *perhaps,* if so thou faine Have Jove thy gracious Lord . VII. vi. 34. 4
which some *perhaps* will mone, . . . *Am.* xxxvi. 13
Perhaps he there may learne, . . . *Am.* lxxiii. 11
Peridure. *Peridure* and Vigent him disthronized. . . . II. x. 44. 9
Or thou, Sir *Peridure,* her sory state, . . . III. viii. 28. 2
Perigot. Tell me, *Perigot,* what shalbe the game, . . . *S.C.* Au. 1
Never shall be sayde that *Perigot* was dared. . . . *S.C.* Au. 24
loe, *Perigot,* the Pledge which I plight, . . . *S.C.* Au. 25
Hey, ho, *Perigot!* . . . *S.C.* Au. 98
Little lacketh *Perigot* of the best, . . . *S.C.* Au. 126
Perigot, so well hath hym payned, . . . *S.C.* Au. 133
Perigot is well pleased with the doome: . . . *S.C.* Au. 135
Peril. Ne runs in *perill* of foes cruell knife, . . . *Gn.* 125
That stout Pendragon to his *perill* felt, . . . *Ti.* 104
when most in *perill* it was brought, . . . *Ti.* 624
The faire Andromeda from *perill* freed: . . . *Ti.* 649
(may it be withouten *perill* spoken?) . . . *Mui.* 97
What needeth *perill* to be sought abroad, . . . *As.* 89
And *perill* without show: . . . I. i. 12. 5
'the *perill* of this place I better wot then you: . . . I. i. 13. 1
the certeine *perill* he stood in, . . . I. i. 24. 2
Ne yet of present *perill* be affraid, . . . I. iv. 49. 3
dwell in *perill* of like painefull plight, . . . I. v. 52. 4
The Marriner yet halfe amazed stares At *perill* past, . . . I. vi. 1. 5
His wandring *perill* closely did lament, . . . I. vi. 32. 2
for such *perill* past Wherewith you to reward? . . . I. viii. 27. 3
found with *perill* and with paine; . . . II. iii. 41. 2
wrought, with *perill* and with payne, . . . II. xi. 15. 4
Then thought the Prince all *peril* sure was past, . . . II. xi. 43. 6
Ne ought save *perill* still as he did pas: . . . II. xii. 2. 3
he gan to feare His toward *perill,* . . . III. i. 9. 7
terrifyde With some late *perill* . . . III. v. 3. 4
Long after she from *perill* was releast: . . . III. vii. 1. 7
She went in *perill,* of each noyse affeard, . . . III. vii. 19. 3
From *peril* free he away her did beare; . . . III. vii. 24. 8
mickle *perill* to bee put to shame. . . . III. x. 39. 4
t' abandon noble chevisaunce For shewe of *perill,* . . . III. xi. 24. 7
having once escaped *perill* neare, . . . IV. i. 34. 8
I, without your *perill* or your cost, Will chalenge . . . IV. i. 35. 7
How to prevent the *perill* that mote rise, . . . IV. ii. 37. 8
for her sake they all that *perill* tooke, . . . IV. ii. 40. 8
Carelesse of *perill* in their fiers affret, . . . IV. iii. 6. 7
Ne either car'd to ward, or *perill* shonne, . . . IV. iii. 36. 4
So worthie of the *perill,* worthy of the paine. . . . IV. iv. 16. 9
Ne any dar'd their *perill* to partake; . . . IV. iv. 29. 5
whatsoever *perill* was prepared, . . . IV. v. 46. 4
Both equall paines and equall *perill* shared; . . . IV. v. 46. 5
Whom without *perill* he cannot invade. . . . IV. vi. 12. 5
I her preserv'd from *perill* and from feare, . . . IV. vi. 35. 6
Withouten dread of *perill* to repaire . . . IV. viii. 5. 2
Withouten *perill* of the stronger pride: . . . IV. viii. 31. 5
Her person, late in *perill,* . . . IV. ix. 18. 3
to the place of *perill* shortly came: . . . IV. x. 5. 2
As if some proved *perill* he did feare, . . . IV. x. 12. 8
shew of *perill* hard . . . IV. x. 17. 4

Peril—*Continued.*
having past all *perill,* . . . IV. x. 21. 1
Till I was throughly past the *perill* of his reach. . . . IV. x. 36. 9
For feare of *perill* which to him mote fall . . . IV. xi. 7. 8
Into redoubted *perill* forth did call; . . . V. i. 3. 5
each Knight, that use of *perill* has, . . . V. ii. 16. 8
all strove with *perill* to winne fame; . . . V. iii. 7. 5
none Against them durst his head to *perill* shew. . . . V. iii. 12. 7
Whom on his *perill* he did undertake . . . to excell: . . . V. iii. 16. 5
Unknowen *perill* of bold womens pride. . . . V. iv. 38. 6
the bold child that *perill* well espying, . . . V. viii. 32. 1
Yet still he strives, ne any *perill* spares, . . . V. xi. 45. 1
when that Knight from *perill* cleare was freed, . . . V. xi. 48. 1
All *perill* ought be lesse, and lesse all paine . . . V. xi. 55. 7
A storme approching that doth *perill* threat, . . . V. xii. 18. 6
I, that knew my selfe from *perill* free, . . . VI. i. 9. 7
Into this bay of *perill* and disgrace? . . . VI. i. 12. 2
never to be recreant for feare Of *perill,* . . . VI. ii. 35. 4
saw his carriage past that *perill* well, . . . VI. iii. 34. 6
shun The *perill* of his pride, . . . VI. iii. 48. 9
for the *perill* of the present stound, . . . VI. iv. 9. 8
And *perill,* by this salvage man pretended, . . . VI. iv. 10. 4
Upon him set, of *perill* nought adrad, . . . VI. v. 16. 3
she thought Her selfe now past the *perill* of her feares: . . . VI. viii. 32. 3
endured for her sake Great *perill* of his life, . . . VI. viii. 33. 9
oft through pride do their owne *perill* weave, . . . VI. ix. 22. 3
Ne any paines ne *perill* did he shonne, . . . VI. x. 32. 7
To leave his love, now *perill* being past, . . . VI. xii. 13. 3
at her *perill* bide the wrathfull Thunders wrack. . . . VII. vi. 12. 9
From feare of *perill* and foule horror free. . . . *Epith.* 322
What brave exploit, what *perill* hardly wrought . . . *H.L.* 220
Perilous. it was a *perilous* beast above all, . . . *S.C.* S. 214
as he that *perilous* game In forreine soyle pursued . . . *As.* 91
Unweeting of the *perillous* wandring wayes, . . . I. v. 18. 3
She fownd not in that *perilous* hous of Pryde, . . . I. vii. 2. 2
Island, that doth ronne And stray in *perilous* gulfe, . . . II. i. 51. 6
glorious spoiles, purchast in *perilous* fight: . . . II. v. 26. 3
My little boat can safely passe this *perilous* bourne.' . . . II. vi. 10. 9
To ferry that old man over the *perlous* foord. . . . II. vi. 19. 9
In Phaedrias flitt barck over that *perlous* shard. . . . II. vi. 38. 9
As Pilot well expert in *perilous* wave, . . . II. vii. 1. 1
counseld him abstaine from *perilous* fight; . . . II. vii. 42. 7
report of that their *perlous* paine, . . . II. ix. 17. 4
Untill he quite had spent his *perlous* store, . . . II. xi. 27. 8
Now comes to point of that same *perilous* sted, . . . II. xii. 1. 7
On thother side they saw that *perilous* Rocke, . . . II. xii. 7. 1
here before a *perlous* passage lyes, . . . II. xii. 17. 8
On th' other side they see that *perilous* Poole, . . . II. xii. 20. 1
After long wayes and *perilous* paines endur'd, . . . III. i. 1. 2
As lay her journey, through that *perlous* Pace, . . . III. i. 19. 7
none durst passen through that *perilous* glade: . . . III. iv. 21. 5
Ne durst assay to wade the *perlous* seas, . . . III. vii. 28. 3
brought through points of many *perilous* swords: . . . III. viii. 17. 3
forth descending to that *perlous* porch . . . III. xii. 42. 6
Scudamour her bought In *perilous* fight . . . IV. i. 2. 2
A *perilous* fight, when he with force her brought . . . IV. i. 2. 3
both did forget The *perilous* present stownd . . . IV. ii. 15. 9
seemd some *perilous* tumult to desine, . . . IV. iii. 37. 7
Approved oft in many a *perlous* fight. . . . IV. iv. 40. 5
through paines and *perlous* jeopardie, . . . IV. x. 28. 7
All change is *perillous,* and all chaunce unsound. . . . V. ii. 36. 7
Those two false brethren on that *perillous* Bridge, . . . V. vi. 36. 6
Till to the *perillous* Bridge she came; . . . V. vi. 38. 3
So to pursue a *perillous* emprize, . . . V. vii. 21. 3
With many wounds full *perilous* and wyde, . . . VI. ii. 40. 8
To visite, after this nights *perillous* passe, . . . VI. iii. 14. 2
Through that same *perillous* foord . . . VI. iii. 31. 4
he remayned in most *perilous* plight, . . . VI. iv. 1. 8
past through many *perillous* assayes, . . . VI. vi. 3. 4
proved oft in many *perillous* fight, . . . VI. vi. 4. 3
in what *perilous* plight He had . . . left that salvage wight . VI. vi. 37. 4
Peril's. Deserved for their *perils* recompense. . . . IV. v. 23. 4
much emmoved at his *perils* vew, . . . VI. iv. 3. 4
Perils. thousand *perills* lie in close awaite . . . *Mui.* 221
'At last, when *perils* all I weened past, . . . I. iv. 47. 1
The house of Pryde, and *perilles* round about; . . . I. vii. 26. 6
how many *perils* doe enfold The righteous man, . . . I. viii. 1. 1
the place where all our *perilles* dwell; . . . I. xi. 2. 2
Of straunge adventures, and of *perils* sad . . . I. xii. 15. 4
through *perils* straunge and hard, . . . I. xii. 31. 8
Guyon, . . . Passing through *perilles* great, . . . II. xii. Arg.
The sacred soile where all our *perils* grow. . . . II. xii. 37. 8
Where daungers dwelt, and *perils* most did wonne, . . . III. i. 3. 2
To hunt out *perilles* and adventures hard, . . . III. ii. 7. 2
many *perilles* past in forreine landes, . . . III. ix. 41. 8
Approved oft in *perils* manifold, . . . IV. ii. 39. 3
rash provoking *perils* all about, . . . IV. ii. 46. 8
thousand *perils* which them still awate, . . . IV. iii. 1. 5
of the *perils* whereto he was bound, . . . IV. vi. 45. 3
pittie is to heare the *perils* which she tride. . . . IV. vii. 2. 9
many *perils* wonne, and many fortunes waide. . . . IV. ix. 38. 9
past *perils* well apay.' . . . IV. ix. 40. 9
often tride In greater *perils* . . . IV. x. 18. 2
to *perils* great for justice sake proceedes. . . . V. ii. 1. 9
The greater prowesse greater *perils* find. . . . V. iii. 9. 2
did her compell To *perils* great; . . . V. iii. 27. 7
So forth he fared . . . Through many *perils;* . . . V. xi. 36. 8
In *perils* strange, in labours long and wide; . . . VI. i. 6. 5
you into such *perils* presently doth call?' . . . VI. i. 6. 9
past through many *perils* by the way, . . . VI. vii. 50. 6

Perils—*Continued.*
Full many pathes and *perils* he hath past, ... VI. ix. 2. 5
Through hidden *perils* round about me plast; . . . . *Am.* xxxiv. 8
by all these *perils* and these paynes, ... *H.L.* 238
Perish. their buds, that *perish* through their harmes. . . . . *T.M.* 78
as things wipt out with a sponge to *perishe,* . . . . *Ti.* 361
'O! helpe, Orgoglio; helpe! or els we *perish* all.' . . . . . . I. viii. 20. 9
Ne suffred them to *perish* through long eld, ... II. ix. 56. 4
If not, die soone; and I with thee will *perish.* . . . . *Am.* ii. 14
be no lenger proud of that shall *perish;* . . . . *Am.* xxvii. 13
Perished. *perished* past all recoverie. . . . . *Pet.*[2] ii. 10
Perissa. young *Perissa* was of other mynd, ... II. ii. 36. 1
Perjured. The recompence of their *perjured* oth; . . . . . . II. x. 40. 4
Perjury. Thou falsed hast thy faith with *perjuree,* . . . . . I. ix. 46. 7
Witnesse . . . guilty heavens of his bold *perjury;* . . . . . I. xii. 27. 6
Perk. *Perke* as a Peacock; . . . . *S.C.* F. 8
Permanent. registred of old In Faery Land mongst records *permanent.* . . . . VII. vi. 2. 4
That only seemes unmov'd and *permanent,* . . . . VII. vii. 17. 7
Nothing doth firme and *permanent* appeare, ... VII. vii. 56. 2
permanent and free From frayle corruption, ... *Am.* lxxix. 7
Permission. by his divine *permission,* . . . . V. ix. 32. 1
Permit. Would not *permit* to make there lenger stay, ... VI. v. 41. 2
she would not him *permit* Once to approch to her . . . . . VI. xi. 8. 1
Perpetual. Which, made *perpetuall,* rose to so great might, . *Ro.* xviii. 9
To damne to death, or dole *perpetuall,* . . . . *Hub.* 1244
thy remembraunce and *perpetuall* band . . . . II. x. 69. 4
A friendly league of love *perpetuall* . . . . III. iv. 4. 4
by succession made *perpetuall,* . . . . III. vi. 47. 6
Some, of deare lovers foes *perpetuall:* . . . . IV. i. 24. 5
to *perpetuall* paine Had damn'd her sonnes . . . . V. vii. 10. 7
Perplex. Could judge what paines doe loving harts *perplexe.* . III. i. 54. 5
Perplexed. deignes to pitie a *perplexed* hart; . . . . *T.M.* 424
seeing her so piteouslie *perplexed,* . . . . *Ti.* 20
Could find no rest in such *perplexed* plight, ... III. i. 59. 5
both her selfe and others eke *perplext.* . . . . V. xii. 35. 9
Perplexity. Doth vex my spirite with *perplexitie,* . . . . . *Pet.*[2] ii. 12
when he heard, in great *perplexitie,* . . . . I. i. 19. 5
Yet is she now in more *perplexitie,* . . . . I. iii. 40. 5
In pensive plight and sad *perplexitie,* . . . . I. viii. 26. 2
The secrete cause of his *perplexitie:* . . . . I. ix. 25. 5
She found her selfe assayld with great *perplexity;* . . . . I. x. 22. 9
soone him overtooke in sad *perplexitye.* . . . . II. iv. 13. 9
in huge *perplexity* The Prince now stood, ... II. viii. 39. 5
In such distresse and sad *perplexity* . . . . III. viii. 33. 8
In heavy plight and sad *perplexitie;* . . . . IV. viii. 57. 2
Him Talus tooke out of *perplexitie,* . . . . V. iv. 25. 3
her selfe in great *perplexity.* . . . . V. vii. 14. 9
Persaunt. *See* **Perceant.**
Perse, Perst. *See* **Pierce, -d.**
Perseline. *See* **Purslane.**
Persephone. There grim *Persephone,* encountring mee, ... *Gn.* 422
Fit for Megera or *Persephone;* . . . . *T.M.* 164
Perseus. Dan *Perseus,* borne of heavenly seed, ... *Ti.* 648
Persevere. Nor to the Lightning; for they still *persever;* . . . *Am.* ix. 9
in her pride she dooth *persever* still. . . . . *Am.* xxxviii. 9
Persevered. much emmov'd, but stedfast still *persevered.* . . . III. xii. 2. 9
I *persever'd* still to knocke and call, ... IV. x. 11. 6
Persia. Ne *Persia* selfe, the nourse of pompous pride, ... I. iv. 7. 6
Persian. A vaine ensample of the *Persian* pride; . . . . . . *Hub.* 750
What of the *Persian* Beares outragiousnesse, ... *Ti.* 66
like a *Persian* mitre on her hed Shee wore, ... I. ii. 13. 4
As the proud *Persian* Queenes accustomed. . . . . III. i. 41. 4
The wealth of th' East, and pompe of *Persian* kings: . . . . III. iv. 23. 4
After the *Persian* Monarks antique guize, ... IV. iii. 38. 8
Persians. flocking *Persians* did the Greeks affray; . . . . . *Gn.* 50
Persist. Doth still *persist* in her rebellious pride: . . . . . *Am.* vi. 2
Persisted. So long *persisted* obstinate and bolde, ... *Hub.* 567
Person. farre unfit it is, that *person* bace . . . . *Hub.* 464
in *person* and in stature Most like a Man, ... *Hub.* 1029
Me seemd I had his *person* seene elsewhere, ... *D.* 52
And in thy *person,* without paragone, ... *Ded. Son.* v. 11
seemde best the *person* to put on Of that good knight, . . . I. ii. 11. 1
His Lady, . . . Did yield her comely *person* to be at my call. I. ii. 36. 9
The Lyon . . . a strong gard Of her chast *person,* . . . . . . I. iii. 9. 3
rugged heare, . . . Was like the *person* selfe whom he did beare: . . . . I. iv. 24. 4
dare not yet committ Her single *person* . . . . I. vi. 12. 2
A Satyre . . . made her *person* thrall unto his beastly kind. . I. vi. 22. 9
A goodly *person,* and could menage faire His stubborne steed . I. vii. 37. 5
Ne yet her *person* such as it was seene; . . . . II. i. 21. 2
Adornes the *person* of her Majestye; . . . . II. ii. 41. 5
supposed him a *person* meet . . . . II. iii. 11. 5
In which that manly *person* late did fade. . . . . II. v. 35. 5
To rest thy weary *person* in the shadow coole?' . . . . . . II. vii. 63. 9
Well knew they both his *person,* . . . . II. viii. 11. 8
The trespass still doth live, albee the *person* dye.' . . . . II. viii. 28. 9
Flesh without blood, a *person* without spright, ... II. xi. 40. 4
A jolly *person,* and of comely vew; . . . . III. i. 45. 2
what so else his *person* most may vaunt?' . . . . III. ii. 16. 7
Portly his *person* was, ... III. ii. 24. 8
Whose shape or *person* yet I never saw, ... III. ii. 38. 4
The rest upon her *person* gave attendance great. . . . . . III. vi. 17. 9
Least salvage beastes her *person* have despoyld: . . . . . . III. x. 39. 8
Without respect of *person* or of port, ... III. xi. 46. 4
His *person* to emperill so in fight; . . . . IV. iv. 10. 6
they so like in *person* did appeare, ... IV. ix. 10. 8
Her *person,* late in perill, ... IV. ix. 18. 3
unto every *person* knew her part; . . . . IV. x. 51. 4
did waite Uppon her *person* for her sure defence, ... V. v. 4. 4

Person—*Continued.*
in her *person* cunningly did shade . . . . V. vii. 3. 3
her proud *person* low prostrated on the plaine. . . . . V. vii. 33. 9
by traytrous traines to spill Her *person,* . . . . V. viii. 19. 4
Then up arose a *person* of deepe reach, ... V. ix. 39. 1
He now t' abhorre and loath her *person* had procured. . . . . V. ix. 39. 9
without sword his *person* to defend: . . . . VI. iv. 17. 5
Some goodly *person,* and of gentle race, ... VI. v. 36. 7
all men did her *person* much admire, ... VI. vii. 28. 6
eeke of *person* huge and hideous, ... VI. vii. 41. 2
rends without regard of *person* or of time. . . . . VI. xii. 40. 9
Angels and Archangels, which attend On Gods owne *person,* . *H.H.B.* 98
Personable. Wise, warlike, *personable,* courteous, and kind. . III. iv. 5. 9
Personage. In whatso please employ his *personage,* . . . . . *Hub.* 778
for the safegard of his *personage,* . . . . *Hub.* 1117
And ye, brave Lord, whose goodly *personage* . . . . *Ded. Son.* vi. 1
With goodly grace and comely *personage,* . . . . I. x. 30. 3
Seemd to have beene a goodly *personage,* . . . . II. i. 41. 6
with selfe-loved *personage* deceiv'd, ... II. iii. 5. 4
At th' upper end there sate . . . a comely *personage,* . . . . II. ix. 27. 6
His goodly reason and grave *personage,* . . . . II. ix. 54. 7
A comely *personage* of stature tall, ... II. xii. 46. 4
The Damzell well did vew his *Personage* . . . . III. ii. 26. 1
a comely *personage* And lovely face, ... III. vii. 46. 2
avizing right Her goodly *personage* and glorious hew, ... III. ix. 23. 6
a grave *personage* That in his hand a braunch of laurell bore, III. xii. 3. 6
zeale Which to thy noble *personage* I beare, ... VI. ii. 26. 6
Personages. taking on himselfe . . . False *personages* . . . . *Hub.* 861
Person's. by his *persons* secret seemlyhed . . . . IV. viii. 14. 3
Persons. of more private *persons* seeke elswhere, ... *Hub.* 522
wretched *persons* to misfortune borne; . . . . *T.M.* 154
Full many *persons* of right worthie parts, ... *Col.* 752
As might become a Squyre so great *persons* to greet. . . . . I. x. 7. 9
The fift had charge sick *persons* to attend, ... I. x. 41. 1
antique praises unto present *persons* fitt. . . . . III. Pr. 3. 9
after them a rude confused rout Of *persons* flockt, ... III. xii. 25. 2
all those *persons* which she saw without: . . . . III. xii. 30. 3
eke of private *persons* many moe, ... IV. i. 24. 1
shrowd their *persons* from that stormie stowre. . . . . . . IV. v. 32. 7
With which she guiltlesse *persons* may accuse, ... IV. viii. 25. 3
error and misthought Of our like *persons,* . . . . IV. viii. 58. 3
How that three warlike *persons* did appeare, ... V. iv. 36. 3
came Many grave *persons* that against her pled. . . . . . . V. ix. 43. 6
all such *persons,* as did late maintayne That Tyrants part . . V. xii. 25. 5
They knew them selves, and both their *persons* rad; . . . . VI. i. 4. 7
all such *persons* as he earst did wrong . . . . VI. xii. 37. 7
Persuade. Her to *persuade* that stubborne fort to yilde: . . . I. vi. 3. 7
gan the . . . thiefe *Perswade* us dye, to stint all further strife: I. ix. 29. 8
Orcus tame, whome nothing can *persuade,* . . . . II. xii. 41. 7
gan fayre *perswade* Not to provoke misfortune, ... III. i. 10. 1
him to sleepe she gently would *perswade,* . . . . III. i. 35. 8
if reason faire might you *perswade* . . . . III. ii. 13. 3
persuade The warlike minds to learne her goodly lore, . . . III. iii. 49. 3
did *perswade* T'endow her sonne . . . . III. iv. 21. 7
gan he her *perswade* to leave that . . . life, ... III. x. 51. 1
Leave nought unpromist that may him *perswade,* . . . . . . V. v. 49. 2
by no meanes could her thereto *perswade;* . . . . V. v. 54. 4
them selves full eath *perswade* To faire accordaunce, ... V. viii. 14. 4
with guilefull words her to *perswade* To banish feare; . . . . V. ix. 12. 5
The which did her commaund without needing *perswade.* . . V. x. 25. 9
To which he easily did them *perswade.* . . . . VI. iv. 13. 4
Him otherwise *perswade* all that she might, ... VI. v. 33. 6
did him halfe *perswade,* . . . . VI. xi. 7. 3
what we see not, who shall us *perswade?* . . . . VII. vii. 49. 5
Persuaded. So he *perswaded* them, ... *Hub.* 1082
He me *perswaded* forth with him to fare. . . . . *Col.* 193
She hardly yet *perswaded* was to stay, ... I. vi. 28. 4
her *perswaded* to disclose the breach . . . . I. vii. 42. 3
till Genuissa gent *Persuaded* him to ceasse, ... II. x. 52. 9
shee at length *persuaded* him to rise, ... III. xi. 20. 1
I . . . *perswaded* long; . . . . VI. ii. 21. 8
Yet would he not *perswaded* be for ought . . . . VI. iii. 43. 1
Persuading. With gentle words *perswading* them to friendly peace. . . . . IV. ix. 32. 9
Persuasions. with *perswasions* myld Did mitigate the fiercenesse . . . . IV. iv. 5. 1
Yet he with strong *perswasions* her asswaged, ... IV. vi. 43. 1
Pert. Or prive or *pert* yf any bene, ... *S.C.* S. 162
Pertain. Her to bethinke of that mote to her selfe *pertaine.* . III. ii. 22. 9
Threatning to chastize me, as doth t' a chyld *pertaine.* . . VI. ii. 11. 9
Pertains. all that els *pertaines* to reveling, ... *Hub.* 694
since now to thee *perteynes* the same . . . . I. xii. 20. 7
perteines in charge particulare, ... II. xii. 47. 4
To you that ornament of hers *pertaines* . . . . IV. ii. 27. 6
this to you, O Britons! most *pertaines,* . . . . IV. xi. 22. 6
Pertake. *See* **Partake.**
Perturbation. no greater enimy Then stubborne *perturbation* . II. v. 1. 4
Peru. Who ever heard of th' Indian *Peru?* . . . . II. Pr. 2. 6
beyond the Africk Ismael Or th' Indian *Peru* . . . . III. i. 6. 8
Perverse. fates *perverse* With guilefull love . . . . IV. vii. 15. 3
Pervert. like a Ram, faire Helle to *pervart,* . . . . III. xi. 30. 5
all which Nature had establisht . . . She did *pervert,* . . . . VII. vi. 5. 4
which mote *pervart* His safe assurance, ... *Am.* xlii. 11
Pestilence. powr'd on th' earth plague, *pestilence,* and death. . *Hub.* 8
Hath powrd on earth this noyous *pestilence,* . . . . *T.M.* 483
harmefull *pestilence,* So sore him noyd, ... I. xi. 45. 1
Pestilent. with plagues and murrins *pestilent* Consume, . . . III. iii. 40. 8
Peter. The bird that warned *Peter* of his fall, ... V. vi. 27. 2
Peter's. Her power to *Peters* successor betooke; . . . . *Ro.* xviii. 12
Phaeax. Great Belus, *Phoeax,* and Agenor best; . . . . IV. xi. 15. 7

Phaedria. Of *Phaedria,* (for so my name is red) . . . . . . II. vi. 9. 7
Of *Phaedria,* thine owne fellow servaunt; . . . . II. vi. 9. 8
Accompanyde with *Phaedria* the faire: . . . . II. vi. 28. 2
fayre *Phaedria,* that beheld That deadly daunger, ... II. vi. 32. 1
That was the wanton *Phaedria,* . . . . II. xii. 17. 1
Phaedria's. In *Phaedrias* flitt barck over that perlous shard. . II. vi. 38. 9
Phaeton. waylde the rash decay Of *Phaeton,* . . . . *Gn.* 199
Phaeton's. drew The Sunnes bright wayne to *Phaetons* decay, V. viii. 40. 2
Phantasies. *See* **Fantasies.**
Phantastes. hight *Phantastes* by his nature trew, ... II. ix. 52. 2
Phantoms. straunge *phantomes* doth lett us ofte foresee, . . . II. xii. 47. 6
Phao. Wherein th' Aegyptian *Phao* long did lurke . . . . III. ii. 20. 3
Fairest Pherusa, *Phao* lilly white, ... IV. xi. 49. 5
Phaon. Guyon . . . Delivers *Phaon,* . . . . II. iv. Arg.
'*Phaon* I hight,' (quoth he) . . . . II. iv. 36. 7
Phasides. Slow Peneus, and tempestuous *Phasides,* . . . . . IV. xi. 21. 3
Phedon. *Guyon . . . Delivers *Phedon,* . . . . II. iv. Arg.
**Phedon* I hight (quoth he) . . . . II. iv. 36. 7
Pherusa. Fairest *Pherusa,* Phao lilly white, ... IV. xi. 49. 5
Phidias. Apelles wit, or *Phidias* his skill, ... *Ro.* xxix. 6
Phidias did make in Paphos Isle of yore, ... IV. x. 40. 4
Philemon. 'My friend, hight *Philemon,* . . . . II. iv. 20. 1
Confest how *Philemon* her wrought to chaunge her weede. . . . II. iv. 29. 9
Philemon, false faytour *Philemon,* . . . . II. iv. 30. 6
Philisides. But was th' Harpe of *Philisides* now dead. . . . *Ti.* 609
Immortall spirite of *Philisides,* . . . . *Ti.* 673
Phillira's. *See* **Philyra's.**
Philomel. *Philomele* her song with teares doth steepe; . . . . *S.C.* N. 141
the dearling of the Summers pryde, Faire *Philomele,* . . . . *T.M.* 236
sorrow all the night With *Philumene,* . . . . *D.* 475
With *Philumene,* the partner of my plight. . . . . *D.* 476
Philosophy. Pourd out his . . . last *Philosophy* To the fayre Critias, ... II. vii. 52. 8
All artes, all science, all *Philosophy,* . . . . II. ix. 53. 8
Witnesse the father of *Philosophie,* . . . . IV. Pr. 3. 6
Or noursle up in lore of learn'd *Philosophy.* . . . . VI. iv. 35. 9
Philotime. fayre *Philotime* she rightly hight, ... II. vii. 49. 1
Philtera. That further mayd, hight *Philtera* the faire, ... V. iv. 8. 7
when *Philtra* saw my lands decay . . . . V. iv. 9. 6
Both Amidas and *Philtra* were displeased; . . . . V. iv. 20. 2
Philumene. *See* **Philomel.**
Philyra's. to compasse *Philliras* hard love, ... III. xi. 43. 7
Phison. *See* **Pison.**
Phlegethon. 'Ne feard the burning waves of *Phlegeton,* . . . *Gn.* 441
Where *Phlegeton* with quenchles flames doth burne; . . . . . *Gn.* 622
They . . . come to fiery flood of *Phlegeton,* . . . . I. v. 33. 3
Acrates, sonne of *Phlegeton* and Jarre; . . . . II. iv. 41. 7
Phlegeton is sonne of Herebus and Night; . . . . II. iv. 41. 8
damned ghoste In flaming *Phlegeton* . . . . II. vi. 50. 9
Firebrand of hell, first tynd in *Phlegeton,* . . . . IV. ii. 1. 1
Phlegraean. When Giants bloud did staine *Phlegraean* ground. *Gn.* 40
triumphes of *Phlegraean* Jove, ... II. x. 3. 4
slaine By thundring Jove in the *Phlegrean* plaine: . . . . . V. vii. 10. 5
Phocas. with a teeme of scaly *Phocas* bownd . . . . III. viii. 30. 8
Phoeax. *See* **Phaeax.**
Phoebe. her angelick face, Like *Phoebe* fayre? . . . . *S.C.* Ap. 65
when *Phoebe* shineth bright: . . . . *S.C.* Jun. 31
the cave where *Phoebe* layed The shepheard . . . . *S.C.* Jul. 63
How *Phoebe* fayles, where Venus sittes, ... *S.C.* D. 84
Phoebe fayre . . . was following the chace, ... I. vii. 5. 1
faire *Phebe* with her silver face . . . . II. ii. 44. 1
Phoebe therewith sore was angered, ... III. vi. 24. 1
Dame *Phoebe* to a Nymphe her babe betooke . . . . III. vi. 28. 3
To thrust faire *Phoebe* from her silver bed, ... VII. vi. 21. 3
Lyke *Phoebe,* from her chamber of the East, ... *Epith.* 149
Phoebe's. like faire *Phebes* garlond shining new, ... *Col.* 342
shone as *Phebes* light Amongst the lesser starres . . . . . . IV. v. 14. 3
Phoebus. my Lute, whom *Phoebus* deignd to give, ... *Ro.* xxxii. 9
In summers day, when *Phoebus* fairly shone, ... *Van.* ii. 1
the welked *Phoebus* gan availe His weary waine; . . . . . . *S.C.* Ja. 73
stouping *Phebus* steepes his face: . . . . *S.C.* Mar. 116
'I saw *Phoebus* thrust out his golden hedde, ... *S.C.* Ap. 73
I heard that Pan with *Phoebus* strove, ... *S.C.* Jun. 68
Bacchus fruite is frend to *Phoebus* wise; . . . . *S.C.* O. 106
Phoebus, weary of his yerely taske, ... *S.C.* N. 14
Phoebus, shall be the author of my song, ... *Gn.* 15
ruddy *Phebus* gins to welke in west, ... I. i. 23. 2
golden *Phoebus,* . . . Hurled his beame so scorching cruell hot, I. ii. 29. 3
Phoebus . . . Came dauncing forth, ... I. v. 2. 3
Phoebus pure . . . his weary wagon did recure. . . . . I. v. 44. 8
Phoebus, . . . His blushing face in foggy cloud implyes, . . . I. vi. 6. 6
Fayre ympe of *Phoebus* and his aged bryde, ... I. xi. 5. 7
gan the golden *Phoebus* for to steepe His fierie face . . . . . I. xi. 31. 1
Scarsely had *Phoebus* . . . Yett harnessed his fyrie-footed teeme, I. xii. 2. 1
now faire *Phoebus* gan decline . . . . II. ix. 10. 1
Daughter of *Phoebus* and of Memorye, ... III. iii. 4. 2
Phoebus with faire beames did her adorne, ... III. vi. 2. 8
Till drouping *Phoebus* gan to hyde his golden hedd. . . . . . III. x. 45. 9
faire *Phoebus,* in thy colours bright . . . . III. xi. 36. 1
For which Dan *Phebus* selfe cannot a salve provide. . . . . . IV. vi. 1. 9
Now when as *Phoebus* with his fiery waine . . . . VI. iii. 29. 1
bade Dan *Phoebus* scribe her Appellation seale. . . . . VII. vi. 35. 9
Phoebus selfe, that god of Poets hight, ... VII. vii. 12. 6
Phoebus selfe, who lightsome is alone, ... VII. vii. 51. 7
Phoebus gins to shew his glorious hed. . . . . *Epith.* 77
O fayrest *Phoebus!* father of the Muse! . . . . *Epith.* 121
Phoebus'. Glaunceth from *Phoebus* face forthright, ... *S.C.* Au. 83
weary thys long lingring *Phoebus* race. . . . . *S.C.* O. 3
(with *Phoebus* friendly leave) . . . . *Gn.* 52
from the force of *Phoebus* boyling ray, ... *Gn.* 167

Phoebus'—*Continued.*
the sad lakes that *Phoebus* sunnie rayes Doo never see, . . . *Gn.* 619
Lawrell, th' ornament of *Phoebus* toyle. . . . . *Gn.* 672
since the time that *Phoebus* foolish sonne Ythundered, . . . *T.M.* 7
their musicke matcheth *Phoebus* quill. . . . . *T.M.* 330
could both *Phoebus* arrowes ward, ... *Mui.* 79
Like *Phoebus* lampe throughout the world doth shine, ... I. Pr. 4. 4
Phoebus fiery carre In hast was climbing . . . . I. ii. 1. 7
Exceeding shone, like *Phoebus* fayrest childe, ... I. iv. 9. 1
That *Phoebus* chearefull face durst never vew, ... I. v. 20. 2
Like glauncing light of *Phoebus* brightest ray; . . . . I. vii. 29. 5
Phoebus golden face it did attaint, ... I. vii. 34. 6
Like *Phoebus* face adornd with sunny rayes, ... II. viii. 5. 6
By *Phoebus* doome the wisest thought alive, ... II. ix. 48. 2
worthy of great *Phoebus* rote, ... II. x. 3. 2
Such as Laomedon of *Phoebus* race did breed. . . . . II. xi. 19. 9
Fayre Daphne *Phoebus* hart with love did gore; . . . . II. xii. 52. 5
Lookt foorth, as *Phoebus* face out of the east . . . . III. ii. 24. 6
Belphoebe was her name, as faire as *Phoebus* sunne. . . . . III. v. 27. 9
nether *Phoebus* beams could through them throng, ... III. vi. 44. 8
Fresh Hyacinthus, *Phoebus* paramoure . . . . III. vi. 45. 3
Phoebus Lamp Bewrayed had the world . . . . III. x. 1. 1
Joves and *Phoebus* kinde; . . . . IV. xi. 52. 7
Mounted in *Phoebus* charet fierie bright, ... V. iii. 19. 2
light then *Phoebus* lampe doth shine more cleare? . . . . . V. xi. 62. 9
for to shrowde in shade from *Phoebus* flame, ... VII. vi. 39. 3
Proud Daphne, scorning *Phoebus* (**Phaebus*) lovely fyre, . . *Am.* xxviii. 9
fly no more, fayre Love, from *Phebus* chace, ... *Am.* xxviii. 13
Phoenicia. costly Oricalche from strange *Phoenice,* . . . . . *Mui.* 78
Phoenix. I saw a *Phoenix* in the wood alone, ... *Pet.* v. 1
the *Phoenix* there alas, Spying the tree destroid, ... *Pet.* v. 8
Phoenix, and Aon, and Pelasgus old; . . . . IV. xi. 15. 6
Pholoe. he thinkes not faire, And *Pholoe* fowle, ... I. vi. 15. 9
Phorcys. *Phorcys,* the father of that fatall brood, ... IV. xi. 13. 1
Phrixus. Ram, which bore *Phrixus* and Helle . . . . V. Pr. 5. 7
Phrygian. more than that great *Phrygian* mother . . . . . . *Ro.* vi. 5
on the *Phrygian* playne . . . He compast Troy . . . . *Gn.* 526
all the purchase of the *Phrigian* pray, ... *Gn.* 591
On *Phrygian* Paris by Plexippus brooke, ... VI. ix. 36. 7
Achilles preassing through the *Phrygian* glaives, ... *H.L.* 233
Phyllis. *Phyllis* is myne for many dayes. . . . . *S.C.* F. 64
Phyllis, Charillis, and sweet Amaryllis. . . . . *Col.* 540
Phyllis, the faire, is eldest of the three: . . . . *Col.* 541
Phyllis, the floure of rare perfection, ... *Col.* 544
Phyllis.' Tho wouldest thou pype of *Phyllis* prayse; . . . . *S.C.* F. 63
Physic. O foolish *physick,* and unfruitfull paine, ... III. v. 42. 1
Physician's. such sweet cordialls passe *Physitions* art. . . . . *Am.* l. 12
Physiognomy. by his like *visnomie* Eathe to be knowen; . . *Mui.* 310
but halfe seene his ugly *visnomie,* . . . . V. iv. 11. 3
certes by her face or *physnomy,* . . . . VII. vii. 5. 5
The goodly ymage of your *visnomy,* . . . . *Am.* xlv. 11
Behold them both in their right *visnomy* . . . . *Com. Son.* ii. 5
Pible stone. *See* **Pebble-stone.**
Picked. choycely *picked* out from all the rest, ... II. vi. 12. 4
A place *pickt* out by choyce of best alyve, ... II. xii. 42. 3
Pictland. Unto the Prince of *Picteland,* bordering nere; . . . VI. xii. 4. 6
Picts. gan the Hunnes and *Picts* invade this land, ... II. x. 61. 6
Those spoylefull *Picts,* and swarming Easterlings, ... II. x. 63. 2
the *Picts* that swarmed over-all, ... IV. xi. 36. 4
Picts'. for those *Picts* annoyes, ... II. x. 64. 6
Picturals. *picturals* Of Magistrates, of courts, of tribunals, . II. ix. 53. 4
Picture. By that which but the *picture* is of thee. . . . . . . *Ro.* v. 4
The *picture* of thy pride in pompous shew: . . . . *Ti.* 82
his deare hart the *picture* gan adore; . . . . II. viii. 43. 5
Beare ye the *picture* of that Ladies head? . . . . II. ix. 2. 8
'if in that *picture* dead Such life ye read, ... II. ix. 3. 1
The glorious *picture* vanisheth away, ... V. iii. 25. 6
The *picture* of his punishment might see, ... VI. vii. 27. 4
Presume to *picture* so divine a wight, ... *H.H.B.* 226
Pictured. Before the Bull she *pictur'd* winged Love, ... *Mui.* 289
Thy selfe thou covet to see *pictured,* . . . . III. Pr. 4. 2
a gracious servaunt *pictured* His Cynthia, ... III. Pr. 4. 5
Next unto him was Neptune *pictured,* . . . . III. xi. 40. 1
Painter . . . Which *pictured* Venus . . . . *H.H.B.* 212
Picture's. Ne *pictures* beautie, nor the glauncing rayes . . . *Gn.* 101
Pictures. Androgeus and Tenantius, *pictures* of his might. . . II. x. 46. 9
why doe not faire *pictures* like powre shew, ... *H.B.* 82
Picturing. *Picturing* that which I in minde embraced, ... *Van.* i. 11
picturing the parts of beauty daynt, ... III. Pr. 2. 7
Pide. *See* **Pied.**
Piece. *See* **Head-piece.**
paying but a *peece.* . . . . *S.C.* May 50
The fairest *peece* that eie beholden can; . . . . I. x. 59. 3
by the ransack of that *peece* they should attayn. . . . . . . II. xi. 14. 9
Argo, which in venturous *peece* First through the Euxine . . II. xii. 44. 8
all the *peece* he shaked from the flore, ... V. ii. 21. 8
no whole *peece* of him was to be seene, ... V. viii. 42. 8
to leave, . . . So fayre a *peece,* . . . . *Am.* xiv. 4
Pieced. Her *peeced* pyneons bene not so in plight: . . . . . . *S.C.* O. 87
Pieces. The skie, in *pieces* seeming to be rent, ... *Gn.* 581
Some on th' Euboick Cliffs in *pieces* rent; . . . . *Gn.* 587
With a plume feather all to *peeces* tore: . . . . *Hub.* 210
T' accept a Benefice in *peeces* riven. . . . . *Hub.* 540
rending them in *pieces,* felly slewe . . . . *Hub.* 1370
Sharpe sorrowe did in thousand *peeces* rive. . . . . *D.* 7
As if his heart in *peeces* would have rent. . . . . *D.* 49
streight him rent in thousand *peeces* small, ... I. iii. 20. 3
high trees overthrew, and rocks in *peeces* tore. . . . . I. xi. 37. 9
Doth belch out flames, and rockes in *peeces* broke, ... I. xi. 44. 6
The sacred Diademe in *peeces* rent, ... II. vii. 13. 6

Pieces—*Continued.*
rend in *peeces* with his ravenous pawes, . . . II. vii. 27. 8
Would him have rent in thousand *peeces* strayt: . . . II. vii. 64. 5
all in *peeces* it was broken fond, . . . II. xii. 57. 4
Shee pownded small, and did in *peeces* bruze; . . . III. v. 33. 2
with blasphemous bannes high God in *peeces* tare. . . . III. vii. 39. 9
as if his hart were *peeces* made, . . . III. xi. 8. 7
Himselfe in thousand *peeces* fondly rent, . . . III. xi. 38. 4
that great brasen pillour broke in *peeces* small. . . . III. xii. 37. 9
Her tender hart in *peeces* would divide: . . . IV. vii. 10. 3
As they the cliffe in *peeces* would have cleft; . . . IV. xi. 3. 7
Her shattered ribs in thousand *peeces* rives, . . . V. ii. 50. 3
His battred ballances in *peeces* lay, . . . V. ii. 50. 7
all his ribs he quite in *peeces* broke, . . . V. iii. 33. 4
To teare his flesh in *peeces* for his sin: . . . V. iv. 37. 5
shattered all to *peeces* round about the plaine. . . . V. v. 10. 9
torne in *pieces* by Alcides great; . . . V. viii. 31. 4
the Prince in *peeces* to have torne . . . V. viii. 31. 6
Of his owne steedes was all to *peeces* torne, . . . V. viii. 43. 4
he to *peeces* would have chopt it quight, . . . V. xi. 5. 5
As if that it she would in *peeces* rend, . . . V. xi. 27. 4
Whom he did all to *peeces* breake, . . . V. xi. 33. 8
they his shield in *peeces* battred have, . . . V. xi. 46. 2
Him rudely rent and all to *peeces* tore; . . . VI. vi. 22. 6
As if he would in *peeces* him have rent: . . . VI. vi. 40. 6
all his launce in *peeces* shivered quite, . . . VI. vii. 8. 3
all his bones in *peeces* nigh he brake. . . . VI. vii. 11. 5
The which amongst them they in *peeces* teare, . . . VI. viii. 41. 4
shooke Nigh all to *peeces*, . . . VII. vi. 47. 8
Pied. An huge great Serpent, all with speckles *pide*, . . . *Gn.* 250
Pierce. *pierce* the cloudes, and with hir wings . . . *Bel.*[1] vi. 7
with a larger flight To *pierce* the cloudes, . . . *Bel.*[2] vii. 6
pierce her heart with poynt of worthy wight, . . . *S.C.* Jun. 100
pierce immortall breasts with mortall smarts? . . . *T.M.* 48
with shrilling cryes *Pierce* the dull heavens . . . *T.M.* 118
pierce his frosen eares? . . . *D.* 249
through their iron sides . . . Does seeke to *perce;* . . . I. ii. 17. 6
Through vainly crossed shield he quite did *perce;* . . . I. iii. 35. 3
enchaunted armes, that none can *perce;* . . . I. iv. 50. 6
stony dart of sencelesse cold *Perce* to my hart, . . . I. vii. 22. 8
point of speare it never *percen* could, . . . I. vii. 33. 8
as a swords poynt through his hart did *perse,* . . . I. ix. 48. 2
cote of steele, so couched neare That nought mote *perce;* . . . I. xi. 9. 3
His harder hyde would nether *perce* nor bight, . . . I. xi. 16. 4
That horrour gan the virgins hart to *perse,* . . . III. xii. 36. 5
passing through the eares would *pierce* the hart, . . . IV. viii. 26. 6
by often beating Doe *pearce* the rockes, . . . IV. xii. 7. 2
no substance . . . But it would *pierce* or cleave, . . . V. i. 10. 7
to make them *pierce* and wound more deepe, . . . V. xii. 42. 6
it can *pierce* through th' eyes unto the hart, . . . *H.B.* 72
Pierceable. Not *perceable* with power of any starr: . . . I. i. 7. 6
Pierced. the steele had *pierced* his pitth, . . . *S.C.* F. 217
I . . . Feele my hart *perst* with so great agony, . . . I. iii. 1. 8
he *perced* through his chaufed chest . . . I. iii. 42. 6
with their force they *perst* both plate and maile, . . . I. vi. 43. 4
steelehead . . . through his shoulder *perst;* . . . II. viii. 32. 8
pierced to the skin, but bit no more; . . . II. viii. 44. 8
point of pitty *perced* through her tender hart. . . . III. v. 30. 9
pierst into her wombe, . . . III. vi. 7. 7
Her hart was *pierst* with pitty at the sight, . . . III. vi. 40. 5
Pierst through his bever quite into his brow, . . . IV. iii. 11. 8
Into his throate and life it *pierced* quight, . . . IV. iii. 30. 4
through his soule like poysned arrow *perst,* . . . IV. v. 31. 4
could have *perst* the hearts of Tigres . . . IV. viii. 4. 9
and *pierst* through either syde; . . . V. x. 35. 7
pearst Her stubborne hart . . . VI. i. 45. 3
both whose sides are *pearst* With wounds, . . . VI. iii. 39. 3
Rest not till they have *pierst* the trembling harts, . . . *H.L.* 123
loves deepe wound, that *pierst* the piteous hart . . . *H.H.L.* 156
Pierceth. as a thonder bolt *Perceth* the yielding ayre, . . . III. xi. 25. 7
Piercing. *See* **Heart-piercing, Thorough-piercing.**
As well can prove the *piercing* levin, . . . *S.C.* Jul. 91
So oft as I record those *piercing* words, . . . *D.* 295
No gate . . . But with that *percing* noise flew open . . . I. viii. 4. 9
percing griefe her stubborne hart did wound, . . . I. viii. 25. 4
with *percing* point Of pitty deare . . . I. viii. 39. 1
The *percing* steele there wrought a wound . . . I. xi. 20. 8
his *percing* speach gan paynt: . . . II. i. 9. 5
dearnly cride With *percing* shriekes . . . II. i. 35. 8
she lefte her *percing* launce, . . . II. iii. 34. 4
With *percing* wordes and pittifull implore, . . . II. v. 37. 5
through his three-square scuchin *percing* quite . . . III. iv. 16. 3
As *percing* levin, which . . . every thing consumes, . . . III. v. 48. 8
those shrieches shrill, *Percing* his hart, . . . VI. iv. 18. 5
Beare off their blowes from *percing* thorough quite: . . . VI. v. 18. 5
through *piercing,* did devowre His vitall breath, . . . VI. vii. 8. 7
The *piercing* points of his avengefull darts; . . . *H.L.* 30
Pierian. the glorie bee Of the *Pierian* streames, . . . *Gn.* 26
Whom the *Pierian* sacred sisters love, . . . *Ti.* 394
Piers. *Piers,* bene not thy teeth on edge, . . . *S.C.* May 35
Now, *Piers,* of felowship, tell us that saying: . . . *S.C.* May 172
Piers, thou art beside thy wit, . . . *S.C.* May 306
Piers, I have pyped erst so long with payne, . . . *S.C.* O. 7
Piety. with sacred *pietie* Hath powred forth for thee, . . . *Mui.* 238
Pight. were *pight* . . . foure great Lyons of gold; . . . *Bel.* iii. 9
The bodie bigge, and mightely *pight,* . . . *S.C.* F. 106
in my face deepe furrowes eld hath *pight:* . . . *S.C.* D. 134
darkesome caves in pleasaunt vallies *pight,* . . . *Gn.* 117
a yong alder hard beside him *pight,* . . . *Gn.* 299
by my wretched lovers side me *pight;* . . . I. ii. 42. 7

Pight—*Continued.*
in the same a little grate was *pight,* . . . I. viii. 37. 6
His dwelling . . . underneath a craggy clift *ypight,* . . . I. ix. 33. 3
As if in Adamant rocke it had beene *pight.* . . . I. xi. 25. 5
hong still on the shield, as it at first was *pight.* . . . I. xi. 43. 9
kist the ground whereon his foot was *pight;* . . . I. xii. 25. 7
Therein an hundred raunges weren *pight,* . . . II. vii. 35. 4
'On thother side an hideous Rocke is *pight* . . . II. xii. 4. 1
there was *pight* A faire Pavilion, . . . III. v. 40. 6
pight Upon the top of Mount Olympus . . . III. vii. 41. 4
here and there were pleasant arbors *pight,* . . . IV. x. 25. 3
farre from where it first was *pight,* . . . V. Pr. 4. 7
in the same are many trap-fals *pight,* . . . V. ii. 7. 8
The earth was in the middle centre *pight,* . . . V. ii. 35. 5
Causd his pavilion to be richly *pight* . . . V. iv. 46. 4
Where was a rich Pavilion ready *pight* . . . V. v. 4. 8
She caused her Pavilion be *pight;* . . . V. vii. 26. 2
on his head unhappily he *pight,* . . . V. viii. 8. 2
he was strong and mightily stiffe *pight,* . . . VI. ix. 44. 2
On top whereof the moon and stars were *pight;* . . . VII. vii. 44. 6
Pike. his threeforkt *Pyke* He stearnly shooke, . . . III. xi. 40. 4
Pike-head. Had riven many a brest with *pikehead* square: . . . I. vii. 37. 4
therein left the *pike-head* of his speare: . . . IV. vii. 27. 7
Pikes. layes forth her threatfull *pikes* . . . *Mui.* 85
Lindus that his *pikes* doth most commend, . . . IV. xi. 39. 7
greedy *pikes* which use therein to feed; . . . *Epith.* 58
pikes all others doo excell;) . . . *Epith.* 59
Pilate. 'I *Pilate* am, the falsest Judge, alas! . . . II. vii. 62. 3
Pile. Against the five great Bulwarkes of that *pyle,* . . . II. xi. 7. 2
Piles. Like to a rancke of *piles* that pitched are awry. . . . V. xi. 9. 9
bounded On everie side, with *pyles* of flaming brands, . . . *H.H.B.* 39
Pilgrim. the *Pilgrim* that the Ploughman playde awhyle; . . . *S.C.* Env. 10
Or like a *Pilgrim,* or a Lymiter, . . . *Hub.* 85
Like to some *Pilgrim* come from farre away. . . . *D.* 42
Then gan the *Pilgrim* thus: . . . I. vi. 38. 1
that false *Pilgrim,* which that leasing told, . . . I. vi. 48. 1
resolving, like a *Pilgrim* pore, . . . III. x. 19. 1
A silly *Pilgrim* driven to distresse, . . . III. x. 25. 6
Pilgrimage. Yode late on *Pilgrimage* To Rome, . . . *S.C.* Jul. 182
'For I will walke this wandring *pilgrimage,* . . . *D.* 372
thy painefull *pilgrimage* To yonder same Hierusalem . . . I. x. 61. 3
Pilgrim's. To walke this way in *Pilgrims* poore estate. . . . I. x. 64. 4
Pilgrims. 'And ye, poore *Pilgrimes!* . . . *D.* 533
Pill. Of which all passers by doo somewhat *pill:* . . . *Ro.* xxx. 12
did he all the kingdome rob and *pill,* . . . *Hub.* 1198
this to adorne, she all the rest did *pill.* . . . VI. x. 5. 9
Sweet is the Nut, but bitter is his *pill;* . . . *Am.* xxvi. 6
Pillage. nightly stelths, and *pillage* severall, . . . I. iii. 16. 8
brought the *pillage* home, whence none could get it out. . . . V. ix. 4. 9
Pillar. Withouten prop or *pillour* it t' upholde, . . . *Ti.* 549
Upon a brazen *pillour* standing hie, . . . *Ti.* 660
Most Noble Lord, the *pillor* of my life, . . . *Ded. Son.* vii. 1
every *pillour* decked was . . . With crownes, . . . II. vii. 43. 7
Of every *pillour* and of every post, . . . III. i. 32. 5
the marble *Pillour* that is pight . . . III. vii. 41. 4
Upon a brasen *pillour,* . . . III. xii. 30. 9
that great brasen *pillour* broke in peeces small. . . . III. xii. 37. 9
in the midst thereof a *piller* placed; . . . IV. x. 8. 2
preacing to the *pillour,* . . . IV. x. 10. 7
seem'd a marble *pillour* it could bow; . . . VI. viii. 16. 3
Pillars. I sawe, an hundred *pillers* eke about, . . . *Bel.*[1] ii. 2
raisde up on *pillers* of Ivorie, . . . *Bel.*[1] iv. 1
hundreth *pillours* fronting faire the same, . . . *Bel.*[2] ii. 3
*I saw raysde up on yvorie *pilloures* tall, . . . *Bel.*[2] iv. 1
postes to dight, And all the Kirke *pillours* . . . *S.C.* May 12
Wrought with faire *pillours* and fine imageries; . . . *Ti.* 96
brasen *Pillours* never to be fired, . . . *Ti.* 410
Whylom the *pillours* of th' earth did sustaine, . . . *Ded. Son.* i. 2
Like two faire marble *pillours* they were seene, . . . II. iii. 28. 1
Many great golden *pillours* did upbeare The massy roofe, . . . II. vii. 43. 5
which two upbeare, Like mightie *pillours,* . . . II. vii. 65. 4
Distaines the *pillours* and the holy grownd, . . . III. iv. 17. 7
all the *pillours* of the one were guilt, . . . IV. x. 5. 8
stately *pillours* fram'd after the Doricke guize. . . . IV. x. 6. 9
Upon an hundred marble *pillors* round . . . IV. x. 37. 4
building . . . Borne uppon stately *pillours,* . . . V. vii. 5. 4
up-held With thousand Crystall *pillors* . . . VII. vi. 10. 4
firmely stayd Upon the *pillours* of Eternity, . . . VII. viii. 2. 4
all the *pillours* deck with girlands trim, . . . *Epith.* 207
First, th' Earth, on adamantine *pillers* founded . . . *H.H.B.* 36
Hercules two *pillors* . . . Did make to quake . . . *Proth.* 148
Pillow. *pillow* was my helmett fayre displayd; . . . I. ix. 13. 4
the hard steele his *pillow.* . . . III. iv. 53. 9
their *pillow* was unsowed: . . . VI. iv. 14. 5
Pillows. raysde up on yvorie *pillowes* tall, . . . *Bel.*[2] iv. 1
Her paps, which like white silken *pillowes* were . . . VI. viii. 42. 2
Pills. pols and *pils* the poore in piteous wize; . . . V. ii. 6. 8
Pilot. now the *Pylote* can no loadstarre see, . . . *Gn.* 573
Withouten helme or *Pilot* her to sway: . . . *T.M.* 142
Withouten oare or *Pilot* it to guide, . . . II. vi. 5. 3
As *Pilot* well expert in perilous wave, . . . II. vii. 1. 1
Love, my lewd *Pilott,* hath a restlesse minde; . . . III. iv. 9. 6
her *Pilott* hath dismayd; . . . III. iv. 53. 4
(The lucky *Pylot* of her passage sad,) . . . V. iv. 11. 7
Pin. not a *pin* Does care for looke of living creatures eye. . . . I. v. 4. 3
Onely she turnd a *pin,* . . . II. vi. 5. 5
Pincers. pluck it out with *pincers* fyrie whott, . . . I. x. 26. 8
A paire of *Pincers* in his hand he had, . . . III. xii. 16. 5
Pinched. *pincht* the haunches of that (this[1]) . . . beast, . . . *Pet.* i. 9
he *pinched* people to the hart, . . . III. xii. 16. 6

Pinched—*Continued.*
hunger . . . Had by the belly oft him *pinched* sore: . . . VII. vii. 30. 5
Pinching. Ys love such *pinching* payne to them that prove? . *S.C.* Ap. 18
Hey, ho, *pinching* payne! . . . *S.C.* Au. 110
Pinckt. *See* **Pinked.**
Pind. *See* **Pinned.**
Pindus. her whilome upon high *Pindus* hill He loved, . . . III. iv. 41. 4
The snow, which doth the top of *Pindus* strew, . . . *Proth.* 40
Pine. With mourning *pyne* I; you with pyning mourne. . . *S.C.* Ja. 48
should they *pynen* in payne and woe? . . . *S.C.* May 149
Pyne, plagues, and dreery death. . . . *S.C.* Jul. 24
I *pyne* for payne, . . . *S.C.* Au. 18
whether in paynefull love I *pyne,* . . . *S.C.* Au. 109
Bene all sterved with *pyne* and penuree: . . . *S.C.* S. 65
Here also grew the rougher rinded *Pine,* . . . *Gn.* 209
To feed on hope, to *pine* with feare and sorrow; . . . *Hub.* 900
pine away in selfe-consuming paine! . . . *D.* 436
The sayling *Pine;* the Cedar proud and tall; . . . I. i. 8. 6
For want whereof poore people oft did *pyne:* . . . I. iv. 21. 7
His raw-bone cheekes, through penurie and *pine,* . . . I. ix. 35. 8
'Whiles thus thy Britons doe in languour *pine,* . . . III. iii. 35. 1
With hatefull thoughts to languish and to *pine,* . . . III. xi. 1. 7
they were forst, through penurie and *pyne,* . . . V. v. 22. 6
by some deadly chaunce be done to *pine* . . . VI. v. 28. 8
having, *pine;* and, having not, complaine. . . . *Am.* xxxv. 4
So doth he *pine* in most satiety; . . . *H.L.* 201
Pined. *See* **Love-pined.**
Pined with griefe of folly late repented: . . . *Mui.* 348
the lad . . . *pyned* away in anguish . . . I. vi. 17. 9
thighes, unable to uphold His *pined* corse, . . . I. viii. 40. 8
pyn'd his flesh to keepe his body low and chast. . . . I. x. 48. 9
She shortly like a *pyned* ghost became . . . III. ii. 52. 5
like a *pined* ghost he soone appeares: . . . IV. vii. 41. 4
pind and wore away, Ne ever laught, . . . IV. viii. 2. 6
pyn'd, and mourn'd, and languisht, . . . IV. xii. 19. 9
Pining. *See* **Long-pining.**
With mourning pyne I; you with *pyning* mourne. . . . *S.C.* Ja. 48
Nor so did Biblis spend her *pining* hart; . . . III. ii. 41. 2
pyning anguish hid in gentle hart, . . . IV. vi. 1. 2
al my dayes in *pining* langour spend, . . . *Am.* xxxvi. 3
My *pining* anguish to appease. . . . *Epig.* iv. 60
Pinioned. With both his hands behinde him *pinnoed* hard, . . V. iv. 22. 2
Pinions. with wide *pinneons* To measure . . . *Bel.*[2] vii. 6
Her peeced *pyneons* bene not so in plight: . . . *S.C.* O. 87
with *pineons* light To mount aloft . . . *Mui.* 43
the pennes, that did his *pineons* bynd, . . . I. xi. 10. 4
His newly-budded *pineons* to assay, . . . I. xi. 34. 7
with golden *pineons* cleave The flitting skyes, . . . II. viii. 2. 3
with her *pineons* cleaves the liquid firmament. . . . III. iv. 49. 9
Pink. 'Bring hether the *Pincke* and purple Cullambine, . . . *S.C.* Ap. 136
Pinked. *Pinckt* upon gold, and paled part per part, . . . VI. ii. 6. 2
Pinks. eyes, lyke *Pincks* but newly spred; . . . *Am.* lxiv. 8
Pinned. With thornes together *pind* and patched was, . . . I. ix. 36. 2
Pionings. Which to outbarre, with painefull *pyonings* . . . II. x. 63. 7
Pipe. *See* **Bagpipe, Conduit-pipe, Hornpipe, Weasand-pipe.**
Well couth he tune his *pipe* and frame his stile: . . . *S.C.* Ja. 10
my *pype,* albee rude Pan thou please, . . . *S.C.* Ja. 67
Both *pype* and Muse shall sore the while abye.' . . . *S.C.* Ja. 71
So broke his oaten *pype,* and downe dyd lye. . . . *S.C.* Ja. 72
Tho wouldest thou *pype* of Phyllis prayse; . . . *S.C.* F. 63
Hys pleasaunt *Pipe,* whych made us meriment, . . . *S.C.* Ap. 14
Made my heart after the *pype* to daunce: . . . *S.C.* May 26
Pan . . . Will *pype* and daunce . . . *S.C.* Jun. 31
tune my *pype* Unto my plaintive pleas . . . *S.C.* Jun. 41
thy oaten *pype* began to sound, . . . *S.C.* Jun. 58
wel could *pype* and singe, . . . *S.C.* D. 3
To Pan his owne selfe *pype* I neede not yield: . . . *S.C.* D. 46
wont to frame my *pype* . . . *S.C.* D. 115
I hang my *pype* upon this tree: . . . *S.C.* D. 141
Was never *pype* of reede did better sounde. . . . *S.C.* D. 142
to match thy *pype* with Tityrus his style. . . . *S.C.* Env. 9
With *pype* of fennie reedes . . . *Gn.* 112
To teach the warbling *pipe* to sound aloft, . . . *T.M.* 290
They to the vulgar sort now *pipe* and sing, . . . *T.M.* 319
To runne thy shrill Arcadian *Pipe* to heare: . . . *Ti.* 328
wont full merrilie to *pipe* and daunce, . . . *D.* 55
to my *pype* to caroll and to daunce. . . . *D.* 105
For he could *pipe,* and daunce, . . . *As.* 31
Soone as his oaten *pipe* began to shrill, . . . *As.* 44
Charming his oaten *pipe* unto his peres, . . . *Col.* 5
Wake then, my *pipe;* my sleepie Muse, awake; . . . *Col.* 48
aemuling my *pipe,* he tooke in hond My *pipe,* . . . *Col.* 72, 73
to mine oaten *pipe* enclin'd her eare, . . . *Col.* 360
carefull *pipe* may make the hearer rew: . . . *Col.* 397
Both did he other, which could *pipe,* maintaine, . . . *Col.* 442
eke could *pipe* himselfe with passing skill. . . . *Col.* 443
ne wont there sound His mery oaten *pipe,* . . . I. ii. 28. 9
on his guilefull *pype* Charmes to the birds . . . V. ix. 13. 1
did *pype* and sing her prayses dew, . . . VI. ix. 8. 6
all agree That Colin Clout should *pipe,* . . . VI. ix. 41. 6
the merry sound Of a shrill *pipe* . . . VI. x. 10. 3
That made him *pipe* so merrily, as never none. . . . VI. x. 15. 9
Pype, jolly shepheard, *pype* thou now . . . VI. x. 16. 6
made me often *pipe,* and now to *pipe* apace. . . . VI. x. 27. 9
The *pipe,* the tabor, and the trembling Croud, . . . *Epith.* 131
Piped. I have *pyped* erst so long with payne, . . . *S.C.* O. 7
when as he *piped* had his fill, . . . *Col.* 10
As ever *piped* on an oaten reed, . . . *Col.* 13
He *pip'd,* I sung; and, when he sung, I *piped;* . . . *Col.* 76
So *piped* we, until we both were weary.' . . . *Col.* 79

Piped—*Continued.*
noblest swaine, That ever *piped* in an oaten quill: . . . *Col.* 441
Was she to whom that shepheard *pypt* alone; . . . VI. x. 15. 8
piped there unto that merry rout; . . . VI. x. 16. 2
That jolly shepheard, which there *piped,* . . . VI. x. 16. 3
He *pypt* apace, whilest they him daunst about. . . . VI. x. 16. 5
Piper. Tom *Piper* makes us better melodie. . . . *S.C.* O. 78
Pipe's. allured with my *pipes* delight, . . . *Col.* 61
Pipes. crowing in *pypes* made of greene corne, . . . *S.C.* F. 40
tune your *pypes* as ruthful as ye may. . . . *S.C.* Au. 150
Then blowe your *pypes,* shepheards, . . . *S.C.* Au. 197
we our slender *pypes* may safely charme. . . . *S.C.* O. 118
Relieve thy Oaten *pypes* that sleepen long. . . . *S.C.* N. 24
Breake we our *pypes,* that shrild . . . *S.C.* N. 71
on *pipes* of oaten reed, Oft times to plaine . . . *As.* Pr. 1
'When thus our *pipes* we both had wearied well, . . . *Col.* 178
they list not their mery *pipes* applie? . . . *Col.* 373
be their *pipes* untunable and craesie, . . . *Col.* 374
when they list to blow Their *pipes* aloud, . . . *Col.* 379
all the way their merry *pipes* they sound, . . . I. vi. 14. 1
up they gan their mery *pypes* to trusse, . . . III. x. 46. 1
Playing on *pipes* and caroling apace, . . . VI. ix. 5. 3
Where wont the shepheards oft their *pypes* resound, . . . VI. xi. 26. 8
Piping. *pyping* lowe in shade of lowly grove, . . . *S.C.* Jun. 71
With *pyping* and dauncing did passe the rest. . . . *S.C.* Au. 10
a Shepheard *piping* he did see. . . . VI. x. 10. 9
Pirates'. Through the Agaean seas from *Pirates* vew, . . . IV. xi. 23. 7
Pirithous. Stout Theseus and *Pirithous* his feare . . . IV. x. 27. 3
Pison. the territories, Which *Phison* and Euphrates floweth by, I. vii. 43. 8
Pit. pitilesse throwne downe in *pit* of fire. . . . *Rev.* iii. 14
And eke that ample *Pitt,* . . . II. x. 11. 1
falne unwares Into some *pit,* . . . IV. xii. 17. 7
Pitch. Who touches *Pitch,* mought needes be defilde; . . . *S.C.* May 74
more black then *pitche,* . . . *S.C.* Jun. 23
aspire Unto so loftie *pitch* of perfectnesse, . . . *T.M.* 394
to the *pitch* of her perfection raised. . . . *Col.* 415
two blacke as *pitch,* And two were browne, . . . I. v. 28. 4
discoloured brest Above his wonted *pitch,* . . . I. xi. 31. 8
Till it the *pitch* of highest praise exceeds: . . . II. ii. 31. 4
far above thy forces *pitch* to sore; . . . V. ii. 34. 4
From *pitch* of higher place . . . VI. ix. 28. 9
My spirit to an higher *pitch* will rayse, . . . *Am.* lxxx. 12
Pitched. He *pitcht* upon a pole on high ordayned; . . . V. ii. 19. 4
Like to a rancke of piles that *pitched* are awry. . . . V. xi. 9. 9
did cause his tent There to be *pitched* . . . V. xii. 10. 2
Pitcher. her *pitcher* downe she threw, And fled away: . . . I. iii. 11. 6
Pitchy. Night, . . . in a foule black *pitchy* mantle clad, . . . I. v. 20. 3
his locks, as blacke as *pitchy* night, . . . VI. vii. 43. 7
Piteous. Greatly aghast with this *piteous* plea, . . . *S.C.* F. 157
poore my *piteous* plaints out . . . *S.C.* Jun. 80
Such play is a *pitteous* plight. . . . *S.C.* Au. 92
My *piteous* plight and losse to amend? . . . *S.C.* S. 245
Thus gan he make of love his *piteous* mone. . . . *S.C.* D. 6
Where the reward of my so *piteous* deed? . . . *Gn.* 357
he heavily departed With *piteous* crie, . . . *Gn.* 640
Those *piteous* plaints and sorrowfull sad tine, . . . *T.M.* 3
pitious lamentation did make; . . . *T.M.* 296
Began her *piteous* plaint, as doth ensew. . . . *T.M.* 360
Now change your praises into *piteous* cries, . . . *T.M.* 371
Much was I mooved at her *piteous* plaint, . . . *Ti.* 29
Let them behold the *piteous* fall of mee, . . . *Ti.* 461
Thus having ended all her *piteous* plaint, . . . *Ti.* 470
For ruth of that same womans *piteous* paine; . . . *Ti.* 480
with your *piteous* layes have learnd . . . *As.* Pr. 3
piteous mone the which she for him made, . . . *As.* 170
when that *pitteous* spectacle they vewed, . . . *As.* 203
Wringing her hands, in wemens *pitteous* wise, . . . I. i. 50. 7
Therewith a *piteous* yelling voice was heard, . . . I. ii. 31. 1
Her *piteous* wordes might not abate his rage, . . . I. iii. 38. 1
with . . . *piteous* plaintes, she filleth his dull eares, . . . I. iii. 44. 2
The *pitteous* mayden, . . . Does throw out thrilling shriekes, I. vi. 6. 1
when they heard that *pitteous* strained voice, . . . I. vi. 8. 1
might her *pitteous* hart be seene to pant and quake. . . . I. vii. 20. 9
The *pitteous* pray of his fiers cruelty have bin. . . . I. vii. 45. 9
At her so *pitteous* cry was much amoov'd . . . I. viii. 21. 1
O heare, how *piteous* he to you for ayd does call!' . . . I. viii. 28. 9
hardest heart would bleede to hear their *piteous* mone. . . . I. viii. 36. 9
These *pitteous* plaintes and dolours did resound: . . . I. viii. 38. 2
piteous spectacle, approving trew The wofull tale . . . I. ix. 37. 1
With *piteous* mone his percing speach gan paynt: . . . II. i. 9. 5
Wringing her handes, and making *piteous* mone: . . . II. i. 13. 7
of his *pitteous* tale he end did make: . . . II. ii. 46. 4
his *pitious* handes gan reare. . . . II. iii. 6. 9
Of fowles and beastes he made the *piteous* prayes, . . . II. v. 26. 7
Crying with *pitteous* voyce, . . . II. vi. 32. 4
eyes endure so *pitteous* sight, . . . II. vi. 32. 6
with their *piteous* cryes, and yelling shrightes, . . . II. vii. 57. 5
sure I rew his *pitteous* plight.' . . . II. viii. 24. 5
nought moved with her *piteous* looke; . . . II. x. 18. 9
pitteous Elidure put in his sted; . . . II. x. 44. 6
made his spright to grone full *piteous;* . . . II. xi. 38. 7
the rich wares to save from *pitteous* spoyle; . . . II. xii. 19. 8
A *piteous* spectacle did represent; . . . II. xii. 45. 7
With . . . plaints, and *piteous* griefe, . . . III. i. 53. 2
Shee made so *piteous* mone and deare wayment, . . . III. iv. 35. 6
much moved at so *pitteous* sight; . . . III. vii. 9. 9
The whiles the *pitteous* Lady up did ryse, . . . III. viii. 32. 1
She was empassioned at that *piteous* act, . . . III. ix. 38. 4
He bound that *pitteous* Lady prisoner, . . . III. xii. 41. 7
Full many *piteous* stories doe remaine, . . . IV. i. 1. 2

Piteous—*Continued.*
none more *piteous* ever was ytold . . . IV. i. 1. 3
They which that *piteous* spectacle beheld . . . IV. iii. 21. 1
that wofull Ladies *piteous* crying, . . . IV. vii. 25. 3
there a *piteous* ditty new deviz'd, . . . IV. viii. 12. 2
most was moved at the *piteous* vew, . . . IV. viii. 20. 3
when my *piteous* plaints he heares, . . . IV. xii. 7. 4
pils the poore in *piteous* wize; . . . V. ii. 6. 8
Unmov'd with praiers or with *piteous* thought, . . . V. ii. 23. 2
Does make her selfe misfortunes *piteous* pray . . . V. ii. 50. 5
that *piteous* storie, which befell . . . V. iii. 31. 1
sent them home to tell a *piteous* tale . . . V. iv. 24. 8
To heare the *piteous* beast pleading . . . V. iv. 40. 9
There then a *piteous* slaughter did begin; . . . V. vii. 35. 5
Come home to her in *piteous* wretchednesse, . . . V. vii. 39. 5
With *piteous* ruth of her so wretched plight, . . . V. ix. 50. 2
Much was he moved with her *piteous* plight, . . . V. x. 22. 1
with *piteous* sound Of his shrill cries . . . VI. i. 11. 5
had reft That *piteous* spoile . . . VI. i. 18. 5
made such *piteous* mourning therewithall, . . . VI. i. 34. 8
Weeping to him in vaine and making *piteous* woe. . . . VI. ii. 10. 9
Drawne with that Ladies loud and *piteous* shright, . . . VI. iv. 2. 3
all the woods with *piteous* plaints did fill, . . . VI. iv. 18. 2
now lie In *piteous* languor . . . VI. vi. 6. 7
triumpest in the *piteous* spoile Of these . . . VI. vi. 25. 3
all her *piteous* plaint they did refuse, . . . VI. vii. 40. 4
her to leave in such a *piteous* plight: . . . VI. viii. 33. 5
O *pittious* worke of Mutability, . . . VII. vi. 6. 7
She meanes at last to make her *pitious* spoyle. . . . *Am.* xli. 12
The *piteous* passion of his dying smart. . . . *Am.* xlviii. 12
they playne, and make ful *piteous* mone . . . *H.L.* 127
pierst the *piteous* hart Of that deare Lord . . . *H.H.L.* 156

Piteously. shee wept and waild so *pityouslie,* . . . *T.M.* 535
seeing her so *piteouslie* perplexed, . . . *Ti.* 20
Would make to melt, or *pitteously* appall; . . . III. vii. 9. 7
mournefull notes full *piteously* did frame, . . . IV. viii. 4. 2
Great sorts of lovers *piteously* complayning, . . . IV. x. 43. 2
piteously complaind her carefull grieffe, . . . IV. xii. 5. 3
His wofull Ladie, *piteously* complayning . . . VI. ii. 41. 2
beat her breast, and *piteously* her selfe torment. . . . VI. v. 4. 9
Unto her prayers *piteously* enclynd, . . . VI. vii. 37. 3
full *pitiously* lamenting, . . . *Epig.* iv. 41

Pith. Shortly within her inmost *pith* there bred . . . *Van.* vii. 6
the steele had pierced his *pitth,* . . . *S.C.* F. 217
Like an old Oke, whose *pith* and sap is seare, . . . IV. iii. 9. 8

Pithy. with *pitthy* words, and counsell sad, . . . II. ii. 28. 5

Pitied. There lyeth the Oake, *pitied* of none! . . . *S.C.* F. 221
All were it of my foe, then fonly *pitied:* . . . *S.C.* May 58
if neede were, *pitied* would be, . . . *S.C.* May 59
pittied is mishappe that nas remedie, . . . *S.C.* May 61
She knew him not, but *pittied* much his case, . . . IV. viii. 12. 8
Well she it markt, and *pittied* the more, . . . VI. xii. 8. 1

Pities. *pities* all this while His mournefull plight, . . . I. v. 18. 7
even to thinke thereof it inly *pitties* mee. . . . IV. xi. 1. 9

Pitieth. none living *pittieth* our paine. . . . *T.M.* 354

Pitiful. So *pitifull* a thing is Suters state! . . . *Hub.* 891
Great pleasure, mixt with *pittiful* regard, . . . I. xii. 16. 1
they his *pittifull* adventures heard; . . . I. xii. 16. 3
Pitifull spectacle of deadly smart, . . . II. i. 40. 1
Pitifull spectacle, as ever eie did vew! . . . II. i. 40. 9
Him stayd from yielding *pitifull* redresse, . . . II. v. 24. 4
With percing wordes and *pittifull* implore, . . . II. v. 37. 5
when those *pittifull* outcries he heard . . . III. viii. 30. 5
your *pitifull* complaint Hath fownd another partner . . . III. ix. 40. 1
Empierced was with *pittifull* regard, . . . V. v. 13. 2
Wayling, and raysing *pittifull* uprore, . . . V. ix. 8. 8
And his sad Ladie left in *pitifull* affright: . . . VI. iv. 1. 9
pittifull complaints which there she made, . . . VI. x. 44. 2
Empierced be with *pittifull* remorse, . . . *H.H.L.* 247

Pitifully. I mourne, and *pitifully* mone, . . . *T.M.* 167
one that wayld and *pittifully* wept, . . . II. xii. 27. 3
all scorcht and *pittifully* brent. . . . III. xi. 26. 9
For which it loudly cald, and *pittifully* cryde. . . . VI. xii. 8. 9

Pitiless. *pitilesse* throwne downe in pit of fire. . . . *Rev.* iii. 14
we mourne and *pittilesse* complaine, . . . *T.M.* 353
with most cruell hand him murdred *pittilesse.* . . . II. x. 35. 9
Guyon broke downe with rigour *pittilesse;* . . . II. xii. 83. 2
with *pitilesse* remorse . . . did wend, . . . IV. ii. 15. 3
Fayre be ye sure, but proud and *pittilesse,* . . . *Am.* lvi. 5

Pits. *See* **Eye-pits.**
dull eies, deepe sunck in hollow *pits,* . . . I. viii. 41. 1

Pit-side. An hundred times about the *pit side* fares . . . IV. xii. 17. 8

Pity. For *pitie* and love my heart yet burnes . . . *Pet.*[1] v. 12
For ruth and *pitie* of so haples plight: . . . *Pet.*[2] v. 13
'Ye Gods of love, that *pitie* lovers payne, . . . *S.C.* Ja. 13
(If any gods the paine of lovers *pitie*) . . . *S.C.* Ja. 14
Pitie the paines that thou thy selfe didst prove. . . . *S.C.* Ja. 18
Ah for *pittie!* wil rancke Winters rage . . . *S.C.* F. 1
Thomalin, I *pittie* thy plight, . . . *S.C.* Mar. 103
Great *pittie* is, he be in such taking, . . . *S.C.* Ap. 156
their fondnesse inly I *pitie:* . . . *S.C.* May 38
That some good body woulde once *pitie* mee!' . . . *S.C.* May 248
breake your sounder sleepe, And *pitie* augment.' . . . *S.C.* Au. 192
The praise of *pitie* vanisht is in vaine, . . . *Gn.* 358
might it you in *pitie* please t' afford, . . . *Hub.* 251
deignes to *pitie* a perplexed hart; . . . *T.M.* 424
All those (O *pitie!*) now are turnd to dust, . . . *Ti.* 97
for *pittie* of the sad wayment . . . *Ti.* 390
in himselfe be moov'd to *pittie* mee.' . . . *Ti.* 469
Was (O great *pitie!*) built of brickle clay, . . . *Ti.* 499

Pity—*Continued.*
Distraught twixt feare and *pitie;* . . . *Ti.* 579
I for *pittie* of his heavie plight . . . *D.* 170
pitie me that living thus doo die; . . . *D.* 383
for pure *pitie* of my sufferance meeke, . . . *D.* 389
Yet *pittie* me in your empassiond spright, . . . *D.* 515
In *pitie* of my undeserv'd distresse, . . . *D.* 531
if in him found *pity* ever place, . . . *As.* Pr. 17
moov'd to *pity* such a case. . . . *As.* Pr. 18
great ruth and *pittie* To travailers, . . . *Col.* 114
Who shall me *pittie,* when thou doest me wrong?' . . . *Col.* 171
tourn Sweet layes of love to endlesse plaints of *pittie.* . . . *Col.* 387
Craving of you, in *pitty* of my state, . . . I. ii. 26. 3
When such I see, . . . all for *pitty* I could dy. . . . I. iii. 1. 9
in *pittie* of my sad estate: . . . I. iii. 7. 5
With *pittie* calmd downe fell his angry mood. . . . I. iii. 8. 5
But full great *pittie,* that so faire a mould . . . I. iv. 5. 3
pitty in her hart was never prov'd Till then, . . . I. v. 24. 8
gin to *pittie* her unhappie state: . . . I. vi. 9. 7
Are wonne with *pitty* and unwonted ruth; . . . I. vi. 12. 7
That it would *pitty* any living eie. . . . I. vi. 43. 6
with percing point Of *pitty* deare his hart . . . I. viii. 39. 2
For *pitty* of his payne . . . I. x. 28. 7
I note whether praise or *pitty* more; . . . I. xii. 17. 4
Great *pitty* is to see you thus dismayd, . . . II. i. 14. 3
deare Lady, which the ymage art Of ruefull *pitty* . . . II. i. 44. 5
in *pitty* of their harmes, . . . II. ii. 27. 3
we may *pitty* such unhappie bale, . . . II. ii. 45. 3
Ne let thy stout hart melt in *pitty* vayne: . . . II. v. 24. 6
pittie could find place, . . . II. vi. 33. 2
helpe, he saw, he needed more Then *pitty,* . . . II. vi. 48. 9
But O great *pitty!* that no lenger time . . . II. ix. 21. 7
stird with *pitty* of the stressed plight . . . II. x. 37. 3
courage hath inclind Through foolish *pitty,* . . . II. xii. 29. 2
it great *pitty* was to see . . . II. xii. 79. 3
Pitty our playnt, and yield us meet reliefe.' . . . III. iii. 21. 3
pitty perced through her tender hart. . . . III. v. 30. 9
'Great *pitty* sure that ye be so forlorne . . . III. vi. 21. 3
Ne ever *pitty* may relent his malice hard. . . . III. vi. 39. 9
Yet *pitty* often did the gods relent, . . . III. vi. 40. 1
Her hart was pierst with *pitty* at the sight, . . . III. vi. 40. 5
pitty did the Virgins hart of patience rob. . . . III. xi. 8. 9
nothing so much *pitty* doth implore . . . III. xi. 18. 5
I with teares full oft doe *pittie* it, . . . IV. i. 1. 8
with passion great And griefull *pittie* . . . IV. i. 16. 4
For *pitie* that ye want a fellow for your ayd.' . . . IV. i. 33. 9
'Alas! for *pittie* that so faire a crew, . . . IV. v. 18. 3
pittie is to heare the perils which she tride. . . . IV. vii. 2. 9
Ne care he had, ne *pittie* of the pray, . . . IV. vii. 8. 4
'Thy ruefull plight I *pitty* as mine owne. . . . IV. vii. 19. 2
Moved with *pity* of her plenteous teares. . . . IV. vii. 23. 4
pitty much his plight, that liv'd like outcast thrall. . . . IV. vii. 43. 9
ah for *pittie!* . . . IV. xi. 1. 1
toucht with soft remorse and *pitty* rare; . . . IV. xii. 12. 5
fowly did array Withouten *pitty* . . . V. ii. 25. 8
Yet for no *pitty* would he change . . . V. ii. 26. 1
through *pittie* of his causelesse smart. . . . V. v. 43. 9
those, whom she to *pitie* had allured, . . . V. ix. 39. 8
came *Pittie* with full tender hart, . . . V. ix. 45. 3
Ne would he spare for *pitty,* . . . VI. i. 17. 9
Neither of other taking *pitty* nor remorse. . . . VI. i. 33. 9
being moov'd with *pittie* of my plight . . . VI. ii. 23. 2
For *pitty* of his Dame whom she saw so diseased. . . . VI. iii. 32. 9
That *pitty* craves, as he of woman was yborne.' . . . VI. iii. 41. 9
But most for *pitty* of his dearest Dame, . . . VI. iii. 43. 7
man, that never . . . Did taste of *pittie,* . . . VI. iv. 3. 2
For *pitty* so to see him overset: . . . VI. v. 22. 5
they to *pitty* turnd their former rage, . . . VI. v. 30. 8
prayd to *pitty* his ill plight. . . . VI. vi. 20. 9
Did counterfeit kind *pittie* . . . VI. vii. 18. 4
Ne ought that foole for *pitty* did him spare, . . . VI. vii. 49. 3
Without regard of *pitty* or of awe? . . . VI. viii. 6. 5
To *pitty* him that list to play the foole; . . . VI. viii. 21. 4
would rew And *pitty* her sad plight, . . . VI. xi. 2. 9
seeing them for tender *pittie* wept; . . . VI. xi. 37. 7
seeing there that did him *pittie* sore, . . . VI. xii. 9. 6
passing joy, which did all into *pitty* melt. . . . VI. xii. 21. 9
Or looke with *pitty* on my payneful smart; . . . *Am.* xviii. 8
To spill were *pitty,* but to save were prayse! . . . *Am.* xxxviii. 12
many thou hast pricked . . . That *pitty* never found: . . . *Epig.* iv. 38
some *pitty* take, When thou doest spoyle of lovers make.' . . . *Epig.* iv. 39
no one drop of *pitie* there doth rest. . . . *H.L.* 147

Pitying. *pittying* hys heavinesse, . . . *S.C.* May 259
pittying this paire of lovers trew, . . . *As.* 182
pittying his peoples ill, . . . III. iii. 35. 8
As *pittying* to see her waile and weepe: . . . III. viii. 21. 8
gazed on their harmes, not *pittying* their estate. . . . IV. ii. 20. 9
Whom *pitying* to heare so sore complaine, . . . VI. iv. 23. 3

Pity's. For *pitties* sake compassion our paine, . . . *T.M.* 346
Percing his hart, with *pities* point did thrill; . . . VI. iv. 18. 5

Place. *See* **Being-place, Commonplace, Dwelling-place, Resting-place.**
The *place* where is the temple of the Gods, . . . *Bel.*[1] vi. 8
joyne There in one *place* all pleasures . . . *Bel.*[1] x. 6
rout . . . assembled on the *place,* . . . *Bel.*[1] x. 12
devoure The spring, the *place,* and all . . . *Pet.* iv. 11
In which all worlds felicitie had *place,* . . . *Bel.*[2] x. 7
A troupe of Satyres in the *place* did rout, . . . *Bel.*[2] xii. 12
Ne suffred him in anie *place* to rest, . . . *Van.* iv. 9
Jove himselfe, the patron of the *place,* . . . *Van.* xi. 10

Place—*Continued.*

'I see Calliope speede her to the *place*, . . . *S.C.* Ap. 100
She shal be a Grace, To fyll the fourth *place*, . . . *S.C.* Ap. 116
when you come whereas shee is in *place*, . . . *S.C.* Ap. 131
Lo! Collin, here the *place* . . . *S.C.* Jun. 1
There is a hyllye *place*, . . . *S.C.* Jul. 58
spake to him in *place*. . . . *S.C.* Jul. 160
'Let stremes of teares supply the *place* of sleepe; . . . *S.C.* Au. 163
O pierlesse Poesye! where is then thy *place?* . . . *S.C.* O. 79
as the springe gives *place* to elder time, . . . *S.C.* D. 73
The verie nature of the *place*, . . . *Gn.* 185
In this so pleasant *place* . . . *Gn.* 233
at his wonted time in that same *place* . . . *Gn.* 249
Lying along before him in that *place*, . . . *Gn.* 267
Abides in highest *place* above the best, . . . *Gn.* 614
Eftsoones he gins to fashion forth a *place;* . . . *Gn.* 650
To anie service, or to anie *place?* . . . *Hub.* 121
not to anie certaine trade or *place*, . . . *Hub.* 130
A good yeoman he was of honest *place*, . . . *Hub.* 230
if that anie other *place* you have, . . . *Hub.* 277
The bread of life powr'd downe from heavenly *place*. . . . *Hub.* 438
Resembling Aarons glorie in his *place:* . . . *Hub.* 463
in highest *place*, t' approach him nigh, . . . *Hub.* 470
in his liking to winne worthie *place*, . . . *Hub.* 776
men, which never came in *place* Of worlds affaires, . . . *Hub.* 834
Ne ever stayd in *place*, ne spake to wight, . . . *Hub.* 938
none shall name the number of his *place?* . . . *Hub.* 982
none, but whom he list, might come in *place*. . . . *Hub.* 1188
Unto the *place* where his prescript did showe. . . . *Hub.* 1261
Each *place* abounding with fowle injuries, . . . *Hub.* 1305
Each *place* defilde with blood of guiltles beasts, . . . *Hub.* 1307
Was ever heard such wayling in this *place*. . . . *T.M.* 18
Those now renew, as fitter for this *place*. . . . *T.M.* 378
Of greatest ones he, greatest in his *place*, . . . *Ti.* 187
Fled back too soone unto his native *place;* . . . *Ti.* 291
Soone after this a Giaunt came in *place*, . . . *Ti.* 533
pastures on the pleasures of each *place*. . . . *Mui.* 176
Before them stands the God of Seas in *place*, . . . *Mui.* 313
The signe by which he chalengeth the *place;* . . . *Mui.* 317
worthie of a better *place* was she: . . . *D.* 366
I will withdraw me to some darksome *place*, . . . *D.* 486
When ye doo heare me in that desert *place* . . . *D.* 508
place my dolefull plaint your plaints emong. . . . *As.* Pr. 6
if in him found pity ever *place*, . . . *As.* Pr. 17
By fate or fortune came unto the *place*, . . . *As.* 141
when I asked from what *place* he came, . . . *Col.* 64
The *place* appointed where it should be doone. . . . *Col.* 127
in the highest *place*, Urania, sister unto Astrofell, . . . *Col.* 486
Well worthie of so honourable *place*, . . . *Col.* 502
Why didst thou ever leave that happie *place*, . . . *Col.* 654
life, . . . to lead in that same *place*, . . . *Col.* 689
Ne is there *place* for any gentle wit, . . . *Col.* 707
Ne mongst true lovers they shall *place* inherit, . . . *Col.* 893
So hie her thoughts as she her selfe have *place*, . . . *Col.* 937
In this same Pageaunt have a worthy *place*, . . . *Ded. Son.* vi. 6
for your worthinesse . . . have your deserved *place* . . . *Ded. Son.* xi. 2
Here eke of right have you a worthie *place*, . . . *Ded. Son.* xi. 5
Whose girland now is set in highest *place*, . . . *Ded. Son.* xiii. 2
You, fairest Lady, leave out of this *place;* . . . *Ded. Son.* xvi. 2
the *place* unknowne and wilde, . . . I. i. 12. 3
'the perill of this *place* I better wot then you: . . . I. i. 13. 1
'this is no *place* for living men.' . . . I. i. 13. 9
Her filthie parbreake all the *place* defiled has. . . . I. i. 20. 9
shall thee well rewarde to shew the *place*, . . . I. i. 31. 6
Then was she fayre alone, when none was faire in *place*. . . . I. ii. 38. 9
Her angels face . . . made a sunshine in the shady *place;* . . . I. iii. 4. 8
to seeke adventure in straunge *place;* . . . I. iii. 29. 2
Deare Sir, what ever that thou be in *place:* . . . I. iii. 37. 3
Great troupes of people . . . of each degree and *place;* . . . I. iv. 3. 2
Which with their presence fayre the *place* much beautifide. . . . I. iv. 7. 9
upriseth from her stately *place* The roiall Dame, . . . I. iv. 16. 1
They backe retourned to the princely *Place;* . . . I. iv. 38. 3
In haste Duessa from her *place* arose, . . . I. v. 14. 1
comes unto the *place* where th' Hethen knight, . . . I. v. 19. 4
dreaded Night in brightest day hath *place*, . . . I. v. 24. 4
I scarse in darksome *place* Could it discerne, . . . I. v. 27. 5
they be come at length Unto the *place* . . . I. v. 29. 2
With smoake and sulphur hiding all the *place*, . . . I. v. 31. 5
They all, beholding worldly wights in *place*, . . . I. v. 36. 1
Unto the *place* they come incontinent: . . . I. vi. 8. 5
The wyld woodgods, arrived in the *place*, . . . I. vi. 9. 1
soone he came, as he the *place* had ghest, . . . I. vi. 40. 4
to tell . . . will need another *place*. . . . I. vi. 48. 9
Upbrayd, for leaving her in *place* unmeet, . . . I. vii. 3. 8
such as she her selfe was then in *place*. . . . I. vii. 5. 7
From top to toe no *place* appeared bare, . . . I. vii. 29. 6
This was the auncient keeper of that *place*, . . . I. viii. 31. 7
'When I awoke, and found her *place* devoyd, . . . I. ix. 15. 1
washed all her *place* with watry eyen. . . . I. ix. 15. 4
'Next to that Ladies love, shalbe the *place*, . . . I. ix. 17. 2
had bene partaker of the *place*. . . . I. ix. 26. 9
when ye arrive in that same *place;* . . . I. ix. 32. 8
Arise, sir Knight; arise, and leave this cursed *place*.' . . . I. ix. 53. 9
That aged Dame, the Lady of the *place*, . . . I. x. 8. 2
an errant knight to see Here in this *place;* . . . I. x. 10. 2
two most goodly virgins came in *place*, . . . I. x. 12. 2
he laid him privily Downe in a darksome lowly *place* . . . I. x. 25. 7
The second was as Almner of the *place:* . . . I. x. 38. 1
shortly back returne unto this *place*, . . . I. x. 64. 3
*many bloudie battailes fought in *place* . . . I. x. 65. 3

Place—*Continued.*

the *place* where all our perilles dwell; . . . I. xi. 2. 2
found no *place* his deadly point to rest. . . . I. xi. 17. 4
Up rose the gentle virgin from her *place*, . . . I. xi. 33. 5
All were she daily with himselfe in *place*, . . . I. xii. 23. 7
signes, here sett in sondrie *place*, . . . II. Pr. 4. 2
from his head no *place* appeared to his feete. . . . II. i. 5. 9
Would God! thy selfe now present were in *place* . . . II. i. 9. 8
Which to avenge he to this *place* me led, . . . II. i. 30. 7
were renowmd, and sought from *place* to *place*. . . . II. ii. 6. 9
turning to that *place*, . . . II. ii. 11. 5
in that *place* straunge knight arrived . . . II. ii. 19. 7
ere they could proceede unto the *place* . . . II. ii. 20. 1
Sith last I left that honorable *place*, . . . II. ii. 44. 3
Still cald upon to kill him in the *place*. . . . II. iv. 9. 4
he came unto th' appointed *place*, . . . II. iv. 28. 1
Abandon this forestalled *place* at erst, . . . II. iv. 39. 3
'Varlet, this *place* most dew to me I deeme, . . . II. iv. 40. 1
to that same *place* where first she wefte. . . . II. vi. 18. 9
pittie could find *place*, . . . II. vi. 33. 2
Of every *place* that was with bruzing harmd, . . . II. vi. 51. 4
'What secret *place* . . . can safely hold . . . II. vii. 20. 1
found no *place* wher safe he shroud him might: . . . II. vii. 22. 7
Ne ever could within one *place* be fownd, . . . II. vii. 31. 6
Another blis before mine eyes I *place*, . . . II. vii. 33. 3
More fitt emongst black fiendes then men to have his *place*. . . . II. vii. 41. 9
The Palmer seeing his lefte empty *place*, . . . II. viii. 9. 1
left his headlesse body bleeding all the *place*. . . . II. viii. 52. 9
Suffise that I have done my dew in *place*.' . . . II. viii. 56. 6
Behold, who list, both one and other in this *place*. . . . II. ix. 1. 9
Nine was the circle sett in heavens *place:* . . . II. ix. 22. 8
Soone as the gracious Alma came in *place*, . . . II. ix. 36. 1
Next Memprise, as unworthy of that *place;* . . . II. x. 21. 3
Arvirage his brothers *place* supplyde . . . II. x. 51. 6
Whose emptie *place* the mightie Oberon Doubly supplide, . . . II. x. 75. 8
round about in fittest steades did *place*, . . . II. xi. 6. 2
In strong entrenchments he did closely *place*, . . . II. xi. 6. 7
The noble Virgin, Ladie of the *Place*, . . . II. xi. 16. 1
groveling to the ground he fell, and fild his *place*. . . . II. xi. 34. 9
A daungerous and detestable *place*, . . . II. xii. 8. 2
A *place* pickt out by choyce of best alyve, . . . II. xii. 42. 3
They in that *place* him Genius did call: . . . II. xii. 47. 1
the fayre aspect Of that sweet *place*, . . . II. xii. 53. 2
The art which all that wrought appeared in no *place*. . . . II. xii. 58. 9
Some goodly swayne of honorable *place*, . . . II. xii. 79. 2
of the fayrest late, now made the fowlest *place*. . . . II. xii. 83. 9
To weet if they would turne backe to that *place;* . . . III. i. 19. 5
rome from *place* to *place* . . . III. i. 22. 4
Mote Princes *place* be seeme so deckt to bee. . . . III. i. 33. 4
go to see that dreadful *place*. . . . III. iii. 8. 2
Was never so great waste in any *place*, . . . III. iii. 34. 5
retourning to his native *place*, . . . III. iii. 41. 5
comming to the *place*, . . . III. iv. 34. 7
Out of her fleshly ferme fled to the *place* of paine. . . . III. v. 23. 9
As did Belphoebe, in the bloody *place*, . . . III. v. 37. 3
Beside the same a dainty *place* there lay, . . . III. v. 40. 1
Thou, a meane Squyre of meeke and lowly *place;* . . . III. v. 47. 3
Whence he it fetcht out of her native *place*, . . . III. v. 52. 4
The higher *place* in her Heroick mynd: . . . III. v. 55. 5
Fayre Amoretta in the second *place:* . . . III. vi. 4. 5
to search from *place* to *place*, . . . III. vi. 25. 8
So faire a *place* as Nature can devize: . . . III. vi. 29. 3
the *place*, to which her hope did guyde, . . . III. vii. 5. 8
She grew familiare in that desert *place*. . . . III. vii. 15. 5
Till her he had attaind and brought in *place*, . . . III. vii. 23. 4
ere the stroke could seize his aymed *place*, . . . III. vii. 40. 3
seeing none in *place*, he gan to make Exceeding mone, . . . III. vii. 45. 3
for want of handsome time and *place*, . . . III. vii. 60. 4
why she could not come in *place;* . . . III. ix. 26. 2
none of those excuses could take *place*, . . . III. ix. 26. 5
in open *place* and commune bord . . . III. x. 6. 5
Nought wants but time and *place*, . . . III. x. 11. 6
Ne wist he how to turne, nor to what *place:* . . . III. x. 14. 8
till he came unto the *place* . . . III. x. 54. 1
the flame; the which eftesoones gave *place*, . . . III. xi. 25. 4
The goodly ordinaunce of this rich *Place*, . . . III. xi. 53. 2
solemne silence over all that *place:* . . . III. xi. 53. 7
His rolling eies did never rest in *place*, . . . III. xii. 15. 6
Soone as that virgin knight he saw in *place*, . . . III. xii. 32. 1
the *place*, where late She left Sir Scudamour . . . III. xii. 43. *or.* 1
The custome of that *place* was such, . . . IV. i. 9. 7
manie by in *place* That present were . . . IV. i. 49. 4
fayrest Florimell was present there in *place*. . . . IV. ii. 22. 9
in privie *place* Did spend her dayes, . . . IV. ii. 44. 8
lightly lept out of his *place* of rest, . . . IV. iii. 22. 6
where so he came in *place*, . . . IV. iv. 4. 4
Unto the *place* of turneyment they came; . . . IV. iv. 13. 6
the hardy Satyrane Appear'd in *place*, . . . IV. iv. 26. 3
So fitly now here commeth next in *place*, . . . IV. v. 2. 1
an hundred Ladies moe Appear'd in *place*, . . . IV. v. 11. 9
Assembled in one *place:* . . . IV. v. 12. 6
Yet not fit *place* he thought it . . . IV. v. 27. 8
Her list no longer in that *place* abide; . . . IV. v. 29. 2
Oft chaunging sides, and oft new *place* electing, . . . IV. v. 40. 3
every *place* seem'd painefull, . . . IV. v. 40. 9
gave *place* to kindly rest, . . . IV. v. 43. 4
a privy *place*, betwixt us hight, . . . IV. vii. 17. 7
in that *place* where I him thought to find, . . . IV. vii. 18. 2
that same gentle Squire arriv'd in *place* . . . IV. vii. 24. 3
The *place* there overflowne seemd . . . IV. vii. 32. 9

Place—*Continued.*

the *place* where late She left the gentle Squire . . . IV. vii. 35. 1
fit solitary *place* For wofull wight, . . . IV. vii. 38. 5
In th' end she her unto that *place* did guide, . . . IV. viii. 11. 8
weend that he had beene some man of *place,* . . . IV. viii. 14. 4
It would have cleft him to the girding *place;* . . . IV. viii. 43. 8
twixt themselves they pointed time and *place:* . . . IV. viii. 51. 1
Having a keeper still with him in *place;* . . . IV. viii. 54. 4
not ever in one *place,* . . . IV. ix. 10. 4
By fortune in that *place* did chance to light: . . . IV. ix. 28. 3
purchase me some *place* amongst the best. . . . IV. x. 4. 5
to the *place* of perill shortly came: . . . IV. x. 5. 2
'That was to weet the Porter of the *place,* . . . IV. x. 12. 1
The onely pleasant and delightfull *place* . . . IV. x. 21. 4
in this joyous *place* they mote have joyance . . . IV. x. 23. 9
Unto that purposd *place* I did me draw, . . . IV. x. 29. 3
most adorne thy *place;* . . . IV. x. 44. 3
That same was fayrest Amoret in *place,* . . . IV. x. 52. 8
They saw it all, and present were in *place;* . . . IV. xi. 40. 6
To view the building of that uncouth *place,* . . . IV. xii. 4. 6
inforced to give *place* Unto the passion . . . IV. xii. 8. 6
When he in *place* his dearest love did spy; . . . IV. xii. 35. 2
Which to another *place* I leave to be perfected. . . . IV. xii. 35. 9
his *place* he shifted hath in sight, . . . V. Pr. 8. 5
Where she hath now an everlasting *place* . . . V. i. 11. 5
In that same *place* whereas it now doth lie. . . . V. i. 18. 7
When to the *place* they came, . . . V. i. 23. 1
place deserved with the Gods on hy. . . . V. ii. 1. 7
Unto the *place* he came within a while, . . . V. ii. 11. 1
whatsoever from one *place* doth fall . . . V. ii. 39. 7
The time and *place* was blazed farre and wide, . . . V. iii. 2. 5
Artegall, arriv'd in *place,* . . . V. iv. 23. 5
with faire words, fit for the time and *place,* . . . V. v. 55. 6
had sought for ease In every *place,* . . . V. vi. 7. 2
every *place* thought best, . . . V. vi. 7. 2
found no *place* that could her liking please, . . . V. vi. 7. 3
Ne would she stay till he in *place* could come, . . . V. vi. 8. 8
By change of *place* seeking to ease her paine; . . . V. vi. 15. 5
one thought, That gave none other *place.* . . . V. vi. 21. 4
kept her *place* with courage confident, . . . V. vi. 28. 4
heavenly honours in the highest *place;* . . . V. vii. 2. 4
change of aire and *place* Would change her paine, . . . V. vii. 45. 3
bringing them to their appointed *place,* . . . V. viii. 27. 1
fled from *place* to *place.* . . . V. viii. 36. 9
Flying from *place* to *place* with cowheard shame; . . . V. viii. 50. 8
resolving now to leave the *place,* . . . V. ix. 3. 3
I would you guyde directly to the *place.'* . . . V. ix. 7. 7
over rockes, and hilles, and every *place* Where so he fled, . . . V. ix. 16. 4
Nigh to the *place* which ye desir'd to see: . . . V. ix. 20. 5
When these two stranger knights arriv'd in *place,* . . . V. ix. 36. 2
A Ladie of great countenance and *place,* . . . V. ix. 38. 2
new accusements to produce in *place:* . . . V. ix. 47. 2
meriteth to have as high a *place,* . . . V. x. 1. 6
Unto some *place* where they mote rest . . . V. x. 22. 7
Some *place* shall us receive . . . V. x. 24. 2
The Ladie counseld him the *place* to shonne, . . . V. x. 30. 8
leveld all against one certaine *place,* . . . V. x. 34. 7
sent . . . unto her *place* of punishment. . . . V. x. 36. 9
prayd the *place* of her abode to learne; . . . V. xi. 21. 3
nigh fild all the *place,* . . . V. xi. 23. 2
Till nigh unto the *place* at length approcht . . . V. xi. 36. 9
time and *place* convenient to areed, . . . V. xii. 9. 3
comming to the *place,* and finding there . . . V. xii. 12. 6
The which in all mens liking gayned *place,* . . . VI. i. 3. 4
in what *place* To find him out, . . . VI. i. 7. 4
thee captyved in this shamefull *place?'* . . . VI. i. 12. 4
he should be soone in *place.'* . . . VI. i. 28. 6
ere he came in *place,* . . . VI. ii. 4. 6
he turned backe Unto the *place* where me he left . . . VI. ii. 21. 3
But wayt on him in every *place* and part: . . . VI. ii. 36. 5
Came to the *place* whereas ye heard afore . . . VI. ii. 40. 4
How thence she might convay him to some *place;* . . . VI. ii. 47. 2
Let none therefore, that is in meaner *place,* Too greatly grieve VI. iii. 5. 8
the *place,* . . . dight With divers flowres . . . VI. iii. 23. 4
Forst to forgoe his pray there in the *place,* . . . VI. iii. 25. 7
the *place* where he his Lady found In dolorous dismay . . . VI. iii. 27. 2
Till to some *place* of rest they mote attaine, . . . VI. iii. 28. 7
He chaunst to spie a faire and stately *place,* . . . VI. iii. 29. 7
An armed Knight approaching to the *place* . . . VI. iii. 30. 7
aunswer'd, that there was no *place* Of lodging . . . VI. iii. 38. 7
the other came in *place* likewise, . . . VI. iii. 48. 1
he him still pursew'd from *place* to *place,* . . . VI. iii. 49. 1
return'd againe With speede unto the *place,* . . . VI. iv. 9. 4
To bring him to the *place* where he would faine, . . . VI. iv. 24. 5
fynd Some *place* of succour to content his mynd, . . . VI. iv. 26. 5
when as she perceived A stranger wight in *place,* . . . VI. iv. 27. 2
Be lacke of children to supply your *place,* . . . VI. iv. 35. 2
Agreeing well both with the *place* and season, . . . VI. iv. 37. 5
she cast to leave the *place,* . . . VI. v. 7. 2
He gan to shrinke and somewhat to give *place,* . . . VI. v. 21. 3
seeke some *place* the which mote yeeld some ease . . . VI. v. 32. 2
Whom when the Hermite present saw in *place,* . . . VI. v. 36. 2
appointed have her *place* Mongst rocks and caves, . . . VI. vi. 11. 3
the Salvage, comming now in *place,* . . . VI. vi. 22. 1
fled from roome to roome, from *place* to *place,* . . . VI. vi. 29. 6
Untill fit time and *place* he mote espy, . . . VI. vii. 3. 4
Backe to the *place* where Turpine late he lore; . . . VI. vii. 14. 2
needs with him streight to the *place* would ryde, . . . VI. vii. 17. 2
he and his fellow there in *place* Were vanquished, . . . VI. vii. 21. 4
out of the wood issew'd Backe to the *place,* . . . VI. vii. 23. 9

Place—*Continued.*

lifted up to honorable *place,* . . . VI. vii. 28. 2
whilest love lackt *place,* . . . VI. vii. 38. 7
The witnesse of his wretchednesse in *place,* . . . VI. viii. 5. 2
Whether to slay her there upon the *place,* . . . VI. viii. 37. 7
round about her they them selves did *place* . . . VI. viii. 39. 1
From pitch of higher *place* unto this low degree.' . . . VI. ix. 28. 9
Tooke Coridon and set him in his *place,* . . . VI. ix. 42. 2
Shall more conveniently in other *place* be ended. . . . VI. ix. 46. 9
Unto a *place* whose pleasaunce did appere . . . VI. x. 5. 4
used to resort Unto this *place,* . . . VI. x. 9. 3
Unto this *place* when as the Elfin Knight . . . VI. x. 10. 1
Thy love is present there with thee in *place;* . . . VI. x. 16. 8
being gone, none can them bring in *place,* . . . VI. x. 20. 4
for more honor brought her to this *place,* . . . VI. x. 26. 8
quite are dimmed when she is in *place:* . . . VI. x. 27. 8
underneath thy feete to *place* her prayse; . . . VI. x. 28. 7
the *place,* whose pleasures rare . . . his sences ravished, . . . VI. x. 30. 6
when faire Pastorell Into this *place* was brought, . . . VI. x. 43. 7
how those marchants were Arriv'd in *place* . . . VI. xi. 10. 2
be his conduct trew Unto the *place,* . . . VI. xi. 35. 4
to the *place* when they approched nye, . . . VI. xi. 36. 5
all the *place* with swarmes do overlay, . . . VI. xi. 48. 3
to his love sometimes he came in *place;* . . . VI. xii. 6. 3
Bedeaw'd with teares there left it in the *place:* . . . VI. xii. 8. 4
Came to the *place;* . . . VI. xii. 9. 4
Through every *place* with restlesse paine and toile . . . VI. xii. 22. 8
now no *place* besides unsought had left, . . . VI. xii. 23. 7
Him in a narrow *place* he overtooke, . . . VI. xii. 26. 1
take what fortune, time, and *place* would lend. . . . VII. vi. 23. 6
beautifull of face As any of the Goddesses in *place,*) . . . VII. vi. 28. 5
seeke by grace and goodnesse to obtaine That *place,* . . . VII. vi. 34. 3
Eftsoones the time and *place* appointed were, . . . VII. vi. 36. 1
parting from the *place,* . . . VII. vi. 55. 2
th' Ocean moveth still from *place* to *place,* . . . VII. vii. 20. 3
To whether side should fall the soveraine *place:* . . . VII. vii. 57. 7
The whiles her foot she in my necke doth *place,* . . . *Am.* xx. 3
Sits downe to rest him in some shady *place,* . . . *Am.* lxvii. 3
there to rest themselves did boldly *place.* . . . *Am.* lxxvi. 12
Lackyng my love, I go from *place* to *place,* . . . *Am.* lxxviii. 1
in their *place* doth now a third appeare, . . . *Com. Son.* iv. 9
Did *place* them all in order, . . . *H.L.* 87
a waste and emptie *place* In His wyde Pallace, . . . *H.H.L.* 101
Fell from the hope of promist heavenly *place,* . . . *H.H.L.* 122
Faire is the heaven where happy soules have *place,* . . . *H.H.B.* 78
All joy, all blisse, all happinesse, have *place;* . . . *H.H.B.* 243
from another *place* I take my name, . . . *Proth.* 130
there standes a stately *place,* . . . *Proth.* 137

Placed. *See* **Overplaced.**

under this great temple *placed* is: . . . *Bel.*[2] i. 10
Joves great Image in Olympus *placed;* . . . *Ro.* ii. 6
On which when as my thought was throghly *placed,* . . . *Van.* i. 9
he them *plac'd* in thy sacred wood . . . saw, . . . *Gn.* 169
Whom ye in goodly seates may *placed* see, . . . *Gn.* 595
Like as a Puppit *placed* in a play, . . . *Hub.* 931
He now hath *placed* his accursed brood, . . . *T.M.* 315
Sith I doo dailie see things highest *placed,* . . . *Ti.* 180
Placed on high upon an Altare faire, . . . *Ti.* 492
placed on a plot of sandie ground: . . . *Ti.* 508
those flowres, . . . She *placed* in her wings, . . . *Mui.* 142
The one upon his hardie head him *plaste,* . . . I. i. 47. 3
Hath thus transformd, and *plast* in open plaines, . . . I. ii. 33. 6
His life was nigh unto deaths dore *yplaste;* . . . I. iv. 28. 1
She is . . . *placed* under stately canapee, . . . I. v. 5. 4
in all mens open vew Duessa *placed* is, . . . I. v. 5. 7
To have her knight into her schoolehous *plaste,* . . . I. x. 18. 4
privy spyals *plast* in all his way, . . . II. i. 4. 3
On every side they *placed* were along; . . . II. vii. 30. 5
castle, *plaste* Foreby a river in a pleasaunt dale; . . . II. ix. 10. 3
Therein two gates were *placed* seemly well: . . . II. ix. 23. 1
There *placed* was a caudron wide and tall . . . II. ix. 29. 5
in another great rownd vessell *plaste,* . . . II. ix. 32. 3
In which accord the Prince was also *plaste,* . . . III. i. 12. 7
plaste for pleasure nigh that forrest syde: . . . III. i. 20. 5
in long Alba *plast* his throne apart; . . . III. ix. 43. 7
al this while was *plast* In secret shade, . . . III. xii. 27. 4
There were rent robes and broken scepters *plast;* . . . IV. i. 21. 4
As seeming *plast* in sole felicity: . . . IV. ii. 11. 4
Before that they in blisse amongst the Gods were *plaste.* . . . IV. iii. 44. 9
shee shall be *placed* here in sight, . . . IV. iv. 9. 5
that snowy Mayd Was in the middest *plast* . . . IV. v. 26. 2
Under a steepe hilles side it *placed* was, . . . IV. v. 33. 1
in the midst thereof a piller *placed;* . . . IV. x. 8. 2
her against sweet Cherefulnesse was *placed,* . . . IV. x. 50. 6
fayld the trust which she in him had *plast,* . . . IV. xii. 23. 3
Ram . . . Hath now forgot where he was *plast* of yore, . . . V. Pr. 5. 8
Amongst them all she *placed* him most low, . . . V. v. 23. 1
his hart was freely *plast.* . . . V. v. 46. 9
by the altars side her selfe to slumber *plaste.* . . . V. vii. 8. 9
placed th' one on th' one, The other on the other side, . . . V. ix. 37. 8
There eke he *placed* a strong garrisone, . . . V. x. 30. 1
the Temple, wherein she was *plast,* Did quake to heare, . . . V. xi. 28. 4
Unto a strangers love, so lightly *placed,* . . . V. xi. 63. 2
seeing in what daunger he was *plast,* . . . VI. i. 39. 7
whether they be *placed* high above Or low beneath, . . . VI. ii. 1. 5
Upon a litle hillocke she was *placed* . . . VI. ix. 8. 1
wish my lot were *plast* in such felicitie.' . . . VI. ix. 19. 9
tooke from her owne head, And *plast* on his, . . . VI. ix. 42. 7
It was an hill *plaste* in an open plaine, . . . VI. x. 6. 1
was *placed* Another Damzell, . . . VI. x. 12. 6

Placed—*Continued.*
Being now *placed* in the firmament, ... VI. x. 13. 6
one, That in the midst was *placed* paravaunt, ... VI. x. 15. 7
To be the fourth with those three other *placed:* . . . . . . VI. x. 25. 7
prises to them *placed* at their pleasure, ... VI. xi. 14. 2
chylde, which in misfortunes mouth was *plaste.* . . . . . . VI. xii. 16. 9
Hecate, in whose almighty hand He *plac't* all rule . . . . . VII. vi. 3. 4
Was *placed* in his principall Estate, ... VII. vi. 19. 4
him *placed* where he close might view . . . . VII. vi. 45. 2
She *placed* was in a pavilion; . . . . VII. vii. 8. 2
In which her glorious ymage *placed* is; . . . . *Am.* xxii. 6
Through hidden perils round about me *plast;* . . . . *Am.* xxxiv. 8
brought . . . By Love himselfe, and in his garden *plaste.* . . *Am.* lxxvii. 12
I blesse my lot, that was so lucky *placed:* . . . . *Am.* lxxxii. 2
that monster *placed* In gentle love, ... *H.L.* 271
he before his eyes had *plast* A goodly Paterne, ... *H.B.* 31
frames her house, in which she will be *placed,* . . . . . . *H.B.* 117
Placer. Thou *placer* of plants both humble and tall, ... *S.C.* F. 164
Places. *See* **Dwelling-places.**
pleasures have we in these *places.* . . . . *S.C.* Jun. 32
forsayd From *places* of delight, ... *S.C.* Jul. 70
how all *places* quake and quiver, ... *Gn.* 340
All *places* they with follie have possest, ... *T.M.* 193
All *places* with our pleasant notes to fill, ... *T.M.* 242
With fearfull howling do all *places* fill; . . . . *T.M.* 284
All *places* they doo with their toyes possesse, ... *T.M.* 325
Through her thin weed their *places* only signifide. . . . . . . II. iii. 29. 9
All other pleasaunt *places* doth excell, ... III. vi. 29. 7
Out of their proper *places* farre away, ... V. Pr. 6. 6
Are not all *places* full of forraine powres? . . . . V. x. 23. 2
still doe flie, and still their *places* vary. . . . . VII. vii. 21. 9
their dew *places* found. . . . . VII. vii. 43. 9
When so ye come into those holy *places,* . . . . *Epith.* 213
Placest. There thou them *placest* in a Paradize . . . . *H.L.* 280
Placidas. Corflambo chaseth *Placidas,* . . . . IV. viii. Arg.
Insteed of whom forth came I, *Placidas,* . . . . IV. viii. 59. 4
Her captive lovers friend, young *Placidas,* . . . . IV. viii. 63. 2
faire Aemylia beheld And *Placidas,* . . . . IV. ix. 9. 2
Plague. powr'd on th' earth *plague,* pestilence, and death. . . *Hub.* 8
To *plague* th' unrighteous which alive remaine; . . . . *D.* 359
The heavie *plague* that for such leachours is prepard. . . . . III. v. 14. 9
The shame of men, and *plague* of womankind: . . . . IV. vii. 18. 5
To be the *plague* and scourge of wretched men, ... VI. i. 8. 7
she will *plague* the man that loves her most, ... *Am.* xli. 6
The scourge of Turkes, and *plague* of infidels, ... *Com.Son.*iii.13
Plagues. Pyne, *plagues,* and dreery death. . . . . *S.C.* Jul. 24
she did pray That *plagues* . . . Might fall on her, ... I. iii. 23. 7
with *plagues* and murrins pestilent Consume, ... III. iii. 40. 8
whereas all the *plagues* and harmes abound . . . . IV. i. 20. 2
all the *plagues,* and horrid paines, of hell . . . . *Am.* lxxxv. 5
Plaid. *See* **Played.**
Plain. downe she fell upon the *plaine.* . . . . *Bel.*[1] vi. 11
That golden Pactol drives upon the *plaine.* . . . . *Bel.*[1] x. 4
I saw her on the *plaine* outstretched . . . . *Bel.*[2] vi. 12
downe she on the *plaine* was felde, ... *Bel.*[2] vii. 11
is in Winter lord of all the *plaine,* . . . . *Ro.* xiv. 2
th' auncient Plot of Rome, displayed *plaine,* . . . . *Ro.* xxvi. 13
'It is not Hobbinol wherefore I *plaine,* . . . . *S.C.* Ja. 55
Shee is my goddesse *plaine,* . . . . *S.C.* Ap. 97
Better is then the lowly *playne,* . . . . *S.C.* Jul. 7
unto his threate Is a *playne* overture. . . . . *S.C.* Jul. 28
That he purchast of me in the *playne* field: . . . . *S.C.* Au. 41
thou speakest to *plaine;* . . . . *S.C.* S. 136
must passe over to th' Elisian *plaine:* . . . . *Gn.* 421
on the Phrygian *playne* . . . He compast Troy . . . . *Gn.* 526
Gan . . . *plaine* his case with words unkinde. . . . . *Hub.* 52
this good Sir did follow the *plaine* word, ... *Hub.* 390
have I not well discourst . . . (though *plaine,* not wourst?) . *Hub.* 542
none durst of him *plaine,* . . . . *Hub.* 1199
He soft arrived on the grassie *plaine,* . . . . *Hub.* 1263
fill with pleasance every wood and *plaine.* . . . . *D.* 56
I spied playing on the grassie *playne* . . . . *D.* 110
miscaried or in *plaine* or wood. . . . . *D.* 140
more *plaine* areade this doubtfull case.' . . . . *D.* 182
Oft times to *plaine* your loves concealed smart; . . . . *As.* Pr. 2
The dowre agreed, the day assigned *plaine,* . . . . *Col.* 126
'Right well he sure did *plaine,* . . . . *Col.* 173
plaine attire such glorious gallantry Disdaines . . . . *Col.* 729
A gentle Knight was pricking on the *plaine,* . . . . I. i. 1. 1
he saw the ugly monster *plaine,* . . . . I. i. 14. 6
plain none might her see, nor she see any *plaine.* . . . . . I. i. 16. 9
waves . . . overflow each *plaine* and lowly dale: . . . . I. i. 21. 4
That path he kept which beaten was most *plaine,* . . . . . . I. i. 28. 3
each wood and *plaine,* Did search, ... I. ii. 8. 7
'Whose borrowed beautie now appeareth *plaine* . . . . I. ii. 39. 2
He leaves the welkin way most beaten *playne,* . . . . I. iv. 9. 7
They, . . . all prostrate upon the lowly *playne,* . . . . I. vi. 12. 8
Plaine, faithfull, true, and enimy of shame, ... I. vi. 20. 7
they the woods are past, and come now to the *plaine.* . . . . I. vi. 33. 9
she bad him tellen *plaine* . . . . I. vi. 37. 7
when in Cymbrian *plaine* An heard of Bulles, . . . complaine, I. viii. 11. 5
painted in a table *plaine,* The damned ghosts . . . . I. ix. 49. 6
court they see, Both *plaine* and pleasaunt . . . . I. x. 6. 3
Long he them bore above the subject *plaine,* . . . . I. xi. 19. 1
overflowed all the fertile *plaine,* . . . . I. xi. 48. 4
was their manner then but bare and *playne;* . . . . I. xii. 14. 7
Whome if ye please for to discover *plaine,* . . . . I. xii. 34. 7
under simple shew, and semblant *plaine,* Lurkt . . . . II. i. 21. 3
did begin To *plaine* of wronges, ... II. iii. 13. 5
easy is the way and passage *plaine* . . . . II. iii. 41. 7

Plain—*Continued.*
I made *plaine* and evident, ... II. iv. 29. 7
on the *plaine* fast pricking Guyon spide One . . . . II. v. 2. 2
layd him downe upon a grassy *playn;* . . . . II. vi. 14. 4
That stretcht itselfe into an ample *playne;* . . . . II. vii. 21. 2
The want thereof now greatly gan to *plaine,* . . . . II. viii. 19. 2
left inglorious on the vanquisht *playne,* . . . . II. x. 58. 2
overflow With suddein fury all the fertile *playne,* . . . . . II. xi. 18. 6
him dismounted on the *plaine* . . . . II. xi. 28. 7
yt rebownds against the lowly *playne,* . . . . II. xi. 43. 4
by the checked wave they did descry It *plaine,* . . . . . . II. xii. 18. 8
A large and spacious *plaine,* . . . . II. xii. 50. 2
through the christall waves appeared *plaine:* . . . . II. xii. 64. 7
Cannot your glorious pourtraict figure *playne,* . . . . III. Pr. 3. 7
as through an open *plaine* they yode, ... III. i. 4. 1
thou wert mett On equall *plaine,* . . . . III. i. 8. 5
faire before the gate a spatious *playne,* . . . . III. i. 20. 6
'now may ye all see *plaine,* . . . . III. i. 29. 7
That *plaine* discovered her incontinence; . . . . III. i. 48. 3
Did use to hide, and *plainc* apparaunce shonne) . . . . . . III. i. 52. 8
To her revealed in a mirrhour *playne;* . . . . III. ii. 17. 4
was loth to let her purpose *plaine* appeare; . . . . III. iii. 17. 9
Both slaine in battaile upon Layburne *playne,* . . . . III. iii. 37. 4
Whose future woes so *plaine* he fashioned; . . . . III. iii. 43. 3
feld Great Ulfin thrise upon the bloody *playne;* . . . . III. iii. 55. 6
made a lake Of Greekish blood so ofte in Trojan *plaine;* . III. iv. 2. 6
plaine In him bewraid great grudge . . . . III. iv. 61. 7
betwixt two marbles *plaine* Shee pownded small, ... III. v. 33. 1
Spreading it selfe into a spatious *plaine:* . . . . III. v. 39. 6
seemd to *plaine* With gentle murmure . . . . III. v. 39. 8
in forest and in *plaine:* . . . . III. vii. 30. 3
largely overflow the fruitfull *plaine,* . . . . III. vii. 34. 4
They spyde a knight fayre pricking on the *playne,* . . . . . III. viii. 44. 7
now it *plaine* display'd; . . . . III. x. 10. 9
One day, as hee forpassed by the *plaine* . . . . III. x. 20. 5
Paridell came pricking fast Upon the *plaine;* . . . . III. x. 35. 3
prayd her wake to heare him *plaine.* . . . . III. x. 49. 6
'What boots it *plaine* that cannot be redrest, ... III. xi. 16. 1
What boots it then to *plaine* that cannot be redrest?' . . . . III. xi. 17. 9
such as she was she *plaine* did shew; . . . . IV. i. 18. 7
As *plaine* as at the first . . . . IV. i. 24. 9
Whom when as Paridel more *plaine* beheld, ... IV. i. 34. 2
is as nigh his end as he that most doth *playne.* . . . . . . IV. iii. 1. 9
downe on the bloudy *plaine* Her selfe she threw, ... IV. iii. 47. 4
both rebutted tumble on the *plaine:* . . . . IV. iv. 18. 5
none perceiv'd it *plaine;* . . . . IV. iv. 25. 2
Full many deedes that day were shewed *plaine:* . . . . IV. iv. 37. 3
shortly was likewise seene lying on the *plaine.* . . . . IV. iv. 44. 9
they *plaine* descryde To be the same . . . . IV. vi. 9. 4
he *plaine* descride That peerelesse paterne . . . . IV. vi. 24. 4
Right *plaine* appeard, though she it would dissemble, ... IV. vi. 29. 7
What mister wight it was that so did *plaine?* . . . . IV. vii. 10. 5
all the accident there hapned *plaine,* . . . . IV. viii. 46. 7
in this storie find approved *plaine;* . . . . IV. ix. 3. 2
'Before that Castle was an open *plaine,* . . . . IV. x. 8. 1
left them groning there upon the *plaine:* . . . . IV. x. 10. 6
By miracle, not yet appearing *playne,* . . . . IV. xi. 1. 7
So went he playing on the watery *plaine;* . . . . IV. xi. 24. 1
Under the which her feet appeared *plaine,* . . . . IV. xi. 47. 5
me seemes of double wrong ye *plaine,* . . . . IV. xii. 30. 2
the truth discover *plaine,* . . . . IV. xii. 30. 7
They all are wandred much; that *plaine* appeares: . . . . . . V. Pr. 5. 5
yet he pricked over yonder *plaine,* . . . . V. i. 19. 5
by signes perceiving *plaine* . . . . V. i. 24. 6
In the wide champian of the Ocean *plaine,* . . . . V. ii. 15. 2
(which *plaine* he shewed there) . . . . V. ii. 32. 3
make them levell with the lowly *plaine;* . . . . V. ii. 38. 2
then *plaine* it did appeare, ... V. ii. 48. 7
Thereby Sir Artegall did *plaine* areed . . . . V. iii. 35. 1
shattered all to peeces round about the *plaine,* . . . . V. v. 10. 9
to her mercie him submitted in *plaine* field. . . . . V. v. 16. 9
ere him she *plaine* descride, ... V. vi. 8. 3
A Knight that softly paced on the *plaine,* . . . . V. vi. 19. 4
sure he weend . . . by many tokens *plaine;* . . . . V. vi. 34. 2
slaine By thundring Jove in the Phlegrean *plaine:* . . . . . . V. vii. 10. 5
her proud person low prostrated on the *plaine.* . . . . V. vii. 33. 9
it *plaine* to them did shew. . . . . V. viii. 37. 9
Then Artegall, himselfe discovering *plaine,* . . . . V. viii. 50. 1
Though *plaine* she saw, by all that she did heare, ... V. ix. 50. 3
They both encounter in the middle *plaine,* . . . . V. x. 32. 1
all the three attonce fell on the *plaine,* . . . . V. xi. 14. 2
foot of man might sound the bottome *plaine,* . . . . V. xii. 5. 3
There to be pitched on the open *plaine;* . . . . V. xii. 10. 2
Like as a tender Rose in open *plaine,* . . . . V. xii. 13. 1
Whom when he saw prostrated on the *plaine,* . . . . V. xii. 23. 8
being matcht with *plaine* Antiquitie, ... VI. Pr. 4. 7
He him pursu'd and chaced through the *plaine,* . . . . VI. i. 22. 7
They bene ymett in middest of the *plaine* . . . . VI. i. 33. 5
By thee no knight; which armes impugneth *plaine?'* . . . . . VI. ii. 7. 5
to meete this knight, . . . passing on the *plaine.* . . . . . . VI. ii. 9. 9
in which *plaine* is showne . . . . VI. iii. 1. 4
And by good fortune the *plaine* champion wonne: . . . . VI. iv. 26. 3
conspiring all together *plaine,* . . . . VI. v. 14. 5
towards night they came unto a *plaine,* . . . . VI. v. 34. 7
with entire affection and appearaunce *plaine.* . . . . VI. v. 38. 9
all her hinder parts did *plaine* expresse . . . . VI. vi. 10. 8
Plaine signes in him of life and livelihead: . . . . VI. vii. 20. 5
Did laugh at those that did lament and *plaine;* . . . . VI. viii. 21. 8
She from her palfrey lighted on the *plaine;* . . . . VI. viii. 32. 6
I gan my follies to my selfe to *plaine,* . . . . VI. ix. 25. 5

Plain—*Continued.*
It was an hill plaste in an open *plaine,* . . . VI. x. 6. 1
on the top thereof a spacious *plaine* . . . VI. x. 8. 1
all them *plaine* may see, . . . VI. x. 24. 4
Ran . . . unto the king of Gods to *plaine.* . . . VII. vi. 14. 9
Till to the *Plaine* she come, whose Valleyes . . . VII. vi. 41. 9
her waves passe through a pleasant *Plaine,* . . . VII. vi. 53. 7
So full they filled every hill and *Plaine;* . . . VII. vii. 4. 5
In a fayre *Plaine* upon an equall Hill . . . VII. vii. 8. 1
'To thee therefore of this same Jove I *plaine,* . . . VII. vii. 15. 1
What is the same but alteration *plaine?* . . . VII. vii. 55. 4
If Saphyres, loe, her eies be Saphyres *plaine;* . . . *Am.* xv. 7
if your selfe in me ye *playne* will see, . . . *Am.* xlv. 13
Was it a dreame, or did I see it *playne;* . . . *Am.* lxxvii. 1
beholding the Idaea *playne,* . . . *Am.* lxxxvii. 9
poure his limbs forth on your pleasant *playne;* . . . *Epith.* 356
they *playne,* and make ful piteous mone . . . *H.L.* 127
As *plaine* as light discovers dawning day. . . . *H.B.* 238
to God . . . even the thoughts of men, do *plaine* appeare; . . . *H.H.B.* 173
Plained. thus him *playnd,* the while his shepe there fedde. . . . *S.C.* Ja. 12
my mishaps, which oft I to him *plained,* . . . *Ti.* 142
breaking foorth at last, thus dearnelie *plained:* . . . *D.* 196
playnd, how that . . . boy Her chaste hart had subdewd . . . I. i. 47. 8
playnd of grievous outrage, . . . II. i. 30. 5
of his lucklesse lott and cruell love thus *playnd:* . . . III. v. 44. 9
despight, Which earst to you I *playnd:* . . . III. xi. 23. 6
Plainer. In *playner* wise to tell her grievaunce . . . III. i. 52. 9
Plainly. *playnely* to speake of shepheards . . . *S.C.* S. 104
doth this Redcrosse knights ensample *plainly* prove. . . . I. iv. 1. 9
through his carcas one might *playnly* see. . . . II. xi. 38. 3
the faire land it selfe did *playnly* sheow. . . . II. xii. 37. 6
she *plainly* was espyde To be a woman-wight, . . . III. ix. 21. 7
plainely did expresse The heavenly pourtraict . . . IV. v. 13. 3
The signes of anguish one mote *plainely* read, . . . IV. v. 45. 8
to let men *plainely* wot . . . IV. xi. 45. 8
doest thou not *plainely* see . . . V. ii. 37. 4
that losell, *plainely* now displayd, . . . V. iii. 35. 5
he *plainely* then descride . . . V. iv. 21. 7
So now *Malfont* was *plainely* to be red, . . . V. ix. 26. 6
By certaine signes he *plainly* him descryde . . . VI. iii. 47. 4
That *plainely* may in this wyld man be red, . . . VI. v. 2. 1
when the Prince had once him *plainely* eyde, . . . VI. vi. 28. 5
plainely gan to him declare the case . . . VI. vii. 21. 2
he *plainely* found It was his owne true groome, . . . VI. viii. 27. 5
In which that rose she *plainely* saw displayd: . . . VI. xii. 19. 5
therby doth find, and *plainly* feele, . . . VII. vi. 1. 3
thy bright radiant eyes shall *plainely* see . . . *H.H.L.* 283
By view whereof it *plainly* may appeare, . . . *H.H.B.* 43
Plains. Your carelesse flocks on hils and open *plaines,* . . . *D.* 520
in open *plaines,* Where Boreas doth blow . . . I. ii. 33. 6
Through woods and *plaines* so long I did her chace, . . . II. iv. 32. 2
overronne The fruitfull *plaines,* . . . III. iii. 46. 8
through mountains and through *playns,* . . . III. iv. 46. 1
doth his course through Blandford *plains* direct, . . . IV. xi. 32. 3
through mountains and through *plains,* . . . VI. vii. 44. 2
through dales, through forests, and through *plaines,* . . . VI. ix. 2. 6
sought the *plaines,* but could no tydings heare: . . . VI. xi. 26. 5
The *playnes* all waste and emptie did appeare; . . . VI. xi. 26. 7
keepe His fleecie flock upon the *playnes* . . . VI. xii. 9. 2
Plaint. tune hir *plaint* to falling rivers sound, . . . *Bel.*[1] viii. 3
Pleaseth you ponder your Suppliants *plaint,* . . . *S.C.* F. 151
badde the Brere in his *plaint* proceede. . . . *S.C.* F. 159
leave this lamentable *plaint* behinde: . . . *Gn.* 635
Began her grievous *plaint,* as doth ensew. . . . *T.M.* 114, 174, 234, 300, 420
fill the Scene with *plaint,* . . . *T.M.* 153
Began her piteous *plaint,* as doth ensew. . . . *T.M.* 360
Began her *plaint,* as doth herein ensew. . . . *T.M.* 480
Began her mournfull *plaint,* as doth ensew. . . . *T.M.* 540
Much was I mooved at her piteous *plaint,* . . . *Ti.* 29
with my mourning plaints your *plaint* increase. . . . *Ti.* 238
Thus having ended all her piteous *plaint,* . . . *Ti.* 470
Let reade the rufull *plaint* herein exprest, . . . *D.* 4
Thus when he ended had his heavie *plaint,* . . . *D.* 540
The heaviest *plaint* that ever I heard sound, . . . *D.* 541
place my dolefull *plaint* your plaints emong. . . . *As.* Pr. 6
waste the wearie night In . . . unpittied *plaint,* . . . I. i. 53. 3
Redounding teares did choke th' end of her *plaint,* . . . I. iii. 8. 1
Now then, your *plaint* appease.' . . . I. iii. 29. 9
Madame, ye have great cause of *plaint;* . . . I. vii. 52. 3
badd tell on the tenor of his *playnt:* . . . II. i. 9. 2
The knight was greatly moved at his *playnt,* . . . II. v. 24. 1
The varlet at his *plaint* was grieved so sore, . . . II. vi. 45. 6
Pitty our *playnt,* and yield us meet reliefe.' . . . III. iii. 21. 3
She shut up all her *plaint* in privy griefe . . . III. iv. 11. 2
in scorne Of her vaine *playnt,* . . . III. vi. 21. 2
With womanish compassion of her *plaint,* . . . III. vii. 10. 2
gan to her her mournfull *plaint* to make, . . . IV. viii. 9. 6
Let then this *plaint* unto his eares be borne, . . . IV. xii. 8. 3
There she began to make her monefull *plaint* . . . V. vi. 12. 1
he regarded neither *playnt* nor teare, . . . VI. ii. 22. 8
To whom approching, . . . her *plaint* she stayd, . . . VI. iv. 27. 2
shut up all his *plaint* in privy paine. . . . VI. v. 24. 5
all her piteous *plaint* they did refuse, . . . VI. vii. 40. 4
in his *Plaint of kinde* describ'd it . . . VII. vi. 9. 7
once vouchsafe my *plaint* to heare, . . . *Am.* xviii. 7
Plaintiff. *See* **Plaintive.**
Plaintive. my *plaintive* pleas in verses made: . . . *S.C.* Jun. 42
In songs and *plaintive* pleas, . . . *S.C.* Au. 185
Choking the remnant of his *plaintife* speach, . . . III. xi. 12. 4

Plaintive—*Continued.*
the piteous beast pleading her *plaintiffe* cause. . . . V. iv. 40. 9
Thus gan her *plaintif* Plea with words to amplifie: . . . VII. vii. 13. 9
Plaints. poore my piteous *plaints* out . . . *S.C.* Jun. 80
my *plaints,* causd of discurtesee, . . . *S.C.* Jun. 97
Wherein my *plaints* did oftentimes resound: . . . *S.C.* Au. 152
Thus all the night in *plaints,* . . . *S.C.* Au. 179
why weary we the Gods with *playnts,* . . . *S.C.* N. 173
all those *plaints* unto him brought Of wronges, . . . *Hub.* 1252
Those piteous *plaints* and sorrowfull sad tine, . . . *T.M.* 3
With equall *plaints* her sorrowe did partake. . . . *T.M.* 298
wont forth to powre Her restles *plaints,* . . . *Ti.* 132
with my mourning *plaints* your plaint increase. . . . *Ti.* 238
into *plaints* convert your joyous playes, . . . *D.* 321
lowd *plaints* have duld mine eares; . . . *D.* 415
place my dolefull plaint your *plaints* emong. . . . *As.* Pr. 6
tourn Sweet layes of love to endlesse *plaints* of pittie. . . . *Col.* 387
In Tragick *plaints* and passionate mischance. . . . *Col.* 427
seemd she to appease Her mournefull *plaintes,* . . . I. i. 54. 7
ruefull *plaints,* me bidding guiltlesse blood to spare?' . . . I. ii. 32. 9
with . . . piteous *plaintes,* she filleth his dull eares, . . . I. iii. 44. 2
With loud *plaintes* importuneth the skyes, . . . I. vi. 6. 4
voyce These pitteous *plaintes* and dolours did resound: . . . I. viii. 38. 2
through the sea resounding *plaints* did fly: . . . II. xii. 27. 4
With sighes, and sobs, and *plaints,* . . . III. i. 53. 2
many *plaintes* to her were brought, . . . III. vi. 15. 3
forth breaking into bitter *plaintes* . . . III. xi. 9. 1
her *plaints* might not prevaile, . . . IV. ix. 7. 8
when my piteous *plaints* he heares, . . . IV. xii. 7. 4
weare the weary night In waylfull *plaints* . . . V. vi. 26. 2
But more enforst my paine, the more my *plaints* to heare. . . . VI. ii. 22. 9
all the woods with piteous *plaints* did fill, . . . VI. iv. 18. 2
Tho when as all her *plaints* she had displayd, . . . VI. viii. 34. 1
Playnts, prayers, vowes, ruth, . . . *Am.* xiv. 11
Ne all the *playnts* and prayers, . . . *Am.* xxxii. 7
all the *playnts* which to her be applyde. . . . *Am.* xxxii. 12
Seek with my *playnts* to match that mournful dove. . . . *Am.* lxxxviii. 8
Planet. To every *planet* point his sundry yeare: . . . *Am.* lx. 2
his *planet* cleare Began in me to move, . . . *Am.* lx. 5
let my loves fayre *Planet* short her wayes, . . . *Am.* lx. 13
Hast thee, O fayrest *Planet,* to thy home, . . . *Epith.* 282
Unto her native *planet* shall retyre; . . . *H.B.* 103
Plant. of Paradise Some noble *plant* I thought . . . *Pet.* iii. 4
To plough, to *plant,* to reap, . . . *Hub.* 263
feedes each living *plant* with liquid sap, . . . II. ii. 6. 4
their bright Squadrons round about us *plant;* . . . II. viii. 2. 7
In Paradize whylome did *plant* this flowre; . . . III. v. 52. 3
to sett or sow, To *plant* or prune; . . . III. vi. 34. 2
Another *plant,* that raught to wondrous hight, . . . III. ix. 47. 7
an oaken *plant,* which lately hee Rent by the root; . . . VI. vii. 24. 7
Planted. Was not I *planted* of thine owne hand, . . . *S.C.* F. 165
He *planted* there, and reard a mount of earth, . . . *Gn.* 685
groves, which *planted* were with paines, . . . *T.M.* 277
Lets none shoot up that nigh him *planted* bee: . . . *Ti.* 453
Great God it *planted* in that blessed stedd . . . I. xi. 46. 7
planted there did bring forth fruit of gold; . . . II. vii. 54. 7
planted there their huge artillery, . . . II. xi. 7. 8
Planted with mirtle trees and laurells greene, . . . III. v. 40. 2
They in that Gardin *planted* bee agayne, . . . III. vi. 33. 2
As fresh as when it first was *planted* . . . IV. iii. 29. 9
there was *planted,* or grew naturall: . . . IV. x. 22. 5
by the Gods with paine *Planted* in earth, . . . VI. Pr. 3. 6
manners mylde were *planted* naturall; . . . VI. i. 2. 4
Planting. In *planting* eeke he took no small delight. . . . VII. vii. 40. 6
Plants. manie yong *plants* spring out of her rinde: . . . *Ro.* xxviii. 11
Thou placer of *plants* both humble and tall, . . . *S.C.* F. 164
wets the little *plants* that lowly dwell. . . . *S.C.* N. 32
yong *plants,* which wont with fruit t' abound, . . . *T.M.* 251
few *plants,* preserv'd through heavenly ayd, . . . IV. viii. 33. 3
with their boughes the gentle *plants* did beat: . . . V. i. 1. 5
Plash. underneath his feet soone made a purple *plesh.* . . . II. viii. 36. 9
Plast(e). *See* **Placed.**
Plasters. Whiles dayly *playsters* to his wownd she layd, . . . III. v. 43. 5
Platan. The fruitfull Olive; and the *Platane* round; . . . I. i. 9. 8
Plate. *See* **Breast-plate, Shoulder-plate.**
with their force they perst both *plate* and maile, . . . I. vi. 43. 4
Disarmed all of yron-coted *Plate;* . . . I. vii. 2. 8
Ne *plate,* ne male, could ward so mighty throwes, . . . II. v. 9. 3
seemd both shield and *plate* it would have riv'd; . . . III. i. 6. 3
Bacchus fruit out of the silver *plate* . . . III. ix. 30. 3
neither *plate* nor mayle . . . could once sustaine . . . IV. iii. 15. 4
So forth he came, all in a cote of *plate* . . . V. viii. 29. 1
All armed in a cote of yron *plate* . . . V. xii. 14. 3
Plated. *See* **Brass-plated, Broad-plated.**
Like *plated* cote of steele, . . . I. xi. 9. 2
Plates. shine all scaly with fine golden *plates.* . . . *Bel.*[1] ii. 10
shine all scaly with great *plates* of golde; . . . *Bel.*[2] ii. 10
mighty brawned bowrs Were wont to rive steele *plates,* . . . I. viii. 41. 7
Some in round *plates* withouten moniment; . . . II. vii. 5. 7
all his mayle yriv'd, and *plates* yrent, . . . IV. vi. 15. 8
Rashing off helmes, and ryving *plates* asonder, . . . V. iii. 8. 6
hew'd their helmes, and *plates* asunder brake, . . . VI. i. 37. 4
Platform. long experience the *platforme* was: . . . *Hub.* 1168
Plato. those Idees . . . which *Plato* so admyred, . . . *H.H.B.* 83
Play. When shepheardes groomes han leave to *playe,* . . . *S.C.* Mar. 62
he, that earst seemd but to *playe,* . . . *S.C.* Mar. 95
So sweetely they *play,* And sing . . . *S.C.* Ap. 106
playen while their flockes be unfedde: . . . *S.C.* May 44
To brouze, or *play,* or what shee thought good: . . . *S.C.* May 179
I *play* to please myselfe, . . . *S.C.* Jun. 72

Play—*Continued.*
Upon the glyttering wave doth *playe,* . . . *S.C.* Au. 91
Such *play* is a pitteous plight. . . . *S.C.* Au. 92
with shepheard sittes not *playe,* . . . *S.C.* S. 232
matter made for Poets on to *play:* . . . *S.C.* O. 64
Nor Pan to herye, nor with love to *playe;* . . . *S.C.* N. 10
leade me forth on Fancies bitte to *playe:* . . . *S.C.* D. 64
to *play* An easie running verse . . . *Gn.* 52
bad the Ape him dight To *play* his part, . . . *Hub.* 234
he could *play,* and daunce, and vaute, and spring, . . . *Hub.* 693
And *play* the Poet oft. . . . *Hub.* 810
Like as a Puppit placed in a *play,* . . . *Hub.* 931
his fine handling, and his cleanly *play,* . . . *Hub.* 1015
A thousand Nymphes . . . Were wont to *play,* . . . *Ti.* 138
Walking abroad with all her Nymphes to *play,* . . . *Mui.* 115
then againe he turneth to his *play,* . . . *Mui.* 185
Where on a sunnie banke the Lambes doo *play,* . . . *Mui.* 402
evermore when I did sleepe or *play,* . . . *D.* 132
There was no pleasure nor delightfull *play,* . . . *As.* 29
The shepheard swaines that did about him *play:* . . . *Col.* 6
Provoked me to *plaie* some pleasant fit; . . . *Col.* 69
what thou didst sing, when he did *plaie;* . . . *Col.* 84
With the sweet Lady Muses for to *play:* . . . *Ded. Son.* i. 6
Thereby a christall streame did gently *play,* . . . I. i. 34. 8
made him dreame of loves and lustfull *play,* . . . I. i. 47. 4
She soone left off her mirth and wanton *play,* . . . I. ii. 14. 4
in ydle pomp, or wanton *play,* . . . I. v. 51. 7
For love of me leave off this dreadfull *play;* . . . I. vi. 28. 7
drops of blood thence like a well did *play:* . . . I. x. 27. 4
the thrise three learned Ladies *play* Their hevenly notes, . . I. x. 54. 8
Their wanton sportes and childish mirth did *play,* . . . I. xii. 7. 2
come too neare, and with his talants *play,* . . . I. xii. 11. 2
apply Her curious skill the warbling notes to *play,* . . . I. xii. 38. 7
a lovely babe did *play* His cruell sport, . . . II. i. 40. 5
with the woody Nymphes when she did *play,* . . . II. iii. 28. 7
queld The salvage beasts in her victorious *play,* . . . II. iii. 29. 4
more enflerced through his currish *play,* . . . II. iv. 8. 6
murmuring wave did *play* Emongst the pumy stones, . . . II. v. 30. 2
did *play* Their wanton follies . . . II. v. 32. 5
water worke and *play* About her little frigot, . . . II. vi. 7. 8
so fiers did *play* On th' others helmett, . . . II. vi. 31. 5
With his faire mother he him dights to *play,* . . . II. viii. 6. 5
The Goddesse, pleased with his wanton *play,* . . . II. viii. 6. 7
Ordinaunce Upon the Bulwarkes cruelly did *play,* . . . II. xi. 14. 4
she saw him bent to cruell *play,* . . . III. i. 37. 3
With whom he ment to make his sport and courtly *play.* . . . III. i. 56. 9
subtile sophismes, which doe *play* With double sences, . . . III. iv. 28. 7
To sorrow huge she turnd her former *play,* . . . III. iv. 30. 3
How diversly love doth his pageaunts *play,* . . . III. v. 1. 2
mortall miseries doth make her *play.* . . . III. vii. 4. 5
who that smites it mars his joyous *play,* . . . III. vii. 41. 8
taught the carefull Mariner to *play,* . . . III. viii. 20. 3
she does joy to *play* emongst her peares, . . . III. ix. 4. 8
all the night did minde his joyous *play:* . . . III. x. 48. 4
In signe of silence, as to heare a *play,* . . . III. xii. 4. 4
it gan againe to *play,* . . . III. xii. 6. 8
at your pleasure *play:* . . . III. xii. 47. *or.* 8
That masked Mock-knight was their sport and *play.* . . . IV. iv. 13. 4
To joyous feast and other gentle *play,* . . . IV. iv. 48. 7
She with the pleasant Graces wont to *play.* . . . IV. v. 5. 6
I with that Elfe did *play,* . . . IV. viii. 61. 6
Sweet springs, in which a thousand Nymphs did *play;* . . . IV. x. 24. 3
The waters *play,* and pleasant lands appeare, . . . IV. x. 44. 8
They all doe learne to *play* the Paramours; . . . IV. x. 45. 5
beasts begin to *play* Their pleasant friskes, . . . IV. x. 46. 1
Ten thousand fishes *play* . . . IV. xi. 29. 9
So did the villaine to her prate and *play,* . . . V. ix. 13. 5
be aveng'd of their unknightly *play.* . . . V. x. 36. 4
both were wondrous practicke in that *play,* . . . VI. i. 36. 3
To pitty him that list to *play* the foole; . . . VI. viii. 21. 4
at pleasure she mote sport and *play;* . . . VI. ix. 37. 5
with the Graces there to *play* and sport; . . . VI. x. 9. 5
Mutability in them doth *play* Her cruell sports . . . VII. vi. 1. 4
with the Nymphes the Satyres love to *play* . . . VII. vi. 39. 9
(After her sweaty chace and toylesome *play*) . . . VII. vi. 42. 2
when I pleade, she bids me *play* my part; . . . *Am.* xviii. 9
they take pleasure in her cruell *play,* . . . *Am.* xlvii. 11
Right so my cruell fayre with me doth *play;* . . . *Am.* liii. 5
Beholding me, that all the pageants *play,* . . . *Am.* liv. 3
let the roring Organs loudly *play* . . . *Epith.* 218
Ye sonnes of Venus, *play* your sports at will! . . . *Epith.* 364
All night therefore attend your merry *play,* . . . *Epith.* 368
making their paine thy *play,* . . . *H.L.* 135
they doe *play* Their hurtlesse sports, . . . *H.L.* 287
So many millions of chaste pleasures *play.* . . . *H.B.* 259
did softly *play* A gentle spirit, . . . *Proth.* 2

Played. to the many a Horne-pype *playd,* . . . *S.C.* May 23
the Pilgrim that the Ploughman *playde* awhyle; . . . *S.C.* Env. 10
We now have *playde* (Augustus) wantonly, . . . *Gn.* 1
Have onely *playde;* . . . *Gn.* 4
the false Foxe most kindly *plaid* his part; . . . *Hub.* 1137
when he hath both *plaid* and fed his fill, . . . *Mui.* 205
he tooke in hond My pipe, . . . And *plaid* thereon; . . . *Col.* 74
glauncing fire out of the yron *plaid,* . . . I. xi. 42. 5
cursed hand, hath *plaid* this cruell part, . . . II. i. 44. 7
he went, and his owne false part *playd,* . . . II. iv. 27. 7
weend it was my love with whom he *playd.* . . . II. iv. 28. 5
litle Cupid *playd* His wanton sportes, . . . II. ix. 34. 6
Some *plaid* with strawes; . . . II. ix. 35. 3
of all that ever *playd* At tilt or tourney, . . . III. ii. 9. 7

Played—*Continued.*
Yet *playd* Pasiphae a more monstrous part, . . . III. ii. 41. 5
playd Amongst her watry sisters by a pond, . . . III. iv. 29. 6
in the midst a little river *plaide* . . . III. v. 39. 7
The sunbeames bright upon her body *playd,* . . . III. vi. 7. 5
The good man selfe, which then the Porter *playd,* . . . III. ix. 10. 2
thus on earth great Jove these pageaunts *playd,* . . . III. xi. 35. 5
Antickes, which their follies *playd* In the rich metall . . . III. xi. 51. 5
shril trompets and loud clarions sweetly *playd.* . . . IV. iii. 5. 9
Yet in his time he wrought as well as *playd,* . . . VII. vii. 35. 3

Player. All in greene leaves, as he a *Player* were; . . . VII. vii. 35. 2

Playfellows. Go, find some other *play-fellowes,* . . . I. vi. 28. 9

Playfellows'. her *play-fellowes* aide to call, . . . *Mui.* 282

Playing. *Playing* on yvorie harp with silver strong. . . . *Gn.* 16
playing on the grassy greene, . . . *Gn.* 177
Playing alone carelesse on hir heavenlie Virginals. . . . *U.V.* 6
I spied *playing* on the grassie playne . . . *D.* 110
babes about her hong, *Playing* their sportes, . . . I. x. 31. 2
Titan, *playing* on the eastern streames, . . . II. iii. 1. 3
playing their wanton toyes, . . . II. xii. 60. 8
The faire Poeana *playing* on a Rote . . . IV. ix. 6. 2
Art, *playing* second natures part, supplyed it. . . . IV. x. 21. 9
like to Angels *playing* heavenly toyes, . . . IV. x. 42. 5
playing on his harpe, . . . IV. xi. 23. 4
So went he *playing* on the watery plaine; . . . IV. xi. 24. 1
Amongst his peres *playing* his childish sport; . . . V. i. 6. 3
Playing on shaumes and trumpets, . . . V. v. 4. 5
Talus did attend, *Playing* his pages part, . . . V. viii. 29. 7
Playing on pipes and caroling apace, . . . VI. ix. 5. 3
the merry sound Of a shrill pipe he *playing* heard . . . VI. x. 10. 3

Plays. When that was done, he might attend his *playes:* . . . *Hub.* 394
into plaints convert your joyous *playes,* . . . *D.* 321
through the trembling leaves full gently *playes,* . . . I. vii. 3. 3
with faire Adonis *playes* his wanton partes. . . . III. vi. 49. 9
his trew love faire Psyche with him *playes,* . . . III. vi. 50. 1
to learne his wanton *playes;* . . . III. xi. 44. 3
sleepes, and sports, and *playes;* . . . IV. i. 47. 6
here with thee doe make their pleasant *playes?* . . . VI. x. 19. 7
the Mavis descant *playes:* . . . *Epith.* 81

Plea. Greatly aghast with this piteous *plea,* . . . *S.C.* F. 157
gan her plaintif *Plea* with words to amplifie: . . . VII. vii. 13. 9

Plead. never meant with words, but swords, to *plead* his right: I. iv. 42. 9
In face of judgement he their right would *plead,* . . . I. x. 43. 4
truth is strong her rightfull cause to *plead,* . . . I. xii. 28. 7
Many grave persons that against her *pled.* . . . V. ix. 43. 6
Rose many advocates for her to *plead:* . . . V. ix. 45. 2
Griefe did *plead,* and many teares forth powre. . . . V. ix. 45. 9
she thereto nould *plead,* nor answere ought, . . . VI. vii. 36. 3
when I *pleade,* she bids me play my part; . . . *Am.* xviii. 9
I weepe, and wayle, and *pleade* in vaine, . . . *Am.* xviii. 13
teach to speak, and my just cause to *plead;* . . . *Am.* xliii. 10
plead thy maisters cause, unjustly payned. . . . *Am.* xlviii. 8

Pleading. To heare the piteous beast *pleading* her plaintiffe cause. . . . V. iv. 40. 9

Pleads. Bold Alteration *pleades* Large Evidence: . . . VII. vii. Arg.

Pleas. my plaintive *pleas* in verses made: . . . *S.C.* Jun. 42
In songs and plaintive *pleas,* . . . *S.C.* Au. 185
hearing *pleas* of people meane and base: . . . V. ix. 36. 5

Pleasance. Puffed up with pryde and vaine *pleasaunce;* . . . *S.C.* F. 223
when all is ycladd With *pleasaunce:* . . . *S.C.* May 7
Such *pleasaunce* makes the Grashopper so poore, . . . *S.C.* O. 11
to pricke them forth with *pleasaunce* of thy vaine, . . . *S.C.* O. 23
For beauties prayse and *pleasaunce* had no peere; . . . *S.C.* N. 94
Such *pleasaunce* now displast by dolors dint: . . . *S.C.* N. 104
bene thy verses meint With doleful *pleasaunce,* . . . *S.C.* N. 204
it with *pleasaunce* mought thy fancie feede) . . . *S.C.* D. 16
My hurtlesse *pleasaunce* did me ill upbraide; . . . *S.C.* D. 51
His witlesse *pleasance,* and ill pleasing vaine. . . . *Hub.* 799
With seasoned wit and goodly *pleasance* graced, . . . *T.M.* 200
cut downe, and all their *pleasaunce* mard, . . . *T.M.* 281
fill with *pleasance* every wood and plaine. . . . *D.* 56
provoke them might To idle *pleasance;* . . . *D.* 327
Faire seemely *pleasaunce* each to other makes, . . . I. ii. 30. 1
With *pleasaunce* of the breathing fields yfed, . . . I. iv. 38. 2
bathe in *pleasaunce* of the joyous shade, . . . I. vii. 4. 2
with sweet *pleasaunce,* and bold blandishment, . . . II. ii. 1. 5
turned all her *pleasaunce* to a scoffing game. . . . II. vi. 6. 9
Whose *pleasaunce* she him shewd, . . . II. vi. 11. 9
Her honest merth and *pleasaunce* to partake; . . . II. vi. 21. 6
All *pleasaunce* was to them griefe and annoy: . . . II. ix. 35. 5
on every side Strowed with *pleasauns;* . . . II. xii. 50. 3
His stubborne brest gan secret *pleasaunce* to embrace. . . . II. xii. 65. 9
After them went Displeasure and *Pleasaunce,* . . . III. xii. 18. 1
with melting *pleasaunce* mollifye Their hardned hearts, . . . V. viii. 1. 8
Allur'd with . . . *pleasaunce* of the place, . . . VI. iii. 23. 4
place whose *pleasaunce* did appere To passe all others . . . VI. x. 5. 4
when she did dispose Her selfe to *pleasaunce,* . . . VI. x. 9. 2
astonished in spright, And rapt with *pleasaunce,* . . . VI. x. 17. 4
The lovely *pleasance;* and the lofty pride; . . . *Am.* xvii. 11
mild *pleasance,* which doth pride displace, . . . *Am.* xxi. 5
A melting *pleasance* ran through every part, . . . *Am.* xxxix. 7
In her unspotted *pleasauns* to delight. . . . *Am.* lxxxviii. 12
For they of joy and *pleasance* to you sing, . . . *Epith.* 90

Pleasant. singing with most *plesant* melodie . . . *Bel.*[1] ix. 7
so *pleasant* (*pleasaunt*[1]) sent did yeld, . . . *Bel.* xi. 13
most *pleasant* notes did sing, . . . *Bel.*[2] xi. 7
pleasant spring appeareth: . . . *S.C.* Mar. 9
Hys *pleasaunt* Pipe, whych made us meriment, . . . *S.C.* Ap. 14
here the place whose *plesaunt* syte . . . *S.C.* Jun. 1
Thou, *pleasaunt* spring, hast luld me oft asleepe, . . . *S.C.* Au. 155

Pleasant—*Continued.*
Fayre fieldes and *pleasaunt* layes there bene; . . . . *S.C.* N. 188
darkesome caves in *pleasaunt* vallies pight, ... *Gn.* 117
O ye *pleasaunt* Springs Of Tempe! . . . . *Gn.* 145
A *pleasant* bowre with all delight abounding . . . . *Gn.* 187
In this so *pleasant* place . . . . *Gn.* 233
pleasant tales (fit for that idle stound) . . . . *Hub.* 26
Our *pleasant* Willy, ah! is dead of late: . . . . *T.M.* 208
All places with our *pleasant* notes to fill, ... *T.M.* 242
Our *pleasant* groves, which planted were with paines, ... *T.M.* 277
Then did I see a *pleasant* Paradize, ... *Ti.* 519
all, that faire or *pleasant* may be found, ... *Mui.* 167
Provoked me to plaie some *pleasant* fit; . . . . *Col.* 69
gave that name unto that *pleasant* vale; . . . . *Col.* 107
seemed to be a goodly *pleasant* lea: . . . . *Col.* 283
Leaping like wanton kids in *pleasant* Spring. . . . . I. vi. 14. 4
court they see, Both plaine and *pleasaunt* . . . . I. x. 6. 3
like that *pleasaunt* Mount, ... I. x. 54. 6
they came at last Into a *pleasant* dale . . . . II. i. 24. 3
on the other syde a *pleasaunt* grove . . . . II. v. 31. 1
she in *pleasaunt* purpose did abound, ... II. vi. 6. 3
in the calme of *pleasaunt* womankind. . . . . II. vi. 8. 9
The flowrs, the fields, and all that *pleasaunt* growes, ... II. vi. 15. 2
Till they arrived in that *pleasaunt* Ile, ... II. vi. 22. 3
all, though *pleasaunt,* yet she made much more: . . . . II. vi. 24. 5
Does yield unto his foe a *pleasaunt* victory. . . . . II. vi. 34. 9
castle, plaste Foreby a river in a *pleasaunt* dale; . . . . . II. ix. 10. 4
seemd so sweet and *pleasaunt* to the eye, ... II. xii. 14. 5
twixt them both a *pleasaunt* port they made, ... II. xii. 30. 6
Their *pleasaunt* tunes they sweetly thus applyde: . . . . . . II. xii. 32. 2
the *pleasaunt* hill Of Rhodope, ... II. xii. 52. 1
As faint through heat, or dight to *pleasant* sin; . . . . . . II. xii. 77. 2
all those *pleasaunt* bowres, and Pallace brave, ... II. xii. 83. 1
Where was their dwelling, in a *pleasant* glade . . . . III. v. 39. 2
All other *pleasaunt* places doth excell, ... III. vi. 29. 7
There was a *pleasaunt* Arber, ... III. vi. 44. 2
Yet should it be a *pleasant* tale, ... IV. i. 5. 1
turning all to game And *pleasaunt* bord, ... IV. iv. 13. 2
She with the *pleasant* Graces wont to play. . . . . IV. v. 5. 6
More hard for hungry steed t' abstaine from *pleasant* lare. . . IV. viii. 29. 9
gladsome countenaunce nor *pleasaunt* glee; . . . . IV. ix. 13. 5
The onely *pleasant* and delightfull place . . . . IV. x. 21. 4
here and there were *pleasant* arbors pight, ... IV. x. 25. 3
The waters play, and *pleasant* lands appeare, ... IV. x. 44. 8
beasts begin to play Their *pleasant* friskes, ... IV. x. 46. 2
decke his *pleasant* streame. . . . . IV. xi. 29. 9
Sture, that parteth with his *pleasant* floods . . . . IV. xi. 33. 3
The *pleasant* Boyne, the fishy fruitfull Ban, ... IV. xi. 41. 4
The *pleasaunt* Bandon crownd with many a wood; . . . . . . IV. xi. 44. 2
talk't of *pleasant* things . . . . V. vi. 22. 9
Charmes to the birds full many a *pleasant* lay, ... V. ix. 13. 2
many *pleasant* tricks before her show, ... V. ix. 13. 6
Out of the *pleasant* soyle and cities glad, ... V. x. 18. 5
all that *pleasant* is to eare or eye, ... VI. Pr. 1. 5
here with thee doe make their *pleasant* playes? . . . . VI. x. 19. 7
begot of faire Eurynome, . . . in this *pleasant* grove, ... VI. x. 22. 3
pitty her sad plight, so chang'd from *pleasaunt* hew. . . . . VI. xi. 2. 9
So now her waves passe through a *pleasant* Plaine, ... VII. vi. 53. 7
in *pleasant* mew To sport my muse, ... *Am.* lxxx. 9
May poure his limbs forth on your *pleasant* playne; . . . . *Epith.* 356
pleasant grace To all things faire, ... *H.B.* 57
by *pleasant* Tempes shore, . . . through Thessaly they streeme, *Proth.* 79

Pleasantly. noise Heard sownd through all the Pallace *pleasantly,* . . . . I. xii. 39. 2
pleasauntly did sing Many faire Ladies . . . . II. xii. 72. 7
pleasauntly . . . Did seeme to overlooke the lowly vale; . . . VI. x. 8. 7

Please. my pype, albee rude Pan thou *please,* . . . . *S.C.* Ja. 67
I play to *please* myselfe, ... *S.C.* Jun. 72
were Hobbinoll as God mought *please,* . . . . *S.C.* S. 252
if thee *please* in bigger notes to sing, ... *S.C.* O. 46
when shall it *please* thee sing, ... *S.C.* N. 1
The loser Lasse I cast to *please* no more; . . . . *S.C.* D. 119
One if I *please,* enough is me therefore. . . . . *S.C.* D. 120
The better *please,* the worse despise; . . . . *S.C.* Env. 12
beleeve that anie thing could *please* Fell Cerberus, ... *Gn.* 439
Therefore (if *please* you) this shalbe our plot: . . . . *Hub.* 154
Which might it you in pitie *please* t' afford, ... *Hub.* 251
(Might it you *please*) . . . . *Hub.* 290
An easie life, and fit high God to *please.* . . . . *Hub.* 395
might *please* you . . . Us to advise, ... *Hub.* 409
To crouche, to *please,* to be a beetle-stock . . . . *Hub.* 507
In whatso *please* employ his personage, ... *Hub.* 778
Let God . . . if *please,* care for the manie, ... *Hub.* 1195
Till *please* the heavens affoord me remedy. . . . . *T.M.* 294
please my selfe with mine owne selfe-delight, ... *T.M.* 525
Mote *please* his fancie, nor him cause t' abide: . . . . *Mui.* 158
No common things may *please* a wavering wit. . . . . *Mui.* 160
To take what ever thing doth *please* the eie? . . . . *Mui.* 214
Made not to *please* the living but the dead. . . . . *As.* Pr. 16
to what course thou *please* thy selfe advance: . . . . *Col.* 425
Unlesse to *please* it selfe it can applie; . . . . *Col.* 708
fed with words that could not chose but *please:* . . . . . . I. i. 54. 8
To doe none ill, if *please* ye not doe well.' . . . . I. ii. 26. 4
excuse, that mote ye *please* Well to accept, ... I. iii. 29. 6
Unseemely man to *please* faire Ladies eye; . . . . I. iv. 24. 6
mayd Did her content to *please* their feeble eyes, ... I. vi. 19. 2
death after life, does greatly *please.'* . . . . I. ix. 40. 9
Whome if ye *please* for to discover plaine, ... I. xii. 34. 7
Each strove to *please,* . . . . II. iv. 19. 9
Was overcome of thing that did him *please;* . . . . II. vi. 13. 8

Please—*Continued.*
Take what thou *please* of all this surplusage; . . . . II. vii. 18. 7
Diverse delights they fownd them selves to *please;* . . . . . II. ix. 35. 1
if *please* you it discure, ... II. ix. 42. 8
wanton pleasures him too much did *please,* . . . . II. x. 17. 7
if ye *please,* to yonder castle turne . . . . III. viii. 51. 9
if *please* ye listen to my lore, ... III. xi. 18. 7
there mote find to *please* it selfe withall; . . . . IV. x. 22. 7
if ye *please* that I your cause decide, ... V. i. 25. 5
Yet found no place that could her liking *please,* . . . . . . V. vi. 7. 3
Which if ye *please* forgive, ... V. viii. 13. 4
sith ye *please* that both our blames shall die, ... V. viii. 14. 1
'Ah! Sir, but mote ye *please,* . . . . V. xi. 18. 2
Fashion'd to *please* the eies of them that pas, ... VI. Pr. 5. 4
To *please* the best, and th' evill to embase; . . . . VI. i. 3. 7
tell, if *please* you, of the good successe . . . . VI. i. 5. 1
Please it you, Ladie, to us to aread . . . . VI. ii. 15. 2
if *please* her make the priefe; . . . . VI. iv. 34. 5
Somewhile with merry purpose, fit to *please,* . . . . VI. v. 32. 7
how to *please* the minds of good and ill, ... VI. vi. 41. 8
learn'd the art to *please,* . . . . VI. vi. 43. 3
if ye *please* to lend me leave awhile, ... VI. viii. 6. 8
seeke to *please;* that now is counted wise mens threasure. . . VI. xii. 41. 9
might delight the smell, or *please* the view, ... VII. vii. 10. 5
As if ye *please* it into parts divide, ... VII. vii. 17. 3
Leaves, lines, and rymes, seeke her to *please* alone, ... *Am.* i. 13
Whom if ye (you[1]) *please,* I care for other none! . . . . . . *Am.* i. 14
wont to *please* Some dainty eares, ... *Am.* xxxviii. 5
Let her, yf *please* her, bynd with adamant chayne: . . . . . *Am.* xlii. 10
rules the members as it selfe doth *please?* . . . . *Am.* l. 8
his spotted hyde Doth *please* all beasts, ... *Am.* liii. 2
Her harts desire with most contentment *please.* . . . . . . *Am.* lxxii. 12
till he *please* My pining anguish to appease. . . . . *Epig.* iv. 59
May *please* her best, and grace unto him gaine; . . . . . . *H.L.* 222
It may so *please,* . . . . *H.B.* 26
to the lookers sight They seeme to *please;* . . . . *H.B.* 54

Pleased. all his plenteous pasture nought him *pleased:* . . . . *Van.* ii. 13
Perigot is well *pleased* with the doome: . . . . *S.C.* Au. 135
Let him rest *pleased* with his owne insight, ... *Gn. Ded.* 9
my sense it greatly *pleased,* . . . . *Hub.* 39
whilst that other like vaine wits he *pleased,* . . . . *Hub.* 709
neither *pleased* was to have the rayne Twixt them divided . . *Hub.* 1023
Who rests not *pleased* with such happines, ... *Mui.* 215
to be *pleased* To turne aside . . . . *D.* 557
He found himselfe full greatly *pleasd* at it: . . . . *Col.* 71
pleasd them all with meete satiety. . . . . II. ii. 39. 2
So *pleased* did his wrathfull purpose faire appease. . . . . . II. vi. 13. 9
she well *pleased* was thence to amove him farre. . . . . . . II. vi. 37. 9
The Goddesse, *pleased* with his wanton play, ... II. viii. 6. 7
As *pleased* them to use that use it might; . . . . III. i. 39. 5
His feeling wordes her feeble sence much *pleased,* . . . . . III. ii. 15. 1
pleased with that seeming goodly-hed, ... III. ii. 38. 8
The which the powres to thee are *pleased* to revele.' . . . . III. iii. 19. 9
in short space She was well *pleasd,* . . . . III. vi. 25. 7
So be ye *pleasd* to pardon all amis. . . . . III. vii. 53. 5
That counsell *pleased* well: . . . . III. viii. 52. 1
That counsell *pleasd:* . . . . III. ix. 9. 8
It *pleased* well: So well they both agree: . . . . III. x. 11. 8
That counsell *pleased* not Malbeccoes mynd, ... III. x. 41. 8
It *pleased;* so he did. . . . . III. x. 42. 9
That offer *pleased* all the company: . . . . IV. iv. 10. 1
As though she wished to have *pleasd* them all, ... IV. v. 26. 7
Therewith he rested, and well *pleased* was: . . . . IV. vi. 39. 1
Well *pleased* with that doome was Sangliere, ... V. i. 27. 1
dowre Of all her gifts, that *pleasde* each living sight, ... VI. viii. 20. 4
There he did see that *pleased* much his sight, ... VI. x. 11. 6
Bellamoure againe so well her *pleased* . . . . VI. xii. 5. 1
Proud Change (not *pleasd* in mortall things . . . to raigne) VII. vi. Arg.
There Faunus saw that *pleased* much his eye, ... VII. vi. 46. 1
all that *pleased* earst now seemes to paine; . . . . *H.H.B.* 270

Pleasest. thou *pleasest* not where most I would: . . . . . . *S.C.* Ja. 68

Pleaseth. *Pleaseth* you ponder your Suppliants plaint, ... *S.C.* F. 151
never thing on earth so *pleaseth* me . . . . *S.C.* Au. 147
Like as himselfe us *pleaseth* save or spill. . . . . *Col.* 814

Pleasing. *See* **Ill-pleasing, Self-pleasing.**
when he ought not *pleasing* would put by . . . . *Hub.* 1169
pleasing sound yshrilled far about, ... *Col.* 62
there is *pleasing* Alcon, could he raise His tunes . . . . . . *Col.* 394
that olde man of *pleasing* wordes had store, ... I. i. 35. 6
th' others *pleasing* service to abate, ... II. ii. 19. 5
A *pleasing* vaine of glory he did fynd, ... II. iii. 4. 5
Did all she might more *pleasing* to appeare. . . . . II. iv. 25. 4
flowes in pleasures and vaine *pleasing* toyes, ... II. v. 28. 8
Such powre have *pleasing* wordes: . . . . II. vi. 36. 5
thy bounteous baytes and *pleasing* charmes, ... II. vii. 10. 3
sweete and *pleasing* unto living sense, ... II. xii. 42. 6
semblaunce *pleasing,* more then naturall, ... II. xii. 46. 5
all that *pleasing* is to living eare . . . . II. xii. 70. 7
As in approvaunce of his *pleasing* wordes. . . . . II. xii. 76. 3
To feed her humor with his *pleasing* style, ... III. ii. 12. 2
pleasing wordes are like to Magick art, ... III. ii. 15. 5
To love the semblaunt *pleasing* most your minde, ... III. ii. 40. 7
with amorous delights And *pleasing* toyes . . . . III. x. 8. 2
with humble pride and *pleasing* guile: . . . . III. x. 9. 3
painefull pleasure turnes to *pleasing* paine. . . . . III. x. 60. 4
Through false allurement of that *pleasing* baite, ... IV. Pr. 1. 7
Or beare her on thy backe with *pleasing* payne, ... VI. iii. 32. 4
she so well applyde Her *pleasing* tongue, ... VI. vi. 43. 5
Burnt in her love, and with sweet *pleasing* payne . . . . . . VI. ix. 10. 3
twixt his *pleasing* tongue, and her faire hew, ... VI. ix. 26. 8

Pleasing—*Continued.*
pleasing gifts for her purvaid, ... VII. vi. 43. 5
Me from these woods and *pleasing* forrests bring, ... VII. vii. 1. 2
So *pleasing* is in my extreamest paine, ... *Am.* xlii. 2
ought that else might to thee *pleasing* bee. . . . . . . *H.L.* 7

Pleasure. Art and Nature had assembled All *pleasure* . . . . *Bel.*² xii. 6
Reapen the fruite thereof, that is *pleasure,* . . . . . . *S.C.* May 65
fynd no part 'Of *pleasure* past. . . . . . . *S.C.* Au. 169
They wander at wil and stay at *pleasure,* . . . . . . *S.C.* S. 144
They han the *pleasure,* I a sclender prise; . . . . . . *S.C.* O. 16
Delight is layd abedde; and *pleasure* past; . . . . . . *S.C.* D. 137
perfect *pleasure* buildes her joyous bowre, ... *Gn.* 135
we will walke about the world at *pleasure* . . . . . . *Hub.* 159
of them slew at *pleasure* what they wolde. . . . . . . *Hub.* 336
Yee shall our pasport at your *pleasure* see, ... *Hub.* 377
Ne, them to *pleasure,* would he sometimes scorne . . . . . . *Hub.* 807
with *pleasure* The listners eyes and eares with melodie; . . . *T.M.* 177
With beawtie kindled, and with *pleasure* fed, ... *T.M.* 364
Now onely seeke for *pleasure,* . . . . . . *T.M.* 468
O short *pleasure,* bought with lasting paine! . . . . . . *Ti.* 526
whoso else in *pleasure* findeth sense, ... *D.* 8
in her workmanship no *pleasure* finde, ... *D.* 394
There was no *pleasure* nor delightfull play, ... *As.* 29
Ne feeling have in any earthly *pleasure,* . . . . . . *Col.* 45
In whose high thoughts *Pleasure* hath built her bowre, . . . *Ded. Son.* viii. 6
foorth they passe, with *pleasure* forward led, ... I. i. 8. 1
in her many troubles did most *pleasure* take. . . . . . . I. ii. 9. 9
since thou bidst, thy *pleasure* shalbe donne. . . . . . . I. x. 52. 1
Great *pleasure,* mixt with pittiful regard, ... I. xii. 16. 1
'Her blis is all in *pleasure,* . . . . . . II. i. 52. 1
The strong through *pleasure* soonest falles, ... II. i. 57. 9
to prepare Their minds to *pleasure,* . . . . . . II. ii. 33. 9
poured out in *pleasure* and delight: . . . . . . II. ii. 36. 5
gazers sence with double *pleasure* fed, ... II. iii. 22. 8
where no *pleasure* is, ... II. iii. 39. 2
swim in *pleasure,* which thou here doest mis: . . . . . . II. iii. 39. 7
others *pleasure* to fulfill. . . . . . . II. iv. 19. 9
In joyous *pleasure* then in grievous paine; . . . . . . II. vi. 1. 2
Ne wind and weather at his *pleasure* call: . . . . . . II. vi. 23. 3
Great *pleasure* had those straunger knightes . . . . . . II. ix. 54. 6
secret *pleasure* did offence empeach, ... II. x. 68. 8
Where *Pleasure* dwelles in sensuall delights, ... II. xii. 1. 8
Rather for *pleasure* then for battery or fight. . . . . . . II. xii. 43. 9
Quite molten into lust and *pleasure* lewd; . . . . . . II. xii. 73. 8
plaste for *pleasure* nigh that forrest syde: . . . . . . III. i. 20. 5
bore withouten paine, that she conceiv'd Withouten *pleasure*; III. vi. 27. 3
here all plenty and all *pleasure* flowes; . . . . . . III. vi. 41. 4
reape sweet *pleasure* of the wanton boy: . . . . . . III. vi. 46. 3
Pleasure, that doth both gods and men aggrate, ... III. vi. 50. 8
Pleasure, the daughter of Cupid and Psyche late. . . . . . . III. vi. 50. 9
daughter *Pleasure,* to whom shee Made her companion, . . . III. vi. 51. 7
Her lothsom *pleasure* there to satisfye; . . . . . . III. vii. 51. 4
In hope unto my *pleasure* to have won; . . . . . . III. vii. 59. 8
painefull *pleasure* turnes to pleasing paine. . . . . . . III. x. 60. 4
gave her leave at *pleasure* forth to passe. . . . . . . III. xii. 43. 6
she, faire Lady, . . . did in *pleasure* melt, ... III. xii. 45. *or.* 6
at your *pleasure* play: . . . . . . III. xii. 47. *or.* 8
chaung'd at *pleasure* for those impes of thine! . . . . . . IV. ii. 51. 7
As if he naught but peace and *pleasure* ment, ... IV. iv. 7. 3
Walkt through the wood, for *pleasure* or for need; . . . . . . IV. vii. 4. 2
when your *pleasure* is to deeme aright, ... IV. viii. 17. 4
For ought will from his greedie *pleasure* spare: . . . . . . IV. viii. 29. 8
solace in soft *pleasure* Those weaker Ladies . . . . . . IV. ix. 12. 7
at *pleasure* Would change his liking, ... IV. ix. 21. 5
'In such luxurious plentie of all *pleasure,* . . . . . . IV. x. 23. 1
She is the nourse of *pleasure* and delight, ... IV. x. 35. 8
thou the same for *pleasure* didst prepayre: . . . . . . IV. x. 47. 5
There leave we them in *pleasure* and repast, ... V. iii. 40. 1
in anothers losse great *pleasure* take, ... V. xii. 32. 8
So downe he sate, and with delightfull *pleasure* . . . . . . VI. iii. 22. 7
Abstaine from *pleasure,* and restraine your will; . . . . . . VI. vi. 14. 5
Thereof by force to take their beastly *pleasure:* . . . . . . VI. viii. 43. 6
The whylest at *pleasure* she mote sport and play; . . . . . . VI. ix. 37. 5
for *pleasure* might Desired be, ... VI. x. 8. 5
prises to them placed at their *pleasure,* . . . . . . VI. xi. 14. 2
ready passage to her *pleasure* did prepaire. . . . . . . VII. vi. 7. 9
(for *pleasure* and for rest) Oft to resort there-to, ... VII. vi. 38. 4
none of all there-in more *pleasure* found Then Cynthia, . . . VII. vi. 38. 6
if shee would him *pleasure* With this small boone, ... VII. vi. 44. 1
The least of which this little *pleasure* should excell. . . . . VII. vi. 44. 9
And eke his learned hand at *pleasure* guide, ... *Am.* xvii. 6
That endlesse *pleasure* shall unto me gaine! . . . . . . *Am.* xxvi. 14
feeds at *pleasure* on the wretched pray: . . . . . . *Am.* xlvii. 8
they take *pleasure* in her cruell play, ... *Am.* xlvii. 11
thinck they dy with *pleasure,* live with payne. . . . . . . *Am.* xlvii. 14
But if it be your *pleasure,* . . . To shew the powre . . . . . *Am.* xlix. 5
no thought of joy, or *pleasure* vaine, ... *Am.* lii. 9
spotlesse *Pleasure* builds her sacred bowre. . . . . . . *Am.* lxv. 14
The bowre of blisse, the paradice of *pleasure,* . . . . . . *Am.* lxxvi. 3
Sweet fruit of *pleasure,* brought from Paradice . . . . . . *Am.* lxxvii. 11
greedy *pleasure,* carelesse of your toyes, ... *Epith.* 365
with thy daughter *Pleasure* they doe play . . . . . . *H.L.* 287
But there their termelesse time in *pleasure* spend; . . . . . *H.H.L.* 75
And feele such joy and *pleasure* inwardly, ... *H.H.B.* 264

Pleasure's. Impatient of *pleasures* faint desires, ... *Ro.* xxiii. 6
Pampred in *pleasures* deepe: . . . . . . *S.C.* Jul. 198
drownded lie in *pleasures* wastefull well, ... *Col.* 762
subdewd to learne Dame *Pleasures* toy. . . . . . . I. i. 47. 9
slaine With *pleasures* poisoned baytes. . . . . . . II. i. Arg.
to melt in *pleasures* whott desyre, ... II. i. 58. 3

Pleasure's—*Continued.*
learne from *pleasures* poyson to abstaine; . . . . . . II. ii. 45. 4
passage plaine To *pleasures* pallace: . . . . . . II. iii. 41. 8
Pleasures porter was devizd to bee, ... II. xii. 48. 8
As Ladies wont, in *pleasures* wanton lap, ... III. ii. 6. 7
In blessed Nectar and pure *Pleasures* well, ... III. xi. 2. 4
Drawne with sweet *pleasures* bayt, ... *Am.* lxxii. 7

Pleasures. in one place all *pleasures* of the eye. . . . . . . *Bel.*¹ x. 6
my sprites were ravisht with these *pleasures* . . . . . . *Pet.*¹ iii. 7
To see such *pleasures* gon so suddenly. . . . . . . *Pet.*² iv. 14
all that doth consume our *pleasures* soone; . . . . . . *Ro.* xix. 4
Such pierlesse *pleasures* have we . . . . . . *S.C.* Jun. 32
ryper age such *pleasures* doth reprove: . . . . . . *S.C.* Jun. 36
all wylde beasts made vassals of his *pleasures,* . . . . . . *Hub.* 1129
fed with *pleasures* sweet, ... *T.M.* 302
The noble hearts to *pleasures* they allure, ... *T.M.* 331
make a tunefull Diapase of *pleasures,* . . . . . . *T.M.* 549
hir *pleasures* were wonte to lull me asleepe: . . . . . . *U.V.* 13
With *pleasures* choyce to feed his cheerefull sprights: . . . *Ti.* 522
joy in *pleasures* vaine, ... *Ti.* 528
Feeding upon their *pleasures* bounteouslie, ... *Mui.* 151
pastures on the *pleasures* of each place. . . . . . . *Mui.* 176
To spoyle the *pleasures* of that Paradise; . . . . . . *Mui.* 186
on their *pleasures* greedily doth pray. . . . . . . *Mui.* 204
made the vassall of his *pleasures* vilde. . . . . . . I. vi. 3. 5
Then serve his Ladies love, and waste in *pleasures* vayne. . I. vi. 21. 9
His heart did seeme to melt in *pleasures* manifold. . . . . I. xii. 40. 9
ydle *pleasures* in her Bowre of Blisse, ... II. v. 27. 3
flowes in *pleasures* and vaine pleasing toyes, ... II. v. 28. 8
Him to aggrate, and greatest *pleasures* shew: . . . . . . II. v. 33. 2
fild with *pleasures* vayn, ... II. vi. 14. 2
Refuse such fruitlesse toile, and present *pleasures* chuse.' . II. vi. 17. 9
told that gardins *pleasures* in their caroling. . . . . . . II. vi. 24. 9
her sweet peace and *pleasures* did annoy, ... II. vi. 37. 7
Her selfe to shroud, and *pleasures* to entreat; . . . . . . II. vii. 53. 5
wanton *pleasures* him too much did please, ... II. x. 17. 7
strong effort Of feeling *pleasures,* . . . . . . II. xi. 13. 8
In which all *pleasures* plenteously abownd, ... II. xii. 58. 3
Ne tastest Princes *pleasures,* . . . . . . III. ii. 31. 6
fraught With *pleasures* manifold. . . . . . . III. vi. Arg.
From her sweete bowres, and beds with *pleasures* fraught? . III. vi. 20. 4
be the vassall of her *pleasures* vile, ... III. vii. 50. 8
timely service to her *pleasures* meet, ... III. ix. 7. 8
her *pleasures* lenger to partake. . . . . . . III. xi. 33. 9
spotlesse *pleasures* and sweet loves content. . . . . . . IV. x. 26. 2
To tast of joy, and to wont *pleasures* to retourne. . . . . V. iii. 1. 9
Such secret comfort and such heavenly *pleasures,* . . . . . . VI. Pr. 2. 1
prov'd the perfect *pleasures* which doe grow . . . . . . VI. x. 3. 5
the place, whose *pleasures* rare . . . his sences ravished, . . VI. x. 30. 6
these her celestial threasures, And unrevealed *pleasures,* . . *Epith.* 201
His *pleasures* with thee wrought. . . . . . . *Epith.* 381
the sweet *pleasures* of theyr loves delight . . . . . . *Epith.* 401
endeere Thy *pleasures* unto those which them partake, . . . *H.L.* 275
So many millions of chaste *pleasures* play. . . . . . . *H.B.* 259
And doest thy mynd in durty *pleasures* moyle, ... *H.H.L.* 220
Whereof such wondrous *pleasures* they conceave, ... *H.H.B.* 256
With whose sweete *pleasures* being so possest, ... *H.H.B.* 300
let your bed with *pleasures* chast abound, ... *Proth.* 103

Pled. *See* **Plead.**

Pledge. loe, Perigot, the *Pledge* which I plight, ... *S.C.* Au. 25
a *pledge* I leave with thee . . . . . . *D.* 288
Which in your noble hands for *pledge* I leave . . . . . . *Ded. Son.* vii. 9
Nereus crownes with cups; his mates him *pledg* around. . . . I. iii. 31. 9
threw his gauntlet, as a sacred *pledge* . . . . . . I. iv. 43. 1
ne yet the warlike *pledge* to yield, ... I. xi. 43. 3
The sacred *pledge* of Christes Evangely. . . . . . . II. x. 53. 5
when so of his hand the *pledge* she raught, ... III. ix. 31. 1
Defil'd the *pledge* committed to thy trust? . . . . . . IV. i. 53. 5
The sacred *pledge* which in his faith was left, ... IV. vi. 8. 3
The *pledge* of faith, her hand, engaged held . . . . . . IV. x. 55. 7
grieved to restore the *pledge* he did possesse. . . . . . . IV. xii. 32. 9
The sacred *pledge* of peace and clemencie, ... V. ix. 30. 3
yield for *pledge* my poore captyved hart; . . . . . . *Am.* xlii. 8
your hand, The *pledge* of all our band! . . . . . . *Epith.* 239

Pledges. as *pledges* firme, right hands together joynd. . . . . I. ix. 18. 9
by him had many *pledges* dere. . . . . . . I. x. 4. 9
sacred *pledges* he both gave, and had, ... I. xii. 27. 3
With right hands plighted, *pledges* of good will. . . . . . . II. i. 34. 2
Thy litle hands . . . I for *pledges* leave. . . . . . . II. i. 37. 9
should bring their names And *pledges,* . . . . . . III. vii. 54. 9
Three hundred *pledges* for my good desartes, ... III. vii. 55. 4
Would me refuse their *pledges* to afford, ... III. vii. 56. 6
pledges pawnd the same to keepe aright: . . . . . . IV. iii. 3. 4

Plenteous. all his *plenteous* pasture nought him pleased: . . . *Van.* ii. 13
looking for *plenteous* praie Of fish, ... *Ti.* 151
all happie peace and *plenteous* store . . . . . . *Col.* 310
On her they poured forth of *plenteous* horne: . . . . . . III. vi. 2. 6
Moved with pity of her *plenteous* teares. . . . . . . IV. vii. 23. 4
he forth would poure so *plenteous* teares, ... IV. viii. 4. 6
the *plenteous* Ouse came far from land, ... IV. xi. 34. 1
With the revenue of her *plenteous* meedes: . . . . . . V. ii. 9. 8
Of which though present age doe *plenteous* seeme, ... VI. Pr. 4. 6
Which she perceiving did with *plenteous* teares . . . . . . VI. iii. 12. 1
Nature me endu'd with *plenteous* dowre Of all her gifts, . . VI. viii. 20. 3
As though he joyed in his *plentious* store, ... VII. vii. 30. 2
blessings . . . With *plenteous* hand by heaven upon you thrown; *Am.* lxvi. 2
spend His *plenteous* vaine in setting forth her prayse, . . . *H.H.B.* 220
through Lillies *plenteous* store, ... *Proth.* 81

Plenteously. flowres, with which so *plenteouslie* Her lap she filled . . . . . . *Mui.* 140

Plenteously—*Continued.*
God his gifts there *plenteously* bestowes, . . . *Col.* 326
heavenly grace so *plenteously* displayd! . . . II. x. 50. 6
In which all pleasures *plenteously* abownd, . . . II. xii. 58. 3
Poure out your blessing on us *plentiously*, . . . *Epith.* 415
Plenteousness. praises in all *plenteousnesse* Powr'd upon her, *D.* 227
Plentiful. Whose pleasaunce she him shewd, and *plentifull* great store. . . . II. vi. 11. 9
poured forth with *plentifull* dispence, . . . II. xii. 42. 8
Plentifully. That vertue should be *plentifully* found, . . . VI. i. 1. 4
Plenty. In forrein costes men sayd was *plentye;* . . . *S.C.* S. 28
plenty, which in all the land did grow: . . . I. iii. 18. 7
Whose welth was want, whose *plenty* made him pore; . . . I. iv. 29. 4
Gluttony, That of his *plenty* poured forth to all: . . . I. iv. 43. 8
of her *plenty* adde unto their need: . . . II. ii. 38. 8
of my *plenty* poure out unto all, . . . II. vii. 8. 3
Abusd her *plenty* and fat swolne encreace . . . II. vii. 16. 7
Pourd out their *plenty* without spight or spare. . . . III. i. 51. 4
here all *plenty* and all pleasure flowes; . . . III. vi. 41. 4
'In such luxurious *plentie* of all pleasure, . . . IV. x. 23. 1
Plenty of pearles to decke his dames withall; . . . IV. xi. 39. 6
Liv'd here on earth, and *plenty* made abound; . . . VII. vii. 37. 7
so *plenty* makes me poore. . . . *Am.* xxxv. 8
Betokening peace and *plenty* to ensew. . . . *Am.* lxii. 4
Begot of *Plentie* and of Penurie, . . . *H.L.* 53
Plentie of riches forth on him will powre, . . . *H.H.B.* 247
blessed *Plentie* wait upon your bord; . . . *Proth.* 102
Plenty's. swolne with *plenties* pride, . . . *Ro.* xxiii. 13
Plesh. *See* **Plash.**
Plexippus. On Phrygian Paris by *Plexippus* brooke, . . . VI. ix. 36. 7
Plied. his false engins fast he *plyde*, . . . III. x. 7. 2
Plies. During which time her gentle wit she *plyes* . . . I. vi. 19. 5
Plight. For ruth and pitie of so haples *plight:* . . . *Pet.*[2] v. 13
Art made a myrrhour to behold my *plight:* . . . *S.C.* Ja. 20
Thomalin, I pittie thy *plight*, . . . *S.C.* Mar. 103
may shee florish long In princely *plight!* . . . *S.C.* Ap. 49
messengers of this my painfull *plight*, . . . *S.C.* Jun. 98
Never knew I lovers sheepe in good *plight:* . . . *S.C.* Au. 20
loe, Perigot, the Pledge which I *plight*, . . . *S.C.* Au. 25
Such play is a pitteous *plight*. . . . *S.C.* Au. 92
Never I wist thee in so poore a *plight*. . . . *S.C.* S. 8
My piteous *plight* and losse to amend? . . . *S.C.* S. 245
Her peeced pyneons bene not so in *plight:* . . . *S.C.* O. 87
Thilke sollein season sadder *plight* doth aske, . . . *S.C.* N. 17
know the purporte of my evill *plight*, . . . *Gn.* Ded. 8
In this ill *plight* there came to visite mee . . . *Hub.* 17
The evill *plight* that doth me sore constraine, . . . *Hub.* 56
hereupon an oath unto me *plight*,' . . . *Hub.* 1055
Might be the cause of so impatient *plight?* . . . *T.M.* 44
for pittie of his heavie *plight* . . . *D.* 170
Alcyon, painfull is thy *plight*, . . . *D.* 174
With Philumene, the partner of my *plight*. . . . *D.* 476
Ne will be helde in anie stedfast *plight*, . . . *D.* 496
when she saw her love in such a *plight*, . . . *As.* 151
'In this sad *plight*, . . . I, Fidessa, dwell, . . . I. ii. 26. 1
'We may not chaunge,' (quoth he,) 'this evill *plight*, . . . I. ii. 43. 3
Sad Una downe her laies in weary *plight*, . . . I. iii. 15. 3
pities all this while His mournefull *plight*, . . . I. v. 18. 8
Whom when she found, as she him left in *plight*, . . . I. v. 19. 7
dwell in perill of like painefull *plight*, . . . I. v. 52. 4
devise to quitt a thrall from such a *plight?* . . . I. vi. 6. 9
In their rude eyes unworthie of so wofull *plight*. . . . I. vi. 9. 9
more heavy *plight* Then that I feele, . . . I. vii. 25. 3
In pensive *plight* and sad perplexitie, . . . I. viii. 26. 2
woman . . . The roote of all your care and wretched *plight*, . I. viii. 45. 5
weighing the decayed *plight* . . . of her chosen knight, . . . I. ix. 20. 4
never knight I saw in such misseeming *plight*.' . . . I. ix. 23. 9
Till he recovered had his late decayed *plight*. . . . I. x. 2. 9
be partakers of their evill *plight*, . . . I. x. 10. 7
well acquainted with that commune *plight*, . . . I. x. 23. 2
much aswag'd the passion of his *plight*, . . . I. x. 24. 8
by the faith which I to armes have *plight*, . . . I. xii. 18. 3
appease your griefe and heavie *plight*, . . . II. i. 14. 5
read who hath ye wrought this shamefull *plight*, . . . II. i. 18. 2
Sir Guyon, mindfull of his vow *yplight*, . . . II. iii. 1. 5
Purfled upon with many a folded *plight*, . . . II. iii. 26. 5
When late he saw his Lord in heavie *plight* . . . II. v. 25. 5
rings of rushes *plight:* . . . II. vi. 7. 5
His owne deare Lord Pyrochles in sad *plight*, . . . II. vi. 43. 4
To save my Lord in wretched *plight* forlore; . . . II. vi. 48. 3
yet in my trouth *yplight*, . . . II. vii. 50. 6
sure I rew his pitteous *plight*.' . . . II. viii. 24. 5
Mote I beseech to succour his sad *plight*, . . . II. viii. 25. 7
sith I armes and knighthood first did *plight*, . . . II. ix. 7. 2
Close rownd about her tuckt with many a *plight:* . . . II. ix. 40. 6
the stressed *plight* Of this sad realme, . . . II. x. 37. 3
the Prince, seeing her wofull *plight*, . . . II. xi. 16. 4
most deadly daunger and distressed *plight*. . . . II. xii. 11. 9
Having their weary limbes to perfect *plight* Restord, . . . III. i. 1. 3
we your liegemen faith unto you *plight*.' . . . III. i. 30. 5
Could find no rest in such perplexed *plight*, . . . III. i. 59. 5
'what evill *plight* Hath thee oppress, . . . III. ii. 30. 7
doth plonge in dolefull *plight*, . . . III. iii. 16. 5
eke him selfe mournd at their mournful *plight*, . . . III. iv. 32. 3
Lamenting his mishap and heavy *plight;* . . . III. iv. 44. 2
To comfort me in my distressed *plight*. . . . III. v. 35. 4
his foule sore reduced to faire *plight:* . . . III. v. 41. 8
came at last in weary wretched *plight* . . . III. vii. 5. 7
ruth of her sad *plight* Would make to melt, . . . III. vii. 9. 6
his sad mother, seeing his sore *plight*, . . . III. vii. 20. 6

Plight—*Continued.*
All wayes shee sought him to restore to *plight*, . . . III. vii. 21. 1
perceive In that fowle *plight* . . . III. vii. 46. 2
their lately bruzed parts to bring in *plight*. . . . III. ix. 19. 9
he emongst the rest crept forth in sory *plight*. . . . III. x. 52. 9
Indians do aray . . . in their proudest *plight:* . . . III. xii. 8. 4
Dissembling his disease and evill *plight;* . . . IV. i. 38. 3
not in *plight* This day to wreake the dammage . . . IV. i. 44. 5
evill *plight*, in which her dearest brother Now stood, . . . IV. iii. 40. 7
Unweeting of thine owne like haplesse *plight:* . . . IV. vii. 10. 8
'Thy ruefull *plight* I pitty as mine owne. . . . IV. vii. 19. 2
wast his wretched daies in wofull *plight;* . . . IV. vii. 39. 8
There he continued in this carefull *plight*, . . . IV. vii. 41. 1
pitty much his *plight*, that liv'd like outcast thrall. . . . IV. vii. 43. 9
seeing his sad *plight*, her tender heart . . . did emmove, . . . IV. viii. 3. 6
Full of discomfort and disquiet *plight*, . . . IV. viii. 8. 4
With mild regard to see his ruefull *plight*, . . . IV. viii. 17. 7
In heavy *plight* and sad perplexitie; . . . IV. viii. 57. 2
fayled oft through faint and feeble *plight:* . . . IV. xi. 25. 5
farre from hearing of my heavy *plight;* . . . IV. xii. 6. 6
In this sad *plight* he walked here and there, . . . IV. xii. 17. 1
For his deare sake, that ill deserv'd that *plight:* . . . IV. xii. 19. 5
To whom complayning her afflicted *plight*, . . . V. i. 4. 3
Artegall him selfe her seemelesse *plight* did rew. . . . V. ii. 25. 9
in the rudenesse of that evill *plight* . . . V. v. 12. 6
his faith had *plight* Her vassall to become, . . . V. v. 23. 8
She chaw'd the cud of lover's carefull *plight;* . . . V. v. 27. 2
For breach of faith to her, which he had firmely *plight*. . . . V. vi. 12. 9
Me to deceive of faith unto me *plight*, . . . V. vi. 16. 8
After that long daies toile and weary *plight:* . . . V. vii. 12. 4
They might perceive she was not well in *plight*, . . . V. vii. 18. 2
leaving there in that dispiteous *plight*, . . . V. viii. 8. 7
With piteous ruth of her so wretched *plight*, . . . V. ix. 50. 2
Much was he moved with her piteous *plight*, . . . V. x. 22. 1
sure to me her faith she first did *plight*, . . . V. xi. 50. 1
Her halfe dismayd they found in doubtfull *plight*, . . . V. xi. 60. 4
With so foule blame as breach of faith once *plight*, . . . V. xi. 62. 4
cast his shield about to be in readie *plight*. . . . V. xii. 16. 9
of him learnes His state and present *plight*. . . . VI. ii. Arg.
he was not presently in *plight* Her to defend, . . . VI. ii. 19. 1
being moov'd with pittie of my *plight* . . . VI. ii. 23. 2
Is now him selfe in much more wretched *plight:* . . . VI. ii. 45. 6
And to salute him, if he were in *plight*, . . . VI. iii. 14. 3
his faith thereto did *plight* It to performe: . . . VI. iii. 16. 1
There left on ground, though in full evill *plight*, . . . VI. iii. 26. 2
In dolorous dismay and deadly *plight*, . . . VI. iii. 27. 3
plight In which this Lady languisheth forlorne, . . . VI. iii. 41. 7
he remayned in most perilous *plight*, . . . VI. iv. 1. 8
feele compassion of his evill *plight*, . . . VI. iv. 3. 6
So much more wofull, as my wofull *plight* . . . VI. iv. 28. 4
Under the greenewoods side in sorie *plight*, . . . VI. iv. 39. 2
some asswagement of their painefull *plight*. . . . VI. v. 40. 4
So shall you soone repaire your present evill *plight*.' . . . VI. vi. 14. 9
prayd to pitty his ill *plight*. . . . VI. vi. 20. 9
in what perilous *plight* He had . . . left that salvage wight . VI. vi. 37. 4
How fortuneth this foule uncomely *plight*, . . . VI. vii. 14. 8
Regarding more his faith which he did *plight*, . . . VI. vii. 23. 3
on his head a roll of linnen *plight*, . . . VI. vii. 43. 5
As her to leave in such a piteous *plight:* . . . VI. viii. 33. 5
would rew And pitty her sad *plight*, . . . VI. xi. 2. 9
The sad remembrance of her wretched *plight:* . . . VI. xi. 50. 7
Rejoyced much to see his captive *plight*, . . . VI. xii. 37. 8
in that *plight* To hunt him with their hounds, . . . VII. vi. 50. 8
the religion of the faith first *plight* . . . *Epith.* 392
Plighted. *See* **Plight, Well-plighted.**
he already *plighted* his right hand Unto another love, . . . I. xii. 26. 8
With right hands *plighted*, pledges of good will. . . . II. i. 34. 2
with solemne oath and *plighted* hand Assurd, . . . II. iv. 23. 8
the vow that to faire Columbell I *plighted* have, . . . III. vii. 51. 7
plighted hands for ever friends to be. . . . IV. iii. 49. 5
dearer then them both your faith once *plighted* hold.' . . . V. xi. 63. 9
Plights. these rent reliques, speaking their ill *plightes?* . . . II. xii. 9. 7
Glistring like gold amongst the *plights* enrold, . . . V. ix. 28. 7
Never abiding in their stedfast *plights:* . . . VII. vii. 21. 3
speake no word to her of these sad *plights*, . . . *Am.* lxxxiii. 11
Plim. meeting *Plim*, to Plimmouth thence declines: . . . IV. xi. 31. 4
Plong, -ed. *See* **Plunge, -d.**
Plot. th' auncient *Plot* of Rome, displayed plaine, . . . *Ro.* xxvi. 13
Therefore (if please you) this shalbe our *plot:* . . . *Hub.* 154
I Did first devise the *plot* by pollicie; . . . *Hub.* 1036
placed on a *plot* of sandie ground: . . . *Ti.* 508
In this faire *plot* dispacing too and fro, . . . *Mui.* 250
It was a chosen *plott* of fertile land, . . . II. vi. 12. 1
Till they arriv'd whereas their purpose they did *plott*. . . . III. xi. 20. 9
all this cursed *plot* . . . discovered was betymes, . . . V. ix. 42. 3
The *plot* of all her practise did display, . . . V. ix. 47. 8
In this small *plot* of your dominion, . . . VI. ix. 28. 4
To prosecute her *plot*. . . . VII. vi. 23. 9
Plots. stragling *plots* which to and fro doe ronne . . . II. xii. 11. 5
diverse *plots* did frame to maske in strange disguise. . . . III. iii. 51. 9
Plotteth. *plotteth* out a tombe by measured space: . . . *Gn.* 652
Plough. To *plough*, to plant, to reap, to rake, to sowe, . . . *Hub.* 263
for to drive The painefull *plough*, . . . VI. viii. 35. 6
never usde to live by *plough* nor spade, . . . VI. x. 39. 4
His *plough* and harnesse fit to till the ground, . . . VII. vii. 43. 6
Ploughed. Streight was the passage, like a *ploughed* ridge, . . V. vi. 36. 8
their bad Stuard neither *plough'd* nor sowed, . . . VI. iv. 14. 7
Ploughing-share. his *ploughing-share* and coulter ready tyde. . VII. vii. 39. 9
Plough-irons. by his *plough-yrons* mote right well appeare. . VII. vii. 35. 4
Ploughman. the Pilgrim that the *Ploughman* playde awhyle; . *S.C.* Env. 10

Ploughman—*Continued.*
thee a *Ploughman* all unweeting fond, . . . I. x. 66. 3
a sturdy *ploughman* with his hynde . . . VI. viii. 12. 1
Ploughman's. The *ploughmans* hope and shepheards labour vaine: . . . *Ro.* xiv. 4
brought thee up in *ploughmans* state to byde, . . . I. x. 66. 5
The Churches part, and *Ploughmans* portion, . . . II. x. 39. 4
Plovers. There now haunt yelling Mewes and whining *Plovers.* *Ti.* 133
Pluck. liker bene they to *pluck* away more, . . . *S.C.* S. 128
Do *pluck* it softly for that shepheards sake. . . . *As.* 198
From Lyons clawes to *pluck* the gryped pray. . . . I. vi. 7. 4
that proud avenging boy Did soone *pluck* downe, . . . I. ix. 12. 4
Amendment . . . did wayt, To *pluck* it out . . . I. x. 26. 8
from Cerberus greedy jaw To *plucke* a bone, . . . I. xi. 41. 5
plucke the pray oftimes out of their greedy hould. . . . VI. v. 15. 9
raught forth her hand To *pluck* her downe . . . VII. vi. 13. 3
Plucked. to frame A girlond . . . He *pluckt* a bough; . . . I. ii. 30. 8
Her from her Palfrey *pluckt,* her visage to behold. . . . I. iii. 40. 9
He *pluckt* from us all hope of dew reliefe, . . . I. ix. 29. 5
pluckt him backe; . . . II. iv. 6. 5
him *pluckt* perforce, Perforse him *pluckt,* . . . III. vii. 43. 2, 3
Unto your part, and *pluckt* from his away, . . . V. iv. 17. 4
And *plucked* quite from all possessors hand, . . . V. iv. 19. 3
Some by the nose him *pluckt,* some by the taile, . . . VII. vi. 49. 4
Plucking. downe him *plucking,* . . . Gan him to hale, . . . VI. viii. 28. 6
Plumed. quite it clove his *plumed* crest in tway, . . . II. vi. 31. 7
Plume-feather. With a *plume feather* all to peeces tore: . . . *Hub.* 210
Plumes. May now goe prune his *plumes* . . . *T.M.* 402
with brave *plumes* doth beate the azure skie, . . . *Ti.* 423
doth her tender *plumes* as yet but trie . . . *Col.* 422
The *plumes* of pride, and winges of vanity, . . . I. x. 39. 3
an Eagle . . . His aery *plumes* doth rouze, . . . I. xi. 9. 6
he hath lefte his *plumes* all hory gray, . . . I. xi. 34. 4
As Peacocke that his painted *plumes* doth pranck, . . . II. iii. 6. 4
She her gay painted *plumes* disorderid: . . . II. iii. 36. 4
two sharpe winged sheares, Decked with diverse *plumes,* . . . II. viii. 5. 8
Puttockes, all in *plumes* arayd; . . . II. xi. 11. 5
paynted *plumes* in goodly order dight, . . . III. xii. 8. 2
as those same *plumes* so seemd he vaine and light, . . . III. xii. 8. 5
with borrowed *plumes* thy selfe endewed, . . . V. iii. 20. 7
The wingd-foot God so fast his *plumes* did beat, . . . VII. vi. 17. 1
On golden *plumes* up to the purest skie, . . . *H.L.* 178
Thence gathering *plumes* of perfect speculation, . . . *H.H.B.* 134
Soyle their fayre *plumes* with water . . . *Proth.* 50
Plumy. with *plumy* wings doth sheare The subtile ayre . . . III. vii. 39. 3
Plunge. Doth *plonge* himselfe in Tethys bosome faire; . . . *Ro.* xx. 4
downe againe Her *plong,* . . . II. xii. 64. 3
Tormenteth and doth *plonge* in dolefull plight, . . . III. iii. 16. 5
Plunged. He, *plongd* in payne, his tressed locks dooth teare. . *S.C.* Ap. 12
hart, so *plungd* in sea of sorrowes deep, . . . I. vii. 39. 2
Which *plonged* had faire Lady in so wretched state. . . . II. i. 56. 9
In those sad waves . . . *Plonged* continually . . . II. vii. 57. 4
Should *plonged* be in such affliction . . . III. viii. 1. 5
the sad distresse In which that boy thee *plonged,* . . . III. xi. 36. 3
Pluto. Of griesly *Pluto* she the daughter was, . . . I. iv. 11. 1
All these before the gates of *Pluto* lay, . . . II. vii. 24. 1
tell To griesly *Pluto* what on earth was donne, . . . VI. xii. 35. 6
Yet *Pluto* and Proserpina were present there. . . . VII. vii. 3. 9
Pluto's. did fetch his dame From *Plutoes* balefull bowre . . . *S.C.* O. 29
He bad awake blacke *Plutoes* griesly Dame; . . . I. i. 37. 4
Have borne him hence to *Plutoes* balefull bowres: . . . I. v. 14. 8
downe to *Plutoes* house are come bilive: . . . I. v. 32. 3
streight did lead to *Plutoes* griesly rayne. . . . II. vii. 21. 4
fly Unto her rest in *Plutoes* griesly land; . . . IV. iii. 13. 3
Ply. sternely bad him other businesse *plie* . . . I. vi. 46. 7
ply himselfe to any honest trade, . . . III. vii. 12. 6
towards them did *ply* With speedie course, . . . IV. i. 38. 5
Yet Talus after them apace did *plie,* . . . V. vi. 30. 4
Plymouth. meeting Plim, to *Plimmouth* thence declines: . . . IV. xi. 31. 4
Po. Nor *Po* nor Tyburs swans so much renowned, . . . *Col.* 412
Pocket. A murdrous knife out of his *pocket* drew, . . . III. xii. 32. 5
Podalyrius. that immortall spright Of *Podalyrius* . . . VI. vi. 1. 8
Poeana. one daughter that is hight The faire *Poeana,* . . . IV. viii. 49. 4
Of faire *Poeana* I received was, . . . IV. viii. 59. 7
*Squire of low degree releast *Poeana* takes to wife . . . IV. ix. Arg.
though *Poeana* were as faire as morne, . . . IV. ix. 3. 6
The faire *Poeana* playing on a Rote . . . IV. ix. 6. 2
That faire *Poeana,* them beholding both, . . . IV. ix. 9. 6
The faire *Poeana,* he enlarged free, . . . IV. ix. 13. 2
Poem. excuse This Gnats small *Poeme,* . . . *Gn.* 5
No braver *Poeme* can be under Sun. . . . *Col.* 411
to let thy name be writt In this base *Poeme,* . . . *Ded. Son.* ii. 5
Yet, till that thou thy *Poeme* wilt make knowne, . . . *Ded.Son.*viii. 13
Poems. with lewd *poems* which he did compyle; . . . V. ix. 25. 7
Poems'. with vaine *poemes* weeds to have their fancies fed. . IV. Pr. 1. 9
Poesy. Bellay, first garland of free *Poesie* . . . *Ro.* Env. 1
any buddes of *Poesie,* . . . *S.C.* O. 73
O pierlesse *Poesye!* where is then thy place? . . . *S.C.* O. 79
for thy worth frame some fit *Poesie:* . . . *Gn.* 12
Have mard the face of goodly *Poesie,* . . . *T.M.* 557
Supports the praise of noble *Poesie;* . . . *T.M.* 574
The pure well head of *Poesie* did dwell) . . . VII. vii. 9. 4
Poet. All otherwise the state of *Poet* stands; . . . *S.C.* O. 97
play the *Poet* oft. . . . *Hub.* 810
Ne anie *Poet* seekes him to revive, . . . *Ti.* 223
hath a *Poet* got To sing his living praises . . . *Ti.* 436
let that same delitious *Poet* lend A little leave . . . III. Pr. 5. 1
As that renowmed *Poet* them compyled . . . IV. ii. 32. 6
the bold title of a *poet* bad He on himselfe had ta'en, . . . V. ix. 25. 8
that whilome that good *Poet* sayd, . . . VI. iii. 1. 1

Poet—*Continued.*
Or that sweete Teian *Poet,* which did spend . . . *H.H.B.* 219
Poetress. is her selfe a peereles *Poetresse.* . . . *T.M.* 576
Most peereles Prince, most peereles *Poetresse,* . . . *T.M.* 577
Poetry. Ne let such verses *Poetrie* be named! . . . *Hub.* 814
They thinke to be chiefe praise of *Poetry;* . . . *T.M.* 555
T' embrace the service of sweete *Poetry,* . . . *Ded. Son.* iv. 7
Poet's. O that I had the Thracian *Poets* harpe, . . . *Ro.* xxv. 1
Who but thy selfe deserves sike *Poetes* prayse? . . . *S.C.* N. 23
with gentle mood Of *Poets* Prince, . . . *Gn.* 18
with sweete *Poets* verse be glorifide. . . . *Ti.* 427
Poets wits are had in peerlesse price: . . . *Col.* 321
whose vertues . . . merit a most famous *Poets* witt . . . *Ded. Son.* ii. 2
That Mantuane *Poetes* incompared spirit, . . . *Ded. Son.* xiii. 1
the verse of famous *Poets* witt He does backebite, . . . I. iv. 32. 6
Poets witt, that passeth Painter farre . . . III. Pr. 2. 6
To whom sweet *Poets* verse hath given endlesse date. . . . III. vi. 45. 9
Ne spareth he the gentle *Poets* rime; . . . VI. xii. 40. 8
Poets. matter made for *Poets* on to play: . . . *S.C.* O. 64
The vaunting *Poets* found nought worth a pease . . . *S.C.* O. 69
the rich fee, which *Poets* wont divide, . . . *T.M.* 471
Yet manie *Poets* honourd him alive. . . . *Ti.* 224
that blessed throng Of heavenlie *Poets* and Heroes . . . *Ti.* 341
whose famous ofspring The antique *Poets* wont . . . to sing; . *Ded. Son.* vi. 5
The Laurell, meed of . . . *Poets* sage; . . . I. i. 9. 2
Phoebus selfe, that god of *Poets* hight, . . . VII. vii. 12. 6
Poets'. Let not sweete *Poets* praise, . . . *Hub.* 811
Through famous *Poets* verse each where renownd, . . . I. x. 54. 7
Whom famous *Poetes* verse so much doth vaunt, . . . I. xi. 27. 2
matter made for famous *Poets* verse, . . . III. iv. 1. 6
they therewith doe *Poetes* heads adorne, . . . *Am.* xxix. 7
Poignant. His *poynant* speare that many made to bleed, . . . I. vii. 19. 7
His *poynant* speare he thrust . . . II. viii. 36. 3
then the Faery quickly raught His *poynant* speare, . . . III. i. 5. 4
his *poynant* speare he fierce aventred . . . IV. iii. 9. 1
Point. *See* **Counterpoint.**
flame, Mounting like waves with triple *point* . . . *Bel.*[1] ix. 2
flame . . . Waving aloft with triple *point* . . . *Bel.*[2] xi. 2
pierce her heart with *poynt* of worthy wight, . . . *S.C.* Jun. 100
Whom, thus at *point* prepared, to prevent, . . . *Gn.* 281
since we passed are Unto this *point,* . . . *Hub.* 1048
one in mayle, Armed to *point,* . . . I. i. 16. 6
A faithlesse Sarazin, all armde to *point,* . . . I. ii. 12. 6
He . . . cared not for God or man a *point.* . . . I. ii. 12. 9
he perced . . . With thrilling *point* of deadly yron brand, . . I. iii. 42. 7
point of speare it never percen could, . . . I. vii. 33. 8
with percing *point* Of pitty deare his hart was thrilled sore; . I. viii. 39. 1
is the *point* of death now turnd fro mee, . . . I. ix. 26. 3
as a swords *poynt* through his hart did perse, . . . I. ix. 48. 2
those in *point* of death which lay; . . . I. x. 41. 2
at the *point* two stinges in fixed arre, . . . I. xi. 11. 8
found no place his deadly *point* to rest. . . . I. xi. 17. 4
From *poynt* to *poynt* . . . Discourst his voyage long, . . . I. xii. 15. 8
with his steedy staffe did *point* his way; . . . II. i. 34. 6
thrild with *point* of thorough-piercing paine: . . . II. i. 38. 5
ere the *point* arrived where it ought, . . . II. viii. 32. 4
Without full *point,* or other Cesure right; . . . II. x. 68. 3
Now comes to *point* of that same perilous sted, . . . II. xii. 1. 7
hungers *poynt* or Venus sting . . . II. xii. 39. 3
For death sate on the *point* of that enchaunted speare: . . . III. i. 9. 9
Threatning the *point* of her avenging blaed; . . . III. i. 63. 8
Me lever were with *point* of foemans speare be dead. . . . III. ii. 6. 9
All which the Redcrosse knight to *point* aredd, . . . III. ii. 16. 8
in each *point* her selfe informd aright, . . . III. iv. 4. 3
The *point* of pitty perced through her tender hart. . . . III. v. 30. 9
her swords *point* directing forward right . . . III. xi. 25. 3
felt the *point* of his hart-percing dart, . . . III. xi. 30. 2
All arm'd to *point,* his chalenge to abet: . . . IV. iii. 6. 2
in his side The mortall *point* most cruelly empight; . . . IV. iii. 10. 4
ythrild With *point* of steele that close his hartbloud spild, . IV. iii. 22. 5
His hart was thrild with *point* of deadly feare, . . . IV. vi. 37. 2
From the first *point* of his appointed sourse; . . . V. Pr. 1. 8
Shall find that from the *point* . . . V. Pr. 5. 3
came Artegal . . . All arm'd to *point,* . . . V. v. 5. 2
three knights he spyde, All arm'd to *point,* . . . V. x. 34. 2
Percing his hart, with pities *point* did thrill; . . . VI. iv. 18. 5
All arm'd to *point* came ryding thetherward; . . . VI. v. 11. 3
He to that *point* fit speaches gan to frame, . . . VI. vi. 6. 2
Ere he attain'd the *point* by him intended, . . . VI. ix. 46. 8
His poysnous *point* deepe fixed in his hart . . . VI. x. 31. 2
To every planet *point* his sundry yeare: . . . *Am.* lx. 2
Pointed. *See* **Appointed, Sharp-pointed, Well-pointed.**
to his Gate he *pointed* a strong gard, . . . *Hub.* 1115
Beyond the compasse of his *pointed* path, . . . *T.M.* 10
Her huge long taile . . . *Pointed* with mortall sting. . . . I. i. 15. 4
With dint of swerd, nor push of *pointed* speare: . . . I. xi. 9. 4
The *pointed* steele, arriving rudely theare, . . . I. xi. 16. 3
many dreadfull feends hath *pointed* to her gard. . . . III. xi. 16. 9
twixt themselves they *pointed* time and place: . . . IV. viii. 51. 1
pointed for the combat twixt them twayne The morrow next, . V. xii. 9. 7
Twixt Peleus and Dame Thetis, *pointed* there; . . . VII. vii. 12. 5
Pointest. thou *pointest* thy Sons poysned arrow, . . . *H.B.* 62
Pointing. *pointing* forth, 'Lo! yonder is . . . The brasen towre, . . . I. xi. 3. 1
Points. he could doo manie other *poynts,* . . . *Hub.* 696
he, that *points* the Centonell his roome, . . . I. ix. 41. 8
They beene ymett, and both theyr *points* arriv'd; . . . III. i. 6. 1
brought through *points* of many perilous swords: . . . III. viii. 17. 3
deadly *points* at eithers breast to bend, . . . IV. ii. 14. 8
More sharpe then *points* of needles, . . . IV. viii. 39. 2

Points—*Continued.*
The which the prisoner *points* unto the free! . . . . IV. xii. 11. 2
The piercing *points* of his avengefull darts; . . . . *H.L.* 30
their *points* rebutted backe againe Are duld, ... *H.H.B.* 122
Poise. *See* **Counterpoise.**
Against a Rocke to breake with dreadfull *poyse:* . . . . *Ro.* xvi. 4
With dreadfull *poyse* is from the mayneland rift, ... I. xi. 54. 7
What was the *poyse* of every part of yore: . . . . V. ii. 34. 7
with such monstrous *poise* adowne descended, ... V. xii. 21. 3
Poison. Did in his drinke shed *poyson* privilie; . . . . *Van.* vi. 8
bowels so with ranckling *poyson* swelde, ... *Mui.* 255
A floud of *poyson* horrible and blacke, ... I. i. 20. 2
all the *poison* ran about his chaw; . . . . I. iv. 30. 4
spightfull *poison* spues . . . on all that ever writt. . . . . I. iv. 32. 7
despeyre did many thereof sup, And secret *poyson* . . . . I. viii. 14. 4
brought unto him swords, ropes, *poison,* fire, ... I. ix. 50. 6
Was swoln with wrath and *poyson,* . . . . I. xi. 8. 9
learne from pleasures *poyson* to abstaine: . . . . II. ii. 45. 4
In *poyson* and in blood of malice and despight. . . . . II. iv. 38. 9
through *poyson* stopped was his breath; . . . . II. x. 67. 8
Pouring out streames of *poyson* and of gall . . . . IV. viii. 24. 6
till she had all her *poyson* spent. . . . . IV. viii. 35. 9
poyson therewith rusht, That him nigh choked . . . . V. xi. 31. 7
The bloudie gore and *poyson* dropping lothsomely. . . . . V. xii. 30. 9
Foming with *poyson* round about her gils, ... V. xii. 36. 2
in fresh *poyson* steepe; . . . . V. xii. 42. 8
he the more his wicked *poyson* forth did poure.' . . . . VI. i. 9. 9
scattering Contagious *poyson* close through every vaine, ... VI. vi. 8. 8
spat out *poyson,* and gore-bloudy gere, ... VI. xii. 28. 3
spitting forth the *poyson* of his spight . . . . VI. xii. 29. 5
Poisoned. him the *poysoned* garment did enchaunt, ... I. xi. 27. 5
slaine With pleasures *poisoned* baytes. . . . . II. i. Arg.
through his soule like *poysned* arrow perst, ... IV. v. 31. 4
poysoned words and spitefull speeches . . . . *Am.* lxxxv. 4
thou pointest thy Sons *poysned* arrow, ... *H.B.* 62
Poisonous. all her blood to *poysonous* rancor turne: . . . . *Mui.* 344
Defended from foule Envies *poisnous* bit. . . . . *Ded. Son.* iii. 4
A thousand yong ones, . . . Sucking upon her *poisnous* dugs; . . . . I. i. 15. 6
all my entrailes flow with *poisnous* gore, ... III. ii. 39. 4
Ne *poysnous* Envy justly can empayre The prayse . . . . III. v. 54. 5
todes and frogs, his pasture *poysonous,* . . . . III. x. 59. 2
poysnous spirit sent From inward parts, ... IV. viii. 26. 3
poysnous bale did breede . . . . IV. viii. 39. 4
Out of her *poysnous* entrails fraught with dire decay.' . . . . V. xi. 20. 9
the *poysnous* sting, which infamy Infixeth . . . . VI. vi. 1. 3
The *poysnous* humour . . . infest Their ranckling wounds, ... VI. vi. 2. 8
pours his *poysnous* gall forth . . . . VI. vi. 12. 5
His *poysnous* point deepe fixed in his hart . . . . VI. x. 31. 2
Poke. like a wide deepe *poke,* downe hanging low, ... IV. vii. 6. 2
Pole. He pitcht upon a *pole* on high ordayned; . . . . V. ii. 19. 4
Pole-ax. in his hand an huge *Polaxe* did beare, ... V. xii. 14. 7
Policies. With these in praise of *pollicies* mote strive. . . . . II. ix. 48. 7
Policy. he is practiz'd well in *policie,* . . . . *Hub.* 783
I Did first devise the plot by *pollicie;* . . . . *Hub.* 1036
No counterpoint of cunning *policie,* . . . . *Hub.* 1140
delay The rugged brow of carefull *Policy,* . . . . *Ded. Son.* i. 12
pollicie, And strong advizement of six wisards old, ... I. iv. 12. 7
Of commen-wealthes, of states, of *pollicy,* . . . . II. ix. 53. 6
dominion By strength was wielded without *pollicy:* . . . . II. x. 39. 8
They have exceld in artes and *pollicy,* . . . . III. ii. 2. 8
eke of Justice, and of *Policie;* . . . . VII. vi. 6. 2
Venice . . . farre exceedes in *policie* of right. . . . . *Com. Son.* iv. 12
Polished. not with skill of craftsman *polished:* . . . . *Gn.* 130
her became, as *polisht* yvory . . . . II. ix. 41. 5
Pollente. 'His name is hight *Pollente,* . . . . V. ii. 7. 1
On which *Pollente* with Artegall did fight. . . . . V. vi. 36. 7
Polls. *pols* and pils the poore in piteous wize; . . . . V. ii. 6. 8
Pollute. Dares to *pollute* her hidden mysterie; . . . . *T.M.* 568
To dare not to *pollute* so sacred threasure . . . . VI. viii. 43. 8
Polluted. he hath *polluted* oft of yore, ... I. xii. 27. 7
Polluted this same gentle soyle long time; . . . . II. x. 9. 2
Polygony. whether yt divine Tobacco were, Or Panachaea,
or *Polygony,* . . . . III. v. 32. 7
Polynome. she that hight of many heastes *Polynome;* . . . . IV. xi. 50. 9
Pomp. see the end of *pompe* and fleshlie pride! . . . . *Ti.* 543
With royall *pomp* and princely majestie She is ybrought . . . . I. v. 5. 2
old Ninus far did pas In princely *pomp,* . . . . I. v. 48. 4
in ydle *pomp,* or wanton play, ... I. v. 51. 7
Such proud luxurious *pompe* is swollen up but late. . . . . I. xii. 14. 9
in *pompe* of prowd estate' . . . . II. iii. 40. 1
The wealth of th' East, and *pompe* of Persian kings: . . . . III. iv. 23. 4
roiall *pompe,* which there long hidden lay, ... V. viii. 51. 5
And all that *pompe* to which proud minds aspyre . . . . *H.H.B.* 277
Pompey. High Caesar, great *Pompey,* and fiers Antonius. . . . . I. v. 49. 9
Pompous. themselves to raise Through *pompous* pride, ... *T.M.* 92
The picture of thy pride in *pompous* shew: . . . . *Ti.* 82
Ne Persia selfe, the nourse of *pompous* pride, Like ever saw. I. iv. 7. 6
decke the world with their rich *pompous* showes; . . . . II. vi. 15. 7
the matter of his huge desire And *pompous* pride . . . . II. vii. 17. 7
His glory did enhaunce, and *pompous* pryde display. . . . . II. vii. 44. 9
like a *pompous* bride Did decke her, ... II. xii. 50. 7
Old Cybele, arayd with *pompous* pride, ... IV. xi. 28. 4
a stately pallace did behold Of *pompous* show, ... V. ix. 21. 5
brought forth with *pompous* showes . . . . VII. vi. 41. 4
entertayne The greatest Prince with *pompous* roialty: . . . . *Am.* lxxvii. 4
Pond. Amongst her watry sisters by a *pond,* . . . . III. iv. 29. 7
underneath him like a *pond* appeare, ... V. xii. 20. 7
Ponder. Pleaseth you *ponder* your Suppliants plaint, ... *S.C.* F. 151
Pontic. yron bands abord The *Pontick* sea . . . . *Gn.* 47
built Nausicle by the *Pontick* shore; . . . . III. ix. 37. 3
Pontoporea. Euagore, and light *Pontoporea,* . . . . IV. xi. 50. 3
Pool. On th' other side they see that perilous *Poole,* . . . . II. xii. 20. 1
Ne *Poole* so small, that can his smoothnesse holde . . . . VII. vii. 20. 6
Poor. *See* **Pour.**
which I your *poore* Vassall dayly endure; . . . . *S.C.* F. 153
'God blesse thee, *poore* Orphane! . . . . *S.C.* May 191
all as a *poore* pedler he did wend, ... *S.C.* May 238
I am a *poore* sheepe, ... *S.C.* May 266
Never I wist thee in so *poore* a plight. . . . . *S.C.* S. 8
my *poore* Muse hath spent her spared store, ... *S.C.* O. 9
Such pleasaunce makes the Grashopper so *poore,* . . . . *S.C.* O. 11
was *poore* shepheards pryde, ... *S.C.* N. 198
Who so loathes not too much the *poore* estate, ... *Gn.* 90
my *poore* wretched ghost Is forst to ferrie . . . . *Gn.* 337
I, *poore* wretch, am forced to retourne . . . . *Gn.* 618
thou art he whom my *poore* ghost complaines . . . . *Gn.* 630
would ye not *poore* fellowship expell, ... *Hub.* 96
he us'd oft to beguile *Poore* suters, ... *Hub.* 878
'And ye, *poore* Pilgrimes! that with restlesse toyle . . . . *D.* 533
I, *poore* swaine, of many, greatest crosse! . . . . *Col.* 18
Therein stil wait *poore* passengers to teare. . . . . *Col.* 203
bountie . . . Which she to Colin her *poore* shepheard shewed.' . *Col.* 647
Those that *poore* Sutors papers do retaine, ... *Col.* 741
Then we *poore* shepheards are accustomd here, ... *Col.* 785
we *poore* shepheards whether rightly so, ... *Col.* 795
Wont to robbe . . . *poore* mens boxes . . . . I. iii. 17. 3
For want whereof *poore* people oft did pyne: . . . . I. iv. 21. 7
Whose welth was want, whose plenty made him *pore;* . . . . I. iv. 29. 4
What hath *poore* Virgin . . . Wherewith you to reward? . . . . I. viii. 27. 3
helpe the helplesse *pore:* . . . . I. x. 3. 7
To call in commers-by that needy were and *pore.* . . . . I. x. 36. 9
some he would give to the *pore.* . . . . I. x. 38. 9
Poore prisoners to relieve with gratious ayd, ... I. x. 40. 2
To walke this way in Pilgrims *poore* estate. . . . . I. x. 64. 4
Poore Orphane! in the wild world scattered, ... II. ii. 2. 5
Unto an aged woman, *poore* and bare, ... II. v. 17. 3
Of the *poore* traveiler that went astray . . . . III. i. 43. 6
both lewd and *poore* attonce him made. . . . . III. vii. 12. 9
In which there slept a fisher old and *pore,* . . . . III. vii. 27. 5
resolving, like a Pilgrim *pore,* . . . . III. x. 19. 1
a little cottage, like some *poore* mans nest. . . . . IV. v. 32. 9
Whose glorie is to aide all suppliants *pore,* . . . . V. i. 4. 6
albee he rich or *poore,* . . . . V. ii. 6. 3
pols and pils the *poore* in piteous wize; . . . . V. ii. 6. 8
all the wealth of rich men to the *poore* will draw.' . . . . V. ii. 38. 9
Sith ye thus farre have tendred my *poore* case, ... V. xi. 18. 3
triumphest in the piteous spoile Of these *poore* folk, ... VI. vi. 25. 4
on the labours of *poore* men to feed, ... VI. viii. 35. 8
maketh wretch or happie, rich or *poore;* . . . . VI. ix. 30. 2
pleasures which doe grow Amongst *poore* hyndes, ... VI. x. 3. 6
That jolly shepheard . . . was *Poore* Colin Clout, ... VI. x. 16. 4
To make one minime of thy *poore* handmayd, ... VI. x. 28. 6
they were *poore* heardgroomes, ... VI. xi. 39. 8
Yet he (*poore* soule!) with patience all did beare; . . . . VII. vi. 49. 6
Of my *poore* life to make unpittied spoile. . . . . *Am.* xi. 8
Yet my *poore* life, . . . I would her yield, ... *Am.* xi. 9
in bloody bath Of such *poor* thralls . . . . *Am.* xxxi. 12
so plenty makes me *poore.* . . . . *Am.* xxxv. 8
yield for pledge my *poore* captyved hart; . . . . *Am.* xlii. 8
Perforce subdude my *poore* captived hart, ... *H.L.* 2
th' evils which *poore* lovers greeve. . . . . *H.L.* 258
Compyld by me, which thy *poore* liegeman am! . . . . *H.B.* 273
Pope. Sometimes she laught, as merry as *Pope* Jone; . . . . II. vi. 3. 4
Popes. He told of Saintes and *Popes,* . . . . I. i. 35. 8
Poplar. Least that the *Poplar* happely should rew Her brothers
strokes, ... *Gn.* 219
The vine-propp Elme; the *Poplar* never dry; . . . . I. i. 8. 7
Poplar-branch. in her hand a *Poplar braunch* did hold: . . . . II. ix. 37. 3
What wight she was that *Poplar* braunch did hold? . . . . II. ix. 39. 7
Popped. He *popt* him in, and his basket did latch: . . . . *S.C.* May 291
Poppy. Dull *Poppie,* and drink-quickning Setuale, ... *Mui.* 196
Dead sleeping *Poppy,* and black Hellebore; . . . . II. vii. 52. 3
Porch. Of hewen stone the *porch* was fayrely wrought, ... II. ix. 24. 1
rownd about the *porch* on every syde . . . . II. ix. 26. 1
in the *Porch* there sate A comely personage . . . . II. xii. 46. 3
So fashioned a *Porch* with rare device. . . . . II. xii. 54. 1
Under that *Porch* a comely dame did rest . . . . II. xii. 55. 7
in the *Porch,* that did them sore amate, ... III. xi. 21. 5
forth descending to that perlous *porch* . . . . III. xii. 42. 6
chokt the *porch* of that enchaunted gate . . . . III. xii. 43. 3
in the *Porch* did evermore abide An hideous Giant, ... IV. x. 16. 5
Unto the *porch* approcht which open stood; . . . . IV. x. 31. 2
Up-lifted in the *porch* of heaven hie: . . . . V. vii. 17. 4
Whose *porch,* that most magnificke did appeare, ... V. ix. 22. 3
even in the *Porch* he him did win, ... VI. i. 23. 4
Porches. Strong walls, rich *porches,* princelie pallaces, ... *Ti.* 93
arched all with *porches,* . . . . IV. x. 6. 8
Pore. *See* **Poor.**
Poris. Wondred Agave, *Poris,* and Nesaea, ... IV. xi. 49. 6
Porphyry. in *Porphyre* and Marble doo appeare, ... *Ro.* xxxii. 7
Porpoises. heard Of stinking Seales and *Porcpisces* . . . . *Col.* 249
Porrex. Stout Ferrex and sterne *Porrex* him in prison threw. . II. x. 34. 9
greedy thirst . . . Stird *Porrex* up . . . . II. x. 35. 3
Port. If too great winde against the *port* him drive, ... *Ro.* xxi. 13
Doth in the *port* it selfe his vessell rive. . . . . *Ro.* xxi. 14
Soone as the *port* from far he has espide, ... I. iii. 31. 7
Sleepe after toyle, *port* after storme seas, ... I. ix. 40. 8
with stately grace and princely *port* . . . . II. iii. 28. 5
knowes her *port,* and thither sayles by ayme, ... II. vi. 10. 3
There her small Gondelay her *port* did make, ... II. vi. 11. 5

Port—*Continued.*
Better safe *port* then be in seas distrest.' . . . II. vi. 23. 8
cleped was *Port* Esquiline, . . . II. ix. 32. 8
Ne made for shipping any certeine *port*, . . . II. xii. 13. 3
twixt them both a pleasaunt *port* they made, . . . II. xii. 30. 6
This is the *Port* of rest from troublous toyle, . . . II. xii. 32. 8
stately *port* of Castle Joyeous, . . . III. i. 31. 2
Unto the gladsome *port* of her intent. . . . III. iv. 10. 5
vouchsafed to embace Her goodly *port*, . . . III. vii. 15. 3
in his *port* appeared manly hardiment. . . . III. viii. 44. 9
Without respect of person or of *port*, . . . III. xi. 46. 4
With stately *port* and proud magnificence, . . . V. v. 4. 2
sayling alwaies in the *port*. . . . VI. x. 2. 9
rest her selfe as in a gladsome *port*, . . . VI. x. 9. 4
With goodly *port* and gracious Majesty, . . . VII. vii. 5. 2
that proud *port*, which her so goodly graceth, . . . *Am.* xiii. 1
That happie *port* for ever to recure! . . . *H.L.* 298
Portamore. Whom they by name there *Portamore* did call; . . . VI. vii. 35. 8
Portance. in court gay *portaunce* he perceiv'd, . . . II. iii. 5. 7
by her stately *portance* borne of heavenly birth. . . . II. iii. 21. 9
His *portaunce* terrible, and stature tall, . . . II. vii. 41. 4
her prowd *portaunce* and her princely gest, . . . III. ii. 27. 3
seemed, by their *portance* and attire, . . . VI. v. 11. 4
Ryding a softly pace with *portance* sad, . . . VI. vii. 6. 8
Portas. in his hand his *Portesse* still he bare, . . . I. iv. 19. 1
Portcullis. over it a fayre *Portcullis* hong, . . . II. ix. 24. 6
Portend. For dread of daunger which it might *portend;* . . . III. iii. 14. 4
huge Orion, that doth tempests still *portend;* . . . IV. xi. 13. 9
To shew that Isis doth the Moone *portend;* . . . V. vii. 4. 7
Porter. charge of them was to a *Porter* hight, . . . I. iv. 6. 3
when they knockt, The *Porter* opened unto them . . . I. x. 5. 4
Within the Barbican a *Porter* sate, . . . II. ix. 25. 1
The *Porter* eke to her did lout with humble gestes. . . . II. ix. 26. 9
Pleasures *porter* was devizd to bee, . . . II. xii. 48. 8
Old Genius the *porter* of them was, . . . III. vi. 31. 8
The good man selfe, which then the *Porter* playd, . . . III. ix. 10. 2
'That was to weet the *Porter* of the place, . . . IV. x. 12. 1
at the *Porter* . . . Threw many threats, . . . V. iv. 37. 3
slew the *Porter* on the flore. . . . VI. i. 23. 9
the rude *Porter* that no manners had . . . VI. iii. 38. 1
Porters. did them *porters* make Of heavens gate . . . VII. vii. 45. 6
Portesse. *See* **Portas.**
Portion. *See* **Coportion.**
sorrowes are Left thee for *porcion* of thy livelyhed; . . . II. ii. 2. 4
Canute had his *portion* from the rest, . . . II. x. 12. 7
each his *portion* peaceably enjoyd, . . . II. x. 14. 6
The Churches part, and Ploughmans *portion*, . . . II. x. 39. 4
That she unto their *portion* might befall. . . . IV. v. 26. 5
The *portion* of that good which Fortune gave her, . . . V. iv. 12. 7
joyne in equall *portion* of thy realme; . . . V. vii. 23. 6
The greatest *portion* of the greedie pray, . . . VI. xi. 17. 4
Th' eternall *portion* of her precious dowre, . . . *H.H.B.* 250
Portions. chalenge to our selves our *portions* dew . . . *Hub.* 137
got large *portions* of land, . . . II. x. 65. 6
Both goodly *portions*, but of both the better she. . . . V. iv. 12. 9
Portliness. Such pride is praise; such *portlinesse* is honor; . *Am.* v. 9
Portly. *Portly* his person was, . . . III. ii. 24. 8
Beares he himselfe with *portly* majestee, . . . III. iii. 32. 4
In finding fault with her too *portly* pride: . . . *Am.* v. 2
where she comes along with *portly* pace, . . . *Epith.* 148
Portrait. when he was requirde To *pourtraict* Venus . . . *Ded.Son.*xvii.2
arrived where that sad *pourtraict* Of death . . . II. i. 39. 3
hevenly *pourtraict* of bright Angels hew, . . . II. iii. 22. 2
Whereon the Faery Queenes *pourtract* was writt,) . . . II. viii. 43. 3
Need but behold the *pourtraict* of her hart; . . . III. Pr. 1. 8
Cannot your glorious *pourtraict* figure playne, . . . III. Pr. 3. 7
For Chian folke to *pourtraict* beauties Queene, . . . IV. v. 12. 7
The heavenly *pourtraict* of bright Angels hew. . . . IV. v. 13. 4
The glorious *pourtraict* of that Angels face, . . . *Am.* xvii. 1
The *pourtraict* of so heavenly hew to paint. . . . *H.H.B.* 231
Portraits. Fashion the *pourtraicts* of these Palacis, . . . *Ro.* xxv. 10
All dreadfull *pourtraicts* of deformitee: . . . II. xii. 23. 5
Many faire *pourtraicts*, and many a faire feate; . . . III. xi. 29. 2
Portraiture. hath not seene that heavens *portracture*. . . . *Hub.* 611
In which sad Death his *pourtraicture* had writ, . . . *D.* 303
calles to mind his *pourtraiture* alive, . . . I. vi. 17. 3
Portray. in her feigning fancie did *pourtray* Him . . . III. iv. 5. 7
Portrayed. On each side *purtraid* (*portraide*[1]) was a Victorie, *Bel.* iv. 5
if thou be, as thou art *pourtrahed* With natures pen, . . . I. viii. 33. 7
nothing *pourtrahed* nor wrought; Not wrought nor *pourtrahed*, II. ix. 33. 8, 9
weren *pourtrayd* Foolish delights, . . . II. xi. 11. 7
If *pourtrayd* it might bee by any living art. . . . III. Pr. 1. 9
was *pourtrahed* The love of Venus and her Paramoure, . . . III. i. 34. 3
Behold them both . . . Here truly *pourtray'd*, (**pourtrayt*) . *Com. Son.* ii. 6
Ne could that Painter . . . Have *purtrayd* this, . . . *H.H.B.* 214
Ports. Finding in it fit *ports* for fishers trade, . . . II. x. 6. 8
Portugese. *See* **Al Portugese.**
Posies. let them make great store of bridale *poses*, . . . *Epith.* 45
vermeil Roses, To decke their Bridegroomes *posies* . . . *Proth.* 34
Possess. The title of the Kingdome to *possesse*. . . . *Hub.* 1046
All places they doo with their toyes *possesse*, . . . *T.M.* 325
Which ye now in securitie *possesse*, . . . *T.M.* 365
doo *possesse* the Empire of the aire, . . . *Mui.* 18
all the countrey wide he did *possesse*, . . . *Mui.* 150
dayly dooth my weaker wit *possesse*, . . . *D.* 30
That man, who doth the whole worlds rule *possesse*, . . . *D.* 179
with your loves do their rude hearts *possesse*, . . . *D.* 527
my dread Lord, that doest liege hearts *possesse*, . . . *Col.* 793
The land which warlike Britons now *possesse*, . . . II. x. 5. 1
Camber did *possesse* the Westerne quart, . . . II. x. 14. 4

Possess—*Continued.*
Yet did *possesse* their horrible intent; . . . III. ii. 43. 7
thee abandond wholy do *possesse*, . . . III. ii. 46. 3
to *possesse* the purpose they desird: . . . III. iii. 51. 7
That ever Greece did boast, or knight *possesse*, . . . III. ix. 34. 8
none was to *possesse* So rich purveyaunce, . . . III. xi. 53. 8
happinesse: . . . that fate n'ould let her yet *possesse*. . . . III. xii. 46. *or.* 9
He should without disturbance her *possesse:* . . . IV. v. 25. 8
happie soules, which doe *possesse* Th' Elysian fields . . . IV. x. 23. 4
frankely there their loves desire *possesse;* . . . IV. x. 28. 6
warlike Amazons, who doe *possesse* the same. . . . IV. xi. 21. 9
grieved to restore the pledge he did *possesse*. . . . IV. xii. 32. 9
Did the most chast Penelope *possesse* . . . V. vii. 39. 2
allure The sence of man, and all his minde *possesse*, . . . V. viii. 1. 2
I do *possesse* the worlds most regiment; . . . VII. vii. 17. 2
from the earth, which they may long *possesse* . . . *Epith.* 418
happie man! might he the same *possesse*, . . . *H.L.* 209
Possessed. *Possest* nigh of the Capitol through slight, . . . *Van.* xi. 7
All places they with follie have *possest*, . . . *T.M.* 193
The which my soule first conquerd and *possest*, . . . *D.* 300
The which art of so rich a spoile *possest*, . . . *Col.* 553
that high powre, wherewith thou art *possest*. . . . *Col.* 826
the faire Fidessa, loe! Is there *possessed* of the traytour vile; I. iv. 42. 3
Whereof he weend *possessed* soone to bee, . . . I. vi. 5. 4
Who . . . was *possessed* of his newfound make. . . . I. vii. 15. 5
Possessed of his Ladies hart and hand; . . . I. xii. 40. 7
Being *possessed* of that spoyle, . . . III. viii. 13. 8
all mens eares *possest*, . . . IV. x. 4. 2
Of puissant Nations which the world *possest*, . . . IV. xi. 15. 2
afterward both sea and land *possest;* . . . IV. xi. 18. 4
what the mighty Sea hath once *possest*, . . . V. iv. 19. 2
Least some new love had him from her *possest:* . . . V. vi. 4. 7
Her minde was whole *possessed* of one thought, . . . V. vi. 21. 3
My pallaces *possessed* of my foe, . . . V. x. 23. 3
Possessed of sweete sleepe that luld him soft in swound. . . . VI. vii. 18. 9
chiefly Calidore, whom griefe had most *possest*. . . . VI. xi. 41. 9
Then shalt thou feele thy spirit so *possest*, . . . *H.H.L.* 267
being thus with her huge love *possest*, . . . *H.H.B.* 237
With whose sweete pleasures being so *possest*, . . . *H.H.B.* 300
Possesseth. she her selfe, when ever that she will, *Possesseth* him, . . . III. vi. 46. 9
Possession. sole *possession* in so chaste a brest! . . . *Col.* 555
them of their unjust *possession* depriv'd. . . . II. x. 9. 9
Possessors. their *possessours* often did dismay: . . . IV. i. 29. 7
Possessors'. plucked quite from all *possessors* hand, . . . V. iv. 19. 3
Post. over the pousse hetheward doth *post*. . . . *S.C.* Au. 46
Lightned with deadly lamps on everie *post?* . . . *Gn.* 341
as a speedie *post* that passeth by. . . . *D.* 413
Of every pillour and of every *post*, . . . III. i. 32. 5
whose tongue was . . . Nayld to a *post*, . . . V. ix. 25. 3
A Bayliefe-errant forth in *post* did passe, . . . VI. vii. 35. 7
Posterities. them to their *posterities* doe still declare. . . . V. x. 5. 9
praise They all were bound to all *posterities* to raise. . . . V. xi. 34. 9
Posterity. *posteritie*, Striving in power their grandfathers to passe, . . . *Ro.* viii. 6
posteritie Of age ensuing shall you ever read? . . . *Ro.* xxxii. 1
that late *posteritie* Should know their names, . . . *T.M.* 441
To be remembred of *posteritie*, . . . *Ti.* 165
raced Out of the knowledge of *posteritie*, . . . *Ti.* 178
engraven . . . That it may live to all *posterity*. . . . *Ded. Son.* vi. 14
That all *posteritie* thy honor may rehearse. . . . *Ded. Son.* xi. 14
Shall Hevenfield be cald to all *posterity*. . . . III. iii. 38. 9
to recount the Seas *posterity:* . . . IV. xii. 1. 7
The course of all her fortune and *posteritie*. . . . V. vii. 12. 9
The gladfull blessing of *posteritie*, . . . VI. iv. 31. 3
tell her prayse to all *posterity*, . . . *Am.* lxix. 11
That we may raise a large *posterity*, . . . *Epith.* 417
That all *posteritie* admyred it, . . . *H.H.B.* 213
Postern. He by a privy *Posterne* tooke his flight, . . . I. v. 52. 7
breaking forth out at a *posterne* dore, . . . V. viii. 48. 8
it the *Posterne* did from closing stay: . . . V. x. 37. 5
them convayd out at a *Posterne* dore. . . . V. x. 38. 4
Posts. home they hasten the *postes* to dight, . . . *S.C.* May 11
The Dorick flames consum'd the Iliack *posts*. . . . *Gn.* 549
Then gan they sprinckle all the *posts* with wine, . . . I. xii. 38. 1
all the *postes* adorne as doth behove, . . . *Epith.* 206
sprinkle all the *postes* and wals with wine, . . . *Epith.* 253
Pot. *See* **Earth-pot.**
a *pot* Made of the mettall that we honour most. . . . *Bel.*[1] iii. 5
leaning on (against[1]) the belly of a *pot*, . . . *Bel.* ix. 5
The top thereof a *pot* did seeme to beare, . . . *Bel.*[2] iii. 5
on her shoulders sad a *pot* of water bore. . . . I. iii. 10. 9
Lay hidden in the bottome of the *pot*. . . . III. ii. 26. 5
All which she in a earthen *Pot* did poure, . . . III. ii. 49. 7
Potentates. match them selfe with mighty *potentates*, . . . *S.C.* May 122
The soveraine Powres and mightie *Potentates*, . . . *H.H.B.* 86
Potion. washt away his guilt with guilty *potion*. . . . II. iv. 30. 9
Pot's. round about the *Pots* mouth bound the thread; . . . III. ii. 50. 3
Potsherds. plates asunder brake, As they had *potshares* bene; VI. i. 37. 5
Pouke. *See* **Puck.**
Pounce. from her griping *pounce* the greedy prey doth rive. V. iv. 42. 9
Pounces. His wearie *pounces* all in vaine doth spend . . . I. xi. 19. 7
Pound. if the living yerely doo arise To fortie *pound*, . . . *Hub.* 529
A dram of sweete is worth a *pound* of sowre. . . . I. iii. 30. 4
All which at once huge strokes on him did *pound*, . . . IV. iv. 31. 8
A *pound* of gall doth over it redound: . . . IV. x. 1. 5
thousand pretious gifts worth many a *pound*, . . . IV. x. 37. 7
if thou now shouldst weigh them new in *pound*, . . . V. ii. 36. 5
Pounded. betwixt two marbles plaine Shee *pownded* small, . . . III. v. 33. 2
Thought sure have *pownded* him to powder soft, . . . VI. viii. 15. 3

Pour. *poore* my piteous plaints out . . . *S.C.* Jun. 80
Let *powre* in lavish cups and thriftie bitts . . . *S.C.* O. 105
shall *powre* into my swollen eyes A sea of teares . . . *T.M.* 115
from her eyes a sea of teares did *powre;* . . . *T.M.* 476
such store of teares shee forth did *powre,* . . . *T.M.* 595
wont forth to *powre* Her restles plaints, . . . *Ti.* 131
powre forth th' offring of his guiltles blood: . . . *Ti.* 300
powre foorth fountaines of incessant teares? . . . *D.* 247
raine Did *poure* into his Lemans lap so fast, . . . I. i. 6. 7
when she list *poure* out her larger spright, . . . I. x. 20. 1
of my plenty *poure* out unto all, . . . II. vii. 8. 3
all attonce their malice forth do *poure:* . . . II. viii. 48. 7
infinite desire into your spirite *poure.* . . . II. ix. 3. 9
Adowne the rolling river she did *poure,* . . . II. x. 19. 7
All which she in a earthen Pot did *poure,* . . . III. ii. 49. 7
The mist of griefe dissolv'd did into vengeance *powre.* . . . III. iv. 13. 9
he forth would *poure* so plenteous teares, . . . IV. viii. 4. 6
Griefe did plead, and many teares forth *powre.* . . . V. ix. 45. 9
he the more his wicked poyson forth did *poure.'* . . . VI. i. 9. 9
For which I thus doe mourne, and *poure* forth ceaselesse teares.' VI. iv. 33. 9
poure that vertue from our heavenly cell . . . VII. vii. 48. 7
And doe myne humbled hart before her *poure;* . . . *Am.* xx. 2
Poure out the wine without restraint or stay, . . . *Epith.* 250
Poure not by cups, but by the belly full, . . . *Epith.* 251
Poure out to all that wull, . . . *Epith.* 252
May *poure* his limbs forth on your pleasant playne; . . . *Epith.* 356
Poure out your blessing on us plentiously, . . . *Epith.* 415
powre Through all the parts, . . . *H.B.* 52
Plentie of riches forth on him will *powre,* . . . *H.H.B.* 247
Poured. Who . . . *Pourd* foorth a water, . . . *Bel.*[2] ix. 6
guilt *Powr'd* vengeance forth on you . . . *Ro.* xxiv. 11
Let streaming teares be *poured* out in store; . . . *S.C.* N. 61
powr'd on th' earth plague, pestilence, and death. . . . *Hub.* 8
The bread of life *powr'd* downe from heavenly place. . . . *Hub.* 438
sorrowfull sad tine, Which late ye *powred* forth . . . *T.M.* 4
she *powred* foorth a brackish flood . . . *T.M.* 415
Hath *powrd* on earth this noyous pestilence, . . . *T.M.* 483
the heavens *powrde* all their gifts upon her. . . . *Ti.* 280
Hath *powred* forth for thee, . . . *Mui.* 239
praises in all plenteousnesse *Powr'd* upon her, . . . *D.* 228
Had *powred* kindly heat and formall feature, . . . *Col.* 862
Through whose large bountie, *poured* on me rife . . . *Ded. Son.* vii. 3
She *poured* forth out of her hellish sinke . . . I. i. 22. 5
Gluttony, That of his plenty *poured* forth to all: . . . I. iv. 43. 8
Pourd out in loosnesse on the grassy grownd, . . . I. vii. 7. 2
what evill starre On you hath . . . *pourd* his influence bad, . . I. viii. 42. 7
Had vertue *pourd* into their waters bace, . . . II. ii. 6. 8
poured out in pleasure and delight: . . . II. ii. 36. 5
now he has *pourd* out his ydle mynd . . . II. v. 28. 5
downe them *poured* through an hole full wide . . . II. vii. 6. 4
Witnesse the guiltlesse blood *pourd* oft on ground, . . . II. vii. 13. 4
Socrates; . . . *Pourd* out his life . . . II. vii. 52. 8
poured forth with plentifull dispence, . . . II. xii. 42. 8
poured forth in sensuall delight, . . . III. i. 48. 6
Pourd out their plenty without spight or spare. . . . III. i. 51. 4
thence *pourd* into men, which men call Love! . . . III. iii. 1. 4
They *pourd* in soveraine balme and Nectar good, . . . III. iv. 40. 8
On her they *poured* forth of plenteous horne: . . . III. vi. 2. 6
in sweete ravishment *pourd* out her spright. . . . III. xii. 45. *or.*7
As thicke as hayle forth *poured* from the skie: . . . IV. iii. 25. 5
pour'd the purple bloud forth on the gras; . . . IV. vi. 15. 7
through many vowes which forth he *pour'd,* . . . IV. vi. 41. 6
being thenceforth *powrd* In three great rivers ran, . . . IV. xi. 42. 8
powred forth over the Castle wall, . . . V. ii. 23. 6
burning all to ashes *powr'd* it downe the brooke. . . . V. ii. 27. 9
From thence *pour'd* down on men by influence of grace. . . . V. x. 1. 9
powred forth his wretched life in deadly dreare. . . . V. x. 35. 9
powred out of her infernall sinke Most ugly filth; . . . V. xi. 31. 6
He saw his life *powrd* forth despiteously; . . . VI. iii. 51. 4
there by her were *poured* forth at fill, . . . VI. x. 5. 8
Poureth. *powreth* forth these oracles so sage . . . *Col.* 825
poureth forth a sudden shoure of raine, . . . IV. iv. 47. 8
Pouring. *powring* foorth to thee . . . great mirth and gladsome glee. . . . *Gn.* 183
forth *powring* His trickling streames, . . . *Gn.* 227
Pouring forth streames of teares abundantly; . . . *T.M.* 230
Pouring out streames of poyson and of gall . . . IV. viii. 24. 6
powring forth their bloud in brutishe wize, . . . V. x. 28. 8
And *powring* balme, . . . Into his wounds, . . . VI. ii. 48. 3
Pours. *Powres* forth sweete odors and alluring sights; . . . *Mui.* 164
poures it selfe forth in a stormy showre: . . . III. iv. 13. 6
pours his poysnous gall forth . . . VI. vi. 12. 5
Pousse. *See* **Pulse.**
Pout. made him scoule, and *pout,* . . . VI. ix. 38. 7
Poverty. the other Peeres, for *povertie,* . . . *Hub.* 1177
And noble Patrone of weake *povertie;* . . . *Ti.* 262
Vile *Poverty;* and, lastly, Death with infamy. . . . III. xii. 25. 9
From youth to eld, from wealth to *poverty,* . . . VII. vii. 19. 5
His paines, his *povertie,* his sharpe assayes, . . . *H.H.L.* 235
Powder. these mountaines, now consum'd to *pouder;* . . . *Ro.* xvii. 12
Thought sure have pownded him to *powder* soft, . . . VI. viii. 15. 3
Powdered. *See* **Fair-powdered.**
Againe on foote to reare her *pouldred* corse. . . . *Ro.* xxvii. 14
He had beene *pouldred* all as thin as flowre: . . . I. vii. 12. 4
Poudred with pearle and stone; . . . IV. x. 31. 8
Power. The mightie Dragon gave to hir his *power.* . . . *Rev.* i. 6
with her mightie *powre* Tam'd all the world, . . . *Ro.* iii. 6
That other earthlie *power* should not resemble Her . . . *Ro.* vi. 12
Striving in *power* their grandfathers to passe, . . . *Ro.* viii. 7
having all parts in their *power,* . . . *Ro.* viii. 9

Power—*Continued.*
Seem'd above heavens *powre* it selfe to advaunce; . . . *Ro.* xi. 4
Her *power* to Peters successor betooke; . . . *Ro.* xviii. 12
Her *power,* disperst through all the world did vade; . . . *Ro.* xx. 13
Her *power* it selfe against it selfe did arme; . . . *Ro.* xxi. 10
all *power* he doth expell; . . . *S.C.* O. 99
The *power* of herbs, both which can hurt and ease, . . . *S.C.* D. 88
through *power* of some divining spright, . . . *Gn.* Ded. 6
my soft Muse, as for her *power* more meete, . . . *Gn.* 51
'Th' Argolicke *power* returning home againe, . . . *Gn.* 561
bends what ever *power* his aged yeares Him lent, . . . *Gn.* 646
had not *power* to doo him good or ill. . . . *Hub.* 890
Subject unto that *powre* imperiall.' . . . *Hub.* 972
to prove whether his *powre* would pas As currant, . . . *Hub.* 1094
The care of Kings and *power* of Empires stand, . . . *Hub.* 1226
Through *power* of that he runnes through enemies swerds; . *Hub.* 1283
Through *power* of that he passeth through the herds . . . *Hub.* 1284
Through *power* of that his cunning theeveries . . . *Hub.* 1287
through the *power* of that, he putteth on What shape . . . *Hub.* 1289
Thy scepter rent, and *power* put to wrack; . . . *T.M.* 400
mortall men have *powre* to deifie: . . . *T.M.* 460
overran the East with greedie *powre,* . . . *Ti.* 69
for warlike *power,* and peoples store, . . . *Ti.* 99
'His blessed spirite, full of *power* divine . . . *Ti.* 288
with *power* of mightie spell . . . *Ti.* 374
bands of impacable fate, And *power* of death, . . . *Ti.* 396
Of wondrous *powre,* and of exceeding stature, . . . *Ti.* 534
By his great lookes and *power* Imperiall. . . . *Mui.* 312
So rich a spoile within his *power* to see. . . . *As.* 102
Religion hath lay *powre* to rest upon her, . . . *Col.* 322
Her *power,* her mercy, and her wisdome, . . . *Col.* 346
Jove himselfe his *powre* began to dread, . . . *Col.* 809
Blaspheme his *powre,* or termes unworthie yield.' . . . *Col.* 822
that high *powre,* wherewith thou art possest. . . . *Col.* 826
needs his priest t' expresse his *powre* divine. . . . *Col.* 838
by his *powre* the world was made of yore, . . . *Col.* 841
Against whose *powre,* nor God nor man can fynd Defence, . . *Col.* 875
And their disloiall *powre* defaced clene, . . . *Ded. Son.* xi. 11
To baser wit his *power* therein to spend, . . . *Ded. Son.* xii.10
Not perceable with *power* of any starr: . . . I. i. 7. 6
The hidden *powre* of herbes, and might of Magick spel? . . . I. ii. 10. 9
from him fled away with all her *powre;* . . . I. ii. 20. 4
fortune false betraide me to thy *powre,* . . . I. ii. 22. 5
true love hath no *powre* To looken backe; . . . I. iii. 30. 7
loving him with all my *powre,* . . . I. iv. 46. 8
sithens . . . enimies *powre,* hath now captived you, Returne . I. iv. 51. 2
she in hell and heaven had *power* equally. . . . I. v. 34. 9
Now in the *powre* of everlasting Night? . . . I. v. 43. 5
for to make his *powre* approved more, . . . I. vi. 26. 1
so exceeding was the villeins *powre,* . . . I. vii. 12. 7
with extorted *powre,* and borrow'd strength, . . . I. vii. 18. 3
Parents deare from tyrants *powre* deliver might. . . . I. vii. 46. 9
ye, the forlorne reliques of his *powre,* . . . I. viii. 48. 1
to weet what suddein stowre . . . dar'd his dreaded *powre.* . I. viii. 5. 9
No *powre* he had to stirre, . . . I. viii. 15. 4
He hath no *powre* to hurt, nor to defend. . . . I. viii. 21. 7
lowd did call With all his *powre,* . . . I. viii. 37. 8
loe! that wicked woman . . . Now in your *powre,* . . . I. viii. 45. 6
His *powre* is reft, and weaknes doth remaine. . . . I. ix. 31. 8
all the good is Gods, both *power* and eke will. . . . I. x. 1. 9
Almightie God her gave such *powre* . . . I. x. 20. 9
Ne ought the *powre* of mighty men did dread . . . I. x. 43. 5
That hill they scale with all their *powre* and might, . . . I. x. 47. 7
prov'd the *powre* of many a puissant knight. . . . I. xi. 17. 9
when he saw no *power* might prevaile, . . . I. xi. 42. 1
with her soveraine *power,* and scepter shene, . . . II. ii. 40. 4
what ever hevenly *powre,* Or earthly wight thou be, . . . II. iii. 34. 8
shee is some *powre* celestiall? . . . II. iii. 44. 4
all his *power* was utterly defaste, . . . II. iv. 14. 3
A knight of wondrous *powre* and great assay, . . . II. iv. 40. 6
Like as a Lyon, whose imperiall *powre* . . . II. v. 10. 1
Such *powre* have pleasing wordes: . . . II. vi. 36. 5
powre of al which them poursew.' . . . II. vii. 19. 9
with his pride all others *powre* deface: . . . II. vii. 41. 8
this weapons *powre* I well have kend . . . II. viii. 19. 8
by your *powre* protect his feeble cace? . . . II. viii. 25. 8
secrete *powre* t' appease inflamed rage: . . . II. viii. 26. 8
With hideous strokes and importable *powre,* . . . II. viii. 35. 2
no'te avoyded be by earthly skill or *powre.* . . . II. viii. 43. 9
so soone as his outrageous *powre* Is layd, . . . II. viii. 48. 4
withstond Oppressours *powre* by armes and puissant hond? . II. viii. 56. 5
mans body, both for *powre* and forme, . . . II. ix. 1. 3
That is, her bounty, and imperiall *powre,* . . . II. ix. 3. 6
To serve that Queene with al my *powre* and might. . . . II. ix. 7. 4
This parts great workemanship and wondrous *powre,* . . . II. ix. 47. 2
three the chiefest and of greatest *powre,* . . . II. ix. 47. 7
her *powre* she did display . . . II. x. 20. 5
with her *powre* her owne selfe overthrew, . . . II. x. 54. 4
gainst the Romanes bent their proper *powre;* . . . II. x. 57. 6
Great was his *power* and glorie . . . II. x. 76. 1
Long mayst thou, Glorian, live in glory and great *powre!* . . II. x. 76. 9
after them did drive with all her *power* and might. . . . II. xii. 15. 9
threatning to devoure all that his *powre* despise. . . . II. xii. 21. 9
Such wondrous *powre* did in that staffe appeare, . . . II. xii. 40. 8
wisedomes *powre,* and temperaunces might, . . . II. xii. 43. 6
Not that celestiall *powre,* . . . II. xii. 47. 2
not thy fault, but secret *powre* unseene: . . . III. i. 7. 8
vowd with all their *power* and witt . . . III. i. 12. 3
sighing softly had no *powre* To speake . . . III. ii. 5. 1
Ybuilded all of glasse, by Magicke *powre,* . . . III. ii. 20. 7

Power—*Continued.*
No shadow but a body hath in *powre*: . . . . III. ii. 45. 7
no *powre* Nor guidaunce of herselfe . . . . III. ii. 49. 2
Ne braver proofe in any of thy *powre* . . . . III. iii. 3. 2
to withstand The *powre* of forreine Paynims . . . . III. iii. 27. 9
Shall well defend, and Saxons *powre* suppresse; . . . . . . III. iii. 33. 2
indewd With heavenly *powre,* . . . . III. iii. 38. 5
with paine Or *powre,* be hable it to remedy, ... III. iii. 40. 4
As overcomen of the spirites *powre,* . . . . III. iii. 50. 2
Both speare and shield of great *powre,* . . . . III. iii. 60. 9
for all was in her *powre*. . . . . III. iv. 18. 9
So feeble is the *powre* of fleshly arme. . . . . III. iv. 27. 6
shewes his *powre* in variable kindes: . . . . III. v. 1. 3
had no *powre* in his soft flesh to bite. . . . . III. v. 19. 5
the Middayes scorching *powre,* Ne the sharp Northerne wind III. v. 51. 4
Eternall God, in his almightie *powre,* . . . . III. v. 52. 1
With so sweet sence and secret *powre* unspide, ... III. vi. 7. 8
with my *power* or skill I might doe service . . . . III. vii. 54. 5
seeming sory that she ever came Into his *powre,* . . . . . . III. viii. 14. 8
he so ofte had tryde The *powre* thereof, ... III. ix. 29. 8
he the *powre* of chaste hands might not beare, ... III. xi. 6. 3
seemes t' exceede the *powre* of patience, ... III. xi. 14. 2
powre of hand, nor skill of learned brest, ... III. xi. 16. 3
To shew Dan Cupids *powre* and great effort: . . . . III. xi. 46. 5
man and beast with *powre* imperious Subdeweth . . . . . . III. xii. 22. 4
In *power* of herbes, and tunes of beasts and burds; . . . . . IV. ii. 35. 6
Had *power* to staunch al wounds that mortally did bleed. . . IV. ii. 39. 9
Which did her *powre* into three parts divyde; . . . . IV. ii. 43. 4
where as their *powre* They felt, ... IV. iii. 15. 4
He can let drive at him with all his *power,* . . . . IV. iii. 20. 4
In which their *powre* all others did excell; . . . . IV. iii. 39. 3
Much more of price and of more gratious *powre,* . . . . . . IV. iii. 45. 1
thereto all his *power* and might applide: . . . . IV. iv. 24. 2
with unwearied *powre* his party still assured. . . . . IV. iv. 37. 9
no *powre* of man Could bide the force . . . . IV. iv. 46. 3
Likewise assayd to prove that girdles *powre;* . . . . IV. v. 19. 3
Ne Judges *powre,* ne reasons rule, mote them restraine. . . . IV. v. 24. 9
when ever in his *powre* He may them catch . . . . IV. vii. 12. 6
to his *powre* we all are subject borne: . . . . IV. viii. 15. 2
Full of sad *powre,* that poysnous bale did breede . . . . . IV. viii. 39. 4
by the *powre* of his infectious sight, ... IV. viii. 47. 8
doe dispart the hart with *powre* extreme, ... IV. ix. 1. 3
gathered had by wrong And tortious *powre,* . . . . IV. ix. 12. 4
Left in the victors *powre,* like vassall bond, ... IV. ix. 18. 7
laid on load with all their might and *powre,* . . . . IV. ix. 22. 7
Passing the measure of my feeble *powre;* . . . . IV. ix. 39. 7
maugre all his *powre,* . . . . IV. x. 58. 2
unlesse some heavenly *powre* her free . . . . IV. xi. 1. 6
The *powre* to rule the billowes, ... IV. xi. 12. 9
wish that in his *powre* it weare Her to redresse: . . . . . . IV. xii. 12. 7
Whose soveraine *powre* is herein most exprest, ... V. Pr. 10. 3
That *powre* he also doth to Princes lend, ... V. Pr. 10. 6
The club of Justice dread with kingly *powre* endewed. . . . . V. i. 2. 9
With wrongfull *powre* oppressing others of their kind. . . . V. i. 7. 9
Through strong oppression of his *powre* extort, ... V. ii. 5. 8
with his *powre* he all doth overgo, ... V. ii. 7. 3
In whose right hands great *power* is contayned, ... V. ii. 19. 7
alwaies doe their *powre* within just compasse pen. . . . . . V. ii. 19. 9
powr of charms, which she against him wrought, ... V. ii. 22. 8
For wight against his *powre* them selves to reare. . . . . . V. ii. 24. 6
All in the *powre* of their great Maker lie: . . . . V. ii. 40. 8
He maketh subjects to their *powre* obay; . . . . V. ii. 41. 6
Ne any may his soveraine *power* shonne, ... V. ii. 42. 3
Such *power* it had, that to no womans wast . . . . V. iii. 28. 6
For *powre* is the right hand of Justice truely hight. . . . . V. iv. 1. 9
to proude oppression Of womens *powre,* . . . . V. iv. 26. 5
A Princesse of great *powre* and greater pride, ... V. iv. 33. 4
for all the *powre* she did apply . . . . V. iv. 41. 8
though *powre* faild, her courage did accrew; . . . . V. v. 7. 4
In signe of true subjection to her *powre,* . . . . V. v. 18. 2
if in his owne *powre* occasion lay, ... V. v. 39. 2
eke of *powre* her owne doome to undo, ... V. v. 41. 8
A Goddesse of great *powre* and soverainty, ... V. vii. 3. 2
To shew that she had *powre* in things divine: . . . . V. vii. 6. 7
Such is the *powre* of that same fruit, ... V. vii. 11. 7
swolne with pride of his owne peerelesse *powre,* . . . . . . V. vii. 15. 7
Lion-like shall shew his *powre* extreame. . . . . V. vii. 23. 8
Drawne with the *powre* of an heart-robbing eye, ... V. viii. 1. 6
Such wondrous *powre* hath wemens faire aspect . . . . V. viii. 2. 8
after her did speed With all their *powre,* . . . . V. viii. 4. 4
A Princesse of great *powre* and majestie, ... V. viii. 16. 8
all his *powre* doth thereunto apply: . . . . V. viii. 18. 5
Gainst tortious *powre* and lawlesse regiment, ... V. viii. 30. 7
Purchast through lawlesse *powre* and tortious wrong . . . . V. viii. 51. 6
feared for their *powre;* . . . . V. ix. 1. 8
her to appose With peremptorie *powre,* . . . . V. ix. 44. 2
High Gods beheast, and *powre* of holy lawes; . . . . V. ix. 44. 6
high alliance unto forren *powre;* . . . . V. ix. 45. 6
So much more, then, is that of *powre* and art . . . . V. x. 2. 5
through his tortious *powre,* . . . . V. x. 8. 1
For his huge *powre* and great oppression, ... V. x. 9. 4
Through his three bodies *powre* in one combynd; . . . . . . V. x. 9. 6
their *powre* against her right oppose: . . . . V. x. 12. 5
gave him soveraine *powre* . . . . V. x. 13. 2
by his *powre* oppressed every one, ... V. x. 30. 3
towards him with all their *powre* did ryde, ... V. x. 34. 3
when he found no more T' oppose against his *powre* . . . . V. x. 38. 6
Through avarice, or *powre,* or guile, or strife, ... V. xi. 1. 3
A Lions clawes, with *powre* and rigour clad, ... V. xi. 24. 3
sought with lawlesse *powre* him to oppresse, ... V. xi. 44. 4

Power—*Continued.*
Did set upon those troupes with all his *powre* and might. . . V. xi. 57. 9
all his *powre* applyed thereunto, ... V. xii. 22. 2
with strong *powre* did them long time oppresse; . . . . . . V. xii. 24. 4
Did nought regard his malice nor his *powre;* . . . . VI. i. 9. 8
through strong *powre* had now her self in hould, ... VI. i. 29. 7
with all his *powre* and might. . . . . VI. i. 32. 9
with all their *powre* and might, ... VI. i. 38. 2
with presumpteous *powre* against that knight streight go'th. VI. ii. 17. 9
couching close his speare and all his *powre,* . . . . VI. iii. 48. 2
threatning his sharpe clawes, now wanting *powre* to traine. . VI. iv. 22. 9
Exceeding all the rest in *powre* and hight; . . . . VI. v. 13. 7
Small praise to prove your *powre* on wight so weake.' . . . VI. v. 30. 5
him against his *powre* gan to prepare; . . . . VI. vi. 27. 3
him smite . . . with so impetuous *powre,* . . . . VI. vii. 8. 2
Ne *powre* had to withstand, ne hope of any ayd. . . . . . VI. vii. 48. 9
Ye gentle Ladies, in whose soveraine *powre* . . . . VI. viii. 1. 1
Ne list the Knight the *powre* thereof assay, ... VI. viii. 8. 7
Sitting like King of fowles in majesty and *powre:* . . . . . VI. x. 6. 9
Sith in his *powre* she was to foe or frend, ... VI. xi. 6. 4
had raught Faire Pastorella from those Brigants *powre,* . . . VI. xii. 3. 2
the more he rag'd, the more his *powre* increast. . . . . . . VI. xii. 32. 9
The proved *powre* of noble Calidore, ... VI. xii. 36. 7
many of them afterwards obtain'd Great *power* . . . . . . VII. vi. 3. 2
sad examples shewed Of her great *power,* . . . . VII. vi. 4. 7
His snaky-wreathed Mace, whose awfull *power* . . . . . . VII. vi. 18. 2
Since thou hast seene her dreadfull *power* belowe, ... VII. vi. 32. 6
(Oppressing them with *power* unequally,) . . . . VII. vii. 14. 7
say, they by your secret *powre* are made: . . . . VII. vii. 49. 4
that *power* and vertue which ye spake, ... VII. vii. 54. 4
His wanton wings and darts of deadly *power*. . . . . *Am.* iv. 8
And yet the Lyon that is Lord of *power,* . . . . *Am.* xx. 5
your *powre,* which I too well have tride. . . . . *Am.* xxv. 8
The *powre* thereof, which ofte in me I find, ... *Am.* xxviii. 5
Such is the *powre* of love in gentle mind, ... *Am.* xxx. 13
Is it because your eyes have *powre* to kill? . . . . *Am.* xlix. 2
To shew the *powre* of your imperious eyes; . . . . *Am.* xlix. 6
assurance that weake flesh reposeth In her owne *powre,* . . . *Am.* lviii. 2
Great both by name, and great in *power* and might, ... *Com. Son.* iii. 11
Love, . . . to thy mighty *powre* Perforce subdude . . . . . *H.L.* 1
Such is the *powre* of that sweet passion, ... *H.L.* 190
through infusion of celestiall *powre,* . . . . *H.B.* 50
Hath white and red in it such wondrous *powre,* . . . . . . *H.B.* 71
why doe not faire pictures like *powre* shew, ... *H.B.* 82
Which *powre* retayning still . . . . *H.B.* 113
Adore the *powre* of thy great Majestie, ... *H.B.* 271
shew what wondrous *powre* your beauty hath, ... *H.B.* 286
That High Eternall *Powre,* which now doth move . . . . . *H.H.L.* 27
His second brood, though not in *powre* so great, ... *H.H.L.* 53
most fit For so great *powre* and peerelesse majesty, ... *H.H.B.* 186
lower creatures all Subjected to her *powre* imperiall. . . . *H.H.B.* 196
Powerful. T' enrich the storehouse of his *powerfull* wit, . . . *Hub.* 790
rules the creatures by his *powrfull* saw: . . . . *Col.* 884
Shee smote them lightly with her *powrefull* wand. . . . . . IV. iii. 48. 2
charg'd his *powrefull* speare At Artegall, ... IV. iv. 44. 1
From *powrefull* eyes close venim doth convay . . . . IV. viii. 39. 8
the Ladie with her *powrefull* speach . . . . IV. x. 36. 6
did his *powrefull* light empeach, ... V. viii. 37. 7
to what I might compare Those *powrefull* eies, ... *Am.* ix. 2
Expressing all thy mothers *powrefull* art. . . . . *Am.* xxxix. 2
Yet being pregnant still with *powrefull* grace, ... *H.H.L.* 50
Powerless. His *powrelesse* arme, benumbd with secret feare, IV. vi. 21. 3
Powers. Where other *powers* farre different I see, ... *Gn.* 420
Stygian *powres* appease: . . . . *Gn.* 440
all the heavenly *powres* Conspire in one . . . . *Gn.* 578
T' appease the *powers;* . . . . *Gn.* 606
Will honour heaven, or heavenlie *powers* adore, ... *D.* 198
she that did my vitall *powres* supplie, ... *D.* 437
At last, when paine his vitall *powres* had spent, ... *As.* 173
th' infernall *powres* . . . Have borne him hence . . . . . . I. v. 14. 6
His chaunged *powres* at first them selves not felt; . . . . . I. vii. 6. 6
All other *powres* and knighthood he did scorne. . . . . . . I. vii. 10. 4
Therefore, deare Sir, your mightie *powres* assay.' . . . . . . I. viii. 2. 6
all his vitall *powres* Decayd, ... I. viii. 41. 8
To rest them selves, and weary *powres* repaire; . . . . . . I. viii. 50. 8
when their *powres* . . . With dew repast they had recured well, I. ix. 2. 1
all his manly *powres* it did disperse, ... I. ix. 48. 7
either hellish feends, or *powres* on hye: . . . . II. iii. 45. 5
doubling all his *powres* redoubled every stroke. . . . . . . II. vi. 30. 9
vitall *powres* gan wexe both weake and wan . . . . II. vii. 65. 2
United all his *powres* to purge him selfe from blame. . . . . II. xi. 31. 9
The which the *powres* to thee are pleased to revele.' . . . . III. iii. 19. 9
fading vitall *powres* gan to fade, ... III. xii. 21. 7
all the *powres* of nature, ... IV. ii. 44. 2
did restore His weakned *powers,* . . . . IV. iii. 24. 4
Ne felt his blood to wast, ne *powres* emperisht, ... IV. iii. 29. 2
all her vitall *powres* . . . gan there assemble; . . . . IV. vi. 29. 4
Privily pricked with thy lustfull *powres,* . . . . IV. x. 45. 7
Are not all places full of forraine *powres?* . . . . V. x. 23. 2
As if her vitall *powers* were at strife . . . . VI. v. 5. 7
Oftimes their sundry *powres* they did employ, ... VI. v. 14. 1
to th' infernall *Powers* her need give lone . . . . VII. vi. 11. 7
'Harken to mee awhile, yee heavenly *Powers!* . . . . VII. vi. 20. 1
even the highest *Powers* of heaven to check) . . . . VII. vi. 22. 4
both heavenly *Powers* and earthly wights, ... VII. vi. 36. 2
Onely th' infernall *Powers* might not appeare; . . . . VII. vii. 3. 6
Then any of the gods or *Powers* on hie: . . . . VII. vii. 5. 4
No eies but joyes, in which al *powers* conspire, ... *Am.* viii. 3
my weak *powres* of passions warreid arre; . . . . *Am.* xliv. 7
So weake my *powres,* so sore my wounds, ... *Am.* lvii. 5

Powers—*Continued.*
all ye *powers* which in the same remayne, . . . *Epith.* 413
The soveraine *Powres* and mightie Potentates, . . . *H.H.B.* 86
Powre. *See* **Pour, Power.**
Poynant. *See* **Poignant.**
Practic. All that Lysippus *practike* arte could forme, . . . *Ro.* xxix. 5
she used hath the *practicke* paine . . . I. xii. 34. 5
His *practick* witt and his fayre fyled tonge, . . . II. i. 3. 6
In cunning sleightes and *practick* knavery. . . . II. iii. 9. 6
Right *practicke* was Sir Priamond in fight, . . . IV. iii. 7. 1
both their skill forgot, And *practicke* use in armes; . . . V. vii. 29. 5
both were wondrous *practicke* in that play, . . . VI. i. 36. 3
Practice. the shepheard his *practise* spyed, . . . *S.C.* S. 202
each *practise* ill Of cosinage . . . *Hub.* 856
no *practise* slie, No counterpoint . . . *Hub.* 1139
Am put from *practise* of my kindlie skill, . . . *T.M.* 383
So well he wrought with *practise* and with paines, . . . *As.* 99
through continuall *practise* and usage . . . II. ix. 54. 4
cut off by *practise* criminall Of secrete foes, . . . III. iii. 28. 8
skil, which *practize* small Wil bring, . . . III. iii. 53. 8
he him selfe through *practise* usuall, Leapes forth . . . V. ii. 8. 5
Least any more such *practise* should proceede. . . . V. vi. 31. 5
The plot of all her *practise* did display, . . . V. ix. 47. 8
Practise. the fawne I *practise* from the Doe, . . . how to convay: . . . VI. ix. 23. 3
To *practise* games and maisteries to try, . . . VI. ix. 43. 2
Practised. he is *practiz'd* well in policie, . . . *Hub.* 783
Which in her cott she daily *practized?* . . . II. vi. 9. 4
whom he could not kill he *practizd* to entrap. . . . III. xii. 11. 9
perfectly *practiz'd* in womans craft, . . . IV. ii. 10. 2
with them *practiz'd*, how for to depryve Mercilla of her crowne, V. ix. 41. 6
Therein well *practisd* was, . . . VI. ix. 43. 8
Practising. *practising* the proofe of warlike deedes, . . . *Hub.* 740
Praise. the great (*om.*[1]) glorie and the auncient *praise*, . . . *Bel.* x. 6
your *praise*, the which shall never die . . . *Ro.* i. 3
Great Babylon her haughtie walls will *praise*, . . . *Ro.* ii. 1
Did fill with her renowmed nourslings *praise* . . . *Ro.* x. 7
thy *prayse* Excelling all that ever went before. . . . *Ro.* Env. 9
His sternesse was his *prayse*, . . . *Van.* x. 5
Tho wouldest thou pype of Phyllis *prayse;* . . . *S.C.* F. 63
Helpe me to blaze Her worthy *praise*, . . . *S.C.* Ap. 44
who my song doth *prayse* or blame, . . . *S.C.* Jun. 73
the *prayse* is better then the price, . . . *S.C.* O. 19
So *praysen* babes the Peacoks spotted traine, . . . *S.C.* O. 31
Sike *prayse* is smoke, . . . *S.C.* O. 35
loatheth sike delightes as thou doest *prayse:* . . . *S.C.* N. 18
Who but thy selfe deserves sike Poetes *prayse?* . . . *S.C.* N. 23
The songs that Colin made you in her *praise*, . . . *S.C.* N. 78
For beauties *prayse* and plesaunce had no peere; . . . *S.C.* N. 94
The *praise* of pitie vanisht is in vaine, . . . *Gn.* 358
the immortall *praise* Of womankinde, . . . *Gn.* 428
here the *praise* of either Scipion Abides . . . *Gn.* 613
'Live they for ever through their lasting *praise!* . . . *Gn.* 617
like desire and *praise* of noble fame, . . . *Hub.* 769
may be matter meete to gaine him *praise:* . . . *Hub.* 779
Let not sweete Poets *praise*, . . . *Hub.* 811
In th' eyes of people they put all their *praise*, . . . *T.M.* 93
The famous witnesse of our wonted *praise*, . . . *T.M.* 274
blazon foorth an earthlie beauties *praise* . . . *T.M.* 369
they him heare, and they him highly *prayse*. . . . *T.M.* 414
Due *praise*, that is the spur of dooing well? . . . *T.M.* 454
onely seeke for pleasure, nought for *praise*. . . . *T.M.* 468
They thinke to be chiefe *praise* of Poetry; . . . *T.M.* 555
Supports the *praise* of noble Poesie; . . . *T.M.* 574
To sing with Angels her immortall *praize*. . . . *T.M.* 588
shepherd groomes, which wont his songs to *praise:* . . . *Ti.* 228
Praise who so list, yet I will him dispraise, . . . *Ti.* 229
shall rehearse His worthie *praise*, . . . *Ti.* 256
I will it spend in speaking of thy *praise*, . . . *Ti.* 310
thine doo better *praise*. . . . *Ti.* 336
Vouchsafe this moniment of his last *praise* . . . *Ti.* 682
They her did *praise*, and my good fortune blesse. . . . *D.* 147
Eternally Him *praise* that hath them blest; . . . *D.* 286
Young Astrophel, the pride of shepheards *praise*, . . . *As.* 7
Thrise happie she, whom he to *praise* did chose. . . . *As.* 36
For her he made hymnes of immortall *praise*, . . . *As.* 63
prick him foorth with proud desire of *praise* . . . *As.* 86
carol made to *praise* thy loved lasse.' . . . *Col.* 87
No whit inferiour to thy Fanchins *praise*, . . . *Col.* 301
'By wondring at thy Cynthiaes *praise*, . . . *Col.* 353
There eke is Palin worthie of great *praise*, . . . *Col.* 392
all I *praise;* but in the highest place, . . . *Col.* 486
Paragone Of peerlesse price, and ornament of *praise*, . . . *Col.* 549
if I all should *praise* as they deserve, . . . *Col.* 578
they themselves for *praise* of fooles do sell, . . . *Col.* 723
Whose *praise* hereby no whit impaired is, . . . *Col.* 755
made amends to her with treble *praise*. . . . *Col.* 924
her honour paravant, And *praise* her worth, . . . *Col.* 942
To patronize the authour of their *praise*, . . . *Ded. Son.* iv. 10
To tast the streames . . . of thy loves *praise;* . . . *Ded.Son.*viii.10
For love of vertue and of Martiall *praise;* . . . *Ded. Son.* x. 6
In bigger tunes to sound your living *prayse*. . . . *Ded.Son.*xiii. 14
lasting baies Of . . . everlasting *praies;* . . . *Ded. Son.* xv. 5
Much can they *praise* the trees so straight and hy, . . . I. i. 8. 5
th' inheritance . . . Of brothers *prayse*, . . . I. iv. 48. 6
all for *praise* and honour he did fight. . . . I. v. 7. 6
Beseeching him with prayer and with *praise*, . . . I. v. 41. 6
Great pains, and greater *praise*, both never to be donne.' . . . I. v. 43. 9
yled with far reported *praise*, . . . I. vii. 46. 1
friendly each did others *praise* devize, . . . I. ix. 1. 7

Praise—*Continued.*
A worke of labour long, and endlesse *prayse:* . . . I. xi. 7. 6
I note whether *praise* or pitty more; . . . I. xii. 17. 4
draw them from pursuit of *praise* and fame . . . II. i. 23. 2
Against his *praise* to stirre up enmitye Of such, . . . II. i. 23. 8
'His be the *praise* that this atchiev'ment wrought, . . . II. i. 33. 2
So double was his paines, so double be his *praise*. . . . II. ii. 25. 9
Ne ought the *praise* of prowesse more doth marre . . . II. ii. 30. 8
Till it the pitch of highest *praise* exceeds: . . . II. ii. 31. 4
Such *prayse* is shame; . . . II. iii. 10. 8
All vertue merits *praise*, . . . II. iii. 37. 9
Trew be thy words, and worthy of thy *praise*, . . . II. iii. 38. 2
proud through *praise* and mad through love, . . . II. iv. 27. 1
Both loosers lott, and victours *prayse* alsoe: . . . II. v. 15. 8
Famous throughout the world for warlike *prayse*, . . . II. v. 26. 2
Unmindfull of thy *praise* and prowest might, . . . II. v. 36. 4
dew *praise* or dew reproch them yield; . . . II. viii. 14. 8
First *prayse* of knighthood is fowle outrage to deface.' . . . II. viii. 25. 9
With these in *praise* of pollicies mote strive. . . . II. ix. 48. 7
did apply Their mindes to *prayse* . . . II. x. 22. 6
In rule succeede, and eke in fathers *praise;* . . . II. x. 41. 2
A woman worthy of immortall *praise*, . . . II. x. 42. 4
O famous moniment of womens *prayse!* . . . II. x. 56. 1
in all godly thewes and goodly *praise* . . . II. x. 59. 6
To pricke of highest *prayse* forth to advaunce, . . . II. xii. 1. 3
the ydle instruments Of sleeping *praise*, . . . II. xii. 80. 2
To sing his mistresse *prayse;* . . . III. Pr. 5. 3
From seeking *praise* and deeds of armes abrode, . . . III. i. 1. 8
To hunt for glory and renowmed *prayse*. . . . III. i. 3. 3
for *prayse*, and proofe of manly might, . . . III. i. 13. 4
in their proper *praise* too partiall bee, . . . III. ii. 1. 2
we foolish men that *prayse* gin eke t' envy. . . . III. ii. 2. 9
faire Britomart, whose *prayse* I wryte; . . . III. ii. 3. 2
O soveraine Queene! whose *prayse* I would endyte, . . . III. ii. 3. 4
here to seek for *praise* and fame. . . . III. ii. 7. 9
through the earth have spredd their living *prayse*, . . . III. iii. 3. 8
Doth *praise* thee oft, . . . III. iv. 56. 7
Of Gods high *praise*, and of their loves sweet teene, . . . III. v. 40. 4
The *prayse* of her fresh flowring Maydenhead; . . . III. v. 54. 6
In so great *prayse* of stedfast chastity . . . III. v. 55. 1
both encreast the *prayse* of woman kynde, . . . III. v. 55. 7
Ne ever cast his mind to covet *prayse*, . . . III. vii. 12. 5
crowne of heavenly *prayse* with Saintes above, . . . III. viii. 42. 7
enterprised *praise* for dread to disavaunce.' . . . III. xi. 24. 9
Even immortal *prayse* and glory wyde, . . . III. xii. 39. 6
that augmented all her other *prayse*, . . . IV. ii. 35. 7
much augmented all their other *praise;* . . . IV. ii. 54. 3
all the more, the more his *praise* increst: . . . IV. iv. 21. 7
make his *praise* before his owne preferd: . . . IV. iv. 36. 8
bore The *prayse* of prowesse from them all away. . . . IV. iv. 48. 4
with the *praise* of armes and chevalrie . . . IV. v. 1. 2
the Paragon to see Of beauties *praise*, . . . IV. v. 9. 9
with blame would blot, and of due *praise* deprive. . . . IV. viii. 25. 9
admyrde her change, and spake her *praise*. . . . IV. ix. 16. 9
of their publicke *praise* had them despoyled, . . . IV. ix. 36. 4
second unto none in prowesse *prayse;* . . . V. iii. 5. 4
the greatest *prayse* redounded To Marinell, . . . V. iii. 6. 8
knights of Maidenhead, whose *praise* she would empaire.' . . . V. iv. 34. 9
all his former *praise* doth fowly spill: . . . V. vi. 1. 5
As it is greater *prayse* to save then spill, . . . V. x. 2. 8
Who then can thee, Mercilla, throughly *prayse*, . . . V. x. 3. 1
thine owne people do thy mercy *prayse* much more. . . . V. x. 3. 9
whose everlasting *praise* They all were bound . . . to raise. V. xi. 34. 8
all my former *praise* hath blemisht sore: . . . V. xi. 49. 4
Is ought on earth so pretious or deare As *prayse* and honour? V. xi. 62. 7
The goodly *praise* of Princely curtesie, . . . VI. Pr. 6. 3
praise likewise deserve good thewes . . . VI. ii. 2. 9
Of all those goodly implements of *prayse*, . . . VI. ii. 39. 2
Small *praise* to prove your powre on wight so weake.' . . . VI. v. 30. 5
praise the feature of her goodly face; . . . VI. vii. 28. 7
Some *praise* her paps; some *praise* her lips and nose; . . . VI. viii. 39. 5
to *praise* th' Almighty that doth send it! . . . VI. ix. 21. 9
underneath thy feete to place her *prayse;* . . . VI. x. 28. 7
The more t' augment her price through *praise* of comlinesse. VI. xi. 11. 9
did her greatly like, and did her greatly *praize*. . . . VI. xi. 13. 9
Such pride is *praise;* such portlinesse is honor; . . . *Am.* v. 9
Their anthemes sweet, devized of loves *prayse*, . . . *Am.* xix. 6
fill the world with her victorious *prayse*. . . . *Am.* xxix. 14
To spill were pitty, but to save were *prayse!* . . . *Am.* xxxviii. 12
tell her *prayse* to all posterity, . . . *Am.* lxix. 11
To speake her *prayse* and glory excellent, . . . *Am.* lxxiv. 11
sport my muse, and sing my loves sweet *praise;* . . . *Am.* lxxx. 10
When I doe *praise* her, say I doe but flatter; . . . *Am.* lxxxiv. 2
joyed in theyr *praise:* . . . *Epith.* 6
carroll of Loves *praise*. . . . *Epith.* 79
we cease your further *prayse* to sing; . . . *Epith.* 407
rapt with wonder of their famous *praise*, . . . *Com. Son.* iii. 5
Then would I sing of thine immortall *praise* . . . *H.L.* 301
song, thus fram'd in *praise* of thee. . . . *H.L.* 307
The wondrous matter of my fyre to *prayse*. . . . *H.B.* 7
in *praise* of thine owne name, . . . *H.B.* 8
In *praise* of that mad fit which fooles call love, . . . *H.H.L.* 9
spend His plenteous vaine in setting forth her *prayse*, . . . *H.H.B.* 220
Of Gods high *praise*, that filles the brasen sky; . . . *H.H.B.* 263
Praised. Loath was the Ape, though *praised*, to adventer, . . . *Hub.* 1005
God himselfe for wisedome most is *praised*, . . . *T.M.* 89
if good were not *praised* more than ill, . . . *T.M.* 455
when her as the worthiest She *praisd'*, . . . *Mui.* 126
Such as the world admyr'd, and *praised* it: . . . *Col.* 191
all the brood of Greece so highly *praised*, . . . *Col.* 413

Praised—*Continued.*
Hath *prais'd* and rais'd above each other starre. . . . . . . *Col.* 535
to be In this or that *praysd* diversly apart, ... *Col.* 569
he *praisd* his divelish arts, ... I. ii. 9. 4
Now *praysd,* hereafter deare thou shalt repent; . . . . . . I. ix. 43. 5
God she *praysd,* and thankt her faithfull knight, ... I. xi. 55. 8
Of merchants farre for profits therein *praysd;* . . . . . . II. x. 5. 7
hardly *praisd* his wedlock good. . . . . . . III. ix. 42. 9
litle *prays'd* his labours evill speed, ... IV. v. 22. 4
Liagore much *praisd* for wise behests; . . . . . . IV. xi. 51. 4
thy great justice, *praysed* over-all: . . . . . . V. Pr. 11. 8
Much more it *praysed* was of those two knights, ... V. x. 4. 1
He *praysd* it much, and much admyred it; . . . . . . VI. ii. 24. 5
such proud looks would make her *praysed* more; . . . . . . VI. vii. 30. 2
Witnesse the world how worthy to be *prayzed!* . . . . . . *Am.* iii. 2
Chose rather to be *praysd* for dooing good, ... *Am.* xxxviii. 13
Of all alive most worthy to be *praysed.* . . . . . . *Am.* lxxiv. 12
the trew fayre . . . is much more *praysd* of me: . . . . . . *Am.* lxxix. 4
Praise-desire. her name was *Prays-desire,* . . . . . . II. ix. 39. 8
Praises. sound their *praises* lowd. . . . . . . *Gn.* 616
Now change your *praises* into piteous cries, ... *T.M.* 371
Whose living *praises* in heroick style, ... *T.M.* 431
know their names, or speak their *praises* dew, ... *T.M.* 442
Be fild with *praises* of divinest wits, ... *T.M.* 581
Doo fawne on you, and your wide *praises* sing; . . . . . . *Ti.* 201
Whose *praises* I to future age doo sing; . . . . . . *Ti.* 277
To sing his living *praises* being dead, ... *Ti.* 437
whose *praises* wide Were spred abroad; . . . . . . *D.* 144
The *praises* of my parted love envy, ... *D.* 226
praises in all plenteousnesse Powr'd upon her, ... *D.* 227
Till I have told her *praises* lasting long: . . . . . . *Col.* 49
nought my *praises* of her needed arre, ... *Col.* 533
To the last *praises* of this Faery Queene; . . . . . . *Ded. Son.* ii. 10
Let thy faire Cinthias *praises* be thus rudely showne. . . . . *Ded.Son.* viii.14
Which of their *praises* have left you the haire; . . . . . . *Ded. Son.* x. 4
Thy gracious Soverains *praises* to compile, ... *Ded. Son.* xii. 6
she might . . . sound their *praises* dew? . . . . . . *Ded. Son.* xiv. 4
gentle deeds; Whose *praises* having slept in silence . . . . I. Pr. 1. 6
spake the *praises* of the workmans witt; . . . . . . I. iv. 5. 2
Ledd with thy *prayses,* . . . . . . I. x. 11. 4
staynd their *prayses* with thy least good part; . . . . . . II. iv. 26. 4
Far reach her mercies, and her *praises* farre, ... II. ix. 4. 8
who can tell the *prayses* of that makers might? . . . . . . II. ix. 46. 9
Which yet their *praises* speake, all be they loth, ... II. x. 40. 7
Bad counsels, *prayses,* and false flatteries: . . . . . . II. xi. 10. 8
antique *praises* unto present persons fitt. . . . . . . III. Pr. 3. 9
Thy selfe thy *prayses* tell, and make them knowen farre. . . III. ii. 3. 9
his *prayses* to compyle, ... III. ii. 12. 5
The *prayses* of high God he faire displayes, ... III. iv. 59. 3
His maistresse *praises* sweetly caroled: . . . . . . III. vii. 17. 4
all thy worthie *prayses* being blent . . . . . . III. ix. 33. 8
The *prayses* of that Prince so manifold; . . . . . . V. ix. 21. 2
all your other *praises* will deface, ... VI. viii. 2. 5
did pype and sing her *prayses* dew, ... VI. ix. 8. 6
my toung would speak her *praises* dew, ... *Am.* iii. 9
mote enlarge her living *prayses,* dead. . . . . . . *Am.* xxxiii. 4
To sing your name and *prayses* over-all: . . . . . . *Am.* lxxiii. 12
let her *prayses* yet be low and meane, ... *Am.* lxxx. 13
setting your immortall *prayses* forth: . . . . . . *Am.* lxxxii. 12
my glad mouth with her sweet *prayses* fill. . . . . . . *Am.* lxxxiv. 12
Helpe me mine owne loves *prayses* to resound; . . . . . . *Epith.* 14
Then I thy soverayne *prayses* loud wil sing, ... *Epith.* 127
But blush to heare her *prayses* sung so loud, ... *Epith.* 163
Nathlesse doe ye still loud her *prayses* sing, ... *Epith.* 165
Then would ye wonder, and her *prayses* sing, ... *Epith.* 202
The *praises* of the Lord in lively notes; . . . . . . *Epith.* 219
I meane to sing the *praises* of thy name, ... *H.L.* 10
The heavenly *prayses* of true love to sing. . . . . . . *H.H.L.* 14
Let Angels, . . . her soveraigne *praises* sing, ... *H.H.B.* 233
Praises'. To be thy living *praises* instrument, ... *Ded. Son.* ii. 3
Thy *praises* everlasting monument Is in this verse . . . . *Ded. Son.* vi. 12
Praiseth. *Praiseth* the thing that doth thy sorrow breed: . . *Hub.* 596
Praiseworthily. grudge at all That ever she sees doen *prays-worthily;* . . . . . . V. xii. 31. 3
Praiseworthy. due reward For her *prais-worthie* workmanship *Mui.* 268
Ne lesse *praise-worthie* I Theana read, ... *Col.* 492
Ne lesse *praise-worthie* is her sister deare, ... *Col.* 504
Ne lesse *praise-worthie* is Mansilia, ... *Col.* 508
Ne lesse *praise-worthie* Galathea seemes, ... *Col.* 516
Ne lesse *praise-worthie* faire Neaera is, ... *Col.* 524
Ne lesse *praise-worthie* Stella do I read, ... *Col.* 532
Ne lesse *praisworthie* are the sisters three, ... *Col.* 536
his own vertues and *praise-worthie* deedes. . . . . . . II. vii. 2. 5
'Well may yee speede in so *praiseworthy* payne! . . . . . . III. viii. 51. 2
Praising. doth sharply wite For *praising* love . . . . . . IV. Pr. 1. 4
Praysing their god, and yeelding him great thankes, ... IV. x. 25. 7
Lauding and *praysing* his renowmed worth . . . . . . V. xi. 33. 3
Prance. towardes him with dreadfull fury *praunce;* . . . . . I. vii. 11. 3
under him he saw his Lybian steed to *praunce;* . . . . . . II. viii. 17. 9
Prank. Long time he used this slippery *pranck,* . . . . . . *S.C.* S. 200
Some *prancke* their ruffes; . . . . . . I. iv. 14. 8
In sumptuous tire she joyd her selfe to *pranck,* . . . . . . II. ii. 36. 8
As Peacocke that his painted plumes doth *pranck,* . . . . . . II. iii. 6. 4
Full farre was I from thinking such a *pranke;* . . . . . . V. i. 15. 4
Prate. Feigning full many a fond excuse to *prate,* . . . . . . IV. x. 14. 7
So did the villaine to her *prate* and play, ... V. ix. 13. 5
Praxiteles. All were it Zeuxis or *Praxiteles,* . . . . . . III. Pr. 2. 3
Pray. *See* **Prey.**
Now I *pray* thee, shepheard, tel it not forth: . . . . . . *S.C.* F. 239
will we . . . *pray* him leaden our daunce. . . . . . . *S.C.* Mar. 24

Pray—*Continued.*
I *pray* thee, Hobbinoll, recorde some one, ... *S.C.* Ap. 30
I you *pray* . . . to fore-stall my neere decay.' . . . . . . *S.C.* May 272
I *pray* thee, lette me thy tale borrowe . . . . . . *S.C.* May 308
I *pray* thee, gall not my old griefe: . . . . . . *S.C.* S. 12
Diggon, I *praye* thee, speake not so dirke; . . . . . . *S.C.* S. 102
mought I thee *praye* Of ayde . . . . . . *S.C.* S. 246
scorning to the sacred Gods to *pray,* . . . . . . *Gn.* 390
Fast much, *pray* oft, looke lowly on the ground, ... *Hub.* 498
tell us (said the Ape) we doo you *pray,* . . . . . . *Hub.* 615
'Ne worse to you, my sillie sheepe! I *pray,* . . . . . . *D.* 351
of friendship I thee *pray,* . . . . . . *Col.* 159
Your first adventure: many such I *pray,* . . . . . . I. i. 27. 8
that old woman . . . did *pray* Upon her beads, ... I. iii. 13. 6
she gan them *pray,* That . . . she rest her may. . . . . . . I. iii. 14. 8
she did *pray* That plagues . . . Might fall on her, ... I. iii. 23. 6
well begonne, end all so well, I *pray!* . . . . . . I. viii. 28. 4
up to heven, as she did *pray,* . . . . . . I. x. 14. 8
made him *pray* both earely and eke late: . . . . . . I. x. 26. 5
first thou must a season fast and *pray,* . . . . . . I. x. 52. 7
To trusse the *pray* too heavy for his flight; . . . . . . I. xi. 19. 8
gan to highest God entirely *pray* . . . . . . I. xi. 32. 4
for his safetie gan devoutly *pray,* . . . . . . I. xi. 50. 8
albe the knight her much did *pray.* . . . . . . II. vi. 4. 9
Of grace I *pray* thee, give to eat and drinke to mee!' . . . . II. vii. 59. 9
watch thou, I *pray,* . . . . . . II. viii. 8. 6
of pardon I you *pray;* . . . . . . II. ix. 42. 6
of grace I *pray,* Pitty our playnt, ... III. iii. 21. 2
Do one or other good, I you most humbly *pray.* . . . . . . III. v. 10. 9
Have care, I *pray,* to guide the cock-bote well, ... III. viii. 24. 4
'Pardon, I *pray,* my heedlesse oversight, ... III. ix. 47. 2
you entyrely *pray* Of pardon for the strife, ... III. ix. 51. 7
of friendship let me now you *pray,* . . . . . . IV. i. 40. 2
I me submit, and you of pardon *pray,* . . . . . . IV. vi. 3. 8
'Sir Knight, of pardon I you *pray,* . . . . . . V. viii. 13. 1
whom he did *pray* To tend them well. . . . . . . VI. v. 41. 4
Thereto, when needed, she could weepe and *pray,* . . . . . VI. vi. 42. 5
This holy season, fit to fast and *pray,* . . . . . . *Am.* xxii. 1
Prayd, Prayes. *See* **Preyed, Preys.**
Prayed. The Priest gan wexe halfe proud to be so *praide,* . . *Hub.* 413
made The holie brethren falslie to have *praid.* . . . . . . *Ti.* 497
all the way he *prayed* as he went, ... I. i. 29. 8
her to save from outrage meekely *prayed* him. . . . . . . III. viii. 15. 9
them of patience gently *prayd.* . . . . . . III. ix. 10. 7
as the rest, he *prayd* for nought; . . . . . . III. ix. 12. 5
Then they Malbecco *prayd* of courtesy, ... III. ix. 25. 7
prayd her wake to heare him plaine. . . . . . . III. x. 49. 6
he her *prayd,* for mercy or for meed, ... III. x. 50. 7
Like as his mother *prayd* the Destinie, ... IV. iii. 13. 7
All on her gazing wisht, and vowd, and *prayd,* . . . . . . IV. v. 26. 3
her of pardon *prayd* more earnestlie, ... IV. vi. 23. 8
she woo'd and *prayd* him fast, ... IV. viii. 52. 8
'She often *prayd,* and often me besought, ... IV. x. 57. 1
streight that boaster *prayd,* . . . . . . V. iii. 10. 8
The more that he with meeke intreatie *prayd* . . . . . . V. v. 14. 8
prayd the place of her abode to learne; . . . . . . V. xi. 21. 3
Chyld Tristram *prayd* that he with him might goe . . . . . . VI. ii. 36. 3
I may not graunt that ye so greatly *prayde.* . . . . . . VI. ii. 37. 9
humbly *praid* to let them in that night; . . . . . . VI. iii. 38. 6
prayd to pitty his ill plight. . . . . . . VI. vi. 20. 9
often him besought, and *prayd,* and vowd, ... VI. vi. 31. 7
entyrely *prayd* T' advize him better . . . . . . VI. vii. 22. 3
with silence mercie *prayd.* . . . . . . VI. vii. 25. 9
They *prayd* high God them farre from them to send. . . . . VI. ix. 6. 5
adowne They *prayd* him sit, ... VI. ix. 7. 3
prayd that those same captives there Mote . . . Be sold, . . . VI. xi. 10. 3
Tho Coridon he *prayd,* . . . To wend with him, ... VI. xi. 35. 1
Prayer. Beseeching him with *prayer* and with praise, ... I. v. 41. 6
for *prayer* nor for meed: . . . . . . V. xi. 61. 7
to his *prayer* nought he would incline, ... VI. vii. 26. 2
But mine, no price nor *prayer* may surcease. . . . . . . *Am.* xi. 14
Prayers. all the peoples *prayers* to present . . . . . . *Hub.* 471
With *praiers* lowd importuning the skie, ... *Col.* 880
when she saw her *prayers* nought prevaile, ... I. iii. 24. 1
Her *prayers* nought prevaile, ... I. iii. 43. 9
doest the *praiers* of the righteous sead Present . . . . . . I. x. 51. 7
by good *prayers,* or by other hap, ... II. ii. 6. 7
Ne would for price or *prayers* once affoord . . . . . . II. vi. 19. 8
their *praiers* to appele With great devotion, ... III. ii. 48. 4
Amongst her teares immixing *prayers* meeke, ... IV. iii. 47. 6
with her *prayers* reasons, to restraine From blouddy strife, IV. iii. 47. 7
Unmov'd with *praiers* or with piteous thought, ... V. ii. 23. 2
Unto her selfe her silent *prayers* did impart. . . . . . . V. vii. 7. 9
With humble *prayers* and intreatfull teares; . . . . . . V. x. 6. 5
with *prayers* meeke . . . lodging did for her beseeke. . . . VI. iii. 37. 8
And called oft with *prayers* loud and shrill, ... VI. iii. 49. 7
Unto her *prayers* piteously enclynd, ... VI. vii. 37. 3
booted nought for *prayers* . . . To hope for to release . . . VI. viii. 3. 6
Playnts, *prayers,* vowes, ruth, ... *Am.* xiv. 11
Ne all the playnts and *prayers,* . . . . . . *Am.* xxxii. 7
Praying. *praying* to be garded from greevance.' . . . . . . *S.C.* F. 188
praying still did wake, and waking did lament. . . . . . . I. xi. 32. 9
instead of *praying* them surcease, . . . Bidding them fight . IV. ii. 19. 4
So *praying* him t' accept her service evermore. . . . . . . V. v. 54. 9
therein he likewise was *praying* now, ... VI. v. 35. 8
Preace, *etc.* *See* **Press,** *etc.*
Preach. She . . . heavenly documents thereout did *preach,* . I. x. 19. 4
Preached. Joseph of Arimathy, Who . . . *preacht* the truth; . II. x. 53. 9
Preasse. *See* **Press.**
Prebendaries. To Lords, to Principalls, to *Prebendaries?* . . *Hub.* 422

Precedent. the *president* Of Noblesse and of chevalree: . . . *To his Booke* 3
Moste noble Lord, the . . . *Precedent* of all that armes ensue? *Ded. Son.* xiv. 7
of all wisedom bee thou *precedent*, ... III. ii. 3. 3
no braver *president* this day Remaines on earth, ... V. iv. 2. 6
Precept. promist to performe his *precept* well, ... VI. i. 43. 3
But she his *precept* proudly disobayes, ... *Am.* xix. 11
Precepts. embrace The *precepts* of my heavenlie discipline; . *T.M.* 518
Precious. His *precious* robe I saw embrued with bloud. . . . *Rev.* iii. 5
the pavement *precious* stone. . . . . *Rev.* iv. 11
incense of *precious* Cedar tree, ... *Bel.* xi. 3
dew . . . gan quench those *precious* flames; . . . . *Bel.*[2] xi. 12
the glauncing rayes Of *precious* stones, ... *Gn.* 102
thy life more deare and *precious* Was . . . . *Gn.* 331
The *precious* store of this celestiall riches? . . . . *T.M.* 146
Adornd with purest golde and *precious* stone; . . . . *Ti.* 86
in it did most *precious* treasure hide, ... *Ti.* 619
bring to her so *precious* a pray. . . . . *Mui.* 112
In glistring gold and perelesse *pretious* stone; . . . . I. iv. 8. 6
coffers . . . With *precious* metall full . . . . I. iv. 27. 4
with stones most *pretious* rare. . . . . I. vii. 29. 9
in the midst thereof one *pretious* stone . . . . I. vii. 30. 1
builded . . . Of perle and *precious* stone, ... I. x. 55. 5
pretious blood, which cruelly was spilt . . . . I. x. 57. 5
pretious Balme, whose vertuous might Did heale his woundes, . I. xi. 50. 5
precious odours fetcht from far away, ... I. xii. 38. 4
His *precious* horne, sought of his enimyes, ... II. v. 10. 7
to remove . . . Those *pretious* hils . . . . II. vii. 6. 3
To trouble my still seate and heapes of *pretious* pelfe. . . . II. vii. 7. 9
Laden from far with *precious* merchandize, ... II. xii. 19. 2
Yt framed was of *precious* yvory, ... II. xii. 44. 1
with great perles and *pretious* stones embost; . . . . III. i. 32. 7
So fell proud Marinell upon the *pretious* shore. . . . . III. iv. 17. 9
pearles and *pretious* stones of great assay, ... III. iv. 18. 5
would not stay For gold, or perles, or *pretious* stones, ... III. iv. 18. 8
Exceeding riches and all *pretious* things, ... III. iv. 23. 2
all that els was *pretious* and deare, ... III. iv. 23. 6
all the ground, with *pretious* deaw bedight, ... III. vi. 43. 8
Lapped in flowres and *pretious* spycery, ... III. vi. 46. 5
The utmost rowme abounding with all *precious* store: . . . . III. xi. 27. 9
There was an Altar built of *pretious* stone . . . . III. xi. 47. 2
Bearing that *precious* relicke in an arke Of gold, ... IV. iv. 15. 2
curiously embost With pearle and *precious* stone, ... IV. iv. 15. 7
Where beauties prize shold win that *pretious* spoyle: . . . . IV. iv. 48. 8
This *pretious* ornament, they say, did make, ... IV. v. 4. 3
about her purple brest That *precious* juell, ... IV. viii. 10. 3
Eftsoones that *pretious* liquour forth he drew, ... IV. viii. 20. 6
thousand *pretious* gifts worth many a pound, ... IV. x. 37. 7
neither *pretious* stone, nor durefull brasse, ... IV. x. 39. 4
much more rare and *pretious* to esteeme, ... IV. x. 39. 6
close with him in *pretious* store That his false Ladie, ... V. iii. 13. 4
Is ought on earth so *pretious* or deare As prayse and honour? V. xi. 62. 6
as a *precious* gemme Amidst a ring . . . . VI. x. 12. 7
Do seeke most *pretious* things . . . . *Am.* xv. 2
all those *pretious* ornaments deface. . . . . *Am.* xxxi. 4
With *pretious* merchandize she forth doth lay; . . . . *Am.* lxxxi. 6
what can prize that thy most *precious* blood? . . . . *H.H.L.* 175
Th' eternall portion of her *precious* dowre, ... *H.H.B.* 250
Preeving. *See* **Proving.**
Prefer. meaning her much better to *preferre*, ... *Col.* 121
to true loves he may us evermore *Preferre*, ... *Col.* 818
her Whose love before their life they doe *prefer*. . . . . . . *H.L.* 140
Preferment. Still wayting to *preferment* up to clime, ... *Hub.* 76
Preferred. her honor, which she more then life *prefard*. . . . III. viii. 14. 9
Shall to that fairest Ladie be *prefard*. . . . . IV. ii. 27. 4
make his praise before his owne *preferd*: . . . . IV. iv. 36. 8
Old love is litle worth when new is more *prefard*. . . . . . VI. ix. 40. 9
Prefixed. the full time, *prefixt* by destiny, ... III. iii. 40. 5
now he hath to her *prefixt* a day, ... V. xi. 40. 1
When my abodes *prefixed* time is spent, ... *Am.* xlvi. 1
Pregnant. in her *pregnant* flesh they shortly fructifide. . . . III. vi. 7. 9
was shed Into her *pregnant* bosome, ... V. vii. 11. 2
hearing th' answeres of his *pregnant* wit, ... VI. ii. 24. 4
Yet being *pregnant* still with powrefull grace, ... *H.H.L.* 50
Preife. *See* **Proof.**
Prejudice. That nought mote hinder his quicke *prejudize*: . . II. ix. 49. 7
Prelates. All jolly *Prelates*, worthie rule to beare, ... *Hub.* 423
Prepare. In the fresh shadowe did for them *prepayre*, ... *Gn.* 188
gins straight to *prepare* The weapons, ... *Gn.* 275
unto rest his wearie joynts *prepare*. . . . . *Gn.* 320
whatso theretoo did neede Each did *prepare*, ... *Hub.* 107
theretoo gan his furnitures *prepare*. . . . . *Mui.* 56
Small needments else need shepheard to *prepare*. . . . . . . *Col.* 195
To you this humble present I *prepare*, ... *Ded. Son.* x. 5
he . . . gan eftsoones *prepare* Himselfe to batteill . . . . . I. iii. 34. 3
A gentle Husher, . . . passage for them did *prepaire*: . . . . I. iv. 13. 4
He . . . did him selfe *prepayre* In sunbright armes, ... I. v. 2. 7
seemely welcome for her did *prepare*: . . . . I. x. 44. 7
to *prepare* Their minds to pleasure, ... II. ii. 33. 8
doest not unto death thyselfe *prepayre*? . . . . II. iii. 7. 7
soone thyselfe *prepaire* To batteile, ... II. vi. 28. 5
gan themselves *prepare* to batteill greedily. . . . . II. viii. 18. 9
unto better fortune doth her selfe *prepayre*. . . . . II. xi. 36. 9
He them espying gan him selfe *prepare*, ... III. i. 4. 7
she did *prepare* Way to her love, ... III. i. 51. 7
unto battaill did her selfe *prepayre*. . . . . III. iv. 14. 3
to the batteill doth her selfe *prepare*: . . . . III. vii. 39. 6
gan him selfe *prepare* Him to receive . . . . IV. i. 41. 5
all things dooe, That might her love *prepare*, ... IV. ii. 8. 9
by one way that passage did *prepare*. . . . . IV. x. 6. 5
thou the same for pleasure didst *prepayre*: . . . . IV. x. 47. 5

Prepare—*Continued.*
pearles which th' Indian seas for her *prepaire*. . . . . IV. xi. 11. 9
seized . . . Uppon some fowle that should her feast *prepare*; . V. iv. 42. 5
as she did her selfe to strike *prepare*, ... V. viii. 48. 3
Himselfe unto his journey gan *prepare*, ... V. x. 16. 2
all his way before him still *prepare*. . . . . V. x. 17. 7
gan him selfe to fight on foote *prepare*: . . . . V. xi. 9. 4
Those warlike armes . . . he gan eftsoones *prepare*, ... VI. v. 8. 5
him against his powre gan to *prepare*; . . . . VI. vi. 27. 3
His bloudy vessels wash, and holy fire *prepare*. . . . . VI. viii. 39. 9
ready passage to her pleasure did *prepaire*. . . . . VII. vi. 7. 9
Prepare your selfe new love to entertaine. . . . . *Am.* iv. 14
Prepare your selves; for he is comming strayt. . . . . . . *Epith.* 113
Prepare your selves, and open wide your harts . . . . *H.L.* 33
Prepare your selves to march amongst his host, ... *H.L.* 40
Prepared. *See* **Well-prepared.**
Whom, thus at point *prepared*, to prevent, ... *Gn.* 281
to what labour els he was *prepar'd*, ... *Hub.* 265
With humble service to her will *prepard*: . . . . I. iii. 9. 7
unto battell sterne themselves *prepar'd*. . . . . II. ii. 19. 9
soone *prepard* to field, his sword forth drew, ... II. vi. 29. 3
all by wrong waies for themselves *prepard*: . . . . II. vii. 47. 5
to his purposd journey him *prepar'd*: . . . . II. xi. 3. 6
freshly, as at first, *prepard* himselfe to fight. . . . . II. xi. 38. 9
The heavie plague that for such leachours is *prepard*. . . . . III. v. 14. 9
the which him selfe *prepar'd* To giust . . . . III. x. 35. 3
whatsoever perill was *prepared*, ... IV. v. 46. 4
him selfe *prepar'd* To tell . . . . IV. ix. 41. 4
both which *prepard* her way. . . . . IV. xi. 47. 9
ready for the gallow-tree *prepard*: . . . . V. iv. 22. 4
to them way to make with weapons well *prepard*. . . . . . . V. iv. 37. 9
Them selves thereto *preparde* in order dew; . . . . V. v. 1. 7
Talus desir'd that he might have *prepared* The way . . . . . V. vi. 38. 4
themselves *prepard* thorough the foord to ride. . . . . VI. iii. 30. 9
being well *prepard* His first assault . . . did ward, ... VI. iv. 5. 4
Dew to thy selfe, that it for me *prepard*! . . . . *Am.* lxxxv. 14
this Lay, *Prepar'd* against that Day, ... *Proth.* 88
Prepares. So to his worke Aragnoll him *prepares*. . . . . . . *Mui.* 408
Preparing. with his yron club *preparing* way, ... VI. viii. 8. 2
Prepense. ever in your noble hart *prepense*, ... III. xi. 14. 5
Prerogative. yours the waift by high *prerogative*. . . . . . . IV. xii. 31. 6
Presage. seek this path that I to thee *presage*, ... I. x. 61. 1
if Sir Calidore could it *presage*, ... III. viii. 28. 8
Prescribed. That is the terme *prescribed* by the spell.' . . . . I. ii. 43. 5
Then what *prescribed* were by lawes of chevalrie. . . . . . . V. vii. 28. 9
With him he raignd, before all time *prescribed*, ... *H.H.L.* 36
Prescript. Unto the place where his *prescript* did showe. . . . *Hub.* 1261
Presence. the wight whose *presence* was our pryde; . . . . . *S.C.* N. 65
The *presence* of your dearest loves delight, ... *D.* 513
from her *presence* faultlesse him debard. . . . . *Col.* 167
Untill that we to Cynthiaes *presence* came: . . . . *Col.* 332
may that blessed *presence* still enjoy, ... *Col.* 661
By them they passe, . . . And to the *Presence* mount; . . . . I. iv. 7. 2
Which with their *presence* fayre the place much beautifide. . . I. iv. 7. 9
Soone as the Elfin knight in *presence* came, ... I. iv. 13. 1
That greatest Princes *presence* might behold. . . . . I. viii. 35. 4
my Lord . . . Whose *presence* I have lackt . . . . I. viii. 43. 2
him beares Forth from her *presence*, ... I. x. 35. 2
At their first *presence* grew agrieved sore, ... I. x. 49. 2
So fairely dight when she in *presence* came, ... I. xii. 24. 1
Her joyous *presence*, and sweet company, ... I. xii. 41. 1
his aged Guide in *presence* came; . . . . II. i. 31. 3
did abase their lofty crests To her faire *presence* . . . . . . II. ii. 32. 5
In which her roiall *presence* is enrold; . . . . II. ii. 44. 4
Ne car'd he greatly for her *presence* vayne, ... II. iii. 43. 6
Least by her *presence* daunger mote befall; . . . . II. iii. 44. 2
When he in *presence* came, ... II. iv. 39. 1
Ne thou for better hope, if thou his *presence* stay.' . . . . . II. iv. 40. 9
that straunger knight in *presence* came, ... II. viii. 23. 1
at these straungers *presence* every one did hush. . . . . II. ix. 35. 9
Ne ever to her *presence* should presume, ... III. vii. 56. 3
Great comfort of her *presence* he conceiv'd, ... III. viii. 23. 3
Ne would they eate till she in *presence* came. . . . . III. ix. 26. 6
Shee came in *presence* with right comely grace, ... III. ix. 26. 7
as one daunted with her *presence* dread, ... IV. viii. 13. 7
In *presence* came, desirous t' understand Tydings . . . . . . IV. viii. 62. 8
In *presence* of them all forth led her thence . . . . IV. x. 56. 7
here and there before his *presence* flew, ... V. ii. 53. 8
Whose *presence* all their troups so much encombred, ... V. v. 19. 5
it should let your pace Towards my Ladies *presence*, ... V. ix. 7. 6
Unto the *presence* of that gratious Queene; . . . . V. ix. 27. 2
knights were to her *presence* brought; . . . . V. ix. 34. 2
Admyr'd of all the rest in *presence* there, ... V. x. 15. 7
From whose sterne *presence* they diffused ran, ... V. xi. 47. 8
when as my *presence* he did spy To be a let, ... VI. ii. 17. 4
'Glad would I surely be, . . . To have thy *presence* . . . . . VI. ii. 37. 2
fiends affrighted bee . . . from her *presence* flee: . . . . . . VI. vi. 10. 5
with her goodly *presence* all the rest much graced. . . . . . VI. x. 12. 9
him bring before his *presence* prest. . . . . VII. vi. 16. 9
Before great Natures *presence* should appeare, ... VII. vi. 36. 3
being lowe before her *presence* feld . . . . VII. vii. 13. 7
to thy *presence* call The rest . . . . VII. vii. 27. 2
if in *presence* of that fayrest proud . . . . *Am.* ii. 9
From *presence* of my dearest deare exylde, ... *Am.* lii. 7
That of her *presens* I my meed may take. . . . . *Am.* lii. 14
her bowre with her late *presence* deckt; . . . . *Am.* lxxviii. 6
Since I did leave the *presence* of my love, ... *Am.* lxxxvi. 1
on his owne dread *presence* to attend, ... *H.H.L.* 68
those whom shee Vouchsafeth to her *presence* to receave, . . *H.H.B.* 254
Present. Goe, little booke! thy selfe *present*, ... *To his Booke* 1

Present—*Continued.*
all the peoples prayers to *present* Before his throne, ... *Hub.* 471
Unto his Church for to *present* a wight, ... *Hub.* 526
to *present* His bodie, as a spotles sacrifise; . . . . *Ti.* 297
never wist I till this *present* day, ... *Col.* 827
As if his godhead thou didst *present* see.' . . . . *Col.* 834
right noble Lord, I send This *present* . . . . *Ded. Son.* iv. 14
ensample to the *present* age Of th' old Heroes, ... *Ded. Son.* vi. 3
Unfitly I these ydle rimes *present,* . . . . *Ded. Son.* ix. 7
To you this humble *present* I prepare, ... *Ded. Son.* x. 5
But to make humble *present* of good will: . . . . *Ded.Son.* xvi. 12
Then that brave court doth to mine eie *present,* *Ded.Son.*xvii.11
For *present* cause was none of dread her to dismay. . . . . I. ii. 20. 9
Ne yet of *present* perill be affraid, ... I. iv. 49. 3
To her makes *present* of his service seene: . . . . I. v. 16. 3
unto their God *present* That flowre of fayth . . . . I. vi. 15. 4
these reliques sad *present* unto mine eye. . . . . I. vii. 24. 9
Thou doest the praiers . . . *Present* before the majesty divine, I. x. 51. 8
nothing may my *present* hope empare.' . . . . I. x. 63. 5
Would God! thy selfe now *present* were in place . . . . . . II. i. 9. 8
chaunst, That you, most noble Sir, had *present* beene . . . . II. i. 10. 2
The which good fortune doth to you *present.* . . . . II. i. 16. 4
I *present* was, and can it witnesse well, ... II. i. 19. 6
He oft finds *present* helpe who does his griefe impart.' . . . . II. i. 46. 9
poursewed fast The *present* offer of faire victory, ... II. v. 12. 2
Refuse such fruitlesse toile, and *present* pleasures chuse.' . . . II. vi. 17. 9
when I thee *present* see In daunger . . . . II. vi. 49. 6
when an earthly wight they *present* saw . . . . II. vii. 37. 1
'Abide the fortune of thy *present* fate; . . . . II. vii. 60. 2
To teach them how to use their *present* state.' . . . . II. vii. 60. 5
The next could of thinges *present* best advize; . . . . II. ix. 49. 2
The one she slew upon the *present* floure; . . . . II. x. 19. 5
antique praises unto *present* persons fitt. . . . . III. Pr. 3. 9
That her . . . Unto his Faery Queene he might *present:* . . . III. i. 2. 6
did them selves *present* Unto her vew, ... III. i. 44. 2
It was a famous *Present* for a Prince, ... III. ii. 21. 6
of each shade that did it selfe *present;* . . . . III. vii. 19. 4
He comming *present,* where the Monster vilde . . . . III. vii. 30. 7
I with me brought, and did to her *present:* . . . . III. vii. 55. 6
those two sought nought but the *present* pray, ... III. x. 34. 4
for the *present* did her anger shrowd, ... IV. i. 10. 7
That *present* were to testifie the case.' . . . . IV. i. 49. 5
fortune doth to you *present* So fayre a spoyle, ... IV. ii. 5. 8
both did forget The perilous *present* stownd . . . . IV. ii. 15. 9
That fayrest Florimell was *present* there in place. . . . . . IV. ii. 22. 9
for this Ladie, *present* in your vew, ... IV. ii. 24. 3
for the *present* they were reconcyld, ... IV. iv. 5. 3
she for the *present* was appeased, ... IV. vi. 44. 1
yet untouched till this *present* day, ... IV. vii. 18. 8
to the *present* neede it wisely usd. . . . . IV. viii. 60. 4
this *present* lucklesse howre, ... IV. ix. 39. 2
there it *present* was, ... IV. x. 22. 9
with him brought a *present* joyfully . . . . IV. xi. 33. 7
They saw it all, and *present* were in place; . . . . IV. xi. 40. 6
present at this great solemnity: . . . . IV. xi. 53. 5
with state of *present* time . . . the antique world compare, . V. Pr. 1. 1
the common line Of *present* dayes, ... V. Pr. 3. 4
'Seest not how badly all things *present* bee, ... V. ii. 37. 2
with this *present* treatise doth agree, ... V. iii. 3. 8
Which when as all that *present* were beheld, ... V. iii. 26. 1
this his *present* guest Was Artegall, ... V. vi. 34. 1
there *present* in her sight Those two false brethren . . . . . V. vi. 36. 5
She for a *present* to their Goddesse brought. . . . . V. vii. 24. 5
when all her warlike traine There *present* saw, ... V. vii. 34. 8
tempred for the time her *present* heavinesse. . . . . V. vii. 44. 9
her to *present* Unto his scornefull Lady . . . . V. viii. 25. 8
comming *present* there, She at her ran . . . . V. viii. 46. 7
many fearefull objects to them to *present.* . . . . V. ix. 46. 9
To whom their sute they humbly did *present* . . . . V. x. 14. 8
her shewed there The *present* of his paines, ... V. xi. 33. 6
Of which though *present* age doe plenteous seeme, ... VI. Pr. 4. 6
of him learnes His state and *present* plight. . . . . VI. ii. Arg.
To have thy presence in my *present* quest, ... VI. ii. 37. 2
did *present* The fearefull Lady to her father . . . . VI. iii. 18. 1
the *present* mischiefe to redresse, ... VI. iii. 44. 2
for the perill of the *present* stound, ... VI. iv. 9. 8
fortune doth to you *present* This litle babe, ... VI. iv. 35. 3
Whom when the Hermite *present* saw in place, ... VI. v. 36. 2
So shall you soone repaire your *present* evill plight.' . . . . VI. vi. 14. 9
in *present* vew, Him rudely rent . . . . VI. vi. 22. 5
Whose share, her guiltlesse bloud, they would *present;* . . . VI. viii. 38. 7
to question of her *present* woe, ... VI. viii. 50. 6
I forbore To finish then, for other *present* hast. . . . . . . VI. ix. 2. 4
when he came in companie Where Calidore was *present,* . . . VI. ix. 39. 2
Thy love is *present* there with thee in place; . . . . VI. x. 16. 8
to *present* her with their labours late; . . . . VI. x. 33. 7
Hither those Brigants brought their *present* pray, ... VI. xi. 43. 1
wishing oft that he were *present* there . . . . VI. xi. 33. 8
Pluto and Proserpina were *present* there. . . . . VII. vii. 3. 9
Be also *present* heere, ... *Epith.* 71
forme, which they *present* Unto their mind, ... *H.B.* 214
Th' Idee of his pure glorie *present* still Before thy face, . . *H.H.L.* 284
Presented. Unto my eyes strange showes *presented* were, . . *Van.* i. 10
Before mine eies strange sights *presented* were, ... *Ti.* 489
when she *presented* was to sight; . . . . II. iii. 26. 2
there was *presented* to her eye A comely knight, ... III. ii. 24. 1
Presented to the fayrest Florimell, ... V. iii. 27. 8
he it *presented* Before the feete of the faire Pastorell; . . . VI. x. 36. 6
Presenting. *Presenting* him with all the rich array . . . . V. viii. 51. 4
The which *presenting* all in trim Array, ... *Proth.* 85
Presently. *presently* was void and wholly vaine: . . . . . . I. viii. 4. 7
this Dame do *presently* Restore unto her health . . . . . . III. xii. 35. 5
Ne into ayre did vanish *presently,* . . . . IV. iii. 13. 4
Whereof I have to treat here *presently:* . . . . V. vii. 3. 5
you into such perils *presently* doth call?' . . . . VI. i. 6. 9
he was not *presently* in plight Her to defend, ... VI. ii. 19. 1
As if they would have slaine them *presently:* . . . . VI. vi. 23. 5
Presents. brought him *presents,* flowers if it were prime, . . *As.* 47
Good lucke *presents* you with yond lovely mayd, ... IV. i. 33. 8
Yet she no whit his *presents* did regard, ... VI. ix. 40. 6
this young Mayd, whom chance to her *presents,* . . . . . . VI. xii. 20. 5
Preserve. so much gold Thou canst *preserve* . . . . II. vii. 20. 4
to *preserve* inviolated right . . . . V. x. 2. 3
still *preserve* your first informed grace, ... *H.B.* 167
Preserved. *Preserved* from being to his foes betrayde; . . . . *Van.* xi. 11
al that life *preserved* did detest; . . . . I. xi. 49. 3
First got with guile, and then *preserv'd* with dread, ... II. vii. 12. 3
such as were through former flight *preserv'd* . . . . II. x. 55. 5
it had beene here *preserv'd* in store, ... III. iii. 60. 4
I her *preserv'd* from perill and from feare, ... IV. vi. 35. 6
few plants, *preserv'd* through heavenly ayd, ... IV. viii. 33. 3
preserv'd from yron rust Of rude oblivion . . . . V. iv. 2. 7
She was *preserved* from their traytrous traine. . . . . V. vi. 34. 7
If her Sir Artegall had not *preserved,* . . . . V. xii. 43. 4
Preserver. the most kind *preserver* Of living wights, ... *H.L.* 156
President. *See* **Precedent.**
Presidents. their rule of yearely *Presidents* Grew great, . . . *Ro.* xviii. 7
Press. To put in *preace* emong the learned troupe: . . . . *S.C.* O. 70
Far from all peoples *preace,* as in exile, ... I. iii. 3. 3
Ne I against the same can justly *preace:* . . . . I. xii. 19. 4
all that *preace* did rownd about her swell . . . . II. vii. 46. 5
What meant that *preace* about that Ladies throne, ... II. vii. 48. 2
Exceld at Athens all the learned *preace,* . . . . II. x. 25. 7
rushing through the thickest *preasse* . . . . III. i. 23. 5
To barre the *prease* of people farre away; . . . . IV. iii. 4. 2
passed through th' unruly *preace* Of people, ... IV. iii. 41. 1
Into the thickest of that knightly *preasse* He thrust, ... IV. iv. 34. 1
thrusting fierce into the thickest *preace* . . . . IV. ix. 32. 6
Artegall . . . Stood in the *preasse* close covered, ... V. iii. 20. 2
Forth from the thickest *preasse* of people came, ... V. iii. 29. 4
round about him *preace* in riotous aray. . . . . V. vi. 29. 9
pressing through the *preace* unto the gate, ... V. vii. 35. 3
passing through the thickest *preasse,* . . . . V. ix. 23. 6
to retyre him hasted Through the thick *prease,* . . . . VI. vi. 28. 4
out of them to *presse* the milke: . . . . VI. ix. 37. 9
covered with confused *preasse* Of carcases, ... VI. xi. 20. 1
in great store Unto the cave gan *preasse,* . . . . VI. xi. 46. 4
Pressed. With her owne weight down *pressed* now shee lies, . . *Ti.* 76
nought but *pressed* gras where she had lyen, ... I. ix. 15. 2
preaced to draw nere To th' upper part, ... II. vii. 44. 3
grudge in so streight prison to be *prest,* . . . . II. xi. 32. 4
through thy darksom dore Unwares have *prest;* . . . . III. iii. 15. 8
after him Sir Palimord forth *prest:* . . . . IV. iv. 21. 5
They *pressed* forward, entraunce to have made; . . . . V. iv. 38. 2
before his horses vew, As they upon him *prest,* . . . . V. viii. 37. 9
as he *pressed* in, him there did slay: . . . . V. x. 36. 7
the Prince hard *preased* in betweene, ... V. x. 37. 6
as she *prest* on him with heavy sway, ... V. xi. 31. 1
He fiercely him pursu'd, and *pressed* sore; . . . . VI. i. 21. 8
from the citties to the townes him *prest,* . . . . VI. ix. 3. 7
further then she willing was he *prest,* . . . . VI. xi. 7. 6
Pressing. *preacing* to the pillour, ... IV. x. 10. 7
From rudely *pressing* to the middle center; . . . . V. v. 5. 7
pressing through the preace unto the gate, ... V. vii. 35. 3
boldly *preacing*-on raught forth her hand . . . . VII. vi. 13. 2
Achilles *preassing* through the Phrygian glaives, ... *H.L.* 233
Prest. to prolong The vengeaunce *prest?* . . . . II. viii. 28. 3
him affronting soone, to fight was readie *prest.* . . . . . . IV. iii. 22. 9
In which his worke he had sixe servants *prest,* . . . . IV. v. 36. 1
hard behind his backe his foe was *prest,* . . . . IV. viii. 41. 6
To warne her foe to battell soone be *prest:* . . . . V. vii. 27. 2
finding there ready *prest* Sir Artegall, ... V. viii. 9. 1
He watcht in close awayt with weapons *prest,* . . . . VI. vi. 44. 3
his salvage page, that wont be *prest,* . . . . VI. vii. 19. 5
him bring before his presence *prest.* . . . . VII. vi. 16. 9
Presume. I never lyst *presume* to Parnasse hyll, ... *S.C.* Jun. 70
Presume the things so sacred to prophane? . . . . *Col.* 349
That did *presume* his fathers fyrie wayne, ... I. iv. 9. 2
Presume so high to stretch mine humble quill? . . . . III. Pr. 3. 3
Ne ever to her presence should *presume,* . . . . III. vii. 56. 3
That beautie durst *presume* to violate, ... III. viii. 36. 2
How then dare I . . . *Presume* to picture . . . . *H.H.B.* 226
Presumed. His prowd *presumed* force increased more, ... II. vi. 30. 3
Presumes. Each idle wit at will *presumes* to make, ... *T.M.* 215
Presumest. 'Thou that *presum'st* to weigh the world anew, . . V. ii. 34. 1
Presuming. Bold men, *presuming* life for gaine to sell, . . . *Col.* 209
presuming to contend With hardy fowle . . . . I. xi. 19. 5
presuming on th' appointed tyde, ... V. xi. 39. 1
Presumption. through *presumption* of his matchlesse might, . I. vii. 10. 3
that proud Knight in his *presumption* . . . . VI. iii. 8. 3
with bold *presumption* doth aspire . . . . VII. vi. 21. 2
Presumptious. ramping forth with proud *presumpteous* gate, . I. viii. 12. 5
with *presumpteous* cheare And countenance sublime . . . . . V. viii. 30. 3
Who came at length with proud *presumpteous* gate . . . . . . V. xii. 14. 1
with *presumpteous* powre against that knight streight go'th. . VI. ii. 17. 9
Presumptiously. *presumpteouslie* By wicked doome . . . . . IV. xii. 29. 8
Presumptuous. those signes of your *presumptuous* boasts . . *Ro.* xv. 3
Heaven had not feare of that *presumptuous* might, ... *Ro.* xvii. 3
punished for their *presumptuous* guile. . . . . *Hub.* 1256
the *presumptuous* Damzell rashly dar'd . . . . *Mui.* 269

Pretence. With flying speede and seeming great *pretence,* . . . I. xii. 24. 7
unto things of valorous *pretence* Seemes to be borne . . . II. iv. 1. 4
aery spirite under false *pretence,* . . . II. xi. 39. 8
with boastfull vaine *pretense,* Stept Braggadochio . . . IV. v. 23. 5
To laugh at me, and favour my *pretence,* . . . IV. x. 56. 4
Without discoverie of my thoughts *pretence,* . . . V. v. 33. 7
For what their speares had fayld of their *pretence:* . . . V. viii. 10. 3
Pretend. never entraunce any durst *pretend,* . . . II. xi. 15. 8
would some rightfull cause *pretend,* . . . IV. xii. 30. 9
to *pretend* Some shew of favour, . . . VI. xi. 6. 5
Seene but a glims of this which I *pretend,* . . . *H.H.B.* 221
Pretended. for memorie Of her *pretended* crime, . . . *Mui.* 143
perill, by this salvage man *pretended,* . . . VI. iv. 10. 4
His target alwayes over her *pretended;* . . . VI. xi. 19. 4
Pretends. *Pretends* . . . To be the Soveraine. . . . VII. vi. Arg.
Pretext. we may coulor it with some *pretext* . . . *Hub.* 988
Pretty. The *pretie* Pawnce, And the Chevisaunce, . . . *S.C.* Ap. 142
See yee the blindfoulded *pretie* God, . . . *Tetrasticon.* 1
the merry birds, thy *prety* pages, . . . IV. x. 45. 6
many a *pretty* Page Attended duely, . . . IV. xi. 29. 1
On her two *pretty* handmaides did attend, . . . IV. xi. 47. 1
Their *prety* stealthes shal worke, . . . *Epith.* 361
Prevail. when she saw her prayers nought *prevaile,* . . . I. iii. 24. 1
Her prayers nought *prevaile,* . . . I. iii. 43. 9
when he saw no power might *prevaile,* . . . I. xi. 42. 1
thought to *prevaile* To bringe her backe againe, . . . III. vii. 21. 8
when all this he nothing saw *prevaile,* . . . III. viii. 40. 6
when as all might nought with them *prevaile,* . . . IV. iii. 48. 1
her plaints might not *prevaile,* . . . IV. ix. 7. 8
Might otherwise *prevaile,* or make him cease for ought. . . . V. ii. 22. 9
'Say and do all that may thereto *prevaile;* . . . V. v. 49. 1
Prevailed. in field against them thrice *prevailed;* . . . *Ti.* 111
Her words *prevaild:* . . . I. v. 44. 1
him gainstriving nought at all *prevaild;* . . . II. iv. 14. 2
Ne to recomfort her at all *prevayld;* . . . III. viii. 34. 6
(so much his force *prevayled*) . . . IV. vi. 12. 8
Prevent. Whom, thus at point prepared, to *prevent,* . . . *Gn.* 281
How to *prevent* this mischiefe ere it fall, . . . *Hub.* 190
For feare of afterclaps, for to *prevent:* . . . *Hub.* 332
he by meanes might cast them to *prevent,* . . . *Hub.* 881
Th' ill to *prevent,* that life ensewen may; . . . I. ix. 44. 3
Which to *prevent* the Prince his mortall speare . . . II. xi. 25. 1
With a strong gard, all reskew to *prevent,* . . . III. i. 2. 3
th' evill thinkes by watching to *prevent:* . . . III. x. 3. 6
How to *prevent* the perill that mote rise, . . . IV. ii. 37. 8
Cambels fate that fortune did *prevent;* . . . IV. iii. 18. 5
did not them *prevent* with vigilant foresight. . . . IV. x. 20. 9
Prevented. *Prevented* him before his stroke could light, . . . VI. i. 38. 7
him thankt that had her death *prevented.* . . . VI. x. 36. 9
Preventing. Like shaft out of a bow *preventing* speed: . . . IV. i. 41. 3
The noble childe, *preventing* his desire, . . . VI. viii. 15. 7
He him *preventing* layes on earth along, . . . VI. viii. 49. 3
Previe. *See* **Privy.**
Prey. The *pray* of time, which all things doth devowre! . . . *Ro.* iii. 8
cram'd with guiltles blood and greedie *pray* . . . *Van.* iii. 4
With *pray* of beasts and spoyle of living blood, . . . *Van.* x. 3
This Wolvish sheepe woulde catchen his *pray,* . . . *S.C.* S. 197
all the purchase of the Phrigian *pray,* . . . *Gn.* 591
there to hunt after the hoped *pray,* . . . *Hub.* 503
looking for plenteous *praie* Of fish, . . . *Ti.* 151
To be the *pray* of Tyme, and Fortunes spoyle! . . . *Ti.* 516
bring to her so precious a *pray.* . . . *Mui.* 112
on their pleasures greedily doth *pray.* . . . *Mui.* 204
Lyes in ambushment of his hoped *pray,* . . . *Mui.* 404
he seized greedelie On the resistles *pray;* . . . *Mui.* 436
borne to heaven, for heaven a fitter *pray;* . . . *D.* 164
Be ye the *pray* of Wolves; . . . *D.* 349
Where store he heard to be of salvage *pray.* . . . *As.* 94
he lept As Lyon fierce upon the flying *pray,* . . . I. i. 17. 2
to the *pray* when as he drew more ny, . . . I. iii. 5. 7
Her selfe a yielded *pray* to save or spill: . . . I. iii. 43. 4
him rencountring fierce, reskewd the noble *pray.* . . . I. iv. 39. 9
a Gryfon, seized of his *pray,* . . . I. v. 8. 2
now the *pray* of fowles in field he lyes, . . . I. v. 23. 3
From Lyons clawes to pluck the gryped *pray.* . . . I. vi. 7. 4
The innocent *pray* in hast he does forsake; . . . I. vi. 10. 7
She fownd not in that perilous hous . . . Her hoped *pray,* . . . I. vii. 2. 4
Fast flying from that Paynims greedy *pray,* . . . I. vii. 20. 3
The pitteous *pray* of his fiers cruelty have bin. . . . I. vii. 45. 9
The knight, then lightly leaping to the *pray,* . . . I. viii. 24. 1
So brought unto his Lord as his deserved *pray.* . . . I. viii. 25. 9
Unaes foe, that all her realme did *pray.* . . . I. ix. 20. 3
as an Eagle, seeing *pray* appeare, . . . I. xi. 9. 5
It booted nought to thinke to robbe him of his *pray.* . . . I. xi. 41. 9
Inflamed was to follow beauties *pray,* . . . II. ii. 7. 7
Whom they in equall *pray* hope to divide, . . . II. ii. 22. 8
threatning to make the *pray* Of the rough rockes, . . . II. ii. 24. 2
Thy carcas for their *pray,* . . . II. vi. 28. 9
that hardy guest . . . Should be his *pray.* . . . II. vii. 27. 5
griev'd so long to lacke his greedie *pray;* . . . II. vii. 34. 2
So goodly did beguile the Guyler of his *pray.* . . . II. vii. 64. 9
murdrous spoiles and bloody *pray,* . . . II. viii. 6. 4
Were to those Pagans made an open *pray,* . . . II. x. 62. 4
deepe engorgeth all this worldes *pray;* . . . II. xii. 3. 5
Dare not adventure on the stubborne *pray,* . . . III. i. 22. 3
yield the *pray* of love to lothsome death at last. . . . III. ii. 17. 9
t' increase thy lover's *pray.* . . . III. iii. 28. 4
had gotten a great *pray* Of Saxon goods; . . . III. iii. 58. 5
more happy were to win so goodly *pray.* . . . III. iv. 46. 9
The Monster, ready on the *pray* to sease, . . . III. vii. 28. 1

Prey—*Continued.*
Him forst to leave his *pray,* . . . III. vii. 32. 4
trembled like a lambe fled from the *pray;* . . . III. vii. 36. 6
trembling stood, and yielded him the *pray;* . . . III. viii. 13. 2
hayle The greedy villein from his hoped *pray,* . . . III. viii. 31. 6
as relique of the *pray.'* . . . III. viii. 49. 9
Waiting advauntage on the *pray* to sease, . . . III. x. 30. 6
all that golden *pray,* . . . I loath . . . III. x. 31. 4
*Fame is my meed, and glory vertues *pray.* . . . III. x. 31. 7
those two sought nought but the present *pray,* . . . III. x. 34. 4
To blot her with dishonor of so faire a *pray.* . . . IV. i. 4. 9
'Lo! sluggish Knight, the victors happie *pray!* . . . IV. ii. 7. 5
that every spoyle or *pray* Should equally be shard . . . IV. ii. 13. 4
a Vulture greedie of his *pray,* . . . IV. iii. 19. 1
To rescue Satyrane out of his *pray,* . . . IV. iv. 31. 7
Ne care he had, ne pittie of the *pray,* . . . IV. vii. 8. 4
trussing me, as Eagle doth his *pray,* . . . IV. vii. 18. 6
Defends him selfe, and saves his gotten *pray:* . . . IV. vii. 25. 7
So tempting her still to pursue the *pray,* . . . IV. viii. 11. 4
Forgoe the purchase of my gotten *pray,* . . . IV. viii. 62. 4
Does make her selfe misfortunes piteous *pray.* . . . V. ii. 50. 5
The other stayd behind to gard the *pray:* . . . V. iii. 11. 7
Yet my good lucke he shall not likewise *pray,* . . . V. iv. 14. 8
from her griping pounce the greedy *prey* doth rive. . . . V. iv. 42. 9
like a greedie Beare unto her *pray,* . . . V. v. 9. 7
of his innocence to make her *pray.* . . . V. v. 52. 4
at spoyling of some hungry *pray,* . . . V. vii. 30. 2
like hound full greedy of his *pray,* . . . V. viii. 7. 1
brought that Damzell as his purchast *pray;* . . . V. viii. 26. 8
Till he himselfe was made their greedie *pray,* . . . V. viii. 31. 3
I . . . all her *pray* and all her diet know. . . . VI. ii. 32. 4
Forst to forgoe his *pray* . . . VI. iii. 25. 7
Like to a Tygre that hath mist his *pray,* . . . VI. iv. 6. 2
the beast enrag'd to loose his *pray* Upon him turned, . . . VI. iv. 20. 5
The litle babe, sweet relickes of his *pray;* . . . VI. iv. 23. 2
plucke the *pray* oftimes out of their greedy hould. . . . VI. v. 15. 9
of the *pray* each one a part doth beare. . . . VI. viii. 41. 5
Amongst the rest, the which they then did *pray,* . . . VI. x. 40. 1
reskue from their *pray,* . . . VI. x. 41. 4
Hither those Brigants brought their present *pray,* . . . VI. x. 43. 1
Of all the other *pray* which they had got, . . . VI. xi. 4. 4
The greatest portion of the greedie *pray,* . . . VI. xi. 17. 4
Disperseth them to catch his choysest *pray,* . . . VI. xi. 49. 2
She bath'd her lovely limbes, for Jove a likely *pray.* . . . VII. vi. 45. 9
makes himself his owne consuming *pray:* . . . VII. vii. 24. 5
For who sees not that Time on all doth *pray?* . . . VII. vii. 47. 5
That ye were blooded in a yeelded *pray.* . . . *Am.* xx. 14
feeds at pleasure on the wretched *pray:* . . . *Am.* xlvii. 8
To let them gaze, whylest he on them may *pray:* . . . *Am.* liii. 4
panting hounds beguiled of their *pray:* . . . *Am.* lxvii. 4
came the tyde, and made my paynes his *pray.* . . . *Am.* lxxv. 4
On the sweet spoyle of beautie they did *pray;* . . . *Am.* lxxvi. 8
Preyed. His loves deare spoile, in which his heart was *prayde,* VI. x. 35. 8
Devouring tyme and changeful chance have *prayd,* . . . *Am.* lviii. 7
Preys. Of fowles and beastes he made the piteous *prayes,* . . . II. v. 26. 7
With warlike spoiles and with victorious *prayes* . . . III. xi. 52. 2
Priam. The day that first of *Priame* she was seene, . . . II. iii. 31. 7
Priamond. the first hight *Priamond,* . . . IV. ii. 41. 8
Stout *Priamond,* but not so strong to strike; . . . IV. ii. 42. 1
Priamond on foote had more delight; . . . IV. ii. 42. 5
speare and curtaxe both usd *Priamond* in field. . . . IV. ii. 42. 9
Sir *Priamond,* with equall worth And equall armes, . . . IV. iii. 6. 3
Right practicke was Sir *Priamond* in fight, . . . IV. iii. 7. 1
Yet one, of many, was so strongly bent By *Priamond,* . . . IV. iii. 8. 2
Priam's. By whose advice old *Priams* cittie fell, . . . II. ix. 48. 6
after Greekes did *Priams* realme destroy, . . . III. ix. 36. 7
Trojan warres and *Priams* citie sackt, . . . III. ix. 38. 2
finally destroy Proud *Priams* towne. . . . IV. xi. 19. 7
Price. All that which Asie ever had of *prise,* . . . *Ro.* xxix. 11
Then paye you the *price* of your surquedrie, . . . *S.C.* F. 49
Least thou the *price* of my displeasure prove.' . . . *S.C.* F. 138
her sonne had sette to deere a *prise* . . . *S.C.* May 299
the prayse is better then the *price,* . . . *S.C.* O. 19
The metall was of rare and passing *price;* . . . *Mui.* 76
and held in passing *price,* . . . *As.* Interl. 220
Poets wits are had in peerlesse *price:* . . . *Col.* 321
the Paragone Of peerlesse *price,* . . . *Col.* 549
With *price* whereof they buy a golden bell, . . . *Col.* 725
some shall pay the *price* of others guilt; . . . I. v. 26. 2
Shall with his owne blood *price* that he hath spilt. . . . I. v. 26. 4
With thine owne blood to *price* his blood, . . . I. ix. 37. 9
owches . . . Whose passing *price* uneath was to be told: . . . I. x. 31. 7
captives to redeeme with *price* of bras . . . I. x. 40. 3
Ne would for *price* or prayers once affoord . . . II. vi. 19. 8
With *price* of silver shall his kingdome buy; . . . III. iii. 39. 6
Ne worldly *price,* cannot redeeme my deare . . . III. xi. 16. 4
Much more of *price* and of more gratious powre, . . . IV. iii. 45. 1
He ment to make them know their follies *prise,* . . . IV. ix. 35. 2
Though vertue then were held in highest *price,* . . . V. i. 1. 1
They have the *price* of their owne folly payd.' . . . V. viii. 23. 6
Adorned all with gemmes of endlesse *price,* . . . V. ix. 27. 6
The more t' augment her *price* through praise of comlinesse. . . . VI. xi. 11. 9
But mine, no *price* nor prayer may surcease. . . . *Am.* xi. 14
Twoo golden apples of unvalewd *price;* . . . *Am.* lxxvii. 6
And pay the *price,* all were his debt extreeme. . . . *H.H.L.* 133
Which also were with selfe-same *price* redeemed That we, . . . *H.H.L.* 202
Priced. Ne ought would buy, how ever *prisd* with measure, . . . VI. xi. 14. 4
Prices. *prises* to them placed at their pleasure, . . . VI. xi. 14. 2
To make the *prises* of the rest more deare. . . . VI. xi. 15. 5
Prick. they that shooten neerest the *pricke* . . . *S.C.* S. 122

Prick—*Continued.*
pricke them forth with pleasaunce of thy vaine, . . . *S.C.* O. 23
Did *prick* him foorth with proud desire of praise . . . *As.* 86
sharp Remorse his hart did *prick* and nip, . . . I. x. 27. 3
seeing him from far so fierce to *pricke,* . . . II. i. 26. 1
Gay steed with spurs did *pricke,* . . . II. i. 49. 9
To *pricke* of highest prayse forth to advaunce, . . . II. xii. 1. 3
Then gan he freshly *pricke* his fomy steed, . . . III. iv. 48. 2
Ne did he spare sometime to *pricke* himselfe, . . . III. xi. 45. 3
like thornes did *pricke* his gealous hart, . . . IV. v. 31. 3
Gan towards them to *pricke* with eger speede, . . . IV. vi. 2. 8
Ne feeles the thornes and thickets *pricke* her tender toes. . . IV. vii. 21. 9
Her spightfull words did *pricke* and wound the inner part. . . IV. viii. 26. 9
Pricked. yond Bullocke beares . . . his *pricked* eares? . . . *S.C.* F. 72
being *prickt* do vanish into noughts. . . . *Col.* 718
his light-foot steede, *Pricked* with wrath . . . I. ii. 8. 4
prickte with pride And hope to winne his Ladies hearte . . . I. ii. 14. 6
the hungry rage, which late Him *prickt,* . . . I. iii. 7. 5
prickt forth with jollitee Of looser life . . . I. ix. 12. 5
prickt with anguish of his sinnes so sore, . . . I. x. 21. 7
prickt with courage, and thy forces pryde, . . . I. x. 66. 7
prickt with courage kene, did cruell battell breath. . . . II. i. 27. 9
He *pricked* forth his puissant force to prove. . . . II. i. 50. 7
prickt so fiers, that underneath his feete . . . II. v. 3. 3
prickt with guiltie shame And inward griefe, . . . II. viii. 44. 2
prickt with proud disdaine . . . II. x. 33. 3
His Beast he felly *prickt* on either syde, . . . II. xi. 24. 3
the Prince, *prickt* with reprochful shame, . . . II. xi. 31. 6
They spide a knight that towards *pricked* fayre; . . . III. i. 4. 2
prickt forth with loves extremity . . . III. x. 22. 4
pricked fiercely forward where she did him vew. . . . III. xi. 4. 9
So forth he fiercely *prickt* that one him scarce could see. . . IV. i. 35. 9
it *prickt* his wanton mind With sting of lust . . . IV. ii. 5. 4
Fiercely forth *prickt* his steed . . . IV. ii. 6. 7
By sundry meanes thereto she *prickt* him forth; . . . IV. ii. 12. 1
two Tygers *prickt* with hungers rage . . . IV. iii. 16. 1
He *pricked* forth in ayd of Satyran; . . . IV. iv. 19. 2
Privily *pricked* with thy lustfull powres, . . . IV. x. 45. 7
yet he *pricked* over yonder plaine, . . . V. i. 19. 5
Knight, That . . . *prickt* with all his might: . . . V. viii. 5. 3
prickt him so that he away it threw: . . . V. ix. 18. 6
Eftsoones forth *pricked* proudly in his might, . . . V. x. 31. 8
Eftsoones they *pricked* forth with forward pryde, . . . VI. vii. 6. 5
When pride of youth forth *pricked* my desire, . . . VI. ix. 24. 2
Full many thou hast *pricked* to the hart, . . . *Epig.* iv. 37
Pricket. joyed oft to chace the trembling *Pricket,* . . . *S.C.* D. 27
Pricketh. So proudly *pricketh* on his courser strong, . . . II. v. 38. 8
Sweet is the Eglantine, but *pricketh* nere; . . . *Am.* xxvi. 3
Pricking. in his throat him *pricking* softly under, . . . *Van.* v. 9
A gentle Knight was *pricking* on the plaine, . . . I. i. 1. 1
One *pricking* towards them with hastie heat, . . . I. iii. 33. 2
on the plaine fast *pricking* Guyon spide One . . . II. v. 2. 2
*His *pricking* armes, entrayld with roses red, . . . II. v. 29. 5
pricking him with his sharp-pointed dart, . . . II. v. 36. 1
They spyde a knight fayre *pricking* on the playne, . . . III. viii. 44. 7
Paridell came *pricking* fast Upon the plaine; . . . III. x. 35. 2
a Knight He spide come *pricking* on . . . VI. i. 32. 9
Prickles. chaw the tender *prickles* in her Cud; . . . *Gn.* 86
Prickling. His *prickling* armes, entrayld with roses red, . . . II. v. 29. 5
Pricks. cruddles the blood and *pricks* the harte: . . . *S.C.* F. 46
Atin ay him *pricks* with spurs of shame . . . II. v. 38. 9
Pride. name of blasphemie Filde hir with *pride.* . . . *Rev.* ii. 4
Puft up with *pride* of Romane hardiehead, . . . *Ro.* xi. 3
have thy *pride* so much abaced, . . . *Ro.* xiii. 12
the ruin'd *pride* Of these old Romane works, . . . *Ro.* xv. 12
swolne with plenties *pride,* . . . *Ro.* xxiii. 13
The antique *pride* which menaced the skie, . . . *Ro.* xxvii. 2
Where all this worlds *pride* once was situate. . . . *Ro.* xxxi. 2
Thought all things lesse than his disdainful *pride.* . . . *Van.* iii. 6
Both borrowed *pride,* and native beautie stained. . . . *Van.* viii. 12
his strength his *pride,* . . . *Van.* x. 5
Puffed up with *pryde* and vaine pleasaunce; . . . *S.C.* F. 223
Now gan he repent his *pryde* to late; . . . *S.C.* F. 229
cannot wel ken, But it be by his *pryde,* . . . *S.C.* S. 43
the wight whose presence was our *pryde;* . . . *S.C.* N. 65
whilome was poore shepheards *pryde,* . . . *S.C.* N. 198
such *pryde* at length was ill repayde: . . . *S.C.* D. 49
bringeth forth the fruite of sommers *pryde;* . . . *S.C.* D. 74
in avengement of his *pride* . . . *Gn.* 389
he through *pride* and fatnes gan despise Their meanesse; . . . *Hub.* 586
A vaine ensample of the Persian *pride;* . . . *Hub.* 750
whose onely *pride* Is virtue to advaunce, . . . *Hub.* 811
sdeignfull *pride,* and wilfull arrogaunce: . . . *Hub.* 1135
Gluttonie, malice, *pride,* and covetize, . . . *Hub.* 1309
themselves to raise Through pompous *pride,* . . . *T.M.* 92
Like as the dearling of the Summers *pryde,* . . . *T.M.* 235
sway in Court with *pride* and rashnes rude; . . . *T.M.* 328
all in sumptuous *pride* They spend, . . . *T.M.* 469
Doth scorne the *pride* of wonted ornaments: . . . *T.M.* 544
that Citie, which the garland wore Of Britaines *pride,* . . . *Ti.* 37
made all nations vassals of her *pride,* . . . *Ti.* 72
The picture of thy *pride* in pompous shew: . . . *Ti.* 82
through *pride* or covetize, . . . *Ti.* 363
see the end of pompe and fleshlie *pride!* . . . *Ti.* 543
The Roses raigning in the *pride* of May, . . . *Mui.* 189
In the *pride* of his freedome principall: . . . *Mui.* 380
flowring *pride,* opprest With early frosts, . . . *D.* 27
Be it riches, beautie, or honors *pride,* . . . *D.* 500
Young Astrophel, the *pride* of shepheards praise, . . . *As.* 7
Amyntas, floure of shepheards *pride* forlorne: . . . *Col.* 439

Pride—*Continued.*
She is the *pride* and primrose of the rest, . . . *Col.* 560
they be puffed up with *pride,* . . . *Col.* 759
that most Heroicke spirit, The hevens *pride,* . . . *Ded. Son.* xv. 2
That the worlds *pride* seemes gathered there to bee. . . . *Ded.Son.*xvii.12
loftie trees, yclad with sommers *pryde,* . . . I. i. 7. 4
father Nilus gins to swell With timely *pride* . . . I. i. 21. 2
prickte with *pride* And hope to winne his Ladies hearte . . . I. ii. 14. 6
two rams, stird with ambitious *pride,* . . . I. ii. 16. 1
yielded *pryde* and proud submission, Still dreading death, . . . I. iii. 6. 6
He now, Lord of the field, his *pride* to fill, . . . I. iii. 43. 5
To sinfull hous of *Pryde* Duessa Guydes . . . I. iv. Arg.
Ne Persia selfe, the nourse of pompous *pride,* Like ever saw. . I. iv. 7. 6
with *pride* so did she swell; . . . I. iv. 11. 4
each others greater *pride* does spight. . . . I. iv. 14. 9
Drawne of fayre Pecocks, that excell in *pride,* . . . I. iv. 17. 8
Duessa . . . Returnd to stately pallace of Dame *Pryde:* . . . I. v. 45. 2
Through wastfull *Pride* and wanton Riotise, . . . I. v. 46. 5
layd Low under all, yet above all in *pride,* . . . I. v. 48. 6
Through wicked *pride* and wasted welthes decay. . . . I. v. 51. 4
al through that great Princesse *pride* did fall, . . . I. v. 53. 5
The dreadfull spectacle of that sad house of *Pryde.* . . . I. v. 53. 9
She fownd not in that perilous hous of *Pryde,* . . . I. vii. 2. 2
The house of *Pryde,* and perilles round about; . . . I. vii. 26. 6
through his own foolish *pride* Or weaknes, . . . I. viii. 1. 6
The plumes of *pride,* and winges of vanity, . . . I. x. 39. 3
prickt with courage, and thy forces *pryde,* . . . I. x. 66. 7
rusht upon him with outragious *pryde;* . . . I. xi. 53. 3
th' antique world excesse and *pryde* did hate: . . . I. xii. 14. 8
All lilly white, withoutten spot or *pride,* . . . I. xii. 22. 7
By which she triumphes over yre and *pride,* . . . II. ii. 31. 6
soone renews her native *pride:* . . . II. iii. 36. 6
well could menage and subdew his *pride,* . . . II. iv. 2. 2
Their blazing *pride* thou wouldest soone have blent, . . . II. iv. 26. 3
spent with *pride* and lavishnesse, . . . II. vii. 12. 4
later ages *pride,* like corn-fed steed, . . . II. vii. 16. 6
the matter of his huge desire And pompous *pride* . . . II. vii. 17. 7
with his *pride* all others powre deface: . . . II. vii. 41. 8
His glory did enhaunce, and pompous *pryde* display. . . . II. vii. 44. 9
all the ornaments of Floraes *pride,* . . . II. xii. 50. 5
soone comes age that will her *pride* deflowre; . . . II. xii. 75. 7
beastes, whose brutish *pryde* Mote breede him scath . . . III. i. 37. 7
upbrayd A dolefull heart with so disdainfull *pride:* . . . III. vi. 21. 8
that faire Maide, the flowre of wemens *pride;* . . . III. vii. 31. 5
a kindly *pride* Of gratious speach . . . III. ix. 32. 6
with humble *pride* and pleasing guile; . . . III. x. 9. 3
cruell Mulciber would not obay His threatfull *pride,* . . . III. xi. 26. 6
smiled at his *pryde.* . . . III. xi. 32. 9
At Artegall, in middest of his *pryde,* . . . IV. iv. 44. 2
That peerelesse paterne of Dame Natures *pride* . . . IV. vi. 24. 5
Withouten perill of the stronger *pride:* . . . IV. viii. 31. 5
she it all did mar with cruelty and *pride.* . . . IV. ix. 14. 9
whose goodly *pride* And costly frame . . . IV. x. 16. 2
Myld Titus and Gesippus without *pryde;* . . . IV. x. 27. 5
Some of their *pride,* some paragons disdayning, . . . IV. x. 43. 4
Nathlesse his *pride* full dearely he did pryse; . . . IV. xi. 5. 5
Old Cybele, arayd with pompous *pride,* . . . IV. xi. 28. 4
if he should through *pride* your doome undo, . . . IV. xii. 10. 4
he, whose spirit was with *pride* upblowne, . . . V. i. 17. 5
with sterne countenance and indignant *pride* . . . V. i. 23. 5
Until that Talus had his *pride* represt, . . . V. i. 29. 5
she them all despiseth for great *pride.'* . . . V. ii. 10. 4
The *pride* of Ladies, and the worth of knights, . . . V. iii. 3. 4
saw that boasters *pride* and gracelesse guile, . . . V. iii. 20. 3
all men wonder at her colours *pride;* . . . V. iii. 25. 4
for to maister wrong and puissant *pride:* . . . V. iv. 1. 5
A Princesse of great powre and greater *pride,* . . . V. iv. 33. 4
Unknowen perill of bold womens *pride.* . . . V. iv. 38. 6
in his kingly *pride* Soring through his wide Empire . . . V. iv. 42. 1
Through vengeful wrath and sdeignfull *pride* half mad; . . . V. iv. 43. 3
With an embrodered belt of mickell *pride;* . . . V. v. 3. 5
So great her *pride* that she such basenesse much abhord. . . V. v. 27. 9
That may pull downe the courage of his *pride;* . . . V. v. 50. 6
To fierce avengement of that womans *pride,* . . . V. vi. 18. 7
swolne with *pride* of his owne peerelesse powre, . . . V. vii. 15. 7
Tho turning all his *pride* to humblesse meeke, . . . V. vii. 16. 1
I see thy *pride* is nought.' . . . V. vii. 40. 9
that discourteous Dame with scornfull *pryde* . . . VI. i. 30. 4
the reproch of *pride* and cruelnesse. . . . VI. i. 41. 4
But he me first through *pride* . . . Assayld, . . . VI. ii. 8. 4
had wounded sore . . . in his despiteous *pryde:* . . . VI. ii. 40. 6
as if his greater *pryde* Did scorne the challenge . . . VI. iii. 36. 3
with such scornefull *pryde* Had him abusde . . . VI. iii. 47. 5
shun The perill of his *pride,* . . . VI. iii. 48. 9
stout Despetto in his greater *pryde* Did front him, . . . VI. v. 20. 7
Eftsoones they pricked forth with forward *pryde,* . . . VI. vii. 6. 5
Did worthily revenge this maydens *pride;* . . . VI. vii. 32. 2
for stubborne *pride* which her restrayned. . . . VI. vii. 36. 4
Through her dispiteous *pride,* . . . VI. vii. 38. 7
his enemies He scorned in his overweening *pryde;* . . . VI. vii. 42. 4
prove the puissaunce of his *pride.* . . . VI. vii. 46. 9
That *pride* doe not to tyranny you lift; . . . VI. viii. 1. 7
As if such *pride* the other could apall; . . . VI. viii. 26. 7
oft through *pride* do their owne perill weave, . . . VI. ix. 22. 3
When *pride* of youth forth pricked my desire, . . . VI. ix. 24. 2
That makes both heaven and earth to tremble at her *pride.* . VII. vi. 3. 9
All were she fraught with *pride* and impudence, . . . VII. vi. 25. 2
Yet gathering spirit of her natures *pride,* . . . VII. vi. 26. 2
Deckt all with dainties of her seasons *pryde,* . . . VII. vii. 34. 2
the *pride* Of hasting Prime did make them burgein round. . VII. vii. 43. 7

Pride—*Continued.*
flowring *pride,* so fading and so fickle, ... VII. viii. 1. 8
In finding fault with her too portly *pride:* . . . . *Am.* v. 2
Such *pride* is praise; such portlinesse is honor; . . . . . . *Am.* v. 9
Without some spark of such self-pleasing *pride.* . . . . . . *Am.* v. 14
Doth still persist in her rebellious *pride:* . . . . *Am.* vi. 2
she doth comptroll All this worlds *pride,* . . . . *Am.* x. 11
The lovely pleasance; and the lofty *pride;* . . . . *Am.* xvii. 11
the Lyon . . . In his most *pride* disdeigneth . . . . *Am.* xx. 7
pride and meeknesse, mixt by equall part, ... *Am.* xxi. 3
mild pleasance, which doth *pride* displace, ... *Am.* xxi. 5
shew the last ensample of your *pride;* . . . . *Am.* xxv. 6
Whose *pryde* depraves each other better part, ... *Am.* xxxi. 3
The more she frieseth in her wilfull *pryde;* . . . . *Am.* xxxii. 10
in her *pride* she dooth persever still. . . . . *Am.* xxxviii. 9
Thrugh stubborn *pride,* amongst themselves did jar, ... *Am.* xliv. 2
Whome, . . . she kills with cruell *pryde,* . . . . *Am.* xlvii. 7
Her glories *pride* that none may it repayre. . . . . *Am.* lviii. 8
T' accuse of *pride,* or rashly blame for ought. . . . . . . *Am.* lxi. 4
pride dare not approch, ... *Am.* lxv. 9
cloud of *pryde,* which oft doth dark Her goodly light, ... *Am.* lxxxi. 7
doe still adorne her beauties *pride,* . . . . *Epith.* 104
no jot Of loves dislike or *pride* was to be found, ... *H.H.L.* 34
But *pride,* impatient of long resting peace, ... *H.H.L.* 78
Through *pride,* (for *pride* and love may ill agree) . . . . . *H.H.L.* 95
Till they decayd through *pride:* . . . . *Proth.* 136

Prides. So fell those two in spight of both their *prydes;* . . . IV. i. 42. 7

Priefe. *See* **Proof.**

Priest. chaunst with a formall *Priest* to meete, ... *Hub.* 361
Which when the *Priest* beheld, he vew'd it nere, ... *Hub.* 379
The *Priest* gan wexe halfe proud to be so praide, ... *Hub.* 413
He is the Shepheard, and the *Priest* is hee; . . . . *Hub.* 443
of the *Priest* eftsoones gan to enquire, ... *Hub.* 481
there (said the *Priest*) is arte indeed: . . . . *Hub.* 483
The *Priest* him wisht good speed, ... *Hub.* 550
craftie Reynold was a *Priest* ordained, ... *Hub.* 556
their next neighbor *Priest,* . . . . *Hub.* 572
now nor Prince nor *Priest* doth her maintayne, ... *T.M.* 565
of that God the *Priest* thou shouldest bee, ... *Col.* 832
needs his *priest* t' expresse his powre divine. . . . . *Col.* 838
The *Priest* him selfe a garland doth compose . . . . VI. viii. 39. 7
them the *Priest* rebuking did advize . . . . VI. viii. 43. 7
the *Priest* with naked armes full net Approching nigh, . . . VI. viii. 45. 4
Hearing the holy *priest* that to her speakes, ... *Epith.* 224

Priest's. often crost with the *priestes* crewe, ... *S.C.* F. 209
Through the *Priests* holesome counsell lately tought, ... *Hub.* 553

Priests. Princes and high *Priests* . . . . *T.M.* 560
spoild the *Priests* of their habiliments; . . . . I. iii. 17. 7
all the *Priests* were damzels in soft linnen dight. . . . . . IV. x. 38. 9
her *Priests* the same . . . labour'd to concele: . . . . IV. x. 41. 2
she received was in goodly wize Of many *Priests,* . . . . . V. vii. 4. 2
other beds the *Priests* there used none, ... V. vii. 9. 1
the *Priestes* she found full busily . . . . V. vii. 17. 7
on those *Priests* bestowed rich reward; . . . . V. vii. 24. 3
mongst the rout Of Bacchus *Priests,* . . . . V. viii. 47. 6
Lyke sacred *priests* that never thinke amisse! . . . . *Am.* xxii. 8

Priests'. linnen stole after those *Priestes* guize, ... V. vii. 13. 3

Prieve. *See* **Prove.**

Prime. Where will he live tyll the lusty *prime?* . . . . *S.C.* F. 16
With flowring blossomes to furnish the *prime,* . . . . *S.C.* F. 167
now passed youngthly *pryme,* . . . . *S.C.* D. 75
Sweet Marjoram, and Daysies decking *prime:* . . . . *Mui.* 192
brought him presents, flowers if it were *prime,* . . . . . . *As.* 47
'In *prime* of youthly yeares, when corage hott . . . . I. ii. 35. 1
Till on a day (that day is everie *Prime,* . . . . I. ii. 40. 4
girlonds gay, That seemd as fresh as Flora in her *prime;* . . I. iv. 17. 3
all as glad as birdes of joyous *Pryme,* . . . . I. vi. 13. 5
Early and late it rong, at evening and at *prime.* . . . . . . II. ix. 25. 9
gan this Realme renew her passed *prime:* . . . . II. x. 58. 8
Gather therefore the Rose whilest yet is *prime,* . . . . . . II. xii. 75. 6
her conception of the joyous *Prime;* . . . . III. vi. 3. 2
with fresh colours decke the wanton *Pryme,* . . . . III. vi. 42. 4
When as mans age was in his freshest *prime,* . . . . V. Pr. 1. 3
'In *prime* of youthly yeares, ... VI. viii. 20. 1
in my first *prime* of yeares, ... VI. ix. 24. 1
of their Winter spring another *Prime,* . . . . VII. vii. 18. 7
pride Of hasting *Prime* did make them burgein round. . . . VII. vii. 43. 8
Make hast, therefore, sweet love, whilest it is *prime;* . . . . *Am.* lxx. 13

Primitiae. have in gage The *Primitias* of your Parsonage: . . *Hub.* 518

Primrose. To be the *primrose* of all thy land; . . . . *S.C.* F. 166
She is the pride and *primrose* of the rest, ... *Col.* 560
The virgin Lillie, and the *Primrose* trew, ... *Proth.* 32
mine the *Primrose* in the lowly shade: . . . . *D.* 233

Primroses. Bay leaves betweene, And *primroses* greene, . . . *S.C.* Ap. 62

Prince. the Troyan *prince* spilt Turnus blood . . . . *Bel.*[2] ix. 8
Nor *prince,* nor peere, nor kin, they would abide. . . . . . *Ro.* xxiii. 14
with gentle mood Of Poets *Prince,* . . . . *Gn.* 18
to have accesse Unto the *Prince,* . . . . *Hub.* 1202
tell their *Prince* that learning is but vaine: . . . . *T.M.* 332
now nor *Prince* nor Priest doth her maintayne, ... *T.M.* 565
Most peereles *Prince,* most peereles Poetresse, ... *T.M.* 577
A mightie *Prince,* of most renowmed race, ... *Ti.* 184
His brother *Prince,* his brother noble Peere, ... *Ti.* 240
Which th' ashes seem'd of some great *Prince* to hold, ... *Ti.* 661
Tanaquill, Whom that most noble Briton *Prince* . . . . Sought . I. Pr. 2. 6
Great Gorgon, *prince* of darknes and dead night; . . . . . . I. i. 37. 8
Was never *Prince* so faithfull and so faire, ... I. ii. 23. 4
Was never *Prince* so meeke and debonaire; . . . . I. ii. 23. 5
The house of mightie *Prince* it seemd to be, ... I. iv. 2. 7
Prince Arthure meets with Una . . . . I. vii. Arg.

Prince—*Continued.*
all he wrought For this young *Prince,* . . . . I. vii. 36. 7
For whose deliverance she this *Prince* doth thither guyd. . . I. viii. 1. 9
Whom when the *Prince,* . . . did see, ... I. viii. 22. 1
the noble *Prince* had marked well, ... I. viii. 34. 3
this good *Prince* redeemd the Redcrosse knight from bands. . I. ix. 1. 9
'Faire virgin,' (said the *Prince,*) . . . . I. ix. 3. 1
Prince Arthure, crowne of Martiall band?' . . . . I. ix. 6. 5
sad remembraunce now the *Prince* amoves . . . . I. ix. 18. 3
Prince Arthur gave a boxe of Diamond sure, ... I. ix. 19. 1
Withhold, O soverayne *Prince!* your hasty hond . . . . . . I. xii. 28. 3
Sith her *Prince* Arthur of proud ornaments . . . spoyld. . . . II. i. 22. 6
the best and noblest knight alive *Prince* Arthur is, ... II. iii. 18. 4
never earthly *Prince* in such aray His glory did enhaunce, . . II. vii. 44. 8
Prince Arthur, flowre of grace and nobilesse, ... II. viii. 18. 4
'Indeed,' then said the *Prince,* . . . . II. viii. 29. 1
the *Prince* would not forsake his sell, ... II. viii. 31. 3
Now was the *Prince* in daungerous distresse, ... II. viii. 34. 1
in huge perplexity The *Prince* now stood, ... II. viii. 39. 6
So rag'd *Prince* Arthur twixt his foemen twaine, ... II. viii. 42. 8
on the haubergh stroke the *Prince* so sore, ... II. viii. 44. 6
Well knew The *Prince,* . . . . II. viii. 47. 7
So did *Prince* Arthur beare himselfe in fight, ... II. viii. 48. 8
him in strength and skill the *Prince* surpast, ... II. viii. 49. 8
Wroth was the *Prince,* and sory yet withall, ... II. viii. 52. 5
to the *Prince,* bowing with reverence dew . . . . II. viii. 55. 3
The Briton *Prince* recov'ring his stolne sword, ... II. ix. 2. 2
him the *Prince* with gentle court did bord: . . . . II. ix. 2. 5
grace of earthly *Prince* so soveraine, ... II. ix. 6. 2
'Certes,' (then said the *Prince*) 'I God avow, ... II. ix. 7. 1
The *Prince* by chaunce did on a Lady light, ... II. ix. 36. 6
the *Prince* in courteous maner sayd; . . . . II. ix. 37. 4
The *Prince* was inly moved at her speach, ... II. ix. 39. 1
From this renowmed *Prince* derived arre, ... II. x. 4. 2
The *Prince* him selfe halfe seemed to offend; . . . . II. x. 68. 7
Prince Arthure them repelles, ... II. xi. Arg.
To see a cruell fight doen by the *prince* this day. . . . . . . II. xi. 4. 9
the *Prince,* seeing her wofull plight, ... II. xi. 16. 4
Soone as the Carle from far the *Prince* espyde . . . . II. xi. 24. 1
the *Prince* his mortall speare Soone to him raught, ... II. xi. 25. 1
Proofe be thou, *Prince,* the prowest man alyve, ... II. xi. 30. 6
the *Prince,* prickt with reprochful shame, ... II. xi. 31. 6
the Briton *Prince* him rouzd Out of his holde, ... II. xi. 33. 1
Then thought the *Prince* all peril sure was past, ... II. xi. 43. 6
The famous Briton *Prince* and Faery knight, ... III. i. 1. 1
seek adventures as he with *Prince* Arthure went. . . . . . . III. i. 2. 9
besought The *Prince* of grace to let him ronne . . . . III. i. 5. 2
eke the *Prince* like treaty handeled, ... III. i. 11. 3
In which accord the *Prince* was also plaste, ... III. i. 12. 7
The *Prince* and Guyon . . . pursewd, ... III. i. 18. 6
It was a famous Present for a *Prince,* . . . . III. ii. 21. 6
Nor *Prince* nor pere it is, ... III. ii. 37. 8
the *Prince* and Faery gent, ... III. iv. 45. 4
fayrest fortune to the *Prince* befell, ... III. iv. 47. 6
Which when the *Prince* beheld, a lothfull sight, ... III. iv. 52. 4
Thus did the *Prince* that wearie night outweare . . . . . . III. iv. 61. 1
Prince Arthure heares of Florimell: . . . . III. v. Arg.
It lettes not scarse this *Prince* to breath at all, ... III. v. 2. 8
To whom the *Prince:* 'Dwarfe, comfort to thee take, ... III. v. 11. 6
from *Prince* Arthure fled with wings of idle feare. . . . . . III. vi. 54. 9
with the *Prince* of Darkenes fell somewhyle . . . . III. viii. 8. 3
The Queene of love, and *Prince* of peace . . . . IV. Pr. 4. 9
His owne deare Lord *Prince* Arthure came that way, ... IV. vii. 42. 2
when the *Prince* unto him spake, ... IV. vii. 44. 6
The *Prince* did wonder much, yet could not ghesse . . . . . IV. vii. 45. 2
his owne deare Lord The noble *Prince,* . . . . IV. viii. 18. 5
Whom when the *Prince* beheld, ... IV. viii. 20. 1
all the way the *Prince* on footpace traced, ... IV. viii. 34. 8
annoyd The *Prince* on foot, not wonted so to fare; . . . . . IV. viii. 37. 6
when he saw the *Prince* in armour bright, ... IV. viii. 40. 6
the *Prince* tooke downe those Ladies twaine . . . . IV. viii. 41. 1
Had not the noble *Prince* his readie stroke represt: . . . . . IV. viii. 41. 9
Whereat the *Prince* full wrath . . . . IV. viii. 43. 1
gan the *Prince* at leasure to inquire . . . . IV. viii. 46. 6
She deare besought the *Prince* of remedie; . . . . IV. viii. 64. 7
Prince Arthur stints their strife. . . . . IV. ix. Arg.
Prince Arthur graunted had To yeeld . . . . IV. ix. 4. 1
Whom straight the *Prince* ensuing in together far'd. . . . . IV. ix. 5. 9
The *Prince* halfe rapt began on her to dote; . . . . IV. ix. 6. 7
the *Prince,* when as he them avized, ... IV. ix. 11. 1
Upon all which the Briton *Prince* made seasure, ... IV. ix. 12. 5
the *Prince,* through his well wonted grace, ... IV. ix. 14. 1
when the *Prince* had perfectly compylde, ... IV. ix. 17. 1
Whom when the Briton *Prince* afarre beheld . . . . IV. ix. 32. 1
The *Prince* yet being fresh untoucht afore; . . . . IV. ix. 34. 2
To whom the *Prince* thus goodly well replied: . . . . IV. ix. 37. 1
Prince Arthure and Sir Artegall Free Samient . . . . V. viii. Arg.
the *Prince:* 'Certes me needeth more To crave the same; . . V. viii. 13. 7
Then Artegall gan of the *Prince* enquire, ... V. viii. 15. 1
(the *Prince* then sayd) . . . . V. viii. 15. 5
Soone after whom the *Prince* arrived there, ... V. viii. 27. 6
The Briton *Prince* him readie did awayte, ... V. viii. 29. 3
the brave *Prince* for honour and for right, . . . did fight: . . V. viii. 30. 6
the *Prince* in peeces to have torne . . . . V. viii. 31. 6
Oft drew the *Prince* unto his charret nigh, ... V. viii. 33. 1
Yet could the *Prince* not nigh unto him goe, ... V. viii. 37. 3
Yet still the *Prince* pursew'd him close behind. . . . . . . V. viii. 42. 1
the *Prince,* as victour of that day, ... V. viii. 51. 2
turne we to the noble *Prince,* . . . . V. ix. 2. 6
The whiles the *Prince* there kept the entrance still. . . . . V. ix. 15. 2

Prince—*Continued.*
The prayses of that *Prince* so manifold; . . . V. ix. 21. 2
The Briton *Prince* was sore empassionate, . . . V. ix. 46. 2
All which when as the *Prince* had heard . . . V. ix. 49. 1
Prince Arthur takes the enterprize . . . V. x. Arg.
The noble *Prince* and righteous Artegall, . . . V. x. 4. 2
The noble Briton *Prince* with his brave Peare; . . . V. x. 15. 2
till that the *Prince* arrived Within the land . . . V. x. 18. 1
There did the *Prince* him leave in deadly swound, . . . V. x. 33. 7
So all attonce they on the *Prince* did thonder, . . . V. x. 35. 1
after them the *Prince* as swiftly sped, . . . V. x. 36. 3
the *Prince* hard preased in betweene, . . . V. x. 37. 6
Long sought the *Prince;* . . . V. x. 38. 5
Prince Arthure overcomes the great Gerioneo . . . V. xi. Arg.
The *Prince* staid not his aunswere to devize, . . . V. xi. 4. 1
the bold *Prince* was forced foote to give . . . V. xi. 5. 6
Which uncouth use when as the *Prince* perceived, . . . V. xi. 7. 1
Which when the *Prince* heard tell, . . . V. xi. 21. 1
The armed *Prince* with shield so blazing bright . . . V. xi. 26. 2
Appointed by that mightie Faerie *Prince,* . . . V. xii. 3. 3
Till she *Prince* Arthure fynd; . . . VI. v. Arg.
Prince Arthur and young Timias, . . . VI. v. 11. 8
Then gan the *Prince* of her for to demand . . . VI. v. 27. 6
the *Prince* sought to appease The bitter anguish . . . VI. v. 32. 4
Wherewith the *Prince* sore moved there avoud . . . VI. v. 34. 1
the *Prince* . . . Was forced there to leave them . . . VI. v. 41. 1
What fortune to the Briton *Prince* did lite, . . . VI. vi. 17. 5
The *Prince* . . . Pursu'd him streight; . . . VI. vi. 18. 1
the *Prince,* him fayning to embase, . . . VI. vi. 20. 5
the bold *Prince* defended him so well, . . . VI. vi. 23. 6
Whereof whenas the *Prince* was well aware, . . . VI. vi. 27. 1
So likewise turnde the *Prince* upon the Knight, . . . VI. vi. 27. 8
when the *Prince* had once him plainely eyde, . . . VI. vi. 28. 5
Ne would the *Prince* him ever foot forsake . . . VI. vi. 29. 4
There did the *Prince* him overtake anone, . . . VI. vi. 30. 4
even the *Prince* his basenesse did despize; . . . VI. vi. 32. 4
Whom when the *Prince* so deadly saw dismayd, . . . VI. vi. 33. 1
Whom when the *Prince* so felly saw to rage, . . . VI. vi. 39. 1
were not that the *Prince* did him appeaze, . . . VI. vi. 40. 7
The *Prince* himselfe there all that night did rest; . . . VI. vi. 41. 2
soone she pacifyde The wrathfull *Prince,* . . . VI. vi. 43. 6
the whyles the *Prince* did rest In carelesse couch, . . . VI. vi. 44. 1
The morrow next the *Prince* did early rize, . . . VI. vi. 44. 8
He of the *Prince* his life received late, . . . VI. vii. 2. 4
The gentle *Prince* not farre away they spyde, . . . VI. vii. 6. 7
the stout *Prince,* with much more steddy stowre, . . . VI. vii. 8. 5
Not so the *Prince;* for his well-learned speare . . . VI. vii. 11. 1
The *Prince* soone hearkned, and his life forgave. . . . VI. vii. 12. 5
The *Prince* much mused at such villenie, . . . VI. vii. 13. 1
Whereas the *Prince* himselfe lay all alone, . . . VI. vii. 18. 7
Whereat the *Prince* awaking, . . . VI. vii. 25. 1
Prince Arthure overcomes Disdaine; . . . VI. viii. Arg.
They met *Prince* Arthure with Sir Enias, . . . VI. viii. 4. 3
to the *Prince* thus sayd: . . . VI. viii. 6. 1
The *Prince* assented; . . . VI. viii. 7. 1
Which when the *Prince* beheld, there standing by, . . . VI. viii. 12. 6
But yet the *Prince* so well enured was . . . VI. viii. 14. 1
Eftsoones the *Prince* to him full nimbly stept, . . . VI. viii. 17. 1
'Certes,' (sayd then the *Prince*) 'the God is just, . . . VI. viii. 23. 1
cry Procur'd the *Prince* his cruell hand to stay, . . . VI. viii. 29. 2
Then thus the *Prince* gan say: . . . VI. viii. 29. 5
in wedlocke to have bound Unto the *Prince* of Picteland, . . . VI. xii. 4. 6
entertayne The greatest *Prince* with pompous roialty: . . . *Am.* lxxvii. 4
Princedom. Deposed was from *princedome* soverayne, . . . II. x. 44. 5
Princely. may shee florish long In *princely* plight! . . . *S.C.* Ap. 49
Her heavenly haveour, her *princely* grace, . . . *S.C.* Ap. 66
Thenceforth proceeding with his *princely* trayne, . . . *Hub.* 1086
them that had purloyn'd his *Princely* honours. . . . *Hub.* 1342
Strong walls, rich porches, *princelie* pallaces, . . . *Ti.* 93
'The Lyon, . . . 'his *princely* puissance doth abate, . . . I. iii. 7. 2
So proud she shyned in her *princely* state, . . . I. iv. 10. 1
All hurtlen forth; and she, with *princely* pace, . . . I. iv. 16. 3
They backe retourned to the *princely* Place; . . . I. iv. 38. 3
With royall pomp and *princely* majestie . . . I. v. 5. 2
old Ninus far did pas In *princely* pomp, . . . I. v. 48. 4
princely gifts of yvory and gold, . . . I. xii. 12. 6
with stately grace and *princely* port . . . II. iii. 28. 5
full of *princely* bounty and great mind, . . . II. viii. 51. 1
her prowd portaunce and her *princely* gest, . . . III. ii. 27. 3
Banisht from *princely* bowre to wastefull wood! . . . III. iii. 42. 6
So goodly grave, and full of *princely* aw, . . . IV. vi. 33. 5
There Justice first her *princely* rule begonne. . . . V. i. 2. 5
a Queene, and come of *Princely* kynd, . . . V. v. 41. 5
of *princely* grace to be inclyn'd thereto. . . . V. v. 41. 9
after all her *princely* entertayne, . . . V. ix. 37. 1
she, whose *Princely* brest was touched nere . . . V. x. 50. 1
The goodly praise of *Princely* curtesie, . . . VI. Pr. 6. 3
Prince's. in *Princes* pallace thou doe sitt, . . . *S.C.* O. 80
yet is *Princes* pallace the most fitt,) . . . *S.C.* O. 81
in his *Princes* service spends his dayes, . . . *Hub.* 773
the *Princes* pallaces fell fast To ruine . . . *Hub.* 1175
That might for anie *Princes* couche be red, . . . *Ti.* 633
can empierce a *Princes* mightie hart. . . . *Col.* 431
As ever else in *Princes* Court thou vewest. . . . *Col.* 738
In living *Princes* court none ever knew . . . I. iv. 7. 4
That greatest *Princes* presence might behold. . . . I. viii. 35. 4
purveyaunce meet Of all, that royall *Princes* court became; I. xii. 13. 6
The large discourse of roiall *Princes* state. . . . I. xii. 14. 6
when that *Princes* wrath was pacifide, . . . I. xii. 36. 6
Whom *Princes* late displeasure left in bands, . . . II. i. 1. 2

Prince's—*Continued.*
'In *Princes* court'—The rest she would have sayd, . . . II. iii. 42. 1
There chaunced to the *Princes* hand to rize . . . II. ix. 59. 5
Mote *Princes* place be seeme so deckt to bee. . . . III. i. 33. 4
Ne tastest *Princes* pleasures, . . . III. ii. 31. 6
Timias, the *Princes* gentle Squyre, . . . III. iv. 47. 1
greatest *Princes* court would welcome fayne; . . . IV. viii. 27. 2
In *Princes* Court doe hap to sprout againe, . . . IV. viii. 33. 4
Sprung of the auncient stocke of *Princes* straine, . . . IV. viii. 33. 7
recoure His Leman from the Stygian *Princes* boure: . . . IV. x. 58. 5
Into the *Princes* shield where it empight, . . . V. x. 32. 7
Not so the *Princes,* but with restlesse force . . . V. x. 33. 1
well beseemeth that in *Princes* hall . . . VI. i. 1. 3
To be a *Princes* Paragone esteemed, . . . VI. ix. 11. 5
in the *Princes* gardin daily wrought: . . . VI. ix. 24. 8
Then had ye sorted with a *princes* pere: . . . *Am.* lxvi. 10
my long fruitlesse stay in *Princes* Court, . . . *Proth.* 7
Princes. To learne the enterdeale of *Princes* strange, . . . *Hub.* 785
Princes and high Priests . . . *T.M.* 560
Provide therefore (ye *Princes*) whilst ye live, . . . *Ti.* 365
'In vaine doo earthly *Princes,* . . . *Ti.* 407
titles vaine, Which mortall *Princes* wore . . . II. vii. 43. 9
all earthly *Princes* she doth far surmount. . . . II. x. 1. 9
Gathered the *Princes* of the people loose . . . II. x. 37. 6
Even seven hundred *Princes,* . . . II. x. 74. 3
greatest *Princes* liking it mote well delight. . . . III. v. 40. 9
Of Alexander, and his *Princes* five . . . IV. i. 22. 8
That powre he also doth to *Princes* lend, . . . V. Pr. 10. 6
of weake *Princes* to be Patronesse, . . . V. i. 4. 7
many *Princes* she in wealth exceedes, . . . V. ii. 9. 6
Upon the thrones of mortall *Princes* tend, . . . V. ix. 32. 2
trayterous desynes Gainst loiall *Princes,* . . . V. ix. 42. 3
herein doest all earthly *Princes* pas? . . . V. x. 3. 2
The spoiles of *Princes* hang'd which were in battel won. . . . VI. viii. 42. 9
Whom greatest *Princes* sought on lowest knee. . . . *H.H.L.* 231
All mortall *Princes* and imperiall States; . . . *H.H.B.* 88
Princes'. Fell from high *Princes* courtes, or Ladies bowres, I. v. 51. 6
The skill whereof to *Princes* hearts he doth reveale, . . . V. vii. 1. 9
in *Princes* courts to worke great scath and hindrance: . . . V. ix. 22. 9
Are wont for *Princes* states to fashion; . . . VII. vii. 8. 4
Princes bowres adorne with painted imagery. . . . VII. vii. 10. 9
Princess. Such for a *Princesse* bene principall. . . . *S.C.* Ap. 126
So I of this small Northerne world was *Princesse.* . . . *Ti.* 84
song, Which he hath of that mightie *Princesse* made? . . . *Col.* 405
other grace vouchsafed them to showe Of *Princesse* worthy; I. iv. 14. 4
Thought . . . that great *Princesse* too exceeding prowd, . . . I. iv. 15. 8
thou, O fayrest *Princesse* under sky! . . . II. Pr. 4. 6
to that mighty *Princesse* did complaine . . . II. ii. 43. 2
made thee soldier of that *Princesse* bright, . . . II. ix. 5. 3
A *Princesse* of great powre and greater pride, . . . V. iv. 33. 4
During which space she there as *Princess* rained, . . . V. vii. 42. 3
A *Princesse* of great powre and majestie, . . . V. viii. 16. 8
as any *Princesse* under sky, . . . V. viii. 18. 7
As their true Liege and *Princesse* naturall; . . . V. xii. 24. 8
Princess'. To have thy *Princes* grace, yet want her Peeres; *Hub.* 901
al through that great *Princesse* pride did fall, . . . I. v. 53. 5
Principal. Such for a Princesse bene *principall.* . . . *S.C.* Ap. 126
In the pride of his freedome *principall:* . . . *Mui.* 380
both him honor'd as their *principall,* . . . IV. xi. 30. 8
Oft spilles the *principall* to save the part; . . . V. x. 2. 4
Was placed in his *principall* Estate, . . . VII. vi. 19. 4
Principality. Riches, renowme, and *principality,* . . . II. vii. 8. 5
He plac't all rule and *principalitie,* . . . VII. vi. 3. 4
As for the gods owne *principality,* . . . VII. vii. 16. 5
Principals. To Lords, to *Principalls,* to Prebendaries? . . . *Hub.* 422
Principle. Doubting sad end of *principle* unsound: . . . V. xi. 2. 7
Printing. Whose image *printing* in his deepest wit, . . . *H.L.* 197
Priscilla. Calidore brings *Priscilla* home; . . . VI. iii. Arg.
But faire *Priscilla* (so that Lady hight) . . . VI. iii. 10. 1
when he saw his faire *Priscilla* by, . . . VI. iii. 11. 4
Prise, *etc. See* **Price, Prize,** *etc.*
Prison. My spirit shaking off her earthly *prison,* . . . *Van.* i. 2
A diverse Dreame out of his *prison* darke, . . . I. i. 44. 2
life does win Unto her native *prison* to retourne; . . . I. vii. 21. 8
overcommen kept in *prison* long, . . . II. x. 32. 8
Stout Ferrex and sterne Porrex him in *prison* threw. . . . II. x. 34. 9
In wretched *prison* long he did remaine, . . . II. x. 45. 1
grudge in so streight *prison* to be prest, . . . II. xi. 32. 4
meant unto her *prison* to have brought, . . . III. vii. 51. 3
Her body, late the *prison* of sad paine, . . . III. xii. 45. or. 3
As if he had in *prison* long bene pent: . . . IV. v. 34. 5
came upon a day Unto the *prison,* . . . IV. viii. 52. 2
secretly out of her *prison* steale; . . . IV. viii. 55. 7
Thence she commaunded me to *prison* new; . . . IV. viii. 56. 7
Who now long time had lyen in *prison* sad; . . . IV. ix. 4. 3
in this *prison* put him here with me; . . . IV. xii. 10. 6
One *prison* fittest is to hold us two. . . . IV. xii. 10. 7
the false mayden shortly turn'd againe Unto the *prison,* . . . V. v. 51. 9
Which had her Lord in her base *prison* pent, . . . V. vi. 18. 8
She for that yron *prison* did enquire, . . . V. vii. 37. 2
the whiles in *prison* she did dwell. . . . VI. xii. 15. 9
So sweet your *prison* you in time shall prove, . . . *Am.* lxxi. 11
Breaking his *prison,* forth to you doth fly. . . . *Am.* lxxiii. 4
Out of my *prison* I will breake anew; . . . *Am.* lxxx. 6
Out of great Chaos ugly *prison* crept, . . . *H.L.* 58
Prison-door. So soone as he the *Prison-dore* did pas, . . . III. x. 53. 1
the keyes of every *prison dore* . . . IV. viii. 54. 6
compeld To open unto him the *prison dore,* . . . IV. ix. 8. 2
Prisoner. He found the meanes that *Prisoner* up to reare; . . . I. viii. 40. 6
He bound that pitteous Lady *prisoner,* . . . III. xii. 41. 7

Prisoner—*Continued.*
In hope to take him *prisoner*, ... IV. iv. 31. 9
The which the *prisoner* points unto the free! . . . . IV. xii. 11. 2
now perforce they have him *prisoner* taken; . . . . V. iii. 9. 6
from the other fiftie soone the *prisoner* fet. . . . . V. iii. 11. 9
requere That Damsell whom he held as wrongfull *prisonere*. . V. viii. 27. 9
kept as *prisonere* By Artegall, ... V. viii. 46. 5
brought, as *prisoner* to the barre, ... V. ix. 38. 1
I goe lyke one that, . . . Is *prisoner* . . . . *Am.* lii. 3
So doe I now my selfe a *prisoner* yeeld To sorrow . . . . *Am.* lii. 5
Prisoners. Poore *prisoners* to relieve with gratious ayd, . . . I. x. 40. 2
One day, as he did all his *prisoners* vew, ... VI. xi. 3. 6
some, which did the sundry *prisoners* knowe, ... VI. xi. 11. 5
Prisonment. joy that for his sake I suffer *prisonment*. . . . . IV. xii. 7. 9
Prisons. shut up fast within her *prisons* blind, ... III. ix. 15. 4
Private. of more *private* persons seeke elswhere, ... *Hub.* 522
eke of *private* men somewhile, ... *Hub.* 787
with their spoyles enlarg'd his *private* treasures. . . . . . *Hub.* 1130
selfe-regard of *private* good or ill . . . . *Col.* 682
that which *private* errours doth pursew; . . . . *Col.* 750
the troublous stormes that tosse The *private* state, ... II. vii. 14. 2
A *private* life ledd in Albania With Gonorill, ... II. x. 29. 7
many a publike state, And many a *private* . . . . IV. i. 19. 4
eke of *private* persons many moe, ... IV. i. 24. 1
Ne *private* jarre, ne spite of enemis, ... IV. ix. 16. 3
of their *private* loves beguyled, ... IV. ix. 36. 5
To feeding of her *private* fire, ... V. v. 53. 7
back to *private* farmes he scorsed. . . . . VI. ix. 3. 9
Privately. each the other gan . . . *privately* bemone. . . . . IV. i. 16. 4
Privily. Did in his drinke shed poyson *privilie;* . . . . *Van.* vi. 8
Prevelie he peeped out through a chinck, ... *S.C.* May 252
Yet not so *previlie* but the Foxe him spyed; . . . . *S.C.* May 253
prively prolling to and froe, ... *S.C.* S. 160
privily his servant thereto hire: . . . . *Hub.* 682
enquiring *privily,* to learne What did . . . . *Hub.* 1249
would steale them *privily* away, ... *Mui.* 111
as he him schooled *privily:* . . . . I. i. 46. 5
spices . . . To kindle heat of corage *privily;* . . . . I. v. 4. 7
he laid him *privily* Downe . . . . I. x. 25. 6
avoided quite, and throwne out *privily*. . . . . II. ix. 32. 9
he perceiving, ever *privily,* . . . . III. ix. 52. 8
the rich metall lurked *privily,* . . . . III. xi. 28. 4
Privily moystening his horrid cheeke: . . . . III. xi. 44. 7
Did *privily* put coles unto his secret fire. . . . . IV. ii. 11. 9
Ate eke provokt him *privily* . . . . IV. iv. 11. 6
'Me when as he had *privily* espide . . . . IV. x. 14. 1
Privily pricked with thy lustfull powres, ... IV. x. 45. 7
kindled *privily,* Into outragious flames unwares did grow, . . V. vii. 14. 6
He found that they had festred *privily;* . . . . VI. vi. 5. 2
Calidore Had, underneath, him armed *privily*. . . . . VI. xi. 36. 4
a fleece of wooll, which *privily* . . . brought, ... *Epith.* 379
privily doth powre Through all the parts, ... *H.B.* 52
Privity. it must be gelt in *privitie*. . . . . *Hub.* 520
Him oft and oft I askt in *privity,* . . . . I. ix. 5. 5
Of all my love and all my *privitie;* . . . . II. iv. 20. 2
Thereat the Elfe did blush in *privitee,* . . . . II. ix. 44. 1
all his dayes he drownes in *privitie,* . . . . III. ix. 3. 8
for reasons speciall *privitie,* . . . . IV. v. 1. 4
neither showed to other their hearts *privity*. . . . . IV. ix. 19. 9
she would not him permit Once to approch to her in *privity,* VI. xi. 8. 2
To see her naked mongst her Nymphes in *privity*. . . . . . . VII. vi. 42. 9
Privy. Or made *previe* to the same? . . . . *S.C.* Mar. 30
The *previe* marks I would bewray, ... *S.C.* Mar. 35
Ye carelesse byrds are *privie* to my cryes, ... *S.C.* Au. 153
Or *prive* (*privie) or pert yf any bene, ... *S.C.* S. 162
yourselfe, that onely *privie* are: . . . . *Gn.* Ded. 4
I meane my Gossip *privie* first to make.' . . . . *Hub.* 70
breach of lawes to *privie* ferme did let: . . . . *Hub.* 1160
He by a *privy* Posterne tooke his flight, ... I. v. 52. 7
At last in *privy* wise . . . . I. vi. 32. 6
privy spyals plast in all his way, ... II. i. 4. 3
She shut up all her plaint in *privy* griefe . . . . III. iv. 11. 2
The *privie* guilt whereof makes him alway Suspect her truth, III. ix. 5. 3
Empoisned was with *privy* lust and gealous dredd. . . . . . III. ix. 28. 9
Ne *privy* bee unto your treasures grave.' . . . . III. x. 42. 8
through *privy* griefe and horrour vaine, ... III. x. 60. 7
privy love his brest empierced had, ... III. xi. 41. 8
in *privie* place Did spend her dayes, ... IV. ii. 44. 8
a *privy* place, betwixt us hight, ... IV. vii. 17. 7
He askt what *privie* tokens he did beare? . . . . V. iii. 32. 6
privie was and partie in the case: . . . . V. ix. 47. 5
A *privy* token which betweene them past, ... VI. i. 29. 3
shut up all his plaint in *privy* paine. . . . . VI. v. 24. 5
Which carrie *privie* message to the spright, ... *H.B.* 236
Prize. They han the pleasure, I a sclender *prise;* . . . . . . *S.C.* O. 16
Who ever casts to compasse weightye *prise,* . . . . *S.C.* O. 103
manie honest men . . . grow to goodly *prize;* . . . . *Hub.* 420
For *prize* of value, or for learned lore: . . . . *T.M.* 466
Who ever gave more honourable *prize* . . . . *Ded. Son.* xiv. 1
His Lady, left as a *prise* martiall, Did yield . . . . I. ii. 36. 8
Labour'd in vaine to have recur'd their *prize,* . . . . II. xii. 19. 7
Britomart winnes the *prize* from all, ... IV. iv. Arg.
The *prize* of her which did in beautie most excell. . . . . . IV. iv. 5. 9
To challenge her anew, as his owne *prize,* . . . . IV. iv. 8. 6
To be the *prize* of beautie and of might; . . . . IV. iv. 16. 2
that glorious *prize* to gaine. . . . . IV. iv. 26. 5
did yeeld the *prize* To Triamond and Cambell . . . . IV. iv. 36. 3
So did the warlike Britomart restore The *prize* . . . . IV. iv. 48. 2
Where beauties *prize* shold win that pretious spoyle: . . . . IV. iv. 48. 8
The *prize* of beautie still hath joyned beene; . . . . IV. v. 1. 3

Prize—*Continued.*
The third dayes *prize* unto that straunger Knight, ... IV. v. 8. 1
left that Turneyment for beauties *prise,* . . . . IV. vii. 3. 2
eke the famous *prize* of beauty from them wonne. . . . . . . IV. ix. 28. 9
the fame of this renowmed *prise* . . . . IV. x. 4. 1
Nathlesse his pride full dearely he did *pryse;* . . . . IV. xi. 5. 5
when Paris brought his famous *prise,* . . . . IV. xi. 19. 3
forst the burden of their *prize* to stay. . . . . V. iii. 11. 4
whose The honour of the *prize* should be adjudg'd . . . . . V. iii. 13. 9
So unto him they did addeeme the *prise* . . . . V. iii. 15. 2
As if the *prize* she gotten had almost, ... V. v. 10. 3
as his purchast *prize* with him convay . . . . V. viii. 25. 7
through his late luckelesse *prise,* . . . . VI. viii. 25. 7
Was his owne purchase and his onely *prize;* . . . . VI. xi. 12. 3
peerelesse beauties *prise,* . . . . *Am.* lxix. 7
what can *prize* that thy most precious blood? . . . . *H.H.L.* 175
Prized. *prizde* with slaughter of their Generall; . . . . *Ti.* 116
Proceed. badde the Brere in his plaint *proceede*. . . . . . . *S.C.* F. 159
laesie Vesper . . . gan *proceede* withall; . . . . *Gn.* 316
On their intended journey to *proceede;* . . . . *Hub.* 105
She stayd; and foorth Duessa gan *proceede:* . . . . I. v. 22. 1
ere they could *proceede* unto the place . . . . II. ii. 20. 1
'So from immortall race he does *proceede,* . . . . II. iv. 42. 1
forth she gan *proceede:* 'Most wretched woman . . . . II. vi. 33. 6
feeble age . . . he saw *proceed,* . . . . II. x. 27. 7
draw from on this journey to *proceed.'* . . . . II. xii. 26. 5
Yet stayd they not, but forward did *proceed,* . . . . II. xii. 37. 3
he forth on his journey did *proceede,* . . . . III. iv. 4. 6
the rest, which in this Quest *proceed,* . . . . III. viii. 50. 8
From his moist eies, and like two streames *procead;* . . . . IV. viii. 13. 4
from that goodly glorious flowre *proceed,* . . . . IV. viii. 33. 6
did *proceede,* Shooting forth farre away . . . . IV. viii. 39. 2
Nereus . . . Did first *proceed,* . . . . IV. xi. 18. 6
she saw him to *proceede* Unmov'd . . . . V. ii. 23. 1
Least any more such practise should *proceede*. . . . . V. vi. 31. 5
whence all this did *proceede;* . . . . V. vi. 31. 7
He purposd to *proceed,* what so befall, ... V. vii. 43. 8
to his voyage gan againe *proceed;* . . . . V. xi. 65. 8
She on her way cast forward to *proceede,* . . . . VI. v. 31. 2
must *proceed* alone . . . From your owne will . . . . VI. vi. 7. 2
from whom al true And perfect beauty did at first *proceed:* . *Am.* lxxix. 12
From whence *proceed* her beames so pure and bright . . . . *H.H.B.* 160
For from th' Eternall Truth it doth *proceed,* . . . . *H.H.B.* 174
Proceeded. wist no creature whence that hevenly sweet *Proceeded,* I. xii. 39. 7
To weet whence all the wealth . . . *Proceeded,* . . . . II. vii. 38. 5
Proceeding. Thenceforth *proceeding* with his princely trayne, *Hub.* 1086
forth *proceeding* with sad sober cheare, ... I. xii. 21. 4
Proceeding to the midst he stil did stand, ... III. xii. 4. 1
Proceeds. *proceedes* Yet on his way, ... II. vii. 2. 2
of no ill *proceeds* But of occasion, ... IV. iv. 1. 6
to perils great for justice sake *proceedes*. . . . . V. ii. 1. 9
proceeds such soule-enchaunting might. . . . . *H.B.* 14
light *proceedes,* which kindleth lovers fire, ... *H.B.* 100
Process. she bad him tellen plaine The further *processe* . . . I. vi. 37. 8
Proclaim. Their Lord and Patrone loud did him *proclame,* . . . I. xii. 6. 3
as through the world I did *proclame,* . . . . I. xii. 20. 2
troublous warre *proclame:* . . . . II. v. 1. 7
did *proclame* That Marinell that day deserved best. . . . . . V. iii. 7. 7
Proclaimed. *See* **Far-proclaimed.**
Proclaymed joy and peace through all his state; . . . . . . I. xii. 3. 8
solemne feast *proclaymd* throughout the land, ... I. xii. 40. 2
caus'd to be *proclaim'd* each where A solemne feast, ... IV. ii. 26. 7
cursed Idole, farre *proclamed,* He hath set up, ... V. x. 28. 4
Procrustes'. bold *Procrustes* hire . . . Would have suffiz'd . . . VII. vi. 29. 5
Procure. Ne let vaine feares *procure* your needlesse smart, . . I. i. 54. 4
Then she began a treaty to *procure,* . . . . II. ii. 32. 6
secretly doth us *procure* to fall . . . . II. xii. 48. 5
doth *procure* Great warriours oft their rigour to represse, . . V. viii. 1. 3
had no meanes to comfort, nor *procure* her glee. . . . . . . VI. iii. 43. 9
liking in her yet untamed heart *procure*. . . . . VI. x. 32. 9
So it the fairer bodie doth *procure* . . . . *H.B.* 129
Procured. th' Ape his Parish Clarke *procur'd* to bee. . . . . *Hub.* 557
Of the faire Alma greatly were *procur'd* . . . . III. i. 1. 5
it was no old sore which his new paine *procured;* . . . . . IV. xii. 23. 9
him entreat for grace that had *procur'd* her paine. . . . . . V. v. 28. 9
He now t' abhorre and loath her person had *procured*. . . . V. ix. 39. 9
cry *Procur'd* the Prince his cruell hand to stay, ... VI. viii. 29. 2
Prodigious. it *prodigious* seemes in common peoples sight. . . IV. i. 13. 9
All that behold so strange *prodigious* sight, ... V. iii. 19. 5
Produce. did Paridell *produce* His false Duessa, ... IV. v. 11. 1
new accusements to *produce* in place: . . . . V. ix. 47. 2
Produced. Whence being forth *produc'd,* . . . . IV. ix. 7. 1
Profane. Presume the things so sacred to *prophane?* . . . . . *Col.* 349
His mightie mysteries they do *prophane,* . . . . *Col.* 788
A sacrament *prophane* in mistery of wine. . . . . III. ix. 30. 9
that bad eyes might it not *prophane:* . . . . IV. iv. 15. 3
which all Asia sought with vowes *prophane,* . . . . IV. x. 30. 3
Profaned. suffer her *prophaned* for to bee . . . . *T.M.* 566
mote not be *prophan'd* of common eyes, ... VI. viii. 43. 2
Profess. Whether shall we *professe* some trade or skill, ... *Hub.* 117
high God himselfe, whom they *professe?* . . . . *Hub.* 843
all noble feates *professe* To register, ... *T.M.* 97
banish me, which do *professe* the skill . . . . *T.M.* 521
none might *professe* But Princes . . . that secret skill; . . . *T.M.* 559
Ne onelie favours them which it *professe,* . . . . *T.M.* 575
I do *professe* to be Vassall to one, ... *Col.* 466
those that skill of medicine *professe,* . . . . *Col.* 742
Vaine votaries of laesie Love *professe,* . . . . *Col.* 766
him they do not serve as they *professe,* . . . . *Col.* 791
To all that armes *professe* and chevalry. . . . . *Ded. Son.* iv. 4

Profess—*Continued.*
Mecaenas . . . to al that civil artes *professe,* — *Ded.Son.*xiii.10
Young knight whatever, that dost armes *professe,* — I. iv. 1. 1
Gainst all that truth or vertue doe *professe;* — IV. viii. 24. 7
greater love to me then her he did *professe.* — IV. viii. 57. 9
though revengefull vow she did *professe,* — V. vii. 36. 3
court'sie doth as well as armes *professe,* — VI. i. 41. 2
her face and former parts *professe* A faire young Mayden, — VI. vi. 10. 6
ne ever knighthood dare Hence to *professe;* — VI. vi. 36. 4
Professed. My part it is and my *professed* skill — *T.M.* 151
his sweet lore *professed* there? — *Col.* 772
Regan greater love to him *profest* Then all the world, — II. x. 28. 3
love is not where most it is *profest;* — II. x. 31. 2
all Ladies, which have it *profest,* — III. Pr. 1. 7
Scorne the faire offer of good will *profest;* — III. i. 55. 2
Friendship *professed* with unfained hart. — III. iii. 62. 8
profest a virgine wife. — IV. i. 6. 9
all those knights, as their *professed* fone, — IV. ii. 28. 8
Profest to her true friendship and affection sweet. — IV. iii. 50. 9
friends *profest* are chaungd to foemen fell: — IV. iv. 1. 3
Each one *profest* to be her paramoure, — IV. v. 24. 7
wonder was to see In friends *profest,* — IV. ix. 27. 7
both his *professed* fone: — IV. ix. 30. 4
from the first that her I love *profest,* — IV. ix. 39. 1
Ne more sincere in word and deed *profest;* — IV. xi. 18. 7
blame it is to him, that armes *profest,* — IV. xii. 8. 4
by vow, which I *profest* To my dread Soveraine, — VI. ii. 37. 5
he which was their Capitaine *profest,* — VI. xi. 3. 4
To shew the courtesie by him *profest* — VI. xii. 2. 4
soveraine Queene *profest* Of woods and forrests — VII. vi. 38. 7
loud *profest* His foolish thought: — VII. vi. 46. 5
Professeth. she her selfe *professeth* mortall foe To Justice, — V. viii. 20. 6
Professing. *Professing* thee I lifted am aloft — *Gn.* 33
Profession. mocke Divines and their *profession.* — *Hub.* 841
It is my chiefe *profession* to compyle; — *T.M.* 432
for *profession* of all learned arts, — *Col.* 754
Professors. there *professours* find small maintenance, — *Col.* 705
gives to their *professors* stipends large. — *Col.* 746
Proffer. To them that covet . . . *Proffer* thy giftes, — II. vii. 9. 9
proffer made by force her to reprize: — IV. iv. 8. 8
Some *proffer* made with him for her to fight. — IV. v. 27. 5
your bounteous *proffer* Be farre fro me, — VI. ix. 33. 3
Proffered. The which thy *proffred* curtesie denayd? — III. vii. 57. 7
Proffers. by *proffers* vaine Of idle hopes — VII. vi. 34. 7
Profit. yeeld them timely *profite* for their paine. — *Hub.* 236
No reach, no breach, that might him *profit* bring, — *Hub.* 1141
each his paynes to others *profit* still employd. — II. x. 14. 9
Profits. Of merchants farre for *profits* therein praysd; — II. x. 5. 7
Progenies. The substaunces of natures fruitfull *progenyes.* — III. vi. 36. 9
Progeny. Renowm'd for fruite of famous *progenie,* — *Ro.* vi. 6
ornament of great Joves *progenie,* — *Gn.* 14
for to purchase for his *progeny.* — *Hub.* 1148
The goodly off-spring of Joves *progenie,* — *T.M.* 429
Then, by like right the noble *Progeny,* — *Ded. Son.* iv. 5
three sonnes, his famous *progeny,* — II. x. 13. 4
happy father of faire *progeny:* — II. x. 22. 2
Here ended Brutus sacred *progeny,* — II. x. 36. 1
famous *Progeny,* Which from them springen shall. — III. iii. Arg.
from thy wombe a famous *Progenee* Shall spring — III. iii. 22. 5
the endlesse *progeny* Of all the weeds — III. vi. 30. 7
To count the seas abundant *progeny,* — IV. xii. 1. 2
the Theban Knight, The father of that fatall *progeny,* — V. xi. 25. 3
should the *progeny* of man Be rooted out, — VII. vi. 31. 8
Till they bring forth the fruitfull *progeny;* — *Epith.* 403
Seekes to enlarge his lasting *progenie;* — *H.L.* 105
Progress. forth they both yfere make their *progresse,* — III. xi. 20. 7
Progression. What else then did he by *progression,* — *Hub.* 842
Project. Before his feet her selfe she did *project;* — VI. i. 45. 5
Prolling. *See* **Prowling.**
Prolong. her husbands daies She did *prolong* — *Gn.* 427
why seeke I to *prolong* My wearie daies — *D.* 439
He would at her request *prolong* her nephews daies. — I. v. 41. 9
Ne may a man *prolong,* nor shorten, it; — I. ix. 41. 3
to *prolong* The vengeaunce prest? — II. viii. 28. 2
Sought by all meanes his dolor to *prolong,* — III. vii. 35. 7
right willing to *prolong* his date: — III. xii. 35. 9
thereby did more *prolong* their paine: — IV. iii. 2. 3
Till then your challenges ye may *prolong;* — IV. iv. 12. 7
then doe it not *prolong,* — IV. xii. 9. 7
though her dome she doe *prolong,* — V. xi. 1. 5
The faire doth it *prolong;* the fowle doth it impaire. — VII. vii. 22. 9
Prolonged. good lucke *prolonged* hath thy date, — I. ix. 45. 7
That so their lives might be *prolonged* late: — IV. ii. 51. 3
Prometheus. how first *Prometheus* did create A man, — II. x. 70. 5
Prometheus'. great *Prometheus* tasting of our ire, — VII. vi. 29. 7
Promise. Did largely *promise,* and to him fore-red, — *Mui.* 29
The flowre of chevalry . . . Doth *promise* fruite — *Ded. Son.* x. 3
honourable sight Doth *promise* hope of helpe — II. viii. 25. 6
with sure *promise* of her good endevour — V. v. 35. 2
Through *promise* to afford her timely aide, — V. xi. 41. 4
for *promise* of great meed, — VI. vii. 12. 7
as ye did *promise* make, — VI. vii. 15. 7
New yeare, . . . Doth seeme to *promise* hope — *Am.* iv. 2
Promised. *promised* of timely fruite such store, — *S.C.* D. 104
The Foxe had *promised* of friendship store, — *Hub.* 1206
they *promised* to dight for him Gay chapelets — *As.* 41
grove . . . That *promist* ayde the tempest to withstand; — I. i. 7. 3
He *promised* to bring me at that howre, — II. iv. 24. 7
Thy Grandsire Nereus *promist* to adorne? — III. iv. 36. 5
She *promist* kisses sweet, and sweeter things, — III. vi. 12. 8

Promised—*Continued.*
for his love him *promist* libertie at last. — IV. viii. 52. 9
promist large amends to make. — IV. viii. 60. 6
promist him, what ever wight she weare, — IV. xii. 27. 5
she *promist* that she would . . . Devize how — V. v. 55. 1
Promist, if she would free him from that case, — V. v. 55. 8
ye *promist,* as ye were a Knight, To meete her — V. xi. 39. 2
promist to performe his precept well, — VI. i. 43. 3
he *promist,* if shee would him pleasure — VII. vi. 44. 1
promist both to recompens; — *Epith.* 431
Fell from the hope of *promist* heavenly place, — *H.H.L.* 122
Promiseth. That *promiseth* the same; — *Proth.* 154
Prone. Of them that to him buxome are and *prone:* — III. ii. 23. 4
Pronoe. Large Lisianassa and *Pronaea* sage, — IV. xi. 50. 2
Pronounced. When he his sentence thus *pronounced* had, — V. iv. 20. 1
Proof. Let thy follye be the *priefe.* — *S.C.* Au. 116
For *priefe* thereof, my death shall weepe, — *S.C.* Au. 119
'Well may appeare by *proofe* of their mischaunce, — *Gn.* 553
readie are of anie to make *preife.* — *Hub.* 408
practising the *proofe* of warlike deedes, — *Hub.* 740
he put in *proofe:* — *Hub.* 1139
Of which, apparaunt *proofe* was to be seene, — *Ded. Son.* xi. 8
Drawne into armes, and *proofe* of mortall fight, — *Mui.* 4
joyd to make *proofe* of her cruelty — I. vi. 31. 6
of his prowesse *proofe* he since hath made — I. vii. 47. 6
good growes of evils *priefe.'* — I. viii. 43. 6
onely worthie you through prowes *priefe,* — I. ix. 17. 8
med'cines, which had passing *prief;* — I. x. 24. 5
now by *proofe* all otherwise I weene, — I. x. 58. 7
whence she might behold that battailles *proof,* — I. xi. 5. 3
tell what fatall *priefe* Hath . . . you opprest; — II. i. 48. 6
To *proofe* of passing wonders hath full often usd: — II. ii. 5. 9
For *proofe* thereof, . . . Aray thyselfe in her most gorgeous geare, — II. iv. 26. 7
Me liefer were ten thousand deathes *priefe* — II. iv. 28. 8
made a *priefe* Of every place — II. vi. 51. 3
Proofe be thou, Prince, the prowest man alyve, — II. xi. 30. 6
for prayse, and *proofe* of manly might, — III. i. 13. 4
had never *priefe* Of such malengine — III. i. 53. 7
Ne braver *proofe* in any of thy powre — III. iii. 3. 2
proofe of thy prow valiaunce — III. iii. 28. 3
Thy daies abridge through *proofe* of puissaunce, — III. viii. 18. 2
with *proofe* of last extremity, — III. xi. 18. 8
After the *proofe* of prowesse ended well, — IV. v. 2. 2
For dread of her displeasures utmost *proofe:* — IV. vii. 37. 5
Did shun the *proofe* thereof, and it avoyded light. — IV. viii. 44. 9
Till he had made of her some better *priefe;* — IV. ix. 15. 5
Streight forth issewd a Knight all arm'd to *proofe,* — IV. x. 9. 6
for the *proofe* of his great puissance, — IV. xi. 16. 2
To deedes of armes and *proofe* of chevalrie — V. iii. 4. 3
For *proofe* shew forth thy sword, — V. iii. 21. 5
For *proofe* whereof he bad them Florimell forth call. — V. iii. 22. 9
with dint of sword And battailes doubtfull *proofe* — V. iv. 6. 2
Consisted much in that adventures *priefe:* — V. vii. 44. 5
to make *proofe* of utmost shame, — V. viii. 22. 6
Ere *proofe* it tooke, — V. ix. 42. 4
loth t' assay The *proofe* of battell now — VI. iii. 41. 4
if please her make the *priefe;* — VI. iv. 34. 5
by *proofe* of that which she hath fylde — VI. xii. 21. 3
shee such *proofe* and sad examples shewed — VII. vi. 4. 6
little *priefe* In deep discovery of the mynds disease; — *Am.* 1. 5
late repentance through thy follies *prief;* — *H.H.B.* 293
Prop. *See* **Vine-prop.**
Withouten *prop* or pillour it t' upholde, — *Ti.* 549
Proper. calling me then by my *propre* name, — *Bel.*[1] i. 7
Didst arme thy hand against thy *proper* hart; — *Ro.* xxxi. 11
I chaunst to see her in her *proper* hew, — I. ii. 40. 6
a science *Proper* to gentle blood: — II. iv. 1. 8
Her *proper* face I not descerned — II. iv. 28. 3
gainst the Romanes bent their *proper* powre; — II. x. 57. 6
each might best offend his *proper* part, — II. xi. 6. 3
in their *proper* praise too partiall bee, — III. ii. 1. 2
To let him loose to save their *proper* stakes, — IV. iv. 34. 8
Out of their *proper* places farre away, — V. Pr. 6. 6
Nor tooke away his love, but his owne *proper* good. — V. i. 23. 9
Of their vaine prowesse turned to their *proper* bale. — V. iv. 24. 9
soone did make To leave his *proper* forme, — V. ix. 16. 9
that is his *proper* owne: — VI. iii. 1. 7
at the last breake forth in his owne *proper* kynd. — VI. v. 1. 9
Properties. Appeared in their native *propertis,* — *Ti.* 284
that old man Eumnestes, by their *propertis.* — II. ix. 58. 9
Property. a waift . . . he claym'd as *propertie:* — IV. xii. 31. 4
Prophecies. Shewes, visions, sooth-sayes, and *prophesies;* — I. xi. 51. 8
'Fond Proteus, father of false *prophecis!* — III. iv. 37. 1
Thereto he was expert in *prophecies,* — IV. xi. 19. 1
Prophecy. sung the *prophecie* Of his owne death — *Ti.* 594
(For Proteus was with *prophecy* inspir'd) — III. iv. 25. 3
It was no time to scan the *prophecie,* — IV. xii. 28. 3
Prophesied. That Proteus *prophecide* should him dismay; — III. iv. 28. 2
'Well hop't he then, when this was *propheside,* — VI. iv. 33. 1
Prophet. the *Prophet* still awhile did stay, — III. iii. 21. 4
Prophets. The hellish Harpyes, *prophets* of sad destiny. — II. xii. 36. 9
Propitious. make thee more *propitious* in my need, — *H.L.* 9
Proportion. Of wondrous length, and streight *proportion,* — *Van.* vii. 2
proportion of the outward part — *H.B.* 75
with his spirits *proportion* to agree, — *H.B.* 227
Proportioned. *See* **Well-proportioned.**
Justly *proportion'd* (*proportionde*[1]) up — *Bel.* iii. 3
Proportiond equally by seven and nine; — II. ix. 22. 7
Proportions. Those two the first and last *proportions* are; — II. ix. 22. 3

Propound. for all the suit I could *propownd,* Would me refuse III. vii. 56. 5
To follow that which he did long *propound,* . . . IV. vi. 42. 5
these conditions doe to him *propound:* . . . V. iv. 49. 1
Began the streight conditions to *propound,* . . . V. vii. 28. 2
With these conditions which I will *propound:* . . . VI. i. 42. 6
Prosecute. Which he so wisely well did *prosecute,* . . . VI. x. 38. 4
To *prosecute* her plot. . . . VII. vi. 23. 9
Prosecuting. From *prosecuting* his revenging rage: . . . III. i. 11. 2
discouraged From *prosecuting* of her first intent, . . . III. xi. 50. 8
Proserpina. horrid house of sad *Proserpina,* . . . *Ti.* 373
sad *Proserpina,* the Queene of hell; . . . I. iv. 11. 2
The Gardin of *Proserpina* this hight; . . . II. vii. 53. 1
Brought thee from balefull house of *Proserpine,* . . . III. xi. 1. 2
Yet Pluto and *Proserpina* were present there. . . . VII. vii. 3. 9
Proserpina's. gan threaten hellish paine, And sad *Proserpines* wrath, . . . I. ii. 2. 7
Prosper. Ill might it *prosper* that ill gotten was; . . . *Hub.* 1149
Prosperity. To greatnes growne, through long *prosperitie,* . . . *Ro.* xxxi. 13
tract of time, and long *prosperitie,* . . . *S.C.* May 117
'For th' heavens, envying our *prosperitie,* . . . VI. iv. 31. 1
envies lovers long *prosperity,* . . . VI. x. 38. 8
Prostrate. downe in dust *prostrate,* . . . *Gn.* 558
Themselves to humble to the Ape *prostrate,* . . . *Hub.* 1083
To her my love I lowly do *prostrate,* . . . *Col.* 474
They, . . . all *prostrate* upon the lowly playne, . . . I. vi. 12. 8
carcases on ground were horribly *prostrate.* . . . II. viii. 54. 9
prostrate she fell unto the grownd. . . . III. xii. 38. 9
Before faire Britomart she fell *prostrate,* . . . III. xii. 39. 1
her selfe uppon the land She did *prostrate,* . . . V. vii. 7. 8
Whylest kings and kesars at her feet did them *prostrate.* . . . V. ix. 29. 9
a storme, that all things doth *prostrate;* . . . *Am.* lvi. 6
Prostrated. *prostrated* fall, And kisse my stirrup; . . . II. iii. 8. 5
Whom when he saw before his foote *prostrated,* . . . V. v. 11. 6
her proud person low *prostrated* on the plaine. . . . V. vii. 33. 9
Belge, with her sonnes, *prostrated* low . . . V. xi. 16. 1
Whom when he saw *prostrated* on the plaine, . . . V. xii. 23. 8
Prostrating. him before themselves *prostrating* low, . . . I. xii. 6. 2
on the ground herselfe *prostrating* low, . . . I. xii. 33. 2
The wretched man . . . low *prostrating* said: . . . III. x. 25. 2
Protect. by the names of Souldiers us *protect:* . . . *Hub.* 197
by your powre *protect* his feeble cace? . . . II. viii. 25. 8
seemed nought could him from death *protect;* . . . V. xii. 21. 4
Protection. Muse . . . craves *protection* of her feeblenesse: . . . *Ded.Son.*xiii.12
All these, I wote, in thy *protection* bee, . . . III. iv. 58. 6
left in his *protection* whileare, . . . IV. ix. 17. 8
Seem'd under her *protection* him to shroud; . . . VI. vi. 31. 4
Protections. Which in their high *protections* doe containe . . . *H.H.B.* 87
Protense. by dew degrees, and long *protense,* . . . III. iii. 4. 8
Protest. The eldest, Gonorill, gan to *protest* . . . II. x. 28. 1
Proteus. *Proteus* eke with him does drive his heard . . . *Col.* 248
As many formes . . . As ever *Proteus* to himselfe could make: I. ii. 10. 4
she inquir'd One day of *Proteus* . . . III. iv. 25. 2
(For *Proteus* was with prophecy inspir'd) . . . III. iv. 25. 3
That *Proteus* prophecide should him dismay; . . . III. iv. 28. 2
'Fond *Proteus,* father of false prophecis! . . . III. iv. 37. 1
wrong'd by Carle, by *Proteus* sav'd, . . . III. viii. Arg.
Proteus abrode did rove, . . . III. viii. 29. 8
Proteus is Shepheard of the seas of yore, . . . III. viii. 30. 1
when *Proteus* she did see her by. . . . III. viii. 33. 9
Unlovely *Proteus,* missing to his mind . . . IV. xi. 2. 2
To *Proteus* selfe to sue for her discharge: . . . IV. xii. 14. 4
Proteus to constraine; . . . IV. xii. 14. 8
Whether old *Proteus* true or false had sayd, . . . IV. xii. 28. 4
To *Proteus* selfe to sew she thought it vaine, . . . IV. xii. 29. 1
Proteus, that hath ordayn'd my sonne to die; . . . IV. xii. 31. 2
Commaunding *Proteus* straight t' enlarge the mayd, . . . IV. xii. 32. 3
Departed straight to *Proteus* therewithall; . . . IV. xii. 32. 7
Proteus'. He comes to *Proteus* hall, . . . IV. xi. Arg.
for the Gods in *Proteus* house be made; . . . IV. xi. 9. 2
All these together marched toward *Proteus* hall. . . . IV. xi. 39. 9
Proteus house they fild even to the dore; . . . IV. xii. 3. 3
being freed from *Proteus* cruell band . . . V. iii. 2. 1
Proto. Swift *Proto,* milde Eucrate, Thetis faire, . . . IV. xi. 48. 7
Protomedaea. Panopae, and wise *Protomedaea,* . . . IV. xi. 49. 8
Protract. nights, that slowly seemd to move Theyr sad *protract* *Am.* lxxxvi. 4
Proud. *Proud* that so manie Gods she brought to light; . . . *Ro.* vi. 3
Proud of his highest service, . . . *Van.* iv. 3
Mongst all the daughters of *proud* Libanon, . . . *Van.* vii. 4
his *proude* heart is fild with fretting ire: . . . *Van.* x. 10
Thy sommer *prowde,* with Daffadillies dight; . . . *S.C.* Ja. 22
With painted words tho gan this *proude* weede . . . *S.C.* F. 160
proud that ever he begot Such a Bellibone; . . . *S.C.* Ap. 91
Is not thilke same a goteheard *prowde,* . . . *S.C.* Jul. 1
As Goteherd *prowd,* that, sitting hye, . . . *S.C.* Jul. 103
he was *proude,* that ill was payd, . . . *S.C.* Jul. 149
with *proud* vaunt his head aloft doth holde; . . . *Gn.* 259
The Priest gan wexe halfe *proud* to be so praide, . . . *Hub.* 413
the *proud* beasts him readily obayd: . . . *Hub.* 1102
Through *prowd* ambition and hart-swelling hate, . . . *Mui.* 5
Did prick him foorth with *proud* desire of praise . . . *As.* 86
And that *proud* people, woxen insolent . . . *Ded. Son.* vi. 10
the Cedar *proud* and tall; . . . I. i. 8. 6
it chaunced this *proud* Sarazin To meete me wandring; . . . I. ii. 25. 1
Who, whiles he livde, was called *proud* Sans foy, . . . I. ii. 25. 6
yielded pryde and *proud* submission, . . . I. iii. 6. 6
mightie *proud* to humble weake does yield, . . . I. iii. 7. 3
proud Paynim forward came so ferce . . . I. iii. 35. 1
Proud of such glory . . . I. iv. 9. 5
So *proud* she shyned in her princely state, . . . I. iv. 10. 1
proud Lucifera men did her call, . . . I. iv. 12. 1

Proud—*Continued.*
Thought . . . that great Princesse too exceeding *prowd,* . . . I. iv. 15. 8
grudged at the great felicitee Of *proud* Lucifera, . . . I. iv. 31. 9
Duessa, next unto the chaire Of *proud* Lucifer', . . . I. iv. 37. 6
'With *proud* foes sight my sorrow to renew, . . . I. iv. 51. 7
with that Pagan *proud* he combatt will that day. . . . I. v. 2. 9
'Goe now, *proud* Miscreant, . . . I. v. 13. 1
by law of that *proud* Tyrannesse, . . . I. v. 46. 6
There was that great *proud* king of Babylon, . . . I. v. 47. 1
proud Antiochus, . . . advaunst His cursed hand gainst God, I. v. 47. 8
Proud Tarquin, and too lordly Lentulus; . . . I. v. 49. 6
Proud wemen, vaine, forgetfull of their yoke: . . . I. v. 50. 2
Whereas that Pagan *proud* him selfe did rest . . . I. vi. 40. 5
Whom all so soone as that *proud* Sarazin Espide, . . . I. vi. 46. 1
of that *proud* Paynim sore afrayd. . . . I. vi. 47. 9
The Redcrosse knight is . . . By Gyaunt *proud* opprest: . . . I. vii. Arg.
after him the *proud* Duessa came, . . . I. viii. 6. 1
Came ramping forth with *proud* presumpteous gate, . . . I. viii. 12. 5
The *proud* Duessa, full of wrathfull spight, . . . I. viii. 13. 1
of his puissaunce *proud* ensample made; . . . I. viii. 16. 3
Whom when his maistresse *proud* perceiv'd to fall, . . . I. viii. 20. 6
prouder vaunt that *proud* avenging boy Did soone pluck downe, I. ix. 12. 3
she was *proud,* and of too high intent, . . . I. ix. 27. 8
In ashes . . . *proud* humors to abate; . . . I. x. 26. 2
Such *proud* luxurious pompe is swollen up but late. . . . I. xii. 14. 9
that *proud* Paynim king that works her teene: . . . I. xii. 18. 8
Sith her Prince Arthur of *proud* ornaments . . . spoyld. . . . II. i. 22. 6
the Scarcrow wexed wondrous *prowd,* . . . II. iii. 7. 1
in pompe of *prowd* estate' . . . II. iii. 40. 1
leave so *proud* disdayne.' . . . II. iii. 43. 9
proud through praise and mad through love, . . . II. iv. 27. 1
prowd corage to provoke, . . . II. v. 3. 2
A *prowd* rebellious Unicorn defyes, . . . II. v. 10. 2
His *prowd* presumed force increased more, . . . II. vi. 30. 3
False Archimage provokte their corage *prowd,* . . . II. viii. 11. 3
match his brother *proud* in battailous aray. . . . II. viii. 22. 9
speare he thrust . . . At *proud* Cymochles, . . . II. viii. 36. 4
that *proud* towre of Troy, . . . II. ix. 45. 8
The king retourned *proud* of victory, . . . II. x. 17. 1
Through *proud* ambition against her rebeld, . . . II. x. 32. 7
prickt with *proud* disdaine . . . II. x. 33. 3
Ruddoc and *proud* Stater, both allyes, . . . II. x. 38. 3
Archigald, who for his *proud* disdayne . . . II. x. 44. 4
Till the *prowde* Romanes him disquieted, . . . II. x. 47. 5
Stoupes at a flying heron with *proud* disdayne, . . . II. xi. 43. 2
the great sea, puft up with *proud* disdaine, . . . II. xii. 21. 7
depriv'd Of their *proud* beautie, . . . II. xii. 31. 4
As the *proud* Persian Queenes accustomed. . . . III. i. 41. 4
her *prowd* portaunce and her princely gest, . . . III. ii. 27. 3
his *proud* foes discomfit in victorious field. . . . III. iii. 31. 9
Proud Etheldred shall from the North arise, . . . III. iii. 35. 2
how stout Debora strake *Proud* Sisera, . . . III. iv. 2. 8
Ythrild with deepe disdaine of his *proud* threat, . . . III. iv. 15. 1
Proud of his dying honor and deare bandes, . . . III. iv. 17. 3
So fell *proud* Marinell upon the pretious shore. . . . III. iv. 17. 9
with *proud* envy and indignant yre . . . III. iv. 47. 3
as a victour *proud,* gan ransack fast . . . III. v. 48. 4
In his *proud* furnitures she freshly dight, . . . III. vii. 18. 8
Proud Braggadocchio, that in vaunting vaine . . . III. viii. 11. 8
Proud man himselfe then Braggadochio deem'd, . . . III. viii. 13. 6
At those *prowd* words that other knight begonne . . . III. viii. 17. 7
The roring billowes in their *proud* disdaine, . . . III. viii. 37. 3
the late ruine of *proud* Marinell, . . . III. viii. 46. 4
proud Encelade, whose wide nosethrils burnd . . . III. ix. 22. 3
proude of that new honour which they redd, . . . III. x. 44. 7
the *proud* Bird, ruffing his fethers wyde . . . III. xi. 32. 6
More sondry colours then the *proud* Pavone Beares . . . III. xi. 47. 7
their *proud* girlonds of tryumphant bayes . . . III. xi. 52. 7
Nought therewith daunted was her courage *prowd,* . . . III. xii. 1. 7
his *proud* spoile of that same dolorous Faire Dame . . . III. xii. 22. 7
Of which ful *prowd,* him selfe up rearing hye . . . III. xii. 23. 1
seeing his so *prowd* And boastfull chalenge, . . . IV. i. 10. 5
Nathlesse *proud* man himselfe the other deemed, . . . IV. ii. 8. 1
this trustie squire with *proud* disdaine . . . IV. ix. 3. 7
the *proud* Nymph would for no worldly meed, . . . IV. xi. 8. 7
finally destroy *Proud* Priams towne. . . . IV. xi. 19. 7
Proud of his Adamants with which he shines . . . IV. xi. 31. 7
Which the *proud* Humber unto them had donne, . . . IV. xi. 38. 3
White hand Eunica, *proud* Dynamene, . . . IV. xi. 49. 1
With *proud* disdaine did scornefull answere make, . . . V. iii. 16. 2
the *proud* boaster gan his doome upbrayd, . . . V. iii. 35. 7
yeelded you to *proude* oppression Of womens powre, . . . V. iv. 26. 4
a *proud* Amazon did late defy All the brave Knights . . . V. iv. 29. 5
her *proud* observaunce will withstand, . . . V. iv. 32. 2
in his necke Her *proud* foote setting, . . . V. iv. 40. 3
With stately port and *proud* magnificence, . . . V. v. 4. 2
There bound t' obay that Amazons *proud* law, . . . V. v. 22. 3
Serving *proud* Radigund with true subjection, . . . V. v. 26. 2
her *proud* mind convert To meeke obeysance . . . V. v. 28. 7
proud rebellious flesh to mortify: . . . V. vii. 9. 5
proud Radigund, with fell despight, . . . V. vii. 32. 1
her *proud* person low prostrated on the plaine. . . . V. vii. 33. 9
Whom that *proud* Amazon subdewed had, . . . V. vii. 41. 6
this *proude* Dame, disdayning all accord, . . . V. viii. 22. 3
that *proud* dame which her so much disdained, . . . V. viii. 24. 4
as his *proud* wife of her had sight, . . . V. viii. 26. 5
the *proud* Souldan . . . Sought onely slaughter . . . V. viii. 30. 3
Of that *proud* Souldan whom he earst did slay. . . . V. viii. 51. 7
came at length with *proud* presumpteous gate . . . V. xii. 14. 1
Glad to be quit from that *proud* Tyrants awe, . . . V. xii. 24. 3

Proud—*Continued.*
proud despight of his selfe-pleasing mynd, . . . VI. i. 15. 2
is the boast of that *proud* Ladies threat, . . . VI. i. 40. 4
put away *proud* looke and usage sterne, . . . VI. i. 40. 8
slay A *proud* discourteous knight: . . . VI. ii. Arg.
Wherewith he wroth, and full of *proud* disdaine, . . . VI. ii. 11. 6
support of count'nance *proud* . . . To wrong the weaker, . . VI. ii. 23. 8
that *proud* Knight in his presumption . . . VI. iii. 8. 3
this *proud* gyant should with brave emprize Quite overthrow; VI. iv. 33. 4
avenge th' abuses of that *proud* And shamefull Knight . . . VI. v. 34. 3
Pursuing that *proud* Knight, . . . VI. vi. 17. 6
she thereof grew *proud* and insolent, . . . VI. vii. 29. 1
such *proud* looks would make her praysed more; . . . VI. vii. 30. 2
For penaunce of my *proud* and hard rebellious hart. . . . VI. viii. 19. 9
could so meekly make *proud* hearts avale, . . . VI. viii. 25. 3
Proud Change (not pleasd in mortall things . . . to raigne) VII. vi. Arg.
Typhons fall, or *proud* Ixions paine, . . . VII. vi. 29. 6
if in presence of that fayrest *proud* . . . *Am.* ii. 9
But her *proud* hart doe thou a little shake, . . . *Am.* x. 9
In that *proud* port, which her so goodly graceth, . . . *Am.* xiii. 1
Faire *Proud!* now tell me, why should faire be *proud,* . . . *Am.* xxvii. 1
be no lenger *proud* of that shall perish; . . . *Am.* xxvii. 13
that *proud* mayd, . . . *Proud* Daphne, . . . *Am.* xxviii. 8, 9
my *proud* one doth worke the greater scath, . . . *Am.* xxxi. 9
a *proud* love, that doth my spirite spoyle. . . . *Am.* xxxiii. 12
my toung with *proud* restraint to tie; . . . *Am.* xliii. 6
But if it be your pleasure, and *proud* will, . . . *Am.* xlix. 5
Fayre be ye sure, but *proud* and pittilesse, . . . *Am.* lvi. 5
Why then doe ye, *proud* fayre, misdeeme . . . *Am.* lviii. 13
So farre from being *proud*. . . . *Epith.* 164
To humble your *proud* faces: . . . *Epith.* 214
my faire love does ly, In *proud* humility! . . . *Epith.* 306
Thou doest emmarble the *proud* hart of her . . . *H.L.* 139
And all that pompe to which *proud* minds aspyre . . . *H.H.B.* 277
Prouder. when him list the *prouder* lookes subdew, . . . I. vii. 35. 8
prouder vaunt that proud avenging boy Did soone pluck downe, I. ix. 12. 3
Then which a *prouder* Lady liveth none: . . . VI. i. 14. 7
Proudest. No lesse, I dare saie, than the *prowdest* wight; . . *Hub.* 62
in paragone of *proudest* men: . . . III. iii. 54. 6
Indians do aray . . . in their *proudest* plight: . . . III. xii. 8. 4
proudest harts base love hath blynded.' . . . V. v. 40. 9
Those engins can the *proudest* love convert: . . . *Am.* xiv. 12
Proudly. yet Love she *proudly* (*proudely*[1]) did forsake: . . *Pet.* vi. 4
Brere, Which *proudly* thrust into Thelement, . . . *S.C.* F. 116
proudlie neighing, from them parted hee. . . . *Hub.* 654
would he laugh it out, and *proudly* looke, . . . *Hub.* 703
thorough them did passe So *proudly,* . . . *Col.* 223
Under his Lordly foot him *proudly* hath supprest. . . . I. iii. 19. 9
And *proudly* said; . . . I. iii. 36. 3
prowdly threw to ground, as things of naught; . . . I. vii. 18. 5
her feathers . . . *Prowdly* to prune, . . . II. iii. 36. 8
So *proudly* pricketh on his courser strong, . . . II. v. 38. 8
proudly did impugne her sentence just: . . . V. iv. 2. 5
Proudly stands over, and a while doth pause . . . V. iv. 40. 8
I him find to be too *proudly* fed: . . . V. v. 50. 2
Eftsoones forth pricked *proudly* in his might, . . . V. x. 31. 8
But she his precept *proudly* disobayes, . . . *Am.* xix. 11
Prove. Pitie the paines that thou thy selfe didst *prove.* . . . *S.C.* Ja. 18
Least thou the price of my displeasure *prove.'* . . . *S.C.* F. 138
Ys love such pinching payne to them that *prove?* . . . *S.C.* Ap. 18
As well can *prove* the piercing levin, . . . *S.C.* Jul. 91
to *prove* whether his powre would pas As currant, . . . *Hub.* 1094
yet to *prove* more true he meant to see, . . . *Hub.* 1277
That he in time would sure *prove* such an one, . . . *Mui.* 31
Came downe to *prove* the truth, . . . *Mui.* 267
To *prove* that death their hearts cannot divide, . . . *As.* 179
his hart did earne To *prove* his puissance . . . I. i. 3. 7
He . . . gan himselfe advise To *prove* his sense, . . . I. i. 50. 6
That doth this Redcrosse knights ensample plainly *prove.* . . I. iv. 1. 9
To *prove* the wide report of her great Majestee. . . . I. iv. 13. 9
joyd weake wemens hearts to tempt, and *prove,* . . . I. iv. 26. 4
thou his errour shalt, I hope, now *proven* trew.' . . . I. vi. 42. 9
prove thy puissant armes, . . . I. x. 66. 9
to *prove* his late-renewed might, . . . I. xi. 35. 5
To *prove* how many acres he did spred of land. . . . I. xii. 11. 9
to *prove* if any drop Of living blood . . . II. i. 43. 4
He pricked forth his puissant force to *prove.* . . . II. i. 50. 7
sith in might thou didst my mercy *prove,* . . . II. v. 16. 7
full bent To *prove* extremities of bloody fight, . . . II. vi. 36. 2
To *proove* he lived il that did thus fowly dye. . . . II. viii. 12. 9
resolv'd likewise to *prove* the rest, . . . II. x. 31. 4
prove his cause.' . . . III. i. 28. 6
prove too well Our faulty weakenes, . . . III. i. 30. 1
Which to *prove,* I (*I to *prove*) this voyage have begonne. . III. ii. 8. 5
well can witnesse who by tryall it does *prove.* . . . III. ii. 51. 9
prove thy selfe, this sad encounter shonne, . . . III. viii. 17. 5
To *prove* some deeds of armes upon an equall pere?' . . . III. x. 24. 9
resolv'd to *prove* her utmost might, . . . III. xi. 25. 1
As he did for Erigone it *prove*) . . . III. xi. 43. 4
A thousand charmes he formerly did *prove,* . . . III. xii. 31. 8
both resolv'd the last extremities to *prove.* . . . IV. ii. 19. 9
whosoever contrarie doth *prove,* . . . IV. v. 3. 3
Likewise assayd to *prove* that girdles powre; . . . IV. v. 19. 3
Without displeasance for to *prove* his spere. . . . IV. vi. 4. 3
Where she, captived long, great woes did *prove;* . . . IV. vi. 34. 8
I me resolv'd the utmost end to *prove;* . . . IV. vii. 16. 7
Which losse her made like passion also *prove:* . . . IV. viii. 3. 5
change his liking, and new Lemans *prove;* . . . IV. ix. 21. 6
an eager mastiffe once doth *prove* The tast of bloud . . . IV. ix. 31. 5
if old sawes *prove* true . . . IV. xi. 35. 2

Prove—*Continued.*
Which well I *prove,* as shall appeare by triall, . . . V. iv. 15. 6
To *prove* her surname true, that she imposed has. . . . V. viii. 49. 9
prove her cleare Of all those crimes . . . V. xi. 40. 4
To *prove* if better foote then horsebacke would ensew. . . . VI. i. 35. 9
prove the finall fortune of the fight; . . . VI. i. 38. 4
In hope he sure would *prove* a doughtie knight: . . . VI. ii. 36. 8
his kyndly courtesie to *prove,* . . . VI. iii. 15. 5
prove thy manhood on the billowes vayne.' . . . VI. iii. 32. 5
Small praise to *prove* your powre . . . VI. v. 30. 5
prove the puissaunce of his pride. . . . VI. vii. 46. 9
Yet ceast he not to sew, and all waies *prove,* . . . VI. xi. 5. 5
to *prove* how pale and weake she was. . . . VI. xi. 12. 9
do surely *prieve* That yond same is your daughter sure, . . VI. xii. 18. 8
what if I can *prove,* that even yee . . . are likewise chang'd, VII. vii. 49. 8
both you and them to me I subject *prove.* . . . VII. vii. 55. 9
prove your powre, which I too well have tride. . . . *Am.* xxv. 8
So sweet your prison you in time shall *prove,* . . . *Am.* lxxi. 11
forgets . . . His mothers heast to *prove.* . . . *Epig.* iv. 58
Proved. *See* **Well-proved.**
you, which the world have *proved,* . . . *Hub.* 409
by that which little while I *prooved,* . . . *Col.* 664
ye have . . . *proov'd* your strength on a strong enimie, . . I. i. 27. 7
pitty in her hart was never *prov'd* Till then, . . . I. v. 24. 8
Againe his wonted angry weapon *proov'd,* . . . I. viii. 21. 3
had he *prov'd* the powre of many a puissant knight. . . . I. xi. 17. 9
stoutly *prov'd* thy puissaunce here in sight. . . . II. iv. 45. 7
Your self his prowesse *prov'd,* . . . II. viii. 13. 9
wife, though alwaies faithful *prov'd.* . . . II. x. 17. 9
when ever it were *proov'd;* . . . II. x. 28. 4
she *proov'd* Whether she slept or wakte: . . . III. i. 60. 5
For his great vertues *proved* long afore: . . . III. iii. 60. 5
many fortunes *prov'd* in th' Ocean mayne, . . . III. ix. 48. 8
So *proov'd* it eke that gratious God of wine, . . . III. xi. 43. 6
Some, of borne brethren *prov'd* unnaturall; . . . IV. i. 24. 4
'Last turne was mine, well *proved* to my paine; . . . IV. ii. 6. 4
prov'd himselfe most foole in what he seem'd most wise. . . IV. ii. 9. 9
babes, that *prov'd* three champions bold. . . . IV. ii. 45. 9
Upon them gladly would have *prov'd* his might, . . . IV. iv. 3. 8
prov'd true by this . . . IV. viii. 1. 1
As if some *proved* perill he did feare, . . . IV. x. 12. 8
Through his too ventrous prowesse *proved* over all. . . . IV. xi. 7. 9
Well *prov'd* in that same day when Jove those Gyants quelled: V. i. 9. 9
swat, and chauf'd, and *proved* every way: . . . V. ii. 46. 8
well-seene in armes, and *prov'd* in many a fight. . . . V. iii. 5. 9
Ne would I it have ween'd, had I not late it *prieved.'* . . . V. iv. 33. 9
one day she thus him *proved.* . . . V. v. 35. 9
For so great prowesse as he there had *proved,* . . . V. x. 39. 2
proved oft in many perillous fight, . . . VI. vi. 4. 3
now have *prov'd* what happinesse ye hold . . . VI. ix. 28. 3
prov'd the perfect pleasures which doe grow . . . VI. x. 3. 5
The *proved* powre of noble Calidore, . . . VI. xii. 36. 7
proved The piercing points of his avengefull darts; . . . *H.L.* 29
I, that have often *prov'd,* too well it know, . . . *H.B.* 87
Provender. Their bodies to his beastes for *provender* did spred,) V. viii. 28. 9
Proves. With which my weaker patience fortune *proves:* . . . IV. viii. 63. 8
Proveth. seldome seene, forejudgment *proveth* true. . . . *Mui.* 320
Provide. let him feede, as Nature did *provide,* . . . *Van.* iii. 11
provide for meanes of maintenaunce, . . . *S.C.* May 79
the toomb he did *provide* . . . *Gn.* 662
huckster man, That wont *provide* his necessaries, . . . *Hub.* 926
Ne new ones could he easily *provide,* . . . *Hub.* 929
Gan to *provide* for all things in assurance, . . . *Hub.* 1113
Provide therefore (ye Princes) whilst ye live, . . . *Ti.* 365
her Love would her *provide;* . . . *Mui.* 108
May them avoyde, or remedie *provide.* . . . *Mui.* 224
The housling fire did kindle and *provide,* . . . I. xii. 37. 4
For which Dan Phebus selfe cannot a salve *provide.* . . . IV. vi. 1. 9
Till time for him should remedy *provide,* . . . IV. vii. 47. 6
how long space Hath he her lent a Champion to *provide?'* . . V. xi. 42. 2
Which to *provide* she hath this Castle dight, . . . VI. i. 15. 6
In hope there for his love some succour to *provyde.* . . . VI. iii. 29. 9
Would for the wretched infants helpe *provyde;* . . . VI. xii. 8. 8
at first *provide* . . . for ever to abide. . . . VII. vi. 5. 8
Provided. *Provided* him a sword of meanest sort; . . . VI. xi. 42. 6
Providence. Eternall *providence,* exceeding thought, . . . I. vi. 7. 1
Led with eternall *providence,* . . . III. iii. 24. 4
Providence hevenly passeth living thought, . . . III. v. 27. 1
submit you to high *providence;* . . . III. xi. 14. 4
Province. Corineus had that *Province* utmost west . . . II. x. 12. 2
Proving. bad him stay at ease till further *preeving.* . . . *Hub.* 1366
Provoke. *provoke* them might To idle pleasaunce; . . . *D.* 326
'Least suddaine mischiefe ye too rash *provoke:* . . . I. i. 12. 2
advise The angry beastes not . . . too much to *provoke;* . . . I. vi. 25. 6
prowd corage to *provoke,* . . . II. v. 3. 2
Him all that while Occasion did *provoke* . . . II. v. 21. 1
just wronges to vengeaunce doe *provoke,* . . . II. viii. 27. 3
gan fayre perswade Not to *provoke* misfortune, . . . III. i. 10. 2
'What monstrous enmity *provoke* we heare? . . . III. xi. 22. 7
Ne list I for revenge *provoke* new fight, . . . IV. i. 35. 3
when he did her *provoke.* . . . IV. xi. 5. 9
to *provoke* the yre Of damned fiends, . . . *H.L.* 234
Provoked. *Provoked* me to plaie some pleasant fit; . . . *Col.* 69
Provokt with Wrath and Envyes false surmise, . . . I. v. 46. 7
death was dew to him that had *provokt* Gods ire. . . . I. ix. 50. 9
provokt her sonne to wreake her wrong; . . . II. iv. 12. 6
False Archimage *provokte* their corage prowd, . . . II. viii. 11. 3
Provoked them the breaches to assay, . . . II. xi. 14. 7
Ate eke *provokt* him privily . . . IV. iv. 11. 6
'To all which cruell tyranny, they say, He is *provokt,* . . . V. viii. 20. 2

Provoked—*Continued.*
where he is *provokt* with peevishnesse, VI. vii. 37. 2
Provokement. Whose sharpe *provokement* them incenst so sore, IV. iv. 4. 6
Provoking. *Provoking* him, by her outrageous talke, II. iv. 5. 3
rash *provoking* perils all about, IV. ii. 46. 8
Prow. proofe of thy *prow* valiaunce III. iii. 28. 3
Prowess. Whose warlike *prowesse* . . . Hath fild sad Belgicke *Ded. Son.* xiv. 8
I hope . . . your *prowesse* can me yield reliefe: I. vii. 42. 8
of his *prowesse* proofe he since hath made I. vii. 47. 6
Can speake his *prowesse* that did earst you beare, I. vii. 48. 4
with his *prowesse* may Defend thine honour, I. ix. 16. 7
Wondrous great *prowesse* and heroick worth He shewd II. ii. 25. 3
Ne ought the praise of *prowesse* more doth marre II. ii. 30. 8
Through deeds of armes and *prowesse* martiall. II. iii. 37. 8
Your self his *prowesse* prov'd, II. viii. 13. 9
Ne canst of *prowesse* ne of knighthood deeme, II. viii. 14. 2
two sonnes, or pearelesse *prowesse* both, II. x. 40. 2
Of their brave gestes and *prowesse* martiall: III. ii. 1. 6
they mervaild at her chevalree And noble *prowesse,* III. ix. 24. 6
through great *prowesse* and bold hardinesse, III. ix. 34. 6
I your vassall, by your *prowesse* freed, III. xii. 39. 7
his utmost *prowesse* there made knowen; IV. iv. 38. 2
bore The prayse of *prowesse* . . . away. IV. iv. 48. 4
After the proofe of *prowesse* ended well, IV. v. 2. 2
Through his too ventrous *prowesse* IV. xi. 7. 9
The greater *prowesse* greater perils find. V. iii. 9. 2
Of their vaine *prowesse* turned to their proper bale. V. iv. 24. 9
so great *prowesse* as he there had proved, V. x. 39. 2
through *prowesse* and their brave emprize VI. vi. 35. 7
knew Calidore right well, And loved for his *prowesse,* VI. xii. 11. 3
through thy *prowesse,* . . . Thy country may be freed *Proth.* 155
Prowess'. onely worthie you through *prowes* priefe, I. ix. 17. 8
Whose *prowesse* paragone saw never living wight. III. ii. 13. 9
second unto none in *prowesse* prayse; V. iii. 5. 4
Prowest. The *prowest* knight that ever field did fight, I. iv. 41. 7
prowest knight, That ever Ladie to her love did chose, I. v. 14. 2
they be two the *prowest* knights on grownd, II. iii. 15. 6
Unmindfull of thy praise and *prowest* might, II. v. 36. 4
yonder comes the *prowest* knight alive, II. viii. 18. 3
the *prowest* and most gent, II. xi. 17. 5
Proofe be thou, Prince, the *prowest* man alyve, II. xi. 30. 6
To love the *prowest* knight that ever was. III. iii. 24. 7
Two of the *prowest* Knights in Faery lond, IV. ii. 31. 6
Prowling. prively *prolling* to and froe, *S.C.* S. 160
Prudent. *prudent* Mutius, Who in his flesh endur'd the scorching flame, *Gn.* 606
Those *prudent* heads, that with theire counsels wise *Ded. Son.* i. 1
Such as that *prudent* Romane well invented, IV. ii. 2. 7
Prune. May now goe *prune* his plumes *T.M.* 402
Prowdly to *prune,* and sett on every side; II. iii. 36. 8
to sett or sow, To plant or *prune;* III. vi. 34. 2
tooles to *prune* the trees, VII. vii. 43. 7
Pruned. Hath *pruned* from the native tree, V. xi. 11. 9
Pryene. *Pryene,* (so she hight,) II. iv. 25. 6
with him brought *Pryene,* II. iv. 28. 2
That was *Pryene;* she did first offend, II. iv. 31. 5
Psalmist. such as that celestiall *Psalmist* was, IV. ii. 2. 1
Psamathe. *Psamathe* for her brode snowy brests; IV. xi. 51. 5
Psyche. Her sonne to *Psyche* secrete love did beare, *Mui.* 131
his trew love faire *Psyche* with him playes, III. vi. 50. 1
Fayre *Psyche* to him lately reconcyld, III. vi. 50. 2
Pleasure, the daughter of Cupid and *Psyche* late. III. vi. 50. 9
unto *Psyche* with great trust and care Committed her, III. vi. 51. 3
Ptolemy. Great *Ptolomaee* it for his lemans sake Ybuilded III. ii. 20. 6
learned *Ptolomaee* his hight did take, V. Pr. 7. 6
Pubidius. Matilda, daughter to *Pubidius,* III. iii. 13. 6
Public. many a *publike* state, . . . oft doth overthrow. IV. i. 19. 3
A solemne feast, with *publike* turneying, IV. ii. 26. 8
of their *publicke* praise had them despoyled, IV. ix. 36. 4
Importune care of their owne *publicke* cause; V. ix. 44. 8
Publish. take great joy to *publish* it to many, V. xii. 35. 3
Published. at the length he *published* to holde A Visitation, *Hub.* 568
Puck. Ne let the *Pouke,* nor other evill sprights, *Epith.* 341
Puddle. Of muddie water, that like *puddle* stanke, IV. v. 33. 4
In which a *puddle* of contagion was, V. xi. 32. 3
Puddles. like to troubled *puddles* have them made. *T.M.* 276
Puff. not one *puffe* of winde there did appeare, II. xii. 22. 5
Loosely disperst with *puff* of every blast: III. i. 16. 4
If any *puffe* of breath or signe of sence shee fond. III. i. 60. 9
At *puffe* of every storme doth stagger here and theare. IV. iii. 9. 9
overspread her like a *puffe* of wind; V. ix. 14. 3
pride . . . Did *puffe* them up *H.H.L.* 79
Puffed. with fine perle and golde *puft* up in heart. *Rev.* ii. 7
Puft up with pride of Romane hardiehead, *Ro.* xi. 3
puffed up with passing surquedrie, *Van.* viii. 7
Puffed up with pryde and vaine pleasaunce; *S.C.* F. 223
puft up with sdeignfull insolence, *T.M.* 71
they be *puffed* up with pride, *Col.* 759
earthly slyme, *Puft* up with emptie wynd, I. vii. 9. 9
puffed up with smoke of vanity, II. iii. 5. 3
the great sea, *puft* up with proud disdaine, II. xii. 21. 7
Puissance. Her that did match the whole earths *puissaunce,* *Ro.* vi. 13
that mortall *puissaunce,* Puft up with pride *Ro.* xi. 2
Nor thou oppos'd against thine owne *puissance;* *Ro.* xiii. 8
Pyrrhus and the *puissaunce* Of Afrike *Ro.* xxi. 1
his hart did earne To prove his *puissance* I. i. 3. 7
Each others equall *puissaunce* envies, I. ii. 17. 4
'The Lyon, . . . 'his princely *puissance* doth abate, I. iii. 7. 2
so great was the *puissance* of his push, I. iii. 35. 6
too weake . . . his *puissance* to withstand; I. iii. 42. 2

Puissance—*Continued.*
of his *puissaunce* proud ensample made; I. viii. 16. 3
Orgoglio with his *puissaunce* fell Had made his caytive thrall: I. viii. 32. 7
Almightie God her gave . . . *puissaunce* great. I. x. 20. 9
nothing seemd the *puissaunce* could withstand: I. xi. 24. 3
nought so wondrous *puissaunce* might sustaine: I. xi. 43. 5
his wrong with greater *puissance* maintaine.' II. i. 14. 9
They were two knights of perelesse *puissaunce,* II. ii. 16. 6
stoutly prov'd thy *puissaunce* here in sight. II. iv. 45. 7
such hideous *puissaunce* on foot to beare; II. v. 3. 9
of his *puissaunce* tryall made extreeme: II. viii. 14. 4
That in advauntage would his *puissaunce* bost: II. viii. 26. 4
neither could his mightie *puissaunce* sustaine. II. viii. 42. 9
As well in state of peace, as *puissaunce* in warre.' II. ix. 4. 9
with such *puissaunce* and impetuous maine II. ix. 14. 5
in semblaunce of his *puissaunce* great, II. x. 23. 3
these twelve troupes with dreadfull *puissaunce* II. xi. 14. 1
he with all his *puissaunce* doth stryve II. xii. 5. 4
That mortall *puissaunce* mote not withstond. III. i. 10. 6
Seeking adventures hard, to exercise Their *puissaunce,* III. i. 14. 4
Of warlike *puissaunce* in ages spent, III. ii. 3. 1
his mighty *puissaunce* And dreaded name III. iii. 28. 1
for memory Of his late *puissaunce,* III. iii. 29. 2
till all their warlike *puissaunce* be spent. III. iii. 40. 9
all that els had *puissaunce,* III. iv. 3. 1
With so fierce furie and great *puissaunce,* III. iv. 16. 2
So long as breath and hable *puissaunce* III. vii. 3. 1
Thy daies abridge through proofe of *puissaunce,* III. viii. 18. 2
T' employ her *puissaunce* to his reskew, III. xi. 4. 8
broke The *puissaunce* of his intended stroke: IV. vii. 26. 5
for the proofe of his great *puissance,* IV. xi. 16. 2
his faint foe no longer could abide His *puissance,* V. ii. 17. 8
strove with *puissance* strong To fill the other scale V. ii. 46. 4
at her strooke with *puissaunce* fearefull fell: V. v. 10. 7
he me first through pride and *puissance* strong Assayld, VI. ii. 8. 4
prove the *puissaunce* of his pride. VI. vii. 46. 9
Putting his *puissaunce* forth, pursu'd so hard, VI. xii. 30. 3
Puissant. on horses white, A *puissant* armie *Rev.* iii. 7
the *puissant* brood Of golden girt Alcmena, *Ti.* 379
so fell and *puissant* he grew, *Col.* 808
increasing more Their *puissant* force, I. vi. 45. 3
a Groome, . . . gan despoile Of *puissant* armes, I. x. 17. 8
prove thy *puissant* armes, I. x. 66. 9
sore amoved with so *puissaunt* push, I. xi. 16. 6
prov'd the powre of many a *puissant* knight. I. xi. 17. 9
He pricked forth his *puissant* force to prove. II. i. 50. 7
'Ah, *puissant* Lords! what cursed evil Spright, II. ii. 29. 1
His *puissant* armes about his noble brest, II. iii. 1. 8
Under Sir Guyons *puissant* stroke to fall, II. v. 25. 6
had never mett before So *puissant* foe, II. vi. 30. 2
that ought those *puissant* hands may marre: II. vi. 44. 8
Three times more furious and more *puissaunt,* II. viii. 34. 8
speare he thrust with *puissant* sway II. viii. 36. 3
withstond Oppressours powre by armes and *puissant* hond? II. viii. 56. 5
puissant kinges which all the world warrayd, II. x. 72. 2
Adowne he kest it with so *puissant* wrest, II. xi. 42. 7
up he caught him twixt his *puissant* hands, II. xi. 46. 1
Her Steed did stagger with that *puissant* strooke; III. vii. 41. 1
on his collar laying *puissant* hand, III. vii. 43. 1
Three such as able were to match a *puissant* host? IV. iii. 24. 9
with *puissant* stroke she downe did beare IV. v. 8. 4
Of *puissant* Nations which the world possest, IV. xi. 15. 2
he is so *puissant* and strong, V. ii. 7. 2
for to maister wrong and *puissant* pride: V. iv. 1. 5
Albe the stroke so strong and *puissant* were, VI. viii. 16. 2
What *puissant* conquest, what adventurous paine, *H.L.* 221
Pull. That may *pull* downe the courage of his pride; V. v. 50. 6
Pulled. Untill that state by strength was *pulled* downe; V. x. 26. 2
But hayld and *puld* with all his might and maine, VI. iv. 7. 4
Pulleth. He *pulleth* downe, he setteth up on hy; V. ii. 41. 7
Pulse. over the *pousse* hetheward doth post. *S.C.* Au. 46
then gan softly feel Her feeble *pulse,* II. i. 43. 4
With trembling hand his troubled *pulse* gan try; II. viii. 9. 6
Did feele his *pulse,* III. iv. 41. 7
Pulse's. feeling by his *pulses* beating rife III. v. 31. 3
Pumice. oft the *pumices* latched. *S.C.* Mar. 93
Pumice-stones. *pumie stones* I hastly hent And threwe; *S.C.* Mar. 89
whose murmuring wave did play Emongst the *pumy stones,* II. v. 30. 3
a little river plaide Emongst the *pumy stones,* III. v. 39. 8
Punching. *Pounching* me with the butt end of his speare, VI. ii. 22. 6
Punish. A judge, that after death doth *punish* sore *Gn.* 447
that vengeable despight To *punish:* II. iv. 30. 4
He cast to *punish* for his hainous fault: III. viii. 36. 3
So doth he *punish* her, and eke him selfe torment. III. x. 3. 9
bownd for to revenge, and *punish* if they may. III. x. 27. 9
punish wicked men that walke amisse: IV. i. 20. 3
To *punish* those that doe deserve the same; VI. i. 26. 5
avenge, and *punish* him with speed?' VI. vii. 5. 9
gan augment Their cruelty, and him to *punish* more, VI. viii. 4. 7
Would for it selfe redresse, and *punish* such despights. VI. viii. 18. 9
Thought not enough to *punish* him in sport, VII. vi. 51. 2
Punished. having worthily him *punished,* *Hub.* 923
Be *punished* for their presumptuous guile. *Hub.* 1256
He sorely *punished* with heavie payne; V. xii. 25. 7
Punishment. Did shrowd her selfe like *punishment* to shonne. *Gn.* 176
punishment is due to the offender. *Gn.* 366
let destruction be the *punishment,* *Gn.* 367
how to scape great *punishment,* or shame, *Hub.* 314
Els surely death should be no *punishment,* *D.* 362
ten thousand sorts of *punishment* . . . torment. I. v. 33. 8

Punishment—*Continued.*

Pure—*Continued.*

Purport—*Continued.*
There written was the *purport* of his sin, V. ix. 26. 2
Purpose. His worke he shortly to good *purpose* brought, *Gn.* 655
The *purpose* of the complot which ye tell; *Hub.* 178
he the same did to his *purpose* wring. *Hub.* 1142
Was fil'd with hope his *purpose* to obtaine: *Mui.* 396
fitting gestures to her *purpose* frame. I. vii. 1. 6
for her humor fitting *purpose* faine, I. vii. 38. 7
nether darkenesse fowle, . . . his *purpose* could withhold, I. viii. 40. 2
On which they lowly sitt, and fitting *purpose* frame. I. xii. 13. 9
she was inly glad her *purpose* so to gaine. II. i. 20. 9
Her *purpose* was not such as she did faine, II. i. 21. 1
all unfitt for so great *purpose,* II. ii. 43. 9
forward he his *purpose* gan pursew, II. ii. 45. 6
poursewing my fell *purpose,* II. iv. 31. 9
Yet mildly him to *purpose* answered; II. iv. 39. 8
With cruell *purpose* bent to wreake on him II. vi. 2. 2
she in pleasaunt *purpose* did abound, II. vi. 6. 3
So pleased did his wrathfull *purpose* faire appease. II. vi. 13. 9
whenas Mammon saw his *purpose* mist, II. vii. 34. 8
goodly *purpose* they together fond II. viii. 56. 7
stead you much your *purpose* to subdew.' II. ix. 9. 4
Them gan to bord, and *purpose* diversely; II. xii. 16. 2
for secret *purpose* did appoynt To lodge III. i. 60. 3
faire *purpose* gan to find, III. ii. 4. 2
to their *purpose* used wicked art: III. ii. 41. 4
The fatall *purpose* of divine foresight III. iii. 2. 5
was loth to let her *purpose* plaine appeare; III. iii. 17. 9
make Way for themselves their *purpose* to pertake?' III. iii. 25. 5
to possesse the *purpose* they desird: III. iii. 51. 7
shield of great powre, for her *purpose* fit. III. iii. 60. 9
T' approve the unknowen *purpose* of eternall fate. III. iv. 28. 9
He gan make gentle *purpose* to his Dame III. viii. 14. 2
Purpose was moved by that gentle Dame III. ix. 32. 2
With *purpose* how they might it best betray; III. x. 34. 7
Till they arriv'd whereas their *purpose* they did plott. III. xi. 20. 9
other-whiles to her she *purpos* made Of love, IV. i. 7. 7
twixt themselves did gentle *purpose* make, IV. ii. 30. 7
to small *purpose* yron wedges made; IV. v. 35. 8
From his revengefull *purpose* shronke abacke, IV. vi. 21. 4
she sundry *purpose* found . . . the time for to delay, IV. vi. 45. 1
see how much her *purpose* was deceaved! V. iv. 10. 5
The last daies *purpose* of their vowed fight, V. v. 1. 6
this further *purpose* to him shope. V. v. 39. 9
comming to this knight, she *purpose* fayned, V. v. 54. 1
least by that art He should his *purpose* misse, V. vi. 24. 3
It would no passage yeeld unto his *purpose* vaine. V. xi. 10. 9
by slights allur'd, and to their *purpose* lad. V. xii. 37. 9
Somewhile with merry *purpose,* fit to please, VI. v. 32. 7
in his mind had closely made A further *purpose,* VI. xi. 38. 8
Of sundry things he *purpose* gan to faine, VI. xi. 39. 2
ymages Of hardest marble are of *purpose* made, *Am.* ii. 2
Purposed. to his *purposd* journey him prepar'd: II. xi. 3. 6
liberty to frame Their *purpost* flight, III. x. 16. 5
Unto that *purposd* place I did me draw, IV. x. 29. 3
He *purposd* to proceed, what so befall, V. vii. 43. 8
Purposes. for their *purposes* none fit espyed. *Hub.* 226
To which he levels all his *purposis,* *Hub.* 772
pleasaunce each to other makes, With goodly *purposes,* I. ii. 30. 2
his *purposes* to breake, III. iii. 36. 4
Oft *purposes,* oft riddles, he devysd, III. x. 8. 6
Purslane. Fat Colworts, and comforting *Perseline,* *Mui.* 199
Pursue. Two eager dogs did her *pursue* in chace, *Pet.* i. 6
cruell fate And angry Gods *pursue* *S.C.* Jun. 15
Have care for to *pursue* his footing light *Gn.* 31
Ah! pensive boy, *pursue* that brave conceipt *Col.* 388
that which private errours doth *pursew;* *Col.* 750
So long they fight, and full revenge *pursue,* I. vi. 44. 1
famous harde atchievements still *pursew;* I. vii. 45. 5
With fresh desire his voyage to *pursew;* I. ix. 18. 4
Would not a while her forward course *pursew,* I. ix. 20. 6
Pursew the end of their strong enmity, II. ii. 28. 3
forward he his purpose gan *pursew,* II. ii. 45. 6
durst he nott *Pursew* her steps II. iii. 43. 3
his voyage to *poursew.* II. v. 25. 3
powre of al which them *poursew.'* II. vii. 19. 9
What straunge adventure doe ye now *pursew?* II. ix. 9. 2
Whom to *poursue* the Infant after hide II. xi. 25. 7
him his foe more fiercely should *poursew:* II. xi. 27. 4
The flying ships with swiftnes to *pursew:* II. xii. 24. 4
Yet did false Archimage her still *pursew,* III. iv. 45. 1
did attonce *pursew* The fearefull damzell III. iv. 46. 2
By the great *persue* which she there perceav'd, III. v. 28. 6
Through thicke and thin her to *poursew* apace, III. vii. 23. 2
had no regard Him to *poursew,* III. viii. 19. 2
behinde The fearefull boy so greedily *poursew,* III. xi. 4. 6
with speedie pace did after them *pursew.* IV. ii. 30. 9
The which, for length, I will not here *pursew,* IV. ii. 54. 8
Which vauntage Cambell did *pursue* so fast, IV. iv. 30. 5
So tempting her still to *pursue* the pray, IV. viii. 11. 4
The more did she *pursue* her lewd intent, IV. viii. 35. 8
Whom after did a mightie man *pursew,* IV. viii. 38. 6
Resolved to *pursue* his former quest; IV. ix. 17. 5
He fear'd least they with shame would him *pursew:* V. ii. 52. 7
mindefull to *pursew* The last daies purpose V. v. 1. 5
he gan fiercely her *pursew.* V. v. 7. 5
eke *pursew,* if he attaine it may.' V. v. 39. 7
So to *pursue* a perillous emprize, V. vii. 21. 3
So cruelly did him *pursew* and chace, V. viii. 36. 6
Artegall him after did *pursew,* V. ix. 15. 1

Pursue—*Continued.*
Nathlesse the yron man did still *pursew* V. xi. 65. 1
'The Blattant Beast' . . . 'I doe *pursew,* VI. i. 7. 1
that Beast' . . . 'Which I *pursue,* VI. i. 10. 2
so him left . . . to *pursue* that villaine, VI. i. 18. 4
Against his foe that did him so *pursew;* VI. iv. 3. 7
Securely he did after him *pursew,* VI. v. 17. 1
Him booted not to thinke them to *pursew,* VI. v. 22. 8
Yet he them still so sharpely did *pursew,* VI. vi. 24. 1
did him fast *pursew.* VI. vii. 2. 9
now your crime with cruelty *pursew!* VI. viii. 7. 7
So sharply he the Monster did *pursew,* VI. ix. 3. 1
the cruell boy . . . Would needs the fly *pursue;* *Epig.* iv. 22
Pursued. as he that perilous game In forreine soyle *pursued* *As.* 92
He left his stond, and her *pursewd* apace, I. vi. 48. 6
all the like, which honor have *pursewd* II. iii. 37. 7
so he me *poursewd* apace, II. iv. 32. 5
poursewed fast The present offer of faire victory, II. v. 12. 1
She list not heare, but her disports *poursewd,* II. vi. 26. 8
she so fast *pursewd,* that him she tooke II. x. 18. 6
As fearing evill that *poursewd* her fast; III. i. 16. 2
The Prince and Guyon equally bylive Her selfe *pursewd,* III. i. 18. 7
whiles his Lord *pursewd* that noble Mayd, III. v. 13. 3
as shee *pursewd* the chace Of some wilde beast, III. v. 28. 1
Her hard *pursewd,* and sought for to suppresse. III. vii. 37. 5
the knight That her *pursewed* III. vii. 43. 7
her the hardy knight *pursewd* so nye III. vii. 44. 5
Sometimes pursewing, and sometimes *pursewed,* IV. vi. 18. 2
her *pursu'd* as fast as she did flie: IV. vii. 21. 7
she speedily *poursewed* With winged feete IV. vii. 30. 1
his cruell foe that him *pursewd* in sight. IV. viii. 40. 9
The Tyrant selfe came forth . . . And me *pursew'd;* IV. viii. 62. 3
Artegall trayn'd in Justice lore Irenaes quest *pursewed;* V. i. Arg.
His yron page, who him *pursew'd* so light, V. i. 20. 2
Artegall *pursewd* him still so neare V. ii. 18. 1
th' other still *pursu'd* the fearefull Mayd; V. viii. 6. 1
for what cause *pursu'd* of them attone. V. viii. 16. 5
Yet still the Prince *pursew'd* him close behind. V. viii. 42. 1
He him *pursewd* where ever that he went; V. ix. 16. 3
with mortall malice him *pursu'd* so nere. V. xi. 48. 9
So well he him *pursew'd,* V. xii. 23. 1
whiles he her *pursued* every where, VI. i. 16. 7
He fiercely him *pursu'd,* and pressed sore; VI. i. 21. 8
He him *pursu'd* and chaced through the plaine, VI. i. 22. 7
he him still *pursew'd* from place to place, VI. iii. 49. 1
with more eager felnesse him *pursew'd;* VI. iii. 50. 2
him *pursewed* with importune speed, VI. iv. 8. 2
by the cry he follow'd, and *pursewed* fast. VI. iv. 18. 9
The Prince . . . *Pursu'd* him streight; VI. vi. 18. 3
so sharpely still he him *pursewd,* VI. vii. 48. 1
There on a day, as he *pursew'd* the chace, VI. ix. 5. 1
them *pursu'd* into their dortours sad, VI. xii. 24. 3
Putting his puissance forth, *pursu'd* so hard, VI. xii. 30. 3
Pursues. Paridell rapeth Hellenore: Malbecco her *poursewes;* III. x. Arg.
Calidore . . . *Pursues* the Blatant Beast: VI. iii. Arg.
For who my passed follies now *pursewes,* *H.H.L.* 20
Pursueth. But greedily her fell intent *poursewth,* *Am.* xi. 7
Pursuing. *poursewing* my fell purpose, II. iv. 31. 9
After *pursewing* death II. vi. 44. 7
pursewing that same foster strong, III. iv. 45. 6
that bold knight, whom ye *pursuing* saw III. vii. 52. 1
Sometimes *pursewing,* and sometimes pursewed, IV. vi. 18. 2
Pursuing that faire Lady full of feare: IV. vii. 24. 5
So as he was *pursuing* of his quest, VI. iii. 20. 1
Pursuing him apace with greedy speede; VI. iii. 46. 7
Pursuing that proud Knight, VI. vi. 17. 6
he him fast *pursuing* soone approched neare. VI. xii. 25. 9
Pursuit. Satyrane him from *pursuit* did let. I. vii. 20. 4
brave *poursuitt* of chevalrous emprize, I. ix. 1. 4
draw them from *pursuit* of praise and fame II. i. 23. 2
In brave *poursuitt* of honorable deed, II. iv. 1. 1
His wearisome *pursuit* perforce he stayd, III. iv. 53. 5
to his first *poursuit* him forward still doth call. III. v. 2. 9
when hee saw him selfe free from *poursute,* III. viii. 14. 1
In which *poursuit* how each one did succeede, IV. v. 28. 5
The Beast, with their *pursuit* incited more, VI. iii. 25. 1
after long *pursuit* . . . The gentle deare returnd *Am.* lxvii. 5
Pursuivant. cleave The flitting skyes, like flying *Pursuivant,* II. viii. 2. 4
Pursuivants. *Pursivants* he often for them sent; *Hub.* 565
Purvey. doe *purvay* Your selfe of sword II. iii. 15. 4
It can *purvay* in twinckling of an eye; II. vii. 11. 4
all thinges did conveniently *purvay.* III. iii. 58. 2
all things did *purvay* which for them needfull weare. V. xii. 10. 9
Purveyance. mounting up, they fynd *purveyaunce* meet I. xii. 13. 5
to the ill *purveyaunce* of his page, III. i. 11. 7
whose royaltee And rich *purveyance* might uneath be red; III. i. 33. 3
none was to possesse So rich *purveyaunce,* III. xi. 53. 9
Purveyed. And powring balme, which he had long *purvayd,* VI. ii. 48. 3
pleasing gifts for her *purvaid,* VII. vi. 43. 5
Push. so great was the puissance of his *push,* I. iii. 35. 6
With dint of swerd, nor *push* of pointed speare: I. xi. 9. 4
sore amoved with so puissaunt *push,* I. xi. 16. 6
His tyreling Jade he fiersly forth did *push* III. i. 17. 4
with the *push* of his sharp-pointed speare VI. iv. 5. 6
Pushed. rudely he him thrust, and *pusht* with paine, I. i. 42. 4
That one did reach the other *pusht* away; IV. i. 29. 2
Put. Such fond fantsies shall soone be *put* to flight. *S.C.* Au. 22
To *put* in preace emong the learned troupe: *S.C.* O. 70
The hatefull darknes now had *put* to flight; *Gn.* 69
put themselves (a Gods name) on their way; *Hub.* 111

Put—*Continued.*
what ever such like paine Ye *put* on me, . . . *Hub.* 288
To speed to day, to be *put* back to morrow; . . . *Hub.* 899
bad him *put* all cowardize away: . . . *Hub.* 958
sith I For it did *put* my life in jeopardie: . . . *Hub.* 1028
he *put* in proofe: . . . *Hub.* 1139
when he ought not pleasing would *put* by . . . *Hub.* 1169
In th' eyes of people they *put* all their praise, . . . *T.M.* 93
Am *put* from practise of my kindlie skill, . . . *T.M.* 383
Thy scepter rent, and power *put* to wrack; . . . *T.M.* 400
When th' heavenlie light of knowledge is *put* out, . . . *T.M.* 488
put us all ashore on Cynthias land. . . . *Col.* 289
At which . . . Styx is *put* to flight. . . . I. i. 37. 9
seemde best the person to *put* on Of that good knight, . . . I. ii. 11. 1
put feare apart, And tel both who ye be, . . . I. ii. 21. 8
To comfort her; and, feare to *put* away, . . . I. vi. 11. 8
His trembling hand he would him force to *put* Upon the Lyon . I. vi. 24. 3
consuming thought To *put* away out of his carefull brest. . . . I. x. 29. 6
with redoubled buffes them backe did *put:* . . . II. ii. 23. 4
Resolv'd to *put* away that loathly blame, . . . II. viii. 44. 4
Stird Porrex up to *put* his brother downe; . . . II. x. 35. 3
pitteous Elidure *put* in his sted; . . . II. x. 44. 6
meet respect of honor *putt* to flight: . . . III. i. 48. 8
whenas all were *put* to shamefull flight, . . . III. i. 67. 1
the same was *put* to flight; . . . III. ii. 29. 5
bad her all things *put* in readinesse anon. . . . III. iii. 57. 9
To scale the skyes and *put* Jove from his right: . . . III. vii. 47. 5
How many fownd'st thou such to *put* in thy record?' . . . III. vii. 56. 9
she *put* a Spright to rule the carcas dead; . . . III. viii. 7. 9
Thus was the ape . . . *put* into Malbeccoes cape. . . . III. ix. 31. 9
mickle perill to bee *put* to shame. . . . III. x. 39. 4
for her sake He then did *put,* . . . III. xi. 33. 9
put away remembrance of late teene; . . . III. xii. 40. 7
he *put* his spurres unto his steed, . . . IV. i. 41. 1
Did privily *put* coles unto his secret fire. . . . IV. ii. 11. 9
in this prison *put* him here with me; . . . IV. xii. 10. 6
So first the right he *put* into one scale, . . . V. ii. 46. 3
put two wrongs together to be tride, . . . V. ii. 48. 3
some hath *put* to shame, . . . V. iv. 29. 9
put to that base service of her band, . . . V. iv. 32. 7
put before his lap a napron white, . . . V. v. 20. 8
all the Temple *put* in jeopardy Of flaming, . . . V. vii. 14. 8
Mal was now *put* in: . . . V. ix. 26. 5
Whom she did *put* to death, deceived like a foole. . . . V. xi. 25. 9
they found A ship all readie . . . To *put* to sea, . . . V. xii. 4. 3
put away proud looke and usage sterne, . . . VI. i. 40. 8
to frolicke, and to *put* away The pensive fit . . . VI. iii. 9. 2
put them all about himselfe unfit, . . . VI. v. 8. 6
T' amend what was amisse, and *put* in right aray. . . . VI. v. 10. 9
Were vanquished, and *put* to foule disgrace; . . . VI. vii. 21. 5
'Here in this bottle . . . 'I *put* the tears . . . VI. viii. 24. 2
in this bag . . . I *put* repentaunce, . . . VI. viii. 24. 5
all which I *put* in fals out anon, . . . VI. viii. 24. 7

Put—*Continued.*
did it *put* on Coridons instead: . . . VI. ix. 42. 8
Bending her horned browes, did *put* her back; . . . VII. vi. 12. 6
So was the Titanesse *put* downe and whist, . . . VII. vii. 59. 6
put you in mind Of that proud mayd, . . . *Am.* xxviii. 7
Putrify. The inner parts now gan to *putrify,* . . . VI. vi. 5. 4
Putteth. he *putteth* on What shape he list . . . *Hub.* 1289
Putting. *putting* all In readinesse, forth to the Towne-gate went; . . . V. iv. 50. 1
putting spurres unto her fiery beast, . . . V. vi. 39. 2
Putting his puissaunce forth, pursu'd so hard, . . . VI. xii. 30. 3
Puttock. a *Puttocke* having spyde in sight A gentle Faulcon . V. v. 15. 1
Puttocks. *Puttockes,* all in plumes arayd; . . . II. xi. 11. 5
Puttocks'. with long nayles over-raught, Like *puttocks* clawes; V. xii. 30. 3
Pylades. *Pylades* and Orestes by his syde; . . . IV. x. 27. 4
Pylian. that sage *Pylian* syre, . . . II. ix. 48. 4
Pypt. *See* **Piped.**
Pyramids. Nylus nurslings their *Pyramides* faire; . . . *Ro.* ii. 4
with *Pyramides* to heaven aspired, . . . *Ti.* 408
Their huge *Pyramids,* which do heaven threat. . . . *Com. Son.* iii. 8
Pyrochles. '*Pyrochles* is his name, . . . II. iv. 41. 2
That shall *Pyrochles* well requite, . . . II. iv. 45. 8
Pyrochles does with Guyon fight, . . . II. v. Arg.
who so bound it findes, As did *Pyrochles,* . . . II. v. 1. 9
dismayd with horror of that dint *Pyrochles* was, . . . II. v. 8. 2
'Fly, O *Pyrochles!* fly the dreadfull warre . . . II. v. 16. 1
streight defyde Both Guyon and *Pyrochles;* . . . II. v. 19. 4
he would algates with *Pyrochles* fight, . . . II. v. 20. 2
Now gan *Pyrochles* wex as wood as hee, . . . II. v. 20. 6
did provoke Against *Pyrochles,* . . . II. v. 21. 2
Whiles sad *Pyrochles* lies on sencelesse ground, . . . II. v. 36. 6
On him, that did *Pyrochles* deare dismay: . . . II. v. 38. 7
He with *Pyrochles* sharp debatement made: . . . II. vi. 39. 2
His owne deare Lord *Pyrochles* in sad plight, . . . II. vi. 43. 4
Pyrochles, O Pyrochles! what is thee betyde?' . . . II. vi. 43. 9
'Ah! be it,' (said he) 'from *Pyrochles* farre . . . II. vi. 44. 6
To see *Pyrochles* there so rudely rage; . . . II. vi. 48. 7
'*Pyrochles!* what is this I see? . . . II. vi. 49. 1
Whom when *Pyrochles* saw, . . . II. viii. 12. 1
fiers *Pyrochles,* lacking his owne sword, . . . II. viii. 19. 1
Pyrochles, should I lend The same to thee, . . . II. viii. 21. 7
Pyrochles gan reply the second tyme, . . . II. viii. 30. 1
to *Pyrochles* many strokes he told; . . . II. viii. 41. 4
ever at *Pyrochles* when he smitt, . . . II. viii. 43. 1
suffred rash *Pyrochles* waste his ydle might. . . . II. viii. 48. 9
Pyrochles'. rash *Pyrochles* varlett, Atin hight, . . . II. v. 25. 4
Pyrrha. stone; Such as . . . Were throwne by *Pyrrha* and Deucalione: . . . V. Pr. 2. 7
Pyrrhus. The same, which *Pyrrhus* . . . could not tame, . . . *Ro.* xxi. 1
Queene Of Amazons, whom *Pyrrhus* did destroy, . . . II. iii. 31. 6
Pythias. Damon and *Pythias,* whom death could not sever: . IV. x. 27. 6
Pyracmon. Farre passing Bronteus or *Pyracmon* great, . . . IV. v. 37. 2

Q

Quadrate. twixt them both a *quadrate* was the base, . . . II. ix. 22. 6
Quaffing. *quaffing* glad, Pourd out his life . . . II. vii. 52. 7
Quail. the budde eke needes must *quaile;* . . . *S.C.* N. 91
To drive him to despaire, and quite to *quaile,* . . . I. ix. 49. 5
Withouten sword or shield, an hoste to *quayle?* . . . II. iii. 16. 7
did he never *quaile,* Ne backward shrinke, . . . II. viii. 35. 6
her prowd portaunce . . . now did *quaile:* . . . III. ii. 27. 4
thinking for to make her stubborne corage *quayle.* . . . III. viii. 40. 9
so to see him made her heart to *quaile;* . . . IV. iii. 46. 7
made ech member quake, and manly hart to *quayle.* . . . IV. vi. 22. 9
quaile in conquest of that land of gold. . . . IV. xi. 22. 5
his force to shrincke And rage to *quaile,* . . . IV. xii. 34. 2
Quailed. furious fitts at earst quite weren *quaild:* . . . II. iv. 14. 4
all her sences with abashment quite were *quayld.* . . . III. viii. 34. 9
Quaint. With *queint* Bellona in her equipage! . . . *S.C.* O. 114
Fashion'd with *queint* devises, never seene In Court . . . *Hub.* 673
kindling new his corage seeming *queint,* . . . II. v. 11. 4
nothing *quaint* Nor 'sdeignfull of so homely fashion, . . . III. vii. 10. 5
thousand spots of colours *queint* elect, . . . III. vii. 22. 5
everie look was coy and wondrous *quaint,* . . . IV. i. 5. 7
In *quyent* disguise, full hard to be descride: . . . IV. iv. 39. 3
his uncouth guise and usage *quaint* . . . IV. vii. 45. 1
nor hart could wish for any *queint* device, . . . IV. x. 22. 8
in *queint* disguise . . . doest maske thy royall blood, . . . V. vii. 21. 1
never had acquainted beene With such *queint* usage, . . . VI. ix. 35. 2
Quake. thinking yet on her I burne and *quake;* . . . *Pet.* vi. 2
His wonderous weight made the ground to *quake,* . . . *S.C.* F. 219
the Heavens did *quake* his verse to here. . . . *S.C.* O. 60
Seest thou not how all places *quake* and quiver, . . . *Gn.* 340
so did he *quake;* . . . *Hub.* 964
The Ape, that earst did nought but chill and *quake,* . . . *Hub.* 993
whereat he gan to *quake,* . . . I. i. 43. 3
of himselfe he ofte for feare would *quake,* . . . I. ii. 10. 7
everie beast for feare of him did fly, and *quake.* . . . I. vi. 24. 9
might her pitteous hart be seene to pant and *quake.* . . . I. vii. 20. 9
stoutest heart, I weene, could cause to *quake:* . . . I. vii. 52. 4
to shake The stedfast globe of earth, as it for feare did *quake.* I. viii. 23. 9
trembling every joynt, did inly *quake,* . . . I. ix. 24. 8
cold that makes the hart to *quake,* . . . I. ix. 44. 7
his hand did *quake* And tremble . . . I. ix. 51. 3
That made the Redcrosse knight nigh *quake* for feare, . . . I. xi. 15. 8
feigning then in every limb to *quake* . . . II. i. 9. 3
that boaster gan to *quake,* . . . II. iii. 18. 8

Quake—*Continued.*
I *quake* and tremble over-all.' . . . II. iii. 44. 7
seemd to tremble evermore and *quake;* . . . II. xi. 22. 5
As if she had a fever fitt, did *quake,* . . . III. ii. 5. 4
Which all that while shee felt to pant and *quake,* . . . III. ii. 42. 8
The feends do *quake* when any him to them does name. . . . III. iii. 12. 9
make The warlike Mertians for feare to *quake:* . . . III. iii. 30. 5
whose victorious Exployts made Rome to *quake;* . . . III. iii. 54. 8
seemd for feare to *quake* in every lim, . . . III. viii. 15. 8
the darts . . . he shooke, that all did *quake,* . . . III. xii. 23. 6
Anon she gan perceive the house to *quake,* . . . III. xii. 37. 1
everie limbe that touched her did *quake;* . . . IV. i. 5. 8
He felt his hart for very paine to *quake,* . . . IV. v. 44. 5
made ech member *quake,* and manly hart to quayle. . . . IV. vi. 22. 9
gan her heart to faint, and *quake,* and earne, . . . IV. xii. 24. 4
The yron man, . . . did inly chill and *quake,* . . . V. vi. 9. 6
her heart did *quake* For very ruth, . . . V. vii. 36. 5
whylome wont to doe so many *quake,* . . . V. ix. 35. 8
Did *quake* to heare, and nigh asunder brast: . . . V. xi. 28. 5
Began to *quake* and tremble with dismay; . . . V. xii. 41. 5
every joynt for dread of death did *quake,* . . . VI. vi. 29. 7
still did lie as dead, and *quake,* and quiver, . . . VI. vi. 32. 3
Her heart does *quake,* . . . VI. viii. 40. 6
dreadfull thunder-claps (that make them *quake*) . . . VII. vii. 23. 8
Yet did he *quake* and quiver, like to quell, . . . VII. vii. 42. 3
Hercules two pillors . . . Did make to *quake* . . . *Proth.* 149
Quaked. *See* **Quook.**
all the Pallace *quaked* at the stound, . . . *Hub.* 1353
The fearefull Dame all *quaked* at the sight, . . . I. vi. 28. 1
all the castle *quaked* from the grownd, . . . I. viii. 5. 2
oftentimes he *quakt,* and fainted oftentimes. . . . I. ix. 48. 9
the stiffe beame *quaked* as affrayd, . . . I. xi. 20. 5
quaked under their so hideous masse; . . . III. ix. 50. 6
Quakes. Gorgon, . . . At which Cocytus *quakes,* . . . I. i. 37. 9
Which, quitt from death, yet *quakes* in every lim . . . I. vi. 10. 8
all the forest *quakes* to heare him rore: . . . II. viii. 42. 7
Quaking. *quaking* hands, and other signes of feare: . . . I. iii. 12. 6
inly *quaking,* seem'd as reft of sense . . . VII. vi. 25. 4
Qualified. in short space he has them *qualifyde,* . . . II. vi. 51. 8
Quality. stryfull mind and diverse *qualitee* . . . II. ii. 13. 5
With two companions of like *qualitie,* . . . IV. i. 32. 7
Of sundry kindes and sundry *quality;* . . . VI. xi. 27. 2
Quantity. shortly grew into so great *quantitie,* . . . II. xii. 62. 4

Quarrel. to the ground the idle *quarrell* fell: . . . . II. xi. 24. 8
his hands Discharged of his bow and deadly *quar'le,* . . . . II. xi. 33. 8
In better *quarell* then defence of right, ... III. x. 28. 4
Perhaps I may all further *quarrell* end, ... V. i. 25. 6
tooke in hand her *quarrell* to maintaine; . . . . VI. i. 33. 2
A wrongfull *quarrell* to maintaine by fight; . . . . VI. vi. 35. 6
Quarrels. unquiet strife . . . great *quarrels* wrought, ... IV. ii. 37. 4
Quarry. The stone-dead *quarrey* falls so forciblye, ... II. xi. 43. 3
The *quarry* throwes to ground with fell despight, ... III. vii. 39. 5
Her from the *quarrey* he away doth drive, ... V. iv. 42. 8
Whilest they together for the *quarrey* strove, ... VI. ii. 20. 2
Quart. Camber did possesse the Westerne *quart,* . . . . . . II. x. 14. 4
Quarter. thereof nigh one *quarter* sheard away; . . . . II. vi. 31. 4
Quartered. He bore a bloodie Crosse that *quartred* all the field.' II. i. 18. 9
in gilden armes, with azure band *Quartred* athwart, ... VI. ii. 44. 8
Quarters. *See* **Three-quarters.**
Is not enough fowre *quarters* of a man, ... II. iii. 16. 6
Quayed. Therewith his sturdie corage soon was *quayd,* . . . I. viii. 14. 8
Quean. Regardlesse of that *queane* so base and vilde . . . . IV. viii. 28. 8
Queen. *Queene* of land and sea her selfe she made. . . . . . *Ro.* xx. 11
Colours meete to clothe a mayden *Queene?* . . . . *S.C.* F. 132
Of fayre Elisa, *Queene* of shepheardes all, ... *S.C.* Ap. 34
Yclad in Scarlot, like a mayden *Queene,* . . . . *S.C.* Ap. 57
his *Queene* attone Was Lady Flora, ... *S.C.* May 30
Well mought it beseme any harvest *Queene.* . . . . *S.C.* Au. 36
The shepheard of Ida that judged beauties *Queene.* . . . . . *S.C.* Au. 138
The *Queene* of hell to move as easily, ... *Gn.* 462
I late was wont to raine as *Queene,* . . . . *T.M.* 179
the Mother of delight, And *Queene* of beautie, ... *T.M.* 398
let the dreadfull *Queene* Of Darkenes deepe come . . . . . . *D.* 19
Ah! my loves *queene,* . . . . *Col.* 170
To the last praises of this Faery *Queene;* . . . . *Ded. Son.* ii. 10
Both for your nearnes to that Faerie *Queene* . . . . *Ded. Son.* xi. 6
to draw the semblant trew Of beauties *Queene,* . . . . *Ded. Son.* xvii. 6
(That greatest Glorious *Queene* of Faery lond) . . . . I. i. 3. 3
of beautie soveraigne *Queene,* Fayre Venus, ... I. i. 48. 1
A mayden *Queene* that shone as Titans ray, ... I. iv. 8. 5
sad Proserpina, the *Queene* of hell; . . . . I. iv. 11. 2
That made her selfe a *Queene,* and crownd to be; . . . . . . I. iv. 12. 2
great *Queene,* . . . Commaunded them their fury to refraine; I. iv. 40. 5
So be, O *Queene!* you equall favour showe.' . . . . I. iv. 42. 7
At last forth comes that far renowmed *Queene:* . . . . I. v. 5. 1
he goeth to that soveraine *Queene;* . . . . I. v. 16. 1
up, dreary Dame, of darknes *Queene!* . . . . I. v. 24. 1
daring tempt the *Queene* of heaven to sin; . . . . I. v. 35. 2
Do worship her as *Queene* with olive girlond cround. . . . . I. vi. 13. 9
the Faery *Queene* it brought To Faerie lond, ... I. vii. 36. 8
th' onely daughter of a King and *Queene,* . . . . I. vii. 43. 3
Gloriane, great *Queene* of glory bright, ... I. vii. 46. 6
at her parting said, She *Queene* of Faeries hight. . . . . . I. ix. 14. 9
'O happy *Queene* of Faeries! . . . . I. ix. 16. 6
Of that great *Queene* may well gaine worthie grace, ... I. ix. 17. 7
In which that fairest Faery *Queene* doth dwell, ... I. x. 58. 3
Twixt that great faery *Queene* and Paynim king, ... I. xi. 7. 4
aged *Queene,* Arayd in antique robes . . . . I. xii. 5. 1
Did seeme . . . a goodly maiden *Queene.* . . . . I. xii. 8. 9
That godly King and *Queene* did passionate, ... I. xii. 16. 2
Backe to retourne to that great Faery *Queene,* . . . . I. xii. 18. 6
Unto his Faery *Queene* backe to retourne; . . . . I. xii. 41. 8
To serve againe his soveraine Elfin *Queene,* . . . . II. i. 1. 6
revive Fresh memory in me of that great *Queene,* . . . . . . II. ii. 40. 2
Great and most glorious virgin *Queene* alive, ... II. ii. 40. 3
as that famous *Queene* Of Amazons, ... II. iii. 31. 5
'Shee is the mighty *Queene* of Faery, ... II. ix. 4. 1
To serve that *Queene* with al my powre and might. . . . . . . II. ix. 7. 4
I would assay Thy name, O soveraine *Queene!* . . . . II. x. 3. 9
Thy name, O soveraine *Queene!* . . . . II. x. 4. 1
Alma, like a virgin *Queene* most bright, ... II. xi. 2. 6
Unto his Faery *Queen* he might present: . . . . III. i. 2. 6
O soveraine *Queene!* whose prayse I would endyte, ... III. ii. 3. 4
Which long'd to Angela, the Saxon *Queene,* . . . . III. iii. 58. 8
so faire a blossome bare, As thee, O *Queene!* . . . . III. iv. 3. 8
His Faery *Queene,* for whom he did complaine, ... III. iv. 54. 7
that his Faery *Queene* were such as shee; . . . . III. iv. 54. 8
that cruell *Queene* avengeresse, ... III. viii. 20. 6
that sacred Saint my soveraigne *Queene,* . . . . IV. Pr. 4. 2
The *Queene* of love, and Prince of peace . . . . IV. Pr. 4. 9
For Chian folke to pourtraict beauties *Queene,* . . . . IV. v. 12. 7
to the *Queene* of beautie close did call, ... IV. v. 26. 4
The *Queene* of beautie, and of love the mother, ... IV. x. 29. 6
Queene of beautie and of grace, ... IV. x. 44. 1
queene of th' ayre, ... IV. x. 47. 7
by his side his *Queene* with coronall, ... IV. xi. 11. 5
Did to the Faery *Queene* her way addresse, ... V. i. 4. 2
That soveraine *Queene,* that mightie Emperesse, ... V. i. 4. 5
The semblant of this false by his faire beauties *Queene.* . . . V. iii. 19. 9
Queene of Amazons, in armes well tride . . . . V. iv. 33. 5
Ere long their *Queene* her selfe . . . Came forth . . . . . . V. iv. 36. 8
a *Queene,* and come of Princely kynd, ... V. v. 41. 5
earnest suit she . . . had made Unto her *Queene,* . . . . . . V. v. 54. 3
I Doe serve a *Queene* . . . . V. viii. 16. 7
a mayden *Queene* of high renowne, ... V. viii. 17. 2
To have bene done against her Lady *Queene* . . . . V. viii. 24. 3
There shall ye see my soverayne Lady *Queene,* . . . . V. ix. 20. 6
foule blaspheme that *Queene* for forged guyle, ... V. ix. 25. 5
Unto the presence of that gratious *Queene;* . . . . V. ix. 27. 2
false Duessa, now untitled *Queene,* . . . . V. ix. 42. 8
to their *Queene* for judgement loudly call, ... V. ix. 49. 8
humbly gan that mightie *Queene* entreat . . . . V. x. 15. 8
Then taking humble leave of that great *Queene,* . . . . V. x. 17. 1

Queen—*Continued.*
Unto his soveraine *Queene* her suite for to commend. . . . . V. xi. 37. 9
O soveraine Lady *Queene?* . . . . VI. Pr. 6. 4
'The widow *Queene* my mother, . . . conceiving then great feare VI. ii. 29. 1
by the Faery *Queene* was on him layd, ... VI. x. 1. 4
the traine of beauties *Queene,* . . . . VI. x. 17. 5
the Faery *Queene* had long afore Bequeath'd . . . . VI. xii. 12. 4
soveraine *Queene* profest Of woods . . . . VII. vi. 38. 7
Supported her like to their soveraigne *Queene:* . . . . VII. vii. 34. 6
Not finishing her *Queene* of Faery, ... *Am.* xxxiii. 3
the daughter of the *Queene* of Love, ... *Am.* xxxix. 1
my sovereigne *Queene* most kind, ... *Am.* lxxiv. 7
Fit for the handmayd of the Faery *Queene.* . . . . *Am.* lxxx. 14
ye three handmayds of the Cyprian *Queene,* . . . . *Epith.* 103
Seeme lyke some mayden *Queene.* . . . . *Epith.* 158
There vertue raynes as *Queene* in royal throne, ... *Epith.* 194
His harts enshrined saint, his heavens *queene,* . . . . *H.L.* 215
her they crowne their Goddesse and their *Queene,* . . . . . . *H.L.* 292
great Goddesse! *Queene* of Beauty, ... *H.B.* 15
thy soveraine might, O Cyprian *Queene!* . . . . *H.B.* 55
A pallace fit for such a virgin *Queene.* . . . . *H.B.* 126
O great Beauties *Queene,* . . . . *H.B.* 267
As King and *Queene,* the heavens Empire sway; . . . . *H.H.B.* 56
Clad like a *Queene* in royall robes, ... *H.H.B.* 185
faire Venus, that is *Queene* of love, ... *Proth.* 96
Beseeming well the bower of anie *Queene,* . . . . *Proth.* 170
Queen-apples. seeke for *Queene-apples* unrype, ... *S.C.* Jun. 43
Queene-apples, and red Cherries from the tree, ... VII. vi. 43. 6
Queen's. Whereon the Faery *Queenes* pourtract was writt,) . . II. viii. 43. 3
Queens. Like virgin *Queenes,* with laurell garlands cround . . *T.M.* 309
Royall lynage . . . Of ancient Kinges and *Queenes,* . . . . . I. i. 5. 4
As the proud Persian *Queenes* accustomed. . . . . III. i. 41. 4
Kings, *Queenes,* Lords, Ladies, ... III. xi. 46. 1
queint usage, fit for *Queenes* and Kings, ... VI. ix. 35. 2
Queint. *See* **Quaint.**
Quell. Winters wrath beginnes to *quell,* . . . . *S.C.* Mar. 8
Such joy he had their stubborne harts to *quell,* . . . . I. vi. 26. 7
bent his enimy to *quell,* . . . . I. vi. 43. 3
so extremely did the buffe him *quell,* . . . . I. xi. 24. 7
They heapt huge strokes the scorned life to *quell,* . . . . . II. ii. 20. 5
Whose father Hercules in Fraunce did *quell,* . . . . II. x. 11. 7
dint of steele his carcas could not *quell;* . . . . III. vii. 35. 8
winnes the prize from all, And Artegall doth *quell.* . . . . . IV. iv. Arg.
him likewise with that same speare he eke did *quell.* . . . . IV. iv. 19. 9
Much did his words the gentle Ladie *quell,* . . . . V. iii. 16. 8
From that sad land where he his syre did *quell,* . . . . . . V. x. 11. 4
ere he could recov'r, he did him *quell,* . . . . VI. x. 36. 5
'How could the death dare ever her to *quell?* . . . . VI. xi. 29. 6
That monstrous Beast by finall force to *quell,* . . . . VI. xii. 22. 7
Yet did he quake and quiver, like to *quell,* . . . . VII. vii. 42. 3
Quelled. wherewith she *queld* The salvage beastes . . . . . . II. iii. 29. 3
when his cruell foes he *queld.* . . . . II. vii. 40. 9
Eftesoones their stubborne corages were *queld,* . . . . II. xii. 40. 4
At sight thereof she was with terror *queld,* . . . . IV. x. 55. 5
in that same day when Jove those Gyants *quelled:* . . . . . . V. i. 9. 9
their faint harts with senselesse horrour *queld,* . . . . . . V. iii. 26. 3
She comming forth . . . was greatly *queld,* . . . . V. xi. 26. 3
Was with his ghastly count'nance nothing *queld;* . . . . . . V. xii. 16. 7
hearts dismay and inward dolour *queld,* . . . . VI. i. 18. 3
kept downe, till he be throughly *queld.* . . . . VI. xii. 30. 9
Yet with the sight thereof was almost *queld;* . . . . VII. vi. 25. 3
Quelling. *See* **Heart-quelling.**
Queme. Such merimake holy Saints doth *queme,* . . . . *S.C.* May 15
Quench. shoure Gan *quench* the glystering flame. . . . . . . *Bel.*[1] ix. 12
dew . . . gan *quench* those precious flames; . . . . *Bel.*[2] xi. 12
Adowne thy cheeke, to *quenche* thy thristye payne. . . . . . . *S.C.* Ap. 8
Which when they thinken agayne to *quenche,* . . . . *S.C.* S. 88
alwayes flow to *quench* his thirstie heate. . . . . *Gn.* 120
quench the flame of furious despight, ... I. v. 14. 5
grace . . . doth *quench* the brond of hellish smart, ... I. ix. 53. 7
The sparks soone *quench,* . . . . II. iv. 35. 7
now *quench* thy whott emboyling wrath: . . . . II. v. 18. 5
Therein did often *quench* his thristy heat, ... II. v. 30. 6
So easie was to *quench* his flamed minde . . . . II. vi. 8. 6
quench the brond of his conceived yre: . . . . II. vi. 27. 6
Yet nought can *quench* mine inly flaming syde, ... II. vi. 44. 3
To seeke young men to *quench* her flaming thrust, ... III. vii. 50. 2
To *quench* the flames which she had tyn'd before, ... III. x. 13. 3
In generation seeke to *quench* their inward fire. . . . . . . IV. x. 46. 9
Offred him drinke to *quench* his thirstie heat, ... VI. ix. 6. 8
So for to *quench* his fire . . . . VI. ix. 34. 9
Thinking to *quench* her thirst at the next brooke: . . . . . . *Am.* lxvii. 8
To *quench* the flame which they in burning fynd; . . . . *H.L.* 102
nought may *quench* his infinite desyre, ... *H.L.* 202
quench the light of your bright shyning starre. . . . . . . *H.B.* 175
Sith now that heat is quenched, *quench* my blame, ... *H.H.L.* 18
Quenched. *See* **Out-quenched.**
Their fervent appetites they *quenched* had, ... I. xii. 15. 2
it should not be *quenched* day nor night, ... I. xii. 37. 8
broke his wanton darts, and *quenched* bace desyre. . . . . . . II. iii. 23. 9
she sought To kindle his *quencht* fyre, ... II. v. 19. 9
the flames which me consume,' . . . 'Ne can be *quencht,* . . . II. vi. 49. 9
having *quencht* her burning fier-brands, ... II. xi. 47. 5
Moystened their fierie beames, . . . yet *quenched* not; . . . . II. xii. 78. 8
whose faire eyes, like lamps of *quenched* fire, ... III. v. 29. 3
Out of the flames which he had *quencht* whylere, ... III. x. 17. 3
neither may This fire be *quencht* by any witt, ... III. xi. 23. 7
quenched quite like a consumed torch, ... III. xii. 42. 8
quenched is with Cupids greater flame: . . . . IV. ix. 2. 2
Ne can be *quenched* quite, ... VII. vii. 24. 2

Quenched—*Continued.*
Sith now that heat is *quenched,* quench my blame, ... *H.H.L.* 18
th' Aire . . . Never consum'd, nor *quencht* with mortall hands; *H.H.B.* 40
Quenching. *Quenching* the gasping furrowes thirst with rayne? *S.C.* Ap. 6
Quenchless. Phlegeton with *quenchles* flames doth burne; . *Gn.* 622
Quest. thrive in that unluckie *quest;* . . . . *Hub.* 916
'Her well beseemes that *Quest,'* . . . . III. vii. 53. 1
what wight he was, and what his *quest,* . . . . III. viii. 45. 2
the rest, which in this *Quest* proceed, ... III. viii. 50. 8
bound Upon an hard adventure yet in *quest,* . . . . IV. vi. 42. 3
Resolved to pursue his former *quest;* . . . . IV. ix. 17. 5
Artegall . . . Irenaes *quest* pursewed; . . . . V. i. Arg.
To follow his old *quest,* . . . . V. iv. 20. 9
Had him misfalne in his adventurous *quest;* . . . . V. vi. 4. 2
Nor hold from suite of his avowed *quest,* . . . . V. viii. 3. 2
streight way went On his first *quest,* . . . . V. xi. 36. 3
Sir Artegall, return'd from his late *quest,* . . . . V. xii. 38. 3
Atchiev'd so hard a *quest,* as few before; . . . . VI. i. 5. 8
'What is that *quest,'* . . . . VI. i. 6. 8
then to his first *quest* he passed forth along. . . . . . . VI. i. 47. 9
on his former way To follow his first *quest,* . . . . . . VI. ii. 3. 6
To have thy presence in my present *quest,* . . . . VI. ii. 37. 2
sleepe all night through weary travell of his *quest.* . . . . VI. iii. 9. 9
as he was pursuing of his *quest,* . . . . VI. iii. 20. 1
went onward still On his first *quest,* . . . . VI. viii. 30. 8
In that same *quest* which fortune on him cast, ... VI. ix. 2. 7
If he for slouth forslackt so famous *quest.* . . . . VI. ix. 3. 5
Although his *quest* were farre afore him gon: . . . . . . VI. ix. 12. 3
His former *quest,* so full of toile and paine: . . . . VI. x. 2. 2
Another *quest,* another game in vew He hath, ... VI. x. 2. 3
delayd This gentle knight from sewing his first *quest,* . . . VI. xii. 2. 2
Tho gan Sir Calidore him to advize Of his first *quest,* . . . VI. xii. 12. 2
He went forth on his *quest,* . . . . VI. xii. 13. 9
Question. Sike *question* ripeth up cause of newe woe, ... *S.C.* S. 13
first gan *question,* whether should assay . . . . *Hub.* 997
Than *question* made of his calamitie, ... *D.* 90
first was *question* made, which of those Knights . . . . . IV. v. 7. 1
staying nought to *question* from aloofe, ... IV. x. 9. 8
not for those she now in *question* came, ... V. ix. 40. 6
to *question* of her present woe, ... VI. viii. 50. 6
gan to *question* streight, how she it knew? . . . . VI. xii. 18. 2
Questioned. Ne let thy learning *question'd* be of anie. . . . . *Hub.* 524
would have *questiond* more; . . . . II. v. 37. 2
Cymochles of her *questioned* Both what she was, ... II. vi. 9. 2
Till he had *questioned* the cause of their dissent. . . . . . V. iv. 6. 9
Though also those mote *question'd* be aright, ... V. ix. 40. 7
the theeves them *questioned* againe, ... VI. xi. 39. 5
Quetch. That once he could not move, nor *quich* at all; . . . V. ix. 33. 7
Quich. *See* **Quetch.**
Quick. Might see the moving of some *quicke,* . . . . *S.C.* Mar. 74
busying his *quicke* eies her face to view, ... I. ii. 26. 6
With windy Nitre and *quick* Sulphur fraught, ... I. vii. 13. 3
wondrous *quick* and persaunt was his spright, ... I. x. 47. 5
lay, halfe dead, halfe *quick;* . . . . II. i. 39. 4
That nought mote hinder his *quicke* prejudize: . . . . . . II. ix. 49. 7
their entrailles, full of *quick* Brimston, ... II. x. 26. 4
he called Elfe, to weet *Quick,* . . . . II. x. 71. 2
turning *quicke* aside His light-foot beast, ... II. xi. 25. 5
Those feeling words so neare the *quicke* did goe, ... III. xi. 15. 7
with readie *quicke* foresight . . . . IV. viii. 44. 8
Calidore, that was more *quicke* of sight . . . . VI. i. 38. 5
Quicken. To *quicken* . . . The stonie joynts of these old walls *Ro.* xxv. 6
Quickened. *quickned* the dull spright with musicall comfort. . II. v. 31. 9
Doe life conceive and *quickned* are by kynd: . . . . III. vi. 8. 6
Quickeneth. The duller earth it *quickneth* with delight, . . . *H.B.* 51
Quickening. *See* **Drink-quickening.**
quickning faith, that earst was woxen weake, ... I. v. 12. 3
Quickly. The Foxe was glad, and *quickly* did agree: . . . . . *Hub.* 102
O! bid me *quicklie* come to thee, ... *Ti.* 307
her awaking bad her *quickly* dight, ... *Ti.* 639
they be all but vaine, and *quickly* fade; . . . . *D.* 395
rouze thy feathers *quickly,* Daniell, ... *Col.* 424
'Goe, caytive Elfe, him *quickly* overtake, ... I. v. 11. 1
he her *quickly* reared up againe: . . . . I. vii. 24. 2
him the Squire made *quickly* to retrate, ... I. viii. 12. 7
The light-foot Squyre her *quickly* turnd around, ... I. viii. 25. 7
can *quickly* ryse From off the earth, ... I. xi. 23. 7
away is *quickly* gone . . . . II. i. 13. 2
he *quickly* does him dight, ... II. v. 38. 1
Forth launched *quickly* as she did desire, ... II. vi. 20. 4
then the Faery *quickly* raught His poynant speare, ... III. i. 5. 3
Betwixt her feeble armes her *quickly* keight, ... III. ii. 30. 4
him likewise he *quickly* downe did smight, ... IV. iv. 21. 3
he her *quickly* stayd, and forst to wend withall. . . . . . V. i. 22. 9
Whom having *quickly* arm'd againe anew, ... V. iii. 12. 2
'Goe, damzell, *quickly,* doe thy selfe addresse . . . . . . V. iv. 48. 4
quickly she it overpast, ... V. v. 45. 6
She *quickly* caught her sword, ... V. vi. 28. 9
'Leave, faytor, *quickely* that misgotten weft . . . . VI. i. 18. 7
Sternely did bid him *quickely* thence avaunt, ... VI. vi. 21. 2
Helpe *quickly* her to dight: . . . . *Epith.* 97
pure complexions, that shall *quickly* fade . . . . *H.B.* 67
Quick-moving. a *quicke moving* Spirit did arret . . . . . . III. viii. 7. 3
Quicksand. by the way there is a great *Quicksand,* . . . . . II. xii. 18. 1
That *quicksand* nigh with water covered; . . . . II. xii. 18. 6
It called was the *quickesand* of Unthriftyhed. . . . . II. xii. 18. 9
Quiet. *See* **Quietage.**
Sweete *quiet* harbours in his harmeless head, ... *Gn.* 134
In *quiet* rest his molten heart did steep, ... *Gn.* 245
drown'd in carelesse *quiet* deepe; . . . . *D.* 136

Quiet—*Continued.*
May come their happie *quiet* to molest; . . . . *D.* 284
cares finde *quiet!* . . . . *D.* 447
Abandon *quiet* home to seeke for it, ... *Col.* 686
carelesse *Quiet* lyes Wrapt in eternall silence . . . . I. i. 41. 8
layes the soule to sleepe in *quiet* grave? . . . . I. ix. 40. 7
we be come unto a *quiet* rode, ... I. xii. 42. 2
ended all her woe in *quiet* death. . . . . II. i. 56. 4
during their *quiet* treague, Into her lodging to repaire . . . II. ii. 33. 3
the *quiet* wombe Of his great Grandmother . . . . II. vii. 17. 1
their *quiet* government annoyd; . . . . II. x. 14. 8
Whose countries he redus'd to *quiet* state, ... II. x. 38. 7
Out of her *quiet* slomber did awake, ... III. i. 61. 8
Her teme at her commaundement *quiet* stands, ... III. iv. 42. 3
to the Castle gate approcht in *quiet* wise. . . . . III. ix. 9. 9
Out of his *quiet* slomber him abrade, ... III. xi. 8. 4
*In stead thereof sweet peace and *quiet* age . . . . IV. iii. 43. 5
Where they might hide their heads in *quiet* rest, ... IV. v. 32. 6
The bellowes noyse disturb'd his *quiet* rest, ... IV. v. 41. 4
his *quiet* slomber brake: . . . . IV. v. 44. 7
did her passed paines in *quiet* rest assoyle. . . . . IV. vii. 3. 9
to afflicted minds sweet rest and *quiet* sends. . . . . . . IV. x. 34. 9
Warn'd man and beast in *quiet* rest be shrowded, ... V. iv. 45. 3
troubled had their *quiet* loves delight: . . . . VI. iii. 21. 5
Ne once my minds unmoved *quiet* grieve; . . . . VI. ix. 22. 7
to love more deare This lowly *quiet* life . . . . VI. ix. 25. 9
in this *quiet* make you safer live.' . . . . VI. ix. 32. 8
in her snowy bosome boldly lay Their *quiet* heads, ... *H.L.* 290
Quietage. *See* **Age, Quiet.**
Instead thereof sweet peace and *quiet-age* . . . . IV. iii. 43. 5
Quieted. With gentle calme the world had *quieted,* . . . . . *Mui.* 50
all things *quieted,* . . . . V. iv. 46. 2
Quietly. By them the Sprite doth passe in *quietly,* . . . . . I. i. 40. 7
suffered them to passen *quietly;* . . . . I. v. 34. 8
And *quietly* doth hold it in his hand, ... VI. iv. 30. 3
Quietness. Bid strange mischance his *quietnes* to spill. . . . *Gn.* 248
closde her eyes with carelesse *quietnesse;* . . . . *D.* 257
joyous peace and *quietnesse* alway . . . . V. ix. 24. 7
Quiet's. How he may flow in *quiets* matchles treasour, ... *Gn.* 139
Quietsome. let the night be calme, and *quietsome,* . . . . . *Epith.* 326
Quight. *See* **Quit, Quite.**
Quill. holden scorne of homely shepheards *quill:* . . . . . . *S.C.* Jun. 67
To sadder times thou mayst attune thy *quill,* . . . . *S.C.* N. 35
their musicke matcheth Phoebus *quill.* . . . . *T.M.* 330
workes with loome, with needle, and with *quill.* . . . . . *Mui.* 272
Ne ever Shepheard sound his Oaten *quill* . . . . *D.* 325
Nought tooke I with me, but mine oaten *quill:* . . . . . . *Col.* 194
Albe he envie at my rustick *quill:* . . . . *Col.* 393
noblest swaine, That ever piped in an oaten *quill:* . . . . *Col.* 441
For thereunto doth need a golden *quill,* *Ded.Son.*xvi.10
Argument worthy of Maeonian *quill;* . . . . II. x. 3. 1
Presume so high to stretch mine humble *quill?* . . . . . . III. Pr. 3. 3
fethered with an unlucky *quill:* . . . . III. v. 20. 5
father Mole, whom Shepheards *quill* Renowmed hath . . . VII. vi. 36. 8
Meane-while, O Clio! lend Calliope thy *quill.* . . . . . . VII. vi. 37. 9
Her worth is written with a golden *quill,* . . . . *Am.* lxxxiv. 10
Painter . . . Which pictured Venus with so curious *quill,* . *H.H.B.* 212
Quilt. Th' embroder'd *quilt* she lightly up did lifte, ... III. i. 61. 3
Quilted. On his horse necke before the *quilted* sell, ... II. v. 4. 5
quilted uppon sattin white as milke; . . . . V. v. 2. 3
in a Jacket, *quilted* richly rare . . . . VI. vii. 43. 3
Quip. The more he laughes, and does her closely *quip,* . . . VI. vii. 44. 8
Quips. with sharp *quips* joy'd others to deface, ... *Hub.* 707
Quire. *See* **Choir.**
Quirinal. Upon her stomacke laid Mount *Quirinal,* . . . . . *Ro.* iv. 11
Quit. Nought from the Romane Empire might be *quight;* . . *Ro.* viii. 10
cast to *quitt* them from their bondage quight: . . . . . . *Van.* xi. 4
For nought mought they *quitten* him from decay, ... *S.C.* F. 213
now nill be *quitt* with baile nor borrowe. . . . . *S.C.* May 131
To *quite* it from the blacke bowre of sorrowe. . . . . . . *S.C.* S. 97
he never should be *quit,* nor stal'd. . . . . *Hub.* 1245
Untill he *quite* him of this guiltie blame. . . . . *Ti.* 230
To *quite* them ill, that me demeand so well: . . . . *Col.* 681
I his shield have *quit* from dying foe.' . . . . I. v. 11. 4
devise to *quitt* a thrall from such a plight? . . . . I. vi. 6. 9
Which, *quitt* from death, yet quakes in every lim . . . . . I. vi. 10. 8
his combred clubbe to *quight* Out of the earth, ... I. viii. 10. 4
How shall I *quite* the paynes ye suffer for my sake? . . . . I. viii. 26. 9
what I cannot *quite* requite with usuree. . . . . I. viii. 27. 9
double *quite* for that he on them spent; . . . . I. x. 37. 7
Till from her cursed foe thou have her freely *quitt.'* . . . . I. x. 63. 9
'how shall I *quight* The many favours . . . . I. x. 67. 1
fairely *quit* (**quite*) him of th' imputed blame; . . . . . II. i. 20. 2
Quit from that danger forth their course they kept; . . . . II. xii. 27. 1
meed, With which her soverain mercy thou doest *quight?* . III. v. 45. 2
wretched Lady, *quitt* from wofull state, ... III. xii. 39. 3
glad to be so *quit:* . . . . V. iv. 25. 2
To loose his shield, . . . But, when he could not *quite* it, . V. xi. 27. 8
Glad to be *quit* from that proud Tyrants awe, ... V. xii. 24. 3
to *quit* her with a better; . . . . VII. vi. 44. 2
Quite (*partial list*). *See* **Quit.**
With sodain fall to dust consumed *quight.* . . . . *Bel.*[2] iv. 14
faire greene Lawrell branch did *quite* decay. . . . . *Bel.*[2] ix. 14
rent this royall tree *quite* by the roote; . . . . *Pet.* iii. 12
and be *quite* undonne: . . . . *Ro.* xxii. 12
which injurious time hath *quite* outworne, ... *Ro.* xxvii. 6
Till that Barbarian hands it *quite* did spill, ... *Ro.* xxx. 10
to quitt them from their bondage *quight:* . . . . *Van.* xi. 4
thou leane, I *quite* forlorne: . . . . *S.C.* Ja. 47
The fayrest floure . . . Is faded *quite,* . . . . *S.C.* N. 76

Quod—*Continued.*
and loe (*quod* he) beholde, . . . *Bel.*[1] i. 9
Where is (*quod* she) this whilome honored face? . . . *Bel.*[1] viii. 5
What one is like (*quod* he) This . . . *Rev.* i. 9
loe, the sea (*quod* he) is now no more. . . . *Rev.* iv. 2
Vayne man, *quod* I, that hast but little priefe . . . *Am.* l. 5
Not so, *quod* I; . . . *Am.* lxxv. 9
(*quod* she) my sonne, how great the smart . . . *Epig.* iv. 35
Quook. *See* **Quaked.**
at the Lyons skin he inly *quooke;* . . . *Hub.* 1060
every member of his body *quooke.* . . . III. x. 24. 5
shooke And tottred, like two towres which through a tempest *quooke.* . . . V. viii. 9. 9
like an hazell wand it quivered and *quooke.* . . . VI. vii. 24. 9
all the world beneath for terror *quooke,* . . . VII. vi. 30. 8
Quoth. *See* **Quod.**
(*quoth* hee) . . . *Bel.*[2] i. 9
(*quoth* she) . . . *Bel.*[2] x. 5
(*quoth* he) . . . *S.C.* F. 127
(*quoth* she and with that gan weepe, . . . *S.C.* May 189
(*quoth* shee) . . . *S.C.* May 215
(*quoth* he) . . . *Hub.* 433, 545
(*quoth* he theretoo) . . . *Hub.* 999
(*quoth* she) . . . *Ti.* 22, 34
(*quoth* I) . . . *D.* 69, 78
quoth he, . . . *D.* 86, 183
(*quoth* he) . . . *Col.* 56, 88, 100, 163
(*Quoth* he) and each an end of singing made . . . *Col.* 179
is the sea (*quoth* Coridon) so fearfull? . . . *Col.* 200
(*quoth* he) . . . *Col.* 201
(*quoth* I) . . . *Col.* 236
(*quoth* he) . . . *Col.* 240
(then *quoth* Colin) . . . *Col.* 292
(*quoth* he) . . . *Col.* 304
more (*Quoth* he) abound . . . *Col.* 309
(*Quoth* he) as that same shepheard . . . *Col.* 331
(*quoth* he) . . . *Col.* 358
'Ah far be it (*quoth* Colin Clout) fro me, . . . *Col.* 464
(*quoth* he) . . . *Col.* 485, 590, 680, 749, 775
some celestiall rage Of Love (*quoth* Cuddy) . . . *Col.* 824
'Be well aware,' *quoth* then that Ladie milde, . . . I. i. 12. 1
'Yea but' (*quoth* she) 'the perill . . . I. i. 13. 1
'Fly, fly!' (*quoth* then The fearefull Dwarfe) . . . I. i. 13. 8
(*quoth* he) . . . I. i. 30. 5; 32. 1
Quoth then that aged man: . . . I. i. 33. 5
(*quoth* he,) . . . I. i. 43. 6; 52. 8
'Curse on that Cross,' (*quoth* then the Sarazin,) . . . I. ii. 18. 1
(*quoth* he,) . . . I. ii. 33. 1
'Say on, Fradubio, . . . *Quoth* then the Knight; . . . I. ii. 34. 2
(*quoth* he,) . . . I. ii. 43. 3
'The Lyon, . . . *Quoth* she, 'his princely puissance doth abate, I. iii. 7. 2
'Ah dearest Dame,' *quoth* then the Paynim bold, . . . I. iv. 41. 1
litle sweet Oft tempred is,' (*quoth* she,) 'with . . . I. iv. 46. 4
'O! but I feare the fickle freakes,' (*quoth* shee) . . . I. iv. 50. 1
'Why, dame,' (*quoth* he) 'what oddes can ever bee, . . . I. iv. 50. 3
(*quoth* she) . . . I. iv. 50. 5
Quoth she, . . . I. v. 26. 7
'Ah Dame, (*quoth* he) 'thou temptest me in vaine, . . . I. v. 42. 1
'Not so,' (*quoth* she) . . . I. v. 43. 1
(*quoth* he) 'well may I rew . . . I. vi. 36. 7
'Ah! dearest Lord,' (*quoth* she) 'how might that bee, . . . I. vi. 39. 1
'Ah! dearest dame,' (*quoth* hee) . . . I. vi. 39. 3
'Not far away,' (*quoth* he) . . . I. vi. 39. 7
'Tell on,' (*quoth* she) 'the wofull Tragedy, . . . I. vii. 24. 8
'Ah Lady deare,' *quoth* then the gentle knight, . . . I. vii. 40. 1
(*quoth* she) . . . I. vii. 41. 1, 5, 8
(*quoth* he) . . . I. vii. 41. 3, 7, 9
'To doe her die,' (*quoth* Una) 'were despight, . . . I. viii. 45. 7
'Full hard it is,' (*quoth* he) . . . I. ix. 6. 6
'Ah! courteous Knight,' (*quoth* she) . . . I. ix. 7. 8
'Dear Dame,' (*quoth* he) 'you sleeping sparkes awake, . . . I. ix. 8. 1

Quoth—*Continued.*
(*quoth* he) . . . I. ix. 26. 1, 5; 31. 3; 32. 5; 38. 1
'Who life did limit by almightie doome,' (*Quoth* he) . . . I. ix. 41. 7
(*quoth* she) . . . I. x. 11. 2; 16. 8; 50. 1
(*quoth* he) . . . I. x. 57. 1; 62. 1
*(*Quoth* he) as wretched, and liv'd in like paine. . . . I. x. 62. 4
(*quoth* he) . . . I. x. 63. 1; 64. 1; 67. 1
'Unhappy falls that hard necessity,' (*Quoth* he) . . . I. xii. 19. 2
(*quoth* he) . . . II. i. 11. 3; 12. 4
if that carelesse hevens,' (*quoth* she) 'despise . . . II. i. 36. 1
quoth he, 'death is an equall doome . . . II. i. 59. 1
(*quoth* he) 'thy destinies withstand My wrathfull will, . . . II. iii. 8. 3
'Who-so in pompe of prowd estate' (*quoth* she) 'Does swim, . . . II. iii. 40. 1
(*quoth* he) . . . II. iv. 17. 2; 36. 7; 43. 5
(*quoth* she) . . . II. vi. 23. 1
(*quoth* he) . . . II. vi. 49. 6; vii. 15. 1; 19. 6; 20. 1, 5
thou Money God,' (*quoth* hee) . . . II. vii. 39. 1
(*quoth* he) . . . II. vii. 60. 1; xii. 85. 6
(*quoth* she) . . . III. i. 28. 2; ii. 36. 1, 9
'Nought like,' (*quoth* shee) . . . III. ii. 45. 1
'Ah! read,' (*quoth* Britomart) 'how is she hight?' . . . III. iii. 56. 1
(*quoth* she) . . . III. iii. 56. 2
(*quoth* he) . . . III. v. 5. 2; 6. 7; 8. 1
'Her well beseemes that Quest,' (*quoth* Satyrane) . . . III. vii. 53. 1
(*quoth* he) . . . III. vii. 53. 4; 56. 8; viii. 49. 2; 50. 6; xi. 23. 5
(*quoth* hee) 'And I, . . . Will chalenge yond same other . . . IV. i. 35. 6
'Then tell,' (*quoth* Blandamour) 'and feare no blame: . . . IV. i. 48. 5
'I saw' (*quoth* she) 'a stranger knight, . . . IV. i. 48. 7
(*quoth* he) . . . IV. ii. 22. 3; 25. 5
(*quoth* she) 'the terme of each mans life . . . IV. ii. 52. 1
(*quoth* he) . . . IV. vi. 5. 1; 6. 1
declare,' (*Quoth* she) 'of all . . . IV. vii. 14. 2
(*quoth* she) . . . IV. vii. 14. 8; 19. 6
(*quoth* he) . . . IV. viii. 47. 1; 63. 6
(*quoth* she) 'a greater wrong remaines: . . . IV. ix. 38. 1
well-away!' (*quoth* hee, Bursting forth teares . . . V. i. 15. 1
(*quoth* he) . . . V. i. 19. 3; ii. 4. 1; 5. 1; iv. 17. 6; 18. 6; 28. 6; 33. 3; v. 39. 5
(*quoth* she) . . . V. vi. 10. 8; 16. 6
(*quoth* he) . . . V. vii. 19. 6
quoth she, . . . V. vii. 40. 1
(*quoth* he) . . . V. xi. 42. 3; 52. 7; 56. 1
'What is that quest,' (*quoth* then Sir Artegall) . . . VI. i. 6. 8
'The Blattant Beast' (*quoth* he) . . . VI. i. 7. 1
God you speed,' (*quoth* then Sir Artegall) . . . VI. i. 10. 6
(*Quoth* he) 'I hold it no indignity; . . . VI. i. 28. 2
'Cowherd!' (*quoth* she) . . . VI. i. 28. 5
(*quoth* he) . . . VI. iii. 39. 1; 40. 1; iv. 28. 6
(*quoth* he halfe wrothfully) . . . VI. vii. 16. 1
The bay (*quoth* she) is of the victours borne, . . . *Am.* xxix. 5
never blush, Cupid, *quoth* I, . . . *Epig.* iii. 7
'Whats this (*quoth* he) that gives so great a voyce . . . *Epig.* iv. 7

R

Rabblement. unfit for that rude *rabblement.* . . . *Hub.* 1270
A rude, mishapen, monstrous *rablement,* . . . I. vi. 8. 7
Heaped together in rude *rablement,* . . . I. xii. 9. 2
a monstrous *rablement* Of fowle misshapen wightes, . . . II. xi. 8. 1
Was, as the rest, a grysie *rablement;* . . . II. xi. 12. 3
Whome soone as that unruly *rablement* . . . did espye, . . . II. xi. 17. 7
mingled with the raskall *rablement,* . . . III. xi. 46. 3
Race. the greatnesse of the stately *race,* . . . *Bel.*[1] v. 7
in their cruell *race* They pincht the haunches . . . *Pet.* i. 8
So sprong her grace Of heavenly *race,* . . . *S.C.* Ap. 53
To renne hys dayly *race,* . . . *S.C.* Jul. 60
weary thys long lingring Phoebus *race.* . . . *S.C.* O. 3
ere that into the *race* We enter, . . . *Hub.* 122
runne on foote a *race,* . . . *Hub.* 744
anie Should of his *race* be voyd of infamie; . . . *Hub.* 1242
the honorable *race* Of mightie Peeres . . . *T.M.* 79
doth degenerate the noble *race,* . . . *T.M.* 436
A mightie Prince, of most renowmed *race,* . . . *Ti.* 184
Of all the *race* of silver-winged Flies . . . *Mui.* 17
of the *race* that all wild beastes do feare, . . . *D.* 123
She did excell, and seem'd of Angels *race,* . . . *D.* 213
robd her *race* of bountie quight. . . . *D.* 221

Race—*Continued.*
Of gentlest *race* that ever shepheard bore, . . . *As.* 2
heavenly borne, And of immortall *race,* . . . *Col.* 257
Go, gather up the reliques of thy *race;* . . . I. v. 24. 2
I the . . . roote of Duessaes *race.* . . . I. v. 27. 7
took her wonted way To ronne her timely *race,* . . . I. v. 44. 8
Satt downe to rest in middest of the *race:* . . . I. vii. 5. 4
wondrous faith, exceeding earthly *race,* . . . I. ix. 17. 4
Whom well she knew to spring from hevenly *race,* . . . I. x. 8. 7
faire ymp, sprong out from English *race,* . . . I. x. 60. 1
thou springst from ancient *race* Of Saxon kinges, . . . I. x. 65. 1
Titan rose to runne his daily *race;* . . . I. xi. 33. 2
He gan rencounter him in equall *race.* . . . II. i. 26. 5
Must now anew begin like *race* to ronne. . . . II. i. 32. 7
His *race* with reason, . . . he ofte did stay, . . . II. i. 34. 7
'So from immortall *race* he does proceede, . . . II. iv. 42. 1
'Most wretched woman and of wicked *race,* . . . II. vi. 33. 7
Like an huge Gyant of the Titans *race;* . . . II. vii. 41. 6
soveraine Queene! thy realme, and *race,* . . . II. x. 4. 1
Madan raignd, unworthie of his *race,* . . . II. x. 21. 1
Such as Laomedon of Phoebus *race* did breed. . . . II. xi. 19. 9
Cormoyraunts, with birds of ravenous *race,* . . . II. xii. 8. 5

Race—*Continued.*
Their banket houses burne; their buildings *race;* . . . . . II. xii. 83. 8
Be it worthy of thy *race* and royall sead, ... III. ii. 33. 4
all thy Citties they shall sacke and *race,* . . . . . III. iii. 34. 7
and bounteous *race* Of woman kind . . . . . III. v. 52. 7
Amphisa, who by *race* A Faerie was, ... III. vi. 4. 2
Retird their steeds, to ronne in even *race;* . . . . . III. viii. 18. 6
from whose *race* . . . was lineally extract; . . . . . III. ix. 38. 6
To have rencountred him in equall *race;* . . . . . IV. vi. 3. 2
More swift then Myrrh' or Daphne in her *race,* . . . . . IV. vii. 22. 8
Gainst wofull Niobes unhappy *race,* . . . . . IV. vii. 30. 8
tell their hidden *race,* . . . . . IV. xi. 40. 8
evermore some of the vertuous *race* Rose up, ... V. i. 1. 6
Return'd to heaven, whence she deriv'd her *race;* . . . . . V. i. 11. 4
drownes Lady Munera, Does *race* her castle quight. . . . . . V. ii. Arg.
of the *race* Of th' old Aegyptian Kings . . . . . V. vii. 2. 5
they both like *race* in equall justice runne. . . . . . V. vii. 4. 9
renound For noble courage and for hardie *race,* . . . . . V. viii. 36. 8
She first was bred, and borne of heavenly *race,* . . . . . V. x. 1. 8
borne and bred Of Gyants *race,* . . . . . V. x. 9. 2
meeting him right in the middle *race* . . . . . V. x. 34. 4
rooted all the relickes out Of that vilde *race,* . . . . . V. xi. 18, 7
Horrible, hideous, and of hellish *race,* . . . . . V. xi. 23. 4
'It is a Monster bred of hellishe *race,'* . . . . . VI. i. 7. 7
he deem'd him borne of noble *race:* . . . . . VI. ii. 5. 5
Of what degree and what *race* he is growne: . . . . . VI. iii. 1. 5
Him overtooke in middest of his *race;* . . . . . VI. iii. 25. 5
Some goodly person, and of gentle *race,* . . . . . VI. v. 36. 7
Doth she exceede the rest of all her *race;* . . . . . VI. x. 26. 6
Her antique *race* and linage ancient, ... VII. vi. 2. 2
some beast of strange and forraine *race* . . . . . VII. vi. 28. 7
all other beastes of bloody *race* . . . . . *Am.* xxxi. 5
The weary yeare his *race* now having run, ... *Am.* lxii. 1
After so long a *race* as I have run . . . . . *Am.* lxxx. 1
forth to run her mighty *race,* . . . . . *Epith.* 150
That same is Beautie, borne of heavenly *race.* . . . . . *H.L.* 112
loves to get Things like himselfe, and to enlarge his *race,* . . . . . *H.H.L.* 52
the daughters of all wemens *race,* . . . doth excell, ... *H.H.B.* 205

Raced. *See* **Rased.**
Crete will boast the Labyrinth, now *raced:* . . . . . *Ro.* ii. 8
hath our dwellings *raced* . . . . . *T.M.* 268
grieve that my remembrance quite is *raced* Out . . . . . *Ti.* 177
fowly *ras't,* that none the signes might see: . . . . . II. xii. 80. 4
quite from off the earth their memory be *raste?'* . . . . . III. iii. 43. 9
Great cities ransackt, and strong castles *rast;* . . . . . IV. i. 21. 7
lastly all that Castle quite he *raced,* . . . . . V. ii. 28. 1
Thinking at once both head and helmet to have *raced.* . . . . . V. v. 11. 9
but *Bon,* that once had written bin, Was *raced* out, ... V. ix. 26. 5
My cities sackt, and their sky-threating towres *Raced* . . . . . V. x. 23. 5

Race's. that brave *races* greatnes . . . . . *Bel.*[2] v. 7
Rack. his feet in fetters to an yron *racke.* . . . . . II. iv. 14. 9
Racked. fild with treasure *rackt* with robberies; . . . . . *Hub.* 1306

Rad. *See* **Read, Rode.**
good . . . may more notably be *rad,* . . . . . III. ix. 2. 3
by his grenning laughter mote farre off be *rad.* . . . . . IV. vii. 24. 9
Which was by him Belphebe rightly *rad.* . . . . . IV. vii. 46. 5
the courser whereuppon he *rad* Could swim . . . . . V. ii. 13. 8
'The tidings sad . . . will needs, I see, be *rad.* . . . . . V. vi. 10. 5
They knew them selves, and both their persons *rad;* . . . . . VI. i. 4. 7

Radegone. citty . . . of her owne name, she called *Radegone.* . V. iv. 35. 9
Radiant. thy bright *radiant* eyes shall plainely see . . . . . *H.H.L.* 283
Like *Radiant* Hesper, when his golden hayre . . . . . *Proth.* 164

Radigund. seeme as Saintlike as Saint *Radegund:* . . . . . *Hub.* 497
'Her name' (quoth he) 'they *Radigund* doe call, ... V. iv. 33. 3
Which when as *Radigund* there comming heard, ... V. iv. 37. 6
Radigund her selfe, when she espide Sir Terpin, ... V. iv. 39. 1
Bold *Radigund* with sound of trumpe on hight, ... V. iv. 45. 4
Radigund, full of heart-gnawing griefe . . . . . V. iv. 47. 1
Artegall fights with *Radigund,* . . . . . V. v. Arg.
Even so did *Radigund* with bootlesse paine . . . . . V. v. 15. 8
Serving proud *Radigund* with true subjection, ... V. v. 26. 2
if thou by faire entreatie can Move *Radigund?* . . . . . V. v. 40. 4
She fights with *Radigund,* . . . . . V. vii. Arg.
Whereof when newes to *Radigund* was brought, ... V. vii. 25. 1
proud *Radigund,* with fell despight, ... V. vii. 32. 1

Raft. *See* **Reft.**
so hath *raft* us of our meriment. . . . . . *S.C.* Au. 14
Colin Clout *rafte* me of his brother, ... *S.C.* Au. 40
He *raft* her hatefull heade without remorse: . . . . . I. i. 24. 8

Rag. Without or robe or *rag* to hide his shame: . . . . . II. x. 58. 3

Rage. roming through the field with greedie *rage* . . . . . *Bel.*[2] vi. 6
Renewing in themselves that *rage* unkinde, ... *Ro.* x. 13
Into the Gothicke colde hot *rage* instil'd. . . . . . *Ro.* xi. 8
Through idlenes would turne to civill *rage,* . . . . . *Ro.* xxiii. 7
grype your hearts with noysome *rage* imbew'd, ... *Ro.* xxiv. 6
'Such *rage* as winters reigneth in my heart, ... *S.C.* Ja. 25
wil rancke Winters *rage* . . . never ginne tasswage? . . . . . *S.C.* F. 1
Enaunter his *rage* mought cooled bee; . . . . . *S.C.* F. 200
when choler is inflamed with *rage,* . . . . . *S.C.* May 136
Thou kenst not, Percie, howe the ryme should *rage,* . . . . . *S.C.* O. 109
bids him clayme with rigorous *rage* hys right: . . . . . *S.C.* D. 130
rime at riot, and doo *rage* in love; . . . . . *T.M.* 395
her owne people led with warlike *rage:* . . . . . *Ti.* 173
Reason with sudden *rage* did overgoe; . . . . . *Mui.* 134
celestiall *rage* Of Love . . . is breath'd into thy brest, . . . *Col.* 823
When that tumultuous *rage* and fearfull deene . . . . . *Ded. Son.* xi. 9
As those that are inspir'd with Martial *rage,* *Ded.Son.*xiii.11
his murdrous spoyles and bloudie *rage* allayd. . . . . . I. Pr. 3. 9
kindling *rage* her selfe she gathered round, ... I. i. 18. 2
all in *rage* to see his skilfull might Deluded so, ... I. ii. 2. 5

Rage—*Continued.*
The eie of reason was with *rage* yblent, ... I. ii. 5. 7
Spurring so hote with *rage* dispiteous, ... I. ii. 15. 2
His bloody *rage* aswaged with remorse, ... I. iii. 5. 8
the hungry *rage,* which late Him prickt, ... I. iii. 7. 4
of his cruell *rage* Nigh dead with feare, ... I. iii. 13. 3
long the dore with *rage* and threats he bett, ... I. iii. 19. 1
Her piteous wordes might not abate his *rage,* . . . . . I. iii. 38. 1
his *rage* is more of might. . . . . . I. iii. 43. 9
Trembling through hasty *rage* . . . . . I. iv. 33. 9
burning all with *rage,* He to him lept, ... I. iv. 39. 4
Who, all in *rage,* his Sea-god syre besought . . . . . I. v. 38. 1
when in *rage* he for revenge did earne. . . . . . I. vi. 25. 9
Lyonesse . . . roaring all with *rage* . . . . . I. vi. 27. 6
increasing more Their puissant force, and cruell *rage* . . . . . I. vi. 45. 3
Bulles, whom kindly *rage* doth sting, ... I. viii. 11. 6
through *rage* more strong then both were erst; . . . . . I. viii. 18. 3
Before their *rage* grew to so great unrest, ... I. ix. 9. 7
redeeme thy woefull parents head From tyrans *rage* . . . . . I. x. 9. 5
Come gently, but not with that mightie *rage,* . . . . . I. xi. 6. 2
So flam'd his eyne with *rage* and rancorous yre; . . . . . I. xi. 14. 7
Exceeding *rage* enflam'd the furious Beast, ... I. xi. 17. 5
with wonted *rage* he him advaunced neare. . . . . . I. xi. 52. 9
Fitt to inflame faire Lady with loves *rage,* . . . . . II. i. 41. 8
with new *rage* their shieldes to hew . . . . . II. ii. 23. 7
fowle revenging *rage,* and base contentious jarre. . . . . . II. ii. 30. 9
With beastly brutish *rage* gan him assay, ... II. iv. 6. 7
rage enforst my flight; . . . . . II. iv. 32. 1
his mother did more *rage* inspyre. . . . . . II. iv. 32. 9
whilest his foe did *rage* most rife: . . . . . II. v. 9. 7
gan to *rage,* and inly frett, ... II. vi. 28. 3
To see Pyrochles there so rudely *rage;* . . . . . II. vi. 48. 7
fiers Vulcans *rage* to tame, ... II. vii. 36. 5
inflam'd with *rage* That sire he fowl bespake: . . . . . II. viii. 12. 1
secrete powre t' appease inflamed *rage:* . . . . . II. viii. 26. 8
Horribly then he gan to *rage* and rayle, ... II. viii. 37. 1
When rancour doth with *rage* him once engore, ... II. viii. 42. 2
had not yet felt Cupides wanton *rage;* . . . . . II. ix. 18. 2
with great spoile and *rage* Forwasted all, ... II. x. 52. 7
infirmity Of the fraile flesh, relenting to their *rage,* . . . . . II. xi. 1. 6
carries into smoake with *rage* and horror great. . . . . . II. xi. 32. 9
halfe in *rage* to be deluded thus, ... II. xi. 38. 5
rule the Furyes when they most doe *rage.* . . . . . II. xii. 41. 8
From prosecuting his revenging *rage:* . . . . . III. i. 11. 2
no usuall fire, no usuall *rage* Yt is, ... III. ii. 37. 3
yielded ready passage, and their *rage* surceast. . . . . . III. iv. 31. 9
deceive Fraile Ladies hart with loves consuming *rage,* . . . . . III. vii. 46. 4
in his *rage* his mother would have slaine, ... III. viii. 4. 2
Broke into open fire and *rage* extreme; . . . . . III. viii. 26. 5
In your avengement and despiteous *rage,* . . . . . III. viii. 28. 6
met Together with impetuous *rage* . . . . . III. ix. 16. 2
(whereat he raves With roring *rage,* . . . . . III. ix. 45. 4
did the more augment His mighty *rage,* . . . . . III. xi. 26. 7
each abacke rebowndes With roaring *rage;* . . . . . IV. i. 42. 4
he the more with furious *rage* was fyred, ... IV. i. 54. 7
with *rage* extreme, Like two mad mastiffes, ... IV. ii. 17. 7
They gan abate the rancour of their *rage,* . . . . . IV. ii. 28. 2
two Tygers prickt with hungers *rage* . . . . . IV. iii. 16. 1
stirs up anguish and contentious *rage:* . . . . . IV. iii. 43. 4
Like as a Lion . . . doth *rage* and rore, ... IV. iv. 32. 6
him saw approching neare With so fell *rage,* . . . . . IV. vi. 10. 4
all the way did *rage* at that same Squire, ... IV. viii. 40. 1
full of *rage* he gan to curse and sweare, ... IV. viii. 44. 2
From all foure parts of heaven doe *rage* full sore, ... IV. ix. 23. 6
seas, when they do sorest *rage,* . . . . . IV. xi. 50. 5
They snuf, they snort, they bounce, they *rage,* . . . . . V. ii. 15. 6
when he saw he greatly grew in *rage,* . . . . . V. ii. 47. 1
by *rage* of waves that never rest, ... V. iv. 19. 4
Her heart for *rage* did grate, ... V. iv. 37. 7
on him ran With furious *rage,* . . . . . V. v. 6. 4
She gan to storme, and *rage,* . . . . . V. v. 47. 2
in *rage* she turn'd from him aside, ... V. vi. 11. 7
they together run With greedy *rage,* . . . . . V. vii. 29. 2
forth did rome whether her *rage* her bore, ... V. viii. 48. 6
Her burning tongue with *rage* inflamed hath, ... V. viii. 49. 2
Doe all attonce their thunders *rage* forth rent, ... V. x. 34. 8
He gan to burne in *rage,* . . . . . V. xi. 2. 6
was forced foote to give To his first *rage,* . . . . . V. xi. 5. 7
as he in his *rage* him overstrooke, ... V. xi. 13. 6
long in vaine their *rage* withstands. . . . . . V. xi. 44. 9
him seeing so to *rage* Willd him to stay, ... V. xii. 8. 1
With bitter *rage* and fell contention, ... V. xii. 41. 3
He . . . in that *rage* gan rove . . . . . VI. ii. 20. 7
such as sudden *rage* him lent to smite; . . . . . VI. iv. 4. 3
they to pitty turnd their former *rage,* . . . . . VI. v. 30. 8
rule the stubborne *rage* of passion blinde: . . . . . VI. vi. 5. 8
whose tempestuous *rage* Makes th' heavens tremble . . . . . VI. vi. 11. 8
Whom when the Prince so felly saw to *rage,* . . . . . VI. vi. 39. 1
in *rage* he on him streight did seaze, ... VI. vi. 40. 5
the beast doth *rage* and loudly rore; . . . . . VI. vii. 47. 6
with great *rage* he stoutly doth denay; . . . . . VI. xi. 15. 6
With cruell *rage* and dreadfull violence, ... VI. xi. 30. 4
In so great *rage* that them in dongeon deepe . . . . . VI. xii. 5. 6
his *rage* to ward Did cast his shield atweene; . . . . . VI. xii. 30. 1
cruelly the Beast did *rage* and rore . . . . . VI. xii. 31. 1
his force to shrincke And rage to quaile, ... VI. xii. 34. 2
Making their cruell *rage* thy scornefull game, ... *H.L.* 47
with such *rage* extreme Fraile men, ... *H.L.* 117
therein stirre such *rage* and restlesse stowre, ... *H.B.* 73
Rapt with the *rage* of mine own ravisht thought, ... *H.H.B.* 1

Raged 682 Raise

Raged. Whilst Hector *raged* with outragious minde, *Gn.* 503
the Bore . . . *raged* sore In bitter words, *Hub.* 1088
how he fum'd, and sweld, and *rag'd*, and panted; *Hub.* 1340
So as he *rag'd* emongst that beastly rout, *As.* 115
And slake the heavenly fire that *raged* evermore. I. v. 40. 9
rudely *rag'd*, and like a cruell tygre far'd. II. v. 8. 9
So *rag'd* Prince Arthur twixt his foemen twaine, II. viii. 42. 8
those wild-beasts that *rag'd* with furie mad; II. xii. 84. 5
Rored and *raged* to be underkept; III. vii. 33. 8
they chaft, and *rag'd*, And woxe nigh mad IV. v. 27. 1
rayl'd and *rag'd*, till she had all her poyson spent. IV. viii. 35. 9
waves, which *rag'd* and ror'd IV. xi. 3. 6
The more she *rag'd*, the more he did abide; V. v. 6. 8
the more he *rag'd*, the more his powre increast. VI. xii. 32. 9
Rage's. in his first *rages* heat, V. viii. 31. 7
Rages. strove their stubborne *rages* to revoke; II. ii. 28. 6
Yet at her speach their *rages* gan relent, II. vi. 36. 3
mother call to coole their kindly *rages*. IV. x. 45. 9
Rageth. ever fickle fortune *rageth* rife; I. ix. 44. 8
in thy troubled bowels raignes and *rageth* ryfe. III. iv. 8. 9
rageth sore in each degree and state, VI. xii. 40. 2
Ragged. My *ragged* rontes all shiver and shake, *S.C.* F. 5
a *ragged* rout Of Faunes and Satyres, *T.M.* 267
Then fittest are these *ragged* rimes for mee, *T.M.* 545
ragged ruines breed great ruth and pittie *Col.* 114
His goodly corps, on *ragged* cliffs yrent, I. v. 38. 6
club . . . All armd with *ragged* snubbes I. viii. 7. 4
trunck, halfe rent with *ragged* rift, I. viii. 22. 8
trees . . . Did hang upon the *ragged* rocky knees I. ix. 34. 3
His garment, nought but many *ragged* clouts, I. ix. 36. 1
Scattred with bushy thornes and *ragged* breares, I. x. 35. 3
The rolling billowes beate the *ragged* shore, I. xi. 21. 3
ragged ribs of mountaines molten new, I. xi. 44. 7
My *ragged* rimes are all too rude and bace I. xii. 23. 4
In *ragged* robes and filthy disaray; II. iv. 4. 2
the *ragged* breaches hong Embost with massy gold II. vii. 28. 3
Vile caitive wretches, *ragged*, rude, deformd, II. ix. 13. 4
threatneth downe to throw his *ragged* rift II. xii. 4. 5
rent his *ragged* heare; III. vii. 20. 5
ragged weed Made of Beares skin, III. xii. 11. 1
hung With *ragged* monuments of times forepast, IV. i. 21. 2
a Snake, . . . Casts off his *ragged* skin IV. iii. 23. 9
His word, which on his *ragged* shield was writ, IV. iv. 39. 8
Upon the ground in *ragged* rude attyre, IV. viii. 23. 6
all to-worne and *ragged*, V. ix. 10. 8
catching her fast by her *ragged* weed V. xi. 61. 3
How to reforme that *ragged* common-weale: V. xii. 26. 4
their garments yet, Being all *rag'd* and tatter'd, V. xii. 28. 8
catching up in hand a *ragged* stone VI. iv. 21. 2
Unmard with *ragged* mosse or filthy mud; VI. x. 7. 3
With *ragged* weedes, and lockes upstaring hye, VI. xi. 27. 4
Raging. Nor the deep wounds of victours *raging* blade, *Ro.* xiii. 2
The *raging* fyre that kindled at his ray. *S.C.* D. 58
The sodain rysing of the *raging* seas, *S.C.* D. 86
those bitter stounds Of *raging* love *T.M.* 374
raging Love dothe appall the weake stomacke: *U.V.* 11
No griesly famine, nor no *raging* sweard, *Col.* 314
As *raging* flames who striveth to suppresse.' I. ii. 34. 6
raging spoile of lawlesse victors will? I. iii. 43. 2
The swelling Splene, and Frenzy *raging* rife, I. iv. 35. 7
Therewith redoubled was his *raging* yre, I. v. 10. 4
Whom when the *raging* Sarazin espyde, I. vi. 8. 6
commaund themselves to . . . throw in *raging* sea I. x. 20. 8
He cryde, as *raging* seas are wont to rore I. xi. 21. 1
Inflam'd with wrath, his *raging* blade he hefte, I. xi. 39. 6
raging passion with fierce tyranny II. i. 57. 4
Whom *raging* windes . . . doe diversly disease, II. ii. 24. 2
whoso will *raging* Furor tame, II. iv. 11. 1
bitt his tawny beard to shew his *raging* yre. II. iv. 15. 9
wel nigh molt his hart in *raging* yre: II. v. 8. 5
with his *raging* armes he rudely flasht II. vi. 42. 6
servaunt stryving with his *raging* Lord. II. vi. 47. 9
arm'd with *raging* flame. II. xi. 23. 9
the *raging* surges reard Up to the skyes, II. xii. 2. 8
yet may it nought appease My *raging* smart, III. ii. 43. 4
in their *raging* surquedry disdaynd III. iv. 7. 6
like to a storme *Raging* within the waves: III. viii. 41. 4
therewith fierce did stryke The *raging* billowes, III. xi. 40. 6
when *raging* heat Doth burne the earth IV. iv. 47. 1
Whose *raging* rigour neither steele nor bras Could stay, IV. vi. 15. 5
raging fire of love to womankind, IV. ix. 1. 6
mollifie, and calme her *raging* heat: IV. ix. 14. 7
their *raging* rigour to relent, IV. ix. 25. 8
The *raging* Buls rebellow through the wood, IV. x. 46. 4
thy smyling looke doest pacifie The *raging* seas, IV. x. 44. 5
all the *raging* seas for joy forgot to rore. IV. xi. 23. 9
Beare off the burden of her *raging* yre: V. v. 16. 4
all the troublous stormes asswage And *raging* flames, V. vii. 23. 2
wound, . . . through *raging* smart of it, V. vii. 33. 4
Like *raging* Ino, when with knife in hand V. viii. 47. 1
inly burnt with flames most *raging* whot, VI. xi. 4. 2
with his *raging* brond divide Their thickest troups, VI. xi. 48. 8
Upon a Lyon *raging* yet with ire VII. vii. 36. 3
a rocke amidst the *raging* floods; *Am.* lvi. 10
strongly part The *raging* waves, *Am.* lix. 6
raging now therein with restlesse stowre, *H.L.* 3
seeking to aslake thy *raging* fyre, *H.B.* 4
Rags. ran away in his rent *rags* by night, *Hub.* 937
ruffin raiment all was . . . to *rags* yrent, I. iv. 34. 2
Their feet unshod, their bodies wrapt in *rags*, II. xi. 23. 4
Rags—*Continued.*
Fury was full ill appareiled In *rags*, III. xii. 17. 2
Rude was his garment, and to *rags* all rent, IV. v. 35. 1
Torne all to *rags*, and rent with many a wound; V. viii. 42. 7
in what *rags*, and in how base aray, *H.H.L.* 228
Raid. *See* **Rayed.**
Raign. *See* **Reign.**
Rail. a spring out of a rocke forth *rayle*, *Bel.*[2] xii. 1
cry, and curse, and *raile*, and rend her heare, I. iii. 25. 2
Large floods of blood adowne their sides did *raile*; I. vi. 43. 7
sober Guyon, hearing him so *rayle*, II. vi. 40. 2
Horribly then he gan to rage and *rayle*, II. viii. 37. 1
saw the red blood *rayle* Adowne so fast, II. viii. 37. 3
All carelesse of his taunt and bitter *rayle*; IV. i. 43. 2
streames of bloud did *rayle* Adowne, IV. ii. 18. 3
Shee with her rod did softly smite the *raile*, IV. iii. 46. 2
rayle at them with grudgefull discontent, IV. viii. 28. 4
Against the stones and trees did *rayle* anew, IV. viii. 36. 8
fouly *rayle* with all she could invent; V. xii. 40. 2
Talus, hearing her so lewdly *raile*, V. xii. 43. 1
sharpely at him to revile and *raile* VI. xii. 33. 3
Railed. Guyon . . . By strife is *rayld* uppon. II. iv. Arg.
a long bloody river through them *rayld*, III. xi. 46. 8
rayl'd and rag'd, till she had all her poyson spent. IV. viii. 35. 9
Railest. Thou *raylest* on, right withouten reason, *S.C.* May 146
Railing. teares from her faire eyes forth *railing*: *Ti.* 12
With *railing* tearmes defied the Jewish hoast, *Ti.* 538
Shamefully at her *rayling* all the way, I. iii. 23. 3
amidst her *rayling*, she did pray That plagues, I. iii. 23. 6
Her bitter *rayling* and foule revilement, II. iv. 12. 5
Instead of rest thou lendest *rayling* teares; III. iv. 57. 4
Reviling me and *rayling* as she lust, V. viii. 22. 5
rayling rymes had sprad. V. ix. 25. 9
Railings. those unknightly *raylinges* which he spoke, II. vi. 30. 6
Rails. In vaine the Pagan bannes, and sweares, and *rayles*, V. viii. 39. 4
Raiment. His ruffin *raiment* all was staind with blood I. iv. 34. 1
in their steede for other *rayment* sought, V. vii. 41. 3
With locks all loose, and *rayment* all to-rent; V. viii. 4. 8
The fields my food, my flocke my *rayment* breed; VI. ix. 20. 8
Raiments. With ruffled *rayments*, and fayre blubbred face, I. vi. 9. 3
Rain. *See* **Reign.**
In *raine*, or snowe, or haile, *Ro.* xx. 8
your teares that from your boughes doe *raine*, *S.C.* Ja. 35
Quenching the gasping furrowes thirst with *rayne*? *S.C.* Ap. 6
When the *rayne* is faln, *S.C.* S. 18
is worne with *raine*: *Ti.* 417
the teares which fro mine eyes do *raine*, *D.* 376
neither car'd for wynd, nor haile, nor *raine*, *Col.* 221
an hideous storme of *raine* Did poure I. i. 6. 6
ever-drizling *raine* upon the loft, I. i. 41. 3
As it had deawed bene with timely *raine*: I. xi. 48. 5
forth her bleeding life does *raine*, II. i. 38. 7
thicke as stormie showre, Their strokes did *raine*: II. viii. 35. 6
In whose sad time blood did from heaven *rayne*. II. x. 34. 2
His watry eies drizling like deawy *rayne*, III. v. 34. 3
Did *raine* into her lap an hony dew; III. xi. 31. 4
poureth forth a sudden shoure of *raine*, IV. iv. 47. 8
At length breakes downe in *raine*, IV. ix. 33. 6
soone as few drops of *raine* Thereon distill V. xii. 13. 3
Rayne, haile, and snowe do pay them sad penance, VII. vii. 23. 7
stormes, which she alone on me doth *raine*. *Am.* xlvi. 14
happy influence upon us *raine*, *Epith.* 416
Rainbow. His hornes bene as broade as *Rainebowe* bent, *S.C.* F. 73
like the coloured *Rainbowe* arched wide: *Ti.* 550
In which all colours of the *rainbow* bee; *Col.* 341
Rained. *See* **Reigned.**
she *raynd* such store of streaming teares, *T.M.* 109
Rainy. No otherwise than *raynie* cloud, *Ro.* xx. 1
Raise. Gods and men my honour up did *raise*? *Bel.*[2] x. 8
Neroes and Caligulaes . . . must dayly *rayse*?' *Bel.*[2] x. 14
It seem'd her top the firmament did *rayse*, *Bel.*[2] xiv. 5
Over all the world did *raise* a Trophee *Bel.*[2] xv. 8
gins Bartas hie to *rayse* His heavenly Muse, *Ro.* Env. 11
Would *rayse* ones mynd above the starry skie, *S.C.* O. 94
did *raise* full busily A little mount, *Gn.* 659
For learning sake to living them to *raise*; *Hub.* 538
for to *raise* Himselfe to high degree, *Hub.* 774
they doo onely strive themselves to *raise* *T.M.* 91
noble Peeres, whom I was wont to *raise*, *T.M.* 467
Care now his idle bagpipe up to *raise*, *Ti.* 226
Thereto doo thou my humble spirite *raise*, *Ti.* 313
His mistresse name, and his owne fame to *raise*. *As.* 88
raise His tunes from laies to matter of more skill. *Col.* 394
thrust downe other . . . Himselfe to *raise*: *Col.* 692
How rashly blame of Rosalind ye *raise*.' *Col.* 926
When so thee list thy lofty Muse to *raise*: *Ded.Son.*viii.12
To like desire of honor may ye *raise*, *Ded. Son.* x. 11
Which if ye yield, perhaps ye may her *rayse* *Ded.Son.*xiii.13
raise my thoughtes, too humble and too vile, I. Pr. 4. 6
charmes, A fordonne wight from dore of death mote *raise*, I. v. 41. 8
doughty knights, whom Faery land did *raise*, I. vii. 46. 3
to kill, And *rayse* againe to life the hart I. x. 19. 9
to my tunes thy second tenor *rayse*, I. xi. 7. 8
my dreaded name to *raise* Above the Moone, II. iii. 38. 7
to *rayse* our house to honour did begin.' II. iv. 36. 9
Some thought to *raise* themselves to high degree II. vii. 47. 1
of them both did foy and tribute *raise*, II. x. 41. 4
Semiramis, Whom antique history so high doth *rayse*, II. x. 56. 3
thou afterwardes did *rayse* Most famous fruites III. iii. 3. 6
What heavenly Muse shall thy great honour *rayse* V. x. 3. 3

Raise—*Continued.*
praise . . . to all posterities to *raise*. . . . . V. xi. 34. 9
'full loth I were To *rayse* a lyving blame . . . . VI. ii. 15. 7
He tooke that Ladie, and her up did *rayse* . . . . VI. ii. 39. 7
all, which did Loves honor *rayse*, ... *Am.* xix. 9
My spirit to an higher pitch will *rayse*, ... *Am.* lxxx. 12
death, or love, or fortunes wreck did *rayse*, ... *Epith.* 8
That we may *raise* a large posterity, ... *Epith.* 417
rich triumphall Arcks which they did *raise*, ... *Com. Son.* iii. 7
name then would I *raise* Bove all the gods, ... *H.L.* 303
rayse The wondrous matter of my fyre . . . . *H.B.* 6
Raised. I saw *raisde* up on pillers of Ivorie, ... *Bel.*[1] iv. 1
She *raisde* a Trophee over all the worlde. . . . . *Bel.*[1] xi. 8
I saw *raysde* up on yvorie pillours [*text,* pillowes] . . . . *Bel.*[2] iv. 1
I the ship saw after *rais'd* againe. . . . . *Bel.*[2] xiii. 14
men to God thereby are nighest *raised*. . . . . *T.M.* 90
Bacchus and Hercules I *raisd* to heaven, ... *T.M.* 461
whilome *raised* they the puissant brood . . . . *Ti.* 379
'So *raisde* they eke faire Ledaes warlick twinnes, ... *Ti.* 386
first was *raisde* for vertuous parts, ... *Ti.* 451
to the pitch of her perfection *raised*. . . . . *Col.* 415
Hath prais'd and *rais'd* above each other starre. . . . . . *Col.* 535
her beastly bodie *raizd* With doubled forces . . . . I. i. 18. 3
by her hellish science *raisd* . . . A foggy mist . . . . . . I. ii. 38. 4
from her settled seat, The house was *raysd*, ... II. ii. 20. 7
therein have their mighty empire *raysd*, ... II. x. 5. 2
Raisd warre, and him in batteill overthrew. . . . . II. x. 33. 6
hellish feend *raysd* up through divelish science. . . . . . II. xi. 39. 9
reysd (*raysd) him up much stronger then before, ... II. xi. 45. 5
So is his soveraine honour *raisde* to hevens hight.' . . . . III. ii. 14. 9
raised from below Out of the dwellings . . . . IV. i. 19. 7
Have *rays'd* this cruell warre and outrage fell, ... IV. ii. 24. 4
This cruell conflict *raised* thereabout, ... IV. ix. 24. 8
The loft was *raysed* againe, that no man could it spie. . . . V. vi. 27. 9
More brave and noble knights have *raysed* beene . . . . . . VI. iv. 36. 3
The hue and cry was *raysed* all about; . . . . VI. xi. 46. 2
by her from basenesse *raysed;* . . . . *Am.* iii. 4
By whom my spirit out of dust was *raysed:* . . . . *Am.* lxxiv. 10
Raising. Wayling, and *raysing* pittifull uprore, ... V. ix. 8. 8
Rake. to plant, to reap, to *rake*, to sowe, ... *Hub.* 263
His body leane and meagre as a *rake*, ... II. xi. 22. 2
Raked. in his ashes *raked* up and hid, ... III. iii. 48. 3
Rake-hell. farre away, amid their *rakehell* bands, ... V. xi. 44. 6
Ram. like a *Ram*, faire Helle to pervart, ... III. xi. 30. 5
For that same golden fleecy *Ram*, ... V. Pr. 5. 6
sturdy March . . . rode upon a *Ram*, ... VII. vii. 32. 4
Rammed. Engin, . . . *ramd* with bollet rownd, ordaind to kill, I. vii. 13. 4
Ramp. trampling the fine element would fiercely *ramp*. . . . . I. v. 28. 9
Rampant. The *rampant* Lyon hunts he fast, ... *S.C.* Jul. 21
Ramped. He *rampt* upon him with his ravenous pawes, ... VI. xii. 29. 8
Ramping. out of the thickest wood A *ramping* Lyon rushed . I. iii. 5. 2
ramping on his shield, did weene the same Have reft away . I. iii. 41. 5
Her dreadfull beast; . . . Came *ramping* forth . . . . I. viii. 12. 5
hundred *ramping* Lions seemd to rore, ... I. xi. 37. 3
Rams. As when two *rams*, . . . Fight for the rule . . . . I. ii. 16. 1
Ran. *See* **Outran, Overran.**
Ran flowing all along the creekie shoare . . . . *Bel.*[1] vii. 7
streame . . . *Ranne* through the mid, ... *Rev.* iv. 13
Ran bathing all the creakie shore . . . . *Bel.*[2] ix. 7
Therewith affrayd, I *ranne* away; . . . . *S.C.* Mar. 94
ranne awaye with him in all hast. . . . . *S.C.* May 293
ranne out as he was wont of yore. . . . . *S.C.* S. 221
The wiser Muses after Colin *ranne*. . . . . *S.C.* D. 48
and *ran* away by night. . . . . *Hub.* 574
ran away in his rent rags by night, ... *Hub.* 937
frosen horror *ran* through everie part. . . . . *Ti.* 483
With gaping mouth at her *ran* greedily, ... I. iii. 5. 5
forth they *ran*, like two amazed deare, ... I. iii. 22. 7
all the poison *ran* about his chaw; . . . . I. iv. 30. 4
ran towardes the far rebownded noyce, ... I. vi. 8. 3
trembling horrour *ran* through every joynt, ... I. viii. 39. 3
Whome when his Lady saw, to him she *ran* . . . . I. viii. 42. 1
The crudled cold *ran* to her well of life, ... I. ix. 52. 2
fiersely *ran* at him with rigorous might: . . . . I. xi. 16. 2
Ran through his mouth with so importune might, ... I. xi. 53. 7
after all the raskall many *ran*, ... I. xii. 9. 1
he *ran* Unto that stead, ... II. ii. 21. 6
upon him *ran*, and him beset . . . . II. ii. 22. 2
The faire Medina . . . Emongst them *ran;* . . . . II. ii. 27. 4
ran away full light. II. iii. 4. 9
nimbly *ran* her wonted course . . . . II. vi. 20. 6
soone atweene them *ran;* . . . . II. vi. 32. 2
knight that towardes him fast *ran;* . . . . II. vi. 41. 2
He *ran* on foot, ... II. vi. 41. 3
the stony feare *Ran* to his hart, ... II. viii. 46. 2
as the winde *ran* underneath his lode, ... II. xi. 20. 5
she to him *ran* hastily; . . . . II. xi. 28. 9
Like two mad dogs they *ran* about the lands, ... II. xi. 47. 2
the hoare waters from his frigot *ran*, ... II. xii. 10. 3
Ran towards to devoure those unexpected guests. . . . . . . II. xii. 39. 9
she *ran* apace Unto his reskew, ... III. i. 22. 7
to her weapon *ran*, ... III. i. 62. 3
eke the Redcrosse knight *ran* to the stownd, ... III. i. 63. 2
Strongly the straunge knight *ran*, and sturdily . . . . III. iv. 15. 7
Knotted with blood in bounches rudely *ran;* . . . . III. v. 29. 6
Unto his reskew *ran*, and greedily him spedd. . . . . III. vii. 30. 9
speare he couched warily, And at her *ran;* . . . . III. vii. 38. 8
So *ran* the Geauntesse unto the fight, ... III. vii. 39. 7
Malbecco, . . . *ran* with fearfull speed, ... III. ix. 18. 3
her husband *ran* with sory haste . . . . III. x. 13. 2

Ran—*Continued.*
ran into her lovers armes right fast; . . . . III. x. 13. 5
He *ran* as fast as both his feet could beare, ... III. x. 53. 2
ran away, *ran* with him selfe away; . . . . III. x. 54. 6
to her *ran* with hasty egernesse, ... III. xii. 44. *or.* 6
They to his succour *ran* with readie ayd; . . . . IV. i. 37. 2
Ran hastily, to weete what did him ayle. . . . . IV. i. 43. 4
the more strong and stiffely that he *ran*, ... IV. iv. 19. 5
ran at him with all his might and maine; . . . . IV. iv. 44. 8
many others at him likewise *ran*, ... IV. iv. 46. 1
against her fiercely *ran*. . . . . IV. vi. 10. 2
in his armes her bearing *Ran*, ... IV. vii. 8. 7
Ran forth in hast with hideous outcry, ... IV. vii. 21. 4
She *ran* in hast his life to have bereft; . . . . IV. vii. 32. 2
his life *ran* foorth in bloudie streame, ... IV. viii. 45. 8
ran, and him with streight embras Enfolding, ... IV. viii. 63. 4
they both unto him *ran*, ... IV. ix. 9. 2
Ran fierce at me that fire glaunst from his horses hoofe. . . . IV. x. 9. 9
In three great rivers *ran*, ... IV. xi. 42. 9
both Together *ran* with ready speares in rest. . . . . V. ii. 12. 4
Eftsoones the people all to harnesse *ran*, ... V. iv. 36. 6
ranne to his redresse: . . . . V. iv. 41. 3
She . . . on him *ran* With furious rage, ... V. v. 6. 3
ran to meete him forth to know his tidings somme. . . . . . V. vi. 8. 9
So *ran* they all, as they had bene at bace, ... V. viii. 5. 4
He *ran* still on, thinking to follow fast . . . . V. viii. 8. 8
He at him *ran* with ready speare in rest; . . . . V. viii. 9. 3
with their ryder *ranne* perforce away: . . . . V. viii. 38. 4
Streight downe she *ranne*, like an enraged cow . . . . V. viii. 46. 1
She at her *ran* with all her force . . . . V. viii. 46. 8
Unto the wyld wood *ranne*, her dolours to deplore. . . . . . V. viii. 48. 9
Ran with her fast away . . . . V. ix. 14. 5
Up to the rocke he *ran*, ... V. ix. 15. 3
ran into the Hall, ... V. x. 37. 8
From whose sterne presence they diffused *ran*, ... V. xi. 47. 8
Unto her *ran* with greedie great desyre, ... V. xi. 61. 2
Against him stoutly *ran*, ... VI. i. 19. 3
coucht his speare, and *ran* at him amaine. . . . . VI. i. 33. 4
like men dismayde, *Ran* after fast to reskue . . . . VI. iii. 24. 9
With that *ran* at him, ... VI. iii. 48. 7
with fierce fury . . . Upon him *ran;* . . . . VI. iv. 5. 4
after him the wyld man *ran* apace, ... VI. iv. 8. 1
after him he *ran* with zealous haste . . . . VI. iv. 18. 6
the bold knight . . . Upon him *ran*, ... VI. iv. 21. 4
both with equall might Against him *ran;* . . . . VI. vii. 7. 6
ran in hast To reskue her; . . . . VI. x. 35. 1
He *ran* at him enraged, ... VI. x. 35. 9
the theefe awaking light Unto the entrance *ran;* . . . . . . VI. xi. 43. 5
streight forth she *ran* in hast . . . . VI. xii. 16. 6
forth in hast *ran* to the straunger Mayd; . . . . VI. xii. 19. 2
ran at him amaine With open mouth, ... VI. xii. 26. 4
by her side there *ran* her Page, ... VII. vi. 9. 5
Ran forth in haste unto the king of Gods to plaine. . . . . . VII. vi. 14. 9
All *ran* together with a great out-cry . . . . VII. vi. 15. 1
A melting pleasance *ran* through every part, ... *Am.* xxxix. 7
the Nymphes, . . . *Ran* all in haste . . . . *Proth.* 56
Ranch. Hasting to *raunch* the arrow out, ... *S.C.* Au. 97
Rancor. Such *rancour* in the harts of mightie men? . . . . . *Mui.* 16
all her blood to poysonous *rancor* turne: . . . . *Mui.* 344
he, enrag'd with *rancor*, nothing heares. . . . . I. iii. 44. 5
fraught with *rancour* and engorged yre, ... I. xi. 40. 5
in bloody fight With *deadly* rancour . . . . II. ii. 21. 4
Her gracious words their *rancour* did appall, ... II. ii. 32. 1
yield he would not, nor his *rancor* slack. . . . . II. iv. 14. 6
when *Rancor* rife Kindles Revenge, ... II. iv. 44. 4
His honour staines with *rancour* and despight, ... II. viii. 29. 8
When *rancour* doth with rage him once engore, ... II. viii. 42. 2
For vile disdaine and *rancour*, which did gnaw . . . . II. viii. 50. 7
with wrath outrageous And cruell *rancour* . . . . II. x. 43. 5
Vyle *rancor* to avoid and cruel surquedry. . . . . III. i. 13. 9
Their direfull *rancour* rather did encreasse; . . . . III. i. 23. 4
Vile *rancour* their rude harts had fild . . . . III. v. 16. 9
Without fell *rancor* or fond gealosy. . . . . III. vi. 41. 6
They gan abate the *rancour* of their rage, ... IV. ii. 28. 2
she was stuft with *rancour* and despight . . . . IV. viii. 24. 3
Burning with inward *rancour* and despight, ... VI. v. 18. 2
Ne ever shewed signe of *rancour* or of jarre. . . . . VI. ix. 39. 9
Rancorous. to aswage The *ranckorous* rigour of his might, . . *S.C.* F. 185
So flam'd his eyne with rage and *rancorous* yre; . . . . . . I. xi. 14. 7
Cruell Revenge, and *rancorous* Despight, ... II. vii. 22. 2
A filthy blood, or humour *rancorous*, ... III. x. 59. 4
His *rancorous* despight did not releasse, ... VI. vi. 43. 8
Rancor's. Bitter despight, with *rancours* rusty knife, ... I. iv. 35. 4
Random. letten them runne at *randon* alone: . . . . *S.C.* May 46
They cherelie chaunt, and rymes at *randon* fling, ... *T.M.* 321
shootes his arrowes . . . at *randon* as he will, ... *Col.* 812
as a blindfold Bull, at *randon* fares, ... II. iv. 7. 8
at *randon* there to raunge: . . . . III. viii. 20. 5
The gentle Lady, loose at *randon* lefte, ... III. x. 36. 1
With which he shot at *randon*, ... III. xi. 48. 3
There might ye see loose steeds at *randon* ronne, ... IV. iv. 38. 6
Ne rov'd at *randon*, after gazers guyse, ... IV. x. 49. 8
and doe at *randon* rove . . . . V. Pr. 6. 5
As thing at *randon* left, ... V. iv. 19. 7
As a mad bytch . . . Doth runne at *randon*, ... V. viii. 49. 3
The fish, still floting, doe at *randon* range, ... VII. vii. 21. 4
Rang. *See* **Rong, Rung.**
with sharp reasons *rang* her such a pele, ... V. ix. 39. 7
Range. *raunge* abroad to seeke her food, ... *Bel.*[2] vi. 5
To *raunge* the fields with wide open throte. . . . . *S.C.* S. 195

Range—*Continued.*
'I wont to *raunge* amydde the mazie thickette, . . . *S.C.* D. 25
now in other state abroad to *range:* . . . *Hub.* 356
joy'd to *range* abroad in fresh attire, . . . *Mui.* 37
as I the fields did *range* . . . *D.* 106
had more joy to *raunge* the forrest wyde, . . . I. vi. 21. 7
the woodes with bow and shaftes did *raunge,* . . . II. ii. 7. 3
doest *raunge* In this wilde forest, . . . II. iii. 39. 1
over all the countrie she did *raunge* . . . III. vii. 50. 1
at randon there to *raunge:* . . . III. viii. 20. 5
To *range* the field, and victorlike to raine, . . . IV. iv. 25. 4
So now all *range,* . . . V. Pr. 6. 5
Whose wandring fancie after lust did *raunge,* . . . V. v. 26. 8
in that rage gan . . . *range* through all the wood, . . . VI. ii. 20. 8
did *raunge* the wood for salvage game, . . . VI. v. 15. 2
One day, as he did *raunge* the fields abroad, . . . VI. x. 5. 1
all this while at will did *range* and raine, . . . VI. xii. 2. 8
The fish, still floting, doe at randon *range,* . . . VII. vii. 21. 4
gan to *raunge* them selves in huge array, . . . *H.L.* 79
Ranged. bevie of Ladies bright, *Raunged* in a rowe? . . . *S.C.* Ap. 119
rang'd each where without suspition. . . . *Mui.* 376
As they the forest *raunged* on a day, . . . *As.* 140
A teme of Dolphins *raunged* in aray . . . III. iv. 33. 1
raungd abrode to seeke adventures wilde, . . . III. vii. 30. 2
All *raunged* in a ring . . . VI. x. 11. 9
All they without were *raunged* in a ring, . . . VI. x. 12. 1
In good estate, and in meet order *ranged,* . . . VII. vi. 5. 3
raunged farre abroad in every border, . . . VII. vii. 4. 8
Ranger. Nor outlawes fell affray the forest *raunger.* . . . *Col.* 319
Rangers. For feare of *raungers* and the great hunt, . . . *S.C.* S. 159
Ranges. Therein an hundred *raunges* weren pight, . . . II. vii. 35. 4
With many *raunges* reard along the wall, . . . II. ix. 29. 2
set with yron teeth in *raunges* twaine, . . . VI. xii. 26. 7
Rangeth. hunt the salvage chace, . . . Of all that *raungeth* . . . VI. ii. 31. 8
he *raungeth* through the world againe, . . . VI. xii. 40. 1
Ranging. In the wilde forrest *raunging* fresh and free. . . . *Hub.* 630
Greedie of mischiefe, *ranging* all about, . . . *D.* 157
Raunging the forest wide on courser free, . . . I. ix. 12. 7
it his *ranging* fancie did refraine, . . . IV. vi. 33. 6
Belphebe, *raunging* in that forrest wide, . . . IV. vii. 29. 2
Rank. An Hercules so *ranke* seed to represse, . . . *Ro.* x. 10
wil *rancke* Winters rage . . . never ginne tasswage? . . . *S.C.* F. 1
doth shrowde Emong the bushes *rancke?* . . . *S.C.* Jul. 4
When folke bene fat, and riches *ranke,* . . . *S.C.* Jul. 211
The fruitfull spawne of their *ranke* fantasies: . . . *T.M.* 322
Nor the *ranke* grassie fennes delights untride. . . . *Mui.* 156
seeing him ryde so *ranck,* . . . II. iii. 6. 7
more for *ranck* despight then for great paine, . . . II. iv. 15. 7
knitting their *rancke* braunches, . . . III. vi. 44. 4
With him went Hope in *rancke,* . . . III. xii. 13. 1
Dissemblaunce and Suspect Marcht in one *rancke,* . . . III. xii. 14. 2
By which few crooked sallowes grew in *ranke:* . . . IV. v. 33. 5
sound Of many yron hammers beating *ranke,* . . . IV. v. 33. 7
Like to a *rancke* of piles that pitched are awry. . . . V. xi. 9. 9
Ranked. Sett by it selfe, and *ranckt* in comely rew; . . . III. vi. 35. 4
Rankle. wound . . . doth *rancle* in my riven brest, . . . I. ix. 7. 4
Inward corruption . . . did *ranckle* yett within, . . . I. x. 25. 4
now gan afresh to *rancle* sore, . . . VI. x. 31. 3
Rankled. *Ranckled* so sore, and festred inwardly, . . . II. iv. 23. 3
on their Paynim foes avenge their *ranckled* ire. . . . III. iii. 36. 9
closely *rankled* under th' orifis: . . . IV. xii. 22. 7
Rankleth. now it *ranckleth* more and more, . . . *S.C.* Mar. 100
There it *ranckleth,* ay more and more, . . . *S.C.* Au. 101
Now *ranckleth* in this same fraile fleshly mould, . . . III. ii. 39. 3
Rankling. *ranckling* wound as yet does rifelye bleede. . . . *S.C.* D. 94
bowels so with *ranckling* poyson swelde, . . . *Mui.* 255
two Bores, with *rancling* malice mett, . . . I. vi. 44. 4
Ne might his *rancling* paine with patience be appeasd. . . . I. xi. 38. 9
could ease his *rankling* maladie, . . . IV. xi. 6. 4
the sharpnesse of her *rankling* wound: . . . VI. iv. 9. 9
did most infest Their *ranckling* wounds, . . . VI. vi. 2. 9
ranckling inward with unruly stounds, . . . VI. vi. 5. 3
Made all of rusty yron *ranckling* sore, . . . VI. vi. 9. 3
Rankly. spring forth *ranckly* under his chinne. . . . *S.C.* May 188
Rankness. with strong hand their fruitful *rancknes* did deface. V. i. 1. 9
Ranks. heavenly *ranks,* where blessed soules do rest; . . . *Gn.* 58
Three *ranckes* of yron teeth enraunged were, . . . I. xi. 13. 2
In endlesse *rancks* along enraunged were, . . . III. vi. 35. 8
divers trees enrang'd in even *rankes;* . . . IV. x. 25. 2
all the host of heaven in *rankes* doost lead, . . . *Epith.* 289
Rank-smelling. *Ranke-smelling* Rue, and Cummin good for eyes, . . . *Mui.* 188
Ransack. Who it to rob and *ransacke* did intend. . . . II. vii. 32. 5
by the *ransack* of that peece they should attayn. . . . II. xi. 14. 9
gan *ransack* fast His inward partes, . . . III. v. 48. 4
rather do not *ransack* all, and him selfe kill?' . . . III. ix. 8. 9
gan they *ransacke* that same Castle strong, . . . IV. ix. 12. 1
ransacke all their dennes from most to least, . . . VI. xii. 24. 8
Ransacked. And win rich spoile of *ransackt* chastitee. . . . I. vi. 5. 5
with sondrie spoiles she hath been *ransacked.* . . . II. x. 23. 9
ransackt Greece wel tryde, when they were wroth; . . . II. x. 40. 5
ransackt all her veines with passion entyre. . . . III. i. 47. 9
with spoiles and cruelty *Ransackt* the world, . . . III. vi. 49. 6
Great cities *ransackt,* and strong castles rast; . . . IV. i. 21. 7
Ransom. For *ransome* leaving him the late-borne childe; . . . I. vi. 23. 6
'then *ransome* of the richest knight, . . . II. v. 7. 2
her lockes for *raunsome* fro me free.' . . . VI. i. 19. 9
Rap. him did *rap* Upon his headpeece . . . IV. v. 42. 3
with my speare upon the shield did *rap,* . . . IV. x. 9. 4
Rape. he liv'd all on ravin and on *rape* . . . IV. vii. 5. 7
Rapeth. Paridell *rapeth* Hellenore: . . . III. x. Arg. 1
Rapt. *rapt* with sweetenes new, . . . *Gn.* 195
I feele my selfe like one *yrapt* in spright. . . . *Col.* 623
rapt with whirling wheeles, inflames the skyen . . . I. iv. 9. 8
Whose circled waters *rapt* with whirling sway, . . . II. xii. 20. 5
Amoret *rapt* by greedie lust Belphebe saves . . . IV. vii. Arg. 1
The Prince halfe *rapt* began on her to dote; . . . IV. ix. 6. 7
Are *rapt* with wonder and with rare affright. . . . V. iii. 19. 7
So was this Souldan *rapt* and all to-rent, . . . V. viii. 43. 8
he was *rapt* with double ravishment, . . . VI. ix. 26. 4
astonished in spright, And *rapt* with pleasaunce, . . . VI. x. 17. 4
rapt with joy resembling heavenly madnes, . . . *Am.* xxxix. 9
rapt with wonder of their famous praise, . . . *Com. Son.* iii. 5
Rapt with the rage of mine own ravisht thought, . . . *H.H.B.* 1
Rare. Ravisht I was to see so *rare* a thing, . . . *Bel.*[1] v. 9
Ravisht I was so *rare* a thing to vew; . . . *Bel.*[2] v. 9
Bearing close envie to these riches *rare,* . . . *Bel.*[2] xiii. 6
To reade the secrete of this riddle *rare,* . . . *Gn. Ded.* 7
his ey-lids twinckling *rare* . . . *Gn.* 284
To tell my riches, and endowments *rare,* . . . *Ti.* 87
Thy father, that good Earle of *rare* renowne, . . . *Ti.* 261
The metall was of *rare* and passing price; . . . *Mui.* 76
mastered with workmanship so *rare,* . . . *Mui.* 338
For *rare* it seemes in reason to be skand, . . . *D.* 178
in her sex more wonderfull and *rare.* . . . *Col.* 491
Phyllis, the floure of *rare* perfection, . . . *Col.* 544
Sends to my doubtful eares these speaches *rare,* . . . I. ii. 32. 8
The God himselfe, vewing that mirrhour *rare,* . . . I. vi. 15. 6
He wondred at her wisedome hevenly *rare,* . . . I. vi. 31. 1
with stones most pretious *rare.* . . . I. vii. 29. 9
store they fownd of al that dainty was and *rare.* . . . I. viii. 50. 9
areedes . . . of adventures *rare:* . . . I. ix. 28. 7
them receives a gentle Squyre, Of . . . *rare* courtesee, . . . I. x. 7. 2
Of wondrous beauty and of bounty *rare,* . . . I. x. 30. 2
to her with reverence *rare* He humbly louted . . . I. x. 44. 5
ravished with *rare* impression in his sprite. . . . I. xii. 39. 9
rare ensample made, . . . II. ii. 25. 4
rare perfection in mortalitye, . . . II. ii. 41. 7
He was a man of *rare* redoubted might, . . . II. v. 26. 1
antique shapes of kings and kesars straunge and *rare.* . . . II. vii. 5. 9
with *rare* delight And gazing wonder . . . II. ix. 33. 2
let him heare some part of their *rare* melody. . . . II. xii. 33. 9
So fashioned a Porch with *rare* device. . . . II. xii. 54. 1
in th' other her *rare* chastitee. . . . III. Pr. 5. 9
A worke of *rare* device and wondrous wit. . . . III. i. 34. 6
woman of great bountihed, And of *rare* beautie, . . . III. i. 41. 6
Nought wanted there that dainty was and *rare,* . . . III. i. 51. 5
the vertues *rare* Which thereof spoken were, . . . III. ii. 22. 7
for pure chastitee and vertue *rare,* . . . III. iv. 3. 4
In stedfast chastitie and vertue *rare,* . . . III. v. 8. 5
Many Restoratives of vertues *rare,* . . . III. v. 50. 3
Of bounty, and of beautie, and all vertues *rare.* . . . III. vi. 4. 9
Need teacheth her this lesson hard and *rare,* . . . III. vii. 4. 3
with *rare* light his bote did beautifye, . . . III. viii. 22. 6
the *rare* sweetnesse of the melody . . . III. xii. 6. 3
Fansy, like a lovely Boy Of *rare* aspect, . . . III. xii. 7. 2
Full many great calamities and *rare* . . . IV. vii. 14. 3
now of dayes such temperance is *rare* . . . IV. viii. 29. 6
with the sweetnesse of her *rare* delight . . . IV. ix. 6. 6
Abounding all with delices most *rare,* . . . IV. x. 6. 2
much more *rare* and pretious to esteeme, . . . IV. x. 39. 6
of a fishes shell was wrought with *rare* delight. . . . IV. xi. 6. 9
toucht with soft remorse and pitty *rare;* . . . IV. xii. 12. 5
The royall banquets, and the *rare* delights, . . . V. iii. 3. 5
Are rapt with wonder and with *rare* affright. . . . V. iii. 19. 7
With all deare delices and *rare* delights, . . . V. iii. 40. 4
could be fram'd by workmans *rare* device; . . . V. ix. 27. 8
Yet did appeare *rare* beautie in her face, . . . V. ix. 38. 4
rare in-sight hard matters to revele; . . . V. ix. 39. 2
Royall examples of her mercies *rare* . . . V. x. 5. 6
gave him roiall giftes and riches *rare,* . . . V. x. 17. 2
nigh ravisht with *rare* thoughts delight, . . . VI. Pr. 1. 6
Him . . . he gan admire For the *rare* hope . . . VI. ii. 34. 3
divers flowres distinct with *rare* delight, . . . VI. iii. 23. 5
one of mickle might And manhood *rare,* . . . VI. iii. 40. 3
in a Jacket, quilted richly *rare* . . . VI. vii. 43. 3
markt her *rare* demeanure, . . . VI. ix. 11. 2
in all that world of beauties *rare,* . . . VI. x. 4. 6
Divine resemblaunce, beauty soveraine *rare,* . . . VI. x. 27. 4
the place, whose pleasures *rare* . . . his sences ravished, . . . VI. x. 30. 6
To cherish her with all things choice and *rare;* . . . VI. xii. 14. 7
rare perfection of each goodly part; . . . *Am.* xxiv. 2
Not ayre; for she is not so light or *rare:* . . . *Am.* lv. 7
admire such worlds *rare* wonderment; . . . *Am.* lxix. 12
he there may learne, with *rare* delight, . . . *Am.* lxxiii. 11
My verse your vertues *rare* shall eternize, . . . *Am.* lxxv. 11
Onely behold her *rare* perfection, . . . *Am.* lxxxiii. 13
Endewd with wisedomes riches, heavenly, *rare.* . . . *H.H.L.* 112
Rascall. As for the *rascall* Commons least he cared, . . . *Hub.* 1193
when him list the *raskall* routes appall, . . . I. vii. 35. 5
after all the *raskall* many ran, . . . I. xii. 9. 1
with his *raskall* routs t' enclose them rownd, . . . II. ix. 15. 4
with his sword disperst the *raskall* flockes, . . . II. xi. 19. 2
mingled with the *raskall* rablement, . . . III. xi. 46. 3
In the base blood of such a *rascall* crew; . . . V. ii. 52. 5
none appear'd of all that *raskall* rout, . . . V. ii. 54. 8
A *raskall* rout, with weapons rudely dight: . . . V. vi. 29. 4
The *raskall* manie soone they overthrew; . . . V. xi. 59. 8
did still pursew That *raskall* many . . . V. xi. 65. 2
Rased. *See* **Raced.**

Rased—*Continued.*
lightly *rased* her soft silken skin, . . . III. i. 65. 7
Rash. waylde the *rash* decay Of Phaeton, . . . *Gn.* 198
to wreake their *rash* contempt, . . . *Gn.* 579
Tickled with glorie and *rash* covetise: . . . *Hub.* 996
Unto the King so *rash* ye may not goe; . . . *Hub.* 1214
Bereave of sence each *rash* beholders sight. . . . *Col.* 547
'Least suddaine mischiefe ye too *rash* provoke: . . . I. i. 12. 2
Least . . . *rash* misweening doe thy hart remove: . . . I. iv. 1. 6
his *rash* syre began to rend His heare, . . . I. v. 39. 4
foolish man, so *rash* a doome to give? . . . I. ix. 38. 2
could have dazd the *rash* beholders sight, . . . I. x. 12. 8
Himselfe in streighter bandes too *rash* implyes, . . . I. xi. 23. 5
he by many *rash* adventures wan, . . . II. ii. 17. 4
bereav'd the *rash* beholders sight: . . . II. iii. 23. 5
As through the flouring forrest *rash* she fled, . . . II. iii. 30. 7
rash Occasion makes unquiet life!' . . . II. iv. 44. 7
T' avoide the *rash* assault . . . II. v. 10. 3
rash Pyrochles varlett, Atin hight, . . . II. v. 25. 4
I read thee *rash* and heedlesse of thy selfe, . . . II. vii. 7. 8
That was Ambition, *rash* desire to sty, . . . II. vii. 46. 8
better reason will aswage The *rash* revengers heat. . . . II. viii. 26. 7
suffred *rash* Pyrochles waste his ydle might. . . . II. viii. 48. 9
Threatning unheedy wrecke and *rash* decay, . . . II. x. 6. 5
So th' other did mens *rash* desires apall, . . . III. i. 46. 4
Carados her hand withheld From *rash* revenge, . . . III. iii. 55. 8
pardon simple man that *rash* did him displease. . . . III. x. 30. 9
shields did share, and mailes did *rash*, . . . IV. ii. 17. 9
rash provoking perils all about, . . . IV. ii. 46. 8
of his owne *rash* hand one wound was to be seene. . . . IV. vii. 35. 9
pardon crav'd for his so *rash* default, . . . VI. iii. 21. 8
Thretning *rash* eies which gaze on her so wide, . . . *Am.* v. 7
At every *rash* beholder passing by. . . . *Am.* xvi. 8
Rashing. *Rashing* off helmes, and ryving plates asonder, . . . V. iii. 8. 6
Rashly. with his hand him *rashly* bruzing slewe . . . *Gn.* 290
Yet he the name on him would *rashly* take, . . . *Hub.* 815
dare their follies forth so *rashlie* throwe, . . . *T.M.* 220
the presumptuous Damzell *rashly* dar'd . . . *Mui.* 269
daring not too *rashly* mount on hight, . . . *Col.* 421
how we *rashly* go To serve that God, . . . *Col.* 797
Rashly to wyten creatures so divine; . . . *Col.* 916
How *rashly* blame of Rosalind ye raise.' . . . *Col.* 926
The angry beastes not *rashly* to despise, . . . I. vi. 25. 5
With him in bloody armes they *rashly* did debate. . . . II. viii. 11. 9
Well weeting trew what she had *rashly* told; . . . II. ix. 39. 2
Rashly out of their rouzed couches sprong, . . . III. i. 62. 8
None of them *rashly* durst to her approch, . . . III. i. 64. 7
Ne durst adventure *rashly* in to wend, . . . III. iii. 14. 2
rashly through thy darksom dore Unwares have prest; . . . III. iii. 15. 7
voyage *rashly* make By this forbidden way . . . III. iv. 14. 5
hond Where ill became him *rashly* would have thrust; . . . III. viii. 25. 7
The wicked weapon *rashly* he did wrest, . . . III. xii. 33. 2
rashly lusted For thing unlawfull, . . . IV. i. 11. 3
As men awaked *rashly* out of dreme, . . . IV. ii. 17. 2
If he too *rashly* to his charet drew, . . . V. viii. 32. 2
valiant Knights doe *rashly* enterprize . . . VI. vi. 35. 4
rashly sought that which I mote not see.' . . . VI. x. 29. 7
stare Henceforth too *rashly* on that guilefull net, . . . *Am.* xxxvii. 10
T' accuse of pride, or *rashly* blame for ought. . . . *Am.* lxi. 4
my frayle thoughts too *rashly* led astray! . . . *Am.* lxxvi. 6
Rashness. sway in Court with pride and *rashnes* rude; . . . *T.M.* 328
Through unadvized *rashnes* woxen wood; . . . I. iv. 34. 3
Rash-witted. some *rash-witted* wight, . . . IV. viii. 29. 2
Rate. the costly *rate* Of riotise, . . . *Gn.* 92
Streight gan he him revyle, and bitter *rate*, . . . II. vi. 39. 3
As if he did a dogge in kenell *rate* . . . III. ix. 14. 7
right feeble through the evill *rate* Of food . . . IV. viii. 19. 5
No words may *rate*, nor rigour him remove . . . IV. ix. 31. 7
'Thus sate they all around in seemely *rate*: . . . IV. x. 52. 1
to revile, and *rate*, and recreant call, . . . VI. vii. 26. 8
Ne spareth he most learned wits to *rate*, . . . VI. xii. 40. 7
Rated. As *rated* Spaniell takes his burden up for feare. . . . V. i. 29. 9
him revil'd, and *rated*, and disdayned, . . . V. iii. 35. 8
Rathe. Sylvanes haunten *rathe*; . . . *S.C.* Jul. 78
Thus is my harvest hastened all to *rathe*; . . . *S.C.* D. 98
Too *rathe* cut off by practise criminall . . . III. iii. 28. 8
Rather. But *rather* wrought by his owne industry, . . . *Bel.* iv. 10
I say *rather*, though not all agreeing . . . *Ro.* ix. 12
The *rather* Lambes bene starved with cold, . . . *S.C.* F. 83
I (as I am) had *rather* be envied, . . . *S.C.* May 57
Rather then other should scorne at me: . . . *S.C.* May 60
rather rule and raigne in soveraign see, . . . *Hub.* 980
rather chose with scornfull shame Him to avenge, . . . *Hub.* 1239
Or *rather* learnd themselves behoves to bee, . . . *T.M.* 83
Doth *rather* choose to sit in idle Cell, . . . *T.M.* 221
rather seekes my sorrow to augment . . . *T.M.* 425
Rather desires to be forgotten quight, . . . *D.* 89
But *rather* riddance from long languishment. . . . *D.* 364
in hunting such felicitie, Or *rather* infelicitie, . . . *As.* 80
rather chose back to my sheep to tourne, . . . *Col.* 672
of spight . . . *rather* then of right . . . *Col.* 678
rather death desire then such despight. . . . I. vii. 49. 6
through his boldnes *rather* feare did reach; . . . I. ix. 25. 8
gives not *rather* cause it to forsake? . . . I. ix. 44. 5
With many *rather* for to goe astray, . . . I. x. 10. 6
me, sad mayd, or *rather* widow sad, . . . I. xii. 27. 1
'There did I find, or *rather* I was fownd . . . I. xii. 32. 1
forgery, *Rather* then matter of just memory; . . . II. Pr. 1. 5
'Or *rather* would, O! would it so had chaunst, . . . II. i. 10. 1
me behoveth *rather* to upbrayd, . . . II. i. 28. 4

Rather—*Continued.*
overcome Of anguish, *rather* then of crime, . . . II. i. 58. 7
Gan smyle on them, that *rather* ought to weepe, . . . II. ii. 1. 6
In daunger *rather* to be drent then brent?' . . . II. vi. 49. 7
Do *rather* choose my flitting houres to spend, . . . II. vii. 33. 7
rather fowler seemed to the *eye;* . . . II. vii. 61. 8
Or *rather* worthy of great Phoebus rote, . . . II. x. 3. 2
not Scuith *guiridh* . . . But *rather y scuith gogh,* . . . II. x. 24. 9
Rather then fly, or be captiv'd, her selfe she slew. . . . II. x. 55. 9
Rather for pleasure then for battery or fight. . . . II. xii. 43. 9
thother *rather* higher did arise, . . . II. xii. 66. 5
was arayd, or *rather* disarayd, . . . II. xii. 77. 3
But *rather* shewd more white, if more might bee: . . . II. xii. 77. 6
Dye *rather* would he then endure that same. . . . III. i. 9. 5
Their direfull rancour *rather* did encreasse; . . . III. i. 23. 4
But *rather* doth my helpelesse griefe augment; . . . III. ii. 43. 5
Dye *rather*, dye, then so disloyally Deeme . . . III. v. 45. 6
Dye *rather*, dye, then ever love disloyally. . . . III. v. 45. 9
Dye *rather*, dye, and dying doe her serve; . . . III. v. 46. 6
Dye *rather*, dye, then ever from her service swerve. . . . III. v. 46. 9
rather, dye, then ever so faire love forsake!' . . . III. v. 47. 9
rather chose to dye for sorow great, . . . III. v. 49. 8
Rather then of the tyrant to be caught: . . . III. vii. 26. 8
rather joyd to bee then seemen sich, . . . III. vii. 29. 8
misery craves *rather* mercy then repriefe. . . . III. viii. 1. 9
Dye had she *rather* in tormenting griefe . . . III. viii. 42. 3
rather do not ransack all, . . . III. ix. 8. 9
rather had he dy . . . III. ix. 14. 8
meant to ravish her, that *rather* had to dy. . . . III. x. 13. 9
Rather let try extremities of chaunce, . . . III. xi. 24. 8
But *rather* stird to cruell enmity, . . . III. xii. 1. 8
rather die then Ladies cause release: . . . IV. ii. 19. 7
rather ought in friendship for her sake To joyne . . . IV. ii. 24. 6
with thy meaning so I may the *rather* meete. . . . IV. ii. 34. 9
But *rather* will reserve it for a Canto new. . . . IV. ii. 54. 9
doe not *rather* wish them soone expire, . . . IV. iii. 1. 3
But *rather* stir'd to vengeance and despight, . . . IV. iii. 14. 4
but *rather* sought Him selfe to save, . . . IV. iii. 32. 3
Who would not to this vertue *rather* yeeld his voice? . . . IV. iii. 45. 9
And *rather* stird by his discordfull Dame, . . . IV. iv. 3. 7
boastful Braggadochio *rather* chose, . . . IV. iv. 14. 4
rather wholly dead Himselfe he wisht have beene, . . . IV. iv. 22. 8
That *rather* seemes, sith knowen armes ye shonne.' . . . IV. vi. 5. 5
And, *rather* then my love abandon so, . . . IV. vii. 16. 8
So had I *rather* to be thrall then free; . . . IV. xii. 10. 8
rather gan in troubled mind devize . . . IV. xii. 28. 8
But *rather* of his hand besought to die. . . . V. i. 18. 4
rather chose his challenge off to breake, . . . V. i. 24. 3
And *rather* guilty chose himselfe to yield: . . . V. i. 24. 5
Did yield she *rather* should with him remaine . . . V. i. 27. 5
rather then his love should suffer paine, He chose . . . V. i. 27. 7
rather in them kindled choler new: . . . V. ii. 13. 4
rather strove extremities to way, . . . V. ii. 49. 3
rather had to lose then trie in armes his right. . . . V. iii. 31. 9
I *rather* chose to die in lives despight, . . . V. iv. 32. 8
Rather then see her people spoiled . . . V. iv. 47. 8
Die *rather* would he . . . V. v. 46. 5
rather how she mote him faster tye. . . . V. v. 56. 6
he would make Her *rather* reade his meaning . . . V. vi. 9. 9
rather bent To peace then needlesse trouble . . . V. vi. 19. 6
desirous *rather* to rest mute, Then termes to entertaine . . . V. vi. 20. 3
rather then she kindnesse would despize, . . . V. vi. 20. 5
will ye sleepe? ah! wake, and *rather* weepe . . . V. vi. 25. 8
rather let, . . . to fall Few perling drops . . . V. ix. 50. 6
Dye, *rather* then doe ought that mote . . . V. xi. 55. 9
rather more enrag'd for those words sake; . . . VI. i. 19. 4
rather did more chearefull seeme therefore: . . . VI. i. 32. 5
Rather then let my selfe of wight be stroken, . . . VI. ii. 7. 8
He *rather* should have taken up behind; . . . VI. ii. 11. 5
but *rather* doe quite clame: . . . for you he spake it, . . . VI. ii. 14. 4
The *rather*, since that fortune hath this day . . . VI. ii. 33. 7
I . . . *rather* wish that some more noble hire . . . VI. ii. 34. 7
That *rather* seem'd the conquest of his might, . . . VI. v. 9. 4
And *rather* needed to be disciplinde . . . VI. vi. 5. 6
That *rather* needes wise read and discipline, . . . VI. vi. 13. 3
Yet *rather* counseld him contrarywize, . . . VI. vii. 22. 6
And *rather* did the more her beate and bruse: . . . VI. vii. 40. 5
Exceeding . . . mans stature, And *rather* like a Gyant . . . VI. vii. 41. 4
Rather then once his burden to sustaine: . . . VI. vii. 46. 7
Rather then hunt still after shadowes vaine . . . VI. x. 2. 7
'But thee, faire Titans child, I *rather* weene, . . . VII. vi. 32. 1
Chose *rather* to be praysd for dooing good, . . . *Am.* xxxviii. 13
Such heavenly formes ought *rather* worshipt be, . . . *Am.* lxi. 13
Rather then envy, let them wonder at her, . . . *Am.* lxxxiv. 7
not seeme . . . of any earthly Seede, But *rather* Angels, . . . *Proth.* 66
Rattle. all the dores to *rattle* round about: . . . III. xii. 37. 2
on his shield did *rattle* like to haile . . . VI. vi. 26. 3
Rattling. thunder which doth ryve The *rattling* heavens, . . . *Gn.* 520
rend the *ratling* skyes with flames of fouldring heat. . . . II. ii. 20. 9
Raught. *See* **Overraught.**
she *raught* the Gods owne mansions: . . . *Bel.*[2] vii. 8
That same hath Jesus Christ now to him *raught*, . . . *Hub.* 441
till ryper years he *raught;* . . . I. vi. 29. 2
to the hous of hevenly gods it *raught:* . . . I. vii. 18. 2
He to him *raught* a dagger sharpe and keene, . . . I. ix. 51. 2
so soone as ryper yeares he *raught*, . . . II. iii. 2. 6
Sometimes she *raught* him stones, . . . II. iv. 5. 5
Sir Guyons sword he lightly to him *raught*, . . . II. viii. 40. 2
from her shoulder to her heele downe *raught;* . . . II. ix. 19. 2
Till ryper yeares he *raught* . . . II. x. 20. 4

Raught—*Continued.*
his long legs nigh *raught* unto the ground. . . . . II. xi. 20. 6
the Prince his mortall speare Soone to him *raught*, . . . II. xi. 25. 2
then the Faery quickly *raught* His poynant speare, ... III. i. 5. 3
fayntly fluttering, scarce his helmet *raught*, ... III. v. 24. 8
To reach the sea ere she of him were *raught*: . . . . . . III. vii. 26. 6
Her golden locks, . . . *raught* unto her heeles; . . . . . III. ix. 20. 6
when so of his hand the pledge she *raught*, ... III. ix. 31. 1
Another plant, that *raught* to wondrous hight, ... III. ix. 47. 7
Her golden cup to them for drinke she *raught*, ... IV. iii. 48. 8
Sternly stept forth and *raught* away his speare, ... IV. iv. 20. 6
raught downe to his waste when up he stood, ... IV. vii. 6. 8
ere unto his hellish den he *raught*, ... IV. vii. 31. 2
raught full low adowne. . . . . IV. x. 31. 9
In which she noursled him till yeares he *raught*, ... V. i. 6. 8
Untill the ripenesse of mans yeares he *raught*; . . . . . V. i. 8. 3
he *raught* her Such an huge stroke, ... V. iv. 41. 4
it *raught* Downe to her lowest heele; . . . . V. v. 2. 7
Did stay her cruell hand ere she her *raught*; . . . . . . V. viii. 48. 2
Eftsoones againe his axe he *raught* on hie, ... V. xi. 10. 1
When Calidore these ruefull newes had *raught*, ... VI. xi. 33. 1
had *raught* Faire Pastorella from those Brigants powre, . . VI. xii. 3. 1
raught forth her hand To pluck her downe . . . . VII. vi. 13. 2

Rauran. His dwelling . . . Under the foot of *Rauran* mossy hore, ... I. ix. 4. 6

Rave. thousand enemies about us *rave*, ... II. ix. 12. 6
With murmurous disdayne doth inly *rave*, ... II. xi. 32. 3
with great terrour *rave*. . . . . II. xii. 5. 9
gainst which doe *rave* The roring billowes . . . . III. viii. 37. 2
he therewith so felly still did *rave*, ... IV. vii. 28. 5
made him *rave*, like to a Lyon wood, ... V. viii. 35. 5

Raved. He *rav'd*, he wept, he stampt, he lowd did cry, . . . III. x. 17. 7

Raven. *See* **Night-raven.**
Then was the Germane *Raven* in disguise . . . . *Ro.* xvii. 9
to dislodge the *Raven* of her nest? . . . . *S.C.* D. 32
be entombed in the *raven* or the kight?' . . . . II. viii. 16. 9
a *Raven*, far from rising Sunne, ... III. iii. 46. 5
They spoile and *ravine* without all remorse; . . . . . . IV. iv. 35. 8

Ravenings. At all that came within his *ravenings*; . . . . VI. xii. 28. 4

Ravenous. bene of *ravenous* Wolves yrent, ... *S.C.* S. 148
the herds Of *ravenous* wilde beasts, ... *Hub.* 1285
No *ravenous* wolves the good mans hope destroy . . . . . *Col.* 318
next to him malicious Envy rode Upon a *ravenous* wolfe, . . I. iv. 30. 2
What ever thing does touch his *ravenous* pawes, ... I. xi. 12. 4
Lions . . . *ravenous* hunger did thereto constraine: . . . . I. xi. 37. 4
rend in peeces with his *ravenous* pawes, ... II. vii. 27. 8
Cormoyraunts, with birds of *ravenous* race, ... II. xii. 8. 5
escaped from a *ravenous* beast, ... III. vii. 1. 2
riding on a Lion *ravenous*, ... III. xii. 22. 2
harbour here in safety from those *ravenous* dogs.' . . . . V. x. 23. 9
A *ravenous* Wolfe amongst the scattered flockes: . . . . . V. xii. 38. 6
Watching to drive the *ravenous* Wolfe away, ... VI. ix. 37. 4
He rampt upon him with his *ravenous* pawes, ... VI. xii. 29. 8

Ravens. *See* **Night-ravens.**

Raves (whereat he *raves* With roring rage, ... III. ix. 45. 3

Ravin. Alike with equall *ravine* to devoure. . . . . . . *Bel.*[2] viii. 8
A Dragon . . . would his rightfull *ravine* rend away: . . . I. v. 8. 5
With murdrous *ravine*, and devouring might, ... I. vii. 44. 4
into his darke abysse all *ravin* fell. . . . . I. xi. 12. 9
he liv'd all on *ravin* and on rape . . . . IV. vii. 5. 7
Full of fell *ravin* and fierce greedinesse; . . . . V. xi. 24. 2

Ravine. *See* **Raven, Ravin.**

Ravish. meant to *ravish* her, that rather had to dy. . . . . III. x. 13. 9
all the sences they doe *ravish* quite; . . . . *Epith.* 136

Ravished. *Ravisht* I was to see so rare a thing, ... *Bel.*[1] v. 9
My sprites were *ravisht* with these pleasures . . . . *Pet.*[1] iii. 7
Ravisht I was so rare a thing to vew; . . . . *Bel.*[2] v. 9
with their sweetnes I was *ravish't* nere. . . . . *Pet.*[2] iii. 7
th' one was *ravisht* of his owne bondmaide, ... *Gn.* 489
Robbed of sense, and *ravished* with joy: . . . . *Ti.* 321
weaker sence it could have *ravisht* quight: . . . . I. i. 45. 5
Was never hart so *ravisht* with delight, ... I. ix. 14. 6
ravished with rare impression in his sprite. . . . . . . I. xii. 39. 9
with her wondrous beauty *ravisht* quight, ... II. iii. 42. 4
At last, quite *ravisht* with delight . . . . II. x. 69. 1
with his melting sweetnes *ravished*, ... III. Pr. 4. 7
All that her saw with wonder *ravisht* weare, ... IV. v. 14. 5
nigh *ravisht* with rare thoughts delight, ... VI. Pr. 1. 6
the place, whose pleasures rare . . . his sences *ravished*, . . VI. x. 30. 7
all the gods were *ravisht* with delight . . . . VII. vii. 12. 8
leapt and daunc't as they had *ravisht* beene! . . . . . . VII. vii. 34. 8
It *ravisht* is with fancies wonderment: . . . . *Am.* iii. 12
My soule was *ravisht* quite as in a traunce; . . . . *Am.* xxxix. 10
How was I *ravisht* with your lovely sight, ... *Am.* lxxvi. 5
The *ravisht* harts of gazefull men . . . . *H.B.* 12
ravisht with devouring great desire Of his deare selfe, . . *H.H.L.* 268
Then shall thy *ravisht* soule inspired bee . . . . *H.H.L.* 281
Rapt with the rage of mine own *ravisht* thought, ... *H.H.B.* 1

Ravishment. with secret *ravishment* He stole away, ... *As.* 21
in sweete *ravishment* pourd out her spright. . . . . III. xii. 45. *or.* 7
he was rapt with double *ravishment*, ... VI. ix. 26. 4

Raw. great lumps of flesh and gobbets *raw*, ... I. i. 20. 3
all his sinewes woxen weake and *raw*, ... I. x. 2. 3
In which yett trickling blood, and gobbets *raw*, ... I. xi. 13. 3
His cheeke-bones *raw*, and eie-pits hollow grew, ... IV. xii. 20. 3
A villaine to them came with scull all *raw*, ... V. ii. 11. 5
Her lips were, like *raw* lether, pale and blew: . . . . . . V. xii. 29. 7

Raw-bone. His *rawbone* armes, . . . Were clene consum'd; . . I. viii. 41. 6
His *raw-bone* cheekes . . . Were shronke into his jawes, . . I. ix. 35. 8
With hollow eyes and *rawbone* cheekes forspent, ... IV. v. 34. 4

Ray. *See* **Array.**
with their villeine feete the streame did *ray* . . . . . . *Bel.*[2] xii. 13
as Dame Cynthias silver *raye*, ... *S.C.* Au. 89
The raging fyre that kindled at his *ray*. . . . . *S.C.* D. 58
from the force of Phoebus boyling *ray*, ... *Gn.* 167
her Bridegrome was in readie *ray* To come to her, ... *Ti.* 640
Dimmed her former beauties shining *ray*, ... I. ii. 38. 7
A mayden Queene that shone as Titans *ray*, ... I. iv. 8. 5
face all tand with scorching sunny *ray*, ... I. vi. 35. 4
armour . . . Like glauncing light of Phoebus brightest *ray*; . I. vii. 29. 5
so exceeding shone his glistring *ray*, ... I. vii. 34. 5
succour from the scorching *ray*, ... II. i. 35. 6
the cleane waves with purple gore did *ray*: . . . . II. i. 40. 4
In secrete shadow from the sunny *ray*, ... II. v. 32. 2
before the Morne with cremosin *ray* . . . . II. xi. 3. 1
Such was the beautie and the shining *ray*, ... III. i. 43. 8
Through influence of th' hevens fruitfull *ray*, ... III. vi. 6. 2
As doth the lilly fresh before the sunny *ray*. . . . . . . III. vi. 38. 9
'Fresh shadowes, fit to shroud from sunny *ray*; . . . . . IV. x. 24. 1
Ne ever evening saw, ne mornings *ray*, ... IV. xi. 4. 7
spoyling all her geares and goodly *ray* . . . . V. ii. 50. 4
flakes of fire, bright as the sunny *ray*, ... V. v. 8. 3
in *ray* Came dauncing forth, ... V. xi. 34. 3
envies cloud still dimmeth vertues *ray*. . . . . V. xii. 27. 7
And from his face the filth that did it *ray*; . . . . . . VI. iv. 23. 5
Like to the Evening starre adorn'd with deawy *ray*. . . . VI. vii. 19. 9
star, that wont with her bright *ray* Me to direct, ... *Am.* xxxiv. 5
Thrugh the broad world doth spred his goodly *ray*; . . . . *Am.* xl. 8
send, Into the glooming world, his gladsome *ray*: . . . . *Am.* lxii. 10
th' onely image of that heavenly *ray*, ... *Am.* lxxxvii. 7
Faire Sun! shew forth thy favourable *ray*, ... *Epith.* 117
lend him light from her owne goodly *ray*; . . . . *H.L.* 73
lampe, from whose celestiall *ray* That light proceedes, . . *H.B.* 99
what booteth that celestiall *ray*, ... *H.B.* 187

Rayed. Ruffled and fowly *raid* with filthy soyle, ... III. viii. 32. 2

Rayne, *etc.* *See* **Rain, Reign, Rein,** *etc.*

Raynold's. *See* **Reynold's.**

Rayons. a thousand *rayons* threw . . . . *Bel.*[2] ii. 7

Rays. *See* **Sun-rays.**
threw forth a thousand *rayes* . . . . *Bel.*[1] ii. 7
Of this faire fire the faire dispersed *rayes* . . . . . . *Bel.*[1] ix. 9
Of this faire fire the scattered *rayes* . . . . *Bel.*[2] xi. 9
'Shewe thyselfe, Cynthia, with thy silver *rayes*, ... *S.C.* Ap. 82
shroude in shady leaves from sonny *rayes*, ... *S.C.* Jun. 54
the glauncing *rayes* Of precious stones, ... *Gn.* 101
lakes that Phoebus sunnie *rayes* Doo never see, ... *Gn.* 619
Through the myld temperance of her goodly *raies*. . . . . *Col.* 551
Like Phoebus face adornd with sunny *rayes*, ... II. viii. 5. 6
before the sunny *rayes* He us'd to slug, ... III. vii. 12. 7
all the earth doest lighten with thy *rayes*, ... VI. x. 28. 2

Raze. *See* **Race, Rase.**

Reach. *See* **Overreach.**
hie as mought an Archer *reache* with sight. . . . . *Bel.*[1] iii. 4
with hir wings to *reache* The place . . . . *Bel.*[1] vi. 7
May *reach* from hence to depth of darkest hell, ... *Ro.* i. 6
things exceeding *reach* of common reason; . . . . *Van.* i. 4
The billowes striving to the heavens to *reach*, ... *Gn.* 575
speach Against Gods holie Ministers oft *reach*, ... *Hub.* 840
both from his *reach*: . . . . *Hub.* 991
No *reach*, no breach, that might him profit bring, ... *Hub.* 1141
for his rough hide He gan to *reach*, ... *Hub.* 1336
Above the *reach* of ruinous decay, ... *Ti.* 422
Being above my slender reasons *reach*; . . . . *Ti.* 487
reatch his hand into his enemies hoast. . . . . *Ti.* 542
Above the *reach* of anie living sight: . . . . *Ti.* 628
passeth reasons *reach*, ... *Col.* 837
joy of living speach, Can hart . . . *reach?* . . . . I. vii. 39. 3
from his arme did *reach* Those keyes, ... I. viii. 34. 6
through his boldnes rather feare did *reach*; . . . . I. ix. 25. 8
That weaker witt of man could never *reach*; . . . . I. x. 19. 5
what within his *reach* he ever drawes. . . . . I. xi. 12. 5
Bad on that Messenger rude hands to *reach*. . . . . I. xii. 35. 3
lower part did *reach* to lowest Hell; . . . . II. vii. 46. 4
did often thinke To *reach* the fruit . . . . II. vii. 58. 5
Far *reach* her mercies, and her praises farre, ... II. ix. 4. 8
To *reach*, when ever he for ought did send; . . . . II. ix. 58. 5
contending to excell The *reach* of men, ... II. x. 26. 9
His wonder far exceeded reasons *reach*, ... II. xi. 40. 1
with her right the riper fruit did *reach*, ... II. xii. 56. 2
yet love can higher stye Then reasons *reach*, ... III. ii. 36. 6
reach into the house that beares the stile . . . . III. iii. 48. 7
To *reach* the sea ere she of him were raught: . . . . . . III. vii. 26. 6
appeare . . . flames and *reach* to hevens hight, ... III. x. 12. 8
As if his dayes were come to their last *reach*: . . . . . . III. xi. 12. 5
That one did *reach* the other pusht away; . . . . IV. i. 29. 2
ere she could him *reach*, ... IV. vii. 32. 3
them seeing past the *reach* of eare, ... IV. viii. 36. 7
Till I was throughly past the perill of his *reach*. . . . . IV. x. 36. 9
These towring rocks, which *reach* unto the skie, ... V. ii. 38. 3
Ill can he rule the great that cannot *reach* the small.' . . V. ii. 43. 9
Their sound did *reach* unto the heavens hight: . . . . . . V. v. 4. 6
Sith shady dampe had dimd the heavens *reach*, ... V. vi. 21. 8
all that ever came within his *reach* . . . . V. vii. 35. 6
That one sure stroke he might unto him *reach*, ... V. viii. 37. 4
Then up arose a person of deepe *reach*, ... V. ix. 39. 1
if I yet him nigh may *reach*, I may avenge him . . . . . . VI. ii. 42. 5
even to the heavens theyr shouting shrill Doth *reach*, . . . *Epith.* 142
Above the *reach* of loathly sinfull lust, ... *H.L.* 179
Farre above feeble *reach* of earthly sight, ... *H.H.L.* 5

Reaches. She it revives, and new occasion *reaches*; . . . . IV. ii. 12. 7

Reaching. at that instant *reaching* forth his sweard . . . . IV. iii. 33. 6
That nothing may escape her *reaching* might, ... V. xi. 24. 8
Read. *See* **Book-read, Fore-read, Over-read, Rad, Rede.**
When ye, these rythmes doo *read,* . . . . *Pet.*[2] vii. 11
posteritie Of age ensuing shall you ever *read?* . . . . *Ro.* xxxii. 2
ye, that *read* these ruines tragicall, ... *Van.* xii. 9
when his honor has thee *redde,* . . . . *To his Booke* 11
reede me what payne doth thee so appall; . . . . *S.C.* Au. 15
To *reade* the secrete of this riddle rare, ... *Gn. Ded.* 7
whether God or Fortune . . . Its hard to *read:* . . . . *Gn.* 303
read he could not evidence, nor will, ... *Hub.* 382
to *read* Homelies upon holidayes; . . . . *Hub.* 393
Much good deep learning one thereout may *reed;* . . . . *Hub.* 484
read (faire Sir, of grace) from whence come yee; . . . . *Hub.* 604
fortunes *read* Out of their hands, ... *Hub.* 698
Harvey, the happy above happiest men I *read;* . . . . *Com. Son.* i. 2
in this halfe happie I doo *read* Good Melibae, ... *Ti.* 435
That might for anie Princes couche be *red,* . . . . *Ti.* 633
Let *reade* the rufull plaint herein exprest, ... *D.* 4
When passing by ye *read* these wofull layes, ... *D.* 536
Shall hap to heare, or covet them to *read:* . . . . *As.* Pr. 14
read now eke, . . . What dittie did . . . . *Col.* 159
None fairer, nor more fruitfull to be *red:* . . . . *Col.* 279
if I her like ought on earth might *read,* . . . . *Col.* 336
His Eliseis would be *redde* anew. . . . . *Col.* 403
Ne lesse praise-worthie I Theana *read,* . . . . *Col.* 492
Ne lesse praise-worthie Stella do I *read,* . . . . *Col.* 532
And, in so faire a land as may be *redd,* . . . . *Ded. Son.* v. 5
Such . . . shapes elswher may no man *reed.* . . . . I. i. 21. 9
words most horrible, (Let none them *read*) . . . . I. i. 37. 2
his Portesse still he bare, . . . but therein little *redd;* . . . . I. iv. 19. 2
could . . . fortunes tell, and *read* in loving bookes, ... I. iv. 25. 8
read her sorrow in her count'nance sad; . . . . I. vi. 11. 4
the sad sight which mine eies have *red;* . . . . I. vi. 36. 8
Whose kingdomes seat Cleopolis is *red;* . . . . I. vii. 46. 7
all in vaine, for he has *redd* his end . . . . I. viii. 21. 4
hast not *red* How ill it sits . . . . I. viii. 33. 4
'to *read* aright The course of heavenly cause, ... I. ix. 6. 6
That none could *reade* except she did them teach, ... I. x. 19. 2
Each bone might through his body well be *red* . . . . I. x. 48. 5
That hast my name and nation *redd* aright, ... I. x. 67. 3
great vertues over-all were *redd;* . . . . I. xi. 46. 4
he disclosing *read* thus, as the paper spake: . . . . I. xii. 25. 9
When he these bitter byting wordes had *red,* . . . . I. xii. 29. 1
of the world least part to us is *red;* . . . . II. Pr. 2. 2
'False traytour certes,' . . . 'I *read* the man, ... II. i. 17. 7
read who hath ye wrought this shamefull plight, ... II. i. 18. 2
grievous outrage, which he *red* A knight had wrought . . . II. i. 30. 5
All good and honour might therein be *red,* . . . . II. iii. 24. 5
read how art thou nam'd, and of what kin?' . . . . II. iv. 36. 6
Of Phaedria, (for so my name is *red*) . . . . II. vi. 9. 7
I *read* thee rash and heedlesse of thy selfe, ... II. vii. 7. 8
'All otherwise' (saide he) 'I riches *read,* . . . . II. vii. 12. 1
whose kinds mote not be *redd:* . . . . II. vii. 51. 5
In whose dead face he *redd* great magnanimity. . . . . II. viii. 23. 9
'Now, felon, sure I *read,* How that thou art . . . . II. viii. 30. 2
read, what wicked hand hath robbed mee . . . . II. viii. 54. 1
'Sir knight, mote I of you this court'sy *read,* . . . . II. ix. 2. 6
'if in that picture dead Such life ye *read,* . . . . II. ix. 3. 2
To *read* those bookes; . . . . II. ix. 60. 9
Guyon all this while his booke did *read,* . . . . II. x. 70. 1
So long they *redd* in those antiquities, ... II. x. 77. 3
here to be *red* By these rent reliques, ... II. xii. 9. 6
more might in that goodly gate Be *red,* . . . . II. xii. 46. 2
To *read* what manner musicke that mote bee: . . . . II. xii. 70. 6
the sage wisard telles, as he has *redd,* . . . . III. i. 16. 8
whose royaltee And rich purveyance might uneath be *red;* . . . III. i. 33. 3
read where I that faytour false may find.' . . . . III. ii. 13. 2
to *read* Where now on earth, or how, he may be fownd; . . . III. ii. 14. 1
who does wonder, that has *red* the Towre . . . . III. ii. 20. 2
as sure I *read* By knowen signes . . . . III. ii. 33. 2
My crime, (if crime it be) I will it *reed.* . . . . III. ii. 37. 7
whence it sprong, I can not *read* aright: But this I *read,* . . III. iii. 16. 7, 8
'Ah! *read,'* (quoth Britomart) 'how is she hight?' . . . . III. iii. 56. 1
when I *reade,* how stout Debora strake Proud Sisera, ... III. iv. 2. 7
can ye *read,* Sir, how I may her finde, ... III. v. 6. 9
of her selfe, her name Belphoebe *red:* . . . . III. vi. 28. 5
As ye may elswhere *reade* that ruefull history. . . . . III. vi. 53. 9
read, thou Squyre of Dames, what vow is this, ... III. vii. 53. 2
I note *read* aright What hard misfortune brought . . . . III. viii. 23. 7
in his eye his meaning wisely *redd,* . . . . III. ix. 28. 6
well she *redd* out of the learned line: . . . . III. ix. 30. 8
proude of that new honour which they *redd,* . . . . III. x. 44. 7
with Sir Satyrane, as earst ye *red,* . . . . III. xi. 3. 1
freely *read* what wicked felon so Hath outrag'd you, ... III. xi. 15. 2
whose names is hard to *read:* . . . . III. xii. 25. 2
names and natures I note *readen* well; . . . . III. xii. 26. 2
dreadfull thinges out of that balefull booke He *red,* . . . . III. xii. 36. 4
all the while he *red,* . . . . III. xii. 36. 8
That she may . . . *reade* this lesson often. . . . . IV. Pr. 5. 9
That by her monstrous shape might easily be *red.* . . . . IV. i. 26. 9
mongst the manie vertues which we *reed,* . . . . IV. ii. 39. 8
A straunger knight, from whence no man could *reed,* . . . . IV. iv. 39. 2
The signes of anguish one mote plainely *read,* . . . . IV. v. 45. 8
reade you, Sir, sith ye my name have hight, ... IV. vi. 4. 4
that same knight, whom by his launce I *read,* . . . . IV. vi. 7. 8
whence he was, . . . I have not *red,* . . . . IV. vii. 7. 8
read to me, by what devise or wit Hast thou . . . . IV. vii. 19. 3
who he whilome was uneath was to be *red.* . . . . IV. vii. 40. 9
when as these rimes be *red* With misregard, ... IV. viii. 29. 1

Read—*Continued.*
Of two full hard to *read* the harder theft: . . . . IV. ix. 36. 6
'Which when I *red,* my heart did inly earne, ... IV. x. 9. 1
(as we in records *reed*) . . . . IV. xi. 8. 5
read the salvage cuntreis thorough which they pace. . . . . IV. xi. 40. 9
wondrous sholes which may of none be *red.* . . . . IV. xii. 2. 5
Nought could she *read* the roote of his disease, ... IV. xii. 22. 1
Which love he *red* to be, ... IV. xii. 25. 9
Read therefore who it is which this hath wrought, ... IV. xii. 30. 6
And if then those may any worse be *red,* . . . . V. Pr. 2. 8
not that arme, nor thou the man, I *reed,* . . . . V. iii. 21. 3
Her rather *reade* his meaning then him selfe it spake. . . . V. vi. 9. 9
Whose like before she never saw nor *red;* . . . . V. vii. 5. 7
what so penaunce shall by you be *red.'* . . . . V. viii. 13. 6
In cyphers strange, that few could rightly *read,* . . . . V. ix. 26. 3
So now *Malfont* was plainely to be *red,* . . . . V. ix. 26. 6
Nor of ought else that may be richest *red,* . . . . V. ix. 28. 3
many high regards and reasons gainst her *red.* . . . . V. ix. 43. 9
That he had *red* her Riddle, ... V. xi. 25. 5
Whether withheld from me . . . I cannot *read* aright. . . . V. xi. 49. 9
Marriner doth *reed* A storme approching . . . . V. xii. 18. 5
all her bones might through her cheekes be *red:* . . . . V. xii. 29. 6
that long the marke was to be *read.* . . . . V. xii. 39. 9
Well may I, certes, such an one thee *read,* . . . . VI. ii. 25. 6
taking counsell of a wise man *red,* . . . . VI. ii. 30. 1
mightst rightly *reed* Me then to be full base . . . . VI. iii. 31. 7
That plainely may in this wyld man be *red,* . . . . VI. v. 2. 1
which he by signes did *reede,* . . . . VI. v. 10. 5
when the roules were *red* . . . . VI. vii. 33. 1
every body two, and two she foure did *read.* . . . . VI. viii. 31. 9
his words, which he with reason *red,* . . . . VI. x. 30. 5
read thou, shepheard, *read* what destiny . . . . VI. xi. 29. 7
Which who will *read* set forth so as it ought, ... VII. vii. 9. 8
reade the sorrowes of my dying spright, ... *Am.* i. 7
Such art of eyes I never *read* in bookes! . . . . *Am.* xxi. 14
Love-learned letters to her eyes to *read;* . . . . *Am.* xliii. 12
lyke to those which *red* Medusaes mazeful hed. . . . . *Epith.* 189
wonders doe they *reede* To their conceipt, ... *H.B.* 246
your faire eyes these fearefull lines shal *read,* . . . . *H.B.* 283
ye that wont . . . To *reade* my fault, ... *H.H.L.* 16
And *read,* through love, his mercies manifold. . . . . *H.H.L.* 224
From thence *reade* on the storie of his life, ... *H.H.L.* 232
therein *reed* The endlesse kinds of creatures . . . . *H.H.B.* 31
To *reade* enregistred in every nooke His goodnesse, ... *H.H.B.* 131
enlumineth the . . . aire, whereby al things are *red;* . . . . *H.H.B.* 165
Readily. the proud beasts him *readily* obayd: . . . . *Hub.* 1102
names I cannot *readily* now ghesse: . . . . *Col.* 740
readily they shut and open might. . . . . II. ix. 46. 8
Of which her selfe avising *readily.* . . . . III. iii. 59. 5
As she had learned *readily* by rote; . . . . IV. ix. 6. 5
The rest my selfe too *readily* can spell.' . . . . V. vi. 11. 6
Readiness. Each did prepare, in *readines* to bee. . . . . *Hub.* 107
bad her all things put in *readinesse* anon. . . . . III. iii. 57. 9
So stood they both in *readinesse* thereby . . . . V. iv. 6. 5
putting all In *readinesse,* forth to the Towne-gate went; . . V. iv. 50. 2
Reading. *reading* it with inward loathfulnesse, ... IV. xii. 32. 8
Reads. Which fame of her shrill trompet worthy *reedes;* . . II. vii. 2. 7
Who wonders not, that *reades* so wonderous worke? . . . . III. ii. 20. 1
Miraculous may seeme to him that *reades* . . . . III. vi. 8. 1
Ready. (Alas! that it so *ready* should stand!) . . . . *S.C.* F. 196
bids make *readie* Maias bowre, ... *S.C.* Mar. 17
come by *readie* meanes unto his end, ... *Hub.* 127
I would be *readie,* both in deed and word, ... *Hub.* 252
bad next day that all should *readie* be: . . . . *Hub.* 329
readie are of anie to make preife. . . . . *Hub.* 408
Bridegrome was in *readie* ray To come . . . . *Ti.* 640
Thus the fresh Clarion, being *readie* dight, ... *Mui.* 145
seeing *readie* tide, He rusheth forth, ... *Mui.* 405
She, all resolv'd, and *ready* to remove, ... *D.* 261
still I may be *readie* on my way . . . . *D.* 458
should it not thy *readie* course restraine, ... *Col.* 82
ready entraunce was not at his call; . . . . I. iii. 16. 6
Redoubted battaile *ready* to darrayne, ... I. iv. 40. 2
twise he reeled, *readie* twise to fall: . . . . I. v. 11. 6
Through mirkesome aire her *ready* way she makes: . . . . I. v. 28. 3
got his *ready* steed, and fast away gan ryde. . . . . I. vi. 8. 9
Amendment *readie* still at hand did wayt, ... I. x. 26. 7
to heaven she teacheth him the *ready* path. . . . . I. x. 33. 9
nothing might his *ready* passage stay: . . . . I. x. 35. 5
ever *ready* for your foeman fell: . . . . I. xi. 2. 5
to battaile *ready* drest, ... I. xi. 15. 7
did himselfe to battaile *ready* dight; . . . . I. xi. 52. 3
in the rest his *ready* speare did sticke: . . . . II. i. 26. 3
They bene ymett, both *ready* to affrap, ... II. i. 26. 6
that brave steed there finding *ready* dight, ... II. iii. 4. 8
yield him *ready* passage to that other part. . . . . II. vi. 36. 9
Ready to drowne him selfe for fell despight: . . . . II. vi. 43. 5
the golden metall, *ready* to be tryde. . . . . II. vii. 35. 9
So *ready* dight fierce battaile to assay, ... II. viii. 22. 8
were enraunged *ready* still for fight. . . . . II. ix. 26. 5
ready dight with drapets festivall, ... II. ix. 27. 3
them awaited *ready* at the ford The Ferriman, ... II. xi. 4. 1
his mischievous bow full *readie* bent, ... II. xi. 24. 4
Ne hedge ne ditch his *readie* passage brake; . . . . II. xi. 26. 5
many Groomes and Squyres *ready* were . . . . II. xi. 49. 1
Sir knight, your *ready* arms about you throw.' . . . . II. xii. 37. 9
bare to *ready* spoyle Of hungry eies, ... II. xii. 78. 1
bandes, which there they *readie* found: . . . . II. xii. 82. 5
ne *ready* answere make, ... III. ii. 5. 2
tooke their *ready* way Unto the Church, ... III. ii. 48. 3

Ready—*Continued.*
Tho to their *ready* Steedes they clombe full light, . . . III. iii. 61. 6
kept her *ready* way Along the strond; . . . III. iv. 18. 2
Them yielded *ready* passage, and their rage surceast. . . . III. iv. 31. 9
His *readie* wound with better salves new drest: . . . III. v. 41. 4
her *ready* to arrest; . . . III. vii. 2. 6
The Monster, *ready* on the pray to sease, . . . III. vii. 28. 1
With greedy jawes her *ready* for to teare: . . . III. viii. 33. 7
they restrained were Of *ready* entraunce, . . . III. viii. 52. 4
So *readie* rype to ill ill wemens counsels bee! . . . III. x. 11. 9
ready seeing him with her to fly, . . . III. x. 14. 2
as on the *readie* flore Of some Theatre, . . . III. xii. 3. 5
They to his succour ran with *readie* ayd; . . . IV. i. 37. 2
Returned *readie* newes, that those same . . . IV. ii. 31. 5
there arresting, *readie* way did yield For bloud . . . IV. iii. 9. 4
him affronting soone, to fight was *readie* prest. . . . IV. iii. 22. 9
One in bright armes, with *ready* speare in rest, . . . IV. iv. 6. 6
Shewing him selfe all *ready* for the field. . . . IV. iv. 17. 5
as it fell, his steed he *ready* found; . . . IV. iv. 23. 3
readie were new battell to darraine. . . . IV. v. 24. 6
Till I thereto had all things *ready* dight. . . . IV. vii. 17. 4
With bow in hand and arrowes *ready* bent, . . . IV. vii. 29. 6
she *ready* shewed The arrow . . . IV. vii. 30. 3
Even as he *ready* was there to have entred, . . . IV. vii. 31. 3
With *ready* hand it to have reft away; . . . IV. viii. 10. 6
They passing forth kept on their *readie* way, . . . IV. viii. 37. 1
Had not the noble Prince his *readie* stroke represt: . . . IV. viii. 41. 9
with *readie* quicke foresight . . . IV. viii. 44. 8
thereto did with *readie* will consent, . . . IV. viii. 64. 8
ready to obay; . . . IV. xi. 29. 2
thitherward forthright his *ready* way did make. . . . V. ii. 10. 9
on the Bridge he *ready* armed saw The Sarazin, . . . V. ii. 11. 2
both Together ran with *ready* speares in rest. . . . V. ii. 12. 4
With weapons in their hands as *ready* for to fight. . . . V. iv. 21. 9
ready for the gallow-tree prepard: . . . V. iv. 22. 4
Where was a rich Pavilion *ready* pight . . . V. v. 4. 8
to his fortunes helpe make *readie* way?' . . . V. v. 39. 4
readie to deserve what grace I found.' . . . V. v. 42. 5
So forth she rode uppon her *ready* way, . . . V. vi. 18. 1
Two Knights all armed *ready* for to fight; . . . V. vi. 29. 2
in his hand his thresher *ready* keight. . . . V. vi. 29. 7
Was to the battell whilome *ready* dight. . . . V. vii. 27. 6
Did forth issue all *ready* for the fight: . . . V. vii. 27. 8
finding there *ready* prest Sir Artegall, . . . V. viii. 9. 1
He at him ran with *ready* speare in rest; . . . V. viii. 9. 3
The Briton Prince him *readie* did awayte, . . . V. viii. 29. 3
ere his *readie* speare He could advance, . . . V. viii. 33. 5
all his armours *readie* dight that day, . . . V. x. 16. 3
When he was *readie* to his steede to mount . . . V. x. 16. 8
Into his shield it *readie* passage found, . . . V. x. 33. 2
Her *ready* to assaile, . . . V. xi. 26. 3
To weete if shipping *readie* he mote there descry. . . . V. xii. 3. 9
they found A ship all *readie* . . . V. xii. 4. 2
Whereas they *readie* found, them to repell, Great hostes of men V. xii. 4. 7
cast his shield about to be in *readie* plight. . . . V. xii. 16. 9
long restrayned of his *ready* course, . . . VI. i. 21. 3
from the battlements she *ready* seem'd to fall. . . . VI. i. 34. 9
this Lady, . . . is *ready* to forgo the ghost; . . . VI. iii. 39. 4
Whom when her Host saw *readie* to depart, . . . VI. v. 8. 1
when as all things *readie* were aright, . . . VI. viii. 45. 1
with a naked knife *Readie* to launch her brest, . . . VI. viii. 48. 9
supper *readie* dight they to it fell . . . VI. ix. 17. 7
Was *readie* oft his owne heart to devoure, . . . VI. ix. 39. 4
Besides a thousand more which *ready* bee . . . VI. x. 21. 7
ready now to rend His loves deare spoile, . . . VI. x. 35. 7
being *readie* met By some of these same theeves . . . VI. xi. 9. 6
his owne flesh he *readie* was to teare: . . . VI. xi. 25. 6
sith he well knew The *readie* way . . . VI. xi. 35. 2
Where all the rest for him did *readie* stay, . . . VI. xi. 47. 7
ready passage to her pleasure did prepaire. . . . VII. vi. 7. 9
his ploughing-share and coulter *ready* tyde. . . . VII. vii. 39. 9
For lusty Spring . . . Is *ready* to come forth, . . . *Am.* iv. 10
her selfe soone *ready* make, To wayt on Love . . . *Am.* lxx. 9
long since *ready* forth his maske to move, . . . *Epith.* 26
All *ready* to her silver coche to clyme; . . . *Epith.* 76
Now is my love all *ready* forth to come: . . . *Epith.* 110

Re-ally. Before they could new counsels *re-allie,* . . . VII. vi. 23. 4

Realm. foule abuses both in *realme* and raine; . . . *Hub.* 1276
Ne ruld her *Realme* with lawes, but pollicie, . . . I. iv. 12. 7
Unaes foe, that all her *realme* did pray. . . . I. ix. 20. 3
soveraine Queene! thy *realme,* and race, . . . II. x. 4. 1
Brute this *Realme* unto his rule subdewd, . . . II. x. 13. 1
her powre she did display Through all this *Realme,* . . . II. x. 20. 6
Next Huddibras his *realme* did not encrease, . . . II. x. 25. 4
his *realme* he equally decreed To have divided. . . . II. x. 27. 5
twixt them shayrd his *realme* by equall lottes; . . . II. x. 29. 3
war on those which him had of his *realme* bereav'd. . . . II. x. 31. 9
Thenceforth this *Realme* was into factions rent, . . . II. x. 36. 6
this sad *realme,* cut into sondry shayres . . . II. x. 37. 4
for this *Realme* found many goodly layes, . . . II. x. 42. 5
Till he surrendered *Realme* and life to fate. . . . II. x. 45. 5
gan this *Realme* renew her passed prime: . . . II. x. 58. 8
Long time in peace his *realme* established, . . . II. x. 63. 3
in the *Realme* ere long they stronger arre . . . II. x. 65. 7
Happy this *Realme,* had it remayned ever since! . . . III. ii. 21. 9
after Greekes did Priams *realme* destroy, . . . III. ix. 36. 7
His soule descended downe into the Stygian *reame.* . . . IV. viii. 45. 9
joyne in equall portion of thy *realme;* . . . V. vii. 23. 6
through all that *realme* he sent . . . V. xii. 26. 6
that *Realme* for to redresse: . . . V. xii. 27. 6

Realm's. The *Realmes* chiefe strength . . . *Hub.* 1185
for his *Realmes* defence, . . . II. x. 15. 8

Realms. *Ne ruld her *Realmes* with lawes, but pollicie, . . . I. iv. 12. 7
thine owne *realmes* in lond of Faery, . . . II. Pr. 4. 8
realmes and rulers thou doest both confound, . . . II. vii. 13. 2
he wonts the Stygian *realmes* invade . . . II. xii. 41. 4
to your willes both royalties and *Reames* Subdew, . . . III. v. 53. 3
so were *realmes* and nations run awry. . . . V. ii. 32. 6

Reame, -s. *See* **Realme, -s.**

Reap. *Reapen* the fruite thereof, . . . *S.C.* May 65
To plough, to plant, to *reap,* to rake, to sowe, . . . *Hub.* 263
hop'd to *reape* the crop of all my care, . . . I. iv. 47. 2
To enter in and *reape* the dew reward. . . . III. i. 30. 8
reape sweet pleasure of the wanton boy: . . . III. vi. 46. 3
Should *reap* the harvest ere it ripened were: . . . VI. ix. 38. 6
To *reape* the ripened fruits . . . VII. vii. 30. 9

Reaped. Nought *reaped* but a weedye crop of care; . . . *S.C.* D. 122
of his love he *reapt* the timely frute, . . . VI. x. 38. 5

Reaping. *Reaping* eternall glorie of his restlesse paines. . . . VI. ix. 2. 9

Reaps. Who *reapes* the harvest sowen by his foe, . . . I. iv. 42. 4

Rear. bad me to *reare* My lookes to heaven . . . *Bel.*[2] i. 7
Upon the Latine Coast herselfe to *reare:* . . . *Bel.*[2] xiii. 4
In spight of time out of the dust doth *reare,* . . . *Ro.* v. 13
Againe on foote to *reare* her pouldred corse. . . . *Ro.* xxvii. 14
reare the Muse on stately stage, . . . *S.C.* O. 112
in the sacred temples he may *reare* A trophee . . . *Gn.* 126
Eftsoones the Ape himselfe gan up to *reare,* . . . *Hub.* 237
reare a trophee for devouring death, . . . *Ti.* 52
in their armes then softly did him *reare:* . . . *As.* 146
to *reare* Her out of carelesse swowne. . . . I. ii. 45. 3
his heavie hand he high gan *reare,* . . . I. v. 13. 5
At them he gan to *reare* his bristles strong, . . . I. v. 34. 5
club, . . . He could not *rearen* up . . . I. viii. 10. 2
He found the meanes that Prisoner up to *reare;* . . . I. viii. 40. 6
As carefull Nourse her child from falling oft does *reare.* . . . I. x. 35. 9
ere the morrow next gan *reare* Out of the sea . . . I. xi. 33. 3
From loathed soile he can him lightly *reare,* . . . I. xi. 39. 3
reare againe The sencelesse corse appointed for the grave: . . . I. xi. 48. 7
Aurora from the deawy bed . . . gan herselfe to *reare* . . . I. xi. 51. 3
he saw himselfe so freshly *reare,* . . . I. xi. 52. 6
her dim eie-lids she up gan *reare,* . . . II. i. 45. 1
'Such and such evil God on Guyon *reare,* . . . II. i. 61. 5
An heavie load, himselfe did lightly *reare;* . . . II. ii. 11. 4
In widest Ocean she her throne does *reare,* . . . II. ii. 40. 6
his pitious handes gan *reare.* . . . II. iii. 6. 9
*As ghastly bug their haire on end does *reare:* . . . II. iii. 20. 5
him move to wrath, and indignation *reare.* . . . II. iv. 5. 9
Her mery fitt shee freshly gan to *reare,* . . . II. vi. 21. 2
He sent to Germany straunge aid to *reare;* . . . II. x. 64. 7
Unweeting what such horrour straunge did *reare.* . . . II. xii. 22. 7
His deawy face out of the sea doth *reare;* . . . II. xii. 65. 2
shewd him many sights that corage cold could *reare.* . . . II. xii. 68. 9
Which by that new rencounter he should *reare;* . . . III. i. 9. 8
none of them himselfe could *reare* againe: . . . III. i. 29. 2
Untill that brasen wall they up doe *reare;* . . . III. iii. 11. 7
all the conquests which them high did *reare,* . . . III. iv. 1. 5
hardines might *reare* Some hard mishap . . . III. iv. 24. 5
their brode flaggy finnes no fome did *reare,* . . . III. iv. 33. 6
Whiles they the corse into her wagon *reare,* . . . III. iv. 42. 4
O Titan! hast to *reare* thy joyous waine; . . . III. iv. 60. 3
thereof she countlesse summes did *reare,* . . . III. x. 12. 4
amongst the hives to *reare* An hony-combe, . . . III. x. 53. 5
her selfe did *reare* Out of her secret stand . . . III. xii. 28. 8
Would afterwards afresh the sleeping evill *reare.* . . . IV. i. 34. 9
They up againe them selves can lightly *reare,* . . . IV. iv. 29. 1
Fro me the honour of that game did *reare;* . . . IV. vi. 6. 7
as his hand he up againe did *reare,* . . . IV. vi. 21. 1
they their bevers up did *reare,* . . . IV. vi. 25. 8
he them from ground did *reare,* . . . IV. viii. 22. 6
The shield it drove, and did the covering *reare:* . . . IV. viii. 42. 7
his murdrous mace he up did *reare,* . . . IV. viii. 44. 4
by the lilly hand her labour'd up to *reare.* . . . IV. x. 53. 9
forced him, maulgre, it up to *reare.* . . . V. i. 29. 6
his head he gan a litle *reare* Above the brincke . . . V. ii. 18. 3
For wight against his powre them selves to *reare.* . . . V. ii. 24. 6
from his rootes doth *reare:* . . . V. vi. 40. 7
flames, that many foes shall *reare* To hinder thee . . . V. vii. 23. 2
Ventailes *reare* each other to behold. . . . V. viii. 12. 5
had he chaunced not his shield to *reare,* . . . V. xi. 10. 4
those crimes that he gainst her doth *reare,* . . . V. xi. 40. 5
her up did *reare* Upon his steede, . . . V. xi. 64. 7
He all his forces streight to him did *reare,* . . . V. xii. 6. 7
No shame to stoupe, ones head more high to *reare;* . . . V. xii. 19. 3
the cursed felon high did *reare* His cruell hand . . . V. xii. 20. 2
by what meanes did they at first it *reare,* . . . VI. i. 14. 3
little bootes against him hand to *reare.* . . . VI. i. 16. 5
since the day that armes I first did *reare,* . . . VI. ii. 26. 8
The Ladie, . . . Gan *reare* her eyes . . . VI. ii. 42. 8
him up thereon did *reare,* . . . VI. ii. 48. 4
Gan him recomfort and from ground to *reare:* . . . VI. vi. 32. 6
this wicked custome, . . . thou dost *reare;* . . . VI. vi. 34. 5
was not able up him selfe to *reare,* . . . VI. viii. 25. 6
Striving in vaine to *rere* him selfe upright: . . . VI. xii. 31. 4
How she at first her selfe began to *reare* . . . VII. vi. 1. 8
I aloft should *reare* My Trophee, . . . VII. vii. 56. 4
More bright then Hesperus his head doth *rere.* . . . *Epith.* 95
Love . . . Gan *reare* his head, . . . *H.L.* 63
harts of gazefull men might *reare* To admiration . . . *H.B.* 12

Reared. *See* **High-reared.**
Sonne hath *reared* up His fyerie-footed teme, . . . *S.C.* Jul. 17

Reared 689 Rebutted

Reared—*Continued.*
He planted there, and *reard* a mount of earth, ... *Gn.* 685
At length out of the River it was *reard* . . . . *Ti.* 610
The knight her lightly *reared* up againe, ... I. vi. 37. 5
he her quickly *reared* up againe: . . . . I. vii. 24. 2
as a Castle, *reared* high and round, ... I. viii. 23. 1
High *reard* their royall throne in Britans land, ... I. x. 65. 4
he *reared* high afore His body monstrous, ... I. xi. 8. 6
Ne *reard* above the earth his flaming creast, ... I. xii. 2. 3
Thrise he her *reard,* and thrise she sunck againe, ... II. i. 46. 3
reared him up light From off the earth . . . . II. iii. 19. 4
my self I boldly *reard.* . . . . II. iii. 45. 9
Had *reard* him selfe againe to cruel fight . . . . II. viii. 34. 7
With many raunges *reard* along the wall, ... II. ix. 29. 2
They *reard* a most outrageous dreadfull yelling cry: . . . . II. xi. 17. 9
the raging surges *reard* Up to the skyes, ... II. xii. 2. 8
Shortly they *reard* out of her frosen swownd; . . . . III. i. 64. 3
His double folded necke she *reard* upright, ... III. v. 31. 6
Till that unweldy burden she had *reard,* . . . . III. vi. 10. 4
He *reard* him up and loosd his yron bands, ... III. vii. 46. 6
having her from Trompart lightly *reard,* . . . . III. viii. 19. 3
Her up betwixt his rugged hands he *reard,* . . . . III. viii. 35. 1
that young Squyre him *reared* from below; . . . . III. ix. 16. 8
Troy againe out of her dust was *reard* . . . . III. ix. 44. 3
light Out of the ruddy East was fully *reard,* . . . . III. x. 52. 7
up his head he *reared* easily, ... III. xi. 15. 8
himself he *reared* light from ground. . . . . III. xii. 43. *or.* 9
They *reared* him on horsebacke and upstayd, ... IV. i. 37. 4
As one that had out of a dreame bene *reard,* . . . . IV. iii. 31. 4
ere his hand he *reard,* he overthrew Seven Knights, ... IV. iv. 41. 1
That headlesse tyrants tronke he *reard* from ground, ... IV. ix. 4. 6
There *reared* was a castle . . . . IV. x. 7. 2
roofe up high was *reared* from the ground, ... IV. x. 37. 5
ere they *reared* hand the Amazone Began . . . . V. vii. 28. 1
The which this Gyant *reared* first on hie, ... V. xi. 19. 3
more fiercely *reard* Uppon her wide great wings, ... V. xi. 30. 5
He *reared* her up from the bloudie ground, ... VI. v. 6. 2
Reareth. findes him almost dead, And *reareth* out of sownd. . . III. v. Arg.
Rearing. *rearing* fercely their upstaring crests, ... II. xii. 39. 8
him selfe up *rearing* hye . . . . III. xii. 23. 1
rearing up his former feete on hight, ... VI. xii. 29. 7
Rears. Upon the naked fields in stackes he *reares:* . . . . . *Ro.* xxx. 8
her faire face she *reares* up to the skie, ... *Am.* xiii. 2
Reascend. I wish that day would shortly *reascend.* . . . . . *Am.* lxxxvi. 8
Reason. things exceeding reach of common *reason;* . . . . . *Van.* i. 4
Thou raylest on, right withouten *reason,* . . . . *S.C.* May 146
her dame, that had good *reason,* . . . . *S.C.* May 177
Depriv'd of sense and ordinarie *reason,* . . . . *Hub.* 11
everie thing that is begun with *reason* . . . . *Hub.* 126
In case his paines were recompenst with *reason.* . . . . . . *Hub.* 887
I with *reason* meete will rest content, ... *Hub.* 1049
No care of justice, nor no rule of *reason,* . . . . *Hub.* 1131
Reason with sudden rage did overgoe; . . . . *Mui.* 134
For rare it seemes in *reason* to be skand, ... *D.* 178
manly courage, Tempred with *reason* . . . . *Ded. Son.* xiv. 9
The eie of *reason* was with rage yblent, ... I. ii. 5. 7
'Flesh may empaire,' . . . 'but *reason* can repaire.' . . . . I. vii. 41. 9
His goodly *reason,* and well-guided speach, ... I. vii. 42. 1
Those creeping flames by *reason* to subdew, ... I. ix. 9. 6
Whose hastie hand so far from *reason* strayd, ... II. i. 28. 5
His race with *reason,* . . . he ofte did stay, ... II. i. 34. 7
Robs *reason* of her dew regalitie, ... II. i. 57. 5
the Palmer gan to bord With goodly *reason,* . . . . II. ii. 5. 2
He hearkned to his *reason,* . . . . II. ii. 11. 1
Above the *reason* of her youthly yeares. . . . . II. ii. 15. 6
reason with foole-hardize over ran; . . . . II. ii. 17. 7
they would strive dew *reason* to exceed, ... II. ii. 38. 6
reason, blent through passion, nought descryde; . . . . . . II. iv. 7. 7
when yeares More rype us *reason* lent . . . . II. iv. 18. 5
cruell battry bend Gainst fort of *Reason,* . . . . II. iv. 34. 8
with strong *reason* maistred passion fraile, ... II. vi. 40. 4
having him with *reason* pacifyde, ... II. vii. 43. 1
better *reason* will aswage The rash revengers heat. . . . . . II. viii. 26. 6
lasht outrageously, Withouten *reason* or regard. . . . . . . II. viii. 47. 6
no time nor *reason* could arize, ... II. ix. 49. 4
His goodly *reason* and grave personage, ... II. x. 54. 7
By *reason* that the Captaines on her syde, ... II. x. 55. 3
Against the forte of *reason* evermore, ... II. xi. 1. 3
His wrathfull will with *reason* to aswage; . . . . III. i. 11. 4
if *reason* faire might you perswade . . . . III. ii. 13. 3
For which no *reason* can finde remedy.' . . . . III. ii. 36. 2
though no *reason* may apply Salve . . . . III. ii. 36. 6
who with *reason* can you aye reprove . . . . III. ii. 40. 6
with *reason* yet represse The growing evill, ... III. ii. 46. 1
With *reason* dew the passion to subdew, ... III. v. 44. 2
reason teacheth that the fruitfull seades . . . . III. vi. 8. 3
So strong is passion that no *reason* heares. . . . . III. vii. 21. 5
When they the *reason* of his words had hard, ... IV. ii. 28. 1
by no *reason* it might be reverst, ... IV. v. 31. 5
I with better *reason* him aviz'd, ... IV. viii. 58. 1
by *reason* of the lode . . . . IV. xi. 26. 2
Ne ever any asketh *reason* why. . . . . V. ii. 41. 2
then all rule and *reason* they withstand . . . . V. v. 25. 5
Not fit mongst men that doe with *reason* mell, ... V. ix. 1. 4
By *reason* of the streight, ... VI. i. 13. 7
before I did attaine Ripe yeares of *reason* . . . . VI. ii. 28. 5
spare her Knight, and rest with *reason* pacifyde: . . . . . . VI. iii. 49. 9
By *reason* that her knight was wounded sore: . . . . VI. iv. 10. 6
T' expresse his passions, which his *reason* did empeach. . . VI. iv. 11. 9
Therefore inclyning to his goodly *reason,* . . . . VI. iv. 37. 4

Reason—*Continued.*
against all *reason* and all law, ... VI. viii. 6. 4
his words, which he with *reason* red, ... VI. x. 30. 5
with better *reason* cast How he might save her life, ... VI. xi. 34. 4
like to one distraught And robd of *reason,* . . . . VI. xi. 45. 8
Ne wilbe moov'd with *reason,* or with rewth, ... *Am.* xi. 5
No skill can stint, nor *reason* can aslake. . . . . *Am.* xliv. 8
What *reason* is it then but she should scorne Base things, . . *Am.* lxi. 11
it can rob both sense, and *reason* blynd? . . . . *H.B.* 77
Him first to love great right and *reason* is, ... *H.H.L.* 190
Reasonable. cope with thee in *reasonable* wise; . . . . *Hub.* 527
Some fitt for *reasonable* sowles t' indew; . . . . III. vi. 35. 5
Reason's. he that is of *reasons* skill bereft, ... *T.M.* 139
Being above my slender *reasons* reach; . . . . *Ti.* 487
passeth *reasons* reach, ... *Col.* 837
man, that had the sparke of *reasons* might . . . . *Col.* 867
great griefe made forgett the raines to hold Of *reasons* rule, I. iv. 41. 4
yeeld His partes to *reasons* rule obedient, ... II. xi. 2. 2
His wonder far exceeded *reasons* reach, ... II. xi. 40. 1
yet love can higher stye Then *reasons* reach, ... III. ii. 36. 6
With sting of lust that *reasons* eye did blind, ... IV. ii. 5. 5
for *reasons* speciall privitie, ... IV. v. 1. 4
ne *reasons* rule, mote them restraine. . . . . IV. v. 24. 9
lawlesse lust to rule with *reasons* lore; . . . . IV. ix. 19. 4
Ne within *reasons* rule her madding mood containe. . . . . . V. vii. 11. 9
Reasons. *reasons,* to restraine From blouddy strife, ... IV. iii. 47. 7
with sharp *reasons* rang her such a pele, ... V. ix. 39. 7
many high regards and *reasons* gainst her red. . . . . . . V. ix. 43. 9
reasons brought that no man could refute: . . . . V. ix. 44. 4
Reave. talke, that might unquiet fancies *reave;* . . . . *Hub.* 24
Sith nothing ever may redeeme, nor *reave* . . . . *Ded. Son.* vii. 6
He to him lept, in minde to *reave* his life, ... I. iii. 36. 2
To *reave* by strength the griped gage away: . . . . I. xi. 41. 6
that false Traytour did my honour *reave?'* . . . . II. i. 17. 5
I will him *reave* of armes, ... II. viii. 15. 7
When the wroth Western wind does *reave* their locks: . . . . II. xi. 19. 5
used her so hard To *reave* her honor, ... III. viii. 14. 9
wreake on him that did her *reave.'* . . . . IV. vi. 38. 9
reave out of the hand that did it hend: . . . . V. xi. 27. 5
Withouten cause, but onely her to *reave* . . . . VI. ii. 43. 6
Great treason to him meant, his life to *reave.* . . . . VI. vii. 12. 4
Reaved. in mind her to have *reav'd* From wight unworthie . IV. v. 28. 3
like a ghastly Gelt whose wits are *reaved,* . . . . IV. vii. 21. 3
The living Lady, which from thee he *reaved,* . . . . V. i. 28. 3
life, which first fro me she *reaved,* . . . . *H.B.* 279
Rebeaten. *Rebeaten* backe upon himselfe againe, ... VI. viii. 10. 6
Rebel. like a *rebell* stout, I will him use; . . . . V. v. 51. 3
Had damn'd her sonnes which gainst them did *rebell,* . . . . V. vii. 10. 8
did *rebell* gainst lawfull government; . . . . V. xii. 26. 8
unlesse she turne to thee . . . let her a *rebell* be! . . . . . *Am.* xix. 14
Rebelled. Through proud ambition against her *rebeld,* . . . . II. x. 32. 7
that whylome *rebelled* Gainst highest heaven: . . . . V. i. 9. 6
Rebellious. A prowd *rebellious* Unicorn defyes, ... II. v. 10. 2
Ne henceforth be *rebellious* unto love, ... IV. vi. 31. 6
proud *rebellious* flesh to mortify: . . . . V. vii. 9. 5
Mote in them stirre up old *rebellious* thought . . . . V. vii. 11. 5
Yet did he murmure with *rebellious* sound, ... V. ix. 33. 8
murdred cruelly by a *rebellious* Mayd. . . . . VI. vii. 34. 9
For penaunce of my proud and hard *rebellious* hart. . . . . VI. viii. 19. 9
Doth still persist in her *rebellious* pride: . . . . *Am.* vi. 2
Love relented their *rebellious* yre. . . . . *H.L.* 84
Ne once move ruth in that *rebellious* Dame, ... *H.L.* 151
Rebellow. The raging Buls *rebellow* through the wood, ... IV. x. 46. 4
Rebellowed. That all the fieldes *rebellowed* againe. . . . . . I. viii. 11. 4
all the aire *rebellowed* againe, ... V. xii. 41. 6
Rebels. that tumultuous rage, . . Of Northerne *rebels* . . . . *Ded. Son.* xi. 10
Rebound. Were wont redoubled Echoes to *rebound,* . . . . . *T.M.* 22
Did now *rebound* with nought but rufull cries, ... *T.M.* 23
sownd, Which through the wood loud bellowing did *rebownd,* I. vii. 7. 5
backe againe it did alofte *rebownd,* . . . . II. xi. 42. 8
dart, which did *rebownd* From her faire eyes . . . . III. v. 42. 5
their report did far away *rebound;* . . . . III. xii. 6. 7
through the woods their Eccho did *rebound.* . . . . VI. x. 10. 5
The woods did nought but ecchoes vaine *rebound;* . . . . . VI. xi. 26. 6
Rebounded. *See* **Far-rebounded.**
all the woods they ecchoes back *rebounded,* . . . . *Am.* xix. 7
Rebounding. backe *rebownding* left the forckhead keene: . . II. iv. 46. 8
Rebounds. yt *rebownds* against the lowly playne, ... II. xi. 43. 4
From under that deepe Rock most horribly *rebowndes.* . . . III. iii. 9. 9
each abacke *rebowndes* With roaring rage; . . . . IV. i. 42. 3
Rebuke. him to much *rebuke* and Daunger drove, ... *S.C.* Jun. 69
Gan at the length them to *rebuke* againe, ... *Hub.* 397
Laies of sweet love, without *rebuke* or blame, ... *Col.* 3
holy righteousnesse, without *rebuke* or blame. . . . . I. x. 45. 9
the Palmer gan full bitterly Her to *rebuke* . . . . II. xii. 16. 6
great *rebuke* it is love to despise, ... III. i. 55. 3
Her sharpe *rebuke* full litle did esteeme; . . . . III. viii. 26. 2
fowle *rebuke* and shame Be theirs . . . . IV. viii. 15. 3
Ne ever for *rebuke* or blame of any balkt. . . . . IV. x. 25. 9
sharpe *rebuke* for being over bold; . . . . IV. x. 54. 2
For the *rebuke* which she sustain'd that day, ... V. iv. 47. 2
Abasht at his *rebuke,* that bit her neare, ... V. xi. 64. 2
hurtlesse sports, without *rebuke* or blame, ... *H.L.* 288
Rebuked. He much *rebukt* those wandring eyes of his, ... II. xii. 69. 2
they her *rebuked* and upbrayded sore. . . . . V. xi. 61. 9
Rebuking. them the Priest *rebuking* did advize . . . . VI. viii. 43. 7
Rebut. And eke themselves, . . . Doe backe *rebutte,* . . . . . I. ii. 15. 9
Their sharp assault right boldly did *rebut,* . . . . II. ii. 23. 2
Rebutted. him rencountring fierce, . . . Perforce *rebutted* backe. I. xi. 53. 5
Coyly *rebutted* his embracement light; . . . . III. viii. 10. 5

Recourse. Here han the holy Faunes *recourse,* . . . . *S.C.* Jul. 77
her late *recourse* to rest, ... III. ix. 26. 3
by the swift *recourse* of flushing blood . . . . IV. vi. 29. 6
As to his memory they had *recourse;* . . . . V. ii. 2. 7
As well as to her minde it had *recourse.* . . . . V. vii. 20. 3
Recover. *See* **Recour.**
Or ever hope *recover* her againe: . . . . I. vi. 33. 6
to *recover* right for such as wrong did grieve. . . . . . . III. i. 3. 9
rest themselves for to *recover* spirits spent. . . . . . . IV. ix. 25. 9
Which never they *recover* might againe; . . . . IV. x. 13. 6
Till I the conquest of my will *recover.'* . . . . V. v. 51. 5
ere he could *recover* foote againe, ... VI. i. 39. 1
least he should *recover* foote againe, ... VI. viii. 17. 2
ere he could *recov'r,* he did him quell, ... VI. x. 36. 5
Recovered. life *recover'd* had the raine, And over-wrestled his strong enimy, ... I. vii. 24. 5
he *recovered* had his former hew; . . . . I. ix. 20. 8
Till he *recovered* had his late decayed plight. . . . . . . I. x. 2. 9
thus *recover'd* by wise Patience . . . . I. x. 29. 1
Till by his death he it *recovered:* . . . . II. x. 44. 8
Could scarce *recovered* bee out of her paine: . . . . III. iv. 35. 2
soone as life *recovered* had the raine, ... III. iv. 35. 5
well *recovered* after long repast, ... III. vii. 18. 7
ere him selfe he had *recovered* well, ... IV. iv. 30. 6
when they both *recovered* were right well, ... IV. viii. 21. 1
soone as she her sence *recover'd* had, ... V. iv. 43. 1
when againe they had *recovered* sence, ... V. viii. 10. 1
they to life *recovered* her at last: . . . . VI. xi. 22. 6
Recovereth. He falleth nigh to ground, and scarse *recovereth* flight. . . . . IV. iii. 19. 9
Recovering. *recovering* hart, he does begin To rubb her temples, ... I. vii. 21. 4
The Briton Prince *recov'ring* his stolne sword, ... II. ix. 2. 2
Himselfe *recovering* was return'd to fight, ... VI. vii. 10. 2
Recovers. The gentle Squire *recovers* grace, ... IV. viii. Arg.
Recovery. perished past all *recoverie.* . . . . *Pet.*² ii. 10
ere he *recovery* could gaine, ... VI. viii. 10. 8
Recreant. to see this *recreaunt* knight, No knight, but treachour I. iv. 41. 4
'Let be that Lady debonaire, Thou *recreaunt* knight, ... II. vi. 28. 5
'Lo! *recreant,'* (sayd he) . . . . IV. i. 51. 1
'Thou *recreant* false traytor, ... V. vi. 37. 4
counted but a *recreant* Knight with endles shame. . . . . . V. xi. 46. 9
'Vile *recreant!* know that I doe much disdaine . . . . . . VI. i. 27. 7
never to be *recreant* for feare Of perill, ... VI. ii. 35. 3
And be for ever held a *recreant* Knight, ... VI. iii. 35. 6
Atwene that Ladie myld and *recreant* knight, ... VI. vi. 37. 2
That *recreant* knight, whose hated life I sought? . . . . . VI. vii. 16. 4
to revile, and rate, and *recreant* call, ... VI. vii. 26. 8
Recreant's. Then taking up that *Recreants* shield and speare, VI. iv. 13. 1
Recuile, Recule. *See* **Recoil.**
Recure. but your goodnes the same *recure,* . . . . *S.C.* F. 154
In westerne waves his weary wagon did *recure.* . . . . . . I. v. 44. 9
that . . . were infected sore It could *recure;* . . . . . . I. xi. 30. 4
medicine, That mote *recure* their wounds; . . . . II. xi. 21. 9
may never it *recure,* But wandreth evermore . . . . II. xii. 12. 8
none but hee . . . could the same *recure* againe. . . . . . III. xii. 34. 7
if I hap to fayle, you shall *recure* my right.' . . . . . . IV. vi. 9. 9
ere his hand he could *recure* againe . . . . IV. viii. 45. 1
ere he could him selfe *recure* againe, ... V. i. 22. 1
Who then can thinke their hedlong ruine to *recure?* . . . . V. x. 26. 9
Her to *recure* out of that stony swound, ... VI. v. 6. 4
to *recure* no skill of Leaches art Mote him availe, ... VI. x. 31. 5
with another doth it streight *recure;* . . . . *Am.* xxi. 11
That happie port for ever to *recure!* . . . . *H.L.* 298
may *recure* my harts long pyning griefe, ... *H.B.* 285
Recured. ease of paine which cannot be *recured.* . . . . . *Col.* 946
when their powres . . . With dew repast they had *recured* well, I. ix. 2. 2
to ease he him *recured* brief, ... I. x. 24. 7
her strength *recur'd* from fraile infirmitis.' . . . . I. x. 52. 9
I him *recured* to a better will, ... II. i. 54. 7
Being at last *recured,* he gan inquyre . . . . II. iv. 16. 7
Right well *recur'd,* and did away that blame . . . . II. x. 23. 4
Labour'd in vaine to have *recur'd* their prize, ... II. xii. 19. 7
sory wounds right well *recur'd,* . . . . III. i. 1. 4
By this he had sweet life *recur'd* agayne, ... III. v. 34. 1
She his hurt thigh to him *recurd* againe, ... III. v. 42. 3
Yet evermore his honour he *recured,* . . . . IV. iv. 37. 8
wearie limmes *recur'd* after late usage bad. . . . . IV. vi. 39. 9
Who when him selfe now well *recur'd* did see, ... V. vii. 43. 7
hence, . . . Convay to be *recur'd.'* . . . . VI. ii. 46. 6
Till she *recured* were of those her woundes wide. . . . . . VI. iii. 28. 9
he had that knightes wound *Recured* well, ... VI. iv. 16. 7
had againe *recured* The favour of Belphebe . . . . VI. v. 12. 1
It ever can *recured* be againe; . . . . VI. vi. 1. 6
Their wounds *recur'd,* and forces reincreast, ... VI. vi. 15. 7
wel *recured* Of that his malady: . . . . *Epig.* iv. 51
Recuyle. *See* **Recoil.**
Recyve. *See* **Receive.**
Red. *See* **Blood-red, Bloody-red, Crimson-red, Fiery-red, Read, Rosy red, Scarlet-red.**
The *Redde* rose medled with the White yfere, ... *S.C.* Ap. 68
Red Amaranthus, luckless Paramour; . . . . *Gn.* 677
with a crosse of *redd* And manie slits, ... *Hub.* 205
From her *red* cheeks the roses rent away; . . . . *As.* 160
one flowre that is both *red* and blew; . . . . *As.* 184
It first growes *red,* and then to blew doth fade, ... *As.* 185
adowne his coursers side The *red* bloud trickling . . . . . I. ii. 14. 9
heathnish shield, wherein with letters *red,* Was writt *Sansjoy,* I. iv. 38. 5
That in his armour bare a croslet *red?* . . . . I. vi. 36. 6
Bespotted as with shieldes of *red* and blacke, ... I. xi. 11. 5

Red—*Continued.*
With rosy cheekes, for shame as blushing *red:* . . . . I. xi. 51. 4
in her cheekes the vermeill *red* did shew . . . . II. iii. 22. 5
opened wide a *red* floodgate. . . . . II. v. 7. 9
His prickling armes, entrayld with roses *red,* . . . . II. v. 29. 5
Out of the wound the *red* blood flowed fresh, ... II. viii. 36. 8
brother saw the *red* blood rayle Adowne so fast, ... II. viii. 37. 3
a large lukewarme flood, *Red* as the Rose, ... II. viii. 39. 2
yclad in *red* Downe to the ground, ... II. ix. 27. 5
deckt with blossoms dyde in white and *red,* . . . . II. xii. 12. 5
Some as the Rubine laughing sweetely *red,* . . . . II. xii. 54. 8
She bath'd with roses *red* and violets blew, ... III. vi. 6. 8
sides empurpled were with smyling *red;* . . . . III. vii. 17. 2
nosethrils burnd . . . like to a furnace *redd,* . . . . III. ix. 22. 4
dyde in sanguine *red* her skin . . . . III. xii. 20. 9
their bloud fresh steeming *red,* . . . . VI. vi. 24. 7
Queene-apples, and *red* Cherries from the tree, ... VII. vi. 43. 6
lyke unto Roses *red;* . . . . *Am.* lxiv. 6
when the rose in her *red* cheekes appeares; . . . . *Am.* lxxxi. 3
How the *red* roses flush up in her cheekes, ... *Epith.* 226
Hath white and *red* in it such wondrous powre, ... *H.B.* 71
that same goodly hew of white and *red,* . . . . *H.B.* 92
Red Cross. The . . . Enchaunter parts The *Redcrosse* Knight from Truth: . . . . I. ii. Arg.
The knight of the *Redcrosse,* . . . Gan fairely couch his speare, I. ii. 15. 1
he . . . saw the *Red-crosse* which the knight did beare, . . . I. iii. 34. 2
That doth this *Redcrosse* knights ensample plainly prove. . . I. iv. 1. 9
she, all vowd unto the *Redcrosse* Knight, ... I. vi. 32. 1
tidings of her knight of the *Redcrosse;* . . . . I. vi. 34. 6
the *Redcrosse* knight was slain with Paynim knife.' . . . . . I. vi. 38. 9
That good knight of the *Redcrosse* to have slain: . . . . . I. vi. 41. 4
That *Redcrosse* knight, perdie, I never slew; . . . . I. vi. 42. 6
The *Redcrosse* knight is captive made . . . . I. vii. Arg.
Where she had left the noble *Redcrosse* knight, ... I. vii. 2. 3
she did love the knight of the *Redcrosse,* . . . . I. vii. 27. 8
O! heavie record of the good *Redcrosse,* . . . . I. vii. 48. 8
Els should this *Redcrosse* knight in bands have dyde, ... I. viii. 1. 8
Despeyre, Whom *Redcros* knight withstands. . . . . I. ix. Arg.
this good Prince redeemd the *Redcrosse* knight from bands. . . I. ix. 1. 9
'Thine, O! then,' said the gentle *Redcrosse* knight, ... I. ix. 17. 1
the *Redcrosse* knight him gave A booke, ... I. ix. 19. 6
The *Redcrosse* knight toward him crossed fast, ... I. ix. 23. 1
Whenas the gentle *Redcrosse* knight did vew, ... I. ix. 37. 3
That made the *Redcrosse* knight nigh quake for feare, ... I. xi. 15. 8
Fayre Una to the *Redcrosse* Knight Betrouthed is . . . . . . I. xii. Arg.
the *Redcrosse* knight this answere sent: . . . . I. xii. 31. 1
Guyon . . . The *Redcrosse* knight awaytes; . . . . II. i. Arg.
the *Redcrosse* knight he understands To beene departed . . . II. i. 1. 4
To see the *Redcrosse* thus advaunced hye; . . . . II. i. 23. 6
said the *Redcrosse* knight; 'Now mote I weet, ... II. i. 29. 5
him answered the *Redcrosse* knight, ... II. i. 33. 1
the *Redcrosse* knight he erst did weet To been with Guyon . . II. iii. 11. 7
By Guyon, and by that false *Redcrosse* knight; . . . . II. iii. 13. 6
The *Redcrosse* Knight was soon disarmed there; . . . . III. i. 42. 6
eke the *Redcrosse* knight ran to the stownd, ... III. i. 63. 2
eke the *Redcrosse* knight gave her good ayd, ... III. i. 66. 7
The *Redcrosse* knight to Britomart Describeth Artegall: . . . III. ii. Arg.
All which the *Redcrosse* knight to point aredd, ... III. ii. 16. 8
meeting with this *Redcrosse* Knight, ... III. iii. 62. 3
The *Redcrosse* Knight diverst, ... III. iii. 62. 9
through speaches with the *Redcrosse* Knight, ... III. iv. 4. 1
the *Redcrosse* knight did earst display Her lovers shape . . . III. iv. 5. 4
By a good knight, the knight of the *Redcrosse;* . . . . . . V. xi. 53. 2
Redder. somewhat *redder* then beseem'd aright, ... IV. vi. 19. 8
Rede. *See* **Read, Star-rede.**
Wherefore soone I *rede* thee hence remove, ... *S.C.* F. 137
This *reede* is ryfe, that oftentime . . . . *S.C.* Jul. 11
'Now *read,* . . . What course ye weene is best . . . . *Hub.* 114
I *read* that we our counsells call, ... *Hub.* 189
Beware therefore, ye groomes, I *read* betimes, ... *Col.* 925
Therefore I *read* beware.' . . . . I. i. 13. 8
a whyle I *read* you rest, and to your bowres recoyle.' . . . . I. x. 17. 5
Abandon soone, I *read,* the caytive spoile . . . . II. viii. 12. 4
read,' . . . 'thou Magitian, What meanes shall she . . . . . III. iii. 25. 1
I *read* thee soone retyre, whiles thou hast might, ... III. iv. 14. 8
I repeated The *read* thereof . . . . IV. x. 10. 8
'Concord she cleeped was in common *reed,* . . . . IV. x. 34. 1
lesse she feared that same fatall *read,* . . . . IV. xii. 27. 1
of so divine a *read* As thy great justice, ... V. Pr. 11. 7
who does dissent from this my *read,* . . . . V. i. 26. 6
To whose wise *read* she hearkning sent me streight . . . . . VI. ii. 30. 7
With holesome *reede* of sad sobriety, ... VI. vi. 5. 7
needes wise *read* and discipline, ... VI. vi. 13. 3
Such mercy he by his most holy *reede* . . . taught, ... *H.H.L.* 211
Redeem. Arise, and doo thyself *redeeme* from shame, ... *Hub.* 1331
Sith nothing ever may *redeeme,* nor reave . . . . *Ded. Son.* vii. 6
soone *redeeme* from his long-wandring woe: . . . . I. v. 11. 2
That he my captive langour should *redeeme:* . . . . I. vii. 49. 2
Faire virgin, to *redeeme* her deare, ... I. viii. Arg.
redeeme thy woefull parents head From tyrans rage . . . . . I. x. 9. 4
captives to *redeeme* with price of bras . . . . I. x. 40. 3
redeeme my deare Out of her thraldome . . . . III. xi. 16. 4
Out of his hands could not *redeeme* her gage, ... IV. viii. 50. 7
life so dearely did *redeeme.'* . . . . VI. vii. 15. 9
But cast out of that bondage to *redeeme,* . . . . *H.H.L.* 132
Redeemed. from his griping pawes He hath his shield *redeemd,* I. iii. 41. 9
this good Prince *redeemd* the Redcrosse knight . . . . I. ix. 1. 9
She you from death, you me from dread, *redeemd;* . . . . . III. vii. 52. 7
When her from deadly thraldome he *redeemed,* . . . . IV. i. 8. 4
By Braggadochio lately was *redeemed;* . . . . IV. ix. 20. 7

Redeemed—*Continued.*
Till he *redeemed* had that Lady thrall: . . . V. vii. 45. 8
ne thence could be *redeemed* By any skill . . . VI. ix. 11. 7
Which also were with selfe-same price *redeemed* That we, . . *H.H.L.* 202
Redeemer. his *redeemer* chalengd for his foe, . . . II. v. 20. 3
Redeemer's. The sacred badge of my *Redeemers* death, . . . II. i. 27. 6
in which he did endosse His deare *Redeemers* badge . . . V. xi. 53. 5
Redeems. Britomart *redeemes* faire Amoret . . . III. xii. Arg.
Her Calidore from them *redeemes,* . . . VI. xi. Arg.
Redemption. Sith no *redemption* nigh she did nor heare nor see. V. xii. 11. 9
Redes. Unto their lodgings then his guestes he *riddes:* . . . I. i. 36. 5
Red-hot. A paire of *red-whot* yron tongs did take . . . IV. v. 44. 2
Redisburse. His borrowed waters forst to *redisbourse,* . . . IV. iii. 27. 7
Redoubled. Were wont *redoubled* Echoes to rebound, . . . *T.M.* 22
Therewith *redoubled* was his raging yre, . . . I. v. 10. 4
redoubled crime with vengeaunce new Thou biddest me to eeke? I. v. 42. 7
with *redoubled* buffes them backe did put: . . . II. ii. 23. 4
doubling all his powres *redoubled* every stroke. . . . II. vi. 30. 9
Weake body wel is chang'd for minds *redoubled* forse. . . . II. ix. 55. 9
With huge *redoubled* strokes she on him layd; . . . V. v. 14. 6
His stroke *redoubled* with such might and maine, . . . VI. i. 39. 3
To her *redoubled* that her undersong, . . . *Proth.* 110
Redoubling. A second fall *redoubling* backe agayne. . . . II. xi. 43. 5
Redoubted. *Redoubted* Lord, in whose corageous mind . . . *Ded. Son.* x. 1
doubtfull words made that *redoubted* knight Suspect her truth: I. i. 53. 5
Redoubted battaile ready to darrayne, . . . I. iv. 40. 2
There to obtaine some such *redoubted* knight, . . . I. vii. 46. 8
'*Redoubted* knight, that for myne only sake . . . I. xii. 29. 7
To be the shield of some *redoubted* knight; . . . II. iv. 38. 6
He was a man of rare *redoubted* might, . . . II. v. 26. 1
Unworthie usage of *redoubted* knight. . . . II. viii. 25. 4
Renowmed Martia; and *redoubted* Emmilen. . . . III. iii. 54. 9
Redoubted knights, and honorable Dames, . . . III. ix. 1. 1
bold he sayd; O most *redoubted* Pere! . . . III. x. 26. 8
dread thereof and his *redoubted* might . . . IV. ii. 40. 2
the most *redoubted* Britonesse . . . IV. v. 13. 1
Into *redoubted* perill forth did call; . . . V. i. 3. 5
The sixt was Lansack, a *redoubted* Knight; . . . V. iii. 5. 8
'O most *redoubted* Knight, . . . V. xi. 16. 4
Redound. lore, which from her sweet lips did *redound.* . . . I. vi. 30. 9
Ay doing things that to his fame *redownd,* . . . III. ii. 14. 5
Of hurt unwist most daunger doth *redound;* . . . III. ii. 26. 6
A pound of gall doth over it *redound:* . . . IV. x. 1. 5
softly royne, when salvage choler gan *redound.* . . . V. ix. 33. 9
Right so in Faery court it did *redound,* . . . VI. i. 1. 7
drizling drops, that often doe *redound,* . . . *Am.* xviii. 3
streames . . . stil do flow, and freshly still *redound,* . . . *H.H.L.* 165
So those likewise doe by degrees *redound,* . . . *H.H.B.* 75
fruitfull issue . . . make your joyes *redound* . . . *Proth.* 106
Redounded. the greatest prayse *redounded* To Marinell, . . . V. iii. 6. 8
Redounding. To rest their limbs with wearines *redounding.* . *Gn.* 189
Redounding teares did choke th' end of her plaint, . . . I. iii. 8. 1
Redress. The silly Flie, that no *redresse* did see, . . . *Van.* iv. 5
to seeke *redresse* mought little boote; . . . *S.C.* S. 127
So seeke we helpe our sorrow to *redresse,* . . . *T.M.* 351
For that Hippolytus rent corse he did *redresse.* . . . I. v. 36. 9
Whereof he crav'd *redresse.* . . . II. ii. 43. 5
devisd *redresse* for such annoyes: . . . II. ii. 43. 8
Him stayd from yielding pitifull *redresse,* . . . II. v. 24. 4
His single speare could doe him small *redresse* . . . II. viii. 34. 3
Yet no'te she find *redresse* for such despight: . . . III. vi. 40. 7
Redresse the wrong of miserable wight, . . . III. x. 28. 2
Of his loves succour, of his owne *redresse,* . . . III. xii. 43. *or.* 4
But-if the heavens helpe to *redresse* her wrong, . . . IV. vii. 23. 3
then none may it *redresse* or blame, . . . IV. viii. 15. 1
Ye may *redresse,* and me restore to light!' . . . IV. viii. 17. 5
wish that in his powre it weare Her to *redresse:* . . . IV. xii. 12. 7
She her besought of gratious *redresse.* . . . V. i. 4. 4
wrong *redresse* in such as wend awry: . . . V. ii. 1. 4
ranne to his *redresse:* . . . V. iv. 41. 3
the wrong'd, whom ye did enterprise Both to *redresse,* . . . V. viii. 11. 5
sent *redresse* thereof by this brave Briton Knight. . . . V. xi. 1. 9
whose sting without *redresse* Full deadly wounds . . . V. xi. 24. 5
that Realme for to *redresse:* . . . V. xii. 27. 6
no remedy . . . the present mischiefe to *redresse,* . . . VI. iii. 44. 2
no herbe he found Which could *redresse,* . . . VI. iv. 16. 9
Which to *redresse* she did th' assistance need . . . VI. v. 10. 4
Would for it selfe *redresse,* . . . VI. viii. 18. 9
Redressed. Untill my cause of sorrow be *redrest.* . . . *T.M.* 228
but to have *redrest* The bitter pangs . . . II. i. 48. 4
redrest This my deare daughters deepe engraffed ill, . . . III. iii. 18. 2
shortly she his dolour hath *redrest,* . . . III. v. 41. 7
'What boots it plaine that cannot be *redrest,* . . . III. xi. 16. 1
What boots it then to plaine that cannot be *redrest?*' . . . III. xi. 17. 9
thought his weake limbs to have *redrest.* . . . IV. v. 39. 5
in short space his hurts he had *redrest,* . . . IV. xi. 7. 3
To let her die whom he might have *redrest.*' . . . IV. xii. 8. 5
Both to redresse, and both *redrest* likewise: . . . V. viii. 11. 5
having there their wounds awhile *redrest,* . . . VI. iv. 15. 8
my wofull plight Cannot *redressed* be by living wight!' . . . VI. iv. 28. 5
For dread of daunger not to be *redrest,* . . . VI. ix. 3. 4
Reduce. He the six Islands . . . Shall to the same *reduce,* . . . III. iii. 32. 8
all things would *reduce* unto equality. . . . V. ii. 32. 9
when they went astray, He could . . . them *reduce* aright, . . VI. vi. 3. 8
Reduced. Till it *reduced* was to one mans governements. . . . II. ix. 59. 9
Whose countries he *redus'd* to quiet state, . . . II. x. 38. 7
his foule sore *reduced* to faire plight: . . . III. v. 41. 8
It she *reduced,* but himselfe destroyed quight. . . . III. v. 41. 9
Reducing. it *reducing* to her first perfection, . . . *H.B.* 216
Re-echo. Did ring againe, and loud *re-eccho* to the skie. . . . VII. vi. 52. 9
Re-echoed. through the wood *re-echoed* againe; . . . II. i. 38. 2
Reed. *See* **Read, Rede.**
the Romish Tityrus . . . left his Oaten *reede,* . . . *S.C.* O. 56
Rude ditties, tund to shepheards Oaten *reede,* . . . *S.C.* D. 14
Was never pype of *reede* did better sounde. . . . *S.C.* D. 142
on pipes of oaten *reed,* Oft times to plaine . . . *As.* Pr. 1
As ever piped on an oaten *reed,* . . . *Col.* 13
on a broken *reed* he still did stay His feeble steps, . . . III. xii. 10. 8
Re-edify. The ruin'd wals he did *reaedifye* Of Troynovant, . . II. x. 46. 4
Reeds. *See* **Reads.**
all mine Oten *reedes* bene rent and wore, . . . *S.C.* O. 8
With pype of fennie *reedes* doth him delight. . . . *Gn.* 112
on shrill *reedes* chaunting his rustick rime, . . . *Gn.* 155
For trumpets sterne to chaunge mine Oaten *reeds,* . . . I. Pr. 1. 4
A little cottage, built of stickes and *reedes* . . . III. vii. 6. 2
Reek. his browes with sweat did *reek* and steem, . . . VII. vii. 40. 4
Reeking. Fewe chymneis *reeking* you shall espye: . . . *S.C.* S. 117
vapour thin and light *Reeking* aloft . . . III. vii. 5. 3
Reel. Sisyphus an huge round stone did *reele* . . . I. v. 35. 3
made him *reele,* and to his brest his bever bent. . . . II. v. 6. 9
horse and man it made to *reele* asyde: . . . II. viii. 31. 2
made him twise to *reele,* that never moov'd afore. . . . II. viii. 44. 9
feeble spirits, that gan faint and *reele,* . . . V. x. 20. 5
That forst him backe recoyle and *reele* areare, . . . VI. iv. 5. 8
Reeled. twise he *reeled,* readie twise to fall: . . . I. v. 11. 6
his feeble feet for faintnesse *reeld,* . . . I. viii. 20. 7
reeled to and fro from east to west. . . . III. vii. 42. 7
too and fro in great amazement *reel'd;* . . . IV. iii. 9. 7
Re-enforced. Oft he *re'nforst,* and oft his forces fayld, . . . II. iv. 14. 5
Refection. feeble spirit inly felt *refection:* . . . IV. xii. 34. 5
Refine. the grosse matter . . . doth *refyne,* . . . *H.B.* 47
Refined. *See* **Well-refined.**
(So pure the metall was and well *refynd,*) . . . V. x. 32. 8
the *refyned* mynd doth newly fashion . . . *H.L.* 192
A more *refyned* forme, . . . *H.B.* 214
Reflection. with their beauties amorous *reflexion.* . . . *Col.* 546
feeles the warmth of sunny beames *reflection,* . . . IV. xii. 34. 7
two mirrours, by opposd *reflexion,* . . . *H.B.* 181
Reflex. With my *reflex* yours shall encreased be. . . . *Am.* lxvi. 14
Reform. better to *reforme* then to cut off the ill. . . . V. x. 2. 9
How to *reforme* that ragged common-weale: . . . V. xii. 26. 4
ere he coulde *reforme* it thoroughly, . . . V. xii. 27. 1
Reformed. thenceforth *reformd* her waies, . . . IV. ix. 16. 8
Whilest he *reformed* that uncivill fo, . . . V. i. 21. 4
wicked customes of that Bridge *refourmed;* . . . V. ii. 28. 8
Refrain. hardly did *refraine,* But that with thunder bolts . *Hub.* 1235
all their flocks from feeding to *refraine:* . . . *Col.* 26
from her most beastly companie I gan *refraine,* . . . I. ii. 41. 6
Commaunded them their fury to *refraine;* . . . I. iv. 40. 7
(O who can then *refrayn?*) . . . I. iv. 41. 8
uneathes it can *refraine* . . . II. vi. 1. 4
to *refraine* From chase of greater beastes, . . . III. i. 37. 6
From love in course of nature to *refraine.* . . . III. iv. 26. 4
the hard rocks could scarse from tears *refraine;* . . . III. iv. 35. 7
Scudamour . . . scarcely did *refraine* . . . IV. i. 52. 2
forced them from fighting to *refraine,* . . . IV. iv. 25. 7
brute beasts, forst to *refraine* fro meat, . . . IV. iv. 47. 3
for nought would from their worke *refraine,* . . . IV. v. 38. 5
it his ranging fancie did *refraine,* . . . IV. vi. 33. 6
Then either care of parents could *refraine,* . . . IV. ix. 3. 4
made *refraine* from meat, . . . IV. ix. 14. 5
nathemore would they from land *refraine:* . . . V. xii. 5. 1
spare for pitty, nor *refraine* for feare. . . . VI. i. 17. 9
did him selfe from fraile impatience *refraine.* . . . VI. i. 30. 9
Albe the wyld-man hardly would *refraine.* . . . VI. v. 27. 5
your outward senses to *refraine* From things . . . VI. vi. 7. 6
warn'd all men by their example to *refraine.* . . . VII. vi. 29. 9
Refrained. Him from his wicked will uneath *refrayned;* . . . IV. x. 36. 7
Refraining. With heavie eyne, from teares uneath *refrayning,* VI. ii. 41. 7
Refresh. doth *refresh* his sprights . . . *T.M.* 138
to *refresh* his sprights: . . . *Mui.* 162
with rest *refresh* my fainting sprights, . . . *D.* 472
the drie withered stocke it gan *refresh,* . . . III. viii. 25. 3
Him to *refresh,* and her late wounds to heale: . . . V. vii. 42. 2
Refreshed. The grasse nowe ginnes to be *refresht,* . . . *S.C.* Mar. 10
ofte *refreshed,* battell oft renue. . . . I. vi. 44. 3
their wearie limbes . . . And bodies were *refresht* . . . I. x. 18. 2
as a steed *refreshed* after toyle, . . . *Am.* lxxx. 5
Refreshing. Colde Lettuce, and *refreshing* Rosmarine. . . . *Mui.* 200
Himselfe *refreshing* with the liquid cold, . . . II. i. 24. 8
Reft. *See* **Raft.**
Makes the world wonder what they from thee *reft.* . . . *Ro.* xiii. 14
when lambes fail'd the old sheepes lives they *reft;* . . . *Hub.* 322
as one whose wits were *reft,* Fled here and there, . . . *Hub.* 1356
reft the spoyle his ornament to bee; . . . *Mui.* 68
reft fro me my sweete companion, . . . *D.* 159
reft fro me my love, my life, my hart: . . . *D.* 160
'Out of the world thus was she *reft* awaie, . . . *D.* 162
with her she *reft* Great hope, . . . *D.* 220
did weene the same Have *reft* away with his sharp . . . clawes: I. iii. 41. 6
That him of life, and us of joy, hath *refte?*' . . . I. vi. 39. 6
had not greater grace Me *reft* from it, . . . I. ix. 26. 9
His powre is *reft,* and weaknes doth remaine. . . . I. ix. 31. 8
From thence a Faery thee unweeting *reft,* . . . I. x. 65. 6
felt secretly Himselfe thereby *refte* of his sences meet, . . . I. xii. 39. 8
whenas use of speach was from her *reft,* . . . II. iv. 13. 1
that faire spectacle from him was *reft,* . . . II. xii. 67. 6
that which *reft* it no lesse faire was fownd. . . . II. xii. 67. 7
refte from men the worldes desired vew, . . . III. ii. 28. 3
Now lyest thou of life and honor *refte;* . . . III. iv. 36. 6

Reft 693 Rehearse

Reft—*Continued.*
cursed night that *reft* from him so goodly scope. . . . . . . III. iv. 52. 9
fro me *reft* both life and light attone. . . . . III. v. 7. 6
chaunce Which *reft* from him so faire a chevisaunce. . . . . III. vii. 45. 5
hath thy lady *reft* and knighthood shent, ... III. x. 32. 4
From whom the Squyre of Dames was *reft* whylere; . . . . III. xi. 3. 8
from Braggadocchio whilome *reft* The snowy Florimell, . . . IV. ii. 4. 6
Out of his headpeece Cambell fiercely *reft*, ... IV. iii. 12. 4
from his shoulders quite his head he *reft*: . . . . IV. iii. 20. 6
notwithstanding that one soule was *reft*, ... IV. iii. 21. 6
having *reft* her from the witches sonne, ... IV. iv. 8. 4
Some thought from him her to have *reft* by might; . . . . . IV. v. 27. 4
The fayrest Ladie *reft*, and ever since withheld.' . . . . . . IV. vi. 6. 9
'For lately he my love hath fro me *reft*, ... IV. vi. 8. 1
What is of her become, or whether *reft*, ... IV. vi. 35. 2
With ready hand it to have *reft* away; . . . . IV. viii. 10. 6
shew'd that she had not that Lady *reft*, ... IV. ix. 36. 8
her lovers which would her have *reft*: . . . . IV. xi. 3. 5
Fro me *reft* mine away by lawlesse might, ... V. i. 17. 8
from her *reft* While she was flying, ... V. iii. 27. 4
Then from him *reft* his shield, ... V. iii. 37. 6
Which had bene *reft* from many a noble Knight, ... V. vii. 41. 5
Ere all her children he from her had *reft*: . . . . V. x. 14. 5
He lightly *reft* his head to ease him of his paine. . . . . . . V. xii. 23. 9
villaine, which had *reft* That piteous spoile . . . . VI. i. 18. 4
a discourteous Knight, who her had *reft* . . . . VI. iii. 18. 6
his love *reft* away, ... VI. xi. 25. 3
The selfe same flocks the which those theeves had *reft* . . . VI. xi. 37. 2
Had *reft* from Meliboe and from his make, ... VI. xi. 51. 7
inly quaking, seem'd as *reft* of sense . . . . VII. vi. 25. 4
Refuge. To finde some *refuge* there, and rest her wearie syde. III. vii. 5. 9
refuge from the Monsters cruelty, ... III. viii. 21. 2
He was compeld to seeke some *refuge* neare, ... III. ix. 13. 2
His hope of *refuge* used to remaine: . . . . VI. i. 22. 5
his . . . *refuge* was still Behind his Ladies back; . . . . . . VI. iii. 49. 5
Hoping unto some *refuge* to withdraw: . . . . VI. vi. 29. 3
Refuse. 'The feeble flocks in field *refuse* their former foode, *S.C.* N. 133
seeing kindly sleep *refuse* to doe His office, ... *Hub.* 21
Minerva did the chalenge not *refuse*, ... *Mui.* 273
heavens *refuse* to heare a wretches cry; . . . . *D.* 355
Will die for thrist, and water doth *refuse*? . . . . II. vi. 17. 8
Refuse such fruitlesse toile, ... II. vi. 17. 9
If thee list not, leave have thou to *refuse*: . . . . II. vii. 18. 8
all thine ydle offers I *refuse*. . . . . II. vii. 39. 2
Ne let his fayrest Cynthia *refuse* . . . . III. Pr. 5. 5
Would me *refuse* their pledges to afford, ... III. vii. 56. 6
entraunce late did not *refuse*. . . . . III. ix. 18. 9
with him To turne she doth *refuse*. . . . . III. x. Arg.
Whom when the rest did see her to *refuse*, ... IV. v. 21. 1
time yet serves that I the same *refuse*; . . . . IV. vi. 4. 8
all her piteous plaint they did *refuse*, ... VI. vii. 40. 4
Nor that thing worst which men do most *refuse*; . . . . . . VI. ix. 29. 7
dooth oft *refuse* This too high flight, ... VII. vii. 1. 3
Doe not thy servants simple boone *refuse*; . . . . *Epith.* 124
Refused. to give largely to the boxe *refused*. . . . . *Hub.* 1224
Greeke, That for his love *refused* deitye. . . . . I. iii. 21. 6
when she saw her offred sweets *refusd*, ... I. v. 37. 6
thing *refused* doe not afterward accuse.' . . . . II. vii. 18. 9
that straunge sword *refusd* to serve his neede, ... II. viii. 49. 2
he so wilfully *refused* grace; . . . . II. viii. 52. 6
their tribute he *refusd* to let be payd. . . . . II. x. 50. 9
'The first which then *refused* me,' . . . . III. vii. 58. 1
flat *refusd* to have adoe with mee, ... III. vii. 58. 3
evermore she him *refused* flat, ... III. viii. 39. 3
flatly he of entrance was *refusd*. . . . . III. ix. 12. 6
she it all *refused* at one word, ... III. x. 51. 7
So much the more as she *refusd* to love, ... IV. ii. 37. 1
for her sake *refus'd* to enterprize The battell, ... IV. iv. 11. 4
my friend that had her long *refus'd*, ... IV. viii. 60. 2
had *refusde* a God that her had sought to wife. . . . . . . IV. xii. 16. 9
Refused hath to yeeld her love againe, ... VI. i. 15. 3
he flat *refused* To take me up . . . . VI. ii. 22. 2
wroth Against her Knight, her gentlenesse *refused*, ... VI. iii. 33. 2
Yet he them all *refusd*, though thankt her as a frend; . . . VI. iv. 39. 9
She in regard hereof *refusde* . . . . VI. x. 9. 9
They all *refused* in regard of her, ... VI. xi. 14. 3
Refusing. Then craving sucke, and then the sucke *refusing*: . V. vi. 14. 8
refusing him to let unlace, ... V. viii. 27. 3
Refute. reasons brought that no man could *refute*: . . . . . V. ix. 44. 4
Regal. The Ape, thus seized of the *Regall* throne, ... *Hub.* 1111
Regality. Robs reason of her dew *regalitie*, ... II. i. 57. 5
Regan. *Regan* greater love to him profest Then all the world, . II. x. 28. 3
to his daughter *Regan* he repayrd, ... II. x. 30. 6
Regard. *See* **Self-regard.**
Those faytours little *regarden* their charge, ... *S.C.* May 39
why should he *regard* . . . . *S.C.* May 83
of their maisters hast no lesse *regarde* . . . . *S.C.* D. 11
meane *regard*, and basest fortunes scorne, ... *Hub.* 60
vertues bare *regard* advaunced bee, ... *Hub.* 638
A noble Gentleman of high *regard*, ... *Hub.* 685
Regard of honour harbours more than ought, ... *Hub.* 718
being one of great *regard* In Court, ... *Hub.* 885
No temperance, nor no *regard* of season, ... *Hub.* 1132
Of men of armes he had but small *regard*, ... *Hub.* 1189
Without *regard*, or due Decorum kept; . . . . *T.M.* 214
with *regard* Their names shall of the later age be heard, . . . *Ti.* 347
of divine *regard* and heavenly hew, ... *Col.* 933
Without *regard* of armes and dreaded fight: . . . . I. ii. 3. 6
Great pleasure, mixt with pittiful *regard*, ... I. xii. 16. 1
not *regard* dew right and just desarts? . . . . II. ii. 29. 7

Regard—*Continued.*
Regard of worldly mucke doth fowly blend, ... II. vii. 10. 5
Others through friendes; others for base *regard*, ... II. vii. 47. 4
why should hevenly God to men have such *regard*? . . . . . II. viii. 2. 9
lasht outrageously, Withouten reason or *regard*. . . . . . . II. viii. 47. 6
in good order, and with dew *regard*; . . . . II. ix. 25. 4
A sweet *regard* and amiable grace, ... II. xii. 79. 5
'He should advaunced bee to high *regard*,' . . . . III. i. 27. 8
Without *regard* of grace or comely amenaunce. . . . . III. i. 41. 9
all *regard* of shame she had discust, ... III. i. 48. 7
Onely for honour and for high *regard*, ... III. ii. 7. 4
Beates downe both leaves and buds without *regard*, ... III. vi. 39. 8
with sterne *regard* Her dreadfull weapon she to him addrest, III. vii. 42. 1
she thereto would lend but light *regard*, ... III. viii. 14. 6
had no *regard* Him to poursew, ... III. viii. 19. 1
Through gratious *regard* of her faire eye, ... III. ix. 25. 4
With vigilant *regard* and dew attent, ... III. ix. 52. 3
without *regard* of gaine or scath, ... III. x. 11. 3
Vouchsafe with mild *regard* a wretches cace to heare.' . . . III. x. 26. 9
mov'd amisse with massy mucks unmeet *regard*. . . . . . . III. x. 31. 9
She, in *regard* thereof, him recompenst With golden words . IV. ii. 9. 1
with their honours and their loves *regard* . . . . IV. ii. 28. 3
a faint affection breeds Without *regard* of good, ... IV. iv. 1. 9
With mild *regard* to see his ruefull plight, ... IV. viii. 17. 7
For his great justice, held in high *regard*, ... V. i. 30. 2
thus unto him spake, without *regard* or feare. . . . . V. ii. 33. 9
Empierced was with pittifull *regard*, ... V. v. 13. 2
For such your kind *regard* I can but rest your detter. . . . V. v. 37. 9
with her joyn'd *Regard* of womanhead; . . . . V. ix. 45. 4
Her fearefull speaches nought he did *regard*, ... V. x. 31. 1
Did nought *regard* his malice nor his powre; . . . . VI. i. 9. 8
Without *regard* of pitty or of awe? . . . . VI. viii. 6. 5
Did litle whit *regard* his courteous guize, ... VI. ix. 35. 6
Yet she no whit his presents did *regard*, ... VI. ix. 40. 6
her owne Cytheron . . . She in *regard* hereof refusde . . . . VI. x. 9. 9
With such *regard* his sences ravished, ... VI. x. 30. 7
like a Diamond of rich *regard*, ... VI. xi. 13. 3
They all refused in *regard* of her, ... VI. xi. 14. 3
rends without *regard* of person or of time. . . . . VI. xii. 40. 9
With mercifull *regard* give mercy too. . . . . *Am.* xlix. 12
thou thyselfe likewise art lyttle made, If thou *regard* the same. *Epig.* iv. 14
Regard of honour, and mild modesty; . . . . *Epith.* 193
baseborne mynds such lamps *regard* the lesse, ... *H.L.* 173
With pure *regard* and spotlesse true intent, ... *H.B.* 212
Regarded. The resty raynes, *regarded* now no more: . . . . V. viii. 39. 6
he *regarded* neither playnt nor teare, ... VI. ii. 22. 8
regarded not her threat, ... VII. vi. 12. 3
Regardful. man, in whom was ought *regardfull* . . . . *Col.* 185
with *regardfull* sight She looking backe . . . . IV. vii. 22. 4
Regarding. Whom nought *regarding* they kept on their gate, . II. xii. 17. 3
nought *regarding* her displeasure, forward goth. . . . . . . II. xii. 57. 9
Regarding neither speare that mote him slay, ... VI. iv. 6. 4
Regarding more his faith which he did plight, ... VI. vii. 23. 3
nought *regarding* her so goodly hew, ... VI. vii. 32. 3
Regarding nought religion, nor their holy heast. . . . . . . VI. xii. 24. 9
Regardless. That is *regardles* of his governaunce. . . . . . . *Mui.* 384
Regardlesse of that queane so base and vilde . . . . IV. viii. 28. 8
Regardlesse of her wounds yet bleeding rife, ... VI. v. 5. 2
Regards. To them that list these base *regardes* I lend; . . . II. vii. 33. 5
knowes no kinred, nor *regardes* no right, ... II. x. 35. 2
many high *regards* and reasons gainst her red. . . . . V. ix. 43. 9
Regent. His liege, his Ladie, and his lifes *Regent*.— . . . . *Col.* 235
Regiment. the *Regiment* Of a great shepheardesse, ... *Col.* 233
when he had resignd his *regiment*, ... II. x. 30. 3
the full time . . . of Britons *regiment*: . . . . III. iii. 40. 6
Then loyall love had royall *regiment*, ... IV. viii. 30. 7
They two enough t' encounter an whole *Regiment*. . . . . . V. i. 30. 9
Gainst tortious powre and lawlesse *regiment*, ... V. viii. 30. 7
strive With Saturnes sonne for heavens *regiment*; . . . . . VII. vi. 2. 7
I do possesse the worlds most *regiment*; . . . . VII. vii. 17. 2
Regiments. this lands . . . old division into *Regiments*, . . . II. ix. 59. 8
Region. With fire and sword the *region* to invade: . . . . . I. xi. 14. 6
Through the wide *region* of the wastfull aire, ... IV. viii. 8. 8
all strangers, in that *region* Arryving, ... V. x. 9. 7
she past the *region* of the ayre And of the fire, ... VII. vi. 7. 6
Regions. through hardy enterprize Many great *Regions* are discovered, ... II. Pr. 2. 4
Register. To *register*, and sound in trump of gold, ... *T.M.* 98
Registered. As I have found it *registred* of old . . . . . . VII. vi. 2. 3
Registers. To be the . . . *Registres* of everlasting fame, . . . *Ded. Son.* iv. 3
enrolled is your glorious name In heavenly *Regesters* . . . . II. i. 32. 4
antique *Regesters* for to avise, ... II. ix. 59. 4
Regret. To tumble into sorrow and *regreet*, ... *T.M.* 304
The rest of her impatient *regret*, ... *As.* 169
She fell to ground for sorrowfull *regret*, ... I. vii. 20. 7
Whereat renfierst with wrath and sharp *regret*, ... II. viii. 45. 1
Much greater griefe and shamefuller *regrett* . . . . III. i. 8. 2
Spake, as was meet, for ease of my *regret*: . . . . VI. ii. 23. 3
By his faire patients side with sorrowfull *regret*. . . . . . VI. xi. 9. 9
Rehearsal. *See* **Hersall.**
Rehearse. ylke can I you *rehearse*. . . . . *S.C.* Au. 142
dolefully his doole thou didst *rehearse*! . . . . *S.C.* Au. 196
Rehearse to me, ye sacred Sisters nine, ... *T.M.* 1
shall *rehearse* His worthie praise, ... *Ti.* 255
In sort as she it sung I will *rehearse*. . . . . *As.* 216
The which I here in order will *rehearse*, ... *As.* Interl. 227
That all posteritie thy honor may *reherse*. . . . . *Ded. Son.* xi. 14
ne you the like need to *reherce*. . . . . I. iv. 50. 9
Well knowing trew all that he did *reherse*, ... I. ix. 48. 4
Hearing him those same bloody lynes *reherse*; . . . . III. xii. 36. 7

Relent—*Continued.*
till she came without *relent* Unto the land of Amazons, . . . V. vii. 24. 8
for great ruth his courage gan *relent:* . . . V. ix. 46. 6
When once he felt his foeman to *relent,* . . . VI. i. 21. 7
Yet he them all withstood, and often made *relent.* . . . VI. v. 20. 9
maugre all his might backe to *relent:* . . . VI. vii. 45. 8
since ye deignd so goodly to *relent* . . . *Am.* lxxxii. 9
Relented. His hand *relented* and the stroke forbore, . . . II. viii. 43. 4
The outrage of his furious fit *relented.* . . . IV. ii. 2. 4
Love *relented* their rebellious yre. . . . *H.L.* 84
Relenting. infirmity Of the fraile flesh, *relenting* to their rage, II. xi. 1. 6
at last *relenting,* she to him was wed. . . . IV. xi. 8. 9
Gives me great hope of your *relenting* mynd: . . . *Am.* xxviii. 2
Relest. *See* **Released.**
Relic. girdle cast astray, . . . as *relique* of the pray.' . . . III. viii. 49. 9
Bearing that precious *relicke* in an arke Of gold, . . . IV. iv. 15. 2
Relics. your last *reliques* marre. . . . *Ro.* vii. 11
Which now their dusty *reliques* do bewray; . . . *Ro.* xv. 4
clad with *reliques* of some Trophees olde, . . . *Ro.* xxviii. 2
As they which gleane, the *reliques* use to gather, . . . *Ro.* xxx. 13
holding idely The broken *reliques* of their former cruelty. . . . I. ii. 16. 9
Go, gather up the *reliques* of thy race; . . . I. v. 24. 2
gathering up the *reliques* (**relicks*) of his smart, . . . I. v. 39. 6
Tragedy, . . . these *reliques* sad present unto mine eye. . . . I. vii. 24. 9
ye, the forlorne *reliques* of his powre, . . . I. vii. 48. 1
leave these *relicks* of his living might . . . II. viii. 16. 6
Her *reliques* Fulgent having gathered, . . . II. x. 57. 1
here to be red By these rent *reliques,* . . . II. xii. 9. 7
Gathred the Trojan *reliques* sav'd from flame, . . . III. ix. 36. 8
Of all . . . some *relicks* did remaine. . . . IV. i. 21. 9
there the *relicks* of the drunken fray, . . . IV. i. 23. 1
the *relickes* of his feast And cruell spoyle, . . . IV. vii. 6. 3
yet with him as *relickes* did abide . . . IV. viii. 6. 3
Till ye have rooted all the *relickes* out Of that vilde race, . . . V. xi. 18. 6
The litle babe, sweet *relickes* of his pray; . . . VI. iv. 23. 2
Amongst thy deerest *relicks* to be kept. . . . *Am.* xxii. 14
Relied. Blandamour to Claribell *relide:* . . . IV. ix. 26. 5
Relief. rob'd of rest and naturall *reliefe.* . . . *Hub.* 16
well dispos'd him some *reliefe* to showe, . . . *Hub.* 261
yeeld us some *reliefe* in this distresse; . . . *T.M.* 347
(Signe of thy love, though nought for my *reliefe,* . . . *D.* 94
my *reliefe* exceedeth living thought;) . . . *D.* 95
they all for their *relief* Wend too and fro . . . *Col.* 246
Such grace sometimes shall give me some *reliefe,* . . . *Col.* 945
Wont to robbe . . . poore mens boxes of their due *reliefe,* . . . I. iii. 17. 3
comforted with curteous kind *reliefe:* . . . I. vi. 37. 6
I hope . . . your prowesse can me yield *reliefe:* . . . I. vii. 42. 8
His long endured famine needed more *reliefe.* . . . I. viii. 43. 9
He pluckt from us all hope of dew *reliefe,* . . . I. ix. 29. 5
he gan apply *relief* Of salves and med'cines, . . . I. x. 24. 4
doe vouchsafe now to receive *reliefe,* . . . II. i. 16. 3
That I may cast to compas your *reliefe,* . . . II. i. 48. 8
she did lend her short *reliefe* And doe her comfort, . . . III. i. 53. 5
nor daunger from thy dew *reliefe* Shall me debarre: . . . III. ii. 33. 8
choicest med'cine for sick harts *reliefe:* . . . III. iii. 5. 5
Pitty our playnt, and yield us meet *reliefe.'* . . . III. iii. 21. 3
Far from the hoped haven of *reliefe,* . . . III. iv. 8. 3
Her to restraine, and give her good *reliefe* . . . III. iv. 11. 5
for wretched mens *reliefe* make way; . . . III. v. 27. 2
Without all hope of comfort or *reliefe;* . . . III. viii. 1. 6
if that hevenly grace some goode *reliefe* You send, . . . III. xi. 14. 3
Could take no rest, ne would receive *reliefe;* . . . V. iv. 47. 3
Gave unto her great comfort and *reliefe;* . . . V. vii. 44. 7
and thinke what *reliefe* Were best devise . . . VI. ii. 46. 3
He gan in mind conceive a fit *reliefe* For all her paine, . . . VI. iv. 34. 4
Fit medecines for my bodies best *reliefe.* . . . *Am.* l. 4
Deigne to let fall one drop of dew *reliefe,* . . . *H.B.* 284
Relieve. *Relieve* thy Oaten pypes that sleepen long. . . . *S.C.* N. 24
Whose onely joy was to *relieve* the needes . . . I. x. 3. 6
Poore prisoners to *relieve* with gratious ayd, . . . I. x. 40. 2
Seeking the weake oppressed to *relieve,* . . . III. i. 3. 8
Relieved. I be *relieved* by your beastlyhead. . . . *S.C.* May 265
the delight thereof me much *releeved.* . . . *Hub.* 32
the noble wits he led Which him *reliev'd,* . . . *Hub.* 822
to be so *reliev'd* is wretchednesse. . . . *T.M.* 348
that late weaker band of chalengers *relieved.* . . . IV. iv. 46. 9
which th' heart mote have *relieved;* . . . V. vi. 24. 8
how he may be *relieved* With grace from her, . . . VI. x. 1. 8
Religion. zealous disposition To God, and so to his *religion.* . . . *Hub.* 492
Religion hath lay powre to rest upon her, . . . *Col.* 322
make *religion* how we rashly go . . . *Col.* 797
of his wonder made *religion,* . . . IV. vi. 22. 3
by the vow of their *religion,* . . . V. vii. 9. 6
neither hath *religion* nor fay, . . . V. viii. 19. 7
Next gan *Religion* gainst her to impute . . . V. ix. 44. 5
religion held even theeves in measure. . . . VI. viii. 43. 9
Regarding nought *religion,* nor their holy heast. . . . VI. xii. 24. 9
the *religion* of the faith first plight . . . *Epith.* 392
Religious. *Religious* reverence doth buriall teene; . . . II. i. 59. 6
In streight observaunce of *religious* vow, . . . VI. v. 35. 6
Religiously. so *religiously* to be esteemed. . . . *Col.* 830
Relish. some *relish* of that hevenly lay . . . II. x. 3. 6
Relive. *Reliven* not for any good. . . . *S.C.* N. 89
Relived. As in a swowne: but, soone *reliv'd* againe, . . . I. ix. 52. 3
Shee should not then have bene *relyv'd* againe; . . . III. iv. 35. 4
Thought with that sight him much to have *reliv'd* . . . III. viii. 3. 2
when they saw her now *reliv'd* againe, . . . VI. xi. 24. 1
Rely. Living, on God and on thy selfe *relie;* . . . *Ti.* 209
either doth on other much *relie.* . . . IV. v. 1. 5
Remain. Under these antique ruines yet *remaine.* . . . *Ro.* xix. 14

Remain—*Continued.*
Looke from above, where you in joyes *remaine,* . . . *S.C.* Ja. 15
Whose drops in drery ysicles *remaine.* . . . *S.C.* Ja. 36
such end, perdie, does all hem *remayne,* . . . *S.C.* May 304
No such countrye as there to *remaine;* . . . *S.C.* S. 35
The more bene the Foxes that here *remaine.* . . . *S.C.* S. 155
whose endles sovenaunce . . . may aye *remaine,* . . . *S.C.* N. 6
let an happie roome *remaine* for thee . . . *Gn.* 57
yet they both doe mortall foes *remaine,* . . . *Gn.* 415
As if his daies for ever should *remaine?* . . . *Ti.* 54
now no remnant doth thereof *remaine:* . . . *Ti.* 415
in the end he breathlesse did *remaine,* . . . *Mui.* 430
Why then should I desire here to *remaine!* . . . *D.* 277
To plague th' unrighteous which alive *remaine;* . . . *D.* 359
many others mo *remaine,* . . . *Col.* 448
Of which among you many yet *remaine,* . . . *Col.* 739
Wherein old dints of deepe woundes did *remaine,* . . . I. i. 1. 3
Ay wont in desert darknes to *remaine,* . . . I. i. 16. 8
His powre is reft, and weaknes doth *remaine.* . . . I. ix. 31. 8
fire and brimstone, which for ever shall *remaine.* . . . I. ix. 49. 9
'What need of armes, where peace doth ay *remaine,* . . . I. x. 62. 7
let me heare for aie in peace *remaine,* . . . I. x. 63. 3
After his foes defeasaunce did *remaine,* . . . I. xii. 12. 4
Of which a store-house did with her *remaine:* . . . II. vi. 6. 5
Ne Mammon would there let him long *remayne,* . . . II. vii. 63. 3
Great guerdon, well I wote, should you *remaine,* . . . II. ix. 6. 7
of his victories Brave moniments *remaine,* . . . II. x. 21. 9
after wild it should to her *remaine,* . . . II. x. 32. 3
A seate in Ireland safely to *remayne,* . . . II. x. 41. 8
In wretched prison long he did *remaine,* . . . II. x. 45. 1
he victor onely did *remayne;* . . . II. xi. 43. 7
Whiles the dredd daunger does behind *remaine.* . . . II. xii. 21. 4
both awhile would covered *remaine,* . . . II. xii. 64. 4
now there do but two of six *remaine,* . . . III. i. 29. 5
nought for me but death there doth *remaine.'* . . . III. ii. 35. 5
if life Yett in his frosen members did *remaine;* . . . III. v. 31. 2
Some thousand yeares so doen they there *remayne,* . . . III. vi. 33. 5
lefte next in *remaine* To Paridas his sonne, . . . III. ix. 37. 4
Till so she doe, she must in doole *remaine,* . . . III. xi. 17. 7
Full many piteous stories doe *remaine,* . . . IV. i. 1. 2
Of all . . . some relicks did *remaine.* . . . IV. i. 21. 9
Where in a maze they both did long *remaine,* . . . IV. iv. 18. 7
Give it to her, for ever to *remaine,* . . . IV. v. 4. 6
Yet did the smart *remaine,* though he himselfe did flee. . . . IV. v. 44. 9
He left him there in languor to *remaine,* . . . IV. vii. 47. 5
any bud thereof doth scarse *remaine,* . . . IV. viii. 33. 2
in a mighty hond Her person . . . did *remaine,* . . . IV. ix. 18. 3
To let faire Florimell in bands *remayne,* . . . IV. xi. 1. 4
In which he long time after did *remaine* . . . IV. xi. 7. 5
stormes which therein still *remaine.* . . . IV. xi. 38. 9
Did yield she rather should with him *remaine* Alive, . . . V. i. 27. 5
Looke what surplus did of each *remaine,* . . . V. ii. 31. 8
In which they doe these many yeares *remaine,* . . . V. ii. 36. 3
We are not sure they would so long *remaine:* . . . V. ii. 36. 6
Who all this while behind him did *remaine,* . . . V. iii. 13. 3
whiles he did in the wood *remaine,* . . . V. iii. 31. 4
Unto the prison, where her hart did thrall *remaine.* . . . V. v. 51. 9
Which still was wont with Artegall *remaine;* . . . V. vi. 34. 4
That mote *remaine* for an eternall token . . . V. viii. 44. 4
nought else but bare life doth *remaine;* . . . V. x. 21. 7
So now all three one sencelesse lumpe *remaine,* . . . V. xi. 14. 5
even that which thou savedst thine still to *remaine?'* . . . V. xi. 16. 9
There he with Belgae did awhile *remaine* . . . V. xi. 35. 1
During which time that he did there *remayne,* . . . V. xii. 26. 1
vertue, which with you doth there *remaine,* . . . VI. Pr. 3. 2
His hope of refuge used to *remaine:* . . . VI. i. 22. 5
Streight to the carkasse . . . where it did *remaine:* . . . VI. iii. 17. 4
posteritie, Which we might see after our selves *remaine* . . . VI. iv. 31. 4
Or understand that she in safetie did *remaine.* . . . VI. iv. 40. 9
'What hope of helpe doth then for us *remaine,* . . . VI. vi. 13. 6
Upon the rest that did alive *remaine;* . . . VI. vi. 38. 4
whilest him list *remaine,* . . . VI. ix. 34. 2
With whom he myndes for ever to *remaine,* . . . VI. x. 2. 5
Where his faire Pastorella did *remaine:* . . . VI. x. 32. 3
They found that life did yet in her *remaine:* . . . VI. xi. 22. 2
So did he eeke long after this *remaine,* . . . VI. xii. 38. 6
Onely the starry skie doth still *remaine:* . . . VII. vii. 55. 5
To knit the knot, that ever shall *remaine.* . . . *Am.* vi. 14
So, as I then disarmed did *remaine,* . . . *Am.* xii. 5
she as steele and flint doth still *remayne.* . . . *Am.* xviii. 14
Ne any mention shall thereof *remaine,* . . . *Am.* xxvii. 10
joy, her thrall for ever to *remayne,* . . . *Am.* xlii. 7
Long-while alone in languor to *remaine.* . . . *Am.* lii. 8
some glance doth in mine eie *remayne.* . . . *Am.* lxxxvii. 8
About the sacred Altare doe *remaine,* . . . *Epith.* 230
The bridale bowre and geniall bed *remaine,* . . . *Epith.* 399
all ye powers which in the same *remayne,* . . . *Epith.* 413
lampe doth yet *remaine* Fresh burning . . . *H.L.* 131
Where they for ever should in bonds *remaine* . . . *H.H.L.* 125
in state *remaine* As their great Maker did at first ordaine, . . . *H.H.B.* 200
Or idle thought of earthly things, *remaine;* . . . *H.H.B.* 268
Remained. Ne of so brave a building ought *remained,* . . . *Ti.* 559
I in minde *remained* sore agast, . . . *Ti.* 578
Lost both his eyes and so *remaynd* long while, . . . *Col.* 922
the cause and root of all his ill, . . . behind *remained* still, . . . I. x. 25. 3
remaynd Some lingring life within his hollow brest, . . . I. xii. 10. 3
he has so long *remained* theare, . . . II. vii. 65. 1
in bands, where he till death *remaind;* . . . II. x. 18. 7
Ne ought in secret from the same *remaynd;* . . . III. ii. 19. 7
Happy this Realme, had it *remayned* ever since! . . . III. ii. 21. 9

Remained—*Continued.*
They which *remaynd* . . . departed thence . . . IV. v. 28. 1
Where many years it afterwards *remayned,* . . . V. ii. 19. 5
Ne of that goodly hew *remayned* ought, . . . V. iii. 24. 8
Thus he long while in thraldome there *remayned,* . . . V. v. 57. 6
There all that night *remained* Britomart, . . . V. vi. 24. 5
She there *remain'd;* but with right wary heede, . . . V. vi. 31. 4
So there a while they afterwards *remained,* . . . V. vii. 42. 1
some life *remayned* secretly; . . . V. xii. 39. 7
There he *remaind* with them right well agreed, . . . VI. i. 47. 7
he *remayned* in most perilous plight, . . . VI. iv. 1. 8
remained in most wretched state, . . . VI. v. 29. 3
that Dame *remayned* With her unworthy knight, . . . VI. vi. 39. 8
Whylest thus she in these hellish dens *remayned,* . . . VI. xi. 3. 1
So ever since they firmely have *remained,* . . . *H.L.* 92
Ne she her selfe, had she *remained* still, . . . *H.H.B.* 215

Remaining. long *remaining,* he did alwaies strive . . . I. v. 40. 7
this old woman, here *remaining* beene, . . . IV. vii. 13. 7
no whit of them *remayning* one may see. . . . V. x. 29. 9
Some sparks *remaining* of that heavenly fyre, . . . *H.L.* 107
Which in it selfe it hath *remaining* still, . . . *H.B.* 219

Remains. Ne ought save Tyber . . . *Remaines* of all. . . . *Ro.* iii. 12
Thereof nought *remaynes* but the memoree; . . . *S.C.* N. 121
manie lost, of whom no moniment *Remaines,* . . . *Gn.* 590
all that in the deepest earth *remaines,* . . . *Hub.* 1230
Of which there now *remaines* no memorie, . . . *Ti.* 4
Ne ought to me *remaines,* . . . *Ti.* 156
yet *remaines* his wide memoriall. . . . II. x. 76. 3
now alone he conquerour *remaines:* . . . II. xi. 48. 1
still *remaines* in everlasting store, . . . III. vi. 36. 4
Where he *remaines,* of all unsuccour'd and unsought. . . . IV. viii. 51. 9
'a greater wrong *remaines:* . . . IV. ix. 38. 1
no braver president this day *Remaines* on earth, . . . V. iv. 2. 7
what *remaines,* That we may compasse this our enterprize? . . . V. v. 48. 1
What then *remaines* but I to ashes burne, . . . *Am.* xxxii. 13
Within my hart, . . . every part *remaines* immortally: . . . *Am.* xlv. 8
whole *remaines* scarse any little part; . . . *H.L.* 144

Remeasure. His late miswandred wayes now to *remeasure* right. . . . III. vii. 18. 9

Remedies. Sharpe Isope, good for greene wounds *remedies,* . . . *Mui.* 190
From whence descend all hopelesse *remedies:* . . . III. v. 34. 5

Remediless. Emprisond was in chaines *remedilesse;* . . . I. v. 36. 8
Remedilesse for aie he doth him hold. . . . I. vii. 51. 8
else her paine Should be *remedilesse;* . . . III. xii. 34. 6
forced to forgoe th' attempt *remedilesse.'* . . . V. xi. 51. 9

Remedy. pittied is mishappe that nas *remedie,* . . . *S.C.* May 61
hope thereof to finde due *remedie?* . . . *Hub.* 57
Till please the heavens afford me *remedy.* . . . *T.M.* 294
none is left to *remedie* my paine, . . . *T.M.* 423
May them avoyde, or *remedie* provide. . . . *Mui.* 224
The cause to weet, and fault to *remedy:* . . . II. xi. 20. 3
For which no reason can finde *remedy.'* . . . III. ii. 36. 2
Ne can my ronning sore finde *remedee,* . . . III. ii. 39. 6
but if *remedee* Thou her afford, . . . III. iii. 16. 8
with paine Or powre, be hable it to *remedy,* . . . III. iii. 40. 4
To seeke for hearbes that mote him *remedy;* . . . III. v. 32. 2
To doe him ease, or doe him *remedy.* . . . III. v. 50. 2
Fond is the feare that findes no *remedie:* . . . III. x. 3. 3
succor . . . the whole worlds commune *remedy.'* . . . III. x. 26. 5
ne no man *remedye.* . . . III. xi. 48. 9
Till time for him should *remedy* provide, . . . IV. vii. 47. 6
She deare besought the Prince of *remedie;* . . . IV. viii. 64. 7
Whom she besought to find some *remedie,* . . . IV. xi. 6. 7
So left her her withouten *remedie.* . . . IV. xii. 24. 3
in vaine; for-why no *remedy* He saw . . . VI. iii. 44. 1
sorrowes of the mynd Find *remedie* unsought, . . . VI. iv. 28. 9
Ne all the skill, . . . Can *remedy* such hurts: . . . VI. vi. 1. 9
In vaine of me ye hope for *remedie,* . . . VI. vi. 6. 8
for want of *remedie* Did languish long . . . VI. vii. 31. 2
seeking all things meete for *remedy;* . . . VI. xi. 8. 5
she resolv'd no *remedy* to fynde, . . . VI. xi. 8. 6
Yet could not *remedie* her wretched case; . . . VI. xii. 8. 2

Remember. So well as I her words *remember* may. . . . *Hub.* 42
Remember yet my undeserved paines; . . . *D.* 522
Well could he him *remember,* . . . II. vi. 39. 1
In those same woods ye well *remember* may . . . III. v. 27. 5
remember well the mighty word . . . III. vi. 34. 4
he said, (if I *remember* right) . . . III. ix. 47. 5
as ye *remember* well, . . . IV. iv. 2. 7
They gan *remember* of the fowle upbraide, . . . IV. ix. 28. 5
Here neede you to *remember,* . . . IV. xi. 2. 1
(as ye lately mote *remember* well) . . . V. i. 3. 3
(as ye mote yet right well *Remember*) . . . V. ix. 41. 2
Ye may *remember* since th' Earths cursed seed . . . VII. vi. 20. 2
through merry feasting . . . did not the cold *remember;* . . . VII. vii. 41. 3
That ye for ever it *remember* may. . . . *Epith.* 264

Remembered. Hereafter many yeares *remembred* be . . . *Gn.* 61
To be *remembred* of posteritie, . . . *Ti.* 165
'How manie great ones may *remembred* be, . . . *Ti.* 358
Ne thenceforth his approved skill . . . *Remembred* he, . . . II. v. 8. 8
The warres he well *remembred* of king Nine, . . . II. ix. 56. 8
he *remembred* both their infancis: . . . II. ix. 57. 3
He then *remembred* well, that had bene sayd, . . . II. xi. 45. 1
Whom he now seeing, her *remembred* well, . . . IV. iv. 8. 3
He well *remembred* that the same was hee, . . . VI. vi. 40. 3
The rosie marke, which she *remembred* well . . . VI. xii. 15. 6

Remembereth. Her minde *remembreth* her mortalitie, . . . *Am.* xiii. 7

Remembering. his owne health *remembring* now no more, . . . II. vi. 45. 8

Remembrance. weake was my *remembrance* it to hold, . . . *Hub.* 1387
grieve that my *remembrance* quite is raced Out . . . *Ti.* 177

Remembrance—*Continued.*
his owne end unto *remembrance* call; . . . *Ti.* 467
in *remembrance* of that glorious bright, . . . *Col.* 46
Remembraunce of that most Heroicke spirit, . . . *Ded. Son.* xv. 1
But with *remembraunce* of your gracious name, . . . *Ded. Son.* xvi. 3
The deare *remembrance* of his dying Lord, . . . I. i. 2. 2
sad *remembraunce* now the Prince amoves . . . I. ix. 18. 3
to his fresh *remembraunce* did reverse The ugly vew . . . I. ix. 48. 5
Greevd with *remembrance* of his wicked wayes, . . . I. x. 21. 6
This man of infinite *remembraunce* was, . . . II. ix. 56. 1
thy *remembraunce* and perpetuall band . . . II. x. 69. 4
Oenone . . . for *remembrance* of her passed joy, . . . III. ix. 36. 5
put away *remembrance* of late teene; . . . III. xii. 40. 7
Now with *remembrance* of those spightfull speaches, . . . IV. ii. 12. 2
in *remembrance* of his friends late harme, . . . IV. iv. 35. 2
wiping out *remembrance* of all ill, . . . IV. vi. 32. 4
have the sterne *remembrance* wypt away . . . IV. viii. 1. 8
At the *remembrance* of their knaverie: . . . V. iii. 39. 5
The sad *remembrance* of her wretched plight: . . . VI. xi. 50. 7
to deprive *Remembrance* of all paines . . . *Am.* lxiii. 12

Remembrances. resemblaunces To her he made, and many kinde *remembraunces.* . . . III. vii. 16. 9

Remercied. She him *remercied* as the Patrone of her life. . . . II. xi. 16. 9

Remission. often treat for pardon and *remission* To suppliants, . . . V. ix. 32. 3

Remit. Would ye *remit* it to some righteous man.' . . . V. iv. 16. 3

Remitted. deserve to have small faults *remitted,* . . . *Gn.* 474
he bad the Lyon be *remitted* Into his seate, . . . *Hub.* 1254

Remnant. now no *remnant* doth thereof remaine: . . . *Ti.* 415
with a *remnant* did to sea repayre; . . . III. ix. 41. 3
Choking the *remnant* of his plaintife speach, . . . III. xi. 12. 4
th' onely *remnant* of that royall breed, . . . IV. viii. 33. 8
rise against the *remnant* at their will: . . . VI. xi. 18. 3

Remora. A little fish, that men called *Remora,* . . . *Van.* ix. 10

Remorse. The heavens doe melt in teares without *remorse;* . . . *S.C.* N. 131
Why then weepes Lobbin so without *remorse?* . . . *S.C.* N. 167
He raft her hatefull heade without *remorse:* . . . I. i. 24. 8
His bloody rage aswaged with *remorse,* . . . I. iii. 5. 8
many corses . . . lay Without *remorse* or decent funerall; . . . I. v. 53. 4
in a Dongeon deepe him threw without *remorse.* . . . I. vii. 15. 9
sharp *Remorse* his hart did prick and nip, . . . I. x. 27. 3
him beset . . . without *remorse,* . . . II. ii. 22. 3
The noble Guyon, mov'd with great *remorse,* . . . II. iv. 6. 1
Drew him through durt and myre without *remorse,* . . . II. v. 23. 4
Him thereinto he threw without *remorse,* . . . II. xi. 46. 7
of that feend was rent without *remorse:* . . . III. vii. 31. 3
with great *remorse* He nere was touched . . . III. vii. 43. 7
with pitilesse *remorse* Through shield . . . did wend, . . . IV. ii. 15. 3
They spoille and ravine without all *remorse;* . . . IV. iv. 35. 8
toucht with soft *remorse* and pitty rare; . . . IV. xii. 12. 5
rudely hayld her forth without *remorse,* . . . V. ii. 26. 3
made them both one masse withouten more *remorse.* . . . V. viii. 32. 9
to banish all *remorse,* . . . V. ix. 43. 3
With more then needfull naturall *remorse,* . . . V. x. 4. 8
brusht and battred them without *remorse,* . . . V. xii. 7. 4
Neither of other taking pitty nor *remorse.* . . . VI. i. 33. 9
did thinke without *remorse* To be aveng'd . . . VI. iv. 20. 8
make one end of him without ruth or *remorse.* . . . VI. viii. 14. 9
Empierced be with pittifull *remorse,* . . . *H.H.L.* 247

Remotest. Searching all lands and each *remotest* part, . . . III. iv. 6. 7

Remoud. *See* **Removed.**

Remounted. *Remounted* up as light as chearefull Larke; . . . I. i. 44. 7
He up *remounted* light, . . . III. x. 38. 9

Remounting. hastily *remounting* to his steed . . . III. ix. 15. 1
Unto her Coch *remounting,* home did ride, . . . IV. iii. 51. 8
On whom *remounting* fiercely forth he rode, . . . IV. iv. 23. 4

Remounts. *Remounts* againe into the open ayre, . . . II. xi. 36. 8

Remove. Wherefore soone I rede thee hence *remove,* . . . *S.C.* F. 137
Where mortall wreakes their blis may not *remove;* . . . *Ti.* 397
She, all resolv'd, and ready to *remove,* . . . *D.* 261
needlesse dread for to *remove* away, . . . I. iii. 14. 6
Least . . . rash misweening doe thy hart *remove:* . . . I. iv. 1. 6
the treachour did *remove* His craftie engin, . . . II. iv. 27. 3
those warriours far *remove,* . . . II. v. 16. 5
he rose for to *remove* aside Those pretious hils . . . II. vii. 6. 2
to *remove* the same I have no might: . . . II. vii. 50. 8
Some to *remove* the scum as it did rise; . . . II. ix. 31. 7
Shall doe unto her service, never to *remove:* . . . III. i. 26. 9
Yet will I not fro mine own love *remove,* . . . III. i. 28. 3
yield your heart whence ye cannot *remove?* . . . III. ii. 40. 8
No ydle charmes so lightly may *remove:* . . . III. ii. 51. 8
loosenes, that she lightly did *remove.* . . . III. viii. 42. 5
thousand charmes could not her stedfast hart *remove.* . . . III. xii. 31. 9
use of awfull Majestie *remove.* . . . IV. Pr. 5. 4
A new unknowen mischiefe did from him *remove.* . . . IV. i. 2. 9
being knit with vertue, never will *remove.* . . . IV. vi. 31. 9
nothing could my fixed mind *remove,* . . . IV. vii. 16. 5
stay Till she drew neare, and then againe *remove;* . . . IV. viii. 11. 3
seeing not how thence he mote *remove,* . . . IV. viii. 53. 3
No words may rate, nor rigour him *remove* . . . IV. ix. 31. 7
May nought at all their setled mindes *remove,* . . . IV. x. 2. 3
'The widow Queene . . . Thought best away me to *remove* . . . VI. ii. 29. 7
Her constant mynd could not a whit *remove,* . . . VI. xi. 5. 2
Remove the cause by which your fayre beames darkned be. . . . *Am.* xlv. 14
captived are So firmely, that ye never may *remove.* . . . *Am.* lxxi. 8
hath vertue to *remove* All Loves dislike, . . . *Proth.* 98

Removed. Her faithfull gard *remov'd,* her hope dismaid, . . . I. iii. 43. 3
breares . . . still before him she *remov'd* away, . . . I. x. 35. 4
therefore was *removed* far behind, . . . II. ix. 55. 2
quite his hart from Guendolene *remov'd,* . . . II. x. 17. 8
had not bene *removed* many a day; . . . II. xi. 35. 8

Removed—*Continued.*
Romulus, renewing it, to Rome *remoud.'* . . . III. ix. 43. 9
fire . . . Ne yet by any meanes *remov'd* away; . . . III. xi. 23. 8
when the cause, whence evill doth arize, *Removed* is, . . . VI. vi. 14. 4
Removes. what mishap thus long him fro my selfe *removes?'* . IV. viii. 63. 9
Removing. out of that same fishers filthy nest *Removing* her, . III. viii. 35. 8
Rencounter. He gan *rencounter* him in equall race. . . . III. i. 26. 5
Which by that new *rencounter* he should reare; . . . III. i. 9. 8
Rencountered. To have *rencountred* him in equall race; . . IV. vi. 3. 2
Rencountred him with so impetuous might, . . . VI. xii. 29. 2
Rencountering. him *rencountring* fierce, reskewd the noble pray. I. iv. 39. 9
him *rencountring* fierce, as hauke in flight, . . . I. xi. 53. 4
Rend. this brave monument with flash did *rend.* . . . *Bel.*[2] iii. 14
rend the greedie mindes of covetous men, . . . *Gn.* 95
with wide wounds their carcases doth *rend;* . . . *Gn.* 414
now I will my golden Clarion *rend,* . . . *T.M.* 463
wound my heart, and *rend* my bleeding chest, . . . *D.* 298
Did *rend* his haire, and beat his blubbred face, . . . *D.* 551
The whiles the captive heard his nets did *rend,* . . . *As.* 125
For anguish great they gan to *rend* their heare, . . . I. iii. 22. 4
cry, and curse, and raile, and *rend* her heare, . . . I. iii. 25. 2
A Dragon . . . would his rightfull ravine *rend* away: . . . I. v. 8. 5
his rash syre began to *rend* His heare, . . . I. v. 39. 4
rend his flesh, and his owne synewes eat. . . . I. x. 28. 3
scratch my sonne, or *rend* his tender hand?' . . . I. xii. 11. 6
Where sate a gentle Lady . . . With garments *rent,* . . . II. i. 13. 6
rend the ratling skyes with flames of fouldring heat. . . . II. ii. 20. 9
rend in peeces with his ravenous pawes, . . . II. vii. 27. 8
As if the rest some wicked hand did *rend,* . . . II. x. 68. 4
from the Daniske Tyrants head shall *rend* Th' usurped crowne, III. iii. 47. 6
many wilde woodmen which robbe and *rend* All travellers: . . III. x. 40. 6
Whilest deadly torments doe her chast brest *rend,* . . . III. xi. 11. 3
speares . . . in their flesh a griesly passage *rend,* . . . IV. ii. 15. 5
their armes away to *rend;* . . . IV. iii. 35. 4
His mighty heart did almost *rend* in tway, . . . IV. iv. 22. 7
Right fit to *rend* the food on which he fared. . . . IV. v. 35. 5
a rocke of Diamond it could rive And *rend* asunder . . . IV. v. 37. 9
knocke his head, and *rend* his rugged heares, . . . IV. viii. 4. 8
seem'd his shrikes would *rend* the brasen skie: . . . IV. viii. 38. 5
She gan to storme, and rage, and *rend* her gall, . . . V. v. 47. 2
To *rend* and teare what so she can oppresse; . . . V. xi. 24. 4
As if that it she would in peeces *rend,* . . . V. xi. 27. 4
ready now to *rend* His loves deare spoile, . . . VI. x. 35. 7
snatch, and byte, and *rend,* and tug, and teare; . . . VI. xi. 17. 6
with one word my whole years work doth *rend.* . . . *Am.* xxiii. 12
Rended. her flank wide *rended.* . . . *Bel.*[2] vi. 11
Out of his breast the very heart have *rended:* . . . V. v. 6. 5
Render. shun'd destruction doth destruction *render:* . . . *Gn.* 364
render up a reckning of their travels . . . *Hub.* 310
Render therefore therein to me my right, . . . IV. ii. 13. 8
Whose smallest minute lost no riches *render* may. . . . IV. x. 14. 9
Rendered. it ought be *rendred* her without deniall.' . . . V. iv. 15. 9
Rending. *rending* them in pieces, felly slewe . . . *Hub.* 1370
Rending her yeolow locks, . . . *Ti.* 10
rending up his helmet, would Have slayne him streight; . . . I. iii. 38. 2
reft away with his . . . *rending* clawes: . . . I. iii. 41. 6
The sharpnesse of his cruel *rending* clawes: . . . I. xi. 12. 2
The God himselfe *rending* his golden heare, . . . III. xi. 37. 7
Rends. all things in his way Full stearnly *rends* . . . *Gn.* 272
She to them runnes in hast, and her haire *rends,* . . . V. viii. 10. 7
rends her golden locks, and snowy brests embrew. . . . VI. viii. 40. 9
rends without regard of person or of time. . . . VI. xii. 40. 9
Renew. Those now *renew,* as fitter for this place. . . . *T.M.* 378
By dubble usurie doth twise *renew* it. . . . *Col.* 39
Therewith she gan her passion to *renew,* . . . I. iii. 25. 1
'With proud foes sight my sorrow to *renew,* . . . I. iv. 51. 7
fates expired could *renew* again, . . . I. v. 40. 3
With like attempt to like end to *renew.* . . . I. v. 42. 4
ofte refreshed, battell oft *renue.* . . . I. vi. 44. 3
Them to *renew,* I wote, breeds no delight, . . . I. viii. 44. 3
Una earnd her traveill to *renew.* . . . I. ix. 18. 5
long decay *Renew,* as one were borne that very day. . . . I. xi. 30. 5
He gan *renew* the late forbidden bains, . . . I. xii. 36. 7
when this breathlesse woxe, that batteil gan *renew.* . . . II. viii. 47. 9
her Host she did *renew,* . . . II. x. 55. 6
gan this Realme *renew* her passed prime: . . . II. x. 58. 8
to him brought, fresh batteill to *renew;* . . . II. xi. 28. 3
Much greater griefe . . . thou wouldst *renew,* . . . III. i. 8. 3
Tho gan she to *renew* her former smart, . . . III. ii. 29. 8
the old sparkes *renew* Of native corage, . . . III. iii. 45. 7
gan his former griefe *renew.* . . . IV. i. 38. 9
Rusht fiercely forth the battell to *renew,* . . . IV. iii. 14. 6
Could stand on foot now to *renew* the fight: . . . IV. iii. 23. 3
gan he all this storie to *renew,* . . . IV. viii. 64. 1
all afresh gan former fight *renew.* . . . IV. ix. 26. 6
She gan afresh thus to *renew* her wretched case. . . . IV. xii. 8. 9
Comaunded them their daily workes *renew,* . . . V. v. 1. 4
gan *renew* her former cruelnesse: . . . V. v. 14. 4
They turne afresh, and oft *renew* their former threat. . . . V. xi. 45. 9
courage chill Kindling afresh, gan battell to *renew,* . . . VI. i. 35. 8
to *renue* the rigour of his smart; . . . VI. x. 31. 4
Dare to *renew* the like bold enterprize, . . . VII. vi. 30. 2
if I speake, her wrath *renew* I shall; . . . *Am.* xliii. 2
griefe *renew,* and passions doe awake . . . *Am.* xliv. 11
Our love shall live, and later life *renew.* . . . *Am.* lxxv. 14
Renewed. *See* **Fresh-renewed, Late-renewed.**
When as ye heare her memory *renewed,* . . . *Col.* 645
she to him her gracious speach *renewd:* . . . II. iii. 37. 5
bad him stay till time the tide *renewd.* . . . II. vi. 26. 9
maystring them, *renewd* his former heat: . . . II. vii. 36. 6

Renewed—*Continued.*
home returne, where all should be *renewd* . . . III. x. 51. 3
Sir Arthegall *renewed* His strength still more, . . . IV. vi. 18. 4
Renew'd her death by timely death denying. . . . VI. xi. 23. 5
Renewer. Breeder of new, *renewer* of old smarts: . . . III. iv. 57. 3
Reneweth. the weary war *renew'th;* . . . *Am.* xi. 4
Renewing. *Renewing* in themselves that rage unkinde, . . . *Ro.* x. 13
Renewing her complaint with passion strong, . . . *Ti.* 479
From needlesse trouble of *renewing* fight . . . II. v. 25. 2
Romulus, *renewing* it, to Rome remoud.' . . . III. ix. 43. 9
a chyld, *renewing* still thy yeares, . . . *H.L.* 55
Renews. *Renewes* herselfe with buildings rich and gay; . . . *Ro.* xxvii. 11
soone *renews* her native pride: . . . II. iii. 36. 6
Beginnes his owne, and my old fault *renewes.* . . . *H.H.L.* 21
Renfierst. Whereat *renfierst* with wrath and sharp regret, . . II. viii. 45. 1
Renforced. twise *renforst* backe to their ships to fly; . . . II. x. 48. 2
Renne, *etc. See* **Run,** *etc.*
Renounce. if thou wilt *renounce* thy miscreaunce, . . . II. viii. 51. 6
All other loves, . . . Thou must *renounce* and utterly displace, *H.H.L.* 264
Renounced. shortly he *renounst* the vassallage Of Rome againe, II. x. 52. 5
Renown. Ne strive to winne *renowne,* . . . *S.C.* Jun. 74
My volume shall *renowne,* . . . *Gn.* 48
So thy *renowme* lives ever by endighting. . . . *Com. Son.* i. 14
Thy father, that good Earle of rare *renowne,* . . . *Ti.* 261
Riches, *renowme,* and principality, . . . II. vii. 8. 5
whom I lust do heape with glory and *renowne?'* . . . II. vii. 11. 9
long had in great *renowne,* . . . II. x. 29. 8
With high *renowme* and great felicity: . . . II. x. 36. 3
'So may ye gaine to you full great *renowme* . . . III. v. 11. 1
the Squire lives with *renowne.* . . . III. v. 25. 9
He lives, but takes small joy of his *renowne;* . . . III. v. 26. 1
'for which is bought Endlesse *renowm,* . . . III. xi. 19. 9
Of passing valew and of great *renowme,* . . . III. xi. 47. 3
a mayden Queene of high *renowne,* . . . V. viii. 17. 2
him did much *renowme,* and far his fame display. . . . VI. i. 2. 9
Renowned. *See* **Far-renowned.**
Renowm'd for fruite of famous progenie, . . . *Ro.* vi. 6
Did fill with her *renowmed* nourslings praise . . . *Ro.* x. 7
Renown'd in choyce of happie marriage . . . *Gn.* 487
brave Knights, and their *renowned* Squires; . . . *Hub.* 29
Of dreadfull battailes of *renowmed* Knights; . . . *Hub.* 767
A mightie Prince, of most *renowmed* race, . . . *Ti.* 184
that great Towre, which is so much *renownd* . . . *Ti.* 509
the wide rule of his *renowmed* sire. . . . *Mui.* 40
Nor Po nor Tyburs swans so much *renowned,* . . . *Col.* 412
Renowmed Lord, that, for your worthinesse . . . *Ded. Son.* xi. 1
that *renowmed* Snake Which great Alcides in Stremona slew, . I. vii. 17. 1
house . . . *Renowmd* throughout the world . . . I. x. 3. 2
Through famous Poets verse each where *renownd,* . . . I. x. 54. 7
That shall ye evermore *renowmed* make . . . I. xi. 2. 8
to demaund of his *renowmed* guest: . . . I. xii. 15. 6
were *renowmd,* and sought from place to place. . . . II. ii. 6. 9
the most *renownd* That may this day . . . be found. . . . II. ii. 42. 4
renowmed farre For his bold feates . . . II. iv. 41. 2
Mars . . . is for Venus loves *renowmed* more . . . II. vi. 35. 8
Throughout the world, *renowmed* far and neare, . . . II. ix. 4. 4
From this *renowmed* Prince derived arre, . . . II. x. 4. 2
men of *renowmed* might; . . . II. x. 65. 3
Elfant was of most *renowmed* fame, . . . II. x. 73. 3
To hunt for glory and *renowmed* prayse. . . . III. i. 3. 3
'*Renowmed* kings, and sacred Emperours, . . . III. iii. 23. 1
for his warlike feates *renowmed* is, . . . III. iii. 27. 3
Renowmed Martia; and redoubted Emmilen. . . . III. iii. 54. 9
Troynovant, . . . Lincolne, both *renowmed* far away; . . . III. ix. 51. 2
As that *renowmed* Poet them compyled . . . IV. ii. 32. 6
Ne more *renowmed* for their chevalrie, . . . IV. iii. 2. 8
the fame of this *renowmed* prise . . . IV. x. 4. 1
Inachus *renowmd* above the rest; . . . IV. xi. 15. 5
Tybris, *renowmed* for the Romaines fame, . . . IV. xi. 21. 6
there the three *renowmed* brethren were, . . . IV. xi. 42. 1
much *renound* For noble courage . . . V. viii. 36. 7
Lauding and praysing his *renowmed* worth . . . V. xi. 33. 3
shall you most *renowmed* make for evermore. . . . VI. i. 5. 9
seem'd the spoile of some right well *renownd:* . . . VI. v. 25. 5
Renowmed much in armes and derring doe; . . . VI. v. 37. 4
father MOLE, whom Shepheards quill *Renowmed* hath . . . VII. vi. 36. 9
those *renoumed* noble Peres of Greece, . . . *Am.* xliv. 1
Rent. *See* **To-rent, Yrent.**
rent this royall tree quite by the roote; . . . *Pet.* iii. 12
The stonie joynts of these old walls now *rent,* . . . *Ro.* xxv. 7
feeble flocke, whose fleece is rough and *rent,* . . . *S.C.* Ja. 43
a sigh had nigh *rent* her heart in twaine) . . . *S.C.* May 194
bene of ravenous Wolves *yrent,* . . . *S.C.* S. 148
all mine Oten reedes bene *rent* and wore, . . . *S.C.* O. 8
limbs, with lightening *rent,* . . . *Gn.* 199
hath his jawes with angrie spirits *rent,* . . . *Gn.* 278
It *rent,* and streight about him gan beholde . . . *Gn.* 300
The skie, in pieces seeming to be *rent,* . . . *Gn.* 581
Some on th' Euboick Cliffs in pieces *rent;* . . . *Gn.* 587
ran away in his *rent* rags by night, . . . *Hub.* 937
thy kingdome from thy head is *rent,* . . . *Hub.* 1329
all her Sisters *rent* their golden heares, . . . *T.M.* 111
Thy scepter *rent,* and power put to wrack; . . . *T.M.* 400
Such one King Edmond, but was *rent* for gaine. . . . *Ti.* 418
As if his heart in peeces would have *rent.* . . . *D.* 49
From her red cheeks the roses *rent* away; . . . *As.* 160
her unruly Page With his rude clawes the wicket open *rent,* I. iii. 13. 2
streight him *rent* in thousand peeces small, . . . I. iii. 20. 3
His ruffin raiment all was . . . to rage *yrent,* . . . I. iv. 34. 2
For that Hippolytus *rent* corse he did redresse. . . . I. v. 36. 9

Rent—*Continued.*
His goodly corps, on ragged cliffs *yrent*, . . . I. v. 38. 6
sorrowfull assay . . . almost *rent* her tender hart in tway, . . . I. vii. 27. 4
Both loftie towres and highest trees hath *rent*, . . . I. viii. 9. 7
trunck, halfe *rent* with ragged rift, . . . I. viii. 22. 8
Which shaking off, he *rent* that yron dore . . . I. viii. 39. 5
Her looser golden lockes he rudely *rent*, . . . II. i. 11. 5
With garments *rent*, and heare discheveled, . . . II. i. 13. 6
Her golden lockes most cruelly she *rent*, . . . II. i. 15. 4
seemd her tender heart was *rent* in twaine, . . . II. i. 38. 4
As budding braunch *rent* from the native tree, . . . II. ii. 2. 6
smott, and bitt, and kickt, and scratcht, and *rent*, . . . II. iv. 6. 8
The sacred Diademe in peeces *rent*, . . . II. vii. 13. 6
Would him have *rent* in thousand peeces strayt: . . . II. vii. 64. 5
His cursed life out of her lodge have *rent*; . . . II. viii. 32. 3
Thenceforth this Realme was into factions *rent*, . . . II. x. 36. 6
Beautie and Money, they that Bulwarke sorely *rent*. . . . II. xi. 9. 9
They on this rock are *rent*, . . . II. xii. 4. 9
here to be red By these *rent* reliques, . . . II. xii. 9. 7
bring my ship, ere it be *rent*, . . . III. iv. 10. 4
gan she gather up her garments *rent*, . . . III. vii. 11. 1
teare His rugged flesh, and *rent* his ragged heare; . . . III. vii. 20. 5
of that feend was *rent* without remorse: . . . III. vii. 31. 3
Himselfe in thousand peeces fondly *rent*, . . . III. xi. 38. 4
Their swerds . . . were broke, and hauberques *rent*, . . . III. xi. 52. 6
from her head ofte *rente* her snarled heare: . . . III. xii. 17. 5
There were *rent* robes and broken scepters plast; . . . IV. i. 21. 4
Their girlonds *rent*, their bowres despoyled all; . . . IV. i. 24. 7
their soules they would attonce have *rent* Out of their brests, . . . IV. ii. 18. 2
For to have *rent* his shield and armes away, . . . IV. iv. 31. 2
Rude was his garment, and to rags all *rent*, . . . IV. v. 35. 1
all his mayle yriv'd, and plates *yrent*, . . . IV. vi. 15. 8
rent his haire and scratcht his face for paine . . . IV. viii. 46. 5
made the rockes to roare as they were *rent*. . . . IV. xi. 12. 5
at the length he has *yrent* the dore, . . . V. ii. 24. 3
Torne all to rags, and *rent* with many a wound; . . . V. viii. 42. 7
Doe all attonce their thunders rage forth *rent*, . . . V. x. 34. 8
Them fouly *rent*, and shamefully defaced had. . . . V. xi. 60. 9
through the yron walles their way they *rent*, . . . V. xii. 17. 7
Gan teare her hayre, and all her garments *rent*, . . . VI. v. 4. 8
Him rudely *rent* and all to peeces tore; . . . VI. vi. 22. 6
As if he would in peeces him have *rent*: . . . VI. vi. 40. 6
an oaken plant, which lately hee *Rent* by the root; . . . VI. vii. 24. 8
As if they would have *rent* the brasen skies. . . . VI. viii. 40. 4
Which they from many long had robd and *rent*, . . . VI. xi. 51. 3
Rent up her brest, and bosome open layd, . . . VI. xii. 19. 4
As if he would have *rent* him with his cruell clawes: . . . VI. xii. 29. 9
He freely gave to be both *rent* and torne . . . *H.H.L.* 150
Renting. *Renting* hir faire visage and golden haire, . . . *Bel.*[1] viii. 4
Renversed. Whose shield he beares *renverst*, . . . I. iv. 41. 9
Then from him reft his shield, and it *renverst*, . . . V. iii. 37. 6
Repaid. such pryde at length was ill *repayde*: . . . *S.C.* D. 49
He is *repayd* with scorne and foule despite, . . . *Col.* 905
What may suffice to be for meede *repayd* . . . II. viii. 55. 7
with their owne *repayed* duely weare, . . . IV. ix. 30. 8
By equall dome *repayd* on his owne pate: . . . IV. xi. 38. 4
them *repaide* againe with double more. . . . V. vii. 31. 4
most gratefull shew'd, and heaped thanks *repayd*. . . . V. viii. 23. 9
all is now *repayd* with interest againe. . . . VI. viii. 21. 9
Repair. thereto aye wonned to *repayre* The shepheards daughters *S.C.* F. 119
wont to *repayre* Unto the flocke, . . . *S.C.* S. 186
Much do I feare back to them to *repayre*, . . . *Gn.* 382
To Morpheus house doth hastily *repaire*. . . . I. i. 39. 3
that good knight would not so nigh *repaire*, . . . I. iv. 37. 7
Unto those native woods for to *repaire*, . . . I. vi. 30. 3
'Flesh may empaire,' . . . but reason can *repaire*.' . . . I. vii. 41. 9
To rest them selves, and weary powres *repaire*; . . . I. viii. 50. 8
their forwasted kingdom to *repayre*: . . . I. xi. 1. 3
he did her deadly wounds *repaire*, . . . II. i. 43. 8
Into her lodging to *repaire* awhile, . . . II. ii. 33. 4
the dying bronds *repayre* With yron tongs, . . . II. vii. 36. 3
Ida, where the Gods lov'd to *repayre*, . . . II. xii. 52. 6
every knight which doth this way *repayre*, . . . III. i. 26. 7
Into her fathers closet to *repayre*; . . . III. ii. 22. 2
A knight that way there chaunced to *repaire* . . . III. viii. 11. 5
with a remnant did to sea *repayre*; . . . III. ix. 41. 3
where list them to *repayre*. . . . III. x. 16. 9
To snaky-locke Medusa to *repayre*, . . . III. xi. 42. 8
Withouten dread of perill to *repaire* Unto his wonne, . . . IV. viii. 5. 2
To which when he according did *repaire*, . . . IV. viii. 51. 2
dayly yet thou doest the same *repayre*; . . . IV. x. 47. 2
All which he undertooke for to *repaire*, . . . V. ii. 32. 7
How Fortune will your ruin'd name *repaire* . . . V. iv. 34. 8
ere he could his weapon backe *repaire*, . . . V. xi. 13. 7
the Nymphs . . . Which daily may to thy sweete lookes *repayre*, VI. ii. 25. 3
So shall you soone *repaire* your present evill plight.' . . . VI. vi. 14. 9
pride that none may it *repayre*. . . . *Am.* lviii. 8
Doe make and still *repayre*: . . . *Epith.* 102
Repaired. Till she *repaired* have her tackles spent, . . . I. xii. 42. 6
to his daughter Regan he *repayrd*, . . . II. x. 30. 6
To which they all *repayr'd*, . . . IV. xi. 9. 3
Repairing. *Repayring* her decayed fashion, . . . *Ro.* xxvii. 10
Reparation. That there mote be no hope of *reparation*, . . . V. ii. 28. 4
Repast. gan now to take more sound *repast*; . . . I. ii. 4. 3
when their powres . . . With dew *repast* they had recured well, I. ix. 2. 2
bodies were refresht with dew *repast*, . . . I. x. 18. 2
His mind was full of spiritual *repast*, . . . I. x. 48. 8
take *repast* For their sharpe wounds . . . II. ix. 16. 6
well recovered after long *repast*, . . . III. vii. 18. 7
There leave we them in pleasure and *repast*, . . . V. iii. 40. 1

Repast—*Continued.*
For beasts and foules to feede upon for their *repast*. . . . V. ix. 19. 9
Repay. life must life, and blood must blood, *repay*. . . . I. ix. 43. 6
Ye will me now with like good turne *repay*, . . . IV. i. 40. 5
That curt'sie with like kindnesse to *repay*, . . . V. xi. 11. 5
tribute backe *repay* as to their King: . . . VI. Pr. 7. 5
That thankfull guerdon may to you *repay*.' . . . VI. ii. 38. 5
Repeal. The liberty of women did *repeale*, . . . V. vii. 42. 5
forepast displeasures to *repeale*. . . . V. viii. 21. 5
Repeat. too painfull to *repeat* The passed fortunes, . . . *Col.* 32
My leasure so long leaves here to *repeat*: . . . II. x. 70. 4
all Cupids warres they did *repeate*, . . . III. xi. 29. 5
who all that passed gan *repeat*: . . . IV. ix. 35. 9
To her, whose name he often did *repeat*; . . . VI. xi. 33. 7
Repeated. I *repeated* The read thereof . . . IV. x. 10. 7
Repel. To joyne your force, their forces to *repell* . . . IV. ii. 24. 7
readie found, them to *repell*, Great hostes of men . . . V. xii. 4. 7
he did *repell* And beat them back, . . . VI. vi. 23. 8
Repels. Prince Arthure them *repelles*, . . . II. xi. Arg.
Repent. Now gan he *repent* his pryde to late; . . . *S.C.* F. 229
The fatall sisters eke *repent* . . . *S.C.* N. 148
knockt his brest, as one that did *repent*. . . . I. i. 29. 9
His cruel facts he often would *repent*; . . . I. iv. 34. 7
Now praysd, hereafter deare thou shalt *repent*; . . . I. ix. 43. 5
Whose chaunce it was, that soone he did *repent*, . . . III. iv. 47. 7
noble knights . . . may sore *repent* with mee, . . . III. viii. 47. 8
that vile knight, . . . ere long shall dearely it *repent*; . . . III. x. 32. 7
The sonne of Climene, he did *repent*; . . . III. xi. 38. 2
Reproch the first, Shame next, *Repent* behinde: . . . III. xii. 24. 2
made *repent* that he had rashly lusted . . . IV. i. 11. 3
will I never of my love *repent*, . . . IV. xii. 7. 8
Gan to *repent* that she had beene so mad . . . V. iv. 11. 4
shortly must *repent* that now so vainely bravest.' . . . V. vii. 32. 9
His former fancies ruth he gan *repent*, . . . V. ix. 49. 2
for what cause, declare; so mote ye not *repent*.' . . . VI. iv. 27. 9
'Vile cowheard dogge! now doe I much *repent*, . . . VI. vi. 33. 4
That it hereafter may you not *repent*, . . . *Am.* lxxiii. 13
Repentance. having learnd *repentance* late, . . . *Col.* 674
late *repentance* which shall long abyde: . . . I. vii. 23. 7
house of Holinesse; Where he is taught *repentaunce*, . . . I. x. Arg.
sad *Repentance* used to embay His blamefull body . . . I. x. 27. 5
thus recover'd by wise Patience And trew *Repentaunce*, . . . I. x. 29. 2
Doe breede *repentaunce* late, and lasting infamy.' . . . II. v. 13. 9
Behinde him was Reproch, *Repentaunce*, Shame; . . . III. xii. 24. 1
Repentaunce feeble, sorrowfull, and lame; . . . III. xii. 24. 3
Shame lowrd, *Repentaunce* sighd, Reproch did scould; . . . III. xii. 24. 6
Reproch sharpe stings, *Repentaunce* whips entwinde, . . . III. xii. 24. 7
in this bag . . . I put *repentaunce* for things past and gon. . . . VI. viii. 24. 5
late *repentance* through thy follies prief; . . . *H.H.B.* 293
Repented. them *repented* much so foolishly . . . *Hub.* 945
Pined with griefe of folly late *repented*: . . . *Mui.* 348
Then that thou hadst *repented* it too late? . . . I. vi. 47. 4
Deserves to taste his follies fruit, *repented* payne.' . . . II. v. 24. 9
she *repented* sore to have him angered. . . . III. vi. 20. 9
Fell into wretched woes, which she *repented* late. . . . VI. viii. 2. 9
Repenting. As her *repenting* so to have missayd, . . . III. ii. 9. 2
repenting That he the fly did mock. . . . *Epig.* iv. 43
Repine. Art at nature did *repine*; . . . II. xii. 59. 4
Lachesis thereat gan to *repine*, . . . IV. ii. 51. 4
sternly gan *repine* at his beheast; . . . V. i. 29. 2
Whence soone upstarting much he gan *repine*, . . . VI. v. 26. 5
in signe Of servile yoke, that nobler harts *repine*: . . . VI. vii. 26. 5
greatly did the Beast *repine* at those Straunge bands, . . . VI. xii. 36. 1
Repined. *Repyned* greatly, and did him miscall . . . II. xi. 86. 8
much *repynd*, that . . . she did him forestall. . . . IV. v. 9. 2
Repining. *repining* courage yields No foote to foe: . . . I. ii. 17. 6
his ghost, freed from *repining* strife, . . . I. iii. 36. 5
Replanted. these weake impes *replanted* by thy might, . . . V. xi. 16. 7
Replenish. Into the world, it to *replenish* more; . . . III. vi. 36. 2
Replete. her golden cup, . . . *replete* with magick artes; . . . I. viii. 14. 2
Replevy. It to *replevie*, and my sonne reprive. . . . IV. xii. 31. 8
Replied. *replyde*: 'How ever, Sir, ye fyle Your courteous tongue . . . III. ii. 12. 4
she was more engrieved, and *replide*; . . . III. vi. 21. 6
To whom the Prince thus goodly well *replied*: . . . IV. ix. 37. 1
'But what so stonie minde,' (she then *replyde*) . . . V. v. 39. 1
(he then *replide*) . . . V. vi. 11. 2
Then thus *replide*: . . . V. xi. 41. 1
'What is that Blattant Beast?' (then he *replide*.) . . . VI. i. 7. 6
all full of wrath she thus *repylde*: . . . VI. i. 27. 6
Sir Calidore . . . thus *replide*: . . . VI. ii. 34. 4
to insinuate his harts desire, He thus *replyde*: . . . VI. ix. 27. 3
So having said, she thus to him *replide*: . . . VII. vi. 34. 6
nought to him *replyde*; . . . I. ix. 24. 7
Replies. The Thrush *replyes*; . . . *Epith.* 81
Reply. To this the Oake cast him to *replie* . . . *S.C.* F. 189
'Good or bad,' gan his brother fiers *reply*, . . . II. viii. 15. 1
Pyrochles gan *reply* the second tyme, . . . II. viii. 30. 1
Ne lenger stayd for th' other to *reply*, . . . III. iv. 15. 5
The Heavens Herald staid not to *reply*, . . . VII. vi. 19. 1
Report. *Report* is, that dame Venus, on a day In spring, . . . *Mui.* 113
Much greater than the rude *report* . . . *D.* 146
through *report* of that lives painted blisse, . . . *Col.* 685
for *report* of spotlesse honestie, . . . *Col.* 753
To prove the wide *report* of her great Majestee. . . . I. iv. 13. 9
the ecchoed *report* Of their new joy, . . . I. xii. 4. 2
home ye may *report* thrise happy newes; . . . II. i. 33. 8
report of that their perlous paine, . . . II. ix. 17. 4
His learned daughters would to me *report* . . . II. x. 3. 7
dreadfull to *report*; . . . II. xi. 13. 2

Report—*Continued.*
'As th' Isle of Delos whylome, men *report,* . . . II. xii. 13. 1
as I largely can *report.* . . . III. ii. 12. 9
Or speake ye of *report,* or did ye see . . . III. viii. 48. 5
their *report* did far away rebound; . . . III. xii. 6. 7
still are led with every light *report:* . . . IV. i. 28. 5
(as Faeries wont *report*) . . . IV. v. 3. 6
I heard *report* that farre abrode did fly, . . . V. iv. 29. 4
report of him much ill, . . . V. vi. 1. 2
To hearke what any one did good *report,* . . . V. xii. 34. 8
of their loves successe they there may make *report;* . . . VI. vii. 32. 9
fed with light *report* Of every blaste, . . . VI. x. 2. 8
Were yrkesome to *report;* . . . VI. xii. 24. 6
Reported. *See* **Far-reported.**
Reported unto all, that he was sure A noble Gentleman . . . *Hub.* 684
To see her Lord, that was *reported* drent . . . V. vii. 39. 3
Reports. The false *reports* that flying tales doe beare, . . . *H.L.* 261
Repose. in their might *repose* their most assurance, . . . *Van.* xi. 13
do those men in golden thrones *repose,* . . . *Ti.* 370
in ought under heaven *repose* assurance, . . . *D.* 499
All night afflict thy naturall *repose;* . . . III. ii. 31. 2
forth she rode, without *repose* or rest, . . . III. iv. 6. 6
if she should her trust in me *repose.* . . . III. vii. 58. 9
His glory did *repose,* and credit did maintaine. . . . III. viii. 11. 9
Homeward to march, themselves there to *repose:* . . . IV. iii. 51. 5
Where better seem'd he mote himselfe *repose;* . . . IV. v. 40. 4
There did the warlike Maide her selfe *repose,* . . . V. vii. 12. 1
I may here with your selfe some small *repose* obtaine. . . . VI. ix. 31. 9
therein to *repose* And rest her selfe . . . VI. x. 9. 3
Reposed. Where all worldes hap [and honour] was *reposed,* *Bel.*[1] viii. 7
confidence The which the Ape *repos'd* in him alone, . . . *Hub.* 1165
Reposedst. in worlds ficklenesse *Reposedst* hope, . . . *D.* 151
Reposeth. Weake is th' assurance that weake flesh *reposeth* *Am.* lviii. 1
Reprehension. Ne fearest foolish *reprehension* Of faulty men, *Com. Son.* i. 7
Represent. A piteous spectacle did *represent;* . . . I. xii. 45. 7
living him in all activity To thee shall *represent.* . . . III. iii. 29. 4
made to *represent* The great Creatours owne resemblance . IV. viii. 32. 1
that same Crocodile doth *represent* The righteous Knight . V. vii. 22. 3
represent Sights never seene, . . . *H.L.* 254
Repress. An Hercules so ranke seed to *represse,* . . . *Ro.* x. 10
represse The streames of Hebrus with his songs, . . . *Gn.* 180
'Deare sonne, thy causelesse ruth *represse,* . . . II. v. 24. 5
represse The growing evill, . . . III. ii. 46. 1
Whose will her weakenesse could no way *represse,* . . . IV. ix. 18. 8
womanish complaints she did *represse,* . . . V. vii. 44. 8
doth procure Great warriours oft their rigour to *represse,* . V. viii. 1. 4
did the rigour of his doome *represse;* . . . VI. vii. 37. 4
And the great Dragon strongly doth *represse,* . . . *H.H.B.* 157
Repressed. Him weening, ere he nigh approcht, to have *represt.* . . . IV. iv. 6. 9
Had not the noble Prince his readie stroke *represt:* . . . IV. viii. 41. 9
wrong *repressed,* and establisht right, . . . V. i. 2. 3
Until that Talus had his pride *represt,* . . . V. i. 29. 5
Repriefe. *See* **Reproof.**
Reprieve. my Lord from her I would *reprive,* . . . II. i. 55. 2
It to replevie, and my sonne *reprive.* . . . IV. xii. 31. 8
doth from death *reprive.* . . . V. iv. Arg.
Reprieved. *See* **Reproved.**
*like one that hopelesse was *repryv'd* From deathes dore, . . V. iv. 35. 1
Reprise. from her womb new spirits to *reprize.* . . . II. xi. 44. 9
proffer made by force her to *reprize:* . . . IV. iv. 8. 8
Reproach. Not yet unmindfull of her olde *reproach.* . . . *Gn.* 224
Brings to *reproach* and common infamie! . . . *Hub.* 222
Behold the fowle *reproach* and open shame, . . . *T.M.* 61
With fowle *reproach,* and cruell banishment? . . . *T.M.* 426
with *reproch* of carelesnes unkynd Upbrayd, . . . I. vii. 3. 7
In fowle *reproch* of knighthoodes fayre degree, . . . I. ix. 22. 6
In fowle *reproch,* and termes of vile despight, . . . II. iv. 5. 2
With whose *reproch,* and odious menace, . . . II. iv. 9. 5
To chaunge love causelesse is *reproch* to warlike knight.' . II. vii. 50. 9
dew praise or dew *reproch* them yield; . . . II. viii. 14. 8
when Cymochles saw the fowle *reproch,* . . . II. viii. 44. 1
they weened fowle *reproch* Was to them doen, . . . II. ix. 11. 1
Forthy this hight The Rocke of vile *Reproch,* . . . II. xii. 8. 1
shame and sad *reproch,* here to be red . . . II. xii. 9. 6
To shunne Rocke of *Reproch,* . . . II. xii. 9. 9
with fowle *reproch* To stirre up strife, . . . III. i. 64. 4
her turne to fowle repriefe And sore *reproch,* . . . III. iii. 5. 8
The worlds *reproch;* the cruell victors scorne; . . . III. iii. 42. 5
drive Their brother to *reproch* and shamefull flight; . . . III. v. 16. 6
farre be such *reproch* fro mee! . . . III. v. 46. 3
Spare, gentle sister, with *reproch* my paine to eeke; . . . III. vi. 22. 9
so fowle *reproch* to shonne, . . . III. ix. 48. 5
Behinde him was *Reproch,* Repentaunce, Shame; . . . III. xii. 24. 1
Reproch the first, Shame next, Repent behinde: . . . III. xii. 24. 2
Reproch despightfull, carelesse, and unkinde; . . . III. xii. 24. 4
Shame lowrd, Repentaunce sighd, *Reproch* did scould; . . . III. xii. 24. 6
Reproch sharpe stings, Repentaunce whips entwinde, . . . III. xii. 24. 7
The badges of *reproch,* he threw away, . . . V. iv. 35. 4
so great honour with so fowle *reproch* had blent. . . . V. vi. 18. 9
her late vile *reproch* though vaunted vaine, . . . V. vii. 34. 4
the *reproch* of pride and cruelnesse. . . . VI. i. 41. 4
he them spotted with *reproch,* or secrete shame. . . . VI. vi. 12. 9
live in *reproch* and scorne, . . . VI. vi. 36. 2
Reproached. him reviled, and *reproched* sore . . . V. v. 23. 3
Reproaches. With foule *reproches* . . . Her vildly entertaines; I. iii. 43. 6
The bold Semiramis . . . her fowle *reproches* spoke: . . . I. v. 50. 4
Slaunderous *reproches,* and fowle infamies, . . . II. xi. 10. 6
every one threw forth *reproches* rife . . . III. vi. 14. 6
These vile *reproches* gan unto her speake: . . . V. vi. 37. 3
Reproachful. with *reproachfull* tearmes gan them revile, . . . *Hub.* 365
with *reprochfull* scorne discountenaunce, . . . *T.M.* 340
He . . . spake *reprochful* shame Of highest God, . . . I. i. 37. 5
lewdnes fild him with *reprochfull* pain Of that foule evill, . I. iv. 26. 6
With foule *reprochfull* words he boldly him defide. . . . I. vi. 40. 9
What meanest thou by this *reprochfull* strife? . . . I. ix. 52. 7
that *reprochfull* fall right fowly he disdaynd; . . . I. xi. 23. 9
with *reprochfull* shame mine honour shent, . . . II. i. 27. 4
First her restraine from her *reprochfull* blame . . . II. iv. 11. 3
with thy blood abolish so *reprochfull* blott.' . . . II. iv. 45. 9
the Prince, prickt with *reprochful* shame, . . . II. xi. 31. 6
For to revenge that fowle *reprochefull* shame, . . . III. i. 9. 2
Late foule dishonour and *reprochfull* spight, . . . III. ii. 8. 8
vile curses and *reprochfull* shame . . . IV. xii. 16. 4
with *reprochfull* blasphemy defide, . . . V. ii. 20. 5
Had stayned with *reprochfull* crueltie . . . V. xii. 40. 6
with *reprochfull* words him thus bespake . . . VI. vi. 24. 9
it was to thee *reprochfull* blame . . . VI. vi. 34. 3
least *reprochfull* blame With foule dishonour him mote blot VI. xii. 12. 6
Without all blemish or *reprochfull* blame, . . . *H.H.L.* 149
Reproachfully. The which erewhile spake so *reprochfully,* . V. ii. 21. 4
tongues of mortall men, Which spake *reprochfully,* . . . VI. xii. 27. 9
Reproach's. Colour thy name with foule *reproaches* rust! . IV. i. 53. 7
Reproof. wounding words, and termes of foule *repriefe,* . . . I. ix. 29. 4
shame of such *repriefe.* . . . II. iv. 28. 9
her turne to fowle *repriefe* And sore reproch, . . . III. iii. 5. 7
gan with sharpe *repriefe* Her to restraine, . . . III. iv. 11. 4
misery craves rather mercy then *repriefe.* . . . III. viii. 1. 9
Right sore agrieved at her sharpe *reproofe,* . . . IV. vii. 37. 2
Reprove. 'Lo! how the least the greatest may *reprove.*' . . . *Van.* iv. 14
Shee deignes not my good will, but doth *reprove,* . . . *S.C.* Ja. 63
ryper age such pleasures doth *reprove:* . . . *S.C.* Jun. 36
pain Of that foule evill, which all men *reprove,* . . . I. iv. 26. 7
who with reason can you aye *reprove* . . . III. ii. 40. 6
When she for ought him sharpely did *reprove,* . . . III. vi. 11. 7
well may she you *reprove* Of falsehood or of slouth, . . . III. viii. 27. 8
any should of falsenesse her *reprove,* . . . III. viii. 42. 4
they ought not thing unknowne *reprove,* . . . IV. Pr. 2. 3
often did my folly fowle *reprove:* . . . IV. vii. 16. 4
none them rightly may *reprove* Of rudenesse . . . VI. ii. 1. 7
his Lady much displeased Did him *reprove,* . . . VI. iii. 32. 7
Him of ungentle usage did *reprove,* . . . VI. iii. 42. 7
But all those follies now I do *reprove,* . . . *H.H.L.* 12
Reproved. shamefully *reproved* for his rudenes fond. . . . III. viii. 25. 9
her eyes she streight *reprieved:* . . . V. vi. 24. 9
Reproves. in the secret darke, that none *reproves,* . . . *Epith.* 360
Repulse. With foule *repulse* from Fraunce was forced . . . II. x. 22. 9
many bold *repulse* and many hard Atchievement wrought, . II. xi. 15. 3
Shall backe *repulse* the valiaunt Brockwell twise, . . . III. iii. 35. 5
to leave, . . . for one *repulse* so light. . . . *Am.* xiv. 4
Repulsed. twise they were *repulsed* backe againe, . . . II. x. 48. 1
Reputed. For feare least we like rogues should be *reputed,* *Hub.* 187
Requere. *See* **Require.**
Request. yelde unto thy lorde a sweete *request,* . . . *Pet.*[1] vii. 3
hether looke, At my *request:* . . . *S.C.* Ap. 40
Open the dore at his *request.*' . . . *S.C.* May 226
did her name of her *request.* . . . *Ti.* 33
I would *request* thee, Colin, for my sake, To tell . . . *Col.* 83
He would at her *request* prolong her nephews daies. . . . I. v. 41. 9
you, Sir knight, whose name mote I *request,* . . . I. ix. 32. 3
They turne themselves, at Unaes meeke *request,* . . . I. x. 15. 6
Fayre Una gan Fidelia fayre *request,* . . . I. x. 18. 3
She was right joyous of her just *request;* . . . I. x. 33. 1
Discourst his voyage long, according his *request.* . . . I. xii. 15. 9
rudely sdeigne a gentle harts *request;* . . . III. i. 55. 4
to shifte their curious *request,* . . . III. ix. 26. 1
Mote I *request* you tydings of my love, . . . IV. vi. 34. 6
At whose *request* he gan him selfe advise . . . IV. ix. 35. 5
So well that Leach did hearke to her *request,* . . . IV. xi. 7. 1
Was glad to yeeld unto his good *request,* . . . V. vi. 22. 2
left his love, albe her strong *request,* . . . V. viii. 3. 4
'Yet let me you of courtesie *request*' . . . V. xi. 57. 1
By which he mote accomplish his *request,* . . . VI. xi. 5. 6
This their *request* the Captaine much appalled, . . . VI. xi. 10. 6
Requested. He him *requested,* . . . To lend him day . . . VI. ii. 19. 3
Requests. stablish terms betwixt both their *requests,* . . . II. ii. 32. 7
neede, that answers not to all *requests,* . . . IV. viii. 27. 3
Requiem. to laie The sacred sod, or *Requiem* to saie. . . . *Ti.* 196
Require. to *require* Respite till morrow . . . *Hub.* 325
Dame Una, weary Dame, . . . entrance did *requere:* . . . I. iii. 12. 9
Lyonesse . . . did lowd *requere* Her children . . . I. vi. 27. 6
'yee me *require* A thing without the compas of my witt; . I. ix. 3. 1
Shee doth thee *require,* To shew it . . . I. x. 50. 8
death will never come when needes *require.* . . . I. xi. 28. 5
marched to the Strond there passage to *require.* . . . II. vi. 27. 9
to *requyre,* Or think, that ought those puissant hands may marre: . . . II. vi. 44. 7
To weete what they so rudely did *require?* . . . II. ix. 11. 8
With hookes and ladles, as need did *requyre;* . . . II. ix. 30. 7
The which to let you weet will further time *requyre.* . . . III. viii. 52. 9
did *require* To see him . . . III. xi. 33. 2
nought but spoyle and vengeance did *require:* . . . IV. vi. 11. 5
So gan the rest him likewise to *require,* . . . IV. ix. 41. 1
The Lady to alight did eft *require,* . . . V. i. 21. 3
passage money did of them *require,* . . . V. ii. 11. 6
To all that shall *require* my comfort . . . V. vii. 19. 9
did of him *requere* That Damsell . . . V. viii. 27. 8
whatsoever else he would *requere.* . . . VI. i. 43. 4
I would thy selfe *require* thee to reveale, . . . VI. ii. 26. 4
(if that ye it *require*) . . . VI. v. 11. 7

Required. in watch did spend, If cause *requir'd,* . . . . . . D. 130
The Chian Peincter, when he was *requirde* . . . . Ded. Son. xvii. 1
lowd and wyde be hard When cause *requyrd,* . . . . II. ix. 25. 8
she *requir'd,* that first fayre Amoret Might be to her allow'd, IV. i. 12. 2
as neede *required,* . . . sought to have assuaged . . . . . IV. i. 54. 2
Whom he *requir'd* his forward hast to stay, ... V. ii. 2. 3
the terme, approching fast, *required* speed. . . . . V. xi. 65. 9
Had he *required* life of us againe, ... H.H.L. 179
Requireth. shall finde friends, if need *requireth* soe. . . . . I. xii. 28. 8
Requit. *See* **Required.**
They lightly her *requit,* . . . . IV. iii. 47. 1
yet soone she it *requit;* . . . . V. vii. 33. 5
Requite. Ah, Hobbinoll! God mought it thee *requite;* . . . . S.C. S. 258
scarce vouchsafte them to *requite.* . . . . Hub. 587
'That ill (said Hobbinol) they him *requite,* . . . . Col. 903
That brothers hand shall dearely well *requight,* . . . . . . I. iv. 42. 6
Behold . . . what I cannot quite *requite* with usuree. . . . . I. viii. 27. 9
Which to *requite,* the Redcrosse knight him gave A booke, . . I. ix. 19. 6
Who, well them greeting, humbly did *requight,* . . . . . . I. x. 49. 8
That shall Pyrochles well *requite,* . . . . II. iv. 45. 8
that I mote you *requite?'* . . . . IV. vi. 4. 5
first I may that wrong to him *requite;* . . . . IV. vi. 9. 8
She would her selfe displease; so him *requite.* . . . . V. vi. 20. 6
yet at length she did *requight,* . . . . V. xi. 1. 8
What other meed, then, need me to *requight,* . . . . V. xi. 17. 7
shame shal thee with shame *requight.'* . . . . VI. i. 25. 9
one stroke or twaine; Which I, . . . Cast to *requite;* . . . . VI. ii. 12. 6
Or curtesie with rudenesse to *requite:* . . . . VI. iii. 41. 5
And offred him, his courtesie to *requite,* . . . . VI. iv. 39. 7
to *requite* him with the like againe, ... VI. viii. 9. 1
And speake her good, though she *requite* it ill. . . . . . . Am. xlviii. 14
How can we thee *requite* for all this good? . . . . H.H.L. 174
Requited. *See* **Requit.**
with his speare *requited* him againe, ... III. v. 21. 7
Requites. them *requites* with court'sies seeming meet, . . . I. x. 32. 3
Requitest. them *requitest* with thy thankfull labours. . . . . Col. 587
Rere. *See* **Rear.**
Resaluted. Whom she saluting faire, faire *resaluted* was: . . . V. vii. 17. 9
Rescue. commen to his *reskew,* ere his bitter bane. . . . . . II. xi. 29. 9
in their mistresse *reskew* whom they lad; . . . . II. xii. 84. 7
With a strong gard, all *reskew* to prevent, ... III. i. 2. 3
To *reskew* her from shamefull villany. . . . . III. i. 18. 5
she ran apace Unto his *reskew,* . . . . III. i. 22. 8
To *reskew* her from shame, and to revenge her wrong. . . . III. iv. 45. 9
doubtfull which to take, her to *reskew,* . . . . III. iv. 46. 7
slew him cruelly ere any *reskew* came. . . . . III. vii. 28. 9
Unto his *reskew* ran, and greedily him spedd. . . . . III. vii. 30. 9
without *reskew* led her quite away. . . . . III. viii. 13. 5
The loving couple neede no *reskew* feare, ... III. x. 16. 3
He gan devise how her he *reskew* mought: . . . . III. x. 18. 8
T' employ her puissaunce to his *reskew,* . . . . III. xi. 4. 8
Unto whose *rescue* forth rode Paridell; . . . . IV. iv. 19. 8
To *rescue* Satyrane out of his pray, ... IV. iv. 31. 7
rescue him, through succour of his might, ... IV. viii. 40. 8
Ne none there was to *reskue* her, ... IV. ix. 7. 9
From which he lately had through *reskew* fled: . . . . V. v. 18. 8
To *reskew* his owne Lord, ... V. v. 19. 9
To *reskue* her from their rude violence; . . . . V. xi. 45. 2
my selfe I long in vaine have bent To *rescue* her, ... V. xi. 51. 4
Yet *rescue* her thence by no meanes I may, ... V. xi. 51. 5
Gainst which no flight nor *rescue* mote avayle, ... V. xi. 59. 5
Vouchsafe to *reskue* her against a Knight, ... VI. i. 29. 6
Ran after fast to *reskue* the distressed mayde. . . . . . . VI. iii. 24. 9
a wondrous chaunce his *reskue* wrought, ... VI. iii. 51. 6
he ran with zealous haste To *rescue* th' infant, ... VI. iv. 18. 7
To *reskue* him, and his weake part abet, ... VI. v. 22. 4
durst her dreaded *reskue* enterprize, ... VI. viii. 18. 7
ran in hast To *reskue* her; . . . . VI. x. 35. 2
reskue from their pray, ... VI. x. 41. 4
Rescued. him rencountring fierce, *reskewd* the noble pray. . I. iv. 39. 9
Whom Arthure soone hath *reskewed,* . . . . II. viii. Arg.
indewd With heavenly powre, and by Angels *reskewd,* . . . III. iii. 38. 5
Her selfe, well as I might, I *reskewd* tho, ... III. v. 6. 4
reskewed out of the heavy stownd. . . . . III. v. 38. 5
reskewed from captivaunce Of his strong foe, ... III. vii. 45. 7
So Marinell by him was *rescu'd* from his fone. . . . . V. iii. 12. 9
Calepine . . . From Turpine *reskewed* is; . . . . VI. iv. Arg.
Rescues. lacke of *reskewes,* will to parley drive; . . . . . . III. x. 10. 4
Reseized. then therein *reseized* was againe, ... II. x. 45. 3
Resemblance. *See* **Self-resemblance.**
living evermore In the divine *resemblaunce* . . . . Ded. Son. xv. 10
The false *resemblaunce* of Deceipt, ... I. v. 27. 3
fayre *resemblance* above all the rest, ... III. viii. 8. 2
In his divine *resemblance* wondrous lyke: . . . . III. xi. 40. 2
The great Creatours owne *resemblance* bright, ... IV. viii. 32. 2
Their like *resemblaunce* much admired there, ... IV. ix. 11. 2
sate thereby, with gyantlike *resemblance,* . . . . V. ix. 22. 6
Divine *resemblaunce,* beauty soveraine rare, ... VI. x. 27. 4
The most *resemblance* of that heavenly light, ... H.B. 121
Resemblances. many *resemblaunces* To her he made, ... III. vii. 16. 8
Resemble. That other earthlie power should not *resemble* Her Ro. vi. 12
He did *resemble* to his lady bright; . . . . III. x. 21. 8
to which I dare *Resemble* th' ymage . . . . Am. ix. 4
Such He him made, that he *resemble* might Himselfe, ... H.H.L. 113
Resembled. The cruell Leopard she *resembled* much: . . . . . Rev. i. 4
Resembleth. *resembleth* more th' immortall flame Of heavenly light, ... H.L. 115
Resembling. *See* **Life-resembling.**
Resembling Aarons glorie in his place: . . . . Hub. 463
Resembling Stella in her freshest yeares, ... As. 189
Resembling—*Continued.*
most *resembling* both in shape and spright Her brother . . . As. 213
The maker selfe *resembling* in her feature! . . . . IV. vi. 17. 5
Therein *resembling* Janus auncient . . . . IV. x. 12. 5
Most sacred vertue . . . *Resembling* God in his imperiall might; V. Pr. 10. 2
rapt with joy *resembling* heavenly madnes, ... Am. xxxix. 9
Resembling heavens glory in her light, ... Am. lxxii. 6
Reserve. *Reserve* her cause to her eternall doome; . . . . . II. i. 58. 8
will *reserve* it for a Canto new. . . . . IV. ii. 54. 9
That we may us *reserve* both fresh and strong . . . . IV. iv. 12. 4
whom he list *reserve* to be afflicted more. . . . . IV. viii. 54. 9
Reserved. nothing he from her *reserv'd* apart, ... III. ii. 22. 3
to save, as thing *reserv'd* from stealth. . . . . IV. i. 6. 7
Resiant. In which her kingdomes throne is chiefly *resiant.* . IV. xi. 28. 9
Resigned. their living they *resigned* quight . . . . Hub. 573
when he had *resignd* his regiment, ... II. x. 30. 3
he soone *resinde* His former suit, ... III. xi. 5. 3
that which he had to Sir Paridel *resynd.* . . . . IV. i. 37. 9
Resinde. *See* **Resigned.**
Resist. Him booteth not *resist,* nor succour call, ... I. iii. 20. 1
which no creature may Long time *resist,* . . . . IV. v. 43. 4
when he saw it bootelesse to *resist,* . . . . V. i. 29. 7
Resistance. Encountring him with small *resistence* slew, . . . VI. xi. 43. 6
Made no *resistance,* ne could her contraire, ... VII. vi. 7. 8
Resistless. he seized greedelie On the *resistles* pray; . . . . Mui. 436
Immoveable, *resistlesse,* without end; . . . . V. i. 12. 7
their *resistlesse* rigour did eschew: . . . . V. viii. 32. 4
with huge *resistlesse* might The dores assayled, ... VI. xi. 43. 2
With which thou armest his *resistlesse* hand. . . . . H.L. 230
Resolution. His *resolution* was, . . . His bodie was her thrall, V. v. 46. 8
Resolve. to *resolve* first hereupon.' . . . . Hub. 123
how Fortune would *resolve* that daungerous dout. . . . . . . V. v. 5. 9
I *resolve* this siege not to give over, ... V. v. 51. 4
whether quite from them for to retrate I shall *resolve,* . . . VI. ix. 31. 8
Resolved. his limbs, *resolv'd* through idle leisour, ... Gn. 141
So both *resolv'd,* . . . to proceede; . . . . Hub. 103
She, all *resolv'd,* and ready to remove, ... D. 261
Resolvd in minde all suddenly to win, ... I. i. 24. 4
resolv'd to work his finall smart, ... I. ix. 51. 8
Resolv'd to put away that loathly blame, ... II. viii. 44. 4
resolv'd likewise to prove the rest, ... II. x. 31. 4
she *resolv'd,* unweeting to her Syre, ... III. iii. 57. 5
seeing them *resolvd* indeed To flame the gates, ... III. ix. 18. 1
Resolv'd to build his balefull mansion . . . . III. x. 58. 2
resolv'd to prove her utmost might, ... III. xi. 25. 1
both *resolv'd* the last extremities to prove. . . . . IV. ii. 19. 9
Resolv'd to end it one or other way, ... IV. iii. 17. 8
I me *resolv'd* the utmost end to prove; . . . . IV. vii. 16. 7
Resolv'd with him to wend, gainst all her friends consent. . IV. viii. 50. 9
Resolved to pursue his former quest; . . . . IV. ix. 17. 5
Resolv'd him to assault with manhood stout, ... IV. x. 19. 4
resolv'd her selfe in single fight To try her Fortune, ... V. iv. 47. 6
then againe *resolv'd* to hunt him out . . . . V. vi. 6. 7
Resolved in one t' assemble all his force, ... VI. viii. 14. 8
she *resolv'd* no remedy to fynde, ... VI. xi. 8. 6
Eftsoones she thus *resolv'd;* . . . . VII. vi. 23. 1
Resolving. At last *resolving* forward still to fare, ... I. i. 11. 1
resolving him to find Alive or dead; . . . . I. vii. 28. 2
resolving, like a Pilgrim pore, ... III. x. 19. 1
resolving to revenge his blood . . . . V. ii. 51. 8
resolving now to leave the place, ... V. ix. 3. 3
resolving what it was to know, ... VI. x. 17. 8
resolving to returne in hast . . . . VI. xii. 13. 1
Resort. to the dales *resort,* . . . . S.C. Jun. 21
'*Resort* of people doth my greefs augment, ... S.C. Au. 157
if to my cotage thou wilt *resort,* . . . . S.C. S. 254
Daylie *resort* to me from farre and neare, ... D. 143
Hermitage . . . Far from *resort* of people . . . . I. i. 34. 3
knights of worth and courage bold *Resort,* . . . . II. ii. 42. 9
honour in their festivall *resort;* . . . . II. iii. 28. 4
Ne suffreth he *resort* of living wight Approch to her, ... III. ix. 5. 6
did *resort* of sinfull people shonne. . . . . IV. vii. 42. 8
every one gan homeward to *resort:* . . . . IV. xii. 18. 2
never there the like *resort* they knew. . . . . V. ii. 29. 7
there did *resort* from every side . . . . V. iii. 2. 7
There let her wonne, farre from *resort* of men, ... V. ix. 2. 1
she used often to *resort* To common haunts, ... V. xii. 34. 6
Unto the which all lovers doe *resort,* . . . . VI. vii. 32. 8
used to *resort* Unto this place, ... VI. x. 9. 2
Oft to *resort* there-to, when seem'd them best, ... VII. vi. 38. 5
where she did *resort* With all her Nymphes . . . . VII. vi. 39. 6
Resorted. unto him all monstrous beasts *resorted* . . . . . . Hub. 1122
Resorts. Thither *resortes,* and . . . with faire Adonis playes III. vi. 49. 8
Resound. Wherein my plaints did oftentimes *resound:* . . . . S.C. Au. 152
The forest wide . . . *resound* The hollow Echo . . . . S.C. Au. 159
the wild woodes, my sorowes to *resound,* . . . . S.C. Au. 166
All which the ayrie Echo did *resound.* . . . . Gn. 232
madest the forrests ring, And fields *resownd,* . . . . Ti. 326
shady woods *resound* with dreadfull yells; . . . . D. 331
all the woodes and forestes did *resownd:* . . . . I. vi. 7. 6
voyce These pitteous plaintes and dolours did *resound:* . . . I. viii. 38. 2
that fame may it *resound* In her eternall tromp, ... II. iii. 38. 8
They made the further shore *resounden* wide. . . . . II. vii. 57. 6
Through all the seas so ruefully *resownd,* . . . . III. viii. 30. 6
That ever shrilling trumpet did *resound;* . . . . IV. ii. 32. 4
Where wont the shepheards oft their pypes *resound,* . . . . VI. xi. 26. 8
Helpe me mine owne loves prayses to *resound;* . . . . Epith. 14
gentle Eccho . . . Their accents did *resound.* . . . . Proth. 113
Resounded. both the shores *resounded,* . . . . Ti. 597
all the fields *resounded* with the ruefull cry. . . . . II. viii. 3. 9

Resounded—*Continued.*
Marinell, whose name the Heralds loud *resounded.* . . . . . V. iii. 6. 9
Don Braggadochios name *resounded* thrise: . . . . V. iii. 15. 4
the quyre of Byrds *resounded,* Their anthemes . . . . . *Am.* xix. 5
Resoundest. none of all their due deserts *resoundest.'* . . . *Col.* 463
Resounding. *resounding* With gentle murmure . . . . *Gn.* 185
through the sea *resounding* plaints did fly: . . . . II. xii. 27. 4
the rolling sea, *resounding* soft, ... II. xii. 33. 1
Resounds. Their merry Musick that *resounds* from far, ... *Epith.* 130
Resource. *Here han the holy Faunes *resourse,* . . . . *S.C.* Jul. 77
Respect. meet *respect* of honor putt to flight: . . . . III. i. 48. 8
Without *respect* of richesse or reward: . . . . III. ii. 7. 5
I graunt to thy great misery Gratious *respect;* . . . . III. x. 32. 2
Without *respect* of person or of port, ... III. xi. 46. 4
by wrong And tortious powre, without *respect* or measure: . IV. ix. 12. 4
to the Moone it mote be like in each *respect.* . . . . V. v. 3. 9
he it well did ward with wise *respect,* . . . . V. xii. 21. 5
With all due thankes and dutifull *respect,* . . . . VI. i. 45. 7
paines are nothing in *respect* of this; . . . . *Am.* lxiii. 13
if you loosely love without *respect,* . . . . *H.B.* 194
All which are made with wondrous wise *respect,* . . . . . . *H.H.B.* 34
Respected. If purest things be not by them *respected?* . . . *D.* 207
had he not that Dame *respected* more, ... I. x. 49. 4
Respire. trample th' earth, the whiles they may *respire,* . . . I. vi. 44. 8
Love! lay down thy bow, the whiles I may *respyre.* . . . . . I. ix. 8. 9
He cast to suffer him no more *respire,* . . . . I. xi. 28. 7
Whom whenas he perceived to *respyre,* . . . . II. iv. 16. 5
Nothing but death can doe me to *respyre.'* . . . . II. vi. 44. 5
he that breathlesse seems shal corage bold *respire.* . . . . . II. viii. 7. 9
From their long vassalage gin to *respire,* . . . . III. iii. 36. 8
whilest here I doe *respire.* . . . . III. xii. 45. 9
ne let him once *respyre,* . . . . V. v. 16. 7
Respite. to require *Respite* till morrow t' answere his desire; *Hub.* 326
Ne once did yield it *respitt* day nor night; . . . . II. xi. 9. 3
To graunt small *respit* to my restlesse toile; . . . . *Am.* xi. 6
Resplendent. With royall arras, and *resplendent* gold, ... I. viii. 35. 2
more illumine your *resplendent* ray, ... *H.B.* 177
Compared to his least *resplendent* sparke? . . . . *H.H.B.* 126
Respondence. voyces made To th' instruments divine *re-spondence* meet; . . . . II. xii. 71. 4
Rest. Ere it be long within the earth to *rest.* . . . . . . *Pet.*[1] vii. 4
rest, soft sliding downe From heavens hight . . . . *Bel.* i. 1
shortly turne unto my happie *rest,* . . . . *Pet.*[2] vii. 6
these rythmes doo read, and vew the *rest,* . . . . *Pet.*[2] vii. 11
shall never die . . . ne in ashes *rest;* . . . . *Ro.* i. 4
My sad desires, *rest* therefore moderate; . . . . *Ro.* vii. 12
the *rest* The which injurious time hath quite outworne, . . . *Ro.* xxvii. 5
Ne suffred him in anie place to *rest,* . . . . *Van.* iv. 9
A sword-fish small him from the *rest* did sunder, ... *Van.* v. 8
My spright was greatly moved in her *rest,* . . . . *Van.* xii. 2
reigne with the *rest* in heaven. . . . . *S.C.* Ap. 117
They sleepen in *rest,* . . . . *S.C.* May 68
If I may *rest,* I nill live in sorrowe. . . . . *S.C.* May 151
to winne renowne, or passe the *rest:* . . . . *S.C.* Jun. 74
all the *rest* did spill. . . . . *S.C.* Jul. 68
sith theyr soules bene now at *rest,* . . . . *S.C.* Jul. 123
With pyping and dauncing did passe the *rest.* . . . . *S.C.* Au. 10
Whatever thing lacketh chaungeable *rest,* . . . . *S.C.* S. 240
Whither thou list in fayre Elisa *rest,* . . . . *S.C.* O. 45
rolle with *rest* in rymes of rybaudrye; . . . . *S.C.* O. 76
the *rest* Under the tree . . . . *S.C.* D. 34
Let him *rest* pleased with his owne insight, ... *Gn.* Ded. 9
heavenly ranks, where blessed soules do *rest;* . . . . *Gn.* 58
To *rest* their limbs with wearines redounding. . . . . *Gn.* 189
Emongst the *rest* the clambring Yvie grew, ... *Gn.* 217
their wearie limbs to *rest,* . . . . *Gn.* 234
by the fountaine side, in shade to *rest,* . . . . *Gn.* 238
In quiet *rest* his molten heart did steep, ... *Gn.* 245
unto *rest* his wearie joynts prepare. . . . . *Gn.* 320
Calling in vaine for *rest,* and can have none. . . . . *Gn.* 392
here wise Curius . . . lives in endles *rest;* . . . . *Gn.* 610
the sloathfull fit of lifes sweete *rest* . . . . *Gn.* 641
Emongst the *rest* a wicked maladie . . . . *Hub.* 9
Was rob'd of *rest* and naturall reliefe. . . . . *Hub.* 16
Amongst the *rest* a good old woman was, ... *Hub.* 33
farre surpas The *rest* in honest mirth, ... *Hub.* 35
all the *rest* doo rob of good and land. . . . . *Hub.* 140
(compar'd to all the *rest* Of each degree) . . . . *Hub.* 179
he will care for all the *rest* to shift, ... *Hub.* 532
heares and sees the follies of the *rest,* . . . . *Hub.* 725
he doth recoyle Unto his *rest,* . . . . *Hub.* 755
I with reason meete will *rest* content, ... *Hub.* 1049
let the *rest* in order thee ensew. . . . . *T.M.* 54
the *rest* That whilome wont to wait . . . . *T.M.* 195
Therefore I mourne and sorrow with the *rest,* . . . . *T.M.* 227
all the *rest* her dolefull din augmented . . . . *T.M.* 357
all the *rest,* her sorrow to supplie, ... *T.M.* 537
all the *rest,* as borne of salvage brood, ... *T.M.* 589
The *rest* untold no living tongue can speake. . . . . *T.M.* 600
tell hir, that my eyes can take no *reste:* . . . . *U.V.* 7
I nightly waste, wanting my kindely *reste:* . . . . *U.V.* 16
shedding teares a while, I still did *rest,* . . . . *Ti.* 32
all the *rest,* that me so honord made . . . . *Ti.* 121
O vainesse! to be added to the *rest,* . . . . *Ti.* 459
all the *rest* downe shortlie fell, ... *Ti.* 558
all the *rest* must needs be left behinde: . . . . *Ti.* 586
Emongst the *rest* a gentle Nymph was found, ... *Mui.* 118
beeing nimbler joynted than the *rest,* . . . . *Mui.* 121
After his dayes long labour drew to *rest,* . . . . *D.* 23
Ne lets it *rest* untill it forth have brought . . . . *D.* 31

Rest—*Continued.*
I goe with gladnesse to my wished *rest,* . . . . *D.* 282
Let *rest* her selfe from her long wearinesse, ... *D.* 338
Ne will I *rest* my feete for feeblenesse, ... *D.* 460
Ne will I *rest* my limmes for frailtie, ... *D.* 461
Ne will I *rest* mine eyes for heavinesse. . . . . *D.* 462
Ne shall with *rest* refresh my fainting sprights, ... *D.* 472
he was not so happie as the *rest.* . . . . *As.* 12
all the *rest* but litle he esteemed. . . . . *As.* 66
The *rest* of her impatient regret, ... *As.* 169
I, among the *rest,* of many least, ... *Col.* 252
Religion hath lay powre to *rest* upon her, ... *Col.* 322
The *rest* of thine adventures, that betyded.' . . . . *Col.* 329
She is the pride and primrose of the *rest,* . . . . *Col.* 560
all the *rest* do most-what fare amis, ... *Col.* 757
had the sparke of reasons might More then the *rest* . . . . *Col.* 868
after him uprose eke all the *rest:* . . . . *Col.* 953
to draw their bleating flocks to *rest.* . . . . *Col.* 955
for pledge I leave Of all the *rest* . . . . *Ded. Son.* vii. 10
And on whose mightie shoulders most doth *rest* . . . . . . *Ded. Son.* ix. 3
from their noyance he no where can *rest;* . . . . I. i. 23. 7
wanting *rest,* will also want of might? . . . . I. i. 32. 7
with the Sunne take, Sir, your timely *rest,* . . . . I. i. 33. 1
Rest is their feast, and all thinges at their will: . . . . . . I. i. 35. 3
to your *rest* depart.' . . . . I. i. 54. 5
He could not *rest;* but did his stout heart eat, ... I. ii. 6. 3
she her weary limbes would never *rest;* . . . . I. ii. 8. 6
a large share it hewd out of the *rest,* . . . . I. ii. 18. 8
'Henceforth in safe assuraunce may ye *rest,* . . . . I. ii. 27. 1
to . . . *rest* their weary limbs a tide. . . . . I. ii. 29. 9
in their cotage small that night she *rest* her may. . . . . . I. iii. 14. 9
In stead of *rest* she does lament and weepe, ... I. iii. 15. 5
the first, that all the *rest* did guyde, ... I. iv. 18. 5
Emongst the *rest* rode that false Lady faire, ... I. iv. 37. 4
the Chamberlain, Slowth, did to *rest* them call. . . . . . . I. iv. 43. 9
Returne from whence ye came, and *rest* a while, ... I. iv. 51. 3
The noble hart . . . Can never *rest,* . . . . I. v. 1. 3
Whereas that Pagan proud him selfe did *rest* . . . . I. vi. 40. 5
he wearie sate To *reste* him selfe . . . . I. vii. 2. 7
Satt downe to *rest* in middest of the race: . . . . I. vii. 5. 4
To *rest* them selves, and weary powres repaire; . . . . . . I. viii. 50. 8
never vowd to *rest* till her I fynd: . . . . I. ix. 15. 8
'hence shall I never *rest,* Till I . . . . I. ix. 32. 1
'He there does now enjoy eternall *rest* . . . . I. ix. 40. 1
here ly downe, and to thy *rest* betake, ... I. ix. 44. 2
He chose an halter from among the *rest,* . . . . I. ix. 54. 4
tyred limbes to *rest,* . . . 'I hither came; . . . . I. x. 11. 1
a whyle I read you *rest,* . . . . I. x. 17. 5
when their wearie limbes with kindly *rest,* . . . . I. x. 18. 1
The *rest* was all in yellow robes arayed . . . . I. x. 30. 9
As Guardian and Steward of the *rest.* . . . . I. x. 37. 3
There she awhile him stayes, himselfe to *rest,* . . . . . . I. x. 45. 1
to the *rest* more hable he might bee; . . . . I. x. 45. 2
Brings them to joyous *rest* and endlesse blis. . . . . I. x. 52. 6
after litle *rest,* . . . . I. x. 68. 7
found no place his deadly point to *rest.* . . . . I. xi. 17. 4
from their journall labours they did *rest;* . . . . I. xi. 31. 4
One, that would wiser seeme then all the *rest,* . . . . I. xii. 10. 2
in his eyes did *rest* Yet sparckling fyre, ... I. xii. 10. 7
Let us devize of ease and everlasting *rest.'* . . . . I. xii. 17. 9
'Of ease or *rest* I may not yet devize; . . . . I. xii. 18. 2
Tounge hates to tell the *rest* . . . . II. i. 11. 9
in the *rest* his ready speare did sticke: . . . . II. i. 26. 3
So give me leave to *rest.'* . . . . II. i. 37. 9
To lett a weary wretch from her dew *rest,* . . . . II. i. 47. 7
To hinder soule from her desired *rest,* . . . . II. i. 48. 2
the common In of *rest;* . . . . II. i. 59. 2
Which whoso wants, wants so much of his *rest:* . . . . . . II. i. 59. 7
all this while were at their wanton *rest,* . . . . II. ii. 16. 4
To *rest* themselves, and grace to reconcile. . . . . II. ii. 33. 5
Ne ever shall I *rest* in house nor hold, ... II. ii. 44. 5
then each to *rest* him hyes. . . . . II. ii. 46. 9
rowze as comming late from *rest.* . . . . II. iii. 35. 9
The *rest* she would have sayd, ... II. iii. 42. 1
my engreeved mind could find no *rest,* . . . . II. iv. 23. 4
choycely picked out from all the *rest,* . . . . II. vi. 12. 4
here a while ye may in safety *rest,* . . . . II. vi. 23. 6
the *rest* of those same ruefull sightes, ... II. vii. 57. 7
To *rest* thy weary person in the shadow coole?' . . . . . . II. vii. 63. 9
Ne man nor beast may *rest,* or take repast . . . . II. ix. 16. 6
The *rest* had severall offices assynd; . . . . II. ix. 31. 6
all the *rest,* that noyous was and nought, ... II. ix. 32. 5
ne once would *rest* a whit. . . . . II. ix. 49. 9
Canute had his portion from the *rest,* . . . . II. x. 12. 7
resolv'd likewise to prove the *rest,* . . . . II. x. 31. 4
though carcas sleepe in *rest.* . . . . II. x. 43. 9
As if the *rest* some wicked hand did rend, ... II. x. 68. 4
Was, as the *rest,* a grysie rablement; . . . . II. xi. 12. 3
halfe the steele behind his backe did *rest;* . . . . II. xi. 37. 5
This is the Port of *rest* from troublous toyle, ... II. xii. 32. 8
So made by art to beautify the *rest,* . . . . II. xii. 55. 2
Under that Porch a comely dame did *rest* . . . . II. xii. 55. 7
The *rest* hidd underneath him more desirous made. . . . . . II. xii. 66. 9
the *rest* Fled all away . . . . II. xii. 81. 6
one above the *rest* in speciall . . . . II. xii. 86. 6
The fayrest vertue, far above the *rest:* . . . . III. Pr. 1. 2
Them to betake unto their kindly *rest:* . . . . III. i. 58. 2
when the Britonesse saw all the *rest* Avoided . . . . III. i. 58. 5
Could find no *rest* in such perplexed plight, ... III. i. 59. 5
any drop of slombring *rest* . . . . III. ii. 29. 1

Rest—*Continued.*

all wilde beastes do *rest*, III. ii. 32. 2
more then all the *rest* may sway, III. iii. 55. 1
forth she rode, without repose or *rest*, III. iv. 6. 6
with sharpe speare the *rest* made dearly knowne. III. iv. 15. 6
after all his warre to *rest* his wearie knife. III. iv. 24. 9
clombe all the *rest*, And forth together went III. iv. 31. 6
The *rest*, of other fishes drawen weare, III. iv. 33. 8
Then all the *rest* into their coches clim, III. iv. 42. 6
gentle Sleepe envyde him any *rest*: III. iv. 54. 1
Instead of *rest* thou lendest rayling teares; III. iv. 57. 4
from the wearie spirit thou doest drive Desired *rest*, III. iv. 57. 9
It lettes not fall, it lettes it not to *rest*; III. v. 2. 7
two of them the *rest* far overpast, III. v. 37. 8
In easie couch his feeble limbes to *rest*. III. v. 41. 2
all the *rest* it seemd they robbed bare Of bounty, III. vi. 4. 8
downe to *rest* Her selfe she set, III. vi. 10. 6
The *rest* upon her person gave attendance great. III. vi. 17. 9
Great enimy to it, and to all the *rest* III. vi. 39. 1
nought that wanteth *rest* can long aby: III. vii. 3. 5
finde some refuge there, and *rest* her wearie syde. III. vii. 5. 9
crave but rowme to *rest* while tempest overblo'th.' III. vii. 8. 9
to *rest* her faint And wearie limbes awhile. III. vii. 10. 4
As glad of that small *rest* as Bird of tempest gon. III. vii. 10. 9
Ne once to stay to *rest*, or breath at large, III. vii. 23. 3
fayre resemblance above all the *rest*, III. viii. 8. 2
From heavens blis and everlasting *rest*: III. viii. 8. 4
never suffred her to be at *rest*; III. viii. 39. 2
Emongst the *rest* my lott (unworthy') is to be one.' III. viii. 46. 9
the *rest*, which in this Quest proceed, III. viii. 50. 8
all were now retyrd Unto their *rest* III. ix. 10. 4
with earnest mone, Like as the *rest*, III. ix. 12. 4
like so as the *rest*, he prayd for nought; III. ix. 12. 5
that straunger knight emongst the *rest* III. ix. 20. 1
to *rest* in glorious victorye. III. ix. 22. 9
her late recourse to *rest*, III. ix. 26. 3
weetlesse wandered . . . Ere *rest* he fownd. III. ix. 41. 7
two rivers bownd the *rest*. III. ix. 46. 4
So huge a mind could not in lesser *rest*, III. ix. 46. 7
after *rest*, they, seeking farre abrode, III. ix. 49. 4
besought Them go to *rest*. III. ix. 53. 9
The *rest* she fyr'd, for sport, or for despight: III. x. 12. 6
The *rest* he leaves in ground: III. x. 19. 4
did the *rest* with grievous sighes suppresse, III. x. 25. 8
with pale eyes fast fixed on the *rest*, III. x. 41. 2
he emongst the *rest* crept forth in sory plight. III. x. 52. 9
His rolling eies did never *rest* in place, III. xii. 15. 6
Amongst the *rest* there was a jolly knight, IV. i. 10. 1
spurres unto his steed, With speare in *rest*, IV. i. 41. 2
the *rest* him seeing lie on ground Ran hastily, IV. i. 43. 3
glad to *rest* withall. IV. ii. 21. 9
fly Unto her *rest* in Plutoes griesly land; IV. iii. 13. 3
He lightly lept out of his place of *rest*, IV. iii. 22. 6
found *rest* Upon the brim of his brode-plated shield, IV. iii. 34. 5
One in bright armes, with ready speare in *rest*, IV. iv. 6. 6
when most us needeth *rest*, IV. iv. 12. 3
his on th' one, the *rest* on th' other side. IV. iv. 14. 3
The *rest* themselves in troupes did else dispose, IV. iv. 14. 7
with no better fortune then the *rest*: IV. iv. 21. 2
all the *rest* it did amazed make, IV. iv. 29. 4
trumpets sound did warne them all to *rest*; IV. iv. 36. 2
with no better fortune then the *rest* afore. IV. iv. 45. 9
Where I with sound of trompe will also *rest* IV. iv. 48. 9
all the *rest* which had the best afore, IV. v. 8. 6
The sight . . . did all the *rest* dismay. IV. v. 13. 9
Whereat the *rest* gan greatly to envie, IV. v. 19. 6
Whom when the *rest* did see her to refuse, IV. v. 21. 1
Amongst the *rest*, with boastfull vaine pretense, IV. v. 23. 5
Since with the *rest* she went not after Florimell. IV. v. 28. 9
hide their heads in quiet *rest*, IV. v. 32. 6
With huge great hammers, that did never *rest* IV. v. 36. 3
in his armour layd him down to *rest*: IV. v. 39. 2
To *rest* he layd him downe upon the flore, IV. v. 39. 3
Her feeble joynts layd eke adowne to *rest*; IV. v. 39. 7
The bellowes noyse disturb'd his quiet *rest*, IV. v. 41. 4
gave place to kindly *rest*, IV. v. 43. 4
ne did it ever *rest*, IV. vi. 13. 5
when they had long time there taken *rest*, IV. vi. 42. 1
T' alight, and *rest* their wearie limbs awhile. IV. vii. 3. 6
did her passed paines in quiet *rest* assoyle. IV. vii. 3. 9
I *rest* his wretched thrall, the sad Aemylia.' IV. vii. 18. 9
Amongst the *rest* a jewell rich he found, IV. viii. 6. 6
to *rest* as seem'd her meet. IV. viii. 9. 4
unto *rest* themselves all onely lent, IV. viii. 28. 7
Amongst the *rest* she chaunced there to see IV. viii. 52. 4
favour she to him hath hight Above the *rest*, IV. viii. 54. 2
Amongst the *rest* that Squire of low degree IV. ix. 8. 8
continu'd there a while To *rest* him selfe, IV. ix. 12. 7
by the *rest* did set in sumptuous chaire IV. ix. 13. 3
These paires of friends in peace and setled *rest*, IV. ix. 17. 2
rest themselves for to recover spirits spent. IV. ix. 25. 9
how ever loth to *rest*; IV. ix. 32. 7
I never joyed happinesse nor *rest*; IV. ix. 39. 3
So gan the *rest* him likewise to require, IV. ix. 41. 1
of my love at length I *rest* assured, IV. x. 2. 8
this same brave emprize for me did *rest*, IV. x. 4. 7
To sit and *rest* the walkers wearie shankes: IV. x. 25. 5
to afflicted minds sweet *rest* and quiet sends. IV. x. 34. 9
Amongst the *rest* some one, IV. x. 43. 7
graver countenance then all the *rest*; IV. x. 49. 2
all the *rest* were eke her equall peares, IV. x. 49. 3
stedfast still her eyes did fixed *rest*, IV. x. 49. 7
her sacrifices let to *rest*." IV. x. 54. 9
Inachus renowmd above the *rest*; IV. xi. 15. 5
th' oldest two of all the *rest*; IV. xi. 18. 2
all the *rest* of those two parents came, IV. xi. 18. 3
no lesse famous then the *rest* they bee, IV. xi. 40. 2
there, amongst the *rest*, IV. xi. 53. 6
Amongst the *rest* was faire Cymodoce, IV. xii. 3. 6
By timely death shall winne her wished *rest*, IV. xii. 8. 2
most is Mars amisse of all the *rest*, V. Pr. 8. 8
she of all the *rest*, V. Pr. 10. 1
Would not so *rest* contented with his right; V. i. 17. 6
both Together ran with ready speares in *rest*. V. ii. 12. 4
So all the *rest* did other parts empaire, V. ii. 32. 5
all men went to *rest*. V. iii. 7. 9
due tryall lend Of all the *rest*; V. iii. 8. 2
When they are all restor'd thou shalt *rest* in disgrace. V. iii. 20. 9
weary barke at last upon mine Isle did *rest*. V. iv. 11. 9
by rage of waves that never *rest*, V. iv. 19. 4
I will not *rest* till I her might doe trie, V. iv. 34. 3
mongst the *rest* the fight did untill evening last. V. iv. 43. 9
Warn'd man and beast in quiet *rest* be shrowded, V. iv. 45. 3
Where he him selfe did *rest* in safety V. iv. 46. 6
Could take no *rest*, ne would receive reliefe; V. iv. 47. 3
Artegall him selfe to *rest* did dight, V. iv. 51. 8
Besides the *rest* dismayd, V. v. 19. 7
For such your kind regard I can but *rest* your detter. V. v. 37. 9
Yet in my truthes assurance I *rest* fixed fast.' V. v. 38. 9
I to your selfe should *rest* for ever bound, V. v. 42. 4
The *rest* my selfe too readily can spell.' V. vi. 11. 6
Forcing in vaine the *rest* to her to tell; V. vi. 11. 8
desirous rather to *rest* mute, V. vi. 20. 3
Thus passing th' evening well, till time of *rest*, V. vi. 23. 1
with sweete *rest* her heavy eyes did close, V. vii. 12. 3
thorough evill *rest* of this last night, V. vii. 18. 7
In which stout Britomart her selfe did *rest*, V. vii. 26. 3
To serve her so as she the *rest* had bound: V. vii. 28. 4
Ne day nor night did ever idly *rest*; V. viii. 3. 7
rode apace With speare in *rest*, V. viii. 5. 3
at him ran with ready speare in *rest*; V. viii. 9. 3
For stint of strife and stablishment of *rest* V. viii. 21. 3
for *rest*, there having stayd not long, V. viii. 51. 8
Whose long *rest* rusted the bright steely brand; V. ix. 30. 7
Amongst the *rest*, which in that space befell, V. x. 6. 1
Admyr'd of all the *rest* in presence there, V. x. 15. 7
Unto some place where they mote *rest* V. x. 22. 7
all the *rest* which in that Castle were, V. x. 38. 1
Full loath to Belgae and to all the *rest*; V. xi. 35. 6
ne ever day did *rest*. V. xi. 35. 9
no lesse Then all the *rest* burst out V. xii. 2. 9
Into the *rest* which round about you ring, VI. Pr. 7. 7
the *rest* the which the Castle kept VI. i. 24. 1
So they the evening past till time of *rest*; VI. iii. 9. 6
In covert shade him selfe did safely *rest*, VI. iii. 20. 3
Till to some place of *rest* they mote attaine, VI. iii. 28. 7
When day is spent, and *rest* us needeth most, VI. iii. 39. 2
spare her Knight, and *rest* with reason pacifyde: VI. iii. 49. 9
Compelled were themselves awhile to *rest*, VI. iv. 15. 6
They mote the abler be to passe unto the *rest*. VI. iv. 15. 9
never . . . His limbes would *rest*, VI. iv. 40. 7
now strong through *rest* so long a space, VI. v. 7. 5
Exceeding all the *rest* in powre and hight; VI. v. 13. 7
fair Serene all night could take no *rest*, VI. v. 39. 6
Upon the *rest* that did alive remaine; VI. vi. 38. 4
The Prince himselfe there all that night did *rest*; VI. vi. 41. 2
the Prince did *rest* In carelesse couch, VI. vi. 44. 1
there in shade himselfe had layd to *rest*, VI. vii. 19. 2
would not let her lite, nor *rest* a little stead: VI. vii. 40. 9
Arthure with the *rest* went onward still VI. viii. 30. 7
she betooke her selfe to *rest*: VI. viii. 34. 5
Each wisheth to him selfe, and to the *rest* envyes:— VI. viii. 41. 9
For love in soft delight thereon to *rest*; VI. viii. 42. 3
to the *rest* his wrathfull hand he bends; VI. viii. 49. 5
The *rest*, that scape his sword VI. viii. 49. 8
day nor night he suffred him to *rest*, VI. ix. 3. 2
Higher then all the *rest*, VI. ix. 8. 2
all the *rest* like lesser lamps did dim: VI. ix. 9. 5
Then all the *rest* about her rose likewise, VI. ix. 15. 3
rest himselfe till supper time befell; VI. ix. 17. 4
Which tosse the *rest* in daungerous disease; VI. ix. 19. 5
to *rest* from toyle, VI. ix. 23. 8
that all contented *rest* With that they hold: VI. ix. 29. 8
in this shore To *rest* my barcke, VI. ix. 31. 4
of all the *rest* which there did dwell, VI. ix. 46. 5
set his *rest* amongst the rusticke sort, VI. x. 2. 6
this to adorne, she all the *rest* did pill. VI. x. 5. 9
therein to repose And *rest* her selfe VI. x. 9. 4
the *rest* them round about did hemme, VI. x. 12. 4
with her goodly presence all the *rest* much graced. VI. x. 12. 9
Seem'd all the *rest* in beauty to excell, VI. x. 14. 4
Doth she exceede the *rest* of all her race; VI. x. 26. 6
Amongst the *rest* . . . They spoyld old Melibee VI. x. 40. 1
had the chiefe commaund of all the *rest*, VI. xi. 3. 5
Ne day nor night he suffred her to *rest*, VI. xi. 5. 8
onely mongst the *rest* by her to sit, VI. xi. 8. 3
with the *rest* they tooke not long agoe; VI. xi. 11. 7
At last when all the *rest* them offred were, VI. xi. 14. 1
The *rest* take if they would; VI. xi. 14. 9

Rest—*Continued.*
with the *rest* be sold before him theare, VI. xi. 15. 4
To make the prises of the *rest* more deare. VI. xi. 15. 5
Scarse yeelding her due food or timely *rest,* VI. xi. 24. 5
askt where were the *rest?* VI. xi. 28. 2
Whereat the knight amaz'd yet did not *rest,* VI. xi. 28. 7
all the *rest* Were dead, VI. xi. 41. 6
they both full glad and blyth did *rest,* VI. xi. 41. 8
In dead of night, when all the theeves did *rest,* VI. xi. 42. 2
Where all the *rest* for him did readie stay, VI. xi. 47. 7
Would have suffiz'd the *rest* for to restraine, VII. vi. 29. 8
likewise Should handle as the *rest* of her allies, VII. vi. 30. 5
wealths and goodnesse, far above the *rest* VII. vi. 38. 2
(for pleasure and for *rest*) Oft to resort VII. vi. 38. 4
He could him not containe in silent *rest;* VII. vi. 46. 4
Cynthia's selfe, more angry then the *rest,* VII. vi. 51. 1
never *rest,* but evermore exchange Their dwelling places, VII. vii. 21. 5
a certaine grange Wherein to *rest,* VII. vii. 21. 8
all the *rest,* which they usurp, VII. vii. 26. 9
The *rest* which doe the world in being hold; VII. vii. 27. 3
King of all the *rest,* as ye doe clame, VII. vii. 53. 2
stedfast *rest* of all things, VII. viii. 2. 3
thence-forth all shall *rest* eternally VII. viii. 2. 7
to lead fraile mindes to *rest* In chast desires, *Am.* viii. 7
with theyr terrour al the *rest* may chace, *Am.* xxxi. 7
All were it, as the *rest,* but rudely writ? *Am.* xxxiii. 8
till she vouchsafe to grawnt me *rest;* *Am.* xxxiii. 13
Be lyke in mercy as in all the *rest.* *Am.* lv. 14
Most happy she, that most assur'd doth *rest;* *Am.* lix. 13
The joyous safety of so sweet a *rest;* *Am.* lxiii. 10
Sits downe to *rest* him in some shady place, *Am.* lxvii. 3
there to *rest* themselves did boldly place. *Am.* lxxvi. 12
Sweet thoughts! I envy your so happy *rest,* *Am.* lxxvi. 13
all the *rest* . . . Shall turne to nought *Am.* lxxix. 5
Give leave to *rest* me being halfe fordonne, *Am.* lxxx. 3
The *rest* be works of natures wonderment: *Am.* lxxxi. 13
so much you graced In this as in the *rest,* *Am.* lxxxii. 6
Goe visit her in her chast bowre of *rest* *Am.* lxxxiii. 7
suffrest neyther gods in sky, Nor men in earth, to *rest:* *Epig.* iv. 16
Let all the *rest* be thine. *Epith.* 126
let the Graces daunce unto the *rest,* *Epith.* 257
Thy tyred steedes long since have need of *rest.* *Epith.* 284
So let us *rest,* sweet love, in hope of this, *Epith.* 424
Rest not till they have pierst the trembling harts, *H.L.* 123
no one drop of pitie there doth *rest.* *H.L.* 147
He nathemore can so contented *rest,* *H.L.* 246
all delight and joyous happie *rest,* *H.L.* 281
Hercules and Hebe, and the *rest* Of Venus dearlings, *H.L.* 283
And carrie all the *rest* with him around; *H.H.B.* 74
attend On Gods owne person, without *rest* or end. *H.H.B.* 98
Fairer then all the *rest* which there appeare, *H.H.B.* 102
In th' only wonder of her selfe to *rest,* *H.H.B.* 238
Thy straying thoughts henceforth for ever *rest.* *H.H.B.* 301
all the *rest* around To her redoubled *Proth.* 109
these twaine, that did excell The *rest,* *Proth.* 121
Above the *rest* were goodly to bee seene *Proth.* 168

Rested. Him *rested* the goodman on the lea, *S.C.* F. 158
So *rested* she; and then the next in rew *T.M.* 173
So *rested* shee; and then the next in rew *T.M.* 233, 299
when as he piped had his fill, He *rested* him: *Col.* 11
when they *rested* had a season dew, II. ix. 20. 6
lively vigour *rested* in his mind, II. ix. 55. 7
Ne *rested* they, till that to Faery lond They came, III. iii. 62. 1
He *rested* him awhile; III. v. 41. 3
Therewith he *rested,* and well pleased was: IV. vi. 39. 1
Nathlesse she *rested* not so satisfide; IV. xii. 25. 1
Ne *rested* till she came without relent V. vii. 24. 8
awhile he *rested* still: VI. i. 35. 5
Sir Calidore . . . Yet *rested* not, VI. ii. 13. 6
being well suffiz'd them *rested* faine. VI. v. 39. 5
Ne *rested* he himselfe, but natures dew, VI. ix. 3. 3
In sommers shade him selfe here *rested* weary: VI. x. 22. 6
He breath'd his sword, and *rested* him till day; VI. xi. 47. 2

Resting. *See* **Long-resting, Never-resting.**
my fraile safetie, *resting* in the might Of him VI. ii. 29. 3

Resting-place. Uprose Duessa from her *resting place,* I. iv. 44. 8
forward thence did pas Unto some *resting place,* IV. vi. 39. 4

Restless. *restles* seas of wretchednes and woe; *Pet.*[2] vii. 4
With sight of such as chaunge the *restlesse* woe. *S.C.* Au. 172
wont t' enrage the *restlesse* sheepe, *S.C.* D. 89
lying *reastlesse* in heavy bedde, *U.V.* 4
wont forth to powre Her *restles* plaints, *Ti.* 132
with *restlesse* toyle Wearie your selves *D.* 533
let not his *restlesse* spright, Be unreveng'd, I. iv. 48. 7
Such *restlesse* passion did all night torment I. v. 1. 5
Against that Castle *restlesse* siege did lay, II. xi. 14. 2
Like to a *restlesse* wheele, still ronning round, II. xii. 20. 6
restlesse walketh all the world arownd, III. ii. 14. 4
Love, . . . hath a *restlesse* minde; III. iv. 9. 6
In *restlesse* anguish and unquiet paine; III. iv. 61. 2
having left that *restlesse* house of Care, IV. vi. 2. 1
Restlesse, recomfortlesse, with heart deepe grieved, V. vi. 24. 6
with *restlesse* force . . . it readie passage found, V. x. 33. 1
restlesse paines did take. VI. viii. 33. 9
Reaping eternall glorie of his *restlesse* paines. VI. ix. 2. 9
had bred his *restlesse* paine; VI. x. 31. 8
with *restlesse* paine and toile VI. xii. 22. 8
turne they still about, and change in *restlesse* wise. VII. vii. 18. 9
small respit to my *restlesse* toile; *Am.* xi. 6
raging now therein with *restlesse* stowre, *H.L.* 3

Restless—*Continued.*
therein stirre such rage and *restlesse* stowre, *H.B.* 73

Restoratives. Many *Restoratives* of vertues rare, III. v. 50. 3

Restore. ought of the gotten good to *restore:* *S.C.* S. 129
Nor failing force to former strength *restore:* *D.* 473
That may *restore* you to your wonted well?' I. ii. 43. 7
to former kynd Shall us *restore;* I. ii. 43. 9
Himselfe with salves to health for to *restore,* I. v. 40. 8
all things see . . . their merites to *restore,* I. viii. 27. 7
they did to health *restore* The man I. x. 27. 8
unto life the dead it could *restore,* I. xi. 30. 1
Whom his victorious handes did earst *restore* To native crowne II. i. 2. 6
Did life with usury to him *restore,* II. xi. 45. 4
when she saw no helpe might him *restore,* III. i. 38. 7
Till he had made amends, and full *restore* III. v. 18. 8
Sith I her dew reward cannot *restore?* III. v. 46. 5
can *restore* A love-sick hart, III. v. 50. 6
shee sought him to *restore* to plight, III. vii. 21. 1
Ne griefe might not his love to him *restore,* III. x. 18. 7
Restore unto her health and former state: III. xii. 35. 6
did *restore* His weakned powres, IV. iii. 24. 3
the warlike Britomart *restore* The prize IV. iv. 48. 1
him *restore* to former grace againe: IV. vii. 47. 7
Ye may redresse, and me *restore* to light!' IV. viii. 17. 5
at his will may whom he list *restore,* IV. viii. 54. 8
unto former liberty *restore.* IV. ix. 8. 7
As if instead thereof they Chaos would *restore.* IV. ix. 23. 9
grieved to *restore* the pledge IV. xii. 32. 9
Chose Artegall to right her to *restore;* V. i. 4. 8
to his owne part *restore* the same againe: V. ii. 31. 9
all things to an equall to *restore,* V. ii. 34. 2
To Braggadochio did his shield *restore,* V. iii. 13. 2
restore Belge unto her right. V. xi. Arg.
light to men *restore,* V. xii. 11. 4
to her kingdomes seat *restore* agayne: V. xii. 25. 4
no salves may us to health *restore?'* VI. vi. 13. 7
Having subdew'd yet did to life *restore;*) VI. viii. 4. 5
since things passed none may now *restore,* VI. x. 20. 8
He did them all to Coridon *restore:* VI. xi. 51. 8
ere thou doest them unto grace *restore,* *H.L.* 164
can *restore* a damned wight from death. *H.B.* 287
him *restore* unto that happie state *H.H.L.* 139

Restored. th' Ausonian light might be *restor'd!* *Ro.* xxv. 8
For that I thee *restor'd* to life *Gn.* 354
him *restor'd* to helth II. vi. 51. 9
to his crowne she him *restord* againe; II. x. 32. 1
shortly it to him *restord* agayne, II. x. 44. 7
He is againe unto his rule *restord;* II. x. 66. 2
their weary limbes to perfect plight *Restord,* III. i. 1. 4
Ere they to former rule *restor'd* shal bee, III. iii. 44. 6
every part . . . was soone *restord.* III. xii. 38. 7
Was to that goodly fellowship *restor'd,* IV. i. 15. 2
unto strength *restor'd* her soone anew. IV. viii. 20. 9
him *restor'd* to healthfull state againe: IV. xi. 7. 4
When they are all *restor'd* V. iii. 20. 9
earst was dead, *restor'd* to life againe, V. xi. 16. 6
he had to her both life and love *restord.* VI. i. 45. 9
Thus having her *restored* trustily, VI. iii. 19. 6
Her tongue to her *restord,* then thus she sayd: VI. viii. 19. 4
He gave us life, he it *restored* lost; *H.H.L.* 181

Restoring. him *restoring* unto living light, V. iv. 25. 6
them *restoring* To mens subjection, V. vii. 42. 6

Restrain. Doo not *restraine* your images still mourning) *Ro.* xv. 8
to *restraine* The lust of lawlesse youth *S.C.* O. 21
should it not thy readie course *restraine,* *Col.* 82
their bootlesse zeale she did *restrayne* I. vi. 19. 8
with outrageous strokes did him *restraine,* I. viii. 13. 8
sad ruth does seeme you to *restraine,* II. ii. 45. 2
First her *restraine* from her reprochfull blame II. iv. 11. 3
*foes of life, she better can *restraine;* II. vi. 1. 7
he espying cast her to *restraine* II. xi. 28. 4
each the other from to rise *restraine;* II. xii. 64. 5
Her to *restraine,* and give her good reliefe III. iv. 11. 5
his cours they did *restraine.* III. v. 39. 9
reasons, to *restraine* From blouddy strife, IV. iii. 47. 7
loose affections streightly to *restraine;* IV. v. 4. 8
ne reasons rule, mote them *restraine.* IV. v. 24. 9
Like to a stubborne steede whom strong hand would *restraine.* IV. vi. 33. 9
dread of shame my doubtfull lips doth still *restraine.'* V. v. 30. 9
The fell contagion may thereof *restraine,* V. vii. 11. 8
bands of nature, that wilde beastes *restraine,* V. xii. 1. 5
Did him reprove, yet could him not *restrayne,* VI. iii. 32. 7
His dear affect with silence did *restraine,* VI. v. 24. 4
did from further violence *restraine,* VI. v. 27. 4
your tongue, your talk *restraine* VI. vi. 7. 8
Abstaine from pleasure, and *restraine* your will; VI. vi. 14. 5
none was him to stop, nor none him to *restraine.* VI. xii. 2. 9
Ne any is that may him now *restraine,* VI. xii. 40. 3
Would have suffiz'd the rest for to *restraine,* VII. vi. 29. 8
from all wandring loves . . . strongly it *restrayne.* *Am.* xlii. 12

Restrained. Hardly, naythles, were they *restrayned* so, *Hub.* 1073
As stubborne steed, that is with curb *restrained,* *D.* 194
hardly was *restreined* of that aged sire. I. ii. 5. 9
him perforce *restraynd,* II. vii. 6. 9
their devouring covetize *restraynd;* III. iv. 7. 8
from such hardy boldnesse was *restraynd,* III. v. 44. 8
they *restrained* were Of ready entraunce, III. viii. 52. 3
Hatred would my entrance have *restrayned,* IV. x. 36. 4
long *restrayned* of his ready course, VI. i. 21. 3
Would he *restrayned* be from his attendement. VI. vi. 18. 9

Restrained—*Continued.*
for stubborne pride which her *restrayned*. . . . . VI. vii. 36. 4
Restraining. *Restraining* stealth and strong extortion, ... II. x. 39. 5
Restrains. *Restraines* those sterne behests and cruell doomes of his. . . . . V. vii. 22. 9
Restraint. enprisonment, . . . he endured in his late *restraint*, I. x. 2. 5
the Palmer, by his grave *restraynt*, Him stayd . . . . . . II. v. 24. 3
to be free from hard *restraynt* . . . . III. ix. 4. 9
with watch and hard *restraynt* . . . . III. ix. 6. 8
my toung with proud *restraint* to tie; . . . . *Am.* xliii. 6
Poure out the wine without *restraint* or stay, ... *Epith.* 250
Rests. there him *rests* in riotous suffisaunce . . . . *Mui.* 207
Who *rests* not pleased with such happines, ... *Mui.* 215
rests not so, but other meanes doth make, ... I. ii. 9. 6
then againe retourned to their *restes:* . . . . II. ix. 26. 8
Ne ever *rests* he in tranquillity, ... III. x. 58. 8
It never *rests* till it have wrought . . . . VI. vi. 8. 9
Resty. with both his hands unto him hayles The *resty* raynes, V. viii. 39. 6
Resume. that I my traveill should *resume*, ... III. vii. 56. 1
My former shield I may *resume* againe: . . . . V. xi. 56. 2
Retain. doo the name of Rome *retaine*, ... *Ro.* vii. 2
Those that poore Sutors papers do *retaine*, ... *Col.* 741
th' other halfe did womans shape *retaine*, ... I. i. 14. 8
he his mothers lore did well *retaine*, ... III. iv. 26. 5
the weake sowle her seat did yett *retaine*, ... III. v. 31. 4
Which vertue it for ever after did *retaine*. . . . . IV. v. 4. 9
taking downe the shield with me did it *retaine*. . . . . . IV. x. 10. 9
sore against his will did him *retaine*, ... IV. xi. 7. 7
Whose bad condition yet it doth *retaine*, ... IV. xi. 38. 8
Till we may be assur'd they shall their course *retaine*.' . . . V. ii. 36. 9
could it not sterne Artegall *retaine*, ... V. viii. 3. 1
Calidore himselfe would not *retaine* . . . . VI. i. 47. 1
skill, which that immortall spright . . . did in it *retaine*, . VI. vi. 1. 8
creatures, What-ever life or motion do *retaine*, ... VII. vii. 4. 2
Retained. Even thrise eleven descents the crowne *retaynd*, . . II. x. 45. 8
th' upper halfe their hew *retayned* still, ... II. xii. 31. 6
retain'd Enough to hold a foole in vaine delight. . . . . . III. viii. 10. 6
to her selfe it secretly *retayned* . . . . V. v. 44. 5
Retaining. Which powre *retayning* still . . . . *H.B.* 113
Retinue. Nymphs, which she doth hold In her *retinew*, ... *Col.* 460
Retire. oft faining to *retire* And oft him to assaile, ... *Gn.* 306
Then home he suffred her for to *retyre*, ... I. vi. 23. 5
Til breathlesse both themselves aside *retire*, ... I. vi. 44. 6
the Gyaunt . . . forst the knight *retyre*. . . . . I. viii. 17. 9
To Una back he cast him to *retyre*, ... I. x. 68. 2
forst him to *retire* A little backeward . . . . I. xi. 45. 2
being entred might not backe *retyre;* . . . . II. vi. 20. 2
were it not for shame, he would *retyre;* . . . . II. vii. 37. 8
life ere long shall to her home *retire*, ... II. viii. 7. 8
from Fraunce was forced to *retyre*. . . . . II. x. 22. 9
I read thee soone *retyre*, ... III. iv. 14. 8
did him selfe to safety *retyre*.' . . . . III. ix. 40. 9
backe *retire*, all scorcht and pittifully brent. . . . . III. xi. 26. 9
from daunger of the throwes Backe to *retire*, ... IV. iii. 26. 4
He bad him stay, and backe with him *retire*, ... V. i. 21. 1
if that he should *retire*, ... V. ii. 52. 6
Nought could he do but . . . backward still *retyre;* . . . . V. v. 16. 2
forst at first those knights backe to *retyre:* . . . . V. xi. 58. 6
turn'd abacke, and to *retyre* him hasted . . . . VI. vi. 28. 3
Be but vaine shadowes to this safe *retyre* Of life, ... VI. ix. 27. 5
they to freedome did *retyre*. . . . . VI. xii. 10. 5
What way is best to drive her to *retire*, ... VII. vi. 21. 7
to get his love *retyre;* . . . . *H.L.* 235
Unto her native planet shall *retyre;* . . . . *H.B.* 103
Retired. would have backe *retyred* to her cave, ... I. v. 21. 6
weapon . . . back *retyrd*, his life blood forth . . . . . . I. xi. 53. 9
Back to the strond *retyrd*, ... II. vi. 40. 6
With lighter hearts unto their home *retird;* . . . . III. iii. 51. 4
a furlongs mountenaunce *Retird* their steeds, ... III. viii. 18. 6
all were now *retyrd* Unto their rest, ... III. ix. 10. 3
he backe *retyred* soft away, ... III. xii. 4. 7
The other backe *retired* and contrarie trode. . . . . IV. i. 28. 9
Backe to that desert forrest they *retyred*, ... IV. vi. 47. 1
though he still *retyr'd*, ... V. v. 14. 5
would have backe *retyred* from that sight, ... VI. vii. 20. 8
Retrait. To stay the steppe, ere forced to *retrate*. . . . . . I. i. 13. 5
him the Squire made quickly to *retrate*, ... I. viii. 12. 7
Working belgardes and amorous *retrate;* . . . . II. iii. 25. 3
Whose faire *retraitt* I in my shield doe beare; . . . . . . II. ix. 4. 2
As fast as forward erst now backward to *retrate*. . . . . . IV. iii. 26. 8
shortly them compelled to *retrate*, ... IV. ix. 34. 8
did me also friend in my *retrate*. . . . . IV. x. 57. 9
ere she would once *retrate*. . . . . V. iv. 45. 9
yet so fast they could not home *retrate*, ... V. vii. 35. 1
sounded the *retraite*, and drew his folke away. . . . . . . V. xii. 9. 9
from them for to *retrate* . . . . VI. ix. 31. 7
Retreat. she him forced backward to *retreat*, ... IV. vi. 15. 3
forst him backe with fowle dishonor to *retreat*. . . . . . IV. vii. 37. 9
Return. then *returne* to his former fall? . . . . *S.C.* F. 14
The time was once, and may againe *retorne*, ... *S.C.* May 103
till safe and sound 'She home *returne*, ... *S.C.* Au. 181
I, poore wretch, am forced to *returne* . . . . *Gn.* 618
doo *returne* from whence he first begun, ... *Hub.* 306
The running waters wept for thy *returne*, ... *Col.* 27
weening to *returne* whence they did stray, ... I. i. 10. 3
To wish you backe *returne* with foule disgrace, ... I. i. 13. 3
Returne from whence ye came, and rest a while, ... I. iv. 51. 3
They gan to fight *retourne*, ... I. vi. 45. 2
life does win Unto her native prison to *retourne;* . . . . . I. vii. 21. 8
shortly back *returne* unto this place, ... I. x. 64. 3

Return—*Continued.*
Backe to *retourne* to that great Faery Queene, ... I. xii. 18. 6
Ye then shall hither backe *retourne* agayne, ... I. xii. 19. 8
Unto his Faery Queene backe to *retourne;* . . . . I. xii. 41. 8
nought that falles . . . May backe *retourne*, ... II. xii. 6. 9
Ne did the other backe his foote *returne*, ... III. i. 5. 7
bownd till his *retourne* their labour not to slake. . . . . . III. iii. 10. 9
vowed never to *returne* againe, ... III. v. 10. 3
they agayn *returne* backe by the hinder gate. . . . . . . III. vi. 32. 9
thither they *retourne* where first they grew: . . . . III. vi. 33. 8
Till we *returne* againe in safety: . . . . III. x. 42. 5
home *returne*, where all should be renewd . . . . III. x. 51. 3
Awayted there for Britomarts *returne*, ... III. xii. 45. 2
Backe to him selfe he gan *returne* the blame, ... IV. xii. 16. 2
Ne former strength *returne* so suddenly, ... IV. xii. 35. 4
of her health . . . And safe *returne*, ... V. ii. 3. 6
tast of joy, and to wont pleasures to *retourne*. . . . . . . V. iii. 1. 9
the utmost date assynde For his *returne* . . . . V. vi. 3. 7
when as yet she saw him not *returne*, ... V. vi. 6. 1
none can backe *returne* that once are gone amis. . . . . . V. ix. 6. 9
to your selfe doe it *returne* againe. . . . . VI. Pr. 7. 3
Till his *returne* unto this tree he bond; . . . . VI. i. 16. 8
To whom the other did this taunt *returne:* . . . . VI. iii. 31. 6
He with him thought backe to *returne* againe; . . . . . . VI. iv. 24. 2
dare not *returne* for all his daily vaunt. . . . . VI. iv. 29. 9
All is in time like to *returne* againe To that foule feend, . VI. iv. 31. 7
no hope of his *retourne* She saw now left, ... VI. v. 7. 1
to *returne* againe To his wounds worker, ... VI. x. 31. 6
resolving to *returne* in hast . . . . VI. xii. 13. 1
(After *returne* of Hermes Embassie) . . . . VII. vi. 23. 2
Whatso is fayrest shall to earth *returne*. . . . . *Am.* xiii. 8
Retourne agayne, my forces late dismayd, ... *Am.* xiv. 1
They ydly back *returne* to me agayne: . . . . *Am.* lxxviii. 10
his *returne* that seemes to linger late: . . . . *Am.* lxxxviii. 4
Returned. My thought *returned* greeved home againe, ... *Ti.* 478
waste wordes *retournd* to him in vaine: . . . . I. i. 42. 2
he backe *returnd* againe. . . . . I. i. 55. 9
Shee backe *retourned* with some labour lost; . . . . I. iii. 24. 2
But few *returned*, having scaped hard, ... I. iv. 3. 3
They backe *retourned* to the princely Place; . . . . I. iv. 38. 3
creature never past, That backe *retourned* . . . . I. v. 31. 7
Returnd to stately pallace of Dame Pryde: . . . . I. v. 45. 2
adowne he looked to the grownd To have *returnd;* . . . . . I. x. 67. 6
fled attonce, he ever backe *retourned* eye; . . . . II. iii. 19. 9
She to her use *returnd*, ... II. v. 19. 3
A while they fled, but soone *retournd* againe . . . . II. ix. 15. 1
then againe *retourned* to their restes: . . . . II. ix. 26. 8
being *retourned* late From his fierce warres, ... II. ix. 34. 7
The king *retourned* proud of victory, ... II. x. 17. 1
The way they came, the same *retourn'd* they right, ... II. xii. 84. 3
Let them *returned* be unto their former state.' . . . . . . II. xii. 85. 9
Retourned home, the royall Infant fell . . . . III. ii. 49. 1
turnd contrary, and *returnd* All contrary; . . . . III. ii. 51. 3
Ne ever to his worke *returnd* againe: . . . . III. iii. 11. 3
with the Dwarfe he back *retourn'd* againe, ... III. v. 12. 1
That hast from darkenes me *returnd* to light, ... III. v. 35. 7
After that they againe *retourned* beene, ... III. vi. 33. 1
was *returnd* againe unto his Dame, ... III. vii. 61. 8
Once having turnd, no more *returnd* his face, ... III. viii. 18. 8
retourned back againe To his first way. . . . . III. viii. 44. 5
(being late *returnd* From slaughter of the Giaunts . . . . . III. ix. 22. 1
She turnd her, and *returned* backe againe; . . . . III. x. 49. 8
then *returned*, having marched thrise, ... III. xii. 26. 8
Returned readie newes, that those same . . . . IV. ii. 31. 5
backe *returned* with right heavie mind . . . . IV. vi. 46. 4
His weary eie *returnd* to him againe, ... IV. viii. 8. 3
when he to himselfe *returnd* againe, ... IV. viii. 44. 1
wish to life *return'd* againe to bee, ... IV. x. 23. 8
Being *returned* to his mothers bowre, ... IV. xii. 19. 1
Return'd to heaven, whence she deriv'd her race; . . . . . V. i. 11. 4
unto his former journey he *retourned:* . . . . V. ii. 28. 9
She unto Talus forth *return'd* againe, ... V. vi. 15. 4
Being *returned* to his former hew; . . . . V. ix. 18. 8
as he backe *returned* from that land, ... V. xii. 28. 1
Sir Artegall, *return'd* from his late quest, ... V. xii. 38. 3
I . . . backe *returned* His scornefull taunts . . . . VI. ii. 12. 1
backe *return'd* againe With speede . . . . VI. iv. 9. 3
soone as he *returned* backe againe, ... VI. v. 34. 2
Himselfe recovering was *return'd* to fight, ... VI. vii. 10. 2
backe *returned* to his rusticke wonne, ... VI. x. 32. 2
when he backe *returned* from the wood, ... VI. xi. 25. 1
The gentle deare *returnd* the selfe-same way, ... *Am.* lxvii. 7
Returnedst. back *returnedst* to this barrein soyle, ... *Col.* 656
Returneth. *Returneth* by continuall successe, ... *Gn.* 30
Returning. Styx, not passable to soules *returning*, ... *Ro.* xv. 6
'Th' Argolicke power *returning* home againe, ... *Gn.* 561
I now depart, *returning* to thee never, ... *Gn.* 634
backe *returning* by the Yvorie dore, ... I. i. 44. 6
Retourning to his bed in torment great, ... I. ii. 6. 1
backe *retourning*, took her wonted way . . . . I. v. 44. 7
returning from the drery Night, ... I. vii. 2. 1
'From whom *retourning* sad and comfortlesse, ... I. ix. 28. 1
'I home *retourning*, fraught with fowle despight, ... II. iv. 29. 1
Into the which *retourning* backe he fell: . . . . II. x. 11. 4
fierce *retourning*, as a faulcon fayre, ... II. xi. 36. 6
brave *retourning*, with his brandisht blade . . . . II. xi. 37. 1
retourning to his native place, ... III. iii. 41. 5
backe *returning* to the former land, ... III. vii. 61. 5
backe *retourning* spyde Tyde with her golden girdle; . . . . III. viii. 2. 6
Returning back, those goodly rowmes, ... III. xii. 42. 1

Returning—*Continued.*
Who backe *returning* told, as he had seene, ... IV. iv. 3. 1
his felonous intent *Returning* disappointed his desire, ... IV. vi. 11. 7
backe *returning* where his Dame did lie, ... V. vi. 30. 7
being forst to abide the daies *returning,* . . . . V. vi. 31. 3
Artegall, *returning* yet halfe sad . . . . VI. i. 4. 4
So all *returning* to the Castle glad, ... VI. i. 46. 1
when the groome *returning* brought . . . . VI. iii. 43. 3
backe *returning* to that sorie Dame, ... VI. v. 4. 1
returning to that Ladie backe, ... VI. viii. 50. 1
backe *returning* to my sheepe againe, ... VI. ix. 25. 7
backe *returning* to his dearest deare, ... VI. xi. 50. 1
back *returning* to Molann' againe, ... VII. vi. 53. 2
Reveal. Such as no carpers may contrayre *reveale;* . . . . *Hub.* 494
Reveale to me, and all the meanes detect, ... *Mui.* 13
I will *revele* what ye so much desire. . . . . I. ix. 8. 8
th' amarous sweet spoiles to greedy eyes *revele.* . . . . . . II. xii. 64. 9
His joyous face did to the world *revele,* . . . . III. ii. 48. 2
which the powres to thee are pleased to *revele.'* . . . . . . III. iii. 19. 9
bad that none their joyous treason should *reveale.* . . . . . III. x. 5. 9
passing beautie did eftsoones *reveale,* . . . . IV. v. 10. 4
till that the Dwarfe did me *reveale,* . . . . IV. viii. 55. 5
If ought lay hidden . . . It to *reveale;* . . . . IV. xii. 24. 9
skill whereof to Princes hearts he doth *reveale,* . . . . . . V. vii. 1. 9
rare in-sight hard matters to *revele;* . . . . V. ix. 39. 2
could *reveale* All hidden crimes, ... V. xii. 26. 5
Revele to me the sacred noursery Of vertue, ... VI. Pr. 3. 1
I would thy selfe require thee to *reveale,* . . . . VI. ii. 26. 4
my lyfes Leach! doe your skill *reveale;* . . . . *Am.* l. 13
Revealed. The thing . . . now is *reveald* to thee. . . . . . . II. vii. 38. 5
sacred lawes, . . . unto him *reveald* in vision; . . . . II. x. 39. 2
To her *revealed* in a mirrhour playne; . . . . III. ii. 17. 4
Yet never he his hart to her *reveald;* . . . . III. v. 49. 7
to her *reveald* By errant Sprights, ... III. viii. 6. 4
Revel. Then made they *revell* route and goodly glee; . . . . *Hub.* 558
Reveling. all that els pertaines to *reveling,* . . . . *Hub.* 694
Dauncing and *reveling* both day and night, ... III. i. 39. 7
Revenge. Wanting *revenge,* is hard to asswage: . . . . *S.C.* May 137
Cruell *revenge,* which he in hart did hyde; . . . . I. iii. 33. 8
when in rage he for *revenge* did earne. . . . . I. vi. 25. 9
So long they fight, and full *revenge* pursue, ... I. vi. 44. 1
would eat His neighbour element in his *revenge:* . . . . . . I. xi. 21. 6
That short *revenge* the man may overtake, ... II. i. 18. 3
'despise The doome of just *revenge,* . . . . II. i. 36. 2
Of his *revenge* to make the instrument; . . . . II. iii. 11. 6
threatning *revenge* in vaine: . . . . II. iv. 15. 4
when Rancor rife Kindles *Revenge,* . . . . II. iv. 44. 5
*for his *revenge* Atin Cymochles finds. . . . . II. v. Arg.
care of vow'd *revenge* and cruell fight, ... II. vi. 8. 4
The hasty heat of his avowd *revenge* delayd. . . . . II. vi. 40. 9
On thother side . . . there sate Cruell *Revenge,* . . . . II. vii. 22. 2
shamefull vaunt Of vile *revenge.* . . . . II. viii. 16. 4
Making advauntage, to *revenge* their spight, ... II. viii. 25. 2
His life for dew *revenge* should deare abye? . . . . II. viii. 28. 8
with *revenge* desyring soone to dye, ... II. viii. 47. 2
casting wronges and all *revenge* behind, ... II. viii. 51. 3
For to *revenge* that fowle reprochefull shame, ... III. i. 9. 2
Carados her hand withheld From rash *revenge,* . . . . III. iii. 55. 8
reskew her from shame, and to *revenge* her wrong. . . . . . . III. iv. 45. 9
al good knights, . . . Are bownd for to *revenge,* . . . . III. x. 27. 9
long'd *revenge* to see: . . . . III. xii. 34. 9
Ne list I for *revenge* provoke new fight, ... IV. i. 35. 3
He for *revenge* had guiltlesse Glauce slaine: . . . . IV. i. 52. 4
from *revenge* their willes they scarce asswag'd: . . . . IV. v. 27. 3
he to fell *reveng* was fully bent: . . . . IV. v. 30. 9
Bent to *revenge* on blamelesse Britomart The crime . . . . . IV. v. 31. 1
nought but dire *revenge* his anger mote defray. . . . . IV. v. 31. 9
a fresh desire Of fell *revenge,* . . . . IV. ix. 29. 2
resolving to *revenge* his blood . . . . V. ii. 51. 8
Them to disable from *revenge* adventuring. . . . . V. iv. 31. 9
what way She mote *revenge* that blot . . . . V. iv. 47. 5
How to *revenge* that blot of honour blent, ... V. vi. 13. 2
till she *revenge* had wrought Of a late wrong . . . . V. vi. 23. 7
in *revenge* both of her loves distresse . . . . V. vii. 34. 3
all, in his *revenge,* of spirite would deprive. . . . . V. vii. 36. 9
What doe ye then devise Of more *revenge?* . . . . V. viii. 11. 8
end your *revenge* on mee.' . . . . V. viii. 11. 9
flaming with *revenge* and furious despight. . . . . V. viii. 46. 9
him to no *revenge* he forth could call, ... VI. iii. 36. 7
Ne secretly from thought of fell *revenge* surceasse: . . . . . VI. vi. 43. 9
Did worthily *revenge* this maydens pride; . . . . VI. vii. 32. 2
if it to *revenge* he were too weake, ... VI. xi. 34. 8
Revenged. To have *revenged* that his villeny; . . . . V. iii. 36. 2
Revengeful. The which conceiv'd in her *revengefull* minde . . *Gn.* 398
From his *revengefull* purpose shronke abacke, ... IV. vi. 21. 4
though *revengefull* vow she did professe, ... V. vii. 36. 3
In cancred malice and *revengefull* spight: . . . . VI. vii. 1. 4
the gods, in theyr *revengefull* yre, ... *Am.* xxviii. 11
Revengement. Seemes that no foes *revengement* he did feare: *Hub.* 216
dwell In her sonnes flesh, to mind *revengement,* . . . . II. ii. 10. 8
in *revengement* of his owne despight; . . . . IV. iv. 35. 3
for *revengement* of those wrongfull smarts, ... VI. viii. 22. 3
Revenger's. better reason will aswage The rash *revengers* heat. II. viii. 26. 7
Revenging. Halfe mad through malice and *revenging* will, . . I. iii. 22. 8
rides fierce *revenging* Wrath, Upon a Lion, ... I. iv. 33. 1
whether the *revenging* steele Were hardned . . . . I. xi. 36. 1
*What direfull chance, armd with *revenging* fate, ... II. i. 44. 6
fowle *revenging* rage, and base contentious jarre. . . . . . . II. ii. 30. 9
satisfy The greedy hunger of *revenging* yre, ... II. viii. 15. 4
From prosecuting his *revenging* rage: . . . . III. i. 11. 2

Revenging—*Continued.*
From dread of her *revenging* fathers hond; . . . . III. vii. 26. 2
Revenue. With the *revenue* of her plenteous meedes: . . . . . V. ii. 9. 8
Revenues. great *revenues* all in sumptuous pride They spend, *T.M.* 469
Reverence. I *reverence* and adore: . . . . *S.C.* Jul. 114
them receives a gentle Squyre, . . . Hight *Reverence.* . . . . . I. x. 7. 6
to her with *reverence* rare He humbly louted . . . . I. x. 44. 5
Whom highly he did *reverence* and adore, ... I. x. 49. 5
She to her Syre made humble *reverence,* . . . . I. xii. 24. 2
Religious *reverence* doth buriall teene; . . . . II. i. 59. 6
Doe her adore with sacred *reverence,* . . . . II. ii. 41. 8
to the Prince, bowing with *reverence* dew . . . . II. viii. 55. 3
The knightes there entring did him *reverence* dew, ... II. ix. 59. 1
sacred *Reverence* yborne of heavenly strene. . . . . V. ix. 32. 9
With trembling steps, and humble *reverence,* . . . . *Epith.* 210
Humbled with feare and awfull *reverence,* . . . . *H.H.B.* 141
Reverend. His *reverend* heares and holy gravitee . . . . . . I. viii. 32. 1
Behold this heavy sight, thou *reverend* Sire! . . . . II. viii. 7. 6
'*Reverend* Syre, What great misfortune hath betidd . . . . . II. viii. 24. 1
Reverse. The bands of th' elements shall backe *reverse* . . . *Ro.* xxii. 11
to his fresh remembraunce did *reverse* The ugly vew . . . . . I. ix. 48. 5
Out of her daughters hart fond fancies to *reverse.* . . . . . III. ii. 48. 9
doen they onely sleepe, and shall againe *reverse?* . . . . . . III. iv. 1. 9
his charmes back to *reverse.* . . . . III. xii. 36. 2
Reversed. by no reason it might be *reverst,* . . . . IV. v. 31. 5
Reversion. As in *reversion* of his brothers right; . . . . . . IV. iii. 14. 7
Revert. Make hast, ye shepheards, thether to *revert:* . . . . *S.C.* N. 191
He unto her would speedily *revert:* . . . . IV. vi. 43. 7
Revest. Her nathelesse Th' enchaunter . . . Did thus *revest,* . II. i. 22. 9
Review. when his meane estate he did *revew,* . . . . III. v. 44. 7
Revile. with reproachfull tearmes gan them *revile,* . . . . . *Hub.* 365
list at will them to *revile* or snib: . . . . *Hub.* 372
one, that fairest Helene did *revile,* . . . . *Col.* 920
Streight gan he him *revyle,* . . . . II. vi. 39. 3
Florimell him fowly gan *revile,* . . . . IV. iv. 11. 3
he falsely did *revyle* And foule blaspheme . . . . V. ix. 25. 4
th' other comming neare gan him *revile,* . . . . V. xii. 40. 1
to *revile,* and rate, and recreant call, ... VI. vii. 26. 8
how they doe that Squire beat and *revile!* . . . . VI. viii. 6. 6
The whiles the foole did him *revile* and flout, ... VI. viii. 11. 8
sharpely at him to *revile* and raile . . . . VI. xii. 33. 3
Reviled. Walk through the world of every one *revilde.* . . . *T.M.* 342
her litle babe *revyld,* . . . . I. xii. 11. 3
with big thundring voice *revyld* him lowd: . . . . II. iii. 7. 3
With which his mother Venus her *revyld,* . . . . III. vi. 50. 4
him in vaine *revild:* . . . . III. viii. 27. 2
To be unjustly blamd, and bitterly *revilde.* . . . . IV. viii. 28. 9
Them follow'd fast, and them *reviled* sore, ... IV. viii. 35. 3
him *revil'd,* and rated, and disdayned, ... V. iii. 35. 8
And him *reviled,* and reproched sore . . . . V. iv. 23. 3
And me in lieu thereof *revil'd* againe, ... VI. ii. 11. 8
both himselfe *revil'd* and eke his love; . . . . VI. iii. 42. 5
He was *revyld,* disgrast, and foule abused; . . . . *H.H.L.* 242
Revilement. Her bitter rayling and foule *revilement,* . . . . II. iv. 12. 5
Reviling. *Reviling* me and rayling as she lust, ... V. viii. 22. 5
Him still *reviling* and afflicting sore, ... VI. viii. 4. 2
Revyling him, that them most vile became, ... *H.H.L.* 152
Revive. Olde Rome out of her ashes to *revive,* . . . . *Ro.* Env. 5
Ne anie Poet seekes him to *revive,* . . . . *Ti.* 223
both woods and fields and floods *revive,* . . . . *Col.* 29
the sleeping spark Of native vertue gan eftsoones *revive;* . . I. ii. 19. 2
wondrous science . . . that could the dead *revive,* . . . . . . I. v. 40. 2
he ginneth to *revive* His ancient love, ... I. vi. 17. 1
he gan *revive* the memory Of his leud lusts, ... I. vi. 46. 2
doth *revive* Fresh memory in me . . . . II. ii. 40. 1
Hable to heale the sicke, and to *revive* the ded. . . . . . . II. iii. 22. 9
Might not *revive* desire of knightly exercize. . . . . II. vi. 25. 9
dying dayly, dayly yet *revive.* . . . . II. vi. 45. 4
shall *revive* the sleeping memoree . . . . III. iii. 22. 7
To wreake the wrath, which he did earst *revive* . . . . III. v. 16. 4
That I thy labours lost may thus *revive,* . . . . IV. ii. 34. 2
So her uneath at last he did *revive* . . . . VI. xi. 50. 8
Revived. thrise he her *reviv'd* with busie paine. . . . . I. vii. 24. 4
His chearefull words *reviv'd* her chearelesse spright, ... I. vii. 52. 8
Wherewith *reviv'd,* this answere forth he threw: . . . . II. iii. 33. 1
a ghost, that lately is *reviv'd* . . . . III. vii. 14. 7
His former griefe with furie fresh *reviv'd* . . . . III. viii. 3. 4
It would have lived, and *revived* eft; . . . . IV. iii. 21. 8
revived with her sweet inspection, ... IV. xii. 34. 4
She was *reviv'd,* and joyd much in his semblance glad. . . . . V. vii. 41. 9
Revived was, and sad dispaire away did cast. . . . . VI. v. 21. 9
She sudden was *revived* therewithall, ... VI. xi. 44. 4
me *revived* with hart-robbing gladnesse. . . . . *Am.* xxxix. 8
Revives. *revives* his toyled spright; . . . . *Hub.* 756
when his passion is allayd, She it *revives,* . . . . IV. ii. 12. 7
Reviving. *Revivyng* thought of glory and of fame, ... II. xi. 31. 8
Revoke. to *revoke* The forward footing for an hidden shade: I. i. 12. 7
strove their stubborne rages to *revoke;* . . . . II. ii. 28. 6
twise him forst his foot *revoke.* . . . . II. viii. 39. 9
Enforced them their forward footing to *revoke.* . . . . III. xi. 21. 9
Talus to *revoke* from the right way . . . . V. xii. 27. 5
the faint sprite he did *revoke* againe . . . . VI. iii. 28. 2
Revoked. *Revoked* life, that would have fled away, ... *D.* 188
with love *revokt* from vaine affright, ... I. vi. 28. 3
Revolt. to her yold the flames, and did their force *revolt.* . . . III. xi. 25. 9
Revolution. if I marked well the starres *revolution,* . . . . . *S.C.* Env. 3
the just *revolution* measured . . . . III. iii. 44. 3
the heavens *revolution* Is wandred farre . . . . V. Pr. 4. 6
Rew. *See* **Row, Rue.**
the next in *rew* Began her grievous plaint, ... *T.M.* 173, 233, 299, 419

Rew—*Continued.*
the next in *rew* Began her piteous plaint, . . . *T.M.* 359
then the next in *rew* Began her plaint, . . . *T.M.* 479
then the next in *rew* Began her mournfull plaint, . . . *T.M.* 539
Sitting beside a fountaine in a *rew;* . . . III. vi. 17. 4
Sett by it selfe, and ranckt in comely *rew;* . . . III. vi. 35. 4
Spinning and carding all in comely *rew,* . . . V. v. 22. 4
Reward. Where the *reward* of my so piteous deed? . . . *Gn.* 357
without *reward* Livings in Court be gotten, . . . *Hub.* 513
Nor yet are sung of others for *reward,* . . . *Ti.* 345
due *reward* For her prais-worthie workmanship . . . *Mui.* 267
shall thee well *rewarde* to shew the place, . . . I. i. 31. 6
What hath poore Virgin . . . Wherewith you to *reward?* . . . I. viii. 27. 4
to that Damsell thankes gave for *reward.* . . . II. vi. 38. 6
high degree By riches and unrighteous *reward;* . . . II. vii. 47. 2
all for love, and nothing for *reward.* . . . II. viii. 2. 8
what *reward* had he that overcame?' . . . III. i. 27. 7
have our Ladies love for his *reward.* . . . III. i. 27. 9
To enter in and reape the dew *reward.* . . . III. i. 30. 8
Without respect of richesse or *reward:* . . . III. ii. 7. 5
worthy worke of infinite *reward,* . . . III. ii. 21. 7
the dew *reward* Of his bad deedes, . . . III. v. 14. 6
Sith I her dew *reward* cannot restore? . . . III. v. 46. 5
to *reward* my trusty true intent, . . . III. vii. 55. 8
reward the wretch for his mesprise, . . . III. ix. 9. 6
my selfe, . . . Your worthy paine shall wel *reward* . . . III. x. 28. 9
ne deeme my dew *reward:* . . . III. x. 31. 6
'If good find grace, and righteousnes *reward,* . . . III. xi. 10. 1
the *reward* for such vile outrage dew. . . . III. xii. 33. 9
Your vertue selfe her owne *reward* shall breed, . . . III. xii. 39. 5
'Gentle Dame, *reward* enough I weene, . . . III. xii. 40. 2
Shall have that golden girdle for *reward;* . . . IV. ii. 27. 2
for want of other meete *reward,* . . . V. i. 30. 4
on those Priests bestowed rich *reward;* . . . V. vii. 24. 3
the vertue selfe, which her *reward* doth pay.' . . . V. xi. 17. 9
you to *reward* with greater dignitie.' . . . VI. ii. 34. 9
Therefore now yeeld . . . My due *reward,* . . . VI. vii. 15. 8
I shall You well *reward,* . . . VI. ix. 32. 6
For slaves to sell them for no small *reward* . . . VI. x. 43. 4
Shame be thy meed, and mischiefe thy *reward,* . . . *Am.* lxxxv. 13
Rewardful. grace was great, and bounty most *rewardfull.* . . . *Col.* 187
Rewards. who *rewards* him ere the more for-thy, . . . *S.C.* O. 33
he For ill *rewards* him well. . . . VI. ix. Arg.
Rewed, Rewing. *See* **Rued, Rueing.**
Rewth. *See* **Ruth.**
Reynard. *See* **Reynold.**
Reynold. 'Now read, Sir *Reynold,* as ye be right wise, . . . *Hub.* 114
craftie *Reynold* was a Priest ordained, . . . *Hub.* 556
his man *Reynold,* with fine counterfesaunce, . . . *Hub.* 667
false *Reynold* would abuse The simple Suter, . . . *Hub.* 883
such as hath a *Reynold* to his man, . . . *Hub.* 917
Reynold's. his man *Raynolds* purchase which he gain'd. . . . *Hub.* 854
Reysd. *See* **Raised.**
Rhene, Rhetaean. *See* **Rhine, Rhoetean.**
Rhoesus'. In working of Strymonian *Rhaesus* fall, . . . *Gn.* 535
Rheusa. the faire Nimph *Rheusa* wandring there. . . . IV. xi. 42. 3
Rhine. the borne Souldier which *Rhine* running drinks: . . . *Ro.* xxxi. 8
Swift *Rhene,* and Alpheus still immaculate . . . IV. xi. 21. 4
Rhodanus. Long *Rhodanus,* whose sourse springs from the skie . . . IV. xi. 20. 4
Rhodian. The antique *Rhodian* will likewise set forth The great Colosse, . . . *Ro.* ii. 9
Rhododaphne. Fresh *Rhododaphne,* and the Sabine flowre, . . . *Gn.* 673
Rhodope. the pleasaunt hill Of *Rhodope,* . . . II. xii. 52. 2
Rhoetean. all the *Rhetaean* shore to ashes turne, . . . *Gn.* 511
Rhy. *See* **Rye.**
Rhyme, -rs. *See* **Rime, -rs.**
Rhythms. When ye, these *rythmes* doo read, . . . *Pet.*[2] vii. 11
Ribald. lewd *rybauld,* with vyle lust advaunst, . . . II. i. 10. 3
Ribaldry. rolle with rest in rymes of *rybaudrye;* . . . *S.C.* O. 76
Rolling in rymes of shameles *ribaudrie* . . . *T.M.* 213
Riband. The golden *ribband,* which that virgin wore . . . III. vii. 36. 1
a *riband* new, In which his Ladies colours were, . . . IV. viii. 7. 1
Bound truelove wize, with a blew silke *riband.* . . . *Epith.* 44
Ribands. with colourd *ribbands* drest: . . . IV. viii. 10. 4
hangd on high with golden *ribbands* laced; . . . IV. x. 8. 5
Trayled with *ribbands* diversly distraught, . . . V. v. 2. 4
Of sundry flowres with silken *ribbands* tyde, . . . VI. ix. 7. 8
Ribs. ragged *ribs* of mountaines molten new, . . . I. xi. 44. 7
On whose sharp cliftes the *ribs* of vessels broke; . . . II. xii. 7. 3
Their wooden *ribs* are shaken nigh asonder. . . . IV. ii. 16. 6
Her shattered *ribs* in thousand peeces rives, . . . V. ii. 50. 3
all his *ribs* he quite in peeces broke, . . . V. iii. 33. 4
makes her *ribs* to cracke as they were torne; . . . V. xi. 29. 4
Rich. With *rich* (*riche*[1]) treasures this gay ship . . . *Pet.* ii. 6
no lesse *rich* than faire, . . . *Bel.*[2] xiv. 6
Renewes herselfe with buildings *rich* and gay; . . . *Ro.* xxvii. 11
his *rich* attire and goodly forme, . . . *Van.* viii. 6
where shepheards *ritch* . . . bene every where to see: . . . *S.C.* Jun. 21
I thought the soyle would have made me *rich,* . . . *S.C.* S. 78
sad cares that *rich* mens hearts devowre. . . . *Gn.* 136
The Mule all deckt in goodly *rich* aray, . . . *Hub.* 582
great he was in grace, and *rich* through gaine. . . . *Hub.* 1200
the *rich* fee, which Poets wont divide, . . . *T.M.* 471
with *rich* bountie, and deare cherishment, . . . *T.M.* 573
Strong walls, *rich* porches, princelie pallaces, . . . *Ti.* 93
'What booteth it to have been *rich* alive? . . . *Ti.* 351
rich spoyles, which late he did purchas . . . *Ti.* 654
So *rich* a spoile within his power to see. . . . *As.* 102
More *rich* then pearles of Ynde, . . . *Col.* 490
About the borders of our *rich* Coshma, . . . *Col.* 522

Rich—*Continued.*
The which art of so *rich* a spoile possest, . . . *Col.* 553
Purfled with gold and pearle of *rich* assay; . . . I. ii. 13. 3
In so *ritch* weedes, and seeming glorious show, . . . I. ii. 21. 5
a most mighty king, most *rich* and sage: . . . I. ii. 23. 3
Saints of their *rich* vestiments He did disrobe, . . . I. iii. 17. 5
on every side With *rich* array . . . dight. . . . I. iv. 6. 6
a *rich* throne, as bright as sunny day; . . . I. iv. 8. 2
to match, in roiall *rich* array, . . . I. iv. 17. 4
And win *rich* spoile of ransackt chastitee. . . . I. vi. 5. 5
all within full *rich* arayd he found, . . . I. viii. 35. 1
writt with golden letters *rich* and brave: . . . I. ix. 19. 8
In which were not *rich* tyres, nor garments gay, . . . I. x. 39. 2
Dame; Who *rich* arayd, and yet in modest guize, . . . II. ii. 14. 6
they fastned were . . . In a *rich* jewell, . . . II. iii. 27. 7
with him brought Pryene, *rich* arayd, . . . II. iv. 28. 2
decke the world with their *rich* pompous showes; . . . II. vi. 15. 7
A worke of *rich* entayle and curious mould, . . . II. vii. 4. 5
these *rich* hils of welth doest hide apart . . . II. vii. 7. 3
with *rich* metall loaded every rifte, . . . II. vii. 28. 5
al men doe ayme, *rich* to be made: . . . II. vii. 32. 8
his broad braunches, laden with *rich* fee, . . . II. vii. 56. 3
with *rich* spoyles and famous victorie . . . II. x. 75. 4
the *rich* wares to save from pitteous spoyle; . . . II. xii. 19. 8
the weake boughes, with so *rich* load opprest . . . II. xii. 55. 5
the *rich* metall was so coloured, . . . II. xii. 61. 3
whose royaltee And *rich* purveyance . . . III. i. 33. 3
A goodly Armour, and full *rich* aray, . . . III. iii. 58. 7
Marinell . . . throwne on the *Rich* strond: . . . III. iv. Arg.
bestrowed all with *rich* aray Of pearles . . . III. iv. 18. 4
suffred by that same *Rich* strond to travell, . . . III. iv. 20. 8
T' endow her sonne with threasure and *rich* store . . . III. iv. 21. 8
upon the brim Of the *Rich* Strond, . . . III. iv. 34. 2
Her faire lockes in *rich* circlet be enrold, . . . III. v. 5. 4
the *rich* furrowes flote, . . . III. vii. 34. 6
it a part Of her *rich* spoyles . . . III. viii. 2. 8
paine shall wel reward with guerdon *rich.*' . . . III. x. 28. 9
the *rich* metall lurked privily, . . . III. xi. 28. 4
Antickes, which their follies playd In the *rich* metall . . . III. xi. 51. 6
The goodly ordinaunce of this *rich* Place, . . . III. xi. 53. 2
none was to possesse So *rich* purveyaunce, . . . III. xi. 53. 9
so *rich* and royally arayd, . . . III. xii. 42. 2
that *rich* Romane of white marble wrought, . . . III. xii. 46. *or.* 3
For that *rich* girdle of faire Florimell, . . . IV. iv. 5. 8
a jewell *rich* he found, . . . IV. viii. 6. 6
stones of *rich* assay, . . . IV. x. 15. 5
The *rich* Cteatus; and Eurytus long; . . . IV. xi. 14. 1
Rich Oranochy, though but knowen late; . . . IV. xi. 21. 7
from all men so *rich* a kingdome hold! . . . IV. xi. 22. 2
adornes *rich* Waterford; . . . IV. xi. 43. 2
albee he *rich* or poore, . . . V. ii. 6. 3
he him selfe uppon the *rich* doth tyrannize. . . . V. ii. 6. 9
'Thereto she is full faire, and *rich* attired, . . . V. ii. 10. 1
wealth of *rich* men to the poore will draw.' . . . V. ii. 38. 9
The bridegromes state, the brides most *rich* aray, . . . V. iii. 3. 3
full *rich* aguiz'd As each one had his furnitures deviz'd. . . . V. iii. 4. 4
Where was a *rich* Pavilion ready pight . . . V. v. 4. 8
They wore *rich* Mitres shaped like the Moone, . . . V. vii. 4. 6
on those Priests bestowed *rich* reward; . . . V. vii. 24. 3
Presenting him with all the *rich* array . . . V. viii. 51. 4
Not of *rich* tissew, nor of cloth of gold, . . . V. ix. 28. 2
Thus did she sit in royall *rich* estate, . . . V. ix. 33. 1
Robbed her people that full *rich* had beene, . . . V. x. 25. 7
Of costly Ivory full *rich* beseene, . . . V. x. 28. 3
they spoile her . . . of all her *rich* array; . . . VI. viii. 41. 3
That so *rich* frute should be from us bereft; . . . VI. ix. 1. 7
maketh wretch or happie, *rich* or poore; . . . VI. ix. 30. 2
in that litle is both *rich* and wise; . . . VI. ix. 30. 6
nought tempted with the offer Of his *rich* mould, . . . VI. ix. 33. 2
like a Diamond of *rich* regard, . . . VI. xi. 13. 3
rich arrayd In garment all of gold . . . VII. vii. 37. 1
none so *rich* or wise, so strong or fayre, . . . *Am.* lviii. 9
rich triumphall Arcks which they did raise, . . . *Com. Son.* iii. 7
Richer. *richer* then that vessell seem'd to bee, . . . *Bel.*[2] xiii. 1
richer seem'd then any tapestry, . . . VII. vii. 10. 8
Riches. So great *riches* as like cannot be found! . . . *Pet.* ii. 14
Bearing close envie to these *riches* rare, . . . *Bel.*[2] xiii. 6
these *riches,* second unto none, . . . *Bel.*[2] xiii. 10
When folke bene fat, and *riches* rancke, . . . *S.C.* Jul. 211
No greedy *riches* knowes nor bloudie strife, . . . *Gn.* 123
abound in *riches* above measure. . . . *Gn.* 128
The precious store of this celestiall *riches?* . . . *T.M.* 146
To tell my *riches,* and endowments rare, . . . *Ti.* 87
whilome wast the worldes chiefst *riches,* . . . *Ti.* 675
Be it *riches,* beautie, or honors pride, . . . *D.* 500
On her he spent the *riches* of his wit: . . . *As.* 62
All heavenly gifts and *riches* locked are; . . . *Col.* 489
*His heart too high through his great *riches* store; . . . I. v. 47. 7
Riches, renowme, and principality, . . . II. vii. 8. 5
Those be the *riches* fit for an advent'rous knight.' . . . II. vii. 10. 9
'All otherwise' (saide he) 'I *riches* read, . . . II. vii. 12. 1
to be Lord of those that *riches* have, . . . II. vii. 33. 8
upbeare The massy roofe, and *riches* huge sustayne; . . . II. vii. 43. 6
high degree By *riches* and unrighteous reward; . . . II. vii. 47. 2
The roiall *riches* and exceeding cost . . . III. i. 32. 4
To doen his Nephew in all *riches* flow; . . . III. iv. 22. 2
Exceeding *riches* and all pretious things, . . . III. iv. 23. 2
great *riches,* gathered manie a day, . . . IV. i. 29. 5
that could so goodly *riches* gaine, . . . IV. iv. 16. 8
Whose smallest minute lost no *riches* render may. . . . IV. x. 14. 9

Riches—*Continued.*
great sackes with endlesse *riches* fraught . . . V. ii. 23. 4
they hoped to have got great good, And wondrous *riches* . . V. ii. 51. 7
gave him roiall giftes and *riches* rare, . . . V. x. 17. 2
doe all worldly *riches* farre excell, . . . VI. Pr. 2. 4
and make her th' others *riches* scorne. . . . VI. iii. 7. 9
wisedome is most *riches:* . . . VI. ix. 30. 7
farre renound For his great *riches* . . . VI. xii. 4. 3
heavy laden with the spoyle Of harvests *riches,* . . . VII. vii. 38. 3
All this worlds *riches* that may farre be found: . . . *Am.* xv. 6
th' heavenly *riches* which she robd erewhyle. . . . *H.B.* 119
That heavenly *riches* which in you ye beare, . . . *H.B.* 185
Endewd with wisedomes *riches,* heavenly, rare. . . . *H.H.L.* 112
The glory of our heavenly *riches* lay, . . . *H.H.L.* 229
Plentie of *riches* forth on him will powre, . . . *H.H.B.* 247
Even heavenly *riches,* which there hidden ly . . . *H.H.B.* 248
Seemes to them basenesse, and all *riches* drosse, . . . *H.H.B.* 279
Riches'. store of cares doth follow *riches* store. . . . VI. ix. 21. 4
Richesse. none ever knew Such endlesse *richesse,* . . . I. iv. 7. 5
still did spare, . . . *richesse* to compare: . . . I. iv. 28. 5
In her the *richesse* of all heavenly grace . . . II. ii. 41. 1
did the house of *Richesse* from hell-mouth divide. . . . II. vii. 24. 9
Here Sleep, ther *Richesse,* and Hel-gate them both betwext. II. vii. 25. 9
shewd of *richesse* such exceeding store, . . . II. vii. 31. 4
Without respect of *richesse* or reward: . . . III. ii. 7. 5
That honour and large *richesse* to me lent: . . . *Am.* lxxiv. 8
Richesse'. through his great *richesse* store; . . . I. v. 47. 7
Richest. the bases were of *richest* golde, . . . *Bel.*[1] iv. 2
bases were of *richest* mettalls warke, . . . *Bel.*[2] iv. 2
Built all of *richest* stone that might bee found, . . . *Ti.* 506
richest substance that on earth might bee, . . . II. xii. 60. 2
'then ransome of the *richest* knight, . . . III. v. 7. 2
Nor of ought else that may be *richest* red, . . . V. ix. 28. 3
The *richest* champian that may else be rid; . . . VII. vi. 54. 8
Fayre bosome! fraught with vertues *richest* tresure, . . . *Am.* lxxvi. 1
Rich-fleeced. two rams, . . . Fight for the rule of the *rich fleeced* flocke, . . . I. ii. 16. 2
Rich-laden. her brest, lyke a *rich laden* barke, . . . *Am.* lxxxi. 5
Richlier. *richlier* by many partes arayd; . . . III. xi. 51. 2
Richly. With sprincled pearle and gold full *richly* drest, . . . I. vii. 32. 3
ornaments that *richly* were displaid; . . . I. viii. 46. 3
Most false Duessa, royall *richly* dight, . . . I. xii. 32. 4
a woman, gorgeous gay And *richly* cladd . . . II. vii. 44. 7
with gold and perle most *richly* wrought, . . . II. ix. 19. 4
with royall arras *richly* dight, . . . II. ix. 33. 7
though *richly* guilt, . . . II. ix. 45. 8
was al within most *richly* dight, . . . III. v. 40. 8
Causd his pavilion to be *richly* pight . . . V. iv. 46. 4
of massy gold Most *richly* made, . . . V. xi. 21. 9
faire she was, and *richly* clad In roiall robes, . . . V. xi. 60. 6
in a Jacket, quilted *richly* rare . . . VI. vii. 43. 3
Amidst a ring most *richly* well enchaced, . . . VI. x. 12. 8
In whose cote-armour *richly* are displayd . . . *Am.* lxx. 2
Her brest that table was, so *richly* spredd; . . . *Am.* lxxvii. 13
The gate with pearles and rubyes *richly* dight; . . . *Am.* lxxxi. 10
Rid. *See* **Ride.**
Seeing at last her selfe from daunger *rid,* . . . II. iii. 36. 5
ridd a wretched man from handes of hellish wight!' . . . II. v. 23. 9
After that foster fowle he fiercely *ridd* . . . III. v. 13. 4
streight that boaster prayd, with whom he *rid,* . . . V. iii. 10. 8
She had not *rid* the mountenance of a flight, . . . V. vi. 36. 4
And with his Lady to the Castle *rid,* . . . VI. iii. 37. 3
though she were right glad so *rid* to bee . . . VI. iv. 10. 1
to be so *rid* Of his young charge . . . VI. iv. 38. 1
The richest champian that may else be *rid;* . . . VII. vi. 54. 8
Riddance. But rather *riddance* from long languishment. . . . *D.* 364
Ridden. They had not *ridden* far, . . . I. iii. 33. 1
ere that litle while they *ridden* had, . . . VI. vii. 6. 6
Riddes. *See* **Redes.**
Riddle. To reade the secrete of this *riddle* rare, . . . *Gn. Ded.* 7
The *riddle* of thy loved Lionesse; . . . *D.* 177
That he had red her *Riddle,* . . . V. xi. 25. 5
Riddles. In rymes, in *ridles,* and in bydding base; . . . *S.C.* O. 5
Oft purposes, oft *riddles,* he devysd, . . . III. x. 8. 6
In wittie *riddles,* and in wise soothsayes; . . . IV. ii. 35. 5
Riddling. By any *ridling* skill, or commune wit. . . . III. xi. 54. 5
Ride. *See* **Rid.**
To fawne, to crowche, to waite, to *ride,* to ronne, . . . *Hub.* 905
in the necke of all the world did *ride?* . . . *Ti.* 74
on Pegasus must *ride,* . . . *Ti.* 426
ye fond men! on fortunes wheele that *ride,* . . . *D.* 498
The red bloud . . . staind the way, as he did *ride.* . . . I. ii. 14. 9
Gan fairely couch his speare, and towards *ride.* . . . I. ii. 15. 3
She . . . towards him gan *ride:* . . . I. iii. 26. 7
Doe *ride* each other upon her to gaze: . . . I. iv. 16. 8
when she does *ride* To Joves high hous . . . I. iv. 17. 6
On which her six sage Counsellours did *ryde,* . . . I. iv. 18. 2
Upon a slouthfull Asse he chose to *ryde,* . . . I. iv. 18. 7
greedy Avarice by him did *ride,* . . . I. iv. 27. 1
erthly wight that with the Night durst *ride.* . . . I. v. 32. 9
his woundes wyde . . . unready were to *ryde.* . . . I. v. 45. 5
got his ready steed, and fast away gan *ryde.* . . . I. vi. 8. 9
Buls . . . To tame, and *ryde* their backes, . . . I. vi. 24. 7
towards him they gan in haste to *ride,* . . . I. vi. 34. 4
'will *ryde* Against my liking backe to doe you grace: . . . I. ix. 32. 5
on her wearie journey she did *ride;* . . . I. xii. 22. 5
Does *ride* on both their backs, . . . II. ii. 24. 9
seeing him *ryde* so ranck, . . . II. iii. 6. 7
gan to *ride* As one unfitt therefore, . . . II. iii. 46. 3
chiefly skill to *ride* seemes a science . . . II. iv. 1. 7

Ride—*Continued.*
well of yore he learned had to *ryde,* . . . II. viii. 31. 4
fierce at him did *ride,* . . . II. xi. 25. 2
Here may thy storme-bett vessell safely *ryde,* . . . II. xii. 32. 7
So goodly all agreed they forth yfere did *ryde.* . . . III. i. 12. 9
a forest wyde, . . . Therein they long did *ryde,* . . . III. i. 14. 7
With hasty gallop towards her did *ryde.* . . . III. iv. 12. 3
horse Whereon faire Florimell was wont to *ride,* . . . III. vii. 31. 2
he was so stund that he n'ote *ryde,* . . . III. vii. 42. 6
To tucke about her short when she did *ryde,* . . . III. ix. 21. 4
Paridell complaynd, . . . *ryde* he could not, . . . III. x. 1. 9
where ever thou do go or *ryde,* . . . IV. i. 51. 8
'Sir knight, why *ride* ye dumpish thus behind, . . . IV. ii. 5. 7
flew ope, and gave her way to *ride.* . . . IV. iii. 46. 3
Unto her Coch remounting, home did *ride,* . . . IV. iii. 51. 8
with her alwaies *ride,* till he another get.' . . . IV. iv. 9. 9
who fiersly forth did *ride.* . . . IV. iv. 17. 9
him against Sir Blandamour did *ride* . . . IV. iv. 19. 3
Upon her first adventure forth did *ride,* . . . IV. v. 29. 4
The next day, as he on his way did *ride,* . . . IV. vi. 2. 2
when on adventures they did *ride,* . . . IV. vi. 44. 8
scarcely she could *ryde,* . . . IV. viii. 37. 4
made it so to *ride* as it alive was found. . . . IV. ix. 4. 9
as we *ride* together on our way, . . . IV. ix. 40. 6
In her great iron charet wonts to *ride,* . . . IV. xi. 28. 2
Till like a victor on his backe he *ride,* . . . IV. xii. 13. 5
as she thus melancholicke did *ride,* . . . V. vi. 19. 1
on his first adventure forward forth did *ride.* . . . V. x. 17. 9
towards him with all their powre did *ryde,* . . . V. x. 34. 3
Rebutting him, which in the midst did *ryde,* . . . V. x. 35. 5
an armed knight that did on horsebacke *ryde.* . . . VI. ii. 3. 9
themselves prepard thorough the foord to *ride.* . . . VI. iii. 30. 9
Being unhable else alone to *ride,* . . . VI. iii. 46. 3
Withouten armes or steede to *ride* upon, . . . VI. iv. 39. 3
Well did he tract his steps as he did *ryde,* . . . VI. vii. 3. 1
needs with him streight to the place would *ryde,* . . . VI. vii. 17. 2
Upon two brethrens shoulders she did *ride,* . . . VII. vii. 34. 4
Upon a dreadfull Scorpion he did *ride,* . . . VII. vii. 39. 6
In an old wagon, for he could not *ride,* . . . VII. vii. 43. 2
towres . . . on Themmes brode aged backe doe *ryde,* . . . *Proth.* 133
Rider. his hot *ryder* spurd his chauffed side: . . . I. iii. 33. 6
His gorgeous *ryder* . . . Would have cast downe, . . . I. viii. 17. 5
to the ground he is . . . constraynd To throw his *ryder;* . . . I. xi. 23. 7
affrap The warlike *ryder* to his most mishap: . . . III. ii. 6. 5
stumble, that his *rider* nigh he cast; . . . IV. iv. 30. 4
layd Before the *ryder,* as he captive were, . . . IV. ix. 5. 2
Through which the *rider* downe doth fall . . . V. ii. 7. 9
with their *ryder* ranne perforce away: . . . V. viii. 38. 4
Did warne his *rider* be uppon his gard; . . . VI. v. 21. 7
Rider's. T' obey their *riders* hest, as seemed good. . . . IV. iii. 39. 5
Riders. Whose lucklesse *riders* late were overthrowen; . . . IV. iv. 38. 7
Rides. him beside *rides* fierce revenging Wrath, . . . I. iv. 33. 1
on a Palfrey *rydes* more white then snow, . . . III. v. 5. 6
'He *rides*' (said Turpine) 'there not farre afore, . . . VI. vii. 6. 1
Ridge. Streight was the passage, like a ploughed *ridge,* . . . V. vi. 36. 8
Riding. Forth *ryding* underneath the castell wall, . . . I. v. 53. 7
A band of Britons, *ryding* on forray . . . III. iii. 58. 4
The gentle Squyre came *ryding* that same way, . . . III. v. 18. 2
Forth *ryding* from Malbeccoes hostlesse hous, . . . III. xi. 3. 2
riding on a Lion ravenous, . . . III. xii. 22. 2
ech of them had *ryding* by his side A Ladie, . . . IV. i. 17. 3
eke those masked Ladies *riding* them beside. . . . IV. iv. 2. 9
Which Blandamour had *riding* by his side: . . . IV. iv. 7. 8
A Knight soft *ryding* towards them they spyde, . . . IV. vi. 9. 2
Both through a forest *ryding* did devise T' alight, . . . IV. vii. 3. 5
Ryding upon a Dromedare on hie, . . . IV. viii. 38. 7
ryding streight under the Castle wall, . . . V. x. 31. 2
All arm'd to point came *ryding* thetherward; . . . VI. v. 11. 3
Ryding a softly pace with portance sad, . . . VI. vii. 6. 8
Whom late we left *ryding* upon an Asse, . . . VI. vii. 27. 8
after them the Monthes all *riding* came. . . . VII. vii. 32. 2
Riding together both with equall pase, . . . VII. vii. 44. 2
Rife. This reede is *ryfe,* that oftentime . . . *S.C.* Jul. 11
where the countrey Nymphs are *rife,* . . . *Gn.* 146
To live in heaven where happines is *rife:* . . . *Ti.* 670
ever and anon, with singults *rife,* . . . *Col.* 168
Through whose large bountie, poured on me *rife* . . . *Ded. Son.* vii. 3
Frenzy raging *rife,* . . . I. iv. 35. 7
ever fickle fortune rageth *rife;* . . . I. ix. 44. 8
threw it to the ground, enraged *rife,* . . . I. ix. 52. 5
when Rancor *rife* Kindles Revenge, . . . II. iv. 44. 4
whilest his foe did rage most *rife:* . . . II. v. 9. 7
Whence foorth it breakes in sighes and anguish *ryfe,* . . . III. ii. 32. 8
in thy troubled bowels raignes and rageth *ryfe.* . . . III. iv. 8. 9
feeling by his pulses beating *rife* . . . III. v. 31. 3
every one threw forth reproches *rife* . . . III. vi. 14. 6
Thence streames of purple bloud issuing *rife* . . . IV. iii. 12. 8
Claribell enraged *rife* With fervent flames, . . . IV. ix. 21. 3
there with guiltie bloudshed charged *ryfe;* . . . V. ix. 48. 4
Regardlesse of her wounds yet bleeding *rife,* . . . VI. v. 5. 2
Rifely. ranckling wound as yet does *rifelye* bleede. . . . *S.C.* D. 94
Rift. out of whose *rifte* there came Smal drops of gory bloud, I. ii. 30. 8
trunck, halfe rent with ragged *rift,* . . . I. viii. 22. 8
With dreadfull poyse is from the mayneland *rift,* . . . I. xi. 54. 7
hart of flint asonder could have *rifte;* . . . II. vii. 23. 8
rich metall loaded every *rifte,* . . . II. vii. 28. 5
threatneth downe to throw his ragged *rift* . . . II. xii. 4. 5
Rifts. through their *rifts* the ruddie bloud did showre, . . . IV. iii. 15. 7
Rigged. *See* **Well-rigged.**
Right. *See* **Birthright, Forthright.**

Right—*Continued.*

no lesse rich than faire, *right* worthie sure . . . *Bel.*[2] xiv. 6
Caelian on the *right;* . . . *Ro.* iv. 13
Him needeth not to seeke for usage *right* Of line, . . . *Ro.* xxvi. 2
blew the winde into her bosome *right;* . . . *Van.* ix. 5
Nought aske I, but onely to hold my *right;* . . . *S.C.* F. 186
Thou raylest on, *right* withouten reason . . . *S.C.* May 146
does the *right* way forsake: . . . *S.C.* May 165
To the waters fall their tunes attemper *right.* . . . *S.C.* Jun. 8
Never dempt more *right* . . . *S.C.* Au. 137
balk the *right* way, and strayen abroad. . . . *S.C.* S. 93
if that Hobbinol *right* judgement bare, . . . *S.C.* D. 45
bids him clayme with rigorous rage hys *right:* . . . *S.C.* D. 130
Sir Reynold, as ye be *right* wise, . . . *Hub.* 114
There is no *right* in this partition, . . . *Hub.* 143
'*Right* well . . . ye advized have, . . . *Hub.* 193
had the use of his *right* arme bereaved. . . . *Hub.* 208
right well this Curdog . . . will serve . . . *Hub.* 294
From the *right* way full eath may wander wide: . . . *Hub.* 404
'It seemes . . . *right* well that ye be Clerks, . . . *Hub.* 415
some good Gentleman, that hath the *right* . . . for to present . *Hub.* 525
the *right* gentle minde would bite his lip, . . . *Hub.* 711
chafte at that indignitie *right* sore: . . . *Hub.* 1338
right tunefull . . . *T.M.* 27
hold by wrong that wee should have by *right.* . . . *T.M.* 318
which have no skill to rule them *right,* . . . *T.M.* 551
Right and loyall did his word maintaine. . . . *Ti.* 189
Robd of all *right* and true nobilitie. . . . *Ti.* 294
Clayming that sea-coast Citie as his *right.* . . . *Mui.* 314
thou *right* wel doest know, . . . *D.* 99
'If this be *right,* why did they then create The world so fayre, *D.* 204
For age to dye is *right,* but youth is wrong; . . . *D.* 243
I know not *right:* . . . *Col.* 63
doth run downe *right* To Buttevant, . . . *Col.* 110
'*Right* well he sure did plaine, . . . *Col.* 173
he himselfe may rewed be more *right,* . . . *Col.* 398
Right noble Nymphs, and high to be commended: . . . *Col.* 577
of spight . . . rather then of *right* . . . *Col.* 678
persons of *right* worthie parts, . . . *Col.* 752
love is Lord of all the world by *right,* . . . *Col.* 883
Which so to doe may thee *right* well befit, . . . *Ded. Son.* iii. 5
Then, by like *right* the noble Progeny, . . . *Ded. Son.* iv. 5
right noble Lord, I send This present . . . *Ded. Son.* iv. 13
To you, *right* noble Lord, whose carefull brest . . . *Ded. Son.* ix. 1
Here eke of *right* have you a worthie place, . . . *Ded. Son.* xi. 5
In vain I thinke, *right* honourable Lord, . . . *Ded. Son.* xii. 1
Right faithfull true he was . . . I. i. 2. 7
'*Right* well . . . ye have advised bin,' . . . I. i. 33. 4
What not by *right* she cast to win by guile; . . . I. ii. 38. 3
all that he by *right* or wrong could find, . . . I. iii. 18. 1
Right glad with him to have increast . . . I. iv. 15. 2
whether *right* he went, or else astray. . . . I. iv. 19. 9
he was *right* fitly clad, . . . I. iv. 22. 1
right and wrong ylike in equall ballaunce waide. . . . I. iv. 27. 9
if that either to that shield had *right,* . . . I. iv. 40. 8
He never meant with words, but swords, to plead his *right:* . I. iv. 42. 9
To you th' inheritance belonges by *right* . . . I. iv. 48. 5
So th' one for wrong, the other strives for *right.* . . . I. v. 8. 1
So th' one for wrong, the other strives for *right,* . . . I. v. 9. 1
the lignage *right* From whence he tooke his weldeserved name: I. vi. 20. 3
He . . . ever lov'd to fight for Ladies *right;* . . . I. vi. 20. 8
was knowne *right* well To have done . . . I. vii. 36. 2
'*Right* so,' (quoth he) . . . I. vii. 41. 3
ne ever . . . Had throwne to ground the unregarded *right:* . I. vii. 47. 5
ye heavens, that all things *right* esteeme, . . . I. vii. 49. 7
the Dwarfe them guiding ever *right.* . . . I. vii. 52. 9
smote off quite his *right* leg by the knee, . . . I. viii. 22. 4
His name Ignaro did his nature *right* aread. . . . I. viii. 31. 9
as pledges firme, *right* hands together joynd. . . . I. ix. 18. 9
What justice can but judge against thee *right,* . . . I. ix. 37. 8
he that once hath missed the *right* way, . . . I. ix. 43. 8
His name was Zele, that him *right* well became: . . . I. x. 6. 6
Right cleanly clad in comely sad attyre; . . . I. x. 7. 3
So few there bee, That . . . seeke the *right:* . . . I. x. 10. 4
With goodly counsell and advisement *right;* . . . I. x. 23. 5
She was *right* joyous . . . I. x. 33. 1
from the *right* to stray, . . . I. x. 35. 7
In face of judgement he their *right* would plead, . . . I. x. 43. 4
that leadeth *right* To that most glorious house, . . . I. x. 50. 4
glauncing by, foorth passed forward *right.* . . . I. xi. 16. 5
right fowly he disdaynd; . . . I. xi. 23. 9
sad habiliments *right* well beseene: . . . I. xii. 5. 3
bowed low, that her *right* well became, . . . I. xii. 24. 3
he for nought would stay his passage *right* . . . I. xii. 25. 4
Ne weene my *right* with strength adowne to tread, . . . I. xii. 28. 5
Right well I wote, . . . II. Pr. 1. 1
he surely is A *right* good knight, . . . II. i. 19. 5
With *right* hands plighted, pledges of good will. . . . II. i. 34. 2
'Ye bene *right* hard amated, . . . II. ii. 5. 3
when the knight arriv'd, he was *right* well Receiv'd, . . . II. ii. 14. 1
Ne ought he car'd whom he . . . bereav'd of *right:* . . . II. ii. 18. 8
Both knightes and ladies forth *right* angry far'd, . . . II. ii. 19. 8
Their sharp assault *right* boldly did rebut, . . . II. ii. 23. 2
not regard dew *right* and just desarts? . . . II. ii. 29. 7
No measure in her mood, no rule of *right,* . . . II. ii. 36. 4
Whose *right* haunch earst my stedfast arrow strake? . . . II. iii. 32. 8
from the *right* way seeke to draw him wide, . . . II. iv. 2. 7
Right well beseemed it . . . II. iv. 38. 5
His am I Atin, his in wrong and *right,* . . . II. iv. 42. 5
to his brest it selfe intended *right:* . . . II. iv. 46. 4

Right—*Continued.*

To which *right* wel the wise doe give that name, . . . II. v. 1. 5
Because he had not well mainteind his *right,* . . . II. v. 20. 4
perdy ye have not doen me *right,* . . . II. vi. 22. 7
Me litle needed from my *right* way to have straid.' . . . II. vi. 22. 9
Him Atin spying knew *right* well of yore, . . . II. vi. 48. 1
his griefe He knew *right* well, . . . II. vi. 51. 2
From the worldes eye, and from her *right* usaunce?' . . . II. vii. 7. 4
Her face *right* wondrous faire did seeme to bee, . . . II. vii. 45. 1
Not to debate the chalenge of your *right,* . . . II. viii. 27. 7
thou thy treasons fruit . . . shalt taste *Right* sowre, . . . II. viii. 31. 9
It seizd in his *right* side, and there the dint did stay. . . . II. viii. 38. 9
right glad he grew, And saide; . . . II. viii. 53. 6
entertained them *right* fairely, as befell. . . . II. ix. 17. 9
They did obeysaunce, as beseemed *right,* . . . II. ix. 26. 7
backe againe faire Alma led them *right,* . . . II. ix. 33. 5
right faire and fresh as morning rose, . . . II. ix. 36. 7
right fayre and modest of demayne, . . . II. ix. 40. 3
He now was growne *right* wise and wondrous sage: . . . II. ix. 54. 5
Right firme and strong, . . . II. ix. 55. 4
though from earth it be derived *right* . . . II. x. 2. 4
Right well recur'd, . . . II. x. 23. 4
knowes no kinred, nor regardes no *right,* . . . II. x. 35. 2
settled he his kingdome, and confirmd his *right:* . . . II. x. 60. 9
Without full point, or other Cesure *right;* . . . II. x. 68. 3
Of whom all Faeryes spring, and fetch their lignage *right.* . II. x. 71. 9
whiles wind and wether *right* Doe serve their turnes: . . . II. xi. 4. 7
many arrowes under his *right* side, . . . II. xi. 21. 2
Fiercely advaunst his valorous *right* arme, . . . II. xi. 34. 7
right well aware To shonne the engin . . . II. xi. 36. 2
lookt still forward *right,* . . . II. xii. 53. 4
with her *right* the riper fruit did reach, . . . II. xii. 56. 2
Right hard it was for wight which did it heare, . . . II. xii. 70. 5
right over him she hong . . . II. xii. 73. 1
The way they came, the same retourn'd they *right,* . . . II. xii. 84. 3
in living colours, and *right* hew, . . . III. Pr. 4. 1
sory wounds *right* well recur'd, . . . III. i. 1. 4
to recover *right* for such as wrong did grieve. . . . III. i. 3. 9
the sword was servaunt unto *right;* . . . III. i. 13. 2
So unto wrong to yield my wrested *right:* . . . III. i. 24. 5
mote I weet of you, *right* courteous knight, Tydings . . . III. ii. 8. 6
Defending Ladies cause and Orphans *right,* . . . III. ii. 14. 6
What time king Ryence raign'd and dealed *right,* . . . III. ii. 18. 5
A looking glasse, *right* wondrously aguiz'd, . . . III. ii. 18. 8
by wrong or *right* To compas thy desire, . . . III. ii. 46. 8
for she the *right* did shunne; . . . III. ii. 51. 4
Who was the lord of Mathraval by *right,* . . . III. iii. 13. 7
the crowne that was his fathers *right,* . . . III. iii. 29. 6
Themselves they forth convaid, and passed forward *right.* . III. iii. 61. 9
ne her *right* course for ought forsooke. . . . III. iv. 44. 9
Right as he entring was into the flood, . . . III. v. 25. 3
Angell, or Goddesse doe I call thee *right?* . . . III. v. 35. 5
tempred *right* With heate and humour, . . . III. vi. 9. 4
Right in the middest of that Paradise . . . III. vi. 43. 1
T' adore thing so divine as beauty were but *right.* . . . III. vii. 11. 9
His late miswandred wayes now to remeasure *right.* . . . III. vii. 18. 9
To scale the skyes and put Jove from his *right:* . . . III. vii. 47. 5
Right sore I feare, . . . III. ix. 1. 3
avizing *right* Her goodly personage . . . III. ix. 23. 5
Shee came in presence with *right* comely grace, . . . III. ix. 26. 7
he said, (if I remember *right*) . . . III. ix. 47. 5
ran into her lovers armes *right* fast; . . . III. x. 13. 5
In better quarell then defence of *right,* . . . III. x. 28. 4
Her swords point directing forward *right* . . . III. xi. 25. 3
hath his *right* way lost. . . . III. xii. 17. 9
Did yield him selfe *right* willing to prolong his date: . . . III. xii. 35. 9
Amoret *right* fearefull was and faint . . . IV. i. 5. 4
Right well deserved, as his duefull meed, . . . IV. i. 6. 3
avow'd That fairest Amoret was his by *right,* . . . IV. i. 10. 3
The Seneschall was cal'd to deeme the *right:* . . . IV. i. 12. 1
found *right* safe assurance theare. . . . IV. i. 15. 9
now himselfe he fitted had *right* well . . . IV. i. 32. 6
that me *right* dearely cost; . . . IV. i. 35. 2
because his love he wonne by *right:* . . . IV. i. 39. 6
the left hand rubs the *right.'* . . . IV. i. 40. 9
Render therefore therein to me my *right,* . . . IV. ii. 13. 8
Thereto she was *right* faire, . . . IV. ii. 44. 6
Right practicke was Sir Priamond in fight, . . . IV. iii. 7. 1
he for paine himselfe n'ote *right* upreare, . . . IV. iii. 9. 6
As in reversion of his brothers *right;* . . . IV. iii. 14. 7
whilst his *right* foot did slyde. . . . IV. iii. 18. 9
who so winnes her may her have by *right:* . . . IV. iv. 9. 7
His life he then would spend to justifie his *right.* . . . IV. iv. 10. 9
certes his *right* name was otherwize, . . . IV. iv. 42. 7
To Britomart was given by good *right;* . . . IV. v. 8. 3
as her dew *right,* It yielded was . . . IV. v. 20. 2
Who was *right* glad to gaine so goodly meed: . . . IV. v. 22. 2
he himselfe his *right* would eke releasse: . . . IV. v. 25. 6
Right fit to rend the food on which he fared. . . . IV. v. 35. 5
He wist *right* well that it was Britomart, . . . IV. vi. 7. 2
if I hap to fayle, you shall recure my *right.'* . . . IV. vi. 9. 9
therewithall at him *right* furiously she strooke. . . . IV. vi. 14. 9
He was therewith *right* wondrously dismayd; . . . IV. vi. 24. 3
Right plaine appeard, though she it would dissemble, . . . IV. vi. 29. 7
backe returned with *right* heavie mind . . . IV. vi. 46. 4
had it bene *right* hard him to withstand, . . . IV. vii. 25. 8
He held the Lady forth before him *right,* . . . IV. vii. 26. 3
Right sore agrieved at her sharpe reproofe, . . . IV. vii. 37. 2
Him seemed oft he heard his owne *right* name. . . . IV. viii. 4. 5
a Ruby of *right* perfect hew, . . . IV. viii. 6. 7

Right—*Continued.*
she formerly Had knowne *right* well, . . . IV. viii. 10. 4
right feeble through the evill rate Of food . . . IV. viii. 19. 5
when they both recovered were *right* well, . . . IV. viii. 21. 1
that same dwarfe *right* sorie seem'd and sad, . . . IV. viii. 46. 3
better him bethinking of the *right,* . . . IV. ix. 6. 8
in that *right* should by all knights be shielded: . . . IV. ix. 37. 8
me . . . Whose *right* she is, . . . IV. ix. 38. 8
The which *right* well her workes divine did shew; . . . IV. x. 34. 5
unto Venus grace the gate doth open *right* . . . IV. x. 35. 9
'*Right* in the midst the Goddesse selfe did stand . . . IV. x. 39. 1
teaching others to doe *right.* . . . IV. xi. 18. 9
To whom the *right* hereof it selfe hath sold, . . . IV. xi. 22. 7
thinke to reckon *right.* . . . IV. xi. 53. 3
if any Gods at all Have care of *right,* . . . IV. xii. 9. 2
Right sorrowfully mourning her bereaved cares. . . . IV. xii. 17. 9
was *right* joyous that she gotten had . . . IV. xii. 33. 6
Right so himselfe did Marinell upreare, . . . IV. xii. 35. 1
Right now is wrong, and wrong that was is *right;* . . . V. Pr. 4. 4
ne keepes his course more *right,* . . . V. Pr. 7. 3
both to good and bad he dealeth *right,* . . . V. Pr. 10. 4
rule his people *right,* . . . V. Pr. 10. 9
wrong repressed, and establisht *right,* . . . V. i. 2. 3
Chose Artegall to *right* her to restore; . . . V. i. 4. 8
she him taught to weigh both *right* and wrong . . . V. i. 7. 1
In all the skill of deeming wrong and *right,* . . . V. i. 8. 2
Would not so rest contented with his *right;* . . . V. i. 17. 6
to approve his *right* with speare and shield, . . . V. i. 24. 4
this doubtfull causes *right* . . . V. i. 25. 1
And both the living Lady claime your *right,* . . . V. i. 26. 2
to defend the feeble in their *right,* . . . V. ii. 1. 3
Right in the midst . . . a trap was letten downe . . . V. ii. 12. 5
In whose *right* hands great power is contayned, . . . V. ii. 19. 7
Instead of *right* me seemes great wrong dost shew, . . . V. ii. 34. 3
not a dram was missing of their *right:* . . . V. ii. 35. 4
The *right* or wrong, the false or else the trew?' . . . V. ii. 44. 6
he could justly weigh the wrong or *right.* . . . V. ii. 45. 3
'Now take the *right* likewise,' . . . V. ii. 46. 1
So first the *right* he put into one scale, . . . V. ii. 46. 3
Yet all the wrongs could not a litle *right* downe way. . . . V. ii. 46. 9
they doe nought but *right* or wrong betoken; . . . V. ii. 47. 5
in the mind the doome of *right* must bee: . . . V. ii. 47. 6
set the truth and set the *right* aside, . . . V. ii. 48. 1
truth is one, and *right* is ever one.' . . . V. ii. 48. 6
right sate in the middest of the beame alone. . . . V. ii. 48. 9
he the *right* from thence did thrust away, . . . V. ii. 49. 1
For it was not the *right* which he did seeke, . . . V. ii. 49. 2
To chalenge all in *right* of Florimell, . . . V. iii. 4. 8
rather had to lose then trie in armes his *right.* . . . V. iii. 31. 9
By law of armes there neede ones *right* to trie, . . . V. iii. 32. 2
further *right* by tokens to descrie, . . . V. iii. 32. 5
Artegall dealeth *right* betwixt Two brethren . . . V. iv. Arg.
By what good *right* doe you withhold this day?' . . . V. iv. 17. 5
'What other *right,*' (quoth he) 'should you esteeme, . . . V. iv. 17. 6
'Your *right* is good,' (sayd he) . . . V. iv. 17. 8
By what *right* doe you claime to be your owne?' . . . V. iv. 18. 5
'What other *right,*' (quoth he) 'should you esteeme, . . . V. iv. 18. 6
'Your *right* is good,' (sayd he) . . . V. iv. 18. 8
'For equall *right* in equall things doth stand; . . . V. iv. 19. 1
so the threasure yours is, Bracidas, by *right.*' . . . V. iv. 19. 9
Bracidas and Lucy were *right* glad, . . . V. iv. 20. 3
each one had his *right.* . . . V. iv. 20. 6
'*Right* true: but faulty men use oftentimes . . . V. iv. 28. 1
In which condition I *right* now did stand: . . . V. iv. 32. 5
From that first flaw him selfe *right* well defended. . . . V. v. 6. 7
Many brave knights, whose names *right* well he knew, . . . V. v. 22. 2
thereto did himselfe *right* well behave Her to obay, . . . V. v. 23. 7
What *right* is it, that he should thraldome find . . . V. v. 32. 4
with gratefull service me *right* well apay. . . . V. v. 33. 9
she was *right* sore bestad, . . . V. vi. 17. 5
ne ever lookt aside, But still *right* downe; . . . V. vi. 18. 5
right fully bent To fierce avengement . . . V. vi. 18. 6
right discontent In minde he grew, . . . V. vi. 24. 1
With sight whereof she was dismayd *right* sore, . . . V. vi. 28. 1
with *right* wary heede, . . . V. vi. 31. 4
this same vertue that doth *right* define: . . . V. vii. 1. 3
whence mortal men implore *Right* in their wrongs, . . . V. vii. 1. 5
with *right* humble hart . . . her silent prayers did impart. . . V. vii. 7. 8
loth to loose her *right* away, . . . V. vii. 30. 5
To breake all bonds of law and rules of *right:* . . . V. viii. 20. 5
led her to the Souldans *right:* . . . V. viii. 26. 4
In glistering armes *right* goodly well-beseene, . . . V. viii. 29. 4
the brave Prince for honour and for *right,* . . . did fight: . . V. viii. 30. 6
behight Unto that Damzell in her Ladies *right,* . . . V. ix. 3. 5
'Loe! now, *right* noble knights, arriv'd ye bee . . . V. ix. 20. 4
(as ye mote yet *right* well Remember) . . . V. ix. 41. 1
she of death was guiltie found by *right,* . . . V. ix. 50. 4
Gerioneos Seneschall He slayes in Belges *right.* . . . V. x. Arg.
to preserve inviolated *right* . . . V. x. 2. 3
never doth from doome of *right* depart, . . . V. x. 2. 7
their powre against her *right* oppose: . . . V. x. 12. 5
thence unto the castle marched *right,* . . . V. x. 33. 8
meeting him *right* in the middle race . . . V. x. 34. 4
Right in the middest of the threshold lay, . . . V. x. 37. 4
with *right* humble thankes him goodly greeting . . . V. x. 39. 1
With her two sonnes, *right* deare of her beloved, . . . V. x. 39. 7
restore Belge unto her *right.* . . . V. xi. Arg.
right long time is overborne of wrong . . . V. xi. 1. 2
Yet at the last she will her owne cause *right:* . . . V. xi. 1. 6
To which they had no *right,* nor any wrongfull state. . . . V. xi. 3. 9

Right—*Continued.*
Full nobly mounted in *right* warlike wize; . . . V. xi. 4. 3
He wox *right* blyth, as he had got thereby, . . . V. xi. 9. 6
But by their trueth and by the causes *right:* . . . V. xi. 17. 5
for triall of her *right* . . . V. xi. 39. 4
right and wrong most cruelly confound: . . . V. xii. 2. 7
to trie the *right* Of fayre Irenaes cause . . . V. xii. 8. 8
Which none durst breake, though many would *right* faine . . V. xii. 10. 5
Right in the flanke him strooke with deadly dreare, . . . V. xii. 20. 5
Talus to revoke from the *right* way . . . V. xii. 27. 5
yet he for nought would swerve From his *right* course, . . . V. xii. 43. 8
Right so from you all goodly vertues well . . . VI. Pr. 7. 6
Right so in Faery court it did redound, . . . VI. i. 1. 7
I am *right* glad To heare these tidings, . . . VI. i. 10. 2
Will it avenge, and pay thee with thy *right;* . . . VI. i. 25. 8
To pay each with his owne is *right* and dew; . . . VI. i. 42. 3
There he remaind with them *right* well agreed, . . . VI. i. 47. 7
he had good *right* gaynst all that it gainesayd. . . . VI. ii. 18. 9
To lend him day his better *right* to trie, . . . VI. ii. 19. 4
'and *right,* Me seemes, that him befell . . . VI. ii. 23. 5
And lost the crowne which should my head by *right* adorne,) VI. ii. 27. 9
Ripe yeares of reason my *right* to maintaine: . . . VI. ii. 28. 5
I may beare armes, and learne to use them *right;* . . . VI. ii. 33. 6
though she were *right* glad so rid to bee . . . VI. iv. 10. 1
That which your selfe have earst ared so *right?* . . . VI. iv. 28. 2
Right glad was Calepine to be so rid. . . . VI. iv. 38. 1
And did *right* noble deedes; the which els where are showne. VI. iv. 38. 9
T' amend what was amisse, and put in *right* aray. . . . VI. v. 10. 9
seem'd the spoile of some *right* well renownd: . . . VI. v. 25. 5
For he *right* well in Leaches craft was seene; . . . VI. vi. 3. 1
greater force there needs to maintaine wrong then *right.* . . . VI. vi. 35. 9
Whom he likewise *right* sorely did constraine, . . . VI. vi. 38. 5
My due reward, the which *right* well I deeme I yearned have, VI. vii. 15. 8
Given to Calidore as his due *right;* . . . VI. ix. 44. 7
right well Did her beseeme: . . . VI. x. 14. 5
Right happy thou that mayst them freely see! . . . VI. x. 19. 8
'*Right* sory I,' (saide then Sir Calidore) . . . VI. x. 20. 6
Right well knew Coridon his owne late sheepe, . . . VI. xi. 37. 6
Whereof *right* glad they seem'd, . . . VI. xi. 40. 1
right so as Coridon had taught: . . . VI. xi. 41. 7
with their litle stings *right* felly fare; . . . VI. xi. 48. 4
Right so it fares with me in this long way, . . . VI. xii. 1. 8
For Bellamour knew Calidore *right* well, . . . VI. xii. 11. 2
he, *right* well aware, his rage to ward . . . VI. xii. 30. 1
fared like a feend *right* horrible in hew: . . . VI. xii. 31. 9
wrong of *right,* and bad of good did make . . . VII. vi. 6. 3
Jove himselfe to shoulder from his *right.* . . . VII. vi. 7. 5
The younger thrust the elder from his *right:* . . . VII. vi. 27. 5
Much lesse the Title of old Titans *Right:* . . . VII. vi. 33. 4
For to betray my *Right* before I have it tride. . . . VII. vi. 34. 9
Of my desert, or of my dewfull *Right;* . . . VII. vi. 35. 2
Seeking for *Right,* which I of thee entreat, . . . VII. vii. 14. 3
Right to all dost deale indifferently, . . . VII. vii. 14. 4
'Then weigh, O soveraigne goddesse! by what *right* . . . VII. vii. 16. 1
by his plough-yrons mote *right* well appeare. . . . VII. vii. 35. 4
As fed with lard, and that *right* well might seeme; . . . VII. vii. 40. 2
'*Right* true it is, . . . VII. vii. 48. 1
Right so my cruell fayre with me doth play; . . . *Am.* liii. 5
Right so your selfe were caught . . . *Am.* lxxi. 5
by *right* deserts, t' attaine, Unto the type of true Nobility; . *Com. Son.* ii. 1
Behold them both in their *right* visnomy . . . *Com. Son.* ii. 5
Venice . . . farre exceedes in policie of *right.* . . . *Com. Son.* iv. 12
Him first to love great *right* and reason is, . . . *H.H.L.* 190

Righteous. Minos *righteous* soules doth sever From wicked ones, *Gn.* 623
the month in which the *righteous* Maide, . . . *Hub.* 1
'The good and *righteous* he away doth take, . . . *D.* 358
how many perils doe enfold The *righteous* man, . . . I. viii. 1. 2
By *righteous* sentence of th' Almighties law. . . . I. ix. 50. 4
his *righteous* soule might save. . . . I. x. 34. 9
the praiers of the *righteous* sead . . . I. x. 51. 7
What booteth then the good and *righteous* deed, . . . III. xi. 9. 8
righteous doome aread, . . . V. Pr. 11. 4
to her he seem'd best skild in *righteous* lore. . . . V. i. 4. 9
next her selfe her *righteous* ballance hanging bee. . . . V. i. 11. 9
Then answered the *righteous* Artegall, . . . V. ii. 39. 2
That which he doth with *righteous* doome decide, . . . V. iv. 1. 4
Would ye remit it to some *righteous* man.' . . . V. iv. 16. 3
are rul'd by *righteous* lore Of highest Jove, . . . V. vii. 1. 5
The *righteous* Knight that is thy faithfull lover, . . . V. vii. 22. 4
Where *righteous* Artegall her late exyled; . . . V. ix. 2. 2
unto them was dealing *righteous* doome: . . . V. ix. 23. 5
begot in loves delight Upon the *righteous* Themis; . . . V. ix. 31. 6
The noble Prince and *righteous* Artegall, . . . V. x. 4. 2
Nature soone Her *righteous* Doome areads. . . . VII. vii. Arg.
the *righteous* Virgin, which of old Liv'd here . . . VII. vii. 37. 6
Ensampled it by his most *righteous* deede, . . . *H.H.L.* 213
That sits upon the *righteous* throne on hy, . . . *H.H.B.* 151

Righteousness. Of love, and *righteousnes,* and well to donne; I. x. 33. 4
frame In holy *righteousnesse,* without rebuke or blame. . . . I. x. 45. 9
If goodnesse find no grace, nor *righteousnes* no meed? . . . III. xi. 9. 9
'If good find grace, and *righteousnes* reward, . . . III. xi. 10. 1
His scepter is the rod of *Righteousnesse,* . . . *H.H.B.* 155

Rightest. Then with a few to walke the *rightest* way. . . . I. x. 10. 8

Rightful. Such is the *rightfull* Courtier in his kinde, . . . *Hub.* 793
rightfull kingdome she had none at all, . . . I. iv. 12. 3
would his *rightfull* ravine rend away: . . . I. v. 8. 5
their *rightfull* causes downe to tread; . . . I. x. 43. 7
truth is strong her *rightfull* cause to plead, . . . I. xii. 28. 7
more to mighty hands then *rightfull* cause doth trust. . . . II. ii. 29. 9
were there *rightfull* cause of difference, . . . II. ii. 30. 1

Rightful—*Continued.*
the *rightfull* owner of that steede, . . . II. iv. 2. 1
thou didst these goods bereave From *rightfull* owner . . . II. vii. 19. 4
Ne forst his *rightful* owner to offend; . . . II. viii. 21. 4
such as claymd themselves Brutes *rightfull* hayres, . . . II. x. 37. 5
would some *rightfull* cause pretend, . . . IV. xii. 30. 9
all the depth of *rightfull* doome was taught . . . V. i. 5. 3
Their greatest glory for their *rightfull* deedes, . . . V. ii. 1. 6
to his damzell, as their *rightfull* meed . . . VI. i. 47. 5
Rightfully. *rightfully* aread so dolefull lay. . . . *T.M.* 52
His name was meeke Obedience, *rightfully* aredd. . . . I. x. 17. 9
Wherefore *Morddure* it *rightfully* is hight. . . . II. viii. 21. 6
Right-hand. *See* **Hand, Right.**
In his *right hand* he bare The tree of peace, . . . *Bel.*[1] vii. 10
At my *right hand* (*hande*[1]) a Hynde appear'd . . . *Pet.* i. 4
His *right hand* did the peacefull olive wield; . . . *Bel.*[2] ix. 11
the stout hynde arm'd his *right hand* with steele: . . . *Ro.* xviii. 6
Scarce this *right hand* the mouth with diet feedeth, . . . *Hub.* 274
In her *right hand* a broken rod she held, . . . *Ti.* 13
in her *right hand* bore a cup of gold, . . . I. x. 13. 2
he already plighted his *right hand* Unto another love, . . . I. xii. 26. 8
Thou litle wotest what this *right-hand* can: . . . II. iii. 16. 8
In his *right hand* an yron club he held, . . . II. vii. 40. 6
'Fayre Sonne, great God thy *right hand* blesse, . . . II. viii. 40. 3
his *right hand* unarmed fearefully did wield. . . . III. xii. 12. 9
In her *right hand* a firebrand shee did tosse . . . III. xii. 17. 6
the darts which his *right hand* did straine . . . III. xii. 23. 5
In her *right hand* a rod of peace shee bore, . . . IV. iii. 42. 1
with his craggy club in his *right hand* . . . IV. vii. 25. 6
his strong *right hand* . . . heaved up on hie, . . . IV. viii. 43. 1
For powre is the *right hand* of Justice truely hight. . . . V. iv. 1. 9
In his *right hand* he held a trembling dart, . . . VI. ii. 6. 4
even as his *right hand* adowne descends, . . . VI. viii. 49. 2
In his *right hand* a tipped staffe he held, . . . VII. vii. 31. 6
Rightly. All Kent can *rightly* boaste: . . . *S.C.* Jul. 44
By whom the flock is *rightly* fed, and taught: . . . *Hub.* 442
whether *rightly* so, Or through our rudenesse . . . *Col.* 795
of his nature *rightly* to define, . . . *Col.* 836
doth need a golden quill, . . . them *rightly* to devise; . . . *Ded.Son.*xvi.11
rightly may I rew The fall . . . I. v. 25. 1
it *rightly* hot The well of life, . . . I. xi. 29. 8
skill them *rightly* to have chusd, . . . II. ii. 5. 8
unto thee dew worship I may *rightly* frame.' . . . II. iii. 33. 9
fayre Philotime she *rightly* hight, . . . II. vii. 49. 1
his large bountie *rightly* doth areed: . . . III. iv. 59. 4
Great father he of generation Is *rightly* cald, . . . III. vi. 9. 2
Which was by him Belphebe *rightly* rad. . . . IV. vii. 46. 5
if one did *rightly* deeme; . . . IV. x. 39. 8
The Ouze, whom men doe Isis *rightly* name; . . . IV. xi. 24. 7
though *rightly* nought.' . . . IV. xii. 30. 9
For worthy thou of her doest *rightly* seeme. . . . V. i. 28. 4
'His name is hight Pollente, *rightly* so, . . . V. ii. 7. 1
In cyphers strange, that few could *rightly* read, . . . V. ix. 26. 3
none them *rightly* may reprove Of rudenesse . . . VI. ii. 1. 7
Yet boldly answer'd, as he *rightly* might, . . . VI. ii. 18. 7
mightst *rightly* reed Me then to be full base . . . VI. iii. 31. 7
Therefore it *rightly* cleeped was mount Acidale. . . . VI. x. 8. 9
yet, being *rightly* wayd, . . . VII. vii. 58. 3
Rights. *See* **Arights.**
Her to demaund and chalenge as their *rights,* . . . IV. v. 23. 3
By all meanes to maintaine that castels ancient *rights.* . . . IV. x. 7. 9
with dint of sword . . . their *rights* to try, . . . V. iv. 6. 2
heavens them selves, that favour feeble *rights,* . . . VI. viii. 18. 8
For triall of their Titles and best *Rights:* . . . VII. vi. 36. 4
Rigor. to aswage The ranckorous *rigour* of his might, . . . *S.C* F. 185
upon his crest With *rigor* so outrageous he smitt, . . . I. ii. 18. 7
at his foe with furious *rigor* smites, . . . I. viii. 18. 5
beare the *rigour* of his bold mesprise; . . . II. vii. 39. 8
Guyon broke downe with *rigour* pittilesse; . . . II. xii. 83. 2
with *rigor* fell Smote him . . . III. v. 23. 4
her besought . . . *rigour* to abate, . . . IV. ii. 50. 2
Whose raging *rigour* neither steele nor bras Could stay, . . . IV. vi. 15. 5
Relent the *rigour* of your wrathfull will, . . . IV. vi. 32. 2
sufferaunce soft, which *rigour* can abate, . . . IV. viii. 1. 7
their raging *rigour* to relent, . . . IV. ix. 25. 8
No words may rate, nor *rigour* him remove . . . IV. ix. 31. 7
When so it needs with *rigour* to dispence: . . . V. i. 7. 5
doth procure Great warriours oft their *rigour* to repress, . . . V. viii. 1. 4
their resistlesse *rigour* did eschew: . . . V. viii. 32. 4
Rebutting him . . . With so huge *rigour,* . . . V. x. 35. 6
A Lions clawes, with powre and *rigour* clad, . . . V. xi. 24. 3
Ne once for ruth their *rigour* they releast, . . . VI. i. 36. 8
did the *rigour* of his doome represse; . . . VI. vii. 37. 4
to renue the *rigour* of his smart; . . . VI. x. 31. 4
Mourning the *rigour* of her malady, . . . VI. xi. 8. 4
with unkind disdaine And cruell *rigour* . . . VI. xi. 24. 4
Somewhat to slacke the *rigour* of my flame? . . . *H.L.* 152
Under the *rigour* of his judgement just; . . . *H.H.B.* 158
Rigorous. bids him clayme with *rigorous* rage hys right: . . . *S.C.* D. 130
And eke themselves, too rudely *rigorous,* . . . I. ii. 15. 7
fiersely ran at him with *rigorous* might: . . . I. xi. 16. 2
It vaine she thought with *rigorous* uprore For to efforce, . . . III. xii. 27. 8
me captiving streight with *rigorous* wrong, . . . *Am.* xii. 11
Rime. Thou kenst not, Percie, howe the *ryme* should rage, . . . *S.C.* O. 109
Up, grieslie ghostes! and up my rufull *ryme!* . . . *S.C.* N. 55
on shrill reedes chaunting his rustick *rime,* . . . *Gn.* 155
rime at riot, and doo rage in love; . . . *T.M.* 395
By this rude *rime* to memorize thy name, . . . *Ded. Son.* xii. 2
Shouting, and singing all a shepheards *ryme;* . . . I. vi. 13. 7
(O too high ditty for my simple *rime!*) . . . II. x. 50. 7

Rime—*Continued.*
Ne spareth he the gentle Poets *rime;* . . . VI. xii. 40. 8
Rimers. With wanton Bardes, and *Rymers* impudent; . . . III. xii. 5. 5
Rimes. to heare thy *rymes* and roundelayes, . . . *S.C.* Jun. 49
my *rymes* bene rough, and rudely drest; . . . *S.C.* Jun. 77
if in *rymes* with me thou dare strive, . . . *S.C.* Au. 21
In *rymes,* in ridles, and in bydding base; . . . *S.C.* O. 5
rolle with rest in *rymes* of rybaudrye; . . . *S.C.* O. 76
if thy *rymes* as rownde and rufull bene . . . *S.C.* N. 43
howe my *rimes* bene rugged . . . *S.C.* N. 51
Rolling in *rymes* of shameles ribaudrie . . . *T.M.* 213
They cherelie chaunt, and *rymes* at randon fling, . . . *T.M.* 321
use to paint in *rimes* the troublous state . . . *T.M.* 381
Then fittest are these ragged *rimes* for mee, . . . *T.M.* 545
all that ever did in *rimes* rejoice, . . . *Ti.* 334
well I wot my *rymes* bene rudely dight. . . . *As.* Pr. 12
Them to vouchsafe emongst his *rimes* to name, . . . *As.* 38
his *rimes,* his songs were all upon her. . . . *As.* 60
Till he recanted had his wicked *rimes,* . . . *Col.* 923
And to these ydle *rymes* lend litle space, . . . *Ded. Son.* i. 13
Rude *rymes,* the which a rustick Muse did weave . . . *Ded.Son.*vii.11
My *rimes* I know unsavory and sowre, . . . *Ded.Son.*viii.8
Unfitly I these ydle *rimes* present, . . . *Ded. Son.* ix. 7
As he were charmed with inchaunted *rimes;* . . . I. ix. 48. 8
My ragged *rimes* are all too rude and bace . . . I. xii. 23. 4
my *rymes* too rude and rugged arre, . . . III. ii. 3. 6
Are still emongst them song, that far my *rymes* exceed. . . . III. viii. 42. 9
This odious argument my *rymes* should shend, . . . III. ix. 1. 4
My looser *rimes* (I wote) doth sharply wite . . . IV. Pr. 1. 3
these *rimes,* so rude as doth appeare, . . . IV. ii. 33. 7
when as these *rimes* be red With misregard, . . . IV. viii. 29. 1
rayling *rymes* had sprad. . . . V. ix. 25. 9
Therefore do you, my *rimes,* keep better measure, . . . VI. xii. 41. 8
happy *rymes!* bath'd in the sacred brooke . . . *Am.* i. 9
Leaves, lines, and *rymes,* seeke her to please alone, . . . *Am.* i. 13
Whom ye thought worthy of your gracefull *rymes,* . . . *Epith.* 3
That may my *rymes* with sweet infuse embrew, . . . *H.H.L.* 47
That all the world shold with his *rimes* be fraught! . . . *H.H.B.* 224
Rinaldo. The which *Rinaldo* drunck in happie howre, . . . IV. iii. 45. 3
Rind. manie yong plants spring out of her *rinde:* . . . *Ro.* xxviii. 11
now the gray mosse marred his *rine;* . . . *S.C.* F. 111
'The carefull cold hath nypt my rugged *rynde,* . . . *S.C.* D. 133
her leafe was greene, and fresh her *rinde,* . . . *D.* 240
My tender sides in this rough *rynd* embard; . . . I. ii. 31. 3
Her wrizled skin, as rough as maple *rind,* So scabby was . . . I. viii. 47. 8
Sweet is the Cypresse, but his *rynd* is tough; . . . *Am.* xxvi. 5
Rinded. *See* **Rougher-rinded.**
Rine. *See* **Rind.**
Ring. Echo made the neyghbour groves to *ring,* . . . *S.C.* Jun. 52
All were Elisa one of thilke same *ring;* . . . *S.C.* O. 53
the nigh aymed *ring* away to beare. . . . *Hub.* 742
with our musick wont so oft to *ring,* . . . *T.M.* 278
madest the forrests *ring,* . . . *Ti.* 325
here no tunes, save sobs and grones, shall *ring.* . . . *D.* 14
all the woods with doubled Eccho *ring;* . . . I. vi. 14. 2
The neighbor woods arownd with hollow murmur *ring.* . . . I. viii. 11. 9
with their horror heven and earth did *ring;* . . . I. xi. 7. 5
made the forrest *ring,* . . . II. iii. 20. 9
When one so oft a night did *ring* his matins bell. . . . III. x. 48. 9
Conceived by a *ring* which she him sent, . . . IV. ii. 39. 7
All was through vertue of the *ring* he wore; . . . IV. iii. 24. 1
Loe! here this *ring,* which shall thy warrant bee, . . . V. v. 34. 2
Into the rest which round about you *ring,* . . . VI. Pr. 7. 7
taking from her hand a *ring* of gould, . . . VI. i. 29. 2
Calidore should lead the *ring,* . . . VI. ix. 41. 7
All raunged in a *ring* and dauncing in delight. . . . VI. x. 11. 9
All they without were raunged in a *ring,* . . . VI. x. 12. 1
as a precious gemme Amidst a *ring* . . . VI. x. 12. 8
Did *ring* againe, and loud re-eccho to the skie. . . . VII. vi. 52. 9
The woods shall to me answer, and my Eccho *ring.* . . . *Epith.* 18
That all the woods may answer, and your eccho *ring.* . . . *Epith.* 36
The woods shall to you answer, and your Eccho *ring.* . . . *Epith.* 55
That all the woods may answer, and your eccho *ring.* . . . *Epith.* 73
That all the woods them answer, and theyr eccho *ring.* . . . *Epith.* 91
The whiles the woods shal answer, and your eccho *ring.* . . . *Epith.* 109
all the woods shal answer, and theyr eccho *ring.* . . . *Epith.* 128
al the woods them answer, and theyr eccho *ring.* . . . *Epith.* 147
That all the woods may answer, and your eccho *ring.* . . . *Epith.* 166
To which the woods did answer, and your eccho *ring?* . . . *Epith.* 184
al the woods should answer, and your echo *ring.* . . . *Epith.* 203
That al the woods may answere, and their echo *ring.* . . . *Epith.* 222
That all the woods may answere, and your eccho *ring.* . . . *Epith.* 241
To which the woods shall answer, and theyr eccho *ring.* . . . *Epith.* 260
Ring ye the bels, ye yong men of the towne, . . . *Epith.* 261
Ring ye the bels, to make it weare away, . . . *Epith.* 274
That all the woods may answer, and your eccho *ring.* . . . *Epith.* 277
all the woods them answer, and their echo *ring!* . . . *Epith.* 295
The woods no more shall answere, nor your echo *ring.* . . . *Epith.* 314
Ne let the woods them answer nor theyr eccho *ring.* . . . *Epith.* 333, 352
Ne will the woods now answer, nor your Eccho *ring.* . . . *Epith.* 371
Ne let the woods us answere, nor our Eccho *ring.* . . . *Epith.* 389
Ne any woods shall answer, nor your Eccho *ring.* . . . *Epith.* 408
The woods no more us answer, nor our eccho *ring!* . . . *Epith.* 426
great Elisaes glorious name may *ring* . . . *Proth.* 157
Ringed. all the castle *ringed* with the clap. . . . IV. x. 9. 5
Ringing. oftentimes loud strokes and *ringing* sowndes . . . III. iii. 9. 8
Ring's. Well was that *rings* great vertue knowen to all; . . . IV. ii. 40. 1
Ne felt his blood to wast, . . . Through that *rings* vertue, . . . IV. iii. 29. 3
Rings. *See* **Rush-rings.**
fame now *rings* Through the wide world, . . . *Gn.* 149

Rings—*Continued.*
Ne spared he to give her gold and *rings;* . . . I. iii. 18. 8
rings of rushes plight: . . . II. vi. 7. 5
Gold, amber, yvorie, perles, owches, *rings,* . . . III. iv. 23. 5
They all gan shout aloud, that all the heaven *rings.* . . . IV. iii. 49. 9
First *rings* his silver Bell t' each sleepy wight, . . . V. vi. 27. 3
Riot. rime at *riot,* and doo rage in love; . . . *T.M.* 395
Riotise. the costly rate Of *riotise,* . . . *Gn.* 93
With courtizans, and costly *riotize,* . . . *Hub.* 805
lawlesnes raigning with *riotize;* . . . *Hub.* 1310
otherwise His life he led in lawlesse *riotise,* . . . I. iv. 20. 5
Through wastfull Pride and wanton *Riotise,* . . . I. v. 46. 5
The image of superfluous *riotize,* . . . III. i. 33. 6
Consuming *Riotise,* and guilty Dread . . . III. xii. 25. 7
Riotous. In *riotous* excesse doth there abound. . . . *Mui.* 168
there him rests in *riotous* suffisaunce . . . *Mui.* 207
In which was nothing *riotous* nor vaine? . . . I. xii. 14. 2
round about him preace in *riotous* aray. . . . V. vi. 29. 9
Rip. *rip* up griefe where it may not availe: . . . I. vii. 39. 8
To *rip* up wrong that battell once hath tried; . . . IV. ix. 37. 3
Ripe. *See* **Mellow-ripe.**
yeeres more *rype* . . . toyes away dyd wype, . . . *S.C.* Jun. 46
Sike follies nowe have gathered as too *ripe,* . . . *S.C.* D. 117
Her deeds were like great clusters of *ripe* grapes, . . . *Col.* 600
when yeares More *rype* us reason lent . . . II. iv. 18. 5
rype of age, And in demeanure sober, . . . II. ix. 27. 8
There sate a man of *ripe* and perfect age, . . . II. ix. 54. 2
ripe age bad him surrender late His life, . . . II. x. 13. 8
he dyde, made *ripe* for death by eld, . . . II. x. 32. 2
Ambrose and Uther, did *ripe* yeares attayne, . . . II. x. 67. 2
So readie *rype* to ill ill wemens counsels bee! . . . III. x. 11. 9
he . . . dyde, before I did attaine *Ripe* yeares . . . VI. ii. 28. 5
He was to weete a man of full *ripe* yeares, . . . VI. iii. 3. 1
Ripened. faire Emeraudes, not yet well *ripened.* . . . II. xii. 54. 9
Till to her dew perfection she were *ripened.* . . . III. vi. 3. 9
Should reap the harvest ere it *ripened* were: . . . VI. ix. 38. 6
To reape the *ripened* fruits . . . VII. vii. 30. 9
Ripeness. when she to perfect *ripenes* grew, . . . III. vi. 52. 1
when to *ripenesse* due they growen arre, . . . IV. i. 25. 6
Till that to *ripenesse* of mans state they grew: . . . IV. ii. 46. 2
Untill the *ripenesse* of mans yeares he raught; . . . V. i. 8. 3
with carefull labour nurst, Till it to *ripenesse* grew, . . . VI. Pr. 3. 9
Till he to perfect *ripenesse* grew; . . . VI. i. 8. 5
Riper. *ryper* age such pleasures doth reprove: . . . *S.C.* Jun. 36
To thinges of *ryper* season selfe applyed, . . . *S.C.* D. 76
till to *ryper* yeares he gan aspyre, . . . I. vi. 23. 7
till *ryper* years he raught; . . . I. vi. 29. 2
so soone as *ryper* yeares he raught, . . . II. iii. 2. 6
Till *ryper* years he raught and stronger stay; . . . II. x. 20. 4
with her right the *riper* fruit did reach, . . . II. xii. 56. 2
seemd of *ryper* yeares then th' other Swayne, . . . III. xii. 9. 2
'The first of them did seeme of *ryper* yeares . . . IV. x. 49. 1
Ripest. Of *rypest* yeares, and heares all hoarie gray, . . . II. i. 7. 3
Ripeth. Sike question *ripeth* up cause of newe woe, . . . *S.C.* S. 13
Riphoean. a shady glade Of the *Riphoean* hils, . . . III. viii. 6. 4
Rippeth. *See* **Ripeth.**
Rise. I saw a fresh spring *rise* out of a rocke, . . . *Bel.*[1] x. 1
I saw her *rise,* and with a larger flight . . . *Bel.* vii. 5
out of a (the[1]) rocke did *rise* A spring . . . *Pet.* iv. 1
the heavens in warre against her *rize:* . . . *Bel.*[2] xv. 12
'Now *ryse* up, Elisa, . . . *S.C.* Ap. 145
ryse, ye blessed Flocks, and home apace, . . . *S.C.* Jun. 118
The nombers flowe as fast as spring doth *ryse.* . . . *S.C.* O. 108
Courtiers, as the tide, doo *rise* and fall.' . . . *Hub.* 614
still somewhat to his share did *rize:* . . . *Hub.* 806
then him waking, forced up to *rize,* . . . *Hub.* 1323
from a golden Censer forth doth *rise,* . . . *Col.* 609
he doth soonest *rise* . . . *Col.* 692
having ended, he from ground did *rise,* . . . *Col.* 952
'*Rise, rise!* unhappy Swaine, . . . I. ii. 4. 6
of those fearfull women none durst *rize,* . . . I. iii. 19. 2
No powre he had to stirre, nor will to *rize.* . . . I. viii. 15. 4
can quickly *ryse* From off the earth, . . . I. xi. 23. 7
knight to battell new did *rise.* . . . I. xi. 34. 9
rise out of your paine, . . . II. i. 20. 6
So up he let him *rise;* . . . II. v. 14. 1
Ne suffred them to *ryse* or greater grow; . . . II. vii. 47. 8
to those brethren sayd; '*Rise, rise* bylive, . . . II. viii. 18. 1
Some to remove the scum as it did *rise;* . . . II. ix. 31. 7
There chaunced to the Princes hand to *rize* . . . II. ix. 59. 5
goodly frame of Temperaunce Fayrely to *rise,* . . . II. xii. 1. 2
The surging waters like a mountaine *rise,* . . . II. xii. 21. 6
each the other from to *rise* restraine; . . . II. xii. 64. 5
A gloomy grove of mirtle trees did *rise,* . . . III. vi. 43. 3
The whiles the pitteous Lady up did *ryse,* . . . III. viii. 32. 1
Paridell did *rise* And to the Castle gate approcht . . . III. ix. 9. 8
shee at length persuaded him to *rise,* . . . III. xi. 20. 1
the inner rowme from whence they first did *rise.* . . . III. xii. 26. 9
How to prevent the perill that mote *rise,* . . . IV. ii. 37. 8
litle lust he had to *rise* againe: . . . IV. iv. 44. 6
bad him *rise,* or surely he should die. . . . IV. vi. 23. 6
rules the Seas and makes them *rise* or fall; . . . IV. xi. 11. 2
where he ought *rise* aright: . . . V. Pr. 8. 7
weigh the light that in the East doth *rise;* . . . V. ii. 43. 3
An hideous tempest seemed from below To *rise* . . . V. vii. 14. 3
Now *rise* againe at this your joyous sight. . . . V. x. 20. 6
suffring him to *rise,* he made him sweare . . . VI. i. 43. 5
That from his sides some noble chyld should *rize,* . . . VI. iv. 33. 2
Who thinkes from me his sorrow all doth *rize.* . . . VI. iv. 33. 7
now come to himselfe yet would not *rize,* . . . VI. vi. 32. 2

Rise—*Continued.*
The morrow next the Prince did early *rize,* . . . VI. vi. 44. 8
Then up he made him *rise,* . . . VI. vii. 49. 1
Whence he assayd to *rise,* but could not for his hurt. . . . VI. viii. 16. 9
he did abstaine streightway, And let him *rise.* . . . VI. viii. 29. 5
wild the damzell *rise;* . . . VI. ix. 13. 9
A Tigre forth out of the wood did *rise,* . . . VI. x. 34. 4
rise against the remnant at their will: . . . VI. xi. 18. 3
And *rise* more faire, till they at last arive . . . *H.H.B.* 76
Risen. Like ghost late *risen* from his grave agryz'd, . . . IV. viii. 12. 7
twice hath *risen* where he now doth West, . . . V. Pr. 8. 6
Riseth. Where Titan *ryseth* from the mayne . . . *S.C.* Jul. 59
Rising. The sodain *rysing* of the raging seas, . . . *S.C.* D. 86
haplesse *rising* of some froward starre, . . . *Gn.* 570
The royall virgin . . . *rising* forth . . . I. ii. 7. 6
As fayre Aurora, *rysing* hastily, . . . III. iii. 20. 4
a Raven, far from *rising* Sunne, . . . III. iii. 46. 5
rising up, gan streight to over-looke Those cursed leaves, . . . III. xii. 36. 1
odours *rising* from the altars flame. . . . IV. x. 37. 3
Calidore *rising* up as fresh as day . . . VI. iii. 13. 8
rising up at last in ghastly wize, . . . VI. vi. 32. 7
Rites. Cybeles franticke *rites* have made them mad: . . . I. vi. 15. 3
With sacred *rites* and vowes for ever to abyde. . . . I. xii. 36. 9
Had with dew *rites* and dolorous lament . . . II. ii. 1. 2
There wanted nought but few *rites* to be donne, . . . II. iv. 21. 5
did attend Uppon the *rites* and daily sacrifize, . . . V. vii. 4. 3
With sacred *rites* hast taught to solemnize; . . . *Epith.* 393
Rivage. Throwes forth upon the *rivage* round about him nere. IV. vi. 20. 9
Rival. The *rivall* slaine, the victour, . . . Escaped hardly, . . . III. ix. 42. 8
Rivallus. His sonne *Rivall'* (**Rivallo*) his dead rowme did supply; . . . II. x. 34. 1
Rivals. even they, the which his *rivals* were, . . . VI. ix. 45. 3
Rive. *See* **Rived, Riven.**
let those deep Abysses open *rive,* . . . *Ro.* i. 7
Doth in the port it selfe his vessell *rive.* . . . *Ro.* xxi. 14
thunder which doth *ryve* The ratling heavens, . . . *Gn.* 519
Sharpe sorrowe did in thousand peeces *rive.* . . . *D.* 7
So hugely stroke, that it the steele did *rive,* . . . I. ii. 19. 4
mighty brawned bowrs Were wont to *rive* steele plates, . . . I. viii. 41. 7
as it would *rive* in twaine. . . . II. iii. 20. 9
his deepe wounded hart in two did *rive;* . . . II. vi. 45. 7
rive with thousand throbs thy thrilled brest: . . . III. ii. 32. 5
a rocke of stone to rew, Or *rive* in twaine: . . . III. v. 30. 3
no wals so strong, But that continuall battery will *rive,* . . . III. x. 10. 2
the sharpe steele doth *rive* her hart in tway, . . . III. xi. 11. 4
What time his people into partes did *rive,* . . . IV. ii. 2. 8
seem'd a rocke of Diamond it could *rive* . . . IV. v. 37. 8
the ghost would *rive* Out of their wretched corses, . . . IV. ix. 22. 8
from her griping pounce the greedy prey doth *rive.* . . . V. iv. 42. 9
For very ruth, which did it almost *rive,* . . . V. vii. 36. 6
seem'd a marble rocke asunder could have *rive.* . . . V. xi. 5. 9
Rived. *See* **Rive.**
it both bone and muscles *ryved* quight. . . . *As.* 120
hart-strings of an Aegle *ryv'd.* . . . II. x. 70. 9
So *ryv'd* her trembling hart, and wicked end did make. . . . II. xi. 47. 9
seemd both shield and plate it would have *riv'd;* . . . III. i. 6. 3
whom late their ladies arrow *ryv'd:* . . . III. v. 37. 5
nathemore the steele asonder *riv'd,* . . . III. vii. 40. 5
would have algates *riv'd* The hart out of his brest: . . . III. viii. 3. 5
rived were like rotten wood asunder; . . . IV. iii. 15. 6
The soule had sure out of his bodie *rived,* . . . IV. iii. 18. 3
all his mayle *yriv'd,* and plates yrent, . . . IV. vi. 15. 8
Riven. *See* **Rive.**
T' accept a Benefice in peeces *riven.* . . . *Hub.* 540
As if it quite were *riven* from the ground, . . . *Hub.* 1354
felt my heart nigh *riven* in my brest . . . *Ti.* 30
stony hart could *riven* have in twaine; . . . I. iii. 44. 3
Had *riven* many a brest with pikehead square: . . . I. vii. 37. 4
Through *riven* cloudes and molten firmament; . . . I. viii. 9. 5
gushed, like fresh water streame from *riven* rocke. . . . I. viii. 10. 9
doth rancle in my *riven* brest, . . . I. ix. 7. 4
These words she breathed forth from *riven* chest: . . . II. i. 47. 5
An open passage through his *riven* brest, . . . II. xi. 37. 4
wound, which . . . *riven* bowels gor'd, . . . III. xii. 38. 4
the *riven* walls were hung With ragged monuments . . . IV. i. 21. 1
Like as the lightning brond from *riven* skie, . . . IV. vi. 14. 1
all adowne their *riven* sides did ronne. . . . IV. ix. 27. 5
soules they wold have *ryven* quight Out of their breasts . . . V. x. 32. 4
from their *riven* sides forth gushed like a flood. . . . VI. i. 37. 9
sighing sore, as if her hart in twaine Had *riven* bene . . . VI. xi. 22. 8
River. I saw a *river* swift, . . . *Bel.*[2] viii. 1
the darksome *river* Of Styx, . . . *Ro.* xv. 5
forst to ferrie over Lethes *river,* . . . *Gn.* 338
doo thou haunt the soft downe-rolling *river,* . . . *Gn.* 636
By that same *River* lurking under greene, . . . *Gn.* 649
that gentle *River* for great griefe Of my mishaps, . . . *Ti.* 141
At length out of the *River* it was reard . . . *Ti.* 610
of my *river* Bregogs love I soong, . . . *Col.* 92
her owne brother *river,* Bregog hight, . . . *Col.* 117
he that *river* for his daughter wonne: . . . *Col.* 125
a *River,* which he was of old, . . . *Col.* 152
the *river* Dee, . . . His tombling billowes rolls . . . I. ix. 4. 7
A gushing *river* of blacke gory blood, . . . I. xi. 22. 4
The Amazon huge *river,* now found trew? . . . II. Pr. 2. 8
Through midst thereof a little *river* rold, . . . II. i. 24. 6
Came to a *river,* by whose utmost brim . . . II. vi. 2. 4
That is the *river* of Cocytus deepe, . . . II. vii. 56. 8
carcas deepe was drent Within the *river,* . . . II. vii. 61. 3
castle, plaste Foreby a *river* in a pleasaunt dale; . . . II. ix. 10. 4
the *River* that whylome was hight The ancient Abus, . . . II. x. 16. 2

River—*Continued.*
Adowne the rolling *river* she did poure, II. x. 19. 7
every *river* eke his course forbeares, III. ii. 32. 3
in the midst a little *river* plaide III. v. 39. 7
a long bloody *river* through them rayld, III. xi. 46. 8
the *river* rolling still With murmure soft, IV. x. 15. 8
that huge *River,* which doth beare his name IV. xi. 21. 8
in the *river* drowned quight IV. xi. 37. 9
same *river,* where he late Had drenched them, IV. xi. 38. 5
nam'd the *river* of his wretched fate IV. xi. 38. 7
underneath the same a *river* flowes V. ii. 8. 1
over side the Bridge she cast Into the *river,* V. vi. 39. 9
And carelesly into the *river* goth, VI. iii. 33. 3
Others would through the *river* him have drive VII. vi. 50. 5
(both combin'd) themselves in one faire *river* spred. VII. vi. 53. 9
every *River* still doth ebbe and flowe; VII. vii. 20. 4
Whose rutty Bancke, the which his *River* hemmes *Proth.* 12
River's. tune hir plaint to falling *rivers* sound *Bel.*[1] viii. 3
that great *rivers* banck, that runnes by Rome; *Bel.* i. 6
Hard by a *rivers* side *Bel.* x. 1
To falling *rivers* sound thus tun'd her sobs. *Bel.*[2] x. 4
by a *rivers* bancke that swift downe slidd, *Bel.*[2] xv. 7
one of that *Rivers* Nymphes, *Ti.* 15
There now no *rivers* course is to be seene, *Ti.* 139
Upon that famous *Rivers* further shore, *Ti.* 589
to the *rivers* syde they both together far'd: II. xi. 3. 9
Downe in a dale forby a *rivers* syde VI. iii. 29. 6
comming to the *rivers* side, he found VI. iii. 30. 1
in a Meadow, by the *Rivers* side, *Proth.* 19
Descended to the *Rivers* open vewing, *Proth.* 166
forth pacing to the *Rivers* side, *Proth.* 175
Rivers. the swift running *rivers* still did stand, *Gn.* 450
When Teucrian soyle with bloodie *rivers* swelde, *Gn.* 500
he along would flie Upon the streaming *rivers,* *Mui.* 47
The woods, the *rivers,* and the medowes green, *Mui.* 153
most goodly *rivers* there appeare, *Col.* 300
Greeke and Asian *rivers* stayned with their blood. III. iii. 22. 9
two *rivers* bownd the rest. III. ix. 46. 4
Adowne their sides like litle *rivers* stremed, IV. iii. 28. 7
Doth burne the earth and boyled *rivers* drie, IV. iv. 17. 2
As that in *rivers* swim, or brookes doe wade; IV. xi. 9. 5
after him the famous *rivers* came, IV. xi. 20. 1
All little *Rivers* which owe vassallage To him, IV. xi. 29. 3
many *rivers* taking under-hand Into his waters IV. xi. 34. 3
Ne thence the Irishe *Rivers* absent were, IV. xi. 40. 1
In three great *rivers* ran, IV. xi. 42. 9
Of Gods, of Nymphs, of *rivers,* yet unred; IV. xii. 2. 7
from the Ocean all *rivers* spring, VI. Pr. 7. 4
Nymphes, of *Rivers* all: For all those *Rivers* to me subject are, VII. vii. 26. 7, 8
Both of the *rivers* and the forrests greene, *Epith.* 38
Rives. Her shattered ribs in thousand peeces *rives,* V. ii. 50. 3
Riving. Rashing off helmes, and *ryving* plates asonder, V. iii. 8. 6
Road. *See* **Rode.**
we be come unto a quiet *rode,* I. xii. 42. 2
making nightly *rode* Into their neighbours borders; VI. viii. 35. 3
Roam. *rome* from place to place III. i. 22. 4
round about did *rome* IV. xii. 4. 5
She forth did *rome* whether her rage her bore, V. viii. 48. 6
better so To lodge then in the salvage fields to *rome.* VI. ix. 16. 7
Roamed. Beares, Lyons, and Buls, which *romed* them arownd. III. i. 14. 9
romed round about the rocke in vaine, IV. xii. 17. 2
as there he *romed* up and downe, VI. xi. 27. 1
Roaming. *roming* through the field with greedie rage *Bel.*[2] vi. 6
still *roming* here and there; As a dismayed Deare III. xii. 17. 7
Roar. all the sea did *roare* like heavens thunder, *Van.* v. 11
he gan full terribly to *rore,* *Hub.* 1337
she made them *roare* againe. *Col.* 223
His tombling billowes rolls with gentle *rore;* I. ix. 4. 8
like a Lyon he would cry and *rore,* I. x. 28. 2
He cryde, as raging seas are wont to *rore* I. xi. 21. 1
hundred ramping Lions seemd to *rore,* I. xi. 37. 3
all the forest quakes to heare him *rore:* II. viii. 42. 7
Doth *rore* at them in vaine, II. xii. 5. 9
the billowes *rore* Outragiously, II. xii. 22. 1
dreadfull noise and hollow rombling *rore* II. xii. 25. 3
gainst the craggy clifts did loudly *rore,* III. iv. 7. 5
the beast, that lowd did *rore* III. vii. 36. 3
Like as a Lion . . . doth rage and *rore,* IV. iv. 32. 6
The Lyons *rore;* the Tygres loudly bray; IV. x. 46. 3
made the rockes to *roare* as they were rent. IV. xi. 12. 5
all the raging seas for joy forgot to *rore.* IV. xi. 23. 9
They snuf, they snort, they bounce, they rage, they *rore,* V. ii. 15. 6
with the noise, whilest he did loudly *rore,* VI. vi. 22. 8
the beast doth rage and loudly *rore;* VI. vii. 47. 6
Full cruelly the Beast did rage and *rore* VI. xii. 31. 1
no more Him liberty was left aloud to *rore:* VI. xii. 36. 5
Roared. all the way he *roared* as he went, *Hub.* 1345
he *roar'd* alowd, as he were wood, *Hub.* 1352
with death opprest He *ror'd* aloud, I. iii. 42. 9
Thereat he *rored* for exceeding paine, I. viii. 17. 1
many beasts, that *roard* outrageously, II. xii. 39. 2
Rored and raged to be underkept; III. vii. 33. 8
waves, which rag'd and *ror'd* IV. xi. 3. 6
Roaring. *Roaring* yet lowder that all harts it daunted, *Hub.* 1368
Horrible, hideous, *roaring* with hoarse crie.' *Col.* 199
wyld *roring* Buls he would him make To tame, I. vi. 24. 6
he would . . . make the Libbard sterne Leave *roaring,* I. vi. 25. 9
Lyonesse . . . *roaring* all with rage I. vi. 27. 6
throw in raging sea with *roaring* threat. I. x. 20. 8
they heard a *roaring* hideous sownd, I. xi. 4. 1

Roaring—*Continued.*
An hideous *roring* far away they heard, II. xii. 2. 6
There shall a Lion . . . come *roring,* III. iii. 47. 3
Eftesoones the *roaring* billowes still abid, III. iv. 32. 7
As shee arrived on the *roring* shore, III. vii. 27. 2
The *roring* billowes in their proud disdaine, III. viii. 37. 3
(whereat he raves With *roring* rage, III. ix. 45. 4
The *roring* billowes beat his bowre so boystrously. III. x. 58. 9
each abacke rebowndes With *roaring* rage; IV. i. 42. 4
fast bound in yron chaine, And, *roring* horribly, VI. xii. 35. 4
let the *roring* Organs loudly play *Epith.* 218
in their *roring* taking great delight; *H.L.* 48
Roast. does not so felly *roste.'* II. vi. 50. 9
Rob. The shepheards there *robben* one another, *S.C.* S. 38
all the rest doo *rob* of good and land. *Hub.* 140
did he all the kingdome *rob* and pill, *Hub.* 1198
Wont to *robbe* churches of their ornaments, I. iii. 17. 2
to thinke to *robbe* him of his pray. I. xi. 41. 9
Who it to *rob* and ransacke did intend. II. vii. 32. 5
woodmen which *robbe* and rend All traveilers: III. x. 40. 6
pitty did the Virgins hart of patience *rob.* III. xi. 8. 9
sacrilege me seem'd the Church to *rob,* IV. x. 53. 3
search out those that usd to *rob* and steale, V. xii. 26. 7
Now comest thou to *rob* my house unmand, VI. i. 25. 4
Thieves should *rob* and spoile that Coast around: VII. vi. 55. 6
smiles, that *rob* sence from the hart; *Am.* xvii. 10
it can *rob* both sense, and reason blynd? *H.B.* 77
Robbed. Was *rob'd* of rest and naturall reliefe. *Hub.* 16
this wretched world, whom he *Robd* of all right *Ti.* 294
Robbed of sense, and ravished with joy: *Ti.* 321
robd her race of bountie quight. *D.* 221
that witch they . . . *robd* of roiall robes, I. viii. 46. 2
Lyon, which hath long time saught His *robbed* whelpes, II. viii. 40. 8
read, what wicked hand hath *robbed* mee II. viii. 54. 1
they *robbed* bare Of bounty, and of beautie, III. vi. 4. 8
robd the world of threasure endlesse deare, IV. ii. 33. 4
hearts quite *robbed* with so glorious sight, IV. iv. 16. 5
As to have *robde* you of that manly hew? V. vii. 40. 7
robbed all the countrie there about, V. ix. 4. 8
Robbed her people that full rich had beene, V. x. 25. 7
like to one distraught And *robd* of reason, VI. xi. 45. 8
Which they from many long had *robd* and rent, VI. xi. 51. 3
robd the Chancell, and the deskes downe threw, VI. xii. 25. 2
th' heavenly riches which she *robd* erewhyle. *H.B.* 119
Robberies. fild with treasure rackt with *robberies;* *Hub.* 1306
Robbers. And lastly, how twixt *robbers* crucifyde, *H.H.L.* 244
Robbery. Thou canst preserve from wrong and *robbery?'* II. vii. 20. 4
Robbing. *See* **Heart-robbing.**
robbing me of the swete sonnes sight? *S.C.* F. 174
Robe. His precious *robe* I saw embrued with bloud. *Rev.* iii. 5
rosy fingred Morning faire, . . . Had spred her purple *robe* I. ii. 7. 3
spoile her of her scarlot *robe,* and let her fly.' I. viii. 45. 9
purple *robe* gored with many a wound, II. vii. 13. 7
In *robe* of lilly white she was arayd, II. ix. 19. 1
tooke on him the *robe* of Emperoure: II. x. 57. 8
Without or *robe* or rag to hide his shame; II. x. 58. 3
Ease, on his *robe* in golden letters cyphered. III. xii. 4. 9
As with a *robe,* with her owne silver haire, IV. xi. 11. 8
All decked in a *robe* of watchet hew, IV. xi. 27. 2
transfigured Her linnen stole to *robe* of scarlet red, V. vii. 13. 5
Robes. White seem'd her *robes,* yet woven so *Pet.* vi. 5
embellished With royall *robes* and gorgeous array, I. iv. 8. 4
roiall *robes,* and purple pall, I. viii. 46. 2
all in yellow *robes* arayed still. I. x. 30. 9
Arayd in antique *robes* downe to the grownd, I. xii. 5. 2
In ragged *robes* and filthy disaray; II. iv. 4. 2
richly cladd in *robes* of royaltye, II. vii. 44. 7
There were rent *robes* and broken scepters plast; IV. i. 21. 4
All clad in linnen *robes* with silver hemd; V. vii. 4. 4
richly clad In roiall *robes,* and many jewels dight; V. xi. 60. 7
Clad like a Queene in royall *robes,* *H.H.B.* 185
Robs. *Robs* reason of her dew regalitie, II. i. 57. 5
robs the harts of those which it admyre; *H.B.* 61
Rock. a fresh spring rise out of a *rocke,* *Bel.*[1] x. 1
a spring out of a *rocke* forth rayle, *Bel.*[2] xii. 1
Under a *Rocke,* where she, alas, opprest, *Pet.* i. 11
Strake on a *rock* (*rocke*[1]), that under water lay, *Pet.* ii. 9
out of a (the[1]) *rocke* did rise A spring *Pet.* iv. 1
Against a *Rocke* to breake with dreadfull poyse: *Ro.* xvi. 4
On everie bush, and everie hollow *rocke,* *Gn.* 235
trickling streame from high *rock* tumbling downe, I. i. 41. 2
So stood these twaine, unmoved as a *rocke,* I. ii. 16. 7
a ship, . . . An hidden *rocke* escaped hath I. vi. 1. 2
As *rock* of Diamond stedfast evermore. I. vi. 4. 5
Hewen out of Adamant *rocke* with engines keene, I. vii. 33. 7
Forth gushed, like fresh water streame from riven *rocke.* I. viii. 10. 9
As if in Adamant *rocke* it had beene pight. I. xi. 25. 5
Built on a *rocke* adjoyning to the seas: II. ii. 12. 7
'On thother syde an hideous *Rocke* is pight II. xii. 4. 1
They on this *rock* are rent, II. xii. 4. 9
On thother side they saw that perilous *Rocke,* II. xii. 7. 1
Forthy this hight The *Rocke* of vile Reproch, II. xii. 8. 1
To shunne *Rocke* of Reproch, II. xii. 9. 9
On th' other side an high *rocke* toured still, II. xii. 30. 5
on the *rocke* the waves breaking aloft II. xii. 33. 3
an hideous hollow cave (they say) Under a *Rock* III. iii. 8. 4
From under that deepe *Rock* III. iii. 9. 9
could have made a *rocke* of stone to rew, III. v. 30. 2
mightie *rocke,* gainst which doe rave III. viii. 37. 2
Sad Clotho held the *rocke,* IV. ii. 48. 5

Rock—*Continued.*
water-sprinkles gainst a *rocke* are dasht. . . . IV. iii. 25. 9
seem'd a *rocke* of Diamond it could rive . . . IV. v. 37. 8
Deepe in the bottome of an huge great *rocke* . . . IV. xi. 3. 1
all about that *rocke* the sea did flow: . . . IV. xii. 15. 5
romed round about the *rocke* in vaine, . . . IV. xii. 17. 2
when a *rocke* Is lightly stricken . . . V. i. 21. 6
beheld a mighty Gyant stand Upon a *rocke,* . . . V. ii. 30. 2
down the *rock* him throwing, . . . V. ii. 49. 9
whom cruell tempest drives Upon a *rocke* . . . V. ii. 50. 2
wonned in a *rocke* not farre away, . . . V. ix. 4. 7
the *rocke,* in which he wonts to dwell, . . . V. ix. 6. 2
ny Unto the *rocke* where was the villains won: . . . V. ix. 8. 2
The Damzell went . . . Unto the *rocke;* . . . V. ix. 9. 7
Up to the *rocke* he ran, . . . V. ix. 15. 3
seem'd a marble *rocke* asunder could have rive. . . . V. xi. 5. 9
hard and obstinate, As is a *rocke* . . . *Am.* lvi. 10
Rocked. dull wearines . . . Having *yrockt* asleepe his irkesome spright, . . . I. i. 55. 5
all the Graces *rockt* her cradle being borne. . . . III. vi. 2. 9
Rock's. continuall feare Of that *rocks* fall, . . . III. x. 58. 4
Rocks. Some on the *rocks* of Caphareus are throwne; . . . *Gn.* 586
strikes the *rockes* with his three-forked mace; . . . *Mui.* 315
lost emong those *rocks* into him rold, . . . *Col.* 154
round about with mightie white *rocks* hemd, . . . *Col.* 274
Doth roll adowne the *rocks,* . . . I. viii. 22. 9
Shee, . . . lurkt in *rocks* and caves, . . . I. viii. 50. 5
high trees overthrew, and *rocks* in peeces tore. . . . I. xi. 37. 9
belch out flames, and *rockes* in peeces broke, . . . I. xi. 44. 6
Lurking in *rockes* and caves far under ground, . . . II. i. 22. 3
threatning to make the pray Of the rough *rockes,* . . . II. ii. 24. 3
both from *rocks* and flats it selfe could wisely save. . . . II. vi. 5. 9
Out of the *rockes* and caves adjoyning nye; . . . II. ix. 13. 3
Learning his ship from those white *rocks* to save, . . . II. x. 6. 3
Ziffius, whom Mariners eschew No lesse then *rockes,* . . . II. xii. 24. 8
On the rough *rocks,* or on the sandy shallowes, . . . III. iv. 9. 4
the hard *rocks* could scarse from tears refraine; . . . III. iv. 35. 7
on the *rockes* he fell so flit and light, . . . III. x. 57. 5
made the *rockes* to roare as they were rent. . . . IV. xi. 12. 5
by often beating Doe pearce the *rockes,* . . . IV. xii. 7. 2
These towring *rocks,* which reach unto the skie, . . . V. ii. 38. 3
Through woods, and *rocks,* and mountaines . . . V. viii. 41. 5
over *rockes,* and hilles, and every place Where so he fled, . . . V. ix. 16. 4
all the woods and *rockes* nigh to that way . . . V. xii. 41. 4
the streight, and *rocks* among) . . . VI. i. 13. 7
appointed have her place Mongst *rocks* and caves, . . . VI. vi. 11. 4
springs out of two marble *Rocks,* . . . VII. vi. 41. 1
Rocky. I saw a Wolfe under a *rockie* cave . . . *Bel.*[2] vi. 1
High growing on the top of *rocky* clift, . . . I. viii. 22. 6
Did hang upon the ragged *rocky* knees; . . . I. ix. 34. 3
huge *rocky* clift, Whose false foundacion waves have washt away, . . . I. xi. 54. 5
Lyke an huge cave hewne out of *rocky* clifte, . . . II. vii. 28. 2
sitting downe upon the *rocky* shore, . . . III. iv. 7. 2
in a *rocky* cave, as wight forlorne, . . . III. iv. 20. 3
a strong *rocky* Cave, . . . Hewen underneath that Mount, . . . III. vi. 48. 8
he came unto a *rocky* hill . . . III. x. 56. 3
ruth it moved in the *rocky* stone, . . . IV. xii. 5. 7
his hard *rocky* hart for no entreating Will yeeld, . . . IV. xii. 7. 3
uppon yond *rocky* hill, . . . VI. i. 13. 1
Rod. with the budding *rod* Did rule the Jewes, . . . *Hub.* 439
In her right hand a broken *rod* she held, . . . *Ti.* 13
On either side disparted with his *rod,* . . . I. x. 53. 4
in his hand a white *rod* menaged: . . . II. ix. 27. 7
Caduceus, the *rod* of Mercury, . . . II. xii. 41. 3
Stretch her white *rod* over the Belgicke shore, . . . III. iii. 49. 7
In her right hand a *rod* of peace shee bore, . . . IV. iii. 42. 1
Like to the *rod* which Maias sonne doth wield, . . . IV. iii. 42. 6
Shee with her *rod* did softly smite the raile, . . . IV. iii. 46. 2
the Goddesse with her *rod* him backe did beat. . . . V. vii. 15. 9
His scepter is the *rod* of Righteousnesse, . . . *H.H.B.* 155
Rode. *See* **Road, Rad.**
And ever as he *rode* his hart did earne . . . I. i. 3. 6
A lovely Ladie *rode* him faire beside, . . . I. i. 4. 1
And after him she *rode,* . . . I. ii. 8. 1
So forth they *rode,* he feining seemely merth, . . . I. ii. 27. 8
With whome, as once I *rode* accompanyde, . . . I. ii. 35. 6
by his side *rode* loathsome Gluttony, . . . I. iv. 21. 1
as he *rode* he somewhat still did eat, . . . I. iv. 22. 5
next to him *rode* lustfull Lechery . . . I. iv. 24. 1
malicious Envy *rode* Upon a ravenous wolfe, . . . I. iv. 30. 1
Still as he *rode* he gnasht his teeth . . . I. iv. 31. 6
after all, upon the wagon beame, *Rode* Sathan . . . I. iv. 36. 2
Emongst the rest *rode* that false Lady faire, . . . I. iv. 37. 4
Upright he *rode,* . . . II. i. 18. 8
rode in golden sell with single spere, . . . II. iii. 12. 3
Upon a Tygre swift and fierce he *rode,* . . . II. xi. 20. 4
him beside an aged Squire there *rode,* . . . III. i. 4. 3
Then to the next she *rode,* . . . III. i. 28. 9
The Redcrosse Knight diverst, but forth *rode* Britomart. . . . III. iii. 62. 9
forth she *rode,* without repose or rest, . . . III. iv. 6. 6
forward *rode,* and kept her ready way . . . III. iv. 18. 2
but to the lady *rode;* . . . III. viii. 19. 2
afterwardes on what adventure now he *rode.* . . . III. viii. 45. 9
Alone he *rode* without his Paragone; . . . III. x. 35. 6
forth he *rode* as his adventure fell; . . . III. x. 38. 4
Lo! thus they *rode,* . . . IV. i. 17. 1
Such was that hag which with Duessa *roade;* . . . IV. i. 31. 1
With whom as they thus *rode* accompanide, . . . IV. ii. 4. 1
So, well accorded, forth they *rode* together . . . IV. ii. 29. 1

Rode—*Continued.*
Two knights that lincked *rode* in lovely wise, . . . IV. ii. 30. 3
all the way they *rode:* . . . IV. iv. 5. 5
So as he *rode* with them accompanide, . . . IV. iv. 7. 6
where so they *rode* or came, . . . IV. iv. 13. 3
Unto whose rescue forth *rode* Paridell; . . . IV. iv. 19. 8
On whom remounting fiercely forth he *rode,* . . . IV. iv. 23. 4
Against her *rode,* full of despiteous ire, . . . IV. vi. 11. 4
as through that wood he *rode,* . . . IV. viii. 19. 1
So forth she *rode* uppon her ready way, . . . V. vi. 18. 1
Sadly she *rode,* and never word did say . . . V. vi. 18. 3
rode him selfe uppon his first intent, . . . V. viii. 3. 6
ever as she *rode* her eye was backeward bent. . . . V. viii. 4. 9
after those two former *rode* apace . . . V. viii. 5. 2
On which long way he *rode,* . . . V. xi. 35. 9
as they *rode* together on their way, . . . V. xi. 43. 6
as he and I together *roade* Upon our way . . . VI. ii. 16. 1
forth together *rode,* a comely couplement. . . . VI. v. 24. 9
So forth they *rode* together all in troupe . . . VI. v. 32. 1
He found the gate wyde ope, and in he *rode,* . . . VI. vi. 19. 2
as they *rode* he saw the way all dyde . . . VI. vii. 17. 5
sturdy March . . . *rode* upon a Ram, . . . VII. vii. 32. 4
Upon a Bull he *rode,* . . . VII. vii. 33. 3
Upon a Crab he *rode,* . . . VII. vii. 35. 5
Upon a Lyon . . . He boldly *rode,* . . . VII. vii. 36. 4
Yet *rode* he not, but led a lovely Mayd . . . VII. vii. 37. 3
Whereon he *rode* not easie was to deeme; . . . VII. vii. 40. 7
Upon a shaggy-bearded Goat he *rode,* . . . VII. vii. 41. 5
Roderick. *Rhodoricke,* whose surname shal be Great, . . . III. iii. 45. 1
Roe. he was long, and swift as any *Roe,* . . . III. xi. 5. 8
Roebuck. The hartlesse Hynd and *Robucke* to dismay, . . . II. ii. 7. 4
flying fast as *Roebucke* through the fen, . . . II. x. 7. 5
overleapes them all, like *Robucke* light, . . . IV. vii. 22. 2
Roebucks. the *Robuckes* in flight to overtake, . . . I. vi. 24. 8
Roffin. what my selfe knowe Chaunced to *Roffynn* . . . *S.C.* S. 171
Roffy. Ere *Roffy* could for his laboure him thanck. . . . *S.C.* S. 201
Roffy is wise, and as Argus eyed,) . . . *S.C.* S. 203
had not *Roffy* renne to the steven, . . . *S.C.* S. 224
Rogues. For feare least we like *rogues* should be reputed, . . . *Hub.* 187
Roin. softly *royne,* when salvage choler gan redound. . . . V. ix. 33. 9
Rold. *See* **Rolled.**
Roll. *See* **Bead-roll.**
rolle with rest in rymes of rybaudrye; . . . *S.C.* O. 76
did *roll* downe from his hill Huge mightie stones, . . . *Col.* 149
trunck, . . . Doth *roll* adowne the rocks, . . . I. viii. 22. 9
Did *roll* too lightly, and too often glaunce, . . . III. i. 41. 8
To stirre and *roll* them like to womens eyes: . . . III. viii. 7. 4
Whom when on ground she groveling saw to *rowle,* . . . IV. vii. 32. 1
on his head a *roll* of linnen plight, . . . VI. vii. 43. 5
Rolled. lost emong those rocks into him *rold,* . . . *Col.* 154
Through midst thereof a little river *rold,* . . . II. i. 24. 6
rolled on an heape, lay still in swound . . . IV. i. 43. 1
rould in clouds to heaven did aspire, . . . IV. x. 38. 4
at her feete a Crocodile was *rold,* . . . V. vii. 6. 8
rudely *rowld* to ground, both man and horse, . . . VI. i. 33. 8
the clouds are also tost and *roll'd,* . . . VII. vii. 20. 8
Rolling. *See* **Down-rolling.**
passing by with *rolling* wreathed pace, . . . *Gn.* 253
Rolling in rymes of shameles ribaudrie . . . *T.M.* 213
Rolling like mountaines in wide wildernesse, . . . *Col.* 198
In *rolling* globes up to the vauted skies. . . . *Col.* 611
The *rolling* billowes beate the ragged shore, . . . I. xi. 21. 3
rolling downe great Neptune doth dismay: . . . I. xi. 54. 8
Adowne the *rolling* river she did poure, . . . II. x. 19. 7
The waves come *rolling,* . . . II. xii. 22. 1
the *rolling* sea, resounding soft, . . . II. xii. 33. 1
His *rolling* eies did never rest in place, . . . III. xii. 15. 6
rolling thence the stone, Which wont to stop the mouth . . . IV. vii. 20. 4
the river *rolling* still With murmure soft, . . . IV. x. 15. 8
There was the Liffy *rolling* downe the lea, . . . IV. xi. 41. 1
And search the courses of the *rowling* spheares, . . . V. Pr. 5. 2
The *rolling* wheele that runneth often round, . . . *Am.* xviii. 1
that mightie bound which doth embrace The *rolling* Spheres, . . . *H.H.L.* 26
Rolls. Against a mountaine *rolls* a mightie stone, . . . *Gn.* 391
Lay forth . . . The antique *rolles,* . . . I. Pr. 2. 4
His tombling billowes *rolls* with gentle rore; . . . I. ix. 4. 8
His chamber all was hangd about with *rolls* . . . II. ix. 57. 6
And *rolls* of Elfin Emperours, . . . II. x. Arg.
those *rolles,* layd up in heaven above, . . . IV. xi. 10. 3
when the *roules* were red . . . VI. vii. 33. 1
Roman. glory of the *Romaine* peares (*Romane* lordes[1]). . . . *Bel.* iv. 8
Seven *Romane* Hils, the worlds Seven Wonderments. . . . *Ro.* ii. 14
Nought from the *Romane* Empire might be quight; . . . *Ro.* viii. 10
Romane palaces Made of some matter no less firme . . . *Ro.* ix. 7
Puft up with pride of *Romane* hardiehead, . . . *Ro.* xi. 3
With which he had those *Romane* spirits fild, . . . *Ro.* xi. 6
Should boast himselfe of the *Romane* Empire, . . . *Ro.* xi. 14
heaped was On these seven *Romane* hils, . . . *Ro.* xii. 10
The *Romane* triumphs glorie to behold, . . . *Ro.* xiv. 12
the ruin'd pride Of these old *Romane* works, . . . *Ro.* xv. 13
That *Romane* Eagle seene to cleave asunder, . . . *Ro.* xvii. 10
He well foresaw how that the *Romane* courage, . . . *Ro.* xxiii. 5
Who list the *Romane* greatnes forth to figure, . . . *Ro.* xxvi. 1
the *Romaine* Daemon Doth yet himselfe . . . enforce, . . . *Ro.* xxvii. 12
So grew the *Romane* Empire by degree, . . . *Ro.* xxx. 9
the *Romaine* Empire bore the raine Of all the world . . . *Van.* xi. 1
delivered unto me By *Romane* Victors, . . . *Ti.* 38
having overcome The *Romane* legion . . . II. x. 60. 8
Whome *Romane* warres . . . could no whit dismay; . . . II. x. 62. 6
that rich *Romane* of white marble wrought, . . . III. xii. 46. *or.* 3

Roman—*Continued.*
Such as that prudent *Romane* well invented, IV. ii. 2. 7
That *Romaine* Monarch built a brasen wall, IV. xi. 36. 2
there flowed forth the *Romane* Flood. VII. vii. 42. 9
Romans. Was this (ye *Romanes*) your hard destinie, *Ro.* xxiv. 9
with the *Romanes* fought, *Ti.* 110
Till the prowde *Romanes* him disquieted, II. x. 47. 5
Soone after this the *Romanes* him warrayd; II. x. 50. 8
Did drive the *Romanes* to the weaker syde, II. x. 51. 8
never king more . . . dredd of *Romanes,* II. x. 52. 2
Romanes daily did the weake subdew: II. x. 54. 5
gainst the *Romanes* bent their proper powre; II. x. 57. 6
Which when the *Romanes* heard, II. x. 59. 1
Romans'. The Antique ruins of the *Romanes* fall: I. v. 49. 4
Tybris, renowmed for the *Romaines* fame, IV. xi. 21. 6
Romble, *etc. See* **Rumble,** *etc.*
Rome. *See* **Roam.**
great rivers banck, that runnes by *Rome;* *Bel.* i. 6
for *Rome* in *Rome* here seekest, *Ro.* iii. 1
nought of *Rome* in *Rome* perceiv'st at all, *Ro.* iii. 2
that which *Rome* men call. *Ro.* iii. 4
Rome now of *Rome* is th' onely funerall, *Ro.* iii. 9
onely *Rome* of *Rome* hath victorie; *Ro.* iii. 10
O *Rome!* thee let him see, *Ro.* v. 2
Rome is no more: but if the shade of *Rome* May . . . yeeld *Ro.* v. 5
The corpes of *Rome* in ashes is entombed, *Ro.* v. 9
Rome onely might to *Rome* compared bee, *Ro.* vi. 9
onely *Rome* could make great *Rome* to tremble: *Ro.* vi. 10
doo the name of *Rome* retaine, *Ro.* vii. 2
Through armes and vassals *Rome* the world subdu'd, *Ro.* viii. 1
so oft thee, (*Rome*) their conquest made; *Ro.* xiii. 4
Rome, in the time of her great ancesters, *Ro.* xix. 7
Rome was th' whole world, and al the world was *Rome;* *Ro.* xxvi. 9
then name ye *Rome;* *Ro.* xxvi. 11
naming *Rome,* ye land and sea comprize: *Ro.* xxvi. 12
th' auncient Plot of *Rome,* displayed plaine, *Ro.* xxvi. 13
Thou that at *Rome* astonisht dost behold *Ro.* xxvii. 1
marke how *Rome* . . . Renewes herselfe *Ro.* xxvii. 9
Rome, living, was the worlds sole ornament, *Ro.* xxix. 13
Olde *Rome* out of her ashes to revive, *Ro.* Env. 5
a Goose great *Rome* from ruine stayde, *Van.* xi. 9
To *Rome,* (if such be *Rome*) *S.C.* Jul. 183
Descended all from *Rome* by linage due; *Gn.* 596
Rome, that holds the world in sovereigntie, *Gn.* 597
'O *Rome!* thy ruine I lament and rue, *Ti.* 78
And taught ambitious *Rome* to tyrannise *Ded. Son.* i. 3
sacked *Rome* too dearely did assay, II. x. 40. 3
this land was tributarie made T' ambitious *Rome,* II. x. 49. 7
shortly he renounst the vassallage Of *Rome* againe, II. x. 52. 6
Who afterward was Emperour of *Rome,* II. x. 60. 2
whose victorious Exployts made *Rome* to quake; III. iii. 54. 8
Romulus, renewing it, to *Rome* remoud.' III. ix. 43. 9
Of fatall Thebes; of *Rome* that raigned long; IV. i. 22. 2
Romish. the *Romish* Tityrus . . . left his Oaten reede, *S.C.* O. 55
Rompe. *See* **Rump.**
Romulus. Great *Romulus,* the Grandsyre of them all; I. v. 49. 5
Romulus, renewing it, to Rome remoud.' III. ix. 43. 9
Rong. *See* **Rang, Rung.**
Early and late it *rong,* at evening and at prime. II. ix. 25. 9
Did shrieke alowd, that through the hous it *rong,* III. i. 62. 6
Gan shout aloud, that unto heaven it *rong;* V. xi. 34. 2
Ronne, *etc. See* **Run,** *etc.*
Ront, -s. *See* **Runt, -s.**
Rood. Deckt all the roofe, and, shadowing the *roode,* VI. v. 35. 3
Roof. Both *roofe,* and floore, and walls, were all of gold, II. vii. 29. 1
golden pillours did upbeare The massy *roofe,* II. vii. 43. 6
The *roofe* hereof was arched over head, II. ix. 46. 1
through the *roofe* of her strong brasen towre III. xi. 31. 3
The *roofe* up high was reared from the ground, IV. x. 37. 5
being all with Yvy overspred Deckt all the *roofe,* VI. v. 35. 3
Rook. skin all withered like a dryed *rooke;* II. xi. 22. 3
Room. *See* **House-room, Kitchen-room.**
Let that *rowme* to my Lady be yeven: *S.C.* Ap. 114
let an happie *roome* remaine for thee *Gn.* 57
From *rowme* to *rowme,* from beam to beame *Hub.* 1373
in her *roome* unseemly Sorrow sits, *T.M.* 184
Full envious that night so long his *roome* did fill: I. ii. 1. 9
A gentle Husher, Vanitie by name, Made *rowme,* I. iv. 13. 4
Through every *rowme* he sought, I. viii. 37. 1
he, that points the Centonell his *roome,* I. ix. 41. 8
yield his *rowme* to sad succeeding night, I. xi. 49. 6
him that raignd into his *rowme* thrust downe, II. vii. 11. 8
In all that *rowme* was nothing to be seene II. vii. 30. 1
shortly brought Unto another *rowme,* II. vii. 35. 2
The *rowme* was large and wyde, II. vii. 43. 3
brought them to the second *rowme,* II. ix. 53. 2
Of those that *rowme* was full; II. ix. 54. 1
led to th' hindmost *rowme* of three. II. ix. 54. 9
His sonne Rivall' his dead *rowme* did supply; II. x. 34. 1
Octavius here lept into his *roome,* II. x. 60. 4
forth were led Into an inner *rowme,* III. i. 33. 2
spare to one, or two, or three, *Rowme* in their writtes; III. ii. 1. 8
yield her *rowme* to day that can it governe well.' III. iv. 60. 9
in her hart finde highest *rowme* III. v. 11. 3
crave but *rowme* to rest while tempest overblo'th.' III. vii. 8. 9
the Championesse now entred has The utmost *rowme,* III. xi. 27. 8
The utmost *rowme* abounding with all precious store: III. xi. 27. 9
at the upper end of that faire *rowme* III. xi. 47. 1
forward with bold steps into the next *roome* went. III. xi. 50. 9
Much fayrer then the former was that *roome,* III. xi. 51. 1

Room—*Continued.*
the inner *rowme* from whence they first did rise. III. xii. 26. 9
Forthy from that same *rowme* not to depart III. xii. 28. 3
Ne living wight she saw in all that *roome,* III. xii. 30. 5
was let adowne to fall Into a lower *roome,* V. vi. 27. 8
Each *rowme* she sought, but them all empty fond. V. vi. 35. 8
Went up the hall, that was a large wyde *roome,* V. ix. 23. 2
He fled from *roome* to *roome,* VI. vi. 29. 6
Room's. she spyde at that *rowmes* upper end III. xi. 54. 6
Rooms. Working her formall *rowmes* in wexen frame, *S.C.* D. 68
purchace highest *rowmes* in bowre and hall: *Col.* 726
Therein were divers *rowmes,* II. ix. 47. 6
These three in these three *rowmes* did sondry dwell, II. ix. 48. 8
those goodly *rowmes,* which erst She saw III. xii. 42. 1
Root. *See* **Heart-root.**
I saw the *roote* in great (hie[1]) disdaine *Bel.* v. 13
rent this royall tree quite by the *roote;* *Pet.* iii. 12
to the *roote* bent his sturdy stroake, *S.C.* F. 201
That art the *roote* of all this ruthfull woe! *S.C.* Jun. 116
The *roote* whereof and tragicall effect, Vouchsafe, *Mui.* 9
I the . . . *roote* of Duessaes race. I. v. 27. 7
wicked woman . . . The *roote* of all your care I. viii. 45. 5
the cause and *root* of all his ill, I. x. 25. 1
Occasion; the *roote* of all wrath and despight. II. iv. 10. 9
deeme them *roote* of all disquietnesse; II. vii. 12. 2
Whose *root* and stalke so bitter yet did taste, III. ii. 17. 6
Thou art the *roote* and nourse of bitter cares, III. iv. 57. 2
it of honor and all vertue is The *roote,* IV. Pr. 2. 7
from one *roote* deriv'd their vitall sap: IV. ii. 43. 6
like that *roote* that doth her life divide, IV. ii. 43. 7
Thou art the *root* of all that joyous is: IV. x. 47. 6
Nought could she read the *roote* of his disease, IV. xii. 22. 1
Who was the *root* and worker of her woe, IV. xii. 29. 2
then I am shee Which was the *roote* of all: V. viii. 11. 9
roote of civill conversation: VI. i. 1. 6
oaken plant, which lately hee Rent by the *root;* VI. vii. 24. 8
sweet is Moly, but his *root* is ill. *Am.* xxvi. 8
Whose *root* from earths base groundworke shold begin. *H.H.L.* 105
Rooted. *See* **Deep-rooted.**
Throughly *rooted,* and of wonderous hight; *S.C.* F. 107
All things not *rooted* well will soone be rotten.' IV. i. 51. 5
Till ye have *rooted* all the relickes out V. xi. 18. 6
shortly should the progeny of man Be *rooted* out, VII. vi. 31. 9
Rooting. thence th' Imperiall Eagle *rooting* tooke, *Ro.* xviii. 10
a sore evill . . . First *rooting* tooke; III. iii. 16. 6
Roots. Shewing her wreathed *rootes,* and naked armes, *Ro.* xxviii. 6
Theyr *rootes* bene dryed up *S.C.* D. 111
moysten their *roots* dry; III. vi. 34. 8
from his *rootes* doth reare; V. vi. 40. 7
Rope. About his neck an hempen *rope* he weares, I. ix. 22. 7
he of *rope* or armes has now no memoree. I. ix. 22. 9
To me he lent this *rope,* to him a rusty knife. I. ix. 29. 9
Led in a *rope* which both his hands did bynd; VI. vii. 49. 2
Ropes. brought unto him swords, *ropes,* poison, fire, I. ix. 50. 6
Rosalind. Colin them gives to *Rosalind* againe. *S.C.* Ja. 60
So nowe fayre *Rosalind* hath bredde hys smart, *S.C.* Ap. 27
Queene-apples unrype, To give my *Rosalind;* *S.C.* Jun. 44
faithlesse *Rosalind* and voide of grace, *S.C.* Jun. 115
Rosalend (who knowes not *Rosalend?*) *S.C.* Au. 141
those that did thy *Rosalind* complayne, *S.C.* N. 44
who has wrought my *Rosalind* this spight, *S.C.* D. 113
Tell *Rosalind,* her Colin bids her adieu.' *S.C.* D. 156
Faire *Rosalind* of divers fowly blamed *Col.* 908
How rashly blame of *Rosalind* ye raise.' *Col.* 926
Rose. *rose* to so great might, *Ro.* xviii. 9
The Redde *rose* medled with the White yfere, *S.C.* Ap. 68
The *Rose* engrained in pure scarlet die; *Gn.* 666
White as the native *Rose* before the chaunge *D.* 108
'She is the *Rose,* the glorie of the day, *D.* 232
kisse thy lips like faded leaves of *rose.* *As.* 138
Then up he *rose,* and clad him hastily: I. ii. 6. 8
Up Una *rose,* up *rose* the lyon eke; I. iii. 21. 2
forth she *rose,* ne lenger would abide, I. v. 19. 3
he no lenger would There dwell . . . But earely *rose;* I. v. 52. 5
The Sarazin, this hearing, *rose* amain, I. vi. 41. 7
up he *rose,* and thence amounted streight. I. ix. 54. 1
Both horse and man up lightly *rose* againe, I. xi. 17. 1
Titan *rose* to runne his daily race; I. xi. 33. 2
Up *rose* the gentle virgin from her place, I. xi. 33. 5
he *rose* for to remove aside Those pretious hils II. vii. 6. 2
a large lukewarme flood, Red as the *Rose,* II. viii. 39. 2
right faire and fresh as morning *rose,* II. ix. 36. 7
see the Virgin *Rose,* how sweetly shee II. xii. 74. 4
Gather therefore the *Rose* whilest yet is prime, II. xii. 75. 6
Gather the *Rose* of love whilest yet is time, II. xii. 75. 8
As hee that hath espide a vermeill *Rose,* III. i. 46. 6
That daintie *Rose,* the daughter of her Morne, III. v. 51. 1
to the Goddesse *rose;* III. vi. 19. 8
in his strength he *rose,* IV. iii. 30. 1
Judges *rose,* and Marshals of the field IV. iii. 35. 3
Faire Canacee, as fresh as morning *rose,* IV. iii. 51. 7
up he *rose,* like heavie lumpe of lead, IV. v. 45. 6
Rose in his strength, and gan her fresh assayle, IV. vi. 16. 4
Therewith she *rose* in hast, IV. viii. 10. 5
evermore some of the vertuous race *Rose* up, V. i. 1. 7
They *rose* in armes, and all in battell order stood. V. ii. 51. 9
Then did the trompets sound, and Judges *rose,* V. iii. 13. 6
To hide the blush which in her visage *rose* V. v. 30. 2
Decking her cheeke with a vermilion *rose;* V. v. 30. 4
Then up she *rose* fraught with melancholy, V. vii. 17. 5

Rose—*Continued.*
then the Law of Nations gainst her *rose,* . . . V. ix. 44. 3
Rose many advocates for her to plead: . . . V. ix. 45. 2
Then up she *rose,* . . . V. xii. 12. 1
Like as a tender *Rose* in open plaine, . . . V. xii. 13. 1
Then up they *rose,* and gan them selves to dight . . . VI. v. 40. 5
The people of the house *rose* forth . . . VI. vi. 22. 9
up he *rose,* and forth streightway he went . . . VI. vii. 14. 1
Then all the rest about her *rose* likewise, . . . VI. ix. 15. 3
Out of the wood he *rose,* . . . VI. x. 17. 9
like a *rose* her silken leaves did faire unfold. . . . VI. xii. 7.9
with these eyes did view The litle purple *rose* . . . VI. xii. 18. 5
In which that *rose* she plainely saw displayd: . . . VI. xii. 19. 5
So forth she *rose,* . . . VII. vi. 23. 7
Sweet is the *Rose,* but grows upon a brere; . . . *Am.* xxvi. 1
when the *rose* in her red cheekes appeares; . . . *Am.* lxxxi. 3
With *rose* and lillies over them displayd. . . . *H.L.* 286
Rosemary. *See* **Rosmarine.**
The knotted rush-ringes, and gilte *Rosemaree?* . . . *S.C.* N. 116
The Marigolde, and cherefull *Rosemarie;* . . . *Gn.* 668
Rosemarys. *See* **Rosmarines.**
throw into the well sweet *Rosemaryes,* . . . III. i. 36. 7
Roses. With Damaske *roses* and Daffadillies set: . . . *S.C.* Ap. 60
girlonds of *roses,* and Sopps in wine. . . . *S.C.* May 14
The *Roses* raigning in the pride of May, . . . *Mui.* 189
From her red cheeks the *roses* rent away; . . . *As.* 160
With *Roses* dight and Goolds and Daffadillies; . . . *Col.* 339
silver deaw upon the *roses* pearling. . . . *Col.* 507
Like *roses* in a bed of lillies shed, . . . II. iii. 22. 6
His prickling armes, entrayld with *roses* red, . . . II. v. 29. 5
Upon a bed of *Roses* she was layd, . . . II. xii. 77. 1
Emongst the *Roses* grow some wicked weeds: . . . III. i. 49. 6
She bath'd with *roses* red and violets blew, . . . III. vi. 6. 8
in her cheekes made *roses* oft appeare: . . . IV. x. 50. 5
As *roses* did with lilies interlace; . . . V. iii. 23. 5
ruddy cheekes, lyke unto *Roses* red . . . *Am.* lxiv. 6
Another gay girland . . . of lillyes and of *roses,* . . . *Epith.* 43
How the red *roses* flush up in her cheekes, . . . *Epith.* 226
With store of vermeil *Roses,* . . . *Proth.* 33
Rosier. crowned with a garland of sweete *Rosiere.* . . . II. ix. 19. 9
Rosmarine. *See* **Rosemary.**
Colde Lettuce, and refreshing *Rosmarine.* . . . *Mui.* 200
Rosmarines. *See* **Rosemarys.**
greedy *Rosmarines* with visages deforme. . . . II. xii. 24. 9
Rosseponte. By faire Kilkenny and *Rosseponte* boord; . . . IV. xi. 43. 4
Rosy. fayre Aurora, with her *rosie* heare, . . . *Gn.* 68
with *rosie* garland crownd! . . . *D.* 312
A *Rosy* girlond was the victors meede. . . . I. ii. 37. 5
With *rosy* cheekes, for shame as blushing red: . . . I. xi. 51. 4
Crownd with a *rosie* girlond . . . VI. x. 14. 5
Chaunst to espy upon her yvory chest The *rosie* marke, . . . VI. xii. 15. 6
The *Rosy* Morne long since left Tithones bed, . . . *Epith.* 75
those sweete *rosy* leaves, so fairely spred . . . *H.B.* 94
lips, like *rosy* buds in May, . . . *H.B.* 258
Rosy-fingered. *rosy fingred* Morning faire, . . . Had spred her purple robe . . . I. ii. 7. 1
Rosy red. Loaden with fruit and apples *rosy redd,* . . . I. xi. 46. 2
rosy red Did paint his chearefull cheekes, . . . II. i. 41. 4
ever and anone with *rosy red* . . . II. ix. 41. 3
the *rosy red* Flasht through her face, . . . III. ii. 5. 6
Spoild of their *rosy red* were woxen pale and wan. . . . III. v. 29. 9
Rot. as superfluous flesh did *rott,* . . . I. x. 26. 6
Rote. worthy of great Phoebus *rote,* . . . II. x. 3. 2
The faire Poeana playing on a *Rote* . . . IV. ix. 6. 2
As she had learned readily by *rote;* . . . IV. ix. 6. 5
Rother. the *Rother,* decked all with woods . . . IV. xi. 33. 1
Rots. that foule evill, . . . That *rotts* the marrow, . . . I. iv. 26. 8
Rotted. Through rusty elde, that hath *rotted* thee: . . . *S.C.* F. 54
rotted ere they were halfe mellow ripe; . . . *S.C.* D. 107
Rotten. on her trunke, all *rotten* and unsound, . . . *Ro.* xxviii. 7
cast hem out as *rotten* and unsoote. . . . *S.C.* D. 118
long while after I am dead and *rotten,* . . . *Col.* 640
Her teeth out of her *rotten* gummes were feld, . . . I. viii. 47. 4
All things not rooted well will soone be *rotten.'* . . . IV. i. 51. 5
rived were like *rotten* wood asunder; . . . IV. iii. 15. 6
Rough. feeble flocke, whose fleece is *rough* and rent, . . . *S.C.* Ja. 43
my rymes bene *rough,* and rudely drest; . . . *S.C.* Jun. 77
for his *rough* hide He gan to reach, . . . *Hub.* 1335
My tender sides in this *rough* rynd embard; . . . I. ii. 31. 3
next her wrinkled skin *rough* sackecloth wore, . . . I. iii. 14. 3
Who *rough,* and blacke, and filthy, did appeare, . . . I. iv. 24. 5
frowning forheades, with *rough* hornes yclad, . . . I. vi. 11. 5
Her wrizled skin, as *rough* as maple rind, . . . I. viii. 47. 8
threatning to make the pray Of the *rough* rockes, . . . II. ii. 24. 3
From whose *rough* vaut the ragged breaches hong . . . II. vii. 28. 3
On the *rough* rocks, or on the sandy shallowes, . . . III. iv. 9. 4
his *rough* hond Where ill became him . . . III. viii. 25. 6
the cold ysickles from his *rough* beard . . . III. viii. 35. 3
rough Masons hand with engines keene . . . III. viii. 37. 6
Embraced of a Satyre *rough* and rude, . . . III. x. 48. 3
A Ladie on *rough* waves row'd in a sommer barge. . . . VI. ii. 44. 9
Sweet is the Firbloome, but his braunche is *rough;* . . . *Am.* xxvi. 4
Rougher-rinded. the *rougher rinded* Pine, . . . *Gn.* 209
Roughly. All were my notes but rude and *roughly* dight; . . . *Col.* 363
And *roughly* wrought in an unlearned Loome: . . . *Ded.Son.*vii.13
When with the maistring spur he did him *roughly* stire. . . . II. v. 2. 9
roughly him bespake: . . . II. vii. 63. 6
Rould. *See* **Rolled.**
Round. Him behooves to vew in compasse *round* . . . *Ro.* xxvi. 5
dirks the beauty of my blossomes *rownd:* . . . *S.C.* F. 134

Round—*Continued.*
his trees of state in compasse *rownd:* . . . *S.C.* F. 146
wandred, I wene, about the world *round,* . . . *S.C.* S. 22
carroll lowde, and leade the Myllers *rownde,* . . . *S.C.* O. 52
if thy rymes as *rownde* and rufull bene . . . *S.C.* N. 43
that most hideous snake Enwrapped *round,* . . . *Gn.* 306
sitting all in seates about me *round,* . . . *Hub.* 25
your silken hyde Fil'd with *round* flesh, . . . *Hub.* 592
Nymphes about them flocking *round,* . . . *Mui.* 295
The Shepheards daughters dauncing in a *rownd!* . . . *D.* 310
Amongst the shepheards daughters dancing *rownd,* . . . *Col.* 641
The fruitfull Olive; and the Platane *round;* . . . I. i. 9. 8
kindling rage her selfe she gathered *round,* . . . I. i. 18. 2
Gathred themselves about her body *round,* . . . I. i. 25. 4
a calme shadowe far in compasse *round:* . . . I. ii. 28. 6
Ne ever wont in field, ne in *round* lists, to fight: . . . I. iii. 38. 9
they passe, all gazing on them *round,* . . . I. iv. 7. 1
Sisyphus an huge *round* stone did reele . . . I. v. 35. 3
Faunes . . . were dauncing in a *rownd,* . . . I. vi. 7. 8
Thence lead her forth, about her dauncing *round,* . . . I. vi. 13. 6
Engin, . . . ramd with bollet *rownd,* ordaind to kill, . . . I. vii. 13. 4
as a Castle, reared high and *round,* . . . I. viii. 23. 1
Disordred hong about his shoulders *round,* . . . I. ix. 35. 5
about him soared *round;* . . . I. xi. 18. 7
A noble crew about them waited *rownd* . . . I. xii. 5. 4
hurtle *rownd* in warlike gyre, . . . II. v. 8. 7
Some in *round* plates withouten moniment; . . . II. vii. 5. 7
a blacke flood, which flow'd about it *round.* . . . II. vii. 56. 7
Sought with his raskall routs t' enclose them *rownd,* . . . II. ix. 15. 4
in another great *rownd* vessell plaste, . . . II. ix. 32. 3
Like many swarmes of Bees assembled *round,* . . . II. ix. 51. 4
Like to a restlesse wheele, still ronning *round,* . . . II. xii. 20. 6
it *round* and hollow shaped was, . . . III. ii. 19. 8
displayd The clothes about her *round* . . . III. ii. 47. 5
When so he counseld with his sprights encompast *round.* . . . III. iii. 7. 9
All fretted *round* with gold, and goodly wel beseene. . . . III. iii. 58. 9
Whiles on his broad *rownd* backe they softly slid, . . . III. iv. 32. 2
Their watchet mantles frindgd with silver *rownd,* . . . III. iv. 40. 5
the Nymphes sitt all about him *rownd,* . . . III. iv. 44. 1
The Christall humor stood congealed *rownd;* . . . III. v. 29. 4
Mount, on whose *round* top A gloomy grove . . . III. vi. 43. 2
all their goodly heardes did gather *rownd;* . . . III. x. 46. 2
dim the brightnesse of the welkin *rownd,* . . . III. x. 46. 7
her small waste girt *rownd* with yron bands . . . III. xii. 30. 8
With thornes and barren brakes environd *round,* . . . IV. i. 20. 5
Now hurtling *round* advantage for to take: . . . IV. iv. 29. 7
An hundred knights had him enclosed *round,* . . . IV. iv. 31. 6
in her wheeling *round,* . . . So sorely he her strooke, . . . IV. vi. 13. 2
Upon an hundred marble pillors *round* . . . IV. x. 37. 4
it encompast *round* as with a golden fret. . . . IV. xi. 27. 9
His charret wheeles about him whirled *round,* . . . V. viii. 36. 2
beat about him *round;* . . . VI. v. 19. 4
were raunged in a ring, And daunced *round;* . . . VI. x. 12. 2
hasting Prime did make them burgein *round.* . . . VII. vii. 43. 8
Now hornd, now *round,* now bright, . . . VII. vii. 50. 8
hir teeth be Pearles, both pure and *round;* . . . *Am.* xv. 9
The rolling wheele that runneth often *round,* . . . *Am.* xviii. 1
(Not this *round* heaven, which we from hence behold, . . . *H.H.L.* 58
On that bright shynie *round* still moving Masse, . . . *H.H.B.* 51
Round about. *See* **About, Round.**
he did himselfe dispace There *round about,* . . . *Gn.* 266
hideous heavinesse Is *round about* me heapt . . . *Gn.* 372
fluttering *round about* them . . . *Gn.* 406
Tost on salt billowes, *round about* doth stray. . . . *Gn.* 592
round about he taught sweete flowres to growe: . . . *Gn.* 665
warders *round about* them stood: . . . *Hub.* 1351
he arriving *round about* doth flie, . . . *Mui.* 169
round about her worke she did empale . . . *Mui.* 297
round about doth goe Like a Mill-wheele . . . *D.* 431
round about us it doth make aboad! . . . *As.* 90
round about them feed at libertie. . . . *Col.* 55
round about with mightie white rocks hemd, . . . *Col.* 274
He sought all *round about,* . . . I. v. 15. 2
house of Pryde, and perilles *round about;* . . . I. vii. 26. 6
sunny beames . . . *round about* her head did shine . . . I. x. 12. 9
Thus flocked all the folke him *rownd about;* . . . I. xii. 12. 1
Before, behind, and *round about* him laies; . . . II. ii. 25. 8
round about a cloud of dust did fly, . . . II. iv. 37. 4
round about the wreath this word was writ, . . . II. iv. 38. 4
round about him threw forth sparkling fire, . . . II. v. 2. 6
The smouldring dust did *rownd about* him smoke, . . . II. v. 3. 4
daintie odours *round about* them threw: . . . II. v. 29. 6
rownd about him dissolute did play . . . II. v. 32. 5
round about him lay on every side . . . II. vii. 5. 1
dead mens bones, which *round about* were flong; . . . II. vii. 30. 7
all that preace did *rownd about* her swell . . . II. vii. 46. 5
their bright Squadrons *round about* us plant; . . . II. viii. 2. 7
*hath the Sunne . . . Walkt *round about* the world, . . . II. ix. 7. 6
A thousand villeins *rownd about* them swarmd . . . II. ix. 13. 2
rownd about the porch on every syde . . . II. ix. 26. 1
Close *rownd about* her tuckt with many a plight: . . . II. ix. 40. 6
round about in fittest steades did place, . . . II. xi. 6. 2
round about him flocke impetuously, . . . II. xi. 18. 3
Goodly it was enclosed *rownd about,* . . . II. xii. 43. 1
strowed *rownd about;* . . . II. xii. 49. 2
all the margent *round about* was sett With . . . II. xii. 63. 1
round about them pleasauntly did sing . . . II. xii. 72. 7
gathering him *rownd about* more neare, . . . III. i. 23. 3
The wals were *round about* appareiled . . . III. i. 34. 1
rownd about it many beds were dight, . . . III. i. 39. 2

Round about—*Continued.*
round about yfretted all with gold, ... III. ii. 25. 4
round about the Pots mouth bound the thread; . . . . . III. ii. 50. 3
her *rownd about* she from her turnd, ... III. ii. 51. 1
round about, as she could well it uze, ... III. v. 33. 5
With mountaines *rownd about* environed, ... III. v. 39. 3
round about the walls yclothed were . . . . III. xi. 28. 1
round about a border was entrayld . . . . III. xi. 46. 6
He looked *round about* with sterne disdayne, ... III. xii. 23. 2
rownd about Shee cast her eies . . . . III. xii. 30. 1
all the dores to rattle *round about:* . . . . III. xii. 37. 2
round about Her tender waste . . . . III. xii. 37. 7
in compasse *round About* her backe . . . . IV. i. 13. 4
round about themselves awhile did gaze; . . . . IV. ii. 17. 3
There she them found all sitting *round about,* . . . . . . IV. ii. 48. 1
looking *round about,* like one dismaid, ... IV. iv. 22. 3
with his brondiron *round about* him layd; . . . . IV. iv. 32. 3
looking *round about* him, none could see, ... IV. v. 44. 8
round about the same her yellow heare, ... IV. vi. 20. 1
Throwes forth upon the rivage *round about* him nere. . . . IV. vi. 20. 9
round about doth stie, ... IV. ix. 33. 5
'An hundred Altars *round about* were set, ... IV. x. 38. 1
round about him many a pretty Page . . . . IV. xi. 29. 1
round about did rome . . . . IV. xii. 4. 5
romed *round about* the rocke in vaine, ... IV. xii. 17. 2
Amongst the flags and covert *round about.* . . . . V. ii. 54. 6
round about her tender wast it fitted well. . . . . . . V. iii. 27. 9
round about his necke an halter tight, ... V. iv. 22. 3
They *round about* him gan to swarme apace, ... V. iv. 23. 7
shattered all to peeces *round about* the plaine. . . . . . V. v. 10. 9
he *round about* him saw Many brave knights, ... V. v. 22. 1
round about him preace in riotous aray. . . . . V. vi. 29.9
ever *round about* he cast his looke: . . . . V. ix. 11. 5
round about before her feet there sate . . . . V. ix. 31. 1
flocking *round about* them, as a swarme Of flyes . . . . V. xi. 58. 1
Which when the people *round about* him saw, ... V. xii. 24. 1
round about her jawes one might descry The bloudie gore . . V. xii. 30. 8
Foming with poyson *round about* her gils, ... V. xii. 36. 2
the rest which *round about* you ring, ... VI. Pr. 7. 7
like a wilde goate *round about* did chace . . . . VI. iii. 49. 3
heaped strokes did *round about* him haile . . . . VI. v. 18. 3
dangerously did *round about* enclose: . . . . VI. v. 20. 3
round about with boystrous strokes oppresse, ... VI. vi. 26. 2
Traceth his ground, and *round about* doth beat, ... VI. vii. 47. 4
Then looking *round about,* . . . . VI. viii. 32. 4
So *round about* her they them selves did place . . . . . VI. viii. 39. 1
round about her flocke, like many flies, ... VI. viii. 40. 2
round about Environ'd with a girland, ... VI. ix. 8. 2
round about was bordered with a wood . . . . VI. x. 6. 2
the rest them *round about* did hemme, ... VI. x. 12. 4
round about her move in order excellent. . . . . VI. x. 13. 9
round about him scattreth wide. . . . . VI. xi. 48. 9
Out of their townes did *round about* him throng, ... VI. xii. 37. 4
the starres, which *round about* her blazed, ... VII. vi. 13. 6
round about such beames of splendor threw, ... VII. vii. 6. 7
sleep and darknesse *round about* did trace: . . . . VII. vii. 44. 7
Through hidden perils *round about* me plast; . . . . . . *Am.* xxxiv. 8
Shall fly and flutter *round about* your bed, ... *Epith.* 359
Rounded. in his eare him *rownded* close behinde: . . . . III. x. 30. 4
Roundel. sike a *roundle* never heard I none: . . . . . *S.C.* Au. 125
Ne bubling *rowndell* they behinde them sent. . . . . . . III. iv. 33. 7
Roundelay. Now gynneth this *roundelay.* . . . . *S.C.* Au. 56
Now endeth our *roundelay.'* . . . . *S.C.* Au. 124
Roundelays. to heare thy rymes and *roundelayes,* . . . . *S.C.* Jun. 49
Roundels. should it not yshend Your *roundels* fresh, . . . *S.C.* Au. 140
Roundly. Her golden lockes she *roundly* did uptye . . . . II. ii. 15. 7
Roundness. Both heaven and earth in *roundnesse* compassing; *Ro.* iv. 4
Both land and sea in *roundnes* had survew'd, ... *Ro.* viii. 3
Rouse. *rouze* thy feathers quickly, Daniell, ... *Col.* 424
an Eagle . . . His aery plumes doth *rouze,* . . . . I. xi. 9. 6
rowze as comming late from rest. . . . . II. iii. 35. 9
Then *rouze* thy selfe, O Earth! out of thy soyle, ... *H.H.L.* 218
Roused. He *rousd* himselfe full blyth, ... I. xi. 4. 9
Such noyse his *rouzed* scales did send unto the knight. . . I. xi. 9. 9
wilde Bores late *rouzd* out of the brakes: . . . . II. xi. 10. 5
the Briton Prince him *rouzd* Out of his holde, ... II. xi. 33. 1
Rashly out of their *rouzed* couches sprong, ... III. i. 62. 8
Rousing. *rouzing* up himselfe, ... *Hub.* 1335
Rout. a naked *rout* of Faunes With hideous cry . . . . . *Bel.*[1] x. 11
A troupe of Satyres in the place did *rout,* . . . . *Bel.*[2] xii. 12
A rulesse *rout* of yongmen which her woo'd, ... *Gn.* 431
Then made they revell *route* and goodly glee; . . . . . . *Hub.* 558
a ragged *rout* Of Faunes and Satyres, ... *T.M.* 267
the listning *rout* Of shepherd groomes, ... *Ti.* 227
So as he rag'd emongst that beastly *rout,* . . . . *As.* 115
A *route* of people there assembled were, ... II. vii. 44. 1
when they had that troublous *rout* disperst, ... II. ix. 17. 1
He them encountred, a confused *rout,* . . . . II. x. 16. 1
after them a rude confused *rout* Of persons flockt, ... III. xii. 25. 1
Did all that youthly *rout* so much appall, ... IV. ii. 40. 3
thorough rude confusion of the *rout,* . . . . IV. iii. 41. 6
rushed forth out of the thickest *rout* . . . . IV. iv. 43. 7
They gan to gather in tumultuous *rout,* . . . . V. ii. 51. 3
none appear'd of all that raskall *rout,* . . . . V. ii. 54. 8
A *rout* of many people farre away; . . . . V. iv. 21. 3
their Queene . . . Came forth into the *rout,* . . . . . . V. iv. 36. 9
Then all that *rout* uppon them rudely laid, ... V. iv. 38. 7
to barre the *rout* From rudely pressing . . . . V. v. 6. 6
amongst the warlike *rout* Of errant Knights, ... V. vi. 6. 5
A raskall *rout,* with weapons rudely dight; . . . . V. vi. 29. 4

Rout—*Continued.*
armed Knights and eke unarmed *rout;* . . . . V. vi. 30. 3
mongst the *rout* Of Bacchus Priests, ... V. viii. 47. 5
gainst all that warlike *rout* Of knights . . . . V. viii. 50. 2
'What is there else' (sayd he) 'left of their *rout?* . . . . . V. xi. 18. 8
A *rout* of people they before them kend, ... V. xi. 43. 7
Of a rude *rout* him chasing to and fro, ... V. xi. 44. 3
that rude *rout* Them also gan assaile . . . . V. xi. 47. 2
The lustie shepheard swaynes sate in a *rout,* . . . . . . VI. ix. 8. 5
Amongst that rusticke *rout* . . . . VI. ix. 45. 2
piped there unto that merry *rout;* . . . . VI. x. 16. 2
the Brigants . . . entred in a *rout:* . . . . VI. xi. 46. 5
Routs. O, how the rurall *routes* to thee doe cleave! . . . . *S.C.* O. 26
Huge *routs* of people did about them band, ... I. iv. 36. 5
the endlesse *routes* of wretched thralles, ... I. v. 51. 1
when him list the raskall *routes* appall, ... I. vii. 35. 5
with his raskall *routs* t' enclose them rownd, ... II. ix. 15. 4
Rouze, *etc. See* **Rouse,** *etc.*
Rove. At that good knight so cunningly didst *rove,* . . . . I. Pr. 3. 3
Still did she *rove* at her with crafty glaunce . . . . . . III. i. 50. 6
Proteus abrode did *rove,* . . . . III. viii. 29. 8
here did *rove* In straunge disguize, ... III. xi. 30. 3
and doe at randon *rove* . . . . V. Pr. 6. 5
He . . . in that rage gan *rove* . . . . VI. ii. 20. 7
he to seeke Serena through the woods did *rove.* . . . . . VI. viii. 46. 9
Roved. She *rovde* at me with glauncing eye, ... *S.C.* Au. 79
He *rov'd* at her, and told his secret care . . . . III. ix. 28. 3
Ne *rov'd* at randon, after gazers guyse, ... IV. x. 49. 8
Even at the marke-white of his hart she *roved,* . . . . . V. v. 35. 8
Roving. His *roving* eie did on the Lady glaunce . . . . . IV. iv. 7. 7
Row. *See* **Rew.**
bevie of Ladies bright, Raunged in a *rowe?* . . . . *S.C.* Ap. 119
Such one vile Envy was, that fifte in *row* did sitt. . . . . I. iv. 32. 9
all dauncing on a *row,* The comely virgins came, ... I. xii. 6. 5
my wandring ship I *row,* . . . . II. vi. 10. 2
he the boteman bad *row* easily, ... II. xii. 33. 8
th' one did *row,* and th' other stifly steare; . . . . . . II. xii. 37. 4
without ship or bote her thence to *row,* . . . . IV. xii. 15. 7
With all her Nymphes enranged on a *rowe,* . . . . VII. vi. 39. 7
Rowed. Ere long they *rowed* were quite out of sight, . . . II. xi. 4. 5
So forth they *rowed;* . . . . II. xii. 10. 1
turnd her bote about, and from them *rowed* quite. . . . . II. xii. 16. 9
A Ladie on rough waves *row'd* in a sommer barge. . . . . VI. ii. 44. 9
Rowels. The yron *rowels* into frothy fome he bitt. . . . . I. vii. 37. 9
Rowing. that wide strond Where she was *rowing,* . . . . . II. vi. 19. 3
Rowme, -s. *See* **Room, -s.**
Rowne. The Cle, the Were, the Grant, the Sture, the *Rowne.* . IV. xi. 34. 5
Rows. bound in sheaves, and layd in comely *rowes,* . . . . *Ro.* xxx. 7
strongly he them *rowes,* . . . . II. xii. 5. 1
love it steres, and fortune *rowes:* . . . . III. iv. 9. 5
Royal. rent this *royall* tree quite by the roote; . . . . . *Pet.* iii. 12
Elisa, decked as thou art In *royall* aray; . . . . *S.C.* Ap. 146
home they bringen in a *royall* throne, ... *S.C.* May 29
'From *royall* Court I lately came (said he) . . . . *Hub.* 607
Those *royall* ornaments to steale away? . . . . *Hub.* 998
He all those *royall* signes had stolne away, ... *Hub.* 1016
freely up those *royall* spoyles he tooke, ... *Hub.* 1059
thy throne *royall* with dishonour blent: . . . . *Hub.* 1330
the *royall* Beast forbore beleeving, ... *Hub.* 1365
our *royall* thrones, which lately stood . . . . *T.M.* 313
her *royall* P'laces Be fild with praises . . . . *T.M.* 580
Twelve Gods doo sit around in *royall* state, ... *Mui.* 307
'Ne let Elisa, *royall* Shepheardesse, . . . envy, ... *D.* 225
found I lyking in her *royall* mynd, ... *Col.* 454
by descent from *Royall* lynage came . . . . I. i. 5. 3
The *royall* virgin shooke off drousy-hed; . . . . I. ii. 7. 5
Soone as the *royall* virgin he did spy, ... I. iii. 5. 4
most brave embellished With *royall* robes and gorgeous array, I. iv. 8. 4
Why they were come her *roiall* state to see, ... I. iv. 13. 8
Suddein upriseth from her stately place The *roiall* Dame, . . I. iv. 16. 2
to match, in *roiall* rich array, Great Junoes golden chayre; I. iv. 17. 4
With *royall* pomp and princely majestie . . . . I. v. 5. 2
the whiles the *royall* Mayd Fledd farre away, ... I. vi. 47. 8
He . . . her endowd with *royall* majestye. . . . . I. vii. 16. 5
The *roiall* Virgin . . . Came running fast . . . . I. viii. 26. 1
full rich arayd he found, With *royall* arras, ... I. viii. 35. 2
robd of *roiall* robes, and purple pall, ... I. viii. 46. 2
a *royall* Mayd Her daintie limbes . . . down did lay: . . . I. ix. 13. 7
Forgoe that *royal* maides bequeathed care, ... I. x. 63. 7
High reard their *royall* throne in Britans land, ... I. x. 65. 4
purveyaunce meet Of all, that *royall* Princes court became; I. xii. 13. 6
The large discourse of *roiall* Princes state. . . . . I. xii. 14. 6
sayd that *royall* Pere in sober wise; . . . . I. xii. 17. 1
Most false Duessa, *royall* richly dight, ... I. xii. 32. 4
Then stepped forth the goodly *royall* Mayd, ... I. xii. 33. 1
In which her *roiall* presence is enrold; . . . . II. ii. 44. 4
Parlour . . . with *royall* arras richly dight, ... II. ix. 33. 7
that *royall* mace Which now thou bear'st, ... II. x. 4. 3
roiall stocke of old Assaracs line, ... II. x. 9. 7
O! the greedy thirst of *royall* crowne, ... II. x. 35. 1
the *roiall* throne forlorne. . . . . II. x. 36. 5
on him tooke the *roiall* Diademe, ... II. x. 47. 3
The *royall* Ofspring of his native land, ... II. x. 69. 2
The *roiall* riches and exceeding cost . . . . III. i. 32. 4
At last the *royall* Mayd . . . did awake, ... III. i. 61. 7
The *royall* Maid woxe inly wondrous glad, ... III. ii. 11. 1
Be it worthy of thy race and *royall* sead, ... III. ii. 33. 4
the *royall* Infant fell Into her former fitt; . . . . III. ii. 49. 1
in this *royall* Maid of yore, ... III. iii. 3. 3
The *royall* seed, the antique Trojan blood, ... III. iii. 42. 8

Royal—*Continued.*
Of *roiall* majesty and soveraine name: . . . III. iii. 48. 8
Then shall a *royall* Virgin raine, . . . III. iii. 49. 6
To heare so often, in that *royall* hous, . . . III. iii. 54. 2
So farre from court and *royall* Citadell, . . . III. vi. 1. 5
In *royall* heart disdaining to be thrall. . . . IV. iv. 32. 7
Then loyall love had *royall* regiment, . . . IV. viii. 30. 7
th' onely remnant of that *royall* breed, . . . IV. viii. 33. 8
The *royall* child with readie quicke foresight . . . IV. viii. 44. 8
after them the *royall* issue came, . . . IV. xi. 12. 6
The *royall* banquets, and the rare delights, . . . V. iii. 3. 5
Virgin, that . . . doest maske thy *royall* blood, . . . V. vii. 21. 2
royall gifts of gold and silver wrought . . . V. vii. 24. 4
grace, with which her *royall* crowne She doth support, . . . V. viii. 17. 4
roiall pompe, which there long hidden lay, . . . V. viii. 51. 5
She, Angel like, . . . in *royall* state, . . . V. ix. 29. 8
Holding a Scepter in her *royall* hand, . . . V. ix. 30. 2
goodly seem'd t' adorne her *royall* state; . . . V. ix. 31. 3
Thus did she sit in *royall* rich estate, . . . V. ix. 33. 1
Royall examples of her mercies rare . . . V. x. 5. 6
gave him *roiall* giftes and riches rare, . . . V. x. 17. 2
clad In *roiall* robes, and many jewels dight; . . . V. xi. 60. 7
Upon him tooke the *roiall* high degree, . . . VI. ii. 28. 8
Seeing his *royall* usage and array . . . VI. v. 41. 7
leaving home, to *roiall* court I sought, . . . VI. ix. 24. 6
in it She used most to keepe her *royall* court, . . . VI. x. 9. 7
There vertue raynes as Queene in *royal* throne, . . . *Epith.* 194
whereas the *royall* Seates . . . are set, . . . *H.H.B.* 89
Clad like a Queene in *royall* robes, . . . *H.H.B.* 185

Royally. '*Royally* clad' (quoth he) 'in cloth of gold, . . . III. v. 5. 2
so rich and *royally* arayd, . . . III. xii. 42. 2
of all men *royally* be seene, . . . V. ix. 27. 4
this, that seem'd so faire And *royally* arayd, . . . V. ix. 40. 2

Royalties. to your willes both *royalties* and Reames Subdew, . III. v. 53. 3

Royalty. richly cladd in robes of *royaltye,* . . . II. vii. 44. 7
whose *royaltee* And rich purveyance might uneath be red; . III. i. 33. 2
entertayne The greatest Prince with pompous *roialty:* . . . *Am.* lxxvii. 4

Royne. *See* **Roin.**

Rub. recovering hart, he does begin To *rubb* her temples, . . . I. vii. 21. 5

Rubbed. Shee softly felt, and *rubbed* busily, . . . III. ii. 34. 4
rubd his temples and each trembling vaine; . . . III. v. 31. 7

Rubies. If *Rubies,* loe, hir lips be *Rubies* sound; . . . *Am.* xv. 8
The gate with pearles and *rubyes* richly dight; . . . *Am.* lxxxi. 10

Rubine. Some as the *Rubine* laughing sweetely red, . . . II. xii. 54. 8

Rubines. twixt the perles and *rubins* softly brake A silver sound, . . . II. iii. 24. 8

Rubs. the left hand *rubs* the right.' . . . IV. i. 40. 9

Ruby. a *Ruby* of right perfect hew, . . . IV. viii. 6. 7

Rudacus, Rudaucus. *See* **Ruddoc.**

Rudded. Her cheekes lyke apples which the sun hath *rudded,* . *Epith.* 173

Rudder. turne thy *rudder* hitherward awhile . . . II. xii. 32. 6

Ruddoc. *Ruddoc* and proud Stater, both allyes, . . . II. x. 38. 3

Ruddock. The Ouzell shrills; the *Ruddock* warbles soft; . . . *Epith.* 82

Ruddy. *ruddy* Phebus gins to welke in west, . . . I. i. 23. 2
His *ruddy* lips did smyle, . . . II. i. 41. 4
light Out of the *ruddy* East was fully reard, . . . III. x. 52. 7
Whilest through their rifts the *ruddie* bloud did showre, . . . IV. iii. 15. 7
Like to the *ruddie* morne appeard in sight, . . . IV. vi. 19. 6
ruddy cheekes, lyke unto Roses red; . . . *Am.* lxiv. 6

Ruddymane. He might . . . Be called *Ruddymane;* . . . II. iii. 2. 8

Rude. my pype, albee *rude* Pan thou please, . . . *S.C.* Ja. 67
I am but *rude* and borrell, . . . *S.C.* Jul. 95
Rude ditties, tund to shepheards Oaten reede, . . . *S.C.* D. 14
unfit for that *rude* rabblement. . . . *Hub.* 1270
sway in Court with pride and rashnes *rude;* . . . *T.M.* 328
Much greater than the *rude* report . . . *D.* 146
with your loves do their *rude* hearts possesse, . . . *D.* 527
All were my notes but *rude* and roughly dight; . . . *Col.* 363
former dayes Had in *rude* fields bene altogether spent, . . . *Col.* 669
Rude rymes, the which a rustick Muse did weave . . . *Ded.Son.*vii.11
By this *rude* rime to memorize thy name, . . . *Ded.Son.*xii.2
the *rude* wench her answerd nought at all: . . . I. iii. 11. 3
her unruly Page With his *rude* clawes the wicket open rent, . I. iii. 13. 2
A *rude,* mishapen, monstrous rablement, . . . I. vi. 8. 7
In their *rude* eyes unworthie of so wofull plight. . . . I. vi. 9. 9
With sharpe intended sting so *rude* him smott, . . . I. xi. 38. 2
Heaped together in *rude* rablement, . . . I. xii. 9. 2
My ragged rimes are all too *rude* and bace . . . I. xii. 23. 4
Bad on that Messenger *rude* hands to reach. . . . I. xii. 35. 3
With stony feare of that *rude* rustick mate, . . . II. ii. 8. 8
In her *rude* heares sweet flowres themselves did lap, . . . II. iii. 30. 8
His *rude* assault and rugged handeling . . . II. iv. 8. 1
would not seeme so *rude,* and thewed ill, . . . II. vi. 26. 3
Not this *rude* kynd of battaill, . . . II. vi. 34. 2
rude owre, not purifide . . . II. vii. 5. 3
That houses forme within was *rude* and strong, . . . II. vii. 28. 1
rude hand upon his shield he laid, . . . II. viii. 17. 1
'Palmer, (said he) 'no knight so *rude,* I weene, . . . II. viii. 26. 1
Vile caitive wretches, ragged, *rude,* deformd, . . . II. ix. 13. 4
Broke their *rude* troupes, and orders did confownd, . . . II. ix. 15. 7
as yet ashamd how *rude* Pan did her dight. . . . II. ix. 40. 9
With their *rude* handes and gryesly graplement; . . . II. xi. 29. 3
the *rude* And scorned partes . . . II. xii. 59. 1
my rymes too *rude* and rugged arre, . . . III. ii. 3. 6
no lesse the knight feard then that villein *rude.* . . . III. iv. 50. 9
Vile rancour their *rude* harts had fild . . . III. v. 16. 9
gentle sprite deforme with *rude* rusticity. . . . III. vi. 1. 9
gan recomfort her in her *rude* wyse, . . . III. vii. 10. 1
Embraced of a Satyre rough and *rude,* . . . III. x. 48. 3
How the *rude* Shepheards after him did stare, . . . III. xi. 34. 7

Rude—*Continued.*
after them a *rude* confused rout Of persons flockt, . . . III. xii. 25. 1
these rimes, so *rude* as doth appeare, . . . IV. ii. 33. 7
thorough *rude* confusion of the rout, . . . IV. iii. 41. 6
Rude was his garment, and to rags all rent, . . . IV. v. 35. 1
entertaind him in so *rude* a wise, . . . IV. vi. 10. 6
All overgrowen with *rude* and rugged haire; . . . IV. vii. 43. 4
close appeard in that *rude* brutishnesse, . . . IV. vii. 45. 5
Upon the ground in ragged *rude* attyre, . . . IV. viii. 23. 6
They breaking forth with *rude* unruliment . . . IV. ix. 23. 5
preserv'd from yron rust Of *rude* oblivion . . . V. iv. 2. 8
to lay about With his *rude* yron flaile, . . . V. vi. 30. 2
Of a *rude* rout him chasing to and fro, . . . V. xi. 44. 3
To reskue her from their *rude* violence; . . . V. xi. 45. 2
that *rude* rout Them also gan assaile . . . V. xi. 47. 2
with *rude* flaring lockes About her eares, . . . V. xii. 38. 8
With which *rude* speach his Lady much displeased . . . VI. iii. 32. 6
to be so fowle abused Of a *rude* churle, . . . VI. iii. 33. 5
But the *rude* Porter that no manners had . . . VI. iii. 38. 1
by *rude* tokens made to her appeare His deepe compassion . . VI. iv. 11. 3
in *rude* wise him asked, what he was . . . VI. vi. 20. 2
rude hand on him did lay, To thrust him out of dore . . . VI. vi. 21. 8
my *rude* musick, which was wont to please . . . *Am.* xxxviii. 5

Rude-flaring. *See* **Flaring, Rude.**

Rudely. my rymes bene rough, and *rudely* drest; . . . *S.C.* Jun. 77
none of them he *rudely* doth disorder, . . . *Mui.* 174
my rymes bene *rudely* dight. . . . *As.* Pr. 12
Let thy faire Cinthias praises be thus *rudely* showne. . . . *Ded.Son.*viii.14
their Parent . . . so *rudely* falling to the ground, . . . I. i. 25. 2
rudely he him thrust, and pusht with paine, . . . I. i. 42. 4
themselves, too *rudely* rigorous, Astonied with the stroke . . I. ii. 15. 7
tombling *rudely* downe, to ground did rush, . . . I. iii. 35. 8
rudely rending up his helmet, . . . I. iii. 38. 2
whenas his soveraine Dame So *rudely* handled . . . he saw, . . I. iii. 41. 3
crowned mitre *rudely* threw asyde: . . . I. viii. 25. 3
His aery plumes doth rouze, full *rudely* dight; . . . I. xi. 9. 6
The pointed steele, arriving *rudely* theare, . . . I. xi. 16. 3
him so *rudely,* passing by, did brush . . . I. xi. 16. 8
Her looser golden lockes he *rudely* rent, . . . II. i. 11. 5
through the thicke they heard one *rudely* rush, . . . II. iii. 21. 1
him to ground he cast, and *rudely* hayld, . . . II. iv. 14. 7
rudely rag'd, and like a cruell tygre far'd. . . . II. v. 8. 9
he *rudely* flasht The waves about, . . . II. vi. 42. 6
To see Pyrochles there so *rudely* rage; . . . II. vi. 48. 7
That vertuous steele he *rudely* snatcht away, . . . II. viii. 22. 6
with his troncheon he so *rudely* stroke Cymochles . . . II. viii. 39. 8
To weete what they so *rudely* did require? . . . II. ix. 11. 8
rudely sdeigne a gentle harts request, . . . III. i. 55. 4
Smote him so *rudely* on the Pannikell, . . . III. v. 23. 5
Knotted with blood in bounches *rudely* ran; . . . III. v. 29. 6
rudely askte her, how she thither came? . . . III. viii. 23. 6
Rudely to her he he lept, . . . III. viii. 25. 6
They *rudely* drove to ground both man and horse, . . . III. ix. 16. 4
A little off his shield was *rudely* throwne, . . . III. xi. 7. 6
rudely tumbling downe under his horse-feete fell. . . . IV. iv. 30. 9
came *rudely* rushing in, . . . IV. vii. 20. 6
he threw her *rudely* on the flore, . . . IV. vii. 28. 1
rudely hayld her forth without remorse, . . . V. ii. 26. 3
His timbered bones all broken *rudely* rumbled: . . . V. ii. 50. 8
rudely stroke at him on every side; . . . V. ii. 53. 3
Then all that rout uppon them *rudely* laid, . . . V. iv. 38. 7
From *rudely* pressing to the middle center; . . . V. v. 5. 7
A raskall rout, with weapons *rudely* dight; . . . V. vi. 29. 4
She her so *rudely* on the helmet smit . . . V. vii. 33. 7
rudely rowld to ground, both man and horse, . . . VI. i. 33. 8
learne Strangers no more so *rudely* to entreat, . . . VI. i. 40. 7
abasht, . . . That he so *rudely* did uppon them light, . . . VI. iii. 21. 4
Mongst salvage beasts both *rudely* borne and bred, . . . VI. v. 2. 3
Him *rudely* rent and all to peeces tore; . . . VI. vi. 22. 6
Rudely thou wrongest my deare harts desire, . . . *Am.* v. 1
All were it, as the rest, but *rudely* writ? . . . *Am.* xxxiii. 8

Rudeness. See that your *rudenesse* doe not you disgrace: . . *S.C.* Ap. 132
the faire Scene with *rudenes* foule disguize. . . . *T.M.* 192
through our *rudenesse* into errour led, . . . *Col.* 796
leave the *rudenesse* of that antique age . . . II. vii. 18. 2
shamefully reproved for his *rudenes* fond. . . . III. viii. 25. 9
let not my *rudenes* be no breach Unto your patience, . . . III. x. 25. 3
I pardon yield, and with thy *rudenes* beare; . . . III. x. 31. 3
that fowle *rudenesse* which did her deface; . . . IV. ix. 14. 3
in the *rudenesse* of that evill plight . . . V. v. 12. 6
reprove Of *rudenesse* for not yeelding . . . VI. ii. 1. 8
Or curtesie with *rudenesse* to requite: . . . VI. iii. 41. 5
our *rudenesse* to your selfe aread.' . . . VI. ix. 33. 9

Ruder. The homely shepheard, nor the *ruder* clowne; . . . *Pet.* iv. 4
To teach the *ruder* shepheard how . . . *S.C.* Env. 5
even his *ruder* hart began to rew, . . . VI. iv. 3. 5
ne mote the *ruder* clowne, Thereto approch; . . . VI. x. 7. 4

Rudest. courtesie amongst the *rudest* breeds Good will . . . VI. ix. 45. 5

Rue. Least that the Poplar happely should *rew* Her brothers strokes, . . . *Gn.* 219
'O Rome! thy ruine I lament and *rue,* . . . *Ti.* 78
Ranke-smelling *Rue,* and Cummin good for eyes, . . . *Mui.* 188
since so much thou seemst to *rue* my griefe, . . . *D.* 92
stinking Smallage, and unsaverie *Rew;* . . . *D.* 347
ne will I *rew* That with your carkasses . . . *D.* 349
heavenly spirits . . . *rue* their miserie. . . . *D.* 385
rue my Daphnes wrong, And mourne for me . . . *D.* 537
carefull pipe may make the hearer *rew:* . . . *Col.* 397
That I must *rue* his undeserved wrong: . . . I. Pr. 2. 8
Die is my dew; yet *rew* my wretched state, . . . I. i. 51. 7

Rue—*Continued.*
'Deare dame, I *rew*, That . . . such griefe unto you grew. . . I. i. 53. 8
hart of flint would *rew* The undeserved woes . . . . I. ii. 26. 8
ever to have touched her I did deadly *rew*. . . . . I. ii. 40. 9
rightly may I *rew* The fall of famous children . . . . I. v. 25. 1
the thing, which daily yet I *rew*, ... I. v. 42. 2
Gan her admire, and her sad sorrowes *rew*, ... I. vi. 31. 4
'well may I *rew* To tell the sad sight . . . . I. vi. 36. 7
This fatall day that shall I ever *rew*, ... I. vi. 38. 2
Th' enchaunter vaine his errour should not *rew:* . . . . . . I. vi. 42. 8
Could make a stony hart his hap to *rew;* . . . . I. viii. 41. 5
As miserable lovers use to *rew*, ... I. ix. 9. 8
But vaine; for ye shall dearely do him *rew*, ... II. i. 25. 5
Mordant and Amavia did *rew*, ... II. ii. 45. 8
Who shall him *rew* . . . . II. vi. 17. 7
sure I *rew* his pitteous plight.' . . . . II. viii. 24. 5
Whose dolefull moniments who list to *rew*, ... II. x. 66. 8
Had gathered *Rew*, and Savine, ... III. ii. 49. 5
the third time shall *rew* his foolhardise: . . . . III. iii. 35. 7
could have made a rocke of stone to *rew*, ... III. v. 30. 2
'These eyes did see that they will ever *rew* . . . . III. viii. 49. 1
to *rue* the others heavy cheare; . . . . IV. vii. 34. 7
he gan to *rew* The evill case . . . . IV. viii. 20. 1
He cald to him aloud his case to *rew*, ... IV. viii. 40. 7
her deare hart full deepely made to *rew*, ... IV. viii. 64. 3
learne to love by learning lovers paines to *rew*. . . . . . . IV. xii. 13. 9
With a fayre love, whose losse I now do *rew*, ... V. i. 16. 7
Artegall him selfe her seemelesse plight did *rew*. . . . . . . V. ii. 25. 9
I *rew* that thus thy better dayes are drowned . . . . V. v. 36. 4
Oft did she blame her selfe, and often *rew*, ... V. vi. 12. 5
she had him done to *rew*. . . . . V. xi. 30. 9
His mightie hart their mournefull case gan *rew*, ... VI. ii. 41. 8
even his ruder hart began to *rew*, ... VI. iv. 3. 5
Complayning *out on me* that would not on them *rew*. . . . . VI. viii. 20. 9
none is nigh to heare that will her *rew*, ... VI. viii. 40. 8
would *rew* And pitty her sad plight, ... VI. xi. 2. 8
whilest none was them to *rew;* . . . . VI. xii. 25. 5
then the more your owne mishap I *rew*, ... *Am.* lxxxii. 3
(aye me, the more to *rew!*) . . . . *H.B.* 148

Rued. he himselfe may *rewed* be more right, ... *Col.* 398
as if his case she *rewd*. . . . . II. xii. 73. 9
his foote slipt, (that slip he dearely *rewd*) . . . . VI. vii. 48. 3
eke all other creatures her bad dooings *rewed*. . . . . VII. vi. 4. 9

Rueful. wounds my soule with *rufull* memorie, ... *Pet.*[2] iv. 13
if thy rymes as rownde and *rufull* bene . . . . *S.C.* N. 43
Up, grieslie ghostes! and up my *rufull* ryme! . . . . *S.C.* N. 55
Did now rebound with nought but *rufull* cries, ... *T.M.* 23
So all with *rufull* spectacles is fild, ... *T.M.* 163
mickle woe Thereof arose, and manie a *rufull* teare, ... *Mui.* 133
Let reade the *rufull* plaint herein exprest, ... *D.* 4
Shee turning backe, with *ruefull* countenaunce, ... I. ii. 21. 1
ruefull plaints, me bidding guiltlesse blood to spare?' . . . . I. ii. 32. 9
A *ruefull* sight as could be seene with eie; . . . . I. v. 46. 1
The *rueful* moniments of heavinesse; . . . . I. vii. 19. 8
the record of his *ruefull* losse, ... I. vii. 48. 6
A *ruefull* spectacle of death and ghastly drere. . . . . I. viii. 40. 9
'Then shall I you recount a *ruefull* cace,' . . . . I. ix. 26. 6
hearing evermore His *ruefull* shriekes . . . . I. x. 28. 5
To tell this *ruefull* tale: . . . . II. i. 9. 9
They heard a *ruefull* voice, ... II. i. 35. 7
deare Lady, which the ymage art Of *ruefull* pitty . . . . . . II. i. 44. 5
the rest of those same *ruefull* sightes, ... II. vii. 57. 7
all the fields resounded with the *ruefull* cry. . . . . II. viii. 3. 9
they heard a *ruefull* cry . . . . II. xii. 27. 2
The *ruefull* Strich, still waiting on the bere; . . . . II. xii. 36. 7
As ye may elswhere reade that *ruefull* history. . . . . III. vi. 53. 9
The *ruefull* story of Sir Paridell, ... III. ix. 38. 3
a wide wound . . . (O *ruefull* sight!) . . . . III. xii. 20. 5
filled were with *rufull* tine And secret feare, ... IV. iii. 37. 4
whose sad *ruefull* cheare Made her to change her hew, ... IV. iii. 46. 8
'Thy *ruefull* plight I pitty as mine owne. . . . . IV. vii. 19. 2
Onely few *ruefull* lookes unto her sent, ... IV. viii. 13. 8
With mild regard to see his *ruefull* plight, ... IV. viii. 17. 7
Like *ruefull* ghost, ... IV. xii. 20. 9
Much was he moved at that *ruefull* sight; . . . . V. i. 14. 6
they heard a *ruefull* shrieke . . . . VI. i. 17. 1
When Calidore this *ruefull* storie had Well understood, ... VI. ii. 44. 1
halfe enraged at that *ruefull* sight; . . . . VI. xi. 25. 4
askt againe, what ment that *rufull* hew: . . . . VI. xi. 28. 8
When Calidore these *ruefull* newes had raught, ... VI. xi. 33. 1

Ruefully. Through all the seas so *ruefully* resownd, ... III. viii. 30. 6
slaine her children *ruefully*, alas! . . . . V. x. 6. 9
Wringing her hands, and *ruefully* loud crying? . . . . VI. xi. 23. 7

Ruefulness. And well could daunce, and sing with *ruefulnesse;* I. iv. 25. 7

Rueing. even then *ruing* her wilfull fall . . . . V. x. 4. 7
Lay in the lap of death, *rewing* his wretched bale. . . . . . VI. vii. 17. 9

Rueless. A *rulesse* rout of yongmen which her woo'd, ... *Gn.* 431

Rues. Delights not in my merth, nor *rues* my smart: . . . . *Am.* liv. 10

Rueth. 'Deare dame, your suddein overthrow Much *rueth* me; I. ii. 21, 8

Ruffed. prune his plumes like *ruffed* Dove. . . . . *T.M.* 402
the fether in her lofty crest, *Ruffed* of love, ... III. ii. 27. 2

Ruffian. His *ruffin* raiment all was staind with blood . . . . I. iv. 34. 1

Ruffing. the proud Bird, *ruffing* his fethers wyde . . . . . . III. xi. 32. 6

Ruffins. fish . . . the which they *Ruffins* call. . . . . . . IV. xi. 33. 9

Ruffled. With *ruffled* rayments, and fayre blubbred face, . . . I. vi. 9. 3
Ruffled and fowly raid with filthy soyle, ... III. viii. 32. 2

Ruffs. Some prancke their *ruffes;* . . . . I. iv. 14. 8

Rugged. howe my rymes bene *rugged* . . . . *S.C.* N. 51
'The carefull cold hath nypt my *rugged* rynde, ... *S.C.* D. 133
delay The *rugged* brow of carefull Policy, ... *Ded. Son.* i. 12

Rugged—*Continued.*
Gote, whose *rugged* heare, . . . Was like the person selfe . . . I. iv. 24. 2
Upon the Lyon and the *rugged* Beare; . . . . I. vi. 24. 4
whelpes she saw how he did . . . lull in *rugged* armes . . . . I. vi. 27. 9
His rude assault and *rugged* handeling . . . . II. iv. 8. 1
Over the waves his *rugged* armes doth lift, ... II. xii. 4. 4
my rymes too rude and *rugged* arre, ... III. ii. 3. 6
with his teeth did teare His *rugged* flesh, ... III. vii. 20. 5
He was all armd in *rugged* steele unfilde, ... III. vii. 30. 4
Her up betwixt his *rugged* hands he reard, ... III. viii. 35. 1
His face was *rugged*, ... III. xi. 40. 3
The *rugged* forhead, that with grave foresight Welds kingdomes . . . . IV. Pr. 1. 1
With *rugged* beard, and hoarie shagged heare, ... IV. v. 34. 8
overgrowen with rude and *rugged* haire; . . . . IV. vii. 43. 4
rend his *rugged* heares, ... IV. viii. 4. 8
In his strong hand their *rugged* teats to hold, ... VI. ix. 37. 8

Ruin. overthrew this frame with *ruine* great. . . . . *Bel.*[2] ii. 14
Beholde what wreake, what *ruine*, and what wast, ... *Ro.* iii. 5
a Goose great Rome from *ruine* stayde, ... *Van.* xi. 9
the Princes pallaces fell fast To *ruine* . . . . *Hub.* 1176
'O Rome! thy *ruine* I lament and rue, ... *Ti.* 78
That of like *ruine* he may warned bee, ... *Ti.* 468
Sith time doth greatest things to *ruine* bring? . . . . *Ti.* 556
Her hastie *ruine* does more heavie make, ... I. viii. 23. 6
heavy *ruine* they did seeme to threatt; . . . . II. vii. 28. 6
That goodly frame from *ruine* to sustaine: . . . . II. xi. 15. 5
Nor bounds nor banks his headlong *ruine* may sustayne. . . . II. xi. 18. 9
for your *ruine* at the last awayt.' . . . . II. xii. 29. 4
the late *ruine* of proud Marinell, ... III. viii. 46. 4
stately towres . . . Brought unto balefull *ruine*, ... III. ix. 34. 4
Threates with huge *ruine* him to fall upon, ... III. x. 58. 5
was the high-aspyring with huge *ruine* humbled. . . . . . . V. ii. 50. 9
How he his nets doth for their *ruine* lay: . . . . V. ix. 13. 4
wretched *ruine* of so high estate; . . . . V. ix. 46. 5
Who then can thinke their hedlong *ruine* to recure? . . . . . V. x. 26. 9
of them all which did his *ruine* seeke, ... VI. v. 13. 1
Whom ye wreck, doe *ruine*, and destroy. . . . . *Am.* lvi. 14

Ruinate. time in time shall *ruinate* Your workes . . . . . *Ro.* vii. 10
state Will without wisedome soone be *ruinate*. . . . . *Hub.* 1040
Threatning it selfe on them to *ruinate*, ... II. xii. 7. 2
Towres, citties, kingdomes, ye would *ruinate* . . . . III. viii. 28. 5
that same citie, so now *ruinate*, ... V. x. 26. 3
Beats on it strongly, it to *ruinate*. . . . . *Am.* lvi. 8

Ruined. the *ruin'd* pride Of these old Romane works, ... *Ro.* xv. 12
To whom the *ruin'd* walls of Carthage vow'd, ... *Gn.* 615
The *ruin'd* wals he did reaedifye Of Troynovant, ... II. x. 46. 4
How Fortune will your *ruin'd* name repaire . . . . V. iv. 34. 8

Ruinous. Above the reach of *ruinous* decay, ... *Ti.* 422
all the hinder partes, . . . Were *ruinous* and old, ... I. iv. 5. 9
That chamber seemed *ruinous* and old, ... II. ix. 55. 1
is the spectacle of *ruinous* decay. . . . . III. vii. 41. 9
Till they arrive at their last *ruinous* decay. . . . . V. Pr. 6. 9
glad of spoyle and *ruinous* decay, ... V. ix. 47. 6

Ruins. Under deep *ruines*, with huge walls opprest, ... *Ro.* i. 2
Ye sacred *ruines*, and ye tragick sights, ... *Ro.* vii. 1
Under these antique *ruines* yet remaine. . . . . *Ro.* xix. 14
ye, that read these *ruines* tragicall, ... *Van.* xii. 9
nought at all but *ruines* now I bee, ... *Ti.* 39
the light of simple veritie Buried in *ruines*, ... *Ti.* 172
ragged *ruines* breed great ruth and pittie . . . . *Col.* 114
Like the old *ruines* of a broken towre, ... I. ii. 20. 2
by my *ruines* thinkes to make them great: . . . . I. v. 25. 8
The Antique *ruins* of the Romanes fall: . . . . I. v. 49. 4
the *ruines* of great Ossa hill, ... II. x. 3. 3
Of all which *ruines* there some relicks did remaine. . . . . . IV. i. 21. 9

Ruins'. Judge, by these ample *ruines* vew, the rest . . . . . *Ro.* xxvii. 5

Rule. to *rule* this croked shore. . . . . *Bel.*[1] viii. 15
their *rule* of yearely Presidents Grew great, ... *Ro.* xviii. 7
Which mear'd her *rule* with Africa, and Byze, ... *Ro.* xxii. 2
line, or lead, or *rule*, or squaire, to measure . . . . *Ro.* xxvi. 3
They reigne and *rulen* over all, ... *S.C.* Jul. 175
thilke same *rule* were too straight, ... *S.C.* S. 236
All jolly Prelates, worthie *rule* to beare, ... *Hub.* 423
with the budding rod Did *rule* the Jewes, ... *Hub.* 440
rule and raigne in soveraign see, ... *Hub.* 980
I claime my selfe more fit Than you to *rule;* . . . . *Hub.* 1039
so his *rule* might lenger have endurance. . . . . *Hub.* 1114
gan he *rule* and tyrannize at will, ... *Hub.* 1127
No care of justice, nor no *rule* of reason, ... *Hub.* 1131
In th' hearts of men to *rule* them carefully, ... *T.M.* 314
So every where they *rule*, and tyrannize, ... *T.M.* 337
I that *rule* in measure moderate . . . . *T.M.* 379
have no skill to *rule* them right, ... *T.M.* 551
the wide *rule* of his renowmed sire. . . . . *Mui.* 40
That man, who doth the whole worlds *rule* possesse, ... *D.* 179
sparke of reasons might . . . to *rule* his passion, ... *Col.* 868
two rams, . . . Fight for the *rule* of the rich fleeced flocke, . I. ii. 16. 2
He that the wide West under his *rule* has, ... I. ii. 22. 8
griefe made forgett the raines to hold Of reasons *rule*, ... I. iv. 41. 4
Did spred their *rule* through all the territories, ... I. vii. 43. 7
that did earst you beare, and well could *rule;* . . . . I. vii. 48. 5
great *rule* of Temp'raunce goodly doth appeare. . . . . . . II. Pr. 5. 9
No measure in her mood, no *rule* of right, ... II. ii. 36. 4
Brute this Realme unto his *rule* subdewd, ... II. x. 13. 1
Madan was young, unmeet the *rule* to sway, ... II. x. 20. 2
nought him griev'd to beene from *rule* deposed downe. . . . . II. x. 29. 9
ambitious sonnes unto them twayne Arraught the *rule*, ... II. x. 34. 8
In *rule* succeede, and eke in fathers praise; . . . . II. x. 41. 2
sonnes, too young to *rule* aright, ... II. x. 46. 8

Rule—*Continued.*
T' ambitious Rome, and did their *rule* obay, II. x. 49. 7
He is againe unto his *rule* restord; II. x. 66. 2
brave ensample, both of martiall And civil *rule,* II. x. 74. 9
yeeld His partes to reasons *rule* obedient, II. xi. 2. 2
afterwards did *rule* the night and day: II. xii. 13. 7
rule the Furyes when they most doe rage. II. xii. 41. 8
In th' one her *rule,* in th' other her rare chastitee. III. Pr. 5. 9
Ere they to former *rule* restor'd shal bee, III. iii. 44. 6
she put a Spright to *rule* the carcas dead; III. viii. 7. 9
strive the *rule* to get Of all the heard, IV. iv. 18. 3
ne reasons *rule,* mote them restraine. IV. v. 24. 9
rule to himselfe did gaine Of many Nations IV. viii. 47. 3
as the soule doth *rule* the earthly masse, IV. ix. 2. 6
lawlesse lust to *rule* with reasons lore; IV. ix. 19. 4
The powre to *rule* the billowes, IV. xi. 12. 9
Nemertea learned well to *rule* her lust. IV. xi. 51. 9
To *rule* his tides, and surges to uprere, IV. xi. 52. 3
And *rule* his people right, V. Pr. 10. 9
There Justice first her princely *rule* begonne. V. i. 2. 5
Ill can he *rule* the great that cannot reach the small.' V. ii. 43. 9
then all *rule* and reason they withstand V. v. 25. 5
Ne within reasons *rule* her madding mood containe. V. vii. 11. 9
neglect The worlds whole *rule* for Cleopatras sight. V. viii. 2. 7
from flying stay With raynes or wonted *rule,* V. viii. 38. 6
To *rule* the stubborne rage of passion blinde: VI. vi. 5. 8
Hecate, in whose almighty hand He plac't all *rule* VII. vi. 3. 4
Rule and dominion to her selfe to gaine; VII. vi. 4. 2
Her selfe of all that *rule* she deemed most condigne. VII. vi. 11. 9
Jove, injuriously hast held The Heavens *rule* VII. vi. 27. 7
rule both sea and land unto their will: VII. vii. 3. 5
do claime the *rule* and soverainty; VII. vii. 26. 3
them we gods do *rule,* and in them also thee. VII. vii. 48. 9
the *rule* of all, all being rul'd by you.' VII. vii. 56. 9
over them Change doth not *rule* and raigne, VII. vii. 58. 8
though she all unworthy were Of the Heav'ns *Rule;* VII. viii. 1. 4
Ruled. *See* **Overruled.**
For-thy, my Kiddie, be *ruld* by mee, *S.C.* May 221
be *rul'd* to doo as I doo teach.' *Hub.* 992
that ye *ruled* bee In all affaires, *Hub.* 1051
he *rul'd* not the Empire, as he ought? *Hub.* 1251
Ne *ruld* her Realme with lawes, but pollicie, I. iv. 12. 7
ruled long with honorable state, II. x. 45. 4
The Knight was *ruled,* II. xii. 29. 5
First ill, and after *ruled* wickedly; III. iii. 46. 3
rul'd her thoughts with goodly governement, IV. ii. 36. 4
are *rul'd* by righteous lore Of highest Jove, V. vii. 1. 5
the rule of all, all being *rul'd* by you.' VII. vii. 56. 9
thee content thus to be *rul'd* by mee, VII. vii. 59. 2
Rulers. realmes and *rulers* thou doest both confound, II. vii. 13. 2
Rule's. envious Men, fearing their *rules* decay, III. ii. 2. 5
Rules. where he *rules* all power he doth expell; *S.C.* O. 99
furies *rules,* and Tartare tempereth. *Hub.* 1294
She solaceth with *rules* of Sapience *T.M.* 135
rules the creatures by his powrfull saw: *Col.* 884
thundering Jove, that *rules* both night and day?' I. v. 42. 9
rules mens waies, and *rules* the thoughts of living wight. I. ix. 6. 9
in her vertuous *rules* to schoole her knight, I. x. 32. 6
rules the Seas and makes them rise or fall; IV. xi. 11. 2
in the *rules* of justice them instructed well. V. i. 5. 9
To breake all bonds of law and *rules* of right: V. viii. 20. 5
hart . . . *rules* the members *Am.* l. 8
With which she *rules* the house of God on hy, *H.H.B.* 193
Ruling. *See* **Overruling, Sky-ruling, Well-ruling.**
But those two most, which, *ruling* night and day, *H.H.B.* 55
Rumble. To *romble* gently downe with murmur soft, *T.M.* 26
Rumbled. His timbered bones all broken rudely *rumbled:* V. ii. 50. 8
Rumbling. *See* **Soft-rumbling.**
A spring of water, mildly *rumbling* (*romblyng*[1]) *Pet.* iv. 2
caerule streame, *rombling* in Pible stone, *Gn.* 163
dreadfull noise and hollow *rombling* rore II. xii. 25. 3
brasen Caudrons thou shalt *rombling* heare, III. iii. 9. 3
Rumors. Fild with false *rumors* and seditious trouble, IV. i. 28. 3
Rump. at her *rompe* she growing had behind A foxes taile, I. viii. 48. 3
Run. *See* **Outrun, Overrun.**
when the compast course of the universe . . . is *ronne,* *Ro.* xxii. 10
letting their sheepe *runne* at large, *S.C.* May 40
letten them *runne* at randon alone: *S.C.* May 46
Renne after hastely thy silver sound; *S.C.* Jun. 61
To *renne* hys dayly race, *S.C.* Jul. 60
bene thy Bagpypes *renne* farre out of frame? *S.C.* Au. 3
had not Roffy *renne* to the steven, *S.C.* S. 224
we shall *ronne* Into great daunger, *Hub.* 183
or *runne* on foote a race, *Hub.* 744
To fawne, to crowche, to waite, to ride, to *ronne,* *Hub.* 905
Now being let to *runne* at libertie *T.M.* 550
To *runne* thy shrill Arcadian Pipe to heare: *Ti.* 328
wise wordes, taught in numbers for to *runne,* *Ti.* 402
doth *run* downe right To Buttevant, *Col.* 110
took her wonted way To *ronne* her timely race, I. v. 44. 8
Her to behold do thither *runne* apace; I. vi. 18. 2
When after him a Lyonesse did *runne,* I. vi. 27. 5
suddein cold did *ronne* through every vaine, I. vi. 37. 2
whiles equal destinies Did *ronne* about, I. vii. 43. 5
Eft looking back would faine have *runne* away; I. ix. 25. 3
Titan rose to *runne* his daily race; I. xi. 33. 2
Some wrestle, some do *run,* some bathe in christall flood. I. xii. 7. 9
Must now anew begin like race to *ronne.* II. i. 32. 7
Island, that doth *ronne* And stray in perilous gulfe, II. i. 51. 5
to and fro doe *ronne* In the wide waters: II. xii. 11. 5

Run—*Continued.*
Her selfe had *ronne* into that hazardize; II. xii. 19. 5
besought The Prince of grace to let him *ronne* that turne. III. i. 5. 2
make him fast out of the forest *ronne;* III. v. 27. 8
every one to *ronne* the swiftest stryv'd; III. v. 37. 7
So, like a wheele, arownd they *ronne* from old to new. III. vi. 33. 9
if thee list to see thy Courser *ronne,* III. viii. 17. 4
Retird their steeds, to *ronne* in even race; III. viii. 18. 6
There might ye see loose steeds at randon *ronne,* IV. iv. 38. 6
all adowne their riven sides did *ronne.* IV. ix. 27. 5
Me seemes the world is *runne* quite out of square V. Pr. 1. 7
so were realmes and nations *run* awry. V. ii. 32. 6
The trompets sound, then all together *ronne.* V. iii. 6. 4
That ye were *runne* so fondly far astray V. iv. 26. 8
they both like race in equall justice *runne.* V. vii. 4. 9
they together *run* With greedy rage, V. vii. 29. 1
As a mad bytch . . . Doth *runne* at randon, V. viii. 49. 3
Then ganne it *runne* away incontinent, V. ix. 18. 7
Toward the same incessantly did *ronne* VI. iv. 2. 4
all the water which doth *ronne* In the next brooke, VI. iv. 32. 8
Did *runne* at Pastorell her to surprize; VI. x. 34. 7
Mars in three-score yeares doth *run* his spheare. *Am.* lx. 4
The weary yeare his race now having *run,* *Am.* lxii. 1
After so long a race as I have *run* *Am.* lxxx. 1
the boyes *run* up and downe the street, *Epith.* 137
forth to *run* her mighty race, *Epith.* 150
Sweete Themmes! *runne* softly, till I end my Song. *Proth.* 18, 36, 54, 72, 90
Sweete Themmes! *runne* softlie, till I end my Song.' *Proth.* 108
Making his streame *run* slow. *Proth.* 118
Sweete Themmes! *run* softly, *Proth.* 126
Sweete Themmes! *runne* softly, till I end my Song. *Proth.* 144, 162, 180
Rung. *See* **Rang, Rong.**
With bells and bosses that full lowdly *rung,* *Hub.* 583
Whose bridle *rung* with golden bels and bosses brave. I. ii. 13. 9
Runners'. False Labyrinthes, fond *runners* eyes to daze; IV. x. 24. 8
Runneth. how fast *renneth* the shepheard swayne *S.C.* Au. 32
The rolling wheele that *runneth* often round, *Am.* xviii. 1
Running. *See* **Swift-running.**
the borne Souldier which Rhine *running* drinks: *Ro.* xxxi. 8
hit me *running* in the heele: *S.C.* Mar. 97
An easie *running* verse with tender feete. *Gn.* 53
In wrestling nimble, and in *renning* swift, *As.* 73
The *running* waters wept for thy returne, *Col.* 27
to him *running* said; 'O! prowest knight, I. v. 14. 2
running Heralds humble homage made, I. v. 15. 7
A Lyon spyes fast *running* towards him, I. vi. 10. 6
The roiall Virgin . . . Came *running* fast I. viii. 26. 4
As it a *ronning* messenger had beene. I. ix. 51. 7
Came *running* in, much like a man dismayd, I. xii. 24. 8
A varlet *ronning* towardes hastily, II. iv. 37. 2
when him *ronning* in full course he spyes, II. v. 10. 5
running to her boat withouten ore, II. xii. 15. 7
Like to a restlesse wheele, still *ronning* round, II. xii. 20. 6
The trembling groves, the christall *running* by, II. xii. 58. 7
silver flood Through every channell *running* II. xii. 60. 4
Ne can my *ronning* sore finde remedee, III. ii. 39. 6
ronning through that same Thicke forest, III. v. 3. 8
with it *ronning* hast'ly to her sonne, III. viii. 3. 1
Trompart, *ronning* hastely, him did stay, III. x. 23. 6
fiercely *running* to that Lady trew, III. xii. 32. 4
running water tempred with his teares, IV. vii. 41. 7
He, *running* downe, the gate to him unbard; IV. ix. 5. 8
running unto them with greedy joyes, V. x. 20. 1
running all with greedie joyfulnesse To faire Irena, V. xii. 24. 5
And, *running* streight into the thickest wood, VI. iv. 12. 5
running streight upon that villaine base, VI. vi. 22. 3
the foole, which did that end awayte, Came *running* in; VI. viii. 11. 2
to him *running* fast, he did not stay VI. xi. 28. 1
Thence *running* forth unto her loved Lord, VI. xii. 22. 1
running straight where-as she heard his voice, VII. vi. 47. 3
Runs. great rivers banck, that *runnes* by Rome; *Bel.* i. 6
whither *rennes* this bevie of Ladies bright, *S.C.* Ap. 118
Ne *runs* in perill of foes cruell knife, *Gn.* 125
Through power of that he *runnes* through enemies swerds; *Hub.* 1283
Forthwith he *runnes* . . . Unto his guest, I. ii. 4. 1
She to them *runnes* in hast, V. viii. 10. 7
Envie first, . . . Towardes him *runs,* V. xii. 38. 8
he sometimes so far *runnes* out of square, VII. vii. 52. 2
Runts. My ragged *rontes* all shiver and shake, *S.C.* F. 5
Rural. of my *rurall* musicke holdeth scorne. *S.C.* Ja. 64
O, how the *rurall* routes to thee doe cleave! *S.C.* O. 26
The *rurall* song of carefull Colinet. *S.C.* D. 18
In haste forsooke their *rurall* meriment, I. vi. 8. 2
in the *rurall* cottages inquir'd; III. vi. 15. 2
Renowmed hath with hymnes fit for a *rurall* skill. VII. vi. 36. 9
Rush. Listening if any thing did *rushe,* *S.C.* Mar. 71
He, tombling rudely downe, to ground did *rush,* I. iii. 35. 8
horse and man to ground did *rush.* I. xi. 16. 9
through the thicke they heard one rudely *rush,* II. iii. 21. 1
Another in her teeth did gnaw a *rush;* II. ix. 35. 8
A goodly Lady did foreby them *rush,* III. i. 15. 3
a griesly foster forth did *rush,* III. i. 17. 2
like a Gote emongst the Gotes did *rush;* III. x. 47. 3
Rushed. Their dam . . . *rushed* forth, I. i. 16. 2
out of the thickest wood A ramping Lyon *rushed* I. iii. 5. 2
rusht upon him with outragious pryde; I. xi. 53. 3
he *rusht* into the thick, II. i. 39. 2
rushed in on foot to ayd her II. iii. 3. 9
suddein forth they on them *rusht,* II. xii. 81. 3
spyde How towards her he *rusht,* III. xi. 32. 9

Rushed—*Continued.*
Rusht fiercely forth the battell to renew, … IV. iii. 14. 6
rushed forth out of the thickest rout A stranger knight, … IV. iv. 43. 7
poyson therewith *rusht,* That him nigh choked … V. xi. 31. 7
Rushes. rings of *rushes* plight: … II. vi. 7. 5
Rusheth. He *rusheth* forth, and snatcheth quite away … *Mui.* 406
rusheth forth Betweene them both … II. ii. 25. 1
Rushing. *rushing* with fierce might Out of his den, … *Mui.* 434
In hast came *rushing* forth from inner bowre, … I. viii. 5. 6
forth *rushing* from the forest nye. … II. ix. 14. 9
Came *rushing,* in the fomy waves enrold, … II. xii. 25. 4
rushing through the thickest preasse … III. i. 23. 5
rushing forth into the emptie field, … IV. iii. 22. 7
One *rushing* forth out of the thickest weed, … IV. vii. 4. 4
came rudely *rushing* in, … IV. vii. 20. 6
The Blatant Beast forth *rushing* unaware … VI. iii. 24. 2
Rush-rings. The knotted *rush-ringes,* and gilte Rosemaree? *S.C.* N. 116
Rushy. ye likewise, which keepe the *rushy* lake, … *Epith.* 60
Russian. Whenas the *Russian* him in fight does chace) … II. xi. 26. 8
Rust. *See* **Iron-rust.**
Ne *rust* of age hating continuance, … *Ro.* xiii. 6
all corrupted through the *rust* of time … *T.M.* 433
overgrowen with blacke oblivions *rust.* … *Ti.* 98
keyes . . . The which unused *rust* did overgrow: … I. viii. 30. 7
His yron cote, all overgrowne with *rust,* … II. vii. 4. 1
Colour thy name with foule reproaches *rust!* … IV. i. 53. 7
in a cote of plate Burnisht with bloudie *rust;* … V. viii. 29. 2
Rusted. Whose long rest *rusted* the bright steely brand; … V. ix. 30. 7
Rustic. As merrie notes upon his *rusticke* Fife, … *Gn.* 148
on shrill reedes chaunting his *rustick* rime, … *Gn.* 155
Of *rustick* muse full hardly to be betterd. … *D.* 231
Young Astrophel, the *rusticke* lasses love: … *As.* 8
Albe he envie at my *rustick* quill: … *Col.* 393
Rude rymes, the which a *rustick* Muse did weave … *Ded.Son.*vii.11
Why doe I send this *rusticke* Madrigale, … *Ded. Son.* viii. 3
frowning forheades, with rough hornes yclad, And *rustick* horror, … I. vi. 11. 6
With stony feare of that rude *rustick* mate, … II. ii. 8. 8
lend A little leave unto a *rusticke* Muse … III. Pr. 5. 2
After his *rusticke* wise, that well he weend, … VI. ix. 6. 7
Amongst that *rusticke* rout … VI. ix. 45. 2
set his rest amongst the *rusticke* sort, … VI. x. 2. 6
He backe returned to his *rusticke* wonne, … VI. x. 32. 2
Rusticity. gentle sprite deforme with rude *rusticity.* … III. vi. 1. 9
Rustling. But then heard no more *rustling:* … *S.C.* Mar. 72
Rusts. doubted Knights, whose woundlesse armour *rusts,* … *S.C.* O. 41
Rusty. Through *rusty* elde, that hath rotted thee: … *S.C.* F. 54
With *rustie* horrour and fowle fashion; … *Gn.* 443
shall in *rustie* darknes ever lie, … *Ti.* 349
Bitter despight, with rancours *rusty* knife, … I. iv. 35. 4
steedes . . . on their *rusty* bits did champ … I. v. 20. 9
Their mournefull charett, fild with *rusty* blood, … I. v. 32. 2
To me he lent this rope, to him a *rusty* knife. … I. ix. 29. 9
In which a *rusty* knife fast fixed stood, … I. ix. 36. 8
threats his *rusty* knife. … II. iv. 44. 5
Some *rusty* knifes, some staves in fier warmd: … II. ix. 13. 7
a *rusty* blade In th' other was; … III. xii. 11. 5
Made all of *rusty* yron ranckling sore, … VI. vi. 9. 3
Rusty-brown. a steele cap he did weare Of colour *rustie-browne,* V. xii. 14. 6

Ruth. O, how great *ruth,* and sorrowfull assay, … *Pet.*² ii. 11
For *ruth* and pitie of so haples plight: … *Pet.*² v. 13
(O great *ruth* for the same!) … *Van.* vii. 10
With inward *ruth* and deare affection, … *Van.* xii. 3
With tender *ruth* to see her sore constraint; … *Ti.* 31
For *ruth* of that same womans piteous paine; … *Ti.* 480
great *ruth* and pittie To travailers, … *Col.* 114
Tho can she weepe, to stirre up gentle *ruth* … I. i. 50. 8
falshood . . . workes him woefull *ruth.* … I. ii. Arg.
Great *ruth* in all the gazers harts did grow, … I. v. 9. 7
Are wonne with pitty and unwonted *ruth;* … I. vi. 12. 7
horrour . . . For *ruth* of gentle knight … I. viii. 39. 4
ruth . . . did constraine His stout courage to stoupe, … II. i. 42. 8
ruth emperced deepe In that knightes hart, … II. ii. 1. 8
sad *ruth* does seeme you to restraine, … II. ii. 45. 2
for memory of that dayes *ruth,* … II. iii. 2. 7
'Deare sonne, thy causelesse *ruth* represse, … II. v. 24.5
With wretched miseryes and woefull *ruth,* … II. x. 62. 3
wondrous *ruth* to all that shall it heare: … III. v. 6. 8
of her errour straunge I have great *ruth* and mone.' … III. v. 7. 9
ruth of her sad plight Would make to melt, … III. vii. 9. 6
with great *ruth* and terrour she was smit, … III. xi. 12. 8
fild the lookers on attonce with *ruth* and wonder. … IV. iii. 15. 9
felt some *ruth* or sence his hand did lacke, … IV. vi. 21. 7
being mov'd with *ruth* she thus bespake: … IV. viii. 14. 6
ruth it moved in the rocky stone, … IV. xii. 5. 7
ruth of wretches wrong, … IV. xii. 9. 2
his stony heart with tender *ruth* Was toucht, … IV. xii. 13. 1
ruth of beautie will it mollifie. … V. v. 13. 6
with *ruth* . . . Of my mishaps … V. v. 37. 7
her heart did quake For very *ruth,* … V. vii. 36. 6
with *ruth* to salve his sad misfortunes sore. … V. vii. 38. 9
Great *ruth* through her misfortunes tragicke stowre; … V. ix. 45. 8
for great *ruth* his courage gan relent: … V. ix. 46. 6
His former fancies *ruth* he gan repent, … V. ix. 49. 2
With piteous *ruth* of her so wretched plight, … V. ix. 50. 2
Ne once for *ruth* their rigour they releast, … VI. i. 36. 8
he inly touched was With tender *ruth* … VI. iv. 34. 2
ruth it was to see him so lament: … VI. v. 4. 6
with the *ruth* of her so wretched case, … VI. vi. 31. 8
wheres no courage, theres no *ruth* nor mone. … VI. vii. 18. 5
make one end of him without *ruth* or remorse. … VI. viii. 14. 9
Ne wilbe moov'd with reason, or with *rewth,* … *Am.* xi. 5
Playnts, prayers, vowes, *ruth,* sorrow, and dismay; … *Am.* xiv. 11
Ne once move *ruth* in that rebellious Dame, … *H.L.* 151
Ruthful. That art the roote of all this *ruthfull* woe! … *S.C.* Jun. 116
tune your pypes as *ruthful* as ye may. … *S.C.* Au. 150
Ruthfully. my deadly cryes 'Most *ruthfully* to tune: … *S.C.* Au. 175
Ruthless. Nor *ruthlesse* spoyle of souldiers blood-desiring, … *Ro.* xiii. 3
shall their *ruthlesse* torment never cease; … *Am.* xxxvi. 2
Rutty. Whose *rutty* Bancke, . . . Was paynted all with variable flowers, … *Proth.* 12
Rybaudry, Rybauld. *See* **Ribaldry, Ribald.**
Rye. flowing fast to *Rhy;* … IV. xi. 33. 2
Ryence. What time king *Ryence* raign'd and dealed right, … III. ii. 18. 5
gave unto king *Ryence* for his gard, … III. ii. 21. 2
King *Ryence* caused to be hanged hy … III. iii. 59. 2
Rythmes. *See* **Rhythms.**

S

Sabaoth. the God of *Sabaoth* (**Sabbaoth*) hight: O! that great *Sabaoth* (**Sabbaoth*) God, … VII. viii. 2. 8, 9
Sabaoth's. O! that great Sabaoth God, grant me that *Sabaoths* sight. … VII. viii. 2. 9
Sabbath-day. once a weeke, upon the *Sabbath day,* … *Hub.* 456
Sabine. Fresh Rhododaphne, and the *Sabine* flowre, … *Gn.* 673
Sable. to decke thy *sable* Herse. … *Ti.* 679
night, Who with her *sable* mantle … I. xi. 49. 7
Griefe all in *sable* sorrowfully clad, … III. xii. 16. 2
Her covered with her *sable* vestiment, … III. xii. 29. 4
in thy *sable* mantle us enwrap, … *Epith.* 321
Sabrina. The faire *Sabrina,* almost dead with feare, … II. x. 19. 3
Sabrina's. Not far from whence *Sabrinaes* streame doth flow, … *D.* 101
Sack. all thy Citties they shall *sacke* and race, … III. iii. 34. 7
Sackcloth. next her wrinkled skin rough *sackecloth* wore, … I. iii. 14. 3
In ashes and *sackcloth* he did array His daintie corse, … I. x. 26. 1
Sacked. Castles surprizd, great cities *sackt* and brent: … II. vii. 13. 8
sacked Rome too dearely did assay, … II. x. 40. 3
Trojan warres and Priams citie *sackt,* … III. ix. 38. 2
My cities *sackt,* and their sky-threating towres Raced … V. x. 23. 4
Sacks. great *sackes* with endlesse riches fraught … V. ii. 23. 4
Sacrament. A *sacrament* prophane in mistery of wine. … III. ix. 30. 9
Can hardly but by *Sacrament* be tride, … V. i. 25. 2
Even he himselfe, in his deare *sacrament,* … *H.H.L.* 195
Sacred. The whiles that I with *sacred* horror sing … *Ro.* i. 13
Ye *sacred* ruines, and ye tragick sights, … *Ro.* vii. 1
Dragons teeth, sowne in the *sacred* sand; … *Ro.* x. 4
Sacred with many a mysteree, … *S.C.* F. 208
sacred unto saints they stond, … *S.C.* Jul. 39
O come, (thou *sacred* childe) … *Gn.* 37
thou, (dread *sacred* child) … *Gn.* 54
in the *sacred* temples he may reare A trophee … *Gn.* 126
thy *sacred* wood (O Delian Goddesse!) … *Gn.* 169
scorning to the *sacred* Gods to pray, … *Gn.* 390
Maugre the *sacred* Muses, … *Hub.* 816
Rehearse to me, ye *sacred* Sisters nine, … *T.M.* 1
The *sacred* springs of horsefoot Helicon, … *T.M.* 271

Sacred—*Continued.*
The *sacred* lawes therein they wont expresse, … *T.M.* 561
Divine Elisa, *sacred* Emperesse! … *T.M.* 579
Some few beside this *sacred* skill esteme, … *T.M.* 583
Large streetes, brave houses, *sacred* sepulchers, … *Ti.* 94
upon his lips to laie The *sacred* sod, … *Ti.* 196
The *sacred* brood of learning and all honour; … *Ti.* 279
into me that *sacred* breath inspire, … *Ti.* 314
Whom the Pierian *sacred* sisters love, … *Ti.* 394
thy old Sire with *sacred* pietie … *Mui.* 238
Ne let the *sacred* Sisters here be hight, … *D.* 11
Presume the things so *sacred* to prophane? … *Col.* 349
they of love, and of his *sacred* lere, … *Col.* 783
The *sacred* Muses have made alwaies clame … *Ded. Son.* iv. 1
Me . . . the *sacred* Muse areeds To blazon broade … I. Pr. 1. 7
streame . . . from a *sacred* fountaine welled forth alway. … I. i. 34. 9
threw his gauntlet, as a *sacred* pledge … I. iv. 43. 1
T' observe the *sacred* lawes of armes … I. v. 4. 9
in *sacred* bandes of wedlocke tyde To Therion, … I. vi. 21. 5
Teaching the Satyres, . . . Trew *sacred* lore, … I. vi. 30. 9
The *sacred* Nymph . . . Was out of Dianes favor, … I. vii. 4. 8
underneath his filthy feet did tread The *sacred* thinges, … I. vii. 18. 7
sacred ashes over it was strowed new. … I. viii. 35. 9
Renowmd throughout the world for *sacred* lore … I. x. 3. 2
her *sacred* Booke, with blood ywritt, … I. x. 19. 1
On top whereof a *sacred* chappell was, … I. x. 46. 3
like that *sacred* hill, whose head full hie, … I. x. 54. 1
O thou *sacred* Muse! most learned Dame, … I. xi. 5. 6
with innocent blood Defyld those *sacred* waves, … I. xi. 29. 8
sacred pledges he both gave, and had, … I. xii. 27. 3
With *sacred* rites and vowes for ever to abyde. … I. xii. 36. 9
sacred lamp in secret chamber hide, … I. xii. 37. 7
The *sacred* badge of my Redeemers death, … II. i. 27. 6
Bynempt a *sacred* vow, which none should ay releace. … II. i. 60. 9
as a *sacred* Symbole, it may dwell … II. ii. 10. 7
lovely concord, and most *sacred* peace, … II. ii. 31. 1
Doe her adore with *sacred* reverence, … II. ii. 41. 8

Sacred—*Continued.*
by that same *sacred* band Betwixt us both, . . . II. iv. 23. 6
The *sacred* Diademe in peeces rent, . . . II. vii. 13. 6
the hid treasures in her *sacred* tombe . . . II. vii. 17. 3
with all shame that *sacred* throne he fild. . . . II. x. 21. 2
Here ended Brutus *sacred* progeny, . . . II. x. 36. 1
Then made he *sacred* lawes, . . . II. x. 39. 1
The *sacred* pledge of Christes Evangely. . . . II. x. 53. 5
all Which, him before, that *sacred* seate did fill, . . . II. x. 76. 2
The *sacred* soile where all our perills grow. . . . II. xii. 37. 8
Then I avow, by this most *sacred* head . . . III. ii. 33. 5
Most *sacred* fyre, that burnest mightily . . . III. iii. 1. 1
Begin then, O my dearest *sacred* Dame! . . . III. iii. 4. 1
'Renowmed kings, and *sacred* Emperours, . . . III. iii. 23. 1
crowne with martiredome his *sacred* head: . . . III. iii. 39. 4
sacred Peace shall lovingly persuade . . . III. iii. 49. 3
from the *sacred* mould Of her immortall womb, . . . III. iv. 11. 8
Like as the *sacred* Oxe that carelesse stands, . . . III. iv. 17. 1
Most *sacred* virgin without spot of sinne. . . . III. iv. 59. 8
Did him, they say, forwarne through *sacred* spell: . . . III. v. 9. 7
in the *sacred* throne Of her chaste bodie; . . . III. vi. 5. 7
that *sacred* Saint my soveraigne Queene, . . . IV. Pr. 4. 2
Of *sacred* Salem; and sad Ilion, . . . IV. i. 22. 3
Then pardon, O most *sacred* happie spirit! . . . IV. ii. 34. 1
The *sacred* pledge which in his faith was left, . . . IV. vi. 8. 3
O! thou *sacred* imp of Jove . . . IV. xi. 10. 1
Most *sacred* vertue . . . Resembling God . . . V. Pr. 10. 1
Nought is on earth more *sacred* or divine, . . . V. vii. 1. 1
her *sacred* selfe to slay: . . . V. viii. 19. 4
Most *sacred* wight, most debonayre and free, . . . V. ix. 20. 7
The *sacred* pledge of peace and clemencie, . . . V. ix. 30. 3
sacred Reverence yborne of heavenly strene. . . . V. ix. 32. 9
O *sacred* hunger of ambitious mindes, . . . V. xii. 1. 1
Ye *sacred* imps, that on Parnasso dwell, . . . VI. Pr. 2. 2
Revele to me the *sacred* noursery Of vertue, . . . VI. Pr. 3. 1
To dare not to pollute so *sacred* threasure . . . VI. viii. 43. 8
by the twinkling of their *sacred* fire, . . . VI. viii. 48. 2
From thence into the *sacred* Church he broke, . . . VI. xii. 25. 1
As those three *sacred* Saints . . . on mount Thabor . . . VII. vii. 7. 6
bath'd in the *sacred* brooke Of Helicon, . . . *Am.* i. 9
Lyke *sacred* priests that never thinke amisse! . . . *Am.* xxii. 8
that most *sacred* Empresse, my dear dred, . . . *Am.* xxxiii. 2
spotlesse Pleasure builds her *sacred* bowre. . . . *Am.* lxv. 14
The *sacred* harbour of that hevenly spright; . . . *Am.* lxxvi. 4
that may her *sacred* peace molest; . . . *Am.* lxxxiii. 2
The *sacred* ceremonies there partake, . . . *Epith.* 216
About the *sacred* Altare doe remaine, . . . *Epith.* 230
That *sacred* Peace may in assurance rayne, . . . *Epith.* 354
With *sacred* rites hast taught to solemnize; . . . *Epith.* 393
all the way this *sacred* hymne do sing, . . . *H.L.* 41
beautifie this *sacred* hymne of thyne: . . . *H.B.* 21
taking flesh of *sacred* virgins wombe, . . . *H.H.L.* 146
Even for his sake, and for his *sacred* word, . . . *H.H.L.* 206
At sight of his most *sacred* heavenly corse, . . . *H.H.L.* 249
And those most *sacred* mysteries unfold . . . *H.H.B.* 234

Sacrifice. of hys keepe A *sacrifice* to bring, . . . *S.C.* Jul. 134
to present His bodie, as a spotles *sacrifise;* . . . *Ti.* 298
To her my life I wholly *sacrifice:* . . . *Col.* 475
He lives that . . . guiltie Elfin blood shall *sacrifice* in hast.' I. iv. 49. 9
offrest *sacrifice* unto the dead: . . . III. viii. 47. 4
did attend Uppon the rites and daily *sacrifize,* . . . V. vii. 4. 3
as she was doing *sacrifize* To Isis, . . . V. vii. 13. 1
to his Idols *sacrifice* their blood, . . . V. x. 8. 4
Offring to him in sinfull *sacrifice* The flesh of men, . . . V. x. 28. 6
He offred up for daily *sacrifize* My children . . . V. xi. 19. 6
feedes on all the carkasses that die In *sacrifize* . . . V. xi. 20. 4
Unto their God they would her *sacrifize,* . . . VI. viii. 38. 6
To offer *sacrifice* divine thereon; . . . VI. viii. 42. 6
on the same my hart will *sacrifise,* . . . *Am.* xxii. 11
Did *sacrifize* unto the greedy fyre. . . . *Am.* xlviii. 4

Sacrificed. unto those alone The which unto him *sacrificed* bee: V. x. 29. 6

Sacrifices. her *sacrifices* let to rest." . . . IV. x. 54. 9

Sacrifices'. All flaming with their *sacrifices* fire, . . . IV. x. 38. 2

Sacrificeth. *sacrifizeth* to th' infernall feends: . . . VI. viii. 49. 4

Sacrified. As if it had to him bene *sacrifide,* . . . II. xii. 49. 4

Sacrilege. the hid treasures . . . With *Sacriledge* to dig. . . . II. vii. 17. 4
To spoile the dead of weed Is *sacrilege,* . . . II. viii. 16. 5
sacrilege me seem'd the Church to rob, . . . IV. x. 53. 3

Sad. to that *sad* Florentine appeare, . . . *Bel.*[2] xiii. 2
having deeply gron'd these Visions *sad,* . . . *Bel.*[2] xiv. 1
My *sad* desires, rest therefore moderate; . . . *Ro.* vii. 12
When these *sad* sights were overpast and gone, . . . *Van.* xii. 1
Of Winters wracke for making thee *sadde.* . . . *S.C.* F. 10
Our bloncket liveryes bene all to *sadde* . . . *S.C.* May 5
With mery thing its good to medle *sadde.* . . . *S.C.* Au. 144
sadde Winter welked hath the day, . . . *S.C.* N. 13
sadde winters wrathe, and season chill, . . . *S.C.* N. 33
No such *sad* cares, as wont to macerate . . . *Gn.* 94
sad cares that rich mens hearts devowre. . . . *Gn.* 136
The Sunnes *sad* daughters waylde . . . *Gn.* 198
in *sad* tearmes gan sorrowfully weepe, . . . *Gn.* 325
safe delivered from *sad* decay, . . . *Gn.* 335
there huge Othos sits in *sad* distresse, . . . *Gn.* 373
Hymen, at your Spousalls *sad,* . . . *Gn.* 395
sad Eurydice . . . no more Must turne to life, . . . *Gn.* 433
sad lakes that Phoebus sunnie rayes Doo never see, . . . *Gn.* 619
sorie my *sad* case to see, . . . *Hub.* 18
Deeply doo your *sad* words my wits awhape, . . . *Hub.* 72
(said the Ape, as sighing wondrous *sad*) . . . *Hub.* 368
To heare their doome, and *sad* ensample see. . . . *Hub.* 1378

Sad—*Continued.*
Those piteous plaints and sorrowfull *sad* tine, . . . *T.M.* 3
When he is *sad,* shee seeks to make him merie, . . . *T.M.* 137
Full *sad* and dreadfull is that ships event; . . . *T.M.* 143
Full of *sad* sights and sore Catastrophees; . . . *T.M.* 158
secret sorrow and *sad* languishment, . . . *T.M.* 376
seeing her *sad* mood, . . . *T.M.* 417
all her sisters, seeing her *sad* stowre, . . . *T.M.* 597
The worlds *sad* spectacle, and fortunes scorne.' . . . *Ti.* 28
The moniment of whose *sad* funerall, . . . *Ti.* 117
O *sad* joy, made of mourning and anoy! . . . *Ti.* 322
horrid house of *sad* Proserpina, . . . *Ti.* 373
for pittie of the *sad* wayment . . . *Ti.* 390
sate long time in sencelesse *sad* affright, . . . *Ti.* 475
At sight of these *sad* spectacles forepast, . . . *Ti.* 576
sad Clarion did at last decline . . . *Mui.* 14
The engines which in them *sad* death doo hyde: . . . *Mui.* 86
Notes *sad* enough t' expresse this bitter throw: . . . *Mui.* 414
(O *sad* hap, and howre unfortunate!) . . . *Mui.* 421
Even *sad* Alcyon, whose empierced brest . . . *D.* 6
whose *sad* hands Doo weave the direfull threds . . . *D.* 16
no worlds *sad* care nor wasting woe . . . *D.* 283
In which *sad* Death his pourtraicture had writ, . . . *D.* 303
Because they breed *sad* balefulnesse in mee; . . . *D.* 410
wishfull thing this *sad* life to forgoe: . . . *D.* 452
To mourne in sorrow and *sad* sufferaunce, . . . *D.* 507
sad Alcyon dyde in lifes disdaine. . . . *D.* 525
sad ensample of mans suddein end: . . . *As.* 134
there is *sad* Alcyon bent to mourne, . . . *Col.* 384
Whose warlike prowesse . . . Hath fild *sad* Belgicke . . . *Ded. Son.* xiv. 10
of his cheere did seeme too solemne *sad;* . . . I. i. 2. 8
As one that inly mournd, so was she *sad,* . . . I. i. 4. 6
His Lady, *sad* to see his sore constraint, . . . I. i. 19. 1
Sober he seemde, and very sagely *sad,* . . . I. i. 29. 5
the *sad* humor loading their eyeliddes, . . . I. i. 36. 2
sad Night over him her mantle black doth spred. . . . I. i. 39. 9
gan threaten hellish paine, And *sad* Proserpines wrath, . . . I. ii. 2. 7
O, how great sorrow my *sad* soule assaid! . . . I. ii. 24. 5
'In this *sad* plight, . . . I, Fidessa, dwell, . . . I. ii. 26. 1
Full of *sad* feare, and ghastly dreriment, . . . I. ii. 44. 4
in pittie of my *sad* estate: . . . I. iii. 7. 5
sad to see her sorrowfull constraint, . . . I. iii. 8. 3
a faythfull mate Of her *sad* troubles and misfortunes hard: I. iii. 9. 4
on her shoulders *sad* a pot of water bore. . . . I. iii. 10. 9
Sad Una downe her laies in weary plight, . . . I. iii. 15. 3
sad Proserpina, the Queene of hell; . . . I. iv. 11. 2
neighbours welth, that made him ever *sad,* . . . I. iv. 30. 6
The wise Southsayer, seeing so *sad* sight, . . . I. v. 8. 8
griesly Night, with visage deadly *sad,* . . . I. v. 20. 1
The trembling ghosts with *sad* amazed mood, . . . I. v. 32. 5
sad Aesculapius far apart Emprisond was . . . I. v. 36. 7
The dreadfull spectacle of that *sad* house of Pryde. . . . I. v. 53. 9
Having escapt so *sad* ensamples in his sight. . . . I. vi. 1. 9
Yet *sad* he was, that his too hastie speed . . . I. vi. 2. 1
read her sorrow in her count'nance *sad;* . . . I. vi. 11. 4
Gan her admire, and her *sad* sorrowes rew, . . . I. vi. 31. 4
'well may I rew To tell the *sad* sight . . . I. vi. 36. 8
sad Una fraught with anguish sore, . . . I. vi. 45. 7
Did to him pace *sad* battaile to darrayne, . . . I. vii. 11. 5
lively breath her *sad* brest did forsake; . . . I. vii. 20. 8
let eternall night so *sad* sight fro me hyde. . . . I. vii. 22. 9
Tragedy . . . these reliques *sad* present unto mine eye. . . . I. vii. 24. 9
Thy *sad* tong cannot tell more heavy plight . . . I. vii. 25. 3
heare the story *sad,* which I shall tell you briefe. . . . I. vii. 42. 9
The *sad* earth, . . . Did grone full grievous . . . I. viii. 8. 7
In pensive plight and *sad* perplexitie, . . . I. viii. 26. 2
Whom these *sad* eyes saw nigh unto deaths dore, . . . I. viii. 27. 2
His *sad* dull eies, deepe sunck in hollow pits, . . . I. viii. 41. 1
sad to view his visage pale and wan, . . . I. viii. 42. 3
sad remembraunce now the Prince amoves . . . I. ix. 18. 3
'From whom retourning *sad* and comfortlesse, . . . I. ix. 28. 1
'With which *sad* instrument of hasty death, . . . I. ix. 30. 1
a gentle Squyre, . . . clad in comely *sad* attyre; . . . I. x. 7. 3
sad Repentance used to embay His blamefull body . . . I. x. 27. 5
In that *sad* house of Penaunce, . . . I. x. 32. 8
after labors long and *sad* delay, . . . I. x. 52. 5
weening that the *sad* end of the warre; . . . I. xi. 32. 3
in her *sad* dreriment, But praying still . . . I. xi. 32. 8
yield his rowme to *sad* succeeding night, . . . I. xi. 49. 6
sad habiliments right well beseene: . . . I. xii. 5. 3
Of straunge adventures, and of perils *sad* . . . I. xii. 15. 4
with utt'rance grave, and count'nance *sad,* . . . I. xii. 15. 7
forth proceeding with *sad* sober cheare, . . . I. xii. 21. 4
widow-like *sad* wimple throwne away, . . . I. xii. 22. 3
Her greeting sends in these *sad* lines addrest . . . I. xii. 26. 2
me, *sad* mayd, or rather widow *sad,* . . . I. xii. 27. 1
To cloke her guile with sorrow and *sad* teene; . . . II. i. 21. 7
To see *sad* pageaunts of mens miseries, . . . II. i. 36. 3
Hath made *sad* witnesse of thy fathers fall, . . . II. i. 37. 2
the *sad* pang approching shee does feele, . . . II. i. 38. 8
arrived where that *sad* pourtraict Of death . . . II. i. 39. 3
death did sitt as *sad* As lump of lead, . . . II. i. 45. 2
hold *sad* life in long captivitee; . . . II. i. 48. 3
In these *sad* wordes she spent her utmost breath: . . . II. i. 49. 4
"*Sad* verse, give death to him that death does give, . . . II. i. 55. 4
with *sad* Cypresse seemely it embrave; . . . II. i. 60. 3
The end of their *sad* Tragedie uptyde, . . . II. ii. 1. 3
his *sad* fathers armes with blood defilde, . . . II. ii. 11. 3
A sober *sad* and comely courteous Dame; . . . II. ii. 14. 5
with pitthy words, and counsell *sad,* . . . II. ii. 28. 5

Sad—*Continued.*
Sad be the sights, and bitter fruites of warre, . . . II. ii. 30. 6
sad ruth does seeme you to restraine, . . . II. ii. 45. 2
At which *sad* stowre Trompart forth stept . . . II. iii. 34. 6
soone him overtooke in *sad* perplexitye. . . . II. iv. 13. 9
Of all my sorrow and of these *sad* teares, . . . II. iv. 18. 2
Which his *sad* speach infixed in my brest, . . . II. iv. 23. 2
The *sad* spectatour of my Tragedie: . . . II. iv. 27. 6
Least thy foolhardize worke thy *sad* confusion.' . . . II. iv. 42. 9
Whiles *sad* Pyrochles lies on sencelesse ground, . . . II. v. 36. 6
where him she byding fond With his *sad* guide: . . . II. vi. 19. 6
Still solemne *sad*, or still disdainfull coy; . . . II. vi. 37. 5
His owne deare Lord Pyrochles in *sad* plight, . . . II. vi. 43. 4
Which with *sad* cares empeach our native joyes. . . . II. vii. 15. 6
over them *sad* horror with grim hew . . . II. vii. 23. 1
Of death and dolor telling *sad* tidings; . . . II. vii. 23. 5
sad Celeno, sitting on a clifte, . . . II. vii. 23. 6
him that walkes in feare and *sad* affright. . . . II. vii. 29. 9
trees of bitter Gall, and Heben *sad;* . . . II. vii. 52. 2
many damned wightes In those *sad* waves, . . . II. vii. 57. 3
Mote I beseech to succour his *sad* plight, . . . II. viii. 25. 7
his hand, more *sad* then lomp of lead, . . . II. viii. 30. 5
gnaw His hart in twaine with *sad* melancholy; . . . II. viii. 50. 8
be no whit *sad* For want of weapons; . . . II. viii. 54. 4
somwhat *sad* and solemne eke in sight, . . . II. ix. 36. 8
Pensive I yeeld I am, and *sad* in mind, . . . II. ix. 38. 6
the *sad* virgin, innocent of all, . . . II. x. 19. 6
did *sad* Brunchildis see The greene shield dyde . . . II. x. 24. 6
y scuith gogh, signe of *sad* crueltee. . . . II. x. 24. 9
In whose *sad* time blood did from heaven rayne. . . . II. x. 34. 2
this *sad* realme, cut into sondry shayres . . . II. x. 37. 4
Through great bloodshed and many a *sad* assay, . . . II. x. 49. 2
daily spectacle of *sad* decay: . . . II. x. 62. 5
Hengist, seeming *sad* for that was donne, . . . II. x. 66. 3
the Palmer eke in habit *sad* . . . II. xi. 3. 7
Gan her recomfort from so *sad* affright, . . . II. xi. 16. 5
the *sad* husbandmans long hope . . . II. xi. 18. 7
shame and *sad* reproch, here to be red . . . II. xii. 9. 6
great sorrow and *sad* agony . . . II. xii. 27. 7
That he might know and ease her sorrow *sad;* . . . II. xii. 28. 3
The hellish Harpyes, prophets of *sad* destiny. . . . II. xii. 36. 9
that knight . . . both sorrowfull and *sad*. . . . II. xii. 84. 2
'*Sad* end,' (quoth he) 'of life intemperate, . . . II. xii. 85. 6
hideous horror and *sad* trembling sownd, . . . III. i. 14. 6
Sad, solemne, sowre, and full of fancies fraile, . . . III. ii. 27. 5
sad sighes and sorrowes deepe Kept watch . . . III. ii. 28. 6
with *sad* drearyhead Chaunged thy lively cheare, . . . III. ii. 30. 8
Certein *sad* words with hollow voice and bace, . . . III. ii. 50. 5
this *sad* evill, which doth her infest, . . . III. iii. 18. 5
'Great ayd . . . shall give in that *sad* day; . . . III. iii. 28. 2
thy *sad* people, utterly fordonne, . . . III. iii. 34. 3
the *sad* end of her sweet Marinell: . . . III. iv. 25. 5
Drew the smooth charett of *sad* Cymoent: . . . III. iv. 33. 2
Supplide her sobbing breaches with *sad* complement. . . . III. iv. 35. 9
Sad life worse then glad death; . . . III. iv. 38. 8
In stead thereof *sad* sorow and disdaine . . . III. iv. 54. 2
'Night! thou foule Mother of annoyaunce *sad,* . . . III. iv. 55. 1
The dreary image of *sad* death appeares: . . . III. iv. 57. 7
with their *sad* instruments Of spoyle and murder . . . III. v. 16. 1
The fearefull end of his avengement *sad,* . . . III. v. 24. 4
There a *sad* cloud of sleepe her overkest, . . . III. vi. 10. 8
whose *sad* annoy The Gods doe dread, . . . III. vi. 24. 7
To which *sad* lovers were transformde of yore; . . . III. vi. 45. 2
Sad Amaranthus, made a flowre but late, . . . III. vi. 45. 6
Sad Amaranthus, in whose purple gore . . . III. vi. 45. 7
laying his *sad* dartes Asyde, . . . III. vi. 49. 8
ruth of her *sad* plight Would make to melt, . . . III. vii. 9. 6
his *sad* mother, seeing his sore plight, . . . III. vii. 20. 6
Full of *sad* feare and doubtfull agony . . . III. vii. 32. 1
this *sad* encounter shonne, And seeke els . . . III. viii. 17. 5
In such distresse and *sad* perplexity . . . III. viii. 33. 8
turned hath great mirth to mourning *sad,* . . . III. viii. 46. 3
'the signes be *sadd;* . . . III. viii. 50. 1
In one *sad* night consumd and throwen downe; . . . III. ix. 39. 5
To save his people *sad* from victours vengefull handes, . . . III. ix. 41. 9
With this *sad* hersall of his heavy stresse . . . III. xi. 18. 1
The soring clouds into *sad* showres ymolt; . . . III. xi. 25. 8
the *sad* distresse In which that boy thee plonged, . . . III. xi. 36. 2
The God himselfe did pensive seeme and *sad,* . . . III. xi. 41. 6
High heven beholdes *sad* lovers nightly theeveryes. . . . III. xi. 45. 9
arrowes . . . Some headed with *sad* lead, . . . III. xi. 48. 4
now *sad* shadowes gan the world to hyde . . . III. xi. 55. 3
every wight dismayd with darkenes *sad* . . . III. xii. 1. 3
inly being more then seeming *sad:* . . . III. xii. 16. 4
He looking lompish and full sullein *sad,* . . . III. xii. 18. 2
Full of *sad* signes, . . . III. xii. 19. 7
measur'd many a *sad* verse, . . . III. xii. 36. 4
he, *sad* man, when he had long . . . Awayted . . . III. xii. 45. 1
Her body, late the prison of *sad* paine, . . . III. xii. 45. *or.* 3
Of lovers *sad* calamities of old . . . IV. i. 1. 1
All which the *sad* effects of discord sung: . . . IV. i. 21. 3
Of sacred Salem; and *sad* Ilion, . . . IV. i. 22. 3
left him now as *sad,* as whilome jollie, . . . IV. i. 36. 8
Sad Clotho held the rocke, . . . IV. ii. 48. 5
Though *sad* and sorie for so heavy sight, . . . IV. iii. 14. 2
whose *sad* ruefull cheare Made her to change her hew, . . . IV. iii. 46. 8
great comfort in her *sad* misfare Was Amoret, . . . IV. v. 30. 4
Full of melancholie and *sad* misfare . . . IV. vi. 2. 3
I rest his wretched thrall, the *sad* Aemylia.' . . . IV. vii. 18. 9
'Ah, *sad* Aemylia!' (then sayd Amoret) . . . IV. vii. 19. 1

Sad—*Continued.*
forth the *sad* Aemylia issewed, . . . IV. vii. 34. 1
Full of *sad* anguish and in heavy case: . . . IV. vii. 38. 4
covered all with shade And *sad* melancholy: . . . IV. vii. 38. 9
with penaunce *sad* And pensive sorrow . . . IV. viii. 2. 5
seeing his *sad* plight, . . . IV. viii. 3. 6
Both in full *sad* and sorrowfull estate: . . . IV. viii. 19. 4
Full of *sad* powre, that poysnous bale did breede . . . IV. viii. 39. 4
that same dwarfe right sorie seem'd and *sad,* . . . IV. viii. 46. 3
In heavy plight and *sad* perplexitie; . . . IV. viii. 57. 2
soone as *sad* Aemylia did espie . . . IV. viii. 63. 1
Who now long time had lyen in prison *sad;* . . . IV. ix. 4. 3
Dislikefull paine so *sad* a taske to take, . . . IV. ix. 40. 3
The which *sad* lovers for their vowes did pay; . . . IV. x. 37. 8
her *sad* semblant and demeanure wyse: . . . IV. x. 49. 6
deckt with smyles that all *sad* humors chaced, . . . IV. x. 50. 8
in *sad* thraldomes chayne; . . . IV. xi. 1. 5
sad Asopus, comely with his hoarie head. . . . IV. xi. 14. 9
those sixe *sad* brethren, like forlorne, . . . IV. xi. 37. 1
Sad Trowis, that once his people over-ran, . . . IV. xi. 41. 7
Soft Spio, sweete Endore, Sao *sad,* . . . IV. xi. 48. 8
In this *sad* plight he walked here and there, . . . IV. xii. 17. 1
away gan chace *Sad* death, . . . IV. xii. 34. 4
Lamenting sore his sorrowfull *sad* tyne, . . . V. i. 13. 8
she feared The *sad* effect of her neare overthrowe; . . . V. ii. 22. 4
(The lucky Pylot of her passage *sad,*) . . . V. iv. 11. 7
the mightie sway Of that *sad* stroke, . . . V. v. 9. 6
thus thy better dayes are drowned In *sad* despaire, . . . V. v. 36. 5
fairely did dissemble her *sad* thoughts unrest. . . . V. v. 44. 9
sad tydings of his balefull smart . . . V. vi. 3. 3
'The tidings *sad* . . . will needs, I see, be rad. . . . V. vi. 10. 4
The whole discourse of his captivance *sad,* . . . V. vi. 17. 2
suffer sleepe to seaze His eye-lids *sad,* . . . V. vi. 26. 6
She sought with ruth to salve his *sad* misfortune sore, . . . V. vii. 38. 9
Full *sad* and sorrowfull was Britomart . . . V. vii. 44. 1
that Damzell, the *sad* Samient, . . . V. viii. 25. 6
Was brought to her *sad* doome, . . . V. ix. 42. 9
Through the *sad* terror of so dreadfull fate, . . . V. ix. 46. 4
streight tooke his flight From that *sad* land . . . V. x. 11. 4
Within the land where dwelt that Ladie *sad;* . . . V. x. 18. 2
Seeing that *sad* ensample them before, . . . V. x. 38. 2
As by *sad* Belge seemes; . . . V. xi. 1. 7
Doubting *sad* end of principle unsound: . . . V. xi. 2. 7
the *sad* steele seizd not, where it was hight, . . . V. xi. 8. 7
With Belge, who watcht all this while full *sad,* . . . V. xi. 32. 8
Those tidings *sad* Did much abash Sir Artegall to heare, . . . V. xi. 40. 6
Lookt up with eyes full *sad* and hart full sore, . . . V. xii. 11. 7
Artegall, returning yet halfe *sad* . . . VI. i. 4. 4
of the Lady selfe in *sad* dismay He was ymett, . . . VI. i. 24. 7
The *sad* Briana which all this beheld; . . . VI. i. 44. 6
her *sad* selfe . . . constrayning, To wype his wounds, . . . VI. ii. 41. 4
'Dame, be no longer *sad;* . . . VI. ii. 45. 4
Both to her love and to her selfe in that *sad* dreare. . . . VI. ii. 46. 9
timely joy . . . now turnd to *sad* annoy? . . . VI. iii. 4. 9
Crying aloud to shew her *sad* misfare . . . VI. iii. 24. 5
And his *sad* Ladie left in pitifull affright: . . . VI. iv. 1. 9
wrapt In *sad* misfortunes foule deformity . . . VI. v. 1. 3
Did wexe exceeding sorrowfull and *sad,* . . . VI. v. 3. 3
sad dispaire away did cast. . . . VI. v. 21. 9
About the *sad* Serena things to dight, . . . VI. v. 25. 3
With holesome reede of *sad* sobriety, . . . VI. vi. 5. 7
Ryding a softly pace with portance *sad,* . . . VI. vii. 6. 8
His mindes *sad* message backe unto him sent; . . . VI. viii. 8. 3
downe themselves doe drive To *sad* decay, . . . VI. ix. 22. 5
Faire Pastorella, sorrowfull and *sad,* . . . VI. x. 40. 5
Most sorrowfull, most *sad,* that ever sight, . . . VI. x. 40. 6
would rew And pitty her *sad* plight, . . . VI. xi. 2. 9
Faire Pastorella, whose *sad* mournefull hew . . . VI. xi. 3. 8
The *sad* remembrance of her wretched plight: . . . VI. xi. 50. 7
them pursu'd into their dortours *sad,* . . . VI. xii. 24. 3
sad examples shewed Of her great power, . . . VII. vi. 4. 6
do pay them *sad* penance, . . . VII. vii. 23. 7
calling forth out of *sad* Winters night . . . *Am.* iv. 5
Such death the *sad* ensample of your might. . . . *Am.* vii. 14
In secret sorow, and *sad* pensivenesse. . . . *Am.* xxxiv. 14
drery *sad* disdayne Of all worlds gladnesse, . . . *Am.* lii. 11
tempests *sad* assay, . . . *Am.* lxiii. 1
speake no word to her of these *sad* plights, . . . *Am.* lxxxiii. 11
slowly seemd to move Theyr *sad* protract . . . *Am.* lxxxvi. 4
could not chose but laugh . . . Though *sad* to see him pained. . . . *Epig.* iv. 34
her *sad* eyes, still fastened on the ground, . . . *Epith.* 234
How slowly does *sad* Time his feathers move? . . . *Epith.* 281
guydest lovers through the nights *sad* dread, . . . *Epith.* 290
Without tempestuous storms or *sad* afray: . . . *Epith.* 327
Make sudden *sad* affrights; . . . *Epith.* 339

Sad-afflicted. To succour the weake state of *sad afflicted* Troy. . . . II. iii. 31. 9

Sadder. Thilke sollein season *sadder* plight doth aske, . . . *S.C.* N. 17
To *sadder* times thou mayst attune thy quill, . . . *S.C.* N. 35
Your string could soone to *sadder* tenor turne, . . . *Epith.* 9

Saddle. from his *sadle* quite he did him beare. . . . I. iii. 35. 7
from his *saddle* forced him to fly; . . . II. viii. 33. 7
Ne her out of the stedfast *sadle* driv'd; . . . III. vii. 40. 7
being forst his *saddle* soone to leave, . . . IV. i. 36. 4
for to winne the *saddle* lost the steed. . . . IV. v. 22. 5
Whiles unawares his *saddle* he forwent, . . . IV. vi. 11. 8
As he with golden *saddle* is arayd, . . . V. iii. 35. 4
bore him quite out of his *saddle,* . . . V. viii. 7. 8
from his *saddle* swarved nought asyde, . . . V. x. 35. 2

Saddle-bow. to his *saddle-bow* thereby He bowed low, . . . IV. viii. 43. 4

Sadly. They *sadly* traveild thus, . . . I. viii. 2. 1

Sadly—*Continued.*
Musing full *sadly* in his sullein mind: . . . . I. ix. 35. 3
sadly soucing on the sandy shore, ... III. iv. 16. 8
who lay the whiles in swoune, full *sadly* set, ... IV. vii. 35. 4
Sadly she rode, and never word did say . . . . V. vi. 18. 3
Now glooming *sadly*, so to cloke her matter; . . . . VI. vi. 42. 8
Sadness. your faire beautie doe with *sadnes* spill? . . . . II. ix. 37. 6
on me thou shinedst late in *sadnesse*, ... *Am.* xxxix. 6
feeling thence, no more her sorowes *sadnesse*, ... *Am.* xxxix. 11
And all mirth *sadnesse*, and all lucre losse. . . . . *H.H.B.* 280
Safe. *See* **Save.**
Safe in his dreadles den him thought to hide: . . . . *Van.* x. 4
till *safe* and sound 'She home returne, ... *S.C.* Au. 180
safe delivered from sad decay, ... *Gn.* 335
meane estate In *safe* assurance, ... *Hub.* 910
'*Safe* then, and safest were my sillie sheepe, ... *D.* 134
'Henceforth in *safe* assuraunce may ye rest, ... I. ii. 27. 1
in minde to slipp away, Soone as appeard *safe* opportunitie: . I. ii. 41. 7
saw his guest Would *safe* depart, ... I. ix. 54. 3
And eke be *safe* from daunger far descryde. . . . . I. xi. 5. 4
the land . . . seemeth *safe* from storms . . . . I. xii. 1. 5
safe ye seised have the shore, ... I. xii. 17. 7
Here she a while may make her *safe* abode, ... I. xii. 42. 5
Better *safe* port then be in seas distrest.' . . . . II. vi. 23. 8
safe I have them kept in secret mew . . . . II. vii. 19. 8
found no place wher *safe* he shroud him might: . . . . II. vii. 22. 7
nothing else might keepe her *safe* and sound: . . . . II. xii. 82. 7
her to Faery court *safe* to convay; . . . . III. i. 2. 4
safe committ to her soft fethered nest, ... III. i. 58. 7
Her tender babe, it seeing *safe* appeare, ... III. ii. 11. 8
Sporting him selfe in *safe* felicity: . . . . III. vi. 49. 4
till *safe* him selfe he see from jeopardy. . . . . III. x. 53. 9
past the fire *Safe* and untoucht, ... III. xi. 26. 2
thought himselfe not *safe* enough thereby, ... III. xii. 12. 2
found right *safe* assurance theare. . . . . IV. i. 15. 9
This happie day . . . In which you *safe* I see, ... IV. ii. 23. 6
Joyous to see her *safe* after long toyle. . . . . IV. vi. 25. 5
yet she may be *safe* though somewhat strayd: . . . . IV. vi. 37. 8
did in *safe* securitie abide, ... IV. viii. 31. 4
shake the *safe* assuraunce of their state: . . . . IV. ix. 16. 4
She was as *safe* as in a Sanctuary. . . . . IV. ix. 19. 6
of her health when Artegall did heare, And *safe* returne, . . V. ii. 3. 6
'All times have wont *safe* passage to afford . . . . V. viii. 22. 1
With *safe* assuraunce and establishment: . . . . V. xi. 35. 4
Where she in *safe* assuraunce mote abide, ... VI. iii. 28. 8
whilest in Morpheus bosome *safe* she lay, ... VI. viii. 34. 6
Be but vaine shadowes to this *safe* retyre Of life, ... VI. ix. 27. 5
which mote pervart His *safe* assurance, ... *Am.* xlii. 12
Safe-conduct. Gave them *safe conduct*, till to end they came. III. x. 16. 7
To *safe-conduct* his love, ... VI. iii. 15. 8
Safe-conducting. For *safe conducting* of his sickely Dame . VI. iii. 31. 3
Safe-guard. for the *safegard* of his personage, ... *Hub.* 1117
ne car'd for his *saufgard*, ... II. v. 8. 8
To *savegard* her ywandred all alone: . . . . III. viii. 46. 8
'out of the flames for *safegard* fled, ... III. ix. 41. 2
since this Ladie . . . needeth *safegard* . . . . VI. ii. 38. 2
watch about her for her *safegard* keepe. . . . . VI. iii. 44. 9
his backe for best *safegard* He lent against a tree, ... VI. v. 18. 8
Safely. our sheepe about us *safely* fedde. . . . . *S.C.* Jun. 88
Here we our slender pypes may *safely* charme. . . . . *S.C.* O. 118
she is gone that *safely* did hem keepe: . . . . *S.C.* N. 137
The shepheards there abroad may *safely* lie, ... *Col.* 316
Under your beames I will me *safely* shrowd . . . . I. iv. 48. 3
My little boat can *safely* passe this perilous bourne.' . . . II. vi. 10. 9
'What secret place' . . . 'can *safely* hold . . . . II. vii. 20. 1
A seate in Ireland *safely* to remayne, ... II. x. 41. 8
Here may thy storme-bett vessell *safely* ryde, ... II. xii. 32. 7
Thus *safely* with my love I thence did wend.' . . . . IV. x. 58. 8
all that while her life she *safely* garded; . . . . V. v. 8. 8
In covert shade him selfe did *safely* rest, ... VI. iii. 20. 3
to keepe him selfe so *safely* as he may. . . . . VI. iii. 47. 9
Safer. in this quiet make you *safer* live.' . . . . VI. ix. 32. 8
Safest. 'Safe then, and *safest* were my sillie sheepe, ... *D.* 134
when he sleepes in most security And *safest* seemes, . . . III. iv. 27. 4
Aread what course of you is *safest* dempt, ... III. xi. 23. 3
Safeties. She warned them to tend their *safeties* well, . . . IV. ii. 53. 8
Safety. left mine owne his *safetie* to tender; . . . . *Gn.* 362
none the holy things in *safety* kept, ... I. iii. 17. 8
none did others *safety* despize, ... I. ix. 1. 5
am I now in *safetie* sure,' (quoth he) . . . . I. ix. 26. 1
she had great doubt of his *safety*, ... I. xi. 33. 8
for his *safetie* gan devoutly pray, ... I. xi. 50. 8
here a while ye may in *safety* rest, ... II. vi. 23. 6
Ne of his *safetie* seemed care he kept; . . . . II. vi. 42. 5
Ne suffred lust his *safety* to betray. . . . . II. vii. 64. 8
'The charge . . . Of his deare *safety*, ... II. viii. 8. 2
For *safety* that same his sea-marke made, ... II. x. 6. 6
Saxons, whom he for his *safety* imployes. . . . . II. x. 64. 9
The Palmer, seeing them in *safetie* past, ... II. xii. 9. 1
of our *safety* good heede to take; . . . . II. xii. 17. 7
when I shall my selfe in *safety* see, ... III. iv. 10. 6
desire No service but thy *safety* and ayd; . . . . III. v. 36. 4
of her *safety* greatly grew afrayd. . . . . III. vii. 25. 3
safety fownd at sea which she fownd not at land. . . . III. vii. 27. 9
am I glad that here I now in *safety* ame. . . . . III. viii. 23. 9
That Ladies *safetie* is sore to be dradd. . . . . III. viii. 50. 3
did him selfe to *safety* retyre.' . . . . III. ix. 40. 9
of her *safety* in great doubt I ame, ... III. x. 39. 7
Here for to stay in *safetie* behynd: . . . . III. x. 41. 6
Till we returne againe in *safety*: . . . . III. x. 42. 5
Safety—*Continued.*
Forgetfull of his *safety*, ... III. xii. 17. 9
every part to *safety* full sownd, ... III. xii. 38. 6
in *safetie* now I have you seene, ... III. xii. 40. 4
she gan to dout Their *safetie*, ... IV. ii. 46. 6
life it selfe seemd loathsome, and long *safetie* ill. . . . IV. iii. 36. 9
Feare of her *safety* did her not constraine; . . . . IV. ix. 18. 1
Where he him selfe did rest in *safety* . . . . V. iv. 46. 6
harbour here in *safety* from those ravenous dogs.' . . . . V. x. 23. 9
Albe that it most *safety* to him *gave*, ... V. xi. 46. 5
conceiving then great feare Of my fraile *safetie*, ... VI. ii. 29. 3
Or understand that she in *safetie* did remaine. . . . . VI. iv. 40. 9
Like scattred sheepe, to seeke for *safetie*, ... VI. vi. 38. 6
for his *safety* he did him constraine To give him ground, . . VI. vii. 46. 5
fled away . . . To seeke for *safety*; . . . . VI. vii. 50. 5
in that villaines health her *safety* lies; . . . . VI. viii. 18. 5
False Fortune did her *safety* betray . . . . VI. viii. 34. 8
minding more her *safety* then himselfe, ... VI. xi. 19. 3
On which he *safety* hopes that earst feard to be lost. . . . VI. xi. 44. 9
The joyous *safety* of so sweet a rest; . . . . *Am.* lxiii. 10
annoy The *safety* of our joy; . . . . *Epith.* 325
Safety's. forst their chiefetain, for his *safeties* sake, ... II. x. 16. 6
Saffron. *Saffron*, sought for in Cilician soyle; . . . . *Gn.* 671
Weary of aged Tithones *saffron* bed, ... I. ii. 7. 2
Sage. The wholesome *Saulge*, and Lavender still gray, ... *Mui.* 187
powreth forth these oracles so *sage* . . . . *Col.* 825
manly courage, Tempred with . . . advizement *sage*, ... *Ded. Son.* xiv. 9
The Laurell, meed of . . . Poets *sage*; . . . . I. i. 9. 2
a most mighty king, most rich and *sage*: . . . . I. ii. 23. 3
On which her six *sage* Counsellours did ryde, ... I. iv. 18. 2
tyred limbes to rest, O matrone *sage*,' (quoth she) . . . . I. x. 11. 2
A noble crew . . . Of *sage* and sober peres, ... I. xii. 5. 5
He seemd to be a *sage* and sober syre; . . . . II. i. 7. 7
Helpe with thy hand, or with thy counsell *sage*: . . . . II. vi. 48. 4
in demeanure sober, and in counsell *sage*. . . . . II. ix. 27. 9
that *sage* Pylian syre, ... II. ix. 48. 4
He now was growne right wise and wondrous *sage*: . . . . II. ix. 54. 5
with speeches *sage* Inquyrd, ... II. x. 27. 8
his *sage* Palmer that him governed; . . . . II. xii. 38. 5
Such vertue in his staffe had eke this Palmer *sage*. . . . . II. xii. 41. 9
a God him *sage* Antiquity Did wisely make, ... II. xii. 48. 1
counsell *sage* in steed thereof to him applyde. . . . . II. xii. 82. 9
the *sage* wisard telles, as he has redd, ... III. i. 16. 8
With comely haveour and count'nance *sage*, ... III. xii. 3. 8
Few men, but such as sober are and *sage*, ... IV. iii. 43. 7
her friends with counsell *sage* Dissuaded her . . . . IV. viii. 50. 4
Large Lisianassa, and Pronaea *sage*, ... IV. xi. 50. 2
First was a *sage* old Syre, ... V. ix. 43. 7
Which with *sage* counsell . . . He could enforme, ... VI. vi. 3. 7
Sagely. Sober he seemde, and very *sagely* sad, ... I. i. 29. 5
Sages. Where be those learned wits and antique *Sages*, ... *Ti.* 59
there dwelt three honorable *sages*, ... II. ix. 47. 8
all the workes of those wise *sages*, ... IV. Pr. 3. 3
Said. *See* **Old-said.**
An Angell . . . cride out aloude, and *sayd*, ... *Rev.* ii. 13
new Earth, new Heaven, *sayde* Saint John. . . . . *Rev.* iv. 1
A voice then *sayde*, beholde . . . . *Rev.* iv. 5
said Jove, 'Lo! how the least the greatest may reprove.' . . . *Van.* iv. 13
Come tell me what was *sayd* of mee, ... *To his Booke* 17
Tho *sayd*, he was a winged lad, ... *S.C.* Mar. 112
*Nay *sayd* I thereto, by my deare borrowe, ... *S.C.* May 150
if that my Grandsire me *sayd* be true, ... *S.C.* May 268
Sike one (*sayd* Algrind) Moses was, ... *S.C.* Jul. 157
shepeheards (*sayd* he) there doen leade, ... *S.C.* Jul. 185
Never shall be *sayde* that Perigot was dared. . . . . *S.C.* Au. 24
In forrein costes men *sayd* was plentye; . . . . *S.C.* S. 28
reigned (as men *sayd*) in Venus seate. . . . . *S.C.* D. 60
Said he, 'What have I, wretch, deserv'd, ... *Gn.* 329
Thus having *said*, he heavily departed . . . . *Gn.* 639
'Whilome (*said* she) . . . . *Hub.* 45
'Certes (*said* he) . . . . *Hub.* 83
'Surely (*said* th' Ape) . . . . *Hub.* 95
'Now surely brother (*said* the Foxe anon) . . . . *Hub.* 124
afterwards with grave advizement *said*: . . . . *Hub.* 176
(*Said* then the Foxe) . . . . *Hub.* 194
to him *said*: 'Good Sir, full glad am I, ... *Hub.* 270
'Gladly (*said* he) . . . . *Hub.* 287
'Ah! (*said* the Ape, as sighing wondrous sad) . . . . *Hub.* 368
Said then the Foxe: . . . . *Hub.* 403
'It seemes (*said* he) . . . . *Hub.* 415
(*said* th' Ape) the charge is wondrous great, ... *Hub.* 431
Therefore *said* he, ... *Hub.* 439
there (*said* the Priest) is arte indeed: . . . . *Hub.* 483
Said; 'Ah! sir Mule, ... *Hub.* 589
'Foolish Foxe (*said* the Mule) . . . . *Hub.* 595
'Ay me! (*said* then the Foxe) . . . . *Hub.* 601
'From royall Court I lately came (*said* he) . . . . *Hub.* 607
tell us (*said* the Ape) . . . . *Hub.* 615
'Marie, (*said* he) . . . . *Hub.* 619
(*said* the Ape) how shall we first come in, ... *Hub.* 643
'How els (*said* he) . . . . *Hub.* 645
'Now (*sayd* he) . . . . *Hub.* 967
(*sayd* the Ape) . . . . *Hub.* 973
'Fond Ape! (*sayd* then the Foxe) . . . . *Hub.* 977
'I am most worthie, (*said* the Ape) . . . . *Hub.* 1027
'Nay (*said* the Foxe) . . . . *Hub.* 1033
The subtile Foxe so well his message *sayd*, ... *Hub.* 1101
Let God, (*said* he) . . . care for the manie, ... *Hub.* 1195
(then *said* the Foxe) . . . . *Hub.* 1213
'Arise, (*said* Mercurie) . . . . *Hub.* 1327

Said—*Continued.*

‘He should advaunced bee to high regard,’ (*Said* they) III. i. 27. 9
(*said* she then) ‘now may ye all see plaine, III. i. 29. 7
‘Too well we see,’ (*saide* they) III. i. 30. 1
(*Said* he) ‘perhaps ye should it better find: III. ii. 13. 5
sayd; ‘Sir knight, these ydle termes forbeare; III. ii. 16. 1
(*sayd* she) ‘what evill plight Hath thee opprest, III. ii. 30. 7
So having *sayd,* her twixt her armes twaine III. ii. 34. 1
‘O daughter deare!’ (*said* she) ‘despeire no whit; III. ii. 35. 6
‘Was never such, but mote the like be fownd,’ (*Said* she) III. ii. 36. 4
Can doe’ (*said* she) ‘that which cannot be donne.’ III. ii. 36. 8
‘These idle wordes’ (*said* she) ‘doe nought aswage III. ii. 37. 1
‘Daughter,’ (*said* she) ‘what need ye be dismayd? III. ii. 40. 1
that old Dame *said* many an idle verse, III. ii. 48. 8
to the virgin sayd, thrise *sayd* she itt; III. ii. 50. 6
That *sayd,* her rownd about she from her turnd, III. ii. 51. 1
to her *said:* ‘Beldame, by that ye tell III. iii. 17. 4
to him *said:* ‘Yf any leaches skill III. iii. 18. 1
brusting forth in laughter, to her *sayd:* III. iii. 19. 2
sayd; ‘Sith then thou knowest all our griefe, III. iii. 21. 1
‘But read,’ (*saide* Glauce) ‘thou Magitian, III. iii. 25. 1
‘Nay but the terme’ (*sayd* he) ‘is limited, III. iii. 44. 1
‘Deare image of my selfe, (she *sayd*) III. iv. 36. 1
‘What mister wight,’ (*saide* he) ‘and how arayd?’ III. v. 5. 1
‘Now certes, swaine,’ (*saide* he) ‘such one, I weene, III. v. 6. 1
me lever were to weeten that,’ (*Saide* he) III. v. 7. 2
‘Mercy, deare Lord!’ (*said* he) ‘what grace is this III. v. 35. 1
Thereat she blushing *saide;* ‘Ah! gentle Squire, III. v. 36. 1
‘Unthankfull wretch,’ (*saide* he) ‘is this the meed, III. v. 45. 1
sayd that hee Was the disturber of all civill life, III. vi. 14. 7
to her scoffing *sayd:* III. vi. 21. 2
sharply *saide:* ‘Goe, Dame; goe, seeke your boy, III. vi. 24. 2
gan relent What shee had *said;* III. vi. 25. 3
(*said* he) ‘one word may tell III. vii. 57. 1
(then laughing *sayd* The knight) III. vii. 57. 5
‘The first which then refused me,’ (*said* hee) III. vii. 58. 1
she knew, she *said,* I would disclose Her counsell, III. vii. 58. 8
‘Perdy’ (*sayd* Satyrane) ‘thou Squyre of Dames, III. vii. 61. 1
(*sayd* he) ‘this Lady is my deare; III. viii. 12. 8
(*said* Braggadochio) ‘needes thou wilt Thy daies abridge III. viii. 18. 1
This *said,* they both a furlongs mountenaunce Retird III. viii. 18. 5
‘Ah!’ (*sayd* she) ‘father, I note read aright III. viii. 23. 7
saide his boat the way could wisely tell; III. viii. 24. 7
then she *said* she lov’d none, but a Faery knight. III. viii. 39. 9
Who thereto answering *said:* III. viii. 46. 1
‘Ah! gentle knight,’ (*said* then Sir Satyrane) III. viii. 47. 1
Then *said:* ‘Fayre Sir, III. viii. 48. 3
(*said* Paridell) ‘the signes be sadd; III. viii. 50. 1
(*said* then the Squyre of Dames) III. viii. 51. 1
is he not more mad,’ (*sayd* Paridell) III. ix. 8. 1
let us first’ (*sayd* Satyrane) ‘entreat III. ix. 9. 1
‘Anchyses sonne, begott of Venus fayre,’ *Said* he, III. ix. 41. 2
(*said* Britomart) ‘afresh appeard The glory III. ix. 44. 1
(*said* Paridell) ‘Pardon, I pray, III. ix. 47. 1
Indeed he *said,* . . . there grew Another plant, III. ix. 47. 5
Said he, ‘Thou man of nought, III. x. 24. 6
low prostrating *said:* ‘Good Sir, III. x. 25. 2
(*said* Trompart) ‘take good hart, III. x. 26. 1
bold he *sayd;* O most redoubted Pere! III. x. 26. 8
‘It is not long,’ (*saide* hee) III. x. 27. 1
sayd: ‘Thy offers base I greatly loth, III. x. 29. 6
(*sayd* Paridell) ‘She wonneth in the forrest III. x. 38. 2
‘Perdy, nay,’ (*said* Malbecco) III. x. 39. 1
‘Ah! but,’ (*said* crafty Trompart) ‘weete ye well, III. x. 40. 2
Said Trompart; ‘You, . . . stay in safetie behynd: III. x. 41. 4
best,’ (*said* he) ‘that ye doe leave Your treasure III. x. 51. 1
He *sayd;* ‘O soverayne Lord! III. xi. 9. 2
sayd; ‘Sir knight, your cause is nothing lesse III. xi. 18. 3
‘Ah! gentlest knight alive,’ (*sayd* Scudamore) III. xi. 19. 1
‘Life is not lost,’ (*said* she) III. xi. 19. 8
thus *sayd:* ‘What . . . provoke we heare? III. xi. 22. 6
‘Perdy not so,’ (*saide* shee) III. xi. 24. 5
winged boy . . . scoffing thus unto his mother *sayd:* III. xi. 35. 7
to him *said:* ‘Thou wicked man, III. xii. 35. 1
Said: ‘Gentle Dame, III. xii. 40. 2
both did and *sayd* Full many things IV. i. 7. 4
sayd, her love to lose she was full loth, IV. i. 10. 8
Was tickled with delight, and jesting *sayd;* IV. i. 33. 6
‘Ah! Sir,’ (*said* Paridell) ‘do not dismay Your selfe IV. i. 40. 7
Which when as Blandamour beheld, he *sayd;* IV. i. 44. 1
‘Ah gentle knight!’ then false Duessa *sayd,* IV. i. 46. 1
‘Vile hag!’ (*sayd* Scudamour) why dost thou lye, IV. i. 48. 1
‘Fond knight,’ (*sayd* she) IV. i. 48. 3
‘Lo! recreant,’ (*sayd* he) IV. i. 51. 1
made him open chalenge, and thus boldly *sayd;* IV. ii. 12. 9
They *said,* it was for love of Florimell. IV. ii. 22. 2
‘Fond Squire,’ full angry then *sayd* Paridell, IV. ii. 22. 5
as he *said,* by that her outward grace IV. ii. 22. 8
Lachesis thereat gan to repine, And *sayd;* IV. ii. 51. 5
said, ‘Sir Knight, sith ye this Lady clame, IV. iv. 9. 1
Braggadochio *said,* he never thought IV. iv. 10. 4
Which when that warriour saw, he *said* no more, IV. v. 39. 1
‘Certes,’ (*sayd* he) ‘ye mote as now excuse Me IV. vi. 4. 6
‘This other day’ (*sayd* he) ‘a stranger knight IV. vi. 5. 6
‘A stranger knight,’ *sayd* he, ‘unknowne by name, IV. vi. 6. 3
thus he sharply *sayd:* IV. vi. 7. 6
Sayd then Sir Scudamour: IV. vi. 9. 6
(*said* she) ‘where am I, or with whom? IV. vii. 11. 1
(then *sayd* Amoret) IV. vii. 19. 1
‘Is this the faith?’ she *said*—and *said* no more, IV. vii. 36. 8

Said—*Continued.*

saw that all he *said* and did was vaine, IV. vii. 47. 2
Well *said* the Wiseman, now prov’d true by this IV. viii. 1. 1
For all his joy, he *said,* IV. viii. 57. 6
said; ‘And lives yet Amyas?’ IV. viii. 63. 5
lesse,’ (*said* she) ‘by all the woe I pas, IV. viii. 63. 7
sooth is *said,* and tride in each degree, IV. ix. 27. 8
Scudamour . . . thus *saide:* IV. ix. 38. 6
‘True he it *said,* what ever man it *sayd,* IV. x. 1. 1
One of the worlds seven wonders *sayd* to bee, IV. x. 30. 4
said no more: IV. x. 55. 6
whether old Proteus true or false had *sayd,* IV. xii. 28. 4
‘it’s *sayd* That all the world V. Pr. 9. 1
‘Who was it then,’ (*sayd* Artegall) V. i. 16. 1
‘A knight,’ (*said* he) ‘if knight he may be thought V. i. 16. 3
‘Aread’ (*sayd* he) ‘which way then did he make? V. i. 19. 1
No sooner *sayd,* but streight he after sent His yron page, V. i. 20. 1
sayd; ‘Now sure this doubtfull causes right V. i. 25. 1
‘Sith then,’ (*sayd* he) ‘ye both the dead deny, V. i. 26. 1
‘Not so, thou Squire,’ (he *sayd*) V. i. 28. 2
‘He is’ (*said* he) ‘a man of great defence, V. ii. 5. 3
‘Now by my life,’ (*sayd* he) ‘and God to guide, V. ii. 10. 5
He *sayd* that he would all the earth uptake V. ii. 31. 1
For-why, he *sayd,* they all unequall were, V. ii. 32. 1
‘Thou foolishe Elfe,’ (*said* then the Gyant wroth) V. ii. 37. 1
Therewith the Gyant much abashed *sayd,* V. ii. 44. 1
‘Which is’ (*sayd* he) ‘more heavy then in weight, V. ii. 44. 5
sayd that words were light, V. ii. 45. 1
‘Well then,’ *sayd* Artegall, ‘let it be tride: V. ii. 45. 4
‘Now take the right likewise,’ *sayd* Artegale, V. ii. 46. 1
said, ‘Be not upon thy balance wroken, V. ii. 47. 4
said, that surely Florimell it was, V. iii. 17. 6
ne ought he *sayd,* Ne ought he did, V. iii. 18. 5
to the boaster *said;* ‘Thou losell base, V. iii. 20. 6
‘If that’ (*said* Guyon) ‘may you satisfie, V. iii. 32. 7
sayd; ‘Lo there! Sir Guyon, V. iii. 35. 2
So having *sayd,* the younger did ensew: V. iv. 15. 1
‘Unto yourselfe,’ *said* they, ‘we give our word, V. iv. 16. 4
Then Artegall thus to the younger *sayd:* V. iv. 17. 1
‘Your right is good,’ (*sayd* he) V. iv. 17. 8
Then turning to the elder thus he *sayd:* V. iv. 18. 1
‘Your right is good,’ (*sayd* he) V. iv. 18. 8
‘How hight that Amazon?’ (*sayd* Artegall) V. iv. 33. 1
‘Now sure,’ (*said* he) ‘. . . I will not rest V. iv. 34. 1
thus to her *sayd:* V. iv. 48. 3
call Her nearest handmayd, . . . And to her *said:* V. v. 29. 3
(*said* then the faithfull Mayd) V. v. 31. 1
‘Clarin,’ (*said* she) ‘thou seest yond Fayry Knight, V. v. 32. 1
not of cancred will,’ (*Sayd* he) ‘nor obstinate V. v. 41. 2
sayd that he was obstinate and sterne, V. v. 46. 1
mute, . . . Till she againe thus *sayd:* V. vi. 10. 1
(*sayd* then the yron man) V. vi. 16. 1
‘*Sayd* I not then’ (quoth she) ‘erwhile aright, V. vi. 16. 6
she had vow’d, she *sayd,* not to forgo V. vi. 23. 6
‘Ye guilty eyes,’ (*sayd* shee) ‘the which with guyle V. vi. 25. 1
‘Certes,’ (*sayd* she) ‘sith ye so well have spide V. vii. 19. 1
thus upbrayding *said:* V. vii. 32. 4
(the Prince then *sayd*) V. viii. 15. 5
So *said* this Damzell, that hight Samient; V. viii. 23. 7
his owne wylie wit, (she *sayd*) V. ix. 5. 1
‘Were not’ (*sayd* she) ‘that it should let your pace V. ix. 7. 5
‘Then let not that’ (*said* they) ‘stay your intent; V. ix. 7. 8
To which when she approched, thus she *sayd:* V. ix. 20. 3
‘Ah! my sweet boyes,’ (*Sayd* she) V. x. 20. 4
‘And you, Sir knight,’ (*Said* she) V. x. 21. 2
‘Ay me!’ (*sayd* she) ‘and whether shall I goe? V. x. 23. 1
‘Nathlesse,’ (*said* he) ‘deare Ladie, with me goe; V. x. 24. 1
thankt him for that wondrous grace, And further *sayd:* V. xi. 18. 2
‘What is there else’ (*sayd* he) ‘left of their rout? V. xi. 18. 8
‘Now turne againe,’ (Sir Artegall then *sayd*) V. xi. 43. 1
why have ye’ (*said* Artegall) ‘forborne Your owne good shield V. xi. 52. 1
‘Fie on such forgerie!’ (*sayd* Artegall) V. xi. 56. 6
‘Yet let me you of courtesie request’ (*Said* Burbon) V. xi. 57. 2
Sayd Artegall: ‘What foule disgrace is this V. xi. 62. 1
thought more the lesse she *sed.* V. xii. 29. 9
whatsoever good by any *sayd* Or doen she heard, V. xii. 34. 1
happy man,’ (*sayd* then Sir Calidore) VI. i. 5. 6
Sayd Artegall, ‘I such a Beast did see, VI. i. 9. 2
‘That surely is that Beast’ (*saide* Calidore) VI. i. 10. 1
afterwards thus to him *saide.* VI. i. 11. 9
‘A shamefull use . . . *Sayd* Calidore, VI. i. 14. 2
Sayd then that Squire; VI. i. 14. 5
‘False traytor Knight!’ (*said* she) VI. i. 25. 1
‘If I doe so,’ (*sayd* he) VI. i. 28. 7
thus he to him *sayd:* VI. i. 40. 3
‘Certes,’ (*said* he) ‘loth were I to have broken VI. ii. 7. 6
‘Perdie great blame’ (then *said* Sir Calidore) VI. ii. 8. 6
‘That shall I, sooth,’ (*said* he) ‘to you declare. VI. ii. 9. 1
Said then Sir Calidore; ‘Neither will I Him charge VI. ii. 14. 3
‘Certes, Sir knight’ (*sayd* she) ‘full loth I were VI. ii. 15. 6
(then *sayd* Sir Calidore) ‘and right, Me seemes, VI. ii. 23. 5
he *said:* ‘Ye dolefull Dame, VI. ii. 42. 1
And to her *said:* ‘Dame, be no longer sad; VI. ii. 45. 4
whilome that good Poet *sayd,* VI. iii. 1. 1
nought weighing what he *sayd* or did, VI. iii. 37. 1
‘Ill seemes,’ (*sayd* he) ‘if he so valiaunt be, VI. iii. 40. 6
Her chearing up, thus gently to her *sayd:* VI. iv. 27. 7
Yet was it *sayd,* there should to him a sonne Be gotten, VI. iv. 32. 6
And, having cheared her, thus *said:* VI. iv. 34. 6
Found nothing that he *said* unmeet nor geason, VI. iv. 37. 2

Said—*Continued.*
soothly it was *sayd* by common fame, . . . VI. v. 37. 1
thus he to them *sayd:* . . . VI. vi. 6. 5
(*sayd* then Serena, sighing sore) . . . VI. vi. 13. 5
sith we need good counsell,' (*sayd* the swaine) . . . VI. vi. 13. 8
'The best' (*sayd* he) 'that I can you advize, . . . VI. vi. 14. 1
Thus having *sayd,* . . . VI. vi. 15. 1
beleev'd that all he *sayd* was trew; . . . VI. vii. 5. 1
Said then the one of them; . . . VI. vii. 5. 7
'He rides' (*said* Turpine) 'there not farre afore, . . . VI. vii. 6. 1
Then thus *said* he: . . . VI. vii. 12. 6
much mused at such villenie, And *sayd:* . . . VI. vii. 13. 2
Yet thus at length he *said:* . . . VI. vii. 14. 6
'Perdie,' (*said* he) 'in evill houre it fell, . . . VI. vii. 15. 1
'He lyes' (*said* he) 'upon the cold bare ground, . . . VI. vii. 16. 6
Like as that other knight to him had *sayd;* . . . VI. vii. 20. 3
Fell flat to ground, ne word unto him *sayd,* . . . VI. vii. 25. 8
to the Prince thus *sayd:* . . . VI. viii. 6. 1
Her tongue to her restord, then thus she *sayd:* . . . VI. viii. 19. 4
'Certes,' (*sayd* then the Prince) 'the God is just, . . . VI. viii. 23. 1
(*sayd* the sory Mayd) . . . VI. viii. 24. 1
Ah! nay, Sir Knight,' (*said* she) . . . VI. viii. 30. 1
sleepe, they *sayd,* would make her battill better: . . . VI. viii. 38. 3
'How much' (*sayd* he) 'more happie is the state . . . VI. ix. 19. 1
(*said* then old Meliboe) . . . VI. ix. 29. 1
in each mans self' (*said* Calidore) 'It is . . . VI. ix. 31. 1
Gave it to Coridon, and *said* he wonne it well. . . . VI. ix. 44. 9
'Right sory I,' (*saide* then Sir Calidore) . . . VI. x. 20. 6
Sayd Calidore: 'Now sure it yrketh mee, . . . VI. x. 29. 2
'Ah, well-away!' (*sayd* he, then sighing sore) . . . VI. xi. 29. 1
they themselves were evill groomes, they *sayd,* . . . VI. xi. 40. 3
'My liefe,' (*sayd* she) 'ye know that long ygo, . . . VI. xii. 17. 5
'Most certaine markes' (*sayd* she) 'do me it teach; . . . VI. xii. 18. 3
She long so held, and softly weeping *sayd;* . . . VI. xii. 19. 7
So having *said,* he ceast; . . . VII. vi. 22. 1
So having *said,* she thus to him replide: . . . VII. vi. 34. 6
Ne ought he *said,* what ever he did heare, . . . VII. vi. 49. 8
'I well consider all that ye have *said,* . . . VII. vi. 58. 1
Then gin I thinke on that which Nature *sayd,* . . . VII. viii. 2. 1
Vayne man, *sayd* she, . . . *Am.* lxxv. 5
Cupid humbly came, And *sayd* to her; 'All hayle, my mother!' *Epig.* iii. 3
closely smiling *sayd,* 'Twixt earnest and twixt game: . . . *Epig.* iv. 11
Which *said* their brydale daye should not be long; . . . *Proth.* 111

Sail. thou seest my lowly *saile,* . . . *S.C.* S. 250
Nor ever ship shall *saile* there anie more. . . . *Ti.* 154
a ship, that flyes fayre under *sayle,* . . . I. vi. 1. 1
seemd the fountaine in that sea did *sayle* upright. . . . II. xii. 62. 9
saile withouten starres gainst tyde and winde: . . . III. iv. 9. 8
went at will withouten card or *sayle,* . . . III. viii. 31. 2
bore so fayre a *sayle,* . . . III. x. 6. 3

Sailed. As he that having long in tempest *sailed,* . . . *Ro.* xxi. 11
Two dayes now in that sea he *sayled* has, . . . II. xii. 2. 1

Sailing. The *sayling* Pine; the Cedar proud and tall; . . . I. i. 8. 6
sayling thence to th' isle of Paros came. . . . III. ix. 36. 9
sayling alwaies in the port. . . . VI. x. 2. 9

Sailers. *sailers* save from wreckes of wrathfull winde. . . . IV. xi. 52. 5

Sailors'. Now hight Palemon, and is *saylers* frend; . . . IV. xi. 13. 6

Sails. The *sailes* of golde, of silke the tackle were: . . . *Pet.* ii. 3
sitting hye, Upon the Mountaine *sayles.* . . . *S.C.* Jul. 104
sayles, in which the hollow wynd Is gathered full, . . . I. xi. 10. 2
With his broad *sayles,* about him soared round; . . . I. xi. 18. 7
strike your *sailes,* yee jolly Mariners, . . . I. xii. 42. 1
knowes her port, and thither *sayles* by ayme, . . . II. vi. 10. 3
Who swelling *sayles* in Caspian sea doth crosse, . . . II. vii. 14. 3
fild their *sayles* with feare: . . . II. xii. 37. 2
To weather his brode *sailes,* . . . V. iv. 42. 3
strikes his *sayles,* and vereth his mainsheat, . . . V. xii. 18. 8

Saine. *See* **Say.**

Saint. new Earth, new Heaven, sayde *Saint* John. . . . *Rev.* iv. 1
Ah, deare Lord! and sweete *Saint* Charitee! . . . *S.C.* May 247
St. Michels Mount who does not know, . . . *S.C.* Jul. 41
of *St.* Brigets bowre . . . can rightly boaste: . . . *S.C.* Jul. 43
was the *saynt* of shepheards light, . . . *S.C.* N. 176
seeme as Saintlike as *Saint* Radegund: . . . *Hub.* 497
she, my love that was, my *Saint* that is . . . *D.* 379
Saint George himselfe ye would have deemed him to be. . . . I. ii. 11. 9
The true *Saint* George, was wandred far away, . . . I. ii. 12. 2
The shaking Palsey, and *Saint* Fraunces fire, . . . I. iv. 35. 8
thou, emongst those Saints . . . Shalt be a *Saint,* . . . I. x. 61. 7
thou *Saint George* shalt called bee, *Saint George* of mery *England,* . . . I. x. 61. 8, 9
you a *Saint* with Saints your seat have wonne: . . . II. i. 32. 5
doe unwilling worship to the *Saint,* . . . II. v. 11. 7
that sacred *Saint* my soveraigne Queene, . . . IV. Pr. 4. 2
Like the true *saint* beside the image set, . . . V. iii. 24. 2
As he is wont at each *Saint* Valentide, . . . VI. vii. 32. 7
For my sweet *Saynt* some service fit will find. . . . *Am.* xxii. 4
My soverayne *saynt,* the Idoll of my thought, . . . *Am.* lxi. 2
For to receyve this *Saynt* with honour dew, . . . *Epith.* 208
His harts enshrined *saint,* his heavens queene, . . . *H.L.* 215

Saintlike. seeme as *Saintlike* as Saint Radegund: . . . *Hub.* 497

Saints. Such merimake holy *Saints* doth queme, . . . *S.C.* May 15
sacred unto *saints* they stond, . . . *S.C.* Jul. 39
The hylls where dwelled holy *saints* . . . *S.C.* Jul. 113
the *sayncts* Which han be dead of yore. . . . *S.C.* Jul. 115
She raignes a goddesse now emong the *saints,* . . . *S.C.* N. 175
Saints and Angels in celestiall thrones . . . *D.* 285
He told of *Saintes* and Popes, . . . I. i. 35. 8
The holy *Saints* of their rich vestiments He did disrobe, . . I. iii. 17. 5
Now are they *Saints* all in that Citty sam, . . . I. x. 57. 8

Saints—*Continued.*
thou, emongst those *Saints* . . . , Shalt be a Saint, . . . I. x. 61. 6
you a Saint with *Saints* your seat have wonne: . . . II. i. 32. 5
crowne of heavenly prayse with *Saintes* above, . . . III. viii. 42. 7
raignst in blis emongst thy blessed *Saintes,* . . . III. xi. 9. 3
Both girlonds of his *Saints* against their foes offence. . . . IV. x. 51. 9
three sacred *Saints* . . . on mount Thabor . . . VII. vii. 7. 6
with the crew of blessed *Saynts* upbrought, . . . *Am.* lxi. 7
Of blessed *Saints* for to increase the count. . . . *Epith.* 423

Sake. For learning *sake* to living them to raise; . . . *Hub.* 538
For pitties *sake* compassion our paine, . . . *T.M.* 346
Both for my selfe and for my Sisters *sake.* . . . *T.M.* 474
Her back againe to life sent for his *sake.* . . . *Ti.* 392
Do pluck it softly for that shepheards *sake.* . . . *As.* 198
I would request thee, Colin, for my *sake,* . . . *Col.* 83
Not for my skill, but for that shepheards *sake.'* . . . *Col.* 455
rymes . . . for their titles *sake* may find more grace. . . . *Ded. Son.* i. 14
For his, and for your owne especial *sake,* . . . *Ded. Son.* xv. 13
For whose sweete *sake* that glorious badge he wore, . . . I. i. 2. 3
'Your owne deare *sake* forst me . . . to leave . . . I. i. 52. 1
for my *sake* unknowne such griefe unto you grew. . . . I. i. 53. 9
For fairest Unaes *sake,* of whom I sing, . . . I. iii. 2. 2
he chalenged essoyne, For contemplation *sake:* . . . I. iv. 20. 4
for his *sake* have felt full many an heavie stowre. . . . I. iv. 46. 9
mov'd with wrath, and shame, and Ladies *sake,* . . . I. v. 12. 5
for his love, and for her own selfe *sake,* . . . I. vi. 2. 6
O! hold thy mortall hand for Ladies *sake;* . . . I. vii. 14. 6
Hold for my *sake,* and doe him not to dye, . . . I. vii. 14. 7
For whose deare *sake* so many troubles her did tosse. . . . I. vii. 27. 9
How shall I quite the paynes ye suffer for my *sake?* . . . I. viii. 26. 9
Those for Gods *sake* his dewty was to entertaine. . . . I. x. 37. 9
these sorrowes suffer for my *sake,* . . . I. xi. 1. 8
for myne only *sake* Thy life and honor late adventurest, . . I. xii. 29. 7
Vouchsafe to stay your steed for humble misers *sake.'* . . . II. i. 8. 9
He stayd his steed for humble misers *sake,* . . . II. i. 9. 1
greatly joyous seemed for my *sake,* . . . II. iv. 20. 3
forst their chiefetain, for his safeties *sake,* . . . II. x. 16. 6
For whose deare *sake* full many a bitter stownd . . . III. i. 24. 8
Great Ptolomaee it for his lemans *sake* Ybuilded . . . III. ii. 20. 6
Both for his griefe, and for her peoples *sake,* . . . III. iii. 43. 2
for her *sake* And love, . . . III. iii. 56. 6
Ill weares he armes, that nill them use for Ladies *sake.'* . . . III. v. 11. 9
dye meekly for her *sake:* . . . III. v. 47. 8
for his dearest *sake* endured sore Sore trouble . . . III. vi. 53. 5
for her *sake* He then did put, . . . III. xi. 33. 8
for her *sake* her cattell fedd awhile, . . . III. xi. 39. 2
for her *sake* a cowheard vile became . . . III. xi. 39. 3
no lesse griefe endured for your gentle *sake.'* . . . III. xii. 40. 9
as I late adventured for your *sake,* . . . IV. i. 40. 3
ought in friendship for her *sake* To joyne your force, . . . IV. ii. 24. 6
Which for her *sake* he wore, . . . IV. ii. 25. 9
with himselfe should combat for her *sake,* . . . IV. ii. 38. 8
for her *sake* they all that perill tooke, . . . IV. ii. 40. 8
Not for thine owne, but for thy sisters *sake,* . . . IV. iii. 11. 3
So cruelly these Knights strove for that Ladies *sake.* . . . IV. iii. 16. 9
for her *sake* refus'd to enterprize The battell, . . . IV. iv. 11. 4
for her *sake* . . . This pretious ornament, they say, did make, IV. v. 4. 1
For vertues onely *sake,* which doth beget True love . . . IV. vi. 46. 8
Midst sorrow showing joyous semblance for his *sake.* . . . IV. vii. 44. 9
tormenting griefe that for her *sake* Her gentle Squire . . . IV. viii. 9. 8
To my friends good more then for mine owne *sake,* . . . IV. viii. 60. 8
For his friends *sake* her offred favours scorne, . . . IV. ix. 3. 8
joy that for his *sake* I suffer prisonment. . . . IV. xii. 7. 9
For his deare *sake,* . . . IV. xii. 19. 5
to perils great for justice *sake* proceedes. . . . V. ii. 1. 9
for his owne deare Ladies *sake,* . . . V. iii. 16. 4
Is for the *sake* of Bellodant the bold, . . . V. iv. 30. 2
for his *sake* vow'd to doe all the ill . . . V. iv. 30. 8
How for Iolas *sake* he did apply . . . V. v. 24. 3
for his *sake* thy life thou gavest.' . . . V. vii. 32. 6
For his loves *sake* his Lions skin undight; . . . V. viii. 2. 5
for his *sake* Diana did lament, . . . V. viii. 43. 6
not for such slaughters *sake* He thether came, . . . V. xii. 8. 7
rather more enrag'd for those words *sake;* . . . VI. i. 19. 4
she for his *sake* had weetingly Now brought . . . VI. iii. 11. 7
dare, for thy deare Ladies *sake* . . . VI. iii. 35. 7
Yet for the feeble Ladies *sake,* . . . VI. iii. 45. 8
The which I earst adventur'd for your *sake:* . . . VI. vii. 15. 4
for his *sake* his deare life had forgone; . . . VI. vii. 18. 2
for her *sake* fell into misery; . . . VI. viii. 3. 5
endured for her *sake* Great perill of his life, . . . VI. viii. 33. 8
Penelope, for her Ulisses *sake,* . . . *Am.* xxiii. 1
for thy *sake* . . . may one another entertayne! . . . *Am.* lxviii. 11
His owne faire mother, for all creatures *sake,* . . . *H.L.* 72
Not for lusts *sake,* but for eternitie, . . . *H.L.* 104
For mans deare *sake* he did a man become. . . . *H.H.L.* 147
Commaunded us to love them for his *sake,* . . . *H.H.L.* 205
Even for his *sake,* and for his sacred word, . . . *H.H.L.* 206

Sale. *See* **Seal.**
They setten to *sale* their shops of shame, . . . *S.C.* S. 36
All which he to the marchants *sale* did showe: . . . VI. xi. 11. 4

Salem. Of sacred *Salem;* and sad Ilion, . . . IV. i. 22. 3

Saliaunce. why with so fierce *saliaunce,* And fell intent, . . . II. i. 29. 6

Sallied. Where gladsome Guyon *salied* forth to land, . . . II. vi. 38. 5
forth the noble Guyon *sallied,* . . . II. xii. 38. 4

Sallow. *See* **Seal.**
the *Sallow* for the mill; . . . I. i. 9. 5

Sallows. By which few crooked *sallowes* grew in ranke: . . . IV. v. 33. 5

Salmons. Great heapes of *salmons* in his deepe bosome: . . . IV. xi. 43. 6
the faire Shure, in which are thousand *Salmons* bred. . . . VII. vi. 54. 9

Salomon. *See* **Solomon.**
Salt. Here has the *salt* Medway his sourse, . . . *S.C.* Jul. 79
The *salt* Medway, that trickling stremis . . . *S.C.* Jul. 81
Tost on *salt* billowes, . . . *Gn.* 592
their faire faces with *salt* humour steep. . . . *T.M.* 112
embay His blamefull body in *salt* water . . . I. x. 27. 6
salt teares bedeawd the hearers cheaks. . . . I. xii. 16. 9
the *salt* brine out of the billowes sprong. . . . II. xii. 10. 5
Salt-bedewed. Hyponeo with *salt-bedewed* wrests; . . . IV. xi. 51. 2
Saltish. Ofte soust in swelling Tethys *saltish* teare; . . . I. iii. 31. 3
Salued. knight in presence came, And goodly *salued* them; . . II. viii. 23. 2
her *salewd* with seemely bel-accoyle, . . . IV. vi. 25. 4
Salute. him *salute* with well beseeming glee; . . . I. x. 15. 7
gan gently her *salute* With curteous words, . . . V. vi. 20. 1
with uncomely shame Gan him *salute,* . . . VI. i. 24. 9
And to *salute* him, if he were in plight, . . . VI. iii. 14. 3
Saluted. Lowly they him *saluted* in meeke wise; . . . *Hub.* 585
He faire the knight *saluted,* louting low, . . . I. i. 30. 1
They him *saluted,* standing far afore, . . . I. x. 49. 7
Him first *saluted* with a sturdy stroke: . . . I. v. 3. 7
Shee came . . . And fairely them *saluted,* . . . III. ix. 26. 8
Salutes. her lowd *salutes* the mounting larke. . . . I. xi. 51. 9
Saluting. him *saluting* as beseemed best, . . . III. viii. 45. 7
She, them *saluting,* there by them sate still . . . IV. ii. 49. 1
Saluting him gan into speach to fall, . . . IV. vii. 43. 8
Whom she *saluting* faire, faire resaluted was: . . . V. vii. 17. 9
Whom by his name *saluting,* thus he gan: . . . V. xi. 38. 1
Whom Calepine *saluting* (as became) . . . VI. iii. 31. 1
Salvage. *See* **Savage.**
Salvagesse. on his ragged shield was writ, *Salvagesse sans finesse,* . . . IV. iv. 39. 9
Salve. Ne can I find *salve* for my sore: . . . *S.C.* Au. 103
skilfull leaches him abide To *salve* his hurts, . . . I. v. 17. 3
Ne was there *salve,* ne was there medicine, . . . II. xi. 21. 8
never sore but might a *salve* obtaine: . . . III. ii. 35. 7
though no reason may apply *Salve* to your sore, . . . III. ii. 36. 5
She did envy that soveraine *salve* in secret store. . . . III. v. 50. 9
Cast how to *salve,* that both the custome showne Were kept, . IV. i. 11. 7
though he could not *salve,* Ne done undoe, . . . IV. iv. 27. 1
for to *salve* his name And purchase honour . . . IV. iv. 27. 2
For which Dan Phoebus selfe cannot a *salve* provide. . . . IV. vi. 1. 9
seeking thus to *salve* the Amazon, . . . V. v. 43. 5
sought with ruth to *salve* his sad misfortune sore. . . . V. vii. 38. 9
How she the blame might *salve* with coloured disguize. . . . VI. iii. 8. 9
With *salve,* or antidote, or other mene, . . . VI. vi. 9. 5
with medicine To goe about to *salve* such kynd of sore, . . . VI. vi. 13. 2
with one *salve,* both hart and body heale. . . . *Am.* l. 14
Seekes . . . to *salve* each others wound: . . . *Am.* lxv. 12
embaulmed wel With *salve* of soveraigne might: . . . *Epig.* iv. 46
Salved. Ebranck *salved* both their infamies . . . II. x. 21. 6
Salves. strive Himselfe with *salves* to health for to restore, . I. v. 40. 8
If either *salves,* or oyles, or herbes, or charmes, . . . I. v. 41. 7
he gan apply relief Of *salves* and med'cines, . . . I. x. 24. 5
Salves to his wounds, and medicines of might; . . . III. iv. 43. 8
with thy hevenly *salves* and med'cines sweete . . . III. v. 35. 8
His readie wound with better *salves* new drest: . . . III. v. 41. 4
many *Salves* did to his sore applie, . . . IV. xi. 6. 2
Give *salves* to every sore, . . . VI. vi. 5. 9
in vaine doe *salves* to you applie; . . . VI. vi. 6. 9
outward *salves* that may augment it more.' . . . VI. vi. 13. 4
If that no *salves* may us to health restore?' . . . VI. vi. 13. 7
Salving. 'see the *salving* of your blotted name.' . . . II. i. 20. 7
Sam. what concord han light and darke *sam?* . . . *S.C.* May 168
Now are they Saints all in that Citty *sam,* . . . I. x. 57. 8
Same (*partial list*). *See* **Selfsame.**
pillours fronting faire the *same,* . . . *Bel.*^{2} ii. 3
I saw a Citie like unto that *same,* . . . *Bel.*^{2} xiv. 2
The *same* yet vaunting Greece will tell the storie . . . *Ro.* ii. 5
These *same* olde walls, . . . *Ro.* iii. 3
her great spirite, . . . is in the *same* enwombed; . . . *Ro.* v. 11
(as fates the *same* foreseeing) . . . *Ro.* xviii. 13
The *same,* which Pyrrhus . . . could not tame, . . . *Ro.* xxi. 1
that same *brave* Citie, . . . *Ro.* xxi. 2
Upon the *same* to set foundation sure? . . . *Ro.* xxiv. 14
That *same* is now nought but a champian . . . *Ro.* xxxi. 1
(O great ruth for the *same!*) . . . *Van.* vii. 10
but your goodnes the *same* recure, Am like . . . *S.C.* F. 154
Seest not thilke *same* Hawthorne studde, . . . *S.C.* Mar. 13
Or made previe to the *same?* . . . *S.C.* Mar. 30
was thilk *same* song of Colins owne making? . . . *S.C.* Ap. 154
all to sadde For thilke *same* season, . . . *S.C.* May 6
Thilke *same* bene shepeheardes . . . *S.C.* May 43
poore my piteous plaints out in the *same.* . . . *S.C.* Jun. 80
Is not thilke *same* a goteheard prowde, . . . *S.C.* Jul. 1
they han sold thilk *same* long agoe, . . . *S.C.* S. 98
thilke *same* rule were too straight, . . . *S.C.* S. 236
Made me by arte more cunning in the *same.* . . . *S.C.* D. 42
loathed Paddocks lording on the *same:* . . . *S.C.* D. 70
Into the *same* mishap I now am cast, . . . *Gn.* 363
The *same* was able with like lovely lay . . . *Gn.* 461
To daunt his foe by ensample of the *same.* . . . *Gn.* 608
Ile write in termes as she the *same* did say, . . . *Hub.* 41
yet doo never thanke them for the *same,* . . . *Hub.* 165
my selfe fit for the *same* will fashion.' . . . *Hub.* 202
(that *same* he weeping sayes) . . . *Hub.* 254
such like paine . . . I will the *same* sustaine; . . . *Hub.* 288
That *same* hath Jesus Christ . . . raught, . . . *Hub.* 441
but by that *same* that seemeth. . . . *Hub.* 650
nor ought like the *same.* . . . *Hub.* 868
for the *same* him fowlie did entreate; . . . *Hub.* 922

Same—*Continued.*
he the *same* did to his purpose wring. . . . *Hub.* 1142
Into his seate, and those *same* treachours vile . . . *Hub.* 1255
that none the *same* espies; . . . *Hub.* 1288
where is that *same* . . . beast, . . . *Ti.* 71
The *same* that bred was of Medusaes blood, . . . *Ti.* 647
Now in the *same* bathing his tender feete; . . . *Mui.* 182
that *same* subtil gin, . . . *Mui.* 369
This *same* he did applie For to entrap . . . *Mui.* 374
with the *same* fill every hill and dale. . . . *D.* 322
to deck the *same* with Cyparesse; . . . *D.* 529
The gods . . . this *same* beheld, . . . *As.* 181
where ever thou doest finde the *same,* . . . *As.* 195
The *same* with bitter teares they all bedewed. . . . *As.* 204
the *same* to heare, . . . *Col.* 161
the daunger of the *same;* . . . *Col.* 215
The *same* aboord us gently did receave, . . . *Col.* 224
that *same* was the Regiment . . . *Col.* 233
Those *same* . . . were the fields . . . *Col.* 276
That *same* is she to whom . . . *Col.* 510
And fill the *same* with store of timely wine. . . . *Col.* 603
Thou much more fit (were leasure to the *same*) . . . *Ded. Son.* xii. 5
but the *same* did hide Under a vele, . . . I. i. 4. 3
So pure and innocent, as that *same* lambe, . . . I. i. 5. 1
The *same* so sore annoyed has the knight, . . . I. i. 22. 1
Smal drops of gory bloud, that trickled down the *same.* . . . I. ii. 30. 9
Ne ever wist but that she was the *same;* . . . I. ii. 40. 3
The *same* she followes, . . . I. iii. 10. 7
Approaching nigh she wist it was the *same;* . . . I. iii. 26. 8
did weene the *same* Have reft away . . . I. iii. 41. 5
this *same* Monster much more ugly was, . . . I. vii. 17. 6
The *same* to wight he never wont disclose, . . . I. vii. 34. 1
he that made the *same* was knowne right well . . . I. vii. 36. 2
Then cryde the Dwarfe, 'Lo! yonder is the *same,* . . . I. viii. 2. 3
ne living wight To warde the *same,* . . . I. viii. 3. 4
The *same* before the Geaunts gate he blew, . . . I. viii. 5. 1
eye mote not the *same* endure to vew. . . . I. viii. 19. 5
How ill it sits with that *same* silver hed, . . . I. viii. 33. 5
in the *same* a little grate was pight, . . . I. viii. 37. 6
hee Did labour lively to expresse the *same,* . . . I. x. 6. 8
a Leach, . . . could cure the *same:* . . . I. x. 23. 9
same end, which every living wight Should make . . . I. x. 50. 2
Such one as that *same* mighty man of God, That . . . I. x. 53. 2
beseemes all knights . . . that *same* to haunt, . . . I. x. 59. 6
pilgrimage To yonder *same* Hierusalem doe bend, . . . I. x. 61. 4
Into the *same* the knight back overthrowen fell. . . . I. xi. 30. 9
The *same* advauncing high above his head, . . . I. xi. 38. 1
Into that *same* he fell, . . . I. xi. 48. 9
Ne I against the *same* can justly preace: . . . I. xii. 19. 4
since now to thee perteynes the *same* . . . I. xii. 20. 7
With cryme doe not it cover, but disclose the *same.*' . . . I. xii. 30. 9
make you good amendment for the *same:* . . . II. i. 20. 4
The *same* by my device I undertake . . . II. iii. 18. 6
darted fyrie beames out of the *same,* . . . II. iii. 23. 3
Those *same* with stately grace and princely port . . . II. iii. 28. 5
That *same* is Furor, . . . II. iv. 10. 6
unto him she would impart the *same.* . . . II. iv. 20. 8
by that *same* sacred band Betwixt us both, . . . II. iv. 23. 6
Then stubborne perturbation to the *same;* . . . II. v. 1. 4
in utt'ring of the *same,* . . . II. vi. 6. 8
deepe him selfe beducked in the *same,* . . . II. vi. 42. 3
was not that *same* her owne native hew, . . . II. vii. 45. 4
the river, which the *same* did hyde; . . . II. vii. 61. 3
Ne sittest downe on that *same* silver stoole, . . . II. vii. 63. 8
none without the *same* enduren can: . . . II. vii. 65. 5
him henceforth the *same* can save no more; . . . II. viii. 43. 7
them leading forth, the *same* did shew. . . . II. ix. 20. 9
A jolly yeoman, Marshall of the *same,* . . . II. ix. 28. 2
Others to beare the *same* away did mynd; . . . II. ix. 31. 8
in your selfe doe not the *same* advise? . . . II. ix. 38. 3
That may unwares bee blotted with the *same:* . . . II. ix. 38. 5
but she the *same* Dissembled faire, . . . II. ix. 44. 2
Yet were the wals, that did the *same* uphold, . . . II. ix. 55. 3
For safety that *same* his sea-marke made, . . . II. x. 6. 6
their filthinesse Polluted this *same* gentle soyle . . . II. x. 9. 2
Who peaceably the *same* long time did weld, . . . II. x. 32. 4
Seven of the *same* . . . he did closely place, . . . II. xi. 6. 6
Those *same* . . . Did lay strong siege . . . II. xi. 9. 1
that *same* third Fort, . . . was cruelly assayd; . . . II. xi. 11. 1
The *same* he snatcht, and with exceeding sway . . . II. xi. 36. 1
those *same* Islands, . . . Are not firme land, . . . II. xii. 11. 3
no'te the *same* amend, ne yet withstond, . . . II. xii. 57. 7
A subtile net, which only for that *same* . . . II. xii. 81. 4
The way they came, the *same* retourn'd they . . . II. xii. 84. 3
that *same* delitious Poet . . . III. Pr. 5. 1
Dye rather would he then endure that *same.* . . . III. i. 9. 5
Badd those *same* six forbeare that single enimy. . . . III. i. 22. 9
Ne ought in secret from the *same* remaynd; . . . III. ii. 19. 7
Not that *same,* which doth . . . III. iii. 1. 5
The *same,* . . . caused to be hanged hy . . . III. iii. 59. 1
by that *same* Rich strond to travell, . . . III. iv. 20. 7
ronning through that *same* Thicke forest, . . . III. v. 3. 8
Beside the *same* a dainty place there lay, . . . III. v. 40. 1
this *same* All . . . places doth excell, . . . III. vi. 29. 6
Did seeme to be the *same* which she escapt . . . III. vii. 1. 9
A litle valley subject to the *same,* . . . III. vii. 4. 8
Into the *same* she lept, . . . III. vii. 27. 7
even Nature selfe envide the *same,* . . . III. viii. 5. 4
What hard misfortune brought me to this *same;* . . . III. viii. 23. 8
but God turne the *same* to good . . . III. viii. 50. 2

Same—*Continued.*
sith he n'ote save both, he sav'd that *same* . . . . . III. x. 15. 7
As those *same* plumes so seemd he vaine . . . . . III. xii. 8. 5
as it were not the *same,* . . . . . III. xii. 43. 5
few that have abusd the *same;* . . . . . IV. Pr. 2. 5
those *same* cursed seedes doe also serve . . . . . IV. i. 26. 1
Will chalenge yond *same* other for my fee.' . . . . . IV. i. 35. 8
I saw, why should I doubt to tell the *same?'* . . . . . IV. i. 48. 4
from the *same* the fierie sparkles flasht, ... IV. iii. 25. 8
in the *same* she farre exceld all other: . . . . . IV. iii. 40. 5
armes, well knowne to be the *same* . . . . . IV. iv. 27. 5
Cambell seeing much the *same* envyde, ... IV. iv. 44. 7
The *same* one day, when she her selfe disposd . . . . . IV. v. 5. 1
He gan to cast how to appease the *same,* . . . . . IV. v. 25. 2
that *same* gentle Squire arriv'd in place Where this *same* cursed caytive . . . . . IV. vii. 24. 3, 4
sensibly compyld, that in the *same* Him seemed . . . . . IV. viii. 4. 4
that *same* dwarfe right sorie seem'd and sad, ... IV. viii. 46. 3
built . . . both long since this *same,* . . . . . IV. x. 5. 7
I spide within the *same* Where one stood . . . . . IV. x. 11. 7
The *same* to all stoode alwaies open wide; . . . . . IV. x. 16. 4
Not that *same* famous Temple of Diane, ... IV. x. 30. 1
That *same* was fayrest Amoret . . . . . IV. x. 52. 8
warlike Amazons, who doe possesse the *same.* . . . . . IV. xi. 21. 9
all those *same* were there . . . . . IV. xii. 2. 9
that *same* former fatall wound of his . . . . . IV. xii. 22. 5
For that *same* golden fleecy Ram, ... V. Pr. 5. 6
that *same* great glorious lampe of light, ... V. Pr. 7. 1
drew his sword; for with the *same* He ment . . . . . V. iii. 29. 7
this *same* other Damzell since hath fained . . . . . V. iv. 13. 4
that she did transport the *same* by sea, ... V. iv. 13. 6
In sort as ye have heard the *same* of late: . . . . . V. vi. 17. 3
I will not seeke the *same* from you to hide; . . . . . V. vii. 19. 3
that *same* citie, . . . Had bene the keye . . . . . V. x. 26. 3
the *same,* Who all that wrong . . . . . V. xi. 4. 4
That *same* is it which fought for you this day. . . . . . V. xi. 17. 6
To blot the *same* with blame, ... V. xii. 34. 9
But this *same* both her selfe and others eke perplext. . . . . . V. xii. 35. 9
To punish those that doe deserve the *same;* . . . . . VI. i. 26. 5
the *same* Which tooke in hand her quarrell . . . . . VI. i. 33. 1
Toward the *same* incessantly did ronne . . . . . VI. iv. 2. 4
And held the *same* so hard, ... VI. iv. 6. 8
To leape into the *same* after our lives end. . . . . . VI. iv. 31. 9
when time shall be to tell the *same.* . . . . . VI. v. 2. 9
He well remembred that the *same* was hee, ... VI. vi. 40. 3
in the middest of those *same* three was placed . . . . . VI. x. 12. 6
prieve That yond *same* is your daughter sure, ... VI. xii. 18. 9
this *same* day when she on Arlo sat, ... VII. vii. 7. 2
The *same* which over Hellespontus swam; . . . . . VII. vii. 32. 5
the *same* which led Europa . . . . . VII. vii. 33. 3
The *same* which . . . Slew great Orion; . . . . . VII. vii. 39. 7
The *same* wherewith Dan Jove . . . was nourisht . . . . . VII. vii. 41. 6
wheresoever they comment the *same,* . . . . . VII. vii. 53. 7
that *same* time when no more Change shall be, ... VII. viii. 2. 2
on the *same* my hart will sacrifise, ... *Am.* xxii. 11
The *same* at night she did againe unreave: . . . . . *Am.* xxiii. 4
thy love we weighing worthily . . . love thee for the *same* againe; . . . . . *Am.* lxviii. 10
Who is the *same,* which at my window peepes? . . . . . *Epith.* 372
That *same* is Beautie, borne of heavenly race. . . . . . *H.L.* 112
that the *same* doth hold . . . . . *H.B.* 136
Cast to supply the *same,* and to enstall . . . . . *H.H.L.* 103
Of that selfe mould, . . . and to the *same* againe shall fade, . *H.H.L.* 199
Not bounded, not corrupt, as these *same* bee, ... *H.H.B.* 66
And in the *same,* as in a brasen booke, ... *H.H.B.* 130
in the *same* these lower creatures all Subjected . . . . . *H.H.B.* 195
That promiseth the *same:* . . . . . *Proth.* 154

Samient. Prince Arthure and Sir Artegall Free *Samient* from feare: . . . . . V. viii. Arg.
So said this Damzell, that hight *Samient;* . . . . . V. viii. 23. 7
that Damzell, the sad *Samient,* . . . . . V. viii. 25. 6

Samite. In silken *samite* she was light arayd, ... III. xii. 13. 3

Samnitis. Mortall *Samnitis,* and Cicuta bad, ... II. vii. 52. 5

Sample. Theyr *sample* onely to us lent, ... *S.C.* Jul. 119

Sanctuary. She was as safe as in a *Sanctuary.* . . . . . IV. ix. 19. 6

Sand. *See* **Quicksand.**
on *sand* was built the goodly frame: . . . . . *Bel.*[2] xiv. 4
Dragons teeth, sowne in the sacred *sand;* . . . . . *Ro.* x. 4
There now is but an heap of lyme and *sand,* . . . . . *Ti.* 129
soone arrived on the shallow *sand,* . . . . . II. vi. 38. 4
The whiles his nets were drying on the *sand.* . . . . . III. vii. 27. 6
it did glister like the golden *sand,* . . . . . IV. vi. 20. 7

Sandals. His *sandales* were with toilsome travell torne, ... I. vi. 35. 3

Sands. Now to become nought els but heaped *sands?* . . . . . *Ro.* xv. 14
Through boyling *sands* of Arabie . . . . . I. vi. 35. 6
From shore to shore emongst the Lybick *sandes,* . . . . . III. ix. 41. 6
Dart, nigh chockt with *sands* of tinny mines. . . . . . IV. xi. 31. 5
To tell the *sands,* or count the starres on hye, ... IV. xi. 53. 2
by being wreckt uppon the *sands,* . . . . . V. iv. 5. 4

Sandy. placed on a plot of *sandie* ground: . . . . . *Ti.* 508
on a *sandie* hill, . . . it mounted was full hie, ... I. iv. 5. 5
lying downe upon the *sandie* graile, ... I. vii. 6. 2
by the *sandy* shore Of swift Eurotas, ... II. iii. 31. 1
shooke His *sandy* lockes, ... II. v. 14. 4
th' utmost *sandy* breach they shortly fetch, ... II. xii. 21. 3
On the rough rocks, or on the *sandy* shallowes, ... III. iv. 9. 4
sadly soucing on the *sandy* shore, ... III. iv. 16. 8
Xanthus *sandy* bankes with blood all overflowne. . . . . . III. ix. 35. 9
The *sandy* Slane, the stony Aubrian, ... IV. xi. 41. 2
all his bones as small as *sandy* grayle He broke, ... V. ix. 19. 4

Sanglamort. By *Sanglamort* my sword, . . . shall dearely it repent; . . . . . III. x. 32. 5

Sanglier. That was to weet the stout Sir *Sangliere,* . . . . . IV. iv. 40. 3
He doth avenge on *Sanglier* His Ladies bloud . . . . . V. i. Arg.
It was not long before he overtooke Sir *Sanglier,* . . . . . V. i. 20. 7
Well pleased with that doome was *Sangliere,* . . . . . V. i. 27. 1
Sangliere disdained much his doome, ... V. i. 29. 1

Sanguine. into a deep *sanguine* dide the grassy grownd. . . . . II. i. 39. 9
like a lively *sanguine* it seemd to the eye. . . . . . III. viii. 6. 9
dyde in *sanguine* red her skin . . . . . III. xii. 20. 9

Sans. on his ragged shield was writ, *Salvagesse sans finesse,* . IV. iv. 39. 9

Sansfoy. In whose great shield was writ . . . *Sans foy;* . . . . I. ii. 12. 8
Who, whiles he livde, was called proud *Sans foy,* . . . . . I. ii. 25. 6
him that slew *Sansfoy* with bloody knife: . . . . . I. iii. 36. 4
Life from *Sansfoy* thou tookst, Sansloy shall from thee take.' I. iii. 36. 9
when the shamed shield of slaine *Sansfoy* He spide . . . . . I. iv. 39. 1
The prowest knight . . . Even stout *Sansfoy,* . . . . . I. iv. 41. 8
'Ah deare Sansjoy, next dearest to *Sansfoy,* . . . . . I. iv. 45. 4
brest was launcht with lovely dart Of deare *Sansfoy,* . . . I. iv. 46. 6
I would not yield that to *Sansfoy* I gave. . . . . . I. iv. 47. 9
Dead is *Sansfoy,* his vitall paines are past, ... I. iv. 49. 6
on a tree *Sansfoy* his shield is hangd . . . . . I. v. 5. 8
I saw . . . The bold *Sansfoy* shrinck . . . . . I. v. 23. 2
he the man that made *Sansfoy* to fall, ... I. v. 26. 3

Sansfoy's. I . . . with *Sansfoyes* dead dowry you endew.' . I. iv. 51. 5

Sansjoy. bred Of one bad sire, whose youngest is *Sans joy;* . . . I. ii. 25. 8
Sansjoy Doth chaleng him to fight. . . . . . I. iv. Arg.
heathnish shield, wherein with letters red, Was writt *Sansjoy,* I. iv. 38. 6
'Ah deare *Sansjoy,* next dearest to Sansfoy, ... I. iv. 45. 4
the stout *Sansjoy* doth sleepe in deadly shade. . . . . . I. v. 22. 9
The combat which he with *Sansjoy* did hould; . . . . . I. vii. 26. 7

Sansloy. twixt them both was born the bloudy bold *Sans loy.* . I. ii. 25. 9
on his shield *Sansloy* in bloody lines was dyde. . . . . . I. iii. 33. 9
Life from Sansfoy thou tookst, *Sansloy* shall from thee take.' I. iii. 36. 9
Till her unwares the fiers *Sansloy* did overtake: . . . . . I. vi. 2. 9
he that lov'd the youngest was *Sansloy;* . . . . . II. ii. 18. 1
Fast by her side did sitt the bold *Sansloy,* . . . . . II. ii. 37. 1

Sao. Soft Spio, sweete Endore, *Sao* sad, ... IV. xi. 48. 8

Sap. on her *sap* and vitall moysture fed: . . . . . *Van.* vii. 8
Now sucking of the *sap* of herbe most meete, ... *Mui.* 180
feedes each living plant with liquid *sap,* . . . . . II. ii. 6. 4
from one roote deriv'd their vitall *sap:* . . . . . IV. ii. 43. 6
Like an old Oke, whose pith and *sap* is seare, ... IV. iii. 9. 8
brave imps . . . fed with heavenly *sap,* . . . . . VI. iv. 36. 8
The durefull Oake, whose *sap* is not yet dride, ... *Am.* vi. 5

Sapience. Despise the brood of blessed *Sapience.* . . . . . *T.M.* 72
She solaceth with rules of *Sapience* . . . . . *T.M.* 135
There in his bosome *Sapience* doth sit, ... *H.H.B.* 183

Sapphires. If *Saphyres,* loe, her eies be *Saphyres* plaine; . . . *Am.* xv. 7
Her goodly eyes lyke *Saphyres* shining bright, ... *Epith.* 171

Sappy. *sappy* liquor, that with fulnesse sweld, ... II. xii. 56. 3

Saracen. him chaunst to meete . . . A faithlesse *Sarazin,* . . I. ii. 12. 6
The *Sarazin,* . . . Snatcheth his sword, ... I. ii. 17. 1
'Curse on that Cross,' (quoth then the *Sarazin,*) . . . . . I. ii. 18. 1
it chaunced this proud *Sarazin* To meete me wandring; . . . I. ii. 25. 1
Soone after comes the cruell *Sarazin,* . . . . . I. v. 4. 1
The *Sarazin* was stout and wondrous strong, ... I. v. 7. 1
Whom when the raging *Sarazin* espyde, ... I. vi. 8. 6
The *Sarazin,* this hearing, rose amain, ... I. vi. 41. 7
Whom all so soone as that proud *Sarazin* Espide, ... I. vi. 46. 1
Bryton fieldes with *Sarazin* blood bedyde, ... I. xi. 7. 3
when as the *Sarazin* perceiv'd . . . . . II. viii. 49. 1
A cursed cruell *Sarazin* doth wonne, ... V. ii. 4. 6
The *Sarazin,* awayting for some spoile: . . . . . V. ii. 11. 3

Saracen's. The *Sarazins* shield, signe of the conquereoure. . . . . II. ii. 20. 7

Saracens. captives to redeeme . . . From Turkes and *Sarazins,* I. x. 40. 4
thousand *Sar'zins* fowly donne to dye.' . . . . . II. viii. 18. 6
those two *Sarazins* confounded late, ... II. viii. 54. 8

Sardonian. with *Sardonian* smyle Laughing on her, ... V. ix. 12. 6

Sat. hundred Nymphes *sate* side by side . . . . . *Bel.* xii. 10
the fountaine, where they *sat* around, ... *S.C.* Jun. 60
One daye he *sat* upon a hyll, ... *S.C.* Jul. 217
The gentle shepheard *satte* beside a springe, ... *S.C.* D. 1
as he *satte* in secreate shade alone, ... *S.C.* D. 5
Shepheard . . . *Sate* by the fountaine side, ... *Gn.* 238
such as *sate* in justice seate, ... *Hub.* 921
Sate in the bosome of his Soveraine, ... *Ti.* 188
sate long time in sencelesse sad affright, ... *Ti.* 475
Sate (as his custome was) upon a day, ... *Col.* 4
I *sat* (as was my trade) . . . . . *Col.* 56
heavie *sate* upon her palfrey slow; . . . . . I. i. 4. 7
he *sate* upon his courser free, ... I. ii. 11. 8
The fearefull shepheard, . . . Under them never *sat,* . . . . . I. ii. 28. 8
her mother blynd *Sate* in eternall night: . . . . . I. iii. 12. 4
On which there *sate,* . . . A mayden Queene . . . . . I. iv. 8. 3
Teaching the Satyres, which her *sat* around, ... I. vi. 30. 8
he wearie *sate* To reste him selfe . . . . . I. vii. 2. 6
nymph . . . *Satt* downe to rest . . . . . I. vii. 5. 4
there *sate* a gentle payre, Of turtle doves, ... I. x. 31. 8
one *sate* wayting ever them before, ... I. x. 36. 8
still he *sate* long time astonished, ... I. xii. 29. 3
They do arrive anone Where *sate* a gentle Lady . . . . . II. i. 13. 5
there *sate* a knight with helme unlaste, ... II. i. 24. 7
where she *sate* Welling out streames of teares, ... II. ii. 8. 6
Yett still he *satt,* . . . . . II. ii. 37. 9
Betwixt them both the faire Medina *sate* . . . . . II. ii. 38. 1
Upon her eyelids many Graces *sate,* . . . . . II. iii. 25. 1
therein *sate* a Lady fresh and fayre, ... II. vi. 3. 1
By that wayes side there *sate* internall Payne, ... II. vii. 21. 5
fast beside him *sat* tumultuous Strife: . . . . . II. vii. 21. 6

Sat—*Continued.*
On thother side . . . there *sate* Cruell Revenge, . . . II. vii. 22. 1
Before the dore *sat* selfe-consuming Care, . . . II. vii. 25. 1
thereon *satt a* woman, . . . II. vii. 44. 6
Beside his head there *satt* a faire young man, . . . II. viii. 5. 1
Now bene they come whereas the Palmer *sate,* . . . II. viii. 11. 6
Within the Barbican a Porter *sate,* . . . II. ix. 25. 1
on every syde Twise sixteene warders *satt,* . . . II. ix. 26. 2
At th' upper end there *sate,* yclad in red . . . II. ix. 27. 5
A lovely bevy of faire Ladies *sate,* . . . II. ix. 34. 2
some ydly *satt* at ease; . . . II. ix. 35. 3
Emongst them all *sate* he which wonned there, . . . II. ix. 52. 1
oblique Saturne *sate* in th' house of agonyes. . . . II. ix. 52. 9
There *sate* a man of ripe and perfect age, . . . II. ix. 54. 2
therein *sat* an old old man, . . . II. ix. 55. 5
still *sat* wayting on that wastfull clift . . . II. xii. 8. 6
in the Porch there *sate* A comely personage . . . II. xii. 46. 3
death *sate* on the point of that enchaunted speare: . . . III. i. 9. 9
Supper was shortly dight, and downe they *satt;* . . . III. i. 51. 1
sat Keeping their fleecy flockes . . . III. vi. 15. 6
Sate downe upon the dusty ground anon; . . . III. vii. 10. 8
They *sate* to meat; . . . III. ix. 27. 1
he him selfe *sate* looking still askaunce . . . III. ix. 27. 3
his embrodered Bonet *sat* awry: . . . III. xii. 9. 6
her before the vile Enchaunter *sate,* . . . III. xii. 31. 1
As she *sate* carelesse by a cristall flood . . . IV. ii. 45. 4
She, them saluting, there by them *sate* still . . . IV. ii. 49. 1
therein *sate* a Ladie, passing faire . . . IV. iii. 39. 6
We did alight, and *sate* in shadow myld, . . . IV. vi. 36. 3
Upon a day as she him *sate* beside, . . . IV. viii. 6. 1
eke the Dove *sate* by the Faulcons side; . . . IV. viii. 31. 2
'On th' one side he, on th' other *sate* Delay, . . . IV. x. 13. 1
therein *sate* an amiable Dame, . . . IV. x. 31. 3
next to her *sate* goodly Shamefastnesse, . . . IV. x. 50. 1
next to her *sate* sober Modestie, . . . IV. x. 51. 1
her against *sate* comely Curtesie, . . . IV. x. 51. 3
'Thus *sate* they all around in seemely rate: . . . IV. x. 52. 1
Even in the lap of Womanhood there *sate,* . . . IV. x. 52. 3
Justice *sate* high ador'd with solemne feasts, . . . V. Pr. 9. 8
This day as I in solace *sate* hereby . . . V. i. 16. 6
right *sate* in the middest of the beame alone. . . . V. ii. 48. 9
sate thereby, with gyantlike resemblance, . . . V. ix. 22. 6
sate on high, that she might all men see . . . V. ix. 27. 3
Encompassed the throne on which she *sate,*— . . . V. ix. 29. 6
there *sate* A bevie of faire Virgins . . . V. ix. 31. 1
Sate goodly Temperance in garments clene, . . . V. ix. 32. 8
underneath her feete, there as she *sate,* . . . V. ix. 33. 3
a Ladie gent *Sate* with a knight . . . VI. ii. 16. 5
beside him *sate* . . . His wofull Ladie, . . . VI. ii. 41. 1
So downe he *sate,* . . . VI. iii. 22. 7
The lustie shepheard swaynes *sate* in a rout, . . . VI. ix. 8. 5
yet did he stay And *sate* there still, . . . VI. ix. 12. 5
to caroll, as they *sate* Keeping their sheepe, . . . VI. x. 33. 5
there *sate* an hory Old aged Sire, . . . VII. vi. 8. 5
this same day when she on Arlo *sat,* . . . VII. vii. 7. 2

Satan. after all, upon the wagon beame, Rode *Sathan* . . . I. iv. 36. 2

Satiety. My mind, full of my thoughts *satietie,* . . . *Col.* 42
voydnesse to seeke full *satietie.* . . . *Col.* 850
pleasd them all with meete *satiety.* . . . II. ii. 39. 2
full *satietie* Of meates and drinkes . . . V. iii. 4. 1
So doth he pine in most *satiety;* . . . *H.L.* 201
And senses fraught with such *satietie,* . . . *H.H.B.* 282

Satin. quilted uppon *sattin* white as milke; . . . V. v. 2. 3

Satisfied. Having his hunger throughly *satisfide* . . . *Van.* x. 2
with sorowe *satisfide* Th' importune fates, . . . *D.* 386
Having all *satisfide* their bloudy thurst, . . . I. i. 26. 4
Not all so *satisfide,* . . . He sought all round about, . . . I. v. 15. 1
their importune fates all *satisfide:* . . . III. iii. 44. 7
Not *satisfyde* so far her to estraunge . . . III. viii. 20. 7
note their hongry vew be *satisfide,* . . . III. ix. 24. 1
Nathlesse she rested not so *satisfide:* . . . IV. xii. 25. 1
Not *satisfyde* till on the fatall ground . . . VI. iii. 51. 3
nathelesse, not therewith *satisfyde,* . . . VI. vi. 43. 7
else his feare could not be *satisfyde.* . . . VI. vii. 17. 4
to it fell With small adoe, and nature *satisfyde,* . . . VI. ix. 17. 8
Still full, yet never *satisfyde* with it; . . . *H.L.* 199
Therefore in flesh it must be *satisfyde;* . . . *H.H.L.* 142

Satisfy. He casts his glutton sense to *satisfie,* . . . *Mui.* 179
floods of blood could not them *satisfie:* . . . I. vi. 43. 8
satisfy The greedy hunger of revenging yre, . . . II. viii. 15. 3
Why should not that dead carrion *satisfye* The guilt . . . II. viii. 28. 6
Her lothsom pleasure there to *satisfye;* . . . III. vii. 51. 4
Ne seeing could her wonder *satisfie,* . . . III. xi. 49. 7
ne could *satisfy* Her greedy eyes . . . III. xi. 53. 3
whose great desire He glad to *satisfie,* . . . IV. ix. 41. 4
'If that' (said Guyon) 'may you *satisfie,* . . . V. iii. 32. 7
Ne could with seeing *satisfie* his great desire. . . . VI. viii. 27. 9

Saturn. That was the golden age of *Saturne* old, . . . *Hub.* 151
oblique *Saturne* sate in th' house of agonyes. . . . II. ix. 52. 9
Next *Saturne* was, . . . III. xi. 43. 1
That sullein *Saturne* ever weend to love? . . . III. xi. 43. 2
most is Mars amisse . . . And next to him old *Saturne,* . . . V. Pr. 8. 9
The seed of *Saturne* and faire Nais, . . . VII. vii. 40. 9
grim Sir *Saturne* oft doth spare His sterne aspect, . . . VII. vii. 52. 7

Saturnal. Upon her head he heapt Mount *Saturnal,* . . . *Ro.* iv. 9

Saturn-like. A grisly forehed and *Saturnlike* face. . . . *Bel.*[1] vii. 4
Sterne face, and front full of *Saturnlike* awe . . . *Bel.*[2] ix. 4
love is sullein, and *Saturnlike* seene, . . . III. xi. 43. 3

Saturn's. during *Saturnes* ancient raigne . . . V. Pr. 9. 1
Titans that did whylome strive With *Saturnes* sonne . . . VII. vi. 2. 7

Saturn's—*Continued.*
Titan . . . Was *Saturnes* elder brother . . . VII. vi. 27. 2
'Ceasse, *Saturnes* sonne, to seeke by proffers vaine . . . VII. vi. 34. 7

Satyr. *See* **Sea-satyr.**
A cruell *Satyre* with his murdrous dart, . . . *D.* 156
A *Satyre* chaunst her wandring for to finde; . . . I. vi. 22. 6
every *Satyre* first did give a busse To Hellenore; . . . III. x. 46. 3
Embraced of a *Satyre* rough and rude, . . . III. x. 48. 3
would have wakt the *Satyre* by her syde; . . . III. x. 50. 6

Satyrane. *Satyrane,* my dearling and my joy, . . . I. vi. 28. 6
To *Satyrane* she shewed her intent; . . . I. vi. 32. 7
'Where is,' (said *Satyrane*) 'that Paynims sonne, . . . I. vi. 39. 5
whom when *Satyrane* espide, . . . he boldly him defide. . . . I. vi. 40. 8
Satyrane, with strokes him turning, staid, . . . I. vi. 46. 6
Satyrane him from pursuit did let. . . . I. vii. 20. 4
Satyrane saves the Squyre of Dames . . . III. vii. Arg.
It was to weete the good Sir *Satyrane,* . . . III. vii. 30. 1
Which whenas *Satyrane* beheld, . . . III. vii. 38. 1
the good Sir *Satyrane* gan awake . . . III. vii. 45. 1
'Her well beseemes that Quest,' (quoth *Satyrane*) . . . III. vii. 53. 1
(Thereat full hartely laughed *Satyrane.*) . . . III. vii. 58. 5
'Perdy' (sayd *Satyrane*) 'thou Squyre of Dames, . . . III. vii. 61. 1
if that thou, Sir *Satyran,* didst weete, . . . III. viii. 28. 1
To tell of *Satyrane* where I him left of late. . . . III. viii. 43. 9
Sir *Satyrane* him towardes did addresse, . . . III. viii. 45. 1
'Ah! gentle knight,' (said then Sir *Satyrane*) . . . III. viii. 47. 1
Ne long shall *Satyrane* behind you stay, . . . III. viii. 50. 7
why *Satyrane* and Paridell Mote not be entertaynd, . . . III. ix. 3. 2
Thereat Sir *Satyrane* gan smyle, . . . III. ix. 6. 6
let us first' (sayd *Satyrane*) 'entreat . . . III. ix. 9. 1
Satyrane forth stepping did them stay, . . . III. ix. 17. 1
Satyrane his chaunce Was her before, . . . III. ix. 27. 1
ever closely eide Sir *Satyrane,* . . . III. ix. 27. 5
with Sir *Satyrane,* as earst ye red, . . . III. xi. 3. 1
Ne was Sir *Satyrane* her far behinde, . . . III. xi. 5. 1
It was not *Satyrane,* whom he did feare, . . . III. xi. 6. 1
Satyran a girdle did uptake . . . IV. ii. 25. 7
Satyrane makes a Turneyment For love of Florimell: . . . IV. iv. Arg.
Then first of all forth came Sir *Satyrane,* . . . IV. iv. 15. 1
Then tooke the bold Sir *Satyrane* in hand . . . IV. iv. 17. 1
He pricked forth in ayd of *Satyran;* . . . IV. iv. 19. 2
Sir *Satyrane* abraid Out of the swowne, . . . IV. iv. 22. 1
Satyrane that day was judg'd to beare the bell. . . . IV. iv. 25. 9
the hardy *Satyrane* Appear'd in place, . . . IV. iv. 26. 2
There *Satyrane* Lord of the field he found, . . . IV. iv. 28. 1
It chaunst Sir *Satyrane* his steed . . . To stumble, . . . IV. iv. 30. 2
To rescue *Satyrane* out of his pray, . . . IV. iv. 31. 7
Satyrane, bove all the other crew, . . . IV. iv. 37. 4
Thus was Sir *Satyrane* with all his band . . . IV. iv. 43. 1
Satyrane the first day best had donne: . . . IV. v. 7. 4
Tho unto *Satyran* she was adjudged, . . . IV. v. 22. 1
To single combat with Sir *Satyrane:* . . . IV. v. 22. 8
Thereat exceeding wroth was *Satyran;* . . . IV. v. 24. 1
wroth with *Satyran* was Blandamour; . . . IV. v. 24. 2
Which troublous stirre when *Satyrane* aviz'd, . . . IV. v. 25. 1

Satyr's. A *Satyres* sonne, yborne in forrest wyld, . . . I. vi. 21. 1
in his Scutchin bore a *Satyres* hedd. . . . III. vii. 30. 6
In *Satyres* shape Antiopa he snatcht; . . . III. xi. 35. 1

Satyrs. A troupe of *Satyres* in the place did rout, . . . *Bel.*[2] xii. 12
Woodgods, and *Satyres,* and swift Dryades, . . . *Gn.* 178
a ragged rout Of Faunes and *Satyres,* . . . *T.M.* 268
A troupe of Faunes and *Satyres* . . . I. vi. 7. 7
all the *Satyres* scorne their woody kind, . . . I. vi. 18. 8
Teaching the *Satyres,* which her sat around, . . . I. vi. 30. 8
on a day, when *Satyres* all were gone . . . I. vi. 33. 1
Too late it was to *Satyres* to be told, . . . I. vi. 33. 5
Malbecco her poursewes; Fynds emongst *Satyres,* . . . III. x. Arg.
the *Satyres* her espide Straying alone . . . III. x. 36. 4
The jolly *Satyres,* full of fresh delight, . . . III. x. 44. 3
none of all the *Satyres* him espyde or heard. . . . III. x. 47. 9
chose emongst the jolly *Satyres* still to wonne. . . . III. x. 51. 9
with the Nymphes the *Satyres* love to play . . . VII. vi. 39. 9

Saulge. *See* **Sage.**

Savage. then came from the sea a *savage* beast, . . . *Rev.* i. 11
Were first enclosures but of *salvage* soyle; . . . *Ro.* xviii. 2
spoyles, by *salvage* beasts committed? . . . *Hub.* 1253
all the rest, as borne of *salvage* brood, . . . *T.M.* 589
salvage nature seemed not to have, . . . *Ti.* 564
In *salvage* forrest by adventure slew, . . . *Mui.* 67
though by kind shee stout and *salvage* were, . . . *D.* 121
where *salvage* beasts do most abound, . . . *As.* 82
No beast so *salvage* but he could it kill; . . . *As.* 83
Where store he heard to be of *salvage* pray. . . . *As.* 94
Of the wilde fruit which *salvage* soyl hath bred; . . . *Ded. Son.* v. 2
of the which a rustick Muse did weave in *savadge* soyle, . . . *Ded. Son.* vii. 12
Lyon . . . Hunting full greedy after *salvage* blood. . . . I. iii. 5. 3
too weake and feeble was the forse Of *salvage* beast . . . I. iii. 42. 2
Una . . . Whom *salvage* nation does adore, . . . I. vi. Arg.
The *salvage* nation feele her secret smart, . . . I. vi. 11. 3
long time with that *salvage* people stayd, . . . I. vi. 19. 3
to raunge the forrest wyde, And chase the *salvage* beast . . . I. vi. 21. 8
her belly sweld, And bore a boy unto that *salvage* syre: . . . I. vi. 23. 4
wherewith she queld The *salvage* beastes . . . II. iii. 29. 4
Hath tracted forth some *salvage* beastes trade: . . . II. vi. 39. 5
An uncouth, *salvage,* and uncivile wight, . . . II. vii. 3. 4
salvage Bull, whom two fierce mastives bayt, . . . II. viii. 42. 1
In antique times was *salvage* wildernesse, . . . II. x. 5. 3
far in land a *salvage* nation dwelt . . . II. x. 7. 1
He fought great batteils with his *salvage* fone; . . . II. x. 10. 3
he brought them to these *salvage* parts, . . . II. x. 25. 8

Savage—*Continued.*
having at a bay The *salvage* beast . . . III. i. 22. 2
To hunt the *salvage* beast in forrest wyde, . . . III. i. 37. 4
indew The *salvage* minds with skill of just and trew: . . . III. iii. 45. 5
Sith that in *salvage* forests she did dwell, . . . III. vi. 1. 4
sought the *salvage* woods and forests wyde, . . . III. vi. 16. 4
Your glory sett to chace the *salvage* beasts, . . . III. vi. 22. 2
none so bestiall Nor *salvage* hart, . . . III. vii. 9. 6
Least *salvage* beastes her person have despoyld: . . . III. x. 39. 8
Seeking adventures in the *salvage* wood, . . . IV. ii. 45. 2
like *salvage* weed With woody mosse bedight, . . . IV. iv. 39. 4
seemed fit For *salvage* wight; . . . IV. iv. 39. 7
him to terme the *Salvage* Knight; . . . IV. iv. 42. 6
The *Salvage* Knight that victour was whileare, . . . IV. v. 8. 5
That was the *Salvage* Knight: . . . IV. v. 21. 6
call ye me the *Salvage* Knight, . . . IV. vi. 4. 9
'Then this, Sir *Salvage* Knight,' (quoth he) 'areede: . . . IV. vi. 5. 1
'Sir *Salvage* knight, Let me this crave, . . . IV. vi. 9. 6
Sir Artegall, the *salvage* knight, . . . IV. vi. 31. 1
In *salvage* forrests and in deserts wide . . . IV. vii. 2. 6
It was to weet a wilde and *salvage* man; . . . IV. vii. 5. 1
any of the Thracian Nimphes in *salvage* chase. . . . IV. vii. 22. 9
toile which she had tride In *salvage* chase, . . . IV. viii. 9. 4
doe the *salvage* beasts begin to play . . . IV. x. 46. 1
read the *salvage* cuntreis thorough which they pace. . . . IV. xi. 40. 9
What Tygre, or what other *salvage* wight, . . . V. ix. 1. 1
mongst wyld beasts, and *salvage* woods, to dwell; . . . V. ix. 1. 5
softly royne, when *salvage* choler gan redound. . . . V. ix. 33. 9
To meete her at the *salvage* Ilands syde, . . . V. xi. 39. 3
since the *salvage* Island I did leave,' . . . VI. i. 9. 1
to launch the *salvage* hart Of many a Lyon . . . VI. ii. 6. 7
I, . . . bend my carelesse wit To *salvage* chace, . . . VI. ii. 9. 5
my most delight . . . To hunt the *salvage* chace, . . . VI. ii. 31. 7
Calepine by a *salvage* man . . . reskewed is; . . . VI. iv. Arg.
A *salvage* man, which in those woods did wonne, . . . VI. iv. 2. 2
The *salvage* man, . . . Was much emmoved . . . VI. iv. 3. 1
The *salvage* nation doth all dread despize, . . . VI. iv. 6. 6
when the *Salvage* saw his labour vaine . . . VI. iv. 9. 1
perill, by this *salvage* man pretended, . . . VI. vi. 10. 4
He made great mone after his *salvage* mood; . . . VI. iv. 12. 4
The *salvage* serves Serena well, . . . VI. v. Arg.
Mongst *salvage* beasts both rudely borne and bred, . . . VI. v. 2. 3
Whom when the *Salvage* saw so sore distrest, . . . VI. v. 6. 1
A *salvage* man matcht with a Ladie fayre, . . . VI. v. 9. 3
When he did raunge the wood for *salvage* game, . . . VI. v. 15. 2
by what traine She fell into that *salvage* villaines hand? . . . VI. v. 27. 8
'In *salvage* forrest I him lost of late, . . . VI. v. 29. 1
In such a *salvage* wight, of brutish kynd, . . . VI. v. 29. 6
went his way, And with him eke the *salvage,* . . . VI. v. 41. 6
whiles the *salvage* man did take his steede, . . . VI. vi. 19. 8
the *Salvage,* comming now in place, . . . VI. vi. 22. 1
that same Knight and *Salvage* standing by, . . . VI. vi. 23. 2
that same Knight And *salvage* . . . VI. vi. 24. 7
left that *salvage* wight Amongst so many foes, . . . VI. vi. 37. 5
Whom when the *Salvage* saw from daunger free, . . . VI. vi. 40. 1
The whyles his *salvage* page . . . Was wandred . . . VI. vii. 19. 5
The *Salvage* forth out of the wood issew'd . . . VI. vii. 23. 8
Like as a Mastiffe having at a bay A *salvage* Bull, . . . VI. vii. 47. 2
Meane-while the *Salvage* man, when he beheld . . . VI. viii. 28. 1
There dwelt a *salvage* nation, . . . VI. viii. 35. 2
better so To lodge then in the *salvage* fields to rome. . . . VI. ix. 16. 7
more cruell, and more *salvage* wylde, . . . *Am.* xx. 9
Savage-minded. nor so *salvage mynded* As that, . . . V. v. 40. 6
Savages. Serena, found of *Salvages,* . . . VI. viii. Arg.
Save. Ne ought *save* Tyber hastning to his fall Remaines . . . *Ro.* iii. 11
shewed his ware . . . All *save* a bell, . . . *S.C.* May 288
them did *save* with bloudy sweat . . . *S.C.* Jul. 55
To *save* the innocent from the beastes pawes, . . . *S.C.* Au. 33
Doest *save* from mischiefe the unwary sheepe, . . . *S.C.* D. 10
might *save* my sheepe and me fro shame. . . . *S.C.* D. 78
I this doubt will *save;* . . . *Hub.* 194
askes small paines, but thriftines to *save,* . . . *Hub.* 278
none, . . . *Save* that which common is, . . . *Hub.* 613
He cloathed them in all colours, *save* white, . . . *Hub.* 1155
Save what in heavens storehouse he uplaid: . . . *Ti.* 212
Could *save* the sonne of Thetis from to die; . . . *Ti.* 429
Who then can *save* what they dispose to spill? . . . *Mui.* 232
Nought may thee *save* from heavens avengement. . . . *Mui.* 240
Like as himselfe us pleaseth *save* or spill. . . . *Col.* 814
Her selfe a yielded pray to *save* or spill: . . . I. iii. 43. 4
A worke of wondrous grace, and hable soules to *save.* . . . I. ix. 19. 9
his righteous soule might *save.* . . . I. x. 34. 9
when he their soules shall *save.* . . . I. x. 42. 5
shewes the way his sinfull soule to *save!* . . . I. x. 51. 3
To *save* his body from the scorching fire, . . . I. xi. 45. 4
not to be fownd, *Save* in that soile, . . . I. xi. 47. 2
Into that same he fell, which did from death him *save.* . . . I. xi. 48. 9
faire her self doth *save.* . . . II. ii. 24. 9
her silly life to *save,* . . . II. iii. 36. 3
both from rocks and flats it selfe could wisely *save.* . . . II. vi. 5. 9
both from drowning for to *save,* . . . II. vi. 47. 3
To *save* my Lord in wretched plight forlore; . . . II. vi. 48. 3
Eternall God thee *save* from such decay! . . . II. vii. 34. 7
Ne canst of prowesse . . . deeme, *Save* as thou seest . . . II. viii. 14. 3
no enchauntment from his dint might *save;* . . . II. viii. 20. 6
him henceforth the same can *save* no more; . . . II. viii. 43. 7
save your selves from neare decay; . . . II. ix. 12. 3
knights slaine that have us sought to *save.'* . . . II. ix. 12. 9
Learning his ship from those white rocks to *save,* . . . II. x. 6. 3
being all defeated, *save* a few, . . . II. x. 55. 8

Save—*Continued.*
Ne ought *save* perill still as he did pas: . . . II. xii. 2. 3
the rich wares to *save* from pitteous spoyle; . . . II. xii. 19. 8
not on living ground, *Save* in this Paradise, be heard . . . II. xii. 70. 4
save Them from the tempest of his wrathfulnesse, . . . II. xii. 83. 3
Madnesse to *save* a part, and lose the whole! . . . III. v. 43. 3
Nor halfe so fast to *save* her maydenhed . . . III. vii. 26. 3
Badd her commaund my life to *save* or spill. . . . III. vii. 54. 2
'*Safe* her, I never any woman found . . . III. vii. 60. 1
her to *save* from outrage meekely prayed him. . . . III. viii. 15. 9
To *save* her honor from that villaine vilde, . . . III. viii. 27. 4
To *save* her selfe from that outrageous spoyle; . . . III. viii. 32. 5
Save one old Nymph, hight Panope, . . . III. viii. 37. 9
To *save* his people sad from victours vengefull handes. . . . III. ix. 41. 9
Save an huge nation of the Geaunts broode . . . III. ix. 49. 8
sith he n'ote *save* both, he sav'd that . . . dearest . . . III. x. 15. 7
he her prayd, . . . To *save* his life, . . . III. x. 50. 8
Ne living wight she saw . . . *Save* that same woefull Lady, . . . III. xii. 30. 6
nought may *save* thee from to dy . . . III. xii. 35. 4
her honor . . . She sought to *save,* . . . IV. i. 6. 7
So could she forge all colours, *save* the trew. . . . IV. i. 18. 5
save her honour with your ventrous paines: . . . IV. ii. 27. 8
wage Gainst all those knights, . . . *save* they alone. . . . IV. ii. 28. 9
He forced was to strike, and *save* himselfe . . . IV. iii. 31. 9
rather sought Him selfe to *save,* . . . IV. iii. 32. 4
was nothing slow Him selfe to *save* . . . IV. iii. 33. 5
Ne either cared life to *save* or spill, . . . IV. iii. 36. 6
To let him loose to *save* their proper stakes, . . . IV. iv. 34. 8
Save that she algates him a while accompanide. . . . IV. vi. 44. 9
forst him flie abacke, himselfe to *save:* . . . IV. vii. 28. 4
sailers *save* from wreckes of wrathfull winde. . . . IV. xi. 52. 5
save all us three alive.' . . . IV. xii. 31. 9
did helpe to *save* her. . . . V. iv. 12. 4
forward set To *save* her from her feare, . . . V. viii. 6. 9
Oft spilles the principall to *save* the part; . . . V. x. 2. 4
seekes to *save* the subject of her skill, . . . V. x. 2. 6
As it is greater prayse to *save* then spill, . . . V. x. 2. 8
where he did weene Him selfe to *save;* . . . V. x. 37. 9
To *save* him selfe from those his furious heats, . . . V. xi. 13. 3
To *save* her selfe, least that he did her slay; . . . V. xi. 26. 8
Fro dangers dread his doubtfull life to *save;* . . . V. xi. 46. 4
had forsaken quight To *save* themselves, . . . V. xi. 60. 3
save my life, which lot before your foot doth lay.' . . . VI. i. 39. 9
I will it graunt, your hopelesse life to *save,* . . . VI. i. 42. 5
And what he did, he did him selfe to *save:* . . . VI. ii. 14. 6
to thinke to *save* himselfe it booted not. . . . VI. ii. 19. 9
How to *save* hole her hazarded estate; . . . VI. iii. 12. 7
Save such as sudden rage him lent to smite; . . . VI. iv. 4. 3
Cryde out aloud for mercie, him to *save;* . . . VI. vii. 12. 2
She could or *save* or spill . . . VI. vii. 31. 8
to *save* his friend from jeopardy. . . . VI. viii. 12. 9
Ne ought, . . . (*Save* onely Glorianaes heavenly hew, . . . VI. x. 4. 7
were gone, . . . All *save* the shepheard, . . . VI. x. 18. 4
cast How he might *save* her life, . . . VI. xi. 34. 5
heavens had her graste To *save* her chylde, . . . VI. xii. 16. 9
yonder Lady, whom high God did *save.'* . . . VI. xii. 17. 9
did them all exceedingly amate, *Save* Jove; . . . VII. vi. 19. 8
That never any saw, *save* onely one, . . . VII. vi. 45. 3
hunt him with their hounds, him selfe *save* how hee might. . . . VII. vi. 50. 9
she can it *save* or spill. To spill were pitty, but to *save* were prayse! . . . *Am.* xxxviii. 11, 12
And greater glory thinke, to *save* then spill. . . . *Am.* xlix. 4
Us wretches from the second death did *save;* . . . *H.H.L.* 193
Saved. To thee, small Gnat, in lieu of his life *saved,* . . . *Gn.* 687
oft the Paynim *sav'd* from deadly stowre: . . . II. viii. 43. 6
Thy life she *saved* by her gratious deed; . . . III. v. 45. 3
wrong'd by Carle, by Proteus *sav'd,* . . . III. viii. Arg.
Her selfe not *saved* yet from daunger dredd . . . III. viii. 33. 1
the Trojan reliques *sav'd* from flame, . . . III. ix. 36. 8
he *sav'd* that same Which was the dearest . . . III. x. 15. 7
he *sav'd* the victour from fordonne: . . . IV. v. 7. 7
Thine honor *sav'd,* though into thraldome throwne?' . . . IV. vii. 19. 5
this dayes honour *sav'd* to Marinell: . . . V. iii. 21. 2
To his owne love his loialtie he *saved:* . . . V. vi. 2. 5
And *saved* from his cruell villany. . . . VI. iii. 51. 7
sav'd from being to that caytive thrall. . . . VI. iv. 15. 4
she had *sav'd* so many loves as she did lose. . . . VI. vii. 37. 9
in all these two yeares space *Saved* but two; . . . VI. vii. 38. 6
the Carle with paine *Saved* him selfe . . . VI. viii. 9. 4
Yet *sav'd* not so, but that the bloud it drew, . . . VI. viii. 9. 5
Till I have *sav'd* so many as I earst did slay.' . . . VI. viii. 22. 9
having *saved* her from dying, . . . VI. xi. 23. 4
was *sav'd* with strong defence; . . . VI. xi. 30. 7
Savedst. even that which thou *savedst* thine still to remaine?' . . . V. xi. 16. 9
Saves. foe; Whom false Duessa *saves,* . . . I. v. Arg.
Satyrane *saves* the Squyre of Dames . . . III. vii. Arg.
Fayre Britomart *saves* Amoret: . . . IV. i. Arg.
Amoret . . . Belphebe *saves* from dread: . . . IV. vii. Arg.
Defends him selfe, and *saves* his gotten pray: . . . IV. vii. 25. 7
Artegall . . . *Saves* Terpine from the gallow tree, . . . V. iv. Arg.
Calidore *saves* from Maleffort A Damzell . . . VI. i. Arg.
Calidore . . . *Saves* Serena, . . . VI. iii. Arg.
whylest an Infant from a Beare He *saves,* . . . VI. iv. Arg.
Savin. Had gathered Rew, and *Savine,* . . . III. ii. 49. 5
Saving. *saving* that askaunce Her wanton eyes, . . . II. i. 41. 6
In *saving* him from daungerous despaire . . . V. xi. 48. 4
all their showes but shadowes, *saving* she. . . . *Am.* xxxv. 14
Savior's. A booke, wherein his *Saveours* testament Was writ . . . I. ix. 19. 7
His *Saviour's* birth his mind so much did glad. . . . VII. vii. 41. 4
Savor. Can no whit *savour* this celestiall food, . . . *T.M.* 591

Savored. *See* **Well-savored.**
Savory. Sound *Savorie,* and Bazil hartie-hale, . . . *Mui.* 198
Saw. a frame an hundred cubites hie I *sawe,* . . . *Bel.*[1] ii. 2
A sodaine tempest from the heaven, I *saw,* . . . *Bel.*[1] iii. 13
I *saw* raisde upon pillers of Ivorie, . . . *Bel.*[1] iv. 1
I *saw* the birde that dares beholde the Sunne, . . . *Bel.*[1] vi. 1
sodenly I *saw* Where tombling . . . *Bel.*[1] vi. 9
I *saw* hir bodie turned all to dust, . . . *Bel.*[1] vi. 12
I *saw* the foule that shunnes the . . . light . . . *Bel.*[1] vi. 13
I *saw* an hideous body big and strong, . . . *Bel.*[1] vii. 2
Upon a hill I *saw* a kindled flame, . . . *Bel.*[1] ix. 1
I *saw* a fresh spring rise . . . *Bel.*[1] x. 1
I *saw* the great Typhaeus sister . . . *Bel.*[1] xi. 4
I *saw* the heavens warre against hir . . . *Bel.*[1] xi. 12
I *saw* an ugly beast come from the sea, . . . *Rev.* i. 1
I *saw* a Woman sitting on a beast . . . *Rev.* ii. 1
seven heads I *saw,* Ten hornes . . . *Rev.* ii. 4
His precious robe I *saw* embrued with bloud. . . . *Rev.* iii. 5
Then *saw* I . . . A puissant armie come . . . *Rev.* iii. 6
I *saw* new Earth, new Heaven, sayde Saint John. . . . *Rev.* iv. 1
I *saw* the roote in great (hie[1]) disdaine . . . *Bel.* v. 13
I *saw* her rise, . . . *Bel.* vii. 5
I *saw* (sawe[1]) . . . the gaping earth devoure . . . *Pet.* iv. 10
I *saw* a Phoenix in the wood alone, . . . *Pet.* v. 1
On high hills top I *saw* a stately frame, . . . *Bel.*[2] ii. 1
I *saw* a tempest from the heaven descend, . . . *Bel.*[2] iii. 13
I *saw* raysde up on yvorie pillours [*text,* pillowes] . . . *Bel.*[2] iv. 1
I *saw* a Wolfe under a rockie cave . . . *Bel.*[2] vi. 1
I *saw* her litle ones . . . *Bel.*[2] vi. 2
I *saw* her raunge abroad . . . *Bel.*[2] vi. 5
I *saw* a thousand huntsmen, . . . *Bel.*[2] vi. 9
I *saw* her on the plaine outstretched . . . *Bel.*[2] vi. 12
on a tree uphang'd I *saw* her spoyle. . . . *Bel.*[2] vi. 14
I *saw* the Bird that can the sun endure, . . . *Bel.*[2] vii. 1
I *saw* the foule, that doth the light dispise, . . . *Bel.*[2] vii. 13
I *saw* a river swift, . . . *Bel.*[2] viii. 1
I *saw* it cover'd all with griesly shadowes, . . . *Bel.*[2] viii. 3
at length I *saw* the wrathfull winde, . . . *Bel.*[2] viii. 11
An hideous bodie big and strong I *sawe,* . . . *Bel.*[2] ix. 2
I *saw* a spring out of a rocke forth rayle, . . . *Bel.*[2] xii. 1
I *saw* both ship and mariners each one, . . . *Bel.*[2] xiii. 12
I the ship *saw* after raisd' againe. . . . *Bel.*[2] xiii. 14
I *saw* a Citie like unto that same, . . . *Bel.*[2] xiv. 2
Which *saw* the messenger of tidings glad; . . . *Bel.*[2] xiv. 3
I *saw* Typhoeus sister comming . . . *Bel.*[2] xv. 4
I *saw* the heavens in warre against her . . . *Bel.*[2] xv. 12
I *saw* a Bull as white as driven snowe, . . . *Van.* ii. 2
I *saw* a little Bird cal'd Tedula, . . . *Van.* iii. 7
I *saw* the fish (if fish I may it cleepe) . . . *Van.* v. 2
Soone after this I *saw* an Elephant, . . . *Van.* viii. 1
I *saw* a wasp, that fiercely him defide, . . . *Van.* x. 7
I *sawe* so fayre a sight as shee: . . . *S.C.* Ja. 52
'I *sawe* Phoebus thrust out his golden hedde, . . . *S.C.* Ap. 73
when he *sawe* how broade her beames did spredde, . . . *S.C.* Ap. 75
I *sawe* a shole of shepeheardes outgoe, . . . *S.C.* May 20
shee *sawe* in the younglings face . . . *S.C.* May 211
she *saw* the merchaundise . . . *S.C.* May 298
I *sawe* Calliope wyth Muses moe, . . . *S.C.* Jun. 57
Has bene an old-sayd *sawe,* . . . *S.C.* Jul. 98
Moses . . . *sawe* hys makers face, . . . *S.C.* Jul. 158
He *saw* thilke misusage; . . . *S.C.* Jul. 184
I *saw* the bouncing Bellibone, . . . *S.C.* Au. 61
you, that *sawe* it, simple shepe, . . . *S.C.* Au. 117
sithence I *sawe* thy head last, . . . *S.C.* S. 19
Yet *saw* I on the beare when it was brought; . . . *S.C.* N. 161
he them plac'd in thy sacred wood . . . *saw,* . . . *Gn.* 170
when he *saw* him slaine himselfe he cheard. . . . *Gn.* 312
'I *saw* anothers fate approaching fast, . . . *Gn.* 361
Which when they *sawe,* the Ape was sore afrayde, . . . *Hub.* 955
Full of the feared sight which late they *sawe.* . . . *Hub.* 1110
he *saw* that sorely griev'd his hart, . . . *Hub.* 1304
when he *saw* no entraunce to him graunted, . . . *Hub.* 1367
he *saw* my cruell foes me pained, . . . *Ti.* 144
'I *saw* him die, I *saw* him die, . . . *Ti.* 190
I *saw* him die, and no man left to mone . . . *Ti.* 192
I *saw* an Image, all of massie gold, . . . *Ti.* 491
I *saw* this Towre fall sodainelie to dust, . . . *Ti.* 517
Since that I *sawe* this gardine wasted quite, . . . *Ti.* 529
I *saw* two Beares, as white as anie milke, . . . *Ti.* 561
I *sawe* an Harpe stroung all with silver twyne, . . . *Ti.* 604
I *saw,* on th' other side, A curious Coffer . . . *Ti.* 617
Looking aside I *saw* a stately Bed, . . . *Ti.* 631
A fairer wight *saw* never summers day. . . . *Ti.* 637
Lastly I *saw* an Arke of purest golde . . . *Ti.* 659
When as the land she *saw* no more appeare, . . . *Mui.* 286
all the Gods, which *saw* his wondrous might, . . . *Mui.* 318
Which when Arachne *saw,* . . . *Mui.* 337
when I *saw* the anguish of his spright . . . *D.* 172
when I *saw* her leade The Shepheards daughters . . . *D.* 309
Which when I *saw,* . . . *D.* 544
(A fairer star *saw* never living eie) . . . *As.* 57
when she *saw* her love in such a plight, . . . *As.* 151
Which when she *saw,* she staied not a whit, . . . *As.* 175
since I *saw* that Angels blessed eie, . . . *Col.* 40
world . . . In which I *saw* no living people dwell. . . . *Col.* 231
A fairer Nymph yet never *saw* mine eie: . . . *Col.* 559
rules the creatures by his powrfull *saw:* . . . *Col.* 884
things celestiall which ye never *saw.* . . . *Col.* 930
he *saw* the ugly monster plaine, . . . I. i. 14. 6
their Parent deare They *saw* so rudely falling . . . I. i. 25. 2

Saw—*Continued.*
Their bellies swolne he *saw* with fulnesse burst, . . . I. i. 26. 5
when he *saw* his labour all was vaine, . . . I. i. 55. 8
when he *saw* his threatning was but vaine, . . . I. ii. 2. 8
Archimago, when his guests He *saw* divided . . . I. ii. 9. 2
she *saw* the knight his speare advaunce, . . . I. ii. 14. 3
when she *saw* her champion fall . . . I. ii. 20. 1
For danger great, . . . I *saw* before mine eyes, . . . I. ii. 41. 9
when she *saw* her prayers nought prevaile, . . . I. iii. 24. 1
saw the Red-crosse which the knight did beare, . . . I. iii. 34. 2
his soveraine Dame So rudely handled by her foe he *saw,* . . . I. iii. 41. 3
Ne Persia selfe, . . . Like ever *saw.* . . . I. iv. 7. 7
Inconstant man, that loved all he *saw,* . . . I. iv. 26. 1
death it was, when any good he *saw;* . . . I. iv. 30. 7
when she *saw* Duessa, sunny bright, . . . I. v. 21. 1
I *saw* . . . The bold Sansfoy shrinck . . . I. v. 23. 1
when she *saw* her offred sweets refusd, . . . I. v. 37. 6
when he *saw* his flatt'ring artes to fayle, . . . I. vi. 5. 1
monstrous rablement, Whose like he never *saw,* . . . I. vi. 8. 8
The Lyon whelpes she *saw* how he did beare, . . . I. vi. 27. 8
when he *saw* the Damsell passe away, . . . I. vi. 48. 5
His living like *saw* never living eye, . . . I. vii. 8. 7
So daunted when the Geaunt *saw* the knight, . . . I. vii. 14. 1
The wofull Dwarfe, which *saw* his maisters fall . . . I. vii. 19. 1
saw the signes that deadly tydinges spake, . . . I. vii. 20. 6
saw The evil stownd that daungerd her estate, . . . I. viii. 12. 1
Whom these sad eyes *saw* nigh unto deaths dore, . . . I. viii. 27. 2
Whome when his Lady *saw,* to him she ran . . . I. viii. 42. 1
More ugly shape yet never living creature *saw.* . . . I. viii. 48. 9
So fayre a creature yet *saw* never sunny day. . . . I. ix. 13. 9
never knight I *saw* in such misseeming plight.' . . . I. ix. 23. 9
nought but death before his eies he *saw,* . . . I. ix. 50. 2
whenas none of them he *saw* him take, . . . I. ix. 51. 1
Which whenas Una *saw,* . . . I. ix. 52. 1
when the carle . . . *saw* his guest Would safe depart, . . . I. ix. 54. 2
Una *saw* That this her knight was feeble, . . . I. x. 2. 1
God he often *saw* from heavens hight: . . . I. x. 47. 2
when he *saw* them come he did them still forsake. . . . I. xi. 24. 9
Which when his pensive Lady *saw* from farre, . . . I. xi. 32. 1
late she *saw* him fall before his enimy. . . . I. xi. 33. 9
she *saw* where he upstarted brave Out of the well, . . . I. xi. 34. 1
when he *saw* no power might prevaile, . . . I. xi. 42. 1
Una *saw* the second fall Of her deare knight, . . . I. xi. 50. 1
now he *saw* himselfe so freshly reare, . . . I. xi. 52. 6
whenas the direfull feend She *saw* not stirre, . . . I. xi. 55. 6
She nigher drew, and *saw* that joyous end: . . . I. xi. 55. 7
Another said, he *saw* him move his eyes indeed. . . . I. xii. 10. 9
'None but that *saw,*' (quoth he) 'would weene . . . II. i. 11. 3
when as still he *saw* him towards pace, . . . II. i. 26. 4
saw no meanes to scape, . . . II. ii. 8. 2
when Sir Guyon *saw,* all were he wroth, . . . II. ii. 12. 1
saw it stirre: . . . II. iii. 34. 4
when the Pesaunt *saw,* amazd he stood, . . . II. iii. 43. 1
He *saw* from far, or seemed for to see, . . . II. iv. 3. 2
when the Palmer *saw,* he loudly cryde, . . . II. iv. 10. 1
he *saw* that wretched Squyre, . . . II. iv. 16. 2
That when the varlett heard and *saw,* . . . II. iv. 45. 1
When late he *saw* his Lord in heavie plight . . . II. v. 25. 5
he *saw* whereas did swim Along the shore, . . . II. vi. 2. 5
when far off Cymochles heard and *saw,* . . . II. vi. 4. 1
when he *saw* her toy, and gibe, and geare, . . . II. vi. 21. 7
Such as he *saw* she gan him lay before, . . . II. vi. 24. 4
of her joy . . . she *saw* he light did pas, . . . II. vi. 37. 3
he *saw* from farre An armed knight . . . II. vi. 41. 1
The varlett *saw,* when to the flood he came, . . . II. vi. 42. 1
Him when the old man *saw,* . . . II. vi. 48. 6
helpe, he *saw,* he needed more Then pitty, . . . II. vi. 48. 8
Soone as he Guyon *saw,* . . . II. vii. 6. 1
whenas Mammon *saw* his purpose mist, . . . II. vii. 34. 8
when an earthly wight they present *saw* . . . II. vii. 37. 1
They never creature *saw* that cam that way: . . . II. vii. 37. 5
Which whenas Guyon *saw,* . . . II. vii. 48. 1
ne living wight Like ever *saw,* . . . II. vii. 54. 4
looking downe *saw* many damned wightes . . . II. vii. 57. 2
Whom when the Palmer *saw,* . . . II. viii. 7. 1
Whom when Pyrochles *saw,* . . . II. viii. 12. 1
under him he *saw* his Lybian steed to praunce; . . . II. viii. 17. 9
Which when his brother *saw,* . . . II. viii. 33. 1
brother *saw* the red blood rayle Adowne so fast, . . . II. viii. 37. 3
Whom when the Palmer *saw* in such distresse, . . . II. viii. 40. 1
when Cymochles *saw* the fowle reproch, . . . II. viii. 44. 1
Which when his german *saw,* . . . II. viii. 46. 1
his shield he lakt And sword *saw* not, . . . II. viii. 53. 4
when he heard, and *saw* the tokens trew, . . . II. viii. 55. 1
Which when they *saw,* . . . II. ix. 11. 1
feeble age . . . he *saw* proceed, . . . II. x. 27. 7
Yet life he *saw,* and felt his mighty mayne, . . . II. xi. 44. 4
streight they *saw* the raging surges reard . . . II. xii. 2. 8
On thother side they *saw* that perilous Rocke, . . . II. xii. 7. 1
Which when she *saw,* she left her lockes undight, . . . II. xii. 15. 6
Eftsoones they *saw* an hideous hoast . . . II. xii. 22. 8
Whom such when Guyon *saw,* he drew him neare, . . . II. xii. 65. 7
On which when gazing him the Palmer *saw,* . . . II. xii. 69. 1
Which when his Palmer *saw,* . . . III. i. 9. 6
when she *saw* them gone she forward went, . . . III. i. 19. 6
On which she *saw* six knights, . . . III. i. 20. 8
When Britomart him *saw,* she ran apace . . . III. i. 22. 7
she *saw* him bent to cruell play, . . . III. i. 37. 3
when she *saw* no helpe might him restore, . . . III. i. 38. 7
Whom when the Lady *saw* so faire a wight, . . . III. i. 47. 1

Saw—*Continued.*

when the Britonesse *saw* all the rest Avoided	III. i. 58. 5
On thother side they *saw* the warlike Mayd	III. i. 63. 6
Whose prowesse paragone *saw* never living wight	III. ii. 13. 9
Whose shape or person yet I never *saw*,	III. ii. 38. 4
I in my fathers wondrous mirrhour *saw*,	III. ii. 38. 7
That when old Glauce *saw*,	III. ii. 52. 7
secretly he *saw*, yet note discoure:	III. iii. 50. 4
When the two fearefull wemen *saw*,	III. iii. 50. 6
I *saw* a Saxon Virgin,	III. iii. 55. 5
She *saw* bestrowed all with rich aray Of pearles	III. iv. 18. 4
Saw never living eie more heavy sight,	III. v. 30. 1
they *saw* that goodly boy with blood Defowled,	III. v. 38. 1
Soone as she Venus *saw* behinde her backe,	III. vi. 19. 1
Whom whenas Venus *saw* so sore displeasd,	III. vi. 25. 1
When walking through the Gardin them she *saw*,	III. vi. 40. 6
Each shade she *saw*, and each noyse she did heare,	III. vii. 1. 8
The fayrest creature that he ever *saw*	III. vii. 13. 2
when she fit season *saw* To leave	III. vii. 18. 1
when all other helpes she *saw* to faile,	III. vii. 21. 6
him he *saw* still stronger grow through strife,	III. vii. 33. 3
Which when the knight That her pursewed *saw*,	III. vii. 43. 7
that bold knight, whom ye pursuing *saw* That Geauntesse,	III. vii. 52. 1
Which when she *saw*, more bent to eke my smartes	III. vii. 55. 7
who so then her *saw* would surely say It was her selfe	III. viii. 9. 3
when hee *saw* him selfe free from poursute,	III. viii. 14. 1
saw his drover drive along the streame,	III. viii. 22. 2
when he *saw* that blazing beauties beame,	III. viii. 22. 5
He therein *saw* that yrkesome sight,	III. viii. 31. 3
when all this he nothing *saw* prevaile,	III. viii. 40. 6
he *saw* him selfe esteemd,	III. viii. 41. 7
saw the fieldes of faire Scamander strowne	III. ix. 35. 6
when she *saw* aloft appeare The Trojane flames	III. x. 12. 7
saw the wicked fire so furiously Consume his hart,	III. x. 14. 5
At last when sorrow he *saw* booted nought,	III. x. 18. 6
Soone as the old man *saw* Sir Paridell, He fainted,	III. x. 37. 6
The silly man . . . *Saw* all this goodly sport,	III. x. 45. 2
Which when Malbecco *saw*,	III. x. 47. 1
Whom when the Gyaunt *saw*, he soone . . . fled	III. xi. 5. 3
when she heard, and *saw* the ghastly fit	III. xi. 12. 6
Whom whenas Scudamour *saw* past the fire	III. xi. 26. 1
when she *saw* The huge seas . . . t' obay	III. xi. 30. 8
living creature none she *saw* appeare.	III. xi. 55. 2
the brave Maid, . . . *saw* both first and last,	III. xii. 27. 5
all those persons which she *saw* without:	III. xii. 30. 3
Ne living wight she *saw* in all that roome,	III. xii. 30. 5
Soone as that virgin knight he *saw* in place,	III. xii. 32. 1
those goodly rowmes, which erst She *saw*	III. xii. 42. 2
Awayted . . . Britomarts returne, Yet *saw* her not,	III. xii. 45. 3
'the thing that with this eye I *saw*,	IV. i. 48. 4
'I *saw*' (quoth she) 'a stranger knight,	IV. i. 48. 7
'I *saw* him have your Amoret at will;	IV. i. 49. 1
I *saw* him kisse; I *saw* him her embrace;	IV. i. 49. 2
I *saw* him sleepe with her all night his fill;	IV. i. 49. 3
Which when their mother *saw*, she gan to dout	IV. ii. 46. 6
when she *saw*, it did her much amate	IV. ii. 50. 7
Which when she *saw*, downe on the bloudy plaine	IV. iii. 47. 4
When all men *saw* this sudden change of things,	IV. iii. 49. 6
when she *saw* that cruell war so ended,	IV. iii. 50. 4
When as he *saw* the mercilesse affray	IV. iv. 22. 4
There where he *saw* the valiant Triamond	IV. iv. 23. 6
All that her *saw* with wonder ravisht weare,	IV. v. 14. 5
soone as she them *saw* to discord set,	IV. v. 29. 1
Which when that warriour *saw*, he said no more,	IV. v. 39. 1
soone as she him *saw* approching neare	IV. vi. 10. 3
when as he *saw* her hastie heat Abate,	IV. vi. 16. 1
in that enchaunted glasse she *saw*;	IV. vi. 26. 6
her modest countenance he *saw* So goodly grave,	IV. vi. 33. 4
Whom when on ground she groveling *saw* to rowle,	IV. vii. 32. 1
Ne creature *saw*, but hearkned now and then	IV. vii. 33. 3
Which when she *saw* with sodaine glauncing eye,	IV. vii. 36. 1
by that he *saw* on every tree,	IV. vii. 46. 1
saw he often how he wexed glad	IV. vii. 46. 7
saw that all he said and did was vaine,	IV. vii. 47. 2
saw her forward still to make her flight,	IV. viii. 8. 2
Whom when she *saw* in wretched weedes disguiz'd,	IV. viii. 12. 5
when he *saw* the Prince in armour bright,	IV. viii. 40. 6
So faire as ever yet *saw* living eie;	IV. viii. 49. 5
Whom when the watch . . . *Saw* comming home,	IV. ix. 5. 7
saw him sencelesse by the Squire upstaide,	IV. ix. 7. 4
when she them *saw* embrace,	IV. ix. 10. 5
a troupe of Knights They *saw* together skirmishing,	IV. ix. 20. 2
Whose like they never *saw* till that same houre	IV. ix. 22. 5
Which when he *saw*,	IV. x. 19. 8
all that else I *saw*,	IV. x. 29. 1
Whom when I *saw*	IV. x. 56. 3
Whenas he *saw* me,	IV. x. 58. 2
Her constant mind could move at all he *saw*,	IV. xi. 2. 8
Ne ever evening *saw*, ne mornings ray,	IV. xi. 4. 7
nought, She *saw*, could ease his rankling maladie,	IV. xi. 6. 4
They *saw* it all, and present were in place;	IV. xi. 40. 6
Which when his mother *saw*,	IV. xii. 21. 1
since she *saw* the streight extremitie,	IV. xii. 28. 1
they *saw* a Squire in squallid weed Lamenting sore	V. i. 13. 7
'Which when his Ladie *saw*, she follow'd fast,	V. i. 18. 1
When as he *saw* she should be cut in twaine,	V. i. 27. 4
when he *saw* it bootelesse to resist,	V. i. 29. 7
on the Bridge he ready armed *saw* The Sarazin,	V. ii. 11. 2
Which when the Pagan *saw* he wexed wroth,	V. ii. 12. 1
He *saw* no way but close with him in hast;	V. ii. 14. 2
she *saw* The daungerous state in which she stood,	V. ii. 22. 2
she *saw* him to proceede Unmov'd with praiers	V. ii. 23. 1
They *saw* before them . . . Full many people	V. ii. 29. 4
Which when he *saw* he greatly grew in rage,	V. ii. 47. 1
saw his sudden desolation,	V. ii. 51. 2
When Talus *saw* they all the field forsooke,	V. ii. 54. 7
saw that boasters pride and gracelesse guile,	V. iii. 20. 3
when Philtra *saw* my lands decay	V. iv. 9. 6
in the midst of them he *saw* a Knight,	V. iv. 22. 1
when she *saw* at last that he ne would . . . be wonne	V. iv. 30. 5
Soone as she *saw* him on the ground to grovell,	V. iv. 40. 1
Whom when he *saw* before his foote prostrated,	V. v. 11. 6
He *saw* . . . A miracle of natures goodly grace	V. v. 12. 2
he round about him *saw* Many brave knights,	V. v. 22. 1
when as yet she *saw* him not returne,	V. vi. 6. 1
She *saw* it vaine to make there lenger stay,	V. vi. 36. 1
she *saw* there . . . Those two false brethren	V. vi. 36. 5
Whose like before she never *saw* nor red;	V. vii. 5. 7
Which when she *saw* her helmet she unlaste,	V. vii. 8. 8
All sodainely she *saw* transfigured Her linnen stole	V. vii. 13. 4
when all her warlike traine There present *saw*,	V. vii. 34. 8
when she *saw* the heapes which he did make	V. vii. 36. 4
when she *saw* that lothly uncouth sight	V. vii. 37. 6
Soone after these he *saw* another Knight,	V. viii. 5. 1
he *saw* the hindmost overtake One of those two,	V. viii. 5. 6
when they *saw* their foes dead out of doubt,	V. viii. 12. 3
Soone as the infants sunlike shield they *saw*,	V. viii. 41. 2
when she *saw* that Damzell there.	V. viii. 47. 9
Him when the damzell *saw* fast by her side,	V. ix. 12. 1
when the villaine *saw* her so affrayd,	V. ix. 12. 4
Which when he *saw*, his yron man he sent	V. ix. 16. 1
never *saw* they there the like array;	V. ix. 24. 5
they *saw* Some one whose tongue was . . . Nayld	V. ix. 25. 1
she *saw* Those two strange knights such homage to her make,	V. ix. 35. 5
Though plaine she *saw*, by all that she did heare,	V. ix. 50. 3
When one in armes she *saw*,	V. x. 19. 6
Whom when his other fellowes *saw*,	V. x. 36. 1
ever, as he *saw* the stroke to land,	V. xi. 7. 4
Which when the Lady from the Castle *saw*,	V. xi. 15. 1
when they *saw* it falne, they eke him greeted all.	V. xi. 15. 9
Whose ugly shape none ever *saw*, nor kend,	V. xi. 20. 5
There he that Idoll *saw* of massy gold	V. xi. 21. 8
when she *saw* that she was forst to fight,	V. xi. 27. 1
Whom when he *saw* on ground, he was full glad,	V. xi. 32. 6
Whom when she *saw* so joyously come forth,	V. xi. 33. 1
When first to Faery court he *saw* her wend,	V. xi. 37. 8
They *saw* a Knight in daungerous distresse	V. xi. 44. 2
in that uprore Ye with those caytives *saw*,	V. xi. 49. 6
When Artegall she *saw* in that array,	V. xii. 13. 8
whiles he him *saw* so ill bested,	V. xii. 23. 5
Whom when he *saw* prostrated on the plaine,	V. xii. 23. 8
Which when the people round about him *saw*,	V. xii. 24. 1
in that painefull stound When he him *saw*,	VI. i. 11. 8
They *saw* that Carle from farre,	VI. i. 17. 5
when Briana *saw* that drery stound,	VI. i. 34. 5
when he *saw* his foe before in vew,	VI. i. 35. 6
And them beside a Ladie faire he *saw*	VI. ii. 4. 1
Which when he *saw*, his hart was inly child	VI. ii. 4. 8
and *saw* to bee A goodly youth	VI. ii. 5. 1
Which when I *saw*, . . . Much was I moved	VI. ii. 11. 1
his Ladie, which this outrage *saw*,	VI. ii. 20. 1
I never *saw* in any greater hope appeare.'	VI. ii. 26. 9
These eyes him *saw* upon the cold earth sprad,	VI. ii. 45. 7
when he *saw* his sonne so ill bedight	VI. iii. 4. 1
when he *saw* his faire Priscilla by,	VI. iii. 11. 4
Since first he *saw* her,	VI. iii. 18. 5
when he the Lady *saw* There left on ground,	VI. iii. 26. 1
For pitty of his Dame whom she *saw* so diseased.	VI. iii. 32. 9
And *saw* his carriage past that perill well,	VI. iii. 34. 6
no remedy He *saw* the present mischiefe to redresse,	VI. iii. 44. 2
He *saw* his life powrd forth despiteouly;	VI. iii. 51. 4
ever as he *saw* him nigh succeed,	VI. iv. 8. 7
when the Salvage *saw* his labour vaine	VI. iv. 9. 1
she *saw* no meanes to be defended,	VI. iv. 10. 5
Whom though he *saw* now somewhat overpast,	VI. iv. 18. 8
Whom when as Calepine *saw* so dismayd,	VI. iv. 27. 5
Ne ever *saw* faire guize,	VI. v. 2. 4
Whom when the Salvage *saw* so sore distrest,	V. v. 6. 1
no hope of his retourne She *saw*	VI. v. 7. 2
Whom when her Host *saw* readie to depart,	VI. v. 8. 1
Whom when the Hermite present *saw* in place,	VI. v. 36. 2
when on ground they *saw* their fellow slaine,	VI. vi. 23. 1
with the dead He *saw* the ground all strow'd,	VI. vi. 24. 6
when his foe he still so eager *saw*,	VI. vi. 29. 1
Which when the Ladie *saw*,	VI. vi. 31. 1
Whom when the Prince so deadly *saw* dismayd,	VI. vi. 33. 1
Whom when the Prince so felly *saw* to rage,	VI. vi. 39. 1
Whom when the Salvage *saw* from daunger free,	VI. vi. 40. 1
when he *saw* his fellow lifelesse ly,	VI. vii. 10. 3
he *saw* the way all dyde With streames of bloud;	VI. vii. 17. 5
Whom when as Turpin *saw* so loosely layd,	VI. vii. 20. 1
when he *saw* those two so neare him stand,	VI. vii. 24. 1
which when at last she *saw*,	VI. vii. 36. 6
saw those villaines her so vildely use,	VI. vii. 45. 2
when he up did looke And *saw* him selfe captiv'd,	VI. vii. 48. 8
when she *saw* him fall Under that villaines club,	VI. vii. 50. 1
when as he *saw* his Lord The witnesse of his wretchednesse	VI. viii. 5. 1
The greatest shame that ever eye yet *saw*,	VI. viii. 6. 2
When all his strokes he *saw* avoyded quite,	VI. viii. 14. 7

Saw—*Continued.*	
Which when the Lady *saw*, she cryde amaine;	VI. viii. 17. 4
Eftsoones he *saw* one with a naked knife	VI. viii. 48. 8
If such a beast they *saw*,	VI. ix. 5. 9
They answer'd him that no such beast they *saw*,	VI. ix. 6. 1
he there besyde *Saw* a faire damzell,	VI. ix. 7. 7
why, when I them *saw*, fled they away	VI. x. 19. 9
when he *saw* the feend,	VI. x. 35. 2
When he the beast *saw* ready now to rend	VI. x. 35. 7
when him she so importune *saw*,	VI. xi. 6. 1
when she *saw* . . . That further then she willing was he prest,	VI. xi. 7. 5
when they *saw* her now reliv'd againe,	VI. xi. 24. 1
saw his shepheards cottage spoyled quight,	VI. xi. 25. 2
Before I *saw* faire Pastorella dye.'	VI. xi. 29. 4
These eyes *saw* die, and dearely did lament;	VI. xi. 31. 7
when he *saw* the theeves which did them keepe,	VI. xi. 37. 8
albe he *saw* them all asleepe.	VI. xi. 37. 9
In which that rose she plainely *saw* displayd:	VI. xii. 19. 5
When she so faire a daughter *saw* survive,	VI. xii. 21. 7
when the Beast *saw* he mote nought availe	VI. xii. 33. 1
though full many a day He *saw* her clad,	VII. vi. 42. 8
close might view That never any *saw*,	VII. vi. 45. 3
There Faunus *saw* that pleased much his eye,	VII. vi. 46. 1
their glorious Lord in strange disguise Transfigur'd *sawe*;	VII. vii. 7. 9
seeke each where, where last I *sawe* her face,	*Am.* lxxviii. 3
he *saw* me stung and cry,	*Epig.* i. 5
I *saw*, . . . How little Cupid humbly came,	*Epig.* iii. 1
when he *saw* me laugh, for shame His face . . . did flame,	*Epig.* iii. 4
wakened with the noyse, And *saw* the beast so small;	*Epig.* iv. 6
if ye *saw* that which no eyes can see,	*Epith.* 185
I *saw* two Swannes	*Proth.* 37
Whom when they *sawe*,	*Proth.* 58
they never *saw* a sight so fayre,	*Proth.* 60
Sawest. *sawst* the secrets of the world unmade,	I. v. 22. 6
Tell what thou *saw'st*, maulgre who so it heares.'	IV. i. 48. 6
all those Ladies, which thou *sawest* late,	VI. x. 21. 3
Saws. if old *sawes* prove true	IV. xi. 35. 2
Saxon. sith the *Saxon* king Never was Woolfe seene,	*S.C.* S. 151
thou springst from ancient race Of *Saxon* kinges,	I. x. 65. 2
Against his *Saxon* foes in bloody field to fight.	III. iii. 29. 9
Saxon kinges his friendship shall intreat;	III. iii. 45. 3
I saw a *Saxon* Virgin,	III. iii. 55. 5
had gotten a great pray Of *Saxon* goods;	III. iii. 58. 6
Which long'd to Angela, the *Saxon* Queene,	III. iii. 58. 8
Saxons. by force I conquered were Of hardie *Saxons*,	*Ti.* 114
arrived here three hoyes Of *Saxons*,	II. x. 64. 9
Shall stoutly him defeat, and thousand *Saxons* kill.	III. iii. 35. 9
T' afflict the other *Saxons* unsubdewd;	III. iii. 38. 2
to the *Saxons* over-give their government.	III. iii. 41. 9
'Ne shall the *Saxons* selves all peaceably Enjoy the crowne,	III. iii. 46. 1
dreaded more then all The other *Saxons*,	III. iii. 56. 6
The Easterne *Saxons* from the Southerne ny,	IV. xi. 33. 4
Saxons'. Shall well defend, and *Saxons* powre suppresse;	III. iii. 33. 2
Say. *See* **Gainsay, Soothsay.**	
O great griefe, I *say*, Thus in one moment	*Pet.*[1] ii. 10
Say boldly that these same SIX VISIONS	*Pet.*[1] vii. 2
What *say* I more?	*Pet.* v. 7
I *say* not, as the common voyce doth *say*,	*Ro.* ix. 9
I *say* rather, though not all agreeing With some	*Ro.* ix. 12
For once I heard my father *say*,	*S.C.* Mar. 106
A shepheards swaine, *saye*, did thee sing	*To his Booke* 9
Say, thou wert base-begot with blame;	*To his Booke* 14
(as Algrind used to *say*)	*S.C.* May 75
Nay, *say* I thereto,	*S.C.* May 150
sooth to *sayne*, nought seemeth sike strife,	*S.C.* May 158
For our Sir John, to *say* to morrowe	*S.C.* May 309
well he meanes, but little can *say*.	*S.C.* May 311
the little what, That Thomalin can *sayne*.	*S.C.* Jul. 32
Sayne most-what, that they dwell	*S.C.* Jul. 46
as holy fathers *sayne*,	*S.C.* Jul. 57
(as I have heard Old Algrind often *sayne*)	*S.C.* Jul. 126
I *saye* as some have seene.	*S.C.* Jul. 180
say me, what is Algrind,	*S.C.* Jul. 213
in a Kirtle of greene *saye*,	*S.C.* Au. 67
Now *say* it, Cuddie, as thou art a ladde:	*S.C.* Au. 143
Now *say* on, Diggon, what ever thou hast.	*S.C.* S. 55
They *saye* they con to heaven the high-way,	*S.C.* S. 90
They *sayne* the world is much war then it wont,	*S.C.* S. 108
Other *sayne*, but how truely I note,	*S.C.* S. 110
Some sticke not to *say*,	*S.C.* S. 112
Sayne, other the fat from their beards doen lick:	*S.C.* S. 123
(the soth to *sayne*)	*S.C.* S. 154
Say it out, Diggon, whatever it hight,	*S.C.* S. 172
Then up, I *say*, thou jolly shepeheard swayne,	*S.C.* N. 47
(that was, a woful word to *sayne!*)	*S.C.* N. 93
Ile write in termes as she the same did *say*,	*Hub.* 41
No lesse, I dare *saie*, than the prowdest wight;	*Hub.* 62
Say, my faire brother now, if this device	*Hub.* 93
All his care was, his service well to *saine*,	*Hub.* 392
Their service and their holie things to *say*,	*Hub.* 450
say their musicke matcheth Phoebus quill.	*T.M.* 330
say: Waking Love suffereth no sleepe:	*U.V.* 10
Say, that raging Love dothe appall the weake stomacke:	*U.V.* 11
Say, that lamenting Love marreth the Musicall.	*U.V.* 12
who will *saye: this was Immerito?*	*U.V.* 21
may warned be to *say*.	*Ti.* 7
to laie The sacred sod, or Requiem to *saie*.	*Ti.* 196
For her departure, had no word to *say;*	*Ti.* 474
say . . . That thou for secret crime thy blood	*D.* 83
ne more endured to *say*, But fell to ground	*D.* 184

Say—*Continued.*	
not mine; amisse I mine did *say:*	*D.* 234
spight . . . Found ought in him, that she could *say* was ill.	*As.* 24
say on further (then said Corylas)	*Col.* 328
say, who else vouchsafed thee of grace?'	*Col.* 484
sooth to *say*, it is no sort of life,	*Col.* 688
he was such an one as thou doest *say*,	*Col.* 829
sooth to *say*, it is foolhardie thing,	*Col.* 915
Untroubled night, they *say*, gives counsell best.'	I. i. 33. 3
wont to *say* His holy thinges each morne	I. i. 34. 6
so dainty, they *say*, maketh derth.	I. ii. 27. 9
'*Say* on, Fradubio, . . . Quoth then the Knight;	I. ii. 34. 1
nought could she *say;*	I. iii. 12. 4
thrise nine hundred *Aves* she was wont to *say*.	I. iii. 13. 9
sooth to *say*, why I lefte you so long,	I. iii. 29. 1
the which, they *say*, The gods stand gazing on,	I. iv. 17. 5
All in a kirtle of discolourd *say* He clothed was,	I. iv. 31. 1
bad *say* on the secrete of her hart:	I. iv. 46. 2
Goe *say*, his foe thy shield with his doth beare.'	I. v. 13. 4
then to him these womanish words gan *say:*	I. vi. 28. 5
Wherewith enmovd, these bleeding words she gan to *say*.	I. vii. 38. 9
gentle Una thus to him gan *say:*	I. ix. 16. 5
so well, they *say*, It governd was,	I. x. 3. 3
to her gossibs gan in counsell *say;*	I. xii. 11. 4
Thus gan to *say*—	I. xii. 24. 6
may I boldly *say*,	II. i. 19. 4
he nought could *say*, Till him the childe bespoke;	II. viii. 7. 2
say, that I not overcome doe dye,	II. viii. 52. 3
some men *say* Were unto him reveald	II. x. 39. 1
brought with him the holy grayle, they *say*,	II. x. 53. 8
Ne what to *say*, ne what to doe at all:	II. xi. 39. 4
the Gulfe of Greedinesse, they *say*,	II. xii. 3. 4
The constant payre heard all that he did *say*,	II. xii. 76. 4
whylome wont (they *say*) To make his wonne,	III. iii. 7. 5
It is an hideous hollow cave (they *say*)	III. iii. 8. 3
The cause, some *say*, is this:	III. iii. 10. 1
men *say* that he was not the sonne	III. iii. 13. 1
Did him, they *say*, forwarne	III. v. 9. 7
since he (they *say*) was slaine,	III. v. 10. 1
(a wondrous thing to *say*)	III. vi. 26. 8
There yet, some *say*, in secret he does ly,	III. vi. 46. 4
sooth, it seemes, they *say;*	III. vi. 47. 1
which is, they *say*, Hewen underneath that Mount,	III. vi. 48. 8
These twinnes, men *say*, (a thing far passing thought)	III. vii. 48. 5
would surely *say* It was her selfe	III. viii. 9. 3
Ne cares what men *say* of him,	III. ix. 3. 7
Thereat Sir Satyrane gan smyle, and *say;*	III. ix. 6. 6
sith that men *sayne* He was not in . . . fyre Consum'd,	III. ix. 40. 7
adventures found, that now were long to *sayne*.	III. ix. 48. 9
so heard I *say* Old Mnemon.	III. ix. 51. 5
False love! why do men *say* thou canst not see,	III. x. 4. 3
durst he not against it doe or *say*,	III. x. 45. 3
From Limbo lake him late escaped sure would *say*.	III. x. 54. 9
Three nights in one, they *say*,	III. xi. 33. 8
As if in minde he somewhat had to *say;*	III. xii. 4. 2
His garment nether was of silke nor *say*,	III. xii. 8. 1
for the words which she heard *say*,	IV. i. 50. 4
so faire indeede, as he did *say*,	IV. ii. 7. 7
This pretious ornament, they *say*, did make,	IV. v. 4. 3
Was fostered by those Graces, (as they *say*)	IV. v. 5. 8
he nought car'd for all that they could *say*,	IV. v. 27. 6
For ought that Glauce could or doe or *say*.	IV. v. 31. 6
But th' other thus can *say:*	IV. vi. 3. 6
And eft againe deviz'd some what to *say*,	IV. vi. 45. 7
When so he heard her *say*,	IV. viii. 16. 1
For ought that ever she could doe or *say;*	IV. x. 15. 2
they *say*, she hath both kinds in one,	IV. x. 41. 6
'So did he *say:*	IV. x. 48. 1
nought That ever she to me could *say* or doe,	IV. x. 57. 4
the mother of the Gods, they *say*,	IV. xi. 28. 1
this of Artegall, which here we have to *say*.	V. iv. 2. 9
whether it be so or no, I can not *say*.	V. iv. 13. 9
This doe I *say*,	V. iv. 14. 2
little had for his excuse to *say*,	V. iv. 27. 4
'The cause, they *say*, of this her cruell hate	V. iv. 30. 1
What ever he shall like to doe or *say*.	V. iv. 49. 5
Say on, my soverayne Ladie, and be bold:	V. v. 31. 5
'*Say* and do all that may thereto prevaile;	V. v. 49. 1
the man, that *say* or doe so dare,	V. vi. 1. 6
Sadly she rode, and never word did *say*	V. vi. 18. 3
for wine, they *say*, is blood,	V. vii. 10. 3
'*Say* on' (quoth he) 'the secret of your hart	V. vii. 19. 6
heare what she to them will *say*.	V. viii. 10. 9
Whom when they heard so *say*,	V. viii. 12. 1
'To all which cruell tyranny, they *say*,	V. viii. 20. 1
they *say* Unto his horses gave his guests for meat,	V. viii. 31. 1
Nought feared they what he could do or *say*.	V. viii. 38. 7
There they doe *say* that she transformed was	V. viii. 49. 6
some doe *say* it goeth downe to hell:	V. ix. 6. 5
those, they *say*, Upon Joves judgement-seat wayt	V. ix. 31. 6
they *say* that he was borne and bred	V. x. 9. 1
they were all, they *say*, of purple hew,	V. x. 10. 1
devoures, they *say*, both flesh and bone.	V. x. 29. 7
of a man, they *say*, It has the voice,	V. xi. 20. 6
every . . . word, that he did *say*, Was like enchantment,	VI. ii. 3. 2
It gladly did accept, as he did *say*;	VI. ii. 38. 7
Fearlesse who ought did thinke or ought did *say*,	VI. iii. 16. 5
fro me *say*, That here is . . . an errant Knight,	VI. iii. 41. 1
eke could doe as well as *say* the same;	VI. vi. 6. 4
Till Mirabellaes fortunes I doe further *say*.	VI. vii. 50. 9

Say—*Continued.*
approching thus he gan to *say:* . . . VI. viii. 7. 3
Then thus the Prince gan *say:* . . . VI. viii. 29. 5
for nought that he could *say* or doe, . . . VI. viii. 50. 8
well could doe and *say,* . . . VI. ix. 18. 4
They *say* that Venus . . . used to resort . . . VI. x. 9. 1
all that ever he could doe or *say* . . . VI. xi. 5. 1
Mongst which he found a sword of better *say,* . . . VI. xi. 47. 5
I will rehearse that whylome I heard *say,* . . . VII. vi. 1. 7
That, some do *say,* was so by skill devized, . . . VII. vii. 6. 1
They *say,* did sing the spousall hymne . . . VII. vii. 12. 7
wherewith Dan Jove . . . They *say,* was nourisht . . . VII. vii. 41. 7
say Whether . . . CHANGE doth not raign . . . VII. vii. 47. 2
say, they by your secret powre are made: . . . VII. vii. 49. 4
'as changefull as the Moone' men use to *say.* . . . VII. vii. 50. 9
Some *say* in Crete . . . VII. vii. 53. 5
even itselfe is mov'd, as wizards *saine:* . . . VII. vii. 55. 7
very sooth to *say,* . . . VII. viii. 1. 4
let none ever *say,* That ye were blooded . . . *Am.* xx. 13
When I doe praise her, *say* I doe but flatter: . . . *Am.* lxxxiv. 2
Now none doth hinder you, that *say* or sing; . . . *Epith.* 370
Leda was (they *say*) as white as he, . . . *Proth.* 44
were they bred of Somers-heat, they *say,* . . . *Proth.* 67
Whose smile, they *say,* hath vertue to remove . . . *Proth.* 98
Sayer. *See* **Soothsayer.**
Sayest. How *saist* thou (friend) have I not well discourst . . . *Hub.* 541
Saying. of felowship, tell us that *saying:* . . . *S.C.* May 172
Such myster *saying* me seemeth to mirke. . . . *S.C.* S. 103
These lookes (nought *saying*) doo a benefice seeke, . . . *Hub.* 500
Saying; 'By wondring at thy Cynthiaes praise, . . . *Col.* 353
Saying: 'Why Colin, . . . *Col.* 652
Saying, that harlott she too lately knew, . . . I. iii. 25. 3
Saying; 'Yet, O thou dreaded Dame! I crave Abyde, . . . I. v. 21. 8
saying, 'In that fayre face . . . Did *closely* lurke; . . . I. v. 27. 2
Saying, he now had boulted all the floure, . . . II. iv. 24. 2
So *saying,* every Nimph full narrowly shee eide. . . . III. vi. 23. 9
Saying, 'Thou foolish knight, . . . III. viii. 17. 1
Saying, but if she Mercie would him give, . . . III. x. 7. 8
Saying; 'Ah noble knight! . . . III. xii. 39. 2
Saying, it was to Knight unseemely shame . . . IV. x. 54. 3
Saying, 'Sir knight, it would dishonour bee . . . V. iii. 36. 6
Saying, 'Sir Knight, of pardon I you pray, . . . V. viii. 13. 1
her recomforted the best he might, *Saying;* . . . V. xi. 17. 3
Saying that he had . . . his honour blent, . . . V. xii. 40. 3
Saying and doing all that mote behove; . . . VI. xi. 5. 7
Sayne. *See* **Say.**
Says. *See* **Soothsays.**
(that same he weeping *sayes*) . . . *Hub.* 254
when I weep, she *sayes,* Teares are but water, . . . *Am.* xviii. 10
when I sigh, she *sayes,* I know the art; . . . *Am.* xviii. 11
Scabby. Her wrizled skin, . . . So *scabby* was . . . I. viii. 47. 9
Scald. head . . . Was overgrowne with scurfe and filthy *scald;* I. viii. 47. 3
Scalding. to slake his *scalding* smart; . . . III. xi. 30. 4
Scaldis. Let *Scaldis* tell, and let tell Hania, . . . II. x. 24. 1
Scale. Heapt hils on hils to *scale* the starrie skie, . . . *Ro.* xii. 2
That hill they *scale* with all their powre and might, . . . I. x. 47. 7
To *scale* the skyes and put Jove from his right: . . . III. vii. 47. 5
then the false he layd In th' other *scale;* . . . V. ii. 45. 7
So first the right he put into one *scale,* . . . V. ii. 46. 3
To fill the other *scale* with so much wrong; . . . V. ii. 46. 5
Scaled. 'How often have I *scaled* the craggie Oke, . . . *S.C.* D. 31
Scales. over all with brasen *scales* was armd, . . . I. xi. 9. 1
Such noyse his rouzed *scales* did send unto the knight. . . . I. xi. 9. 9
shoke his *scales* to battaile ready drest, . . . I. xi. 15. 7
Bright Scolopendraes arm'd with silver *scales;* . . . II. xii. 23. 8
Her garments gay with *scales* of fish . . . III. viii. 26. 9
Scalp. sitting so with bared *scalpe,* . . . *S.C.* Jul. 221
His monstrous *scalpe* downe to his teeth it tore, . . . I. viii. 16. 4
Upon his crested *scalp* so sore did smite, . . . I. xi. 35. 7
Whose *scalp* is bare, that bondage doth bewray, . . . V. ii. 6. 7
Scaly. *See* **Brass-scaly.**
the seeling . . . Did shine all *scaly* . . . *Bel.* ii. 10
armed be with clawes, or *scalie* creasts, . . . *Ro.* xxiv. 4
wrapt his *scalie* boughts with fell despight, . . . *Gn.* 255
On everie side did shine like *scalie* golde; . . . *Gn.* 261
The *scalie* backe of that most hideous snake . . . *Gn.* 305
An yron brest, and back of *scaly* bras, . . . I. vii. 17. 8
scaly tayle was stretcht adowne his back full low. . . . I. vii. 31. 9
glauncing from his *scaly* necke . . . I. xi. 20. 6
with a teeme of *scaly* Phocas bownd . . . III. viii. 30. 8
The silver *scaly* trouts doe tend full well, . . . *Epith.* 57
Scamander. the fieldes of faire *Scamander* strowne With carcases III. ix. 35. 6
Divine *Scamander,* purpled yet with blood . . . IV. xi. 20. 6
Scan. Colin fittes such famous flight to *scanne;* . . . *S.C.* O. 88
It was no time to *scan* the prophecie, . . . IV. xii. 28. 3
Scanderbeg. Thy acts, O *Scanderbeg,* this volume tels. . . . *Com.Son.*iii.14
Scanned. For rare it seemes in reason to be *skand,* . . . *D.* 178
Where they mote heare the matter throughly *scand* . . . V. ix. 37. 7
deedes ought not be *scand* By th' authors manhood, . . . V. xi. 17. 3
till she the highest stage had *scand,* . . . VII. vi. 8. 8
equall gave to each as Justice duly *scann'd.* . . . VII. vii. 38. 9
Scanted. Use *scanted* diet, and forbeare your fill; . . . VI. vi. 14. 7
Scape. never might his luckie *scape* forget. . . . *Gn.* 664
how to *scape* great punishment, or shame, . . . *Hub.* 314
he them all might kill, That none might *scape,* . . . *As.* 110
Ne let that wicked woman *scape* away; . . . I. viii. 28. 5
often semblaunce made to *scape* out of their hand. . . . I. xii. 35. 9
saw no meanes to *scape,* . . . II. ii. 8. 2
may not hope by flight to *scape* alive, . . . II. viii. 50. 3
when he with Asterie did *scape;* . . . III. xi. 34. 3

Scape—*Continued.*
who can *scape* what his owne fate hath wrought? . . . V. iv. 27. 8
they were fayne to let him *scape* away, . . . V. v. 19. 3
The rest, that *scape* his sword and death eschew, . . . VI. viii. 49. 8
Scaped. But few returned, having *scaped* hard, . . . I. iv. 3. 3
That cursed wight, from whom I *scapt* whyleare, . . . I. ix. 28. 4
none ever saw, nor kend, That ever *scap'd:* . . . V. xi. 20. 6
I onely *scapt* through great confusione . . . VI. xi. 32. 3
Yet as it was, I hardly *scap't* with paine. . . . *Am.* xvi. 14
Scarab. Bird . . . One day did scorne the simple *Scarabee,* . . . *Van.* iv. 2
Scarce. Is graunted *scarce* to Gods above. . . . *S.C.*Mar.Emb.2
Scarce this right hand the mouth . . . feedeth, . . . *Hub.* 274
Scarse can a Bishoprick forpas them by, . . . *Hub.* 519
scarce vouchsafte them to requite. . . . *Hub.* 587
scarse thy legs uphold thy feeble gate.' . . . *Hub.* 600
Scarse could the Ape yet speake, . . . *Hub.* 964
Scarse anie left to close his eylids . . . *Ti.* 194
Scarse anie left upon his lips to laie . . . *Ti.* 195
where it was *scarce* seemed anie sight? . . . *Ti.* 530
scarce the skin the strong contagion helde. . . . *Mui.* 256
So finely sponne that *scarce* they could be spide. . . . *Mui.* 360
scarse them bad arise. . . . I. iv. 14. 4
Scarse could he once uphold his heavie hedd, . . . I. iv. 19. 5
His dronken corse he *scarse* upholden can: . . . I. iv. 22. 8
Ne *scarse* good morsell all his life did taste, . . . I. iv. 28. 3
I *scarse* . . . Could it discerne, . . . I. v. 27. 5
Scarse could he footing find . . . I. v. 53. 1
Whose feeble thighes . . . him *scarse* to light could beare; . . . I. vii. 40. 8
vew of eye could *scarse* him overtake, . . . II. xi. 26. 2
Ne *scarse* his feet on ground were seene to tred: . . . II. xi. 26. 3
Scarse had he saide, when hard at hand they spy . . . II. xii. 18. 5
scarse them leasure gave her passing to behold. . . . III. i. 15. 9
Scarse do they spare to one . . . Rowme in their writtes; . . . III. ii. 1. 7
Could *scarce* recovered bee out of her paine: . . . III. iv. 35. 2
the hard rocks could *scarse* from tears refraine; . . . III. iv. 35. 7
It lettes not *scarse* this Prince to breath at all, . . . III. v. 2. 8
fayntly fluttering, *scarce* his helmet raught, . . . III. v. 24. 8
one him *scarce* could see. . . . IV. i. 35. 9
He falleth nigh to ground, and *scarse* recovereth flight. . . . IV. iii. 19. 9
Close underneath his shield, that *scarce* did show, . . . IV. iii. 33. 7
scarse he him upheld from falling in a swound. . . . IV. iv. 24. 9
from revenge their willes they *scarce* asswag'd: . . . IV. v. 27. 3
scarse the Squire his hand could once upreare, . . . IV. vii. 28. 6
any bud thereof doth *scarse* remaine, . . . IV. viii. 33. 2
almost blind through eld, that *scarce* her way could see. . . . IV. xi. 24. 9
his *scarse* diet somewhat was amended, . . . V. v. 57. 2
Scarse so conceived in her jealous thought, . . . V. vi. 3. 2
she her shield . . . Could *scarse* uphold: . . . V. vii. 33. 5
scarse an hound by smell Can follow out . . . V. ix. 6. 7
whether man or monster one could *scarse* discerne. . . . V. xii. 15. 9
that *scarse* did see Yet seventeene yeares, . . . VI. ii. 5. 3
Ne *scarse* wyld beasts durst come, . . . VI. iv. 13. 9
Scarse yeelding her due food or timely rest, . . . VI. xi. 24. 5
scarse his loosed limbes he hable was to weld. . . . VII. vii. 31. 9
which is gold, or heare, may *scarse* be told? . . . *Am.* xxxvii. 4
whole remaines *scarse* any little part? . . . *H.L.* 144
Scarcely. They both, deformed, *scarsely* could bee known. . . . I. vi. 45. 6
scarsely could he weeld his bootlesse single blade. . . . I. vii. 11. 9
Scarsely had Phoebus . . . harnessed his fyrie-footed teeme, . . . I. xii. 2. 1
A faire Pavilion, *scarcely* to bee seene, . . . III. v. 40. 7
never looked who behind him was, Ne *scarsely* who before: . . . III. x. 53. 4
When her weake feete could *scarcely* her sustaine, . . . III. xii. 21. 6
what of them became themselves did *scarsly* weete. . . . IV. i. 41. 9
But Scudamour, . . . *scarcely* did refraine . . . IV. i. 52. 2
Yet *scarcely* once to breath would they relent, . . . IV. ii. 18. 7
scarcely she could ryde, . . . IV. viii. 37. 4
he which way to turne him *scarcely* wist: . . . VI. viii. 13. 5
scarcely yet from former feare exempted, . . . VI. x. 36. 8
scarsely suffring her infestred wound . . . to be drest. . . . VI. xi. 24. 6
Arlo *scarsly* could them all containe, . . . VII. vii. 4. 4
Scarecrow. the *Scarcrow* wexed wondrous prowd, . . . II. iii. 7. 1
Scared. *scared* nations doest with horror sterne astownd. . . . I. xi. 6. 9
were from approaching *scard;* . . . IV. x. 17. 7
those two losels *scared;* . . . V. vi. 38. 5
Scarf. She with her *scarf* did bind the wound . . . III. v. 33. 9
finding in the way the scattred *scarfe,* . . . V. ii. 3. 3
Scarlet. She seemde with glorie of the *scarlet* faire, . . . *Rev.* ii. 6
scarlot berries in Sommer time? . . . *S.C.* F. 168
Yclad in *Scarlot,* like a mayden Queene, . . . *S.C.* Ap. 57
The Rose engrained in pure *scarlet* die; . . . *Gn.* 666
he gave in charge unto his Squyre, That *scarlot* whore . . . I. viii. 29. 2
spoile her of her *scarlot* robe, and let her fly.' . . . I. viii. 45. 9
Bespredd with costly *scarlott* of great name, . . . I. xii. 13. 8
Her with a *scarlott* mantle covered . . . III. i. 59. 8
Scarlet-red. A goodly Lady clad in *scarlot red,* . . . I. ii. 13. 2
transfigured Her linnen stole to robe of *scarlet red,* . . . V. vii. 13. 5
Scarmoges. *See* **Skirmishes.**
Scars. many *scarres* and many hoary heares, . . . V. vii. 39. 8
Scater. *See* **Scatter.**
Scathe. all my hoped gaine is turnd to *scathe:* . . . *S.C.* D. 100
many mischiefes follow cruell Wrath: . . . unthrifty *scath,* . . . I. iv. 35. 3
To worke new woe and improvided *scath,* . . . I. xii. 34. 3
Whose freedom shall thee turne to greatest *scath!* . . . II. v. 18. 4
Mote breede him *scath* unwares; . . . III. i. 37. 8
Tryde often to the *scath* of many Deare, . . . III. iv. 24. 2
without regard of gaine or *scath,* . . . III. x. 11. 3
Tygres *scath* In crueltie and outrage she did pas, . . . V. viii. 49. 7
in Princes courts to worke great *scath* and hindrance: . . . V. ix. 22. 9
Where he mote worke him *scath* and villeny. . . . VI. vii. 3. 5
Thenceforth more mischiefe and more *scath* he wrought . . . VI. xii. 39. 1

Scathe—*Continued.*
my proud one doth worke the greater *scath*, . . . *Am.* xxxi. 9
Scatter. Which th' husbandman behind him chanst to *scater*. . *Ro.* xxx. 14
Scattered. Of this faire fire the *scattered* rayes . . . *Bel.*[2] xi. 9
Some *scattred* on the Hercaean shores unknowne; . . . *Gn.* 588
but *scattred* all to nought; . . . *Col.* 153
Her *scattered* (**scattred*) brood, . . . Gathred themselves about her body . . . I. i. 25. 1
underneath their feet, all *scattered* lay Dead sculls . . . I. iv. 36. 8
his members chast *Scattered* on every mountaine . . . I. v. 38. 8
carcases were *scattred* on the greene, . . . I. ix. 34. 5
a narrow way, *Scattred* with bushy thornes . . . I. x. 35. 3
Poore Orphane! in the wild world *scattered,* . . . II. ii. 2. 5
low behinde her backe were *scattered:* . . . II. iii. 30. 5
all the ground with sculs was *scattered,* . . . II. vii. 30. 6
forst them fly, Like *scattered* Sheepe, . . . II. ix. 14. 7
Out of the Trojans *scattered* ofspring, . . . III. ix. 44. 7
His weapons which lay *scattered* all abrode, . . . IV. iv. 23. 2
By *scattered* shields, was easie to be showen. . . . IV. iv. 38. 5
With filthy lockes about her *scattered* wide, . . . IV. viii. 23. 7
all about her altar *scattered* lay . . . IV. x. 43. 1
finding in the way the *scattred* scarfe, . . . V. ii. 3. 3
here and there like *scattred* sheepe they lay: . . . V. vi. 30. 6
scattred all about, and strow'd upon the greene. . . . V. viii. 42. 9
Her brothers bones she *scattered* all about; . . . V. viii. 47. 4
shivered all about, and *scattered* in the wynd: . . . V. x. 32. 9
Like *scattred* chaffe the which the wind away doth fan. . . . V. xi. 47. 9
her keepers had forsaken . . . and *scattered* were abrode. . . V. xi. 60. 3
all their *scattred* crew Into the sea he drove . . . V. xi. 65. 3
they lay *scattred* over all the land, . . . V. xii. 7. 8
to reclayme with speed His *scattred* people, . . . V. xii. 9. 2
A ravenous Wolfe amongst the *scattered* flockes: . . . V. xii. 38. 6
Like *scattred* sheepe, to seeke for safetie, . . . VI. vi. 38. 6
scattered all about fell on the flowre: . . . VI. vii. 8. 4
Bynd up the locks the which hang *scatterd* light, . . . *Epith.* 62
Tempes shore, *Scattred* with Flowres, . . . *Proth.* 80
Scattereth. round about him *scattreth* wide. . . . VI. xi. 48. 9
Scattering. *scattering* Contagious poyson close through every vaine, . . . VI. vi. 8. 7
Scatterlings. neighbour Scots, and forrein *Scatterlings* . . . II. x. 63. 5
Scene. fill the *Scene* with plaint, . . . *T.M.* 153
the faire *Scene* with rudenes foule disguize. . . . *T.M.* 192
Scent. so pleasant *sent* (*scent*[1]) did yeld, . . . *Bel.* xi. 13
A fit false dreame, that can delude the sleepers *sent*. . . . I. i. 43. 9
vew Of hunter swifte and *sent* of howndes trew. . . . III. iv. 46. 5
through his perfect *sent* And passing speede, . . . III. vii. 23. 8
at *sent* of stranger guest: . . . IV. v. 41. 7
Tenne thousand mores of sundry *sent* and hew, . . . VII. vii. 10. 4
Sceptre. His Crowne and *Scepter* lying him beside, . . . *Hub.* 953
when his Crowne and *scepter* both he wanted, . . . *Hub.* 1339
Thy *scepter* rent, and power put to wrack; . . . *T.M.* 400
did usurpe . . . Upon the *scepter* which she now did hold: . . I. iv. 12. 6
with her soveraine power, and *scepter* shene, . . . II. ii. 40. 4
had seven hundred yeares this *scepter* borne . . . II. x. 36. 2
The first and eldest, which that *scepter* swayd, . . . II. x. 72. 4
mightily that *scepter* did sustayne, . . . II. x. 75. 3
letteth her that ought the *scepter* weeld, . . . II. xi. 2. 3
Holding a *Scepter* in her royall hand, . . . V. ix. 30. 2
the might Of him that did the kingly *Scepter* beare, . . . VI. ii. 29. 4
His *scepter* is the rod of Righteousnesse, . . . *H.H.B.* 155
in her hand a *scepter* she doth hold, . . . *H.H.B.* 192
Sceptre's. Day did beare upon his *scepters* hight The goodly Sun VII. vii. 44. 8
Sceptres. Their *scepters* stretcht from East to Westerne shore, I. i. 5. 5
'Ne thine be kingdomes, ne the *scepters* thine; . . . II. vii. 13. 1
There were rent robes and broken *scepters* plast; . . . IV. i. 21. 4
Scerne. *scerne* that it was not his sweetest sweet, . . . III. x. 22. 8
Scholars. (need makes good *schollers*) . . . III. iii. 53. 3
School. Find entertainment or in Court or *Schoole;* . . . *T.M.* 410
they that scorne the *schoole* of arts divine, . . . *T.M.* 520
No art of *schoole,* but Courtiers schoolery. . . . *Col.* 702
arts of *schoole* have there small countenance, . . . *Col.* 703
in her vertuous rules to *schoole* her knight, . . . I. x. 32. 6
To many a one which came unto her *schoole,* . . . V. xi. 25. 8
To love my selfe I learned had in *schoole*. . . . VI. viii. 21. 5
Schooled. So *schooled* the Gate her wanton sonne, . . . *S.C.* May 227
he was *school'd* by kinde in all the skill . . . *Hub.* 855
In sort as he him *schooled* privily: . . . I. i. 46. 5
Schoolery. No art of schoole, but Courtiers *schoolery*. . . . *Col.* 702
Schoolhouse. To have her knight into her *schoolehous* plaste, . I. x. 18. 4
Schoolmaster. Love wont to be *schoolmaster* of my skill, . . *T.M.* 385
Schoolmistress. The great *schoolmaistresse* of all courtesy: . III. vi. 1. 6
Schools. The *schooles* they fill with fond new fanglenesse, . . *T.M.* 327
School-trick. if one could, it were but a *schoole trick*. . . . *Hub.* 512
Science. by his mighty *science* he could take As many formes I. ii. 10. 2
by her hellish *science* raisd . . . A foggy mist . . . I. ii. 38. 4
Such wondrous *science* in mans witt to rain . . . I. v. 40. 1
a *science* Proper to gentle blood: . . . II. iv. 1. 7
All artes, all *science,* all Philosophy, . . . II. ix. 53. 8
with sweet *science* mollifide their stubborne harts. . . . II. x. 25. 9
hellish feend raysd up through divelish *science*. . . . II. xi. 39. 9
by his mightie *Science* he had seene The secrete vertue . . . III. i. 10. 4
By his deepe *science* and hell-dreaded might, . . . III. ii. 18. 7
Well seene in everie *science* that mote bee, . . . IV. ii. 35. 3
Sciences. Cynthia doth in *sciences* abound, . . . *Col.* 745
Scimitar. Uppon her thigh her *Cemitare* was tide . . . V. v. 3. 4
With her sharpe *Cemitare* at him she flew, . . . V. v. 9. 8
Scion. cropt the branches of the *sient* base, . . . V. i. 1. 8
Scipio. here the praise of either *Scipion* Abides . . . *Gn.* 613
Stout *Scipio,* and stubborne Hanniball; . . . I. v. 49. 7
Scoff. To face, to forge, to *scoffe,* to companie, . . . *Hub.* 506

Scoff—*Continued.*
So would he *scoffe* them out with mockerie, . . . *Hub.* 705
he would *scoffe* at learning, . . . *Hub.* 832
Who scornes thy ydle *scoffe,* and bids thee be defyde.' . . . VI. i. 27. 9
Scoffed. Whose *scoffed* words he taking halfe in scorne, . . . IV. ii. 6. 6
Scoffing. In stead thereof *scoffing* Scurrilitie, . . . *T.M.* 211
Scoffing at him that did her justly wite, . . . II. xii. 16. 8
to her *scoffing* sayd: . . . III. vi. 21. 2
scoffing thus unto his mother sayd: . . . III. xi. 35. 7
Scoffing-game. turned all her pleasaunce to a *scoffing game*. . II. vi. 6. 9
Scold. to *scold* And snebbe the good Oake, . . . *S.C.* F. 125
Shame lowrd, Repentaunce sighd, Reproch did *scould;* . . . III. xii. 24. 6
arm'd her tongue, and thought at him to *scold;* . . . IV. vi. 27. 7
the Hag did *scold* And rayle at them . . . IV. viii. 28. 3
gan first to *scold* And chyde at him . . . IV. xii. 26. 3
So much the more at him still did she *scold,* . . . V. xii. 43. 6
Scolopendras. Bright *Scolopendraes* arm'd with silver scales; II. xii. 23. 8
Scope. doe misse the marked *scope;* . . . *S.C.* N. 155
To ayme their counsels to the fairest *scope,* . . . *Hub.* 960
cursed night that reft from him so goodly *scope*. . . . III. iv. 52. 9
So huge a *scope* at first him seemed best, . . . III. ix. 46. 5
graunt more *scope* to me to walke at large. . . . IV. viii. 61. 4
Which speaches she applying to the *scope* Of her intent, . . V. v. 39. 8
And Eagles wings, for *scope* and speedinesse, . . . V. xi. 24. 7
ere they come unto their aymed *scope,* . . . VI. iii. 5. 3
come . . . unto the wished *scope* Of my desire, . . . *H.L.* 296
Scorch. Be it where the yerely starre doth *scortch* the ground, *Ro.* xxvi. 7
Joves dreaded thunder light Does *scorch* not halfe so sore, . . II. vi. 50. 8
saw the wicked fire . . . *scorch* his Idoles face, . . . III. x. 14. 6
erst all entrers wont so cruelly to *scorch*. . . . III. xii. 42. 9
Scorched. nets, which oft we woven see Of *scorched* deaw, . . II. xii. 77. 9
retire, all *scorcht* and pittifully brent. . . . III. xi. 26. 9
left their *scorched* path yet in the firmament. . . . V. viii. 40. 9
Scorching. *scortching* Sunne had brent His wings . . . *Ro.* xvii. 5
Agaynst his cruell *scortching* heate, . . . *S.C.* Jul. 25
Were not better to shunne the *scortching* heate? . . . *S.C.* Au. 48
In some coole shadow from the *scorching* heat, . . . *Gn.* 143
in his flesh endur'd the *scorching* flame, . . . *Gn.* 607
Hurled his beame so *scorching* cruell hot, . . . I. ii. 29. 5
scorching Sunne does dry my secret vaines; . . . I. ii. 33. 8
scorching flames of fierce Orions hound; . . . I. iii. 31. 6
face all tand with *scorching* sunny ray, . . . I. vi. 35. 4
This nymph, quite tyr'd with heat of *scorching* ayre, . . . I. vii. 5. 3
The *scorching* flame sore swinged all his face, . . . I. xi. 26. 6
To save his body from the *scorching* fire, . . . I. xi. 45. 4
Did heale his woundes, and *scorching* heat alay; . . . I. xi. 50. 6
succour from the *scorching* ray, . . . II. i. 35. 6
for heat of *scorching* aire, . . . II. iii. 26. 3
Yt now devoures with flames and *scorching* heat, . . . II. xi. 32. 8
Nor *scorching* heat, nor cold intemperate, . . . II. xii. 51. 5
the Middayes *scorching* powre, Ne the sharp Northerne wind III. v. 51. 4
Others lay shaded from the *scorching* heat, . . . III. vi. 17. 8
From *scorching* heat her daintie limbes to shade; . . . III. xi. 32. 5
What time the dayes with *scorching* heat abound, . . . IV. i. 13. 7
else some woodman shrowded there from *scorching* sunne. . . IV. vii. 42. 9
Score. *See* **Threescore.**
above a *score* Of Knights and Squires . . . IV. ix. 8. 4
My lambes doe every yeare increase their *score,* . . . VI. ix. 21. 7
Scored. Upon his shield the like was also *scor'd,* . . . I. i. 2. 5
on your shield, so goodly *scord,* . . . II. ix. 2. 7
Scorn. Bird . . . One day did *scorne* the simple Scarabee, . . *Van.* iv. 2
how great vainnesse is it then to *scorne* The weake, . . . *Van.* vi. 13
shortly gan all other beasts to *scorne*. . . . *Van.* viii. 8
To *scorne* all difference of great and small, . . . *Van.* xii. 6
of my rurall musicke holdeth *scorne*. . . . *S.C.* Ja. 64
Tho gynne you, fond flyes! the cold to *scorne,* . . . *S.C.* F. 39
Ah, foolish old man! I *scorne* thy skill, . . . *S.C.* F. 51
Nowe loves a lasse that all his love doth *scorne*. . . . *S.C.* Ap. 11
Rather then other should *scorne* at me: . . . *S.C.* May 60
their foes done eache of hem *scorne*. . . . *S.C.* May 161
holden *scorne* of homely shepheards quill: . . . *S.C.* Jun. 67
Ne would she *scorne* the simple shepheards swaine; . . . *S.C.* N. 97
meane regard, and basest fortunes *scorne,* . . . *Hub.* 60
Let us all servile base subjection *scorne;* . . . *Hub.* 134
make them seeke for that they wont to *scorne,* . . . *Hub.* 257
Of thy great Masters will, to *scorne,* or mock. . . . *Hub.* 508
makes the *scorne* of other beasts to bee: . . . *Hub.* 603
Did ever after *scorne* on foote to goe. . . . *Hub.* 752
would he sometimes *scorne* A Pandares coate . . . *Hub.* 807
eke *scorne* The Sectaries thereof, . . . *Hub.* 832
not contented us themselves to *scorne,* . . . *T.M.* 65
laughing stocke of all that list to *scorne;* . . . *T.M.* 224
with reprochfull *scorne* discountenaunce, . . . *T.M.* 340
name of learning utterly doo *scorne*. . . . *T.M.* 438
they that *scorne* the schoole of arts divine, . . . *T.M.* 520
Doth *scorne* the pride of wonted ornaments: . . . *T.M.* 544
The worlds sad spectacle, and fortunes *scorne*.' . . . *Ti.* 28
glorie of the world your high thoughts *scorne,* . . . *Ti.* 681
sdeignfull *scorne* endure; . . . *Mui.* 7
and *scorne* their shamefull sin, . . . *Mui.* 373
cruell Death doth *scorne* to come at call, . . . *D.* 356
He is repayd with *scorne* and foule despite, . . . *Col.* 905
Seemd in their song to *scorne* the cruell sky. . . . I. i. 8. 4
who shall not great Nightes children *scorne,* . . . I. v. 23. 8
all the Satyres *scorne* their woody kind, . . . I. vi. 18. 8
All other powres and knighthood he did *scorne*. . . . I. vii. 10. 4
Vaine Braggadocchio, . . . is made the *scorne* Of knighthood . II. iii. Arg.
The *scorne* of knighthood and trew chevalrye, . . . II. iii. 10. 5
'lett be thy bitter *scorne,* . . . II. vii. 18. 1
made him *scorne* all creatures great and small, . . . II. vii. 41. 7

Scorn—*Continued.*
as in *scorne* of his spent stormy spight, ... II. viii. 48. 6
halfe in *scorne* Of niggard Nature, ... II. xii. 50. 6
Scorne the faire offer of good will profest; . . . . III. i. 55. 2
The worlds reproch; the cruell victors *scorne;* . . . . . . III. iii. 42. 5
in *scorne* Of her vaine playnt, ... III. vi. 21. 1
To *scorne* the joy that Jove is glad to seeke: . . . . III. vi. 22. 6
we *scorne* his foolish joy, ... III. vi. 24. 4
she with angry *scorne* did him withstond, ... III. viii. 25. 8
To keepe us out in *scorne,* . . . . III. ix. 8. 8
Griefe, and despight, and gealosy, and *scorne,* . . . . . . III. x. 55. 5
Whose scoffed words he taking halfe in *scorne,* . . . . . . IV. ii. 6. 6
inward griefe or wilfull *scorne* Of life . . . . IV. viii. 15. 5
For his friends sake her offred favours *scorne,* . . . . . IV. ix. 3. 8
at one stroke cropt off her head with *scorne,* . . . . . . V. i. 18. 6
full of *scorne* to be commaunded so, ... V. i. 21. 2
made the *scorne* of Knighthod . . . . V. iv. 27. 7
albe all love of men she *scorne,* . . . . V. v. 40. 7
trampled downe in dust his thoughts disdained *scorne.* . . . . V. viii. 31. 9
That is the greatest shame and foulest *scorne,* . . . . . . V. xi. 52. 3
no Knight at all, But *scorne* of armes, ... VI. i. 25. 2
Tooke in foule *scorne* that I such fault did find, ... VI. ii. 11. 7
and make her th' others riches *scorne.* . . . . VI. iii. 7. 9
If I would beare behinde a burden of such *scorne.* . . . . . . VI. iii. 31. 9
Did *scorne* the challenge of so base a thrall; . . . . VI. iii. 36. 4
live in reproch and *scorne,* . . . . VI. vi. 36. 2
that same foole . . . Was *Scorne;* . . . . VI. vii. 44. 6
with bitter mockes and mowes He would him *scorne,* . . . . VI. vii. 49. 7
two lewd companions, . . . Disdaine and *Scorne,* . . . . . VI. viii. 22. 8
is behinde me trodden downe of *Scorne,* . . . . VI. viii. 24. 8
They mocke and *scorne* him, ... VII. vi. 49. 3
is close implide, *Scorn* of base things, ... *Am.* v. 6
seemes to *scorne* Base thing, ... *Am.* xiii. 9
deprave My simple meaning with disdaynfull *scorne;* . . . . *Am.* xxix. 2
What reason is it then but she should *scorne* Base things, . . *Am.* lxi. 11
The Fly, that I so much did *scorne,* . . . . *Epig.* iv. 29
even the greatest did not greatly *scorne* . . . . *Epith.* 4
Love doest laugh and *scorne* At their complaints, ... *H.L.* 134
the bait of sinne, and sinners *scorne,* . . . . *H.B.* 152
Scorned. now these *scorned* fields bemone her fall, ... *Ro.* xii. 13
a Brize, a *scorned* little creature, ... *Van.* ii. 10
scorned bene dedes of fond foolerie. . . . . *S.C.* May 62
the fires *scorn'd* furie to detest; . . . . *Gn.* 612
he sdeignfully it *scorn'd* In his great heart, ... *Hub.* 1234
the man, of whom the Muse is *scorned,* . . . . *Ti.* 454
Scorned of everie one, which by it went; . . . . *Ti.* 503
As if it *scornd* the daunger of the same; . . . . *Col.* 215
Not then to her that *scorned* thing so base, ... *Col.* 935
scornd of God and man, a shamefull death he dide. . . . . . I. v. 48. 9
'That ydle name of love . . . I ever *scornd,* . . . . I. ix. 10. 3
They heapt huge strokes the *scorned* life to quell, ... II. ii. 20. 5
though he *scornd* his ydle vanitee, ... II. iv. 39. 7
the rude And *scorned* partes . . . . II. xii. 59. 2
Paridell her *scornd,* and set at nought, ... IV. ii. 3. 4
To be so *scorned* of a base-borne thrall, ... V. v. 47. 4
scornd all former law: . . . . V. viii. 41. 4
scornd them all that love unto her ment: . . . . VI. vii. 29. 3
Glauncing askew, as if his enemies He *scorned* . . . . VI. vii. 42. 4
Scorner's. sitting carelesse on the *scorners* stoole, ... VI. viii. 21. 7
Scorneth. reposeth In her owne powre, and *scorneth* others ayde; . . . . *Am.* lviii. 2
Scornful. chose with *scornfull* shame Him to avenge, ... *Hub.* 1239
scornfull Follie with Contempt is crept, ... *T.M.* 212
Blind Error, *scornefull* Follie, and base Spight, ... *T.M.* 317
late he sung unto a *scornfull* lasse. . . . . *Col.* 419
underneath her *scornefull* feete was layne A dreadfull Dragon I. iv. 10. 4
Inflamd with *scornefull* wrath and high disdaine, ... I. viii. 7. 2
scornefull eyeglaunce at him shot. . . . . II. iv. 37. 9
with *scornefull* eye They sdeigned . . . . III. i. 40. 7
quite devourd her beauties *scornefull* grace. . . . . III. vii. 23. 5
drag'd him through the waves in *scornfull* state, ... III. viii. 36. 7
it was *scornefull* Braggadochio, ... III. x. 23. 1
Which *scornefull* offer Blandamour gan soone despize; . . . . IV. iv. 8. 9
Which when that *scornefull* Squire of Dames did vew, ... IV. v. 18. 1
With proud disdaine did *scornefull* answere make, ... V. iii. 16. 2
her to present Unto his *scornefull* Lady . . . . V. viii. 25. 9
that discourteous Dame with *scornfull* pryde . . . . VI. i. 30. 4
I . . . backe returned His *scornefull* taunts . . . . VI. ii. 12. 2
the man that with such *scornefull* pryde . . . . VI. iii. 47. 5
issue forth t' attach that *scornefull* lasse. . . . . VI. vii. 35. 5
downe he kept him with his *scornefull* sway, ... VI. viii. 11. 4
Making their cruell rage thy *scornefull* game, ... *H.L.* 47
How with most *scornefull* taunts, and fell despights, ... *H.H.L.* 241
Scornfully. Lettice . . . That *scornefully* lookes askaunce; . . *S.C.* Mar. 21
more *scornfully* Scoffing at him . . . . II. xii. 16. 7
he on it lookt *scornefully* askew, ... III. x. 29. 3
Scorning. thend of this Ambitious brere, For *scorning* Eld— . *S.C.* F. 238
For *scorning* to the sacred Gods to pray, ... *Gn.* 390
Scorning the boldnes of such base-borne men, ... *T.M.* 219
Scorning the let of so unequall foe: . . . . I. viii. 13. 5
scorning both their spights, does make wide way, ... II. ii. 24. 7
The hot-spurre youth so *scorning* to be crost, ... IV. i. 35. 5
As *scorning* his unmanly cowardize: . . . . IV. iv. 11. 2
the Porter, *skorning* them so few, ... IV. vi. 37. 3
Scorning her offers and conditions vaine; . . . . V. v. 46. 2
Words sharpely wound, but greatest griefe of *scorning* growes. VI. vii. 49. 9
Of her freewill, *scorning* both thee and me? . . . . *Am.* x. 4
Proud Daphne, *scorning* Phoebus lovely fyre, ... *Am.* xxviii. 9
Scorns. *Scorns* th' one and th' other in his deeper skill. . . . *Ti.* 448
Who *scornes* thy ydle scoffe, and bids thee be defyde.' . . . . VI. i. 27. 9

Scorns—*Continued.*
The gentle heart *scornes* base disparagement. . . . . VI. x. 37. 5
Scorpion. Soone as they did the monstrous *Scorpion* vew . . . V. viii. 40. 3
Upon a dreadfull *Scorpion* he did ride, ... VII. vii. 39. 6
Scorse. recompenst them with a better *scorse:* . . . . II. ix. 55. 8
Could not arise the counterchaunge to *scorse,* . . . . III. ix. 16. 7
Scorsed. from the country back to private farmes he *scorsed.* . VI. ix. 3. 9
Scotch. Upon his head an old *Scotch* cap he wore, ... *Hub.* 209
Scots. wedded th' one to Maglan king of *Scottes,* . . . . . II. x. 29. 1
neighbour *Scots,* and forrein Scatterlings . . . . II. x. 63. 5
many a band Of *Scots* and English both, ... IV. xi. 36. 9
Scour. his blustring blast eche coste dooth *scoure.* . . . . . . *S.C.* D. 132
with good speed the fomie billowes *scowre:* . . . . *Gn.* 564
after her as hastily gan *scowre,* . . . . I. ii. 20. 5
to forray the land, or *scoure* the deepe. . . . . VI. xi. 40. 5
Scoured. In three great rivers ran, and many countreis *scowrd.* IV. xi. 42. 9
Scourge. therewith *scourge* the buxome aire so sore, ... I. xi. 37. 6
To be the plague and *scourge* of wretched men, ... VI. i. 8. 7
she to wicked men a *scourge* should bee, ... *Am.* xxiv. 11
since ye are my *scourge,* . . . . *Am.* xxiv. 13
The *scourge* of Turkes, and plague of infidels, ... *Com.Son.*iii.13
Scourged. out of court him *scourged* openly. . . . . V. iii. 38. 5
Him often *scourg'd,* and forst his feete to fynd: . . . . . . VI. vii. 49. 5
How *scourgd,* how crownd, how buffeted, how brused; . . . . *H.H.L.* 243
Scourgeth. So sore him *scourgeth* that the bloud downe followeth . . . . VI. viii. 28. 9
Scourging. *scourging* th' emptie ayre with his long trayne, . . I. viii. 17. 3
Scourging and haling him more vehement; . . . . VI. viii. 4. 8
Scouring. the slimie *scowring* Of the moist moores, ... *Gn.* 229
Scouts. forth issuing with his *scouts* afore, ... V. xii. 6. 8
Scowl. made him *scoule,* and pout, ... VI. ix. 38. 7
Scowled. She *scould,* and frownd with froward countenaunce; II. ii. 35. 8
Scraped. The which her sire had *scrap't* by hooke and crooke, . V. ii. 27. 8
Scratch. his talants may Yet *scratch* my sonne, ... I. xii. 11. 6
Gan him to hale, and teare, and *scratch,* and bite; . . . . . VI. viii. 28. 7
Scratched. *scratcht* her face with ghastly dreriment; . . . . II. i. 15. 5
smott, and bitt, and kickt, and *scratcht,* and rent, ... II. iv. 6. 8
scratcht his face, and with his teeth did teare . . . . III. vii. 20. 4
With briers and bushes all to-rent and *scratcht;* . . . . . . IV. vii. 8. 3
rent his haire and *scratcht* his face for paine. . . . . . . IV. viii. 46. 5
with th' one of which she *scratcht* Her cursed head, ... V. xii. 30. 3
He grind, hee bit, he *scratcht,* he venim threw, ... VI. xii. 31. 8
Scratching. Now *scratching* her, and her loose locks misusing, V. vi. 14. 6
Screech-owl. *See* **Shritch-owl.**
Screen. as they entred at the *Scriene,* . . . . V. ix. 25. 1
he there slew him at the *skreene.* . . . . V. x. 37. 9
Scribe. bade Dan Phoebus *scribe* her Appellation seale. . . . VII. vi. 35. 9
Scried. *See* **Descry.**
two shepheards curres had *scryde* A ravenous Wolfe . . . . . V. xii. 38. 5
Scriene. *See* **Screen.**
Scrike. The litle babe did loudly *scrike* and squall, ... VI. iv. 18. 1
Scrine. Lay forth out of thine everlasting *scryne* . . . . . . I. Pr. 2. 3
laid them up in his immortall *scrine,* . . . . II. ix. 56. 6
Scrip. eke behind His *scrip* did hang, ... I. vi. 35. 9
Scrolls. old records . . . some in long parchment *scrolls,* . . II. ix. 57. 8
Scruze. Into his wound the juice thereof did *scruze;* . . . . . III. v. 33. 4
Scruzed. having *scruzd* out of his carrion corse The lothfull life, ... II. xi. 46. 2
Whose sappy liquor . . . Into her cup she *scruzd* . . . . . . II. xii. 56. 4
Scuchin. *See* **Scutcheon.**
Scudamour. the noble knight Sir *Scudamore,* . . . . III. vi. 53. 2
Britomart chaceth Ollyphant; Findes *Scudamour* distrest: . . . III. xi. Arg.
All for she *Scudamore* will not denay. . . . . III. xi. 11. 5
thou, vile man, vile *Scudamore,* art sound, ... III. xi. 11. 6
'Ah! gentlest knight alive,' (sayd *Scudamore*) . . . . III. xi. 19. 1
turning backe to *Scudamour,* . . . . III. xi. 22. 6
Scudamore here die with sorrowing.' . . . . III. xi. 24. 4
Whom whenas *Scudamour* saw past the fire . . . . III. xi. 26. 1
Where late she left the pensife *Scudamore* . . . . III. xii. 44. 2
She left Sir *Scudamour* in great distresse, ... III. xii. 43. *or.* 2
discord breedes Twixt *Scudamour* and Blandamour: . . . . . IV. i. Arg.
Scudamour her bought In perilous fight . . . . IV. i. 2. 1
he perfectly descride To be Sir *Scudamour,* . . . . IV. i. 39. 2
Scudamour was shortly well aware Of his approch, ... IV. i. 41. 4
Scudamour himselfe did soone upryse, ... IV. i. 42. 8
'False faitour *Scudamour,* that hast by slight . . . . IV. i. 44. 2
Ne be ye wroth, Sir *Scudamour,* . . . . IV. i. 46. 5
'Vile hag!' (sayd *Scudamour*) why dost thou lye, ... IV. i. 48. 1
Which when as *Scudamour* did heare, ... IV. i. 49. 6
So stood Sir *Scudamour* when this he heard, ... IV. i. 50. 1
Scudamour . . . Staid not to answer; . . . . IV. i. 52. 1
Scudamour, comming to Cares House, ... IV. v. Arg.
her lover long miswent, The gentle *Scudamour,* . . . . . . IV. v. 30. 7
Sir *Scudamour* there entring much admired . . . . IV. v. 38. 1
There lay Sir *Scudamour* long while . . . . IV. v. 40. 1
Both *Scudamour* and Arthegall Doe fight with Britomart: . . . IV. vi. Arg.
Such was the wound that *Scudamour* did gride, ... IV. vi. 1. 8
Which *Scudamour* perceiving forth issewed . . . . IV. vi. 3. 1
'Ah, gentle *Scudamour!* unto your grace I me submit, . . . IV. vi. 3. 7
Whereto thus *Scudamour:* 'Small harme it were . . . . . . IV. vi. 4. 1
When *Scudamour* heard mention of that speare, ... IV. vi. 7. 1
Sayd then Sir *Scudamour:* . . . . IV. vi. 9. 6
Scudamour, who now abrayd, Beheld, ... IV. vi. 24. 1
Scudamour, now woxen inly glad . . . . IV. vi. 28. 1
Scudamour . . . Her thus bespake: . . . . IV. vi. 34. 1
When *Scudamour* those heavie tydings heard, ... IV. vi. 37. 1
To *Scudamour,* whom she had left behind: . . . . IV. vi. 46. 5
Britomart and gentle *Scudamour;* . . . . IV. ix. 22. 2
Scudamour and that same Briton maide . . . . IV. ix. 28. 2
Paridell and Druon fiercely laid At *Scudamour,* . . . . . . IV. ix. 30. 4

Scudamour—*Continued.*
Scudamour, then sighing deepe, IV. ix. 38. 6
were it not, sir *Scudamour,* IV. ix. 40. 2
Scudamour doth his conquest tell IV. x. Arg.
Scuith. *See* **Scuith guiridh, Y scuith gogh.**
Scuith guiridh. not *Scuith guiridh* it mote seeme to bee, II. x. 24. 8
Scull. *See* **Skull.**
Scum. *See* **Offscum.**
Some to remove the *scum* as it did rise; II. ix. 31. 7
Scummed. Some *scumd* the drosse that from the metall came; II. vii. 36. 7
Scurf. Her crafty head . . . Was overgrowne with *scurfe* I. viii. 47. 3
Scurrility. In stead thereof scoffing *Scurrilitie,* *T.M.* 211
Scutcheon. through his three-square *scuchin* percing quite III. iv. 16. 3
in his *Scutchin* bore a Satyres hedd. III. vii. 30. 6
did those armes and that same *scutchion* weld, IV. i. 34. 5
That bloudie *scutchin,* being battered sore, V. xi. 54. 4
Scutcheons. With *scutchins* gilt and banners broad displayd; IV. iii. 5. 6
Scylla. greedie *Scilla,* under whom there bay Manie great bandogs *Gn.* 539
Scythe. Of him his God is worshipt with his *sythe,* *Gn.* 129
with his *scyth* addrest Does mow the flowring herbes III. vi. 39. 3
Behinde his back a *sithe,* . . . he bore VII. vii. 36. 8
Scythia. One hand on *Scythia,* th' other on the More, *Ro.* iv. 3
Scythian. wrathfull winde . . . burst out of *Scithian* mew, *Bel.*[2] viii. 12
a *Scythian* king, that Humber hight, IV. xi. 37. 8
Sdeign. Yet doe not *sdeigne* to let thy name be writt *Ded. Son.* ii. 4
rudely *sdeigne* a gentle harts request, III. i. 55. 4
So she departed full or griefe and *sdaine,* V. v. 51. 6
is close implide, . . . *sdeigne* of foule dishonor: *Am.* v. 6
Sdeigned. *sdeign'd* the low degree; *Hub.* 679
They *sdeigned* such lascivious disport, III. i. 40. 8
for doubt of being *sdayned,* V. v. 44. 2
Sdeignful. *sdeignfull* pride, and wilfull arrogaunce: *Hub.* 1135
puft up with *sdeignfull* insolence, *T.M.* 71
sdeignfull scorne endure; *Mui.* 7
casting up a *sdeinfull* eie at me, *D.* 549
Nor *s'deignfull* of so homely fashion, III. vii. 10. 6
In *sdeignfull* wize he drew unto him neare, V. ii. 33. 8
Through vengeful wrath and *sdeignfull* pride half mad; V. iv. 43. 3
Sdeignfully. he *sdeignfully* it scorn'd In his great heart, *Hub.* 1234
Sdeigns. either *sdeignes* with other to partake: IV. iii. 16. 8
Sea. *See* **Main sea.**
an ugly beast come from the *sea,* *Rev.* i. 1
then came from the *sea* a savage beast, *Rev.* i. 11
loe, the *sea* (quod he) is now no more. *Rev.* iv. 2
at *sea* a tall ship did appeare, *Pet.* ii. 1
Milde was the winde, calme seem'd the *sea* *Pet.* ii. 4
did so turmoyle the aire, And tumbled up the *sea,* *Pet.* ii. 8
Both land and *sea* in roundnes had survew'd, *Ro.* viii. 3
Like as ye see the wrathfull *Sea* from farre *Ro.* xvi. 1
Queene of land and *sea* her selfe she made. *Ro.* xx. 11
When land and *sea* ye name, *Ro.* xxvi. 11
naming Rome, ye land and *sea* comprize: *Ro.* xxvi. 12
Toward the *sea* turning my troubled eye, *Van.* v. 1
fish . . . That makes the *sea* before his face to flye, *Van.* v. 3
all the *sea* did roare like heavens thunder, *Van.* v. 11
once sea-beate, will to *sea* againe: *S.C.* F. 34
yron bands abord The Pontick *sea* *Gn.* 47
A *sea* of teares that never may be dryde, *T.M.* 116
from her eyes a *sea* of teares did powre; *T.M.* 476
Then did I see a Bridge . . . Over the *Sea* *Ti.* 548
The *sea,* the aire, the fire, the day, the night, *Mui.* 228
on his backe Her through the *sea* did beare; *Mui.* 279
it true *Sea,* and true Bull, ye would weene. *Mui.* 280
I hate the *Sea,* because it teares supplyes. *D.* 406
Of Cynthia the Ladie of the *Sea,* *Col.* 166
to the *sea* we came; the *sea,* that is A world of waters *Col.* 196
is the *sea* (quoth Coridon) so fearfull?' *Col.* 200
Let him to *sea,* and he shall see it there. *Col.* 207
nought but *sea* and heaven to us appeare. *Col.* 227
the shepheards which my Cynthia serve At *sea,* *Col.* 261
land and *sea* my Cynthia doth deserve *Col.* 262
Floting amid the *sea* in jeopardie, *Col.* 273
An high headland thrust far into the *sea,* *Col.* 281
hart, so plungd in *sea* of sorrowes deep, I. vii. 39. 2
A *sea* of blood gusht from the gaping wownd, I. viii. 16. 6
She would commaund themselves to . . . throw in raging *sea* I. x. 20. 8
Out of the *sea* faire Titans deawy face, I. xi. 33. 4
In *sea* of deadly daungers was distrest: I. xii. 17. 6
swimming in that *sea* of blisfull joy, I. xii. 41. 5
'In this wide Inland *sea,* II. vi. 10. 1
Who fares on *sea* may not commaund his way, II. vi. 23. 2
The *sea* is wide, and easy for to stray; II. vi. 23. 4
calme the *sea* of their tempestuous spight. II. vi. 36. 4
Nor *sea* of licour cold, nor lake of myre: II. vi. 44. 4
Who swelling sayles in Caspian *sea* doth crosse, II. vii. 14. 3
it doth, as cloud from *sea,* aryse. II. ix. 42. 5
By *sea* to have bene from the Celticke maynland brought. II. x. 5. 9
When him at *sea* found wandring from their waies, II. x. 41. 7
From *sea* to *sea* he heapt a mighty mound, II. x. 63. 8
upon the glassy *See* A bridge of bras, II. x. 73. 8
Two dayes now in that *sea* he sayled has, II. xii. 2. 1
With his stiffe oares did brush the *sea* so strong, II. xii. 10. 2
Amid th' Aegaean *sea* long time did stray, II. xii. 13. 2
Islands, which doe fleet In the wide *sea,* II. xii. 14. 4
descry It plaine, and by the *sea* discoloured: II. xii. 18. 8
the great *sea,* puft up with proud disdaine, II. xii. 21. 7
He smote the *sea,* which calmed was II. xii. 26. 7
through the *sea* resounding plaints did fly: II. xii. 27. 4
the rolling *sea,* resounding soft, II. xii. 33. 1

Sea—*Continued.*
seemd the fountaine in that *sea* did sayle upright. II. xii. 62. 9
His deawy face out of the *sea* doth reare; II. xii. 65. 2
By *sea,* by land, where so they may be mett, III. ii. 7. 3
The Land to *sea,* and *sea* to maineland dry, III. iii. 12. 3
where the day out of the *sea* doth spring, III. iii. 27. 4
Shall overswim the *sea,* III. iii. 33. 8
'Huge *sea* of sorrow and tempestuous griefe, III. iv. 8. 1
which the *sea* below Had . . . devoured deepe, III. iv. 22. 5
The *sea* unto him voluntary brings; III. iv. 23. 7
griesly Monsters of the *See* Stood gaping III. iv. 32. 8
with their finny oars the swelling *sea* did sheare. III. iv. 33. 9
Deepe in the bottome of the *sea* III. iv. 43. 1
To reach the *sea* ere she of him were raught: III. vii. 26. 6
in the *sea* to drowne herselfe she fond, III. vii. 26. 7
safety fownd at *sea* which she fownd not at land. III. vii. 27. 9
to chaunge The land for *sea,* III. viii. 20. 5
sith far in *sea* we bee, III. viii. 24. 1
Least worse on *sea* then us on land befell.' III. viii. 24. 5
To fetch from *sea* that ye at land lost late! III. viii. 28. 4
the wide *sea* importuned long space III. viii. 29. 7
with a remnant did to *sea* repayre; III. ix. 41. 3
with him ledd to *sea* an youthly trayne; III. ix. 48. 6
To seeke her endlong both by *sea* and lond. III. x. 19. 5
a rocky hill Over the *sea* suspended dreadfully, III. x. 56. 4
filleth all the *sea* with fome, IV. i. 42. 5
As when two warlike Brigandines at *sea,* IV. ii. 16. 1
He sends the *sea* his owne with double gaine, IV. iii. 27. 8
whylome they have conquerd *sea* and land, IV. vi. 31. 4
Upon the *sea* to wreake his fell intent; IV. ix. 23. 4
afterward both *sea* and land possest; IV. xi. 18. 4
The spacious Shenan spreading like a *sea,* IV. xi. 41. 3
ere to the *sea* they come; IV. xi. 43. 8
have the *sea* in charge to them assinde, IV. xi. 52. 2
Venus of the fomy *sea* was bred, IV. xii. 2. 2
all about that rocke the *sea* did flow: IV. xii. 15. 5
all the *sea,* disturbed with their traine, V. ii. 15. 7
Till that at length nigh to the *sea* they drew; V. ii. 29. 2
he would all the earth uptake And all the *sea,* V. ii. 31. 2
Like as the *sea* . . . Had worne the earth; V. ii. 32. 3
The *sea* it selfe doest thou not plainely see V. ii. 37. 4
though the *sea* with waves continuall Doe eate the earth, V. ii. 39. 4
in the *sea* him dround. V. ii. 49. 9
which ye there before you see Not farre in *sea;* V. iv. 7. 6
this devouring *Sea,* that naught doth spare, V. iv. 8. 2
Into the *Sea* her selfe did headlong throw, V. iv. 10. 3
she did transport the same by *sea,* V. iv. 13. 6
Your brothers land the which the *sea* hath layd V. iv. 17. 3
the *sea* it to my share did lay?' V. iv. 17. 7
what the *sea* unto you sent your own should seeme.' V. iv. 17. 9
But that the *sea* hath it unto me throwne?' V. iv. 18. 7
what the *sea* unto you sent your own should seeme. V. iv. 18. 9
what the mighty *Sea* hath once possest, V. iv. 19. 2
all the shores, which to the *sea* accoste, V. xi. 42. 6
all their scattred crew Into the *sea* he drove V. xi. 65. 4
they found A ship all readie . . . To put to *sea,* V. xii. 4. 3
Talus into the *sea* did forth issew V. xii. 5. 4
rule both *sea* and land unto their will: VII. vii. 3. 5
of the *sea* that neighbours to her neare: *Epith.* 39
th' Earth, . . . founded Amid the *Sea,* *H.H.B.* 37
Sea-beat. once *sea-beate,* will to sea againe: *S.C.* F. 34
Sea-beaten. catching hold of this *Sea-beaten* chest, V. iv. 11. 6
Seaboard. a Lion from the *sea-bord* wood Of Neustria III. iii. 47. 2
Southwinde, from the *seabord* coste Upblowing, III. iv. 13. 4
Sea-coast. Clayming that *sea-coast* Citie as his right. *Mui.* 314
all along the Southerne *sea-coast* lay II. x. 6. 4
to the *sea-coast* at length she her addrest. III. iv. 6. 9
when they came to the *sea coast* V. xii. 4. 1
Sead, -es. *See* **Seed, -s.**
Sea-god. Who, all in rage, his *Sea-god* syre besought I. v. 38. 1
Her *Sea-god* syre she dearely did perswade III. iv. 21. 7
Sea-god's. Under the *Sea-gods* seale autenticall, IV. xii. 32. 2
Sea-gods. Tryphon of *sea gods* the soveraine leach is hight. III. iv. 43. 9
And feasts the *Sea-gods* all. IV. xi. Arg.
all the *Sea-gods* and their fruitfull seede, IV. xi. 8. 2
the *Sea-gods,* which to themselves doe clame The powre IV. xi. 12. 8
Sea-gods'. (This Tryphon is the *seagods* surgeon hight,) IV. xi. 6. 6
Sea-gulls. *Seagulles* hoars and bace, II. xii. 8. 4
Sea-horses. His *seahorses* did seeme to snort amayne, III. xi. 41. 1
Seal. to entrappe the fish in winding *sale* *S.C.* D. 81
Under the Sea-gods *seale* autenticall, IV. xii. 32. 2
As when a Dolphin and a *Sele* are met V. ii. 15. 1
bade Dan Phoebus scribe her Appellation *seale.* VII. vi. 35. 9
Sealed. *seald* up in the threasure of her hart. *Col.* 571
A booke, that was both signd and *seald* with blood; I. x. 13. 8
virgin wex that never yet was *seald,* III. viii. 6. 7
So firmely she had *sealed* up her brest. III. viii. 39. 5
Seals. heard Of stinking *Seales* and Porcpisces *Col.* 249
Seam. through the *seame,* which did his hauberk close, IV. iii. 30. 3
Sea-mark. For safety that same his *sea-marke* made, II. x. 6. 6
Sea-monsters. huge *Sea monsters,* such as living sence dismayd: II. xii. 22. 9
Sea-nymph's. he must do battail with the *Sea-nymphes* sonne. III. iv. 20. 9
'A *Sea-nymphes* sonne, that Marinell is hight, III. v. 9. 1
Sea-nymphs. after these the *Sea Nymphs* marched all, IV. xi. 48. 1
Sear. Like an old Oke, whose pith and sap is *seare,* IV. iii. 9. 8
Search. she . . . each wood and plaine, Did *search,* I. ii. 8. 8
By further *search* had passage found elsewhere; II. viii. 3. 4
She secretly would *search* each daintie lim, III. i. 36. 6
They softly gan to *search* his griesly wownd: III. iv. 40. 2
She made those Damzels *search;* III. v. 38. 8

Search—*Continued.*
To *search* the secret haunts of Dianes company. . . . III. vi. 16. 9
to *search* from place to place, ... III. vi. 25. 8
To *search* the God of love her Nimphes she sent . . . . III. vi. 26. 1
To *search* her forth where so she might be fond, ... III. x. 19. 2
My Lord and I will *search* the wide forest.' . . . . III. x. 41. 7
The wood they enter, and *search* everie where, ... III. xi. 6. 8
To *search* each secrete of that goodly sted, ... III. xi. 50. 2
Ne could by *search* nor any meanes out find . . . . IV. xii. 21. 3
And *search* the courses of the rowling spheares, ... V. Pr. 5. 2
gotten by her slight And earnest *search*, ... V. i. 9. 3
To *search* out those that usd to rob and steale, ... V. xii. 26. 7
After long *search* and chauff he turned backe . . . . VI. ii. 21. 2
I the measure of her flight doe *search*, ... VI. ii. 32. 3
lighting candles new, gan *search* anone, ... VI. xi. 20. 8
Searched. He cast about, and *searcht* his baleful bokes againe. I. ii. 2. 9
all that noyd his heavie spright Well *searcht*, ... I. x. 24. 4
Then *searcht* his secret woundes, ... II. vi. 51. 3
after having *searcht* the intuse deepe, ... III. v. 33. 8
searched everie way through which his wings Had borne him, III. vi. 12. 6
They *searched* diversely, so both divided were. . . . . III. xi. 6. 9
And every litle limbe he *searcht* around, ... VI. iv. 23. 6
searched all their cels and secrets neare: . . . . VI. xii. 24. 4
Searcheth. His subtile tong . . . *searcheth* every vaine; . . . I. ix. 31. 6
Searching. by *searching* daungers new, ... IV. ii. 46. 7
Searching all lands and each remotest part, ... III. iv. 6. 7
searching every part, ... IV. xii. 23. 8
as he was *searching* of their wounds, ... VI. vi. 5. 1
Seare. *See* **Sere.**
Seared. flame . . . through his armour all his body *seard*, . . . I. xi. 26. 7
His cole-blacke hands did seeme to have ben *seard* . . . . II. vii. 3. 8
Sea's. Against the *seas* encroching crueltie. . . . . *Col.* 275
Of that *seas* nature did him not avise: . . . . II. vi. 46. 5
Compared to the creatures in the *seas* entrall. . . . . II. xii. 25. 9
To count the *seas* abundant progeny, ... IV. xii. 1. 2
to recount the *Seas* posterity: . . . . IV. xii. 1. 7
none but to the *seas* sole Soveraine. . . . . IV. xii. 30. 5
Seas. restles *seas* of wretchednes and woe; . . . . *Pet.*^{2} vii. 4
The soveraigne of *seas* he blames in vaine, ... *S.C.* F. 33
The sodain rysing of the raging *seas*, ... *S.C.* D. 86
from Indian *seas* brought far away; . . . . *Gn.* 106
Nereis to the *Seas* a token gave, ... *Gn.* 567
skies and *seas* doo make most dreadfull warre; . . . . *Gn.* 574
Before them stands the God of *Seas* in place, ... *Mui.* 313
My . . . service, that by land and *seas* Have vowd you to defend. I. iii. 29. 8
Sleepe after toyle, port after stormie *seas*, ... I. ix. 40. 8
He cryde, as raging *seas* are wont to rore . . . . I. xi. 21. 1
Built on a rocke adjoyning to the *seas:* . . . . II. ii. 12. 7
As a tall ship tossed in troublous *seas*, ... II. ii. 24. 1
Better safe port then be in *seas* distrest.' . . . . II. vi. 23. 8
all the *seas* for feare doe seeme away to fly. . . . . II. xii. 3. 9
Sucking the *seas* into his entralles deepe, ... II. xii. 6. 2
through the Euxine *seas* bore all the flowr of Greece. . . . . II. xii. 44. 9
'Thou God of windes, that raignest in the *seas*, ... III. iv. 10. 1
Ne durst assay to wade the perlous *seas*, ... III. vii. 28. 3
Proteus is Shepheard of the *seas* of yore, ... III. viii. 30. 1
Through all the *seas* so ruefully resownd, ... III. viii. 30. 6
Confounds both land and *seas*, ... III. ix. 15. 9
when she saw The huge *seas* under her . . . . III. xi. 30. 9
thy smyling looke doest pacifie The raging *seas*, ... IV. x. 44. 5
rules the *Seas* and makes them rise or fall; . . . . IV. xi. 11. 2
pearles which th' Indian *seas* for her prepaire. . . . . IV. xi. 11. 9
the which became A God of *seas* . . . . IV. xi. 13. 5
Through the Agaean *seas* from Pirates vew, ... IV. xi. 23. 7
all the raging *seas* for joy forgot to rore. . . . . IV. xi. 23. 9
with her least word can asswage The surging *seas*, ... IV. xi. 50. 5
the *seas* by her are most augmented: . . . . IV. xii. 2. 3
greedy *seas* doe in the spoile of life delight. . . . . IV. xii. 6. 9
the *seas* . . . Doe pearce the rockes, ... IV. xii. 7. 1
'Ye Gods of *seas*, ... IV. xii. 9. 1
the which by fortune came Upon your *seas*, ... IV. xii. 31. 4
wandring on his *seas* imperiall . . . . IV. xii. 32. 4
After long tossing in the *seas* distrest, ... V. iv. 11. 8
From all the tempests of these worldly *seas*, ... VI. ix. 19. 4
In *seas* of troubles and of toylesome paine; . . . . VI. ix. 31. 6
Neptune, of *seas;* . . . . VII. vii. 26. 7
He forth was thrown into the greedy *seas;* . . . . *Am.* xxxviii. 2
Through *seas*, through flames, ... *H.L.* 228
As these are fairer then the land and *seas?* . . . . *H.H.B.* 63
Sea-satyr. The horrible *Sea-satyre*, ... II. xii. 24. 5
Sease, etc. *See* **Seize, etc.**
Sea-shore. she gan approch to the *sea shore*, ... III. vii. 25. 4
as he did passe by the *sea shore*, ... V. iv. 4. 1
To the *sea-shore* he gan his way apply, ... V. xii. 3. 8
Sea-shouldering. Spring-headed Hydres; and *sea-shouldring* Whales; . . . . II. xii. 23. 6
Season. as in *season* due the husband mowes . . . . *Ro.* xxx. 5
brought forth in her last declining *season*, ... *Van.* i. 7
all to sadde For thilke same *season*, ... *S.C.* May 6
on a tyme, in Sommer *season*, ... *S.C.* May 176
All the cold *season* to wach and waite; . . . . *S.C.* S. 237
Thilke sollein *season* sadder plight doth aske, ... *S.C.* N. 17
sadde winters wrathe, and *season* chill, ... *S.C.* N. 33
Sommer *season* sped him to display . . . . *S.C.* D. 56
To thinges of ryper *season* selfe applyed, ... *S.C.* D. 76
season more secure Shall bring forth fruit, ... *Gn.* 9
Ye have this matter motioned in *season;* . . . . *Hub.* 125
No temperance, nor no regard of *season*, ... *Hub.* 1132
season milde With gentle calme the world had quieted, . . . *Mui.* 49
In the first *season* of my feeble age, ... *Ded. Son.* vii. 4

Season—*Continued.*
first thou must a *season* fast and pray, ... I. x. 52. 7
Till *season* serve new passage to assay: . . . . II. vi. 23. 7
when they rested had a *season* dew, ... II. ix. 20. 6
the milde ayre with *season* moderate . . . attempred, . . . II. xii. 51. 7
when she fit *season* saw To leave . . . . III. vii. 18. 1
Faire lawnds, to take the sunne in *season* dew; . . . . IV. x. 24. 2
washeth Winborne meades in *season* drye. . . . . IV. xi. 32. 4
One day, as she to shunne the *season* whot . . . . IV. xi. 42. 4
Agreeing well both with the place and *season*, ... VI. iv. 37. 5
now long *season* past Had never joyance felt . . . . VI. xi. 45. 1
yet the *season* was full sharp and breem: . . . . VII. vii. 40. 5
Drawne of two fishes, for the *season* fitting, ... VII. vii. 43. 3
This holy *season*, fit to fast and pray, ... *Am.* xxii. 1
bred . . . In sweetest *Season*, ... *Proth.* 68
Seasoned. With *seasoned* wit and goodly pleasance graced, . . *T.M.* 200
Season's. Deckt all with dainties of her *seasons* pryde, ... VII. vii. 34. 2
Seasons. times and *seasons* of the yeare that fall: . . . . VII. vii. 27. 4
forth issew'd the *Seasons* of the yeare. . . . . VII. vii. 28. 1
doe the *seasons* of the yeare allot, ... *Epith.* 100
Seat. *See* **Judgment-seat, Mercy-seat.**
streame, . . . sprong from triumphant *seat*. . . . . *Rev.* iv. 13
shooke the hill from lowest *seat*, ... *Bel.*^{2} ii. 13
you up to call To honours *seat*, ... *Van.* xii. 12
reigned (as men sayd) in Venus *seate*. . . . . *S.C.* D. 60
such as sate in justice *seate*, ... *Hub.* 921
he bad the Lyon be remitted Into his *seate*, ... *Hub.* 1255
Lifting the Good up to high Honours *seat*, ... *Com. Son.* i. 11
sits in highest *seate* Of this worlds glorie, ... *Ti.* 463
on his *seat* His dronken corse he scarse upholden can: . . . . I. iv. 22. 7
Which fast is tyde to Joves eternall *seat?* . . . . I. v. 25. 6
Whose kingdomes *seat* Cleopolis is red; . . . . I. vii. 46. 7
huge mountaines from their native *seat* . . . to beare away, I. x. 20. 6
they the earth would shoulder from her *seat;* . . . . I. xi. 21. 4
you a Saint with Saints your *seat* have wonne: . . . . II. i. 32. 5
all on uprore from her settled *seat*, ... II. ii. 20. 6
set in highest *seat* of dignitee, ... II. iv. 19. 4
Whom nether wind out of their *seat* could forse . . . . II. vi. 20. 8
To trouble my still *seate*, ... II. vii. 7. 9
in the midst thereof a silver *seat*, ... II. vii. 53. 2
Whom fortune hath already laid in lowest *seat*.' . . . . II. viii. 27. 9
Which blott his sonne succeeding in his *seat*, ... II. x. 23. 1
A *seate* in Ireland safely to remayne, ... II. x. 41. 8
all Which, him before, that sacred *seate* did fill, ... II. x. 76. 2
strives to mount unto his native *seat;* . . . . II. xi. 32. 6
the weake sowle her *seat* did yett retaine, ... III. v. 31. 4
Out of his wavering *seat* him pluckt perforse, ... III. vii. 43. 2
To sitt in second *seat* of soveraine king . . . . III. ix. 44. 4
To be the compasse of his kingdomes *seat:* . . . . III. ix. 46. 6
finding no fit *seat*, the lifelesse corse it left. . . . . IV. iii. 21. 9
To sit in his own *seate*, ... V. Pr. 10. 8
highest sit In *seate* of judgement . . . . V. Pr. 11. 2
he was mounted in his *seat* so high, ... V. viii. 33. 3
Sith in th' Almighties everlasting *seat* She first was bred, . . V. x. 1. 7
to her kingdomes *seat* restore agayne: . . . . V. xii. 25. 4
vertues *seat* is deepe within the mynd, ... VI. Pr. 5. 8
to the folds, where sheepe at night doe *seat*, ... VI. ix. 4. 7
had to her that soveraigne *seat* By highest Jove assign'd, . . VII. vi. 12. 1
Was striving with faire Cynthia for her *seat;* . . . . VII. vi. 17. 3
To honors *seat* and chastities sweet bowre. . . . . *Epith.* 180
meriting a meere triumphant *seate*. *Com.Son.*iii.12
He gan to move out of his idle *seate;* . . . . *H.L.* 66
And sit in Gods owne *seat* without commission; . . . . *H.H.L.* 82
His *seate* is Truth, to which the faithfull trust, ... *H.H.B.* 159
Seated. it was *seated* in an Island strong, ... IV. x. 6. 1
her before was *seated* overthwart Soft Silence, ... IV. x. 51. 5
Seats. *See* **Judgment-seats.**
The *seates* and benches shone as yvorie, ... *Bel.* xii. 9
Threw down the *seats*, ... *Bel.* xii. 14
to the *seates* of happie soules admitted: . . . . *Gn.* 478
Whom ye in goodly *seates* may placed see, ... *Gn.* 595
sitting all in *seates* about me round, ... *Hub.* 25
Emongst the *seats* of Angels . . . . *Col.* 614
They all attonce out of their *seates* arose, ... II. ix. 36. 2
shadie *seates*, and sundry flowring bankes, ... IV. x. 25. 4
touch celestiall *seates* with earthly mire? . . . . VII. vi. 29. 4
whereas the royall *Seates* . . . are set, ... *H.H.B.* 89
Sea-walled. leave his love in that *sea-walled* fort. . . . . IV. xii. 18. 5
Second. these riches, *second* unto none, ... *Bel.*^{2} xiii. 10
give a *second* life to dead decayes! . . . . *Ro.* Env. 6
to those ashes gave a *second* life, ... *Ti.* 669
Such one was Gluttony, the *second* of that crew. . . . . I. iv. 23. 9
The *second* was as Almner of the place: . . . . I. x. 38. 1
to my tunes thy *second* tenor rayse, ... I. xi. 7. 8
the *second* fall Of her deare knight, ... I. xi. 50. 1
second sister, who did far excell The other two: . . . . II. ii. 14. 3
both did at their *second* sister grutch . . . . II. ii. 34. 6
Pyrochles gan reply the *second* tyme, ... II. viii. 30. 1
brought them to the *second* rowme, ... II. ix. 53. 2
The *second* Brute, the *second* both in name . . . . II. x. 23. 2
They crownd the *second* Constantine with joyous teares. . . . II. x. 62. 9
The *second* Bulwarke was the Hearing sence, ... II. xi. 10. 1
Gainst which the *second* troupe assignment makes; . . . . II. xi. 10. 2
gan him selfe to *second* battaill bend, ... II. xi. 35. 5
A *second* fall redoubling backe agayne. . . . . II. xi. 43. 5
The *second* was Parlante, a bold knight; . . . . III. i. 45. 3
Fayre Amoretta in the *second* place: . . . . III. vi. 4. 5
'The *second* was an holy Nunne to chose, ... III. vii. 58. 6
To sitt in *second* seat of soveraine king . . . . III. ix. 44. 4
Both first and *second* Troy shall dare to equalise, ... III. ix. 44. 9

Second—*Continued.*
This *second* Helene, fayre Dame Hellenore, . . . III. x. 13. 1
the *second* evening Her covered . . . III. xii. 29. 3
when the *second* watch was almost past, . . . III. xii. 29. 6
The *second* Dyamond, the youngest Triamond. . . . IV. ii. 41. 9
The *second* was to Triamond behight, . . . IV. v. 7. 6
the judges did arret her Unto the *second* best . . . IV. v. 21. 5
Hath conquered you anew in *second* fight: . . . IV. vi. 31. 3
she went to seeke faire Amoret, Her *second* care, . . . IV. vi. 46. 7
'Thence forth I passed to the *second* gate, . . . IV. x. 16. 1
Art, playing *second* natures part, supplyed it. . . . IV. x. 21. 9
It seem'd a *second* paradise to ghesse, . . . IV. x. 23. 2
The *second* had to name Sir Bellisont, . . . V. iii. 5. 3
second unto none in prowesse prayse; . . . V. iii. 5. 4
The *second* day, so soone as morrow light . . . V. iii. 7. 1
The *second*, not so strong but wise, Decetto; . . . VI. v. 13. 8
He stayd his *second* strooke, . . . VI. vi. 31. 9
with the *second* stroke thought certainely To have supplyde
the first, . . . VI. viii. 9. 8
Her selfe sole left a *second* spoyle to bee . . . VI. xi. 23. 3
The *second* is my sovereigne Queene . . . *Am.* lxxiv. 7
Agayne, I wrote it with a *second* hand; . . . *Am.* lxxv. 3
stoutly will that *second* worke assoyle, . . . *Am.* lxxx. 7
second Babell, tyrant of the West, . . . *Com. Son.* iv. 3
His *second* brood, though not in powre so great, . . . *H.H.L.* 53
Us wretches from the *second* death did save; . . . *H.H.L.* 193

Secrecy. By creeping close into his *secrecie;* . . . *Col.* 698
Shun *secresie,* and talke in open sight: . . . VI. vi. 14. 8

Secret. they gang in more *secrete* wise, . . . *S.C.* S. 156
as he satte in *secreate* shade alone, . . . *S.C.* D. 5
To reade the *secrete* of this riddle rare, . . . *Gn.* Ded. 7
fortune doth you *secret* favour give.' . . . *Hub.* 594
By *secrete* meanes gan of his state enquire, . . . *Hub.* 681
Of all the which there came a *secret* fee, . . . *Hub.* 875
The Lyon sleeping lay in *secret* shade, . . . *Hub.* 952
them borne aside Into a *secret* corner unespide. . . . *Hub.* 1018
He gan enquire of some in *secret* wize, . . . *Hub.* 1272
Thenceforth he past into each *secrete* part, . . . *Hub.* 1303
those *secret* causes to display; . . . *T.M.* 50
secret sorrow and sad languishment, . . . *T.M.* 376
none might professe . . . that *secret* skill; . . . *T.M.* 560
they in *secret* harts envying sore, . . . *Mui.* 124
Did lend her *secret* aide, . . . *Mui.* 127
Her sonne to Psyche *secrete* love did beare, . . . *Mui.* 131
in their *secret* doome Ordained have, . . . *Mui.* 225
with *secret* joy therefore Did tickle inwardly . . . *Mui.* 393
for *secret* crime thy blood hast spilt.' . . . *D.* 84
with *secret* ravishment He stole away, . . . *As.* 21
not so *secret,* but it was descride, . . . *Col.* 146
Through *secret* sence which thereto doth them draw. . . . *Col.* 886
seeming to mistrust Some *secret* ill, or hidden foe . . . I. i. 49. 4
waste the wearie night In *secret* anguish . . . I. i. 53. 3
Those twoo he tooke, and in a *secrete* bed, . . . I. ii. 3. 7
Who soone him brought into a *secret* part, . . . I. ii. 5. 3
scorching Sunne does dry my *secret* vaines; . . . I. ii. 33. 8
In *secrete* shadow, far from all mens sight: . . . I. iii. 4. 4
he . . . learned had to love with *secret* lookes; . . . I. iv. 25. 6
Lo! his Fidessa, to thy *secret* faith I flye.' . . . I. iv. 45. 9
bad say on the *secrete* of her hart: . . . I. iv. 46. 2
my *secret* aide Shall follow you.' . . . I. iv. 51. 8
Who all that while lay hid in *secret* shade. . . . I. v. 15. 4
he learned had in *secret* wise The hidden cause . . . I. v. 46. 2
The salvage nation feele her *secret* smart, . . . I. vi. 11. 3
in *secret* cabin there he held Her captive . . . I. vi. 23. 1
all her witt in *secret* counsels spent, . . . I. vi. 32. 5
did rest In *secret* shadow by a fountaine side: . . . I. vi. 40. 6
did stay In *secret* shadow . . . I. vi. 48. 3
he knew Some *secret* sorrow did her heart distraine; . . . I. vii. 38. 4
despeyre did many thereof sup, And *secret* poyson . . . I. viii. 14. 4
Whose *secret* filth good manners biddeth not be told. . . . I. viii. 46. 9
The *secret* meaning of th' eternall might, . . . I. ix. 6. 8
'what *secret* wound Could ever find to grieve the gentlest hart I. ix. 7. 8
The *secrete* cause of his perplexitie: . . . I. ix. 25. 5
ere one be aware, by *secret* stealth His powre is reft, . . . I. ix. 31. 7
in his conscience made a *secrete* breach, . . . I. ix. 48. 3
other *secret* vertue did ensew; . . . I. xi. 36. 5
The *secret* treasons, which of late I know . . . I. xii. 33. 5
sacred lamp in *secret* chamber hide, . . . I. xii. 37. 7
Himselfe he frees by *secret* meanes unseene; . . . II. i. 1. 8
feele some *secret* ease. . . . II. i. 16. 9
he doth himselfe in *secret* shrowd, . . . II. i. 25. 3
tell the *secrete* of your mortall smart: . . . II. i. 46. 8
Their blood with *secret* filth infected hath, . . . II. ii. 4. 7
secret vertues are infusd In every fountaine, . . . II. ii. 5. 6
in *secret* cave . . . her selfe hath hid, . . . II. iii. 36. 1
told for *secret,* how he understood . . . II. iv. 22. 5
Me leading, in a *secret* corner layd, . . . II. iv. 27. 5
In *secrete* shadow from the sunny ray, . . . II. v. 32. 2
within my *secret* bowelles bee. . . . II. vi. 49. 9
Then searcht his *secret* woundes, . . . II. vi. 51. 3
led downe To see his *secrete* store. . . . II. vii. Arg.
found in *secret* shade An uncouth . . . wight, . . . II. vii. 3. 3
in *secret* mew From hevens sight, . . . II. vii. 19. 8
'What *secret* place . . . can safely hold . . . II. vii. 20. 1
secrete powre t' appease inflamed rage: . . . II. viii. 26. 8
By *secret* wayes, that none might it espy, . . . II. ix. 32. 6
in the *secret* of your hart close lyes, . . . II. ix. 42. 4
seeth with *secret* fire eternally, . . . II. x. 26. 3
secret pleasure did offence empeach, . . . II. x. 68. 8
ofte of *secret* ill bids us beware: . . . II. xii. 47. 7

Secret—*Continued.*
His stubborne brest gan *secret* pleasaunce to embrace. . . . II. xii. 65. 9
The *secrete* signes of kindled lust appeare, . . . II. xii. 68. 6
In *secret* shade after long wanton joyes, . . . II. xii. 72. 6
not thy fault, but *secret* powre unseene: . . . III. i. 7. 8
The *secrete* vertue of that weapon keene, . . . III. i. 10. 5
Now leading him into a *secret* shade . . . III. i. 35. 6
joyd his love in *secret* unespyde: . . . III. i. 37. 2
secret darts did throw; . . . III. i. 51. 8
for *secret* purpose did appoynt To lodge . . . III. i. 60. 3
Such *secrete* ease felt gentle Britomart, . . . III. ii. 15. 7
Ne ought in *secret* from the same remaynd; . . . III. ii. 19. 7
To let the *secret* of her hart to her appeare. . . . III. ii. 34. 9
Through deepe impression of thy *secret* might, . . . III. iii. 2. 7
in *secrete* store Were from him hidden, . . . III. iii. 15. 4
cut off by practise criminall Of *secrete* foes, . . . III. iii. 28. 9
Where they in *secret* counsell close conspird, . . . III. iii. 51. 5
Covered with *secret* cloud of silent night, . . . III. iii. 61. 8
Finding the Nymph asleepe in *secret* wheare, . . . III. iv. 19. 7
She did envy that soveraine salve in *secret* store. . . . III. v. 50. 9
With so sweet sence and *secret* powre unspide, . . . III. vi. 7. 8
To search the *secret* haunts of Dianes company. . . . III. vi. 16. 9
To lurke emongst your Nimphes in *secret* wize, . . . III. vi. 23. 2
There yet, some say, in *secret* he does ly, . . . III. vi. 46. 4
In *secret* wize herselfe thence to withdraw, . . . III. vii. 18. 3
She with her bringes into a *secret* Ile, . . . III. vii. 50. 6
Had she not fled into a *secret* mew, . . . III. viii. 4. 3
Infixt such *secrete* sting of greedy lust, . . . III. viii. 25. 2
told his *secret* care . . . III. ix. 28. 3
they *secret* way did make Unto their wils, . . . III. ix. 31. 5
seest every *secret* of the minde; . . . III. x. 4. 7
none espyde His *secret* drift, . . . III. x. 6. 4
in *secret* den My Lady and my love so cruelly to pen! . . . III. xi. 10. 8
To search each *secrete* of that goodly sted, . . . III. xi. 50. 2
for feare Of *secret* daunger, . . . III. xi. 55. 6
al this while was plast In *secret* shade, . . . III. xii. 27. 5
her selfe did reare Out of her *secret* stand . . . III. xii. 28. 9
every one gan grow in *secret* dout . . . IV. i. 14. 3
His mightie indignation . . . was not yet so *secret,* . . . IV. i. 45. 3
His hart with *secret* envie gan to swell, . . . IV. ii. 7. 8
Did privily put coles unto his *secret* fire. . . . IV. ii. 11. 9
As if they *secret* counsels did partake; . . . IV. ii. 30. 4
every *secret* worke of natures wayes; . . . IV. ii. 35. 4
watcht on every side, of *secret* foes affrayd, . . . IV. ii. 36. 9
a Fay, and had the skill Of *secret* things, . . . IV. ii. 44. 2
Through *secret* understanding of their feature. . . . IV. ii. 44. 5
durst Come see the *secret* of the life of man, . . . IV. ii. 49. 7
Through *secret* feeling of his generous spright, . . . IV. iii. 14. 5
filled were with rufull tine And *secret* feare, . . . IV. iii. 37. 5
shewing *secret* wit. . . . IV. iv. 39. 9
left behind her in her *secret* bowre . . . IV. v. 5. 4
by *secret* skill With golden foyle doth finely over-spred . . . IV. v. 15. 1
fell away, as feeling *secret* blame. . . . IV. v. 16. 7
touched was with *secret* wrath and shame . . . IV. v. 17. 4
His powrelesse arme, benumbd with *secret* feare, . . . IV. vi. 21. 3
For sudden joy and *secret* feare withall; . . . IV. vi. 29. 3
Which *secret* fate hath in this Ladie wrought . . . IV. vi. 30. 4
Artegall close smyling joy'd in *secret* hart. . . . IV. vi. 32. 9
I sought by *secret* meanes . . . IV. vii. 17. 1
by *secret* signes of manlinesse . . . IV. vii. 45. 4
by his persons *secret* seemlyhed . . . IV. viii. 14. 3
casting *secret* flakes of lustfull fire . . . IV. viii. 48. 8
Of his old love conceav'd in *secret* brest, . . . IV. ix. 17. 4
secret theft Of all her lovers . . . IV. xi. 3. 4
The *secret* cause and nature of his teene, . . . IV. xii. 21. 4
Ne lesse was she in *secret* hart affected, . . . IV. xii. 35. 6
all things *secrete* wisely could bewray, . . . V. ii. 25. 4
suffred all his *secret* marke to see: . . . V. iii. 34. 6
Gan cast a *secret* liking to this captive straunge. . . . V. v. 26. 9
Unto her selfe in *secret* she did call . . . V. v. 29. 1
'Say on' (quoth he) 'the *secret* of your hart . . . V. vii. 19. 6
abasht with *secrete* shame . . . V. vii. 38. 3
Such *secret* comfort and such heavenly pleasures, . . . VI. Pr. 2. 1
unarm'd and set in *secret* shade. . . . VI. iii. 8. 5
he them spotted with reproch, or *secrete* shame. . . . VI. vi. 12. 9
Gan mutter close a certaine *secret* charme, . . . VI. viii. 45. 6
with *secret* wound . . . empierced were, . . . VI. xii. 4. 7
through grace Or *secret* guifts, . . . VI. xii. 6. 2
Mote not bewray the *secret* of her lode, . . . VI. xii. 7. 3
Her to discover for some *secret* hire: . . . VII. vi. 43. 3
that he might *secret* bee. . . . VII. vi. 43. 9
say, they by your *secret* powre are made: . . . VII. vii. 49. 4
In *secret* sorow, and sad pensivenesse. . . . *Am.* xxxiv. 14
I saw, in *secret* to my Dame How little Cupid humbly came, . *Epig.* iii. 1
in the *secret* darke, that none reproves, . . . *Epith.* 360
With *secret* ayde doest succour and supply, . . . *Epith.* 402
Out of thy silver bowres and *secret* blisse, . . . *H.L.* 23
Through *secret* sparks of his infused fyre, . . . *H.L.* 97
Whether in earth layd up in *secret* store, . . . *H.B.* 37
For she, out of her *secret* threasury . . . *H.H.B.* 246

Secretly. one of you Yet here . . . *secretly* doth hide) . . . *Ro.* xv. 10
he would learne their busines *secretly,* . . . *Hub.* 879
Ladie faire . . . him *secretly* envide, . . . *Mui.* 106
So *secretly* did he his love enjoy . . . *Col.* 145
in his bosome *secretly* there lay An hatefull Snake, . . . I. iv. 31. 3
with his breath . . . Her hollow womb did *secretly* inspyre, I. vii. 9. 4
each one felt *secretly* . . . I. xii. 39. 7
Lurkt false Duessa *secretly* unseene, . . . II. i. 21. 4
secretly doth us procure to fall . . . II. xii. 48. 5
She *secretly* would search each daintie lim, . . . III. i. 36. 6

Secretly—Continued.

secretly he saw, yet note discoure:	III. iii. 50. 4
secretly their hoste did on them lowre,	III. ix. 19. 3
secretly did glyde Into his heart,	III. ix. 29. 4
secretly from thence that night her bore away.	IV. v. 27. 9
With guilefull love did *secretly* agree	IV. vii. 15. 4
secretly his enemies did slay:	IV. viii. 39. 6
secretly out of her prison steale;	IV. viii. 55. 7
to her selfe it *secretly* retayned	V. v. 44. 5
secretly afflict with jealous feare,	V. vi. 4. 6
some life remayned *secretly*;	V. xii. 39. 7
Ne *secretly* from thought of fell revenge surcease:	VI. vi. 43. 9
secretly Will teach to speak,	Am. xliii. 9

Secrets.

sawst the *secrets* of the world unmade,	I. v. 22. 6
brought You to inquere the *secrets* of my griefe,	I. vii. 42. 6
Utterers of *secrets* he from thence debard,	II. ix. 25. 5
dared of all sinnes the *secrets* to unfold.	IV. viii. 31. 9
how canst thou those greater *secrets* know,	V. ii. 43. 7
all the *secrets* of their entrayles sought.	VI. xi. 41. 4
searched all their cels and *secrets* neare:	VI. xii. 24. 4

Sect. now is thought a civile begging *sect*.   Hub. 198

Sectaries.

eke scorne The *Sectaries* thereof,	Hub. 833
The *sectaries* of my celestiall skill,	T.M. 73

Sects. From whence arise diversitie of *sects*,   Hub. 388

Secure.

Gods *secure* feare not her force at all.	Ro. xii. 14
he, that of himselfe is most *secure*,	Van. xii. 13
season more *secure* Shall bring forth fruit.	Gn. 9
But was *secure*; the liker he to fall.	Mui. 382
the whiles he was thereof *secure*.	VI. v. 16. 9

Securely.

Unto sweete sleepe he may *securely* lend	Gn. 142
all the while the fisher did *securely* sleepe.	III. viii. 21. 9
Securely he did after him pursew,	VI. v. 17. 1
Love, that had now long time *securely* slept	H.L. 61

Security.

Lulled the shepheards in such *securitie*,	S.C. May 119
how we may, with most *securitie*,	Hub. 191
Which ye now in *securitie* possesse,	T.M. 365
when he sleepes in most *security*	III. iv. 27. 3
leave Your treasure here in some *security*,	III. x. 42. 2
Where he is shrowded in *security*.	III. xi. 6. 7
did in safe *securitie* abide,	IV. viii. 31. 4

Sedition. Then brought he forth *Sedition*,   V. ix. 48. 5

Seditious. Fild with false rumors and *seditious* trouble,   IV. i. 28. 3

Seduce. did *seduce* The hearts of some   IV. v. 11. 3

See. *See* Sea.

Ravisht I was to *see* so rare a thing,	Bel.¹ v. 9
to *see* th' inconstance of the heavens:	Bel.¹ xi. 3
Then might I *see* . . . The faithfull man	Rev. iii. 1
Then did I *see* the beast and Kings	Rev. iii. 11
Let me no more *see* faire thing	Bel. iv. 12
So manie strange things happened me to *see*,	Pet. i. 2
in a (one¹) moment to *see* lost and drown'd,	Pet. ii. 13
heavenly branches did I *see* arise	Pet. iii. 1
Some noble plant I thought myselfe to *see*:	Pet. iii. 4
each thing at last (length¹) we *see* Doth passe	Pet. v. 7
far as Archer might his level *see*:	Bel.² iii. 4
Much was I mazde, to *see* this monsters kinde	Bel.² viii. 9
a bright flame I did *see* Waving aloft	Bel.² xi. 1
Casting mine eyes farre off, I chaunst to *see*:	Bel.² xiii. 3
Much wondred I to *see* so faire a wall:	Bel.² xiv. 9
to *see* the heavens still wavering	Bel.² xv. 3
To *see* such pleasures gon so suddenly.	Pet.² iv. 14
O let mine eyes no more *see* such a sight !	Pet.² v. 14
Who lists to *see* what ever nature,	Ro. v. 1
O Rome ! thee let him *see*,	Ro. v. 2
her equall match could *see*.	Ro. vi. 8
you to *see* doth th' heaven it selfe appall;	Ro. vii. 6
Like as ye *see* the wrathfull Sea from farre	Ro. xvi. 1
Like as ye *see* fell Boreas with sharpe blast	Ro. xvi. 5
as ye *see* huge flames spred diverslie,	Ro. xvi. 9
these old wals, which ye *see*,	Ro. xviii. 1
they which *see* the dawning day arize;	Ro. xxii. 4
All that which Asie had of prise, Was here to *see*.	Ro. xxx. 12
left of it but these olde markes to *see*,	Ro. xxx. 11
Griefe of good mindes, to *see* goodnesse disgraced !	Van. i. 8
The silly Flie, that no redresse did *see*,	Van. iv. 5
To *see* so goodly thing so soone decayed.	Van. vii. 14
To *see* so great things by so small distrest.	Van. xii. 4
I *see* your teares that from your boughes doe raine,	S.C. Ja. 35
I longd the neighbour towne to *see*,	S.C. Ja. 50
See howe he venteth into the wynd;	S.C. F. 75
sighed to *see* his neare overthrow.	S.C. F. 216
Might *see* the moving of some quicke,	S.C. Mar. 74
But *see*, the Welkin thicks apace,	S.C. Mar. 115
'*See*, where she sits upon the grassie greene,	S.C. Ap. 55
He blusht to *see* another Sunne belowe,	S.C. Ap. 77
'I *see* Calliope speede her to the place,	S.C. Ap. 100
See that your rudenesse doe not you disgrace:	S.C. Ap. 132
To *see* those folkes make such jovysaunce.	S.C. May 25
now I *see* thou speakest of spight,	S.C. May 55
both fresh and lovely to *see*,	S.C. May 183
To *see* the braunche of his body displaie.	S.C. May 196
To *see* thee succeede in thy fathers steade,	S.C. May 203
for the love of the glasse he did *see*.	S.C. May 283
see the dore stand open wyde.	S.C. May 295
where harbrough nis to *see*,	S.C. Jun. 19
fruictfull flocks, bene every where to *see*:	S.C. Jun. 22
Shepheard to *see* them in theyr art outgoe.	S.C. Jun. 64
I *see* thou doest but clatter.	S.C. Jul. 207
I pyne for payne, and they my payne to *see*.	S.C. Au. 18
see, how fast renneth the shepheard swayne	S.C. Au. 32

See—Continued.

When I them *see* so waist,	S.C. Au. 168
All were they lustye as thou didst *see*,	S.C. S. 64
I *see* thou speakest to plaine;	S.C. S. 136
I *see* thee, blessed soule, I *see*	S.C. N. 178
Tode-stoole growne there mought I *se*,	S.C. D. 69
Where other powers farre different I *see*,	Gn. 420
durst those lowest shadowes goe to *see*,	Gn. 438
now the Pylote can no loadstarre *see*,	Gn. 573
Whom ye in goodly seates may placed *see*,	Gn. 595
the sad lakes that Phoebus sunnie rayes Doo never *see*,	Gn. 620
sorie my sad case to *see*,	Hub. 18
no lenger hope I *see*,	Hub. 65
so soone as one might *see* Light	Hub. 108
small oddes I often *see* Twixt them that aske;	Hub. 373
Yee shall our pasport at your pleasure *see*,	Hub. 377
How manie honest men *see* ye arize.	Hub. 419
I *see* you so goodly and so gay In your attyres,	Hub. 590
all the braverie that eye may *see*,	Hub. 608
So wilde a beast so tame ytaught . . . is joy to *see*;	Hub. 626
so brave beasts she loveth best to *see*	Hub. 629
full few which follow them, I *see*,	Hub. 637
all which did such strangenesse in him *see*	Hub. 680
here arriv'd, to *see* if like he found.	Hub. 688
rule and raigne in soveraign *see*,	Hub. 980
yet to prove more true he meant to *see*,	Hub. 1277
To heare their doome, and sad ensample *see*.	Hub. 1378
doo not *see* their owne unhappinesse.	T.M. 150
no where now to *see*;	T.M. 183
To *see* thee, and thy mercie measurelesse !	T.M. 516
See yee the blindfoulded pretie God,	Tetrasticon 1
Nor anie little moniment to *see*,	Ti. 5
With tender ruth to *see* her sore constraint;	Ti. 31
lye in mine owne ashes, as ye *see*,	Ti. 40
To *see* the light of simple veritie Buried	Ti. 171
Sith I doo dailie *see* things highest placed,	Ti. 180
That happie there I maie thee alwaies *see*.	Ti. 308
no word we heare, nor signe now *see*,	Ti. 360
To *see* that vertue should dispised bee	Ti. 450
they *see* not the way of their confusion.	Ti. 458
in my case their owne ensample *see*.	Ti. 462
Then did I *see* a pleasant Paradize,	Ti. 519
see the end of pompe and fleshlie pride !	Ti. 543
did I *see* a Bridge, made all of golde,	Ti. 547
what bootes it to *see* earthlie thing	Ti. 554
Behold (said it) and by ensample *see*,	Ti. 582
all that him so horrible did *see* . . .	Mui. 70
heaped spoyles of bleeding harts to *see*,	Mui. 100
from farre and neare, To *see* my Lyonesse,	D. 144
My good to heare, and toward joyes to *see* !	D. 280
To *see* all things, and not my love to *see*;	D. 408
I hate to *see*, mine eyes are dimd with teares;	D. 417
Why doo I longer *see* this loathsome light	D. 444
ever as I *see* the starres to fall,	D. 477
For all I *see* is vaine and transitorie,	D. 495
I sore griev'd to *see* his wretched case.	D. 553
So rich a spoile within his power to *see*.	As. 102
The dolefull beare that ever man did *see*,	As. 149
the fairest face that eye mote *see*,	As. 155
The gods, which all things *see*,	As. 181
thether flock to *see* what they did heare	As. 202
wend with him, his Cynthia to *see*;	Col. 186
Let him to sea, and he shall *see* it there.	Col. 207
Where may I the hills and pastures *see*,	Col. 238
In which all pure perfection one may *see*.	Col. 343
that elsewhere I ever yet did *see*,	Col. 558
In her thou maist them all assembled *see*,	Col. 570
Some part of those enormities did *see*,	Col. 665
their owne misfaring will not *see*:	Col. 758
As if his godhead thou didst present *see*.'	Col. 834
Excelling all that ever ye did *see*.	Col. 934
doe *see* And heare the languors	Col. 947
In which trew honor yee may fashioned *see*,	Ded. Son. x. 10
A fairer crew yet no where could I *see*	Ded. Son. xvii. 10
plain none might her *see*, nor she *see* any plaine.	I. i. 16. 9
His Lady, sad to *see* his sore constraint,	I. i. 19. 1
To *see* th' unkindly Impes, . . . Devoure	I. i. 26. 2
Who see your vanquisht foes before you lye,	I. i. 27. 4
cleane dismayd to *see* so uncouth sight,	I. i. 50. 1
all in rage to *see* his skilfull might Deluded so,	I. ii. 2. 5
see where your false Lady doth her honor staine.'	I. ii. 4. 9
gan she wail and weepe to *see* that woeful stowre.	I. ii. 7. 9
Art thou misshaped thus, as now I *see* ?	I. ii. 34. 3
whome ye *see* Now not a Lady, but a seeming tree;	I. ii. 35. 4
I chaunst to *see* her in her proper hew,	I. ii. 40. 6
'Her neather partes . . . I could not *see*;	I. ii. 41. 2
When such I *see*, . . . all for pitty I could dy.	I. iii. 1. 9
sad to *see* her sorrowfull constraint,	I. iii. 8. 3
they might *see* One pricking towards them	I. iii. 33. 1
'Why Archimago, lucklesse syre, What doe I *see* ?	I. iii. 39. 2
her selfe so mockt to *see* By him,	I. iii. 40. 2
till at last they *see* A goodly building	I. iv. 2. 5
Why they were come her roiall state to *see*,	I. iv. 13. 8
gnasht his teeth to *see* Those heapes of gold	I. iv. 31. 6
to *see* this recreaunt knight, No knight, but treachour	I. iv. 41. 4
Joyous to *see* his ymage in mine eye,	I. iv. 45. 6
warlike feates of both those knights to *see*.	I. v. 5. 5
The sonnes of Day he favoureth, I *see*,	I. v. 25. 7
O welcome, child ! whom I have longd to *see*,	I. v. 27. 8
heavens ! that doe . . . heavenly virgin thus outraged *see*,	I. vi. 5. 7

See—*Continued.*

yet quakes . . . to *see* the Lyon looke so grim.	I. vi. 10. 9
Sometimes dame Venus selfe he seemes to *see;*	I. vi. 16. 6
Flocke all about to *see* her lovely face;	I. vi. 18. 4
loving mother came . . . to *see* her little sonne;	I. vi. 27. 2
To *see* his syre and ofspring auncient.	I. vi. 30. 4
These eies did *see* that knight	I. vi. 36. 9
'I chaunst this day, . . . To *see* two knights,	I. vi. 38. 3
To *see* their blades so greedily imbrew,	I. vi. 38. 7
'how might I *see* The thing	I. vi. 39. 3
none can breath, nor *see,* nor heare at will,	I. vii. 13. 7
To *see* what end of fight should him befall	I. viii. 2. 9
To *see* his loved Squyre into such thraldom brought:	I. viii. 15. 9
the Prince, . . . threatning high his dreadfull stroke, did *see,*	I. viii. 22. 2
all things *see* With equall eye,	I. viii. 27. 6
to *see* him made her glad,	I. viii. 42. 2
my selfe now mated, as ye *see;*	I. ix. 12. 2
joyd to *see* her lover languish and lament:	I. ix. 27. 9
lever had I die then *see* his deadly face.'	I. ix. 32. 9
entred in, a spatious court they *see,*	I. x. 6. 2
'Straunge thing it is an errant knight to *see* Here	I. x. 10. 1
'Thy selfe to *see,* . . . 'I hither came;	I. x. 11. 1
greatly joy each other for to *see:*	I. x. 15. 4
her to *see* should be but troublesome.'	I. x. 16. 7
come, thou man of earth, and *see* the way,	I. x. 52.2
he might *see* The blessed Angels	I. x. 56. 1
emongst those Saints whom thou doest *see,*	I. x. 61. 6
Una, who him joyd to *see;*	I. x. 68. 6
Whom I from far *see* on the walles appeare,	I. xi. 3. 4
The knight was wroth to *see* his stroke beguyld,	I. xi. 25. 1
Behold! I *see* the haven nigh at hand	I. xii. 1. 1
To *see* the face of that victorious man,	I. xii. 9. 3
Tounge hates to tell the rest that eye to *see* abhord.'	II. i. 11. 9
Great pitty is to *see* you thus dismayd,	II. i. 14. 3
Ne would she speake, ne *see,* ne yet be seene,	II. i. 15. 6
desyre To *see* faire heavens face,	II. i. 17. 4
see the salving of your blotted name.'	II. i. 20. 7
To *see* the Redcrosse thus advaunced hye;	II. i. 23. 6
To *see* sad pageaunts of mens miseries,	II. i. 36. 3
childe, whom thus ye *see* with blood defild.	II. i. 50. 9
three valiaunt knights to *see* Three combates joine	II. ii. 26. 1
Did *see* and grieve at his bold fashion;	II. ii. 37. 7
none might *see* How they . . . enwrapped bee:	II. iii. 27. 8
didst not thou *see* a bleeding Hynde,	II. iii. 32. 7
Such wounded beast as that I did not *see,*	II. iii. 33. 5
There maist thou best be seene, and best maist *see:*	II. iii. 39. 8
all might *see* He had not trayned bene	II. iii. 46. 4
He saw from far, or seemed for to *see,*	II. iv. 3. 2
Ne ever thing that she could think or *see,*	II. iv. 20. 7
I should *see* that would me nearer move,	II. iv. 24. 8
That on his shield depainted he did *see:*	II. v. 11. 8
ill beseemes thee, such as I thee *see,*	II. v. 17. 6
where he them bound did *see,*	II. v. 18. 8
Guyon standing by their uncouth strife does *see.*	II. v. 20. 9
should he but his owne deare Lord there *see,*	II. vi. 43. 3
To *see* my Lord so deadly damnifyde?	II. vi. 43. 8
Burning in flames, yet no flames can I *see,*	II. vi. 45. 3
To *see* Pyrochles there so rudely rage;	II. vi. 48. 7
'Pyrochles! what is this I *see?*	II. vi. 49. 1
when I thee present *see* In daunger	II. vi. 49. 6
led downe To *see* his secrete store.	II. vii. Arg.
'Come thou,' (quoth he) 'and *see.*'	II. vii. 20. 5
As eie of man did never *see* before,	II. vii. 31. 5
That living eye before did never *see;*	II. vii. 38. 2
that all men might it *see.*	II. vii. 45. 3
Clothed with leaves, that none the wood mote *see,*	II. vii. 53. 8
if that thou be such as I thee *see,*	II. vii. 59. 8
Soone shalt thou *see,* and then beleeve for troth,	II. viii. 22. 3
With so fresh hew uprysing him to *see,*	II. viii. 54. 3
I live this day, and *see* my foes subdewd,	II. viii. 55. 6
even heven rejoyced her sweete face to *see.*	II. ix. 18. 9
to *see* the mayd So straungely passioned,	II. ix. 41. 8
to *see* His goodly reason	II. ix. 54. 6
did sad Brunchildis *see* The greene shield dyde	II. x. 24. 6
To *see* a cruell fight doen by the prince	II. xi. 4. 9
through his carcas one might playnly *see.*	II. xi. 38. 3
Like did he never heare, like did he never *see.*	II. xi. 40. 9
that grisely mouth did *see* Sucking the seas	II. xii. 6. 1
a goodly Ship did *see*	II. xii. 19. 1
On th' other side they *see* that perilous Poole,	II. xii. 20. 1
Suddeine they *see* from midst of all the Maine	II. xii. 21. 5
Such as Dame Nature selfe mote feare to *see,*	II. xii. 23. 2
whom though we do not *see,*	II. xii. 47. 8
Through guilefull semblants which he makes us *see:*	II. xii. 48. 6
Through every channell running one might *see;*	II. xii. 60. 4
sweet and faire to *see,*	II. xii. 62. 2
through the waves one might the bottom *see,*	II. xii. 62. 7
see, whoso fayre thing doest faine to *see,*	II. xii. 74. 2
see the Virgin Rose, how sweetly shee	II. xii. 74. 4
That fairer seemes the lesse ye *see* her may.	II. xii. 74. 6
see soone after how more bold and free	II. xii. 74. 7
see soone after how she fades and falls away.	II. xii. 74. 9
nets, which oft we woven *see* Of scorched deaw,	II. xii. 77. 8
to *see* Him his nobility so fowle deface:	II. xii. 79. 3
that none the signes might *see:*	II. xii. 80. 4
some for wrath to *see* their captive Dame:	II. xii. 86. 5
'*See* the mind of beastly man,	II. xii. 87. 1
Thy selfe thou covet to *see* pictured,	III. Pr. 4. 2
In mirrours more then one her selfe to *see;*	III. Pr. 5. 6
Which outrage when those gentle knights did *see,*	III. i. 18. 1
'now may ye all *see* plaine,	III. i. 29. 7
'Too well we *see,*' (saide they)	III. i. 30. 1
Which stately manner whenas they did *see,*	III. i. 33. 5
By knowen signes and passions which I *see,*	III. ii. 33. 3
go to *see* that dreadful place.	III. iii. 8. 2
full shortly I her dead shall *see.*'	III. iii. 16. 9
If ay more goodly creature thou didst *see?*	III. iii. 32. 2
that men them faire may *see.*	III. iii. 44. 9
when I shall my selfe in safety *see,*	III. iv. 10. 6
gaping at their gate, and wondred them to *see.*	III. iv. 32. 9
greater crosse To *see* frends grave,	III. iv. 38. 9
ne lettest *see* The beautie of his worke?	III. iv. 56. 3
all that lewdnesse love doe hate the light to *see.*	III. iv. 58. 9
Wonder it is to *see* in diverse mindes	III. v. 1. 1
That ever living eye, I weene, did *see.*	III. v. 8. 3
Els shall thy loving Lord thee *see* no more;	III. v. 26. 7
To succor wretched wights whom we captived *see.*'	III. v. 36. 9
Jove laught on Venus from his soverayne *see,*	III. vi. 2. 7
Wondred to *see* her belly so upblone,	III. vi. 9. 8
everie one did aske, did he him *see?*	III. vi. 14. 2
To *see* so faire thinges mard and spoiled	III. vi. 40. 2
Me seemes I *see* Amintas wretched fate,	III. vi. 45. 8
To *see* his whole yeares labor lost so soone,	III. vii. 34. 8
brutishly brought up, that nev'r did fashions *see.*'	III. vii. 57. 9
grudg'd to *see* the counterfet should shame The thing	III. viii. 5. 5
if thee list to *see* thy Courser ronne,	III. viii. 17. 4
As pittying to *see* her waile and weepe:	III. viii. 21. 8
no more we can the mayn-land *see,*	III. viii. 24. 3
See how the heavens . . . Doe succor send	III. viii. 29. 2
when Proteus she did *see* her by.	III. viii. 33. 9
did ye *see* Just cause of dread,	III. viii. 48. 5
'These eyes did *see* that they will ever rew T' have seene,'	III. viii. 49. 1
they dissembled what they did not *see,*	III. ix. 19. 5
The fairest woman-wight that ever eie did *see.*	III. ix. 21. 9
seeing still the more desir'd to *see,*	III. ix. 24. 2
False love! why do men say thou canst not *see,*	III. x. 4. 3
To *see* th' unkindnes of his Hellenore.	III. x. 45. 5
till safe him selfe he *see* from jeopardy.	III. x. 53. 9
to *see* what new successe Mote him befall	III. xi. 20. 2
To *see* him in his soverayne majestee	III. xi. 33. 3
to *see* what was become Of all those persons	III. xii. 30. 2
long'd revenge to *see:*	III. xii. 34. 9
There did he *see,* that most on earth him joy'd,	III. xii. 44. *or.* 1
hope, . . . to *see* her own deare knight,	III. xii. 44. 8
Was then assembled deeds of armes to *see:*	IV. i. 9. 4
Her face most fowle and filthy was to *see,*	IV. i. 27. 1
one him scarce could *see.*	IV. i. 35. 9
desir'd their cause of strife to *see:*	IV. ii. 22. 1
Glad man was he to *see* that joyous sight,	IV. ii. 23. 1
This happie day . . . In which you safe I *see,*	IV. ii. 23. 6
durst Come *see* the secret of the life of man,	IV. ii. 49. 7
she might *see* her childrens thrids forth brought,	IV. ii. 50. 3
To *see* their thrids so thin as spiders frame,	IV. ii. 50. 8
is of them the shortest, as I *see,*	IV. ii. 52. 5
none did ever *see* More happie creatures	IV. iii. 2. 4
Did ever *see* upon this world to shine,	IV. iii. 3. 6
to *see* the fortune of that fray,	IV. iii. 4. 7
amaz'd the headlesse tronke to *see* Stand up	IV. iii. 21. 2
to *see* their fatall fine,	IV. iii. 37. 5
so to *see* him made her heart to quaile;	IV. iii. 46. 7
Wonder it is that sudden change to *see:*	IV. iii. 49. 2
Triamond, halfe wroth to *see* him staid,	IV. iv. 20. 5
There might ye *see* loose steeds at randon ronne,	IV. iv. 38. 6
the Paragon to *see* Of beauties praise,	IV. v. 9. 8
So many faire did *see*	IV. v. 12. 9
all were glad there Florimell to *see,*	IV. v. 14. 8
Whom when the rest did *see* her to refuse,	IV. v. 21. 1
looking round about him, none could *see;*	IV. v. 44. 8
Weening some heavenly goddesse he did *see,*	IV. vi. 22. 4
Joyous to *see* her safe after long toyle.	IV. vi. 25. 5
I joy to *see* you lout so low	IV. vi. 28. 7
sith meanes, ye *see,* there wants theretoo.	IV. vi. 30. 9
'To tell' (quoth she) 'that what ye *see,* needs not;	IV. vii. 14. 8
Where hardly eye mote *see* bright heavens face	IV. vii. 38. 7
With mild regard to *see* his ruefull plight,	IV. viii. 17. 7
To *see* his foe breath out his spright in vaine:	IV. viii. 46. 2
howld aloud to *see* his Lord there slaine,	IV. viii. 46. 4
she chaunced there to *see* This lovely swaine,	IV. viii. 52. 4
never two so like did living creature *see.*	IV. viii. 55. 9
To *see* the sight perforce that both her eyes were loth.	IV. ix. 9. 9
the other Knights and Squires which them (*him) did *see.*	IV. ix. 11. 9
Such mortall malice wonder was to *see*	IV. ix. 27. 6
to *see* that gentle maide so tost!'	IV. ix. 38. 5
Should happen this with living eye to *see,*	IV. x. 23. 6
to be th' Almighties *see;*	IV. x. 30. 7
soone as they *see* The spring breake forth	IV. x. 45. 3
scarce her way could *see.*	IV. xi. 24. 9
shall *see* Stamford, though now homely hid,	IV. xi. 35. 4
joy likewise this solemne day to *see?*	IV. xi. 40. 5
to learne and *see* The manner of the Gods	IV. xii. 3. 8
vaine, I *see,* my sorrowes to unfold,	IV. xii. 6. 1
the seas, I *see,* by often beating	IV. xii. 7. 1
mourn'd to *see* her losse before her eyne,	IV. xii. 21. 7
To *see* an helplesse evill double griefe doth lend.	IV. xii. 21. 9
those twelve signes, which nightly we doe *see*	V. i. 11. 6
'That ever I this dismall day did *see!*	V. i. 15. 3
his blasphemous head, that all might *see,*	V. ii. 19. 3
All which when Artegall did *see* and heare,	V. ii. 33. 6
doest thou not plainely *see*	V. ii. 37. 4

See—*Continued.*

To *see* the thing, that seem'd so excellent, ... V. iii. 26. 4
suffred all his secret marke to *see:* . . . . V. iii. 34. 6
It's punishment enough that all his shame doe *see.'* . . . . V. iii. 36. 9
Two Ilands, which ye there before you *see* . . . . V. iv. 7. 5
see how much her purpose was deceaved! . . . . V. iv. 10. 5
wend with me, that ye may *see* and know . . . . V. iv. 34. 7
Rather then *see* her people spoiled quight, ... V. iv. 47. 8
From time to time, when thou it best shalt *see,* . . . . V. v. 34. 4
'The tidings sad . . . will needs, I *see,* be rad. . . . . V. vi. 10. 5
By outward signes (as well he might) did *see,* . . . . V. vi. 21. 5
by your change of cheare is easie for to *see.'* . . . . V. vii. 18. 9
doe thy love forlorne in womens thraldome *see.* . . . . V. vii. 21. 9
she the face of her new foe might *see:* . . . . V. vii. 25. 7
To *see* her Lord, that was reported drent . . . . V. vii. 39. 3
I *see* thy pride is nought.' . . . . V. vii. 40. 9
Who when him selfe now well recur'd did *see,* . . . . V. vii. 43. 7
whom ye may *see* There dead on ground. . . . . V. viii. 11. 6
two false Knights, whom there ye lying *see,* . . . . V. viii. 23. 3
all men, which that spectacle did *see,* . . . . V. viii. 44. 8
to *see* her Ladie thence not farre away. . . . . V. ix. 3. 9
To *see* her Ladie, as they did agree; . . . . V. ix. 20. 2
Nigh to the place which ye desir'd to *see:* . . . . V. ix. 20. 5
shall ye *see* my soverayne Lady Queene, ... V. ix. 20. 6
Straunge there to *see,* it did them much amaze, ... V. ix. 24. 3
sate on high, that she might all men *see* . . . . V. ix. 27. 3
when he none of all those knights did *see* . . . . V. x. 15. 3
And that so wretched one, as ye do *see,* . . . . V. x. 21. 8
any yron eyes to *see* it would agrize. . . . . V. x. 28. 9
no whit of them remayning one may *see.* . . . . V. x. 29. 9
To *see* if entrance there as yet obtaine he might. . . . . V. x. 33. 9
did about them throng To *see* the man, ... V. xi. 34. 8
Sith no redemption nigh she did nor heare nor *see.* . . . . V. xii. 11. 9
see not perfect things but in a glas: . . . . VI. Pr. 5. 5
'I such a Beast did *see,* . . . . VI. i. 9. 2
that scarse did *see* Yet seventeene yeares, ... VI. ii. 5. 3
'The knight, as ye did *see,* on horsebacke was, ... VI. ii. 10. 1
'Whom when my knight did *see* so lovely faire, ... VI. ii. 17. 1
(as this young man did *see*) . . . . VI. ii. 22. 3
Most joyfull man her sire was her to *see,* . . . . VI. iii. 19. 1
the Lady was full faire to *see,* . . . . VI. iii. 20. 8
and mockt to *see* him like to swim: . . . . VI. iii. 34. 4
seldome yet did living creature *see* . . . . VI. iii. 40. 8
Whom now in deadly daunger he did *see,* . . . . VI. iii. 43. 8
to *see* that chearefull sight. . . . . VI. iii. 45. 5
no lesse encombrance she did *see,* . . . . VI. iv. 10. 3
posteritie, Which we might *see* after our selves remaine . . . . VI. iv. 31. 4
ruth it was to *see* him so lament: . . . . VI. v. 4. 6
For pitty so to *see* him overset: . . . . VI. v. 22. 5
as now ye *see,* . . . . VI. v. 28. 1
Whom Gods doe hate, and heavens abhor to *see;* . . . . VI. vi. 10. 2
To *see* him so bedight with bloodie gore, ... VI. vii. 14. 4
What meaneth this which here I *see* before? . . . . VI. vii. 14. 7
Which ye may *see* yet all about me steeme. . . . . VI. vii. 15. 6
as ye may *see* there in the stound.' . . . . VI. vii. 16. 9
Where he himselfe might *see* his foeman slaine; . . . . VI. vii. 17. 3
The picture of his punishment might *see,* . . . . VI. vii. 27. 4
That he might *see* his men, ... VI. vii. 33. 9
To *see* her sore lament . . . . VI. vii. 44. 9
As if it them should grieve to *see* his punishment. . . . . VI. viii. 4. 9
As loth to *see* or to be seene at all: . . . . VI. viii. 5. 6
'*See* you, Sir Knight, The greatest shame . . . . VI. viii. 6. 1
See, how they doe that Squire beat . . . . VI. viii. 6. 6
See, how they doe the Lady hale and draw! . . . . VI. viii. 6. 7
face Like the faire yvory shining they did *see,* . . . . VI. viii. 37. 3
in the midst a Shepheard piping he did *see.* . . . . VI. x. 10. 9
There he did *see* that pleased much his sight, ... VI. x. 11. 6
Right happy thou that mayst them freely *see!* . . . . VI. x. 19. 8
all them plaine may *see,* . . . . VI. x. 24. 4
'Such were those Goddesses which ye did *see;* . . . . VI. x. 25. 1
rashly sought that which I mote not *see.'* . . . . VI. x. 29. 7
that sore she griev'd to *see,* . . . . VI. xi. 23. 1
sought the woods, but no man could *see* there; . . . . VI. xi. 26. 4
'That ever I did live this day to *see,* . . . . VI. xi. 29. 2
here to *see* all desolate and wast, ... VI. xi. 32. 7
to *see* what should be donne; . . . . VI. xi. 35. 4
did him compell To *see* the hatefull sunne, ... VI. xii. 35. 5
To *see* him leade that Beast in bondage strong; . . . . VI. xii. 37. 5
Rejoyced much to *see* his captive plight, ... VI. xii. 37. 8
To *see* that mortall eyes have never seene; . . . . VII. vi. 32. 3
a fayrer flood may no man *see.* . . . . VII. vi. 40. 9
longed foolishly To *see* her naked . . . . VII. vi. 42. 9
what time he might her Lady *see* . . . . VII. vi. 43. 8
Yet *see* we soone decay; . . . . VII. vii. 18. 3
We daily *see* new creatures to arize, ... VII. vii. 18. 6
The beasts we daily *see* massacred dy . . . . VII. vii. 19. 2
We *see* his parts, . . . To lose their heat . . . . VII. vii. 24. 3
To thousand sorts of Change we subject *see:* . . . . VII. vii. 25. 3
must, Which he was treading in the wine-fats *see,* . . . . VII. vii. 39. 3
Ne ought to *see,* but like a shade to weene, ... VII. vii. 46. 4
we *see* not how they are mov'd and swayd . . . . VII. vii. 49. 2
what we *see* not, who shall us perswade? . . . . VII. vii. 49. 5
her face and countenance every day We changed *see* . . . . VII. vii. 50. 7
According as thy selfe doest *see* and heare, ... VII. vii. 56. 7
none no more change shal *see.'* . . . . VII. vii. 59. 5
Jove confirm'd in his imperiall *see.* . . . . VII. vii. 59. 7
Whose light doth lighten all that here we *see.* . . . . *Am.* ix. 14
See! how the Tyrannesse doth joy to *see* . . . . *Am.* x. 5
I thinke that I a new Pandora *see,* . . . . *Am.* xxiv. 8
See! how the stubborne damzell doth deprave . . . . *Am.* xxix. 1

See—*Continued.*

if your selfe in me ye playne will *see,* . . . . *Am.* xlv. 13
ye high hevens, that all this sorowe *see,* . . . . *Am.* xlvi. 9
Doe I not *see* that fayrest ymages . . . . *Am.* li. 1
in theyr Maker ye them best may *see.* . . . . *Am.* liii. 14
Strange thing, me seemd, to *see* a beast so wyld, ... *Am.* lxvii. 13
I joy to *see* how, in your drawen work, ... *Am.* lxxi. 1
all thensforth eternall peace shall *see* . . . . *Am.* lxxi. 13
Was it a dreame, or did I *see* it playne; . . . . *Am.* lxxvii. 1
when I hope to *see* theyr trew object, ... *Am.* lxxviii. 11
Ceasse then, myne eyes, to seeke her selfe to *see;* . . . . *Am.* lxxviii. 13
For that your selfe ye dayly such doe *see:* . . . . *Am.* lxxix. 2
Ne ought I *see,* though in the clearest day, ... *Am.* lxxxvii. 5
'*See!* thou thyselfe likewise art lyttle made, ... *Epig.* iv. 13
sad to *see* him pained. . . . . *Epig.* iv. 34
The joyfulst day that ever sunne did *see.* . . . . *Epith.* 116
did ye *see* So fayre a creature . . . . *Epith.* 167
if ye saw that which no eyes can *see,* . . . . *Epith.* 185
at last I *see* it gloome, ... *Epith.* 285
That no man may us *see;* . . . . *Epith.* 320
hob Goblins, names whose sence we *see* not, ... *Epith.* 343
with equall insight *see* The ods twixt both, ... *Com. Son.* ii. 9
Fraile men, whose eyes seek heavenly things to *see,* . . . . *H.L.* 118
They deigne to *see,* and seeing it still dye. . . . . *H.L.* 133
Thou, being blind, letst him not *see* his feares, ... *H.L.* 226
no man may it *see* With sinfull eyes, ... *H.B.* 38
we nature *see* of art Exceld, ... *H.B.* 83
they did *see* And know ech other . . . . *H.B.* 202
all, that like the beautie which they *see,* . . . . *H.B.* 208
See more then any other eyes can *see,* . . . . *H.B.* 234
Therein they *see,* through amorous eye-glaunces, ... *H.B.* 239
wonders . . . that others never *see!* . . . . *H.B.* 247
Where I may *see* those admirable things . . . . *H.H.L.* 3
For Love doth love the thing belov'd to *see,* . . . . *H.H.L.* 118
When him the silly Shepheards came to *see,* . . . . *H.H.L.* 230
plainely *see* Th' Idee of his pure glorie . . . . *H.H.L.* 283
Which in my weake distraughted mynd I *see;* . . . . *H.H.B.* 14
Endure their Captains flaming head to *see?* . . . . *H.H.B.* 60
For farre above these heavens, which here we *see,* . . . . *H.H.B.* 64
That are unable else to *see* his face, ... *H.H.B.* 117
how can we *see* with feeble eyne . . . . *H.H.B.* 123
Angels, which her goodly face behold And *see* at will, ... *H.H.B.* 233
And letteth them her lovely face to *see,* . . . . *H.H.B.* 255
In which they *see* such admirable things, ... *H.H.B.* 260
Is fixed all on that which now they *see;* . . . . *H.H.B.* 272
Two fairer Birds I yet did never *see;* . . . . *Proth.* 39
Ran all in haste to *see* that silver brood, ... *Proth.* 56

Seed. An Hercules so ranke *seed* to represse, ... *Ro.* x. 10
I will not match her with Latonaes *seede,* . . . . *S.C.* Ap. 86
the *seede* that in my youth was sowne . . . . *S.C.* D. 101
before That Ceres *seede* of mortall men were knowne, ... *Gn.* 207
Dan Perseus, borne of heavenly *seed,* . . . . *Ti.* 648
creatures . . . of his fruitful *seed;* . . . . I. i. 21. 8
The hight of three the tallest sonnes of mortall *seed.* . . . . I. vii. 8. 9
as a stocke he left unto his *seede.* . . . . I. x. 38. 7
the praiers of the righteous *sead* . . . . I. x. 51. 7
nest Of many Dragonettes, his fruitfull *seede:* . . . . I. xii. 10. 6
Doth beare the fayrest flowre in honourable *seed.* . . . . II. iii. 10. 9
difference Betweene the vulgar and the noble *seed,* . . . . II. iv. 1. 3
The fire of sparkes, the weede of little *seede,* . . . . II. iv. 35. 4
sparks, *seed,* drops, and filth, do thus delay; . . . . II. iv. 35. 6
the springing *seed* outweed, ... II. iv. 35. 7
all his *seede* the curse doth often cleave, ... II. viii. 29. 4
all that seemed fitt for kingly *seed:* . . . . II. x. 27. 4
The fierce Spumador, borne of heavenly *seed,* . . . . II. xi. 19. 8
Be it worthy of thy race and royall *sead,* . . . . III. ii. 33. 4
sprong of *seed* terrestriall, ... III. iii. 26. 5
The royall *seed,* the antique Trojan blood, ... III. iii. 42. 8
of immortall *seed* To beene ybredd . . . . III. iv. 38. 1
her wombe did fill With hevenly *seed,* . . . . III. iv. 41. 6
Dayes dearest children be the blessed *seed* . . . . III. iv. 59. 5
noble kind at first was sure of heavenly *seed.* . . . . IV. viii. 33. 9
the Basiliske, of serpents *seede,* . . . . IV. viii. 39. 7
both borne of heavenly *seed,* . . . . IV. x. 34. 3
all the Sea-gods and their fruitfull *seede,* . . . . IV. xi. 8. 2
to this feast with Neptunes *seed* was dight. . . . . IV. xi. 16. 9
three thousand more there were Of th' Oceans *seede,* . . . . IV. xi. 52. 7
Whose fruitfull *seede* farre passeth those in land, ... IV. xii. 1. 3
being ment of mortall creatures *sead,* . . . . IV. xii. 27. 3
the wicked *seede* of vice Began to spring; . . . . V. i. 1. 3
their lives did strow, Like fruitles *seede,* . . . . V. vii. 31. 9
As thicke as doth the *seede* after the sowers hand: . . . . V. xii. 7. 9
Or surely borne of some Heroicke *sead,* . . . . VI. ii. 25. 8
The *seede* of all this evill first doth spring, ... VI. vi. 8. 2
since th' Earths cursed *seed* Sought to assaile . . . . VII. vi. 20. 2
'Of that bad *seed* is this bold woman bred, ... VII. vi. 21. 1
As well those that are sprung of heavenly *seed,* . . . . VII. vii. 3. 3
Nought leaving but their barren ashes without *seede.* . . . . VII. vii. 24. 9
The *seed* of Saturne and faire Nais, ... VII. vii. 40. 9
divine, and borne of heavenly *seed;* . . . . *Am.* lxxix. 10
the chast wombe informe with timely *seed,* . . . . *Epith.* 386
When she in fleshly *seede* is eft enraced, ... *H.B.* 114
Fit to receive the *seede* of vertue strewed; . . . . *H.B.* 138
begot of any earthly *Seede,* . . . . *Proth.* 65

Seeded. Like as the *seeded* field greene grasse first showes, ... *Ro.* xxx. 1

Seeds. The *seedes,* of which all things at first were bred, ... *Ro.* xxii. 13
the fruitfull *seades* Of all things living, ... III. vi. 8. 3
Now growen great, at first of little *seedes,* . . . . IV. i. 25. 4
The *seedes* of evill wordes and factious deedes; . . . . IV. i. 25. 5
those same cursed *seedes* doe also serve To her for bread, ... IV. i. 26. 1

Seeds—*Continued.*
dyes like ill grounded *seeds*. . . . IV. iv. 1. 9
heavenly *seedes* of bounty soveraine, . . . VI. Pr. 3. 7
in her mynde the *seeds* Of perfect love did sow, . . . VI. ix. 45. 7
in a bag all sorts of *seeds* ysame, . . . VII. vii. 32. 7

Seeing. *seing* hir striken fall . . . *Bel.*[1] xi. 13
Nay, but thy *seeing* will not serve, . . . *S.C.* Mar. 43
That *seeing*, I levelde againe . . . *S.C.* Mar. 85
the shepheard, *seeing* (**seing*) day appeare, . . . *Gn.* 70
Seeing the doubled shadowes low to fall, . . . *Gn.* 318
Narcisse, that, in a well *Seeing* his beautie, . . . *Gn.* 680
seeing kindly sleep refuse to doe His office, . . . *Hub.* 21
Seeing them wander loosly, . . . *Hub.* 244
Seeing the world, in which they bootles boad, Had wayes enough . . . *Hub.* 400
all her sisters, *seeing* her doo soe, . . . *T.M.* 297
her Sisters, *seeing* her sad mood, . . . *T.M.* 417
all her sisters, *seeing* her sad stowre, . . . *T.M.* 597
seeing her so piteouslie perplexed, . . . *Ti.* 20
I, it *seeing*, dearelie did lament. . . . *Ti.* 504
Who, *seeing* him, with secret joy therefore . . . *Mui.* 393
seeing readie tide, He rusheth forth, . . . *Mui.* 405
She lookt about, and *seeing* one in mayle, . . . I. i. 16. 5
His Lady, *seeing* all that chaunst from farre, . . . I. i. 27. 1
seeing . . . The doubtfull ballaunce equally to sway, . . . I. ii. 38. 1
seeing by her side the Lyon stand, . . . I. iii. 11. 5
Whome *seeing* such, . . . hee durst not show Him selfe . . . I. iii. 26. 3
The wise Southsayer, *seeing* so sad sight, . . . I. v. 8. 8
Seeing the gored woundes to gape so wyde, . . . I. v. 9. 8
His cruell step-dame, *seeing* what was donne, . . . I. v. 39. 1
They, *seeing* Una, towardes her gan wend, . . . I. x. 15. 1
seeing Mercie, that his steps upbare . . . I. x. 44. 4
as an Eagle, *seeing* pray appeare, . . . I. xi. 9. 5
seeing him from far so fierce to pricke, . . . II. i. 26. 1
That *seeing*, good Sir Guyon could uneath . . . II. i. 56. 5
seeing him ryde so ranck, . . . II. iii. 6. 7
seeing one, that shone in armour fayre, . . . II. iii. 11. 3
Seeing at last her selfe from daunger rid, . . . II. iii. 36. 5
Whom Guyon *seeing* stoup, . . . II. v. 12. 1
The knight, him *seeing* labour so in vaine, . . . II. vii. 59. 1
The Palmer *seeing* his lefte empty place, . . . II. viii. 9. 1
Which *seeing*, stout Bunduca up arose, . . . II. x. 54. 6
gentle Alma, *seeing* it so late, . . . II. x. 77. 5
the Prince, *seeing* her wofull plight, . . . II. xi. 16. 4
The Palmer, *seeing* them in safetie past, . . . II. xii. 9. 1
Which *seeing*, good Sir Guyon deare besought . . . III. i. 5. 1
Her tender babe, it *seeing* safe appeare, . . . III. ii. 11. 8
The doubtfull Mayd, *seeing* her selfe descryde, . . . III. iii. 20. 1
The which his mother *seeing* gan to feare . . . III. iv. 24. 4
That *seeing*, now the only last of three . . . III. v. 24. 1
Which *seeing* fayre Belphoebe gan to feare, . . . III. v. 49. 1
his sad mother, *seeing* his sore plight, . . . III. vii. 20. 6
seeing none in place, he gan to make Exceeding mone, . . . III. vii. 45. 3
Who *seeing* her gan streight upstart, . . . III. viii. 9. 8
seeing with that Chorle so faire a wight, . . . III. viii. 12. 1
seeing nigh him jeopardy extreme, . . . III. viii. 16. 8
The knight, him *seeing* flie, . . . III. viii. 19. 1
seeing them resolvd indeed To flame the gates, . . . III. ix. 18. 1
seeing still the more desir'd to see, . . . III. ix. 24. 2
th' old man *seeing* wel, . . . III. ix. 53. 6
Cupid selfe, it *seeing*, close did smyle . . . III. x. 5. 7
ready *seeing* him with her to fly, . . . III. x. 14. 2
Malbecco, *seeing* how his losse did lye, . . . III. x. 17. 2
seeing him behind a stranger knight, . . . III. xi. 13. 3
Which the bold Virgin *seeing* . . . III. xi. 13. 8
Ne *seeing* could her wonder satisfie, . . . III. xi. 49. 7
Th' Enchaunter . . . *Seeing* his worke now wasted, . . . III. xii. 43. 9
seeing his so prowd And boastfull chalenge, . . . IV. i. 10. 5
the rest him *seeing* lie on ground Ran hastily, . . . IV. i. 43. 3
The aged Dame, him *seeing* so enraged, . . . IV. i. 54. 1
whom Paridell *Seeing* so faire indeede, . . . IV. ii. 7. 7
Till *seeing* her, that Florimell did seme, In doubt . . . IV. ii. 17. 4
seeing both bent to so bloudy games, . . . IV. ii. 20. 4
seeing it at hand, he swarv'd asyde, . . . IV. iii. 18. 6
Which Cambell *seeing* come . . . IV. iii. 33. 4
Which th' other *seeing* gan his course relent, . . . IV. iv. 7. 1
Whom he now *seeing*, her remembred well, . . . IV. iv. 8. 3
Braggadochio *seeing* had no will To hasten . . . IV. iv. 20. 1
Which Cambell *seeing*, though he could not salve, . . . IV. iv. 27. 1
seeing him come on so furiously, . . . IV. iv. 28. 7
Which Cambell *seeing* much the same envyde, . . . IV. iv. 44. 7
Glauce, *seeing* all that chaunced there, . . . IV. vi. 25. 1
Whom *seeing* flie she speedily poursewed . . . IV. vii. 30. 1
He *seeing* her depart arose up light, . . . IV. vii. 37. 1
seeing his sad plight, her tender heart . . . did emmove, . . . IV. viii. 3. 6
she, them *seeing* past the reach of eare, . . . IV. viii. 36. 7
seeing not how thence he mote remove, . . . IV. viii. 53. 3
Seeing her selfe all soly succourlesse, . . . IV. ix. 18. 6
seeing them through suffrance hartned more, . . . IV. ix. 34. 5
Which *seeing*, Marinell was sore offended . . . IV. xii. 18. 3
Whom *seeing* fit, and with no crime defilde, . . . V. i. 6. 4
seeing then her selfe forsaken so, . . . V. iv. 10. 1
now *seeing* night at dore, . . . V. vi. 22. 1
They *seeing* that let drive at him streightway, . . . V. vi. 29. 8
Seeing his honor . . . Consisted much in that adventures priefe . . . V. vii. 44. 4
seeing her approch gan forward set . . . V. viii. 6. 8
seeing him come still so fiercely on, . . . V. viii. 9. 4
'Which my liege Lady *seeing*, . . . V. viii. 21. 1
seeing all in armour bright as day, . . . V. ix. 24. 2
Seeing that sad ensample them before, . . . V. x. 38. 2

Seeing—*Continued.*
Which Burbon *seeing* her againe assayd; . . . V. xi. 64. 6
Artegall, *seeing* his cruell deed, . . . V. xi. 65. 6
him *seeing* so to rage Willd him to stay, . . . V. xii. 8. 1
seeing him from farre, . . . VI. i. 11. 5
seeing him so fiercely towardes make, . . . VI. i. 19. 2
from the wall him *seeing* so aghast, . . . VI. i. 23. 1
seeing in what daunger he was plast, . . . VI. i. 39. 7
Seeing his face so lovely sterne and coy, . . . VI. ii. 24. 3
his brother, *seeing* mee An infant, . . . VI. ii. 28. 6
Seeing his sharpe assault and cruell stoure, . . . VI. iv. 3. 3
Seeing the ugly Monster passing by, . . . VI. v. 16. 2
seeing one in so great daunger set . . . VI. v. 22. 2
he it *seeing* lightly to him lept, . . . VI. v. 25. 8
Seeing his royall usage and array . . . VI. v. 41. 7
his Dame, him *seeing* in such guize, . . . VI. vi. 32. 5
Where *seeing* him so lie, he left his steed, . . . VI. vii. 11. 6
Ne could with *seeing* satisfie his great desire. . . . VI. viii. 27. 9
seeing nought Which doubt of daunger to her offer mought, . . . VI. viii. 32. 4
one of them, him *seeing* so to sweat, . . . VI. ix. 6. 6
Now *seeing* Calidore left all alone, . . . VI. ix. 16. 2
Which *seeing* Coridon, . . . much was troubled . . . VI. ix. 38. 1
seeing him to mourne, Drew neare, . . . VI. x. 18. 8
seeing them for tender pittie wept; . . . VI. xi. 37. 7
seeing there that did him pittie sore, . . . VI. xii. 9. 6
Seeing her weake and wan . . . VI. xii. 11. 6
The sober mother *seeing* such her mood, . . . VI. xii. 17. 1
seeing Calidore, away he flew, . . . VI. xii. 25. 7
seeing now no more His liberty was left . . . VI. xii. 36. 4
seeing it much wondred at the sight: . . . VI. xii. 37. 6
*and *seeing* it, they gaze on it the more: . . . *Am.* xxxv (*lxxxiii). 6
Seeing my hart through-launced every where . . . *Am.* lvii. 7
Seeing the game from him escapt away, . . . *Am.* lxvii. 2
They deigne to see, and *seeing* it still dye. . . . *H.L.* 133
Which *seeing* now so inly faire to be, . . . *H.B.* 225
seeing her faire eyes so sharpe effect, . . . *H.B.* 244
Th' Almighty, *seeing* their so bold assay, . . . *H.H.L.* 85
Now *seeing* left a waste and emptie place . . . *H.H.L.* 101
Seeing him lie like creature long accurst . . . *H.H.L.* 129

Seek. *See* **Outseek.**
raunge abroad to *seeke*, her food, . . . *Bel.*[2] vi. 5
Him needeth not to *seeke* for usage right Of line, . . . *Ro.* xxvi. 2
Albee my love he *seeke* with dayly suit; . . . *S.C.* Ja. 56
seeke for Queene-apples unrype, . . . *S.C.* Jun. 43
who will *seeke* for unknowne gayne, . . . *S.C.* S. 72
to *seeke* redresse mought little boote; . . . *S.C.* S. 127
I was wont to *seeke* the honey Bee, . . . *S.C.* D. 67
seeke to glose upon the text; . . . *Gn.* Ded. 10
His sense to *seeke* for ease turnes every way: . . . *Gn.* 388
the ships which they did *seeke* to burne. . . . *Gn.* 512
determined to *seeke* Their fortunes farre abroad, . . . *Hub.* 47
To *seeke* my fortune, where I may it mend: . . . *Hub.* 88
I driven am to *seeke* some meanes to live: . . . *Hub.* 250
make them *seeke* for that they wont to scorne, . . . *Hub.* 257
seeke some other way to gaine by giving, . . . *Hub.* 350
These lookes (nought saying) doo a benefice *seeke*, . . . *Hub.* 500
Doo not thou therefore *seeke* a living there, . . . *Hub.* 521
of more private persons *seeke* elswhere, . . . *Hub.* 522
We may *seeke* favour of the best of all?' . . . *Hub.* 618
after we may favour *seeke* to win?' . . . *Hub.* 644
will to Court for shadowes vaine to *seeke*, . . . *Hub.* 912
To come so farre to *seeke* for misery, . . . *Hub.* 946
seeke with slaunder his good name to blot; . . . *Hub.* 1219
cast to *seeke* the Lion where he may, . . . *Hub.* 1316
Doo *seeke* to make us of the world forlorne, . . . *T.M.* 66
So *seeke* we helpe our sorrow to redresse, . . . *T.M.* 351
Now onely *seeke* for pleasure, . . . *T.M.* 468
Seeke . . . To make their memories for ever live; . . . *Ti.* 408
To come to her, and *seeke* her loves delight. . . . *Ti.* 641
'To *seeke* to heare that which cannot be tolde, . . . *D.* 72
seeke alone to weepe, and dye alone.' . . . *D.* 77
Her now I *seek* throughout this earthlie soyle, . . . *D.* 167
Th' importune fates, which vengeance on me *seeke*, . . . *D.* 387
why *seeke* I to prolong My wearie daies . . . *D.* 439
To *seek* abroad, of daunger nought ydrad, . . . *As.* 87
in those wandring stremes *Seek* waies unknowne, . . . *Col.* 211
Abandon quiet home to *seeke* for it, . . . *Col.* 686
voydnesse to *seeke* full satietie. . . . *Col.* 850
seeke to be medicynd Of her that first did stir . . . *Col.* 877
If all the world to *seeke* I overwent, . . . *Ded.Son.* xvii. 9
Enforst to *seeke* some covert nigh at hand, . . . I. i. 7. 1
through their iron sides . . . Does *seeke* to perce; . . . I. ii. 17. 6
In wildernesse . . . strayd, To *seeke* her knight; . . . I. iii. 3. 5
To *seeke* her strayed Champion if she might attayne. . . . I. iii. 8. 9
pas, In waies unknowne, her wandring knight to *seeke*, . . . I. iii. 21. 4
to *seeke* adventure in straunge place; . . . I. iii. 29. 2
from one to other Ynd, Him for to *seeke*, . . . I. vi. 2. 8
to that forrest came To *seeke* his kindred, . . . I. vi. 20. 3
to the wood she goes, to . . . *seeke* her spouse . . . I. vi. 22. 4
forth she went to *seeke* him far and wide. . . . I. vii. 2. 5
To *seek* her out with labor and long tyne, . . . I. ix. 15. 7
Nyne monethes I *seek* in vain, . . . I. ix. 15. 9
Arthur on his way To *seeke* his love, . . . I. ix. 20. 2
So few there bee, That . . . *seeke* the right: . . . I. x. 10. 4
seek this path that I to thee presage, . . . I. x. 61. 1
To Faery court thou cam'st to *seek* for fame, . . . I. x. 66. 8
'Fayre sonne of Mars, that *seeke* with warlike spoyle, . . . II. i. 8. 7
is quickly gone To *seeke* that knight, . . . II. i. 13. 3
all I *seeke* is but to have redrest . . . II. i. 48. 4
As wont ye knightes to *seeke* adventures wilde, . . . II. i. 50. 6

Seek—*Continued.*
cast to *seek* him forth through danger . . . II. i. 52. 9
To *seeke* her game: . . . II. iii. 31. 5
from the right way *seeke* to draw him wide, . . . II. iv. 2. 7
To *seeke* Occasion, where so she bee: . . . II. iv. 43. 6
'that does *seeke* Occasion to wrath, . . . II. iv. 44. 1
every way did *seeke* into his life; . . . II. v. 9. 2
So evill thing to *seeke* unto their ayd, . . . II. vii. 14. 8
seek adventures as he with Prince Arthure went. . . . III. i. 2. 9
To *seeke* her lover . . . III. i. 8. 8
here to *seek* for praise and fame. . . . III. ii. 7. 9
spight, The which I *seeke* to wreake, . . . III. ii. 8. 9
Making her *seeke* an unknowne Paramoure, . . . III. iii. 3. 4
To *seeke* adventures which mote him befall, . . . III. iv. 4. 7
Her now I *seeke;* . . . III. v. 4. 8
Of whom ye *seeke* to be most magnifide; . . . III. v. 11. 4
To *seeke* his Lady where he mote her finde; . . . III. v. 12. 2
To *seeke* for hearbes that mote him remedy; . . . III. v. 32. 2
Him for to *seeke,* she left her heavenly hous, . . . III. vi. 12. 1
scorne the joy that Jove is glad to *seeke:* . . . III. vi. 22. 6
'Goe, Dame; goe, *seeke* your boy, . . . III. vi. 24. 2
To *seeke* the fugitive both farre and nere. . . . III. vi. 26. 4
wandring for to *seeke* her lover deare, . . . III. vi. 54. 6
raungd abrode to *seeke* adventures wilde, . . . III. vii. 30. 2
To *seeke* young men to quench her flaming thrust, . . . III. vii. 50. 2
seeke els without hazard of thy hedd.' . . . III. viii. 17. 6
fals to ground to *seeke* for succor theare, . . . III. viii. 33. 5
He was compeld to *seeke* some refuge neare, . . . III. ix. 13. 2
who from East to West will endlong *seeke,* . . . III. ix. 51. 3
To *seeke* her endlong both by sea and lond. . . . III. x. 19. 5
A silly Pilgrim . . . That *seeke* a Lady'— . . . III. x. 25. 7
To *seeke* his wife that was far wandered: . . . III. x. 34. 3
from her went to *seeke* another lott, . . . III. x. 37. 3
let us goe to *seeke* my dearest Dame, . . . III. x. 39. 5
did not *seeke* t' appease their deadly hate, . . . IV. ii. 20. 8
seeke perforce her from you both to take, . . . IV. ii. 24. 8
restraine From bloudy strife, and blessed peace to *seeke,* . . . IV. iii. 47. 8
Which Ladies ought to love, and *seeke* for to obtaine. . . . IV. v. 2. 9
forth did ride, To *seeke* her lov'd, . . . IV. v. 29. 5
Unluckie Mayd, to *seeke* her enemie! . . . IV. v. 29. 6
Unluckie Mayd, to *seeke* him farre and wide, . . . IV. v. 29. 7
forced them to *seeke* some covert bowre, . . . IV. v. 32. 5
That where ye left I may her *seeke,* . . . IV. vi. 34. 9
she went to *seeke* faire Amoret, . . . IV. vi. 46. 6
To *seeke* by flight her fellowship t' eschew, . . . IV. viii. 56. 5
To *seeke* their loves dispersed diversly, . . . IV. ix. 19. 8
forst to *seeke* my lifes deare patronnesse: . . . IV. x. 28. 8
In generation *seeke* to quench their inward fire. . . . IV. x. 46. 9
what doe I their names *seeke* to reherse, . . . IV. xi. 17. 1
Whereby to *seeke* some meanes it to appease. . . . IV. xii. 22. 3
it was not the right which he did *seeke,* . . . V. ii. 49. 2
who list to *seeke* it there.' . . . V. iii. 32. 9
She goes to *seeke* him, . . . V. vi. Arg.
thought to send some one to *seeke* him out; . . . V. vi. 6. 2
to *seeke* her errant Knight; . . . V. vi. 6. 6
To *seeke* her Knight, as Talus her did guide. . . . V. vi. 18. 2
comming downe to *seeke* them where they wond, . . . V. vi. 35. 6
gan for grace and love of her to *seeke;* . . . V. vii. 16. 3
I will not *seeke* the same from you to hide; . . . V. vii. 19. 3
she forward went To *seeke* her love, . . . V. vii. 24. 7
To *seeke* for succour of her and her Peares, . . . V. x. 6. 4
To *seeke* for succour of this Ladies gieft; . . . V. x. 14. 7
it was she the which for helpe did *seeke.* . . . VI. i. 17. 3
his love, which thus ye *seeke* t' obtaine.' . . . VI. i. 27. 5
For his sicke charge some harbour there to *seeke;* . . . VI. iii. 37. 6
To *seeke* if he perchance asleepe were layd, . . . VI. v. 3. 7
To *seeke* some comfort in that sorie case. . . . VI. v. 7. 4
of them all which did his ruine *seeke,* . . . VI. v. 13. 1
To *seeke* some place the which mote yeeld . . . VI. v. 32. 2
If therefore health ye *seeke,* observe this one: . . . VI. vi. 7. 5
Like scattred sheepe, to *seeke* for safetie, . . . VI. vi. 38. 6
him where so he were would *seeke.* . . . VI. vii. 13. 9
fled away . . . To *seeke* for safety; . . . VI. vii. 50. 5
wandring every way To *seeke* for booty, . . . VI. viii. 36. 7
he to *seeke* Serena through the woods did rove. . . . VI. viii. 46. 9
seeke to please; that now is counted wise mens threasure. . VI. xii. 41. 9
seeke by grace and goodnesse to obtaine That place, . . . VII. vi. 34. 2
'Ceasse, Saturnes sonne, to *seeke* by proffers vaine . . . VII. vi. 34. 7
Go *seek* he out that Alane where he may be sought. . . . VII. vii. 9. 9
Leaves, lines, and rymes, *seeke* her to please alone, . . . *Am.* i. 13
seeke some succour both to ease my smart, . . . *Am.* ii. 7
Dayly when I do *seeke* and sew for peace, . . . *Am.* xi. 1
Do *seeke* most pretious things . . . *Am.* xv. 2
What needeth you to *seeke* so farre . . . *Am.* xv. 4
In vaine I *seeke* and sew to her for grace, . . . *Am.* xx. 1
Mongst whome the more I *seeke* to settle peace, . . . *Am.* xliv. 13
seeke first to appease The inward languor . . . *Am.* l. 9
ne favour *seek* of friends: . . . *Am.* lix. 10
seeke each where, where last I sawe her face, . . . *Am.* lxxviii. 3
I *seeke* the fields . . . I *seeke* her bowre . . . *Am.* lxxviii. 5, 6
Ceasse then, myne eyes, to *seeke* her selfe to see; . . . *Am.* lxxviii. 13
Seek with my playnts to match that mournful dove. . . . *Am.* lxxxviii. 8
the wylde wolves, which *seeke* them to devoure, . . . *Epith.* 69
Let no false treason *seeke* us to entrap, . . . *Epith.* 323
wil *seeke,* . . . t' attaine, Unto the type of true Nobility; . . *Com. Son.* ii. 1
Faine would I *seeke* to ease my bitter smart . . . *H.L.* 5
they *seeke* onely, without further care, . . . *H.L.* 101
Fraile men, whose eyes *seek* heavenly things to see, . . . *H.L.* 118
every one doth *seeke* and sew to have it, . . . *H.B.* 153
every one doth *seeke* but to deprave it. . . . *H.B.* 154

Seekest. for Rome in Rome here *seekest,* . . . *Ro.* iii. 1
falsly *seekst* a vertuous wight to shame?' . . . IV. i. 48. 2
thy decay thou *seekst* by thy desire; . . . VII. vii. 59. 3

Seeketh. The stubborne mettall *seeketh* to subdew, . . . V. v. 7. 7
In vaine he *seeketh* others to suppresse, . . . VI. i. 41. 5

Seeking. *Seeking* to kisse her, brok'st the Gods decree, . . . *Gn.* 471
seeking to take occasion . . . to make invasion: . . . *Hub.* 1089
seeking all the forrest busily, . . . *Hub.* 1319
seeking misse, and missing doe lament.' . . . *D.* 168
Still *seeking* him, that from her still did flye; . . . I. iii. 21. 8
Seeking for daunger and adventures vaine? . . . II. vi. 17. 5
seeking medicine whence she was stong, . . . II. xii. 73. 3
From *seeking* praise and deeds of armes abrode, . . . III. i. 1. 8
Seeking the weake oppressed to relieve, . . . III. i. 3. 8
Seeking adventures hard, to exercise Their puissaunce, . . . III. i. 14. 3
seeking him adowne to tread, . . . III. iii. 39. 7
Seeking to match the chaste with th' unchaste Ladies traine.' III. vii. 60. 9
after rest, they, *seeking* farre abrode, . . . III. ix. 49. 4
Seeking adventures in the salvage wood, . . . IV. ii. 45. 2
Seeking adventures where they anie knew. . . . IV. ii. 46. 5
in *seeking* for her children three Long life, . . . IV. iii. 2. 2
In *seeking* him that should her paine assoyle; . . . IV. v. 30. 3
Seeking adventures where he mote heare tell; . . . IV. vii. 42. 3
Him *seeking* evermore, yet no where him descride. . . . IV. viii. 18. 9
seeking long to weet which way she straid, . . . IV. ix. 24. 4
seeking ever since with endlesse paines . . . IV. ix. 38. 3
seeking often entraunce afterwards in vaine. . . . IV. x. 13. 9
By all meanes *seeking* to asswage their ires; . . . V. iv. 4. 7
From *seeking* favour where it doth abound; . . . V. v. 42. 2
seeking thus to salve the Amazon, . . . V. v. 43. 5
Now *seeking* darkenesse, and now *seeking* light, . . . V. vi. 14. 7
By change of place *seeking* to ease her paine; . . . V. vi. 15. 5
Seeking by every way to make some breach; . . . V. viii. 37. 2
Seeking to drive away deepe-rooted dreede . . . V. x. 22. 4
In *seeking* all the woods . . . VI. iv. 16. 3
Find remedie unsought, which *seeking* cannot fynd.' . . . VI. iv. 28. 9
seeking all things meete for remedy; . . . VI. xi. 8. 5
seeking . . . That monstrous Beast by finall force to quell, . VI. xii. 22. 6
Seeking for Right, which I of thee entreat, . . . VII. vii. 14. 3
seeking to aslake thy raging fyre, . . . *H.B.* 4

Seeks. When he is sad, shee *seeks* to make him merie, . . . *T.M.* 137
rather *seekes* my sorrow to augment . . . *T.M.* 425
Ne anie Poet *seekes* him to revive, . . . *Ti.* 223
each one *seeks* with malice, and with strife, . . . *Col.* 690
He *seekes* out mighty charmes . . . I. i. 36. 9
Forsaken Truth long *seekes* her love, . . . I. iii. Arg.
In vaine he *seekes* that having cannot hold. . . . I. vi. 33. 7
him to offend, . . . by open fight, He *seekes,* . . . II. i. 3. 4
Who *seekes* with painfull toile shall honor soonest fynd: . . . II. iii. 40. 9
In vaine *seekes* wonders out of Magick spell.' . . . III. iii. 17. 7
Vaine is the art that *seekes* it selfe for to deceive. . . . IV. vi. 40. 9
seekes to know anothers griefe in vaine, . . . IV. vii. 10. 7
Dolon . . . *seekes* her to entrap. . . . V. vi. Arg.
Seekes to subvert her Crowne and dignity, . . . V. viii. 18. 4
he *seekes* by traytrous traines to spill Her person, . . . V. viii. 19. 3
seekes to save the subject of her skill, . . . V. x. 2. 6
But then she *seeks,* . . . To force me live, . . . *Am.* xi. 11
mutuall good-will, *Seekes* . . . to salve each others wound: *Am.* lxv. 12
Seekes to enlarge his lasting progenie; . . . *H.L.* 105

Seel. Braies out her latest breath, and up her eies doth *seele.* II. i. 38. 9

Seeled. eyes . . . *seeled* up with death . . . I. vii. 23. 9

Seeling. *See* **Ceiling.**

Seely. The *seely* man, seeing him ryde so ranck, . . . II. iii. 6. 7
'Me, *seely* wretch, she so at vauntage caught, . . . III. vii. 51. 1

Seem. *See* **Beseem.**
The top therof a pot did *seeme* to beare, . . . *Bel.*[2] iii. 5
Did *seeme* to match the Gods in Majestie. . . . *Bel.*[2] xv. 6
doth *seeme* to sweepe The fomie waves . . . *Van.* v. 4
she did *seeme* to daunce, as in delight, . . . *Van.* ix. 7
May *seeme* he lovd, or els some care he tooke; . . . *S.C.* Ja. 9
hanging heads did *seeme* his carefull case to weepe. . . . *S.C.* Ja. 78
lighter *seeme* than this Gnats idle name. . . . *Gn.* 8
seeme to flame out flakes of flashing fyre, . . . *Gn.* 263
we are as honest as we *seeme,* . . . *Hub.* 376
seeme as Saintlike as Saint Radegund: . . . *Hub.* 497
Then would he *seeme* a Farmer, . . . *Hub.* 871
nought but dread and death do *seeme* in show? . . . *Hub.* 966
Of all alive did *seeme* the fairest wight. . . . *Mui.* 24
fields with faded flowers did *seem* to mourne, . . . *Col.* 25
in simple eie *Seeme* greatest, when their garments are most gay. *Col.* 722
Ne any there doth brave or valiant *seeme,* . . . *Col.* 779
Venus selfe doth soly couples *seeme,* . . . *Col.* 801
Well may it *seeme,* by this thy deep insight, . . . *Col.* 831
of his cheere did *seeme* too solemne sad; . . . I. i. 2. 8
a black stole, most like to *seeme* for Una fit. . . . I. i. 45. 9
though a tree I *seme,* yet cold and heat me paines.' . . . I. ii. 33. 9
they did *seeme* more foule and hideous, . . . I. ii. 41. 3
Ne dare to weepe, nor *seeme* to understand . . . I. iii. 20. 7
May *seeme* the wayne was very evill ledd, . . . I. iv. 19. 7
'I, that do *seeme* not I, Duessa ame,' . . . I. v. 26. 6
cast her coulours . . . To *seeme* like truth, . . . I. vii. 1. 5
Ne let it *seeme* that credence this exceedes; . . . I. vii. 36. 1
My loyalty, not such as it did *seeme,* . . . I. vii. 49. 5
That strongest Oake might *seeme* to overthrow. . . . I. viii. 18. 6
The fields . . . Did *seeme* to laugh on me, . . . I. ix. 12. 9
signe of last outbreathed life did *seeme* . . . I. xii. 2. 5
Did *seeme,* such as she was, a goodly maiden Queene. . . . I. xii. 8. 9
One, that would wiser *seeme* then all the rest, . . . I. xii. 10. 2
His heart did *seeme* to melt in pleasures manifold. . . . I. xii. 40. 9
Wherewith above all knights ye goodly *seeme* aguizd! . . . II. i. 31. 9

Seem—*Continued.*
evermore did *seeme* As discontent . . . . II. ii. 35. 3
sad ruth does *seeme* you to restraine, ... II. ii. 45. 2
that day too farre did *seeme*. . . . . II. iv. 21. 6
that harme, which thou dost *seeme* To threat . . . . . . II. iv. 40. 3
Therby thine armes *seem* strong, ... II. v. 5. 6
would not *seeme* so rude, and thewed ill, ... II. vi. 26. 3
His cole-blacke hands did *seeme* to have ben seard . . . . II. vii. 3. 8
heavy ruine they did *seeme* to threatt; . . . . II. vii. 28. 6
Her face right wondrous faire did *seeme* to bee, ... II. vii. 45. 1
gold al is not that doth golden *seeme;* . . . . II. viii. 14. 5
though they bodies *seem,* yet substaunce from them fades. . . II. ix. 15. 9
as a cloud doth *seeme* to dim the skies; . . . . II. ix. 16. 5
not *Scuith guiridh* it mote *seeme* to bee, ... II. x. 24. 8
all the seas for feare doe *seeme* away to fly. . . . . II. xii. 3. 9
well they *seeme* to him, that farre doth vew, ... II. xii. 12. 1
starry light . . . does *seeme* more bright. . . . . II. xii. 78. 9
Whose face did *seeme* as cleare as Christall stone, ... III. i. 15. 4
'Things ofte impossible' (quoth she) '*seeme,* ere begonne. . . III. ii. 36. 9
To order them as best to thee doth *seeme,* . . . . III. iii. 2. 3
disloyally Deeme of her high desert, or *seeme* so light; . . . III. v. 45. 7
Miraculous may *seeme* to him that reades . . . . III. vi. 8. 1
seeme to labour under their fruites lode: . . . . III. vi. 42. 6
Did *seeme* to be the same which she escapt whileare. . . . . III. vii. 1. 9
rather joyd to bee then *seemen* sich, ... III. vii. 29. 8
both to be and *seeme* to him was labor lich. . . . . III. vii. 29. 9
the more to *seeme* such as she hight, ... III. viii. 10. 4
That challenge did too peremptory *seeme,* . . . . III. viii. 16. 6
seeme Such as no doubt of him he neede misdeeme.' . . . . . III. ix. 6. 4
seeme too suddeinly him to invade. . . . . III. xi. 8. 5
hart Did lively *seeme* to tremble, ... III. xi. 30. 8
all the walles did *seeme* to flame: . . . . III. xi. 38. 6
His seahorses did *seeme* to snort amayne, ... III. xi. 41. 1
The God himselfe did pensive *seeme* and sad, ... III. xi. 41. 6
Made him *seeme* happie for so glorious theft; . . . . IV. ii. 4. 8
Till seeing her, that Florimell did *seme,* In doubt . . . . . IV. ii. 17. 4
makes it *seeme* to have some other sourse; . . . . IV. iii. 27. 5
some, that would *seeme* wise, their wonder turnd to dout. . . IV. iii. 41. 9
ye *seemen* much to blame . . . . IV. ix. 37. 2
seeme . . . to them most sweet; . . . . IV. x. 2. 4
The which did *seeme,* unto my simple doome, ... IV. x. 21. 3
likest glasse did *seeme*. . . . . IV. x. 39. 9
'The first of them did *seeme* of ryper yeares . . . . IV. x. 49. 1
Albe they endlesse *seeme* in estimation, ... IV. xii. 1. 6
made it *seeme* to feele her grievous paine, ... IV. xii. 5. 8
For worthy thou of her doest rightly *seeme*. . . . . V. i. 28. 4
Another, that would *seeme* to have more wit, ... V. iii. 33. 6
what the sea unto you sent your own should *seeme.'* V.iv.17.9;18.9
Doth *seeme* to be her selfe, ... V. v. 12. 9
to make them *seeme* more few; . . . . V. vi. 5. 7
Each hour did *seeme* a moneth, ... V. vi. 5. 9
To so faire Ladie, as ye *seeme* in sight, ... V. xi. 62. 2
With her dull eyes did *seeme* to looke askew, ... V. xii. 29. 2
Of which though present age doe plenteous *seeme,* . . . . . VI. Pr. 4. 6
The which did *seeme* a thousand tongues to have, ... VI. i. 9. 3
rather did more chearefull *seeme* therefore: . . . . VI. i. 32. 5
let it not you *seeme* disgrace To beare this burden . . . . . VI. ii. 47. 7
to all vertue it may *seeme* unapt, ... VI. v. 1. 7
That mote to all men *seeme* an uncouth sight; . . . . VI. v. 9. 2
Much did the Craven *seeme* to mone his case, ... VI. vii. 18. 1
standing on his tiptoes, to *seeme* tall, ... VI. viii. 26. 5
did *seeme* so farre From malicing, ... VI. ix. 39. 6
Did *seeme* to overlooke the lowly vale; . . . . VI. x. 8. 8
they alwaies smoothly *seeme* to smile, ... VI. x. 24. 1
To make it *seeme* more deare and dainty, ... VI. xi. 1. 9
make even that dimmed light *Seeme* much more lovely . . . VI. xi. 21. 7
Tygres, that did *seeme* to gren And snar at all . . . . . . VI. xii. 27. 6
sure thy worth no lesse then hers doth *seem* to showe. . . . VII. vi. 32. 9
in thine owne behalfe maist partiall *seeme:* . . . . VII. vi. 35. 3
That well may *seemen* true; . . . . VII. vii. 7. 1
Did *seeme* to bow their bloosming heads . . . . VII. vii. 8. 8
even the gods to thee, as men to gods, do *seeme*. . . . . . VII. vii. 15. 9
As fed with lard, and that right well might *seeme;* . . . . VII. vii. 40. 2
though he . . . alwayes *seeme* as one, ... VII. vii. 51. 2
he his way doth *seem* quite to have lost, ... VII. vii. 52. 3
New yeare, . . . Doth *seeme* to promise hope . . . . *Am.* iv. 2
Ye . . . doe *seeme* to me inclind: . . . . *Am.* xxviii. 4
maketh every minute *seeme* a myle. . . . . *Am.* lxxxvi. 12
So sorrow still doth *seeme* too long to last; . . . . *Am.* lxxxvi. 13
Seeme lyke some mayden Queene. . . . . *Epith.* 158
nought more divine doth *seeme,* . . . . *H.L.* 114
to the lookers sight They *seeme* to please; . . . . *H.B.* 54
An outward shew of things that onely *seeme*. . . . . *H.B.* 91
seeme like twinckling starres in frostie night; . . . . . . *H.B.* 257
all earthes glorie, . . . *Seeme* durt and drosse . . . . . . *H.H.L.* 276
And make her native brightnes *seem* more cleare. . . . . . *H.H.B.* 189
did not *seeme* To be begot of any earthly Seede, ... *Proth.* 64
like old Peneus Waters they did *seeme,* . . . . *Proth.* 78

Seemed. *See* **Meseemed.**
It *seemed* that arte and nature strived . . . . *Bel.*[1] x. 5
In majestie she *seemde* to matche the Gods. . . . . *Bel.*[1] xi. 6
She *seemde* with glorie of the scarlet faire, ... *Rev.* ii. 6
fierce and fell this woman *seemde* to me. . . . . *Rev.* ii. 11
calme *seem'd* the sea to bee, ... *Pet.* ii. 4
White *seem'd* her robes, ... *Pet.* vi. 5
No worke it *seem'd* of earthly craftsmans wit, ... *Bel.*[2] iv. 9
seem'd . . . with equall ravine to devoure. . . . . *Bel.*[2] viii. 7
It *seem'd* that Art and Nature had assembled . . . . *Bel.*[2] xii. 5
richer then that vessell *seem'd* to bee, ... *Bel.*[2] xiii. 1
It *seem'd* her top the firmament did rayse, ... *Bel.*[2] xiv. 5

Seemed—*Continued.*
Seem'd above heavens powre it selfe to advaunce; . . . . . . *Ro.* xi. 4
seemed to threat the Firmament: . . . . *S.C.* F. 117
Semed, the sencelesse yron dyd feare, ... *S.C.* F. 205
Thearth shronke under him, and *seemed* to shake:— . . . . *S.C.* F. 220
he, that earst *seemd* but to playe, ... *S.C.* Mar. 95
Seemed shee sawe in the younglings face . . . . *S.C.* May 211
all things *seem'd* appalled at his sight. . . . . *Gn.* 256
it to Leaches *seemed* strange and geason. . . . . *Hub.* 12
honest mirth, that *seem'd* her well: . . . . *Hub.* 35
Well *seemd* the Ape to like this ordinaunce; . . . . *Hub.* 173
all that els *seemd* faire and fresh . . . . *T.M.* 39
Hath mard the face of all that *semed* fayre. . . . . *T.M.* 258
towards heaven shee *seemd* on high to weld. . . . . *Ti.* 14
where it was scarce *seemed* anie sight? . . . . *Ti.* 530
salvage nature *seemed* not to have, ... *Ti.* 564
whylome *seemed* to have been The Harpe . . . . *Ti.* 606
Which th' ashes *seem'd* of some great Prince to hold, ... *Ti.* 661
Seemed the heavens with the earth did disagree, ... *Ti.* 664
She *seem'd* still backe unto the land to looke, ... *Mui.* 281
seem'd to live, so like it was in sight: . . . . *Mui.* 332
well he *seemd* to be sum wight forlorne; . . . . *D.* 45
She did excell, and *seem'd* of Angels race, ... *D.* 213
he himselfe *seemed* made for meriment, ... *As.* 27
Yet *seemed* to be a goodly pleasant lea: . . . . *Col.* 283
seemd amid the surges for to fleet, ... *Col.* 286
followd those which happie *seemd* to bee. . . . . *Col.* 667
Full jolly knight he *seemd,* . . . . I. i. 1. 8
Seemed in heart some hidden care she had, ... I. i. 4. 8
Behind her . . . a Dwarfe did lag, That lasie *seemd,* . . . . I. i. 6. 2
Seemd in their song to scorne the cruell sky. . . . . I. i. 8. 4
path . . . that beaten *seemd* most bare, ... I. i. 11. 3
Sober he *seemde,* and very sagely sad, ... I. i. 29. 5
Then *seemed* him his Lady by him lay, ... I. i. 47. 7
she . . . *seemde* unto his bed to bring Her, ... I. i. 48. 2
the Graces *seemed* all to sing, . . . dauncing all around; . . I. i. 48. 7
Her swollen hart her speech *seemd* to bereave, ... I. i. 52. 3
seemd she to appease Her mournefull plaintes, ... I. i. 54. 6
seemde best the person to put on Of that good knight, . . . I. ii. 11. 1
Full jolly knight he *seemde,* and wel addrest; . . . . I. ii. 11. 7
Both *seemde* to win, and both *seemde* won to bee, ... I. ii. 37. 6
ever false Duessa *seemde* as faire as shee. . . . . I. ii. 37. 9
Much *seemed* he to mone her haplesse chaunce, ... I. iii. 25. 6
His lovely words her *seemd* due recompence . . . . I. iii. 30. 1
th' enchaunter joyous *seemde* no lesse Then the glad marchant, I. iii. 32. 2
His looke . . . *seemed* still to threat Cruell revenge, ... I. iii. 33. 7
The house of mightie Prince it *seemd* to be, ... I. iv. 2. 7
girlonds gay, That *seemd* as fresh as Flora in her prime; . . I. iv. 17. 3
fellowship *seemd* far unfitt for warlike swaine. . . . . I. iv. 37. 9
He *seemd* in hart to harbour thoughts unkind, ... I. iv. 38. 8
gan to turne aside For feare, as *seemd,* . . . . I. vi. 34. 8
all the earth for terror *seemd* to shake, ... I. vii. 7. 6
with his tallnesse *seemd* to threat the skye; . . . . I. vii. 8. 5
seemd to throw . . . bright sparckles fiery redd, ... I. vii. 31. 6
heares . . . Did shake, and *seemd* to daunce for jollity, . . . I. vii. 32. 4
all that was not such as *seemd* . . . did fade, ... I. vii. 35. 3
seemd himselfe as conquered to yield. . . . . I. viii. 20. 5
Gyaunts fall, that *seemd* to shake The stedfast globe . . . I. viii. 23. 8
That *seemed* from some feared foe to fly, ... I. ix. 21. 3
of him selfe he *seemd* to be afrayd; . . . . I. ix. 23. 4
foltring tongue, at last, these words *seemd* forth to shake; . I. ix. 24. 9
Not all so chearefull *seemed* she . . . . I. x. 14. 3
Panthea, *seemd* the brightest thing that was; . . . . I. x. 58. 6
seemd uneath to shake the stedfast ground. . . . . I. xi. 4. 3
nothing *seemd* the puissaunce could withstand: . . . . I. xi. 24. 3
hundred ramping Lions *seemd* to rore, ... I. xi. 37. 3
So huge and horrible a masse it *seemd;* . . . . I. xi. 55. 2
That *seemd* like silke and silver woven neare; . . . . I. xii. 22. 8
He *seemd* to be a sage and sober syre; . . . . II. i. 7. 7
Full loth she *seemd* thereto, ... II. i. 20. 8
that *seemed* ill bested, ... II. i. 30. 4
seemd her tender heart was rent in twaine, ... II. i. 38. 4
Seemd to have beene a goodly personage, ... II. i. 41. 6
all his sences *seemd* berefte attone: . . . . II. i. 42. 4
Seemd that lowde thunder . . . Did rend . . . . II. ii. 20. 8
suddeinly he *seemd* enragd, ... II. iii. 14. 1
seemd to be a woman of great worth, ... II. iii. 21. 8
Her face so faire as flesh it *seemed* not, ... II. iii. 22. 1
heavenly musicke *seemd* to make. . . . . II. iii. 24. 9
thousand thousand times more faire, She *seemd,* . . . . . . II. iii. 26. 2
He saw from far, or *seemed* for to see, ... II. iv. 3. 2
Straunge *seemed* to the knight, ... II. iv. 8. 2
seemd no lesse to love then lov'd to bee: . . . . II. iv. 19. 5
greatly joyous *seemed* for my sake, ... II. iv. 20. 3
seemd him to enflame on every side: . . . . II. v. 2. 7
Him deeming dead, as then he *seemd* in sight, ... II. v. 25. 7
(That day it selfe him *seemed* all too long) . . . . II. v. 38. 6
like a litle forrest *seemed* outwardly. . . . . II. vi. 2. 9
Yet *seemed,* nothing well they her became; . . . . II. vi. 6. 6
He *seemed* breathlesse, hartlesse, faint, and wan; . . . . . II. vi. 41. 5
Ne of his safetie *seemed* care he kept; . . . . II. vi. 42. 5
lives, it *seemed,* whilome there were shed, ... II. vii. 30. 8
rather fowler *seemed* to the eye; . . . . II. vii. 61. 8
nothing *seemd* mote beare so monstrous might: . . . . II. viii. 38. 2
The frame thereof *seemd* partly circulare, ... II. ix. 22. 1
Tall yeomen *seemed* they and of great might, ... II. ix. 26. 4
Another *seemed* envious or coy, ... II. ix. 35. 7
eyes, That mad or foolish *seemd;* . . . . II. ix. 52. 7
That chamber *seemed* ruinous and old, ... II. ix. 55. 1
all that *seemed* fitt for kingly seed: . . . . II. x. 27. 4

Seemed—*Continued.*
As for her Syre and king her *seemed* best; . . . II. x. 31. 7
The Prince him selfe halfe *seemed* to offend; . . . II. x. 68. 7
whose sound hevens thunder *seem'd* to bee, . . . II. x. 73. 9
As every one *seem'd* meetest in that cace. . . . II. xi. 6. 5
like a ghost he *seem'd* . . . II. xi. 20. 9
seemd to tremble evermore and quake; . . . II. xi. 22. 5
a dead mans skull, that *seemd* a ghastly sight. . . . II. xi. 22. 9
Some land-marke *seemd* to bee, . . . II. xi. 35. 9
could not die, yet *seemd* a mortall wight, . . . II. xi. 40. 7
seemd more horrible then hell to bee, . . . II. xii. 6. 3
seemd so sweet and pleasaunt to the eye, . . . II. xii. 14. 5
seem'd to fly for feare them to behold. . . . II. xii. 25. 5
Seemed some great misfortune to deplore, . . . II. xii. 27. 8
this great Universe *seemd* one confused mas. . . . II. xii. 34. 9
seemd a worke of admirable witt; . . . II. xii. 44. 2
seemd the waves were into yvory . . . sent; . . . II. xii. 45. 3
Yt *seemd* thenchaunted flame which did Creusa wed. . . . II. xii. 45. 9
traveilers to him *seemd* to entize: . . . II. xii. 46. 6
seemd to entice All passers by . . . II. xii. 54. 3
garments loose that *seemd* unmeet for womanhed. . . . II. xii. 55. 9
some *seemd* with lively jollitee To fly about, . . . II. xii. 60. 7
drops of Christall *seemd* for wantones to weep. . . . II. xii. 61. 9
like a litle lake it *seemd* to bee; . . . II. xii. 62. 5
seemd the fountaine in that sea did sayle upright. . . . II. xii. 62. 9
seemed to contend And wrestle wantonly, . . . II. xii. 63. 7
Such *seemed* they, . . . II. xii. 65. 5
whence that Musick *seemed* heard to bee, . . . II. xii. 72. 1
seemd to be Some goodly swayne . . . II. xii. 79. 1
seemd to couch under his shield threesquare, . . . III. i. 4. 4
seemd both shield and plate it would have riv'd; . . . III. i. 6. 3
Whose hideous horror . . . Full griesly *seemd:* . . . III. i. 14. 7
She *seemd* a woman of great bountihed, . . . III. i. 41. 5
they all *seemed* courteous and gent, . . . III. i. 44. 4
fierce Bacchante *seemd* too fell and keene; . . . III. i. 45. 6
High time it *seemed* then for everie wight . . . III. i. 58. 1
Faire Lady she him *seemd,* like Lady drest. . . . III. ii. 4. 8
Like to the world itselfe, and *seemd* a world of glas. . . . III. ii. 19. 9
all his armour *seemd* of antique mould, . . . III. ii. 25. 2
Thrise shined faire, and thrise *seemd* dim and wan, . . . III. iii. 16. 3
His steed eke *seemd* t' apply his steps to his intent. . . . III. iv. 61. 9
He met a Dwarfe that *seemed* terrifyde . . . III. v. 3. 3
seemd to plaine With gentle murmure . . . III. v. 39. 8
seemed those two vertues strove to fynd . . . III. v. 55. 4
all the rest it *seemd* they robbed bare Of bounty, . . . III. vi. 4. 8
seemd the Ocean could not containe them there. . . . III. vi. 35. 9
Busie (as *seem'd*) about some wicked gin: . . . III. vii. 7. 3
is not such as she *seemd,* But a faire virgin . . . III. vii. 52. 2
ill they *seemed* sure avizd to bee, . . . III. vii. 57. 8
like a lively sanguine it *seemd* to the eye. . . . III. viii. 6. 9
seem'd The fairest wight on ground, . . . III. viii. 13. 8
Seemed to thunder, and did nigh affray . . . III. viii. 15. 5
seemd for feare to quake in every lim, . . . III. viii. 15. 8
dissembled well, and light *seemd* to esteeme . . . III. viii. 16. 9
Paridell . . . *seemd* dismaid to bee; . . . III. viii. 48. 2
entertaynd, as *seemed* meet, . . . III. ix. 3. 3
So huge a scope at first him *seemed* best, . . . III. ix. 46. 5
the smart . . . *seemd* more grievous then it was before. . . . III. x. 18. 5
Him *seemed* more their maner did agree; . . . III. x. 21. 3
seemd no help for him was left in living sight. . . . III. x. 56. 9
As *seemed* by their semblaunt, . . . III. xi. 29. 4
Straunge thing it *seem'd,* . . . III. xi. 53. 8
As those same plumes so *seemd* he vaine . . . III. xii. 8. 5
seemd of ryper yeares then th' other Swayne, . . . III. xii. 9. 2
That evill matched paire they *seemd* to bee: . . . III. xii. 18. 6
So *seemd* those two, . . . III. xii. 46. *or.* 5
a man, such as indeed he *seemed;* . . . IV. i. 8. 2
since he *seemed* valiant, though unknowne, . . . IV. i. 11. 5
That *seem'd* full hard t' accord two things . . . IV. i. 11. 9
Perceiv'd to be such as they *seemd* in vew, . . . IV. i. 38. 8
the fayrest Florimell him *seemed* To him was fallen . . . IV. ii. 8. 3
He *seemed* brought to bed in Paradise, . . . IV. ii. 9. 8
prov'd himselfe most foole in what he *seem'd* most wise. . . . IV. ii. 9. 9
Combing her golden lockes, as *seemd* her good; . . . IV. ii. 45. 5
thrids . . . so short, that *seemd* their ends out shortly came. . IV. ii. 50. 9
More happie creatures then they *seem'd* to bee; . . . IV. iii. 2. 5
mightie strokes . . . *seemed* death in them to beare; . . . IV. iii. 7. 7
So fresh he *seemed* and so fierce in sight: . . . IV. iii. 23. 6
Then he halfe vanquisht, then the other *seemed,* . . . IV. iii. 28. 4
each to other *seemd* the victorie to yield. . . . IV. iii. 34. 9
life it selfe *seemd* loathsome, and long safetie ill. . . . IV. iii. 36. 9
seemd some perilous tumult to desine, . . . IV. iii. 37. 7
T' obey their riders hest, as *seemed* good. . . . IV. iii. 39. 5
seemed borne of Angels brood, . . . IV. iii. 39. 7
toward them his course *seem'd* to apply: . . . IV. iv. 6. 7
such an Hag, that *seemed* worse then nought, . . . IV. iv. 10. 5
Like as it *seemed* best to every one; . . . IV. iv. 14. 8
Them *seemd* that could so goodly riches gaine, . . . IV. iv. 16. 8
As one that *seemed* doubtfull or dismayd. . . . IV. iv. 20. 4
seemed fit For salvage wight; . . . IV. iv. 39. 6
Most answerable to his wyld disguize It *seemed* . . . IV. iv. 42. 6
all afore that *seemed* fayre and bright, . . . IV. v. 14. 1
Florimell her selfe . . . She *seem'd* to passe: . . . IV. v. 15. 9
dreadfull *seem'd* to every living wight, . . . IV. v. 32. 3
seemed some blacksmith dwelt in that desert ground. . . . IV. v. 33. 9
He like a monstrous Gyant *seem'd* in sight, . . . IV. v. 37. 1
seem'd to dust he shortly would it drive: . . . IV. v. 37. 6
seem'd a rocke of Diamond it could rive . . . IV. v. 37. 8
Where better *seem'd* he mote himselfe repose; . . . IV. v. 40. 4
every place *seem'd* painefull, and ech changing vaine. . . . IV. v. 40. 9

Seemed—*Continued.*
seem'd he was full bent to some mischievous deede. . . . IV. vi. 2. 9
seemed nought but death mote be her destinie. . . . IV. vi. 18. 9
The feare whereof *seem'd* much her to affray; . . . IV. vi. 45. 4
The place there overflowne *seemd* like a sodaine flood. . . . IV. vii. 32. 9
Him *seemed* oft he heard his owne right name. . . . IV. viii. 4. 5
to rest as *seem'd* her meet. . . . IV. viii. 9. 4
seem'd his shrikes would rend the brasen skie: . . . IV. viii. 38. 5
seemed nought the souse thereof could beare, . . . IV. viii. 44. 5
that same dwarfe right sorie *seem'd* and sad, . . . IV. viii. 46. 3
together skirmishing, as *seemed:* . . . IV. ix. 20. 2
seem'd to serve the workmans will. . . . IV. x. 15. 9
It *seem'd* a second paradise to ghesse, . . . IV. x. 23. 2
seem'd to be of very sober mood, . . . IV. x. 31. 4
shapes *seem'd* not like to terrestriall boyes, . . . IV. x. 42. 4
folly *seem'd* to leave the thing undonne . . . IV. x. 53. 4
Full weake and crooked creature *seemed* shee, . . . IV. xi. 24. 8
seem'd full aged by his outward sight, . . . IV. xi. 25. 7
seem'd to stoupe afore With bowed backe, . . . IV. xi. 26. 1
seemed strange to common vew, . . . IV. xi. 27. 7
seem'd like silver, sprinckled here and theare . . . IV. xi. 45. 4
no mortall worke, that *seem'd* and yet was not. . . . IV. xi. 45. 9
seem'd unlike unto his earthly home: . . . IV. xii. 4. 7
nothing like himselfe he *seem'd* in sight. . . . IV. xii. 20. 5
to her he *seem'd* best skild in righteous lore. . . . V. i. 4. 9
'He, whether mine *seem'd* fayrer in his eye, . . . V. i. 17. 1
As that it *seem'd* above the ground he went; . . . V. i. 20. 3
To see the thing, that *seem'd* so excellent, . . . V. iii. 26. 4
Seem'd that for it these Squires at ods did fall, . . . V. iv. 5. 6
the one him *seem'd* a Knight all armed, . . . V. iv. 36. 4
Well shot in yeares he *seem'd,* . . . V. vi. 19. 6
As sundry chaunge her *seemed* best to ease. . . . V. vi. 26. 4
Her *seem'd,* as she was doing sacrifize To Isis, . . . V. vii. 13. 1
An hideous tempest *seemed* from below To rise . . . V. vii. 14. 2
Seem'd to awake in horrible dismay, . . . V. vii. 15. 3
one of them, who *seem'd* in sight To be the greatest . . . V. vii. 18. 4
(as *seemed* best) . . . V. vii. 26. 1
deadly daunger *seem'd* in all mens sight To tempt . . . V. ix. 15. 6
seemed to outshine the dimmed skye, . . . V. ix. 21. 8
Seemed those litle Angels did uphold The cloth of state, . . V. ix. 29. 1
goodly *seem'd* t' adorne her royall state; . . . V. ix. 31. 3
this, that *seem'd* so faire And royally arayd, . . . V. ix. 40. 1
seem'd their soules they wold have ryven quight . . . V. x. 32. 4
seem'd a marble rocke asunder could have rive. . . . V. xi. 5. 9
seem'd to be of infinite great strength: . . . V. xi. 23. 3
seemed nought could him from death protect; . . . V. xii. 21. 4
seem'd of them to take no keepe. . . . V. xii. 42. 9
from the battlements she ready *seem'd* to fall. . . . VI. i. 34. 9
He burst into these wordes, as to him *seemed* good: . . . VI. ii. 24. 9
sith ye so courteous *seemed* late, . . . VI. ii. 27. 4
the onely helpe . . . *Seem'd* to be Calidore: . . . VI. iii. 12. 9
as sure to them he *seemed,* A courteous Knight . . . VI. iii. 13. 1
him *seemed* fit that wounded Knight To visite, . . . VI. iii. 14. 1
The dastard, . . . *Seem'd* not to weigh his threatfull words . VI. iii. 36. 2
Him *seem'd* his feet did fly and in their speed delight. . . . VI. iv. 19. 9
A voice, that *seemed* of some woman kynd, . . . VI. iv. 26. 7
rather *seem'd* the conquest of his might, . . . VI. v. 9. 4
seemed . . . To be two errant knights, . . . VI. v. 11. 4
seemed nothing might Beare off their blowes . . . VI. v. 18. 4
As to them *seemed* fit time to entertaine; . . . VI. v. 24. 7
seem'd the spoile of some right well renownd: . . . VI. v. 25. 5
Seem'd like a grove faire braunched over-hed: . . . VI. v. 35. 4
well it *seem'd* that whilome he had beene Some goodly person, VI. v. 36. 6
quite they *seem'd* past helpe of surgery; . . . VI. vi. 5. 5
Seem'd under her protection him to shroud; . . . VI. vi. 31. 4
So different from that which earst ye *seem'd* in sight?' . . . VI. vii. 14. 9
To doe some thing that *seemed* to him best; . . . VI. vii. 19. 7
bootelesse thing him *seemed* to abide So mighty blowes, . . VI. vii. 46. 8
seemed nought the course thereof could stay, . . . VI. viii. 8. 5
seem'd a marble pillour it could bow; . . . VI. viii. 16. 3
seem'd the soyle both fayre and frutefull eft, . . . VI. ix. 1. 5
seemed So farre the meane of shepheards to excell, . . . VI. ix. 11. 2
Then Coridon woxe frollicke, that earst *seemed* dead. . . . VI. ix. 42. 9
hight, that *seem'd* th' earth to disdaine; . . . VI. x. 6. 3
him *seemed* that the merry sound . . . he playing heard . . . VI. x. 10. 2
Seem'd all the rest in beauty to excell, . . . VI. x. 14. 4
two of them still froward *seem'd* to bee, . . . VI. x. 24. 7
seem'd to be some sorie simple clowne, . . . VI. xi. 27. 3
Whereof right glad they *seem'd,* . . . VI. xi. 40. 1
seemed to containe A full good pecke . . . VI. xii. 26. 5
inly quaking, *seem'd* as reft of sense . . . VII. vi. 25. 4
Oft to resort there-to, when *seem'd* them best, . . . VII. vi. 38. 5
that *seem'd* penaunce light: . . . VII. vi. 50. 6
richer *seem'd* then any tapestry, . . . VII. vii. 10. 8
wet he *seem'd* in sight With waves, . . . VII. vii. 33. 8
More sweet than Nectar . . . *Seemd* every bit . . . *Am.* xxxix. 14
seemd the longer for my greater paines. . . . *Am.* lx. 12
Whose harvest *seemd* to hasten now apace,) . . . *Am.* lxxvi. 10
slowly *seemd* to move Theyr sad protract . . . *Am.* lxxxvi. 3
all that earst *seemd* sweet seemes now offense, . . . *H.H.B.* 269
streame, . . . *Seem'd* foule to them, . . . *Proth.* 48
Them *seem'd* they never saw a sight so fayre, . . . *Proth.* 60
So fresh they *seem'd* as day, . . . *Proth.* 70
like the twins of Jove they *seem'd* . . . *Proth.* 173

Seemest. So *semest* thou like Good Fryday to frowne: . . . *S.C.* F. 30
since so much thou *seemst* to rue my griefe, . . . *D.* 92
seemst to laugh atweene thy twinkling light, . . . *Epith.* 292

Seemeth. *See* **Meseemeth.**
Seemeth thy flocke thy counsell can, . . . *S.C.* F. 77
nought *seemeth* sike strife, . . . *S.C.* May 158

Seemeth—*Continued.*
starre *Seemeth* ay greater when it is farre: . . . *S.C.* S. 77
Seemeth thou dost their soule of sence bereave; . . . *S.C.* O. 27
but by that same that *seemeth.* . . . *Hub.* 650
it *seemeth* I was made to raigne, . . . *Hub.* 1031
Such loftie flight base shepheard *seemeth* not, . . . *Col.* 618
'as she *seemeth* here, Such is the face of falshood: . . . I. viii. 49. 3
seemeth safe from storms that may offend; . . . I. xii. 1. 5
seemeth by your troubled cheare, . . . II. ix. 42. 1
*The Prince him selfe halfe *seemeth* to offend, . . . II. x. 68. 7
Seemeth that such wilde woodes should far expell . . . III. vi. 1. 7
seemeth well to answere to your weede, . . . IV. vi. 5. 3
I, . . . Strooke him, as *seemeth,* underneath the hart, . . . VI. ii. 12. 8
his high head, that *seemeth* alwayes hore . . . VII. vii. 11. 3
All this worlds glory *seemeth* vayne to me, . . . *Am.* xxxv. 13
it *seemeth,* in my simple wit, . . . *Am.* xl. 5
herein eke thy glory *seemeth* more, . . . *H.L.* 162

Seeming. *See* **Dead-seeming, Fair-seeming, Gay-seeming, Like-seeming, True-seeming.**
May of the bodie yeeld a *seeming* sight, . . . *Ro.* v. 6
Both *seeming* now full glad and joyeous . . . *Gn.* 483
The skie, in pieces *seeming* to be rent, . . . *Gn.* 581
Like tragicke Pageants *seeming* to appeare. . . . *Ti.* 490
Most like Alcyon *seeming* at a glaunce; . . . *D.* 53
seeming to mistrust Some secret ill, or hidden foe . . . I. i. 49. 3
he spred A *seeming* body of the subtile aire, . . . I. ii. 3. 3
As many formes and shapes in *seeming* wise, . . . I. ii. 10. 3
In so ritch weedes, and *seeming* glorious show, . . . I. ii. 21. 5
the *seeming* simple maid Let fal her eien, . . . I. ii. 27. 5
whome ye see Now not a Lady, but a *seeming* tree; . . . I. ii. 35. 5
Th' one *seeming* such, the other such indeede, . . . I. ii. 37. 2
Her *seeming* dead he fownd with feigned feare, . . . I. ii. 45. 1
false Duessa, *seeming* Lady fayre, . . . I. iv. 13. 2
As ashes pale of hew, and *seeming* ded; . . . I. iv. 33. 7
him amoves with speaches *seeming* fitt: . . . I. iv. 45. 3
he his paine endur'd, as *seeming* now more light. . . . I. x. 24. 9
them requites with court'sies *seeming* meet, . . . I. x. 32. 3
With flying speede, and *seeming* great pretence, . . . I. xii. 24. 7
seeming sorely chauffed at his band, . . . I. xii. 35. 6
Who feigning . . . and *seeming* pale and faynt, . . . II. i. 9. 4
kindling new his corage *seeming* queint, . . . II. v. 11. 4
As to despise so curteous *seeming* part . . . II. vi. 26. 4
Now *seeming* flaming whott, . . . II. ix. 39. 5
Hengist, *seeming* sad for that was donne, . . . II. x. 66. 3
those same Islands, *seeming* now and than, . . . II. xii. 11. 3
'These *seeming* beasts are men indeed, . . . II. xii. 85. 1
Was usd of knightes and Ladies *seeming* gent: . . . III. i. 67. 6
pleased with that *seeming* goodly-hed, . . . III. ii. 38. 8
her *seeming* griev'd Out of her heavie swowne not to awake . . . III. vi. 27. 7
seeming sory that she ever came Into his powre, . . . III. viii. 14. 7
A couple, *seeming* well to be his twaine, . . . III. x. 20. 7
Courteous to all and *seeming* debonaire, . . . III. xii. 14. 4
inly being more then *seeming* sad: . . . III. xii. 16. 4
Sorrow *seeming* dead; . . . III. xii. 25. 5
Seeming transfixed with a cruell dart; . . . III. xii. 31. 5
A Ladie, *seeming* in so farre a space: . . . IV. i. 17. 4
As *seeming* plast in sole felicity: . . . IV. ii. 11. 4
as *seeming* wondrous glad, . . . IV. vii. 24. 8
seeming still to smile, Glauconome, . . . IV. xi. 50. 8
seeming to have suffred mickle wrong, . . . V. iv. 5. 3
as best was *seeming* for a Knight, . . . V. v. 1. 8
still *seeming* faine When ought he did, . . . VI. iv. 16. 4

Seemless. Artegall him selfe her *seemelesse* plight did rew. . . . V. ii. 25. 9

Seemlihead. by his persons secret *seemlyhed* . . . IV. viii. 14. 3

Seemly. (O *seemely* sight!) . . . *S.C.* Ap. 56
to the Court in *seemly* sort they come; . . . *Hub.* 662
Delight, and Laughter, deckt in *seemly* sort. . . . *T.M.* 198
In all that *seemly* shepheard might behove. . . . *As.* 10
So forth they rode, he feining *seemely* merth, . . . I. ii. 27. 8
Faire *seemely* pleasaunce each to other makes, . . . I. ii. 30. 1
she up arose with *seemely* grace, . . . I. x. 8. 4
naked nature *seemely* to aray; . . . I. x. 39. 5
In *seemely* sort their corses to engrave, . . . I. x. 42. 2
seemely welcome for her did prepare: . . . I. x. 44. 7
with sad Cypresse *seemely* it embrave; . . . II. i. 60. 3
Seemely to entertaine her new-come guest, . . . II. ii. 16. 2
Therein two gates were placed *seemly* well: . . . II. ix. 23. 1
Did order all th' Achates in *seemely* wise, . . . II. ix. 31. 4
A *seemely* Maiden sitting by the shore, . . . II. xii. 27. 6
Dwelt simple truth in *seemely* fashion, . . . III. vii. 59. 6
in that horror shewd a *seemely* grace, . . . III. xii. 19. 8
her salewd with *seemely* bel-accoyle, . . . IV. vi. 25. 4
'Thus sate they all around in *seemely* rate: . . . IV. x. 52. 1
in order *seemly* good Did on the Thamis attend, . . . IV. xi. 44. 7
her attending in full *seemly* sort, . . . IV. xii. 18. 7
them beside two *seemely* damzells stood, . . . V. iv. 4. 6
they received were In *seemely* wise, . . . V. vi. 22. 7
In gentle thewes and such like *seemly* leres: . . . VI. ii. 31. 5
When Calidore in *seemly* good array . . . VI. iii. 9. 7
Set all your things in *seemely* good aray, . . . *Epith.* 114
now so faire and *seemely* they appeare, . . . *H.B.* 34

Seemly-well. *See* **Seemly, Well.**

Seems. *See* **Meseems.**
Whatever thing *seems* small in common eyes. . . . *Van.* v. 14
Seemes that no foes revengement he did feare: . . . *Hub.* 216
'It *seemes* . . . right well that ye be Clerks, . . . *Hub.* 415
Seemes that in fruitfull pastures ye doo live, . . . *Hub.* 593
'*Seemes,* that that gentle River . . . farre fled, . . . *Ti.* 141
For rare it *seemes* in reason to be skand, . . . *D.* 178
as ghastly dreadfull, as it *seemes,* . . . *Col.* 208

Seems—*Continued.*
That *seems,* with none of them thou favor foundest, . . . *Col.* 461
Ne lesse praise-worthie Galathea *seemes,* . . . *Col.* 516
it *seemes* of spight Thou speakest thus . . . *Col.* 676
it *seemes* that some celestiall rage . . . *Col.* 823
That the worlds pride *seemes* gathered there to bee. . . . *Ded.Son.* xvii.12
Faire harbour that them *seems,* . . . I. i. 7. 9
Sometimes dame Venus selfe he *seemes* to see; . . . I. vi. 16. 6
'Old syre, it *seemes* thou hast not red . . . I. viii. 33. 4
prove thy puissant armes, as *seemes* thee best became.' . . . I. x. 66. 9
it *seemes,* that she suborned hath . . . I. xii. 34. 1
the stone her semblance *seemes* to show, . . . II. ii. 9. 4
Seemes that through many yeares thy wits thee faile, . . . II. iii. 16. 2
Seemes to be borne by native influence; . . . II. iv. 1. 5
chiefly skill to ride *seemes* a science . . . II. iv. 1. 7
he that breathlesse *seems* shal corage bold respire. . . . II. viii. 7. 9
whose valorous great might, It *seemes,* . . . II. viii. 27. 3
That fairer *seemes* the lesse ye see her may. . . . II. xii. 74. 6
certes *seemes* bestowed not amis: . . . III. ii. 42. 4
seemes some cursed witches deed, . . . III. iii. 18. 8
Whereof she *seemes* ashamed inwardly: . . . III. iii. 20. 7
one of th' old Heroes *seemes* to bee! . . . III. iii. 32. 5
when he sleepes in most security And safest *seemes,* . . . III. iv. 27. 4
sooth, it *seemes,* they say; . . . III. vi. 47. 1
all the countrey *seemes* to be a Maine, . . . III. vii. 34. 5
seemes rough Masons hand . . . Had long while laboured . . . III. viii. 37. 6
white *seemes* fayrer macht with blacke attone; . . . III. ix. 2. 4
seemes t' exceede the powre of patience, . . . III. xi. 14. 2
it prodigious *seemes* in common peoples sight. . . . IV. i. 13. 9
he that happie *seemes,* and least in payne, . . . IV. iii. 1. 8
from his force *seemes* nought may it defend; . . . IV. iii. 19. 4
That rather *seemes,* sith knowen armes ye shonne.' . . . IV. vi. 5. 5
faire Poeana, who *seemes* outwardly So faire . . . IV. viii. 49. 4
'Sir Knight, it *seemes* to me . . . V. vii. 18. 6
Alreadie *seemes* that fortunes headlong wheele . . . V. x. 20. 7
As by sad Belge *seemes;* . . . V. xi. 1. 7
Of Court, it *seemes,* men Courtesie doe call, . . . VI. i. 1. 1
In whom, it *seemes,* that gentlenesse of spright . . . VI. i. 2. 3
My knight hers soone, as *seemes,* to daunger drove, . . . VI. ii. 20. 5
'Ill *seemes,*' (sayd he) 'if he so valiaunt be, . . . VI. iii. 40. 6
as a girlond *seemes* to deck the locks . . . VII. vi. 41. 3
That only *seemes* unmov'd and permanent, . . . VII. vii. 17. 7
Ne any Lake, that *seems* most still and slowe, . . . VII. vii. 20. 5
seemes to scorne Base thing, . . . *Am.* xiii. 9
Fayre soyle it *seemes* from far, . . . *Am.* lxiii. 7
further *seemes* his terme still to extend, . . . *Am.* lxxxvi. 11
his returne that *seemes* to linger late: . . . *Am.* lxxxviii. 4
Clad all in white, that *seemes* a virgin best. . . . *Epith.* 151
seems more fayre, The more they on it stare. . . . *Epith.* 232
seemes on earth most heavenly to embrace, . . . *H.L.* 111
this, That *seemes* in it all blisses to containe, . . . *H.L.* 207
In sight whereof all other blisse *seemes* vaine: . . . *H.L.* 208
Nothing on earth *seemes* fayre to fleshly sight, . . . *H.B.* 18
It *seemes* that he before his eyes had plast . . . *H.B.* 31
all that earst seemd sweet *seemes* now offense, . . . *H.H.B.* 269
all that pleased earst now *seemes* to paine; . . . *H.H.B.* 270
lampe . . . Thenceforth *seemes* fowle, and full of sinfull blame; *H.H.B.* 276
And all that pompe . . . *Seemes* to them basenesse, . . . *H.H.B.* 279

Seen. *See* **Well-seen.**
I have *seene* so faire a thing as this, . . . *Bel.*[1] iv. 13
mine eyes have *seene* so faire a sight . . . *Bel.*[2] iv. 13
was the faire Dodonian tree far *seene,* . . . *Bel.*[2] v. 1
Thrice having *seene* under the heavens veale . . . *Ro.* i. 9
That Romane Eagle *seene* to cleave asunder, . . . *Ro.* xvii. 10
Is now no more *seen* flying, nor alighting. . . . *Ro.* xvii. 14
Was never *seene,* that anie fortunes wreakes . . . *Ro.* xxi. 7
He that hath *seene* a great Oke drie and dead, . . . *Ro.* xxviii. 1
Who such an Oke hath *seene,* let him record . . . *Ro.* xxviii. 12
Which *seene,* the pensife boy . . . Arose, . . . *S.C.* Ja. 76
nowe no succoure was *seene* him nere. . . . *S.C.* F. 228
Now tell us what thou hast *seene.* . . . *S.C.* Mar. 60
'Tell me, have ye *seene* her angelick face, . . . *S.C.* Ap. 64
Where have you *seene* the like but there? . . . *S.C.* Ap. 72
Well is it *seene* . . . *S.C.* May 45
I saye as some have *seene.* . . . *S.C.* Jul. 180
such a cup hast thou ever *sene?* . . . *S.C.* Au. 35
sith the Saxon king Never was Woolfe *seene,* . . . *S.C.* S. 152
Who to entrappe the fish . . . Was better *seene,* . . . *S.C.* D. 82
Whereas continuall shade is to be *seene,* . . . *Gn.* 118
With many Fairies oft were dauncing *seene.* . . . *Gn.* 179
hath not *seene* that heavens portracture. . . . *Hub.* 611
devises, never *seene* In Court before, . . . *Hub.* 673
seene the manners of all beasts on ground; . . . *Hub.* 687
that he might be *seene* Of the wilde beasts . . . *Hub.* 1065
There now no rivers course is to be *seene,* . . . *Ti.* 139
ships were *seene* . . . to cut their fomie waie, . . . *Ti.* 148
Dan Orpheus was *seene* Wylde beasts . . . to lead, . . . *Ti.* 607
so lively *seene,* That it true Sea . . . ye would weene. . . . *Mui.* 279
seldome *seene,* forejudgment proveth true. . . . *Mui.* 320
Such as she oft is *seene* in warlicke field: . . . *Mui.* 323
Me seemd I had his person *seene* elsewhere, . . . *D.* 52
Whose like before mine eye had seldome *seene,* . . . *D.* 114
As if that death he in the face had *seene,* . . . *D.* 565
was not like mourning *seen.* . . . *As.* 210
hast not *seene* least part of natures worke: . . . *Col.* 293
Nought hast thou, foolish boy, *seene* in thy daies.' . . . *Col.* 303
Of which, apparaunt proofe was to be *seene,* . . . *Ded. Son.* xi. 8
So many pathes, so many turnings *seene,* . . . I. i. 10. 8
To her makes present of his service *seene:* . . . I. v. 16. 3
let be *seene* That dreaded Night . . . hath place, . . . I. v. 24. 3

Seen—*Continued.*
child! whom I . . . now have *seene* unwares. . . . I. v. 27. 9
Which having *seene,* from thence arose away The mother . . I. v. 44. 4
A ruefull sight as could be *seene* with eie; . . . . . I. v. 46. 1
might her pitteous hart be *seene* to pant and quake. . . . I. vii. 20. 9
Ne might of mortall eye be ever *seene;* . . . . . I. vii. 33. 2
it may be *seene,* if sought: . . . . . I. vii. 36. 9
'The forlorne Maiden, whom your eies have *seene* . . . . I. vii. 43. 1
Nor voice was heard, nor wight was *seene* . . . . . I. viii. 29. 9
trees, Whereon nor fruit nor leafe was ever *seene,* . . . . I. ix. 34. 2
troubled blood through his pale face was *seene* . . . . I. ix. 51. 5
every sinew *seene,* through his long fast: . . . . . I. x. 48. 6
That never yet was *seene* of Faeries sonne; . . . . . I. x. 52. 3
The fairest citty was that might be *seene;* . . . . . I. x. 58. 4
To tell how he had *seene* the Dragons fatall fall. . . . . I. xii. 2. 9
Oft had he *seene* her faire, but never so faire dight. . . . I. xii. 23. 9
nothing is but that which he hath *seene?* . . . . . II. Pr. 3. 5
With living eye more fayre was never *seene* . . . . . II. i. 10. 7
Ne would she speake, ne see, ne yet be *seene,* . . . . II. i. 15. 6
Ne yet her person such as it was *seene;* . . . . . II. i. 21. 2
still the litle hands were bloody *seene:* . . . . . II. ii. 3. 7
Was lightnesse *seene* or looser vanitie, ... II. ii. 15. 4
over all the earth it may be *seene,* . . . . . II. ii. 40. 7
Thrise *seene* the shadowes of the neather world, ... II. ii. 44. 2
Like two faire marble pillours they were *seene,* . . . . II. iii. 28. 1
The day that first of Priame she was *seene,* . . . . II. iii. 31. 7
There maist thou best be *seene,* and best maist see: . . . II. iii. 39. 8
Eftsoones he fled away, and might no where be *seene.* . . . II. iv. 46. 9
nothing to be *seene* But . . . chests, ... II. vii. 30. 1
Ne was there ever noble corage *seene,* . . . . . II. viii. 26. 3
never had they *seene* so straunge a sight. . . . . II. ix. 33. 4
Some daily *seene* and knowen by their names, ... II. ix. 50. 6
lost his sword, yet to be *seene* this day. . . . . II. x. 49. 5
in his hand a bended bow was *seene,* . . . . . II. xi. 21. 1
Ne scarse his feet on ground were *seene* to tred: . . . . II. xi. 26. 3
Ye might have *seene* the frothy billowes fry . . . . . II. xii. 45. 1
Whose image shee had *seene* in Venus looking glas. . . . III. i. 8. 9
he had *seene* The secrete vertue of that weapon keene, . . . III. i. 10. 4
it was *seene* To gore her side; . . . . . III. i. 65. 5
emongst the which was *seene* A goodly Armour, ... III. iii. 58. 6
Whose like in Faery lond were seldom *seene,* . . . . III. iv. 51. 2
A foule ill-favoured foster, I have *seene:* . . . . . III. v. 6. 3
By tract of blood, which she had freshly *seene* . . . . III. v. 28. 4
A faire Pavilion, scarcely to bee *seene,* . . . . . III. v. 40. 7
too late He had him *seene,* . . . . . III. vi. 14. 4
as they had never *seene* Fleshly corruption, ... III. vi. 33. 3
ne living wight was *seene* Save one old Nymph, ... III. viii. 37. 8
'These eyes did see that they will ever rew T' have *seene,'* III. viii. 49. 2
who so straungely had him *seene* bestadd, ... III. x. 54. 7
Twise was he *seene* in soaring Eagles shape, ... III. xi. 34. 1
ye mote have lively *seene* The God . . . . . III. xi. 37. 6
love is sullein, and Saturnlike *seene,* . . . . . III. xi. 43. 3
a wide wound . . . was to be *seene,* . . . . . III. xii. 20. 8
Which *seene,* he much rejoyced in his cruell minde. . . . III. xii. 22. 9
in safetie now I have you *seene,* . . . . . III. xii. 40. 4
Had ye them *seene,* . . . . . III. xii. 46. *or.* 1
Bove all her sexe that ever yet was *seene.* . . . . . IV. Pr. 4. 5
Witnesse their broken bandes there to be *seene,* . . . . IV. i. 24. 6
to see the fortune of that fray, And to be *seene,* . . . . IV. iii. 4. 8
had ye then him forth advauncing *seene,* . . . . . IV. iii. 23. 4
Is often *seene* full freshly to have florisht, ... IV. iii. 29. 7
halfe affeard . . . as he some ghost had *seene,* . . . . IV. iii. 31. 6
Who backe returning told, as he had *seene,* . . . . . IV. iv. 3. 1
he came where he had Cambell *seene* . . . . . IV. iv. 34. 4
shortly was likewise *seene* lying on the plaine. . . . . IV. iv. 44. 9
It hath bene through all ages ever *seene,* . . . . . IV. v. 1. 1
produce His false Duessa, that she might be *seene;* . . . . IV. v. 11. 2
So many heavenly faces were not *seene* . . . . . IV. v. 12. 5
The sight of whom once *seene* did all the rest dismay. . . . IV. v. 13. 9
As like can not be *seene* from East to West, ... IV. v. 18. 4
all his haire was like a garment *seene;* . . . . . IV. vii. 7. 3
these sory eies have *seen* Seaven women . . . . . IV. vii. 13. 4
of his owne rash hand one wound was to be *seene.* . . . . IV. vii. 35. 9
strange wight, whom he had *seene* no where, ... IV. vii. 43. 7
he him had *seene* To weld his naked sword, ... IV. vii. 45. 8
full oft she both of them had *seene* Asunder, ... IV. ix. 10. 3
by one patterne, *seene* somewhere, She had them made . . . IV. ix. 11. 5
Which he had lately *seene,* . . . . . IV. xii. 26. 9
A sorie sight as ever *seene* with eye, ... V. i. 14. 2
seene The semblant of this false by his faire beauties Queene. . V. iii. 19. 8
tasted had, And but halfe *seene* his ugly visnomie, ... V. iv. 11. 3
As she had *seene* that day, ... V. iv. 47. 9
Out of her steely armes were flashing *seene,* . . . . . V. v. 8. 4
Who had him *seene* imagine mote thereby . . . . . V. v. 24. 1
sooth oft *seene,* that proudest harts base love hath blynded.' . V. v. 40. 9
those deadly ends Of both her foes had *seene,* . . . . . V. viii. 10. 5
having throughly heard and *seene* Al those great wrongs, . . V. viii. 24. 1
no whole peece of him was to be *seene,* . . . . . V. viii. 42. 8
That ever yet upon this earth was *seene,* . . . . . V. ix. 20. 8
of all men royally be *seene,* . . . . . V. ix. 27. 4
Was brought to her sad doome, as here was to be *seene.* . . V. ix. 42. 9
All which when as the Prince had heard and *seene,* . . . . V. ix. 49. 1
When they had *seene* and heard her doome . . . . . V. x. 4. 3
had *seene* In their first flowre, ... V. x. 7. 4
Whose dreadfull shape was never *seene* of none . . . . . V. x. 29. 4
what she had not *seene* within unto her shewed: . . . . V. x. 38. 9
all his teeth wide bare One might have *seene* . . . . . V. xi. 9. 8
oft had *seene* like sight, ... V. xii. 16. 6
where may be *seene* The goodly praise . . . . . VI. Pr. 6. 2
none is to me unknowne that ev'r was *seene.* . . . . . VI. ii. 31. 9

Seen—*Continued.*
For seldome *seene* a trotting Stalion get . . . . . VI. iii. 1. 6
So seldome *seene* that one in basenesse set . . . . . VI. iii. 1. 8
'And, certes, it hath oftentimes bene *seene,* . . . . . VI. iv. 36. 1
Having oft *seene* it tryde as he did teach: . . . . . VI. iv. 37. 3
he right well in Leaches craft was *seene;* . . . . . VI. vi. 3. 1
As loth to see or to be *seene* at all: . . . . . VI. viii. 5. 6
Unwilling to be knowne or *seene* at all, ... VI. viii. 27. 3
Ne ever had such knightly service *seene,* . . . . . VI. ix. 35. 3
who had *seene* him then, would have bethought . . . . VI. ix. 36. 6
if he were *seene;* . . . . . VI. x. 11. 3
Whose like before his eye had never *seene;* . . . . . VI. x. 17. 2
not so well *seene* as felt. . . . . VI. x. 42. 9
but hardly *seene* by candle-light, ... VI. xi. 13. 2
To see that mortall eyes have never *seene;* . . . . . VII. vi. 32. 3
Since thou hast *seene* her dreadfull power belowe, ... VII. vi. 32. 6
Ne could be *seene* but like an image in a glass. . . . . VII. vii. 6. 9
the love of some new Nymph, late *seene,* . . . . . VII. vii. 11. 6
Death with most grim and griesly visage *seene,* . . . . VII. vii. 46. 2
still throw betweene Some graces to be *seene;* . . . . *Epith.* 107
Had ye once *seene* these her celestial threasures, ... *Epith.* 200
thing on earth so heavenly to have *seene* . . . . . *H.L.* 214
Sights never *seene,* and thousand shadowes vaine, ... *H.L.* 255
it may well be *seene* A pallace . . . . . *H.B.* 125
And tell me then, what hast thou ever *seene* . . . . . *H.H.B.* 57
his grace, . . . through which he may Be *seene* . . . . *H.H.B.* 116
Teian Poet . . . *Seene* but a glims of this which I pretend, . . *H.H.B.* 221
were goodly to bee *seene* Two gentle Knights . . . . . *Proth.* 168

Sees. heares and *sees* the follies of the rest, ... *Hub.* 725
when he *sees* his age, And hoarie head of Archimago old, . . I. iii. 38. 3
Thou seest all, yet none at all *sees* thee: . . . . . III. x. 4. 8
He *sees* her face; doth fall in love, ... IV. vi. Arg.
shee strange visions *sees:* . . . . . V. vii. Arg.
grudge at all That ever she *sees* doen prays-worthily; . . . V. xii. 31. 3
Calidore *sees* young Tristram slay . . . . . VI. ii. Arg.
Which when she *sees* with ghastly griefful eies, ... VI. viii. 40. 5
Calidore *sees* the Graces daunce . . . . . VI. x. Arg.
who them *sees* would wonder at their fray, ... VI. xi. 17. 7
who *sees* not would be affrayd to heare: . . . . . VI. xi. 17. 8
What man that *sees* the ever-whirling wheele, Of Change, . . VII. vi. 1. 1
For who *sees* not that Time on all doth pray? . . . . . VII. vii. 47. 5
the more she fervent *sees* my fit, ... *Am.* xxxii. 9
When once the Crab behind his back he *sees.* . . . . . *Epith.* 269

Seest. These same olde walls, olde arches, which thou *seest,* . . *Ro.* iii. 3
Seest howe brag yond Bullocke beares, ... *S.C.* F. 71
Seest how fresh my flowers bene spredde, ... *S.C.* F. 129
Seest not thilke same Hawthorne studde, ... *S.C.* Mar. 13
thou *seest* my lowly saile, ... *S.C.* S. 250
Seest thou not how all places quake and quiver, ... *Gn.* 340
Save as thou *seest* or hearst. . . . . II. viii. 14. 3
seest every secret of the minde; . . . . . III. x. 4. 7
Thou *seest* all, yet none at all sees thee: . . . . . III. x. 4. 8
'*Seest* not the Ladie there before thy face?' . . . . . IV. ii. 22. 6
'*Seest* not how badly all things present bee, ... V. ii. 37. 2
'thou *seest* yond Fayry Knight, ... V. v. 32. 1

Seethe. *seeth* with secret fire eternally, ... II. x. 26. 3

Seewing. *See* **Suing.**

Seisin. As of her owne by liverey and *seisin;* . . . . . VI. iv. 37. 7

Seize. With that he causeth sleep to *seize* the eyes, ... *Hub.* 1295
beast, Who on his neck his bloody clawes did *seize,* . . . . I. viii. 15. 2
To *seize* upon his foe flatt lying on the marle. . . . . II. xi. 33. 9
by no meanes the high banke he could *sease,* . . . . . III. v. 19. 8
The Monster, ready on the pray to *sease,* . . . . . III. vii. 28. 1
ere the stroke could *seize* his aymed place, ... III. vii. 40. 3
Waiting advauntage on the pray to *sease,* . . . . . III. x. 30. 6
suffer sleepe to *seaze* His eye-lids sad, ... V. vi. 26. 5
Tho all in rage he on him streight did *seaze,* . . . . . VI. vi. 40. 5
flyes . . . Do *seize* upon some beast whose flesh is bare, . . VI. xi. 48. 2

Seized. sleep . . . *seized* everie lim. . . . . *Gn.* 240
The Ape, thus *seized* of the Regall throne, ... *Hub.* 1111
he *seized* greedelie On the resistles pray; . . . . . *Mui.* 435
a Gryfon, *seized* of his pray, ... I. v. 8. 2
in his shoulder *seasd,* Where fast it stucke, ... I. xi. 38. 6
safe ye *seised* have the shore, ... I. xii. 17. 7
cold Have not all *seized* on your frozen hart, ... II. i. 46. 6
It *seizd* in his right side, and there the dint did stay. . . . II. viii. 38. 9
seized every sence with sorrow sore opprest. . . . . III. vi. 10. 9
Him in his iron paw he *seized* had; . . . . . V. i. 22. 2
on the threasure by that judgement *seased,* . . . . . V. iv. 20. 4
seiz'd her cruell clawes Uppon the carkasse . . . . . V. iv. 40. 6
hath *seized* for her share Uppon some fowle . . . . . V. iv. 42. 4
the sad steele *seizd* not, where it was hight, ... V. xi. 8. 7
'So is my Lord now *seiz'd* of all the land, ... VI. iv. 30. 1
of her love he was entyrely *seized,* . . . . . VI. xii. 5. 3

Seizing. *seizing* cruell clawes on trembling brest, ... I. iii. 19. 8
On which it *seizing* no way enter might, ... II. iv. 46. 7
th' one hand *seizing* on his golden bit, ... V. iii. 29. 6
thereon *seizing* tooke no great effect; . . . . . V. xii. 21. 7

Seizure. Upon all which the Briton Prince made *seasure,* . . . IV. ix. 12. 5

Selcouth. wondred much at his so *selcouth* case; . . . . IV. viii. 14. 2

Seldom. levin, That *seeldome* falles bynethe. . . . . *S.C.* Jul. 92
seeldome chaunge the better brought: . . . . . *S.C.* S. 69
Sildome but some good commeth ere the end.' . . . . . *Hub.* 172
seldome seene, forejudgment proveth true. . . . . *Mui.* 320
Whose like before mine eye had *seldome* seene, ... *D.* 114
th Maple *seeldom* inward sound. . . . . I. i. 9. 9
from his frend he *seeldome* knew his fo. . . . . I. iv. 23. 5
True loves are often sown, but *seldom* grow on grownd.' . . I. ix. 16. 9
'*Seldom*' (said Guyon) 'yields to vertue aide, ... II. ix. 8. 2
Whose like in Faery lond were *seldom* seene, ... III. iv. 51. 2

Seldom—*Continued.*
With which he *seldome* fished at the brooke, . . . V. ix. 11. 7
Yet spake she *seldom,* but thought more . . . V. xii. 29. 9
whose like hereafter *seldome* may, . . . VI. ii. 33. 2
For *seldome* seene a trotting Stalion get . . . VI. iii. 1. 6
So *seldome* seene that one in basenesse set . . . VI. iii. 1. 8
For *seldome* yet did living creature see . . . VI. iii. 40. 8
Select. the glorious Features of beautie, and all shapes *select,* III. vi. 12. 4
likest to your selves ye them *select,* . . . *H.B.* 191
Selected. The judges, which thereto *selected* were, . . . IV. v. 6. 7
Self. *See* **Herself, Himself, Itself, Myself, Themselves, Thyself, Yourself.**
Selfe have I worne out thrise threttie yeares, . . . *S.C.* F. 17
The Hus-bandman *selfe* to come that way, . . . *S.C.* F. 144
The while the shepheard *selfe* did spill. . . . *S.C.* Au. 60
Colin Clout, I wene, be his *selfe* boye, . . . *S.C.* S. 176
As if it the old man *selfe* had bene: . . . *S.C.* S. 218
To Pan his owne *selfe* pype I . . . *S.C.* D. 46
To thinges of ryper season *selfe* applyed, . . . *S.C.* D. 76
the Shepheard *self,* tending his stocke, . . . *Gn.* 237
Ida *selfe,* in ayde of that fierce fight, . . . *Gn.* 505
the man whom Nature *selfe* had made . . . *T.M.* 205
The Goddesse *selfe* to chalenge . . . *Mui.* 270
Worthie of Colin *selfe,* that did it make. . . . *Col.* 158
Made by the Maker *selfe* to be admired; . . . *Col.* 561
That Cupid *selfe* of them ashamed is, . . . *Col.* 768
Venus *selfe* doth soly couples seeme, . . . *Col.* 801
Hast Cupid *selfe* depainted in his kynd, . . . *Col.* 898
The maker *selfe,* . . . Was nigh beguiled . . . I. i. 45. 6
Ne Persia *selfe,* the nourse of pompous pride, . . . I. iv. 7. 6
Was like the person *selfe* whom he did beare: . . . I. iv. 24. 4
for his love, and for her own *selfe* sake, . . . I. vi. 2. 6
old Sylvanus *selfe* bethinkes . . . I. vi. 16. 3
dame Venus *selfe* he seemes to see; . . . I. vi. 16. 6
The Gyaunt *selfe,* dismaied with that sownd, . . . I. viii. 5. 4
Accept therefore My simple *selfe,* . . . I. viii. 27. 5
strive your excellent *selfe* to excell: . . . I. xi. 2. 7
As *selfe* to dyen bad, unburied bad to beene.' . . . II. i. 59. 9
Vaine others overthrowes who *selfe* doth overthrow. . . . II. v. 15. 9
her sweete *selfe* . . . She sett beside, . . . II. vi. 14. 5
th' Author *selfe* could not at least attend . . . II. x. 68. 5
Such as Dame Nature *selfe* mote feare . . . II. xii. 23. 2
That is our *Selfe,* . . . each doth in him selfe it well perceive II. xii. 47. 8
Eden *selfe,* if ought with Eden mote compayre. . . . II. xii. 52. 9
But Guyon *selfe,* ere well he was aware, . . . III. i. 6. 6
see frends grave, then dead the grave *self* to engrosse. . . . III. iv. 38. 9
even Nature *selfe* envide the same, . . . III. viii. 5. 4
She was the Lady *selfe* whom he so long had sought. . . . III. viii. 9. 9
The good man *selfe,* . . . Him answered, . . . III. ix. 10. 2
Cupid *selfe,* it seeing, close did smyle . . . III. x. 5. 7
Your vertue *selfe* her owne reward shall breed, . . . III. xii. 39. 5
Th' Enchaunter *selfe,* which all that fraud did frame . . . III. xii. 43. 7
eke the Ladie *selfe* he brought away, . . . IV. i. 2. 7
even th' Almightie *selfe* . . . IV. i. 30. 2
Love is free, and led with *selfe* delight, . . . IV. i. 46. 8
Such as the maker *selfe* could best by art devize. . . . IV. iii. 38. 9
to Braggadochio *selfe* alone She came . . . IV. v. 26. 8
entring in, they found the goodman *selfe* . . . IV. v. 34. 1
For which Dan Phebus *selfe* cannot a salve provide. . . . IV. vi. 1. 9
The maker *selfe* resembling in her feature! . . . IV. vi. 17. 5
Selfe to forget to mind another is over-sight.' . . . IV. vii. 10. 9
Loe! where the villaine *selfe,* . . . Came . . . IV. vii. 20. 3
that *selfe* arrow which the Carle had kild; . . . IV. vii. 36. 5
The Tyrant *selfe* came forth . . . IV. viii. 62. 2
did nature *selfe* amaze. . . . IV. x. 24. 9
'Right in the midst the Goddesse *selfe* did stand . . . IV. x. 39. 1
To Proteus *selfe* to sue for her discharge: . . . IV. xii. 14. 4
To Proteus *selfe* to sew she thought it vaine, . . . IV. xii. 29. 1
unto great king Neptune *selfe* did goe, . . . IV. xii. 29. 4
Braggadochio *selfe* with dreriment So daunted was . . . V. iii. 26. 7
Untill that Guyon *selfe* unto him spake, . . . V. iii. 34. 2
lo! the Damzell *selfe,* whence all did grow, . . . V. viii. 15. 8
spill Her person, and her sacred *selfe* to slay: . . . V. viii. 19. 4
Uppon the Souldan *selfe,* . . . V. viii. 24. 7
the vertue *selfe,* which her reward doth pay.' . . . V. xi. 17. 9
Belge *selfe* was therewith stonied sore, . . . V. xi. 30. 3
Grandtorto *selfe* I did appall, . . . V. xi. 53. 8
A wicked hag, and Envy *selfe* excelling In mischiefe; . . . V. xii. 35. 7
of the Lady *selfe* in sad dismay He was ymett, . . . VI. i. 24. 7
great helpe dame Nature *selfe* doth lend; . . . VI. ii. 2. 1
her sad *selfe* . . . constrayning, To wype his wounds, . . . VI. ii. 41. 4
did with his smarting toole Oft whip her dainty *selfe,* . . . VI. vii. 39. 9
'Since then in each mans *self'* . . . VI. ix. 31. 1
him esteemed nought, No more then Cynthia's *selfe;* . . . VII. vi. 18. 9
But Cynthia's *selfe,* more angry . . . VII. vi. 51. 1
Where Phoebus *selfe,* . . . did sing . . . VII. vii. 12. 6
that to be My heritage Jove's *selfe* cannot denie, . . . VII. vii. 16. 7
Cupid *selfe* about her fluttred all in greene. . . . VII. vii. 34. 9
Phoebus *selfe,* who lightsome is alone, . . . VII. vii. 51. 7
Natur's *selfe* did vanish, . . . VII. vii. 59. 9
to the Maker *selfe* they likest be, . . . *Am.* ix. 13
Your goodly *selfe* for evermore to vew: . . . *Am.* xlv. 2
in my selfe, my inward *selfe,* I meane, . . . *Am.* xlv. 3
vile adders sting, Of that *selfe* kynd . . . *Am.* lxxxv. 2
In whom He might His mightie *selfe* behould; . . . *H.H.L.* 117
onely man himselfe, who *selfe* did slyde: . . . *H.H.L.* 145
our brethren, that were made Of that *selfe* mould, . . . *H.H.L.* 198
made Of that selfe mould, and that *selfe* Makers hand, . . . *H.H.L.* 198
great desire Of his deare *selfe,* . . . *H.H.L.* 269
Self-assurance. Such *selfe-assurance* need not feare . . . *Am.* lix. 9
Self-consuming. pine away in *selfe-consuming* paine! . . . *D.* 436
Before the dore sat *selfe-consuming* Care, . . . II. vii. 25. 1
feed it selfe with *selfe-consuming* smart? . . . III. xi. 1. 8
inflame The hearts of men with *selfe-consuming* fyre . . . *H.H.B.* 275
Self-deceiver. So did deceipt the *selfe-deceiver* fayle. . . . V. ix. 19. 7
Self-delight. please my selfe with mine owne *selfe-delight,* . . . *T.M.* 525
Self-despite. He driven was to ground in *selfe despight;* . . . VI. viii. 10. 7
Self-disliked. *selfe-disliked* life, doth thee thus wretched make? . . . IV. viii. 14. 9
Self-feeling. by *self-feeling* of her feeble sexe, . . . III. i. 54. 2
Self-loved. in her *selfe-lov'd* semblance took delight; . . . I. iv. 10. 8
with *selfe-loved* personage deceiv'd, . . . II. iii. 5. 4
Self-murdering. through long anguish and *selfe-murdring* thought, . . . III. x. 57. 1
Self-pleasing. With such *selfe-pleasing* thoughts her wound she fedd, . . . III. iv. 6. 1
proud despight of his *selfe-pleasing* mynd, . . . VI. i. 15. 2
Without some spark of such *self-pleasing* pride. . . . *Am.* v. 14
Self-regard. *selfe-regard* of private good or ill . . . *Col.* 682
Self-resemblance. in her *self-resemblance* well beseene, . . . I. xii. 8. 8
Self's. thine owne *selfes* valiance, . . . *Ti.* 324
Yet he it tooke in his owne *selfes* despight, . . . V. v. 23. 6
Selfsame. A puissant armie come the *selfe same* way. . . . *Rev.* iii. 7
The very *selfe same* day that she was wedded, . . . IV. i. 3. 2
in the *selfe same* river, where he late . . . IV. xi. 38. 5
The *selfe same* evening fortune hether drove, . . . VI. viii. 46. 8
Pastorell, who, with the *selfe same* wound . . . VI. xi. 19. 8
The *selfe same* flocks the which those theeves had reft . . . VI. xi. 37. 2
The gentle deare returnd the *selfe-same* way, . . . *Am.* lxvii. 7
Which also were with *selfe-same* price redeemed That we, . . *H.H.L.* 202
Self-willed. pynd away in anguish and *selfe-wild* annoy. . . . I. vi. 17. 9
Selinis. an almond tree ymounted hye On top of greene *Selinis* I. vii. 32. 6
Sell. *sell* fee-simples in his Masters name, . . . *Hub.* 867
A Farmer, that would *sell* Bargaines of woods, . . . *Hub.* 871
himselfe to mockerie to *sell.* . . . *T.M.* 222
Bold men, presuming life for gaine to *sell,* . . . *Col.* 209
they themselves for praise of fooles do *sell,* . . . *Col.* 723
He left his loftie steed with golden *sell* . . . II. ii. 11. 6
rode in golden *sell* with single spere, . . . II. iii. 12. 3
On his horse necke before the quilted *sell,* . . . II. v. 4. 5
the Prince would not forsake his *sell,* . . . II. viii. 31. 3
Nathelesse it bore his foe not from his *sell,* . . . III. i. 6. 4
never wight so fast in *sell* could sit, . . . III. iii. 60. 6
the Boaster from his loftie *sell* Faynd to alight, . . . III. x. 38. 5
To *sell* her borrowed beautie to abuse: . . . IV. i. 31. 4
forced him to leave his loftie *sell,* . . . IV. iv. 30. 8
it chynd his backe behind the *sell,* . . . IV. vi. 13. 8
So hard a taske as life for hyre to *sell;* . . . VI. vii. 15. 3
Where I did *sell* my selfe for yearely hire, . . . VI. ix. 24. 7
For slaves to *sell* them for no small reward . . . VI. x. 43. 4
Selves. 'Ne shall the Saxons *selves* all peaceably Enjoy . . . III. iii. 46. 1
To your faire *selves* a faire ensample frame . . . III. v. 54. 1
That th' Angels *selves* can not endure his sight. . . . *H.H.B.* 119
Semblably. Is in this verse engraven *semblably,* . . . *Ded. Son.* vi. 13
Semblance. you likest are For manly *semblance,* . . . *Hub.* 200
semblance she did carrie under feigned hew. . . . I. i. 46. 9
in her selfe-lov'd *semblance* took delight; . . . I. iv. 10. 8
gently grenning, shew a *semblance* glad . . . I. vi. 11. 7
often *semblaunce* made to scape out of their hand. . . . I. xii. 35. 9
the stone her *semblance* seemes to show, . . . II. ii. 9. 4
in *semblaunce* of his puissaunce great, . . . II. x. 23. 3
semblaunce pleasing, more then naturall, . . . II. xii. 46. 5
to faire *semblaunce* doth light faith annexe: . . . III. i. 54. 7
semblaunce of faire fight did make, . . . III. vii. 44. 8
in face And outward shew faire *semblance* they did beare; . IV. i. 17. 6
made good *semblance* to his companie, . . . IV. i. 38. 2
Midst sorrow showing joyous *semblance* for his sake. . . . IV. vii. 44. 9
joyd much in his *semblance* glad. . . . V. vii. 41. 9
under shew oftimes of fayned *semblance* . . . V. ix. 22. 8
To whom faire *semblance,* as he could, he shewed . . . VI. iv. 14. 2
Semblances. with soft sighes and lovely *semblaunces* . . . III. vii. 16. 6
Semblant. by the *semblant* of his countenaunce . . . *D.* 51
to draw the *semblant* trew Of beauties Queene, . . . *Ded. Son.* xvii. 5
the knight whose *semblaunt* he did beare, . . . I. ii. 12. 1
under simple shew, and *semblant* plaine Lurkt . . . II. i. 21. 3
Full lively is the *semblaunt,* . . . II. ix. 2. 9
with faire *semblaunt* sought to hyde the breach, . . . II. ix. 39. 3
th' only shade and *semblant* of a knight, . . . III. ii. 38. 3
To love the *semblaunt* pleasing most your minde, . . . III. ii. 40. 7
As seemed by their *semblaunt,* . . . III. xi. 29. 4
in her *semblant* shew'd great womanhood: . . . IV. x. 31. 5
her sad *semblant* and demeanure wyse: . . . IV. x. 49. 6
The *semblant* of this false by his faire beauties Queene. . . V. iii. 19. 9
So daily he faire *semblant* did her shew, . . . V. v. 56. 1
by his modest *semblant* that no evill ment. . . . V. vi. 19. 9
in that wretched *semblant* . . . V. ix. 38. 8
shewed *semblant* of exceeding mone . . . VI. v. 4. 2
Sweete *semblaunt,* friendly offices that bynde, . . . VI. x. 23. 5
Most lively lyke behold your *semblant* trew. . . . *Am.* xlv. 4
with the goodly *semblant* of her hew, . . . *Am.* liii. 6
Unto like goodly *semblant* to aspyre; . . . *H.L.* 109
Semblants. *semblants* outward brave! . . . *Gn.* 93
Through guilefull *semblants* which he makes us see: . . . II. xii. 48. 6
broke his staffe with which he charmed *semblants* sly. . . . II. xii. 49. 9
the sights of *semblants* vaine. . . . III. iv. 54. 5
Semele. the Thebane *Semelee,* Deceivd of gealous Juno, . . . III. xi. 33. 1
Seminary. there is the first *seminary* Of all things that are borne . . . III. vi. 30. 4
Semiramis. The bold *Semiramis* . . . her fowle reproches spoke: I. v. 50. 3
Matchable either to *Semiramis,* . . . II. x. 56. 2

Send. *See* **After-send.**
roote . . . *Sende* forth againe a twinne . . . *Bel.*[1] v. 14
I saw . . . *send* (*Sende*[1]) forth againe. . . . *Bel.* v. 14
I will *send* more after thee. . . . *To his Booke* 18
their God his good does them *send*, . . . *S.C.* May 64
send thee joy of thy jollitee. . . . *S.C.* May 192
Shepheards sich, God mought us many *send*, . . . *S.C.* S. 178
send out Lowder (for so his dog hote) . . . *S.C.* S. 194
Content with any food that God doth *send;* . . . *Gn.* 140
That curse God *send* unto mine enemie! . . . *Hub.* 914
She . . . Will *send* for me; . . . *D.* 390
bad me stay, till she for me did *send*. . . . *D.* 455
right noble Lord, I *send* This present . . . *Ded. Son.* iv. 13
Why doe I *send* this rusticke Madrigale, . . . *Ded. Son.* viii. 3
He bids thee to him *send* . . . A fit false dreame, . . . I. i. 43. 8
path . . . after all to heaven shall thee *send*, . . . I. x. 61. 2
Such noyse his rouzed scales did *send* unto the knight. . . . I. xi. 9. 9
Beacons . . . *Send* forth their flames . . . I. xi. 14. 4
So far as Ewghen bow a shaft may *send*, . . . I. xi. 19. 2
God ye speed and *send* you good successe, . . . II. i. 25. 6
when ever he for ought did *send;* . . . II. ix. 58. 5
they to direfull death their groning ghosts did *send*. . . . II. xi. 15. 9
for him in hast did *send;* . . . III. iii. 10. 7
mightie cause, us two did hither *send*.' . . . III. iii. 15. 9
To *send* thine Angell from her bowre of blis . . . III. v. 35. 3
Which chearefull signe did *send* unto her sight . . . III. vii. 5. 4
succor *send* to her distressed cace; . . . III. viii. 29. 4
if that hevenly grace some goode reliefe You *send*, . . . III. xi. 14. 4
God *send* you better gaine!' . . . IV. ii. 6. 5
Each other horse and man to ground did *send;* . . . IV. ii. 15. 7
out of his streame doth *send* Plenty of pearles . . . IV. xi. 39. 5
We on his first adventure may him forward *send*. . . . V. iii. 40. 9
She thought to *send* some one to seeke him out; . . . V. vi. 6. 2
So both agreed to *send* that mayd afore, . . . V. ix. 8. 6
she take comfort which God now did *send:* . . . V. x. 22. 8
speaches forth doth *send*, . . . V. xi. 20. 7
She was by him adviz'd to *send* me . . . VI. ii. 30. 2
whom she did oft implore To *send* her succour, . . . VI. iv. 10. 9
prayd high God them farre from them to *send*. . . . VI. ix. 6. 5
to praise th' Almighty that doth *send* it! . . . VI. ix. 21. 9
Into this sinfull world from heaven to *send;* . . . *Am.* xxiv. 10
Then shall the new yeares joy forth freshly *send*, . . . *Am.* lxii. 9
Send us the timely fruit of this same night. . . . *Epith.* 404
When he them on his messages doth *send*, . . . *H.H.L.* 67
Sendest. Instead of sleepe thou *sendest* troublous feares . . . III. iv. 57. 5
Sendeth. firme is fixt, and *sendeth* light from farre . . . I. ii. 1. 4
sendeth forth to live in mortall state, . . . III. vi. 32. 8
Sending. *sending* to the Souldan in despight A bold defyance, V. viii. 27. 7
Sends. 'What voice . . . *Sends* to my doubtful eares these speaches rare, . . . I. ii. 32. 8
Her greeting *sends* . . . The wofull daughter . . . I. xii. 26. 2
blessed Angels he *sends* to and fro, . . . II. viii. 1. 8
He *sends* the sea his owne with double gaine, . . . IV. iii. 27. 8
Sends forth the winds out of his hidden threasure . . . IV. ix. 23. 3
to afflicted minds sweet rest and quiet *sends*. . . . IV. x. 34. 9
swarmes of damned soules to hell he *sends:* . . . VI. viii. 49. 7
in her songs, *sends* many a wishfull vow . . . *Am.* lxxxviii. 3
when her words embassade forth she *sends*, . . . *H.B.* 251
Seneschal. The *Seneschall* was cal'd to deeme the right: . . . IV. i. 12. 1
Gerioneos *Seneschall* He slayes . . . V. x. Arg.
set a *Seneschall* of dreaded might, . . . V. x. 30. 2
forth to call Into the field their Tyrants *Seneschall:* . . . V. x. 31. 5
laid his *Seneschall* low on the ground, . . . V. xi. 2. 4
therein hath a *Seneschall* assynd, Cald Maleffort, . . . VI. i. 15. 7
Murdred my men, and slaine my *Seneschall*, . . . VI. i. 25. 3
Having late slaine her *Seneschall* in fight, . . . VI. i. 29. 8
Whom from her *Seneschall* he lately freed, . . . VI. i. 47. 4
Seneschals. Yet could the *Seneschals* no entrance find . . . V. x. 32. 6
Sens. *See* **Since.**
Sense. Seemeth thou dost their soule of *sence* bereave; . . . *S.C.* O. 27
bigger notes, that may thy *sense* allure, . . . *Gn.* 11
feare and yre Had blent so much his *sense*, . . . *Gn.* 311
Into whose *sense* so soone as lighter sleepe Was entered, . . . *Gn.* 321
His *sense* to seeke for ease turnes every way: . . . *Gn.* 388
the shrill woods, which were of *sense* bereav'd, . . . *Gn.* 455
Depriv'd of *sense* and ordinarie reason, . . . *Hub.* 11
sought my troubled *sense* how to deceave . . . *Hub.* 23
my *sense* it greatly pleased, . . . *Hub.* 39
men depriv'd of *sense* and minde. . . . *T.M.* 156
A stonie coldnesse hath benumbd the *sence* . . . *T.M.* 253
With horrid sound though having little *sence*, . . . *T.M.* 554
Robbed of *sense*, and ravished with joy: . . . *Ti.* 321
His choicefull *sense* with every change doth flit: . . . *Mui.* 159
He casts his glutton *sense* to satisfie, . . . *Mui.* 179
whoso else in pleasure findeth *sense*, . . . *D.* 8
Bereave of *sence* each rash beholders sight. . . . *Col.* 547
Through secret *sence* which thereto doth them draw. . . . *Col.* 886
Yet if their deeper *sence* be inly wayd, . . . *Ded. Son.* ix. 9
me needs . . . To sharpe my *sence* with sundry beauties vew, . *Ded. Son.* xvii. 7
with that dint her *sence* was dazd; . . . I. i. 18. 1
weaker *sence* it could have ravisht quight: . . . I. i. 45. 5
gan himselfe advise To prove his *sense*, . . . I. i. 50. 6
doubting much his *sence*, he thus bespake: . . . I. ii. 32. 4
the Paynim lay, Devoid of outward *sence* . . . I. v. 29. 3
an Enchaunter bad His *sence* abusd, . . . I. vii. 49. 4
every *sence* the humour sweet embayd, . . . I. ix. 13. 5
did quite confound His feeble *sence*, . . . I. x. 67. 8
bitter *sence* of his deepe rooted ill, . . . I. xi. 22. 8
let that man with better *sence* advize, . . . II. Pr. 2. 1
yield his *sence* to bee too blunt and bace, . . . II. Pr. 4. 4

Sense—*Continued.*
so far all *sence* they pas. . . . II. i. 49. 6
gazers *sence* with double pleasure fed, . . . II. iii. 22. 8
her sweete words that all his *sence* dismayd, . . . II. iii. 42. 3
sweetnesse doth allure the weaker *sence* . . . II. vi. 1. 3
had both life and *sence*, . . . II. vii. 40. 8
stony feare . . . all his *sence* dismayd, . . . II. viii. 46. 2
The second Bulwarke was the Hearing *sence*, . . . II. xi. 10. 1
doe that *sence* besiege with light illusions. . . . II. xi. 11. 9
Illusion that did beguile his *sense*, . . . II. xi. 39. 6
huge Sea monsters, such as living *sence* dismayd: . . . II. xii. 22. 9
sweete and pleasing unto living *sense*, . . . II. xii. 42. 6
suffred no delight To sincke into his *sence*, . . . II. xii. 53. 3
If any puffe of breath or signe of *sence* shee fond. . . . III. i. 60. 9
His feeling wordes her feeble *sence* much pleased, . . . III. ii. 15. 1
a litle creeping sleepe Surprisd her *sence:* . . . III. ii. 47. 7
With so sweet *sence* and secret powre unspide, . . . III. vi. 7. 8
seized every *sence* with sorrow sore opprest. . . . III. vi. 10. 9
They were through wonder nigh of *sence* berev'd, . . . III. vi. 27. 5
shewd by outward signes that dread her *sence* did daze. . . . III. vii. 7. 9
some extasye Assotted had his *sence*, . . . III. viii. 22. 9
Him bett so sore, that life and *sence* did much dismay . . . III. viii. 31. 9
So lively and so like that living *sence* it fayld. . . . III. xi. 46. 9
could not find what *sence* it figured: . . . III. xi. 50. 5
as if the steele had *sence*, . . . IV. vi. 21. 6
felt some ruth or *sence* his hand did lacke, . . . IV. vi. 21. 7
Whilest trembling horrour did his *sense* assayle, . . . IV. vi. 22. 8
Ne signe of *sence* did shew, ne common wit, . . . IV. vii. 44. 3
gainst common *sence*, . . . IV. x. 2. 4
sense of man so coy and curious nice, . . . IV. x. 22. 6
did fraile *sense* entice. . . . IV. x. 22. 9
huge stroke, that it of *sence* distraught her; . . . V. iv. 41. 5
soone as she her *sence* recover'd had, . . . V. iv. 43. 1
albe he wanted *sence* And sorrowes feeling, . . . V. vi. 9. 4
By outward shew her inward *sence* desining: . . . V. vii. 8. 3
each one of *sence* bereft Fled fast . . . V. vii. 34. 8
Nought under heaven so strongly doth allure The *sence* of man, V. viii. 1. 2
when againe they had recovered *sence*, . . . V. viii. 10. 1
So did the sight thereof their *sense* dismay, . . . V. viii. 38. 2
candle-light, which delt A doubtfull *sense* of things, . . . VI. x. 42. 9
inly quaking, seem'd as reft of *sense* . . . VII. vi. 25. 4
which who feeles not by *sense* . . . To flit still, . . . VII. vii. 22. 1
(For of all *sense* it is the middle meane) . . . VII. vii. 22. 2
smiles, that rob *sence* from the hart; . . . *Am.* xvii. 10
hob Goblins, names whose *sence* we see not, . . . *Epith.* 343
doth so much excell All mortall *sence*, . . . *H.B.* 42
it can rob both *sense*, and reason blynd? . . . *H.B.* 77
to the *sense* most daintie odours yield, . . . *H.B.* 80
With *sence* whereof, . . . Lift up thy mind . . . *H.H.L.* 253
Whose glorious beames all fleshly *sense* doth daze . . . *H.H.L.* 278
it doth bereave Their soule of *sense*, . . . *H.H.B.* 258
Ne from thenceforth doth any fleshly *sense*, . . . remaine; . . . *H.H.B.* 267
That to the *sense* did fragrant odours yeild, . . . *Proth.* 75
Senseful. The Ladie, hearkning to his *sensefull* speach, . . . VI. iv. 37. 1
Whose *sensefull* words empierst his hart so neare, . . . VI. ix. 26. 3
Senseless. Semed, the *sencelesse* yron dyd feare, . . . *S.C.* F. 205
beast, That here liest *senseles*, like the corpse deceast, . . . *Hub.* 1328
sate long time in *sencelesse* sad affright, . . . *Ti.* 475
both stand *sencelesse* as a blocke, . . . I. ii. 16. 5
Most *sencelesse* man he, that himselfe doth hate, . . . I. vi. 47. 5
up he tooke the slombred *sencelesse* corse, . . . I. vii. 15. 6
let the stony dart of *sencelesse* cold Perce to my hart, . . . I. vii. 22. 7
Whose *sencelesse* speach, and doted ignorance, . . . I. viii. 34. 2
There him he findes all *sencelesse* and aghast, . . . I. ix. 23. 3
The *sencelesse* corse appointed for the grave: . . . I. xi. 48. 8
Being diffused through the *senceless* tronck, . . . II. ii. 4. 8
Whiles sad Pyrochles lies on *sencelesse* ground, . . . II. v. 36. 6
still he stood as *sencelesse* stone. . . . II. vi. 31. 9
slumbring fast In *senceles* dreame; . . . II. viii. 4. 9
all his sences drowned in deep *sencelesse* wave: . . . II. viii. 24. 9
Life having maystered her *sencelesse* foe, . . . II. viii. 53. 2
kest The lumpish corse unto the *sencelesse* grownd; . . . II. xi. 42. 6
fownd Their lady lying on the *sencelesse* grownd: . . . III. i. 63. 5
Inglorious now lies in *sencelesse* swownd, . . . III. iv. 29. 3
each awhile lay like a *sencelesse* corse. . . . III. ix. 16. 5
like two *senceles* stocks in long embracement dwelt. . . . III. xii. 45. *or.* 9
senselesse stood, like to a mazed steare . . . IV. vi. 37. 4
Having his carrion corse quite *sencelesse* left . . . IV. vii. 32. 4
lay long while in *senselesse* swowne. . . . IV. viii. 42. 9
saw him *sencelesse* by the Squire upstaide, . . . IV. ix. 7. 4
on the ground he layd him like a *sencelesse* blocke. . . . V. i. 21. 9
their faint harts with *senselesse* horrour queld, . . . V. iii. 26. 3
In *sencelesse* swoune, as if her life forsooke, . . . V. v. 11. 4
with soft delight Of *sencelesse* sleepe . . . V. vii. 12. 6
tombling downe upon the *senselesse* ground . . . V. x. 33. 4
So now all three one *sencelesse* lumpe remaine, . . . V. xi. 14. 5
his foe lay fast in *sencelesse* swound; . . . VI. i. 34. 2
confused sound Of *senselesse* words, . . . VI. iv. 11. 8
to the ground he fell in *senselesse* swone: . . . VI. vi. 30. 7
falleth downe to ground like *senselesse* thing; . . . VI. vii. 9. 7
yse, which is congeald with *sencelesse* cold, . . . *Am.* xxx. 11
She is no woman, but a *sencelesse* stone. . . . *Am.* liv. 14
Sense's. All those this *sences* Fort assayle incessantly. . . . II. xi. 12. 9
his *senses* straunge astonishment, . . . V. v. 12. 2
Senses. To this his minde and *senses* he doth bend, . . . *Gn.* 138
streight the spirite out of his *senses* flew, . . . *Gn.* 292
all my *senses* were bereaved quight, . . . *Ti.* 577
may allure the *senses* to delight, . . . *D.* 324
So all my *senses* from me are bereft. . . . *D.* 420
sences all were straight benumbd and starke. . . . I. i. 44. 5

Senses—*Continued.*
all my *senses* were bereaved quight: I. ii. 42. 5
whose glorious vew Their frayle amazed *senses* did confound: I. iv. 7. 3
stony horrour all her *sences* fild I. vi. 37. 3
all his *sences* stound that still he lay full low. I. vii. 12. 9
all his *sences* were with suddein dread dismayd. I. viii. 14. 9
Became stark blind, and all his *sences* dazd, I. viii. 20. 3
dimmes the dazed eyen, and daunts the *sences* quight. I. viii. 21. 9
The deadly dint his dulled *sences* all dismaid. I. xi. 35. 9
refte of his *sences* meet, I. xii. 39. 8
all his *sences* seemd berefte attone: II. i. 42. 4
Thus when shee had his eyes and *sences* fed II. vi. 14. 1
all his *sences* were with deadly fit opprest. II. vii. 66. 9
all his *sences* drowned in deep sencelesse wave: II. viii. 24. 9
That all their *sences* filled with affright; II. xii. 2. 7
Guyons *senses* softly tickeled, II. xii. 33. 7
My *sences* lulled are in slomber of delight. III. Pr. 4. 9
With double *sences*, and with false debate, III. iv. 28. 8
to their *senses* vyld Her gentle speach applyde, III. vii. 15. 3
Least his fraile *senses* were emperisht quight, III. vii. 20. 8
her sonne whose *senses* were decayd. III. viii. 4. 9
fild his *senses* with abashment great; III. viii. 16. 7
all her *sences* with abashment quite were quayld. III. viii. 34. 9
whiles sleepe their *sences* did invade. III. x. 46. 9
the passing brightnes her fraile *sences* dazd. III. xi. 49. 9
sweetnesse . . . The feeble *sences* wholy did confound, III. xii. 6. 4
hammers sound his *senses* did molest, IV. v. 41. 2
all his *senses* did full soone arrest: IV. v. 43. 5
all thy *senses* swowned In stupid sorow, V. v. 36. 5
your outward *senses* to refraine From things VI. vi. 7. 6
from those outward *sences*, ill affected, VI. vi. 8. 1
With such regard his *sences* ravished, VI. x. 30. 7
Like lyfull heat to nummed *senses* brought, VI. xi. 45. 4
all the *sences* they doe ravish quite; *Epith.* 136
And *senses* fraught with such satietie, *H.H.B.* 282
Sensibly. a lamentable lay, So *sensibly* compyld, IV. viii. 4. 4
Sensual. there he held Her captive to his *sensuall* desyre, I. vi. 23. 2
To slug in slouth and *sensuall* delights, II. i. 23. 3
With one sweete drop of *sensuall* delight. II. vi. 8. 7
Armed with dartes of *sensuall* Delight, II. xi. 13. 6
Where Pleasure dwelles in *sensuall* delights, II. xii. 1. 8
swimming deepe in *sensuall* desyres; III. i. 39. 8
poured forth in *sensuall* delight, III. i. 48. 6
It stirreth up to *sensuall* desire, III. v. 1. 6
all that might not slake her *sensuall* desyre: III. vii. 49. 9
Ne one light glance of *sensuall* desyre *Am.* lxxxiii. 3
Sent. *See* **Outsent, Scent.**
forth *sent* That antique horror, *Ro.* xvii. 7
a gentle murmure *sent;* *Gn.* 228
him to death unfaithfull Paris *sent;* *Gn.* 530
as on ambassage *sent* Both too and fro, *Hub.* 472
Pursivants he often for them *sent;* *Hub.* 565
sent the Foxe to them streightway, *Hub.* 1095
Her back againe to life *sent* for his sake. *Ti.* 392
'Hether' (quoth he) 'me Archimago *sent*, I. i. 43. 6
damned sprights *sent* forth to make ill men aghast. I. v. 31. 9
Cursing high Jove, the which them thither *sent*. I. v. 33. 6
In evill houre thy foes thee hither *sent* I. vi. 42. 2
a little grate . . . Through which he *sent* his voyce, I. viii. 37. 7
Me hither *sent* for cause to me unghest; I. ix. 7. 2
sent with carefull diligence, To fetch a Leach, I. x. 23. 6
from his wide devouring oven *sent* A flake of fire, I. xi. 26. 3
Trompets . . . *sent* to heven the ecchoed report I. xii. 4. 2
victorious man, Whom all admired as from heaven *sent*, I. xii. 9. 4
the Redcrosse knight this answere *sent:* I. xii. 31. 1
'My Lord,' (quoth he) 'me *sent*, II. iv. 43. 5
the wise Cordelia Was *sent* to Aggannip of Celtica. II. x. 29. 5
hither hastly *sent* Vespasian, II. x. 52. 6
they hither *sent* Constantius, II. x. 59. 1
He *sent* to Germany straunge aid to reare; II. x. 64. 7
at him a cruell shaft he *sent:* II. xi. 24. 5
yvory into the waves were *sent;* II. xii. 45. 4
the captiv'd Acrasia he *sent*, . . . a nigher way, III. i. 2. 1
Which forth he *sent*, with felonous despight III. i. 65. 3
Ne bubling rowndell they behinde them *sent*. III. iv. 33. 7
sent in haste for Tryphon, III. iv. 43. 7
sent out of the thicket neare A cruell shaft, III. v. 20. 3
headlesse him into the foord he *sent:* III. v. 25. 5
forth her damzells *sent* Through all the woods, III. vi. 25. 7
To search the God of love her Nimphes she *sent* III. vi. 26. 1
sent into the chaungefull world agayne, III. vi. 33. 7
daily forth are *sent* Into the world, III. vi. 36. 1
when the Beast . . . Late foorth she *sent*, III. viii. 2. 6
sent close messages of love to her at will. III. ix. 27. 9
Shee *sent* at him one fyrie dart, III. ix. 28. 8
thy wife shall backe be *sent:* III. x. 32. 2
sent away So many Centaures drunken soules to hell, IV. i. 23. 3
to Sir Paridell these words he *sent:* IV. ii. 5. 6
They *sent* that Squire afore, IV. ii. 31. 3
Conceived by a ring which she him *sent*, IV. ii. 39. 7
Full many mightie strokes on either side Were *sent*, IV. iii. 7. 7
So thicke they fell, and forcibly were *sent*, IV. iii. 26. 2
Sent forth their Squire to have them both descride, IV. iv. 2. 8
She *sent* an arrow forth with mighty draught, IV. vii. 31. 4
Onely few ruefull lookes unto her *sent*, IV. viii. 13. 8
poysnous spirit *sent* From inward parts, IV. viii. 26. 3
streight he after *sent* His yron page, V. i. 20. 1
Therefore he Talus to them *sent* V. ii. 52. 8
what the sea unto you *sent* your own should seeme.' V. iv. 17. 9; 18. 9
he Talus *sent* To wrecke on them their follies hardyment: V. iv. 24. 4

Sent—*Continued.*
sent them home to tell a piteous tale V. iv. 24. 8
Unto those warlike Knights she warning *sent*. V. iv. 50. 4
sent her winged thoughts, more swift then wind, V. vi. 7. 8
it was one *sent* from her love indeede; V. vi. 8. 4
So me in message unto her she *sent*, V. viii. 21. 6
soone after me she *sent* These two false Knights, V. viii. 23. 2
Unto his scornefull Lady that for her had *sent*. V. viii. 25. 9
sent to him a Page that mote direct his way. V. viii. 26. 9
his yron man he *sent* To follow him; V. ix. 16. 1
Sent by their mother, who, a widow, was V. x. 6. 6
these two, her eldest sonnes, she *sent* V. x. 14. 6
sent His groning soule unto her place of punishment. V. x. 36. 8
sent redresse thereof by this brave Briton Knight. V. xi. 1. 9
now he hath this troupe of villains *sent* V. xi. 51. 1
through all that realme he *sent* V. xii. 26. 6
Into this wicked world he forth was *sent* VI. i. 8. 6
He *sent* to her his basenet as a faithfull band. VI. i. 31. 9
Whose fellow he before had *sent* apart; VI. ii. 6. 5
And *sent* me, where him list, instructed for to bee. VI. ii. 28. 9
she . . . *sent* me streight Into this land, VI. ii. 30. 7
They *sent* that Blatant Beast to be a baite VI. v. 15. 3
His mindes sad message backe unto him *sent;* VI. viii. 8. 3
since by grace of God she there was *sent*, VI. viii. 38. 5
Eftsoones the sonne of Maia forth he *sent* VII. vi. 16. 1
sent forth odours sweet; VII. vii. 10. 3
from heaven most hideous stormes are *sent*, Am. xlvi. 3
Sentence. By righteous *sentence* of th' Almighties law. I. ix. 50. 4
proudly did impugne her *sentence* just: V. iv. 2. 5
then you shall my *sentence* understand.' V. iv. 16. 8
When he his *sentence* thus pronounced had, V. iv. 20. 1
most agreed, and did this *sentence* give, VII. vi. 50. 7
Sentinel. he, that points the *Centonell* his roome, I. ix. 41. 8
Sentinels. like to warie *Centonels* well stayd, Still watcht IV. ii. 36. 8
September. Next him *September* marched, VII. vii. 38. 1
Sepulchres. Large streetes, brave houses, sacred *sepulchers*, *Ti.* 94
Seraphim. And those eternall burning *Seraphins*, *H.H.B.* 94
Sere. 'All so my lustfull leafe is drye and *sere*, *S.C.* Ja. 37
His honor decayed, his braunches *sere*. *S.C.* F. 114
this faded Oake, Whose bodie is *sere*, *S.C.* F. 170
Now bringen bitter Eldre braunches *seare;* *S.C.* N. 147
A cloud of smoothering smoke, and sulphure *seare*, I. xi. 13. 7
Serena. Calidore . . . Saves *Serena*, VI. iii. Arg.
The faire *Serena* (so his Lady hight) VI. iii. 23. 2
Serena full of dolorous dismay, VI. iii. 45. 3
The salvage serves *Serena* well, VI. v. Arg.
About the sad *Serena* things to dight, VI. v. 25. 3
aloude the faire *Serena* cryde Unto the Knight, VI. v. 27. 1
Serena did to him relate The foule discourt'sies VI. v. 33. 1
fair *Serene* all night could take no rest, VI. v. 39. 6
(sayd then *Serena*, sighing sore) VI. vi. 13. 5
token Which faire *Serene* to him delivered had, VI. vi. 18. 2
the gentle Squire, with faire *Serene*, VI. vii. 39. 2
The faire *Serena* . . . thought That slaine he was, VI. vii. 50. 1
Serena, found of Salvages, By Calepine is freed. VI. viii. Arg.
first it falleth me by course to tell Of faire *Serena;* VI. viii. 31. 2
he to seeke *Serena* through the woods did rove. VI. viii. 46. 9
Sergeant. had not Natures *Sergeant* . . . Them well disposed VII. vii. 4. 6
Sergis. 'Haile, good Sir *Sergis*, truest Knight alive, V. xi. 38. 2
aread, Sir *Sergis*, how long space V. xi. 42. 1
yet old *Sergis* did so well him paine, V. xii. 10. 7
Sermon. By that he ended had his ghostly *sermon*, *Hub.* 479
Serpent. A stinging *serpent* by the heele her caught: *Pet.* vi. 8
An huge great *Serpent*, all with speckles pide, *Gn.* 250
monster . . . Halfe like a *serpent* horribly displaide, I. i. 14. 7
a cup . . . In which a *Serpent* did himselfe enfold, I. x. 13. 4
like a *Serpent* to the Thracian mayd. III. xi. 35. 4
The cursed *Serpent* . . . was not all so dead V. xii. 39. 5
Serpent's. the Basiliske, of *serpents* seede, IV. viii. 39. 7
Serpents. Fast bound with *serpents* that him oft invades; *Gn.* 374
fruitfull cursed spawne of *serpents* small, I. i. 22. 6
About the which two *Serpents* weren wound, IV. iii. 42. 2
The tongues of *Serpents*, with three forked stings, VI. xii. 28. 2
Servant. *See* **Fellow-servant.**
privily his *servant* thereto hire: *Hub.* 682
A *servant* to the vile affection *Hub.* 817
So am I made the *servant* of the manie, *T.M.* 223
her fiers *servant* . . . full greedy at him came, I. iii. 41. 1
makes it *servaunt* to her basest part, II. i. 57. 6
The carefull *servaunt* stryving with his raging Lord. II. vi. 47. 9
a gracious *servaunt* pictured His Cynthia, III. Pr. 4. 5
the sword was *servaunt* unto right; III. i. 13. 2
with his *servant* Trompart hoverd there, III. x. 23. 2
The *servant* of Admetus, cowheard vile, III. xi. 39. 4
bad his *servant* Talus to invent Which way V. ii. 20. 8
of her *servant* make her soverayne Lord: V. v. 27. 8
His trustie sword, the *servant* of his might, VI. vii. 25. 4
Servant's. ignorant of *servants* bad abuse III. ix. 18. 6
t' obay her *servaunts* law. III. xi. 30. 9
Doe not thy *servants* simple boone refuse; *Epith.* 124
Servants. Proffer thy giftes, and fitter *servaunts* entertaine. II. vii. 9. 9
Doth blesse her *servaunts*, and them high advaunce. II. ix. 5. 5
for his trusty *servaunts* doth so strongly fight.' III. i. 29. 9
In which his worke he had sixe *servants* prest, IV. v. 36. 1
Serve. Nay, but thy seeing will not *serve*, *S.C.* Mar. 43
will *serve* my sheepe to gather, *Hub.* 295
all men, which anie master *serve*, *Hub.* 467
slaine to *serve* the Apes beheasts: *Hub.* 1308
So made by nature for to *serve* their will, *T.M.* 40
Do *serve* to them, *Mui.* 230

Serve—*Continued.*
serve and honour her with faithfull mind. . . . *Col.* 255
the shepheards which my Cynthia *serve* At sea, . . . *Col.* 260
be the shepheards which do *serve* her laesie, . . . *Col.* 372
Vassall to one, whom all my dayes I *serve;* . . . *Col.* 467
Besides yet many mo that Cynthia *serve,* . . . *Col.* 576
him do sue and *serve* all otherwise: . . . *Col.* 786
him they do not *serve* as they professe, . . . *Col.* 791
make him *serve* to them for sordid uses: . . . *Col.* 792
how we rashly go To *serve* that God, . . . *Col.* 798
Then *serve* his Ladies love, and waste in pleasures vayne. . . I. vi. 21. 9
to the wood she goes, to *serve* her turne, . . . I. vi. 22. 3
sold thy selfe to *serve* Duessa vild, . . . I. ix. 46. 8
her to *serve* sixe yeares in warlike wize, . . . I. xii. 18. 7
To *serve* againe his soveraine Elfin Queene, . . . II. i. 1. 6
To *serve* at court in view of vaunting eye; . . . II. iii. 10. 2
To *serve* his Lemans love: . . . II. v. 28. 2
For thou to *serve* Acrasia thy selfe doest vaunt. . . . II. vi. 9. 9
Both slow and swift alike do *serve* my tourne; . . . II. vi. 10. 6
Till season *serve* new passage to assay: . . . II. vi. 23. 7
if for me ye fight, or me will *serve,* . . . II. vi. 34. 1
if me thou deigne to *serve* and sew, . . . II. vii. 9. 1
To *serve* to wicked man, to *serve* his wicked foe. . . . II. viii. 1. 9
that straunge sword refusd to *serve* his neede, . . . II. viii. 49. 2
To *serve* that Queene with al my powre and might. . . . II. ix. 7. 4
whiles wind and wether right Doe *serve* their turnes: . . . II. xi. 4. 8
Dye rather, dye, and dying doe her *serve;* . . . III. v. 46. 6
Dying her *serve,* and living her adore, . . . III. v. 46. 7
To her to whom the hevens doe *serve* and sew? . . . III. v. 47. 2
Whom so she fittest findes to *serve* her lust, . . . III. vii. 50. 4
That gentle Lady whom I love and *serve,* . . . III. vii. 53. 6
Because his sinfull lust she would not *serve,* . . . IV. i. 4. 2
doe also *serve* To her for bread, . . . IV. i. 26. 1
Therefore he her did court, did *serve,* did wooe, . . . IV. ii. 8. 6
most fit the faire to *serve,* . . . IV. v. 1. 6
seem'd to *serve* the workmans will. . . . IV. x. 15. 9
as his Squire him offred evermore To *serve,* . . . V. i. 30. 4
To *serve* the lowly vassall of her might, . . . V. v. 27. 7
none she found so fit to *serve* that turne, . . . V. vi. 6. 3
To *serve* her so as she the rest had bound: . . . V. vii. 28. 4
I Doe *serve* a Queene that not far hence doth wone, . . . V. viii. 16. 7
so let his Idols *serve* the Elfe! . . . V. viii. 19. 9
when time doth *serve,* . . . V. xi. 56. 1
faithfully did *serve* both day and night . . . VI. v. 9. 7
serve their owne necessities with others need. . . . VI. viii. 35. 9
to *serve* to all delight, . . . VI. x. 8. 2
To *serve* the vengeaunce of his wrathfull will; . . . VI. x. 36. 2
made unfit to *serve* his lawlesse mindes behest. . . . VI. xi. 7. 9
so hard handling those which best thee *serve,* . . . *H.L.* 163
That they might *serve* him in eternall blis, . . . *H.H.L.* 62
Served. little them *served* for their mayntenaunce. . . . *S.C.* May 112
The which in Court him *served* to good stead; . . . *Hub.* 697
Long I her *serv'd,* . . . II. iv. 19. 6
with fresh corage on the victor *servd:* . . . II. x. 55. 7
his feeble vaines . . . *served* not his need, . . . II. xi. 48. 4
Where they were *served* with all sumptuous fare, . . . III. i. 51. 2
Served a gentle Lady of great sway . . . III. v. 4. 5
servd of all things that mote needfull bee; . . . III. ix. 19. 2
So had he *served* many one. . . . III. x. 35. 9
The winde and weather *served* them so well, . . . V. xii. 4. 5
noblest she that *served* is of noblest knight. . . . VI. vii. 29. 9
Serves. the foule, that *serves* to beare the lightning, . . . *Ro.* xvii. 13
That when time *serves* may bring things better forth. . . . *Van.* i. 14
Nor for fruict nor for shadowe *serves* thy stocke; . . . *S.C.* F. 128
he that *serves* the Lord of hoasts most high, . . . *Hub.* 469
let us hence depart whilest wether *serves* and winde.' . . . II. xii. 87. 9
time yet *serves* that I the same refuse; . . . IV. vi. 4. 8
her good Knights, of which so brave a band *Serves* her . . . V. viii. 18. 7
makes his God of his ungodly pelfe, And Idols *serves:* . . . V. viii. 19. 9
The salvage *serves* Serena well, . . . VI. v. Arg.
Such homely what as *serves* the simple clowne, . . . VI. ix. 7. 4
Service. Proud of his highest *service,* . . . *Van.* iv. 3
Dooing my Countrey *service* as I might, . . . *Hub.* 61
To anie *service,* or to anie place? . . . *Hub.* 121
As if good *service* he were fit to doo; . . . *Hub.* 239
in long *service* lost both limbs and good; . . . *Hub.* 248
To doo you faithfull *service* all my dayes. . . . *Hub.* 253
All his care was, his *service* well to saine, . . . *Hub.* 392
Their *service,* and their holie things to say, . . . *Hub.* 450
Good garments for their *service* should deserve; . . . *Hub.* 468
in his Princes *service* spends his dayes, . . . *Hub.* 773
The faithfull *service* of my learned skill, . . . *T.M.* 428
to her ghost doo *service* day by day. . . . *D.* 371
To her he vowd the *service* of his daies, . . . *As.* 61
with brave deeds to her sole *service* vowed, . . . *As.* 69
In faithfull *service* of faire Cynthia: . . . *Col.* 381
service high so basely they ensew, . . . *Col.* 767
T' embrace the *service* of sweete Poetry, . . . *Ded. Son.* iv. 7
Awaite whereto their *service* he applyes, . . . I. i. 38. 4
a loose Leman to vile *service* bound: . . . I. i. 48. 6
With humble *service* to her will prepard: . . . I. iii. 9. 7
evermore embrace My faithfull *service,* . . . I. iii. 29. 8
Like to an holy Monck, the *service* to begin. . . . I. iv. 18. 9
To her makes present of his *service* seene: . . . I. v. 16. 3
To do their *service* to Sylvanus old, . . . I. vi. 33. 2
Accept therefore My simple selfe, and *service* evermore: . . . I. viii. 27. 5
vowed all Their life to *service* of high heavens King, . . . I. x. 36. 4
doen their *service* to that soveraigne Dame, . . . I. x. 59. 7
Well worthy doest thy *service* for her grace, . . . I. x. 60. 3
To be her Squire, and do her *service* well aguisd. . . . II. i. 21. 9

Service—*Continued.*
th' others pleasing *service* to abate, . . . II. ii. 19. 5
'To her I homage and my *service* owe, . . . II. ii. 42. 1
By faithfull *service* and meete amenaunce, . . . II. ix. 5. 7
Damsels which were taught That *service* well. . . . II. ix. 19. 6
Offring his *service,* and his dearest life . . . II. xi. 16. 6
Shall doe unto her *service,* . . . III. i. 26. 9
Ne to your Lady will I *service* done, . . . III. i. 28. 4
her knights *service* ought, to hold of her in fee. . . . III. i. 44. 9
the stubborne feendes he to his *service* bownd. . . . III. iii. 14. 9
What *service* may I doe unto thee meete, . . . III. v. 35. 6
desire No *service* but thy safety and ayd; . . . III. v. 36. 4
Dye rather, dye, then ever from her *service* swerve. . . . III. v. 46. 9
'But, foolish boy, what bootes thy *service* bace . . . III. v. 47. 1
The love and *service* of the basest crew? . . . III. v. 47. 7
never learned he such *service* till that day. . . . III. vii. 36. 9
I might doe *service* unto gentle Dames, . . . III. vii. 54. 6
'So well I to faire Ladies *service* did, . . . III. vii. 55. 1
hast a thanklesse *service* on thee ta'ne, . . . III. viii. 47. 3
Unfit faire Ladies *service* to supply; . . . III. ix. 5. 2
timely *service* to her pleasures meet, . . . III. ix. 7. 8
hath himselfe unto such *service* sold, . . . III. ix. 8. 2
He did her *service* dewtifull, . . . III. x. 9. 2
Her love, her *service,* and her utmost wealth: . . . IV. i. 6. 4
For which no *service* she too much esteemed: . . . IV. i. 8. 5
Yet he to her did dayly *service* more, . . . IV. ii. 11. 1
to her *service* bind each living creature, . . . IV. ii. 44. 4
she most fit his *service* doth deserve, . . . IV. v. 1. 8
with meeke *service* and much suit . . . IV. vi. 40. 3
Kings and Keasars to thy *service* bound; . . . IV. vii. 1. 4
No *service* lothsome to a gentle kind, . . . IV. viii. 22. 7
all the *service* of the bodie frame, . . . IV. ix. 2. 7
with meet *service* waited him about, . . . IV. xi. 30. 4
To doe their dueful *service,* . . . IV. xi. 44. 9
To doe her *service* so as I am bond: . . . V. ii. 4. 4
The goodly *service,* the devicefull sights, . . . V. iii. 3. 2
Which didst that *service* unto Florimell. . . . V. iii. 21. 4
put to that base *service* of her band, . . . V. iv. 32. 7
To be her thrall and *service* her afford: . . . V. v. 17. 5
with gratefull *service* me right well apay. . . . V. v. 33. 9
So praying him t' accept her *service* evermore. . . . V. v. 54. 9
Offred his *service* to disarme the Knight; . . . V. viii. 27. 2
Himselfe and *service* to her offered, . . . V. x. 12. 3
'Unarm'd . . . as then more meete For Ladies *service,* . . . VI. ii. 18. 2
The noble ympe, of such new *service* fayne, . . . VI. ii. 38. 6
wont doe suit and *service* to his might, . . . VI. vii. 34. 2
sude and sought with all the *service* dew: . . . VI. viii. 20. 6
Ne ever had such knightly *service* seene, . . . VI. ix. 35. 3
He daily did apply him selfe to donne All dewfull *service,* . . . VI. x. 32. 6
With humble *service,* and with daily sute, . . . VI. x. 38. 2
With dayly *service* and attendance dew, . . . VI. xii. 5. 2
For my sweet Saynt some *service* fit will find. . . . *Am.* xxii. 4
Forget their *service* and about her fly, . . . *Epith.* 231
any *service* I might do to thee, . . . *H.L.* 6
their best *service* lend . . . *Proth.* 124
Serviceable. Not good nor *serviceable* elles for ought, . . . II. ix. 32. 2
Services. To doo their kindly *services* as needeth . . . *Hub.* 273
Of comely *services,* or courtly trayne? . . . I. xii. 14. 4
vain sheows . . . And courtly *services,* . . . III. vii. 29. 7
After long suit and wearie *servicis,* . . . III. vii. 53. 7
unto Venus *services* was sold. . . . IV. x. 54. 5
ill your goddesse *services* are drest By virgins, . . . IV. x. 54. 8
yeeld theyr *services* unto her will; . . . *Epith.* 197
Servile. Let us all *servile* base subjection scorne; . . . *Hub.* 134
Her *servile* beast yet would not leave her so, . . . I. iii. 44. 6
them to have my selfe, and be their *servile* sclave.' . . . II. vii. 33. 9
Good turnes be counted as a *servile* bond . . . II. viii. 56. 2
he had brought it now in *servile* bond, . . . V. x. 27. 1
foot he set on his vile necke, in signe Of *servile* yoke, . . . VI. vii. 26. 5
My hart, (whom none with *servile* bands can tye, . . . *Am.* lxxiii. 2
Serving. *Serving* th' ambitious will of Augustine, . . . III. iii. 35. 3
serving her in her malitious use . . . IV. i. 31. 2
Serving proud Radigund with true subjection, . . . V. v. 26. 2
Servitors. Denies them quite for *servitors* of his.' . . . *Col.* 770
Set. *See* **Onset, Overset.**
Upon the top therof was *set* a pot . . . *Bel.*[1] iii. 5
set on hie upon triumphing chaire, . . . *Bel.*[1] iv. 7
upon a white horse *set* The faithfull man . . . *Rev.* iii. 1
His head did shine with crounes *set* therupon. . . . *Rev.* iii. 3
in triumphant chayre was *set* on hie, . . . *Bel.*[2] iv. 7
set forth The great Colosse, . . . *Ro.* ii. 9
Upon the same to *set* foundation sure? . . . *Ro.* xxiv. 14
a fowling net, Which he for carrion Crowes had *set* . . . *S.C.* Mar. 110
With Damaske roses and Daffadillies *set:* . . . *S.C.* Ap. 60
Shee *set* her youngling before her knee, . . . *S.C.* May 182
her sonne had *sette* to deere a prise . . . *S.C.* May 299
They *setten* to sale their shops of shame, . . . *S.C.* S. 36
Wherewith they *sette* all the world on fire; . . . *S.C.* S. 87
They never *sette* foote in that same troade, . . . *S.C.* S. 92
Soone as thou gynst to *sette* thy notes in frame, . . . *S.C.* O. 25
Of smoothest marble stone in order *set,* . . . *Gn.* 663
my weake bodie, *set* on fire with griefe, . . . *Hub.* 15
Adventure which might them a working *set;* . . . *Hub.* 224
They were in doubt, and flatly *set* abord. . . . *Hub.* 324
He chaffred Chayres in which Churchmen were *set,* . . . *Hub.* 1159
Upon his head his glistering Burganet . . . he did *set:* . . . *Mui.* 75
every flowre and herbe there *set* in order: . . . *Mui.* 172
No toong can tell, nor any forth can *set,* . . . *As.* 171
Whose girland now is *set* in highest place, . . . *Ded. Son.* xiii. 2
the Northerne wagoner had *set* His sevenfold teme . . . I. ii. 1. 1

Set—*Continued.*
high hath *set* his throne where Tiberis doth pas. I. ii. 22. 9
He *set* her on her steede, I. ii. 45. 9
Lordes and Ladies . . . devise Themselves to *setten* forth I. iv. 14. 6
triple crowne *set* on her head full hye, I. vii. 16. 4
Upon this dreadfull Beast . . . He *sett* the false Duessa, I. vii. 18. 9
when her eyes she on the Dwarf had *set,* I. vii. 20. 5
two broad Beacons, *sett* in open fieldes, I. xi. 14. 3
Those glaring lampes were *sett* that made a dreadfull shade, I. xi. 14. 9
high her burning torch *set* up in heaven bright. I. xi. 49. 9
on her head they *sett* a girlond greene, I. xii. 8. 6
signes, here *sett* in sondrie place, II. Pr. 4. 2
on your shield is *set* for ornament!' II. i. 27. 7
She *set* her downe to weepe II. ii. 8. 3
Prowdly to prune, and *sett* on every side; II. iii. 36. 8
set in highest seat of dignitee, II. iv. 19. 4
To chaunge thy will, and *set* Occasion free, II. v. 17. 8
Emongst wide waves *sett,* like a litle nest, II. vi. 12. 2
without dread or disdayn She *sett* beside, II. vi. 14. 6
Nine was the circle *sett* in heavens place: II. ix. 22. 8
It might breake out and *set* the whole on fyre, II. ix. 30. 2
set them forth, as well he could devise. II. ix. 31. 5
Two goodly Beacons, *set* in watches stead, II. ix. 46. 3
set in silver sockets bright, II. ix. 46. 6
Amidst them all he in a chaire was *sett,* II. ix. 58. 1
To which whiles absent he his mind did *sett,* II. x. 60. 3
The other five five sondry wayes he *sett* II. xi. 7. 1
A mighty Mazer bowle of wine was *sett,* II. xii. 49. 3
sett With shady Laurell trees, II. xii. 63. 1
from Britayne *sett* To seeke her lover III. i. 8. 7
'All my delight on deedes of armes is *sett,* III. ii. 7. 1
Imperious Love hath highest *set* his throne, III. ii. 23. 2
'Not so th' Arabian Myrrhe did *set* her mynd, III. ii. 41. 1
sett her by to watch, and *sett* her by to weepe. III. ii. 47. 9
All her delight is *set* on Marinell, III. v. 9. 4
themselves they *set* There in await III. v. 17. 6
They did him *set* theron, and forth with them convayd. III. v. 38. 9
downe to rest Her selfe she *set,* III. vi. 10. 7
Your glory *sett* to chace the salvage beasts, III. vi. 22. 2
Ne needs there Gardiner to *sett* or sow, III. vi. 34. 1
Sett by it selfe, and ranckt in comely rew; III. vi. 35. 4
set his triumphes hye, III. vi. 49. 7
He *sett* upon her Palfrey tired lame, III. vii. 28. 8
two burning lampes she *set* In silver sockets, III. viii. 7. 1
Upon his Courser *sett* the lovely lode, III. viii. 19. 4
all his minde is *set* on mucky pelfe, III. ix. 4. 1
On which their eies and harts were wholly *sett,* III. x. 34. 6
That did her win and free from chalenge *set:* IV. i. 12. 4
set it all on fire by force unknowen, IV. ii. 1. 4
Paridell her scornd, and *set* at nought, IV. ii. 3. 4
perilous present stownd in which their lives were *set.* IV. ii. 15. 9
The day was *set,* that all might understand, IV. iii. 3. 3
Fayre Canacee upon a stately stage Was *set,* IV. iii. 4. 7
Sir Priamond, . . . himselfe did forward *set.* IV. iii. 6. 4
Through working of the stone therein *yset.* IV. iii. 24. 5
Together with this Hag beside her *set,* IV. iv. 9. 6
having it about her middle *set,* IV. v. 19. 4
First in the midst to *set* that fayrest Dame, IV. v. 25. 4
soone as she them saw to discord *set,* IV. v. 29. 1
she by her did *set.* IV. vi. 46. 9
in swoune, full sadly *set,* IV. vii. 35. 4
if she should him freely *set,* IV. viii. 53. 8
did *set* in sumptuous chaire To feast IV. ix. 13. 3
Venus Temple is describ'd; And lovers life forth *set.* IV. x. Arg.
all were they *set* together. IV. x. 29. 9
'An hundred Altars round about were *set,* IV. x. 38. 1
In which were many towres and castels *set,* IV. xi. 27. 8
on his steed her *set* to beare her out of sight. V. i. 17. 9
First in one ballance *set* the true aside.' V. ii. 45. 5
set the truth and *set* the right aside, V. ii. 48. 1
Of which th' one halfe upon himselfe did *set,* V. iii. 11. 6
To *set* afresh on all the other crew: V. iii. 12. 4
Then did he *set* her by that snowy one, V. iii. 24. 1
Like the true saint beside the image *set,* V. iii. 24. 2
Soone as the gates were open to them *set,* V. iv. 38. 1
With froward will doth *set* him selfe to weepe, V. vi. 14. 3
One foote was *set* uppon the Crocodile, V. vii. 7. 1
gan forward *set* To save her from her feare, V. viii. 6. 8
cursed Idole, farre proclamed, He hath *set* up, V. x. 28. 5
set a Seneschall of dreaded might, V. x. 30. 2
long since aside had *set* The use of armes, V. xi. 37. 3
Did *set* upon those troupes with all his powre V. xi. 57. 9
Talus sternely did upon them *set,* V. xii. 7. 3
there arriv'd againe whence forth he *set,* V. xii. 28. 2
By the way side being together *set;* V. xii. 28. 5
the Blatant Beast, by them *set* on, V. xii. 41. 1
Did *set* uppon us flying both for feare; VI. i. 16. 4
That mote thy kindled courage *set* on fire, VI. ii. 37. 3
that one in basenesse *set* Doth noble courage shew VI. iii. 1. 8
unarm'd and *set* in secret shade. VI. iii. 8. 5
By straunge occasion that her needs forth be *set.* VI. v. 11. 9
Upon him *set,* of perill nought adrad, VI. v. 16. 3
seeing one in so great daunger *set* VI. v. 22. 2
Upon a mangy jade unmeetely *set,* VI. vi. 16. 8
in some stable neare did *set* him up to feede. VI. vi. 19. 9
His foot he *set* upon his vile necke, VI. vii. 26. 4
therewith flesht upon him *set* anew, VI. viii. 9. 7
He in his necke had *set* his foote VI. viii. 10. 9
The Damzell was before the altar *set,* VI. viii. 45. 2
Tooke Coridon and *set* him in his place, VI. ix. 42. 2

Set—*Continued.*
set his rest amongst the rusticke sort, VI. x. 2. 6
set for stales T' entrap unwary fooles VI. x. 3. 8
was *set* By his faire patients side VI. xi. 9. 8
All *set* with yron teeth in raunges twaine, VI. xii. 26. 7
To *set* upon them in that extasie, VII. vi. 23. 5
Long lov'd the Fanchin, who by nought did *set* her, VII. vi. 44. 4
in some snare or gin *set* close behind, Entrapped him, VII. vi. 48. 6
Which who will read *set* forth so as it ought, VII. vii. 9. 8
And doth his ydle message *set* at nought. *Am.* xix. 12
Most sorts of men doe *set* but little store. *Am.* xxvi. 12
Set all your things in seemely good aray, *Epith.* 114
and *set* thee all on fire With burning zeale, *H.H.L.* 270
And heavenly Dominations are *set,* *H.H.B.* 90
on her head a crowne of purest gold Is *set,* *H.H.B.* 191
And onely thinke on that before them *set.* *H.H.B.* 266
Sets. Then *sets* she forth, *Mui.* 324
In other none, but him, she *sets* delight; III. v. 9. 3
he *sets* nought at all by Florimell; III. v. 9. 5
Settest. *setst* thy kingdome in the captive harts Of Kings IV. vii. 1. 3
Setteth. He pulleth downe, he *setteth* up on hy; V. ii. 41. 7
fully *setteth* his felicitie; *H.B.* 229
Setting. in *setting* of hir image up. *Rev.* i. 14
From the uprising to the *setting* Sunne, III. i. 3. 5
in his necke Her proud foote *setting,* V. iv. 40. 3
setting up an Idole of his owne, V. x. 13. 8
And *setting* on his steede her did sustaine VI. iii. 28. 5
At last, about the *setting* of the Sunne, VI. iv. 26. 1
setting your immortall prayses forth: *Am.* lxxxii. 12
spend His plenteous vaine in *setting* forth her prayse, *H.H.B.* 220
Setting-forth. from the point where they first tooke Their *setting forth,* V. Pr. 5. 4
Settle. well-guided speach, So deepe did *settle* in her gracious thought, I. vii. 42. 2
settle patience in so furious heat? II. viii. 27. 6
Ne suffred sleepe to *settle* in his brest. IV. v. 41. 5
Mongst whome the more I seeke to *settle* peace, *Am.* xliv. 13
Settled. all on uprore from her *settled* seat, II. ii. 20. 6
So *settled* he his kingdome, II. x. 60. 9
setled there in sure establishment. II. xi. 2. 5
grounded and fast *setteled* On firme foundation II. xii. 1. 4
in peace and *setled* rest, IV. ix. 17. 2
May nought at all their *setled* mindes remove, IV. x. 2. 3
Untill he had her *settled* in her raine V. xi. 35. 3
assured Unto her selfe, and *setled* so in hart, *Am.* lix. 2
Settling. There whilest he thus was *setling* things above, VI. vi. 37. 1
Setual. Dull Poppie, and drink-quickning *Setuale,* *Mui.* 196
Seven. *seven* springing heds of monstrous crimes, *Bel.*[1] viii. 13
seven heads, ten crounes, ten hornes did beare, *Rev.* i. 2
seven heads I saw, Ten hornes *Rev.* ii. 4
faire Dodonian tree . . . Upon *seaven* (*seven*[1]) hills *Bel.* v. 2
a strange beast with *seven* heads *Bel.*[2] viii. 5
seven heads, budding monstrous crimes *Bel.*[2] x. 12
Seven Romane Hils, the worlds *Seven* Wonderments. *Ro.* ii. 14
these *seven* hils, which be nowe Tombes *Ro.* iv. 7
heaped was On these *seven* Romane hils, *Ro.* xii. 10
Charlemaine amongst the Starris *seaven.* *T.M.* 462
in a siege *seaven* yeres about me dwelt. *Ti.* 105
seven great heads out of his body grew, I. vii. 17. 7
seven Bead-men . . . Did spend their daies I. x. 36. 3
The first and chiefest of the *seven,* I. x. 44. 2
with one sword *seven* knightes I brought to end, II. iii. 17. 7
seven times dipped in the bitter wave II. viii. 20. 8
Seven times the Sunne, with his lamp-burning light, II. ix. 7. 5
Seven yeares this wize they us besieged have, II. ix. 12. 8
Proportiond equally by *seven* and nine: II. ix. 22. 7
Seven of the same against the Castle gate II. xi. 6. 6
these *seven* monethes day, III. xi. 10. 8
Seven moneths he so her kept in bitter smart, IV. i. 4. 1
ere his hand he reard, he overthrew *Seven* Knights, IV. iv. 41. 2
Seaven women by him slaine, IV. vii. 13. 5
One of the worlds *seven* wonders sayd to bee, IV. x. 30. 4
There did this lucklesse mayd *seven* months abide, IV. xi. 4. 6
Sevenfold. 'The *sevenfold* yron gates of grislie Hell, *Ti.* 372
His *sevenfold* teme behind the stedfast starre I. ii. 1. 2
this dreadfull Beast with *sevenfold* head I. vii. 18. 8
seven fold shield, which he from Guyon brought, II. viii. 32. 5
on his shield enveloped *sevenfold* III. ii. 25. 7
Sevenfolded. the upper marge Of his *sevenfolded* shield II. v. 6. 3
Seven-headed. where is that same great *seven-headded* beast, *Ti.* 71
Seven hundred. had *seven hundred* yeares this scepter borne II. x. 36. 2
Even *seven hundred* Princes, II. x. 74. 3
Seven-mouthed. muddy shore of broad *seven-mouthed* Nile, I. v. 18. 2
Seventeen. Even *seventeene* goodly sonnes; V. x. 7. 4
seventeene yeares, but tall and faire of face, VI. ii. 5. 4
Seventh. The *seventh* . . . Had charge the tender Orphans I. x. 43. 1
Sever. Minos righteous soules doth *sever* From wicked ones, *Gn.* 623
let the flitting aire my vaine words *sever.*' *Gn.* 638
Though death his soule doo from his bodie *sever;* *Ti.* 257
Damon and Pythias, whom death could not *sever:* IV. x. 27. 6
so soone as they do *sever,* VII. vii. 24. 3
chast affects that naught but death can *sever;* *Am.* vi. 12
Nor unto Cristall; for nought may them *sever;* *Am.* ix. 11
Whose sundrie parts he from themselves did *sever* *H.L.* 76
Several. load . . . Of nightly stelths, and pillage *severall,* I. iii. 16. 8
The rest had *severall* offices assynd; II. ix. 31. 6
call Their sondry kings to do their homage *severall.* III. iii. 32. 9
both tooke goodly leave, and parted *severall.* VI. i. 10. 9
they did employ . . . *several* deceipts, but all in vaine; VI. v. 14. 2
each his sundrie sheepe with *severall* care Gathered together, VI. ix. 15. 4

Severe. approved The feends to be too cruell and *severe,* . . . *Gn.* 466
Severn. quart, Which *Severne* now from Logris doth depart: . II. x. 14. 5
of her name now *Severne* men do call: . . . II. x. 19. 8
them unwares besides the *Severne* did enclose. . . . II. x. 54. 9
not the stately *Severne* grudg'd at all, . . . IV. xi. 30. 6
Severus. Fought with *Severus,* and him overthrew, . . . II. x. 57. 2
Sew. *See* **Sue.**
To spin, to card, to *sew,* to wash, to wring; . . . V. iv. 31. 6
Sewde, *etc. See* **Sued,** *etc.*
Sex. Which in her *sexe* doth all excell. . . . *S.C.* Ap. 45
in her *sex* more wonderfull and rare. . . . *Col.* 491
the glory of her *sex,* . . . II. x. 20. 6
All ignorant of her contrary *sex,* . . . III. i. 47. 2
her *sexe* under that straunge purport Did use to hide, . . . III. i. 52. 7
by self-feeling of her feeble *sexe,* . . . III. i. 54. 2
So he surpassed his *sex* masculine, . . . III. xi. 4. 3
Bove all her *sexe* that ever yet was seene. . . . IV. Pr. 4. 5
for to hide her fained *sex* the better . . . IV. i. 7. 3
That shamefull Hag, the slaunder of her *sexe,* . . . IV. viii. 35. 2
Sex's. that Emperesse, . . . her *sexes* grace: . . . *Ded. Son.* xi. 4
Shackles. the strong *shackles* of fraile flesh,' . . . *D.* 86
His *shackles* emptie lefte, himselfe escaped cleene. . . . II. i. 1. 9
Shade. Dodonian tree . . . throw forth his gladsome *shade,* . . *Bel.*[1] v. 2
Chaunting in *shade* their sundrie melodie, . . . *Pet.* iii. 6
if the *shade* of Rome May . . . yeeld a seeming sight, . . . *Ro.* v. 5
This Citie, which was first but shepheards *shade,* . . . *Ro.* xx. 9
to awake out of th' infernall *shade* . . . *Ro.* xxv. 2
Hindering with his *shade* my lovely light, . . . *S.C.* F. 173
we close shrowded in thys *shade* alone. . . . *S.C.* Ap. 32
in Sommer *shade* Dight gaudy Girlonds . . . *S.C.* Jun. 44
pyping lowe in *shade* of lowly grove, . . . *S.C.* Jun. 71
content us in thys humble *shade,* . . . *S.C.* O. 116
summer *shade,* under the cocked hay. . . . *S.C.* N. 12
as he satte in secreate *shade* alone, . . . *S.C.* D. 5
Whereas continuall *shade* is to be seene, . . . *Gn.* 118
by the fountaine side, in *shade* to rest, . . . *Gn.* 238
The Lyon sleeping lay in secret *shade,* . . . *Hub.* 952
With kindly counter under Mimick *shade,* . . . *T.M.* 207
of that brightnes now appeares no *shade,* . . . *Ti.* 124
mine the Primrose in the lowly *shade:* . . . *D.* 233
Or some deepe cave, or solitarie *shade;* . . . *D.* 487
amongst the cooly *shade* Of the greene alders . . . *Col.* 58
sitting me beside in that same *shade,* . . . *Col.* 68
To let thy fame lie so in hidden *shade:* . . . *Col.* 407
to revoke The forward footing for an hidden *shade:* . . . I. i. 12. 8
A litle glooming light, much like a *shade;* . . . I. i. 14. 5
For the coole *shade* him thither hastly got: . . . I. ii. 29. 2
Who all that while lay hid in secret *shade.* . . . I. v. 15. 4
the stout Sansjoy doth sleepe in deadly *shade.* . . . I. v. 22. 9
Hee feedes upon the cooling *shade,* . . . I. vii. 3. 1
bathe in pleasaunce of the joyous *shade,* . . . I. vii. 4. 2
Those glaring lampes were sett that made a dreadfull *shade.* . I. xi. 14. 9
with her sable mantle gan to *shade* The face of earth . . . I. xi. 49. 7
The valley did with coole *shade* overcast: . . . II. i. 24. 5
now in *shade* he shrowded yonder lies.' . . . II. iii. 35. 5
I not descerned in that darkesome *shade,* . . . II. iv. 28. 4
'Cymochles; oh! no, but Cymochles *shade* . . . II. v. 35. 4
As Shepheardes curre, that in darke eveninges *shade* . . . II. vi. 39. 4
found in secret *shade* An uncouth . . . wight, . . . II. vii. 3. 3
beam great brightnes threw Through the dim *shade,* . . . II. vii. 45. 3
to th' infernall *shade* Fast flying, . . . II. viii. 45. 7
As one awakte out of long slombring *shade,* . . . II. xi. 31. 8
usd to bath themselves in that deceiptfull *shade.* . . . II. xii. 30. 9
Through ghastly horror and eternall *shade:* . . . II. xii. 41. 5
The dales for *shade,* the hilles for breathing space, . . . II. xii. 58. 6
The joyous birdes, shrouded in chearefull *shade* . . . II. xii. 71. 1
In secret *shade* after long wanton joyes, . . . II. xii. 72. 6
Now leading him into a secret *shade* . . . III. i. 35. 6
ere the grosse Earthes gryesy *shade* Was all disperst . . . III. i. 67. 7
th' only *shade* and semblant of a knight, . . . III. ii. 38. 3
I, fonder, love a *shade,* the body far exyld.' . . . III. ii. 44. 9
So straungely vewed her straunge lovers *shade,* . . . III. iii. 6. 3
from the Sun their forheads fayr to *shade;* . . . III. iv. 29. 9
mightie woodes which did the valley *shade* . . . III. v. 39. 4
The state of life out of the griesly *shade.* . . . III. vi. 37. 5
in the thickest covert of that *shade* . . . III. vi. 44. 1
Each *shade* she saw, and each noyse she did heare, . . . III. vii. 1. 8
He us'd to slug, or sleepe in slothfull *shade:* . . . III. vii. 12. 8
of each *shade* that did it selfe present; . . . III. vii. 19. 4
her face did with a Lawrell *shade.* . . . III. x. 44. 9
th' Earthes gloomy *shade* Did dim the brightnesse . . . III. x. 46. 6
As if he had beene slombring in the *shade;* . . . III. xi. 8. 2
From scorching heat her daintie limbes to *shade;* . . . III. xi. 32. 5
Straunge horrour to deforme his griesly *shade:* . . . III. xii. 11. 4
al this while was plast In secret *shade,* . . . III. xii. 27. 5
Doe hunt for *shade,* where shrowded they may lie, . . . IV. iv. 47. 4
Sitting in *shade* beside his grazing steede; . . . IV. vi. 2. 6
covered all with *shade* And sad melancholy: . . . IV. vii. 38. 8
Siting in covert *shade* of arbors sweet, . . . IV. viii. 9. 2
cunningly did *shade* That part of Justice . . . V. vii. 3. 3
long in captive *shade* Had shrowded bene, . . . V. vii. 43. 1
full eath perswade . . . both faults to *shade,* . . . V. viii. 14. 5
his false intent to *shade,* . . . V. ix. 12. 7
out of an hidden *shade* There forth issewd . . . V. xi. 22. 8
unarm'd and set in secret *shade.* . . . VI. iii. 8. 5
In covert *shade* him selfe did safely rest, . . . VI. iii. 20. 3
Did underneath them make a gloomy *shade,* . . . VI. iv. 13. 7
his three foes shrowded in guilefull *shade* . . . VI. v. 17. 8
He there in *shade* himselfe had layd to rest, . . . VI. vii. 19. 2
I downe doe lay My limbes in every *shade* . . . VI. ix. 23. 8

Shade—*Continued.*
In the woods *shade* which did the waters crowne, . . . VI. x. 7. 7
In sommers *shade* him selfe here rested weary: . . . VI. x. 22. 6
the thicke shrubs, which did them alwaies *shade* . . . VI. x. 42. 3
Her wretched life shut up in deadly *shade,* . . . VI. x. 44. 4
Lay sleeping soundly in the bushes *shade,* . . . VI. xi. 38. 4
for to shrowde in *shade* from Phoebus flame, . . . VII. vi. 39. 3
her dainty limbes to lay In covert *shade,* . . . VII. vi. 42. 5
Ne ought to see, but like a *shade* to weene, . . . VII. vii. 46. 4
in the *shade* of death it selfe shall shroud, . . . *Am.* xxvii. 3
appeare An hundred Graces as in *shade* to sit. . . . *Am.* xl. 4
passe away, like to a sommers *shade;* . . . *H.B.* 68
Shaded. Others lay *shaded* from the scorching heat, . . . III. vi. 17. 8
shaded oft from sunne, . . . IV. Pr. 3. 7
Shades. From other *shades* hath weand my wandring mynde: *S.C.* Jun. 2
Waste wildernes, amongst Cymerian *shades,* . . . *Gn.* 370
greislie *shades,* such as doo haunt in hell . . . *Ti.* 125
Hewing and slashing at their idle *shades;* . . . II. ix. 15. 8
To wander in the griesly *shades* of night. . . . V. x. 33. 6
Shading. With fayned colours *shading* a true case; . . . V. vii. 2. 7
Shadow. no such *shadow* shalbe had againe. . . . *Pet.* iii. 14
for succoure flee Under the *shadow* of his wing; . . . *To his Booke* 7
Nor for fruict nor for *shadowe* serves thy stocke; . . . *S.C.* F. 128
All in the *shadowe* of a bushye brere, . . . *S.C.* D. 2
In some coole *shadow* from the scorching heat, . . . *Gn.* 143
In the fresh *shadowe* did for them prepayre, . . . *Gn.* 188
Under the *shadow* of thy countenaunce . . . *Ti.* 268
their greene leaves, . . . Made a calme *shadowe* . . . I. ii. 28. 6
In secrete *shadow,* far from all mens sight: . . . I. iii. 4. 4
eke my night of death the *shadow* is; . . . I. iii. 27. 8
did rest In secret *shadow* by a fountaine side: . . . I. vi. 40. 6
did stay In secret *shadow* . . . I. vi. 48. 3
made wide *shadow* under his huge waste, . . . I. xi. 8. 4
Under the *shadow* of her even browes, . . . II. iii. 25. 2
In secrete *shadow* from the sunny ray, . . . II. v. 32. 2
a faint *shadow* of uncertein light: . . . II. vii. 29. 6
To rest thy weary person in the *shadow* coole?' . . . II. vii. 63. 9
Against this lifelesse *shadow* so to fight: . . . II. xi. 44. 3
the brode *shadow* of an hoarie hill; . . . II. xii. 30. 4
I in colourd showes may *shadow* itt, . . . III. Pr. 3. 8
like a *shadowe* wexe, . . . III. ii. 44. 4
lov'st the *shadow* of a warlike knight; . . . III. ii. 45. 6
No *shadow* but a body hath in powre: . . . III. ii. 45. 7
In whose enclosed *shadow* there was pight A faire Pavilion, . III. v. 40. 6
feard each *shadow* moving too or froe; . . . III. xii. 12. 3
We did alight, and sate in *shadow* myld, . . . IV. vi. 36. 3
'Under one hood to *shadow* faces twaine: . . . V. xi. 56. 7
them in that *shadow* found . . . VI. ii. 43. 2
for *shadow* to pretend Some shew of favour, . . . VI. xi. 6. 5
In doubtfull *shadow* of the darkesome night . . . VI. xi. 13. 4
overspred Me with the *shadow* of thy gentle wing, . . . *H.L.* 20
shadow yet shynes in your beauteous face. . . . *H.B.* 168
And darkes the earth with *shadow* of her sight? . . . *H.H.B.* 229
Shadowed. tree, So fayre and great that *shadowed* all the ground, . . . II. vii. 56. 2
Shadowing. Deckt all the roofe, and, *shadowing* the roode, . . VI. v. 35. 3
Shadows. wall . . . cover'd all with griesly *shadowes,* . . . *Bel.*[2] viii. 3
Into thick *shadowes,* there themselves to lay. . . . *Gn.* 168
Seeing the doubled *shadowes* low to fall, . . . *Gn.* 318
To the black *shadowes* of the Stygian shore, . . . *Gn.* 383
durst those lowest *shadowes* goe to see, . . . *Gn.* 438
will to Court for *shadowes* vaine to seeke, . . . *Hub.* 912
enfold In covert vele, and wrap in *shadowes* light, . . . II. Pr. 5. 2
Thrise seene the *shadowes* of the neather world, . . . II. ii. 44. 2
Disperst the *shadowes* of the misty night, . . . II. iii. 1. 2
Through griesly *shadowes* by a beaten path, . . . II. vii. 51. 3
to faire Britomart they all but *shadowes* beene. . . . III. i. 45. 9
feed on *shadowes* whiles I die for food, . . . III. ii. 44. 3
griesly *shadowes* covered heaven bright, . . . III. iv. 52. 2
Him long she so with *shadowes* entertain'd, . . . III. viii. 10. 8
sad *shadowes* gan the world to hyde . . . III. xi. 55. 3
'Fresh *shadowes,* fit to shroud from sunny ray; . . . IV. x. 24. 1
yclowded With fearefull *shadowes* of deformed night, . . . V. iv. 45. 2
both with hope of *shadowes* vaine inspyred) . . . V. ix. 41. 5
Be but vaine *shadowes* to this safe retyre Of life, . . . VI. ix. 27. 5
The whiles their flockes in *shadowes* shrouded bee, . . . VI. ix. 41. 4
hunt still after *shadowes* vaine Of courtly favour, . . . VI. x. 2. 7
all their showes but *shadowes,* saving she. . . . *Am.* xxxv. 14
When others gaze upon theyr *shadowes* vayne, . . . *Am.* lxxxvii. 6
Sights never seene, and thousand *shadowes* vaine, . . . *H.L.* 255
All other sights but fayned *shadowes* bee. . . . *H.H.B.* 273
Hast after vaine deceiptfull *shadowes* sought, . . . *H.H.B.* 291
doe fly away, Like empty *shaddowes,* . . . *Proth.* 9
Shady. 'You naked trees, whose *shady* leaves are lost, . . . *S.C.* Ja. 31
shroude in *shady* leaves . . . *S.C.* Jun. 54
shady woods resound with dreadfull yells; . . . *D.* 331
Both christall wells and *shadie* groves forsooke, . . . *As.* 45
Under a *shady* vele is therein writ, . . . *Ded. Son.* iii. 7
A *shadie* grove not farr away they spide, . . . I. i. 7. 2
Her angels face . . . made a sunshine in the *shady* place; . . I. iii. 4. 8
Whiles old Sylvanus slept in *shady* arber sownd: . . . I. vi. 7. 9
Beholdes her nymphes enraung'd in *shady* wood, . . . I. xii. 7. 8
Fayre marching underneath a *shady* hill, . . . II. i. 5. 7
Into a *shady* dale she soft him led, . . . II. vi. 14. 3
to that *shady* delve him brought at last, . . . II. viii. 4. 6
sett With *shady* Laurell trees, . . . II. xii. 63. 2
Betwixt two *shady* mountaynes doth arize: . . . III. ii. 24. 7
till they arrived were In that same *shady* covert . . . III. vi. 26. 6
Emongst the *shady* leaves, their sweet abode, . . . III. vi. 42. 8
Whose *shady* boughes sharp steele did never lop, . . . III. vi. 43. 4

Shady—*Continued.*
a *shady* glade Of the Riphoean hils, III. viii. 6. 3
the *shady* damp Out of the goodly heven amoved quight, III. x. 1. 3
shadie seates, and sundry flowring bankes, IV. x. 25. 4
Under Slewbloome in *shady* grove was got, IV. xi. 42. 5
Sith *shady* dampe had dimd the heavens reach, V. vi. 21. 8
Where he with boughes hath built his *shady* stand, V. viii. 35. 8
Through many woods and *shady* coverts flowes, VII. vi. 41. 7
Sits downe to rest him in some *shady* place, *Am.* lxvii. 3
Shaft. A *shaft* in earnest snatched, *S.C.* Mar. 96
So far as Ewghen bow a *shaft* may send, I. xi. 19. 2
towards gan a deadly *shafte* advaunce, II. iii. 34. 5
at him a cruell *shaft* he sent: II. xi. 24. 5
A cruell *shaft,* headed with deadly ill, III. v. 20. 4
with that wicked *shafte* him wounded had, III. v. 24. 2
with a *shaft* was shot through either eye, III. xi. 48. 8
Like *shaft* out of a bow preventing speed: IV. i. 41. 3
The wicked *shaft* . . . Stayd not, V. viii. 34. 6
Shafts. bowe and *shafts* as then none had, *S.C.* Mar. 113
The one his bowe and *shafts,* *Mui.* 292
Then got he bow and *shafts* of gold and lead, *Col.* 807
The Birch for *shaftes;* I. i. 9. 5
Diana he her takes to be, But misseth bow and *shaftes,* I. vi. 16. 9
she the woodes with bow and *shaftes* did raunge, II. ii. 7. 3
keepe his standing, and his *shaftes* eschew, II. xi. 27. 7
with his killing bow And cruell *shafts,* IV. x. 55. 4
in his hand he bore A boawe and *shaftes,* VII. vii. 29. 7
One of his *shafts* she stole away. *Epig.* ii. 4
Shagged. With rugged beard, and hoarie *shagged* heare, IV. v. 34. 8
long curld locks that downe his shoulders *shagged;* V. ix. 10. 6
Shaggy-bearded. Upon a *shaggy-bearded* Goat he rode, VII. vii. 41. 5
Shake. My ragged rontes all shiver and *shake,* *S.C.* F. 5
Thearth shronke under him, and seemed to *shake:*— *S.C.* F. 220
for he was but slowe, did slowth off *shake* *Gn.* 309
shake and shiver Her flaming fire-brond, *Gn.* 342
shake off this vile harted cowardree. *Hub.* 986
clash their shields, and *shake* their swerds on hy, I. iv. 40. 3
faith . . . The creeping deadly cold away did *shake:* I. v. 12. 4
every tender part for feare does *shake.* I. vi. 10. 2
all the earth for terror seemd to *shake,* I. vii. 7. 6
heares . . . Did *shake,* and seemd to daunce for jollity, I. vii. 32. 4
fall, that seemd to *shake* The stedfast globe I. viii. 23. 8
foltring tongue, at last, these words seemd forth to *shake;* I. ix. 24. 9
seemd uneath to *shake* the stedfast ground. I. xi. 4. 3
his lofty crest Did fiercely *shake,* II. iii. 35. 9
Ne all good knights that *shake* well speare and shield. II. viii. 14. 6
every daintie limbe with horrour *shake;* III. ii. 5. 5
though all the world do *shake;* III. iii. 25. 7
himselfe so shall he *shake;* III. iii. 30. 2
make him *shake,* and shortly learn to fall. III. iii. 49. 9
they gan their shivering speares to *shake,* IV. ii. 14. 7
He all enrag'd his shivering speare did *shake,* IV. iii. 10. 8
shake the safe assuraunce of their state: IV. ix. 16. 4
makes them all to shiver and to *shake:* VII. vii. 23. 6
But her proud hart doe thou a little *shake,* *Am.* x. 9
Shaked. *See* **Off-shaked.**
Whose warlike prowesse . . . *shakt* the Lusitanian soile. *Ded. Son.* xiv. 12
every breath of heaven *shaked* itt: I. iv. 5. 7
So *shaked* he, that horror was to heare: I. xi. 9. 7
Shakt his long locks colourd like copper-wyre, II. iv. 15. 8
all the peece he *shaked* from the flore, V. ii. 21. 8
Shaken. Their wooden ribs are *shaken* nigh asonder. IV. ii. 16. 6
When they have *shaken* off the shamefast band, V. v. 25. 2
Shakes. She *shakes* off shame, II. iii. 36. 9
it *shakes* the bottome of the bulke, V. xi. 29. 3
Shaketh. every leafe, that *shaketh* III. vii. 1. 4
Shaking. *See* **Off-shaking.**
A sodein earthquake . . . *Shaking* the hill *Bel.*[1] ii. 13
My spirit *shaking* off her earthly prison, *Van.* i. 2
in his lustlesse limbs, . . . A *shaking* fever raignd I. iv. 20. 8
The *shaking* Palsey, and Saint Fraunces fire. I. iv. 35. 8
Phoebus . . . Came dauncing forth, *shaking* his deawie hayre, I. v. 2. 4
Which *shaking* off, he rent that yron dore I. viii. 39. 5
with stiffe force *shaking* his mortall launce, II. iii. 14. 4
To laugh at *shaking* of the leaves light II. vi. 7. 7
shaking off his drowsy dreriment, II. vi. 27. 3
shaking off all doubt and shamefast feare IV. x. 53. 6
Shalbe (*partial list*).
For no such shadow *shalbe* had againe. *Pet.*[2] iii. 14
*She *shalbe* a grace, *S.C.* Ap. 115
Tell me, Perigot, what *shalbe* the game, *S.C.* Au. 1
Or thrive in welth, she *shalbe* mine, *S.C.* Au. 111
Therefore . . this *shalbe* our plot: *Hub.* 154
said he, . . . *All shalbe taught of God.* *Hub.* 440
they themselves *shalbe* forgot ere long. *T.M.* 444
Next to that Ladies love, *shalbe* the place, I. ix. 17. 2
thy pleasure *shalbe* donne. I. x. 52. 1
twise fowre hundreth yeares *shalbe* supplide, III. iii. 44. 5
Ere they to former rule restor'd *shal bee,* III. iii. 44. 6
Shall (*partial list*). *See* **Shalbe.**
For he *shall* be their God, *Rev.* iv. 6
Die *shall* all flesh? I. ix. 47. 6
brimstone, which for ever *shall* remaine. I. ix. 49. 9
'Old man great sure *shal* be thy meed, II. iii. 14. 6
Who meanes no guile be guiled soonest *shall,* III. i. 54. 6
'Perdy, nay,' (said Malbecco) '*shall* ye not; III. x. 39. 1
Yet my good lucke he *shall* not likewise pray, V. iv. 14. 8
Shallop. Did thrust the *shallop* from the floting strand: III. vii. 27. 8
Shallow. Eftsoones her *shallow* ship away did slide, II. vi. 5. 1
soone arrived on the *shallow* sand, II. vi. 38. 4

Shallow—*Continued.*
These after came the stony *shallow* Lone, IV. xi. 39. 1
Shallows. On the rough rocks, or on the sandy *shallowes,* III. iv. 9. 4
Shalt (*partial list*).
thou thy selfe herein *shalt* also live: *Ti.* 258
when thou of none *shalt* be maintained, *D.* 83
Now praysd, hereafter deare thou *shalt* repent; I. ix. 43. 5
Shame. For-thy thereof thou takest *shame.* *To his Booke* 15
But yeelded, with *shame* and greefe adawed, *S.C.* F. 141
for *shame* of thy swete layes. *S.C.* Jun. 56
as halfe with *shame* confound *S.C.* Jun. 64
They setten to sale their shops of *shame,* *S.C.* S. 36
they holden *shame* of theyr cote: *S.C.* S. 111
Cuddie, for *shame!* hold up thy heavye head, *S.C.* O. 1
save my sheepe and me fro *shame.* *S.C.* D. 78
Shame light on him, *Hub.* 219
how to scape great punishment, or *shame,* *Hub.* 314
ah! for *shame,* Let not sweete Poets praise, *Hub.* 810
a thousand deathes, and *shame* beside?' *Hub.* 976
chose with scornfull *shame* Him to avenge, *Hub.* 1239
the avengement for this *shame* *Hub.* 1317
Arise, and doo thyself redeeme from *shame,* *Hub.* 1331
forth with *shame* unto his judgement brought. *Hub.* 1376
Behold the fowle reproach and open *shame,* *T.M.* 61
shame and sorrow and accursed case *T.M.* 519
at length awake for *shame!* *Ti.* 231
The *shame* of Nature, the bondslave of spight, *Mui.* 245
wrought her *shame,* and sorrow never ended. *Mui.* 264
'*shame* were to revoke The forward footing I. i. 12. 7
fearefull more of *shame* Then of the certeine perill I. i. 24. 1
He . . . spake reprochful *shame* Of highest God, I. i. 37. 5
To thinke that knighthood I so much should *shame,* I. iii. 28. 3
no greater *shame* Then . . . inconstancie in love: I. iv. 1. 7
each to deadly *shame* would drive his foe: I. v. 9. 2
mov'd with wrath, and *shame,* and Ladies sake, I. v. 12. 5
Duessa I, the daughter of Deceipt and *Shame.*' I. v. 26. 9
Phoebus, . . . hydes for *shame.* I. vi. 6. 8
Plaine, faithfull, true, and enimy of *shame,* I. vi. 20. 7
Ne *shame* he thought to shonne so hideous might: I. viii. 8. 1
shame t' avenge so weake an enimy; I. viii. 45. 8
Her neather parts, the *shame* of all her kind, I. viii. 48. 1
My chaster Muse for *shame* doth blush to write; I. viii. 48. 2
From living eies her open *shame* to hide, I. viii. 50. 4
with dread of *shame* sore terrifide. I. xi. 45. 9
With rosy cheekes, for *shame* as blushing red: I. xi. 51. 4
Either for grievous *shame,* or for great teene. II. i. 15. 8
All wrongs have mendes, but no amendes of *shame.* II. i. 20. 5
hide her *shame* and loathly filthinesse, II. i. 22. 5
end their daies with irrenowmed *shame,* II. i. 23. 4
with reprochfull *shame* mine honour shent, II. i. 27. 4
'well mote I *shame* to tell The fond encheason II. i. 30. 1
foule *shame* him follow wher he went!' II. i. 30. 9
For all so great *shame* after death I weene, II. i. 59. 8
of *shame* affrayd, She set her downe to weepe II. ii. 8. 2
Such prayse is *shame;* II. iii. 10. 8
She shakes off *shame,* II. iii. 36. 9
unto knighthood workes much *shame* and woe; II. iv. 10. 7
shame of such repriefe. II. iv. 28. 9
knights and knighthood doest with *shame* upbray, II. iv. 45. 3
Losse is no *shame,* nor to bee lesse then foe; II. v. 15. 6
To worke such *shame.* II. v. 17. 7
Atin ay him pricks with spurs of *shame* II. v. 38. 9
Tho up she started, stird with *shame* extreme, II. vi. 27. 7
whither dost thou flye The *shame* and death, II. vi. 39. 7
shame his ugly face did hide from living eye. II. vii. 22. 8
were it not for *shame,* he would retyre; II. vii. 37. 8
with fowle cowardize his carcas *shame,* II. viii. 13. 4
prickt with guiltie *shame* And inward griefe, II. viii. 44. 2
the third for *shame* did blush, II. ix. 35. 6
more abasht for *shame* II. ix. 43. 1
All naked without *shame* or care of cold, II. x. 7. 6
with all *shame* that sacred throne he fild. II. x. 21. 2
Without or robe or rag to hide his *shame:* II. x. 58. 3
the Prince, prickt with reprochful *shame,* II. xi. 31. 6
shame and sad reproch, here to be red II. xii. 9. 6
shame that ever should so fowle defects II. xii. 23. 3
for feare of fowler *shame.* II. xii. 81. 7
And stared ghastly; some for inward *shame,* II. xii. 86. 4
Great *shame* and sorrow of that fall he tooke; III. i. 7. 1
For to revenge that fowle reprochefull *shame,* III. i. 9. 2
For knight to leave his Lady were great *shame* III. i. 25. 3
all regard of *shame* she had discust, III. i. 48. 7
Such love is hate, and such desire is *shame.* III. i. 50. 5
such *shame* Should ever enter in his bounteous thought, III. ii. 10. 1
worke so hainous tort, In *shame* of knighthood, III. ii. 12. 9
To reskew her from *shame,* and to revenge her wrong. III. iv. 45. 9
To bene avenged of the *shame* he did III. v. 13. 5
They three be dead with *shame,* III. v. 25. 9
Fayre death it is, to shonne more *shame,* to dy: III. v. 45. 8
Whereof conceiving *shame* and foule disgrace, III. vi. 10. 1
greatest *shame* was to that maiden twin, III. vii. 49. 3
for feare of *shame* and fowle disgrace. III. vii. 60. 5
the counterfet should *shame* The thing it selfe: III. viii. 5. 5
For *shame,* but more for feare of his grim sight, III. viii. 32. 8
He fled . . . for *shame,* so fowle reproch to shonne, III. ix. 48. 5
shame of all that doe for honor strive, III. x. 27. 4
were it not for *shame*'— III. x. 29. 9
mickle perill to bee put to *shame.* III. x. 39. 4
Behinde him was Reproch, Repentaunce, *Shame;* III. xii. 24. 1
Reproch the first, *Shame* next, Repent behinde: III. xii. 24. 2

Shame—*Continued.*
Shame most ill-favourd, bestiall, and blinde: . . . III. xii. 24. 5
Shame lowrd, Repentaunce sighd, Reproch did scould; . . . III. xii. 24. 6
Shame burning brond-yrons in her hand did hold: . . . III. xii. 24. 8
dread of *shame* and doubt of fowle dishonor . . . IV. i. 8. 6
with wondrous griefe of mynd And *shame*, . . . IV. i. 37. 7
falsly seekst a vertuous wight to *shame?*' . . . IV. i. 48. 2
Let ugly *shame* and endlesse infamy Colour thy name . . . IV. i. 53. 6
To let them passe at will, for dread of *shame*. . . . IV. iv. 3. 5
(For so to lose a Lady were great *shame*) . . . IV. iv. 9. 3
With love of her, and *shame* of such mesprize. . . . IV. iv. 11. 7
cast t' avenge the *shame* doen to his freend: . . . IV. iv. 45. 2
touched was with secret wrath and *shame* . . . IV. v. 17. 4
To *shame* us all with this *Ungirt unblest!* . . . IV. v. 18. 7
Shame and dishonour hath unto me donne, . . . IV. vi. 5. 7
'*Shame* be his meede,' (quoth he) 'that meaneth *shame!* . . . IV. vi. 6. 1
In *shame* of knighthood and fidelitie; . . . IV. vi. 8. 4
The *shame* of men, and plague of womankind: . . . IV. vii. 18. 5
fowle rebuke and *shame* Be theirs . . . IV. viii. 15. 4
now in feare of *shame* she more did stond, . . . IV. ix. 18. 5
Wherein the honor both of Armes ye *shame*, . . . IV. ix. 37. 4
sooth it was not sure for womanish *shame*, . . . IV. x. 41. 4
it was to Knight unseemely *shame* . . . IV. x. 54. 3
Astraeus, that did *shame* Himselfe . . . IV. xi. 13. 7
shame on you, O men! . . . IV. xi. 22. 3
vile curses and reprochfull *shame* . . . IV. xii. 16. 4
who now is fled with *shame*.' . . . V. i. 15. 9
He chose with *shame* to beare that Ladies head: . . . V. i. 27. 8
True love despiseth *shame*, . . . V. i. 27. 9
to tell abrode your *shame*.' . . . V. i. 28. 9
He fear'd least they with *shame* would him pursew: . . . V. ii. 52. 7
He much was mov'd at so unworthie *shame*, . . . V. iii. 10. 7
turn'd aside for *shame* to heare what he did tell. . . . V. iii. 16. 9
It's punishment enough that all his *shame* doe see.' . . . V. iii. 36. 9
So ought all faytours that true knighthood *shame*, . . . V. iii. 38. 6
him selfe did *shame* on womankinde His mighty hand to shend, V. iv. 24. 3
Partly with *shame*, and partly with dismay, . . . V. iv. 27. 2
to this *shame* am brought, . . . V. iv. 27. 6
'Then sith ye needs' (quoth he) 'will know my *shame*, . . . V. iv. 28. 6
some hath put to *shame*, . . . V. iv. 29. 9
venge the *shame* that she to Knights doth show. . . . V. iv. 34. 4
T' avenge that *shame* they did on him commit, . . . V. iv. 39. 4
dight In womans weedes, that is to manhood *shame*, . . . V. v. 20. 7
that mote his *shame* bewray; . . . V. v. 21. 7
dread of *shame* my doubtfull lips doth still restraine.' . . . V. v. 30. 9
Great *shame* to lose so long employed paines, . . . V. v. 48. 3
greater *shame* t' abide so great misprize, . . . V. v. 48. 4
badly doest thou hide Thy maisters *shame*, . . . V. vi. 11. 5
many brought to *shame* by treason treacherous. . . . V. vi. 32. 9
abasht with secrete *shame* . . . V. vii. 38. 3
to make proofe of utmost *shame*, . . . V. viii. 22. 6
that no *shame* might wanting be, . . . V. viii. 23. 1
Flying from place to place with cowheard *shame;* . . . V. viii. 50. 8
for vyld treasons and outrageous *shame*, . . . V. ix. 40. 8
To whom he wont shew all the *shame* he might, . . . V. x. 30. 5
all the world spake *shame*. . . . V. xi. 4. 7
for endlesse horrour of his *shame*, . . . V. xi. 19. 5
counted but a recreant Knight with endles *shame*. . . . V. xi. 46. 9
That is the greatest *shame* and foulest scorne, . . . V. xi. 52. 3
Sir Burbon, blushing halfe for *shame:* . . . V. xi. 52. 6
stouped oft his head from *shame* to shield: . . . V. xii. 19. 2
No *shame* to stoupe, ones head more high to reare; . . . V. xii. 19. 3
misfortune, which did me abase Unto this *shame*, . . . VI. i. 12. 8
with uncomely *shame* Gan him salute, . . . VI. i. 24. 8
shame shal thee with *shame* requight.' . . . VI. i. 25. 9
'Not unto me the *shame*, . . . VI. i. 26. 2
No greater *shame* to man then inhumanitie. . . . VI. i. 26. 9
for dread of *shame*, forgoe This evill manner . . . VI. i. 27. 1
shame he weend a sleeping wight to wound. . . . VI. i. 34. 4
to increase his *shame*, . . . Would thumpe her forward . . . VI. ii. 10. 5
that knight wrought knightlesse *shame;* . . . VI. ii. 14. 7
tooke with him the head, the signe of *shame*. . . . VI. iii. 17. 6
as thou hast thy steed forlorne with *shame*, . . . VI. iii. 32. 1
With wrathfull fury for so foule a *shame*, . . . VI. iii. 43. 5
Withouten thought of *shame* or villeny, . . . VI. v. 9. 8
To worke his utter *shame*, . . . VI. v. 14. 9
Turpine doth defeate, and *shame* For his late villanies. . . . VI. vi. Arg.
he them spotted with reproch, or secrete *shame*. . . . VI. vi. 12. 9
by what meanes that *shame* to her befell, . . . VI. vi. 17. 1
so boldly, without let or *shame*, . . . VI. vi. 20. 3
meede whereof shall shortly be thy *shame*, . . . VI. vi. 25. 6
further hast thou heaped *shame* to *shame*, . . . VI. vi. 34. 1
To shew such faintnesse . . . Is greatest *shame;* . . . VI. vi. 35. 3
shame is to adorne . . . one so basely borne: . . . VI. vi. 36. 4
that *shame*, which kindled inward hate: . . . VI. vii. 2. 7
Great *shame* in lieges blood to be embrew'd! . . . VI. vii. 23. 6
Shame would be hid. . . . VI. viii. 5. 7
The greatest *shame* that ever eye yet saw, . . . VI. viii. 6. 2
inward *shame* of her uncomely case She did conceive, . . . VI. viii. 51. 1
that were too great a *shame*, . . . VI. ix. 1. 6
worke his foe great *shame*. . . . VI. ix. 43. 9
gentle Shepheard, pardon thou my *shame*, . . . VI. x. 29. 6
of her *shame* to make a gamesome jest; . . . VII. vi. 51. 3
Great *shame* it is to leave, like one afrayd, . . . *Am.* xiv. 3
Great *shame* it is, thing so divine in view, . . . *Am.* liii. 9
Shame be thy meed, and mischiefe thy reward, . . . *Am.* lxxxv. 13
for *shame* His face . . . did flame, . . . *Epig.* iii. 4
Their quiet heads, devoyd of guilty *shame*, . . . *H.L.* 290
through guilty *shame* May be corrupt, . . . *H.B.* 157
And in her ashes shrowd my dying *shame;* . . . *H.H.L.* 19

Shame—*Continued.*
with despightfull *shame* Revyling him, . . . *H.H.L.* 151
Shamed. when the *shamed* shield of slaine Sansfoy He spide . I. iv. 39. 1
Miscreaunt, That hast . . . Faire knighthood fowly *shamed*, . I. vi. 41. 3
For suffering such abuse as knighthood *sham'd*, . . . II. v. 21. 5
Ne all are *shamed* by the fault of one: . . . III. ix. 2. 5
what is he by whom ye *shamed* were? . . . IV. vi. 6. 2
Had him abusde and *shamed* yesterday; . . . VI. iii. 47. 6
all knights hast *shamed* with this knightlesse part. . . . VI. vi. 33. 9
so fayre beauty was so fowly *shamed*. . . . *Am.* xli. 14
Shamefast. Let fal her eien, as *shamefast*, to the earth, . . . I. ii. 27. 6
to the knight with *shamefast* modestie They turne themselves, I. x. 15. 5
You *shamefast* are, but Shamefastnes it selfe is shee.' . . . II. ix. 43. 9
shaking off all doubt and *shamefast* feare . . . IV. x. 53. 6
When they have shaken off the *shamefast* band, . . . V. v. 25. 2
Shamefastness. You shamefast are, but *Shamefastnes* it selfe is shee.' . . . II. ix. 43. 9
next to her sate goodly *Shamefastnesse*, . . . IV. x. 50. 1
Whereto her bashful *shamefastnesse* ywrought A great increase V. iii. 23. 3
Shameful. Their armes in *shamefull* wise bounde . . . *Bel.*[1] xi. 10
armes bound at their backs in *shamefull* wize. . . . *Bel.*[2] xv. 10
sonne-bright honour pend in *shamefull* coupe. . . . *S.C.* O. 72
and scorne their *shamefull* sin, . . . *Mui.* 373
wights Have knit themselves in Venus *shameful* chaine: . . . I. ii. 4. 8
No knight, but treachour full of . . . *shameful* treason, . . . I. iv. 41. 6
whom he . . . slew, and brought to *shamefull* grave: . . . I. iv. 47. 6
scornd of God and man, a *shamefull* death he dide. . . . I. v. 48. 9
came to *shamefull* end. . . . I. v. 53. 6
Phoebus, flying so most *shamefull* sight, . . . I. vi. 6. 6
them conjure t' avenge this *shamefull* injury. . . . I. xii. 27. 9
read who hath ye wrought this *shamefull* plight, . . . II. i. 18. 2
Yonder he,' . . . 'That wrought the *shamefull* fact . . . II. i. 25. 2
shamefull vaunt Of vile revenge. . . . II. viii. 16. 3
Hengist eke soon brought to *shamefull* death. . . . II. x. 67. 6
To reskew her from *shamefull* villany. . . . III. i. 18. 5
whenas all were put to *shamefull* flight, . . . III. i. 67. 1
Such *shamefull* lustes who loaths not, . . . III. ii. 41. 7
they, how ever *shamefull* and unkinde, . . . III. ii. 43. 6
Shamefull deceipt, and daunger imminent, . . . III. iv. 58. 4
he would have hid His *shamefull* head . . . III. v. 13. 8
drive Their brother to reproch and *shamefull* flight; . . . III. v. 16. 6
in all *shamefull* sort him selfe with her defile, . . . III. vii. 50. 9
How suffrest thou such *shamefull* cruelty . . . III. xi. 9. 4
shameful thing Yt were t' abandon . . . chevisaunce . . . III. xi. 24. 5
with *shamefull* spot of sinfull lust . . . IV. i. 53. 4
He with his *shamefull* lust doth first deflowre, . . . IV. vii. 12. 8
For horrour of his *shamefull* villany: . . . IV. vii. 21. 5
That *shamefull* Hag, the slaunder of her sexe, . . . IV. viii. 35. 2
lead that *shamefull* life, unworthy of a Knight.' . . . V. iv. 32. 9
Most *shamefull*, most unrighteous, most untrew, . . . V. xii. 42. 2
thee captyved in this *shamefull* place?' . . . VI. i. 12. 4
'A *shamefull* use as ever I did heare,' . . . VI. i. 14. 1
to the *shamefull* doer it afford. . . . VI. i. 26. 3
avenge th' abuses of that proud And *shamefull* Knight . . . VI. v. 34. 4
With bitter termes of *shamefull* infamy; . . . VI. xii. 33. 4
Shamefuller. Much greater griefe and *shamefuller* regrett . III. i. 8. 2
Shamefully. *Shamefully* at her rayling all the way, . . . I. iii. 23. 3
With Elfin sword most *shamefully* betrade? . . . I. v. 22. 8
How *shamefully* that Mayd he did torment: . . . II. i. 11. 4
Would him disarme and treaten *shamefully;* . . . II. viii. 25. 3
shamefully reproved for his rudenes fond. . . . III. viii. 25. 9
So *shamefully* forlorne of womankynd, . . . III. x. 55. 8
she had them both *shamefully* fordonne, . . . IV. ix. 28. 8
Where he full *shamefully* was hanged by the hed. . . . V. v. 18. 9
Them fouly rent, and *shamefully* defaced had. . . . V. xi. 60. 9
He for such basenesse *shamefully* him shent, . . . VI. vi. 33. 2
On him that had so *shamefully* him shent: . . . VI. vi. 44. 5
Shameless. small gaines, but *shameles* flatterie, . . . *Hub.* 850
Rolling in rymes of *shameles* ribaudrie . . . *T.M.* 213
half enraged at her *shamelesse* guise, . . . I. i. 50. 2
So *shamelesse* beauty soone becomes a loathly sight. . . . III. i. 48. 9
Shames. those *shames*, that erst ye spake me to deface.' . . . VI. i. 28. 9
Shames not to be with guiltlesse bloud defylde, . . . *Am.* xx. 11
Good *shames* to be to ill an instrument! . . . *Am.* liii. 12
Shaming. *shaming* to have given so great head To his off-spring, . . . *Ro.* xi. 1
Shanks. crooked crawling *shankes*, of marrowe empted; . . . *Mui.* 350
To sit and rest the walkers wearie *shankes:* . . . IV. x. 25. 5
Shannon. Flowes up the *Shenan* with contrarie forse, . . . IV. iii. 27. 2
The spacious *Shenan* spreading like a sea, . . . IV. xi. 41. 3
Shape. *See* **Misshape.**
This dreadfull *shape* was vanished to nought. . . . *Bel.*[2] viii. 14
some quick Whose *shape* appeared not; . . . *S.C.* Mar. 75
for outward *shape* Most like a man, . . . *Hub.* 1041
gan he to himselfe new *shape* to frame; . . . *Hub.* 1266
What *shape* he list in apparition. . . . *Hub.* 1290
from the *shape* of womanhed, . . . *Mui.* 345
She grew to hideous *shape* of dryrihed, . . . *Mui.* 347
excelling far each other, In comely *shape*, . . . *As.* 16
Ah! wretched boy, the *shape* of dreryhead, . . . *As.* 133
most resembling both in *shape* and spright . . . *As.* 213
The image of the heavens in *shape* humane.' . . . *Col.* 351
th' other halfe did womans *shape* retaine, . . . I. i. 14. 8
more foule . . . Then womans *shape* man would beleeve to bee. I. ii. 41. 4
In *shape* and life more like a monster then a man. . . . I. iv. 22. 9
truth, whose *shape* she well can faine, . . . I. vii. 1. 5
that misformed *shape* misshaped more. . . . I. viii. 16. 5
More ugly *shape* yet never living creature saw. . . . I. viii. 48. 9
What *shape*, what shield, what armes, . . . III. ii. 16. 6
Whose *shape* or person yet I never saw, . . . III. ii. 38. 4

Shape—*Continued.*
Her lovers *shape* and chevalrous aray: . . . III. iv. 5. 5
for thy bad And brutish *shape* . . . III. iv. 55. 4
That ugly *shape* so sore her terrifide, . . . III. vii. 24. 3
in *shape* and looke So lively and so like, . . . III. viii. 5. 8
every *shape* on him he could endew; . . . III. viii. 40. 2
as he better did their *shape* avize, . . . III. x. 21. 2
Twise was he seene in soaring Eagles *shape*, . . . III. xi. 34. 1
In Satyres *shape* Antiopa he snatcht; . . . III. xi. 35. 1
That by her monstrous *shape* might easily be red. . . . IV. i. 26. 9
some celestiall *shape* that flesh did beare: . . . IV. v. 14. 7
was no man, but onely like in *shape*, . . . IV. vii. 5. 2
oft admir'd his monstrous *shape*, . . . IV. vii. 32. 7
He wilfully did cut and *shape* anew; . . . IV. vii. 40. 2
it in *shape* and beautie did excell All other Idoles . . . IV. x. 40. 1
of his *shape* appear'd no litle moniment. . . . V. viii. 43. 9
leave his proper forme, and other *shape* to take. . . . V. ix. 16. 9
Whose dreadfull *shape* was never seene of none . . . V. x. 29. 4
Whose ugly *shape* none ever saw, nor kend, . . . V. xi. 20. 5
So hideous is her *shape*, so huge her hed, . . . VI. vi. 10. 3
That like itselfe in lovely *shape* may bee. . . . *H.H.L.* 119

Shaped. *See* **Shope, Well-shaped.**
stone . . . *Shapt* like a Ladies head, exceeding shone, . . . I. vii. 30. 3
Shapt like a maide, . . . II. ii. 9. 5
All *shap't* according their conditions: . . . II. xi. 11. 6
it round and hollow *shaped* was, . . . III. ii. 19. 8
Him *shaped* thus she deckt in garments gay, . . . III. viii. 9. 1
Shap'd like a heart yet bleeding of the wound, . . . IV. viii. 6. 8
blacke spot doth appeare, *Shapt* like a horses shoe, . . . V. iii. 32. 9
They wore rich Mitres *shaped* like the Moone, . . . V. vii. 4. 6

Shapes. each one Of sundrie *shapes*, yet all ill-favored: . . . I. i. 15. 7
Such ugly monstrous *shapes* . . . I. i. 21. 9
he could take As many formes and *shapes* . . . I. ii. 10. 3
The antique *shapes* of kings and kesars straunge and rare. . . . II. vii. 5. 9
And ugly *shapes* did nigh the man dismay, . . . II. vii. 37. 7
Infinite *shapes* of thinges dispersed thin; . . . II. ix. 50. 3
hideous *shapes* were like to feendes of hell, . . . II. xi. 11. 3
Most ugly *shapes* and horrible aspects, . . . II. xii. 23. 1
into these fearefull *shapes* disguiz'd . . . II. xii. 26. 3
curious ymageree . . . and *shapes* of naked boyes, . . . II. xii. 60. 6
Infinite *shapes* of creatures men doe fynd . . . III. vi. 8. 8
Disguiz'd in thousand *shapes*, that none might him bewray.) III. vi. 11. 9
the glorious Features of beautie, and all *shapes* select, . . . III. vi. 12. 4
Infinite *shapes* of creatures there are bred, . . . III. vi. 35. 1
To dreadfull *shapes* he did him selfe transforme; . . . III. viii. 41. 1
she could d'on so manie *shapes* in sight, . . . IV. i. 18. 3
Cast into sundry *shapes* by wondrous skill, . . . IV. x. 15. 6
shapes seem'd not like to terrestriall boyes, . . . IV. x. 42. 4
In thousand dreadful *shapes* doth mongst them stalke, . . . VI. xi. 16. 7

Shard. *See* **Shared.**
In Phaedrias flitt barck over that perlous *shard*. . . . II. vi. 38. 9

Share. *See* **Ploughing-share.**
still somewhat to his *share* did rize: . . . *Hub.* 806
Now Parasites and Sycophants doo *share:* . . . *T.M.* 472
The victorie did yeeld her as her *share:* . . . *Mui.* 342
their judgments *share* Mongst earthlie wightes, . . . *D.* 199
a large *share* it hewd out of the rest, . . . I. ii. 18. 8
her dew loves deryv'd to that vile witches *shayre*. . . . I. iii. 2. 9
Debons *shayre* was that is Devonshyre: . . . II. x. 12. 6
twixt the other twain his kingdom whole did *shayre*. . . . II. x. 28. 9
To whom no *share* in armes and chevalree They doe impart, . III. ii. 1. 4
did *share* The heritage of all celestiall grace; . . . III. vi. 4. 6
shields did *share*, and mailes did rash, . . . IV. ii. 17. 9
Whether of them in her should have the greater *share*. . . . IV. iii. 39. 9
He part of his small feast to her would *share;* . . . IV. viii. 5. 7
each of either take his *share* aright: . . . V. i. 26. 5
had encroched upon others *share;* . . . V. ii. 32. 2
two falses, of each equall *share*, . . . V. ii. 48. 4
throwne it up unto my brothers *share:* . . . V. iv. 8. 4
the sea it to my *share* did lay?' . . . V. iv. 17. 7
hath seized for her *share* Uppon some fowle . . . V. iv. 42. 4
And wish that he part of his spoyle might *share:* . . . VI. ii. 17. 3
Whose *share*, her guiltlesse bloud, they would present; . . . VI. viii. 38. 7
did their labours *share*, . . . VI. ix. 15. 7
wisht that with that shepheard he mote dwelling *share*. . . . VI. x. 30. 9
all the rest, which they usurp, be all my *share*. . . . VII. vii. 26. 9

Shared. not so common was his bountie *shared:* . . . *Hub.* 1194
First into many parts his streame he *shar'd*, . . . *Col.* 138
twixt them *shayrd* his realme by equall lottes; . . . II. x. 29. 3
Alexander, . . . *shar'd* to them the spoiles . . . IV. i. 22. 9
pray Should equally be *shard* betwixt us tway. . . . IV. ii. 13. 5
Both equall paines and equall perill *shared;* . . . IV. v. 46. 5
Her ventayle *shard* away, . . . IV. vi. 19. 3
Wheresoever it did light, it throughly *shard*. . . . V. i. 10. 9
to him selfe be *shared* dead; . . . V. i. 27. 6
Halfe of her shield he *shared* quite away, . . . V. v. 9. 2
mongst them *shared* equally. . . . VI. xi. 10. 5

Shares. did divide this fort To them by equall *shares* . . . II. ii. 13. 4
this sad realme, cut into sondry *shayres* . . . II. x. 37. 4

Sharp. fell Boreas with *sharpe* blast Tossing huge tempests . . *Ro.* xvi. 5
beare of the *sharpe* showres; . . . *S.C.* May 157
with *sharpe* teeth the bramble leaves doth lop, . . . *Gn.* 85
the Shepheard after this *sharpe* stowre, . . . *Gn.* 317
with *sharp* quips joy'd others to deface. . . . *Hub.* 707
The *sharpe* dislikes of each condition: . . . *Com. Son.* i. 4
Like two *sharpe* speares his enemies to gore: . . . *Mui.* 83
Sharpe Isope, good for greene wounds remedies, . . . *Mui.* 190
Sharpe sorrowe did in thousand peeces rive. . . . *D.* 7
Now with his *sharp* bore-spear, . . . *As.* 108
me needs . . . To *sharpe* my sence with sundry beauties vew, *Ded.Son.*xvii.7

Sharp—*Continued.*
the *sharpe* yron did for anger eat, . . . I. iii. 33. 5
the same Have reft away with his *sharp* . . . clawes: . . . I. iii. 41. 6
ghosts . . . with *sharp* shrilling shriekes doe bootlesse cry, . I. v. 33. 5
He to him raught a dagger *sharpe* and keene, . . . I. ix. 51. 2
sharp Remorse his hart did prick and nip, . . . I. x. 27. 3
Both deadly *sharp*, that sharpest steele exceeden farre. . . . I. xi. 11. 9
So many furies and *sharpe* fits did haunt . . . I. xi. 27. 4
With *sharpe* intended sting so rude him smott, . . . I. xi. 38. 2
his *sharpe* sword Against her snowy brest . . . II. i. 11. 6
Sharpe be thy wounds, but sweete the medicines be, . . . II. i. 36. 8
Their *sharp* assault right boldly did rebut, . . . II. ii. 23. 2
a *sharpe* bore-speare she held, . . . II. iii. 29. 1
'The gnawing anguish, and *sharp* gelosy, . . . II. iv. 23. 1
two dartes, exceeding flit And deadly *sharp*, . . . II. iv. 38. 8
the *sharpe* steele, arriving forcibly On his broad shield, . . II. v. 4. 3
He with Pyrochles *sharp* debatement made: . . . II. vi. 39. 2
two *sharpe* winged sheares, Decked with diverse plumes, . II. viii. 5. 7
Whereat renfierst with wrath and *sharp* regret, . . . II. viii. 45. 1
their *sharpe* wounds and noyous injuries, . . . II. ix. 16. 7
He had a *sharpe* foresight . . . II. ix. 49. 8
sharpe staring eyes, That mad or foolish seemd: . . . II. ix. 52. 6
On whose *sharp* cliftes the ribs of vessels broke; . . . II. xii. 7. 3
in his clownish hand a *sharp* bore speare he shooke. . . . III. i. 17. 9
sharp thornes and breres the way forstall, . . . III. i. 46. 7
with *sharpe* fits thy tender hart oppresseth sore: . . . III. iii. 21. 9
gan with *sharpe* repriefe Her to restraine, . . . III. iv. 11. 4
with *sharpe* speare the rest made dearly knowne. . . . III. iv. 15. 6
Ne the *sharp* Northerne wind thereon to showre; . . . III. v. 51. 5
his *sharpe* dartes and whot artilleree: . . . III. vi. 14. 5
Whose shady boughes *sharp* steele did never lop, . . . III. vi. 43. 4
Nor Aeolus *sharp* blast could worke them any wrong. . . . III. vi. 44. 9
Her *sharpe* rebuke full litle did esteeme; . . . III. viii. 26. 2
the *sharpe* hauke which her attached neare, . . . III. viii. 33. 4
with *sharpe* threates her often did assayle; . . . III. viii. 40. 8
the *sharpe* steele doth rive her hart in tway, . . . III. xi. 11. 4
Reproch *sharpe* stings, Repentaunce whips entwinde, . . . III. xii. 24. 7
Whose *sharpe* provokement them incenst so sore, . . . IV. iv. 4. 6
Britomart with *sharpe* avizefull eye . . . IV. vi. 26. 1
Right sore agrieved at her *sharpe* reproofe, . . . IV. vii. 37. 2
More *sharpe* then points of needles, . . . IV. viii. 39. 2
sharpe rebuke for being over bold; . . . IV. x. 54. 2
with which thou diddest sway So *sharpe* a battell, . . . V. iii. 21. 9
with *sharpe* threats, but threats the more increast their mood. V. iv. 4. 9
When as their *sharpe* contention he had ceased, . . . V. iv. 20. 7
they were ymet With a *sharpe* showre of arrowes, . . . V. iv. 38. 4
With her *sharpe* Cemitare at him she flew, . . . V. v. 9. 8
his *sharpe* sword he threw from him apart, . . . V. v. 13. 3
in peeces to have torne With his *sharp* wheeles, . . . V. viii. 31. 7
with *sharp* reasons rang her such a pele, . . . V. ix. 39. 7
their *sharpe* speares doe both together smite . . . V. x. 32. 2
her cursed tongue, full *sharpe* and short, . . . V. xii. 36. 3
oft recuile to shunne his *sharpe* despight: . . . VI. i. 20. 4
And in his left he held a *sharpe* bore-speare, . . . VI. ii. 6. 6
forth at last did breake in speaches *sharpe* . . . VI. iii. 34. 9
Seeing his *sharpe* assault and cruell stoure, . . . VI. iv. 3. 3
threatning his *sharpe* clawes, now wanting powre to traine. VI. iv. 22. 9
Least that the beasts *sharpe* teeth had any wound Made . . VI. iv. 23. 8
doe him *sharpe* assay On every side, . . . VI. v. 19. 3
The bitter anguish of their *sharpe* disease . . . VI. v. 32. 5
with *sharpe* words did bitterly upbrayd: . . . VI. vi. 33. 3
With his *sharpe* sword he fiercely at him flew, . . . VI. viii. 9. 2
the *sharpe* passion being overpast, . . . VI. viii. 19. 3
when he him strooke With his *sharpe* steele, . . . VI. xii. 26. 4
yet the season was full *sharp* and breem: . . . VII. vii. 40. 5
Sweet is the Junipere, but *sharpe* his bough; . . . *Am.* xxvi. 2
With his *sharpe* dart of love: . . . *Epig.* iv. 56
Through the *sharpe* sorrowes which thou hast me bred, . . . *H.L.* 16
therwith tip his *sharp* empoisned darts, . . . *H.L.* 121
Who, seeing her faire eyes so *sharpe* effect, . . . *H.B.* 244
His paines, his povertie, his *sharpe* assayes, . . . *H.H.L.* 235
can the sight that is most *sharpe* and keene . . . *H.H.B.* 59

Sharped. a *sharped* spyre of Diamond . . . *Bel.* iii. 1
sharped steeples high shot up in ayre; . . . *Ro.* ii. 2

Sharpen. O . . . *sharpen* my dull tong! . . . I. Pr. 2. 9
those hags them selves did paine To *sharpen* him, . . . V. xii. 41. 9
Did *sharpen* them, and in fresh poyson steepe; . . . V. xii. 42. 8

Sharpened. knottie snags were *sharpned* all afore, . . . IV. vii. 7. 5

Sharper. or *sharper* edge did feele, . . . I. xi. 36. 3

Sharpest. Both deadly sharp, that *sharpest* steele exceeden farre. I. xi. 11. 9
sharpest steele did far exceed The sharpnesse of his . . . clawes: I. xi. 12. 1
with thy charmes the *sharpest* sight doest binde, . . . III. x. 4. 5

Sharp-head. with his *sharphead* speare, Through . . . shield he quite did perce; . . . I. iii. 35. 2

Sharply. my soule was *sharply* gryde, . . . *S.C.* Au. 95
sharply gan to spurne His fomy steed, . . . III. i. 5. 4
When she for ought him *sharpely* did reprove, . . . III. vi. 11. 7
sharply saide: 'Goe, Dame; goe, seeke your boy, . . . III. vi. 24. 2
doth *sharply* wite For praising love . . . IV. Pr. 1. 3
Triamond . . . *sharpely* him assayld, . . . IV. iii. 25. 3
thus he *sharply* sayd: . . . IV. vi. 7. 6
layd at them so *sharpely* and so sore, . . . IV. ix. 34. 7
him *sharpely* twight For breach of faith to her, . . . V. vi. 12. 8
now they doe so *sharpely* him assay, . . . V. xi. 46. 1
Sharpely they all attonce did him assaile, . . . VI. v. 18. 1
Yet he them still so *sharpely* did pursew, . . . VI. vi. 24. 1
so *sharpely* still he him pursewd, . . . VI. vii. 48. 1
Words *sharpely* wound, but greatest griefe of scorning growes. VI. vii. 49. 9
So *sharply* he the Monster did pursew, . . . VI. ix. 3. 1
sharpely at him to revile and raile . . . VI. xii. 33. 3

Sharply—*Continued.*
Yet shoot ye *sharpely* still, . . . *Am.* lvii. 9
lovers eyes more *sharply* sighted bee . . . *H.B.* 232
And, *sharply* launching every inner part, . . . *H.H.L.* 158
Sharpness. Did more increase the *sharpnes* of her showre. . . *T.M.* 478
The *sharpnesse* of his cruell rending clawes: . . . I. xi. 12. 2
the *sharpnesse* of her rankling wound: . . . VI. iv. 9. 9
Sharp-pointed. Shot her *sharp pointed* beames through purest aire. . . . *As.* 58
pricking him with his *sharp-pointed* dart, . . . II. v. 36. 1
with the push of his *sharp-pointed* speare . . . VI. iv. 5. 6
Sharp-staring. *See* **Sharp, Staring.**
Shattered. Her *shattered* ribs in thousand peeces rives, . . . V. ii. 50. 3
shattered all to peeces round about the plaine. . . . V. v. 10. 9
Shaumes. *See* **Shawms.**
Shave. First he his beard did *shave,* . . . V. iii. 37. 5
they that Ladies lockes doe *shave* away, . . . VI. i. 13. 8
Shawms. With *shaumes,* and trompets, and with Clarions sweet; . . . I. xii. 13. 2
Playing on *shaumes* and trumpets, . . . V. v. 4. 5
She (*partial list*).
I sawe so fayre a sight as *shee:* . . . *S.C.* Ja. 52
If *shee* were thine, and thou as now am I? . . . III. xi. 19. 4
Where *shee* strange visions sees: . . . V. vii. Arg.
all their showes but shadowes, saving *she.* . . . *Am.* xxxv. 14
Sheaf. when I thought have thresht in swelling *sheave,* . . . *S.C.* D. 123
Shear. *See* **Sheer.**
with their finny oars the swelling sea did *sheare.* . . . III. iv. 33. 9
through the brackish waves their passage *sheare;* . . . III. iv. 42. 7
with plumy wings doth *sheare* The subtile ayre . . . III. vii. 39. 3
The which he never wont to combe, or comely *sheare.* . . . IV. v. 34. 9
Sheared. thereof nigh one quarter *sheard* away; . . . II. vi. 31. 4
Shearing-feast. Emongst the shepheards in their *shearing feast;* *As.* 32
Shears. More swift then swallow *sheres* the liquid skye, . . . II. vi. 5. 2
two sharpe winged *sheares,* Decked with diverse plumes, . . . II. viii. 5. 7
Sheath. yvory *sheath,* ycarv'd with curious slights, . . . I. vii. 30. 7
The dead knights sword out of his *sheath* he drew, . . . II. i. 61. 1
Sheaves. bound in *sheaves,* and layd in comely rowes, . . . *Ro.* xxx. 7
She-bear's. from the *she Beares* teats her whelps to teare; . . . I. vi. 24. 5
Shed. He *shed* a water, . . . *Bel.*[1] vii. 6
Did in his drinke *shed* poyson privilie; . . . *Van.* vi. 8
teache the trees their trickling teares to *shedde.* . . . *S.C.* Jun. 96
shed his whirling flames on either side, . . . *Gn.* 159
blood Which she with cursed hands had *shed* before; . . . *Gn.* 174
Having the blood of vanquisht Hector *shedd,* . . . *Gn.* 527
as if that he had *shedd* Much blood . . . *Hub.* 206
Shed thy faire beames into my feeble eyne, . . . I. Pr. 4. 5
Dame . . . For whose defence he was to *shed* his blood. . . . I. i. 55. 3
drizling teares did *shed* for pure affection. . . . I. iii. 6. 9
that harlott . . . That causd her *shed* so many a bitter teare; I. iii. 25. 4
his blood, here *shed* in sight?' . . . I. ix. 37. 9
With snowy lockes adowne his shoulders *shed;* . . . I. x. 48. 2
Her golden locks . . . were loosely *shed* About her eares, . . . I. xi. 51. 5
Like roses in a bed of lillies *shed,* . . . II. iii. 22. 6
Sweete wordes like dropping honny she did *shed;* . . . II. iii. 24. 7
About her shoulders weren loosely *shed,* . . . II. iii. 30. 2
To *shed* your lives on ground? . . . II. vi. 32. 7
lives, it seemed, whilome there were *shed,* . . . II. vii. 30. 8
Ne drop of blood appeared *shed* to bee, . . . II. xi. 38. 1
like the boyes blood therein *shed,* . . . II. xii. 45. 6
leafe and fruite, both too untimely *shed,* . . . III. ii. 31. 8
To fly for succour to a little *shed,* . . . III. ix. 11. 8
to that *shed,* to shrowd him from the showre, . . . III. ix. 13. 3
in her lap did *shed* her idle draught, . . . III. ix. 31. 3
The blood hath of so many thousands *shedd,* . . . III. x. 32. 6
gan the humid vapour *shed* the grownd With perly deaw, . . . III. x. 46. 5
teares gan *shed* amaine, . . . IV. iii. 47. 5
He much more goodly glosse thereon doth *shed* . . . IV. v. 15. 5
the deawy humour *shed* Did tricle downe . . . IV. xi. 46. 7
With many bitter teares *shed* from his blubbred eyne. . . . V. i. 13. 9
neither he did *shed* that Ladies bloud, . . . V. i. 23. 8
of their vitall bloud, the which was *shed* . . . V. vii. 11. 1
wicked sclaunders by him *shed.* . . . V. ix. 26. 9
Her deawy humour gan on th' earth to *shed,* . . . VI. ix. 13. 2
Lillyes, ere theyr leaves be *shed;* . . . *Am.* lxiv. 11
Vouchsafe to *shed* into my barren spright . . . *H.H.L.* 45
Vouchsafe . . . To *shed* into my breast some sparkling light *H.H.B.* 10
Sheddeth. smoke, that *sheddeth* in the skye; . . . *S.C.* O. 35
Ne *sheddeth* teares from lamentable eie; . . . *Ti.* 163
Doth weepe full sore, and *sheddeth* tender teares; . . . I. v. 18. 6
all about him *sheddeth* glorious light: . . . *H.H.B.* 161
Shedding. *shedding* teares a while, I still did rest, . . . *Ti.* 32
So *shedding* many teares they closd the earth agayne. . . . II. i. 61. 9
shedding few soft teares from tender eyne, . . . VI. v. 24. 3
Sheder. He would have devoured both hidder and *shidder.* . . . *S.C.* S. 211
Sheen. Dido! the greate shepehearde his daughter *sheene.* . . . *S.C.* N. 38
in his new glory *sheene.* . . . *Hub.* 1066
To spoyle her dainty corps, so faire and *sheene* . . . II. i. 10. 5
with her soveraine power, and scepter *shene,* . . . II. ii. 40. 4
Dioclesians fifty daughters *shene* . . . II. x. 8. 4
fell intent, against the virgin *sheene:* . . . III. i. 65. 4
Was mounted high in top of heaven *sheene,* . . . III. iv. 51. 7
His Lucida, that was full faire and *sheene:* . . . IV. v. 11. 7
past through heven *sheene,* . . . IV. vii. 13. 2
Laomedia like the christall *sheene;* . . . IV. xi. 51. 3
shone as bright as doth the heaven *sheene:* . . . V. viii. 29. 5
Upon a throne of gold full bright and *sheene,* . . . V. ix. 27. 5
Her stately towres and buildings sunny *sheene,* . . . V. x. 25. 5
as in a mirrour *sheene,* . . . VI. Pr. 6. 5
Her garment was so bright and wondrous *sheene,* . . . VII. vii. 7. 3

Sheen—*Continued.*
her faire hands are Silver *sheene:* . . . *Am.* xv. 12
Sheep. All as the *Sheepe,* such was the shepeheards looke, . . . *S.C.* Ja. 7
the while his *shepe* there fedde. . . . *S.C.* Ja. 12
Arose, and homeward drove his sonned *sheepe,* . . . *S.C.* Ja. 77
Keeping his *sheepe* on the hils of Kent? . . . *S.C.* F. 93
were not that my *sheepe* would stray, . . . *S.C.* Mar. 34
My *sheepe* for that may chaunce to swerve, . . . *S.C.* Mar. 44
letting their *sheepe* runne at large, . . . *S.C.* May 40
theyr *sheepe* bene not their owne, . . . *S.C.* May 45
what might arise of the bare *sheepe,* . . . *S.C.* May 107
often devoured their owne *sheepe,* . . . *S.C.* May 128
I am a poore *sheepe,* . . . *S.C.* May 266
our *sheepe* about us safely fedde. . . . *S.C.* Jun. 88
O blessed *sheepe!* O shepheard great! . . . *S.C.* Jul. 53
My seely *sheepe* like well belowe, . . . *S.C.* Jul. 105
Simple as simple *sheepe;* . . . *S.C.* Jul. 130
Nowe with a Kidde, now with a *sheepe,* . . . *S.C.* Jul. 135
Theyr Pan theyr *sheepe* to them has sold, . . . *S.C.* Jul. 179
Theyr *sheepe* han crustes, . . . *S.C.* Jul. 187
(O, seely *sheepe,* the while!) . . . *S.C.* Jul. 190
Never knew I lovers *sheepe* in good plight: . . . *S.C.* Au. 20
My *sheepe* did leave theyr wonted food, . . . *S.C.* Au. 73
Hey, ho, seely *sheepe!* . . . *S.C.* Au. 74
you, that sawe it, simple *shepe,* . . . *S.C.* Au. 117
My *sheepe* bene wasted; . . . *S.C.* S. 25
they will buy his *sheepe* out of the cote, . . . *S.C.* S. 40
My seely *sheepe* (ah, seely *sheepe!*) . . . *S.C.* S. 62
ledde of theyr *sheepe* what way they wyll, . . . *S.C.* S. 81
sike bene her *sheepe,* . . . *S.C.* S. 141
Ycladde in clothing of seely *sheepe,* . . . *S.C.* S. 188
As if a Woolfe were emong the *sheepe:* . . . *S.C.* S. 192
This Wolvish *sheepe* woulde catchen his pray, . . . *S.C.* S. 197
the Wolves, that chase the wandring *sheepe,* . . . *S.C.* N. 136
Does save from mischiefe the unwary *sheepe,* . . . *S.C.* D. 10
save my *sheepe* and me fro shame. . . . *S.C.* D. 78
wont t' enrage the restlesse *sheepe,* . . . *S.C.* D. 89
Adieu, my little Lambes and loved *sheepe;* . . . *S.C.* D. 153
how to feede his *sheepe,* . . . *S.C.* Env. 5
To keep his *sheep,* or to attend his swyne, . . . *Hub.* 285
I of your fleecie *sheepe* . . . would take on me the keep. . . *Hub.* 289
Unto my fathers *sheepe* I usde to looke, . . . *Hub.* 292
will serve my *sheepe* to gather, . . . *Hub.* 295
The *Sheepe* and th' Asse, . . . *Hub.* 1068
the *Sheepe,* to whom of yore The Foxe had promised . . . *Hub.* 1205
'Soft, Gooddie *Sheepe!* (then said the Foxe) . . . *Hub.* 1213
So went the *Sheepe* away with heavie hart: . . . *Hub.* 1222
all my joy was on my gentle *sheepe,* . . . *D.* 104
'Safe then, and safest were my sillie *sheepe,* . . . *D.* 134
'Ne worse to you, my sillie *sheepe!* I pray, . . . *D.* 351
Did keepe his *sheep,* his litle stock and store: . . . *As.* 4
since first on grassie greene Shepheards kept *sheep,* . . . *As.* 210
Keeping my *sheepe* amongst the cooly shade . . . *Col.* 58
pastures . . . On which she useth for to feed her *sheepe?'* . . . *Col.* 239
wash faire Cynthiaes *sheep,* when they be shorne, . . . *Col.* 258
Here to keep *sheepe,* . . . *Col.* 658
rather chose back to my *sheep* to tourne, . . . *Col.* 672
innocents trew, . . . slaine as *sheepe* out of the fold, . . . I. viii. 35. 7
forst them fly, Like scattered *Sheepe,* . . . II. ix. 14. 7
Great heapes of them, like *sheepe* in narrow fold, . . . IV. iii. 41. 4
like a sort of *sheepe* dispersed farre . . . V. iv. 44. 7
here and there like scattred *sheepe* they lay: . . . V. vi. 30. 6
Like scattred *sheepe,* to seeke for safetie, . . . VI. vi. 38. 6
this Lady, like a *sheepe* astray, . . . VI. viii. 36. 8
to the folds, where *sheepe* at night doe seat, . . . VI. ix. 4. 7
sundrie *sheepe* with severall care Gathered together, . . . VI. ix. 15. 4
To follow *sheepe* and shepheards base attire: . . . VI. ix. 24. 4
backe returning to my *sheepe* againe, . . . VI. ix. 25. 7
kept her *sheepe* with diligent attent, . . . VI. ix. 37. 3
as they sate Keeping their *sheepe,* . . . VI. x. 33. 6
Fit to keepe *sheepe,* unfit for loves content: . . . VI. x. 37. 4
Some flockes of *sheepe* and shepheards to espy; . . . VI. xi. 36. 7
Right well knew Coridon his owne late *sheepe,* . . . VI. xi. 37. 6
Unwont with heards to watch, or pasture *sheepe,* . . . VI. xi. 40. 4
Sheepcote. oft in the night came to the *shepe-cote,* . . . *S.C.* S. 216
Sheep-hook. with his *shepe-hooke* hath him slayne. . . . *S.C.* Au. 34
Sheep's. with *sheepes* clothing doen hem disguise. . . . *S.C.* S. 157
let out the *sheepes* bloud at his throte. . . . *S.C.* S. 207
when lambes fail'd the old *sheepes* lives they reft; . . . *Hub.* 322
Sheer. having vewed in a fountaine *shere* His face, . . . III. ii. 44. 7
she at last came to a fountaine *sheare,* . . . III. xi. 7. 2
which Pactolus with his waters *shere* Throwes forth . . . IV. vi. 20. 8
th' Ayre to Water *sheere,* . . . VII. vii. 25. 6
Sheet. *See* **Main-sheet.**
her Belamour, the partner of his *sheet:* . . . III. x. 22. 9
Sheets. odourd *sheetes,* and Arras coverlets. . . . *Epith.* 304
Shell. of a fishes *shell* was wrought with rare delight. . . . IV. xi. 6. 9
Shell-fish. A *shell-fish* downe let flye: . . . *S.C.* Jul. 224
She weend the *shell-fishe* to have broke, . . . *S.C.* Jul. 225
Sheltered. calmy bay, on th' one side *sheltered* . . . II. xii. 30. 3
Shenan. *See* **Shannon.**
Shend. *See* **Yshend.**
Such simplesse mought them *shend:* . . . *S.C.* Jul. 172
Her fawning love . . . He would not *shend;* . . . I. i. 53. 8
The famous name of knighthood fowly *shend;* . . . II. vi. 35. 2
This odious argument my rymes should *shend,* . . . III. ix. 1. 4
Whereby the name of knight-hood thou dost *shend,* . . . IV. i. 51. 3
A stranger knight, that did his glorie *shend:* . . . IV. iv. 43. 8
on womankinde His mighty hand to *shend,* . . . V. iv. 24. 4
Cynthia doth *shend* The lesser starres. . . . *Proth.* 121

Shendst. with thy brutenesse *shendst* thy comely age, ... II. viii. 12. 3
Shent. 'That knight should knighthood ever so have *shent?*' . . II. i. 11. 2
with reprochfull shame mine honour *shent,* . . . . II. i. 27. 4
all enraged thus him loudly *shent;* . . . . II. v. 5. 2
former feare of being fowly *shent* . . . . III. iv. 50. 4
light doe shonne for feare of being *shent;* . . . . III. iv. 58. 7
Their ofspring hath . . . later glory *shent?* . . . . III. ix. 33. 9
hath thy lady reft and knighthood *shent,* . . . . III. x. 32. 4
hath this day so many so unmanly *shent.'* . . . . IV. v. 18. 9
First he his beard did shave, and fowly *shent,* . . . . V. iii. 37. 5
To be by them dishonoured and *shent:* . . . . V. viii. 23. 4
nor for being *shent,* Would be restrayned be . . . . VI. vi. 18. 8
He for such basenesse shamefully him *shent,* . . . . VI. vi. 33. 2
On him that had so shamefully him *shent:* . . . . VI. vi. 44. 5
his deare Ladie *shent:* . . . . VI. vii. 4. 5
Else had he surely there bene slaine, or fowly *shent.* . . . . VI. vii. 45. 9
Shepherd. The homely *shepheard* (*shepherde*[1]), nor the clowne; . . . . Pet. iv. 4
Now I pray thee, *shepheard,* tel it not forth: . . . . *S.C.* F. 239
Hye thee home, *shepheard,* . . . . *S.C.* F. 246
shepheard must walke another way, ... *S.C.* May 81
Shepheard, I list none accordaunce make . . . . *S.C.* May 164
With *shepheard* that does the right way forsake: . . . . . . *S.C.* May 165
Shepheard to see them in theyr art outgoe. . . . . *S.C.* Jun. 64
With *shepheard* sittes not followe flying fame, ... *S.C.* Jun. 75
O blessed sheepe! O *shepheard* great! . . . . *S.C.* Jul. 53
the cave where Phoebe layed The *shepheard* . . . . *S.C.* Jul. 64
Alsoone may *shepheard* clymbe to skye . . . . *S.C.* Jul. 101
whilome was the first *shepheard,* . . . . *S.C.* Jul. 127
nothing such thilk *shepehearde* was . . . . *S.C.* Jul. 145
shepheard mought be meeke and mylde, ... *S.C.* Jul. 153
A *shepheard* trewe, yet not so true . . . . *S.C.* Jul. 163
He is a *shepheard* great in gree, ... *S.C.* Jul. 215
Now farwell, *shepheard,* . . . . *S.C.* Jul. 231
The while the *shepheard* selfe did spill. . . . . *S.C.* Au. 60
The *shepheard* of Ida that judged beauties Queene. . . . . . *S.C.* Au. 138
The jolly *shepheard* that was of yore . . . . *S.C.* S. 26
Is nowe nor jollye, nor *shepeheard* more. . . . . *S.C.* S. 27
Thilk same *shepheard* mought I well marke, ... *S.C.* S. 180
Never had *shepheard* so kene a kurre, ... *S.C.* S. 182
the *shepheard* would breake his sleepe, ... *S.C.* S. 193
the *shepheard* his practise spyed, ... *S.C.* S. 202
with *shepheard* sittes not playe, ... *S.C.* S. 232
the *shepheard* that did fetch his dame . . . . *S.C.* O. 28
Dido! the greate *shepehearde* his daughter sheene. . . . . . *S.C.* N. 38
'O thou greate *shepheard,* Lobbin, ... *S.C.* N. 113
No daunger there the *shepheard* can astert; . . . . *S.C.* N. 187
Ay, francke *shepheard,* how bene thy verses meint . . . . . *S.C.* N. 203
The gentle *shepheard* satte beside a springe, ... *S.C.* D. 1
A good old *shephearde,* Wrenock was his name, ... *S.C.* D. 41
To teach the ruder *shepheard* . . . . *S.C.* Env. 5
the *shepheard,* seeing day appeare, ... *Gn.* 70
each *shepheard* sings As merrie notes . . . . *Gn.* 147
his carelesse time This *Shepheard* drives, ... *Gn.* 154
gan the *shepheard* gather into one His stragling Goates, . . . *Gn.* 161
the *Shepheard* self, tending his stocke, ... *Gn.* 237
A Gnat, unto the sleepie *Shepheard* went; . . . . *Gn.* 283
the *Shepheard* after this sharpe stowre, ... *Gn.* 317
the sloathfull fit . . . Had left the heavie *Shepheard,* . . . . *Gn.* 642
The *Shepheard* hath thy deaths record engraved. . . . . . . *Gn.* 688
drew the wicked *Shepheard* to his will. . . . . *Hub.* 320
He is the *Shepheard,* and the Priest is hee; . . . . *Hub.* 443
Whether he *shepheard* be, or shepheards swaine, ... *Ti.* 234
Then stay, Alcyon, gentle *shepheard!* . . . . *D.* 68
her own *Shepheard,* Colin, her owne *Shepherd,* . . . . *D.* 229
Weepe, *Shepheard!* weepe, to make my undersong. . . . . . . *D.* 245
Weep, *Shepheard!* weep, to make mine undersong. . . . . . . *D.* 294
Ne ever *Shepheard* sound his Oaten quill . . . . *D.* 325
Weepe, *Shepheard!* weepe, to make my undersong. . . . *D.* 343, 392, 441, 490
Cease, *Shepheard!* cease, and end thy undersong.' . . . . . *D.* 539
A gentle *shepheard* borne in Arcady, ... *As.* 1
Of gentlest race that ever *shepheard* bore, ... *As.* 2
In all that seemly *shepheard* might behove. . . . . *As.* 10
lov'd this *shepheard* dearest in degree, ... *Col.* 14
To whom the *shepheard* gently answered thus; . . . . *Col.* 36
a straunge *shepheard* chaunst to find me out, ... *Col.* 60
The *Shepheard* of the Ocean by name, ... *Col.* 66
In sort as I it to that *shepheard* told: . . . . *Col.* 101
What dittie did that other *shepheard* sing: . . . . *Col.* 160
Small needments else need *shepheard* to prepare. . . . . . . *Col.* 195
That *shepheard* I besought to me to tell, ... *Col.* 229
the *shepheard* which hath charge in chief, ... *Col.* 244
Those same, the *shepheard* told me, ... *Col.* 276
as that same *shepheard* still us guyded, ... *Col.* 331
I, base *shepheard,* bold and blind, ... *Col.* 348
how that *shepheard* strange thy cause advanced.' . . . . . . *Col.* 357
'The *Shepheard* of the Ocean . . . . *Col.* 358
joyd that country *shepheard* ought could fynd . . . . *Col.* 366
there is a new *shepheard* late up sprong, ... *Col.* 416
there that *Shepheard* of the Ocean is, ... *Col.* 428
A gentler *shepheard* may no where be found: . . . . *Col.* 445
'*Shepheard,* enough of shepheards thou hast told, ... *Col.* 457
verse of noblest *shepheard* lately dead . . . . *Col.* 534
Shepheard, what ever thou hast heard . . . . *Col.* 568
Such loftie flight base *shepheard* seemeth not, ... *Col.* 618
Which she to Colin her poore *shepheard* shewed.' . . . . . . *Col.* 647
'*Shepheard,* (said Thestylis) . . . . *Col.* 676
life, For *shepheard* fit to lead . . . . *Col.* 689
Ne is there *shepheard,* ne yet shepheards swaine, ... *Col.* 819
'*Shepheard,* it seemes that some celestiall rage . . . . *Col.* 823

Shepherd—*Continued.*
As gentle *shepheard* in sweete eventide, ... I. i. 23. 1
The fearefull *shepheard,* . . . Under them never sat, ... I. ii. 28. 7
Proteus is *Shepheard* of the seas of yore, ... III. viii. 30. 1
Whiles yet on Ida he a *shepeheard* hight, ... III. ix. 36. 3
A *shepeheard,* when Mnemosyne he catcht; . . . . III. xi. 35. 3
the *shepheard* Coridon For her did languish, ... VI. ix. 10. 5
This new-come *shepheard* had his market mard. . . . . VI. ix. 40. 8
in the midst a *Shepheard* piping he did see. . . . . VI. x. 10. 9
Was she to whom that *shepheard* pypt alone; . . . . VI. x. 15. 8
That jolly *shepheard,* which there piped, ... VI. x. 16. 3
Pype, jolly *shepheard,* pype thou now apace . . . . VI. x. 16. 6
All save the *shepheard,* who . . . broke his bag-pipe quight, . VI. x. 18. 4
'Haile, jolly *shepheard,* . . . . VI. x. 19. 2
Tho gan that *shepheard* thus for to dilate: . . . . VI. x. 21. 1
'Then wote, thou *shepheard,* whatsoever thou bee, ... VI. x. 21. 2
Pardon thy *shepheard,* . . . . VI. x. 28. 4
When thus that *shepheard* ended had his speach, ... VI. x. 29. 1
gentle *Shepheard,* pardon thou my shame, ... VI. x. 29. 6
wisht that with that *shepheard* he mote dwelling share. . . . VI. x. 30. 9
the *shepheard* Coridon . . . Did strive to match . . . . VI. x. 33. 1
the *Shepheard* streight with jealousie did frize. . . . . . . VI. x. 33. 9
read thou, *shepheard,* read what destiny . . . . VI. xi. 29. 7
when the *Shepheard* breathed had awhyle, ... VI. xi. 30. 1
At length a *Shepheard* . . . Came to the place; . . . . VI. xii. 9. 1
That *Shepheard* Colin dearely did condole, ... VII. vi. 40. 5
The Latmian *shepherd* (**shephard*) once unto thee brought, . *Epith.* 380
Shepherdess. 'Ne let Elisa, royall *Shepheardesse,* . . . envy, . . *D.* 225
The gentlest *shepheardesse* that lives this day, ... *As.* 212
a great *shepheardesse,* that Cynthia hight, ... *Col.* 234
'If then (quoth I) a *shepheardesse* she bee, ... *Col.* 236
shee That is so great a *shepheardesse* her selfe, ... *Col.* 369
Gan to inquire for that faire *shepherdesse,* . . . . VI. xi. 11. 6
Shepherd-grooms. the listning rout Of *shepherd groomes,* . . . *Ti.* 228
He chaunst to spy a sort of *shepheard groomes,* . . . . VI. ix. 5. 2
Shepherd-lasses. Well may the *shepheard lasses* now lament; *D.* 222
ye *Shepheard lasses!* who shall lead Your wandring troupes, . *D.* 316
Shepherd-like. Peters successor . . . Who, *shepheardlike,* (as fates the same foreseeing) . . . . *Ro.* xviii. 13
Shepherd peers. I to much beleeved my *shepherd peeres,*) . . *S.C.* D. 39
where were ye this while his *shepheard peares,* . . . . *As.* 127
Shepherd's. The ploughmans hope and *shepheards* labour vaine: *Ro.* xiv. 4
This Citie, which was first but *shepheards* shade, ... *Ro.* xx. 9
A *shepheards* swaine, saye, did thee sing . . . . *To his Booke* 9
A *shepeheards* boye . . . Led forth his flock, ... *S.C.* Ja. 1
All as the Sheepe, such was the *shepeheards* looke, ... *S.C.* Ja. 7
Shepheards devise she hateth as the snake, ... *S.C.* Ja. 65
Colin thou kenst, the Southerne *shepheardes* boye; . . . . . *S.C.* Ap. 21
I her *shepherds* swayne, ... *S.C.* Ap. 98
holden scorne of homely *shepheards* quill: . . . . *S.C.* Jun. 67
she the truest *shepheards* hart made bleede, ... *S.C.* Jun. 111
What, ho! thou jollye *shepheards* swayne, ... *S.C.* Jul. 5
to holden chat With seely *shepherds* swayne, ... *S.C.* Jul. 30
never was abhord The simple *shepheards* kynd. . . . . *S.C.* Jul. 140
O Colin, Colin! the *shepheards* joye, ... *S.C.* Au. 193
they will carven the *shepheards* throte. . . . . *S.C.* S. 41
The *sheperdes* swayne you cannot wel ken, ... *S.C.* S. 42
they nill listen to the *shepheards* voyce, ... *S.C.* S. 142
had he cond the *shepherds* call, ... *S.C.* S. 215
Ne would she scorne the simple *shepheards* swaine; . . . . . *S.C.* N. 97
Rude ditties, tund to *shepheards* Oaten reede, ... *S.C.* D. 14
in derring-doe compare With *shepheards* swayne . . . . *S.C.* D. 44
Unto the shifting of the *shepheards* foote, ... *S.C.* D. 116
ever creepe into the *shepheards* den. . . . . *Gn.* 96
this *Shepheards* flocke Lay everie where, ... *Gn.* 233
Wake, *shepheards* boy, at length awake for shame! . . . . . . *Ti.* 231
Whether he shepheard be, or *shepheards* swaine, ... *Ti.* 234
Do pluck it softly for that *shepheards* sake. . . . . *As.* 198
The *shepheards* boy (best knowen by that name) . . . . *Col.* 1
told her father by a *shepheards* boy, ... *Col.* 147
Not for my skill, but for that *shepheards* sake.' . . . . . . *Col.* 455
Ne is there shepheard, ne yet *shepheards* swaine, ... *Col.* 819
Muse whylome did maske . . . in lowly *Shephards* weeds, . . . I. Pr. 1. 2
As *Shepheardes* curre, that in darke eveninges shade . . . . II. vi. 39. 4
the *Shepherds* swaine A Lyon and a Tigre doth espye, ... II. ix. 14. 7
love a *Shephards* daughter for his dearest Dame. . . . . . . III. xi. 38. 9
As it had bene two *shepheards* curres . . . . V. xii. 38. 5
ne was there *shepheards* swayne, But did her honour; . . . . VI. ix. 10. 1
With *shepheards* hooke in hand, and fit attyre, ... VI. ix. 13. 8
To follow sheepe and *shepheards* base attire: . . . . VI. ix. 24. 4
being bred under base *shepheards* wings, ... VI. ix. 35. 4
himselfe addrest In *shepheards* weed; . . . . VI. ix. 36. 4
Instead of steele-head speare, a *shepheards* hooke . . . . . . VI. ix. 36. 5
She was, to weete, that jolly *Shepheards* lasse, ... VI. x. 16. 1
He had no weapon but his *shepheards* hooke . . . . VI. x. 36. 1
saw his *shepheards* cottage spoyled quight, ... VI. xi. 25. 2
Coridon it was, the silly *shepheards* hynd. . . . . VI. xi. 27. 9
old father MOLE, whom *Shepheards* quill Renowmed hath . . VII. vi. 36. 8
Shepherds. *See* **Fellow-shepherds.**
Then tooke the *shepheards* Kingly ornaments, ... *Ro.* xviii. 5
Such an one *shepeheards* would make full faine; . . . . *S.C.* F. 67
Of fayre Elisa, Queene of *shepheardes* all, ... *S.C.* Ap. 34
I sawe a shole of *shepeheardes* outgoe . . . . *S.C.* May 20
shepeheardes for the Devils stedde, ... *S.C.* May 43
When great Pan account of *shepeherdes* shall aske. . . . . . *S.C.* May 54
What shoulden *shepheards* other things tend, ... *S.C.* May 63
shepheards (as Algrind used to say) . . . . *S.C.* May 75
When *shepeheards* had none inheritaunce, ... *S.C.* May 105
Well ywis was it with *shepheards* thoe: . . . . *S.C.* May 109
Lulled the *shepheards* in such securitie, ... *S.C.* May 119

Shepherds—*Continued.*
under colour of *shepeheards,* . . . *S.C.* May 126
the *shepheards* that did hem keepe: . . . *S.C.* May 129
How shoulden *shepheardes* live, . . . *S.C.* May 148
That *shepheardes* so witen ech others life, . . . *S.C.* May 159
Much needeth all *shepheards* hem to knowe. . . . *S.C.* May 313
where *shepheards* ritch . . . bene every where to see: . . . *S.C.* Jun. 21
The God of *shepheards,* Tityrus, is dead, . . . *S.C.* Jun. 81
was the soveraigne head Of *shepheards* all . . . *S.C.* Jun. 84
Ye gentle *Shepheards,* which your flocks do feede, . . . *S.C.* Jun. 106
used *shepheards* all To feede theyr flocks . . . *S.C.* Jul. 65
shepheardes bene forsayd From places of delight, . . . *S.C.* Jul. 69
Shepheards they weren of the best, . . . *S.C.* Jul. 121
(No such mought *shepheards* bee) . . . *S.C.* Jul. 150
(Mought they good *sheepeheards* bene?) . . . *S.C.* Jul. 178
shepeheards (sayd he) there doen leade, . . . *S.C.* Jul. 185
Sike syrlye *shepheards* han we none, . . . *S.C.* Jul. 203
wont to make the jolly *shepeheards* gladde, . . . *S.C.* Au. 9
ye jolly *shepheards* twayne: . . . *S.C.* Au. 51
tell me, *shepherds,* . . . *S.C.* Au. 139
blowe your pypes, *shepheards,* til you be at home; . . . *S.C.* Au. 197
The *shepheards* there robben one another, . . . *S.C.* S. 38
the *shepeheards* bene ydle and still, . . . *S.C.* S. 80
playnely to speake of *shepheards* most what, . . . *S.C.* S. 104
All for her *shepheards* bene beastly and blont. . . . *S.C.* S. 109
Sike as the *shepheards,* sike bene her sheepe, . . . *S.C.* S. 141
heedy *shepheards* to discerne their face; . . . *S.C.* S. 167
Shepheards sich, God mought us many send, . . . *S.C.* S. 178
'*Shepheards,* that by your flocks on Kentish downes abyde, . . . *S.C.* N. 63
So well she couth the *shepherds* entertayne . . . *S.C.* N. 95
Make hast, ye *shepheards,* thether to revert: . . . *S.C.* N. 191
'O soveraigne Pan! thou god of *shepheards* all, . . . *S.C.* D. 7
O! the great happines, which *shepheards* have, . . . *Gn.* 89
Mongst simple *shepheards* they do boast their skill, . . . *T.M.* 329
shepheards leave their lambs unto mischaunce, . . . *Ti.* 327
'Oft did the *Shepeheards* . . . Daylie resort to me . . . *D.* 141
flocks and *shepheards* caused to rejoyce. . . . *D.* 315
Shepheards, that wont, on pipes of oaten reed, . . . *As.* Pr. 1
Hearken, ye gentle *shepheards,* to my song, . . . *As.* Pr. 5
Emongst the *shepheards* in their shearing feast; . . . *As.* 32
all the sports that *shepheards* are emong. . . . *As.* 76
A sort of *shepheards,* sewing of the chace, . . . *As.* 139
Had not good hap those *shepheards* thether led. . . . *As.* 144
The *shepheards* all which loved him full deare, . . . *As.* 200
since first on grassie greene *Shepheards* kept sheep, . . . *As.* 210
Harke then, ye jolly *shepheards,* to my song.' . . . *Col.* 51
the *shepheards* which my Cynthia serve At sea, . . . *Col.* 260
The *shepheards* there abroad may safely lie, . . . *Col.* 316
hath so many *shepheards* in her fee, . . . *Col.* 370
be the *shepheards* which do serve her laesie, . . . *Col.* 372
better *shepheards* be not under skie, . . . *Col.* 377
Helpe, O ye *shepheards,* helpe ye all in this, . . . *Col.* 436
enough of *shepheards* thou hast told, . . . *Col.* 457
Then we poore *shepheards* are accustomd here, . . . *Col.* 785
we poore *shepheards* whether rightly so, . . . *Col.* 795
'Ah! *shepheards,* (then said Colin) . . . *Col.* 927
How the rude *Shepheards* after him did stare, . . . III. xi. 34. 7
shepherds singing to their flockes . . . VI. ix. 4. 3
to the litle cots, where *shepherds* lie . . . VI. ix. 4. 8
So farre the meane of *shepheards* to excell, . . . VI. ix. 11. 3
warn'd the *shepheards* to their homes to hast . . . VI. ix. 13. 3
to commend the happie life Which *Shepheards* lead, . . . VI. ix. 18. 9
This simple sort of life that *shepheards* lead, . . . VI. ix. 33. 8
oft complaine Of Pastorell to all the *shepheards* . . . VI. ix. 38. 8
The dwelling of these *shepheards* did invade, . . . VI. x. 39. 7
Where wont the *shepheards* oft their pypes resound, . . . VI. xi. 26. 8
Which with those gentle *shepherds* here I wont to lead.' . . . VI. xi. 32. 9
Some flockes of sheepe and *shepheards* to espy; . . . VI. xi. 36. 7
When him the silly *Shepheards* came to see, . . . *H.H.L.* 230

Shepherds'. Pallaces . . . were *shepheards* cottages somewhile. *Ro.* xviii. 4
Pan, thou *shepheards* God that once didst love, . . . *S.C.* Ja. 17
thereto aye wonned to repayre The *shepheards* daughters . . . *S.C.* F. 120
When *shepheardes* groomes han leave to playe, . . . *S.C.* Mar. 62
Shepheards delights he dooth them all forsweare; . . . *S.C.* Ap. 13
Which Pan, the *shepheards* God, of her begot: . . . *S.C.* Ap. 51
'Ye *shepheards* daughters, that dwell on the greene, . . . *S.C.* Ap. 127
The *shepheards* God so wel them guided, . . . *S.C.* May 113
Tho gan *shepheards* swaines to looke aloft, . . . *S.C.* May 124
This was the first sourse of *shepheards* sorowe, . . . *S.C.* May 130
To wyten *shepheards* welth: . . . *S.C.* Jul. 210
thou wont the *shepheards* laddes to leade . . . *S.C.* O. 4
endles sovenaunce Emong the *shepeheards* swaines . . . *S.C.* N. 6
Sing now, ye *shepheards* daughters, . . . *S.C.* N. 77
shepherds wonted solace is extinct. . . . *S.C.* N. 106
was the saynt of *shepheards* light, . . . *S.C.* N. 176
whilome was poore *shepheards* pryde, . . . *S.C.* N. 198
The *shepheards* God (perdie God was he none) . . . *S.C.* D. 50
'Now leave, ye *shepheards* boyes, your merry glee; . . . *S.C.* D. 139
the *Shepheards* swaines Were wont . . . to sing, . . . *T.M.* 279
The *Shepheards* daughters dauncing in a rownd! . . . *D.* 310
faire Damsels! *Shepheards* dere delights, . . . *D.* 526
Young Astrophel, the pride of *shepheards* praise, . . . *As.* 7
how great a losse Had all the *shepheards* nation . . . *Col.* 17
Amyntas, floure of *shepheards* pride forlorne: . . . *Col.* 439
Of all the *shepheards* daughters which there bee, . . . *Col.* 556
Amongst the *shepheards* daughters dancing rownd, . . . *Col.* 641
to warne yong *shepheards* wandring wit, . . . *Col.* 684
the other crew Of *shepheards* daughters . . . *Col.* 932
Shouting, and singing all a *shepheards* ryme; . . . I. vi. 13. 7
Both clad in *shepheards* weeds agreeably, . . . VI. xi. 36. 2

Shepherds'—*Continued.*
both with *shepheards* hookes: . . . VI. xi. 36. 3

Shepherd-swain. how fast renneth the *shepheard swayne* . . . *S.C.* Au. 32
Then up, I say, thou jolly *shepeheard swayne,* . . . *S.C.* N. 47
Thus is this Ape become a *shepheard swaine,* . . . *Hub.* 303
Alcyon he, the jollie *Shepheard swaine* . . . *D.* 54

Shepherd-swains. We but his *shepheard swaines* ordain'd to bee. *Hub.* 444
The *shepheard swaines* that did about him play: . . . *Col.* 6
them fond Emongst the *shepeheard swaynes,* . . . II. viii. 40. 9
the gentle *Shepheard swaynes,* . . . III. vi. 15. 6
The lustie *shepheard swaynes* sate in a rout, . . . VI. ix. 8. 5
when as the *shepheard swaynes* together Were met . . . VI. ix. 41. 1

Shidder. *See* **Sheder.**

Shield. God *shield,* man, that I should clime, . . . *S.C.* Jul. 9
God *shield,* man, he should so ill have thrive, . . . *S.C.* S. 226
thwarting his huge *shield,* Them battell bad, . . . *Gn.* 514
that which Vulcane made to *sheild* Achilles life . . . *Mui.* 63
to her selfe she gives her Aegide *shield,* . . . *Mui.* 321
Ycladd in mightie armes and silver *shielde,* . . . I. i. 1. 2
Upon his *shield* the like was also scor'd, . . . I. i. 2. 5
she . . . Lept fierce upon his *shield,* . . . I. i. 18. 6
In mighty armes he was yclad anon, And silver *shield;* . . . I. ii. 11. 4
In whose great *shield* was writ with letters gay . . . I. ii. 12. 7
glauncing downe his *shield* from blame him fairly blest. . . . I. ii. 18. 9
The Sarazins *shield,* signe of the conqueroure. . . . I. ii. 20. 7
she him spyde, By his like seeming *shield* . . . I. iii. 26. 6
on his *shield* Sansloy in bloody lines was dyde. . . . I. iii. 33. 9
Through vainly crossed *shield* he quite did perce; . . . I. iii. 35. 3
Through *shield* and body eke he should him beare: . . . I. iii. 35. 5
ramping on his *shield,* did weene the same Have reft away . . . I. iii. 41. 5
from his griping pawes He hath his *shield* redeemd, . . . I. iii. 41. 9
heathnish *shield,* wherein with letters red, Was writt . . . I. iv. 38. 5
the shamed *shield* of slaine Sansfoy . . . I. iv. 39. 1
if that either to that *shield* had right, . . . I. iv. 40. 8
Whose *shield* he beares renverst, . . . I. iv. 41. 9
who unworthie ware His worthie *shield,* . . . I. iv. 47. 5
'he beares a charmed *shield,* . . . I. iv. 50. 5
his *shield* is hangd with bloody hew; . . . I. v. 5. 8
his brothers *shield,* which hong thereby: . . . I. v. 10. 3
here thy *shield* is hangd for victors hyre? . . . I. v. 10. 7
I his *shield* have quit from dying foe.' . . . I. v. 11. 4
'Thine the *shield,* and I, and all!' . . . I. v. 11. 9
Goe say, his foe thy *shield* with his doth beare.' . . . I. v. 13. 4
The conquest yours; I yours; the *shield,* and glory yours.' . . . I. v. 14. 9
the *shield,* the cause of enmitie. . . . I. v. 15. 9
catching up in hast his three-square *shield* . . . I. vi. 41. 8
ere he could . . . gett his *shield,* . . . I. vii. 8. 2
His silver *shield,* now idle, maisterlesse; . . . I. vii. 19. 6
His warlike *shield* all closely cover'd was, . . . I. vii. 33. 1
Before that *shield* did fade, and suddeine fall: . . . I. vii. 35. 4
Both *shield* and sword, and armour all he wrought . . . I. vii. 36. 6
his mightie *shild* Upon his manly arme . . . I. viii. 6. 6
The stroke upon his *shield* so heavie lites, . . . I. viii. 18. 7
his *shield,* that covered was, Did loose his vele . . . I. viii. 19. 1
amazd At flashing beames of that sunshiny *shield,* . . . I. viii. 20. 2
he has redd his end In that bright *shield,* . . . I. viii. 21. 5
high emongst all knights hast hong thy *shield,* . . . I. x. 60. 6
his angry needle shott Quite through his *shield,* . . . I. xi. 38. 6
did fiercely fall Upon his sunne-bright *shield,* . . . I. xi. 40. 9
The other foote, fast fixed on his *shield,* . . . I. xi. 43. 1
The paw . . . hong still on the *shield,* . . . I. xi. 43. 9
in his silver *shield* He bore a bloodie Crosse . . . II. i. 18. 8
on your *shield* is set for ornament!' . . . II. i. 27. 7
That decks and armes your *shield* with faire defence: . . . II. i. 28. 8
that deare Crosse uppon your *shield* devizd, . . . II. i. 31. 8
His sunbroad *shield* about his wrest he bond, . . . II. ii. 21. 5
on his *shield* like yron sledges bet: . . . II. ii. 22. 4
many-folded *shield* he bound about his wrest. . . . II. iii. 1. 9
Withouten sword or *shield,* an hoste to quayle? . . . II. iii. 16. 7
Behind his backe he bore a brasen *shield,* . . . II. iv. 38. 1
To be the *shield* of some redoubted knight; . . . II. iv. 38. 6
advaunst his *shield* atweene, . . . II. iv. 46. 6
arriving forcibly On his broad *shield,* bitt not, . . . II. v. 4. 4
the upper marge Of his sevenfolded *shield* . . . II. v. 6. 3
That on his *shield* depainted he did see: . . . II. v. 11. 8
Cymochles sword on Guyons *shield* yglaunst, . . . II. vi. 31. 3
Ne all good knights that shake well speare and *shield.* . . . II. viii. 14. 6
And of that *shield,* more worthy of good knight; . . . II. viii. 15. 8
rude hand upon his *shield* he laid, . . . II. viii. 17. 1
bore after him an heben launce And coverd *shield.* . . . II. viii. 17. 7
Guyons *shield* about his wrest he bond: . . . II. viii. 22. 7
seven fold *shield,* which he from Guyon brought, . . . II. viii. 32. 5
in his *shield* . . . Their strokes did raine: . . . II. viii. 35. 5
whiles his *shield* was wyde, . . . II. viii. 36. 4
The one upon his covered *shield* did fall, . . . II. viii. 38. 3
Ne *shield* defend the thunder of his throwes: . . . II. viii. 41. 3
(Who Guyons *shield* cast ever him before, . . . II. viii. 43. 2
his *shield* he lakt And sword saw not, . . . II. viii. 53. 3
robbed mee Of my good sword and *shield?*' . . . II. viii. 54. 2
recov'ring his stolne sword, And Guyon his lost *shield,* . . . II. ix. 2. 3
on your *shield,* so goodly scord, . . . II. ix. 2. 7
Whose faire retraitt I in my *shield* doe beare; . . . II. ix. 4. 2
The greene *shield* dyde in dolorous vermell? . . . II. x. 24. 7
Upon his *shield* their heaped hayle he bore, . . . II. xi. 19. 1
it warded well Upon his *shield,* . . . II. xi. 24. 7
his bright *shield* that nought him now avayld, . . . II. xi. 41. 8
his brave *shield,* full of old moniments, . . . II. xii. 80. 3
on his arme addresse his goodly *shield* . . . III. i. 4. 8
seemd to couch under his *shield* threesquare, . . . III. i. 4. 4
seemd both *shield* and plate it would have riv'd; . . . III. i. 6. 3

Shield—*Continued.*
To tossen speare and *shield,* . . . III. ii. 6. 4
What shape, what *shield,* what armes, . . . III. ii. 16. 6
on his *shield* enveloped sevenfold . . . III. ii. 25. 7
Avenge his fathers losse with speare and *shield,* . . . III. iii. 31. 8
The dreadful speare and *shield* to exercize: . . . III. iii. 53. 4
Both speare she tooke and *shield* . . . III. iii. 60. 8
Both speare and *shield* of great powre, . . . III. iii. 60. 9
Where be the batteiles, where the *shield* and speare, . . . III. iv. 1. 4
her goodly *shield* addressing fayre, . . . III. iv. 14. 1
she againe him in the *shield* did smite . . . III. iv. 16. 1
His uncouth *shield* and straunge armes her dismayd, . . . III. iv. 51. 1
His speare amids her sun-brode *shield* arriv'd: . . . III. vii. 40. 4
her Gorgonian *shield* gins to untye . . . III. ix. 22. 8
I expected one with *shield* and spere . . . III. x. 24. 8
A little off his *shield* was rudely throwne, . . . III. xi. 7. 6
Her ample *shield* she threw before her face, . . . III. xi. 25. 2
Gainst whom he alwayes bent a brasen *shield,* . . . III. xii. 12. 8
the *shield* of love . . . he brought away, . . . IV. i. 2. 6
with *shield* and armour fit; . . . IV. i. 14. 7
in his *shield* he beares . . . the heads . . . IV. i. 48. 8
Through *shield* and mayle and haberjeon did wend, . . . IV. ii. 15. 4
Triamond to handle speare and *shield,* . . . IV. ii. 42. 8
throughly skild in use of *shield* and speare; . . . IV. iii. 7. 2
forced him his *shield* to disadvaunce . . . IV. iii. 8. 4
aventred With doubled force close underneath his *shield,* . . . IV. iii. 9. 2
reaching forth his sweard Close underneath his *shield,* . . . IV. iii. 33. 7
Upon the brim of his brode-plated *shield,* . . . IV. iii. 34. 6
addrest his maiden-headed *shield,* . . . IV. iv. 17. 4
The *shield* and armes, well knowne to be the same . . . IV. iv. 27. 5
For to have rent his *shield* and armes away, . . . IV. iv. 31. 2
His word, which on his ragged *shield* was writ, . . . IV. iv. 39. 8
vow'd with speare and *shield* it to maintaine; . . . IV. v. 24. 8
Unto her sword and *shield* her soone betooke; . . . IV. vi. 14. 8
the deadly brunt did beare Upon his *shield,* . . . IV. viii. 42. 3
hard unto his crowne The *shield* it drove, . . . IV. viii. 42. 7
this *shield* of love I late have wonne, . . . IV. x. 3. 2
both *shield* and she whom I behold . . . IV. x. 4. 8
this *shield,* of many sought in vaine, . . . IV. x. 8. 3
The *shield* of Love, whose guerdon me hath graced, . . . IV. x. 8. 4
Whose ever be the shield, faire Amoret be his. . . . IV. x. 8. 9
with my speare upon the *shield* did rap, . . . IV. x. 9. 4
taking downe the *shield* with me did it retaine . . . IV. x. 10. 9
Bearing the *shield* which I had conquerd late, . . . IV. x. 14. 2
advauncing that enchaunted *shield,* . . . IV. x. 19. 6
my *shield* I forth to her did show, . . . IV. x. 55. 1
evermore my *shield* did me defend . . . IV. x. 58. 6
bore upon his *shield* . . . A broken sword . . . V. i. 19. 6
by the other markes which of his *shield* he tooke . . . V. i. 20. 9
to approve his right with speare and *shield,* . . . V. i. 24. 4
To change his *shield* with him, to be the better hid . . . V. iii. 10. 9
To Braggadochio did his *shield* restore, . . . V. iii. 13. 2
Came Braggadochio, and did shew his *shield,* . . . V. iii. 14. 8
'That *shield,* which thou doest beare, . . . V. iii. 21. 1
this the arme the which that *shield* did beare, . . . V. iii. 22. 2
Then from him reft his *shield,* . . . V. iii. 37. 6
on her shoulder hung her *shield,* . . . V. v. 3. 6
with her *shield* so well her selfe she warded . . . V. v. 8. 6
Halfe of her *shield* he shared quite away, . . . V. v. 9. 2
Yet with her *shield* she warded it againe, . . . V. v. 10. 8
Having her thus disarmed of her *shield,* . . . V. v. 11. 1
with his single *shield* . . . Beare off the burden . . . V. v. 16. 3
Till he to her delivered had his *shield,* . . . V. v. 16. 8
quickly caught her sword, and *shield* about her bound . . . V. vi. 28. 9
she her *shield* . . . Could scarse uphold: . . . V. vii. 33. 4
from his victorious *shield* he drew The vaile, . . . V. viii. 37. 6
Soone as the infants sunlike *shield* they saw, . . . V. viii. 41. 2
Onely his *shield* and armour, which there lay, . . . V. viii. 44. 1
purchase it to us with speare and *shield:* . . . V. x. 24. 4
no entrance find Into the Princes *shield* . . . V. x. 32. 7
Into his *shield* it readie passage found, . . . V. x. 33. 2
Past through his *shield* and pierst through . . . V. x. 35. 7
had he chaunced not his *shield* to reare, . . . V. xi. 10. 4
th' Adamantine *shield* which he did beare . . . V. xi. 10. 7
his bright *shield* display . . . V. xi. 21. 5
The armed Prince with *shield* so blazing bright . . . V. xi. 26. 2
on his *shield* tooke hold with all her might, . . . V. xi. 27. 3
strove out of her greedy gripe To loose his *shield,* . . . V. xi. 27. 7
thrown his *shield* atween, . . . V. xi. 30. 9
they his *shield* in peeces battred have, . . . V. xi. 46. 2
'forborne Your owne good *shield* in daungerous dismay? . . . V. xi. 52. 2
when he gave me armes . . . Gave me a *shield,* . . . V. xi. 53. 4
for that many did that *shield* envie, . . . V. xi. 54. 1
Your honours stile, that is, your warlike *shield* . . . V. xi. 55. 6
My former *shield* I may resume againe: . . . V. xi. 56. 2
Artegall . . . blames for changing *shield:* . . . V. xii. Arg.
cast his *shield* about to be in readie plight . . . V. xii. 16. 9
stouped oft his head from shame to *shield:* . . . V. xii. 19. 2
twixt him and the blow his *shield* did cast, . . . V. xii. 21. 6
His axe he could not from his *shield* undoe; . . . V. xii. 22. 5
loosing soone his *shield* did it forgoe; . . . V. xii. 22. 7
So off he did his *shield,* . . . VI. ii. 48. 1
Tho on his *shield* he griple hold did lay, . . . VI. iv. 6. 7
having now no . . . force his *shield* to straine, . . . VI. iv. 7. 7
Both speare and *shield,* . . . He quite forsooke, . . . VI. iv. 7. 8
Then taking up that Recreants *shield* and speare, . . . VI. iv. 13. 1
His *shield,* his helmet, and his curats bare; . . . VI. v. 8. 7
on his *shield* did rattle like to haile . . . VI. vi. 26. 3
did him smite Full in the *shield* . . . VI. vii. 8. 2
his *shield* about him threw, . . . VI. viii. 7. 2

Shield—*Continued.*
Did cast his *shield* atweene; . . . VI. xii. 30. 2
His *shield* he on him threw, . . . VI. xii. 30. 6
Despoyld of warlike armes and knowen *shield* . . . *Am.* iii. 4
Shielded. shade, Which *shielded* them against the boyling heat, I. vii. 4. 3
in that right should by all knights be *shielded:* . . . IV. ix. 37. 8
Shields. *shields* of brasse that shone like burnisht golde, . . . *Van.* vi. 3
fier flies, . . . out of their burning *shields;* . . . I. ii. 17. 8
clash their *shields,* and shake their swerds on hy, . . . I. iv. 40. 3
Their shining *shieldes* about their wrestes they tye, . . . I. v. 6. 3
from their *shields* forth flyeth firie light, . . . I. v. 7. 8
Bespotted as with *shieldes* of red and blacke, . . . I. xi. 11. 5
His blazing eyes, like two bright shining *shieldes,* . . . I. xi. 14. 1
Gan with new rage their *shieldes* to hew . . . II. ii. 23. 7
Faire *shields,* gay steedes, bright armes be my delight; . . . II. vii. 10. 8
Sheilds, steeds, and armes, and all things for thee meet, . . . II. vii. 11. 3
Disshivered speares, and *shields* ytorn in twaine; . . . IV. i. 21. 6
shields did share, and mailes did rash, . . . IV. ii. 17. 9
gan their *shields* addresse them selves afore: . . . IV. iv. 4. 8
By scattered *shields,* was easie to be showen . . . IV. iv. 38. 5
Hewing and slashing *shields* and helmets bright, . . . IV. iv. 41. 6
doe both together smite Amid their *shields,* . . . V. x. 32. 3
Shift. he will care for all the rest to *shift,* . . . *Hub.* 532
then assayle him fresh, ere he could *shift* for more . . . II. xi. 27. 9
none from it can *shift:* . . . II. xii. 4. 7
with easy *shifte* . . . she lightly up did lifte, . . . III. i. 61. 1
to *shifte* their curious request, . . . III. ix. 26. 1
He could his weapon *shift* from side to syde, . . . V. xi. 6. 5
One time when he his weapon faynd to *shift,* . . . V. xi. 7. 6
To give him ground, and *shift* to every side, . . . VI. vii. 46. 6
Shifted. So well they *shifted,* . . . *Hub.* 659
his place he *shifted* hath in sight, . . . V. Pr. 8. 5
Shifting. *See* **Nimble-shifting.**
Unto the *shifting* of the shepheards foote, . . . *S.C.* D. 116
to maligne, t' envie, t' use *shifting* slight, . . . VI. vii. 1. 5
Shifts. filthie brocage, and unseemly *shifts,* . . . *Hub.* 851
by his *shifts* his Master furnish can . . . *Hub.* 918
handle his deceitfull wit In subtil *shifts,* . . . *Col.* 694
with slie *shiftes* and wiles did underminde . . . V. vi. 32. 7
Shine. *See* **Outshine, Sunshine.**
His head did *shine* with crounes set therupon . . . *Rev.* iii. 3
the seeling bright (eke[1]) Did *shine* all scaly . . . *Bel.* ii. 10
On everie side did *shine* like scalie golde; . . . *Gn.* 261
ne heaven doth *shine* so bright, . . . *Mui.* 93
Like Phoebus lampe throughout the world doth *shine,* . . . I. Pr. 4. 4
did then *shine* as the Morning starre . . . I. ii. 36. 4
not made to burne, but fayrely for to *shyne* . . . I. iv. 9. 9
Then gan her beautie *shyne* as brightest skye, . . . I. vi. 4. 8
all embrewd in blood his eyes did *shine* as glas . . . I. vii. 17. 9
beames . . . did *shine* like hevens light . . . I. x. 12. 9
opened his dull eyes, that light mote in them *shine* . . . I. x. 18. 9
hevenly throne, where thousand Angels *shine?* . . . I. x. 51. 6
brightnes, which did . . . too exceeding *shyne* . . . I. x. 67. 8
like to orient perles did purely *shyne* . . . III. vii. 9. 3
the white fomy creame Did *shine* with silver, . . . III. xi. 41. 5
Did ever see upon this world to *shine,* . . . IV. iii. 3. 6
These warlike Champions, all in armour *shine,* . . . IV. iii. 3. 8
Whose beauties beame eftsoones did *shine* so bright, . . . IV. v. 10. 8
Doest fayrest *shine,* and most adorne thy place; . . . IV. x. 44. 3
see Stamford . . . Then *shine* in learning, . . . IV. xi. 35. 5
sunne to *shine* more bright Then it was wont, . . . V. x. 20. 8
goodly light then Phoebus lampe doth *shine* more cleare? . . . V. xi. 62. 9
Not to the Sun; for they doo *shine* by night; . . . *Am.* ix. 5
the lodestar of my lyfe, Will *shine* again, . . . *Am.* xxxiv. 11
The Suns bright beames when he on us doth *shyne,* . . . *H.H.B.* 121
But that immortall light, which there doth *shine,* . . . *H.H.B.* 169
Shined. *See* **Shone.**
my fair Starre (that *shinde* on me so bright) . . . *D.* 480
Her angels face, . . . *shyned* bright, . . . I. iii. 4. 7
So proud she *shyned* in her princely state, . . . I. iv. 10. 1
His glitterand armour *shined* far away, . . . I. vii. 29. 4
a bauldrick . . . That *shind,* like twinkling stars, . . . I. vii. 29. 9
as the Sunny beames . . . so *shined* bright, . . . II. v. 2. 5
Thrise *shined* faire, and thrise seemd dim and wan, . . . III. iii. 16. 3
Informed in the mud on which the Sunne hath *shynd* . . . III. vi. 8. 9
yet this much fairer *shined,* . . . IV. x. 40. 6
bedeckt Uppon the bosse with stones that *shined* wide, . . . V. v. 3. 7
Dark is the world, where your light *shined* never; . . . *Am.* viii. 13
Shinedst. on me thou *shinedst* late in sadnesse, . . . *Am.* xxxix. 6
Shines. to the place, Where my Goddesse *shines;* . . . *S.C.* Ap. 101
No sonne now *shines;* . . . *S.C.* D. 138
Sunne that *shines* so wide and faire, . . . II. x. 2. 1
his Adamants with which he *shines* And glisters wide, . . . IV. xi. 31. 7
whose is that faire face that *shines* so bright? . . . *Epith.* 373
shadow yet *shynes* in your beauteous face . . . *H.B.* 168
Shineth. when Phoebe *shineth* bright: . . . *S.C.* Jun. 31
beautie *shyneth* as the morning cleare, . . . *Col.* 506
Whose glory *shineth* as the morning starre, . . . II. ix. 4. 6
Shining. *See* **Bright-shining, Fair-shining.**
Threw forth . . . a thousand *shining* leames, . . . *Bel.*[1] ix. 10
bottome yellow like the *shining* land, . . . *Bel.*[1] x. 3
Then cried a *shining* Angell . . . *Rev.* iii. 8
shining Christall, which from top to base . . . *Bel.* ii. 6
On everie side a thousand *shining* beames: . . . *Bel.*[2] xi. 10
when the *shining* sunne laugheth once, . . . *S.C.* F. 37
like faire Phebes garlond *shining* new, . . . *Col.* 342
Dimmed her former beauties *shining* ray, . . . I. ii. 38. 7
my light, and *shining* lampe of blis!' . . . I. iii. 27. 9
Their *shining* shieldes about their wrestes they tye, . . . I. v. 6. 3
shyning lampes in Joves high house were light; . . . I. v. 19. 2

Shining—*Continued.*
Adornd with gold and jewels *shining* cleare, I. v. 21. 2
catching up in hast his . . . *shining* helmet, I. vi. 41. 9
shut up heavens windowes *shyning* wyde; I. vii. 23. 5
all armd in *shyning* bras. II. ii. 17. 9
shyning blade unsheathd, II. ii. 21. 6
on whom the *shining* Sunne Did shew his face, II. iv. 21. 7
His *shining* Helmet he gan soone unlace, II. viii. 52. 8
All pav'd beneath with Jaspar *shining* bright, II. xii. 62. 8
Such was the beautie and the *shining* ray, III. i. 43. 8
Defaste the beautie of the *shyning* skye, III. ii. 28. 2
silver sockets, *shyning* like the skyes, III. viii. 7. 2
doth blend The *shyning* glory of your soveraine light; III. ix. 1. 8
Like as the *shining* skie in summers night, IV. i. 13. 6
Nor *shining* gold, nor mouldring clay it was; IV. x. 39. 5
her *shyning* face Hath . . . itselfe bewray'd: IV. x. 52. 6
Shyning with beauties light IV. x. 52. 9
all dispred With *shining* gold, V. vii. 5. 5
the bright mettall *shyning* like Sunne rayes, VI. ii. 39. 4
her face Like the faire yvory *shining* VI. viii. 37. 3
With starrie beames about her *shining* bright, VI. xi. 13. 5
Her goodly eyes lyke Saphyres *shining* bright, *Epith.* 171
Light . . . which, *shyning* in the face, *H.B.* 59
And with ten thousand gemmes of *shyning* gold,) *H.H.L.* 60
And, last, that mightie *shining* christall wall, *H.H.B.* 41

Shiny. beautefie the *shinie* firmament, *Hub.* 1269
Lastly his *shinie* wings as silver bright, *Mui.* 89
to the *shiny* Mulla he did beare, *Col.* 93
Aldeboran . . . Above the *shinie* Cassiopeias chaire, I. iii. 16. 2
a fountaine . . . So pure and *shiny* II. xii. 60. 3
It was upon a Sommers *shinie* day, III. vi. 6. 4
To frame such subtile wire, so *shinie* cleare; IV. vi. 20. 6
Unto the *shinie* heaven in haste she hide, IV. xii. 25. 3
On that bright *shynie* round still moving Masse, *H.H.B.* 51

Shiny beam. daies faire *shinie-beame,* yclowded V. iv. 45. 1

Shiny beams. death out of theyr *shiny beames* doe dart; *Am.* xxiv. 7

Shiny-clear. *See* **Clear, Shiny.**

Ship. at sea a tall *ship* did appeare, *Pet.* ii. 1
With rich treasures this gay *ship* fraighted was: *Pet.* ii. 6
gan assaile this *ship* with dreadfull threat, *Bel.*[2] xiii. 7
ship to which none other might compare: *Bel.*[2] xiii. 8
both *ship* and mariners each one, *Bel.*[2] xiii. 12
I the *ship* saw after rais'd againe. *Bel.*[2] xiii. 14
her *ship,* tost with so manie freakes, *Ro.* xxi. 5
A goodly *ship* with banners bravely dight, *Van.* ix. 2
My *shippe* unwont in stormes to be tost. *S.C.* F. 32
Is like a *ship* in midst of tempest left *T.M.* 141
Nor ever *ship* shall saile there anie more. *Ti.* 154
Thereto our *ship* her course directly bent, *Col.* 268
There did our *ship* her fruitfull wombe unlade, *Col.* 288
His *ship* far come from watrie wildernesse; I. iii. 32. 4
As when a *ship,* . . . An hidden rocke escaped hath I. vi. 1. 1
As wetherbeaten *ship* arryv'd on happie shore. II. i. 2. 9
As a tall *ship* tossed in troublous seas, II. ii. 24. 1
Eftsoones her shallow *ship* away did slide, II. vi. 5. 1
my wandring *ship* I row, II. vi. 10. 2
Learning his *ship* from those white rocks to save, II. x. 6. 3
a goodly *Ship* did see II. xii. 19. 1
bravely furnished as *ship* might bee, II. xii. 19. 3
the frothy billowes fry Under the *ship* II. xii. 45. 2
bring my *ship,* ere it be rent, III. iv. 10. 4
a *ship,* whose Lodestar suddeinly Covered with cloudes III. iv. 53. 3
without *ship* or bote her thence to row, IV. xi. 15. 7
Like as a *ship,* whom cruell tempest drives V. ii. 50. 1
they found A *ship* all readie V. xii. 4. 2
Like as a *ship* with dreadfull storme long tost, VI. iv. 1. 1
Like as a *ship,* that through the Ocean wyde VI. xii. 1. 1
Lyke as a *ship,* that through the Ocean wyde, *Am.* xxxiv. 1
a *ship,* of succour desolate, Doth suffer wreck *Am.* lvi. 11
That *ship,* that tree, and that same beast, am I, *Am.* lvi. 13
like a steddy *ship,* doth strongly part The raging waves, *Am.* lix. 5

Shipping. Ne made for *shipping* any certeine port, II. xii. 13. 3
To weete if *shipping* readie he mote there descry. V. xii. 3. 9

Ship's. Full sad and dreadfull is that *ships* event; *T.M.* 143

Ships. from th' Argolick *ships* with furious yre *Gn.* 495
the *ships* which they did seeke to burne. *Gn.* 512
To cut the *ships* from turning home againe To Argos; *Gn.* 522
where the winged *ships* were seene *Ti.* 148
twise renforst backe to their *ships* to fly; II. x. 48. 2
shivered *ships,* which had beene wrecked late, II. xii. 7. 4
The flying *ships* with swiftnes to pursew: II. xii. 24. 4

Ships'. The great Argoan *ships* brave ornament, *Gn.* 210

Shipwreck. Did afterwards make *shipwrack* violent II. xii. 7. 8
suffred cruell *shipwracke* by the way: V. iv. 13. 8

Shire. Send forth their flames far off to every *shyre,* I. xi. 14. 4
of him selfe doth name the *shire* thereby: IV. xi. 32. 7

Shiver. My ragged rontes all *shiver* and shake, *S.C.* F. 5
shake and *shiver* Her flaming fire-brond, *Gn.* 342
makes them all to *shiver* and to shake: VII. vii. 23. 6

Shivered. *shivered* ships, which had beene wrecked late, II. xii. 7. 4
broken bowes and arrowes *shivered* short; III. xi. 46. 7
By *shivered* speares, and swords all under strowen, IV. iv. 38. 4
shivered all about, and scattered in the wynd: V. x. 32. 9
all his launce in peeces *shivered* quite, VI. vii. 8. 3

Shivering. *shivering* speare in bloody field first shooke, III. i. 7. 3
The Parthian strikes a stag with *shivering* dart, IV. i. 49. 8
they gan their *shivering* speares to shake, IV. ii. 14. 7
He all enrag'd his *shivering* speare did shake, IV. iii. 10. 8
threw A *shivering* dart with so impetuous force, V. viii. 32. 6

Shivers. glauncing . . . brast In thousand *shivers,* III. vii. 40. 9

Shoal. I sawe a *shole* of shepeheardes outgoe, *S.C.* May 20
this Molanna, were she not so *shole,* VII. vi. 40. 7

Shoals. wondrous *sholes* which may of none be red. IV. xii. 2. 5

Shock. Sustein'd the *shocke* of common enmitie; *Ro.* xxi. 4
with the terror of the *shocke,* Astonied, both stand I. ii. 16. 4
with the *shocke* of their owne heedlesse might IV. ii. 16. 5

Shod. *See* **Dry-shod.**

Shoe. blacke spot doth appeare, Shapt like a horses *shoe,* V. iii. 32. 9

Shoes. his *shooes* beaten out with traveling. *Hub.* 214
thred-bare cote, and cobled *shoes,* hee ware; I. iv. 28. 2
over *shoes* in blood he waded on the grownd. I. viii. 16. 9

Shole. *See* **Shoal.**

Shone. *See* **Shined.**
The seates and benches *shone* as yvorie, *Bel.* xii. 9
In summers day, when Phoebus fairly *shone,* *Van.* ii. 1
shields of brasse that *shone* like burnisht golde, *Van.* vi. 3
A gilden towre, which *shone* exceedinglie; *Van.* viii. 4
when the Welkin *shone* faire, *S.C.* S. 187
as a glasse upon the water *shone,* *Ti.* 220
Her yellow locks that *shone* so bright and long, *As.* 157
Soone as that uncouth light upon them *shone,* I. i. 15. 8
ere my hoped day of spousall *shone,* I. ii. 23. 6
A mayden Queene that *shone* as Titans ray, I. iv. 8. 5
As envying her selfe, that too exceeding *shone:* I. iv. 8. 9
Exceeding *shone,* like Phoebus fayrest childe, I. iv. 9. 1
stone . . . exceeding *shone,* Like Hesperus I. vii. 30. 3
so exceeding *shone* his glistring ray, I. vii. 34. 5
flashing fire about him *shone:* I. x. 53. 9
seeing one, that *shone* in armour fayre, II. iii. 11. 3
On th' others helmett, which as Titan *shone,* II. vi. 31. 6
His snowy front . . . Divinely *shone;* II. viii. 5. 7
all her steed with tinsell trappings *shone,* III. i. 15. 7
unwares It shewd it selfe and *shone* unwillingly; III. xi. 28. 7
an Image . . . which with his owne light *shone;* III. xi. 47. 5
The morow next, so soone as Titan *shone,* IV. i. 16. 5
Compar'd to her that *shone* as Phebes light IV. v. 14. 3
shone as bright as doth the heaven sheene: V. viii. 29. 5
That *shone* as heavens light, *Proth.* 52

Shook. An earthquake *shooke* the hill *Bel.*[2] ii. 13
how she in everie member *shooke,* *Mui.* 285
Shooke him so hard, that forced him to speake. I. i. 42. 6
The royall virgin *shooke* off drousy-hed; I. ii. 7. 5
shoke his scales to battaile ready drest, I. xi. 15. 7
shooke His sandy lockes, II. v. 14. 3
With that he stifly *shooke* his steelhead dart: II. vi. 40. 1
with the noise it *shooke* as it would fall. II. ix. 11. 5
shivering speare in bloody field first *shooke,* III. i. 7. 3
in his clownish hand a sharp bore speare he *shooke.* III. i. 17. 9
his threeforkt Pyke He stearnly *shooke,* III. xi. 40. 5
the darts . . . Full dreadfully he *shooke,* III. xii. 23. 6
ever when the Squire his javelin *shooke,* IV. vii. 26. 2
well perceiving how her wand she *shooke,* V. vii. 8. 4
yet to and fro long *shooke* V. viii. 9. 8
his head at him *shooke,* V. xi. 12. 8
her long taile and fethers strongly *shooke,* V. xi. 22. 7
With trembling joynts, as he for terrour *shooke;* V. xi. 28. 8
He *shooke* off luskishnesse; VI. i. 35. 7
which he so sternely *shooke,* VI. vii. 24. 8
he *shooke* His Nectar-deawed locks, VII. vi. 30. 6
shooke Nigh all to peeces, VII. vi. 47. 7

Shoot. His Vellet head began to *shoote* out, *S.C.* May 185
they that *shooten* nearest the pricke *S.C.* S. 122
gan to *shoote* agayne, *S.C.* O. 74
high *shoote* up their heads into the skyes. *Gn.* 192
learned Impes that wont to *shoote* up still, *T.M.* 75
Now ginnes to *shoote* up fast, *Ti.* 269
Lets none *shoot* up that nigh him planted bee: *Ti.* 453
through the persant aire *shoote* forth their azure streames. III. ix. 20. 9
the white fomy creame Did . . . *shoot* forth his beame. III. xi. 41. 5
So many learned impes, that *shoote* abrode, IV. xi. 26. 5
the blinded guest *Shoot* out his darts *Am.* viii. 6
Yet *shoot* ye sharpely still, and spare me not, *Am.* lvii. 9

Shooting. Drerily *shooting* his stormy darte, *S.C.* F. 45
I cast to goe a *shooting.* *S.C.* Mar. 63
shooting wide, doe misse the marked scope; *S.C.* N. 155
In *shooting* steddie, and in swimming strong: *As.* 74
shooting in the earth, castes up a mount of clay. I. viii. 9. 9
Shooting forth farre away two flaming streames, IV. viii. 39. 3
broke their bowes, and did their *shooting* marre, V. iv. 44. 4
here and there *shooting* forth silver streames, V. ix. 28. 8
Most dainty trees, that, *shooting* up anon, VII. vii. 8. 7

Shoots. thence he *shootes* his arrowes every where *Col.* 811

Shop. To call backe life to her forsaken *shop.* II. i. 43. 7

Shope. *See* **Shaped.**
this further purpose to him *shope.* V. v. 39. 9

Shops. They setten to sale their *shops* of shame, *S.C.* S. 36

Shore. *See* **Sea-shore.**
flowing all along the creekie *shoare* *Bel.*[1] vii. 7
to rule this croked *shore.* *Bel.*[1] viii. 15
on the *shore,* harde by a violent streame, *Bel.*[1] xi. 7
bathing all the creakie *shore* aflot, *Bel.*[2] ix. 7
Beside the fruitfull *shore* of muddie Nile, *Van.* iii. 1
To the black shadowes of the Stygian *shore,* *Gn.* 383
all the Rhetaean *shore* to ashes turne, *Gn.* 511
beside the *shore* Of silver streaming Thamesis *Ti.* 1
Upon that famous Rivers further *shore,* *Ti.* 589
greene alders by the Mullaes *shore;* *Col.* 59
Their scepters stretcht from East to Westerne *shore,* I. i. 5. 5
muddy *shore* of broad seven-mouthed Nile, I. v. 18. 2
The rolling billowes beate the ragged *shore,* I. xi. 21. 3

Shore—*Continued.*
safe ye seised have the *shore*, ... I. xii. 17. 7
As wetherbeaten ship arryv'd on happie *shore*. . . . . II. i. 2. 9
by the sandy *shore* Of swift Eurotas, ... II. iii. 31. 1
did swim Along the *shore* . . . A litle Gondelay, ... II. vi. 2. 6
The little barke unto the *shore* to draw, ... II. vi. 4. 3
painted bote streightway Turnd to the *shore*, ... II. vi. 4. 7
that gay payre, issewing on the *shore*, ... II. vi. 11. 6
issewd forth on *shore;* . . . . . II. vi. 24. 2
Upon that *shore* he spyed Atin stand, ... II. vi. 38. 7
Lo! to that *shore* one in an auncient gowne, ... II. vi. 47. 4
he in hast approched to the *shore*, ... II. vi. 48. 9
They made the further *shore* resounden wide. . . . . . II. vii. 57. 6
spred his empire to the umost *shore*, ... II. x. 10. 2
with blood they all the *shore* did staine, ... II. x. 48. 3
Bidding them nigher draw unto the *shore*, ... II. xii. 15. 2
A seemely Maiden sitting by the *shore*, ... II. xii. 27. 6
Stretch her white rod over the Belgicke *shore*, ... III. iii. 49. 7
sitting downe upon the rocky *shore*, ... III. iv. 7. 2
sadly soucing on the sandy *shore*, ... III. iv. 16. 8
So fell proud Marinell upon the pretious *shore*. . . . . . III. iv. 17. 9
upon that *shore* there heaped was Exceeding riches . . . . . III. iv. 23. 1
Along the margent of the fomy *shore*, ... III. iv. 34. 4
Stoutly foorth stepping on the further *shore*, ... III. v. 18. 6
Foolish Narcisse, that likes the watry *shore;* . . . . . III. vi. 45. 5
As shee arrived on the roring *shore*, ... III. vii. 27. 2
cast him up upon the *shore;* . . . . . III. viii. 36. 8
built Nausicle by the Pontick *shore;* . . . . . III. ix. 37. 3
From *shore* to *shore* emongst the Lybick sandes, ... III. ix. 41. 6
from *shore* behold the dreadfull sight . . . . . IV. ii. 16. 7
I by chaunce then wandring on the *shore* . . . . . V. iv. 12. 1
usd to fish for fooles on the dry *shore*, ... V. ix. 11. 8
From th' utmost brinke of the Americke *shore* . . . . . V. x. 3. 6
when as nigh unto the *shore* they drew . . . . . V. xii. 5. 2
darts from *shore* and stones they at him threw; . . . . . V. xii. 5. 5
Did win the *shore;* . . . . . V. xii. 5. 8
Meant them to have encountred ere they left the *shore:* . . . V. xii. 6. 9
in this *shore* To rest my barcke, ... VI. ix. 31. 3
Like as the wounded Whale to *shore* flies . . . . . VI. x. 31. 9
On the Thessalian *shore* from him did flie: . . . . . *Am.* xxviii. 10
the happy *shore*, In which I hope . . . to arryve: . . . . . *Am.* lxiii. 5
the *shoare* of silver streaming Themmes; . . . . . *Proth.* 11
by pleasant Tempes *shore* . . . through Thessaly they streeme, *Proth.* 79
Shores. Out of these crooked *shores* . . . . . *Bel.*[2] x. 14
wide Sigaean *shores* were spred with corses, ... *Gn.* 501
Some scattred on the Hercaean *shores* unknowne; . . . . . *Gn.* 588
by the wayling *shores* to waste my dayes, ... *Gn.* 621
both the *shores* resounded, ... *Ti.* 597
From wandring Stygian *shores*, where it doth endlesse move.' I. iv. 48. 9
From Stygian *shores* where late it wandered: . . . . . III. vii. 14. 8
all the *shores*, which to the sea accoste, ... V. xi. 42. 6
Shorn. So soone as Fates their vitall thred have *shorne*, . . . *Ti.* 181
To wash faire Cynthiaes sheep, when they be *shorne*, ... *Col.* 258
Short. at the last, and in *short* (*shorte*[1]) time, ... *Pet.* i. 10
in so *short* as thought, ... *Bel.*[2] viii. 13
Better a *short* tale than a bad long shriving: . . . . . *Hub.* 543
O *short* pleasure, bought with lasting paine! . . . . . *Ti.* 526
Is not *short* payne well borne, that bringes long ease, . . . I. ix. 40. 6
in *short* space they did to health restore The man . . . . . I. x. 27. 8
That *short* revenge the man may overtake, ... II. i. 18. 3
in *short* space he has them qualifyde, ... II. vi. 51. 8
Nether unseemely *short*, nor yet exceeding long. . . . . . II. ix. 24. 9
the same enjoyed but *short* happy howre: . . . . . II. x. 57. 9
some like ugly Urchins thick and *short:* . . . . . II. xi. 13. 4
but if she did lend her *short* reliefe . . . . . III. i. 53. 5
in *short* space their foes they have quite terrifyde. . . . . . III. i. 66. 9
Short end of sorrowes they therby did finde; . . . . . III. ii. 43. 8
my *short* blis maligne, ... III. iv. 39. 2
in *short* space She was well pleasd, ... III. vi. 25. 6
in *short* space She grew familiare . . . . . III. vii. 15. 4
To tucke about her *short* when she did ryde, ... III. ix. 21. 4
broken bowes and arrowes shivered *short;* . . . . . III. xi. 46. 7
th' one long, the other *short*, ... IV. i. 28. 7
She in *short* space did often bring to nought, ... IV. i. 29. 6
so thin as spiders frame, And eke so *short*, ... IV. ii. 50. 9
in *short* time his face they overgrew, ... IV. vii. 40. 7
in *short* space his hurts he had redrest, ... IV. xi. 7. 3
offended That his departure thence should be so *short*, . . . IV. xii. 18. 4
in *short* space his wonted chearefull hew Gan fade, ... IV. xii. 20. 1
Which was *short* tucked for light motion . . . . . V. v. 2. 6
somewhat *short* did fall, ... V. xi. 8. 8
in *short* space, whiles there with her he stayd, ... V. xii. 25. 8
her cursed tongue, full sharpe and *short*, ... V. xii. 36. 3
They fall too *short* of our fraile reckonings, ... VI. iii. 5. 4
in *short* space their malady was ceast, ... VI. vi. 15. 4
to her confessed *short* That 'twas Molanna . . . . . VII. vi. 51. 7
Some in *short* space, and some in longer yeares, ... VII. vii. 55. 3
Short Time shall soon cut down . . . . . VII. viii. 1. 9
In one *short* houre I find by her undonne. . . . . . *Am.* xxiii. 8
short her wayes . . . or else *short* my dayes. . . . . . *Am.* lx. 13, 14
All sorrowes *short* that gaine eternall blisse. . . . . . *Am.* lxiii. 14
for *short* time an endlesse moniment. . . . . . *Epith.* 433
Shorten. Ne may a man prolong, nor *shorten*, it; . . . . . I. ix. 41. 3
Shortest. is of them the *shortest*, as I see, ... IV. ii. 52. 5
shortest night, when longest fitter weare: . . . . . *Epith.* 272
Shortly. *shortly* turne unto my happie rest, ... *Pet.*[2] vii. 6
Which eare the frutefull graine doth *shortly* bring; . . . . . *Ro.* xxx. 4
Shortly within her inmost pith there bred . . . . . *Van.* vii. 6
shortly balde and bared she became. . . . . . *Van.* vii. 12
shortly gan all other beasts to scorne. . . . . . *Van.* viii. 8

Shortly—*Continued.*
His worke he *shortly* to good purpose brought, ... *Gn.* 655
as ye shall *shortly* heare.' . . . . . *Hub.* 549
shortly brought to hopelesse wretchednesse. . . . . . *Hub.* 934
He *shortly* met the Tygre, and the Bore, ... *Hub.* 1087
King indeed himselfe he *shortly* thought, ... *Hub.* 1105
shortly the foundation decaid, ... *Ti.* 500
the rest downe *shortlie* fell, ... *Ti.* 558
shortly from the shape of womanhed, ... *Mui.* 345
shortly was of all the Gods the first. . . . . . *Col.* 806
shortly after, everie living wight Crept forth . . . . . *Col.* 859
Shortly therein so perfect he became, ... I. x. 45. 6
shortly back returne unto this place, ... I. x. 64. 3
The which he *shortly* did, ... I. xii. 41. 9
'Nathlesse he *shortly* shall againe be tryde, ... II. i. 20. 1
'That shall I *shortly* purchase . . . . . II. iii. 18. 2
me poursewd apace, And *shortly* overtooke: . . . . . II. iv. 32. 6
shortly gaynd that losse exceeded farre. . . . . . II. v. 15. 5
awaiting *shortly* to obtayn Thy carcas . . . . . II. vi. 28. 8
Thereof devising *shortly* to be wroke, ... II. vi. 30. 8
shortly brought Unto another rowme, ... II. vii. 35. 1
shortly he forgot the jeopardy, ... II. x. 17. 3
fierce Cundah gan *shortly* to envy His brother Morgan, . . . II. x. 33. 2
shortly brought to civile governaunce, ... II. x. 38. 8
shortly it to him restord agayne, ... II. x. 44. 7
shortly he renounst the vassallage Of Rome . . . . . II. x. 52. 5
This good king *shortly* without issew dide, ... II. x. 54. 1
shortly was by Coyll in batteill slaine: . . . . . II. x. 58. 5
Of these a mighty people *shortly* grew, ... II. x. 72. 1
th' utmost sandy breach they *shortly* fetch, ... II. xii. 21. 3
shortly gan descry The land . . . . . II. xii. 34. 3
they *shortly* doe arryve . . . . . II. xii. 42. 1
shortly grew into so great quantitie, ... II. xii. 62. 4
shortly brent into extreme desyre, ... III. i. 47. 8
Supper was *shortly* dight, ... III. i. 51. 1
Shortly they reard out of her frosen swownd; . . . . . III. i. 64. 3
Her *shortly* answered: 'Faire martiall Mayd, ... III. ii. 9. 4
She *shortly* like a pyned ghost became . . . . . III. ii. 52. 5
full *shortly* I her dead shall see.' . . . . . III. iii. 16. 9
make him shake, and *shortly* learn to fall. . . . . . III. iii. 49. 9
shortly make you a mayd Martiall. . . . . . III. iii. 53. 9
She *shortly* thus: 'Fly they, that need to fly; . . . . . III. iv. 15. 2
Shortly upon that shore there heaped was . . . . . III. iv. 23. 1
shortly he a great Lord did appeare, ... III. iv. 23. 8
shortly he from daunger was releast, ... III. v. 14. 4
Shortly she came whereas that wofull Squire, ... III. v. 29. 1
They wondred much; and *shortly* understood . . . . . III. v. 38. 3
shortly she his dolour hath redrest, ... III. v. 41. 7
in her pregnant flesh they *shortly* fructifide. . . . . . III. vi. 7. 9
Shortly unto the wastefull woods she came, ... III. vi. 17. 1
shortly asked her, what cause her brought . . . . . III. vi. 20. 2
shortly grew into outrageous fire; . . . . . III. vii. 16. 2
shortly he her overhent. . . . . . III. vii. 23. 9
Peece, . . . Will *shortly* yield it selfe, ... III. x. 10. 6
time and place, which *shortly* shee Devized hath, ... III. x. 11. 6
shortly doen be dedd.' . . . . . III. x. 32. 9
shortly she Malbecco has forgott, ... III. x. 37. 1
Scudamour was *shortly* well aware Of his approch, ... IV. i. 41. 4
shortly friends them make: . . . . . IV. ii. 1. 9
seemd their ends out *shortly* came. . . . . . IV. ii. 50. 9
cared not to spare that should be *shortly* spent. . . . . . IV. iii. 6. 9
shortly was likewise seene lying on the plaine. . . . . . IV. iv. 44. 9
thought in mind it *shortly* to amend: . . . . . IV. iv. 45. 7
seem'd to dust he *shortly* would it drive: . . . . . IV. v. 37. 6
Her dearest love full loth so *shortly* to forsake. . . . . . IV. vi. 42. 9
having *shortly* tride The traines of wit, ... IV. viii. 31. 7
He would her *shortly* leave, ... IV. viii. 53. 9
shortly them compelled to retrate, ... IV. ix. 34. 8
to the place of perill *shortly* came: . . . . . IV. x. 5. 2
by good fortune *shortly* him unseated. . . . . . IV. x. 10. 2
she her love to him would *shortly* gaine. . . . . . IV. xii. 27. 6
the wicked seede of vice . . . *shortly* grew full great, ... V. i. 1. 4
I *shortly* will to you rehearse the same, ... V. iv. 28. 8
the false mayden *shortly* turn'd againe . . . . . V. v. 51. 8
shortly did all other beasts subdew. . . . . . V. vii. 16. 7
shortly must repent that now so vainely bravest.' . . . . . V. vii. 32. 9
shortly forst him to forsake The hight, ... V. ix. 16. 6
through the wound his spirit *shortly* did depart.' . . . . . VI. ii. 12. 9
The meede whereof shall *shortly* be thy shame, ... VI. vi. 25. 6
shortly brought Unto the barre . . . . . VI. vii. 36. 1
an altar *shortly* they erected To slay her on. . . . . . VI. viii. 44. 3
they for better hyre did *shortly* looke: . . . . . VI. xi. 40. 8
Where *shortly* they in great acquaintance grew, ... VI. xi. 41. 3
Then *shortly* should the progeny of man Be rooted out, . . . VII. vi. 31. 8
To lose their heat and *shortly* to decay; . . . . . VII. vii. 24. 4
then my body shall have *shortly* ease: . . . . . *Am.* l. 11
I wish that day would *shortly* reascend. . . . . . *Am.* lxxxvi. 8
The wanton boy was *shortly* wel recured . . . . . *Epig.* iv. 51
Shot. sharped steeples high *shot* up in ayre; . . . . . *Ro.* ii. 2
manfully thereat *shotte*. . . . . . *S.C.* Mar. 78
shott at him with might and maine, ... *S.C.* Mar. 86
So long I *shott*, that al was spent; . . . . . *S.C.* Mar. 88
It was a desperate *shot*. . . . . . *S.C.* Au. 100
shot each where Out of his golden Charet . . . . . *Gn.* 66
Shot her sharp pointed beames through purest aire. . . . . *As.* 58
Their God . . . *Shott* many a dart . . . . . I. ix. 10. 8
his angry needle *shott* Quite through his shield, ... I. xi. 38. 5
he heard her wrath, and threatned *shott*, ... II. iii. 43. 4
scornefull eyeglaunce at him *shot*. . . . . . II. iv. 37. 9
a pleasaunt grove Was *shott* up high, ... II. v. 31. 2

Shot—*Continued.*
To be avenged of that *shot* whyleare; II. xi. 25. 3
shot at him apace. II. xi. 26. 9
Apace he *shot,* and yet he fled apace, II. xi. 27. 1
the false Archer, which that arrow *shot* III. ii. 26. 7
therewith *shott* an arrow at the lad; III. v. 24. 7
with his empoysned *shot* Their wofull harts he wounded had III. vi. 13. 7
march not past the mountenaunce of a *shott,* III. xi. 20. 8
With which he *shot* at randon, III. xi. 48. 3
with a shaft was *shot* through either eye, III. xi. 48. 8
Well *shot* in yeares he seem'd, V. vi. 19. 6
thousand arrowes, which your eies have *shot:* *Am.* lvii. 8
Should (*partial list*).
That birdes . . . *Should* warre upon the kings, *Rev.* iii. 10
yet canst not when thou *should;* *S.C.* Ja. 70
She *shoulde* have neede no more spell; *S.C.* Mar. 54
What *shoulden* shepheards other things tend, *S.C.* May 63
How *shoulden* shepheardes live, if not so? *S.C.* May 148
as if it *shold* Be for some bride, *Ti.* 634
By which . . . her wandring knight *shold* pas, I. iii. 10. 2
As time . . . the truth to light *should* bring.' I. ix. 5. 9
he *should* dye who merites not to live? I. ix. 38. 4
That her to see *should* be but troublesome.' I. x. 16. 7
even dead we honour *should.* I. x. 42. 8
Trembling . . . least down he fallen *should,* And III. xi. 34. 8
next stroke him *should* have slaine, Had not III. xii. 34. 2
For feare her mistresse *shold* have knowledge V. v. 44. 4
such blot his honour blemish *should.* V. vi. 2. 9
Shoulder. So on thy corbe *shoulder* it leanes amisse. *S.C.* F. 56
The stroke . . . from her head unto her *shoulder* glaunst. I. i. 17. 9
they the earth would *shoulder* from her seat; I. xi. 21. 4
in his *shoulder* seasd, Where fast it stucke, I. xi. 38. 6
steelehead . . . through his *shoulder* perst; II. viii. 32. 8
from her *shoulder* to her heele downe raught; II. ix. 19. 2
Through Cambels *shoulder* it unwarely went, IV. iii. 8. 3
by the *shoulder* him so sore he bit, V. iii. 33. 8
he him maymed quite, and all his *shoulder* split. V. iii. 33. 9
on her *shoulder* hung her shield, V. v. 3. 6
with his spere Strooke through his *shoulder,* VI. iii. 50. 7
Jove himselfe to *shoulder* from his right. VII. vi. 7. 5
he on her *shoulder* laid His snaky-wreathed Mace, VII. vi. 18. 1
Shouldered. Eftsoones of thousand billowes *shouldred* narre, *Ro.* xvi. 3
shouldred is, or out of doore quite shit, *Col.* 709
And *shouldred* hath the Bull which fayre Europa bore: V. Pr. 5. 9
He *shouldered* him from off the higher ground, V. ii. 49. 8
Shouldering. *See* **Sea-shouldering.**
Some by close *shouldring;* some by flatteree; II. vii. 47. 3
Shoulder-plate. He smote so manly on his *shoulder plate,* II. v. 7. 6
glauncing on her *shoulder-plate* it bit Unto the bone, V. vii. 33. 2
Shoulders. beares on his *shoulders* the heavens height. *S.C.* May 143
with our *shoulders* beare of the sharpe showres; *S.C.* May 157
on his *shoulders* high his bat to beare, *Hub.* 238
About her *shoulders* careleslie downe trailing, *Ti.* 11
about his *shoulders* broad he threw An hairie hide *Mui.* 65
And on whose mightie *shoulders* most doth rest *Ded. Son.* ix. 3
On Atlas mighty *shoulders* is upstayd, *Ded. Son.* ix. 6
on her *shoulders* sad a pot of water bore. I. iii. 10. 9
Disordred hong about his *shoulders* round, I. ix. 35. 5
With snowy lockes adowne his *shoulders* shed; I. x. 48. 2
About her *shoulders* weren loosely shed, II. iii. 30. 2
Full large he was of limbe, and *shoulders* brode, II. xi. 20. 7
Upon his *shoulders* carried him II. xi. 46. 4
Now loose about her *shoulders* hong undight, III. vi. 18. 8
from his *shoulders* quite his head he reft: IV. iii. 20. 6
over all his *shoulders* did dispred, IV. vii. 40. 8
all about her necke and *shoulders* IV. x. 42. 1
Whose yvorie *shoulders* weren covered all, IV. xi. 11. 7
all her *shoulders* spred As a new spring; IV. xi. 46. 4
long curld locks that downe his *shoulders* shagged; V. ix. 10. 6
His head meant from his *shoulders* to have swept. VI. viii. 17. 3
Upon two brethrens *shoulders* she did ride, VII. vii. 34. 4
Shouldst (*partial list*).
the Priest thou *shouldest* bee, *Col.* 832
Why *shouldst* thou then despeire, I. ix. 53. 5
had not grace thee blest, thou *shouldest* not survive. II. xi. 30. 9
Shout. Some laught for sport, some did for wonder *shout,* IV. iii. 41. 8
They all gan *shout* aloud, that all the heaven rings. IV. iii. 49. 9
Gan *shout* aloud, that unto heaven it rong; V. xi. 34. 2
oft rejoyce, and oft for wonder *shout,* VI. ix. 8. 7
Hymen, io Hymen, Hymen, they do *shout;* *Epith.* 140
Shouted. They *shouted* loud, and signes of gladnesse all did shew. V. iii. 23. 9
They *shouted* all for joy of his successe, V. xii. 24. 2
Whereat they *shouted* all, and made a loud alarme. VI. viii. 45. 9
Shouting. With singing, and *shouting,* and jolly chere: *S.C.* May 21
Huge routs of people . . . *Showting* for joy; I. iv. 36. 6
Shouting, and clapping all their hands on hight, I. v. 16. 8
Shouting, and singing all a shepheards ryme; I. vi. 13. 7
Shouting as they the heavens would have brast; VII. vi. 52. 7
to the heavens theyr *shouting* shrill Doth reach, *Epith.* 141
Shouts. Confusd with womens cries and *shouts* of boyes, IV. iii. 37. 8
Show. *See* **Outshow.**
The worke did *shew* it selfe not wrought by man, *Bel.*[1] iv. 9
To *shewe* the greatnesse of the stately race, *Bel.*[1] v. 7
The skie eachwhere did *show* (*shew*[1]) full bright *Pet.* ii. 5
many a spoyle, and many a goodly *show,* *Bel.*[2] v. 6
Now on these ashie tombes *shew* boldnesse vaine, *Ro.* xiv. 13
Doth *shew* that all things turne to their first being. *Ro.* xviii. 14
To *shew* that all in th' end to nought shall fade. *Ro.* xx. 14
Ewe, Whose clouted legge her hurt doth *shewe,* *S.C.* Mar. 50
'*Shewe* thyselfe, Cynthia, with thy silver rayes, *S.C.* Ap. 82

Show—*Continued.*
how he could *shewe* many a fine knack: *S.C.* May 286
where thou thy skill didst *showe,* *S.C.* Jun. 62
Death on hym such outrage *showe?*) *S.C.* Jun. 90
Till fayrer Fortune *shewe* forth her head. *S.C.* S. 257
well dispos'd him some reliefe to *showe,* *Hub.* 261
not a lambe . . . Had they to *shew;* *Hub.* 317
wisely did maintaine With gallant *showe,* *Hub.* 691
Where nought but dread and death do seeme in *show?* *Hub.* 966
Unto the place where his prescript did *showe.* *Hub.* 1261
The picture of thy pride in pompous *shew:* *Ti.* 82
To *shew* in Heaven his brightnes orient; *Ti.* 389
mournfull tunes enough my griefe to *show?* *Mui.* 412
soone as day doth *shew* his deawie face, *D.* 484
meanes deviz'd to *shew* his sorrow best. *As.* 208
Next gan the earth to *shew* her naked head, *Col.* 857
when he list *shew* grace, *Col.* 881
And perill without *show:* I. i. 12. 5
Sir knight, *shew* what ye bee; I. i. 19. 2
Simple in *shew,* and voide of malice bad; I. i. 29. 7
I . . . shall thee well rewarde to *shew* the place, I. i. 31. 6
'Mercy, mercy, Sir, vouchsafe to *show* On silly Dame, I. ii. 21. 2
In so ritch weedes, and seeming glorious *show,* I. ii. 21. 5
hart of flint would rew The . . . sorrowes, which ye *shew.* I. ii. 26. 9
never *shew* of living wight espyde; I. iii. 10. 3
hee durst not *show* Him selfe too nigh at hand, I. iii. 26. 3
In living Princes court none ever knew . . . so sumpteous *shew;* I. iv. 7. 5
Ne other grace vouchsafed them to *showe* I. iv. 14. 3
to Duess' each one himselfe did payne All kindnesse . . . to *shew,* I. iv. 15. 4
So be, O Queene! you equall favour *showe.*' I. iv. 42. 7
hewen helmets deepe *shew* marks of eithers might. I. v. 7. 9
the armes, that earst so bright did *show,* I. v. 9. 5
shew thy famous might In medicine, I. v. 43. 7
gently grenning, *shew* a semblance glad I. vi. 11. 7
suddeine horrour to faint hartes did *show;* I. vii. 31. 8
earth, . . . did like an erthquake *show.* I. viii. 8. 9
The golden Sunne his glistring head gan *shew,* I. ix. 18. 2
narrow was the way which he did *show.* I. x. 5. 9
Ne wanted ought to *shew* her bounteous I. x. 11. 9
To *shew* it to this knight, according his desire.' I. x. 50. 9
he unto him did *shew* A little path I. x. 55. 1
pardon me . . . to *sheow* The secret treasons, I. xii. 33. 4
Which I so much doe vaunt, yet no where *show,* II. Pr. 1. 8
later times thinges more unknowne shall *show.* II. Pr. 3. 3
'That shall I *shew,*' (sayd he) II. i. 12. 8
under simple *shew,* and semblant plaine, Lurkt II. i. 21. 3
'That wrought the shamefull fact which I did *shew;* II. i. 25. 2
His stout courage to stoupe, and *shew* his inward paine. II. i. 42. 9
To *shew* how sore bloodguiltinesse he hat'th; II. ii. 4. 5
the stone her semblance seemes to *show,* II. ii. 9. 4
No solace could her Paramour intreat Her once to *show,* II. ii. 35. 6
gallant *shew* to be in greatest gree, II. iii. 5. 8
in her cheekes the vermeill red did *shew* II. iii. 22. 5
Did *shew* her selfe in great triumphant joy, II. iii. 31. 8
doubted whether he himselfe should *shew,* II. iii. 32. 3
nether doth thy face terrestriall *shew,* II. iii. 33. 3
bitt his tawny beard to *shew* his raging yre. II. iv. 15. 9
on whom the shining Sunne Did *shew* his face, II. iv. 21. 8
painted colors *shew.* II. v. 29. 9
Him to aggrate, and greatest pleasures *shew:* II. v. 33. 2
show to him that walkes in feare and sad affright. II. vii. 29. 9
wrought by art and counterfetted *shew,* II. vii. 45. 5
Such life ye read, and vertue in vaine *shew;* II. ix. 3. 2
gan Sir Guyon all the story *shew* II. ix. 9. 5
them leading forth, the same did *shew.* II. ix. 20. 9
him full of melancholy did *shew;* II. ix. 52. 5
some did like spyders *shew,* II. xi. 13. 3
doth *shew* His fearefull face II. xii. 24. 5
the faire land it selfe did playnly *sheow.* II. xii. 37. 6
First did it *shew* the bitter balefull stowre, III. i. 34. 7
glistred all with gold and glorious *shew,* III. i. 41. 3
Basciante did him selfe most courteous *shew;* III. i. 45. 5
It vertue had to *shew* in perfect sight III. ii. 19. 1
Shall of him selfe a brave ensample *shew,* III. iii. 45. 2
chearfull looks as earst did *shew.* III. iii. 50. 9
did her *shew* Pure and unspotted III. vi. 3. 3
Both *shew* their auncestry. III. ix. Arg.
like sunny beames, . . . *shewe* their golden gleames, III. ix. 20. 8
Was never better time to *shew* thy smart III. x. 26. 3
t' abandon noble chevisaunce For *shewe* of perill, III. xi. 24. 7
To *shew* Dan Cupids powre and great effort: III. xi. 46. 5
To *shew* the victors might and mercilesse intent. III. xi. 52. 9
did great liking *sheowe,* III. xii. 13. 8
in face And outward *shew* faire semblance they did beare; IV. i. 17. 6
such as she was she plaine did *shew;* IV. i. 18. 7
Close underneath his shield, that scarce did *show,* IV. iii. 33. 7
their deedes of armes to *shew.* IV. iv. 37. 2
Then did Sir Ferramont unto them *shew* His Lucida, IV. v. 11. 6
Her lovely Amoret did open *shew;* IV. v. 13. 2
so forged things do fairest *shew.* IV. v. 15. 9
To come and *shew* themselves before the light, IV. vii. 33. 8
Ne signe of sence did *shew,* ne common wit, IV. vii. 44. 3
goodly grace she him did *shew:* IV. viii. 6. 5
Shew gladsome countenaunce nor pleasaunt glee; IV. ix. 13. 5
shew of perill hard IV. x. 17. 4
The which right well her workes divine did *shew:* IV. x. 34. 5
my shield I forth to her did *show,* IV. x. 55. 1
Whose like none else could *shew,* IV. xi. 33. 9
for no cause, but as I shall you *shew.* V. i. 16. 5

Show—*Continued.*
Instead of right me seems great wrong dost *shew*, ... V. ii. 34. 3
if the weight of these thou canst not *show*, ... V. ii. 43. 5
There Marinell great deeds of armes did *shew*, ... V. iii. 8. 4
none Against them durst his head to perill *shew*. . . . . . V. iii. 12. 7
Came Braggadochio, and did *shew* his shield, ... V. iii. 14. 8
For proofe *shew* forth thy sword, ... V. iii. 21. 5
shew the wounds which unto thee befell; . . . . V. iii. 21. 7
shew the sweat with which thou diddest sway . . . . V. iii. 21. 8
signes of gladnesse all did *shew*. . . . . V. iii. 23. 9
what a glorious *shew* he made in all their sights. . . . . . V. iii. 39. 9
venge the shame that she to Knights doth *show*. . . . . . V. iv. 34. 4
halfe her side it selfe did naked *show*, ... V. v. 9. 3
With daily *shew* of courteous kind behaviour, ... V. v. 35. 7
So daily he faire semblant did her *shew*, ... V. v. 56. 1
thus much friendship she to him did *show*, ... V. v. 57. 1
To *shew* that Isis doth the Moone portend; . . . . V. vii. 4. 7
To *shew* that she had powre in things divine: . . . . V. vii. 6. 7
By outward *shew* her inward sence desining: . . . . V. vii. 8. 3
To *shew* that clemence oft, ... V. vii. 22. 8
Lion-like shall *shew* his powre extreame. . . . . V. vii. 23. 8
it plaine to them did *shew*. . . . . V. viii. 37. 9
many pleasant trickes before her *show*, ... V. ix. 13. 6
a stately pallace did behold Of pompous *show*, ... V. ix. 21. 5
under *shew* oftimes of fayned semblance . . . . V. ix. 22. 8
To whom he wont *shew* all the shame he might, ... V. x. 30. 5
She gan rejoyce and *shew* triumphant chere, ... V. xi. 33. 2
doe instead thereof mild curt'sie *showe* . . . . VI. i. 27. 3
'Who will not mercie unto others *shew*, ... VI. i. 42. 1
To *show* her thankefull mind . . . . VI. i. 46. 4
And unto him did *shew* all lovely courtesyes. . . . . VI. ii. 16. 9
Doth noble courage *shew* with curteous manners met. . . . . VI. iii. 1. 9
Crying aloud to *shew* her sad misfare . . . . VI. iii. 24. 5
so soone as joyous day Did *shew* it selfe . . . . VI. iii. 45. 2
will it *shew* some sparkes of gentle mynd, ... VI. v. 1. 8
The covert was so thicke that did no passage *shew*. . . . . VI. v. 22. 9
Those evill tidings to their Lord to *shew*: . . . . VI. vi. 24. 3
To *shew* such faintnesse and foule cowardize . . . . VI. vi. 35. 2
delight in painted *show* Of such false blisse, ... VI. x. 3. 7
never more they should endure the *shew* . . . . VI. x. 4. 4
Nymphes, or Faeries, or enchaunted *show*, ... VI. x. 17. 6
To make them lovely or well-favoured *show*; . . . . VI. x. 23. 3
Like the faire Morning . . . did *shew*. . . . . VI. xi. 3. 9
to pretend Some *shew* of favour, ... VI. xi. 6. 6
Nor better cheare to *shew* in misery, ... VI. xi. 8. 7
All which he to the marchants sale did *showe*: . . . . . . VI. xi. 11. 4
To *shew* the courtesie by him profest . . . . VI. xii. 2. 4
thy worth no lesse then hers doth seem to *showe*. . . . . . VII. vi. 32. 9
her face did like a Lion *shew*, ... VII. vii. 6. 4
like a throne did *showe*. (**shew*) . . . . VII. vii. 8. 9
shew the last ensample of your pride; . . . . *Am.* xxv. 6
A close intent at last to *shew* me grace: . . . . *Am.* xxv. 10
though hardly it can *shew* Thing so divine . . . . *Am.* xlv. 5
To *shew* the powre of your imperious eyes; . . . . *Am.* xlix. 6
then no mercy will unto me *shew*. . . . . *Am.* liii. 8
With *shew* of morning mylde he hath begun, ... *Am.* lxii. 3
Phoebus gins to *shew* his glorious hed. . . . . *Epith.* 77
now *shew* theyr goodly beams . . . . *Epith.* 94
Faire Sun! *shew* forth thy favourable ray, ... *Epith.* 117
They . . . *shew* their kindly might. . . . . *H.L.* 91
Since thou doest *shew* no favour unto mee, ... *H.L.* 150
why doe not faire pictures like powre *shew*, ... *H.B.* 82
An outward *shew* of things that onely seeme. . . . . *H.B.* 91
shew what wondrous powre your beauty hath, ... *H.B.* 286
That we the like should to the wretches *shew*, ... *H.H.L.* 215
that I may *show* Some litle beames . . . . *H.H.B.* 11
And *shew* himselfe in th' image of his grace, ... *H.H.B.* 114
The snow, . . . Did never whiter *shew*, ... *Proth.* 41
did by signes his glad affection *show*, ... *Proth.* 117
Showed. a savage beast . . . *shewde* his force by fire, ... *Rev.* i. 12
Tho *shewed* his ware . . . . *S.C.* May 287
his ey-lids . . . *Shewd* the two pearles . . . . *Gn.* 285
Muttred of matters as their bookes them *shewd*, ... *Hub.* 836
let us heare what grace she *shewed* thee, ... *Col.* 356
bountie . . . Which she to Colin her poore shepheard *shewed*.' . *Col.* 647
As goodlie well ye *shew'd* in late assaies, ... *Ded. Son.* x. 8
To Satyrane she *shewed* her intent; . . . . I. vi. 32. 7
so soone as life . . . *shewed* hevens light, ... I. ix. 3. 6
Hee *shewd* him . . . The damned ghosts . . . . I. ix. 49. 6
In word and deede that *shewd* great modestee, ... I. x. 7. 4
So faire and fresh that Lady *shewd* herselfe in sight. . . . I. xii. 21. 9
great prowesse and heroick worth He *shewd* . . . . II. ii. 25. 4
'There this old Palmer *shewd* himselfe that day, ... II. ii. 43. 1
shewd them naked, deckt with many ornaments. . . . . . . II. v. 32. 9
Whose pleasaunce she him *shewd*, ... II. vi. 11. 9
nought but desert wildernesse *shewed* all around. . . . . . II. vii. 2. 9
shewd of richesse such exceeding store, ... II. vii. 31. 4
all the wealth late *shewd* by mee . . . . II. vii. 38. 4
so great graces as ye have me *shewd*, ... II. viii. 55. 8
Whom Alma having *shewed* to her guestes, ... II. ix. 53. 1
shewd him many sights that corage cold could reare. . . . . II. xii. 68. 9
rather *shewd* more white, if more might bee: . . . . II. xii. 77. 6
'what grace is this That thou hast *shewed* to me . . . . . . III. v. 35. 2
shewd by outward signes that dread her sence did daze. . . . III. vii. 7. 9
shewd her selfe in all a gentle courteous Dame. . . . . . . III. ix. 26. 9
unwares It *shewd* it selfe and shone unwillingly; . . . . . . III. xi. 28. 7
shewd it how the Thebane Semelee, ... III. xi. 33. 1
in that horror *shewd* a seemely grace, ... III. xii. 19. 8
he *shewd* him selfe to be dismayd . . . . IV. i. 37. 7
Which Clotho graunting *shewed* her the same. . . . . IV. ii. 50. 6

Showed—*Continued.*
So soone as heavens window *shewed* light, ... IV. iii. 3. 7
Whereat they *shewed* curteous countenaunce. . . . . IV. iv. 7. 5
He open *shewd*, that all men it mote marke: . . . . IV. iv. 15. 5
Full many deedes that day were *shewed* plaine: . . . . . . IV. iv. 37. 3
Shew'd all his bodie bare unto the cruell dent. . . . . . . IV. vi. 15. 9
shew'd themselves to her such as indeed they were. . . . . IV. vi. 25. 9
Shew'd change of better cheare: . . . . IV. vi. 38. 3
she ready *shewed* The arrow . . . . IV. vii. 30. 3
Ne ever laught, ne once *shew'd* countenance glad, ... IV. viii. 2. 7
Whose bloudie corse they *shew'd* him there beside, ... IV. viii. 21. 7
him aviz'd, And *shew'd* him how, ... IV. viii. 58. 2
neither *showed* to other their hearts privity. . . . . IV. ix. 19. 9
shew'd that she had not that Lady reft, ... IV. ix. 36. 8
in her semblant *shew'd* great womanhood: . . . . IV. x. 31. 5
the virgin lad, And *shewed* her to him, ... IV. xii. 33. 9
chearefull signes he *shewed* outwardly. . . . . IV. xii. 35. 5
Next Hercules his like ensample *shewed*, ... V. i. 2. 6
(which plaine he *shewed* there) . . . . V. ii. 32. 3
unto all himselfe there open *shewed*, ... V. iii. 20. 5
(so *shewed* forth his wounds) . . . . V. iii. 22. 3
shew'd that with his Lord she would emparlaunce make. . . V. iv. 50. 9
Dolon had . . . *shewd* his cankred hate. . . . . V. vi. 33. 9
Her selfe most gratefull *shew'd*, ... V. viii. 23. 9
were Directed in, and *shewed* all the sight; . . . . V. ix. 22. 2
what she had not seene within unto her *shewed*: . . . . . . V. x. 38. 9
Which being *shew'd*, he gan him selfe streightway . . . . V. xi. 21. 4
her *shewed* there The present of his paines, ... V. xi. 33. 5
she *shew'd*, how that discourteous knight, ... VI. ii. 43. 1
Witnesse thereof he *shew'd* his head there left, ... VI. iii. 18. 8
To whom faire semblance, as he could, he *shewed* . . . . VI. iv. 14. 2
Yet *shewd* some token of his gentle blood . . . . VI. v. 2. 5
He *shewed* semblant of exceeding mone . . . . VI. v. 4. 2
Ne ever *shewed* signe of foule disloyalty. . . . . VI. v. 9. 9
Which Turpine had unto her *shewed* late, ... VI. v. 33. 3
Ne ever *shewed* signe of rancour . . . . VI. ix. 39. 9
one still towards *shew'd* her selfe afore; . . . . VI. x. 24. 8
he kyndnesse to her *showed*, ... VI. xi. 4. 6
they *shewed*, how those marchants were Arriv'd . . . . . . VI. xi. 10. 1
So *shew'd* them her, to prove how pale . . . . VI. xi. 12. 9
sad examples *shewed* Of her great power, ... VII. vi. 4. 6
when ye have *shewd* (**shewed*) all extremityes, ... *Am.* xxxvi. 9
Showedst. Ne braver proofe in any of thy powre *Shewd'st* thou, III. iii. 3. 3
Shower. sodain dropping of a golden *shoure* . . . . *Bel.*[1] ix. 11
Like April *shoure* so stremes the trickling teares . . . . . *S.C.* Ap. 7
Did more increase the sharpnes of her *showre*. . . . . . . *T.M.* 478
everie *shower* will wash and wipe away; . . . . *Ti.* 205
To tast the streames that, like a golden *showre*, ... *Ded. Son.* viii. 9
as thicke as stormie *showre*, Their strokes did raine: . . . . II. viii. 35. 5
they fiercely then begin to *showre*; . . . . II. viii. 48. 5
poures it selfe forth in a stormy *showre*: . . . . III. iv. 13. 6
Like to thicke clouds that threat a stormy *showre*, ... III. iv. 43. 3
Ne the sharp Northerne wind thereon to *showre*; . . . . . . III. v. 51. 5
With *showre* and hayle so horrible and dred, ... III. ix. 11. 6
to that shed, to shrowd him from the *showre*, ... III. ix. 13. 3
into a golden *showre* Him selfe he chaung'd, ... III. xi. 31. 1
through their rifts the ruddie bloud did *showre*, ... IV. iii. 15. 7
poureth forth a sudden *shoure* of raine, ... IV. iv. 47. 8
Covered with cloudie storme and bitter *showre*, ... IV. v. 32. 2
Heaping huge strokes as thicke as *showre* of hayle, ... IV. vi. 16. 5
they were ymet With a sharpe *showre* of arrowes, ... V. iv. 38. 4
Showers. beare of the sharpe *showres*; . . . . *S.C.* May 157
haile, and harmful *showres*, ... *Gn.* 582
with storming *showers* be washt away, ... *Ti.* 404
With *showres* of heaven and tempests . . . . *Ti.* 501
Powr'd upon her, like *showers* of Castaly, ... *D.* 228
The soring clouds into sad *showres* ymolt; . . . . III. xi. 25. 8
Showest. *shewst* th' example of thy childishe might, ... II. iv. 45. 4
Showeth. *sheweth* each thing as it is in deed: . . . . III. iv. 59. 2
speaking token *sheweth* at the least Her certeine losse, . . . III. viii. 49. 5
this Ladie, which he *sheweth* here, ... V. iii. 22. 5
Showing. *Shewing* her wreathed rootes, and naked armes, . . *Ro.* xxviii. 6
Shewing her selfe both wise and liberall. . . . . II. ix. 20. 5
Shewing desire her inward flame to slake. . . . . III. ix. 31. 4
Shewing his nature in his countenaunce: . . . . III. xii. 15. 5
shewing her, did Paridell upbray; . . . . IV. ii. 7. 4
shewing forth signes of their fathers blood, ... IV. ii. 46. 3
Shewing him selfe all ready for the field. . . . . IV. iv. 17. 5
Salvagesse sans finesse, shewing secret wit. . . . . IV. iv. 39. 9
Midst sorrow *shewing* joyous semblance . . . . IV. vii. 44. 9
shewing, by their heapes, how great they were. . . . . . . *Com. Son.* iv. 8
Shewing us mercie (miserable crew!) . . . . *H.H.L.* 214
Shown. what so by my selfe may not be *showen*, ... *Gn. Ded.* 13
nor memorie is to be *showne*: . . . . *Gn.* 590
An island, which the first to west was *showne*. . . . . . . *Col.* 271
Let thy faire Cinthias praises be thus rudely *showne*. . . . *Ded.Son.*viii.14
that path, which first was *showne*, ... I. i. 10. 4
all her filthy feature open *showne*, ... I. viii. 49. 8
therein write to lett his love be *showne*; . . . . III. ix. 30. 7
where ever it in field was *showne*. . . . . III. xi. 7. 9
that mask of love which late was *showen*; . . . . IV. i. 3. 6
that both the custome *showne* Were kept, ... IV. i. 11. 7
was easie to be *showen*. . . . . IV. iv. 38. 5
have so done, as she to me hath *showne*; . . . . IV. vii. 19. 7
when as fortune all her spight hath *showne*, ... V. iii. 1. 3
Bracidas, let this likewise be *showne*; . . . . V. iv. 18. 2
in which plaine is *showne* Of what degree . . . . VI. iii. 1. 4
(As their victorious deedes have often *showen*, ... VI. iv. 36. 4
right noble deedes; the which els where are *showne*. . . . . VI. iv. 38. 9
Shows. seeded field greene grasse first *showes*, ... *Ro.* xxx. 1

Shows—*Continued.*
Unto my eyes strange *showes* presented were, . . . *Van.* i. 10
with false *shewes* abuse his fantasy, . . . I. i. 46. 4
to my loathed life now *shewes* some light, . . . I. iv. 48. 2
Yet outwardly some little comfort *shewes*. . . . I. vii. 21. 3
shewes the way his sinfull soule to save! . . . I. x. 51. 3
where Titan his face never *shewes*. . . . II. v. 27. 9
Guyon in them all *shewes* goodly maysteries. . . . II. vi. 1. 9
decke the world with their rich pompous *showes;* . . . II. vi. 15. 7
With such vaine *shewes* . . . abuse; . . . II. vii. 39. 5
Shewes, visions, sooth-sayes, and prophesies; . . . II. ix. 51. 8
I in colourd *showes* may shadow itt, . . . III. Pr. 3. 8
shews the famous Progeny Which from them springen shall. . . . III. iii. Arg.
shewes his powre in variable kindes: . . . III. v. 1. 3
vain *sheows,* that wont yong knights bewitch, . . . III. vii. 29. 6
of ydle *showes,* nor of false charmes aghast. . . . III. xii. 29. 9
al the world *shews* joyous cheare. . . . IV. x. 44. 9
Ye will them all but fayned *showes* esteeme, . . . VI. Pr. 4. 8
not in outward *shows,* but inward thoughts defynd. . . . VI. Pr. 5. 9
In whose pure minde . . . It *showes,* . . . VI. Pr. 6. 6
Not with such forged *showes,* . . . VI. v. 38. 7
'To them that list the worlds gay *showes* I leave, . . . VI. ix. 22. 1
all this worlds gay *showes,* which we admire, . . . VI. ix. 27. 4
brought forth with pompous *showes* Out of her bowre, . . . VII. vi. 41. 4
all their *showes* (**shewes*) but shadowes, saving she. . . . *Am.* xxxv. 14
by right deserts, t' attaine . . . And not by painted *shewes,* . . . *Com. Son.* ii. 3
The vaine surmizes, the distrustfull *showes,* . . . *H.L.* 260
which fondly here admyre Faire seeming *shewes,* . . . *H.H.B.* 17
Shred. when ye *shred* with fatall knife His line, . . . IV. ii. 52. 3
Shriche-, Shriech Oule. *See* **Shritch-owl.**
Shriek. *See* **Shrike.**
a deadly *shrieke* she forth did throw . . . II. i. 38. 1
Did *shrieke* alowd, that through the hous it rong, . . . III. i. 62. 6
For many other Nymphes, he sore did *shreek,* . . . III. xi. 44. 5
they heard a ruefull *shrieke* . . . VI. i. 17. 1
She starting up began to *shrieke* aloud; . . . VI. vi. 31. 2
to shrill And *shrieke* aloud, . . . VI. viii. 46. 2
Shrieked. Some fearing *shriekt,* some being harmed hould, . . . IV. iii. 41. 7
Feebly she *shriekt,* but so feebly indeed . . . IV. vii. 4. 7
'Thereat he *shriekt* aloud, . . . IV. viii. 62. 1
And *shrieked* out, a thing uncomely for a knight. . . . VI. iv. 8. 9
Shrieking. That ye may understand my *shreiking* yell. . . . *Ro.* i. 8
byrds, whose *shrieking* sound Ys signe of dreery death, . . . *S.C.* Au. 173
Does throw out thrilling shriekes, and *shrieking* cryes, . . . I. vi. 6. 2
the ghastly Owle, *Shrieking* his balefull note, . . . I. ix. 33. 7
yelling outcries, and with *shrieking* sowne; . . . III. iv. 30. 8
shrieking Hububs them approching nere, . . . III. x. 43. 3
Shriek-owls. fowle Goblins and *Shriekowles* . . . *T.M.* 283
Shrieks. yelling *shrieks* throwne up into the skies. . . . *T.M.* 24
lowd *shrieks* and drerie dolefull cries. . . . *T.M.* 172
Did throw forth *shrieks* and cries . . . *T.M.* 538
the ghastly owle, With drery *shriekes* . . . I. v. 30. 7
with sharp shrilling *shriekes* doe bootlesse cry, . . . I. v. 33. 5
Does throw out thrilling *shriekes,* and shrieking cryes, . . . I. vi. 6. 2
Her shrill outcryes and *shrieks* so loud did bray, . . . I. vi. 7. 5
His ruefull *shriekes* and gronings, . . . I. x. 28. 5
dearnly cride With percing *shriekes* . . . II. i. 35. 8
importuned long space With shrilling *shriekes,* . . . III. viii. 29. 8
kicks, and squals, and *shriekes* for fell despight; . . . V. vi. 14. 5
Shrieve. *See* **Shrive.**
Shrifts. Their Diriges, their Trentals, and their *shrifts,* . . . *Hub.* 453
Shright. she hid her face, and lowdly *shright.* . . . III. viii. 32. 9
that Ladies loud and piteous *shright,* . . . VI. iv. 3. 2
Shrights. with their piteous cryes, and yelling *shrightes,* . . . II. vii. 57. 5
Shrike. she lowdly did lament and *shrike,* . . . *T.M.* 229
she lowdly gan to waile and *shrike,* . . . *T.M.* 475
Shrikes. With *shrikes* and groanes and grievous agonie. . . . *T.M.* 358
With dolefull *shrikes* shee vanished away, . . . *Ti.* 471
seem'd his *shrikes* would rend the brasen skie: . . . IV. viii. 38. 5
Shriking. the Owle Lowde *shriking,* . . . IV. v. 41. 9
Shrill. on *shrill* reedes chaunting his rustick rime, . . . *Gn.* 155
shrill grashoppers chirped them around; . . . *Gn.* 231
the *shrill* woods, which were of sense bereav'd, . . . *Gn.* 455
outcries *shrill* Of wretched persons . . . *T.M.* 153
The dreadfull accents of their outcries *shrill.* . . . *T.M.* 286
To runne thy *shrill* Arcadian Pipe to heare: . . . *Ti.* 328
with the suddein *shrill* I was appalled. . . . *Ti.* 581
'Let Bagpipe never more be heard to *shrill,* . . . *D.* 323
Soone as his oaten pipe began to *shrill,* . . . *As.* 44
she might immortalize In her *shril* tromp, . . . *Ded. Son.* xiv. 4
chearefull Chaunticlere with his note *shrill* . . . I. ii. 1. 6
Her *shrill* outcryes and shrieks so loud did bray, . . . I. vi. 7. 5
No bird but did her *shrill* notes sweetely sing; . . . II. vi. 13. 3
Which fame of her *shrill* trompet worthy reedes; . . . II. vii. 2. 7
The whistler *shrill,* that whoso heares doth dy; . . . II. xii. 36. 8
They heard a noyse of many bagpipes *shrill,* . . . III. x. 43. 2
shrill trompets lowd did bray, . . . III. xii. 6. 6
The whiles *shril* trompets and loud clarions sweetly playd. . . . IV. iii. 5. 9
Triton his trompet *shrill* before them blew, . . . IV. xi. 12. 3
the trompets *shrill* Don Braggadochios name resounded . . . V. iii. 15. 3
caused streight a Trumpet loud to *shrill* . . . V. vii. 27. 1
with piteous sound Of his *shrill* cries . . . VI. i. 11. 6
And called oft with prayers loud and *shrill,* . . . VI. iii. 49. 7
those shrieches *shrill,* Percing his hart, . . . VI. iv. 18. 4
Then gan the bagpypes and the hornes to *shrill* . . . VI. viii. 46. 1
the merry sound Of a *shrill* pipe he playing heard . . . VI. x. 10. 3
They after follow'd all with *shrill* out-cry, . . . VII. vi. 52. 6
His trompet *shrill* hath . . . sounded, . . . *Am.* xix. 2
Fame in her *shrill* trump shal thunder, . . . *Am.* lxxxiv. 13
how the Minstrils gin to *shrill* aloud . . . *Epith.* 129

Shrill—*Continued.*
to the heavens theyr shouting *shrill* Doth reach, . . . *Epith.* 141
Shrilled. pypes, that *shrild* as lowde as Larke; . . . *S.C.* N. 71
their mightie strokes so *shrild,* . . . *Gn.* 518
they heard a horne that *shrilled* cleare . . . II. iii. 20. 7
Shrilling. *shrilling* voyce of wight alive . . . *Ro.* i. 5
with *shrilling* cryes Pierce the dull heavens . . . *T.M.* 117
A *shrilling* trompett sownded from on hye, . . . I. v. 6. 1
ghosts . . . with sharp *shrilling* shriekes doe bootlesse cry, . . . I. v. 33. 5
Was never wight that heard that *shrilling* sownd, . . . I. viii. 4. 1
importuned long space With *shrilling* shriekes, . . . III. viii. 29. 8
She heard a *shrilling* Trompet sound alowd, . . . III. xii. 1. 5
That ever *shrilling* trumpet did resound; . . . IV. ii. 32. 4
shrilling trompets loudly gan to bray, . . . IV. iv. 48. 5
Britomart heard not the *shrilling* sound, . . . IV. vii. 4. 8
The Ouzell *shrills;* the Ruddock warbles soft; . . . *Epith.* 82
Shrined. All heavenly grace and vertue *shrined* is, . . . *Pet.*[2] vii. 10
bounteous deeds and noble favours *shrynd,* . . . *Col.* 582
Sith it is *shrined* in my Soveraines brest, . . . III. Pr. 1. 5
Shrines. *Shrines* made of the mettall most desired, . . . *Ti.* 411
Shrink. Whose corage when the feend perceivd to *shrinke,* . . . I. i. 22. 4
I saw . . . The bold Sansfoy *shrinck* . . . I. v. 23. 2
when his feet . . . gan to *shrinke,* . . . I. x. 35. 7
yet did he never quaile, Ne backward *shrinke,* . . . II. viii. 35. 7
the fates are firme, And may not *shrinck,* . . . III. iii. 25. 7
the flore to *shrinke* he did avyse; . . . III. xii. 10. 7
when he felt him *shrinke,* . . . VI. i. 20. 8
He gan to *shrinke* and somewhat to give place, . . . VI. v. 21. 3
Ne would him suffer once to *shrinke* asyde, . . . VI. vi. 28. 7
when as he found his force to *shrincke* . . . VI. xii. 34. 1
Shritches. those *shrieches* shrill, Percing his hart, . . . VI. iv. 18. 4
Shritch-owl. See **Shriek-owls.**
For the *Shriche-owle* to build her balefull bowre: . . . *Ti.* 130
Let not the *shriech Oule* nor the Storke be heard, . . . *Epith.* 345
Shrive. When holy fathers wont to *shrieve;* . . . *S.C.* Au. 55
afterwards she gan him soft to *shrieve,* . . . IV. xii. 26. 5
Shriving. Better a short tale than a bad long *shriving:* . . . *Hub.* 543
Shronk. *See* **Shrunk.**
Thearth *shronke* under him, . . . *S.C.* F. 220
had his staggering steed not *shronke* for feare, . . . I. iii. 35. 4
all still *shronke,* and still he greater grew: . . . I. vii. 45. 7
al his flesh *shronk* up like withered flowres. . . . I. viii. 41. 9
His raw-bone cheekes . . . Were *shronke* into his jawes, . . . I. ix. 35. 9
with stayed stedfastnesse, Ne ever *shroncke,* (*shruncke) . . . II. xii. 29. 7
From his revengefull purpose *shronke* abacke, . . . IV. vi. 21. 4
Shroud. in his small bushes used to *shrowde* . . . *S.C.* F. 122
to *shroude* my locklesse pate. . . . *S.C.* Jun. 16
byrds, which . . . Did *shroude* in shady leaves . . . *S.C.* Jun. 54
Whose straying heard them selfe doth *shrowde* . . . *S.C.* Jul. 3
Did *shrowd* her selfe like punishment to shonne. . . . *Gn.* 176
everie wight to *shrowd* it did constrain; . . . I. i. 6. 8
faire couple eke to *shroud* themselves were fain. . . . I. i. 6. 9
Under your beames I will me safely *shrowd* . . . I. iv. 48. 3
the darknes him does *shrowd.* . . . I. v. 13. 9
he doth himselfe in secret *shrowd,* . . . II. i. 25. 3
they *shrowd* themselves from causeles feare; . . . II. iii. 20. 2
Therein to *shrowd* her sumptuous Belamoure; . . . II. vi. 16. 7
found no place wher safe he *shroud* him might: . . . II. vii. 22. 7
Her selfe to *shroud,* and pleasures to entreat; . . . II. vii. 53. 5
to that shed, to *shrowd* him from the showre, . . . III. ix. 13. 3
every bird and beast awarned made To *shrowd* themselves, . . . III. x. 46. 9
In silence and in sleepe themselves did *shrowd,* . . . III. xii. 1. 4
for the present did her anger *shrowd,* . . . IV. i. 10. 7
shrowd their persons from that stormie stowre. . . . IV. v. 32. 7
'Fresh shadowes, fit to *shroud* from sunny ray; . . . IV. x. 24. 1
Seem'd under her protection him to *shroud;* . . . VI. vi. 31. 4
to *shrowde* in shade from Phoebus flame, . . . VII. vi. 39. 3
in the shade of death it selfe shall *shroud,* . . . *Am.* xxvii. 3
And in her ashes *shrowd* my dying shame; . . . *H.H.L.* 19
Shrouded. store of birds therein *yshrowded* (*yshrouded*[1]) were, . . . *Pet.* iii. 5
Above the wast a darke clowde *shrouded* her, . . . *Pet.* vi. 7
when all *shrouded* were in silent night, . . . *Van.* xi. 5
(There *shrouded* was the little God) . . . *S.C.* Mar. 68
we close *shrowded* in thys shade alone. . . . *S.C.* Ap. 32
sorrow close *shrouded* in hart, . . . *S.C.* S. 15
when all *shrowded* were In careles sleep, . . . *Hub.* 333
therein *shrouded* from the tempest dred, . . . I. i. 8. 3
every creature *shrowded* is in sleepe. . . . I. iii. 15. 2
now in shade he *shrowded* yonder lies.' . . . II. iii. 35. 5
The joyous birdes, *shrouded* in chearefull shade . . . II. xii. 71. 1
the world in silence deepe *Yshrowded* was, . . . III. i. 59. 2
Where he is *shrowded* in security. . . . III. xi. 6. 7
hunt for shade, where *shrowded* they may lie, . . . IV. iv. 47. 4
woodman *shrowded* there from scorching sunne. . . . IV. vii. 42. 9
Warn'd man and beast in quiet rest be *shrowded,* . . . V. iv. 45. 3
long in captive shade Had *shrowded* bene, . . . V. vii. 43. 2
his three foes *shrowded* in guilefull shade . . . VI. v. 17. 8
whiles their flockes in shadowes *shrouded* bee, . . . VI. ix. 41. 4
Shrouds. Wherein the lightsome levin *shroudes,* . . . *S.C.* Au. 87
Shrubby. Island . . . Covered with *shrubby* woods, . . . VI. x. 41. 7
Shrubs. the bushie *shrubs* which growe thereby. . . . *Gn.* 80
Cover'd with boughes and *shrubs* from heavens light, . . . II. vii. 3. 2
a hollow glade Covered with mossie *shrubs,* . . . VI. iv. 13. 6
thicke *shrubs,* which did them alwaies shade . . . VI. x. 42. 3
Shrunk. *See* **Shronk.**
broken reed . . . *shrunck* when hard thereon he lay. . . . III. xii. 10. 9
Shrunken. weighing the . . . *shrunken* synewes of her chosen knight, . . . I. ix. 20. 5
Shun. Were not better to *shunne* the scortching heate? . . . *S.C.* Au. 48
Did shrowd her selfe like punishment to *shonne.* . . . *Gn.* 176

Shun—*Continued.*
for to *shunne* the horrible mischiefe, ... *Ti.* 143
'I hate all men, and *shun* all womankinde; . . . . . *D.* 421
Ne shame he thought to *shonne* so hideous might: . . . . . I. viii. 8. 1
shunne the death ordaynd by destinie? . . . . . I. ix. 42. 8
wrath and hatred warely to *shonne,* . . . . . I. x. 33. 5
Thenceforth the suitt of earthly conquest *shonne,* . . . . . I. x. 60. 7
shonne The cursed land where many wend amis, ... II. i. 51. 7
'what man can *shun* the hap, ... II. iv. 17. 2
To *shonne* the engin of his meant decay; . . . . . II. xi. 36. 3
To *shunne* Rocke of Reproch, ... II. xii. 9. 9
Therefore doe them *shonne;* . . . . . II. xii. 11. 7
who can *shun* the chance that dest'ny doth ordaine? . . . . . III. i. 37. 9
Did use to hide, and plaine apparaunce *shonne*) . . . . . III. i. 52. 8
for she the right did *shunne;* . . . . . III. ii. 51. 4
light doe *shonne* for feare of being shent; . . . . . III. iv. 58. 7
Fayre death it is, to *shonne* more shame, to dy: . . . . . III. v. 45. 8
this sad encounter *shonne,* And seeke els . . . . . III. viii. 17. 5
'In vaine he feares that which he cannot *shonne;* . . . . . III. ix. 7. 1
He fled . . . so fowle reproch to *shonne,* . . . . . III. ix. 48. 5
Which he to *shun,* and stop vile envies sting, ... IV. ii. 26. 6
Ne either car'd to ward, or perill *shonne,* . . . . . IV. iii. 36. 4
every one gan *shun* his dreadfull sight, ... IV. iv. 41. 8
rather seemes, sith knowen armes ye *shonne.'* . . . . . IV. vi. 5. 5
shun his mightie strokes, gainst which no armes avayled. . . . . . IV. vi. 12. 9
did resort of sinfull people *shonne,* . . . . . IV. vii. 42. 8
Did *shun* the proofe thereof, and it avoyded light. . . . . . IV. viii. 44. 9
My hard mishaps that ye may learne to *shonne;* . . . . . IV. x. 3. 7
One day, as she to *shunne* the season whot . . . . . IV. xi. 42. 4
makes all men for feare that passage for to *shonne.'* . . . . . V. ii. 4. 9
Ne any may his soveraine power *shonne,* . . . . . V. ii. 42. 3
shun the dred despight Of her fierce wrath, ... V. v. 16. 1
Ne either sought the others strokes to *shun,* . . . . . V. vii. 29. 3
The Ladie counseld him the place to *shonne,* . . . . . V. x. 30. 8
oft recuile to *shunne* his sharpe despight: . . . . . VI. i. 20. 4
nought could do but *shun* The perill . . . . . VI. iii. 48. 8
Shun secresie, and talke in open sight: . . . . . VI. vi. 14. 8
Ne any paines ne perill did he *shonne,* . . . . . VI. x. 32. 7
by all meanes the daunger knowne did *shonne:* . . . . . VI. xi. 35. 7
day-light doth *shonne:* . . . . . VI. xii. 35. 8
Th' importune suit of my desire to *shonne:* . . . . . *Am.* xxiii. 6
warne to *shun* the daunger of theyr wrath. . . . . . *Am.* xxxi. 8
Shunned. *shun'd* destruction doth destruction render: . . . . . *Gn.* 364
The fearefull shepheard, . . . *shund* th' unlucky ground. . . . . . I. ii. 28. 9
greatly *shunned* manly exercise; . . . . . I. iv. 20. 2
from thenceforth he *shund* the like to take, ... I. xi. 24. 8
he descryde and *shonned* still his slight: . . . . . II. i. 4. 8
comes unsought, and *shonned* followes eke. . . . . . II. iv. 44. 3
lightly *shunned* it; and, passing by, ... II. v. 4. 1
shund the marke at which it should be ment; . . . . . II. v. 5. 5
shund dishonor which as death she feard: . . . . . III. vi. 10. 5
it she *shund* no lesse then dread to die; . . . . . III. vii. 24. 4
she the way *shund* nathemore forthy, ... III. vii. 38. 5
had he not it *shun'd* with heedfull vew, ... V. viii. 32. 7
with warie heed He *shund* his strokes, ... V. xii. 18. 3
shund to match with any forrein fere. . . . . . VI. xii. 4. 9
Shunneth. Upon her fist the bird, which *shonneth* vew, ... II. ix. 40. 7
Shunning. *See* **Light-shunning.**
The warie fowle . . . avoydes it, *shunning* light, ... IV. iii. 19. 6
Shuns. the foule that *shunnes* the cherefull light . . . . . *Bel.*[1] vi. 13
Shure. *See* **Suir.**
Shut. *See* **Outshut.**
better dayes death hath *shut* up in woe? . . . . . *S.C.* N. 74
shouldred is, or out of doore quite *shit,* . . . . . *Col.* 709
full of ghastly fright . . . Gan *shut* the dore. . . . . . I. iii. 12. 8
shut up heavens windowes shyning wyde; . . . . . I. vii. 23. 5
Whose gates he fownd fast *shutt,* . . . . . I. viii. 3. 3
Thy life *shutt* up for death so oft did call; . . . . . I. ix. 45. 6
gate, Which long time had beene *shut,* . . . . . I. xii. 3. 7
the dore streight way Did *shutt,* . . . . . II. vii. 26. 6
readily they *shut* and open might. . . . . . II. ix. 46. 8
She *shut* up all her plaint in privy griefe . . . . . III. iv. 11. 2
dore Was *shut* to all which lodging did desyre: . . . . . III. viii. 52. 8
shut up fast within her prisons blind, ... III. ix. 15. 4
Cambell thus did *shut* up all in jest: . . . . . IV. iv. 12. 1
to *shut* up all in friendly love, ... IV. ix. 15. 1
Shut up her haven, mard her marchants trade, ... V. x. 25. 6
within the dore . . . That it could not be *shut;* . . . . . VI. i. 23. 8
whose silken leaves small Long *shut* up in the bud . . . . . VI. ii. 35. 8
the rude Porter . . . Did *shut* the gate . . . . . VI. iii. 38. 2
shut up all his plaint in privy paine. . . . . . VI. v. 24. 5
Her wretched life *shut* up in deadly shade, ... VI. x. 44. 4
therein *shut* up his blasphemous tong, ... VI. xii. 34. 5
Shutting. in close hart *shutting* up her payne, ... I. iii. 8. 6
Shuttlecocks. With *shuttelcocks,* misseeming manlie wit, ... *Hub.* 804
Sib. I am very *sybbe* to you: . . . . . *S.C.* May 269
ne *sib* at all To Elfes, ... III. iii. 26. 4
huge and hideous . . . And *sib* to great Orgolio, ... VI. vii. 41. 8
Sic. *See* **Such.**
sike fancies weren foolerie, ... *S.C.* F. 211
Sike worldly sovenance he must forsay. . . . . . *S.C.* May 82
Sike mens follie I cannot compare . . . . . *S.C.* May 95
nought seemeth *sike* strife, ... *S.C.* May 158
Sike one . . . Moses was, ... *S.C.* Jul. 157
Sike mister men bene all misgone, ... *S.C.* Jul. 201
Sike syrlye shepheards han we none, ... *S.C.* Jul. 203
Of all my flocke there nis *sike* another, ... *S.C.* Au. 38
Sike a song never heardest thou . . . . . *S.C.* Au. 50
Sike a judge as Cuddie were for a king. . . . . . *S.C.* Au. 52
sike a roundle never heard I none: . . . . . *S.C.* Au. 125

Sic—*Continued.*
That *sike* mischiefe graseth hem emong, ... *S.C.* S. 113
of *sike* pastoures howe done the flocks creepe? . . . . . *S.C.* S. 140
Sike as the shepheards, *sike* bene her sheepe, ... *S.C.* S. 141
If *sike* bene Wolves, as thou hast told, ... *S.C.* S. 228
Sike prayse is smoke, . . . *Sike* words bene wynd, ... *S.C.* O. 35, 36
Sike myrth in May is meetest for to make, ... *S.C.* N. 11
loatheth *sike* delightes as thou doest prayse: . . . . . *S.C.* N. 18
Who but thy selfe deserves *sike* Poetes prayse? . . . . . *S.C.* N. 23
sike happy cheere is turnd to heavie chaunce, ... *S.C.* N. 103
Sike follies nowe have gathered as too ripe, ... *S.C.* D. 117
Sick. *See* **Love-sick.**
'*Sicke, sicke,* alas! and little lack of dead, ... *S.C.* May 264
The fift had charge *sick* persons to attend, ... I. x. 41. 1
Hable to heale the *sicke,* . . . . . II. iii. 22. 9
cheard the feeble spright Of the *sicke* virgin, ... III. ii. 47. 2
choicest med'cine for *sick* harts reliefe: . . . . . III. iii. 5. 5
the *sicke* Damosell . . . vewed her straunge lovers shade, ... III. iii. 6. 2
humid evening ill for *sicke* folkes cace; . . . . . III. ix. 26. 4
so weake of limbe, and *sicke* of love He woxe, ... IV. xii. 20. 6
For his *sicke* charge some harbour there to seeke; . . . . . VI. iii. 37. 6
yeeld some ease To these *sicke* twaine, ... VI. v. 32. 3
Their hearts were *sicke;* their sides were sore; . . . . . VI. v. 40. 9
During which space that she thus *sicke* did lie, ... VI. xi. 9. 1
Sicker. *sicker* thy head veray tottie is, ... *S.C.* F. 55
Sicker, Willye, thou warnest well; . . . . . *S.C.* Mar. 7
Sicker I hold him for a greater fon, ... *S.C.* Ap. 158
Sicker this morrowe, no lenger agoe, ... *S.C.* May 19
Sicker, now I see thou speakest of spight, ... *S.C.* May 55
Sicker, I am very sybbe to you: . . . . . *S.C.* May 269
Syker, thous but a laesie loord, ... *S.C.* Jul. 33
Syker, thou speakes lyke a lewde lorrell, ... *S.C.* Jul. 93
Now, *sicker,* I see . . . . . *S.C.* Jul. 207
Sicker, make like account . . . . . *S.C.* Au. 43
Sicker, sike a roundle never heard I none: . . . . . *S.C.* Au. 125
But, *sicker,* so it is, ... *S.C.* S. 76
Content with little in condition *sicker.* . . . . . *Hub.* 430
Sickerness. to her feet betooke her doubtfull *sickernesse.* . . . . . III. vii. 25. 9
drew her selfe aside in *sickernesse,* . . . . . III. xi. 55. 8
Sickle. in his hand a *sickle* he did holde, ... VII. vii. 30. 8
Under his belt he bore a *sickle* circling wide. . . . . . VII. vii. 36. 9
Time shall soon cut down with his consuming *sickle.* . . . . . VII. viii. 1. 9
Sickly. soone forgot his former *sickely* payne: . . . . . III. viii. 10. 3
For safe conducting of his *sickely* Dame . . . . . VI. iii. 31. 3
his *sickely* patients Did gladly hearken . . . . . VI. vi. 15. 1
his Lady, though she *sickely* were, ... VI. vi. 17. 8
Sickness. Feare, *sicknesse,* age, losse, labour, sorrow, strife, ... I. ix. 44. 6
Those that with *sicknesse* were infected sore . . . . . I. xi. 30. 3
to faine A sodaine *sickenesse* . . . . . VI. xi. 7. 8
Her *sickenesse* was not of the body, ... VI. xi. 8. 9
through *sicknesse* now so wan and weake, ... VI. xi. 12. 7
Side. *See* **Foreside, Forest-side, Fountain-side, Garden-side, North-side, Overside, Pit-side, Wayside.**
and *side* did hang his hair, ... *Bel.*[1] vii. 3
On each *side* purtraid was a Victorie, ... *Bel.* iv. 5
Hard by a rivers *side* . . . . . *Bel.* x. 1
hundred Nymphes sate *side* by *side* about; . . . . . *Bel.* xii. 10
On everie *side* a thousand shining beames: . . . . . *Bel.*[2] xi. 10
Hard by his *side* grewe a bragging Brere, ... *S.C.* F. 115
So beate his old boughes my tender *side,* . . . . . *S.C.* F. 175
shed his whirling flames on either *side,* . . . . . *Gn.* 159
On everie *side* did shine like scalie golde; . . . . . *Gn.* 261
Throwing his firie eyes on everie *side,* . . . . . *Gn.* 270
On this *side* them there is a yongman layd, ... *Gn.* 493
The heavens on everie *side* enclowded bee: . . . . . *Gn.* 571
death on everie *side* to them appeares . . . . . *Gn.* 583
Enclosing it with banks on everie *side,* . . . . . *Gn.* 658
gan the Courtiers gaze on everie *side,* . . . . . *Hub.* 669
if that wrong on eyther *side* there were, ... *Hub.* 1097
on the other *side,* I did behold A Woman sitting, ... *Ti.* 8
About whose flowrie bankes on either *side* . . . . . *Ti.* 136
Over the Sea from one to other *side,* . . . . . *Ti.* 548
to the other *side* To cast mine eye, ... *Ti.* 587
I saw, on th' other *side,* A curious Coffer . . . . . *Ti.* 617
Strongly outlaunced towards either *side,* . . . . . *Mui.* 82
Full closely creeping by the hinder *side,* . . . . . *Mui.* 403
Hermitage . . . hard by a forests *side,* . . . . . I. i. 34. 2
adowne his coursers *side* The red bloud trickling . . . . . I. ii. 14. 8
Their horned fronts so fierce on either *side* Doe meete, ... I. ii. 16. 3
That had a like faire Lady by his *syde;* . . . . . I. ii. 35. 8
by my wretched lovers *side* me pight; . . . . . I. ii. 42. 7
seeing by her *side* the Lyon stand, ... I. iii. 11. 5
his hot ryder spurd his chauffed *side:* . . . . . I. iii. 33. 6
was on every *side* With rich array . . . dight. . . . . . I. iv. 6. 5
a noble crew Of Lords and Ladies stood on every *side,* . . . . . I. iv. 7. 8
by his *side* rode loathsome Gluttony, ... I. iv. 21. 1
Two iron coffers hong on either *side,* . . . . . I. iv. 27. 3
On th' other *side* . . . Duessa placed is, ... I. v. 5. 6
victory they dare not wish to either *side.* . . . . . I. v. 9. 9
softly gan embalme on everie *side:* . . . . . I. v. 17. 5
on every *side* them stood The trembling ghosts . . . . . I. v. 32. 4
all the hellish brood . . . flockt on every *side,* . . . . . I. v. 32. 8
by his *side* his steed the grassy forage ate. . . . . . I. vii. 2. 9
Perce to my hart, and pas through everie *side,* . . . . . I. vii. 22. 8
an horne . . . Which hong adowne his *side* . . . . . I. viii. 3. 6
Me seemed, by my *side* a royall Mayd . . . . . I. ix. 13. 7
by her *syde* there sate a gentle payre, ... I. x. 31. 8
On either *side* disparted with his rod, ... I. x. 53. 4
he lay upon the sunny *side* Of a great hill, ... I. xi. 4. 5
him assayle on everie *side.* . . . . . II. ii. 22. 9

Sight—*Continued.*
That th' Angels selves can not endure his *sight*. . . . *H.H.B.* 119
But we, fraile wights! whose *sight* cannot sustaine . . . *H.H.B.* 120
In *sight* of whom both Sun and Moone are darke, . . . *H.H.B.* 125
hid . . . from the *sight* Of all . . . *H.H.B.* 178
And darkes the earth with shadow of her *sight?* . . . *H.H.B.* 229
wight Who of her selfe can win the wishfull *sight*. . . . *H.H.B.* 245
So full their eyes are of that glorious *sight*, . . . *H.H.B.* 281
never saw a *sight* so fayre, . . . *Proth.* 60
like the twins of Jove they seem'd in *sight*, . . . *Proth.* 173
Sighted. *See* **Pure-sighted.**
lovers eyes more sharply *sighted* bee . . . *H.B.* 232
Sights. *See* **Oversights.**
Be vext with *sights*, that doo her peace molest. . . . *Pet.*[2] vii. 8
Ye sacred ruines, and ye tragick *sights*, . . . *Ro.* vii. 1
yet those *sights* empassion me full nere. . . . *Van.* i. 12
When these sad *sights* were overpast and gone, . . . *Van.* xii. 1
Full of sad *sights* and sore Catastrophees; . . . *T.M.* 158
Before mine eies strange *sights* presented were, . . . *Ti.* 489
where other *sights* I spide. . . . *Ti.* 588
Powres forth sweete odors and alluring *sights;* . . . *Mui.* 164
When as my hearse shall happen to your *sightes*, . . . *D.* 528
As one . . . whose dryer braine Is tost with troubled *sights* . . . I. i. 42. 8
after troublous *sights* And dreames, . . . I. ii. 4. 2
strove for to amaze the weaker *sights:* . . . I. vii. 30. 5
Sad be the *sights*, and bitter fruites of warre, . . . II. ii. 30. 6
horribly misshapes with ugly *sightes*, . . . II. v. 27. 7
the rest of those same ruefull *sightes*, . . . II. vii. 57. 7
'Behold th' ensamples in our *sights* . . . II. xii. 9. 2
shewd him many *sights* that corage cold could reare. . . . II. xii. 68. 9
the *sights* of semblants vaine. . . . III. iv. 54. 5
all those *sights*, and all that else I saw, . . . IV. x. 29. 1
Braggadochio is uncas'd In all the Ladies *sights*. . . . V. iii. Arg.
The goodly service, the devicefull *sights*, . . . V. iii. 3. 2
what a glorious shew he made in all their *sights*. . . . V. iii. 39. 9
That is the highest head (in all mens *sights*) . . . VII. vi. 36. 7
fill your selfe with those most joyous *sights*, . . . *Am.* lxxxiii. 9
no deluding dreames, nor dreadfull *sights*, . . . *Epith.* 338
Sights never seene, and thousand shadowes vaine, . . . *H.L.* 255
Through contemplation of those goodly *sights*, . . . *H.H.B.* 2
All other *sights* but fayned shadowes bee. . . . *H.H.B.* 273
Sign. It is a *signe* of helth. . . . *S.C.* Jul. 212
whose shrieking sound Ys *signe* of dreery death, . . . *S.C.* Au. 174
Whom golden Fleece did make an heavenly *signe;* . . . *Gn.* 211
the sweete Cypresse, *signe* of deadly bale. . . . *Gn.* 216
No *signe* of storme, no feare of future paine, . . . *Gn.* 565
crueltie, the *signe* of currish kinde, . . . *Hub.* 1134
no word we heare, nor *signe* now see, . . . *Ti.* 360
Where now he is become an heavenly *signe*, . . . *Ti.* 601
So now in heaven a *signe* it doth appeare, . . . *Ti.* 615
The *signe* by which he chalengeth the place; . . . *Mui.* 317
her silence, *signe* of one dismaid, . . . *Mui.* 341
(*Signe* of thy love, though nought for my reliefe, . . . *D.* 94
The Sarazins shield, *signe* of the conqueroure. . . . I. ii. 20. 7
whally eies (the *signe* of gelosy,) . . . I. iv. 24. 3
Saint George of mery *England*, the *signe* of victoree.' . . . I. x. 61. 9
That *signe* of last outbreathed life . . . I. xii. 2. 5
Glad *signe* of victory and peace in all their land. . . . I. xii. 5. 9
y scuith gogh, *signe* of sad crueltee. . . . II. x. 24. 9
land-marke seemd to bee, or *signe* of sundry way: . . . II. xi. 35. 9
If any puffe of breath or *signe* of sence shee fond. . . . III. i. 60. 9
The surest *signe*, whereby ye may her know, . . . III. v. 5. 8
Which chearefull *signe* did send unto her sight . . . III. vii. 5. 4
Signe of nigh battaill, or got victory: . . . III. xii. 1. 6
In *signe* of silence, as to heare a play, . . . III. xii. 4. 4
saw her not, nor *signe* of her good speed, . . . III. xii. 45. 3
There was the *signe* of antique Babylon; . . . IV. i. 22. 1
A *signe* which did to him the victorie assure. . . . IV. iii. 32. 9
The *signe* whereof yet stain'd his bloudy lips afore. . . . IV. vii. 5. 9
Ne *signe* of sence did shew, ne common wit, . . . IV. vii. 44. 3
In *signe* of true subjection to her powre, . . . V. v. 18. 2
signe of truce did make: . . . V. xii. 8. 2
tooke with him the head, the *signe* of shame. . . . VI. iii. 17. 6
Ne ever shewed *signe* of foule disloyalty. . . . VI. v. 9. 9
His foot he set on his vile necke, in *signe* Of servile yoke, . . . VI. vii. 26. 4
Ne ever shewed *signe* of rancour or of jarre. . . . VI. ix. 39. 9
Made *signe* to them in their degrees to speake, . . . VII. vi. 22. 5
That is a *signe* to know the gentle blood. . . . *H.B.* 140
crowne . . . in *signe* of highest soveraignty; . . . *H.H.B.* 191
Signed. A booke, that was both *signd* and seald with blood; . . . I. x. 13. 8
I seeke the fields with her late footing *synd;* . . . *Am.* lxxviii. 5
Signified. Through her thin weed their places only *signifide*. . . . II. iii. 29. 9
Signifies. Like as Osyris *signifies* the Sunne: . . . V. vii. 4. 8
Signs. Many a spoile, and many goodly *signes*, . . . *Bel.*[1] v. 6
With wondrous *signes* to make all wights adore . . . *Rev.* i. 13
Brought foorth those *signes* of your presumptuous boasts . . . *Ro.* xv. 3
as *signes* of ill luck, . . . *S.C.* May 232
I learned als the *signes* of heaven to ken, . . . *S.C.* D. 83
He all those royall *signes* had stolne away, . . . *Hub.* 1016
quaking hands, and other *signes* of feare: . . . I. iii. 12. 6
saw the *signes* that deadly tydinges spake, . . . I. vii. 20. 6
goodly gifts, the *signes* of gratefull mynd, . . . I. ix. 18. 8
Suffice it heare by *signes* to understand . . . I. xii. 40. 4
By certein *signes* . . . He may it fynd; . . . II. Pr. 4. 2
With her two crooked handes she *signes* did make, . . . II. iv. 13. 2
signes of grudge and discontentment vaine. . . . II. viii. 23. 5
The secrete *signes* of kindled lust appeare, . . . II. xii. 68. 6
that none the *signes* might see: . . . II. xii. 80. 4
Her wanton eyes, ill *signes* of womanhed, . . . III. i. 41. 7
By knowen *signes* and passions which I see, . . . III. ii. 33. 3

Signs—*Continued.*
shewd by outward *signes* that dread her sence did daze. . . . III. vii. 7. 9
'the *signes* be sadd; . . . III. viii. 50. 1
By such close *signes* they secret way did make . . . III. ix. 31. 5
With other *signes* of sorrow and impatient teene. . . . III. xi. 37. 9
Full of sad *signes*, . . . III. xii. 19. 7
shewing forth *signes* of their fathers blood, . . . IV. ii. 46. 3
The *signes* of anguish one mote plainely read, . . . IV. v. 45. 8
by secret *signes* of manlinesse . . . IV. vii. 45. 4
At which he wondred much when all those *signes* he fond. . . . IV. viii. 21. 9
chearefull *signes* he shewed outwardly. . . . IV. xii. 35. 5
Mongst those twelve *signes*, which nightly we doe see . . . V. i. 11. 6
by *signes* perceiving plaine . . . V. i. 24. 6
And these the *signs*' (so shewed forth his wounds) . . . V. iii. 22. 3
signes of gladnesse all did shew. . . . V. iii. 23. 9
Bewrayd the *signes* of feature excellent; . . . V. v. 12. 7
By outward *signes* (as well he might) did see, . . . V. vi. 21. 5
to ghesse streightway, By many *signes* . . . VI. ii. 45. 2
By certaine *signes* he plainly him descryde . . . VI. iii. 47. 4
he *signes* unto them made . . . VI. iv. 13. 2
he shewed By *signes*, by lookes, . . . VI. iv. 14. 3
He shewed semblant of exceeding mone By speaking *signes*, . . . VI. v. 4. 3
which he by *signes* did reede, . . . VI. v. 10. 5
sought by making *signes* him to asswage; . . . VI. vi. 39. 3
Plaine *signes* in him of life and livelihead: . . . VI. vii. 20. 5
He mote perceive by *signes* which he did fynd, . . . VI. xi. 27. 8
She found at last, by very certaine *signes* . . . VI. xii. 20. 3
the Starres and *Signes* therein still move, . . . VII. vii. 55. 6
by *signes* his glad affection show, . . . *Proth.* 117
Silence. her solein *silence* she broke, . . . *S.C.* May 213
Doo mone my miserie with *silence* soft: . . . *T.M.* 292
her *silence*, signe of one dismaid, . . . *Mui.* 341
all their birds with *silence* to complaine: . . . *Col.* 24
Till Thestylis at last their *silence* brake, . . . *Col.* 651
spirit, . . . Might long perhaps have lien in *silence* . . . *Ded. Son.* xiii. 5
like a stupid stock in *silence* die! . . . *Am.* xliii. 8
my hart with *silence* secretly Will teach to speak, . . . *Am.* xliii. 9
let stil *Silence* trew night-watches keepe, . . . *Epith.* 353
deeds; Whose praises having slept in *silence* long, . . . I. Pr. 1. 6
carelesse Quiet lyes Wrapt in eternall *silence* . . . I. i. 41. 9
He . . . would not all his *silence* breake. . . . I. i. 42. 9
Thence turning backe in *silence* softe they stole, . . . I. v. 31. 1
There raignd a solemne *silence* over all; . . . I. viii. 29. 8
sithens *silence* lesseneth not my fire, . . . I. ix. 8. 6
forst, at last he made through *silence* suddein breach. . . . I. ix. 25. 9
At last his solemn *silence* thus he brake, . . . I. xii. 29. 5
the world in *silence* deepe Yshrowded was, . . . III. i. 59. 1
solemne *silence* over all that place: . . . III. xi. 53. 7
In *silence* and in sleepe themselves did shrowd, . . . III. xii. 1. 4
In signe of *silence*, as to heare a play, . . . III. xii. 4. 4
His sodaine *silence* which he long had pent, . . . IV. viii. 16. 2
Soft *Silence*, and submisse Obedience, . . . IV. x. 51. 6
In solitary *silence*, far from wight, . . . IV. xii. 19. 2
by his *silence* he would make Her rather reade his meaning . . . V. vi. 9. 8
His dear affect with *silence* did restraine, . . . VI. v. 24. 4
with *silence* mercie prayd. . . . VI. vii. 25. 9
So having ended, *silence* long ensewed; . . . VII. vii. 57. 1
At length she . . . The *silence* brake, . . . VII. vii. 57. 9
Silent. when all shrouded were in *silent* night, . . . *Van.* xi. 5
Before him sits the Titmose *silent* bee; . . . *S.C.* N. 26
'Let birds be *silent* on the naked spray, . . . *D.* 330
Uprose Duessa . . . And to the Paynims lodging comes with *silent* pace. . . . I. iv. 44. 9
sparckling on the *silent* waves, . . . II. xii. 78. 9
Covered with secret cloud of *silent* night, . . . III. xi. 61. 8
doth thy justice sleepe and *silent* ly? . . . III. xi. 9. 7
Unto her selfe her *silent* prayers did impart. . . . V. vii. 7. 9
He could him not containe in *silent* rest; . . . VII. vi. 46. 4
Shall I then *silent* be, or shall I speake? . . . *Am.* xliii. 1
if I *silent* be, my hart will breake, . . . *Am.* xliii. 3
Silk. The sailes of golde, of *silke* the tackle were: . . . *Pet.* ii. 3
haire as soft as *silke*, . . . *Ti.* 563
That seemd like *silke* and silver woven neare; . . . I. xii. 22. 8
neither *silke* nor silver therein did appeare. . . . I. xii. 22. 9
All in a vele of *silke* and silver thin, . . . II. xii. 77. 4
goodly arras . . . Woven with gold and *silke*, . . . III. xi. 28. 3
His garment nether was of *silke* nor say, . . . III. xii. 8. 1
alwaies in her hand two clewes of *silke* she twynd. . . . III. xii. 14. 9
All in a Camis light of purple *silke* . . . V. v. 2. 1
Bound truelove wize, with a blew *silke* riband. . . . *Epith.* 44
Silken. your *silken* hyde Fil'd with round flesh, . . . *Hub.* 591
two such fannes, so *silken* soft . . . *Mui.* 107
Ne with his feete their *silken* leaves deface, . . . *Mui.* 175
The *silken* downe with which his backe is dight, . . . *Mui.* 334
In skilfull knitting of soft *silken* twyne, . . . *Mui.* 362
in a *silken* Camus lilly whight, . . . II. iii. 26. 4
With *silkin* curtens and gold coverletts, . . . II. vi. 16. 6
the downy heare Did . . . *silken* blossoms beare. . . . II. xii. 79. 9
lightly rased her soft *silken* skin, . . . III. i. 65. 7
lapped up her *silken* leaves most chayre, . . . III. v. 51. 6
In *silken* samite she was light arayd, . . . III. xii. 13. 3
like a *silken* veile in compasse round . . . IV. i. 13. 4
all her *silken* garments did with bloud bestaine. . . . IV. vii. 27. 9
a flowre, whose *silken* leaves small . . . VI. ii. 35. 7
Her paps, which like white *silken* pillowes were . . . VI. viii. 42. 2
a crowne Of sundry flowres with *silken* ribbands tyde, . . . VI. ix. 7. 8
like a rose her *silken* leaves did faire unfold. . . . VI. xii. 7. 9
a thin *silken* cassock coloured greene, . . . VII. vii. 29. 2
silken courteins over her display, . . . *Epith.* 303
spare To wet their *silken* feathers, . . . *Proth.* 49

Silks. with the finest *silkes* us to aray, ... *Hub.* 461
Silly. The *silly* Flie, that no redresse did see, ... *Van.* iv. 5
a little Ant, a *silly* worme, ... *Van.* viii. 9
to holden chat With *seely* shepherds swayne, ... *S.C.* Jul. 30
My *seely* sheepe like well belowe, ... *S.C.* Jul. 105
(O, *seely* sheepe, the while!) . . . . *S.C.* Jul. 190
Hey, ho, *seely* sheepe! . . . . *S.C.* Au. 74
My *seely* sheepe (ah, *seely* sheepe!) . . . . *S.C.* S. 62
Ycladde in clothing of *seely* sheepe, ... *S.C.* S. 188
So would he worke the *silly* man by treason . . . . *Hub.* 888
we *silly* Maides, whom they dispize . . . . *T.M.* 339
'Safe then, and safest were my *sillie* sheepe, ... *D.* 134
'Ne worse to you, my *sillie* sheepe! I pray, ... *D.* 351
To heare thee sing, a simple *silly* Elfe? . . . . *Col.* 371
I, *silly* man, whose former dayes Had in rude fields . . . . *Col.* 668
Silly old man, that lives in hidden cell, ... I. i. 30. 6
'Mercy, mercy, Sir, vouchsafe to show On *silly* Dame, . . . I. ii. 21. 3
Me, *silly* maid, away with him he bare, ... I. iv. 47. 7
A *seely* Lamb . . . does take, ... I. vi. 10. 4
A *silly* man, in simple weeds forworne, ... I. vi. 35. 1
her *silly* life to save, ... II. iii. 36. 3
With *silly* weake old woman that did fight! . . . . II. iv. 45. 5
She wist not, *silly* Mayd, what she did aile, ... III. ii. 27. 7
'Beldame, be not wroth With *silly* Virgin, ... III. vii. 8. 7
boldly bent Against the *silly* clowne, ... III. viii. 12. 6
The *silly* virgin strove him to withstand . . . . III. viii. 27. 1
A *silly* Pilgrim driven to distresse, ... III. x. 25. 6
The *silly* man that in the thickett lay . . . . III. x. 45. 1
Litle for him to have one *silly* lasse; . . . . VI. xi. 12. 6
Coridon it was, the *silly* shepherds hynd. . . . . VI. xi. 27. 9
So did Diana and her maydens all Use *silly* Faunus, ... VII. vi. 49. 2
disdeigneth to devoure The *silly* lambe . . . . *Am.* xx. 8
my *silly* barke was tossed sore: . . . . *Am.* lxiii. 4
When him the *silly* Shepheards came to see, ... *H.H.L.* 230
Siloam. Both *Silo* this, and Jordan, did excell, ... I. xi. 30. 6
Silver. a Nimph, that wings of *silver* weares, ... *Bel.*² iv. 6
sudden dropping of a *silver* dew . . . . *Bel.*² xi. 11
The *silver* swanne doth sing . . . . *Frag.*
silver bowe, which was but slacke, ... *S.C.* Mar. 83
'Of fayre Elisa be your *silver* song, ... *S.C.* Ap. 46
'Shewe thyselfe, Cynthia, with thy *silver* rayes, ... *S.C.* Ap. 82
Renne after hastely thy *silver* sound; . . . . *S.C.* Jun. 61
as Dame Cynthias *silver* raye, ... *S.C.* Au. 89
voyces *silver* sound . . . can chaunge my cherelesse cryes. . . . *S.C.* Au. 181
Playing on yvorie harp with *silver* strong. . . . . *Gn.* 16
a *silver* Spring, forth powring . . . . *Gn.* 227
Through their hard barke his *silver* sound receav'd . . . . *Gn.* 456
Into her *silver* bowre the Sunne received; . . . . *Hub.* 4
Beside the *silver* Springs of Helicone, ... *T.M.* 5
th' hollow hills, from which their *silver* voyces . . . . . . *T.M.* 21
in Venus *silver* bowre were bred, ... *T.M.* 362
beside the shore Of *silver* streaming Thamesis . . . . *Ti.* 2
to slide In *silver* channell, ... *Ti.* 135
All happinesse in Hebes *silver* bowre, ... *Ti.* 384
an Harpe stroong all with *silver* twyne, ... *Ti.* 604
Lastly his shinie wings as *silver* bright, ... *Mui.* 89
flowrie bancks with *silver* liquor steepe; . . . . *D.* 102
brought away fast bound with *silver* chaine. . . . . *D.* 119
silver deaw upon the roses pearling. . . . . *Col.* 507
doth need a golden quill, And *silver* leaves, ... *Ded. Son.* xvi. 11
Ycladd in mightie armes and *silver* shielde, ... I. i. 1. 2
Cynthia . . . doth steepe In *silver* deaw his ever-drouping hed, I. i. 39. 8
The other all with *silver* overcast; . . . . I. i. 40. 3
In mighty armes he was yclad anon, And *silver* shield; . . . I. ii. 11. 4
His *silver* shield, now idle, maisterlesse; . . . . I. vii. 19. 6
silver Cynthia wexed pale and faynt, ... I. vii. 34. 8
How ill it sits that same *silver* hed, ... I. viii. 33. 5
the river Dee, as *silver* cleene, ... I. ix. 4. 7
Upon her arme a *silver* anchor lay, ... I. x. 14. 6
take assured hold Upon her *silver* anchor, ... I. x. 22. 3
From which fast trickled forth a *silver* flood, ... I. xi. 29. 4
That seemd like silke and *silver* woven neare; . . . . . . I. xii. 22. 8
neither silke nor *silver* therein did appeare. . . . . I. xii. 22. 9
in his *silver* shield He bore a bloodie Crosse . . . . II. i. 18. 8
faire Phebe with her *silver* face . . . . II. ii. 44. 1
twixt the perles and rubins softly brake A *silver* sound, . . . II. iii. 24. 9
Fountaines of gold and *silver* to abownd, ... II. vii. 17. 5
in the midst thereof a *silver* seat, ... II. vii. 53. 2
Ne sittest downe on that same *silver* stoole, ... II. vii. 63. 8
How oft do they their *silver* bowers leave, ... II. viii. 2. 1
set in *silver* sockets bright, ... II. ix. 46. 6
Bright Scolopendraes arm'd with *silver* scales; . . . . II. xii. 23. 8
the *silver* flood Through every channell running . . . . . . II. xii. 60. 3
themselves dipping in the *silver* dew . . . . II. xii. 61. 7
All in a vele of silke and *silver* thin, ... II. xii. 77. 4
Breakes forth her *silver* beames, ... III. i. 43. 4
With price of *silver* shall his kingdome buy; . . . . III. iii. 39. 6
Their watchet mantles frindgd with *silver* rownd, ... III. iv. 40. 5
had unlaste Her *silver* buskins . . . . III. vi. 18. 3
silver sockets, shyning like the skyes, ... III. viii. 7. 2
Bacchus fruit out of the *silver* plate . . . . III. ix. 30. 3
the white fomy creame Did shine with *silver*, ... III. xi. 41. 5
Without adorne of gold or *silver* bright, ... III. xii. 20. 2
in *silver* basin layd, ... III. xii. 21. 2
did take His *silver* Harpe in hand . . . . IV. ii. 1. 9
Deawed with *silver* drops through sweating sore, ... IV. vi. 19. 7
With *silver* streames amongst the linnen stray'd; . . . . . . IV. x. 52. 5
As with a robe, with her owne *silver* haire, ... IV. xi. 11. 8
Deawed with *silver* drops that trickled downe alway. . . . . IV. xi. 25. 9
seem'd like *silver*, sprinckled here and theare . . . . IV. xi. 45. 4

Silver—*Continued.*
Her *silver* feet, faire washt against this day: . . . . IV. xi. 47. 6
With golden hands and *silver* feete beside, ... V. ii. 10. 2
eke her feete, those feete of *silver* trye, ... V. ii. 26. 7
silke Woven uppon with *silver*, subtly wrought, ... V. v. 2. 2
First rings his *silver* Bell t' each sleepy wight, ... V. vi. 27. 3
Like coles that through a *silver* Censer sparkle bright. . . . V. vi. 38. 9
All clad in linnen robes with *silver* hemd; . . . . V. vii. 4. 4
was framed all of *silver* fine, ... V. vii. 6. 2
Hemd all about with fringe of *silver* twine: . . . . V. vii. 6. 5
royall gifts of gold and *silver* wrought . . . . V. vii. 24. 4
here and there shooting forth *silver* streames, ... V. ix. 28. 8
a sage old Syre, . . . with a white *silver* hed, ... V. ix. 43. 8
it in *silver* bowre does hidden ly . . . . VI. Pr. 3. 3
jacket . . . Of Lincolne greene, belayd with *silver* lace; . . . VI. ii. 5. 7
The whiles his Lord in *silver* slomber lay, ... VI. vii. 19. 8
Whose *silver* lockes bedeckt his beard and hed, ... VI. ix. 13. 7
all the night in *silver* sleepe I spend, ... VI. ix. 22. 8
flud His *silver* waves did softly tumble downe, ... VI. x. 7. 2
Whose *silver* gates . . . she entred, ... VII. vi. 8. 5
To bid her leave faire Cynthias *silver* bower; . . . . VII. vi. 18. 7
To thrust faire Phoebe from her *silver* bed, ... VII. vi. 21. 3
(That on each side her *silver* channell crowne) . . . . . . VII. vi. 41. 8
If *Silver*, her faire hands are *Silver* sheene: . . . . *Am.* xv. 12
in a *silver* dish did ly Twoo golden apples . . . . *Am.* lxxvii. 5
The *silver* scaly trouts doe tend full well, ... *Epith.* 57
All ready to her *silver* coche to clyme; . . . . *Epith.* 76
Out of thy *silver* bowres and secret blisse, ... *H.L.* 23
to see that *Silver* brood, ... *Proth.* 56
through the Skie draw Venus *silver* Teeme; . . . . *Proth.* 63
Silver-dropping. With some few *silver-dropping* teares t' adorne; . . . . *Ti.* 683
Silver-scaly. *See* **Scaly, Silver.**
Silver-sounding. The *silver sounding* instruments did meet . II. xii. 71. 5
Silver-streaming. the shoare of *silver streaming* Themmes; . *Proth.* 11
Silver-winged. Of all the race of *silver-winged* Flies . . . *Mui.* 17
Simois. *Simois* and Xanthus blood outwelde; . . . . *Gn.* 502
Simple. Bird . . . One day did scorne the *simple* Scarabee, . *Van.* iv. 2
The base kinred of so *simple* swaine. . . . . *S.C.* May 271
The *simple* ayre, the gentle warbling wynde, ... *S.C.* Jun. 4
Simple as *simple* sheepe; . . . . *S.C.* Jul. 130
never was abhord The *simple* shepheards kynd. . . . . . . *S.C.* Jul. 140
simple was theyr weede: . . . . *S.C.* Jul. 168
you, that sawe it, *simple* shepe, ... *S.C.* Au. 117
Ne would she scorne the *simple* shepheards swaine; . . . . . *S.C.* N. 97
A *simple* husbandman in garments gray; . . . . *Hub.* 228
simple men, which never came in place Of worlds affaires, . . *Hub.* 834
false Reynold would abuse The *simple* Suter, ... *Hub.* 884
with the *simple* Camell raged sore . . . . *Hub.* 1088
Mongst *simple* shepheards they do boast their skill, ... *T.M.* 329
the light of *simple* veritie Buried in ruines, ... *Ti.* 171
glorie greater then my *simple* thought, ... *Col.* 333
she mott my *simple* song, ... *Col.* 365
To heare thee sing, a *simple* silly Elfe? . . . . *Col.* 371
glorie that in *simple* eie Seeme greatest, ... *Col.* 721
single Truth and *simple* Honestie . . . . *Col.* 727
grace let her vouchsafe to grant To *simple* swaine, ... *Col.* 940
This *simple* trophe of her great conquest.'— . . . . *Col.* 951
Receive, most noble Lord, a *simple* taste . . . . *Ded. Son.* v. 1
Simple in shew, and voide of malice bad; . . . . I. i. 29. 7
the seeming *simple* maid Let fal her eien, ... I. ii. 27. 5
Her up he tooke, (too *simple* and too trew) . . . . I. ii. 45. 7
O, how can . . . *simple* truth subdue avenging wrong! . . . . I. iii. 6. 5
A silly man, in *simple* weeds forworne, ... I. vi. 35. 1
Accept therefore My *simple* selfe, ... I. viii. 27. 5
But *simple*, trew, and eke unfained sweet, ... I. x. 7. 8
Too high a ditty for my *simple* song. . . . . I. x. 55. 7
under *simple* shew, and semblant plaine Lurkt . . . . II. i. 21. 3
simple answere, wanting colours fayre . . . . II. x. 28. 6
(O too high ditty for my *simple* rime!) . . . . II. x. 50. 7
to beguyle A *simple* maide, ... III. ii. 12. 8
in her countenaunce Dwelt *simple* truth . . . . III. vii. 59. 6
hee too *simple* ever to surprise The jolly Paridell, ... III. x. 20. 3
eke my selfe, albee I *simple* such, ... III. x. 28. 8
pardon *simple* man that rash did him displease. . . . . . . III. x. 30. 9
In *simple* truth and blamelesse chastitie, ... IV. viii. 30. 3
unto my *simple* doome, ... IV. x. 21. 3
simple Truth did rayne, ... V. Pr. 3. 9
How he mis-led the *simple* peoples traine, ... V. ii. 33. 7
loved *simple* truth and stedfast honesty. . . . . VI. i. 3. 9
Sith he cannot expresse his *simple* minde, ... VI. v. 30. 3
Such homely what as serves the *simple* clowne, ... VI. ix. 7. 4
began Him to invite unto his *simple* home; . . . . VI. ix. 16. 4
This *simple* sort of life that shepheards lead, ... VI. ix. 33. 8
Simple and true, from covert malice free; . . . . VI. x. 24. 5
seem'd to be some sorie *simple* clowne, ... VI. xi. 27. 3
The *simple* mayd did yield to him anone; . . . . VII. vi. 45. 1
doth deprave My *simple* meaning . . . . *Am.* xxix. 2
Sufficient worke for one mans *simple* head, ... *Am.* xxxiii. 7
it seemeth, in my *simple* wit, ... *Am.* xl. 5
simple truth, and mutuall good-will, ... *Am.* lxv. 11
To heare theyr names sung in your *simple* layes, ... *Epith.* 5
Doe not thy servants *simple* boone refuse; . . . . *Epith.* 124
vouchsafe to take of me This *simple* song, ... *H.L.* 307
In *simple* cratch, wrapt in a wad of hay, ... *H.H.L.* 226
Simpleness. this false footman, clokt with *simplenesse*, . . . I. xii. 34. 6
Simples. *See* **Fee-simples.**
Simplesse. Such *simplesse* mought them shend; . . . . *S.C.* Jul. 172
Simplicity. craft, coloured with *simplicitie*: . . . . *S.C.* May 303
Sin. Was this . . . your hard destinie, Or some old *sinne*, . . . *Ro.* xxiv. 10

Sin—*Continued.*
The vassals of Gods wrath, and slaves of *sin*. *T.M.* 126
Through fleshes frailtie, and deceipt of *sin*. *T.M.* 492
and scorne their shamefull *sin*, *Mui.* 373
her body, full of filthie *sin*, I. i. 24. 7
the first, . . . Was sluggish Idlenesse, the nourse of *sin*; I. iv. 18. 6
daring tempt the Queene of heaven to *sin*; I. v. 35. 2
With beastly *sin* thought her to have defilde, I. vi. 3. 4
his leud lusts, and late attempted *sin*, I. vi. 46. 3
for want of faith, or guilt of *sin*, I. vii. 45. 8
'The lenger life, I wote, the greater *sin*; I. ix. 43. 1
The greater *sin*, the greater punishment: I. ix. 43. 2
'Why then doest thou, O man of *sin*! desire I. ix. 46. 1
Inward corruption and infected *sin*, I. x. 25. 2
The filthy blottes of *sin* to wash away. I. x. 27. 7
sin, and hell, and death, doe most dismay I. x. 41. 4
blood can nought but *sin*, and wars but sorrows yield. I. x. 60. 9
As faint through heat, or dight to pleasant *sin*; II. xii. 77. 2
Most sacred virgin without spot of *sinne*. III. iv. 59. 8
Where wicked ghosts doe waile their former *sin*. III. v. 22. 4
'So liv'd they ever after in like *sin*, III. vii. 49. 1
As may be worthy of his haynous *sin*.' III. ix. 9. 7
Gan dight him selfe unto his wonted *sinne*; IV. vii. 20. 8
when the world with *sinne* gan to abound, V. i. 11. 1
To teare his flesh in peeces for his *sin*: V. iv. 37. 5
There written was the purport of his *sin*, V. ix. 26. 2
Did choke the entraunce with a lumpe of *sin*, VI. i. 23. 7
Knowing his voice, although not heard long *sin*, VI. xi. 44. 3
make thy triumph over death and *sin*; *Am.* lxviii. 2
with thy deare blood clene washt from *sin*, *Am.* lxviii. 7
the bait of *sinne*, and sinners scorne, *H.B.* 152
now of *sinne* to all ensample bee: *H.H.L.* 96

Sinai. Of *Synah* can I tell thee more, *S.C.* Jul. 73

Sinamon. *See* **Cinnamon.**

Since (*partial list*).
since, I saw the roote in great disdaine *Bel.* v. 13
Since of all workmen helde in reckning best; *Ro.* xxvii. 7
since I am not as I wish I were, *S.C.* Jun. 105
ever *since* my hart did greve, *S.C.* Au. 123
I hate the house, *since* thence my love did part, *S.C.* Au. 161
Since when thou hast measured much grownd, *S.C.* S. 21
My volume shall renowne, so long *since* past. *Gn.* 48
since their souldiers pas no better spedd, *Hub.* 357
Nath'les . . . *since* we passed are Unto this point, *Hub.* 1047
Since which all Apes . . . their eares have left, *Hub.* 1383
For *since* the time that Phoebus *T.M.* 7
tunes were never *since* invented. *T.M.* 12
Nor *since* that faire Calliope did lose *T.M.* 13
'It is not long, *since* these two eyes beheld *Ti.* 183
Since that I sawe this gardine wasted quite, *Ti.* 529
Since which that flie . . . doth beare. *Mui.* 144
since so much thou seemst to rue my griefe, *D.* 92
'No age hath bred (*since* fayre Astraea left *D.* 218
' "I, *since* the messenger is come for mee, *D.* 267
Since whose departure, day is turnd to night, *D.* 482
Since round about us it doth make aboad! *As.* 90
since first on grassie greene Shepheards kept sheep, *As.* 209
since I saw that Angels blessed eie, *Col.* 40
Since that same day in nought I take delight, *Col.* 44
since I said he is, he quite is gone, *Col.* 433
Since which she doth . . . dread;— *Col.* 567
since thou foundst such grace *Col.* 652
since no' untruth he knew, I. i. 53. 6
since mine eie your joyous sight did mis, I. iii. 27. 6
since my brest was launcht with lovely dart I. iv. 46. 5
ever *since* hath kept in darksom cave, I. iv. 47. 8
since faire Sunne hath sperst I. iv. 48. 1
since his late luckelesse fray. I. v. 29. 5
of his prowesse proofe he *since* hath made I. vii. 47. 6
since that glauncing sight, He hath no powre I. viii. 21. 6
thrice hid . . . *Since* I the heavens chearefull face did vew. I. viii. 38. 8
since thou bidst, thy pleasure shalbe donne. I. x. 52. 1
Since late she saw him fall I. xi. 33. 9
since now safe ye seised have the shore, I. xii. 17. 7
since that band ye cannot now release, I. xii. 19. 5
since now to thee perteynes the same I. xii. 20. 7
'Therefore, *since* mine he is, I. xii. 28. 1
Since errant armes to sew he first began: II. ii. 17. 5
since the Redcrosse knight he erst did weet II. iii. 11. 7
Since he this hardy enterprize began: II. vii. 65. 7
since no way is lefte to wreake my spight, II. viii. 15. 6
since it greatly did decay. II. x. 53. 9
since Lucies tyme, Was of the Britons first crownd II. x. 58. 6
had it remayned ever *since*! III. ii. 21. 9
since thy faithful zele lets me not hyde III. ii. 37. 6
'Five daies there be *since* he . . . was slaine, And fowre *since* Florimell III. v. 10. 1, 2
Since so good fortune doth to you present IV. ii. 5. 8
Her claym'd, by him in battell wonne long *sens*: IV. v. 23. 7
ever *since* withheld.' IV. vi. 6. 9
Long *since* in that enchaunted glasse she saw; IV. vi. 26. 6
Since I was brought into this dolefull den; IV. vii. 13. 3
Whom seeking ever *since* with endlesse paines IV. ix. 38. 3
since the day that first IV. x. 1. 7
Since of my love at length I rest assured, IV. x. 2. 8
since ye so desire, IV. x. 3. 5
in Cyprus, both long *since* this same, IV. x. 5. 7
since he meanes found none, IV. xii. 12. 8
since she saw the streight extremitie, IV. xii. 28. 1
Since he himselfe it us'd in that great fight V. i. 9. 5

Since—*Continued.*
this same other Damzell *since* hath fained V. iv. 13. 4
loth she was, *since* she no ill did heare, V. vi. 4. 8
Since that he was not forst, nor overcome V. vi. 16. 9
dead long *since* in dolorous distresse, V. vii. 39. 4
Since neither is endamadg'd much V. viii. 14. 3
long *since* aside had set The use of armes, V. xi. 37. 3
Sith which she hath me ever *since* abhord, V. xi. 50. 7
having *since* Taken in hand th' exploit, V. xii. 3. 2
Since it at first was by the Gods VI. Pr. 3. 5
since the salvage Island I did leave,' VI. i. 9. 1
since ye mercie now doe need to crave, VI. i. 42. 4
Since I him lately lost, VI. v. 28. 9
since ye hither came, VI. vi. 6. 7
since thy life . . . I given have, VI. vi. 36. 1
since by grace of God she there was sent, VI. viii. 38. 5
'*Since* then in each mans self' VI. ix. 31. 1
since things passed none may now restore, VI. x. 20. 8
they twaine Long *since* had fought in field: VI. xii. 11. 4
since th' Earths cursed seed Sought to assaile VII. vi. 20. 2
Since which thou, Jove, injuriously hast held VII. vi. 27. 6
Since thou hast seene her dreadfull power VII. vi. 32. 6
that lands in-dwellers *since* have found. VII. vi. 55. 9
since that lyfe is more then death desyred, *Am.* vii. 9
Have ever *since* me kept in cruell bands. *Am.* xii. 12
Since I did leave the presence of my love, *Am.* lxxxvi. 1
And long *since* ready forth his maske to move, *Epith.* 26
long *since* left Tithones bed, *Epith.* 75
Thy tyred steedes long *since* have need of rest. *Epith.* 284
Love, that long *since* hast to thy mighty powre *H.L.* 1
ever *since* they firmely hath remained, *H.L.* 92
Since thou doest shew no favour *H.L.* 150
they have harbourd *since* their first descent *H.B.* 201
since that loving Lord Commaunded us *H.H.L.* 204

Sincere. with cleane minde, and heart *sincere*, *Gn.* 122
Ne more *sincere* in word and deed profest; IV. xi. 18. 7

Sinew. every *sinew* seene, through his long fast: I. x. 48. 6

Sinews. weighing the . . . shrunken *synewes* of her chosen knight, I. ix. 20. 5
all his *sinewes* woxen weake and raw, I. x. 2. 3
rend his flesh, and his owne *synewes* eat. I. x. 28. 3

Sinful. Caried to heaven, from *sinfull* bondage losed; *Ro.* xix. 12
for disdaine of *sinfull* worlds upbraide *Hub.* 2
through unnoble sloth, or *sinfull* crime, *T.M.* 435
all that lives on face of *sinfull* earth! *Ti.* 44
Loathing this *sinfull* earth and earthlie slime *Ti.* 290
loath this drosse of *sinfull* worlds desire! *Ti.* 686
(since fayre Astraea left The *sinfull* world) *D.* 219
soule assoyld from *sinfull* fleshlinesse. *D.* 259
To *sinfull* hous of Pryde Duessa Guydes I. iv. Arg.
masse of earthly slyme, . . . fild with *sinfull* cryme. I. vii. 9. 9
So oft as he, . . . is to *sinfull* bands made thrall: I. viii. 1. 7
the measure of thy *sinfull* hire I. ix. 46. 3
the dart of *sinfull* guilt the soule dismayes. I. x. 21. 9
sinfull horror workes in wounded hart, I. x. 23. 3
shewes the way his *sinfull* soule to save! I. x. 51. 3
His chosen people, purg'd from *sinful* guilt I. x. 57. 4
guilt of *sinfull* crimes cleane wash away; I. xi. 30. 2
In frayle intemperaunce through *sinfull* bayt; II. vii. 64. 2
To purge away the guilt of *sinfull* crime. II. x. 50. 4
No wretchednesse is like to *sinfull* vellenage. II. xi. 1. 9
The lothfull life, now loosd from *sinfull* bands, II. xi. 46. 3
she was pure from blame of *sinfull* blott; III. ii. 23. 8
His *sinfull* sowle with desperate disdaine III. v. 23. 8
hast shewed to me *sinfull* wight, III. v. 35. 2
Hast drest my *sinfull* wounds? III. v. 35. 9
he clothes with *sinfull* mire, III. vi. 32. 7
Because his *sinfull* lust she would not serve, IV. i. 4. 2
with shamefull spot of *sinfull* lust IV. i. 53. 4
the *sinfull* sowle . . . Was fled to hell, IV. vii. 32. 3
did resort of *sinfull* people shonne, IV. vii. 42. 8
To *sinfull* men with darknes overdight, IV. viii. 34. 2
Offring to him in *sinfull* sacrifice The flesh of men, V. x. 28. 6
Into this *sinfull* world from heaven to send; *Am.* xxiv. 10
Exceeding sweet, yet voyd of *sinfull* vice; *Am.* lxxvii. 9
Above the reach of loathly *sinfull* lust, *H.L.* 179
no man may it see With *sinfull* eyes, *H.B.* 39
sonne . . . Eternall, pure, and voide of *sinfull* blot, *H.H.L.* 32
How then can *sinfull* flesh itselfe assure, *H.H.L.* 97
To heale the sores of *sinfull* soules unsound, *H.H.L.* 166
lampe . . . Thenceforth seemes fowle, and full of *sinfull* blame; *H.H.B.* 276

Sing. most pleasant notes did *sing*, *Bel.*[2] xi. 7
The whiles that I with sacred horror *sing* *Ro.* i. 13
I will *sing* . . . Seven Romane Hils, *Ro.* ii. 13
The silver swanne doth *sing* *Frag.*
A shepheards swaine, saye, did thee *sing* *To his Booke* 9
will I *singe* his laye Of fayre Elisa, *S.C.* Ap. 33
They dauncen deffly, and *singen* soote, *S.C.* Ap. 111
they play, And *sing* all the way, *S.C.* Ap. 107
Tho couth I *sing* of love, *S.C.* Jun. 41
thou were wont on wastfull hylls to *singe*, *S.C.* Jun. 50
never heardest thou but Colin *sing*, *S.C.* Au. 50
sing of bloody Mars, of wars, of giusts; *S.C.* O. 39
if thee please in bigger notes to *sing*, *S.C.* O. 46
Of love and lustihead tho mayst thou *sing*, *S.C.* O. 51
eft did *sing* of warres and deadly drede, *S.C.* O. 59
sing as soote as Swanne. *S.C.* O. 90
when shall it please thee *sing*, *S.C.* N. 1
Now somewhat *sing*, whose endles sovenaunce *S.C.* N. 5
sing of sorrowe and deathes dreeriment; *S.C.* N. 36

Sit—*Continued.*
as ye did *sit* Beside the silver Springs . . . *T.M.* 4
Doth rather choose to *sit* in idle Cell, . . . *T.M.* 221
Like wofull Culvers, doo *sit* wayling now, . . . *T.M.* 246
in the bosome of all blis did *sit*, . . . *T.M.* 308
So to their worke they *sit*, . . . *Mui.* 275
On which the clowde of ghastly night did *sit*, . . . *D.* 305
Twelve Gods doo *sit* around in royall state, . . . *Mui.* 307
Full jolly knight he seemd, and faire did *sitt*, . . . I. i. 1. 8
I warne thee now assured *sitt*, . . . I. ii. 18. 5
pleasaunce each to other makes . . . there as they *sit*; . . . I. ii. 30. 2
Thrise every weeke in ashes she did *sitt*, . . . I. iii. 14. 2
on those . . . eyes of his The clowde of death did *sit*. . . . I. iii. 39. 8
so faire a mould Did on so weake foundation ever *sitt*: . . . I. iv. 5. 4
Such one vile Envy was, that fifte in row did *sitt*. . . . I. iv. 32. 9
Doest thou *sit* wayling by blacke Stygian lake, . . . I. v. 10. 6
Acheron, Where many soules *sit* wailing woefully, . . . I. v. 33. 2
The doubtfull Damzell . . . amazd does *sitt*, . . . I. vi. 12. 3
steed . . . chauft that any on his backe should *sitt*: . . . I. vii. 37. 8
he that high does *sit*, and all things see . . . I. viii. 27. 6
On which they lowly *sitt*, and fitting purpose frame. . . . I. xii. 13. 9
death did *sitt* as sad As lump of lead, . . . II. i. 45. 2
Fast by her side did *sitt* the bold Sansloy, . . . II. ii. 37. 1
No braunch whereon a fine bird did not *sitt*; . . . II. vi. 13. 2
as in glistring glory she did *sitt*, . . . II. vii. 46. 1
Upon her fist the bird . . . Did *sitt*, . . . II. ix. 40. 9
the first did in the forepart *sit*, . . . II. ix. 49. 6
never wight so fast in sell could *sit*, . . . III. iii. 60. 6
all her sisters that with her did *sitt* . . . III. iv. 31. 3
the Nymphes *sitt* all about him rownd, . . . III. iv. 44. 1
sit downe, to rest her faint And wearie limbes . . . III. vii. 10. 4
Troy . . . was reard To *sitt* in second seat of soveraine king . III. ix. 44. 4
To *sit* and rest the walkers wearie shankes: . . . IV. x. 25. 5
To *sit* in his own seate, . . . V. Pr. 10. 8
Goddesse, that doest highest *sit* In seate of judgment. . . . V. Pr. 11. 1
He maketh Kings to *sit* in soverainty; . . . V. ii. 41. 5
to no womans wast . . . it would *sit*, . . . V. iii. 28. 7
where he did *sit* Beholding all that womanish weake fight; . . V. iv. 25. 7
henceforth he oft shall hungry *sit*.' . . . V. iv. 49. 9
Where she might *sit* nigh to the den alone, . . . V. ix. 8. 7
Thus she did *sit* in soverayne Majestie, . . . V. ix. 30. 1
Thus did she *sit* in royall rich estate, . . . V. ix. 33. 1
he besought him downe by him to *sit*, . . . VI. iii. 22. 3
without sword upon his thigh to *sit*: . . . VI. v. 8. 8
adowne They prayd him *sit*, . . . VI. ix. 7. 3
most in Pastorellaes grace did *sit*: . . . VI. ix. 41. 8
Nymphes and Faeries by the bancks did *sit* . . . VI. x. 7. 6
in her soveraine Majesty to *sit*, . . . VI. x. 9. 8
onely mongst the rest by her to *sit*, . . . VI. xi. 8. 3
Where Cynthia did *sit*, that never still did stand. . . . VII. vi. 8. 9
appeare An hundred Graces as in shade to *sit*. . . . *Am.* xl. 4
Where thou doest *sit* in Venus lap above, . . . *H.L.* 24
And *sit* in Gods owne seat without commission; . . . *H.H.L.* 82
There in his bosome Sapience doth *sit*, . . . *H.H.B.* 183
Site. here the place whose plesaunt *syte* . . . *S.C.* Jun. 1
in his costly Bath causd to bee *site*. . . . III. xii. 46. *or.* 4
Sited. It *sited* was in fruitfull soyle of old, . . . III. vi. 31. 1
Sith (*partial list*). *See* **Sithe.**
Sith onely God surmounts all times decay, . . . *Bel.* i. 13
Sith that mine eyes have seene so faire a sight . . . *Bel.* iv. 13
(*sith* the darksome river Of Styx, not passable to soules . *Ro.* xv. 5
Sith that so small so mightie can constraine? . . . *Van.* iii. 14
Sith so small thing his happines may varie. . . . *Van.* viii. 14
Sith nought on earth can chalenge . . . *Van.* xi. 14
Sith that the greatest often are opprest, . . . *Van.* xii. 7
sith their God his good does them send, . . . *S.C.* May 64
sith I heard that Pan with Phoebus strove, . . . *S.C.* Jun. 68
sith theyr soules bene now at rest, . . . *S.C.* Jul. 123
sith thys hyll Thou hast . . . *S.C.* Jul. 231
sith the Saxon king Never was Woolfe seene, . . . *S.C.* S. 151
Sith each with brothers bloudie hand was slaine. . . . *Gn.* 416
sith then we are free borne, . . . *Hub.* 133
'I am most worthie, . . . *sith* I . . . *Hub.* 1027
Sith ignorance our kingdome did confound, . . . *T.M.* 311
Sith none is left to remedie my paine, . . . *T.M.* 423
Sith I no more finde worthie to commend . . . *T.M.* 465
Sith now I am but weedes . . . *Ti.* 42
Sith all that in this world is great . . . *Ti.* 55
Sith I doo dailie see things highest placed, . . . *Ti.* 180
sith she eke did spring Out of his stocke . . . *Ti.* 275
Sith time doth greatest things to ruine bring? . . . *Ti.* 556
Sith morning faire may bring fowle evening . . . *Mui.* 219
sith fairenesse is neglected? . . . *D.* 205
sith she is dead That was the Lady . . . *D.* 318
Sith then they so have ordred, . . . *D.* 369
Sith she that did my vitall powres supplie, . . . *D.* 437
Sith all my sorrow should have end . . . *D.* 446
Sith that my fairest flower is faded quight; . . . *D.* 494
sith daie was overcast, . . . *D.* 556
sith thy Muse . . . Was heard to sound . . . *Col.* 19
Sith thou art come, . . . *Col.* 30
sith I my selfe was there, . . . *Col.* 735
sith her I may not love: . . . *Col.* 940
Sith th' antique glory . . . is therein writ, . . . *Ded. Son.* iii. 6
'but, *sith* that heavens king . . . I. v. 43. 1
Sith cruell fates the carefull threds unfould, . . . I. vii. 22. 5
sith the heavens . . . Have made you master . . . I. viii. 28. 1
'avouchen good, *Sith* to thee is unknowne . . . I. x. 64. 9
Sith none . . . does know . . . II. Pr. 1. 6
Sith Una now he algates must forgoe, . . . II. i. 2. 5

Sith—*Continued.*
Sith that false Traytour did my honour reave?' . . . II. i. 17. 5
Sith her Prince Arthur of proud ornaments . . . spoyld. . . II. i. 22. 6
sith I know your goodly governaunce, . . . II. i. 29. 8
Sith him in Faery court he late avizd; . . . II. i. 31. 6
Sith heven thee deignes to hold . . . II. i. 37. 3
sith this wretched woman overcome Of anguish, . . . II. i. 58. 6
Sith last I left that honorable place, . . . II. ii. 44. 3
Sith his good steed is lately from him gone; . . . II. iii. 3. 2
Sith earst into this forrest wild I came. . . . II. iii. 33. 6
'*sith* thou hast Falne into mischiefe . . . II. iv. 36. 1
sith in might thou didst my mercy prove, . . . II. v. 16. 7
sith for me ye fight, . . . II. vi. 33. 4
sith of late He with Pyrochles sharp debatement made: . . . II. vi. 39. 1
Sith late with him I batteill vaine would boste; . . . II. vi. 50. 6
sith thou hast found favour in mine eye, . . . II. vii. 49. 7
sith of late . . . they rashly did debate. . . . II. viii. 11. 8
'What doe I recke, *sith* that he dide entire? . . . II. viii. 15. 2
Sith wrathfull hand wrought not her owne desire? . . . II. viii. 15. 5
sith his fate so cruelly did fall, . . . II. viii. 52. 7
sith I armes and knighthood first did plight, . . . II. ix. 7. 2
Sith of that Goddesse I have sought the sight, . . . II. ix. 7. 7
Sith now he is far from his monstrous swarme, . . . II. xi. 34. 4
sith warlike armes he bore . . . III. i. 7. 2
sith they warlike armes have laide away, . . . III. ii. 2. 7
sith it is uneath to finde his haunt, . . . III. ii. 16. 2
Sith him whylome in Britayne she did vew, . . . III. ii. 17. 3
Sith a sore evill, which . . . Tormenteth . . . III. iii. 16. 4
'*Sith* then thou knowest all our griefe, . . . III. iii. 21. 1
sith fates can make Way for themselves . . . III. iii. 25. 4
Sith which it had beene here preserv'd . . . III. iii. 60. 4
sith both are bold and blinde? . . . III. iv. 9. 9
Sith other offices . . . They would not graunt— . . . III. iv. 39. 6
sith we no more shall meet!' . . . III. iv. 39. 9
Sith her whilome upon high Pindus hill He loved, . . . III. iv. 41. 4
Sith I her dew reward cannot restore? . . . III. v. 46. 5
Sith that in salvage forests she did dwell, . . . III. vi. 1. 4
Sith brought she was now to so hard constraint, . . . III. vii. 10. 7
sith her dedd He surely dempt, . . . III. viii. 3. 6
'*Sith* then,' (said Braggadochio) . . . III. viii. 18. 1
Sith late mischaunce had her compeld . . . III. viii. 20. 4
sith far in sea we bee, . . . III. viii. 24. 1
tooke he him, yet trembling *sith* of late, . . . III. viii. 36. 4
sith the Sunne now ginnes to slake his beames . . . III. viii. 51. 3
Sith all thy worthie prayses being blent . . . III. ix. 33. 8
sith that men sayne . . . III. ix. 40. 7
sith he n'ote save both, . . . III. x. 15. 7
Sith late he fled from his too earnest foe: . . . III. x. 23. 3
'*Sith* I enjoyd the gentlest Dame alive; . . . III. x. 27. 2
sith the howre that first he did them lett . . . behold, . . . III. x. 34. 8
Sith that more bounteous creature never far'd . . . III. xi. 10. 3
Sith powre of hand, . . . cannot redeeme my deare . . . III. xi. 16. 3
sith none but hee . . . could the same recure . . . III. xii. 34. 6
sith all of loves were fitted. . . . IV. i. 12. 9
Sith she her selfe was of his grace indigne; . . . IV. i. 30. 5
Sith each of them his Ladie had him by, . . . IV. iv. 6. 2
sith meanes, ye see, there wants theretoo. . . . IV. vi. 30. 9
sith this gentle crew Is now so well accorded . . . IV. ix. 40. 4
sith they cannot . . . Comprised be, . . . IV. ix. 41. 8
sith all by lot we hold. . . . IV. x. 4. 9
Sith no lesse famous then the rest they bee, . . . IV. xi. 40. 2
'*Sith* then,' . . . 'ye both the dead deny, . . . V. i. 26. 1
Sith neither force of stones . . . V. ii. 22. 7
'*Sith* thou misdeem'st so much of things . . . V. ii. 39. 3
Sith of things subject to thy daily vew . . . V. ii. 42. 8
sith ye needs' . . . 'will know my shame, . . . V. iv. 28. 6
sith he his faith had plight . . . V. v. 23. 8
sith I thee fostred first, . . . V. v. 29. 4
sith thy juster merit Might . . . bene crowned: . . . V. v. 36. 6
Sith shady dampe had dimd the heavens reach, . . . V. vi. 21. 8
'*sith* ye so well have spide . . . V. vii. 19. 1
sith ye please that both our blames shall die, . . . V. viii. 14. 1
Sith . . . She first was bred, . . . V. x. 1. 7
sith he heard but one that did appeare, . . . V. xi. 2. 8
Sith ye thus farre have tendred my poore case, . . . V. xi. 18. 3
Sith which she hath me ever since abhord, . . . V. xi. 50. 7
Sith no redemption nigh she did nor heare nor see. . . . V. xii. 11. 9
Sith he cannot expresse his simple minde, . . . VI. v. 30. 3
sith we need good counsell,' . . . VI. vi. 13. 8
sith that I did forgive.' . . . VI. vi. 36. 6
Sith he likewise did wrong by him sustaine, . . . VI. vii. 22. 7
sith your fortunes thus dispose, . . . VI. viii. 29. 6
sith I left him last Sewing . . . VI. ix. 2. 2
Sith they know best what is the best for them; . . . VI. ix. 29. 3
Sith each unto himselfe his life may fortunize.' . . . VI. ix. 30. 9
Sith in his powre she was . . . VI. xi. 6. 4
Sith they that were the cause of all were gone: . . . VI. xi. 20. 6
Sith otherwise he could not mend thing past; . . . VI. xi. 34. 7
sith he well knew The readie way . . . VI. xi. 35. 1
sith they twaine Long since had fought . . . VI. xii. 11. 3
which so long *sith* past She . . . had loosely layd . . . VI. xii. 16. 3
Sith shee his Jove and him esteemed nought, . . . VII. vi. 18. 8
sith I needs must follow thy behest, . . . VII. vii. 2. 1
Sith of them all thou art the equall mother, . . . VII. vii. 14. 8
Sith heaven and earth are both alike to thee, . . . VII. vii. 15. 7
sith of wemens labours thou hast charge, . . . *Epith.* 383
Sithe. The woods were heard to waile full many a *sythe*, . . . *Col.* 23
humbly thanked him a thousand *sith* . . . III. x. 33. 3
Sithence. *See* **Since.**
Why have your hands long *sithence* traveiled . . . *Ro.* ix. 5

Sithence—*Continued.*
For *sithens* is but the third morowe . . . *S.C.* Mar. 46
sithens shepheardes bene forsayd . . . *S.C.* Jul. 69
That *sithens* never was abhord . . . *S.C.* Jul. 139
nowe, *sithence* I sawe thy head last, . . . *S.C.* S. 19
Had *sithence* slaine her Lambe most cruellie, . . . *Hub.* 1210
sithens fortunes guile, . . . hath now captived you, . . . I. iv. 51. 1
sithens silence lesseneth not my fire, . . . I. ix. 8. 6
Yet *sithens* helpe, he saw, he needed . . . II. vi. 48. 8
Sithence I loathed have my life to lead, . . . III. ii. 6. 6
'*Sithens* it hath infixed faster hold . . . III. ii. 39. 1
lately tooke, and *sithence* kept as thrall. . . . IV. xii. 32. 5
Great threasure *sithence* we did finde . . . V. iv. 13. 2

Sithes. 'A thousand *sithes* I curse that carefull hower . . . *S.C.* Ja. 49
tenne thousand *sithes* I blesse the stoure . . . *S.C.* Ja. 51

Sits. 'See, where she *sits* upon the grassie greene, . . . *S.C.* Ap. 55
With them it *sits* to care for their heire, . . . *S.C.* May 77
sittes not followe flying fame, . . . *S.C.* Jun. 75
sittes on yonder bancke, . . . *S.C.* Jul. 2
with shepheard *sittes* not playe, . . . *S.C.* S. 232
Before him *sits* the Titmose silent bee; . . . *S.C.* N. 26
where Venus *sittes,* and when. . . . *S.C.* D. 84
there huge Othos *sits* in sad distresse, . . . *Gn.* 373
in her roome unseemly Sorrow *sits,* . . . *T.M.* 184
him beside *sits* ugly Barbarisme, . . . *T.M.* 187
sits in highest seate Of this worlds glorie, . . . *Ti.* 463
All goodly bountie and true honour *sits.* . . . *Ded. Son.* v. 12
With holy father *sits* not with such thinges to mell. . . . I. i. 30. 9
How ill it *sits* with that same silver hed, . . . I. viii. 33. 5
'Then loe! wher bound she *sits,* . . . II. iv. 44. 8
each bird that *sits* on spray, . . . *Am.* xl. 9
My love, . . . ydly *sits;* Beholding me, . . . *Am.* liv. 2
Sits downe to rest him in some shady place, . . . *Am.* lxvii. 3
the Culver, on the bared bough, *Sits* mourning . . . *Am.* lxxxviii. 2
That *sits* upon the righteous throne on hy; . . . *H.H.B.* 151

Sittest. Ne *sittest* downe on that same silver stoole, . . . II. vii. 63. 8
'O soverayne Lord! that *sit'st* on hye . . . III. xi. 9. 2

Sitting. a Woman *sitting* on a beast . . . *Rev.* ii. 1
sitting hye, Upon the Mountaine sayles. . . . *S.C.* Jul. 103
sitting so with bared scalpe, . . . *S.C.* Jul. 221
Sitting upon a hill so hye, . . . *S.C.* Au. 57
sitting all in seates about me round, . . . *Hub.* 25
Sitting one day within his turret hye, . . . *Hub.* 1227
Sitting so cheerlesse at the cheerfull boorde, . . . *U.V.* 5
sitting like a Looker-on Of this worldes Stage, . . . *Com. Son.* i. 2
A Woman *sitting,* sorrowfullie wailing, . . . *Ti.* 9
sitting then around, One of those groomes . . . *Col.* 11
sitting me beside in that same shade, . . . *Col.* 68
her father, *sitting* still on hie, . . . *Col.* 132
sitting high, for lowly she did hate: . . . I. iv. 10. 3
That cursed man, low *sitting* on the ground, . . . I. ix. 35. 2
she *sitting* in an yvory chayre. . . . I. x. 31. 9
One *sitting* ydle on a sunny banck, . . . II. iii. 6. 2
he *sitting* found in secret shade An uncouth . . . wight, . . . II. vii. 3. 3
Gealosy, out of their sight *Sitting* alone, . . . II. vii. 22. 5
sad Celeno, *sitting* on a clifte, . . . II. vii. 23. 6
all *sitting* at his bord; . . . II. x. 66. 7
they *sitting* did espy A daintie damsell . . . II. xii. 14. 7
A seemely Maiden *sitting* by the shore, . . . II. xii. 27. 6
Whom they found *sitting* on a sumptuous bed . . . III. i. 41. 2
sitting downe upon the rocky shore, . . . III. iv. 7. 2
Sitting beside a fountaine in a rew; . . . III. vi. 17. 4
sitting on the flore the Hag she found . . . III. vii. 7. 2
Sitting beside his mother on the ground; . . . III. vii. 13. 3
There she them found all *sitting* round about, . . . IV. ii. 48. 1
Sitting in shade beside his grazing steede; . . . IV. vi. 2. 6
Shee *sitting* by him, as on ground he lay, . . . IV. viii. 4. 1
Sitting in covert shade of arbors sweet, . . . IV. viii. 9. 2
one old woman *sitting* there beside . . . IV. viii. 23. 5
A gentle Faulcon *sitting* on an hill, . . . V. v. 15. 2
Now walking soft, now *sitting* still upright, . . . V. vi. 26. 3
So *sitting* high in dreaded soverayntie, . . . V. ix. 34. 1
Who, *sitting* with his Lady then at bord, . . . VI. iii. 42. 3
Whereas his love was *sitting* all alone, . . . VI. vi. 30. 2
Sitting beside his Ladie there at ease, . . . VI. vi. 40. 2
sitting carelesse on the scorners stoole, . . . VI. viii. 21. 7
sitting downe, her selfe awhile bethought . . . VI. viii. 32. 7
Whom by the Altar he doth *sitting* find . . . VI. viii. 50. 2
Sitting like King of fowles in majesty and powre: . . . VI. x. 6. 9
sitting downe by them upon the greene, . . . VI. xi. 39. 1
Her *sitting* on an Ivory throne shee found, . . . VII. vi. 9. 1
Thus *sitting* in her throne, as I have teld, . . . VII. vii. 13. 5
February, *sitting* In an old wagon, . . . VII. vii. 43. 1

Situate. Where all this worlds pride once was *situate.* . . . *Ro.* xxxi. 2
Whereas the Bowre of Blisse was *situate;* . . . II. xii. 42. 2

Six. SIX VISIONS Do yelde unto thy lorde . . . *Pet.*[1] vii. 2
sixe months greater a great deele; . . . *Ro.* xviii. 8
In *sixe* and thirtie thousand yeares is ronne, . . . *Ro.* xxii. 10
strong advizement of *six* wisards old, . . . I. iv. 12. 8
this was drawne of *six* unequall beasts, . . . I. iv. 18. 1
On which her *six* sage Counsellours did ryde, . . . I. iv. 18. 2
her to serve *sixe* yeares in warlike wize, . . . I. xii. 18. 7
Soone as the terme of those *six* yeares shall cease, . . . I. xii. 19. 7
On which she saw *six* knights, . . . III. i. 20. 8
none of all the *six* before him durst assay. . . . III. i. 21. 9
Badd those same *six* forbeare that single enimy. . . . III. i. 22. 9
'These *six* would me enforce by oddes of might . . . III. i. 24. 2
'Certes,' (said she) 'then beene ye *sixe* to blame, . . . III. i. 25. 1
Then spake one of those *six;* . . . III. i. 26. 1
now there do but two of *six* remaine, . . . III. i. 29. 5

Six—*Continued.*
those *six,* which lately with her fought, . . . III. i. 44. 1
all *sixe* brethren, borne of one parent, . . . III. i. 44. 5
those *sixe* knights, that ladies Champions . . . III. i. 63. 1
one of those *sixe* knights, Gardante hight, . . . III. i. 65. 1
He the *six* Islands . . . Shall to the same reduce, . . . III. iii. 32. 6
Thus marched these *six* couples forth in faire degree. . . . III. xii. 18. 9
at th' one side *sixe* judges were dispos'd, . . . IV. iii. 4. 3
In which his worke he had *sixe* servants prest, . . . IV. v. 36. 1
All *sixe* strong groomes, but one then other more; . . . IV. v. 36. 5
Sixe they were all, all full of fell despight, . . . IV. ix. 20. 3
Bearing his *sixe* deformed heads on hye, . . . IV. xi. 32. 2
those *sixe* sad brethren, like forlorne, . . . IV. xi. 37. 1
Sixe valiant Knights of one faire Nymphe yborne, . . . IV. xi. 37. 3
with him *sixe* knights more, . . . V. iii. 4. 7
All *sixe* well-seene in armes, and prov'd in many a fight. . . . V. iii. 5. 9
Sixe of thy fellowes of the best array, . . . V. iv. 49. 7
which those *six* books compile, . . . *Am.* lxxx. 2

Sixteen. on every syde Twise *sixteene* warders satt, . . . II. ix. 26. 2

Sixth. The *sixt* had charge of them now being dead, . . . I. x. 42. 1
From the fourth howre of night untill the *sixt;* . . . III. xii. 2. 7
is the Virgin, *sixt* in her degree, . . . V. i. 11. 8
The *sixt* was Lansack, a redoubted Knight; . . . V. iii. 5. 8
The *sixt* was August, . . . VII. vii. 37. 1

Skand. *See* Scanned.

Skell. High Swale, unquiet Nide, and troublous *Skell;* . . . IV. xi. 37. 7

Skies. Tombes of her greatnes which did threate the *skies:* . . . *Ro.* iv. 8
high shoote up their heads into the *skyes.* . . . *Gn.* 192
skies and seas doo make most dreadfull warre; . . . *Gn.* 574
yelling shrieks throwne up into the *skies.* . . . *T.M.* 24
Betwixt the centred earth and azure *skies,* . . . *Mui.* 19
pardon that unto the cruell *skies,* . . . *As.* 113
As fairly formd as any star in *skyes;* . . . *As.* 188
In rolling globes up to the vauted *skies.* . . . *Col.* 611
the glooming *skies* Warnd them . . . *Col.* 954
inflames the *skyen* With fire not made to burne, . . . I. iv. 9. 8
with loud plaintes importuneth the *skyes,* . . . I. vi. 6. 4
Like Eyas hauke up mounts unto the *skies,* . . . I. xi. 34. 6
The hell-bred beast threw forth unto the *skies,* . . . I. xi. 40. 3
rend the ratling *skyes* with flames of fouldring heat. . . . II. ii. 20. 9
when they had markt the chaunged *skyes,* . . . II. ii. 46. 8
cleave The flitting *skyes,* like flying Pursuivant, . . . II. viii. 2. 4
as a cloud doth seeme to dim the *skies;* . . . II. ix. 16. 5
borne with ill-disposed *skyes,* . . . II. ix. 52. 8
lift it selfe unto the highest *skyes?* . . . II. x. 1. 5
the raging surges reard Up to the *skyes,* . . . III. xii. 2. 9
Her mantle, colour'd like the starry *skyes,* . . . III. i. 36. 2
He up gan lifte toward the azure *skies,* . . . III. v. 34. 4
To scale the *skyes* and put Jove from his right: . . . III. vii. 47. 5
silver sockets, shyning like the *skyes,* . . . III. viii. 7. 2
with his furious blast . . . *skyes* doth overcast. . . . III. ix. 15. 9
Up to the *skies,* whence first deriv'd it was, . . . V. x. 3. 4
As if they would have rent the brasen *skies.* . . . VI. viii. 40. 4
the *skyes* And all the world beneath for terror quooke, . . . VII. vi. 30. 7
Either with nimble wings to cut the *skies,* . . . *H.H.L.* 66

Skilful. made by his owne *skilfull* hande . . . *Bel.*[1] iv. 10
unfitte to thrust in *skilfull* thronge, . . . *S.C.* N. 27
In *skilfull* knitting of soft silken twyne, . . . *Mui.* 362
Himselfe as *skilfull* in that art as any. . . . *Col.* 75
all in rage to see his *skilfull* might Deluded so, . . . I. ii. 2. 5
many *skilfull* leaches him abide To salve his hurts, . . . I. v. 17. 2
wondrous strong by nature, and by *skilfull* frame. . . . II. ii. 12. 9
passe . . . Their native musicke by her *skilful* art: . . . II. vi. 25. 4
The *skilfull* Palmer formally did frame: . . . II. xii. 81. 5
Artegall in swimming *skilfull* was, . . . V. ii. 16. 6
As when a *skilfull* Marriner doth reed A storme approching . . . V. xii. 18. 5
Ne *skilfull* of the uncouth jeopardy; . . . VI. v. 16. 4
Most happy letters! fram'd by *skilfull* trade, . . . *Am.* lxxiv. 1

Skill. By Magicke *skill* out of eternall night. . . . *Ro.* v. 8
Apelles wit, or Phidias his *skill,* . . . *Ro.* xxix. 6
Ah, foolish old man! I scorne thy *skill,* . . . *S.C.* F. 51
hath he *skill* to make so excellent, . . . *S.C.* Ap. 19
Yet hath so little *skill* to brydle love? . . . *S.C.* Ap. 20
where thou thy *skill* didst showe, . . . *S.C.* Jun. 62
Of Muses, Hobbinol, I conne no *skill,* . . . *S.C.* Jun. 65
hys passing *skil* with him is fledde, . . . *S.C.* Jun. 91
they that con of Muses *skill* . . . *S.C.* Jul. 45
not with *skill* of craftsman polished: . . . *Gn.* 130
Whether shall we professe some trade or *skill,* . . . *Hub.* 117
small *skill* in warre: . . . *Hub.* 200
yet the *skill* thereof I have not loste: . . . *Hub.* 293
little els (God wote) could thereof *skill;* . . . *Hub.* 381
with sweete delight Of Musicks *skill* . . . *Hub.* 756
all the *skill* Of close conveyance, . . . *Hub.* 855
Like as the Foxe did guide his graceles *skill;* . . . *Hub.* 1128
Through the divine infusion of their *skill,* . . . *T.M.* 38
The sectaries of my celestiall *skill,* . . . *T.M.* 73
he that is of reasons *skill* bereft, . . . *T.M.* 139
My part it is and my professed *skill* . . . *T.M.* 151
Mongst simple shepheards they do boast their *skill,* . . . *T.M.* 329
Am put from practise of my kindlie *skill,* . . . *T.M.* 383
Love wont to be schoolmaster of my *skill,* . . . *T.M.* 385
The faithfull service of my learned *skill,* . . . *T.M.* 428
banish me, which do professe the *skill* . . . *T.M.* 521
have no *skill* to rule them right. . . . *T.M.* 551
none might professe . . . that secret *skill;* . . . *T.M.* 560
Some few beside this sacred *skill* esteme, . . . *T.M.* 583
Scorns th' one and th' other in his deeper *skill.* . . . *Ti.* 448
passing farre All Painters *skill,* . . . *Mui.* 91
in her owne *skill* confound, . . . *Mui.* 262

Skill—*Continued.*
in curious *skill* Of workes with loome, . . . *Mui.* 271
To heare the charmes of his enchanting *skill;* . . . *As.* 46
No chace so hard, but he therein had *skill.* . . . *As.* 84
Such *skill,* matcht with such courage as he had, . . . *As.* 85
stand astonisht at his curious *skill,* . . . *Col.* 8
(for well that *skill* he cond;) . . . *Col.* 74
Besides her peerlesse *skill* in making well, . . . *Col.* 188
raise His tunes from laies to matter of more *skill.* . . . *Col.* 395
this *skill,* though knowen yet to few; . . . *Col.* 401
could pipe himselfe, with passing *skill.* . . . *Col.* 443
Not for my *skill,* but for that shepheards sake.' . . . *Col.* 455
those that *skill* of medicine professe, . . . *Col.* 742
with wondrous *skill,* Hast Cupid selfe depainted . . . *Col.* 897
her kindly *skil* To bring forth fruit, . . . I. iii. 28. 7
that divelish yron Engin, . . . framd by Furies *skill,* . . . I. vii. 13. 2
Ne let the man ascribe it to his *skill,* . . . I. x. 1. 6
by her wicked arts and wylie *skill,* . . . I. xii. 32. 6
Too false and strong for earthly *skill* or might, . . . I. xii. 32. 7
apply Her curious *skill* the warbling notes to play, . . . I. xii. 38. 7
transformed from his former *skill,* . . . II. i. 54. 4
hath *skill* them rightly to have chusd, . . . II. ii. 5. 8
through want of *skill,* . . . II. iii. 25. 9
chiefly *skill* to ride seemes a science . . . II. iv. 1. 7
his approved *skill,* to ward, Or strike, . . . II. v. 8. 6
no'te avoyded be by earthly *skill* or powre. . . . II. viii. 43. 9
him in strength and *skill* the Prince surpast, . . . II. viii. 49. 8
goodly order and great workmans *skill* . . . II. ix. 33. 1
most famous hight For *skil* in Musicke . . . II. x. 59. 8
Ne like in grace, ne like in learned *skill;* . . . II. x. 76. 7
their sweet *skill* in wonted melody; . . . II. xii. 31. 7
skill That whilome in divinest wits did rayne, . . . III. Pr. 3. 1
Nought so of love this looser Dame did *skill,* . . . III. i. 50. 1
Whence he indued was with *skill* so merveilous. . . . III. iii. 13. 9
More neede of leach-crafte . . . Then of my *skill:* . . . III. iii. 17. 6
any leaches *skill,* Or other learned meanes, . . . III. iii. 18. 1
indew The salvage minds with *skill* of just and trew: . . . III. iii. 45. 5
Ne ought ye want but *skil,* . . . III. iii. 53. 8
through foresight of his eternall *skill,* . . . III. iv. 25. 6
had learned *skill* In leaches craft, . . . III. iv. 41. 2
hid from the world, and from the *skill* Of Stygian Gods, . . . III. vi. 46. 6
with my power or *skill* I might doe service . . . III. vii. 54. 5
has no *skill* of Court nor courtesie, . . . III. ix. 3. 6
skill his words to frame . . . III. ix. 32. 7
powre of hand, nor *skill* of learned brest, . . . III. xi. 16. 3
O wondrous *skill!* and sweet wit of the man, . . . III. xi. 32. 3
By any ridling *skill,* or commune wit. . . . III. xi. 54. 5
his sisters *skill* unto him lent Most confidence . . . IV. ii. 39. 5
a Fay, and had the *skill* Of secret things, . . . IV. ii. 44. 1
By wondrous *skill* and many hidden wayes . . . IV. ii. 47. 3
Ne lesse his *skill* in weapons did appeare; . . . IV. iii. 7. 4
by secret *skill* With golden foyle doth finely over-spred . . . IV. v. 15. 1
whether it through *skill* or errour were. . . . IV. ix. 11. 7
Cast into sundry shapes by wondrous *skill,* . . . IV. x. 15. 6
which by surpassing *skill* Phidias did make . . . IV. x. 40. 3
In all the *skill* of deeming wrong and right, . . . V. i. 8. 2
So feeble *skill* of perfect things the vulgar has. . . . V. iii. 17. 9
By any *skill* or labour it would sit, . . . V. iii. 28. 7
Whoso upon him selfe will take the *skill* . . . V. iv. 1. 1
(though now it little *skill*) . . . V. iv. 14. 7
The *skill* whereof to Princes hearts he doth reveale, . . . V. vii. 1. 9
She wondred at the workemans passing *skill,* . . . V. vii. 5. 6
through great fury both their *skill* forgot, . . . V. vii. 29. 4
seekes to save the subject of her *skill,* . . . V. x. 2. 6
he had great *skill* in single fight: . . . V. xii. 15. 5
Great *skill* it is such duties timely to bestow. . . . VI. ii. 1. 9
others that have greater *skill* . . . cannot attaine; . . . VI. ii. 2. 5
Ne all the *skill* . . . Can remedy such hurts: . . . VI. vi. 1. 7
Through tempering of her words and lookes by wondrous *skill.* VI. vi. 41. 9
ne thence could be redeemed By any *skill* . . . VI. ix. 11. 8
by natures *skill* Devized to worke delight . . . VI. x. 5. 6
which *skill* men call Civility. . . . VI. x. 23. 9
no *skill* of Leaches art Mote him availe, . . . VI. x. 31. 5
from *skill* of any wight. . . . VI. x. 37. 9
leaves no *skill* nor difference of wight. . . . VI. xi. 16. 9
Renowmed hath with hymnes fit for a rurall *skill.* . . . VII. vi. 36. 9
Do thou my weaker wit with *skill* inspire, . . . VII. vii. 2. 2
That, some do say, was so by *skill* devized, . . . VII. vii. 6. 1
by their idle *skill* Are wont . . . to fashion; . . . VII. vii. 8. 3
to amaze weake mens confused *skil,* . . . *Am.* xvii. 2
Of natures *skill* the onely complement; . . . *Am.* xxiv. 3
her great triumph, which my *skill* exceeds, . . . *Am.* xxix. 11
with sly *skill* so cunningly them dresses, . . . *Am.* xxxvii. 3
my rude musick, . . . cannot, with any *skill,* . . . *Am.* xxxviii. 6
she may it mend with *skill:* . . . *Am.* xli. 3
No *skill* can stint, nor reason can aslake. . . . *Am.* xliv. 8
my lyfes Leach! doe your *skill* reveale; . . . *Am.* l. 13
they that *skill* not of so heavenly matter, . . . *Am.* lxxxiv. 5
Thereof he fashions in his higher *skill* . . . *H.B.* 221
Yet form'd by wondrous *skill,* and by His might, . . . *H.H.L.* 107
With heavenly thoughts farre above humane *skil,* . . . *H.H.L.* 282
Ne could that Painter . . . Have purtrayd this, for all his
    maistring *skill;* . . . *H.H.B.* 214

Skilled. *See* **Well-skilled.**
Corinth *skil'd* in curious workes to grave; . . . *Ro.* xxix. 4
I that in true Tragedies am *skild,* . . . *T.M.* 165
Nor anie *skil'd* in workmanship embost, . . . *Mui.* 365
Nor anie *skil'd* in loupes of fingring fine, . . . *Mui.* 366
Elfinor, who was in magicke *skild;* . . . II. x. 73. 7
throughly *skild* in use of shield and speare; . . . IV. iii. 7. 2

Skilled—*Continued.*
A Painim knight that well in armes was *skild,* . . . IV. iv. 17. 7
Let them record them that are better *skild,* . . . IV. xi. 17. 5
to her he seem'd best *skild* in righteous lore. . . . V. i. 4. 9
both were *skild* in that experiment, . . . V. ii. 17. 3
The fift Armeddan, *skild* in lovely layes; . . . V. iii. 5. 7
better *skild* in Tilt and Turnament, . . . V. viii. 7. 7
his young charge whereof he *skilled* nought, . . . VI. iv. 38. 2
They, that in course of heavenly spheares are *skild,* . . . *Am.* lx. 1

Skim. were wount To *skim* those coastes . . . VI. xi. 9. 3

Skin. We han great Bandogs will teare their *skinne.* . . . *S.C.* S. 163
his *skinne,* the terror of the wood, . . . *Hub.* 969
at the Lyons *skin* he inly quooke; . . . *Hub.* 1060
on his backe the *skin* he did, . . . *Hub.* 1062
Thinke him Alcides with the Lyons *skin,* . . . *Mui.* 71
scarce the *skin* the strong contagion helde. . . . *Mui.* 256
next her wrinkled *skin* rough sackecloth wore, . . . I. iii. 14. 3
Her wrizled *skin,* . . . So scabby was . . . I. viii. 47. 8
Close creeping twixt the marow and the *skin:* . . . I. x. 25. 5
pierced to the *skin,* but bit no more; . . . II. viii. 44. 8
skin all withered like a dryed rooke; . . . II. xi. 22. 3
hid no whit her alablaster *skin,* . . . II. xii. 77. 5
staynes his snowy *skin* with hatefull hew: . . . III. i. 38. 6
lightly rased her soft silken *skin,* . . . III. i. 65. 7
deckt the azure field with her fayre pouldred *skin.* . . . III. ii. 25. 9
looke on her faire face and marke her snowy *skin.* . . . III. viii. 24. 9
ragged weed Made of Beares *skin,* . . . III. xii. 11. 2
dyde . . . red her *skin* all snowy cleene. . . . III. xii. 20. 9
a Snake, . . . Casts off his ragged *skin* . . . IV. iii. 23. 9
His Lyons *skin* chaungd to a pall of gold, . . . V. v. 24. 7
For his loves sake his Lions *skin* undight; . . . V. viii. 2. 5
Him in Deares *skin* to clad; . . . VII. vi. 50. 8
him . . . With a Deeres-*skin* they covered, . . . VII. vi. 52. 2

Skip. faire sun-shine, that makes all *skip* and daunce; . . . VII. vii. 23. 4

Skippet. By whom a little *skippet* floting did appeare. . . . II. xii. 14. 9

Skirmishes. Such cruell game my *scarmoges* disarmes. . . . II. vi. 34. 5

Skirmishing. troupe of Knights . . . together *skirmishing,* IV. ix. 20. 2

Skirt. all the *skirt* about Was hemd with golden fringe. . . . II. iii. 26. 8
skirt with gold Was fretted all about, . . . II. ix. 37. 1

Skirts. *skirts* were bordred with bright sunny beames, . . . V. ix. 28. 6

Skull. to the *scull* a yawning wound it made: . . . I. xi. 35. 8
an Helmet light, Made of a dead mans *skull,* . . . II. xi. 22. 9
A villaine to them came with *scull* all raw, . . . V. ii. 11. 5

Skulls. underneath their feet, all scattered lay Dead *sculls* . . . I. iv. 36. 9
all the grownd with *sculs* was scattered, . . . II. vii. 30. 6

Sky. no more see faire thing under *sky,* . . . *Bel.*[2] iv. 12
Waving aloft with triple point to *skie,* . . . *Bel.*[2] xi. 2
The *skie* eachwhere did show full bright . . . *Pet.* ii. 5
The *skie* gan everie where to overcast, . . . *Pet.* iii. 9
Triumphant Arcks, spyres, neighbours to the *skie,* . . . *Ro.* vii. 5
Heapt hils on hils to scale the starrie *skie,* . . . *Ro.* xii. 2
Tossing huge tempests through the troubled *skie,* . . . *Ro.* xvi. 6
The antique pride which menaced the *skie,* . . . *Ro.* xxvii. 2
Upon whose toppe . . . all the *skie* doth leane; . . . *S.C.* Jul. 62
Alsoone may shepheard clymbe to *skye* . . . *S.C.* Jul. 101
smoke, that sheddeth in the *skye;* . . . *S.C.* O. 35
Would rayse ones mynd above the starry *skie,* . . . *S.C.* O. 94
Betwixt the forrest wide and starrie *sky:* . . . *Gn.* 34
Drawing in teemes along the starrie *skie;* . . . *Gn.* 458
The *skie,* in pieces seeming to be rent, . . . *Gn.* 581
they began to threat the neighbour *sky;* . . . *Hub.* 1174
Most miserable creature under *sky* . . . *T.M.* 127
Above the compasse of the arched *skie;* . . . *T.M.* 370
From hence wee mount aloft unto the *skie,* . . . *T.M.* 505
loathing earth, I looke up to the *sky,* . . . *T.M.* 527
Upreard her buildinges to the threatned *skie:* . . . *Com. Son.* iv. 2
with brave plumes doth beate the azure *skie,* . . . *Ti.* 423
The Arke did beare with him above the *skie,* . . . *Ti.* 668
To mount aloft unto the Cristall *skie,* . . . *Mui.* 44
To raine in th' aire from th' earth to highest *skie,* . . . *Mui.* 212
having overrun The compast *skie,* . . . *D.* 25
Stella the faire, the fairest star in *skie,* . . . *As.* 55
Under what *skie,* or in what world we were, . . . *Col.* 230
better shepheards be not under *skie,* . . . *Col.* 377
yet there be the fairest under *skie,* . . . *Col.* 557
From flocks and fields, to angels and to *skie.'* . . . *Col.* 619
With praiers lowd importuning the *skie,* . . . *Col.* 880
Seemd in their song to scorne the cruell *sky.* . . . I. i. 8. 4
faire Hesperus in highest *skie* Had spent his lampe, . . . I. ii. 6. 6
purest *skye* with brightnesse they dismaid: . . . I. iv. 4. 5
night had all displayd Her coleblacke curtein over brightest
    skye; . . . I. iv. 44. 2
Then gan her beautie shyne as brighest *skye,* . . . I. vi. 4. 8
with his tallnesse seemd to threat the *skye;* . . . I. vii. 8. 5
'O great Orgoglio! greatest under *skye,* . . . I. vii. 14. 5
thou, O fayrest Princesse under *sky!* . . . II. Pr. 4. 6
The great earthes wombe they open to the *sky,* . . . II. i. 60. 2
Vaine-glorious man . . . is lifted up to *skye;* . . . II. iii. 10. 4
Cleare as the *skye,* . . . II. iii. 22. 3
'O fairest under *skie!* . . . II. iii. 38. 1
Weening it had beene thunder in the *skye,* . . . II. iii. 45. 7
More swift then swallow sheres the liquid *skye,* . . . II. vi. 5. 2
Great Mammon, greatest god below the *skye,* . . . II. vii. 8. 2
Of every sort and nation under *skye,* . . . II. vii. 44. 2
The fairest wight that wonneth under *skie,* . . . II. vii. 49. 2
'Most cursed of all creatures under *skye,* . . . II. vii. 59. 4
Two Paynim knights al armd as bright as *skie,* . . . II. viii. 10. 2
Defaste the beautie of the shyning *skye,* . . . III. ii. 28. 2
neither God of love nor God of *skye* . . . III. ii. 36. 7
Emongst th' eternall spheres and lamping *sky,* . . . III. iii. 1. 3

Sky—*Continued.*
could call out of the *sky* Both Sunne and Moone, . . . III. iii. 12. 1
vauted all within, like to the *Skye,* . . . III. iv. 43. 4
When so the froward *skye* began to lowre; . . . III. v. 51. 7
Reeking aloft uprolled to the *sky:* . . . III. vii. 5. 3
th' ayre was milde and cleared was the *skie,* . . . III. viii. 21. 5
angry Gods and cruell *skie* . . . III. ix. 33. 4
doe thinke it threates the *skye* . . . III. ix. 45. 9
Like as the shining *skie* in summers night, . . . IV. i. 13. 6
it all the *skie* doth overcast With darknes dred, . . . IV. i. 45. 8
Ne chaunged was into a starre in *sky;* . . . IV. iii. 13. 5
As thicke as hayle forth poured from the *skie:* . . . IV. iii. 25. 5
As Jove will have advaunced to the *skie,* . . . IV. iii. 44. 2
A watry cloud doth overcast the *skie,* . . . IV. iv. 47. 7
Like as the lightning brond from riven *skie,* . . . IV. vi. 14. 1
seem'd his shrikes would rend the brasen *skie:* . . . IV. viii. 38. 5
She were as faire as any under *skie:* . . . IV. viii. 49. 7
Like to a storme which hovers under *skie,* . . . IV. ix. 33. 4
under *skie* Doest fayrest shine, . . . IV. x. 44. 2
Long Rhodanus, whose sourse springs from the *skie;* . . . IV. xi. 20. 4
also those which wonne in th' azure *sky:* . . . IV. xii. 1. 4
These towring rocks, which reach unto the *skie,* . . . V. ii. 38. 3
As when two sunnes appeare in the azure *skye,* . . . V. iii. 19. 1
as any Princesse under *sky,* . . . V. viii. 18. 7
seemed to outshine the dimmed *skye,* . . . V. ix. 21. 8
furthest from the *skie* And from the earth, . . . VI. vi. 11. 2
No more then lightening from the lofty *sky:* . . . VI. viii. 8. 6
'Sunne of the world, great glory of the *sky,* . . . VI. x. 28. 1
till light the *sky* forsooke . . . VI. xi. 40. 9
in th' highest *sky,* Was placed in his principall Estate, . . . VII. vi. 19. 3
through the purest *sky* . . . cast to ascend, . . . VII. vi. 23. 7
chalenge th' heritage of this our *skie;* . . . VII. vi. 30. 3
Did ring againe, and loud re-eccho to the *skie* . . . VII. vi. 52. 9
Unlesse the kingdome of the *sky* yee make Immortall . . . VII. vii. 54. 2
Onely the starry *skie* doth still remaine: . . . VII. vii. 55. 5
her faire face she reares up to the *skie,* . . . *Am.* xiii. 2
needs another Element . . . that is, the *skye* . . . *Am.* lv. 10
In mind to mount up to the purest *sky;* . . . *Am.* lxxii. 2
suffrest neyther gods in *sky,* Nor men in earth, to rest: . . . *Epig.* iv. 15
On golden plumes up to the purest *skie,* . . . *H.L.* 178
Being a parcell of the purest *skie* . . . *H.B.* 105
To contemplation of th' immortall *sky;* . . . *H.H.B.* 25
The house of blessed God, which men call *Skye,* . . . *H.H.B.* 52
And menageth the ever-moving *sky,* . . . *H.H.B.* 194
Of Gods high praise, that filles the brasen *sky;* . . . *H.H.B.* 263
through the *Skie* draw Venus silver Teeme; . . . *Proth.* 63

Sky-ruling. 'They are the daughters of *sky-ruling* Jove, . . . VI. x. 22. 1

Sky-threating. their *sky-threating* towres Raced . . . V. x. 23. 4

Slack. silver bowe, which was but *slacke,* . . . *S.C.* Mar. 83
it forst him *slacke* His grasping hold, . . . I. i. 20. 4
thick entangled knots adown does *slack,* . . . I. xi. 11. 4
yield he would not, nor his rancor *slack* . . . II. iv. 14. 6
when they spyde the knight to *slacke* his pace . . . II. xii. 68. 4
woxe halfe wroth against her damzels *slacke,* . . . III. vi. 19. 3
Nor wearinesse to *slack* her hast, . . . III. vii. 2. 4
slacke attendaunce unto straungers call . . . III. ix. 18. 7
slack her threatfull hand for daungers dout: . . . III. xii. 37. 4
cruell sword out of his fingers *slacke* Fell downe . . . IV. vi. 21. 5
neither would their fiendlike fury *slacke,* . . . IV. ix. 25. 5
Ne ever Artegall his griple strong . . . wold *slacke,* . . . V. ii. 14. 9
Somewhat to *slacke* the rigour of my flame? . . . *H.L.* 152

Slacked. Has somewhat *slackt* the tenor of thy string, . . . *S.C.* O. 50

Slain. with his shepe-hooke hath him *slayne* . . . *S.C.* Au. 34
Lowder had be *slaine* thilke same even . . . *S.C.* S. 225
she halfe frantick, having *slaine* her sonne, . . . *Gn.* 175
when he saw him *slaine* himselfe he cheard . . . *Gn.* 312
each with brothers bloudie hand was *slaine* . . . *Gn.* 416
All *slaine* with darts, lie wallowed in their blood . . . *Gn.* 432
slaine her Lambe most cruellie, . . . *Hub.* 1210
with thunder bolts he had him *slaine,* . . . *Hub.* 1236
had been *slaine* to serve the Apes beheasts: . . . *Hub.* 1308
when ye heare that I am dead or *slaine,* . . . *D.* 523
His foes have *slaine* themselves, . . . I. i. 26. 9
He thought have *slaine* her in his fierce despight; . . . I. i. 50. 3
he . . . would have *slaine* them . . . I. ii. 5. 8
My dearest Lord . . . cruelly was *slaine;* . . . I. ii. 23. 9
'O! leave her soone, or let her soone be *slaine."* . . . I. ii. 39. 3
finding Kirkrapine there *slayne,* . . . I. iii. 22. 3
rending up his helmet, would Have *slayne* him streight; . . . I. iii. 38. 3
when the shamed shield of *slaine* Sansfoy He spide . . . I. iv. 39. 1
who through guile hath *slayn* The prowest knight . . . I. iv. 41. 6
his heavie hand . . . Him to have *slaine;* . . . I. v. 13. 6
the Redcrosse knight was *slain* with Paynim knife.' . . . I. vi. 38. 9
vaunt That good knight of the Redcrosse to have *slain:* . . . I. vi. 41. 4
Him thought at first encounter to have *slaine* . . . I. viii. 7. 5
weapon . . . that heaved was on hye For to have *slain* the man, . . . I. viii. 19. 9
innocents trew, Which there were *slaine* . . . I. viii. 35. 7
Guyon . . . Fyndes Mordant and Amavia *slaine* . . . II. i. Arg.
Had *slayne* Sir Mordant and his Lady bright: . . . II. iii. 13. 8
The crowned often *slaine,* the slayer cround; . . . II. vii. 13. 5
knights *slaine* that have us sought to save.' . . . II. ix. 12. 9
of him was *slaine* anon . . . II. x. 11. 9
the king was by a Treachetour Disguised *slaine,* . . . II. x. 51. 4
in the chace was *slaine* of them that fled, . . . II. x. 57. 3
shortly was by Coyll in batteill *slaine:* . . . II. x. 58. 5
flying from his guilt, by them was *slayne;* . . . II. x. 67. 5
Full litle wanted but he had him *slaine,* . . . II. xi. 29. 6
Till both the sonnes of Edwin he have *slayne,* . . . III. iii. 37. 2
Both *slaine* in battaile upon Layburne playne, . . . III. iii. 37. 4
she had him surely *slayne:* . . . III. iii. 55. 8

Slain—*Continued.*
how Camill' hath *slaine* The huge Orsilochus, . . . III. iv. 2. 8
of a forreine foe He is *yslaine,* . . . III. v. 9. 9
'Five daies there be since he (they say) was *slaine,* . . . III. v. 10. 1
dronke with blood of men *slaine* by his might, . . . III. vii. 47. 7
in his rage his mother would have *slaine,* . . . III. viii. 4. 2
finding not th' Hyena to be *slayne,* . . . III. viii. 44. 4
The rivall *slaine,* the victour, . . . Escaped hardly, . . . III. ix. 42. 8
Whom having *slain* through luckles arrowes glaunce, . . . III. ix. 48. 3
next stroke him should have *slaine,* . . . III. xii. 34. 2
Nations captived, and huge armies *slaine:* . . . IV. i. 21. 8
He for revenge had guiltlesse Glauce *slaine:* . . . IV. i. 52. 4
Seaven women by him *slaine,* and eaten clene: . . . IV. vii. 13. 5
Corflambo chaseth Placidas, And is by Arthure *slaine* . . . IV. viii. Arg.
vow by Mahoune that he should be *slaine* . . . IV. viii. 44. 3
howld aloud to see his Lord there *slaine,* . . . IV. viii. 46. 4
'This mightie man,' (quoth he) 'whom you have *slaine,* . . . IV. viii. 47. 1
his mortall part by great mischance Was *slaine;* . . . IV. xi. 16. 8
offred streight the Lady to be *slaine;* . . . V. i. 27. 2
About that wofull couple which were *slaine,* . . . V. iii. 31. 2
To have him *slaine,* or dearely doen aby: . . . V. iii. 36. 4
The eldest of the which was *slaine* erewhile . . . V. vi. 33. 4
therefore ment him surely to have *slaine:* . . . V. vi. 34. 5
by thee *slaine,* and murdred by thy slight.' . . . V. vi. 37. 9
Even the bloud of Gyants, which were *slaine* . . . V. vii. 10. 4
Which late her folke had *slaine,* . . . V. vii. 25. 9
slaine her children ruefully, alas! . . . V. x. 6. 9
Them to have stricken, and thrise to have *slaine* . . . V. xi. 14. 4
sure he had her *slaine,* had she not turnd her way . . . V. xi. 26. 9
ere they all were *slaine,* . . . V. xii. 9. 2
Murdred my men, and *slaine* my Seneschall, . . . VI. i. 25. 3
Having late *slaine* her Seneschall in fight, . . . VI. i. 29. 8
In blood of knight, the which by thee is *slaine,* . . . VI. ii. 7. 4
this knight, who there lyes *slaine,* . . . VI. ii. 9. 8
The cause of all this evill, who was *slaine* . . . VI. iii. 17. 2
Thought therewithall forthwith him to have *slaine;* . . . VI. v. 26. 7
when on ground they saw their fellow *slaine,* . . . VI. vi. 23. 1
As if they would have *slaine* them presently: . . . VI. vi. 23. 5
Hast *slaine* my men in this unmanly maner, . . . VI. vi. 25. 2
whom sure he thought By this quite *slaine* . . . VI. vi. 37. 7
slaughtred bodies which his hand had *slaine,* . . . VI. vi. 38. 2
Slayne of that errant knight . . . VI. vii. 16. 7
Where he himselfe might see his foeman *slaine;* . . . VI. vii. 17. 3
sib to great Orgolio, which was *slaine* By Arthure, . . . VI. vii. 41. 8
Else had he surely there bene *slaine,* . . . VI. vii. 45. 9
then surely thought That *slaine* he was, . . . VI. vii. 50. 3
Slay not that Carle, though worthy to be *slaine,* . . . VI. viii. 17. 7
Whilest Melibee is *slaine:* . . . VI. xi. Arg.
Old Meliboe is *slaine;* . . . VI. xi. 18. 4
He at the length was *slaine* . . . VI. xi. 19. 6
How many of their friends were *slaine,* . . . VI. xi. 20. 9
Were by them *slaine* by generall consent: . . . VI. xi. 31. 5
that he were present there When she was *slaine,* . . . VI. xi. 33. 9
Pastorell, were she alive or *slaine:* . . . VI. xi. 39. 4
sure I had bene *slayne;* . . . *Am.* xvi. 13

Slake. *slake* the winters sorowe . . . *S.C.* Mar. 6
lightly *slake* The flames which love . . . *S.C.* Jun. 85
doest thy forces *slake* To after-send his foe, . . . I. v. 10. 8
slake the heavenly fire . . . I. v. 40. 9
Ne ever will their fervent fury *slake,* . . . I. ix. 8. 3
To *slake* your wrath, and mollify your mind' . . . III. ii. 13. 4
Ne *slake* the fury of her cruell flame, . . . III. ii. 52. 2
their labour not to *slake* . . . III. iii. 10. 9
will hevens fury never *slake,* . . . III. iii. 43. 5
all that might not *slake* her sensuall desyre: . . . III. vii. 49. 9
sith the Sunne now ginnes to *slake* his beames . . . III. viii. 51. 3
Shewing desire her inward flame to *slake* . . . III. ix. 31. 4
to *slake* his scalding smart; . . . III. xi. 30. 4
None but a God or godlike man can *slake;* . . . IV. ii. 1. 6
she his fury willed him to *slake:* . . . V. vii. 36. 7
However loth he were his way to *slake,* . . . V. viii. 5. 8
asswage Their forces furie, and their terror *slake;* . . . V. xii. 8. 4
nought mote *slake* Their greedy vengeaunces . . . VI. i. 37. 5

Slaked. when fervent sorrow *slaked* was, She up arose, . . . I. vii. 28. 1
they *slaked* had the fervent heat Of appetite . . . III. i. 52. 1
Soone as the cruell flames *yslaked* were, . . . III. x. 17. 1
when they had their hunger *slaked* well, . . . VI. ix. 18. 1

Slander. seeke with *slaunder* his good name to blot; . . . *Hub.* 1219
Sclaunder her guests doth staine: . . . IV. viii. Arg.
Her name men *Sclaunder* call . . . IV. viii. 24. 9
That shamefull Hag, the *slaunder* of her sexe, . . . IV. viii. 35. 2

Slandering. by *slaundring* his well-deemed name, . . . *Col.* 695

Slanderous. *Slaunderous* reproches, and fowle infamies . . . II. xi. 10. 6

Slanderously. How to deprave and *slaunderously* upbrayd, . . . V. xii. 34. 3

Slanders. wicked *sclaunders* by him shed . . . V. ix. 26. 9
To her, that so false *sclaunders* at him threw: . . . V. xii. 42. 5

Slaney. The sandy *Slane,* the stony Aubrian, . . . IV. xi. 41. 2

Slashing. Hewing and *slashing* at their idle shades; . . . II. ix. 15. 8
Hewing and *slashing* shields and helmets bright, . . . IV. iv. 41. 6

Slaughter. Mow'd downe themselves with *slaughter* mercilesse; . . . *Ro.* x. 12
prizde with *slaughter* of their Generall; . . . *Ti.* 116
To *slaughter* them, and worke their finall bale, . . . *As.* 105
From *slaughter* of the Giaunts conquered; . . . III. ix. 22. 2
he left the bloudy *slaughter* In which he swam, . . . V. iv. 41. 2
There then a piteous *slaughter* did begin; . . . V. vii. 35. 5
Sought onely *slaughter* and avengement; . . . V. viii. 30. 5
Commaunded him from *slaughter* to recoyle, . . . V. xi. 65. 7
glad he was the *slaughter* so to stay; . . . V. xii. 9. 6
To stay their cruell hands from *slaughter* fell, . . . VI. xi. 20. 5

Slaughtered. the heapes . . . Of *slaughtred* carkasses, . . . V. vii. 36. 5

Slaughtered—*Continued.*
through fell tyranny He *slaughtred* had, . . . V. viii. 28. 8
With *slaughtred* bodies which his hand had slaine, . . . VI. vi. 38. 2
Slaughter's. not for such *slaughters* sake He thether came, . . V. xii. 8. 7
Slave. *See* **Bondslave.**
them to have my selfe, and be their servile *sclave.*' . . . II. vii. 33. 9
So hard it is to be a womans *slave.* . . . V. v. 23. 5
Slavered. as she spake therewith she *slavered;* . . . V. xii. 29. 8
Slaves. The vassals of Gods wrath, and *slaves* of sin. . . . *T.M.* 126
For *slaves* to sell them for no small reward . . . VI. x. 43. 4
Arrived . . . T' inquire for *slaves;* . . . VI. xi. 9. 6
streight the *slaves* should forth be called, . . . VI. xi. 10. 8
Slay. Joinyng their force to *slea* the faithfull man. . . . *Rev.* iii. 12
With bitter woundes her owne deere babes to *slay,* . . . *Gn.* 399
The Conquerour nought cared him to *slay;* . . . II. viii. 51. 2
conquered, and cruelly did *slay.* . . . II. x. 10. 9
hardy Nennius, whom he yet did *slay,* . . . II. x. 49. 4
For perdy one shall other *slay,* or daunt: . . . III. ii. 16. 5
him shall *slay,* and on a gallowes bleak . . . III. iii. 36. 5
secretly his enemies did *slay:* . . . IV. viii. 39. 6
those which he did wound and *slay,* . . . V. v. 19. 6
They *slay* the Soudan, . . . V. viii. Arg.
her sacred selfe to *slay:* . . . V. viii. 19. 4
that proud Souldan whom he earst did *slay.* . . . V. viii. 51. 7
as he pressed in, him there did *slay:* . . . V. x. 36. 7
Prince Arthure . . . Doth *slay* the Monster, . . . V. xi. Arg.
To save her selfe, least that he did her *slay;* . . . V. xi. 26. 8
'Ah mercie, Sir! doe me not *slay,* . . . VI. i. 39. 8
sees young Tristram *slay* A proud discourteous knight: . . . VI. ii. Arg.
this was he whom Tristram earst did *slay,* . . . VI. ii. 45. 3
Regarding neither speare that mote him *slay,* . . . VI. iv. 6. 4
with many a wound Did *slay* againe, . . . VI. vii. 16. 9
Slay not that Carle, though worthy to be slaine, . . . VI. viii. 17. 7
Till I have sav'd so many as I earst did *slay.*' . . . VI. viii. 22. 9
Whether to *slay* her there upon the place, . . . VI. viii. 37. 7
an altar shortly they erected To *slay* her on. . . . VI. viii. 44. 4
would not so them *slay,* . . . VI. xi. 38. 8
all that nere him came did hew and *slay,* . . . VI. xi. 49. 4
to *slay* he would have sought.) . . . VI. xii. 6. 7
all that are of others bredd doth *slay;* . . . VII. vii. 24. 7
whylst her bloody hands them *slay,* . . . *Am.* xlvii. 9
Slayer. The crowned often slaine, the *slayer* cround; . . . II. vii. 13. 5
Slayeth. fights, And *slaieth* him in field. . . . V. xii. Arg.
Slaying. his title justifide by might, *Slaying* Traherne, . . . II. x. 60. 7
how litle glory ye have gayned By *slaying* him, . . . *Am.* xxxvi. 11
In *slaying* him that would live gladly yours! . . . *Am.* lvii. 12
Slays. Arthure . . . *slayes* the Gyaunt, . . . I. viii. Arg.
Does with the Pagan fight: Him *slaies,* . . . V. ii. Arg.
either both them drownes, or trayterously *slaies.* . . . V. ii. 8. 9
She fights with Radigund, her *slaies,* . . . V. vii. Arg.
Gerioneos Seneschall He *slayes* in Belges right. . . . V. x. Arg.
Slea. *See* **Slay.**
Sledge. With his great yron *sledge* doth strongly on it beat. . V. v. 7. 9
with his heavy *sledge* he can it beat, . . . *Am.* xxxii. 3
Sledges. on his shield like yron *sledges* bet: . . . II. ii. 22. 4
Sleep. *See* **Asleep.**
In the forgetfulnes of *sleepe* (*slepe*[1]) . . . *Bel.* i. 3
a noyse alluring *sleepe* (*slepe*[1]) . . . *Bel.* xii. 7
whiles that my daylie cares did *sleepe,* . . . *Van.* i. 1
They *sleepen* in rest, . . . *S.C.* May 68
debarres myne eyes from *sleepe.* . . . *S.C.* Au. 162
'Let stremes of teares supply the place of *sleepe;* . . . *S.C.* Au. 163
till my last *sleepe* Doe close mine eyes: . . . *S.C.* Au. 170
when nature craveth *sleepe,* . . . *S.C.* Au. 177
spends her time of *sleepe* In songs . . . *S.C.* Au. 184
Let breake your sounder *sleepe,* . . . *S.C.* Au. 191
When the good old man used to *sleepe.* . . . *S.C.* S. 189
the shepheard would breake his *sleepe,* . . . *S.C.* S. 193
sleepe, as some doen, all the long day; . . . *S.C.* S. 233
thou in *sleepe* art dead. . . . *S.C.* O. 6
Relieve thy Oaten pypes that *sleepen* long. . . . *S.C.* N. 24
wont to worke eternall *sleepe.* . . . *S.C.* D. 90
Unto sweete *sleepe* he may securely lend . . . *Gn.* 142
gentle slumbring *sleep* oppressed him . . . *Gn.* 239
His dearest life did trust to careles *sleep;* . . . *Gn.* 243
so soone as lighter *sleepe* Was entered, . . . *Gn.* 321
Thy careles limbs in loose *sleep* dost display. . . . *Gn.* 336
seeing kindly *sleep* refuse to doe His office, . . . *Hub.* 21
when all shrowded were In careles *sleep,* . . . *Hub.* 334
With that he causeth *sleep* to seize the eyes, . . . *Hub.* 1295
Waking Love suffereth no *sleepe:* . . . *U.V.* 10
in watch . . . If cause requir'd, or els in *sleepe,* . . . *D.* 130
Shee would all night by mee or watch or *sleepe* . . . *D.* 131
evermore when I did *sleepe* or play, . . . *D.* 132
as if to *sleepe* she went, . . . *D.* 256
sleepe (the harbenger of wearie wights) . . . *D.* 470
Sweet slombring deaw, the which to *sleep* them biddes. . . . I. i. 36. 4
when all drownd in deadly *sleepe* he findes, . . . I. i. 36. 6
Care . . . Who oft is wont to trouble gentle *Sleepe.* . . . I. i. 40. 6
'Love of your selfe,' . . . Lets me not *sleepe,* . . . I. i. 53. 2
you in carelesse *sleepe* are drowned quight.' . . . I. i. 53. 4
unhappy Swaine, That here wex old in *sleepe,* . . . I. ii. 4. 7
every creature shrowded is in *sleepe.* . . . I. iii. 15. 2
all in deadly *sleepe* did drowned lye . . . I. iii. 16. 3
Still drownd in *sleepe,* and most of his daies dedd: . . . I. iv. 19. 4
Did chace away sweet *sleepe* from sluggish eye, . . . I. iv. 44. 4
the stout Sansjoy doth *sleepe* in deadly shade. . . . I. v. 22. 9
downe to *sleepe* me layd, . . . I. ix. 13. 2
layes the soule to *sleepe* in quiet grave? . . . I. ix. 40. 7
Sleepe after toyle, port after stormie seas, . . . I. ix. 40. 8

Sleep—*Continued.*
sleepe never he so sownd; . . . I. xi. 6. 8
slyding soft, as downe to *sleepe* her layd, . . . II. i. 56. 3
bid them *sleepe* in everlasting peace. . . . II. i. 60. 6
did beguyle their eyes Of kindly *sleepe* . . . II. ii. 46. 7
Sometimes he falsely faines himselfe to *sleepe,* . . . II. v. 34. 4
In slouthfull *sleepe* his molten hart to steme, . . . II. vi. 27. 5
Ne would he suffer *Sleepe* . . . II. vii. 25. 5
next to death is *Sleepe* to be compard; . . . II. vii. 25. 7
Here *Sleep,* ther Richesse, and Hel-gate them both betwext. . II. vii. 25. 9
sleepe his eie-strings did untye, . . . II. vii. 27. 4
weake and wan For want of food and *sleepe,* . . . II. vii. 65. 3
Suffers her selfe through *sleepe* beguild to bee, . . . II. viii. 6. 8
lives his memorie, though carcas *sleepe* in rest. . . . II. x. 43. 9
him to *sleepe* she gently would perswade, . . . III. i. 35. 8
Was drowned in the depth of deadly *sleepe;* . . . III. i. 59. 3
She with her Nourse adowne to *sleepe* did lye; . . . III. ii. 28. 4
sleepe full far away from her did fly: . . . III. ii. 28. 5
In her warme bed to *sleepe,* if that she might; . . . III. ii. 47. 3
a litle creeping *sleepe* Surprisd her sence: . . . III. ii. 47. 6
Or doen they onely *sleepe,* and shall againe reverse? . . . III. iv. 1. 9
if they *sleepe,* O let them soone awake! . . . III. iv. 2. 2
Upon the grassy ground to *sleepe* a throw: . . . III. iv. 53. 8
gentle *Sleepe* envyde him any rest: . . . III. iv. 54. 1
in *sleepe* . . . doth love to steepe His lustlesse limbes, . . . III. iv. 56. 4
Instead of *sleepe* thou sendest troublous feares . . . III. iv. 57. 5
Upon the grassy ground her selfe she layd To *sleepe,* . . . III. vi. 7. 3
There a sad cloud of *sleepe* her overkest, . . . III. vi. 10. 8
in her *sleepe* . . . Unwares had borne two babes, . . . III. vi. 26. 8
Ne did she let dull *sleepe* once to relent, . . . III. vii. 2. 3
sleepe in slothfull shade: . . . III. vii. 12. 8
all the while the fisher did securely *sleepe.* . . . III. viii. 21. 9
whiles *sleepe* their sences did invade. . . . III. x. 46. 9
At night, when all they went to *sleepe,* . . . III. x. 48. 1
wearie of their sport to *sleepe* they fell, . . . III. x. 49. 2
he dare never *sleepe,* . . . III. x. 58. 6
doth thy justice *sleepe* and silent ly? . . . III. xi. 9. 7
ne let *sleepe* oppresse Her heavy eyes . . . III. xi. 55. 6
In silence and in *sleepe* themselves did shrowd, . . . III. xii. 1. 4
saw him *sleepe* with her all night his fill; . . . IV. i. 49. 3
comming to Cares House, Doth *sleepe* from him expell. . . . IV. v. Arg.
When gentle *sleepe* his heavie eyes would close; . . . IV. v. 40. 2
when he to *sleepe* did thinke, . . . IV. v. 41. 1
Ne suffred *sleepe* to settle in his brest. . . . IV. v. 41. 5
So oftentimes he out of *sleepe* abrayd, . . . IV. v. 42. 8
in his soundest *sleepe* his dayly feare . . . IV. v. 43. 6
Where fearelesse I to *sleepe* me downe did lay: . . . IV. vi. 36. 4
when as I did out of *sleepe* abray, . . . IV. vi. 36. 5
heavie *sleepe* the eye-lids did surprise . . . IV. vii. 3. 7
Ne dayly food did take, ne nightly *sleepe,* . . . IV. xii. 19. 8
whose sounder *sleepe* Is broken . . . V. vi. 14. 1
the least twinckling *sleepe* to start Into her eye, . . . V. vi. 24. 7
now needes will ye *sleepe?* . . . V. vi. 25. 6
Now will ye *sleepe?* . . . V. vi. 25. 8
suffer *sleepe* to seaze His eye-lids sad, . . . V. vi. 26. 5
Ne suffred slothfull *sleepe* her eyelids to oppresse. . . . V. vi. 34. 9
with soft delight Of sencelesse *sleepe* . . . V. vii. 12. 6
under Isis feete doth *sleepe* for ever; . . . V. vii. 22. 7
Bad doe away the dampe of drouzie *sleepe,* . . . V. vii. 26. 8
(for she ful ill Could *sleepe* all night, . . . V. vii. 27. 4
Ne day nor night did *sleepe* t' attend them on, . . . V. x. 10. 4
Did *sleepe* all night through weary travell . . . VI. iii. 9. 9
Would to no bed, nor take no kindely *sleepe,* . . . VI. iii. 10. 2
layd her underneath a bush to *sleepe,* . . . VI. iii. 44. 6
sweete *sleepe* that luld him soft in swound. . . . VI. vii. 18. 9
Now drowned in the depth of *sleepe* all fearelesse lay. . . . VI. viii. 36. 9
suffer her out of her *sleepe* to wake, . . . VI. viii. 37. 8
to let her *Sleepe* out her fill . . . VI. viii. 38. 2
sleepe, they sayd, would make her battill better: . . . VI. viii. 38. 3
all the night in silver *sleepe* I spend, . . . VI. ix. 22. 8
sleep and darknesse round about did trace: . . . VII. vii. 44. 7
Theyr *sleepe* thou doost molest. . . . *Epig.* iv. 18
why doe ye *sleepe* thus long, . . . *Epith.* 85
Twixt *sleepe* and wake, after she weary was, . . . *Epith.* 309
Breake gentle *sleepe* with misconceived dout. . . . *Epith.* 337
tymely *Sleep,* when it is tyme to *sleepe,* . . . *Epith.* 355
To breake his *sleepe,* and waste his ydle braine: . . . *H.L.* 256
Sleeper's. dreame, that can delude the *sleepers* sent.' . . . I. i. 43. 9
Sleepeth. That nowe *sleepeth* in Lethe lake, . . . *S.C.* Mar. 23
lustie Love still *sleepeth* not, . . . *S.C.* Mar. 26
whiles the Lyon *sleepeth* sound, . . . *Hub.* 967
Sleeping. *See* **Dead-sleeping.**
Those antique Caesars, *sleeping* long in darke, . . . *Ro.* xxv. 3
The Lyon *sleeping* lay in secret shade, . . . *Hub.* 952
he found, where *sleeping* he did ly. . . . *Hub.* 1320
these Beares lay *sleeping* sound, . . . *Ti.* 570
Therein a goodly Virgine *sleeping* lay; . . . *Ti.* 636
Mars *sleeping* with his wife to compasse in, . . . *Mui.* 371
the *sleeping* spark Of native vertue . . . I. ii. 19. 1
'Dear Dame,' (quoth he) 'you *sleeping* sparkes awake, . . . I. ix. 8. 1
Where *sleeping* late she lefte her other knight. . . . II. vi. 22. 4
envy base to barke at *sleeping* fame. . . . II. viii. 13. 7
to doen outrage to a *sleeping* ghost; . . . II. viii. 26. 2
Her other sonne fast *sleeping* did oppresse, . . . II. x. 35. 8
The young man, *sleeping* by her, . . . II. xii. 79. 1
Yet *sleeping,* in his well proportiond face; . . . II. xii. 79. 7
the ydle instruments Of *sleeping* praise, . . . II. xii. 80. 2
the *sleeping* memoree Of those same antique Peres, . . . III. iii. 22. 7
her in daffadillies *sleeping* made . . . III. xi. 32. 4
Would afterwards afresh the *sleeping* evill reare. . . . IV. i. 34. 9

Sleeping—*Continued.*
through weary travel she lay *sleeping* sound. . . . IV. vii. 4. 9
the Crocodile, which *sleeping* lay Under the Idols feete . . . V. vii. 15. 1
shame he weend a *sleeping* wight to wound. . . . VI. i. 34. 4
time did offer meanes him *sleeping* to surprize. . . . VI. vii. 22. 9
whereas his Lord he *sleeping* vew'd. . . . VI. vii. 23. 9
Lay *sleeping* soundly in the bushes shade, . . . VI. xi. 38. 4
Sleeps. All musick *sleepes,* . . . *S.C.* N. 105
sleepes in dust, dead and inglorious, . . . *Ti.* 355
when he *sleepes* in most security . . . III. iv. 27. 3
sleepes, and sports, and playes; . . . IV. i. 47. 6
Is it not Cinthia, she that never *sleepes,* . . . *Epith.* 374
Sleepy. A Gnat, unto the *sleepie* Shepheard went; . . . *Gn.* 283
my *sleepie* Muse, awake; . . . *Col.* 48
mighty charmes to trouble *sleepy* minds. . . . I. i. 36. 9
drownd in *sleepie* night, . . . I. ii. 42. 2
Whose *sleepie* head she in her lap did soft dispose. . . . II. xii. 76. 9
rings his silver Bell t' each *sleepy* wight, . . . V. vi. 27. 3
Sleet. raine, and haile and *sleet,* . . . IV. ix. 33. 6
Sleeves. *sleeves* dependaunt Albanese-wyse: . . . III. xii. 10. 4
Sleight. Possest nigh of the Capitol through *slight,* . . . *Van.* xi. 7
he usde another slipprie *slight,* . . . *Hub.* 859
With excellent device and wondrous *slight,* . . . *Mui.* 330
wily lover did devise this *slight:* . . . *Col.* 137
Castle, . . . By subtile engins and malitious *slight* Is undermined . . . I. viii. 23. 2
guest Would safe depart, for all his subtile *sleight,* . . . I. ix. 54. 3
By subtilty, nor *slight,* nor might, . . . I. xi. 36. 9
he descryde and shonned still his *slight:* . . . II. i. 4. 8
With such faire *sleight* him Guyon often fayld, . . . II. v. 11. 1
well perceived his deceiptfull *sleight,* . . . II. vii. 64. 7
through his nimble *sleight* did under him down cast. . . . II. viii. 49. 9
by *slight* And foule advantage this good Knight dismayd, . . . IV. i. 44. 2
Was so expert in every subtile *slight,* . . . IV. ii. 10. 8
he sought by *slight* It forth to wrest, . . . IV. iii. 10. 5
Which subtill *sleight* did him encumber much, . . . IV. vii. 27. 1
gotten by her *slight* And earnest search, . . . V. i. 9. 2
by *sleight* the truth thereout to straine; . . . V. i. 24. 9
some by *sleight* he eke doth underfong. . . . V. ii. 7. 5
by might extort, or else by *slight* deceaved? . . . V. iii. 30. 9
by thee slaine, and murdred by thy *slight.'* . . . V. vi. 37. 9
Least by such *slight* he were unwares deceived; . . . V. xi. 7. 3
the hatchets *slight* Hath pruned . . . V. xi. 11. 8
So also did this Monster use like *slight* . . . V. xi. 25. 7
By guilefull treason and by subtill *slight* . . . V. xi. 39. 7
He can devize this counter-cast of *slight,* . . . VI. iii. 16. 8
not onely sought . . . To overthrow, but to supplant by *slight:* VI. v. 13. 5
to maligne, t' envie, t' use shifting *slight,* . . . VI. vii. 1. 5
whether by force, or *sleight,* . . . away convayd? . . . VI. vii. 34. 5
by unjust And guilefull meanes, through Corybantes *slight,* VII. vi. 27. 4
Sleights. all their *sleights* espyed. . . . *Hub.* 346
that, which Merlin by his magicke *slights* Made . . . *Ti.* 523
and finest *sleights* devise, . . . *Col.* 694
he by conning *sleights* in at the window crept. . . . I. iii. 17. 9
yvory sheath, ycarv'd with curious *slights,* . . . I. vii. 30. 7
by subtile *sleights* she him betraid . . . I. vii. 51. 1
false Duessa, . . . Her false *sleightes* doe imploy. . . . I. xii. Arg.
With thousand other *sleightes;* . . . II. i. 3. 7
In cunning *sleightes* and practick knavery. . . . II. iii. 9. 6
Tryde all her arts and all her *sleights* . . . II. xii. 81. 9
with what *sleights* and sweet allurements she Entyst . . . III. i. 35. 1
all the *sleights* unbosomd in his hart: . . . III. x. 7. 3
there *sleights* and art She cast to use, . . . III. xii. 28. 1
He them abused through his subtill *slights,* . . . V. iii. 39. 8
Through these his *slights* he many doth confound: . . . V. ix. 6. 1
he in *slights* and jugling feates did flow, . . . V. ix. 13. 8
Warning him hold it fast for feare of *slights:* . . . V. ix. 18. 3
by *slights* allur'd, and to their purpose lad. . . . V. xii. 37. 9
Yet are they chang'd (by other wondrous *slights*) . . . VII. vii. 25. 4
Slender. They han the pleasure, I a *sclender* prise; . . . *S.C.* O. 16
Here we our *slender* pypes may safely charme. . . . *S.C.* O. 118
Being above my *slender* reasons reach; . . . *Ti.* 487
A *sclender* swaine, excelling far each other, . . . *As.* 15
sparkes of fire which fall in *sclender* flex, . . . III. i. 47. 7
wore About her *sclender* waste, . . . III. vii. 36. 2
covered with a *slender* veile afore; . . . IV. x. 40. 7
Her selfe then tooke he by the *sclender* wast, . . . V. ii. 27. 1
She stretched forth a long white *sclender* wand. . . . V. vii. 7. 5
A goodly youth . . . Yet but a *slender* slip, . . . VI. ii. 5. 3
with a *slender* dart, . . . Strooke him, . . . VI. ii. 12. 6
Slenderly. like a cobweb weaving *slenderly,* . . . *Gn.* 3
Slepst. thou *slepst* in tender swadling band, . . . I. x. 65. 7
Slept. deeds; Whose praises having *slept* in silence long, . . . I. Pr. 1. 6
So sound he *slept,* that nought mought him awake. . . . I. i. 42. 3
he *slept* soundly void of evil thought, . . . I. i. 46. 3
when she *slept,* he kept both watch and ward; . . . I. iii. 9. 5
Saints . . . He did disrobe, when all men carelesse *slept,* . . . I. iii. 17. 6
Whiles old Sylvanus *slept* in shady arber sownd: . . . I. vi. 7. 9
whilst he *slept* she over him would spred Her mantle, . . . III. i. 36. 1
She soundly *slept,* and carefull thoughts did quite assoile. . . . III. i. 58. 9
she proov'd Whether she *slept* or wakte: . . . III. i. 60. 6
in drowsie cave Hath long time *slept,* . . . III. iii. 30. 2
there *slept* a fisher old and pore, . . . III. vii. 27. 5
to his wife, that now full soundly *slept,* . . . III. x. 49. 3
She *slept;* yet . . . closely spyde . . . III. xi. 32. 8
it fell, and deadly *slept.* . . . IV. iii. 20. 9
Ere he had *slept* his fill, . . . VI. i. 35. 3
he *slept* full fast; . . . VI. viii. 47. 6
theeves did rest, . . . and *slept* full sound, . . . VI. xi. 42. 3
that long hath *slept* in cheerlesse bower, . . . *Am.* iv. 6

Slept—*Continued.*
Love, that had now long time securely *slept* . . . *H.L.* 61
Slew. Witnesse shee *slewe* me with her eye, . . . *S.C.* Au. 115
people *slew* with sword, . . . *Gn.* 44
with his hand him rashly bruzing *slewe* . . . *Gn.* 290
wretched boy, they *slew* with guiltie blades; . . . *Gn.* 403
also him that false Ulysses *slewe,* . . . *Gn.* 531
He lately *slue* his dreadfull foe in fight. . . . *Gn.* 648
ever as they bred, They *slue* them, . . . *Hub.* 318
of them *slew* at pleasure what they wolde. . . . *Hub.* 336
felly *slewe* Those warders strange, . . . *Hub.* 1370
In salvage forrest by adventure *slew,* . . . *Mui.* 67
the Lyon, which with toyle Alcides *slew,* . . . *D.* 166
him that *slew* Sansfoy with bloody knife: . . . I. iii. 36. 4
with guilefull snare Entrapped *slew,* . . . I. iv. 47. 6
how he *slew* with glauncing dart amisse . . . I. vi. 17. 5
That Redcrosse knight, perdie, I never *slew;* . . . I. vi. 42. 6
Snake Which great Alcides in Stremona *slew,* . . . I. vii. 17. 2
With wrathfull hand I *slew* her innocent, . . . II. iv. 29. 4
The one she *slew* upon the present floure; . . . II. x. 19. 5
there him *slew:* . . . II. x. 33. 8
Ymner *slew* of Logris miscreate; . . . II. x. 38. 2
Rather then fly, or be captiv'd, her selfe she *slew.* . . . II. x. 55. 9
him Allectus treacherously *slew,* . . . II. x. 57. 7
three hundred Lords he *slew* Of British blood, . . . II. x. 66. 6
Whom with his brethren Timias *slew,* . . . III. vi. 54. 4
slew him cruelly ere any reskew came. . . . III. vii. 28. 9
The Palfrey whereon she did travell *slew,* . . . III. viii. 49. 3
All whom a Scythian king . . . *Slew* cruelly, . . . IV. xi. 37. 9
A cruell carle, the which all strangers *slew,* . . . V. x. 10. 3
he there *slew* him at the skreene. . . . V. x. 37. 9
slew the Porter on the flore. . . . VI. i. 23. 9
This knight, whom Tristram *slew,* . . . VI. ii. 40. 5
that discourteous knight, (Whom Tristram *slew*) . . . VI. ii. 43. 2
So miserably him all helpelesse *slew,* . . . VI. vi. 22. 7
Saved him selfe but that he there him *slew;* . . . VI. viii. 9. 4
Encountring him with small resistence *slew,* . . . VI. xi. 43. 6
slew the formost that came first to hand . . . VI. xi. 46. 8
till th' Amphytrionide Him *slew,* . . . VII. vii. 36. 7
by Dianaes doom unjust *Slew* great Orion; . . . VII. vii. 39. 8
And *slew* the Just by most unjust decree. . . . *H.H.L.* 154
Slewbloome, Slewlogher. *See* **Slieve Bloom, Slieve Lougher.**
Slid. a rivers bancke that swift downe *slidd,* . . . *Bel.*[2] xv. 7
Whiles on his broad rownd backe they softly *slid,* . . . III. iv. 32. 2
next to him the Nene downe softly *slid;* . . . IV. xi. 35. 7
Slide. With liquid foote doth *slide* downe easily. . . . *Gn.* 24
where the christall Thamis wont to *slide* . . . *Ti.* 134
One of his feete unwares from him did *slide,* . . . *Ti.* 544
Till they into the Mullaes water *slide.* . . . *Col.* 144
His nigh forweried feeble feet did *slide,* . . . I. xi. 45. 8
suffred not his wandring feete to *slide;* . . . II. iv. 2. 5
Eftsoones her shallow ship away did *slide,* . . . II. vi. 5. 1
they avoyded were, and vainely by did *slyde.* . . . IV. iii. 7. 9
whilst his right foot did *slyde.* . . . IV. iii. 18. 9
tombling backe he downe did *slyde* . . . IV. iv. 44. 4
not a drop can *slide:* . . . V. ii. 35. 8
still it downe did *slide,* . . . V. ii. 45. 7
through the flood before did softly *slyde* . . . VII. vii. 43. 4
onely man himselfe, who selfe did *slyde:* . . . *H.H.L.* 145
Sliding. *See* **Soft-sliding.**
Sweetely *sliding* into the eyes of men, . . . *Bel.*[1] i. 2
rest, soft *sliding* downe From heavens hight . . . *Bel.*[2] i. 1
(thou sacred childe) come *sliding* soft, . . . *Gn.* 37
slyding softly forth, she turnd as to her ease. . . . I. i. 54. 9
slyding soft, as downe to sleepe her layd, . . . II. i. 56. 3
Slieve Bloom. Under *Slewbloome* in shady grove was got, . . IV. xi. 42. 5
Slieve Lougher. Strong Allo tombling from *Slewlogher* steep, IV. xi. 41. 8
Slight. *See* **Sleight.**
fire, whose substance thin and *slight* Made no resistance, . . VII. vi. 7. 7
Slime. To drench himselfe in moorish *slime* did trace, . . . *Gn.* 251
Shall die in darknesse, and lie hid in *slime:* . . . *T.M.* 106
Loathing this sinfull earth and earthlie *slime,* . . . *Ti.* 290
Of fleshly *slime* and fraile mortalitie; . . . *D.* 403
His fattie waves doe fertile *slime* outwell, . . . I. i. 21. 3
Brought forth this monstrous masse of earthly *slyme,* . . . I. vii. 9. 8
of thing like to that Aegyptian *slime,* . . . II. ix. 21. 5
All were they borne of her owne native *slime:* . . . II. x. 9. 5
th' eternall Lord in fleshly *slime* Enwombed was, . . . II. x. 50. 2
Had she not beene devoide of mortall *slime,* . . . III. iv. 35. 3
That is ingenerate in fleshly *slime.* . . . III. vi. 3. 5
To turne againe unto their earthly *slime:* . . . VII. vii. 18. 4
hinders heavenly thoughts with drossy *slime.* . . . *Am.* xiii. 12
cryme Which was enrooted in all fleshly *slyme.* . . . *H.H.L.* 168
Slimy. the *slimie* scowring Of the moist moores, . . . *Gn.* 229
like wormes out of her *slimie* nature. . . . *Col.* 860
Slip. *slipp* away, Soone as appeard safe opportunitie: . . . I. ii. 41. 6
we must surprise, Els she will *slip* away, . . . II. xii. 69. 9
A goodly youth . . . Yet but a slender *slip,* . . . VI. ii. 5. 3
When his foote slipt, (that *slip* he dearely rewd) . . . VI. vii. 48. 3
Slipped. He would have *slipt* the coller handsomly, . . . *Hub.* 269
When his foote *slipt,* (that slip he dearely rewd) . . . VI. vii. 48. 3
Slipper. *See* **Slippery.**
slipper hope Of mortal men, . . . *S.C.* N. 153
Slippery. *See* **Slipper.**
Long time he used this *slippery* pranck, . . . *S.C.* S. 200
The chaungfull turning of mens *slipperie* state, . . . *Gn.* 554
he usde another *slipprie* slight, . . . *Hub.* 859
Through *slipperie* footing fell into the brooke, . . . V. v. 43. 3
Slipping. lightly *slipping* by, Unwares defrauded . . . VI. viii. 8. 8
Slips. He *slips* aside; . . . II. v. 10. 6

Slits. with a crosse of redd And manie *slits,* . . . *Hub.* 206
Slombry. *See* **Slumbery.**
Sloth. for he was but slowe, did *slowth* off shake . . . *Gn.* 309
begot amisse By yawning *Sloth* . . . *T.M.* 263
through unnoble *sloth,* or sinfull crime, . . . *T.M.* 435
to subject his desire To loathsome *sloth,* . . . *Mui.* 36
oft as *Slowth* still in the mire did stand. . . . I. iv. 36. 4
the Chamberlain, *Slowth,* did to rest them call. . . . I. iv. 43. 9
Theseus condemned to endlesse *slouth* by law; . . . I. v. 35. 8
To slug in *slouth* and sensuall delights, . . . II. i. 23. 3
in lewd *slouth* to wast his carelesse day; . . . III. v. 1. 7
well may she you reprove Of falsehood or of *slouth,* . . . III. viii. 27. 9
To banish *sloth* that oft doth noble mindes annoy. . . . IV. vii. 23. 9
If he for *slouth* forslackt so famous guest. . . . VI. ix. 3. 5
Slothful. the *sloathfull* fit of lifes sweete rest . . . *Gn.* 641
Upon a *slouthfull* Asse he chose to ryde, . . . I. iv. 18. 7
The *slouthfull* wave of that great griesy lake: . . . II. vi. 18. 7
In *slouthfull* sleepe his molten hart to steme, . . . II. vi. 27. 5
The *slouthfull* body . . . Doth praise thee oft, . . . III. iv. 56. 5
to slug, or sleepe in *slothfull* shade: . . . III. vii. 12. 8
Ne suffred *slothfull* sleepe her eyelids to oppresse. . . . V. vi. 34. 9
Slothfulness. Through their bad dooings, or base *slothfulnesse,* *T.M.* 99
Slow. for he was but *slowe,* did slowth off shake . . . *Gn.* 309
heavie sate upon her palfrey *slow;* . . . I. i. 4. 7
so much speede As her *slowe* beast could make; . . . I. ii. 8. 2
A damzel spyde, *slow* footing her before, . . . I. iii. 10. 8
Abessa, daughter of Corceca *slow,* . . . I. iii. 18. 4
where Una traveild *slow,* . . . I. iii. 26. 1
Thenceforth her waters wexed dull and *slow,* . . . I. vii. 5. 8
all hory gray, With . . . gate full *slow,* . . . I. x. 5. 6
with *slow* pace the knight did lead, . . . II. i. 7. 8
Sore bruzed with the fall he *slow* uprose, . . . II. v. 5. 1
Tempring the passion with advizement *slow,* . . . II. v. 13. 2
whether swift I wend, or whether *slow:* . . . II. vi. 10. 5
Both *slow* and swift alike do serve . . . II. vi. 10. 6
The waves thereof so *slow* and sluggish were, . . . II. vi. 46. 6
And his *slow* eies beguiled of their sight, . . . II. viii. 9. 2
by the grim floud of Cocytus *slow,* . . . III. iv. 55. 5
was nothing *slow* Him selfe to save . . . IV. iii. 33. 4
drew her far, and led with *slow* delay. . . . IV. viii. 11. 7
Slow Peneus, and tempestuous Phasides, . . . IV. xi. 21. 3
Ne any Lake, that seems most still and *slowe,* . . . VII. vii. 20. 5
Making his streame run *slow.* . . . *Proth.* 118
Slowly. *slowly* seemd to move Theyr sad protract . . . *Am.* lxxxvi. 3
How *slowly* do the houres theyr numbers spend? . . . *Epith.* 280
How *slowly* does sad Time his feathers move? . . . *Epith.* 281
Slue. *See* **Slew.**
Slug. To *slug* in slouth and sensuall delights, . . . II. i. 23. 3
He us'd to *slug,* or sleepe in slothfull shade: . . . III. vii. 12. 8
Sluggish. 'Arise, (said Mercurie) thou *sluggish* beast, . . . *Hub.* 1327
sluggish Idlenesse, the nourse of sin; . . . I. iv. 18. 6
chace away sweet sleepe from sluggish *eye,* . . . I. iv. 44. 4
sluggish german, doest thy forces slake . . . I. v. 10. 8
did drive out of their *sluggish* sourse. . . . II. vi. 20. 9
The waves thereof so slow and *sluggish* were, . . . II. vi. 46. 6
In his free thought to build her *sluggish* nest, . . . III. v. 2. 2
'Lo! *sluggish* Knight, the victors happie pray! . . . IV. ii. 7. 5
Sluices. Now like great Hills, and streight like *sluces* them unfold. . . . VII. vii. 20. 9
Slumber. hast thy selfe his *slomber* broke, . . . *S.C.* Mar. 29
more to lulle him in his *slumber* soft, . . . I. i. 41. 1
comming where the knight in *slomber* lay . . . I. i. 47. 2
creeping *slomber* made him to forget . . . II. v. 30. 8
My sences lulled are in *slomber* of delight. . . . III. Pr. 4. 9
Out of her quiet *slomber* did awake, . . . III. i. 61. 8
doth the charmed Snake in *slomber* lay. . . . III. ii. 15. 6
Out of his quiet *slomber* him abrade, . . . III. xi. 8. 4
at the last they brake His *slomber,* . . . IV. i. 43. 9
Upon the ground awhile in *slomber* lay; . . . IV. ii. 7. 2
the which his quiet *slomber* brake: . . . IV. v. 44. 7
Soft rombling brookes, that gentle *slomber* drew; . . . IV. x. 24. 4
by the altars side her selfe to *slumber* plaste. . . . V. vii. 8. 9
whyles his Lord in silver *slomber* lay, . . . VI. vii. 19. 8
Slumbered. up he tooke the *slombred* sencelesse corse, . . . I. vii. 15. 6
Where soone he *slumbred* fearing not be harmd: . . . II. vi. 14. 8
Keeping that *slombred* corse to him assind: . . . II. viii. 11. 7
Slumbereth. Thy Muse to long *slombreth* in sorrowing, . . . *S.C.* N. 3
Slumbering. *See* **Aslumbering, Long-slumbering, Sweet-slumbering.**
Where gentle *slumbring* sleep oppressed him . . . *Gn.* 239
In *slombring* swownd, nigh voyd of vitall spright, . . . I. v. 19. 5
slombring soft my hart did steale away, . . . I. ix. 13. 6
the good Guyon he found *slumbring* fast . . . II. viii. 4. 8
any drop of *slombring* rest . . . III. ii. 29. 1
a gentle *slombring* swowne Upon her fell, . . . III. vi. 7. 3
As if he had beene *slombring* in the shade; . . . III. xi. 8. 2
Love lay sweetly *slumbring* . . . *Epig.* iv. 1
Slumbery. whereas lay Faire Crysogone in *slombry* traunce . . . III. vi. 26. 7
Sly. the *slie* Foxe, as like to be his groome, . . . *Hub.* 661
my *slie* wyles and subtill craftinesse, . . . *Hub.* 1045
no practise *slie,* . . . *Hub.* 1139
stroke his weapon *slie* Into his heart, . . . *Mui.* 437
with usage *sly* He taught to imitate . . . I. i. 46. 7
meeting earst with Archimago *slie* . . . II. viii. 10. 7
with pacience and sufferaunce *sly* . . . to subdew: . . . II. viii. 47. 7
Cover'd with lids deviz'd of substance *sly,* . . . II. ix. 46. 7
staffe with which he charmed semblants *sly.* . . . II. xii. 49. 9
entertaine with her occasions *sly:* . . . IV. x. 13. 4
Next him went Wylibourne with passage *slye,* . . . IV. xi. 32. 5
with *slie* shiftes and wiles did underminde . . . V. vi. 32. 7

Sly—*Continued.*
with such nimblesse *sly* Could wield about, . . . V. xi. 6. 6
with *sly* skill so cunningly them dresses, . . . *Am.* xxxvii. 3
Slyly. that arrow shot So *slyly* . . . III. ii. 26. 8
Smack. Began some *smacke* of comfort new to tast, . . . VI. xi. 45. 3
Small. lukewarme blood Of the *small* heards, . . . *Bel.*[2] vi. 8
So by the *small* the great is oft diseased. . . . *Van.* ii. 14
so *small* so mightie can constraine? . . . *Van.* iii. 14
A sword-fish *small* him from the rest did sunder, . . . *Van.* v. 8
Whatever thing seems *small* in common eyes. . . . *Van.* v. 14
Sith so *small* thing his happines may varie. . . . *Van.* viii. 14
that so *small* a thing Should able be . . . *Van.* ix. 13
To see so great things by so *small* distrest . . . *Van.* xii. 4
To scorne all difference of great and *small,* . . . *Van.* xii. 6
in his *small* bushes used to shrowde . . . *S.C.* F. 122
blamest hem much for *small* encheason. . . . *S.C.* May 147
Let not my *small* demaund be so contempt. . . . *S.C.* N. 48
excuse This Gnats *small* Poeme, . . . *Gn.* 5
the *small* Birds, in their wide boughs embowring, . . . *Gn.* 225
deserve to have *small* faults remitted, . . . *Gn.* 474
To thee, *small* Gnat, in lieu of his life saved, . . . *Gn.* 687
small skill in warre: . . . *Hub.* 200
askes *small* paines, but thriftines to save, . . . *Hub.* 278
small oddes I often see Twixt them that aske, . . . *Hub.* 373
It is enough to doo our *small* devotion, . . . *Hub.* 457
He made *small* choyce; . . . *Hub.* 849
sure his honestie Got him *small* gaines, . . . *Hub.* 850
Of men of armes he had but *small* regard, . . . *Hub.* 1189
So I of this *small* Northerne world was Princesse. . . . *Ti.* 84
(*small* joy to him, alas!) . . . *Ti.* 652
from *small* jarre . . . broke into open warre. . . . *Mui.* 7
With fine *small* cords about it stretched wide, . . . *Mui.* 359
th' onely usance Of a *small* time, . . . *D.* 504
Small needments else need shepheard to prepare. . . . *Col.* 195
arts of schoole have there *small* countenance, . . . *Col.* 703
there professours find *small* maintenance, . . . *Col.* 705
Vouchsafe in worth this *small* guift to receave, . . . *Ded. Son.* vii. 8
fruitfull cursed spawne of serpents *small,* . . . I. i. 22. 6
there came *Smal* drops of gory bloud, . . . I. ii. 30. 9
in their cotage *small* that night she rest her may. . . . I. iii. 14. 9
streight him rent in thousand peeces *small,* . . . I. iii. 20. 3
Then tooke that Squire an horne of bugle *small,* . . . I. viii. 3. 5
her *small* Gondelay her port did make, . . . II. vi. 11. 5
with how *small* allowaunce . . . II. vii. 15. 3
made him scorne all creatures great and *small,* . . . II. vii. 41. 7
His single speare could doe him *small* redresse . . . II. viii. 34. 3
Their murmuring *small* trompetts sownden wide, . . . II. ix. 16. 3
the same writing *small* Does all their deedes deface, . . . III. ii. 1. 8
skil, which practize *small* Wil bring, . . . III. iii. 53. 8
He lives, but takes *small* joy of his renowne; . . . III. v. 26. 1
betwixt two marbles plaine Shee pownded *small,* . . . III. v. 33. 2
As glad of that *small* rest as Bird of tempest gon. . . . III. vii. 10. 9
To get *small* thankes, and therewith many blames, . . . III. vii. 61. 3
Ne in *small* meares containe his glory great, . . . III. ix. 46. 8
at the last he found a cave with entrance *small.* . . . III. x. 57. 9
her *small* waste girt rownd with yron bands . . . III. xii. 30. 8
that great brasen pillour broke in peeces *small.* . . . III. xii. 37. 9
He had *small* lust to buy his love so deare, . . . IV. i. 34. 6
wicked discord; whose *small* sparkes once blowen . . . IV. ii. 1. 5
Great matter growing of beginning *small,* . . . IV. ii. 54. 7
(for *small* delight They had . . . IV. iii. 47. 1
about her middle *small* They thought to gird, . . . IV. v. 16. 3
to *small* purpose yron wedges made; . . . IV. v. 35. 8
'*Small* harme it were For any knight . . . IV. vi. 4. 1
He part of his *small* feast to her would share; . . . IV. viii. 5. 7
Where one stood peeping through a crevis *small,* . . . IV. x. 11. 8
in *small* compasse hild? . . . IV. xi. 17. 4
she was sustained Of two *smal* grooms, . . . IV. xi. 25. 2
The Churne and Charwell, two *small* streames, . . . IV. xi. 25. 3
Eden, though but *small,* . . . IV. xi. 36. 7
Ill can he rule the great that cannot reach the *small.*' . . . V. ii. 43. 9
like a little Mount of *small* degree, . . . V. iv. 7. 7
all his bones as *small* as sandy grayle He broke, . . . V. ix. 19. 4
Such loathly matter were *small* lust to speake or thinke. . . . V. xi. 31. 9
a flowre, whose silken leaves *small* . . . VI. ii. 35. 7
some *small* continuance He there did make, . . . VI. iii. 19. 7
Glad of that easement, though it were but *small;* . . . VI. iv. 15. 7
Small praise to prove your powre on wight so weake.' . . . VI. v. 30. 5
Small was his house, and like a little cage, . . . VI. v. 38. 3
they to it fell With *small* adoe, . . . VI. ix. 17. 8
having *small* yet doe I not complaine Of want, . . . VI. ix. 20. 3
In this *small* plot of your dominion, . . . VI. ix. 28. 4
I may here with your selfe some *small* repose obtaine. . . . VI. ix. 31. 9
For slaves to sell them for no *small* reward . . . VI. x. 43. 4
Some shew of favour, by him gracing *small,* . . . VI. xi. 6. 6
through that *small* favours gaine, . . . VI. xi. 7. 5
Encountring him with *small* resistence slew, . . . VI. xi. 43. 6
would him pleasure With this *small* boone, . . . VII. vi. 44. 2
Ne Poole so *small,* that can his smoothnesse holde . . . VII. vii. 20. 6
In planting eeke he took no *small* delight. . . . VII. vii. 40. 6
To graunt *small* respit to my restlesse toile; . . . *Am.* xi. 6
needeth greater might Then those *small* forts . . . *Am.* xiv. 6
wakened with the noyse, And saw the beast so *small;* . . . *Epig.* iv. 6
Certes *small* glory doest thou winne hereby, . . . *H.L.* 153
all my woes to be but penance *small.* . . . *H.L.* 300
Yet being malist both of great and *small.* . . . *H.H.L.* 238
Smallage. stinking *Smallage,* and unsaverie Rew; . . . *D.* 347
Smallest. Whose *smallest* minute lost no riches render may. . . . IV. x. 14. 9
Smart. Such stormy stoures doo breede my balefull *smart,* . . . *S.C.* Ja. 27
For then I little *smart* did feele, . . . *S.C.* Mar. 98

Smart—*Continued.*
So nowe fayre Rosalind hath bredde hys *smart*, . . . *S.C.* Ap. 27
to kepe is a burdenous *smart:* . . . *S.C.* S. 16
As in avengement of his heedles *smart*, . . . *Gn.* 291
tell the anguish of my inward *smart*, . . . *T.M.* 422
Gave her the fatall wound of deadlie *smart*, . . . *D.* 158
Oft times to plaine your loves concealed *smart;* . . . *As.* Pr. 2
spends his wit in loves consuming *smart:* . . . *Col.* 429
Ne let vaine feares procure your needlesse *smart*, . . . I. i. 54. 4
litle sweet Oft tempred is,' . . . 'with muchell *smart:* . . . I. iv. 46. 4
Leave off their worke, unmindfull of their *smart*, . . . I. v. 36. 2
gathering up the reliques of his *smart*, . . . I. v. 39. 6
The salvage nation feele her secret *smart*, . . . I. vi. 11. 3
wound That launched hath my brest with bleeding *smart*. . . . I. vii. 25. 7
counsell mitigates the greatest *smart:* . . . I. vii. 40. 8
all enrag'd with *smart* and frantick yre, . . . I. viii. 17. 8
resolv'd to work his finall *smart*, . . . I. ix. 51. 8
grace . . . doth quench the brond of hellish *smart*, . . . I. ix. 53. 7
came to Caelia to declare her *smart;* . . . I. x. 23. 1
with the uncouth *smart* the Monster lowdly cryde. . . . I. xi. 20. 9
With heat, toyle, wounds, armes, *smart*, and inward fire, . . . I. xi. 28. 2
the grievous *smart* which him did wring, . . . I. xi. 39. 2
Pitifull spectacle of deadly *smart*, . . . II. i. 40. 1
Of ruefull pitty and impatient *smart*, . . . II. i. 44. 5
tell the secrete of your mortall *smart:* . . . II. i. 46. 8
through pleasure soonest falles, the weake through *smart*.' . . . II. i. 57. 9
She last should *smart:* . . . II. iv. 31. 6
Therewith to doen his foes eternall *smart*. . . . II. viii. 20. 4
With hope of thing that may allegge his *smart;* . . . III. ii. 15. 4
Tho gan she to renew her former *smart*, . . . III. ii. 29. 8
'doe nought aswage My stubborne *smart*, . . . III. ii. 37. 2
yet may it nought appease My raging *smart*, . . . III. ii. 43. 4
thought so to beguile her grievous *smart;* . . . III. iv. 6. 2
so her *smart* was much more grievous bredd, . . . III. iv. 6. 3
Full of soft passion and unwonted *smart:* . . . III. v. 30. 8
long enlargement of her painefull *smart*. . . . III. viii. 2. 4
still the *smart* thereof increased more, . . . III. x. 18. 4
Was never better time to shew thy *smart* . . . III. x. 26. 3
Cros-cuts the liver with internall *smart*, . . . III. x. 59. 8
feed it selfe with selfe-consuming *smart?* . . . III. xi. 1. 8
to slake his scalding *smart;* . . . III. xi. 30. 4
was thy love her death, and her death was thy *smart*. . . . III. xi. 36. 9
In wilfull languor and consuming *smart*, . . . III. xii. 16. 8
who can love the worker of her *smart?* . . . III. xii. 31. 7
Seven moneths he so her kept in bitter *smart*, . . . IV. i. 4. 1
The beast astonisht stands in middest of his *smart*. . . . IV. i. 49. 9
Smart daunts not mighty harts, . . . IV. iii. 8. 9
pacifie the strife, which causd so deadly *smart*. . . . IV. iii. 40. 9
did the *smart* remaine, though he himselfe did flee. . . . IV. v. 44. 9
nourisheth her owne consuming *smart?* . . . IV. vi. 1. 4
martyrest with sorow and with *smart*, . . . IV. vii. 2. 5
she gan mone his undeserved *smart*, . . . IV. viii. 3. 8
like the stings of aspes that kill with *smart*, . . . IV. viii. 26. 8
Besought her to graunt ease unto my *smart*, . . . IV. x. 48. 4
through great abundance of her *smart*. . . . IV. xii. 11. 9
The more she still augmented her owne *smart*, . . . V. v. 28. 4
through pittie of his causelesse *smart*. . . . V. v. 43. 9
Touching her loves successe, her lingring *smart*. . . . V. v. 45. 3
sad tydings of his balefull *smart* . . . V. vi. 3. 3
for what cause so great mischievous *smart* Was ment . . . V. vi. 31. 8
all that shall require my comfort in their *smart*.' . . . V. vii. 19. 9
griesly wound, . . . through raging *smart* of it, . . . V. vii. 33. 4
Yet wisely moderated her owne *smart*, . . . V. vii. 44. 3
what reliefe . . . for this your lovers *smart;* . . . VI. ii. 46. 4
Of all his mischiefe and late lucklesse *smart;* . . . VI. vii. 21. 3
Did languish long in life-consuming *smart*, . . . VI. vii. 31. 3
damned to endure this direfull *smart*, . . . VI. viii. 19. 8
to renue the rigour of his *smart;* . . . VI. x. 31. 4
seeke some succour both to ease my *smart*, . . . *Am.* ii. 7
Or looke with pitty on my payneful *smart;* . . . *Am.* xviii. 8
when I feele the bitter balefull *smart*, . . . *Am.* xxiv. 5
To be acquit fro my continual *smart;* . . . *Am.* xlii. 6
The piteous passion of his dying *smart*. . . . *Am.* xlviii. 12
Delights not in my merth, nor rues my *smart:* . . . *Am.* liv. 10
how great the *smart* Of those whom thou dost wound: . . . *Epig.* iv. 35
often called art Of women in their *smart;* . . . *Epith.* 395
Faine would I seeke to ease my bitter *smart* . . . *H.L.* 5
to augment the anguish of my *smart*, . . . *H.L.* 145
After long sorrow and consuming *smart*. . . . *H.B.* 28
nought but death can stint his dolours *smart?* . . . *H.B.* 74

Smarted. With piteous crie, that anie would have *smarted*. . . *Gn.* 640

Smarting. Rode Sathan with a *smarting* whip in hand, . . . I. iv. 36 .2
*embay His bodie in salt water *smarting* sore, . . . I. x. 27. 6
The beast, impatient of his *smarting* wound . . . I. xi. 25. 6
did with his *smarting* toole Oft whip . . . VI. vii. 39. 8

Smarts. pierce immortall breasts with mortall *smarts?* . . . *T.M.* 48
in midst of worldlie *smarts:* . . . *T.M.* 136
How he may worke unto her further *smarts;* . . . I. ii. 9. 7
'The author . . . 'of all my *smarts*, Is . . . I. ii. 34. 7
stird you up to worke your wilfull *smarts?* . . . II. ii. 29. 4
tyrannizeth in the bitter *smarts* . . . III. ii. 23. 3
Breeder of new, renewer of old *smarts:* . . . III. iv. 57. 3
more bent to eke my *smartes* . . . III. vii. 55. 7
did shreek, . . . with unwarlike *smarts*, . . . III. xi. 44.6
Without compassion of her cruell *smarts:* . . . VI. v. 33. 4
for revengement of those wrongfull *smarts*, . . . VI. viii. 22. 3
The cruell worker of your kindly *smarts*, . . . *H.L.* 32

Smear. The one my madding kiddes to *smere*, . . . *S.C.* Jul. 87

Smell. Of Sulphure now did breathe corrupted *smel*. . . . *Bel.*[1] ix. 14
My Sinamon *smell* too much annoieth: . . . *S.C.* F. 136

Smell—*Continued.*
I hate to *smell*, no sweet on earth is left; . . . *D.* 418
breathed ever forth a filthie banefull *smell*. . . . I. viii. 39. 9
nether darkenesse fowle, . . . Nor noyous *smell*, . . . I. viii. 40. 2
that same third Fort, that is the *Smell*, . . . II. xi. 11. 1
breathed forth sweet spirit and holesom *smell:* . . . II. xii. 51. 9
scarse an hound by *smell* Can follow out . . . V. ix. 6. 7
sweete flowres that far did *smell* . . . VI. x. 14. 7
might delight the *smell*, or please the view, . . . VII. vii. 10. 5
Her lips did *smell* lyke unto Gillyflowers; . . . *Am.* lxiv. 5
flowers doe give most odorous *smell;* . . . *Am.* lxiv. 13

Smelled. *See* **Smelt.**
Of nothing now but noyous sulphure *smeld*. . . . *Bel.*[2] xi. 14
her sowre breath abhominably *smeld;* . . . I. viii. 47. 5

Smelling. *See* **Rank-smelling.**
To gather May bus-kets and *smelling* brere: . . . *S.C.* May 10
with painted blossomes drest And *smelling* sweete, . . . II. vi. 12. 8

Smells. Did breath out bounteous *smels*, . . . II. v. 29. 9
throwe her sweete *smels* al arownd. . . . II. vi. 12. 9

Smelt. *See* **Smelled.**
I *smelt* a gardin of sweet flowres, . . . *Am.* lxiv. 2

Smere. *See* **Smear.**

Smile. at her owne felicitie did *smile*. . . . *Van.* ix. 8
match with that sweet *smile* and chearfull brow, . . . *D.* 306
His ruddy lips did *smyle*, . . . II. i. 41. 4
The litle babe . . . Gan *smyle* on them, . . . II. ii. 1. 6
Did *smyle* full smoothly at her weetlesse wofull stound. . . . III. ii. 26. 9
Therewith th' Enchaunter softly gan to *smyle* . . . III. iii. 17. 1
yet she did *smile* thereat. . . . III. vi. 15. 9
Thereat Diana gan to *smile*, . . . III. vi. 21. 1
Thereat Sir Satyrane gan *smyle*, . . . III. ix. 6. 6
Cupid selfe, it seeing, close did *smyle* . . . III. x. 5. 7
At which his vaine excuse they all gan *smile*, . . . IV. iv. 11. 1
seeming still to *smile*, Glauconome, . . . IV. xi. 50. 8
with Sardonian *smyle* Laughing on her, . . . V. ix. 12. 6
they alwaies smoothly seeme to *smile*, . . . VI. x. 24. 1
Her *smile* me drawes; . . . *Am.* xxi. 12
Sweet *Smile!* the daughter of the Queene of Love, . . . *Am.* xxxix. 1
Her eyes looke lovely, and upon them *smyle;* . . . *Am.* xlvii. 10
let faire Venus, . . . upon you *smile*, . . . *Proth.* 97
Whose *smile*, they say, hath vertue to remove . . . *Proth.* 98

Smiled. all the heavens on lower creatures *smilde*, . . . *Mui.* 53
Thereat Sir Guyon *smylde;* . . . II. v. 18. 1
Therewith she sweetly *smyld*. . . . II. vi. 36. 1
smiled at his pryde. . . . III. xi. 32. 9
She alway *smyld*, . . . III. xii. 13. 5

Smiles. deckt with *smyles* that all sad humors chaced, . . . IV. x. 50. 8
Sometime with witching *smyles;* . . . IV. x. 57. 3
The charming *smiles*, that rob sence . . . *Am.* xvii. 10
Mark when she *smiles* with amiable cheare, . . . *Am.* xl. 1
with flattring *smyles* weake harts doth guyde . . . *Am.* xlvii. 5
cloud of pryde . . . with *smiles* she drives away. . . . *Am.* lxxxi. 8
her *smiles*, with which their soules they feede, . . . *H.B.* 248

Smiling. her faire eyes, sweet *smyling* in delight, . . . II. xii. 78. 6
sides empurpled were with *smyling* red; . . . III. vii. 17. 2
thy sweete *smyling* mother from above, . . . IV. Pr. 5. 7
Artegall close *smyling* joy'd in secret hart. . . . IV. vi. 32. 9
with thy *smyling* looke doest pacifie The raging seas, . . . IV. x. 44. 4
To whom God Neptune, softly *smyling*, thus: . . . IV. xii. 30. 1
and brode displayes his *smyling* hew. . . . VI. ii. 35. 9
Now *smyling* smoothly, like to sommers day, . . . VI. vi. 42. 7
Trust not the treason of those *smyling* lookes, . . . *Am.* xlvii. 1
his mother closely *smiling* . . . *Epig.* iv. 11

Smirk. yond Bullocke . . . So *smirke*, so smoothe, . . . *S.C.* F. 72

Smit. *See* **Smitten, Smot, Smote.**
upon his crest With rigor so outrageous he *smitt*, . . . I. ii. 18. 7
ever at Pyrochles when he *smitt*, . . . II. viii. 43. 1
When first her tender hart was with his beautie *smit*. . . . III. i. 34. 9
blinded God, which hath ye blindly *smit*, . . . III. ii. 35. 8
with great ruth and terrour she was *smit*, . . . III. xi. 12. 8
all were with amazement *smit*, . . . IV. i. 14. 2
being doubly smitten likewise doubly *smit*. . . . IV. ix. 29. 9
He ment the thiefe there deadly to have *smit:* . . . V. iii. 29. 8
on his head-peece him so fiercely *smit*, . . . V. iv. 39. 7
She her so rudely on the helmet *smit* . . . V. vii. 33. 7
quite *smit* off his arme . . . V. xi. 7. 9
he no word could speake, but *smit* his brest, . . . VI. xi. 28. 5
the harder she is *smit* With all the playnts . . . *Am.* xxxii. 11

Smite. With hideous horror both together *smight*, . . . I. v. 8. 6
Upon his crested scalp so sore did *smite*, . . . I. xi. 35. 7
on him they freshly gan to *smight*. . . . II. ii. 23. 9
she raught him stones, wherwith to *smite*, . . . II. iv. 5. 5
With his bright blade did *smite* at him . . . II. v. 4. 2
thother did upon his troncheon *smyte*, . . . II. viii. 38. 5
with their wicked wings them ofte did *smight*, . . . II. xii. 35. 8
Which two did yield before she did them *smight*. . . . III. i. 29. 6
the great Castle *smite* so sore withall, . . . III. iii. 49. 8
she againe him in the shield did *smite* . . . III. iv. 16. 1
so deadly *smight* Her dearest sonne, . . . III. iv. 44. 4
him he could not come to *smite;* . . . III. v. 19. 7
With burning charet wheeles it nigh to *smite;* . . . III. vii. 41. 7
With curtaxe used Diamond to *smite*, . . . IV. ii. 42. 7
with her rod did softly *smite* the raile, . . . IV. iii. 46. 2
him likewise he quickly downe did *smight*, . . . IV. iv. 21. 3
Oft making offer him to *smite*, . . . V. viii. 42. 2
their sharpe speares doe both together *smite* . . . V. x. 32. 2
reare His cruell hand to *smite* him mortally, . . . V. xii. 20. 3
did him *smite* with all his might and maine, . . . V. xii. 23. 6
such as sudden rage him lent to *smite;* . . . VI. iv. 4. 3
with his sword him on the head did *smyte*, . . . VI. vi. 30. 6

Smite—*Continued.*
did him *smite* Full in the shield . . . VI. vii. 8. 1
When they their tymbrels *smyte,* . . . *Epith.* 134
Smites. at his foe with furious rigor *smites,* . . . I. viii. 18. 5
who that *smites* it mars his joyous play, . . . III. vii. 41. 8
Smith. the wicked carle, the maister *Smith,* . . . IV. v. 44. 1
a *Smith* that . . . The stubborne mettall seeketh to subdew, . . . V. v. 7. 6
The paynefull *smith,* with force of fervent heat, . . . *Am.* xxxii. 1
Smith's. seard In *smythes* fire-spitting forge, . . . II. vii. 3. 9
Smitten. *See* **Smit, Smot.**
Thereat he *smitten* was with great affright, . . . II. xi. 39. 1
they *smitten* were With great amazement . . . III. ix. 23. 1
being doubly *smitten* likewise doubly smit. . . . IV. ix. 29. 9
Smock. in her snow-white *smocke,* with locks unbownd, . . . III. i. 63. 7
did her lilly *smock* with staines of vermeil steep. . . . III. i. 65. 9
wrapt him in her *smock:* . . . *Epig.* iv. 42
Smoke. She climbed up to heaven in the *smoke.* . . . *Bel.*[1] ix. 8
in the *smoake* she unto heaven did stie. . . . *Bel.*[2] xi. 8
Sike prayse is *smoke,* that sheddeth in the skye; . . . *S.C.* O. 35
Is turnd to *smoake,* that doth to nothing fade; . . . *Ti.* 123
Nought else but *smoke,* and fumeth soone away; . . . *Col.* 720
Oft fire is without *smoke,* . . . I. i. 12. 4
With *smoake* and sulphur hiding all the place, . . . I. v. 31. 5
smouldry cloud of duskish stincking *smoke;* . . . I. vii. 13. 8
Till living moysture into *smoke* do flow, . . . I. ix. 8. 4
hide the *smoke* that did his fire display, . . . I. ix. 16. 4
A cloud of smoothering *smoke,* and sulphure seare, . . . I. xi. 13. 7
all the ayre about with *smoke* and stench did fill. . . . I. xi. 13. 9
With fowle enfouldred *smoake* and flashing fire, . . . I. xi. 40. 2
Enrold in duskish *smoke* and brimstone blew: . . . I. xi. 44. 4
Enwrapt in coleblacke clowds and filthy *smoke,* . . . I. xi. 44. 8
That vanisht into *smoke* and cloudes swift; . . . I. xi. 54. 2
the last deadly *smoke* aloft did steeme, . . . I. xii. 2. 4
puffed up with *smoke* of vanity, . . . II. iii. 5. 3
The smouldring dust did rownd about him *smoke,* . . . II. v. 3. 4
His face with *smoke* was tand, . . . II. vii. 3. 6
fowle *smoke* and clouds more black then Jett. . . . II. vii. 28. 9
long tonnell thence The *smoke* forth threw. . . . II. ix. 29. 4
carries into *smoake* with rage and horror great. . . . II. xi. 32. 9
from like inward fire that outward *smoke* had steemd. . . . III. i. 55. 9
As *smoke* and sulphure mingled with confused stryfe. . . . III. ii. 32. 9
she did descry A litle *smoke,* . . . III. vii. 5. 2
The inward *smoke,* that did before but steeme, . . . III. viii. 26. 4
A flaming fire, ymixt with smouldry *smoke* . . . III. xi. 21. 6
made the sparckling waves to *smoke* agayne, . . . III. xi. 41. 3
A direfull stench of *smoke* and sulphure mixt . . . III. xii. 2. 5
Besmeard with *smoke* that nigh his eye-sight blent; . . . IV. v. 34. 7
Smoky. As in the *smoky* forge it was compilde, . . . III. vii. 30. 5
Smook. There forth issewd from under th' Altars *smooke* . . . V. xi. 22. 4
Smooth. yond Bullocke . . . So smirke, so *smoothe,* . . . *S.C.* F. 72
with *smooth* flattering Doo fawne on you, . . . *Ti.* 200
well could file his tongue as *smooth* as glas: . . . I. i. 35. 7
more *smooth* and fine, Then Jett or Marble . . . II. ix. 24. 2
softly gan to smyle At her *smooth* speeches, . . . III. iii. 17. 2
Drew the *smooth* charett of sad Cymoent: . . . III. iv. 33. 2
With such *smooth* termes her error I abusd . . . IV. viii. 60. 7
So *smooth* of tongue, and subtile in his tale, . . . V. ix. 5. 6
made *smooth* fields now full of flowres? . . . V. x. 23. 5
Smoothest. Of *smoothest* marble stone in order set, . . . *Gn.* 663
Smoothly. Did smyle full *smoothly* . . . III. ii. 26. 9
Now smyling *smoothly,* like to sommers day, . . . VI. vi. 42. 7
they alwaies *smoothly* seeme to smile, . . . VI. x. 24. 1
Smoothness. Ne Poole so small, that can his *smoothnesse* holde VII. vii. 20. 6
Smot. *See* **Smit, Smitten, Smote.**
He *smott* off his left arme, . . . I. viii. 10. 6
With mortall steele him *smot* againe . . . I. viii. 24. 2
smot againe with more outrageous might; . . . I. xi. 25. 2
With sharpe intended sting so rude him *smott,* . . . I. xi. 38. 2
He *smott* thereat with all his might and maine, . . . I. xi. 43. 4
smott, and bitt, and kickt, and scratcht, and rent. . . . II. iv. 6. 8
him so sore *smott* with his yron mace, . . . II. xi. 34. 8
downe him *smot* ere well aware he weare; . . . III. i. 28. 8
Til thou in open fielde adowne be *smott:* . . . III. ii. 46. 5
with terrour and with aw So inly *smot,* . . . III. vii. 13. 6
with their faulchins *smot;* . . . V. vii. 29. 2
But at him flew, and with his speare him *smot;* . . . VI. ii. 19. 8
Smote. *See* **Smit, Smot.**
Himselfe *smote* with his beake, as in disdaine, . . . *Pet.* v. 10
He *smote* his steed, . . . *Ti.* 657
with her weapon dredd She *smote* the ground, . . . *Mui.* 325
smote off quite his right leg by the knee, . . . I. viii. 22. 4
He *smote* his courser in the trembling flanck, . . . II. iii. 6. 5
He *smote* so manly on his shoulder plate, . . . II. v. 7. 6
he *smote* his haughty crest so hye, . . . II. v. 12. 4
Smote him so hugely on his haughtie crest, . . . II. viii. 33. 6
He *smote* the sea, which calmed was . . . II. xii. 26. 7
Smote him so rudely on the Pannikell, . . . III. v. 23. 5
sight, which *smote* Deepe indignation . . . III. viii. 31. 3
So mightily she *smote* him, . . . He fell halfe dead: . . . III. xii. 34. 1
with his axe him *smote* in evill hower, . . . IV. iii. 20. 5
smote the other with so wondrous might, . . . IV. iii. 30. 2
Shee *smote* them lightly with her powrefull wand. . . . IV. iii. 48. 2
smote downe all that was betweene, . . . IV. iv. 34. 2
Him at the first encounter downe he *smote,* . . . IV. iv. 40. 6
smote him on his Umbriere So sore, . . . IV. iv. 44. 3
to the ground she *smote* both horse and man; . . . IV. vi. 10. 7
smote at him with all his might; . . . IV. viii. 44. 6
He *smote* at him with all his might and maine, . . . IV. viii. 45. 3
He *smote* it off, that tumbling on the strand . . . V. ii. 18. 5
smote at him with so importune might, . . . V. xi. 11. 6

Smote—*Continued.*
on the helmet *smote* him formerlie, . . . VI. i. 38. 8
smote him on the knee that never yet was bent. . . . VI. viii. 15. 9
Smothering. A cloud of *smoothering* smoke, and sulphure seare, I. xi. 13. 7
Smouldering. Enrold in flames, and *smouldring* dreriment, . . . I. viii. 9. 4
The *smouldring* dust did rownd about him smoke, . . . II. v. 3. 4
Smouldery. *smouldry* cloud of duskish stincking smoke; . . . I. vii. 13. 8
A flaming fire, ymixt with *smouldry* smoke . . . III. xi. 21. 6
Snaggy. his stalking steps are stayde Upon a *snaggy* Oke, . . . I. vii. 10. 7
Snags. with a staffe, all full of litle *snags,* . . . II. xi. 23. 7
knottie *snags* were sharpned all afore, . . . IV. vii. 7. 5
Snails. some like *Snailes,* some did like spyders shew, . . . II. xi. 13. 3
Snake. Shepheards devise she hateth as the *snake,* . . . *S.C.* Ja. 65
were it faerie, feend, or *snake,* . . . *S.C.* Mar. 76
The scalie backe of that most hideous *snake* . . . *Gn.* 305
her he hated as the hissing *snake,* . . . I. ii. 9. 8
in his bosome secretly there lay An hatefull *Snake,* . . . I. iv. 31. 4
that renowmed *Snake* Which great Alcides in Stremona slew, . . . I. vii. 17. 1
creeping close, as *Snake* in hidden weedes, . . . I. ix. 28. 8
Orion, flying fast from hissing *snake,* . . . II. ii. 46. 2
as cold and drery as a *snake,* . . . II. xi. 22. 4
doth the charmed *Snake* in slomber lay. . . . III. ii. 15. 6
as a *Snake,* still lurked in his wounded mynd. . . . III. x. 55. 9
O hatefull hellish *Snake!* . . . III. xi. 1. 1
Like a discolourd *Snake,* . . . III. xi. 28. 8
a *Snake,* whom wearie winters teene Hath worne . . . IV. iii. 23. 7
a *snake,* whose head and tail were fast combyned. . . . IV. x. 40. 9
to a *snake* againe Have turn'd himselfe, . . . V. ix. 19. 1
The other held a *snake* with venime fraught, . . . V. xii. 30. 5
even that halfe-gnawen *snake,* . . . V. xii. 39. 3
Snakes. Ten thousand *snakes* cralling about his hed . . . *Gn.* 348
fiends of hell, Girt with long *snakes,* . . . *Gn.* 626
some like to *Snakes,* . . . II. xi. 10. 4
Snaky. He tooke Caduceus, his *snakie* wand, . . . *Hub.* 1292
the Furies fell Theyr *snaky* heads doe combe, . . . *Am.* lxxxv. 3
Snaky-lock. To *snaky-locke* Medusa to repayre, . . . III. xi. 42. 8
Snaky-paced. Nor swelling streames of that God *snakie-paced,* . . . *Ro.* xiii. 10
Snaky-wreathed. on her shoulder laid His *snaky-wreathed* Mace, VII. vi. 18. 2
Snar. Tygres, that did seeme to gren And *snar* at all . . . VI. xii. 27. 7
Snare. whom he with guilefull *snare* Entrapped slew, . . . I. iv. 47. 5
Cupids wanton *snare* As hell she hated; . . . I. x. 30. 5
he, at first or last, was trapt in womens *snare.* . . . V. vi. 1. 9
in some *snare* or gin set close behind, Entrapped . . . VII. vi. 48. 6
entangle in that golden *snare;* . . . *Am.* xxxvii. 6
caught in cunning *snare* Of a deare foe, . . . *Am.* lxxi. 5
Snares. wrapt his winges twaine In lymie *snares* . . . *Mui.* 429
brought t'unworthie wretchednesse Through envies *snares,* . . . I. iii. 1. 4
To ketch him at a vauntage in his *snares.* . . . II. i. 4. 5
a discolourd Snake, whose hidden *snares* . . . III. xi. 28. 8
For freeing from their *snares* Irena thrall: . . . V. xii. 37. 5
stealthes shal worke, and *snares* shal spread . . . *Epith.* 361
Snarled. from her head ofte rente her *snarled* heare: . . . III. xii. 17. 5
Snatch. To steale a *snatch* of amorous conceipt, . . . II. v. 34. 6
To get a *snatch* when turned is his face. . . . III. i. 22. 5
snatch, and byte, and rend, and tug, and teare; . . . VI. xi. 17. 6
Snatched. A shaft in earnest *snatched,* . . . *S.C.* Mar. 96
gage Of victors glory from him *snacht* away: . . . I. iv. 39. 6
He *snatcht* the vele that hong her face before: . . . I. vi. 4. 7
Out of his hand she *snatcht* the cursed knife, . . . I. ix. 52. 4
Snatcht up both horse and man, . . . I. xi. 18. 9
with his cruell clawes he *snatcht* the wood, . . . I. xi. 22. 2
the cruell steel He lightly *snatcht,* . . . II. i. 43. 2
Had he so doen, he had him *snatcht* away, . . . II. vii. 34. 5
That vertuous steele he rudely *snatcht* away, . . . II. viii. 22. 6
Snatcht first the one, and then the other Jade, . . . II. xi. 31. 2
The same he *snatcht,* and with exceeding sway . . . II. xi. 36. 1
Twixt his two mighty armes him up he *snatcht,* . . . II. xi. 42. 1
Trojane boy so fayre He *snatcht* from Ida hill, . . . III. xi. 34. 5
In Satyres shape Antiopa he *snatcht;* . . . III. xi. 35. 1
Had unawares her *snatched* up from ground: . . . IV. vii. 4. 6
This ugly creature in his armes her *snatcht,* . . . IV. vii. 8. 1
lightly *snatcht* him up and with me bore away. . . . IV. viii. 61. 9
Snatches. To filch away sweet *snatches* of delight, . . . *Epith.* 362
Snatcheth. *snatcheth* quite away One of the litle yonglings . . . *Mui.* 406
The Sarazin, . . . *Snatcheth* his sword, . . . I. ii. 17. 2
Snatching. *snatching* his bright sword began to close With her III. i. 9. 3
snatching from her hand halfe angrily The belt . . . IV. v. 19. 8
snatching forth his direfull deadly blade . . . IV. vi. 12. 2
with furious bit *Snatching* at every thing . . . V. viii. 49. 4
snatching her soone up, ere well she knew, . . . V. ix. 14. 4
snatching neare his syde His trustie sword, . . . VI. vii. 25. 3
Snebbe. *See* **Snib.**
Snib. to scold And *snebbe* the good Oake, . . . *S.C.* F. 126
list at will them to revile or *snib:* . . . *Hub.* 372
Snort. His seahorses did seeme to *snort* amayne, . . . III. xi. 41. 1
They snuf, they *snort,* they bounce, they rage, . . . V. ii. 15. 6
Snow. As *snowe* and golde together had been wrought: . . . *Pet.* vi. 6
In raine, or *snowe,* or haile, he forth is horld; . . . *Ro.* xx. 8
I saw a Bull as white as driven *snowe,* . . . *Van.* ii. 2
heaped *snowe* burdned him so sore, . . . *S.C.* F. 233
a lowly Asse more white then *snow,* . . . I. i. 4. 2
An old old man, with beard as white as *snow,* . . . I. viii. 30. 2
it is chaste and pure as purest *snow,* . . . II. ii. 9. 7
Their fluttring arrowes, thicke as flakes of *snow,* . . . II. xi. 18. 2
on a Palfrey rydes more white then *snow,* . . . III. v. 5. 6
Yet still he wasted, as the *snow* congeald . . . III. v. 49. 5
purest *snow* in massy mould congeald, . . . III. viii. 6. 2
Rayne, haile, and *snowe* do pay them sad penance, . . . VII. vii. 23. 7
The pure *snow,* with goodly vermill stayne . . . *Epith.* 227
The *snow,* . . . Did never whiter shew, . . . *Proth.* 40

Snow-white. in her *snow-white* smocke, with locks unbownd, III. i. 63. 7
Snowy. There stood a *snowie* Swan of heavenly hiew, *Ti.* 590
to her *snowy* Palfrey got agayne, I. iii. 8. 8
With *snowy* lockes adowne his shoulders shed; I. x. 48. 2
his sharpe sword Against her *snowy* brest II. i. 11. 7
forelay Athwart her *snowy* brest, II. iii. 29. 6
His *snowy* front, curled with golden heares, II. viii. 5. 5
The bashfull blood her *snowy* cheekes did dye, II. ix. 41. 4
otherwhere the *snowy* substaunce sprent With vermell, II. xii. 45. 5
their *snowy* limbes, as through a vele, II. xii. 64. 6
Her *snowy* brest was bare II. xii. 78. 1
staynes his *snowy* skin with hatefull hew: III. i. 38. 6
did purely shyne Upon her *snowy* cheeke; III. vii. 9. 4
The Witch creates a *snowy* Lady III. viii. Arg.
marke her *snowy* skin. III. viii. 24. 9
Then was he turnd into a *snowy* Swan, III. xi. 32. 1
dyde . . . red her skin all *snowy* cleene, III. xii. 20. 9
Unwares it strooke into her *snowie* chest, III. xii. 33. 4
from Braggadocchio whilome reft The *snowy* Florimell, IV. ii. 4. 7
It was to weete that *snowy* Florimell, IV. iv. 8. 1
that *snowy* Mayd Was in the middest plast IV. v. 26. 1
the love of that same *snowy* maid, IV. ix. 24. 2
In that late Turney for the *snowy* maide; IV. ix. 28. 7
Psamathe for her brode *snowy* brests; IV. xi. 51. 5
met Upon the way with that his *snowy* Dame: V. iii. 10. 4
Then forth he brought his *snowy* Florimele, V. iii. 17. 1
He gazed still upon that *snowy* mayd; V. iii. 18. 7
Then did he set her by that *snowy* one, V. iii. 24. 1
Her *snowy* substance melted as with heat, V. iii. 24. 7
all her garments from her *snowy* brest, VI. i. 17. 7
rends her golden locks, and *snowy* brests embrew. VI. viii. 40. 9
having her *snowy* brest As yet not laced, VI. xii. 15. 2
snowy browes, like budded Bellamoures; *Am.* lxiv. 7
Her *snowie* necke lyke to a marble towre; *Epith.* 177
in her *snowy* bosome boldly lay *H.L.* 289
Their *snowie* Foreheads therewithall they crownd, *Proth.* 86
Snowy-necked. *snowy neckd* Doris, and milkewhite Galathaea: IV. xi. 49. 9
Snubs. club . . . All armd with ragged *snubbes* I. viii. 7. 4
Snuff. They *snuf,* they snort, they bounce, they rage, V. ii. 15. 6
So (*partial list*). *See* **How-so, If so be, Whatso, Whatsoever, Whenso, Whereso, Wheresoever, Whomso, Whoso, Whosoever.**
seing hir striken . . . With *so* great noyse I start *Bel.*[1] xi. 14
So I, that know this worlds inconstancies, *Bel.* i. 12
Sith that mine eyes have seene *so* faire a sight *Bel.* iv. 13
so in their cruell race They pincht *Pet.* i. 8
sudden storme did *so* turmoyle the aire, *Pet.* ii. 7
woven *so* they were, As snowe and golde *Pet.* vi. 5
To see such pleasures gon *so* suddenly. *Pet.*[2] iv. 14
sowne in the sacred sand; *So* this *Ro.* x. 5
So did that haughtie front, *Ro.* xii. 9
So long as Joves great Bird did make his flight, *Ro.* xvii. 1
So, when the compast course . . . is ronne, *Ro.* xxii. 9
Sith that *so* small *so* mightie can constraine? *Van.* iii. 14
'All *so* my lustfull leafe is drye and sere, *S.C.* Ja. 37
Thomalin, why sytten we *soe,* *S.C.* Mar. 1
What fallen the flocke, *so* they han the fleece, *S.C.* May 49
How shoulden shepheardes live, if not *so?* *S.C.* May 148
if foxes bene *so* crafty as *so,* *S.C.* May 312
Forsake the soyle that *so* doth thee bewitch: *S.C.* Jun. 18
Of heaven to demen *so;* *S.C.* Jul. 94
That als we mought doe *soe.* *S.C.* Jul. 120
So hath theyr god them blist; *S.C.* Jul. 174
sitting *so* with bared scalpe, *S.C.* Jul. 221
so there is, but all of miserye: *S.C.* S. 29
sicker, *so* it is, as the bright starre Seemeth *S.C.* S. 76
So high to sore and make *so* large a flight; *S.C.* O. 86
*All *so* my age . . . To thinges of ryper reason *S.C.* D. 75
So nowe he stormes . . . *So* now his *S.C.* D. 131, 132
So well as I her words remember may. *Hub.* 42
Ne was it *so* by institution Ordained *Hub.* 144
they which call them *so* more beggers bee; *Hub.* 162
so will wander free Where so us listeth, *Hub.* 168
Nath'les perhaps ye things may handle *soe,* *Hub.* 641
So that it seemeth I was made to raigne, *Hub.* 1031
So that it wholly springeth from my wit: *Hub.* 1037
so he got it, little did he pas. *Hub.* 1150
So much as they were able well to beare, *Hub.* 1157
'Soft, Goddie Sheepe! . . . not *soe:* *Hub.* 1213
So shall succeeding ages have no light *T.M.* 103
So is the man that wants intendiment. *T.M.* 144
seeing her doo *soe,* *T.M.* 297
My Daphne hence departing bad me *so;* *D.* 454
'Ah! nay (said Colin) neither *so,* nor *so:* *Col.* 376
So Ennius . . . *So* Maro . . . *So* you, great Lord, *Ded.Son.*i.7,8,9
sith thou maist not *so,* give leave a while *Ded. Son.* xii. 9
on whom while *so* he gazd, I. i. 26. 3
So lively and *so* like in all mens sight, I. i. 45. 4
So, slyding softly forth, I. i. 54. 9
knighthood I *so* much should shame, I. iii. 28. 3
sooth to say, why I lefte you *so* long, I. iii. 29. 1
He left him lying *so,* I. iii. 39. 9
Amased stands, her selfe *so* mockt to see I. iii. 40. 2
would not leave her *so,* I. iii. 44. 6
Called Fidess', and *so* supposd to be, I. iv. 2. 4
pittie, that *so* faire a mould Did on *so* weake foundation I. iv. 5. 3, 4
Such endlesse richesse, and *so* sumpteous shew; I. iv. 7. 5
mind in meat and drinke was drowned *so,* I. iv. 23. 4
So, having solaced themselves a space I. iv. 38. 1
And souce *so* sore that they the heavens affray; I. v. 8. 7

So—*Continued.*
The wise Southsayer, seeing *so* sad sight, I. v. 8. 8
her abhorred face, *so* filthy and *so* fowle. I. v. 30. 9
'Not *so,*' (quoth she) 'but, sith that I. v. 43. 1
so fearlesse and *so* fell he grew, I. vi. 25. 1
gentle Dame, *so* hurtlesse and *so* trew: I. vi. 31. 7
What man *so* wise, what earthly witt *so* ware, I. vii. 1. 1
hart, *so* plungd . . . And heaped with *so* huge misfortunes I. vii. 39. 2, 3
'Right *so,*' (quoth he) I. vii. 41. 3
No gate *so* strong, no locke *so* firme I. viii. 4. 8
sad earth, wounded with *so* sore assay, I. viii. 8. 7
With mortall steele him smot againe *so* sore, I. viii. 24. 2
well begonne, end all *so* well, I pray! I. viii. 28. 4
So fayre a creature yet saw never sunny day. I. ix. 13. 9
her encrease *so* evermore!' I. x. 16. 9
So in short space they did to health restore, I. x. 27. 8
besought, to be *so* good As . . . to schoole her knight, I. x. 32. 5
as the tree does fall, *so* lyes it ever low. I. x. 41. 9
shall I soone,' . . . '*so* God me grace, I. x. 64. 1
sore amoved with *so* puissaunt push, I. xi. 16. 6
So far as Ewghen bow a shaft may send, I. xi. 19. 2
With which he stroke *so* furious and *so* fell, I. xi. 24. 2
So downe he fell, I. xi. 54. 1, 3, 5, 9
shall finde friends, if need requireth *soe.* I. xii. 28. 8
spoyle her dainty corps, *so* faire and sheene, II. i. 10. 5
So God ye speed and send you good successe, II. i. 25. 6
'Him *so* I sought; and *so* at last I fownd, II. i. 54. 1
For all *so* great shame after death II. i. 59. 8
So both agree their bodies to engrave: II. i. 60. 1
some were *so* from their sourse indewd II. ii. 6. 1
So double was his paines, *so* double be his praise. II. ii. 25. 9
beames . . . *So* passing persant, and *so* wondrous bright, II. iii. 23. 4
Was he abashed now, not fighting *so;* II. iv. 8. 5
'Not *so,* O Guyon! never thinke that *so* II. iv. 10. 2
So easie is t' appease the stormy winde II. vi. 8. 8
thunder light Does scorch not halfe *so* sore, II. vi. 50. 8
ghoste In flaming Phlegeton does not *so* felly roste.' II. vi. 50. 9
so fond and undiscreet *So* evill thing to seeke II. vii. 14. 7, 8
him seeing labour *so* in vaine, II. vii. 59. 1
was the force *so* furious and *so* fell, II. viii. 31. 1
'Not *so* th' Arabian Myrrhe . . . Nor *so* did Biblis III. ii. 41. 1, 2
Not *so;* for what the Fates do once decree, IV. ii. 51. 8
living thus a wretch, and loving *so,* IV. ix. 39. 8
So all that ever yet I have endured IV. x. 2. 6
(*so* young mens thoughts are bold) IV. x. 4. 6
Loose *so* immortall glory, and *so* endlesse gaines. IV. xi. 22. 9
So ever loose, *so* ever happy be! IV. xii. 11. 5
Such as behind their backs (*so* backward bred) V. Pr. 2. 6
'His name is hight Pollente, rightly *so,* V. ii. 7. 1
whether it be *so* or no, I can not say. V. iv. 13. 9
whether it indeede be *so* or no, V. iv. 14. 1
Even *so* did Radigund with bootlesse paine V. v. 15. 8
making all her Knights and people to doe *so.* V. viii. 20. 9
When *so* she lagged, as she needs mote *so* VI. ii. 10. 6
Ne cared as a coward *so* to be condemned VI. iii. 36. 9
'*So* is my Lord now seiz'd of all the land, VI. iv. 30. 1
glooming sadly, *so* to cloke her matter; VI. vi. 42. 8
what the matter was that mov'd her *so?* VI. xii. 17. 4
Made him *so* frollick and *so* full of lust: VII. vii. 39. 5
So nothing heere long standeth in one stay: VII. vii. 47. 7
were they *so,* as ye them faine to be, VII. vii. 49. 6
So that 'as changefull as the Moone' men use to say. VII. vii. 50. 9
So many turning cranks these have, *so* many crookes. VII. vii. 52. 9
So sundry wayes and fashions as clerkes faine, VII. vii. 55. 2
Do worke their owne perfection *so* by fate: VII. vii. 58. 7
So was the Titanesse put downe and whist, VII. vii. 59. 6
state of life *so* tickle, And love of things *so* vaine VII. viii. .1 6, 7
flowring pride, *so* fading and *so* fickle, VII. viii. 1. 8
So, when I thinke to end *Am.* xxiii. 9
So every sweet with soure is tempred still, *Am.* xxvi. 9
her cold *so* great Is not dissolv'd through my *so* hot desyre, *Am.* xxx. 2. 3
to *so* hard a hart Given *so* goodly giftes *Am.* xxxi. 1, 2
so plenty makes me poore. *Am.* xxxv. 8
So my storme-beaten hart likewise is cheared *Am.* xl. 13
if her nature and her wil be *so,* *Am.* xli. 5
beleeve me there is more then *so,* *H.B.* 85
Th' Almighty, seeing their *so* bold assay, *H.H.L.* 85
So that next off-spring of the Makers love, *H.H.L.* 92
So, taking flesh of sacred virgins wombe, *H.H.L.* 146
that deare Lord with *so* entyre affection, *H.H.L.* 157
What hart can feele least touch of *so* sore launch, *H.H.L.* 162
Of the soare faulcon *so* I learne to fly, *H.H.B.* 26
so still more cleare And faire it growes, *H.H.B.* 45
So those likewise doe by degrees redound, *H.H.B.* 75
Soak. T' abate all spasme, and *soke* the swelling bruze; III. v. 33. 7
So and so. didst thou . . . *so and so* to noble Britomart: IV. vii. 2. 2
Soar. whose high top above the starres did *sore,* *Ro.* iv. 1
So high to *sore* and make so large a flight; *S.C.* O. 86
fluttering round about them still does *sore:* *Gn.* 406
sad horror with grim hew Did alwaies *sore,* II. vii. 23. 2
far above thy forces pitch to *sore;* V. ii. 34. 4
Soared. An Eagle *sored* hye, *S.C.* Jul. 222
all the champain o're he *soared* light; *Mui.* 149
With his broad sayles, about him *soared* round; I. xi. 18. 7
Soar-falcon. Of the *soare faulcon* so I learne to fly, *H.H.B.* 26
Soaring. *See* **High-soaring.**
For dread of *soring* hauke her selfe hath hid, II. iii. 36. 2
The *soring* clouds into sad showres ymolt; III. xi. 25. 8
Twise was he seene in *soaring* Eagles shape, III. xi. 34. 1
Soring through his wide Empire of the aire V. iv. 42. 2

Soaring—*Continued.*
in their tops the *soring* hauke did towre, VI. x. 6. 8
So as. *So as* thou can many thinges relate; *S.C.* S. 23
So as I can I wil thee comfort; *S.C.* S. 255
So as the Heavens did quake his verse to here. *S.C.* O. 60
so as I ne wotte Whether rejoyce or weepe *S.C.* N. 204
So as their begging now them failed quyte, *Hub.* 347
Yet *so as* him their terrour more adornes. *Mui.* 88
So as he rag'd emongst that beastly rout, *As.* 115
so as I found, to tell *Col.* 683
like *so as* the rest, he prayd III. ix. 12. 5
full of guests . . . *So as* he was not let to enter III. ix. 13. 5
To doe her service *so as* I am bond: V. ii. 4. 4
So as ere long he had that knightes wound Recured well, VI. iv. 16. 6
right *so as* Coridon had taught: VI. xi. 41. 7
Sob. with most painefull pangs to sigh and *sob*, III. xi. 8. 8
Sobbed. He sigh'd, he *sobd*, he swownd, III. x. 7. 4
Sobbing. Supplide her *sobbing* breaches with sad complement. III. iv. 35. 9
one close by her side Sighing and *sobbing* sore, IV. vii. 10. 2
So be. *See* **If so be.**
So be your goodlihead doe not disdayne *S.C.* May 270
(*so be* thou deigne to heare Rude ditties, *S.C.* D. 13
So be, O Queene! you equall favour showe.' I. iv. 42. 7
'That shall I you recount, . . . *So be* ye pleasd III. vii. 53. 5
Sober. There thou must walke in *sober* gravitee, *Hub.* 496
Sober he seemde, and very sagely sad, I. i. 29. 5
Venus never had so *sober* mood: I. vi. 16. 7
With *sober* gladnesse and myld modestie; I. viii. 26. 5
The eldest two, most *sober*, chast, and wise, I. x. 4. 5
sober lookes her wisedome well descryde: I. x. 34. 3
A noble crew . . . Of sage and *sober* peres, I. xii. 5. 5
sayd that royall Pere in *sober* wise; I. xii. 17. 1
forth proceeding with sad *sober* cheare, I. xii. 21. 4
With *sober* countenance thus to him sayd: I. xii. 33. 3
He seemd to be a sage and *sober* syre; II. i. 7. 7
Therewith amoved from his *sober* mood, II. i. 12. 1
A *sober* sad and comely courteous Dame; II. ii. 14. 5
hearken to the *sober* speaches which she spoke. II. ii. 28. 9
With *sober* grace and goodly carriage: II. ii. 38. 2
sober Guyon, hearing him so rayle, II. vi. 40. 2
in which Doth *sober* Alma dwell, II. ix. Arg.
Whiles it is kept in *sober* government; II. ix. 1. 4
in demeanure *sober*, and in counsell sage. II. ix. 27. 9
It selfe doth offer to his *sober* eye, II. xii. 58. 2
With *sober* words, that sufferance desired, IV. i. 54. 4
Few men, but such as *sober* are and sage, IV. iii. 43. 7
seem'd to be of very *sober* mood, IV. x. 31. 4
next to her sate *sober* Modestie, IV. x. 51. 1
The *sober* mother seeing such her mood, VI. xii. 17. 1
Sobriety. With holesome reede of sad *sobriety*, VI. vi. 5. 7
Sobs. To falling rivers sound thus tun'd her *sobs*. *Bel.*[2] x. 4
here no tunes, save *sobs* and grones, shall ring. *D.* 14
With sighes, and *sobs*, and plaints, and piteous griefe, III. i. 53. 2
Sock. with Comick *sock* to beautefie The painted Theaters, *T.M.* 176
Sockets. set in silver *sockets* bright, II. ix. 46. 6
silver *sockets*, shyning like the skyes, III. viii. 7. 2
Socrates. th' unjust Atheniens made to dy Wise *Socrates*; II. vii. 52. 7
Sod. upon his lips to laie The sacred *sod*, *Ti.* 196
Sodain, -ly. *See* **Sudden, -ly.**
Sods. To dig up *sods* out of the flowrie grasse, *Gn.* 654
A little cottage . . . wald with *sods* around; III. vii. 6. 3
Soft. rest, *soft* sliding downe From heavens hight *Bel.*[2] i. 1
a noyse alluring sleepe *soft* trembled. *Bel.*[2] xii. 7
the *soft* sounding of the waters fall: *Pet.*[2] iv. 7
leave to live hard, and learne to ligge *soft*: *S.C.* May 125
(thou sacred childe) come sliding *soft*, *Gn.* 37
my *soft* Muse, as for her power more meete, *Gn.* 51
on the *soft* greene grasse feeding their fills, *Gn.* 78
some *soft* Willow, or new growen stud; *Gn.* 84
On the *soft* grasse his limbs doth oft display, *Gn.* 108
doo thou haunt the *soft* downe-rolling river, *Gn.* 636
'*Soft*, Gooddie Sheepe! (then said the Foxe) *Hub.* 1213
He *soft* arrived on the grassie plaine, *Hub.* 1263
To romble gently downe with murmur *soft*, *T.M.* 26
Doo mone my miserie with silence *soft*: *T.M.* 292
in the lap of *soft* delight Beene long time luld, *T.M.* 301
haire as *soft* as silke, *Ti.* 563
two such fannes, so silken *soft* *Mui.* 107
In skilfull knitting of *soft* silken twyne, *Mui.* 362
He sighed *soft*, and inly deepe did grone, *D.* 48
The whiles *soft* death away her spirit hent, *D.* 258
Out of his lips like lilies pale and *soft*: *As.* 166
In loves *soft* laies and looser thoughts delight. *Col.* 423
more to lulle him in his slumber *soft*. I. i. 41. 1
As one then in a dreame, . . . He mumbled *soft*, I. i. 42. 9
yeelding *soft*, in that she nought gainsaid, I. ii. 27. 7
Then, sighing *soft*; 'I learne that litle sweet I. iv. 46. 3
Thence turning backe in silence *softe* they stole, I. v. 31. 1
soft withdrew His weapon huge, I. viii. 19. 7
Who answerd him full *soft*, I. viii. 32. 5
slombring *soft* my hart did steale away, I. ix. 13. 6
slyding *soft*, as downe to sleepe her layd, II. i. 56. 3
soft himselfe inclyning on his knee II. ii. 3. 1
algates mote he *soft* himselfe appease, II. ii. 12. 2
To lull him *soft* asleepe that by it lay: II. v. 30. 4
did *soft* embrew The sugred licour II. v. 33. 5
Into a shady dale she *soft* him led, II. vi. 14. 3
turning *soft* aside, II. ix. 39. 6
the rolling sea, resounding *soft*, II. xii. 33. 1
Th' Angelicall *soft* trembling voyces II. xii. 71. 3

Soft—*Continued.*
Now *soft*, now loud, unto the wind did call; II. xii. 71. 8
Wherewith she sighed *soft*, as if his case she rewd. II. xii. 73. 9
Whose sleepie head she in her lap did *soft* dispose. II. xii. 76. 9
her *soft* arme lay underneath his hed, III. i. 36. 3
With her *soft* garment wipes away the gore III. i. 38. 5
panting *softe*, and trembling every joynt, III. i. 60. 1
with her *softe* hand She softely felt III. i. 60. 6
lightly rased her *soft* silken skin, III. i. 65. 7
Her alablaster brest she *soft* did kis, III. ii. 42. 7
had no powre in his *soft* flesh to bite. III. v. 19. 5
Full of *soft* passion and unwonted smart: III. v. 30. 8
therewithall She sighed *soft*, III. vii. 9. 5
with *soft* sighes and lovely semblaunces III. vii. 16. 6
soft knocking entrance he desyrd. III. ix. 10. 1
sighing *soft* awhile, III. ix. 39. 1
he backe retyred *soft* away, III. xii. 4. 7
himselfe he *soft* withdrew Out of the field, IV. iv. 25. 1
A Knight *soft* ryding towards them they spyde, IV. vi. 9. 2
her enhaunced hand she downe can *soft* withdraw. IV. vi. 26. 9
Some litle whispering, and *soft* groning sound. IV. vii. 33. 4
handling *soft* the hurts which she did get; IV. vii. 35. 7
sufferaunce *soft*, which rigour can abate, IV. viii. 1. 7
still from her escaping *soft* away: IV. viii. 11. 5
With easie steps so *soft* as foot could stryde, IV. viii. 37. 2
solace in *soft* pleasure Those weaker Ladies IV. ix. 12. 7
the river rolling still With murmure *soft*, IV. x. 15. 9
all the Priests were damzels in *soft* linnen dight. IV. x. 38. 9
I with murmure *soft*, IV. x. 48. 1
Soft Silence, and submisse Obedience, IV. x. 51. 6
Yar, *soft* washing Norwitch wall, IV. xi. 33. 6
Soft Spio, sweete Endore, Sao sad, IV. xi. 48. 8
toucht with *soft* remorse and pitty rare; IV. xii. 12. 5
afterwards she gan him *soft* to shrieve, IV. xii. 26. 5
Now walking *soft*, now sitting still upright, V. vi. 26. 3
with *soft* delight Of sencelesse sleepe V. vii. 12. 5
on his steede her did sustaine . . . *soft* footing her beside; VI. iii. 28. 6
a *soft* murmure and confused sound VI. iv. 11. 7
From his *soft* eyes the teares he wypt away, VI. iv. 23. 4
Being now *soft* and fit them to embrace; VI. iv. 35. 7
none of them in his *soft* flesh did bite; VI. v. 18. 7
shedding few *soft* teares from tender eyne, VI. v. 24. 3
soft dismounting, like a weary lode, VI. vi. 19. 4
With a wyld man *soft* footing by his syde; VI. vii. 6. 2
Possessed of sweete sleepe that luld him *soft* in swound. VI. vii. 18. 9
as ye *soft* and tender are by kynde, VI. viii. 2. 1
So be ye *soft* and tender eeke in mynde; VI. viii. 2. 3
Thought sure have pownded him to powder *soft*, VI. viii. 15. 3
For love in *soft* delight thereon to rest; VI. viii. 42. 3
Mongst these sterne stounds to mingle *soft* delights; VII. vi. 37. 4
on the *soft* And downy grasse her dainty limbes to lay VII. vi. 42. 3
Shall handle you, and hold in loves *soft* (swete[1]) bands, *Am.* i. 3
cannot all these flames, in which I fry, Her hart . . . *soft* a whit; *Am.* xxxii. 6
The Ouzell shrills; the Ruddock warbles *soft*; *Epith.* 82
Soften. haughtie courage *soften*, IV. Pr. 5. 8
Yet cannot I, . . . *soften* her hard hart; *Am.* xviii. 6
Mote *soften* it and to his will allure; *Am.* li. 10
Softened. To you whose *softened* hearts it may empierse *As.* Pr. 9
My *softened* heart so sorely doth constraine, IV. i. 1. 7
whilest so thy *softened* spirit Is inly toucht, *H.H.L.* 253
Soft-feathered. safe committ to her *soft fethered* nest, III. i. 58. 7
Soft-footing. *See* **Footing, Soft.**
Soft-groaning. *See* **Groaning, Soft.**
Softly. in his throat him pricking *softly* under, *Van.* v. 9
I *softlie* sayd, Alcyon! *D.* 58
So having said, away she *softly* past: *D.* 293
softly tread The tender grasse, *D.* 311
in their armes then *softly* did him reare: *As.* 146
Do pluck it *softly* for that shepheards sake. *As.* 198
honny . . . which doth *softly* trickle from the hive, *Col.* 597
slyding *softly* forth, she turnd as to her ease. I. i. 54. 9
her plaint, Which *softly* ecchoed I. iii. 8. 2
softly gan embalme on everie side: I. v. 17. 5
Her twyfold Teme, . . . Did *softly* swim away, I. v. 28. 6
His cruell wounds, . . . handle *softly*, I. v. 29. 8
Whome having *softly* disaraid of armes, I. v. 41. 4
Her daintie limbes full *softly* down did lay: I. ix. 13. 8
gan *softly* feel Her feeble pulse, II. i. 43. 3
The gentle knight her . . . *softly* did uphold: II. i. 46 .2
twixt the perles and rubins *softly* brake A silver sound, II. iii. 24. 8
there trickled *softly* downe A gentle streame, II. v. 30. 1
On a sweet bed of lillies *softly* laid, II. v. 32. 3
In her loose lap, it *softly* to sustayn, II. vi. 14. 7
Guyons senses *softly* tickeled, II. xii. 33. 7
She *softely* felt if any member moov'd, III. i. 60. 7
by her side her selfe she *softly* layd, III. i. 61. 4
she sighing *softly* had no powre To speake III. ii. 5. 1
softly sunck into her molten hart: III. ii. 15. 2
Shee *softly* felt, and rubbed busily, III. ii. 34. 4
Therewith th' Enchaunter *softly* gan to smyle III. iii. 17. 1
sighing *softly* sore, and inly deepe, III. iv. 11. 1
Whiles on his broad rownd backe they *softly* slid, III. iv. 32. 2
let their temed fishes *softly* swim III. iv. 34. 3
They *softly* gan to search his griesly wownd: III. iv. 40. 2
They *softly* wipt away the gelly blood III. iv. 40. 6
Upon great Neptunes necke they *softly* swim, III. iv. 42. 8
Few trickling teares she *softly* forth let fall, III. vii. 9. 2
Softly at last he gan his mother aske, III. vii. 14. 1
with his frory lips full *softly* kist, III. viii. 35. 2

Softly—*Continued.*
The cruell steele . . . Fell *softly* forth, III. xii. 38. 2
Shee with her rod did *softly* smite the raile, IV. iii. 46. 2
Which drawing *softly* forth out of the darke, IV. iv. 15. 4
To lend an eare, and *softly* to relent. IV. vi. 41. 5
softly askt againe What mister wight it was IV. vii. 10. 4
wiping the deawy wet Which *softly* stild, IV. vii. 35. 6
with few drops thereof did *softly* dew, Her wounds, IV. viii. 20. 8
forward *softly* paced, IV. viii. 34. 6
next to him the Nene downe *softly* slid; IV. xi. 35. 7
To whom God Neptune, *softly* smyling, thus: IV. xii. 30. 1
A Knight that *softly* paced on the plaine, V. vi. 19. 4
softly royne, when salvage choler gan redound. V. ix. 33. 9
Ryding a *softly* pace with portance sad, VI. vii. 6. 8
softly whispering him, VI. vii. 22. 3
flud His silver waves did *softly* tumble downe, VI. x. 7. 2
he *softly* it unbound; VI. xii. 9. 5
She long so held, and *softly* weeping sayd; VI. xii. 19. 7
These, marching *softly*, thus in order went; VII. vii. 32. 1
through the flood before did *softly* slyde VII. vii. 43. 4
She wrapt him *softly*, *Epig.* iv. 43
Come *softly*, and my feeble breast inspire *H.L.* 27
did *softly* play A gentle spirit, *Proth.* 2
Sweete Themmes! runne *softly*, till I end my Song. *Proth.* 18, 36
two Swannes . . . Come *softly* swimming *Proth.* 38
Sweete Themmes! runne *softly*, till I end my Song. *Proth.* 54, 72, 90
Sweete Themmes! runne *softlie*, till I end my Song.' *Proth.* 108
Sweete Themmes! run *softly*, till I end my Song. *Proth.* 126
Sweete Themmes! runne *softly*, till I end my Song. *Proth.* 144, 162, 180

Soft-rumbling. *Soft rombling* brookes, that gentle slomber drew; IV. x. 24. 4

Soft-sliding. *See* **Sliding, Soft.**
The morish Cole, and the *soft sliding* Breane, IV. xi. 29. 6

Soft-trembling. *See* **Soft, Trembling.**

Soft-washing. *See* **Soft, washing.**

Soil. thousand throbs in her owne *soyle*; *Bel.*[2] vi. 13
Were first enclosures but of salvage *soyle*; *Ro.* xviii. 2
the *soyle* that so doth thee bewitch: *S.C.* Jun. 18
I thought the *soyle* would have made me rich, *S.C.* S. 78
When Teucrian *soyle* with bloodie rivers swelde, *Gn.* 500
Saffron, sought for in Cilician *soyle*; *Gn.* 671
He fed his cubs with fat of all the *soyle*, *Hub.* 1151
buildes so stronglie on so frayle a *soyle*, *Ti.* 513
Her now I seek throughout this earthlie *soyle*, *D.* 167
as he that perilous game In forreine *soyle* pursued *As.* 92
back returnedst to this barrein *soyle*, *Col.* 656
Of the wilde fruit which salvage *soyl* hath bred; *Ded. Son.* v. 2
Such, therefore, as that wasted *soyl* doth yield, *Ded. Son.* v. 13
In savadge *soyle*, far from Parnasso Mount, *Ded. Son.* vii. 12
Whose warlike prowesse . . . shakt the Lusitanian *soile*. *Ded. Son.* xiv. 12
'Now are we come unto my native *soyle*, I. xi. 2. 1
From loathed *soile* he can him lightly reare, I. xi. 39. 3
in that *soile*, where all good things did grow, I. xi. 47. 2
Polluted this same gentle *soyle* long time; II. x. 9. 2
Androgeus, false to native *soyle*, II. x. 48. 6
The sacred *soile* where all our perills grow. II. xii. 37. 8
Far fro my native *soyle*, III. ii. 7. 8
To this his native *soyle* thou backe shalt bring, III. iii. 27. 7
a straunger king, from unknowne *soyle* Arriving, III. iii. 33. 3
soyle, which did deforme their lively hew; III. vi. 17. 7
It sited was in fruitfull *soyle* of old, III. vi. 31. 1
Ruffled and fowly raid with filthy *soyle*, III. viii. 32. 2
for . . . glories gaine, My native *soile* have lefte, III. ix. 37. 8
Found it the fittest *soyle* for their abode, III. ix. 49. 5
a Deare, that greedily embayes In the cool *soile*, III. xii. 44. *or.* 8
Whiles neither lets the other touch the *soyle*, IV. iii. 16. 7
As fresh as when it first was planted in the *soyle*. IV. iii. 29. 9
Like warie Hynd within the weedie *soyle*, IV. x. 55. 8
water all the English *soile* throughout: IV. xi. 30. 2
upon the *soyle* Having her selfe in wretched wize abjected, V. ix. 9. 7
Out of the pleasant *soyle* and cities glad, V. x. 18. 5
left so in the loathely *soyle*. V. xi. 33. 9
Into the sea he drove quite from that *soyle*, V. xi. 65. 4
through many a *soyle* Had traveld still on foot VI. viii. 47. 1
Yet seem'd the *soyle* both fayre and frutefull eft, VI. ix. 1. 5
him enricht with bounty of the *soyle*: VII. vii. 38. 4
Fayre *soyle* it seemes from far, *Am.* lxiii. 7
Then rouze thy selfe, O Earth! out of thy *soyle*, *H.H.L.* 218
least they might *Soyle* their fayre plumes *Proth.* 50

Soiled. *soild* with dust of the long dried way; I. vi. 35. 2
upon the *soiled* gras The dead corse II. i. 41. 1
made to spoile Themselves of *soiled* armes, II. ii. 33. 8
all *soild* with blood and myre: II. iv. 16. 4
all so *soyld* that none could him descry: II. iv. 37. 7
with blood, And *soyld* with durtie gore, II. vi. 41. 7
my soule was *soyld* with fowle iniquity.' II. vii. 62. 9

Sojourn. To make there lenger *sojourne* and abode; III. i. 1. 6

Sojourned. he there *sojourned* his woundes to heale; III. x. 5. 6

Sojourning. There Atin fownd Cymochles *sojourning*, II. v. 28. 1

Solace. shepherds wonted *solace* is extinct. *S.C.* N. 106
meanes of gladsome *solace* to devise: *Hub.* 20
where yong Clarion Was wont to *solace* him, *Mui.* 243
Nor suffer *solace* to approach him nie, *D.* 548
forth they marchen . . . To take the *solace* of the open aire, I. iv. 37. 2
Unkindnesse past, they gan of *solace* treat, I. vii. 4. 1
No *solace* could her Paramour intreat Her once to show, II. ii. 35. 5
Making sweet *solace* to herselfe alone: II. vi. 3. 2
Themselves did *solace* each one with his Dame, II. ix. 44. 5
Where goodly *solace* was unto them made, IV. vi. 39. 6
Did greatly *solace* his engrieved mind. IV. viii. 7. 4

Solace—*Continued.*
solace in soft pleasure Those weaker Ladies IV. ix. 12. 7
Delightfull bowres, to *solace* lovers trew; IV. x. 24. 7
This day as I in *solace* sate hereby V. i. 16. 6
As if him selfe to *solace* he were faine: V. vi. 19. 5
To *solace* with his Lady in delight: VI. iii. 20. 4
Each gan his fellow *solace* and embrace VI. viii. 37. 4
no thought of joy, . . . that may my *solace* breed; *Am.* lii. 10
Doe ye to her of joy and *solace* sing, *Epith.* 35

Solaced. having *solaced* themselves a space . . . They backe retourned I. iv. 38. 1
Well *solast* in that Souldans late delight, V. ix. 3. 2

Solaceth. She *solaceth* with rules of Sapience *T.M.* 135

Solacing. her selfe now *solacing* With a new Lover, II. xii. 72. 2

Sold. Theyr Pan theyr sheepe to them has *sold*, *S.C.* Jul. 179
they han *sold* thilk same long agoe, *S.C.* S. 98
Justice he *solde* injustice for to buy, *Hub.* 1147
unto hell him selfe for money *sold*: I. iv. 27. 7
sold thy selfe to serve Duessa vild, I. ix. 46. 8
they from hence were *sold*; II. vii. 54. 4
were your will her *sold* to entertaine, II. ix. 6. 5
hath himselfe unto such service *sold*, III. ix. 8. 2
she her love and hart hath wholy *sold* To him, III. x. 11. 2
unto Venus services was *sold*. IV. x. 54. 5
To whom the right hereof it selfe hath *sold*, IV. xi. 22. 7
sought unrighteousnesse, and justice *sold*, V. ii. 26. 8
Fie on the pelfe for which good name is *sold*, V. xi. 63. 6
them kept in bondage hard, Or *sold* againe. VI. x. 43. 6
to them for their most commodity Be *sold*, VI. xi. 10. 5
sold for most advantage, VI. xi. 10. 9
his love should not be *sold*; VI. xi. 14. 8
with the rest be *sold* before him theare, VI. xi. 15. 4
how faire Pastorell should have bene *sold* To marchants, VI. xi. 30. 6
after Wrong was lov'd, and Justice *solde*, VII. vii. 37. 8

Soldan. They slay the *Soudan*, V. viii. Arg.
to worke avengement strong Uppon the *Souldan* selfe, V. viii. 24. 7
sending to the *Souldan* in despight A bold defyance, V. viii. 27. 7
the *Souldan* all with furie fraught, V. viii. 28. 1
the proud *Souldan* . . . Sought onely slaughter V. viii. 30. 3
So thought the *Souldan*, V. viii. 31. 5
Ne could the *Souldan* them from flying stay V. viii. 38. 5
So was this *Souldan* rapt and all to-rent, V. viii. 43. 8
maintaine The Ladies part, and to the *Souldan* lout: V. viii. 50. 4
Of that proud *Souldan* whom he earst did slay. V. viii. 51. 7
after that he had foyled The cruell *Souldan*, V. ix. 2. 8

Soldan's. with him convay Unto the *Souldans* court, V. viii. 25. 8
led her to the *Souldans* right: V. viii. 26. 4
Well solast in that *Souldans* late delight, V. ix. 3. 2

Soldier. the borne *Souldier* which Rhine running drinks: *Ro.* xxxi. 8
Be you the *Souldier*, for you likest are *Hub.* 199
To whom the Ape, 'I am a *Souldiere*, *Hub.* 246
The *souldier* may not move from watchfull sted, I. ix. 41. 4
made thee *soldier* of that Princesse bright, II. ix. 5. 3

Soldier-like. The Ape clad *Souldierlike*, *Hub.* 204

Soldier's. Nor ruthlesse spoyle of *souldiers* blood-desiring, *Ro.* xiii. 3
since their *souldiers* pas no better spedd, *Hub.* 357

Soldiers. by the names of *Souldiers* us protect: *Hub.* 197
turne the name of *Souldiers* to abusion, *Hub.* 220

Sole. one would weene that one *sole* Cities strength *Ro.* viii. 2
Rome, living, was the worlds *sole* ornament, *Ro.* xxix. 13
Rome, . . . dead, is now the worlds *sole* moniment. *Ro.* xxix. 14
My lifes *sole* blisse, *Col.* 47
sole possession in so chaste a brest! *Col.* 555
with brave deeds to her *sole* service vowed, *As.* 69
that Emperesse, The worlds *sole* glory *Ded. Son.* xi. 4
Of beauties Queene, the worlds *sole* wonderment, *Ded. Son.* xvii. 6
The builder Oake, *sole* king of forrests all; I. i. 8. 8
Borne the *sole* daughter of an Emperour, I. ii. 22. 7
As seeming plast in *sole* felicity: IV. ii. 11. 4
By his *sole* manhood and atchievement stout Dismay'd, IV. iv. 43. 2
Well knowing her to be his deaths *sole* instrument. IV. vii. 29. 9
kist the ground on which her *sole* did tread, IV. viii. 13. 2
For whose *sole* libertie I love and life did stake. IV. viii. 60. 9
none but to the seas *sole* Soveraine. IV. xii. 30. 5
Even from the *sole* of his foundation, V. ii. 28. 2
her *sole* victor left. V. vii. 34. 9
recommended To Gods *sole* grace, VI. iv. 10. 8
Her selfe *sole* left a second spoyle to bee VI. xi. 23. 3
sole aspect he counts felicitye. *H.L.* 217

Solein. *See* **Sullen.**

Solely. Venus selfe doth *soly* couples seeme, *Col.* 801
Seeing her selfe all *soly* succourlesse, IV. ix. 18. 6

Solemn. of his cheere did seeme too *solemne* sad; I. i. 2. 8
in the wine a *solemne* oth they bynd I. v. 4. 8
There raignd a *solemne* silence over all; I. viii. 29. 8
people, as in *solemne* feast, To him assembled I. xii. 4. 6
At last his *solemn* silence thus he brake, I. xii. 29. 5
solemne feast proclaymd throughout the land, I. xii. 40. 2
An yearely *solemne* feast she wontes to hold, II. ii. 42. 6
with *solemne* oath and plighted hand Assurd, II. iv. 23. 8
Still *solemne* sad, or still disdainfull coy; II. vi. 37. 5
As it some Gyeld or *solemne* Temple weare. II. vii. 43. 4
somwhat sad and *solemne* eke in sight, II. ix. 36. 8
A *solemne* Meane unto them measured; II. xii. 33. 4
Sad, *solemne*, sowre, and full of fancies fraile, III. ii. 27. 5
solemne silence over all that place: III. xi. 53. 7
caus'd to be proclaim'd each where A *solemne* feast, IV. ii. 26. 8
a *solemne* feast was there IV. xi. 8. 1
joy likewise this *solemne* day to see? IV. xi. 40. 5
ador'd with *solemne* feasts, V. Pr. 9. 8

Solemn—*Continued.*
solemne feasts and giusts ordain'd therefore: V. iii. 2. 6
To celebrate the *solemne* bridall cheare VII. vii. 12. 4
Solemnity. present at this great *solemnity:* IV. xi. 53. 5
Solemnize. Though spousd, yet wanting wedlocks *solemnize;* I. x. 4. 7
made great feast to *solemnize* that day: I. xii. 38. 2
With sacred rites hast taught to *solemnize;* *Epith.* 393
Solemnized. through the wyde worlde soone were *solemniz'd.* III. ii. 18. 9
when her bridale cheare Should be *solemniz'd;* V. ii. 3. 8
Solemnly. By which he lyes entombed *solemnly.* II. x. 46. 7
Solemn-sad. *See* **Sad, Solemn.**
Soles. ceassest not thy weary *soles* to lead; I. x. 9. 7
Solitary. beate upon the *solitarie* Brere; *S.C.* F. 227
Or some deepe cave, or *solitarie* shade; *D.* 487
she, . . . all this while Forsaken, wofull, *solitarie* mayd, I. iii. 3. 2
choosing *solitarie* to abide Far from all neighbours, III. vii. 6. 6
fit *solitary* place For wofull wight, IV. vii. 38. 5
In *solitary* silence, far from wight, IV. xii. 19. 2
to her chamber went like *solitary* cell. V. vi. 11. 9
All *solitarie* without living wight; V. x. 19. 2
yeeld To sorrow and to *solitary* paine; *Am.* lii. 6
Sollein. *See* **Sullen.**
Solomon. did grieve the noble spright Of *Salomon* *Ti.* 444
Soly. *See* **Solely.**
Some. *See* **All and Some.**
Some noble plant I thought myselfe to see: *Pet.* iii. 4
That of *some* heavenly wight I had the vewe; *Pet.* v. 4
Some greater learned wit will magnifie: *Ro.* ii. 12
Made of *some* matter no less firme and strong? *Ro.* ix. 8
With *some* that weene the contrarie *Ro.* ix. 13
(for perhaps *some* one of you *Ro.* xv. 9
your hard destinie, Or *some* old sinne, *Ro.* xxiv. 10
clad with reliques of *some* Trophees olde, *Ro.* xxviii. 2
May seeme he lovd, or els *some* care he tooke; *S.C.* Ja. 9
worne out thrise threttie yeares, *Some* in much joy, *S.C.* F. 18
And *some* of love, and *some* of chevalrie; *S.C.* F. 99
And fall into *some* mischiefe: *S.C.* Mar. 45
Might see the moving of *some* quicke, *S.C.* Mar. 74
hath *some* Wolfe thy tender Lambes ytorne? *S.C.* Ap. 2
I pray thee, Hobbinoll, recorde *some* one, *S.C.* Ap. 30
Some gan to gape for greedie governaunce, *S.C.* May 121
some old sorowe that made a newe breache: *S.C.* May 210
That *some* good body woulde once pitie mee!' *S.C.* May 248
if on me *some* little drops would flowe *S.C.* Jun. 93
I saye as *some* have seene. *S.C.* Jul. 180
Some sticke not to say, *S.C.* S. 112
Never was Woolfe seene, many nor *some,* *S.C.* S. 152
Or sleepe, as *some* doen, all the long day; *S.C.* S. 233
As thou were wont, songs of *some* jouisaunce? *S.C.* N. 2
As if *some* evill were to her betight? *S.C.* N. 174
through power of *some* divining spright, *Gn.* Ded. 6
for thy worth frame *some* fit Poesie: *Gn.* 12
Some on the soft greene grasse . . . *Some,* clambring through *Gn.* 78, 79
doth catch the utmost top Of *some* soft Willow, *Gn.* 84
In *some* coole shadow from the scorching heat, *Gn.* 143
Or haplesse rising of *some* froward starre, *Gn.* 570
'*Some* in the greedie flouds . . . *Some* on the rocks *Gn.* 585, 586
Some on th' Euboick Cliffs . . . *Some* scattred on the Hercaean shores *Gn.* 587, 588
Some friends, who, sorie my sad case to see, *Hub.* 18
Some tolde of Ladies, . . . *Some* of brave Knights, *Hub.* 28, 29
Some of the Faeries . . . And *some* of Giaunts, *Hub.* 30, 31
I meane me to disguize In *some* straunge habit, *Hub.* 84
Whether shall we professe *some* trade or skill, *Hub.* 117
Free men *some* beggers call, *Hub.* 161
Light not on *some* that may our state amend; *Hub.* 171
Sildome but *some* good commeth ere the end.' *Hub.* 172
I driven am to seeke *some* meanes to live: *Hub.* 250
well dispos'd him *some* reliefe to showe, *Hub.* 261
seeke *some* other way to gaine by giving, *Hub.* 350
As if therein *some* text he studying were, *Hub.* 380
Of *some* good course *Hub.* 411
Might unto *some* of those in time arise? *Hub.* 426
Being *some* honest Curate, or *some* Vicker *Hub.* 429
Then to *some* Noble-man your selfe applye, *Hub.* 489
For *some* good Gentleman, . . . Will cope with thee *Hub.* 525
Newes may perhaps *some* good unweeting *Hub.* 606
To *some* of these thou must thy selfe apply; *Hub.* 633
either for *some* gainfull benefit, *Hub.* 639
As if he were *some* great Magnifico, *Hub.* 665
some good Ladies gifts: *Hub.* 852
with him far'd *some* better chaunce to fynde. *Hub.* 942
For we may coulor it with *some* pretext *Hub.* 988
Now gan *some* courage unto him to take, *Hub.* 994
He gan enquire of *some* in secret wize, *Hub.* 1272
yeeld us *some* reliefe in this distresse; *T.M.* 347
Some few beside this sacred skill esteme, *T.M.* 583
Which did the losse of *some* dere love lament, *Ti.* 16
as if it shold Be for *some* bride, *Ti.* 635
Which th' ashes seem'd of *some* great Prince *Ti.* 661
With *some* few silver-dropping teares t' adorne; *Ti.* 683
An hairie hide of *some* wilde beast, *Mui.* 66
he pearcheth on *some* braunch thereby, *Mui.* 183
th' armies of their creatures all and *some* Do serve *Mui.* 229
some ungracious blast, out of the gate Of Aeoles *Mui.* 419
Like to *some* Pilgrim come from farre away. *D.* 42
he seemd to be *sum* wight forlorne; *D.* 45
Griefe findes *some* ease by him that like *D.* 67
As if to me had chanst *some* evill tourne! *D.* 266
to *some* darksome place, Or *some* deepe cave, *D.* 486, 487

Some—*Continued.*
That hearbe of *some* Starlight is cald by name, *As.* 193
Provoked me to plaie *some* pleasant fit; *Col.* 69
Whether it were *some* hymne, *Col.* 86
Glewed togither with *some* subtile matter. *Col.* 217
Some part of those enormities did see, *Col.* 665
else by breeding him *some* blot of blame, *Col.* 697
Unlesse that *some* gay Mistresse badge he *Col.* 780
it seemes that *some* celestiall rage *Col.* 823
Such grace shall be *some* guerdon for the griefe, *Col.* 943
grace sometimes shall give me *some* reliefe, *Col.* 945
And steale from each *some* part of ornament. *Ded.Son.*xvii.8
Seemed in heart *some* hidden care she had, I. i. 4. 8
Enforst to seeke *some* covert nigh at hand, I. i. 7. 1
Till that *some* end they finde, I. i. 11. 2
seeming to mistrust *Some* secret ill, or hidden foe I. i. 49. 4
Shee backe retourned with *some* labour lost; I. iii. 24 .2
Some frounce their curled heare in courtly guise; I. iv. 14. 7
Some prancke their ruffes; I. iv. 14. 8
to my loathed life now shewes *some* light, I. iv. 48. 2
Her feeling speaches *some* compassion mov'd I. v. 24. 6
some shall pay the price of others guilt; I. v. 26. 2
besought *Some* cursed vengeaunce on his sonne to cast. I. v. 38. 2
Go, find *some* other play-fellowes, I. vi. 28. 9
For feare, as seemd, or for *some* feigned losse: I. vi. 34. 8
Yet outwardly *some* little comfort shewes. I. vii. 21. 3
Some secret sorrow did her heart distraine; I. vii. 38. 4
There to obtaine *some* such redoubted knight, I. vii. 46. 8
after charmes and *some* enchauntments said, I. viii. 14. 6
That seemed from *some* feared foe to fly, I. ix. 21. 3
What if *some* little payne the passage have, I. ix. 40. 4
some he would give to the pore. I. x. 38. 9
Some wrestle, *some* do run, *some* bathe in christall flood. I. xii. 7. 9
Some feard, and fledd; *some* feard, and well it faynd; I. xii. 10. 1
remaynd *Some* lingring life within his hollow brest, I. xii. 10. 4
in his wombe might lurke *some* hidden nest I. xii. 10. 5
some more bold to measure him nigh stand, I. xii. 11. 8
rode, Where we must land *some* of our passengers, I. xii. 42. 3
Of *some* th' aboundance of an ydle braine Will judged be, II. Pr. 1. 3
such to *some* appeare. II. Pr. 3. 9
He weened well to worke *some* uncouth wyle: II. i. 8. 2
feele *some* secret ease. II. i. 16. 9
as if *some* new mishap, Had him betide, II. i. 26. 2
Great cause, I weene, you guided, or *some* uncouth chaunce.' II. i. 29. 9
some were so from their sourse indewd II. ii. 6. 1
But other *some,* by guifte of later grace, II. ii. 6. 6
shee is *some* powre celestiall? II. iii. 44. 4
some others faine To menage steeds, II. iv. 1. 8
Some troublous uprore or contentious fray, II. iv. 3. 3
Least worse betide thee by *some* later chaunce. II. iv. 36. 5
To be the shield of *some* redoubted knight; II. iv. 38. 6
Yet in himselfe *some* comfort he did find, II. v. 14. 7
Some framd faire lookes, . . . *Some* bathed kisses, II. v. 33. 3, 5
Hath tracted forth *some* salvage beastes trade: II. vi. 39. 5
some were rude owre, not purifide II. vii. 5. 3
Some others were new driven, II. vii. 5. 5
Some in round plates withouten moniment; II. vii. 5. 7
Some scumd the drosse that from the metall came; II. vii. 36. 7
Some stird the molten owre with ladles great; II. vii. 36. 8
As it *some* Gyeld or solemne Temple weare. II. vii. 43. 4
Some thought to raise themselves to high degree II. vii. 47. 1
Some by close shouldring; *some* by flatteree; II. vii. 47. 3
Some with unweldy clubs, *some* with long speares, II. ix. 13. 6
Some rusty knifes, *some* staves in fier warmd: II. ix. 13. 7
Some to remove the scum as it did rise; II. ix. 31. 7
Some song in sweet consort; *some* laught for joy; *Some* plaid with strawes; *some* ydly satt II. ix. 35. 2, 3, 4
other *some* could not abide to toy; II. ix. 35. 4
As if *some* pensive thought constraind her II. ix. 36. 9
Some such as in the world were never yit, II. ix. 50. 4
Some daily seene and knowen by their names, II. ix. 50. 6
Some made in books, *some* in long parchment scrolls, II. ix. 57. 8
if *some* relish of that hevenly lay II. x. 3. 6
of *some* thought By sea to have bene II. x. 5. 8
That monstrous error, which doth *some* assott, II. x. 8. 3
lawes, which *some* men say Were unto him reveald II. x. 39. 1
As if the rest *some* wicked hand did rend, II. x. 68. 4
wightes, of which *some* were Headed II. xi. 8. 2
some had wings, and *some* had clawes to teare: II. xi. 8. 5
Some having heads like Harts, *some* like to Snakes, II. xi. 10. 4
Some like wilde Bores II. xi. 10. 5
Some like to houndes, *some* like to Apes, II. xi. 11. 4
Some like to Puttockes, all in plumes arayd; II. xi. 11. 5
Some mouth'd . . . *some* faste Like loathly Toades; II. xi. 12. 4
some fashioned in the waste Like swine: II. xi. 12. 5
For *some* like Snailes, *some* did like spyders shew, II. xi. 13. 3
some like ugly Urchins thick and short: II. xi. 13. 4
Some land-marke seemd to bee, II. xi. 35. 9
least it were *some* magicall Illusion II. xi. 39. 5
Forthy he gan *some* other wayes advize, II. xi. 44. 6
Seemed *some* great misfortune to deplore, II. xii. 27. 8
heare *some* part of their rare melody. II. xii. 33. 9
Some deepe empurpled as the Hyacine, *Some* as the Rubine . . . *Some* like faire Emeraudes, II. xii. 54. 7, 8, 9
some were of burnisht gold, II. xii. 55. 1
some seemd with lively jollitee To fly II. xii. 60. 7
Some goodly swayne of honorable place, II. xii. 79. 2
some for inward shame, And *some* for wrath II. xii. 86. 4, 5
in a fountaine by *some* covert glade: III. i. 35. 9
Some for untimely ease, *some* for delight, III. i. 39. 4

Some—*Continued.*

Emongst the Roses grow *some* wicked weeds: . . . . III. i. 49. 6
Some fell to daunce, *some* fel to hazardy, ... III. i. 57. 1
Some to make love, *some* to make meryment, ... III. i. 57. 2
Tell me *some* markes by which he may appeare, ... III. ii. 16. 3
thought it was not love, but *some* melancholy. . . . . III. ii. 27. 9
then *some* hope I might unto me draw; . . . . III. ii. 38. 2
The cause, *some* say, is this: . . . . III. iii. 10. 1
That either seemes *some* cursed witches deed, ... III. iii. 18. 8
the brave atchievements doen by *some?* . . . . III. iv. 1. 3
At last blow up *some* gentle gale of ease, ... III. iv. 10. 3
Some hard mishap in hazard of his life. . . . . III. iv. 24. 6
Some litle life his feeble sprites emong; . . . . III. iv. 41. 8
To finde *some* issue thence; . . . . III. v. 3. 2
terrifyde With *some* late perill . . . . III. v. 3. 4
shee pursewd the chace Of *some* wilde beast, ... III. v. 28. 2
for *some* light displeasure . . . . III. vi. 11. 3
the love of *some* of them him tyde: . . . . III. vi. 16. 7
Some of them washing with the liquid dew . . . . III. vi. 17. 5
Some thousand yeares so doen they there remayne, ... III. vi. 33. 5
Some fitt for reasonable sowles t' indew; . . . . III. vi. 35. 5
Some made for beasts, *some* made for birds to weare; . . . . III. vi. 35. 6
There yet, *some* say, in secret he does ly, ... III. vi. 46. 4
in the same did wonne *some* living wight. . . . . III. vii. 5. 5
To finde *some* refuge there, ... III. vii. 5. 9
He was compeld to seeke *some* refuge neare, ... III. ix. 13. 2
To prove *some* deeds of armes . . . . III. x. 24. 9
Your treasure here in *some* security, ... III. x. 42. 2
fast closed in *some* hollow greave, ... III. x. 42. 3
if that hevenly grace *some* goode reliefe You send, ... III. xi. 14. 3
Some headed with sad lead, *some* with pure gold; . . . . . III. xi. 48. 4
when *some* foe she might descry. . . . . III. xii. 1. 9
as on the readie flore Of *some* Theatre, ... III. xii. 3. 6
Some argument of matter passioned: . . . . III. xii. 4. 6
found *some* beasts fresh spoyle, ... IV. iii. 16. 2
that he had beene *some* man of place, ... IV. viii. 14. 4
To speake to them, and *some* emparlance move; . . . . IV. ix. 31. 2
The tast of bloud of *some* engored beast, ... IV. ix. 31. 6
To winne me honour by *some* noble gest, ... IV. x. 4. 4
purchase me *some* place amongst the best. . . . . IV. x. 4. 5
As if *some* proved perill he did feare, Or did misdoubt *some* ill IV. x. 12. 8, 9
Through which *some* lost great hope . . . . IV. x. 13. 5
Againe, *some* other, . . . Crept in . . . . IV. x. 18. 6
Upon an altar of *some* costly masse, ... IV. x. 39. 2
Some of their losse, *some* of their loves delay, *Some* of their pride, *some* paragons disdayning, *Some* fearing fraud, *some* fraudulently fayning, ... IV. x. 43. 3, 4, 5
As if *some* blame of evill she did feare, ... IV. x. 50. 4
unlesse *some* heavenly powre her free . . . . IV. xi. 1. 6
Whom she besought to find *some* remedie, ... IV. xi. 6. 7
There also *some* most famous founders were . . . . IV. xi. 15. 1
T' expresse *some* part of that great equipage . . . . IV. xi. 17. 8
whose calfe is falne unwares Into *some* pit, ... IV. xii. 17. 7
Whereby she might apply *some* medicine; . . . . IV. xii. 21. 5
to seeke *some* meanes it to appease. . . . . IV. xii. 22. 3
it was *some* other maladie, Or grief . . . . IV. xii. 24. 1
he did languish of *some* inward thought, ... IV. xii. 25. 7
would *some* rightfull cause pretend, ... IV. xii. 30. 9
some of the vertuous race Rose up, ... V. i. 1. 6
Is lightly stricken with *some* stones throw; . . . . V. i. 21. 7
some by sleight he eke doth underfong. . . . . V. ii. 7. 5
The Sarazin, awayting for *some* spoile: . . . . V. ii. 11. 3
That she might win *some* time, ... V. ii. 23. 7
from the most that *some* were given to the least? . . . . . V. ii. 37. 9
Some blisfull houres at last . . . . V. iii. 1. 4
Unlesse *some* succour had in time him overtaken. . . . . . . V. iii. 9. 9
some fayre Franion, fit for such a fere, ... V. iii. 22. 7
Would ye remit it to *some* righteous man.' . . . . V. iv. 16. 3
wrought unwares *some* villanous assay. . . . . V. iv. 23. 9
Which *some* hath put to shame, ... V. iv. 29. 9
Uppon the carkasse of *some* beast too weake, ... V. iv. 40. 7
seized for her share Uppon *some* fowle . . . . V. iv. 42. 5
Was lately broken by *some* fortune ill; . . . . V. v. 15. 4
Give her great comfort and *some* harts content. . . . . . . V. v. 35. 3
or *some* guilefull traine did weave, ... V. v. 37. 4
Gan to demaund of her *some* tydings good, ... V. v. 45. 2
'*Some* of his diet doe from him withdraw, ... V. v. 50. 1
Some men, I wote, will deeme in Artegall . . . . V. vi. 1. 1
she feared least *some* hard mishap . . . . V. vi. 4. 1
Least *some* new love had him from her possest: . . . . V. vi. 4. 7
sleepe Is broken with *some* fearefull dreames . . . . V. vi. 14. 2
that *some* pensivenesse to heart she tooke: . . . . V. vii. 18. 3
Like one adawed with *some* dreadfull spright: . . . . V. vii. 20. 8
Are met at spoyling of *some* hungry pray, ... V. vii. 30. 2
In hope *some* stroke to fasten on him neare, ... V. viii. 33. 2
guyded . . . By *some* bad spirit . . . . V. viii. 34. 7
Seeking by every way to make *some* breach; . . . . V. viii. 37. 2
But *some* doe say it goeth downe to hell: . . . . V. ix. 6. 5
As if she did *some* great calamitie deplore. . . . . V. ix. 8. 9
Should issue forth, in hope to find *some* spoyle, ... V. ix. 9. 2
With hope of her *some* wishfull boot to have. . . . . V. ix. 10. 3
as if that there were *some* Which unto them was dealing . . . V. ix. 23. 4
countenance . . . tempred with *some* majestie imperiall. . . . V. ix. 34. 9
Some Clarkes doe doubt . . . . V. x. 1. 1
to wend Unto *some* place where they mote rest . . . . V. x. 22. 7
Some place shall us receive and harbour yield; . . . . V. x. 24. 2
Mongst joyes mixing *some* tears, ... V. xi. 16. 3
As when the Mast of *some* well-timbred hulke Is with the blast of *some* outragious storme Blowne downe, ... V. xi. 29. 1, 2
As if that there were *some* tumultuous affray. . . . . V. xi. 43. 9

Some—*Continued.*

some life remayned secretly; . . . . V. xii. 39. 7
Yet now *some* hope your words unto me add.' . . . . VI. i. 10. 5
thorough *some* more mighty enemies wrong . . . . VI. i. 11. 3
Yet doubt thou not, but that *some* better Knight . . . . . . VI. i. 25. 6
Till to *some* place of rest they mote attaine, ... VI. iii. 28. 7
there for his love *some* succour to provyde. . . . . VI. iii. 29. 9
For his sicke charge *some* harbour there to seeke; . . . . . VI. iii. 37. 6
Whom well he wist to be *some* enemy, ... VI. iii. 46. 8
His former malice to *some* new assay, ... VI. iii. 47. 8
As bent to *some* malicious enterprise, ... VI. iii. 48. 3
Yet will it shew *some* sparkes of gentle mynd, ... VI. v. 1. 8
Yet shewd *some* token of his gentle blood . . . . VI. v. 2. 5
As he of *some* misfortune were afrayd; . . . . VI. v. 3. 4
To seeke *some* comfort in that sorie case. . . . . VI. v. 7. 4
It chaunst *some* furniture about her steed To be disordred by *some* accident, ... VI. v. 10. 2, 3
There they awhile *some* gracious speaches spent, ... VI. v. 24. 6
the spoile of *some* right well renownd: . . . . VI. v. 25. 5
by *some* deadly chaunce be done to pine . . . . VI. v. 28. 8
To seeke *some* place the which mote yeeld *some* ease . . . VI. v. 32. 2
that whilome he had beene *Some* goodly person, ... VI. v. 36. 7
brought . . . *some* asswagement of their painefull plight. . . VI. v. 40. 4
some counsell that may us sustaine.' . . . . VI. vi. 13. 9
in *some* stable neare did set him up to feede. . . . . VI. vi. 19. 9
Feeling *some* curre behinde his heeles to bite, ... VI. vi. 27. 6
Hoping unto *some* refuge to withdraw: . . . . VI. vi. 29. 3
After he gotten had . . . *Some* of their weapons . . . . . . VI. vi. 38. 8
lookes but false and fayned, To *some* hid end . . . . VI. vi. 42. 2
Or by *some* other violence despoyled: . . . . VI. vii. 33. 5
To spy where he may *some* advauntage get, ... VI. vii. 47. 5
He flew . . . like a greedy kight Unto *some* carrion . . . . . VI. viii. 28. 5
Some with their eyes the daintest morsels chose; . . . . . . VI. viii. 39. 4
Some praise her paps; *some* praise her lips and nose; . . . VI. viii. 39. 5
Some whet their knives, ... VI. viii. 39. 6
some of them gan mongst themselves devize . . . . VI. viii. 43. 5
As if *some* miracle of heavenly hew . . . . VI. ix. 8. 8
Who, her admiring as *some* heavenly wight, ... VI. ix. 9. 6
some, that hath abundance . . . Hath not enough, ... VI. ix. 30. 3
here with your selfe *some* small repose obtaine. . . . . . . VI. ix. 31. 9
to pretend *Some* shew of favour, ... VI. xi. 6. 6
met By *some* of these same theeves . . . . VI. xi. 9. 7
Till *some,* . . . Gan to inquire . . . . VI. xi. 11. 5
some other of the chiefest theeves . . . . VI. xi. 15. 1
hungry dogs, ymet About *some* carcase . . . . VI. xi. 17. 2
That seem'd to be *some* sorie simple clowne, ... VI. xi. 27. 3
As if he did from *some* late daunger fly, ... VI. xi. 27. 5
Some flockes of sheepe and shepheards . . . . VI. xi. 36. 7
misdoubting least of-new *Some* uprore were like that . . . . VI. xi. 43. 9
Began *some* smacke of comfort new to tast, ... VI. xi. 45. 3
flyes, . . . Do seize upon *some* beast . . . . VI. xi. 48. 2
Some were of dogs, that barked day and night; And *some* of cats, that wrawling still did cry; And *some* of Beares, that groynd continually; And *some* of Tygres, that did seeme to gren VI.xii.27.3,4,5,6
which *some* wicked tongues did it backebite, ... VI. xii. 41. 5
some beast of strange and forraine race . . . . VII. vi. 28. 7
Through *some* vaine errour, . . . To see . . . . VII. vi. 32. 2
seemes to deck the locks Of *som* faire Bride, ... VII. vi. 41. 4
Her to discover for *some* secret hire: . . . . VII. vi. 43. 3
some wicked beast unware That breakes into . . . . VII. vi. 48. 3
Hath, in *some* snare or gin . . . Entrapped him, ... VII. vi. 48. 6
Some by the nose him pluckt, *some* by the taile, ... VII. vi. 49. 4
by his goatish beard *some* did him haile: . . . . VII. vi. 49. 5
Some would have gelt him; . . . . VII. vi. 50. 3
That, *some* do say, was so by skill devized, ... VII. vii. 6. 1
As if the love of *some* new Nymph, ... VII. vii. 11. 6
seeke *some* succour both to ease my smart, ... *Am.* ii. 7
his death, which *some* perhaps will mone, ... *Am.* xxxvi. 13
invent *Som* hevenly wit, ... *Am.* lxxxii. 7
throw betweene *Some* graces to be seene; . . . . *Epith.* 107
ye would weene *Some* angell she had beene. . . . . *Epith.* 153
being crowned . . . Seeme lyke *some* mayden Queene. . . . . *Epith.* 158
Some sparks remaining of that heavenly fyre, ... *H.L.* 107
she at length will streame *Some* deaw of grace into . . . . . *H.B.* 27
Which it assumed of *some* stubborne grownd, ... *H.B.* 145
deform'd with *some* foule imperfection. . . . . *H.B.* 147
They gathered *some;* . . . . *Proth.* 30

Somedeal. thou lackest *somedele* their delight. . . . . *S.C.* May 56
Somedele ybent to song . . . . *S.C.* D. 40
the anguish of his spright *Some deale* alaid, ... *D.* 173

Some one. *See* **One.**
Unlesse *some one* perhaps of gentle kin, ... *T.M.* 345
Some one, that would with grace be gratifide, ... *Mui.* 110
some one did chaunt this lovely lay: . . . . II. xii. 74. 1
she heard *some one* close by her side Sighing . . . . IV. vii. 10. 1
some one, through Loves constrayning . . . . IV. x. 43. 7
sure she weend it was *some one* of those, ... IV. xii. 26. 8
to send *some one* to seeke him out; . . . . V. vi. 6. 2
Some one whose tongue was . . . Nayld to a post, ... V. ix. 25. 2

Something. *something* amisse to mend; . . . . III. x. 38. 6
To doe *some thing* that seemed to him best; . . . . VI. vii. 19. 7

Sometime. A goodly Oake *sometime* had it bene, ... *S.C.* F. 103
Sometime a fowle, *sometime* a fish in lake, ... I. ii. 10. 5
Ne did he spare *sometime* to pricke himselfe, ... III. xi. 45. 3
me besought, *Sometime* with tender teares . . . . IV. x. 57. 2
Sometime with witching smyles; . . . . IV. x. 57. 3
Sometime she feared least some hard mishap Had him misfalne V. vi. 4. 1
Sometime least his false foe did him entrap . . . . V. vi. 4. 3
Sometime the fawne I practise from the Doe, ... VI. ix. 23. 3

Sometimes. When ye *sometimes* behold the ruin'd pride . . . *Ro.* xv. 12
would he *sometimes* scorne A Pandares coate . . . *Hub.* 807
Such grace *sometimes* shall give me some reliefe, . . . *Col.* 945
With like delightes *sometimes* . . . delay The rugged brow . . . *Ded. Son.* i. 11
Sometimes dame Venus selfe he seemes to see; . . . I. vi. 16. 6
Sometimes Diana he her takes to be, . . . I. vi. 16. 8
Sometimes great hostes of men she could dismay; . . . I. x. 20. 4
Sometimes she raught him stones, . . . *Sometimes* her staffe, II. iv. 5. 5, 6
Sometimes athwart, *sometimes* he strook him strayt, . . . II. v. 9. 8
sometimes had the worse, and lost by warre, . . . II. v. 15. 4
Sometimes he falsely faines himselfe to sleepe, . . . II. v. 34. 4
Sometimes she song . . . *Sometimes* she laught, . . . II. vi. 3. 3, 4
Sometimes her head she fondly would aguize . . . II. vi. 7. 3
Sometimes, to do him laugh, she would assay . . . II. vi. 7. 6
throw the crowne *Sometimes* to him . . . II. vii. 11. 7
Sometimes with threats, *sometimes* with hope of gayn, . . . II. xi. 14. 8
Sometimes the one would lift the other . . . II. xii. 64. 1
Girlonds of flowres *sometimes* for her faire hed . . . III. vii. 17. 5
Sometimes he boasted that a God he hight, . . . III. viii. 39. 6
Sometimes him blessing with a light eyeglance, . . . IV. ii. 9. 4
Sometimes estranging him in sterner wise; . . . IV. ii. 9. 6
Sometimes pursewing, and *sometimes* pursewed, . . . IV. vi. 18. 2
he *sometimes* may space And walke about . . . IV. viii. 54. 2
sometimes Paridell and Blandamour The better had, . . . IV. ix. 25. 1
Sometimes aloft he layd, *sometimes* alow, . . . VI. viii. 13. 6
'*Sometimes* I hunt the Fox, . . . VI. ix. 23. 1
to his love *sometimes* he came in place; . . . VI. xii. 6. 3
he *sometimes* so far runnes out of square, . . . VII. vii. 52. 2
Those lamping eyes will deigne *sometimes* to look, . . . *Am.* i. 6
Sometimes I joy when glad occasion fits, . . . *Am.* liv. 5
Sometimes upon her forhead they behold . . . *H.B.* 253
Sometimes within her eye-lids they unfold . . . *H.B.* 255

Somewhat. Of which all passers by doo *somewhat* pill: . . . *Ro.* xxx. 12
Her stombling steppe *some what* her amazed, . . . *S.C.* May 231
Has *somewhat* slackt the tenor of thy string, . . . *S.C.* O. 50
Now *somewhat* sing, whose endles sovenaunce . . . *S.C.* N. 5
Whereof still *somewhat* to his share did rize: . . . *Hub.* 806
Tho when the pang was *somewhat* overpast, . . . *D.* 554
as he rode he *somewhat* still did eat, . . . I. iv. 22. 5
Below her ham her weed did *somewhat* trayne, . . . II. iii. 27. 1
Though *somewhat* moved in his mightie hart, . . . II. vi. 40. 3
somwhat sad and solemne eke in sight, . . . II. ix. 36. 8
though *somwhat* they declind; . . . II. ix. 55. 4
somewhat gan relent his earnest pace; . . . II. xii. 65. 8
therewith *somewhat* starting, up gan looke, . . . III. xi. 13. 2
As if in minde he *somewhat* had to say; . . . III. xii. 4. 2
forst . . . *somewhat* to relent, . . . IV. iii. 26. 4
somewhat redder then beseem'd aright, . . . IV. vi. 19. 8
she may be safe though *somewhat* strayd: . . . IV. vi. 37. 8
eft againe deviz'd *some what* to say, . . . IV. vi. 45. 7
he *somewhat* seem'd to stoupe afore . . . IV. xi. 26. 1
his scarse diet *somewhat* was amended, . . . V. v. 57. 2
Would change her paine, and sorrow *somewhat* ease, . . . V. vii. 45. 4
fervour of his flames *somewhat* adaw . . . V. ix. 35. 4
Bate *somewhat* of that Majestie and awe . . . V. ix. 35. 7
but *somewhat* short did fall, . . . V. xi. 8. 8
having *somewhat* calm'd his wrathfull heat . . . VI. i. 40. 2
Whom though he saw now *somewhat* overpast, . . . VI. iv. 18. 8
gan to shrinke and *somewhat* to give place, . . . VI. v. 21. 3
for great joy of *some-what* he did spy, . . . VII. vi. 46. 3
He *somewhat* loseth of his heat and light, . . . *Epith.* 268
Somewhat to slacke the rigour of my flame? . . . *H.L.* 152

Somewhere. Whom sure he weend, that he *some-wher* tofore had eide. . . . IV. iv. 7. 9
one patterne, seene *somewhere,* . . . IV. ix. 11. 5
me to remove *somewhere* Into some forrein land, . . . VI. ii. 29. 7

Somewhile. Pallaces . . . were shepheards cottages *somewhile.* . *Ro.* xviii. 4
somewhile There crept in Wolves, . . . *S.C.* May 126
and eke of private men *somewhile,* . . . *Hub.* 787
suters, that in Court did haunt *some while;* . . . *Hub.* 878
with the Prince of Darkenes fell *somewhyle* . . . III. viii. 8. 3
though *some while* Fortune from him withdrew, . . . IV. iv. 37. 7
Some while he thought, . . . IV. xii. 14. 3
Somewhile with merry purpose, fit to please, . . . VI. v. 32. 7

Son. As that brave *sonne* of Aeson, . . . *Ro.* x. 1
The *sonne* of his loines why should he regard . . . *S.C.* May 83
a motherly care Of her young *sonne,* . . . *S.C.* May 181
'My *Sonne,* . . . 'God blesse thee, . . . *S.C.* May 189
So schooled the Gate her wanton *sonne,* . . . *S.C.* May 227
her *sonne* had sette to deere a prise . . . *S.C.* May 299
she halfe frantick, hairing slaine her *sonne,* . . . *Gn.* 175
'Gainst which the noble *sonne* of Telamon Oppos'd himselfe, . *Gn.* 513
from him Laertes *sonne* his vewe Doth turne aside, . . . *Gn.* 533
then his yongest *sonne* Shall twentie have, . . . *Hub.* 529
The *Sonne* of Maia, . . . *Hub.* 1257
since the time that Phoebus foolish *sonne* Ythundered, . . . *T.M.* 7
thy gay *Sonne,* that winged God of Love, . . . *T.M.* 401
left his *sonne* t' ensue those steps of his. . . . *Ti.* 266
Could save the *sonne* of Thetis from to die; . . . *Ti.* 429
Clarion, the eldest *sonne* and haire Of Muscaroll; . . . *Mui.* 22
The Archer God, the *sonne* of Cytheree, . . . *Mui.* 98
Her *sonne* to Psyche secrete love did beare, . . . *Mui.* 131
dreaded impe of highest Jove, Faire Venus *sonne,* . . . I. Pr. 3. 2
'Ah! my dear *sonne,*' (quoth he) . . . I. i. 30. 5
'Ah! wretched *sonne* of wofull syre, . . . I. v. 10. 5
besought Some cursed vengeaunce on his *sonne* to cast. . . . I. v. 38. 2
In death avowing th' innocence of her *sonne.* . . . I. v. 39. 3
O thou far renowmed *sonne* Of great Apollo! . . . I. v. 43. 6
let stay Aveugles *sonne* there . . . I. v. 44. 6
would as Ammons *sonne* be magnifide, . . . I. v. 48. 8

Son—*Continued.*
A Satyres *sonne,* yborne in forrest wyld, . . . I. vi. 21. 1
His loving mother came . . . to see her little *sonne;* . . . I. vi. 27. 2
'Where is,' (said Satyrane) 'that Paynims *sonne,* . . . I. vi. 39. 5
'O foolish faeries *sonne!* . . . I. vi. 47. 1
That I was *sonne* and heire unto a king, . . . I. ix. 5. 8
die soone, O faeries *sonne!*' . . . I. ix. 47. 9
hath encreast the world with one *sonne* more, . . . I. x. 16. 6
taking by the hand that Faeries *sonne,* . . . I. x. 33. 2
never yet was seene of Faeries *sonne;* . . . I. x. 52. 3
How ever now accompted Elfins *sonne,* . . . I. x. 60. 2
Whom all a Faeries *sonne* doen nominate?' . . . I. x. 64. 7
his talants may Yet scratch my *sonne,* . . . I. xii. 11. 6
'Deare *Sonne,* great beene the evils which ye bore . . . I. xii. 17. 2
'Fayre *sonne* of Mars, that seeke with warlike spoyle, . . . II. i. 8. 7
'Fayre *sonne,* God give you happy chaunce, . . . II. i. 31. 7
this their wretched *sonne,* . . . II. ii. 44. 8
with which she doth enrage Her frantick *sonne,* . . . II. iv. 11. 5
provokt her *sonne* to wreake her wrong; . . . II. iv. 12. 6
gan her *sonne* to flye Full fast away, . . . II. iv. 13. 6
Acrates, *sonne* of Phlegeton and Jarre; . . . II. iv. 41. 7
Phlegeton is *sonne* of Herebus and Night; . . . II. iv. 41. 8
Herebus *sonne* of Aeternitie is hight. . . . II. iv. 41. 9
to her captive *sonne* yield his first libertee. . . . II. v. 17. 9
Before her *sonne* could well assoyled bee, . . . II. v. 19. 2
'Deare *sonne,* thy causelesse ruth represse, . . . II. v. 24. 5
t' Olympick Jove, And to his *sonne* Alcides, . . . II. v. 31. 4
What is become of great Acrates *sonne?* . . . II. v. 35. 6
'*Sonne,*' (said he then) 'lett be thy bitter scorne, . . . II. vii. 18. 1
'Behold, thou Faeries *sonne,* with mortall eye, . . . II. vii. 38. 1
Sir Guyon, . . . is by Acrates *sonne* despoyld; . . . II. viii. Arg.
from the grandsyre to the Nephewes *sonne,* . . . II. viii. 29. 3
'Fayre *Sonne,* great God thy right hand blesse, . . . II. viii. 40. 3
'Fayre *sonne,* be no whit sad . . . II. viii. 54. 4
that huge *sonne* of hideous Albion, . . . II. x. 11. 6
her *sonne,* which she to Locrin bore, . . . II. x. 20. 1
when her *sonne* to mans estate did wex, . . . II. x. 20. 8
Which blott his *sonne* succeeding in his seat, . . . II. x. 23. 1
His *sonne,* king Leill, . . . II. x. 25. 1
His *sonne* Rivall' his dead rowme did supply; . . . II. x. 34. 1
Her other *sonne* fast sleeping did oppresse, . . . II. x. 35. 8
Gurgiunt, great Belinus *sonne,* . . . II. x. 41. 1
Her *sonne* Sisillus after her did rayne; . . . II. x. 43. 1
by the helpe of Vortimere his *sonne,* . . . II. x. 66. 1
'His *sonne,* hight Vortipore, shall him succeede . . . III. iii. 31. 1
'O thou fayre *sonne* of gentle Faery, . . . III. xii. 32. 3
he was not the *sonne* Of mortall Syre . . . III. iii. 13. 1
'But sooth he is the *sonne* of Gorlois, . . . III. iii. 27. 1
'His *sonne,* hight Vortipore, shall him succeede . . . III. iii. 31. 1
his *sonne* Malgo shall full mightily Avenge . . . III. iii. 31. 7
'All which his *sonne* Careticus awhile Shall well defend, . . III. iii. 33. 1
On his *sonne* Edwin all those wrongs shall wreake; . . . III. iii. 36. 2
did beare This warlike *sonne* unto an earthly peare, . . . III. iv. 19. 5
he must do battail with the Sea-nymphes *sonne.* . . . III. iv. 20. 9
T' endow her *sonne* with threasure and rich store . . . III. iv. 21. 8
To bring her *sonne* unto his last decay. . . . III. iv. 28. 5
The wretched *sonne* of wretched mother borne, . . . III. iv. 36. 2
Farewell, my sweetest *sonne,* sith we no more shall meet!' . . . III. iv. 39. 9
Her dearest *sonne,* her dearest harts delight: . . . III. iv. 44. 5
'A Sea-nymphes *sonne,* that Marinell is hight, . . . III. v. 9. 1
faire Venus having lost Her little *sonne,* . . . III. vi. 11. 2
both how and what Her *sonne* had to them doen; . . . III. vi. 15. 9
she her dearest *sonne* Cupido sought, . . . III. vi. 20. 7
your gay *sonne,* that gives ye so good ayd . . . III. vi. 21. 4
tell me, if that ye my *sonne* have heard . . . III. vi. 23. 1
The witches *sonne* loves Florimell: . . . III. vii. Arg.
This wicked woman had a wicked *sonne,* . . . III. vii. 12. 1
by the witch or by her *sonne* compast. . . . III. vii. 18. 5
that vile hag, or her uncivile *sonne;* . . . III. vii. 19. 6
with it ronning hast'ly to her *sonne,* . . . III. viii. 3. 1
How she might heale her *sonne* whose senses were decayd. . III. viii. 4. 9
her *sonne* that lay in feeble state; . . . III. viii. 9. 7
lefte next in remaine To Paridas his *sonne,* . . . III. ix. 37. 5
'Anchyses *sonne,* begott of Venus fayre,' . . . III. ix. 41. 1
His *sonne* Iulus did from thence depart . . . III. ix. 43. 5
that same Brute, . . . was Sylvius his *sonne,* . . . III. ix. 48. 2
for his owne deare *sonne,* . . . he did repent; . . . III. xi. 38. 1
The *sonne* of Climene, he did repent; . . . III. xi. 38. 2
Like to the rod which Maias *sonne* doth wield, . . . IV. iii. 42. 6
having reft her from the witches *sonne,* . . . IV. iv. 8. 4
This Gyants *sonne,* that lies there on the laire . . . IV. viii. 51. 5
tragicke Inoes *sonne,* . . . IV. xi. 13. 4
Albion the *sonne* of Neptune was, . . . IV. xi. 16. 1
he their *sonne* full fresh and jolly was, . . . IV. xi. 27. 1
Brutus warlicke *sonne,* Locrinus, . . . IV. xi. 36. 1
Dame Venus *sonne,* that tameth stubborne youth . . . IV. xii. 13. 3
To cure her *sonne,* as he his faith had lent, . . . IV. xii. 23. 4
comming to her *sonne,* . . . IV. xii. 26. 3
Proteus, that hath ordayn'd my *sonne* to die; . . . IV. xii. 31. 2
It to replevie, and my *sonne* reprive. . . . IV. xii. 31. 8
So faire a wife for her *sonne* Marinell. . . . IV. xii. 33. 7
afterwards a *sonne* to him shalt beare, . . . V. vii. 23. 7
Like as the cursed *son* of Theseus, . . . V. viii. 43. 1
borne and bred Of Gyants race, the *sonne* of Geryon; . . . V. x. 9. 2
His *sonne* was this Geryoneo hight; . . . V. x. 11. 1
repayre, . . . unto Latonaes *sonne* After his chace . . . VI. ii. 25. 4
I am a Briton borne, *Sonne* of a King, . . . VI. ii. 27. 7
when he saw his *sonne* so ill bedight . . . VI. iii. 4. 1
there should to him a *sonne* Be gotten, not begotten; . . . VI. iv. 32. 6
'Faire daughter Dame, And you, faire *Sonne,* . . . VI. vi. 6. 6

Son—*Continued.*
The *sonne* of Venus, who is myld by kynd . . . VI. vii. 37. 1
'Surely, my *sonne*,' (then answer'd he againe) . . . VI. ix. 20. 1
Titans that did whylome strive With Saturnes *sonne* . . . VII. vi. 2. 7
Eftsoones the *sonne* of Maia forth he sent . . . VII. vi. 16. 1
'Ceasse, Saturnes *sonne*, to seeke by proffers vaine . . . VII. vi. 34. 7
'Think now (quod she) my *sonne*, . . . *Epig.* iv. 35
begot, Like to it selfe his eldest *sonne* and heire, . . . *H.H.L.* 31
faire Venus, . . . With her heart-quelling *Sonne* . . . *Proth.* 97
Sonder. *See* **Asunder.**
Song. *See* **Sung.**
My *song* thus now in thy Conclusions . . . *Pet.*[1] vii. 1
accords more sweete than Mermaids *song:* . . . *Bel.* xii. 8
That thou art first, which of thy Nation *song* . . . *Ro.* xxxii. 13
'Of fayre Elisa be your silver *song*, . . . *S.C.* Ap. 46
Let dame Elisa thanke you for her *song:* . . . *S.C.* Ap. 150
was thilk same *song* of Colins owne making? . . . *S.C.* Ap. 154
Frame to thy *songe* their chereful cheriping, . . . *S.C.* Jun. 55
Nought weigh I who my *song* doth prayse . . . *S.C.* Jun. 73
Sike a *song* never heardest thou . . . *S.C.* Au. 50
if thou this *song* areede; . . . *S.C.* Au. 146
The Nightingale is sovereigne of *song*, . . . *S.C.* N. 25
Philomele her *song* with teares doth steepe; . . . *S.C.* N. 141
Ceasse now, my *song*, . . . *S.C.* N. 201
if I ever sonet *song* so cleare, . . . *S.C.* D. 15
The rurall *song* of carefull Colinet. . . . *S.C.* D. 18
ybent to *song* and musicks mirth, . . . *S.C.* D. 40
Tuning our *song* unto a tender Muse, . . . *Gn.* 2
Phoebus, shall be the author of my *song*, . . . *Gn.* 15
the devicefull matter of my *song;* . . . *T.M.* 386
A dolefull case desires a dolefull *song*, . . . *T.M.* 541
Awake, and to his *Song* a part applie: . . . *Ti.* 236
here thou livest, being ever *song* Of us, . . . *Ti.* 338
even their heavie *song* would breede delight; . . . *D.* 13
Hearken, ye gentle shepheards, to my *song*, . . . *As.* Pr. 5
larke . . . with her *song* doth greet The dawning day . . . *As.* 33
made the Muses in his *song* to mourne. . . . *As.* Interl. 222
Harke then, ye jolly shepheards, to my *song*.' . . . *Col.* 51
of my river Bregogs love I *soong*, . . . *Col.* 92
His *song* was all a lamentable lay . . . *Col.* 164
she mott my simple *song*, . . . *Col.* 365
Who lives that can match that heroick *song*, . . . *Col.* 404
Appearing well in that well tuned *song*, . . . *Col.* 418
Fierce warres and faithful loves shall moralize my *song*. . . . I. Pr. 1. 9
Seemd in their *song* to scorne the cruell sky. . . . I. i. 8. 4
Too high a ditty for my simple *song*. . . . I. x. 55. 7
song (*sung) In well attuned notes a joyous lay, . . . I. xii. 7. 3
one sung a *song* of love and jollity. . . . I. xii. 38. 9
Sometimes she *song* (*sung) as lowd as larke in ayre, . . . II. vi. 3. 3
No *song* but did containe a lovely ditt. . . . II. vi. 13. 4
A *song* of bale and bitter sorrow sings, . . . II. vii. 23. 7
Some *song* in sweet consort; . . . II. ix. 35. 2
To decke my *song* withall, . . . II. x. 3. 8
ever mixt their *song* with light licentious toyes. . . . II. xii. 72. 9
thee, O Queene! the matter of my *song*, . . . III. iv. 3. 8
the birds *song* many a lovely lay . . . III. v. 40. 3
Are still emongst them *song*, that far my rymes exceed. . . . III. viii. 42. 9
Fit *song* of Angels caroled to bee! . . . III. viii. 43. 1
it a wonder of the world is *song* In forreine landes; . . . III. ix. 45. 7
All which together *song* full chearefully A lay . . . III. xii. 5. 6
To her this *song* most fitly is addrest, . . . IV. Pr. 4. 8
for guerdon of her *song*, . . . IV. viii. 5. 6
fit matter for another *song*. . . . V. viii. 51. 9
Came dauncing forth, and joyous carrols *song:* . . . V. xi. 34. 4
To take the ayre and heare the thrushes *song*, . . . VI. iv. 17. 3
Faire Pastorell, of whom is now my *song:* . . . VI. xi. 2. 2
ravisht with delight Of his celestiall *song*, . . . VII. vii. 12. 9
The whiles doe ye this *song* unto her sing, . . . *Epith.* 54
hearken to the birds love-learned *song*, . . . *Epith.* 88
Song! made in lieu of many ornaments, . . . *Epith.* 427
vouchsafe to take of me This simple *song*, . . . *H.L.* 307
runne softly, till I end my *Song*. . . . *Proth.* 18, 36, 54, 72, 90
runne softlie, till I end my *Song*.' . . . *Proth.* 108
run softly, till I end my *Song*. . . . *Proth.* 126
runne softly, till I end my *Song*. . . . *Proth.* 144, 162, 180
Songs. laughes the *songs* that Colin Clout doth make. . . . *S.C.* Ja. 66
doth forbeare His wonted *songs*, . . . *S.C.* Ap. 16
in your *songs* were wont to make a part: . . . *S.C.* Au. 154
To cheerefull *songs* can chaunge my cherelesse cryes. . . . *S.C.* Au. 182
In *songs* and plaintive pleas, . . . *S.C.* Au. 185
sing . . . *songs* of some jouisaunce? . . . *S.C.* N. 2
looser *songs* of love to underfong, . . . *S.C.* N. 22
The *songs* that Colin made you in her praise, . . . *S.C.* N. 78
he of Tityrus his *songs* did lere: . . . *S.C.* D. 4
represse The streames of Hebrus with his *songs*, . . . *Gn.* 181
shepherd groomes, which wont his *songs* to praise: . . . *Ti.* 228
his rimes, his *songs* were all upon her. . . . *As.* 60
Trees, braunches, birds, and *songs*, were framed fitt . . . II. vi. 13. 5
in her *songs*, sends many a wishfull vow . . . *Am.* lxxxviii. 3
Sonnet. if I ever *sonet* song so cleare, . . . *S.C.* D. 15
Son's. So hee his *sonnes* both Syre and brother hight. . . . *T.M.* 264
Semiramis, whose sides transfixt With *sonnes* own blade . . . I. v. 50. 4
it may dwell In her *sonnes* flesh, . . . II. ii. 10. 8
Her deare *sonnes* destiny to her to tell, . . . III. iv. 25. 4
To graunt to her her *sonnes* life, . . . IV. xii. 29. 7
And Aldus was his name; and his *sonnes*, Aladine. . . . VI. iii. 3. 9
thou pointest thy *Sons* poysned arrow, . . . *H.B.* 62
Sons. 'There be the two stout *sonnes* of Aeacus, . . . *Gn.* 481
as we bee *sonnes* of the world so wide, . . . *Hub.* 135
The *sonnes* of darknes and of ignoraunce, . . . *T.M.* 68

Sons—*Continued.*
If old Aveugles *sonnes* so evill heare? . . . I. v. 23. 7
The *sonnes* of Day he favoureth, I see, . . . I. v. 25. 7
The hight of three the tallest *sonnes* of mortall seed. . . . I. vii. 8. 9
The *sonnes* of old Acrates and Despight; . . . II. iv. 41. 6
Those were the two *sonnes* of Acrates old, . . . II. viii. 10. 6
That *sonnes* of men amazd their sternnesse to behold. . . . II. x. 7. 9
He left three *sonnes*, his famous progeny, . . . II. x. 13. 4
Of which were twentie *sonnes*, . . . II. x. 22. 5
his ambitious *sonnes* unto them twayne Arraught the rule, . . . II. x. 34. 7
two *sonnes*, of pearelesse prowesse both, . . . II. x. 40. 2
Five *sonnes* he left, . . . II. x. 44. 1
all the *sonnes* of these five brethren raynd . . . II. x. 45. 6
He had two *sonnes*, . . . II. x. 46. 1
He left two *sonnes*, too young to rule . . . II. x. 46. 8
Three *sonnes* he dying left, all under age; . . . II. x. 64. 1
the *sonnes* of Constantine, which fled, . . . II. x. 67. 1
He left three *sonnes*, . . . II. x. 74. 1
He left two *sonnes*, . . . II. x. 75. 6
Till both the *sonnes* of Edwin he have slayne, . . . III. iii. 37. 2
Bove all the *sonnes* that were of earthly wombes ybore. . . . III. iv. 21. 9
daies, by which the *sonnes* of men Divide their works, . . . IV. vii. 13. 1
sonnes of Neptune, now assembled here: . . . IV. xi. 15. 3
she in time forth brought These three faire *sons*, . . . IV. xi. 42. 8
He had three *sonnes*, all three like fathers *sonnes*, . . . V. vi. 33. 1
had deviz'd of late With these his wicked *sons*, . . . V. vi. 33. 9
Nor sire, nor *sonnes*, nor any could she spie: . . . V. vi. 35. 7
to perpetuall paine Had damn'd her *sonnes* . . . V. vii. 10. 8
Even seventeene goodly *sonnes;* . . . V. x. 7. 4
these two, her eldest *sonnes*, she sent . . . V. x. 14. 6
when her owne two *sonnes* she had in sight, . . . V. x. 19. 7
Thenceforth into that Castle he her led With her two *sonnes*, . . . V. x. 39. 7
Where she with her two *sonnes* did looking stand, . . . V. xi. 15. 2
Belge, with her *sonnes*, prostrated low . . . V. xi. 16. 1
Areed, ye *sonnes* of God, as best ye can devise.' . . . VII. vi. 21. 9
Both *sonnes* of Uranus; . . . VII. vi. 27. 3
hast held The Heavens rule from Titans *sonnes* . . . VII. vi. 27. 7
Ye *sonnes* of Venus, play your sports at will! . . . *Epith.* 364
Sons'. Agape Doth lengthen her *sonnes* lives. . . . IV. ii. Arg.
Soon. *See* **Soon as, So soon as.**
Soone on a tree uphang'd I saw her spoyle. . . . *Bel.*[2] vi. 14
soone her bodie turn'd to ashes colde. . . . *Bel.*[2] vii. 12
all that doth consume our pleasures *soone;* . . . *Ro.* xix. 4
grose disease *Soone* growes through humours . . . *Ro.* xxiii. 12
see so goodly thing so *soone* decayed. . . . *Van.* vii. 14
Soone after this I saw an Elephant, . . . *Van.* viii. 1
soone I rede thee hence remove, . . . *S.C.* F. 137
But *soone* it sore encreased; . . . *S.C.* Mar. 99
Soone as my younglings cryen for the dam . . . *S.C.* Ap. 95
will be *soone* wasted . . . *S.C.* May 90
So conteck *soone* by concord mought be ended. . . . *S.C.* May 163
I *soone* would learne . . . *S.C.* Jun. 95
They *soone* myght be corrupted, . . . *S.C.* Jul. 110
Such fond fantsies shall *soone* be put to flight. . . . *S.C.* Au. 22
Such woundes *soone* wexen wider. . . . *S.C.* Au. 96
Diggon should *soone* find favour . . . *S.C.* S. 253
wasten *soone* in vayne. . . . *S.C.* O. 36
Her vitall threde so *soone* was spent. . . . *S.C.* N. 149
future paine, Which *soone* ensued them . . . *Gn.* 566
government of state Will without wisedome *soone* be ruinate. *Hub.* 1040
enraged, *soone* he gan upstart, . . . *Hub.* 1333
Fled back too *soone* unto his native place; . . . *Ti.* 291
Too *soone* for all that did his love embrace, . . . *Ti.* 292
Too *soone* for all this wretched world, . . . *Ti.* 293
Soone after this a Giaunt came in place, . . . *Ti.* 533
Soone after this I saw, . . . A curious Coffer . . . *Ti.* 617
O that so faire a flower so *soone* should fade, . . . *D.* 237
he of them great troups did *soone* entrap. . . . *As.* 100
Nought else but smoke, and fumeth *soone* away, . . . *Col.* 720
Which gives them life, that els would *soone* have dide, . . . *Ded. Son.* iv. 11
soone to loose her wicked bands did her constraine. . . . I. i. 19. 9
Resolvd . . . to win, Or *soone* to lose, . . . I. i. 24. 5
Who *soone* him brought into a secret part, . . . I. ii. 5. 3
She *soone* left off her mirth . . . I. ii. 14. 4
Soone meete they both, . . . I. ii. 15. 4
Her *soone* he overtooke, . . . I. ii. 20. 8
'O! leave her *soone*, or let her *soone* be slaine." . . . I. ii. 39. 4
Soone after comes the cruell Sarazin, . . . I. v. 4. 1
soone redeeme from his long-wandring woe: . . . I. v. 11. 2
Whereof he weend possessed *soone* to bee, . . . I. vi. 5. 4
soone he came, as he the place had ghest, . . . I. vi. 40. 4
soone him buckled to the field. . . . I. vi. 41. 9
Such earthly mettals *soon* consumed beene, . . . I. vii. 33. 4
his mightie shild Upon his manly arme he *soone* addrest, . . . I. viii. 6. 7
Therewith his sturdie corage *soon* was quayd, . . . I. viii. 14. 8
Had not the Gyaunt *soone* her succoured; . . . I. viii. 17. 7
Did *soone* pluck downe, . . . I. ix. 12. 4
die *soone*, O faeries sonne!' . . . I. ix. 47. 9
As in a swowne: but, *soone* reliv'd againe, . . . I. ix. 52. 3
soone in him was lefte no one corrupted jott. . . . I. x. 26. 9
'Then shall I *soone*,' . . . Abett that virgins cause . . . I. x. 64. 1
Soone after them, all dauncing on a row, . . . I. xii. 6. 5
and *soone* upon him light.' . . . II. i. 18. 4
come *soone;* come sweetest death, to me, . . . II. i. 36. 6
he rusht into the thick, And *soone* arrived . . . II. i. 39. 3
The gentle knight her *soone* with carefull paine Uplifted . . . II. i. 46. 1
They *soone* consent: . . . II. ii. 33. 6
'that shall I *soone*, . . . II. iii. 15. 1
soone renews her native pride: . . . II. iii. 36. 6
Soone into other fitts he was transmewd, . . . II. iii. 37. 4

Soon—*Continued.*

it may *soone* be spide,	II. iii. 41. 8
Let us *soone* hence depart.' They *soone* agree:	II. iii. 46. 2
gan *soone* unbrace His grasping hold:	II. iv. 9. 7
soone him overtooke	II. iv. 13. 9
Their blazing pride thou wouldest *soone* have blent,	II. iv. 26. 3
soone her selfe arayd,	II. iv. 27. 2
after *soone* I dearely did lament;	II. iv. 29. 5
all your hurts may *soone* through temperance be easd.'	II. iv. 33. 9
soone through suff'rance growe	II. iv. 34. 4
The sparks *soone* quench,	II. iv. 35. 7
He *soone* approched,	II. iv. 37. 6
soone his dreadfull blade about he cast,	II. v. 12. 3
'that shall I *soone* declare.	II. v. 17. 1
The merry mariner unto his word *Soone* hearkned,	II. vi. 4. 6
Carelesse the man *soone* woxe,	II. vi. 13. 7
Where *soone* he slumbred	II. vi. 14. 8
soone leave off this toylsome weary stoure:	II. vi. 16. 4
Soone shee that Island far behind her lefte,	II. vi. 18. 8
shee *soone* to hond Her ferry brought,	II. vi. 19. 4
soone thyselfe prepaire To batteile,	II. vi. 28. 5
Who, *soone* prepard to field, his sword forth drew,	II. vi. 29. 3
soone atweene them ran;	II. vi. 32. 2
soone arrived on the shallow sand,	II. vi. 38. 4
death, which will thee *soone* invade?	II. vi. 39. 7
Whom Arthure *soone* hath reskewed,	II. viii. Arg.
Abandon *soone,* I read, the caytive spoile	II. viii. 12. 4
Soone shalt thou see, and then beleeve for troth,	II. viii. 22. 3
underneath his feet *soone* made a purple plesh.	II. viii. 36. 9
with revenge desyring *soone* to dye,	II. viii. 47. 2
So hasty heat *soone* cooled to subdew:	II. viii. 47. 8
His shining Helmet he gan *soone* unlace,	II. viii. 52. 8
they shall *soone* be had.'	II. viii. 54. 5
A while they fled, but *soone* retournd againe	II. ix. 15. 1
soone the knights . . . Broke their rude troupes,	II. ix. 15. 6
Soone it must turne to earth;	II. ix. 21. 9
soone into a goodly Parlour brought,	II. ix. 33. 6
Soone after this the Romanes him warrayd;	II. x. 50. 8
Who *soone* by meanes thereof the Empire wan,	II. x. 61. 4
Soone after which three hundred Lords he slew	II. x. 66. 6
Hengist eke *soon* brought to shamefull death.	II. x. 67. 6
the Prince his mortall speare *Soone* to him raught,	II. xi. 25. 2
He *soone* in vomit up againe doth lay,	II. xii. 3. 7
Lo! see *soone* after how	II. xii. 74. 7, 9
soone comes age that will her pride deflowre;	II. xii. 75. 7
Verdant (so he hight) he *soone* untyde,	II. xii. 82. 8
But them the Palmer *soone* did pacify.	II. xii. 84. 8
That hath so *soone* forgot the excellence	II. xii. 87. 2
soone compeld to hearken unto peace.	III. i. 23. 7
soone as maistery comes sweet Love anone . . . *soone* away is gone.'	III. i. 25. 8, 9
Redcrosse Knight was *soon* disarmed there;	III. i. 42. 6
shamelesse beauty *soone* becomes a loathly sight.	III. i. 48. 9
Whose vertues . . . *soone* were solemniz'd.	III. ii. 18. 9
O let them *soone* awake!	III. iv. 2. 2
Her dolour *soone* she ceast,	III. iv. 12. 4
I read thee *soone* retyre,	III. iv. 14. 8
findeth dew effect or *soone* or late;	III. iv. 27. 5
that *soone* he did repent,	III. iv. 47. 7
Soone her garments loose Upgath'ring,	III. vi. 19. 6
so her she *soone* appeasd	III. vi. 25. 3
doth *soone* withdraw His feeble eyne,	III. vii. 13. 7
To see his whole yeares labor lost so *soone,*	III. vii. 34. 8
soone forgot his former sickely payne:	III. viii. 10. 3
heat that *soone* in flame forth brust:	III. viii. 25. 4
How *soone* would yee assemble many a fleete,	III. viii. 28. 3
soone arryving they restrained were	III. viii. 52. 3
soone after they were gone,	III. ix. 12. 1
Yet was *soone* wonne his malice to relent,	III. ix. 25. 3
soone he shal be fownd,	III. x. 32. 9
his journey bring too *soone* to evill end.'	III. x. 40. 9
he *soone* resinde His former suit,	III. xi. 5. 3
Soone after that, . . . Him selfe he chaung'd,	III. xi. 31. 1
soone they life conceiv'd,	III. xii. 9. 9
every part . . . was *soone* restord.	III. xii. 38. 7
that same younker *soone* was overthrowne,	IV. i. 11. 2
Ne for light Ladies love that *soone* is lost.'	IV. i. 35. 4
The warlike Britonesse her *soone* addrest,	IV. i. 36. 1
That being forst his saddle *soone* to leave,	IV. i. 36. 4
Scudamour himselfe did *soone* uprayse,	IV. i. 42. 8
All things not rooted well will *soone* be rotten.'	IV. i. 51. 5
Ate *soone* discovering his desire,	IV. ii. 11. 6
doe not rather wish them *soone* expire,	IV. iii. 1. 3
Soone after did the brethren three advance	IV. iii. 5. 4
His foe was *soone* addrest:	IV. iii. 14. 9
Who, him affronting *soone,*	IV. iii. 22. 9
He *soone* her lost:	IV. iv. 8. 5
offer Blandamour gan *soone* despize;	IV. iv. 8. 9
his wound he *soone* forgot,	IV. iv. 33. 2
soone enforced beene To let him loose	IV. iv. 34. 7
by his friend himselfe eke *soone* he fond	IV. iv. 45. 3
he was *soone* awaked therewithall,	IV. v. 42. 5
That all his senses did full *soone* arrest:	IV. v. 43. 5
doth fall in love, And *soone* from her depart.	IV. vi. Arg.
Unto her sword and shield her *soone* betooke;	IV. vi. 14. 8
like a pined ghost he *soone* appeares:	IV. vii. 41. 4
unto strength restor'd her *soone* anew.	IV. viii. 20. 9
For naturall affection *soone* doth cesse,	IV. ix. 2. 1
she that wrongfull challenge *soone* assoyled,	IV. ix. 36. 7
They *soone* would loath their lesser happinesse,	IV. x. 23. 7

Soon—*Continued.*

Soone after whom the lovely Bridegroome came,	IV. xi. 24. 2
soone he gan such folly to forthinke againe.	IV. xii. 14. 9
'To hope' (quoth he) 'him *soone* to overtake	V. i. 19. 3
soone them over-hent,	V. iii. 11. 1
from the other fiftie *soone* the prisoner fet.	V. iii. 11. 9
with sore havocke *soone* they overthrew,	V. iii. 12. 5
he was *soone* aware of their ill minde,	V. iv. 24. 1
Soone after eke came she,	V. v. 5. 3
her sunshynie helmet *soone* unlaced,	V. v. 11. 8
soone she did her countenance compose,	V. v. 30. 5
Where *soone* arriving they received were	V. vi. 22. 6
of his game she *soone* enwombed grew,	V. vii. 16. 5
To warne her foe to battell *soone* be prest:	V. vii. 27. 2
her foe appeared *soone* in sight.	V. vii. 27. 9
yet *soone* she it requit;	V. vii. 33. 5
Soone after these he saw another Knight,	V. viii. 5. 1
Amends may for the trespasse *soone* be made,	V. viii. 14. 2
soone after me she sent	V. viii. 23. 2
Soone after whom the Prince arrived there,	V. viii. 27. 6
snatching her *soone* up,	V. ix. 14. 4
soone did make To leave his proper forme,	V. ix. 16. 8
Talus *soone* him overtooke,	V. ix. 18. 9
The raskall manie *soone* they overthrew;	V. xi. 59. 8
loosing *soone* his shield did it forgoe;	V. xii. 22. 7
turne thee *soone* to him of whom thou art defyde.'	VI. i. 18. 9
The gate *soone* opened	VI. i. 23. 2
he should be *soone* in place.'	VI. i. 28. 6
having *soone* his armes about him dight,	VI. i. 32. 6
My knight hers *soone,* as seemes, to daunger drove,	VI. ii. 20. 5
He *soone* allayd that Knights conceiv'd displeasure,	VI. iii. 22. 2
His weapons *soone* from him he threw away,	VI. iii. 27. 6
Compeld him *soone* the spoyle adowne to lay.	VI. iv. 20. 4
soone upstarting much he gan repine,	VI. v. 26. 5
Who to them stepping did them *soone* divide,	VI. v. 27. 3
shall you *soone* repaire your present evill plight.'	VI. vi. 14. 9
that *soone* she pacifyde The wrathfull Prince,	VI. vi. 43. 5
The Prince *soone* hearkned,	VI. vii. 12. 5
th' one is dead, and th' other *soone* shall die,	VI. vii. 13. 3
Gathered him selfe together *soone* againe,	VI. vii. 46. 2
I will them *soone* acquite, and both of blame assoile.'	VI. viii. 6. 9
buckling *soone* him selfe, gan fiercely fly	VI. viii. 12. 8
an altar *soone* they fayned,	VI. viii. 44. 8
The knight full gladly *soone* agreed thereto,	VI. ix. 16. 8
'With sight whereof *soone* cloyd,	VI. ix. 25. 1
he did it *soone* displace,	VI. ix. 42. 7
Calidore *soone* comming to her ayde,	VI. x. 35. 6
Thereto they *soone* agreed,	VI. xi. 40. 6
he him fast pursuing *soone* approched neare.	VI. xii. 25. 9
men onely (whom she *soone* subdewed)	VII. vi. 4. 8
That *soone* he came where-as the Titanesse	VII. vi. 17. 2
could the greatest wrath *soone* turne to grace,	VII. vi. 31. 3
Nature *soone* Her righteous Doome areads.	VII. vii. Arg.
Yet see we *soone* decay;	VII. vii. 18. 3
Short Time shall *soon* cut down	VII. viii. 1. 9
If not, die *soone;* and I with thee will perish.	*Am.* ii. 14
soone about him dight His wanton wings	*Am.* iv. 7
Such cruelty she would have *soone* abhord.	*Am.* xxxi. 14
The hardest yron *soone* doth mollify;	*Am.* xxxii. 2
Wil *soon* conceive, and learne to construe well.	*Am.* xliii. 14
Soone after, when my joy to sorrow flits, I waile,	*Am.* liv. 7
Bid her therefore her selfe *soone* ready make,	*Am.* lxx. 9
he, *soone* after, fresh againe enured His former cruelty.	*Epig.* iv. 53
Your string could *soone* to sadder tenor turne,	*Epith.* 9
Bid her awake therefore, and *soone* her dight,	*Epith.* 30
now *soon* her disaray.	*Epith.* 300
For it will *soone* be day:	*Epith.* 369

Soon as (*partial list*). *See* **So soon as.**

Soone as thy oaten pype began to sound,	*S.C.* Jun. 58
Soone as thou gynst to sette thy notes in frame,	*S.C.* O. 25
soone as spring his mantle hath displayde,	*S.C.* N. 85
Soone as the chaffe should in the fan be fynd,	*S.C.* D. 125
Soone as he them plac'd in thy sacred wood	*Gn.* 169
soone as they this mock-King did espy,	*Hub.* 1091
soone as he receiv'd That word,	*Hub.* 1257
soone as day doth shew his deawie face,	*D.* 484
Soone as his oaten pipe began to shrill,	*As.* 44
Soone as on them the Suns life-giving light	*Col.* 861
Soone as that uncouth light upon them shone,	I. i. 15. 8
soone as their Parent deare They saw	I. i. 25. 1
soone as he them can spie,	I. ii. 29. 1
Soone as appeard safe opportunitie:	I. ii. 41. 7
Soone as the royall virgin he did spy,	I. iii. 5. 4
Soone as she parted thence,	I. iii. 22. 1
Soone as the port from far he has espide,	I. iii. 31. 7
Soone as the Elfin knight in presence came,	I. iv. 13. 1
Soone as the Faerie heard his Ladie speake,	I. v. 12. 1
Soone as I thinke upon my bitter bale.	I. vii. 39. 6
soone as breath out of his brest did pas,	I. viii. 24. 6
Soone as thy dreadfull trompe begins	I. xi. 6. 6
Soone as the terme of those six yeares shall cease,	I. xii. 19. 7
Soone as the Redcrosse knight he understands	II. i. 1. 4
soone as on that knight his eye did glaunce,	II. i. 31. 4
Soone as the morrow fayre with purple beames	II. iii. 1. 1
Soone as my loathed love appeard	II. iv. 29. 3
Soone as Occasion felt her selfe untyde,	II. v. 19. 1
soone as Furor was enlargd,	II. v. 19. 8
Soone as he Guyon saw,	II. vii. 6. 1
Soone as he entred was, the dore streight way	II. vii. 26. 5
Soone as those glitterand armes he did espye,	II. vii. 42. 1

Sore—*Continued.*
urged *sore* . . . Him hasty to arise. . . . . II. v. 37. 4
The varlet at his plaint was grieved so *sore,* . . . . II. vi. 45. 6
he wondred *sore* To see Pyrochles there . . . . II. vi. 48. 6
Joves dreaded thunder light Does scorch not halfe so *sore,* . II. vi. 50. 8
which sight at first him *sore* aghast. . . . . II. viii. 4. 9
The Palmer . . . Woxe *sore* affraid, ... II. viii. 9. 3
on the haubergh stroke the Prince so *sore,* . . . . II. viii. 44. 6
What warre so cruel, or what siege so *sore,* . . . . II. xi. 1. 1
him so *sore* smott with his yron mace, ... II. xi. 34. 8
sore annoyed, groping in that griesly night. . . . . II. xii. 35. 9
He fownd him selfe dishonored so *sore*. . . . . III. i. 7. 4
sore beset on every side arownd, ... III. i. 21. 2
never *sore* but might a salve obtaine: . . . . III. ii. 35. 7
though no reason may apply Salve to your *sore,* . . . . . . III. ii. 36. 5
so *sore* Now ranckleth in this same fraile fleshly mould, . . III. ii. 39. 2
Ne can my ronning *sore* finde remedee, ... III. ii. 39. 6
her turne to fowle repriefe And *sore* reproch, ... III. iii. 5. 8
a *sore* evill, which this virgin bright Tormenteth . . . . . III. iii. 16. 4
with sharpe fits thy tender hart oppresseth *sore:* . . . . . III. iii. 21. 9
sighing *sore,* at length him thus bespake: . . . . III. iii. 43. 4
the great Castle smite so *sore* withall, ... III. iii. 49. 8
all too long I burne with envy *sore* . . . . III. iv. 2. 3
the fast earth affronted them so *sore,* . . . . III. iv. 7. 7
sighing softly *sore,* and inly deepe, ... III. iv. 11. 1
surbate *sore* Their tender feete . . . . III. iv. 34. 5
For *sore* he swat, and . . . was bescracht . . . . III. v. 3. 8
That stroke the hardy Squire did *sore* displease, ... III. v. 19. 6
the third brother him did *sore* assay, ... III. v. 21. 3
of that cruell wound he bled so *sore,* . . . . III. v. 26. 2
his foule *sore* reduced to faire plight: . . . . III. v. 41. 8
his hart woxe *sore,* and health decayd: . . . . III. v. 43. 2
sore affright, Wondred to see her belly so upblone, ... III. vi. 9. 7
seized every sence with sorrow *sore* opprest. . . . . III. vi. 10. 9
sore accus'd His falshood, ... III. vi. 13. 3
she repented *sore* to have him angered. . . . . III. vi. 20. 9
Phoebe therewith *sore* was angered, ... III. vi. 24. 1
Whom whenas Venus saw so *sore* displeasd, ... III. vi. 25. 1
endured *sore Sore* trouble of an hainous enimy, ... III. vi. 53. 5, 6
his sad mother, seeing his *sore* plight, ... III. vii. 20. 6
That ugly shape so *sore* her terrifide, ... III. vii. 24. 3
dismayd At that same last extremity ful *sore,* . . . . III. vii. 25. 2
did him *sore* apall. . . . . III. vii. 31. 9
therewith *sore* enrag'd, ... III. vii. 42. 1
Him bett so *sore,* that life and sence did much dismay. . . . III. viii. 31. 9
The virgin whom he had abusde so *sore;* . . . . III. viii. 36. 6
noble knights . . . may *sore* repent with mee, ... III. viii. 47. 8
makes ye doubt so *sore?* . . . . III. viii. 48. 6
That Ladies safetie is *sore* to be dradd. . . . . III. viii. 50. 3
wondrous *sore* Thereat displeasd they were, ... III. viii. 52. 5
Right *sore* I feare, ... III. ix. 1. 3
How to avenge himselfe so *sore* abusd, ... III. ix. 12. 8
Paridell *sore* brused with the blow . . . . III. ix. 16. 6
sore him selfe does throng) . . . . III. ix. 45. 4
his late fight . . . so *sore* did him offend, ... III. x. 1. 8
did consume his gall with anguish *sore:* . . . . III. x. 18. 2
Then sighing *sore,* 'It is not long,' . . . . III. x. 27. 1
Saw all this goodly sport, and grieved *sore;* . . . . III. x. 45. 2
him assayling *sore* his carkas teare, ... III. x. 53. 7
For whom so faire a Lady feeles so *sore* a wound!' . . . . . III. xi. 11. 9
The warlike Damzell was empassiond *sore,* . . . . III. xi. 18. 2
in the Porch, that did them *sore* amate, ... III. xi. 21. 5
Did beat and bounse his head and brest ful *sore:* . . . . . . III. xi. 27. 6
For many other Nymphes, he *sore* did shreek, ... III. xi. 44. 5
th' enchaunter which had her distrest So *sore,* . . . . III. xii. 41. 5
Thereat her noble hart was stonisht *sore;* . . . . III. xii. 44. 5
too long absence him had *sore* annoyd, ... III. xii. 44. *or.* 3
many of them mov'd to eye her *sore*. . . . . IV. i. 9. 6
it grieved him full *sore,* . . . . IV. i. 39. 7
'Why do ye strive for Ladies love so *sore,* . . . . IV. i. 46. 2
with the sudden stroke astonisht *sore,* . . . . IV. ii. 7. 1
So mortall was their malice, and so *sore* Become, ... IV. ii. 18. 8
Whereat she *sore* affrayd, yet her besought . . . . IV. ii. 50. 1
sore bestedde With heapes of strokes, ... IV. iii. 25. 3
he yet was *sore* of his late lucklesse fight. . . . . IV. iv. 3. 9
Whose sharpe provokement them incenst so *sore,* . . . . . . IV. iv. 4. 6
With which so *sore* he Ferramont assaid, ... IV. iv. 20. 7
went away *sore* wounded of his haplesse hand. . . . . IV. iv. 21. 9
So *sore* he sowst him on the compast creast, ... IV. iv. 30. 7
They have him taken captive, though it grieve him *sore*. . . IV. iv. 32. 9
so *sore* that none him life behote. . . . . IV. iv. 40. 9
therewith smote him on his Umbriere So *sore,* . . . . IV. iv. 44. 4
he woxe therewith displeased *sore,* . . . . IV. iv. 45. 6
all those stranger knights full *sore* agrieved, ... IV. iv. 46. 8
heaping stroakes which thereon soused *sore:* . . . . IV. v. 36. 4
such a *sore,* that doth her grievance hide, ... IV. vi. 1. 6
Deawed with silver drops through sweating *sore,* . . . . . . IV. vi. 19. 7
He blest himselfe as one *sore* terrifide: . . . . IV. vi. 24. 7
so *sore* a breach That sudden newes had made . . . . IV. vi. 38. 3
her therewith full *sore* displeasd he found, ... IV. vi. 42. 7
In feeble Ladies tyranning so *sore,* . . . . IV. vii. 1. 6
Sighing and sobbing *sore,* . . . . IV. vii. 10. 2
With dreadfull strokes let drive at him so *sore,* . . . . . . IV. vii. 28. 3
held her wrathfull hand from vengeance *sore:* . . . . IV. vii. 36. 6
Right *sore* agrieved at her sharpe reproofe, ... IV. vii. 37. 2
the Squire, in her defense, her *sore* astound. . . . . IV. viii. 19. 9
Them follow'd fast, and them reviled *sore,* . . . . IV. viii. 35. 3
sore annoyd The Prince on foot, ... IV. viii. 37. 5
stroke the Pagan with his steely brand So *sore,* . . . . . . IV. viii. 43. 4
sigh full *sore* to heare the miserie . . . . IV. viii. 64. 4

Sore—*Continued.*
From all foure parts of heaven doe rage full *sore,* . . . . . IV. ix. 23. 6
layd at them so sharpely and so *sore,* . . . . IV. ix. 34. 7
through Loves constrayning Tormented *sore,* . . . . IV. x. 43. 8
many salves did to his *sore* applie, ... IV. xi. 6. 2
sore against his will did him retaine, ... IV. xi. 7. 7
Marinell was *sore* offended . . . . IV. xii. 18. 3
she in her mind Was troubled *sore,* . . . . IV. xii. 21. 2
it was no old *sore* which his new paine procured; . . . . . . IV. xii. 23. 9
Which of the Nymphes his heart so *sore* did mieve; . . . . . IV. xii. 26. 7
then being *sore* bestad. . . . . IV. xii. 33. 9
present dayes, which are corrupted *sore,* . . . . V. Pr. 3. 4
Lamenting *sore* his sorrowfull sad tyne, ... V. i. 13. 8
The sight whereof the Lady *sore* adrad, ... V. i. 22. 7
all the warders it did *sore* amate, ... V. ii. 21. 3
Whom with *sore* havocke soone they overthrew, ... V. iii. 12. 5
by the shoulder him so *sore* he bit, ... V. iii. 33. 8
threatned *sore* Her to have swallow'd up, ... V. iv. 12. 3
him reviled, and reproched *sore* . . . . V. iv. 23. 3
she was right *sore* bestad, ... V. vi. 17. 5
With sight whereof she was dismayd right *sore,* . . . . . . V. vi. 28. 1
thy sire lamenting *sore* for thee, ... V. vii. 21. 8
dealt her blowes unmercifully *sore;* . . . . V. vii. 31. 2
sore engriev'd to heare, ... V. vii. 32. 7
of her wound which *sore* did paine, ... V. vii. 34. 5
She sought with ruth to salve his sad misfortune *sore*. . . . V. vii. 38. 9
all unweeting have you wrong'd thus *sore,* . . . . V. viii. 13. 2
The dreadfull sight did them so *sore* affray, ... V. viii. 40. 5
The Briton Prince was *sore* empassionate, ... V. ix. 46. 2
lewd Impietie, that her accused *sore*. . . . . V. ix. 48. 9
He that whylome in Spaine so *sore* was dred . . . . V. x. 9. 3
now his cruelty so *sore* she drad, ... V. x. 18. 7
Belge selfe was therewith stonied *sore,* . . . . V. xi. 30. 3
grieved *sore* that . . . she had Fallen into that Tyrants hand . V. xi. 40. 8
all my former praise hath blemisht *sore:* . . . . V. xi. 49. 4
That bloudie scutchin, being battered *sore,* . . . . V. xi. 54. 4
they her rebuked and upbrayded *sore*. . . . . V. xi. 61. 9
wherewith troubled *sore* . . . . V. xii. 6. 6
Lookt up with eyes full sad and hart full *sore,* . . . . . . V. xii. 11. 7
with his burdenous blowes him *sore* did overlade. . . . . . . V. xii. 19. 9
whiles he combred was therewith so *sore,* . . . . V. xii. 22. 8
full *sore* aghast He staggered to and fro . . . . V. xii. 23. 3
Uppon an hard adventure *sore* bestad, ... VI. i. 4. 2
He *sore* doth wound, and bite, and cruelly torment.' . . . . VI. i. 8. 9
He fiercely him pursu'd, and pressed *sore;* . . . . VI. i. 21. 8
hers . . . to daunger drove, And left *sore* wounded: . . . . VI. ii. 20. 6
This knight, . . . had wounded *sore* Another knight . . . . VI. ii. 40. 5
So *sore* her sides, so much her wounds . . . . VI. iii. 46. 4
the bitter stoure Of his *sore* vengeaunce, ... VI. iii. 48. 5
By reason that her knight was wounded *sore:* . . . . VI. iv. 10. 6
Whom pitying to heare so *sore* complaine, ... VI. iv. 23. 3
Whom when the Salvage saw so *sore* distrest, ... VI. v. 6. 1
Wherewith the Prince *sore* moved there avoud . . . . VI. v. 34. 1
whose griefe through suffraunce *sore* increast. . . . . VI. v. 39. 9
hearts were sicke; their sides were *sore;* their feete were lame. VI. v. 40. 9
heales both Squire and dame Of their *sore* maladies: . . . . VI. vi. Arg.
No wound . . . so *sore* doth light . . . . VI. vi. 1. 2
Give salves to every *sore,* but counsell to the minde. . . . VI. vi. 5. 9
Made all of rusty yron ranckling *sore,* . . . . VI. vi. 9. 3
with medicine To goe about to salve such kynd of *sore,* . . VI. vi. 13. 2
(sayd then Serena, sighing *sore*) . . . . VI. vi. 13. 5
Full on his bever did him strike so *sore,* . . . . VI. vii. 8. 6
gainst the cold hard earth so *sore* him strake, ... VI. vii. 11. 4
griesly wounds that him appalled *sore;* . . . . VI. vii. 14. 5
What cared she who sighed for her *sore,* . . . . VI. vii. 30. 5
To see her *sore* lament and bite her tender lip. . . . . . . VI. vii. 44. 9
The villaine, wroth for greeting him so *sore,* . . . . VI. vii. 46. 1
Him still reviling and afflicting *sore,* . . . . VI. viii. 4. 2
Addeem'd me to endure this penaunce *sore;* . . . . VI. viii. 22. 5
So *sore* him scourgeth that the bloud downe followeth. . . . VI. viii. 28. 9
groning *sore* from grieved hart entire . . . . VI. viii. 48. 7
whose love his heart hath *sore* engrieved. . . . . VI. x. 1. 9
what were they all, whose lacke thee grieves so *sore?*' . . . VI. x. 20. 9
now gan afresh to rancle *sore,* . . . . VI. x. 31. 3
A sodaine sickenesse which her *sore* opprest, ... VI. xi. 7. 8
sighing *sore,* as if her hart in twaine Had riven bene . . . VI. xi. 22. 7
that *sore* her griev'd to see, ... VI. xi. 23. 1
her infestred wound, That *sore* her payn'd, ... VI. xi. 24. 7
(sayd he, then sighing *sore*) . . . . VI. xi. 29. 1
do him assayle on every side, And *sore* oppresse, ... VI. xi. 48. 7
seeing there that did him pittie *sore,* . . . . VI. xii. 9. 6
that enterprize . . . forslacked had so *sore;* . . . . VI. xii. 12. 5
rageth *sore* in each degree and state, ... VI. xii. 40. 2
so *sore* him dread aghast. . . . . VII. vi. 52. 5
From mortall eyes that should be *sore* agrized; . . . . VII. vii. 6. 3
his limbes with labor heated *sore*. . . . . VII. vii. 29. 9
oft him pinched *sore:* . . . . VII. vii. 30. 5
so *sore* my wounds, ... *Am.* lvii. 5
my silly barke was tossed *sore:* . . . . *Am.* lxiii. 4
I wounded am full *sore:* . . . . *Epig.* iv. 28
bleeding hart . . . thou mangled hast so *sore,* . . . . *H.L.* 143
What hart can feele least touch of so *sore* launch, ... *H.H.L.* 162

Sorely. being downe, is . . . brouzed, and *sorely* hurt. . . . *S.C.* F. 236
With painfull torments to be *sorely* beaten. . . . . *Gn.* 352
sorely griev'd his hart, ... *Hub.* 1304
seeming *sorely* chauffed at his band, ... I. xii. 35. 6
They did about their businesse sweat, and *sorely* toyld. . . II. ix. 30. 9
Beautie and Money, they that Bulwarke *sorely* rent. . . . . II. xi. 9. 9
Sorely thereat he was displeased, ... III. iv. 12. 7
Into his heart, which it did *sorely* gryde. . . . . III. ix. 29. 5

Sorely—*Continued.*
My softened heart so *sorely* doth constraine, . . . IV. i. 1. 7
with their axes both so *sorely* bet, . . . IV. iii. 15. 3
So much more *sorely* to the ground he fell, . . . IV. iv. 19. 6
So *sorely* he her strooke, . . . IV. vi. 13. 3
of that Carle she *sorely* bruz'd had beene, . . . IV. vii. 35. 8
From whom he now so *sorely* was bestad, . . . IV. vii. 46. 4
with his heeles so *sorely* he him strake, . . . V. iii. 33. 3
Them *sorely* vext, and courst, and overran, . . . V. iv. 44. 3
Even so did Radigund . . . *sorely* him constraine. . . . V. v. 15. 9
He *sorely* punished with heavie payne; . . . V. xii. 25. 7
There he that knight full *sorely* bleeding found, . . . VI. iv. 9. 6
For fell despight to be so *sorely* crost; . . . VI. iv. 40. 4
Whom he likewise right *sorely* did constraine, . . . VI. vi. 38. 5
his old foes that once him *sorely* fear'd. . . . VII. vi. 15. 9
Will both together me too *sorely* wracke. . . . *Am.* xlvi. 12
Sorer. Ne *sorer* vengeance wish on you to fall . . . *D.* 352
Sores. To heale the *sores* of sinfull soules unsound, . . . *H.H.L.* 166
Sorest. seas, when they do *sorest* rage, . . . IV. xi. 50. 5
Sorrow. slake the winters *sorowe.* . . . *S.C.* Mar. 6
I chaunst to fall asleepe with *sorowe* . . . *S.C.* Mar. 47
Such follie great *sorow* to Niobe did breede: . . . *S.C.* Ap. 87
This was the first sourse of shepheards *sorowe,* . . . *S.C.* May 130
If I may rest, I nill live in *sorrowe.* . . . *S.C.* May 151
Sorrowe ne neede be hastened on, . . . *S.C.* May 152
some old *sorowe* that made a newe breache: . . . *S.C.* May 210
Love is a curelesse *sorrowe.* . . . *S.C.* Au. 104
sorrow close shrouded in hart, . . . *S.C.* S. 15
To quite it from the blacke bowre of *sorrowe.* . . . *S.C.* S. 97
sing of *sorrowe* and deathes dreeriment; . . . *S.C.* N. 36
with pure brest from carefull *sorrow* free, . . . *Gn.* 107
That balefull *sorrow* he no longer beares . . . *Gn.* 644
the thing that doth thy *sorrow* breed: . . . *Hub.* 596
To feed on hope, to pine with feare and *sorrow;* . . . *Hub.* 900
in her roome unseemly *Sorrow* sits, . . . *T.M.* 184
Therefore I mourne and *sorrow* with the rest, . . . *T.M.* 227
Untill my cause of *sorrow* be redrest. . . . *T.M.* 228
My spirits now dismayd with *sorrow* dull . . . *T.M.* 291
With equall plaints her *sorrowe* did partake. . . . *T.M.* 298
To tumble into *sorrow* and regreet, . . . *T.M.* 304
So seeke we helpe our *sorrow* to redresse, . . . *T.M.* 351
secret *sorrow* and sad languishment, . . . *T.M.* 376
rather seekes my *sorrow* to augment . . . *T.M.* 425
Therefore I mourne and endlesse *sorrow* make, . . . *T.M.* 473
shame and *sorrow* and accursed case . . . *T.M.* 519
her *sorrow* to supplie, . . . *T.M.* 537
Ne tell his *sorrow* to the listning rout . . . *Ti.* 227
through inward *sorrowe* wexen faint, . . . *Ti.* 472
for great *sorrow* of their sudden fate, . . . *Ti.* 573
There now the joy is his, here *sorrow* mine. . . . *Ti.* 602
wrought both joy and *sorrow* in my mind: . . . *Ti.* 614
wrought her shame, and *sorrow* never ended. . . . *Mui.* 264
Sharpe *sorrowe* did in thousand peeces rive. . . . *D.* 7
Though they of *sorrowe* heavilie can sing; . . . *D.* 12
harts deep *sorrow* hates both life and light. . . . *D.* 91
with *sorowe* satisfide Th' importune fates, . . . *D.* 386
Sith all my *sorrow* should have end thereby, . . . *D.* 446
I will wake and *sorrow* all the night . . . *D.* 474
There will I sigh, and *sorrow* all day long, . . . *D.* 488
To mourne in *sorrow* and sad sufferaunce, . . . *D.* 507
he whose heart like *sorrow* did invade. . . . *As.* 172
meanes deviz'd to shew his *sorrow* best. . . . *As.* 208
O, how great *sorrow* my sad soule assaid! . . . I. ii. 24. 5
one loving howre For many yeares of *sorrow* can dispence; . . . I. iii. 30. 3
'With proud foes sight my *sorrow* to renew, . . . I. iv. 51. 7
read her *sorrow* in her count'nance sad; . . . I. vi. 11. 4
Una, . . . Could not for *sorrow* follow him so fast; . . . I. vi. 40. 3
earthly sight can nought but *sorrow* breed, . . . I. vii. 23. 6
thrilling *sorrow* throwne his utmost dart: . . . I. vii. 25. 2
when fervent *sorrow* slaked was, She up arose, . . . I. vii. 28. 1
he knew Some secret *sorrow* did her heart distraine; . . . I. vii. 38. 4
The chearelesse man, whom *sorrow* did dismay, . . . I. viii. 43. 7
Feare, sicknesse, age, losse, labour, *sorrow,* strife, . . . I. ix. 44. 6
Great woe and *sorrow* did her soule assay, . . . I. xi. 32. 2
'Fayre Lady, through fowle *sorrow* ill bedight, . . . II. i. 14. 2
She wilfully her *sorrow* did augment, . . . II. i. 15. 2
As if her hart with *sorrow* had transfixed beene: . . . II. i. 15. 9
To cloke her guile with *sorrow* and sad teene; . . . II. i. 21. 7
play His cruell sport, in stead of *sorrow* dew; . . . II. i. 40. 6
die with you in *sorrow,* . . . II. i. 48. 9
Of all my *sorrow* and of these sad teares, . . . II. iv. 18. 2
his *sorrow* sought through wilfulnesse, . . . II. v. 24. 7
doolefull *sorrow* heape with deadly harmes: . . . II. vi. 34. 4
Lamenting *Sorrow* did in darknes lye, . . . II. vii. 22. 8
A song of bale and bitter *sorrow* sings, . . . II. vii. 23. 7
great *sorrow* and sad agony . . . II. xii. 27. 7
That he might know and ease her *sorrow* sad; . . . II. xii. 28. 3
Great shame and *sorrow* of that fall he tooke; . . . III. i. 7. 1
Least that too farre ye have your *sorrow* sought: . . . III. ii. 10. 7
Sorrow is heaped in thy hollow chest, . . . III. ii. 32. 7
'Huge sea of *sorrow* and tempestuous griefe, . . . III. iv. 8. 1
Her former *sorrow* into suddein wrath, . . . III. iv. 12. 6
To *sorrow* huge she turnd her former play, . . . III. iv. 30. 3
forth together went with *sorow* fraught. . . . III. iv. 31. 7
For great compassion of their *sorow,* . . . III. iv. 32. 5
In stead thereof sad *sorow* and disdaine . . . III. iv. 54. 2
sorrow and despeyre without aleggeaunce! . . . III. v. 42. 9
rather chose to dye for *sorow* great, . . . III. v. 49. 8
seized every sence with *sorrow* sore opprest. . . . III. vi. 10. 9
At last when *sorrow* he saw booted nought, . . . III. x. 18. 6

Sorrow—*Continued.*
doth himselfe with *sorrow* new sustaine, . . . III. x. 60. 2
all the *sorrow* in the world is lesse Then vertues might . . . III. xi. 14. 6
wreake your *sorrow* on your cruell foe; . . . III. xi. 15. 5
sow vaine *sorrow* in a fruitlesse eare, . . . III. xi. 16. 2
your cause is nothing lesse Then is your *sorrow* certes, . . . III. xi. 18. 4
More for great *sorrow* that he could not pas . . . III. xi. 27. 2
With other signes of *sorrow* and impatient teene. . . . III. xi. 37. 9
As if no *sorrow* she ne felt ne drad; . . . III. xii. 18. 5
Sorrow seeming dead; . . . III. xii. 25. 5
Yet leave unto his *sorrow* did not yeeld, . . . IV. iii. 14. 3
'Great cause of *sorrow* certes, Sir, ye have; . . . IV. vi. 38. 6
martyrest with *sorow* and with smart, . . . IV. vii. 2. 5
Midst *sorrow* shewing joyous semblance for his sake. . . . IV. vii. 44. 9
with penaunce sad And pensive *sorrow* . . . IV. viii. 2. 6
singing all her *sorrow* to the note, . . . IV. ix. 6. 4
Hath me much *sorrow* and much travell cost: . . . IV. ix. 38. 4
her losse ought me to *sorrow* most, . . . IV. ix. 38. 7
That none might heare the *sorrow* of my hart, . . . IV. x. 48. 2
to her selfe her *sorrow* did bemone: . . . IV. xii. 5. 5
all thy senses swowned In stupid *sorow,* . . . V. v. 36. 6
Would change her paine, and *sorrow* somewhat ease, . . . V. vii. 45. 4
There he her found in *sorrow* and dismay, . . . V. x. 19. 1
Who thinkes from me his *sorrow* all doth rize. . . . VI. iv. 33. 7
Nor cease her *sorrow* and impatient stound, . . . VI. v. 6. 7
it forth doth bring *Sorrow,* and anguish, . . . VI. vi. 8. 6
to the dore of death for *sorrow* drew, . . . VI. viii. 20. 8
being tyrde with travell, and opprest With *sorrow,* . . . VI. viii. 34. 5
Playnts, prayers, vowes, ruth, *sorrow,* and dismay; . . . *Am.* xiv. 11
In secret *sorow,* and sad pensivenesse. . . . *Am.* xxxiv. 14
all the more my *sorrow* it augmenteth, . . . *Am.* xlii. 3
With *sorrow* dimmed and deform'd it were, . . . *Am.* xlv. 10
ye high hevens, that all this *sorowe* see, . . . *Am.* xlvi. 9
yeeld To *sorrow* and to solitary paine; . . . *Am.* lii. 6
Soone after, when my joy to *sorrow* flits, I waile, . . . *Am.* liv. 7
So *sorrow* still doth seeme too long to last; . . . *Am.* lxxxvi. 13
After long *sorrow* and consuming smart. . . . *H.B.* 28
Sorrowed. I *sorrowed* all so much as earst I joyd, . . . I. ix. 15. 3
Thus when they all had *sorowed* their fill, . . . III. iv. 40. 1
But sigh'd and *sorrow'd* for her lover deare, . . . VI. iii. 6. 7
Sorrowful. O, how great ruth, and *sorrowfull* assay, . . . *Pet.*[2] ii. 11
bitter griefe and *sorrowfull* annoy: . . . *Pet.*[2] vi. 12
Those piteous plaints and *sorrowfull* sad tine, . . . *T.M.* 3
When ye doo heare my *sorrowfull* annoy, . . . *D.* 514
sad to see her *sorrowfull* constraint, . . . I. iii. 8. 3
She fell to ground for *sorrowfull* regret, . . . I. vii. 20. 7
She . . . strove to maister *sorrowfull* assay, . . . I. vii. 27. 2
with *sorrowfull* demayne And deadly hew, . . . II. viii. 23. 7
that knight . . . both *sorrowfull* and sad. . . . II. xii. 84. 2
Repentaunce feeble, *sorrowfull,* and lame; . . . III. xii. 24. 3
The cause of that his *sorrowfull* constraint; . . . IV. vii. 45. 3
Both in full sad and *sorrowfull* estate: . . . IV. viii. 19. 4
Lamenting sore his *sorrowfull* sad tyne, . . . V. i. 13. 8
Full sad and *sorrowfull* was Britomart . . . V. vii. 44. 1
She forth was brought in *sorrowfull* dismay . . . V. xii. 12. 4
forth he cald from *sorrowfull* dismay . . . VI. i. 44. 5
Did wexe exceeding *sorrowfull* and sad, . . . VI. v. 3. 3
Faire Pastorella, *sorrowfull* and sad, . . . VI. x. 40. 5
Most *sorrowfull,* most sad, that ever sight, . . . VI. x. 40. 6
By his faire patients side with *sorrowfull* regret. . . . VI. xi. 9. 9
Now lay those *sorrowfull* complaints aside; . . . *Epith.* 12
Sorrowfully. in sad tearmes gan *sorrowfully* weepe, . . . *Gn.* 325
A Woman sitting, *sorrowfullie* wailing, . . . *Ti.* 9
Griefe all in sable *sorrowfully* clad, . . . III. xii. 16. 2
Right *sorrowfully* mourning her bereaved cares. . . . IV. xii. 17. 9
Sorrowing. Thy Muse to long slombreth in *sorrowing,* . . . *S.C.* N. 3
Therefore I mourne with deep harts *sorrowing,* . . . *T.M.* 107
to thee sings with deepe harts *sorrowing,* . . . *Ti.* 318
Sorrowing tempered with deare delight, . . . *Ti.* 319
When he thus ended had his *sorrowing,* . . . II. iv. 33. 7
Scudamore here die with *sorrowing.'* . . . III. xi. 24. 4
Sorrowings. bring us bale and bitter *sorrowings,* . . . VI. iii. 5. 5
Sorrow's. now cease thy *sorrowes* sourse; . . . *S.C.* N. 171
lovers heaven must passe by *sorrowes* hell.' . . . IV. vi. 32. 7
the villaine selfe, their *sorrowes* sourse, . . . IV. vii. 20. 3
made her understand His *sorrowes* cause, . . . IV. viii. 12. 4
albe he wanted sence And *sorrowes* feeling, . . . V. vi. 9. 5
Of former daies mishap, his *sorrowes* wicked sourse. . . . VI. iii. 14. 9
feeling thence, no more her *sorowes* sadnesse, . . . *Am.* xxxix. 11
Sorrows. the wild woodes, my *sorowes* to resound, . . . *S.C.* Au. 166
To tell my *sorrowes* that exceeding bee. . . . *T.M.* 546
hart of flint would rew The undeserved woes and *sorrowes,* . . . I. ii. 26. 9
'Faire Dame, be nought dismaid For *sorrowes* past; . . . I. iv. 49. 2
Gan her admire, and her sad *sorrowes* rew, . . . I. vi. 31. 4
hart, so plungd in sea of *sorrowes* deep, . . . I. vii. 39. 2
thus I heare you of your *sorrowes* treat. . . . I. vii. 40. 4
blood can nought but sin, and wars but *sorrows* yield. . . . I. x. 60. 9
all these *sorrowes* suffer for my sake, . . . I. xi. 1. 8
the *sorrowes* that uneath My tong can tell, . . . II. i. 49. 5
Full little weenest thou what *sorrowes* are Left thee . . . II. ii. 2. 3
sad sighes and *sorrowes* deepe Kept watch . . . III. ii. 28. 6
Short end of *sorrowes* they therby did finde; . . . III. ii. 43. 8
after all these *sorrowes,* . . . III. iii. 41. 1
after many teares and *sorrowes* spent, . . . IV. viii. 64. 6
vaine, I see, my *sorrowes* to unfold, . . . IV. xii. 6. 1
After long *sorrowes* suffered whyleare, . . . V. iii. 1. 7
Or loth to let her *sorrowes* be bewrayd: . . . VI. iv. 27. 4
haps that *sorrowes* of the mynd Find remedie . . . VI. iv. 28. 8
In sad misfortunes foule deformity And wretched *sorrowes,* . . . VI. v. 1. 4
sorrowes heapt on her in greater throng; . . . VI. xi. 2. 7

Sorrows—*Continued.*
reade the *sorrowes* of my dying spright, . . . *Am.* i. 7
Unquiet thought! . . . with sighes and *sorrowes* fed, . . . *Am.* ii. 3
Yet my poore life, all *sorrowes* to assoyle, . . . *Am.* xi. 9
All *sorrowes* short that gaine eternall blisse. . . . *Am.* lxiii. 14
for all the paynes and *sorrowes* past, . . . *Epith.* 32
Through the sharpe *sorrowes* which thou hast me bred, . . . *H.L.* 16
Cures all their *sorrowes* with one sweete aspect. . . . *H.B.* 245
And let thy soule, whose sins his *sorrows* wrought, . . . *H.H.L.* 251

Sorry. who, *sorie* my sad case to see, Began to comfort . . . *Hub.* 18
Where towards me a *sory* wight did cost, . . . *D.* 39
why should he, that loves me, *sorie* bee . . . *D.* 278
two knights, . . . (A *sory* sight) . . . I. vi. 38. 4
Wroth was the Prince, and *sory* yet withall, . . . II. viii. 52. 5
sory wounds right well recur'd, . . . III. i. 1. 4
Shee inly *sory* was, and gan relent . . . III. vi. 25. 2
seeming *sory* that she ever came Into his powre, . . . III. viii. 14. 7
didst weete . . . her *sory* state, . . . III. viii. 28. 2
Thither he brought the *sory* Florimell, . . . III. viii. 38. 1
all faire Ladies may for ever *sory* bee.' . . . III. viii. 47. 9
The whiles her husband ran with *sory* haste . . . III. x. 13. 2
he emongst the rest crept forth in *sory* plight. . . . III. x. 52. 9
Though sad and *sorie* for so heavy sight, . . . IV. iii. 14. 2
full *sorie* to his vew. . . . IV. iv. 33. 9
Where *sorie* Britomart had lost her late; . . . IV. vi. 47. 2
these *sory* eies have seen Seaven women . . . IV. vii. 13. 4
Which *sory* words her mightie hart did mate . . . IV. viii. 17. 6
that same dwarfe right *sorie* seem'd and sad, . . . IV. viii. 46. 3
Full inly *sorie,* for the fervent zeale . . . IV. viii. 55. 2
Whereof I *sorie,* yet myselfe did bend . . . IV. viii. 57. 3
A *sorie* sight as ever seene with eye, . . . V. i. 14. 2
neither glad nor *sorie* for their sight; . . . V. xi. 60. 5
Whereof she now more glad then *sory* earst, . . . VI. i. 45. 1
Which *sorie* sight when Calidore did vew . . . VI. ii. 41. 6
And from her *sory* hart few heavie words forth sight: . . . VI. ii. 42. 9
these words burst forth: 'Ah, *sory* boy! . . . VI. iii. 4. 6
Under the greenewoods side in *sorie* plight, . . . VI. iv. 39. 2
backe returning to that *sorie* Dame, . . . VI. v. 4. 1
To seeke some comfort in that *sorie* case. . . . VI. v. 7. 4
(sayd the *sory* Mayd) . . . VI. viii. 24. 1
though no lesse *sory* wight For that mishap, . . . VI. x. 18. 7
'Right *sory* I,' (saide then Sir Calidore) . . . VI. x. 20. 6
seem'd to be some *sorie* simple clowne, . . . VI. xi. 27. 3
she entred, were he liefe or *sory*; . . . VII. vi. 8. 7
made you merie oft when ye were *sorie.* . . . *H.L.* 35

Sort. Goe . . . emongste the meaner *sorte:* . . . *S.C.* Env. 8
After which *sort* they wandered long while, . . . *Hub.* 343
to the Court in seemly *sort* they come; . . . *Hub.* 662
Delight, and Laughter, deckt in seemly *sort.* . . . *T.M.* 198
They to the vulgar *sort* now pipe and sing, . . . *T.M.* 319
Hath writ my record in true-seeming *sort.* . . . *Ti.* 168
A *sort* of shepheards, sewing of the chace, . . . *As.* 139
In *sort* as she it sung I will rehearse. . . . *As.* 216
In *sort* as I it to that shepheard told: . . . *Col.* 101
sooth to say, it is no *sort* of life, . . . *Col.* 688
In *sort* as he him schooled privily: . . . I. i. 46. 5
So forth they marchen in this goodly *sort,* . . . I. iv. 37. 1
In seemely *sort* their corses to engrave, . . . I. x. 42. 2
In *sort* as through the world I did proclame, . . . I. xii. 20. 2
Therein three sisters dwelt of sundry *sort,* . . . II. ii. 13. 1
Straunge *sort* of fight, three valiaunt knights to see . . . II. ii. 26. 1
the mery birdes of every *sorte* . . . II. v. 31. 6
Of every *sort* and nation under skye, . . . II. vii. 44. 2
she in merry *sort* Them gan to bord, . . . II. xii. 16. 1
loath'd the loose demeanure of that wanton *sort.* . . . III. i. 40. 9
with meates of every *sort,* . . . III. i. 52. 2
It ill beseemes a knight of gentle *sort,* . . . III. ii. 12. 6
every *sort* is in a sondry bed Sett by it selfe, . . . III. vi. 35. 3
all about grew every *sort* of flowre, . . . III. vi. 45. 1
in all shamefull *sort* him selfe with her defile. . . . III. vii. 50. 9
heap'd together with the vulgar *sort,* . . . III. xi. 46. 2
Bred in assemblies of the vulgar *sort,* . . . IV. i. 28. 4
In friendly *sort* that lasted but a while; . . . IV. ii. 29. 2
What time she usd to live in wively *sort,* . . . IV. v. 3. 8
another *sort* Of lovers . . . IV. x. 26. 3
her attending in full seemly *sort,* . . . IV. xii. 18. 7
Whiles through the world she walked in this *sort,* . . . V. i. 6. 1
In *sort* as they were formed aunciently, . . . V. ii. 32. 8
like a *sort* of Bees in clusters swarmed: . . . V. iv. 36. 7
like a *sort* of sheepe dispersed farre . . . V. iv. 44. 7
In *sort* as ye have heard the same of late: . . . V. vi. 17. 3
To blot the same in blame, or wrest in wicked *sort.* . . . V. xii. 34. 9
He chaunst to spy a *sort* of shepheard groomes, . . . VI. ix. 5. 2
This simple *sort* of life that shepheards lead, . . . VI. ix. 33. 8
set his rest amongst the rusticke *sort,* . . . VI. x. 2. 6
in *sort* as he at first begonne, . . . VI. x. 32. 4
a *sort* of merchants . . . Arrived in this Isle, . . . VI. xi. 9. 2
Like as a *sort* of hungry dogs, . . . VI. xi. 17. 1
Provided him a sword of meanest *sort;* . . . VI. xi. 42. 6
Stood all astonied; like a *sort* of steeres, . . . VII. vi. 28. 6
In this bold *sort* to Heaven claime to make, . . . VII. vi. 29. 3
gan examine him in straighter *sort,* . . . VII. vi. 51. 4
With ears of corne of every *sort,* . . . VII. vii. 30. 7
That I may laugh at her in equall *sort,* . . . *Am.* x. 13
Of every *sort,* which in that Meadow grew, . . . *Proth.* 29

Sorted. Then had ye *sorted* with a princes pere: . . . *Am.* lxvi. 10

Sorts. Infinite *sortes* of people did abide There waiting long, . I. iv. 6. 7
ten thousand *sorts* of punishment . . . torment. . . . I. v. 33. 8
Great *sorts* of lovers piteously complayning, . . . IV. x. 43. 2
thirty *sorts* of fish, . . . IV. xi. 35. 9

Sorts—*Continued.*
did in strength most *sorts* of men surpas, . . . V. xii. 15. 3
To thousand *sorts* of Change we subject see: . . . VII. vii. 25. 3
in a bag all *sorts* of seeds ysame, . . . VII. vii. 32. 7
Most *sorts* of men doe set but little store. . . . *Am.* xxvi. 12
richly are displayd All *sorts* of flowers, . . . *Am.* lxx. 3

So soon as. *See* **Soon as.**
so soone as scortching Sunne had brent His wings . . . *Ro.* xvii. 5
so soone as lighter sleepe Was entered, . . . *Gn.* 321
So soone as day appeard to peoples vewing, . . . *Hub.* 104
so soone as one might see Light . . . *Hub.* 108
So soone as Fates their vitall thred have shorne, . . . *Ti.* 181
Which vanisht quite, *so soone as* it was sought: . . . *Ti.* 221
So soone as Clarion he did beholde, . . . *Mui.* 355
So soone as on them blowes the Northern winde, . . . *D.* 396
Whom all *so soone as* that proud Sarazin Espide, . . . I. vi. 46. 1
all *so soone as* life did me admitt . . . I. ix. 3. 5
all *so soone as* it doth come to fight . . . I. x. 1. 3
all *so soone as* he from far descryde . . . I. xi. 4. 7
so soone as day he spyde, . . . I. xi. 52. 5
"*So soone as* Bacchus with the Nymphe . . . II. i. 55. 6
so soone as ryper yeares he raught, . . . II. iii. 2. 6
So soon as Mammon there arrivd, . . . II. vii. 26. 1
so soone as his enfeebled spright Gan sucke . . . II. vii. 66. 5
so soone as his outrageous powre Is layd, . . . II. viii. 48. 4
so soone as Guyon thence was gon . . . II. xi. 5. 1
So soone as he unto her wombe did fall: . . . II. xi. 45. 6
So soone as Night had with her pallid hew . . . III. ii. 28. 1
so soone as Phoebus Lamp Bewrayed had . . . III. x. 1. 1
So soone as they were in, . . . III. xii. 27. 1
So soone as she was entred, . . . Shee cast . . . III. xii. 30. 1
so soone as Titan shone, They both uprose . . . IV. i. 16. 5
So soone as heavens window shewed light, . . . IV. iii. 3. 7
so soone as they once tasted had, . . . IV. iii. 49. 1
so soone as they perceiv'd That she was gone, . . . IV. v. 28. 1
so soone as by wit or art Could that atchieve . . . IV. vi. 43. 5
So soone as she . . . Had left . . . IV. vii. 3. 1
so soone as morrow light Appear'd . . . V. iii. 7. 1
So soone as day forth dawning . . . V. v. 1. 1
so soone As she her face had wypt . . . V. v. 45. 6
so soone as dawning houre Discovered had . . . V. vi. 35. 1
so soone as dawning light Bad doe away . . . V. vii. 26. 7
So soone as it did to the world display . . . V. xii. 11. 3
So soone as passage is unto him lent, . . . VI. i. 21. 4
Earely, *so soone as* Titans beames forth brust . . . VI. iii. 13. 5
so soone as joyous day Did shew it selfe . . . VI. iii. 45. 1
so soone as he was out of vew, . . . VI. vii. 2. 8
so soone as they convenient may, . . . VI. x. 43. 3
so soone as they do sever, . . . VII. vii. 24. 3

Souce, Soucing. *See* **Souse,** *etc.*

Soudan. *See* **Soldan.**

Sought. nys on earth assuraunce to be *sought;* . . . *S.C.* N. 157
Saffron, *sought* for in Cilician soyle; . . . *Gn.* 671
They *sought* my troubled sense how to deceave . . . *Hub.* 23
manie waies they *sought,* and manie tryed, . . . *Hub.* 225
Unto their master, which it of them *sought,* . . . *Hub.* 311
Fled here and there, and everie corner *sought,* . . . *Hub.* 1357
vanish quite, so soone as it was *sought:* . . . *Ti.* 221
Although the compast world were *sought* around. . . . *Ti.* 567
as the mother of the Gods, that *sought* For faire Eurydice, *D.* 463
forest . . . He *sought,* where salvage beasts do most abound. *As.* 82
What needeth perill to be *sought* abroad, . . . *As.* 89
Tanaquill, Whom that most noble Briton Prince . . . *Sought* I. Pr. 2. 7
She . . . *sought* backe to turne againe; . . . I. i. 16. 6
creeping *sought* way in the weedy gras: . . . I. i. 20. 8
with the Lady backward *sought* to wend. . . . I. i. 28. 2
He passed forth, and new adventure *sought:* . . . I. i. 28. 8
She, . . . Through woods and wastnes wide him daily *sought;* I. iii. 3. 8
subtill Archimag, that Una *sought* . . . I. iii. 24. 6
with greedy eye He *sought* all round about, . . . I. v. 15. 2
far abroad for straunge adventures *sought;* . . . I. vi. 29. 7
it may be seene, if *sought:* . . . I. vii. 36. 9
Through every rowme he *sought,* . . . I. viii. 37. 1
while so my deare I *sought.* . . . II. i. 53. 9
'Him so I *sought;* and so at last I fownd, . . . II. i. 54. 1
were renowmd, and *sought* from place to place. . . . II. ii. 6. 9
Accord of friendes, consent of Parents *sought,* . . . II. iv. 21. 3
I *sought* Upon myselfe that vengeable despight To punish: . II. iv. 30. 2
wher bound she sits, whom thou hast *sought,'* . . . II. iv. 44. 8
His precious horne, *sought* of his enimyes, . . . II. v. 10. 7
she *sought* To kindle his quencht fyre, . . . II. v. 19. 8
his sorrow *sought* through wilfulnesse, . . . II. v. 24. 7
for passage *sought.* . . . II. vi. 19. 3
she *sought* for helps to cloke her crime withall. . . . II. vii. 45. 9
he had long time *sought* with fruitlesse suit: . . . II. vii. 55. 3
Lyon, which hath long time *saught* His robbed whelpes, . . . II. viii. 40. 7
Sith of that Goddesse I have *sought* the sight, . . . II. ix. 7. 7
knights slaine that have us *sought* to save.' . . . II. ix. 12. 9
evermore their cruell Capitaine *Sought* . . . II. ix. 15. 4
sought with her to lincke in marriage: . . . II. ix. 18. 5
each one *sought* his Lady to aggrate: . . . II. ix. 34. 5
have three years *sought* one, . . . II. ix. 38. 9
with faire semblaunt *sought* to hyde the breach, . . . II. ix. 39. 3
by well doing *sought* to honour to aspyre. . . . II. ix. 39. 9
that great Lady thence away them *sought* . . . II. ix. 44. 6
That boy them *sought* and unto him did lend: . . . II. ix. 58. 7
sought Of merchants farre . . . II. x. 5. 6
they which *sought* at first their helping hand, . . . II. x. 65. 8
ne ever *sought* to bayt His tyred armes . . . II. xii. 29. 7
earst was *sought* to deck both bed and bowre . . . II. xii. 75. 4

Sought—*Continued.*
(love far *sought* alas!) . . . III. i. 8. 8
Least that too farre ye have your sorrow *sought:* . . . III. ii. 10. 7
Full many waies she *sought,* but none could find, . . . III. iii. 5. 3
Him forth through infinite endevour to have *sought.* . . . III. iii. 6. 9
Bad eke attonce their charetts to be *sought:* . . . III. iv. 31. 4
First she him *sought* in Court, . . . III. vi. 13. 1
She then the Cities *sought* from gate to gate, . . . III. vi. 14. 1
in the countrey she abroad him *sought,* . . . III. vi. 15. 1
sought the salvage woods and forests wyde, . . . III. vi. 16. 4
she her dearest sonne Cupido *sought,* . . . III. vi. 20. 7
So long they *sought,* till they arrived were . . . III. vi. 26. 5
All wayes shee *sought* him to restore to plight, . . . III. vii. 21. 1
Sought by all meanes his dolor to prolong, . . . III. vii. 35. 7
Her hard pursewd, and *sought* for to suppresse. . . . III. vii. 37. 5
wrong'd by Carle, by Proteus sav'd, Is *sought* by Paridell. III. viii. Arg.
the Lady selfe whom he so long had *sought.* . . . III. viii. 9. 9
to her he *sought* to intimate His inward griefe, . . . III. ix. 30. 1
th' inland folke, which *sought* him backe to drive, . . . III. ix. 42. 3
Long he her *sought,* he *sought* her far and nere, . . . III. x. 19. 6
those two *sought* nought but the present pray, . . . III. x. 34. 4
renowm, that, more then death, is to be *sought.'* . . . III. xi. 19. 9
her honor . . . She *sought* to save, . . . IV. i. 6. 7
each of life *sought* others to deprive, . . . IV. i. 23. 8
sought to bring all things unto decay; . . . IV. i. 29. 4
His flaming furie *sought* to have assuaged . . . IV. i. 54. 3
evermore *sought* Britomart to cleare: . . . IV. i. 54. 6
So much the more she loved was and *sought,* . . . IV. ii. 37. 2
he *sought* by slight It forth to wrest, . . . IV. iii. 10. 5
rather *sought* Him selfe to save, . . . IV. iii. 32. 3
if to match that Lady they had *sought* Another like, . . . IV. iv. 10. 7
starting up streight for his armour *sought:* . . . IV. iv. 33. 3
In vaine he *sought,* for there he found it not; . . . IV. iv. 33. 4
to winne the same So many Ladies *sought,* . . . IV. v. 6. 4
So many faire did see as here he might have *sought.* . . . IV. v. 12. 9
likewise *sought* her lover long miswent, . . . IV. v. 30. 6
I cal'd her loud, I *sought* her farre and neare, . . . IV. vi. 36. 8
There they her *sought,* and every where inquired . . . IV. vi. 47. 3
many a knight had *sought* so many a day. . . . IV. vii. 8. 5
I *sought* by secret meanes to worke Time to my will, . . . IV. vii. 17. 1
this shield, of many *sought* in vaine, . . . IV. x. 8. 3
which all Asia *sought* with vowes prophane, . . . IV. x. 30. 3
farre and neare the Nymph his mother *sought,* . . . IV. xi. 6. 1
him had *sought* through trouble and long strife, . . . IV. xii. 16. 8
had refusde a God that her had *sought* to wife. . . . IV. xii. 16. 9
soone as he had *sought* . . . IV. xii. 25. 5
all men *sought* their owne, . . . V. Pr. 3. 7
he entrance *sought,* but was denide, . . . V. ii. 20. 4
Long they her *sought,* . . . V. ii. 25. 1
sought unrighteousnesse, and justice sold, . . . V. ii. 26. 8
For there is nothing lost, that may be found if *sought.* . . . V. ii. 39. 9
least she him *sought* t' appeach Of treason, . . . V. v. 37. 3
all the wayes she *sought* his love for to have wonne: . . . V. v. 45. 9
The more that she it *sought* to cover and to hyde. . . . V. v. 53. 9
Brought in untimely houre, ere it was *sought:* . . . V. vi. 3. 5
she long had *sought* for ease In every place, . . . V. vi. 7. 1
Each rowme she *sought,* but them all empty fond. . . . V. vi. 35. 8
To seeke her love, where he was to be *sought;* . . . V. vii. 24. 7
Ne either *sought* the others strokes to shun, . . . V. vii. 29. 3
She *sought* with ruth to salve his sad misfortunes sore. . . . V. vii. 38. 9
in their steede for other rayment *sought,* . . . V. vii. 41. 3
Souldan, . . . *Sought* onely slaughter and avengement; . . . V. viii. 30. 5
Still when he *sought* t' approch unto him ny . . . V. viii. 36. 1
when as foes enforst, or friends *sought* ayde, . . . V. ix. 30. 8
Long *sought* the Prince; . . . V. x. 38. 5
her imprisond hath, and her life often *sought.* . . . V. xi. 39. 9
sought with lawlesse powre him to oppresse, . . . V. xi. 44. 4
sought his life for to empaire: . . . V. xi. 48. 5
all she *sought* was mens good name to have bereaved. . . . V. xii. 33. 9
sought to win his love by all the meanes she might. . . . VI. i. 14. 9
He woxe halfe mad; . . . and *sought* her . . . VI. ii. 20. 9
who *sought* her to affy To a great pere; . . . VI. iii. 7. 2
He *sought* him farre and neare, yet him no where he spyde. VI. v. 3. 9
sought by all the meanes that he could . . . VI. v. 6. 3
sought by open might To overthrow, . . . VI. v. 13. 4
his three foes *Sought* to encompasse him . . . VI. v. 20. 2
each *sought* to supply the office of her page. . . . VI. v. 30. 9
the Prince *sought* to appease The bitter anguish . . . VI. v. 32. 4
he *sought* If yet he were alive, . . . VI. vi. 37. 8
sought by making signes him to asswage; . . . VI. vi. 39. 3
lately *sought* his Lord for to displease: . . . VI. vi. 40. 4
That recreant knight, whose hated life I *sought?* . . . VI. vii. 16. 4
which long time she *sought,* . . . VI. vii. 50. 5
sude and *sought* with all the service dew: . . . VI. viii. 20. 6
Long had he *sought* her, . . . VI. viii. 47. 1
leaving home, to roiall court I *sought,* . . . VI. ix. 24. 6
When he the love of fayre Oenone *sought,* . . . VI. ix. 36. 8
wanton squirrels in the woods farre *sought,* . . . VI. ix. 40. 3
rashly *sought* that which I mote not see.' . . . VI. x. 29. 7
sought her love by all the meanes he mote; . . . VI. xi. 4. 7
He *sought* the woods, but no man could see there; . . . VI. xi. 26. 4
He *sought* the plaines, but could no tydings heare: . . . VI. xi. 26. 5
whilest one *sought* her to hold, . . . VI. xi. 30. 8
now *sought* hyre elswhere. . . . VI. xi. 39. 9
all the secrets of their entrayles *sought.* . . . VI. xi. 41. 4
that long for death had *sought.* . . . VI. xi. 45. 5
to slay he would have *sought,*) . . . VI. xii. 6. 7
whylest he that monster *sought* Throughout the world, . . . VI. xii. 13. 4
th' empire *sought* from them to beare. . . . VII. vi. 1. 9
on earth she *sought* it to obtaine; . . . VII. vi. 4. 5

Sought—*Continued.*
all their kingdoms *sought.* . . . VII. vi. 18. 9
Sought to assaile the heavens eternall towers, . . . VII. vi. 20. 3
On her whose sight before so much he *sought.* . . . VII. vi. 47. 6
him of heavens Empire *sought* to dispossesse? . . . VII. vii. 1. 9
Go seek he out that Alane where he may be *sought.* . . . VII. vii. 9. 9
I *sought* to what I might compare . . . *Am.* ix. 1
One day I *sought* . . . To make a truce, . . . *Am.* xii. 1
false enimies, Which *sought* me to entrap . . . *Am.* xii. 4
Sought not to fly, but fearelesse still did bide; . . . *Am.* lxvii. 10
many *sought,* yet none could ever taste; . . . *Am.* lxxvii. 10
Whom greatest Princes *sought* on lowest knee. . . . *H.H.L.* 231
Hast after vaine deceiptfull shadowes *sought,* . . . *H.H.B.* 291
Soul. wounds my *soule* with rufull memorie, . . . *Pet.*[2] iv. 13
who can counsell a thristie *soule,* . . . *S.C.* May 138
So cleaves thy *soule* asonder: . . . *S.C.* Au. 88
Therewith my *soule* was sharply gryde, . . . *S.C.* Au. 95
Fayth of my *soule,* I deeme ech have gayned: . . . *S.C.* Au. 131
Fayth of my *soule,* thou shalt ycrouned be . . . *S.C.* Au. 145
by my *soule,* I dare undersaye . . . *S.C.* S. 91
by my *soule,* Diggon, I lament . . . *S.C.* S. 248
Seemeth thou dost their *soule* of sence bereave; . . . *S.C.* O. 27
Her *soule* unbodied of the burdenous corpse. . . . *S.C.* N. 166
I see thee, blessed *soule,* . . . *S.C.* N. 178
To fret thy *soule* with crosses and with cares; . . . *Hub.* 903
Though death his *soule* doo from his bodie sever; . . . *Ti.* 257
ere his happie *soule* to heaven went . . . *Ti.* 295
do my *soule* with inward griefe infest: . . . *Ti.* 460
yet my *soule* it deepely doth empassion. . . . *D.* 35
soule assoyld from sinfull fleshlinesse. . . . *D.* 259
The which my *soule* first conquerd and possest, . . . *D.* 300
O, how great sorrow my sad *soule* assaid! . . . I. ii. 24. 5
layes the *soule* to sleepe in quiet grave? . . . I. ix. 40. 7
hellish anguish did his *soule* assaile; . . . I. ix. 49. 4
the dart of sinfull guilt the *soule* dismayes. . . . I. x. 21. 9
his righteous *soule* might save. . . . I. x. 34. 9
The feeble *soule* departing hence away. . . . I. x. 41. 5
shewes the way his sinfull *soule* to save! . . . I. x. 51. 3
Whose sight my feeble *soule* doth greatly cheare: . . . I. xi. 3. 5
Great woe and sorrow did her *soule* assay, . . . I. xi. 32. 2
To hinder *soule* from her desired rest, . . . II. i. 48. 2
The weary *sowle* from thence it would discharge; . . . II. v. 6. 7
my *soule* was soyld with fowle iniquity.' . . . II. vii. 62. 9
To bring the *sowle* into captivity? . . . II. xi. 1. 4
the disdainfull *sowle* he thence dispatcht, . . . II. xi. 42. 3
His sinfull *sowle* with desperate disdaine . . . III. v. 23. 8
the weake *sowle* her seat did yett retaine, . . . III. v. 31. 4
doth transfixe the *soule* with deathes eternall dart. . . . III. x. 59. 9
an huge heape of singultes did oppresse His strugling *soule,* III. xi. 12. 2
Fearing least from her cage the wearie *soule* would flit. . . . III. xi. 12. 9
the frayle *soule* in deepe delight nigh drownd: . . . III. xii. 6. 5
As if but one *soule* in them all did dwell, . . . IV. ii. 43. 3
The *soule* had sure out of his bodie rived, . . . IV. iii. 18. 3
notwithstanding that one *soule* was reft, . . . IV. iii. 21. 6
that same *soule* which therein dwelt . . . IV. iii. 22. 1
So did one *soule* out of his bodie flie . . . IV. iii. 30. 8
through his *soule* like poysned arrow perst, . . . IV. v. 31. 4
him afflicted to the very *sowle.* . . . IV. v. 41. 9
As if he thought her *soule* to disentrayle. . . . IV. vi. 16. 7
the sinfull *sowle* . . . Was fled to hell, . . . IV. vii. 32. 3
wound the *soule* it selfe with griefe unkind; . . . IV. viii. 26. 7
His *soule* descended downe into the Stygian reame. . . . IV. viii. 45. 9
zeale Which I to him as to my *soule* did beare, . . . IV. viii. 55. 3
as the *soule* doth rule the earthly masse, . . . IV. ix. 2. 6
love of *soule* doth love of bodie passe, . . . IV. ix. 2. 8
Griev'd to the *soule,* and groning inwardly, . . . V. iv. 22. 8
sent His groning *soule* unto her place of punishment. . . . V. x. 36. 9
To call the *soule* backe to her home againe; . . . VI. xi. 22. 4
Yet he (poore *soule!*) with patience all did beare; . . . VII. vi. 49. 6
Then is my *soule* with life and love inspired: . . . *Am.* vii. 6
My *soule* was ravisht quite as in a traunce; . . . *Am.* xxxix. 10
Thence to the *soule* darts amorous desyre, . . . *H.B.* 60
the *soule,* the which derived was, . . . *H.B.* 106
of the *soule* the bodie forme doth take; . . . *H.B.* 132
soule is forme, and doth the bodie make. . . . *H.B.* 133
A beauteous *soule,* with faire conditions thewed, . . . *H.B.* 137
the *soule* is faire and beauteous still, . . . *H.B.* 159
Dolours of death into his *soule* did dart, . . . *H.H.L.* 159
And let thy *soule* . . . Melt into teares, . . . *H.H.L.* 251
With all thy hart, with all thy *soule* and mind, . . . *H.H.L.* 260
Then shall thy ravisht *soule* inspired bee . . . *H.H.L.* 281
this darke world, whose damps the *soule* do blynd, . . . *H.H.B.* 137
it doth bereave Their *soule* of sense, . . . *H.H.B.* 258
Ah, then, my hungry *soule!* which long hast fed . . . *H.H.B.* 288
Soul-diseased. comming to that *sowle-diseased* knight, . . . I. x. 24. 1
Soul-enchanting. proceeds such *soule-enchaunting* might. . . . *H.B.* 14
Soul's. trouble dying *soules* tranquilitee; . . . II. i. 47. 8
My *soules* long-lacked foode, my heavens blis; . . . *Am.* i. 12
Souls. Styx, not passable to *soules* returning, . . . *Ro.* xv. 6
sith theyr *soules* bene now at rest, . . . *S.C.* Jul. 123
the leane *soules* treaden under foote, . . . *S.C.* S. 126
heavenly ranks, where blessed *soules* do rest; . . . *Gn.* 58
to the seates of happie *soules* admitted: . . . *Gn.* 478
where *soules* doo alwaies mourne; . . . *Gn.* 620
Minos righteous *soules* doth sever From wicked ones, . . . *Gn.* 623
the charge is wondrous great, To feed mens *soules,* . . . *Hub.* 432
'To feede mens *soules* . . . is not in man; . . . *Hub.* 433
thence the *soules* to bring awaie . . . *Ti.* 375
summons *soules* unto the bridale feast . . . *D.* 268
at last it flitted is, Whither the *soules* doe fly . . . I. ii. 19. 9

Souls—*Continued.*
Acheron, Where many *soules* sit wailing woefully, ... I. v. 33. 2
A worke of wondrous grace, and hable *soules* to save. . . . . I. ix. 19. 9
to relieve the needes Of wretched *soules,* . . . . I. x. 3. 7
many *soules* in dolours had fordonne: . . . . I. x. 33. 7
The faulty *soules* . . . brought to his heavenly bowre. . . . I. x. 40. 9
when he their *soules* shall save. . . . . I. x. 42. 5
long captived *soules* from weary thraldome free. . . . . . II. i. 36. 9
full many *soules* do endlesse wayle and weepe. . . . . . . II. vii. 56. 9
In which the damned *soules* he did behold, ... II. vii. 63. 5
Some fitt for reasonable *sowles* t' indew; . . . . III. vi. 35. 5
sent away So many Centaures drunken *soules* to hell, ... IV. i. 23. 4
As if their *soules* they would attonce have rent . . . . . . IV. ii. 18. 2
the happie *soules,* which doe possesse Th' Elysian fields . . . IV. x. 23. 4
seem'd their *soules* they wold have ryven quight . . . . . . V. x. 32. 4
whose *soules* with black dishonor . . . doe decke thy bloudy baner? . . . . VI. vi. 25. 4
swarmes of damned *soules* to hell he sends: . . . . VI. viii. 49. 7
Therof it comes that these faire *soules,* . . . . *H.B.* 120
smiles, with which their *soules* they feede, ... *H.B.* 248
To heale the sores of sinfull *soules* unsound, ... *H.H.L.* 166
himselfe, . . . To feede our hungry *soules,* unto us lent. . . . *H.H.L.* 196
Faire is the heaven where happy *soules* have place, ... *H.H.B.* 78

Sound. tune hir plaint to falling rivers *sound,* . . . . . . *Bel.*[1] viii. 3
To falling rivers *sound* thus tun'd her sobs. . . . . *Bel.*[2] x. 4
Cease not to *sound* these olde antiquities; . . . . *Ro.* xxxii. 10
thy oaten pype began to *sound,* . . . . *S.C.* Jun. 58
Renne after hastely thy silver *sound;* . . . . *S.C.* Jun. 61
whose shrieking *sound* Ys signe of dreery death, ... *S.C.* Au. 173
till safe and *sound* 'She home returne, ... *S.C.* Au. 180
voyces silver *sound* . . . can chaunge my cherelesse cryes. . . *S.C.* Au. 181
the *sound* Of these my nightly cryes . . . . *S.C.* Au. 188
So mought our Cuddies name to heaven *sownde.* . . . . *S.C.* O. 54
Was never pype of reede did better *sounde.* . . . . *S.C.* D. 142
Through their hard barke his silver *sound* receav'd. . . . . *Gn.* 456
sound their praises lowd. . . . . *Gn.* 616
whiles the Lyon sleepeth *sound,* . . . . *Hub.* 967
everie *sound* that under heaven blew; . . . . *Hub.* 1011
Of their sweete instruments were wont to *sound,* . . . . . . *T.M.* 20
To register, and *sound* in trump of gold, ... *T.M.* 98
To teach the warbling pipe to *sound* aloft, ... *T.M.* 290
With horrid *sound* though having little sence, ... *T.M.* 554
So brave a Trompe, thy noble acts to *sound!* . . . . *Ti.* 434
these Beares lay sleeping *sound,* . . . . *Ti.* 570
Sound Savorie, and Bazil hartie-hale, ... *Mui.* 198
manie Tritons which their hornes did *sound.* . . . . *Mui.* 296
he saide, with hollow *sound,* . . . . *D.* 61
Ne ever Shepheard *sound* his Oaten quill . . . . *D.* 325
The heaviest plaint that ever I heard *sound,* . . . . *D.* 541
Like hartlesse deare, dismayd with thunders *sound.* . . . . . *Col.* 9
heard to *sound* as she was wont on hye, ... *Col.* 20
pleasing *sound* yshrilled far about, ... *Col.* 62
his wreathed horne: At *sound* whereof, ... *Col.* 246
Doth like himselfe Heroically *sound.* . . . . *Col.* 447
In bigger tunes to *sound* your living prayse. . . . . *Ded.Son.* xiii. 14
she might . . . *sound* their praises dew? . . . . *Ded.Son.* xiv. 4
the Maple seeldom inward *sound.* . . . . I. i. 9. 9
winde, much like the *sowne* Of swarming Bees, ... I. i. 41. 4
So *sound* he slept, that nought mought him awake. . . . . . I. i. 42. 3
guest, . . . gan now to take more *sound* repast; . . . . . . I. ii. 4. 3
ne wont there *sound* His mery oaten pipe, ... I. ii. 28. 8
His chearfull whistle merily doth *sound,* . . . . I. iii. 31. 8
At last the trumpets Triumph *sound* on hie; . . . . I. v. 15. 6
giving warning of th' unwonted *sound,* . . . . I. v. 30. 3
old Sylvanus slept in shady arber *sownd:* . . . . I. vi. 7. 9
all the way their merry pipes they *sound.* . . . . I. vi. 14. 1
at the last he heard a dreadfull *sownd,* . . . . I. vii. 7. 4
Was never wight that heard that shrilling *sownd,* . . . . . . I. viii. 4. 1
The Gyaunt selfe, dismaied with that *sownd,* . . . . I. viii. 5. 4
He loudly brayd with beastly yelling *sownd,* . . . . I. viii. 11. 3
Ne fleshly brest can armed be so *sownd,* . . . . I. ix. 11. 2
Doth license him depart at *sound* of morning droome.' . . . . I. ix. 41. 9
they heard a roaring hideous *sownd,* . . . . I. xi. 4. 1
Soone as thy dreadfull trompe begins to *sownd,* . . . . . . I. xi. 6. 6
sleepe never he so *sownd;* . . . . I. xi. 6. 8
Then gan triumphant Trompets *sownd* on hye, ... I. xii. 4. 1
tall young men, all hable armes to *sownd;* . . . . I. xii. 5. 7
there was an heavenly noise Heard *sownd* . . . . I. xii. 39. 2
began these words aloud to *sownd.* . . . . II. ii. 39. 9
twixt the perles and rubins softly brake A silver *sound,* . . . II. iii. 24. 9
Nor voyce *sound* mortall; . . . . II. iii. 33. 4
I heard her horn *sound* with such ghastlinesse. . . . . . . II. iii. 44. 9
made a *sowne,* To lull him soft asleepe . . . . II. v. 30. 3
ledd with the troublous *sowne:* . . . . II. vi. 47. 7
Their murmuring small trompetts *sownden* wide, ... II. ix. 16. 3
buzzed all about, and made such *sound* . . . . II. ix. 51. 2
Who now shall give unto me words and *sound* . . . . II. x. 1. 1
whose *sound* hevens thunder seem'd to bee. . . . . II. x. 73. 9
gave against his mother earth a gronefull *sownd.* . . . . . . II. xi. 42. 9
Eftsoones they heard a most melodious *sound,* . . . . II. xii. 70. 1
nothing else might keepe her safe and *sound:* . . . . II. xii. 82. 7
hideous horror and sad trembling *sownd,* . . . . III. i. 14. 6
wondrous massy and assured *sownd,* . . . . III. ii. 25. 3
With yelling outcries, and with shrieking *sowne;* . . . . . . III. iv. 30. 8
hurt his hart, the which before was *sound,* . . . . III. v. 42. 4
did abide for ever chaste and *sound."* . . . . III. vii. 56. 7
were for other causes firme and *sound;* . . . . III. vii. 60. 3
That dreadfull *sound* the bosters hart did thrill . . . . . . III. x. 43. 5
thou, vile man, vile Scudamore, art *sound,* . . . . III. xi. 11. 6
She heard a shrilling Trompet *sound* alowd, ... III. xii. 1. 5

Sound—*Continued.*
harmony . . . was sweetly heard to *sound,* . . . . III. xii. 6. 2
every part to safety full *sownd,* . . . . III. xii. 38. 6
whose voices knowen *sound* Soon as he heard, ... III. xii. 43. *or.* 8
With warlike numbers and Heroicke *sound,* . . . . IV. ii. 32. 7
trumpets *sound* to cease did them compell: . . . . IV. iv. 25. 8
trumpets *sound* did warne them all to rest; . . . . IV. iv. 36. 2
Where I with *sound* of trompe will also rest a whyle. . . . . IV. iv. 48. 9
they heard the *sound* Of many yron hammers . . . . IV. v. 33. 6
hammers *sound* his senses did molest, ... IV. v. 41. 2
Britomart heard not the shrilling *sound,* . . . . IV. vii. 4. 8
through weary travel she lay sleeping *sound.* . . . . IV. vii. 4. 9
Some litle whispering, and soft groning *sound.* . . . . IV. vii. 33. 4
a most celestiall *sound* Of dainty musicke, ... IV. xi. 23. 1
no dreadfull trompets *sound;* . . . . V. Pr. 9. 5
durst the depth of any water *sownd.* . . . . V. ii. 16. 7
The trompets *sound,* then all together ronne. . . . . V. iii. 6. 4
Then did the trompets *sound,* . . . . V. iii. 13. 6
Bold Radigund with *sound* of trumpe on hight, ... V. iv. 45. 4
Their *sound* did reach unto the heavens hight: . . . . V. v. 4. 6
It was not long before she heard the *sound* . . . . V. vi. 28. 6
would no lenger treat, but bad them *sound;* . . . . V. vii. 28. 7
The Trumpets *sound,* and they together run . . . . V. vii. 29. 1
Yet did he murmure with rebellious *sound,* . . . . V. ix. 33. 8
As if the onely *sound* thereof she feard. . . . . V. xi. 30. 4
'She liveth sure and *sound,* . . . . V. xi. 38. 8
foot of man might *sound* the bottome plaine, ... V. xii. 5. 3
The trompets *sound,* and they together goe . . . . V. xii. 17. 1
For his faire usage and conditions *sound,* . . . . VI. i. 3. 3
with piteous *sound* Of his shrill cries . . . . VI. i. 11. 5
confused *sound* Of senselesse words, ... VI. iv. 11. 7
that curre, barking with bitter *sownd,* . . . . VI. v. 19. 5
the merry *sound* Of a shrill pipe he playing heard . . . . . VI. x. 10. 2
when all the theeves . . . slept full *sound,* . . . . VI. xi. 42. 3
Untill the Damzell gan to wex more *sound* and strong. . . . . VI. xii. 11. 9
drad Bellona, that doth *sound* on hie Warres . . . . VII. vi. 3. 7
If Rubies, loe, hir lips be Rubies *sound;* . . . . *Am.* xv. 8

Sounded. A shrilling trompett *sownded* from on hye, ... I. v. 6. 1
The trumpets *sounded,* and they all arose. . . . . IV. iii. 51. 2
The Trumpets *sounded,* and the field began; . . . . V. v. 6. 1
So *sounded* the retraite, and drew his folke away. . . . . . V. xii. 9. 9
eke her champions glorie *sounded* overall. . . . . V. xii. 24. 9
His trompet shrill hath thrise already *sounded,* . . . . . . *Am.* xix. 2

Sounder. Let breake your *sounder* sleepe, ... *S.C.* Au. 191
Like as a wayward childe, whose *sounder* sleepe Is broken . . V. vi. 14. 1

Soundest. in his *soundest* sleepe his dayly feare . . . . . . IV. v. 43. 6

Sounding. *See* **Silver-sounding.**
the soft (gentle[1]) *sounding* of the waters fall: . . . . *Pet.* iv. 7
the sweete waves of *sounding* Castaly . . . . *Gn.* 23
to the Maydens *sounding* tymbrels song . . . . I. xii. 7. 3
sounding loud a Trumpet from the wall, ... V. iv. 50. 3
To weeten what that trumpets *sounding* ment: . . . . V. iv. 50. 7

Soundly. he slept *soundly* void of evil thought, ... I. i. 46. 3
She *soundly* slept, and carefull thoughts did quite assoile. . . III. i. 58. 9
to his wife, that now full *soundly* slept, ... III. x. 49. 3
Lay sleeping *soundly* in the bushes shade, ... VI. xi. 38. 4

Sounds. is thy Bagpype broke, that *soundes* so sweete? . . . *S.C.* Ap. 3
oftentimes loud strokes and ringing *sowndes* . . . . III. iii. 9. 8
As when two billowes in the Irish *sowndes,* . . . . IV. i. 42. 1

Sour. Sweet without *sowre,* and honny without gall: . . . . *As.* 26
My rimes I know unsavory and *sowre,* . . . . *Ded. Son.* viii. 8
A dram of sweete is worth a pound of *sowre.* . . . . I. iii. 30. 4
With fowle words tempring faire, *soure* gall with hony sweet. I. vii. 3. 9
her *sowre* breath abhominably smeld; . . . . I. viii. 47. 5
thou thy treasons fruit . . . shalt taste Right *sowre,* . . . . II. viii. 31. 9
Sad, solemne, *sowre,* and full of fancies fraile, ... III. ii. 27. 5
Sweet is the Broome-flowre, but yet *sowre* enough; . . . . . *Am.* xxvi. 7
every sweet with *soure* is tempred still, ... *Am.* xxvi. 9

Source. This was the first *sourse* of shepheards sorowe, . . . *S.C.* May 130
Here has the salt Medway his *sourse,* . . . . *S.C.* Jul. 79
flouds do gaspe, for dryed is theyr *sourse,* . . . . *S.C.* N. 126
now cease thy sorrowes *sourse;* . . . . *S.C.* N. 171
some were so from their *sourse* indewd . . . . II. ii. 6. 1
the *sourse* Of all my sorrow . . . . II. iv. 18. 1
Nor timely tides did drive out of their sluggish *sourse.* . . . II. vi. 20. 9
makes it seeme to have some other *sourse;* . . . . IV. iii. 27. 5
the villaine selfe, their sorrowes *sourse,* . . . . IV. vii. 20. 3
Long Rhodanus, whose *sourse* springs from the skie; . . . . . IV. xi. 20. 4
From the first point of his appointed *sourse;* . . . . V. Pr. 1. 8
whose swelling *sourse* Shall drive a Mill, ... VI. i. 21. 1
Of former daies mishap, his sorrowes wicked *sourse.* . . . . VI. iii. 14. 9
Began to mitigate his swelling *sourse,* . . . . VI. xi. 34. 3
The which your forms first *sourse* may sympathize, ... *H.B.* 192
Whose bleeding *sourse* their streames yet never staunch . . . *H.H.L.* 164
gave this Lifes first native *sourse,* . . . . *Proth.* 129

Sours. A thousand *sowres* hath tempred with one sweet, . . . VI. xi. 1. 8

Souse. both . . . *souce* so sore that they the heavens affray; . . I. v. 8. 7
once hath failed of her *souse* full neare, ... II. xi. 36. 7
spies him toward bend His dreadfull *souse,* . . . . IV. iii. 19. 6
seemed nought the *souse* thereof could beare, ... IV. viii. 44. 5
with his *souce,* which none enduren dare, ... V. iv. 42. 7
with the *souse* thereof full sore aghast He staggered . . . . V. xii. 23. 3
Fayles of her *souse,* and passing by doth hurt no more. . . . VI. vii. 9. 9

Soused. Ofte *soust* in swelling Tethys saltish teare; . . . . . I. iii. 31. 3
He stroke, he foynd, he *soust,* he hewd, he lasht, ... IV. iii. 25. 6
So sore he *sowst* him on the compast creast, ... IV. iv. 30. 7
heaping strokes which thereon *soused* sore: . . . . IV. v. 36. 4
when she felt Her selfe downe *soust,* . . . . IV. vii. 9. 3

Souses. with few *sowces* of his yron flale . . . . V. iv. 24. 6

Sousing. sadly *soucing* on the sandy shore, ... III. iv. 16. 8

South. shall spred his banner brave Over the troubled *South*, III. iii. 30. 4
Southern. Colin thou kenst, the *Southerne* shepheardes boye; *S.C.* Ap. 21
all along the *Southerne* sea-coast lay II. x. 6. 4
The Easterne Saxons from the *Southerne* ny, IV. xi. 33. 4
He is declyned . . . to the *Southerne* lake; V. Pr. 7. 8
South Wales. In Deheubarth, that now *South-wales* is hight, III. ii. 18. 4
South wind. The watry *Southwinde*, from the seabord coste Upblowing, III. iv. 13. 4
Souvenance. Sike worldly *sovenance* he must forsay. *S.C.* May 82
endles *sovenaunce* Emong the shepeheards swaines *S.C.* N. 5
To dwell in darkenesse without *sovenance?* *T.M.* 486
of his way he had no *sovenaunce*, II. vi. 8. 3
all thy wronges will wipe out of my *sovenaunce*.' II. viii. 51. 9
Sovereign. The *soveraigne* of seas he blames in vaine, *S.C.* F. 33
'Ah, my *soveraigne!* Lord of creatures all, *S.C.* F. 163
was the *soveraigne* head Of shepheards all *S.C.* Jun. 83
The Nightingale is *sovereigne* of song, *S.C.* N. 25
'O *soveraigne* Pan! thou god of shepheards all, *S.C.* D. 7
rule and raigne in *soveraign* see, *Hub.* 980
borne to be a Kingly *soveraigne*.' *Hub.* 1032
Whom not their kindly *Sovereigne* did welde, *Hub.* 1232
O *soveraigne* Lord! O *soveraigne* happinesse, *T.M.* 515
Then was shee held in *soveraigne* dignitie, *T.M.* 563
Sate in the bosome of his *Soveraine*, *Ti.* 188
straight obay his *soveraine* beheast; *D.* 270
Thy *soveraine* Goddesses most deare delight, *Ded. Son.* viii. 2
soveraine hope which in his helpe he had. I. i. 2. 6
of beautie *soveraigne* Queene, Fayre Venus, I. i. 48. 1
The Fort, that Ladies hold in *soveraigne* dread. I. ii. 25. 4
his *soveraine* Dame So rudely handled by her foe he saw, I. iii. 41. 2
he goeth to that *soveraine* Queene; I. v. 16. 1
They, in . . . wonder of her beautie *soverayne*, I. vi. 12. 6
doen their service to that *soveraigne* Dame, I. x. 59. 7
A trickling streame of Balme, most *soveraine* I. xi. 48. 2
Withhold, O *soverayne* Prince! your hasty hond I. xii. 28. 3
'O! pardon me, my *soveraine* Lord, I. xii. 33. 4
Right well I wote, most mighty *Soveraine*, II. Pr. 1. 1
To serve againe his *soveraine* Elfin Queene, II. i. 1. 6
with her *soveraine* power, and scepter shene, II. ii. 40. 4
My *Soveraine*, Whose glory is in gracious deeds, II. ii. 43. 5
soveraine moniment of mortall vowes, II. iii. 25. 7
eke of nature *Soveraine*, II. vi. 17. 2
The guifts of *soveraine* bounty did embrace: II. vii. 16. 4
him thus bespake their *soveraine* Lord and syre; II. vii. 37. 9
A stately siege of *soveraine* majestye; II. vii. 44. 5
My liefe, my liege, my *Soveraine*, my deare, II. ix. 4. 5
grace of earthly Prince so *soveraine*, II. ix. 6. 2
auncestryes Of my most dreaded *Soveraigne* I recount, II. x. 1. 8
Conceive such *soveraine* glory and great bountyhed? II. x. 2. 9
I would assay Thy name, O *soveraine* Queene! II. x. 3. 9
Thy name, O *soveraine* Queene! II. x. 4. 1
Locrine was left the *soveraine* Lord of all: II. x. 14. 1
Deposed was from princedome *soverayne*, II. x. 44. 5
of the Britons first crownd *Soveraine*. II. x. 58. 7
O dredd *Soverayne!* III. Pr. 3. 5
Whose *soveraine* beautie hath no living pere; III. i. 26. 3
O *soveraine* Queene! whose prayse I would endyte, III. ii. 3. 4
So is his *soveraine* honour raisde to hevens hight.' III. ii. 14. 9
Of roiall majesty and *soveraine* name: III. iii. 48. 8
They pourd in *soveraine* balme and Nectar good, III. iv. 40. 8
Tryphon of sea gods the *soveraine* leach is hight. III. iv. 43. 9
The *soveraine* weede . . . Shee pownded small, III. v. 33. 1
Her *soveraine* bountie and celestiall hew, III. v. 44. 5
With which her *soverain* mercy thou doest quight? III. v. 45. 2
She did envy that *soveraine* salve in secret store. III. v. 50. 9
Jove laught on Venus from his *soverayne* see, III. vi. 2. 7
soveraine favor towards chastity, III. viii. 29. 3
doth blend The shyning glory of your *soveraine* light; III. ix. 1. 8
of all Asie bore the *soveraine* crowne, III. ix. 39. 4
To sitt in second seat of *soveraine* king III. ix. 44. 4
bad before his *soveraine* Lord appere. III. x. 23. 7
'O *soverayne* Lord! that sit'st on hye III. xi. 9. 2
To see him in his *soverayne* majestee III. xi. 33. 3
that sacred Saint my *soveraigne* Queene, IV. Pr. 4. 2
And tribute eke withall, as to his *Soveraine*. IV. iii. 27. 9
Nepenthe is a drinck of *soverayne* grace, IV. iii. 43. 1
The controverse of beauties *soveraine* grace; IV. v. 2. 3
Held vertue for it selfe in *soveraine* awe: IV. viii. 30. 6
Dew'd with her drops of bountie *Soveraine*, IV. viii. 33. 5
none but to the seas sole *Soveraine*. IV. xii. 30. 5
Whose *soveraine* powre is herein most exprest, V. Pr. 10. 3
Dread *Soverayne* Goddesse, that doest highest sit In seate of judgement V. Pr. 11. 1
That *soveraine* Queene, that mightie Emperesse, V. i. 4. 5
Ne any may his *soveraine* power shonne, V. ii. 42. 3
of her servant make her *soverayne* Lord: V. v. 27. 8
Say on, my *soverayne* Ladie, and be bold: V. v. 31. 5
Justice was a God of *soveraine* grace, V. vii. 2. 2
soveraine grace, with which her royall crowne She doth support, V. viii. 17. 4
There shall ye see my *soverayne* Lady Queene, V. ix. 20. 6
Thus she did sit in *soverayne* Majestie. V. ix. 30. 1
gave him *soveraine* powre V. x. 13. 2
Unto his *soveraine* Queene her suite for to commend. V. xi. 37. 9
heavenly seedes of bounty *soveraine*, VI. Pr. 3. 7
O *soveraine* Lady Queene? VI. Pr. 6. 4
pardon me, most dreaded *Soveraine*, VI. Pr. 7. 1
by vow, which I profest To my dread *Soveraine*, VI. ii. 37. 6
in her *soveraine* lyking he dwelt evermore VI. v. 12. 9
Did boast her beautie had such *soveraine* might, VI. vii. 31. 6

Sovereign—*Continued.*
Ye gentle Ladies, in whose *soveraine* powre VI. viii. 1. 1
Did for their *soveraine* goddesse her esteeme, VI. ix. 9. 7
in her *soveraine* Majesty to sit, VI. x. 9. 8
Divine resemblaunce, beauty *soveraine* rare, VI. x. 27. 4
as well of Gods as Men To be the *Soveraine*. VII. vi. Arg.
had to her that *soveraigne* seat By highest Jove assign'd, VII. vi. 12. 1
in his *soveraine* throne gan straight dispose Himselfe, VII. vi. 24. 7
by conquest, of our *soveraine* might, VII. vi. 33. 5
Have Jove thy gracious Lord and *Soveraine*.' VII. vi. 34. 5
soveraine Queene profest Of woods and forrests VII. vi. 38. 7
heavens King (Thy *soveraine* Sire) VII. vii. 1. 6
'Then weigh, O *soveraigne* goddesse! by what right VII. vii. 16. 1
Supported her like to their *soveraigne* Queene: VII. vii. 34. 6
To whether side should fall the *soveraine* place: VII. vii. 57. 7
The *soverayne* beauty which I doo admyre, *Am.* iii. 1
My *soverayne* saynt, the Idoll of my thought, *Am.* lxi. 2
when that *soverayne* beauty it doth spy, *Am.* lxxii. 5
my *sovereigne* Queene most kind, *Am.* lxxiv. 7
salve of *soveraigne* might: *Epig.* iv. 46
Then I thy *soverayne* prayses loud wil sing, *Epith.* 127
Made in the honor of your *Soveraigne* king. *H.L.* 42
the *soveraine* Lord of all, *H.L.* 157
whose *soverayne* grace and kindly dewty *H.B.* 17
That is thy *soveraine* might, *H.B.* 54
by a *soveraine* might Tempers so trim, *H.B.* 124
graunt, O great *Soveraine!* *H.B.* 274
Which there thou workest by thy *soveraine* might, *H.H.L.* 4
That thou his *soveraine* bountie mayst behold, *H.H.L.* 223
And to his *soveraine* mercie doe appeale; *H.H.L.* 257
The *soveraine* Powres and mightie Potentates, *H.H.B.* 86
The *soveraine* dearling of the Deity, *H.H.B.* 184
Could once come neare this beauty *soverayne*. *H.H.B.* 217
Let Angels, . . . her *soveraigne* praises sing, *H.H.B.* 233
And looke at last up to that *Soveraine* Light, *H.H.B.* 295
Sovereign's. Thy gracious *Soverains* praises to compile, *Ded. Son.* xii. 6
it is shrined in my *Soveraines* brest, III. Pr. 1. 5
My glorious *Soveraines* goodly auncestrye, III. iii. 4. 7
Sovereignty. The nations gan their *soveraigntie* disdaine, *Van.* xi. 3
nowe is in his chiefe *sovereigntee*, *S.C.* S. 50
Whilst each does for the *Soveraignty* contend, *Gn.* 410
Rome, that holds the world in *sovereigntie*, *Gn.* 597
she had none . . . Ne heritage of native *soveraintie;* I. iv. 12. 4
To have a pere in part of *soverainty;* II. x. 33. 4
envious of Uncles *soveraintie*, II. x. 48. 7
He maketh Kings to sit in *soverainty;* V. ii. 41. 5
Unlesse the heavens them lift to lawfull *soveraintie*. V. v. 25. 9
A Goddesse of great powre and *soverainty*, V. vii. 3. 2
So sitting high in dreaded *soverayntie*, V. ix. 34. 1
These gods do claime the worlds whole *soverainty*, VII. vii. 16. 2
do claime the rule and *soverainty;* VII. vii. 26. 3
crowne . . . in signe of highest *soveraignty;* *H.H.B.* 191
Sow. To plough, to plant, to reap, to rake, to *sowe*, *Hub.* 263
As incorrupted Nature did them *sow*, I. xi. 47. 4
Ne needs there Gardiner to sett or *sow*, III. vi. 34. 1
sow vaine sorrow in a fruitlesse eare, III. xi. 16. 2
in her mynde the seeds Of perfect love did *sow*, VI. ix. 45. 8
Sowces. *See* **Souses.**
Sowed. their bad Stuard neither plough'd nor *sowed*, VI. iv. 14. 7
All *sowd* with glistring stars more thicke then grasse, *H.H.B.* 53
Sower's. As thicke as doth the seede after the *sowers* hand: V. xii. 7. 9
Sowing. *sowing* in th' Aemathian fields thy spight, *Ro.* xxxi. 10
Sown. Dragons teeth, *sowne* in the sacred sand; *Ro.* x. 4
the seede that in my youth was *sowne* *S.C.* D. 101
first Triptoleme taught how to be *sowne*. *Gn.* 208
Who reapes the harvest *sowen* by his foe, I. iv. 42. 4
Sowen in bloodie field, and bought with woe: I. iv. 42. 5
Arriv'd wher they in erth their fruitles blood had *sown*. I. vi. 45. 9
True loves are often *sown*, but seldom grow on grownd.' I. ix. 16. 9
fruitlesse lives were under furrow *sowne*, III. ix. 35. 8
weedes, Which she her selfe had *sowen* all about, IV. i. 25. 3
thought that those brave imps were *sowen* Here by the Gods, VI. iv. 36. 7
Sownd. *See* **Sound, Swoon.**
Sowne. *See* **Sound.**
Sowst. *See* **Soused.**
Spa. th' English Bath, and eke the German *Spau;* I. xi. 30. 7
Space. plotteth out a tombe by measured *space:* *Gn.* 652
Whom all the Muses did bewaile long *space*, *T.M.* 17
And to these ydle rymes lend litle *space*, *Ded. Son.* i. 13
such a cursed creature lives so long a *space*.' I. i. 31. 9
having solaced themselves a *space* . . . They backe retourned I. iv. 38. 1
knight now grew in litle *space*, . . . To such perfection I. x. 21. 1
in short *space* they did to health restore The man I. x. 27. 8
cruell combat joynd in middle *space:* II. ii. 20. 3
me met in middle *space*. II. iv. 32. 4
to stay your deadly stryfe a *space*.' II. vi. 33. 5
in short *space* he has them qualifyde, II. vi. 51. 8
At length they came into a larger *space*, II. vii. 21. 1
standing still a *space* Gaz'd after him, II. viii. 9. 3
Well kend him so far *space* II. viii. 17. 7
The dales for shade, the hilles for breathing *space*, II. xii. 58. 6
them awayted there a certaine *space*, III. i. 19. 4
in short *space* their foes they have quite terrifyde. III. i. 66. 9
having whispered a *space* Certein sad words III. ii. 50. 4
lyes a litle *space* From the swift Barry, III. iii. 8. 4
during eight yeares *space*, III. iii. 41. 2
She fled into the wildernesse a *space*, III. vi. 10. 3
in short *space* She was well pleasd, III. vi. 25. 6
in short *space* She grew familiare III. vii. 15. 4
importuned long *space* With shrilling shriekes, III. viii. 29. 7

Space—*Continued.*
he them both outran a wondrous *space,* . . . III. xi. 5. 7
did it selfe divide with equall *space,* . . . III. xi. 25. 5
ne could satisfy . . . with gazing a long *space:* . . . III. xi. 53. 4
A Ladie, seeming in so farre a *space:* . . . IV. i. 17. 4
She in short *space* did often bring to nought, . . . IV. i. 29. 6
lov'd in forests wyld to *space.* . . . IV. ii. 44. 9
Thereat the Champions both stood still a *space,* . . . IV. iii. 38. 1
No longer *space* thereto he did desire, . . . IV. vi. 43. 8
During which *space* these sory eies have seen . . . IV. vii. 13. 4
it did astonish him long *space.* . . . IV. viii. 43. 9
he sometimes may *space* And walke about her gardens . . . IV. viii. 54. 2
Within the compasse of that Islands *space;* . . . IV. x. 21. 2
in short *space* his hurts he had redrest, . . . IV. xi. 7. 3
after she had wept and wail'd a *space,* . . . IV. xii. 8. 8
in short *space* his wonted chearefull hew Gan fade, . . . IV. xii. 20. 1
Astraea loathing lenger here to *space* Mongst wicked men, . . . V. i. 11. 2
During which *space* she there as Princess rained, . . . V. vii. 42. 3
There she continu'd for a certaine *space,* . . . V. vii. 45. 1
with Sir Artegall a *space* Well solast . . . V. ix. 3. 1
Amongst the rest, which in that *space* befell, . . . V. x. 6. 1
how long *space* Hath he her lent a Champion to provide?' . . . V. xi. 42. 1
in short *space,* whiles there with her he stayd, . . . V. xii. 25. 8
In travelling on foote so long a *space,* . . . VI. iii. 29. 4
now strong through rest so long a *space,* . . . VI. v. 7. 5
in short *space* their malady was ceast, . . . VI. vi. 15. 4
in all these two yeares *space* Saved but two; . . . VI. vii. 38. 5
As each thought best to spend the lingring *space:* . . . VI. viii. 39. 3
During which *space* that she thus sicke did lie, . . . VI. xi. 9. 1
drew a litle *space* Behind the bushes, . . . VI. xii. 8. 5
where she was wont to *space,* . . . VII. vi. 55. 4
Some in short *space,* . . . VII. vii. 55. 3
Ne Nature to or fro spake for a *space,* . . . VII. vii. 57. 2
al my wounds wil heale in little *space.* . . . *Am.* lvii. 14
mightie bound which . . . parts their houres by *space,* . . . *H.H.L.* 26

Spacious. entred in, a *spatious* court they see, . . . I. x. 6. 2
A large and *spacious* plaine, . . . II. xii. 50. 2
faire before the gate a *spatious* playne, . . . III. i. 20. 6
through a Chamber long and *spacious,* . . . III. i. 31. 7
Spreading it selfe into a *spatious* plaine: . . . III. v. 39. 6
an Island *spatious* and brode, . . . III. ix. 49. 2
stopt the entraunce with his *spacious* stride, . . . IV. x. 16. 7
The *spacious* Shenan spreading like a sea, . . . IV. xi. 41. 3
The waies . . . Are so exceeding *spacious* and wyde, . . . VI. Pr. 1. 3
on the top thereof a *spacious* plaine . . . VI. x. 8. 1

Spade. His yron-headed *spade* tho making cleene, . . . *Gn.* 653
never usde to live by plough nor *spade,* . . . VI. x. 39. 4
Yet in his hand a *spade* he also hent, . . . VII. vii. 32. 6

Spain. Ne Afrike thereof guiltie is, nor *Spaine,* . . . *Ro.* xxxi. 5
He also gave to fugitives of *Spayne,* . . . II. x. 41. 6
He that whylome in *Spaine* so sore was dred . . . V. x. 9. 3
through all *Spaine* did thunder, . . . *Proth.* 147

Spake. *See* **Spoke.**
So *spake* this bold brere with great disdaine: . . . *S.C.* F. 139
(that word she *spake* with payne, . . . *S.C.* May 193
spake to him in place. . . . *S.C.* Jul. 160
Ne ever *spake,* ne cause of speaking mooved; . . . *Gn.* 469
Ne ever stayd in place, ne *spake* to wight, . . . *Hub.* 938
Then *spake* a lovely lasse, . . . *Col.* 456
so feelingly he *spake:* . . . *Col.* 649
So having said, Melissa *spake* at will; . . . *Col.* 895
He . . . *spake* reprochful shame Of highest God, . . . I. i. 37. 5
The Messenger approching to him *spake;* . . . I. i. 42. 1
It . . . *spake* the praises of the workmans witt; . . . I. iv. 5. 2
To gayne so goodly guerdon as she *spake:* . . . I. vii. 15. 2
saw the signes that deadly tydinges *spake,* . . . I. vii. 20. 6
Thus as he *spake,* his visage wexed pale, . . . I. ix. 16. 1
he disclosing read thus, as the paper *spake:* . . . I. xii. 25. 9
ne word to creature *spake.* . . . I. xii. 29. 4
with delight of that he wisely *spake* . . . II. ii. 46. 5
when she *spake,* . . . II. iii. 24. 6
whiles she *spake* her great words did appall . . . II. iii. 44. 5
Thus as he *spake,* lo! far away they spyde . . . II. iv. 37. 1
to Guyon first He boldly *spake;* . . . II. iv. 39. 2
They were far past the passage which he *spake,* . . . II. vi. 11. 2
they passing *spake* unto them nought; . . . II. vii. 24. 2
Then *spake* one of those six; . . . III. i. 26. 1
Ne any noise she made, ne word she *spake,* . . . III. i. 61. 6
To heare the warlike feates which Homere *spake* . . . III. iv. 2. 4
Full myld to her he *spake,* . . . III. iv. 48. 8
Paridell . . . thus *spake,* . . . III. ix. 32. 9
the bold Virgin . . . *spake* thus courtesly:— . . . III. xi. 13. 9
No word they *spake,* . . . III. xii. 45. *or.* 8
everie word did tremble as she *spake,* . . . IV. i. 5. 6
Als as she double *spake,* so heard she double, . . . IV. i. 28. 1
yet so mazed that he nothing *spake.* . . . IV. i. 43. 9
when the Prince unto him *spake,* . . . IV. vii. 44. 6
Yet *spake* no word, whereby she might aread . . . IV. viii. 13. 5
admyrde her change, and *spake* her praise. . . . IV. ix. 16. 9
Whilest thus I *spake,* . . . IV. x. 48. 6
No more he *spake,* . . . V. ii. 10. 8
The which erewhile *spake* so reprochfully, . . . V. ii. 21. 4
thus unto him *spake,* without regard or feare. . . . V. ii. 33. 9
Untill that Guyon selfe unto him *spake,* . . . V. iii. 34. 2
his owne mouth . . . *spake* so warelesse word, . . . V. v. 17. 4
Her rather reade his meaning then him selfe it *spake.* . . . V. vi. 9. 9
all the world *spake* shame. . . . V. xi. 4. 7
Till he an Herauld cald, and to him *spake,* . . . V. xii. 8. 5
as she *spake* therewith she slavered; . . . V. xii. 29. 8
Yet *spake* she seldom, but thought more the lesse she sed. . . . V. xii. 29. 9

Spake—*Continued.*
among most bitter wordes they *spake,* . . . V. xii. 42. 1
whiles they *spake* they heard a ruefull shrieke . . . VI. i. 17. 1
with sterne count'naunce thus unto him *spake:* . . . VI. i. 19. 5
those shames, that erst ye *spake* me to deface.' . . . VI. i. 28. 9
For what he *spake,* for you he *spake* it, Dame; . . . VI. ii. 14. 5
this young man . . . *Spake,* as was meet, . . . VI. ii. 23. 3
first him greeting, thus unto him *spake:* . . . VI. x. 19. 1
the mayd of whom they *spake* Was his owne purchase, . . . VI. xi. 12. 2
tongues of mortall men, Which *spake* reprochfully, . . . VI. xii. 27. 9
spake licentious words and hatefull things . . . VI. xii. 28. 5
Whil'st she thus *spake,* . . . VII. vi. 28. 1
that power and vertue which ye *spake,* . . . VII. vii. 54. 4
Ne Nature to or fro *spake* for a space, . . . VII. vii. 57. 2
Which in his last bequest he to us *spake,* . . . *H.H.L.* 207

Spalls. naked made each others manly *spalles;* . . . II. vi. 29. 6

Span. *See* **Spun.**
Beholding how the thrids of life they *span:* . . . IV. ii. 49. 2
eke in stature higher by a *span;* . . . IV. vii. 5. 3

Spangles. frost with *spangles* doth attire The mossy braunches I. x. 48. 3

Spangs. glittering *spangs* that did like starres appeare, . . . IV. xi. 45. 5

Spaniel. As rated *Spaniell* takes his burden up for feare. . . . V. i. 29. 9
Like to a *Spaniell* wayting carefully . . . V. vi. 26. 8

Spaniels. the hungry *Spaniells* she does spye . . . III. viii. 33. 6

Spar. *Sperre* the yate fast . . . *S.C.* May 224
laboured fast To *sperre* the gate; . . . V. x. 37. 2
opening streight the *Sparre,* forth to him came, . . . V. xi. 4. 2

Spare. nought to learning they may *spare;* . . . *T.M.* 470
do not *spare* the best or fayrest, . . . *D.* 202
'O! *spare* with guilty hands to teare My tender sides . . . I. ii. 31. 2
ruefull plaints, me bidding guiltlesse blood to *spare?*' . . . I. ii. 32. 9
hee . . . both from backe and belly still did *spare,* . . . I. iv. 28. 4
if that no *spare* clothes to give he had, . . . I. x. 39. 8
th' Enchaunter would not *spare* his payne, . . . II. i. 5. 1
As if that age badd him that burden *spare,* . . . III. i. 4. 5
mischievous mischaunce his life and limbs did *spare.* . . . III. i. 6. 9
Pourd out their plenty without spight or *spare.* . . . III. i. 51. 4
spare to one, or two, or three, Rowme in their writtes; . . . III. ii. 1. 7
no paines did *spare* To doe him ease, . . . III. v. 50. 1
Spare, gentle sister, with reproch my paine to eeke; . . . III. vi. 22. 9
spare thy happy daies, and them apply To better boot; . . . III. xi. 19. 5
Ne did he *spare* . . . His owne deare mother, . . . III. xi. 45. 1
Ne did he *spare* sometime to pricke himselfe, . . . III. xi. 45. 3
cared not to *spare* that should be shortly spent. . . . IV. iii. 6. 9
Yet neither toyle nor griefe she once did *spare,* . . . IV. v. 30. 2
For ought will from his greedie pleasure *spare:* . . . IV. viii. 29. 8
all the way from trotting hard to *spare;* . . . IV. viii. 37. 8
Ne helmets bright ne hawberks strong did *spare,* . . . IV. ix. 27. 3
this devouring Sea, that naught doth *spare,* . . . V. iv. 8. 2
Ne would he *spare* for pitty, nor refraine for feare. . . . VI. i. 17. 9
To *spare* her Knight, and rest with reason pacifyde: . . . VI. iii. 49. 9
Ne ought that foole for pitty did him *spare,* . . . VI. vii. 49. 3
ne any him doth *spare;* . . . VI. xi. 48. 7
grim Sir Saturne oft doth *spare* His sterne aspect, . . . VII. vii. 52. 7
Yet shoot ye sharpely still, and *spare* me not, . . . *Am.* lvii. 9
bad his billowes *spare* To wet their silken feathers, . . . *Proth.* 48

Spared. To leave enriched with that he hath *spard?* . . . *S.C.* May 84
my poore Muse hath spent her *spared* store, . . . *S.C.* O. 9
Ne *spared* he to give her gold and rings; . . . I. iii. 18. 8
Ne *spared* they to strip her naked all. . . . I. viii. 46. 4
ne *spard* for nicenesse none. . . . II. ix. 28. 9
neither day nor night from working *spared,* . . . IV. v. 35. 7
Shall for another canticle be *spared:* . . . IV. v. 46. 7
cruell spoyle, which he had *spard,* . . . IV. vii. 6. 4
ne *spared* not Their dainty parts, . . . V. vii. 29. 5
still his spirite *spar'd,* . . . VI. i. 20. 6
Ne Kesars *spared* he a whit, . . . VI. xii. 28. 7

Sparely. time, that should be *sparely* spent, . . . *S.C.* May 41

Spares. Yet still he strives, ne any perill *spares,* . . . V. xi. 45. 1

Spareth. Ne *spareth* he most learned wits to rate, . . . VI. xii. 40. 7
Ne *spareth* he the gentle Poets rime; . . . VI. xii. 40. 8

Sparing. nought for nicenesse nor for envy *sparing,* . . . IV. x. 56. 6
for *sparing* little cost or paines, . . . IV. xi. 22. 8
Ne *sparing* him the more for all his grievous wound. . . . VI. iv. 2. 9
Not *sparing* him with bitter words to taunt, . . . VI. vi. 21. 7
Not *sparing* wight, ne leaving any balke, . . . VI. xi. 16. 4
Nought *sparing* them, the more did tosse and teare, . . . VI. xii. 24. 7

Sparingly. such fond favours *sparingly* dispenst: . . . IV. ii. 9. 3

Spark. man, that had the *sparke* of reasons might . . . *Col.* 867
the sleeping *spark* Of native vertue gan eftsoones revive; . . . I. ii. 19. 1
The *sparke* of noble corage now awake, . . . I. xi. 2. 6
There shall a *sparke* of fire, . . . III. iii. 48. 2
Like *sparke* of fire that from the andvile glode, . . . IV. iv. 23. 5
Glaunst swiftly by; like to that heavenly *sparke,* . . . VI. vii. 7. 8
To *sparke* out litle beames, . . . VI. xi. 21. 9
Without some *spark* of such self-pleasing pride. . . . *Am.* v. 14
in her eyes the fyre of love does *sparke.* . . . *Am.* lxxxi. 4
Let not one *sparke* of filthy lustfull fyre Breake out, . . . *Am.* lxxxiii. 1
Compared to his least resplendent *sparke?* . . . *H.H.B.* 126
Light, farre exceeding that bright blazing *sparke* . . . *H.H.B.* 162

Sparkle. from his bloodie eyes doth *sparkle* fire: . . . *Van.* x. 12
Did *sparckle* forth great light, . . . III. i. 32. 9
Like coles that through a silver Censer *sparkle* bright. . . . V. vi. 38. 9

Sparkled. The beame of beautie *sparkled* from above, . . . *Col.* 468
Did burne with wrath, and *sparkled* living fyre: . . . I. xi. 14. 2
beautie . . . *Sparkled* on her from Gods owne glorious face, . *H.H.B.* 207

Sparkles. His eies did hurle forth *sparcles* fiery red, . . . I. iv. 33. 5
From flaming mouth bright *sparckles* fiery redd, . . . I. vii. 31. 7
As *sparkles* from the Andvile use to fly, . . . I. xi. 42. 6
from the same the fierie *sparkles* flasht, . . . IV. iii. 25. 8

Sparkles—*Continued.*
The glauncing *sparkles* through her bever glared, ... V. vi. 38. 7

Sparkling. *See* **Wide-sparkling.**
His *sparkling* blade about his head he blest, ... I. viii. 22. 3
backe againe the *sparcling* steele recoyld, ... I. xi. 25. 3
in his eyes did rest Yet *sparckling* fyre, ... I. xii. 10. 8
round about him threw forth *sparkling* fire, ... II. v. 2. 6
staring eyes *sparckling* with fervent fyre . . . . II. vii. 37. 6
in his *sparkling* face The secrete signes of kindled lust . . . II. xii. 68. 5
sparckling on the silent waves, ... II. xii. 78. 9
made the *sparckling* waves to smoke agayne, ... III. xi. 41. 3
sparkling fire out of his furious eyne, ... VI. v. 26. 2
That golden wyre, those *sparckling* stars so bright, ... *H.B.* 97
light . . . yet *sparckling* in his sight, ... *H.B.* 220
some *sparkling* light Of thine eternall Truth, ... *H.H.B.* 10

Sparks. with *sparks* of hevenlie beautie fired. . . . . . . *Col.* 563
'Dear Dame,' (quoth he) 'you sleeping *sparkes* awake, ... I. ix. 8. 1
threw forth *sparkes* of fyre; . . . . II. iv. 15. 6
The fire of *sparkes*, the weede of little seede, ... II. iv. 35. 4
sparks, seed, drops, and filth, do thus delay; . . . . II. iv. 35. 6
The *sparks* soone quench, ... II. iv. 35. 7
Like *sparkes* of fire which fall in sclender flex, ... III. i. 47. 7
The outward *sparkes* of her inburning fire; . . . . III. i. 53. 3
the old *sparkes* renew Of native corage, ... III. iii. 45. 7
Her fyrie eyes with furious *sparkes* did stare, ... III. vii. 39. 8
Twixt both his hands few *sparks* he close did strayne, ... III. xii. 9. 7
whose small *sparkes* once blowen None but a God . . . can slake; . . . . IV. ii. 1. 5
Yet will it shew some *sparkes* of gentle mynd, ... VI. v. 1. 8
Kindle fresh *sparks* of that immortall fire . . . . VII. vii. 2. 4
The *sparkes* whereof let kindle thine own fyre, ... *Am.* lxxxv. 9
Through secret *sparks* of his infused fyre, ... *H.L.* 97
Some *sparks* remaining of that heavenly fyre, ... *H.L.* 107

Sparred. Kiddie the dore *sperred* after her fast. . . . . . *S.C.* May 234

Sparrows. litle *sparrowes* stolen from their nest, ... VI. ix. 40. 2

Spartan. The *Spartan* Mirtle, whence sweet gumb does flowe; . *Gn.* 669

Spasm. T' abate all *spasme*, and soke the swelling bruze; . . . III. v. 33. 7

Spat. *spat* out poyson, and gore-bloudy gere, ... VI. xii. 28. 3

Spau. *See* **Spa.**

Spawn. The fruitfull *spawne* of their ranke fantasies: . . . . *T.M.* 322
fruitfull cursed *spawne* of serpents small, ... I. i. 22. 6
all the fruitfull *spawne* of fishes hew . . . . III. vi. 35. 7

Speak. Anger nould let him *speake* to the tree, ... *S.C.* F. 199
Diggon, I praye thee, *speake* not so dirke; . . . . *S.C.* S. 102
playnely to *speake* of shepheards most what, ... *S.C.* S. 104
this Muse shall *speak* to thee In bigger notes, ... *Gn.* 10
Scarse could the Ape yet *speake*, ... *Hub.* 964
none durst *speake*, ne none durst of him plaine, ... *Hub.* 1199
know their names, or *speak* their praises dew, ... *T.M.* 442
The rest untold no living tongue can *speake*. . . . . *T.M.* 600
'I hate to *speake*, my voyce is spent with crying; . . . . . . *D.* 414
gan a gentle bonylasse to *speake*, ... *Col.* 172
want I words to *speake* it fitly forth: . . . . *Col.* 625
when I *speake* of her what I have thought, ... *Col.* 626
Yet will I thinke of her, yet will I *speake*, ... *Col.* 628
'Of loves perfection perfectly to *speake*, ... *Col.* 835
he . . . Shooke him so hard, that forced him to *speake*. . . . I. i. 42. 6
'Nor guileful sprite to thee these words doth *speake*; . . . . I. ii. 33. 2
She could not heare, nor *speake*, nor understand; . . . . . . I. iii. 11. 4
Soone as the Faerie heard his Ladie *speake*, ... I. v. 12. 1
Ne word to *speake*, ne joynt to move, she had; . . . . I. vi. 11. 2
Can *speake* his prowesse that did earst you beare, ... I. vii. 48. 4
Ne would she *speake*, ne see, ne yet be seene, ... II. i. 15. 6
When she her Squyre heard *speake*, ... II. i. 16. 8
when he heard him *speake*, ... II. i. 28. 1
Speake, O dear Lady, *speake!* help never comes too late.' . . II. i. 44. 9
Ne ought would *speake*, ... II. ii. 35. 3
Speake they which have beheld . . . . II. iii. 16. 9
Which yet their praises *speake*, all be they loth, ... II. x. 40. 7
no powre To *speake* a while, ne ready answere make, ... III. ii. 5. 2
Ne word did *speake*, but lay as in a swowne, ... III. iv. 30. 6
Ne had one word to *speake* for great amaze, ... III. vii. 7. 8
Ne how to *speake*, ne how to use his gest; . . . . III. viii. 8. 7
Or *speake* ye of report, or did ye see . . . . III. viii. 48. 5
Ne word he had to *speake* his griefe to tell, ... III. x. 37. 8
both the parts did *speake*, and both contended; . . . . . . IV. i. 27. 7
Ne word had he to *speake* for great dismay, ... IV. i. 50. 2
Content to heare him *speake*, ... IV. ii. 21. 9
Ne ever word to *speake* to woman more; . . . . IV. vii. 39. 4
did Britomart assay To *speake* to them, ... IV. ix. 31. 2
These vile reproches gan unto her *speake*: . . . . V. vi. 37. 3
They stayd their hands, when she thus gan to *speake*: . . . . V. viii. 11. 1
Such loathly matter were small lust to *speake* or thinke. . . . V. xi. 31. 9
speake so ill of him that well deserved, ... V. xii. 43. 2
cannot expresse . . . me but by tokens *speake*: . . . . VI. v. 30. 4
she, for nought . . . One word durst *speake*, ... VI. viii. 50. 9
was so opprest, That he no word could *speake*, ... VI. xi. 28. 5
Whose like he never once did *speake*, nor heare, ... VI. xii. 33. 6
Made signe to them in their degrees to *speake*, ... VII. vi. 22. 5
'*Speake*, thou fraile woman, *speake* with confidence; . . . . . VII. vi. 25. 7
my toung would *speak* her praises dew, ... *Am.* iii. 9
I then both *speake* and write The wonder . . . . *Am.* iii. 13
and teach my hart to *speake*; . . . . *Am.* viii. 10
shall I *speake?* And, if I *speake*, ... *Am.* xliii. 1, 2
That nether I may *speake* nor thinke at all, ... *Am.* xliii. 7
teach to *speak*, and my just cause to plead; . . . . *Am.* xliii. 10
And *speake* her good, though she requite it ill. . . . . *Am.* xlviii. 14
To *speake* her prayse and glory excellent, ... *Am.* lxxiv. 11
speake no word to her of these sad plights, ... *Am.* lxxxiii. 11
murmurde low, As he would *speake*, ... *Proth.* 116

Speakest. now I see thou *speakest* of spight, ... *S.C.* May 55
I see thou *speakest* to plaine; . . . . *S.C.* S. 136
Thou *speakest* thus gainst their felicitie, ... *Col.* 677

Speaking. Ne ever spake, ne cause of *speaking* mooved; . . . *Gn.* 469
speaking streames of pure Castalion, ... *T.M.* 273
I will it spend in *speaking* of thy praise, ... *Ti.* 310
The *speaking* woods, and murmuring waters fall, ... *Col.* 636
these rent reliques, *speaking* their ill plightes? . . . . II. xii. 9. 7
speaking token sheweth at the least . . . . III. viii. 49. 5
With *speaking* lookes, that close embassage bore, ... III. ix. 28. 2
In *speaking* many false belgardes at her let fly. . . . . . . III. ix. 52. 9
Then *speaking* to the Ladie thus he said: . . . . VI. ii. 42. 1
shewed semblant of exceeding mone By *speaking* signes, ... VI. v. 4. 3
speaking markes of passed monuments, ... VI. xii. 20. 4

Speaks. thou *speakes* lyke a lewde lorrell, ... *S.C.* Jul. 93
she *speakes* no more Of past: . . . . I. iii. 30. 6
calles and *speakes*, yet nought avayles; . . . . V. viii. 39. 7
Hearing the holy priest that to her *speakes*, ... *Epith.* 224

Spear. *See* **Boar-spear.**
backe was arm'd against the dint of *speare* . . . . *Van.* vi. 2
Now his bright armes assaying, now his *speare*, ... *Hub.* 741
steelhed *speare*, and morion on her hedd, ... *Mui.* 322
to the Dwarfe a while his needlesse *spere* he gave. . . . . . I. i. 11. 9
she saw the knight his *speare* advaunce, ... I. ii. 14. 3
The knight of the Redcrosse, . . . Gan fairely couch his *speare*, I. ii. 15. 3
his harder fortune was to fall Under my *speare*: . . . . I. ii. 36. 7
prepare Himselfe to batteill with his couched *speare*. . . . . I. iii. 34. 4
bent his *speare*, and spurd his horse with yron heele. . . . . I. iii. 34. 9
with his sharphead *speare*, Through . . . shield he quite did perce; . . . . I. iii. 35. 2
mightie corse, As ever wielded *speare* in warlike hand, . . . I. iii. 42. 4
I saw . . . Sansfoy shrinck underneath his *speare*: . . . . . I. v. 23. 2
His poynant *speare* that many made to bleed, ... I. vii. 19. 7
point of *speare* it never percen could, ... I. vii. 33. 8
youth . . . His *speare* of heben wood behind him bare, ... I. vii. 37. 2
His biting sword, and his devouring *speare*, ... I. vii. 48. 2
With dint of swerd, nor push of pointed *speare*: . . . . . . I. xi. 9. 4
The knight gan fayrely couch his steady *speare*, ... I. xi. 16. 1
The knight his thrillant *speare* againe assayd . . . . I. xi. 20. 2
streight against that knight his *speare* he did addresse. . . II. i. 25. 9
in the rest his ready *speare* did sticke: . . . . II. i. 26. 3
that warriour gan abace His threatned *speare*, ... II. i. 26. 8
He left his steed without, and *speare* besyde, ... II. iii. 3. 8
Purloynd both steed and *speare*, ... II. iii. 4. 9
to him threatned his hart-thrilling *speare*: . . . . II. iii. 6. 6
rode in golden sell with single *spere*, ... II. iii. 12. 3
That *speare* is him enough to doen a thousand grone.' . . . II. iii. 12. 9
fayrly couching his steeleheaded *speare*, ... II. v. 3. 6
Ne all good knights that shake well *speare* and shield. . . . II. viii. 14. 6
his balefull *speare* he fiercely bent . . . . II. viii. 32. 1
His single *speare* could doe him small redresse . . . . II. viii. 34. 3
His poynant *speare* he thrust . . . . II. viii. 36. 3
the Prince his mortall *speare* Soone to him raught, ... II. xi. 25. 1
then the Faery quickly raught His poynant *speare*, ... III. i. 5. 4
bent his dreadful *speare* against the others head. . . . . . III. i. 5. 9
shivering *speare* in bloody field first shooke, ... III. i. 7. 3
That *speare* enchaunted was which layd thee on the greene. . III. i. 7. 9
For death sate on the point of that enchaunted *speare*: . . . III. i. 9. 9
in his clownish hand a sharp bore *speare* he shooke. . . . . III. i. 17. 9
her mortall *speare* She mightily aventred . . . . III. i. 28. 6
To tossen *speare* and shield, ... III. ii. 6. 4
Me lever were with point of foemans *speare* be dead. . . . . III. ii. 6. 9
Avenge his fathers losse with *speare* and shield, ... III. iii. 31. 8
The dreadful *speare* and shield to exercize: . . . . III. iii. 53. 4
Beside those armes there stood a mightie *speare*, ... III. iii. 60. 1
Both *speare* she tooke and shield . . . . III. iii. 60. 8
Both *speare* and shield of great powre, ... III. iii. 60. 9
Where be the batteilles, where the shield and *speare*, ... III. iv. 1. 4
That mortall *speare* she in her hand did take, ... III. iv. 14. 2
with sharpe *speare* the rest made dearly knowne. . . . . . . III. iv. 15. 6
with his *speare* requited him againe, ... III. v. 21. 7
His mighty *speare* he couched warily, ... III. vii. 38. 7
His *speare* amids her sun-brode shield arriv'd: . . . . III. vii. 40. 4
His bloody *speare* eftesoones he boldly bent . . . . III. viii. 12. 5
Transfixed with her *speare* downe tombled dedd . . . . III. ix. 22. 5
I expected one with shield and *spere* . . . . III. x. 24. 8
Cannot employ your most victorious *speare* . . . . III. x. 28. 3
His haberjeon, his helmet, and his *speare*: . . . . III. xi. 7. 5
he put his spurres unto his steed, With *speare* in rest, ... IV. i. 41. 2
Triamond to handle *speare* and shield, ... IV. ii. 42. 8
speare and curtaxe both usd Priamond in field. . . . . IV. ii. 42. 9
throughly skild in use of shield and *speare*; . . . . IV. iii. 7. 2
his poynant *speare* he fierce aventred . . . . IV. iii. 9. 1
He all enrag'd his shivering *speare* did shake, ... IV. iii. 10. 8
One in bright armes, with ready *speare* in rest, ... IV. iv. 6. 6
vaunted *speare* eftsoones to disadvaunce, ... IV. iv. 7. 2
An huge great *speare*, such as he wont to wield, ... IV. iv. 17. 2
him likewise with that same *speare* he eke did quell. . . . . IV. iv. 19. 9
Sternly stept forth and raught away his *speare*, ... IV. iv. 20. 6
at him his beam-like *speare* he aimed, ... IV. iv. 24. 1
A mightie *speare* eftsoones at him he bent; . . . . IV. iv. 28. 6
charg'd his *spere* At him that first appeared . . . . IV. iv. 40. 1
when his *speare* was brust, his sword he drew, ... IV. iv. 41. 3
charg'd his powrefull *speare* At Artegall, ... IV. iv. 44. 1
His *speare* he feutred, and at him it bore, ... IV. iv. 45. 8
Could bide the force of that enchaunted *speare*, ... IV. iv. 46. 4
Whom all men term'd Knight of the Hebene *speare*, ... IV. v. 8. 2
the Knight That bore the Hebene *speare*, ... IV. v. 20. 5
vow'd with *speare* and shield it to maintaine; . . . . IV. v. 24. 8
his *speare* he gan abase And voide his course: . . . . IV. vi. 3. 4

Spear—*Continued.*
Without displeasance for to prove his *spere*. . . . . IV. vi. 4. 3
knowne by fame, and by an Hebene *speare*, ... IV. vi. 6. 4
When Scudamour heard mention of that *speare*, ... IV. vi. 7. 1
he his threatfull *speare* Gan fewter, ... IV. vi. 10. 1
therein left the pike-head of his *speare:* . . . . IV. vii. 27. 7
with my *speare* upon the shield did rap, ... IV. x. 9. 4
to approve his right with *speare* and shield, ... V. i. 24. 4
Uppon her *speare* she bore before her breast, ... V. vi. 39. 5
after those two former rode apace With *speare* in rest, ... V. viii. 5. 3
Thought with his *speare* him quight have overwent. . . . . . V. viii. 7. 4
He at him ran with ready *speare* in rest; . . . . V. viii. 9. 3
ere his readie *speare* He could advance, ... V. viii. 33. 5
purchase it to us with *speare* and shield: . . . . V. x. 24. 4
his mortall *speare* Past through his shield . . . . V. x. 35. 6
coucht his *speare*, and ran at him amaine. . . . . VI. i. 33. 4
He with his *speare*, . . . Would thumpe her forward . . . . . VI. ii. 10. 7
he . . . with his *speare* strooke me one stroke . . . . VI. ii. 12. 4
But at him flew, and with his *speare* him smot; . . . . VI. ii. 19. 8
Pounching me with the butt end of his *speare*, ... VI. ii. 22. 6
And him unarm'd, . . . Charg'd with his *speare*, ... VI. ii. 43. 5
With *speare* in th' one hand stayd him selfe upright, ... VI. iii. 33. 8
couching close his *speare* and all his powre, ... VI. iii. 48. 2
with his *spere* Strooke through his shoulder, ... VI. iii. 50. 6
He cared not for dint of sword nor *speere*, ... VI. iv. 4. 6
with the push of his sharp-pointed *speare* . . . . VI. iv. 5. 6
Regarding neither *speare* that mote him slay, ... VI. iv. 6. 4
having now no use of his long *speare* . . . . VI. iv. 7. 6
Both *speare* and shield, . . . He quite forsooke, ... VI. iv. 7. 8
Then taking up that Recreants shield and *speare*, ... VI. iv. 13. 1
his well-learned *speare* Tooke surer hould, ... VI. vii. 11. 1
Instead of steele-head *speare*, a shepheards hooke; . . . . . VI. ix. 36. 5
A lustie knight as ever wielded *speare*, ... VI. xii. 3. 6

Spear's. Nigh a *speares* length behind his crouper fell; . . . III. i. 6. 7
His *speares* default to mend with cruell blade; . . . . III. i. 10. 3

Spears. with an hundred *speares* her flank wide rended. . . . *Bel.*[2] vi. 11
Like two sharpe *speares* his enemies to gore: . . . . *Mui.* 83
Some with unweldy clubs, some with long *speares*, ... II. ix. 13. 6
Their steel-hed *speares* they strongly coucht, ... III. ix. 16. 1
Their swerds and *speres* were broke, ... III. xi. 52. 6
Disshivered *speares*, and shields ytorne in twaine; . . . . . IV. i. 21. 6
the heads of many broken *speares;* . . . . IV. i. 48. 9
they gan their shivering *speares* to shake, ... IV. ii. 14. 7
both their *speares* with pitilesse remorse . . . . IV. ii. 15. 3
By shivered *speares*, and swords all under strowen, ... IV. iv. 38. 4
both Together ran with ready *speares* in rest. . . . . V. ii. 12. 4
strongly either strooke And broke their *speares;* . . . . . . V. viii. 9. 7
For what their *speares* had fayld of their pretence: . . . . . V. viii. 10. 3
their sharpe *speares* doe both together smite . . . . V. x. 32. 2
Did all their *speares* attonce on him enchace. . . . . V. x. 34. 5
both at once with equall spight Did bend their *speares*, . . . VI. vii. 7. 5
through thousand swords and *speares;* . . . . *H.L.* 228

Spears'. bore him . . . longer Then two *speares* length: . . . . V. viii. 7. 9

Special. They her besought of favour *speciall* . . . . II. ix. 20. 7
one above the rest in *speciall* . . . . II. xii. 86. 6
for reasons *speciall* privitie, ... IV. v. 1. 4
committed be, of *speciall* grace, ... IV. viii. 54. 7

Specked. all his backe was *spect* With thousand spots . . . . III. vii. 22. 4

Speckled. turning fierce her *speckled* taile advaunst, ... I. i. 17. 6
Forelifting up a-loft his *speckled* brest, ... I. xi. 15. 2

Speckles. An huge great Serpent, all with *speckles* pide, . . . *Gn.* 250

Spectacle. The worlds sad *spectacle*, and fortunes scorne.' . . *Ti.* 28
His bodie left the *spectacle* of care. . . . . *Mui.* 440
when that pitteous *spectacle* they vewed, ... *As.* 203
The dreadfull *spectacle* of that sad house of Pryde. . . . . I. v. 53. 9
instruments . . . That doe this deadly *spectacle* behold, . . . I. vii. 22. 2
A ruefull *spectacle* of death and ghastly drere. . . . . . . I. viii. 40. 9
piteous *spectacle*, approving trew The wofull tale . . . . . I. ix. 37. 1
Pitifull *spectacle* of deadly smart, ... II. i. 40. 1
Pitifull *spectacle*, as ever eie did vew! . . . . II. i. 40. 9
daily *spectacle* of sad decay: . . . . II. x. 62. 5
A piteous *spectacle* did represent; . . . . II. xii. 45. 7
that faire *spectacle* from him was reft, ... II. xii. 67. 6
other ghastly *spectacle* dismayd, ... III. iii. 50. 3
for that *spectacle* bad . . . their cruell vengeaunce blin, . . . III. v. 22. 6
is the *spectacle* of ruinous decay. . . . . III. vii. 41. 9
They which that piteous *spectacle* beheld . . . . IV. iii. 21. 1
To have beheld a *spectacle* so bad; . . . . V. vii. 38. 5
all men, which that *spectacle* did see, ... V. viii. 44. 8

Spectacles. So all with rufull *spectacles* is fild, ... *T.M.* 163
At sight of these sad *spectacles* forepast, ... *Ti.* 576

Spectator. The sad *spectatour* of my Tragedie: . . . . II. iv. 27. 6
My love, lyke the *Spectator*, ydly sits; . . . . *Am.* liv. 2

Spectators. To be *spectators* of this uncouth fit, ... IV. vi. 30. 3

Speculation. Thence gathering plumes of perfect *speculation*, *H.H.B.* 134

Sped. Sommer season *sped* him to display . . . . *S.C.* D. 56
since their souldiers pas no better *spedd*, ... *Hub.* 357
th' Ape and Foxe ere long so well them *sped*, ... *Hub.* 552
So well they *sped*, that they be come . . . . I. v. 29. 1
Forthwith to court of Gloriane I *sped*, ... I. vii. 46. 5
thy cruell hond, That twise hath *spedd;* . . . . II. viii. 37. 7
the nimble bote so well her *sped*, ... II. xii. 38. 2
Nathlesse the villein *sped* himselfe so well, ... III. v. 14. 1
Unto his reskew ran, and greedily him *spedd*. . . . . III. vii. 30. 9
after him eke fearefull Trompart *spedd:* . . . . III. x. 43. 8
when he *spedd* His nimble feet, ... III. x. 55. 3
inly grudge at him that he had *sped* so well. . . . . IV. ii. 7. 9
So well she *sped* her, and so far she ventred, ... IV. vii. 31. 1
after them the Prince as swiftly *sped*, ... V. x. 36. 3
So well he *sped* him, that the wearie Beare . . . . VI. iv. 20. 1

Sped—*Continued.*
hearing how his people badly *sped*, ... VI. vi. 24. 4

Speech. his impudent lewde *speach* . . . . *Hub.* 839
deepelie muzing at her doubtfull *speach*, ... *Ti.* 485
milde of *speach*, and meeke of nature: . . . . *Ti.* 536
the whole assembly of those heards Moov'd at his *speech*, . . *Col.* 649
a savage beast, With Dragons *speche*, ... *Rev.* i. 12
So longe have I listened to thy *speche*, ... *S.C.* F. 241
interrupted all her other *speache* . . . . *S.C.* May 209
Her swollen hart her *speech* seemd to bereave, ... I. i. 52. 3
When all this *speech* the living tree had spent, ... I. ii. 44. 5
the witches *speach* she gan to heare, ... I. v. 21. 7
'What worlds delight, or joy of living *speach*, Can hart . . . reach? . . . . I. vii. 39. 1
His goodly reason, and well-guided *speach*, ... I. vii. 42. 1
Whose senceless *speach*, and doted ignorance, ... I. viii. 34. 2
nathemore by his bold hartie *speach* . . . . I. ix. 25. 6
'How may a man,' . . . 'with idle *speach* Be wonne . . . . . I. ix. 31. 1
The knight was much enmoved with his *speach*, ... I. ix. 48. 1
wonder was to heare her goodly *speach:* . . . . I. x. 19. 7
The king was greatly moved at her *speach;* . . . . I. xii. 35. 1
his percing *speach* gan paynt: . . . . II. i. 9. 5
Ne in her *speach*, ne in her haviour, ... II. ii. 15. 3
she to him her gracious *speach* renewd: . . . . II. iii. 37. 5
whenas use of *speach* was from her reft, ... II. iv. 13. 1
Which his sad *speach* infixed in my brest, ... II. iv. 23. 2
Yet at her *speach* their rages gan relent, ... II. vi. 36. 3
The Prince was inly moved at her *speach*, ... II. ix. 39. 1
wonder of antiquity long stopt his *speach*. . . . . II. x. 68. 9
to their senses vyld Her gentle *speach* applyde, ... III. vii. 15. 4
a kindly pride Of gratious *speach* . . . . III. ix. 32. 7
much he did advaunce In all his *speach*, ... III. ix. 48. 2
with commune *speach* He courted her; . . . . III. x. 6. 6
The wretched man at his imperious *speach* . . . . III. x. 25. 1
Choking the remnant of his plaintife *speach*, ... III. xi. 12. 4
lookt a little up at that his *speech*, ... IV. ii. 21. 3
hardly of her chearefull *speech* Did comfort take, ... IV. vi. 38. 1
Saluting him gan into *speach* to fall, ... IV. vii. 43. 8
to his *speach* he aunswered no whit, ... IV. vii. 44. 1
she did not her spightfull *speach* forbeare, ... IV. viii. 36. 2
the Ladie with her powrefull *speach* . . . . IV. x. 36. 6
Much did he marvell at her uncouth *speach*, ... V. v. 37. 1
He list no lenger to use lothfull *speach*, ... V. vi. 21. 6
and time his *speach* To all assayes; . . . . V. ix. 39. 3
comely guize withall And gracious *speach*, ... VI. i. 2. 6
Much did Sir Calidore admyre his *speach* . . . . VI. ii. 13. 1
The Ladie, hearing his so courteous *speach*, ... VI. ii. 42. 7
And moved *speach* to him of things of course, ... VI. iii. 14. 6
With which rude *speach* his Lady much displeased . . . . . VI. iii. 32. 6
For other language had he none, nor *speach*, ... VI. iv. 11. 6
The Ladie, hearkning to his sensefull *speach*, ... VI. iv. 37. 1
for all his *speach* the gentle knight Would not be tempted . VI. vii. 23. 1
evermore his *speach* he did apply To th' heards, ... VI. ix. 12. 8
drawing thence his *speach* another way, ... VI. ix. 18. 7
his *speach*, that wrought him great content, ... VI. ix. 26. 5
When thus that shepheard ended had his *speach*, ... VI. x. 29. 1
Much was the Lady troubled at that *speach*, ... VI. xii. 18. 1
reft of sense And voyd of *speach* . . . . VII. vi. 25. 5
that *speech* whyleare Of Mutabilitie, ... VII. viii. 1. 1

Speeches. the best *speaches* with ill meaning spill, ... *Hub.* 716
through wise *speaches* and grave conference . . . . *Hub.* 791
With those sweet sugred *speaches* doo compare, ... *D.* 299
with lewd *speeches*, and licentious deeds, ... *Col.* 787
'What voice . . . Sends to my doubtful eares these *speaches* rare, ... I. ii. 32. 8
him amoves with *speaches* seeming fitt: . . . . I. iv. 45. 3
Her feeling *speaches* some compassion mov'd . . . . I. v. 24. 6
he al enrag'd these bitter *speaches* said. . . . . I. vi. 46. 9
God you never let his charmed *speaches* heare!' . . . . I. ix. 30. 9
in his *speaches* . . . hee Did labour lively . . . . I. x. 6. 7
He them with *speaches* meet Does faire entreat; . . . . . . I. x. 7. 6
Many kind *speeches* they betweene them spend, ... I. x. 15. 3
hearken to the sober *speaches* which she spoke. . . . . II. ii. 28. 9
with *speeches* sage Inquyrd, ... II. x. 27. 8
softly gan to smyle At her smooth *speeches*, ... III. iii. 17. 2
through *speaches* with the Redcrosse Knight, ... III. iv. 4. 1
he could well his glozing *speaches* frame . . . . III. viii. 14. 4
he endevored with *speaches* milde . . . . III. viii. 34. 1
all the while that he these *speeches* spent, ... III. ix. 52. 1
Now with remembrance of those spightfull *speaches*, ... IV. ii. 12. 2
Ne let his *speeches* come unto their eare. . . . . IV. v. 38. 6
brought forth *speeches* myld when she would have missayd. . IV. vi. 27. 9
to his *speeches* was content To lend an eare, ... IV. vi. 41. 4
when all her *speeches* she had spent, ... IV. vi. 46. 1
framed *speaches* fit for his behoofe, ... IV. vii. 37. 7
with good thewes and *speaches* well applyde . . . . IV. ix. 14. 6
them with *speaches* milde gan first disswade . . . . IV. ix. 34. 3
Now with faire *speches*, now with threatnings sterne, ... IV. xii. 24. 7
She did allure with gifts and *speaches* milde . . . . V. i. 6. 5
did uncomely *speaches* crake. . . . . V. iii. 16. 7
With spightfull *speaches*, fitting with her well; . . . . . . V. v. 10. 4
Armies of lovely lookes, and *speeches* wise, ... V. v. 34. 8
Which *speaches* she applying to the scope Of her intent, . . . V. v. 39. 8
with bold *speaches* which he blazed had, ... V. ix. 25. 6
With such his chearefull *speaches* he doth wield Her mind . . V. x. 24. 7
Her fearefull *speaches* nought he did regard, ... V. x. 31. 1
speaches forth doth send, ... V. xi. 20. 7
fowle blasphemous *speaches* forth did cast, ... V. xi. 28. 2
forth at last did breake in *speaches* sharpe . . . . VI. iii. 34. 9
There they awhile some gracious *speaches* spent, ... VI. v. 24. 6

Speeches—*Continued.*
He to that point fit *speaches* gan to frame, . . . VI. vi. 6. 2
afterwards to cheare with *speaches* kind; . . . VI. viii. 50. 7
With gladfull *speaches* and with lovely cheare; . . . VI. xi. 50. 3
Did unto them at length these *speeches* wise unfold; . . . VII. vi. 19. 9
gave her doome in *speeches* few. . . . VII. vii. 57. 9
poysoned words and spitefull *speeches* . . . *Am.* lxxxv. 4
Speed. 'I see Calliope *speede* her to the place, . . . *S.C.* Ap. 100
Tho to the greene Wood they *speeden* hem all, . . . *S.C.* May 27
to the wood would he *speede* him fast. . . . *S.C.* S. 199
with good *speed* the fomie billowes scowre: . . . *Gn.* 564
The Priest him wisht good *speed,* . . . *Hub.* 550
To *speed* to day, to be put back to morrow; . . . *Hub.* 899
bad him flie with never-resting *speed* . . . *Hub.* 1247
with good *speed* began to take his flight. . . . *Mui.* 147
with so much *speede* As her slowe beast could make; . . . I. ii. 8. 1
speed The fayre Duess' had forst him leave behind; . . . I. vi. 2. 1
Uprose with hasty joy, and feeble *speed,* . . . I. xii. 3. 1
With flying *speede* . . . Came running in, . . . I. xii. 24. 7
Well may she *speede,* and fairely finish her intent! . . . I. xii. 42. 9
God ye *speed* and send you good successe, . . . II. i. 25. 6
his good Squyre, him helping up with *speed,* . . . II. xi. 48. 7
He smote the sea, which calmed was with *speed,* . . . II. xii. 26. 7
Yet shall he long time warre with happy *speed,* . . . III. iii. 31. 3
Farre better I it deeme to die with *speed* . . . III. iv. 38. 3
So evermore he did increase his *speed,* . . . III. iv. 48. 4
Speed thee to spred abroad thy beames bright, . . . III. iv. 60. 4
through his perfect sent And passing *speede,* . . . III. vii. 23. 9
gan encrease his *speed* as she encreast her flight. . . . III. vii. 43. 9
be partaker of their *speed.'* . . . III. viii. 50. 9
'Well may yee *speede* in so praiseworthy payne! . . . III. viii. 51. 2
ran with fearfull *speed,* . . . III. ix. 18. 3
now made better *speed* t' escape his feared foe . . . III. xi. 5. 9
saw her not, nor signe of her good *speed,* . . . III. xii. 45. 3
Like shaft out of a bow preventing *speed:* . . . IV. i. 41. 3
Most confidence and hope of happie *speed,* . . . IV. ii. 39. 6
litle prays'd his labours evill *speed,* . . . IV. v. 22. 4
departed thence with *speed,* And follow'd them, . . . IV. v. 28. 2
Gan towards them to pricke with eger *speede,* . . . IV. vi. 2. 8
towards them with *speed* A Squire came gallopping, . . . IV. viii. 38. 1
One comming towards her with hasty *speede.* . . . V. vi. 8. 2
Before two Knights that after her did *speed* . . . V. viii. 4. 3
the terme, approching fast, required *speed.* . . . V. xi. 65. 9
for to reclayme with *speed* His scattred people, . . . V. xii. 9. 1
way did give unto their gracelesse *speed:* . . . V. xii. 18. 4
'Now God you *speed,'* . . . VI. i. 10. 6
Bad him to flie with all the *speed* he could . . . VI. i. 29. 4
Pursuing him apace with greedy *speede;* . . . VI. iii. 46. 7
him pursewed with importune *speed,* . . . VI. iv. 8. 2
return'd againe With *speede* unto the place, . . . VI. iv. 9. 4
armes . . . Whose burden mote empeach his needfull *speed,* . . . VI. iv. 19. 2
Him seem'd his feet did fly and in their *speed* delight. . . . VI. iv. 19. 9
Thinking by *speed* to overtake his flight; . . . VI. v. 17. 2
That we may it avenge, and punish him with *speed?'* . . . VI. vii. 5. 9
Unlesse to me thou hether bring with *speed* The wretch . . . VI. vii. 13. 4
fled away with all the *speede* she mought, . . . VI. vii. 50. 4
With which her winged *speed* is let and crost, . . . VI. xii. 1. 4
chast With all their hounds that after him did *speed;* . . . VII. vi. 52. 3
Speedeth. to the field alone he *speedeth,* . . . *S.C.* F. 197
Speedily. He unto her would *speedily* revert: . . . IV. vi. 43. 7
she *speedily* poursewed With winged feete . . . IV. vii. 30. 1
Speediness. And Eagles wings, for scope and *speedinesse,* . . . V. xi. 24. 7
Speedy. in their *speedie* course and nimble flight . . . *Hub.* 621
as a *speedie* post that passeth by. . . . *D.* 413
He, making *speedy* way through spersed ayre, . . . I. i. 39. 1
to the Easterne coast of heaven makes *speedy* way: . . . I. v. 19. 9
Is gathered full, and worketh *speedy* way: . . . I. xi. 10. 3
Through hils and dales he *speedy* way did make, . . . II. xi. 26. 4
Not fitt for *speedy* pace, or manly exercize. . . . II. xii. 46. 9
Carried away with wings of *speedy* feare.' . . . III. v. 6. 6
through swiftnesse of his *speedie* beast, . . . III. v. 14. 2
towards them did ply With *speedie* course, . . . IV. i. 38. 6
with *speedie* pace did after them pursew. . . . IV. ii. 30. 9
Lo! where they spyde with *speedie* whirling pace, . . . IV. iii. 38. 3
There was the *speedy* Tamar, . . . IV. xi. 31. 1
Speedy Hippothoe, and chaste Actea, . . . IV. xi. 50. 1
Ne once for ought her *speedy* passage stayd, . . . V. viii. 6. 3
Gave way unto his horses *speedie* flying, . . . V. viii. 32. 3
made him evermore increase his *speedie* pace. . . . VI. vi. 29. 9
he, more *speedy,* from them fled more fast Then any Deere, . . . VII. vi. 52. 4
Spell. She shoulde have neede no more *spell;* . . . *S.C.* Mar. 54
with power of mightie *spell* . . . *Ti.* 374
who can tell The . . . might of Magick *spel?* . . . I. ii. 10. 9
That is the terme prescribed by the *spell.'* . . . I. ii. 43. 5
Merlin . . . did excell All living wightes in might of magicke
spell: . . . I. vii. 36. 5
In vaine seekes wonders out of Magick *spell.'* . . . III. iii. 17. 7
by his mighty *spell* (For Proteus was with prophecy inspir'd) III. iv. 25. 2
Did him, they say, forwarne through sacred *spell:* . . . III. v. 9. 7
The rest my selfe too readily can *spell.'* . . . V. vi. 11. 6
her deep wit, that true harts thought can *spel,* . . . *Am.* xliii. 13
Spells. other *spelles* like terrible, . . . I. i. 37. 3
evermore with mightie *spels* them charmd; . . . II. vi. 51. 7
damned ghosts, cald up with mighty *spels,* . . . *Epith.* 347
Spend. *See* **Spent.**
Good is no good, but if it be *spend;* . . . *S.C.* May 71
To *spend,* to give, to want, to be undonne. . . . *Hub.* 906
doth his life in so long tendance *spend!* . . . *Hub.* 908
all in sumptuous pride They *spend,* . . . *T.M.* 470
I will it *spend* in speaking of thy praise, . . . *Ti.* 310

Spend—*Continued.*
all the night that I in watch did *spend,* . . . *D.* 129
To baser wit his power therein to *spend,* . . . *Ded.Son.*xii.10
Now needeth him no lenger labour *spend,* . . . I. i. 26. 8
all their forces *spend* Them selves in vaine: . . . I. viii. 21. 5
Many kind speeches they betweene them *spend,* . . . I. x. 15. 3
His wearie pounces all in vaine doth *spend* . . . I. xi. 19. 7
Did *spend* their daies in doing godly thing. . . . I. x. 36. 5
in Amours the passing howres to *spend,* . . . II. vi. 35. 4
that in . . . honours suit my vowed daies do *spend,* . . . II. vii. 10. 2
choose my flitting houres to *spend,* . . . II. vii. 33. 7
His dayes, his goods, his bodie, he did *spend:* . . . II. xii. 80. 8
Nor so did Biblis *spend* her pining hart; . . . III. ii. 41. 2
muchell blood did *spend,* Yet might not doe him die: . . . III. vii. 32. 7
has full large to live and *spend* at libertie. . . . III. ix. 3. 9
my dayes to *spend* In seewing deeds of armes, . . . III. ix. 37. 8
in privie place Did *spend* her dayes, . . . IV. ii. 44. 9
maketh him his wing in vaine to *spend;* . . . IV. iii. 19. 7
life and labour both in vaine to *spend.* . . . IV. iii. 32. 5
His life he then would *spend* to justifie his right. . . . IV. iv. 10. 9
Though I this dearest life for her doe *spend.'* . . . V. xi. 43. 4
Doe *spend* my dayes and bend my carelesse wit . . . VI. ii. 9. 4
So all that day in wandring vainely he did *spend.* . . . VI. iv. 25. 9
As each thought best to *spend* the lingring space: . . . VI. viii. 39. 3
For her did languish, and his deare life *spend;* . . . VI. ix. 10. 6
all the night in silver sleepe I *spend,* . . . VI. ix. 22. 8
al my dayes in pining langour *spend,* . . . *Am.* xxxvi. 3
Thus I the time with expectation *spend,* . . . *Am.* lxxxvi. 9
How slowly do the houres theyr numbers *spend?* . . . *Epith.* 280
But there their termelesse time in pleasure *spend;* . . . *H.H.L.* 75
spend His plenteous vaine in setting forth her prayse, . . . *H.H.B.* 219
Spending. *Spending* his daies in dolour and despaire, . . . IV. vii. 43. 2
Spending their joyous dayes and gladfull nights, . . . V. iii. 40. 2
Spends. *spends* her time of sleepe In songs . . . *S.C.* Au. 184
in his Princes service *spends* his dayes, . . . *Hub.* 773
spends his wit in loves consuming smart: . . . *Col.* 429
Spent. *See* **Overspent, Spend.**
having his wide wings *spent* in wast, . . . *Ro.* xvi. 7
When Winters wastful spight was almost *spent,* . . . *S.C.* Ja. 2
So long I shott, that al was *spent;* . . . *S.C.* Mar. 88
their time, that should be sparely *spent,* . . . *S.C.* May 41
what they *spent* in cost, . . . *S.C.* May 69
Thrise three Moones bene fully *spent* and past; . . . *S.C.* S. 20
my poore Muse hath *spent* her spared store, . . . *S.C.* O. 9
Her vitall threde so soone was *spent.* . . . *S.C.* N. 149
My spring is *spent,* . . . *S.C.* D. 128
yeares . . . have *spent* and worne In meane regard, . . . *Hub.* 59
late in warres have *spent* my deerest blood, . . . *Hub.* 247
To loose good dayes, that might be better *spent;* . . . *Hub.* 897
by my foes are now all *spent* and gone; . . . *Ti.* 88
spent his vitall spirite, . . . *Ti.* 382
all his yongthly forces idly *spent,* . . . *Mui.* 431
my voyce is *spent* with crying; . . . *D.* 414
On her he *spent* the riches of his wit: . . . *As.* 62
At last, when paine his vitall powres had *spent,* . . . *As.* 173
former dayes Had in rude fields bene altogether *spent,* . . . *Col.* 669
now day is *spent:* . . . I. i. 33. 6
faire Hesperus . . . Had *spent* his lampe, . . . I. ii. 6. 7
When all this speech the living tree had *spent,* . . . I. ii. 44. 5
The day is *spent;* and commeth drowsie night, . . . I. iii. 15. 1
all the way they *spent* Discoursing . . . I. iii. 32. 6
After long labours and adventures *spent,* . . . I. vi. 30. 2
all her witt in secret counsels *spent,* . . . I. vi. 32. 5
'Tempestuous fortune hath *spent* all her spight, . . . I. vii. 25. 1
All night she *spent* in bidding of her bedes, . . . I. x. 3. 8
double quite for that he on them *spent;* . . . I. x. 37. 7
Till she repaired have her tackles *spent,* . . . I. xii. 42. 6
In these sad wordes she *spent* her utmost breath: . . . II. i. 49. 4
Night was far *spent;* . . . II. ii. 46. 1
They wist their houre was *spent;* . . . II. ii. 46. 9
Therein I have (* have I) *spent* all my youthly daies, . . . II. iii. 38. 4
Diverse discourses in their way they *spent;* . . . II. vi. 9. 1
by this Cymochles howre was *spent,* . . . II. vi. 27. 1
Great heapes of gold that never could be *spent;* . . . II. vii. 5. 2
And after *spent* with pride and lavishnesse, . . . II. vii. 12. 4
as in scorne of his *spent* stormy spight, . . . II. viii. 48. 6
when the oyle is *spent,* The light goes out, . . . II. x. 30. 1
Untill he quite had *spent* his perlous store, . . . II. xi. 27. 8
having all their substance *spent* . . . II. xii. 7. 6
spent their looser daies in leud delightes, . . . II. xii. 9. 5
Which *spent* in vaine, at last she told her briefe, . . . III. i. 53. 4
th' eternall lampes . . . were halfe *yspent,* . . . III. i. 57. 7
Of warlike puissaunce in ages *spent,* . . . III. ii. 3. 1
till all their warlike puissaunce be *spent.* . . . III. iii. 40. 9
Yet is the stocke not lessened nor *spent,* . . . III. vi. 36. 3
All that same evening she in flying *spent,* . . . III. vii. 2. 1
having through incessant traveill *spent* His force, . . . III. vii. 3. 6
the night was forward *spent,* . . . III. ix. 11. 3
all the while that he these speeches *spent,* . . . III. ix. 52. 1
now the humid night was farforth *spent,* . . . III. ix. 53. 4
Laught at his foolish labour *spent* in waste, . . . III. x. 13. 4
as if their springs of life were *spent;* . . . IV. ii. 18. 4
cared not to spare that should be shortly *spent.* . . . IV. iii. 6. 9
Till th' heat of his fierce furie he had *spent;* . . . IV. iii. 26. 5
when the floud is *spent,* then backe againe, . . . IV. iii. 27. 6
theire daies they *spent* In perfect love, . . . IV. iii. 52. 1
when all her speeches she had *spent,* . . . IV. vi. 46. 1
all that evening . . . they together *spent;* . . . IV. viii. 28. 2
till she had all her poyson *spent.* . . . IV. viii. 35. 9
after many teares and sorrowes *spent,* . . . IV. viii. 64. 6

Spent—*Continued.*
rest themselves for to recover spirits *spent*. . . . . IV. ix. 25. 9
my daies I have not lewdly *spent*, ... VI. ii. 31. 1
When day is *spent*, and rest us needeth most, ... VI. iii. 39. 2
Having *spent* all her mastes and her ground-hold, ... VI. iv. 1. 2
So that he now has almost *spent* his spright, ... VI. v. 17. 5
There they awhile some gracious speaches *spent*, ... VI. v. 24. 6
whylest all the night was *spent*. . . . . VI. vi. 44. 7
untill the flying day Was farre forth *spent*, ... VI. ix. 12. 6
spent my youth in vaine, ... VI. ix. 25. 4
In such discourses they together *spent* Long time, ... VI. x. 30. 1
griefe . . . *spent* it selfe in mourning, ... VI. xi. 34. 2
When my abodes prefixed time is *spent*, ... *Am.* xlvi. 1
one yeare is *spent*: . . . . *Am.* lx. 6
That little, that I am, shall all be *spent* . . . . *Am.* lxxxii. 11
Speranza. Fidelia and *Speranza*, virgins were; . . . . I. x. 4. 6
Her younger sister, that *Speranza* hight, ... I. x. 14. 1
wise *Speranza* gave him comfort sweet, ... I. x. 22. 1
Sperre, -d. *See* **Spar, -red.**
Spersed. *sperst* these cloudes; . . . . *Bel.*^{2} viii. 13
sperst in the aire The weake foundations . . . . *Bel.*^{2} xiv. 13
He, making speedy way through *spersed* ayre, ... I. i. 39. 1
faire Sunne hath *sperst* that lowring clowd, ... I. iv. 48. 1
broke his sword in twaine, and all his armour *sperst*. . . . V. iii. 37. 9
Spew. His wide Abysse him forced forth to *spewe*, ... *Van.* v. 10
Spewed. she *spewd* out of her filthie maw . . . . I. i. 20. 1
most like a brutish beast, He *spued* up his gorge, ... I. iv. 21. 9
Spews. spightfull poison *spues* . . . on all that ever writt. . . I. iv. 32. 7
Sphere. extend Her lofty towres unto the starry *sphere*, . . . I. x. 56. 8
within the Moones fayre shining *spheare*, ... II. Pr. 3. 6
cleane without his usuall *spheere* to fare; . . . . VII. vii. 52. 4
Mars in three-score yeares doth run his *spheare*. . . . . . . *Am.* lx. 4
The *spheare* of Cupid fourty yeares containes: . . . . *Am.* lx. 10
Spheres. Emongst th' eternall *spheres* and lamping sky, . . . III. iii. 1. 3
search the courses of the rowling *spheares*, ... V. Pr. 5. 2
is miscaried with the other *Spheares*: . . . . V. Pr. 7. 4
the sundry motions of your *Spheares*, ... VII. vii. 55. 1
in course of heavenly *spheares* are skild, ... *Am.* lx. 1
mightie bound which doth embrace The rolling *Spheres*, . . . *H.H.L.* 26
That need no Sunne t' illuminate their *spheres*, ... *H.H.B.* 69
Spheres'. The Starres pure light, the *Spheres* swift movement, . *T.M.* 508
Spials. privy *spyals* plast in all his way, ... II. i. 4. 3
Spicery. With balme, and wine, and costly *spicery*, ... II. xi. 49. 4
cheared well with wine and *spiceree*: . . . . III. i. 42. 5
Lapped in flowres and pretious *spycery*, ... III. vi. 46. 5
Spices. daintie *spices* fetch from furthest Ynd, ... I. v. 4. 6
Spider. Strove with a *Spider* his unequall peare; . . . . *Van.* vi. 5
the *Spyder*, that doth lurke In close awayt, ... *Am.* lxxi. 3
peace shall see Betweene the *Spyder* and the gentle Bee. . . *Am.* lxxi. 14
Spider's. To see their thrids so thin as *spiders* frame, ... IV. ii. 50. 8
Such labour like the *Spyders* web I fynd, ... *Am.* xxiii. 13
Spiders. some like Snailes, some did like *spyders* shew, ... II. xi. 13. 3
Spied. at the last, and in short time, I *spide* (*spied*[1]), ... *Pet.* i. 10
Spide where the Eagle built his towring nest, ... *Van.* iv. 6
No: but happely I hym *spyde*, ... *S.C.* Mar. 31
the Foxe him *spyed*; . . . . *S.C.* May 253
the shepheard his practise *spyed*, ... *S.C.* S. 202
when as at last he *spide*, ... *Gn.* 266
He *spide* his foe with felonous intent, ... *Gn.* 295
they *spide*, how, in a gloomy glade, ... *Hub.* 951
if he be *spide*, ... *Hub.* 975
through the watchmen, who him never *spide*: . . . . *Hub.* 1302
him at last the Lyon *spide*, and caught, ... *Hub.* 1375
where other sights I *spide*. . . . . *Ti.* 588
when he *spide* the joyous Butterflie . . . . *Mui.* 249
So finely sponne that scarce they could be *spide*. . . . . . *Mui.* 360
having *spide* Where . . . the Lambes doo play, ... *Mui.* 401
I *spied* playing on the grassie playne . . . . *D.* 110
A shadie grove not farr away they *spide*, ... I. i. 7. 2
when him he *spide* Spurring so hote with rage . . . . I. ii. 15. 1
she has A damzel *spyde*, slow footing her before, ... I. iii. 10. 8
she him *spyde*, By his like seeming shield . . . . I. iii. 26. 5
the shamed shield of slaine Sansfoy He *spide* . . . . I. iv. 39. 2
his wary Dwarfe had *spyde* . . . . I. v. 45. 7
of no envious eyes he mote be *spyde*; . . . . I. v. 52. 8
A Donghill of dead carcases he *spyde*; . . . . I. v. 53. 8
when the knight he *spyde*, he gan advaunce . . . . I. vii. 11. 1
Which when the Gyaunt *spyde* with staring eye, ... I. viii. 19. 6
Whose grievous fall when false Duessa *spyde*, ... I. viii. 25. 1
so soone as day he *spyde*, ... I. xi. 52. 5
it may soone be *spide*, ... II. iii. 41. 8
far away they *spyde* A varlet . . . . II. iv. 37. 1
on the plaine fast pricking Guyon *spide* One . . . . II. v. 2. 2
Atin, arriving there, when him he *spyde* . . . . II. v. 35. 1
Upon that shore he *spyed* Atin stand, ... II. vi. 38. 7
he *spide* where towards him did pace . . . . II. viii. 10. 1
spyde where towards them did pace An armed knight, ... II. viii. 17. 4
at last, when he advantage *spyde*, ... II. viii. 36. 2
when the Paynym *spyde* the streaming blood, ... II. viii. 39. 3
the Palmer . . . he by him *spyde*, ... II. viii. 53. 6
Whenas they *spide* a goodly castle, ... II. ix. 10. 3
when they *spyde* the knight to slacke his pace . . . . II. xii. 68. 4
They *spide* a knight that towards pricked . . . . III. i. 4. 2
A stately Castle far away she *spyde*, ... III. i. 20. 2
she *spyde* Where far away one, all in armour bright, ... III. iv. 12. 1
The goodly Maide . . . he by him *spide*, ... III. v. 34. 8
*When walking through the Gardin, them she *spyde*, ... III. vi. 40. 6
He *spide* far off a mighty Giauntesse . . . . III. vii. 37. 2
which when he *spyde*, His mighty speare he couched . . . . III. vii. 38. 6
having *spide* on hight An Eagle . . . . III. vii. 39. 2

Spied—*Continued.*
he *spyde* whereas that wofull Squyre, ... III. vii. 45. 6
she backe retourning *spyde* . . . . III. viii. 2. 6
They *spyde* a knight fayre pricking on the playne, ... III. viii. 44. 7
Whom such whenas Malbecco *spyed* clere, ... III. x. 23. 4
They *spide* where Paridell came pricking fast . . . . III. x. 35. 2
twixt her eielids closely *spyde* . . . . III. xi. 32. 8
she *spyde* at that rowmes upper end . . . . III. xi. 54. 6
they *spide* Two armed Knights . . . . IV. i. 17. 1
Which faire adventure when Cambello *spide*, ... IV. iii. 20. 1
they *spyde* with speedie whirling pace, ... IV. iii. 38. 3
They *spide* a little cottage, ... IV. v. 32. 9
A Knight soft ryding towards them they *spyde*, ... IV. vi. 9. 2
A litle cotage farre away they *spide*, ... IV. viii. 23. 2
spide where towards them with speed A Squire . . . . IV. viii. 38. 1
at the last I *spide* within the same . . . . IV. x. 11. 7
I *spyde* where at the Idoles feet apart . . . . IV. x. 48. 7
soone as they him nigh approching *spide*, ... V. ii. 53. 1
he *spide* A rout of many people farre away; . . . . V. iv. 21. 2
by chaunce hath *spide* A Goshauke, ... V. iv. 42. 3
having *spyde* in sight A gentle Faulcon . . . . V. v. 15. 1
she *spide* One comming towards her . . . . V. vi. 8. 1
Whom soone as Talus *spide* . . . . V. vi. 29. 5
Untill she *spide* the lampe of lightsome day . . . . V. vii. 17. 3
'sith ye so well have *spide* The troublous passion . . . . . V. vii. 19. 1
as he nigher drew, three knights he *spyde*, ... V. x. 34. 1
They *spide* a Lady left all succourlesse, ... V. xi. 44. 7
a Knight He *spide* come pricking on . . . . VI. i. 32. 9
he *spyde* A tall young man, ... VI. ii. 3. 6
yet him no where he *spyde*. . . . . VI. v. 3. 9
he *spide* a Knight approching nye; . . . . VI. v. 22. 1
gentle Prince not farre away they *spyde*, ... VI. vii. 6. 7
when he *spyde* The traytour Turpin . . . . VI. vii. 25. 1
Soone as they *spide* her, Lord! what gladfull glee . . . . . VI. viii. 37. 1
a woman spoyld of all attire He *spyde* . . . . VI. viii. 48. 6
he *spyde* upon the earth t' encroch, ... VI. xi. 47. 3
how all creatures laught when her they *spide* . . . . VII. vii. 34. 7
Spies. with cruell *spies* Does seeke to perce; . . . . I. ii. 17. 5
a greedy Wolfe, . . . A Lyon *spyes* . . . . I. vi. 10. 6
when him ronning in full course he *spyes*, ... II. v. 10. 5
with her two crafty *spyes* She secretly would search . . . . . III. i. 36. 5
Nor brasen walls, nor many wakefull *spyes*, ... III. ix. 7. 5
spies him toward bend His dreadfull souse, ... IV. iii. 19. 5
Sate with a knight . . . free from all gealous *spyes*. . . . . VI. ii. 16. 6
closely tempted with their craftie *spyes*; . . . . VI. viii. 43. 4
Spill. Till that Barbarian hands it quite did *spill*, ... *Ro.* xxx. 10
wouldest me my springing youngth to *spil*: . . . . *S.C.* F. 52
all the rest did *spill*. . . . . *S.C.* Jul. 68
The while the shepheard selfe did *spill*. . . . . *S.C.* Au. 60
To *spil* the flowres that should her girlond dight? . . . . . *S.C.* D. 114
Bid strange mischance his quietnes to *spill*. . . . . *Gn.* 248
his vowed life to *spill* For Countreyes health, ... *Gn.* 603
that disguised Dog lov'd blood to *spill*, ... *Hub.* 319
the best speaches with ill meaning *spill*. . . . . *Hub.* 716
Who then can save what they dispose to *spill*? . . . . *Mui.* 232
spight it selfe, that all good things doth *spill*, ... *As.* 23
his water-courses *spill*. . . . . *Col.* 151
Like as himselfe us pleaseth save or *spill*. . . . . *Col.* 814
Her selfe a yielded pray to save or *spill*: . . . . I. iii. 43. 4
your faire beautie doe with sadnes *spill*? . . . . II. ix. 37. 6
many drops of milk and blood through it did *spill*. . . . . III. ii. 49. 9
Badd her commaund my life to save or *spill*. . . . . III. vii. 54. 2
ne car'd to *spill* Her garments gay . . . . III. viii. 26. 8
Ne either cared life to save or *spill*, ... IV. iii. 36. 6
all his former praise doth fowly *spill*: . . . . V. vi. 1. 5
by traytrous traines to *spill* Her person, ... V. viii. 19. 3
As it is greater prayse to save then *spill*, ... V. x. 2. 8
could or save or *spill* whom she would hight: . . . . VI. vii. 31. 8
that same would *spill* The Wood-gods breed, ... VII. vi. 50. 3
Least, trembling, it his workmanship should *spill*; . . . . . *Am.* xvii. 7
she can it save or *spill*. To *spill* were pitty, ... *Am.* xxxviii. 11, 12
And greater glory thinke, to save then *spill*. . . . . *Am.* xlix. 4
pride dare not approch, nor discord *spill* The league . . . . *Am.* lxv. 9
Spilled. With point of steele that close his hartbloud *spild*, . . IV. iii. 22. 5
all his vitall spirites thereby *spild*, ... IV. vii. 31. 8
Spilling. blam'd for *spilling* guiltlesse blood. . . . . *Am.* xxviii. 14
Spills. Oft *spilles* the principall to save the part; . . . . . . V. x. 2. 4
A distaffe . . . Upon the which she litle spinnes, but *spils*; . . V. xii. 36. 7
with one looke she *spils* that long I sponne; . . . . *Am.* xxiii. 11
Spilt. the Troyan prince *spilt* Turnus blood . . . . *Bel.*^{2} ix. 8
blood, the which at first was *spilt* . . . . *Ro.* xxiv. 12
for secret crime thy blood hast *spilt*.' . . . . *D.* 84
staind with blood Which he had *spilt*, ... I. iv. 34. 2
Shall with his owne blood price that he hath *spilt*. . . . . . I. v. 26. 4
Altare, . . . On which trew Christians blood was often *spilt*, . I. viii. 36. 3
blood, which cruelly was *spilt* On cursed tree, ... I. x. 57. 5
young Hectors blood by cruell Greekes was *spilt*. . . . . . . II. ix. 45. 9
all the others pavement were with yvory *spilt*. . . . . IV. x. 5. 9
Nor *spilt* the blossome of my tender yeares . . . . VI. ii. 31. 2
Spin. *See* **Span.**
More subtile web Arachne cannot *spin*; . . . . II. xii. 77. 7
To *spin*, to card, to sew, to wash, ... V. iv. 31. 6
he thereon should *spin* both flax and tow; . . . . V. v. 23. 3
Spinning. *Spinning* and carding all in comely rew, ... V. v. 22. 4
Spins. nether *spinnes* nor cards, ne cares nor fretts, ... II. vi. 16. 8
A distaffe . . . Upon the which she litle *spinnes*, ... V. xii. 36. 7
Spio. Soft *Spio*, sweete Endore, Sao sad, ... IV. xi. 48. 8
Spire. a sharped *spyre* (*spire*[1]) of Diamond . . . . *Bel.* iii. 1
flames . . . Gathered in one up to the heavens to *spyre*, . . . *Ro.* xvi. 10
looked from the highest *spire* The watch, ... II. ix. 11. 6

Spire—*Continued.*
it fayrest Flowre doth *spyre,* . . . . III. v. 52. 8
Spires. Triumphant Arcks, *spyres,* neighbours to the skie, . . *Ro.* vii. 5
Spirit. Doth vex my *spirite* with perplexitie, ... *Pet.*[2] ii. 12
my free *spirite* might not . . . Be vext . . . . *Pet.*[2] vii. 7
her great *spirite* . . . is in the same enwombed; . . . . *Ro.* v. 10
rejoyned to the *spirite* Of this great masse, ... *Ro.* v. 10
By paterne of great Virgils *spirit* divine! . . . . *Ro.* xxv. 11
My *spirit* shaking off her earthly prison, ... *Van.* i. 2
streight the *spirite* out of his senses flew, ... *Gn.* 292
Bold sure he was, and worthie *spirite* bore, ... *Gn.* 437
All were my *spirite* heavie and diseased, ... *Hub.* 40
In his chiefe parts, that is, in wit and *spirite;* . . . . *Hub.* 1043
that same gentle *Spirit,* . . . . *T.M.* 217
I, whose joy was earst with *Spirit* full . . . . *T.M.* 289
'Most gentle *spirite,* breathed from above . . . . *Ti.* 281
'His blessed *spirite,* full of power divine . . . . *Ti.* 288
'O noble *spirite!* live there ever blessed, ... *Ti.* 302
Thereto doo thou my humble *spirite* raise, ... *Ti.* 313
spent his vitall *spirite,* . . . . *Ti.* 382
griefe thereof my *spirite* greatly pained. . . . . *Ti.* 560
Immortall *spirite* of Philisides, ... *Ti.* 673
soft death away her *spirit* hent, ... *D.* 258
That Mantuane Poetes incompared *spirit,* . . . . *Ded. Son.* xiii. 1
Remembraunce of that most Heroicke *spirit,* . . . . *Ded. Son.* xv. 1
infinite desire into your *spirite* poure. . . . . II. ix. 3. 9
More ample *spirit* then hitherto was wount . . . . II. x. 1. 6
aery *spirite* under false pretence, ... II. xi. 39. 8
breathed forth sweet *spirit* and holesom smell: . . . . II. xii. 51. 9
then his *spirite* thus gan foorth display: . . . . III. iii. 21. 5
from the wearie *spirit* thou doest drive Desired rest, ... III. iv. 57. 8
a quicke moving *Spirit* did arret . . . . III. viii. 7. 3
From her high *spirit* chase imperious feare, ... IV. Pr. 5. 3
Then pardon, O most sacred happie *spirit!* . . . . IV. ii. 34. 1
infusion sweete Of thine owne *spirit* . . . . IV. ii. 34. 7
poysnous *spirit* sent From inward parts, ... IV. viii. 26. 3
feeble *spirit* inly felt refection: . . . . IV. xii. 34. 5
he, whose *spirit* was with pride upblowne, ... V. i. 17. 5
pangs of death her *spirit* overtooke. . . . . V. v. 11. 5
Looke up at last, and wake thy dulled *spirit* . . . . V. v. 36. 8
all, in his revenge, of *spirite* would deprive. . . . . V. vii. 36. 9
guyded through th' ayrie wyde By some bad *spirit* . . . . V. viii. 34. 7
still his *spirite* spar'd, ... VI. i. 20. 6
through the wound his *spirit* shortly did depart.' . . . . VI. ii. 12. 9
This litle babe, of . . . spotlesse *spirit* . . . . VI. iv. 35. 5
gathering *spirit* of her natures pride, ... VII. vi. 26. 2
my fraile *spirit* . . . Lift up aloft, ... VII. viii. 1. 3
with subtill influence Of his thin *spirit* . . . . VII. vii. 22. 4
kindled heavenly fyre In my fraile *spirit,* . . . . *Am.* iii. 4
a proud love, that doth my *spirite* spoyle. . . . . *Am.* xxxiii. 12
when my *spirit* doth spred her bolder winges, ... *Am.* lxxii. 1
By whom my *spirit* out of dust was raysed: . . . . *Am.* lxxiv. 10
Deriv'd from that fayre *Spirit,* . . . . *Am.* lxxix. 11
My *spirit* to an higher pitch will rayse, ... *Am.* lxxx. 12
So every *spirit,* as it is most pure, ... *H.B.* 127
O most blessed *Spirit!* pure lampe of light, ... *H.H.L.* 43
Nor *spirit,* nor Angell, though they man surpas, ... *H.H.L.* 143
whilest so thy softened *spirit* Is inly toucht, ... *H.H.L.* 253
Then shalt thou feele thy *spirit* so possest, ... *H.H.L.* 267
A gentle *spirit,* that lightly did delay . . . . *Proth.* 3
Spirit's. As overcomen of the *spirites* powre, ... III. iii. 50. 2
with his *spirits* proportion to agree, ... *H.B.* 227
Spirits. Ye heavenly *spirites,* whose ashie cinders lie . . . . *Ro.* i. 1
With which he had those Romane *spirits* fild, ... *Ro.* xi. 6
Ye pallid *spirits,* and ye ashie ghoasts, ... *Ro.* xv. 1
Tell me, ye *spirits,* . . . . *Ro.* xv. 5
All that doth feede our *spirits* and our eies, ... *Ro.* xix. 3
Live, happie *spirits,* th' honour of your name, ... *Ro.* Env. 13
hath his jawes with angrie *spirits* rent, ... *Gn.* 278
livelie *spirits* of each living wight, ... *T.M.* 254
My *spirits* now dismayd with sorrow dull . . . . *T.M.* 291
Ye gentle *Spirits,* breathing from above, ... *T.M.* 361
The *Spirites* and Intelligences fayre, ... *T.M.* 509
wandring *spirits* walke untimely howres. . . . . *D.* 336
heavenly *spirits* have compassion On mortall men, ... *D.* 384
feeble *spirits* in their force maintaine, ... *D.* 438
And is there love In heavenly *spirits* . . . . II. vii. 1. 2
from her womb new *spirits* to reprize. . . . . II. xi. 44. 9
let her with the damned *spirits* dwell, ... III. iv. 60. 8
with vaine hope his *spirits* faint supply, ... III. x. 26. 7
restore His weakned powers, and dulled *spirits* whet, ... IV. iii. 24. 4
mighty *spirites* bound with mightier band, ... IV. iii. 48. 7
haughtie *spirits* meekely to adaw, ... IV. vi. 26. 8
all his vitall *spirites* thereby spild, ... IV. vii. 31. 8
rest themselves for to recover *spirits* spent. . . . . IV. ix. 25. 9
in their *spirits* kindling zealous fire, ... IV. x. 26. 8
lively *spirits* deaded quight: . . . . IV. xii. 20. 2
feeble *spirits,* that gan faint and reele, ... V. x. 20. 5
wondrous joy felt in her *spirits* thrall: . . . . VI. xi. 44. 5
life-full *spirits* privily doth powre . . . . *H.B.* 52
when the vitall *spirits* doe expyre, ... *H.B.* 102
it then tooke light And lively *spirits* . . . . *H.B.* 111
thy *spirits* shall fill With sweete enragement . . . . *H.H.L.* 285
Spiritual. it doth come to fight Against *spirituall* foes, ... I. x. 1. 4
His mind was full of *spiritual* repast, ... I. x. 48. 8
Spit. 'Come daughter, come; come, *spit* upon my face; . . . III. ii. 50. 7
Spitt thrise upon me, thrise upon me *spitt;* . . . . III. ii. 50. 8
Spite. In *spight* of time out of the dust doth reare, ... *Ro.* v. 13
Nor wrath of Gods, nor *spight* of men unstable, ... *Ro.* xiii. 7
sowing in th' Aemathian fields thy *spight,* . . . . *Ro.* xxxi. 10

Spite—*Continued.*
When Winters wastful *spight* was almost spent, ... *S.C.* Ja. 2
to worke me more *spight;* . . . . *S.C.* F. 180
now I see thou speakest of *spight,* . . . . *S.C.* May 55
false Fortune such joy did him *spight,* . . . . *S.C.* May 198
that wrought so deadly *spight.* . . . . *S.C.* Jun. 101
the more bene fraight with fraud and *spight,* . . . . *S.C.* S. 84
death, and dreaded sisters deadly *spight,* . . . . *S.C.* N. 163
who has wrought my Rosalind this *spight,* . . . . *S.C.* D. 113
lying all at ease from guile or *spight,* . . . . *Gn.* 111
yeeld (for *spight*) Store of firebronds . . . . *Gn.* 507
yet *spite* bites neare. . . . . *Hub.* 424
The fatall Sisters, did for *spight* destroy, ... *T.M.* 16
Feareles through his own fault or Fortunes *spight* . . . . *T.M.* 303
Blind Error, scornefull Follie, and base *Spight,* . . . . *T.M.* 317
How ever yet they mee despise and *spight,* . . . . *T.M.* 523
Spite bites the dead, that living never baid. . . . . *Ti.* 215
In *spight* of envie that his deeds would spot: . . . . *Ti.* 439
all those flowres, . . . that bred her *spight,* . . . . *Mui.* 141
The shame of Nature, the bondslave of *spight,* . . . . *Mui.* 245
with fell *spight,* Under the left wing stroke his weapon . . *Mui.* 436
spight it selfe, that all good things doth spill, ... *As.* 23
old Palemon free from *spight* . . . . *Col.* 396
it seemes of *spight* Thou speakest thus . . . . *Col.* 676
love with foule disdainefull *spight* He would not shend; . . . I. i. 53. 7
With . . . disdaineful *spight* Her vildly entertaines; . . . . I. iii. 43. 6
each others greater pride does *spight.* . . . . I. iv. 14. 9
From dreaded storme of his disdainfull *spight:* . . . . I. iv. 48. 4
'Tempestuous fortune hath spent all her *spight,* . . . . I. vii. 25. 1
The proud Duessa, full of wrathfull *spight,* . . . . I. viii. 13. 1
object of his *spight* And deadly food he makes: . . . . II. i. 3. 1
Against themselves turning their wrathfull *spight,* . . . . II. ii. 23. 6
hath (maugre her *spight*) thus low me laid in dust.' . . . . II. v. 12. 9
more to augment his *spight,* . . . . II. v. 22. 5
calme the sea of their tempestuous *spight.* . . . . II. vi. 36. 4
Kindled through his infernall brond of *spight,* . . . . II. vi. 50. 5
no way is lefte to wreake my *spight,* . . . . II. viii. 15. 6
Making advauntage, to revenge their *spight,* . . . . II. viii. 25. 2
as in scorne of his spent stormy *spight,* . . . . II. viii. 48. 6
Pourd out their plenty without *spight* or spare. . . . . III. i. 51. 4
Late foule dishonour and reprochfull *spight,* . . . . III. ii. 8. 8
Such happinesse did, maulgre, to me *spight,* . . . . III. v. 7. 5
though *spite* did oft assay To blot her with dishonor . . . . IV. i. 4. 8
fell those two in *spight* of both their prydes; . . . . IV. i. 42. 7
To stirre up strife twixt love and *spight* and ire, ... IV. ii. 11. 8
gan therefore close *spight* to him to beare; . . . . IV. ii. 26. 5
she her selfe did thinke it doen for *spight,* . . . . IV. v. 17. 3
She came of her accord, in *spight* of all his fone. . . . . IV. v. 26. 9
Ne private jarre, ne *spite* of enemis, ... IV. ix. 16. 3
when as fortune all her *spight* hath showne, ... V. iii. 1. 3
both Knights envide, and Ladies eke did *spight.* . . . . V. vi. 6. 9
all in *spight* and malice did agree; . . . . VI. i. 9. 4
far from envious eyes that mote him *spight;* . . . . VI. iii. 20. 7
Or house to hide his head from heavens *spight,* . . . . VI. iv. 39. 4
To weary him the more and waste his *spight,* . . . . VI. v. 17. 4
In cancred malice and revengefull *spight:* . . . . VI. vii. 1. 4
they both at once with equall *spight* Did bend . . . . VI. vii. 7. 4
nought abating of his former *spight,* . . . . VI. vii. 10. 5
Firme Chastity, that *spight* ne blemish dare: . . . . VI. x. 27. 5
spitting forth the poyson of his *spight* . . . . VI. xii. 29. 5
Bellona, whose great glory thou doost *spight,* . . . . VII. vi. 32. 5
need not feare the *spight* Of grudging foes, ... *Am.* lix. 9
Spiteful. Him when the *spitefull* brere had espyed, ... *S.C.* F. 147
spightfull poison spues . . . on all that ever writt. . . . . I. iv. 32. 7
thy cruell wrath and *spightfull* wrong . . . . III. iv. 8. 7
Now with remembrance of those *spightfull* speaches, . . . IV. ii. 12. 2
Her *spightfull* words did pricke and wound . . . . IV. viii. 26. 9
she did not her *spightfull* speach forbeare, ... IV. viii. 36. 2
With *spightfull* speaches, fitting with her well; . . . . V. v. 10. 4
Which *spitefull* words she . . . Thus answer'd: . . . . V. vii. 32. 7
poysoned words and *spitefull* speeches . . . . *Am.* lxxxv. 4
Spitefulest. nor strong nor wise, but *spightfullest,* . . . . VI. v. 13. 9
Spites. scorning both their *spights,* does make wide way, . . . II. ii. 24. 7
how Arlo, through Dianaes *spights,* . . . Was made . . . . VII. vi. 37. 5
Spiting. the heavens unjust, *Spighting* my happie freedome, . V. v. 29. 8
Spitting. *See* **Fire-spitting.**
spitting forth the poyson of his spight . . . . VI. xii. 29. 5
Spleen. many evils moe haunt ire, The swelling *Splene,* . . . I. iv. 35. 7
Splendor. round about such beames of *splendor* threw, . . . VII. vii. 6. 7
Split. he him maymed quite, and all his shoulder *split.* . . . V. iii. 33. 9
Spoil. me the *spoile* and bootie of the world, ... *Bel.*[1] viii. 10
And many a *spoyle* (*spoile*[1]), ... *Bel.* v. 6
on a tree uphang'd I saw her *spoyle.* . . . . *Bel.*[2] vi. 14
The whole worlds *spoile,* . . . . *Bel.*[2] x. 10
death shall *spoyle* your goodly features. . . . . *Pet.*[2] vii. 14
The peoples fable, and the *spoyle* of all: . . . . *Ro.* vii. 8
Nor ruthlesse *spoyle* of souldiers blood-desiring, ... *Ro.* xiii. 3
Harten against her selfe her conquer'd *spoile,* . . . . *Ro.* xxii. 6
Carthage towres from *spoile* should be forborne, ... *Ro.* xxiii. 2
pray of beasts and *spoyle* of living blood, ... *Van.* x. 3
beguile Their greedie mouthes of the expected *spoyle;* . . . *Hub.* 1286
now to nought through *spoyle* of time is wasted. . . . . *Ti.* 119
To be the pray of Tyme, and Fortunes *spoyle!* . . . . *Ti.* 516
after greedie *spoyle* of bloud to crave: . . . . *Ti.* 565
reft the *spoyle* his ornament to bee; . . . . *Mui.* 68
To *spoyle* the pleasures of that Paradise; . . . . *Mui.* 186
the world, unworthie such a *spoyle,* . . . . *D.* 163
So rich a *spoile* within his power to see. . . . . *As.* 102
The which art of so rich a *spoile* possest, ... *Col.* 553
Hath fild sad Belgicke with victorious *spoile;* . . . . *Ded. Son.* xiv. 10

Spoil—*Continued.*
raging *spoile* of lawlesse victors will? . . . I. iii. 43. 2
And win rich *spoile* of ransackt chastitee. . . . I. vi. 5. 5
spoile her of her scarlot robe, and let her fly.' . . . I. viii. 45. 9
to *spoyle* the Castle of his health?' . . . I. ix. 31. 2
Here hauntes that feend, and does his dayly *spoyle;* . . . I. xi. 2. 3
sonne of Mars, that seeke with warlike *spoyle,* . . . II. i. 8. 7
To *spoyle* her dainty corps, so faire and sheene . . . II. i. 10. 5
made to *spoile* Themselves of soiled armes, . . . II. ii. 33. 7
all in blood and *spoile* is his delight. . . . II. iv. 42. 4
gay *spoile,* sure hast thou gott, . . . II. iv. 45. 6
his frayle eye with *spoyle* of beauty feedes: . . . II. v. 34. 3
spoile the treasure there in gard: . . . II. vii. 25. 4
the caytive *spoile* Of that same outcast carcas, . . . II. viii. 12. 4
To *spoile* the dead of weed Is sacrilege, . . . II. viii. 16. 4
Betrayd his countrey unto forreine *spoyle.* . . . II. x. 48. 8
with great *spoile* and rage Forwasted all, . . . II. x. 52. 7
In hope thereof to win victorious *spoile.* . . . II. xi. 7. 5
still sat wayting . . . For *spoile* of wretches, . . . II. xii. 8. 7
the rich wares to save from pitteous *spoyle;* . . . II. xii. 19. 8
bare to ready *spoyle* Of hungry eies, . . . II. xii. 78. 1
their gardins did deface; Their arbers *spoyle;* . . . II. xii. 83. 7
Ne in so glorious *spoile* themselves embosse: . . . III. i. 64. 8
the *spoile* of the countrey conquered . . . III. iii. 47. 8
The *spoyle* of all the world; . . . III. iv. 23. 3
sad instruments Of *spoyle* and murder . . . III. v. 16. 2
yield herselfe to *spoile* of greedinesse: . . . III. vii. 25. 6
Being possessed of that *spoyle,* . . . III. viii. 13. 8
To save her selfe from that outrageous *spoyle;* . . . III. viii. 32. 5
like a Lyon hunting after *spoile;* . . . III. xi. 39. 7
his proud *spoile* of that same dolorous Faire Dame . . . III. xii. 22. 7
spoile of love misgotten, . . . IV. i. 51. 2
good fortune doth to you present So fayre a *spoyle,* . . . IV. ii. 5. 9
that every *spoyle* or pray Should equally be shard . . . IV. ii. 13. 4
of your gotten *spoyle* their owne triumph to make.' . . . IV. ii. 24. 9
by good fortune found some beasts fresh *spoyle,* . . . IV. iii. 16. 2
They *spoile* and ravine without all remorse; . . . IV. iv. 35. 8
Where beauties prize should win that pretious *spoyle:* . . . IV. iv. 48. 8
nought but *spoyle* and vengeance did require: . . . IV. vi. 11. 5
To *spoyle* so goodly workmanship of nature, . . . IV. vi. 17. 4
the relickes of his feast And cruell *spoyle,* . . . IV. vii. 6. 4
on the *spoile* of women he doth live, . . . IV. vii. 12. 5
will not he the lovely *spoile* downe lay, . . . IV. vii. 25. 5
surcharg'd with *spoile* and theft: . . . IV. vii. 32. 5
spoyle to make, and wast them unto nought, . . . IV. viii. 48. 7
divide part of his purchast *spoile.* . . . IV. ix. 12. 9
purchased this peerelesse beauties *spoile,* . . . IV. x. 3. 3
no intreatie would forgoe so glorious *spoyle.* . . . IV. x. 55. 9
That glorious *spoyle* of beautie with me lead, . . . IV. x. 58. 3
greedy seas doe in the *spoile* of life delight. . . . IV. xii. 6. 9
'Then doth he take the *spoile* of them . . . V. ii. 9. 1
The Sarazin, awayting for some *spoile:* . . . V. ii. 11. 3
The *spoile* of peoples evil gotten good, . . . V. ii. 27. 7
The which of all her *spoyle* was onely left; . . . V. iii. 27. 2
in hope to find some *spoyle,* . . . V. ix. 9. 2
glad of *spoyle* and ruinous decay, . . . V. ix. 47. 6
The present of his paines, that Monsters *spoyle,* . . . V. xi. 33. 6
pursew That raskall many with unpitied *spoyle;* . . . V. xi. 65. 2
had reft That piteous *spoile* . . . VI. i. 18. 5
spoile by selfe that can not thee withstand? . . . VI. i. 25. 5
wish that he part of his *spoyle* might share: . . . VI. ii. 17. 3
fortune hath this day Given to me the *spoile* . . . VI. ii. 33. 8
Compeld him soone the *spoyle* adowne to lay. . . . VI. iv. 20. 4
his lovely litle *spoile* Crying for food . . . VI. iv. 25. 7
the conquest of his might, Gotten by *spoyle* . . . VI. v. 9. 5
seem'd the *spoile* of some right well renownd: . . . VI. v. 25. 5
hanging up his armes and warlike *spoyle,* . . . VI. v. 37. 8
triumphest in the piteous *spoile* . . . VI. vi. 25. 3
taketh vengeaunce of his peoples *spoile;* . . . VI. viii. 23. 2
nation, which did live Of stealth and *spoile,* . . . VI. viii. 35. 3
first they *spoile* her of her jewels deare, . . . VI. viii. 41. 2
ready now to rend His loves deare *spoile,* . . . VI. x. 35. 8
fed on *spoile* and booty, . . . VI. x. 39. 5
Now made the *spoile* of theeves . . . VI. x. 40. 7
Her selfe sole left a second *spoyle* to bee . . . VI. xi. 23. 3
all unwares, and take the *spoyle* away; . . . VI. xi. 38. 6
when he wrapped found Th' abandond *spoyle,* . . . VI. xii. 9. 5
She in the open fields had loosely layd To fortunes *spoile,* . . . VI. xii. 16. 5
Him follow'd by the tract of his outragious *spoile.* . . . VI. xii. 22. 9
such *spoile,* such havocke, and such theft . . . VI. xii. 23. 4
Thieves should rob and *spoile* that Coast around: . . . VII. vi. 55. 6
heavy laden with the *spoyle* Of harvests riches, . . . VII. vii. 38. 2
Of my poore life to make unpittied *spoile.* . . . *Am.* xi. 8
both the Indias of their treasure *spoile;* . . . *Am.* xv. 3
a proud love, that doth my spirite *spoyle.* . . . *Am.* xxxiii. 12
She meanes at last to make her pitious *spoyle.* . . . *Am.* xli. 12
The happy purchase of my glorious *spoile,* . . . *Am.* lxix. 13
On the sweet *spoyle* of beautie they did pray; . . . *Am.* lxxvi. 8
thou doest *spoyle* of lovers make.' . . . *Epig.* iv. 40
adorning it with *spoyle* Of th' heavenly riches . . . *H.B.* 118

Spoiled. Of all the world was *spoyl'd* within a while: . . . *Ro.* xxii. 8
spoyld of Charon too and fro am tost. . . . *Gn.* 339
She *spoyld* thereof, and filled with annoy. . . . *As.* 162
'His blessed body, *spoild* of lively breath, . . . I. ii. 24. 1
spoild the Priests of their habiliments; . . . I. iii. 17. 7
Dragon . . . Their kingdome *spoild,* and countrey wasted quight: . . . I. vii. 44. 5
her Prince Arthur of . . . borrowd beauty *spoyld.* . . . II. i. 22. 7
Spoild of their rosy red were woxen pale . . . III. v. 29. 9
To see so faire thinges mard and *spoiled* quight; . . . III. vi. 40. 2

Spoiled—*Continued.*
Rather then see her people *spoiled* quight, . . . V. iv. 47. 8
The infant, so for want of nourture *spoyld;* . . . V. v. 53. 4
was bearing her apace For to have *spoyled* her, . . . VI. iii. 25. 3
a woman *spoyld* of all attire . . . VI. viii. 48. 5
spoyld their houses, and them selves did murder, . . . VI. x. 39. 8
They *spoyld* old Melibee of all he had, . . . VI. x. 40. 2
saw his shepheards cottage *spoyled* quight, . . . VI. xi. 25. 2
Spoyld all our cots, and caried us from hence; . . . VI. xi. 30. 5

Spoilful. Those *spoylefull* Picts, and swarming Easterlings, II. x. 63. 2

Spoiling. By hunting and by *spoiling* liveden; . . . II. x. 7. 7
spoyling all her geares and goodly ray . . . V. ii. 50. 4
Are met at *spoyling* of some hungry pray, . . . V. vii. 30. 2

Spoils. A trophee of his glittering *spoyles* and treasure, . . . *Gn.* 127
Enricht with *spoyles* of th' Ericthonian towre, . . . *Gn.* 562
freely up those royall *spoyles* he tooke, . . . *Hub.* 1059
with their *spoyles* enlarg'd his private treasures. . . . *Hub.* 1130
spoyles, by salvage beasts committed? . . . *Hub.* 1253
Are heapt with *spoyles* of fortune . . . *T.M.* 161
rich *spoyles,* which late he did purchas . . . *Ti.* 654
heaped *spoyles* of bleeding harts to see, . . . *Mui.* 100
After his murdrous *spoyles* and bloudie rage allayd. . . . I. Pr. 3. 9
glorious *spoiles,* purchast in perilous fight: . . . II. v. 26. 3
more Then all his wars and *spoiles,* . . . II. vi. 35. 9
murdrous *spoiles* and bloody pray, . . . II. viii. 6. 4
with sondrie *spoiles* she hath been ransacked. . . . II. x. 23. 9
with rich *spoyles* and famous victorie . . . II. x. 75. 4
th' amarous sweet *spoiles* to greedy eyes revele. . . . II. xii. 64. 9
with *spoiles* and cruelty Ransackt the world, . . . III. vi. 49. 5
pledges, as the *spoiles* of my victorious games. . . . III. vii. 54. 9
it a part Of her rich *spoyles* . . . III. viii. 2. 8
house of Busyrane, Where loves *spoyles* are exprest. . . . III. xi. Arg.
spoiles wherewith he all the ground did strow, . . . III. xi. 45. 7
the glistring walles were hong With warlike *spoiles* . . . III. xi. 52. 2
shar'd to them the *spoiles* that he had got alive. . . . IV. i. 22. 9
To lay his *spoiles* before his lemans traine: . . . V. viii. 2. 3
He either *spoiles* . . . Or to his part allures, . . . V. viii. 18. 8
The *spoiles* of Princes hang'd which were in battel won. . . . VI. viii. 42. 9
Whom they before in diverse *spoyles* had caught; . . . VI. xi. 11. 3
thence did all the *spoyles* and threasures take, . . . VI. xi. 51. 2

Spoke. *See* **Spake.**
The bold Semiramis . . . her fowle reproches *spoke:* . . . I. v. 50. 4
hearken to the sober speaches which she *spoke.* . . . II. ii. 28. 9
those unknightly raylinges which he *spoke,* . . . II. vi. 30. 6
They forward passe; ne Guyon yet *spoke* word, . . . II. vii. 31. 1
Thus as he *spoke,* . . . II. ix. 13. 1
never word from that day forth he *spoke.* . . . V. iii. 33. 5
whether what he *spoke* Were soothly so, . . . VI. ii. 13. 7
Altars fouled, and blasphemy *spoke,* . . . VI. xii. 25. 3

Spoken. At everie thing which they heare *spoken* ill, . . . *Hub.* 715
(may it be withouten perill *spoken?*) . . . *Mui.* 97
oft I heard it *spoken,* How one, . . . *Col.* 919
the vertues rare Which thereof *spoken* were, . . . III. ii. 22. 8
first was *spoken* by th' Almighty Lord, . . . III. vi. 34. 5
As if the word so *spoken* were halfe donne, . . . III. x. 33. 2
To stay their hands, till he awhile had *spoken;* . . . IV. ii. 21. 2
likewise of words, the which be *spoken,* . . . V. ii. 47. 7
To all mongst whom this storie should be *spoken,* . . . V. viii. 44. 5
Ne ever was the name of warre there *spoken,* . . . V. ix. 24. 6

Spon. *See* **Spun.**

Sponge. as things wipt out with a *sponge* . . . *Ti.* 361

Sport. Making his *sport,* that manie makes to weep: . . . *Van.* v. 7
Tho shall we *sporten* in delight, . . . *S.C.* Mar. 19
to thinke How great *sport* they gaynen . . . *S.C.* May 36
it good *sport* had been him to have eyde: . . . *Hub.* 1013
Fine Counterfesaunce, and unhurtfull *Sport,* . . . *T.M.* 197
Upon the streaming rivers, *sport* to finde; . . . *Mui.* 47
With his yong brother *Sport,* . . . *Mui.* 290
in fresh flowring fields themselves to *sport:* . . . I. iv. 37. 3
a lovely babe did play His cruell *sport,* . . . II. i. 40. 6
*with the wooddie Nymphes when she did *sport,* (editors' conject.) . . . II. iii. 28. 7
Now faining dalliaunce and wanton *sport,* . . . II. xii. 16. 3
with delightfull *sport* To loose her warlike limbs . . . III. i. 52. 4
he ment to make his *sport* and courtly play. . . . III. i. 56. 9
The rest she fyr'd, for *sport,* or for despight: . . . III. x. 12. 6
The silly man . . . Saw all this goodly *sport,* . . . III. x. 45. 2
wearie of their *sport* to sleepe they fell, . . . III. x. 49. 2
By way of *sport,* as oft in maskes is knowen, . . . IV. i. 3. 8
Some laught for *sport,* some did for wonder shout, . . . IV. iii. 41. 8
That masked Mock-knight was their *sport* . . . IV. iv. 13. 4
layd aside when so she usd her looser *sport.* . . . IV. v. 3. 9
by themselves did *sport* Their spotlesse pleasures . . . IV. x. 26. 1
amongst the wanton Nymphs to *sport* and toy. . . . IV. xi. 19. 9
Amongst his peres playing his childish *sport;* . . . V. i. 6. 3
at pleasure she mote *sport* and play; . . . VI. ix. 37. 5
with the Graces there to play and *sport;* . . . VI. x. 9. 5
with the Nymphes the Satyres love to play and *sport.* . . . VII. vi. 39. 9
Thought not enough to punish him in *sport,* . . . VII. vi. 51. 2
and makes my pain her *sport.* . . . *Am.* x. 14
sport my muse, and sing my loves sweet praise; . . . *Am.* lxxx. 10

Sporting. *Sporting* him selfe in safe felicity: . . . III. vi. 49. 4

Sports. who such *sports* and sweet delights doth blame, . . . *Gn.* 7
with Loves, and Ladies gentle *sports,* . . . *Hub.* 757
Her youthfull *sports* and kindlie wantonnesse, . . . *D.* 111
His *sports* were faire, his joyance innocent, . . . *As.* 25
all the *sports* that shepheards are emong. . . . *As.* 76
After his *sportes* and cruell pastime donne; . . . I. vi. 27. 4
'Forwearied with my *sportes,* . . . I. ix. 13. 1
babes about her hong, Playing their *sportes,* . . . I. x. 31. 2

Sport—*Continued.*
Their wanton *sportes* and childish mirth did play, ... I. xii. 7. 2
litle Cupid playd His wanton *sportes,* . . . . . II. ix. 34. 7
sleepes, and *sports,* and playes; . . . . . IV. i. 47. 6
litle loves, and *sports,* and joyes, ... IV. x. 42. 2
to make their *sports* and merrie glee, ... VI. ix. 41. 2
doth play Her cruell *sports* to many mens decay? . . . . . VII. vi. 1. 5
sonnes of Venus, play your *sports* at will! . . . . . *Epith.* 364
they doe play Their hurtlesse *sports,* . . . . . *H.L.* 288
Spot. shee is Syrinx daughter without *spotte,* . . . . . *S.C.* Ap. 50
Faire Ladies loves they *spot* with thoughts impure, ... *T.M.* 333
In spight of envie that his deeds would *spot:* . . . . . Ti. 439
All lilly white, withoutten *spot* or pride, ... I. xii. 22. 7
Most sacred virgin without *spot* of sinne. . . . . . III. iv. 59. 8
His cruell deedes and wicked wyles did *spot:* . . . . . III. vi. 13. 5
that could deserve No *spot* of blame, ... IV. i. 4. 8
with shamefull *spot* of sinfull lust . . . . . IV. i. 53. 4
Within his mouth a blacke *spot* doth appeare, ... V. iii. 32. 8
So faire and tender without staine or *spot* . . . . . V. vii. 29. 7
Spotless. pure and *spotles,* as at first he sprong . . . . . *T.M.* 388
to present His bodie, as a *spotles* sacrifise; . . . . . *Ti.* 298
for report of *spotlesse* honestie, ... *Col.* 753
pure and *spotlesse* Cupid forth she brought, ... *Col.* 803
perfect love and *spotlesse* fame Of chastitie, ... III. v. 54. 3
spotlesse pleasures and sweet loves content. . . . . . IV. x. 26. 2
This litle babe, of . . . *spotlesse* spirit . . . . . VI. iv. 35. 5
spotlesse Pleasure builds her sacred bowre. . . . . . *Am.* lxv. 14
pure affections bred in *spotlesse* brest, ... *Am.* lxxxiii. 5
With pure regard and *spotlesse* true intent, ... *H.B.* 212
heavens . . . Unmoving, uncorrupt, and *spotlesse* bright, . . . *H.H.B.* 68
Spots. thousand *spots* of colours queint elect, ... III. vii. 22. 5
Spotted. *See* **Eye-spotted.**
sprong forth a naked swayne With *spotted* winges, ... *S.C.* Mar. 80
Thereto will I pawne yonder *spotted* Lambe, ... *S.C.* Au. 37
So praysen babes the Peacoks *spotted* traine, ... *S.C.* O. 31
His creste above, *spotted* with purple die, ... *Gn.* 260
The *spotted* Panther, and the tusked Bore, ... I. vi. 26. 3
he them *spotted* with reproch, or secrete shame. . . . . . VI. vi. 12. 9
his *spotted* hyde Doth please all beasts, ... *Am.* liii. 1
Spousal. ere my hoped day of *spousall* shone, ... I. ii. 23. 6
Doubly supplide, in *spousall* and dominion. . . . . . II. x. 75. 9
He would be there, and honor to her *spousall* ad. . . . . . V. ii. 3. 9
sing the *spousall* hymne full cleere, ... VII. vii. 12. 7
Spousals. Hymen, at your *Spousalls* sad, ... *Gn.* 395
In honour of the *spousalls* . . . . . IV. xi. 8. 3
The *spousals* of faire Florimell, ... V. iii. Arg.
Spouse. garnisht as a loved *spouse.* . . . . . *Rev.* iv. 4
His noble *Spouse,* and Paragon of fame. . . . . . *Ti.* 245
to the wood she goes, to . . . seeke her *spouse* . . . . . I. vi. 22. 4
to their heavenly *spouse* . . . They might appeare, ... I. x. 42. 4
I that Lady to my *spouse* had wonne; . . . . . II. iv. 21. 2
Thy *spouse* I will her make, ... II. vii. 49. 8
ordaynd to bee The *spouse* of Britomart, ... III. iii. 26. 2
musicke, which did next ensew Before the *spouse:* . . . . . IV. xi. 23. 3
Spoused. Though *spousd,* yet wanting wedlocks solemnize; . I. x. 4. 7
How she was found againe, and *spousde* to Marinell. . . . . V. ii. 2. 9
he her *spous'd,* and made his joyous bride. . . . . . V. iii. 2. 4
Sprad. *See* **Spread.**
Spray. 'Let birds be silent on the naked *spray,* . . . . . *D.* 330
from the trees did lop the needlesse *spray:* . . . . . VII. vii. 42. 7
each bird that sits on *spray,* . . . . . *Am.* xl. 9
Spread. *See* **Overspread.**
to *spread* his gladsome gleame, ... *Bel.*[2] v. 2
as ye see huge flames *spred* diverslie, ... *Ro.* xvi. 9
As waves, as winde, as fire, *spred* over all, ... *Ro.* xvi. 13
Seest how fresh my flowers bene *spredde,* . . . . . *S.C.* F. 129
when he sawe how broade her beames did *spredde,* . . . . . *S.C.* Ap. 75
over them *spred* a goodly wild vine, ... *S.C.* Au. 29
Spread themselves farre abroad . . . . . *Gn.* 77
wide Sigaean shores were *spred* with corses, ... *Gn.* 501
Olyve tree, with berries *spredd,* . . . . . *Mui.* 326
whose praises wide Were *spred* abroad; . . . . . *D.* 145
loftie trees . . . Did *spred* so broad, ... I. i. 7. 5
sad Night over him her mantle black doth *spred.* . . . . . I. i. 39. 9
on whom he *spred* A seeming body of the subtile aire, ... I. ii. 3. 2
rosy fingred Morning faire, . . . Had *spred* her purple robe . I. ii. 7. 3
trees, that faire did *spred* Their armes abroad, ... I. ii. 28. 3
High above all a cloth of State was *spred,* . . . . . I. iv. 8. 1
Dragon . . . over all did *spredd* His golden winges: . . . . . I. vii. 31. 4
Did *spred* their rule through all the territories, ... I. vii. 43. 7
fame throughout the world had *spred,* . . . . . I. vii. 46. 2
her charet, all with flowers *spred,* . . . . . I. xi. 51. 7
To prove how many acres he did *spred* of land. . . . . . I. xii. 11. 9
spred his glory through all countryes wide. . . . . . II. i. 35. 4
The dead corse of an armed knight was *spred,* . . . . . II. i. 41. 2
fragrant Eglantine did *spred* His prickling armes, ... II. v. 29. 4
Arachne high did . . . *spred* her subtile nett, ... II. vii. 28. 8
spred his empire to the utmost shore, ... II. x. 10. 2
Upon the waves to *spred* her trembling light, ... II. xii. 2. 5
was *spred* A trayle of yvie . . . . . II. xii. 61. 1
a spatious playne, . . . it selfe did *spredden* wyde, ... III. i. 20. 7
she over him would *spred* Her mantle, ... III. i. 36. 1
the false instilled fire Did *spred* it selfe, ... III. i. 56. 5
spred Abroad thy fresh youths fayrest flowre, ... III. ii. 31. 6
through the earth have *spredd* their living prayse, ... III. iii. 3. 8
comming forth shall *spred* his banner brave . . . . . III. iii. 30. 3
Speed thee to *spred* abroad thy beames bright, ... III. iv. 60. 4
was forg'd and *spred* with golden foyle, ... IV. ii. 29. 4
with their braunches *spred* all Britany, ... IV. xi. 26. 6
all her shoulders *spred* As a new spring; . . . . . IV. xi. 46. 4

Spread—*Continued.*
gins to *spread* his leafe before the faire sunshine. . . . . . IV. xii. 34. 9
Their bodies to his beastes for provender did *spred,*) . . . . V. viii. 28. 9
rayling rymes had *sprad.* . . . . . V. ix. 25. 9
All over her a cloth of state was *spred,* . . . . . V. ix. 28. 1
Did *spred* abroad and throw in th' open wynd: . . . . . V. xii. 33. 7
on his head an hood with aglets *sprad,* . . . . . VI. ii. 5. 8
These eyes him saw upon the cold earth *sprad,* . . . . . VI. ii. 45. 7
a spacious plaine Did *spred* it selfe, ... VI. x. 8. 2
themselves in one faire river *spred.* . . . . . VII. vi. 53. 9
Thrugh the broad world doth *spred* his goodly ray; . . . . *Am.* xl. 8
Pincks but newly *spred;* . . . . . *Am.* lxiv. 8
when my spirit doth *spred* her bolder winges, ... *Am.* lxxii. 1
A goodly table . . . All *spred* with juncats, ... *Am.* lxxvii. 3
Her brest that table was, so richly *spredd;* . . . . . *Am.* lxxvii. 13
His golden beame upon the hils doth *spred,* . . . . . *Epith.* 20
Spread thy broad wing over my love and me, ... *Epith.* 319
stealthes shal worke, and snares shal *spread* . . . . . *Epith.* 361
rosy leaves, so fairely *spred* Upon the lips, ... *H.B.* 94
spred thy lovely kingdome over-all. . . . . . *H.B.* 266
Spreadest. when thou *spredst* thy mantle forth on hie, . . . IV. x. 44. 7
Spreading. *See* **Broad-spreading.**
through his entrailes *spredding* diversly, ... *Van.* vi. 9
with their *spredding* armes Do beat their buds, ... *T.M.* 77
hairie hide . . . Which, *spredding* all his backe, ... *Mui.* 69
spreading forth at large, ... *Col.* 111
Faire *spreading* forth her leaves . . . . . *Col.* 545
spredding on the grownd Their watchet mantles . . . . . III. iv. 40. 4
Spreading it selfe into a spatious plaine: . . . . . III. v. 39. 6
spredding over all the flore alone, ... IV. vii. 20. 7
The spacious Shenan *spreading* like a sea, ... IV. xi. 41. 3
The *spreading* Lee that, like an Island fayre, ... IV. xi. 44. 3
both behind upheld her *spredding* traine; . . . . . IV. xi. 47. 4
Covered with mossie shrubs, which *spredding* brode . . . VI. iv. 13. 6
Spredding pavilions for the birds to bowre, ... VI. x. 6. 6
Spreads. With his great bellie *spreds* the dimmed world, . . *Ro.* xx. 6
When her discolourd bow she *spreds* through hevens hight. . III. xi. 47. 9
spreds it selfe through all civilitie: . . . . . VI. Pr. 4. 5
a goodly banner, *Spreds* in defiaunce . . . . . *Am.* v. 12
Spredde. *See* **Spread.**
Sprent. Hath powred forth for thee, and th' altars *sprent:* . . *Mui.* 239
otherwhere the snowy substaunce *sprent* With vermell, . . . II. xii. 45. 5
all the ground with purple bloud was *sprent,* . . . . . IV. ii. 18. 5
Spright. *See* **Sprite.**
Spring. *See* **Day-spring, Offspring, Well-spring.**
a fresh *spring* rise out of a rocke, ... *Bel.*[1] x. 1
a *spring* out of a rocke forth rayle, ... *Bel.*[2] xii. 1
A *spring* of water, mildly rumbling downe, ... *Pet.* iv. 2
devoure The *spring,* the place, and all . . . . . *Pet.* iv. 11
to the *Spring,* that late devoured was. . . . . . *Pet.* v. 6
manie yong plants *spring* out of her rinde: . . . . . *Ro.* xxviii. 11
Then from greene grasse into a stalke doth *spring;* . . . . . *Ro.* xxx. 2
Whilome thy fresh *spring* flowrd, ... *S.C.* Ja. 21
alas! but now my *spring* begonne, ... *S.C.* Ja. 29
You deemen the *Spring* is come attonce; . . . . . *S.C.* F. 38
pleasant *spring* appeareth: . . . . . *S.C.* Mar. 9
Which once he made as by a *spring* he laye, ... *S.C.* Ap. 35
spring forth ranckly under his chinne. . . . . . *S.C.* May 188
in the lower *spring* Did shroude . . . . . *S.C.* Jun. 53
the *spring* was in his learned hedde, ... *S.C.* Jun. 94
Thou, pleasaunt *spring,* hast luld me oft asleepe, ... *S.C.* Au. 155
The nombers flowe as fast as *spring* doth ryse. . . . . . *S.C.* O. 108
soone as *spring* his mantle hath displayde, ... *S.C.* N. 85
The gentle shepheard satte beside a *springe,* . . . . . *S.C.* D. 1
when flowrd my joyfull *spring,* . . . . . *S.C.* D. 19
Tho deemed I my *spring* would ever laste. . . . . . *S.C.* D. 30
'Tho gan my lovely *Spring* bid me farewel, ... *S.C.* D. 55
as the *springe* gives place to elder time, ... *S.C.* D. 73
My *spring* is spent, ... *S.C.* D. 128
a silver *Spring,* forth powring His trickling streames, . . . *Gn.* 227
The joyous *Spring* out of the ground brings forth, ... *Gn.* 683
he could play, and daunce, and vaute, and *spring,* . . . . . *Hub.* 693
sith she eke did *spring* Out of his stocke . . . . . *Ti.* 275
In *spring,* when flowres doo clothe the fruitful ground, . . *Mui.* 114
gathering Into her lap the children of the *spring.* . . . . . *Mui.* 128
the other *Spring* A burning Teade about his head did move, . *Mui.* 292
'She fell away in her first ages *spring,* . . . . . *D.* 239
first did *spring* From heaven, ... *Col.* 917
when his later *spring* gins to avale, ... I. i. 21. 5
the chastest flowre that aye did *spring* . . . . . I. i. 48. 4
Leaping like wanton kids in pleasant *Spring.* . . . . . I. vi. 14. 4
askt . . . Of what loines and what lignage I did *spring;* . . . I. ix. 5. 6
Whom well she knew to *spring* from hevenly race, ... I. x. 8. 7
Their welheads *spring,* and are with moisture deawd; . . . II. ii. 6. 3
No tree whose braunches did not bravely *spring;* . . . . . II. vi. 13. 1
They *spring,* they bud, they blossome fresh . . . . . II. vi. 15. 6
the flowres did freshly *spring,* . . . . . II. vi. 24. 6
Of whom all Faeryes *spring,* . . . . . II. x. 71. 9
the downy heare Did now but freshly *spring,* . . . . . II. xii. 79. 9
Progeny, Which from them *springen* shall. . . . . . III. iii. Arg.
Whence *spring* all noble deedes . . . . . III. iii. 1. 9
from thy wombe a famous Progenee Shall *spring* . . . . . III. iii. 22. 6
where the day out of the sea doth *spring,* . . . . . III. iii. 27. 4
There is continuall *Spring,* . . . . . III. vi. 42. 1
The glory of the later world to *spring,* . . . . . III. ix. 44. 2
see The *spring* breake forth . . . . . IV. x. 45. 4
all her shoulders spred As a new *spring;* . . . . . IV. xi. 46. 5
the wicked seede of vice Began to *spring;* . . . . . V. i. 1. 4
from the Ocean all rivers *spring,* . . . . . VI. Pr. 7. 4
The seede of all this evill first doth *spring,* . . . . . VI. vi. 8. 2

Spring—*Continued.*
drew To this sweet *spring*; . . . VII. vi. 45. 8
of their Winter *spring* another Prime, . . . VII. vii. 18. 7
lusty *Spring*, all dight in leaves of flowres . . . VII. vii. 28. 2
For lusty *Spring* now in his timely howre . . . *Am.* iv. 9
The merry Cuckow, messenger of *Spring*, . . . *Am.* xix. 1
Fresh *Spring*, the herald of loves mighty king, . . . *Am.* lxx. 1
All sorts of flowers, the which on earth do *spring*, . . . *Am.* lxx. 3
a *spring* Of poysoned words and spitefull speeches well; . . . *Am.* lxxxv. 3
Eternall *spring* of grace and wisedome trew, . . . *H.H.L.* 44
Springalds. There came two *Springals* of full tender yeares, . V. x. 6. 2
Springest. thou *springst* from ancient race . . . I. x. 65. 1
Springeth. oft the bloud *springeth* from woundes wyde; . . . *S.C.* F. 176
it wholly *springeth* from my wit: . . . *Hub.* 1037
Spring-headed. *Spring-headed* Hydres; and sea-shouldring Whales; . . . II. xii. 23. 6
Springing. *See* **Fresh-springing.**
seven *springing* heds of monstrous crimes, . . . *Bel.*[1] viii. 13
wouldest me my *springing* youngth to spil: . . . *S.C.* F. 52
As if her eyes had beene two *springing* wells; . . . *T.M.* 536
springing out of Mole, doth run downe right . . . *Col.* 110
you, fresh budd of vertue *springing* fast, . . . I. viii. 27. 1
Of auncient time there was a *springing* well, . . . I. xi. 29. 3
Gan cleare the deawy ayre with *springing* light, . . . II. iii. 1. 4
the *springing* seed outweed, . . . II. iv. 35. 7
In *springing* flowre the image of thy day. . . . II. xii. 74. 3
two babes, as faire as *springing* day. . . . III. vi. 26. 9
Springs. O ye pleasaunt *Springs* Of Tempe! . . . *Gn.* 145
Beside the silver *Springs* of Helicone, . . . *T.M.* 5
The sacred *springs* of horsefoot Helicon, . . . *T.M.* 271
That in the Gardin of Adonis *springs*, . . . III. vi. 39. 2
as if their *springs* of life were spent; . . . IV. ii. 18. 4
Sweet *springs*, in which a thousand Nymphs did play; . . . IV. x. 24. 3
Long Rhodanus, whose sourse *springs* from the skie; . . . IV. xi. 20. 4
Bursting forth teares like *springs* out of a banke), . . . V. i. 15. 2
first, she *springs* out of two marble Rocks, . . . VII. vi. 41. 1
all that from her *springs*, and is ybredde, . . . VII. vii. 18. 1
From whose pure beams al perfect beauty *springs*, . . . *H.H.B.* 296
Springtime. In sweete *spring time*, . . . *Gn.* 109
Sprinkle. *See* **Holy-water sprinkle.**
ever *sprinckle* brackish teares among, . . . *D.* 530
Then gan they *sprinckle* all the posts with wine, . . . I. xii. 38. 1
with sweet Nectar she did *sprinkle* him. . . . III. i. 36. 9
Sprinckle her heart, and haughtie courage soften, . . . IV. Pr. 5. 8
sprinkle all the postes and wals with wine, . . . *Epith.* 253
Sprinkled. Faire Xanthus *sprincled* with Chimaeras blood, . . *Gn.* 19
With sundrie colours paints the *sprinckled* lay: . . . *Gn.* 110
With *sprincled* pearle and gold full richly drest, . . . I. vii. 32. 3
She lightly *sprinkled* on his weaker partes: . . . I. viii. 14. 7
holy water thereon *sprinckled* wide; . . . I. xii. 37. 5
all his armour *sprinckled* was with blood, . . . II. vi. 41. 6
sprinckled ofte the same With liquid waves, . . . II. vii. 36. 4
that sweete verse, with Nectar *sprinckeled*, . . . III. Pr. 4. 4
sprinckled frost upon his deawy beard: . . . III. viii. 30. 4
she *sprinckled* favours manifold On whom she list, . . . III. xii. 13. 7
sprinckled here and theare With glittering spangs . . . IV. xi. 45. 4
sprinckled with such sweet variety . . . VI. Pr. 1. 4
Sprinkled with wholsom waters more then most on ground: . VII. vi. 38. 9
Sprinckled with perle, and perling flowres atweene, . . . *Epith.* 155
hew . . . With which the cheekes are *sprinckled*, . . . *H.B.* 93
Sprinkles. *See* **Water-sprinkles.**
Sprinkling. With pearly dew *sprinkling* the morning grasse: . IV. v. 45. 5
Sprite. My *spright* was greatly moved in her rest, . . . *Van.* xii. 2
through power of some divining *spright*, . . . *Gn.* Ded. 6
the Foxe, deep groning in his *sprite*, . . . *Hub.* 588
revives his toyled *spright*; . . . *Hub.* 756
I feele my feeble *spright* Robbed of sense, . . . *Ti.* 320
did grieve the noble *spright* Of Salomon . . . *Ti.* 443
Much was I troubled in my heavie *spright*, . . . *Ti.* 575
his deepe-groning *spright* In bloodie streames foorth fled . *Mui.* 438
the anguish of his *spright* Some deale alaid, . . . *D.* 172
Yet pittie me in your empassiond *spright*, . . . *D.* 515
resembling both in shape and *spright* Her brother . . . *As.* 213
Whose gentle *spright* for Daphnes death . . . *Col.* 386
I feele my selfe like one yrapt in *spright*. . . . *Col.* 623
By them the *Sprite* doth passe in quietly, . . . I. i. 40. 7
The *Sprite* then gan more boldly him to wake, . . . I. i. 43. 1
made a Lady of that other *Spright*, . . . I. i. 45. 2
wearines . . . Having yrockt asleepe his irkesome *spright*, . I. i. 55. 5
With that misformed *spright* he backe returnd againe. . . . I. i. 55. 9
That feigning dreame, and that faire-forged *Spright*, . . . I. ii. 2. 2
Eftsoones he tooke . . . that false other *Spright*, . . . I. ii. 3. 2
Or guilefull *spright* wandring in empty aire, . . . I. ii. 32. 6
'Nor guileful *sprite* to thee these words doth speake; . . . I. ii. 33. 2
let not his restlesse *spright*, Be unreveng'd, . . . I. iv. 48. 7
In slombring swownd, nigh voyd of vitall *spright*, . . . I. v. 19. 5
wondrous great griefe groneth in my *spright*, . . . I. vii. 40. 3
His chearefull words reviv'd her chearelesse *spright*, . . . I. vii. 52. 8
Ne divelish thoughts dismay thy constant *spright*: . . . I. ix. 53. 3
when she list poure out her larger *spright*, . . . I. x. 20. 1
all that noyd his heavie *spright* . . . I. x. 24. 3
his *spright* Had past the paines of hell . . . I. x. 32. 8
wondrous quick and persaunt was his *spright*, . . . I. x. 47. 5
Till from her bands the *spright* assoiled is, . . . I. x. 52. 8
ravished with rare impression in his *sprite*. . . . I. xii. 39. 9
what cursed evil *Spright*, Or fell Erinnys, . . . II. ii. 29. 1
his flowing toung and troublous *spright* . . . II. iii. 4. 6
when the frantick fitt inflamd his *spright*, . . . II. iv. 7. 3
quickned the dull *spright* with musicall comfort. . . . II. v. 31. 9
groneth out his utmost grudging *spright* . . . II. v. 36. 7

Sprite—*Continued.*
In his owne flesh, and make way to the living *spright*! . . II. vi. 32. 9
low abase the high heroicke *spright*, . . . II. vii. 10. 6
The charge thereof unto a covetous *Spright* . . . II. vii. 32. 1
his enfeebled *spright* Gan sucke this vitall ayre . . . II. vii. 66. 5
As if some pensive thought constraind her gentle *spright*. . . II. ix. 36. 9
either *Spright*, Or Angell, . . . II. x. 71. 6
made his *spright* to grone full piteous; . . . II. xi. 38. 7
nathemore forth fled his groning *spright*, . . . II. xi. 38. 8
Flesh without blood, a person without *spright*, . . . II. xi. 40. 4
through his humid eyes did sucke his *spright*, . . . II. xii. 73. 7
whose engrieved *spright* Could find no rest . . . III. i. 59. 4
Did chaunce to still into her weary *spright*, . . . III. ii. 29. 2
cheard the feeble *spright* Of the sicke virgin, . . . III. ii. 47. 1
By false illusion of a guilefull *Spright* . . . III. iii. 13. 4
seemes some cursed witches deed, Or evill *spright*, . . . III. iii. 18. 9
Both coosen passions of distroubled *spright*, . . . III. iv. 12. 7
Was earst impressed in her gentle *spright*. . . . III. iv. 49. 3
in brave *sprite* it kindles goodly fire, . . . III. v. 1. 8
gentle *sprite* deforme with rude rusticity. . . . III. vi. 1. 9
thought her to adore with humble *spright*: . . . III. vii. 11. 8
He nere was touched in his noble *spright*, . . . III. vii. 43. 8
she put a *Spright* to rule the carcas dead; . . . III. viii. 7. 9
A wicked *Spright*, yfraught with fawning guyle . . . III. viii. 8. 1
gin awake, and stir his frosen *spright*: . . . III. viii. 23. 5
all the passions . . . vex his caytive *spright*. . . . III. x. 17. 9
All desperate of his fore-damned *spright*, . . . III. x. 56. 8
nothing left but like on aery *Spright*, . . . III. x. 57. 4
like a dreary *Spright* Cald by strong charmes . . . III. xii. 19. 4
freshly bleeding forth her fainting *spright*, . . . III. xii. 20. 7
gentle *spright* Now gan to feede on hope, . . . III. xii. 44. 6
in sweete ravishment pourd out her *spright*. . . . III. xii. 45. *or.* 7
Was much empassiond in her gentle *sprite*, . . . III. xii. 46. *or.* 7
that false *spright* . . . Was so expert . . . IV. ii. 10. 6
Through secret feeling of his generous *spright*, . . . IV. iii. 14. 5
As all men do, that lose the living *spright*. . . . IV. iii. 30. 7
The other breathing now another *spright*, . . . IV. iii. 35. 8
Blandamour full of vainglorious *spright*, . . . IV. iv. 3. 6
his wearie *sprite*, opprest With fleshly weaknesse, . . . IV. v. 43. 2
breach That sudden newes had made into his *spright*, . . . IV. vi. 38. 4
hard to finde, that heat of youthfull *spright* . . . IV. viii. 29. 7
To see his foe breath out his *spright* in vaine: . . . IV. viii. 46. 2
that which is th' immortall *spright* Lives still, . . . IV. xi. 16. 8
Being fast fixed in her wounded *spright*, . . . V. v. 27. 4
with thy bloud thou shalt appease the *spright* . . . V. vi. 37. 8
appeare unto her heavenly *spright* A wondrous vision, . . . V. vii. 12. 7
Like one adawed with some dreadfull *spright*: . . . V. vii. 20. 8
it much appald her troubled *spright*: . . . V. viii. 45. 5
with dull countenance and with doleful *spright* . . . V. xii. 12. 3
chears my dulled *spright*. . . . VI. Pr. 1. 9
gentlenesse of *spright* And manners mylde . . . VI. i. 2. 3
Of all this day on ground that breathen living *spright*! . . . VI. i. 4. 9
he nould let him breath, nor gather *spright*, . . . VI. iii. 26. 7
the faint *sprite* he did revoke againe . . . VI. iii. 28. 2
Doe it disclose to ease your grieved *spright*: . . . VI. iv. 28. 7
he now has almost spent his *spright*, . . . VI. v. 17. 5
that immortall *spright* Of Podalyrius . . . VI. vi. 1. 7
passions heale which wound the weaker *spright*. . . . VI. vi. 3. 9
being fresh and full of youthly *spright*, . . . VI. vii. 5. 2
standing long astonished in *spright*, . . . VI. x. 17. 3
gan to burne in her ambitious *spright*, . . . VII. vi. 10. 5
in his *spright* Did inly grudge, . . . VII. vi. 35. 7
(in whose gentle *spright*, The pure well head of Poesie did dwell) . . . VII. vii. 9. 3
reade the sorrowes of my dying *spright*, . . . *Am.* i. 7
Bids all old thoughts to die in dumpish *spright*: . . . *Am.* iv. 4
powrefull eies, which lighten my dark *spright*; . . . *Am.* ix. 2
cheare you your heavy *spright*, . . . *Am.* lxii. 13
The sacred harbour of that hevenly *spright*; . . . *Am.* lxxvi. 4
To beare the message of her gentle *spright*. . . . *Am.* lxxxi. 12
The inward beauty of her lively *spright*, . . . *Epith.* 186
in his deducted *spright* Some sparks remaining . . . *H.L.* 106
out of that great immortall *Spright*, . . . *H.B.* 107
carrie privie message to the *spright*, . . . *H.B.* 236
Most wise, most holy, most almightie *Spright*! . . . *H.H.L.* 39
Vouchsafe to shed into my barren *spright* . . . *H.H.L.* 45
and breathd a living *spright* Into his face . . . *H.H.L.* 110
Blinding the eyes, and lumining the *spright*. . . . *H.H.L.* 280
Vouchsafe then, O thou most Almightie *Spright*! . . . *H.H.B.* 8
And them transport from flesh into the *spright*. . . . *H.H.B.* 259
That kindleth love in every godly *spright* . . . *H.H.B.* 297
Sprites. My *sprites* were ravisht with these pleasures . . . *Pet.*[1] iii. 7
Olde moniments, which of so famous *sprights* . . . *Ro.* vii. 3
he kindleth his ambitious *sprights* . . . *Hub.* 768
into their noble *sprights* Desire of honor . . . *Hub.* 824
doth refresh his *sprights* . . . *T.M.* 138
With pleasures choyce to feed his cheerefull *sprights*: . . . *Ti.* 522
to refresh his *sprights*: . . . *Mui.* 162
with rest refresh my fainting *sprights*, . . . *D.* 472
sprights began to faint, . . . *D.* 542
forth he cald . . . Legions of *Sprights*, . . . I. i. 38. 2
He that the stubborne *Sprites* can wisely tame, . . . I. i. 43. 7
As one aghast with feends or damned *sprights*, . . . I. ii. 4. 5
damned *sprights* sent forth to make ill men aghast. . . . I. v. 31. 9
blessed *sprites*, . . . To God for vengeance cryde . . . I. viii. 36. 6
the feeble *sprightes* Can call out . . . II. v. 27. 4
Plonged continually of cruell *Sprightes*, . . . II. vii. 57. 4
companing with feends and filthy *Sprights* . . . II. x. 8. 6
When so he counseld with his *sprights* encompast round. . . . III. iii. 7. 9
thousand *sprights* with long enduring paines . . . III. iii. 9. 4

Sprites—*Continued.*
did it commend Unto these *Sprights* . . . . . III. iii. 10. 5
Some litle life his feeble *sprites* emong; . . . . . III. iv. 41. 8
Where she was wont her *Sprightes* to entertaine, ... III. viii. 4. 4
to her reveald By errant *Sprights,* . . . . . III. viii. 6. 5
a whole legione Of wicked *Sprightes* . . . . . III. ix. 2. 8
Now singing sweetly to surprize her *sprights,* . . . . . III. x. 8. 3
Out of the dwellings of the damned *sprights,* . . . . . IV. i. 19. 8
Therewith their dulled *sprights* they edgd anew, ... IV. ii. 17. 6
turne we here . . . to gather fresher *sprights,* . . . . . V. iii. 40. 7
modest thoughts breathd from weltempred *sprites,* . . . . . *Am.* lxxxiii. 6
the Pouke, nor other evill *sprights,* . . . . . *Epith.* 341
Do kindle love in high conceipted *sprights;* . . . . . *H.H.B.* 5
Sprong. *See* **Sprung, Upsprong.**
streame, . . . *sprong* from triumphant seat. . . . . . *Rev.* iv. 13
With that *sprong* forth a naked swayne . . . . . *S.C.* Mar. 79
So *sprong* her grace Of heavenly race, ... *S.C.* Ap. 52
as it *sprong,* it wither must agayne: . . . . . *S.C.* O. 77
as at first he *sprong* Out of th' Almighties bosome, ... *T.M.* 388
die forgot from whence at first they *sprong,* . . . . . *T.M.* 443
the certein Sire, From which I *sprong,* . . . . . I. ix. 3. 4
faire ymp, *sprong* out from English race, ... I. x. 60. 1
freely *sprong* out of the fruitfull grownd, ... I. xi. 47. 3
Here also *sprong* that goodly golden fruit, ... II. vii. 55. 1
whence they *sprong,* or how they were begott, ... II. x. 8. 1
the salt brine out of the billowes *sprong.* . . . . . II. xii. 10. 5
Rashly out of their rouzed couches *sprong,* . . . . . III. i. 62. 8
whence it *sprong,* I can not read aright: . . . . . III. iii. 16. 7
sprong of seed terrestriall, ... III. iii. 26. 5
Well worthie stock from which the branches *sprong* . . . III. iv. 3. 6
whereof wise Paeon *sprong*) . . . . . III. iv. 41. 6
So *sprong* these twinnes in womb of Chrysogone; . . . . . III. vi. 9. 6
noble Britons *sprong* from Trojans bold, ... III. ix. 38. 8
Sprout. His wreathed hornes gan newly *sprout:* . . . . . *S.C.* May 186
In Princes Court doe hap to *sprout* againe, ... IV. viii. 33. 4
Sprung. *See* **Outsprung, Sprong.**
Sprung of the auncient stocke of Princes straine, ... IV. viii. 33. 7
of them *sprung* by lineall descent: . . . . . IV. xi. 12. 7
As well those that are *sprung* of heavenly seed, ... VII. vii. 3. 3
Spumador. The fierce *Spumador,* trode them downe like docks; II. xi. 19. 7
The fierce *Spumador,* borne of heavenly seed, ... II. xi. 19. 8
Spun. *See* **Outspun, Span.**
So finely *sponne* that scarce they could be spide. . . . . . *Mui.* 360
the thrid By griesly Lachesis was *spun* with paine, ... IV. ii. 48. 6
with one looke she spils that long I *sponne;* . . . . . *Am.* xxiii. 11
Spur. *See* **Hotspur.**
Due praise, that is the *spur* of dooing well? . . . . . *T.M.* 454
with the maistring *spur* he did him roughly stire. . . . . . II. v. 2. 9
makes her feare a *spur* to hast her flight: . . . . . IV. vii. 22. 7
Spurn. sharply gan to *spurne* His fomy steed, ... III. i. 5. 4
Spurned. *bent his speare, and *spurned* his horse with yron heele. . . . . . I. iii. 34. 9
Spurred. He, prickte with pride . . . Forth *spurred* fast: . . . I. ii. 14. 8
his hot ryder *spurd* his chauffed side: . . . . . I. iii. 33. 6
bent his speare, and *spurd* his horse with yron heele. . . . . I. iii. 34. 9
all *spurd* after, fast as they mote fly, ... III. i. 18. 4
Spurring. when him he spide *Spurring* so hote with rage . . . I. ii. 15. 2
Spurs. Gay steed with *spurs* did pricke, ... II. i. 49. 9
Atin ay him pricks with *spurs* of shame . . . . . II. v. 38. 9
he put his *spurres* unto his steed, ... IV. i. 41. 1
putting *spurres* unto her fiery beast, ... V. vi. 39. 2
Spy. so faire a Ladie did I *spie,* . . . . . *Pet.* vi. 1
ought in them blameworthie thou doest *spie.'* . . . . . *Col.* 679
this good knight, soone as he them can *spie,* . . . . . I. ii. 29. 1
Soone as the royall virgin he did *spy,* . . . . . I. iii. 5. 4
the hinder partes, that few could *spie,* Were ruinous . . . . I. iv. 5. 8
she might *spy* Her loved knight . . . . . I. xi. 33. 6
Whom when the damned feend so fresh did *spy,* . . . . . I. xi. 35. 1
he gan *spy* Where at his feet, ... II. viii. 23. 6
Which when those wicked Hags from far did *spye,* . . . . . II. xi. 47. 1
far off they many Islandes *spy* . . . . . II. xii. 10. 6
they *spy* That quicksand . . . . . II. xii. 18. 5
the hungry Spaniells she does *spye* . . . . . III. viii. 33. 6
keepe continuall *spy* Upon her . . . . . III. ix. 5. 4
Over the dore thus written she did *spye,* . . . . . III. xi. 50. 3
his owne armes when glittering he did *spy* . . . . . III. xii. 12. 4
When he in place his dearest love did *spy;* . . . . . IV. xii. 35. 2
Soone as the knight she there by her did *spy* . . . . . V. v. 14. 1
loft was raysd againe, that no man could it *spie.* . . . . . V. vi. 27. 9
Where ever in the darke he could them *spie,* . . . . . V. vi. 30. 5
Nor sire, nor sonnes, nor any could she *spie:* . . . . . V. vi. 35. 7
she did before her *spie* Sir Artegall; . . . . . V. viii. 6. 4
Which when the Damzell neare at hand did *spy,* . . . . . V. ix. 8. 3
when as fit advantage he did *spy,* . . . . . V. xii. 20. 1
when as my presence he did *spy* To be a let, ... VI. ii. 17. 4
He chaunst to *spie* a faire and stately place, ... VI. iii. 29. 7
chaunst far off an armed Knight to *spy* . . . . . VI. iii. 46. 6
To *spy* where he may some advauntage get, ... VI. vii. 47. 5
chaunst to *spy* a sort of shepheard groomes, ... VI. ix. 5. 2
chaunst one comming towards him to *spy,* . . . . . VI. xi. 27. 2
for great joy of some-what he did *spy,* . . . . . VII. vi. 46. 3
One of those archers closely I did *spy,* . . . . . *Am.* xvi. 9
when that soverayne beauty it doth *spy,* . . . . . *Am.* lxxii. 5
a byrd, that in ones hand doth *spy* Desired food, ... *Am.* lxxiii. 5
No blemish she may *spie.* . . . . . *Epith.* 66
do thou not envy My love with me to *spy:* . . . . . *Epith.* 377
Spyals. *See* **Spials.**
Spying. the Phoenix there alas, *Spying* the tree destroid, . . *Pet.* v. 9
The Foxe him *spying,* bad the Ape him dight . . . . . *Hub.* 233
he them *spying* gan to turne aside . . . . . I. vi. 34. 7

Spying—*Continued.*
him *spying,* both . . . upon him ran, ... II. ii. 22. 1
him *spying* thus bespake: . . . . . II. iii. 32. 6
all breathlesse, weary, faint, Him *spying,* . . . . . II. v. 11. 3
Him Atin *spying* knew right well of yore, ... II. vi. 48. 1
Squadrons. furious *squadrons* downe to ground did fall, . . . *Ro.* xii. 6
their bright *Squadrons* round about us plant; . . . . . II. viii. 2. 7
Squalid. Lastly the *squalid* lakes of Tartarie, ... *Gn.* 543
squallid Fortune, into basenes flong, ... *T.M.* 543
they saw a Squire in *squallid* weed Lamenting sore . . . . . V. i. 13. 7
from you lightly throw This *squalid* weede, ... V. iv. 34. 6
on her selfe did dight Most *squalid* garments, ... V. xii. 12. 2
Squall. The litle babe did loudly scrike and *squall,* . . . . . VI. iv. 18. 1
Squalls. kicks, and *squals,* and shriekes for fell despight; . . . V. vi. 14. 5
Square. *See* **Three-square.**
Square was this Citie, ... *Rev.* iv. 9
Ten feete each way in *square* . . . . . *Bel.* iii. 2
line, or lead, or rule, or *squaire,* to measure . . . . . *Ro.* xxvi. 3
Had riven many a brest with pikehead *square:* . . . . . I. vii. 37. 4
'with golden *squire* . . . can measure out a meane; . . . . . II. i. 58. 1
distent Into great Ingowes and to wedges *square;* . . . . . II. vii. 5. 6
Me seemes the world is runne quite out of *square* . . . . . V. Pr. 1. 7
he sometimes so far runnes out of *square,* . . . . . VII. vii. 52. 2
Squared. A stately Pallace built of *squared* bricke, ... I. iv. 4. 1
Squaring. *squaring* it in compasse well beseene, ... *Gn.* 651
Squib. asked for their pas by everie *squib,* . . . . . *Hub.* 371
Squint. I fear me, thou have a *squint* eye: . . . . . *S.C.* Au. 129
Squinted. With *squinted* eyes contrarie wayes intended, . . . IV. i. 27. 2
Squire. *See* **Square.**
the gentle *Squire,* to entertaine His fayre Belphoebe, ... *Ti.* 524
he spred A seeming body . . . Like a young *Squire,* . . . . . I. ii. 3. 4
Together with his *Squyre,* arayed meet: . . . . . I. vii. 29. 3
A gentle youth, his dearely loved *Squire,* . . . . . I. vii. 37. 1
So with his *Squire,* . . . He marched forth . . . . . I. viii. 3. 1
tooke that *Squire* an horne of bugle small, ... I. viii. 3. 5
him the *Squire* made quickly to retrate, ... I. viii. 12. 7
see his loved *Squyre* into such thraldom brought: . . . . . I. viii. 15. 9
The light-foot *Squyre* her quickly turnd around, ... I. viii. 25. 7
gave in charge unto his *Squyre,* That scarlot whore . . . . . I. viii. 29. 1
There fayrely them receives a gentle *Squyre,* . . . . . I. x. 7. 1
As might become a *Squyre* so great persons to greet. . . . . . I. x. 7. 9
where him that crafty *Squyre* Supposd to be. . . . . . II. i. 13. 3
Till her that *Squyre* bespake: . . . . . II. i. 16. 1
When she her *Squyre* heard speake, ... II. i. 16. 8
'Ah! gentle trustie *Squyre,* . . . . . II. i. 17. 1
himselfe had craftily devisd To be her *Squire,* . . . . . II. i. 21. 9
he saw that wretched *Squyre,* . . . . . II. iv. 16. 2
'It was a faithlesse *Squire,* . . . . . II. iv. 18. 1
'*Squyre,* sore have ye beene diseasd, ... II. iv. 33. 8
this *Squyre* have laide thus low. . . . . . II. iv. 34. 9
'Unlucky *Squire,*' . . . Henceforth take heede . . . . . II. iv. 36. 1
Whose *squire* bore after him an heben launce . . . . . II. viii. 17. 6
the *Squire* gan nigher to approch, ... II. ix. 11. 3
With his gay *Squyre* issewing did espye, ... II. xi. 17. 8
Had not his gentle *Squire* beheld his paine, ... II. xi. 29. 8
The *Squyre* arriving fiercely in his armes . . . . . II. xi. 31. 1
cumming to his *Squyre* that kept his steed, ... II. xi. 48. 2
his good *Squyre,* him helping up with speed, ... II. xi. 48. 7
him beside an aged *Squire* there rode, ... III. i. 4. 3
every knight, and every gentle *Squire,* . . . . . III. i. 56. 7
as her *Squyre* attend her carefully. . . . . . III. iii. 61. 5
Badd her old *Squyre* unlace her lofty creast: . . . . . III. iv. 7. 3
Timias, the Princes gentle *Squyre,* . . . . . III. iv. 47. 1
want of his good *Squire* late lefte behinde, ... III. v. 12. 4
bold, as ever *Squyre* that waited by knights side: . . . . . III. v. 12. 9
Had used beene of that foolehardie *Squyre:* . . . . . III. v. 15. 8
that *Squyre* unknowne Mote algates passe: . . . . . III. v. 17. 5
The gentle *Squyre* came ryding that same way, ... III. v. 18. 2
That stroke the hardy *Squire* did sore displease, ... III. v. 19. 6
the *Squire* lives with renowne. . . . . . III. v. 25. 9
Now God thee keepe, thou gentlest *squire* alive, ... III. v. 26. 6
that wofull *Squire,* With blood deformed, ... III. v. 29. 1
'Ah! gentle *Squire,* Nor Goddesse I, nor Angell; . . . . . III. v. 36. 1
Thither they brought that wounded *Squyre,* . . . . . III. v. 41. 1
Thou, a meane *Squyre* of meeke and lowly place; . . . . . III. v. 47. 3
Satyrane saves the *Squyre* of Dames . . . . . III. vii. Arg.
She bore before her lap a dolefull *Squire,* . . . . . III. vii. 37. 6
that wofull *Squyre,* Whom he had reskewed . . . . . III. vii. 45. 6
trembling yet through feare the *Squire* bespake: . . . . . III. vii. 47. 1
Call me the *Squyre* of Dames; . . . . . III. vii. 51. 9
read, thou *Squyre* of Dames, what vow is this, ... III. vii. 53. 2
'Ah! gentle *Squyre,*' (quoth he) 'tell at one word, ... III. vii. 56. 8
'Perdy' (sayd Satyrane) 'thou *Squyre* of Dames, ... III. vii. 61. 1
having ended with that *Squyre* of Dames . . . . . III. viii. 44. 1
With that same *Squyre* retourned back againe . . . . . III. viii. 44. 5
(said then the *Squyre* of Dames) . . . . . III. viii. 51. 1
that young *Squyre* Gan them informe the cause, ... III. viii. 52. 6
(as that *Squyre* does tell.) . . . . . III. ix. 3. 4
that young *Squyre* him reared from below; . . . . . III. ix. 16. 8
From whom the *Squyre* of Dames was reft whylere; . . . . . III. xi. 3. 8
With her own trusty *Squire,* . . . . . III. xii. 44. 3
gan advize with her old *Squire,* . . . . . III. xii. 45. 6
'False traitour *squire!* false *squire* of falsest knight! . . . . IV. i. 52. 6
Yet thou, false *Squire,* his fault shalt deare aby, ... IV. i. 53. 8
a *Squire,* even he the *Squire* of Dames, ... IV. ii. 20. 2
'Fond *Squire,*' full angry then sayd Paridell, ... IV. ii. 22. 5
'Aread, thou *Squire,* that I the man may learne, ... IV. ii. 25. 3
They sent that *Squire* afore, to understand . . . . . IV. ii. 31. 3
Sent forth their *Squire* to have them both descride, ... IV. iv. 2. 8
when that scornefull *Squire* of Dames did vew, ... IV. v. 18. 1

Squire—*Continued.*
that old aged Dame, his faithfull *Squire,* . . . IV. v. 39. 6
with him eke that aged *Squire* attone; . . . IV. v. 46. 3
The *Squire* her loves; . . . IV. vii. Arg.
was he but a *Squire* of low degree; . . . IV. vii. 15. 7
I with that *Squire* agreede away to flit, . . . IV. vii. 17. 6
that same gentle *Squire* arriv'd in place . . . IV. vii. 24. 3
Which drery sight the gentle *Squire* espying . . . IV. vii. 25. 1
ever when the *Squire* his javelin shooke, . . . IV. vii. 26. 2
scarse the *Squire* his hand could once upreare, . . . IV. vii. 28. 6
She left the gentle *Squire* with Amoret: . . . IV. vii. 35. 2
albeit his owne dear *Squire* he were, . . . IV. vii. 43. 5
The gentle *Squire* recovers grace, . . . IV. viii. Arg.
to this gentle *Squire* did happen late, . . . IV. viii. 1. 2
Her gentle *Squire* through her displeasure did pertake. . . . IV. viii. 9. 9
the *Squire,* in her defence, her sore astound. . . . IV. viii. 19. 9
towards them with speed A *Squire* came gallopping, . . . IV. viii. 38. 2
He all the way did rage at that same *Squire,* . . . IV. viii. 40. 1
Came to that *Squire,* yet trembling every vaine; . . . IV. viii. 41. 3
both *Squire* and dwarfe did tomble downe . . . IV. viii. 42. 8
Which when that *Squire* beheld, he woxe full glad . . . IV. viii. 46. 1
which was thus to him declared by that *Squire.* . . . IV. viii. 46. 9
a gentle *Squire* That lov'd a Ladie . . . IV. viii. 50. 1
This lovely swaine, the *Squire* of low degree; . . . IV. viii. 52. 5
her *Squire* of low degree Did secretly . . . IV. viii. 55. 6
For me he did mistake that *Squire* to bee, . . . IV. viii. 55. 8
The *Squire* of low degree, releast, Aemylia takes to wife: . . . IV. ix. Arg.
this trustie *squire* with proud disdaine . . . IV. ix. 3. 7
Then did he take that chaced *Squire,* . . . IV. ix. 5. 1
saw him sencelesse by the *Squire* upstaide, . . . IV. ix. 7. 4
that same *Squire* of treason to upbraide; . . . IV. ix. 7. 7
that *Squire* of low degree Came forth . . . IV. ix. 8. 8
the captive *Squire* she lov'd so deare, . . . IV. ix. 10. 6
That trusty *Squire* he wisely well did move . . . IV. ix. 15. 3
they saw a *Squire* in squallid weed Lamenting sore . . . V. i. 13. 7
By that same carefull *Squire* did then abide, . . . V. i. 23. 2
all That did betwixt him and that *Squire* betide: . . . V. i. 23. 4
Well did the *Squire* perceive him selfe too weake . . . V. i. 24. 1
that same *Squire,* to whom she was more dere, . . . V. i. 27. 3
'Not so, thou *Squire,*' (he sayd) . . . V. i. 28. 2
Much did that *Squire* Sir Artegall adore . . . V. i. 30. 1
as his *Squire* him offred evermore To serve, . . . V. i. 30. 3
by chaunce a comely *Squire* he found, . . . VI. i. 11. 2
'Unhappy *Squire!* what hard mishap thee brought . . . VI. i. 12. 1
Sayd then that *Squire;* . . . VI. i. 14. 5
Eftsoones he loosd that *Squire,* . . . VI. i. 18. 2
gave them streight unto that *Squire* againe, . . . VI. i. 47. 3
He makes him *Squire,* . . . VI. ii. Arg.
Let me this crave, . . . That ye will make me *Squire* . . . VI. ii. 33. 4
So he him dubbed, and his *Squire* did call. . . . VI. ii. 35. 5
'Glad would I surely be, thou courteous *Squire,* . . . VI. ii. 37. 1
his *Squyre,* With th' Hermit leaves behynd. . . . VI. v. Arg.
a knight, together with his *squire,* . . . VI. v. 11. 2
they wist that *Squire* to be so bold, . . . VI. v. 15. 6
So did that *Squire* his foes disperse . . . VI. v. 19. 9
the *Squire,* now nigh aghast, Revived was, . . . VI. v. 21. 8
To be his Timias, his owne true *Squire;* . . . VI. v. 23. 2
To whom the *Squire* nought aunswered againe, . . . VI. v. 24. 2
Which when that *Squire* beheld, he to them stept . . . VI. v. 25. 6
eke this *Squire,* who likewise wounded was . . . VI. v. 31. 6
Ne yet that gentle *Squire,* . . . VI. v. 39. 7
that *Squire* and Dame So faint and feeble were, . . . VI. v. 40. 6
The Hermite heales both *Squire* and dame . . . VI. vi. Arg.
Made in the bodies of that *Squire* and Dame; . . . VI. vi. 2. 2
The *Squire,* for that he courteous was indeed, . . . VI. vi. 16. 4
In th' harts of . . . many a gentle *squire.* . . . VI. vii. 28. 9
the gentle *Squire,* with faire Serene, . . . VI. vii. 39. 2
Whose cruell handling when that *Squire* beheld, . . . VI. vii. 45. 1
So did the *Squire,* the whiles the Carle did fret . . . VI. vii. 47. 7
after thraldome of the gentle *Squire,* . . . VI. viii. 3. 1
The *Squire* him selfe, when as he saw his Lord . . . VI. viii. 5. 1
Yond Lady and her *Squire* with foule despight Abusde, . . . VI. viii. 6. 3
See, how they doe that *Squire* beat and revile! . . . VI. viii. 6. 6
It was his owne true groome, the gentle *Squire,* . . . VI. viii. 27. 6
When first the gentle *Squire* at variaunce fell . . . VI. viii. 31. 3
Squires. brave Knights, and their renowned *Squires;* . . . *Hub.* 29
a goodly traine Of *Squires* and Ladies equipaged well, . . . II. ix. 17. 8
many Groomes and *Squyres* ready were . . . II. xi. 49. 1
all was full of Damzels and of *Squyres,* . . . III. i. 39. 6
squiers make hast to helpe their Lords fordonne. . . . IV. iv. 38. 8
these *Squires* true friendship more did sway . . . IV. ix. 3. 3
Knights and *Squires* to him unknowne afore: . . . IV. ix. 8. 5
the other Knights and *Squires* which them did see. . . . IV. ix. 11. 9
two comely *Squires,* Both brethren, . . . V. iv. 4. 2
for it these *Squires* at ods did fall, . . . V. iv. 5. 6
Squirrel. the *squirrell* wild He brought to her in bands, . . . III. vii. 17. 6
Squirrels. all about the fields like *Squirrels* hunt; . . . V. xi. 59. 3
wanton *squirrels* in the woods farre sought, . . . VI. ix. 40. 3
Stable. in some *stable* neare did set him up to feede. . . . VI. vi. 19. 9
Stabled. *Ystabled* hath his steedes . . . *S.C.* N. 15
Stablish. *stablish* terms betwixt both their requests, . . . II. ii. 32. 7
Stablished. *stablished* my peace. . . . V. xi. 18. 7
Stablishment. For stint of strife and *stablishment* of rest . . . V. viii. 21. 3
Stacks. Upon the naked fields in *stackes* he reares: . . . *Ro.* xxx. 8
Staddle. governing . . . aged limbs on cypresse *stadle* stout, . . . I. vi. 14. 8
Staff. *See* **Jacob's staff.**
wants the *staffe* of wisedome him to stay, . . . *T.M.* 140
on a *staffe* his feeble steps did frame, . . . I. viii. 30. 3
Wont on a *staffe* his feeble steps to stay, . . . I. x. 5. 7
with a *staffe* his feeble steps did stire, . . . II. i. 7. 4

Staff—*Continued.*
with his steedy *staffe* did point his way; . . . II. i. 34. 6
on a *staffe* her feeble steps did stay: . . . II. iv. 4. 4
Sometimes her *staffe,* though it her one leg were, . . . II. iv. 5. 6
with a *staffe,* all full of litle snags, . . . II. xi. 23. 7
lifting up his vertuous staffe on *hye,* . . . II. xii. 26. 6
The Palmer over them his *staffe* upheld, . . . II. xii. 40. 2
His mighty *staffe,* that could all charmes defeat. . . . II. xii. 40. 3
Such wondrous powre did in that *staffe* appeare, . . . II. xii. 40. 8
Such vertue in his *staffe* had eke this Palmer sage. . . . II. xii. 41. 9
Holding a *staffe* in hand for mere formalitee. . . . II. xii. 48. 9
broke his *staffe* with which he charmed semblants sly. . . . II. xii. 49. 9
Streight way he with his vertuous *staffe* them strooke, . . . II. xii. 86. 1
with his *staffe,* that drives his heard astray, . . . III. viii. 31. 8
the *staffe* asunder brake, And left the head behinde: . . . IV. iii. 10. 6
in his hand an huge long *staffe* he held, . . . V. ix. 11. 1
In his right hand a tipped *staffe* he held, . . . VII. vii. 31. 6
Stag. Now, like a *stag;* now, like a faulcon flit: . . . III. xi. 39. 8
The Parthian strikes a *stag* with shivering dart, . . . IV. i. 49. 8
Stage. How I could reare the Muse on stately *stage,* . . . *S.C.* O. 112
The *Stage* with Tragick buskin to adorne, . . . *T.M.* 152
all that els the Comick *Stage* . . . graced, . . . *T.M.* 199
like a Looker-on Of this worldes *Stage,* . . . *Com. Son.* i. 3
wontst the tragick *stage* for to direct, . . . *Mui.* 11
th' honorable *stage* of womanhead, . . . III. v. 54. 8
Yclad in costly garments fit for tragicke *Stage.* . . . III. xii. 3. 9
Fayre Canacee upon a stately *stage* Was set, . . . IV. iii. 4. 6
Ne staide till she the highest *stage* had scand, . . . VII. vi. 8. 8
Stages. Therein were divers rowmes, and divers *stages;* . . . II. ix. 47. 6
Stagger. Their steeds doe *stagger,* and amazed stand; . . . I. ii. 15. 6
made him *stagger,* as he were not well: . . . III. i. 6. 5
Her Steed did *stagger* with that puissaunt strooke; . . . III. vii. 41. 1
At puffe of every storme doth *stagger* here and theare. . . . IV. iii. 9. 9
It made her *stagger* oft, . . . V. iv. 41. 9
makes the wals to *stagger* with astonishment: . . . V. x. 34. 9
made him *stagger* with uncertaine sway, . . . V. xi. 11. 2
made him *stagger* and stand halfe agast, . . . V. xi. 28. 7
oft he made him *stagger* as unstayd, . . . VI. i. 20. 3
Staggered. He *staggered* to and fro in doubtfull sted. . . . V. xii. 23. 4
Staggering. With *staggring* pace and dismall lookes dismay, . . . *D.* 564
had his *staggering* steed not shronke for feare, . . . I. iii. 35. 4
rushing forth from inner bowre, With . . . *staggering* steps, . . . I. viii. 5. 8
staggering steps thy steady hand doth lead, . . . I. x. 51. 2
Stags. both as swift on foot as chased *Stags;* . . . II. xi. 23. 5
Staid. With *stayed* steps and grave beseeming grace: . . . VI. v. 36. 5
The villaine *stayd* not aunswer to invent, . . . VI. viii. 8. 1
Stain. When Giants bloud did *staine* Phlegraean ground. . . . *Gn.* 40
could this gardine *staine.* . . . *Ti.* 525
That did all other Beasts in beawtie *staine.* . . . *D.* 112
Come, see where your false Lady doth her honor *staine.'* . . . I. ii. 4. 9
His burning eyen, whom bloody strakes did *staine,* . . . II. iv. 15. 5
whiles with blood they all the shore did *staine,* . . . II. x. 48. 3
devoure Her native flesh and *staine* her brothers bowre, . . . III. vii. 49. 5
Sclaunder her guests doth *staine:* . . . IV. viii. Arg.
So faire and tender without *staine* or spot . . . V. vii. 29. 7
the pure snow, with goodly vermill *stayne* . . . *Epith.* 227
Without blemish or *staine;* . . . *Epith.* 400
Stained. all the waves were *stain'd* with filthie hewe. . . . *Van.* v. 12
Both borrowed pride, and native beautie *stained.* . . . *Van.* viii. 12
all his tract with bloudie drops is *stained* . . . *Gn.* 279
With brutishnesse and beastlie filth hath *stained.* . . . *T.M.* 270
his pure streames with guiltles blood oft *stained;* . . . *Ti.* 145
The red bloud trickling *staind* the way, . . . I. ii. 14. 9
His ruffin raiment all was *staind* with blood . . . I. iv. 34. 1
Una, his deare dreed, Her truth had *staynd* with treason . . . I. vi. 2. 4
when her face is *staynd* with magicke arts constraint. . . . I. vii. 34. 9
A sea of blood . . . her gay garments *staynd* . . . I. viii. 16. 7
That all her goodly garments *staind* arownd, . . . II. i. 39. 8
staynd their prayses with thy least good part; . . . II. iv. 26. 4
with the liquor *stained* all the lond: . . . II. xii. 57. 5
Greeke and Asian rivers *stayned* with their blood. . . . III. iii. 22. 9
all their armours *staynd* with bloudie gore; . . . IV. ii. 18. 6
signe whereof yet *stain'd* his bloudy lips afore. . . . IV. vii. 5. 9
often *stainde* with bloud of many a band . . . IV. xi. 36. 8
balefull Oure, late *staind* with English blood, . . . IV. xi. 44. 5
Whose waters with his filthy bloud it *stayned;* . . . V. ii. 19. 2
Had *stayned* with reprochfull crueltie In guiltlesse blood . . . V. xii. 40. 6
Stains. His honour *staines* with rancour and despight, . . . II. viii. 29. 8
staynes his snowy skin with hatefull hew: . . . III. i. 38. 6
did her lilly smock with *staines* of vermeil steep. . . . III. i. 65. 9
Stair. From highest *staire* to lowest step me drave, . . . *Ti.* 25
fall on lowest *staire.* . . . *Ti.* 494
My dearest Lord fell from high honors *staire* . . . I. ii. 23. 7
So goodly brought them to the lowest *stayre* . . . I. iv. 13. 5
Forthy she standeth on the highest *stayre* . . . III. v. 54. 7
he, that standeth on the hyghest *stayre,* . . . *Am.* lviii. 11
Ascending up, with many a stately *stayre,* . . . *Epith.* 179
Stake. the white beare to the *stake* did bring. . . . *S.C.* O. 48
both her handes fast bound unto a *stake,* . . . II. iv. 13. 5
For whose sole libertie I love and life did *stake.* . . . IV. viii. 60. 9
Eftsoones he stood as still as any *stake,* . . . V. iii. 34. 5
As she had got thereby and gayned a great *stake.* . . . V. xii. 32. 9
Stakes. To let him loose to save their proper *stakes,* . . . IV. iv. 34. 8
Stale. No leasing new, nor Grandams fable *stale,* . . . *Col.* 102
Stales. Still as he went he craftie *stales* did lay, . . . II. i. 4. 1
set for *stales* T' entrap unwary fooles . . . VI. x. 3. 8
Stalk. Then from greene grasse into a *stalke* doth spring, . . . *Ro.* xxx. 2
from a *stalke* into an eare forth-growes, . . . *Ro.* xxx. 3
The byting frost nipt his *stalke* dead, . . . *S.C.* F. 231
him behynd a wicked Hag did *stalke,* . . . II. iv. 4. 1

Stalk—*Continued.*
which with monstrous *stalke* behind him stept, ... II. vii. 26. 8
Whose root and *stalke* so bitter yet did taste, ... III. ii. 17. 6
though it on a lowly *stalke* doe bowre, ... VI. Pr. 4. 3
In thousand dreadful shapes doth mongst them *stalke,* . . . VI. xi. 16. 7
Stalketh. Upon his tiptoes, *stalketh* stately by, ... *Hub.* 664
Stalking. enimy With sturdie steps came *stalking* in his sight, I. vii. 8. 3
his *stalking* steps are stayde Upon a snaggy Oke, ... I. vii. 10. 6
stalking stately, like a Crane, did stryde . . . . VI. vii. 42. 5
Stalks. cropt full feateously The tender *stalkes* on hye. . . . . *Proth.* 28
Stall. *See* **Forestall, Head-stall, Laystall.**
The fatte Oxe, that wont ligge in the *stal,* . . . . *S.C.* S. 118
Like carkases of beastes in butchers *stall.* . . . . I. v. 49. 2
Bound like a beast appointed to the *stall:* . . . . V. i. 22. 6
in bloudy *stall* Of butchers balefull hand to ground is feld, VI. xii. 30. 7
Stalled. Is nowe fast *stalled* in her crumenall. . . . . *S.C.* S. 119
he never should be quit, nor *stal'd.* . . . . *Hub.* 1245
Stallion. a trotting *Stalion* get An ambling Colt, ... VI. iii. 1. 6
Stalls. His little Goats gan drive out of their *stalls,* . . . . . *Gn.* 71
Stamford. shall see *Stamford,* though now homely hid, ... IV. xi. 35. 4
Stamp. Teme . . . Did softly swim away, ne ever *stamp* . . . . I. v. 28. 6
Stamped. most were *stampt,* . . . . II. vii. 5. 8
he *stampt,* he lowd did cry, ... III. x. 17. 7
Stanch. Whose bleeding sourse their streames yet never *staunch* *H.H.L.* 164
Stand. *See* **Upstand.**
(Alas! that it so ready should *stand!*) . . . . *S.C.* F. 196
nowe upright he can *stand* no more; . . . . *S.C.* F. 234
see the dore *stand* open wyde. . . . . *S.C.* May 295
sacred unto saints they *stond,* . . . . *S.C.* Jul. 39
uneth may I *stand* any more: . . . . *S.C.* S. 48
the swift running rivers still did *stand,* . . . . *Gn.* 450
you . . . doo in order *stand.* . . . . *Gn.* 480
The care of Kings and power of Empires *stand,* . . . . . . *Hub.* 1226
'Where my high steeples whilom usde to *stand,* . . . . . . *Ti.* 127
Did *stand* astonisht at his curious skill, ... *Col.* 8
is there other then whereon we *stand?*' . . . . *Col.* 291
Their steeds doe stagger, and amazed *stand;* . . . . I. ii. 15. 6
both *stand* sencelesse as a blocke, ... I. ii. 16. 5
I in defence of mine did likewise *stand,* . . . . I. ii. 36. 3
seeing by her side the Lyon *stand,* . . . . I. iii. 11. 5
thy foe doth vanquisht *stand* Now at thy mercy: . . . . . . I. iii. 37. 4
the which, . . . The gods *stand* gazing on, ... I. iv. 17. 6
When fairer faces were bid *standen* by: . . . . I. iv. 24. 8
well he could not touch, nor goe, nor *stand.* . . . . I. iv. 29. 8
So oft as Slowth still in the mire did *stand.* . . . . I. iv. 36. 4
All *stand* amazed at so uncouth sight, ... I. vi. 9. 6
All *stand* astonied at her beautie bright, ... I. vi. 9. 8
He left his *stond,* and her pursewd apace, ... I. vi. 48. 6
the Squire . . . did like a bulwarke *stand.* . . . . I. viii. 12. 9
The souldier may not . . . leave his *stand* . . . . I. ix. 41. 5
Ne ought his sturdy strokes might *stand* afore, ... I. xi. 37. 8
some more bold to measure him nigh *stand,* . . . . I. xii. 11. 8
her dores to all *stand* open wide. . . . . II. iii. 41. 9
the Blacke Palmer suffred still to *stond,* . . . . II. vi. 19. 7
Upon that shore he spyed Atin *stand,* . . . . II. vi. 38. 7
his cruell foes, that *stand* hereby, ... II. viii. 25. 1
dreadfull Death behynd thy backe doth *stond.*' . . . . II. viii. 37. 9
constant keepe the way in which ye *stand;* . . . . II. ix. 8. 6
in assuraunce it may never *stand,* . . . . II. xi. 30. 4
At sight whereof the people *stand* aghast; . . . . III. i. 16. 7
may emongst Alcides labours *stand.*' . . . . III. vii. 61. 4
Proceeding to the midst he stil did *stand,* . . . . III. xii. 4. 1
her selfe did reare Out of her secret *stand* . . . . III. xii. 28. 9
Do greatly *stand* amaz'd at such unwonted wonder. . . . . . IV. ii. 16. 9
much amaz'd the headlesse tronke to see *Stand* up . . . . . IV. iii. 21. 3
Could *stand* on foot now to renew the fight: . . . . IV. iii. 23. 3
they, like men astonisht, still did *stand.* . . . . IV. iii. 48. 5
none of them against his strokes could *stand,* . . . . IV. iv. 21. 6
Gainst whom none able was to *stand* on ground; . . . . IV. iv. 28. 3
none of them in field durst *stand,* . . . . IV. iv. 43. 3
still over him did *stand,* . . . . IV. vi. 23. 4
now in feare of shame she more did *stond,* . . . . IV. ix. 18. 5
turn'd his face away, as he did *stand,* . . . . IV. x. 33. 4
the Goddesse selfe did *stand* Upon an altar . . . . IV. x. 39. 1
lenger he note *stand* upright, ... IV. xii. 20. 7
There they beheld a mighty Gyant *stand* Upon a rocke, . . . V. ii. 30. 1
what on earth can alwayes happie *stand?* . . . . V. iii. 9. 1
not for it this ods twixt us doth *stand,* . . . . V. iv. 15. 4
for assurance to my doome to *stand,* . . . . V. iv. 16. 6
'For equall right in equall things doth *stand;* . . . . V. iv. 19. 1
In which condition I right now did *stand:* . . . . V. iv. 32. 5
Be well adviz'd that he *stand* stedfast still; . . . . V. vi. 1. 7
Uppon two stubborne oakes, which *stand* so neare . . . . . V. vi. 40. 2
on the ground the other fast did *stand;* . . . . V. vii. 7. 2
Doth in defence thereof full stoutly *stond:* . . . . V. vii. 30. 6
if they against him *stand,* . . . . V. viii. 18. 8
Where he with boughes hath built his shady *stand,* . . . . . V. viii. 35. 8
He there did *stand* That would his doings justifie . . . . . . V. xi. 4. 8
Where she with her two sonnes did looking *stand,* . . . . . V. xi. 15. 2
Declare it boldly, Dame, and doe not *stand* in dout.' . . . . V. xi. 18. 9
made him stagger and *stand* halfe agast, ... V. xi. 28. 7
that of him she mote assured *stand,* . . . . VI. i. 31. 8
He bad him *stand* t' abide the bitter stoure . . . . VI. iii. 48. 4
of her grace did *stand* againe assured, ... VI. v. 12. 3
when he saw those two so neare him *stand,* . . . . VI. vii. 24. 1
she that in the midst of them did *stand* . . . . VI. x. 14. 3
Calidore in th' entry close did *stand,* . . . . VI. xi. 46. 6
Where Cynthia did sit, that never still did *stand.* . . . . . VII. vi. 8. 9
the Moones bright wagon still did *stand,* . . . . VII. vi. 13. 7
he did assoyle . . . where it in doubt did *stand,* . . . . . . VII. vii. 38. 8

Stand—*Continued.*
looking still on her, I *stand* amazed . . . . *Am.* iii. 7
Why *stand* ye still ye virgins in amaze, ... *Epith.* 181
wonder at that sight, And *stand* astonisht . . . . *Epith.* 189
How ever here on higher steps we *stand,* . . . . *H.H.L.* 201
Standest. 'Why *standst* there (quoth he) thou brutish blocke? *S.C.* F. 127
Standeth. never *standeth* in one certaine state, ... *D.* 430
all the day it *standeth* full of deow, ... *As.* 191
Forthy she *standeth* on the highest stayre . . . . III. v. 54. 7
So nothing heere long *standeth* in one stay: . . . . VII. vii. 47. 7
he, that *standeth* on the hyghest stayre, ... *Am.* lviii. 11
Standing. *standing* by the gates in strange disguize, ... *Hub.* 1271
Upon a brazen pillour *standing* hie, ... *Ti.* 660
They him saluted, *standing* far afore, ... I. x. 49. 7
Before her *standing* she espied had, ... II. i. 45. 5
her two other sisters, *standing* by, ... II. ii. 28. 1
standing stoutly up, his lofty crest Did fiercely shake, . . . II. iii. 35. 8
Guyon *standing* by their uncouth strife does see. . . . . . . II. v. 20. 9
standing still a space Gaz'd after him, ... II. viii. 9. 3
keepe his *standing,* and his shaftes eschew, ... II. xi. 27. 7
Until he came unto a *standing* lake; . . . . II. xi. 46. 6
standing high aloft low lay thine eare, ... III. iii. 9. 1
The noble Mayd still *standing* all this vewd, ... III. xii. 5. 1
The direfull distaffe *standing* in the mid, ... IV. ii. 48. 2
About the Andvile *standing* evermore . . . . IV. v. 36. 2
Standing with emptie hands all weaponlesse, ... V. v. 14. 2
a Ladie faire he saw *Standing* alone . . . . VI. ii. 4. 2
that same Knight and Salvage *standing* by, ... VI. vi. 23. 2
Which when the Prince beheld, there *standing* by, ... VI. viii. 12. 6
him supported *standing* neare. . . . . VI. viii. 25. 9
standing on his tiptoes, to seeme tall, ... VI. viii. 26. 5
standing long astonished in spright, ... VI. x. 17. 3
the people *standing* all about, ... *Epith.* 143
Hercules two pillors *standing* neere . . . . *Proth.* 148
Stands. Now *stands* the Brere like a lord alone, ... *S.C.* F. 222
All otherwise the state of Poet *stands;* . . . . *S.C.* O. 97
He *stands* on tearmes of honourable minde, ... *Hub.* 721
Before them *stands* the God of Seas in place, ... *Mui.* 313
Before her *stands* her knight, ... I. iii. 30. 9
the virgin . . . who all this while Amased *stands,* . . . . . I. iii. 40. 2
He *standes* amazed how he thence should fade: . . . . I. v. 15. 5
none did . . . aid envy to him in need that *stands;* . . . . . I. ix. 1. 6
Their stedfast *stonds* did mightily maintaine, ... II. xi. 15. 2
Like as the sacred Oxe that carelesse *stands,* . . . . III. iv. 17. 1
Her teme at her commaundement quiet *stands,* . . . . III. iv. 42. 3
Troynovant . . . which *stands* so hy, ... III. ix. 45. 6
Upon a brasen pillour, by the which she *stands.* . . . . . . III. xii. 30. 9
The beast astonisht *stands* in middest of his smart. . . . . . IV. i. 49. 9
all the world in state unmoved *stands,* . . . . IV. x. 35. 2
Proudly *stands* over, and a while doth pause . . . . V. iv. 40. 8
As now in miserable state he *stands;* . . . . V. v. 33. 3
in this Church hereby There *stands* an Idole . . . . V. xi. 19. 2
Whilest still she *stands,* as stonisht and forlorne: . . . . . V. xi. 29. 5
there *stands* a castle strong, ... VI. i. 13. 2
abide the death that hard before you *stands.*' . . . . VI. viii. 7. 9
gazing still on others *stands.* . . . . VI. ix. 11. 9
whiles she before the altar *stands,* . . . . *Epith.* 223
there *standes* a stately place, ... *Proth.* 137
Stank. *See* **Stunk.**
I am so stiffe and so *stanck,* . . . . *S.C.* S. 47
sad waves, which direfull deadly *stancke,* . . . . II. vii. 57. 3
Of muddie water, that like puddle *stanke,* . . . . IV. v. 33. 4
Star. *See* **Evening-star, Lodestar, Morning-star, Northern star, Venus-star.**
where the yerely *starre* doth scortch the ground, ... *Ro.* xxvi. 7
he, that strives to touch a *starre,* . . . . *S.C.* Jul. 99
the bright *starre* Seemeth ay greater . . . . *S.C.* S. 76
haplesse rising of some froward *starre,* . . . . *Gn.* 570
So now it is transform'd into that *starre,* . . . . *Ti.* 629
Distinguished with manie a twinckling *starre;* . . . . *Mui.* 94
My love . . . that wont to be their *Starre:* . . . . *D.* 424
my fair *Starre* (that shinde on me so bright) . . . . *D.* 480
Stella the faire, the fairest *star* in skie, ... *As.* 55
(A fairer *star* saw never living eie,) . . . . *As.* 57
in the midst thereof a *star* appeares, ... *As.* 187
As fairly formd as any *star* in skyes; . . . . *As.* 188
prais'd and rais'd above each other *starre.* . . . . *Col.* 535
Not perceable with power of any *starr:* . . . . I. i. 7. 6
'Faire knight, borne under happie *starre,* . . . . I. i. 27. 3
His sevenfold teme behind the stedfast *starre* . . . . I. ii. 1. 2
what evill *starre* On you hath frownd, ... I. viii. 42. 6
in every other *starre* unseene . . . . II. Pr. 3. 7
'Ah! lucklesse babe, borne under cruell *starre,* . . . . . . II. ii. 2. 1
Death is for wretches borne under unhappy *starre.*' . . . . . II. vi. 44. 9
to a stedfast *starre* his course hath bent, ... II. vii. 1. 2
that faire *Starre,* the messenger of morne, ... II. xii. 65. 1
as a blazing *starre* doth farre outcast His hearie beames, . . III. i. 16. 5
Ne chaunged was into a *starre* in sky; . . . . IV. iii. 13. 5
By conduct of some *star,* doth make her way; . . . . *Am.* xxxiv. 2
star, that wont with her bright ray Me to direct, ... *Am.* xxxiv. 5
flowing from the beame Of thy bright *starre,* . . . . *H.B.* 56
that fayrest *starre* Which lights the world . . . . *H.B.* 111
the light of your bright shyning *starre.* . . . . *H.B.* 175
Stare. Fellie he hisseth, and doth fiercely *stare,* . . . . . . *Gn.* 277
stare on him, with big lookes basen wide, ... *Hub.* 670
with fast fixed eyes on her did *stare,* . . . . *Mui.* 340
Her fyrie eyes with furious sparkes did *stare,* . . . . III. vii. 39. 8
How the rude Shepheards after him did *stare,* . . . . III. xi. 34. 7
It made her . . . *stare* with ghastly eye. . . . . V. iv. 41. 9
Take heed . . . myne eyes, how ye doe *stare* . . . . *Am.* xxxvii. 9

Stare—*Continued.*
So many gazers as on her do *stare,* . . . . *Epith.* 160
seems more fayre, The more they on it *stare.* . . . . *Epith.* 233
Stared. *See* **Upstared.**
His eies . . . *stared* sterne on all that him beheld; . . . . . I. iv. 33. 6
his hollow eyne . . . *stared* as astound; . . . . I. ix. 35. 7
Stared full wide, and threw forth sparkes of fyre; . . . . . II. iv. 15. 6
they did unmanly looke, And *stared* ghastly; . . . . II. xii. 86. 4
Stared on her awhile, as one astound, ... III. vii. 7. 7
So *stared* he on her, and stood long while amaz'd. . . . . . III. vii. 13. 9
she *star'd* A while about her with confused eye; . . . . . . V. v. 13. 7
stifly *stared* Like one adawed . . . . V. vii. 20. 7
He gaz'd about and *stared* horriblie, ... VI. vii. 42. 8
with sterne eye-browes *stared* at him oft, ... VI. viii. 26. 3
Stares. The Marriner yet halfe amazed *stares* At perill past, . . I. vi. 1. 4
Star-gazers. even these *Star-gazers* stonisht are . . . . . VII. vii. 52. 5
Staring. So stood these twaine, . . . Both *staring* fierce, . . . I. ii. 16. 8
The trembling ghosts . . . *staring* wide With stony eies; . . . I. v. 32. 6
With *staring* countenance sterne, as one astownd, ... I. viii. 5. 7
Which when the Gyaunt spyde with *staring* eye, ... I. viii. 19. 6
staring wyde With stony eyes . . . . I. ix. 24. 2
with *staring* eyes fixed askaunce, ... II. vii. 7. 5
Their *staring* eyes sparckling with fervent fyre . . . . II. vii. 37. 6
Staring with hollow eies, and stiffe upstanding heares. . . . . II. ix. 13. 9
sharpe *staring* eyes, That mad or foolish seemd: . . . . II. ix. 52. 6
With upstart haire and *staring* eyes dismay, ... III. x. 54. 8
All looking on, and like astonisht *staring,* . . . . IV. x. 56. 8
stood long *staring* on him mongst uncertaine feares. . . . . . V. vii. 39. 9
Stark. as he were *starke* lame: . . . . *S.C.* May 279
sences all were straight benumbd and *starke.* . . . . I. i. 44. 5
the fruitfull-headed beast, . . . Became *stark* blind, ... I. viii. 20. 3
His hart gan wexe as *starke* as marble stone, ... II. i. 42. 2
Starlight. That hearbe of some *Starlight* is cald by name, . . . *As.* 193
Star-rede. wisards old, Which in *Star-read* . . . have best insight, ... V. Pr. 8. 2
Starry. Heapt hils on hils to scale the *starrie* skie, ... *Ro.* xii. 2
Would rayse ones mynd above the *starry* skie, ... *S.C.* O. 94
Betwixt the forrest wide and *starrie* sky: . . . . *Gn.* 34
Drawing in teemes along the *starrie* skie; . . . . *Gn.* 458
extend Her lofty towres unto the *starry* sphere, ... I. x. 56. 8
like *starry* light, Which, sparckling . . . . II. xii. 78. 8
Her mantle, colour'd like the *starry* skyes, ... III. i. 36. 2
by th' uncertaine glims of *starry* night, ... VI. viii. 48. 1
With *starrie* beames about her shining bright, ... VI. xi. 13. 5
Onely the *starry* skie doth still remaine: . . . . VII. vii. 55. 5
with *starry* light, Those lamping eyes will . . . look, ... *Am.* i. 5
Stars. She, whose high top above the *starres* did sore, ... *Ro.* iv. 1
Ye cruell *starres,* and eke ye Gods unkinde, ... *Ro.* ix. 1
twincling *starres* the daylight hence chase. . . . . *S.C.* Ap. 161
Upon whose toppe the *starres* bene stayed, ... *S.C.* Jul. 61
*And he that strives to touch the *starres,* . . . . *S.C.* Jul. 99
To make the mountaines touch the *starres* divine, ... *Gn.* 213
Sun and *starres* and all the heavenly powres . . . . *Gn.* 578
Charlemaine amongst the *Starris* seaven. . . . . *T.M.* 462
Starres conspiring wretched men t' afflict, ... *T.M.* 482
ever as I see the *starres* to fall, ... *D.* 477
molten *starres* doe drop like weeping eyes; . . . . I. vi. 6. 5
a bauldrick . . . That shind, like twinkling *stars,* . . . . . . I. vii. 29. 9
burning *starres* and everliving fire, ... I. x. 50. 6
glistred bright Like twinckling *starres;* . . . . II. iii. 26. 8
saile withouten *starres* gainst tyde and winde: . . . . III. iv. 9. 8
with thousand *starres* was decked fayre: . . . . III. iv. 52. 3
shone as Phebes light Amongst the lesser *starres* . . . . . . IV. v. 14. 4
eyes, like twinkling *stars* in evening cleare, ... IV. x. 50. 7
glittering spangs that did like *starres* appeare, ... IV. xi. 45. 5
To tell the sands, or count the *starres* on hye, ... IV. xi. 53. 2
much more eath to tell the *starres* on hy, ... IV. xii. 1. 5
As he on whom the lucklesse *stars* did lowre, ... V. v. 18. 5
is unto the *starres* an ornament, ... VI. x. 13. 8
like *starres* in foggie night. . . . . VI. xi. 21. 9
Environd with tenne thousand *starres* around . . . . VII. vi. 9. 3
the *starres,* which round about her blazed, ... VII. vi. 13. 6
On top whereof the moon and *stars* were pight; . . . . VII. vii. 44. 6
the *Starres* and Signes therein still move, ... VII. vii. 55. 6
Nor to the *Starres;* for they have purer sight; . . . . *Am.* ix. 7
like *stars* that dimmed were With darksome cloud, ... *Epith.* 93
That golden wyre, those sparckling *stars* so bright, ... *H.B.* 97
twinckling *starres* in frostie night; . . . . *H.B.* 257
All sowd with glistring *stars* more thicke then grasse, ... *H.H.B.* 53
gemmes and jewels . . . that brighter then the *starres* appeare, *H.H.B.* 188
Cynthia doth shend The lesser *starres.* . . . . *Proth.* 122
Stars'. if I marked well the *starres* revolution, ... *S.C.* Env. 3
The *Starres* pure light, the Spheres swift movement, ... *T.M.* 508
likely harts composd of *starres* concent, ... *H.B.* 198
Start. *See* **Started, Upstart.**
With so great noyse I *start* in sodaine wonder. . . . . *Bel.*[1] xi. 14
now from me hys madding mynd is *starte,* . . . . *S.C.* Ap. 25
He lifted up his hand, that backe againe did *start.* . . . . . . I. ix. 51. 9
with sterne horror backward gan to *start;* . . . . III. v. 30. 6
the least twinckling sleepe to *start* Into her eye, ... V. vi. 24. 7
from just verdict will for nothing *start,* . . . . V. x. 2. 2
vowing not to *start,* But wayt on him . . . . VI. ii. 36. 4
that same knight would not once let him *start,* . . . . VI. vii. 21. 1
that it from her may never *start,* . . . . *Am.* xlii. 9
Ne feard with worse to any chaunce to *start;* . . . . *Am.* lix. 4
Started. *See* **Start.**
she *started* up with cherefull sight, ... *Ti.* 642
*He *started* up, as seeming to mistrust . . . . I. i. 49. 3
streight way, He *started* up, and did him selfe prepayre . . . I. v. 2. 7
She weakely *started,* yet she nothing drad: . . . . II. i. 45. 7

Started—*Continued.*
Tho up he *started,* stird with shame extreme, ... II. vi. 27. 7
All unawares he *started* up anon, ... IV. iii. 31. 3
lightly *started* up as one affrayd, ... IV. v. 42. 6
started up avenged for to be . . . . IV. v. 44. 6
Lightly he *started* up out of that stound, ... IV. vi. 12. 1
He *started* up, there where on ground he lay, ... V. vi. 29. 6
He *started* up; and . . . Like a fell Lyon leaped . . . . VI. vii. 25. 3
He lightly *started* up like one aghast, ... VI. viii. 47. 8
In haste forth *started* from the guilty brooke; . . . . VII. vi. 47. 2
Starteth. In this great passion . . . He *starteth* up, ... I. i. 49. 3
Starting. *See* **Back-starting.**
to his *starting* steed that swarv'd asyde, ... III. i. 11. 6
therewith somewhat *starting,* up gan looke, ... III. xi. 13. 2
starting up streight for his armour sought: . . . . IV. iv. 33. 3
Whereat the other *starting* up dismayd, ... VI. ii. 18. 6
Hastily *starting* up, . . . Ran after fast . . . . VI. iii. 24. 8
She *starting* up began to shrieke aloud; . . . . VI. vi. 31. 2
Starve. Nowe doe I dayly *starve,* wanting my lively foode: . . *U.V.* 17
if I *starve,* who will record my cursed end? . . . . *U.V.* 20
these armes . . . the which doe men in bale to *sterve,* . . . . II. vi. 34. 3
was like to *sterve* Through cruell knife . . . . IV. i. 4. 4
life it is to her, when others *sterve* . . . . IV. i. 26. 3
I *starve* my body, and mine eyes doe blynd. . . . . *Am.* lxxxvii. 14
sterve their harts that needeth nourture most, ... *H.L.* 39
Starved. The rather Lambes bene *starved* with cold, ... *S.C.* F. 83
Bene all *sterved* with pyne and penuree: . . . . *S.C.* S. 65
almost *sterv'd* did much lament and mourne. . . . . *Hub.* 580
he *sterv'd* with hunger, and with drouth, ... II. vii. 58. 8
the wilde beast shall dy in *starved* den. . . . . III. iii. 34. 9
Narcissus vaine, Whose eyes him *starv'd:* . . . . *Am.* xxxv. 8
Like Tantale, that in store doth *sterved* ly, ... *H.L.* 200
Starving. driven be perforce to *sterving,* . . . . *Hub.* 370
State. tickle trustles *state* Of vaine worlds glorie, ... *Pet.*[2] vii. 1
Shall finde his *state* most fickle and unsure. . . . . *Van.* xii. 14
now is come thy wynters stormy *state,* . . . . *S.C.* Ja. 23
his trees of *state* in compasse rownd: . . . . *S.C.* F. 146
entrap in thy tender *state:* . . . . *S.C.* May 218
I blesse thy *state,* . . . . *S.C.* Jun. 9
so stiffe and so *state,* As cocke on his dunghill . . . . *S.C.* S. 45
Content who lives with tryed *state* . . . . *S.C.* S. 70
All otherwise the *state* of Poet stands; . . . . *S.C.* O. 97
'O! trustlesse *state* of earthly things, ... *S.C.* N. 153
The chaungfull turning of mens slipperie *state,* . . . . *Gn.* 554
Light not on some that may our *state* amend; . . . . *Hub.* 171
Brings downe the stowtest hearts to lowest *state;* . . . . . . *Hub.* 255
now in other *state* abroad to range: . . . . *Hub.* 356
on us taken anie *state* of life, ... *Hub.* 407
By secrete meanes gan of his *state* enquire, ... *Hub.* 681
So pitifull a thing is Suters *state!* . . . . *Hub.* 891
government of *state* Will without wisedome soone be ruinate. . *Hub.* 1039
Heare, and behold the miserable *state* Of us, ... *T.M.* 59
use to paint in rimes the troublous *state* . . . . *T.M.* 381
Unhappie Verse, the witnesse of my unhappie *state,* . . . . . *U.V.* 1
unstedfast *state* Of all that lives . . . . *Ti.* 43
'O! trustlesse *state* of miserable men, ... *Ti.* 197
In *state* of blis, or stedfast happinesse? . . . . *Ti.* 569
what on earth can long abide in *state,* . . . . *Mui.* 217
Twelve Gods doo sit around in royall *state,* . . . . *Mui.* 307
never standeth in one certaine *state,* . . . . *D.* 430
Die is my dew; yet rew my wretched *state,* . . . . I. i. 51. 7
Craving of you, in pitty of my *state,* To doe none ill, ... I. ii. 26. 3
High above all a cloth of *State* was spred, ... I. iv. 8. 1
So proud she shyned in her princely *state,* . . . . I. iv. 10. 1
Why they were come her roiall *state* to see, ... I. iv. 13. 8
gin to pittie her unhappie *state:* . . . . I. vi. 9. 7
blisse may not abide in *state* of mortall men. . . . . I. viii. 44. 9
holds the world in his still chaunging *state,* . . . . I. ix. 42. 7
in true ballaunce thou wilt weigh thy *state;* . . . . I. ix. 45. 2
brought thee up in ploughmans *state* to byde, ... I. x. 66. 5
Proclaymed joy and peace through all his *state;* . . . . I. xii. 3. 8
The large discourse of roiall Princes *state.* . . . . I. xii. 14. 6
oft they did lament his lucklesse *state,* . . . . I. xii. 16. 4
the Gard, which on his *state* did wait, ... I. xii. 35. 4
He was an Elfin borne of noble *state* . . . . II. i. 6. 5
heven thee deignes to hold in living *state,* . . . . II. i. 37. 3
Which plonged had faire Lady in so wretched *state.* . . . . . II. i. 56. 9
Such is the *state* of men: . . . . II. ii. 2. 8
Transformd her to a stone from stedfast virgins *state.* . . . . II. ii. 8. 9
To succour the weake *state* of sad afflicted Troy. . . . . . . II. iii. 31. 9
the troublous stormes that tosse The private *state,* . . . . . II. vii. 14. 2
them that liv'd therin in *state* forlorne: . . . . II. vii. 18. 3
To teach them how to use their present *state.'* . . . . II. vii. 60. 5
As well in *state* of peace, as puissaunce in warre.' . . . . . . II. ix. 4. 9
he parted his imperiall *state,* . . . . II. x. 13. 6
Too truely tryde in his extremest *state.* . . . . II. x. 31. 3
Whose countries he redus'd to quiet *state,* . . . . II. x. 38. 7
ruled long with honorable *state* . . . . II. x. 45. 4
naturall desire of countryes *state,* . . . . II. x. 77. 2
So feeble is mans *state,* . . . . II. xi. 30. 3
whatever in this worldly *state* Is sweete . . . . II. xii. 42. 5
still in stedfast *state,* . . . . II. xii. 51. 2
Let them returned be unto their former *state.'* . . . . II. xii. 85. 9
Exceeding much the *state* of meane degree, ... III. i. 33. 7
bewrayes to Britomart The *state* of Arthegall; . . . . III. iii. Arg.
So ticle be the termes of mortall *state,* . . . . III. iv. 28. 6
sendeth forth to live in mortall *state,* . . . . III. vi. 32. 8
The *state* of life out of the griesly shade. . . . . III. vi. 37. 5
in stedfast love and happy *state* . . . . III. vi. 50. 6
her sonne that lay in feeble *state;* . . . . III. viii. 9. 7

State—*Continued.*	
didst weete . . . her sory *state,*	III. viii. 28. 2
drag'd him through the waves in scornfull *state,*	III. viii. 36. 7
Yt yrkes me leave thee in this wofull *state,*	III. viii. 43. 8
makes ensample of mans wretched *state,*	III. ix. 39. 8
Restore unto her health and former *state:*	III. xii. 35. 6
wretched Lady, quitt from wofull *state,*	III. xii. 39. 3
Welds kingdomes causes and affaires of *state,*	IV. Pr. 1. 2
many a publike *state,* . . . oft doth overthrow	IV. i. 19. 3
Long may you live in health and *happie* state!'	IV. ii. 23. 8
Till that to ripenesse of mans *state* they grew:	IV. ii. 46. 2
To overthrow my *state* and dignitie	IV. vii. 15. 5
him receiv'd againe to former favours *state*	IV. viii. 17. 9
shake the safe assurance of their *state:*	IV. ix. 16. 4
stronger in his *state* Then th' elder,	IV. x. 32. 8
all the world in *state* unmoved stands,	IV. x. 35. 2
him restor'd to healthfull *state* againe:	IV. xi. 7. 4
So oft as I with *state* of present time . . . compare,	V. Pr. 1. 1
she saw The daungerous *state* in which she stood,	V. ii. 22. 3
The bridegromes *state,* the brides most rich aray,	V. iii. 3. 3
how fell ye in this *state?'*	V. iv. 28. 5
all the wounded, and the weake in *state,*	V. iv. 45. 8
As now in miserable *state* he stands;	V. v. 33. 3
upon whose hopelesse *state* Fortune . . . hath felly frowned,	V. v. 36. 1
in the streightnesse of that captive *state*	V. vi. 2. 1
what he did, and in what *state* he stood,	V. vi. 15. 8
he is not the while in *state* to woo;	V. vi. 16. 2
To hide thy *state* from being understood?	V. vii. 21. 5
'Mongst many which maligne her happy *state,*	V. viii. 18. 1
Had utterly subverted his unrighteous *state.*	V. ix. 2. 9
All over her a cloth of *state* was spred,	V. ix. 28. 1
Seemed those litle Angels did uphold The cloth of *state,*	V. ix. 29. 2
She, Angel-like, . . . in royall *state,*	V. ix. 29. 8
goodly seem'd t' adorne her royall *state;*	V. ix. 31. 3
That Castle was the strength of all that *state,*	V. x. 26. 1
Untill that *state* by strength was pulled downe;	V. x. 26. 2
To which they had no right, nor any wrongfull *state.*	V. xi. 3. 9
of him learnes His *state* and present plight	VI. ii. Arg.
in this her needfull *state,* To succour her	VI. ii. 38. 3
So tickle is the *state* of earthly things,	VI. iii. 5. 2
This is the *state* of Keasars and of Kings!	VI. iii. 5. 7
this ill *state* in which she stood;	VI. iii. 11. 6
Such was the *state* of this most courteous knight	VI. iv. 1. 6
remained in most wretched *state,*	VI. v. 29. 3
from the high degree of happy *state* Fell	VI. viii. 2. 8
Would not bewray the *state* in which she stood.	VI. viii. 51. 5
'How much' (sayd he) 'more happie is the *state*	VI. ix. 19. 1
rageth sore in each degree and *state,*	VI. xii. 40. 2
In that still happy *state* for ever to abide.	VII. vi. 5. 9
unto Gods, whose *state* she did maligne,	VII. vi. 11. 6
all creatures to maintaine In *state* of life?	VII. vii. 22. 5
loath this *state* of life so tickle,	VII. viii. 1. 6
Why did ye stoup unto so lowly *state?*	*Am.* lxvi. 8
That they gan cast their *state* how to increase	*H.H.L.* 80
him restore unto that happie *state*	*H.H.L.* 139
of her fulnesse . . . They all partake, and do in *state* remaine	*H.H.B.* 200
Stately. shewe the greatnesse of the *stately* race,	*Bel.*[1] v. 7
Ten hornes also the *stately* beast did beare	*Rev.* ii. 5
a *stately* frame, An hundred cubits high	*Bel.*[2] ii. 1
How I could reare the Muse on *stately* stage,	*S.C.* O. 112
How have I wearied . . . The *stately* Walnut-tree,	*S.C.* D. 34
with big words, and with a *stately* pace,	*Hub.* 646
Upon his tiptoes, stalketh *stately* by,	*Hub.* 664
Sure gates, sweete gardens, *stately* galleries,	*Ti.* 95
Next unto this a *statelie* Towre appeared,	*Ti.* 505
Looking aside I saw a *stately* Bed,	*Ti.* 631
did a *stately* heape of stones upreare,	*Col.* 285
A *stately* Pallace built of squared bricke,	I. iv. 4. 1
Suddein upriseth from her *stately* place The roiall Dame,	I. iv. 16. 1
She is . . . placed under *stately* canapee,	I. v. 5. 4
Duessa . . . Returnd to *stately* pallace of Dame Pryde:	I. v. 45. 2
Which in that *stately* building wont to dwell:	I. viii. 32. 4
What *stately* building durst so high extend	I. x. 56. 7
by her *stately* portance borne of heavenly birth.	II. iii. 21. 9
with *stately* grace and princely port	II. iii. 28. 5
full of the *stately* tree	II. v. 31. 2
A *stately* siege of soveraine majestye;	II. vii. 44. 5
Thence she them brought into a *stately* Hall,	II. ix. 27. 1
Up to a *stately* Turret she them brought,	II. ix. 44. 8
A *stately* Castle far away she spyde,	III. i. 20. 2
stately port of Castle Joyeous,	III. i. 31. 2
Which *stately* manner whenas they did see,	III. i. 33. 5
like a *stately* Theatre it made,	III. v. 39. 5
There stood a *stately* Mount,	III. vi. 43. 2
stately towres of Ilion	III. ix. 34. 3
Fayre Canacee upon a *stately* stage Was set,	IV. iii. 4. 6
With *stately* steps and fearelesse countenance,	IV. iii. 5. 2
stately pillours fram'd after the Doricke guize	IV. x. 6. 9
not the *stately* Severne grudg'd at all,	IV. xi. 30. 6
Avon marched in more *stately* path,	IV. xi. 31. 6
With *stately* port and proud magnificence,	V. v. 4. 2
building . . . Borne uppon *stately* pillours,	V. vii. 5. 4
Where they a *stately* pallace did behold	V. ix. 21. 4
Taking them up unto her *stately* throne,	V. ix. 37. 6
defaced cleene Her *stately* towres	V. x. 25. 5
He chaunst to spie a faire and *stately* place,	VI. iii. 29. 7
stalking *stately,* like a Crane,	VI. vii. 42. 5
In which all trees of honour *stately* stood,	VI. x. 6. 4
Trophees to erect in *stately* wize;	*Am.* lxix. 2
Ascending up, with many a *stately* stayre,	*Epith.* 179
Stately—*Continued.*	
there standes a *stately* place,	*Proth.* 137
Stater. Ruddoc and proud *Stater,* both allyes,	II. x. 38. 3
States. Lovers of Lordship, and troublers of *states,*	*S.C.* May 123
th' intent of Counsells, and the change Of *states,*	*Hub.* 787
all mens *states* alike unstedfast be.	*D.* 518
still are wont most happie *states* t' annoy:	*Col.* 663
Inquireth of our *states,* and of our knightly deedes.	I. ix. 28. 9
Of commen-wealthes, of *states,* of pollicy,	II. ix. 53. 6
brave ensample, . . . to kinges and *states* imperiall.	II. x. 74. 9
When those gainst *states* and kingdomes do conjure,	V. x. 26. 8
tosseth *states,* and under foot doth tread	VI. ix. 27. 8
Are wont for Princes *states* to fashion;	VII. vii. 8. 4
do their *states* maintaine	VII. vii. 58. 9
All mortall Princes and imperiall *States;*	*H.H.B.* 88
Statues. Admire their *statues,* their Colossoes great:	*Com. Son.* iii. 6
Stature. in person and in *stature* Most like a Man,	*Hub.* 1029
Of wondrous powre, and of exceeding *stature,*	*Ti.* 534
his *stature* did exceed The hight of three	I. vii. 8. 8
His portaunce terrible, and *stature* tall,	II. vii. 41. 4
Of *stature* huge, and eke of corage bold,	II. x. 7. 8
A comely personage of *stature* tall,	II. xii. 46. 4
she was right faire . . . and of goodly *stature:*	IV. ii. 44. 7
eke in *stature* higher by a span;	IV. vii. 5. 3
Of *stature* huge, and horrible of hew,	IV. viii. 38. 8
Of *stature* huge and hideous he was,	V. xii. 15. 1
now growen to *stature* strong	VI. ii. 30. 9
Him thus describ'd; to be of *stature* large,	VI. ii. 44. 6
Exceeding much the measure of mans *stature,*	VI. vii. 41. 3
'Beeing of *stature* tall as any there	VII. vi. 28. 3
Being far greater and more tall of *stature*	VII. vii. 5. 3
Fit for so goodly *stature,*	*Proth.* 172
Statute. No *statute* so established might bee,	*Hub.* 1161
Statutes. wholesome *Statutes* to her husband brought	II. x. 42. 6
all their *statutes* burst:	VII. vi. 5. 4
Staunch. Had power to *staunch* al wounds	IV. ii. 39. 9
staunch the bleeding of her dreary wound:	VI. v. 6. 5
Staunched. And stopt the bleeding straight, ere he it *staunched* thought	VI. iv. 12. 9
Staves. The Aspine good for *staves;*	I. i. 8. 9
Some rusty knifes, some *staves* in fier warmd:	II. ix. 13. 7
Stay. In God alone do *stay* my confidence	*Bel.*[1] i. 14
In God alone my confidence do *stay.*	*Bel.*[2] i. 14
that is flitting doth abide and *stay.*	*Ro.* iii. 14
the good man noulde *stay* his leasure,	*S.C.* F. 192
They wander at wil and *stay* at pleasure,	*S.C.* S. 144
Taking to hoste, it quite from him did *stay;*	*Gn.* 196
all things . . . that might his passage *stay.*	*Gn.* 272
eke the Moone her hastie steedes did *stay,*	*Gn.* 457
him the Foxe with hardy words did *stay,*	*Hub.* 957
in the Kings name bad them both to *stay,*	*Hub.* 1071
bad him *stay* at ease till further preeving	*Hub.* 1366
wants the staffe of wisedome him to *stay,*	*T.M.* 140
Then *stay,* Alcyon, gentle shepheard! *stay,*	*D.* 68
Let streaming floods their hastie courses *stay,*	*D.* 332
me unworthie willed here to *stay,*	*D.* 367
mocking such as thinke they long will *stay.*	*D.* 399
I must *stay;* I may it not amend,	*D.* 453
bad me *stay,* till she for me did send	*D.* 455
whilest I in this wretched vale doo *stay*	*D.* 456
staie with me, till he were better eased	*D.* 559
Ne longer him intreate with me to *staie,*	*D.* 562
The *staie* whereof shall nought these eares annoy,	*Col.* 98
wisedome warnes, . . . To *stay* the steppe,	I. i. 13. 5
with his trenchand blade . . . forced her to *stay:*	I. i. 17. 4
Her soone he overtooke, and bad to *stay;*	I. ii. 20. 8
He would no lenger *stay* him to advize,	I. iii. 19. 4
He left him lying so, ne would no lenger *stay:*	I. iii. 39. 9
To wayle his wofull case she would not *stay,*	I. v. 19. 8
let *stay* Aveugles sonne there	I. v. 44. 5
She hardly yet perswaded was to *stay,*	I. vi. 28. 4
a Jacobs staffe, to *stay* His weary limbs upon;	I. vi. 35. 7
did *stay* In secret shadow	I. vi. 48. 2
He hearkned, and did *stay* from further harmes,	I. vii. 15. 1
The noble knight . . . badd the Ladie *stay,*	I. viii. 2. 8
all that might his angry passage *stay;*	I. viii. 9. 8
. . . by hard meanes enforcing her to *stay,*	I. viii. 25. 8
'For Gods deare love, Sir knight, doe me not *stay;*	I. ix. 25. 1
he him forst to *stay,*	I. ix. 25. 4
th' other forst him *staye,* and comforted in feare	I. ix. 34. 9
meetes a flood that doth his passage *stay,*	I. ix. 39. 3
Wont on a staffe his feeble steps to *stay,*	I. x. 5. 7
She would commaund the hasty Sunne to *stay,*	I. x. 20. 2
nothing might his ready passage *stay:*	I. x. 35. 5
There eke my feeble barke a while may *stay,*	I. xii. 1. 8
he for nought would *stay* his passage right,	I. xii. 25. 4
Vouchsafe to *stay* your steed	II. i. 8. 9
his fierce foe his steed could *stay* uneath,	II. i. 27. 8
From fowle intemperaunce he ofte did *stay,*	II. i. 34. 8
to attend awhile their forward steps they *stay.*	II. i. 35 .9
Great favour I thee graunt for aunswere thus to *stay.'*	II. iii. 7. 9
to *stay* the mortall chaunce,	II. iii. 34. 7
'O! *stay* thy hand;	II. iii. 35. 1
on a staffe her feeble steps did *stay:*	II. iv. 4. 4
wishe me *stay* till I more truth should fynd	II. iv. 22. 9
Sore chauffed at my *stay* in such a cace,	II. iv. 32. 7
Ne thou for better hope, if thou his presence *stay.'*	II. iv. 40. 9
Appease his heat, or hastie passage *stay;*	II. v. 38. 4
The wind unstable, and doth never *stay.*	II. vi. 23. 5
bad him *stay* till time the tide renewd	II. vi. 26. 9

Stay—*Continued.*

grace Both yield, to *stay* your deadly stryfe . . . II. vi. 33. 5
How without stop or *stay* he fiersly lept, . . . II. vi. 42. 2
no living wight . . . might suffred be to *stay:* . . . II. vii. 66. 3
seizd in his right side, and there the dint did *stay*. . . . II. viii. 38. 9
ne can I *stay* to tell, . . . II. ix. 47. 1
Till ryper years he raught and stronger *stay;* . . . II. x. 20. 4
wearie wax of his continuall *stay*. . . . II. x. 30. 5
here I a while must *stay,* To see a cruell fight . . . II. xi. 4. 8
With stedfast hand upon his horse did *stay,* . . . II. xi. 48. 8
of whom no memorie did *stay:* . . . II. xii. 20. 4
th' other by his bote behind did *stay*. . . . II. xii. 38. 6
faire Britomart . . . did *stay* behynd, . . . III. i. 19. 3
Ne did she *stay* till three on ground she layd . . . III. i. 29. 1
the Prophet still awhile did *stay,* . . . III. iii. 21. 4
would not *stay* For gold, or perles, . . . III. iv. 18. 7
meeke wordes to *stay* and comfort her withall. . . . III. iv. 48. 9
'Sir, ill mote I *stay* To tell the same: . . . III. v. 4. 2
could not *stay,* so fast she did foregoe, . . . III. v. 6. 5
Him boldly bad his passage there to *stay,* . . . III. v. 18. 7
Ne once to *stay* to rest, or breath at large, . . . III. vii. 23. 3
On Tromparts steed her mounted without *stay,* . . . III. viii. 13. 4
Ne long shall Satyrane behind you *stay,* . . . III. viii. 50. 7
with watch and hard restraynt to *stay* A womans will, . . . III. ix. 6. 8
Satyrane forth stepping did them *stay,* . . . III. ix. 17. 1
in a cloud their light did long time *stay,* . . . III. ix. 20. 7
Trompart, ronning hastely, him did *stay,* . . . III. x. 23. 6
Here for to *stay* in safetie behynd: . . . III. x. 41. 6
Ne banck nor bush could *stay* him, . . . III. x. 55. 3
mighty be th' enchauntments which the same do *stay*. . . . III. xi. 23. 9
on a broken reed he still did *stay* His feeble steps, . . . III. xii. 10. 8
The hurts whereof me now from battell *stay,* . . . IV. i. 40. 4
To *stay* their hands, till he awhile had spoken; . . . IV. ii. 21. 2
nought mote *stay* the steele, . . . IV. iii. 10. 3
Yet not fit place he thought it there to *stay,* . . . IV. v. 27. 8
raging rigour neither steele nor bras Could *stay,* . . . IV. vi. 15. 6
I here will *stay* Untill another tyde . . . IV. vi. 47. 8
swarv'd aside, and there againe did *stay* . . . IV. viii. 10. 8
stay Till she drew neare, . . . IV. viii. 11. 2
they for nought their cruell hands would *stay,* . . . IV. ix. 31. 3
gan him selfe advise To *stay* his hand, . . . IV. ix. 35. 6
Whose manner was all passengers to *stay* . . . IV. x. 13. 3
thought my steps to *stay,* . . . IV. x. 14. 6
Thame was stronger, and of better *stay;* . . . IV. xi. 25. 6
bad him *stay,* and backe with him retire, . . . V. i. 21. 1
Whom he requir'd his forward hast to *stay,* . . . V. ii. 2. 3
Loth was the Dwarfe, yet did he *stay* perforse, . . . V. ii. 2. 5
forst the burden of their prize to *stay* . . . V. iii. 11. 4
He nigh them drew to *stay* th' avengers forse, . . . V. iii. 30. 7
Did *stay* a while their greedy bickerment, . . . V. iv. 6. 8
he gently did desyre To *stay* her stroks, . . . V. v. 16. 6
Ne would she *stay* till he in place could come, . . . V. vi. 8. 8
She saw it vaine to make there lenger *stay,* . . . V. vi. 36. 1
Crying to them their cruell hands to *stay,* . . . V. viii. 10. 8
Ne could the Souldan them from flying *stay* . . . V. viii. 38. 5
Did *stay* her cruell hand ere she her raught; . . . V. viii. 48. 2
'Then let not that' (said they) '*stay* your intent; . . . V. ix. 7. 8
They doe his anger calme, and cruell vengeance *stay*. . . . V. ix. 31. 9
That nought the morrow next mote *stay* his fare. . . . V. x. 16. 4
th' one did th' other *stay,* . . . V. x. 36. 5
it the Posterne did from closing *stay:* . . . V. x. 37. 5
him seeing so to rage Willd him to *stay,* . . . V. xii. 8. 2
glad he was the slaughter so to *stay;* . . . V. xii. 9. 6
His course of Justice he was forst to *stay,* . . . V. xii. 27. 4
Or *stay* till he his armes, . . . Might lightly fetch: . . . VI. ii. 19. 5
so after little *stay,* . . . VI. iii. 16. 2
in his tender armes her forced up to *stay*. . . . VI. iii. 27. 9
ne did the other *stay,* . . . VI. iii. 37. 4
full loth To make there lenger *stay,* . . . VI. iii. 45. 9
Ere long he overtooke and forst to *stay;* . . . VI. iv. 20. 2
Would not permit to make there lenger *stay,* . . . VI. v. 41. 2
seemed nought the course thereof could *stay,* . . . VI. viii. 8. 5
'*Stay, stay,* Sir Knight! for love of God abstaine . . . VI. viii. 17. 5
his cruell hand to *stay,* . . . VI. viii. 29. 2
after he had fed, yet did he *stay* . . . VI. ix. 12. 4
To *stay* their cruell hands from slaughter fell, . . . VI. xi. 20. 5
he did not *stay* To greet him first, . . . VI. xi. 28. 1
all the rest for him did readie *stay,* . . . VI. xi. 47. 7
So nothing heere long standeth in one *stay:* . . . VII. vii. 47. 7
willing me against her will to *stay*. . . . *Am.* xlvi. 4
Of this worlds Theatre in which we *stay,* . . . *Am.* liv. 1
in the *stay* of her owne stedfast might, . . . *Am.* lix. 11
Poure out the wine without restraint or *stay,* . . . *Epith.* 250
Ye would not *stay* your dew time to expect, . . . *Epith.* 430
my long fruitlesse *stay* In Princes Court, . . . *Proth.* 6

Stayed. a Goose great Rome from ruine *stayde,* . . . *Van.* xi. 9
Ne *stayed* he once the dore to make fast, . . . *S.C.* May 292
from former follies move To *stayed* steps; . . . *S.C.* Jun. 38
Upon whose toppe the starres bene *stayed,* . . . *S.C.* Jul. 61
that faire troupe of woodie Goddesses *Staied* thee, . . . *Gn.* 183
As pausing in great doubt, awhile he *staid,* . . . *Hub.* 175
Ne ever *stayd* in place, ne spake to wight, . . . *Hub.* 938
Ne *staid,* till that he came . . . *Hub.* 1260
th' Altare, on the which this Image *staid,* . . . *Ti.* 498
stayed not, till I againe did call: . . . *D.* 60
may not *stayed* bee, . . . *D.* 412
she *staied* not a whit, . . . *As.* 175
Knight could not . . . be *staide;* . . . I. i. 14. 2
The other by him selfe *staide,* . . . I. i. 38. 9
He *stayde* his hand; and gan himselfe advise . . . I. i. 50. 5

Stayed—*Continued.*

Staid not to waile his woefull funerall, . . . I. ii. 20. 3
She *stayd;* and foorth Duessa gan proceede: . . . I. v. 22. 1
long time with that salvage people *stayd,* . . . I. vi. 19. 3
Satyrane, with strokes him turning, *staid,* . . . I. vi. 46. 6
his stalking steps are *stayde* Upon a snaggy Oke, . . . I. vii. 10. 6
'Despaire breeds not,' . . . 'where faith is *staid.*' . . . I. vii. 41. 7
him . . . hardly he from flying forward *stayd,* . . . I. ix. 23. 5
Turkes and Sarazins, which them had *stayd:* . . . I. x. 40. 4
He *stayd* his steed for humble misers sake, . . . II. i. 9. 1
He *stayd* not lenger talke, . . . II. i. 13. 1
He *stayd* not for more bidding, . . . II. iii. 19. 1
Trompart stoutly *stayd* . . . II. iii. 21. 5
She *staid:* with that he crauld out . . . II. iii. 35. 6
goodly peace of *staied* mindes Does overthrow, . . . II. v. 1. 6
he never *staid* to greete, . . . II. v. 3. 1
Yet there the steel *stayd* not, . . . II. v. 7. 8
Eftsoones his cruel hand Sir Guyon *stayd,* . . . II. v. 13. 1
Him *stayd* from yielding pitifull redresse, . . . II. v. 24. 4
Ne *staied* for his Damsell to inquire, . . . II. vi. 27. 8
They *stayd* a while, and forth she gan proceede: . . . II. vi. 33. 6
Back to the strond retyrd, and there still *stayd,* . . . II. vi. 40. 6
him strongly *stayd* From drowning. . . . II. vi. 46. 3
Guyon . . . *stayd* His hand . . . II. vii. 6. 6
Whereby her course is stopt and passage *staid:* . . . II. ix. 8. 4
Him backeward overthrew, and downe him *stayd* . . . II. xi. 29. 2
shee . . . al the while his wounds were dressing by him *stayd*. II. xi. 49. 9
Held on his course with *stayed* stedfastnesse, . . . II. xii. 29. 6
Yet *stayd* they not, but forward did proceed, . . . II. xii. 37. 3
They *stayd* not to avise who first should bee, . . . III. i. 18. 3
The mortall steele *stayd* not . . . III. i. 65. 5
For nothing would she lenger there be *stayd,* . . . III. i. 67. 4
They, here arriving, *staid* awhile without, . . . III. iii. 14. 1
Shal be by vision *staide* from his intent: . . . III. iii. 41. 6
There Merlin *stayd,* As overcomen . . . III. iii. 50. 1
Ne lenger *stayd* for th' other to reply, . . . III. iv. 15. 5
The martiall Mayd *stayd* not him to lament, . . . III. iv. 18. 1
shee knew there *staied* still Some litle life . . . III. iv. 41. 7
His wearisome pursuit perforce he *stayd,* . . . III. iv. 53. 5
stayd not till it did light In his left thigh, . . . III. v. 20. 6
which being *stayd,* They did him set theron, . . . III. v. 38. 8
when he *stayd,* to flight againe she did her take. . . . III. vii. 44. 9
All that I ever fownd so wisely *stayd,* . . . III. vii. 57. 2
foorth they far'd; but he behind them *stayd,* . . . III. x. 2. 1
There he suddein *staid,* . . . III. x. 25. 7
Ne *stayd* he, till he came unto the place . . . III. x. 54. 1
Ne *stayd* his flight nor fearefull agony, . . . III. x. 56. 2
Therewith she *stayd* her hand, loth *stayd* to bee; . . . III. xii. 34. 8
But Scudamour, . . . *Staid* not to answer; . . . IV. i. 52. 2
like to warie Centonels well *stayd,* . . . IV. ii. 36. 8
Triamond, halfe wroth to see him *staid,* . . . IV. iv. 20. 5
Staid not till it arrived in his side, . . . IV. iv. 24. 5
He *stayed* not, but in his armes her bearing Ran, . . . IV. vii. 8. 6
She *staid* not th' utmost end thereof to try, . . . IV. vii. 21. 2
Ne *stayed* further newes thereof to learne, . . . IV. x. 9. 3
he her quickly *stayd,* and forst to wend withall. . . . V. i. 22. 9
by no meane could in the weight be *stayd;* . . . V. ii. 45. 8
The other *stayd* behind to gard the pray: . . . V. iii. 11. 7
With a sharpe showre of arrowes, which them *staid,* . . . V. iv. 38. 4
Her wrathful hand from greedy vengeance to have *stayd*. . . . V. v. 14. 9
Yet *stayd* she not for them, but forward fared, . . . V. vi. 38. 2
She *stayd* not to advise which way to take, . . . V. vi. 39. 1
Stayd not till she came to her selfe againe, . . . V. vii. 34. 2
when she had his execution *stayd,* . . . V. vii. 37. 1
Ne once for ought her speedy passage *stayd,* . . . V. viii. 6. 3
They *stayd* their hands, when she thus gan to speake: . . . V. viii. 11. 1
Stayd not, till through his curat it did glyde, . . . V. viii. 34. 8
there having *stayd* not long, . . . V. viii. 51. 8
Ne *stayed* step, till that he came at last . . . V. xi. 3. 3
The Prince *staid* not his aunswere to devize, . . . V. xi. 4. 1
whiles there with her he *stayd,* . . . V. xii. 25. 8
for no demaunds he *staide,* . . . VI. i. 11. 8
Where long he *stayed* not, . . . VI. i. 32. 8
Ne *stayd* to aske if it were he by name, . . . VI. i. 33. 3
his mortall hand a while he *stayd;* . . . VI. i. 40. 1
cheare his guests whom he had *stayd* that night, . . . VI. iii. 6. 3
Staide not to succour her in that affright, . . . VI. iii. 26. 4
With speare in th' one hand *stayd* him selfe upright, . . . VI. iii. 33. 8
With th' other *staide* his Lady up . . . VI. iii. 33. 9
Wherefore he *stayd,* till that he nearer drew. . . . VI. iii. 47. 1
He *stayed* not t' advize which way were best . . . VI. iv. 5. 1
To whom approching . . . her plaint she *stayd,* . . . VI. iv. 27. 2
greedily him griping his avengement *stayd*. . . . VI. v. 26. 9
They *stayd* not there, but streightway in did pas: . . . VI. v. 36. 1
Ne *stayd,* till that he came into the hall; . . . VI. vi. 19. 3
He *stayd* his second strooke, . . . VI. vi. 31. 9
Approching to him neare, his hand he *stayd,* . . . VI. vi. 39. 2
He *staide* his hand according her desire, . . . VI. viii. 18. 1
awhile she *stayd;* Till the sharpe passion being overpast, . . . VI. viii. 19. 2
So, being *stayd,* they her from thence directed . . . VI. viii. 44. 1
Whose course is often *stayd,* yet never is astray. . . . VI. xii. 1. 9
The matrone *stayd* no lenger to enquire, . . . VI. xii. 19. 1
th' outrage of his violence he *stayd,* . . . VI. xii. 29. 3
Ne *staide* till she the highest stage had scand, . . . VII. vi. 8. 8
The Heavens Herald *staid* not to reply, . . . VII. vi. 19. 1
He *staid* his hand; . . . VII. vi. 31. 5
With which his feeble steps he *stayed* still; . . . VII. vii. 31. 7
firmely *stayd* Upon the pillours of Eternity, . . . VII. viii. 2. 3
Tell her the joyous time wil not be *staid,* . . . *Am.* lxx. 7
The more they *stayed* be on stedfastnesse; . . . *H.L.* 172

Stayeth. Ne *stayeth* leave to take before his friends doe dye. . VI. xi. 18. 9
Staying. *staying* nought to question from aloofe, ... IV. x. 9. 8
Stays. There she awhile him *stayes,* himselfe to rest, ... I. x. 45. 1
Ne *stayes,* till safe him selfe he see from jeopardy. . . . . . III. x. 53. 9
nor hill, nor dale she *staies,* . . . . IV. vii. 22. 1
Stead. *See* **Instead.**
shepeheardes for the Devils *stedde,* . . . . *S.C.* May 43
To see thee succeede in thy fathers *stede,* . . . . *S.C.* May 203
thou shalt ycrouned be in Colins *stede,* . . . . *S.C.* Au. 146
flouds of teares flowe in theyr *stead* . . . . *S.C.* N. 127
which in Court him served to good *stead;* . . . . *Hub.* 697
False personages fit for everie *sted,* . . . . *Hub.* 861
Into whose *stead* faire falshood steps, ... I. ii. Arg.
false Duessa in her *sted* had borne, ... I. iv. 2. 3
The souldier may not move from watchfull *sted,* . . . . I. ix. 41. 4
Great God it planted in that blessed *stedd* . . . . I. xi. 46. 7
he ran Unto that *stead,* . . . . II. ii. 21. 7
fly this fearefull *stead* anon, ... II. iv. 42. 8
Mote *stead* you much your purpose to subdew.' . . . . II. ix. 9. 4
Two goodly Beacons, set in watches *stead,* . . . . II. ix. 46. 3
pitteous Elidure put in his *sted;* . . . . II. x. 44. 6
by the people chosen in their *sted,* . . . . II. x. 47. 2
afterwards he in his *stead* did raigne, ... II. x. 58. 4
Now comes to point of that same perilous *sted,* . . . . II. xii. 1. 7
the *sted* Whereas those Mermayds dwelt: . . . . II. xii. 30. 1
he ne wonneth in one certeine *stead,* . . . . III. ii. 14. 3
what shield, what armes, what steed, what *stedd,* . . . . . . III. ii. 16. 6
crowne himselfe in th' others *stead:* . . . . III. iii. 29. 7
in her litle loves *stead,* which was strayd, ... III. vi. 28. 8
in the *stead* Of life, she put a Spright . . . . III. viii. 7. 8
in his *stead* let Love for ever dwell; . . . . III. xi. 2. 2
To search each secrete of that goodly *sted,* . . . . III. xi. 50. 2
whose noyaunce fild the fearefull *sted* . . . . III. xii. 2. 6
rather wholly dead . . . then in so bad a *stead.* . . . . IV. iv. 22. 9
She in my *stead* supplide his bestiall desire.' . . . . IV. vii. 19. 9
mounting in their *stead* Came to that Squire, ... IV. viii. 41. 2
Goddesse, that doest highest sit . . . in th' Almighties *stead,* V. Pr. 11. 2
in their *steede* for other rayment sought, ... V. vii. 41. 3
He staggered to and fro in doubtfull *sted.* . . . . V. xii. 23. 4
Ladies ayde in every *stead* and stound,' . . . . VI. i. 42. 9
in that wofull *stead* Kept and delivered me . . . . VI. v. 29. 4
Yet would not let her lite, nor rest a little *stead:* . . . . . VI. vii. 40. 9
Still mooving, yet unmoved from her *sted;* . . . . VII. vii. 13. 3
ne in one *stead* do tarry; . . . . VII. vii. 21. 8
one of hers did close convay Into the others *stead:* . . . . . *Epig.* ii. 6
Steadfast. walkes upright with comely *stedfast* pace, ... *Hub.* 728
In state of blis, or *stedfast* happinesse? . . . . *Ti.* 569
Ne will be helde in anie *stedfast* plight, ... *D.* 496
His sevenfold teme behind the *stedfast* starre . . . . I. ii. 1. 2
As rock of Diamond *stedfast* evermore. . . . . I. vi. 4. 5
stedfast truth acquite him out of all. . . . . I. viii. 1. 4
fall, that seemd to shake The *stedfast* globe . . . . I. viii. 23. 9
ever up to heven, . . . Her *stedfast* eyes were bent, ... I. x. 14. 9
seemd uneath to shake the *stedfast* ground. . . . . I. xi. 4. 3
To move the world from off his *stedfast* henge, ... I. xi. 21. 8
Transformd her to a stone from *stedfast* virgins state. . . . . II. ii. 8. 9
Whose right haunch earst my *stedfast* arrow strake? . . . . . II. iii. 32. 8
Who ever doth to temperaunce apply His *stedfast* life, ... II. v. 1. 2
to a *stedfast* starre his course hath bent, ... II. vii. 1. 2
as a *stedfast* towre, Whom foe . . . doth assaile, ... II. viii. 35. 7
Their *stedfast* stonds did mightily maintaine, ... II. xi. 15. 2
With *stedfast* hand upon his horse did stay, ... II. xi. 48. 8
still in *stedfast* state, ... II. xii. 51. 2
With *stedfast* corage and stout hardiment: . . . . III. i. 19. 8
In *stedfast* chastitie and vertue rare, ... III. v. 8. 5
In so great prayse of *stedfast* chastity . . . . III. v. 55. 1
in *stedfast* love and happy state . . . . III. vi. 50. 6
Her former love and *stedfast* loialty, ... III. vi. 53. 8
Ne her out of the *stedfast* sadle driv'd; . . . . III. vii. 40. 7
much emmov'd, but *stedfast* still persevered. . . . . III. xii. 2. 9
thousand charmes could not her *stedfast* hart remove. . . . . III. xii. 31. 9
still with *stedfast* eye and courage stout . . . . III. xii. 37. 5
stedfast still her eyes did fixed rest, ... IV. x. 49. 7
Alwayes to execute her *stedfast* doome, ... V. i. 12. 3
Ne loose that he hath bound with *stedfast* band, ... V. ii. 42. 4
Be well adviz'd that he stand *stedfast* still; . . . . V. vi. 1. 7
They tied were to *stedfast* chastity . . . . V. vii. 9. 7
wading through the waves with *stedfast* sway, ... V. xii. 5. 6
loved simple truth and *stedfast* honesty. . . . . VI. i. 3. 9
the steele-head no *stedfast* hold could fynd, ... VI. vii. 10. 8
Never abiding in their *stedfast* plights: . . . . VII. vii. 21. 3
stedfast rest of all things, ... VII. viii. 2. 3
it then more *stedfast* will endure: . . . . *Am.* li. 12
in the stay of her owne *stedfast* might, ... *Am.* lix. 11
The more of *stedfast* mynds to be admyred, ... *H.L.* 171
Let endlesse Peace your *steadfast* hearts accord, ... *Proth.* 101
Steadfastly. vow . . . I plighted have, and yet keepe *stedfastly.* III. vii. 51. 7
Him *stedfastly* he markt, ... VI. ii. 5. 1
Steadfastness. through temperaunce and *stedfastnesse,* . . . . II. iv. 2. 8
Held on his course with stayed *stedfastnesse,* . . . . II. xii. 29. 6
At last he bade her (with bold *stedfastnesse*) . . . . VII. vi. 17. 7
all things *stedfastnesse* do hate And changed be; . . . . . . VII. vii. 58. 2
The more they stayed be on *stedfastnesse;* . . . . *H.L.* 172
Steads. Thus chatten the people in theyr *steads,* . . . . . . *S.C.* S. 120
round about in fittest *steades* did place, ... II. xi. 6. 2
Steady. In shooting *steddie,* and in swimming strong: . . . . *As.* 74
staggering steps thy *steady* hand doth lead, ... I. x. 51. 2
The knight gan fayrely couch his *steady* speare, ... I. xi. 16. 1
with his *steedy* staffe did point his way; . . . . II. i. 34. 6
to them does the *steddy* helme apply, ... II. vii. 1. 8

Steady—*Continued.*
steadie hand was faine his steede to guyde, ... IV. viii. 37. 7
staide his Lady up with *steddy* might. . . . . VI. iii. 33. 9
with much more *steddy* stowre, ... VI. vii. 8. 5
like a *steddy* ship, ... *Am.* lix. 5
Steal. Those royall ornaments to *steale* away? . . . . *Hub.* 998
to *steale* the Diademe away Were the worke . . . . *Hub.* 1034
From him would *steale* them privily away, ... *Mui.* 111
And *steale* from each some part of ornament. *Ded.Son.*xvii.8
slombring soft my hart did *steale* away, ... I. ix. 13. 6
To *steale* a snatch of amorous conceipt, ... II. v. 34. 6
So did she *steale* his heedelesse hart away, ... III. i. 37. 1
Her love-sicke hart to other thoughts did *steale;* . . . . . . III. ii. 48. 7
To *steale* away that I with blowes have wonne, ... III. viii. 17. 2
To weet how he her love away did *steale,* . . . . III. x. 5. 8
steale from thee the meede of thy due merit, ... IV. ii. 34. 3
able was weake harts away to *steale.* . . . . IV. v. 10. 5
steale away the crowne of their good name: . . . . IV. viii. 25. 4
secretly out of her prison *steale;* . . . . IV. vii. 55. 7
time to *steale,* the threasure of mans day, ... IV. x. 14. 8
Then did he cast to *steale* her thence away, ... IV. xii. 15. 1
from her self unwares he might her *steale* the whyle. . . . . V. ix. 12. 9
search out those that usd to rob and *steale,* . . . . V. xii. 26. 7
did *steale* mens hearts away: . . . . VI. i. 2. 6
enchantment, that . . . did *steale* the hart away. . . . . . . VI. ii. 3. 4
Steale. *See* **Stele.**
Stealing. night with *stealing* steppes doe you forsloe, ... *S.C.* Jun. 119
Crept in by stouping low, or *stealing* of the kaies. . . . . . . IV. x. 18. 9
Stealth. *See* **Love-stealth.**
ere one be aware, by secret *stealth* His powre is reft, ... I. ix. 31. 7
Restraining *stealth* and strong extortion, ... II. x. 39. 5
the Evening, fit for lovers *stealth,* . . . . III. x. 12. 1
as thing reserv'd from *stealth.* . . . . IV. i. 6. 7
salvage nation, which did live Of *stealth* and spoile, ... VI. viii. 35. 3
Stealths. load . . . Of nightly stelths, and pillage severall, . I. iii. 16. 8
Their prety *stealthes* shal worke, ... *Epith.* 361
Steam. the last deadly smoke aloft did *steeme,* . . . . I. xii. 2. 4
In slouthfull sleepe his molten hart to *steme,* . . . . II. vi. 27. 5
The inward smoke, that did before but *steeme,* . . . . III. viii. 26. 4
with the *steme* thereof the Temple swet, ... IV. x. 38. 3
Which ye may see yet all about me *steeme.* . . . . VI. vii. 15. 6
his browes with sweat did reek and *steem,* . . . . VII. vii. 40. 4
Steamed. Out of his stinking gorge forth *steemed* still, ... I. xi. 13. 8
from like inward fire that outward smoke had *steemd.* . . . . III. i. 55. 9
Steaming. *See* **Fresh-steaming.**
in her blood yet *steeming* fresh embayd: . . . . III. xii. 21. 4
cruell blades, yet *steeming* with whot bloud, ... IV. ix. 29. 4
Steane. *See* **Steen.**
Sted. *See* **Stead, Steed.**
Steed. *See* **Instead.**
stoute as *steede* of brasse. . . . . *S.C.* Jul. 156
A Knight all arm'd, upon a winged *steed;* . . . . *Ti.* 646
He smote his *steed,* . . . . *Ti.* 657
Whenceforth issues a warlike *steed* in sight, ... *Mui.* 316
As stubborne *steed,* that is with curb restrained, ... *D.* 194
His angry *steede* did chide his foming bitt, ... I. i. 1. 6
Then mounted he upon his *Steede* againe, ... I. i. 28. 1
The dwarfe him brought his *steed;* . . . . I. ii. 6. 9
For him so far had borne his light-foot *steede,* . . . . I. ii. 8. 3
He set her on her *steede,* and forward forth did beare. . . . I. ii. 45. 9
he forward gan advaunce His fair enchaunted *steed,* . . . . . I. iii. 25. 9
had his staggering *steed* not shronke for feare, ... I. iii. 35. 4
Dismounting lightly from his loftie *steed,* . . . . I. iii. 36. 1
got his ready *steed,* and fast away gan ryde. . . . . I. vi. 8. 9
by his side his *steed* the grassy forage ate. . . . . I. vii. 2. 9
Whiles he had keeping of his grasing *steed.* . . . . I. vii. 19. 2
His stubborne *steed* with curbed canon bitt, ... I. vii. 37. 6
noble knight alighted . . . From loftie *steed,* . . . . I. viii. 2. 8
His gorgeous ryder from her loftie *sted* Would have cast downe, I. viii. 17. 5
I did alight From loftie *steed,* . . . . I. ix. 13. 2
Als flew his *steed* as he his bandes had brast, ... I. ix. 21. 7
enwrapt the nimble thyes Of his froth-fomy *steed,* . . . . . . I. xi. 23. 3
Who taught his trampling *steed* with equall steps to tread. . II. i. 7. 9
Vouchsafe to stay your *steed* . . . . II. i. 8. 9
He stayd his *steed* for humble misers sake, ... II. i. 9. 1
under him a gray *steede* he did wield, ... II. i. 18. 6
his fierce foe his *steed* could stay uneath, ... II. i. 27. 8
dismounting straict From his tall *steed,* . . . . II. i. 39. 2
Gay *steed* with spurs did pricke, ... II. i. 49. 9
He left his loftie *steed* . . . . II. ii. 11. 6
Sith his good *steed* is lately from him gone; . . . . II. iii. 3. 2
He left his *steed* without, ... II. iii. 3. 8
that brave *steed* there finding ready dight, ... II. iii. 4. 8
Purloynd both *steed* and speare, ... II. iii. 4. 9
he from his loftie *steed* Downe fell . . . . II. iii. 21. 2
So to his *steed* he gott, ... II. iii. 46. 3
the rightfull owner of that *steede,* . . . . II. iv. 2. 1
His *steed* was bloody red, and fomed yre, ... II. v. 2. 8
His forlorne *steed* from him the victour wan: . . . . II. vi. 41. 4
later ages pride, like corn-fed *steed,* . . . . II. vii. 16. 6
To decke his herce, and trap his tomb-blacke *steed.'* . . . . II. viii. 16. 7
'What herce or *steed'* . . . 'should he have dight, ... II. viii. 16. 8
under him he saw his Lybian *steed* to praunce; . . . . II. viii. 17. 9
underneath him his courageous *steed,* . . . . II. xi. 19. 6
cumming to his Squyre that kept his *steed,* . . . . II. xi. 48. 2
To take him from his *steed* full tenderly: . . . . II. xi. 49. 2
sharply gan to spurne His fomy *steed,* . . . . III. i. 5. 5
to his starting *steed* that swarv'd asyde, ... III. i. 11. 6
all her *steed* with tinsell trappings shone, ... III. i. 15. 7
what shield, what armes, what *steed,* what stedd, ... III. ii. 16. 6

Steed—*Continued.*
Then gan he freshly pricke his fomy *steed*, ... III. iv. 48. 2
from his loftie *steed* dismounting low . . . . III. iv. 53. 6
clombe unto his *steed*. . . . . III. iv. 61. 6
His *steed* eke seemd t' apply his steps to his intent. . . . III. iv. 61. 9
from his *steed* he fell in deadly swowne: . . . . III. v. 26. 3
Her *Steed* did stagger with that puissaunt strooke; . . . . III. vii. 41. 1
On Tromparts *steed* her mounted without stay, ... III. viii. 13. 4
turne his *steede* about, or sure he should be dedd. . . . . III. viii. 17. 9
hastily remounting to his *steed* . . . . III. ix. 15. 1
begonne His stolen *steed* to thunder furiously, ... III. x. 33. 6
She . . . his forwandred *steed* unto him gott: . . . . . . III. xi. 20. 6
he put his spurres unto his *steed*, ... IV. i. 41. 1
Fiercely forth prickt his *steed* . . . . IV. ii. 6. 7
as it fell, his *steed* he ready found; . . . . IV. iv. 23. 3
It chaunst Sir Satyrane his *steed* . . . To stumble, . . . IV. iv. 30. 2
Lightly Cambello leapt downe from his *steed* . . . . IV. iv. 31. 1
all his *steed* With oaken leaves attrapt, ... IV. iv. 39. 5
for to winne the saddle lost the *steed*. . . . . IV. v. 22. 5
Unto his lofty *steede* he clombe anone, ... IV. v. 46. 1
Sitting in shade beside his grazing *steede;* . . . . IV. vi. 2. 6
Yet she no whit dismayd her *steed* forsooke, ... IV. vi. 14. 6
Like to a stubborne *steede* whom strong hand would restraine. IV. vi. 33. 9
More hard for hungry *steed* t' abstaine from pleasant lare. . IV. viii. 29. 9
steadie hand was faine his *steede* to guyde, ... IV. viii. 37. 7
Bearing a litle Dwarfe before his *steed*, ... IV. viii. 38. 3
tooke downe those Ladies twaine From loftie *steede*, ... IV. viii. 41. 2
from my lofty *steede* dismounting low . . . . IV. x. 15. 3
on his *steed* her set to beare her out of sight. . . . . . V. i. 17. 9
Either the other from his *steede* to cast; . . . . V. ii. 14. 7
His owne good *steed*, which he had stolne, to clame; . . . . V. iii. 29. 5
gan inquire how was that *steed* bereaved, ... V. iii. 30. 8
'Lo there! Sir Guyon, take to you the *steed*, ... V. iii. 35. 3
mounting to her *steede* bad Talus guide her on. . . . . . . V. vi. 17. 9
tooke her *steede;* and thereon mounting light . . . . V. vi. 36. 2
his good *steed* . . . Durst not endure their sight, ... V. viii. 36. 7
When he was readie to his *steede* to mount . . . . V. x. 16. 8
low dismounting from his loftie *steede* . . . . V. x. 22. 2
Downe streight to ground fell his astonisht *steed*, ... V. xi. 9. 1
streight dismounting from his *steed*, ... V. xi. 61. 1
her up did reare Upon his *steede*, ... V. xi. 64. 8
He . . . downe from his *steed* me throw'th . . . . VI. ii. 17. 8
refused To take me up . . . Upon his *steed*, ... VI. ii. 22. 4
and her up did rayse Upon the *steed* . . . . VI. ii. 39. 8
setting on his *steede* her did sustaine . . . . VI. iii. 28. 5
To take him up behinde upon his *steed;* . . . . VI. iii. 31. 5
as thou hast thy *steed* forlorne with shame, ... VI. iii. 32. 1
Turned his *steede* about another way, ... VI. iii. 37. 2
Upstaying still her selfe uppon her *steede*, ... VI. iii. 46. 2
his fierce *steed* that mote him much dismay: . . . . VI. iv. 6. 5
from his *steed* him nigh he drew againe: . . . . VI. iv. 7. 5
helped through the swiftnesse of his *steed*, ... VI. iv. 8. 5
Withouten armes or *steede* to ride upon, ... VI. iv. 39. 3
His *steede*, now strong through rest so long a space, ... VI. v. 7. 5
some furniture about her *steed* To be disordred . . . . . . VI. v. 10. 2
he in the forrest heard A trampling *steede*, ... VI. v. 21. 6
The whiles the salvage man did take his *steede*, ... VI. vi. 19. 8
Where seeing him so lie, he left his *steed*, ... VI. vii. 11. 6
He left his lofty *steede* to aide him neare; . . . . VI. viii. 12. 7
as a *steed* refreshed after toyle, ... *Am.* lxxx. 5

Steede. *See* **Stead.**

Steeds. Ystabled hath his *steedes* . . . . *S.C.* N. 15
Night . . . her teemed *steedes* gan call, ... *Gn.* 314
eke the Moone her hastie *steedes* did stay, ... *Gn.* 457
menaging the mouthes of stubborne *steedes*, ... *Hub.* 739
sweatie *steeds* . . . gan water in the west, ... *D.* 24
The Sunne . . . doth baite his *steedes* . . . . I. i. 32. 9
Their *steeds* doe stagger, and amazed stand; . . . . I. ii. 15. 6
flaming mouthes of *steedes*, unwonted wilde, . . . to rayne: . I. iv. 9. 3
cole blacke *steedes* yborne of hellish brood, ... I. v. 20. 8
his chacing *steedes* aghast Both charett swifte and huntsman overcast: . . . . I. v. 38. 4
his faint *steedes* watred in Ocean deepe, ... I. xi. 31. 3
some others faine To menage *steeds*, ... II. iv. 1. 9
Faire shields, gay *steedes*, bright armes be my delight; . . . II. vii. 10. 8
Sheilds, *steeds*, and armes, and all things for thee meet, . . III. vii. 11. 3
They tooke their *steeds*, and forth upon their journey went. . III. i. 67. 9
Tho to their ready *Steedes* they clombe full light, ... III. iii. 61. 6
Turne we our *steeds;* . . . . III. viii. 18. 3
they both a furlongs mountenaunce Retird their *steeds*, . . . III. viii. 18. 6
Their firie *steedes* with so untamed forse . . . . IV. ii. 15. 1
There might ye see loose *steeds* at randon ronne, ... IV. iv. 38. 6
They tooke their *steeds*, and forward thence did pas . . . . IV. vi. 39. 3
cruell *steedes* which he had fed With flesh of men, ... V. viii. 28. 6
So long as in his *steedes* the flaming breath did last. . . . V. viii. 33. 9
his *steedes*, like to an hungry hound . . . . V. viii. 36. 4
the firie-mouthed *steedes*, which drew The Sunnes bright wayne V. viii. 40. 1
Such was the furie of these head-strong *steeds*, ... V. viii. 41. 1
Of his owne *steedes* was all to peeces torne, ... V. viii. 43. 4
up to their *steedes* they went, ... VI. v. 24. 8
Letting their *steedes* to graze upon the greene. . . . . . . VI. v. 38. 2
Drawne of two *steeds*, th' one black, the other white, ... VII. vi. 9. 2
Thy tyred *steedes* long since have need of rest. . . . . . . *Epith.* 284

Steedy. *See* **Steady.**

Steel. the stout hynde arm'd his right hand with *steele:* . . . *Ro.* xviii. 6
the *steele* had pierced his pitth, ... *S.C.* F. 217
That *steele* in strength, . . . shall outweare; . . . . *S.C.* Env. 2
against the others bodie bend His cursed *steele*, ... *Gn.* 413
The bit of balefull *steele* and bitter stownd, ... *Mui.* 62
Not Bilbo *steele*, nor brasse from Corinth fet, ... *Mui.* 77

Steel—*Continued.*
So hugely stroke, that it the *steele* did rive, ... I. ii. 19. 4
Loth . . . To taste th' untryed dint of deadly *steele:* . . . . I. iii. 34. 6
The cruell *steele* . . . doth bight In tender flesh, ... I. v. 9. 3
his bloody wounds, that through the *steele* were cleft.' . . . I. vi. 39. 9
deadly dint of *steele* endanger may. . . . . I. vii. 29. 7
shield . . . Not made of *steele*, nor of enduring bras, ... I. vii. 33. 3
Whose hartstrings with keene *steele* nigh hewen be; . . . . . I. viii. 22. 7
With mortall *steele* him smot againe so sore, ... I. viii. 24. 2
mighty brawned bowrs Were wont to rive *steele* plates, . . . I. viii. 41. 7
cote of *steele*, so couched neare That nought mote perce; . . I. xi. 9. 2
Both deadly sharp, that sharpest *steele* exceeden farre. . . . I. xi. 11. 9
sharpest *steele* did far exceed The sharpnesse of his . . . clawes: I. xi. 12. 1
The pointed *steele*, arriving rudely theare, ... I. xi. 16. 3
The percing *steele* there wrought a wound full wyde, ... I. xi. 20. 8
backe againe the sparcling *steele* recoyld, ... I. xi. 25. 3
Whom fyrie *steele* now burnt, that erst him armd; . . . . . I. xi. 27. 8
whether the revenging *steele* Were hardned . . . . I. xi. 36. 1
Upon the joint the lucky *steele* did light, ... I. xi. 43. 6
cursed *steele* against that badge I bent, ... II. i. 27. 5
whose sides with cruell *steele* Through launched, ... II. i. 38. 6
the cruell *steel* He lightly snatcht, ... II. i. 43. 1
him beset With strokes of mortall *steele* . . . . II. ii. 22. 3
eke of surest *steele* that may be fownd, ... II. iii. 15. 8
As *steele* can wound, or strength can overthroe. . . . . . . II. iv. 10. 5
The quivering *steele* his aymed end wel knew, ... II. iv. 46. 3
the sharpe *steele*, arriving forcibly On his broad shield, . . II. v. 4. 3
Yet there the *steel* stayd not, ... II. v. 7. 8
The mortall *steele* despiteously entayld . . . . II. vi. 29. 7
teach the cursed *steele* to bight In his owne flesh, ... II. vi. 32. 8
the quiet wombe . . . with *steele* to wound, ... II. vii. 17. 2
Ne mortall *steele* emperce his miscreated mould. . . . . . . II. vii. 42. 9
nether *steele* nor stone The stroke thereof . . . . II. viii. 21. 1
That vertuous *steele* he rudely snatcht away, ... II. viii. 22. 6
The faithfull *steele* such treason no'uld endure, ... II. viii. 30. 8
through his thigh the mortall *steele* did gryde: . . . . . . II. viii. 36. 5
cleaving the hard *steele*, ... II. viii. 45. 4
all armed bright In glistring *steele*, ... II. ix. 26. 3
most gent, That ever brandished bright *steele* on hye! . . . . II. xi. 17. 6
halfe the *steele* behind his backe did rest; . . . . II. xi. 37. 5
The mortall *steele* stayd not . . . . III. i. 65. 5
about her swayd Her wrathfull *steele*, ... III. i. 66. 6
The wicked *steele* through his left side did glaunce. . . . . III. iv. 16. 5
the hard *steele* his pillow. . . . . III. iv. 53. 9
The wicked *steele* stayd not till it did light . . . . III. v. 20. 6
that the wicked *steele* empoysned were: . . . . III. v. 49. 3
Whose shady boughes sharp *steele* did never lop, ... III. vi. 43. 4
He was all armd in rugged *steele* unfilde, ... III. vii. 30. 4
dint of *steele* his carcas could not quell; . . . . III. vii. 35. 8
nathemore the *steele* asonder riv'd, ... III. vii. 40. 5
the sharpe *steele* doth rive her hart in tway, ... III. xi. 11. 4
The cruell *steele*, which thrild her dying hart, ... III. xii. 38. 1
nought mote stay the *steele*, ... IV. iii. 10. 3
With point of *steele* that close his hartbloud spild, ... IV. iii. 22. 5
The wicked *steele*, for mischiefe first ordained, ... IV. iv. 24. 3
Whose raging rigour neither *steele* nor bras Could stay, . . . IV. vi. 15. 5
as if the *steele* had sence, ... IV. vi. 21. 6
beath'd in fire for *steele* to be in sted. . . . . IV. vii. 7. 6
the sad *steele* seizd not, where it was hight, ... V. xi. 8. 7
with his mortal *steel* quite through the body strooke. . . . . V. xi. 13. 9
on his head a *steele* cap he did weare . . . . V. xii. 14. 5
The tempred *steele* did not into his braynepan byte. . . . . VI. vi. 30. 9
the cold *steele*, through piercing, did devowre . . . . VI. vii. 8. 7
the mad *steele* about doth fiercely fly, ... VI. xi. 16. 3
when he him strooke With his sharpe *steele*, ... VI. xii. 26. 4
The hardest *steele*, in tract of time doth teare: . . . . . . *Am.* xviii. 2
Whiles she as *steele* and flint . . . . *Am.* xviii. 14
With your *steele* darts doo chace from comming neer; . . . . *Epith.* 70
More firme and durable then *steele* or brasse, ... *H.H.B.* 153

Steel-head. *steelhed* speare, and morion on her hedd, ... *Mui.* 322
With that he stifly shooke his *steelhead* dart: . . . . II. vi. 40. 1
Through all those foldes the *steelehead* passage wrought, . . . II. viii. 32. 7
Their *steel-hed* speares they strongly coucht, ... III. ix. 16. 1
the *steele-head* no stedfast hold could fynd, ... VI. vii. 10. 8
Instead of *steele-head* speare, a shepheards hooke; . . . . . VI. ix. 36. 5

Steel-headed. quiver gay, Stuft with *steele-headed* dartes, . . II. iii. 29. 3
fayrly couching his *steeleheaded* speare, ... II. v. 3. 6
eft aventring his *steele-headed* launce, ... IV. vi. 11. 3

Steely. The *steely* head stuck fast still in his flesh, ... I. xi. 22. 1
stroke the Pagan with his *steely* brand . . . . IV. viii. 43. 3
When so he list in wrath lift up his *steely* brand, ... V. i. 8. 9
Which *steely* brand, to make him dreaded more, ... V. i. 9. 1
Out of her *steely* armes were flashing seene, ... V. v. 8. 4
Whose long rest rusted the bright *steely* brand; . . . . V. ix. 30. 7

Steemed. *See* **Esteemed.**
Dame Venus girdle, by her *steemed* deare . . . . IV. v. 3. 7
His life he *steemed* dearer then his frend: . . . . VI. x. 35. 5

Steen. Upon an huge great Earth-pot *steane* he stood, ... VII. vii. 42. 8

Steep. cloud . . . to *steepe* his hed, Doth plonge himselfe . . . *Ro.* xx. 3
Philomele her song with teares doth *steepe;* . . . . *S.C.* N. 141
In quiet rest his molten heart did *steep*, ... *Gn.* 245
Sweete slumbring deaw in carelesnesse did *steepe*, ... *Gn.* 323
till that he came with *steep* descent . . . . *Hub.* 1260
their faire faces with salt humour *steep*. . . . . *T.M.* 112
flowrie bancks with silver liquor *steepe;* . . . . *D.* 102
Could not abstaine mine eyes with teares to *steepe;* . . . . . *D.* 171
the bowels of the earth full *steepe*, ... I. i. 39. 4
Cynthia . . . doth *steepe* In silver deaw his ever-drouping hed, I. i. 39. 7
my frayle eies these lines with teares do *steepe*, ... I. iii. 2. 3
Under the *steepe* foot of a mountaine hore: . . . . I. iii. 10. 6

Steep—*Continued.*
does *steepe* Her tender brest in bitter teares . . . . I. iii. 15. 7
in my heart his yron arrow *steep*, ... I. vii. 39. 5
an hill that was both *steepe* and hy, ... I. x. 46. 2
A little path that was both *steepe* and long, ... I. x. 55. 2
steepe His fierie face in billowes of the west, ... I. xi. 31. 1
wordes with bitter teares did *steepe:* . . . . II. ii. 1. 9
His flaming head did hasten for to *steep*, ... II. ii. 46. 3
His wandring thought in deepe desire does *steepe*, ... II. v. 34. 2
Then she with liquors strong his eies did *steepe*, ... II. vi. 18. 3
they themselves did *steepe* In a blacke flood, ... II. vii. 56. 6
all his armour *steepe*, ... II. viii. 37. 4
that darke dreadfull hole of Tartare *steepe* . . . . II. xii. 6. 4
Their fleecy flowres they fearefully did *steepe*, ... II. xii. 61. 8
did her lilly smock with staines of vermeil *steep*. . . . . . . III. i. 65. 9
often *steepe* Her dainty couch with teares . . . . III. ii. 28. 8
The dronken lamp down in the oyl did *steepe*, ... III. ii. 47. 8
doth love to *steepe* His lustlesse limbes, ... III. iv. 56. 5
The flesh therewith shee suppled and did *steepe*, ... III. v. 33. 6
Under a *steepe* hilles side it placed was, ... IV. v. 33. 1
Strong Allo tombling from Slewlogher *steep*, ... IV. xi. 41. 8
in fresh poyson *steepe;* . . . . V. xii. 42. 8
with her teares his wounds did wash and *steepe:* . . . . . . VI. iii. 10. 5
Ne cared she her wound in teares to *steepe*, ... VI. xi. 23. 8
Steeped. Be not twice *steeped* in Assyrian dye; . . . . . . *Gn.* 98
in the lake his loftie crest was *stept*, ... II. vi. 42. 4
Through the thicke clouds in which they *steeped* lay . . . . . VI. iii. 13. 6
Steeple. With dreadfull force falles on some *steeple* hie; . . . VI. vi. 14. 3
Steeples. sharped *steeples* high shot up in ayre; . . . . . . *Ro.* ii. 2
'Where my high *steeples* whilom usde to stand, ... *Ti.* 127
Steeps. stouping Phebus *steepes* his face: . . . . *S.C.* Mar. 116
Steer. with a staffe his feeble steps did *stire*, ... II. i. 7. 4
'Palmer, *stere* aright, And keepe an even course; . . . . . . II. xii. 3. 1
To *stere* the bote towards that dolefull Mayd, ... II. xii. 28. 8
th' one did row, and th' other stifly *steare;* . . . . II. xii. 37. 4
For whom he turnd him selfe into a *Steare*, ... III. xi. 42. 3
senselesse stood, like to a mazed *steare* . . . . IV. vi. 37. 4
a *Steare*, in heat of sommers day, ... VI. i. 24. 4
By strength have overthrowne a stubborne *steare*, ... VI. viii. 12. 2
Steered. His charett swifte in hast he thither *steard*, ... III. viii. 30. 7
Steers. Sterne was their looke; like wild amazed *steares*, . . . II. ix. 13. 8
love it *steres*, and fortune rowes: . . . . III. iv. 9. 5
Stood all astonied; like a sort of *steeres*, ... VII. vi. 28. 6
Stele. Whose *steale* was yron-studded, but not long, ... V. xii. 14. 8
Stella. *Stella* the faire, the fairest star in skie, ... *As.* 55
Resembling *Stella* in her freshest yeares, ... *As.* 189
Ne lesse praise-worthie *Stella* do I read, ... *Col.* 532
Stem. They *stemme* ech other with so fell despight, ... IV. ii. 16. 4
like a girlond did in compasse *stemme:* . . . . VI. x. 12. 5
Yet many of their *stemme* long after did survive: . . . . . . VII. vi. 2. 9
Stench. all the ayre about with smoke and *stench* did fill. . . I. xi. 13. 9
That al the land with *stench* and heven with horror choke. . . I. xi. 44. 9
A direfull *stench* of smoke and sulphure mixt Ensewd, . . . III. xii. 2. 5
Stent. *See* **Stint.**
Step. Her stombling *steppe* some what her amazed, ... *S.C.* May 231
From highest staire to lowest *step* me drave, ... *Ti.* 25
wisedome warnes . . . To stay the *steppe*, ... I. i. 13. 5
every linck thereof a *step* of dignity. . . . . II. vii. 46. 9
Ne stayed *step*, till that he came at last . . . . V. xi. 3. 3
did stryde At every *step* uppon the tiptoes hie: . . . . . . VI. vii. 42. 6
From so high *step* to stoupe unto so low; . . . . VI. x. 3. 2
Stepdame. Heaven envious, and bitter *stepdame* Nature! . . . *Ro.* ix. 2
A *stepdame* eke, as whott as fyre, ... *S.C.* Mar. 41
No nurse, but *Stepdame*, cruell, mercilesse. . . . . *D.* 342
His wanton *stepdame* loved him the more; . . . . I. v. 37. 5
of Hippolytus was lefte no moniment . . . His cruell *step-dame* I. v. 39. 1
Stepdame's. Phrixus and Helle from their *stepdames* feares, . V. Pr. 5. 7
To fly his *stepdames* loves outrageous, ... V. viii. 43. 3
Stepped. Whilest others alwayes have before me *stept*, ... *Hub.* 77
*Now went, now *stept*, now crept, now backward drew, . . . *Hub.* 1012
Then *stepped* forth the goodly royall Mayd, ... I. xii. 33. 1
there *stepped* foorth A goodly Ladie . . . . II. iii. 21. 6
Trompart forth *stept* . . . . II. iii. 34. 7
The which with monstrous stalke behind him *stept*, ... II. vii. 26. 8
Sternly *stept* forth and raught away his speare, ... IV. iv. 20. 6
Stept Braggadochio forth, and as his thrall Her claym'd, . . . IV. v. 23. 6
I to her *stepped* neare, ... IV. x. 53. 8
He *stepped* forth with courage bold and great, ... V. x. 15. 6
Which when that Squire beheld, he to them *stept* . . . . . . VI. v. 25. 6
Eftsoones the Prince to him full nimbly *stept*, ... VI. viii. 17. 1
Stepping. (*stepping* to him light) . . . . *D.* 544
the noble Prince . . . to him *stepping*, ... I. viii. 34. 6
Stoutly foorth *stepping* on the further shore, ... III. v. 18. 6
Satyrane forth *stepping* did them stay, ... III. ix. 17. 1
to him *stepping* neare . . . . V. xii. 20. 4
to them *stepping* did them soone divide, ... VI. v. 27. 3
to him *stepping*, such a stroke him lent, ... VI. vii. 45. 6
Coridon forth *stepping* openly Did chalenge Calidore . . . . . VI. ix. 43. 5
Steps. an hundred *steps* of purest golde. . . . . *Bel.*[2] ii. 8
hundred *steps* of Afrike golds enchase: . . . . *Bel.*[2] ii. 8
from former follies move To stayed *steps;* . . . . *S.C.* Jun. 38
night with stealing *steppes* doe you forsloe, ... *S.C.* Jun. 119
their high *steppes* adore: . . . . *S.C.* Env. 11
stoutly forward he his *steps* did straine, ... *Hub.* 241
left his sonne t' ensue those *steps* of his. . . . . *Ti.* 266
This lowly Muse, that learns like *steps* to trace, ... *Ded. Son.* xiii. 7
Into whose stead faire falshood *steps*, ... I. ii. Arg.
his weake *steps* governing . . . on cypresse stadle stout, . . . I. vi. 14. 7
Then hunt the *steps* of pure unspotted Maid: . . . . I. vi. 46. 8
monstrous enimy With sturdie *steps* came stalking . . . . . . I. vii. 8. 3

Steps—*Continued.*
his stalking *steps* are stayde Upon a snaggy Oke, ... I. vii. 10. 6
rushing forth from inner bowre, With . . . staggering *steps*, . I. viii. 5. 8
on a staffe his feeble *steps* did frame, ... I. viii. 30. 3
Wont on a staffe his feeble *steps* to stay, ... I. x. 5. 7
any other wight, That hither turnes his *steps*. . . . . I. x. 10. 3
They numbred even *steps* and equall pace; . . . . I. x. 12. 5
his weaker wandring *steps* to guyde, ... I. x. 34. 1
Mercie, that his *steps* upbare And alwaies led, ... I. x. 44. 4
staggering *steps* thy steady hand doth lead, ... I. x. 51. 2
with a staffe his feeble *steps* did stire, ... II. i. 7. 4
Who taught his trampling steed with equall *steps* to tread. . . II. i. 7. 9
suffred not in wrath his hasty *steps* to stray. . . . . II. i. 34. 9
to attend awhile their forward *steps* they stay. . . . . II. i. 35. 9
durst he nott Pursew her *steps* . . . . II. iii. 43. 3
on a staffe her feeble *steps* did stay: . . . . II. iv. 4. 4
Ascending by ten *steps* of Alablaster wrought. . . . . II. ix. 44. 9
To which her *steps* directly she did frame. . . . . III. i. 20. 3
His steed eke seemd t' apply his *steps* to his intent. . . . . III. iv. 61. 9
Eftsoones her *steps* she thereunto applyd, ... III. vii. 5. 6
with bold *steps* into the next roome went. . . . . III. xi. 50. 9
on a broken reed he still did stay His feeble *steps*, ... III. xii. 10. 9
those two villeins, which her *steps* upstayd, ... III. xii. 21. 5
With stately *steps* and fearelesse countenance, ... IV. iii. 5. 2
With easie *steps* so soft as foot could stryde, ... IV. viii. 37. 2
thought my *steps* to stay, ... IV. x. 14. 6
Might not my *steps* withhold, ... IV. x. 29. 2
gan he make him tread his *steps* anew, ... IV. xii. 13. 8
deadly daunger seem'd . . . To tempt such *steps*, ... V. ix. 15. 7
The waies, through which my weary *steps* I guyde . . . . . VI. Pr. 1. 1
To which he meant his weary *steps* to guyde, ... VI. iii. 29. 8
With stayed *steps* and grave beseeming grace: . . . . VI. v. 36. 5
Well did he tract his *steps* as he did ryde, ... VI. vii. 3. 1
With which his feeble *steps* he stayed still; . . . . VII. vii. 31. 7
With crooked crawling *steps* an uncouth pase, ... VII. vii. 35. 6
With trembling *steps*, and humble reverence, ... *Epith.* 210
How ever here on higher *steps* we stand, ... *H.H.L.* 201
Stept. *See* **Steeped.**
Stern. *Sterne* face, and front full of . . . awe . . . . *Bel.*[2] ix. 4
stirring up *sterne* strife. . . . . *S.C.* F. 149
My harveste hasts to stirre up Winter *sterne*, ... *S.C.* D. 129
with *sterne* lookes to threaten kindled yre. . . . . *Gn.* 264
What did of late chaunce happen to the Lyon *stearne*, ... *Hub.* 1250
For trumpets *sterne* to chaunge mine Oaten reeds, ... I. Pr. 1. 4
Upon his foe, a Dragon horrible and *stearne*. . . . . I. i. 3. 9
wrapping up her wrethed *sterne* arownd, ... I. i. 18. 5
His looke was *sterne*, and seemed still to threat . . . . . . I. iii. 33. 7
His eies . . . stared *sterne* on all that him beheld; . . . . . I. iv. 33. 6
Ambitious Sylla, and *sterne* Marius; . . . . I. v. 49. 8
make the Libbard *sterne* Leave roaring, ... I. vi. 25. 8
With staring countenance *sterne*, as one astownd, ... I. viii. 5. 7
scared nations doest with horror *sterne* astownd. . . . . . . I. xi. 6. 9
gan his sturdy *sterne* about to weld, ... I. xi. 28. 8
so *sterne* and terrible in sight, ... II. i. 6. 3
Sterne melancholy did his courage pas, ... II. ii. 17. 8
unto battell *sterne* themselves prepar'd. . . . . II. ii. 19. 9
chaufd and fom'd with corage fiers and *sterne*, ... II. iii. 46. 8
with grim looke And count'naunce *sterne*, ... II. v. 14. 2
Sterne was his looke, and full of stomacke vayne; . . . . . . II. vii. 41. 3
with *sterne* lookes, and stomachous disdaine, ... II. viii. 23. 4
Sterne was their looke; like wild amazed steares, ... II. ix. 13. 8
Stout Ferrex and *sterne* Porrex him in prison threw. . . . . . II. x. 34. 9
which he did earst revive In their *sterne* brests, ... III. v. 16. 5
with *sterne* horror backward gan to start; . . . . III. v. 30. 6
fledd so fast from that same foster *stearne* . . . . III. vi. 54. 3
with *sterne* regard Her dreadfull weapon she to him addrest, . III. vii. 42. 1
He looked round about with *sterne* disdayne, ... III. xii. 23. 2
Emongst them was *sterne* Strife, ... III. xii. 25. 3
with countenance *sterne* All full of wrath, ... IV. ii. 25. 1
looking *sterne*, still over him did stand, ... IV. vi. 23. 4
have the *sterne* remembrance wypt away . . . . IV. viii. 1. 8
had With one *sterne* looke so daunted, ... IV. viii. 2. 3
sterne Druon, and lewd Claribell, ... IV. ix. 20. 8
with faire speches, now with threatnings *sterne*, ... IV. xii. 24. 7
with *sterne* countenance and indignant pride . . . . V. i. 23. 5
sayd that he was obstinate and *sterne*, ... V. v. 46. 1
Restraines those *sterne* behests and cruell doomes of his. . . V. vii. 22. 9
Yet could it not *sterne* Artegall retaine, ... V. viii. 3. 1
From whose *sterne* presence they diffused ran, ... V. xi. 47. 8
His face was ugly and his countenance *sterne*, ... V. xii. 15. 6
with *sterne* count'naunce thus unto him spake: . . . . VI. i. 19. 5
put away proud looke and usage *sterne*, ... VI. i. 40. 8
wherefore Betwixt you two began this . . . *sterne* uprore.' . . VI. ii. 8. 9
Seeing his face so lovely *sterne* and coy, ... VI. ii. 24. 3
but terrible and *stearne* In all assaies . . . . VI. iii. 40. 3
'Ill seemes,' . . . That he should be so *sterne* . . . . VI. iii. 40. 7
For he was *sterne* and terrible by nature, ... VI. vii. 41. 1
with *sterne* eye-browes stared at him oft, ... VI. viii. 26. 3
with *sterne* count'naunce and disdainfull cheare, ... VII. vi. 12. 5
on her uncouth habit and *sterne* looke still gazed. . . . . . VII. vi. 13. 9
Mongst these *sterne* stounds to mingle soft delights; . . . . . VII. vi. 37. 4
grim Sir Saturne oft doth spare His *sterne* aspect, ... VII. vi. 52. 8
with *sterne* countenance, ... *Am.* xxi. 7
Sterner. Sometimes estranging him in *sterner* wise; . . . . . IV. ii. 9. 6
Sternly. all things in his way Full *stearnly* rends . . . . . . *Gn.* 272
sternly lookes at him, ... I. v. 4. 3
sternely bad him other businesse plie . . . . I. vi. 46. 7
Him *sternly* grypt, ... II. iv. 8. 7
strooke at him so *sternely*, ... II. xi. 37. 3
The knight, approching, *sternely* her bespake: . . . . III. iv. 14. 4

Sternly—*Continued.*
The Boaster at him *sternely* bent his browe, III. x. 24. 1
his threeforkt Pyke He *stearnly* shooke, III. xi. 40. 5
Sternly stept forth and raught away his speare, IV. iv. 20. 6
sternly gan repine at his beheast; V. i. 29. 2
she *sternely* bade His miserie to be augmented more, V. v. 54. 5
she *sternly* frownd For high disdaine V. vii. 28. 5
She could it *sternely* draw, that all the world dismayde. V. ix. 30. 9
He *sternely* marcht before the Castle gate, V. xi. 3. 6
sternely him beheld with grim and ghastly looke. V. xi. 12. 9
Talus *sternely* did upon them set, V. xii. 7. 3
still the tyrant *sternely* at him layd, V. xii. 19. 6
the stroke That . . . had so *sternely* wroke His wrath VI. ii. 13. 4
sternely with strong hand it from his handling kept. VI. v. 25. 9
Sternely did bid him quickely thence avaunt, VI. vi. 21. 2
which he so *sternely* shooke, VI. vii. 24. 8
so *sternely* he the monster strooke, VI. x. 36. 3
Sternely he turnd againe, VI. xii. 26. 3
Where-at the Titanesse did *sternly* lower, VII. vi. 18. 4
sturdy March, with brows full *sternly* bent VII. vii. 32. 3
Sternness. His *sternesse* was his prayse, *Van.* x. 5
That sonnes of men amazd their *sternnesse* to behold. II. x. 7. 9
amiable grace, Mixed with manly *sternesse,* II. xii. 79. 6
Tempred with *sternesse* and stout majestie, IV. vi. 26. 3
Durst not the *sternnesse* of his looke abide; IV. x. 18. 3
I would abate the *sternenesse* of my stile, VII. vi. 37. 3
Sterve, *etc. See* **Starve,** *etc.*
Steven. had not Roffy renne to the *steven,* *S.C.* S. 224
Stew. burning Aetna from his boyling *stew* I. xi. 44. 5
Steward. For *Steward* was excessive Gluttony, I. iv. 43. 7
As Guardian and *Steward* of the rest. I. x. 37. 3
He *Steward* was, hight Diet; II. ix. 27. 8
As him the *Steward* badd. II. ix. 28. 6
their bad *Stuard* neither plough'd nor sowed, VI. iv. 14. 7
Sthenoboea. Fayre *Sthenoboea,* that her selfe did choke I. v. 50. 5
Stick. Some *sticke* not to say, *S.C.* S. 112
everie *stick* that underneath did ly, *Hub.* 1008
free his feet that in the myre *sticke* fast? I. ix. 39. 5
in the rest his ready speare did *sticke:* I. i. 26. 3
In whose white alabaster brest did *stick* A cruell knife II. i. 39. 5
byting deepe therein did *sticke* so fast V. xii. 21. 8
Sticketh. if thy galage once *sticketh* fast, *S.C.* S. 131
Sticking. The other halfe, behind yet *sticking* fast, IV. iii. 12. 3
Sticks. in me yet *stickes* the mortall sting, II. iv. 33. 5
A little cottage, built of *stickes* and reedes III. vii. 6. 2
Stie. *See* **Sty.**
Stiff. so *stiffe* and so state, As cocke on his dunghill *S.C.* S. 45
I am so *stiffe* and so stanck, *S.C.* S. 47
his *stiffe* armes to stretch with Eughen bowe, *Hub.* 747
curld uncombed heares Upstaring *stiffe,* I. ix. 22. 3
the *stiffe* beame quaked as affrayd, I. xi. 20. 5
with *stiffe* force shaking his mortall launce, II. iii. 14. 4
A sturdie villein, stryding *stiffe* and bold, II. vii. 40. 4
though they both stood *stiffe,* yet could not both withstond. II. viii. 41. 9
Staring with hollow eies, and *stiffe* upstanding heares. II. ix. 13. 9
that Ferryman With his *stiffe* oares II. xii. 10. 2
her faire locks up stared *stiffe* on end, III. xii. 36. 6
To moderate *stiffe* mindes disposd to strive: IV. ii. 2. 6
he was strong and mightily *stiffe* pight, VI. ix. 44. 2
Stiffly. Curtius, Who, *stifly* bent his vowed life to spill *Gn.* 603
In his strong armes he *stifly* him embraste, II. iv. 14. 1
With that he *stifly* shooke his steelhead dart: II. vi. 40. 1
th' one did row, and th' other *stifly* steare; II. xii. 37. 4
whilest thus she *stifly* strove, III. viii. 29. 6
the more strong and *stiffely* that he ran, IV. iv. 19. 5
stifly stared Like one adawed V. vii. 20. 7
Stiffness. With all the strength and *stifnesse* that he can. IV. iv. 19. 4
Through such her stubborne *stifnesse* and hard hart, VII. vii. 31. 1
her too constant *stiffenesse* doth constrayn. *Am.* lxxxiii. 12
Still. *Still* folowing th' example *Bel.*[1] vi. 4
Must *still* bring forth to rule *Bel.*[1] viii. 15
Still freshly bleeding of a grievous wounde. *Rev.* i. 8
to see the heavens *still* wavering thus, *Bel.*[2] xv. 3
Doo not restraine your images *still* mourning) *Ro.* xv. 8
For lustie Love *still* sleepeth not, *S.C.* Mar. 26
the shepeheards bene ydle and *still,* *S.C.* S. 80
Why livest thou *stil,* *S.C.* D. 95
Why dyest thou *stil,* *S.C.* D. 96
fluttering round about them *still* does sore: *Gn.* 406
swift running rivers *still* did stand, *Gn.* 450
Oxeye *still* greene, *Gn.* 678
still I hoped to be up advaunced, *Hub.* 63
but *still* it has mischaunced. *Hub.* 64
froward fortune *still* to follow mee, *Hub.* 66
Still wayting to preferment up to clime, *Hub.* 76
times delay new hope of helpe *still* breeds. *Hub.* 327
manly legs, *still* passing too and fro, *Hub.* 748
still somewhat to his share did rize: *Hub.* 806
still his eare he lent To everie sound *Hub.* 1010
th' Ape *still* flying he no where might get: *Hub.* 1372
learned Impes that wont to shoote up *still,* *T.M.* 75
be companions *still,* *T.M.* 407
shedding teares a while, I *still* did rest, *Ti.* 32
Looking *still,* if I might of her have sight. *Ti.* 476
Still as I gazed, I beheld where stood *Ti.* 645
Lavender *still* gray, *Mui.* 187
Coole Violets, and Orpine growing *still,* *Mui.* 193
She seem'd *still* backe unto the land to looke, *Mui.* 281
Yet *still* Aragnoll . . . Lay lurking *Mui.* 385
still unstedfast, round about doth goe *D.* 431

Still—*Continued.*
That dying lives, and living *still* does dye. *D.* 434
That *still* I may be readie *D.* 458
Yet bleeding lay, and yet would *still* have bled, *As.* 143
her father, sitting *still* on hie, *Col.* 132
warily *still* watch which way she went, *Col.* 133
Therin *stil* wait poore passengers to teare. *Col.* 203
doo *still* attend To wash faire Cynthiaes sheep, *Col.* 257
as that same shepheard *still* us guyded, *Col.* 331
ye, who so ye be, that *still* survive, *Col.* 644
may that blessed presence *still* enjoy, *Col.* 661
still are wont most happie states t' annoy: *Col.* 663
like Moldwarps nousling *still* they lurke, *Col.* 763
doest their bountie *still* so much commend. *Col.* 902
The antique rolles, which there lye hidden *still,* I. Pr. 2. 4
the Firre that weepeth *still:* I. i. 9. 2
resolving forward *still* to fare, I. i. 11. 1
still did follow one unto the end, I. i. 28. 5
and Cynthia *still* doth steepe In silver deaw I. i. 39. 7
As *still* are wont t' annoy the walled towne, I. i. 41. 7
was wandred far away, *Still* flying from his thoughts I. ii. 12. 3
Still dreading death, I. iii. 6. 7
Still, when she slept, he kept both watch and ward; I. iii. 9. 5
Still seeking him, that from her *still* did flye; I. iii. 21. 8
still, amidst her rayling, she did pray I. iii. 23. 6
you to leave that have me loved *stil,* I. iii. 28. 4
His looke was sterne, and seemed *still* to threat I. iii. 33. 7
He answered nought, but in a traunce *still* lay, I. iii. 39. 6
a sandie hill, that *still* did flitt And fall away, I. iv. 5. 5
still to all the gates stood open wide: I. iv. 6. 2
to the highest she did *still* aspyre, I. iv. 11. 8
his Portesse *still* he bare, I. iv. 19. 1
Still drownd in sleepe, I. iv. 19. 4
Still as he rode he somewhat *still* did eat, I. iv. 22. 5
both from backe and belly *still* did spare, I. iv. 28. 4
still did chaw . . . a venomous tode, I. iv. 30. 2
Still as he rode he gnasht his teeth I. iv. 31. 6
on his dagger *still* his hand he held, I. iv. 33. 8
So oft as Slowth *still* in the mire did stand. I. iv. 36. 4
still before their way A foggy mist I. iv. 36. 6
Still did he wake, and *still* did watch I. v. 1. 9
his hurts, that yet *still* freshly bled. I. v. 17. 3
still twixt feare and hope amazd does sitt, I. vi. 12. 3
seeke her spouse that from her *still* does fly, I. vi. 22. 4
goodly court he made *still* to his Dame, I. vii. 7. 1
his sences stound that *still* he lay full low. I. vii. 12. 9
famous harde atchievements *still* pursew; I. vii. 45. 5
all *still* shronke, and *still* he greater grew: I. vii. 45. 7
her golden cup, Which *still* she bore, I. viii. 14. 2
he could not them use, but kept them *still* in store. I. viii. 30. 9
backward *still* was turnd his wrincled face: I. viii. 31. 4
bad me *still* assured bee, I. ix. 5. 7
still wex old in woe, whiles wo *stil* wexeth new. I. ix. 9. 9
Yett *still* he strove to cloke his inward bale, I. ix. 16. 3
Still as he fledd his eye was backward cast, I. ix. 21. 5
eye was backward cast, As if his feare *still* followed I. ix. 21. 6
grave, That *still* for carrion carcases doth crave: I. ix. 33. 5
sin, Not purg'd nor heald, behind remained *still,* I. x. 25. 3
Amendment readie *still* at hand did wayt, I. x. 26. 7
all in yellow robes arayed *still.* I. x. 30. 9
A multitude of babes . . . *still* she fed I. x. 31. 3
still before him she remov'd away, I. x. 35. 4
The grace of God he layd up *still* in store, I. x. 38. 6
Who him awaited *still* with pensive mynd. I. x. 68. 3
the hevens stood *still* I. xi. 10. 9
Out of his stinking gorge forth steemed *still,* I. xi. 13. 8
steely head stuck fast *still* in his flesh, I. xi. 22. 1
when he saw them come he did them *still* forsake. I. xi. 24. 9
praying *still* did wake, and waking did lament. I. xi. 32. 9
Eyas hauke . . . marveiles at himselfe *stil* as he flies: I. xi. 34. 8
The paw . . . hong *still* on the shield, I. xi. 43. 9
on the ground *still* fell, I. xi. 48. 3
That *still* he sate long time astonished, I. xii. 29. 3
Still as he went he craftie stales did lay, II. i. 4. 1
he descryde and shonned *still* his slight: II. i. 4. 8
to all good he enimy was *still.* II. i. 5. 5
when as *still* he saw him towards pace, II. i. 26. 4
his blacke Palmer, that him guided *still:* II. i. 34. 4, 5
he honour *still* away did beare, II. i. 35. 3
Still he strove; Yet *still* the litle hands were bloody II. ii. 3. 6, 7
let them *still* be bloody, II. ii. 10. 4
Still did they strive II. ii. 13. 7
still . . . on him they freshly gan to smight. II. ii. 23. 8
Still strove their stubborne rages to revoke; II. ii. 28. 6
Full of disport, *still* laughing, II. ii. 36. 2
Yett *still* he satt, II. ii. 37. 9
feare them followes *still* II. iii. 20. 3
to be easd of that base burden *still* did erne. II. iii. 46. 9
Still cald upon to kill him II. iv. 9. 4
still provokt her sonne II. iv. 12. 6
nathelesse he did her *still* torment, II. iv. 12. 7
his great yron teeth he *still* did grind II. iv. 15. 3
found her faithfull *still,* II. iv. 19. 6
Their fell contention *still* increased more, II. v. 22. 1
Thus in *still* waves of deepe delight to wade, II. v. 35. 2
the Blacke Palmer suffred *still* to stond, II. vi. 19. 7
Yet she *still* followed her former style, II. vi. 22. 1
still he stood as sencelesse stone. II. vi. 31. 9
Still as he stood, II. vi. 32. 1
Still solemne sad, or *still* disdainfull coy; II. vi. 37. 5

Still—*Continued.*

Back to the strond retyrd, and there *still* stayd, . . . II. vi. 40. 6
Yet *still* he bet the water, . . . II. vi. 42. 9
still he traveild . . . II. vii. 2. 8
To trouble my *still* seate, . . . II. vii. 7. 9
trembling Feare *still* to and fro did fly, . . . II. vii. 22. 6
still on hye He over him did hold . . . II. vii. 27. 5
gaped *still* as coveting to drinke . . . II. vii. 58. 2
standing *still* a space Gaz'd after him, . . . II. viii. 9. 3
The trespass *still* doth live, albee the person dye.' . . . II. viii. 28. 9
Nought could he hurt, but *still* at warde did ly: . . . II. viii. 39. 7
Long trembling *still* he stoode: . . . II. viii. 46. 5
Still waytes for death . . . II. viii. 50. 4
Still open to their friendes, . . . II. ix. 23. 9
were enraunged ready *still* for fight. . . . II. ix. 26. 5
Which he recorded *still* as they did pas, . . . II. ix. 56. 3
A litle boy did on him *still* attend To reach, . . . II. ix. 58. 4
each his paynes to others profit *still* enployd. . . . II. x. 14. 9
Still as the greedy knight nigh to him drew; . . . II. xi. 27. 2
still as abroad he strew His wicked arrowes, . . . II. xi. 28. 1
whiles he marveild *still*, did *still* him payne; . . . II. xi. 44. 5
Whom *still* he marked freshly to arize . . . II. xi. 44. 8
Ne ought save perill *still* as he did pas: . . . II. xii. 2. 3
still sat wayting on that wastfull clift . . . II. xii. 8. 6
Like to a restlesse wheele, *still* ronning round, . . . II. xii. 20. 6
it was a *still* And calmy bay, . . . II. xii. 30. 2
On th' other side an high rocke toured *still*, . . . II. xii. 30. 5
th' upper halfe their hew retayned *still*, . . . II. xii. 31. 6
The ruefull Strich, *still* waiting on the bere; . . . II. xii. 36. 7
still in stedfast state, . . . II. xii. 51. 2
still it breathed forth sweet spirit and holesom smell: . . . II. xii. 51. 9
lookt *still* forward right, . . . II. xii. 53. 4
Still as she fledd her eye she backward threw, . . . III. i. 16. 1
Cupid *still* emongest them kindled lustfull fyres. . . . III. i. 39. 9
Still did she rove at her with crafty glaunce . . . III. i. 50. 6
her wound *still* inward freshly bledd, . . . III. i. 56. 3
they *still* the girlond bore away; . . . III. ii. 2. 4
hard Tydings thereof, and so them *still* debar'd. . . . III. ii. 21. 5
Did chaunce to *still* into her weary spright, . . . III. ii. 29. 2
shee *still* did waste, and *still* did wayle, . . . III. ii. 52. 3
the Prophet *still* awhile did stay, . . . III. iii. 21. 4
Eftsoones the roaring billowes *still* abid, . . . III. iv. 32. 7
shee knew there staied *still* Some litle life . . . III. iv. 41. 7
Yet did false Archimage her *still* pursew, . . . III. iv. 45. 1
of each turning *still* kept wary heed: . . . III. iv. 48. 5
Yet he her followd *still* . . . III. iv. 51. 5
to his first poursuit him forward *still* doth call. . . . III. v. 2. 9
still the foster . . . Him kept from landing . . . III. v. 20. 1
still the blood forth gusht in so great store, . . . III. v. 26. 4
To commun accidents *stil* open layd, . . . III. v. 36. 7
Still as his wound did gather, . . . III. v. 43. 1
So *still* his hart woxe sore, . . . III. v. 43. 2
Still whenas he beheld the heavenly Mayd, . . . III. v. 43. 4
So *still* his Malady the more increast, . . . III. v. 43. 6
Still when her excellencies he did vew, . . . III. v. 44. 4
Yet *still* he wasted, as the snow congeald . . . III. v. 49. 5
still increast till she her terme had full outgone. . . . III. vi. 9. 9
still remaines in everlasting store, . . . III. vi. 36. 4
still she feared to be overhent . . . III. vii. 19. 5
more fresh And fierce he *still* appeard, . . . III. vii. 32. 9
still stronger grow through strife, . . . III. vii. 33. 3
still, when him at hand she did espy, . . . III. vii. 44. 7
still, with gentle countenaunce, . . . III. viii. 10. 6
hymmes . . . Are *still* emongst them song, . . . III. viii. 42. 9
still anew With wonder of her beauty . . . III. ix. 23. 8
seeing *still* the more desir'd to see, . . . III. ix. 24. 2
looking *still* askaunce Gainst Britomart, . . . III. ix. 27. 3
Still when he mused on his late mischiefe, . . . III. x. 18. 3
still the smart thereof increased more, . . . III. x. 18. 4
lay *still* in the winde, . . . III. x. 30. 5
chose emongst the jolly Satyres *still* to wonne. . . . III. x. 51. 9
as treading *still* on thorne: . . . III. x. 55. 4
as a Snake, *still* lurked in his wounded mynd. . . . III. x. 55. 9
Still fled he forward, looking backward *still*; . . . III. x. 56. 1
one eye *Still* ope he keepes . . . III. x. 58. 7
Still as she stood, she heard . . . Him grone, . . . III. xi. 8. 6
much emmov'd, but stedfast *still* persevered. . . . III. xii. 2. 9
Proceeding to the midst he *stil* did stand, . . . III. xii. 4. 1
The noble Mayd *still* standing all this vewd, . . . III. xii. 5. 1
For *still* he far'd as dauncing in delight, . . . III. xii. 8. 7
in the ydle ayre he mov'd *still* here and theare. . . . III. xii. 8. 9
Which *still* he blew and kindled busily, . . . III. xii. 9. 8
he *still* did stay His feeble steps, . . . III. xii. 10. 8
Under his eiebrowes looking *still* askaunce; . . . III. xii. 15. 2
Holding a lattis *still* before his face, . . . III. xii. 15. 8
Through which he *still* did peep as forward he did pace. . . . III. xii. 15. 9
still roming here and there; . . . III. xii. 17. 7
Her forward *still* with torture did constraine, . . . III. xii. 21. 8
still with stedfast eye and courage stout . . . III. xii. 37. 5
her golden lockes, that were upbound *Still* in a knot, . . . IV. i. 13. 3
never thoght one thing, but doubly *stil* was guided. . . . IV. i. 27. 9
still are led with every light report: . . . IV. i. 28. 5
rolled on an heape, lay *still* in swound . . . IV. i. 43. 1
still when any Knight Is weakned, . . . IV. i. 44. 7
lying *still* awhile, both did forget . . . IV. ii. 15. 8
Still watcht on every side, of secret foes affrayd, . . . IV. ii. 36. 9
She, them saluting, there by them sate *still* . . . IV. ii. 49. 1
thousand perills which them *still* awate, . . . IV. iii. 1. 5
still the life stood fearelesse of her foe; . . . IV. iii. 17. 5
Stood *still* awhile, and his fast footing kept, . . . IV. iii. 20. 8

Still—*Continued.*

Cambell *still* more strong and greater grew, . . . IV. iii. 29. 1
Still when as he enfeebled was, him cherisht, . . . IV. iii. 29. 4
Stood *still* amaz'd, holding his idle sweard; . . . IV. iii. 31. 7
Yet *still* that direfull stroke kept on his way, . . . IV. iii. 34. 1
Thereat the Champions both stood *still* a space, . . . IV. iii. 38. 1
they, like men astonisht, *still* did stand. . . . IV. iii. 48. 5
Whether shall have the Hag, or hold the Lady *still*.' . . . IV. iv. 12. 9
stood there *still*, As one that seemed doubtfull . . . IV. iv. 20. 3
with unwearied powre his party *still* assured. . . . IV. iv. 37. 9
still the Knights of Maidenhead the better wonne; . . . IV. iv. 38. 9
The prize of beautie *still* hath joyned beene; . . . IV. v. 1. 3
Still as advantage they espyde thereto: . . . IV. vi. 18. 3
renewed His strength *still* more, but she *still* more decrewed. . . . IV. vi. 18. 5
still over him did stand, . . . IV. vi. 23. 4
fayned *still* her former angry mood, . . . IV. vi. 29. 8
he therewith so felly *still* did rave, . . . IV. vii. 28. 5
stood *still* mute, as if he had beene dum, . . . IV. vii. 44. 2
saw her forward *still* to make her flight, . . . IV. viii. 8. 2
So tempting her *still* to pursue the pray, . . . IV. viii. 11. 4
still from her escaping soft away: . . . IV. viii. 11. 5
loath this life, *still* longing for to die. . . . IV. viii. 16. 9
after them did barke, and *still* backbite, . . . IV. viii. 36. 3
she him *still* detaines in captive hold, . . . IV. viii. 53. 7
Having a keeper *still* with him in place; . . . IV. viii. 54. 4
still with care was moved. . . . IV. x. 1. 9
I persever'd *still* to knocke and call, . . . IV. x. 11. 6
the river rolling *still* With murmure soft, . . . IV. x. 15. 8
him maystred *still* in all debate. . . . IV. x. 32. 9
could not containe it *still*, . . . IV. x. 43. 8
stedfast *still* her eyes did fixed rest, . . . IV. x. 49. 7
huge Orion, that doth tempests *still* portend; . . . IV. xi. 13. 9
that which is th' immortall spright Lives *still*, . . . IV. xi. 16. 9
Swift Rhene, and Alpheus *still* immaculate . . . IV. xi. 21. 4
Stood *still* by him astonisht at his lore, . . . IV. xi. 23. 8
the *still* Darent, in whose waters cleane . . . IV. xi. 29. 8
doth make His way *still* under ground, . . . IV. xi. 32. 9
Still Ure, swift Werfe, and Oze the most of might, . . . IV. xi. 37. 6
stormes which therein *still* remaine. . . . IV. xi. 38. 9
seeming *still* to smile, Glauconome, . . . IV. xi. 50. 8
still bemoning her unworthy paine. . . . IV. xii. 17. 5
who *still* her answered, there was nought. . . . IV. xii. 24. 9
With which his daughter doth him *still* support; . . . V. ii. 5. 6
By which he *stil* them holds, . . . V. ii. 5. 9
still upon him hong. . . . V. ii. 14. 9
Artegall pursewd him *still* so neare . . . V. ii. 18. 1
Yet *still* he bet and bounst uppon the dore, . . . V. ii. 21. 6
still continu'd his assault the more, . . . V. ii. 24. 1
Still holding up her suppliant hands on hye, . . . V. ii. 26. 4
still it downe did slide, . . . V. ii. 45. 7
He gazed *still* upon that snowy mayd; . . . V. iii. 18. 7
Eftsoones he stood as *still* as any stake, . . . V. iii. 34. 5
I hold mine owne, and so will hold it *still*. . . . V. iv. 14. 5
Yet *still* her blowes he bore, . . . V. v. 7. 1
Yet *still* her crueltie increased more, . . . V. v. 7. 3
though he *still* retyr'd, . . . V. v. 14. 5
With many idle stoups her troubling *still*: . . . V. v. 15. 7
Nought could he do but . . . backward *still* retyre; . . . V. v. 16. 2
So much the greater *still* her anguish grew, . . . V. v. 28. 1
still the more she strove it to subdew. . . . V. v. 28. 3
The more she *still* augmented her owne smart, . . . V. v. 28. 4
dread of shame my doubtfull lips doth *still* restraine.' . . . V. v. 30. 9
as bound to me he may continue *still*: . . . V. v. 32. 9
though she *still* have worne Her dayes in warre, . . . V. v. 40. 4
to her Dame him *still* she discommended, . . . V. v. 57. 4
Be well adviz'd that he stand stedfast *still*; . . . V. vi. 1. 7
With which those Amazons his love *still* craved, . . . V. vi. 2. 4
when she reckned them, *still* drawing neare, . . . V. vi. 5. 8
stood *still* mute, as one in great suspence; . . . V. vi. 9. 7
ne ever lookt aside, But *still* right downe; . . . V. vi. 18. 5
Now walking soft, now sitting *still* upright, . . . V. vi. 26. 3
Which *still* was wont with Artegall remaine; . . . V. vi. 34. 4
thereuppon long while stood gazing *still*, . . . V. vii. 5. 8
With which she used *still* to tye her fone, . . . V. vii. 28. 3
th' other *still* pursu'd the fearefull Mayd; . . . V. viii. 6. 1
still from him as fast away did flie, . . . V. viii. 6. 2
like hound . . . Continu'd *still* his course, . . . V. viii. 7. 3
He ran *still* on, thinking to follow fast . . . V. viii. 8. 8
seeing him come *still* so fiercely on, . . . V. viii. 9. 4
against her *still* doth fight, . . . V. viii. 20. 7
Kept himselfe *still* in his straunge armour dight: . . . V. viii. 27. 5
Yet *still* he him did follow every where, . . . V. viii. 33. 7
Still when he sought t' approch unto him ny . . . V. viii. 36. 1
Yet *still* the Prince pursew'd him close behind. . . . V. viii. 42. 1
Where *still* the stronger doth the weake devoure, . . . V. ix. 1. 6
The whiles the Prince there kept the entrance *still*. . . . V. ix. 15. 2
them to their posterities doe *still* declare. . . . V. x. 5. 9
all his way before him *still* prepare. . . . V. x. 17. 7
stil, when fit occasion did betyde, . . . V. xi. 6. 4
even that which thou savedst thine *still* to remaine?' . . . V. xi. 16. 9
stretcht it selfe as it had long lyen *still*; . . . V. xi. 22. 6
Whilest *still* she stands, as stonisht and forlorne: . . . V. xi. 29. 5
Yet *still* he strives, ne any perill spares, . . . V. xi. 45. 1
she by force is *still* fro me detayned, . . . V. xi. 54. 8
Nathlesse the yron man did *still* pursew . . . V. xi. 65. 1
still the tyrant sternely at him layd, . . . V. xii. 19. 6
envies cloud *still* dimmeth vertues ray. . . . V. xii. 27. 7
And *still* among most bitter wordes they spake, . . . V. xii. 42. 1
So much the more at him *still* did she scold, . . . V. xii. 43. 6
still the way did hold To Faerie Court; . . . V. xii. 43. 8

Still—*Continued.*
still I forward trace.' VI. i. 7. 5
still his spirite spar'd, VI. i. 20. 6
as he *still* decayd so he encreased more. VI. i. 21. 9
awhile he rested *still:* VI. i. 35. 5
as it *still* encreast, so *still* increast VI. i. 36. 6
Subject to fortunes chance, *still* chaunging new: VI. i. 41. 8
But *still* his passion grew more violent VI. ii. 21. 9
Yet was he courteous *still* to every wight, VI. iii. 3. 5
Therefore there *still* he stood as in a stound, VI. iii. 30. 3
Upstaying *still* her selfe uppon her steede, VI. iii. 46. 2
he him *still* pursew'd from place to place, VI. iii. 49. 1
refuge was *still* Behind his Ladies back; VI. iii. 49. 5
But chaste him *still* for all his Ladies cry; VI. iii. 51. 2
still seeming faine When ought he did, VI. iv. 16. 4
though he were *still* in this desert wood, VI. v. 2. 2
creeping *still* behinde, doth him incomber, VI. v. 19. 6
Creeping behinde him *still* to have destroyde; VI. v. 20. 5
when the cause . . . Removed is, th' effect surceaseth *still.* VI. vi. 14. 4
Yet he them *still* so sharpely did pursew, VI. vi. 24. 1
wretched end which *still* attendeth on her.' VI. vi. 25. 7
cowardize doth *still* in villany delight. VI. vi. 26. 9
flying *still* did ward, and warding fly away. VI. vi. 28. 9
when his foe he *still* so eager saw, VI. vi. 29. 1
Still looking after him that did him chace, VI. vi. 29. 8
still did lie as dead, and quake, and quiver, VI. vi. 32. 3
Where *still* he bathed lay in his owne bloody gore. VI. vii. 8. 9
still, when she complaines, The more he laughes, VI. vii. 44. 7
so sharpely *still* he him pursewd, VI. vii. 48. 1
Where *still* he lay, ne out of swoune awooke, VI. vii. 48. 5
Him *still* reviling and afflicting sore, VI. viii. 4. 2
still suppressing, gan of her inquire, VI. viii. 18. 3
Arthure with the rest went onward *still* VI. viii. 30. 7
Had traveld *still* on foot in heavie armes, VI. viii. 47. 2
gazing *still* on others stands. VI. ix. 11. 9
So stood he *still* long gazing thereupon, VI. ix. 12. 1
yet did he stay And sate there *still,* VI. ix. 12. 5
Hong *still* upon his melting mouth attent; VI. ix. 26. 2
hunt *still* after shadowes vaine Of courtly favour, VI. x. 2. 7
two of them *still* froward seem'd to bee, VI. x. 24. 7
one *still* towards shew'd her selfe afore; VI. x. 24. 8
Bad them be *still;* VI. xi. 14. 8
Still slew the formost that came first to hand VI. xi. 46. 8
Still winneth way, ne hath her compasse lost: VI. xii. 1. 7
cats, that wrawling *still* did cry; VI. xii. 27. 4
still, the more he strove, the more the Knight Did him VI. xii. 31. 5
crop his thousand heads, which *still* new Forth budded, VI. xii. 32. 4
In that *still* happy state for ever to abide. VII. vi. 5. 9
Where Cynthia did sit, that never *still* did stand. VII. vi. 8. 9
with his Torche, *still* twinkling like twylight, VII. vi. 9. 7
the Moones bright wagon *still* did stand, VII. vi. 13. 7
on her uncouth habit and sterne looke *still* gazed. VII. vi. 13. 9
if Jove should do *still* what he can. VII. vi. 31. 9
Still mooving, yet unmoved from her sted; VII. vii. 13. 3
So turne they *still* about, and change in restlesse wise. VII. vii. 18. 9
Still change and vary thoughts, as new occasions fall. VII. vii. 19. 9
th' Ocean moveth *still* from place to place, VII. vii. 20. 3
every River *still* doth ebbe and flowe; VII. vii. 20. 4
Ne any Lake, that seems most *still* and slowe, VII. vii. 20. 5
Still tost and turned with continuall change, VII. vii. 21. 2
The fish, *still* floting, doe at randon range, VII. vii. 21. 4
flitting *still* doe flie, and *still* their places vary. VII. vii. 21. 9
which who feeles not by sense . . . To flit *still,* VII. vii. 22. 3
With which his feeble steps he stayed *still;* VII. vii. 31. 7
subject *still* to Mutability?' VII. vii. 47. 9
still compell To keepe his course? VII. vii. 48. 5
Onely the starry skie doth *still* remaine: VII. vii. 55. 5
the Starres and Signes therein *still* move, VII. vii. 55. 6
with firme eyes affixt the ground *still* viewed. VII. vii. 57. 3
But, looking *still* on her, I stand amazed *Am.* iii. 7
her unmoved mind Doth *still* persist *Am.* vi. 2
Nor to the Lightning; for they *still* persever; *Am.* ix. 9
Yet lowly *still* vouchsafe to looke on me; *Am.* xiii. 13
she as steele and flint doth *still* remayne. *Am.* xviii. 14
every sweet with soure is tempred *still,* *Am.* xxvi. 9
still, the more she fervent sees my fit, *Am.* xxxii. 9
Still to behold the object of their paine, *Am.* xxxv. 2
their cruelty doth *still* increace, *Am.* xxxvi. 7
in her pride she dooth persever *still.* *Am.* xxxviii. 9
Yet shoot ye sharpely *still,* *Am.* lvii. 9
Sought not to fly, but fearelesse *still* did bide; *Am.* lxvii. 10
further seemes his terme *still* to extend, *Am.* lxxxvi. 11
So sorrow *still* doth seeme too long to last; *Am.* lxxxvi. 13
Doe make and *still* repayre: *Epith.* 102
doe *still* adorne her beauties pride, *Epith.* 104
still throw betweene Some graces to be seene; *Epith.* 106
Nathlesse doe ye *still* loud her prayses sing, *Epith.* 165
Why stand ye *still* ye virgins in amaze, *Epith.* 181
her sad eyes, *still* fastened on the ground, *Epith.* 234
the night Raven, that *still* deadly yels; *Epith.* 346
th' unpleasant Quyre of Frogs *still* croking *Epith.* 349
let *stil* Silence trew night-watches keepe, *Epith.* 353
The lawes of wedlock *still* dost patronize; *Epith.* 391
a chyld, renewing *still* thy yeares, *H.L.* 55
see, and seeing it *still* dye. *H.L.* 133
beholding *still* with constant sight, *H.L.* 195
Still full, yet never satisfyde *H.L.* 199
striveth *still* T' approch *H.L.* 247
Which powre retayning *still* *H.B.* 113
the soule is faire and beauteous *still,* *H.B.* 159

Still—*Continued.*
mindfull *still* of your first countries sight, *H.B.* 166
Doe *still* preserve your first informed grace, *H.B.* 167
Which in it selfe it hath remaining *still,* *H.B.* 219
Armies of Loves *still* flying too and fro, *H.B.* 240
Yet being pregnant *still* with powrefull grace, *H.H.L.* 50
For he his beames doth *still* to them extend, *H.H.L.* 72
Still flowing forth His goodnesse unto all, *H.H.L.* 100
streames . . . *stil* do flow, and freshly *still* redound, *H.H.L.* 165
glorie present *still* Before thy face, *H.H.L.* 284
Then th' Aire *still* flitting, but yet firmely bounded *H.H.B.* 38
still as every thing doth upward tend, *H.H.B.* 44
so *still* more cleare And faire it growes, *H.H.B.* 45
And as these heavens *still* by degrees arize, *H.H.B.* 71
Whence they doe *still* behold the glorious face *H.H.B.* 80
By which they first were made, and *still* increast. *H.H.B.* 203
Ne she her selfe, had she remained *still,* *H.H.B.* 215
idle hopes, which *still* doe fly away, *Proth.* 8
they stood amazed *still,* *Proth.* 58

Still-changing. holds the world in his *still chaunging* state. I. ix. 42. 7

Stilled. wiping the deawy wet Which softly *stild,* IV. vii. 35. 6
Ne can be *stild* for all his nurses might, V. vi. 14. 4

Still-moving. this worlds *still moving* mightie masse *H.L.* 57
On that bright shynie round *still moving* Masse, *H.H.B.* 51

Sting. Through his faire hide his angrie *sting* did threaten, *Van.* ii. 11
forkhed *sting* that death in it did beare, *Van.* vi. 4
heate of heedlesse lust me so did *sting,* *S.C.* D. 21
Her huge long taile . . . Pointed with mortall *sting.* I. i. 15. 4
Threatning her angrie *sting,* him to dismay; I. i. 17. 7
Snake, the which his . . . mortall *sting* implyes. I. iv. 31. 5
Cleopatra . . . with stroke Of Aspes *sting* I. v. 50. 8
An heard of Bulles, whom kindly rage doth *sting,* I. viii. 11. 6
With sharpe intended *sting* so rude him smott, I. xi. 38. 2
The mortall *sting* his angry needle shott I. xi. 38. 5
strove to loose the far infixed *sting:* I. xi. 39. 4
in me yet stickes the mortall *sting,* II. iv. 33. 5
hungers poynt or Venus *sting* II. xii. 39. 3
Infixt such secrete *sting* of greedy lust, III. viii. 25. 2
it prickt his wanton mind With *sting* of lust IV. ii. 5. 5
stop vile envies *sting,* IV. ii. 26. 6
the *sting* which in her tongs end grew. IV. viii. 36. 9
whose *sting* without redresse Full deadly wounds V. xi. 24. 5
Appear'd like Aspis *sting* that closely kils, V. xii. 36. 4
with the *sting* which in her vile tongue grew V. xii. 42. 7
the poysnous *sting,* which infamy Infixeth VI. vi. 1. 3
envenimd *sting* . . . now gan afresh to rancle sore, VI. x. 31. 1
Venemous toung, tipt with vile adders *sting,* *Am.* lxxxv. 1

Stinging. A *stinging* serpent by the heele her caught: *Pet.* vi. 8

Stings. All striving to infixe their feeble *stinges,* I. i. 23. 6
at the point two *stinges* in fixed arre, I. xi. 11. 8
stinges and sharpest steele I. xi. 12. 1
With *stinges* of carnall lust, II. xi. 13. 7
Reproch sharpe *stings,* Repentaunce whips entwinde, III. xii. 24. 7
like the *stings* of aspes that kill with smart, IV. viii. 26. 8
with their little *stings* right felly fare; VI. xi. 48. 4
The tongues of Serpents, with three forked *stings,* VI. xii. 28. 2

Stink. welnigh choked with the deadly *stinke,* I. i. 22. 2
him nigh choked with the deadly *stinke.* V. xi. 31. 8

Stinking. *stinking* Smallage, and unsaverie Rew; *D.* 347
heard Of *stinking* Seales and Porcpisces *Col.* 249
smouldry cloud of duskish *stincking* smoke; I. vii. 13. 8
Out of his *stinking* gorge forth steemed still, I. xi. 13. 8
smouldry smoke And *stinking* sulphure, III. xi. 21. 7

Stint. Perswade us dye, to *stint* all further strife: I. ix. 29. 8
They *stint* their strife II. ii. 22. 9
n'ould she *stent* Her bitter rayling II. iv. 12. 4
Yet nathemore did it his fury *stint,* II. v. 8. 3
allay, and *stint* thy stormy strife, III. iv. 8. 8
To *stint* all strife and foster friendly peace, IV. ii. 19. 2
For *stint* of strife and stablishment of rest V. viii. 21. 3
To *stint* all strife and troublous enmitie, V. xi. 54. 3
No skill can *stint,* nor reason can aslake. *Am.* xliv. 8
nought but death can *stint* his dolours smart? *H.B.* 74

Stinted. Their troublous strife they *stinted* by and by, *Hub.* 1092
stinted all the strife incontinent: IV. iii. 18. 4
so *stinted* all their strife. IV. ix. 15. 9

Stints. Prince Arthur *stints* their strife. IV. ix. Arg.

Stipends. gives to their professors *stipends* large. *Col.* 746

Stir. waketh and if but a leafe *sturre.* *S.C.* S. 183
My harveste hasts to *stirre* up Winter sterne, *S.C.* D. 129
her that first did *stir* that mortall stownd. *Col.* 878
hand or foot to *stirr* he strove in vaine. I. i. 18. 8
Tho can she weepe, to *stirre* up gentle ruth I. i. 50. 8
he was . . . unhable once to *stirre* or go; I. iv. 23. 2
with their *sturre* they troubled all the traine; I. iv. 40. 4
No powre he had to *stirre,* I. viii. 15. 4
joyd to *stirre* up strife, I. ix. 10. 3
whenas the direfull feend She saw not *stirre,* I. xi. 55. 6
Against his praise to *stirre* up enmitye Of such, II. i. 23. 8
saw it *stirre:* II. iii. 34. 4
her handes fast bound . . . That she note *stirre.* II. iv. 13. 6
stirre him up to strife and cruell fight. II. iv. 42. 7
When with the maistring spur he did him roughly *stire.* II. v. 2. 9
To *stirre* up strife, and garre them disagree: II. v. 19. 7
bellowes, which did *styre* Continually, II. ix. 30. 4
To *stirre* up strife, and troublous contecke broch: III. i. 64. 5
to forbeare The bloody batteill and to *stirre* up strife, III. iv. 24. 8
Unable to arise, or foote or hand to *styre.* III. vii. 45. 9
To *stirre* and roll them like to womens eyes: III. viii. 7. 4
To gin awake, and *stir* his frosen spright: III. viii. 23. 5

Stir—*Continued.*
strive and storme with *stirre* outrageous For her, IV. i. 47. 3
both you here . . . *stirre* up bloudie frayes, IV. i. 47. 8
To *stirre* up strife twixt love and spight and ire, IV. ii. 11. 8
Both falling out doe *stirre* up strifefull broyle, IV. iii. 16. 5
ye doe wrong To *stirre* up strife, IV. iv. 12. 3
Which troublous *stirre* when Satyrane aviz'd, IV. v. 25. 1
unable once to *stirre* or move. IV. xii. 20. 9
mutining to *stirre* up civill faction V. ii. 51. 4
Which troublous *stirre* when Artegall perceived, V. iii. 30. 6
With which he wont to *stirre* up battailous alarmes. V. v. 21. 9
Mote in them *stirre* up old rebellious thought V. vii. 11. 5
To *stirre* up strife and many a tragicke stowre; V. x. 13. 5
From things that *stirre* up fraile affection; VI. vi. 7. 7
looser lookes that *stir* up lustes impure; *Am.* xxi. 8
In my true love did *stirre* up coles of yre; *Am.* lxxxv. 8
therein *stirre* such rage and restlesse stowre, *H.B.* 73
loves, with which the world doth . . . *stirre* up affections base, *H.H.L.* 263
Stire. *See* **Steer, Stir.**
Stirred. A comett *stird* up that unkindly heate, *S.C.* D. 59
Afraid of everie leafe that *stir'd* him by, *Hub.* 1007
Hath *stirred* up so mischievous despight? *T.M.* 46
the strings, *stirred* with the warbling wind, *Ti.* 613
Stir'd up through wrathfull Nemesis despight, *Mui.* 2
To judge the strife betweene them *stirred* late: *Mui.* 309
two rams, *stird* with ambitious pride, I. ii. 16. 1
stird you up to worke your wilfull smarts? II. ii. 29. 4
Tho up he started, *stird* with shame extreme, II. vi. 27. 7
Some *stird* the molten owre with ladles great; II. vii. 36. 8
greedy thirst . . . *Stird* Porrex up II. x. 35. 3
stird with pitty II. x. 37. 3
Ne *stird,* till hope of life did him forsake: II. xi. 46. 8
as the one *stird* up affections bace, III. i. 46. 3
them with bitter words he *stird* to bloodie yre. III. v. 15. 9
her courage . . . rather *stird* to cruell enmity, III. xii. 1. 8
rather *stir'd* to vengeance and despight, IV. iii. 14. 4
now a new debate *Stird* up IV. iv. 2. 4
rather *stird* by his discordfull Dame, IV. iv. 3. 7
Thereto him Ate *stird,* new discord to maintaine. IV. v. 22. 9
So all together *stird* up strifull stoure, IV. v. 24. 5
what dreadfull stoure, it *stird* this day; V. iii. 21. 6
stirred up with different desires, V. iv. 4. 4
Yet *stirred* not at all for doubt of more, V. vi. 28. 3
stird up day and night V. viii. 20. 2
Stirredst. *stirredst* up th' Heroes high intents, III. iii. 2. 8
Stirreth. Ne *stirreth* limbe; *Mui.* 405
It *stirreth* up to sensuall desire, III. v. 1. 6
Stirring. *stirring* up sterne strife. *S.C.* F. 149
him *stirring* to bee wroke Of his late wronges, II. v. 21. 3
stirring up their stormy enmity, III. viii. 21. 7
Having through *stirring* loosd their wonted band, IV. vi. 20. 2
Stirrup. prostrated fall, And kisse my *stirrup;* II. iii. 8. 6
by his *stirrup* Talus did attend, V. viii. 29. 6
Stirs. *stirs* up anguish and contentious rage: IV. iii. 43. 4
Stock. *See* **Beetle-stock, Laughing-stock.**
Nor for fruict nor for shadowe serves thy *stocke;* *S.C.* F. 128
any buddes of Poesie, Yet of the old *stocke,* *S.C.* O. 74
the Shepheard self, tending his *stocke,* *Gn.* 237
The glorie of the *stock* of Tantalus, *Gn.* 546
Out of his *stocke* and famous familie, *Ti.* 276
Did keepe his sheep, his litle *stock* and store: *As.* 4
streames of blood out of the truncked *stock* Forth gushed, I. viii. 10. 8
grace of God . . . as a *stocke* he left unto his seede. I. x. 38. 7
Strikes in the *stocke,* ne thence can be releast, II. v. 10. 8
roiall *stocke* of old Assaracs line, II. x. 9. 7
The noble braunch from th' antique *stocke* was torne II. x. 36. 4
Well worthie *stock,* from which the branches sprong III. iv. 3. 6
did in *stocke* of earthly flesh enrace, III. v. 52. 5
Yet is the *stocke* not lessened nor spent, III. vi. 36. 3
the drie withered *stocke* it gan refresh, III. viii. 25. 3
of the antique Trojan *stocke* there grew Another plant, III. ix. 47. 6
Sprung of the auncient *stocke* of Princes straine, IV. viii. 33. 7
like a stupid *stock* in silence die! *Am.* xliii. 8
Stocks. They han great stores and thriftye *stockes,* *S.C.* Jul. 193
all about old *stockes* and stubs of trees, I. ix. 34. 1
As withered leaves drop from their dryed *stockes,* II. xi. 19. 4
like two senceles *stocks* in long embracement dwelt. III. xii. 45. *or.* 9
Stoic. these *Stoicke* censours cannot well deny. IV. Pr. 3. 9
Stole. They *stole* away, and tooke their hastie flight, *Hub.* 339
mens hearts . . . He *stole* away, *As.* 22
mourning *stole* of carefull wydowhead, *Col.* 494
Of each a part I *stole* by cunning thefte: *Ded.Son.*xvii.13
over all a blacke *stole* shee did throw: I. i. 4. 5
a black *stole,* most like to seeme for Una fit. I. i. 45. 9
Under blacke *stole* hyding her bayted hooke; I. i. 49. 6
she . . . layd her *stole* aside. I. iii. 4. 6
Thence turning backe in silence softe they *stole,* I. v. 31. 1
she had layd her mournefull *stole* aside, I. xii. 22. 2
stole fire from heven to animate His worke, II. x. 70. 7
linnen *stole* after those Priestes guize, V. vii. 13. 3
sodainely she saw transfigured Her linnen *stole* V. vii. 13. 5
Unto whose bed false Bregog whylome *stole,* VII. vi. 40. 4
One of his shafts she *stole* away. *Epig.* ii. 4
Stolen. He all those royall signes had *stolne* away, *Hub.* 1016
he to her brought part of his *stolen* things. I. iii. 18. 9
The Briton Prince recov'ring his *stolne* sword, II. ix. 2. 2
whylome by false Faries *stolne* away, III. iii. 26. 6
begonne His *stolen* steed to thunder furiously, III. x. 33. 6
stolne away from her beloved mate, IV. vi. 47. 7
So *stolen* from their fancies wonderment V. iii. 26. 5
Stolen—*Continued.*
His owne good steed, which he had *stolne,* to clame; V. iii. 29. 5
with lone Of armes hast knighthood *stolne,* V. vi. 37. 5
litle sparrowes *stolen* from their nest, VI. ix. 40. 2
Whose whelpes are *stolne* away, VI. xi. 25. 9
Stomach. Upon her *stomacke* laid Mount Quirinal, *Ro.* iv. 11
the Ape in wondrous *stomack* woxe, *Hub.* 1103
raging Love dothe appall the weake *stomacke:* *U.V.* 11
Sterne was his looke, and full of *stomacke* vayne; II. vii. 41. 3
Corrupts the *stomacke* with gall vitious, III. x. 59. 7
Stomachous. with sterne lookes, and *stomachous* disdaine, II. viii. 23. 4
Stonck. *See* **Stunk.**
Stond, -s. *See* **Stand, -s.**
Stone. *See* **Altar-stone, Corner-stone, Crystal-stone, Magnes-stone, Marble-stone, Pebble-stone.**
Threwe downe this building to the lowest *stone.* *Bel.*[1] ii. 14
the pavement precious *stone.* *Rev.* iv. 11
sorow to Niobe did breede: Now she is a *stone,* *S.C.* Ap. 88
Against a mountaine rolls a mightie *stone,* *Gn.* 391
Adornd with purest golde and precious *stone;* *Ti.* 86
Built all of richest *stone* that might bee found, *Ti.* 506
Queene . . . In glistring gold and perelesse pretious *stone;* I. iv. 8. 6
Sisyphus an huge round *stone* did reele I. v. 35. 3
in the midst thereof one pretious *stone* I. vii. 30. 1
from underneath the *stone,* To God for vengeance cryde I. viii. 36. 6
writt in *stone* With bloody letters I. x. 53. 6
builded . . . Of perle and precious *stone,* I. x. 55. 5
Transformd her to a *stone* II. ii. 8. 9
'Lo! now she is that *stone;* II. ii. 9. 1
the *stone* her semblance seemes to show, II. ii. 9. 4
still he stood as sencelesse *stone.* II. vi. 31. 9
nether steele nor *stone* The stroke thereof II. viii. 21. 1
Not built of bricke, ne yet of *stone* and lime, II. ix. 21. 4
Of hewen *stone* the porch was fayrely wrought, II. ix. 24. 1
Stone more of valew, and more smooth and fine, II. ix. 24. 2
He of his name Coylchester built of *stone* and lime. II. x. 58. 9
An huge great *stone,* which stood upon one end, II. xi. 35. 7
could have made a rocke of *stone* to rew, III. v. 30. 2
the hardest hart of *stone* Would hardly finde III. viii. 1. 7
There was an Altar built of pretious *stone* III. xi. 47. 2
Through working of the *stone* therein yset. IV. iii. 24. 5
curiously embost With pearle and precious *stone,* IV. iv. 15. 7
rolling thence the *stone,* Which wont to stop the mouth IV. vii. 20. 4
The *stone* which passed straunger at him threw: IV. viii. 36. 6
Poudred with pearle and *stone;* IV. x. 31. 8
neither pretious *stone,* nor durefull brasse, IV. x. 39. 4
ruth it moved in the rocky *stone,* IV. xii. 5. 7
men . . . Are now transformed into hardest *stone;* V. Pr. 2. 5
bake their sides uppon the cold hard *stone,* V. vii. 9. 3
like a *stone* it fell upon the land; V. ix. 17. 8
catching up in hand a ragged *stone* VI. iv. 21. 2
Now beating his hard head upon a *stone,* VI. v. 4. 5
She is no woman, but a sencelesse *stone.* *Am.* liv. 14
Stone-dead. The *stone-dead* quarrey falls so forciblye, II. xi. 43. 3
Stonehenge. Th' eternall marks of treason may at *Stonheng* vew. II. x. 66. 9
now entombed lies at *Stoneheng* by the heath. II. x. 67. 9
Stone's. rocke Is lightly stricken with some *stones* throw; V. i. 21. 7
Stones. *See* **Pumice-stones.**
These heapes of *stones,* these old wals, *Ro.* xviii. 1
the glauncing rayes Of precious *stones,* *Gn.* 102
stones, the which encomber might His passage, *Col.* 150
did a stately heape of *stones* upreare, *Col.* 285
fill with *stones,* that all men may it know. *Col.* 635
a bauldrick . . . with *stones* most pretious rare. I. vii. 29. 9
Men into *stones* therewith he could transmew, I. vii. 35. 6
transmew . . . *stones* to dust, I. vii. 35. 7
Sometimes she raught him *stones,* II. iv. 5. 5
those three monstrous *stones* doe most excell, II. x. 11. 5
with great perles and pretious *stones* embost; III. i. 32. 7
pearles and pretious *stones* of great assay, III. iv. 18. 5
would not stay For gold, or perles, or pretious *stones,* III. iv. 18. 8
Against the *stones* and trees did rayle anew, IV. viii. 36. 8
stones of rich assay, IV. x. 15. 5
Beaten with *stones* downe from the battilment, V. ii. 20. 6
force of *stones* which they did throw, V. ii. 22. 7
all the hewen *stones* thereof defaced, V. ii. 28. 3
bedeckt Uppon the bosse with *stones* that shined wide, V. v. 3. 7
he then *stones* at it so long did cast, V. ix. 17. 7
darts from shore and *stones* they at him threw; V. xii. 5. 5
still did she scold, And *stones* did cast; V. xii. 43. 7
there Her whelm'd with *stones.* VII. vi. 53. 4
she to *stones* at length all frosen turne! *Am.* xxxii. 14
For feare the *stones* her tender foot should wrong, *Epith.* 49
Stong. *See* **Stung.**
Stonied. Belge selfe was therewith *stonied* sore, V. xi. 30. 3
Stonished. Thereat her noble hart was *stonisht* sore; III. xii. 44. 5
Whilest still she stands, as *stonisht* and forlorne: V. xi. 29. 5
these Star-gazers *stonisht* are At sight thereof, VII. vii. 52. 5
The whiles my *stonisht* hart stood in amaze, *Am.* xvi. 3
Stonishment. Whiles thus he lay in deadly *stonishment,* III. iv. 19. 1
Stony. The *stonie* joynts of these old walls now rent, *Ro.* xxv. 7
could have made a *stonie* heart to weep; *T.M.* 110
A *stonie* coldnesse hath benumbd the sence *T.M.* 253
Amooved him out of his *stonie* swound, *D.* 545
stony hart could riven have in twaine; I. iii. 44. 3
ghosts . . . staring wide With *stony* eies; I. v. 32. 7
stony horrour all her sences fild I. vi. 37. 3
could have overthrowne a *stony* towre; I. vii. 12. 2
let the *stony* dart of sencelesse cold Perce to my hart, I. vii. 22. 7

Stony—*Continued.*
Could make a *stony* hart his hap to rew; . . . I. viii. 41. 5
staring wyde With *stony* eyes . . . I. ix. 24. 3
if the *stony* cold Have not all seized . . . II. i. 46. 5
With *stony* feare of that rude rustick mate, . . . II. ii. 8. 8
the *stony* feare Ran to his hart, . . . II. viii. 46. 1
Now seeming flaming whott, now *stony* cold: . . . II. ix. 39. 5
Their tender feete upon the *stony* grownd: . . . III. iv. 34. 6
What *stony* hart, that heares thy haplesse fate, . . . III. ix. 39. 6
along whose *stony* bancke . . . IV. xi. 36. 1
These after came the *stony* shallow Lone, . . . IV. xi. 39. 1
The sandy Slane, the *stony* Aubrian, . . . IV. xi. 41. 2
his *stony* heart with tender ruth Was toucht, . . . IV. xii. 13. 1
the golden age, . . . It's now at earst become a *stonie* one; . . . V. Pr. 2. 2
'But what so *stonie* minde,' (she then replyde) . . . V. v. 39. 1
Ne could he brooke the coldnesse of the *stony* masse. . . . VI. iv. 21. 9
Her to recure out of that *stony* swound, . . . VI. v. 6. 4
Stony-cold. yet would live with heart halfe *stonie cold,* . . . *Col.* 206
Stony-hard. 'What hart so *stony hard* but that would weepe, . . . *D.* 246
Stood. if in his wayes he *stood?* . . . *S.C.* May 86
manie warders round about them *stood:* . . . *Hub.* 1351
our royall thrones, which lately *stood* In th' hearts . . . *T.M.* 313
Nigh where the goodly Verlame *stood* . . . *Ti.* 3
There *stood* a snowie Swan of heavenly hiew, . . . *Ti.* 590
I beheld where *stood* A Knight . . . *Ti.* 645
She *stood* astonied long, . . . *Mui.* 339
as we *stood* there waiting on the strond, . . . *Col.* 212
stood awhile astonisht at his words, . . . *Col.* 650
the certeine perill he *stood* in, . . . I. i. 24. 2
So *stood* these twaine, unmoved as a rocke, . . . I. ii. 16. 7
Astond he *stood,* and up his heare did hove; . . . I. ii. 31. 8
The kingly beast upon her gazing *stood:* . . . I. iii. 8. 4
still to all the gates *stood* open wide: . . . I. iv. 6. 2
a noble crew Of Lords and Ladies *stood* on every side, . . . I. iv. 7. 8
Before the dore her yron charet *stood,* . . . I. v. 20. 6
all the while she *stood* upon the ground, . . . I. v. 30. 1
on every side them *stood* The trembling ghosts . . . I. v. 32. 4
The God himselfe, . . . *Stood* long amazd, . . . I. vi. 15. 7
Sylvanus . . . *stood* In doubt . . . I. vi. 16. 4
captiv'd, of life or death he *stood* in doubt. . . . I. vii. 26. 9
Astonisht *stood,* as one that had aspyde Infernall furies . . . I. ix. 24. 4
In which a rusty knife fast fixed *stood,* . . . I. ix. 36. 8
that long hath *stood* Upon the bancke, . . . I. ix. 39. 8
when they *stood* in most necessitee, . . . I. x. 43. 8
As he thereon *stood* gazing, . . . I. x. 56. 1
all the hevens *stood* still amazed with his threat. . . . I. xi. 10. 9
drowned all the land whereon he *stood;* . . . I. xi. 22. 5
Behynd his backe, unweeting, where he *stood,* . . . I. xi. 29. 2
they came where that faire virgin *stood:* . . . I. xii. 7. 6
All in the open hall amazed *stood* . . . I. xii. 25. 1
when the Pesaunt saw, amazd he *stood,* . . . II. iii. 43. 1
still he *stood* as sencelesse stone. . . . II. vi. 31. 9
Still as he *stood,* . . . II. vi. 32. 1
Whylest there the varlet *stood,* . . . II. vi. 41. 1
He never *stood,* But bent his hastie course . . . II. vi. 41. 8
in huge perplexity The Prince now *stood,* . . . II. viii. 39. 6
though they both *stood* stiffe; . . . II. viii. 41. 9
Long trembling still he *stoode:* . . . II. viii. 46. 5
An huge great stone, which *stood* upon one end, . . . II. xi. 35. 7
Awhile he *stood* in this astonishment, . . . II. xi. 41. 1
ever open *stood* to all Which thither came; . . . II. xii. 46. 2
in the midst of all a fountaine *stood,* . . . II. xii. 60. 1
The wanton Maidens, him espying, *stood* Gazing . . . II. xii. 66. 1
Whose empire lenger here then ever any *stood?'* . . . III. iii. 42. 9
Beside those armes there *stood* a mightie speare, . . . III. iii. 60. 1
Great Neptune *stoode* amazed at their sight, . . . III. iv. 32. 1
Stood gaping at their gate, and wondred them to see. . . . III. iv. 32. 9
The Christall humor *stood* congealed rownd; . . . III. v. 29. 4
There *stood* a stately Mount, . . . III. vi. 43. 2
stared he on her, and *stood* long while amaz'd. . . . III. vii. 13. 9
trembling *stood,* and yielded him the pray; . . . III. viii. 13. 2
they all on her, *Stood* gazing, . . . III. ix. 23. 4
faire it florished and long time *stoud,* . . . III. ix. 43. 8
stood aloofe, unweeting what to doe; . . . III. x. 22. 3
teares *stood* in his eies, . . . III. x. 25. 9
Still as she *stood,* she heard . . . Him grone, . . . III. xi. 8. 6
on every syde They trembling *stood,* . . . III. xi. 40. 7
there *stood* an Image all alone . . . III. xi. 47. 4
the Lady, which by him *stood* bound, . . . III. xii. 34. 3
So *stood* Sir Scudamour when this he heard, . . . IV. i. 50. 1
still the life *stood* fearelesse of her foe; . . . IV. iii. 17. 5
The headlesse tronke, . . . *Stood* still awhile, . . . IV. iii. 20. 8
Sir Triamond at last full faint and feeble *stood.* . . . IV. iii. 28. 9
Stood still amaz'd, holding his idle sweard; . . . IV. iii. 31. 7
there among *Stood* gazing, . . . IV. iii. 37. 4
Thereat the Champions both *stood* still a space, . . . IV. iii. 38. 1
evill plight, in which her dearest brother Now *stood,* . . . IV. iii. 40. 8
stood there still, As one that seemed doubtfull . . . IV. iv. 20. 3
In hope to take him prisoner, where he *stood* on ground. . . . IV. iv. 31. 9
whereas he *stood* not farre aside, . . . IV. vi. 24. 2
senselesse *stood,* like to a mazed steare . . . IV. vi. 37. 4
raught downe to his waste when up he *stood,* . . . IV. vii. 6. 8
over him she there long gazing *stood,* . . . IV. vii. 32. 6
stood still mute, as if he had beene dum, . . . IV. vii. 44. 2
I, who *stood* all fearelesse free, . . . IV. viii. 58. 6
those two other, which beside them *stoode,* . . . IV. ix. 22. 1
Where one *stood* peeping through a crevis small, . . . IV. x. 11. 8
The same to all *stoode* alwaies open wide; . . . IV. x. 16. 4
Unto the porch approcht which open *stood;* . . . IV. x. 31. 2
On either side of her two young men *stood,* . . . IV. x. 32. 1

Stood—*Continued.*
Stood still by him astonisht at his lore, . . . IV. xi. 23. 8
of all he guiltlesse *stood,* . . . V. i. 23. 6
she saw The daungerous state in which she *stood,* . . . V. ii. 22. 3
They rose in armes, and all in battell order *stood.* . . . V. ii. 51. 9
men *stood* amaz'd, and at his might did wonder. . . . V. iii. 8. 9
He long astonisht *stood,* ne ought he sayd, . . . V. iii. 18. 5
So *stood* Sir Marinell, . . . V. iii. 19. 8
Artegall . . . *Stood* in the preasse close covered, . . . V. iii. 20. 2
like a lifelesse corse immoveable he *stood.* . . . V. iii. 26. 9
Eftsoones he *stood* as still as any stake, . . . V. iii. 34. 5
them beside two seemely damzells *stood,* . . . V. iv. 4. 6
there before them *stood* a Coffer strong . . . V. iv. 5. 1
So *stood* they both in readinesse thereby . . . V. iv. 6. 5
As one adaw'd, and halfe confused *stood;* . . . V. v. 45. 5
stood still mute, as one in great suspence; . . . V. vi. 9. 7
what he did, and in what state he *stood,* . . . V. vi. 15. 8
thereuppon long while *stood* gazing still, . . . V. vii. 5. 8
stood long staring on him mongst uncertaine feares. . . . V. vii. 39. 9
Stood open wyde to all men day and night; . . . V. ix. 22. 4
Thus there he *stood,* . . . V. ix. 26. 1
there *stood* gazing from the Citties wall . . . V. xi. 15. 6
Stood long amaz'd as she amated weare: . . . V. xi. 64. 5
There where she *stood* uppon the Castle wall, . . . VI. i. 34. 6
lake Of bloody gore congeal'd about them *stood,* . . . VI. i. 37. 8
And when he long had him beholding *stood,* . . . VI. ii. 24. 8
this ill state in which she *stood;* . . . VI. iii. 11. 6
there still he *stood* as in a stound, . . . VI. iii. 30. 3
discourteous Knight *Stood* on the further bancke . . . VI. iii. 34. 2
nigh thereto a little Chappell *stoode,* . . . VI. v. 35. 1
all this while *stood* there beside them bound, . . . VI. viii. 27. 2
Would not bewray the state in which she *stood.* . . . VI. viii. 51. 5
So *stood* he still long gazing thereupon, . . . VI. ix. 12. 1
In which all trees of honour stately *stood,* . . . VI. x. 6. 4
Stood all astonied; . . . VII. vi. 28. 6
Upon an huge great Earth-pot steane he *stood,* . . . VII. vii. 42. 8
my stonisht hart *stood* in amaze, . . . *Am.* xvi. 3
state In which he *stood* before his haplesse fate. . . . *H.H.L.* 140
they *stood* amazed still, . . . *Proth.* 58
Stool. *See* **Footstool, Toadstool.**
Ne sittest downe on that same silver *stoole,* . . . II. vii. 63. 8
sitting carelesse on the scorners *stoole,* . . . VI. viii. 21. 7
Stoop. after vertue gan for age to *stoope,* (**stoupe*) . . . *S.C.* O. 67
forced him to *stoupe* upon his knee: . . . I. v. 12. 8
he would learne The Lyon *stoup* to him . . . I. vi. 25. 7
fraile affection did constraine His stout courage to *stoupe,* . . . II. i. 42. 9
make him *stoup* so low, . . . II. v. 7. 3
He made him *stoup* perforce unto his knee, . . . II. v. 11. 6
Whom Guyon seeing *stoup,* . . . II. v. 12. 1
meekely *stoup* unto the victor strong . . . III. vii. 35. 4
seem'd to *stoupe* afore With bowed backe, . . . IV. xi. 26. 1
made him *stoupe,* till he did him bestride: . . . IV. xii. 13. 7
made them *stoupe* that looked earst so hie, . . . V. ii. 21. 5
gan to *stoupe,* and her proud mind convert . . . V. v. 28. 7
Who will not *stoupe* with good shall be made *stoupe* with harme. . . . V. v. 49. 9
As a faire *stoupe* of her high soaring thought, . . . V. ix. 34. 7
No shame to *stoupe,* ones head more high to reare; . . . V. xii. 19. 3
made him *stoupe* to ground with meeke humilitie: . . . VI. i. 38. 9
Her stubborne hart . . . Gan *stoupe;* . . . VI. vii. 36. 8
From so high step to *stoupe* unto so low; . . . VI. x. 3. 2
Why did ye *stoup* unto so lowly state? . . . *Am.* lxvi. 8
Stooped. when the Kidde *stooped* downe to catch, . . . *S.C.* May 290
Had he not *stouped* so, he should have cloven bee. . . . I. v. 12. 9
coming to this well, he *stoupt* to drincke: . . . II. i. 55. 8
Yet *stoupt* he not, but lay still in the winde, . . . III. x. 30. 5
Could so great courage *stouped* have to ought? . . . V. vii. 40. 8
stouped oft his head from shame to shield: . . . V. xii. 19. 2
Stoop-gallant. *stoope-gallaunt* Age, the hoste of Greevaunce. . . . *S.C.* F. 90
Stooping. *stouping* Phebus steepes his face: . . . *S.C.* Mar. 116
stouping, like an arrowe from a bowe, . . . *Hub.* 1262
They passe in, *stouping* low; . . . I. x. 5. 8
At last, low *stouping* with unweldy sway, . . . I. xi. 18. 8
sheare The subtile ayre *stouping* with all his might, . . . III. vii. 39. 4
stouping downe she him amoved light; . . . III. xi. 13. 1
Crept in by *stouping* low, . . . IV. x. 18. 9
stouping downe to her in drery swound . . . VI. iii. 27. 7
Stoops. *Stoupes* at a flying heron with proud disdayne, . . . II. xi. 43. 2
With many idle *stoups* her troubling still: . . . V. v. 15. 7
Stop. To *stop* his wearie cariere suddenly: . . . *Ro.* xvi. 8
To *stop* his wound that wondrously did bleed! . . . *As.* 132
They stopt his wound, (too late to *stop* it was!) . . . *As.* 145
That *stop* out of the way to overthroe, . . . I. viii. 13. 4
no barre to *stop,* nor foe him to empeach. . . . I. viii. 34. 9
did the floodgate *stop* With his faire garment; . . . II. i. 43. 2
How without *stop* or stay he fiersly lept, . . . II. vi. 42. 2
he that strives to *stop* a suddein flood, . . . III. vii. 34. 1
stop vile envies sting, . . . IV. ii. 26. 6
stop the mouth thereof, that none Might issue forth, . . . IV. vii. 20. 5
Whilst none was him to *stop,* . . . VI. xii. 2. 9
You *stop* my toung, and teach my hart . . . *Am.* viii. 10
Stopped. *stopt* her course, and held her by the heele, . . . *Van.* ix. 11
Now went, now *stopt,* now crept, . . . *Hub.* 1012
They *stopt* his wound, . . . *As.* 145
There she *stopt* with teares; . . . I. i. 52. 2
when *stopped* is the flood.' . . . II. iv. 11. 9
Whereby her course is *stopt* and passage staid: . . . II. ix. 8. 4
through poyson *stopped* was his breath; . . . II. x. 67. 8
wonder of antiquity long *stopt* his speach. . . . II. x. 68. 9
Malbecco *stopt* in great astonishment, . . . III. x. 41. 1

Story—*Continued.*
in this *storie* find approved plaine; . . . IV. ix. 3. 2
that piteous *storie,* which befell . . . V. iii. 31. 1
He to her told the *story* of that fray, . . . V. vi. 30. 8
(as they the *story* tell) . . . V. vii. 10. 6
To all mongst whom this *storie* should be spoken, . . . V. viii. 44. 5
When Calidore this ruefull *storie* had Well understood, . . . VI. ii. 44. 1
All fairely deckt with heavens goodly *storie;* . . . VII. vi. 8. 4
From thence reade on the *storie* of his life, . . . *H.H.L.* 232
Stound. I curse the *stounde* . . . *S.C.* S. 56
My Muse is hoarse and wearie of thys *stounde:* . . . *S.C.* D. 140
not these leaves do sing that dreadfull *stound,* . . . *Gn.* 39
pleasant tales (fit for that idle *stound*) . . . *Hub.* 26
complayning his unhappy *stound,* . . . *Hub.* 940
all the Pallace quaked at the *stound,* . . . *Hub.* 1353
The bit of balefull steele and bitter *stownd,* . . . *Mui.* 62
the drerie *stownd* is now arrived, . . . *Mui.* 415
that strong *stownd* which him so sore beset. . . . *D.* 560
he endured not the direfull *stound,* . . . *As.* 123
her that first did stir that mortall *stownd.* . . . *Col.* 878
all his sences *stound* that still he lay full low. . . . I. vii. 12. 9
Begin, and end the bitter balefull *stound;* . . . I. vii. 25. 8
saw The evil *stownd* that daungerd her estate, . . . I. viii. 12. 2
she could not endure that doleful *stound* . . . I. viii. 25. 5
that here lye dying every *stound,* . . . I. viii. 38. 4
till that *stownd* could never wight him harme . . . I. xi. 36. 8
He cast betwen to ward the bitter *stownd:* . . . II. viii. 32. 6
was not so hardy to abide That bitter *stownd,* . . . II. xi. 25. 5
he turned in his wrathfull *stownd,* . . . III. i. 21. 7
full many a bitter *stownd* I have endurd, . . . III. i. 24. 8
eke the Redcrosse knight ran to the *stownd,* . . . III. i. 63. 2
smyle full smoothly at her weetlesse wofull *stound.* . . . III. ii. 26. 9
his sweete lips, on which before that *stownd* . . . III. v. 29. 7
reskewed out of the heavy *stownd.* . . . III. v. 38. 5
soone as she beheld that suddein *stound,* . . . III. vii. 7. 4
Ne in that *stownd* wist how her selfe to beare; . . . III. xi. 22. 2
both did forget The perilous present *stownd* . . . IV. ii. 15. 9
Much was he daunted with that direfull *stound,* . . . IV. iv. 24. 8
Lightly he started up out of that *stound,* . . . IV. vi. 12. 1
of mortall stroke the *stound* doth beare, . . . IV. vi. 37. 5
ward his bodie from the balefull *stound,* . . . IV. viii. 45. 2
at which dreadfull *stound* She quickly caught her sword, . . . V. vi. 28. 8
So was he *stound* with stroke of her huge taile; . . . V. xi. 29. 6
in that painefull *stound* When he him saw, . . . VI. i. 11. 7
when Briana saw that drery *stound,* . . . VI. i. 34. 5
Ladies ayde in every stead and *stound.'* . . . VI. i. 42. 9
piteously complayning . . . that most unluckie *stound,* . . . VI. ii. 41. 3
drove away the *stound* which mortally attacht him. . . . VI. iii. 10. 9
there still he stood as in a *stound,* . . . VI. iii. 30. 3
for the perill of the present *stound,* . . . VI. iv. 9. 8
His deepe compassion of her dolefull *stound,* . . . VI. iv. 11. 4
Nor cease her sorrow and impatient *stound,* . . . VI. v. 6. 7
hath me driven to this drery *stound.* . . . VI. v. 28. 5
as ye may see there in the *stound.'* . . . VI. vii. 16. 9
Stounds. keepe your corpse from the carefull *stounds* . . . *S.C.* May 257
the stubborne stroke of stronger *stounds* . . . *S.C.* O. 49
those bitter *stounds* Of raging love . . . *T.M.* 373
oftentimes great grones, and grievous *stounds,* . . . III. iii. 9. 6
this the sword which wrought those cruell *stounds,* . . . V. iii. 22. 1
With sodaine *stounds* of wrath and griefe attone; . . . V. vi. 17. 6
ranckling inward with unruly *stounds,* . . . VI. vi. 5. 3
Mongst these sterne *stounds* to mingle soft delights; . . . VII. vi. 37. 4
Stour. tenne thousand sithes I blesse the *stoure* . . . *S.C.* Ja. 51
The Woodes can witnesse many a wofull *stowre.* . . . *S.C.* D. 66
he stormes with many a sturdy *stoure;* . . . *S.C.* D. 131
the Shepheard after this sharpe *stowre,* . . . *Gn.* 317
soone ensued them with heavie *stowre.* . . . *Gn.* 566
far more bitter storme than winters *stowre* . . . *T.M.* 247
all her sisters, seeing her sad *stowre,* . . . *T.M.* 597
Fitter, perhaps, to thonder Martiall *stowre,* . . . *Ded. Son.* viii. 11
gan she wail and weepe to see that woeful *stowre.* . . . I. ii. 7. 9
how many a woeful *stowre* For him she late endurd; . . . I. iii. 30. 5
have felt full many an heavie *stowre.* . . . I. iv. 46. 9
he was wary of that deadly *stowre,* . . . I. vii. 12. 5
Which have endured many a dreadfull *stowre,* . . . I. vii. 48. 3
to weet what suddein *stowre* Had wrought . . . I. viii. 5. 8
he, that harrowd hell with heavie *stowre,* . . . I. x. 40. 8
At which sad *stowre* Trompart forth stept . . . II. iii. 34. 6
rash assault and wrathful *stowre* Of his fiers foe, . . . II. v. 10. 3
soone leave off this toylsome weary *stoure:* . . . II. vi. 16. 4
wisely watch to ward that deadly *stowre;* . . . II. viii. 35. 4
oft the Paynim sav'd from deadly *stoure:* . . . II. viii. 43. 6
nothing may withstand his stormy *stowre,* . . . II. viii. 48. 2
*The one she slew in that impatient *stoure,* . . . II. x. 19. 5
First did it shew the bitter balefull *stowre,* . . . III. i. 34. 7
with hart-thrilling throbs and bitter *stowre,* . . . III. ii. 5. 3
I have been trained up in warlike *stowre,* . . . III. ii. 6. 3
through many a bitter *stowre:* . . . III. iii. 3. 5
suddein fitt, and halfe extatick *stoure,* . . . III. iii. 50. 5
disclo'ste Her clowdy care into a wrathfull *stowre,* . . . III. iv. 13. 8
to avoyde th' intollerable *stowre,* . . . III. ix. 13. 1
could once sustaine the hideous *stowre,* . . . IV. iii. 15. 5
The headlesse tronke, as heedlesse of that *stower,* . . . IV. iii. 20. 7
So all together stird up strifull *stoure,* . . . IV. v. 24. 5
shrowd their persons from that stormie *stowre.* . . . IV. v. 32. 7
wondred at their impacable *stoure,* . . . IV. ix. 22. 4
thus turmoild from one to other *stowre* . . . IV. ix. 39. 4
the storme of every dreadfull *stoure:* . . . IV. x. 58. 7
there came *Stoure* with terrible aspect, . . . IV. xi. 32. 1
Sture, that parteth with his pleasant floods . . . IV. xi. 33. 3

Stour—*Continued.*
The Cle, the Were, the Grant, the *Sture,* the Rowne. . . . IV. xi. 34. 5
He gan record the lamentable *stowre,* . . . IV. xii. 19. 3
what dreadfull *stoure,* it stird this day; . . . V. iii. 21. 6
t' abide the balefull *stowre* . . . V. v. 18. 7
As being troubled with that stormy *stowre;* . . . V. vii. 15. 4
Great ruth through her misfortunes tragicke *stowre;* . . . V. ix. 45. 8
To stirre up strife and many a tragicke *stowre;* . . . V. x. 13. 5
the bitter *stoure* Of his sore vengeaunce, . . . VI. iii. 48. 4
Seeing his sharpe assault and cruell *stoure,* . . . VI. iv. 3. 3
with much more steddy *stowre,* . . . VI. vii. 8. 5
had endured many a dreadfull *stoure* . . . VI. xii. 3. 7
raging now therein with restlesse *stowre,* . . . *H.L.* 3
therein stirre such rage and restlesse *stowre,* . . . *H.B.* 73
Stours. Such stormy *stoures* do breede my balefull smart, . . . *S.C.* Ja. 27
when approchen the stormie *stowres,* . . . *S.C.* May 156
lastly thrown themselves into these heavy *stowres.* . . . I. v. 51. 9
(as fit for warlike *stoures*) . . . VII. vii. 28. 7
glory thinke to make these cruel *stoures.* . . . *Am.* lvii. 10
Stout. His left the palme tree *stout,* . . . *Bel.*[2] ix. 10
the *stout* hynde arm'd his right hand with steele: . . . *Ro.* xviii. 6
with *stout* courage arm'd against mischaunce, . . . *Ro.* xxi. 3
stoute as steede of brasse. . . . *S.C.* Jul. 156
with theyr hornes butten the more *stoute;* . . . *S.C.* S. 125
'There be the two *stout* sonnes of Aeacus, . . . *Gn.* 481
blacke Laestrigones, a people *Stout:* . . . *Gn.* 538
the antique fame of *stout* Camill Doth ever live; . . . *Gn.* 601
stout Flaminius, whose devotion Taught him . . . *Gn.* 611
armd with blindnesse and with boldnes *stout,* . . . *T.M.* 265
That *stout* Pendragon to his perill felt, . . . *Ti.* 104
though by kind shee *stout* and salvage were, . . . *D.* 121
(despeyre makes cowards *stout,*) . . . *As.* 117
The Champion *stout* Eftsoones dismounted . . . I. i. 11. 7
He . . . did his *stout* heart eat, . . . I. ii. 6. 3
Her humblesse . . . Did much emmove his *stout* heroicke heart; I. ii. 21. 6
He was, to weete, a *stout* and sturdy thiefe, . . . I. iii. 17. 1
he was *stout,* and lust did now inflame His corage . . . I. iii. 41. 7
the *stout* Faery . . . Thought all their glorie vaine . . . I. iv. 15. 6
The prowest knight . . . Even *stout* Sansfoy, . . . I. iv. 41. 8
The Sarazin was *stout* and wondrous strong, . . . I. v. 7. 1
the *stout* Sansjoy doth sleepe in deadly shade. . . . I. v. 22. 9
Stout Scipio, and stubborne Hanniball; . . . I. v. 49. 7
his weake steps governing . . . on cypresse stadle *stout,* . . . I. vi. 14. 8
He led away with corage *stout* and bold. . . . I. vi. 33. 4
The lucklesse conflict with the Gyaunt *stout,* . . . I. vii. 26. 8
'Full many knights, adventurous and *stout,* . . . I. vii. 45. 1
At her so pitteous cry was much amoov'd Her champion *stout;* I. viii. 21. 2
his froth-fomy steed, whose courage *stout* . . . I. xi. 23. 3
where that champion *stout* . . . did remaine, . . . I. xii. 12. 3
fraile affection did constraine His *stout* courage to stoupe, . . . II. i. 42. 9
Ne let thy *stout* hart melt in pitty vayne: . . . II. v. 24. 6
Goemot, whome in *stout* fray Corineus conquered, . . . II. x. 10. 8
with courage *stout* He them defeated . . . II. x. 16. 3
Stout Ferrex and sterne Porrex him in prison threw. . . . II. x. 34. 9
Which seeing, *stout* Bunduca up arose, . . . II. x. 54. 6
With stedfast corage and *stout* hardiment: . . . III. i. 19. 8
stout Guendolen; Renowmed Martia; . . . III. iii. 54. 8
generous *stout* courage did inspyre, . . . III. iii. 57. 4
how *stout* Debora strake Proud Sisera, . . . III. iv. 2. 7
A virgin straunge and *stout* him should dismay . . . III. iv. 25. 9
sterne Strife, and Anger *stout;* . . . III. xii. 25. 3
the *stout* Damzell, to him leaping light, . . . III. xii. 32. 8
still with stedfast eye and courage *stout* . . . III. xii. 37. 5
She, that no lesse was courteous then *stout,* . . . IV. i. 11. 6
of those Knights, who is most *stout* on ground, . . . IV. ii. 27. 3
Couragious Cambell, and *stout* Triamond, . . . IV. ii. 31. 8
Cambell, that was *stout* and wise, . . . IV. ii. 37. 6
Stout Priamond, but not so strong to strike; . . . IV. ii. 42. 1
Strong Diamond, but not so *stout* a knight; . . . IV. ii. 42. 2
Triamond was *stout* and strong alike: . . . IV. ii. 42. 3
Their days mote be abridged through their corage *stout.* . . . IV. ii. 46. 9
with *stout* courage turnd upon them all, . . . IV. iv. 32. 2
That was to weet the *stout* Sir Sangliere, . . . IV. iv. 40. 3
By his sole manhood and atchievement *stout* Dismay'd, . . . IV. iv. 43. 2
Tempred with sternesse and *stoute* majestie, . . . IV. vi. 26. 3
In greater perils to be *stout* and bold, . . . IV. x. 18. 2
Resolv'd him to assault with manhood *stout,* . . . IV. x. 19. 4
Stout Theseus and Pirithous his feare . . . IV. x. 27. 3
Ne storming Humber, though he looked *stout;* . . . IV. xi. 30. 7
Cymodoce, and *stout* Autonoe, . . . IV. xi. 50. 6
through *stout* disdaine of manly mind . . . V. iv. 32. 1
like a rebell *stout,* I will him use; . . . V. v. 51. 3
In which *stout* Britomart her selfe did rest, . . . V. vii. 26. 3
Which Britomart withstood with courage *stout,* . . . V. vii. 31. 3
neither Ino, nor Medea *stout,* . . . V. viii. 47. 7
All which he did assault with courage *stout,* . . . V. viii. 50. 5
To weet, a wicked villaine, bold and *stout,* . . . V. ix. 4. 6
how ever strong and *stout* They were, . . . V. xi. 47. 4
Nathlesse thereto he was full *stout* and tall, . . . VI. i. 2. 7
'Faire gentle swayne, and yet as *stout* as fayre, . . . VI. ii. 25. 1
stout Despetto in his greater pryde Did front him, . . . VI. v. 20. 7
laying yet afresh, with courage *stout,* Upon the rest . . . VI. vi. 38. 3
the *stout* Prince, with much more steddy stowre, . . . VI. vii. 8. 5
yoke them two and tame their corage *stout.* . . . VI. viii. 11. 9
entertayning them with courage *stout,* . . . VI. xi. 46. 7
threatens all with corage *stout.* . . . *Epig.* iv. 10
stout Aeneas in the Trojane fyre, . . . *H.L.* 232
Stouter. yield it those that *stouter* could it wield. . . . III. i. 4. 6
Stoutest. Brings downe the *stowtest* hearts to lowest state; . . . *Hub.* 255
he the *stoutest* knight that ever wonne?' . . . I. vi. 39. 2

Stoutest—*Continued.*
stoutest heart, I weene, could cause to quake: I. vii. 52. 4
So love does raine In *stoutest* minds, II. ii. 26. 6
could the *stoutest* corage have appald; III. vii. 22. 3
They by consent should chose the *stoutest* three IV. ii. 38. 7
So *stoutest* knights doen oftentimes in field. V. xii. 19. 5

Stoutly. *stoutly* forward he his steps did straine, *Hub.* 241
Cleopatra . . . her selfe did *stoutly* kill; I. v. 50. 8
double blowes about him *stoutly* laid, I. xi. 42. 4
Trompart *stoutly* stayd II. iii. 21. 5
standing *stoutly* up, II. iii. 35. 8
stoutly prov'd thy puissaunce here in sight. II. iv. 45. 7
So *stoutly* he withstood their strong assay; II. viii. 36. 1
defend The walles so *stoutly* with their sturdie mayne, II. xi. 15. 7
stoutly forward came: III. i. 9. 4
stoutly dealt his blowes, III. i. 21. 6
Shall *stoutly* him defeat, III. iii. 35. 9
Stoutly foorth stepping on the further shore, III. v. 18. 6
stoutly came unto the Castle gate, III. xi. 21. 2
them *stoutly* well withstood; IV. ix. 29. 7
Doth in defence thereof full *stoutly* stond: V. vii. 30. 6
Against him *stoutly* ran, VI. i. 19. 3
Which had himselfe so *stoutly* well acquit, VI. ii. 24. 2
with great rage he *stoutly* doth denay; VI. xi. 15. 6
did sternly lower, And *stoutly* answer'd, VII. vi. 18. 5
stoutly will that second worke assoyle, *Am.* lxxx. 7

Stow. In which he wont the relickes of his feast . . . to *stow:* IV. vii. 6. 4

Stower, Stowre. *See* **Stour.**

Straggling. gan the shepheard gather into one His *stragling* Goates, *Gn.* 162
stragling plots which to and fro doe ronne II. xii. 11. 5

Straict. *See* **Straight.**

Straight. *See* **Strait.**
Of wondrous length, and *streight* proportion, *Van.* vii. 2
gins *straight* to prepare The weapons, *Gn.* 275
streight the spirite out of his senses flew, *Gn.* 292
and *streight* about him gan beholde *Gn.* 300
streight with his azure wings he cleav'd *Hub.* 1258
his steed, that *straight* to heaven him bore, *Ti.* 657
streight foorth did yield A fruitfull Olyve tree, *Mui.* 325
Eftsoones her white *streight* legs were altered *Mui.* 349
weaving *straight* a net *Mui.* 357
straight obay his soveraine beheast; *D.* 270
the trees so *straight* and hy, I. i. 8. 5
sences all were *straight* benumbd I. i. 44. 5
Who *streight* him rent in thousand peeces small, I. iii. 20. 3
would Have slayne him *streight;* I. iii. 38. 3
From surging gulf two Monsters *streight* were brought, I. v. 38. 3
streight deliver'd to a Fary knight, I. ix. 3. 8
up he rose, and thence amounted *streight.* I. ix. 54. 1
I bownden am *streight* after this emprize, . . . to retourne I. xii. 18. 4
the Gard, . . . bound him *strait;* I. xii. 35. 5
streight did enterpris Th' adventure II. i. 19. 7
streight against that knight his speare he did addresse. II. i. 25. 9
dismounting *straict* From his tall steed, II. i. 39. 1
Streight downe againe herselfe . . . threw to ground, II. i. 45. 8
The Miser threw him selfe, . . . *Streight* at his foot II. iii. 8. 8
her *streight* legs most bravely were embayld II. iii. 27. 2
streight behight To seeke Occasion, II. iv. 43. 5
Sometimes athwart, sometimes he strook him *strayt,* II. v. 9. 8
streight on grownd made him full low to lye; II. v. 12. 5
streight defyde Both Guyon and Pyrochles; II. v. 19. 3
Streight gan he him revyle, II. vi. 39. 3
That *streight* did lead to Plutoes griesly rayne. II. vii. 21. 4
Would him have rent in thousand peeces *strayt:* II. vii. 64. 5
him *streight* did choose Their king, II. x. 37. 8
she marched *streight* against her foes, II. x. 54. 8
Those could he well direct and *streight* as line, II. xi. 21. 6
streight they saw the raging surges II. xii. 2. 8
streight his Palmer bad To stere the bote II. xii. 28. 1
the Boteman *strayt* Held on his course II. xii. 29. 5
streight of beastes they comely men became; II. xii. 86. 2
ever what she did was *streight* undonne. III. ii. 51. 5
the *streight* course of hevenly destiny, III. iii. 24. 3
gave it *streight* in charge III. vii. 23. 1
seeing her gan *streight* upstart, III. viii. 9. 8
Fell *streight* to ground in great astonishment. III. viii. 12. 7
streight did he hayle The greedy villein III. viii. 31. 5
streight would lose The worlds foundations III. xii. 2. 3
they *streight* were vanisht all and some; III. xii. 30. 4
gan *streight* to over-looke Those cursed leaves, III. xii. 36. 1
Straight he upstarted from the loathed layes, III. xii. 44. *or.* 5
Which *straight* to her was yeelded without let. IV. i. 12. 5
Streight entring into Triamond IV. iii. 22. 2
Which *straight* flew ope, IV. iii. 46. 3
starting up *streight* for his armour sought: IV. iv. 33. 3
she waked out of dread *Streight* into griefe, IV. vii. 9. 4
Whom *straight* the Prince ensuing in together far'd. IV. ix. 5. 9
Streight forth issewd a Knight IV. x. 9. 6
He kend it *streight,* IV. x. 14. 3
streight he closd the gate: IV. x. 14. 4
streight his warrant made, IV. xii. 32. 1
Commaunding Proteus *straight* t' enlarge the mayd, IV. xii. 32. 3
Departed *straight* to Proteus therewithall; IV. xii. 32. 7
So home with her she *streight* the virgin lad, IV. xii. 33. 8
streight he after sent His yron page, V. i. 20. 1
streight at him with all his force did go, V. i. 21. 5
offred *streight* the Lady to be slaine; V. i. 27. 2
streight he did expire. V. ii. 11. 9
streight him selfe unto the fight addrest, V. ii. 12. 2

Straight—*Continued.*
streight leapt the Carle unblest, V. ii. 12. 7
He answered that he would try it *streight;* V. ii. 44. 7
streight the winged words out of his ballaunce flew. V. ii. 44. 9
streight that boaster prayd, V. iii. 10. 8
by the watchman were Descried *streight;* V. iv. 36. 2
She bad that *streight* the gates should be unbard, V. iv. 37. 8
Goe *streight,* and take with thee V. iv. 49. 6
The Damzell *streight* obayd, V. iv. 50. 1
So he them *streight* conducted to his Lord; V. iv. 51. 1
would not strike him *strayt,* V. v. 42. 8
streight her selfe did dight, and armor don, V. vi. 17. 8
her eyes she *streight* reprieved: V. vi. 24. 9
did *streight* devoure Both flames and tempest: V. vii. 15. 5
caused *streight* a Trumpet loud to shrill V. vii. 27. 1
Thenceforth she *streight* into a bowre him brought, V. vii. 41. 1
to whom she *straight* did hie With gladfull hast, V. viii. 6. 5
She weened *streight* it was her Paynim Knight, V. viii. 26. 7
Commaunded *straight* his armour to be brought; V. viii. 28. 3
mounting *straight* uppon a charret hye, V. viii. 28. 4
Streight downe she ranne, like an enraged cow V. viii. 46. 1
The Damzell *straight* went, as she was directed, V. ix. 9. 6
streight tooke his flight From that sad land V. x. 11. 3
Fell *straight* about their neckes as they did kneele, V. x. 20. 2
ryding *streight* under the Castle wall, V. x. 31. 2
he *streight* Cals for his armes, V. x. 31. 6
Streight th' other fled away, V. x. 37. 7
opening *streight* the Sparre, forth to him came, V. xi. 4. 2
As if he would have over-run him *streight;* V. xi. 5. 2
Downe *streight* to ground fell V. xi. 9. 1
streight went forth his gladnesse to partake V. xi. 32. 7
streight dismounting from his steed, V. xi. 61. 1
He all his forces *streight* to him did reare, V. xii. 6. 7
Willing him wend unto the Tyrant *streight,* V. xii. 8. 6
gan him *streight* to buckle to the fight, V. xii. 16. 8
streight her leading with meete majestie V. xii. 25. 1
streight he tooke his flight Toward the Castle, VI. i. 22. 3
full blyth the Lady *streight* became, VI. i. 32. 1
weend he *streight* that he should be the same VI. i. 33. 1
gave them *streight* unto that Squire againe, VI. i. 47. 3
with presumpteous powre against that knight *streight* go'th. VI. ii. 17. 9
he taking oddes, *streight* bids him dight Himselfe VI. ii. 18. 4
she . . . sent me *streight* Into this land, VI. ii. 30. 7
Streight to the carkasse of that Knight he went, VI. iii. 17. 1
running *streight* into the thickest wood, VI. iv. 12. 5
stopt the bleeding *streight,* ere he it staunched thought. VI. iv. 12. 9
Would *streight* dislodge the wretched wearie life. VI. v. 5. 5
streight his combrous armes aside did lay VI. v. 10. 6
From his devotion *streight* he troubled was; VI. v. 36. 3
The Prince . . . Pursu'd him *streight;* VI. vi. 18. 3
running *streight* upon that villaine base, VI. vi. 22. 3
them perceiving *streight* to him obayd, VI. vi. 39. 4
all in rage he on him *streight* did seaze, VI. vi. 40. 5
streight he held his hand at his commaundement. VI. vi. 40. 9
with him *streight* to the place would ryde, VI. vii. 17. 2
Therefore a Jurie was impaneld *streight* VI. vii. 34. 4
The warrant *straight* was made, VI. vii. 35. 6
streight to the noise forth past. VI. viii. 47. 9
streight unto her litle flocke did fare: VI. ix. 15. 2
the Shepheard *streight* with jealousie did frize. VI. x. 33. 9
streight the slaves should forth be called, VI. xi. 10. 8
he *streight* went to the Captaines nest: VI. xi. 42. 7
streight she gan to cast In her conceiptfull mynd VI. xii. 16. 1
full of joy, *streight* forth she ran in hast VI. xii. 16. 6
gan to question *streight,* how she it knew? VI. xii. 18. 2
To whose bright shining palace *straight* she came, VII. vi. 8. 3
straight gan cast their counsell grave and wise. VII. vi. 22. 6
To Joves high Palace *straight* cast to ascend, VII. vi. 23. 8
in his soveraine throne gan *straight* dispose Himselfe, VII. vi. 24. 7
running *straight* where-as she heard his voice, VII. vi. 47. 3
Now like great Hills, and *streight* like sluces VII. vii. 20. 9
Now boyling hot, *streight* friezing deadly cold; VII. vii. 23. 3
Streight bitter stormes, and balefull countenance VII. vii. 23. 5
Who, me captiving *streight* *Am.* xii. 11
with another doth it *streight* recure; *Am.* xxi. 11
My cruell fayre *streight* bids me wend my way: *Am.* xlvi. 2
Unto his mother *straight* he weeping came, *Epig.* iv. 31
She tooke him *streight* full pitiously lamenting, *Epig.* iv. 41
For she will waken *strayt;* *Epith.* 53
Prepare your selves; for he is comming *strayt.* *Epith.* 113
all, that like the beautie . . . *Streight* do not love; *H.B.* 209
Love is not so light As *streight* to burne *H.B.* 210

Straightway. The man *straightway* his choler up did move, *Hub.* 364
sent the Foxe to them *streightway,* *Hub.* 1095
Fled closely forth, *streightway* of death afeard, *Hub.* 1360
calling forth *straight way* A diverse Dreame I. i. 44. 1
by her hellish science raisd *streight way* A foggy mist I. ii. 38. 4
streight way, He started up, and did him selfe prepayre I. v. 2. 6
The Porter opened unto them *streight way.* I. x. 5. 4
streightway sent with careful diligence, I. x. 23. 6
streightway on that last long voiage fare, I. x. 63. 4
streight way he knew His errour; II. i. 28. 1
all on fire *streight way,* II. iv. 6. 5
streight way He wexed wondrous wroth, II. iv. 45. 1
her painted bote *streightway* Turnd to the shore, II. vi. 4. 6
the dore *streight way* Did shutt, II. vii. 26. 5
Streight way he with his vertuous staffe them strooke, II. xii. 86. 1
Streight-way with dreames, and with fantastick sight III. ii. 29. 4
the dore *streightway* Fast locked, III. xii. 27. 1
Streight-way, so soone as both together met, V. iii. 24. 5

Straightway—*Continued.*
to my brother did ellope *streight way,* . . . V. iv. 9. 8
They seeing that let drive at him *streightway,* . . . V. vi. 29. 8
he *straightway* Himselfe unto his journey gan prepare, . . . V. x. 16. 1
he gan him selfe *streightway* Thereto addresse, . . . V. xi. 21. 4
streight way went On his first quest, . . . V. xi. 36. 2
they *streightway* ghest That it was she . . . VI. i. 17. 2
he *streightway* with haughtie choler burned, . . . VI. ii. 12. 3
Then gan Sir Calidore to ghesse *streightway,* . . . VI. ii. 45. 1
The groome went *streight way* in, . . . VI. iii. 42. 1
Went forth *streightway* into the forrest wyde . . . VI. v. 3. 6
They stayd not there, but *streightway* in did pas: . . . VI. v. 36. 1
So up he rose, and forth *streightway* he went . . . VI. vii. 14. 1
streightway Dismounting light, his shield about him threw, . VI. viii. 7. 1
being checkt he did abstaine *streightway,* . . . VI. viii. 29. 4
Which she *streightway* . . . Delivered to her handmayd, . . . VI. xii. 6. 6
Straightways. she would *streightwayes* invent How to deprave V. xii. 34. 2
Strain. when Winter doth her *straine.* . . . *S.C.* O. 12
Yet, as I conne, my conning I will *strayne.* . . . *S.C.* N. 52
stoutly forward he his steps did *straine,* . . . *Hub.* 241
The one in hand an yron whip did *strayne,* . . . II. vii. 21. 7
all his bodie *straine,* . . . II. xii. 21. 2
after her his nimble winges doth *straine,* . . . III. iv. 49. 7
A forest-bill, which both his hands did *strayne;* . . . III. v. 21. 5
Twixt both his hands few sparks he close did *strayne,* . . . III. xii. 9. 7
the darts which his right hand did *straine* : . . . III. xii. 23. 5
Sprung of the auncient stocke of Princes *straine,* . . . IV. viii. 33. 7
by sleight the truth thereout to *straine;* . . . V. i. 24. 9
sacred Reverence yborne of heavenly *strene.* . . . V. ix. 32. 9
their owne cursed tongs did *straine.* . . . V. xii. 41. 9
having now no . . . force his shield to *straine,* . . . VI. iv. 7. 7
that same beast was bred of hellish *strene,* . . . VI. vi. 9. 7
Strained. *See* **Outstrained.**
kept them lowe, and *streigned* verie hard. . . . *Hub.* 1190
when they heard that pitteous *strained* voice, . . . I. vi. 8. 1
Shee streightly *straynd,* and colled tenderly; . . . III. ii. 34. 2
strained him so streightly that he chokt him neare. . . . VI. xii. 33. 9
Straint. with the *straint* his wesand nigh he brast. . . . V. ii. 14. 5
Strait. *See* **Straight.**
with her hard hold, and *straight* embracing, . . . *S.C.* May 99
thilke same rule were too *straight,* . . . *S.C.* S. 236
ne halfe so *streight* and sore. . . . *Hub.* 448
streight and narrow was the way . . . I. x. 5. 9
with *streight* diet tame his stubborne malady. . . . I. x. 25. 9
through a darksom narrow *strayt,* . . . II. vii. 40. 1
grudge in so *streight* prison to be prest, . . . II. xi. 32. 4
Gan coyne *streight* lawes to curb their liberty: . . . III. ii. 2. 6
streight embraced she to him did cry . . . III. x. 13. 6
him with *streight* embras Enfolding, . . . IV. viii. 63. 4
since she saw the *streight* extremitie, . . . IV. xii. 28. 1
Of strong compulsion and *streight* violence, . . . V. v. 33. 2
Streight was the passage, like a ploughed ridge, . . . V. vi. 36. 8
Began the *streight* conditions to propound, . . . V. vii. 28. 2
That it to such a *streight* mote you constraine) . . . V. xi. 55. 4
he had given *streight* commaundement . . . V. xii. 10. 3
uppon yond rocky hill, Hard by a *streight,* . . . VI. i. 13. 2
must passe that way, By reason of the *streight,* . . . VI. i. 13. 7
In *streight* observaunce of religious vow, . . . VI. v. 35. 6
Laide heavy hands on him and held so *strayte,* . . . VI. viii. 11. 3
In whose *streight* bands ye now captived are . . . *Am.* lxxi. 7
Straiter. Himselfe in *streighter* bandes too rash implyes, . . . I. xi. 23. 5
Give him more labour, and with *streighter* law, . . . V. v. 50. 3
gan examine him in *straighter* sort, . . . VII. vi. 51. 4
Straitly. So *streightly* God doth judge. . . . II. viii. 29. 6
Shee *streightly* straynd, and colled tenderly; . . . III. ii. 34. 2
streightly did embrace her body bright, . . . III. xii. 45. *or.* 2
loose affections *streightly* to restraine; . . . IV. v. 4. 8
Yet did so *streightly* them asunder keepe, . . . VI. xii. 5. 8
strained him so *streightly* that he chokt him neare. . . . VI. xii. 33. 9
Straitness. in the *streightnesse* of that captive state . . . V. vi. 2. 1
Strake. *See* **Stroke.**
Strake on a rock, that under water lay, . . . *Pet.* ii. 9
he fiercely *strake* Whereas his temples did . . . *Gn.* 307
with so' exceeding furie at him *strake,* . . . I. v. 12. 7
Whose right haunch earst my stedfast arrow *strake?* . . . II. iii. 32. 8
how stout Debora *strake* Proud Sisera, . . . III. iv. 2. 7
almost in the backe he oft her *strake;* . . . III. vii. 44. 6
with his heeles so sorely he him *strake,* . . . V. iii. 33. 3
gainst the cold hard earth so sore him *strake,* . . . VI. vii. 11. 4
Strakes. His burning eyen, whom bloody *strakes* did staine, . . . II. iv. 15. 5
Strand. as we stood there waiting on the *strond,* . . . *Col.* 212
his corse left on the *strand.* . . . I. iii. 20. 5
Unto the other side of that wide *strond* . . . II. vi. 19. 2
marched to the *Strond* there passage to require. . . . II. vi. 27. 9
Forthwith directed to that further *strand;* . . . II. vi. 38. 2
Back to the *strond* retyrd, . . . II. vi. 40. 6
Archimago slie Foreby that idle *strond,* . . . II. viii. 10. 8
long hath waited by the Stygian *strond.* . . . III. ii. 52. 6
Marinell of Britomart Is throwne on the Rich *strond:* . . . III. iv. Arg. 2
kept her ready way Along the *strond;* . . . III. iv. 18. 3
suffred by that same Rich *strond* to travell, . . . III. iv. 20. 8
on that wealthy *Strond* Inglorious now lies . . . III. iv. 29. 2
upon the brim Of the Rich *Strond,* . . . III. iv. 34. 2
Fled fearfull Daphne on th' Aegaean *strond,* . . . III. vii. 26. 4
Did thrust the shallop from the floting *strand:* . . . III. vii. 27. 8
all the way him followd on the *strand,* . . . III. vii. 36. 7
Scots and English both, that tyned on his *strand.* . . . IV. xi. 36. 9
It will be at the Castle of the *Strond;* . . . V. ii. 4. 2
tumbling on the *strand* It bit the earth . . . V. ii. 18. 5
Departed from the Castle of the *Strond* . . . V. iv. 3. 5

Strand—*Continued.*
for this threasure throwne uppon his *strand;* . . . V. iv. 15. 5
on Colchicke *strand* Her brothers bones she scattered . . . V. viii. 47. 3
He had not passed farre upon the *strand,* . . . V. xii. 28. 3
One day I wrote her name upon the *strand;* . . . *Am.* lxxv. 1
Strands. come from the Stygian *strands,* . . . *D.* 20
Strange. So manie *strange* things happened me to see, . . . *Pet.* i. 2
Strange (*straunge*[1]) bird he was, . . . *Pet.* v. 3
a *strange* beast with seven heads . . . *Bel.*[2] viii. 5
All that which Afrike ever brought forth *strange;* . . . *Ro.* xxix. 10
Unto my eyes *strange* showes presented were, . . . *Van.* i. 10
Straunge thing, me seemeth, . . . *Van.* ix. 13
Bid *strange* mischance his quietnes to spill. . . . *Gn.* 248
both of them, by *strange* occasion, Renown'd . . . *Gn.* 486
it to Leaches seemed *strange* and geason. . . . *Hub.* 12
the Faeries and their *strange* attires; . . . *Hub.* 30
a *strange* adventure, that betided . . . *Hub.* 37
In some *straunge* habit, after uncouth wize; . . . *Hub.* 84
full of fortunes, and adventures *straunge,* . . . *Hub.* 91
he was clad in *strange* accoustrements, . . . *Hub.* 672
To learne the enterdeale of Princes *strange,* . . . *Hub.* 785
tyrannie is with *strange* ayde supported. . . . *Hub.* 1121
standing by the gates in *strange* disguize, . . . *Hub.* 1271
felly slewe Those warders *strange,* . . . *Hub.* 1371
Before mine eies *strange* sights presented were, . . . *Ti.* 489
costly Oricalche from *strange* Phoenice, . . . *Mui.* 78
a *straunge* shepheard chaunst to find me out, . . . *Col.* 60
Strange thing! how bold and swift the monster was, . . . *Col.* 220
how that shepheard *strange* thy cause advanced.' . . . *Col.* 357
The ledden of *straunge* languages in charge: . . . *Col.* 744
straunge adventures, which abroad did pas. . . . I. i. 30. 4
Of a *straunge* man I can you tidings tell, . . . I. i. 31. 3
musing at the *straunge* occasion, . . . I. ii. 32. 3
to seeke adventure in *straunge* place; . . . I. iii. 29. 2
That to *strange* knight no better countenance allowd. . . . I. iv. 15. 9
yborne in forrest wyld, By *straunge* adventure . . . I. vi. 21. 2
far abroad for *straunge* adventures sought; . . . I. vi. 29. 7
Straunge Lady in so *straunge* habiliment, . . . I. vi. 30. 7
what suddein stowre Had wrought that horror *strange,* . . . I. viii. 5. 9
earth, . . . trembling with *strange* feare . . . I. viii. 8. 9
fayre areedes Of tydinges *straunge,* . . . I. ix. 28. 7
'*Straunge* thing it is an errant knight to see Here . . . I. x. 10. 1
Of *straunge* adventures, and of perils sad . . . I. xii. 15. 4
The tydings *straunge* did him abashed make, . . . I. xii. 29. 2
through perils *straunge* and hard, . . . I. xii. 31. 8
'Such is this well, wrought by occasion *straunge,* . . . II. ii. 7. 1
in that place *straunge* knight arrived late, . . . II. ii. 19. 7
Straunge sort of fight, three valiaunt knights to see . . . II. ii. 26. 1
to heare of *straunge* adventures to be told. . . . II. ii. 42. 9
Straunge seemed to the knight, . . . II. iv. 8. 2
never in this *straunge* astonishment.' . . . II. vi. 49. 4
shapes of kings and kesars *straunge* and rare. . . . II. vii. 5. 9
that *straunge* sword refusd to serve his neede, . . . II. viii. 49. 2
debate, Which that *straunge* knight for him sustained had, . . II. viii. 54. 7
How may *straunge* knight hope ever to aspire, . . . II. ix. 5. 6
What *straunge* adventure doe ye now pursew? . . . II. ix. 9. 2
All threatning death, all in *straunge* manner armd; . . . II. ix. 13. 5
never had they seene so *straunge* a sight. . . . II. ix. 33. 4
Straunge was her tyre, . . . II. ix. 40. 5
a nation *straunge,* with visage swart, . . . II. x. 15. 1
He sent to Germany *straunge* aid to reare; . . . II. x. 64. 7
Deformed creatures, in *straunge* difference, . . . II. xi. 10. 3
Unweeting what such horrour *straunge* did reare. . . . II. xii. 22. 7
a *straunge* kinde of harmony, . . . II. xii. 33. 6
straunge phantomes doth lett us ofte foresee, . . . II. xii. 47. 6
Whom *straunge* adventure did from Britayne sett . . . III. i. 8. 7
her sexe under that *straunge* purport Did use to hide, . . . III. i. 52. 7
many *straunge* adventures to bee fond, . . . III. ii. 8. 3
By *straunge* occasion she did him behold, . . . III. ii. 18. 1
this affection nothing *straunge* I finde; . . . III. ii. 40. 5
Though *straunge* beginning had, . . . III. ii. 41. 2
So straungely vewed her *straunge* lovers shade, . . . III. iii. 6. 3
disguising both in *straunge* And base atyre, . . . III. iii. 7. 1
writing *straunge* characters in the grownd, . . . III. iii. 14. 8
diverse plots did frame to maske in *strange* disguise. . . . III. iii. 51. 9
Strongly the *straunge* knight ran, and sturdily . . . III. iv. 15. 7
A virgin *straunge* and stout him should dismay . . . III. iv. 25. 9
His uncouth shield and *straunge* armes her dismayd, . . . III. vi. 51. 1
of her errour *straunge* I have great ruth . . . III. v. 7. 9
By what *straunge* accident faire Chrysogone Conceiv'd . . . III. vi. 5. 2
So *straunge* ensample of conception; . . . III. vi. 8. 2
wandred in the world in *straunge* aray, . . . III. vi. 11. 8
That suddein chaunge she *straunge* adventure thought. . . . III. vi. 20. 5
in so *straunge* disguizement there did maske, . . . III. vii. 14. 3
Driven to great distresse by fortune *straunge,* . . . III. viii. 20. 2
Malbecco will no *straunge* knights host, . . . III. ix. Arg.
discoursed diversly Of *straunge* affaires, . . . III. ix. 53. 2
here did rove In *straunge* disguize, . . . III. xi. 30. 4
Straunge thing it seem'd, . . . III. xi. 53. 8
marveild at his *straunge* intendiment. . . . III. xi. 54. 2
harmony In full *straunge* notes . . . III. xii. 6. 2
a discolour'd cote of *straunge* disguyse, . . . III. xii. 10. 2
Straunge horrour to deforme his griesly shade: . . . III. xii. 11. 4
Figuring *straunge* characters of his art: . . . III. xii. 31. 2
since that *strange* Knights love from him was quitted, . . . IV. i. 12. 6
it was a maske of *strange* disguise: . . . IV. i. 14. 8
in a charet of *straunge* furniment . . . IV. iii. 38. 4
deeds of armes abrode, And *strange* adventures, . . . IV. iv. 5. 5
For that *strange* Dame, whose beauties wonderment . . . IV. v. 20. 8
The hard adventures and *strange* haps to tell, . . . IV. v. 28. 8

Strange—*Continued.*
Attyr'd in forraine armes and *straunge* aray: IV. vi. 9. 3
like *strange* wight, whom he had seene no where, IV. vii. 43. 7
Strange was her tyre; IV. x. 31. 6
seemed *strange* to common vew, IV. xi. 27. 7
not which that Lady kild, But that *strange* Knight, V. i. 24. 8
All that behold so *strange* prodigious sight, V. iii. 19. 5
With his *strange* weapon, never wont in warre, V. iv. 44. 2
his senses *straunge* astonishment, V. v. 12. 2
Gan cast a secret liking to this captive *straunge*. V. v. 26. 9
Whose life and manners *straunge* she never knew; V. vi. 12. 7
Strange were the words in Britomartis eare, V. vi. 38. 1
shee *strange* visions sees: V. vii. Arg.
Through great astonishment of that *strange* sight; V. vii. 20. 6
Kept himselfe still in his *straunge* armour dight: V. viii. 27. 5
did to them bewray A *straunge* adventure, V. ix. 4. 5
an uncouth vestiment Made of *straunge* stuffe, V. ix. 10. 8
with their brightnesse daz'd the *straunge* beholders eye. V. ix. 21. 9
Straunge there to see, it did them much amaze, V. ix. 24. 3
In cyphers *strange,* that few could rightly read, V. ix. 26. 3
Those two *strange* knights were to her presence brought; V. ix. 34. 2
Those two *strange* knights such homage to her make, V. ix. 35. 6
through sudden *strange* affright V. x. 19. 5
conduct me well In these *strange* waies VI. Pr. 2. 8
In perils *strange,* in labours long and wide; VI. i. 6. 5
By *straunge* occasion that here needs forth be set. VI. v. 11. 9
It is most *straunge* and wonderfull VI. v. 29. 8
a *straunge* knight, that neare afore him went, VI. vii. 4. 4
Unto a *strange* mischaunce that menac'd her decay. VI. viii. 34. 9
what *straunge* fortunes unto him befell, VI. ix. 46. 7
Much wondred Calidore at this *straunge* sight, VI. x. 17. 1
She should it cause be fostred under *straunge* attyre. VI. xii. 6. 9
wondring long at those so *straunge* events, VI. xii. 20. 7
greatly did the Beast repine at those *Straunge* bands, VI. xii. 36. 2
Was troubled much at their so *strange* affright, VII. vi. 15. 7
to knowe The cause of this so *strange* astonishment, VII. vi. 16. 3
At whose *strange* sight and haughty hardinesse He wondred VII. vi. 17. 4
some beast of *strange* and forraine race VII. vi. 28. 8
they their glorious Lord in *strange* disguise Transfigur'd sawe; VII. vii. 7. 8
Unlike in forme, and chang'd by *strange* disguise: VII. vii. 18. 8
With such *strange* termes her eyes she doth inure, *Am.* xxi. 9
Strange thing, me seemd, to see a beast so wyld, *Am.* lxvii. 13
Strangely. to see the mayd So *straungely* passioned, II. ix. 41. 9
much more *straungely* gan to love his sight, III. ii. 18. 2
So *straungely* vewed her straunge lovers shade, III. iii. 6. 3
who so *straungely* had him seene bestadd, III. x. 54. 7
in a Jacket, quilted richly rare . . . he was *straungely* dight; VI. vii. 43. 4
Strangeness. all which did such *strangenesse* in him see *Hub.* 680
Stranger. Thou *stranger,* which for Rome in Rome here seekest, *Ro.* iii. 1
To weet what end to *straunger* knights may fall. I. v. 3. 3
Una faire besought That *straunger* knight his name . . . tell; I. ix. 2. 7
The noyse thereof cald forth that *straunger* knight, II. ii. 21. 1
yielded had to that same *straunger* knight. II. v. 20. 5
wouldest be reckoned A *straunger* in thy home, II. vi. 9. 6
that *straunger* knight in presence came, II. viii. 23. 1
foes, whom *straunger* knightes to flight compell. II. ix. Arg.
Great pleasure had those *straunger* knightes II. ix. 54. 6
Abasht that her a *straunger* did avise; II. xii. 66. 4
These *stranger* knights, through passing, forth were led III. i. 33. 1
a *straunger* king, from unknowne soyle Arriving, III. iii. 33. 3
Fiercely that *straunger* forward came: III. viii. 16. 1
that *straunger* knight emongst the rest III. ix. 20. 1
To giust with that brave *straunger* knight a cast, III. x. 35. 4
seeing him behind a *stranger* knight, III. xi. 13. 3
'I saw' (quoth she) 'a *stranger* knight, IV. i. 48. 7
there entered on the other side A *straunger* knight, IV. iv. 39. 2
A *stranger* knight, that did his glorie shend: IV. iv. 43. 8
all those *stranger* knights full sore agrieved, IV. iv. 46. 8
The third dayes prize unto that *straunger* Knight, IV. v. 8. 1
at sent of *stranger* guest: IV. v. 41. 7
'a *stranger* knight Shame and dishonour hath unto me donne, IV. vi. 5. 6
'A *stranger* knight,' sayd he, 'unknowne by name, IV. vi. 6. 3
The stone which passed *straunger* at him threw: IV. viii. 36. 6
Then for that *stranger* knight they loud did call, V. iii. 14. 5
Goe thou unto that *stranger* Faery Knight, V. iv. 48. 6
these two *stranger* knights arriv'd in place, V. ix. 36. 2
him to trouble . . . That was a *straunger* VI. ii. 47. 4
By a faire Lady and a *straunger* Knight, VI. iii. 4. 3
That he should be so sterne to *stranger* wight; VI. iii. 40. 7
when as she perceived A *stranger* wight in place, VI. iv. 27. 2
'There is a *straunger* knight, VI. vii. 12. 6
much griev'd against that *straunger* knight, VI. vii. 20, 6
Him to betray unto a *straunger* swaine: VI. vii. 22. 5
she did love a *stranger* swayne then him more dere. VI. ix. 38. 9
forth in hast ran to the *straunger* Mayd; VI. xii. 19. 2
Stranger's. devise Themselves to setten forth to *straungers* sight: I. iv. 14. 6
Those pretious hils from *straungers* envious sight, II. vii. 6. 3
slacke attendaunce unto *straungers* call. III. ix. 18. 7
For yeelding to a *straungers* love so light, V. vi. 12. 6
Unto a *strangers* love, so lightly placed, V. xi. 63. 2
much was troubled at that *straungers* guize, VI. ix. 38. 3
Strangers. It was her guise all *Straungers* goodly so to greet. II. xii. 56. 9
they as *Straungers* shal be notifide: III. iii. 44. 4
all *strangers,* in that region Arryving, V. x. 9. 7
A cruell carle, the which all *strangers* slew, V. x. 10. 3
learne *Strangers* no more so rudely to entreat, VI. i. 40. 6
straungers to devoure, which on their border Were brought VI. viii. 36. 3
Strangers'. at these *straungers* presence every one did hush. II. ix. 35. 9
Strangle. *Strangle* her, els she sure will *strangle* thee.' I. i. 19. 4

Stratagem. That *stratageme* had oftentimes assayd This crafty Paramoure, III. x. 10. 8
Straw. Oft stombles at a *strawe*. *S.C.* Jul. 100
Strawberries. went To the greene wood to gather *strawberies,* VI. x. 34. 2
Strawberry. bosome, lyke a *Strawberry* bed; *Am.* lxiv. 9
Strawen. Let him lodge hard, and lie in *strawen* bed, V. v. 50. 5
Straws. Some plaid with *strawes;* II. ix. 35. 3
No more then for the stroke of *strawes* or bents: VI. iv. 4. 7
Stray. were not that my sheepe would *stray,* *S.C.* Mar. 34
balk the right way, and *strayen* abroad. *S.C.* S. 93
Tost on salt billowes, round about doth *stray*. *Gn.* 592
In this wide world in which they, wretches, *stray,* *T.M.* 493
weening to returne whence they did *stray,* I. i. 10. 3
danger . . . I saw before mine eyes, if I were knowne to *stray*. I. ii. 41. 9
pray . . . that in endlesse error she might ever *stray*. I. iii. 23. 9
The further he doth goe, the further he doth *stray*. I. ix. 43. 9
doe no further goe, no further *stray,* I. ix. 44. 1
doen thy feeble feet unweeting hither *stray?* I. x. 9. 9
from the right to *stray,* I. x. 35. 7
suffred not in wrath his hasty steps to *stray*. II. i. 34. 9
Island, that doth ronne And *stray* in perilous gulfe, II. i. 51. 6
that no looser heares Did out of order *stray* II. ii. 15. 9
The sea is wide, and easy for to *stray;* II. vi. 23. 4
Amid th' Aegaean sea long time did *stray,* II. xii. 13. 2
as he through the wandring wood did *stray,* IV. vii. 42. 4
Suffring my hand against my heart to *stray;* V. viii. 13. 3
I through the world should *stray,* VI. viii. 22. 8
Strayed. after that long *straied* here and there, *Hub.* 577
many yeares throughout the world I *straid,* I. ii. 24. 7
In wildernesse and wastfull deserts *strayd,* I. iii. 3. 4
To seeke her *strayed* Champion if she might attayne. I. iii. 8. 9
unwares I *strayd* Out of my way, I. xii. 31. 7
Whose hastie hand so far from reason *strayd,* II. i. 28. 5
Me litle needed from my right way to have *straid.'* II. vi. 22. 9
The traine whereof loose far behind her *strayd,* II. ix. 19. 3
to and fro at disaventure *strayd;* III. iv. 53. 2
strayd Farre in the woodes III. v. 38. 6
in her litle loves stead, which was *strayd,* III. vi. 28. 8
yet three yeares I now abrode have *strayd,* III. vii. 57. 4
I unwares this way by fortune *straid,* III. x. 25. 5
yet she may be safe though somewhat *strayd:* IV. vi. 37. 8
long did mark which way she *straid*. IV. viii. 7. 9
seeking long to weet which way she *straid,* IV. ix. 24. 4
where ever she be *straide,* IV. ix. 38. 8
With silver streames amongst the linnen *stray'd;* IV. x. 52. 5
Your brothers threasure, which from him is *strayd,* V. iv. 18. 3
As by the way unweetingly I *strayd:* V. viii. 15. 7
The good Sir Calepine, that farre was *strayd,* VI. v. 3. 2
Straying. All as his *straying* flocke he fedde: *To his Booke* 10
keepe both our flockes from *straying*. *S.C.* May 173
Whose *straying* heard them selfe doth shrowde *S.C.* Jul. 3
Gathering his *straying* flocke, *Gn.* 319
Straying alone withouten groome or guide: III. x. 36. 5
far *straying* from his peeres: VII. vi. 28. 8
Thy *straying* thoughts henceforth for ever rest. *H.H.B.* 301
Strays. wearie traveiler, that *strayes* By muddy shore I. v. 18. 1
Strayt. *See* **Straight, Strait.**
Stream. *See* **Water-stream.**
the bankes of the Italian *streame*. *Bel.*[1] v. 4
a water, whose outgushing *streame* *Bel.*[1] vii. 6
harde by a violent *streame,* *Bel.*[1] xi. 7
A lively *streame,* more cleere than Christall *Rev.* iv. 12
bancks of the Ausonian *streame:* *Bel.*[2] v. 4
with their villeine feete the *streame* did ray *Bel.*[2] xii. 13
So love into thy hart did *streame:* *S.C.* Au. 84
caerule *streame,* rombling in Pible stone, *Gn.* 163
Out of the swelling *streame* it lightly caught, *Ti.* 626
from whence Sabrinaes *streame* doth flow, *D.* 101
into many parts his *streame* he shar'd, *Col.* 138
Her words were like a *streame* of honny fleeting, *Col.* 596
A *streame* of cole-black blood forth gushed I. i. 24. 9
Thereby a christall *streame* did gently play, I. i. 34. 8
trickling *streame* from high rock tumbling downe, I. i. 41. 2
who can turne the *stream* of destinee, I. v. 25. 4
the *streame,* as cleare as christall glas: I. vii. 6. 3
The *streame* thereof would drive a water-mill: I. xi. 22. 6
A trickling *streame* of Balme, most soveraine I. xi. 48. 2
To tell were as to strive against the *streame:* I. xii. 23. 3
forth gusht a *stream* of gore blood thick, II. i. 39. 7
there trickled softly downe A gentle *streame,* II. v. 30. 2
a large purple *streame* adowne their giambeux falles. II. vi. 29. 9
Unto the mighty *streame* him be betake, II. x. 16. 8
hope doth throw Adowne the *streame,* II. xi. 18. 8
streame more violent and greedy growes: II. xii. 3. 5
a large *streame* of blood out of the wound did flow. III. v. 21. 9
The carcas with the *streame* was carried downe, III. v. 25. 6
saw his drover drive along the *streame,* III. viii. 22. 2
from their nosethrilles blow the brynie *streame,* III. xi. 41. 2
A *streame* of coleblacke bloud thence gusht amaine, IV. vii. 27. 8
his life ran foorth in bloudie *streame,* IV. viii. 45. 8
by the flowrie marge Of a fresh *streame* IV. viii. 61. 6
decke his pleasant *streame*. IV. xi. 29. 9
out of his *streame* doth send Plenty of pearles IV. xi. 39. 5
the *streame* washt away her guilty blood. V. ii. 27. 5
In whose sweet *streame,* before that bad occasion, VII. vi. 54. 3
she at length will *streame* Some deaw of grace *H.B.* 26
thou into them doest *streame*. *H.B.* 56
the gentle *streame,* the which them bare, *Proth.* 47
through Thessaly they *streeme,* *Proth.* 80
Making his *streame* run slow. *Proth.* 118

Streamed. blood Adowne their sides like litle rivers *stremed,* . IV. iii. 28. 7
Streaming. *See* **Fast-streaming, Silver-streaming.**
Let *streaming* teares be poured out in store; . . . *S.C.* N. 61
she raynd such store of *streaming* teares, . . . *T.M.* 109
beside the shore Of silver *streaming* Thamesis . . . *Ti.* 2
along would flie Upon the *streaming* rivers, . . . *Mui.* 47
Let *streaming* floods their hastie courses stay, . . . *D.* 332
in her *streaming* blood he did embay . . . II. i. 40. 7
Through many a stroke and many a *streaming* wound, . . . II. v. 36. 8
when the Paynym spyde the *streaming* blood, . . . II. viii. 39. 3
with his *streaming* gore Distaines the pillours . . . III. iv. 17. 6
Streams. That bright Pactolus washeth with his *streames;* . *Bel.*[2] xii. 4
Nor swelling *streames* of that God snakie-paced, . . . *Ro.* xiii. 10
with his tumbling *streames* doth beare aboord . . . *Ro.* xiv. 3
Like April shoure so *stremes* the trickling teares . . . *S.C.* Ap. 7
stremis Adowne the dales of Kent, . . . *S.C.* Jul. 81
Whose *streames* my tricklinge teares did ofte augment. . . . *S.C.* Au. 156
'Let *stremes* of teares supply the place of sleepe; . . . *S.C.* Au. 163
Tho gan the *streames* of flowing wittes to cease, . . . *S.C.* O. 71
the glorie bee Of the Pierian *streames,* . . . *Gn.* 26
represse The *streames* of Hebrus with his songs, . . . *Gn.* 181
forth powring His trickling *streames,* . . . *Gn.* 228
The trembling *streames,* which wont in chanels cleare . . . *T.M.* 25
Large *streames* of honnie and sweete Nectar flowe, . . . *T.M.* 218
Pouring forth *streames* of teares abundantly; . . . *T.M.* 230
speaking *streames* of pure Castalion, . . . *T.M.* 273
streames of teares from her faire eyes forth railing: . . . *Ti.* 12
pure *streames* with guiltles blood oft stained; . . . *Ti.* 145
streames of blood foorth flowed on the gras. . . . *Ti.* 651
In bloodie *streames* foorth fled . . . *Mui.* 439
Driven with *streames* of wretchednesse and woe, . . . *D.* 433
so huge *streames* of blood thereout did flow, . . . *As.* 122
those little *streames* so broken . . . *Col.* 141
in those wandring *stremes* Seek waies unknowne, . . . *Col.* 210
To tast The *streames* that, like a golden showre, . . . *Ded. Son.* viii. 9
streams of purple bloud new die the verdant fields. . . . I. ii. 17. 9
streames of blood down flow; . . . I. v. 9. 4
Large *streames* of blood . . . Forth gushed, . . . I. viii. 10. 8
Welling out *streames* of teares, . . . II. ii. 8. 7
fresh *streames* do flow, . . . II. ii. 9. 2
Titan, playing on the eastern *streames,* . . . II. iii. 1. 3
At the well-head the purest *streames* arise; . . . II. vii. 15. 7
Infinit *streames* continually did well . . . II. xii. 62. 1
through the persant aire shoote forth their azure *streames.* . . III. ix. 20. 9
streames of bloud did rayle Adowne, . . . IV. ii. 18. 3
Thence *streames* of purple bloud issuing rife . . . IV. iii. 12. 8
streames of blood his armour all bedide. . . . IV. iv. 24. 7
From his moist eies, and like two *streames* procead; . . . IV. viii. 13. 4
Pouring out *streames* of poyson and of gall . . . IV. viii. 24. 6
Shooting forth farre away two flaming *streames,* . . . IV. viii. 39. 3
With silver *streames* amongst the linnen stray'd; . . . IV. x. 52. 5
Tygris fierce, whose *streames* of none may be withstood; . . . IV. xi. 20. 9
The Churne and Charwell, two small *streames,* . . . IV. xi. 25. 3
thirty sundry *streames.* . . . IV. xi. 35. 9
here and there shooting forth silver *streames,* . . . V. ix. 28. 8
When he beheld the *streames* of purple blood . . . VI. iv. 12. 2
he saw the way all dyde With *streames* of bloud; . . . VI. vii. 17. 6
In her sweet *streames* Diana used oft . . . To bathe . . . VII. vi. 42. 1
exchange Their dwelling places, as the *streames* them carrie: . VII. vii. 21. 6
Whose bleeding sourse their *streames* yet never staunch . . . *H.H.L.* 164
Street. everie *streete* Is full of fortunes, . . . *Hub.* 90
with their garments strowes the paved *street;* . . . I. xii. 13. 4
The whyles the boyes run up and downe the *street,* . . . *Epith.* 137
Streets. Large *streetes,* brave houses, sacred sepulchers, . . . *Ti.* 94
him they led through all their *streetes* along . . . V. xi. 34. 5
Streight, -er, *etc.* *See* **Straight, Strait, -er,** *etc.*
Streigned. *See* **Strained.**
Stremona. that renowmed Snake Which great Alcides in *Stremona* slew, . . . I. vii. 17. 2
Strene. *See* **Strain.**
Strength. one would weene that one sole Cities *strength* . . . *Ro.* viii. 2
his *strength* his pride, . . . *Van.* x. 5
That steele in *strength,* . . . shall outweare; . . . *S.C.* Env. 2
The Realmes chiefe *strength* and girlond of the crowne. . . . *Hub.* 1185
Nor failing force to former *strength* restore: . . . *D.* 473
proov'd your *strength* on a strong enimie, . . . I. i. 27. 7
the Paynim lay, Devoid of . . . native *strength,* . . . I. v. 29. 3
with extorted powre, and borrow'd *strength,* . . . I. vii. 18. 3
'Henceforth, Sir knight, take to you wonted *strength,* . . . I. viii. 45. 1
If any *strength* we have, it is to ill, . . . I. x. 1. 8
her *strength* recur'd from fraile infirmitis.' . . . I. x. 52. 9
three mens *strength* unto the stroake he layd; . . . I. xi. 20. 4
To reave by *strength* the griped gage away: . . . I. xi. 41. 6
no *strength* nor stroks mote him constraine To loose, . . . I. xi. 43. 2
Ne weene my right with *strength* adowne to tread, . . . I. xii. 28. 5
More huge in *strength* then wise in workes he was, . . . II. ii. 17. 6
As steele can wound, or *strength* can overthroe. . . . II. iv. 10. 5
when they once to perfect *strength* do grow, . . . II. iv. 34. 6
him in *strength* and skill the Prince surpast, . . . II. viii. 49. 8
depriv'd Of native *strength* . . . II. ix. 57. 5
the chiefe dominion By *strength* was wielded . . . II. x. 39. 8
trust unto his *strength* and manhood meare, . . . II. xi. 34. 3
The growing evill, ere it *strength* have gott, . . . III. ii. 46. 2
*our weake hands (whom need new *strength* shall teach) . . III. iii. 53. 3
whilest his breath did *strength* to him supply, . . . III. vii. 24. 7
her maine *strength,* in which she most doth trust, . . . III. vii. 50. 5
now he *strength* gan adde unto his will, . . . III. viii. 26. 6
Both light of heven and *strength* of men relate: . . . III. viii. 51. 8
in his *strength* he rose, . . . IV. iii. 30. 1
With all the *strength* and stifnesse that he can. . . . IV. iv. 19. 4

Strength—*Continued.*
Rose in his *strength,* and gan her fresh assayle, . . . IV. vi. 16. 4
Sir Arthegall renewed His *strength* still more, . . . IV. vi. 18. 5
unto *strength* restor'd her soone anew. . . . IV. viii. 20. 9
by his *strength* rule to himselfe did gaine . . . IV. viii. 47. 3
of *strength* and beautie his desire Was spoyle to make, . . . IV. viii. 48. 6
strength and wealth and happinesse she lends, . . . IV. x. 34. 6
Ne former *strength* returne so suddenly, . . . IV. xii. 35. 4
That Castle was the *strength* of all that state, . . . V. x. 26. 1
Untill that state by *strength* was pulled downe; . . . V. x. 26. 2
Besides the double *strength* which in them was: . . . V. xi. 6. 3
seem'd to be of infinite great *strength:* . . . V. xi. 23. 3
did in *strength* most sorts of men surpas, . . . V. xii. 15. 3
It *strength* to me supplies, . . . VI. Pr. 1. 9
Wasting the *strength* of her immortall age: . . . VI. vi. 11. 6
By *strength* have overthrowne a stubborne steare, . . . VI. viii. 12. 2
All flesh is frayle, and all her *strength* unstayd, . . . *Am.* lviii. 5
up aloft above my *strength* . . . *H.B.* 6
Strengthen. the weak to *strengthen,* and the strong suppresse. . II. iv. 2. 9
Strengthened. With those himselfe he *strengthned* mightelie, . *Hub.* 1125
Strength's. Whereby his *strengthes* assay he might him teach. V. viii. 37. 5
Stress. With this sad hersall of his heavy *stresse* . . . III. xi. 18. 1
Stressed. the *stressed* plight Of this sad realme, . . . II. x. 37. 3
Stretch. *See* **Outstretch.**
Whose naked Armes *stretch* unto the fyre, . . . *S.C.* F. 171
stretch her selfe at large from East to West; . . . *S.C.* O. 44
his stiffe armes to *stretch* with Eughen bowe, . . . *Hub.* 747
Stretch his strong thighes, and th' Ocean overstride, . . . *Ti.* 541
Whereat he gan to *stretch;* . . . I. i. 42. 5
his broad braunches . . . Did *stretch* themselves . . . II. vii. 56. 4
doth it selfe *stretch* forth to hevens hight, . . . II. x. 2. 5
Boteman strongly forth did *stretch* His brawnie armes, . . . II. xii. 21. 1
Presume so high to *stretch* mine humble quill? . . . III. Pr. 3. 3
Stretch her white rod over the Belgicke shore, . . . III. iii. 49. 7
gan to *stretch* his limbs; . . . VI. i. 35. 4
Stretched. *See* **Outstretched.**
With fine small cords about it *stretched* wide, . . . *Mui.* 359
Their scepters *stretcht* from East to Westerne shore, . . . I. i. 5. 5
Were *stretcht* now forth at length . . . I. i. 16. 4
Typhoeus joynts were *stretched* on a gin; . . . I. v. 35. 7
His tayle was *stretched* out in wondrous length, . . . I. vii. 18. 1
scaly tayle was *stretcht* adowne his back full low. . . . I. vii. 31. 9
Loe! where your foe lies *strecht* in monstrous length; . . . I. viii. 45. 3
stretcht he lay upon the sunny side Of a great hill, . . . I. xi. 4. 5
Then gan he tosse aloft his *stretched* traine, . . . I. xi. 37. 5
Dragon . . . *Stretcht* on the ground in large extent, . . . I. xii. 9. 7
With feeble hands then *stretched* forth on hye, . . . II. i. 49. 1
space, That *stretcht* itselfe into an ample playne; . . . II. vii. 21. 2
to hevens hight forth *stretched* bee: . . . III. iii. 22. 4
stretched forth in ydlenesse alwayes, . . . III. vii. 12. 4
She *stretched* forth a long white sclender wand. . . . V. vii. 7. 5
stretcht it selfe as it had long lyen still; . . . V. xi. 22. 6
when it in length Was *stretched* forth, . . . V. xi. 23. 2
Stretching. *stretching* forth his hand . . . II. vii. 58. 4
Strew. *Strowe* me the ground with Daffadowndillies, . . . *S.C.* Ap. 140
little needes to *strow* my store, . . . *S.C.* Jul. 75
still as abroad he *strew* His wicked arrowes, . . . II. xi. 28. 1
strowe with flowres the lamentable beare. . . . III. iv. 42. 5
spoiles wherewith he all the ground did *strow,* . . . III. xi. 45. 7
did the Championesse those two there *strow,* . . . V. vi. 40. 8
all the embers *strow* Uppon the ground; . . . V. vii. 14. 5
on the ground their lives did *strow,* . . . V. vii. 31. 8
The snow, which doth the top of Pindus *strew,* . . . *Proth.* 40
And all the Waves did *strew,* . . . *Proth.* 77
Strewed. He *strowd* an *Ave-Mary* after and before. . . . I. i. 35. 9
corses . . . Of murdred men, which therein *strowed* lay . . . I. v. 53. 3
sacred ashes over it was *strowed* new. . . . I. viii. 35. 9
flowres . . . *strowed* rownd about; . . . II. xii. 49. 2
on every side *Strowed* with pleasauns; . . . II. xii. 50. 3
ground was *strow'd* with flowres as fresh as May. . . . IV. x. 37. 9
scattred all about, and *strow'd* upon the greene. . . . V. viii. 42. 9
with the dead He saw the ground all *strow'd,* . . . VI. vi. 24. 6
Till he had *strowd* with bodies all the way; . . . VI. xi. 49. 5
Which on the earth he *strowed* as he went, . . . VII. vii. 32. 8
Be *strewed* with fragrant flowers all along, . . . *Epith.* 50
Fit to receive the seede of vertue *strewed;* . . . *H.B.* 138
Strewing. with greene braunches *strowing* all the ground, . . I. vi. 13. 8
Strewn. in another corner wide were *strowne* . . . I. v. 49. 3
the fieldes of faire Scamander *strowne* With carcases . . . III. ix. 35. 6
By shivered speares, and swords all under *strowen,* . . . IV. iv. 38. 4
Strews. with their garments *strowes* the paved street; . . . I. xii. 13. 4
Out of her bowre, that many flowers *strowes:* . . . VII. vi. 41. 5
Strich. The ruefull *Strich,* still waiting on the bere; . . . II. xii. 36. 7
Stricken. *See* **Stroken.**
seing hir *striken* fall . . . *Bel.*[1] xi. 13
Then downe she *stricken* fell . . . *Bel.*[2] xv. 13
The Sheepe and th' Asse, who, *striken* both with feare, . . . *Hub.* 1068
With love long time did languish, as the *striken* hind. . . . I. ii. 24. 9
Both *stricken* stryke, and beaten both doe beat, . . . I. v. 7. 7
to the earth him drove, as *stricken* dead; . . . I. xi. 38. 3
Againe she *stricken* was with sore affright, . . . I. xi. 50. 7
'as sure as hound The *stricken* Deare doth chalenge . . . II. i. 12. 9
having often by him *stricken* beene, . . . IV. iii. 31. 8
rocke Is lightly *stricken* with some stones throw; . . . V. i. 21. 7
They *stricken* were with great astonishment, . . . V. iii. 26. 2
Them to have *stricken,* and thrise to have slaine. . . . V. xi. 14. 4
Stride. *See* **Overstride.**
Betwixt them both was but a litle *stride,* . . . II. vii. 24. 8
Over his horses taile above a *stryde;* . . . IV. iv. 44. 5
With easie steps so soft as foot could *stryde,* . . . IV. viii. 37. 2

Stride—*Continued.*
stopt the entraunce with his spacious *stride*, IV. x. 16. 7
did *stryde* At every step uppon the tiptoes hie: VI. vii. 42. 5
Striding. A sturdie villein, *stryding* stiffe and bold, II. vii. 40. 4
Strife. stirring up sterne *strife*. *S.C.* F. 149
nought seemeth sike *strife*, *S.C.* May 158
fell all for nuts at *strife?* *S.C.* D. 35
No greedy riches knowes nor bloudie *strife*, *Gn.* 123
That there might be no difference nor *strife*, *Hub.* 148
without *strife* or hate, Findes all things needfull *Hub.* 910
The Ape was glad to end the *strife* so light, *Hub.* 1056
Their troublous *strife* they stinted by and by, *Hub.* 1092
Commaunding them their cause of *strife* bewray; *Hub.* 1096
From heaven descending to appease their *strife*, *Ti.* 667
To judge the *strife* betweene them *Mui.* 309
seeks with malice, and with *strife*, *Col.* 690
his ghost, freed from repining *strife*, I. iii. 36. 5
many mischiefes follow . . . tumultuous *strife*, I. iv. 35. 2
My feareful flesh did tremble at their *strife*, I. vi. 38. 6
joyd to stirre up *strife*, I. ix. 10. 3
Perswade us dye, to stint all further *strife:* I. ix. 29. 8
battels, which thou boasts to win Through *strife*, I. ix. 43. 4
Feare, sicknesse, age, losse, labour, sorrow, *strife*, I. ix. 44. 6
What meanest thou by this reprochfull *strife?* I. ix. 52. 7
their *strife* to understond; II. ii. 21. 7
They stint their *strife* II. ii. 22. 9
Guyon . . . By *strife* is rayld uppon. II. iv. Arg.
stirre him up to *strife* and cruell fight. II. iv. 42. 7
'that does seek Occasion to wrath, and cause of *strife:* II. iv. 44. 2
Guyon, in the heat of all his *strife*, II. v. 9. 5
To stirre up *strife*, and garre them disagree: II. v. 19. 7
Guyon standing by their uncouth *strife* does see. II. v. 20. 9
to stay your deadly *stryfe* a space.' II. vi. 33. 5
'Debatefull *strife*, and cruell enmity, II. vi. 35. 1
Strife and debate, bloodshed and bitternesse, II. vii. 12. 7
fast beside him sat tumultuous *Strife:* II. vii. 21. 6
That breathed *strife* and troublous enmitie. II. viii. 10. 5
their chiefe and th' authour of that *strife:* II. xi. 16. 8
To stirre up *strife*, and troublous contecke broch: III. i. 64. 5
As smoke and sulphure mingled with confused *stryfe*. III. ii. 32. 9
stint thy stormy *strife*, III. iv. 8. 8
to forbeare The bloody batteill and to stirre up *strife*, III. iv. 24. 8
The enimy of peace, and authour of all *strife*. III. vi. 14. 9
still stronger grow through *strife*, III. vii. 33. 3
you entyrely pray Of pardon for the *strife*, III. ix. 51. 8
Emongst them was sterne *Strife*, III. xii. 25. 3
So did they all their former *strife* accord; IV. i. 15. 5
strife was growen Amongst those famous ympes of Greece, IV. ii. 1. 7
stirre up *strife* twixt love and spight and ire, IV. ii. 11. 8
stint all *strife* and foster friendly peace, IV. ii. 19. 2
he desir'd their cause of *strife* to see: IV. ii. 22. 1
oftentimes unquiet *strife* did move Amongst her lovers, IV. ii. 37. 3
true friendships bond Doth their long *strife* agree. IV. iii. Arg.
made an end of *strife*. IV. iii. 12. 9
stinted all the *strife* incontinent: IV. iii. 18. 4
pacifie the *strife*, which causd so deadly smart. IV. iii. 40. 9
reasons, to restraine From blouddy *strife*, IV. iii. 47. 8
In perfect love, devoide of hatefull *strife*, IV. iii. 52. 2
ye doe wrong To stirre up *strife*, IV. iv. 12. 3
Prince Arthur stints their *strife*. IV. ix. Arg.
so stinted all their *strife*. IV. ix. 15. 9
strife and warre and anger does subdew: IV. x. 34. 7
him had sought through trouble and long *strife*, IV. xii. 16. 8
'Certes, your *strife* were easie to accord, V. iv. 16. 2
For stint of *strife* and stablishment of rest V. viii. 21. 3
Then brought he forth Sedition, breeding *stryfe* V. ix. 48. 5
To stirre up *strife* and many a tragicke stowre; V. x. 13. 5
Through avarice, or powre, or guile, or *strife*, V. xi. 1. 3
have her drawne to all this troublous *strife*, V. xi. 41. 3
To stint all *strife* and troublous enmitie, V. xi. 54. 3
wherefore Betwixt you two began this *strife* VI. ii. 8. 9
As if her vitall powers were at *strife* With stronger death, VI. v. 5. 7
lamenting her unluckie *strife*, VI. viii. 48. 6
life Which Shepheards lead, without debate or bitter *strife*. VI. ix. 18. 9
Orpheus with his harp theyr *strife* did bar. *Am.* xliv. 4
His cancred foes, his fights, his toyle, his *strife*, *H.H.L.* 234
Strifeful. th' Ape was *stryfull*, and ambicious; *Hub.* 1021
stryfull mind and diverse qualitee II. ii. 13. 5
stryful Atin in their stubborne mind II. viii. 11. 4
Her list in *stryfull* termes with him to balke, III. ii. 12. 3
falling out doe stirre up *strifefull* broyle, IV. iii. 16. 5
So all together stird up *strifull* stoure, IV. v. 24. 5
That *stryfull* hag with gealous discontent Had fild, IV. v. 30. 8
Strike. *See* **Strake.**
that dreerie Death should *strike* so mortall stroke, *S.C.* N. 123
Well made to *strike*, to throw, to leape, to lift, *As.* 75
strike so fiercely, that they do impresse Deepe . . . furrowes I. v. 6. 7
Both stricken *stryke*, and beaten both doe beat, I. v. 7. 7
strike your sailes, yee jolly Mariners, I. xii. 42. 1
his approved skill, to ward, Or *strike*, II. v. 8. 7
broken hast The law of armes to *strike* foe undefide: II. viii. 31. 7
bid them *strike* the marke which he had eyde; II. xi. 21. 7
doth stryve To *strike* his oares, II. xii. 5. 5
therewith fierce did *stryke* The raging billowes, III. xi. 40. 5
Stout Priamond, but not so strong to *strike;* IV. ii. 42. 1
forced was to *strike*, and save himselfe from teene. IV. iii. 31. 9
as he his hand to *strike* upreard, IV. iii. 33. 8
Threatning to *strike* unlesse he would withstand: IV. vi. 23. 5
oft, when he would *strike*, forbeare; IV. vii. 27. 2
Ne thenceforth ever *strike* in battell stroke, IV. vii. 39. 3

Strike—*Continued.*
would not *strike* him strayt, V. v. 42. 8
as she did her selfe to *strike* prepare, V. viii. 48. 3
Full on his bever did him *strike* so sore, VI. vii. 8. 6
whyles they *strike* at him with heedlesse might, VI. vii. 9. 3
Threatned to *strike* her if she did with-stand: VII. vi. 13. 5
Strikes. *strikes* the rockes with his three-forked mace; *Mui.* 315
Attonce he wards and *strikes;* II. ii. 25. 6
Strikes in the stocke, ne thence can be releast, II. v. 10. 8
The Parthian *strikes* a stag with shivering dart, IV. i. 49. 8
a Vulture . . . *Strikes* at an Heron IV. iii. 19. 3
strikes his sayles, and vereth his mainsheat, V. xii. 18. 8
String. Has somewhat slackt the tenor of thy *string*, *S.C.* O. 50
lett downe that haughtie *string*, I. xi. 7. 7
the knotty *string* Of his huge taile I. xi. 39. 7
Your *string* could soone to sadder tenor turne, *Epith.* 9
And turned have the tenor of my *string*, *H.H.L.* 13
Strings. *See* **Eye-strings, Heart-strings.**
most heavenly noyse was heard Of the *strings*, *Ti.* 613
Strip. Ne spared they to *strip* her naked all. I. viii. 46. 4
Some whet their knives, and *strip* their elboes bare: VI. viii. 39. 6
Stripe. with one *stripe* Her Lions clawes he . . . away did wipe. V. xi. 27. 8
Stripling. Drew by the heare . . . A handsom *stripling* II. iv. 3. 7
cleard that *stripling* of th' imputed blame, VI. ii. 14. 2
Strips. Arthure . . . *strips* Duessa quight. I. viii. Arg.
Another her out boastes, and all for tryall *strips*. II. v. 33. 9
Strive. *See* **Gainstrive.**
Ne *strive* to winne renowne, *S.C.* Jun. 74
if in rymes with me thou dare *strive*, *S.C.* Au. 21
Let everlasting lightsome glory *strive*, *Gn.* 55
they doo onely *strive* themselves to raise *T.M.* 91
strive in vertue others to excell, *T.M.* 452
his grudging ghost did *strive* With the fraile flesh; I. ii. 19. 7
strive Himselfe with salves to health for to restore, I. v. 40. 7
Who then can *strive* with strong necessitie, I. ix. 42. 6
strive your excellent selfe to excell: I. xi. 2. 7
To tell were as to *strive* against the streame: I. xii. 23. 3
Her sisters, . . . *Strive* her to banish cleane. II. ii. Arg.
strive you it to withstand, II. ii. 10. 3
Still did they *strive* and daily disagree; II. ii. 13. 7
they would *strive* dew reason to exceed, II. ii. 38. 6
both doe *strive* their fearefulnesse to faine. II. iii. 20. 6
strive to passe . . . Their native musicke II. vi. 25. 3
every one did *strive* his fellow downe to throw. II. vii. 47. 9
blis, For which ye men doe *strive;* II. vii. 48. 9
Nought booted it the Paynim then to *strive;* II. viii. 50. 1
With these in praise of pollicies mote *strive*. II. ix. 48. 7
he with all his puisaunce doth *stryve* II. xii. 5. 4
after the foule foster Timias did *strive*. III. i. 18. 9
Against it strongly *strive*, and yield thee nott III. ii. 46. 4
when both nations gan to *strive* III. ix. 43. 3
shame of all that doe for honor *strive*, III. x. 27. 4
each did *strive* the other to outgoe; III. xi. 5. 6
For which the three faire Goddesses did *strive:* IV. i. 22. 6
All mindlesse of the Golden fleece, which made them *strive*. IV. i. 23. 9
'Why do ye *strive* for Ladies love so sore, IV. i. 46. 3
strive and storme with stirre outrageous For her, IV. i. 47. 3
To moderate stiffe mindes disposd to *strive:* IV. ii. 2. 6
in vaine yet many *strive:* IV. ii. 34. 5
strive the rule to get Of all the heard, IV. iv. 18. 3
The Ladies for the girdle *strive* Of famous Florimell: IV. v. Arg.
if he thereto list *strive*. IV. v. 37. 9
she would *strive* With forged cause IV. viii. 25. 6
I glad did not gaine say nor *strive*, IV. viii. 56. 8
Two brethren that doe *strive:* V. iv. Arg.
everie one with helping hands did *strive*, VI. ix. 15. 6
Did *strive* to match with strong contention, VI. x. 33. 3
Titans that did whylome *strive* With Saturnes sonne VII. vi. 2. 6
if Gods should *strive* with flesh yfere, VII. vi. 31. 7
at last arive To the most faire, whereto they all do *strive*. *H.H.B.* 77
Strived. *See* **Strove.**
arte and nature *strived* to joyne *Bel.*[1] x. 5
they fondly *striv'd* With th' Heliconian maides II. xii. 31. 1
every one to ronne the swiftest *stryv'd;* III. v. 37. 7
Strives. he, that *strives* to touch a starre, *S.C.* Jul. 99
So th' one for wrong, the other *strives* for right. I. v. 8. 1: 9. 1
strives to mount unto his native seat; II. xi. 32. 6
he that *strives* to stop a suddein flood, III. vii. 34. 1
Blandamour winnes false Florimell; Paridell for her *strives:* IV. ii. Arg.
Yet still he *strives*, ne any perill spares, V. xi. 45. 1
Striveth. As raging flames who *striveth* to suppresse.' I. ii. 34. 6
striveth still T' approch more neare, *H.L.* 247
Striving. *Striving* in power their grandfathers to passe, *Ro.* viii. 7
Emongst themselves with cruell furie *striving*, *Ro.* x. 11
The billowes *striving* to the heavens to reach, *Gn.* 575
th' heavens *striving* them for to impeach. *Gn.* 576
striving more, the more in laces strong Himselfe he tide, *Mui.* 427
All *striving* to infixe their feeble stinges, I. i. 23. 6
Striving to loose the knott that fast him tyes, I. xi. 23. 4
art, *stryving* to compayre With nature, II. v. 29. 1
The carefull servaunt *stryving* with his raging Lord. II. vi. 47. 9
So *striving* each th' other to undermine, II. xii. 59. 5
striving fit to make, I feare, doe marre: III. ii. 3. 8
So *striving* each did other more augment, III. v. 55. 6
Striving to comfort him all that they can, IV. ix. 9. 4
Stryving long time in vaine it to withstond; V. x. 27. 3
Stryving in vaine that nigh his bowels brast, VI. iv. 22. 2
stryving each to get The greatest portion VI. xi. 17. 3
Striving in vaine to rere him selfe upright: VI. xii. 31. 4
Was *striving* with faire Cynthia for her seat; VII. vi. 17. 3

Striving—*Continued.*
Behold them . . . *striving* both for termes of dignitie, . . . *Com. Son.* ii. 7

Stroke. *See* **Counterstroke, Strake, Strook.**
With flushe *stroke* downe this noble monument. . . . . *Bel.*[1] iii. 14
Ne *stroke* on *stroke* of fortune variable, ... *Ro.* xiii. 5
to the roote bent his sturdy *stroake,* . . . . *S.C.* F. 201
gan his newe-budded beard to *stroke.* . . . . *S.C.* May 214
astonied with the *stroke,* . . . . *S.C.* Jul. 227
the stubborne *stroke* of stronger stounds . . . . *S.C.* O. 49
that dreerie Death should strike so mortall *stroke,* . . . *S.C.* N. 123
How have I wearied with many a *stroke* . . . . *S.C.* D. 33
stroke his weapon slie Into his heart, ... *Mui.* 437
therefore your *stroke,* Sir Knight, with-hold, ... I. i. 12. 5
The *stroke* down from her head . . . glaunst. . . . . I. i. 17. 9
stroke at her with more then manly force, ... I. i. 24. 6
Astonied with the *stroke* of their owne hand, ... I. ii. 15. 8
So hugely *stroke,* that it the steele did rive, ... I. ii. 19. 4
he *stroke* him so, That twise he reeled, ... I. v. 11. 5
Cleopatra . . . with *stroke* Of Aspes sting her selfe did stoutly kill; . . . . I. v. 50. 7
th' only breath him daunts, who hath escapt the *stroke.* . . . I. vii. 13. 9
The ydle *stroke,* . . . Did fall to ground, ... I. viii. 8. 2
Stroke one of those deformed heades so sore, ... I. viii. 16. 2
The *stroke* upon his shield so heavie lites, ... I. viii. 18. 7
the Prince, . . . threatning high his dreadfull *stroke,* . . . . I. viii. 22. 2
th' ydle *stroke* yet backe recoyld in vaine, ... I. xi. 17. 3
three mens strength unto the *stroake* he layd; . . . . I. xi. 20. 4
he *stroke* so furious and so fell, ... I. xi. 24. 2
The knight was wroth to see his *stroke* beguyld, ... I. xi. 25. 1
him so strongly *stroke,* that to the ground him feld. . . . . I. xi. 28. 9
They gan abstaine from dint of direfull *stroke,* . . . . . . II. ii. 28. 8
Him first saluted with a sturdy *stroke:* . . . . II. v. 3. 7
that *stroke* of living arme Should him dismay, ... II. v. 7. 2
Under Sir Guyons puissaunt *stroke* to fall, ... II. v. 25. 6
Through many a *stroke* and many a streaming wound, . . . II. v. 36. 8
doubling all his powres redoubled every *stroke.* . . . . . . II. vi. 30. 9
The *stroke* thereof from entraunce may defend; . . . . II. viii. 21. 2
That direfull *stroke* thou dearely shalt aby:' . . . . II. viii. 33. 4
with his troncheon he so rudely *stroke* Cymochles twise, . . II. viii. 39. 8
His hand relented and the *stroke* forbore, ... II. viii. 43. 4
on the haubergh *stroke* the Prince so sore, ... II. viii. 44. 6
He *stroke* so hugely with his borrowd blade, ... II. viii. 45. 2
when he *stroke* most strong the dint deceiv'd, ... II. viii. 49. 3
with mortall *stroke* astownd, ... III. iv. 17. 5
Through heavy *stroke* of Britomartis hond. . . . . III. iv. 29. 4
That *stroke* the hardy Squire did sore displease, ... III. v. 19. 6
ere the *stroke* could seize his aymed place, ... III. vii. 40. 3
Her Steed did stagger with that puissaunt *strooke;* . . . . III. vii. 41. 1
thrise his brest he *stroke,* . . . . III. viii. 22. 3
next *stroke* him should have slaine, ... III. xii. 34. 2
with the sudden *stroke* astonisht sore, ... IV. ii. 7. 1
The dreadfull *stroke,* in case it had arrived . . . . IV. iii. 18. 1
He *stroke,* he soust, he foynd, he hewd, he lasht, ... IV. iii. 25. 6
Stroke him, as he his hand to strike upreard, ... IV. iii. 33. 8
still that direfull *stroke* kept on his way, ... IV. iii. 34. 1
with puissant *stroke* she downe did beare . . . . IV. v. 8. 4
therewith *stroke* at her so hideouslie, ... IV. vi. 18. 8
The wicked *stroke* upon her helmet chaunst, ... IV. vi. 19. 1
full of wrath for that late *stroke,* . . . . IV. vi. 23. 1
of mortall *stroke* the stound doth beare, ... IV. vi. 37. 5
broke The puissance of his intended *stroke:* . . . . IV. vii. 26. 5
Ne thenceforth ever strike in battell *stroke,* . . . . IV. vii. 39. 3
Had not the noble Prince his readie *stroke* represt: . . . . IV. viii. 41. 9
stroke the Pagan with his steely brand . . . . IV. viii. 43. 3
that cruell *stroke* Which Britomart him gave, ... IV. xi. 5. 8
at one *stroke* cropt off her head with scorne, ... V. i. 18. 6
rudely *stroke* at him on every side; . . . . V. ii. 53. 3
Dismayd so with the *stroke* that he no colours knew. . . . . V. iv. 39. 9
he raught her Such an huge *stroke,* . . . . V. iv. 41. 5
the mightie sway Of that sad *stroke,* . . . . V. v. 9. 6
Nath'lesse that *stroke* so cruell passage found, ... V. vii. 33. 1
She with one *stroke* both head and helmet cleft. . . . . . . V. vii. 34. 6
In hope some *stroke* to fasten on him neare, ... V. viii. 33. 2
That one sure *stroke* he might unto him reach, ... V. viii. 37. 4
The wicked *stroke* did wound his enemy . . . . V. xi. 6. 8
ere he saw the *stroke* to land, ... V. xi. 7. 4
Ere that huge *stroke* arrived on him neare, ... V. xi. 10. 5
Yet was the *stroke* so forcibly applide, ... V. xi. 11. 1
So was he stound with *stroke* of her huge taile; . . . . V. xi. 29. 6
Under his *stroke* he to him stepping neare . . . . V. xii. 20. 4
the huge *stroke,* which he before intended, ... V. xii. 21. 1
He *stroke* him with Chrysaor on the hed, ... V. xii. 23. 2
neither could the others *stroke* sustaine, ... VI. i. 33. 7
Prevented him before his *stroke* could light, ... VI. i. 38. 7
His *stroke* redoubled with such might and maine, ... VI. i. 39. 3
he . . . strooke me one *stroke* or twaine; . . . . VI. ii. 12. 4
Sir Calidore . . . more admyr'd the *stroke* . . . . VI. ii. 13. 2
No more then for the *stroke* of strawes or bents: . . . . . . VI. iv. 4. 7
He stayd his second *strooke,* . . . . VI. vi. 31. 9
such a *stroke* him lent, ... VI. vii. 45. 6
with the second *stroke* thought certainely . . . . VI. viii. 9. 8
ere his *stroke* attayned his intent, ... VI. viii. 15. 6
Albe the *stroke* so strong and puissant were, ... VI. viii. 16. 2

Stroken. *See* **Stricken.**
Rather then let my selfe of wight be *stroken,* . . . . . . VI. ii. 7. 8

Strokes. the Poplar happely should rew Her brothers *strokes,* . *Gn.* 220
their mightie *strokes* so shrild, ... *Gn.* 518
doubled *strokes,* like dreaded thunders threat; . . . . . . I. v. 7. 5
heaped *strokes* more hugely then before; . . . . I. vi. 45. 4
Satyrane, with *strokes* him turning, staid, ... I. vi. 46. 6

Strokes—*Continued.*
with outrageous *strokes* did him restraine, ... I. viii. 13. 8
Ne ought his sturdy *strokes* might stand afore, ... I. xi. 37. 8
nor *stroks* mote him constraine To loose, ... I. xi. 43. 2
They heapt huge *strokes* the scorned life to quell, ... II. ii. 20. 5
him beset With *strokes* of mortall steele . . . . II. ii. 22. 3
Through wounds, and *strokes,* and stubborne handeling, . . II. iv. 33. 2
Their mightie *strokes* their haberjeons dismayld, ... II. vi. 29. 5
With hideous *strokes* and importable powre, ... II. viii. 35. 2
as thicke as stormie showre, Their *strokes* did raine: . . . II. viii. 35. 6
to Pyrochles many *strokes* he told; . . . . II. viii. 41. 4
the Carle as fast Gan heap huge *strokes* on him, ... II. xi. 43. 9
Ne ought the more their mightie *strokes* surceasse. . . . . III. i. 23. 2
with her dreadfull *strokes* were all dismayd: . . . . III. i. 66. 4
oftentimes loud *strokes* and ringing sowndes . . . . III. iii. 9. 8
with huge *strokes* and cruell battery . . . . III. vii. 32. 3
him held, and *strokes* upon him hept. . . . . III. vii. 33. 9
many mightie *strokes* on either side Were sent, ... IV. iii. 7. 6
Full many *strokes,* that mortally were ment, ... IV. iii. 17. 1
sore bestedde With heapes of *strokes,* . . . . IV. iii. 25. 4
Strokes, wounds, wards, weapons, all they did despise, . . IV. iii. 36. 3
Instead of *strokes,* each other kissed glad, ... IV. iii. 49. 3
none of them against his *strokes* could stand, ... IV. iv. 21. 6
So dreadfull were his *strokes,* so deadly was his hond. . . IV. iv. 23. 9
All which at once huge *strokes* on him did pound, ... IV. iv. 31. 8
heaping *stroakes* which thereon soused sore: . . . . IV. v. 36. 4
shun his mightie *strokes,* gainst which no armes avayled. . IV. vi. 12. 9
Heaping huge *strokes* as thicke as showre of hayle, ... IV. vi. 16. 5
With dreadfull *strokes* let drive at him so sore, ... IV. vii. 28. 3
The hideous noise of their huge *strokes* did heare, ... IV. vii. 29. 3
So dreadfull *strokes* each did at other drive, ... IV. ix. 22. 6
thundred *strokes* thereon so hideouslie, ... V. ii. 21. 7
So terribly his dreadfull *strokes* did thonder, ... V. iii. 8. 8
What *strokes,* what dreadfull stoure, it stird this day; . . . V. iii. 21. 6
heaped *strokes* so fast on every side, ... V. iv. 38. 8
With bitter *strokes* it both began and ended. . . . . V. v. 6. 2
With huge redoubled *strokes* she on him layd; . . . . V. v. 14. 6
he gently did desyre To stay her *stroks,* . . . . V. v. 16. 6
Ne either sought the others *strokes* to shun, ... V. vii. 29. 3
their huge *strokes* full daungerously bestow, ... V. xii. 17. 3
with warie heed He shund his *strokes,* . . . . V. xii. 18. 3
layd On hideous *strokes* . . . . VI. i. 20. 2
Their cruell *strokes* and terrible affright; . . . . VI. i. 36. 7
heaped *strokes* did round about him haile . . . . VI. v. 18. 3
round about with boystrous *strokes* oppresse, ... VI. vi. 26. 2
when he once his dreadfull *strokes* had tasted, ... VI. vi. 28. 1
so well enured was With such huge *strokes,* . . . . VI. viii. 14. 2
When all his *strokes* he saw avoyded quite, ... VI. viii. 14. 7
They fall to *strokes,* the frute of too much talke, ... VI. xi. 16. 2

Strong. *See* **Strung.**
An hideous bodie big and *strong* . . . . *Bel.* ix. 2
Made of some matter no less firme and *strong?* . . . . . . *Ro.* ix. 8
The weake, that hath the *strong* so oft forlorne! . . . . . *Van.* vi. 14
With armes full *strong* and largely displayd, ... *S.C.* F. 104
buildest *strong* warke upon a weake ground: . . . . *S.C.* May 145
the *strong* divorces Of that great warre, ... *Gn.* 497
Ne to *strong* labour can it selfe enure: . . . . *Hub.* 276
by wrestling to wex *strong* and heedfull, ... *Hub.* 746
with his wicked charmes And *strong* conceipts . . . . *Hub.* 827
to his Gate he pointed a *strong* gard, ... *Hub.* 1115
fantasie is *strong.* . . . . *Hub.* 1326
Strong walls, rich porches, princelie pallaces, ... *Ti.* 93
throng Of heavenlie Poets and Heroes *strong.* . . . . *Ti.* 341
Renewing her complaint with passion *strong,* . . . . *Ti.* 479
Stretch his *strong* thighes, and th' Ocean overstride, . . . *Ti.* 541
scarce the skin the *strong* contagion helde. . . . . *Mui.* 256
the more in laces *strong* Himselfe he tide, ... *Mui.* 427
the *strong* shackles of fraile flesh,' . . . . *D.* 86
Of that *strong* stownd which him so sore beset. . . . . *D.* 560
In shooting steddie, and in swimming *strong:* . . . . *As.* 74
proov'd your strength on a *strong* enimie, ... I. i. 27. 7
what so *strong,* But, wanting rest, will also want of might? I. i. 32. 6
O, how can beautie maister the most *strong,* . . . . I. iii. 6. 4
The Lyon . . . a *strong* gard Of her chast person, ... I. iii. 9. 2
a felon *strong* To many knights did daily worke disgrace; . . I. iii. 29. 3
he was *strong,* and of so mightie corse, ... I. iii. 42. 3
Whose wals were high, but nothing *strong* nor thick, ... I. iv. 4. 3
strong advizement of six wisards old, ... I. iv. 12. 8
The Sarazin was stout and wondrous *strong,* . . . . I. v. 7. 1
breake the chayne of *strong* necessitee, ... I. v. 25. 5
At them he gan to reare his bristles *strong,* . . . . I. v. 34. 5
mightie *strong* was turnd to feeble frayle. . . . . I. vii. 6. 5
life recover'd had the raine, And over-wrestled his *strong* enimy, ... I. vii. 24. 6
hilts were burnisht gold, and handle *strong* Of mother perle; I. vii. 30. 8
He forst to castle *strong* to take their flight; . . . . I. vii. 44. 7
Nigh to a castle builded *strong* and hye: . . . . I. viii. 2. 2
No gate so *strong,* no locke so firme . . . . I. viii. 4. 8
left hand . . . is through rage more *strong* then both were erst; I. viii. 18. 3
With cruell malice and *strong* tyranny: . . . . I. viii. 36. 5
that weake captive wight now wexed *strong,* . . . . I. ix. 2. 3
no fort can be so *strong,* . . . . I. ix. 11. 1
Who then can strive with *strong* necessitie, ... I. ix. 42. 6
By this Charissa, . . . Was woxen *strong,* . . . . I. x. 29. 8
wals and towres were builded high and *strong* . . . . I. x. 55. 4
with *strong* flight did forcibly divyde The yielding ayre, . . I. xi. 18. 3
struggling *strong* did him at last constraine . . . . I. xi. 19. 3
truth is *strong* her rightfull cause to plead, ... I. xii. 28. 7
Too false and *strong* for earthly skill or might, ... I. xii. 32. 7
The *strong* it weakens with infirmitie, ... II. i. 57. 7

Strong—*Continued.*
The *strong* through pleasure soonest falles, . . . II. i. 57. 9
wondrous *strong* by nature, . . . II. ii. 12. 9
Through *strong* opinion of his matchlesse might; . . . II. ii. 18. 6
Pursew the end of their *strong* enmity, . . . II. ii. 28. 3
Weake she makes *strong*, and *strong* thing does increace, . . II. ii. 31. 3
The *strong* extremities of their outrage. . . . II. ii. 38. 4
strong passion, or weake fleshlinesse, . . . II. iv. 2. 6
the weak to strengthen, and the *strong* suppresse. . . . II. iv. 2. 9
when she is withdrawne or *strong* withstood, . . . II. iv. 11. 6
an yron lock did fasten firme and *strong*. . . . II. iv. 12. 9
In his *strong* armes he stifly him embraste, . . . II. iv. 14. 1
Strong warres they make, . . . II. iv. 34. 7
One in bright armes embatteiled full *strong*, . . . II. v. 2. 3
Therby thine armes seem *strong*, . . . II. v. 5. 6
thralled her in chaines with *strong* effort, . . . II. v. 17. 4
gan that villein wex so fiers and *strong*, . . . II. v. 23. 1
proudly pricketh on his courser *strong*, . . . II. v. 38. 8
she with liquors *strong* his eies did steepe, . . . II. vi. 18. 3
with *strong* reason maistred passion fraile, . . . II. vi. 40. 4
Weake handes, but counsell is most *strong* in age.' . . . II. vi. 48. 5
That houses forme within was rude and *strong*, . . . II. vii. 28. 1
huge great yron chests, and coffers *strong*, . . . II. vii. 30. 2
stoutly he withstood their *strong* assay, . . . II. viii. 36. 1
when he stroke most *strong* the dint deceiv'd, . . . II. viii. 49. 3
With comely compasse and compacture *strong*, . . . II. ix. 24. 8
the *strong* passion mard her modest grace, . . . II. ix. 43. 4
Right firme and *strong*, . . . II. ix. 55. 4
Did head against them make and *strong* munificence. . . . II. x. 15. 9
built Cairleill, and built Cairleon *strong*. . . . II. x. 25. 3
after all an army *strong* she leav'd, . . . II. x. 31. 8
her sisters children, woxen *strong*, . . . II. x. 32. 6
Restraining stealth and *strong* extortion, . . . II. x. 39. 5
that which *strong* affections doe apply . . . II. xi. 1. 2
lay *strong* siege about it far and wyde. . . . II. xi. 5. 5
In *strong* entrenchments he did closely place, . . . II. xi. 6. 7
strong siege and battailous assault, . . . II. xi. 9. 2
strong effort Of feeling pleasures, . . . II. xi. 13. 7
most *strong* in most infirmitee; . . . II. xi. 40. 8
With his stiffe oares did brush the sea so *strong*, . . . II. xii. 10. 2
With a *strong* gard, all reskew to prevent, . . . III. i. 2. 3
see plaine, That truth is *strong*, . . . III. i. 29. 8
To loose her warlike limbs and *strong* effort; . . . III. i. 52. 5
Did easely beleeve her *strong* extremitye. . . . III. i. 53. 9
make *Strong* warre upon the Paynim brethren, . . . III. iii. 52. 6
thy cruel billowes beat so *strong*, . . . III. iv. 8. 4
thy *strong* buffets and outrageous blowes, . . . III. iv. 9. 2
pursewing that same foster *strong*, . . . III. iv. 45. 6
hid His shamefull head from his avengement *strong*, . . . III. v. 13. 8
emprisoned for ay . . . In a *strong* rocky Cave, . . . III. vi. 48. 8
So *strong* is passion that no reason heares. . . . III. vii. 21. 5
in *strong* bancks his violence enclose, . . . III. vii. 34. 2
meekely stoup unto the victor *strong*: . . . III. vii. 35. 4
from captivaunce Of his *strong* foe, . . . III. vii. 45. 8
An armed knight upon a courser *strong*, . . . III. viii. 15. 3
all men feare to tempt his billowes *strong*, . . . III. ix. 45. 5
the great Goemagot of *strong* Corineus, . . . III. ix. 50. 3
No fort so fensible, no wals so *strong*, . . . III. x. 10. 1
By *strong* enchauntments and blacke Magicke leare, . . . III. xi. 16. 7
through the roofe of her *strong* brasen towre . . . III. xi. 31. 3
mightie Conquerours and Captaines *strong*, . . . III. xi. 52. 3
Cald by *strong* charmes out of eternall night, . . . III. xii. 19. 5
laid the noble Championesse *strong* hond Upon th' enchaunter III. xii. 41. 3
Great cities ransackt, and *strong* castles rast; . . . IV. i. 21. 7
There also was the name of Nimrod *strong*; . . . IV. i. 22. 7
battell *strong* to wage Gainst all those knights, . . . IV. ii. 28. 7
Stout Priamond, but not so *strong* to strike; . . . IV. ii. 42. 1
Strong Diamond, but not so stout a knight; . . . IV. ii. 42. 2
Triamond was stout and *strong* alike: . . . IV. ii. 42. 3
Cambell still more *strong* and greater grew, . . . IV. iii. 29. 1
That we may us reserve both fresh and *strong* . . . IV. iv. 12. 4
the more *strong* and stiffely that he ran, . . . IV. iv. 19. 5
All sixe *strong* groomes, but one then other more; . . . IV. v. 36. 5
a stubborne steede whom *strong* hand would restraine. . . . IV. vi. 33. 9
Yet he with *strong* perswasions her asswaged, . . . IV. vi. 43. 1
his *strong* right hand In full avengement . . . IV. viii. 43. 1
Ne was there man so *strong*, but he downe bore; . . . IV. viii. 48. 3
To yeeld *strong* succour to that gentle swayne, . . . IV. ix. 4. 2
gan they ransacke that same Castle *strong*, . . . IV. ix. 12. 1
Ne helmets bright ne hawberks *strong* did spare, . . . IV. ix. 27. 3
it was seated in an Island *strong*, . . . IV. x. 6. 1
a castle faire and *strong* . . . IV. x. 7. 2
with so *strong* attempt I had begonne. . . . IV. x. 53. 5
Mightie Chrysaor; and Caicus *strong*; . . . IV. xi. 14. 3
O men! which boast your *strong* And valiant hearts, . . . IV. xi. 22. 3
Strong Allo tombling from Slewlogher steep, . . . IV. xi. 41. 8
Deliver hence out of this dungeon *strong*, . . . IV. xii. 9. 4
with *strong* hand their fruitful rancknes did deface. . . . V. i. 1. 9
Whom a *strong* tyrant did unjustly thrall, . . . V. i. 3. 7
Did with *strong* hand withhold; . . . V. i. 3. 9
strong as Lyon in his lordly might. . . . V. i. 20. 5
keepes a Bridges passage by *strong* hond, . . . V. ii. 4. 7
Through *strong* oppression of his powre extort, . . . V. ii. 5. 8
he stil them holds, and keepes with *strong* effort. . . . V. ii. 5. 9
he is so puissant and *strong*, . . . V. ii. 7. 2
Ne ever Artegall his griple *strong* . . . wold slacke, . . . V. ii. 14. 8
strove with puissance *strong* To fill the other scale . . . V. ii. 46. 4
there before them stood a Coffer *strong* . . . V. iv. 5. 1
Of *strong* compulsion and streight violence, . . . V. v. 33. 2
Not by *strong* hand compelled thereunto, . . . V. vi. 16. 4

Strong—*Continued.*
left his love, albe her *strong* request, . . . V. viii. 3. 4
With all their force to worke avengement *strong* . . . V. viii. 24. 6
Is wondrous *strong* and hewen farre under ground, . . . V. ix. 6. 3
With a *strong* yron chaine and coller bound, . . . V. ix. 33. 6
Till *strong* constraint did her thereto enforce: . . . V. x. 4. 6
By a *strong* Tyrant, who invaded has Her land, . . . V. x. 6. 8
now needing *strong* defence, . . . V. x. 12. 6
extort out of her hand By her *strong* foe, . . . V. x. 25. 4
There eke he placed a *strong* garrisone, . . . V. x. 30. 1
weakens her, and makes her party *strong*; . . . V. xi. 1. 4
how ever *strong* and stout They were, . . . V. xi. 47. 4
No faith so firme, no trust can be so *strong*, . . . V. xii. 1. 8
Of colour rustie-browne, but sure and *strong*; . . . V. xii. 14. 6
with *strong* powre did them long time oppresse; . . . V. xii. 24. 4
there stands a castle *strong*, . . . VI. i. 13. 2
within *strong* bancks is pent, . . . VI. i. 21. 2
through *strong* powre had now her self in hould, . . . VI. i. 29. 7
However *strong* and fortunate in fight, . . . VI. i. 41. 3
of his wounds he wexed hole and *strong*; . . . VI. i. 47. 8
But he me first through . . . puissance *strong* Assayld, . . . VI. ii. 8. 4
the stroke That . . . had made so *strong* a breach . . . VI. ii. 13. 3
He with *strong* hand downe from his steed me throw'th . . . VI. ii. 17. 8
But still his passion grew more violent and *strong*. . . . VI. ii. 21. 9
now growen to stature *strong*. . . . VI. ii. 30. 9
now high time these *strong* joynts to imploy. . . . VI. ii. 32. 9
Full on the breast him strooke, so *strong* and hard . . . VI. iv. 5. 7
when as Calepine was woxen *strong*, . . . VI. iv. 17. 1
now *strong* through rest so long a space, . . . VI. v. 7. 5
The second, not so *strong* but wise, Decetto; . . . VI. v. 13. 8
The third, nor *strong* nor wise, but spightfullest, . . . VI. v. 13. 9
sternely with *strong* hand it from his handling kept. . . . VI. v. 25. 9
the *strong* course of their displeasure breake, . . . VI. v. 30. 7
being growen *strong* it forth doth bring Sorrow, . . . VI. vi. 8. 5
strong And valiant Knights doe rashly enterprize . . . VI. vi. 35. 3
That cursed caytive, my *strong* enemy, . . . VI. vii. 16. 3
Albe the stroke so *strong* and puissant were, . . . VI. viii. 16. 2
In his *strong* hand their rugged teats to hold, . . . VI. ix. 37. 8
he was *strong* and mightily stiffe pight, . . . VI. ix. 44. 2
Did strive to match with *strong* contention, . . . VI. x. 33. 3
her in bondage *strong* Detaynd, . . . VI. xi. 2. 4
was sav'd with *strong* defence; . . . VI. xi. 30. 7
Untill the Damzell gan to wex more sound and *strong*. . . . VI. xii. 11. 9
he tooke a muzzel *strong* Of surest yron, . . . VI. xii. 34. 2
Like as whylome that *strong* Tirynthian swaine . . . VI. xii. 35. 1
To see him leade that Beast in bondage *strong*; . . . VI. xii. 37. 5
He growen is so great and *strong* of late, . . . VI. xii. 40. 4
Strong thrugh your cause, but by your vertue weak. . . . *Am.* viii. 12
Too feeble I t' abide the brunt so *strong*, . . . *Am.* xii. 9
Gaynst such *strong* castles needeth greater might . . . *Am.* xiv. 5
none so rich or wise, so *strong* or fayre, . . . *Am.* lviii. 9
With *strong* endevour and attention dew. . . . *Am.* lxxx. 8
Crying aloud with *strong* confused noyce, . . . *Epith.* 138
Ne ought so *strong* that may his force withstand, . . . *H.L.* 229

Stronger. the stubborne stroke of *stronger* stounds . . . *S.C.* O. 49
Till ryper years he raught and *stronger* stay; . . . II. x. 20. 4
ere long they *stronger* arre . . . II. x. 65. 7
reysd him up much *stronger* then before, . . . II. xi. 45. 5
still *stronger* grow through strife, . . . III. vii. 33. 3
Withouten perill of the *stronger* pride: . . . IV. viii. 31. 5
was the younger *stronger* in his state . . . IV. x. 32. 8
Thame was *stronger*, and of better stay; . . . IV. xi. 25. 6
Artegall was *stronger*, And better skild in Tilt . . . V. viii. 7. 6
Where still the *stronger* doth the weake devoure, . . . V. ix. 1. 6
vitall powers were at strife With *stronger* death, . . . VI. v. 5. 8
Till she her selfe for *stronger* flight can breath. . . . *H.H.B.* 28

Strongest. That *strongest* Oake might seeme to overthrow. . . I. viii. 18. 6

Strongly. *Strongly* encorag'd by the crafty Foxe; . . . *Hub.* 1104
buildes so *stronglie* on so frayle a soyle, . . . *Ti.* 513
two deadly weapons . . . *Strongly* outlaunced . . . *Mui.* 82
Full *strongly* armd, and on a courser . . . I. iii. 33. 3
him so *strongly* stroke, that to the ground him feld. . . . I. xi. 28. 9
And strooke so *strongly*, . . . I. xi. 39. 7
To overthrow him *strongly* did assay, . . . II. iv. 8. 8
doth allure the weaker sence So *strongly*, . . . II. vi. 1. 4
catching hold him *strongly* stayd From drowning. . . . II. vi. 46. 3
armed bright . . . and *strongly* fortifyde: . . . II. ix. 26. 3
oft the Briton kings against them *strongly* swayd. . . . II. x. 49. 9
strongly challenged The crowne . . . II. x. 67. 3
strongly he them rowes, . . . II. xii. 5. 1
Boteman *strongly* forth did stretch His brawnie armes, . . II. xii. 21. 1
both them *strongly* bound In captive bandes, . . . II. xii. 82. 4
for his trusty servaunts doth so *strongly* fight.' . . . III. i. 29. 9
Against it *strongly* strive, and yield thee nott . . . III. ii. 46. 4
Strongly to ayde his countrey . . . III. iii. 27. 8
Strongly the straunge knight ran, and sturdily . . . III. iv. 15. 7
The same to love he *strongly* was constraynd; . . . III. v. 44. 6
Shee strugled *strongly* both with foote and hand . . . III. viii. 27. 3
Their steel-hed speares they *strongly* coucht, . . . IV. ix. 16. 1
Yet one, of many, was so *strongly* bent By Priamond, . . . IV. iii. 8. 1
Both *strongly* arm'd, as fearing one another; . . . IV. x. 32. 2
Which mote the feebled Britons *strongly* flancke . . . IV. xi. 36. 3
to him driving *strongly* downe the tide . . . V. ii. 14. 3
With his great yron sledge doth *strongly* on it beat. . . . V. v. 7. 9
With which wise Nature did them *strongly* bynd . . . V. v. 25. 3
To which the Lion *strongly* doth gainesay, . . . V. vii. 30. 7
Nought under heaven so *strongly* doth allure . . . V. viii. 1. 1
strongly either strooke And broke their speares; . . . V. viii. 9. 6
strongly beateth downe The malice of her foes, . . . V. viii. 17. 5
He gan that Ladie *strongly* to appele . . . V. ix. 39. 5

Strongly—*Continued.*
Strongly did Zele her haynous fact enforce, ... V. ix. 43. 1
her long taile and fethers *strongly* shooke, ... V. xi. 22. 7
Strongly he strove out of her greedy gripe To loose . . . . V. xi. 27. 6
strongly flew With all her body at his head . . . . V. xi. 30. 6
strongly wading through the waves unused, ... VI. iii. 33. 7
That doth thus *strongly* ward the Castle . . . . VI. iii. 39. 9
fiercely at him flew, and strooke so *strongly,* . . . . . . VI. viii. 9. 3
with brows full sternly bent And armed *strongly,* . . . . . . VII. vii. 32. 4
His safe assurance, *strongly* it restrayne. . . . . *Am.* xlii. 12
storme, . . . Beats on it *strongly,* it to ruinate. . . . . . . *Am.* lvi. 8
doth *strongly* part The raging waves, ... *Am.* lix. 5
And the great Dragon *strongly* doth represse, ... *H.H.B.* 157

Strook. *See* **Overstrook, Strake, Stroke.**
The Geaunt *strooke* so maynly mercilesse, ... I. vii. 12. 1
his raging blade he hefte, And *strooke* so strongly, ... I. xi. 39. 7
strooke more often wyde, ... II. iv. 7. 4
strooke At him so fiercely, ... II. v. 6. 1
Sometimes athwart, sometimes he *strook* him strayt, ... II. v. 9. 8
Strooke him so hugely, ... II. v. 11. 5
he *strooke,* and thother *strooke* withall, ... II. viii. 38. 1
strooke, and foynd, and lasht outrageously, ... II. viii. 47. 5
strooke at him so sternely, ... II. xi. 37. 3
through both the sides he *strooke* him quight, ... II. xi. 38. 6
with her crooked keele the land she *strooke:* . . . . II. xii. 38. 3
Streight way he with his vertuous staffe them *strooke,* . . . . II. xii. 86. 1
Strooke her full on the brest, ... III. iv. 15. 8
strooke at him with force so violent, ... III. v. 25. 4
suddein *strook* with great astonishment; . . . . III. vii. 3. 9
awfull terror deepe into him *strooke,* . . . . III. x. 24. 4
th' earth with his faire forhead *strooke:* . . . . III. xi. 13. 7
Unwares it *strooke* into her snowie chest, ... III. xii. 33. 4
Strooke him so hugely that in swowne he lay, ... IV. iii. 34. 3
So sorely he her *strooke,* . . . . IV. vi. 13. 3
therewithall at him right furiously she *strooke.* . . . . . . IV. vi. 14. 9
So furiously she *strooke* in her first heat, ... IV. vi. 15. 1
with that word him *strooke,* . . . . V. ii. 11. 9
at her *strooke* with puissance fearefull fell: . . . . V. v. 10. 7
Upon her helmet he againe her *strooke,* . . . . V. v. 11. 2
Tho with her sword on him she flatling *strooke,* . . . . . . V. v. 18. 1
strongly either *strooke* And broke their speares; . . . . . . V. viii. 9. 6
Thenceforth he car'd no more which way he *strooke,* . . . . V. xi. 12. 6
with his mortal steel quite through the body *strooke.* . . . . V. xi. 13. 9
Through all three bodies he him *strooke* attonce, ... V. xi. 14. 1
Three times, as in defiance, there he *strooke;* . . . . . . V. xi. 22. 2
Tho with her huge long taile she at him *strooke,* . . . . . V. xi. 28. 6
He with his sword it *strooke,* . . . . V. xi. 29. 8
Right in the flanke him *strooke* with deadly dreare, ... V. xii. 20. 5
Which Artegall perceiving *strooke* no more, ... V. xii. 22. 6
he . . . with his speare *strooke* me one stroke . . . . . . VI. ii. 12. 4
I, . . . *Strooke* him, as seemeth, underneath the hart, ... VI. ii. 12. 8
with his spere *Strooke* through his shoulder, ... VI. iii. 50. 7
Full on the breast him *strooke,* . . . . VI. iv. 5. 7
Him with his fist unwares on th' head he *strooke,* . . . . . VI. v. 26. 3
with his yron club to ground him *strooke;* . . . . VI. vii. 48. 4
fiercely at him flew, And *strooke* so strongly, ... VI. viii. 9. 3
so sternely he the monster *strooke,* . . . . VI. x. 36. 3
when he him *strooke* With his sharpe steele, ... VI. xii. 26. 3

Strove. *See* **Strived.**
Strove with a Spider his unequall peare; . . . . *Van.* vi. 5
I heard that Pan with Phoebus *strove,* . . . . *S.C.* Jun. 68
They never *stroven* to be chiefe, ... *S.C.* Jul. 167
th' other *strove* for to defend The force of Vulcane . . . . *Gn.* 523
strove to mitigate The stormie passion . . . . *D.* 191
hand or foot to stirr he *strove* in vaine. . . . . I. i. 18. 8
strove to match, . . . Great Junoes golden chayre; . . . . . I. iv. 17. 4
strove to maister sorrowfull assay, ... I. vii. 27. 2
strove for to amaze the weaker sights: . . . . I. vii. 30. 5
whiles he *strove* his combred clubbe to quight . . . . . . I. viii. 10. 4
still he *strove* to cloke his inward bale, ... I. ix. 16. 3
strove to loose the far infixed sting: . . . . I. xi. 39. 4
Still he *strove;* . . . . II. ii. 3. 6
to his mistresse each himselfe *strove* to advaunce. . . . . . II. ii. 16. 9
Still *strove* their stubborne rages to revoke; . . . . II. ii. 28. 6
Each *strove* to please, ... II. iv. 19. 9
strove with most delights Him to aggrate, ... II. v. 33. 1
strove in vaine, the one him selfe to drowne, ... II. vi. 47. 2
her lover *strove,* but all in vaine; . . . . II. xii. 82. 1
strove Into the Ocean deepe to drive their weary drove. . . . III. i. 57. 8
Long while he *strove* in his corageous brest . . . . III. v. 44. 1
those two vertues *strove* to fynd The higher place . . . . . III. v. 55. 4
The silly virgin *strove* him to withstand . . . . III. viii. 27. 1
whilest thus she stifly *strove,* . . . . III. viii. 29. 6
With busie care they *strove* him to awake, ... IV. i. 43. 6
strove in vaine him long to have withstood, ... IV. ii. 45. 7
So cruelly these Knights *strove* for that Ladies sake. . . . . IV. iii. 16. 9
There they together *strove* and struggled long . . . . V. ii. 14. 6
strove with puissance strong To fill the other scale . . . . . V. ii. 46. 4
rather *strove* extremities to way, ... V. ii. 49. 3
all *strove* with perill to winne fame; . . . . V. iii. 7. 5
Together *strove,* and kindled wrathfull fires: . . . . V. iv. 4. 5
still the more she *strove* it to subdew. . . . . V. v. 28. 3
Strongly he *strove* out of her greedy gripe To loose his shield, V. xi. 27. 6
Long while he tug'd and *strove* to get it out, ... V. xii. 22. 1
Whilest they together for the quarrey *strove,* . . . . VI. ii. 20. 2
I . . . *Strove* to appease him, ... VI. ii. 21. 8
the more he *strove,* the more the Knight Did him suppresse, . VI. xii. 31. 5

Strow, *etc.* *See* **Strew,** *etc.*

Struck. *See* **Strake, Stroke, Strook.**

Struggled. There the fond Flie, entangled, *strugled* long, . . . *Mui.* 425

Struggled—*Continued.*
Whiles thus they *strugled* in that ydle wave, ... II. vi. 47. 1
Shee *strugled* strongly both with foote and hand . . . . . III. viii. 27. 3
There they together strove and *struggled* long . . . . V. ii. 14. 6
when long she *struggled* had in vaine, ... V. v. 28. 6

Struggling. *struggling* strong did him at last constraine . . . I. xi. 19. 3
Which when in vaine he tryde with *struggeling,* . . . . . . I. xi. 39. 5
an huge heape of singultes did oppresse His *strugling* soule, . III. xi. 12. 2

Strung. Playing on yvorie harp with silver *strong.* . . . . . . *Gn.* 16
an Harpe *stroong* all with silver twyne, ... *Ti.* 604

Stryfull. *See* **Strifeful.**

Strymon. *See* **Stremona.**

Strymonian. In working of *Strymonian* Rhaesus fall, ... *Gn.* 535
the goodlie criew Of white *Strimonian* brood . . . . *Ti.* 593

Stuard. *See* **Steward.**

Stubborn. the *stubborne* stroke of stronger stounds . . . . . *S.C.* O. 49
menaging the mouthes of *stubborne* steedes, ... *Hub.* 739
As *stubborne* steed, that is with curb restrained, ... *D.* 194
He that the *stubborne* Sprites can wisely tame, ... I. i. 43. 7
life forsooke his *stubborne* brest. . . . . I. iii. 42. 9
she chaunst their *stubborne* mouths to twitch; . . . . I. v. 28. 7
Stout Scipio, and *stubborne* Hanniball; . . . . I. v. 49. 7
Her to persuade that *stubborne* fort to yilde: . . . . I. vi. 3. 7
Such joy he had their *stubborne* harts to quell, ... I. vi. 26. 7
His *stubborne* steed with curbed canon bitt, ... I. vii. 37. 6
Such percing griefe her *stubborne* hart did wound, ... I. viii. 25. 4
with streight diet tame his *stubborne* malady. . . . . I. x. 25. 9
strove their *stubborne* rages to revoke; . . . . II. ii. 28. 6
Through wounds, and strokes, and *stubborne* handeling, . . II. iv. 33. 2
no greater enimy Then *stubborne* perturbation . . . . II. v. 1. 4
stryful Atin in their *stubborne* mind . . . . II. viii. 11. 4
with sweet science mollifide their *stubborne* harts. . . . . . II. x. 25. 9
Your *stubborne* hart t' affect with fraile infirmity. . . . . . II. xii. 28. 9
Eftesoones their *stubborne* corages were queld, ... II. xii. 40. 4
His *stubborne* brest gan secret pleasaunce to embrace. . . . II. xii. 65. 9
Dare not adventure on the *stubborne* pray, ... III. i. 22. 3
'doe nought aswage My *stubborne* smart, ... III. ii. 37. 2
the *stubborne* feendes he to his service bownd. . . . . . . III. iii. 14. 9
To mitigate his *stubborne* malady: . . . . III. v. 50. 5
thinking for to make her *stubborne* corage quayle. . . . . . III. viii. 40. 9
Upon whose *stubborne* neck, . . . She fastned hath her foot; . III. ix. 45. 3
bad the *stubborne* flames to yield him way: . . . . III. xi. 26. 4
a *stubborne* steede whom strong hand would restraine. . . . IV. vi. 33. 9
The next, the *stubborne* Newre . . . . IV. xi. 43. 3
His *stubborne* heart, that never felt misfare, ... IV. xii. 12. 4
tameth *stubborne* youth With iron bit, ... IV. xii. 13. 3
The *stubborne* mettall seeketh to subdew, ... V. v. 7. 7
Through *stubborne* handling of her love-sicke hart; . . . . . V. v. 28. 2
haps to light Uppon two *stubborne* oakes, ... V. vi. 40. 2
pearst Her *stubborne* hart with inward deepe effect, ... VI. i. 45. 4
To rule the *stubborne* rage of passion blinde: . . . . VI. vi. 5. 8
Through such her *stubborne* stifnesse and hard hart, ... VI. vii. 31. 1
Even for *stubborne* pride which her restrayned. . . . . . . VI. vii. 36. 4
Her *stubborne* hart, which love before disdayned, ... VI. vii. 36. 7
By strength have overthrowne a *stubborne* steare, ... VI. viii. 12. 2
the *stubborne* damzell doth deprave . . . . *Am.* xxix. 1
beat on th' andvile of her *stubberne* wit . . . . *Am.* xxxii. 8
move the Dolphin from her *stubborn* will, ... *Am.* xxxviii. 8
Thrugh *stubborn* pride, amongst themselves did jar, ... *Am.* xliv. 2
So doe I hope her *stubborne* hart to bend, ... *Am.* li. 11
stubborne grownd, That will not yield . . . . *H.B.* 145

Stubs. all about old stockes and *stubs* of trees, ... I. ix. 34. 1

Stuck. The steely head *stuck* fast still in his flesh, ... I. xi. 22. 1
fast it *stucke,* ne would thereout be gott: . . . . I. xi. 38. 7
stuck with carkases exanimate . . . . II. xii. 7. 5

Stud. Seest not thilke same Hawthorne *studde,* . . . . *S.C.* Mar. 13
some soft Willow, or new growen *stud;* . . . . *Gn.* 84

Studded. *See* **Iron-studded.**

Studies. Perforce their *studies* broke, ... II. x. 77. 6

Studious. Abroad in armes, at home in *studious* kynd, ... II. iii. 40. 8
the *studious* Lawyers have their bowers, ... *Proth.* 134

Studs. His hornes were gilden all with golden *studs,* . . . . . VII. vii. 33. 5

Study. all their talke and *studie* is of it. . . . . *Col.* 778
He to his *studie* goes; . . . . I. i. 36. 7
all her *studie* was . . . How she might overthrow . . . . . . IV. i. 29. 8
His *studie* was true Justice how to deale, ... V. xii. 26. 2

Studying. As if therein some text he *studying* were, ... *Hub.* 380

Stuff. an uncouth vestiment Made of straunge *stuffe,* . . . . . V. ix. 10. 8
nor finde like *stuffe* to that: . . . . VII. vii. 7. 5

Stuffed. quiver gay, *Stuft* with steele-headed dartes, ... II. iii. 29. 3
she was *stuft* with rancour and despight . . . . IV. viii. 24. 3

Stumble. chaunst to *stomble* at the threshold flore: . . . . . *S.C.* May 230
To *stumble,* that his rider nigh he cast; . . . . IV. iv. 30. 4

Stumbles. Oft *stombles* at a strawe. . . . . *S.C.* Jul. 100

Stumbling. Her *stombling* steppe some what her amazed, . . . *S.C.* May 231

Stump. Five joints thereof he hewd, and but the *stump* him lefte. . . . . I. xi. 39. 9

Stun. it will *stonn* thy feeble braines; . . . . III. iii. 9. 5

Stung. Sore he him *stong,* . . . . *Van.* x. 9
hardly could bee hurt who was already *stong.* . . . . II. i. 3. 9
seeking medicine whence she was *stong,* . . . . II. xii. 73. 3
he saw me *stung* and cry, ... *Epig.* i. 5
The Bee him *stung* therefore: . . . . *Epig.* iv. 26
Who would not oft be *stung* as this, To be so bath'd . . . . *Epig.* iv. 49

Stunk. *See* **Stank.**
gobbets raw, Which *stunck* so vildly, ... I. i. 20. 4
through the great contagion direful deadly *stonck.* (**stunck*) II. ii. 4. 9

Stunned. he was so *stund* that he n'ote ryde, ... III. vii. 42. 6

Stupefied. With great amazement they were *stupefide;* . . . . V. iii. 17. 5

Stupid. all thy senses swowned In *stupid* sorow, ... V. v. 36. 6

Stupid—*Continued.*
like a *stupid* stock in silence die! . . . . *Am.* xliii. 8
Sturdily. *sturdily* Strooke her full on the brest, ... III. iv. 15. 7
Sturdy. to the roote bent his *sturdy* stroake, ... *S.C.* F. 201
he stormes with many a *sturdy* stoure; . . . . *S.C.* D. 131
He was, to weete, a stout and *sturdy* thiefe, ... I. iii. 17. 1
sturdie courage tame with dreadfull aw, ... I. vi. 26. 8
monstrous enimy With *sturdie* steps came stalking . . . . . I. vii. 8. 3
Therewith his *sturdie* corage soon was quayd, ... I. viii. 14. 8
gan his *sturdy* sterne about to weld, ... I. xi. 28. 8
Ne ought his *sturdy* strokes might stand afore, ... I. xi. 37. 8
Him first saluted with a *sturdy* stroke: . . . . II. v. 3. 7
A *sturdie* villein, stryding stiffe and bold, ... II. vii. 40. 4
defend The walles so stoutly with their *sturdie* mayne, . . . II. xi. 15. 7
As when a *sturdy* ploughman with his hynde . . . . VI. viii. 12. 1
sturdy March, with brows full sternly bent . . . . VII. vii. 32. 3
Sture. *See* **Stour.**
Sturre. *See* **Stir.**
Sty. in the smoake she unto heaven did *stie.* . . . . *Bel.*[2] xi. 8
he dared to *stie* Up to the clowdes, ... *Mui.* 42
my Muse . . . With bolder wing shall dare alofte to *sty* . . *Ded. Son.* ii. 9
with his winges to *stye* above the ground; . . . . I. xi. 25. 8
That was Ambition, rash desire to *sty,* . . . . II. vii. 46. 8
yet love can higher *stye* Then reasons reach, ... III. ii. 36. 5
round about doth *stie,* . . . . IV. ix. 33. 5
Stygian. To the black shadowes of the *Stygian* shore, ... *Gn.* 383
Stygian powres appease: . . . . *Gn.* 440
come from the *Stygian* strands, ... *D.* 20
From wandring *Stygian* shores, where it doth endlesse move.' I. iv. 48. 9
Doest thou sit wayling by blacke *Stygian* lake, ... I. v. 10. 6
in *Stygian* lake, ay burning bright, Had kindled: . . . . . . II. v. 22. 7
If ever he transgrest the fatall *Stygian* lawes. . . . . II. vii. 27. 9
he wonts the *Stygian* realmes invade . . . . II. xii. 41. 4
long hath waited by the *Stygian* strond. . . . . III. ii. 52. 6
oft from *Stygian* deepe Calles thee his goddesse, ... III. iv. 56. 7
By *Stygian* lake I vow, ... III. vi. 24. 7
hid from the world, and from the skill Of *Stygian* Gods, . . III. vi. 46. 7
From *Stygian* shores where late it wandered: . . . . III. vii. 14. 8
As one in feare the *Stygian* gods t' offend, ... IV. iii. 32. 2
His soule descended downe into the *Stygian* reame. . . . . . IV. viii. 45. 9
recoure His Leman from the *Stygian* Princes boure: . . . . . IV. x. 58. 5
More loathd then Lerna, or then *Stygian* lake, ... V. xi. 32. 4
he was fostred long in *Stygian* fen, ... VI. i. 8. 4
long in darksome *Stygian* den upbrought, ... VI. vi. 9. 8
Style. To builde, with levell of my loftie *style,* . . . . *Ro.* xxv. 13
Well couth he tune his pipe and frame his *stile:* . . . . . . *S.C.* Ja. 10
to match thy pype with Tityrus his *style.* . . . . *S.C.* Env. 9
Base is the *style,* and matter meane withall. . . . . *Hub.* 44
Whose living praises in heroick *style,* . . . . *T.M.* 431
In loftie numbers and heroicke *stile.* . . . . *Ded. Son.* xii. 8
The argument of mine afflicted *stile:* . . . . I. Pr. 4. 8
with faire countenance and flattring *style* . . . . II. i. 8. 5
Yet she still followed her former *style,* . . . . II. vi. 22. 1
crownd his coward crest with knightly *stile;* . . . . II. viii. 12. 7
To feed her humor with his pleasing *style,* . . . . III. ii. 12. 2
the house that beares the *stile* Of roiall majesty . . . . . . III. iii. 48. 7
However gay and goodly be the *style,* . . . . IV. ii. 29. 7
As to abandon that which doth containe Your honours *stile,* V. xi. 55. 6
I would abate the sternenesse of my *stile,* . . . . VII. vi. 37. 3
not so fayre her buildinges to behold As Lewkenors *stile* . *Com. Son.* iv. 14
Styre. *See* **Stir.**
Styx. *Styx,* not passable to soules returning, ... *Ro.* xv. 6
At which . . . *Styx* is put to flight. . . . . I. i. 37. 9
dipped in the bitter wave Of hellish *Styx,* . . . . II. viii. 20. 9
In which old *Styx* her aged bones alway . . . doth lay. . . . IV. xi. 4. 4
Old *Styx* the Grandame of the Gods, ... IV. xi. 4. 5
Subdue. Rome . . . doth all Nations unto her *subdue:* . . . . . *Gn.* 598
O, how can . . . simple truth *subdue* avenging wrong! . . . . I. iii. 6. 5
Till morrow next that I the Elfe *subdew,* . . . . I. iv. 51. 4
many heades . . . Did breed him endlesse labor to *subdew.* . I. vii. 17. 5
when him list the prouder lookes *subdew,* . . . . I. vii. 35. 8
many knights . . . Have enterpriz'd that Monster to *subdew.* I. vii. 45. 2
Those creeping flames by reason to *subdew,* . . . . I. ix. 9. 6
well could menage and *subdew* his pride, ... II. iv. 2. 2
So hasty heat soone cooled to *subdew:* . . . . II. viii. 47. 8
stead you much your purpose to *subdew.'* . . . . II. ix. 9. 4
Those germans did *subdew* all Germany, ... II. x. 22. 7
Romanes daily did the weake *subdew:* . . . . II. x. 54. 5
made them victors whome he did *subdew.* . . . . II. x. 57. 4
to them selves all Nations did *subdew.* . . . . II. x. 72. 3
All monsters to *subdew* to him that did it beare. . . . . . . II. xii. 40. 9
he godly Oswald shall *subdew,* . . . . III. iii. 39. 3
'Yet shall a third both these and thine *subdew.* . . . . . . III. iii. 47. 1
Which darknesse shall *subdue* and heaven win: . . . . III. iv. 59. 6
With reason dew the passion to *subdew,* . . . . III. v. 44. 2
to your willes both royalties and Reames *Subdew,* . . . . . III. v. 53. 4
With harder meanes he cast her to *subdew,* . . . . III. viii. 40. 7
strife and warre and anger does *subdew:* . . . . IV. x. 34. 7
by force or guile She doth *subdue,* . . . . V. iv. 31. 2
The stubborne mettall seeketh to *subdew,* . . . . V. v. 7. 7
still the more she strove it to *subdew,* . . . . V. v. 28. 3
shortly did all other beasts *subdew.* . . . . V. vii. 16. 7
great hoastes to *subdew?* . . . . V. vii. 40. 5
the two knights themselves their captains did *subdew.* . . . V. xi. 59. 9
Till I him overtake, or else *subdew:* . . . . VI. i. 7. 3
Who hath not learnd him selfe first to *subdew:* . . . . . . VI. i. 41. 6
Subdue desire, and bridle loose delight; . . . . VI. vi. 14. 6
Calidore doth the Blatant Beast *Subdew,* . . . . VI. xii. Arg.
Did him suppresse, and forcibly *subdew,* . . . . VI. xii. 31. 6
whenas death shall all the world *subdew,* . . . . *Am.* lxxv. 13

Subdue—*Continued.*
in his hand . . . Him caught for to *subdue.* . . . . *Epig.* iv. 24
Subdued. Through armes and vassals Rome the world *subdu'd,* . *Ro.* viii. 1
all the world *subdued* unto it, ... *D.* 307
ye . . . in *subdued* harts do tyranyse; . . . . *Ded. Son.* xvi. 9
that false winged boy Her chaste hart had *subdewd* . . . . . I. i. 47. 9
that thus ye now *subdewed* arre: . . . . II. v. 15. 2
subdewde in equall frayes . . . . II. v. 26. 5
fairly tempring, fond desire *subdewd,* . . . . II. vi. 26. 6
I live this day, and see my foes *subdewd,* . . . . II. viii. 55. 6
Brute this Realme unto his rule *subdewd,* . . . . II. x. 13. 1
He Easterland *subdewd,* and Denmarke wonne, ... II. x. 41. 3
having with huge mightinesse Ireland *subdewd,* . . . . . . III. iii. 33. 6
He had *subdew'd,* and them his vassals made . . . . III. iv. 21. 2
Subdewd with losse of many Britons bold: . . . . III. ix. 50. 2
he many weake harts had *subdewd* Of yore, ... III. x. 9. 7
monstrous tyrants with his club *subdewed:* . . . . V. i. 2. 8
Artegall . . . is *subdewd* by guile: . . . . V. v. Arg.
By her *subdewed* in victorious fray: . . . . V. v. 21. 5
club, which had *subdew'd* of old So many monsters . . . . . V. v. 24. 5
Whom that proud Amazon *subdewed* had, ... V. vii. 41. 6
Having *subdew'd* yet did to life restore;) . . . . VI. viii. 4. 5
not men onely (whom she soone *subdewed*) . . . . VII. vi. 4. 8
Perforce *subdude* my poore captived hart, ... *H.L.* 2
by thy cruell darts to thee *subdewed.* . . . . *H.L.* 14
Subduer. Victor of gods, *subduer* of mankynd, ... *H.L.* 45
Subdues. The faithfull knight . . . *Subdewes* his faithlesse foe; I. v. Arg.
Subdueth. *Subdeweth* to his kingdome tyrannous. . . . . III. xii. 22. 5
Subject. Are temporall, and *subject* to decay: . . . . *Ro.* ix. 11
Continuallie *subject* unto chaunge. . . . . *Hub.* 92
Subject unto that powre imperiall.' . . . . *Hub.* 972
to *subject* his desire To loathsome sloth, ... *Mui.* 35
On silly Dame, *subject* to hard mischaunce, ... I. ii. 21. 3
Long he them bore above the *subject* plaine, ... I. xi. 19. 1
O miserable men that to him *subject* arre! . . . . II. ii. 26. 9
he, now *subject* to the victours law, ... II. viii. 50. 5
hold of him, as *subject* to Britayne. . . . . II. x. 41. 9
all that lives is *subject* to that law; . . . . III. vi. 40. 8
All be he *subject* to mortalitie, ... III. vi. 47. 4
A litle valley *subject* to the same, ... III. vii. 4. 8
to his powre we all are *subject* borne: . . . . IV. viii. 15. 2
makes them *subject* to his mighty wrong; . . . . V. ii. 7. 4
Tyrants, that make men *subject* to their law, ... V. ii. 38. 6
things *subject* to thy daily vew . . . . V. ii. 42. 8
seekes to save the *subject* of her skill, ... V. x. 2. 6
Subject to fortunes chance, still chaunging new: . . . . VI. i. 41. 8
we all are *subject* to that curse, ... VII. vi. 6. 8
To thousand sorts of Change we *subject* see: . . . . VII. vii. 25. 3
all those Rivers to me *subject* are, ... VII. vii. 26. 8
Whether to me they are not *subject* all.' . . . . VII. vii. 27. 7
subject still to Mutability?' . . . . VII. vii. 47. 9
likewise chang'd, and *subject* unto mee? . . . . VII. vii. 49. 9
Are you not *subject* eeke to this misfare? . . . . VII. vii. 53. 3
both you and them to me I *subject* prove. . . . . VII. vii. 55. 9
this base world, *subject* to fleshly eye, ... *H.H.B.* 23
Subjected. *subjected* France and Germany, ... II. x. 40. 6
Hath me *subjected* to loves cruell law: . . . . III. ii. 38. 5
Subjected hath to my unequall might. . . . . V. v. 32. 3
lower creatures all *Subjected* to her powre imperiall. . . . . *H.H.B.* 196
Subjection. Let us all servile base *subjection* scorne; . . . . *Hub.* 134
all the world in their *subjection* held; . . . . I. i. 5. 6
womens powre, that boast of mens *subjection?* . . . . V. iv. 26. 5
In signe of true *subjection* to her powre, ... V. v. 18. 2
Serving proud Radigund with true *subjection,* . . . . V. v. 26. 2
them restoring To mens *subjection,* . . . . V. vii. 42. 7
brought that land to his *subjection,* . . . . V. x. 9. 5
Subjects. He maketh *subjects* to their powre obay; . . . . . . V. ii. 41. 6
on thy *subjects* most dost tyrannize? . . . . *H.L.* 161
Sublime. Souldan, with . . . countenance *sublime* and insolent . V. viii. 30. 4
Submiss. Soft Silence, and *submisse* Obedience, ... IV. x. 51. 6
Submission. yielded pryde and proud *submission,* Still dreading death, ... I. iii. 6. 6
Yet glad at last to make most base *submission,* . . . . V. x. 27. 4
Gan him entreat even with *submission* base, ... VI. iii. 38. 5
Submissively. kneeling at his feete *submissively:* . . . . V. ii. 26. 5
Submit. Therefore *submit* thy wayes unto his will, ... III. iii. 24. 8
submit you to high providence; . . . . III. xi. 14. 4
I me *submit,* and you of pardon pray, ... IV. vi. 3. 8
Submitted. to her mercie him *submitted* in plaine field. . . . . V. v. 16. 9
Submitting. *Submitting* me to your good sufferance, ... *S.C.* F. 187
Suborned. an usurping Ape, with guile *suborn'd,* . . . . *Hub.* 1233
she *suborned* hath This crafty messenger . . . . I. xii. 34. 1
For falsed letters, and *suborned* wyle, ... II. i. 1. 3
Substance. His breastplate first, that was of *substance* pure, . . *Mui.* 57
Ne dint of direfull sword divide the *substance* would. . . . . I. vii. 33. 9
lively is the semblaunt, though the *substance* dead.' . . . . . II. ix. 2. 9
though they bodies seem, yet *substaunce* from them fades. . . II. ix. 15. 9
of more worthy *substance* fram'd it was: . . . . II. ix. 23. 5
Cover'd with lids deviz'd of *substance* sly, ... II. ix. 46. 7
of such subtile *substance* and unsound, ... II. xi. 20. 8
having all their *substance* spent . . . . II. xii. 7. 6
the gate was wrought of *substaunce* light, ... II. xii. 43. 8
otherwhere the snowy *substaunce* sprent With vermell, ... II. xii. 45. 5
richest *substance* that on earth might bee, ... II. xii. 60. 2
she may finde the *substance* thin and light, ... III. i. 43. 3
That *substaunce* is eterne, and bideth so; . . . . III. vi. 37. 6
The *substaunce* is not chaungd nor altered, ... III. vi. 38. 1
every *substaunce* is conditioned To chaunge her hew, ... III. vi. 38. 3
The *substance,* whereof she the body made, ... III. viii. 6. 1
all his *substance* was consum'd to nought, ... III. x. 57. 3

Substance—*Continued.*
frame in earth, and forme of *substance* base, . . . IV. x. 21. 7
Whose *substance* was uneath to understand: . . . IV. x. 39. 3
there no *substance* was so firme and hard, . . . V. i. 10. 6
Her snowy *substance* melted as with heat, . . . V. iii. 24. 7
whose *substance* thin and slight Made no resistance, . . . VII. vi. 7. 7
Made of the heavens *substance,* . . . VII. vi. 10. 3
I marvaile of what *substance* was the mould, . . . *Am.* lv. 3
through unaptnesse in the *substance* fownd, . . . *H.B.* 144
Substances. The *substaunces* of natures fruitfull progenyes. . . III. vi. 36. 9
Subtile. *See* **Subtle.**
Subtle. The *subtill* vermin, creeping closely neare, . . . *Van.* vi. 7
efte in Dolons *subtile* surprysall. . . . *Gn.* 536
they more *subtill* meaning had than he; . . . *Hub.* 330
my slie wyles and *subtill* craftinesse, . . . *Hub.* 1045
The *subtile* Foxe so well his message sayd, . . . *Hub.* 1101
Ne doo I thinke, that that same *subtil* gin, . . . *Mui.* 369
In lymie snares the *subtill* loupes among; . . . *Mui.* 429
There his welwoven toyles, and *subtil* traines, . . . *As.* 97
Glewed togither with some *subtile* matter. . . . *Col.* 217
handle his deceitfull wit In *subtil* shifts, . . . *Col.* 694
spred A seeming body of the *subtile* aire, . . . I. ii. 3. 3
subtill Archimago, . . . praisd his divelish arts, . . . I. ii. 9. 1
subtill Archimag, that Una sought . . . I. iii. 24. 6
his flatt'ring artes to fayle, And *subtile* engines . . . I. vi. 5. 2
The *subtile* traines of Archimago old; . . . I. vii. 26. 2
by *subtile* sleights she him betraid Unto his foe, . . . I. vii. 51. 1
Castle, . . . By *subtile* engins and malitious slight Is undermined . . . I. viii. 23. 2
His *subtile* tong . . . mealt'h Into the heart, . . . I. ix. 31. 5
guest Would safe depart, for all his *subtile* sleight, . . . I. ix. 54. 3
by his *subtile* trains He could escape fowle death . . . I. xii. 36. 4
Thereto his *subtile* engins he does bend, . . . II. i. 3. 5
Arachne high did . . . spred her *subtile* nett, . . . II. vii. 28. 8
of such *subtile* substance and unsound, . . . II. xi. 20. 8
More *subtile* web Arachne cannot spin; . . . II. xii. 77. 7
on them rusht, and threw A *subtile* net, . . . II. xii. 81. 4
full of *subtile* sophismes, . . . III. iv. 28. 7
with plumy wings doth sheare The *subtile* ayre . . . III. vii. 39. 4
Was so expert in every *subtile* slight, . . . IV. ii. 10. 8
all the artes, that *subtill* wits discover, . . . IV. iii. 40. 2
To frame such *subtile* wire, so shinie cleare; . . . IV. vi. 20. 6
Which *subtill* sleight did him encumber much, . . . IV. vii. 27. 1
His horse purloyned was by *subtill* traine, . . . V. iii. 31. 5
He them abused through his *subtill* slights, . . . V. iii. 39. 8
There all her *subtill* nets she did unfold, . . . V. v. 52. 1
notwithstanding all the *subtill* bait . . . V. vi. 2. 3
A man of *subtill* wit and wicked minde, . . . V. vi. 32. 2
So smooth of tongue, and *subtile* in his tale, . . . V. ix. 5. 6
By guilefull treason and by *subtill* slight . . . V. xi. 39. 7
Ne yet entrap in treasons *subtill* traine. . . . VI. v. 14. 4
in *subtile* bands Of the blynd boy; . . . VI. ix. 11. 6
with *subtill* influence Of his thin spirit . . . VII. vii. 22. 3
Such *subtile* craft my Damzell doth conceave, . . . *Am.* xxiii. 5
Subtleties. womans *subtiltyes* Can guylen Argus, . . . III. ix. 7. 2
Subtlety. could never wight him harme By *subtilty,* . . . I. xi. 36. 9
Subtly. *subtily* betrayd Through that late vision . . . I. iii. 3. 5
they of living fire most *subtilly* Were made, . . . II. ix. 46. 5
silke Woven uppon with silver, *subtly* wrought, . . . V. v. 2. 2
Subversed. an usurping Ape . . . Had all *subverst,* . . . *Hub.* 1234
vanisht utterly and cleane *subverst* She found, . . . III. xii. 42. 3
Subvert. Seekes to *subvert* her Crowne and dignity, . . . V. viii. 18. 4
abase Unto this shame, and my young hope *subvert,* . . . VI. i. 12. 8
Subverted. Had utterly *subverted* his unrighteous state. . . . V. ix. 2. 9
Succeed. To see thee *succeede* in thy fathers steade, . . . *S.C.* May 203
With better fortune than did me *succeed,* . . . *D.* 521
the noble Progeny, Which them *succeed* . . . *Ded. Son.* iv. 6
henceforth ever wish that like *succeed* it may!' . . . I. i. 27. 9
had no issue male him to *succeed,* . . . II. x. 27. 2
In rule *succeede,* and eke in fathers praise; . . . II. x. 41. 2
Him to *succeede* therein, by his last will: . . . II. x. 76. 5
shall him *succeede* In kingdome, . . . III. iii. 31. 1
'well may it you *succeed!* . . . III. viii. 50. 6
In which poursuit how each one did *succeede,* . . . IV. v. 28. 5
Like belles in greatnesse orderly *succeed,* . . . IV. v. 36. 8
kept the crowne in which she should *succeed:* . . . V. i. 13. 5
ever as he saw him nigh *succeed,* . . . VI. iv. 8. 7
there did *succeed* An off-spring of their bloud, . . . VII. vi. 20. 7
Succeeded. He dide, and him *succeeded* Marius, . . . II. x. 53. 1
Succeeding. *See* **Ill-succeeding, Late-succeeding.**
succeeding ages have no light Of things forepast, . . . *T.M.* 103
Succeeding them in true nobility: . . . *Ded. Son.* iii. 9
yield his rowme to sad *succeeding* night, . . . I. xi. 49. 6
Which blott his sonne *succeeding* in his seat, . . . II. x. 23. 1
Uther, which Pendragon hight, *Succeeding*— . . . II. x. 68. 2
Success. Returneth by continuall *successe,* . . . *Gn.* 30
In hope to finde there happier *successe.* . . . *Hub.* 658
God ye speed and send you good *successe,* . . . II. i. 25. 6
raynd By dew *successe,* . . . II. x. 45. 7
Not with so good *successe* as shee deserv'd; . . . II. x. 55. 2
heven it selfe shall their *successe* envy, . . . III. iii. 40. 7
Of his *successe* and gladfull victory: . . . III. iii. 59. 4
to see what new *successe* Mote him befall . . . III. xi. 20. 2
of the hardie Britomarts *successe:* . . . III. xii. 43. *or.* 5
dangerous *successe* depended yet in doubt: . . . IV. ix. 24. 9
With great *successe,* that her hath glorifide, . . . V. iv. 33. 7
Touching her loves *successe,* . . . V. v. 45. 3
Whilest Fortune favourd her *successe* in fight: . . . V. vii. 41. 7
hope of his *successe,* . . . V. vii. 44. 6
They shouted all for joy of his *successe,* . . . V. xii. 24. 2

Success—*Continued.*
the good *successe* Which ye have had . . . VI. i. 5. 1
of their loves *successe* they there may make report; . . . VI. vii. 32. 9
to tell of heavens King . . . his fortunate *successe;* . . . VII. vii. 1. 6
Successes. good *successes* which their foes ensew: . . . I. v. 25. 3
Succession. by *succession* made perpetuall, . . . III. vi. 47. 6
Fates divine decree For lifes *succession* in those brethren three. IV. iii. 21. 5
Successively. All which *successively* by turnes did rayne: . . II. x. 44. 2
Successor. Her power to Peters *successor* betooke; . . . *Ro.* xviii. 12
Succor. for *succoure* flee Under the shadow of his wing; . . . *To his Booke* 6
nowe no *succoure* was seene him nere. . . . *S.C.* F. 228
'My weaker yeares, . . . Fly to your fayth for *succour* . . . I. i. 52. 6
Him booteth not resist, nor *succour* call, . . . I. iii. 20. 1
succour from the scorching ray, . . . II. i. 35. 6
To *succour* the weake state of sad afflicted Troy. . . . II. iii. 31. 9
Voide of all *succour* and needfull comfort; . . . II. v. 17. 5
gan him dight to *succour* his distresse, . . . II. v. 24. 2
To come to *succour* us that *succour* want! . . . II. viii. 2. 2
evermore him *succour,* and defend . . . II. viii. 8. 5
Mote I beseech to *succour* his sad plight, . . . II. viii. 25. 7
my *succour* or advizement meete . . . II. ix. 9. 3
far from all *succoure;* . . . II. x. 19. 4
yielding *succour* to that cursed Swaine, . . . II. xi. 28. 5
beare him farre from hope of *succour* usuall. . . . II. xi. 45. 9
lowd to them for *succour* called evermore. . . . II. xii. 27. 9
Hath hither brought for *succour* to appele; . . . III. iii. 19. 8
Or *succour* her, or me direct the way, . . . III. v. 10. 8
To *succor* wretched wights whom we captived see.' . . . III. v. 36. 9
succor send to her distressed cace; . . . III. viii. 29. 4
fals to ground to seeke for *succor* theare, . . . III. viii. 33. 5
To fly for *succour* to a little shed, . . . III. ix. 11. 8
now that noble *succor* is thee by, . . . III. x. 26. 4
Of his loves *succour,* of his owne redresse, . . . III. xii. 43. *or.* 4
They to his *succour* ran with readie ayd; . . . IV. i. 37. 2
This hand may helpe, or *succour* ought supplie, . . . IV. vi. 8. 7
with motion nimble To *succour* it, . . . IV. vi. 29. 5
Himselfe by them on foot to *succour* them from feare. . . . IV. viii. 22. 9
rescue him, through *succour* of his might, . . . IV. viii. 40. 8
To yeeld strong *succour* to that gentle swayne, . . . IV. ix. 4. 2
That was to *succour* a distressed Dame . . . V. i. 3. 6
Unlesse some *succour* had in time him overtaken. . . . V. iii. 9. 9
to get *Succour* against her greedy enimy: . . . V. viii. 6. 7
To seeke for *succour* of her and her Peares, . . . V. x. 6. 4
th' armes and legs of three to *succour* him in fight. . . . V. x. 8. 9
To seeke for *succour* of this Ladies gieft; . . . V. x. 14. 7
well she wist this knight came *succour* to supply. . . . V. x. 19. 9
Both man and beast doe fly, and *succour* doe inquyre. . . . V. xi. 58. 9
ere he tasted bread He would her *succour,* . . . VI. i. 31. 5
To *succour* her from daunger of dismay, . . . VI. ii. 38. 4
Staide not to *succour* her in that affright, . . . VI. iii. 26. 4
there for his love some *succour* to provyde. . . . VI. iii. 29. 9
But his best *succour* and refuge was still . . . VI. iii. 49. 5
whom she did oft implore To send her *succour,* . . . VI. iv. 10. 9
fynd Some place of *succour* to content his mynd, . . . VI. iv. 26. 5
had bene to her *succour* nere. . . . VI. xi. 33. 9
seeke some *succour* both to ease my smart, . . . *Am.* ii. 7
a ship, of *succour* desolate, Doth suffer wreck . . . *Am.* lvi. 11
With secret ayde doest *succour* and supply, . . . *Epith.* 402
Succored. Had not the Gyaunt soone her *succoured;* . . . I. viii. 17. 7
Her *succourd* eke the Champion of the bloody Crosse. . . . III. i. 64. 9
Succorless. Seeing her selfe all soly *succourlesse,* . . . IV. ix. 18. 6
They spide a Lady left all *succourlesse,* . . . V. xi. 44. 7
Such (*partial list*). *See* **Sic.**
Even by an hundred *such* as Hercules, . . . *Bel.*[1] viii. 12
A worthy tombe for *such* a worthy wight. . . . *Bel.* iii. 11
Such store of birds therein yshrowded were, . . . *Pet.* iii. 5
no *such* shadow shalbe had againe. . . . *Pet.* iii. 14
To see *such* pleasures gon so suddenly. . . . *Pet.*[2] iv. 14
O let mine eyes no more see *such* a sight! . . . *Pet.*[2] v. 14
Such as the Berecynthian Goddesse bright, . . . *Ro.* vi. 1
Such was this Citie in her good daies fownd: . . . *Ro.* vi. 4
grewe to *such* height, . . . *Ro.* xx. 10
Who *such* an Oke hath seene, let him record That *such* this Cities . . . *Ro.*xxviii.12,13
Such as this age, in which all good is geason, . . . *Van.* i. 5
Such as they were . . . *Van.* i. 13
such was the shepeheards looke, . . . *S.C.* Ja. 7
'*Such* rage as winters reigneth in my heart, . . . *S.C.* Ja. 25
Such stormy stoures do breede . . . *S.C.* Ja. 27
such sight hath bred my bane. . . . *S.C.* Ja. 53
Such an one shepeheards would make full faine; *Such* an one would make thee younge againe. . . . *S.C.* F. 67, 68
Unto *such* tyrannie doth aspire; . . . *S.C.* F. 172
For this, and many more *such* outrage, . . . *S.C.* F. 183
Had kindled *such* coles of displeasure, . . . *S.C.* F. 191
Such was thend of this Ambitious brere, . . . *S.C.* F. 237
Ys love *such* pinching payne to them . . . *S.C.* Ap. 18
Such follie great sorow to Niobe did breede: . . . *S.C.* Ap. 87
that ever he begot *Such* a Bellibone; . . . *S.C.* Ap. 92
her lot To beare *such* an one. . . . *S.C.* Ap. 94
Such for a Princesse bene principall. . . . *S.C.* Ap. 126
Great pittie is, he be in *such* taking, . . . *S.C.* Ap. 156
Such merimake holy Saints doth queme, . . . *S.C.* May 15
For Younkers, Palinode, *such* follies fitte, . . . *S.C.* May 17
To see those folkes make *such* jovysaunce, . . . *S.C.* May 25
such cause hath she none) . . . *S.C.* May 98
Lulled the shepheards in *such* securitie, . . . *S.C.* May 119
I wene the Geaunt has not *such* a weight, . . . *S.C.* May 142
Such faitors, . . . Will doe as did the Foxe . . . *S.C.* May 170
false Fortune *such* joy did him spight, . . . *S.C.* May 198

Such—*Continued.*

(For *such*, . . . bene dispraised;) . . . *S.C.* May 232
Such end had the Kidde, . . . *S.C.* May 302
such end, perdie, does all hem remayne, That of *such* falsers freendship bene fayne. . . . *S.C.* May 304, 305
Such pierlesse pleasures have we in these places. . . . *S.C.* Jun. 32
In *such* delights did joy amongst my peeres: . . . *S.C.* Jun. 35
But ryper age *such* pleasures doth reprove: . . . *S.C.* Jun. 36
why should Death on hym *such* outrage showe?) . . . *S.C.* Jun. 90
for *such* thy villanee. . . . *S.C.* Jun. 104
Such one he was . . . *S.C.* Jul. 125
Such favour couth he fynd, . . . *S.C.* Jul. 138
such, I weene, the brethren were . . . *S.C.* Jul. 141
But nothing *such* thilk shepheard was . . . *S.C.* Jul. 145
(No *such* mought shepheards bee) . . . *S.C.* Jul. 150
Such simplesse mought them shend: . . . *S.C.* Jul. 172
To Rome, (if *such* be Rome) . . . *S.C.* Jul. 183
Thou hast *such* doubt to climbe. . . . *S.C.* Jul. 232
Such fond fantsies shall soone be put to flight . . . *S.C.* Au. 22
Tell me, *such* a cup hast thou ever sene? . . . *S.C.* Au. 35
Such play is a pitteous plight. . . . *S.C.* Au. 92
Such woundes soone wexen wider. . . . *S.C.* Au. 96
With sight of *such* as chaunge my restlesse woe. . . . *S.C.* Au. 172
such eeking hath made my hart sore. . . . *S.C.* S. 31
But for *such*, as of guile maken gayne, No *such* countrye as there to remaine; . . . *S.C.* S. 34, 35
nowe I wote it is nothing *sich;* . . . *S.C.* S. 79
Such myster saying me seemeth to mirke. . . . *S.C.* S. 103
For *such* encheason, if you goe nye, . . . *S.C.* S. 116
Such ill, . . . mought nedes be endured. . . . *S.C.* S. 139
Shepheards *sich*, God mought us many send, . . . *S.C.* S. 178
Why should we be bound to *such* miseree? . . . *S.C.* S. 239
Diggon on fewe *such* freends did ever lite. . . . *S.C.* S. 259
Such pleasaunce makes the Grashopper . . . *S.C.* O. 11
For Colin fittes *such* famous flight to scanne; . . . *S.C.* O. 88
Such immortal mirrhor, as he doth admire, . . . *S.C.* O. 93
For lordly love is *such* a Tyranne fell, . . . *S.C.* O. 98
Where no *such* troublous tydes han us assayde; . . . *S.C.* O. 117
Such cause of mourning never hadst afore; . . . *S.C.* N. 54
such country chere: . . . *S.C.* N. 96
Such pleasaunce now displast by dolors dint: . . . *S.C.* N. 104
such pryde at length was ill repayde: . . . *S.C.* D. 49
Such as might save my sheepe . . . *S.C.* D. 78
promised of timely fruite *such* store, . . . *S.C.* D. 104
who *such* sports and sweet delights doth blame, . . . *Gn.* 7
No *such* sad cares, . . . *Gn.* 94
In *such* delights whilst thus . . . *Gn.* 153
transformd to *such* an one; . . . *Gn.* 205
Much do I feare among *such* fiends to sit; . . . *Gn.* 381
being *such* as through their might . . . *Gn.* 647
Let *such* vile vassals, . . . Drudge . . . *Hub.* 156
Such will we fashion both our selves to bee, . . . *Hub.* 167
what ever *such* like paine Ye put on me, . . . *Hub.* 287
Of *such* deep learning little had he neede, . . . *Hub.* 385
Such grace did God unto his creatures give. . . . *Hub.* 402
such strangenesse in him see . . . *Hub.* 680
Such is the rightfull Courtier in his kinde, But unto *such* the Ape lent not his minde: . . . *Hub.* 793, 794
Such were for him no fit companions, *Such* would descrie his lewd conditions; . . . *Hub.* 795, 796
Ne let *such* verses Poetrie be named! . . . *Hub.* 814
Of *such*, as he depended most upon; . . . *Hub.* 818
To *such* delights the noble wits he led . . . *Hub.* 821
Or corne, or cattle, or *such* other ware, . . . *Hub.* 873
For none but *such* as this bold Ape, . . . *Hub.* 915
Or *such* as hath a Reynold to his man, . . . *Hub.* 917
by *such* as sate in justice seate, . . . *Hub.* 921
Such followes those . . . *Hub.* 1136
By *such* as hate the honour of our name, . . . *T.M.* 63
such store of streaming teares, . . . *T.M.* 109
Scorning the boldnes of *such* base-borne men, . . . *T.M.* 219
Such as ye wont, . . . *T.M.* 373
Such high conceipt of that celestiall fire, . . . *T.M.* 391
Such happinesse have they that doo embrace . . . *T.M.* 517
such store of teares shee forth did powre, . . . *T.M.* 595
greislie shades, *such* as doo haunt in hell . . . *Ti.* 125
such as neither of themselves can sing, . . . *Ti.* 344
'*Such* one Mausolus made, . . . *Ti.* 414
Such one Marcellus, . . . *Ti.* 416
Such one Lisippus, but is worne with raine: *Such* one King Edmond, but was rent for gaine. . . . *Ti.* 417, 418
All *such* vaine moniments of earthlie masse, . . . *Ti.* 419
Such as on earth man could not more devize, . . . *Ti.* 521
Such rancour in the harts of mightie men? . . . *Mui.* 16
That he in time would sure prove *such* an one, . . . *Mui.* 31
such as could both Phoebus arrowes ward, . . . *Mui.* 79
two *such* fannes, so silken soft . . . *Mui.* 107
Such as Dame Pallas, such as Envie pale, . . . devowres, . . . *Mui.* 301
unworthie *such* a spoyle, . . . *D.* 163
mocking *such* as thinke they long will stay. . . . *D.* 399
thinke that *such* mishap, . . . May happen . . . *D.* 516
that *such* are for *such* ones most fit, . . . *As.* Pr. 15
such felicitie, Or rather infelicitie, . . . *As.* 79
Such skill, matcht with *such* courage as he had, . . . *As.* 85
Such greatnes I cannot compare to ought: . . . *Col.* 335
Such loftie flight base shepheard seemeth not, . . . *Col.* 618
since thou foundst *such* grace . . . *Col.* 652
Even *such* is all their vaunted vanitie, . . . *Col.* 719
Such is their glorie . . . *Col.* 721
he was *such* an one as thou doest say, . . . *Col.* 829

Such—*Continued.*

Such grace shall be some guerdon for the griefe, . . . *Col.* 943
Such grace sometimes shall give me some reliefe, . . . *Col.* 945
Such, therefore, as that wasted soyl doth yield, . . . *Ded. Son.* v. 13
Such as they be, vouchsafe them to receave, . . . *Ded. Son.* ix. 13
many *such* I pray, . . . I. i. 27. 8
'Of *such*,' (saide he,) 'I chiefly doe inquere, . . . I. i. 31. 5
such a cursed creature lives so long a space.' . . . I. i. 31. 9
such is the dye of warre. . . . I. ii. 36. 7
Th' one seeming *such*, the other *such* indeede, . . . I. ii. 37. 2
Eftsoones I thought her *such* as she me told, . . . I. ii. 39. 6
When *such* I see, . . . all for pitty I could dy. . . . I. iii. 1. 9
Did never mortall eye behold *such* heavenly grace. . . . I. iii. 4. 9
Such were the labours of this Lady meeke, . . . I. iii. 21. 7
If that of *such* a Lady shee could tellen ought. . . . I. iii. 24. 9
Whome seeing *such*, . . . hee durst not show Him selfe . . . I. iii. 26. 3
Such joy made Una, when her knight she found; . . . I. iii. 32. 1
In living Princes court none ever knew *Such* endlesse richesse, I. iv. 7. 5
When *such* an one had guiding of the way, . . . I. iv. 19. 8
Such one was Idlenesse, first of this company. . . . I. iv. 20. 9
Such one was Gluttony, the second of that crew. . . . I. iv. 23. 9
Such one was Lechery, the third of all this traine. . . . I. iv. 26. 9
Such one was Avarice, the fourth of this faire band. . . . I. iv. 29. 9
Such one vile Envy was, that fifte in row did sitt. . . . I. iv. 32. 9
Such one was Wrath, the last of this ungodly tire. . . . I. iv. 35. 9
Such restlesse passion did all night torment . . . I. v. 1. 5
Such wondrous science in mans witt to rain . . . I. v. 40. 1
devise to quitt a thrall from *such* a plight? . . . I. vi. 6. 9
Such fearefull fitt assaid her trembling hart, . . . I. vi. 11. 1
Blaming of Fortune, which *such* troubles threw, . . . I. vi. 31. 5
such as she her selfe was then in place. . . . I. vii. 5. 7
Such now he marcheth to this man forlorne, . . . I. vii. 10. 5
Such one it was, as that renowmed Snake . . . I. vii. 17. 1
Such earthly mettals soon consumed beene, . . . I. vii. 33. 4
all that was not *such* as seemd . . . did fade, . . . I. vii. 35. 3
There to obtaine some *such* redoubted knight, . . . I. vii. 46. 8
rather death desire then *such* despight. . . . I. vii. 49. 6
To see his loved Squyre into *such* thraldom brought: . . . I. viii. 15. 9
Such blazing brightnesse through the ayer threw, . . . I. viii. 19. 4
Such was this Gyaunts fall, . . . I. viii. 23. 8
Such percing griefe her stubborne hart did wound, . . . I. viii. 25. 4
'*Such* . . . 'as she seemeth here, *Such* is the face of falshood: I. viii. 49. 3, 4
such the sight Of fowle Duessa, . . . I. viii. 49. 4
Pupill fitt for *such* a Tutors hand! . . . I. ix. 6. 2
never knight I saw in *such* misseeming plight.' . . . I. ix. 23. 9
Almightie God her gave *such* powre and puissaunce great. . . I. x. 20. 9
To *such* perfection of all hevenly grace, . . . I. x. 21. 3
Not unto *such* as could him feast againe, . . . I. x. 37. 6
such as want of harbour did constraine: . . . I. x. 37. 8
'What end' . . . 'should cause us take *such* paine, . . . I. x. 50. 1
Such one as that same mighty man of God, . . . I. x. 53. 2
Such, men do Chaungelings call, . . . I. x. 65. 9
Did seeme, *such* as she was, . . . I. xii. 8. 9
His owne two hands, for *such* a turne most fitt, . . . I. xii. 37. 3
such to some appeare. . . . II. Pr. 3. 9
Such whenas Archimago them did view, . . . II. i. 8. 1
Her purpose was not *such* as she did faine, . . . II. i. 21. 1
Ne yet her person *such* as it was seene, . . . II. i. 21. 2
Against his praise to stirre up enmitye Of *such*, . . . II. i. 23. 9
'*Such* and *such* evil God on Guyon reare, . . . II. i. 61. 5
Such is the state of men: . . . II. ii. 2. 8
'*Such* is this well, wrought by occasion straunge, . . . II. ii. 7. 1
Shapt like a maide, that *such* ye may her know: . . . II. ii. 9. 5
Fitt mate for *such* a mincing mineon, . . . II. ii. 37. 2
devisd redresse for *such* annoyes: . . . II. ii. 43. 8
pitty *such* unhappie bale, . . . II. ii. 45. 3
For *such* as he him thought, . . . II. iii. 5. 6
Such prayse is shame; . . . II. iii. 10. 8
Such when as hartlesse Trompart her did vew, . . . II. iii. 32. 1
Goddesse, (for *such* I thee take to bee) . . . II. iii. 33. 2
Such wounded beast as that I did not see, . . . II. iii. 33. 5
All vertue merits praise, but *such* the most of all.' . . . II. iii. 37. 9
her horn sound with *such* ghastlinesse. . . . II. iii. 44. 9
he is not *such* a foe, . . . II. iv. 10. 4
What hard mishap him brought to *such* distresse, . . . II. iv. 16. 8
Unweeting and unware of *such* mishap, . . . II. iv. 17. 7
'At last *such* grace I found, . . . II. iv. 21. 1
shame of *such* repriefe. . . . II. iv. 28. 9
death were better then *such* agony . . . II. iv. 33. 3
With *such* faire sleight . . . II. v. 11. 1
such as I thee see, To worke *such* shame. . . . II. v. 17. 6, 7
For suffering *such* abuse as knighthood sham'd, . . . II. v. 21. 5
He lowdly cald to *such* as were abord . . . II. vi. 4. 2
Such as he saw she gan him lay before, . . . II. vi. 24. 4
Such superfluities they would despise, . . . II. vii. 15. 5
shewd of richesse *such* exceeding store, . . . II. vii. 31. 4
Eternall God thee save from *such* decay! . . . II. vii. 34. 7
With *such* vaine shewes thy worldlinges vyle abuse; . . . II. vii. 39. 5
never earthly Prince in *such* aray His glory did enhaunce, . . II. vii. 44. 8
Whom all that folke with *such* contention . . . II. vii. 48. 5
Unworthy match for *such* immortall mate . . . II. vii. 50. 4
Not *such* as earth out of her fruitfull woomb . . . II. vii. 51. 6
if that thou be *such* as I thee see, . . . II. vii. 59. 8
nothing cleaner were for *such* intent, . . . II. vii. 61. 7
why should hevenly God to men have *such* regard? . . . II. viii. 2. 9
Whom when the Palmer saw in *such* distresse, . . . II. viii. 40. 1
with *such* puissaunce and impetuous maine . . . II. ix. 14. 5
made *such* sound . . . II. ix. 51. 2
How shall fraile pen . . . Conceive *such* soveraine glory . . . II. x. 2. 9
such dreadful wights As far exceeded . . . II. x. 8. 8

Sudden—*Continued.*
through *sudden* strange affright . . . . . V. x. 19. 5
Save such as *sudden* rage him lent to smite; . . . . . VI. iv. 4. 3
to faine A *sodaine* sickenesse . . . . . VI. xi. 7. 8
She *sudden* was revived therewithall, ... VI. xi. 44. 4
Yet knowing not what meant that *sodaine* thro, ... VI. xii. 17. 2
know what meant that *suddaine* lacke of light. . . . . VII. vi. 15. 5
At sight of her they *suddaine* all arose . . . . . VII. vi. 24. 4
But *sudden* dumps, . . . my torment feed. . . . . *Am.* lii. 11
Make *sudden* sad affrights; . . . . . *Epith.* 339
Suddenly. *sodenly* I saw Where tombling . . . . . *Bel.*[1] vi. 9
sodenly the Palme and Olive fell, ... *Bel.*[1] vii. 13
suddenly arose a tempest great, ... *Bel.*[2] xiii. 5
To see such pleasures gon so *suddenly.* . . . . . *Pet.*[2] iv. 14
All *suddenly* with lightning overthrowne, ... *Ro.* xii. 5
To stop his wearie cariere *suddenly:* . . . . . *Ro.* xvi. 8
All *sodainely* there clove unto her keele . . . . . *Van.* ix. 9
suddenly casting aside his vew, ... *Gn.* 294
All *suddenly* dismaid, and hartles quight, ... *Gn.* 297
'*Suddenly,* whether through the Gods decree, ... *Gn.* 569
I saw this Towre fall *sodainelie* (**sodainlie*) to dust, ... *Ti.* 517
When *suddeinly* both bed and all was gone, ... *Ti.* 643
my fair Starre . . . Fell *sodainly* and faded . . . . . *D.* 481
her huge traine All *suddenly* about his body wound, ... I. i. 18. 7
Resolvd in minde all *suddenly* to win, ... I. i. 24. 4
Whom *suddenly* he wakes with fearful frights, ... I. ii. 4. 4
All in amaze he *suddenly* up start . . . . . I. ii. 5. 1
A ramping Lyon rushed *suddeinly,* . . . . . I. iii. 5. 2
suddeinly that warriour gan abace His threatned speare, . . . II. i. 26. 7
dead *suddeinly* he downe did sincke. . . . . II. i. 55. 9
all *suddeinly* he seemd enragd, ... II. iii. 14. 1
Suddeinly out of his delightfull dreame The man awoke, . . . II. v. 37. 1
suddeinly He heard a voyce . . . . . II. viii. 3. 6
suddeinly a grosse fog over-spred . . . . . II. xii. 34. 5
Suddeinly an innumerable flight . . . . . II. xii. 35. 6
suddeinly both would themselves unhele, ... II. xii. 64. 8
All *suddenly* out of the thickest brush, ... III. i. 15. 1
All *suddeinly* . . . Doth groveling fall, ... III. iv. 17. 5
All *suddeinly* dim wox the dampish ayre, ... III. iv. 52. 1
a ship, whose Lodestar *suddeinly* Covered with cloudes . . . III. iv. 53. 3
All *suddeinly* abasht shee chaunged hew, ... III. v. 30. 5
seeme too *suddeinly* him to invade. . . . . III. xi. 8. 5
All *suddeinly* a stormy whirlwind blew . . . . . III. xii. 3. 1
All *suddenly* they both upstarted light, ... IV. iii. 35. 6
All *suddenly* they heard a troublous noyes, ... IV. iii. 37. 6
Then *suddenly,* as if their hearts did faile, ... IV. iii. 48. 3
as if one him *suddenly* did call: . . . . . IV. v. 42. 7
Yet durst he not make love so *suddenly,* . . . . . IV. vi. 33. 1
suddenly behind her backe she heard One rushing . . . . . IV. vii. 4. 3
Ne former strength returne so *suddenly,* . . . . . IV. xii. 35. 4
All *suddenly,* ere one can looke aside, ... V. iii. 25. 5
All *sodainely* enflam'd with furious fit . . . . . V. iv. 39. 5
Like one that from his dreame is waked *suddenlye.* . . . . . V. v. 13. 9
All *sodainely* the bed . . . was let adowne to fall . . . . . V. vi. 27. 6
All *sodainely* she saw transfigured Her linnen stole . . . . . V. vii. 13. 4
To rise through all the Temple *sodainely,* . . . . . V. vii. 14. 3
He *suddenly* his net upon her threw, ... V. ix. 14. 2
sodainely, t' avenge him selfe againe . . . . . V. xi. 8. 3
loth My loves owne part to leave so *suddenly,* . . . . . VI. ii. 17. 7
All *sodainely* out of the forrest nere . . . . . VI. iii. 24. 1
When *suddenly,* with twincle of her eye, ... *Am.* xvi. 11
Suddenness. amazed stood At *suddeinnesse* of that unwary sight, ... I. xii. 25. 2
Sude. *See* **Sued.**
Sue. he casts to *sew* the chace . . . . . *Hub.* 743
to *sue* for had ywist, That few have found, ... *Hub.* 893
greatest ones did *sue* to gaine his grace; . . . . . *Ti.* 186
him do *sue* and serve all otherwise: . . . . . *Col.* 786
Since errant armes to *sew* he first began: . . . . . II. ii. 17. 5
if me thou deigne to serve and *sew,* . . . . . II. vii. 9. 1
To her to whom the hevens doe serve and *sew?* . . . . . III. v. 47. 2
two Barkes, . . . contrary courses *sew,* . . . . . IV. ix. 26. 8
To Proteus selfe to *sue* for her discharge: . . . . . IV. xii. 14. 4
To Proteus selfe to *sew* she thought it vaine, ... IV. xii. 29. 1
he meanes no more to *sew* His former quest, ... VI. x. 2. 1
Yet ceast he not to *sew,* . . . . . VI. xi. 5. 5
Dayly when I do seeke and *sew* for peace, ... *Am.* xi. 1
In vaine I seeke and *sew* to her for grace, ... *Am.* xx. 1
Which I no lenger can endure to *sue,* . . . . . *Am.* lvii. 3
every one doth seeke and *sew* to have it, ... *H.B.* 153
Sued. it was a knight which now her *sewde,* . . . . . III. iv. 50. 8
sewd At hand with humble pride . . . . . III. x. 9. 2
worthie is for to be *sewd* unto, ... V. v. 41. 6
sude and sought with all the service dew: . . . . . VI. viii. 20. 6
Suffer. Who will not *suffer* the stormy time, ... *S.C.* F. 15
and *suffer* endles paine. . . . . *Gn.* 408
Ne *suffer* it to house there halfe a day. . . . . *Hub.* 828
suffer her prophaned for to bee . . . . . *T.M.* 566
Nor *suffer* solace to approach him nie, ... *D.* 548
How shall I quite the paynes ye *suffer* . . . . . I. viii. 26. 9
all these sorrowes *suffer* for my sake, ... I. xi. 1. 8
He cast to *suffer* him no more respire, ... I. xi. 28. 7
Besought that Damzell *suffer* him depart, ... II. vi. 36. 8
Ne would he *suffer* Sleepe . . . . . II. vii. 25. 5
we *suffer* this same dotard old . . . . . III. ix. 8. 7
Ne doth he *suffer* her, . . . Out of his sight . . . . . III. x. 3. 7
Ne none can *suffer* to approchen neare: . . . . . III. xi. 22. 5
wonne her will to *suffer* him depart; . . . . . IV. vi. 43. 2
joy that for his sake I *suffer* prisonment. . . . . IV. xii. 7. 9
rather then his love should *suffer* paine, ... V. i. 27. 7

Suffer—*Continued.*
suffer sleepe to seaze His eye-lids sad, ... V. vi. 26. 5
He would not *suffer* her alone to fare, ... VI. v. 8. 2
Ne would him *suffer* once to shrinke asyde, ... VI. vi. 28. 7
suffer her out of her sleepe to wake, ... VI. viii. 37. 8
Doth *suffer* wreck both of her selfe and goods. . . . . *Am.* lvi. 12
Sufferance. Submitting me to your good *sufferance,* . . . . . *S.C.* F. 187
Ne of land, nor fee in *sufferaunce,* . . . . . *S.C.* May 106
for pure pitie of my *sufferance* meeke, ... *D.* 389
To mourne in sorrow and sad *sufferaunce,* . . . . . *D.* 507
hastie heat tempring with *sufferance* wise, ... I. i. 50. 4
soone through *suff'rance* growe to fearefull end: . . . . . II. iv. 34. 4
with pacience and *sufferaunce* sly . . . to subdew: . . . . . II. viii. 47. 7
With sober words, that *sufferance* desired, ... IV. i. 54. 4
through long *sufferance* growing now more great, ... IV. vi. 16. 3
sufferaunce soft, which rigour can abate, ... IV. viii. 1. 7
seeing them through *suffrance* hartned more, ... IV. ix. 34. 5
T' enure them selves to *sufferaunce* thereby, ... V. vii. 9. 4
whose griefe through *suffraunce* sore increast. . . . . VI. v. 39. 9
Suffered. Ne *suffred* him in anie place to rest, ... *Van.* iv. 9
mickle want and hardnesse *suffered;* . . . . . *Hub.* 944
Nought *suffered* he the Ape to give or graunt, ... *Hub.* 1143
Briton Prince . . . *suffered* so much ill, ... I. Pr. 2. 7
suffered them to passen quietly; . . . . . I. v. 34. 8
Then home he *suffred* her for to retyre, ... I. vi. 23. 5
suffred not in wrath his hasty steps to stray. . . . . II. i. 34. 9
suffred not their blowes to byte him nere, ... II. ii. 23. 3
suffred not his wandring feete to slide; . . . . . II. iv. 2. 5
the Blacke Palmer *suffred* still to stond, ... II. vi. 19. 7
Ne *suffred* them to ryse or greater grow; . . . . . II. vii. 47. 8
Ne *suffred* lust his safety to betray. . . . . II. vii. 64. 8
no living wight . . . might *suffred* be to stay: . . . . . II. vii. 66. 3
suffred rash Pyrochles waste his ydle might. . . . . II. viii. 48. 9
Ne *suffred* them to perish through long eld, ... II. ix. 56. 4
Ne *suffred* storme nor frost on them to fall, ... II. xii. 51. 3
suffred no delight To sincke into his sence, ... II. xii. 53. 2
suffered him to passe, all were she loth; . . . . . II. xii. 57. 8
suffred by that same Rich strond to travell, ... III. iv. 20. 7
Ne *suffred* she the Middayes scorching powre, ... III. v. 51. 4
suffred her so carelesly disguiz'd Be overtaken. . . . . III. vi. 19. 5
suffred beastes her body to deflowre, ... III. vii. 49. 7
never *suffred* her to be at rest; . . . . . III. viii. 39. 2
never any knight Is *suffred* here to enter, ... III. ix. 6. 4
Much there he *suffered,* And many perilles past . . . . . III. ix. 41. 7
Why then is Busirane with wicked hand *Suffred,* . . . . . III. xi. 10. 8
Whiles that from heaven he *suffered* exile. . . . . III. xi. 39. 5
Ne *suffred* sleepe to settle in his brest: . . . . . IV. v. 41. 5
suffred that same Dwarfe me to her dongeon drive. . . . . IV. viii. 56. 9
After long sorrowes *suffered* whyleare, ... V. iii. 1. 7
suffred all his secret marke to see: . . . . . V. iii. 34. 6
seeming to have *suffred* mickle wrong, ... V. iv. 5. 3
suffred cruell shipwracke by the way: . . . . . V. iv. 13. 8
never had she *suffred* such despight: . . . . . V. iv. 43. 4
Ne *suffred* slothfull sleepe her eyelids to oppresse. . . . . V. vi. 34. 9
whose wrongs though long She *suffred,* . . . . . V. xi. 1. 8
suffred deadly doole: . . . . . V. xi. 25. 6
onely *suffred* him this wretched life to live. . . . . VI. vi. 36. 9
Yet nathemore him *suffred* to arize; . . . . . VI. viii. 18. 2
Then *suffred* he Disdaine up to arise, ... VI. viii. 25. 5
day nor night he *suffred* him to rest, ... VI. ix. 3. 2
Ne day nor night he *suffred* her to rest, ... VI. xi. 5. 8
Sufferedst. Why *suffredst* thou thy Nephewes deare to fall, . . I. v. 22. 7
Sufferest. How *suffrest* thou such shamefull cruelty . . . . . III. xi. 9. 4
thou *suffrest* neyther gods in sky, Nor men in earth, to rest: . *Epig.* iv. 15
Suffereth. Waking Love *suffereth* no sleepe: . . . . . *U.V.* 10
Ne *suffereth* it uncomely idlenesse . . . . . III. v. 2. 1
Ne *suffereth* it thought of ungentlenesse . . . . . III. v. 2. 3
Ne *suffreth* he the resort of living wight Approch to her, . . . III. ix. 5. 6
Suffering. For *suffering* such abuse as knighthood sham'd, . . II. v. 21. 5
Nor *suffering* the least twinckling sleepe to start . . . . . V. vi. 24. 7
Suffring my hand against my heart to stray; . . . . . V. viii. 13. 3
suffring him to rise, he made him sweare . . . . . VI. i. 43. 5
scarsely *suffring* her infestred wound . . . to be drest. . . . . VI. xi. 24. 6
Suffers. *Suffers* her selfe through sleepe beguild to bee, . . . II. viii. 6. 8
suffers not one looke to glaunce awry, ... *Epith.* 236
Suffice. *Suffice* this hill of our. . . . . *S.C.* Jul. 76
Most wretched wight, whom nothing might *suffise;* . . . . . I. iv. 29. 1
Suffice it heare by signes to understand . . . . . I. xii. 40. 4
All these may not *suffise,* . . . . . II. vii. 9. 4
Untroubled Nature doth her selfe *suffise,* . . . . . II. vii. 15. 4
'*Suffise* it then, thou Money God,' . . . . . II. vii. 39. 1
What may *suffice* to be for meede repayd . . . . . II. viii. 55. 7
Suffise that I have done my dew in place.' . . . . . II. viii. 56. 6
With no contentment can themselves *suffize;* . . . . . *Am.* xxxv. 3
Sufficed. Alas, *suffisde* it not that civile bate . . . . . *Bel.*[1] viii. 9
Suffisd it not that civill warres . . . . . *Bel.*[2] x. 9
'Time and *suffised* fates to former kynd Shall us restore; . . I. ii. 43. 8
When all men had . . . their appetites *suffiz'd,* . . . . . V. iii. 4. 2
being well *suffiz'd* them rested faine. . . . . VI. v. 39. 5
Would have *suffiz'd* the rest for to restraine, ... VII. vi. 29. 8
Sufficeth. 'Ne him *sufficeth* all the wrong and ill, ... V. viii. 19. 1
delight *sufficeth* to deprive Remembrance of all paines . . . *Am.* lxiii. 11
Sufficient. *sufficient* were that hire For losse of thousand lives, II. ix. 5. 8
himselfe thereto did want *sufficient* might.' . . . . . VI. vii. 12. 9
Sufficient worke for one mans simple head, ... *Am.* xxxiii. 7
Suffisance. there him rests in riotous *suffisaunce* . . . . . *Mui.* 207
Suffused. Wiping the teares from her *suffused* eyes, ... III. vii. 10. 3
Sugared. With those sweet *sugred* speaches doo compare, . . . *D.* 299
The *sugred* licour through his melting lips: . . . . . II. v. 33. 6
With *sugred* words and gentle blandishment, ... III. vi. 25. 4

Sundered—*Continued.*
Glad from his companie to be so *sondred;* . . . . V. v. 19. 4
Sundry. Chaunting in shade their *sundrie* (*sundry*[1]) melodie, . *Pet.* iii. 6
Theyr *sondry* colours tourne. . . . . *S.C.* N. 129
With *sundrie* colours paints the sprinckled lay: . . . . *Gn.* 110
sundrie flowers in wilde fieldes gathered; . . . . *Gn.* 132
Chaunted their *sundrie* tunes with sweete consent; . . . . . *Gn.* 226
Not halfe so manie *sundrie* colours . . . . *Mui.* 92
a faire border wrought of *sundrie* flowres, ... *Mui.* 298
All these do florish in their *sundry* kynd, ... *Col.* 452
me needs . . . To sharpe my sence with *sundry* beauties vew, . *Ded.Son.*xvii.7
each one Of *sundrie* shapes, yet all ill-favored: . . . . . . I. i. 15. 7
amiddes His magick bookes, and artes of *sundrie* kindes, . . I. i. 36. 8
chearefull birds of *sundry* kynd . . . . I. vii. 3. 4
Thus as they gan of *sondrie* thinges devise, ... I. x. 12. 1
signes, here sett in *sondrie* place, ... II. Pr. 4. 2
Therein three sisters dwelt of *sundry* sort, ... II. ii. 13. 1
These three in these three rowmes did *sondry* dwell, ... II. ix. 48. 8
dispainted all within With *sondry* colours, ... II. ix. 50. 2
with *sondrie* spoiles she hath been ransacked. . . . . II. x. 23. 9
this sad realme, cut into *sondry* shayres . . . . II. x. 37. 4
did her selfe in *sondry* parts divide, ... II. x. 54. 3
oft annoyd with *sondry* bordragings, ... II. x. 63. 4
maintaynd With mightie deedes their *sondry* governments; . II. x. 74. 4
The other five five *sondry* wayes he sett . . . . II. xi. 7. 1
land-marke seemd to bee, or signe of *sundry* way: . . . . . . II. xi. 35. 9
Of *sondry* thinges faire purpose gan to find, ... III. ii. 4. 2
call Their *sondry* kings to do their homage severall. . . . . III. iii. 32. 9
So beene they three three *sondry* wayes ybent; . . . . III. iv. 47. 5
every sort is in a *sondry* bed Sett by it selfe, ... III. vi. 35. 3
To chaunge her hew, and *sondry* formes to don, ... III. vi. 38. 4
winges it had with *sondry* colours dight, ... III. xi. 47. 6
More *sondry* colours then the proud Pavone Beares . . . . . III. xi. 47. 7
So diversely each one did *sundrie* doubts devise. . . . . . . IV. i. 14. 9
By *sundry* meanes thereto she prickt him forth; . . . . IV. ii. 12. 1
she *sundry* purpose found . . . . IV. vi. 45. 1
Cast into *sundry* shapes by wondrous skill, ... IV. x. 15. 6
shadie seates, and *sundry* flowring bankes, ... IV. x. 25. 4
all their *sundry* kinds, and all their hid abodes. . . . . . . IV. xi. 10. 9
thirty *sundry* streames. . . . . IV. xi. 35. 9
A Chapelet of *sundry* flowers she wore, ... IV. xi. 46. 6
gan of *sundry* newes his store to tell, ... V. ii. 2. 6
sundry battels, which she hath atchieved . . . . V. iv. 33. 6
As *sundry* chaunge her seemed best to ease. . . . . V. vi. 26. 4
(As often falles) of *sundry* things did commen: . . . . . . V. ix. 4. 3
Oftimes their *sundry* powres they did employ, ... VI. v. 14. 1
crowne Of *sundry* flowres with silken ribbands tyde, ... VI. ix. 7. 8
discoursing diversly Of *sundry* things as fell, ... VI. ix. 12. 7
each his *sundrie* sheepe with severall care Gathered together, . VI. ix. 15. 4
Whose *sundry* parts were here too long to tell; . . . . VI. x. 14. 2
some, which did the *sundry* prisoners knowe, ... VI. xi. 11. 5
Of *sundrie* things he purpose gan to faine, ... VI. xi. 39. 2
Tho further asking her of *sundry* things, ... VI. xii. 20. 1
Of *sundry* kindes and *sundry* quality; . . . . VI. xii. 27. 2
According to their *sundry* kinds of features, ... VII. vii. 4. 3
Tenne thousand mores of *sundry* sent and hew, ... VII. vii. 10. 4
her face . . . We changed see and *sundry* formes partake, . . . VII. vii. 50. 7
the *sundry* motions of your Spheares, ... VII. vii. 55. 1
sundry wayes and fashions as clerkes faine, ... VII. vii. 55. 2
To every planet point his *sundry* yeare: . . . . *Am.* lx. 2
Whose *sundrie* parts he from themselves did sever . . . . . *H.L.* 76
To keepe them selves within their *sundrie* raines, ... *H.L.* 88
Sung. *See* **Song.**
Nor yet are *sung* of others for reward, ... *Ti.* 345
sung the prophecie Of his owne death . . . . *Ti.* 594
Of onely her he *sung,* he thought, he writ. . . . . *As.* 64
In sort as she it *sung* I will rehearse. . . . . *As.* 216
after Tityrus first *sung* his lay, ... *Col.* 2
He pip'd, I *sung;* and, when he *sung,* I piped; . . . . *Col.* 76
sung so long untill quite hoarse he grew. . . . . *Col.* 399
late he *sung* unto a scornfull lasse. . . . . *Col.* 419
sung by them with flowry gyrlonds crownd. . . . . *Col.* 643
one *sung* a song of love and jollity. . . . . I. xii. 38. 9
*Sometimes she *sung,* as loud as larke in aire, ... II. vi. 3. 3
All which the sad effects of discord *sung:* . . . . IV. i. 21. 3
Wayting when as the Antheme should be *sung* on hye. . . . . IV. x. 48. 9
in their lower braunches *sung* aloud; . . . . VI. x. 6. 7
mongst so many layes As he hath *sung* of thee . . . . VI. x. 28. 5
a thousand birds . . . That sweetly *sung* . . . . VII. vii. 28. 5
To heare theyr names *sung* in your simple layes, ... *Epith.* 5
But blush to heare her prayses *sung* so loud, ... *Epith.* 163
Sunk. storme impetuous *Sunke* up these riches, ... *Bel.*[2] xiii. 10
'Some in the greedie flouds are *sunke* and drent; . . . . . . *Gn.* 585
His sad dull eies, deepe *sunck* in hollow pits, ... I. viii. 41. 1
Thrise he her reard, and thrise she *sunck* againe, ... II. i. 46. 3
suncke so deepe into their boyling brests, ... II. ii. 32. 2
on this rock are rent, and *sunck* in helples wawes.' . . . . . II. xii. 4. 9
full many had with haplesse doole Beene *suncke,* . . . . . . II. xii. 20. 4
softly *sunck* into her molten hart: . . . . III. ii. 15. 2
into the mynd Of the yong Damzell *sunke,* . . . . III. iii. 57. 2
Sun-like. Soone as the infants *sunlike* shield they saw, ... V. viii. 41. 2
Sunned. Arose, and homeward drove his *sonned* sheepe, ... *S.C.* Ja. 77
Sunning. Mamon in a delve *Sunning* his threasure hore; . . . II. vii. Arg.
Sunny. as Christall gainst the *Sunnie* (*Sunny*) beames, . . . *Bel.* xii. 2
Upon a *sunnie* banke outstretched lay, ... *Van.* iii. 2
shroude in shady leaves from *sonny* rayes, ... *S.C.* Jun. 54
All as the *Sunnye* beame so bright, ... *S.C.* Au. 81
the sad lakes that Phoebus *sunnie* rayes Doo never see, ... *Gn.* 619
Where on a *sunnie* banke the Lambes doo play, ... *Mui.* 402
As *Sunny* beames in fairest somers day, ... *As.* 158

Sunny—*Continued.*
a rich throne, as bright as *sunny* day; . . . . I. iv. 8. 2
face all tand with scorching *sunny* ray, ... I. vi. 35. 4
So fayre a creature yet saw never *sunny* day. . . . . I. ix. 13. 9
Like *sunny* beames threw from her Christall face . . . . . . I. x. 12. 7
he lay upon the *sunny* side Of a great hill, ... I. xi. 4. 5
One sitting ydle on a *sunny* banck, ... II. iii. 6. 2
as the *Sunny* beames do glaunce and glide . . . . II. v. 2. 4
In secrete shadow from the *sunny* ray, ... II. v. 32. 2
Like Phoebus face adornd with *sunny* rayes, ... II. viii. 5. 6
The *sunny* beames which on the billowes bett, ... II. xii. 63. 3
As doth the lilly fresh before the *sunny* ray. . . . . III. vi. 38. 9
before the *sunny* rayes He us'd to slug, ... III. vii. 12. 7
like *sunny* beames, . . . shewe their golden gleames, ... III. ix. 20. 6
'Fresh shadowes, fit to shroud from *sunny* ray; . . . . IV. x. 24. 1
feeles the warmth of *sunny* beames reflection, ... IV. xii. 34. 7
flakes of fire, bright as the *sunny* ray, ... V. v. 8. 3
Whose skirts were bordred with bright *sunny* beames, ... V. ix. 28. 6
Her stately towres and buildings *sunny* sheene, ... V. x. 25. 5
joyous day . . . in *sunny* beames bedight, ... VI. iii. 45. 2
as her manner was on *sunny* day, ... VII. vi. 45. 6
Sunny-bright. when she saw Duessa, *sunny bright,* . . . . . . I. v. 21. 1
Sun-rays. the bright mettall shyning like *Sunne rayes,* . . . . VI. ii. 39. 4
Sun's. The firie *sunnes* both one and other hous: . . . . *Ro.* x. 8
robbing me of the swete *sonnes* sight? . . . . *S.C.* F. 174
The *Sunnes* sad daughters waylde . . . . *Gn.* 198
on them the *Suns* life-giving light Had powred . . . . *Col.* 861
since the time they first tooke the *Sunnes* hight, ... V. Pr. 8. 4
firie-mouthed steedes, which drew The *Sunnes* bright wayne . V. viii. 40. 2
The *Suns* bright beames when he on us doth shyne, ... *H.H.B.* 121
Suns. As when two *sunnes* appeare in the azure skye, ... V. iii. 19. 1
Sunshine. All in a *sunneshine* day, as did befall, ... *S.C.* Ja. 3
Her angels face . . . made a *sunshine* in the shady place; . . I. iii. 4. 8
gins to spread his leafe before the faire *sunshine.* . . . . . . IV. xii. 34. 9
in the *sunshine* of her countenance cleare . . . . V. v. 38. 4
that *sunne-shine* that makes them looke askew: . . . . VI. x. 4. 5
faire *sun-shine,* that makes all skip and daunce; . . . . . . VII. vii. 23. 4
the fayre *sunshine* in somers day; . . . . *Am.* xl. 6
that *sunshine,* when cloudy looks are cleared. . . . . *Am.* xl. 14
Sunshiny. amazd At flashing beames of that *sunshiny* shield, . I. viii. 20. 2
glorious light of her *sunshyny* face, ... I. xii. 23. 2
her *sunshynie* helmet soone unlaced, ... V. v. 11. 8
As they are wont in faire *sunshynie* weather, ... VI. ix. 41. 3
For feare of burning her *sunshyny* face, ... *Epith.* 119
Sup. Death and despeyre did many thereof *sup,* . . . . I. viii. 14. 3
nought was given them to *sup* or dyne, ... V. v. 22. 8
Superfluities. Such *superfluities* they would despise, ... II. vii. 15. 5
Superfluity. Soone growes through humours *superfluitie.* . . *Ro.* xxiii. 12
Vaine feastes, and ydle *superfluity:* . . . . II. xi. 12. 8
belcheth forth his *superfluity,* . . . . II. xii. 3. 8
Superfluous. as *superfluous* flesh did rott, ... I. x. 26. 6
The image of *superfluous* riotize, ... III. i. 33. 6
Supped. a bouzing can, Of which he *supt* so oft, ... I. iv. 22. 7
Supper. which doe byte their hasty *supper* best; . . . . I. i. 23. 4
To thinke how *supper* did them long awaite: . . . . II. x. 77. 7
Supper was shortly dight, ... III. i. 51. 1
Supper was dight; . . . . III. ix. 25. 6
supper readie dight they to it fell . . . . VI. ix. 17. 7
Supper-time. rest himselfe till *supper time* befell; . . . . . VI. ix. 17. 4
Supplant. not onely sought . . . To overthrow, but to *supplant* by slight: . . . . VI. v. 13. 5
Supplanted. *Supplanted* by fine falshood and faire guile; . . . *Hub.* 788
Suppled. The flesh therewith shee *suppled* and did steepe, . . III. v. 33. 6
Suppliant. 'Fayr Sir,' said then the Palmer *suppliaunt,* . . . . II. viii. 16. 1
Still holding up her *suppliant* hands on hye, ... V. ii. 26. 4
her *suppliant* hands, those hands of gold, ... V. ii. 26. 6
An humble *suppliant* loe! I lowely fly, ... VII. vii. 14. 2
Suppliant's. Pleaseth you ponder your *Suppliants* plaint, . . . *S.C.* F. 151
Suppliants. Whose glorie is to aide all *suppliants* pore, ... V. i. 4. 6
often treat for pardon and remission To *suppliants,* . . . . . V. ix. 32. 4
Supplied. repaired have her tackles spent, And wants *supplide;* . . . . I. xii. 42. 7
Arvirage his brothers place *supplyde* . . . . II. x. 51. 6
Whose emptie place the mightie Oberon Doubly *supplide,* . . II. x. 75. 9
twise fowre hundreth yeares shalbe *supplide,* . . . . III. iii. 44. 5
Supplide her sobbing breaches with sad complement. . . . . . III. iv. 35. 9
She in my stead *supplide* his bestiall desire.' . . . . IV. vii. 19. 9
Art, playing second natures part, *supplyed* it. . . . . IV. x. 21. 9
thought certainely To have *supplyde* the first, ... VI. viii. 9. 9
Supplies. Out of her mountaines ministred *supplies;* . . . . . *Gn.* 506
I hate the Sea, because it teares *supplyes.* . . . . *D.* 406
supplyes The substaunces of natures fruitfull progenyes. . . . III. vi. 36. 8
It strength to me *supplies,* . . . . VI. Pr. 1. 9
Supply. 'Let stremes of teares *supply* the place of sleepe; . . . *S.C.* Au. 163
not a lambe of all their flockes *supply* . . . . *Hub.* 316
The breaches of her singults did *supply.* . . . . *T.M.* 232
her sorrow to *supplie,* . . . . *T.M.* 537
she that did my vitall powres *supplie,* . . . . *D.* 437
He did *supply* their want, ... I. x. 43. 9
money can thy wantes at will *supply?* . . . . II. vii. 11. 2
His sonne Rivall' his dead rowme did *supply;* . . . . II. x. 34. 1
native corage unto him *supply,* . . . . III. vii. 3. 2
whilest his breath did strength to him *supply,* . . . . III. vii. 24. 7
Unfit faire Ladies service to *supply;* . . . . III. ix. 5. 2
with vaine hope his spirits faint *supply,* . . . . III. x. 26. 7
with thy punishment his penance shalt *supply.'* . . . . IV. i. 53. 9
This hand may helpe, or succour ought *supplie,* . . . . IV. vi. 8. 7
well she wist this knight came succour to *supply.* . . . . . . V. x. 19. 9
Be lacke of children to *supply* your place, ... VI. iv. 35. 2
each sought to *supply* the office of her page. . . . . VI. v. 30. 9

Supply—*Continued.*
With secret ayde doest succour and *supply*, . . . *Epith.* 402
Cast to *supply* the same, and to enstall . . . *H.H.L.* 103
Support. doe the temple of the Gods *support*, . . . II. iii. 28. 2
Which with a staffe . . . She did *support*, . . . II. xi. 23. 8
With which his daughter doth him still *support*; . . . V. ii. 5. 6
soveraine grace, with which her royall crowne She doth *support*, V. viii. 17. 5
through *support* of count'nance proud . . . VI. ii. 23. 8
unable to *support* So huge a burden . . . VI. viii. 16. 6
Supported. tyrannie is with strange ayde *supported*. . . . *Hub.* 1121
him *supported* standing neare. . . . VI. viii. 25. 9
Supported her like to their soveraigne Queene: . . . VII. vii. 34. 6
Supports. Onely *supports* herselfe for meate of wormes; . . . *Ro.* xxviii. 8
Supports his credite and his countenaunce. . . . *Hub.* 668
Supports the praise of noble Poesie; . . . *T.M.* 574
Supposed. Duessa . . . Called Fidess', and so *supposd* to be, . . I. iv. 2. 4
where him that crafty Squyre *Supposd* to be. . . . II. i. 13. 4
supposed him a person meet . . . II. iii. 11. 5
wrong Which he *supposed* donne to Florimell, . . . III. vii. 35. 6
(As they *suppos'd*) . . . IV. ix. 36. 9
many a one *suppos'd* to be a mayd: . . . V. iii. 28. 3
Supposeth. when as she most *supposeth* Her selfe assurd, . . . *Am.* lviii. 3
Suppress. As raging flames who striveth to *suppresse*.' . . . I. ii. 34. 6
the weak to strengthen, and the strong *suppresse*. . . . II. iv. 2. 9
their gardins did deface; . . . their Cabinets *suppresse*; . . . II. xii. 83. 7
Shall well defend, and Saxons powre *suppresse*; . . . III. iii. 33. 2
Her hard pursewd, and sought for to *suppresse*. . . . III. vii. 37. 5
all men busie to *suppresse* the flame, . . . III. x. 16. 2
did the rest with grievous sighes *suppresse*, . . . III. x. 25. 8
faithfull friendship doth them both *suppresse*, . . . IV. ix. 2. 3
I will *suppresse*, that they no more may raine; . . . V. ii. 38. 7
meaning to *suppresse* both forged guile And open force: . . . V. vii .7. 3
In vaine he seeketh others to *suppresse*, . . . VI. i. 41. 5
the more the Knight Did him *suppresse*, . . . VI. xii. 31. 6
Suppressed. Under his Lordly foot him proudly hath *suppresst*. I. iii. 19. 9
he it was, that earst would have *suppresst* Faire Una; . . . I. vi. 40. 7
when death hath both *suppresst*, . . . II. i. 59. 5
long bene underkept and down *suppresst*, . . . II. xi. 32. 2
Mote easie be *suppresst* with little thing; . . . VI. vi. 8. 4
Thus was this Monster . . . *suppresst* and tamed, . . . VI. xii. 38. 2
Suppressing. Advancing vertue and *suppressing* vice. . . . *Col.* 323
suppressing fury mad, They gan abstaine . . . II. ii. 28. 7
still *suppressing*, gan of her inquire, . . . VI. viii. 18. 3
Surbate. *See* **Surbet.**
surbate sore Their tender feete . . . III. iv. 34. 5
Surbet. *See* **Surbate.**
Espye a traveiler with feet *surbet*, . . . II. ii. 22. 7
Surcease. peace, When wars doe *surcease*: . . . *S.C.* Ap. 125
surcease, good Dame, and hence depart.' . . . *Hub.* 1221
Ne ought the more their mightie strokes *surceasse*. . . . III. i. 23. 2
He mote *surceasse* his suit, . . . III. iv. 52. 6
instead of praying them *surcease*, . . . Bidding them fight . . IV. ii. 19. 4
would them faine from battell to *surceasse*, . . . IV. ix. 32. 8
Causd all her people to *surcease* from fight; . . . V. iv. 45. 5
Ne secretly from thought of fell revenge *surceasse*: . . . VI. vi. 43. 9
neither day nor weeke He would *surceasse*, . . . VI. vii. 13. 9
But mine, no price nor prayer may *surcease*. . . . *Am.* xi. 14
Surceased. Them yielded ready passage, and their rage *surceast*. III. iv. 31. 9
Were it not good that wrong were then *surceast*, . . . V. ii. 37. 8
the which now she Had long *surceast*, . . . V. vii. 25. 6
Surceaseth. when the cause . . . Removed is, th' effect *surceaseth* still. . . . VI. vi. 14. 4
Surcharged. *Surcharg'd* with wine, were heedlesse and ill-hedded, . . . IV. i. 3. 4
surcharg'd with spoile and theft: . . . IV. vii. 32. 5
Foure charged two, and two *surcharged* one; . . . IV. ix. 30. 5
Sure. right worthie *sure* . . . of immortall dayes, . . . *Bel.*[2] xiv. 6
if that time make ende of things so *sure*, . . . *Ro.* vii. 13
Upon the same to set foundation *sure*? . . . *Ro.* xxiv. 14
As *sure* it will, . . . *To his Booke* 6
Bold *sure* he was, and worthie spirite bore, . . . *Gn.* 437
(Both two *sure* bands in friendship to be tide) . . . *Hub.* 54
be thou *sure* one not to lacke or long. . . . *Hub.* 501
'Now *sure*, and by my hallidome, . . . *Hub.* 545
he was *sure* A noble Gentleman . . . *Hub.* 684
sure his honestie Got him small gaines, . . . *Hub.* 849
all that els did come were *sure* to faile. . . . *Hub.* 1203
Sure gates, sweete gardens, stately galleries, . . . *Ti.* 95
he in time would *sure* prove such . . . *Mui.* 31
Yet *sure* those wings were fairer . . . *Mui.* 104
Be *sure* that they shall have no long endurance, . . . *D.* 501
sure full deare of all he loved was, . . . *As.* 201
'Right well he *sure* did plaine, . . . *Col.* 173
I weened *sure* he was our God alone, . . . *Col.* 773
nothing ever may redeeme, . . . so *sure* a gage, . . . *Ded. Son.* vii. 7
Strangle her, els she *sure* will strangle thee.' . . . I. i. 19. 4
Fly to your fayth for . . . *sure* ayde: . . . I. i. 52. 6
Nothing is *sure* that growes on earthly grownd; . . . I. ix. 11. 5
dearely *sure* her love was to me bent, . . . I. ix. 14. 3
Prince Arthur gave a boxe of Diamond *sure*, . . . I. ix. 19. 1
am I now in safetie *sure*,' (quoth he) . . . I. ix. 26. 1
in his eternall booke of fate Are written *sure*, . . . I. ix. 42. 5
Dead was it *sure*, as *sure* as death in deed, . . . I. xi. 12. 3
Where she enjoyes *sure* peace for evermore, . . . II. i. 2. 8
as *sure* as hound The stricken Deare doth chalenge . . . II. i. 12. 8
be ye *sure*, he dearely shall abyde, . . . II. i. 20. 3
by the knighthood which they *sure* had sworn, . . . II. ii. 27. 7
great *sure* shal be thy meed, . . . II. iii. 14. 6
(and *sure* I feare it ill) . . . II. iii. 44. 3
sure he was a man of mickle might, . . . II. iv. 7. 1

Sure—*Continued.*
Great glory and gay spoile, *sure* hast thou gott, . . . II. iv. 45. 6
Great mercy, *sure*, for to enlarge a thrall, . . . II. v. 18. 3
For *sure* yt would deceive thy labor and thy might' . . . II. viii. 21. 9
sure I rew his pitteous plight.' . . . II. viii. 24. 5
'Now, felon, *sure* I read, . . . II. viii. 30. 2
no earthly thing is *sure*. . . . II. ix. 21. 9
What ever bee the cause, it *sure* beseemes you ill.' . . . II. ix. 37. 9
setled there in *sure* establishment. . . . II. xi. 2. 5
Then thought the Prince all peril *sure* was past, . . . II. xi. 43. 6
'Love have I *sure*,' (quoth she) 'but Lady none; . . . III. i. 28. 2
as *sure* I read By knowen signes . . . III. ii. 33. 2
'Great pitty *sure* that ye be so forlorne . . . III. vi. 21. 3
did her footing trace So *sure* and swiftly, . . . III. vii. 23. 8
how she might be *sure* that I would never swerve? . . . III. vii. 53. 9
ill they seemed *sure* avizd to bee, . . . III. vii. 57. 8
sure, I weene, the hardest hart of stone . . . III. viii. 1. 7
thereby deeming *sure* the thing as donne, . . . III. viii. 3. 3
turne his steede about, or *sure* he should be dedd. . . . III. viii. 17. 9
if not her *sure* decay: . . . III. viii. 49. 6
sure a foole I doe him firmely hold, . . . III. ix. 8. 4
From Limbo lake him late escaped *sure* would say. . . . III. x. 54. 9
Be *sure* that nought may save thee from to dy . . . III. xii. 35. 4
Misdeeming *sure* that her those flames did burne; . . . III. xii. 45. 5
For *sure* the fayrest Florimell him seemed To him was fallen IV. ii. 8. 3
vertue is the band that bindeth harts most *sure*. . . . IV. ii. 29. 9
The soule had *sure* out of his bodie rived, . . . IV. iii. 18. 3
Yet dead he was not, yet he *sure* did die, . . . IV. iii. 30. 6
weened *sure* He gan to faint toward the battels end, . . . IV. iii. 32. 6
sure . . . It would have cleft his braine . . . IV. iii. 34. 5
They weened *sure* the warre was at an end; . . . IV. iii. 35. 2
Whom *sure* he weend, that he some-wher tofore had eide. . . IV. iv. 7. 9
Him needeth *sure* a golden pen, I weene, . . . IV. v. 12. 2
Some gladfull newes and *sure* intelligence, . . . IV. vi. 34. 4
of us three to morrow he will *sure* eate one.' . . . IV. vii. 13. 9
A foule and loathly creature *sure* in sight, . . . IV. viii. 24. 1
noble kind at first was *sure* of heavenly seed. . . . IV. viii. 33. 9
sure, had not his massie yron mace . . . IV. viii. 43. 6
cause of feare, *sure*, had she none . . . IV. ix. 19. 1
which I found *sure* lockt and chained fast. . . . IV. x. 11. 3
sooth it was not *sure* for womanish shame, . . . IV. x. 41. 4
sure she weend it was some one of those, . . . IV. xii. 26. 8
'Now *sure* this doubtfull causes right . . . V. i. 25. 1
sure they ween'd she was escapt away; . . . V. ii. 25. 2
We are not *sure* they would so long remaine: . . . V. ii. 36. 6
'Now *sure*' . . . I will not rest till I her might doe trie, . . . V. iv. 34. 1
did waite Uppon her person for her *sure* defence, . . . V. v. 4. 4
with sweet love and *sure* benevolence, . . . V. v. 33. 4
with *sure* promise of her good endevour . . . V. v. 35. 2
'Unworthy *sure*' (quoth he) 'of better day, . . . V. v. 39. 5
Which she would *sure* performe, betide her wele or wo. . . . V. vi. 23. 9
For *sure* he weend that this his present guest Was Artegall, . V. vi. 34. 1
else he *sure* had left not one alive, . . . V. vii. 36. 8
That one *sure* stroke he might unto him reach, . . . V. viii. 37. 4
she did *sure* The peoples great compassion unto her allure. . V. ix. 38. 8
This well I wote, that *sure* she is as great, . . . V. x. 1. 5
sure he had her slaine, had she not turnd her way. . . . V. xi. 26. 9
'She liveth *sure* and sound, . . . V. xi. 38. 8
She death shall *sure* aby.' . . . V. xi. 40. 6
'Now *sure* and by my life, . . . V. xi. 41. 1
sure to me her faith she first did plight . . . V. xi. 50. 1
Of colour rustie-browne, but *sure* and strong; . . . V. xii. 14. 6
She deem'd him *sure* to have bene dead on ground; . . . VI. i. 34. 7
That *sure* he deem'd him borne of noble race: . . . VI. ii. 5. 5
Faire was the Ladie, *sure*, . . . VI. ii. 16. 7
'Now *sure*,' . . . 'and right, Me seemes, that him befell . . . VI. ii. 23. 5
sure he weend him borne of noble blood, . . . VI. ii. 24. 6
In hope he *sure* would prove a doughtie knight: . . . VI. ii. 36. 8
as *sure* to them he seemed, A courteous Knight . . . VI. iii. 13. 1
whom *sure* he thought By this quite slaine . . . VI. vi. 37. 6
'Now *sure* ye well have earn'd your meed; . . . VI. vii. 13. 2
Thought *sure* have pownded him to powder soft, . . . VI. viii. 15. 3
sure I weene, . . . VI. viii. 29. 1
soothly *sure* she was full fayre of face, . . . VI. ix. 9. 1
Thought *sure* t' avenge his grudge, . . . VI. ix. 43. 9
His dearest joynt he *sure* had broken quight. . . . VI. ix. 44. 5
so *sure* she was, she worthy was . . . VI. x. 25. 6
Sayd Calidore: 'Now *sure* it yrketh mee, . . . VI. x. 29. 2
here on earth is no *sure* happinesse, . . . VI. xi. 1. 7
do surely prieve That yond same is your daughter *sure*, . . . VI. xii. 18. 9
sure thy worth no lesse then hers doth seem to showe. . . . VII. vi. 32. 9
Had she not so doon, *sure* I had bene slayne; . . . *Am.* xvi. 13
Fayre ye be *sure*, but cruell and unkind, . . . *Am.* lvi. 1
Fayre be ye *sure*, but proud and pittilesse, . . . *Am.* lvi. 5
Fayre be ye *sure*, but hard and obstinate, . . . *Am.* lvi. 9
sure of all that in this mortall frame Contained is, . . . *H.L.* 113
they *sure* did deeme Them heavenly borne, . . . *Proth.* 61
For *sure* they did not seeme . . . *Proth.* 64
Surely. '*Surely* . . . it likes me wondrous well; . . . *Hub.* 95
'Now *surely* brother (said the Foxe anon) . . . *Hub.* 124
this verse Shall live, and *surely* it shall live . . . *Ti.* 254
Did *surely* deeme the victorie his due: . . . *Mui.* 319
Els *surely* death should be no punishment, . . . *D.* 362
he *surely* is A right good knight, . . . II. i. 19. 4
surely deeme it to bee yvie trew: . . . II. xii. 61. 5
she had him *surely* slayne: . . . III. iii. 55. 8
sith her dedd He *surely* dempt, . . . III. viii. 3. 7
would *surely* say It was her selfe . . . III. viii. 9. 3
I *surely* doubt, thou maist aread . . . III. viii. 47. 5
'Extremely mad the man I *surely* deeme, . . . III. ix. 6. 7

Surely—*Continued.*
ye would have *surely* thought . . . III. xii. 46. *or.* 1
him she *surely* thought To be a man, . . . IV. i. 8. 1
So did they *surely* during all their dayes, . . . IV. ii. 54. 1
As if the conquest his he *surely* wist. . . . IV. iii. 5. 3
Some newborne wight ye would him *surely* weene; . . . IV. iii. 23. 5
she should *surely* beare the bell away; . . . IV. v. 13. 6
bad him rise, or *surely* he should die. . . . IV. vi. 23. 6
Such thraldome or such freedome let it *surely* be. . . . IV. xii. 10. 9
said, that *surely* Florimell it was, . . . V. iii. 17. 6
all on fire ye would her *surely* weene; . . . V. v. 8. 5
therefore ment him *surely* to have slaine: . . . V. vi. 34. 5
More happie mother would her *surely* weene . . . V. x. 7. 7
He had him *surely* cloven quite in twaine: . . . V. xi. 10. 6
whom all the bands . . . had *surely* bound, . . . V. xii. 2. 2
'That *surely* is that Beast' . . . VI. i. 10. 1
Ne wote I *surely* whether her he yet have fond.' . . . VI. i. 16. 9
Ne *surely* thus unarm'd I likely were; . . . VI. ii. 8. 3
Or *surely* borne of some Heroicke sead, . . . VI. ii. 25. 8
'Glad would I *surely* be, . . . To have thy presence . . . VI. ii. 37. 1
She made him think it *surely* was his owne; . . . VI. iv. 38. 6
Where I had *surely* long ere this bene dead, . . . VI. v. 29. 2
Else had he *surely* there bene slaine, . . . VI. vii. 45. 9
then *surely* thought That slaine he was, . . . VI. vii. 50. 2
'*Surely*, my sonne,' (then answer'd he againe) . . . VI. ix. 20. 1
He thus replyde: 'Now *surely*, syre, I find, . . . VI. ix. 27. 3
So it *surely* wrought With this faire Mayd, . . . VI. ix. 45. 6
do *surely* prieve That yond same is your daughter sure, . . . VI. xii. 18. 8
Surer. often to him calling to take *surer* hould. . . . III. xi. 34. 9
his well-learned speare Tooke *surer* hould, . . . VI. vii. 11. 2
Surest. eke of *surest* steele that may be fownd, . . . II. iii. 15. 8
The *surest* signe, whereby ye may her know, . . . III. v. 5. 8
he tooke a muzzel strong Of *surest* yron, . . . VI. xii. 34. 3
Surfeit. *Surfeat,* misdiet, and unthriftie waste, . . . II. xi. 12. 7
Surgeon. (This Tryphon is the seagods *surgeon* hight,) . . . IV. xi. 6. 6
Surgery. quite they seem'd past helpe of *surgery;* . . . VI. vi. 5. 5
Surges. their crooked keeles the *surges* clave. . . . *Gn.* 568
'These be the hills (quoth he) the *surges* hie, . . . *Col.* 240
seemd amid the *surges* for to fleet, . . . *Col.* 286
the raging *surges* reard Up to the skyes, . . . II. xii. 2. 8
having vewd awhile the *surges* hore . . . III. iv. 7. 4
To rule his tides, and *surges* to uprere, . . . IV. xi. 52. 3
Doth frie with fome above the *surges* hore. . . . V. ii. 15. 8
she her selfe in stormie *surges* tost; . . . VI. xii. 1. 5
Surging. From *surging* gulf two Monsters streight were brought, I. v. 38. 3
The *surging* waters like a mountaine rise, . . . II. xii. 21. 6
with her least word can asswage The *surging* seas, . . . IV. xi. 50. 5
Surly. Sike *syrlye* shepheards han we none, . . . *S.C.* Jul. 203
Surmise. Provokt with Wrath and Envyes false *surmise,* . . . I. v. 46. 7
The more to be true Florimell he did *surmize.* . . . V. iii. 18. 9
Surmises. The vaine *surmizes,* the distrustfull showes, . . . *H.L.* 260
Surmount. *Surmount* the toppes even of the hiest hilles, . . . *Bel.*[1] vi. 6
all earthly Princes she doth far *surmount.* . . . II. x. 1. 9
though their numbers do much more *surmount,* . . . IV. xii. 2. 8
Surmounts. onely God *surmountes* the force of ty[me,] . . . *Bel.*[1] i. 13
Sith onely God *surmounts* all times decay, . . . *Bel.*[2] i. 13
perfect gold *surmounts* the meanest brasse. . . . IV. ix. 2. 9
Surname. Rhodoricke, whose *surname* shal be Great, . . . III. iii. 45. 1
To prove her *surname* true, that she imposed has. . . . V. viii. 49. 9
Surpass. did farre *surpas* The rest in honest mirth, . . . *Hub.* 34
doth all afore him far *surpasse;* . . . *Col.* 417
He all his Peeres in beauty did *surpas,* . . . I. v. 37. 3
this great Citty that does far *surpas,* . . . I. x. 58. 8
beauty doth her bounty far *surpasse;* . . . III. ix. 4. 5
So much her malice did her might *surpas,* . . . IV. i. 30. 1
did in strength most sorts of men *surpas,* . . . V. xii. 15. 3
Nor spirit, nor Angell, though they man *surpas,* . . . *H.H.L.* 143
Surpassed. him in strength and skill the Prince *surpast,* . . . II. viii. 49. 8
So he *surpassed* his sex masculine, . . . III. xi. 4. 3
Surpasseth. The worke of heavens will *surpasseth* humaine thought.' . . . V. iv. 27. 9
Surpassing. which by *surpassing* skill Phidias did make . . . IV. x. 40. 3
high worths *surpassing* paragon . . . *Am.* lxvi. 5
Surplus. looke what *surplus* did of each remaine, . . . V. ii. 31. 8
Surplusage. Take what thou please of all this *surplusage;* . . . II. vii. 18. 7
Surprisal. efte in Dolons subtile *surprysall.* . . . *Gn.* 536
Surprise. where none might them *surprize;* . . . *Hub.* 576
Lay lurking covertly him to *surprise;* . . . *Mui.* 386
that disdainfull beast . . . him suddein doth *surprize;* . . . I. iii. 19. 7
hidden lyes unwares him to *surpryse?* . . . II. iv. 17. 3
Acrasia, whom we must *surprise,* . . . II. xii. 69. 8
Now singing sweetly to *surprize* her sprights, . . . III. x. 8. 3
hee too simple ever to *surprise* The jolly Paridell, . . . III. x. 20. 3
heavie sleepe the eye-lids did *surprise* Of Britomart, . . . IV. vii. 3. 7
time did offer meanes him sleeping to *surprize.* . . . VI. vii. 22. 9
did runne at Pastorell her to *surprize;* . . . VI. x. 34. 7
Surprised. him disarmed, . . . Unwares *surprised,* . . . I. vii. 51. 4
Castles *surprizd,* great cities sackt and brent: . . . II. vii. 13. 8
a litle creeping sleepe *Surprisd* her sence: . . . III. ii. 47. 7
He was *surprisd,* and buried under beare, . . . III. iii. 11. 2
She was asham'd to be so loose *surpriz'd;* . . . III. vi. 19. 2
as if suddein great affright Had them *surprizd.* . . . III. ix. 23. 5
Yet now he was *surpriz'd:* . . . IV. ii. 10. 6
Surprized was, and to Grantorto brought, . . . V. xi. 39. 8
him with treacherie And traynes having *surpriz'd,* . . . V. xii. 40. 9
He was unwares *surprisd* in subtile bands . . . VI. ix. 11. 6
Surquidry. puffed up with passing *surquedrie,* . . . *Van.* viii. 7
Then paye you the price of your *surquedrie,* . . . *S.C.* F. 49
Transformd to fish for their bold *surquedry;* . . . II. xii. 31. 5
them enraged with fell *surquedry:* . . . II. xii. 39. 4

Surquidry—*Continued.*
Vyle rancor to avoid and cruel *surquedry.* . . . III. i. 13. 9
tread downe the victors *surquedry.* . . . III. iii. 46. 9
in their raging *surquedry* disdaynd . . . III. iv. 7. 6
Might wanting measure moveth *surquedry.* . . . III. x. 2. 5
he boasted, in his *surquedrie,* . . . V. ii. 30. 4
with the weight of their own *surquedry,* They both are fallen, *Com. Son.* iv. 5
Surrender. ripe age bad him *surrender* late His life, . . . II. x. 13. 8
Surrendered. She it *surrendred,* ne her selfe would lenger vex. . II. x. 20. 9
Till he *surrendered* Realme and life to fate. . . . II. x. 45. 5
Survey. takes *survey,* with curious busie eye, . . . *Mui.* 171
did *survay* his goodly company; . . . III. xi. 23. 3
Surview. Of custome for to *survewe* his grownd, . . . *S.C.* F. 145
till they the top *survew,* . . . *Gn.* 221
Surviewed. Both land and sea in roundnes had *survew'd,* . . . *Ro.* viii. 3
Which it *survewd* as hils doen lower ground; . . . II. ix. 45. 4
Survive. Needes must he all eternitie *survive,* . . . *Ro.* Env. 7
Through the worlds endles ages to *survive.* . . . *Gn.* 56
after death no token doth *survive* . . . *Ti.* 353
ye, who so ye be, that still *survive,* . . . *Col.* 644
Pylian syre, which did *survive* Three ages, . . . II. ix. 48. 4
had not grace thee blest, thou shouldest not *survive.* . . . II. xi. 30. 9
he victour did *survive,* . . . III. ix. 43. 1
Of thine owne spirit which doth in me *survive,* . . . IV. ii. 34. 7
is she thrall, or doth she not *survive?'* . . . V. xi. 38. 7
When she so faire a daughter saw *survive,* . . . VI. xii. 21. 7
Yet many of their stemme long after did *survive:* . . . VII. vi. 2. 9
Survived. now that he them *surviv'd.* . . . II. ix. 57. 5
Into his other brethren that *survived,* . . . IV. iii. 13. 8
Suspect. doubtfull words made that redoubted knight *Suspect* her truth: . . . I. i. 53. 6
walketh forth without *suspect* of crime. . . . I. vi. 13. 4
makes him alway *Suspect* her truth, . . . III. ix. 5. 4
Dissemblaunce and *Suspect* Marcht in one rancke, . . . III. xii. 14. 1
Jealous *suspect* as true untruely drad: . . . V. vii. 38. 7
Without *suspect* of ill or daungers . . . VI. iii. 23. 9
Suspended. a rocky hill Over the sea *suspended* dreadfully, . . . II. x. 56. 4
Suspense. hung all this while *suspence,* . . . IV. vi. 34. 2
stood still mute, as one in great *suspence;* . . . V. vi. 9. 7
Did hang in long *suspence* what would ensew, . . . VII. vii. 57. 6
Suspicion. as one carelesse of *suspition,* . . . *Com. Son.* i. 5
rang'd each where without *suspition.* . . . *Mui.* 376
Suspition of friend, nor feare of foe . . . *Mui.* 377
their trew loves without *suspition* tell abrode. . . . III. vi. 42. 9
that more *suspicion* encreast, . . . III. viii. 49. 7
Suspicious. Matter of doubt and dread *suspitious,* . . . III. x. 59. 5
Sustain. such like paine . . . I will the same *sustaine;* . . . *Hub.* 288
true wisedome to *sustaine,* . . . *T.M.* 80
Whylom the pillours of th' earth did *sustaine,* . . . *Ded. Son.* i. 2
nought so wondrous puissaunce might *sustaine:* . . . I. xi. 43. 5
All Faery lond does peaceably *sustene.* . . . II. ii. 40. 5
nothing might *sustaine* his furious forse: . . . II. v. 23. 2
In her loose lap, it softly to *sustayn,* . . . II. vi. 14. 7
upbeare The massy roofe, and riches huge *sustayne;* . . . II. vii. 43. 6
neither could his mightie puissaunce *sustaine.* . . . II. viii. 42. 9
Unhable their encounter to *sustaine;* . . . II. ix. 14. 4
combrous conflict which they did *sustaine,* . . . II. ix. 17. 5
Next whom Morindus did the crowne *sustayne;* . . . II. x. 43. 3
mightily that scepter did *sustayne,* . . . II. x. 75. 3
That goodly frame from ruine to *sustaine:* . . . II. xi. 15. 5
Nor bounds nor banks his headlong ruine may *sustayne.* . . . II. xi. 18. 9
doth himselfe with sorrow new *sustaine,* . . . III. x. 60. 2
When her weake feete could scarcely her *sustaine,* . . . III. xii. 21. 6
plate nor mayle, . . . could once *sustaine* the hideous stowre, . IV. iii. 15. 5
neither could the others force *sustaine;* . . . IV. iv. 18. 2
For so great travell as you doe *sustaine!* . . . V. x. 21. 5
Whenas the Carle no longer could *sustaine,* . . . VI. i. 22. 2
That yron heart it hardly could *sustaine:* . . . VI. i. 30. 6
neither could the others stroke *sustaine,* . . . VI. i. 33. 7
An infant, weake a kingdome to *sustaine,* . . . VI. ii. 28. 7
her did *sustaine* With carefull hands, . . . VI. iii. 28. 5
such as hee Did use his feeble body to *sustaine,* . . . VI. v. 39. 2
'Aread, good Sire, some counsell that may us *sustaine.'* . . . VI. vi. 13. 9
Sith he likewise did wrong by him *sustaine,* . . . VI. vii. 22. 7
Rather then once his burden to *sustaine:* . . . VI. vii. 46. 7
also to *sustayne* thy selfe with food. . . . *Am.* ii. 8
lacking it, they cannot lyfe *sustayne;* . . . *Am.* xxxv. 5
Enough it is for one man to *sustaine* The stormes, . . . *Am.* xlvi. 13
With light thereof I doe my selfe *sustayne,* . . . *Am.* lxxxvii. 11
whose sight cannot *sustaine* The Suns bright beames . . . *H.H.B.* 120
Sustained. *Sustein'd* the shocke of common enmitie; . . . *Ro.* xxi. 4
the best helpe, which chiefly him *sustain'd,* . . . *Hub.* 853
debate, Which that straunge knight for him *sustained* had, . . . II. viii. 54. 7
on either side she was *sustained* Of two smal grooms, . . . IV. xi. 25. 1
For the rebuke which she *sustain'd* that day, . . . V. iv. 47. 2
Sustenance. Furies milke for *sustenaunce* Of his weake infancie, *T.M.* 261
Sute, -r. *See* **Suit, -or.**
Swaddling. thou slepst in tender *swadling* band, . . . I. x. 65. 7
Swain. *See* **Shepherd-swain.**
A shepheards *swaine,* saye, did thee sing . . . *To his Booke* 9
With that sprong forth a naked *swayne* . . . *S.C.* Mar. 79
I her shepherds *swayne,* . . . *S.C.* Ap. 98
The base kinred of so simple *swaine.* . . . *S.C.* May 271
What, ho! thou jollye shepheards *swayne,* . . . *S.C.* Jul. 5
to holden chat With seely shepherds *swayne,* . . . *S.C.* Jul. 30
then, sitte thee downe, *swayne:* . . . *S.C.* Au. 49
The shepheardes *swayne* you cannot wel ken, . . . *S.C.* S. 42
Ne would she scorne the simple shepheards *swaine;* . . . *S.C.* N. 97
in derring-doe compare With shepheards *swayne* . . . *S.C.* D. 44
like a handsome *swaine* it him became. . . . *Hub.* 242

Swain—*Continued.*
Whether he shepheard be, or shepheards *swaine,* . . . *Ti.* 234
A sclender *swaine,* excelling far each other, . . . *As.* 15
another *swaine* Of gentle wit . . . *As.* Interl. 217
I, poore *swaine,* of many, greatest crosse! . . . *Col.* 18
a bonie *swaine,* That Cuddy hight, . . . *Col.* 80
He whilest he lived was the noblest *swaine,* . . . *Col.* 440
Thrise happie do I hold thee, noble *swaine,* . . . *Col.* 552
Ne is there shepheard, ne yet shepheards *swaine,* . . . *Col.* 819
being to that *swaine* too cruell hard, . . . *Col.* 909
grace let her vouchsafe to grant To simple *swaine,* . . . *Col.* 940
'Rise, rise! unhappy *Swaine,* . . . I. ii. 4. 6
Whose fellowship seemd far unfitt for warlike *swaine.* . . . I. iv. 37. 9
Therion, a loose unruly *swayne,* . . . I. vi. 21. 6
nathemore would that corageous *swayne* To her yeeld passage . I. viii. 13. 6
the Shepherds *swaine* A Lyon and a Tigre doth espye, . . . II. ix. 14. 7
yielding succour to that cursed *Swaine,* . . . II. xi. 28. 5
How to take life from that dead-living *swayne,* . . . II. xi. 44. 7
Some goodly *swayne* of honorable place, . . . II. xii. 79. 2
So deepe the deadly feare of that foule *swaine* . . . III. iv. 49. 2
'Now certes, *swaine,*' (saide he) 'such one, I weene, . . . III. v. 6. 1
Yt was a goodly *Swaine,* and of great might, . . . III. vii. 29. 4
knight he was not, but a boastfull *swaine* . . . III. viii. 11. 6
the fresh *Swayne* would not his leasure dwell, . . . III. x. 38. 7
There dwels he ever, miserable *swaine,* . . . III. x. 60. 5
seemd of ryper yeares then th' other *Swayne,* . . . III. xii. 9. 2
Yet was that other *swayne* this elders syre, . . . III. xii. 9. 3
full many a warlike *swaine* Assembled were, . . . IV. iv. 26. 4
It was my lot to love a gentle *swaine,* . . . IV. vii. 15. 6
he whilome some gentle *swaine* had beene, . . . IV. vii. 45. 6
she chaunced there to see This lovely *swaine,* . . . IV. viii. 52. 5
To yeeld strong succour to that gentle *swayne,* . . . IV. ix. 4. 2
So whylome learnd that mighty Jewish *swaine,* . . . V. viii. 2. 1
th' Elfin *swayne,* that oft had seene like sight, . . . V. xii. 16. 6
As then the guize was for each gentle *swayne:* . . . VI. ii. 6. 3
'What meanes this, gentle *Swaine,* . . . VI. ii. 7. 2
'Faire gentle *swayne,* and yet as stout as fayre, . . . VI. ii. 25. 1
And fitteth most for noble *swayne* to know, . . . VI. ii. 32. 7
Then turning to that *swaine* . . . VI. v. 23. 1
sith we need good counsell,' (sayd the *swaine*) . . . VI. vi. 13. 8
The fearfull *swayne* beholding death so nie, . . . VI. vii. 12. 1
That other *swayne,* like ashes deadly pale, . . . VI. vii. 17. 8
Him to betray unto a straunger *swaine:* . . . VI. vii. 22. 5
Now turne againe my teme, thou jolly *swayne,* . . . VI. ix. 1. 1
ne was there shepheards *swayne,* But her did honour; . . . VI. ix. 10. 1
she did love a stranger *swayne* then him more dere. . . . VI. ix. 38. 9
answerd then that *swaine,* . . . VI. x. 20. 1
taking leave of that same gentle *Swaine,* . . . VI. x. 32. 1
Like as whylome that strong Tirynthian *swaine* . . . VI. xii. 35. 1
Swains. *See* **Fellow-swains, Shepherd-swains.**
Tho gan shepheards *swaines* to looke aloft, . . . *S.C.* May 124
endles sovenaunce Emong the shepeheards *swaines* . . . *S.C.* N. 6
the Shepheards *swaines* Were wont . . . to sing, . . . *T.M.* 279
ye, faire *Swayns,* . . . cease your worke, . . . III. xii. 47. *or.* 7
Swale. High *Swale,* unquiet Nide, and troublous Skell; . . . IV. xi. 37. 7
Swallow. The *Swallow* peepes out of her nest, . . . *S.C.* Mar. 11
Like *Swallow* swift I wandred here and there; . . . *S.C.* D. 20
boast to *swallow* her in greedy grave; . . . II. ii. 24. 6
More swift then *swallow* sheres the liquid skye, . . . II. vi. 5. 2
gaping wide to *swallow* them alyve . . . II. xii. 5. 7
Threatning to *swallow* up my fearefull lyfe? . . . III. iv. 8. 6
he was swift as *swallow* in her flight, . . . V. i. 20. 4
Swallowed. With which he *swallowed* up excessive feast, . . . I. iv. 21. 6
The foolish man . . . is *swallowed* up unwares, . . . I. v. 18. 8
He thought attonce him to have *swallowd* quight, . . . I. xi. 53. 2
Which having *swallowd* up excessively, . . . II. xii. 3. 6
Unwares the hidden hooke with baite I *swallowed.* . . . III. ii. 38. 9
threatned sore Her to have *swallow'd* up, . . . V. iv. 12. 4
Swallows. As swifte as *swallowes* on the waves they went, . . . III. iv. 33. 5
Swam. he left the bloudy slaughter In which he *swam,* . . . V. iv. 41. 3
The same which over Hellespontus *swam;* . . . VII. vii. 32. 5
Swan. mount as high, and sing as soote as *Swanne.* . . . *S.C.* O. 90
The silver *swanne* doth sing before her dying day, . . . *Frag.*
There stood a snowie *Swan* of heavenly hiew, . . . *Ti.* 590
Then was he turnd into a snowy *Swan,* . . . III. xi. 32. 1
Jove himselfe, when he a *Swan* would be, . . . *Proth.* 42
Swans. Nor Po nor Tyburs *swans* so much renowned, . . . *Col.* 412
two *Swannes* of goodly hewe . . . *Proth.* 37
Sware. *See* **Swore.**
He knocked fast, and often curst, and *sware,* . . . I. iii. 16. 5
Swarm. As when a *swarme* of Gnats at eventide . . . II. ix. 16. 1
Sith now he is far from his monstrous *swarme,* . . . II. xi. 34. 4
He like a *swarme* of flyes them overthrew; . . . V. ii. 53. 6
They round about him gan to *swarme* apace, . . . V. iv. 23. 7
flocking round about them, as a *swarme* Of flyes . . . V. xi. 58. 1
Swarmed. A thousand villeins rownd about them *swarmd* . . . II. ix. 13. 2
through the world then *swarmd* in every part, . . . II. x. 15. 3
the Picts that *swarmed* over-all, . . . IV. xi. 36. 4
like a sort of Bees in clusters *swarmed:* . . . V. iv. 36. 7
Swarming. *swarming* all about his legs did crall, . . . I. i. 22. 8
winde, much like the sowne Of *swarming* Bees, . . . I. i. 41. 5
Those spoylefull Picts, and *swarming* Easterlings, . . . II. x. 63. 2
So many theeves about him *swarming* are, . . . VI. xi. 48. 5
Swarms. Like many *swarmes* of Bees assembled round, . . . II. ix. 51. 4
swarmes of damned soules to hell he sends: . . . VI. viii. 49. 7
all the place with *swarmes* do overlay, . . . VI. xi. 48. 3
Swart. Of *swarth* complexion, and of crabbed hew, . . . II. ix. 52. 4
a nation straunge, with visage *swart,* . . . II. x. 15. 1
Swarved, Swarving. *See* **Swerved,** *etc.*
Swat. See **Sweat.**

Swat—*Continued.*
For sore he *swat,* and . . . was bescracht . . . III. v. 3. 8
yet he did labour long, And *swat,* and chauf'd, . . . V. ii. 46. 8
Swathbands. And every part that under *sweath-bands* lay, . . . VI. iv. 23. 7
Sway. now in Court doth beare the greatest *sway,* . . . *Hub.* 616
Withouten helme or Pilot her to *sway:* . . . *T.M.* 142
sway in Court with pride and rashnes rude; . . . *T.M.* 328
what ever man bearst worldlie *sway,* . . . *Ti.* 208
So you, great Lord, that with your counsell *sway* . . . *Ded. Son.* i. 9
The doubtfull ballaunce equally to *sway,* . . . I. ii. 38. 2
his heavy *sway* So deepely dinted in the driven clay, . . . I. viii. 8. 4
At last, low stouping with unweldy *sway* . . . I. xi. 18. 8
both attonce their huge blowes down did *sway.* . . . II. vi. 31. 2
speare he thrust with puissant *sway* . . . II. viii. 36. 3
The which dividing with importune *sway,* . . . II. viii. 38. 8
with their importune *sway,* . . . II. x. 15. 5
Madan was young, unmeet the rule to *sway,* . . . II. x. 20. 2
with exceeding *sway* Threw at his foe, . . . II. xi. 36. 1
Whose circled waters rapt with whirling *sway,* . . . II. xii. 20. 5
wemen wont in warres to beare most *sway,* . . . III. ii. 2. 2
ye both in armes shall beare great *sway,* . . . III. iii. 28. 5
more then all the rest may *sway,* . . . III. iii. 55. 1
Served a gentle Lady of great *sway* . . . III. v. 4. 5
fortune all in equall launce doth *sway,* . . . III. vii. 4. 4
with imperious *sway* Him forst, . . . III. xi. 26. 7
bore great *sway* in armes and chivalrie, . . . IV. i. 32. 2
heav'd his murdrous axe at him with mighty *sway.* . . . IV. iii. 17. 9
Strikes at an Heron with all his bodies *sway,* . . . IV. iii. 19. 3
all unwares he felt an hideous *sway* . . . IV. iv. 31. 4
despiteous dreare And heavie *sway* . . . IV. viii. 42. 6
these Squires true friendship more did *sway* . . . IV. ix. 3. 3
enjoyes the wide kingdome . . . with lordly *sway,* . . . IV. x. 42. 8
with which thou diddest *sway* So sharpe a battell, . . . V. iii. 21. 8
the mightie *sway* Of that sad stroke, . . . V. v. 9. 5
made him stagger with uncertaine *sway,* . . . V. xi. 11. 2
as she prest on him with heavy *sway,* . . . V. xi. 31. 1
wading through the waves with stedfast *sway,* . . . V. xii. 5. 6
And borne great *sway* in armes amongst his peares; . . . VI. iii. 3. 3
The which descended with such dreadfull *sway,* . . . VI. viii. 8. 4
downe he kept him with his scornefull *sway,* . . . VI. viii. 11. 4
Change, the which all mortall things doth *sway,* . . . VII. vi. 1. 2
(Such *sway* doth beauty even in Heaven beare) . . . VII. vi. 31. 4
raign and bear the greatest *sway;* . . . VII. vii. 47. 4
In all things else she beares the greatest *sway:* . . . VII. viii. 1. 5
as she will, whose will my life doth *sway,* . . . *Am.* xlvi. 7
As King and Queene, the heavens Empire *sway;* . . . *H.H.B.* 56
Swayed. When heavy hammers on the wedge are *swaid:* . . . I. xi. 42. 7
so cruelly have *swayd* Against that knight! . . . II. viii. 46. 7
oft the Briton kings against them strongly *swayd.* . . . II. x. 49. 9
The first and eldest, which that scepter *swayd,* . . . II. x. 72. 4
about her *swayd* Her wrathfull steele, . . . III. i. 66. 5
we see not how they are mov'd and *swayd* . . . VII. vii. 49. 2
Swear. who would not oft *sweare,* And oft unsweare, . . . *Hub.* 1057
gan devoutly *sweare;* . . . II. i. 61. 4
'Once I did *sweare,* . . . II. iii. 17. 6
Shall yield him selfe his liegeman, and *sweare* fealty. . . . III. iii. 37. 9
I *sweare,* ere long shall dearely it repent; . . . III. x. 32. 7
both . . . with many a cursed oth *Sweare* she is yours, . . . IV. i. 47. 8
when we friendship first did *sweare,* . . . IV. ii. 13. 3
full of rage he gan to curse and *sweare,* . . . IV. viii. 44. 2
So ye will *sweare* my judgement to abide.' . . . V. i. 25. 7
Made them *sweare* fealty to Artegall; . . . V. vii. 43. 6
he made him *sweare* By his owne sword, . . . VI. i. 43. 5
There him he . . . made to *sweare* . . . VI. ii. 35. 1
as he did on his Knighthood *sweare,* . . . VI. iii. 18. 4
fiercely drawing forth his blade, doth *sweare* . . . VI. xi. 15. 7
Sweard. *See* **Sword.**
Swearing. *swearing* faith to either on his blade, . . . V. viii. 14. 7
Swearing and banning most blasphemously, . . . V. viii. 28. 2
Swears. In vaine the Pagan bannes, and *sweares,* and rayles, . V. viii. 39. 4
Sweat. *See* **Swat.**
them did save with bloudy *sweat* . . . *S.C.* Jul. 55
when with Wine the braine begins to *sweate,* . . . *S.C.* O. 107
that swincke and *sweate* for nought, . . . *S.C.* N. 154
they doo swinke and *sweate* to feed the other, . . . *Hub.* 163
through his fiersnesse fomed all with *sweat,* . . . I. iii. 33. 4
From under which fast trickled downe the *sweat.* . . . I. iv. 22. 4
all the house did *sweat* with great aray: . . . I. xii. 38. 5
After their weary *sweat* and bloody toile, . . . II. ii. 33. 2
Before her gate high God did *Sweate* ordaine, . . . II. iii. 41. 5
mingled all with *sweate,* . . . II. iv. 37. 5
wypt away his toilsom *sweat.* . . . II. v. 30. 9
For which men swinck and *sweat* incessantly, . . . II. vii. 8. 7
every one did swincke, and every one did *sweat.* . . . II. vii. 36. 9
did about their businesse *sweat,* and sorely toyld. . . . II. ix. 30. 9
From off their dainty limbs the dusty *sweat* . . . III. vi. 17. 6
To be embaulm'd, and *sweat* out dainty dew, . . . IV. vii. 40. 4
with the steme thereof the Temple *swet,* . . . IV. x. 38. 3
the *sweat* with which thou diddest sway So sharpe a battell, V. iii. 21. 8
bath'd in bloud and *sweat* together ment; . . . V. v. 12. 5
gan to chaufe and *sweat,* . . . V. xi. 12. 7
For which he long in vaine did *sweate* and swincke, . . . VI. iv. 32. 4
Then one of them, him seeing so to *sweat,* . . . VI. ix. 6. 6
from which, as he had chauffed been, The *sweat* did drop; . . VII. vii. 29. 6
his browes with *sweat* did reek and steem, . . . VII. vii. 40. 4
I burne much more in boyling *sweat,* . . . *Am.* xxx. 7
they may *sweat,* and drunken be withall. . . . *Epith.* 254
Sweating. with the sweete of others *sweating* toyle; . . . *Hub.* 1152
Deawed with silver drops through *sweating* sore, . . . IV. vi. 19. 7
To whom Sir Calidore yet *sweating* comes, . . . VI. ix. 5. 7

Sweaty. *sweatie* steeds . . . gan water in the west, *D.* 24
bayes His *sweatie* forehead in the breathing wynd, I. vii. 3. 2
from their *sweaty* Coursers did avale, II. ix. 10. 7
I will their *sweatie* yokes assoyle III. xii. 47. *or.* 5
(After her *sweaty* chace and toylesome play) VII. vi. 42. 2

Sweep. *sweepe* The fomie waves out of the dreadfull deep, *Van.* v. 4
with his oares did *sweepe* the watry wildernesse. II. xii. 29. 9

Sweepeth. It *sweepeth* all the land behind him farre, I. xi. 11. 6

Sweet. *See* **Soot.**
yelde unto thy lorde a *sweete* request, *Pet.*[1] vii. 3
more *sweete* (*swete*[1]) than Mermaids song: *Bel.* xii. 8
The *sweete* Nightingale singing so lowde; *S.C.* F. 123
robbing me of the *swete* sonnes sight? *S.C.* F. 174
Bagpype broke, that soundes so *sweete?* *S.C.* Ap. 3
Embellish the *sweete* Violet. *S.C.* Ap. 63
With Hawthorne buds, and *swete* Eglantine, *S.C.* May 13
joyed at this *sweete* sight! *S.C.* May 197
Ah, deare Lord! and *sweete* Saint Charitee! *S.C.* May 247
'Jesus blesse that *sweete* face I espye, *S.C.* May 256
for shame of thy *swete* layes. *S.C.* Jun. 56
Of *sweete* Violets therein was store, *S.C.* Au. 71
Let all, that *sweete* is, voyd: *S.C.* Au. 164
who such sports and *sweet* delights doth blame, *Gn.* 7
the *sweete* waves of sounding Castaly *Gn.* 23
In *sweete* spring time, *Gn.* 109
Sweete quiet harbours in his harmeless head, *Gn.* 134
Unto *sweete* sleepe he may securely lend *Gn.* 142
with *sweete* teares did lament. *Gn.* 200
the *sweete* Cypresse, signe of deadly bale. *Gn.* 216
Chaunted their sundrie tunes with *sweete* consent; *Gn.* 226
sweete love of pardon worthie is, *Gn.* 473
the slothfull fit of lifes *sweete* rest *Gn.* 641
round about he taught *sweete* flowres to growe: *Gn.* 665
The Spartan Mirtle, whence *sweet* gumb does flowe; *Gn.* 669
At morne and even, besides their Anthemes *sweete,* *Hub.* 451
with *sweete* delight Of Musicks skill *Hub.* 755
Sweete Ladie Muses, Ladies of delight, *Hub.* 761
Let not *sweete* Poets praise, *Hub.* 811
with the sugrie *sweete* thereof allure *Hub.* 819
Who ever leaves *sweete* home, *Hub.* 909
with the *sweete* of others sweating toyle; *Hub.* 1152
the heavenly noyses Of their *sweete* instruments *T.M.* 20
thether came to heare their musick *sweet,* *T.M.* 32
Where be the *sweete* delights of learnings treasure *T.M.* 175
those *sweete* wits, which wont the like to frame, *T.M.* 203
Large streames of honnie and *sweete* Nectar flowe, *T.M.* 218
in *sweet* accord All places . . . to fill, *T.M.* 241
arbors *sweet,* in which the Shepheards swaines *T.M.* 279
fed with pleasures *sweet,* *T.M.* 302
Sweete Love devoyd of villanie or ill, *T.M.* 387
The *sweete* companions of the Muses late, *T.M.* 404
I feede on *sweet* contentment of my thought, *T.M.* 524
the *sweet* numbers and melodious measures, *T.M.* 547
hir *sweete* Tongue was wonte to make me mirth. *U.V.* 15
Sure gates, *sweete* gardens, stately galleries, *Ti.* 95
his *sweete* waters away with him led. *Ti.* 147
with *sweete* Poets verse be glorifide. *Ti.* 427
Full of *sweete* flowres and daintiest delights, *Ti.* 520
none of these, how ever *sweete* they beene, *Mui.* 157
Powres forth *sweete* odors and alluring sights; *Mui.* 164
(for all change is *sweete*) *Mui.* 178
In stead of them, and their *sweet* harmonie, *D.* 15
reft fro me my *sweete* companion, *D.* 159
With those *sweet* sugred speaches doo compare, *D.* 299
I match with that *sweet* smile and chearfull brow, *D.* 306
to smell, no *sweet* on earth is left; *D.* 418
Sweet without sowre, and honny without gall: *As.* 26
For he could pipe, and daunce, and caroll *sweet,* *As.* 31
with *sweet* kisses suckt the wasting breath *As.* 165
Of gentle wit and daintie *sweet* device, *As.* Interl. 218
Laies of *sweet* love, without rebuke or blame, *Col.* 3
feed on *sweet* contentment of that sight: *Col.* 43
tourn *Sweet* layes of love to endlesse plaints of pittie. *Col.* 387
In thy *sweete* Eglantine of Meriflure; *Col.* 389
The blossome of *sweet* joy and perfect love, *Col.* 470
Phyllis, Charillis, and *sweet* Amaryllis. *Col.* 540
sweet Charillis is the Paragone Of peerlesse price, *Col.* 548
throwing forth *sweet* odours *Col.* 610
his *sweet* lore professed there? *Col.* 772
With the *sweet* Lady Muses for to play: *Ded. Son.* i. 6
T' embrace the service of *sweete* Poetry, *Ded. Son.* iv. 7
Nor one Helicone, Left for *sweete* Muses *Ded. Son.* v. 7
gave more honourable prize To the *sweet* Muse *Ded. Son.* xiv. 2
To sing his *sweet* delights in lowlie laies; *Ded. Son.* xv. 7
For whose *sweete* sake that glorious badge he wore, I. i. 2. 3
Joying to heare the birdes *sweete* harmony, I. i. 8. 2
As gentle shepheard in *sweete* eventide, I. i. 23. 1
Sweet slombring deaw, the which to sleep them biddes. I. i. 36. 4
A dram of *sweete* is worth a pound of sowre. I. iii. 30. 4
Did chace away *sweet* sleepe from sluggish eye, I. iv. 44. 4
litle *sweet* Oft tempred is,' . . . 'with muchell smart: I. iv. 46. 3
most heavenly melody . . . *sweet* musicke did divide, I. v. 17. 7
find some other play-fellowes, mine own *sweet* boy.' I. vi. 28. 9
Trew sacred lore, which from her *sweet* lips did redound. I. vi. 30. 9
Doe chaunt *sweet* musick to delight his mynd. I. vii. 3. 5
With fowle words tempring faire, soure gall with hony *sweet.* I. vii. 3. 9
with her witchcraft, and misseeming *sweete,* I. vii. 50. 8
with *sweet* joyous cheare him thus bespake: I. viii. 26. 6
every sence the humour *sweet* embayd, I. ix. 13. 5
But simple, trew, and eke unfained *sweet,* I. x. 7. 8

Sweet—*Continued.*
wise Speranza gave him comfort *sweet,* I. x. 22. 1
both *sweet* and brave They might appeare, I. x. 42. 4
sweet Timbrels all upheld on hight. I. xii. 6. 9
With shaumes, and trompets, and with Clarions *sweet;* I. xii. 13. 2
sweete Musicke did apply Her curious skill I. xii. 38. 6
wist no creature whence that hevenly *sweet* Proceeded, I. xii. 39. 6
Her joyous presence and *sweet* company, I. xii. 41. 1
Sharpe be thy wounds, but *sweete* the medicines be, II. i. 36. 8
sweete Babe, . . . Long maist thou live, II. i. 37. 1
goodly counsell, . . . tempred with *sweete* voice: II. i. 44. 3
with *sweet* pleasaunce, and bold blandishment, II. ii. 1. 5
Sweete wordes like dropping honny she did shed; II. iii. 24. 7
In her rude heares *sweet* flowres themselves did lap, II. iii. 30. 8
fild with delight Of her *sweete* words II. iii. 42. 3
made emongst them selves a *sweete* consort, II. v. 31. 8
On a *sweet* bed of lillies softly laid, II. v. 32. 3
sweet wordes, dropping like honny dew; II. v. 33. 4
Ne Ladies loves, ne *sweete* entreaties, II. v. 38. 3
Making *sweet* solace to herselfe alone: II. vi. 3. 2
With one *sweete* drop of sensuall delight. II. vi. 8. 7
with painted blossomes drest And smelling *sweete,* II. vi. 12. 8
throwe her *sweete* smels al arownd. II. vi. 12. 9
her *sweete* selfe . . . She sett beside, II. vi. 14. 5
she, more *sweete* then any bird on bough, II. vi. 25. 1
love does give his *sweet* Alarmes Without bloodshed, II. vi. 34. 7
her *sweet* peace and pleasures did annoy, II. vi. 37. 7
fruits . . . *sweet* and well savored, II. vii. 51. 7
even heven rejoyced her *sweete* face to see. II. ix. 18. 9
crowned with a garland of *sweete* Rosiere. II. ix. 19. 9
Some song in *sweet* consort; II. ix. 35. 2
with *sweet* science mollifide their stubborne harts. II. x. 25. 9
this *sweet* Island never conquered, II. x. 47. 7
seemd so *sweet* and pleasaunt to the eye, II. xii. 14. 5
their *sweet* skill in wonted melody; II. xii. 31. 7
The worldes *sweet* In from paine and wearisome turmoyle.' II. xii. 32. 9
sweet Zephyrus lowd whisteled His treble, II. xii. 33. 5
sweete and pleasing unto living sense, II. xii. 42. 6
still it breathed forth *sweet* spirit and holesom smell: II. xii. 51. 9
More *sweet* and holesome then the pleasaunt hill Of Rhodope, II. xii. 52. 1
sweet Parnasse, the haunt of Muses fayre; II. xii. 52. 8
the fayre aspect Of that *sweet* place, II. xii. 53. 2
so faire winepresse made the wine more *sweet:* II. xii. 56. 6
all agreed, through *sweete* diversity, II. xii. 59. 8
Infinit streames . . . *sweet* and faire to see, II. xii. 62. 2
th' amarous *sweet* spoiles to greedy eyes revele. II. xii. 64. 9
Their notes unto the voice attempred *sweet;* II. xii. 71. 2
through languour of her late *sweet* toyle, II. xii. 78. 3
her faire eyes, *sweet* smyling in delight, II. xii. 78. 6
A *sweet* regard and amiable grace, II. xii. 79. 5
that *sweete* verse, with Nectar sprinckeled, III. Pr. 4. 4
sweet Love anone Taketh his nimble winges, III. i. 25. 8
with what sleights and *sweet* allurements she Entyst III. i. 35. 1
throw into the well *sweet* Rosemaryes, III. i. 36. 7
with *sweet* Nectar she did sprinkle him. III. i. 36. 9
sweet Musicke did divide Her looser notes III. i. 40. 1
sweet birdes thereto applide Their daintie layes III. i. 40. 3
Let not her fault your *sweete* affections marre, III. i. 49. 3
Sweete love such lewdnes bands from his faire companee. III. ii. 41. 9
that *sweete* fit that doth true beautie love, III. iii. 1. 7
the sad end of her *sweet* Marinell: III. iv. 25. 5
Gathering *sweete* daffadillyes, III. iv. 29. 8
farewell, my sweetest *sweet!* III. iv. 39. 8
his *sweete* lips, on which before that stownd III. v. 29. 7
By this he had *sweet* life recur'd agayne, III. v. 34. 1
with thy hevenly salves and med'cines *sweete* III. v. 35. 8
Of Gods high praise, and of their loves *sweet* teene, III. v. 40. 4
that *sweet* Cordiall, which can restore A love-sick hart, III. v. 50. 6
With so *sweet* sence and secret powre unspide, III. vi. 7. 8
She promist kisses *sweet,* and sweeter things, III. vi. 12. 8
were with *sweet* Ambrosia all besprinckled light. III. vi. 18. 9
From her *sweete* bowres, and beds with pleasures fraught? III. vi. 20. 4
as a fountaine from her *sweete* lips went. III. vi. 25. 5
sweete love gentle fitts emongst them throwes, III. vi. 41. 5
Emongst the shady leaves, their *sweet* abode, III. vi. 42. 8
from their fruitfull sydes *sweet* gum did drop, III. vi. 43. 7
Threw forth most dainty odours and most *sweet* delight. III. vi. 43. 9
To whom *sweet* Poets verse hath given endlesse date. III. vi. 45. 9
reape *sweet* pleasure of the wanton boy: III. vi. 46. 3
That her *sweet* love his malice mote avoyd, III. vi. 48. 7
most *sweet* hymmes of this thy famous deed III. viii. 42. 8
scerne that it was not his sweetest *sweet,* III. x. 22. 8
Sweete Love, that doth his golden wings embay III. xi. 2. 3
sweet wit of the man, III. xi. 32. 3
That he might taste the *sweet* consuming woe, III. xi. 45. 4
A lay of loves delight with *sweet* concent: III. xii. 5. 7
the *sweet* lodge of love and deare delight: III. xii. 45. *or.* 4
in *sweete* ravishment pourd out her spright. III. xii. 45. *or.* 7
those lovers, with *sweet* countervayle, III. xii. 47. *or.* 1
thy *sweete* smyling mother from above, IV. Pr. 5. 7
through infusion *sweete* Of thine owne spirit IV. ii. 34. 6
Instead thereof *sweet* peace and quiet-age IV. iii. 43. 5
Profest to her true friendship and affection *sweet.* IV. iii. 50. 9
Sweete is the love that comes alone with willingnesse. IV. v. 25. 9
With faire entreatie and *sweet* blandishment, IV. vi. 41. 2
wont with ointment *sweet* To be embaulm'd, IV. vii. 40. 3
that *sweet* bird departing flew forthright, IV. viii. 8. 7
Sitting in covert shade of arbors *sweet,* IV. viii. 9. 2
The deare affection unto kindred *sweet,* IV. ix. 1. 5
So litle did they hearken to her *sweet* beheast. IV. ix. 31. 9

Swelling—*Continued.*
T' abate all spasme, and soke the *swelling* bruze; III. v. 33. 7
swelling throbs empeach His foltring toung III. xi. 12. 2
let their *swelling* waters low before him fall. IV. xi. 30. 9
whose *swelling* sourse Shall drive a Mill, VI. i. 21. 1
Began to mitigate his *swelling* sourse, VI. xi. 34. 3

Swelt. *See* **Swelled.**
His heart with vengefull malice inly *swelt;* *Mui.* 356
like a fever fit through all his bodie *swelt.* I. vii. 6. 9
With huge impatience he inly *swelt,* III. xi. 27. 1
griefe, that her deare hart nigh *swelt,* IV. vii. 9. 4
nigh she *swelt* For passing joy, VI. xii. 21. 8

Swept. from my beard the fat away have *swept;* *Hub.* 78
Into the hole, the which the Badger *swept.* *Ti.* 217
all his armour *swept,* That all the blood II. vi. 42. 7
he them all from him full lightly *swept,* VI. i. 24. 3
His head meant from his shoulders to have *swept.* VI. viii. 17. 3

Swerve. My sheepe for that may chaunce to *swerve,* *S.C.* Mar. 44
Dye rather, dye, then ever from her service *swerve.* III. v. 46. 9
how she might be sure that I would never *swerve?* III. vii. 53. 9
from her faith will never *swerve.* IV. v. 1. 9
To temporize is not from truth to *swerve,* V. xi. 56. 3
he for nought would *swerve* From his right course, V. xii. 43. 7
Thou mayest well trie if they will ever *swerve,* *H.L.* 165

Swerved. Her stedfast eyes were bent, ne *swarved* other way. I. x. 14. 9
the Captaines on her syde . . . from her *swerv'd:* II. x. 55. 4
Yet *swarved* not, but kept their forward way II. xii. 76. 5
to his starting steed that *swarv'd* asyde, III. i. 11. 6
seeing it at hand, he *swarv'd* asyde, IV. iii. 18. 6
swarv'd aside, and there againe did stay IV. viii. 10. 8
from his saddle *swarved* nought asyde, V. x. 35. 2
To free his foes, that from his heast had *swerved!* *H.H.L.* 161

Swerving. *swarving* backe, her Javelin bright Against him bent, II. iii. 42. 7
swarving from the marke, II. viii. 30. 9
He, *swarving* with the force, II. viii. 36. 6

Swift. a river *swift,* whose fomy billowes *Bel.*[2] viii. 1
by a rivers bancke that *swift* downe slidd, *Bel.*[2] xv. 7
In her *swifte* charret with high turrets crownde, *Ro.* vi. 2
Nor the *swift* furie of the flames aspiring, *Ro.* xiii. 1
Like Swallow *swift* I wandred here and there; *S.C.* D. 20
Woodgods, and Satyres, and *swift* Dryades, *Gn.* 178
Time, flying with winges *swift,* *Hub.* 308
to sew the chace Of *swift* wilde beasts, *Hub.* 744
The Starres pure light, the Spheres *swift* movement, *T.M.* 508
Two Angels, downe descending with *swift* flight, *Ti.* 625
he so *swift* and nimble was of flight, *Mui.* 41
With violent *swift* flight forth caried *Mui.* 422
In wrestling nimble, and in renning *swift,* *As.* 73
how bold and *swift* the monster was, *Col.* 220
steedes aghast Both charett *swifte* and huntsman overcast: I. v. 38. 5
The Pardale *swift,* and the Tigre cruell, I. vi. 26. 4
That vanisht into smoke and cloudes *swift;* I. xi. 54. 2
by the sandy shore Of *swift* Eurotas, II. iii. 31. 2
carries thee so *swifte* and light.' II. iv. 43. 4
as *swift* as glaunce of eye, A litle Gondelay, II. vi. 2. 6
More *swift* then swallow sheres the liquid skye, II. vi. 5. 2
whether *swift* I wend, or whether slow: II. vi. 10. 5
Both slow and *swift* alike do serve my tourne; II. vi. 10. 6
her *swift* bote Forthwith directed to that further strand; II. vi. 38. 1
after him she flyeth *swifte.* II. vii. 23. 9
with which th' Euboean young man wan *Swift* Atalanta, II. vii. 54. 9
Upon a Tygre *swift* and fierce he rode, II. xi. 20. 4
both as *swift* on foot as chased Stags; II. xi. 23. 5
lyes a litle space From the *swift* Barry, III. iii. 8. 5
Like a *swift* Otter, fell through emptinesse, III. iii. 33. 7
As *swifte* as swallowes on the waves they went, III. iv. 33. 5
vew Of hunter *swifte* and sent of howndes trew. III. iv. 46. 5
Thereto so *swifte* that it all beasts did pas: III. vii. 22. 6
swifte as word that from her went, III. vii. 23. 6
His charett *swifte* in hast he thither steard, III. viii. 30. 7
he was long, and *swift* as any Roe, III. xi. 5. 8
That his *swift* charet might have passage wyde III. xi. 40. 8
by the *swift* recourse of flushing blood IV. vi. 29. 6
as *swift* as wind, IV. vii. 18. 7
More *swift* then Myrrh' on Daphne in her race, IV. vii. 22. 8
the *swift* bird obayd not her behest, IV. viii. 10. 7
Swift Rhene, and Alpheus still immaculate IV. xi. 21. 4
swift Werfe, and Oze the most of might, IV. xi. 37. 6
Swift Awniduff, which of the English man Is cal'de Blackewater, IV. xi. 41. 5
Swift Proto, milde Eucrate, Thetis faire, IV. xi. 48. 7
he was *swift* as swallow in her flight, V. i. 20. 4
That is both *swift* and dangerous deepe withall; V. ii. 8. 2
her winged thoughts, more *swift* then wind, V. vi. 7. 8
swift Talus did the formost win; V. vii. 35. 2
to follow him that was so *swift* and light. V. ix. 15. 9
he was *swift* in chace. V. ix. 16. 2
He met him with a counterstroke so *swift,* V. xi. 7. 8
Who was more light of foote and *swift* in chace, VI. iii. 25. 4
(For he was *swift* as any Bucke in chace) VI. iv. 8. 3
th' other, not so *swift* as she before, VI. vii. 9. 8

Swifter. *swifter* then thought, . . . the Wolfe Lowder caught; *S.C.* S. 222

Swiftest. the wilde beasts, that *swiftest* are in chase; *Hub.* 620
every one to ronne the *swiftest* stryv'd; III. x. 37. 7

Swiftly. to her watry chamber *swiftly* carry him. III. iv. 42. 9
did her footing trace So sure and *swiftly,* III. vii. 23. 8
Through both whose borders *swiftly* downe it glides, IV. xi. 31. 3
after them the Prince as *swiftly* sped, V. x. 36. 3
carried with his force forthright Glaunst *swiftly* by; VI. vii. 7. 8

Swiftness. The flying ships with *swiftnes* to pursew: II. xii. 24. 4
through *swiftnesse* of his speedie beast, III. v. 14. 2
helped through the *swiftnesse* of his steed, VI. iv. 8. 5

Swift-running. the *swift running* rivers still did stand, *Gn.* 450

Swim. *See* **Overswim.**
Unlesse he *swim* in love up to the eares. *Col.* 782
Her twyfold Teme . . . Did softly *swim* away, I. v. 28. 6
swim in pleasure, which thou here doest mis: II. iii. 39. 7
'Who-so in pompe of prowd estate' . . . 'Does *swim,* II. iii. 40. 2
did *swim* Along the shore . . . A litle Gondelay, II. vi. 2. 5
let their temed fishes softly *swim* III. iv. 34. 3
Upon great Neptunes necke they softly *swim,* III. iv. 42. 8
As that in rivers *swim,* or brookes doe wade; IV. xi. 9. 5
Could *swim* like to a fish, V. ii. 13. 9
mockt to see him like to *swim:* VI. iii. 34. 4
did softly slyde And *swim* away: VII. vii. 43. 5

Swimming. I saw an Harpe . . . *Swimming,* *Ti.* 606
In shooting steddie, and in *swimming* strong: *As.* 74
swimming in that sea of blisfull joy, I. xii. 41. 5
swimming in the maine Will die for thrist, II. vi. 17. 7
swimming deepe in sensuall desyres; III. i. 39. 8
to his handy *swimming* him betake. V. ii. 16. 3
Artegall in *swimming* skilfull was, V. ii. 16. 6
So ought each Knight . . . In *swimming* be expert, V. ii. 16. 9
two Swannes . . . Come softly *swimming* *Proth.* 38

Swine. with his nuts larded many *swine:* *S.C.* F. 110
To keep his sheep, or to attend his *swyne,* *Hub.* 285
rode loathsome Gluttony, . . . on a filthie *swyne.* I. iv. 21. 2
some fashioned in the waste Like *swine:* II. xi. 12. 6
The which beside the gate for *swyne* was ordered. III. ix. 11. 9
soyle, In which thou wallowest like to filthy *swyne,* *H.H.L.* 219

Swinged. The scorching flame sore *swinged* all his face, I. xi. 26. 6

Swinging. mard the *swinging* of her flaile. V. xi. 29. 9

Swink. How great sport they gaynen with little *swinck?* *S.C.* May 36
rekes much of thy *swinck,* *S.C.* Jul. 34
The more to wind it out thou doest *swinck,* *S.C.* S. 132
that *swincke* and sweate for nought, *S.C.* N. 154
they doo *swinke* and sweate to feed the other, *Hub.* 163
For which men *swinck* and sweat incessantly, II. vii. 8. 7
every one did *swincke,* and every one did sweat. II. vii. 36. 9
made him vainely *swincke;* II. vii. 58. 7
For which he long in vaine did sweate and *swinke,* VI. iv. 32. 4

Swollen. *swolne* with plenties pride, *Ro.* xxiii. 13
powre into my *swollen* eyes A sea of teares *T.M.* 115
Their bellies *swolne* he saw with fulnesse burst, I. i. 26. 5
Her *swollen* hart her speech seemd to bereave, I. i. 52. 3
eke with fatnesse *swollen* were his eyne; I. iv. 21. 4
who, *swolne* with blood of late, Came ramping forth I. viii. 12. 4
Was *swoln* with wrath and poyson, I. xi. 8. 9
Such proud luxurious pompe is *swollen* up but late. I. xii. 14. 9
Her *swollen* eyes were much disfigured, II. i. 13. 8
Abusd her plenty and fat *swolne* encreace II. vii. 16. 7
swolne with pride of his owne peerelesse powre, V. vii. 15. 7

Swoon. Amooved him out of his stonie *swound,* *D.* 545
ever-drizling raine . . . did cast him in a *swowne.* I. i. 41. 5
pâynd himselfe . . . to reare Her out of carelesse *swowne.* I. ii. 45. 4
In slombring *swownd,* nigh voyd of vitall spright, I. v. 19. 5
ere he could out of his *swowne* awake, I. vii. 15. 7
Thrise did she sinke adowne in deadly *swownd,* I. vii. 24. 3
cold ran to her well of life, As in a *swowne:* I. ix. 52. 3
Sir Guyon, layd in *swowne,* II. viii. Arg.
the villeine overthrowne Out of his *swowne* arose, II. xi. 35. 4
Shortly they reard out of her frosen *swownd;* III. i. 64. 3
Inglorious now lies in sencelesse *swownd,* III. iv. 29. 3
lay as in a *swowne,* III. iv. 30. 6
The lucklesse Marinell lying in deadly *swownd,* III. iv. 34. 9
findes him almost dead, And reareth out of *sownd.* III. v. Arg.
from his steed he fell in deadly *swowne:* III. v. 26. 3
With blood deformed, lay in deadly *swownd;* III. v. 29. 2
whiles that he lay in *swownd,* III. v. 38. 7
a gentle slombring *swowne* Upon her fell, III. vi. 7. 3
Out of her heavie *swowne* not to awake III. vi. 27. 8
rolled on an heape, lay still in *swound* IV. i. 43. 1
Strooke him so hugely that in *swowne* he lay, IV. iii. 34. 3
out of the *swownd,* which him did blend, IV. iii. 35. 7
Sir Satyrane abraid Out of the *swowne,* IV. iv. 22. 1
scarse he him upheld from falling in a *swound.* IV. iv. 24. 9
She almost fell againe into a *swound,* IV. vii. 9. 8
Who lay the whiles in *swoune,* full sadly set, IV. vii. 35. 4
lay long while in senselesse *swowne.* IV. viii. 42. 9
In sencelesse *swoune,* as if her life forsooke, V. v. 11. 4
upstarting from her *swoune,* V. v. 13. 7
There did the Prince him leave in deadly *swound,* V. x. 33. 7
his foe lay fast in sencelesse *swound;* VI. i. 34. 2
the deadly *swound,* in which full deepe VI. iii. 10. 7
stouping downe to her in drery *swound* VI. iii. 27. 7
Her to recure out of that stony *swound,* VI. v. 6. 4
to the ground he fell in senselesse *swone:* VI. vi. 30. 7
Possessed of sweete sleepe that luld him soft in *swound.* VI. vii. 18. 9
ne out of *swoune* awooke, VI. vii. 48. 5
fell down with him in drerie *swound.* VI. xi. 19. 9

Swooned. His mother *swowned* thrise, III. iv. 35. 1
he *swownd,* he perdy dyde, III. x. 7. 4
all thy senses *swowned* In stupid sorow, V. v. 36. 5

Swooning. Out of his *swowning* dreame he gan awake; I. v. 12. 2

Sword. people slew with *sword,* *Gn.* 44
neither *sword* nor dagger he did beare; *Hub.* 215
No griesly famine, nor no raging *sweard,* *Col.* 314
he suddenly up start With *sword* in hand, I. ii. 5. 2
The Sarazin . . . Snatcheth his *sword,* I. ii. 17. 2

Sword—*Continued.*
forth his *swerd* he drawes. . . . . I. iii. 41. 9
With Elfin *sword* most shamefully betrade? . . . . I. v. 22. 8
the world with *sword* and fire warrayd; . . . . I. v. 48. 2
Ne dint of direfull *sword* divide the substance would. . . . . I. vii. 33. 9
shield and *sword,* and armour all he wrought . . . . I. vii. 36. 6
His biting *sword,* and his devouring speare, ... I. vii. 48. 2
Encountring fiers with single *sword* in hand; . . . . I. viii. 12. 8
With dint of *swerd,* nor push of pointed speare: . . . . I. xi. 9. 4
With fire and *sword* the region to invade: . . . . I. xi. 14. 6
His trusty *sword* he cald to his last aid, ... I. xi. 42. 2
his sharpe *sword* Against her snowy brest . . . . II. i. 11. 6
The dead knights *sword* out of his sheath he drew, ... II. i. 61. 1
thousand furies wait on wrathfull *sword;* . . . . II. ii. 30. 7
wanted *sword* to wreake his enmitee? . . . . II. iii. 12. 4
hath his *sword* through hard assay forgone, ... II. iii. 12. 6
doe purvay Your selfe of *sword* . . . . II. iii. 15. 5
To measure manhood by the *sword* or mayle. . . . . II. iii. 16. 5
Withouten *sword* or shield, an hoste to quayle? . . . . . . II. iii. 16. 7
with one *sword* seven knightes I brought to end, ... II. iii. 17. 7
Thenceforth in battaile never *sword* to beare, ... II. iii. 17. 8
He hath a *sword* that flames like burning brond. . . . . . . II. iii. 18. 5
With that he drew his flaming *sword,* . . . . II. v. 6. 1
his *sword* forth drew, ... II. vi. 29. 3
Cymochles *sword* on Guyons shield yglaunst, ... II. vi. 31. 3
Holding in hand a goodly arming *sword,* . . . . II. vi. 47. 6
fiers Pyrochles, lacking his owne *sword,* . . . . II. viii. 19. 1
Beteeme to you this *sword,* you to defend, ... II. viii. 19. 6
that same knights owne *sword* this is, ... II. viii. 20. 1
His owne good *sword* Morddure, ... II. viii. 30. 7
Wanting his *sword* when he on foot should fight: . . . . . . II. viii. 34. 2
Sir Guyons *sword* he lightly to him raught, ... II. viii. 40. 2
To use that *sword* so well as he it ought!' . . . . II. viii. 40. 4
With his owne *swerd* he fierce at him did flye, ... II. viii. 47. 4
that straunge *sword* refusd to serve his neede, ... II. viii. 49. 2
his shield he lakt And *sword* saw not, ... II. viii. 53. 4
robbed mee Of my good *sword* and shield?' . . . . II. viii. 54. 2
The Briton Prince recov'ring his stolne *sword,* . . . . . . II. ix. 2. 2
with his victour *sword* . . . . II. x. 23. 6
lost his *sword,* yet to be seene this day. . . . . II. x. 49. 5
with his *sword* disperst the raskall flockes, ... II. xi. 19. 2
His owne good *sword* Mordure, ... II. xi. 41. 6
snatching his bright *sword* began to close With her . . . . III. i. 9. 3
the *sword* was servaunt unto right; . . . . III. i. 13. 2
by dint of *sword* approve, That she is fairer . . . . III. i. 27. 3
with her flaming *sword* about her layd, ... III. i. 66. 2
Hurling his *sword* away he lightly lept . . . . III. vii. 33. 6
Then drew he his bright *sword,* . . . . III. ix. 16. 9
By Sanglamort my *sword,* . . . shall dearely it repent; . . . III. x. 32. 5
she did extend Her *sword* high over him, ... III. xii. 36. 9
Stood still amaz'd, holding his idle *sweard;* . . . . IV. iii. 31. 7
at that instant reaching forth his *sweard* . . . . IV. iii. 33. 6
when his speare was brust, his *sword* he drew, ... IV. iv. 41. 3
Unto her *sword* and shield her soone betooke; . . . . IV. vi. 14. 8
cruell *sword* out of his fingers slacke Fell downe . . . . . IV. vi. 21. 5
weld his naked *sword,* and try the edges keene. . . . . . . IV. vii. 45. 9
perforce with *sword* and targe Her forth to fetch, ... IV. xii. 14. 7
his *sword* he drew all wrathfully, ... V. i. 18. 5
A broken *sword* within a bloodie field; . . . . V. i. 19. 8
For proofe shew forth thy *sword,* . . . . V. iii. 21. 5
this the *sword* which wrought those cruell stounds, ... V. iii. 22. 1
With th' other drew his *sword;* . . . . V. iii. 29. 7
thrise did lay his hand upon his *sword,* . . . . V. iii. 36. 3
broke his *sword* in twaine, ... V. iii. 37. 9
with dint of *sword* . . . their rights to try, ... V. iv. 6. 1
Under my foote let each lay downe his *sword;* . . . . V. iv. 16. 7
So each of them layd downe his *sword* . . . . V. iv. 16. 9
his sharpe *sword* he threw from him apart, ... V. v. 13. 3
by abandoning his *sword,* . . . . V. v. 17. 7
Tho with her *sword* on him she flatling strooke, ... V. v. 18. 1
broke his *sword,* for feare of further harmes, ... V. v. 21. 8
She quickly caught her *sword,* . . . . V. vi. 28. 9

Sword—*Continued.*
at her feet her *sword* was likewise layde, ... V. ix. 30. 6
He with his *sword* it strooke, ... V. xi. 29. 8
Under her wombe his fatall *sword* he thrust, ... V. xi. 31. 2
that bright *sword,* the *sword* of Justice lent, ... V. xii. 40. 5
were he here, that would it with his *sword* Abett, ... VI. i. 28. 3
By his owne *sword,* and by the crosse thereon, ... VI. i. 43. 6
He cared not for dint of *sword* nor speere, ... VI. iv. 4. 6
without *sword* his person to defend: . . . . VI. iv. 17. 5
this land, late conquer'd by his *sword* . . . . VI. iv. 29. 5
without *sword* upon his thigh to sit: . . . . VI. v. 8. 8
Inflicts with dint of *sword,* . . . . VI. vi. 1. 2
with his *sword* him on the head did smyte, ... VI. vi. 30. 6
flaming *sword* in hand his terror more to breed. . . . . . . VI. vii. 11. 9
Swore by his *sword* . . . would seeke. . . . . VI. vii. 13. 8
snatching neare his syde His trustie *sword,* . . . . VI. vii. 25. 4
With his sharpe *sword* he fiercely at him flew, ... VI. viii. 9. 2
The rest, that scape his *sword* and death eschew, ... VI. viii. 49. 8
Provided him a *sword* of meanest sort; . . . . VI. xi. 42. 6
He breath'd his *sword,* and rested him till day; . . . . . . VI. xi. 47. 2
Mongst which he found a *sword* of better say, ... VI. xi. 47. 5

Swordfish. A *sword-fish* small him from the rest did sunder, . *Van.* v. 8

Sword's. as a *swords* poynt through his hart did perse, ... I. ix. 48. 2
her *swords* point directing forward right . . . . III. xi. 25. 3

Swords. Through power of that he runnes through enemies *swerds:* . . . . *Hub.* 1283
deadly accents, which like *swords* Did wound . . . . *D.* 297
clash their shields, and shake their *swerds* on hy, ... I. iv. 40. 3
never meant with words, but *swords,* to plead . . . . I. iv. 42. 9
brought unto him *swords,* ropes, poison, fire, ... I. ix. 50. 6
underneath her feet their *swords* they mard, ... III. i. 30. 6
brought through points of many perilous *swords:* . . . . . . III. viii. 17. 3
Their *swerds* and speres were broke, ... III. xi. 52. 6
drawing both their *swords,* . . . on other flew, ... IV. ii. 17. 7
to their tryed *swords* them selves betake; . . . . IV. iv. 29. 2
many *swords* that lode on him did lay. . . . . IV. iv. 31. 5
shivered speares, and *swords* all under strowen, ... IV. iv. 38. 4
Chrysaor, that all other *swords* excelled, ... V. i. 9. 8
They drew their *swords,* . . . . V. viii. 10. 2
through thousand *swords* and speares; . . . . *H.L.* 228

Swore. *See* **Sware.**
thereto *swore;* for who would not oft sweare, ... *Hub.* 1057
Witnesse the burning Altars, which he *swore,* . . . . I. xii. 27. 5
I present was . . . When armes he *swore,* . . . . II. i. 19. 7
when he knighthood *swore,* . . . . II. viii. 20. 3
swore him fealty to win or loose. . . . . II. x. 37. 9
swore that he would lodge with them yfere, ... III. ix. 13. 7
swore to him true fealtie for aye. . . . . VI. i. 44. 4
Swore by his sword . . . him where so he were would seeke. . VI. vii. 13. 8
oftentimes by Turmagant and Mahound *swore.* . . . . VI. vii. 47. 9

Sworn. He nought forgott how he whilome had *sworne,* . . . . I. xii. 41. 6
by the knighthood which they sure had *sworn,* . . . . II. ii. 27. 7
Some, of *sworne* friends that did their faith forgoe; . . . . IV. i. 24. 3

Swownd. *See* **Swoon.**

Sybbe. *See* **Sib.**

Sycophants. Now Parasites and *Sycophants* doo share: . . . . *T.M.* 472

Syker. *See* **Sicker.**

Sylla. Ambitious *Sylla,* and sterne Marius; . . . . I. v. 49. 8

Sylvans. the holy Faunes . . . And *Sylvanes* haunten rathe; *S.C.* Jul. 78

Sylvanus. Whiles old *Sylvanus* slept in shady arber sownd: . . I. vi. 7. 9
So towards old *Sylvanus* they her bring; . . . . I. vi. 14. 5
old *Sylvanus* selfe bethinkes not what To thinke . . . . . . I. vi. 16. 3
To do their service to *Sylvanus* old, ... I. vi. 33. 2

Sylvius. that same Brute, . . . was *Sylvius* his sonne, ... III. ix. 48. 2

Symbol. as a sacred *Symbole,* it may dwell . . . . II. ii. 10. 7

Sympathize. The which your forms first sourse may *sympathize,* *H.B.* 192

Sympathy. joyne together in sweete *sympathie,* . . . . *H.B.* 199

Synah, Synd, Syrian. *See* **Sinai, Signed, Sirian.**

Syrinx. *Syrinx* rejoyse that ever was her lot To beare . . . . *S.C.* Ap. 93

Syrinx'. shee is *Syrinx* daughter without spotte, ... *S.C.* Ap. 50

Sysillius. *See* **Caecily.**

Sythe, Sytten. *See* **Sithe, Sit.**

T

Tabernacle. mynd Dwels in deformed *tabernacle* drownd, . . *H.B.* 142

Tabernacles. May heavenly *tabernacles* there inherit, ... *Epith.* 422

Table. painted in a *table* plaine, The damned ghosts . . . . . I. ix. 49. 6
Like a broad *table* did it selfe dispred, ... II. iii. 24. 2
A *table,* for eternall moniment Of thy great grace . . . . . III. iv. 10. 7
Bacchus fruit . . . He on the *table* dasht, ... III. ix. 30. 4
the fayre mayd the *table* ta'ne away, ... VI. ix. 18. 2
A goodly *table* of pure yvory, ... *Am.* lxxvii. 2
Her brest that *table* was, so richly spredd; . . . . *Am.* lxxvii. 13

Tables. Wherein were many *tables* fayre dispred, ... II. ix. 27. 2
Tho were the *tables* taken all away; . . . . III. i. 56. 6

Tabor. Yet on mount *Thabor* quite their wits forgat, ... VII. vii. 7. 7
The pipe, the *tabor,* and the trembling Croud, ... *Epith.* 131

Taborer. Before them yode a lusty *Tabrere,* . . . . *S.C.* May 22

Tabrere. *See* **Taborer.**

Tackle. The sailes of golde, of silke the *tackle* were: . . . . . *Pet.* ii. 3

Tackles. Till she repaired have her *tackles* spent, ... I. xii. 42. 6

Tail. he threats his teeth, his *tayle,* his pawes, ... *Van.* x. 11
His *tayle* he clapt betwixt his legs . . . . *S.C.* May 280
th' Apes long *taile* . . . he quight Cut off, ... *Hub.* 1381
had it armes and wings, and head and *taile,* . . . . *Col.* 218
Her huge long *taile* her den all overspred, ... I. i. 15. 2
hurling her hideous *taile* About her cursed head; . . . . . . I. i. 16. 2
turning fierce her speckled *taile* advaunst, ... I. i. 17. 6

Tail—*Continued.*
An hatefull Snake, the which his *taile* uptyes In many folds, . I. iv. 31. 4
then downe his *taile* he hong, ... I. v. 34. 7
His *tayle* was stretched out in wondrous length, ... I. vii. 18. 1
scaly *tayle* was stretcht adowne his back full low. . . . . . I. vii. 31. 9
at her rompe she growing had behind A foxes *taile,* . . . . . I. viii. 48. 4
His huge long *tayle,* wownd up in hundred foldes, ... I. xi. 11. 1
passing by, did brush With his long *tayle,* . . . . I. xi. 16. 9
His hideous *tayle* then hurled he about, ... I. xi. 23. 1
his huge *taile* he quite a sonder clefte; . . . . I. xi. 39. 8
He, turning *taile,* Back to the strond retyrd, ... II. vi. 40. 5
the villein turn'd his face . . . Unto his Tygres *taile,* . . . . II. xi. 26. 9
hideous *tayle* his lefte foot did enfold, ... III. xi. 48. 7
Over his horses *taile* above a stryde; . . . . IV. iv. 44. 5
a snake, whose head and *tail* were fast combyned. . . . . . . IV. x. 40. 9
Crocodile . . . with her wreathed *taile* her middle did enfold. V. vii. 6. 9
her long *taile* and fethers strongly shooke, ... V. xi. 22. 7
A Dragons *taile,* whose sting . . . Full deadly wounds . . . . V. xi. 24. 5
Tho with her huge long *taile* she at him strooke, ... V. xi. 28. 6
So was he stound with stroke of her huge *taile;* . . . . . . V. xi. 29. 6
With his long *taile* the bryzes brush away. . . . . VI. i. 24. 5
Some by the nose him pluckt, some by the *taile,* . . . . VII. vi. 49. 4

Tails. They wont in the wind wagge their wrigle *tayles,* . . . *S.C.* F. 7
of their *tailes* are utterlie bereft. . . . . *Hub.* 1384

Take—*Continued.*
take what fortune, time, and place would lend. . . . . . . VII. vi. 23. 6
whence she her name did *take;* . . . . VII. vii. 50. 4
doth many changes *take,* . . . . VII. vii. 54. 5
thou of then mayst mightie vengeance *take,* . . . . *Am.* x. 8
Take heed, therefore, myne eyes, ... *Am.* xxxvii. 9
take delight t' encrease a wretches woe; . . . . *Am.* xli. 7
when in hand my tunelesse harp I *take,* . . . . *Am.* xliv. 9
they *take* pleasure in her cruell play, ... *Am.* xlvii. 11
That of her presens I my meed may *take.* . . . . *Am.* lii. 14
Unlesse she doe him by the forelock *take;* . . . . *Am.* lxx. 8
Doe you him *take,* and . . . Gently encage, ... *Am.* lxxiii. 9
some pitty *take,* When thou doest spoyle of lovers make.' . . *Epig.* iv. 39
Where none doo fishes *take;* . . . . *Epith.* 61
through the world his way he gan to *take,* . . . . *H.L.* 74
Which at first blowing *take* not hastie fyre; . . . . *H.L.* 174
vouchsafe to *take* of me This simple song, ... *H.L.* 306
of the soule the bodie forme doth *take;* . . . . *H.B.* 132
things immortall no corruption *take.* . . . . *H.B.* 161
from another place I *take* my name, ... *Proth.* 130

Taken. *See* **Take.**
taken up his ynne in Fishes haske. . . . . *S.C.* N. 16
on us *taken* anie state of life, ... *Hub.* 407
my Daphne they have *tane* away; . . . . *D.* 365
From mothers pap I *taken* was unfitt, ... I. ix. 3. 7
Tho were the tables *taken* all away; . . . . III. i. 56. 6
from the howre I *taken* was from nourses tender pap, . . . III. ii. 6. 2
Was *taken* with her love, and by her closely lay. . . . . . III. iv. 19. 9
upon thy selfe hast lately *ta'ne?'* . . . . III. vii. 53. 3
hast a thanklesse service on thee *ta'ne,* . . . . III. viii. 47. 3
Of two grim lyons, *taken* from the wood, ... IV. iii. 39. 2
They have him *taken* captive, though it grieve him sore. . . IV. iv. 32. 9
when they had long time there *taken* rest, ... IV. vi. 42. 1
'Then was I *taken* and before her brought, ... IV. viii. 56. 1
I, having armes then *taken,* . . . . IV. x. 4. 3
now perforce they have him prisoner *taken;* . . . . V. iii. 9. 6
Which long agoe he *taken* had in hond: . . . . V. iv. 3. 7
the bold title of a poet bad He on himselfe had *ta'en,* . . . V. ix. 25. 9
Had hid themselves, or *taken* further flight: . . . . V. x. 19. 4
taken have this toylesome paine For wretched woman, ... V. x. 21. 2
long having since *Taken* in hand th' exploit, ... V. xii. 3. 2
He rather should have *taken* up behind; . . . . VI. ii. 11. 5
the fayre mayd the table *ta'ne* away, ... VI. ix. 18. 2
With them also was *taken* Coridon, ... VI. x. 41. 1
He *taken* was, betrayd, and false accused; . . . . *H.H.L.* 240

Takes. Unwisely weaves, that *takes* two webbes in hand. . . . *S.C.* O. 102
takes survey, with curious busie eye, ... *Mui.* 171
Of everie one he *takes,* and tastes at will, ... *Mui.* 203
of nothing he *takes* keepe. . . . . I. i. 40. 9
he her *takes* To be the fairest wight that lived yit; . . . . . I. ii. 30. 3
he . . . marcheth home, and by her *takes* the knight, ... I. v. 16. 6
Sometimes Diana he her *takes* to be, ... I. vi. 16. 8
To weete what course he *takes,* . . . . II. i. 4. 4
Your court'sie *takes* on you anothers dew offence.' . . . . . II. i. 28. 9
he *takes* and paies; . . . . II. ii. 25. 6
He lives, but *takes* small joy of his renowne; . . . . III. v. 26. 1
of his sweetnesse *takes* her fill. . . . . III. vi. 46. 9
So *takes* in hond To seeke her . . . . III. x. 19. 4
from one a weapon fiercely *takes.* . . . . IV. iv. 34. 9
The Squire of low degree, releast, Aemylia *takes* to wife: . . IV. ix. Arg.
nathlesse he *takes* great joy . . . . IV. xi. 19. 8
As rated Spaniell *takes* his burden up for feare. . . . . . . V. i. 29. 9
He gives to this, from that he *takes* away, ... V. ii. 41. 8
takes the enterprize For Belgee for to fight: . . . . V. x. Arg.

Takest. For-thy thereof thou *takest* shame. . . . . *To his Booke* 15
of our tender Lambkins *takest* keepe, ... *S.C.* D. 8
Why *takest* not of that same fruite of gold? . . . . II. vii. 63. 7
Whom to thy selfe thou *takest* quite away? . . . . IV. ii. 13. 7

Taketh. Yet no man for them *taketh* paines or care, ... II. vi. 15. 8
Taketh his nimble winges, and soone away is gone.' . . . . . III. i. 25. 9
of all love *taketh* equall vew; . . . . III. v. 47. 5
taketh vengeaunce of his peoples spoile; . . . . VI. viii. 23. 2
But *taketh* glory in her cruelnesse. . . . . *Am.* xx. 12

Taking. Great pittie is, he be in such *taking,* . . . . *S.C.* Ap. 156
Taking to hoste, it quite from him did stay; . . . . *Gn.* 196
In *taking* on himselfe, in common sight, ... *Hub.* 860
Where *taking* Conge, each one by and by Departed . . . . . *Hub.* 1108
without *taking* leave he foorth did goe . . . . *D.* 563
taking up to heaven, him godded new. . . . . *Col.* 810
taking by the hand that Faeries sonne, ... I. x. 33. 2
The weapon bright, *Taking* advantage of his open jaw, . . . I. xi. 53. 6
taking Conge of that virgin pure, ... II. iii. 2. 1
taking armes the Britons to her drew; . . . . II. x. 54. 7
taking courteous conge, ... II. xi. 17. 3
taking his full course Until he came . . . . II. xi. 46. 5
taking it out of her tender hond, ... II. xii. 57. 2
taking thrise three heares from off her head, ... III. ii. 50. 1
that same Armory Downe *taking,* . . . . III. iii. 59. 8
up him *taking* in their tender hands, ... III. iv. 42. 1
she passed forth, not *taking* leave, ... IV. i. 36. 7
Whose scoffed words he *taking* halfe in scorne, ... IV. ii. 6. 6
wise Cambina, *taking* by her side Faire Canacee, ... IV. iii. 51. 6
taking with her lovely Amoret, ... IV. v. 29. 3
With Beares and Tygers *taking* heavie part, ... IV. vii. 2. 7
taking leave of all, with him did beare Faire Amoret, . . . IV. ix. 17. 6
each one *taking* part in others aide . . . . IV. ix. 24. 7
taking downe the shield with me did it retaine. . . . . . . IV. x. 10. 9
many rivers *taking* under-hand Into his waters . . . . IV. xi. 34. 3
taking usurie of time fore-past, ... V. iii. 40. 3
taking her from me, his owne love left astray. . . . . V. iv. 9. 9

Taking—*Continued.*
Yet *taking* leave of her he did depart. . . . . V. vi. 24. 4
Then *taking* leave of them, she forward went . . . . V. vii. 24. 6
taking with him, as his vanquisht thrall, That Damzell, . . . V. viii. 26. 3
Taking them up unto her stately throne, ... V. ix. 37. 6
of her widowhed *Taking* advantage, ... V. x. 12. 2
Then *taking* humble leave of that great Queene, ... V. x. 17. 1
Of whom yet *taking* leave thence forth he went, ... V. xi. 35. 7
taking from her hand a ring of gould, ... VI. i. 29. 2
Neither of other *taking* pitty nor remorse. . . . . VI. i. 33. 9
Whereof he *taking* oddes, ... VI. ii. 18. 4
taking counsell of a wise man red, ... VI. ii. 30. 1
So *taking* courteous leave they parted twayne, ... VI. ii. 38. 8
Of which occasion Aldine *taking* hold . . . . VI. iii. 15. 1
Then *taking* up that Recreants shield and speare, ... VI. iv. 13. 1
For want of *taking* heede unto the same, ... VI. vi. 2. 4
taking them apart into his cell, ... VI. vi. 6. 1
from him *taking* his owne whip, ... VI. viii. 28. 8
So humbly *taking* leave she turnd aside; . . . . VI. viii. 30. 6
taking up, brought home and noursed well . . . . VI. ix. 14. 7
taking leave of that same gentle Swaine, ... VI. x. 32. 1
taking leave of his faire Pastorell, ... VI. xii. 13. 6
taking litle paine To knit the knot, ... *Am.* vi. 13
in their roring *taking* great delight; . . . . *H.L.* 48
taking to him wings of his owne heate, ... *H.L.* 64
So, *taking* flesh of sacred virgins wombe, ... *H.H.L.* 146

Talaunts. *See* **Talons.**

Tale. But shall I tel thee a *tale* of truth, ... *S.C.* F. 91
Here is a long *tale,* and little worth. . . . . *S.C.* F. 240
But little ease of thy lewd *tale* I tasted: . . . . *S.C.* F. 245
lette me thy *tale* borrowe . . . . *S.C.* May 308
this long *tale* Nought easeth the care . . . . *S.C.* S. 242
when her turne was come her *tale* to tell, ... *Hub.* 36
Better a short *tale* than a bad long shriving: . . . . *Hub.* 543
'Heare then . . . the tenor of my *tale,* . . . . *Col.* 100
Alexis broke his *tale* asunder, ... *Col.* 352
The wofull *tale* that Trevisan had told, ... I. ix. 37. 2
To tell this ruefull *tale:* . . . . II. i. 9. 9
'Tell on, fayre Sir, . . . 'that dolefull *tale,* . . . . II. ii. 45. 1
of his pitteous *tale* he end did make: . . . . II. ii. 46. 4
Yet should it be a pleasant *tale,* . . . . IV. i. 5. 1
So ended he his *tale,* where I this Canto end. . . . . . . IV. x. 58. 9
sent them home to tell a piteous *tale* . . . . V. iv. 24. 8
So smooth of tongue, and subtile in his *tale,* . . . . . . V. ix. 5. 6
The Infant hearkned wisely to her *tale,* . . . . VI. viii. 25. 1
'Where shall I then commence This wofull *tale?* . . . . . VI. xi. 30. 3

Tales. Many meete *tales* of youth did he make, ... *S.C.* F. 98
tell us mery *tales* to keepe us wake, ... *S.C.* Jun. 87
pleasant *tales* (fit for that idle stound) . . . . *Hub.* 26
greatly joyed merry *tales* to faine, ... II. vi. 6. 4
leasings, *tales,* and lies. . . . . II. ix. 51. 9
faynes to weave false *tales* and leasings bad, ... V. xii. 36. 8
The false reports that flying *tales* doe beare, ... *H.L.* 261

Talk. a fooles *talke* to beare and to heare. . . . . *S.C.* May 141
medled his *talke* with many a teare: . . . . *S.C.* May 263
Tho may we *talke* and tellen our fill, ... *S.C.* S. 53
talke, that might unquiet fancies reave; . . . . *Hub.* 24
so much to *talke* Of labour, ... *Hub.* 267
all their *talke* and studie is of it. . . . . *Col.* 778
He stayd not lenger *talke,* . . . . II. i. 13. 1
Provoking him, by her outrageous *talke,* . . . . II. iv. 5. 3
to occasion him to further *talke,* . . . . III. ii. 12. 1
little lust had she to *talke* of ought, ... V. vi. 21. 1
your tongue, your *talk* restraine From that they most affect, VI. vi. 7. 8
Shun secresie, and *talke* in open sight: . . . . VI. vi. 14. 8
They fall to strokes, the frute of too much *talke,* . . . . . VI. xi. 16. 2

Talked. Whiles thus she *talked,* and whiles thus she toyd, . . II. vi. 11. 1
So *talked* they, the whiles They wasted had much way, . . . II. ix. 9. 8
Thus as they *talked,* loe! where nigh at hand . . . . . . IV. viii. 62. 6
Ne ever ought but of their true loves *talkt,* . . . . IV. x. 25. 8
talk't of pleasant things the night away to weare. . . . . . V. vi. 22. 9
Whylest thus he *talkt,* . . . . VI. ix. 26. 1

Tall. at sea a *tall* ship did appeare, ... *Pet.* ii. 1
raysde up on yvorie pillours [*text,* pillowes] *tall,* . . . . . *Bel.*[2] iv. 1
Thou placer of plants both humble and *tall,* . . . . *S.C.* F. 164
the Cedar proud and *tall;* . . . . I. i. 8. 6
his foe, a Gyaunt huge and *tall;* . . . . I. vii. 51. 2
tall young men, all hable armes to sownd; . . . . I. xii. 5. 7
dismounting straict From his *tall* steed, ... II. i. 39. 2
As a *tall* ship tossed in troublous seas, ... II. ii. 24. 1
His portaunce terrible, and stature *tall,* . . . . II. vii. 41. 4
Tall yoemen seemed they and of great might, ... II. ix. 26. 4
There placed was a caudron wide and *tall* . . . . II. ix. 29. 5
the *tall* trees with leaves appareled . . . . II. xii. 12. 4
A comely personage of stature *tall,* . . . . II. xii. 46. 4
for ye beene *tall.* And large of limbe . . . . III. iii. 53. 6
in his hand a *tall* young oake he bore, ... IV. vii. 7. 4
From lowest Juniper to Ceder *tall,* . . . . IV. x. 22. 2
Nathlesse thereto he was full stout and *tall,* . . . . VI. i. 2. 7
he spyde A *tall* young man, ... VI. ii. 3. 7
a slender slip, . . . but *tall* and faire of face, ... VI. ii. 5. 4
standing on his tiptoes, to seeme *tall,* . . . . VI. viii. 26. 5
Beeing of stature *tall* as any there . . . . VII. vi. 28. 3
Being far greater and more *tall* of stature . . . . VII. vii. 5. 3

Tallest. The hight of three the *tallest* sonnes of mortall seed. . I. vii. 8. 9

Tallness. with his *tallnesse* seemd to threat the skye; . . . . I. vii. 8. 5

Talons. With griping *talaunts* armd to greedy fight, ... I. viii. 48. 7
Ne wist yett how his *talaunts* to unfold; . . . . I. xi. 41. 3
come too neare, and with his *talants* play, ... I. xii. 11. 2
his *talants* may Yet scratch my sonne, ... I. xii. 11. 5

Talus. His name was *Talus,* made of yron mould, V. i. 12. 6
Until that *Talus* had his pride represt, V. i. 29. 5
Ne wight with him but onely *Talus* went; V. i. 30. 8
bad his servant *Talus* to invent Which way V. ii. 20. 8
Talus, that could like a lime-hound winde her, V. ii. 25. 3
All which when *Talus* throughly had perfourmed, V. ii. 28. 6
Whom when so lewdly minded *Talus* found, V. ii. 49. 6
Therefore he *Talus* to them sent V. ii. 52. 8
When *Talus* saw they all the field forsooke, V. ii. 54. 7
Talus by the backe the boaster hent, V. iii. 37. 2
he *Talus* sent To wrecke on them their follies hardyment: V. iv. 24. 4
Him *Talus* tooke out of perplexitie, V. iv. 25. 3
Talus usde . . . To keepe a nightly watch V. iv. 46. 8
Then *Talus* forth issuing from the tent V. iv. 50. 5
when they thought on *Talus* hands to lay, V. v. 19. 1
Talus brings newes to Britomart V. vi. Arg.
sad tydings . . . *Talus* to her brought; V. vi. 3. 4
it was *Talus,* Artegall his groome: V. vi. 8. 6
'*Talus,* be bold, And tell what ever it be, V. vi. 10. 1
She unto *Talus* forth return'd againe, V. vi. 15. 4
bad *Talus* guide her on. V. vi. 17. 9
To seeke her Knight, as *Talus* her did guide. V. vi. 18. 2
Ne lesse did *Talus* suffer sleepe to seaze His eye-lids sad, V. vi. 26. 5
Whom soone as *Talus* spide by glims of night, V. vi. 29. 5
Yet *Talus* after them apace did plie, V. vi. 30. 4
Talus desir'd that he might have prepared The way V. vi. 38. 4
Talus mote not be admitted to her part. V. vii. 3. 9
Whiles *Talus* watched at the dore all night. V. vii. 26. 4
swift *Talus* did the formost win; V. vii. 35. 2
Ne wight but onely *Talus* with him went, V. viii. 3. 8
by his stirrup *Talus* did attend, V. viii. 29. 6
Talus soone him overtooke, and backward drew. V. ix. 18. 9
With onely *Talus* wayting diligent, V. xi. 36. 7
chiefly *Talus* with his yron flayle, V. xi. 59. 4
Talus into the sea did forth issew V. xii. 5. 4
Talus sternely did upon them set, V. xii. 7. 3
Talus to revoke from the right way V. xii. 27. 5
Talus, hearing her so lewdly raile, V. xii. 43. 1
Talus'. Of Justice, which in *Talus* hand did lye; V. ii. 26. 2
Tamar. There was the speedy *Tamar,* IV. xi. 31. 1
Tambourines. Theyr yvory Luyts and *Tamburins* forgoe, *S.C.* Jun. 59
Tame. The same, which Pyrrhus . . . could not *tame,* *Ro.* xxi. 2
His musicks might the hellish hound did *tame.* *S.C.* O. 30
hunt the hartlesse hare til shee were *tame.* *S.C.* D. 28
So wilde a beast so *tame* ytaught to bee, *Hub.* 625
He that the stubborne Sprites can wisely *tame,* I. i. 43. 7
wyld roring Buls he would him make To *tame,* I. vi. 24. 7
sturdie courage *tame* with dreadfull aw, I. vi. 26. 8
with streight diet *tame* his stubborne malady. I. x. 25. 9
whoso will raging Furor *tame,* II. iv. 11. 1
fiers Vulcans rage to *tame,* II. vii. 36. 5
Orcus *tame,* whome nothing can persuade, II. xii. 41. 7
them with maystring discipline doth *tame,* IV. ix. 2. 4
the waves to *tame.* IV. xi. 12. 9
no one beast in forrest, wylde or *tame,* VI. v. 15. 7
did his best, . . . to *tame* The poysnous humour VI. vi. 2. 7
Threatning to yoke them two and *tame* their corage stout. VI. viii. 11. 9
doest the Lions and fell Tigers *tame,* *H.L.* 46
Tamed. *Tam'd* all the world, hath *tam'd* herselfe *Ro.* iii. 7
Thus was this Monster . . . supprest and *tamed,* VI. xii. 38. 2
Tameth. *tameth* stubborne youth With iron bit, IV. xii. 13. 3
Tanaquill. Faerie knights, and fayrest *Tanaquill,* I. Pr. 2. 5
He dying left the fairest *Tanaquill,* II. x. 76. 4
Tane. *See* **Taken.**
Tanned. having *tand* his tawney hide With . . . breath of Heaven, I. iii. 31. 4
face all *tand* with scorching sunny ray, I. vi. 35. 4
His face with smoke was *tand,* II. vii. 3. 6
Tantalus. The glorie of the stock of *Tantalus,* *Gn.* 546
There thristy *Tantalus* hong by the chin; I. v. 35. 5
Lo! *Tantalus,* I here tormented lye: II. vii. 59. 5
'Nay, nay, thou greedy *Tantalus,*' II. vii. 60. 1
Like *Tantale,* that in store doth sterved ly, *H.L.* 200
Tapestry. richer seem'd then any *tapestry,* VII. vii. 10. 8
Tapet. What storie she will for her *tapet* take. *Mui.* 276
Tapets. in those *Tapets* weren fashioned Many faire pourtraicts, III. xi. 29. 1
Tar. foming *tarre,* their bridles they would champ, I. v. 28. 8
Tare. *See* **Tore.**
with blasphemous bannes high God in peeces *tare.* III. vii. 39. 9
Targe. his *targe* That broke the violence of his intent, II. v. 6. 5
perforce with sword and *targe* Her forth to fetch, IV. xii. 14. 7
bearing in his *targe* A Ladie VI. ii. 44. 8
Target. His *target* alwayes over her pretended; VI. xi. 19. 4
Tarquin. Proud *Tarquin,* and too lordly Lentulus; I. v. 49. 6
Tarras. *See* **Terraces.**
Tarry. They *tarrie* not, but flit and fall away, *D.* 397
So will I travell whilest I *tarrie* heere, *D.* 466
ne in one stead do *tarry;* VII. vii. 21. 8
Tartar. *See* **Tartarus.**
(As wonts the *Tartar* by the Caspian lake, II. xi. 26. 7
Tartarus. *Tartar* covered With bloodie night, *Gn.* 444
Lastly the squalid lakes of *Tartarie,* *Gn.* 543
furies rules, and *Tartare* tempereth. *Hub.* 1294
Dragon . . . Bred in the loathly lakes of *Tartary,* I. vii. 44. 3
that darke dreadfull hole of *Tartare* steepe II. xii. 6. 4
Tartary. *See* **Tartarus.**
Task. for leaving his Lords *taske,* *S.C.* May 53
Phoebus, weary of his yerely *taske,* *S.C.* N. 14
doth the Learneds *taske* upon him take. *T.M.* 216
Am now enforst, a farre unfitter *taske,* I. Pr. 1. 3

Task—*Continued.*
Dislikefull paine so sad a *taske* to take, IV. ix. 40. 3
So hard a *taske* as life for hyre to sell; VI. vii. 15. 3
Tassels. an horne . . . in twisted gold And *tasselles* gay. I. viii. 3. 7
Tasswage. *See* **Assuage.**
Taste. *Taste* no one hower of happines or merth; *Ti.* 46
Well worthy he to *taste* of wretchednes. *Mui.* 216
I hate to *tast,* for food withholds my dying; *D.* 416
Receive, most noble Lord, a simple *taste* *Ded. Son.* v. 1
To *tast* the streames that, like a golden showre, *Ded. Son.* viii. 9
Loth . . . To *taste* th' untryed dint of deadly steele: I. iii. 34. 6
That hath thee . . . brought to *taste* mine yre? I. iii. 39. 3
scarse good morsell all his life did *taste,* I. iv. 28. 3
of her heavenly learning he might *taste,* I. x. 18. 5
Deserves to *taste* his follies fruit, repented payne.' II. v. 24. 9
thou thy treasons fruit, I hope, shalt *taste* II. viii. 31. 8
the fourth Bulwarke, that is the *Taste,* II. xi. 12. 2
All passers by to *taste* their lushious wine, II. xii. 54. 4
she to Guyon offred it to *tast,* II. xii. 57. 1
Whose root and stalke so bitter yet did *taste,* III. ii. 17. 6
After her heat the breathing cold to *taste:* III. vi. 18. 5
That he might *taste* the sweet consuming woe, III. xi. 45. 4
So did those olde Heroes hereof *taste,* IV. iii. 44. 8
Ne other drinke there did he ever *tast* IV. vii. 41. 6
The *tast* of bloud of some engored beast, IV. ix. 31. 6
To *tast* of joy, and to wont pleasures to retourne. V. iii. 1. 9
Therefore they mote not *taste* of fleshly food, V. vii. 10. 1
man, that never . . . Did *taste* of pittie, VI. iv. 3. 2
ne ever of wyld beast Did *taste* the bloud, VI. iv. 14. 9
Began some smacke of comfort new to *tast,* VI. xi. 45. 3
many sought, yet none could ever *taste;* *Am.* lxxvii. 10
Tasted. But little ease of thy lewd tale I *tasted:* *S.C.* F. 245
never *tasted* grace, nor goodnes felt; II. x. 7. 3
tasted many a bloody wownd.' III. i. 24. 9
Of which so soone as they once *tasted* had, IV. iii. 49. 1
no joy . . . He ever *tasted;* IV. viii. 2. 5
I, that never *tasted* blis IV. x. 28. 1
When as the paine of death she *tasted* had, V. iv. 11. 2
before she *tasted* Latonaes childrens wrath V. x. 7. 8
ere he *tasted* bread He would her succour, VI. i. 31. 4
the use of armes, . . . I have not *tasted* yet; VI. ii. 32. 8
when he once his dreadfull strokes had *tasted,* VI. vi. 28. 1
had *tasted* once (as oft did he) The happy peace VI. x. 3. 3
Tastes. Of everie one he takes, and *tastes* at will, *Mui.* 203
Tastest. Ne *tastest* Princes pleasures, III. ii. 31. 6
Tasteth. Now this, now that, he *tasteth* tenderly, *Mui.* 173
Tasting. great Prometheus *tasting* of our ire, VII. vi. 29. 7
Tattered. their garments yet, Being all rag'd and *tatter'd,* V. xii. 28. 8
Tattling. Ne after everie *tattling* fable flie; *Hub.* 724
Taught. Whose Echo . . . *taught* the byrds, *S.C.* Jun. 53
taught me homely, as I can, to make; *S.C.* Jun. 82
I am *taught,* by Algrinds ill, *S.C.* Jul. 219
now by thy losse art *taught,* *S.C.* S. 68
Whereon he earst had *taught* his flocks to feede, *S.C.* O. 57
tryed time yet *taught* me greater thinges; *S.C.* D. 85
first Triptoleme *taught* how to be sowne. *Gn.* 208
devotion *Taught* him the fires scorn'd furie to detest; *Gn.* 612
round about he *taught* sweete flowres to growe: *Gn.* 665
All shalbe *taught* of God. *Hub.* 440
By whom the flock is rightly fed, and *taught:* *Hub.* 442
Through the Priests holesome counsell lately *tought,* *Hub.* 553
So wilde a beast so tame *ytaught* to bee, *Hub.* 625
taught to beare A Bases part *T.M.* 27
Fortunes freakes, is wisely *taught* to beare: *T.M.* 130
wise wordes, *taught* in numbers for to runne, *Ti.* 402
Him forth did bring, and *taught* her lambs to feed; *As.* 14
Alabaster throughly *taught* In all this skill, *Col.* 400
And *taught* in such accordance to agree? *Col.* 846
And *taught* ambitious Rome to tyrannise *Ded. Son.* i. 3
whose Muse whylome did maske, As time her *taught,* I. Pr. 1. 2
with usage sly He *taught* to imitate that Lady trew, I. i. 46. 8
being *taught,* he forward gan advaunce His . . . steed, I. iii. 25. 8
sage Counsellours . . . *Taught* to obay their bestiall beheasts, I. iv. 18. 3
he *taught* the tender ymp . . . To banish cowardize I. vi. 24. 1
whom he had not *taught* To feare his force: I. vi. 29. 4
What justice ever other judgement *taught,* I. ix. 38. 3
house of Holinesse; Where he is *taught* repentaunce, I. x. Arg.
she him *taught* celestiall discipline, I. x. 18. 8
Speranza . . . *taught* him how to take assured hold I. x. 22. 2
taught the way that does to heaven bownd!' I. x. 67. 4
Who *taught* his trampling steed with equall steps to tread. II. i. 7. 9
taught T' avenge his Parents death II. iii. 2. 8
She *taught* to tread, II. iii. 28. 6
For it was *taught* the way which she would have, II. vi. 5. 8
open, as it had beene *taught.* II. vii. 35. 3
Damsels which were *taught* That service well. II. ix. 19. 5
first *taught* men a woman to obay: II. x. 20. 7
taught her first how to be conquered; II. x. 23. 8
taught the land from wearie wars to cease: II. x. 25. 5
Aegerie that Numa *tought:* II. x. 42. 8
goodly *taught* to tilt and turnament: III. i. 44. 7
They were all *taught* by Triton to obay III. iv. 33. 3
Taught of the Nymphe which from her infancy Her nourced III. v. 32. 4
young birds, which he had *taught* to sing, III. vii. 17. 3
fear gave her wings, and need her corage *taught.* III. vii. 26. 9
taught the carefull Mariner to play, III. viii. 20. 3
a Lion . . . *Taught* to obay the menage of that Elfe III. xii. 22. 3
Mulla mine, whose waves I whilom *taught* to weep. IV. xi. 41. 9
all the depth of rightfull doome was *taught* V. i. 5. 3
all the discipline of justice there him *taught.* V. i. 6. 9

Taught—*Continued.*
she him *taught* to weigh both right and wrong . . . . . . V. i. 7. 1
Thus she him trayned, and thus she him *taught* . . . . V. i. 8. 1
Like as the workeman had their courses *taught;* . . . . . . V. v. 2. 5
Ne would be *taught* with any termes . . . . V. v. 46. 3
Ne none can find but who was *taught* them by the Muse. . . . VI. Pr. 2. 9
as in bookes is *taught*. . . . . VI. vi. 9. 9
So *taught* of nature, ... VI. ix. 20. 6
right so as Coridon had *taught:* . . . . VI. xi. 41. 7
Love is the lesson which the Lord us *taught*. . . . . . . *Am.* lxviii. 14
With sacred rites hast *taght* to solemnize; . . . . *Epith.* 393
mercy . . . Unto us *taught,* and to approve it trew, ... *H.H.L.* 212
Taugment. *See* **Augment.**
Taunt. All carelesse of his *taunt* and bitter rayle; . . . . . . IV. i. 43. 2
To whom that other did this *taunt* returne: . . . . VI. iii. 31. 6
Not sparing him with bitter words to *taunt,* . . . . VI. vi. 21. 7
Taunts. With bitter *taunts* and termes of vile disgrace. . . . . V. iv. 23. 4
I . . . backe returned His scornefull *taunts* . . . . VI. ii. 12. 2
How with most scornefull *taunts,* and fell despights, ... *H.H.L.* 241
Tawdry. gird in your waste . . . with a *tawdrie* lace. . . . . . *S.C.* Ap. 135
Tawny. having tand his *tawney* hide With . . . breath of Heaven, ... I. iii. 31. 4
bitt his *tawny* beard to shew his raging yre. . . . . II. iv. 15. 9
the sunburnt Indians do aray Their *tawney* bodies . . . . . III. xii. 8. 4
Teach. *teache* the trees their trickling teares to shedde. . . . . *S.C.* Jun. 96
love does *teach* him climbe so hie, ... *S.C.* O. 91
teache her tread aloft in buskin fine, ... *S.C.* O. 113
To *teach* the ruder shepheard how . . . . *S.C.* Env. 5
be rul'd to doo as I doo *teach*.' . . . . *Hub.* 992
To *teach* the warbling pipe to sound aloft, ... *T.M.* 290
by demonstration me to *teach,* . . . . *Ti.* 488
Her name Ile *teach* in knowen terms to frame: . . . . . . *Col.* 637
lambs . . . Ile *teach* to call for Cynthia by name. . . . . . *Col.* 639
all things els the which his art did *teach:* . . . . I. v. 44. 3
Their backward bent knees *teach* her humbly to obay. . . . . I. vi. 11. 9
her gentle wit she plyes To *teach* them truth, ... I. vi. 19. 6
'I wote,' (quoth he) 'whom tryall late did *teach,* . . . . . I. ix. 31. 3
That none could reade except she did them *teach,* . . . . . I. x. 19. 2
Teach him the weak to strengthen, ... II. iv. 2. 9
teach the cursed steele to bight In his owne flesh, ... II. vi. 32. 8
To *teach* them how to use their present state.' . . . . . . II. vii. 60. 5
our weake hands (need makes good schollers) *teach* . . . . III. iii. 53. 3
*our weake hands (whom need new strength shall *teach*) . III. iii. 53. 3
Hard is to *teach* an old horse amble trew; . . . . III. viii. 26. 3
Whereby his strengthes assay he might him *teach*. . . . . . V. viii. 37. 5
senselesse words, which nature did him *teach* . . . . VI. iv. 11. 8
Having oft seene it tryde as he did *teach:* . . . . VI. iv. 37. 3
teach us how . . . We should our selves demeane, ... VI. x. 23. 7
'Most certaine markes' (sayd she) 'do me it *teach;* . . . . VI. xii. 18. 3
and *teach* my hart to speake; . . . . *Am.* viii. 10
traine and *teach* me with her lookes; . . . . *Am.* xxi. 13
Will *teach* to speak, and my just cause to plead; . . . . . . *Am.* xliii. 10
teach the woods and waters to lament . . . . *Epith.* 10
Teaches. as that Hag him *teaches:* . . . . IV. ii. 12. 5
Teacheth. to heaven she *teacheth* him the ready path. . . . . I. x. 33. 9
reason *teacheth* that the fruitfull seades . . . . III. vi. 8. 3
Need *teacheth* her this lesson hard and rare, ... III. vii. 4. 3
Teaching. *Teaching* the Satyres, which her sat around, ... I. vi. 30. 8
teaching others to doe right. . . . . IV. xi. 18. 9
Tead. *See* **Tede.**
Team. hath reared up His fyerie-footed *teme,* . . . . *S.C.* Jul. 18
Titan draweth neere To loose his *teeme,* . . . . *D.* 469
His sevenfold *teme* behind the stedfast starre . . . . I. ii. 1. 2
With which he forward lasht the laesy *teme,* . . . . I. iv. 36. 3
Her twyfold *Teme* . . . Did softly swim away, ... I. v. 28. 4
them constraine in equall *teme* to draw. . . . . I. vi. 26. 6
his toylesome *teme* that way did guyde, ... I. x. 66. 4
Phoebus . . . Yett harnessed his fyrie-footed *teeme,* . . . . . I. xii. 2. 2
A *teme* of Dolphins raunged in aray . . . . III. iv. 33. 1
Her *teme* at her commaundement quiet stands, ... III. iv. 42. 3
with a *teeme* of scaly Phocas bownd . . . . III. viii. 30. 8
lose the *teme* out of his weary wayne, ... III. viii. 51. 5
Unfitly yokt together in one *teeme*. . . . . III. ix. 6. 2
now my *teme* begins to faint and fayle, ... III. xii. 47. *or.* 3
Her angrie *teame* breaking their bonds of peace . . . . . . IV. iii. 41. 3
my wearie *teeme,* nigh over spent, ... IV. v. 46. 8
his fierie *teme* Towards the westerne brim begins to draw, . V. ix. 35. 1
Now turne againe my *teme,* thou jolly swayne, ... VI. ix. 1. 1
through the Skie draw Venus silver *Teeme;* . . . . *Proth.* 63
Teamed. Night . . . her *teemed* steedes gan call, ... *Gn.* 314
let their *temed* fishes softly swim . . . . III. iv. 34. 3
Teams. Drawing in *teemes* along the starrie skie; . . . . *Gn.* 458
Teamwise. Which foure great Hippodames did draw in *temewise* tyde. . . . . III. xi. 40. 9
Tear. He, plongd in payne, his tressed locks dooth *teare*. . . . *S.C.* Ap. 12
medled his talke with many a *teare:* . . . . *S.C.* May 263
Wolves that would them *teare*. . . . . *S.C.* Jul. 56
We han great Bandogs will *teare* their skinne. . . . . . . *S.C.* S. 163
mickle woe Thereof arose, and manie a rufull *teare,* . . . . *Mui.* 133
Therein stil wait poore passengers to *teare*. . . . . *Col.* 203
'O! spare with guilty hands to *teare* My tender sides . . . . I. ii. 31. 2
gan to . . . beat their brests, and naked flesh to *teare:* . . . I. iii. 22. 5
that harlott . . . That causd her shed so many a bitter *teare;* I. iii. 25. 4
Ofte soust in swelling Tethys saltish *teare;* . . . . I. iii. 31. 3
from the she Beares teats her whelps to *teare;* . . . . I. vi. 24. 5
some had clawes to *teare:* . . . . II. xi. 8. 5
every one did *teare* her girlond from her crowne. . . . . . III. iv. 30. 9
with his teeth did *teare* His rugged flesh, ... III. vii. 20. 4
With greedy jawes her ready for to *teare:* . . . . III. viii. 33. 7
him assayling sore his carkas *teare,* . . . . III. x. 53. 7

Tear—*Continued.*
He wailed womanlike with many a *teare,* . . . . III. xii. 7. 7
from her backe her garments she did *teare,* . . . . III. xii. 17. 4
it would loose, or else asunder *teare*. . . . . IV. v. 3. 5
doth felly bite and *teare* The stone . . . . IV. viii. 36. 5
tosse the deepes, and *teare* the firmament, ... IV. ix. 23. 7
To *teare* his flesh in peeces for his sin: . . . . V. iv. 37. 5
doth *teare* Th' one from the earth, ... V. vi. 40. 4
they did draw The yron charet, and the wheeles did *teare,* . . V. viii. 41. 6
her owne deare flesh did *teare:* . . . . V. viii. 47. 6
To rend and *teare* what so she can oppresse; . . . . V. xi. 24. 4
teare Her flesh for felnesse, ... V. xii. 32. 3
from her head her lockes he nigh did *teare,* . . . . VI. i. 17. 8
he regarded neither playnt nor *teare,* . . . . VI. ii. 22. 8
Gan *teare* her hayre, and all her garments rent, ... VI. v. 4. 8
So did these two this Knight oft tug and *teare*. . . . . . . VI. viii. 12. 5
Gan him to hale, and *teare,* and scratch, and bite; . . . . . VI. viii. 28. 7
The which amongst them they in peeces *teare,* . . . . VI. viii. 41. 4
snatch, and byte, and rend, and tug, and *teare;* . . . . . . VI. xi. 17. 6
his owne flesh he readie was to *teare:* . . . . VI. xi. 25. 6
With many a joyfull kisse and many a melting *teare*. . . . . VI. xii. 20. 9
Nought sparing them, the more did tosse and *teare*. . . . . VI. xii. 24. 7
The hardest steele, in tract of time doth *teare:* . . . . . . *Am.* xviii. 2
with many a dropping *teare* And long intreaty, ... *Am.* xviii. 5
Tearmes. *See* **Termes.**
Tears. all their *teares* he shall wipe cleane away. . . . . . . *Rev.* iv. 7
I see your *teares* that from your boughes doe raine, ... *S.C.* Ja. 35
from mine eyes the drizling *teares* descend, ... *S.C.* Ja. 41
Some in much joy, many in many *teares,* . . . . *S.C.* F. 18
Like April shoure so stremes the trickling *teares* . . . . . *S.C.* Ap. 7
teache the trees their trickling *teares* to shedde. . . . . . *S.C.* Jun. 96
Thy *teares* would make the hardest flint to flowe! . . . . . *S.C.* Jun. 114
Whose streames my tricklinge *teares* did ofte augment. . . *S.C.* Au. 156
'Let stremes of *teares* supply the place of sleepe; . . . . . *S.C.* Au. 163
Let streaming *teares* be poured out in store; . . . . *S.C.* N. 61
now morne with *teares* besprint; . . . . *S.C.* N. 111
flouds of *teares* flowe in theyr stead . . . . *S.C.* N. 127
The heavens doe melt in *teares* without remorse; . . . . . . *S.C.* N. 131
Philomele her song with *teares* doth steepe; . . . . *S.C.* N. 141
dewed with *teares* they han be ever among. . . . . *S.C.* D. 112
In clowdie *teares* my case I thus complaine . . . . *Gn.* Ded. 3
with sweete *teares* did lament. . . . . *Gn.* 200
forst to overflow with brackish *teares,* . . . . *T.M.* 29
she raynd such store of streaming *teares,* . . . . *T.M.* 109
A sea of *teares* that never may be dryde, ... *T.M.* 116
Pouring forth streames of *teares* abundantly; . . . . *T.M.* 230
a brackish flood Of bitter *teares,* . . . . *T.M.* 416
from her eyes a sea of *teares* did powre; . . . . *T.M.* 476
such store of *teares* shee forth did powre, ... *T.M.* 595
teares from her faire eyes forth railing: . . . . *Ti.* 12
shedding *teares* a while, I still did rest, ... *Ti.* 32
Ne sheddeth *teares* from lamentable eie; . . . . *Ti.* 163
Could not from *teares* my melting eyes withholde. . . . . . *Ti.* 532
With some few silver-dropping *teares* t' adorne; . . . . . . *Ti.* 683
(Whilst oft his heart did melt in tender *teares*) . . . . . . *Mui.* 30
give unto my heavie eyes A well of *teares,* . . . . *Mui.* 410
Could not abstaine mine eyes with *teares* to steepe; . . . . . *D.* 171
poure foorth fountaines of incessant *teares?* . . . . *D.* 247
teares, whose brackish bitter well, I wasted have, ... *D.* 250
My drink the *teares* which fro mine eyes do raine, ... *D.* 376
I hate the Sea, because it *teares* supplyes. . . . . *D.* 406
mine eyes are dimd with *teares;* . . . . *D.* 417
ever sprinckle brackish *teares* among, ... *D.* 530
She bathed oft with *teares,* . . . . *As.* 164
the *teares,* that from her eyes did flow. . . . . *As.* 192
The same with bitter *teares* they all bedewed. . . . . *As.* 204
There she stopt with *teares;* . . . . I. i. 52. 2
Let me not die in languor and long *teares*.' . . . . I. i. 52. 7
Melting in *teares,* then gan shee thus lament. . . . . I. ii. 22. 1
my frayle eies these lines with *teares* do steepe, ... I. iii. 2. 3
drizling *teares* did shed for pure affection. . . . . I. iii. 6. 9
Redounding *teares* did choke th' end of her plaint, ... I. iii. 8. 1
does steepe Her tender brest in bitter *teares* all night; . . . I. iii. 15. 8
all the way she wetts with flowing *teares;* . . . . I. iii. 44. 4
Doth weepe full sore, and sheddeth tender *teares;* . . . . . I. v. 18. 6
when her well of *teares* she wasted had, ... I. viii. 42. 5
salt *teares* bedeawd the hearers cheaks. . . . . I. xii. 16. 9
her faire face with *teares* was fowly blubbered. . . . . . . II. i. 13. 9
Sir Guyon could uneath From *teares* abstayne; . . . . II. i. 56. 7
So shedding many *teares* they closd the earth agayne. . . . . II. i. 61. 9
wordes with bitter *teares* did steepe: . . . . II. ii. 1. 9
Welling out streames of *teares,* . . . . II. ii. 8. 7
cheekes with *teares,* and sydes with blood, did all abownd. . II. iv. 3. 9
Of all my sorrow and of these sad *teares,* . . . . II. iv. 18. 2
They crownd the second Constantine with joyous *teares*. . . . II. x. 62. 9
often steepe Her dainty couch with *teares* . . . . III. ii. 28. 9
the hard rocks could scarse from *tears* refraine; . . . . . . III. iv. 35. 7
Instead of rest thou lendest rayling *teares;* . . . . III. iv. 57. 4
Few trickling *teares* she softly forth let fall, ... III. vii. 9. 2
Wiping the *teares* from her suffused eyes, ... III. vii. 10. 3
With herbs, with charms, with counsel, and with *teares;* . . III. vii. 21. 2
tears, nor charms, nor herbs, nor counsell, ... III. vii. 21. 3
Asswage the fury which his entrails *teares:* . . . . III. vii. 21. 4
blubbred face with *teares* of her faire eyes: . . . . III. viii. 32. 3
teares stood in his eies, ... III. x. 25. 9
did shreek, With womanish *teares,* . . . . III. xi. 44. 6
I with *teares* full oft doe pittie it, ... IV. i. 1. 8
teares gan shed amaine; . . . . IV. iii. 47. 5
Amongst her *teares* immixing prayers meeke, ... IV. iii. 47. 6
lightning brond . . . *teares* it all with terrible mischance. . . IV. vi. 14. 5

Tears—*Continued.*
eft gan into tender *teares* to melt. . . . IV. vii. 9. 5
Moved with pity of her plenteous *teares*. . . . IV. vii. 23. 4
running water tempred with his *teares,* . . . IV. vii. 41. 7
he forth would poure so plenteous *teares,* . . . IV. viii. 4. 6
after many *teares* and sorrowes spent, . . . IV. viii. 64. 6
Sometime with tender *teares* to let her goe, . . . IV. x. 57. 2
hardned more with my aboundant *teares:* . . . IV. xii. 7. 5
With many bitter *teares* shed from his blubbred eyne. . . . V. i. 13. 9
Bursting forth *teares* like springs out of a banke), . . . V. i. 15. 2
Griefe did plead, and many *teares* forth powre. . . . V. ix. 45. 9
With humble prayers and intreatfull *teares;* . . . V. x. 6. 5
bursting forth in *teares,* . . . V. x. 20. 3
Mongst joyes mixing some *tears,* . . . V. xi. 16. 3
With heavie eyne, from *teares* uneath refrayning, . . . VI. ii. 41. 7
And with her *teares* his wounds did wash . . . VI. iii. 10. 5
did with plenteous *teares* His care . . . compassionate, . . . VI. iii. 12. 1
From his soft eyes the *teares* he wypt away, . . . VI. iv. 23. 4
I thus doe mourne, and poure forth ceaselesse *teares.'* . . . VI. iv. 33. 9
shedding few soft *teares* from tender eyne, . . . VI. v. 24. 3
Yet were her words but wynd, and all her *teares* but water. . . . VI. vi. 42. 9
Wasting her goodly hew in heavie *teares,* . . . VI. vii. 38. 3
Then bursting forth in *teares,* . . . VI. viii. 19. 1
'Here in this bottle . . . 'I put the *tears* of my contrition, . . . VI. viii. 24. 2
Ne cared she her wound in *teares* to steepe, . . . VI. xi. 23. 8
full of fresh dismay, And gushing forth in *teares,* . . . VI. xi. 28. 4
Bedeaw'd with *teares* there left it in the place: . . . VI. xii. 8. 4
the sorrowes . . . Written with *teares* . . . *Am.* i. 8
when I weep, she sayes, *Teares* are but water, . . . *Am.* xviii. 10
Let no lamenting cryes, nor dolefull *teares,* Be heard . . . *Epith.* 334
And let thy soule . . . Melt into *teares,* . . . *H.H.L.* 252
Teat. In wanton dalliance the *teate* to crave, . . . *Bel.*[2] vi. 3
Teats. from the she Beares *teats* her whelps to teare; . . . I. vi. 24. 5
In his strong hand their rugged *teats* to hold, . . . VI. ix. 37. 8
Tede. A burning *Teade* about his head did move, . . . *Mui.* 293
the bushy *Teade* a groome did light, . . . I. xii. 37. 6
With his bright *Tead* that flames with many a flake, . . . *Epith.* 27
Tedious. to what end they clomb that *tedious* hight? . . . I. x. 49. 9
the *tedious* toyle ye for me take! . . . I. xi. 1. 9
Britomart, after long *tedious* toyle, . . . IV. vii. 3. 8
My *tedious* travell doe forget thereby; . . . VI. Pr. 1. 7
To passe the *tedious* travell of the way, . . . VI. v. 34. 6
Thinck ever to endure so *taedious* toyle! . . . *Am.* xxxiii. 10
Tedula. I saw a little Bird cal'd *Tedula,* . . . *Van.* iii. 7
Teem, -ed. *See* **Team, -ed.**
Teen. *See* **Tine.**
if thou wilt bewayle my wofull *tene,* . . . *S.C.* N. 41
grisly Ghosts, to heare the dolefull *teene.* . . . *D.* 21
That bare-head knight, for dread and dolefull *teene,* . . . I. ix. 34. 7
that proud Paynim king that works her *teene:* . . . I. xii. 18. 8
Either for grievous shame, or for great *teene,* . . . II. i. 15. 8
To cloke her guile with sorrow and sad *teene;* . . . II. i. 21. 7
frye in hartlesse griefe and dolefull *tene:* . . . II. i. 58. 4
Religious reverence doth buriall *teene:* . . . II. i. 59. 6
Of Gods high praise, and of their loves sweet *teene,* . . . III. v. 40. 4
With other signes of sorrow and impatient *teene.* . . . III. xi. 37. 9
put away remembrance of late *teene;* . . . III. xii. 40. 7
whom wearie winters *teene* Hath worne to nought, . . . IV. iii. 23. 7
He forced was to strike, and save himselfe from *teene.* . . . IV. iii. 31. 9
The secret cause and nature of his *teene,* . . . IV. xii. 21. 4
before this fatall *teene* Them overtooke . . . V. x. 7. 5
Teeth. T' embrew her *teeth* and clawes . . . *Bel.*[2] vi. 7
engendred men of armes Of Dragons *teeth,* . . . *Ro.* x. 4
Whetting their *teeth,* and with vaine foolhardise . . . *Ro.* xiv. 7
he threats his *teeth,* his tayle, his pawes, . . . *Van.* x. 11
bene not thy *teeth* on edge, . . . *S.C.* May 35
with sharpe *teeth* the bramble leaves doth lop, . . . *Gn.* 85
Grinding his *teeth,* and grating his great hart; . . . *Hub.* 1334
did chaw Between his cankred *teeth* a venemous tode, . . . I. iv. 30. 3
he gnasht his *teeth* to see Those heapes of gold . . . I. iv. 31. 6
The trembling ghosts . . . Chattring their iron *teeth,* . . . I. v. 32. 6
His monstrous scalpe downe to his *teeth* it tore, . . . I. viii. 16. 4
Her *teeth* out of her rotten gummes were feld, . . . I. viii. 47. 4
Three ranckes of yron *teeth* enraunged were, . . . I. xi. 13. 2
his great yron *teeth* he still did grind . . . II. iv. 15. 3
gan to grind His grated *teeth* . . . II. v. 14. 3
both did gnash their *teeth,* and both did threten life. . . . II. vii. 21. 9
the feend his gnashing *teeth* did grate, . . . II. vii. 34. 1
Another in her *teeth* did gnaw a rush; . . . II. ix. 35. 8
with gnashing *teeth* did bite The bitter earth, . . . III. v. 22. 1
with his *teeth* did teare His rugged flesh, . . . III. vii. 20. 4
huge great *teeth,* like to a tusked Bore: . . . IV. vii. 5. 6
gnashed with his *teeth,* . . . V. ii. 18. 7
Her heart for rage did grate, and *teeth* did grin. . . . V. iv. 37. 7
all his *teeth* wide bare One might have seene . . . V. xi. 9. 7
gnasht his *teeth,* and his head at him shooke, . . . V. xi. 12. 8
all her *teeth* arew, . . . V. xii. 29. 5
backe returned His scornefull taunts unto his *teeth* . . . VI. ii. 12. 2
Gnashing his cruell *teeth* at him in vaine, . . . VI. iv. 22. 8
Least that the beasts sharpe *teeth* had any wound Made . . . VI. iv. 23. 8
Gnashing his grinded *teeth* with griesly looke, . . . VI. v. 26. 1
that beastes *teeth,* which wounded you tofore, . . . VI. vi. 9. 1
with his *teeth* and nailes . . . Him rudely rent . . . VI. vi. 22. 5
with his nayles and *teeth* Gan him to hale, . . . VI. viii. 28. 6
All set with yron *teeth* in raunges twaine, . . . VI. xii. 26. 7
bit them with his banefull *teeth* of injury. . . . VI. xii. 28. 9
Chattering his *teeth* for cold . . . VII. vii. 31. 2
hir *teeth* be Pearles, both pure and round; . . . *Am.* xv. 9
Teian. Or that sweete *Teian* Poet, which did spend . . . *H.H.B.* 219
Teise. One cald the *Theise,* the other cald the Crane, . . . IV. xi. 47. 2

Telamon. Fierce Peleus, and the hardie *Telamon,* . . . *Gn.* 482
'Gainst which the noble sonne of *Telamon* Oppos'd himselfe, . . . *Gn.* 513
Tell. The same yet vaunting Greece will *tell* the storie . . . *Ro.* ii. 5
Tell me, ye spirits, . . . *Ro.* xv. 5
Tell me then, . . . Doo ye not feele . . . *Ro.* xv. 9
Come *tell* me what was sayd of mee, . . . *To his Booke* 17
But shall I *tel* thee a tale of truth, . . . *S.C.* F. 91
Now I pray thee, shepheard, *tel* it not forth: . . . *S.C.* F. 239
Now *tell* us what thou hast seene. . . . *S.C.* Mar. 60
Tell me, good Hobbinoll, what garres thee greete? . . . *S.C.* Ap. 1
'*Tell* me, have ye seene her angelick face, . . . *S.C.* Ap. 64
of felowship, *tell* us that saying: . . . *S.C.* May 172
tell many lesinges of this and that, . . . *S.C.* May 285
Tell me, what wants me here . . . *S.C.* Jun. 3
tell us mery tales . . . *S.C.* Jun. 87
tell the lasse, . . . *S.C.* Jun. 109
Of Synah can I *tell* thee more, . . . *S.C.* Jul. 73
Tell me, Perigot, what shalbe the game, . . . *S.C.* Au. 1
Tell me, such a cup hast thou ever sene? . . . *S.C.* Au. 35
tell me, shepherds, . . . *S.C.* Au. 139
tell me first of thy flocks estate. . . . *S.C.* S. 24
Tho may we talke and *tellen* our fill, . . . *S.C.* S. 53
shall I *tell* thee what my selfe knowe . . . *S.C.* S. 170
Tell Rosalind, her Colin bids her adieu.' . . . *S.C.* D. 156
Cause of my death and just complaint to *tell:* . . . *Gn.* 629
when her turne was come her tale to *tell,* . . . *Hub.* 36
The purpose of the complot which ye *tell;* . . . *Hub.* 178
Through manie haps, which needs not here to *tell,* . . . *Hub.* 360
Ne *tell* a written word, ne write a letter, . . . *Hub.* 383
tell us (said the Ape) we doo you pray, . . . *Hub.* 615
and merie leasings *tell,* . . . *Hub.* 699
tell them that they greatly him mistooke. . . . *Hub.* 704
tell their Prince that learning is but vaine: . . . *T.M.* 332
tell the anguish of my inward smart, . . . *T.M.* 422
To *tell* my sorrowes that exceeding bee. . . . *T.M.* 546
tell hir, that my eyes can take no reste: . . . *U.V.* 7
tell hir, that my mouth can eate no meate: . . . *U.V.* 8
tell hir, I can heare no mirth. . . . *U.V.* 9
Tell hir, that hir pleasures were wonte to lull me asleepe: . . . *U.V.* 13
Tell hir, that hir beautie was wonte to feede mine eyes: . . . *U.V.* 14
Tell hir, that hir sweete Tongue was wonte . . . *U.V.* 15
'To *tell* the beawtie of my buildings fayre, . . . *Ti.* 85
To *tell* my riches, and endowments rare, . . . *Ti.* 87
To *tell* my forces, matchable to none, . . . *Ti.* 89
Ne *tell* his sorrow to the listning rout . . . *Ti.* 227
To *tell* the cause which thee theretoo constrained, . . . *D.* 81
tell your fellow-swaines That sad Alcyon dyde . . . *D.* 524
The mournfulst verse that ever man heard *tell:* . . . *As.* Pr. 8
onely by his lookes did *tell* his thought. . . . *As.* 168
No toong can *tell,* nor any forth can set, . . . *As.* 171
Now at thy leisure them to us to *tell.'* . . . *Col.* 35
To *tell* what thou didst sing, . . . *Col.* 84
But *tell* on further, Colin, as befell . . . *Col.* 176
That shepheard I besought to me to *tell,* . . . *Col.* 229
Most wretched he, that is and cannot *tell.'* . . . *Col.* 659
to *tell* And eke to warne . . . *Col.* 683
who can *tell* what cause had that faire Mayd . . . *Col.* 911
Tydings of warre and worldly trouble *tell?* . . . I. i. 30. 8
Of a straunge man I can you tidings *tell,* . . . I. i. 31. 3
messengers of hell, . . . gan *tel* Their bootelesse paines, . . . I. ii. 2. 3
who can *tell* The hidden powre of herbes, . . . I. ii. 10. 8
tel both who ye be, and who that tooke your part.' . . . I. ii. 21. 9
busying . . . his dull eares to heare what shee did *tell;* . . . I. ii. 26. 7
of such a Lady shee could *tellen* ought. . . . I. iii. 24. 9
could . . . fortunes *tell,* and read in loving bookes, . . . I. iv. 25. 8
'well may I rew To *tell* the sad sight . . . I. vi. 36. 8
wonne from death, she bad him *tellen* plaine . . . I. vi. 37. 7
to *tell* her lamentable cace, . . . I. vi. 48. 8
with them all departes to *tell* his great distresse. . . . I. vii. 19. 9
'*Tell* on,' (quoth she) 'the wofull Tragedy, . . . I. vii. 24. 8
Thy sad tong cannot *tell* more heavy plight . . . I. vii. 25. 3
heare the story sad, which I shall *tell* you briefe. . . . I. vii. 42. 9
Who answerd him full soft, *he could not tell.* . . . I. viii. 32. 5
againe he sayde, *He could not tell;* . . . I. viii. 32. 9
He could not tell, againe he answered. . . . I. viii. 33. 2
His answere likewise was, he could not *tell:* . . . I. viii. 34. 1
Una faire besought That straunger knight his . . . nation *tell;* I. ix. 2. 7
tellen free The secrete cause of his perplexitie: . . . I. ix. 25. 4
That I may *tell* this haplesse history?' . . . I. ix. 26. 4
whether dread did dwell . . . is hard to *tell.* . . . I. x. 14. 5
Could hardly him intreat to *tell* his grief: . . . I. x. 24. 2
nor wit of man can *tell;* . . . I. x. 55. 6
his most hideous head my tongue to *tell* Does tremble; . . . I. xi. 12. 6
To *tell* how he had seene the Dragons fatall fall. . . . I. xii. 2. 9
'How can I *tell,* but that his talants may Yet scratch . . . I. xii. 11. 5
What needes me *tell* their feast and goodly guize, . . . I. xii. 14. 1
To *tell* that dawning day is drawing neare, . . . I. xii. 21. 7
To *tell* were as to strive against the streame: . . . I. xii. 23. 3
badd *tell* on the tenor of his playnt: . . . II. i. 9. 2
To *tell* this ruefull tale: . . . II. i. 9. 9
Tounge hates to *tell* the rest that eye to see abhord.' . . . II. i. 11. 9
tell the cause of your conceived payne; . . . II. i. 14. 6
he hath great glory wonne, as I heare *tell.* . . . II. i. 19. 9
'well mote I shame to *tell* The fond encheason . . . II. i. 30. 1
tell the secrete of your mortall smart: . . . II. i. 46. 8
Tell then, O Lady! *tell* what fatall priefe . . . II. i. 48. 6
the sorrowes that uneath My tong can *tell,* . . . II. i. 49. 6
they his mothers innocence may *tell,* . . . II. ii. 10. 5
how, or where, here fits not *tell.* . . . II. ii. 11. 9
To *tell* from whence he came through jeopardy, . . . II. ii. 39. 5

Tell—*Continued.*
'*Tell* on, fayre Sir,' . . . 'that dolefull tale, ... II. ii. 45. 1
If thou didst, *tell* me, ... II. iii. 32. 9
who can *tell* . . . But that shee is some powre celestiall? . . . II. iii. 44. 3
to *tell* his funerall Unto his brother, ... II. v. 25. 8
'Long were to *tell* the troublous stormes . . . . . . II. vii. 14. 1
never eie did vew, Ne tong did *tell*, ... II. vii. 19. 7
who can *tell* the prayses of that makers might? . . . . . . II. ix. 46. 9
Ne can I *tell*, ne can I stay to *tell*, ... II. ix. 47. 1
Let Scaldis *tell*, and let *tell* Hania, ... II. x. 24. 1
let the marsh of Esthambruges *tell*, ... II. x. 24. 2
to *tell* the sumptuous aray Of that great chamber . . . . . . III. i. 32. 1
In playner wise to *tell* her grievaunce she begonne. . . . . . . III. i. 52. 9
Thy selfe thy prayses *tell*, and make them knowen farre. . . . III. ii. 3. 9
Tell me some markes by which he may appeare, ... III. ii. 16. 3
tell me therefore, my liefest liefe!' . . . . . . III. ii. 33. 9
tell Under what coast of heaven the man did dwell, ... III. iii. 6. 4
He bad *tell* on; . . . . . . III. iii. 16. 1
'Beldame, by that ye *tell* . . . . . . III. iii. 17. 4
Doth by her blushing *tell* . . . . . . III. iii. 20. 5
'Behold the man! and *tell* me, Britomart, ... III. iii. 32. 1
Bards *tell* of many wemen valorous, ... III. iii. 54. 4
Her deare sonnes destiny to her to *tell*, ... III. iv. 25. 4
'Sir, ill mote I stay To *tell* the same: . . . . . . III. v. 4. 3
good Sir, *tell* out of hand.' . . . . . . III. v. 4. 9
tell me, if that ye my sonne have heard . . . . . . III. vi. 23. 1
their trew loves without suspition *tell* abrode. . . . . . . III. vi. 42. 9
tell the idle tidings to his Dame: . . . . . . III. vii. 28. 6
As for my name, it mistreth not to *tell*: . . . . . . III. vii. 51. 8
'*tell* at one word, How many fownd'st thou . . . . . . III. vii. 56. 8
'one word may *tell* All that I ever fownd . . . . . . III. vii. 57. 1
To *tell* what tydings of fayre Florimell became. . . . . . . III. vii. 61. 9
so her selfe did alwaies to him *tell*; . . . . . . III. viii. 19. 8
saide his boat the way could wisely *tell*; . . . . . . III. viii. 24. 7
To *tell* of Satyrane where I him left of late. . . . . . . III. viii. 43. 9
now in Faery court all men doe *tell*, ... III. viii. 46. 2
That ye doe *tell* in such uncerteintee? . . . . . . III. viii. 48. 4
(as that Squyre does *tell*.) . . . . . . III. ix. 3. 4
to *tell* Of deeds of armes . . . . . . III. ix. 32. 3
the noble Britomart heard *tell* Of Trojan warres . . . . . . III. ix. 38. 1
forgot that whylome I heard *tell* From aged Mnemon; . . . . III. ix. 47. 3
tell thy griefe, if any hidden lye: . . . . . . III. x. 26. 2
Ne word he had to speake his griefe to *tell*, ... III. x. 37. 8
did her *tell* That it was he . . . . . . III. x. 49. 4
Long were to *tell* each other lovely fitt; . . . . . . III. xi. 39. 6
Long were to *tell* the amorous assayes, ... III. xi. 44. 1
phantasies . . . that none can *tell*, ... III. xii. 26. 4
to *tell* The diverse usage, and demeanure daint, ... IV. i. 5. 1
none . . . to them tydings *tell* that mote their harts delight. . IV. i. 16. 9
whether were more false full hard it is to *tell*. . . . . . . IV. i. 32. 9
why should I doubt to *tell* the same?' . . . . . . IV. i. 48. 4
'Then *tell*,' (quoth Blandamour) 'and feare no blame: . . . . IV. i. 48. 5
Tell what thou saw'st, maulgre who so it heares.' . . . . IV. i. 48. 6
she so farre astray, as none can *tell*?' . . . . . . IV. ii. 22. 4
as antique stories *tellen* us, ... IV. ii. 32. 1
Her cause of comming she to *tell* began. . . . . . . IV. ii. 49. 5
how their lives were eekt, she did not *tell*; . . . . . . IV. ii. 53. 6
(that wonder is to *tell*) . . . . . . IV. iii. 39. 1
The which by course befals me here to *tell*: . . . . . . IV. iv. 2. 5
which some doe *tell* That glorious belt did in it selfe containe, IV. v. 2. 7
To *tell* the feature of each goodly face: . . . . . . IV. v. 12. 3
The hard adventures and strange haps to *tell*, ... IV. v. 28. 8
Were long to *tell*; therefore, I here will stay . . . . . . IV. vi. 47. 8
So doest thou now to her of whom I *tell*, ... IV. vii. 2. 3
'To *tell*' (quoth she) 'that what ye see, needs not; . . . . IV. vii. 14. 8
Seeking adventures where he mote heare *tell*; . . . . . . IV. vii. 42. 3
tell the course of his captivitie, ... IV. viii. 64. 2
To *tell* through what misfortune he had far'd . . . . . . IV. ix. 41. 5
I will them in another *tell*. . . . . . . IV. ix. 41. 9
Scudamour doth his conquest *tell* . . . . . . IV. x. Arg.
'Long were to *tell* the travell and long toile . . . . . . IV. x. 3. 1
not if an hundred tongues to *tell*, ... IV. xi. 9. 6
Helpe me to *tell* the names of all those floods . . . . . . IV. xi. 10. 6
(as antique fathers *tell*) . . . . . . IV. xi. 37. 2
tell their hidden race, ... IV. xi. 40. 8
With many more whose names no tongue can *tell*: . . . . IV. xi. 44. 6
To *tell* the sands, or count the starres on hye, ... IV. xi. 53. 2
much more eath to *tell* the starres on hy, ... IV. xii. 1. 5
Whose names and nations were too long to *tell*, ... IV. xii. 3. 2
I will them *tell* though unto no man neare: . . . . . . IV. xii. 6. 4
such was he of whom I have to *tell*, ... V. i. 3. 1
to *tell* abrode your shame.' . . . . . . V. i. 28. 9
gan of sundry newes his store to *tell*, ... V. ii. 2. 6
To *tell* the glorie of the feast that day, ... V. iii. 3. 1
turn'd aside for shame to heare what he did *tell*. . . . . . . V. iii. 16. 9
let it *tell* What strokes . . . it stird this day; . . . . . . V. iii. 21. 5
all that piteous storie . . . to him gan *tell*; . . . . . . V. iii. 31. 3
'Now *tell* me, Amidas, if that ye may, ... V. iv. 17. 2
sent them home to *tell* a piteous tale . . . . . . V. iv. 24. 8
tell, Sir Terpin, ne let you amate Your misery, ... V. iv. 28. 4
Tell, that to morrow I with him wil fight, ... V. iv. 48. 8
Tho gan she *tell* her all that she had donne, ... V. v. 45. 8
'Talus, be bold, And *tell* what ever it be, ... V. vi. 10. 2
Forcing in vaine the rest to her to *tell*; . . . . . . V. vi. 11. 8
(as they the story *tell*) . . . . . . V. vii. 10. 6
tell him for his sake thy life thou gavest.' . . . . . . V. vii. 32. 6
how deepe no man can *tell*, ... V. ix. 6. 4
First gan he *tell* how this . . . Duessa hight; . . . . . . V. ix. 40. 1
Which when the Prince heard *tell*, ... V. xi. 21. 1
bitter curses, horrible to *tell*; . . . . . . V. xi. 28. 3

Tell—*Continued.*
To passe them over where them list to *tell*. . . . . . . V. xii. 4. 4
tell him that not for such slaughters sake He thether came, . V. xii. 8. 7
tell, if please you, of the good successe . . . . . . VI. i. 5. 1
tell, if thou have it knowne.' . . . . . . VI. i. 14. 4
should it not displease thee it to *tell*, ... VI. ii. 26. 1
let not your griefe empeach To *tell* . . . . . . VI. ii. 42. 3
tell with all the lamentable plight . . . . . . VI. iii. 41. 7
ne could *tell* Which way to take: . . . . . . VI. iv. 25. 1
To whom she thus: 'What need me, Sir, to *tell* . . . . . . VI. iv. 28. 1
As ye may know when time shall be to *tell* the same. . . . VI. v. 2. 9
Tell me what worlds despight, or heavens yre, ... VI. v. 23. 7
I must awhile forbeare to you to *tell*; . . . . . . VI. vi. 17. 3
tell me, Lady, wherefore doe you beare This bottle . . . . VI. viii. 23. 6
first it falleth me by course to *tell* Of faire Serena; . . . . VI. viii. 31. 1
them to *tell* him courteously besought, ... VI. ix. 5. 8
as old stories *tell*, ... VI. ix. 14. 4
Whose sundry parts were here too long to *tell*; . . . . . . VI. x. 14. 2
Tell me, what mote these dainty Damzels be, ... VI. x. 19. 6
Tell me what were they all, ... VI. x. 20. 9
for to *tell* the dolefull dreriment . . . . . . VI. x. 44. 1
doe feare away, and *tell*.' . . . . . . VI. xi. 29. 9
Whose heavy tydings now I have to *tell*. . . . . . . VI. xi. 31. 3
ere I doe his adventures *tell* . . . . . . VI. xii. 14. 1
To *tell* her how the heavens had her graste . . . . . . VI. xii. 16. 8
let us *tell* Of Calidore; . . . . . . VI. xii. 22. 5
That endlesse were to *tell*. . . . . . . VI. xii. 23. 6
tell To griesly Pluto what on earth was donne, ... VI. xii. 35. 5
tell how Arlo . . . Was made the most unpleasant . . . . . . VII. vi. 37. 5
To *tell* what time he might her Lady see . . . . . . VII. vi. 43. 8
For many moe good turnes then he would *tell*, ... VII. vi. 44. 8
to *tell* of heavens King . . . his fortunate successe; . . . . VII. vii. 1. 5
Can *tell* things doen in heaven so long ygone, ... VII. vii. 2. 8
others *tell* that it so beautious was, ... VII. vii. 6. 6
All her array and vestiments to *tell*, ... VII. vii. 9. 2
But who is it (to me *tell*) . . . . . . VII. vii. 48. 4
tell me, why should faire be proud, ... *Am.* xxvii. 1
Tell me, when shall these wearie woes have end, ... *Am.* xxxvi. 1
tell me whereto can ye lyken it; . . . . . . *Am.* xl. 2
tell her prayse to all posterity, ... *Am.* lxix. 11
Tell her the joyous time wil not be staid, ... *Am.* lxx. 7
false forged lyes, which thou didst *tel*, ... *Am.* lxxxv. 7
Tell me, ye merchants daughters, ... *Epith.* 167
thousands more then any tongue can *tell*, ... *H.L.* 264
none the same may *tell*. . . . . . . *H.B.* 42
To *tell* the marveiles by thy mercie wrought. . . . . . . *H.H.L.* 49
I faine to *tell* the things that I behold, ... *H.H.B.* 6
And *tell* me then, what hast thou ever seene . . . . . . *H.H.B.* 57
The fairenesse of her face no tongue can *tell*; . . . . . . *H.H.B.* 204
here fits not well Olde woes, but joyes, to *tell* . . . . . . *Proth.* 142

Telled. *See* **Told.**
to her *teld* All this accord . . . . . . VI. i. 44. 8
Witnesse, ye Heavens, the truth of all that I have *teld!*' . VII. vi. 27. 9
Thus sitting in her throne, as I have *teld*, ... VII. vii. 13. 5

Tellest. what art thou, that *telst* of Nephews kilt?' . . . . . I. v. 26. 5

Telling. good matter Lost for lacke of *telling*: . . . . . . *S.C.* Jul. 206
telling them to blazon out their blames. . . . . . . *T.M.* 102
Of death and dolor *telling* sad tidings; . . . . . . II. vii. 23. 5
make much worse by *telling*, ... V. xii. 35. 2
Yet is that Highest farre beyond all *telling*, ... *H.H.B.* 101

Tells. The wise Southsayer . . . *telles* of warres . . . . . . I. v. 8. 9
His loves and lignage Arthure *tells*: . . . . . . I. ix. Arg.
the sage wisard *telles*, as he has redd, ... III. i. 16. 8
Thy acts, O Scanderbeg, this volume *tels*. . . . . . . *Com. Son.* iii. 14

Tempe. O ye pleasaunt Springs Of *Tempe!* . . . . . . *Gn.* 146
More sweet and holesome then . . . the Thessalian *Tempe*, . . II. xii. 52. 4
when as Jove her took In *Tempe*, ... *Epith.* 308

Temper. Meet for her *temper* and complexion: . . . . . . III. vi. 38. 5
did that good old Knight *Temper* his griefe, ... VI. iii. 6. 2
she wants to *temper* angry Jove, ... *Am.* xxxix. 3

Temperament. goodly *temp'rament* Of pure complexions, . . . *H.B.* 66

Temperance. No *temperance*, nor no regard of season, ... *Hub.* 1132
Through the myld *temperance* of her goodly raies. . . . . . . *Col.* 551
calmd his wrath with goodly *temperance*. . . . . . . I. viii. 34. 5
great rule of *Temp'raunce* goodly doth appeare. . . . . . . II. Pr. 5. 9
Through goodly handling and wise *temperaunce*. . . . . . . II. i. 31. 2
temperaunce' . . . can measure out a meane; . . . . . . II. i. 58. 1
through *temperaunce* and stedfastnesse, ... II. iv. 2. 8
all your hurts may soone through *temperance* be easd.' . . . II. iv. 33. 9
Who ever doth to *temperaunce* apply His stedfast life, . . . II. v. 1. 1
The house of *Temperance*, . . . Besiegd of many foes, ... II. ix. Arg.
The enimies of *Temperaunce* Besiege her dwelling place: . . . II. xi. Arg.
that goodly frame of *Temperaunce* . . . . . . II. xii. 1. 1
Through goodly *temperaunce* and affection chaste; . . . . . . III. i. 12. 2
now of dayes such *temperance* is rare . . . . . . IV. viii. 29. 6
Sate goodly *Temperance* in garments clene, ... V. ix. 32. 8

Temperance's. wisedomes powre, and *temperaunces* might, . . II. xii. 43. 6

Temperate. His countenance demure and *temperate*; . . . . . II. i. 6. 2
With *temperate* advice discounselled, ... II. xii. 34. 2

Temperature. Most goodly *temperature* ye may descry; . . . . *Am.* xiii. 4

Tempered. *See* **Well-tempered.**
Sorrowing *tempered* with deare delight, ... *Ti.* 319
Full sweetly *tempred* is that Muse of his, ... *Col.* 430
manly courage, *Tempred* with reason . . . . . . *Ded. Son.* xiv. 9
litle sweet Oft *tempred* is,' . . . 'with muchell smart: . . . I. iv. 46. 4
goodly counsell, . . . *tempred* with sweete voice: . . . . . . II. i. 44. 3
Tempred with grace and goodly modesty, ... III. v. 55. 3
tempred right With heate and humour, ... III. vi. 9. 4
glauncing on the *tempred* metall, ... III. vii. 40. 8
The same she *tempred* with fine Mercury . . . . . . III. viii. 6. 6

Tempered 854 Tender

Tempered—*Continued.*
Tempred with sternesse and stout majestie, ... IV. vi. 26. 3
running water *tempred* with his teares, ... IV. vii. 41. 7
'Nathlesse that Dame so well them *tempred* both, ... IV. x. 33. 1
Tempred with Adamant amongst the same, ... V. i. 10. 2
tempred for the time her present heavinesse. . . . . V. vii. 44. 9
Yet *tempred* with some majestie imperiall. . . . . V. ix. 34. 9
by her *tempred* without griefe or gall, ... V. x. 4. 5
th' Adamantine shield which he did beare So well was *tempred*, V. xi. 10. 8
his speach *Tempred* so well, ... VI. ii. 13. 2
The *tempred* steele did not into his braynepan byte. . . . . VI. vi. 30. 9
A thousand sowres hath *tempred* with one sweet, ... VI. xi. 1. 8
tempred so the feature of her face, ... *Am.* xxi. 2
every sweet with soure is *tempred* still, ... *Am.* xxvi. 9
Tempereth. furies rules, and Tartare *tempereth.* . . . . *Hub.* 1294
Tempering. hastie heat *tempring* with sufferance wise, ... I. i. 50. 4
With fowle words *tempring* faire, ... I. vii. 3. 9
Tempring the passion with advizement slow, ... II. v. 13. 2
fairly *tempring*, fond desire subdewd, ... II. vi. 26. 6
coy lookes *tempring* with loose dalliance; . . . . IV. ii. 9. 5
Through *tempering* of her words and lookes by wondrous skill. VI. vi. 41. 9
tempering . . . Their contrary dislikes with loved meanes, . . *H.L.* 85
Tempers. by a soveraine might *Tempers* so trim, ... *H.B.* 125
Tempe's. by pleasant *Tempes* shore, . . . through Thessaly they streeme, ... *Proth.* 79
Tempest. A sodaine *tempest* from the heaven, ... *Bel.*[1] iii. 13
a *tempest* from the heaven descend, ... *Bel.*[2] iii. 13
suddenly arose a *tempest* great, ... *Bel.*[2] xiii. 5
As he that having long in *tempest* sailed, ... *Ro.* xxi. 11
Is like a ship in midst of *tempest* left . . . . *T.M.* 141
The *tempest* of that stormie passion, ... *T.M.* 380
through untimely *tempest* fall away! . . . . *D.* 238
grove . . . That promist ayde the *tempest* to withstand; . . . I. i. 7. 3
therein shrouded from the *tempest* dred, ... I. i. 8. 3
calme the *tempest* of his passion wood: . . . . II. iv. 11. 8
As when a windy *tempest* bloweth hye, ... II. viii. 48. 1
save Them from the *tempest* of his wrathfulnesse, ... II. xii. 83. 4
crave but rowme to rest while *tempest* overblo'th.' . . . . . III. vii. 8. 9
As glad of that small rest as Bird of *tempest* gon. . . . . . III. vii. 10. 9
Another knight, whom *tempest* thither brought, ... III. ix. 12. 2
To calme the *tempest* of his troubled thought: . . . . IV. ii. 3. 2
Till time the *tempest* doe thereof delay . . . . IV. viii. 1. 6
whom cruell *tempest* drives Upon a rocke . . . . V. ii. 50. 1
An hideous *tempest* seemed from below To rise . . . . V. vii. 14. 2
did streight devoure Both flames and *tempest*: . . . . V. vii. 15. 6
tottred, like two towres which through a *tempest* quooke. . . V. viii. 9. 9
Nought may abide the *tempest* of his yre; . . . . V. xi. 58. 8
Ne once to breath awhile their angers *tempest* ceast. . . . . VI. i. 36. 9
did rattle like to haile In a great *tempest;* . . . . VI. vi. 26. 4
being long in *tempest* tost, ... VI. xi. 44. 6
The dreadfull *tempest* of her wrath appease, ... *Am.* xxxviii. 7
being long in her loves *tempest* tost, ... *Am.* xli. 11
Ne ought for *tempest* doth from it depart, ... *Am.* lix. 7
Tempest's. through *tempests* cruel wracke, ... *Am.* xxxviii. 1
Tempests. Tossing huge *tempests* through the troubled skie, . . *Ro.* xvi. 6
With showres of heaven and *tempests* worne away; . . . . . *Ti.* 501
cloudy *tempests* have The faithfull light . . . yblent, ... II. vii. 1. 3
huge Orion, that doth *tempests* still portend; . . . . IV. xi. 13. 9
After long stormes and *tempests* overblowne . . . . V. iii. 1. 1
he, that had like *tempests* often tride, ... V. v. 6. 6
From all the *tempests* of these worldly seas, ... VI. ix. 19. 4
all your *tempests* cannot hold me backe, ... *Am.* xlvi. 10
Tempests'. long stormes and *tempests* sad assay, ... *Am.* lxiii. 1
Tempestuous. '*Tempestuous* fortune hath spent all her spight, . I. vii. 25. 1
calme the sea of their *tempestuous* spight. . . . . II. vi. 36. 4
'Huge sea of sorrow and *tempestuous* griefe, ... III. iv. 8. 1
Slow Peneus, and *tempestuous* Phasides, ... IV. xi. 21. 3
whose *tempestuous* rage Makes th' heavens tremble . . . . . VI. vi. 11. 8
With stormes of fortune and *tempestuous* fate . . . . VI. ix. 31. 5
Without *tempestuous* storms or sad afray: . . . . *Epith.* 327
Thunder, and lightning, and *tempestuous* fyre, ... *H.H.B.* 181
Templar. There whylome wont the *Templer* Knights to byde, . *Proth.* 135
Temple. The place where is the *temple* of the Gods, ... *Bel.*[1] vi. 8
under this great *temple* . . . . *Bel.* i. 10
doe the *temple* of the Gods support, ... II. iii. 28. 2
As it some Gyeld or solemne *Temple* weare. . . . . II. vii. 43. 4
for Apolloes *temple* highly herried.' . . . . II. xii. 13. 9
Great Venus *Temple* is describ'd; . . . . IV. x. Arg.
That was a *temple* faire and auncient, ... IV. x. 5. 3
The *temple* of great Venus, ... IV. x. 29. 5
'Not that same famous *Temple* of Diane, ... IV. x. 30. 1
'Into the inmost *Temple* thus I came, ... IV. x. 37. 1
with the steme thereof the *Temple* swet, ... IV. x. 38. 3
all the *temple* it did fill . . . . IV. x. 43. 9
Unto whose *temple* when as Britomart Arrived, ... V. vii. 3. 6
Was thence by them into the *Temple* led; . . . . V. vii. 5. 2
To rise through all the *Temple* sodainely, ... V. vii. 14. 3
all the *Temple* put in jeopardy Of flaming, ... V. vii. 14. 8
all the *Temple* did with terrour fill; . . . . V. xi. 22. 8
the *Temple*, wherein she was plast, Did quake to heare, . . . V. xi. 28. 4
Her *temple* fayre is built within my mind, ... *Am.* xxii. 5
ye high heavens, the *temple* of the gods, ... *Epith.* 409
Temple-gate. forth I led her through the *Temple gate*, ... IV. x. 57. 6
Temple-gates. Open the *temple gates* unto my love, ... *Epith.* 204
Temples. these arcks, these baths, these *temples* hie; . . . . . *Ro.* xxvii. 4
All that which Greece their *temples* to embrave . . . . . . *Ro.* xxix. 2
if my *temples* were distaind with wine, ... *S.C.* O. 110
in the sacred *temples* he may reare A trophee . . . . *Gn.* 126
Whereas his *temples* did his creast-front tyre; . . . . *Gn.* 308
'High towers, faire *temples*, goodly theaters, ... *Ti.* 92
Temples—*Continued.*
recovering hart, he does begin To rubb her *temples*, ... I. vii. 21. 5
rubd his *temples* and each trembling vaine; . . . . III. v. 31. 7
altars unto him and *temples* lent, ... V. vii. 2. 3
Temporal. *temporall*, and subject to decay: . . . . *Ro.* ix. 11
Temporize. To *temporize* is not from truth to swerve, ... V. xi. 56. 3
Tempt. to that I choose thou doest me *tempt;* . . . . *S.C.* N. 49
oft would dare to *tempt* the troublous winde. . . . . *Mui.* 48
Bold men . . . Dare *tempt* that gulf, ... *Col.* 210
He . . . gan himselfe advise To . . . *tempt* her faigned truth. I. i. 50. 6
joyd weake wemens hearts to *tempt*, and prove, ... I. iv. 26. 4
daring *tempt* the Queene of heaven to sin; . . . . I. v. 35. 2
Her constant hart did *tempt* with diverse guile: . . . . . . I. vi. 4. 3
To *tempt* the cause it selfe for to bewray, ... I. vii. 38. 8
tempt his guest to take thereof assay; . . . . II. vii. 34. 4
it would *tempt* a man to touchen there: . . . . II. xii. 14. 6
all men feare to *tempt* his billowes strong, ... III. ix. 45. 5
Great store of treasure, therewith him to *tempt;* . . . . . . III. x. 29. 2
tempt the deepest flood To come . . . . IV. x. 46. 5
deadly daunger seem'd in all mens sight To *tempt* such steps, . V. ix. 15. 7
weake harts doth . . . *tempte* to theyr decay; . . . . *Am.* xlvii. 6
Thereto approch to *tempt* her mind to ill. . . . . *Epith.* 199
Tempted. Guyon findes Mamon . . . Is by him *tempted*, ... II. vii. Arg.
tempted with the name Of this sweet Island . . . . II. x. 47. 6
Dayly he *tempted* her with this or that, ... III. viii. 39. 1
he was nothing mov'd nor *tempted* therewithall: . . . . . . V. ii. 23. 9
Till thou have tride againe, and *tempted* him more neare. . . V. v. 48. 9
O! who may not with gifts and words be *tempted?* . . . . . V. xi. 50. 6
the gentle knight Would not be *tempted* to such villenie, . . VI. vii. 23. 2
closely *tempted* with their craftie spyes; . . . . VI. viii. 43. 4
nought *tempted* with the offer Of his rich mould, ... VI. ix. 33. 1
Temptest. 'Hobbin, thou *temptest* me to that I covet: . . . . *Col.* 37
'Ah Dame,' (quoth he) 'thou *temptest* me in vaine, ... I. v. 42. 1
Tempting. So *tempting* her still to pursue the pray, ... IV. viii. 11. 4
Ten. seven heads, *ten* crounes, *ten* hornes did beare, ... *Rev.* i. 2
Ten hornes also the stately beast did beare. . . . . *Rev.* ii. 5
a sharped spyre . . . *Ten* feete each way . . . . *Bel.* iii. 2
there shall to thee *Ten* times so much be nombred . . . . . II. vii. 9. 5
Ascending by *ten* steps of Alablaster wrought. . . . . II. ix. 44. 9
long before the *ten* yeares siege of Troy, ... III. ix. 36. 2
'*Ten* daies,' (quoth he) 'he graunted hath of grace, ... V. xi. 42. 3
if I live till those *ten* daies have end, ... V. xi. 43. 2
where I have wond . . . Since I was *ten* yeares old, ... VI. ii. 30. 9
After I had *ten* yeares my selfe excluded From native home, . VI. ix. 25. 3
Tenantius. Androgeus and *Tenantius*, pictures of his might. . II. x. 46. 9
Next him *Tenantius* raignd; . . . . II. x. 50. 1
Tenants. 'As for her *tenants*, that is, man and beasts, ... VII. vii. 19. 1
Tend. What shoulden shepheards other things *tend*, ... *S.C.* May 63
doen so carefully theyr flocks *tend*. . . . . *S.C.* S. 179
Ne ought that did to his advauncement *tend;* . . . . II. xii. 80. 6
tend our charges with obeisaunce meeke. . . . . III. vi. 22. 8
She warned them to *tend* their safeties well, ... IV. ii. 53. 8
Dee . . . that doth by Chester *tend;* . . . . IV. xi. 39. 4
when as time to Artegall shall *tend*, ... V. iii. 40. 8
They mote the better *tend* to their devotion. . . . . V. vii. 9. 9
Upon the thrones of mortall Princes *tend*, ... V. ix. 32. 2
whom he did pray To *tend* them well. . . . . VI. v. 41. 5
The silver scaly trouts doe *tend* full well, ... *Epith.* 57
ye fresh boyes, that *tend* upon her groome, ... *Epith.* 112
still as every thing doth upward *tend*, ... *H.H.B.* 44
Tendance. doth his life in so long *tendance* spend! . . . . . *Hub.* 908
Tender. So beate his old boughes my *tender* side, ... *S.C.* F. 175
utter his *tender* head? . . . . *S.C.* Mar. 15
hath some Wolfe thy *tender* Lambes ytorne? . . . . *S.C.* Ap. 2
entrap in thy *tender* state: . . . . *S.C.* May 218
your *tender* Lambes that by you trace. . . . . *S.C.* Jun. 120
of our *tender* Lambkins takest keepe, ... *S.C.* D. 8
Tuning our song unto a *tender* Muse, ... *Gn.* 2
An easie running verse with *tender* feete. . . . . *Gn.* 53
chaw the *tender* prickles in her Cud; . . . . *Gn.* 86
left mine owne his safetie to *tender*; . . . . *Gn.* 362
With *tender* ruth to see her sore constraint; . . . . *Ti.* 31
(Whilst oft his heart did melt in *tender* teares) . . . . . . *Mui.* 30
Now in the same bathing his *tender* feete; . . . . *Mui.* 182
softly tread The *tender* grasse, ... *D.* 312
doth her *tender* plumes as yet but trie . . . . *Col.* 422
their *tender* wings He brusheth oft, ... I. i. 23. 8
fram'd of liquid ayre her *tender* partes, ... I. i. 45. 3
ruth . . . for her noble blood, and for her *tender* youth. . . I. i. 50. 9
'O! spare with guilty hands to teare My *tender* sides . . . . I. ii. 31. 3
To have attonce devourd her *tender* corse; . . . . I. iii. 5. 6
does steepe Her *tender* brest in bitter teares all night; . . . I. iii. 15. 8
The cruell steele . . . doth bight In *tender* flesh, ... I. v. 9. 4
Doth weepe full sore, and sheddeth *tender* teares; . . . . . . I. v. 18. 6
every *tender* part for feare does shake. . . . . I. vi. 10. 2
They, in compassion of her *tender* youth, ... I. vi. 12. 5
he taught the *tender* ymp . . . To banish cowardize . . . . I. vi. 24. 1
That cruell word her *tender* hart so thrild, ... I. vi. 37. 1
everie *tender* part does tosse and turne: . . . . I. vii. 21. 6
sorrowfull assay . . . almost rent her *tender* hart in tway; . . I. vii. 27. 4
tree . . . Whose *tender* locks do tremble every one . . . . I. vii. 32. 8
the *tender* Orphans of the dead . . . . I. x. 43. 2
thou slepst in *tender* swadling band, ... I. x. 65. 7
scratch my sonne, or rend his *tender* hand?' . . . . I. xii. 11. 6
seemd her *tender* heart was rent in twaine, ... II. i. 38. 4
in her streaming blood he did . . . *tender* joints embrew: . . II. i. 40. 8
In vertuous lore to traine his *tender* youth, ... II. iii. 2. 4
from *tender* dug of commune nourse . . . . II. iv. 18. 3
Her dainty limbes above her *tender* hips; . . . . II. v. 33. 8
Whose *tender* bud to blossome new began, ... II. viii. 5. 3

Tender—*Continued.*
Their *tender* buds or leaves to violate; II. xii. 51. 4
taking it out of her *tender* hond, II. xii. 57. 2
on his *tender* lips the downy heare II. xii. 79. 8
When first her *tender* hart was with his beautie smit. III. i. 34. 9
from the howre I taken was from nourses *tender* pap, III. ii. 6. 2
nine monethes did beare . . . Her *tender* babe, III. ii. 11. 8
with sharpe fits thy *tender* hart oppresseth sore: III. iii. 21. 9
surbate sore Their *tender* feete III. iv. 34. 6
up him taking in their *tender* hands, III. iv. 42. 1
The point of pitty perced through her *tender* hart. III. v. 30. 9
from her loving side the *tender* babes to take. III. vi. 27. 9
Nor wicked beastes their *tender* buds did crop, III. vi. 43. 5
the fearefull Ladies *tender* hart III. xi. 30. 7
round about Her *tender* waste was wound, III. xii. 37. 8
About their *tender* loynes to knit the same; IV. v. 17. 7
to the *tender* flesh it went, IV. vi. 15. 6
eft gan into *tender* teares to melt. IV. vii. 9. 5
Her *tender* hart in peeces would divide: IV. vii. 10. 3
Ne feeles the thornes and thickets pricke her *tender* toes. IV. vii. 21. 9
tender heart the faire Belphebe had . . . daunted, IV. viii. 2. 2
her *tender* heart . . . deeply did emmove, IV. viii. 3. 6
corsive, which did eat Her *tender* heart IV. ix. 14. 5
Sometime with *tender* teares to let her goe, IV. x. 57. 2
his stony heart with *tender* ruth Was toucht, IV. xii. 13. 1
round about her *tender* wast it fitted well. V. iii. 27. 9
The more thereby her *tender* hart was payned; V. v. 44. 7
So faire and *tender* without staine or spot V. vii. 29. 7
First there came Pittie with full *tender* hart, V. ix. 45. 3
in *tender* hart The Briton Prince was sore empassionate, V. ix. 46. 1
There came two Springals of full *tender* yeares, V. x. 6. 2
Like as a *tender* Rose in open plaine, V. xii. 13. 1
Nor spilt the blossome of my *tender* yeares VI. ii. 31. 2
in his *tender* armes her forced up to stay. VI. iii. 27. 9
wound Made in his *tender* flesh; VI. iv. 23. 9
he inly touched was With *tender* ruth VI. iv. 34. 2
shedding few soft teares from *tender* eyne, VI. v. 24. 3
To see her sore lament and bite her *tender* lip. VI. vii. 44. 9
as ye soft and *tender* are by kynde, VI. viii. 2. 1
So be ye soft and *tender* eeke in mynde; VI. viii. 2. 3
Her *tender* sides; her bellie white and clere, VI. viii. 42. 4
fed, and nipt the *tender* bloomes; VI. ix. 5. 5
to their homes to hast Their *tender* flocks, VI. ix. 13. 4
seeing them for *tender* pittie wept; VI. xi. 37. 7
Claribell Ne lesse did *tender* the faire Pastorell, VI. xii. 11. 5
wherewith Dan Jove in *tender* yeares . . . was nourisht VII. vii. 41. 6
Nor to the Diamond; for they are more *tender;* *Am.* ix. 10
For feare the stones her *tender* foot should wrong, *Epith.* 49
cropt full feateously The *tender* stalkes on hye. *Proth.* 28

Tendered. More deare then life she *tendered,* III. v. 51. 2
no lesse carefully her *tendered* Then her owne daughter III. vi. 51. 6
his honor, which she *tendred* chiefe, V. vii. 44. 4
Sith ye thus farre have *tendred* my poore case, V. xi. 18. 3
For first, next after life, he *tendered* her good. VI. iii. 11. 9

Tenderly. Now this, now that, he tasteth *tenderly,* *Mui.* 173
They lay therein their corses *tenderly,* II. i. 60. 5
He much rejoyst, and courd it *tenderly,* II. viii. 9. 8
To take him from his steed full *tenderly;* II. xi. 49. 2
*Their fleecy flowres they *tenderly* did steepe, II. xii. 61. 8
Shee streightly straynd, and colled *tenderly;* III. ii. 34. 2

Tending. the Shepheard self, *tending* his stocke, *Gn.* 237

Tene. *See* **Teen.**

Tenor. Has somewhat slackt the *tenor* of thy string, *S.C.* O. 50
Now change the *tenor* of your joyous layes, *T.M.* 367
'Heare then . . . the *tenor* of my tale, *Col.* 100
to my tunes thy second *tenor* rayse, I. xi. 7. 8
badd tell on the *tenor* of his playnt: II. i. 9. 2
Ne ought mote make him change his wonted *tenor,* IV. vii. 47. 3
Your string could soone to sadder *tenor* turne, *Epith.* 9
And turned have the *tenor* of my string, *H.H.L.* 13

Tent. Both were full loth to leave that needfull *tent,* III. ix. 14. 1
Then Talus forth issuing from the *tent* V. iv. 50. 5
Then forth came Artegall out of his *tent,* V. v. 5. 1
Sir Artegall did cause his *tent* There to be pitched V. xii. 10. 1

Ten thousand. *tenne thousand* sithes I blesse the stoure *S.C.* Ja. 51
Ten thousand snakes cralling about his hed *Gn.* 348
Ten thousand kindes of creatures, partly male And partly femall, I. i. 21. 7
ten thousand sorts of punishment . . . torment. I. v. 33. 8
Me liefer were *ten thousand* deathes priefe II. iv. 28. 8
Mongst thousand dangers, and *ten thousand* Magick mights. II. xii. 1. 9
Ten thousand wayes he cast in his confused thought. III. x. 18. 9
Ten thousand thankes did yeeld her for her meed, IV. i. 15. 3
ten thousand monsters foule abhor'd IV. xi. 3. 8
Ten thousand fishes play IV. xi. 29. 9
Environd with *tenne thousand* starres around VII. vi. 9. 3
Tenne thousand mores of sundry sent and hew, VII. vii. 10. 4
Ten thousand sweet belgards, *H.B.* 256
And with *ten thousand* gemmes of shyning gold,) *H.H.L.* 60

Tercel. Having farre off espyde a *Tassell* gent, III. iv. 49. 6

Terebinth. *Teribinth,* good for Gotes: *S.C.* Jul. 86

Term. my yeare drawes to his latter *terme,* *S.C.* D. 127
whenas Time . . . Expired had the *terme,* *Hub.* 309
That is the *terme* prescribed by the spell.' I. ii. 43. 5
time in her just *term* the truth to light should bring.' I. ix. 5. 9
'The *terme* of life is limited, I. ix. 41. 2
Soone as the *terme* of those six yeares shall cease, I. xii. 19. 7
guyde the heavenly causes to their constant *terme.* III. iii. 25. 9
'Nay but the *terme'* (sayd he) 'is limited, III. iii. 44. 1
when the *terme* is full accomplishid, III. iii. 48. 1

Term—*Continued.*
still increast till she her *terme* had full outgone. III. vi. 9. 9
'the *terme* of each mans life IV. ii. 52. 1
him to *terme* the Salvage Knight; IV. iv. 42. 6
since the *terme* of fourteene hundred yeres, V. Pr. 7. 5
'Most haplesse well ye may Me justly *terme,* V. iv. 27. 6
Ne for advantage *terme* to entertaine, V. xi. 56. 4
the *terme,* approching fast, required speed. V. xi. 65. 9
further seemes his *terme* still to extend, *Am.* lxxxvi. 11

Termagant. by *Termagaunt* thou shalt be dead.' II. viii. 30. 4
oftentimes by *Turmagant* and Mahound swore. VI. vii. 47. 9

Termed. Whom all men *term'd* Knight of the Hebene speare, IV. v. 8. 2
A wofull dame ye have me *termed* well; VI. iv. 28. 3

Termless. But there their *termelesse* time in pleasure spend; *H.H.L.* 75

Terms. with fond *termes,* and witlesse words, *S.C.* Jul. 35
in sad *tearmes* gan sorrowfully weepe, *Gn.* 325
Ile write in *termes* as she the same did say, *Hub.* 41
with reproachfull *tearmes* gan them revile, *Hub.* 365
He stands on *tearmes* of honourable minde, *Hub.* 721
With railing *tearmes* defied the Jewish hoast, *Ti.* 538
Her name Ile teach in knowen *terms* to frame: *Col.* 637
A filed toung, furnisht with *tearmes* of art, *Col.* 701
Blaspheme his powre, or *termes* unworthie yield.' *Col.* 822
with her gealous *termes* his open eares abusd: I. v. 37. 9
wounding words, and *termes* of foule repriefe, I. ix. 29. 4
'knowes best the *termes* established; I. ix. 41. 7
Here heaped up with *termes* of love unkynd, I. xii. 30. 4
stablish *termes* betwixt both their requests, II. ii. 32. 7
In fowle reproch, and *termes* of vile despight, II. iv. 5. 2
into *terms* of open outrage brust, III. i. 48. 2
Her list in stryfull *termes* with him to balke, III. ii. 12. 3
'Sir knight, these ydle *termes* forbeare; III. ii. 16. 1
frends to *termes* of gentle truce entize, III. ii. 24. 5
So ticle be the *termes* of mortall state, III. iv. 28. 6
with dishonorable *termes* her to entreat. III. v. 49. 9
With *termes* of love and lewdnesse dissolute; III. viii. 14. 3
there with many gentle *termes* her faire besought. III. viii. 35. 9
Blandamour with *termes* of foule despight, IV. ii. 3. 3
With which vaine *termes* so much they did them move, IV. ii. 19. 8
with lewd *termes* their lovers to deface. IV. iv. 4. 5
With such smooth *termes* her error I abusd IV. viii. 60. 7
To better *termes* of myldnesse did entreat IV. ix. 14. 2
of a truce to treat In milder *tearmes,* IV. ix. 35. 7
With bitter taunts and *termes* of vile disgrace. V. iv. 23. 4
Ne would be taught with any *termes* V. v. 46. 3
termes to entertaine of common guize, V. vi. 20. 4
her no other *termes* should ever tie V. vii. 28. 8
into bitter *termes* forth brust, V. viii. 22. 4
Ne time would give, nor any *termes* aby, VI. ii. 19. 7
From that they most affect, and in due *termes* containe. VI. vi. 7. 9
With all the evill *termes* and cruell meane VI. vii. 39. 5
With better *tearmes* she did him entertaine, VI. xi. 7. 2
With bitter *termes* of shamefull infamy; VI. xii. 33. 4
To make a truce, and *termes* to entertaine: *Am.* xii. 2
With such strange *termes* her eyes she doth inure, *Am.* xxi. 9
wast and weare away in *termes* unsure, *Am.* xxv. 3
striving both for *termes* of dignitie, *Com. Son.* ii. 7

Terpin. *See* **Turpine.**
Artegall . . . Saves *Terpine* from the gallow tree, V. iv. Arg.
tell, Sir *Terpin,* ne let you amate Your misery, V. iv. 28. 4
Sir *Terpin,* from you lightly throw This squalid weede, V. iv. 34. 5
when she espide Sir *Terpin,* V. iv. 39. 2
Together with Sir *Terpin* all that night: V. iv. 46. 7
Terpine, borne to' a more unhappy howre, V. v. 18. 4

Terraces. With many towres, and *tarras* mounted hye, V. ix. 21. 6

Terrestrial. O vaine labours of *terrestriall* wit, *Ti.* 512
nether doth thy face *terrestriall* shew, II. iii. 33. 3
Far passing th' hight of men *terrestriall,* II. vii. 41. 5
Ne him committ to grave *terrestriall,* II. xi. 45. 8
sprong of seed *terrestriall,* III. iii. 26. 5
shapes seem'd not like to *terrestriall* boyes, IV. x. 42. 4

Terrible. Adowne whose necke, in *terrible* array, *Gn.* 347
other spelles like *terrible,* I. i. 37. 3
so sterne and *terrible* in sight, II. i. 6. 3
His portaunce *terrible,* and stature tall, II. vii. 41. 4
Large were his limbes, and *terrible* his looke, III. i. 17. 8
No whit lesse fayre then *terrible* in fight: III. iii. 56. 3
teares it all with *terrible* mischance. IV. vi. 14. 5
there came Stoure with *terrible* aspect, IV. xi. 32. 1
Did them assault with *terrible* allarme; V. xi. 58. 3
Their cruell strokes and *terrible* affright; VI. i. 36. 7
but *terrible* and stearne In all assaies VI. iii. 40. 3
For he was sterne and *terrible* by nature, VI. vii. 41. 1

Terribly. he gan full *terribly* to rore, *Hub.* 1337
'There he tormenteth her most *terribly* III. xi. 17. 1
So *terribly* his dreadfull strokes did thonder, V. iii. 8. 8

Terrified. with dread of shame sore *terrifide.* I. xi. 45. 9
His hand that trembled as one *terrifyde;* II. vii. 6. 7
in short space their foes they have quite *terrifyde.* III. i. 66. 9
He met a Dwarfe that seemed *terrifyde* III. v. 3. 3
That ugly shape so sore her *terrifide,* III. vii. 24. 3
He blest himselfe as one sore *terrifide:* IV. vi. 24. 7
Yet him nought *terrified* that feared nothing ill. V. xi. 22. 9
nought was *terrifide,* but greater courage tooke. V. xi. 28. 9
terrifide his foes, and armed him, VI. xii. 26. 8

Terrify. With their bright firebronds me to *terrifie.* *Gn.* 424
griesly Feends of hell him *terrifie.* *Gn.* 544
living creature it would *terrify* To looke adowne, III. x. 56. 5
terrifie from Fortunes faire adward: IV. x. 17. 5
As if he with his lookes would all men *terrifie.* VI. vii. 42. 9

Terrify—*Continued.*
mote encheare his friends, and foes mote *terrifie*. . . . . . . VII. vi. 24. 9
Territories. all the *territories,* Which Phison and Euphrates floweth by, ... I. vii. 43. 7
Terror. would have fled with *terror* all dismayde. . . . . . . *Hub.* 956
his skinne, the *terror* of the wood, ... *Hub.* 969
Yet so as him their *terrour* more adornes. . . . . *Mui.* 88
with the *terror* of the shocke, Astonied, both stand . . . . . I. ii. 16. 4
Let now abate the *terrour* of your might, ... I. v. 14. 4
all the earth for *terror* seemd to shake, ... I. vii. 7. 6
peoples hartes with awfull *terror* tye, ... I. vii. 16. 7
haughtie Helmet . . . Both glorious brightnesse and great *terrour* bredd: . . . . I. vii. 31. 2
once abide the *terror* of that blast, ... I. viii. 4. 6
sownd . . . all the ayre with *terror* filled wyde, ... I. xi. 4. 2
The cloudes before him fledd for *terror* great, ... I. xi. 10. 8
was, for *terrour* more, all armd in shyning bras. . . . . . . II. ii. 17. 9
for *terrour* of his name, ... II. v. 26. 6
Troubled with *terrour* and unquiet jarre, ... II. vi. 37. 8
For *terrour* of the tortures manifold, ... II. vii. 63. 4
trembling *terror* did his hart apall; . . . . II. xi. 39. 2
with great *terrour* rave. . . . . II. xii. 5. 9
manly *terror* mixed therewithall; . . . . III. i. 46. 2
with so troublous *terror* they were all dismayd. . . . . . . III. i. 63. 9
for *terror* of his fame, ... III. iii. 12. 8
her *terror* hath encreast; . . . . III. vii. 1. 5
with *terrour* and with aw So inly smot, ... III. vii. 13. 5
with the *terrour* of their fierce affret . . . . III. ix. 16. 3
awfull *terror* deepe into him strooke, ... III. x. 24. 4
with great ruth and *terrour* she was smit, ... III. xi. 12. 8
with the *terrour* of his countenance bold . . . . IV. x. 16. 8
At sight thereof she was with *terror* queld, ... IV. x. 55. 5
with unwonted *terror* halfe affray, ... V. ix. 24. 4
Through the sad *terror* of so dreadfull fate, ... V. ix. 46. 4
with huge *terrour,* to be more ydrad, ... V. xi. 3. 5
all the Temple did with *terrour* fill; . . . . V. xi. 22. 8
With trembling joynts, as he for *terrour* shooke; . . . . . V. xi. 28. 8
asswage Their forces furie, and their *terror* slake; . . . . . V. xii. 8. 4
With dreadfull *terror* and with fell intent; . . . . V. xii. 17. 2
With flaming sword in hand his *terror* more to breed. . . . . VI. vii. 11. 9
did the ayre with *terror* fill, ... VI. viii. 46. 3
all the world beneath for *terror* quooke, ... VII. vi. 30. 8
To hide the *terror* of her uncouth hew . . . . VII. vii. 6. 2
fills the darkned world with *terror* and dismay. . . . . . . VII. vii. 51. 9
with theyr *terrour* al the rest may chace, ... *Am.* xxxi. 7
Terwin. Sir *Terwin* hight, that well himselfe advaunst . . . . I. ix. 27. 3
Testament. A booke, wherein his Saveours *testament* Was writt I. ix. 19. 7
As she bequeathd in her last *testament;* . . . . II. ii. 10. 6
Testified. Yet shall it not by none be *testifyde.*' . . . . . . VI. i. 6. 7
Testifies. by her heaps her hugenesse *testifies.* . . . . *Ti.* 77
Testify. That present were to *testifie* the case.' . . . . IV. i. 49. 5
Tethys. there *Tethys* his wet bed Doth ever wash, ... I. i. 39. 6
the aged Ocean and his Dame Old *Tethys,* . . . . IV. xi. 18. 2
Tethys'. Doth plonge himselfe in *Tethys* bosome faire; . . . *Ro.* xx. 4
Ofte soust in swelling *Tethys* saltish teare; . . . . I. iii. 31. 3
fast gan flye Into great *Tethys* bosome, ... II. xii. 26. 9
Tetra. Cold Coloquintida, and *Tetra* mad; . . . . II. vii. 52. 4
Teucrian. When *Teucrian* soyle with bloodie rivers swelde, . . *Gn.* 500
Text. seeke to glose upon the *text;* . . . . *Gn.* Ded. 10
As if therein some *text* he studying were, ... *Hub.* 380
Texts. breede Doubts mongst Divines, and difference of *texts,* . *Hub.* 387
Thabor. *See* **Tabor.**
Thalia. Joyous *Thalia,* goodly Amphitrite, ... IV. xi. 49. 2
Next faire Aglaia, last *Thalia* merry; . . . . VI. x. 22. 8
Thame. His auncient parents, namely th' auncient *Thame.* . . IV. xi. 24. 5
Thame was stronger, and of better stay; . . . . IV. xi. 25. 6
Oxford, thine doth *Thame* most glorify. . . . . IV. xi. 26. 9
Thames. with his elder brother *Themis* . . . . *S.C.* Jul. 83
beside the shore Of silver streaming *Thamesis* . . . . *Ti.* 2
where the christall *Thamis* wont to slide . . . . *Ti.* 134
with the waves Of wealthy *Thamis* washed is along, ... III. ix. 45. 2
Where *Thames* doth the Medway wedd, ... IV. xi. Arg.
Betwixt the Medway and the *Thames* agreed. . . . . IV. xi. 8. 4
Long had the *Thames* . . . her wooed . . . . IV. xi. 8. 5
The noble *Thamis,* with all his goodly traine; . . . . IV. xi. 24. 3
With such an one was *Thamis* beautifide; . . . . IV. xi. 28. 7
till *Thamis* he overtake. . . . . IV. xi. 32. 9
in order seemly good Did on the *Thamis* attend, ... IV. xi. 44. 8
Along the shoare of silver streaming *Themmes;* . . . . . *Proth.* 11
Sweete *Themmes!* runne softly, till I end my Song. . . *Proth.* 18, 36, 54, 72, 90
Sweete *Themmes!* runne softlie, till I end my Song.' . . . . *Proth.* 108
Sweete *Themmes!* run softly, ... *Proth.* 126
Sweete *Themmes!* runne softly, ... *Proth.* 144, 162, 180
Thames'. With *Thames* inhabitants of noble fame, ... *Ro.* xxii. 3
the bolde people by the *Thamis* brincks, ... *Ro.* xxxi. 6
on *Themmes* brode aged backe . . . . *Proth.* 133
Thamesis. *See* **Thames.**
Thamis. *See* **Thames.**
Than (*partial list*).
accordes more swete *than* Mermaids song, ... *Bel.*[1] x. 8
Hir brightnesse greater was *than* can be founde, ... *Rev.* iv. 8
A lively streame, more cleere *than* Christall is, ... *Rev.* iv. 12
manie accords more sweete *than* Mermaids song: . . . . . . *Bel.* xii. 8
Much richer *then* that vessell seem'd to bee, ... *Bel.*[2] xiii. 1
no lesse rich *than* faire, ... *Bel.*[2] xiv. 6
This Citie, more *than* that great Phrygian mother Renowm'd . *Ro.* vi. 5
No otherwise *than* raynie cloud, first fed . . . . *Ro.* xx. 1
Thought all things lesse *than* his disdainful pride. . . . . . *Van.* iii. 6
To nought more, Thenot, my mind is bent *Then* to heare . . . *S.C.* F. 95
pitied would be, Rather *then* other should scorne . . . . . . *S.C.* May 60

Than—*Continued.*
other things tend, *Then* . . . Reapen the fruite . . . . *S.C.* May 64
cannot compare Better *then* to the Apes folish care, ... *S.C.* May 96
Had lever my foe *then* my freend he be; . . . . *S.C.* May 167
more black *then* pitche, ... *S.C.* Jun. 23
I more delight *then* larke in Sommer dayes: . . . . *S.C.* Jun. 51
the hyll . . . Better is *then* the lowly playne, ... *S.C.* Jul. 7
His face, more cleare *then* Christall glasse, ... *S.C.* Jul. 159
Thou medlest more *then* shall have thanke, ... *S.C.* Jul. 209
She sweeter *then* the Violet. . . . . *S.C.* Au. 72
More meete to wayle my woe . . . *Then* bedde, ... *S.C.* Au. 167
They sayne the world is much war *then* it wont, ... *S.C.* S. 108
liker bene they to pluck away more, *Then* . . . restore: . . . *S.C.* S. 129
better leave of with a little losse, *Then* . . . leese the grosse. . *S.C.* S. 135
swifter *then* thought, ... *S.C.* S. 222
prayse is better *then* the price, ... *S.C.* O. 19
The glory eke much greater *then* the gayne: . . . . *S.C.* O. 20
greater gyfts . . . *Then* Kidde or Cosset, ... *S.C.* N. 46
no lesse regarde *Then* of the flocks, ... *S.C.* D. 12
lighter seeme *than* this Gnats idle name. . . . . *Gn.* 8
lead, then, a more happie life *Than* he, ... *Gn.* 122
thy life more deare . . . Was *than* mine owne, ... *Gn.* 332
No lesse, I dare saie, *than* the prowdest wight; . . . . . . *Hub.* 62
two is better *than* one head.' . . . . *Hub.* 82
more for thrift did care *than* for gay clothing: . . . . . . *Hub.* 231
they more subtill meaning had *than* he; . . . . *Hub.* 330
A garment better *than* of wooll or heare. . . . . *Hub.* 474
Better a short tale *than* a bad long shriving: . . . . *Hub.* 543
rather rule and raigne . . . *Than* dwell in dust . . . . *Hub.* 981
none more tragick matter I can finde *Than* this, ... *T.M.* 156
far more bitter storme *than* winters stowre . . . . *T.M.* 247
Darknesse more *than* Cymerians daylie night: . . . . *T.M.* 256
if good were not praised more *than* ill, ... *T.M.* 455
mercie more *than* mortall men can vew. . . . . *T.M.* 514
count of wisedome more *than* of thy Countie. . . . . *Ti.* 273
who can better sing *Than* thine owne sister, ... *Ti.* 317
Was none more favourable, . . . *Then* Clarion, ... *Mui.* 22
No lesse *than* that which Vulcane made to sheild . . . . . . *Mui.* 63
What more felicitie . . . *Then* to enjoy delight with libertie, . *Mui.* 210
Much fitter *than* the Lyon, ... *D.* 165
spare the best or fayrest, more *Than* worst or fowlest, ... *D.* 203
With better fortune *than* did me succeed, ... *D.* 521
'Fearful much more (quoth he) *then* hart can fear: . . . . . *Col.* 201
fields, *then* which Armulla yields None fairer, ... *Col.* 278
Much greater *then* that frame, ... *Col.* 287
other *then* whereon we stand?' . . . . *Col.* 291
Much more there is unkend *then* thou doest kon, ... *Col.* 294
Whose glorie greater *then* my simple thought, ... *Col.* 333
I found much greater *then* the former fame; . . . . *Col.* 334
More rich *then* pearles of Ynde, ... *Col.* 490
Ne lesse praise-worthie Galathea seemes, *Then* best . . . . *Col.* 517
best to hold eternally . . . *Then* by discourse them to in-dignifie.' . . . . *Col.* 583
all otherwise devise, *Then* we . . . are accustomd . . . . . . *Col.* 785
a lowly Asse more white *then* snow, ... I. i. 4. 2
stroke at her with more *then* manly force, ... I. i. 24. 6
Better new friend *then* an old foe . . . . I. ii. 27. 4
more foule and hideous, *Then* womans shape man would beleeve I. ii. 41. 4
moves more deare compassion of mind, *Then* beautie . . . . . I. iii. 1. 3
joyous seemde no lesse *Then* the glad marchant, ... I. iii. 32. 3
More mild in beastly kind *then* that her beastly foe. . . . . I. iii. 44. 9
no greater shame *Then* lightnesse . . . in love: . . . . I. iv. 1. 8
more like a monster *then* a man. . . . . I. iv. 22. 9
Grandmother of all, More old *then* Jove, ... I. v. 22. 3
greater conquest of hard love he gaynes, . . . *then* he . . . . I. vi. 3. 9
more joy to raunge . . . *Then* serve his Ladies love, ... I. vi. 21. 9
more heavy plight *Then* that I feele, ... I. vii. 25. 4
never Lady loved dearer day *Then* she did love . . . . I. vii. 27. 8
yts better hidden keep, *Then* rip up griefe . . . . I. vii. 39. 8
can more easily be thought *then* said.' . . . . I. vii. 41. 2
rather death desire *then* such despight. . . . . I. vii. 49. 6
my cause of griefe, more great *then* may be told.' . . . . . . I. vii. 51. 9
lever had I die *then* see his deadly face.' . . . . I. ix. 32. 9
forgiveth every howre Much more *then* that . . . . I. x. 40. 7
Who better can . . . aread *Then* thou thyselfe, ... I. x. 51. 5
More dear unto their God *then* younglings to their dam.' . . . I. x. 57. 9
Nor harder was . . . *then* from his cruell claw To reave . . . I. xi. 41. 5
More *then* goodwill to me attribute nought; . . . . II. i. 33. 4
Of anguish, rather *then* of crime, ... II. i. 58. 7
More huge in strength *then* wise in workes . . . . II. ii. 17. 6
more to mighty hands *then* rightfull cause doth trust. . . . . II. ii. 29. 9
better fayre it to accord *Then* . . . to heape offence, ... II. ii. 30. 3
seemd no lesse to love *then* lov'd to bee: . . . . II. iv. 19. 5
liefer were ten thousand deathes priefe *Then* . . . gealous . . II. iv. 28. 9
death were better *then* such agony . . . . II. iv. 33. 3
no greater enimy *Then* stubborne perturbation . . . . II. v. 1. 4
Whose bounty more *then* might, ... II. v. 14. 9
to bee lesser *then* himselfe doth marre . . . . II. v. 15. 7
More swift *then* swallow . . . . II. vi. 5. 2
Better safe port *then* be in seas distrest.' . . . . II. vi. 23. 8
she, more sweete *then* any bird . . . . II. vi. 25. 1
Of love they greater glory bore *Then* of their armes; . . . . II. vi. 35. 7
for Venus loves renowmed more *Then* all his wars . . . . . . II. vi. 35. 9
She no lesse glad *then* he . . . . II. vi. 37. 1
more happy he *then* wise, ... II. vi. 46. 4
In daunger rather to be drent *then* brent?' . . . . II. vi. 49. 7
ugly feend, more fowle *then* dismall day, ... II. vii. 26. 7
clouds more black *then* Jett. . . . . II. vii. 28. 9
More light *then* Culver in the Faulcons fist. . . . . II. vii. 34. 6
To covet more *then* I have cause to use? . . . . II. vii. 39. 4

Than—*Continued.*
More fitt emongst black fiendes *then* men to have his place. . . II. vii. 41. 9
his hand, more sad *then* lomp of lead, ... II. viii. 30. 5
More glory thought to give life *then* decay, ... II. viii. 51. 4
more faire and excellent *Then* is mans body, ... II. ix. 1. 3
none *then* it more fowle and indecent, ... II. ix. 1. 5
Thousand times fairer *than* her mortall hew, ... II. ix. 3. 7
With greater fury *then* before was fownd; . . . . II. ix. 15. 2
more smooth and fine, *Then* Jett or Marble . . . . II. ix. 24. 3
More whott *then* Aetn', or flaming Mongiball . . . . II. ix. 29. 7
she much more *than* her owne life him lov'd; . . . . II. x. 28. 2
greater love to him profest *Then* all the world, ... II. x. 28. 4
never king more highly magnifide, . . . *then* was Arvirage; . II. x. 52. 2
two *then* all more huge . . . . II. xi. 9. 8
No sooner thought, *then* that the Carle . . . Gan heap . . . II. xi. 43. 8
more horrible *then* hell . . . . II. xii. 6. 3
whom Mariners eschew No lesse *then* rockes, ... II. xii. 24. 8
Worse is the daunger hidden *then* descride. . . . . II. xii. 35. 5
Rather for pleasure *then* for battery or fight. . . . . II. xii. 43. 9
semblaunce pleasing, more *then* naturall, ... II. xii. 46. 5
More . . . holesome *then* the pleasaunt hill Of Rhodope, . . II. xii. 52. 1
Few drops, more cleare *then* Nectar, ... II. xii. 78. 4
Dye rather would he *then* endure that same. . . . . III. i. 9. 5
death me liefer were *then* such despight, ... III. i. 24. 4
All losse is lesse, . . . *Then* losse of love . . . . III. i. 25. 6
That she is fairer *then* our fairest Dame; . . . . III. i. 27. 4
love can higher stye *Then* reasons reach, ... III. ii. 36. 6
Other *then* my hard fortune to deplore, ... III. ii. 39. 7
fonder *then* Cephisus foolish chyld, ... III. ii. 44. 6
Ne braver proofe . . . *then* in this royall Maid . . . . III. iii. 3. 3
more insight *Then* ever . . . living wight: . . . . III. iii. 11. 9
More hidden are *then* Sunne in cloudy vele; . . . . III. iii. 19. 6
Whose empire lenger here *then* ever any stood?' . . . . . . III. iii. 42. 9
No whit lesse fayre *then* terrible in fight: . . . . III. iii. 56. 3
dreaded more *then* all The other Saxons, ... III. iii. 56. 5
better . . . to die with speed *Then* waste in woe . . . . . . III. iv. 38. 4
Sad life worse *then* glad death; . . . . III. iv. 38. 8
no lesse afrayd *Then* . . . she had chaced beene; . . . . . . III. iv. 51. 4
on a Palfrey rydes more white *then* snow, ... III. v. 5. 6
lever were to weeten that,' . . . '*then* ransome . . . . III. v. 7. 2
Dye rather, dye, *then* so disloyally Deeme . . . . III. v. 45. 6
Dye rather, dy, *then* ever love disloyally. . . . . III. v. 45. 9
What can I lesse doe *then* her love therefore, ... III. v. 46. 4
Dye rather, dye, *then* ever from her service swerve. . . . . III. v. 46. 9
Dye rather, dye, *then* ever so faire love forsake!' . . . . . III. v. 47. 9
rather chose to dye . . . *Then* with dishonorable termes . . . III. v. 49. 9
More deare *then* life she tendered, ... III. v. 51. 2
it she shund no lesse *then* dread to die; . . . . III. vii. 24. 4
rather joyd to bee *then* seemen sich, ... III. vii. 29. 8
no more was moved . . . *Then* it had lighted . . . . III. vii. 41. 3
me lever were to dye *Then* breake the vow . . . . III. vii. 51. 6
her honor, which she more *then* life prefard. . . . . III. viii. 14. 9
rather . . . *Then* any should of falsenesse her reprove, ... III. viii. 42. 4
rather had he dy *Then* . . . in coward corner ly. . . . . . . III. ix. 14. 9
welcomde more for feare *then* charitee; . . . . III. ix. 19. 4
Was never better time to shew thy smart *Then* now . . . . . III. x. 26. 4
is lesse *Then* vertues might . . . . III. xi. 14. 7
renowm, that, more *then* death, is to be sought.' . . . . . . III. xi. 19. 9
Lesse she thee lov'd *then* was thy just desart, ... III. xi. 36. 8
More sondry colours *then* the proud Pavone Beares . . . . . III. xi. 47. 7
inly being more *then* seeming sad: . . . . III. xii. 16. 4
none more piteous . . . *Then* that of Amorets . . . . IV. i. 1. 4
her honor, dearer *then* her life, ... IV. i. 6. 6
Die had she lever . . . *Then* to be false in love, ... IV. i. 6. 9
none more faire *then* shee, ... IV. i. 9. 5
no lesse was courteous *then* stout, ... IV. i. 11. 6
discord harder is to end *then* to begin. . . . . IV. i. 20. 9
rather die *then* Ladies cause release: . . . . IV. ii. 19. 7
more of price . . . Is this, *then* that same water . . . . . . IV. iii. 45. 2
more swift *then* Myrrh' or Daphne in her race, ... IV. vii. 22. 8
is *Then* death it selfe more dread . . . . IV. viii. 1. 4
two fierie beames, More sharpe *then* points of needles, ... IV. viii. 39. 2
No lesse *then* perfect gold surmounts the meanest brasse. . . IV. ix. 2. 9
harder may be ended, *then* begonne: . . . . IV. x. 3. 4
the paine thereof much greater *then* the fee. . . . . IV. x. 3. 9
Much more *then* that which was in Paphos built, ... IV. x. 5. 6
'No lesse did Daunger threaten me . . . *Then* Cerberus, ... IV. x. 58. 4
then which none more upright, ... IV. xi. 18. 6
ought more hard, *then* thinke to reckon right. . . . . IV. xi. 53. 3
more eath . . . *Then* to recount . . . . IV. xii. 1. 7
had I rather to be thrall *then* free; . . . . IV. xii. 10. 8
was of no lesse vertue *then* of fame; . . . . V. i. 10. 5
mov'd no more therewith, *then* when a rocke . . . . V. i. 21. 6
Ne better doth beseeme brave chevalry, *Then* to defend . . . V. ii. 1. 3
Whereof no braver president . . . *Then* this of Artegall, . . . V. iv. 2. 9
Who more *then* losse of life ydreaded it; . . . . V. iv. 25. 5
rather chose to die . . . *Then* lead that shamefull life, ... V. iv. 32. 9
made her famous, more *then* is believed; . . . . V. iv. 33. 8
No fayrer conquest *then* that . . . . V. v. 17. 9
Die rather . . . *Then* his foes love or liking entertaine. . . . . V. v. 46. 7
her winged thoughts, more swift *then* wind, ... V. vi. 7. 8
rather bent To peace *then* needlesse trouble . . . . V. vi. 19. 7
rather *then* she kindnesse would despize, She would . . . . . V. vi. 20. 5
Nought is on earth more sacred . . . *Then* this same vertue . . V. vii. 1. 3
longer *Then* two speares length: . . . . V. viii. 7. 9
More in his causes truth he trusted *then* in might. . . . . . V. viii. 30. 9
it is greater prayse to save *then* spill, ... V. x. 2. 8
better to reforme *then* to cut off the ill. . . . . V. x. 2. 9
More happie mother . . . *Then* famous Niobe, ... V. x. 7. 8
more bright *Then* it was wont, ... V. x. 20. 9

Than—*Continued.*
liker lingring death *then* loathed life to bee.' . . . . V. x. 21. 9
Much greater *then* was ever in her weeting, ... V. x. 39. 3
puddle . . . More loathd *then* Lerna, or *then* Stygian lake, . . V. xi. 32. 4
lesse all paine *Then* losse of fame . . . . V. xi. 55. 8
Dye, rather *then* doe ought that mote dishonour yield.' . . . V. xi. 55. 9
goodly light *then* Phoebus lampe doth shine more cleare? . . V. xi. 62. 9
Dearer is love *then* life, and fame *then* gold; . . . . V. xi. 63. 8
dearer *then* them both your faith once plighted hold.' . . . . V. xi. 63. 9
The other nothing better was *then* shee, ... V. xii. 33. 1
not a fayrer flowre *Then* is the bloosme of comely courtesie; . VI. Pr. 4. 2
was none more courteous *Then* Calidore, ... VI. i. 2. 2
Then which a prouder Lady liveth none: . . . . VI. i. 14. 7
No greater shame to man *then* inhumanitie. . . . . VI. i. 26. 9
nothing is more blamefull . . . *Then* the reproch of pride . . VI. i. 41. 4
Whereof she now more glad *then* sory earst, ... VI. i. 45. 1
cared not for dint of sword . . . No more *then* for . . . . . . VI. iv. 4. 7
greater force there needs to maintaine wrong *then* right. . . VI. vi. 35. 9
Devizing of his love more *then* of daunger drad. . . . . . . VI. vii. 6. 9
No more *then* lightening from the lofty sky: . . . . VI. viii. 8. 6
more on him doth *then* him selfe depend: . . . . VI. viii. 17. 8
Yet never Turtle truer . . . *Then* he . . . . VI. viii. 33. 7
by chaunce more *then* by choyce, ... VI. viii. 46. 7
better . . . *then* in the salvage fields to rome. . . . . VI. ix. 16. 7
cared more for Colins carolings *Then* all that he could doe, . VI. ix. 35. 8
did love a stranger swayne *then* him more dere. . . . . . . VI. ix. 38. 9
His life he steemed dearer *then* his frend: . . . . VI. x. 35. 5
Liker to heaven *then* mortall wretchednesse: . . . . VI. xi. 1. 5
minding more her safety *then* himselfe, ... VI. xi. 19. 3
better were . . . *Then* here to see all desolate . . . . VI. xi. 32. 7
No more *then* Cynthia's selfe; . . . . VII. vi. 18. 9
I greater am . . . *Then* all the Gods, ... VII. vi. 26. 9
Sprinkled with wholsom waters more *then* most on ground: . . VII. vi. 38. 9
fled more fast *Then* any Deere, ... VII. vi. 52. 5
more tall of stature *Then* any of the gods . . . . VII. vii. 5. 4
That richer seem'd *then* any tapestry, ... VII. vii. 10. 8
gods no more *then* men thou doest esteeme; . . . . VII. vii. 15. 8
Her hart more harde *then* yron . . . . *Am.* xxxii. 6
More sweet *than* Nectar, ... *Am.* xxxix. 13
Clearer *then* cristall, would therein appere. . . . . *Am.* xlv. 12
More bright *then* Hesperus his head doth rere. . . . . *Epith.* 95
Never had man more joyfull day *then* this, ... *Epith.* 246
More *then* we men can fayne! . . . . *Epith.* 414
sweeter farre *then* any Nectar is; . . . . *H.L.* 26
Fairer *then* fairest, ... *H.L.* 216
with more *then* hellish paine! . . . . *H.L.* 253
With thousands more *then* any tongue can tell, ... *H.L.* 264
Yet is there one more cursed *then* they all, ... *H.L.* 266
there is more *then* so, That workes . . . . *H.B.* 85
Counting it fairer *then* it is indeede, ... *H.B.* 230
lovers eyes more sharply sighted bee *Then* other mens, . . . *H.B.* 233
See more *then* any other eyes can see, ... *H.B.* 234
forgetfull of his Makers grace No lesse *then* Angels . . . . . *H.H.L.* 121
sowd with glistring stars more thicke *then* grasse, ... *H.H.B.* 53
More firme and durable *then* steele or brasse, ... *H.H.B.* 153

Thank. Let dame Elisa *thanke* you for her song: . . . . . . *S.C.* Ap. 150
Thou medlest more then shall have *thanke,* . . . . *S.C.* Jul. 209
Ere Roffy could for his laboure him *thanck.* . . . . *S.C.* S. 201
yet doo never *thanke* them for the same, ... *Hub.* 165
(litle have she *thanck!*) . . . . II. ii. 36. 9
Yet litle losse it were, and mickle *thanke,* . . . . V. i. 15. 5
Gan greatly *thanke* his host and his good wife; . . . . VI. ix. 18. 6

Thanked. (*thanked* be God therefore) . . . . *S.C.* Jul. 169
She *thancked* them in her disdainefull wise; . . . . I. iv. 14. 2
thankt be God, and her encrease so evermore!' . . . . I. x. 16. 9
God she praysd, and *thankt* her faithfull knight, ... I. xi. 55. 8
humbly *thanked* him a thousand sith . . . . III. x. 33. 3
thankt be God, and your good hardiment, ... V. viii. 23. 5
She humbly *thankt* him for that wondrous grace, ... V. xi. 18. 1
She *thankt* him deare . . . . VI. ii. 46. 6
Sir Calepine her *thanckt;* . . . . VI. iii. 33. 1
They tooke it well, and *thanked* God for all, ... VI. iv. 15. 2
Yet he them all refusd, though *thankt* her as a frend; . . . . VI. iv. 39. 9
A thousand times him *thankt* that had her death prevented. . VI. x. 36. 9

Thankful. So long as *thankfull* will may it relent. . . . . *Gn.* 368
in closure of a *thankfull* mynd, ... *Col.* 580
them requitest with thy *thankfull* labours. . . . . *Col.* 587
As tokens of her *thankefull* mind beseene, ... V. x. 17. 3
To show her *thankefull* mind and meaning faine, ... VI. i. 46. 4
That *thankfull* guerdon may to you repay.' . . . . VI. ii. 38. 5

Thankfulness. Which she receiving with meete *thankefulnesse,* IV. xii. 32. 6

Thankless. Least so great good . . . buried be in *thankles* thought. . . . . I. ix. 2. 9
hast a *thanklesse* service on thee ta'ne, ... III. viii. 47. 3
will not use his gifts for *thanklesse* nigardise.' . . . . . . IV. viii. 15. 9
Shall to you purchas with her *thankles* paine! . . . . *Am.* xxvii. 12

Thanks. that *thankes* so much should faile of meed; . . . . . *Gn.* 353
Great *thankes* I yeeld you for your discipline, ... *Hub.* 547
she accepts with *thankes* and goodly gree, ... I. v. 16. 4
Great *thankes,* and goodly meed, ... I. x. 68. 4
thousand *thankes* him yeeldes for all his paine. . . . . I. xii. 12. 7
to that Damsell *thankes* gave for reward . . . . II. vi. 38. 6
with glad *thankes,* and unreproved truth, ... II. vii. 16. 3
thrice three hundred *thanks* for my good partes, ... III. vii. 55. 5
To get small *thankes,* and therewith many blames, ... III. vii. 61. 3
Ten thousand *thankes* did yeeld her for her meed, ... IV. i. 15. 3
Praysing their god, and yeelding him great *thankes,* . . . . . IV. x. 25. 7
thousand *thankes* him yeeld, ... V. iii. 15. 8
Can yeeld great *thankes* for such her curtesie; . . . . V. v. 55. 5
Her selfe most gratefull shew'd, and heaped *thanks* repayd. . V. viii. 23. 9

Thanks—*Continued.*
with right humble *thankes* him goodly greeting . . . . . . V. x. 39. 1
yeeld great *thankes* for their so goodly deed, ... V. xi. 48. 3
With all due *thankes* and dutifull respect, ... VI. i. 45. 7
thousand *thankes* to Calidore . . . Did yeeld: . . . . . . VI. iii. 19. 3
Yet no lesse *thankes* to you for your good will.' . . . . . . VI. viii. 30. 5
With *thanks* to Bellamour and Claribell, ... VI. xii. 13. 8
thanks to him, that it deserves, behight; . . . . . . *Com. Son.* ii. 12
That (*partial list*). *See* **Now that.**
From worse unto *that* is worst of all, ... *S.C.* F. 13
But gently tooke *that* ungently came; . . . . . . *S.C.* F. 22
soveraigne of seas . . . *That,* once sea-beate, will to sea . . . . . . *S.C.* F. 34
Let be, as may be, *that* is past: . . . . . . *S.C.* Mar. 58
That is to come, let be forecast: . . . . . . *S.C.* Mar. 59
Nor thys, nor *that,* so muche doeth make . . . . . . *S.C.* Ap. 9
That nource of vice, this of insolencie, ... *S.C.* May 118
Let none mislike of *that* may not be mended: . . . . . . *S.C.* May 162
if *that* my Grandsire me sayd be true, ... *S.C.* May 268
tell many lesinges of this and *that,* . . . . . . *S.C.* May 285
Of *that* the spring was in his learned hedde, ... *S.C.* Jun. 94
for love of *that* is to thee moste leefe, ... *S.C.* S. 11
to *that* I choose thou doest me tempt; . . . . . . *S.C.* N. 49
Now therefore *that* no lenger hope I see, ... *Hub.* 65
For worse than *that* I have I cannot meete. . . . . . . *Hub.* 89
ne by the law of Nature, But *that* she gave . . . . . . *Hub.* 146
make them seeke for *that* they wont to scorne, ... *Hub.* 257
Loving *that* love, and hating those *that* hate; . . . . . . *Hub.* 428
this, or *that, that* may excuse the cryme: . . . . . . *Hub.* 989
'Seemes, *that that* gentle River for great griefe . . . . . . *Ti.* 141
'What land is *that* thou meant, ... *Col.* 290
Before *that* angry heavens list to lowre, ... I. ii. 22. 4
Least to you hap *that* happened to me heare, ... I. ii. 31. 5
As all unweeting of *that* well she knew; . . . . . . I. ii. 45. 2
forth he called *that* his daughter . . . . . . I. xii. 21. 1
take heede of *that* thou now hast past, ... II. iv. 36. 3
Yet shortly gaynd *that* losse exceeded farre. . . . . . . II. v. 15. 5
when this breathlesse woxe, *that* batteil gan renew. . . . . . . II. viii. 47. 9
Dayly he tempted her with this or *that,* . . . . . . III. viii. 39. 1
What boots it then to plaine *that* cannot be redrest?' . . . . . . III. xi. 17. 9
Till evening *that* the Sunne gan downward bend. . . . . . . IV. iv. 43. 6
Barkes, this caried with the tide, *That* with the wind, ... IV. ix. 26. 8
To see *that* mortall eyes have never seene; . . . . . . VII. vi. 32. 3
my fraile wit cannot . . . finde like stuffe to *that:* . . . . . . VII. vii. 7. 5
each of you, *That* vertue have or this or *that* to make, ... VII. vii. 54. 7
the rest around To her redoubled *that* her undersong, ... *Proth.* 110
Thatch. To hedge, to ditch, to thrash, to *thetch,* to mowe? . . . *Hub.* 264
That is. Till he should die his last, *that is,* eternally. . . . . . . I. ix. 54. 9
'As for her tenants, *that is,* man and beasts, ... VII. vii. 19. 1
That's. For all *thats* good is beautifull and faire. . . . . . . *H.H.B.* 133
Thaumantes. the daughter of *Thaumantes* faire . . . . . . V. iii. 25. 1
The (*partial list*).
The fytter they my carefull case to frame: . . . . . . *S.C.* Jun. 78
What *the* foule evill hath thee so bestadde? . . . . . . *S.C.* Au. 7
'*The* lenger life, I wote, *the* greater sin; . . . . . . I. ix. 43. 1
all his wars and spoiles, *the* which he did of yore.' . . . . . . II. vi. 35. 9
change his shield with him to be *the* better hid . . . . . . V. iii. 10. 9
The more she rag'd, *the* more he did abide; . . . . . . V. v. 6. 8
the more she fervent sees my fit, *The* more she frieseth . . . . . . *Am.* xxxii. 9, 10
Whose rutty Bancke, *the* which his River hemmes . . . . . . *Proth.* 12
Theame. *See* **Theme.**
Theana. Ne lesse praise-worthie I *Theana* read, ... *Col.* 492
Theatre. did like an halfe *Theatre* fulfill: . . . . . . II. xii. 30. 7
like a stately *Theatre* it made, ... III. v. 39. 5
as on the readie flore Of some *Theatre,* . . . . . . III. xii. 3. 6
Of this worlds *Theatre* in which we stay, ... *Am.* liv. 1
Theatres. with Comick sock to beautefie The painted *Theaters,* *T.M.* 177
'High towers, faire temples, goodly *theaters,* . . . . . . *Ti.* 92
Such as the troubled *Theatres* oftimes annoyes. . . . . . . IV. iii. 37. 9
Theban. the *Thebane* Semelee, Deceivd of gealous Juno, ... III. xi. 33. 1
that Monster, whom the *Theban* Knight . . . Made kill her selfe V. xi. 25. 2
Thebes. that, which antique Cadmus whylome built In *Thebes,* II. ix. 45. 7
Of fatall *Thebes;* of Rome that raigned long; . . . . . . IV. i. 22. 2
Some say in Crete . . . Others in *Thebes,* . . . . . . VII. vii. 53. 6
Thee (*partial list of pron.*).
Who lists to see . . . *thee* let him see, ... *Ro.* v. 2
Well mote yee *thee,* . . . That home ye may report . . . . . . II. i. 33. 7
If *thee* list not, leave have thou to refuse: . . . . . . II. vii. 18. 8
Life will I graunt *thee* . . . . . . II. viii. 51. 8
Fayre mote he *thee,* the prowest and most gent, ... II. xi. 17. 5
Theft. Of each a part I stole by cunning *thefte:* *Ded.Son.*xvii.13
do Chaungelings call, so chaung'd by Faeries *theft.* . . . . . . I. x. 65. 9
So hidd in lockes and waves from lookers *theft,* . . . . . . II. xii. 67. 8
Light-shonning *thefte,* and traiterous intent, ... III. iv. 58. 2
Made him seeme happie for so glorious *theft;* . . . . . . IV. ii. 4. 8
from that time I from enchaunters *theft* Her freed, ... IV. vi. 35. 4
surcharg'd with spoile and *theft:* . . . . . . IV. vii. 32. 5
Of two full hard to read the harder *theft:* . . . . . . IV. ix. 36. 6
secret *theft* Of all her lovers . . . . . . IV. xi. 3. 4
For ayde against that cruell Tyrants *theft,* . . . . . . V. x. 14. 4
reft That piteous spoile by so injurious *theft;* . . . . . . VI. i. 18. 5
wretched life forlorne for vengement of his *theft.* . . . . . . VI. ii. 18. 9
such spoile, such havocke, and such *theft* He wrought, ... VI. xii. 23. 4
Their (*partial list*). *See* **Her.**
Should warre upon the kings, and eate *their* flesh. . . . . . . *Rev.* iii. 10
theyr sheepe bene not *their* owne, ... *S.C.* May 45
dryed is *theyr* sourse, And floods of teares flowe in *theyr* stead *S.C.* N. 126, 127
every beast . . . lift up *theyr* drooping hed. . . . . . . *Am.* xl. 12
Theirs (*partial list*).
The corne is *theyrs,* let other thresh, ... *S.C.* Jul. 191
Neaera ours, not *theirs,* though there she be; . . . . . . *Col.* 525

Theirs—*Continued.*
shame Be *theirs* that have so cruell thee forlorne! . . . . . . IV. viii. 15. 4
that marke of *theirs* . . . . . . V. Pr. 7. 7
theirs that do abuse it . . . . . . *H.B.* 156
But their owne native light farre passing *theirs.* . . . . . . *H.H.B.* 70
Theise. *See* **Teise.**
Thelf. *See* **Elf.**
Them (*partial list*). *See* **Hem.**
Faire harbour that *them* seems, ... I. i. 7. 9
recompenst *them* (**him*) with a better scorse: . . . . . . II. ix. 55. 8
prayd high God *them* (**him*) farre from *them* to send. . . . VI. ix. 6. 5
Theme. that wofull *theame* For to dilate at large, ... II. v. 37. 3
Then Paridell began to chaunge his *theme,* . . . . . . III. ix. 10. 8
Themis. *See* **Thames.**
by him begot in loves delight Upon the righteous *Themis;* . . V. ix. 31. 6
Themisto. Cymo, Eupompe, and *Themiste* just; . . . . . . IV. xi. 51. 6
Themmes. *See* **Thames.**
Themselves (*partial list*).
match *them selfe* with mighty potentates, ... *S.C.* May 122
Whose straying heard *them selfe* doth shrowde . . . . . . *S.C.* Jul. 3
adore: Not for *themselfe,* but for the sayncts . . . . . . *S.C.* Jul. 115
They, not contented us *themselves* to scorne, ... *T.M.* 65
all their forces spend *Them selves* in vaine: . . . . . . I. viii. 21. 6
To rest *them selves,* and weary powres repaire; . . . . . . I. viii. 50. 8
with shamefast modestie They turne *themselves,* . . . . . . I. x. 15. 6
themselves to beare away, ... I. x. 20. 7
evill That by *themselves* unto *themselves* is wrought. . . . IV. ii. 3. 7
victors both *them selves* alwayes esteemed: . . . . . . IV. iii. 28. 5
The which, for want of heards, *themselves* then kept. . . . VI. xi. 37. 5
men *themselves* do change continually, ... VII. vii. 19. 4
these, that Gods *themselves* do call, ... VII. vii. 26. 2
Then (*partial list*). *See* **Now and then, Than.**
Then did a Ghost before mine eyes appeare, ... *Bel.* i. 5
Then let those deep Abysses open rive, ... *Ro.* i. 7
there being *then* not living An Hercules . . . . . . *Ro.* x. 9
Tell me *then,* (for perhaps . . . . . . *Ro.* xv. 9
Thou *then* adowne might'st fall . . . . . . *Ro.* xxxi. 14
how great vainnesse is it *then* to scorne . . . . . . *Van.* vi. 13
If *then* a Goose great Rome from ruine stayde, ... *Van.* xi. 9
How falls it *then* that this faded Oake, ... *S.C.* F. 169
then, will I singe his laye . . . . . . *S.C.* Ap. 33
How falles it, *then,* we no merrier bene, ... *S.C.* May 3
Of mercye and favour, *then,* I you pray . . . . . . *S.C.* May 272
and *then* He saw thilke misusage; . . . . . . *S.C.* Jul. 183
Abandon, *then,* the base and viler clowne; . . . . . . *S.C.* O. 37
where is *then* thy place? . . . . . . *S.C.* O. 79
Then make thee winges . . . . . . *S.C.* O. 83
'*Then* as the springe gives place to elder time, ... *S.C.* D. 73
let thus much *then* excuse . . . . . . *Gn.* 4
Where *then* is now the guerdon of my paine? . . . . . . *Gn.* 356
sith *then* we are free borne, ... *Hub.* 133
thrice happie *then* Was the condition . . . . . . *Hub.* 149
And *then* ye will (I hope) well mooved bee.' . . . . . . *Hub.* 378
Then must thou thee dispose another way: . . . . . . *Hub.* 504
Then, when he was all dight, he tooke his way . . . . . . *Hub.* 1064
Then, when he saw no entraunce to him graunted, ... *Hub.* 1367
then the next in rew Began . . . . *T.M.* 173, 233, 299, 359, 419, 479, 539
vainly thinke your selves halfe happie *then,* . . . . . . *Ti.* 199
when th' one dies, th' other *then* beginnes . . . . . . *Ti.* 388
And is there *then* Such rancour . . . . . . *Mui.* 15
then about his shoulders broad he threw . . . . . . *Mui.* 65
Who *then* can save what they dispose to spill? . . . . . . *Mui.* 232
'*Then* be it so,' (quoth I) . . . . . . *D.* 78
why did they *then* create The world so fayre, ... *D.* 204
Why *then* should I desire here to remaine! . . . . . . *D.* 277
How happie was I *then,* . . . . . . *D.* 308
Sith *then* they so have ordred, ... *D.* 369
will till *then* my painful penance eeke. . . . . . . *D.* 391
It first growes red, and *then* to blew doth fade, ... *As.* 185
I *then* did sing, as *then* occasion fell: . . . . . . *Col.* 89
And *then,* besides, those little streames . . . . . . *Col.* 141
Then thus Melissa said; 'Thrise happie . . . . . . *Col.* 480
She there *then* waited upon Cynthia, ... *Col.* 520
Not *then* to her that scorned thing so base, ... *Col.* 935
Helpe *then,* O holy virgin! . . . . . . I. Pr. 2. 1
Furthest from end *then,* when they neerest weene, ... I. i. 10. 6
Then rudely be him thrust, ... I. i. 42. 4
Then up he rose, and clad him hastily: . . . . . . I. ii. 6. 8
Now *then,* your plaint appease.' . . . . . . I. iii. 29. 9
was never prov'd Till *then,* . . . . . . I. v. 24. 9
Then gan the Pilgrim thus: . . . . . . I. vi. 38. 1
love another: Lo! *then,* for thine ayd, ... I. vi. 47. 6
Then gins her grieved ghost thus to lament . . . . . . I. vii. 21. 9
'Such *then,'* . . . is the face of falshood: . . . . . . I. viii. 49. 3
'Thine, O! *then,'* . . . shalbe the place, ... I. ix. 17. 1
Why shouldst thou *then* despeire, ... I. ix. 53. 5
said *then* the father grave, ... I. x. 51. 1
Then when his daughter deare he does behold, ... I. xii. 12. 8
Who *then* would thinke . . . . . . I. xii. 36. 4
'Heare *then,* O man! . . . . . . II. i. 49. 5
then dead through great affright They both . . . . . . II. iii. 19. 7
With hart *then* throbbing, ... II. iv. 17. 1
then with solemne oath . . . . . . II. iv. 23. 8
Then gan the Palmer thus: . . . . . . II. iv. 34. 1
'Why *then* doest thou, O man! that of them all . . . . . . II. vi. 17. 1
Then Mammon wexing wroth; . . . . . . II. vii. 14. 6
'Suffise it *then,* thou Money God,' (quoth hee) . . . . . . II. vii. 39. 1
Soone shalt thou see, and *then* beleeve for troth, ... II. viii. 22. 3
Then, (*there) when they rested had a season dew, ... II. ix. 20. 6
Ne wonder *then,* if that he were depriv'd . . . . . . II. ix. 57. 4

Then—*Continued.*
And *then* Kimarus; and *then* Danius: II. x. 43. 2
Then he another and another did expell. II. xi. 24. 9
Snatcht first the one, and *then* the other Jade, II. xi. 31. 2
wide Labyrinth, and *then* to have them dround. II. xii. 20. 9
Then suddeinly both would themselves unhele, II. xii. 64. 8
thy hard fortune *then* thou wouldst renew, That III. i. 8. 3
and *then* in they all together far'd. III. i. 30. 9
The Damzell pauzd; and *then* thus fearfully: III. ii. 35. 1
Then Glauce thus: III. iii. 15. 6
Shall I *then* hate her III. v. 46. 2
How *then?* of all love taketh equall vew; III. v. 47. 5
Then (*there) gan they change their sides, IV. ix. 26. 1
'"*Then* doth the daedale earth throw forth to thee IV. x. 45. 1
It fortun'd *then,* a solemne feast was there IV. xi. 8. 1
'Which is' (sayd he) 'more heavy *then* in weight, V. ii. 44. 5
'Well *then,*' . . . 'let it be tride: V. ii. 45. 4
Then Artegall thus to the younger sayd: V. iv. 17. 1
then with threat Doth them compell V. iv. 31. 4
Then craving sucke, and *then* the sucke refusing: V. vi. 14. 8
Then gan the other further to devize V. vi. 20. 7
Who *then* can thee, Mercilla, throughly prayse, V. x. 3. 1
than When her that Tyrant did of Crowne deprive; V. xi. 38. 3
And *then* and there for triall of her right V. xi. 39. 4
Its now so farre from that which *then* it was, VI. Pr. 5. 2
and *then* Into this wicked world VI. i. 8. 5
There *then* began a fearefull cruell fray VI. i. 36. 1
'Of that commixtion they did *then* beget VI. vi. 12. 1
Said *then* the one of them; 'Where is that wight, VI. vii. 5. 7
Then turning backe VI. viii. 27. 1
whose like till *then* he never bore, VI. xii. 36. 2
cease till *then* our tymely joyes to sing: *Epith.* 425
Then would I sing of thine immortall praise *H.L.* 301
Till *then,* dread Lord! vouchsafe *H.L.* 306
Shall find by tryall, and confesse it *then,* *H.B.* 89

Thence (*partial list*). *See* **Fro thence.**
That *thence* th' Imperiall Eagle rooting tooke, *Ro.* xviii. 10
That winde nor tide could move her *thence* away. *Van.* ix. 12
And *thence* the passage ethe; *S.C.* Jul. 90
I hate the house, since *thence* my love did part, *S.C.* Au. 161
sad Eurydice *thence* now no more Must turne *Gn.* 433
From *thence* infused into mortall brests. *T.M.* 390
driven hence, I thether fly. *Thence* I behold *T.M.* 529
and *thence* the soules to bring awaie *Ti.* 375
thence with pineons light To mount aloft *Mui.* 43
From *thence* another world of land we kend, *Col.* 272
Soone as she parted *thence,* I. iii. 22. 1
Thence to the hall, I. iv. 6. 5
amazed how he *thence* should fade: I. v. 15. 5
Thence turning backe in silence softe they stole, I. v. 31. 1
found the Faery knight Departed *thence;* I. v. 45. 4
Good cause he had to hasten *thence* away; I. v. 45. 6
Thence lead her forth, I. vi. 13. 6
How with that pensive Maid he best might *thence* arise. I. vi. 32. 9
Therewith the knight *thence* marched forth I. vi. 40. 1
up he rose, and *thence* amounted streight. I. ix. 54. 1
drops of blood *thence* like a well did play: I. x. 27. 4
From *thence* to heaven . . . the ready path. I. x. 33. 9
Thence forward by that painfull way they pas I. x. 46. 1
'*Thence* she thee brought into this Faery lond, I. x. 66. 1
Great thankes, . . . He *thens* departing gave I. x. 68. 5
Till mery wynd and weather call her *thence* away. I. xii. 1. 9
The weary sowle from *thence* it would discharge; II. v. 6. 7
Strikes in the stocke, ne *thence* can be releast, II. v. 10. 8
desirous was Of his departure *thence;* II. vi. 37. 2
she well pleased was *thence* to amove him farre. II. vi. 37. 9
Thence forward he him ledd, II. vii. 35. 1
And *thence* him forward ledd II. vii. 39. 9
him forth *thence* ledd, II. vii. 51. 2
cleft his head in twaine, and life *thence* dispossest. II. viii. 33. 9
flood, . . . *thence* gushed grievously; II. viii. 39. 2
Utterers of secrets he from *thence* debard, II. ix. 25. 5
Thence she them brought into a stately Hall, II. ix. 27. 1
great chimney . . . *thence* The smoke forth threw. II. ix. 29. 3
Till by a conduit pipe it *thence* were brought: II. ix. 32. 4
Thence backe againe faire Alma led them right, II. ix. 33. 5
Till that great Lady *thence* away them sought II. ix. 44. 6
Thence brought them to the second rowme, II. ix. 53. 2
Almo *thence* them led II. ix. 54. 9
so soone as Guyon *thence* was gon II. xi. 5. 1
the disdainfull sowle he *thence* dispatcht, II. xi. 42. 3
Thence passing forth, they shortly doe arryve II. xii. 42. 1
thence to defend The sunny beames II. xii. 63. 2
counseld well him forward *thence* did draw. II. xii. 69. 3
Tryde all her arts and all her sleights *thence* out to wrest. II. xii. 81. 9
Thence they were brought to that great Ladies vew, III. i. 41. 1
thence pourd into men, which men call Love! III. iii. 1. 4
From *thence* him, . . . thou backe shalt bring, III. iii. 27. 6
To finde some issue *thence;* III. v. 3. 2
But Venus hers *thence* far away convayd, III. vi. 28. 6
All things from *thence* doe their first being fetch, III. vi. 37. 1
In secret wize herselfe *thence* to withdraw, III. vii. 18. 3
Thence backe returning to the former land, III. vii. 61. 5
His sonne Iulus did from *thence* depart III. ix. 43. 5
From *thence* he threw him selfe despiteously, III. x. 56. 7
I will, . . . Deliver her fro *thence,* III. xi. 18. 9
Thence forth descending to that perlous porch III. xii. 42. 6
from *thence* out throwen Into this world IV. ii. 1. 2
brought with her from *thence* that goodly belt away. IV. v. 5. 9
secretly from *thence* that night her bore away. IV. v. 27. 9

Thence—*Continued.*
oft in wrath he *thence* againe uprose, IV. v. 40. 5
and *thence* forth glaunst Adowne in vaine, IV. vi. 19. 3
sith you her freed fro *thence* Where she, IV. vi. 34. 7
tooke their steeds, and forward *thence* did pas IV. vi. 39. 3
Thence forth she past into his dreadfull den, IV. vii. 33. 1
To know what Virgin did them *thence* unbind, IV. viii. 22. 2
Thence forth were brought to him IV. ix. 8. 4
'*Thence* forth I passed to the second gate, IV. x. 16. 1
not gotten but from *thence,* IV. x. 51. 8
forth led her *thence* IV. x. 56. 7
Ne *thence* the Irishe Rivers absent were, IV. xi. 40. 1
without ship or bote her *thence* to row, He wist not how her *thence* away to bere, IV. xii. 15. 7, 8
So *thence* him farre she brought V. i. 6. 6
he the right from *thence* did thrust away, V. ii. 49. 1
Which was from *thence* not past a mile V. iv. 35. 7
forth into the field she marched *thence,* V. v. 4. 7
ever could Bereave it *thence:* V. vi. 2. 9
Thence forth unto the Idoll they her brought; V. vii. 6. 1
to see her Ladie *thence* not farre away. V. ix. 3. 9
Thence forth they passed V. ix. 20. 1
From *thence* pour'd down on men V. x. 1. 9
thence forth he went, V. xi. 35. 7
to banishe them from *thence;* V. xi. 45. 7
Thence passing forth into the hall he came, VI. i. 24. 6
A tall young man, from *thence* not farre away, VI. ii. 3. 7
ere he *thence* had traveild many a mile, VI. ii. 40. 3
How *thence* she might convay him to some place; VI. ii. 47. 2
Thence they him carried to a Castle neare, VI. ii. 48. 7
A certaine herbe from *thence* unto him brought, VI. iv. 12. 6
He *thence* them led into his Hermitage, VI. v. 38. 1
did bid him quickely *thence* avaunt, VI. vi. 21. 2
Thence passing forth, VI. vii. 18. 6
they her from *thence* directed VI. viii. 44. 1
From *thence* into the open fields he fled, VI. ix. 4. 1
From *thence* into the sacred Church he broke, VI. xii. 25. 1
Thence forth they drew him VII. vi. 47. 7
Thence breaking forth, did . . . throng. *Am.* xii. 8
feeling *thence,* no more her sorowes sadnesse, *Am.* xxxix. 11
having harrowd hell, didst bring away Captivity *thence* *Am.* lxviii. 4
From *thence* reade on the storie of his life, *H.H.L.* 232
From *thence* to mount aloft, by order dew, *H.H.B.* 24
Thence gathering plumes of perfect speculation, *H.H.B.* 134

Thenceforth. *See* **Forth, Thence.**
Thenceforth her garland . . . Began to die, *Van.* vii. 9
Thenceforth I gan . . . To scorne all difference *Van.* xii. 5
Thenceforth proceeding with his princely trayne, *Hub.* 1086
Did *thenceforth* ever enter in his minde; *Hub.* 1133
Thenceforth he past into each secrete part, *Hub.* 1303
The which to leave, *thenceforth* he counseld mee, *Col.* 184
she *thenceforth* therein gan take delight; *Col.* 361
Thenceforth they gan each one his like to love, *Col.* 863
'*Thensforth* I tooke Duessa for my Dame, I. ii. 40. 1
Thensforth from her most beastly companie I. ii. 41. 5
Thenceforth he kept her goodly company, I. vi. 31. 8
Thenceforth her waters wexed dull and slow, I. vii. 5. 8
'*Thenceforth* me desolate he quite forsooke, I. vii. 50. 1
Thenceforth the suitt of earthly conquest shonne, I. x. 60. 7
That from *thenceforth* he shund the like to take, I. xi. 24. 8
And *thenceforth* were renowmd, II. ii. 6. 9
Thenceforth in battaile never sword to beare, II. iii. 17. 8
Ne *thenceforth* his approved skill . . . Remembred he, II. v. 8. 6
Thenceforth she sought for helps II. vii. 45. 9
Ne *thenceforth* life ne corage did appeare; II. viii. 46. 3
Thenceforth this Realme was into factions rent, II. x. 36. 6
Thenceforth this land was tributarie made II. x. 49. 6
Thenceforth Aurelius peaceably did rayne, II. x. 67. 7
Thenceforth it firmely was established, II. xii. 13. 8
Thenceforth the fether in her lofty crest, III. ii. 27. 1
'*Thenceforth* eternall union shall be made III. iii. 49. 1
Into the woods *thenceforth* in haste shee went, III. v. 32. 1
Thenceforth to her he sought to intimate III. ix. 30. 1
thenceforth there Resolv'd to build III. x. 58. 1
from *thenceforth* a wretched life they ladd, III. xii. 16. 7
Like faithfull friends *thenceforth* to joyne in one IV. ii. 28. 6
Yet from *thenceforth* more warily he fought, IV. iii. 32. 1
Ne *thenceforth* feare the thing IV. vi. 30. 6
'*Thenceforth* I sought by secret meanes to worke IV. vii. 17. 1
Ne *thenceforth* ever strike in battell stroke, IV. vii. 39. 3
'*Thenceforth* I found more favour at her hand, IV. viii. 61. 1
thenceforth reformd her waies, IV. ix. 16. 8
Thenceforth they much more furiously gan fare, IV. ix. 27. 1
being *thenceforth* powrd IV. xi. 42. 8
And *thenceforth* unto daunger opened way. V. v. 9. 4
from her parting, she *thenceforth* did labour V. v. 35. 4
gan *thenceforth* to cast affection, V. v. 43. 7
thenceforth not like a lover, . . . I will him use; V. v. 51. 2
Thenceforth she streight into a bowre him brought, V. vii. 41. 1
Never *thenceforth* to nourish enmity, V. viii. 14. 8
Thenceforth into that Castle he her led V. x. 39. 6
Thenceforth he car'd no more which way he strooke, V. xi. 12. 6
thenceforth with warie heed He shund his strokes, V. xii. 18. 2
I from *thenceforth* have learn'd to love VI. ix. 25. 8
So from *thenceforth,* when love he to her made, VI. xi. 7. 1
Thenceforth they joy'd in happinesse together, VI. xii. 10. 6
Thenceforth more mischiefe and more scath he wrought VI. xii. 39. 1
Thence-forth abandond her delicious brooke, VII. vi. 54. 2
Thence-forth she left; and, parting from the place, VII. vi. 55. 2
from *thenceforth* none no more change shal see.' VII. vii. 59. 5

Thenceforth—*Continued.*
thence-forth all shall rest eternally . . . . VII. viii. 2. 7
every bit which *thenceforth* I did eat. . . . *Am.* xxxix. 14
all *thensforth* eternall peace shall see . . . . *Am.* lxxi. 13
Thenceforth they playne, ... *H.L.* 127
Thenceforth all worlds desire will in thee dye, ... *H.H.L.* 274
Ne from *thenceforth* doth any fleshly sense, . . . remaine; . *H.H.B.* 267
lampe . . . *Thenceforth* seemes fowle, and full of sinfull blame; *H.H.B.* 276
Thend. *See* **End.**
Thenot. No marveile, *Thenot,* if thou can beare . . . . *S.C.* F. 25
To nought more, *Thenot,* my mind is bent . . . . *S.C.* F. 94
Thenot, now nis the time of merimake, ... *S.C.* N. 9
Thenot, to that I choose thou doest me tempt; . . . . *S.C.* N. 49
There (*partial list*). *See* **Here and there.**
There many an auncient Trophee was addrest, ... *Bel.* v. 5
All pleasure *there,* . . . And *there* a noyse . . . . *Bel.* xii. 6, 7
there being then not living An Hercules . . . . *Ro.* x. 9
within her inmost pith *there* bred A litle wicked worme, . . . *Van.* vii. 6
Where have you seene the like but *there?* . . . . *S.C.* Ap. 72
Hye you *there* apace: Let none come *there* . . . . *S.C.* Ap.128,129
(O that I were *there,* To helpen . . . . *S.C.* May 33
There is a hyllye place, ... *S.C.* Jul. 58
I dempt *there* much to have eeked my store, ... *S.C.* S. 30
No such countrye as *there* to remaine; . . . . *S.C.* S. 35
That here by *there* I whilome usd to keepe, ... *S.C.* S. 63
There lives shee with the blessed Gods . . . *There* drincks . . *S.C.* N. 194, 195
Into thick shadowes, *there* themselves to lay. . . . . *Gn.* 168
For *there* huge Othos sits in sad distresse, ... *Gn.* 373
'And *there* is mournfull Tityus, ... *Gn.* 377
'*There* chast Alceste lives inviolate, ... *Gn.* 425
Scilla, under whom *there* bay Manie great bandogs . . . . *Gn.* 539
Ne wants *there* pale Narcisse, ... *Gn.* 679
there came to visite mee Some friends, ... *Hub.* 17
In riotous excesse doth *there* abound. *There* he arriving . . . *Mui.* 168, 169
sith I my selfe was *there,* Full many . . . . *Col.* 735
Arrived *there,* the litle house they fill, ... I. i. 35. 1
there before his face his Ladie is, ... I. i. 49. 5
each to other makes, . . . *there* as they sit; . . . . I. ii. 30. 2
By this arrived *there* Dame Una, ... I. iii. 12. 8
'Lo! *there* the worthie meed . . . . I. iii. 36. 3
Arrived *there,* they passed in forth right; . . . . I. iv. 6. 1
There was Ixion turned on a wheele, ... I. v. 35. 1
There thristy Tantalus hong by the chin; . . . . I. v. 35. 5
There auncient Night arriving did alight . . . . I. v. 41. 1
There all within full rich arayd he found, ... I. viii. 35. 1
Arrived *there,* . . . Would faine have fled, ... I. ix. 34. 6
Arrived *there,* the dore they find fast lockt, ... I. x. 5. 1
There when the Elfin knight arrived was, ... I. x. 44. 1
There as thou slepst in tender swadling band, ... I. x. 65. 7
The pointed steele, arriving rudely *theare,* . . . . I. xi. 16. 3
him found not *theare:* . . . . II. ii. 11. 7
'And were *there* rightfull cause of difference, ... II. ii. 30. 1
Here Sleep, *ther* Richesse, and Hel-gate them both betwext. II. vii. 25. 9
So soon as Mammon *there* arrivd, ... II. vii. 26. 1
now he has so long remained *theare,* . . . . II. vii. 65. 1
And is *there* care in heaven? And is *there* love . . . . II. viii. 1. 1
Here, *there,* and every where, about her swayd . . . . III. i. 66. 5
not so much rejoyce as she rejoyced *theare.* . . . . III. ii. 11. 9
the Ocean could not containe them *there* . . . . III. vi. 35. 9
'She wonneth in the forrest *there* before.' . . . . III. x. 38. 3
here, and *there,* and every where, . . . It shewd . . . . III. xi. 28. 6
found right safe assurance *theare.* . . . . IV. i. 15. 9
Tracing and traversing, now here, now *there,* . . . . IV. vii. 28. 8
who list to seeke it *there.'* . . . . V. iii. 32. 9
the Prince arrived *there,* And sending . . . . V. viii. 27. 6
all the rest in presence *there,* . . . . V. x. 15. 7
Ne was *there* Knight ne was *there* Lady found . . . . VI. i. 3. 1
Now here, now *there,* and oft him neare he mist; . . . . VI. viii. 13. 7
Ne was *there* heard, ne was *there* shepheards swayne, ... VI. ix. 10. 1
all . . . was gathered *there,* And *there* by her were . . . . VI. x. 5. 7
blaming her for comming *there,* . . . . VII. vi. 12. 7
the solemne bridall cheare . . . pointed *there;* . . . . VII. vii. 12. 5
That no one drop of pitie *there* doth rest. . . . . *H.L.* 147
that immortall beautie, *there* with thee, ... *H.H.B.* 13
Thereabout. This cruell conflict raised *thereabout,* . . . . IV. ix. 24. 8
the people, which had *there about* Long wayted, ... V. ii. 51. 1
robbed all the countrie *there about,* . . . . V. ix. 4. 8
Thereafter. *Thereafter* all that mucky pelfe he tooke, ... V. ii. 27. 6
grosse matter . . . Which clotheth it *thereafter* doth refyne. . *H.B.* 47
Thereamong. mens eyes and hearts, which *there among* Stood, IV. iii. 37. 3
Thereas. newes to Triamond was brought *There as* he lay, . . IV. iv. 33. 2
Thereat. That my glad hart *thereat* did much rejoyce. . . . *Pet.*[2] iv. 8
And manfully *thereat* shotte . . . . *S.C.* Mar. 78
Yet forth shee yode, *thereat* halfe aghast: . . . . *S.C.* May 233
Thereat enraged, soone he gan upstart, ... *Hub.* 1333
Thereat I wondred much, ... *Col.* 264
Who, *thereat* wondrous wroth, ... I. ii. 19. 1
Thereat he rored for exceeding paine, ... I. viii. 17. 1
Thereat the courteous knight displeased was, ... I. viii. 33. 3
He smott *thereat* with all his might and maine, ... I. xi. 43. 4
Thereat the Scarcrow wexed wondrous prowd, ... II. iii. 7. 1
Thereat Sir Guyon smylde; . . . . II. v. 18. 1
Thereat he, wondrous glad, out of the path Did lightly leape, II. v. 18. 7
Thereat, with staring eyes fixed askaunce, ... II. vii. 7. 5
Thereat the feend his gnashing teeth did grate, ... II. vii. 34. 1
Thereat the Elfe did blush in privitee, ... II. ix. 44. 1
Thereat he smitten was with great affright, ... II. xi. 39. 1
all the three *thereat* woxe much afrayd, ... II. xii. 22. 6
Thereat they greatly were dismayd, ... II. xii. 35. 1
Thereat she sighing softly had no powre . . . . III. ii. 5. 1

Thereat—*Continued.*
Thereat she sighed deepe, ... III. iv. 7. 9
Thereat she blushing said; . . . . III. v. 36. 1
yet she did smile *thereat.* . . . . III. vi. 15. 9
Thereat Diana gan to smile, ... III. vi. 21. 1
Thereat was suddein strook with great astonishment; . . . . III. vii. 3. 9
(*Thereat* full hartely laughed Satyrane.) . . . . III. vii. 58. 5
Much merveiled *thereat,* as well he might, ... III. viii. 12. 3
Thereat th' old man did nought but fondly grin, ... III. viii. 24. 6
Thereat displeasd they were, ... III. viii. 52. 6
Thereat Sir Satyrane gan smyle, ... III. ix. 6. 6
Sorely *thereat* he was displeased, ... III. ix. 12. 7
The foolish man *thereat* woxe wondrous blith, ... III. x. 33. 1
Greatly *thereat* was Britomart dismayd, ... III. xi. 22. 1
Thereat her noble hart was stonisht sore; . . . . III. xii. 44. 5
gan *thereat* to triumph without victorie. . . . . IV. i. 50. 9
Exceeding wroth *thereat* was Blandamour, ... IV. ii. 14. 1
Thereat Sir Blandamour . . . fiercely him bespake: . . . . IV. ii. 25. 1
Thereat did greatly grudge, ... IV. ii. 26. 3
But Lachesis *thereat* gan to repine, ... IV. ii. 51. 4
Thereat the Champions both stood still a space, ... IV. iii. 38. 1
But *thereat* greatly grudged Arthegall, ... IV. v. 9. 1
Thereat all Knights gan laugh, ... IV. v. 19. 1
But Blandamour *thereat* full greatly grudged, ... IV. v. 22. 3
Ne lesse *thereat* did Paridell complaine, ... IV. v. 22. 6
Thereat exceeding wroth was Satyran; . . . . IV. v. 24. 1
Thereat full inly blushed Britomart, ... IV. vi. 32. 8
'*Thereat* he shriekt aloud, ... IV. viii. 62. 1
'*Thereat* that formost matrone me did blame, ... IV. x. 54. 1
She gan *thereat* to fret . . . . IV. xii. 26. 2
Thereat she gan to triumph with great boast, ... V. v. 10. 1
But she *thereat* was wroth, ... V. vi. 38. 6
Were moved much *thereat;* . . . . V. viii. 24. 5
Thereat he brayed loud, ... V. xii. 20. 9
the bold knight no whit *thereat* dismayd, ... VI. iv. 21. 1
He *thereat* wext exceedingly astound, ... VI. viii. 27. 7
Thereat frown'd Coridon, ... VI. ix. 41. 9
There-at Jove wexed wroth, ... VII. vi. 35. 7
Therebeside. *there beside* of marble stone was built An Altare, I. viii. 36. 1
bloudie corse they shew'd him *there beside,* . . . . IV. viii. 21. 7
one old woman sitting *there beside* Upon the ground . . . IV. viii. 23. 5
Whom Trompart had in keeping *there beside,* . . . . V. iii. 17. 2
he *there besyde* Saw a faire damzell, ... VI. ix. 7. 6
Thereby. *Thereby* is a Lambe in the Wolves jawes: . . . *S.C.* Au. 31
The while my flocke did feede *thereby;* . . . . *S.C.* Au. 59
Nibble the bushie shrubs which growe *thereby.* . . . . *Gn.* 80
And *thereby* mad'st her ever damn'd to be. . . . . *Gn.* 472
thereby willing to affoord them aide; . . . . *Hub.* 414
honest men see ye arize Daylie *thereby,* . . . . *Hub.* 420
Thereby to coosin men not well aware; . . . . *Hub.* 874
And lifted up his loftie towres *thereby,* . . . . *Hub.* 1173
men to God *thereby* are nighest raised. . . . . *T.M.* 90
affliction he *thereby,* . . . is wisely taught to beare: . . . . *T.M.* 129
And, *thereby* wanting due intelligence, ... *T.M.* 556
Are *thereby* fild with happie influence; . . . . *T.M.* 586
then he pearcheth on some braunch *thereby,* . . . . *Mui.* 183
But he *thereby* was more empassionate; . . . . *D.* 193
Sith all my sorrow should have end *thereby,* . . . . *D.* 446
Thereby a christall streame did gently play, ... I. i. 34. 8
Upon his brothers shield, which hong *thereby:* . . . . I. v. 10. 3
The house of endlesse paine is built *thereby,* . . . . I. v. 33. 7
Thereby so fearlesse and so fell he grew, ... I. vi. 25. 1
Thereby his mortall blade full comely hong . . . . I. vii. 30. 6
But death he could not worke himselfe *thereby,* . . . . I. ix. 54. 6
And eke a litle Hermitage *thereby,* . . . . I. x. 46. 4
him to defend *thereby.* . . . . I. xi. 42. 9
Another like faire tree eke grew *thereby,* . . . . I. xi. 47. 6
Who *thereby* dead that balefull Beast did deeme, ... I. xii. 2. 7
Himselfe *thereby* reft of his sences meet, ... I. xii. 39. 8
thereby taught T' avenge his Parents death . . . . II. iii. 2. 8
Therby thine armes seem strong, ... II. v. 5. 6
And more *thereby* increased Furors might, ... II. v. 22. 2
a covetous Spright . . . who *thereby* did attend, ... II. vii. 32. 2
Thereby more lovers unto her to call: . . . . II. vii. 45. 6
thereby To climbe aloft, ... II. vii. 46. 6
Askt who he was, and what he ment *thereby?* . . . . II. vii. 59. 2
Thereby there lay An huge great stone, ... II. xi. 35. 6
Her selfe pursewd, in hope to win *thereby* . . . . III. i. 18. 7
thereby esteemd . . . that outward smoke had steemd. . . . III. i. 55. 8
Short end of sorrowes they *therby* did finde; . . . . III. ii. 43. 8
Who, *thereby* forst his workemen to forsake, ... III. iii. 10. 8
Another harnesse which did hang *thereby* . . . . III. iii. 61. 2
And *thereby* deemd the beast had bene depriv'd . . . . III. v. 37. 4
Who, *thereby* deeming sure the thing as donne, ... III. viii. 3. 3
*when *Proteus* she did see *thereby.* . . . . III. viii. 33. 9
thereby he weend Her will to win . . . . III. viii. 41. 4
That he *thereby* receiv'd no hurt at all; . . . . III. x. 57. 6
his shield was rudely throwne, . . . And he *thereby,* . . . . III. xi. 7. 9
She was no whit *thereby* discouraged . . . . III. xi. 50. 7
Yet thought himselfe not safe enough *thereby,* . . . . III. xii. 12. 2
He woxe full blithe, as he had got *thereby,* . . . . IV. i. 50. 8
And dayly more deceived was *thereby;* . . . . IV. ii. 11. 2
thereby did more prolong their paine: . . . . IV. iii. 2. 3
Disgracing them, him selfe *thereby* to grace, ... IV. iv. 4. 2
Thereby to make their loves beginning their lives end. . . . IV. vi. 17. 9
That all his vitall spirites *thereby* spild, ... IV. vii. 31. 8
that to his saddle-bow *thereby* He bowed low, ... IV. viii. 43. 4
him the more agreev'd I found *thereby:* . . . . IV. viii. 57. 5
I *thereby* my former love have lost; . . . . IV. ix. 38. 2
In hope *thereby* her to his bent to draw: . . . . IV. xi. 2. 6

Thereby—*Continued.*
of him selfe doth name the shire *thereby:* . . . IV. xi. 32. 7
got *thereby* Their greatest glory . . . V. ii. 1. 5
to his daughter brings, that dwels *thereby;* . . . V. ii. 9. 2
Thereby Sir Artegall did plaine areed . . . V. iii. 35. 1
So stood they both in readinesse *thereby* . . . V. iv. 6. 5
Who had him seene imagine mote *thereby* . . . V. v. 24. 1
The more *thereby* her tender hart was payned; . . . V. v. 44. 7
T' enure them selves to sufferaunce *thereby,* . . . V. vii. 9. 4
Since neither is endamadg'd much *thereby.'* . . . V. viii. 14. 3
one of mickle might That sate *thereby,* . . . V. ix. 22. 6
He wox right blyth, as he had got *thereby,* . . . V. xi. 9. 6
Hoping *thereby* to have my love obtayned; . . . V. xi. 54. 6
Her name was Envie, knowen well *thereby,* . . . V. xii. 31. 1
As she had got *thereby* and gayned a great stake. . . . V. xii. 32. 9
My tedious travell doe forget *thereby;* . . . VI. Pr. 1. 7
his armes, which were *thereby,* . . . VI. ii. 19. 5
a noble Lord Which dwelt *thereby,* . . . VI. iii. 7. 2
Them much abasht, but more him selfe *thereby,* . . . VI. iii. 21. 3
But he the more *thereby* enraged was, . . . VI. iii. 50. 1
a ragged stone Which lay *thereby* . . . VI. iv. 21. 3
Maintaine this evil use, thy foes *thereby* to foile. . . . VI. vi. 34. 9
Some of their weapons which *thereby* did lie, . . . VI. vi. 38. 8
They, that have much, feare much to loose *thereby,* . . . VI. ix. 21. 3
That she *thereby* mought either freely wend, . . . VI. xi. 6. 7
a Shepheard, which *there by* did keepe His fleecie flock . . . VI. xii. 9. 1
As through the world *thereby* should glorifie his name. . . . VI. xii. 12. 9
What man that sees . . . But that *therby* doth find, . . . VII. vi. 1. 3
from all the brooks *thereby* Had gathered, . . . VII. vii. 10. 6
ye *thereby* much greater glory gate, . . . *Am.* lxvi. 9
Thereby they all do live, . . . *H.L.* 99
And love our brethren; *thereby,* to approve . . . *H.H.L.* 216
lovely Daughters of the Flood *thereby,* . . . *Proth.* 21

Therefore. My sad desires, rest *therefore* moderate; . . . *Ro.* vii. 12
Thy dayes *therefore* are endles, . . . *Ro.* Env. 9
Let *therefore* nought, that great is, therein glorie, . . . *Van.* viii. 13
But now (thanked be God *therefore*) . . . *S.C.* Jul. 169
Here will I dwell apart In gastfull grove *therefore,* . . . *S.C.* Au. 170
My sheepe bene wasted; (wae is me *therefore!*) . . . *S.C.* S. 25
But aske hem *therefore* what they han paund: . . . *S.C.* S. 95
enough is me *therefore.* . . . *S.C.* D. 120
Therefore from him . . . vewe Doth turne aside, . . . *Gn.* 533
Himselfe *therefore* to heaven should elevate; . . . *Gn.* 556
'Me *therefore* thus the cruell fiends of hell, . . . *Gn.* 625
'Them *therefore* as bequeathing to the winde, . . . *Gn.* 633
Now *therefore* that no lenger hope I see, . . . *Hub.* 65
Therefore to me, my trustie friend, aread . . . *Hub.* 81
Thus *therefore* I advize upon the case, . . . *Hub.* 129
Therefore (if please you) this shalbe our plot: . . . *Hub.* 154
Therefore, I read that we our counsells call, . . . *Hub.* 189
Therefore might please you, . . . Us to advise, . . . *Hub.* 409
Therefore said he, . . . *All shalbe taught of God.* . . . *Hub.* 439
Therefore herewith doo not your selfe dismay; . . . *Hub.* 445
First, *therefore,* . . . your selfe applye, . . . *Hub.* 487
Doo not thou *therefore* seeke a living there, . . . *Hub.* 521
Therefore if fortune thee in Court to live, . . . *Hub.* 631
Be *therefore* counselled herein by me, . . . *Hub.* 985
Therefore be rul'd to doo as I doo teach.' . . . *Hub.* 992
Therefore, my owne deare brother, take good hart, . . . *Hub.* 1003
And *therefore* dreadles bad them come to Corte, . . . *Hub.* 1077
And *therefore* crav'd to come unto the King, . . . *Hub.* 1211
Therefore surcease, good Dame, and hence depart.' . . . *Hub.* 1221
Therefore I mourne . . . *T.M.* 107, 167, 227, 293
Therefore we mourne and pittilesse complaine, . . . *T.M.* 353
Therefore the nurse of vertue I am hight, . . . *T.M.* 457
Therefore I mourne and endlesse sorrow make, . . . *T.M.* 473
Therefore, . . . on God and on thy selfe relie; . . . *Ti.* 208
Provide *therefore* (ye Princes) whilst ye live, . . . *Ti.* 365
'*Therefore* in this halfe happie I doo read . . . *Ti.* 435
with secret joy *therefore* Did tickle inwardly . . . *Mui.* 393
Therefore more plaine areade this doubtfull case.' . . . *D.* 182
'*Therefore,* my Daphne they have tane away; . . . *D.* 365
Therefore to dye must needes be joyeous, . . . *D.* 451
Therefore great Cynthia her in chiefest grace Doth hold, . . . *Col.* 500
Therefore, . . . I deeme it best . . . *Col.* 580
Therefore I, silly man, . . . Durst not . . . *Col.* 668
Therefore unjustly thou doest wyte them all, . . . *Col.* 747
Beware *therefore,* ye groomes, I read betimes, . . . *Col.* 925
To thee, *therefore,* . . . I send This present . . . *Ded. Son.* iv. 13
Such, *therefore,* as that wasted soyl doth yield, . . . *Ded. Son.* v. 13
Receive it, Lord, *therefore,* as it was ment, . . . *Ded. Son.* x. 13
therefore your stroke, Sir Knight, with-hold, . . . I. i. 12. 5
Therefore I read beware.' . . . I. i. 13. 8
Therefore with me ye may take up your In . . . I. i. 33. 7
therefore, of life him not deprive.' . . . I. iii. 37. 9
Therefore, deare Sir, your mightie powres assay.' . . . I. viii. 2. 6
Accept *therefore* My simple selfe, . . . I. viii. 27. 4
Therefore, . . . She cast to bring him . . . I. x. 2. 7
therefore, a whyle I read you rest, . . . I. x. 17. 4
Therefore, henceforth bee at your keeping well, . . . I. xi. 2. 4
Therefore I ought crave pardon, . . . I. xii. 18. 9
Therefore, since now to thee perteynes the same . . . I. xii. 20. 7
'*Therefore,* since mine he is, . . . I. xii. 28. 1
Him *therefore* now the object of his spight . . . II. i. 3. 1
Now *therefore,* Lady, rise out of your paine, . . . II. i. 20. 6
Therefore this craftie engine he did frame, . . . II. i. 23. 7
Be, *therefore,* O my deare Lords! pacifide, . . . II. ii. 31. 8
I give thee life: *therefore* prostrated fall, . . . II. iii. 8. 5
gan to ride As one unfitt *therefore,* . . . II. iii. 46. 4
Delivers Phaon, and *therefore* By strife is rayld uppon. . . . II. iv. Arg.

Therefore—*Continued.*
And *therefore* wisht me stay . . . II. iv. 22. 9
Fly *therefore,* fly this fearefull stead anon, . . . II. iv. 42. 8
Therefore, I thee exhort To chaunge thy will, . . . II. v. 17. 7
Therefore his house is unto his annext: . . . II. vii. 25. 8
And *therefore* still on hye . . . did hold . . . II. vii. 27. 5
Now, *therefore,* if thou wilt enriched bee, . . . II. vii. 38. 7
Bad *therefore* I him deeme . . . II. viii. 14. 9
In vaine *therefore,* Pyrochles, should I lend . . . II. viii. 21. 7
Therefore, by Termagaunt thou shalt be dead.' . . . II. viii. 30. 4
therefore was removed far behind, . . . II. ix. 55. 2
Therefore he Anamnestes cleped is; . . . II. ix. 58. 8
Therefore he first wore crowne of gold . . . II. x. 39. 9
Therefore a Fay he her according hight, . . . II. x. 71. 8
Therefore they Glorian call that glorious flowre: . . . II. x. 76. 8
Therefore to grownd he would him cast no more, . . . II. xi. 45. 7
Therefore, old Syre, thy course doe thereunto apply.' . . . II. xii. 10. 9
therefore are they hight The Wandring Islands. *Therefore* doe them shonne; . . . II. xii. 11. 6, 7
Therefore, Sir Palmer, keepe an even hand, . . . II. xii. 18. 3
Therfore, Sir knight, your ready arms about you throw.' . . . II. xii. 37. 9
Therefore a God him sage Antiquity Did wisely make, . . . II. xii. 48. 1
Gather *therefore* the Rose whilest yet is prime, . . . II. xii. 75. 6
'*Therefore* aread, Sir, if thou have a love.' . . . III. i. 28. 1
Therefore, faire Damzell, be ye well aware, . . . III. ii. 10. 6
'Let bee *therefore* my vengeaunce to disswade, . . . III. ii. 13. 1
Therefore away doe dread; . . . III. ii. 33. 7
tell me *therefore,* my liefest liefe!' . . . III. ii. 33. 9
Therefore submit thy wayes unto his will, . . . III. iii. 24. 8
'That, *therefore,* nought our passage may empeach, . . . III. iii. 53. 1
Therefore, faire Infant, her ensample make . . . III. iii. 56. 8
If they be dead, then woe is me *therefore;* . . . III. iv. 2. 1
Therefore, faire Sir, for love of knighthood gent, . . . III. v. 10. 5
What can I lesse doe then her love *therefore,* . . . III. v. 46. 4
Therfore needs mote he live, that living gives to all. . . . III. vi. 47. 9
And *therefore* them of patience gently prayd. . . . III. ix. 10. 7
Therefore, Sir, I greet you well . . . III. ix. 51. 6
therefore advise ye well . . . III. x. 40. 7
therefore prayd her wake to heare him plaine. . . . III. x. 49. 6
'*Therefore,* faire Sir, doe comfort to you take, . . . III. xi. 15. 1
therefore, Sir knight, Aread . . . III. xi. 23. 2
And *therefore* gan advize with her old Squire, . . . III. xii. 45. 6
Therefore I will their sweatie yokes assoyle . . . III. xii. 47. *or.* 5
To such *therefore* I do not sing at all; . . . IV. Pr. 4. 1
Ne be ye wroth, Sir Scudamour, *therefore* . . . IV. i. 46. 5
Therefore he her did court, did serve, did wooe, . . . IV. ii. 8. 6
Yet Paridell him envied *therefore,* . . . IV. ii. 11. 3
Render *therefore* therein to me my right, . . . IV. ii. 13. 8
gan *therefore* close spight to him to beare; . . . IV. ii. 26. 5
Since *therefore* she her selfe is now your ward, . . . IV. ii. 27. 5
Therefore desirous . . . To know, . . . IV. ii. 47. 1
Therefore this Fay I hold but fond and vaine, . . . IV. iii. 2. 1
therefore wisht them . . . To let them passe . . . IV. iv. 3. 4
Cambelloes armes *therefore* he on him threw, . . . IV. iv. 33. 6
To her *therefore* The fayrest Ladie was adjudgd . . . IV. v. 8. 8
therefore, I here will stay . . . IV. vi. 47. 8
'*Therefore* Corflambo was he cald aright, . . . IV. viii. 49. 1
Helpe, *therefore,* O! thou sacred imp of Jove . . . IV. xi. 10. 1
Therefore on either side she was sustained . . . IV. xi. 25. 1
Therefore the antique wisards well invented . . . IV. xii. 2. 1
Therefore to Tryphon she againe doth hast, . . . IV. xii. 23. 1
Read *therefore* who it is . . . IV. xii. 30. 6
Therefore I humbly crave . . . IV. xii. 31. 7
Therefore me thither lead.' . . . V. ii. 10. 8
Therefore the vulgar did about him flocke, . . . V. ii. 33. 1
Therefore leave off to weigh them all againe, . . . V. ii. 36. 8
'*Therefore* I will throw downe these mountaines hie, . . . V. ii. 38. 1
In vaine *therefore* doest thou now take in hand . . . V. ii. 42. 5
Therefore resolving to revenge his blood . . . V. ii. 51. 8
Therefore he Talus to them sent t' inquire . . . V. ii. 52. 8
solemne feasts and giusts ordain'd *therefore:* . . . V. iii. 2. 6
Therefore whylome to knights of great emprise . . . V. iv. 2. 1
Therefore it ought be rendred her without deniall.' . . . V. iv. 15. 9
Therefore, Sir Terpin, from you lightly throw . . . V. iv. 34. 5
Therefore I cast how I may him unbind, . . . V. v. 32. 7
That she *therefore* would him here long forstall. . . . V. v. 47. 7
Therefore unto her mistresse most unkind . . . V. v. 56. 7
And *therefore* ment him surely to have slaine: . . . V. vi. 34. 5
Well *therefore* did the antique world invent . . . V. vii. 2. 1
Therefore they mote not taste of fleshly food, . . . V. vii. 10. 1
Therefore thus one of them, who seem'd . . . V. vii. 18. 4
And *therefore,* loth to loose her right away, . . . V. vii. 30. 5
therefore ought it have where ever she it fond. . . . V. vii. 30. 9
I will *therefore* Yeeld . . . V. viii. 13. 4
Therefore by name Malengin they him call, . . . V. ix. 5. 8
Therefore these two, her eldest sonnes, she sent . . . V. x. 14. 6
Least ye *therefore* mote happily me blame, . . . V. xi. 52. 8
Therefore she used often to resort . . . V. xii. 34. 6
Therefore he wild her doe away all dread; . . . VI. i. 31. 7
rather did more chearefull seeme *therefore:* . . . VI. i. 32. 5
'*Therefore,* . . . sith now occasion fit Doth fall, . . . VI. ii. 33. 1
'*Therefore,* faire Lady, lay aside this griefe, . . . VI. ii. 46. 1
Let none *therefore,* that is in meaner place, . . . VI. iii. 5. 8
Therefore to him their cause they best esteemed . . . VI. iii. 13. 3
Therefore there still he stood . . . VI. iii. 30. 3
Therefore, misdoubting least he should . . . VI. iii. 47. 7
Therefore her selfe she wholy recommended . . . VI. iv. 10. 7
Therefore some thought that those brave imps were sowen . . . VI. iv. 36. 7
Therefore inclyning to his goodly reason, . . . VI. iv. 37. 4
Though many foes did him maligne *therefore,* . . . VI. v. 12. 6

Therefore—*Continued.*
Therefore, conspiring all together plaine, . . . VI. v. 14. 5
'Let me *therefore* this favour for him finde, . . . VI. v. 30. 1
Therefore the Prince, . . . Was forced . . . VI. v. 41. 1
If *therefore* health ye seeke, . . . VI. vi. 7. 5
'In vaine *therefore* it were . . . VI. vi. 13. 1
And *therefore* lightly bad him packe away, . . . VI. vi. 21. 6
Therefore descending backe in haste he sought . . . VI. vi. 37. 8
Therefore, so soone as he was out of vew, . . . VI. vii. 2. 8
Therefore now yeeld, as ye did promise make, . . . VI. vii. 15. 7
'Where is the bootie, which *therefore* I bought, . . . VI. vii. 16. 2
Therefore a Jurie was impaneld streight . . . VI. vii. 34. 4
how could her love make half amends *therefore?* . . . VI. vii. 38. 9
Causde me be called to accompt *therefore;* . . . VI. viii. 22. 2
'*Therefore* I doe not any one envy, . . . VI. ix. 21. 1
Nor am envyde of any one *therefore:* . . . VI. ix. 21. 2
wisedome is most riches: fooles *therefore* They are . . . VI. ix. 30. 7
Therefore it rightly cleeped was mount Acidale. . . . VI. x. 8. 9
Therefore, . . . Out of the wood he rose, . . . VI. x. 17. 8
'*Therefore* they alwaies smoothly seeme to smile, . . . VI. x. 24. 1
Therefore the winged God, to let men weet . . . VI. xi. 1. 6
therefore prayd that those same captives there . . . VI. xi. 10. 3
With foule dishonour him mote blot *therefore;* . . . VI. xii. 12. 7
Therefore, resolving to returne in hast . . . VI. xii. 13. 1
Therefore do you, my rimes, keep better measure, . . . VI. xii. 41. 8
'To thee *therefore* of this same Jove I plaine, . . . VII. vii. 15. 1
Therefore both you and them to me I subject prove. . . . VII. vii. 55. 9
'Cease *therefore,* daughter, further to aspire, . . . VII. vii. 59. 1
Bring *therefore* all the forces . . . *Am.* xiv. 9
Therefore, O Love, unlesse she turne to thee . . . *Am.* xix. 13
Therefore, I lykewise, on so holy day, . . . *Am.* xxii. 3
Take heed, *therefore,* myne eyes, . . . *Am.* xxxvii. 9
Make peace *therefore,* . . . *Am.* lvii. 13
Bid her *therefore* her selfe soone ready make, . . . *Am.* lxx. 9
Make hast, *therefore,* sweet love, . . . *Am.* lxx. 13
The Bee him stung *therefore:* . . . *Epig.* iv. 26
Therefore, henceforth some pitty take, . . . *Epig.* iv. 39
Bid her awake *therefore,* . . . *Epith.* 30
Let all the virgins *therefore* well awayt: . . . *Epith.* 111
Make feast *therefore* now all this live-long day; . . . *Epith.* 248
All night *therefore* attend your merry play, . . . *Epith.* 368
Therefore to us be favorable now; . . . *Epith.* 382
Therefore in choice of love he doth desyre . . . *H.L.* 110
Therefore where-ever that thou doest behold . . . *H.B.* 134
Therefore, to make your beautie more appeare, . . . *H.B.* 183
Whom he *therefore* with equall honour crownd. . . . *H.H.L.* 35
Therefore of clay, base, vile, and next to nought, . . . *H.H.L.* 106
Therefore in flesh it must be satisfyde; . . . *H.H.L.* 142
The meanes, *therefore,* which unto us is lent . . . *H.H.B.* 127

Therein. Such store of birds *therein* yshrowded were, . . . *Pet.* iii. 5
Let therefore nought, that great is, *therein* glorie, . . . *Van.* viii. 13
Of sweete Violets *therein* was store, . . . *S.C.* Au. 71
throgh many wounds *therein* receaved, . . . *Hub.* 207
As if *therein* some text he studying were, . . . *Hub.* 380
Had wayes enough for all *therein* to live; . . . *Hub.* 401
And that *therein* thou maist maintained bee. . . . *Hub.* 534
For he *therein* had great felicitie; . . . *Hub.* 706
But I *therein* most like to him doo merite, . . . *Hub.* 1044
the beasts *therein* Fled fast away . . . *Hub.* 1347
Ah, wretched world! and all that is *therein,* . . . *T.M.* 125
The sacred lawes *therein* they wont expresse, . . . *T.M.* 561
Therein a goodly Virgine sleeping lay; . . . *Ti.* 636
Enclosde *therein* for endles memorie . . . *Ti.* 662
Therein two deadly weapons fixt he bore, . . . *Mui.* 81
No chace so hard, but he *therein* had skill. . . . *As.* 84
wyld beasts . . . *Therin* stil wait . . . *Col.* 203
she thenceforth *therein* gan take delight; . . . *Col.* 361
And all that *therein* wondrous doth appeare. . . . *Col.* 842
To baser wit his power *therein* to spend, . . . *Ded.Son.*xii.10
therein shrouded from the tempest dred, . . . I. i. 8. 3
That much was worne, but *therein* little redd; . . . I. iv. 19. 2
murdred men, which *therein* strowed lay . . . I. v. 53. 3
The sacred Nymph, which *therein* wont to dwell, . . . I. vii. 4. 8
Shortly *therein* so perfect he became, . . . I. x. 45. 6
deeper dint *therein* it would not make; . . . I. xi. 24. 6
neither silke nor silver *therein* did appeare. . . . I. xii. 22. 9
They lay *therein* their corses tenderly, . . . II. i. 60. 5
Therein three sisters dwelt of sundry sort, . . . II. ii. 13. 1
All good and honour might *therein* be red, . . . II. iii. 24. 5
and *therein* entrayld The ends of all the knots, . . . II. iii. 27. 7
Therein I have spent all my youthly daies, . . . II. iii. 38. 4
made a large And open gash *therein:* . . . II. v. 6. 5
Therein did often quench his thristy heat, . . . II. v. 30. 6
Therein the mery birdes of every sorte . . . II. v. 31. 6
therein sate a Lady fresh and fayre, . . . II. vi. 3. 1
her little frigot, *therein* making way. . . . II. vi. 7. 9
Therein to shrowd her sumptuous Belamoure; . . . II. vi. 16. 7
Therein he fownd Fountaines of gold . . . II. vii. 17. 4
To them that liv'd *therin* in state forlorne: . . . II. vii. 18. 3
Therein an hundred raunges weren pight, . . . II. vii. 35. 4
therein did wayt A sturdie villein, . . . II. vii. 40. 3
Therein two gates were placed seemly well: . . . II. ix. 23. 1
Ne ought, I weene, are ye *therein* behynd, . . . II. ix. 38. 8
Two goodly Beacons, . . . *Therein* gave light, . . . II. ix. 46. 4
Therein were divers rowmes, . . . II. ix. 47. 6
therein sat an old old man, halfe blind, . . . II. ix. 55. 5
And *therein* have their mighty empire raysd, . . . II. x. 5. 2
sought Of merchants farre for profits *therein* praysd; . . . II. x. 5. 7
With blood of Henalois which *therein* fell. . . . II. x. 24. 5
And then *therein* reseized was againe, . . . II. x. 45. 3

Therein—*Continued.*
left the fairest Tanaquill, Him to succeede *therein,* . . . II. x. 76. 5
therein all the famous history Of Jason . . . II. xii. 44. 3
With vermell, like the boyes blood *therein* shed, . . . II. xii. 45. 6
T' afflict the creatures which *therein* did dwell; . . . II. xii. 51. 6
And those which *therein* bathed mote offend. . . . II. xii. 63. 4
naked Damzelles he *therein* espyde, Which *therein* bathing . . . II. xii. 63. 6, 7
Therein they long did ryde, . . . III. i. 14. 7
Whatever foe had wrought, . . . *Therein* discovered was, . . . III. ii. 19. 6
Her selfe awhile *therein* she vewd in vaine: . . . III. ii. 22. 6
Ireland subdewd, and *therein* fixt his throne, . . . III. iii. 33. 6
Armory Downe taking, her *therein* appareled . . . III. iii. 59. 8
He *therein* saw that yrkesome sight, . . . III. viii. 31. 3
Therein is eaten out an hollow cave, . . . III. viii. 37. 5
'*Therein* a cancred crabbed Carle does dwell, . . . III. ix. 3. 5
Or *therein* write to lett his love be showne; . . . III. ix. 30. 7
Therein was writt how often thondring Jove . . . III. xi. 30. 1
But what so were *therein* or writ or ment, . . . III. xi. 50. 6
A thousand monstrous formes *therein* were made, . . . III. xi. 51. 7
And a wide wound *therein* (O ruefull sight!) . . . III. xii. 20. 5
That though *therein* himselfe he thought to pas, . . . IV. ii. 10. 3
Render therefore *therein* to me my right, . . . IV. ii. 13. 8
but that same soule which *therein* dwelt . . . IV. iii. 22. 1
Through working of the stone *therein* yset. . . . IV. iii. 24. 5
And *therein* sate a Ladie, passing faire . . . IV. iii. 39. 6
Having *therein* bene trained many a yeare, . . . IV. iii. 40. 3
And *therein* made a very griesly wound, . . . IV. iv. 24. 6
therein left the pike-head of his speare: . . . IV. vii. 27. 7
Weening *therein* some holy Hermit lay, . . . IV. vii. 42. 7
bitter thoughts, which deepe *therein* infixed lay. . . . IV. viii. 1. 9
entring in found none *therein* abide, . . . IV. viii. 23. 4
For every dram of hony *therein* found . . . IV. x. 1. 4
therein wonned twenty valiant Knights, . . . IV. x. 7. 6
Therein resembling Janus auncient . . . IV. x. 12. 5
therein thousand payres of lovers walkt, . . . IV. x. 25. 6
therein sate an amiable Dame, . . . IV. x. 31. 3
Greeks and Trojans which *therein* did die; . . . IV. xi. 20. 7
stormes which *therein* still remaine. . . . IV. xi. 38. 9
all the wrongs that he *therein* could lay . . . V. ii. 46. 6
Both it and all the wealth *therein* behight . . . V. ix. 3. 4
Eyther for th' evill which he did *therein,* . . . V. ix. 26. 7
byting deepe *therein* did sticke so fast . . . V. xii. 21. 8
Did her *therein* establish peaceablie, . . . V. xii. 25. 3
therein hath a Seneschall assynd, . . . VI. i. 15. 7
Therein the Hermite, which his life here led . . . VI. v. 35. 5
And *therein* he likewise was praying now, . . . VI. v. 35. 8
Therein he them full faire did entertaine . . . VI. v. 38. 6
a cottage clad with lome, And all things *therein* meane, . . . VI. ix. 16. 6
Therein well practisd was, . . . VI. ix. 43. 8
ne filth mote *therein* drowne: . . . VI. x. 7. 5
Unto this place, and *therein* to repose . . . VI. x. 9. 3
therein were a thousand tongs empight . . . VI. xii. 27. 1
therein shut up his blasphemous tong, . . . VI. xii. 34. 5
assign'd, *therein* to beare Nights burning lamp, . . . VII. vi. 12. 2
But none of all *there-in* more pleasure found . . . VII. vi. 38. 6
Of woods and forrests which *therein* abound, . . . VII. vi. 38. 8
'*Therein* the changes infinite beholde, . . . VII. vii. 23. 1
the Starres and Signes *therein* still move, . . . VII. vii. 55. 6
The goodly ymage . . . would *therein* appere. . . . *Am.* xlv. 12
greedy pikes which use *therein* to feed; . . . *Epith.* 58
raging now *therein* with restlesse stowre, . . . *H.L.* 3
Of that faire beame which *therein* is empight. . . . *H.B.* 49
therein stirre such rage and restlesse stowre, . . . *H.B.* 73
Therein they see, through amorous eye-glaunces, . . . *H.B.* 239
enstall A new unknowen Colony *therein,* . . . *H.H.L.* 104
therein reed The endlesse kinds of creatures . . . *H.H.B.* 31
that great Lord, which *therein* wont to dwell, . . . *Proth.* 139
Yet *therein* now doth lodge a noble Peer, . . . *Proth.* 145

Thereinto. Like Astrophel, which *thereinto* was made. . . . *As.* 186
Him *thereinto* he threw without remorse, . . . II. xi. 46. 7

Thereof. The top *thereof* a pot did seeme to beare, . . . *Bel.* iii. 5
Ne Afrike *thereof* guiltie is, nor Spaine, . . . *Ro.* xxxi. 5
For-thy *thereof* thou takest shame. . . . *To his Booke* 15
Reapen the fruite *thereof,* that is pleasure, . . . *S.C.* May 65
For priefe *thereof,* my death shall weepe, . . . *S.C.* Au. 119
What good *thereof* to Cuddie can arise? . . . *S.C.* O. 18
Thereof nought remaynes but the memoree; . . . *S.C.* N. 121
Yet was the guilt *thereof,* Orpheus, in thee. . . . *Gn.* 436
That the delight *thereof* me much releeved. . . . *Hub.* 32
And hope *thereof* to finde due remedie? . . . *Hub.* 57
That yet the skill *thereof* I have not loste: . . . *Hub.* 293
For manie beg which are *thereof* ashamed. . . . *Hub.* 352
But little els (God wote) could *thereof* skill; . . . *Hub.* 381
And *thereof* gathers for himselfe the best. . . . *Hub.* 726
with the sugrie sweete *thereof* allure . . . *Hub.* 819
scoffe at learning, and eke The Sectaries *thereof,* . . . *Hub.* 833
Upon the payne that *thereof* follow may. . . . *Hub.* 1072
That the complaints *thereof* could not be tolde. . . . *Hub.* 1313
with astonishment *Thereof* did tremble, . . . *Hub.* 1347
In stead *thereof* scoffing Scurrilitie, . . . *T.M.* 211
But now no remnant doth *thereof* remaine: . . . *Ti.* 415
That nigh with griefe *thereof* my heart was brust. . . . *Ti.* 518
That griefe *thereof* my spirite greatly pained. . . . *Ti.* 560
That sight *thereof* much griev'd my pensive thought. . . . *Ti.* 623
till mickle woe *Thereof* arose, . . . *Mui.* 133
the threasury of joy, She spoyld *thereof,* . . . *As.* 162
in the midst *thereof* a star appeares, . . . *As.* 187
choosing out few words . . . *thereof* did verses frame; . . . I. i. 37. 2
In stead *thereof* he kist her wearie feet, . . . I. iii. 6. 1
all that drinke *thereof* do faint and feeble grow. . . . I. vii. 5. 9

Thereof—*Continued.*
in the midst *thereof* one pretious stone . . . I. vii. 30. 1
her golden cup, . . . despeyre did many *thereof* sup, . . . I. viii. 14. 3
That ay *thereof* her babes might sucke their fill; . . . I. x. 30. 8
That sight *thereof* bredd cold congealed feare; . . . I. xi. 13. 5
The streame *thereof* would drive a water-mill: . . . I. xi. 22. 6
The griefe *thereof* him wondrous sore diseasd, . . . I. xi. 38. 8
Five joints *thereof* he hewd, . . . I. xi. 39. 9
For griefe *thereof* and divelish despight, . . . I. xi. 44. 1
and badd *thereof* take heed; . . . I. xii. 10. 8
Through midst *thereof* a little river rold, . . . II. i. 24. 6
The noyse *thereof* cald forth that straunger knight, . . . II. ii. 21. 1
That none *thereof* could ever taken hold; . . . II. iv. 4. 8
Till that the truth *thereof* I did out wrest; . . . II. iv. 23. 5
For proofe *thereof,* . . . Aray thyselfe . . . II. iv. 26. 7
Thereof devising shortly to be wroke, . . . II. vi. 30. 8
And *thereof* nigh one quarter sheard away; . . . II. vi. 31. 4
that no man can Discerne the hew *thereof.* . . . II. vi. 41. 8
The waves *thereof* so slow and sluggish were, . . . II. vi. 46. 6
that none could behold The hew *thereof;* . . . II. vii. 29. 4
charge *thereof* unto a covetous Spright Commaunded was, . . II. vii. 32. 1
Would tempt his guest to take *thereof* assay; . . . II. vii. 34. 4
And every linck *thereof* a step of dignity. . . . II. vii. 46. 9
Wise Socrates; who, *thereof* quaffing glad, . . . II. vii. 52. 7
in the midst *thereof* a silver seat, . . . II. vii. 53. 2
not forgoe, ne yet forgett The care *thereof* . . . II. viii. 8. 4
The want *thereof* now greatly gan to plaine, . . . II. viii. 19. 2
The stroke *thereof* from entraunce may defend; . . . II. viii. 21. 2
The frame *thereof* seemd partly circulare, . . . II. ix. 22. 1
in the midst *thereof* . . . faire Ladies sate, . . . II. ix. 34. 1
slaine, ere any *thereof* thought: . . . II. x. 51. 4
soone by meanes *thereof* the Empire wan, . . . II. x. 61. 4
In hope *thereof* to win victorious spoile. . . . II. xi. 7. 5
Yet was the fence *thereof* but weake and thin: . . . II. xii. 43. 4
Thereof she usd to give to drinke to each, . . . II. xii. 56. 7
counsell sage in steed *thereof* to him applyde. . . . II. xii. 82. 9
before he hard Tydings *thereof,* . . . III. ii. 21. 5
vertues rare Which *thereof* spoken were, . . . III. ii. 22. 8
In stead *thereof* sad sighes . . . III. ii. 28. 6
Joy *thereof* have thou and eternall blis!' . . . III. ii. 42. 5
was with the love *thereof* beguyld; . . . III. ii. 44. 8
In stead *thereof* sad sorow and disdaine . . . III. iv. 54. 2
Into his wound the juice *thereof* did scruze; . . . III. v. 33. 4
Yet wist she nought *thereof,* . . . III. vi. 9. 7
That had not her *thereof* before aviz'd, . . . III. vi. 19. 4
Yet none of all them her *thereof* amov'd . . . III. ix. 24. 8
he so ofte had tryde The powre *thereof,* . . . III. ix. 29. 8
And Hygate made the meare *thereof* by West, . . . III. ix. 46. 2
thereof she countlesse summes did reare, . . . III. x. 12. 4
Then still the smart *thereof* increased more, . . . III. x. 18. 4
Insted *thereof,* know that your loving Make . . . III. xii. 40. 8
Being *thereof* beguyld, was fild with new affright. . . . III. xii. 44. 9
Insted *thereof* with drops of melting love, . . . IV. Pr. 5. 5
some part *Thereof* did . . . appeare: . . . IV. i. 45. 4
She, in regard *thereof,* him recompenst . . . IV. ii. 9. 1
That dread *thereof* and his redoubted might . . . IV. ii. 40. 2
Yet nought *thereof* was Triamond adredde, . . . IV. iii. 25. 1
Instead *thereof* sweet peace and quiet-age . . . IV. iii. 43. 5
Are by the Gods to drinck *thereof* assynd; . . . IV. iii. 43. 8
at last enquired The cause and end *thereof,* . . . IV. v. 38. 4
the stone, Which wont to stop the mouth *thereof,* . . . IV. vii. 20. 5
staid not th' utmost end *thereof* to try, . . . IV. vii. 21. 2
heart with sight *thereof* was fild With deepe disdaine . . . IV. vii. 36. 2
Till time the tempest doe *thereof* delay . . . IV. viii. 1. 6
And *thereof* made a lamentable lay, . . . IV. viii. 4. 3
with few drops *thereof* did softly dew, . . . IV. viii. 20. 8
That any bud *thereof* doth scarse remaine, . . . IV. viii. 33. 2
That seemed nought the souse *thereof* could beare, . . . IV. viii. 44. 5
Did shun the proofe *thereof,* . . . IV. viii. 44. 9
As if instead *thereof* they Chaos would restore. . . . IV. ix. 23. 9
till nought *thereof* be drie, . . . IV. ix. 33. 7
Yet is the paine *thereof* much greater then the fee. . . . IV. x. 3. 9
for defence *thereof* . . . There reared was a castle . . . IV. x. 7. 1
in the midst *thereof* a piller placed; . . . IV. x. 8. 2
Ne stayed further newes *thereof* to learne, . . . IV. x. 9. 3
I repeated The read *thereof* . . . IV. x. 10. 8
Unto whose trust the charge *thereof* was lent: . . . IV. x. 12. 2
with the steme *thereof* the Temple swet, . . . IV. x. 38. 3
At sight *thereof* she was with terror queld, . . . IV. x. 55. 5
even to thinke *thereof* it inly pitties mee. . . . IV. xi. 1. 9
in the midst *thereof* did horror dwell, . . . IV. xi. 4. 1
yet *thereof* Gualsever they doe call: . . . IV. xi. 36. 5
And all the hewen stones *thereof* defaced, . . . V. ii. 28. 3
Nor memory *thereof* to any nation. . . . V. ii. 28. 5
how much it doth overflow Or faile *thereof,* . . . V. ii. 34. 9
Ne any token doth *thereof* abide: . . . V. iii. 25. 7
Thereof great hurly-burly moved was . . . V. iii. 30. 1
At sight *thereof* his cruell minded hart . . . V. v. 13. 1
Thereof make tryall in my greatest need. . . . V. v. 29. 6
But that instead *thereof* she sternely bade . . . V. v. 54. 5
The fell contagion may *thereof* restraine, . . . V. vii. 11. 8
Doth in defence *thereof* full stoutly stond: . . . V. vii. 30. 6
At sight *thereof* abasht . . . V. vii. 38. 3
So did the sight *thereof* their sense dismay, . . . V. viii. 38. 2
But Artegall, being *thereof* aware, . . . V. viii. 48. 1
She warn'd the knights *thereof;* . . . V. ix. 8. 4
let, instead *thereof,* to fall Few perling drops . . . V. ix. 50. 6
To whom when tydings *thereof* came, . . . V. x. 31. 6
sent redresse *thereof* by this brave Briton Knight. . . . V. xi. 1. 9
As if the onely sound *thereof* she feard. . . . V. xi. 30. 4

Thereof—*Continued.*
with the souse *thereof* full sore aghast . . . V. xii. 23. 3
doe instead *thereof* mild curt'sie showe . . . VI. i. 27. 3
Thereof full blyth the Lady streight became, . . . VI. i. 32. 1
And me in lieu *thereof* revil'd againe, . . . VI. ii. 11. 8
There he the necke *thereof* did cut in twaine, . . . VI. iii. 17. 5
Witnesse *thereof* he shew'd his head there left, . . . VI. iii. 18. 8
Him selfe *thereof* he labour'd to acquite, . . . VI. iii. 21. 7
That he could not *thereof* avenged bee; . . . VI. iii. 43. 6
To weet what issue would *thereof* betyde: . . . VI. iii. 47. 2
the whiles he was *thereof* secure. . . . VI. v. 16. 9
affrighted bee At sight *thereof,* . . . VI. vi. 10. 5
And how *thereof* her selfe she did acquite, . . . VI. vi. 17. 2
Thereof false Turpin was full glad and faine, . . . VI. vii. 17. 1
But she *thereof* grew proud and insolent, . . . VI. vii. 29. 1
That seemed nought the course *thereof* could stay, . . . VI. viii. 8. 5
Ne list the Knight the powre *thereof* assay, . . . VI. viii. 8. 7
gan mongst themselves devize *Thereof* by force to take . . VI. viii. 43. 6
at the foote *thereof* a gentle flud . . . VI. x. 7. 1
on the top *thereof* a spacious plaine . . . VI. x. 8. 1
(for dread least if her syre Should know *thereof* . . . VI. xii. 6. 7
to take *thereof* a sight: . . . VI. xii. 7. 5
But Calidore, *thereof* no whit afrayd, . . . VI. xii. 29. 1
For she her selfe more worthy *thereof* wend, . . . VII. vi. 11. 3
Yet with the sight *thereof* was almost queld; . . . VII. vi. 25. 3
these Star-gazers stonisht are At sight *thereof,* . . . VII. vii. 52. 6
However now *thereof* ye little weene! . . . *Am.* xxvii. 4
Ne any mention shall *thereof* remaine, . . . *Am.* xxvii. 10
The powre *thereof,* which ofte in me I find, . . . *Am.* xxviii. 5
this verse . . . Shall be *thereof* immortall moniment; . . . *Am.* lxix. 10
With light *thereof* I doe my selfe sustayne, . . . *Am.* lxxxvii. 11
At sight *thereof* so much enravisht bee? . . . *H.L.* 119
Thereof as every earthly thing partakes . . . *H.B.* 43
Therof it comes that these faire soules, . . . *H.B.* 120
Thereof he fashions in his higher skill . . . *H.B.* 221
That I *thereof* an heavenly Hymne may sing . . . *H.H.L.* 6
all those which *thereof* worthy bee. . . . *H.H.B.* 252
None *thereof* worthy be, but those . . . *H.H.B.* 253

Thereon. Having *theron* the vile blaspheming name. . . . *Rev.* i. 3
As much it grieveth me to thinke *thereon.* . . . *Pet.* i. 3
tooke in hond My pipe, . . . And plaid *thereon;* . . . *Col.* 74
Of that deare Lord who oft *thereon* was fownd, . . . I. x. 54. 4
As he *thereon* stood gazing, . . . I. x. 56. 1
For happy life to all which *thereon* fedd, . . . I. xi. 46. 5
And holy water *thereon* sprinckled wide; . . . I. xii. 37. 5
Thereon an yron lock did fasten firme and strong. . . . II. iv. 12. 9
And *thereon* satt a woman, gorgeous gay . . . II. vii. 44. 6
whosoever once hath fastened His foot *thereon,* . . . II. xii. 12. 8
burne The verdant gras as he *thereon* did tread; . . . III. i. 5. 6
They did him set *theron,* . . . III. v. 38. 9
When the bright sunne his beams *theron* doth beat: . . . III. v. 49. 6
Ne the sharp Northerne wind *thereon* to showre; . . . III. v. 51. 5
His feeble steps, which shrunck when hard *thereon* he lay. . . III. xii. 10. 9
much more goodly glosse *thereon* doth shed . . . IV. v. 15. 5
heaping stroakes which *thereon* soused sore: . . . IV. v. 36. 4
And thundred strokes *thereon* so hideouslie, . . . V. ii. 21. 7
That he *thereon* should spin both flax and tow; . . . V. v. 23. 3
tooke her steede; and *thereon* mounting light . . . V. vi. 36. 2
thought that she *thereon* could never gaze her fill. . . . V. vii. 5. 9
But first the Tygre clawes *thereon* did lay, . . . V. vii. 30. 4
Up to the rocke he ran, and *thereon* flew . . . V. ix. 15. 3
drops of raine *Thereon* distill . . . V. xii. 13. 4
Which *thereon* seizing tooke no great effect; . . . V. xii. 21. 7
though she hungrily Earst chawd *thereon,* . . . V. xii. 39. 6
The eyes of all which *thereon* fixed beene, . . . VI. Pr. 6. 7
By his owne sword, and by the crosse *thereon,* . . . VI. i. 43. 6
where I *thereon* may hit In all this forrest . . . VI. ii. 9. 5
him up *thereon* did reare, . . . VI. ii. 48. 4
being *thereon* mounted forth did pace . . . VI. v. 7. 7
in soft delight *thereon* to rest; . . . VI. viii. 42. 3
To offer sacrifice divine *thereon;* . . . VI. viii. 42. 6
The little purple rose which *thereon* grew, . . . VI. xii. 18. 5
There-on an heavy haplesse curse did lay; . . . VII. vi. 55. 3
the guests, which would *thereon* have fedd. . . . *Am.* lxxvii. 14
thereon feed my love-affamisht hart. . . . *Am.* lxxxvii. 12
He *thereon* feeds his hungrie fantasy, . . . *H.L.* 198
Thereon his mynd affixed wholly is, . . . *H.L.* 204
He *thereon* fixeth all his fantasie, . . . *H.B.* 228
The greatest wisards which *thereon* do gaze. . . . *H.H.B.* 168
sight Of all that looke *thereon* with eyes unsound; . . . *H.H.B.* 179

Thereout. *Thereout* a strange beast with seven heads arose, . . *Bel.*[2] viii. 5
Much good deep learning one *thereout* may reed; . . . *Hub.* 484
strugled long, Himselfe to free *thereout;* . . . *Mui.* 426
so huge streames of blood *thereout* did flow, . . . *As.* 122
heavenly documents *thereout* did preach, . . . I. x. 19. 4
Where fast it stucke, ne would *thereout* be gott: . . . I. xi. 38. 7
drops of purple blood *thereout* did weepe, . . . III. i. 65. 8
And *there out* sucking venime to her parts entyre. . . . IV. viii. 23. 9
cast about by sleight the truth *thereout* to straine; . . . V. i. 24. 9
Whose grudging ghost was *thereout* fled and past, . . . V. x. 37. 3

There's. wheres no courage, *theres* no ruth nor mone. . . . VI. vii. 18. 5

Thereto. And *thereto* aye wonned to repayre . . . *S.C.* F. 119
Nay, say I *thereto,* . . . *S.C.* May 150
Thereto will I pawne yonder spotted Lambe, . . . *S.C.* Au. 37
Thereto the frogs, . . . their jarring voyces bent, . . . *Gn.* 229
whatso *theretoo* did neede Each did prepare, . . . *Hub.* 106
Thereto right well this Curdog, . . . will serve . . . *Hub.* 294
duly to encline My wits *theretoo,* . . . *Hub.* 549
ye well can fashion Your selves *theretoo,* . . . *Hub.* 652
And privily his servant *thereto* hire: . . . *Hub.* 682

Thereto—*Continued.*
he disdaines himselfe t' embase *theretoo.* . . . *Hub.* 732
And *thereto* doth his Courting most applie: . . . *Hub.* 784
Thereto he could fine loving verses frame, . . . *Hub.* 809
(quoth he *theretoo*) . . . *Hub.* 999
Thereto I am . . . Most like a Man, . . . *Hub.* 1029
And *thereto* swore; . . . *Hub.* 1057
all her Sisters, *thereto* answering, . . . *T.M.* 171
Yet little wote what doth *thereto* behove. . . . *T.M.* 396
'*Theretoo* for warlike power, . . . was none to match . . . *Ti.* 99
Thereto doo thou my humble spirite raise, . . . *Ti.* 313
theretoo gan his furnitures prepare. . . . *Mui.* 56
To tell the cause which thee *theretoo* constrained, . . . *D.* 81
by no meanes I could him win *thereto,* . . . *D.* 561
Thereto our ship her course directly bent, . . . *Col.* 268
Through secret sence which *thereto* doth them draw. . . . *Col.* 886
He *thereto* meeting said, 'My dearest Dame, . . . I. iii. 28. 1
Thereto said he, 'Faire Dame, . . . I. iv. 49. 1
And *thereto* added wordes of wondrous might. . . . I. x. 24. 6
Whom ravenous hunger did *thereto* constraine: . . . I. xi. 37. 4
For nigh *thereto* . . . Durst not approch, . . . I. xi. 49. 1
Thereto his subtile engins he does bend, . . . II. i. 3. 5
Full loth she seemd *thereto,* . . . II. i. 20. 8
he balmes and herbes *thereto* applyde, . . . II. vi. 51. 6
Thereto as cold and drery as a snake, . . . II. xi. 22. 4
his feeble vaines Him faild *thereto,* . . . II. xi. 48. 4
That mote the passengers *thereto* allure; . . . II. xii. 12. 6
**Thereto* the Heavens alwayes Joviall, . . . II. xii. 51. 1
But when *thereto* they might not be allur'd, . . . III. i. 1. 7
Thereto so bounteous and so debonayre, . . . III. i. 26. 4
sweet birdes *thereto* applide Their daintie layes . . . III. i. 40. 3
'Great ayd *thereto* . . . shall give . . . III. iii. 28. 1
Thereto he was a doughty dreaded knight, . . . III. iv. 24. 1
Thereto so swifte that it all beasts did pas: . . . III. vii. 22. 6
Thereto fear gave her wings, . . . III. vii. 26. 9
But she *thereto* would lend but light regard, . . . III. viii. 14. 6
Who *thereto* answering said: . . . III. viii. 46. 1
Thereto her feare was made so much the greater . . . IV. i. 7. 1
That might her love prepare, and liking win *theretoo.* . . . IV. ii. 8. 9
By sundry meanes *thereto* she prickt him forth; . . . IV. ii. 12. 1
Thereto she was right faire, . . . IV. ii. 44. 6
Thereto she learned was in Magicke leare, . . . IV. iii. 40. 1
And *thereto* all his power and might applide: . . . IV. iv. 24. 2
and *thereto* well agreed His word, . . . IV. iv. 39. 7
The judges, which *thereto* selected were, . . . IV. v. 6. 7
But by no meanes they could it *thereto* frame; . . . IV. v. 16. 5
But Britomart would not *thereto* assent, . . . IV. v. 20. 6
Thereto him Ate stird, new discord to maintaine. . . . IV. v. 22. 9
rend asunder quite, if he *thereto* list strive. . . . IV. v. 37. 9
pursewed, Still as advantage they espyde *thereto:* . . . IV. vi. 18. 3
Feared in vaine, sith meanes, ye see, there wants *theretoo.* . . . IV. vi. 30. 9
No longer space *thereto* he did desire, . . . IV. vi. 43. 8
Till I *thereto* had all things ready dight. . . . IV. vii. 17. 4
Thereto the villaine used craft in fight; . . . IV. vii. 26. 1
Belphebe, . . . drew *thereto,* making her eare her guide: . . . IV. vii. 29. 4
his garment, to be *thereto* meet, He wilfully did cut . . . IV. vii. 40. 1
thereto she did annexe False crimes . . . IV. viii. 35. 5
Who *thereto* did with readie will consent, . . . IV. viii. 64. 8
Thereto he offred for to make him chiefe . . . IV. ix. 15. 7
Hatred was *thereto* full loth, . . . IV. x. 33. 3
Thereto he was expert in prophecies, . . . IV. xi. 19. 1
Do you by duresse him compell *thereto,* . . . IV. xii. 10. 5
Thereto they both did franckly condiscend, . . . V. i. 25. 8
But he *thereto* would by no meanes consent, . . . V. i. 30. 6
Thereto he hath a groome of evill guize, . . . V. ii. 6. 6
'*Thereto* she is full faire, and rich attired, . . . V. ii. 10. 1
But he for nought could him *thereto* constraine; . . . V. iii. 31. 7
Them selves *thereto* preparde in order dew; . . . V. v. 1. 7
And *thereto* did himselfe right well behave . . . V. v. 23. 7
Yet would she not *thereto* yeeld free accord . . . V. v. 27. 6
Thereto compelled through hart-murdring paine; . . . V. v. 30. 8
And als' of princely grace to be inclyn'd *thereto.* . . . V. v. 41. 9
'Say and do all that may *thereto* prevaile; . . . V. v. 49. 1
Thereto adde art, even womens witty trade, . . . V. v. 49. 5
But by no meanes could her *thereto* perswade; . . . V. v. 54. 4
Thereto both his owne wylie wit, (she sayd) . . . V. ix. 5. 1
Till strong constraint did her *thereto* enforce: . . . V. x. 4. 6
Thereto a great advauntage eke he has . . . V. xi. 6. 1
gan him selfe streightway *Thereto* addresse, . . . V. xi. 21. 5
Thereto the body of a dog she had, . . . V. xi. 24. 1
(being *theretoo* Appointed by that mightie Faerie Prince, . . . V. xii. 3. 2
Thereto he had great skill in single fight: . . . V. xii. 15. 5
Thereto her hew Was wan and leane, . . . V. xii. 29. 4
Thereto the Blatant Beast, by them set on, . . . V. xii. 41. 1
Nathlesse *thereto* he was full stout and tall, . . . VI. i. 2. 7
Thereto great helpe dame Nature selfe doth lend; . . . VI. ii. 2. 1
his faith *thereto* did plight It to performe: . . . VI. iii. 16. 1
Whatever formes ye list *thereto* apply, . . . VI. iv. 35. 6
And nigh *thereto* a little Chappell stoode, . . . VI. v. 35. 1
So long as age enabled him *thereto,* . . . VI. v. 37. 2
Thereto, when needed, she could weepe and pray, . . . VI. vi. 42. 5
For that himselfe *thereto* did want sufficient might.' . . . VI. vii. 12. 9
But she *thereto* nould plead, . . . VI. vii. 36. 3
Thereto they usde one most accursed order, . . . VI. viii. 36. 1
durst speake, or answere him awhit *thereto.* . . . VI. viii. 50. 9
The knight full gladly soone agreed *thereto,* . . . VI. ix. 16. 8
ne mote the ruder clowne, *Thereto* approch; . . . VI. x. 7. 5
Thereto they all attonce agreed well; . . . VI. xi. 20. 7
Thereto they soone agreed, . . . VI. xi. 40. 6
There to thou maist perhaps, if so thou faine . . . VII. vi. 34. 4

Thereto—*Continued.*
us'd . . . Oft to resort *there-to,* . . . VII. vi. 38. 5
There-to he promist, if shee would him pleasure . . . VII. vi. 44. 1
Nature did yeeld *thereto;* . . . VII. vii. 27. 8
A greater craftesmans hand *thereto* doth neede, . . . *Am.* xvii. 13
doe *thereto* applaud, . . . *Epith.* 144
Thereto approch to tempt her mind to ill. . . . *Epith.* 199
Therto do thou, great Goddesse! Queene of Beauty, . . . *H.B.* 15
And bound *therto* with an eternall band, . . . *H.H.L.* 187

Thereunto. For *thereunto* doth need a golden quill, . . . *Ded.Son.*xvi.10
Next *thereunto* did grow a goodly tree, . . . II. vii. 53. 6
Therefore, old Syre, thy course doe *thereunto* apply.' . . . II. xii. 10. 9
But when shee mote not *thereunto* be wonne, . . . III. i. 52. 6
Eftsoones her steps she *thereunto* applyd, . . . III. vii. 5. 6
Not by strong hand compelled *thereunto,* . . . V. vi. 16. 4
all his powre doth *thereunto* apply: . . . V. viii. 18. 5
Ne ought to answere *thereunto* did find; . . . V. xi. 64. 3
And all his powre applyed *thereunto,* . . . V. xii. 22. 2
Unlesse that I were *thereunto* enforst: . . . VI. iii. 39. 7
And *thereunto* a great long chaine he tight, . . . VI. xii. 34. 8
when myne eyes I *thereunto* direct, . . . *Am.* lxxviii. 9
And *thereunto* doe daunce and carrol sweet, . . . *Epith.* 135

Thereupon. His head did shine with crounes set *therupon.* . . . *Rev.* iii. 3
thereupon did raise full busily A little mount, . . . *Gn.* 659
he himselfe, long gazing *thereupon,* . . . IV. vi. 22. 1
And his accuser *thereuppon* defide; . . . V. i. 23. 7
and *thereuppon* She wore for her defence . . . V. v. 2. 8
thereuppon long while stood gazing still, . . . V. vii. 5. 8
thereuppon long while she musing lay, . . . V. vii. 17. 1
warn'd the knights thereof; who *thereupon* Gan to advize . . . V. ix. 8. 4
triumphal Arch, and *thereupon* The spoiles of Princes hang'd . . . VI. viii. 42. 8
So stood he still long gazing *thereupon,* . . . VI. ix. 12. 1

Therewith. *Therewith* affrayd, I ranne away; . . . *S.C.* Mar. 94
therewith bruzd his brayne; . . . *S.C.* Jul. 226
Therewith my soule was sharply gryde, . . . *S.C.* Au. 95
Therewith he gan full terribly to rore, . . . *Hub.* 1337
Therewith she lowdly did lament and shrike, . . . *T.M.* 229
Therewith shee wayled with exceeding woe, . . . *T.M.* 295
Therewith he gan afresh to waile and weepe, . . . *D.* 169
Therewith enrag'd she loudly gan to bray, . . . I. i. 17. 5
Therewith she spewd . . . A floud of poyson . . . I. i. 20. 1
Therewith upon his crest . . . he smitt, . . . I. ii. 18. 6
Therewith a piteous yelling voice was heard, . . . I. ii. 31. 1
Therewith she gan her passion to renew, . . . I. iii. 25. 1
Therewith in haste his helmet gan unlace, . . . I. iii. 37. 1
Therewith they gan to hurtlen greedily, . . . I. iv. 40. 1
Therewith redoubled was his raging yre, . . . I. v. 10. 4
Therewith upon his crest he stroke him so, . . . I. v. 11. 5
Therewith his heavie hand he high gan reare, . . . I. v. 13. 5
Therewith the knight thence marched forth . . . I. vi. 40. 1
Therewith they gan, . . . To thunder blowes, . . . I. vi. 43. 1
Th' Elfe, *therewith* astownd, Upstarted . . . I. vii. 7. 7
Men into stones *therewith* he could transmew, . . . I. vii. 35. 6
Therewith the Gyant buckled him to fight, . . . I. viii. 7. 1
Therewith his sturdie corage soon was quayd, . . . I. viii. 14. 8
Therewith an hollow, dreary, murmuring voyce . . . I. viii. 38. 1
And *therewith* all enwrapt the nimble thyes . . . I. xi. 23. 2
And *therewith* scourge the buxome aire so sore, . . . I. xi. 37. 6
Therewith at last he forst him to unty . . . I. xi. 42. 8
Therewith amoved from his sober mood, . . . II. i. 12. 1
Therewith her dim eie-lids she up gan reare, . . . II. i. 45. 1
Therewith all suddeinly he seemd enragd, . . . II. iii. 14. 1
Therewith Sir Guyon left his first emprise, . . . II. iv. 12. 1
Therewith she laught, . . . II. vi. 23. 9
Therewith she sweetly smyld. . . . II. vi. 36. 1
Therewith to doen his foes eternall smart. . . . II. viii. 20. 4
Therewith out of his hond . . . he rudely snatcht . . . II. viii. 22. 5
therewith thought His cursed life . . . have rent; . . . II. viii. 32. 2
*And *therewith* all attonce at him let fly . . . II. xi. 18. 1
And *therewith* lowdly laught: . . . II. xi. 15. 4
Therewith (*thereto) the Heavens alwayes joviall . . . II. xii. 51. 1
hungry eies, which n'ote *therewith* be fild; . . . II. xii. 78. 2
Therewith a while she her flit fancy fedd, . . . III. i. 56. 1
the whole family, *therewith* adredd, . . . III. i. 62. 7
Shee, *therewith* well apayd, . . . III. ii. 47. 7
Therewith th' Enchaunter softly gan to smyle . . . III. iii. 17. 1
therewith crowne himselfe in th' others stead: . . . III. iii. 29. 7
And *therewith* shott an arrow at the lad; . . . III. v. 24. 7
The flesh *therewith* she suppled and did steepe, . . . III. v. 33. 6
Therewith he sigh'd; and, turning him aside, . . . III. v. 34. 6
But Phoebe *therewith* sore was angered, . . . III. vi. 24. 1
Yet, *therewith* sore enrag'd, with sterne regard . . . III. vii. 42. 1
To get small thankes, and *therewith* many blames, . . . III. vii. 61. 3
He was *therewith* distressed diversely, . . . III. x. 14. 7
Great store of treasure, *therewith* him to tempt; . . . III. x. 29. 2
The same behold, *therewith* their keene desires were whett. . . . III. x. 34. 9
Who, *therewith* somewhat starting, up gan looke, . . . III. xi. 13. 2
Therewith, resolv'd to prove her utmost might, . . . III. xi. 25. 1
Pyke He stearnly shooke, and *therewith* fierce did stryke . . . III. xi. 40. 5
Nought *therewith* daunted was her courage prowd, . . . III. xii. 1. 7
Exceeding wroth *therewith* the virgin grew, . . . III. xii. 33. 6
Therewith she stayd her hand, . . . III. xii. 34. 8
Therewith their dulled sprights they edgd anew, . . . IV. ii. 17. 6
Therewith asunder in the midst it brast, . . . IV. iii. 12. 1
And *therewith* smote him on his Umbriere . . . IV. iv. 44. 3
he woxe *therewith* displeased sore, . . . IV. iv. 45. 6
Therewith to bind lascivious desire, . . . IV. v. 4. 7
touched was with secret wrath and shame *Therewith,* . . . IV. v. 17. 5
and *therewith,* Under his side him nipt; . . . IV. v. 44. 3
And *therewith* stroke at her so hideouslie, . . . IV. vi. 18. 8

Therewith—*Continued.*
He was *therewith* right wondrously dismayd; . . . . IV. vi. 24. 3
Therewith her wrathfull courage gan appall, ... IV. vi. 26. 7
Therewith he rested, and well pleased was: . . . . IV. vi. 39. 1
But her *therewith* full sore displeasd he found, ... IV. vi. 42. 7
Yet he *therewith* so felly still did rave, ... IV. vii. 28. 5
His greedy throte, *therewith* in two distraught, ... IV. vii. 31. 7
Therewith she rose in hast, ... IV. viii. 10. 5
Therewith both Squire and dwarfe did tomble downe . . . . IV. viii. 42. 8
And *therewith* smote at him with all his might; . . . . . IV. viii. 44. 6
Who mov'd no more *therewith,* then when a rocke . . . . V. i. 21. 6
all that comes doth take, and *therewith* fill The coffers . . . V. ii. 9. 3
Therewith the Gyant much abashed sayd, ... V. ii. 44. 1
He was *therewith* exceedingly dismayd, ... V. iii. 18. 2
Therewith much comforted she gan unfold . . . . V. v. 31. 7
Therewith she gan at first to change her mood, ... V. v. 45. 4
Therewith containes his heavenly Commonweale: . . . . . . V. vii. 1. 8
For that *therewith* he falsely did revyle . . . . V. ix. 25. 4
Therewith all fraught with fury and disdaine, ... V. xi. 8. 1
And Belge selfe was *therewith* stonied sore, ... V. xi. 30. 3
poyson *therewith* rusht, That him nigh choked . . . . V. xi. 31. 7
Therewith Grandtorto selfe I did appall, ... V. xi. 53. 8
That he *therewith* the knight drew all about . . . . V. xii. 22. 3
And, whiles he combred was *therewith* so sore, ... V. xii. 22. 8
And as she spake *therewith* she slavered; . . . . V. xii. 29. 8
Who nathelesse, not *therewith* satisfyde, ... VI. vi. 43. 7
He, *therewith* much abashed and affrayd, ... VI. vii. 22. 1
Therewith the cowheard, deaded with affright, ... VI. vii. 25. 7
having in his hand a whip, Her *therewith* yirks; . . . . . . VI. vii. 44. 7
Who *therewith* flesht upon him set anew, ... VI. viii. 9. 7
taking his owne whip, *therewith* So sore him scourgeth . . . VI. viii. 28. 8
Therewith some other of the chiefest theeves . . . . VI. xi. 15. 1
Therewith he mured up his mouth along, ... VI. xii. 34. 4
there-with lifting up her golden wand, Threatned . . . . . VII. vi. 13. 4
they *therewith* doe Poetes heads adorne, ... *Am.* xxix. 7
beauty doe behold, And *therewith* doe her cruelty compare, . . *Am.* lv. 2
Doth *therwith* tip his sharp empoisned darts, ... *H.L.* 121
Therewith thou pointest thy Sons poysned arrow, ... *H.B.* 62

Therewithal. *There-with-all* He lookt aside . . . . *D.* 58
therewithall he fiersly at him flew, ... II. vi. 29. 1
therewithall (**therewith all*) attonce at him let fly . . . . . II. xi. 18. 1
And manly terror mixed *therewithall;* . . . . III. i. 46. 2
therewithall She sighed soft, ... III. vii. 9. 4
he was soone awaked *therewithall,* . . . . IV. v. 42. 5
therewithall at him right furiously she strooke. . . . . . . IV. vi. 14. 9
To whom I cald aloud, halfe angry *therewithall.* . . . . . . IV. x. 11. 9
Departed straight to Proteus *therewithall;* . . . . IV. xii. 32. 7
he was nothing mov'd nor tempted *therewithall:* . . . . . . V. ii. 23. 9
I bore, and *therewithall* Fought many battels . . . . V. xi. 53. 6
made such piteous mourning *therewithall,* . . . . VI. i. 34. 8
Thought *therewithall* forthwith him to have slaine; . . . . VI. v. 26. 7
therewithall rude hand on him did lay, ... VI. vi. 21. 8
warrant straight was made, and *therewithall* . . . did passe, . VI. vii. 35. 6
His manly mynde was much emmoved *therewithall;* . . . . . VI. viii. 5. 9
She sudden was revived *therewithall,* . . . . VI. xi. 44. 4
therewithall Putting his puissaunce forth, ... VI. xii. 30. 2
there-with-all he on her shoulder laid His snaky-wreathed Mace, VII. vi. 18. 1
Their snowie Foreheads *therewithall* they crownd, ... *Proth.* 86

Therewithin. if living wight Were housed *therewithin,* . . . . I. viii. 37. 9

Therion. That was in sacred bandes of wedlocke tyde To *Therion,* . . . . I. vi. 21. 6

These (*partial list*).
the wrathfull winde, . . . That sperst *these* cloudes; . . . . *Bel.* viii. 13
'Yet shall a third both *these* and thine subdew. . . . . . . III. iii. 47. 1
Whether those same on high, or *these* belowe; . . . . VII. vii. 20. 2

Theseus. *Theseus* condemned to endlesse slouth by law; . . . I. v. 35. 8
Stout *Theseus* and Pirithous his feare . . . . IV. x. 27. 3
Like as the cursed son of *Theseus,* . . . . V. viii. 43. 1
that same day That *Theseus* her unto his bridale bore, . . . VI. x. 13. 3

Thessalian. sweet and holesome then . . . the *Thessalian* Tempe, II. xii .52. 4
On the *Thessalian* shore from him did flie: . . . . *Am.* xxviii. 10

Thessaly. through *Thessaly* they streeme, ... *Proth.* 80

Thestylis. another swaine . . . Hight *Thestylis,* . . . . . . *As.* Interl. 221
him *Thestylis* bespake; . . . . *Col.* 156
Till *Thestylis* at last their silence brake, ... *Col.* 651
'Shepheard, (said *Thestylis*) . . . . *Col.* 676

Thetch. *See* **Thatch.**

Thetis. One foote on *Thetis,* th' other on the Morning, ... *Ro.* iv. 2
Could save the sonne of *Thetis* from to die; . . . . *Ti.* 429
The chaulky Kenet, and the *Thetis* gray, ... IV. xi. 29. 5
Swift Proto, milde Eucrate, *Thetis* faire, ... IV. xi. 48. 7
the solemne bridall cheare Twixt Peleus and Dame *Thetis* . . VII. vii. 12. 5

Thetis'. th' other was with *Thetis* love assaid, ... *Gn.* 491
Thetis wedding with Aeacidee, ... VI. x. 22. 5

Thewed. *See* **Well-thewed.**
would not seeme so rude, and *thewed* ill, ... II. vi. 26. 3
A beauteous soule, with faire conditions *thewed,* . . . . . . *H.B.* 137

Thews. upbrought in gentle *thewes* and martiall might. . . . I. ix. 3. 9
well upbrought In goodly *thewes,* and godly exercise: . . . . I. x. 4. 4
well ye worthy bene for worth and gentle *thewes.'* . . . . . II. i. 33. 9
in all godly *thewes* and goodly praise . . . . II. x. 59. 6
with good *thewes* and speaches well applyde . . . . IV. ix. 14. 6
praise likewise deserve good *thewes* . . . . VI. ii. 2. 9
Have trayned bene . . . In gentle *thewes* . . . . VI. ii. 31. 5
And it in goodly *thewes* so well upbrought, ... VI. iv. 38. 7

They (*partial list*).
fashiond were *they* all in Dorike wise. . . . . *Bel.*[1] ii. 4

They're. As for loose loves, *they 're* vaine, ... I. x. 62. 9

Thick. peeping close into the *thicke,* . . . . *S.C.* Mar. 73
As *thicke* as it had hayled. . . . . *S.C.* Mar. 87

Thick—*Continued.*
Into *thick* shadowes, there themselves to lay. . . . . *Gn.* 168
Whose wals were high, but nothing strong nor *thick,* . . . . I. iv. 4. 3
he rusht into the *thick,* . . . . II. i. 39. 2
forth gusht a stream of gore blood *thick,* . . . . II. i. 39. 7
through the *thicke* they heard one rudely rush, ... II. iii. 21. 1
Through the dull billowes *thicke* as troubled mire, ... II. vi. 20. 7
Through that *thick* covert he him led, ... II. vii. 20. 6
a *thick* Arber goodly over-dight, ... II. vii. 53. 3
loaden all with fruit as *thick* as it might bee. . . . . II. vii. 53. 9
as *thicke* as stormie showre, Their strokes did raine: . . . . II. viii. 35. 5
some like ugly Urchins *thick* and short: . . . . II. xi. 13. 4
Their fluttring arrowes, *thicke* as flakes of snow, ... II. xi. 18. 2
flowing low and *thick* her cloth'd arownd, ... II. xii. 67. 4
Through *thicke* and thin, both over banck and bush, ... III. i. 17. 5
Like to *thicke* clouds that threat a stormy showre, ... III. iv. 43. 3
Through *thick* and thin, through mountains and through playns, ... III. iv. 46. 1
ronning through that same *Thicke* forest, ... III. v. 3. 9
Through the *thicke* woods wherein he would have hid . . . . III. v. 13. 7
with *thicke* woods overgrowne, ... III. v. 17. 7
All coverd with *thick* woodes that quite it overcame. . . . . III. vii. 4. 9
Through *thicke* and thin her to poursew apace, ... III. vii. 23. 2
As *thicke* as hayle forth poured from the skie: . . . . IV. iii. 25. 5
So *thicke* they fell, and forcibly were sent, ... IV. iii. 26. 2
thronging *thicke* her to behold, ... IV. iii. 41. 2
Heaping huge strokes as *thicke* as showre of hayle, ... IV. vi. 16. 5
cluster *thicke* unto his leasings vaine, ... V. ii. 33. 2
arrowes haild so *thicke,* that they could not abide. . . . . . V. iv. 38. 9
As *thicke* as doth the seede after the sowers hand. . . . . . V. xii. 7. 9
The Tyrant thundred his *thicke* blowes so fast, ... V. xii. 17. 6
his Ladie . . . did pas Through *thicke* and thin, ... VI. ii. 10. 4
Through the *thicke* clouds in which they steeped lay . . . . VI. iii. 13. 6
through *thicke* woods and brakes and briers him drew, . . . VI. v. 17. 3
The covert was so *thicke* that did no passage shew. . . . . . VI. v. 22. 9
to retyre him hasted Through the *thick* prease, ... VI. vi. 28. 4
led that Ladies horse Through *thick* and thin, ... VI. vii. 44. 2
the *thicke* shrubs, which did them alwaies shade . . . . . . VI. x. 42. 3
breaking forth, did *thick* about me throng. . . . . *Am.* xii. 8
All sowd with glistring stars more *thicke* then grasse, ... *H.H.B.* 53

Thick-entangled. *thick entangled* knots adown does slack, . . . I. xi. 11. 4

Thickest. Where *thickest* grasse did cloath the open hills. . . *Gn.* 74
a hollowe cave Amid the *thickest* woods. . . . . I. i. 11. 7
out of the *thickest* wood A ramping Lyon rushed . . . . . . I. iii. 5. 1
All suddenly out of the *thickest* brush, ... III. i. 15. 1
rushing through the *thickest* preasse . . . . III. i. 23. 5
in the *thickest* covert of that shade . . . . III. vi. 44. 1
when amid the *thickest* woodes they were, ... III. x. 43. 1
Into the *thickest* of that knightly preasse . . . . IV. iv. 34. 1
rushed forth out of the *thickest* rout . . . . IV. iv. 43. 7
One rushing forth out of the *thickest* weed, ... IV. vii. 4. 4
through the *thickest* makes her nighest waies; . . . . IV. vii. 22. 3
thrusting fierce into the *thickest* preace . . . . IV. ix. 32. 6
through the *thickest* like a Lyon flew, ... V. iii. 8. 5
Forth from the *thickest* preasse of people came, ... V. iii. 29. 4
passing through the *thickest* preasse, ... V. ix. 23. 6
running streight into the *thickest* wood, ... VI. iv. 12. 5
he thrusts into the *thickest* throng . . . . VI. viii. 49. 1
with his raging brond divide Their *thickest* troups, ... VI. xi. 48. 9

Thicket. 'I wont to raunge amydde the mazie *thickette,* . . . *S.C.* D. 25
sent out of the *thicket* neare A cruell shaft, ... III. v. 20. 3
The silly man that in the *thickett* lay . . . . III. x. 45. 1

Thickets. They now amongst the woods and *thickets* ment, . . *Gn.* 75
Through many covert groves and *thickets* close, ... II. xii. 76. 6
Ne feeles the thornes and *thickets* pricke her tender toes. . . IV. vii. 21. 9

Thicks. But see, the Welkin *thicks* apace, ... *S.C.* Mar. 115

Thief. He was, to weete, a stout and sturdy *thiefe,* . . . . . I. iii. 17. 1
hopelesse, hartlesse, gan the cunning *thiefe* Perswade us dye, I. ix. 29. 7
'By Mahoune, cursed *thiefe,* . . . . II. viii. 33. 3
when that *theefe* approching nigh espide . . . . IV. vii. 29. 5
Him calling *theefe,* them whores; . . . . IV. viii. 35. 4
He ment the *thiefe* there deadly to have smit: . . . . V. iii. 29. 8
he chalenged the *thiefe* to fight: . . . . V. iii. 31. 6
whereas the *thiefe* Lay sleeping soundly . . . . VI. xi. 38. 3
the *theefe* awaking light Unto the entrance ran; . . . . . . VI. xi. 43. 4

Thies. *See* **Thighs.**

Thieveries. his cunning *theeveries* He wonts to worke, ... *Hub.* 1287
High heven beholdes sad lovers nightly *theeveryes.* . . . . . . III. xi. 45. 9

Thievery. For their false treason and vile *theeverie:* . . . . . *Hub.* 315

Thieves. religion held even *theeves* in measure. . . . . VI. viii. 43. 9
Now made the spoile of *theeves* and Brigants bad, ... VI. x. 40. 7
carried captive by those *theeves* away; . . . . VI. x. 41. 2
kept with gard Of griesly *theeves,* . . . . VI. x. 43. 8
The *Theeves* fall out for Pastorell, ... VI. xi. Arg.
in dreadfull darknesse layd Amongst those *theeves,* . . . . . VI. xi. 2. 4
being readie met By some of these same *theeves* . . . . . . VI. xi. 9. 7
some other of the chiefest *theeves* . . . . VI. xi. 15. 1
how those *theeves* . . . Fell all at ods, ... VI. xi. 30. 8
The selfe same flocks the which those *theeves* had reft . . . VI. xi. 37. 2
certaine of the *theeves* there by them left, ... VI. xi. 37. 4
when he saw the *theeves* which did them keepe, ... VI. xi. 37. 8
the *theeves* them questioned againe, ... VI. xi. 39. 5
Unto their hellish dens those *theeves* them brought; . . . . VI. xi. 41. 2
In dead of night, when all the *theeves* did rest, ... VI. xi. 42. 2
So many *theeves* about him swarming are, ... VI. xi. 48. 5
Thieves should rob and spoile that Coast around: . . . . . VII. vi. 55. 6
Doth to this day with Wolves and *Thieves* abound: . . . . . VII. vi. 55. 8

Thievish. what befell her in that *theevish* wonne, ... VI. x. 44. 8
The readie way unto that *theevish* wonne, ... VI. xi. 35. 2
into those *theevish* dens he went, ... VI. xi. 51. 1

Thigh. Launched his *thigh* with so mischievous might, . . . *As.* 119
through his *thigh* the mortall steele did gryde: . . . II. viii. 36. 5
stayd not till it did light In his left *thigh,* . . . III. v. 20. 7
She his hurt *thigh* to him recurd againe, . . . III. v. 42. 3
unlaste Her silver buskins from her nimble *thigh,* . . . III. vi. 18. 3
through the mayles into his *thigh* it entred, . . . IV. iii. 9. 3
Uppon her *thigh* her Cemitare was tide . . . V. v. 3. 4
glauncing downe his *thigh* the purple bloud forth drew. . . . V. v. 9. 9
without sword upon his *thigh* to sit: . . . VI. v. 8. 8

Thighs. Stretch his strong *thighes,* and th' Ocean overstride, . *Ti.* 541
His broad outstretched hornes, his hayrie *thies,* . . . *Mui.* 335
Whose feeble *thighes,* . . . him scarse to light could beare; . I. viii. 40. 7
his fraile *thighes,* nigh weary and fordonne, . . . I. x. 47. 8
enwrapt the nimble *thyes* Of his froth-fomy steed, . . . I. xi. 23. 2
Forth creeping on his caitive hands and *thies;* . . . II. iii. 35. 7
Her goodly *thighes,* whose glorie did appeare . . . VI. viii. 42. 7

Thilk. 'I love *thilke* lasse, . . . *S.C.* Ja. 61
Seest not *thilke* same Hawthorne studde, . . . *S.C.* Mar. 13
thilke same unhappye Ewe, . . . *S.C.* Mar. 49
was *thilk* same song of Colins owne making? . . . *S.C.* Ap. 154
Is not *thilke* the mery moneth of May, . . . *S.C.* May 1
all to sadde For *thilke* same season, . . . *S.C.* May 6
thilke God, that gave him that good, . . . *S.C.* May 85
Thilke same Kidde . . . *S.C.* May 174
Is not *thilke* same a goteheard . . . *S.C.* Jul. 1
nothing such *thilk* shepheard was Whom . . . *S.C.* Jul. 145
He saw *thilke* misusage; . . . *S.C.* Jul. 184
Yet should *thilk* lasse not from my thought, . . . *S.C.* Au. 107
Hardly my selfe escaped *thilke* payne, . . . *S.C.* S. 66
they han sold *thilk* same long agoe, . . . *S.C.* S. 98
Thilk same shepheard mought I well marke, . . . *S.C.* S. 180
Lowder had be slaine *thilke* same even. . . . *S.C.* S. 225
thilke same rule were too straight, . . . *S.C.* S. 236
All were Elisa one of *thilke* same ring; . . . *S.C.* O. 53
Thilke sollein season sadder plight doth aske, . . . *S.C.* N. 17
I was in *thilke* same looser yeares, . . . *S.C.* D. 37

Thin. Through their *thin* coverings appearing fayre, . . . *Gn.* 286
Idlenesse, . . . Arayd in habit blacke, and amis *thin,* . . . I. iv. 18. 8
He had beene pouldred all as *thin* as flowre: . . . I. vii. 12. 4
His bare *thin* cheekes for want of better bits, . . . I. viii. 41. 3
Through her *thin* weed their places only signifide. . . . II. iii. 29. 9
Infinite shapes of thinges dispersed *thin;* . . . II. ix. 50. 3
All in a canvas *thin* he was bedight, . . . II. xi. 22. 6
was the fence thereof but weake and *thin:* . . . II. xii. 43. 4
All in a vele of silke and silver *thin,* . . . II. xii. 77. 4
Through thicke and *thin,* both over banck and bush, . . . III. i. 17. 5
Where she may finde the substance *thin* and light, . . . III. i. 43. 3
Through thick and *thin,* through mountains and through playns, . . . III. iv. 46. 1
A litle smoke, whose vapour *thin* and light . . . III. vii. 5. 2
Through thicke and *thin* her to poursew apace, . . . III. vii. 23. 2
To see their thrids so *thin* as spiders frame, . . . IV. ii. 50. 8
He with his yron flale did thresh so *thin,* . . . V. vii. 35. 7
his Ladie . . . did pas Through thicke and *thin,* . . . VI. ii. 10. 4
led that Ladies horse Through thick and *thin,* . . . VI. vii. 44. 2
whose substance *thin* and slight Made no resistance, . . . VII. vi. 7. 7
with subtill influence Of his *thin* spirit . . . VII. vii. 22. 4
a *thin* silken cassock . . . VII. vii. 29. 2

Thine (*partial list*).
Nor ought cald mine or *thine:* . . . *Hub.* 149
they heare *thine,* and *thine* doo better praise. . . . *Ti.* 336
'Yet shall a third both these and *thine* subdew. . . . III. iii. 47. 1
If shee were *thine,* and thou as now am I? . . . III. xi. 19. 4
beautifie this sacred hymne of *thyne:* . . . *H.B.* 21
Unmindfull of that dearest Lord of *thyne;* . . . *H.H.L.* 221
thine owne name . . . *Proth.* 153

Thing. *See* **Allthing, Anything, Everything, Something.**
so faire a *thing* as this, . . . *Bel.*[1] iv. 13
to see so rare a *thing,* . . . *Bel.*[1] v. 9
Let me no more see faire *thing* . . . *Bel.* iv. 12
so rare a *thing* to vew; . . . *Bel.*[2] v. 9
each *thing* at last (length[1]) Doth passe . . . *Pet.* v. 7
Your glorie, fairest of all earthly *thing!* . . . *Ro.* i. 14
Whatever *thing* seems small in common eyes. . . . *Van.* v. 14
To see so goodly *thing* so soone decayed. . . . *Van.* vii. 14
Sith so small *thing* his happines may varie. . . . *Van.* viii. 14
Straunge *thing,* me seemeth, that so small a *thing* Should . . . *Van.* ix. 13
loves the *thing* he cannot purchase. . . . *S.C.* Ap. 159
With mery *thing* its good to medle sadde. . . . *S.C.* Au. 144
never *thing* on earth so pleaseth me . . . *S.C.* Au. 147
Eche *thing* imparted is more eath to beare: . . . *S.C.* S. 17
Whatever *thing* lacketh chaungeable rest, . . . *S.C.* S. 240
But *thing* on earth that is of most availe, . . . *S.C.* N. 87
each *thing* fained ought more warie bee. . . . *Hub.* 495
the *thing* that doth thy sorrow breed: . . . *Hub.* 596
So pitifull a *thing* is Suters state! . . . *Hub.* 891
(for what *thing* can ever last?) . . . *Hub.* 1176
To let him knowe the order of the *thing.* . . . *Hub.* 1212
an ey-witnes of each *thing* to bee. . . . *Hub.* 1278
what *thing* on earth . . . Might be the cause . . . *T.M.* 43
to be learned it a base *thing* deeme: . . . *T.M.* 87
loath'd of losels as a *thing* forlorne: . . . *T.M.* 226
what ever *thing* is goodly thought, . . . *T.M.* 405
what delight (quoth she) in earthlie *thing,* . . . *Ti.* 22
builde your blis on hope of earthly *thing,* . . . *Ti.* 198
as the *thing* Which never was, . . . *Ti.* 346
what bootes it to see earthlie *thing* . . . *Ti.* 554
To take what ever *thing* doth please the eie? . . . *Mui.* 214
Yet was by them as *thing* impure rejected; . . . *D.* 209
Nature, nurse of every living *thing,* . . . *D.* 337

Thing—*Continued.*
wishfull *thing* this sad life to forgoe: . . . *D.* 452
shall never more behold Faire *thing* on earth, . . . *D.* 492
In one *thing* onely fayling of the best, . . . *As.* 11
As men use most to covet forreine *thing.'* . . . *Col.* 162
Strange *thing!* how bold and swift the monster was, . . . *Col.* 220
sooth to say, it is foolhardie *thing,* . . . *Col.* 915
Not then to her that scorned *thing* so base, . . . *Col.* 935
loath each lowly *thing* with loftie eie. . . . *Col.* 938
Unfit he was for any worldly *thing,* . . . I. iv. 23. 1
the *thing,* which daily yet I rew, . . . I. v. 42. 2
Why fearest thou, that canst not hope for *thing;* . . . I. v. 43. 3
'how might I see The *thing* . . . I. vi. 39. 4
A *thing* without the compas of my witt; . . . I. ix. 3. 2
other griesly *thing* that him aghast. . . . I. ix. 21. 4
what ever *thing* is donne In heaven and earth? . . . I. ix. 42. 1
Each goodly *thing* is hardest to begin; . . . I. x. 6. 1
'Straunge *thing* it is an errant knight to see Here . . . I. x. 10. 1
mortall life gan loath as *thing* forlore, . . . I. x. 21. 5
Did spend their daies in doing godly *thing.* . . . I. x. 36. 5
Panthea, seemd the brightest *thing* that was; . . . I. x. 58. 6
What ever *thing* does touch his ravenous pawes, . . . I. xi. 12. 4
To weet what dreadfull *thing* was there in hond, . . . II. ii. 21. 2
strong *thing* does increace, . . . II. ii. 31. 3
earthly *thing* may not my corage brave Dismay . . . II. iii. 45. 3
Ne ever *thing* could cause us disagree. . . . II. iv. 19. 7
Ne ever *thing* that she could think or see, . . . II. iv. 20. 7
Was overcome of *thing* that did him please; . . . II. vi. 13. 8
of no worldly *thing* he carę did take: . . . II. vi. 18. 2
every weighty *thing* they did upbeare, . . . II. vi. 46. 8
So evill *thing* to seeke unto their ayd, . . . II. vii. 14. 8
thing refused doe not afterward accuse.' . . . II. vii. 18. 9
'Me list not' . . . 'receave *Thing* offred, . . . II. vii. 19. 2
lips he layd on *thing* that likte him best, . . . II. vii. 27. 3
The *thing,* that thou didst crave so earnestly, . . . II. vii. 38. 3
of *thing* like to that Aegyptian slime, . . . II. ix. 21. 5
no earthly *thing* is sure. . . . II. ix. 21. 9
each *thing* by which the eyes may fault: . . . II. xi. 9. 7
greatest and most glorious *thing* on ground . . . II. xi. 30. 1
whoso fayre *thing* doest faine to see, . . . II. xii. 74. 2
Ne evil *thing* she feard, ne evill *thing* she ment. . . . III. i. 19. 9
For hardie *thing* it is, to weene by might . . . III. ii. 13. 6
With hope of *thing* that may allegge his smart; . . . III. ii. 15. 4
Whatever *thing* was in the world contaynd, . . . III. ii. 19. 2
Of much more uncouth *thing* I was affrayd, . . . III. ii. 40. 3
what *thing* it mote bee, Or whence it sprong, . . . III. iii. 16. 6
sheweth each *thing* as it is in deed: . . . III. iv. 59. 2
(a wondrous *thing* to say) . . . III. vi. 26. 8
T' adore *thing* so divine as beauty were but right. . . . III. vii. 11. 9
(a *thing* far passing thought) . . . III. vii. 48. 5
thereby deeming sure the *thing* as donne, . . . III. viii. 3. 3
the connterfet should shame The *thing* it selfe: . . . III. viii. 5. 6
That *thing* of course he counted love to entertaine. . . . III. ix. 29. 9
shameful *thing* Yt were t' abandon . . . chevisaunce . . . III. xi. 24. 5
"Straunge *thing* it seem'd, . . . III. xi. 53. 8
No word they spake, nor earthly *thing* they felt, . . . III. xii. 45. *or.* 8
they ought not *thing* unknowne reprove, . . . IV. Pr. 2. 3
as *thing* reserv'd from stealth. . . . IV. i. 6. 7
rashly lusted For *thing* unlawfull, that was not his owne: . IV. i. 11. 4
never thoght one *thing,* but doubly stil was guided. . . . IV. i. 27. 9
'the *thing* that with this eye I saw, . . . IV. i. 48. 3
as *thing* deviz'd her to defame. . . . IV. v. 17. 5
Ne thenceforth feare the *thing* . . . IV. vi. 30. 6
bootlesse *thing* it was to think such blowes to beare. . . . IV. vii. 28. 9
Ne ever *thing* so well was doen alive, . . . IV. viii. 25. 8
lov'd me deare, as dearest *thing* alive. . . . IV. viii. 56. 6
folly seem'd to leave the *thing* undonne . . . IV. x. 53. 4
of no worldly *thing* he tooke delight; . . . IV. xii. 19. 7
doe what ever *thing* he did intend: . . . V. i. 12. 5
to enquire What *thing* so many nations met did there desire. V. ii. 29. 9
'What ever *thing* is done by him is donne, . . . V. ii. 42. 1
doest not know the least *thing* of them all? . . . V. ii. 43. 8
To see the *thing,* that seem'd so excellent, . . . V. iii. 26. 4
As *thing* at randon left, . . . V. iv. 19. 7
Ne doth she give them other *thing* to eat . . . V. iv. 31. 7
bread and water or like feeble *thing,* . . . V. iv. 31. 8
this heavenly *thing* whereof I treat, to weeten Mercie, . . . V. x. 1. 2
when she wanteth other *thing* to eat, . . . V. xii. 31. 6
turne to ill the *thing* that well was ment; . . . V. xii. 34. 5
unryper yeares . . . unfit For *thing* of weight . . . VI. ii. 9. 3
him to beare she thought it *thing* too base. . . . VI. ii. 47. 5
And shrieked out, a *thing* uncomely for a knight. . . . VI. iv. 8. 9
O what an easie *thing* is to descry The gentle bloud, . . . VI. v. 1. 1
Mote easie be supprest with little *thing;* . . . VI. vi. 8. 4
falleth downe to ground like senselesse *thing;* . . . VI. vii. 9. 7
bootelesse *thing* him seemed to abide So mighty blowes, . VI. vii. 46. 8
Nor that *thing* worst which men do most refuse; . . . VI. ix. 29. 7
other daintie *thing* for her addrest, . . . VI. ix. 40. 4
What ever *thing* he did her to aggrate, . . . VI. x. 33. 2
Sith otherwise he could not mend *thing* past; . . . VI. xi. 34. 7
Nor ever thought *thing* so unworthily: . . . VI. xii. 33. 7
O weake life! that does leane On *thing* so tickle . . . VII. vii. 22. 6
Base *thing* I can no more endure to view: . . . *Am.* iii. 6
The *thing* which I doo most in her admire, . . . *Am.* v. 3
seemes to scorne Base *thing,* . . . *Am.* xiii. 10
What more miraculous *thing* may be told, . . . *Am.* xxx. 9
shew *Thing* so divine to vew of earthly eye, . . . *Am.* xlv. 6
Great shame it is, *thing* so divine in view, . . . *Am.* liii. 9
Strange *thing,* me seemd, to see a beast so wyld, . . . *Am.* lxvii. 13
A mortall *thing* so to immortalize; . . . *Am.* lxxv. 6

Thing—*Continued.*
sing the *thing* that mote thy mynd delight, . . . *Epith.* 123
Ne thought of *thing* uncomely ever may Thereto approch . . *Epith.* 198
As *thing* on earth so heavenly . . . *H.L.* 214
Thereof as every earthly *thing* partakes . . . *H.B.* 43
the *thing* which giveth pleasant grace . . . *H.B.* 57
resemble . . . as mortall *thing* immortall could; . . . *H.H.L.* 114
For Love doth love the *thing* belov'd to see, . . . *H.H.L.* 118
That in no earthly *thing* thou shalt delight, . . . *H.H.L.* 272
Enough is me t' admyre so heavenly *thing,* . . . *H.H.B.* 236
Things. So manie strange *things* happened me to see, . . . *Pet.* i. 2
time, which all *things* doth devowre! . . . *Ro.* iii. 8
if that time make ende of *things* so sure, . . . *Ro.* vii. 13
all *things* which beneath the Moone have being . . . *Ro.* ix. 10
Doth shew that all *things* turne to their first being. . . . *Ro.* xviii. 14
The seedes, of which all *things* at first were bred, . . . *Ro.* xxii. 13
if *things* nam'd their names doo equalize, . . . *Ro.* xxvi. 10
things exceeding reach of common reason; . . . *Van.* i. 4
That when time serves may bring *things* better forth. . . . *Van.* i. 14
Thought all *things* lesse than his disdainful pride. . . . *Van.* iii. 6
greatest *things* the least disdaine; . . . *Van.* iii. 13
Why do vaine men mean *things* so much deface, . . . *Van.* xi. 12
To see so great *things* by so small distrest. . . . *Van.* xii. 4
What shoulden shepheards other *things* tend, . . . *S.C.* May 63
Three *thinges* to beare bene very burdenous, . . . *S.C.* May 132
Tway *things* doen ill agree. . . . *S.C.* Jul. 152
So as thou can many *thinges* relate; . . . *S.C.* S. 23
'O! trustlesse state of earthly *things,* . . . *S.C.* N. 153
To *thinges* of ryper season selfe applyed, . . . *S.C.* D. 76
tryed time yet taught me greater *thinges;* . . . *S.C.* D. 85
Ne measures all *things* . . . *Gn.* 92
all *things* seem'd appalled at his sight. . . . *Gn.* 256
all *things* in his way Full stearnly rends . . . *Gn.* 271
things lightly done amis Knew how to pardon, . . . *Gn.* 475
things miscounselled must needs miswend. . . . *Hub.* 128
Their service and their holie *things* to say, . . . *Hub.* 450
perhaps ye *things* may handle soe, . . . *Hub.* 641
Findes all *things* needfull for contentment meeke, . . . *Hub.* 911
Gan to provide for all *things* in assurance, . . . *Hub.* 1113
Of *things* forepast, nor moniments of time; . . . *T.M.* 104
doth all fairest *things* on earth deface, . . . *T.M.* 434
How *things* she formed of a formelesse mas: . . . *T.M.* 502
In contemplation of *things* heavenlie wrought: . . . *T.M.* 526
treadeth under foote hir holie *things,* . . . *T.M.* 569
Sith I doo dailie see *things* highest placed, . . . *Ti.* 180
All *things* doo change that under heaven abide, . . . *Ti.* 206
as *things* wipt out with a sponge . . . *Ti.* 361
welds all *things* at his will, . . . *Ti.* 447
Sith time doth greatest *things* to ruine bring? . . . *Ti.* 556
No common *things* may please a wavering wit. . . . *Mui.* 160
The foe of faire *things,* th' author of confusion, . . . *Mui.* 244
al good *things* with venemous tooth devowres, . . . *Mui.* 302
If purest *things* be not by them respected? . . . *D.* 207
cease henceforth *things* kindly forth to bring, . . . *D.* 339
To see all *things,* and not my love to see; . . . *D.* 408
spight it selfe, that all good *things* doth spill, . . . *As.* 23
The gods, which all *things* see, this same beheld, . . . *As.* 181
all *things* else that living creatures need. . . . *Col.* 299
by paragone Of earthly *things,* to judge of *things* divine: . . *Col.* 345
Presume the *things* so sacred to prophane? . . . *Col.* 349
how should else *things* so far from attone, . . . *Col.* 843
things celestiall which ye never saw. . . . *Col.* 930
Which of all earthly *thinges* he most did crave: . . . I. i. 3. 5
With holy father sits not with such *thinges* to mell. . . . I. i. 30. 9
wont to say His holy *thinges* each morne and eventyde: . . . I. i. 34. 7
Rest is their feast, and all *thinges* at their will: . . . I. i. 35. 3
none the holy *things* in safety kept, . . . I. iii. 17. 8
he to her brought part of his stolen *things.* . . . I. iii. 18. 9
all *things* els the which his art did teach: . . . I. v. 44. 3
prowdly threw to ground, as *things* of naught; . . . I. vii. 18. 5
underneath his filthy feet did tread The sacred *thinges,* . . . I. vii. 18. 7
ye heavens, that all *things* right esteeme, . . . I. vii. 49. 7
high does sit, and all *things* see With equall eye, . . . I. viii. 27. 6
The *things,* that grievous were to doe, or beare, . . . I. viii. 44. 2
Thus as they gan of sondrie *thinges* devise, . . . I. x. 12. 1
Wherein darke *things* were writt, hard to be understood. . . I. x. 13. 9
So darke are earthly *thinges* compard to *things* divine. . . . I. x. 67. 9
in that soile, where all good *things* did grow, . . . I. xi. 47. 2
later times *thinges* more unknowne shall show. . . . II. Pr. 3. 3
unto *things* of valorous pretence Seemes to be borne . . . II. iv. 1. 4
Sheilds, steeds, and armes, and all *things* for thee meet, . . II. vii. 11. 3
The hatefull messengers of heavy *things,* . . . II. vii. 23. 4
The clowdes, as *thinges* affrayd, before him flye; . . . II. viii. 48. 3
The first of them could *things* to come foresee; . . . II. ix. 49. 1
The next could of *thinges* present best advize; . . . II. ix. 49. 2
The third *things* past could keep in memoree: . . . II. ix. 49. 3
Infinite shapes of *thinges* dispersed thin; . . . II. ix. 50. 3
things foregone through many ages held, . . . II. ix. 56. 2
As all *things* els the which this world doth weld; . . . II. ix. 56. 5
when *thinges* were lost, or laid amis, . . . II. ix. 58. 6
all *things* one, and one as nothing was, . . . II. xii. 34. 8
the mightiest *things* efforced bin: . . . II. xii. 43. 7
wondrous *things* concerning our welfare, . . . II. xii. 47. 5
As diverse witts to diverse *things* apply; . . . III. i. 57. 3
Of sondry *thinges* faire purpose gan to find, . . . III. ii. 4. 2
Ay doing *thinges* that to his fame redownd, . . . III. ii. 14. 5
with fantastick sight Of dreadfull *things,* . . . III. ii. 29. 5
'*Things* ofte impossible' (quoth she) 'seeme, ere begonne. . . III. ii. 36. 9
hostes of men of meanest *thinges* could frame, . . . III. iii. 12. 6
'For so must all *things* excellent begin; . . . III. iii. 22. 1

Things—*Continued.*
bad her all *things* put in readinesse anon. . . . III. iii. 57. 9
all *thinges* did conveniently purvay. . . . III. iii. 58. 2
Of diverse *thinges* discourses to dilate, . . . III. iii. 62. 4
Exceeding riches and all pretious *things,* . . . III. iv. 23. 2
doest all *thinges* deface, . . . III. iv. 56. 3
the fruitfull seades Of all *things* living, . . . III. vi. 8. 4
She promist kisses sweet, and sweeter *things,* . . . III. vi. 12. 8
Of all *things* that are borne to live and dye, . . . III. vi. 30. 5
All *things,* as they created were, doe grow, . . . III. vi. 34. 3
All *things* from thence doe their first being fetch, . . . III. vi. 37. 1
Does mow the flowring herbes and goodly *things,* . . . III. vi. 39. 4
To see so faire *thinges* mard and spoiled quight; . . . III. vi. 40. 2
All *things* decay in time, . . . III. vi. 40. 9
In balefull night where all *thinges* are forgot; . . . III. vi. 47. 3
The knights were willing all *things* to excuse, . . . III. ix. 18. 8
servd of all *things* that mote needfull bee; . . . III. ix. 19. 2
Fruitfull of all *thinges* fitt for living foode, . . . III. ix. 49. 6
Two *things* he feared, but the third was death; . . . III. x. 2. 6
whilest all *things* in troublous uprore were, . . . III. x. 16. 1
That cruell element, which all *things* feare, . . . III. xi. 22. 4
Full dreadfull *thinges* out of that balefull booke He red, . . III. xii. 36. 3
call to count the *things* that then were donne, . . . IV. Pr. 3. 2
sayd Full many *things* so doubtfull to be wayd, . . . IV. i. 7. 5
hard t' accord two *things* so far in dout. . . . IV. i. 11. 9
Altars defyld, and holy *things* defast; . . . IV. i. 21. 5
sought to bring all *things* unto decay; . . . IV. i. 29. 4
How she might overthrow the *things* that Concord wrought. . IV. i. 29. 9
All *things* not rooted well will soone be rotten.' . . . IV. i. 51. 5
all *things* did devise, and all *things* dooe, . . . IV. ii. 8. 8
a Fay, and had the skill Of secret *things,* . . . IV. ii. 44. 2
deem'st of *things* divine As of humane, . . . IV. ii. 51. 5
When all men saw this sudden change of *things,* . . . IV. iii. 49. 6
so forged *things* do fairest shew. . . . IV. v. 15. 9
The *things,* that day most minds, at night doe most appeare. . IV. v. 43. 9
Till I thereto had all *things* ready dight. . . . IV. vii. 17. 4
From all forbidden *things* his liking to withdraw. . . . IV. viii. 30. 9
Much dearer be the *things* which come through hard distresse. IV. x. 28. 9
all *things* else, that nourish vitall blood, . . . IV. x. 46. 7
on her waited *things* amisse to mend, . . . IV. xi. 47. 3
all *things* else in time are chaunged quight: . . . V. Pr. 4. 5
all *things* freely grew . . . V. Pr. 9. 7
all *things* secrete wisely could bewray, . . . V. ii. 25. 4
all *things* would reduce unto equality. . . . V. ii. 32. 9
all *things* to an equall to restore, . . . V. ii. 34. 2
'Seest not how badly all *things* present bee, . . . V. ii. 37. 2
'Of *things* unseene how canst thou deeme aright,' . . . V. ii. 39. 1
'Sith thou misdeem'st so much of *things* in sight? . . . V. ii. 39. 3
things subject to thy daily vew . . . V. ii. 42. 8
he of little *things* made reckoning light; . . . V. ii. 44. 2
So feeble skill of perfect *things* the vulgar has. . . . V. iii. 17. 9
vaine it is to deeme of *things* aright, . . . V. iv. 1. 6
tract of time, that all *things* doth decay, . . . V. iv. 8. 1
'For equall right in equall *things* doth stand; . . . V. iv. 19. 1
all *things* quieted, . . . V. iv. 46. 2
gave them gifts and *things* of deare delight. . . . V. iv. 51. 6
this is *things* compacte betwixt you two, . . . V. vi. 16. 7
Then gan the other further to devize Of *things* abrode, . . . V. vi. 20. 8
many *things* demaund, to which she answer'd light. . . . V. vi. 20. 9
talk't of pleasant *things* the night away to weare. . . . V. vi. 22. 9
To shew that she had powre in *things* divine: . . . V. vii. 6. 7
full busily About their holy *things* . . . V. vii. 17. 8
To shew that clemence oft, in *things* amis, . . . V. vii. 22. 8
(As often falles) of sundry *things* did commen: . . . V. ix. 4. 3
sings Hymns to high God, and carols heavenly *things,* . . . V. ix. 29. 5
Of all *things,* to dissemble, fouly may befall!' . . . V. xi. 56. 9
He all *things* did purvay which for them needfull weare. . . V. xii. 10. 9
see not perfect *things* but in a glas: . . . VI. Pr. 5. 5
So tickle is the state of earthly *things,* . . . VI. iii. 5. 2
And moved speach to him of *things* of course, . . . VI. iii. 14. 6
they mote treat of *things* abrode at leasure, . . . VI. iii. 22. 4
speare and shield, as *things* that needlesse were, . . . VI. iv. 7. 8
About the sad Serena *things* to dight, . . . VI. v. 25. 3
having all *things* well about her dight, . . . VI. v. 31. 1
Was wont his howres and holy *things* to bed; . . . VI. v. 35. 7
From *things* that stirre up fraile affection; . . . VI. vi. 7. 7
There whilest he thus was setling *things* above, . . . VI. vi. 37. 1
Thus having all *things* well in peace ordayned, . . . VI. vi. 41. 1
Having his armes and warlike *things* undight, . . . VI. vii. 19. 3
repentaunce for *things* past and gon. . . . VI. viii. 24. 5
when as all *things* readie were aright, . . . VI. viii. 45. 1
discoursing diversly Of sundry *things* as fell, . . . VI. ix. 12. 7
all *things* therein meane, . . . VI. ix. 16. 6
Had ever learn'd to love the lowly *things,* . . . VI. ix. 35. 5
Keeping all noysome *things* away from it, . . . VI. x. 7. 8
since *things* passed none may now restore, . . . VI. x. 20. 8
delt A doubtfull sense of *things,* . . . VI. x. 42. 9
seeking all *things* meete for remedy; . . . VI. xi. 8. 5
Of sundrie *things* he purpose gan to faine, . . . VI. xi. 39. 2
To cherish her with all *things* choice and rare; . . . VI. xii. 14. 7
Tho further asking her of sundry *things,* . . . VI. xii. 20. 1
spake licentious words and hatefull *things* . . . VI. xii. 28. 5
(not pleasd in mortall *things* . . . to raigne) . . . VII. vi. Arg.
Of Change, the which all mortall *things* doth sway, . . . VII. vi. 1. 2
she the face of earthly *things* so changed, . . . VII. vi. 5. 1
learned minds inflameth with desire Of heavenly *things;* . . VII. vii. 2. 6
Can tell *things* doen in heaven so long ygone, . . . VII. vii. 2. 8
all *things* else that under heaven dwell . . . VII. vii. 48. 2
'The *things,* Which we see not how they are mov'd . . . VII. vii. 49. 1
all *things* tost and turned by transverse . . . VII. vii. 56. 3

Things—*Continued.*
all *things* stedfastnesse do hate . . . VII. vii. 58. 2
In all *things* else she beares the greatest sway: . . . VII. viii. 1. 5
love of *things* so vaine to cast away; . . . VII. viii. 1. 7
stedfast rest of all *things,* . . . VII. viii. 2. 3
is close implide, Scorn of base *things,* . . . *Am.* v. 6
Do seeke most pretious *things* . . . *Am.* xv. 2
Yet many wondrous *things* there are beside: . . . *Am.* xvii. 8
That can expresse the life of *things* indeed. . . . *Am.* xvii. 14
easie *things,* that may be got at will, . . . *Am.* xxvi. 11
fire, which all *things* melts, . . . *Am.* xxx. 10
lothe the *things* which they did like before, . . . *Am.* xxxv. 11
a storme, that all *things* doth prostrate; . . . *Am.* lvi. 6
Base *things,* that to her love too bold aspire! . . . *Am.* lxi. 12
It down is weighd with thoght of earthly *things,* . . . *Am.* lxxii. 3
let baser *things* devize To dy in dust, . . . *Am.* lxxv. 9
cannot deeme of worthy *things,* . . . *Am.* lxxxiv. 1
Set all your *things* in seemely good aray, . . . *Epith.* 114
Fray us with *things* that be not: . . . *Epith.* 344
things that are contained Within this goodly cope, . . . *H.L.* 94
Fraile men, whose eyes seek heavenly *things* to see, . . . *H.L.* 118
things hard gotten men more dearely deeme. . . . *H.L.* 168
those heavenly beauties be enfyred As *things* divine, . . . *H.L.* 170
To make al *things* such as we now behold, . . . *H.B.* 30
pleasant grace To all *things* faire, . . . *H.B.* 58
An outward shew of *things* that onely seeme. . . . *H.B.* 91
things immortall no corruption take. . . . *H.B.* 161
Where I may see those admirable *things* . . . *H.H.L.* 3
worlds great frame, in which al *things* Are now containd, . *H.H.L.* 22
Powre, which now doth move In all these *things,* . . . *H.H.L.* 28
loves to get *Things* like himselfe, and to enlarge his race, . *H.H.L.* 52
love, Kindled through sight of those faire *things* above. . . . *H.H.L.* 287
I faine to tell the *things* that I behold, . . . *H.H.B.* 6
enlumineth the . . . aire, whereby al *things* are red; . . . *H.H.B.* 165
In which they see such admirable *things,* . . . *H.H.B.* 260
Or idle thought of earthly *things,* remaine; . . . *H.H.B.* 268
this vile world and these gay-seeming *things;* . . . *H.H.B.* 299

Think. much it grieveth me to *thinke* thereon. . . . *Pet.* i. 3
thinke of heavens blis: . . . *Pet.*[2] vii. 12
thinke, that death shall spoyle your . . . features. . . . *Pet.*[2] vii. 14
You *thinken* to be Lords of the yeare; . . . *S.C.* F. 41
to *thinke* How great sport they gaynen . . . *S.C.* May 35
To blere mine eyes doest *thinke.* . . . *S.C.* Jul. 36
Which when they *thinken* agayne to quench, . . . *S.C.* S. 88
they, that *thinke* themselves the best of all, . . . *Hub.* 181
That men may *thinke* of you in generall, . . . *Hub.* 647
(if we *thinke* good) . . . *Hub.* 970
ever *thinke* a Kingdome is your part.' . . . *Hub.* 1004
Making them *thinke* it but a vision. . . . *Hub.* 1282
They *thinke* to be chiefe praise of Poetry; . . . *T.M.* 555
vainly *thinke* your selves halfe happie then, . . . *Ti.* 199
Thinke him Alcides with the Lyons skin, . . . *Mui.* 71
Ne doo I *thinke,* that that same subtil gin, . . . *Mui.* 369
To *thinke* to ground how that faire blossome fell. . . . *D.* 252
mocking such as *thinke* they long will stay. . . . *D.* 399
thinke that such mishap, as chaunst to me, . . . *D.* 516
Thinke he, that such are for such ones most fit, . . . *As.* Pr. 15
Did *thinke* to match her with the neighbour flood, . . . *Col.* 122
vaine it is to *thinke,* by paragone Of earthly things, . . . *Col.* 344
when I *thinke* of her, as oft I ought, . . . *Col.* 624
I cannot *thinke* according to her worth: . . . *Col.* 627
Yet will I *thinke* of her, yet will I speake, . . . *Col.* 628
In vain I *thinke* . . . to memorize thy name, . . . *Ded. Son.* xii. 1
raise my thoughtes . . . To *thinke* of that true glorious type I. Pr. 4. 7
Much griev'd to *thinke* that gentle Dame so light, . . . I. i. 55. 2
To *thinke* how she through guyleful handeling, . . . I. iii. 2. 4
To *thinke* that knighthood I so much should shame, . . . I. iii. 28. 3
Yet did she *thinke* her pearelesse worth to pas That parentage, I. iv. 11. 3
greevd to *thinke* how foe did him destroy, . . . I. iv. 45. 7
old Sylvanus selfe bethinkes not what To *thinke* . . . I. vi. 16. 4
Soone as I *thinke* upon my bitter bale. . . . I. vii. 39. 6
So thought I eke of him, and *think* I thought aright. . . . I. vii. 49. 9
It booted nought to *thinke* such thunderbolts to beare. . . . I. viii. 7. 9
How dare I *thinke* such glory to attaine?' . . . I. x. 62. 2
To *thinke* of those her captive Parents deare, . . . I. xi. 1. 2
Hart cannot *thinke* what outrage . . . I. xi. 40. 1
It booted nought to *thinke* to robbe him of his pray. . . . I. xi. 41. 9
Who then would *thinke* . . . He could escape fowle death . . . I. xii. 36. 4
To *thinke,* without desert of gentle deed . . . II. iii. 10. 6
never *thinke* that so . . . II. iv. 10. 2
Ne ever thing that she could *think* or see, . . . II. iv. 20. 7
To *thincke* such hideous puissaunce on foot to beare; . . . II. v. 3. 9
think, that ought those puissant hands may marre: . . . II. vi. 44. 8
thinke with how small allowaunce . . . II. vii. 15. 3
did often *thinke* To reach the fruit . . . II. vii. 58. 4
To *thinke* how supper did them long awaite: . . . II. x. 77. 7
It booted not to *thinke* that throw to beare, . . . II. xi. 36. 4
Ne wist he what to *thinke* of that same sight, . . . II. xi. 39. 3
thinke of that fayre visage written in her hart. . . . III. ii. 29. 9
To *thinke* how causelesse, of her owne accord, . . . III. viii. 1. 3
So made him *thinke* him selfe in heven that was in hell. . . III. viii. 19. 9
all . . . doe *thinke* it threates the skye. . . . III. ix. 45. 9
I *thinke* best Here for to stay . . . III. x. 41. 5
Must not here *thinke* to live; . . . III. xi. 14. 9
That dare fro me *thinke* Florimell to take!' . . . IV. ii. 25. 4
Once *thinke* to match three such on equall cost, . . . IV. iii. 24. 8
All which who so dare *thinke* for to enchace, . . . IV. v. 12. 1
she her selfe did *thinke* it doen for spight, . . . IV. v. 17. 3
when he to sleepe did *thinke,* . . . IV. v. 41. 1
thinke with hands impure To spoyle so goodly workmanship . IV. vi. 17. 3

Think—*Continued.*
both of them did *thinke* obedience To doe . . . IV. vi. 21. 8
Ne *thinke* th' affection of her hart to draw . . . IV. vi. 33. 2
bootlesse thing it was to *think* such blowes to beare. . . . IV. vii. 28. 9
even to *thinke* thereof it inly pitties mee. . . . IV. xi. 1. 9
thinke to reckon right. . . . IV. xi. 53. 3
Then gan he *thinke,* . . . IV. xii. 14. 7
Most did she *thinke,* but most she thought amis, . . . IV. xii. 22. 4
Least did she *thinke,* . . . IV. xii. 22. 8
Ne wist he what to *thinke,* or to devise; . . . V. iii. 18. 3
vaine it was to *thinke* from him to flie; . . . V. iii. 38. 2
To *thinke* with how great vaunt of braverie He them abused . V. iii. 39. 7
To *thinke* how this long death thou mightest disinherit.' . . V. v. 36. 9
To *thinke* of him so ill; . . . V. vi. 4. 9
weepe To *thinke* of your nights want, . . . V. vi. 25. 9
There they did *thinke* them selves on her to wreake; . . . V. vi. 37. 1
To *thinke* to follow him that was so swift and light. . . . V. ix. 15. 9
Who then can *thinke* their hedlong ruine to recure? . . . V. x. 26. 9
Such loathly matter were small lust to speake or *thinke.* . . V. xi. 31. 9
to *thinke* gold that is bras; . . . VI. Pr. 5. 7
to *thinke* to save himselfe it booted not. . . . VI. ii. 19. 9
and *thinke* what reliefe Were best devise . . . VI. ii. 46. 3
and groaned inwardly, To *thinke* of this ill state . . . VI. iii. 11. 6
Fearlesse who ought did *thinke* or ought did say, . . . VI. iii. 16. 5
the beast . . . did *thinke* without remorse To be aveng'd . . VI. iv. 20. 8
And makes exceeding mone, when he does *thinke* . . . VI. iv. 32. 2
She made him *think* it surely was his owne; . . . VI. iv. 38. 6
Him booted not to *thinke* them to pursew, . . . VI. v. 22. 8
Asham'd to *thinke* how he that enterprize . . . forslacked had VI. xii. 12. 3
Then gin I *thinke* on that which Nature sayd, . . . VII. viii. 2. 1
thinke not long in taking litle paine . . . *Am.* vi. 13
and *thinke* how she to heaven may clime; . . . *Am.* xiii. 10
Lyke sacred priests that never *thinke* amisse! . . . *Am.* xxii. 8
when I *thinke* to end that I begonne, . . . *Am.* xxiii. 9
I *thinke* that I a new Pandora see, . . . *Am.* xxiv. 8
Do ye not *thinck* th' accomplishment of it Sufficient . . . *Am.* xxxiii. 6
Thinck ever to endure so taedious toyle! . . . *Am.* xxxiii. 10
thinke how litle glory ye have gayned . . . *Am.* xxxvi. 10
That nether I may speake nor *thinke* at all, . . . *Am.* xliii. 7
thinck they dy with pleasure, live with payne. . . . *Am.* xlvii. 14
And greater glory *thinke,* to save then spill. . . . *Am.* xlix. 4
glory *thinke* to make these cruel stoures. . . . *Am.* lvii. 10
'*Think* now . . . how great the smart Of those . . . *Epig.* iv. 35
would I *thinke* these paines no paines at all, . . . *H.L.* 299
What . . . thought can *think* the depth of so deare wound? . . . *H.H.L.* 163
And onely *thinke* on that before them set. . . . *H.H.B.* 266

Thinking. in *thinking* on hir I burne and quake. . . . *Pet.*[1] vi. 2
That *thinking* yet on her I burne and quake; . . . *Pet.*[2] vi. 2
Thinking that their disgracing did him grace: . . . *Hub.* 708
Thinking indeed that it the Lyon was. . . . *Hub.* 1093
thinking of those braunches greene to frame A girlond . . . I. ii. 30. 6
Thinking to overthrowe and downe him tred: . . . II. viii. 49. 7
thinking for to make her stubborne corage quayle. . . . III. viii. 40. 9
Thinking to worke on her his utmost wracke, . . . IV. vi. 21. 2
Thinking to hide the depth by troubling of the flood. . . . IV. vi. 29. 9
thinking to let her weet The great tormenting griefe . . . IV. viii. 9. 7
Full farre was I from *thinking* such a pranke; . . . V. i. 15. 4
Thinking to have her griefe by death bereaved: . . . V. iv. 10. 4
Thinking at once both head and helmet to have raced. . . . V. v. 11. 9
thinking to follow fast His other fellow Pagan . . . V. viii. 8. 8
thinking best by counterfet disguise . . . V. viii. 25. 1
Thinking to pay him with that one for all: . . . V. xi. 8. 6
Thinking the utmost of their force to trie, . . . VI. i. 38. 3
With *thinking* to what case her name should now be brought: VI. iii. 6. 9
Thinking by speed to overtake his flight; . . . VI. v. 17. 2
Thinking to take them from that hylding hound; . . . VI. v. 25. 7
there *thinking* him to hyde: . . . VI. vi. 28. 4
Thinking to quench her thirst at the next brooke: . . . *Am.* lxvii. 8

Thinks. *thinkes* to throwe out thondring words . . . *S.C.* O. 104
All night she *thinks* too long, and often lookes for light. . I. iii. 15. 9
by my ruines *thinkes* to make them great: . . . I. v. 25. 8
His owne fayre Dryope now he *thinkes* not faire, . . . I. vi. 15. 8
Then *thinkes* what punishment were best assign'd, . . . VII. vi. 48. 8
Ne *thinks* of other heaven, . . . *Am.* lxxii. 11
Thinks more upon her paradise of joyes, . . . *Epith.* 366
Ne *thinks* on ought but how it to attaine; . . . *H.L.* 205
ne *thinks* how erst she did her hide. . . . II. iii. 36. 9
th' evill *thinkes* by watching to prevent: . . . III. x. 3. 6
Who ever *thinkes* through confidence of might, . . . VI. ii. 23. 7
Who *thinkes* from me his sorrow all doth rize. . . . VI. iv. 33. 7
Thinks of her Dairy to make wondrous gaine, . . . VII. vi. 48. 2

Third. sithens is but the *third* morowe . . . *S.C.* Mar. 46
Such one was Lechery, the *third* of all this traine. . . . I. iv. 26. 9
The *third* had of their wardrobe custody, . . . I. x. 39. 1
fights Two days incessantly: The *third* him overthrowes, . . . I. xi. Arg.
I meant to purge both with a *third* mischiefe, . . . II. iv. 31. 3
the *third* brunt of this my fatall brond: . . . II. viii. 37. 8
the *third* for shame did blush, . . . II. ix. 35. 6
The *third* things past could keep in memoree: . . . II. ix. 49. 3
that same *third* Fort, that is the Smell, . . . II. xi. 11. 1
Of that *third* troupe was cruelly assayd; . . . II. xi. 11. 2
when appeared the *third* Morrow bright . . . II. xii. 2. 4
the *third* time shall fayre accordaunce make: . . . III. iii. 30. 7
the *third* time shall rew his foolhardise: . . . III. iii. 35. 7
'Yet shall a *third* both these and thine subdew. . . . III. iii. 47. 1
the *third* time Could scarce recovered bee . . . III. iv. 35. 1
the *third* brother him did sore assay, . . . III. v. 21. 3
'The *third* a Damzell was of low degree, . . . III. vii. 59. 1
a *third* kingdom yet is to arise . . . III. ix. 44. 6
Two things he feared, but the *third* was death; . . . III. x. 2. 6

Third—*Continued.*
both their lives may likewise be annext Unto the *third*, . . . IV. ii. 52. 9
The *third* dayes prize unto that straunger Knight, ... IV. v. 8. 1
The *third*, the goodly Barow . . . . . IV. xi. 43. 5
The *third* was Brunell, famous in his dayes; . . . . . V. iii. 5. 5
The *third* day came, that should due tryall lend . . . . . V. iii. 8. 1
the *third* time out of an hidden shade . . . . . V. xi. 22. 3
The *third*, nor strong nor wise, but spightfullest, Defetto. . . VI. v. 13. 9
The *third*, my love, my lifes last ornament, ... *Am.* lxxiv. 9
in their place doth now a *third* appeare, ... *Com. Son.* iv. 9
Together with that *third* from them derived, ... *H.H.L.* 38

Thirst. lukewarm blood . . . her *thirst* for to asswage. . . . *Bel.*² vi. 8
Quenching the gasping furrowes *thirst* with rayne? . . . . *S.C.* Ap. 6
throat through *thirst* to nought nigh being dride . . . . . *Gn.* 387
Having all satisfide their bloudy *thurst*, ... I. i. 26. 4
Will die for *thrist*, (**thirst*) and water doth refuse? . . . II. iv. 17. 8
For *thirst* of single kingdom him he kild. . . . . II. x. 21. 5
O! the greedy *thirst* of royall crowne, ... II. x. 35. 1
To seeke young men to quench her flaming *thrust*, ... III. vii. 50. 2
full glad for *thirst*, ech drunk an harty draught; . . . . . IV. iii. 48. 9
drinke of every brooke when *thirst* my throte doth boyle. . . VI. ix. 23. 9
Thinking to quench her *thirst* at the next brooke: . . . . *Am.* lxvii. 8

Thirsted. dronke with blood, yet *thristed* after life: . . . . . I. vi. 38. 8

Thirstiness. embayes In the cool soile, after long *thirstinesse*, III. xii. 44. *or.* 8

Thirsty. *See* **Bloodthirsty.**
Adowne thy cheeke, to quenche thy *thristye* payne. . . . . *S.C.* Ap. 8
who can counsell a *thristie* soule, ... *S.C.* May 138
alwayes flow to quench his *thirstie* heate. . . . . *Gn.* 120
the *thirsty* land Dronke up his life; . . . . . I. iii. 20. 4
his *thristy* (**thirstie*) blade To bathe in blood . . . . . I. v. 15. 2
There *thristy* (**thirstie*) Tantalus hong by the chin; . . . . I. v. 35. 5
His office was the . . . *thristy* give to drinke; . . . . . I. x. 38. 3
Therein did often quench his *thristy* heat, ... II. v. 30. 6
Offred him drinke to quench his *thirstie* heat, ... VI. ix. 6. 8

Thirty. In sixe and *thirtie* thousand yeares is ronne, ... *Ro.* xxii. 10
Selfe have I worne out thrise *threttie* yeares, ... *S.C.* F. 17
thirty sorts of fish, and *thirty* sundry streames. . . . . . IV. xi. 35. 9
Nigh *thirtie* minutes to the Southerne lake; . . . . . V. Pr. 7. 8

This (*partial list*).
Threwe downe *this* building to the lowest stone. . . . . . *Bel.*¹ ii. 14
Nor *thys*, nor that, so muche doeth make me mourne, . . . *S.C.* Ap. 9
tell many lesinges of *this* and that, ... *S.C.* May 285
Beare witnesse all of *thys* so wicked deede: . . . . . *S.C.* Jun. 108
some pretext Of *this*, or that, ... *Hub.* 989
The precious store of *this* celestiall riches? . . . . . *T.M.* 146
what hard mishap is *this*, That hath . . . . . I. iii. 39. 2
when *this* breathlesse woxe, that batteil gan renew. . . . . II. viii. 47. 9
tempted her with *this* or that, ... III. viii. 39. 1
Barkes, *this* caried with the tide, That with the wind, . . . IV. ix. 26. 7
to corrupt Molanna, *this* her maid, ... VII. vi. 43. 2
vertue have or *this* or that to make, ... VII. vii. 54. 7

Thistle-down. as a *thistle-downe* in th' ayre doth flie, ... *Hub.* 634

Thiswise. *this wise* You to molest, ... II. ix. 42. 2

Thither. Make hast, ye shepheards, *thether* to revert: . . . . *S.C.* N. 191
holde A Visitation, and them cyted *thether*: . . . . . *Hub.* 569
For *thither* they themselves meant to addresse, ... *Hub.* 657
Which *thether* came to heare their musick sweet, ... *T.M.* 32
being driven hence, I *thether* fly. . . . . . *T.M.* 528
Had not good hap those shepheards *thether* led. . . . . . *As.* 144
Did *thether* flock to see what they did heare . . . . . *As.* 202
Whether allured . . . Or *thither* led by chaunce, ... *Col.* 63
For the coole shade him *thither* hastly got: . . . . . I. ii. 29. 2
All bare through peoples feet which *thether* traveiled. . . . I. iv. 2. 9
Thether Duessa badd him bend his pace, ... I. iv. 3. 7
Cursing high Jove, the which them *thither* sent. . . . . I. v. 33. 6
Which *thither* were assembled day by day . . . . . I. v. 51. 2
Her to behold do *thither* runne apace; . . . . . I. vi. 18. 2
And now he *thither* came for like intent; . . . . . I. vi. 30. 5
From every coast . . . Have *thither* come . . . . . I. vii. 45. 4
For whose deliverance she this Prince doth *thither* guyd. . . I. viii. 1. 9
'*Thither* the great magicien Merlin came, ... I. ix. 5. 1
thought From heaven to come, or *thither* to arise; . . . . . I. x. 4. 2
ship . . . knowes her port, and *thither* sayles by ayme, . . . II. vi. 10. 3
Which choosing . . . They *thither* marcht: . . . . . II. ix. 10. 6
open stood to all Which *thither* came; . . . . . II. xii. 46. 3
Lover, whom, . . . she from farre did *thither* bring: . . . . II. xii. 72. 4
old Glauce *thither* led Faire Britomart, ... III. iii. 59. 6
fortune *thither* brought Comfort to him . . . . . III. v. 27. 3
Thither they brought that wounded Squyre, ... III. v. 41. 1
Forthy she *thither* cast her course t' apply, ... III. vi. 16. 8
Till *thither* they retourne where first they grew: . . . . . III. vi. 33. 8
With many . . . Which *thither* haunt, ... III. vi. 49. 3
Thither resortes, and, . . . playes his wanton partes. . . . III. vi. 49. 8
askt, what devill had her *thither* brought, ... III. vii. 8. 2
rudely askte her, how she *thither* came? . . . . . III. viii. 23. 6
His charett swifte in hast he *thither* steard, ... III. viii. 30. 7
Thither he brought the sory Florimell, ... III. viii. 38. 1
Another knight, whom tempest *thither* brought, ... III. ix. 12. 2
passage bard to all that *thither* came, ... III. xii. 43. 4
unhappy houre me *thither* brought, ... IV. vii. 18. 1
what evill guide Them *thether* brought, ... IV. viii. 21. 3
I *thether* went; where I did long conceale . . . . . IV. viii. 55. 4
thither with her came, ... IV. xii. 3. 8
Therefore me *thither* lead.' . . . . . V. ii. 10. 8
thether also came in open sight . . . . . V. viii. 14. 1
for triall of her right . . . Did *thither* come; . . . . . V. xi. 39. 6
not for such slaughters sake He *thether* came, ... V. xii. 8. 8
Thether he brought these unacquainted guests, ... VI. iv. 14. 1
Him *thether* eke, . . . He followed fast, ... VI. ix. 4. 5
beast they saw, which he had *thether* brought. . . . . VI. ix. 5. 9

Thither—*Continued.*
Till time that Calidore brought Pastorella *thether*. . . . . VI. xii. 10. 9
Which of her Nymphes, . . . Him *thither* brought, ... VII. vi. 51. 6
thither also came all other creatures, ... VII. vii. 4. 1

Thitherward. Great troupes of people traveild *thetherward* . . I. iv. 3. 1
suffer Sleepe once *thither-ward* Approch, ... II. vii. 25. 5
thitherward forthright his ready way did make. . . . . V. ii. 10. 9
All arm'd to point came ryding *thetherward*; . . . . . VI. v. 11. 3

Tho. I saw the heavens warre against hir *tho*, ... *Bel.*¹ xi. 12
Tho to a hill his faynting flocke he ledde, ... *S.C.* Ja. 11
Tho gynne you, fond flyes! . . . . . *S.C.* F. 39
Tho wouldest thou learne to caroll of Love, ... *S.C.* F. 61
Tho wouldest thou pype of Phyllis prayse; . . . . . *S.C.* F. 63
tho gan this proude weede . . . . . *S.C.* F. 160
Tho downe . . . he fell forthwith. . . . . . *S.C.* F. 218
Tho shall we sporten in delight, ... *S.C.* Mar. 19
Tho will we little Love awake, ... *S.C.* Mar. 22
Tho, peeping close . . . , Might see . . . . . *S.C.* Mar. 73
Tho pumie stones I hastly hent . . . . . *S.C.* Mar. 89
Tho sayd, he was a winged lad, ... *S.C.* Mar. 112
Tho to the greene Wood they speeden hem all, ... *S.C.* May 27
Tho with them wends what they spent . . . . . *S.C.* May 69
Well ywis was it with shepheards *thoe*: . . . . . *S.C.* May 109
Tho gan shepheards swaines to looke aloft, ... *S.C.* May 124
Tho, . . . somewhile There crept in Wolves, ... *S.C.* May 126
Tho marking him with melting eyes, ... *S.C.* May 207
Tho went the pensife Damme out of dore, ... *S.C.* May 229
Tho . . . Prevelie he peeped out . . . . . *S.C.* May 251
Tho he . . . Thus medled his talke . . . . . *S.C.* May 262
Tho out of his packe a glasse he tooke, ... *S.C.* May 274
Tho opened he the dore, ... *S.C.* May 278
Tho shewed his ware . . . . . *S.C.* May 287
Tho . . . she saw the merchaundise . . . . . *S.C.* May 298
Tho couth I sing of love, ... *S.C.* Jun. 41
Tho would I seeke for Queene-apples . . . . . *S.C.* Jun. 43
In *tho* countryes, whereas I have bene, ... *S.C.* S. 32
Tho may we talke and tellen our fill, ... *S.C.* S. 53
Tho at midnight he would barke . . . . . *S.C.* S. 190
Tho . . . This Wolvish sheepe woulde catchen his pray, . . . *S.C.* S. 196
Of love and lustihead *tho* mayst thou sing, ... *S.C.* O. 51
Tho gan the streames . . . to cease, ... *S.C.* O. 71
Tho deemed I my spring would ever laste. . . . . . *S.C.* D. 30
'*Tho* gan my lovely Spring bid me farewel, ... *S.C.* D. 55
His yron-headed spade *tho* making cleene, ... *Gn.* 653
Tho on his head his dreadfull hat he dight, ... *Hub.* 1279
Lord! how he gan for to bestirre him *tho*, ... *Mui.* 252
Tho when the pang was somewhat overpast, ... *D.* 554
Tho (as he wild) unto his loved lasse, ... *As.* 147
Tho, wrapping up her wrethed sterne arownd, ... I. i. 18. 5
Tho can she weepe, ... I. i. 50. 8
End of the doubtfull battaile deemed *tho* . . . . . I. v. 11. 7
Tho mov'd with wrath, . . . he cast avengd to be, ... I. v. 12. 5
Tho, gathering up the reliques . . . . . I. v. 39. 6
Tho gan to him discover . . . . . I. v. 41. 5
Tho, when her well of teares she wasted had, She said; . . . I. viii. 42. 5
Tho, when he saw no power . . . . . I. xi. 42. 1
Tho to him louting lowly . . . . . II. iii. 13. 4
Tho, hurling high his yron braced arme, ... II. v. 7. 5
Tho gan that villein wex so fiers and strong, ... II. v. 23. 1
Tho up he started, stird with shame extreme, ... II. vi. 27. 7
Tho him she brought abord, ... II. vi. 38. 1
Tho, turning to those brethren, thus bespoke: . . . . . II. viii. 27. 1
Tho, when this breathlesse woxe, that batteil gan renew. . . II. viii. 47. 9
Tho, turning soft aside, he did inquyre . . . . . II. ix. 39. 6
Tho Madan raignd, unworthie of his race, ... II. x. 21. 1
Tho, when feeble age . . . he saw proceed, ... II. x. 27. 6
Tho to his daughter Regan he repayrd, ... II. x. 30. 6
Tho, when he felt him dead, adowne he kest . . . . . II. xi. 42. 5
Tho up he caught him twixt his puissant hands, ... II. xi. 46. 1
Tho, cumming to his Squyre that kept his steed, ... II. xi. 48. 2
Tho, when appeared the third Morrow bright . . . . . II. xii. 2. 4
Tho lifting up his vertuous staffe on hye. . . . . . II. xii. 26. 6
Tho gan she myldly of them to inquyre . . . . . III. i. 23. 8
Tho were the tables taken all away; . . . . . III. i. 56. 6
Tho, when the Britonesse saw all the rest Avoided . . . . III. i. 58. 5
Tho, whenas all were put to shamefull flight, ... III. i. 67. 1
Tho, her avizing of the vertues rare . . . . . III. ii. 22. 7
Tho gan she to renew her former smart, ... III. ii. 29. 8
'*Tho*, when the terme is full accomplishid, ... III. iii. 48. 1
Tho to their ready Steedes they clombe full light, ... III. iii. 61. 6
Tho having vewd awhile the surges hore . . . . . III. iv. 7. 4
Tho, full of bitter griefe and pensife thought, ... III. iv. 31. 5
Tho when the lilly handed Liagore . . . Did feele his pulse, III. iv. 41. 1
Tho, up him taking in their tender hands, ... III. iv. 42. 1
Tho, when her wayes he could no more descry, ... III. iv. 53. 1
Her selfe, well as I might, I reskewd *tho*, ... III. v. 6. 4
Tho to his brethren came, ... III. v. 15. 5
Tho gan the battaile freshly to begin; . . . . . III. v. 22. 5
Tho when that villayn he aviz'd, ... III. vii. 23. 1
Tho gan she gather up her garments rent, ... III. vii. 11. 1
Tho when all other helpes she saw to faile, ... III. vii. 21. 6
Tho fast her clipping twixt his armes . . . . . III. viii. 10. 1
Tho rudely askte her, ... III. viii. 23. 6
Tho to him yode, ... III. viii. 45. 6
Tho hastily remounting . . . . . III. ix. 15. 1
Tho, whenas vailed was her lofty crest, ... III. ix. 20. 3
Tho, when againe he him bethought to live, ... III. x. 7. 6
Tho forth the Boaster marching brave begonne . . . . . III. x. 33. 5
Tho up they gan their mery pypes to trusse, ... III. x. 46. 1
Tho gan he her perswade to leave . . . . . III. x. 51. 1

Tho—*Continued.*
Tho stouping downe she him amoved light; . . . . III. xi. 13. 1
Tho, as she backward cast her busie eye . . . . III. xi. 50. 1
Tho, whenas chearelesse Night ycovered had . . . . III. xii. 1. 1
Tho, blinding him againe, his way he forth did take. . . . . III. xii. 23. 9
Tho, when she felt her selfe to be unbownd . . . . III. xii. 38. 8
Tho each to other did his faith engage, ... IV. ii. 28. 5
Tho unto Satyran she was adjudged, ... IV. v. 22. 1
Tho gan he swell in every inner part . . . . IV. vi. 7. 4
Tho, when they had long time there taken rest, ... IV. vi. 42. 1
Tho, when he long had marked his demeanor, ... IV. vii. 47. 1
Tho, when they both recovered were . . . . IV. viii. 21. 1
Tho, soone as day discovered heavens face . . . . IV. viii. 34. 1
Tho, shaking off all doubt . . . . IV. x. 53. 6
Tho with her sword on him she flatling strooke, ... V. v. 18. 1
Tho gan she tell her all that she had donne, ... V. v. 45. 8
Tho turning all his pride to humblesse meeke, ... V. vii. 16. 1
Tho, when she had his execution stayd, ... V. vii. 37. 1
Tho when as Artegall did Arthure vew, ... V. viii. 12. 6
Tho, when she saw that she was forst to fight, ... V. xi. 27. 1
Tho with her huge long taile she at him strooke, ... V. xi. 28. 6
Tho, as they rode together on their way, ... V. xi. 43. 6
Tho when they came to the sea coast . . . . V. xii. 4. 1
Tho, as he backe returned from that land, ... V. xii. 28. 1
Tho, looking up . . . . VI. i. 17. 4
Tho wexing weary . . . . VI. iii. 29. 3
Tho on his shield he griple hold did lay, ... VI. iv. 6. 7
Tho, backe returning to that sorie Dame, ... VI. v. 4. 1
Tho when they did perceave Their wounds recur'd, ... VI. vi. 15. 6
Tho all in rage he on him streight did seaze, ... VI. vi. 40. 5
Tho, when he up did looke . . . . VI. vii. 48. 7
Tho when as all her plaints she had displayd, ... VI. viii. 34. 1
Tho, when as all things readie were aright, ... VI. viii. 45. 1
Tho, having fed his fill, ... VI. ix. 7. 6
Tho when they had their hunger slaked well, ... VI. ix. 18. 1
Tho, backe returning to my sheepe againe, ... VI. ix. 25. 7
Tho gan that shepheard thus for to dilate: . . . . VI. x. 21. 1
Tho, when as he was dead, the fray gan ceasse; . . . . . . VI. xi. 20. 3
Tho, to him running fast, ... VI. xi. 28. 1
Tho, when the Shepheard breathed had awhyle, ... VI. xi. 30. 1
Tho Coridon he prayd . . . To wend with him, ... VI. xi. 35. 1
Tho, to the place when they approched nye, ... VI. xi. 36. 5
Tho, sitting downe by them upon the greene, ... VI. xi. 39. 1
Tho, when as towards darksome night it drew, ... VI. xi. 41. 1
Tho, when no more could nigh to him approch, ... VI. xi. 47. 1
Tho gan Sir Calidore him to advize Of his first quest, . . . VI. xii. 12. 1
A little mayde, the which ye chylded *tho;* . . . . VI. xii. 17. 7
Tho further asking her of sundry things, ... VI. xii. 20. 1
Tho, wondring long at those so straunge events, ... VI. xii. 20. 7
Tho, rearing up his former feete on hight, ... VI. xii. 29. 7
Tho, when the Beast saw he mote nought availe By force, . . VI. xii. 33. 1
Tho, as her manner was on sunny day, ... VII. vi. 45. 6

Thomalin. *Thomalin,* why sytten we soe, ... *S.C.* Mar. 1
Thomalin, have no care for-thy; . . . . *S.C.* Mar. 37
Thomalin, I pittie thy plight, ... *S.C.* Mar. 103
the little what, That *Thomalin* can sayne. . . . . *S.C.* Jul. 32

Thomiris. *See* **Tomyris.**

Thorn. as treading still on *thorne:* . . . . III. x. 55. 4

Thorns. With *thornes* together pind and patched was, ... I. ix. 36. 2
Scattred with bushy *thornes* and ragged breares, ... I. x. 35. 3
sharp *thornes* and breres the way forstall, ... III. i. 46. 7
nycely trode, as *thornes* lay in his way, ... III. xii. 10. 6
With *thornes* and barren brakes environd round, ... IV. i. 20. 5
like *thornes* did pricke his gealous hart, ... IV. v. 31. 3
Ne feeles the *thornes* and thickets pricke her tender toes. . . IV. vii. 21. 9

Thorough. *See* **Through.**
waves, but *thorough* them did passe . . . . *Col.* 222
no living wight May ever passe, but *thorough* great distresse.' I. i. 32. 3
thorough daily care . . . He led a wretched life, ... I. iv. 28. 7
thorough grace hath gained victory: . . . . I. x. 1. 7
when it locked none might *thorough* pas, ... II. ix. 23. 7
as *thorough* them she went, ... II. xii. 45. 2
none might *thorough* breake, nor overstride. . . . . III. vi. 31. 4
thorough rude confusion of the rout, Some fearing shriekt, . IV. iii. 41. 6
Nor read the salvage cuntreis *thorough* which they pace. . . IV. xi. 40. 9
Thorough the midst of them . . . . V. vi. 39. 3
That, *thorough* evill rest of this last night, ... V. vii. 18. 7
thorough some more mighty enemies wrong . . . . VI. i. 11. 3
thorough fate . . . I my countrie have forlorne, ... VI. ii. 27. 7
passed *thorough* that daies paine, ... VI. iii. 17. 7
themselves prepard *thorough* the foord to ride. . . . . . . VI. iii. 30. 9
Beare off their blowes from percing *thorough* quite: . . . . VI. v. 18. 5
a lewd foole her leading *thorough* dry and wet. . . . . . . VI. vi. 16. 9

Thoroughly. Yet could it not so *thoroughly* digest, ... V. v. 27. 3
ere he coulde reforme it *thoroughly,* . . . . V. xii. 27. 1

Thorough-piercing. thrild with point of *thorough-piercing* paine: . . . . II. i. 38. 5

Those (*partial list*).
let *those* deep Abysses open rive, ... *Ro.* i. 7
Those, those thy foes, *those* warriours far remove, ... II. v. 16. 5
The honour of the prize should be adjudg'd by *those.* . . . . V. iii. 13. 9
Whether *those* same on high, or these belowe; . . . . VII. vii. 20. 2

Thou (*partial list*). *See* **Thous.**
Thyne be the cossette, well hast *thow* it gotte. . . . . . . *S.C.* N. 206
If shee were thine, and *thou* as now am I? . . . . III. xi. 19. 4
Is this the hope . . . *Thou* brings? . . . . VI. iii. 4. 8

Though (*partial list*).
though ye be the fairest of Gods creatures, ... *Pet.*[2] vii. 13
though your frames do for a time make warre . . . . *Ro.* vii. 9
though she owe her fall to the first winde, ... *Ro.* xxviii. 9

Though—*Continued.*
France brought forth, *though* fruitfull of brave wits, ... *Ro.* Env. 2
Is but a jest, *though* envie it abuse: . . . . *Gn.* 6
Backe to be borne, *though* it unlawfull were. . . . . *Gn.* 464
Yet *though* his vesture were but meane and bace, ... *Hub.* 229
Livings in Court be gotten, *though* full hard; . . . . *Hub.* 514
Upon this Common-place, (*though* plaine, not wourst?) . . . *Hub.* 542
For, *though* the vulgar yeeld an open eare, ... *Hub.* 713
Though all men him uncased gan deride, ... *Hub.* 930
Though eating hipps, and drinking watry fome. . . . . . . *Hub.* 948
Loath was the Ape, *though* praised, to adventer, ... *Hub.* 1005
For *though* to steale the Diademe away . . . . *Hub.* 1034
hee Would violate, *though* not with violence, ... *Hub.* 1163
With horrid sound *though* having little sence, ... *T.M.* 554
Though nought at all but ruines now I bee, ... *Ti.* 39
Ne Troynovant, *though* elder sister shee, ... *Ti.* 102
though at last by force I conquered were . . . . *Ti.* 113
though Time all moniments obscure, ... *Ti.* 174
Though death his soule doo from his bodie sever; . . . . . . *Ti.* 257
for memorie Of her pretended crime, *though* crime none were: *Mui.* 143
Not thou, O Clarion! *though* fairest thou . . . . *Mui.* 233
Though of sorrowe heavilie can sing; . . . . *D.* 12
(Signe of thy love, *though* nought for my reliefe, ... *D.* 94
though by kind shee stout and salvage were, ... *D.* 121
cald . . . Of others Penthia, *though* not so well: . . . . . . *As.* 194
And there is Corydon *though* meanly waged, ... *Col.* 382
Though fit to frame an everlasting dittie, ... *Col.* 385
skill, *though* knowen yet to few; . . . . *Col.* 401
there, *though* last not least, is Aetion, ... *Col.* 444
Whose goodly beames *though* they be overdight . . . . . . *Col.* 493
Neaera ours, not theirs, *though* there she be; . . . . *Col.* 525
Though nought my praises of her needed arre, ... *Col.* 533
praise her worth, *though* far my wit above. . . . . *Col.* 942
though nowe too late To wish you backe returne . . . . . . I. i. 13. 2
For *though* a tree I seme, yet cold and heat me paines.' . . . I. ii. 33. 9
Though true as touch, *though* daughter of a king, ... I. iii. 2. 5
Though faire as ever living wight was fayre, ... I. iii. 2. 6
Though nor in word nor deede ill meriting, ... I. iii. 2. 7
truest knight alive, *Though* conquered now he lye . . . . . I. iii. 37. 7
the old man well knew he, *though* untold, ... I. iii. 38. 7
though good lucke prolonged hath thy date, ... I. ix. 45. 7
virgins were; *Though* spousd, ... I. x. 4. 7
though they faulty were, yet well he wayd, ... I. x. 40. 5
Though false Duessa, . . . Her false sleightes doe imploy. . . I. xii. Arg.
Which *though* he hath polluted oft of yore, ... I. xii. 27. 7
Tho' she thy Lady be, ... II. iv. 26. 6
And, *though* he scornd his ydle vanitee, ... II. iv. 39. 7
Though otherwise it did him litle harme: . . . . II. v. 7. 4
Matter of merth enough, *though* there were none, ... II. vi. 3. 7
And all, *though* pleasaunt, yet she made much more: . . . . II. vi. 24. 5
They, *though* full bent To prove extremities . . . . II. vi. 36. 1
Though somewhat moved in his mightie hart, ... II. vi. 40. 3
though himselfe were at the sight dismayd, ... II. vii. 6. 8
Though all the wealth . . . Could gathered be . . . . II. vii. 31. 7
And *though* they both stood stiffe, ... II. viii. 41. 9
lively is the semblaunt, *though* the substance dead.' . . . . II. ix. 2. 9
Here may ye not have entraunce, *though* we would: . . . . . II. ix. 12. 4
though they bodies seem, yet substaunce from them fades. . . II. ix. 15. 9
that proud towre of Troy, *though* richly guilt, ... II. ix. 45. 8
though somewhat they declind; . . . . II. ix. 55. 4
Ne yet Mathusalem, *though* longest liv'd; . . . . II. ix. 57. 2
Which *though* from earth it be derived right . . . . II. x. 2. 4
From Guendolene his wife, *though* alwaies faithful prov'd. . . II. x. 17. 9
Yet lives his memorie, *though* carcas sleepe in rest. . . . . II. x. 43. 9
though overcome in haplesse fight, ... II. x. 56. 8
our Selfe, whom *though* we do not see, Yet . . . . II. xii. 47. 8
though no reason may apply Salve . . . . III. ii. 36. 4
Though straunge beginning had, yet fixed is . . . . III. ii. 42. 2
For *though* my love be not so lewdly bent . . . . III. ii. 43. 2
So was their fortune good, *though* wicked were their minde. . III. ii. 43. 9
'But wicked fortune mine, *though* minde be good, ... III. ii. 44. 1
though beyond the Africk Ismael . . . he were, ... III. iii. 6. 7
may not shrinck, *though* all the world do shake; . . . . . . III. iii. 25. 7
And *though,* oft looking backward, well she vewde . . . . . III. iv. 50. 6
That loves his fetters, *though* they were of gold. . . . . . . III. ix. 8. 5
willing all things to excuse, *Though* nought belev'd, ... III. ix. 18. 9
And Paridell, *though* partly discontent . . . . III. ix. 25. 1
Though whilome far much greater then thy fame, ... III. ix. 33. 3
whereto *though* she did bend Her earnest minde, ... III. xi. 54. 8
was nought ydred, *Though* much emmov'd, ... III. xii. 2. 9
For *though* sweet love to conquer glorious bee, ... IV. x. 3. 8
Though all the pillours of the one were guilt, ... IV. x. 5. 8
'But I, *though* meanest man of many moe, ... IV. x. 19. 1
Though of contrarie natures each to other: . . . . IV. x. 32. 5
Rich Oranochy, *though* but knowen late; . . . . IV. xi. 21. 7
Ne storming Humber, *though* he looked stout; . . . . IV. xi. 30. 7
And shall see Stamford, *though* now homely hid, ... IV. xi. 35. 4
Eden, *though* but small, Yet often stainde with bloud . . . IV. xi. 36. 7
Though I them all . . . Cannot recount, ... IV. xi. 40. 7
For *though* their numbers do much more surmount, ... IV. xii. 2. 8
bred Of mortall sire, *though* of immortall wombe, ... IV. xii. 4. 2
'*Though* vaine, I see, my sorrowes to unfold, ... IV. xii. 6. 1
I will them tell *though* unto no man neare: . . . . IV. xii. 6. 4
Yet *though* he never list to me relent, ... IV. xii. 7. 6
And *though* unto his will she given were, ... IV. xii. 15. 6
would some rightfull cause pretend, *though* rightly nought.' . IV. xii. 30. 9
though his limbs could not his bodie beare, ... IV. xii. 35. 3
Though vertue then were held in highest price, ... V. i. 1. 1
That she might win some time, *though* dearly bought, ... V. ii. 23. 7
What *though* the sea . . . Doe eate the earth, ... V. ii. 39. 4

Though—*Continued.*
(*though* no more . . . there neede ones right to trie, ... V. iii. 32. 1
so mad For any death to chaunge life, *though* most bad: . . V. iv. 11. 5
And *though* my land he first did winne away, ... V. iv. 14. 6
And then my love, (*though* now it little skill) . . . . . . V. iv. 14. 7
Yet, *though* him selfe did shame . . . His mighty hand to shend, V. iv. 24. 3
And, *though* powre faild, her courage did accrew; . . . . . V. v. 7. 4
Doth seeme to be her selfe, *though* darkned be her light. . . V. v. 12. 9
And *though* he still retyr'd, yet nathelesse . . . . V. v. 14. 5
For *though* that he first victorie obtayned, ... V. v. 17. 6
For *though* this cloud have now me overcast, ... V. v. 38. 6
And *though* (unlike) they should for ever last, ... V. v. 38. 8
who, *though* she still have worne Her dayes in warre, . . . V. v. 40. 4
Who *though* desirous rather to rest mute, ... V. vi. 20. 3
Ne doffe her armes, *though* he her much besought: . . . . V. vi. 23. 5
Wherewith *though* wondrous wroth, and inly burning . . . V. vi. 31. 1
And her late vile reproch *though* vaunted vaine, ... V. vii. 34. 4
Where, *though* revengefull vow she did professe, ... V. vii. 36. 3
his shield . . . *Though* nothing whole, but all to-brusd . . . V. viii. 44. 2
Though also those mote question'd be aright, ... V. ix. 40. 7
Though plaine she saw, by all that she did heare, ... V. ix. 50. 3
But Justice, *though* her dome she doe prolong, ... V. xi. 1. 5
whose wrongs *though* long She suffred, ... V. xi. 1. 7
Though I this dearest life for her doe spend.' . . . . V. xi. 43. 4
Is mine owne love, *though* me she have forlore, ... V. xi. 49. 7
Though darts from shore and stones they at him threw; . V. xii. 5. 5
Which none durst breake, *though* many would right faine . . V. xii. 10. 5
though she hungrily Earst chawd thereon, ... V. xii. 39. 5
though it on a lowly stalke doe bowre, ... VI. Pr. 4. 3
Wilt give thy beard, *though* it but little bee? . . . . VI. i. 19. 8
Who, *though* he were still in this desert wood, ... VI. v. 2. 2
wend abrode, *though* feeble and forlorne, ... VI. v. 7. 3
Though many foes did him maligne therefore, ... VI. v. 12. 6
And eke his Lady, *though* she sickely were, ... VI. vi. 17. 8
that wylde man; whom *though* he oft forbad, ... VI. vi. 18. 7
Though of meane parentage and kindred base, ... VI. vii. 28. 4
Who, *though* she were with wearinesse nigh dead, ... VI. vii. 40. 8
Slay not that Carle, *though* worthy to be slaine, ... VI. viii. 17. 7
That *though* the night did cover her disgrace, ... VI. viii. 51. 3
Though meane her lot, yet higher did her mind ascend. . . . VI. ix. 10. 9
Which *though* it were a cottage clad with lome, ... VI. ix. 16. 5
The fruite of joy and blisse, *though* long time dearely bought. VI. ix. 45. 9
though in it She used most to keepe . . . . VI. x. 9. 6
But Calidore, *though* no lesse sory wight . . . . VI. x. 18. 7
this Isle, *though* bare and blunt, ... VI. xi. 9. 5
The sight of whom, *though* now decayd and mard, ... VI. xi. 13. 1
recomforting his griefe, *Though* not his feare, ... VI. xi. 38. 2
Though out of course, yet hath not bene missayd, ... VI. xii. 2. 3
Whom *though* high Jove of kingdome did deprive, ... VII. vi. 2. 8
thogh she nought did reck Of Hermes message, ... VII. vi. 22. 7
though wrongfully from heaven exil'd. . . . . VII. vi. 26. 9
though full many a day He saw her clad, ... VII. vi. 42. 7
As those three sacred Saints, *though* else most wise, ... VII. vii. 7. 6
Autumne all in yellow clad, As *though* he joyed. . . . . . . VII. vii. 30. 2
Long *though* it be, at last I see it gloome, ... *Epith.* 285
For thou likewise didst love, *though* now unthought, ... *Epith.* 378
Though elder then thine owne nativitie, ... *H.L.* 54
And *though* he do not win his wish to end, ... *H.L.* 211
Though from another place I take my name, ... *Proth.* 130
Thought. Then cried a shining Angell as me *thought*, ... *Rev.* iii. 8
Some noble plant I *thought* myselfe to see: . . . . *Pet.* iii. 4
in so short as *thought*, ... *Bel.*[2] viii. 13
I *thought* anone, That of some heavenly wight . . . . *Pet.* v. 3
some that weene the contrarie in *thought*, ... *Ro.* ix. 13
On which when as my *thought* was throghly placed, ... *Van.* i. 9
Thought all things lesse than his disdainful pride. . . . . . *Van.* iii. 6
Safe in his dreadles den him *thought* to hide: . . . . *Van.* x. 4
what shee *thought* good: . . . . *S.C.* May 179
Yet should thilk lasse not from my *thought*, ... *S.C.* Au. 107
I *thought* the soyle would have made me rich, ... *S.C.* S. 78
swifter then *thought* . . . the Wolfe Lowder caught; . . . . *S.C.* S. 222
when I *thought* have thresht in swelling sheave, ... *S.C.* D. 123
Like as he had conceiv'd it in his *thought*. . . . . *Gn.* 656
now is *thought* a civile begging sect. . . . . *Hub.* 198
Exceedingly they troubled were in *thought*, ... *Hub.* 312
in whose beauteous *thought* Regard of honour . . . . *Hub.* 717
Desire of honor or brave *thought* of armes . . . . *Hub.* 825
into whose brest Never crept *thought* of honor, ... *Hub.* 978
King indeed himselfe he shortly *thought*, ... *Hub.* 1105
To hide himselfe from his owne feared *thought*. . . . . . . *Hub.* 1358
The foes of learning and each gentle *thought*; . . . . *T.M.* 64
what ever thing is goodly *thought*, ... *T.M.* 405
I feede on sweet contentment of my *thought*, ... *T.M.* 524
fluttring wings of thy fast flying *Thought*, ... *U.V.* 3
lifting up her brave heroick *thought* . . . . *Ti.* 109
His name is worne alreadie out of *thought*, ... *Ti.* 222
My *thought* returned greeved home againe, ... *Ti.* 478
sight thereof much griev'd my pensive *thought*. . . . . . . *Ti.* 623
There came unto my minde a troublous *thought*, ... *D.* 29
my reliefe exceedeth living *thought*;) . . . . *D.* 95
with wofull heavie *thought*; . . . . *D.* 465
Of onely her he sung, he *thought*, he writ. . . . . *As.* 64
onely by his lookes did tell his *thought*. . . . . *As.* 168
glorie greater then my simple *thought*, ... *Col.* 333
My *thought*, my heart, my love, my life is shee, ... *Col.* 476
she beholds, with high aspiring *thought*, ... *Col.* 612
when I speake of her what I have *thought*, ... *Col.* 626
he slept soundly void of evil *thought*, ... I. i. 46. 3
He *thought* have slaine her in his fierce despight; . . . . . I. i. 50. 3
Eftsoones I *thought* her such as she me told, ... I. ii. 39. 6

Thought—*Continued.*
'The divelish hag . . . Perceiv'd my *thought*; . . . . I. ii. 42. 2
By which she *thought* her wandring knight shold pas, . . . I. iii. 10. 2
Far be it from your *thought*, and fro my wil, ... I. iii. 28. 2
the stout Faery . . . *Thought* all their glorie vaine . . . . . I. iv. 15. 7
The noble hart that harbours vertuous *thought*, ... I. v. 1. 1
With beastly sin *thought* her to have defilde, ... I. vi. 3. 4
Eternall providence, exceeding *thought*, ... I. vi. 7. 1
him to dust *thought* to have battred quight, ... I. vii. 14. 3
'great griefe . . . can more easily be *thought* then said.' . . . I. vii. 41. 2
well-guided speach, So deepe did settle in her gracious *thought*, I. vii. 42. 2
your wisedome will direct my *thought*, ... I. vii. 42. 7
So *thought* I eke of him, and think I *thought* aright. . . . . I. vii. 49. 9
Him *thought* at first encounter to have slaine. . . . . I. viii. 7. 5
Ne shame he *thought* to shonne so hideous might: . . . . . . I. viii. 8. 1
Least so great good . . . buried be in thankles *thought*. . . . I. ix. 2. 9
Caelia men did her call, as *thought* From heaven to come, . . I. x. 4. 1
consuming *thought* To put away . . . . I. x. 29. 5
Thought with his winges to stye above the ground; . . . . I. xi. 25. 8
thought his armes to leave, and helmet to unlace. . . . . . . I. xi. 26. 9
He *thought* attonce him to have swallowd quight, ... I. xi. 53. 2
Well mote ye thee, as well can wish your *thought*, ... II. i. 33. 7
One *thought* her cheare too litle, ... II. ii. 34. 9
th' other *thought* too mutch. . . . . II. ii. 34. 9
Ne *thought* of honour ever did assay His baser brest, ... II. iii. 4. 3
For such as he him *thought*, or faine would be: . . . . II. iii. 5. 6
Thought in his bastard armes her to embrace. . . . . II. iii. 42. 6
I,' (said Braggadocchio) '*thought* no lesse, ... II. iii. 44. 8
better first I *thought* To wreake my wrath on him . . . . . II. iv. 30. 4
His wandring *thought* in deepe desire does steepe, ... II. v. 34. 2
Withdraw from *thought* of warlike enterprize, ... II. vi. 25. 6
fild his inner *thought*. . . . . II. vii. 24. 4
Some *thought* to raise themselves to high degree . . . . . II. vii. 47. 1
thought His cursed life out of her lodge have rent; . . . . . II. viii. 32. 2
More glory *thought* to give life then decay, ... II. viii. 51. 4
easie to be *thought*. II. ix. 33. 9
As if some pensive *thought* constrained her gentle spright. . . II. ix. 36. 9
By Phoebus doome the wisest *thought* alive, ... II. ix. 48. 2
all that in the world was ay *thought* wittily. . . . . II. ix. 53. 9
of some *thought* By sea to have bene . . . brought. . . . . . II. x. 5. 8
Those yet of her be Mertian lawes both nam'd and *thought*. . . II. x. 42. 9
ere any thereof *thought*: . . . . II. x. 51. 4
her attaching *thought* her hands to tye; . . . . II. xi. 28. 6
Revivyng *thought* of glory and of fame, ... II. xi. 31. 8
Then *thought* the Prince all peril sure was past, ... II. xi. 43. 6
No sooner *thought*, then that the Carle as fast . . . . II. xi. 43. 8
thought his labor lost, and travell vayne, ... II. xi. 44. 2
Thought to have mounted; but his feeble vaines . . . . . . II. xi. 48. 3
One would have *thought*, ... II. xii. 59. 1
Should ever enter in his bounteous *thought*, ... III. ii. 10. 2
That may unworthy of it selfe be *thought*. . . . . III. ii. 10. 5
So *thought* this Mayd (as maydens use to done) . . . . III. ii. 23. 5
thought it was not love, but some melancholy. . . . . III. ii. 27. 9
So *thought* she to undoe her daughters love; . . . . III. ii. 51. 6
thought so to beguile her grievous smart; . . . . III. iv. 6. 2
full of bitter griefe and pensife *thought*, ... III. iv. 31. 5
ment To her no evill *thought* nor evill deed; . . . . III. iv. 50. 3
In his free *thought* to build her sluggish nest, ... III. v. 2. 2
Ne suffereth it *thought* of ungentlenesse . . . . III. v. 2. 3
Providence hevenly passeth living *thought*, ... III. v. 27. 1
That suddein chaunge she straunge adventure *thought*. . . . III. vi. 20. 5
Perforce her carried where ever he *thought* best. . . . . . . III. vii. 2. 9
the Damzell, full of doubtfull *thought*, ... III. vii. 8. 5
thought her to adore with humble spright: . . . . III. vii. 11. 8
his base *thought* with terrour and with aw So inly smot, . . III. vii. 13. 5
His caytive *thought* durst not so high aspire: . . . . III. vii. 16. 5
thought to prevaile To bringe her backe againe, ... III. vii. 21. 8
(a thing far passing *thought*) . . . . III. vii. 48. 5
Thought with that sight him much to have reliv'd . . . . . . III. viii. 3. 2
himselfe he *thought* depriv'd Quite of all hope . . . . III. viii. 3. 7
With *thought* whereof exceeding mad he grew, ... III. viii. 4. 1
thought She was the Lady selfe . . . . III. viii. 9. 8
thought that match a fowle disparagement: . . . . III. viii. 12. 4
thought he yet did dreame Not well awakte; . . . . III. viii. 22. 7
Her selfe not saved yet from daunger dredd She *thought*, . . III. viii. 33. 2
thought How to avenge himselfe . . . . III. ix. 12. 7
too long *thought* Every discourse, ... III. ix. 53. 6
Ten thousand wayes he cast in his confused *thought*. . . . . III. x. 18. 9
through long anguish and selfe-murdring *thought*, ... III. x. 57. 1
thought himselfe not safe enough thereby, ... III. xii. 12. 2
It vaine she *thought* with rigorous uprore For to efforce, . . III. xii. 27. 8
he *thought*, for villeinous despight, ... III. xii. 32. 6
ye would have surely *thought* . . . . III. xii. 46. *or.* 1
him she surely *thought* To be a man, ... IV. i. 8. 1
Some *thought* that some enchantment faygned it; . . . . . . IV. i. 14. 5
never *thoght* one thing, but doubly stil was guided. . . . . . IV. i. 27. 9
all her studie was and all her *thought* . . . . IV. i. 29. 8
Which when he *thought*, it grieved him full sore, ... IV. i. 39. 7
To calme the tempest of his troubled *thought*: . . . . IV. ii. 3. 2
though therein himselfe he *thought* to pas, ... IV. ii. 10. 3
Whose beautie each of them *thought* excellent, ... IV. iv. 6. 3
he never *thought* For such an Hag . . . His person to emperill IV. iv. 10. 4
Ne was there Knight that ever *thought* of armes, ... IV. iv. 38. 1
thought in mind it shortly to amend: . . . . IV. iv. 45. 7
pearelesse she was *thought* that did it beare. . . . . IV. v. 6. 5
inly *thought* of that despightfull deede . . . . IV. v. 9. 5
thought For Chian folke to pourtraict beauties Queene, . . . IV. v. 12. 6
thought he had the trew And very Florimell, ... IV. v. 13. 7
Yet *thought* that Florimell was not so faire as shee. . . . . IV. v. 14. 9
about her middle small They *thought* to gird, ... IV. v. 16. 4

Thought—*Continued.*

each one *thought* as to their fancies came. . . . IV. v. 17. 2
when they *thought* it fast, eftsoones it was untide. . . . IV. v. 17. 9
thought t' appeale from that which was decreed . . . IV. v. 22. 7
Some *thought* from him her to have reft by might; . . . IV. v. 27. 4
Yet not fit place he *thought* it there to stay, . . . IV. v. 27. 8
thought his wearie limbs to have redrest. . . . IV. v. 39. 5
As if he *thought* her soule to disentrayle. . . . IV. vi. 16. 7
She arm'd her tongue, and *thought* at him to scold; . . . IV. vi. 27. 7
Hath troubled both your mindes with idle *thought,* . . . IV. vi. 30. 7
thought she wandred was, or gone astray: . . . IV. vi. 36. 7
in that place where I him *thought* to find, . . . IV. vii. 18. 2
There was I found, contrary to my *thought,* . . . IV. vii. 18. 3
in her wrath she *thought* them both have thrild . . . IV. vii. 36. 4
She follow'd her, and *thought* againe it to assay. . . . IV. viii. 10. 9
looser *thought* will lightly be misled, . . . IV. viii. 29. 3
brought Unto his bay, and captived her *thought:* . . . IV. viii. 48. 5
Being likewise beguiled in her *thought,* . . . IV. viii. 56. 3
I boldly *thought,* . . . IV. x. 4. 6
thought my steps to stay, . . . IV. x. 14. 6
I *thought* there was none other heaven then this; . . . IV. x. 28. 3
He *thought* her to compell by crueltie and awe. . . . IV. xi. 2. 9
thought it all one night that did no houres divide. . . . IV. xi. 4. 9
Some while he *thought,* . . . IV. xii. 14. 3
The *thought* whereof empierst his hart so deepe, . . . IV. xii. 19. 6
most she *thought* amis, . . . IV. xii. 22. 4
If ought lay hidden in his grieved *thought,* . . . IV. xii. 24. 8
languish of some inward *thought,* . . . IV. xii. 25. 7
For love of Nymphes she *thought* she need not care, . . . IV. xii. 27. 4
To Proteus selfe to sew she *thought* it vaine, . . . IV. xii. 29. 1
never wight so evill did or *thought,* . . . IV. xii. 30. 8
'A knight,' (said he) 'if knight he may be *thought* . . . V. i. 16. 3
Unmov'd with praiers or with piteous *thought,* . . . V. ii. 23. 2
weigh the *thought* that from mans mind doth flow: . . . V. ii. 43. 4
Which as our owne we tooke, and so it *thought;* . . . V. iv. 13. 3
The worke of heavens will surpasseth humaine *thought.'* . . . V. iv. 27. 9
Whom she *thought* fittest for that businesse; . . . V. iv. 48. 2
when they *thought* on Talus hands to lay, . . . V. v. 19. 1
thought it just t' obay. . . . V. v. 19. 9
Scarse so conceived in her jealous *thought,* . . . V. vi. 3. 2
She *thought* to send some one to seeke him out; . . . V. vi. 6. 2
every place *thought* best, . . . V. vi. 7. 2
in her *thought* did hide The felnesse of her heart, . . . V. vi. 18. 5
Her minde was whole possessed of one *thought,* . . . V. vi. 21. 3
thought that she thereon could never gaze her fill. . . . V. vii. 5. 9
Mote in them stirre up old rebellious *thought* . . . V. vii. 11. 5
She much was eased in her troublous *thought,* . . . V. vii. 24. 2
She was confused in her troublous *thought;* . . . V. vii. 25. 3
Thought with his speare him quight have overwent. . . . V. viii. 7. 4
thought it best With that his wife in friendly wise to deale, . V. viii. 21. 1
So *thought* the Souldan, . . . V. viii. 31. 5
As a faire stoupe of her high soaring *thought,* . . . V. ix. 34. 7
To doe whatever he *thought* good or fit: . . . V. x. 13. 3
of his owne vaine fancies *thought* did frame: . . . V. xi. 19. 4
thought more the lesse she sed. . . . V. xii. 29. 9
his hart was inly child . . . and his *thought* with wonder fild. VI. ii. 4. 9
'The widow Queene . . . *Thought* best away me to remove . VI. ii. 29. 7
him to trouble she it *thought* unfit, . . . VI. ii. 47. 3
him to beare she *thought* it thing too base. . . . VI. ii. 47. 5
inly did afflict her pensive *thought* . . . VI. iii. 6. 8
Sith his own *thought* he knew most cleare from wite: . . . VI. iii. 16. 6
him selfe he *thought* from daunger free, . . . VI. iii. 20. 6
Such chaunces oft exceed all humaine *thought!* . . . VI. iii. 51. 8
And stopt the bleeding straight, ere he it staunched *thought.* . VI. iv. 12. 9
He with him *thought* backe to returne againe; . . . VI. iv. 24. 2
Therefore some *thought* that those brave imps were sowen . VI. iv. 36. 7
day and night did vexe her carefull *thought,* . . . VI. v. 6. 8
Withouten *thought* of shame or villeny, . . . VI. v. 9. 8
Thought therewithall forthwith him to have slaine; . . . VI. v. 26. 7
whom sure he *thought* By this quite slaine . . . VI. vi. 37. 6
Ne secretly from *thought* of fell revenge surceasse: . . . VI. vi. 43. 9
to him leaping vengeance *thought* to take . . . VI. vii. 11. 7
none she worthie *thought* to be her fere, . . . VI. vii. 29. 2
this coy Damzell *thought* contrariwize, . . . VI. vii. 30. 1
then surely *thought* That slaine he was, . . . VI. vii. 50. 2
thought certainely To have supplyde the first, . . . VI. viii. 9. 8
Thought sure have pownded him to powder soft, . . . VI. viii. 15. 3
she *thought* Her selfe now past the perill of her feares: . . . VI. viii. 32. 2
diversely dispose As each *thought* best . . . VI. viii. 39. 3
There I beheld such vainenesse as I never *thought.* . . . VI. ix. 24. 9
thought it best To chaunge the manner of his loftie looke; . VI. ix. 36. 1
Thought sure t' avenge his grudge, . . . VI. ix. 43. 9
She in regard hereof refusde and *thought* unfit. . . . VI. x. 9. 9
she *thought* her self in hell, . . . VI. x. 43. 8
She *thought* it best, for shadow to pretend Some shew . . VI. xi. 6. 5
they find, contrarie to their *thought,* That Pastorell yet liv'd; VI. xi. 41. 5
Sir Calidore him arm'd as he *thought* best, . . . VI. xi. 42. 4
Had never joyance felt nor chearefull *thought,* . . . VI. xi. 45. 2
This daughter *thought* in wedlocke to have bound . . . VI. xii. 4. 5
having *thought* long dead she fyndes alive, . . . VI. xii. 21. 2
Nor ever *thought* thing so unworthily: . . . VI. xii. 33. 7
She gan to cast in her ambitious *thought* . . . VII. vi. 7. 3
I would have *thought* that bold Procrustes hire, . . . VII. vi. 29. 5
loud profest His foolish *thought:* . . . VII. vi. 46. 6
Thought not enough to punish him in sport, . . . VII. vi. 51. 2
who he *thought* Had in his *Plaint of kinde* describ'd it well: . VII. vii. 9. 6
Unquiet *thought!* whom at the first I bred . . . *Am.* ii. 1
her deep wit, that true harts *thought* can spel, . . . *Am.* xliii. 13
not on him that never *thought* you ill, . . . *Am.* xlix. 7
There let no *thought* of joy, . . . Dare to approch, . . . *Am.* lii. 9

Thought—*Continued.*

My soverayne saynt, the Idoll of my *thought,* . . . *Am.* lxi. 2
It down is weighd with *thoght* of earthly things, . . . *Am.* lxxii. 3
Whom ye *thought* worthy of your gracefull rymes, . . . *Epith.* 3
Ne *thought* of thing uncomely ever may Thereto approch . . *Epith.* 198
Which may let in a little *thought* unsownd. . . . *Epith.* 237
forme, which now doth dwell In his high *thought,* . . . *H.L.* 194
forth he casts in his unquiet *thought,* . . . *H.L.* 218
The mirrour of his owne *thought* doth admyre. . . . *H.B.* 224
no *thought* of earthly wight Can comprehend, . . . *H.H.L.* 40
And give me words equall unto my *thought,* . . . *H.H.L.* 48
What . . . *thought* can think the depth of so deare wound? *H.H.L.* 163
Melt into teares, and grone in grieved *thought.* . . . *H.H.L.* 252
Rapt with the rage of mine own ravisht *thought,* . . . *H.H.B.* 1
That it doth farre exceed all humane *thought,* . . . *H.H.B.* 209
Above that Idole of his fayning *thought,* . . . *H.H.B.* 223
Or idle *thought* of earthly things, remaine; . . . *H.H.B.* 268
fed On idle fancies of thy foolish *thought,* . . . *H.H.B.* 289

Thought's. My mind, full of my *thoughts* satietie, . . . *Col.* 42
Muse, full of high *thoughts* invention, . . . *Col.* 446
Without discoverie of my *thoughts* pretence, . . . V. v. 33. 7
fairely did dissemble her sad *thoughts* unrest. . . . V. v. 44. 9
trampled downe in dust his *thoughts* disdained scorne. . . V. viii. 31. 9
nigh ravisht with rare *thoughts* delight, . . . VI. Pr. 1. 6
It stopped is with *thoughts* astonishment; . . . *Am.* iii. 10

Thoughts. The carefull *thoughts* of mortall miseries; . . . *Bel.*[2] i. 4
carefull *thoughts* in her heart did creepe) . . . *S.C.* May 190
Faire Ladies loves they spot with *thoughts* impure, . . . *T.M.* 333
Thoughts halfe devine, full of the fire of love, . . . *T.M.* 363
Ne ever dare their dunghill *thoughts* aspire . . . *T.M.* 393
lowly *thoughts* lift up to heavens hight, . . . *T.M.* 459
with base *thoughts* are into blindnesse led, . . . *T.M.* 592
thoughts of men do as themselves decay; . . . *Ti.* 401
glorie of the world your high *thoughts* scorne, . . . *Ti.* 681
His *thoughts,* his rimes, his songs were all upon her. . . . *As.* 60
In loves soft laies and looser *thoughts* delight. . . . *Col.* 423
To her my *thoughts* I daily dedicate, . . . *Col.* 472
Her *thoughts* are like the fume of Franckincence, . . . *Col.* 608
Nor haughtie words most full of highest *thoughts:* . . . *Col.* 716
So hie her *thoughts* as she her selfe have place, . . . *Col.* 937
In whose high *thoughts* Pleasure hath built her bowre, . . *Ded. Son.* viii. 6
raise my *thoughtes,* too humble and too vile, . . . I. Pr. 4. 6
Still flying from his *thoughts* and gealous feare: . . . I. ii. 12. 3
He seemd in hart to harbour *thoughts* unkind, . . . I. iv. 38. 8
th' eternall might, That . . . rules the *thoughts* of living wight. I. ix. 6. 9
Ne divelish *thoughts* dismay thy constant spright: . . . I. ix. 53. 3
forst him lay his hevenly *thoughts* aside; . . . I. x. 49. 3
without gealous feares Or faultie *thoughts,* . . . II. iv. 18. 8
how great wonder would your *thoughts* devoure, . . . II. ix. 3. 8
All those were idle *thoughtes* and fantasies, . . . II. ix. 51. 6
with vaine *thoughts* her falsed fancy vex: . . . III. i. 47. 5
carefull *thoughts* did quite assoile. . . . III. i. 58. 9
Her love-sicke hart to other *thoughts* did steale; . . . III. ii. 48. 7
A thousand *thoughts* she fashiond in her mind, . . . III. iv. 5. 6
With such selfe-pleasing *thoughts* her wound she fedd, . . III. iv. 6. 1
ydle *thoughts* . . . cleave unto the lowly clay, . . . III. v. 1. 4
did his hart with bitter *thoughts* engore, . . . III. x. 45. 4
With hatefull *thoughts* to languish and to pine, . . . III. xi. 1. 7
wicked Time that all good *thoughts* doth waste, . . . IV. ii. 33. 1
rul'd her *thoughts* with goodly governement, . . . IV. ii. 36. 4
Those be unquiet *thoughts* that carefull minds invade. . . IV. v. 35. 9
inly feeds it selfe with *thoughts* unkind, . . . IV. vi. 1. 3
looser *thoughts* to lawfull bounds withdraw; . . . IV. vi. 33. 7
bitter *thoughts,* which deepe therein infixed lay. . . . IV. viii. 1. 9
Through *thoughts* aspyring to eternall fame: . . . IV. ix. 2. 5
(so young mens *thoughts* are bold) . . . IV. x. 4. 6
Brave *thoughts* and noble deedes did evermore aspire. . . IV. x. 26. 9
in *thoughts* lesse hard and bold, . . . IV. xi. 22. 4
her winged *thoughts,* more swift then wind, . . . V. vi. 7. 8
With thousand *thoughts* feeding her fantasie, . . . V. vii. 17. 2
not in outward shows, but inward *thoughts* defynd. . . . VI. Pr. 5. 9
Me no such cares nor cumbrous *thoughts* offend, . . . VI. ix. 22. 6
many gealous *thoughts* conceiv'd in vaine, . . . VI. ix. 38. 4
All dewfull service, voide of *thoughts* impure; . . . VI. x. 32. 6
'Will never mortall *thoughts* ceasse to aspire . . . VII. vi. 29. 2
Still change and vary *thoughts,* as new occasions fall. . . VII. vii. 19. 9
Bids all old *thoughts* to die in dumpish spright: . . . *Am.* iv. 4
You frame my *thoughts,* and fashion me within; . . . *Am.* viii. 9
hinders heavenly *thoughts* with drossy slime. . . . *Am.* xiii. 12
my *thoughts* doo day and night attend, . . . *Am.* xxii. 7
Not earth, for her high *thoghts* more heavenly are: . . . *Am.* lv. 5
my frayle *thoughts* too rashly led astray! . . . *Am.* lxxvi. 6
Sweet *thoughts!* I envy your so happy rest, . . . *Am.* lxxvi. 13
My *thoughts* the guests, which would thereon have fedd. . . *Am.* lxxvii. 14
let my *thoughts* behold her selfe in mee. . . . *Am.* lxxviii. 14
modest *thoughts* breathd from weltempred sprites, . . . *Am.* lxxxiii. 6
was wont to lead my *thoughts* astray; . . . *Am.* lxxxvii. 2
His dunghill *thoughts* . . themselves enure To dirtie drosse, *H.L.* 183
soule inspired bee With heavenly *thoughts* . . . *H.H.L.* 282
to God . . . even the *thoughts* of men, do plaine appeare; . . *H.H.B.* 173
Thy straying *thoughts* henceforth for ever rest. . . . *H.H.B.* 301

Thous. Syker, *thous* but a laesie loord, . . . *S.C.* Jul. 33
Cuddy . . . *thous* a fon, . . . *Col.* 292

Thousand. *See* **Ten thousand, Three thousand, Twelve thousand, Two hundred thousand.**

threw forth a *thousand* rayes . . . *Bel.*[1] ii. 7
Folding, hir armes with *thousand* sighs . . . *Bel.*[1] viii. 2
Threw forth abrode a *thousand* shining leames, . . . *Bel.*[1] ix. 10
a *thousand* rayons threw . . . *Bel.*[2] ii. 7
I saw a *thousand* huntsmen, . . . *Bel.*[2] vi. 9

Thousand—*Continued.*
Throwing out *thousand* throbs . . . *Bel.*^{2} vi. 13
Folding her armes . . . with *thousand* throbs, . . . *Bel.*^{2} x. 2
On everie side a *thousand* shining beames: . . . *Bel.*^{2} xi. 10
Eftsoones of *thousand* billowes shouldred narre, . . . *Ro.* xvi. 3
In sixe and thirty *thousand* yeares is ronne, . . . *Ro.* xxii. 10
'A *thousand* sithes I curse that carefull hower . . . *S.C.* Ja. 49
death . . . to them appeares In *thousand* formes, . . . *Gn.* 584
Girt with long snakes, and *thousand* yron chaynes, . . . *Gn.* 626
A *thousand* wayes he them could entertaine, . . . *Hub.* 800
a *thousand* deathes, and shame beside?' . . . *Hub.* 976
threatned death, and *thousand* deadly dolours, . . . *Hub.* 1341
A *thousand* Nymphes, with mirthfull jollitee, . . . *Ti.* 137
thousand Fishers numbred to have been, . . . *Ti.* 150
Painted with *thousand* colours, . . . *Mui.* 90
thousand perills lie in close awaite . . . *Mui.* 221
Sharpe sorrowe did in *thousand* peeces rive. . . . *D.* 7
Thousand wyld beasts with deep mouthes . . . *Col.* 202
Her heards be *thousand* fishes with their frie, . . . *Col.* 242
beside a *thousand* moe at land: . . . *Col.* 261
Of her there bred A *thousand* yong ones, . . . I. i. 15. 5
streight him rent in *thousand* peeces small, . . . I. iii. 20. 3
thousand other waies to bait his fleshly hookes. . . . I. iv. 25. 9
Curled with *thousand* adders venemous, . . . I. v. 34. 3
thousand feends that doe them endlesse paine . . . I. ix. 49. 8
thousand times he so him selfe had drest, . . . I. ix. 54. 7
hevenly throne, where *thousand* Angels shine? . . . I. x. 51. 6
thousand thankes him yeeldes for all his paine. . . . I. xii. 12. 7
With *thousand* other sleightes; . . . II. i. 3. 7
thousand furies wait on wrathfull sword; . . . II. ii. 30. 7
That speare is him enough to doen a *thousand* grone.' . . . II. iii. 12. 9
thousand thousand times more faire, . . . II. iii. 26. 1
thousand causes wrought. . . . II. v. 19. 9
thousand waies invent To feede her foolish humour . . . II. vi. 3. 8
Would him have rent in *thousand* peeces strayt: . . . II. vii. 64. 5
thousand Sar'zins fowly donne to dye.' . . . II. viii. 18. 6
Thousand times fairer than her mortall hew, . . . II. ix. 3. 7
sufficient were that hire For losse of *thousand* lives, . . . II. ix. 5. 9
thousand enemies about us rave, . . . II. ix. 12. 6
A *thousand* villeins rownd about them swarmd . . . II. ix. 13. 2
Mongst *thousand* dangers, and ten thousand Magick mights. . . . II. xii. 1. 9
All these, and *thousand* thousands many more, . . . II. xii. 25. 1
With *thousand* blessings she is heried. . . . III. i. 43. 7
rive with *thousand* throbs thy thrilled brest: . . . III. ii. 32. 5
thousand sprights with long enduring paines . . . III. iii. 9. 4
Shall stoutly him defeat, and *thousand* Saxons kill. . . . III. iii. 35. 9
A *thousand* thoughts she fashiond in her mind, . . . III. iv. 5. 6
with *thousand* starres was decked fayre: . . . III. iv. 52. 3
thousand Fancies bett his ydle brayne . . . III. iv. 54. 4
Disguiz'd in *thousand* shapes, that none might him bewray.) . . . III. vi. 11. 9
A *thousand thousand* naked babes attend About him . . . III. vi. 32. 3
Some *thousand* yeares so doen they there remayne, . . . III. vi. 33. 5
thousand spots of colours queint elect, . . . III. vii. 22. 5
brast In *thousand* shivers, . . . III. vii. 40. 9
thousand deathes me lever were to dye . . . III. vii. 51. 5
humbly thanked him a *thousand* sith . . . III. x. 33. 3
Himselfe in *thousand* peeces fondly rent, . . . III. xi. 38. 4
A *thousand* monstrous formes therein were made, . . . III. xi. 51. 7
love in *thousand* monstrous formes doth oft appeare. . . . III. xi. 51. 9
A *thousand* charmes he formerly did prove, . . . III. xii. 31. 8
thousand charmes could not her stedfast hart remove. . . . III. xii. 31. 9
first tynd in Phlegeton, By *thousand* furies, . . . IV. ii. 1. 2
Had *thousand* women of their love beraft, . . . IV. ii. 10. 5
first laide on those Ladies *thousand* blames, . . . IV. ii. 20. 7
whom *thousand* late Misdoubted lost . . . IV. ii. 23. 6
thousand perills which them still awate, . . . IV. iii. 1. 5
thousand vowes from bottome of his hart, . . . IV. vi. 43. 4
Sweet springs, in which a *thousand* Nymphs did play; . . . IV. x. 24. 3
therein *thousand* payres of lovers walkt, . . . IV. x. 25. 6
thousand pretious gifts worth many a pound, . . . IV. x. 37. 7
in these few *thousand* yeares . . . V. Pr. 5. 4
Her shattered ribs in *thousand* peeces rives, . . . V. ii. 50. 3
thousand thankes him yeeld, . . . V. iii. 15. 8
She gan to cast in her misdoubtfull mynde A *thousand* feares, V. vi. 3. 9
With *thousand* thoughts feeding her fantasie, . . . V. vii. 17. 2
a *thousand* more of such as sings Hymns to high God, . . . V. ix. 29. 4
The which did seeme a *thousand* tongues to have, . . . VI. i. 9. 3
Handling and turning them a *thousand* wayes: . . . VI. ii. 39. 5
thousand thankes to Calidore . . . Did yeeld: . . . VI. iii. 19. 3
Besides a *thousand* more which ready bee . . . VI. x. 21. 7
A *thousand* times him thankt that had her death prevented. . . . VI. x. 36. 9
A *thousand* sowres hath tempred with one sweet, . . . VI. xi. 1. 8
In *thousand* dreadful shapes doth mongst them stalke, . . . VI. xi. 16. 7
A *thousand* times embrast, and kist a *thousand* more. . . . VI. xi. 45. 9
A *thousand* times she her embraced nere, . . . VI. xii. 20. 8
therein were a *thousand* tongs empight . . . VI. xii. 27. 1
labourd long in vaine To crop his *thousand* heads, . . . VI. xii. 32. 4
up-held With *thousand* Crystall pillors . . . VII. vi. 10. 4
thousand deathes deviseth in her vengefull mind. . . . VII. vi. 48. 9
the faire Shure, in which are *thousand* Salmons bred. . . . VII. vi. 54. 9
it the Sunne a *thousand* times did pass, . . . VII. vii. 6. 8
flashing lights that *thousand* changes make. . . . VII. vii. 23. 9
To *thousand* sorts of Change we subject see: . . . VII. vii. 25. 3
a *thousand* birds had built their bowres . . . VII. vii. 28. 4
thousand arrowes, which your eies have shot: . . . *Am.* lvii. 8
a *thousand* torches flaming bright Doe burne, . . . *Epith.* 410
whose yet bleeding hart With *thousand* wounds . . . *H.L.* 143
through *thousand* swords and speares; . . . *H.L.* 228
Sights never seene, and *thousand* shadowes vaine, . . . *H.L.* 255
A *thousand* Graces masking in delight; . . . *H.B.* 254

Thousand—*Continued.*
Adornd with *thousand* lamps of burning light, . . . *H.H.L.* 59
Is many *thousand* times more bright, more cleare, . . . *H.H.B.* 170
Thousandfold. more deformed Monsters *thousand fold*, . . . II. xii. 25. 2
Thousands. The least of *thousands* which on earth abide, . . . *Van.* iii. 8
ye may better thrive than *thousands* moe.' . . . *Hub.* 642
With which he *thousands* cleanly coosined: . . . *Hub.* 862
thousands moe the like that did that dongeon fill. . . . I. v. 50. 9
All which, and *thousands* mo, do make a loathsome life. . . . I. ix. 44. 9
His cruel bow, wherewith he *thousands* hath dismayd. . . . II. ix. 34. 9
All these, and thousand *thousands* many more, . . . II. xii. 25. 1
'Mongst *thousands* good one wanton Dame to find: . . . III. i. 49. 5
thousands like which flowed in his braine, . . . III. x. 8. 7
The blood hath of so many *thousands* shedd, . . . III. x. 32. 6
thousands more then any tongue can tell, . . . *H.L.* 264
those . . . and *thousands* more Thy handmaides be, . . . *H.B.* 260
Thracian. O that I had the *Thracian* Poets harpe, . . . *Ro.* xxv. 1
For whome the *Thracian* king lamenting sore, . . . *Gn.* 404
like a Serpent to the *Thracian* mayd. . . . III. xi. 35. 4
any of the *Thracian* Nimphes in salvage chase. . . . IV. vii. 22. 9
Like to the *Thracian* Tyrant, . . . V. viii. 31. 1
Thraldom. To see his loved Squyre into such *thraldom* brought: I. viii. 15. 9
long captived soules from weary *thraldome* free. . . . II. i. 36. 9
To live in *thraldome* of his fathers foe! . . . III. iii. 42. 3
in this *thraldome* Britons shall abide; . . . III. iii. 44. 2
Eternall *thraldome* was to her more liefe . . . III. viii. 42. 1
In dolefull *thraldome* all his dayes to dwell? . . . III. ix. 8. 3
redeeme my deare Out of her *thraldome* . . . III. xi. 16. 5
mighty kings and kesars into *thraldome* brought. . . . III. xi. 29. 9
When her from deadly *thraldome* he redeemed, . . . IV. i. 8. 4
Thine honor sav'd, though into *thraldome* throwne?' . . . IV. vii. 19. 5
how from *thrcldome* vile they were untide, . . . IV. viii. 21. 5
many Nations into *thraldome* led, . . . IV. viii. 47. 4
Should wilfully be into *thraldome* brought, . . . IV. viii. 58. 7
Such *thraldome* or such freedome let it surely be. . . . IV. xii. 10. 9
as her vassall him to *thraldome* tooke: . . . V. v. 18. 3
What right is it, that he should *thraldome* find . . . V. v. 32. 4
Thus he long while in *thraldome* there remayned, . . . V. v. 57. 6
lies in wretched *thraldome*, weake and wan, . . . V. vi. 16. 3
They doe thy love forlorne in womens *thraldome* see. . . . V. vii. 21. 9
she did from *thraldome* free, . . . V. vii. 43. 2
Gave leave unto his ghost from *thraldome* bound . . . V. x. 33. 5
by that Tyrant is in wretched *thraldome* bound: . . . V. xi. 38. 9
For ye into like *thraldome* me did throw, . . . V. xi. 41. 8
What cruell hand thy wretched *thraldome* wrought, . . . VI. i. 12. 3
after *thraldome* of the gentle Squire, . . . VI. viii. 3. 1
So leave we her in wretched *thraldome* bound, . . . VI. xi. 24. 8
all his off-spring into *thraldome* threw, . . . *H.H.L.* 124
Thraldom's. in sad *thraldomes* chayne; . . . IV. xi. 1. 5
Thrall. became their *thrall*, . . . *Ti.* 114
'Who is it that dooth name me, wofull *thrall*, . . . *D.* 62
whom unhappy howre Hath now made *thrall* . . . I. ii. 22. 3
devise to quitt a *thrall* from such a plight? . . . I. vi. 6. 9
A Satyre . . . made her person *thrall* unto his beastly kind. . . . I. vi. 22. 9
valiant knight become a caytive *thrall*, . . . I. vii. 19. 3
He has them now fowr years besiegd to make them *thrall*. . . . I. vii. 44. 9
now in darkesome dungeon, wretched *thrall*, . . . I. vii. 51. 7
So oft as he, . . . is to sinfull bands made *thrall*: . . . I. viii. 1. 7
Thrall to that Gyaunts hatefull tyranny: . . . I. viii. 2. 5
Whom great Orgoglio . . . Had made his caytive *thrall*: . . . I. viii. 32. 8
no where could he find that wofull *thrall*: . . . I. viii. 37. 2
'I am your humble *thrall*.' . . . II. iii. 8. 2
that caytives *thrall*, the *thrall* of wretchednesse. . . . II. iv. 16. 9
Great mercy, sure, for to enlarge a *thrall*, . . . II. v. 18. 3
Wilfully make thyselfe a wretched *thrall*, . . . II. vi. 17. 3
as conquered To be her *thrall*, . . . III. vii. 17. 8
Whom she did meane to make the *thrall* of her desire. . . . III. vii. 37. 9
threatned there to make her his eternall *thrall*. . . . III. viii. 41. 9
In royall heart disdaining to be *thrall*. . . . IV. iv. 32. 7
Like captive *thral* two other Knights atweene: . . . IV. iv. 34. 5
as his *thrall* Her claym'd, . . . IV. v. 23. 6
now become to live a Ladies *thrall*, . . . IV. vi. 28. 8
I rest his wretched *thrall*, the sad Aemylia.' . . . IV. vii. 18. 9
pitty much his plight, that liv'd like outcast *thrall*. . . . IV. vii. 43. 9
Him wretched *thrall* unto his dongeon brought, . . . IV. viii. 51. 8
like her *thrall*: . . . IV. xi. 7. 6
me, woefull *thrall*, Deliver hence . . . IV. xii. 9. 3
So had I rather to be *thrall* then free; . . . IV. xii. 10. 8
tooke, and sithence kept as *thrall*. . . . IV. xii. 32. 5
the boldnesse of thy basest *thrall*, . . . V. Pr. 11. 6
Whom a strong tyrant did unjustly *thrall*, . . . V. i. 3. 7
fain'd to fly for feare of being *thrall*; . . . V. i. 22. 8
To be her *thrall* and service her afford: . . . V. v. 17. 5
have agreed To *thrall* my looser life, . . . V. v. 29. 9
His bodie was her *thrall*, . . . V. v. 46. 9
To be so scorned of a base-borne *thrall*, . . . V. v. 47. 4
Unto the prison, where her hart did *thrall* remaine. . . . V. v. 51. 9
For yeelding so himselfe a wretched *thrall* . . . V. vi. 1. 3
Till he redeemed had that Lady *thrall*: . . . V. vii. 45. 8
taking with him, as his vanquisht *thrall*, . . . V. viii. 26. 3
mote appall An hardie courage, like captived *thrall* . . . V. ix. 33. 5
call, Unto Mercilla myld, for Justice gainst the *thrall*. . . . V. ix. 49. 9
is she *thrall*, or doth she not survive?' . . . V. xi. 38. 7
For freeing from their snares Irena *thrall*: . . . V. xii. 37. 5
scorne the challenge of so base a *thrall*; . . . VI. iii. 36. 4
sav'd from being to that caytive *thrall*. . . . VI. iv. 15. 4
letting him arise like abject *thrall*, . . . VI. vii. 26. 6
slaine he was, or made a wretched *thrall*, . . . VI. vii. 50. 3
Beheld two such, of two such villaines *thrall*, . . . VI. viii. 5. 8
Then turning backe unto that captive *thrall*, . . . VI. viii. 27. 1

Thrall—*Continued.*
at more ease continue there his *thrall:* VI. xi. 6. 8
wondrous joy felt in her spirits *thrall:* VI. xi. 44. 5
Thus long continu'd Claribell a *thrall,* VI. xii. 10. 1
unto Mutabilitie not *thrall,* VII. vii. 17. 8
'Then are ye mortall borne, and *thrall* to me VII. vii. 54. 1
Let her accept me as her faithfull *thrall;* *Am.* xxix. 10
joy, her *thrall* for ever to remayne, *Am.* xlii. 7
my hart to *thrall,* And eke my toung *Am.* xliii. 5
him take, and . . . Gently encage, that he may be your *thrall:* *Am.* lxxiii. 10
your *thrall,* in whom is little worth; *Am.* lxxxii. 10
That I her bounden *thrall* by her may live, *H.B.* 278
like a most demisse And abject *thrall,* *H.H.L.* 137
Free that was *thrall,* and blessed that was band; *H.H.L.* 184

Thralled. Where him that witch had *thralled* to her will, II. i. 54. 2
thralled her in chaines with strong effort, II. v. 17. 4
what wicked felon . . . *thrald* your gentle make. III. xi. 15. 3
have with treason *thralled* unto you These two, VI. viii. 7. 5
Him to have bound and *thrald* without delay; VI. viii. 11. 7
thralled to her might, VII. vi. 7. 2
thralled to his love; *Am.* lxxi. 6

Thralls. made all other Foules his *thralls* to bee: *Van.* iv. 4
caytive wretched *thralls,* that wayled night and day: I. v. 45. 9
the endlesse routes of wretched *thralles,* I. v. 51. 1
To view the *thrals* which there in bondage lay: IV. viii. 52. 3
forth to bring those *thrals* which there he held. IV. ix. 8. 3
dy As *thralls* and vassals unto mens beheasts; VII. vii. 19. 3
in bloody bath Of such poor *thralls* *Am.* xxxi. 12
they lye languishing like *thrals* forlorne, *H.L.* 136

Thrash. *See* **Thresh.**

Thread. Her vitall *threde* so soone was spent. *S.C.* N. 149
So soone as Fates their vitall *thred* have shorne, *Ti.* 181
To finger the fine needle and nyce *thread,* III. ii. 6. 8
round about the Pots mouth bound the *thread;* III. ii. 50. 3
the whiles the *thrid* By griesly Lachesis was spun IV. ii. 48. 5
his lives *threed* to breake. VI. xi. 34. 9

Threadbare. *thred-bare* cote, and cobled shoes, hee ware; I. iv. 28. 2

Threads. Doo weave the direfull *threds* of destinie, *D.* 17
cruell fates the carefull *threds* (**threeds*) unfould, I. vii. 22. 5
Most wretched men, whose dayes depend on *thrids* so vaine! IV. ii. 48. 9
Beholding how the *thrids* of life they span: IV. ii. 49. 2
eke thy childrens *thrids* to be asunder burst!' IV. ii. 49. 9
That she might see her childrens *thrids* forth brought, IV. ii. 50. 3
To see their *thrids* so thin as spiders frame, IV. ii. 50. 8

Threasure, *etc.* *See* **Treasure,** *etc.*

Threat. *See* **Threaten.**
assaile this ship with dreadfull *threat,* *Bel.*[2] xiii. 7
Tombes of her greatnes which did *threate* the skies: *Ro.* iv. 8
Of Sommers flame, nor of Winters *threat,* *S.C.* F. 20
seemed to *threat* the Firmament: *S.C.* F. 117
Encreasing his wrath with many a *threate:* *S.C.* F. 194
unto his *threate* Is a playne overture. *S.C.* Jul. 27
throwe out thondring words of *threate,* *S.C.* O. 104
the charge . . . hath an heavie *threat.'* *Hub.* 432
they began to *threat* the neighbour sky; *Hub.* 1174
faulty men, which daunger to thee *threat:* *Com. Son.* i. 8
Ne feareth change of time, nor fortunes *threate,* *Ti.* 465
His looke . . . seemed still to *threat* Cruell revenge, I. iii. 33. 7
doubled strokes, like dreaded thunders *threat;* I. v. 7. 5
with his tallnesse seemd to *threat* the skye I. vii. 8. 5
throw in raging sea with roaring *threat.* I. x. 20. 8
all the hevens stood still amazed with his *threat.* I. xi. 10. 9
wintry storme his wrathful wreck does *threat;* I. xi. 21. 2
the blustring brethren boldly *threat* To move the world I. xi. 21. 7
with bent lowring browes, as she would *threat,* II. ii. 35. 7
the Hag, with many a bitter *threat,* II. iv. 9. 3
that harme, which thou dost seeme To *threat* to him II. iv. 40. 4
heavy ruine they did seeme to *threatt;* II. vii. 28. 6
soone as they approcht with deadly *threat,* II. xii. 40. 1
Ythrild with deepe disdaine of his proud *threat,* III. iv. 15. 1
Like to thicke clouds that *threat* a stormy showre, III. iv. 43. 3
with bold words and bitter *threat* III. viii. 16. 2
afterwardes affray with cruell *threat,* III. ix. 9. 3
Frame thunderbolts for Joves avengefull *threate.* IV. v. 37. 4
Her mortall arrowes she at him did *threat,* IV. vii. 37. 8
with *threat* Doth them compell to worke, V. iv. 31. 4
well to beare The storme of fortunes frowne or heavens *threat,* V. v. 38. 3
with many a cursed *threat,* V. v. 47. 6
So thought the Souldan, in his follies *threat,* V. viii. 31. 5
fire to them did *threat,* V. xi. 12. 4
They turne afresh, and oft renew their former *threat.* V. xi. 45. 9
A storme approching that doth perill *threat,* V. xii. 18. 6
is the boast of that proud Ladies *threat,* VI. i. 40. 4
Bull, whose cruell hornes doe *threat* Desperate daunger, VI. vii. 47. 2
for prayers nor for *threat* To hope for to release VI. viii. 3. 6
for all his fearefull *threat,* VI. ix. 4. 5
death it selfe unto himselfe did *threat;* VI. xi. 33. 5
regarded not her *threat,* VII. vi. 12. 3
huge Pyramids, which do heaven *threat.* *Com. Son.* iii. 8
From the just wrath of his avengefull *threate* *H.H.B.* 150

Threaten. *See* **Threat.**
Through his faire hide his angrie sting did *threaten,* *Van.* ii. 11
with sterne lookes to *threaten* kindled yre. *Gn.* 264
He oftentimes me dreadfullie doth *threaten* *Gn.* 351
wicked maister, . . . gan *threaten* hellish paine, I. ii. 2. 6
both did gnash their teeth, and both did *threten* life. II. vii. 21. 9
threaten batteill to the Faery knight; II. vii. 42. 4
now it gan to *threaten* neare decay: II. xi. 14. 5
To heare him *threaten* so despightfully, III. ix. 14. 6
'No lesse did Daunger *threaten* me with dread, IV. x. 58. 1

Threaten—*Continued.*
He gan to *threaten* her likewise to eat, V. vii. 15. 8
eke him selfe did *threaten* to confound; V. xi. 2. 5

Threatened. *threatned* death, and thousand deadly dolours, *Hub.* 1341
That vainly *threatned* kingdomes to displace, *Ded. Son.* vi. 8
The Sprite . . . *threatned* . . . the dreaded name Of Hecate: I. i. 43. 2
threatned all his heades like flaming brandes. I. viii. 12. 6
threatned death with many a bloodie word: II. i. 11. 8
that warriour gan abace His *threatned* speare, II. i. 26. 8
to him *threatned* his hart-thrilling speare: II. iii. 6. 6
threatned death with dreadfull countenaunce, II. iii. 14. 2
he feard her wrath, and *threatned* shott, II. iii. 43. 4
them perforce withheld with *threatned* blade, II. xi. 31. 4
threatned death for his outrageous wrong. III. v. 13. 9
threatned there to make her his eternall thrall. III. viii. 41. 9
threatned him with force and punishment extreme: III. ix. 10. 9
With th' one his foes he *threatned* to invade, III. xii. 11. 7
with his club me *threatned* to have brayned, IV. x. 36. 5
threatned sore Her to have swallow'd up, V. iv. 12. 3
The comming of that so much *threatned* Knight; VI. i. 30. 3
Threatned to strike her if she did with-stand: VII. vi. 13. 5
Upreard her buildinges to the *threatned* skie: *Com. Son.* iv. 2

Threateneth. *threatneth* downe to throw his ragged rift. II. xii. 4. 5

Threatening. *Threatning* her angrie sting, him to dismay; I. i. 17. 7
when he saw his *threatning* was but vaine, I. ii. 2. 8
the Prince, . . . *threatning* high his dreadfull stroke, I. viii. 22. 2
threatning to make the pray Of the rough rockes, II. ii. 24. 2
threatning revenge in vaine: II. iv. 15. 4
Threatning with greedy gripe to doe him dye, II. vii. 27. 7
All *threatning* death, all in straunge manner armd; II. ix. 13. 5
Threatning unheedy wrecke and rash decay, II. x. 6. 5
Threatning it selfe on them to ruinate, II. xii. 7. 2
threatning to devoure all that his powre despise. II. xii. 21. 9
Threatning the point of her avenging blaed; III. i. 63. 8
Threatning to swallow up my fearefull lyfe? III. iv. 8. 6
Threatning into his life to make a breach, III. xi. 12. 7
Threatning to strike unlesse he would withstand: IV. vi. 23. 5
then came Daunger, *threatning* hidden dread V. ix. 45. 5
with bold vaunts and ydle *threatning,* V. xi. 3. 7
Threatning to chastize me, VI. ii. 11. 9
threatning his sharpe clawes, now wanting powre to traine. VI. iv. 22. 9
Threatning to yoke them two and tame their corage stout. VI. viii. 11. 9
bet abacke, *threatning* in vaine to bite, VI. xii. 29. 4
Thretning rash eies which gaze on her so wide, *Am.* v. 7
Threatning their owne confusion and decay: *H.L.* 82

Threatenings. after him full many *threatnings* threw, IV. viii. 40. 2
Now with faire speches, now with *threatnings* sterne, IV. xii. 24. 7

Threatens. *threatens* all the world to wast. IV. i. 45. 9
threatens all with corage stout. *Epig.* iv. 10

Threatful. layes forth her *threatfull* pikes *Mui.* 85
drive The hollow vessell through the *threatfull* wave; II. xii. 5. 6
cruell Mulciber would not obay His *threatfull* pride, III. xi. 26. 6
slack her *threatfull* hand for daungers dout: III. xii. 37. 4
he his *threatfull* speare Gan fewter, IV. vi. 10. 1
She chang'd that *threatfull* mood, V. v. 47. 9
Seem'd not to weigh his *threatfull* words VI. iii. 36. 2

Threating. *See* **Sky-threating.**

Threats. In vaine he *threats* his teeth, his tayle, his pawes, *Van.* x. 11
long the dore with rage and *threats* he bett, I. iii. 19. 1
'What meane these bloody vowes and idle *threats,* I. xii. 30. 1
when Rancor rife . . . *threats* his rusty knife. II. iv. 44. 5
Sometimes with *threats,* sometimes with hope of gayn, II. xi. 14. 8
great water flood, that . . . *threates* to overflow II. xi. 18. 5
their malice they did whet With cruell *threats* III. v. 17. 9
with sharpe *threates* her often did assayle; III. viii. 40. 8
doe thinke it *threates* the skye. III. ix. 45. 9
Threates with huge ruine him to fall upon, III. x. 58. 5
with sharpe *threats,* but *threats* the more increast their mood. V. iv. 4. 9
Threw many *threats,* if they the towne did win, V. iv. 37. 4
threates of any to be wroken. V. ix. 24. 9
when in wrath he *threats* the worlds decay, V. xi. 31. 8
Nought fear'd the childe his lookes, ne yet his *threats,* V. xi. 13. 1
threats his horns, and bellowes like the thonder: VI. v. 19. 8
mixed *threats* among, and much unto her vowed. VI. xi. 4. 9
all the gods he *threats* with thundring dart: *Am.* xxxix. 4

Three. Enclosing you in thrice *three* wards for ever, *Ro.* xv. 7
Three thinges to beare bene very burdenous, *S.C.* May 132
Thrise *three* Moones bene fully spent *S.C.* S. 20
ye *three* Twins, to light by Venus brought, *T.M.* 403
one of those *three* fatall Impes *Ti.* 17
Let those *three* fatall Sisters . . . Approach hereto; *D.* 16
Ne lesse praisworthie are the sisters *three,* *Col.* 536
Phyllis, the faire, is eldest of the *three:* *Col.* 541
eldest of *three* brethren; all *three* bred Of one bad sire, I. ii. 25. 7
thrise *three* times did fast from any bitt; I. iii. 14. 4
two of *three* her Nephewes are so fowle forlorne? I. v. 23. 9
dreadfull Cerberus His *three* deformed heads did lay along, I. v. 34. 2
The hight of *three* the tallest sonnes of mortall seed. I. vii. 8. 9
Three miles it might be easy heard arownd, I. viii. 4. 3
Ecchoes *three* aunswer'd it selfe againe: I. viii. 4. 4
three yardes deepe a furrow up did throw. I. viii. 8. 6
three Moones have changed thrice their hew, I. viii. 38. 6
The mother of *three* daughters, well upbrought I. x. 4. 3
the thrise *three* learned Ladies play Their hevenly notes, I. x. 54. 8
leave they take of Caelia and her daughters *three.* I. x. 68. 9
of *three* furlongs does but litle lacke; I. xi. 11. 7
Three ranckes of yron teeth enraunged were, I. xi. 13. 2
three mens strength unto the stroake he layd; I. xi. 20. 4
thrise *three* tymes had fild her crooked hornes, I. i. 53. 3
Therein *three* sisters dwelt II. ii. 13. 1

Three—*Continued.*
The children of one syre by mothers *three;* II. ii. 13. 2
three valiaunt knights to see *Three* combates joine in one, II. ii. 26. 1, 2
three dayes of men were full outwrought, II. vii. 65. 6
with his goodly sisters, Graces *three:* II. viii. 6. 6
Three times more furious and more puissaunt, II. viii. 34. 8
have *three* years (*twelve moneths) sought one, yet no where II. ix. 38. 9
three the chiefest and of greatest powre, II. ix. 47. 7
there dwelt *three* honorable sages, II. ix. 47. 8
Three ages, such as mortall men contrive, II. ix. 48. 5
These *three* in these *three* rowmes did sondry dwell, II. ix. 48. 8
led to th' hindmost rowme of *three.* II. ix. 54. 9
those *three* monstrous stones doe most excell, II. x. 11. 5
He left *three* sonnes, II. x. 13. 4
three faire daughters, which were well uptraind II. x. 27. 3
Three sonnes he dying left, II. x. 64. 1
arrived here *three* hoyes Of Saxons, II. x. 64. 8
The one of which had two heades, th' other *three:* II. x. 73. 6
He left *three* sonnes, II. x. 74. 1
carried him perforse Above *three* furlongs, II. xi. 46. 5
all the *three* thereat woxe much afrayd, II. xii. 22. 6
depth exceeded not *three* cubits hight, II. xii. 62. 6
Ne did she stay till *three* on ground she layd III. i. 29. 1
spare to one, or two, or *three,* Rowme in their writtes; III. ii. 1. 7
taking thrise *three* heares from off her head, III. ii. 50. 1
three Moones with borrowd brothers light III. iii. 16. 2
So beene they *three three* sondry wayes ybent; III. iv. 47. 5
Three fosters Timias wound; III. v. Arg.
they were *three* Ungratious children III. v. 15. 5
the only last of *three* III. v. 24. 1
They *three* be dead with shame, III. v. 25. 9
onely *three* they were disposd so well; III. vii. 57. 3
yet *three* yeares I now abrode have strayd, III. vii. 57. 4
'inquire of thee what were those *three,* III. vii. 57. 6
Thus long they *three* together traveiled, III. x. 34. 1
Three nights in one, . . . He then did put, III. xi. 33. 8
All *three* to each unlike, III. xii. 24. 9
For which the *three* faire Goddesses did strive: IV. i. 22. 6
They by consent should chose the stoutest *three* IV. ii. 38. 7
Amongst those knights there were *three* brethren bold, IV. ii. 41. 1
Three bolder brethren never were yborne, IV. ii. 41. 2
bore *three* such, *three* such not to be fond! IV. ii. 41. 6
whose children werne All *three* as one; IV. ii. 41. 8
These *three* did love each other dearely well, IV. ii. 43. 1
Which did her powre into *three* parts divyde; IV. ii. 43. 4
Like *three* faire branches budding farre and wide, IV. ii. 43. 5
These *three* so noble babes to bring forth at one clap. IV. ii. 43. 9
Got these *three* lovely babes, that prov'd *three* champions bold. IV. ii. 45. 9
To the *three* fatall sisters house she went. IV. ii. 47. 4
the eldest of the *three,* IV. ii. 52. 4
all *three* according to their kynd: IV. ii. 53. 4
battell twixt *three* brethren with Cambell for Canacee: IV. iii. Arg.
in seeking for her children *three* Long life, IV. iii. 2. 2
These *three* that hardie chalenge tooke in hand, IV. iii. 3. 1
Soone after did the brethren *three* advance IV. iii. 5. 4
For lifes succession in those brethren *three.* IV. iii. 21. 5
Once thinke to match *three* such on equall cost, IV. iii. 24. 8
Three such as able were to match a puissant host? IV. iii. 24. 9
till the horned moone *three* courses did expire. IV. vi. 43. 9
of us *three* to morrow he will sure eate one.' IV. vii. 13. 9
When all *three* kinds of love together meet IV. ix. 1. 2
there the *three* renowmed brethren were, IV. xi. 42. 1
she in time forth brought These *three* faire sons, IV. xi. 42. 8
In *three* great rivers ran, IV. xi. 42. 9
save all us *three* alive.' IV. xii. 31. 9
'Within *three* daies,' (quoth he) V. ii. 4. 1
How that *three* warlike persons did appeare, V. iv. 36. 3
He had *three* sonnes, all *three* like fathers sonnes, V. vi. 33. 1
had *three* bodies in one wast empight, V. x. 8. 8
th' armes and legs of *three* to succour him in fight. V. x. 8. 9
Through his *three* bodies powre in one combynd; V. x. 9. 6
as he nigher drew, *three* knights he spyde, V. x. 34. 1
As *three* great Culverings for battrie bent, V. x. 34. 6
Through his *three* double hands thrise multiplyde, V. xi. 6. 2
Through all *three* bodies he him strooke attonce, V. xi. 14. 1
all the *three* attonce fell on the plaine, V. xi. 14. 2
So now all *three* one sencelesse lumpe remaine, V. xi. 14. 5
Three times, as in defiance, there he strooke; V. xi. 22. 2
And in *three* battailes did so deadly daunt, VI. iv. 29. 8
Three mightie enemies did him most despight, VI. v. 13. 2
Three mightie ones, and cruell minded eeke, VI. v. 13. 3
his *three* foes shrowded in guilefull shade VI. v. 17. 8
his *three* foes Sought to encompasse him VI. v. 20. 1
Whom soone as his *three* enemies did vew, VI. v. 22. 6
Three other Ladies did both daunce and sing, VI. x. 12. 3
in the middest of those same *three* VI. x. 12. 6
most of all those *three* did her with gifts endew. VI. x. 14. 9
Those *three* to men all gifts of grace do graunt; VI. x. 15. 4
those *three* in the midst doe chiefe on her attend. VI. x. 21. 9
Sweete Goddesses all *three,* VI. x. 22. 9
'These *three* on men all gracious gifts bestow, VI. x. 23. 1
To be the fourth with those *three* other placed: VI. x. 25. 7
as they all *three* together went To the greene wood VI. x. 34. 1
As those *three* sacred Saints . . . quite their wits forgat, VII. vii. 7. 6
which *three* times thrise happy hath me made, *Am.* lxxiv. 3
Ye *three* Elizabeths! . . . That *three* such graces did unto me give. *Am.* lxxiv. 13, 14
ye *three* handmayds of the Cyprian Queene, *Epith.* 103
Threefold. trebly breaded in a *threefold* lace, III. ii. 50. 2
Three-forked. strikes the rockes with his *three-forked* mace; *Mui.* 315
Three-forked—*Continued.*
The fiers *threeforked* engin, . . . highest trees hath rent, I. viii. 9. 6
his *threeforkt* Pyke He stearnly shooke, III. xi. 40. 4
great Neptune, with his *threeforkt* mace, IV. xi. 11. 1
The tongues of Serpents, with *three forked* stings, VI. xii. 28. 2
Three hundred. *three hundred* Lords he slew Of British blood, II. x. 66. 6
Three hundred pledges for my good desartes, III. vii. 55. 4
thrice *three hundred* thanks for my good partes, III. vii. 55. 5
Three-quarters. Full measured *three quarters* of her yeare, II. i. 53. 2
Threescore. Mars in *three-score* yeares doth run his spheare. *Am.* lx. 4
Three-square. catching up in hast his *three-square* shield I. vi. 41. 8
seemd to couch under his shield *threesquare,* III. i. 4. 4
through his *three-square* scuchin percing quite III. iv. 16. 3
Three thousand. *three thousand* more there were Of th' Oceans seede, IV. xi. 52. 6
Thresh. The corne is theyrs, let other *thresh,* *S.C.* Jul. 191
To hedge, to ditch, to *thrash,* to thetch, to mowe? *Hub.* 264
the more he did him *thresh.* III. vii. 32. 9
He with his yron flale did *thresh* so thin, V. vii. 35. 7
Threshed. when I thought have *thresht* in swelling sheave, *S.C.* D. 123
With which he *thresht* out falshood, V. i. 12. 9
Thresher. in his hand his *thresher* ready keight. V. vi. 29. 7
Threshold. to stomble at the *threshold* flore: *S.C.* May 230
Before the *threshold* dreadfull Cerberus I. v. 34. 1
Him at the *threshold* mett, II. ii. 14. 9
His carkasse, tumbling on the *threshold,* V. x. 36. 8
Right in the middest of the *threshold* lay, V. x. 37. 4
Threttie. *See* **Thirty.**
Threw. *See* **Overthrew.**
threw forth a thousand rayes *Bel.*[1] ii. 7
Threwe downe this building to the lowest stone. *Bel.*[1] ii. 14
Threw forth abrode a thousand . . . leames, *Bel.*[1] ix. 10
Threw down the seats, and drove the Nymphes *Bel.* xii. 14
a thousand rayons *threw* *Bel.*[2] ii. 7
The honour of these noble boughs down *threw:* *Bel.*[2] v. 11
forth *threw* . . . a thousand shining beames: *Bel.*[2] xi. 9
Cedar . . . That farre abroad her daintie odours *threwe;* *Van.* vii. 3
pumie stones I hastly hent And *threwe;* *S.C.* Mar. 90
Threw forth lowd shrieks and drerie dolefull cries. *T.M.* 172
about his shoulders broad he *threw* An hairie hide *Mui.* 65
her pitcher downe she *threw,* And fled away: I. iii. 11. 6
threw his gauntlet, as a sacred pledge I. iv. 43. 1
Blaming of Fortune, which such troubles *threw,* I. vi. 31. 5
he . . . in a Dongeon deepe him *threw* without remorse. I. vii. 15. 9
prowdly *threw* to ground, as things of naught; I. vii. 18. 5
The light . . . Such blazing brightnesse through the ayer *threw,* I. viii. 19. 4
she . . . crowned mitre rudely *threw* asyde: I. viii. 25. 3
threw it to the ground, enraged rife, I. ix. 52. 5
Like sunny beames *threw* from her Christall face I. x. 12. 7
flames of fire he *threw* forth from his large nosethril. I. xi. 22. 9
cries . . . The hell-bred beast *threw* forth unto the skies, I. xi. 40. 3
forth he *threw* Huge flames I. xi. 44. 2
herselfe . . . She groveling *threw* to ground, II. i. 45. 9
he *threw* Into the grave, II. i. 61. 3
The Miser *threw* him selfe, as an Offall, II. iii. 8. 7
ambrosiall odours from them *threw,* II. iii. 22. 7
this answere forth he *threw:* II. iii. 33. 1
to the ground her *threw:* II. iv. 12. 4
threw forth sparkes of fyre; II. iv. 15. 6
With that one of his thrillant darts he *threw,* II. iv. 46. 1
round about him *threw* forth sparkling fire, II. v. 2. 6
daintie odours round about them *threw:* II. v. 29. 6
beam great brightnes *threw* Through the dim shade, II. vii. 45. 2
Apple . . . emongst the gods false Ate *threw;* II. vii. 55. 5
long tonnell thence The smoke forth *threw.* II. ix. 29. 4
Great Godmer *threw* . . . At bold Canutus; II. x. 11. 8
him she tooke And *threw* in bands, II. x. 18. 7
Stout Ferrex and sterne Porrex him in prison *threw.* II. x. 34. 9
with exceeding sway *Threw* at his foe, II. xi. 36. 2
Mordure . . . he lightly *threw* away, II. xi. 41. 7
Him thereinto he *threw* without remorse, II. xi. 46. 7
on them rusht, and *threw* A subtile net, II. xii. 81. 3
Still as she fledd her eye she backward *threw,* III. i. 16. 1
Shee *threw* her selfe downe on the Continent, III. iv. 30. 5
at him a quiv'ring dart he *threw,* III. v. 19. 1
every one *threw* forth reproches rife III. vi. 14. 6
Threw forth most dainty odours and most sweet delight. III. vi. 43. 9
Her selfe to fight addrest, and *threw* her lode aside. III. vii. 38. 9
She *threw* away her burden angrily; III. vii. 44. 2
Beastly he *threwe* her downe, III. viii. 26. 8
far abroad his mightie braunches *threw* III. ix. 47. 8
From thence he *threw* him selfe despiteously, III. x. 56. 7
Her ample shield she *threw* before her face, III. xi. 25. 2
downe on the bloudy plaine Her selfe she *threw,* IV. iii. 47. 5
all men *threw* out vowes and wishes vaine. IV. iv. 16. 6
Cambelloes armes therefore he on him *threw,* IV. iv. 33. 6
there he *threw* her in, nought feeling, ne nought fearing. IV. vii. 8. 9
he *threw* her rudely on the flore, IV. vii. 28. 1
all he broke And *threw* away, IV. vii. 39. 2
all the bounty which Belphebe *threw* On him, IV. viii. 6. 4
The stone which passed straunger at him *threw:* IV. viii. 36. 6
after him full many threatnings *threw,* IV. viii. 40. 2
Her *threw* into a dongeon deepe and blind, IV. xi. 2. 4
Into his mouth his maystring bridle *threw,* IV. xii. 13. 6
So he the words into his ballaunce *threw,* V. ii. 44. 8
of those words, the which that boaster *threw,* V. iii. 23. 6
The badges of reproch, he *threw* away, V. iv. 35. 4
Threw many threats, if they the towne did win, V. iv. 37. 4
his sharpe sword he *threw* from him apart, V. v. 13. 3
she *threw* Her selfe uppon her bed, and did lament: V. vi. 13. 6

Threw—*Continued.*
Him selfe before her feete he lowly *threw*, . . . V. vii. 16. 2
the Pagan *threw* A shivering dart . . . V. viii. 32. 5
Againe the Pagan *threw* another dart, . . . V. viii. 34. 1
She *threw* her husbands murdred infant out; . . . V. viii. 47. 2
He suddenly his net upon her *threw*, . . . V. ix. 14. 2
He *threw* his burden downe, and fast away did fly. . . . V. ix. 14. 9
prickt him so that he away it *threw*: . . . V. ix. 18. 6
blasphemies forth *threw* Against his Gods, . . . V. xi. 12. 3
Though darts from shore and stones they at him *threw*; . . . V. xii. 5. 5
To her, that so false sclaunders at him *threw*: . . . V. xii. 42. 5
His weapons soone from him he *threw* away, . . . VI. iii. 27. 6
On the cold ground maugre himselfe he *threw* . . . VI. iv. 40. 3
Upon the ground her selfe she fiercely *threw*, . . . VI. v. 5. 1
his shield about him *threw*, . . . VI. viii. 7. 2
fragrant odours they upon her *threw*; . . . VI. x. 14. 8
greater mischiefe on her *threw*, . . . VI. xi. 2. 6
up to heaven his eyes fast-streming *threw*: . . . VI. xi. 28. 6
in dongeon deepe Without compassion cruelly he *threw*; . . . VI. xii. 5. 7
robd the Chancell, and the deskes downe *threw*, . . . VI. xii. 25. 2
His shield he on him *threw*, . . . VI. xii. 30. 6
He grind, hee bit, he scratcht, he venim *threw*, . . . VI. xii. 31. 8
Whilest Calidore him under him downe *threw*; . . . VI. xii. 32. 7
round about such beames of splendor *threw*, . . . VII. vii. 6. 7
(*which) they at her foot-stoole *threw*; . . . VII. vii. 10. 7
flowres, That dainty odours from them *threw* . . . *Am.* lxiv. 3
all his off-spring into thraldome *threw*, . . . *H.H.L.* 124
All which upon those goodly Birds they *threw* . . . *Proth.* 76

Thrice. *Thrice* having seene . . . *Ro.* i. 9
Thrice unto you with lowd voyce I appeale, . . . *Ro.* i. 11
Enclosing you in *thrice* three wards for ever, . . . *Ro.* xv. 7
have I worne out *thrise* threttie yeares, . . . *S.C.* F. 17
Thrise three Moones . . . *S.C.* S. 20
He compast Troy *thrice* with his bodie dedd. . . . *Gn.* 528
thrice happie then . . . the condition of mortall men. . . . *Hub.* 149
in field against them *thrice* prevailed; . . . *Ti.* 111
happie were those dayes, *thrice* happie were! . . . *Ti.* 329
Thrise happie she, whom he to praise did chose. . . . *As.* 36
'*Thrise* happie Mayd, . . . *Col.* 480
Thrise happie do I hold thee, noble swaine, . . . *Col.* 552
And *thrise* nine hundred *Aves* . . . I. iii. 13. 9
Thrise every weeke in ashes shee did sitt, . . . I. iii. 14. 2
And *thrise* three times did fast from any bitt; . . . I. iii. 14. 4
Thrise did she sinke adowne in deadly swownd, . . . I. vii. 24. 3
thrise he her reviv'd . . . I. vii. 24. 4
harmeful head, *thrise* heated in the fire, . . . I. vii. 37. 3
three Moones have changed *thrice* their hew, . . . I. viii. 38. 6
three Moones . . . have been *thrice* hid . . . I. viii. 38. 7
'*Thrise* happy man,' said then the father grave, . . . I. x. 51. 1
thrise three learned Ladies play Their hevenly notes, . . . I. x. 54. 8
Thrise he assayd it from his foote to draw, . . . I. xi. 41. 7
thrise in vaine to draw it did assay; . . . I. xi. 41. 8
Thrise happy man the knight himselfe did hold, . . . I. xii. 40. 6
home ye may report *thrise* happy newes; . . . II. i. 33. 8
Thrise he her reard, and *thrise* she sunck againe, . . . II. i. 46. 3
thrise three tymes had fild her crooked hornes, . . . II. i. 53. 3
Thrise happy man, who fares them both atweene! . . . II. i. 58. 5
'Now hath faire Phebe . . . *Thrise* seene the shadowes . . . II. ii. 44. 2
Thrise happy man,' (said then the Briton knight) . . . II. ix. 5. 1
Even *thrise* eleven descents the crowne retaynd, . . . II. x. 45. 8
taking *thrise* three heares from off her head, . . . III. ii. 50. 1
Shee to the virgin sayd, *thrise* sayd she itt; . . . III. ii. 50. 6
Spitt *thrise* upon me, *thrise* upon me spitt; . . . III. ii. 50. 8
Thrise she her turnd contrary, and returnd . . . III. ii. 51. 3
Thrise shined faire, and *thrise* seemd dim and wan, . . . III. iii. 16. 3
Thrise shall he fight with them, and twise shall win; . . . III. iii. 30. 6
feld Great Ulfin *thrise* . . . III. iii. 55. 6
His mother swowned *thrise*, . . . III. iv. 35. 1
thrice three hundred thanks for my good partes, . . . III. vii. 55. 5
not so yellow *thryse* As Florimells fayre heare: . . . III. viii. 7. 7
thrise his brest he stroke, . . . III. viii. 22. 3
then returned, having marched *thrise*, . . . III. xii. 26. 8
thrise his hand to kill her did upreare, . . . IV. i. 54. 8
thrise he drew it backe; . . . IV. i. 54. 9
Thrise happie mother, and *thrise* happie morne, . . . IV. ii. 41. 5
marching *thrise* in warlike ordinance, . . . IV. iii. 5. 7
Thrise lowted lowly to the noble Mayd, . . . IV. iii. 5. 8
Thrise happie Ladie, and *thrise* happie knight, . . . IV. iv. 16. 7
Ah, cruell hand! and *thrise* more cruell hart, . . . IV. vi. 16. 8
Don Braggadochios name resounded *thrise*: . . . V. iii. 15. 4
thrise did lay his hand upon his sword, . . . V. iii. 36. 3
Through his three double hands *thrise* multiplyde, . . . V. xi. 6. 2
thrise have needed for the nonce Them to have stricken, . . . V. xi. 14. 3
Them to have stricken, and *thrise* to have slaine. . . . V. xi. 14. 4
His trompet shrill hath *thrise* already sounded, . . . *Am.* xix. 2
Thrise happie she! that is so well assured . . . *Am.* lix. 1
which three times *thrise* happy hath me made, . . . *Am.* lxxiv. 3
Thrise happie man! . . . *H.L.* 209
But who so may, *thrise* happie man him hold, . . . *H.H.B.* 239

Thrid, -s. *See* **Thread, -s.**

Thrift. more for *thrift* did care than for gay clothing: . . . *Hub.* 231
little *thrift* for him he did it too: . . . *Hub.* 240
They shall him make an ill accompt of *thrift*. . . . *Hub.* 307
care of *thrift*, and husbandry, . . . *Hub.* 1170
After lost credit and consumed *thrift*, . . . II. xii. 8. 8

Thriftiness. askes small paines, but *thriftines* to save, . . . *Hub.* 278

Thriftless. With all the *thriftless* games that may be found; . . . *Hub.* 801
Consumed had their goods and *thriftlesse* howres, . . . I. v. 51. 8
lustfull luxurie and *thriftlesse* wast. . . . II. xii. 9. 3

Thrifty. *teares . . . to quenche thy *thriftye* payne. . . . *S.C.* Ap. 8

Thrifty—*Continued.*
They han great stores and *thriftye* stockes, . . . *S.C.* Jul. 193
lavish cups and *thriftie* bitts of meate, . . . *S.C.* O. 105

Thrill. *See* **Thrall.**
the hart that she did *thrill*. . . . I. x. 19. 9
did light In his left thigh, and deepely did it *thrill*: . . . III. v. 20. 7
the bosters hart did *thrill* With such amazment, . . . III. x. 43. 5
shrieches shrill, Percing his hart, with pities point did *thrill*; . . . VI. iv. 18. 5

Thrillant. The knight his *thrillant* speare againe assayd . . . I. xi. 20. 2
With that one of his *thrillant* darts he threw, . . . II. iv. 46. 1

Thrilled. That cruell word her tender hart so *thrild*, . . . I. vi. 37. 1
eger greedinesse through every member *thrild*. . . . I. viii. 6. 9
with percing point Of pitty deare his hart was *thrilled* sore; . . . I. viii. 39. 2
thrild with point of thorough-piercing paine: . . . II. i. 38. 5
with which she *thrild* Fraile harts, . . . II. xii. 78. 7
rive with thousand throbs thy *thrilled* brest: . . . III. ii. 32. 5
Ythrild with deepe disdaine of his proud threat, . . . III. iv. 15. 1
both his sides were *thrilled* with the throw, . . . III. v. 21. 8
Forthy he *thrild* thee with a leaden dart . . . III. xi. 36. 6
The cruell steele, which *thrild* her dying hart, . . . III. xii. 38. 1
his heart Was *thrild* with inward griefe: . . . IV. i. 49. 7
As one whose inner parts had bene *ythrild* . . . IV. iii. 22. 4
His hart was *thrild* with point of deadly feare, . . . IV. vi. 37. 2
through it *thrild* His greedy throte, . . . IV. vii. 31. 6
thrild With that selfe arrow . . . IV. vii. 36. 4

Thrilling. *See* **Heart-thrilling.**
A *thrilling* throbbe from her hart did aryse, . . . *S.C.* May 208
he perced . . . With *thrilling* point of deadly yron brand, . . . I. iii. 42. 7
The pitteous mayden, . . . Does throw out *thrilling* shriekes, . . . I. vi. 6. 2
thrilling sorrow throwne his utmost dart: . . . I. vii. 25. 2
make agreement with her *thrilling* eyes; . . . *Am.* xxxvi. 6

Thrist- ed, -y. *See* **Thirst -ed, -y.**

Thrive. *See* **Thrived.**
ill may they *thrive!* . . . *S.C.* Au. 19
Or *thrive* in welth, she shalbe mine, . . . *S.C.* Au. 111
God shield, man, he should so ill have *thrive*, . . . *S.C.* S. 226
In case thou ever there wilt hope to *thrive*, . . . *Hub.* 632
ye may better *thrive* than thousands moe.' . . . *Hub.* 642
ever *thrive* in that unluckie quest; . . . *Hub.* 916
whilest him fortune favourd, fayre did *thrive* In bloudy field; . . . I. iii. 37. 8
Long maist thou live, and better *thrive* withall . . . II. i. 37. 4
by adventrous marchandize to *thrive*,) . . . VI. viii. 35. 7

Thrived. fairely well shee *thryvd*, . . . III. iv. 44. 8

Thro. *See* **Throe.**
Yet knowing not what meant that sodaine *thro*, . . . VI. xii. 17. 2

Throat. Feete of a beare, a Lions *throte* she had. . . . *Rev.* i. 5
in his *throat* him pricking softly under, . . . *Van.* v. 9
they will carven the shepheards *throte*. . . . *S.C.* S. 41
To raunge the fields with wide open *throte*. . . . *S.C.* S. 195
let out the sheepes bloud at his *throte*. . . . *S.C.* S. 207
called Lowder, with a hollow *throte*, . . . *S.C.* S. 217
throat through thirst to nought nigh being dride . . . *Gn.* 387
Into his *throate* and life it pierced quight, . . . IV. iii. 30. 4
through it thrild His greedy *throte*, . . . IV. vii. 31. 7
stuft with rancour and despight Up to the *throat*, . . . IV. viii. 24. 4
and thrust it all attone Into his gaping *throte*, . . . VI. iv. 21. 5
and, laying mightie hold Upon his *throte*, . . . VI. iv. 22. 4
drinke of every brooke when thirst my *throte* doth boyle. . . . VI. ix. 23. 9

Throats. The next to heale theyr *throtes*. . . . *S.C.* Jul. 88
with hollow *throates*, The Choristers . . . sing, . . . *Epith.* 220

Throb. A thrilling *throbbe* from her hart did aryse, . . . *S.C.* May 208
she heard with grievous *throb* Him grone, . . . III. xi. 8. 6
my heart gan *throb* . . . IV. x. 53. 1

Throbbing. With hart then *throbbing*, . . . II. iv. 17. 1

Throbs. Throwing out thousand *throbs* . . . *Bel.*[2] vi. 13
Folding her armes . . . with thousand *throbs*, . . . *Bel.*[2] x. 2
many bitter *throbs* did throw, . . . II. i. 47. 3
with hart-thrilling *throbs* and bitter stowre, . . . III. ii. 5. 3
rive with thousand *throbs* thy thrilled brest: . . . III. ii. 32. 5
swelling *throbs* empeach His foltring toung . . . III. xi. 12. 2

Throe. *See* **Thro, Throw.**
Notes sad enough t' expresse this bitter *throw*: . . . *Mui.* 414
have mind of that last bitter *throw*; . . . I. x. 41. 8

Throes. *See* **Throws.**

Throghly. *See* **Throughly.**

Throne. flie up to the *throne* of Gods, . . . *Bel.*[1] ix. 6
up to the *throne* of Gods did flie, . . . *Bel.*[2] xi. 6
home they bringen in a royall *throne*, . . . *S.C.* May 29
all the peoples prayers to present Before his *throne*, . . . *Hub.* 472
The Ape, thus seized of the Regall *throne*, . . . *Hub.* 1111
thy *throne* royall with dishonour blent: . . . *Hub.* 1330
As should be worthie of his fathers *throne*. . . . *Mui.* 32
When she beholds from her celestiall *throne* . . . *D.* 380
high hath set his *throne* where Tiberis doth pas. . . . I. ii. 22. 9
a rich *throne*, as bright as sunny day; . . . I. iv. 8. 2
To dim the brightnesse of her glorious *throne*, . . . I. iv. 8. 8
the lowest stayre Of her high *throne*; . . . I. iv. 13. 6
hevenly *throne*, where thousand Angels shine? . . . I. x. 51. 6
High reard their royall *throne* in Britans land, . . . I. x. 65. 4
In widest Ocean she her *throne* does reare, . . . II. ii. 40. 6
What meant that preace about that Ladies *throne*, . . . II. vii. 48. 2
ere he had established his *throne*, . . . II. x. 10. 1
with all shame that sacred *throne* he fild. . . . II. x. 21. 2
the roiall *throne* forlorne. . . . II. x. 36. 5
Imperious Love hath highest set his *throne*, . . . III. ii. 23. 2
therein fixt his *throne*, . . . III. iii. 33. 6
in the sacred *throne* Of her chaste bodie; . . . III. vi. 5. 7
in long Alba plast his *throne* apart; . . . III. ix. 43. 7
The winged boy did thrust into his *throne*, . . . III. xi. 35. 6
In which her kingdomes *throne* is chiefly resiant. . . . IV. xi. 28. 9

Throne—*Continued.*
Upon a *throne* of gold full bright and sheene, ... V. ix. 27. 5
Encompassed the *throne* on which she sate,— . . . . V. ix. 29. 6
Those did upon Mercillaes *throne* attend, ... V. ix. 32. 5
Taking them up unto her stately *throne,* . . . . V. ix. 37. 6
Her sitting on an Ivory *throne* shee found, ... VII. vi. 9. 1
let her selfe into that Ivory *throne;* . . . . VII. vi. 11. 2
in his soveraine *throne* gan straight dispose Himselfe, ... VII. vi. 24. 7
like a *throne* did showe. . . . . VII. vii. 8. 9
Thus sitting in her *throne,* as I have teld, ... VII. vii. 13. 5
There vertue raynes as Queene in royal *throne,* . . . . *Epith.* 194
in mens harts thou mayst thy *throne* enstall, ... *H.B.* 265
Whose kingdomes *throne* no thought of earthly wight Can comprehend, ... *H.H.L.* 40
That sits upon the righteous *throne* on hy, ... *H.H.B.* 151
His *throne* is built upon Eternity, ... *H.H.B.* 152
His *throne* is all encompassed around, ... *H.H.B.* 177
Thrones. our royall *thrones,* which lately stood . . . . . . *T.M.* 313
do those men in golden *thrones* repose, ... *Ti.* 370
Saints and Angels in celestiall *thrones* . . . . *D.* 285
Upon the *thrones* of mortall Princes tend, ... V. ix. 32. 2
Throng. unfitte to thrust in skilfull *thronge,* . . . . *S.C.* N. 27
if thee list unto the Court to *throng,* . . . . *Hub.* 502
that blessed *throng* Of heavenlie Poets . . . . *Ti.* 340
they all gan *throng* about him neare, ... *Col.* 52
emongst the learned *throng.'* . . . . *Col.* 367
To blazon broade emongst her learned *throng:* . . . . I. Pr. 1. 8
to the troubled chamber all in armes did *throng.* . . . . . . III. i. 62. 9
thy moyst mountaines each on others *throng,* . . . . III. iv. 8. 5
nether Phoebus beams could through them *throng,* . . . . . III. vi. 44. 8
sore him selfe does *throng*) . . . . III. ix. 45. 4
Them guyded through the *throng,* . . . . V. ix. 23. 9
all the vulgar did about them *throng* . . . . V. xi. 34. 7
he thrusts into the thickest *throng* . . . . VI. viii. 49. 1
sorrowes heapt on her in greater *throng;* . . . . VI. xi. 2. 7
Out of their townes did round about him *throng,* . . . . . . VI. xii. 37. 4
breaking forth, did thick about me *throng.* . . . . *Am.* xii. 8
Thronging. The heapes of people, *thronging* in the hall, . . . I. iv. 16. 7
thronging thicke her to behold, ... IV. iii. 41. 2
Through (*partial list*). *See* **Thorough.**
A lively streame, . . . Ranne *through* the mid, ... *Rev.* iv. 13
Throgh the wide woods and groves, ... *Gn.* 32
Much blood *throgh* many wounds therein receaved, ... *Hub.* 207
throgh their owne faire handling wisely wroght, ... *Hub.* 554
Through power of that he passeth *through* the herds . . . . *Hub.* 1284
Trembling *through* hasty rage . . . . I. iv. 33. 9
through his own foolish pride Or weaknes, ... I. viii. 1. 6
'For whether he, *through* fatal deepe foresight, ... I. ix. 7. 1
But *through* his boldnes rather feare did reach; . . . . I. ix. 25. 8
at last he made *through* silence suddein breach. . . . . . . I. ix. 25. 9
And troubled blood *through* his pale face was seene . . . . . I. ix. 51. 5
Through wisedome of a matrone grave and hore; . . . . I. x. 3. 5
Each bone might *through* his body well be red; . . . . I. x. 48. 5
And every sinew seene, *through* his long fast; . . . . I. x. 48. 6
Through famous Poets verse each where renownd, ... I. x. 54. 7
Proclaymed joy and peace *through* all his state; . . . . . . I. xii. 3. 8
sides with cruell steele *Through* launched, ... II. i. 38. 7
Through thicke and thin, both over banck and bush, ... III. i. 17. 5
These stranger knights, *through* passing, forth were led . . . III. i. 33. 1
through her bones the false instilled fire Did spred . . . . III. i. 56. 4
Through thick and thin, *through* mountains and *through* playns, III. iv. 46. 1
That *through* she passed, as a thonder bolt . . . . III. xi. 25. 6
wide woundes launched *through* his inner partes. . . . . . . III. xi. 44. 9
her discolourd bow she spreds *through* hevens hight. . . . . . III. xi. 47. 9
Quite *through* transfixed with a deadly dart, ... III. xii. 21. 3
quite *through* (**throgh*) the body strooke. . . . . V. xi. 13. 9
through his yeares . . . aside had set The use of armes, . . . V. xi. 37. 3
And wading *through* the waves with stedfast sway, ... V. xii. 5. 6
He *through* occasion called was away . . . . V. xii. 27. 2
spreds it selfe *through* all civilitie: . . . . VI. Pr. 4. 5
him pursu'd and chaced *through* the plaine, ... VI. i. 22. 7
through lives despeire Untimely dyde, ... VI. ii. 28. 3
Having both sides *through* grypt with griesly wound. . . . . VI. iii. 27. 5
now strong *through* rest so long a space, ... VI. v. 7. 5
further could not pas *Through* feeblenesse, ... VI. v. 31. 9
whose griefe *through* suffraunce sore increast. . . . . VI. v. 39. 9
past *through* many perillous assayes, ... VI. vi. 3. 4
which was fall'n into this feeble case *Through* many wounds, VI. vi. 20. 8
him hasted *Through* the thick prease, ... VI. vi. 28. 4
had no life him left *through* former feare. . . . . VI. vi. 32. 9
Through tempering of her words and lookes . . . . VI. vi. 41. 9
through piercing, did devowre His vitall breath, ... VI. vii. 8. 7
Through thick and thin, *through* mountains and *through* plains, VI. vii. 44. 2
Through hils, *through* dales, *through* forests, and *through* plaines, ... VI. ix. 2. 6
Through hils and dales, *through* bushes and *through* breres, . VI. viii. 32. 1
Through every place with restlesse paine and toile . . . . . VI. xii. 22. 8
Knights to byde, Till they decayed *through* pride: . . . . . *Proth.* 136
through all Spaine did thunder, ... *Proth.* 147
Through-lanced. Seeing my hart *through-launced* every where . *Am.* lvii. 7
Through-launched. *seeing my hart *through launched* every where *Am.* lvii. 7
Throughly. *See* **Thoroughly.**
my thought was *throghly* placed, ... *Van.* i. 9
Having his hunger *throughly* satisfide . . . . *Van.* x. 2
A goodly Oake . . . *Throughly* rooted, ... *S.C.* F. 107
throughly arm'd against such coverture, ... *Hub.* 683
Alabaster *throughly* taught In all this skill, ... *Col.* 400
his woundes wyde Not *throughly* heald . . . . I. v. 45. 5
The sight whereof so *throughly* him dismaid, ... I. ix. 50. 1
He daily dyde, yet never *throughly* dyen couth. . . . . . . II. vii. 58. 9

Throughly—*Continued.*
throughly skild in use of shield and speare; . . . . IV. iii. 7. 2
now his courage being *throughly* fired, ... IV. ix. 35. 1
Till I was *throughly* past the perill of his reach. . . . . . IV. x. 36. 9
now by this the feast was *throughly* ended, ... IV. xii. 18. 1
Whyleare by Tryphon was not *throughly* healed, ... IV. xii. 22. 6
his old hurt, which was not *throughly* cured. . . . . IV. xii. 23. 6
wheresoever it did light, it *throughly* shard. . . . . V. i. 10. 9
both in armes well traind, and *throughly* tride: . . . . V. ii. 17. 4
All which when Talus *throughly* had perfourmed, ... V. ii. 28. 6
Whom when discovered they had *throughly* eide, ... V. iii. 17. 4
having *throughly* heard and seene Al those great wrongs, . . V. viii. 24. 1
Where they mote heare the matter *throughly* scand . . . . . V. ix. 37. 7
Who then can thee, Mercilla, *throughly* prayse, ... V. x. 3. 1
Ere he were *throughly* buckled to his geare, ... V. xi. 10. 2
To worke his utter shame, and *throughly* him confound. . . . VI. v. 14. 9
the biting of that harmefull Beast Was *throughly* heal'd. . . VI. vi. 15. 6
Is forcibly kept downe, till he be *throughly* queld. . . . . . VI. xii. 30. 9
Throughout. an universall night *Throughout* the world . . . . *Hub.* 1298
Throughout (**throghout*) the world, with wofull heavie thought; *D.* 465
when by tract they hunted had *throughout,* . . . . I. i. 11. 5
Renowmd *throughout* the world . . . . I. x. 3. 2
proclaymd *throughout* the land, ... I. xii. 40. 2
shrilled cleare *Throughout* the wood . . . . II. iii. 20. 8
Which all above besprinckled was *throughout* . . . . II. iii. 26. 6
Famous *throughout* the world . . . . II. v. 26. 2
high accompt *through out* all Elfin land, ... III. v. 4. 6
a stormy whirlwind blew *Throughout* the house, ... III. xii. 3. 2
So he continued all that day *throughout,* . . . . IV. iv. 43. 5
water all the English soile *throughout:* . . . . IV. xi. 30. 2
To Artegall he turn'd and went with him *throughout.* . . . . V. ii. 54. 9
hurly-burly moved was *Throughout* the hall . . . . V. iii. 30. 2
wandring two whole yeares *Throughout* the world . . . . . . VI. vii. 38. 2
It crackt *throughout,* (yet did no bloud appeare,) . . . . . . VI. viii. 16. 5
he that monster sought *Throughout* the world, ... VI. xii. 13. 5
Throw, *etc.* *See* **Overthrow,** *etc.,* **Throe.**
Upon seven hilles *throw* forth his gladsome shade, ... *Bel.*[1] v. 2
to *throwe* out thondring words of threate, ... *S.C.* O. 104
meane for better winde about to *throwe.* . . . . *Hub.* 80
dare their follies forth so rashlie *throwe,* . . . . *T.M.* 220
Did *throw* forth shrieks and cries . . . . *T.M.* 538
Well made to strike, to *throw,* to leape, to lift, ... *As.* 75
on the cold deare earth himselfe did *throw;* . . . . *As.* 124
over all a blacke stole shee did *throw:* . . . . I. i. 4. 5
The pitteous mayden, . . . Does *throw* out thrilling shriekes, . I. vi. 6. 2
seemd to *throw* . . . bright sparckles fiery redd, ... I. vii. 31. 6
three yardes deepe a furrow up did *throw.* . . . . I. viii. 8. 6
She would commaund themselves to . . . *throw* in raging sea . I. x. 20. 8
to the ground he is . . . constraynd To *throw* his ryder; . . . I. xi. 23. 7
at his feet their lawrell boughes did *throw.* . . . . I. xii. 6. 4
did *throw* This gentle knight into so great distresse, ... I. xii. 33. 7
a deadly shrieke she forth did *throw* . . . . II. i. 38. 1
many bitter throbs did *throw,* . . . . II. i. 47. 3
throwe her sweete smels al arownd. . . . . II. vi. 12. 9
Do not I . . . *throw* the crowne . . . . II. vii. 11. 6
every one did strive his fellow downe to *throw.* . . . . . . II. vii. 47. 9
hope doth *throw* Adowne the streame, ... II. xi. 18. 7
It booted not to thinke that *throw* to beare, ... II. xi. 36. 4
threatneth downe to *throw* his ragged rift . . . . II. xii. 4. 5
Sir knight, your ready arms about you *throw.'* . . . . II. xii. 37. 9
throw into the well sweet Rosemaryes, ... III. i. 36. 7
secret darts did *throw;* . . . . III. i. 51. 8
forth to *throw* All the huge threasure, ... III. iv. 22. 4
Upon the grassy ground to sleepe a *throw:* . . . . III. iv. 53. 8
both his sides were thrilled with the *throw,* . . . . III. v. 21. 8
drew he his bright sword, and gan about him *throw.* . . . . . III. ix. 16. 9
He from that deadly *throw* made no defence, ... III. ix. 29. 1
Him selfe to save from that so deadly *throw;* . . . . IV. iii. 33. 5
his shield, which lightly he did *throw* Over his head . . . . IV. viii. 42. 3
doth the daedale earth *throw* forth to thee . . . . IV. x. 45. 1
The which ambrosiall odours forth did *throw* . . . . IV. xi. 46. 3
Is lightly stricken with some stones *throw;* . . . . V. i. 21. 7
force of stones which they did *throw,* . . . . V. ii. 22. 7
'Therefore I will *throw* downe these mountaines hie, ... V. ii. 38. 1
Into the Sea her selfe did headlong *throw,* . . . . V. iv. 10. 3
Or God or Fortune unto me did *throw,* . . . . V. iv. 14. 3
from you lightly *throw* This squalid weede, ... V. iv. 34. 5
Much was he grieved with that haplesse *throe,* . . . . V. viii. 35. 1
For ye into like thraldome me did *throw,* . . . . V. xi. 41. 8
forced him to *throw* it quite away, ... V. xi. 46. 3
Did spred abroad and *throw* in th' open wynd: . . . . V. xii. 33. 7
To *throw* amongst the good which others had disprad. . . . . V. xii. 36. 9
Him to attache, and downe to hell to *throwe;* . . . . VII. vi. 16. 7
still *throw* betweene Some graces to be seene; . . . . *Epith.* 106
Throw thy selfe downe, with trembling innocence, ... *H.H.B.* 143
Throweth. He . . . downe from his steed me *throw'th* . . . . VI. ii. 17. 8
Throwing. *Throwing* out thousand throbs . . . . *Bel.*[2] vi. 13
Hyperion, *throwing* foorth his beames full hott, ... *Gn.* 156
Throwing his firie eyes on everie side, ... *Gn.* 270
throwing forth sweet odours . . . . *Col.* 610
Throwing away her broken chaines and bands, ... II. xi. 47. 4
Now *throwing* forth lewd wordes immodestly; . . . . II. xii. 16. 4
wilfully him *throwing* on the gras . . . . III. xi. 27. 5
down the rock him *throwing,* . . . . V. ii. 49. 9
throwing downe his load out of his hand, ... VI. vii. 24. 3
throwing flowres out of her lap around: . . . . VII. vii. 34. 3
Thrown. pitilesse *throwne* downe in pit of fire. . . . . *Rev.* iii. 14
Some on the rocks of Caphareus are *throwne;* . . . . *Gn.* 586
yelling shrieks *throwne* up into the skies. . . . . *T.M.* 24
Downe to the earth his heavie eyes were *throwne,* . . . . . . *D.* 46

Thrown—*Continued.*
through celestiall doome *thrown* out of dore, ... I. v. 47. 4
All these together in one heape were *throwne,* . . . . I. v. 49. 1
lastly *thrown* themselves into these heavy stowres. . . . . I. v. 51. 9
their noise which through the aire was *thrown,* . . . . I. vi. 45. 8
thrilling sorrow *throwne* his utmost dart: . . . . I. vii. 25. 2
ne ever . . . Had *throwne* to ground the unregarded right: . I. vii. 47. 5
carcases were . . . *throwne* about the cliffs. . . . . I. ix. 34. 6
widow-like sad wimple *throwne* away, ... I. xii. 22. 3
idle threats, *Throwne* out . . . . I. xii. 30. 2
As budding braunch . . . *throwen* forth, till it be withered. . II. ii. 2. 7
was avoided quite, and *throwne* out privily. . . . . II. ix. 32. 9
The light goes out, and weeke is *throwne* away: . . . . II. x. 30. 2
Marinell of Britomart Is *throwne* on the Rich strond: . . . . III. iv. Arg.
In one sad night consumd and *throwen* downe: . . . . III. ix. 39. 5
A little off his shield was rudely *throwne,* . . . . III. xi. 7. 6
There on the cold earth him now *thrown* she found, ... III. xii. 43. *or.* 6
from thence out *throwen* Into this world . . . . IV. ii. 1. 2
Throwne out by angry Jove in his vengeance, ... IV. vi. 14. 2
Thine honor sav'd, though into thraldome *throwne?'* . . . IV. vii. 19. 5
stone; Such as . . . Were *throwne* by Pyrrha and Deucalione: V. Pr. 2. 7
having from his courser her downe *throwne,* . . . . V. i. 17. 7
throwne it up unto my brothers share: . . . . V. iv. 8. 4
for this threasure *throwne* uppon his strand; . . . . V. iv. 15. 5
the sea hath it unto me *throwne?'* . . . . V. iv. 18. 7
thrown his shield atween, ... V. xi. 30. 9
a slender dart, . . . *throwne* not in vaine, ... VI. ii. 12 .7
He forth was *thrown* into the greedy seas; . . . . *Am.* xxxviii. 2
blessings, which ye have . . . upon you *thrown;* . . . . *Am.* lxvi. 2

Throws. The skie . . . *Throwes* lightning forth, ... *Gn.* 582
Against the bitter *throwes* of dolours darts: . . . . *T.M.* 134
Ne plate, ne male, could ward so mighty *throwes,* . . . . II. v. 9. 3
Whiles nothing envious nature them forth *throwes* . . . . II. vi. 15. 4
earth out of her fruitfull woomb *Throwes* forth to men, . . . II. vii. 51. 7
Ne shield defend the thunder of his *throwes:* . . . . II. viii. 41. 3
in her way *throwes* mischiefe and mischaunce, ... II. ix. 8. 3
sweete love gentle fitts emongst them *throwes,* . . . . III. vi. 41. 5
The quarry *throwes* to ground with fell despight, ... III. vii. 39. 5
from daunger of the *throwes* Backe to retire, ... IV. iii. 26. 3
Throwes forth upon the rivage round about him nere. . . . IV. vi. 20. 9
No flowre in field, that daintie odour *throwes,* . . . . IV. x. 22. 3
at him *throwes* it most despightfully: . . . . V. xii. 39. 4

Thrush. The *Thrush* replyes; . . . . *Epith.* 81

Thrush's. To take the ayre and heare the *thrushes* song, . . . VI. iv. 17. 3

Thrust. *See* **Thirst.**
Brere, Which proudly *thrust* into Thelement, ... *S.C.* F. 116
'I sawe Phoebus *thrust* out his golden hedde, ... *S.C.* Ap. 73
unfitte to *thrust* in skilfull thronge, ... *S.C.* N. 27
All these through fained crimes he *thrust* adowne, ... *Hub.* 1186
Full greedily into the heard he *thrust,* . . . . *As.* 104
An high headland *thrust* far into the sea, ... *Col.* 281
To *thrust* downe other into foule disgrace, ... *Col.* 691
as Exuls out of his court be *thrust.'* . . . . *Col.* 894
rudely he him *thrust,* and pusht with paine, ... I. i. 42. 4
the good knight, . . . The bleeding bough did *thrust* into the ground, ... I. ii. 44. 6
unto hell did *thrust* him downe alive, ... I. v. 40. 5
thrust from heaven dew, ... I. v. 42. 5
thrust them forth still as they wexed old: . . . . I. x. 31. 4
after blood to *thrust,* . . . . II. ii. 29. 6
first the Hag did *thrust* away; . . . . II. iv. 6. 2
on his brest his victor foote he *thrust:* . . . . II. v. 12. 6
him that raignd into his rowme *thrust* downe, ... II. vii. 11. 8
From whence the gods have her for envy *thrust:* . . . . II. vii. 49. 6
speare he *thrust* with puissant sway . . . . II. viii. 36. 3
thrust downe to hell below, ... III. iv. 55. 4
Did *thrust* the shallop from the floting strand: . . . . III. vii. 27. 8
hond Where ill became him rashly would have *thrust;* . . . III. viii. 25. 7
The winged boy did *thrust* into his throne, ... III. xi. 35. 6
Into the thickest of that knightly preasse He *thrust,* . . . IV. iv. 34. 2
as doth an eger hound *Thrust* to an Hynd . . . . IV. vi. 12. 4
I will *thrust* downe into the deepest maine, ... V. ii. 38. 4
he the right from thence did *thrust* away, ... V. vii. 49. 1
Me like a dog she out of dores did *thrust,* . . . . V. viii. 22. 7
Under her wombe his fatall sword he *thrust,* . . . . V. xi. 31. 2
and *thrust* it all attone Into his gaping throte, ... VI. iv. 21. 4
To *thrust* him out of dore doing his worst assay. . . . . VI. vi. 21. 9
did *thrust* it farre away, ... VI. ix. 33. 2
To *thrust* faire Phoebe from her silver bed, ... VII. vi. 21. 3
The younger *thrust* the elder from his right: . . . . VII. vi. 27. 5

Thrusting. *thrusting* boldly twixt him and the blow, ... IV. viii. 42. 1
thrusting fierce into the thickest preace . . . . IV. ix. 32. 6

Thrusts. he *thrusts* into the thickest throng . . . . VI. viii. 49. 1

Thump. He with his speare, . . . Would *thumpe* her forward VI. ii. 10. 8

Thumping. many feete fast *thumping* th' hollow ground, . . VI. x. 10. 4

Thunder. seing hir striken fall with clap of *thunder,* . . . *Bel.*[1] xi. 13
downe she stricken fell with clap of *thonder,* . . . . *Bel.*[2] xv. 13
all the sea did roare like heavens *thunder,* . . . . *Van.* v. 11
as the *thonder* cleaves the cloudes, ... *S.C.* Au. 85
Hey, ho, the *Thonder!* . . . . *S.C.* Au. 86
As the great clap of *thunder* which doth ryve . . . . *Gn.* 519
Such one Marcellus, but was torne with *thunder:* . . . . *Ti.* 416
Fitter, perhaps, to *thonder* Martiall stowre, ... *Ded.Son.*viii.11
they gan, . . . To *thunder* blowes, ... I. vi. 43. 2
lowde *thunder* . . . Did rend the ratling skyes . . . . II. ii. 20. 8
Weening it had beene *thunder* in the skye, ... II. iii. 45. 7
Ne shield defend the *thunder* of his throwes: . . . . II. viii. 41. 3
whose sound hevens *thunder* seem'd to bee. . . . . II. x. 73. 9
Seemed to *thunder,* and did nigh affray . . . . III. viii. 15. 5
begonne His stolen steed to *thunder* furiously, ... III. x. 33. 6

Thunder—*Continued.*
With dreadfull *thunder* and lightning atwixt, ... III. xii. 2. 2
heare the ordenance *thonder,* . . . . IV. ii. 16. 8
fire did flash, like lightning after *thunder,* . . . . IV. iii. 15. 8
So terribly his dreadfull strokes did *thonder,* . . . . V. iii. 8. 8
So all attonce they on the Prince did *thonder,* . . . . V. x. 35. 1
threats his horns, and bellowes like the *thonder:* . . . . VI. v. 19. 8
Fame in her shrill trump shal *thunder,* . . . . *Am.* lxxxiv. 13
Thunder, and lightning, and tempestuous fyre, ... *H.H.B.* 181
through all Spaine did *thunder,* . . . . *Proth.* 147

Thunderbolt. With flashing *thunderbolt* ywounded sore: . . . I. v. 40. 6
as a *thonder bolt* Perceth the yielding ayre, ... III. xi. 25. 6

Thunderbolts. To dart abroad the *thunder bolts* of warre, . . *Ro.* xi. 10
Whiles Jove at them his *thunderbolts* let flie, ... *Ro.* xii. 4
with *thunder bolts* he had him slaine, ... *Hub.* 1236
It booted nought to thinke such *thunderbolts* to beare, . . . I. viii. 7. 9
Armd with his *thunderbolts* and lightning fire, ... III. xi. 33. 4
Frame *thunderbolts* for Joves avengefull threate. . . . . IV. v. 37. 4

Thunder-clap. The kingly Bird, that beares Joves *thunder-clap,* *Van.* iv. 1

Thunder-claps. dreadfull *thunder-claps* (that make them quake) VII. vii. 23. 8

Thunder-darts. *thunder-dartes* (*thunder dartes*[1]) for Jove his syre . . . . *Bel.* iv. 11
most art dreaded for thy *thunder darts;* . . . . *T.M.* 56

Thunder-drive. And *thunder-drive* to hell?' . . . . VII. vi. 30. 6

Thundered. Phoebus foolish sonne *Ythundered,* . . . was lamented, ... *T.M.* 8
He hewd, and lasht, and foynd, and *thondred* blowes, ... II. v. 9. 1
thundred strokes thereon so hideouslie, ... V. ii. 21. 7
He with his yron flaile amongst them *thondred,* . . . . V. v. 19. 2
The Tyrant *thundred* his thicke blowes so fast, ... V. xii. 17. 6

Thundering. *See* **Loud-thundering.**
With *thondring* voice cride out aloude, ... *Rev.* ii. 13
throwe out *thondring* words of threate, ... *S.C.* O. 104
thundring Jove, . . . she claymed for her syre, ... I. iv. 11. 5
thundring Jove, that rules both night and day? . . . . I. v. 42. 9
the heavens it doth fill With *thundring* noyse, ... I. vii. 13. 6
almightie Jove, . . . Hurles forth his *thundring* dart . . . . I. viii. 9. 3
with big *thundring* voice revyld him lowd: . . . . II. iii. 7. 3
On goodly courser *thondring* with his feet, ... II. iii. 11. 4
often *thondring* Jove Had felt the point . . . . III. xi. 30. 1
slaine By *thundring* Jove in the Phlegrean plaine: . . . . V. vii. 10. 5
all the gods he threats with *thundring* dart: . . . . *Am.* xxxix. 4

Thunder-light. Joves dreaded *thunder light* Does scorch not halfe so sore, ... II. vi. 50. 7

Thunder's. Like hartlesse deare, dismayd with *thunders* sound. *Col.* 9
doubled strokes, like dreaded *thunders* threat; . . . . I. v. 7. 5
Doe all attonce their *thunders* rage forth rent, ... V. x. 34. 8
at her perill bide the wrathfull *Thunders* wrack. . . . . VII. vi. 12. 9

Thus (*partial list*).
Thus in a moment to see lost and drown'd, ... *Pet.* ii. 13
Whiles *thus* I did behold, An earthquake shooke . . . . *Bel.*[2] ii. 12
To falling rivers sound *thus* tun'd her sobs. . . . . *Bel.*[2] x. 4
Wearie to see the heavens still wavering *thus,* . . . . *Bel.*[2] xv. 3
And *thus* him playnd, the while his shepe there fedde. . *S.C.* Ja. 12
Thus medled his talke with many a teare: . . . . *S.C.* May 263
thou hentest in hond *Thus* holy hylles to blame, ... *S.C.* Jul. 38
'*Thus* is my sommer worne . . . *Thus* is my harvest hastened *S.C.* D. 97, 98
thus of all my harvest-hope I have Nought reaped . . . . *S.C.* D. 121
In clowdie teares my case I *thus* complaine . . . . *Gn.* Ded. 3
let *thus* much then excuse This Gnats small Poeme, ... *Gn.* 4
In such delights whilst *thus* his carelesse time . . . . *Gn.* 153
Whom, *thus* at point prepared, to prevent, ... *Gn.* 281
that *thus* Into this bitter bale I am outcast, ... *Gn.* 329
'Me therefore *thus* the cruell fiends of hell, . . . compell . . *Gn.* 625
This hard adventure, *thus* began . . . . *Hub.* 113
Thus therefore I advize . . . . *Hub.* 129
man, that heard him *thus* complaine, Was griev'd . . . . *Hub.* 259
Thus is this Ape become a shepheard swaine, ... *Hub.* 303
Thus as they them complayned too and fro, ... *Hub.* 949
Thus the fresh Clarion, being readie dight, ... *Mui.* 145
'Long *thus* I joyed in my happinesse, ... *D.* 148
Thus, deare! adieu, whom I expect ere long."— . . . . *D.* 292
And pitie me that living *thus* doo die; . . . . *D.* 383
The which, I, wretch, endured have *thus* long. . . . . *D.* 532
Thus when he ended had his heavie plaint, ... *D.* 540
gan *thus* to him areed. . . . . *Col.* 15
To whom the shepheard gently answered *thus;* . . . . *Col.* 36
Then *thus* Melissa said; . . . . *Col.* 480
Thou speakest *thus* gainst their felicitie, ... *Col.* 677
Or the blind God that doth me *thus* amate, ... I. i. 51. 4
Yet *thus* perforce he bids me do, or die. . . . . I. i. 51. 6
Melting in teares, then gan shee *thus* lament. . . . . I. ii. 22. 1
Long time they *thus* together traveiled; . . . . I. ii. 28. 1
he *thus* bespake: . . . . I. ii. 32. 4
Hath *thus* transformd, ... I. ii. 33. 6
Art thou misshaped *thus,* as now I see? . . . . I. ii. 34. 3
And heavenly virgin *thus* outraged see, ... I. vi. 5. 7
To dally *thus* with death is no fit toy: . . . . I. vi. 28. 8
Then gan the Pilgrim *thus:* . . . . I. vi. 38. 1
They sadly traveild *thus,* . . . . I. viii. 2. 1
That of your selfe ye *thus* berobbed arre, ... I. viii. 42. 8
Thus when they had the witch disrobed quight, ... I. viii. 49. 7
Thus as he spake, his visage wexed pale, ... I. ix. 16. 1
Till gentle Una *thus* to him gan say: . . . . I. ix. 16. 5
Thus beene they parted; . . . . I. ix. 20. 1
Then Una *thus:* 'But she, ... I. x. 16. 1
Thus gan to say—But, eare he *thus* had sayd, ... I. xii. 24. 6
read *thus,* as the paper spake: . . . . I. xii. 25. 9
To them approching, *thus* the knight bespake; . . . . II. i. 8. 6
To see the Redcrosse *thus* advaunced hye; . . . . II. i. 23. 6

Thus—*Continued.*
childe, whom *thus* ye see with blood defild. . . . II. i. 50. 9
Thus when Sir Guyon with his faithful guyde . . . II. ii. 1. 1
Thus enter we Into this life with woe, . . . II. ii. 2. 8
Whom *thus* at gaze the Palmer gan to bord . . . II. ii. 5. 1
To whom she *thus*—but ere her words ensewd, . . . II. iii. 34. 1
To whom he *thus:* 'O fairest under skie! . . . II. iii. 38. 1
He woo'd her *thus:* . . . II. iv. 25. 6
Then gan the Palmer *thus;* . . . II. iv. 34. 1
griefe, love, this Squyre have laide *thus* low. . . . II. iv. 34. 9
griefe, love, do *thus* expell: . . . II. iv. 35. 1
Thus as he spake, lo! . . . II. iv. 37. 1
Whiles *thus* she talked, and whiles *thus* she toyed, . . . II. vi. 11. 1
Furor hath me *thus* bedight: . . . II. vi. 50. 2
him *thus* bespake their soveraine Lord . . . II. vii. 37. 9
lifting up his head, him answerd *thus;* . . . II. vii. 62. 2
therefore I him deeme that *thus* lies dead on field.' . . . II. viii. 14. 9
Tho, turning to those brethren, *thus* bespoke: . . . II. viii. 27. 1
To whom the Infant *thus;* 'Fayre Sir, . . . II. viii. 56. 1
halfe in rage to be deluded *thus,* . . . II. xi. 38. 5
Their pleasaunt tunes they sweetly *thus* applyde: . . . II. xii. 32. 2
Thus being entred, they behold . . . II. xii. 50. 1
When *thus* the Palmer: 'Now, Sir, . . . II. xii. 69. 6
Whom this Enchauntresse hath transformed *thus;* . . . II. xii. 85. 2
To whom the Palmer *thus:* . . . II. xii. 87. 6
and then *thus* fearfully: 'Ah! Nurse, . . . III. ii. 35. 1
Then Glauce *thus:* 'Let not it thee offend, That we *thus* rashly III. iii. 15. 6, 7
And then his spirite *thus* gan foorth display: . . . III. iii. 21. 5
Then Merlin *thus:* 'Indeede . . . III. iii. 25. 6
She shortly *thus:* 'Fly they, . . . III. iv. 15. 2
That through this forrest wandreth *thus* alone? . . . III. v. 7. 8
thus we suffer this same dotard . . . III. ix. 8. 7
Then, sighing soft awhile, at last she *thus:* . . . III. ix. 39. 1
At last he *thus;* 'Thou clod . . . III. x. 31. 2
And hatefull outrage long him chaced *thus;* . . . III. xi. 3. 5
and spake *thus* courtesly:— . . . III. xi. 13. 9
And underneath his feet was written *thus,* . . . III. xi. 49. 1
then sighing deepe, *thus* saide: . . . IV. ix. 38. 6
That living *thus* a wretch, and loving so, . . . IV. ix. 39. 8
Neptune, softly smyling, *thus:* 'Daughter, . . . IV. xii. 30. 1
Thus she him trayned, and *thus* she him taught . . . V. i. 8. 1
had for his excuse to say, But onely *thus:* . . . V. iv. 27. 5
Therefore *thus* one of them, . . . V. vii. 18. 4
thus upbrayding said: 'This token beare . . . V. vii. 32. 4
when she *thus* gan to speake: . . . V. iii. 11. 1
what meane ye *thus* unwise Upon your selves . . . V. viii. 11. 2
have you wrong'd *thus* sore, . . . V. viii. 13. 2
To whom she *thus:* 'Then . . . V. viii. 16. 6
Thus goe they both together . . . V. viii. 30. 1
To whom he *thus:* 'She . . . V. xi. 38. 8
To whom he *thus:* 'My . . . V. xi. 49. 1
To whom *thus* Artegall: 'Certes, Sir knight, . . . V. xi. 55. 1
When Calidore *thus* first: 'Haile, . . . VI. i. 4. 8
whilest he was busied *thus* hard, . . . VI. v. 11. 1
Him *thus* bespake: 'My liefe, . . . VI. v. 23. 5
Why have ye me alone *thus* long yleft? . . . VI. v. 23. 6
Hath you *thus* long away from me bereft? . . . VI. v. 23. 8
To whom she *thus:* 'I am, . . . VI. v. 28. 1
There whilest he *thus* was setling things above, . . . VI. vi. 37. 1
Long *thus* she fled, till that at last . . . VI. viii. 32. 2
Thus to bereave thy loves deare sight from thee: . . . VI. x. 29. 5
There they a while together *thus* did dwell . . . VI. xii. 11. 7
So having said, she *thus* to him replide: . . . VII. vi. 34. 6
Thuswise. *Thus wise* long time he did himselfe dispace . . . *Gn.* 265
Thwart. ye my cousin Wolfe so fowly *thwart,* . . . *Hub.* 1218
laying *thwart* her horse, . . . III. vii. 43. 4
whether *thwart* or flatly it did lyte, . . . VI. vi. 30. 8
Thwarting. *thwarting* his huge shield, Them battell bad, . . . *Gn.* 514
Thy (*partial list*). *See* **Forthy.**
The instrument whereof loe! here *thy* Artegall. . . . V. Pr. 11. 9
Thyamis. Fayre *Thyamis,* the daughter of Labryde; . . . I. vi. 21. 4
Thyes. *See* **Thighs.**
Thyme. Faire Marigoldes, and Bees-alluring *Thime* . . . *Mui.* 191
Bathing her selfe in origane and *thyme:* . . . I. ii. 40. 7
Thyself (*partial list*).
Now *thy selfe* hast lost both lopp and topp, . . . *S.C.* F. 57
Deare as thou art unto *thy selfe,* . . . *Ded. Son.* iii. 13
where *thy selfe* hast thy brave mansione: . . . *Ded. Son.* v. 8
Anothers wrongs to wreak upon *thy selfe:* . . . I. vi. 42. 3
wilt *thy selfe* not pas the flood? . . . I. ix. 39. 9
sold *thy selfe* to serve Duessa vild, . . . I. ix. 46. 8
'*Thy selfe* to see, . . . 'I hither came; . . . I. x. 11. 1
Would God! *thy selfe* now present were in place . . . II. i. 9. 8
I read thee rash and heedlesse of *thy selfe,* . . . II. vii. 7. 8
Thy selfe thou (*your selfe you) covet to see pictured, . . . III. Pr. 4. 2
According as *thy selfe* doest see and heare, . . . VII. vii. 56. 7
Tiber. Ne ought save *Tyber* hastning to his fall . . . *Ro.* iii. 11
He that . . . high hath set his throne where *Tiberis* doth pas. . I. ii. 22. 9
Tybris, renowmed for the Romaines fame, . . . IV. xi. 21. 6
Tiber's. Nor Po nor *Tyburs* swans so much renowned, . . . *Col.* 412
Tickle. this *tickle* trustles state Of vaine worlds glorie, . . . *Pet.*[2] vii. 1
The trode is not so *tickle:* . . . *S.C.* Jul. 14
Did *tickle* inwardly in everie vaine; . . . *Mui.* 394
So *ticle* be the termes of mortall state, . . . III. iv. 28. 6
So *tickle* is the state of earthly things, . . . VI. iii. 5. 2
made his hart to *tickle* in his brest, . . . VII. vi. 46. 2
On thing so *tickle* as th' unsteady ayre, . . . VII. vii. 22. 6
loath this state of life so *tickle,* . . . VII. viii. 1. 6
Tickled. *Tickled* with glorie and rash covetise: . . . *Hub.* 996
Guyons senses softly *tickeled,* . . . II. xii. 33. 7

Tickled—*Continued.*
Was inly *tickled* with that golden vew. . . . III. x. 30. 3
his wanton hart Was *tickled* with delight, . . . IV. i. 33. 6
Tide. *See* **Eventide, Tied, Valentide.**
winde nor *tide* could move her thence away. . . . *Van.* ix. 12
Courtiers, as the *tide,* doo rise and fall.' . . . *Hub.* 614
seeing readie *tide,* He rusheth forth, . . . *Mui.* 405
rest their weary limbs a *tide.* . . . I. ii. 29. 9
bad him stay till time the *tide* renewd. . . . II. vi. 26. 9
saile withouten starres gainst *tyde* and winde: . . . III. iv. 9. 8
The like that mine may be your paine another *tide.* . . . III. vi. 21. 9
with the *tide* drove forward carelesly; . . . III. viii. 21. 4
so fitte *tide* Him to commend to her, . . . III. ix. 32. 8
The learned lover lost no time nor *tyde* . . . III. x. 6. 1
Like as the *tide,* that comes fro th' Ocean mayne, . . . IV. iii. 27. 1
I here will stay Untill another *tyde* . . . IV. vi. 47. 9
I will deferre the end untill another *tide.* . . . IV. vii. 47. 9
this caried with the *tide,* That with the wind, . . . IV. ix. 26. 7
If wind and *tide* doe change, . . . IV. ix. 26. 9
to him driving strongly downe the *tide* . . . V. ii. 14. 3
Is with the *tide* unto another brought: . . . V. ii. 39. 8
presuming on th' appointed *tyde,* . . . Did thither come; . . . V. xi. 39. 1
before that *tide* None can have tidings . . . V. xi. 42. 4
Ye may him overtake in timely *tyde.*' . . . VI. vii. 6. 4
in evill *tyde* That other swayne . . . Lay in the lap of death, . . . VI. vii. 17. 7
Is met of many a counter winde and *tyde,* . . . VI. xii. 1. 3
But came the *tyde,* and made my paynes his pray. . . . *Am.* lxxv. 4
at th' appointed *tyde,* Each one did make his Bryde . . . *Proth.* 177
Tides. Where no such troublous *tydes* han us assayde; . . . *S.C.* O. 117
Nor timely *tides* did drive out of their sluggish sourse. . . . II. vi. 20. 9
Forcibly driven with contrarie *tydes,* . . . IV. i. 42. 2
To rule his *tides,* and surges to uprere, . . . IV. xi. 52. 3
Tidings. saw the messenger of *tidings* glad; . . . *Bel.*[2] xiv. 3
Tydings of death and massacre unkinde; . . . *Gn.* 396
What of *tidings* you abroad doo heare? . . . *Hub.* 605
tidings there is none, I you assure, . . . *Hub.* 612
Hereof when *tydings* far abroad did passe, . . . *As.* 199
Tydings of warre and worldly trouble tell? . . . I. i. 30. 8
Of a straunge man I can you *tidings* tell, . . . I. i. 31. 3
of whose most innocent death When *tidings* came to mee, . . . I. ii. 24. 4
wished *tydinges* none of him unto her brought. . . . I. iii. 3. 9
Of that old woman *tidings* he besought, . . . I. iii. 24. 8
To weete of . . . *tidings* of her knight . . . I. vi. 34. 6
of him inquerd *Tidings* of warre, . . . I. vi. 36. 2
saw the signes that deadly *tydinges* spake, . . . I. vii. 20. 6
O! welcome thou, that doest of death brings *tydings* trew.' . . . I. viii. 38. 9
fayre areedes Of *tydinges* straunge, . . . I. ix. 28. 7
To come and goe with *tidings* from the heart, . . . I. ix. 51. 6
The watchman wayting *tydings* glad to heare; . . . I. xi. 3. 7
looked forth, to weet if trew indeed Those *tydinges* were, . . . I. xii. 3. 4
The *tydings* straunge did him abashed make, . . . I. xii. 29. 2
Of death and dolor telling sad *tidings;* . . . II. vii. 23. 5
Tydings of one that hath unto me donne Late foule dishonour . . . III. ii. 8. 7
he it knew at home before he hard *Tydings* thereof, . . . III. ii. 21. 5
Tydings hereof came to his mothers eare: . . . III. iv. 19. 2
heavy *tidings* heard, whereas she playd . . . III. iv. 29. 6
till thou *tidings* learne what her betide, . . . III. v. 11. 7
the man that of him *tydings* to her brings. . . . III. vi. 12. 9
If any tract of him or *tidings* they mote trace. . . . III. vi. 25. 9
tell the idle *tidings* to his Dame: . . . III. vii. 28. 6
To tell what *tydings* of fayre Florimell became. . . . III. vii. 61. 9
Gan first inquire of *tydinges* farre abrode, . . . III. viii. 45. 8
'The *tydinges* bad, Which now in Faery court . . . III. viii. 46. 1
of each one he mett he *tidings* did inquere. . . . III. x. 19. 9
none . . . to them *tydings* tell that mote their harts delight. . IV. i. 16. 9
To weet what sudden *tidings* was befeld: . . . IV. iii. 50. 3
Mote I request you *tydings* of my love, . . . IV. vi. 34. 6
no where could her find, nor *tydings* of her heare.' . . . IV. vi. 36. 9
When Scudamour those heavie *tydings* heard, . . . IV. vi. 37. 1
Where they might *tydings* get of her estate; . . . IV. vi. 47. 4
dreadfull *tidings* which thou doest declare,' . . . IV. vii. 14. 1
tydings what did unto him betide, . . . IV. viii. 18. 6
when *tydings* came unto mine eare, . . . IV. viii. 55. 1
Tydings of all which there had hapned on the land. . . . IV. viii. 62. 9
Till he of *tidings* mote with him discourse. . . . V. ii. 2. 4
Gan to demaund of her some *tydings* good, . . . V. v. 45. 2
sad *tydings* of his balefull smart . . . V. vi. 3. 3
'The *tidings* sad . . . will needs, I see, be rad. . . . V. vi. 10. 4
To whom when *tydings* thereof came, . . . V. x. 31. 6
Those *tidings* sad Did much abash Sir Artegall to heare, . . . V. xi. 40. 6
before that tide None can have *tidings* . . . V. xi. 42. 5
By this came *tydings* to the Tyrants eare, . . . V. xii. 6. 4
The heavy Mayd, to whom none *tydings* bore . . . V. xii. 11. 5
I am right glad To heare these *tidings,* . . . VI. i. 10. 3
Those evill *tidings* to their Lord to shew: . . . VI. vi. 24. 3
Wayting what *tydings* of her folke became. . . . VI. vi. 30. 3
He sought the plaines, but could no *tydings* heare: . . . VI. xi. 26. 5
Whose heavy *tydings* now I have to tell. . . . VI. xi. 31. 3
That he by them might certaine *tydings* weene . . . VI. xi. 39. 3
Tidings'. ran to meete him forth to know his *tidings* somme. V. vi. 8. 9
Tie. shall we *tie* our selves for certaine yeares . . . *Hub.* 120
With which I wont the winged words to *tie,* . . . *T.M.* 548
Their shining shieldes about their wrestes they *tye,* . . . I. v. 6. 3
peoples hartes with awfull terror *tye,* . . . I. vii. 16. 7
her attaching thought her hands to *tye;* . . . II. xi. 28. 6
about her body gan it *tie.* . . . IV. v. 19. 9
how she mote him faster *tye.* . . . V. v. 56. 6
With which she used still to *tye* her fone, . . . V. vii. 28. 3
her no other termes should ever *tie* . . . V. vii. 28. 8
eke my toung with proud restraint to *tie;* . . . *Am.* xliii. 6

Tie—*Continued.*
true love doth *tye* Without constraynt, *Am.* lxv. 5
My hart, (whom none with servile bands can *tye*, *Am.* lxxiii. 2
Tied. Far of beholding Ephialtes *tide*, *Gn.* 375
(Both two sure bands in friendship to be *tide*) *Hub.* 54
Ne are we *tyde* to fast, but when we list; *Hub.* 459
We be not *tyde* to wilfull chastitie, *Hub.* 477
the more in laces strong Himselfe he *tide*, *Mui.* 428
were in love so firmly *tide*. *As.* 180
are *tyde* T' embrace the service of sweete Poetry, *Ded. Son.* iv. 6
Of all the rest that I am *tyde* t' account: *Ded.Son.*vii.10
Ne would his looser life be *tide* to law, I. iv. 26. 3
the chayne . . . Which fast is *tyde* I. v. 25. 6
That was in sacred bandes of wedlocke *tyde* To Therion, I. vi. 21. 5
threds . . . The which my life and love together *tyde?* I. vii. 22. 6
to the knight his daughter deare he *tyde* I. xii. 36. 8
being *tide* . . . their places only signifide. II. iii. 29. 8
her in chaines of adamant he *tyde;* II. xii. 82. 6
had his furnitures not firmely *tyde*. III. i. 11. 8
with that golden chaine of concord *tyde*. III. i. 12. 8
the love of some of them him *tyde:* III. vi. 16. 7
retourning spyde *Tyde* with her golden girdle; III. viii. 2. 7
tyde behind his charet, to aggrate The virgin III. viii. 36. 5
Which foure great Hippodames did draw in temewise *tyde*. III. xi. 40. 9
With which it blessed Concord hath together *tide*. IV. i. 30. 9
tyde In bands of friendship, IV. x. 27. 7
round about his necke an halter *tight*, V. iv. 22. 3
Uppon her thigh her Cemitare was *tide* V. v. 3. 4
Cold yron chaines with which let him be *tide;* V. v. 50. 8
hide Thy maisters shame, in harlots bondage *tide:* V. vi. 11. 5
They *tied* were to stedfast chastity V. vii. 9. 7
a crowne Of sundry flowres with silken ribbands *tyde*, VI. ix. 7. 8
After her flocke she in their fold had *tyde:* VI. ix. 17. 6
thereunto a great long chaine he *tight*, VI. xii. 34. 8
He had his ploughing-share and coulter ready *tyde*. VII. vii. 39. 9
with her owne goodwill hir fyrmely *tyde*. *Am.* lxvii. 12
Ties. Striving to loose the knott that fast him *tyes*, I. xi. 23. 4
Tiger. He shortly met the *Tygre*, and the Bore, *Hub.* 1087
The Pardale swift, and the *Tigre* cruell, I. vi. 26. 4
As when a Beare and *Tygre*, being met II. ii. 22. 5
like a cruell *tygre* far'd. II. v. 8. 9
A Lyon and a *Tigre* doth espye, II. ix. 14. 8
Upon a *Tygre* swift and fierce he rode, II. xi. 20. 4
as the winged wind his *Tigre* fled, II. xi. 26. 1
Now had the Carle Alighted from his *Tigre*, II. xi. 33. 7
As when a *Tygre* and a Lionesse Are met V. vii. 30. 1
first the *Tygre* clawes thereon did lay, V. vii. 30. 4
she transformed was Into a *Tygre*, V. viii. 49. 7
What *Tygre*, or what other salvage wight, V. ix. 1. 1
Like to a *Tygre* that hath mist his pray, VI. iv. 6. 2
A *Tigre* forth out of the wood did rise, VI. x. 34. 4
cruell and unkind, As is a *Tygre*, *Am.* lvi. 2
Tiger's. the villein turn'd his face . . . Unto his *Tygres* taile, II. xi. 26. 9
Tygres scath In crueltie and outrage she did pas, V. viii. 49. 7
Tigers. many a fayre sight Of Beres and *Tygres*, *S.C.* Au. 28
two *Tygers* prickt with hungers rage IV. iii. 16. 1
With Beares and *Tygers* taking heavie part, IV. vii. 2. 7
certes was with milke of Wolves and *Tygres* fed. IV. vii. 7. 9
could have perst the hearts of *Tigres* and of Beares. IV. viii. 4. 9
The Lyons rore; the *Tygres* loudly bray; IV. x. 46. 3
was not borne Of Beares and *Tygres*, V. v. 40. 6
Tygres, that did seeme to gren And snar at all VI. xii. 27. 6
doest the Lions and fell *Tigers* tame, *H.L.* 46
Tight. *See* **Tied.**
Tigris. By Nyle, or Gange, or *Tygre*, or Euphrate; *Ro.* xxxi. 4
Tygris fierce, whose streames of none may be withstood; IV. xi. 20. 9
Till (*partial list*).
spred over all, *Till* it . . . adowne did fall. *Ro.* xvi. 14
Till at the last, . . . he forth is horld; *Ro.* xx. 7
Till that Barbarian hands it quite did spill, *Ro.* xxx. 10
Till that a Brize, . . . his angrie sting did threaten, *Van.* ii. 10
Till that a little Ant, a silly worme, *Van.* viii. 9
Where will he live *tyll* the lusty prime? *S.C.* F. 16
Till by his foly one did fall, *S.C.* Jul. 67
till my last sleepe Doe close mine eyes: *S.C.* Au. 170
till safe and sound 'She home returne, *S.C.* Au. 180
blowe your pypes, shepheards, *til* you be at home; *S.C.* Au. 197
Till fayrer Fortune shewe forth her head. *S.C.* S. 257
hunt the hartlesse hare *til* shee were tame. *S.C.* D. 28
enfold With her lythe twigs, *till* they the top survew, *Gn.* 221
Respite *till* morrow t' answere his desire; *Hub.* 326
Till at the length he published to holde *Hub.* 568
ne spake to wight, *Till* that the Foxe, . . . found, *Hub.* 939
Till that the Foxe forth toward them did goe, *Hub.* 1074
Ne staid, *till* that he came . . . Unto the place *Hub.* 1260
Till that unto the Pallace nigh he came. *Hub.* 1265
But bad him stay at ease *till* further preeving. *Hub.* 1366
Till please the heavens affoord me remedy. *T.M.* 294
Ne stirreth limbe; *till*, seeing readie tide, He rusheth *Mui.* 405
stayed not, *till* I againe did call: *D.* 60
till thou have to my trustie eare Committed *D.* 69
And will *till* then my painful penance eeke. *D.* 391
She bad me stay, *till* she for me did send. *D.* 455
Till that you come where ye your vowes assoyle, *D.* 535
till he were better eased Of that strong stownd *D.* 559
awake; *Till* I have told her praises lasting long: *Col.* 49
Till they into the Mullaes water slide. *Col.* 144
I wondred much, *till*, . . . we land far off descryde: *Col.* 264
But never wist I *till* this present day, *Col.* 827
Yet armes *till* that time did he never wield. I. i. 1. 5

Till—*Continued.*
Till that some end they finde, I. i. 11. 2
with-hold, *till* further tryall made.' I. i. 12. 6
traveiled; *Til*, weary of their way, they came I. ii. 28. 2
Till on a day . . . I chaunst to see her I. ii. 40. 4
Till we be bathed in a living well: I. ii. 43. 4
Till that at length she found the troden gras, I. iii. 10. 4
Till, seeing by her side the Lyon stand, I. iii. 11. 5
Till Una cride, 'O! hold that heavie hand, I. iii. 37. 2
traveild; *till* at last they see A goodly building I. iv. 2. 5
rest a while, *Till* morrow next I. iv. 51. 4
Abyde, *till* I have told the message which I have.' I. v. 21. 9
never prov'd *Till* then, I. v. 24. 9
handle softly, *till* they can be heald: I. v. 29. 8
Till they be come unto the furthest part; I. v. 36. 4
Till, scornd of God and man, a shamefull death he dide. I. v. 48. 9
Till that with timely fruit her belly sweld, I. vi. 23. 3
Whom, *till* to ryper yeares he gan aspyre, I. vi. 23. 7
He trayned was, *till* ryper years he raught; I. vi. 29. 2
Til breathlesse both themselves aside retire, I. vi. 44. 6
Till at the last he heard a dreadfull sownd, I. vii. 7. 4
'*Till* that their cruell cursed enemy, I. vii. 44. 1
Till, . . . an Enchaunter bad His sence abusd, I. vii. 49. 3
For *till* I have acquitt your captive knight, I. vii. 52. 6
Till living moysture into smoke do flow, I. ix. 8. 4
never vowd to rest *till* her I fynd: I. ix. 15. 8
Till he recovered had his former hew; I. ix. 20. 8
Till he these wordes to him deliver might: I. ix. 23. 6
Till I that treachours art have heard and tryde; I. ix. 32. 2
Then linger *till* the glas be all out ronne? I. ix. 47. 8
Till he should die his last, that is, eternally. I. ix. 54. 9
Till he recovered had his late decayed plight. I. x. 2. 9
did them guide, *till* to the Hall they came. I. x. 6. 9
Till from her bands the spright assoiled is, I. x. 52. 8
Till that his army dry-foot through them yod, I. x. 53. 5
'*Till* now . . . I weened well, I. x. 58. 1
Till from her cursed foe thou have her freely quitt.' I. x. 63. 9
Till prickt with courage . . . thou cam'st I. x. 66. 7
Till I of warres and bloody Mars doe sing, I. xi. 7. 2
Till with his cruell clawes he snatcht the wood, I. xi. 22. 2
till that stownd I. xi. 36. 8
Till that dredd Dragon all did overthrow. I. xi. 47. 5
Till mery wynd and weather call her thence away. I. xii. 1. 9
till I there have beene.' I. xii. 18. 9
Till fast before the king he did alight; I. xii. 25. 5
Till well ye wote by grave intendiment, I. xii. 31. 3
Till she repaired have her tackles spent, I. xii. 42. 6
Till her that Squyre bespake: 'Madame, II. i. 16. 1
till they came at last Into a pleasant dale II. i. 24. 2
Till he his armes about her sides gan fold, II. i. 46. 4
Till, coming to this well, he stoupt to drincke: II. i. 55. 8
Till guiltie blood her guerdon doe obtayne!' II. i. 61. 8
throwen forth, *till* it be withered. II. ii. 2. 7
Till that at last they to a Castle came, II. ii. 12. 6
Till I that false Acrasia have wonne; II. ii. 44. 6
Till that at length with Archimage they meet: II. iii. 11. 2
till he avenged bee Of that despight, II. iii. 12. 7
Till that they come unto a forrest greene, II. iii. 20. 1
till I more truth should fynd. II. iv. 22. 9
Till that the truth thereof I did out wrest; II. iv. 23. 5
Till this mad man, . . . me met in middle space. II. iv. 32. 3
Till at the last all breathlesse, weary, faint, II. v. 11. 2
Such homage *till* that instant never learned hee. II. v. 11. 9
Till that the Palmer, by his grave restraynt, II. v. 24. 3
Till they arrived in that pleasaunt Ile, II. vi. 22. 3
Till season serve new passage to assay: II. vi. 23. 7
bad him stay *till* time the tide renewd. II. vi. 26. 9
Till that they came unto an yron dore, II. vii. 31. 2
till that day They never II. vii. 37. 4
Till that him thus bespake their soveraine Lord II. vii. 37. 9
most hevenly faire . . . was, *till* she did fall; II. vii. 45. 8
Till partiall Paris dempt it Venus dew, II. vii. 55. 7
Till him the childe bespoke; II. viii. 7. 3
Till that they spyde where towards them did pace II. viii. 17. 4
Till vengeaunce utterly the guilt bereave: II. viii. 29. 5
Till by a conduit pipe it thence were brought: II. ix. 32. 4
Till it reduced was II. ix. 59. 9
where he *till* death remaind; II. x. 18. 7
Till ryper yeares he raught II. x. 20. 4
Till that her sisters children, woxen strong, II. x. 32. 6
Till weary of that wretched life her selfe she hong. II. x. 32. 9
till far in years he grew: II. x. 34. 6
For *till* his dayes, . . . By strength was wielded II. x. 39. 7
Till by his death he it recovered: II. x. 44. 8
Till they outraigned had their utmost date, II. x. 45. 2
Till murdred by the freends of Gratian. II. x. 61. 5
Til, by consent of Commons and of Peares, II. x. 62. 8
Till that through poyson stopped was his breath; II. x. 67. 8
Til it dissolved be from earthly band. II. xi. 30. 5
that never fayld At need *till* now, II. xi. 41. 7
Till that the Palmer gan full bitterly II. xii. 16. 5
They were faire Ladies, *till* they fondly striv'd II. xii. 31. 1
Till that he came unto another gate; II. xii. 53. 6
Till that she rushing through the thickest preasse III. i. 23. 5
Ne did she stay *till* three on ground she layd III. i. 29. 1
Till she mote winne fit time for her desire; III. i. 56. 2
stayd not *till* it was seene To gore her side; III. i. 65. 5
Till envious Men, fearing their rules decay, III. ii. 2. 5
Till death make one end of my daies and miseree!' III. ii. 39. 9
Til thou in open fielde adowne be smott: III. ii. 46. 5

Till—*Continued.*
Till that by dew degrees, . . . Thou have it lastly . . . . . . III. iii. 4. 8
Them bownd *till* his retourne their labour not to slake. . . . III. iii. 10. 9
Till they to hevens hight forth stretched bee: . . . . III. iii. 22. 4
Till universall peace compound all civill jarre. . . . . . . III. iii. 23. 9
Till both the sonnes of Edwin he have slayne, ... III. iii. 37. 2
till all their warlike puissaunce be spent. . . . . III. iii. 40. 9
till that to Faery lond They came, ... III. iii. 62. 1
For, *till* thou tidings learne what her betide, ... III. v. 11. 7
to stay, *Till* he had made amends, ... III. v. 18. 8
Till to her dew perfection she were ripened. . . . . III. vi. 3. 9
increast *till* she her terme had full outgone. . . . . III. vi. 9. 9
Till thither they retourne . . . . III. vi. 33. 8
long she traveild, *till* at length she came . . . . III. vii. 4. 6
never learned he such service *till* that day. . . . . III. vii. 36. 9
till morrow next againe . . . . III. viii. 51. 7
Ne would they eate *till* she in presence came. . . . . III. ix. 26. 6
Till on a day the Satyres her espide . . . . III. x. 36. 4
He wooed her *till* day-spring he espyde, ... III. x. 52. 1
Ne stayes, *till* safe him selfe he see . . . . III. x. 53. 9
Till so she doe, she must in doole remaine, ... III. xi. 17. 7
not to depart *Till* morrow next . . . . III. xii. 28. 4
their sweatie yokes assoyle . . . *till* a new day; . . . . . . III. xii. 47. *or.* 6
Till that to ripenesse of mans state they grew: . . . . IV. ii. 46. 2
Till, feeling life to fayle, it fell, ... IV. iii. 20. 9
with her alwaies ride, *till* he another get.' . . . . IV. iv. 9. 9
Till then your challenges ye may prolong; . . . . IV. iv. 12. 7
Staid not *till* it arrived in his side, ... IV. iv. 24. 5
Till evening that the Sunne gan downward bend. . . . . . . IV. iv. 43. 6
nought may be esteemed happie *till* the end. . . . . IV. iv. 43. 9
ne did it ever rest, *Till* . . . it fell; . . . . IV. vi. 13. 6
Till Glauce thus: '. . . be nought dismayd . . . *till* certaintie ye heare; . . . . IV. vi. 37. 6, 7
Ran, *till* he came to th' end . . . . IV. vii. 8. 7
Where yet untouched *till* this present day, ... IV. vii. 18. 8
Till on a day, . . . there chaunst . . . . IV. viii. 3. 1
till that the Dwarfe did me reveale, ... IV. viii. 55. 5
never saw *till* that same houre . . . . IV. ix. 22. 5
Till that uneath they forced were, ... IV. ix. 25. 7
Till Scudamour . . . in that place did chance to light: . . . IV. ix. 28. 2
till nought thereof be drie, ... IV. ix. 33. 7
till all the world it weet. . . . . IV. ix. 33. 9
Till to the Bridges utter gate I came; . . . . IV. x. 11. 2
Till at the last I spide . . . . IV. x. 11. 7
Till I was throughly past the perill . . . . IV. x. 36. 9
Till now, at last relenting, she to him was wed. . . . . . . IV. xi. 8. 9
till Thamis he overtake. . . . . IV. xi. 32. 9
Till like a victor on his backe he ride, ... IV. xii. 13. 5
Till they arrive at their last ruinous decay. . . . . V. Pr. 6. 9
noursled him *till* yeares he raught, ... V. i. 6. 8
Till he of tidings mote with him discourse. . . . . V. ii. 2. 4
Till we may be assur'd . . . . V. ii. 36. 9
fare on foot, *till* he an horse have gayned.' . . . . V. iii. 35. 6
I will not rest *till* I her might doe trie, ... V. iv. 34. 3
Her to receive, *till* time they should begin . . . . V. v. 4. 9
Till I the conquest of my will recover.' . . . . V. v. 51. 5
Ne would she stay *till* he in place could come, ... V. vi. 8. 8
passing th' evening well, *till* time of rest, ... V. vi. 23. 1
Which *till* this day mongst many living are, ... V. x. 5. 8
It was not long *till* that the Prince arrived . . . . V. x. 18. 1
Till nigh unto the place at length approcht he has. . . . . . V. xi. 36. 9
if I live *till* those ten daies have end, ... V. xi. 43. 2
wayting for the Tyrant *till* it was farre day. . . . . V .xii. 13. 9
pursew, . . . *Till* I him overtake, ... VI. i. 7. 3
Till his returne unto this tree he bond; . . . . VI. i. 16. 8
Or stay *till* he his armes, . . . Might lightly fetch: . . . . . VI. ii. 19. 5
'So passed we *till* this young man us met; . . . . VI. ii. 23. 1
till that he . . . Untimely dyde, ... VI. ii. 28. 3
Whom on his backe he bore, *till* he him brought . . . . VI. iii. 2. 6
they the evening past *till* time of rest; . . . . VI. iii. 9. 6
till to her fathers house he had her brought. . . . . VI. iii. 15. 9
Till to that Ladies fathers house he came; . . . . VI. iii. 17. 8
Till to some place of rest they mote attaine, ... VI. iii. 28. 7
Till she recured were of those her woundes wide. . . . . . . VI. iii. 28. 9
So fare on foote *till* thou another gayne, ... VI. iii. 32. 2
crave leave *till* morne, ... VI. iii. 41. 6
Till that at length, in his extreamest neede, ... VI. iii. 46. 5
he stayd, *till* that he nearer drew, ... VI. iii. 47. 1
never *till* this houre . . . . VI. iv. 3. 1
Till that his Ladies sight he mote attaine, ... VI. iv. 40. 8
Till she Prince Arthure fynd; . . . . VI. v. Arg.
never rests *till* it have wrought his finall bane. . . . . . . VI. vi. 8. 9
Till they him force the buxome yoke to beare: . . . . VI. viii. 12. 4
Till to the brim I have it full defrayd: . . . . VI. viii. 24. 3
she fled, *till* that at last . . . . VI. viii. 32. 2
rest himselfe *till* supper time befell; . . . . VI. ix. 17. 4
Till Fortune would her captive bonds unbynde: . . . . VI. xi. 8. 8
there all day they bode, *till* light the sky forsooke. . . . . VI. xi. 40. 9
So long *till* all the entry was with bodies mand. . . . . . . VI. xi. 46. 9
He breath'd his sword, and rested him *till* day; . . . . VI. xi. 47. 2
Till time that Calidore brought Pastorella thether. . . . . . VI. xii. 10. 9
kept downe, *till* he be throughly queld. . . . . VI. xii. 30. 9
Till, having pauz'd awhile, Jove thus bespake: . . . . VII. vi. 29. 1
they him follow'd *till* they weary were; . . . . VII. vi. 53. 1
till th' Amphytrionide Him slew, ... VII. vii. 36. 6
His plough and harnesse fit to *till* the ground, ... VII. vii. 43. 6
Till greater then my wombe thou woxen art: . . . . *Am.* ii. 4
till she vouchsafe to grawnt me rest; . . . . *Am.* xxxiii. 13
Till then I wander carefull, comfortlesse, ... *Am.* xxxiv. 13
did bide; *Till* I in hand her yet halfe trembling tooke, . . . *Am.* lxvii. 11

Till—*Continued.*
Till then give leave to me . . . To sport my muse, ... *Am.* lxxx. 9
I languish, *till* he please My pining anguish to appease. . . . *Epig.* iv. 59
Till which we cease our hopefull hap to sing; . . . . *Epith.* 388
Til which we cease your further prayse to sing; . . . . . . *Epith.* 407
And cease *till* then our tymely joyes to sing: . . . . *Epith.* 425
The world, that was not *till* he did it make, ... *H.L.* 75
Till then, dread Lord! vouchsafe to take of me . . . . *H.L.* 306
Till that great Lord of Love, which him at first . . . . . . *H.H.L.* 127
Till she her selfe for stronger flight can breath. . . . . . *H.H.B.* 28
till to his perfect end . . . it at last ascend; . . . . *H.H.B.* 46
till they at last arive To the most faire, ... *H.H.B.* 76
runne softly, *till* I end my Song. . . . . *Proth.* 18, 36, 54, 72, 90, 144
Tilt. goodly taught to *tilt* and turnament: . . . . III. i. 44. 7
tilt or tourney, or like warlike game, ... III. ii. 9. 8
both in equall *tilt* May meete againe, ... III. viii. 18. 3
better skild in *Tilt* and Turnament, ... V. viii. 7. 7
Tilt-yard. Sir Artegall into the *Tilt-yard* came, ... V. iii. 10. 2
Timber. learnd of lighter *timber* cotes to frame, ... *S.C.* D. 77
Timbered. *See* **Well-timbered.**
His *timbered* bones all broken rudely rumbled: . . . . V. ii. 50. 8
Timbrels. sweet *Timbrels* all upheld on hight. . . . . I. xii. 6. 9
to the Maydens sownding *tymbrels* song . . . . I. xii. 7. 3
When they their *tymbrels* smyte, ... *Epith.* 134
Time. *See* **Mean time, Spring-time, Summer-time, Supper-time.**
onely God surmountes the force of *ty*[*me*,] . . . . *Bel.*[1] i. 13
It was the *time,* when rest, soft sliding downe, ... *Bel.* i. 1
even at the *time,* when Morpheus . . . . *Bel.* xv. 1
at the last, and in short *time,* I spide, ... *Pet.* i. 10
The pray of *time,* which all things doth devowre! . . . . . . *Ro.* iii. 8
In spight of *time* out of the dust doth reare, ... *Ro.* v. 13
for a *time* make warre Gainst *time,* . . . . *Ro.* vii. 9, 10
time in *time* shall ruinate Your workes . . . . *Ro.* vii. 10
if that *time* make ende of things so sure, ... *Ro.* vii. 13
though *time* doth Commonwealths devowre, ... *Ro.* viii. 11
no *time* should so low embase their hight, ... *Ro.* viii. 12
these brave Pallaces, which maystred bee Of *time,* . . . . . . *Ro.* xviii. 4
Rome, in the *time* of her great ancesters, ... *Ro.* xix. 7
The which injurious *time* hath quite outworne, ... *Ro.* xxvii. 6
if that *time* doo let thy glorie live, ... *Ro.* xxxii. 11
That when *time* serves may bring things better forth. . . . . *Van.* i. 14
What *time* the Romaine Empire bore the raine . . . . *Van.* xi. 1
Who will not suffer the stormy *time,* . . . . *S.C.* F. 15
on a *time* he cast him to scold . . . . *S.C.* F. 125
The joyous *time* now nighes fast, ... *S.C.* Mar. 4
Yts *time* to hast us homeward. . . . . *S.C.* Mar. 117
Passen their *time* . . . In lustihede . . . . *S.C.* May 41
The *time* was once, and may againe retorne, ... *S.C.* May 103
tract of *time,* and long prosperitie, ... *S.C.* May 117
on a *tyme,* in Sommer season, ... *S.C.* May 176
time in passing weares, ... *S.C.* Jun. 38
time, I gesse, homeward to goe: . . . . *S.C.* Jun. 117
shall be better in *time.* . . . . *S.C.* Jul. 230
spends her *time* of sleepe In songs . . . . *S.C.* Au. 184
yts *time* to be gone. . . . . *S.C.* Au. 198
Long *time* he used this slippery pranck, ... *S.C.* S. 200
Thenot, now nis the *time* of merimake, ... *S.C.* N. 9
Nowe is *time* to dye: Nay, *time* was long ygoe: . . . . . . *S.C.* N. 81
as the springe gives place to elder *time,* . . . . *S.C.* D. 73
tryed *time* yet taught me greater thinges; . . . . *S.C.* D. 85
and *time* in durance, shall outweare; . . . . *S.C.* Env. 2
his carelesse *time* This Shepheard drives, ... *Gn.* 153
at his wonted *time* in that same place . . . . *Gn.* 249
Thus wise *long* time he did himselfe dispace . . . . *Gn.* 265
I likewise have wasted much good *time,* . . . . *Hub.* 75
Time, flying with winges swift, ... *Hub.* 308
lost their *time* in wandring loose abroad; . . . . *Hub.* 399
unto some of those in *time* arise? . . . . *Hub.* 426
ere long *time* had passed, ... *Hub.* 559
Then was high *time* their wits about to geather. . . . . . . *Hub.* 570
in the world long *time* they wandered, ... *Hub.* 943
now was *time* (if ever . . . . *Hub.* 959
on a *time* the Sheepe, ... *Hub.* 1205
What *time* the Ape the kingdome first did gaine, ... *Hub.* 1207
since the *time* that Phoebus foolish sonne . . . . *T.M.* 7
Of things forepast, nor moniments of *time;* . . . . *T.M.* 104
During the *time* of that her widowhead: . . . . *T.M.* 240
in the lap of soft delight Beene long *time* luld, ... *T.M.* 302
all corrupted through the rust of *time* . . . . *T.M.* 433
now to nought through spoyle of *time* is wasted. . . . . . . *Ti.* 119
though *Time* all moniments obscure, ... *Ti.* 174
Devour'd of *Time,* in *time* to nought doo passe. . . . . . . *Ti.* 420
Ne feareth change of *time,* . . . . *Ti.* 465
sate long *time* in sencelesse sad affright, ... *Ti.* 475
To be the pray of *Tyme,* and Fortunes spoyle! . . . . *Ti.* 516
Sith *time* doth greatest things to ruine bring? . . . . *Ti.* 556
That he in *time* would sure prove such an one, ... *Mui.* 31
th' onely usance Of a small *time,* . . . . *D.* 504
from the *time* that first the Nymph his mother . . . . *As.* 13
Or mellow fruit if it were harvest *time.* . . . . *As.* 48
With dolefull layes unto the *time* addrest: . . . . *As.* Interl. 226
these ydle rimes . . . The labor of lost *time,* . . . . *Ded. Son.* ix. 8
whose Muse whylome did maske, As *time* her taught, ... I. Pr. 1. 2
Yet armes till that *time* did he never wield. . . . . I. i. 1. 5
whose deepe wounded mind . . . long *time* did languish, . . . I. ii. 24. 9
Long *time* they thus together traveiled; . . . . I. ii. 28. 1
in the witch unweeting joyd long *time,* . . . . I. ii. 40. 2
how long *time,'* . . . 'Are you in this misformed hous to dwell?' I. ii. 43. 1
'*Time* and suffised fates to former kynd Shall us restore; . . . I. ii. 43. 8

Time—*Continued.*

long *time* having tand his tawney hide	I. iii. 31. 4
Ladies love as losse of *time* forbore:	I. v. 37. 4
them long *time* before, great Nimrod was,	I. v. 48. 1
she . . . yieldes her to extremitie of *time:*	I. vi. 13. 2
long *time* with that salvage people stayd,	I. vi. 19. 3
During which *time* her gentle wit she plyes	I. vi. 19. 5
the dew *time* In which the wombes of wemen doe expyre,	I. vii. 9. 6
beast . . . which he had kept long *time* in darksom den.	I. vii. 16. 9
time . . . the truth to light should bring.'	I. ix. 5. 9
lovers life, As losse of *time* . . . I ever scornd,	I. ix. 10 .2
As, when just *time* expired, should appeare.	I. ix. 14. 4
During which *time* . . . Shee him instructed	I. x. 45. 3
High *time* now gan it wex	I. xi. 1. 1
The Nourse of *time* and everlasting fame,	I. xi. 5. 8
Of auncient *time* there was a springing well,	I. xi. 29. 3
gate, Which long *time* had beene shut,	I. xii. 3. 7
He was affyaunced long *time* before,	I. xii. 27. 2
still he sate long *time* astonished,	I. xii. 29. 3
fained cheare, as for the *time* behoves,	II. ii. 34. 3
In which we long *time* . . . contynewd as was fitt;	II. iv. 18. 7
By this *time* was the worthy Guyon brought	II. vi. 19. 1
bad him stay till *time* the tide renewd.	II. vi. 26. 9
lover trew, Whom he had long *time* sought	II. vii. 55. 3
lenger *time* then that no living wight	II. vii. 66. 2
Pyrochles gan reply the second *tyme,*	II. viii. 30. 1
Lyon, which hath long *time* saught His robbed whelpes,	II. viii. 40. 7
no lenger *time* . . . workemanship should not endure:	II. ix. 21. 7
When cause requyrd, but never out of *time;*	II. ix. 25. 8
no *time* nor reason could arize,	II. ix. 49. 4
Elfin Emperours, Till *time* of Gloriane.	II. x. Arg.
Polluted this same gentle soyle long *time;*	II. x. 9. 2
During which *time*	II. x. 20. 5
peaceably the same long *time* did weld,	II. x. 32. 4
In whose sad *time* blood did from heaven rayne.	II. x. 34. 2
goodly well long *time* it governed;	II. x. 47. 4
What *time* th' eternall Lord in fleshly slime Enwombed was,	II. x. 50. 2
O joyous memorie of happy *time,*	II. x. 50. 5
since Lucies *tyme,* Was of the Britons first crownd	II. x. 58. 6
Long *time* in peace his realme established,	II. x. 63. 3
how the *time* was fled they quite forgate;	II. x. 77. 4
Amid th' Aegaean sea long *time* did stray,	II. xii. 13. 2
in *time* of greatest storme;	II. xii. 24. 6
Gather the Rose of love whilest yet is *time,*	II. xii. 75. 8
Till she mote winne fit *time* for her desire;	III. i. 56. 2
High *time* it seemed then for everie wight	III. i. 58. 1
What *time* king Ryence raign'd and dealed right,	III. ii. 18. 5
'The *time* that mortall men their weary cares Do lay away,	III. ii. 32. 1
Long *time* ye both in armes shall beare great sway,	III. iii. 28. 5
in drowsie cave Hath long *time* slept,	III. iii. 30. 2
the third *time* shall fayre accordaunce make:	III. iii. 30. 7
Yet shall he long *time* warre with happy speed,	III. iii. 31. 3
the third *time* shall rew his foolhardise:	III. iii. 35. 7
the full *time,* prefixt by destiny,	III. iii. 40. 5
of the *time* doth dew advauntage take.	III. iii. 52. 4
(so *time* their turne did fitt)	III. iii. 58. 3
Long *time* she fostred up,	III. iv. 20. 4
the third *time* Could scarce recovered bee	III. iv. 35. 1
long *time* wandred through the forest wyde	III. v. 3. 1
Thus warreid he long *time* against his will;	III. v. 48. 1
So was she trayned up from *time* to *time*	III. vi. 3. 7
Great enimy to it . . . Is wicked *Tyme;*	III. vi. 39. 3
All things decay in *time,*	III. vi. 40. 9
were it not that *Time* their troubler is,	III. vi. 41. 1
both meeting at one *tyme;*	III. vi. 42. 2
During which *time* the Chorle . . . conceiv'd affection	III. vii. 15. 6
for want of handsome *time* and place,	III. vii. 60. 4
fedd His foolish malady, and long *time* had misledd.	III. viii. 3. 9
Her to disport and idle *time* to pas	III. viii. 11. 3
The which to let you weet will further *time* requyre.	III. viii. 52. 9
in a cloud their light did long *time* stay,	III. ix. 20. 7
faire it florished and long *time* stoud,	III. ix. 43. 8
Where wearie wandring they long *time* did wonne,	III. ix. 48. 7
The learned lover lost no *time* nor tyde	III. x. 6. 1
Nought wants but *time* and place,	III. x. 11. 6
Was never better *time* to shew thy smart	III. x. 26. 3
Lewd Losse of *Time,*	III. xii. 25. 5
from the *time* that Scudamour her bought	IV. i. 2. 1
Untill such *time* as noble Britomart Released her,	IV. i. 4. 3
What *time* the dayes with scorching heat abound,	IV. i. 13. 7
Till *time* the tryall of her truth expyred;	IV. i. 54. 5
Such Musicke is wise words, with *time* concented,	IV. ii. 2. 5
What *time* his people into partes did rive,	IV. ii. 2. 8
on a *time,* as they together way'd,	IV. ii. 12. 8
wicked *Time* that all good thoughts doth waste,	IV. ii. 33. 1
evermore, when she fit *time* could fynd,	IV. ii. 53. 7
What *time* she usd to live in wively sort,	IV. v. 3. 8
Fit *time* t' awaite avenged for to bee.	IV. v. 9. 6
all, which her that *time* did vew,	IV. v. 13. 5
which no creature may Long *time* resist,	IV. v. 43. 4
time yet serves that I the same refuse;	IV. vi. 4. 8
long *time* his grieved hart did wound,	IV. vi. 28. 5
from that *time* I from enchaunters theft Her freed,	IV. vi. 35. 4
In all which *time* Sir Artegall made way	IV. vi. 40. 1
when they had long *time* there taken rest,	IV. vi. 42. 1
Fit *time* for him thence to depart it found,	IV. vi. 42. 4
the *time* for to delay,	IV. vi. 45. 2
to worke *Time* to my will,	IV. vii. 17. 2
in all this *time,* from him unknowne, Thine honor sav'd,	IV. vii. 19. 4
in short *time* his face they overgrew,	IV. vii. 40. 7

Time—*Continued.*

Till *time* for him should remedy provide,	IV. vii. 47. 6
Till *time* the tempest doe thereof delay	IV. viii. 1. 6
he long *time* afterwards did lead An happie life	IV. viii. 18. 1
antique age, yet in the infancie Of *time,*	IV. viii. 30. 2
twixt themselves they pointed *time* and place:	IV. viii. 51. 1
Who now long *time* had lyen in prison sad;	IV. ix. 4. 3
'What *time* the fame of this renowmed prise	IV. x. 4. 1
time to steale, the threasure of mans day,	IV. x. 14. 8
In which he long *time* after did remaine	IV. xi. 7. 5
she in *time* forth brought These three faire sons,	IV. xi. 42. 7
It was no *time* to scan the prophecie,	IV. xii. 28. 3
with state of present *time* . . . the antique world compare,	V. Pr. 1. 1
all things else in *time* are chaunged quight:	V. Pr. 4. 5
in *time* he will us quite forsake.	V. Pr. 7. 9
the *time* they first tooke the Sunnes hight,	V. Pr. 8. 4
The fortune of her life long *time* did feare:	V. ii. 3. 4
if *time* he had, He would be there,	V. ii. 3. 8
What *time,* if naught me let, I will be there	V. ii. 4. 3
That she might win some *time,*	V. ii. 23. 7
The *time* and place was blazed farre and wide,	V. iii. 2. 5
Unlesse some succour had in *time* him overtaken.	V. iii. 9. 9
taking usurie of *time* fore-past,	V. iii. 40. 3
when as *time* to Artegall shall tend,	V. iii. 40. 8
tract of *time,* that all things doth decay,	V. iv. 8. 1
Before which *time* I lov'd . . . That further mayd,	V. iv. 8. 6
till *time* they should begin the fight.	V. v. 4. 9
During which *time* the warlike Amazon,	V. v. 26. 7
Now is the *time* that I untimely must Thereof make tryall	V. v. 29. 5
From *time* to *time,* when thou it best shalt see,	V. v. 34. 4
Yet to awayt fit *time* she weened best,	V. v. 44. 8
with faire words, fit for the *time* and place,	V. v. 55. 6
What *time* sad tydings . . . Talus to her brought;	V. vi. 3. 3
She fayn'd to count the *time* againe anew,	V. vi. 5. 4
Thus passing th' evening well, till *time* of rest,	V. vi. 23. 1
What *time* the native Belman of the night,	V. vi. 27. 1
tempred for the *time* her present heavinesse.	V. vii. 44. 9
what *time* his fierie teme Towards the westerne brim	V. ix. 35. 1
and *time* his speach To all assayes;	V. ix. 39. 3
Stryving long *time* in vaine it to withstond;	V. x. 27. 3
right long *time* is overborne of wrong	V. xi. 1. 2
One *time* when he his weapon faynd to shift,	V. xi. 7. 6
the third *time* out of an hidden shade	V. xi. 22. 3
when *time* doth serve,	V. xi. 56. 1
now *time* drawing ny	V. xii. 3. 6
time and place convenient to areed,	V. xii. 9. 3
with strong powre did them long *time* oppresse;	V. xii. 24. 4
During which *time* that he did there remayne,	V. xii. 26. 1
She long *time* hath deare lov'd a doughty Knight,	VI. i. 14. 8
Ne *time* would give, nor any termes aby,	VI. ii. 19. 7
yet past a boy, And being now high *time*	VI. ii. 32. 9
Yet for the *time* this answere he to him behight.	VI. ii. 36. 9
So they the evening past till *time* of rest;	VI. iii. 9. 6
During which *time* that wyld man did apply	VI. iv. 16. 1
having long *time,* as his daily weed,	VI. iv. 19. 4
And like in *time* to further ill to grow,	VI. iv. 30. 8
All is in *time* like to returne againe	VI. iv. 31. 7
As ye may know when *time* shall be to tell the same.	VI. v. 2. 9
long *time* he lacked had The good Sir Calepine,	VI. v. 3. 1
as they the *time* did waite,	VI. v. 15. 1
As to them seemed fit *time* to entertaine;	VI. v. 24. 7
Untill fit *time* and place he mote espy,	VI. vii. 3. 4
For to avenge in *time* convenient,	VI. vii. 4. 7
Whylest *time* did offer meanes him sleeping to surprize.	VI. vii. 22. 9
which long *time* she sought,	VI. vii. 50. 5
was the *tyme* ordayned For such a dismall deed,	VI. viii. 44. 6
where shepherds lie In winters wrathfull *time,*	VI. ix. 4. 9
she in tract of *time* accompted was his owne.	VI. ix. 14. 9
'The *time* was once, in my first prime of yeares,	VI. ix. 24. 1
During which *time* he did her entertaine	VI. ix. 34. 5
What *time* the golden apple was unto him brought.	VI. ix. 36. 9
Long *time* had lov'd, and hop'd her love to gaine,	VI. ix. 38. 2
Another *time,* when as they did dispose To practise games	VI. ix. 43. 1
though long *time* dearely bought.	VI. ix. 45. 9
Thus Calidore continu'd there long *time*	VI. ix. 46. 1
In such discourses they together spent Long *time,*	VI. x. 30. 2
he in *time* her joyance should obtaine:	VI. xi. 7. 4
gently waking them gave them the *time* of day.	VI. xi. 38. 9
in dew *time* a mayden child forth brought:	VI. xii. 6. 5
Till *time* that Calidore brought Pastorella thether.	VI. xii. 10. 9
long *time* after Calidore,	VI. xii. 39. 5
rends without regard of person or of *time.*	VI. xii. 40. 9
Old aged Sire, with hower-glasse in hand, Hight *Time,*)	VII. vi. 8. 7
take what fortune, *time,* and place would lend.	VII. vi. 23. 6
Eftsoones the *time* and place appointed were,	VII. vi. 36. 1
To tell what *time* he might her Lady see	VII. vi. 43. 8
at the *time* that was before agreed,	VII. vii. 3. 1
How-ever faire it flourish for a *time,*	VII. vii. 18. 2
Yet in his *time* he wrought as well as playd,	VII. vii. 35. 3
For who sees not that *Time* on all doth pray?	VII. vii. 47. 5
all things . . . Are chaung'd of *Time,*	VII. vii. 48. 3
who is it . . . That *Time* himselfe doth move,	VII. vii. 48. 5
But *time* shall come that all shall changed bee,	VII. vii. 59. 4
Short *Time* shall soon cut down	VII. viii. 1. 9
that same *time* when no more Change shall be,	VII. viii. 2. 2
The hardest steele, in tract of *time* doth teare:	*Am.* xviii. 2
doe me not before my *time* to dy.	*Am.* xlii. 14
When my abodes prefixed *time* is spent,	*Am.* xlvi. 1
High *time* it is this warre now ended were	*Am.* lvii. 2
Devouring *tyme* and changeful chance have prayd,	*Am.* lviii. 7

Time—*Continued.*
Tell her the joyous *time* wil not be staid, ... *Am.* lxx. 7
none can call againe the passed *time*. . . . . *Am.* lxx. 14
So sweet your prison you in *time* shall prove, ... *Am.* lxxi. 11
Thus I the *time* with expectation spend, ... *Am.* lxxxvi. 9
since that *time* he wounded hath my selfe. . . . . *Epig.* iv. 55
awake! for it is *time;* . . . . *Epith.* 74
for this *time* it ill ordained was, ... *Epith.* 270
How slowly does sad *Time* his feathers move? . . . . *Epith.* 281
tymely Sleep, when it is *tyme* to sleepe, ... *Epith.* 355
Ye would not stay your dew *time* to expect, ... *Epith.* 430
for short *time* an endlesse moniment. . . . . *Epith.* 433
Love, that had now long *time* securely slept . . . . *H.L.* 61
What *time* this worlds great Workmaister did cast . . . . . *H.B.* 29
Ere flitting *Time* could wag his eyas wings . . . . *H.H.L.* 24
With him he raignd, before all *time* prescribed, ... *H.H.L.* 36
But there their termelesse *time* in pleasure spend; . . . . *H.H.L.* 75
Timely. My *timely* buds with wayling all are wasted; . . . . *S.C.* Ja. 38
to yield the *timely* eare, ... *S.C.* O. 58
promised of *timely* fruite such store, ... *S.C.* D. 104
after Winter commeth *timely* death. . . . . *S.C.* D. 150
Vesper in his *timely* howre From golden Oeta . . . . *Gn.* 315
yeeld them *timely* profite for their paine. . . . . *Hub.* 236
dye, wanting thy *timely* mirth. . . . . *U.V.* 18
untill that *timelie* death . . . doo ende my earthlie daies: . . *Ti.* 311
it desir'd at *timely* houres to heare, ... *Col.* 362
fill the same with store of *timely* wine. . . . . *Col.* 603
whenas *timely* meanes it purchase may, ... *Ded.Son.*xvi.13
father Nilus gins to swell With *timely* pride . . . . I. i. 21. 2
with the Sunne take, Sir, your *timely* rest, ... I. i. 33. 1
on the top a Diall told the *timely* howres. . . . . I. iv. 4. 9
Bardes, that . . . Can tune their *timely* voices . . . . . . I. v. 3. 7
took her wonted way To ronne her *timely* race, ... I. v. 44. 8
with *timely* fruit her belly sweld, And bore a boy . . . . . I. vi. 23. 3
As it had deawed bene with *timely* raine: . . . . I. xi. 48. 5
Nor *timely* tides did drive out of their sluggish sourse. . . . II. vi. 20. 9
hope of helpe and *timely* grace, ... II. viii. 25. 6
timely service to her pleasures meet, ... III. ix. 7. 8
Upon them fell, before her *timely* howre; . . . . IV. v. 32. 4
By *timely* death shall winne her wished rest, ... IV. xii. 8. 2
Timely to joy and carrie comely cheare: . . . . V. v. 38. 5
Through promise to afford her *timely* aide, ... V. xi. 41. 4
such duties *timely* to bestow. . . . . VI. ii. 1. 9
is this the *timely* joy, Which I expected long, ... VI. iii. 4. 8
being now attacht with *timely* age, ... VI. vi. 4. 6
Ye may him overtake in *timely* tyde.' . . . . VI. vii. 6. 4
of his love he reapt the *timely* frute, ... VI. x. 38. 5
Renew'd her death by *timely* death denying. . . . . VI. xi. 23. 5
Scarse yeelding her due food or *timely* rest, ... VI. xi. 24. 5
daughters of high Jove And *timely* Night; . . . . VII. vii. 45. 2
For lusty Spring now in his *timely* howre . . . . *Am.* iv. 9
graunt me *timely* grace, ... *Am.* lvii. 13
stormes, . . . Shall turne to caulmes, and *tymely* cleare away. *Am.* lxii. 12
tymely Sleep, when it is tyme to sleepe, ... *Epith.* 355
the chast wombe informe with *timely* seed, ... *Epith.* 386
Send us the *timely* fruit of this same night. . . . . *Epith.* 404
cease till then our *tymely* joyes to sing: . . . . *Epith.* 425
Time's. Sith onely God surmounts all *times* decay, ... *Bel.*^{2} i. 13
times delay new hope of helpe still breeds. . . . . *Hub.* 327
times decay, and envies cruell tort, ... *Ti.* 167
Of rude oblivion and long *times* decay, ... V. iv. 2. 8
Times. *See* **Oftentimes, Oft-times.**
All the good hap of th' oldest *times* afore, ... *Ro.* xix. 6
While *times* enduren of tranquillitie, ... *S.C.* May 154
To sadder *times* thou mayst attune thy quill, ... *S.C.* N. 35
At other *times* he casts to sew the chace . . . . *Hub.* 743
favourable *times* did us afford Free libertie . . . . *T.M.* 243
I hate all *times,* because, all *times* doo flye . . . . *D.* 411
thrise three *times* did fast from any bitt; . . . . I. iii. 14. 4
Their *times* in his eternall booke of fate . . . . I. ix. 42. 4
thousand *times* he so him selfe had drest, ... I. ix. 54. 7
later *times* thinges more unknowne shall show. . . . . II. Pr. 3. 3
thrise three *tymes* had fild her crooked hornes, ... II. i. 53. 3
thousand thousand *times* more faire, ... II. iii. 26. 1
there shall to thee Ten *times* so much be nombred . . . . . . II. vii. 9. 5
Thou, that doest live in later *times,* . . . . II. vii. 18. 4
seven *times* dipped in the bitter wave . . . . II. viii. 20. 8
Three *times* more furious and more puissaunt, ... II. viii. 34. 8
Thousand *times* fairer than her mortall hew, ... II. ix. 3. 7
Seven *times* the Sunne, with his lamp-burning light, ... II. ix. 7. 5
old records from auncient *times* derivd, ... II. ix. 57. 7
In antique *times* was salvage wildernesse, ... II. x. 5. 3
O! goodly usage of those antique *tymes,* . . . . III. i. 13. 1
by record of antique *times* I finde . . . . III. ii. 2. 1
comprovinciall In auncient *times* unto great Britainee, . . . III. iii. 32. 7
Nine *times* he heard him come aloft ere day, ... III. x. 48. 5
hung With ragged monuments of *times* forepast, ... IV. i. 21. 2
*And know the moniments of passed *times:* . . . . IV. xi. 17. 6
An hundred *times* about the pit side fares . . . . IV. xii. 17. 8
Foure *times* . . . he shifted hath . . . . V. Pr. 8. 5
In those old *times* of which I doe entreat, ... V. i. 1. 2
in *times* of jeopardy, To keepe a nightly watch . . . . V. iv. 46. 8
Yet doe I not of better *times* despeyre; . . . . V. v. 38. 7
'All *times* have wont safe passage to afford . . . . V. viii. 22. 1
twelve of them he did by *times* devoure, ... V. x. 8. 3
Three *times,* as in defiance, there he strooke; . . . . V. xi. 22. 2
A thousand *times* him thankt that had her death prevented. . VI. x. 36. 9
A thousand *times* embrast, and kist a thousand more. . . . . VI. xi. 45. 9
times comparing with their accidents, ... VI. xii. 20. 2
A thousand *times* she her embraced nere, ... VI. xii. 20. 8

Times—*Continued.*
it the Sunne a thousand *times* did pass, ... VII. vii. 6. 8
times and seasons of the yeare that fall: . . . . VII. vii. 27. 4
Times do change and move continually: . . . . VII. vii. 47. 6
which three *times* thrise happy hath me made, ... *Am.* lxxiv. 3
Is many thousand *times* more bright, more cleare, ... *H.H.B.* 170
Timias. after the foule foster *Timias* did strive. . . . . . III. i. 18. 9
Timias, the Princes gentle Squyre, ... III. iv. 47. 1
Three fosters *Timias* wound; . . . . III. v. Arg.
Timias him lightly overhent, ... III. v. 25. 2
Whom with his brethren *Timias* slew, ... III. vi. 54. 4
Prince Arthur and young *Timias,* . . . . VI. v. 11. 8
After that *Timias* had againe recured The favour of Belphebe VI. v. 12. 1
him well he knew To be his *Timias,* . . . . VI. v. 23. 2
Timon. What *Timon* but would let compassion creepe Into his
brest, ... *D.* 248
'Unto Old *Timon* he me brought bylive; . . . . I. ix. 4. 1
Old *Timon,* . . . In warlike feates th' expertest man alive, . . I. ix. 4. 2
Timon's. me had warnd old *Timons* wise behest, ... I. ix. 9. 5
Tinct. the greene in gray is *tinct;* . . . . *S.C.* N. 107
Tindarid. *See* **Tyndarid.**
Tine. *See* **Teen.**
Those piteous plaints and sorrowfull sad *tine,* . . . . *T.M.* 3
In funerall complaints and waylfull *tyne,* . . . . *Mui.* 12
To seek her out with labor and long *tyne,* . . . . I. ix. 15. 7
recure their wounds; so inly they did *tine.* . . . . II. xi. 21. 9
fostred up with bitter milke of *tine,* . . . . III. xi. 1. 4
filled were with rufull *tine* And secret feare, ... IV. iii. 37. 4
As withered weed through cruell winters *tine,* . . . . IV. xii. 34. 6
Lamenting sore his sorrowfull sad *tyne,* . . . . V. i. 13. 8
he sighed deepe for inward *tyne:* . . . . VI. v. 24. 1
As th' onely author of her wofull *tine;* . . . . VI. viii. 33. 3
Tined. bridale torches foule Erynnis *tynde;* . . . . *Gn.* 394
Flames, weapons, wounds, in Greeks fleete to have *tynde.* . . . *Gn.* 504
Coles of contention and whot vengeaunce *tind.* . . . . II. viii. 11. 5
great desire . . . in her forthwith they *tynd,* . . . . III. iii. 57. 3
brutish lust, that was so beastly *tind.* . . . . III. vii. 15. 9
To quench the flames which she had *tyn'd* before, ... III. x. 13. 3
Firebrand of hell, first *tynd* in Phlegeton, ... IV. ii. 1. 1
With fell despight her cruell arrowes *tynde* . . . . IV. vii. 30. 7
Scots and English both, that *tyned* on his strand. . . . . . IV. xi. 36. 9
Tinny. Dart, nigh chockt with sands of *tinny* mines. . . . . IV. xi. 31. 5
Tinsel. Her wanton palfrey all was overspred With *tinsell*
trappings, ... I. ii. 13. 8
all her steed with *tinsell* trappings shone, ... III. i. 15. 7
Tip. therwith *tip* his sharp empoisned darts, ... *H.L.* 121
Tipped. In his right hand a *tipped* staffe he held, ... VII. vii. 31. 6
Venemous toung, *tipt* with vile adders sting, ... *Am.* lxxxv. 1
Tiptoes. himselfe uprearing hy Upon his *tiptoes,* . . . . . . *Hub.* 664
Upon his *tiptoes* nicely he up went, ... *Hub.* 1009
did stryde At every step uppon the *tiptoes* hie: . . . . . . VI. vii. 42. 6
standing on his *tiptoes,* to seeme tall, ... VI. viii. 26. 5
Tire. Whereas his temples did his creast-front *tyre;* . . . . *Gn.* 308
Such one was Wrath, the last of this ungodly *tire.* . . . . . I. iv. 35. 9
when they had despoyld her *tire* and call, ... I. viii. 46. 5
on her head she wore a *tyre* of gold, ... I. x. 31. 5
Least his long way his aged limbes should *tire:* . . . . . . II. i. 7. 5
feeble nature cloth'd with fleshly *tyre.* . . . . II. i. 57. 3
In sumptuous *tire* she joyd her selfe to pranck, ... II. ii. 36. 8
Ne other *tire* she on her head did weare, ... II. ix. 19. 8
Straunge was her *tyre,* . . . . II. ix. 40. 5
After so long a travell which them both did *tire.* . . . . . . IV. v. 39. 9
Strange was her *tyre;* . . . . IV. x. 31. 6
He with an Oaken girlond now did *tire,* . . . . VII. vii. 11. 5
Tired. This nymph, quite *tyr'd* with heat of scorching ayre, . . I. vii. 5. 3
tyred limbes to rest, . . . 'I hither came; . . . . I. x. 11. 1
to bayt His *tyred* armes for toylesome wearinesse, ... II. xii. 29. 8
He sett upon her Palfrey *tired* lame, ... III. vii. 28. 8
my Muse her selfe now *tyred* has, ... IV. xi. 53. 8
at length, nigh *tyrd* with former chace, ... VI. v. 21. 1
being *tyrde* with travell, ... VI. viii. 34. 4
Ne ought was *tyred* with his endlesse toyle, ... VI. viii. 47. 3
Thy *tyred* steedes long since have need of rest. . . . . *Epith.* 284
Tireling. His *tyreling* Jade he fiersly forth did push . . . . III. i. 17. 4
the former villaine, which did lead Her *tyreling* jade, ... VI. vii. 40. 7
Tires. In which were not rich *tyres,* nor garments gay, . . . I. x. 39. 2
Tirynthian. Like as whylome that strong *Tirynthian* swaine . VI. xii. 35. 1
When he begot the great *Tirynthian* groome: . . . . *Epith.* 329
Tisiphone. *Tisiphone* each where doth shake and shiver . . . *Gn.* 342
Tissue. Not of rich *tissew,* nor of cloth of gold, ... V. ix. 28. 2
Titan. Where Titan ryseth from the mayne . . . . *S.C.* Jul. 59
when as drouping *Titan* draweth neere . . . . *D.* 468
the high hils *Titan* discovered, ... I. ii. 7. 4
Titan rose to runne his daily race; . . . . I. xi. 33. 2
Titan, playing on the eastern streames, ... II. iii. 1. 3
where *Titan* his face never shewes. . . . . II. v. 27. 9
On th' others helmett, which as *Titan* shone, ... II. vi. 31. 6
soone as *Titan* gan his head exault, ... II. xi. 9. 4
O *Titan!* hast to reare thy joyous waine; . . . . III. iv. 60. 3
When *Titan* faire his beames did display, ... III. vi. 6. 5
The morow next, so soone as *Titan* shone, ... IV. i. 16. 5
'For *Titan* . . . Was Saturnes elder brother . . . . VII. vi. 27. 1
That place, from which by folly *Titan* fell: . . . . VII. vi. 34. 3
From my great Grandsire *Titan* unto mee Deriv'd . . . . . . VII. vii. 16. 8
Titaness. So likewise did this *Titanesse* aspire . . . . VII. vi. 4. 1
when the hardy *Titanesse* beheld The goodly building . . . . VII. vi. 10. 1
soone he came where-as the *Titanesse* Was striving . . . . . VII. vi. 17. 2
Where-at the *Titanesse* did sternly lower, ... VII. vi. 18. 4
when the haughty *Titanesse* beheld, ... VII. vi. 25. 1
wote thou this, thou hardy *Titanesse,* . . . . VII. vi. 33. 1

Titaness—*Continued.*
Which he obtain'd against that *Titanesse*, VII. vii. 1. 8
thus gan the *Titanesse:* VII. vii. 47. 1
So was the *Titanesse* put downe and whist, VII. vii. 59. 6
Titan's. A mayden Queene that shone as *Titans* ray, I. iv. 8. 5
Out of the sea faire *Titans* deawy face, I. xi. 33. 4
Earely, so soone as *Titans* beames forth brust VI. iii. 13. 5
hast held The Heavens rule from *Titans* sonnes VII. vi. 27. 7
thee, faire *Titans* child, I rather weene, VII. vi. 32. 1
Much lesse the Title of Old *Titans* Right: VII. vi. 33. 4
sparke Which darted is from *Titans* flaming head, *H.H.B.* 163
did delay Hot *Titans* beames, *Proth.* 4
Titans. the *Titans* which did make Warre against heven, III. vii. 47. 3
it us'd in that great fight Against the *Titans,* V. i. 9. 6
a daughter by descent Of those old *Titans* VII. vi. 2. 6
Titans'. Like an huge Gyant of the *Titans* race; II. vii. 41. 6
Tithonus. the deawy bed Of aged *Tithone* I. xi. 51. 3
Tithonus'. Weary of aged *Tithones* saffron bed, I. ii. 7. 2
she did lye All night in old *Tithonus* frozen bed, III. iii. 20. 6
The Rosy Morne long since left *Tithones* bed, *Epith.* 75
Title. Ne make one *title* worse, ne make one better: *Hub.* 384
The *title* of the Kingdome to possesse. *Hub.* 1046
he his *title* justifide by might, II. x. 60. 6
Into their names the *title* to convart, III. ix. 43. 4
the bold *title* of a poet bad He on himselfe had ta'en, V. ix. 25. 8
Unto the type of kingdomes *title* clymes! V. ix. 42. 7
Much lesse the *Title* of Old Titans Right: VII. vi. 33. 4
Title's. rymes . . . for their *titles* sake may find more grace. *Ded. Son.* i. 14
Titles. crownes, and Diademes, and *titles* vaine, II. vii. 43. 8
honour did obscure, And *titles* of nobilitie deface: V. ix. 38. 7
For triall of their *Titles* and best Rights: VII. vi. 36. 4
my pen would write her *titles* true, *Am.* iii. 11
not by . . . *titles* vaine, Derived farre from famous Auncestrie: *Com. Son.* ii. 3
Titmouse. Before him sits the *Titmose* silent bee; *S.C.* N. 26
Titus. Myld *Titus* and Gesippus without pryde; IV. x. 27. 5
Tityrus. Which I cond of *Tityrus* in my youth, *S.C.* F. 92
The God of shepheards, *Tityrus,* is dead, *S.C.* Jun. 81
the Romish *Tityrus* . . . left his Oaten reede, *S.C.* O. 55
he of *Tityrus* his songs did lere: *S.C.* D. 4
to match thy pype with *Tityrus* his style. *S.C.* Env. 9
mournfull *Tityrus,* mindefull yet Of thy displeasure, *Gn.* 377
after *Tityrus* first sung his lay, *Col.* 2
Tityus fed a vultur on his maw; I. v. 35. 6
To (*partial list*). *See* **For to, Thereto, To and fro, Whereto.**
He cride *to* me, *Bel.*[1] i. 9
T' embrew her teeth and clawes with lukewarm blood *Bel.*[2] vi. 7
fayre Naiades, Go *too,* *Gn.* 27
But little thrift for him he did it *too:* *Hub.* 240
ought could fynd Worth harkening *to,* *Col.* 367
The one of them he gave a message *too,* I. i. 38. 8
Retourning *to* his bed in torment great, I. ii. 6. 1
Goe *to* then . . . shew thy famous might I. v. 43. 6
Whereof the keies are *to* thy hand behight I. x. 50. 7
Whereof Georgos he thee gave *to* name; I. x. 66. 6
love In heavenly spirits *to* these creatures bace, II. viii. 1. 2
to Paynim knights wrought gret distresse, II. viii. 18. 5
too or froe; III. xii. 12. 3
multitude him coming *too* In warlike wise V. ii. 52. 1
Too much am I *too* blame V. xi. 41. 2
What fortune *to* the Briton Prince did lite, VI. vi. 17. 5
Ne Nature *to* or fro spake VII. vii. 57. 2
Toad. malicious Envy . . . did chaw . . . a venemous *tode,* I. iv. 30. 3
Toads. loathly frogs and *toades,* which eyes did lacke, I. i. 20. 7
some faste Like loathly *Toades;* II. xi. 12. 5
todes and frogs, his pasture poysonous, III. x. 59. 2
Toadstool. The grieslie *Tode-stoole* growne there *S.C.* D. 69
To and fro. *See* **Fro, To.**
flitting *too and fro,* *Pet.*[2] vii. 2
prolling *to and froe,* *S.C.* S. 160
my poore wretched ghost . . . *too and fro* am tost. *Gn.* 339
as on ambassage sent Both *too and fro,* *Hub.* 473
as a thistle-downe . . . *too and fro* be tost, *Hub.* 635
stretch . . . manly legs, still passing *too and fro,* *Hub.* 748
they them complayned *too and fro,* *Hub.* 949
Butterflie . . . dispacing *too and fro,* *Mui.* 250
walkt at will, and wandred *too and fro,* *Mui.* 379
it changeth ever *too and fro,* *D.* 429
Wend *too and fro* at evening and at morne. *Col.* 247
wander *too and fro* in waies unknowne, I. i. 10. 5
people that did pas In traveill *to and froe:* I. i. 34. 4
his wearie gate both *too and fro,* I. viii. 30. 4
see The blessed Angels *to and fro* descend I. x. 56. 2
Him sternly grypt, and hailing *to and fro,* II. iv. 8. 7
trembling Feare still *to and fro* did fly, II. vii. 22. 6
blessed Angels he sends *to and fro,* II. viii. 1. 8
whom wandring *to and fro* I long have lackt, II. viii. 53. 7
there walked *to and fro* A jolly yeoman, II. ix. 28. 1
stragling plots which *to and fro* doe ronne II. xii. 11. 5
But *to and fro* at disaventure strayd; III. iv. 53. 2
chaunged is, and often altred *to and froe.* III. vi. 37. 9
reeled *to and fro* from east to west. III. vii. 42. 7
But *too and fro* in great amazement reel'd; IV. iii. 9. 7
doubtfull fortune wavering *to and fro,* IV. iii. 17. 7
Thus did the battell varie *to and fro,* IV. iii. 28. 1
Now cuffing close, now chacing *to and fro,* IV. iv. 29. 6
long they trac'd and traverst *to and fro,* IV. vi. 18. 1
as he *to and fro* by chaunce did trace, IV. xii. 4. 8
Twixt life and death long *to and fro* she weaved, V. iv. 10. 7
to and fro long shooke And tottred, V. viii. 9. 8
long they trast and traverst *to and fro,* V. viii. 37. 1

To and fro—*Continued.*
a rude rout him chasing *to and fro,* V. xi. 44. 3
He staggered *to and fro* in doubtfull sted. V. xii. 23. 4
they trac'd and traverst *to and fro,* VI. i. 37. 1
when they long had treated *to and fro,* VI. ii. 36. 1
Long did he wrest and wring it *to and fro,* VI. iv. 7. 1
Armies of Loves still flying *too and fro,* *H.B.* 240
Tobacco. whether yt divine *Tobacco* were, Or Panachaea, III. v. 32. 6
To-bruised. Though nothing whole, but all *to-brusd* and broken, V. viii. 44. 2
Tod. *See* **Ivy-tod.**
To-day. To speed *to day,* to be put back to morrow; *Hub.* 899
What haps *to day* to me to morrow may to you. VI. i. 41. 9
Toe. From top to *toe* no place appeared bare, I. vii. 29. 6
Feare, all arm'd from top to *toe,* III. xii. 12. 1
Toes. Ne feeles the thornes and thickets pricke her tender *toes.* IV. vii. 21. 9
Tofore. Whom sure he weend, that he some-wher *tofore* had eide. IV. iv. 7. 9
that which *tofore* Jealous suspect as true untruely drad: V. vii. 38. 6
that beastes teeth, which wounded you *tofore,* VI. vi. 9. 1
hunger, which *to-fore* Had . . . oft him pinched sore: VII. vii. 30. 4
Together. As snowe and golde *together* had been wrought: *Pet.* vi. 6
'Gather *together* ye (*ye *together*) my little flocke, *S.C.* D. 145
two Beares, . . . Lying *together* in a mightie cave. *Ti.* 562
Glewed *togither* with some subtile matter. *Col.* 217
Proteus eke with him does drive his heard . . . *together,* *Col.* 249
So long as life my limbs doth hold *together;* *Col.* 629
drawne *together* into one *Col.* 845
Them both *together* laid to joy in vaine delight. I. ii. 3. 9
Long time they thus *together* traveiled, I. ii. 28. 1
With hideous horror both *together* smight, I. v. 8. 6
All these *together* in one heape were throwne, I. v. 49. 1
The which my life and love *together* tyde? I. vii. 22. 6
A goodly knight, *Together* with his Squyre, I. vii. 29. 3
as pledges firme, right hands *together* joynd I. ix. 18. 9
As on the way *together* we did fare, I. ix. 28. 2
With thornes *together* pind and patched was, I. ix. 36. 2
Heaped *together* in rude rablement, I. xii. 9. 2
So both *together* fiers engrasped bee, II. v. 20. 8
goodly purpose they *together* fond II. viii. 56. 7
to the rivers syde they both *together* far'd: III. xi. 3. 9
They courteous conge tooke, and forth *together* yode. III. i. 1. 9
then in they all *together* far'd. III. i. 30. 9
Together with the king of Louthiane, III. iii. 37. 5
forth *together* went with sorow fraught. III. iv. 31. 7
Unfitly yokt *together* in one teeme. III. ix. 6. 2
met *Together* with impetuous rage III. ix. 16. 2
Thus long they three *together* traveiled, III. x. 34. 1
It fortuned, as they *together* far'd, III. x. 35. 1
heap'd *together* with the vulgar sort, III. xi. 46. 2
All which *together* song full chearefully III. xii. 5. 6
growne *together* quite, III. xii. 46. *or.* 5
So foorth they went, and both *together* giusted; IV. i. 11. 1
With which it blessed Concord hath *together* tide. IV. i. 30. 9
As when two billowes . . . Do meete *together,* IV. i. 42. 3
on a time, as they *together* way'd, IV. ii. 12. 8
Do meete *together* on the watry lea, IV. ii. 16. 3
So, well accorded, forth they rode *together* IV. ii. 29. 1
A trompet blew; they both *together* met IV. iii. 6. 5
they both *together* fiercely met, IV. iii. 15. 1
by the tailes *together* firmely bound, IV. iii. 42. 4
both *together* chose Homeward to march, IV. iii. 51. 4
Together with this Hag beside her set, IV. iv. 9. 6
So furiously they both *together* met, IV. iv. 18. 1
forcibly to ground they both *together* went. IV. iv. 28. 9
As two wild Boares *together* grapling go, IV. iv. 29. 8
So both *together* give a new allarme, IV. iv. 35. 4
So all *together* stird up strifull stoure, IV. v. 24. 5
on their common harmes *together* did devise. IV. vi. 10. 9
all that evening . . . they *together* spent; IV. viii. 28. 2
The Ladies both on horse, *together* fast embraced. IV. viii. 34. 9
When all three kinds of love *together* meet IV. ix. 1. 2
Whom straight the Prince ensuing in *together* far'd. IV. ix. 5. 9
when awhile they had *together* beene, IV. ix. 10. 1
They liv'd *together* long without debate; IV. ix. 16. 2
many miles they two *together* wore, IV. ix. 19. 7
a troupe of Knights They saw *together* skirmishing, IV. ix. 20. 2
Met here *together,* where, through lewd upbraide IV. ix. 24. 5
as we ride *together* on our way, IV. ix. 40. 6
'All these *together* by themselves did sport IV. x. 26. 1
all were they set *together.* IV. x. 29. 9
both her feete and legs *together* twyned IV. x. 40. 8
Both linckt *together* never to dispart; IV. x. 51. 7
All these *together* marched toward Proteus hall. IV. xi. 39. 9
now *together* on their way they bin, V. i. 13. 6
both *Together* ran with ready speares in rest. V. ii. 12. 4
There being both *together* in the floud, V. ii. 13. 1
There they *together* strove and struggled long V. ii. 14. 6
Then would he ballaunce heaven and hell *together,* V. ii. 31. 5
put two wrongs *together* to be tride, V. ii. 48. 3
then *together* doe them both compare; V. ii. 48. 5
The trompets sound, then all *together* ronne. V. iii. 6. 4
then this warlike crew *Together* met V. iii. 8. 3
They both *together* joyned might and maine, V. iii. 12. 3
so soone as both *together* met, V. iii. 24. 5
Both brethren, whom one wombe *together* bore, V. iv. 4. 3
Together strove, and kindled wrathfull fires: V. iv. 4. 5
Together with her selfe in dowry free; V. iv. 12. 8
Together with Sir Terpin all that night: V. iv. 46. 7
bath'd in bloud and sweat *together* ment; V. v. 12. 5
they *together* run With greedy rage, V. vii. 29. 1

Together—*Continued.*
So both *together,* ylike felly bent, Like fiercely met. V. viii. 7. 5
So both anon *Together* met, V. viii. 9. 6
Thus goe they both *together* to their geare, V. viii. 30. 1
their sharpe speares doe both *together* smite V. x. 32. 2
as they rode *together* on their way, V. xi. 43. 6
Flocking *together* in confusde array; V. xi. 43. 8
The trompets sound, and they *together* goe V. xii. 17. 1
By the way side being *together* set; V. xii. 28. 5
linckt *together* gainst Sir Artegall; V. xii. 37. 2
I chaunst to meete this knight, . . . *Together* with this Ladie, VI. ii. 9. 9
as he and I *together* roade VI. ii. 16. 1
Whilest they *together* for the quarrey strove, VI. ii. 20. 2
Joying *together* in unblam'd delight; VI. ii. 43. 3
They met *together* in that lucklesse glade; VI. iii. 8. 2
as they past *together* on their way, VI. iii. 16. 7
whilest they discoursed both *together,* VI. iii. 23. 1
Who her, *together* with his Squyre, . . . leaves behynd. VI. v. Arg.
a knight, *together* with his squire, VI. v. 11. 2
conspiring all *together* plaine, VI. v. 14. 5
forth *together* rode, a comely couplement. VI. v. 24. 9
So forth they rode *together* all in troupe VI. v. 32. 1
So both *together* traveld, VI. vi. 16. 6
Gathered him selfe *together* soone againe, VI. vii. 46. 2
each his sundrie sheepe with severall care Gathered *together,* VI. ix. 15. 5
when as the shepheard swaynes *together* Were met VI. ix. 41. 1
In such discourses they *together* spent Long time, VI. x. 30. 1
as they all three *together* went To the greene wood VI. x. 34. 1
Like a sort of hungry dogs . . . Doe fall *together,* VI. xi. 17. 3
So forth they goe *together* VI. xi. 36. 1
Thenceforth they joy'd in happinesse *together,* VI. xii. 10. 6
There they a while *together* thus did dwell VI. xii. 11. 7
All ran *together* with a great out-cry VII. vi. 15. 1
Riding *together* both with equall pase, VII. vii. 44. 2
Will both *together* me too sorely wracke. *Am.* xlvi. 12
Together linkt with Adamantine chaines; *H.L.* 89
joyne *together* in sweete sympathie, *H.B.* 199
Together with that third from them derived, *H.H.L.* 38
Though all their beauties joynd *together* were; *H.H.B.* 103

Toil. Free from all troubles and from worldly *toyle,* *Gn.* 151
Lawrell, th' ornament of Phoebus *toyle.* *Gn.* 672
have no wit to live withouten *toyle;* *Hub.* 158
with *toyle* Himselfe hath wearied, *Hub.* 753
with the sweete of others sweating *toyle;* *Hub.* 1152
the fruit of all your travailes *toyle* *Ti.* 515
the Lyon, which with *toyle* Alcides slew, *D.* 165
with restlesse *toyle* Wearie your selves *D.* 533
Least that his *toyle* should of their troups be brust. *As.* 106
to keep sheepe, with hunger and with *toyle?* *Col.* 658
Sleepe after *toyle,* port after stormie seas, I. ix. 40. 8
I wote that of youre *toyle* . . . Ye both forwearied be: I. x. 17. 2
the tedious *toyle* ye for me take! I. xi. 1. 9
With heat, *toyle,* wounds, armes, smart, and inward fire, I. xi. 28. 2
After their weary sweat and bloody *toile,* II. ii. 33. 2
Who seekes with painfull *toile* shall honor soonest fynd: II. iii. 40. 9
Refuse such fruitlesse *toile,* II. vi. 17. 9
With greedie malice and importune *toyle,* II. xi. 7. 7
with much *toyle* Labour'd in vaine II. xii. 19. 6
neither *toyle* nor traveill might her backe recoyle. II. xii. 19. 9
This is the Port of rest from troublous *toyle,* II. xii. 32. 8
through languour of her late sweet *toyle,* II. xii. 78. 3
through long watch, and late daies weary *toile,* III. i. 58. 8
When too huge *toile* and labour them constraines, III. iii. 9. 7
there doe *toyle* and traveile day and night, III. iii. 11. 6
what needes her to *toyle,* III. iii. 25. 4
"Her heart nigh broken was with weary *toyle,* III. viii. 32. 4
All woxen weary of their journall *toyle:* III. xii. 47. *or.* 4
gaine a feastfull guerdon of their *toyle,* IV. iii. 16. 4
Like as a withered tree, through husbands *toyle,* IV. iii. 29. 6
by chaunce doth fall Into the hunters *toile,* IV. iv. 32. 6
bad them leave their labours and long *toyle* IV. iv. 48. 6
So much the more her griefe, the more her *toyle;* IV. v. 30. 1
Yet neither *toyle* nor griefe she once did spare, IV. v. 30. 2
Joyous to see her safe after long *toyle.* IV. vi. 25. 6
Britomart, after long tedious *toyle,* IV. vii. 3. 8
After late wearie *toile* which she had tride IV. viii. 9. 3
So was his *toyle* the more, the more that was his care. IV. viii. 37. 9
Those weaker Ladies after weary *toile;* IV. ix. 12. 8
'Long were to tell the travell and long *toile* IV. x. 3. 1
Weary of *toile* and travell of that day, V. iv. 46. 3
After that long daies *toile* and weary plight: V. vii. 12. 4
With weary travell and uncertaine *toile,* VI. iv. 25. 5
Of warres delight and worlds contentious *toyle,* VI. v. 37. 6
wherefore doe you beare This bottle . . . with such *toile,* VI. viii. 23. 7
Ne ought was tyred with his endlesse *toyle,* VI. viii. 47. 3
Great travell . . . And *toyle* endured, VI. ix. 2. 2
to rest from *toyle,* VI. ix. 23. 8
His former quest, so full of *toile* and paine: VI. x. 2. 2
with restlesse paine and *toile* VI. xii. 22. 8
fit for harvests *toyle,* VII. vii. 38. 5
small respit to my restlesse *toile;* *Am.* xi. 6
with weary *toyle,* Do seeke most pretious things *Am.* xv. 1
Thinck ever to endure so taedious *toyle!* *Am.* xxxiii. 10
Gotten at last with labour and long *toyle.* *Am.* lxix. 14
as a steed refreshed after *toyle,* *Am.* lxxx. 5
His cancred foes, his fights, his *toyle,* his strife, *H.H.L.* 234

Toiled. revives his *toyled* spright; *Hub.* 756
as one *toyld* with travaile downe doth lye, *D.* 255
Before her stands her knight, for whom she *toyld* so sore I. iii. 30. 9
They did about their businesse sweat, and sorely *toyld.* II. ix. 30. 9

Toiled—*Continued.*
all the world is lost, and we in vaine have *toyld.'* III. x. 39. 9

Toilful. Betweene the *toylefull* Oxe and humble Asse, *H.H.L.* 227

Toils. There his welwoven *toyles,* and subtil traines, *As.* 97
*Ne ought was tyred with his endlesse *toyles,* VI. viii. 47. 3

Toilsome. calls foorth men unto their *toylsome* trade, *D.* 485
she is wearie of the *toilsom* way, I. iv. 3. 8
His sandales were with *toilsome* travell torne, I. vi. 35. 3
his *toylesome* teme that way did guyde, I. x. 66. 4
wypt away his *toilsom* sweat. II. v. 30. 9
that *toilesome* paines doest take, II. vi. 15. 1
soone leave off this *toylsome* weary stoure: II. vi. 16. 4
to bayt His tyred armes for *toylesome* wearinesse, II. xii. 29. 8
Through *toylesome* heate and labour of her weary fight. IV. vi. 19. 9
taken have this *toylesome* paine For wretched woman, V. x. 21. 2
Tho wexing weary of that *toylesome* paine, VI. iii. 29. 3
In seas of troubles and of *toylesome* paine; VI. ix. 31. 6
(After her sweaty chace and *toylesome* play) VII. vi. 42. 2

Token. I know him by a *token;* *S.C.* Mar. 105
Nereis to the Seas a *token* gave, *Gn.* 567
after death no *token* doth survive *Ti.* 353
Beares in his wings so manie a changefull *token.* *Mui.* 101
of their passage doth appeare no *token,* *Col.* 143
Vouchsafe from him this *token* in good worth to take. *Ded. Son.* xv. 14
Here take thy lovers *token* on thy pate.' I. vi. 47. 7
Imprinted had that *token* of his wrath, II. ii. 4. 4
speaking *token* sheweth at the least III. viii. 49. 5
them conjur'd by some well knowen *token,* IV. ii. 21. 7
Ne any *token* doth thereof abide: V. iii. 25. 7
token true to old Eumenias, V. v. 34. 3
It as a *token* of good fortune tooke. V. vii. 8. 5
'This *token* beare Unto the man V. vii. 32. 4
That mote remaine for an eternall *token* V. viii. 44. 4
A privy *token* which betweene them past, VI. i. 29. 3
Yet shewd some *token* of his gentle blood VI. v. 2. 5
the former *token* Which faire Serene to him delivered had, VI. vi. 18. 1

Tokens. when he heard, and saw the *tokens* trew, II. viii. 55. 1
further right by *tokens* to descrie, V. iii. 32. 5
He askt what privie *tokens* he did beare? V. iii. 32. 6
For sure he weend . . . by many *tokens* plaine; V. vi. 34. 2
As *tokens* of her thankefull mind beseene, V. x. 17. 3
by rude *tokens* made to her appeare His deepe compassion VI. iv. 11. 3
expresse his simple minde, . . . ne but by *tokens* speake: VI. v. 30. 4

Told. *See* **Telled.**
If sike bene Wolves, as thou hast *told,* *S.C.* S. 228
Some *tolde* of Ladies, and their Paramoures; *Hub.* 28
Tolde of a strange adventure, *Hub.* 37
the complaints thereof could not be *tolde.* *Hub.* 1313
bad her tongue that it so bluntly *tolde.* *Hub.* 1388
Finde nothing worthie to be writ, or *told;* *T.M.* 100
If ought against thine honour I have *tolde;* *Mui.* 103
they in secret harts envying sore, *Tolde* Venus, *Mui.* 125
'To seeke to heare that which cannot be *tolde,* *D.* 72
Till I have *told* her praises lasting long: *Col.* 49
In sort as I it to that shepheard *told:* *Col.* 101
told her father by a shepheards boy, *Col.* 147
Told me that that same was the Regiment *Col.* 233
Those same, the shepheard *told* me, *Col.* 276
enough of shepheards thou hast *told,* *Col.* 457
He *told* of Saintes and Popes, I. i. 35. 8
Eftsoones I thought her such as she me *told,* I. ii. 39. 6
so forth *told* the story of her feare I. iii. 25. 5
he . . . *told* her all that fell, in journey as she went. I. iii. 32. 9
on the top a Diall *told* the timely howres. I. iv. 4. 9
in his lap an heap of coine he *told;* I. iv. 27. 5
Abyde, till I have *told* the message which I have.' I. v. 21. 9
Whose case whenas the careful Dwarfe had *tould,* I. v. 52. 1
Too late it was to Satyres to be *told,* I. vi. 33. 5
that false Pilgrim, which that leasing *told,* I. vi. 48. 1
'great griefe will not be *tould,* I. vii. 41. 1
my cause of griefe, more great then may be *told.'* I. vii. 51. 9
wonders . . . Of that same hornes great vertues weren *told,* I. viii. 3. 8
all the floore (too filthy to be *told*) I. viii. 35. 5
Whose secret filth good manners biddeth not be *told.* I. viii. 46. 9
told, it flames; and, hidden, it does glow, I. ix. 8. 7
The wofull tale that Trevisan had *told,* I. ix. 37. 2
Made him forget all that Fidelia *told.* I. x. 22. 5
Whose passing price uneath was to be *told:* I. x. 31. 7
their exceeding merth may not be *told:* I. xii. 40. 3
to heare of straunge adventures to be *told.* II. ii. 42. 9
fowle deedes, too hideous to bee *told,* II. ii. 44. 7
told the story of the mortall payne, II. ii. 45. 7
told for secret, how he understood II. iv. 22. 5
told that gardins pleasures in their caroling. II. vi. 24. 9
in his lap a masse of coyne he *told,* II. vii. 4. 7
too long here to be *told:* II. vii. 63. 2
of him were *told* That he which earst them combatted II. viii. 10. 8
Was never wight that treason of him *told:* II. viii. 13. 8
to Pyrochles many strokes he *told;* II. viii. 41. 4
Well weeting trew what she had rashly *told;* II. ix. 39. 2
As in that old mans booke they were in order *told.* II. x. 4. 9
It *told* how first Prometheus did create A man, II. x. 70. 5
told her meaning in her countenaunce; III. i. 50. 8
at last she *told* her briefe, III. i. 53. 4
Through hope of those, which Merlin had her *told* III. iv. 11. 6
Which to his mother *told,* despeyre she from her flong. III. iv. 41. 9
birth of fayre Belphoebe and Of Amorett is *told:* III. vi. Arg.
Nor doubt himselfe; and who he was her *told:* III. viii. 34. 4
told his secret care III. ix. 28. 3
time and place, . . . to her lover *told.* III. x. 11. 7

Told—*Continued.*
none more piteous ever was *ytold* . . . IV. i. 1. 3
(as it is *told*) Got these three lovely babes, . . . IV. ii. 45. 8
Who backe returning *told*, as he had seene, . . . IV. iv. 3. 1
they *told*, as then befell, Of that great turney . . . IV. iv. 5. 6
Shall else be *told* in order, as it fell. . . . IV. v. 28. 6
To whom they *told* all that did them betide, . . . IV. viii. 21. 4
the Dwarfe did me reveale, And *told* his Dame . . . IV. viii. 55. 6
told at large how that same errant Knight, . . . IV. ix. 36. 1
hoping griefe may lessen being *told*, . . . IV. xii. 6. 3
Which when he had unto his mother *told*, . . . IV. xii. 26. 1
So he her *told:* . . . IV. xii. 27. 7
it is by them *told* . . . V. Pr. 8. 3
Till they had *told* their message word by word: . . . V. iv. 51. 3
That whylome hath of Hercules bene *told*, . . . V. v. 24. 2
She daily *told* her love he did defye; . . . V. v. 56. 8
him she *told* her Dame his freedome did denye. . . . V. v. 56. 9
for weekes that passed were, She *told* but moneths, . . . V. vi. 5. 7
He to her *told* the story of that fray, . . . V. vi. 30. 8
when they of that yron man had *told*, . . . V. vii. 25. 8
To weete if it were true as she had *told;* . . . V. viii. 12. 2
much more then she had *told;* . . . V. ix. 21. 5
like a cloud, as likest may be *told*, . . . V. ix. 28. 4
where it was *told* The Monster underneath the Altar lay: . . . V. xi. 21. 6
where what him fell shall else be *told*. . . . V. xii. 43. 9
To whom when Hermes had his message *told*, . . . VII. vi. 19. 6
'Which to approven true, as I have *told*, . . . VII. vii. 27. 1
What more miraculous thing may be *told*, . . . *Am.* xxx. 9
which is gold, or heare, may scarse be *told?* . . . *Am.* xxxvii. 4
Lewkenors stile that hath her beautie *told*. . . . *Com. Son.* iv. 14
Toll. *toll* which they for passage pay.' . . . VI. i. 13. 9
Tom. *Tom* Piper makes us better melodie. . . . *S.C.* O. 78
Tomb. A worthy *tombe* for such a worthy wight (corps[1]). . . . *Bel.* iii. 11
It's like a corse drawne forth out of the *tombe* . . . *Ro.* v. 7
plotteth out a *tombe* by measured space: . . . *Gn.* 652
the *toomb* he did provide Of smoothest marble . . . *Gn.* 662
So wailing backe go to their wofull *toomb*. . . . *Ti.* 49
vouchsafe her honorable *toombe*.' . . . II. i. 58. 9
the hid treasures in her sacred *tombe* . . . II. vii. 17. 3
Fitt to . . . deck the drery *toombe*. . . . II. vii. 51. 9
Tomb-black. To decke his herce, and trap his *tomb-blacke* steed.' II. viii. 16. 7
Tomble, *etc.* *See* **Tumble,** *etc.*
Tombs. *Tombes* of her greatnes which did threate the skies: . *Ro.* iv. 8
Now on these ashie *tombes* shew boldnesse vaine, . . . *Ro.* xiv. 13
Tombs'. Your *toombs* devoted compasse over-all, . . . *Ro.* i. 10
To-morrow. to say *to morrowe* At the Kerke, . . . *S.C.* May 309
To speed to day, to be put back *to morrow;* . . . *Hub.* 899
Shall by *to morrow* by thy side be fond.' . . . II. iii. 18. 7
to morrow is an holy day." . . . III. xii. 47. *or.* 9
of us three *to morrow* he will sure eate one.' . . . IV. vii. 13. 9
to morrow I with him wil fight, . . . V. iv. 48. 8
What haps to day to me *to morrow* may to you. . . . VI. i. 41. 9
Tomyris. to Hypsiphil,' or to *Thomiris*. . . . II. x. 56. 4
Tongs. fell Erynnis, with hot burning *tongs*, . . . *Ro.* xxiv. 5
the dying bronds repayre With yron *tongs*, (*toungs) . . . II. vii. 36. 4
A paire of red-whot yron *tongs* did take . . . IV. v. 44. 2
Tongue. (whote cole on her *tongue!*) . . . *S.C.* S. 112
With brandisht *tongue* the emptie aire did gride, . . . *Gn.* 254
bad her *tongue* that it so bluntly tolde. . . . *Hub.* 1388
The rest untold no living *tongue* can speake. . . . *T.M.* 600
hir sweete *Tongue* was wonte to make me mirth. . . . *U.V.* 15
no *tongue* can well unfold; . . . *D.* 74
No *toong* can tell, nor any forth can set, . . . *As.* 171
A filed *toung*, furnisht with tearmes of art, . . . *Col.* 701
O . . . sharpen my dull *tong!* . . . I. Pr. 2. 9
well could file his *tongue* as smooth as glas: . . . I. i. 35. 7
he . . . lickt her lilly hands with fawning *tong*, . . . I. iii. 6. 2
Cerberus . . . lilled forth his bloody flaming *tong:* . . . I. v. 34. 4
hasty *tong* that did offend: . . . I. v. 39. 5
With foltring *tong*, and trembling everie vaine, . . . I. vii. 24. 7
Thy sad *tong* cannot tell more heavy plight . . . I. vii. 25. 3
buckled with a golden *tong*. . . . I. vii. 30. 9
every head with fyrie *tongue* did flame, . . . I. viii. 6. 3
foltring *tongue*, at last, these words seemd forth to shake; I. ix. 24. 9
His subtile *tong* . . . mealt'h Into the heart, . . . I. ix. 31. 5
earthly *tong* Cannot describe, . . . I. x. 55. 5
hideous head my *tongue* (*toung) to tell Does tremble; . . . I. xi. 12. 6
His practick witt and his fayre fyled *tonge*, . . . II. i. 3. 6
Tounge hates to tell the rest that eye to see abhord.' . . . II. i. 11. 9
With lips full pale and foltring *tong* opprest, . . . II. i. 47. 4
the sorrowes that uneath My *tong* can tell, . . . II. i. 49. 6
his flowing *toung* and troublous spright . . . II. iii. 4. 6
her *toung* did walke In fowle reproch, . . . II. iv. 5. 1
catching hold of her ungratious *tonge* . . . II. iv. 12. 8
never eie did vew, Ne *tong* did tell, . . . II. vii. 19. 7
'How ever, Sir, ye fyle Your courteous *tongue* . . . III. ii. 12. 5
swelling throbs empeach His foltring *toung* . . . III. xi. 12. 3
Her lying *tongue* was in two parts divided, . . . IV. i. 27. 6
as her *tongue* so was her hart discided, . . . IV. i. 27. 8
She arm'd her *tongue*, and thought at him to scold; . . . IV. vi. 27. 7
Nathlesse her *tongue* not to her will obayd, . . . IV. vi. 27. 8
his babling *tongue* did yet blaspheme . . . IV. viii. 45. 6
With many more whose names no *tongue* can tell: . . . IV. xi. 44. 6
from thy *tongue* thy hearts intent doth hold.' . . . V. vi. 10. 3
Her burning *tongue* with rage inflamed hath, . . . V. viii. 49. 2
So smooth of *tongue*, and subtile in his tale, . . . V. ix. 5. 6
Some one whose *tongue* was . . . Nayld to a post, . . . V. ix. 25. 2
well could charme his *tongue*, . . . V. ix. 39. 3
her cursed *tongue*, full sharpe and short, . . . V. xii. 36. 3
with the sting which in her vile *tongue* grew . . . V. xii. 42. 7

Tongue—*Continued.*
with vile *tongue* and venemous intent . . . VI. i. 8. 8
your *tongue*, your talk restraine From that they most affect, . VI. vi. 7. 8
his *tongue* doth whet Gainst all, . . . VI. vi. 12. 3
she so well applyde Her pleasing *tongue*, . . . VI. vi. 43. 5
Her *tongue* to her restord, then thus she sayd: . . . VI. viii. 19. 4
twixt his pleasing *tongue*, and her faire hew, . . . VI. ix. 26. 8
therein shut up his blasphemous *tong*, . . . VI. xii. 34. 5
endammadge wight With his vile *tongue*, . . . VI. xii. 38. 4
when my *toung* would speak her praises dew, . . . *Am.* iii. 9
You stop my *toung*, and teach my hart . . . *Am.* viii. 10
my *toung* with proud restraint to tie; . . . *Am.* xliii. 6
Venemous *toung*, tipt with vile adders sting, . . . *Am.* lxxxv. 1
thousands more then any *tongue* can tell, . . . *H.L.* 264
But feele my wits to faile, and *tongue* to fold. . . . *H.H.B.* 7
How then can mortall *tongue* hope to expresse . . . *H.H.B.* 104
Cease then, my *tongue!* and lend unto my mynd . . . *H.H.B.* 106
The fairenesse of her face no *tongue* can tell; . . . *H.H.B.* 204
would speake, but that he lackt a *tong*, . . . *Proth.* 116
Tongue's. the sting which in her *tongs* end grew. . . . IV. viii. 36. 9
Tongues. not if an hundred *tongues* to tell, . . . IV. xi. 9. 6
So dreadfully his hundred *tongues* did bray: . . . V. xii. 41. 7
their owne cursed *tongs* did straine. . . . V. xii. 41. 9
The which did seeme a thousand *tongues* to have, . . . VI. i. 9. 3
therein were a thousand *tongs* empight . . . VI. xii. 27. 1
most of them were *tongues* of mortall men, . . . VI. xii. 27. 8
The *tongues* of Serpents, with three forked stings, . . . VI. xii. 28. 2
he gan his hundred *tongues* apply, . . . VI. xii. 33. 2
some wicked *tongues* did it backebite, . . . VI. xii. 41. 5
Tongues'. renownd For *tongues* confusion in Holie Writ, . . . *Ti.* 510
Too. *See* **To.**
cannot for the storme, If *too* great winde . . . *Ro.* xxi. 13
My Sinamon smell *too* much annoieth: . . . *S.C.* F. 136
gan he repent his pryde *to* late; . . . *S.C.* F. 229
I have troubled your troupes *to* longe: . . . *S.C.* Ap. 149
Our bloncket liveryes bene all *to* sadde . . . *S.C.* May 5
too very foolish and unwise; . . . *S.C.* May 175
her sonne had sette *to* deere a prise . . . *S.C.* May 299
Whose love he bought *to* deare; . . . *S.C.* Jul. 148
may buye golde *to* deere. . . . *S.C.* Au. 108
Such myster saying me seemeth *to* mirke. . . . *S.C.* S. 103
they casten *too* much of worlds care, . . . *S.C.* S. 114
thou speakest *to* plaine; . . . *S.C.* S. 136
Too good for him had bene a great deale worse; . . . *S.C.* S. 213
thilke same rule were *too* straight, . . . *S.C.* S. 236
all *to* weake and wanne, . . . *S.C.* O. 85
Thy Muse *to* long slombreth . . . *S.C.* N. 3
to well I wote my humble vaine, . . . *S.C.* N. 50
shee deemed nothing *too* deere for thee. . . . *S.C.* N. 117
I *to* much beleeved my shepherd peeres,) . . . *S.C.* D. 39
Thus is my harvest hastened all *to* rathe; . . . *S.C.* D. 98
Sike follies nowe have gathered as *too* ripe, . . . *S.C.* D. 117
loathes not *too* much the poore estate, . . . *Gn.* 90
Displeasure *too* implacable was it, . . . *Gn.* 379
The feends to be *too* cruell and severe, . . . *Gn.* 466
Ne are we tyde *to* fast, . . . *Hub.* 459
Fled back *too* soone . . . *Ti.* 291
Both wise and hardie, (*too* hardie, alas!) . . . *As.* 72
They stopt his wound, (*too* late to stop it was!) . . . *As.* 145
were it not *too* painfull to repeat The . . . *Col.* 32
As daring not *too* rashly mount on hight, . . . *Col.* 421
thou hast forgot Thy selfe, me seemes, *too* much, . . . *Col.* 617
the blame . . . is *too* generall, . . . *Col.* 732
being to that swaine *too* cruell hard, . . . *Col.* 909
my *too* long dying, . . . *Col.* 948
Me, all *too* meane, . . . I. Pr. 1. 7
my thoughtes, *too* humble and *too* vile, . . . I. Pr. 4. 6
of his cheere did seeme *too* solemne . . . I. i. 2. 8
'Least suddaine mischiefe ye *too* rash provoke: . . . I. i. 12. 2
nowe *too* late To wish . . . I. i. 13. 2
Yrkesome of life, and *too* long lingring night. . . . I. ii. 6. 5
themselves, *too* rudely rigorous, . . . I. ii. 15. 7
O, *too* deare love, love bought with death *too* deare!' . . . I. ii. 31. 7
Her up he tooke, (*too* simple and *too* trew) . . . I. ii. 45. 7
All night she thinks *too* long, . . . I. iii. 15. 9
that harlott she *too* lately knew, . . . I. iii. 25. 3
Him selfe *too* nigh . . . I. iii. 26. 4
O! then, *too* weake and feeble was the forse . . . I. iii. 42. 1
Least thou of her believe *too* lightly blame, . . . I. iv. 1. 5
As envying her selfe, that *too* exceeding shone: . . . I. iv. 8. 9
that great Princesse *too* exceeding prowd, . . . I. iv. 15. 8
Alone he, wandring, thee *too* long doth want: . . . I. v. 13. 3
That whylome was to me *too* dearely deare. . . . I. v. 25. 5
His hart *too* high through his great richesse store; . . . I. v. 47. 7
Proud Tarquin, and *too* lordly Lentulus; . . . I. v. 49. 6
that his *too* hastie speed . . . had forst him . . . I. vi. 2. 1
Nor *too* much to provoke; . . . I. vi. 25. 6
Too late it was to Satyres to be told, . . . I. vi. 33. 5
Then that thou hadst repented it *too* late? . . . I. vi. 47. 4
But all the floore (*too* filthy to be told) . . . I. viii. 35. 5
Whose presence I have lackt *too* long a day: . . . I. viii. 43. 2
For she was proud, and of *too* high intent, . . . I. ix. 27. 8
That this her knight was feeble, and *too* faint; . . . I. x. 2. 2
Too high a ditty for my simple song. . . . I. x. 55. 7
passing brightnes, which did . . . *too* exceeding shyne. . . . I. x. 67. 8
which nigh *too* feeble found Her flitting parts, . . . I. xi. 18. 4
To trusse the pray *too* heavy for his flight; . . . I. xi. 19. 8
Himselfe in streighter bandes *too* rash implyes, . . . I. xi. 23. 5
her foolehardy chyld Did come *too* neare, . . . I. xii. 11. 2
And often blame the *too* importune fate . . . I. xii. 16. 5

Too—*Continued.*
My ragged rimes are all *too* rude and bace . . . . I. xii. 23. 4
Too false and strong for earthly skill or might, ... I. xii. 32. 7
One thought her cheare *too* litle, th' other . . . *too* mutch. . . II. ii. 34. 9
too long here to be told: . . . . II. vii. 63. 2
ye bene *too* much to blame, ... II. viii. 13. 2
Too truely tryde in his extremest state. . . . . II. x. 31. 3
two sonnes, *too* young to rule . . . . II. x. 46. 8
(O *too* high ditty for my simple rime!) . . . . II. x. 50. 7
'*Too* well we see,' . . . 'and prove *too* well . . . . III. i. 30. 1
Did roll *too* lightly, and *too* often glaunce, ... III. i. 41. 8
my rymes *too* rude and rugged arre, ... III. ii. 3. 6
Both leafe and fruite, both *too* untimely shed, ... III. ii. 31. 8
too huge toile and labour . . . . III. iii. 9. 7
A lesson *too too* hard for living clay . . . . III. iv. 26. 3
froward fortune, and *too* forward Night . . . . III. v. 7. 4
on which was writ, *Be not too bold;* . . . . III. xi. 54. 8
all that night, that *too* long night, ... IV. v. 45. 2
My Sire, who me *too* dearely well did love, ... IV. vii. 16. 2
And eke *too* loose of life, and eke of love *too* light. . . . . IV. viii. 49. 9
I *too* true by triall have approved; . . . . IV. x. 1. 6
will ye betray My life now *too*, ... V. vi. 25. 3
Too much am I too blame . . . . V. xi. 41. 2
aged now, and weary *to* Of warres delight . . . . VI. v. 37. 5
Of every wight, that were not *too* infest; . . . . VI. vi. 41. 7
were here *too* long to tell; . . . . VI. x. 14. 2
strokes, the frute of *too* much talke, ... VI. xi. 16. 2
too-too true that lands in-dwellers since have found. . . . . VII. vi. 55. 9
my fraile spirit . . . refuse This *too* high flight, ... VII. vii. 1. 4
With mercifull regard give mercy *too*. . . . . *Am.* xlix. 12
seeme *too* long to last; . . . . *Am.* lxxxvi. 13

Took. herein I *tooke* (*toke* herein[1]) my chiefe delight, ... *Pet.* iv. 9
Then *tooke* the shepheards Kingly ornaments, ... *Ro.* xviii. 5
thence th' Imperiall Eagle rooting *tooke*, ... *Ro.* xviii. 10
May seeme he lovd, or els some care he *tooke;* . . . . *S.C.* Ja. 9
gently *tooke* that ungently came; . . . . *S.C.* F. 22
out of his packe a glasse he *tooke*, ... *S.C.* May 274
tooke out the Woolfe in his counterfect cote, ... *S.C.* S. 206
Of trecherie or traines nought *tooke* he keep, ... *Gn.* 241
Both their habiliments unto them *tooke*, ... *Hub.* 110
They stole away, and *tooke* their hastie flight, ... *Hub.* 339
freely up those royall spoyles he *tooke*, ... *Hub.* 1059
he *tooke* his way Into the forest, ... *Hub.* 1064
He *tooke* Caduceus, his snakie wand, ... *Hub.* 1292
Thus dight, into the Court he *tooke* his way, ... *Hub.* 1300
wicked weed . . . From underneath his head he *tooke* away, . *Hub.* 1322
up she *tooke* Her daintie feete, ... *Mui.* 283
he *tooke* in hond My pipe, ... *Col.* 72
Nought *tooke* I with me, ... *Col.* 194
like that virgin true which for her knight him *took*. . . . . I. i. 49. 9
Eftsoones he *tooke* that miscreated faire, ... I. ii. 3. 1
Those twoo he *tooke*, and in a secrete bed, ... I. ii. 3. 7
tel both who ye be, and who that *tooke* your part.' . . . . . I. ii. 21. 9
'Thensforth I *tooke* Duessa for my Dame, ... I. ii. 40. 1
with trembling cheare Her up he *tooke*, ... I. ii. 45. 7
From her fayre eyes he *tooke* commandement, ... I. iii. 9. 8
in her selfe-lov'd semblance *took* delight; . . . . I. iv. 10. 8
backe retourning, *took* her wonted way . . . . I. v. 44. 7
He by a privy Posterne *tooke* his flight, ... I. v. 52. 7
the lignage right From whence he *tooke* his weldeserved name: I. vi. 20. 4
up he *tooke* the slombred sencelesse corse, ... I. vii. 15. 6
The wofull Dwarfe . . . *tooke* up his forlorne weed; . . . . . I. vii. 19. 4
Then *tooke* that Squire an horne of bugle small, ... I. viii. 3. 5
Then *tooke* the angrie witch her golden cup, ... I. viii. 14. 1
fercely *tooke* his trenchand blade in hand, ... I. xi. 24. 1
knighthood *tooke* of good Sir Huons hand, ... II. i. 6. 8
in her loosenesse *tooke* exceeding joy: . . . . II. ii. 37. 3
the upper marge . . . away it *tooke*, ... II. v. 6. 3
him selfe she *tooke* aboord, ... II. vi. 19. 6
him she *tooke* And threw in bands, ... II. x. 18. 6
on him *tooke* the roiall Diademe, ... II. x. 47. 3
tooke on him the robe of Emperoure: . . . . II. x. 57. 8
He hearkned, and his armes about him *tooke*, ... II. xii. 38. 1
They *tooke* them both, and both them strongly bound . . . . II. xii. 82. 4
They courteous conge *tooke*, and forth together yode. . . . . III. i. 1. 9
Great shame and sorrow of that fall he *tooke;* . . . . III. i. 7. 1
They *tooke* their steeds, and forth upon their journey went. . III. i. 67. 9
tooke their ready way Unto the Church, ... III. ii. 48. 3
great care she *tooke*, and greater feare, ... III. iii. 5. 6
they *tooke* their way: . . . . III. iii. 7. 4
a sore evill . . . First rooting *tooke;* . . . . III. iii. 16. 6
Both speare she *tooke* and shield . . . . III. iii. 60. 8
Conge *tooke* withall; . . . . III. iv. 4. 5
lately left the same, and *tooke* this way. . . . . III. v. 4. 7
Up they them *tooke;* each one a babe uptooke, ... III. vi. 28. 1
All which she of him *tooke* with countenance meeke and mild. III. vii. 17. 9
in vain sheows . . . *tooke* no delight; . . . . III. vii. 29. 7
he *tooke* in hand, And with it bownd the beast, ... III. vii. 36. 2
In hand she boldly *tooke* To make another . . . . III. viii. 5. 6
Then *tooke* he him, yet trembling sith of late, ... III. viii. 36. 4
they *tooke* delight In their first error, ... III. ix. 23. 7
the Satyres her espide . . . Her up they *tooke*, ... III. x. 36. 6
like a winged horse he *tooke* his flight . . . . III. xi. 42. 7
for her sake they all that perill *tooke*, ... IV. ii. 40. 8
These three that hardie chalenge *tooke* in hand, ... IV. iii. 3. 1
Cambel *tooke* Cambina to his fere, ... IV. iii. 52. 6
Then *tooke* the bold Sir Satyrane in hand . . . . IV. iv. 17. 1
They *tooke* their steeds, and forward thence did pas . . . . . IV. vi. 39. 3
The same he *tooke*, and with a riband new, ... IV. viii. 7. 1
the Prince *tooke* downe those Ladies twaine . . . . IV. viii. 41. 1

Took—*Continued.*
tooke he that same Dwarfe, ... IV. ix. 8. 1
He yeelded, and her *tooke;* . . . . IV. ix. 15. 9
his hindparts, whereof heed I *tooke*, ... IV. x. 20. 3
of no worldly thing he *tooke* delight; . . . . IV. xii. 19. 7
He lately *tooke*, and sithence kept as thrall. . . . . IV. xii. 32. 5
from the point where they first *tooke* Their setting forth, . . V. Pr. 5. 3
they first *tooke* the Sunnes hight, ... V. Pr. 8. 4
whereof it *tooke* his name, ... V. i. 10. 4
by the other markes which of his shield he *tooke*. . . . . . . V. i. 20. 9
Nor *tooke* away his love, but his owne proper good. . . . . V. i. 23. 9
He *tooke* it up, and thence with him did beare, ... V. i. 29. 8
Her selfe then *tooke* he by the sclender wast, ... V. ii. 27. 1
Thereafter all that mucky pelfe he *tooke*, ... V. ii. 27. 6
Him by the bright embrodered hed-stall *tooke;* . . . . V. iii. 33. 7
Which as our owne we *tooke*, ... V. iv. 13. 3
Him Talus *tooke* out of perplexitie, ... V. iv. 25. 3
as her vassall him to thraldome *tooke:* . . . . V. v. 18. 3
Then *tooke* the Amazon this noble knight, ... V. v. 20. 1
Yet he it *tooke* in his owne selfes despight, ... V. v. 23. 6
tooke her steede; and thereon mounting light . . . . V. vi. 36. 2
It as a token of good fortune *tooke*. . . . . V. vii. 8. 5
some pensivenesse to heart she *tooke:* . . . . V. vii. 18. 3
she to hunt the beast first *tooke* in hond; . . . . V. vii. 30. 8
in the compasse of his clouches *tooke;* . . . . V. ix. 11. 4
he then *tooke* it up, and held fast in his hand. . . . . V. ix. 17. 9
Ere proofe it *tooke*, ... V. ix. 42. 4
streight *tooke* his flight From that sad land . . . . V. x. 11. 3
He *tooke* her up forby the lilly hand, ... V. xi. 17. 1
on his shield *tooke* hold with all her might, ... V. xi. 27. 3
nought was terrifide, but greater courage *tooke*. . . . . . . V. xi. 28. 9
thereon seizing *tooke* no great effect; . . . . V. xii. 21. 7
He *tooke* his leave of her there left in heavinesse. . . . . . V. xii. 27. 9
both *tooke* goodly leave, and parted severall. . . . . VI. i. 10. 9
Me first he *tooke* unhable to withstond, ... VI. i. 16. 6
streight he *tooke* his flight Toward the Castle, ... VI. i. 22. 3
tooke in hand her quarrell to maintaine; . . . . VI. i. 33. 2
Tooke in foule scorne that I such fault did find, ... VI. ii. 11. 7
Upon him *tooke* the roiall high degree, ... VI. ii. 28. 8
He *tooke* that Ladie, and her up did rayse . . . . VI. ii. 39. 7
tooke with him the head, the signe of shame. . . . . VI. iii. 17. 6
Then up he *tooke* her twixt his armes twaine, ... VI. iii. 28. 4
So downe he *tooke* his Lady . . . . VI. iii. 44. 5
They *tooke* it well, and thanked God for all, ... VI. iv. 15. 2
Then *tooke* he up betwixt his armes twaine The litle babe, . VI. iv. 23. 1
He *tooke* him selfe unto this Hermitage, ... VI. vi. 4. 8
Of that good Hermite both they *tooke* their leave, ... VI. vi. 15. 8
his well-learned speare *Tooke* surer hould, ... VI. vii. 11. 2
at advantage him at last he *tooke*, ... VI. vii. 48. 2
tooke their gentle offer: . . . . VI. ix. 7. 2
in his hand he *tooke* . . . a shepheards hooke; . . . . VI. ix. 36. 4
Tooke Coridon and set him in his place, ... VI. ix. 42. 2
Her flowry garlond *tooke* from her owne head, ... VI. ix. 42. 6
with the rest they *tooke* not long agoe; . . . . VI. xi. 11. 7
earnest *tooke* To keepe their flockes . . . . VI. xi. 40. 6
He *tooke* it up and in his mantle wound; . . . . VI. xii. 9. 7
he *tooke* a muzzel strong Of surest yron, ... VI. xii. 34. 2
The good Sir Pelleas him *tooke* in hand, ... VI. xii. 39. 6
his burning levin-brond in hand he *tooke*. . . . . VII. vi. 30. 9
Enclos'd the bush about, and there him *tooke*, ... VII. vi. 47. 4
So much delight to bathe her limbes she *tooke:* . . . . VII. vi. 54. 4
In planting eeke he *took* no small delight. . . . . VII. vii. 40. 6
I in hand her yet halfe trembling *tooke*, ... *Am.* lxvii. 11
He *tooke* his wings and away did fly. . . . . *Epig.* i. 6
She *tooke* him streight full pitiously lamenting, ... *Epig.* iv. 41
Like unto Maia, when as Jove her *took* . . . . *Epith.* 307
He then them *tooke*, ... *H.L.* 85
it then *tooke* light And lively spirits . . . . *H.B.* 110

Tookest. Life from Sansfoy thou *tookst*, Sansloy shall from thee take.' . . . . I. iii. 36. 9

Tool. did with his smarting *toole* Oft whip her dainty selfe, . VI. vii. 39. 8

Tools. Those deadly *tooles* which in her hand she held, ... II. iii. 37. 3
tooles to prune the trees, ... VII. vii. 43. 7

Tooth. al good things with venemous *tooth* devowres, ... *Mui.* 302
with fell *tooth* accustomed to blood, ... *As.* 118
he with his *tooth* impure Him heedlesse bit, ... VI. v. 16. 8

Tooting. For birds in bushes *tooting*, ... *S.C.* Mar. 66

Too-too. *See* **Too.**

Top. Upon the *top* therof was set a pot . . . . *Bel.*[1] iii. 5
shining Christall, which from *top* to base . . . . *Bel.* ii. 6
On high hills *top* I saw a stately frame, ... *Bel.*[2] ii. 1
The *top* thereof a pot did seeme to beare, ... *Bel.*[2] iii. 5
It seem'd her *top* the firmament did rayse, ... *Bel.*[2] xiv. 5
She, whose high *top* above the starres did sore, ... *Ro.* iv. 1
Now thy selfe hast lost both lopp and *topp*, ... *S.C.* F. 57
His *toppe* was bald, and wasted with wormes, ... *S.C.* F. 113
Upon whose *toppe* the starres bene stayed, ... *S.C.* Jul. 61
To an high mountaines *top* he with them went, ... *Gn.* 73
the utmost *top* Of some soft Willow, ... *Gn.* 83
Into the highest *top* of heaven gan clime, ... *Gn.* 157
till they the *top* survew, ... *Gn.* 221
on the *top* of all, ... *Gn.* 661
on the *top* a Diall told the timely howres. . . . . I. iv. 4. 9
From *top* to toe no place appeared bare, ... I. vii. 29. 6
Upon the *top* of all his loftie crest, ... I. vii. 32. 1
ymounted hye On *top* of greene Selinis . . . . I. vii. 32. 6
tree, High growing on the *top* of rocky clift, ... I. viii. 22. 6
On *top* whereof ay dwelt the ghastly Owle, ... I. ix. 33. 6
an hill . . . On *top* whereof a sacred chappell was, ... I. x. 46. 3
by her helpe the *top* at last he wonne. . . . . I. x. 47. 9

Top—*Continued.*
on the *top* of all I do espye The watchman . . . I. xi. 3. 6
Was mounted high in *top* of heaven sheene, . . . III. iv. 51. 7
Mount, on whose round *top* A gloomy grove . . . III. vi. 43. 2
Upon the *top* of Mount Olympus hight, . . . III. vii. 41. 5
From *top* of Hemus by him heaped hye;) . . . III. ix. 22. 6
Feare, all arm'd from *top* to toe, . . . III. xii. 12. 1
Whose *top* was arm'd with many an yron hooke, . . . V. ix. 11. 2
on the *top* thereof a spacious plaine . . . VI. x. 8. 1
a mace, On *top* whereof the moon and stars were pight; . . . VII. vii. 44. 6
from the *top* of purest heavens hight . . . *H.B.* 109
The snow, which doth the *top* of Pindus strew, . . . *Proth.* 40
Top-gallant. And flag in her *top-gallant,* . . . *Van.* ix. 3
Top's. coveting, with his high *tops* extent, . . . *Gn.* 212
Tops. the *toppes* even of the hiest hilles, . . . *Bel.*[1] vi. 6
Through the *tops* of the high trees . . . III. vii. 5. 1
all their *tops* bright glistering with gold, . . . V. ix. 21. 7
in their *tops* the soring hauke did towre, . . . VI. x. 6. 8
Topsy-turvy. all overthrowne to ground Quite *topside turvey,* . V. viii. 42. 5
Torch. high her burning *torch* set up in heaven bright. . . . I. xi. 49. 9
quenched quite like a consumed *torch,* . . . III. xii. 42. 8
with his *Torche,* still twinkling like twylight, . . . VII. vi. 9. 7
Torches. Whose bridale *torches* foule Erynnis tynde; . . . *Gn.* 394
Eftesoones long waxen *torches* weren light . . . III. i. 58. 3
a thousand *torches* flaming bright Doe burne, . . . *Epith.* 410
Tore. *See* **Tare, Torn.**
With a plume feather all to peeces *tore:* . . . *Hub.* 210
Her yellow locks . . . She fiersly *tore,* . . . *As.* 159
His monstrous scalpe downe to his teeth it *tore,* . . . I. viii. 16. 4
often *tore* Her guiltlesse garments . . . I. x. 28. 5
high trees overthrew, and rocks in peeces *tore.* . . . I. xi. 37. 9
As it with mighty levers had bene *tore;* . . . III. xii. 3. 4
Him rudely rent and all to peeces *tore;* . . . VI. vi. 22. 6
To-rent. With briers and bushes all *to-rent* and scratcht; . IV. vii. 8. 3
With locks all loose, and rayment all *to-rent;* . . . V. viii. 4. 8
So was this Souldan rapt and all *to-rent,* . . . V. viii. 43. 8
Torment. first gan you to *torment,* . . . *T.M.* 374
Retourning to his bed in *torment* great, . . . I. ii. 6. 1
passion did . . . *torment* The flaming corage . . . I. v. 1. 5
ten thousand sorts of punishment . . . *torment.* . . . I. v. 33. 9
her deare heart with anguish did *torment,* . . . I. vi. 32. 4
his *torment* often was so great, . . . I. x. 28. 1
all his *torment* well withstood . . . I. x. 32. 7
never man such mischiefes did *torment:* . . . I. xi. 28. 3
How shamefully that Mayd he did *torment:* . . . II. i. 11. 4
the weake minde with double woe *torment?'* . . . II. i. 16. 7
inly did him selfe *torment.* . . . II. ii. 37. 9
nathelesse he did her still *torment,* . . . II. iv. 12. 7
'These flames, these flames' (he cryde) 'doe me *torment.'* . . . II. vi. 49. 5
there eternall *torment* found For all the sinnes . . . II. viii. 45. 8
ghosts doen often creepe . . . bad livers to *torment:* . . . II. xii. 6. 6
in her doth such *torment* breed.' . . . III. iii. 18. 9
punish her, and eke him selfe *torment.* . . . III. x. 3. 9
the burning *torment* which he felt; . . . III. xi. 27. 3
What equall *torment* to the griefe of mind . . . IV. vi. 1. 1
then againe she did her selfe *torment,* . . . V. vi. 13. 4
bite, and cruelly *torment.'* . . . VI. i. 8. 9
beat her breast, and piteously her selfe *torment.* . . . VI. v. 4. 9
To make them to endure the pains did them *torment.* . . . VI. v. 32. 9
with *torment* and turmoyle, To force me live, . . . *Am.* xi. 11
to *torment* me thus with cruelty, . . . *Am.* xxv. 7
shall their ruthlesse *torment* never cease; . . . *Am.* xxxvi. 2
But sudden dumps, . . . my *torment* feed. . . . *Am.* lii. 12
O how doth it *torment* His troubled mynd . . . *H.L.* 252
Tormented. with her lacke I might *tormented* be. . . . *D.* 368
in foote and hand A grievous gout *tormented* him full sore, . I. iv. 29. 7
Lo! Tantalus, I here *tormented* lye: . . . II. vii. 59. 5
Infinite moe *tormented* in like paine He there beheld, . . . II. vii. 63. 1
In her *tormented* bodie to embrew: . . . III. xii. 32. 7
when the wicked feend his Lord *tormented,* . . . IV. ii. 2. 2
All travellers *tormented* are with paine: . . . IV. iv. 47. 6
through Loves constrayning *Tormented* sore, . . . IV. x. 43. 8
it *tormented* her both day and night: . . . V. v. 27. 5
That me thou makest thus *tormented* be, . . . *Am.* x. 2
Tormenteth. *Tormenteth* and doth plonge in dolefull plight, . III. iii. 16. 5
'There he *tormenteth* her most terribly . . . III. xi. 17. 1
The love which me so cruelly *tormenteth,* . . . *Am.* xlii. 1
Tormenting. *See* **Great-tormenting.**
what horrour and *tormenting* griefe . . . II. iv. 28. 6
Dye had she rather in *tormenting* griefe . . . III. viii. 42. 3
Torments. Doo ye not feele your *torments* to accrewe, . . . *Ro.* xv. 11
With painfull *torments* to be sorely beaten. . . . *Gn.* 352
Phlegeton, Whereas the damned ghosts in *torments* fry, . . . I. v. 33. 4
The damned ghosts that doe in *torments* waile, . . . I. ix. 49. 7
Whilest deadly *torments* doe her chast brest rend, . . . III. xi. 11. 3
Torn. *See* **Tore, To-torn.**
hath some Wolfe thy tender Lambes *ytorne?* . . . *S.C.* Ap. 2
Such one Marcellus, but was *torne* with thunder: . . . *Ti.* 416
His sandales were with toilsome travell *torne,* . . . I. vi. 35. 3
Oke, which he had *torne* Out of his mothers bowelles, . . . I. vii. 10. 7
The faire Medina with her tresses *torne* . . . II. ii. 27. 2
The noble braunch from th' antique stocke was *torne* Through discord, . . . II. x. 36. 4
Disshivered speares, and shields *ytorne* in twaine; . . . IV. i. 21. 6
torne in pieces by Alcides great; . . . V. viii. 31. 4
in peeces to have *torne* With his sharpe wheeles, . . . V. viii. 31. 6
Torne all to rags, and rent with many a wound; . . . V. viii. 42. 7
Of his owne steedes was all to peeces *torne,* . . . V. viii. 43. 4
makes her ribs to cracke as they were *torne;* . . . V. xi. 29. 4
having from his craven bodie *torne* Those goodly armes, . . . VI. vi. 36. 7

Torn—*Continued.*
Yet is the bottle leake, and bag so *torne,* . . . VI. viii. 24. 6
He freely gave to be both rent and *torne* . . . *H.H.L.* 150
sacred heavenly corse, So *torne* and mangled . . . *H.H.L.* 250
Tort. no wild beasts should do them any *torte* . . . *Hub.* 1078
times decay, and envies cruell *tort,* . . . *Ti.* 167
him, that had them long oppresst with *tort,* . . . I. xii. 4. 4
thou hadst done great *tort* Unto an aged woman, . . . II. v. 17. 2
worke so hainous *tort,* In shame of knighthood, . . . III. ii. 12. 8
Ne each of other feared fraud or *tort,* . . . IV. viii. 31. 3
Tortious. whom he endamaged By *tortious* wrong, . . . II. ii. 18. 8
gathered had by wrong And *tortious* powre, . . . IV. ix. 12. 4
Gainst *tortious* powre and lawlesse regiment, . . . V. viii. 30. 7
Purchast through lawlesse powre and *tortious* wrong . . . V. viii. 51. 6
this fell Tyrant, through his *tortious* powre, . . . V. x. 8. 1
she cast by force and *tortious* might Her to displace, . . . VII. vi. 10. 7
Damning all Wrong and *tortious* Injurie, . . . VII. vii. 14. 5
Torture. With bitter *torture,* and impatient paines, . . . *Gn.* 628
by *torture* he would her constraine . . . III. xi. 17. 5
Her forward still with *torture* did constraine, . . . III. xii. 21. 8
Tortures. For terrour of the *tortures* manifold, . . . II. vii. 63. 4
With all the *tortures* that he could devize, . . . V. xi. 19. 8
Toss. they unto their fortunes change to *tosse:* . . . *Hub.* 342
That troublous dreame gan freshly *tosse* his braine . . . I. i. 55. 6
everie tender part does *tosse* and turne: . . . I. vii. 21. 6
For whose deare sake so many troubles her did *tosse.* . . . I. vii. 27. 9
your lord that could so well you *tosse?* . . . I. vii. 48. 9
Then gan he *tosse* aloft his stretched traine, . . . I. xi. 37. 5
the troublous stormes that *tosse* The private state, . . . II. vii. 14. 1
To *tossen* speare and shield, . . . III. ii. 6. 4
with long enduring paines Doe *tosse,* . . . III. iii. 9. 5
a firebrand shee did *tosse* About her head, . . . III. xii. 17. 6
tosse the deepes, and teare the firmament, . . . IV. ix. 23. 7
Which *tosse* the rest in daungerous disease; . . . VI. ix. 19. 5
Nought sparing them, the more did *tosse* and teare, . . . VI. xii. 24. 7
Tossed. *Tossed* with stormes of fortune variable! . . . *Pet.*[2] vi. 14
mortall men *tossed* by troublous fate . . . *Pet.*[2] vii. 3
her ship, *tost* with so manie freakes, . . . *Ro.* xxi. 5
My shippe unwont in stormes to be *tost.* . . . *S.C.* F. 32
Withouten dreade of Wolves to bene *ytost:* . . . *S.C.* Jun. 12
tost in th' ayre with everie windie blast: . . . *Gn.* 334
spoyld of Charon too and fro am *tost.* . . . *Gn.* 339
Tost on salt billowes, round about doth stray. . . . *Gn.* 592
So vainly shalt thou too and fro be *tost,* . . . *Hub.* 635
As one . . . whose dryer braine Is *tost* with troubled sights . I. i. 42. 8
By traynes into new troubles to have *toste:* . . . I. iii. 24. 7
Long *tost* with stormes, and bet with bitter wind, . . . I. vii. 28. 7
So *tossed* was in fortunes cruell freakes: . . . I. xii. 16. 8
As a tall ship *tossed* in troublous seas, . . . II. ii. 24. 1
One night, when she was *tost* with such unrest, . . . III. ii. 30. 1
Wherein my feeble barke is *tossed* long . . . III. iv. 8. 2
to see that gentle maide so *tost!'* . . . IV. ix. 38. 5
Oft *tossed* with his stormes which therein still remaine. . IV. xi. 38. 9
tossed in her troublous minde . . . V. iv. 47. 4
tost the Paynim without feare or awe; . . . V. viii. 41. 7
From side to side they *tost* him here and there, . . . V. viii. 41. 8
Like as a ship with dreadfull storme long *tost,* . . . VI. iv. 1. 1
And there all night himselfe in anguish *tost,* . . . VI. iv. 40. 5
had in many fortunes *tossed* beene . . . VI. vi. 3. 3
being long in tempest *tost,* . . . VI. xi. 44. 6
she her selfe in stormie surges *tost;* . . . VI. xii. 1. 5
the clouds are also *tost* and roll'd, . . . VII. vii. 20. 8
Still *tost* and turned with continuall change, . . . VII. vii. 21. 2
all things *tost* and turned by transverse, . . . VII. vii. 56. 3
tost with troublous fit Of a proud love, . . . *Am.* xxxiii. 11
being long in her loves tempest *tost,* . . . *Am.* xli. 11
my silly barke was *tossed* sore: . . . *Am.* lxiii. 4
Tosseth. *tosseth* states, and under foot doth tread The mightie VI. ix. 27. 8
Tossing. *Tossing* huge tempests through the troubled skie, . . *Ro.* xvi. 6
Tossing and turning them withouten end; . . . II. ix. 58. 2
perills . . . *Tossing* them like a boate amid the mayne, . . . IV. iii. 1. 6
After long *tossing* in the seas distrest, . . . V. iv. 11. 8
To-torn. underneath, his breech was all *to-torne* and jagged. . V. ix. 10. 9
Tottered. yet to and fro long shooke And *tottred,* . . . V. viii. 9. 9
As if he would have *tottered* to one side: . . . V. xi. 11. 3
Totty. sicker thy head veray *tottie* is, . . . *S.C.* F. 55
For yet his noule was *totty* of the must, . . . VII. vii. 39. 2
Touch. he, that strives to *touch* a starre, . . . *S.C.* Jul. 99
To make the mountaines *touch* the starres divine, . . . *Gn.* 213
Though true as *touch,* though daughter of a king, . . . I. iii. 2. 5
A grievous gout . . . That well he could not *touch,* . . . I. iv. 29. 8
What ever thing does *touch* his ravenous pawes, . . . I. xi. 12. 4
Ne durst approch him nigh to *touch,* or once assay. . . . I. xii. 9. 9
Warnd him not *touch,* . . . I. xii. 10. 3
The inner garment frett, not th' utter *touch:* . . . II. ii. 34. 8
it would tempt a man to *touchen* there: . . . II. xii. 14. 6
Of every finest fingers *touch* affrayd; . . . III. i. 61. 5
Decline her head, and *touch* her crouper with her crown. . III. iv. 15. 9
Whiles neither lets the other *touch* the soyle, . . . IV. iii. 16. 7
hardly could he come the carle to *touch,* . . . IV. vii. 27. 3
him to *touch* with falshoods fowle attaint, . . . V. vi. 12. 3
With the neare *touch* whereof in tender hart . . . V. ix. 46. 1
touch celestiall seats with earthly mire? . . . VII. vi. 29. 4
What hart can feele least *touch* of so sore launch, . . . *H.H.L.* 162
Touched. eke because my selfe am *touched* neare: . . . *Hub.* 74
what he *toucht* came not to light againe; . . . *Hub.* 702
ever to have *toucht* her I did deadly rew. . . . I. ii. 40. 9
He nere was *touched* in his noble spright, . . . III. vii. 43. 8
everie limbe that *touched* her did quake; . . . IV. i. 5. 8
touched was with secret wrath and shame . . . IV. v. 17. 4

Touched—*Continued.*
most she *touched* was with griefe entire . . . IV. ix. 13. 8
toucht with soft remorse and pitty rare; . . . IV. xii. 12. 5
his stony heart with tender ruth Was *toucht*, . . . IV. xii. 13. 2
touched with intire affection nigh him drew; . . . V. viii. 12. 9
brest was *touched* nere With piteous ruth . . . V. ix. 50. 1
Was inly *touched* with compassion deare, . . . VI. iii. 4. 4
he inly *touched* was With tender ruth . . . VI. iv. 34. 1
Was *touched* with compassion entire, . . . VI. viii. 3. 3
whilest so thy softened spirit Is inly *toucht*, . . . *H.H.L.* 254
Touches. Who *touches* Pitch, mought needes be defilde; . . . *S.C.* May 74
Touching. *Touching* her loves successe, . . . V. v. 45. 3
Tough. Sweet is the Cypresse, but his rynd is *tough;* . . . *Am.* xxvi. 5
Tought. *See* **Taught.**
Toured. *See* **Towered.**
Tournament. Devizing how that doughtie *turnament* . . . he achieven might: . . . I. v. 1. 7
goodly taught to tilt and *turnament:* . . . III. i. 44. 7
Satyrane makes a *Turneyment* For love of Florimell: . . . IV. iv. Arg.
Against the *Turneiment* which is not long, . . . IV. iv. 12. 5
Unto the place of *turneyment* they came; . . . IV. iv. 13. 6
left that *Tourneyment* for beauties prise, . . . IV. vii. 3. 2
lost in *Turneyment* of late; . . . IV. ix. 24. 3
better skild in Tilt and *Turnament*, . . . V. viii. 7. 7
Tourney. Well could he *tourney*, and in lists debate, . . . II. i. 6. 7
At tilt or *tourney*, or like warlike game, . . . III. ii. 9. 8
Of that great *turney* which was blazed brode, . . . IV. iv. 5. 7
The morrow next the *Turney* gan anew: . . . IV. iv. 26. 1
in an open *Turney* lately held, . . . IV. vi. 6. 6
In that late *Turney* for the snowy maide; . . . IV. ix. 28. 7
them late had foyled In open *turney*, . . . IV. ix. 36. 3
The spousals of faire Florimell, Where *turney* many knights: V. iii. Arg.
Tourneyed. as they courst, and *turneyd* here and theare, . . . IV. iv. 30. 1
those Knights That lately *turneyd* . . . IV. v. 7. 2
Tourneying. A solemne feast, with publike *turneying*, . . . IV. ii. 26. 8
Tours. With costly clothes of Arras and of *Toure;* . . . III. i. 34. 2
Toused. a Beare, whom angry curres have *touzd*, . . . II. xi. 33. 3
Tow. That he thereon should spin both flax and *tow;* . . . V. v. 23. 3
Toward (*partial list of prep.*).
Toward the sea turning my troubled eye, . . . *Van.* v. 1
Till that the Foxe forth *toward* them did goe, . . . *Hub.* 1074
He *toward* his owne Pallace forth did pas; . . . *Hub.* 1344
which his yong *toward* yeares . . . Did largely promise, . . . *Mui.* 26
Toward those parts came flying carelesslie, . . . *Mui.* 391
My good to heare, and *toward* joyes to see! . . . *D.* 280
'Now,' (saide the Ladie,) 'draweth *toward* night, . . . I. i. 32. 4
The Redcrosse knight *toward* him crossed fast, . . . I. ix. 23. 1
envying my *toward* good, . . . II. iv. 22. 2
he gan to feare His *toward* perill, . . . III. i. 9. 7
He up gan lifte *toward* the azure skies, . . . III. v. 34. 4
that is the bownd *Toward* the land; . . . III. ix. 46. 4
Two armed Knights that *toward* them did pace, . . . IV. i. 17. 2
and *toward* him did fare, . . . IV. i. 41. 2
spies him *toward* bend His dreadfull souse, . . . IV. iii. 19. 5
He gan to faint *toward* the battels end, . . . IV. iii. 32. 7
That *toward* them his course seem'd to apply: . . . IV. iv. 6. 7
But *toward* th' end Sir Arthegall renewed . . . IV. vi. 18. 4
she them brought *toward* the place . . . IV. vii. 35. 1
All these together marched *toward* Proteus hall. . . . IV. xi. 39. 9
toward his dissolution. . . . V. Pr. 4. 9
She chaunst to meete, *toward* the even-tide, . . . V. vi. 19. 3
streight he tooke his flight *Toward* the Castle, . . . VI. i. 22. 4
A salvage man, . . . *Toward* the same incessantly did ronne . . . VI. iv. 2. 4
So forth he drew much gold, and *toward* him it drive. . . . VI. ix. 32. 9
Out of the wood he rose, and *toward* them did go. . . . VI. x. 17. 9
Towards (*partial list*).
And *towards* heaven freshly to arise . . . *Ro.* xvii. 11
weapons . . . outlaunced *towards* either side, . . . *Mui.* 82
Gan fairely couch his speare, and *towards* ride. . . . I. ii. 15. 3
with faire fearefull humblesse *towards* him shee came: . . . I. iii. 26. 9
One pricking *towards* them . . . I. iii. 33. 2
And ran *towardes* the far rebownded noyce, . . . I. vi. 8. 3
towards old Sylvanus they her bring; . . . I. vi. 14. 5
And *towards* him they gan in haste to ride, . . . I. vi. 34. 4
towardes him with dreadfull fury praunce; . . . I. vii. 11. 3
He marched forth *towardes* that castle wall, . . . I. viii. 3. 2
espy An armed knight *towards* them gallop fast, . . . I. ix. 21. 2
They, seeing Una, *towardes* her gan wend, . . . I. x. 15. 1
The first . . . *towardes* him did pas; . . . I. x. 44. 3
So dreadfully he *towardes* him did pas, . . . I. xi. 15. 1
And fresh encounter *towardes* him addrest; . . . I. xi. 17. 2
when as still he saw him *towards* pace, . . . II. i. 26. 4
towards gan a deadly shafte advaunce, . . . II. iii. 34. 5
A varlet ronning *towardes* hastily, . . . II. iv. 37. 2
To stere the bote *towards* that dolefull Mayd, . . . II. xii. 28. 2
Ran *towards* to devoure those unexpected guests. . . . II. xii. 39. 9
They spide a knight that *towards* pricked fayre; . . . III. i. 4. 2
hasting *towards* him gan fayre perswade . . . III. i. 10. 1
mortall speare She mightily aventred *towards* one, . . . III. i. 28. 7
Her fearfull feete *towards* the bowre she mov'd, . . . III. i. 60. 2
With hasty gallop *towards* her did ryde. . . . III. iv. 12. 3
of . . . soveraine favor *towards* chastity, . . . III. viii. 29. 3
Sir Satyrane him *towardes* did addresse, . . . III. viii. 45. 1
ever faine he *towards* them would goe, . . . III. x. 22. 1
her eielids closely spyde How *towards* her he rusht, . . . III. xi. 32. 9
that *towards* them did ply With speedie course, . . . IV. i. 38. 5
One in a charet . . . *Towards* them driving, . . . IV. iii. 38. 5
Gan *towards* them to pricke with eger speede, . . . IV. vi. 2. 8
A Knight soft ryding *towards* them they spyde, . . . IV. vi. 9. 2
they spide where *towards* them . . . came gallopping, . . . IV. viii. 38. 1

Towards—*Continued.*
And *towards* th' end grew greater in his might, . . . V. ii. 17. 6
And by which way they *towards* it should trace. . . . V. ix. 7. 4
Towards the westerne brim begins to draw, . . . V. ix. 35. 2
She *towards* him in hast her selfe did draw . . . V. xi. 15. 3
Envie first, . . . *Towardes* him runs, . . . V. xii. 38. 8
seeing him so fiercely *towardes* make, . . . VI. i. 19. 2
to blame him for such cruelty *Towards* a Ladie, . . . VI. ii. 11. 4
Towards all womenkind them kindly to behave. . . . VI. ii. 14. 9
towards night they came unto a plaine, . . . VI. v. 34. 7
They, *towards* evening wandring every way . . . VI. viii. 36. 6
one still *towards* shew'd her selfe afore; . . . VI. x. 24. 8
He chaunst one comming *towards* him to spy, . . . VI. xi. 27. 2
Tho, when as *towards* darksome night it drew, . . . VI. xi. 41. 1
towards her him bore; . . . VI. xi. 45. 8
Tower. A gilden *towre*, which shone exceedinglie; . . . *Van.* viii. 4
Enricht with spoyles of th' Ericthonian *towre*, . . . *Gn.* 562
On which the lordly Faulcon wont to *towre* . . . *Ti.* 128
Next unto this a statelie *Towre* appeared, . . . *Ti.* 505
that great *Towre*, which is so much renownd . . . *Ti.* 509
I saw this *Towre* fall sodainelie to dust, . . . *Ti.* 517
Like the old ruines of a broken *towre*, . . . I. ii. 20. 2
The Geaunt . . . could have overthrowne a stony *towre;* . . . I. vii. 12. 2
that bright *towre*, all built of christall clene, . . . I. x. 58. 5
this bright Angels *towre* quite dims that *towre* of glas.' . . . I. x. 58. 9
brasen *towre*, in which my parents . . . emprisond be; . . . I. xi. 3. 2
as a stedfast *towre*, Whom foe . . . doth assaile, . . . II. viii. 35. 7
king Nine whilome built Babell *towre*. . . . II. ix. 21. 6
that proud *towre* of Troy, . . . II. ix. 45. 8
that heavenly *towre* That God hath built . . . II. ix. 47. 4
the *Towre* Wherein th' Aegyptian Phao long did lurke . . . III. ii. 20. 2
through the roofe of her strong brasen *towre* . . . III. xi. 31. 3
in their tops the soring hauke did *towre*, . . . VI. x. 6. 8
Fayth doth fearlesse dwell in brasen *towre*, . . . *Am.* lxv. 13
on the hoary mountayne usd to *towre;* . . . *Epith.* 68
Her snowie necke lyke to a marble *towre;* . . . *Epith.* 177
Towered. On th' other side an high rocke *toured* still, . . . II. xii. 30. 5
Towering. where the Eagle built his *towring* nest, . . . *Van.* iv. 6
These *towring* rocks, which reach unto the skie, . . . V. ii. 38. 3
Whether high *towring* or accoasting low, . . . VI. ii. 32. 2
Towers. Carthage *towres* from spoile should be forborne, . . . *Ro.* xxiii. 2
casting downe his *towres*, . . . *Van.* viii. 11
As doen high *Towers* in an earthquake: . . . *S.C.* F. 6
the East . . . Burnt th' Attick *towres*, . . . *Gn.* 44
Up to the heavenly *towers*, . . . *Gn.* 66
downe on them to fall from highest *towres:* . . . *Gn.* 580
lifted up his loftie *towres* thereby, . . . *Hub.* 1173
'High *towers*, faire temples, goodly theaters, . . . *Ti.* 92
High lifted up were many loftie *towres*, . . . I. iv. 4. 6
Both loftie *towres* and highest trees hath rent, . . . I. viii. 9. 7
wals and *towres* were builded high and strong . . . I. x. 55. 4
extend Her lofty *towres* unto the starry sphere, . . . I. x. 56. 8
Towres, citties, kingdomes, ye would ruinate . . . III. viii. 28. 5
stately *towres* of Ilion . . . Brought unto balefull ruine, . . . III. ix. 34. 3
Which they far off beheld from Trojan *toures*, . . . III. ix. 35. 5
In which were many *towres* and castels set, . . . IV. xi. 27. 8
tottred, like two *towres* which through a tempest quooke. . . . V. viii. 9. 9
With many *towres*, and tarras mounted hye, . . . V. ix. 21. 6
My cities sackt, and their sky-threating *towres* Raced . . . V. x. 23. 4
defaced cleene Her stately *towres* . . . V. x. 25. 5
Sought to assaile the heavens eternall *towers*, . . . VII. vi. 20. 3
second Babell . . . Her ayry *Towers* upraised much more high. . . . *Com. Son.* iv. 4
bricky *towres* The which on Themmes brode aged backe . . . *Proth.* 132
From those high *Towers* this noble Lord issuing, . . . *Proth.* 163
To wit. *See* **Weet.**
Town. So this brave *Towne*, that in her youthlie daies . . . *Ro.* x. 5
I longd the neighbour *towne* to see, . . . *S.C.* Ja. 50
a gulph . . . Amidst the *Towne* with his owne corps did fill, . . . *Gn.* 605
in countrey and in *towne*, . . . *Ti.* 263
cryes, As still are wont t' annoy the walled *towne*, . . . I. i. 41. 7
'O lamentable fall of famous *towne!* . . . III. ix. 39. 2
finally destroy Proud Priams *towne*. . . . IV. xi. 19. 7
By many a city and by many a *towne* . . . IV. xi. 34. 2
Threw many threats, if they the *towne* did win, . . . V. iv. 37. 4
they of the *towne* . . . good watch and ward did keepe. . . . V. vii. 26. 5
Fled fast into the *towne*, . . . V. vii. 34. 9
Both goodly Castle, and both goodly *Towne*, . . . V. x. 26. 5
all the people, both of *towne* and land, . . . V. xi. 15. 5
all the damzels of that *towne* . . . V. xi. 34. 3
forward marched to a *towne* in sight. . . . V. xii. 6. 3
doth despise the dainties of the *towne*. . . . VI. ix. 7. 5
did ye see So fayre a creature in your *towne* before; . . . *Epith.* 168
Ring ye the bels, ye yong men of the *towne*, . . . *Epith.* 261
Town-gate. forth to the *Towne-gate* went; . . . V. iv. 50. 2
Towns. *townes* and castles under her brest did coure, . . . *Bel.*[2] viii. 6
The walled *townes* doe worke my greater woe; . . . *S.C.* Au. 158
from the citties to the *townes* him prest, . . . VI. ix. 3. 7
from the *townes* into the countrie forsed, . . . VI. ix. 3. 8
Out of their *townes* did round about him throng, . . . VI. xii. 37. 4
To-worn. all *to-worne* and ragged, . . . V. ix. 10. 8
Toy. subdewd to learne Dame Pleasures *toy*. . . . I. i. 47. 9
To dally thus with death is no fit *toy:* . . . I. vi. 28. 8
when he saw her *toy*, and gibe, and geare, . . . II. vi. 21. 7
A foe of folly and immodest *toy*, . . . II. vi. 37. 4
other some could not abide to *toy;* . . . II. ix. 35. 4
Ne lend we leisure to his idle *toy:* . . . III. vi. 24. 5
amongst the wanton Nymphs to sport and *toy*. . . . IV. xi. 19. 9
Toyed. Whiles thus she talked, and whiles thus she *toyd*, . . . II. vi. 11. 1
with his mistresse *toyed*. . . . V. v. 24. 9

Toys. Those weary wanton *toyes* away dyd wype, ... *S.C.* Jun. 48
with vaine *toyes* the vulgare entertaine; . . . . *T.M.* 194
All places they doo with their *toyes* possesse, ... *T.M.* 325
Counted but *toyes* to busie ydle braines; . . . . *Col.* 704
flowes in pleasures and vaine pleasing *toyes,* . . . . II. v. 28. 8
other whiles vaine *toyes* she would devize, ... II. vi. 7. 1
playing their wanton *toyes,* . . . . II. xii. 60. 8
ever mixt their song with light licentious *toyes.* . . . . . . II. xii. 72. 9
with amorous delights And pleasing *toyes* . . . . III. x. 8. 2
like to Angels playing heavenly *toyes,* . . . . IV. x. 42. 5
fild his ballaunce full of idle *toys:* . . . . V. ii. 30. 8
greedy pleasure, carelesse of your *toyes,* . . . . *Epith.* 365
Trace. after her the other Muses *trace,* . . . . *S.C.* Ap. 102
your tender Lambes that by you *trace.* . . . . *S.C.* Jun. 120
To drench himselfe in moorish slime did *trace,* . . . . *Gn.* 251
How trimly would she *trace* and softly tread . . . . *D.* 311
This lowly Muse, that learns like steps to *trace,* . . . . . *Ded. Son.* xiii. 7
Unlike to men, who ever, as they *trace,* . . . . I. viii. 31. 5
no'te without an hound fine footing *trace.* . . . . II. Pr. 4. 5
Through which a beaten broad high way did *trace,* . . . . II. vii. 21. 3
them beside an aged Sire did *trace,* . . . . II. viii. 10. 3
the same along did *trace* By tract of blood, ... III. v. 28. 3
If any tract of him or tidings they mote *trace.* . . . . . . III. vi. 25. 9
did her footing *trace* So sure and swiftly, ... III. vii. 23. 7
she mervaild that no footings *trace* Nor wight appeard, . . III. xi. 53. 5
ever troden was of footings *trace:* . . . . IV. x. 21. 5
as he to and fro by chaunce did *trace,* . . . . IV. xii. 4. 8
by which way they towards it should *trace.* . . . . V. ix. 7. 4
now I begin To tread an endlesse *trace,* . . . . VI. i. 6. 2
still I forward *trace.'* . . . . VI. i. 7. 5
Not wont on foote with heavy armes to *trace,* . . . . VI. iii. 29. 5
Had vow'd unto the victor him to *trace* . . . . VI. vii. 21. 7
Coridon could daunce, and trimly *trace:* . . . . VI. ix. 42. 4
sleep and darknesse round about did *trace:* . . . . VII. vii. 44. 7
Traced. golden lockes, . . . unto her heeles downe *traced,* . . . IV. i .13. 3
long they *trac'd* and traverst to and fro, ... IV. vi. 18. 1
all the way the Prince on footpace *traced,* . . . . IV. viii. 34. 8
Thus long they *trast* and traverst to and fro, ... V. viii. 37. 1
Thus long they *trac'd* and traverst to and fro, ... VI. i. 37. 1
that fourth Mayd, which there amidst them *traced,* . . . . VI. x. 25. 2
Traces. With Heydeguyes, and trimly trodden *traces,* . . . . *S.C.* Jun. 27
Traceth. *Traceth* his ground, and round about doth beat, . . VI. vii. 47. 4
Tracing. *Tracing* and traversing, now here, now there; . . . IV. vii. 28. 8
Tract. *tract* of time, and long prosperitie, ... *S.C.* May 117
all his *tract* with bloudie drops is stained . . . . *Gn.* 279
We have not yet the *tract* of anie troad, ... *Hub.* 406
from this lower *tract* he dared to stie . . . . *Mui.* 42
when by *tract* they hunted had throughout . . . . I. i. 11. 5
gras, In which the *tract* of peoples footing was, ... I. iii. 10. 5
by what meanes may I his footing *tract?'* . . . . II. i. 12. 7
nowhere could espye *Tract* of his foot: . . . . II. iii. 19. 7
tract of living creature none they fownd, ... III. i. 14. 8
the same along did trace By *tract* of blood, ... III. v. 28. 4
Forthy the bloody *tract* they followd fast, ... III. v. 37. 6
his *tract* she mote detect: . . . . III. vi. 12. 7
If any *tract* of him or tidings they mote trace. . . . . . . III. vi. 25. 9
Farre under ground from *tract* of living went, ... IV. ii. 47. 5
tract of time, that all things doth decay, ... V. iv. 8. 1
He could no path nor *tract* of foot descry, ... VI. iv. 24. 6
Well did he *tract* his steps as he did ryde, ... VI. vii. 3. 1
she in *tract* of time accompted was his owne. . . . . . . VI. ix. 14. 9
Him follow'd by the *tract* of his outragious spoile. . . . . VI. xii. 22. 9
The hardest steele, in *tract* of time doth teare: . . . . . . *Am.* xviii. 2
Tracted. Hath *tracted* forth some salvage beastes trade: . . . II. vi. 39. 5
Tracting. So as they rode . . . *tracting* by the traile, ... VI. vii. 17. 6
Trade. Dight gaudy Girlonds was my common *trade,* . . . . *S.C.* Jun. 45
Whether shall we professe some *trade* or skill, ... *Hub.* 117
not to anie certaine *trade* or place, ... *Hub.* 130
constrain'd that *trade* to overgive, ... *Hub.* 249
following that *trade* so base and vile; . . . . *Hub.* 366
no good *trade* of life did entertaine, ... *Hub.* 398
They trampled have with their fowle footings *trade,* . . . . *T.M.* 275
calls foorth men unto their toylsome *trade,* . . . . *D.* 485
I sat (as was my *trade*) . . . . *Col.* 56
Accursed usury was all his *trade,* . . . . I. iv. 27. 8
Hath tracted forth some salvage beastes *trade:* . . . . . . II. vi. 39. 5
Finding in it fit ports for fishers *trade,* . . . . II. x. 6. 8
There those five sisters had continuall *trade,* . . . . II. xii. 30. 8
so loose life, and so ungentle *trade,* . . . . III. i. 67. 5
ply himselfe to any honest *trade,* . . . . III. vii. 12. 6
To win faire Leda to his lovely *trade:* . . . . III. xi. 32. 2
His name was Care; a blacksmith by his *trade,* . . . . . . IV. v. 35. 6
cursed usage and ungodly *trade* The heavens abhorre, . . . IV. vii. 12. 3
As well which in the mightie Ocean *trade,* . . . . IV. xi. 9. 4
Thereto adde art, even womens witty *trade,* . . . . V. v. 49. 5
Shut up her haven, mard her marchants *trade,* . . . . V. x. 25. 6
ne did give Them selves to any *trade,* . . . . VI. viii. 35. 5
Was hunting in the woods, (as was his *trade*) . . . . VI. x. 39. 2
Why then doe I, untrainde in lovers *trade,* Her hardnes blame, *Am.* li. 5
Most happy letters! fram'd by skilfull *trade,* . . . . *Am.* lxxiv. 1
Tradeful. Ye *tradefull* Merchants, that, with weary toyle, . . *Am.* xv. 1
Traduction. through *traduction* was eftsoones derived, . . . IV. iii. 13. 6
Traffic. by such *trafficke* after gaines to hunt, ... VI. xi. 9. 4
Tragedies. I that in true *Tragedies* am skild, ... *T.M.* 165
To make new matter fit for *Tragedies;* . . . . *D.* 154
to declare the mournfull *Tragedyes* . . . . III. xi. 45. 6
Tragedy. all mans life me seemes a *Tragedy,* . . . . *T.M.* 157
'Tell on,' (quoth she) 'the wofull *Tragedy,* . . . . I. vii. 24. 8
In middest of their mournfull *Tragedy,* . . . . I. ix. 10. 4
The end of their sad *Tragedie* uptyde, ... II. ii. 1. 3

Tragedy—*Continued.*
The sad spectatour of my *Tragedie:* . . . . II. iv. 27. 6
I waile, and make my woes a *Tragedy.* . . . . *Am.* liv. 8
Tragic. Ye sacred ruines, and ye *tragick* sights, ... *Ro.* vii. 1
The Stage with *Tragick* buskin to adorne, ... *T.M.* 152
none more *tragick* matter I can finde . . . . *T.M.* 155
Like *tragicke* Pageants seeming to appeare. . . . . *Ti.* 490
wontst the *tragick* stage for to direct, ... *Mui.* 11
Helpe, O thou *Tragick* Muse! . . . . *Mui.* 413
In *Tragick* plaints and passionate mischance. . . . . *Col.* 427
Yclad in costly garments fit for *tragicke* Stage. . . . . . . III. xii. 3. 9
tragicke Inoes sonne, ... IV. xi. 13. 4
Great ruth through her misfortunes *tragicke* stowre; . . . . V. ix. 45. 8
To stirre up strife and many a *tragicke* stowre; . . . . . . V. x. 13. 5
Tragical. ye, that read these ruines *tragicall,* . . . . *Van.* xii. 9
The roote whereof and *tragicall* effect, Vouchsafe, ... *Mui.* 9
Traherne. his title justifide by might, Slaying *Traherne,* . . . II. x. 60. 7
Trail. Enwoven with an Yvie-winding *trayle:* . . . . *Mui.* 299
A *trayle* of yvie in his native hew; . . . . II. xii. 61. 2
So as they rode . . . tracting by the *traile,* . . . . VI. vii. 17. 6
Trailed. *Trayled* with ribbands diversly distraught, ... V. v. 2. 4
Trailing. About her shoulders careleslie downe *trailing,* . . . *Ti.* 11
Train. this fierce hatefull beast and all hir *traine* . . . . . *Rev.* iii. 13
With spotted winges, like Peacocks *trayne,* . . . . *S.C.* Mar. 80
Lest he should be descried by his *trayne.* . . . . *S.C.* May 281
So praysen babes the Peacoks spotted *traine,* . . . . *S.C.* O. 31
Thenceforth proceeding with his princely *trayne,* . . . . . . *Hub.* 1086
wont to wait upon my *traine,* . . . . *T.M.* 196
Junoes Bird in her ey-spotted *traine* . . . . *Mui.* 95
that his deceitfull *traine* . . . might not be bewraid, ... *Mui.* 398
So hight because of this deceitfull *traine,* . . . . *Col.* 118
Best knowne by bearing up great Cynthiaes *traine:* . . . . *Col.* 509
her huge *traine* All suddenly about his body wound, ... I. i. 18. 6
the man so wrapt in Errours endlesse *traine!* . . . . I. i. 18. 9
A dreadfull Dragon with an hideous *trayne;* . . . . I. iv. 10. 5
Such one was Lechery, the third of all this *traine.* . . . . . I. iv. 26. 9
Emongst the rest rode . . . as one of the *traine:* . . . . . . I. iv. 37. 6
with their sturre they troubled all the *traine;* . . . . I. iv. 40. 4
hast with . . . trecherous *train,* Faire knighthood fowly shamed, I. vi. 41. 2
to discry the crafty cunning *traine,* . . . . I. vii. 1. 2
No . . . deceiptfull *traine,* Might once abide . . . . I. viii. 4. 5
scourging th' emptie ayre with his long *trayne,* . . . . . . I. viii. 17. 3
O! never, Sir, desire to try his guilefull *traine.'* . . . . . . I. ix. 31. 9
Then gan he tosse aloft his stretched *traine,* . . . . I. xi. 37. 5
hoarie king, with all his *traine,* . . . . I. xii. 12. 2
Of comely services, or courtly *trayne?* . . . . I. xii. 14. 4
In vertuous lore to *traine* his tender youth, ... II. iii. 2. 4
Below her ham her weed did somewhat *trayne,* . . . . II. iii. 27. 1
a goodly *traine* Of Squires and Ladies . . . . II. ix. 17. 7
The *traine* whereof loose far behind her strayd, ... II. ix. 19. 3
through that false Ladies *traine* He was surprisd, ... III. iii. 11. 1
Seeking to match the chaste with th' unchaste Ladies *traine.'* . III. vii. 60. 9
with him ledd to sea an youthly *trayne;* . . . . III. ix. 48. 6
marshalling the evill-ordered *trayne,* . . . . III. xii. 23. 4
them to warlike discipline did *trayne,* . . . . IV. viii. 27. 7
The noble Thamis, with all his goodly *traine;* . . . . IV. xi. 24. 3
both behind upheld her spredding *traine;* . . . . IV. xi. 47. 4
all the sea, disturbed with their *traine,* . . . . V. ii. 15. 7
How he mis-led the simple peoples *traine,* . . . . V. ii. 33. 7
His horse purloyned was by subtill *traine,* . . . . V. iii. 31. 5
some guilefull *traine* did weave, ... V. v. 37. 4
least his false foe did him entrap In traytrous *traine,* . . . V. vi. 4. 4
She was preserved from their traytrous *traine.* . . . . V. vi. 34. 7
when all her warlike *traine* There present saw, ... V. vii. 34. 7
To lay his spoiles before his lemans *traine:* . . . . V. viii. 2. 3
threatning his sharpe clawes, now wanting powre to *traine.* VI. iv. 22. 9
Whether ye list him *traine* in chevalry, ... VI. iv. 35. 8
Ne yet entrap in treasons subtill *traine.* . . . . VI. v. 14. 4
by what *traine* She fell into that salvage villaines hand? . . VI. v. 27. 7
by such a *traine* Him to betray . . . . VI. vii. 22. 4
the *traine* of beauties Queene, ... VI. x. 17. 5
Entrapped him, and caught into her *traine;* . . . . VII. vi. 48. 7
Which sought me to entrap in treasons *traine.* . . . . *Am.* xii. 4
traine and teach me with her lookes; . . . . *Am.* xxi. 13
With a great *traine* ensuing. . . . . *Proth.* 167
Trained. *See* **Mistrained.**
Whereto thou list their *trayned* willes entice. . . . . *S.C.* O. 24
In these and like delightes . . . He *trayned* was, ... I. vi. 29. 2
all my daies he traind mee up in vertuous *lore.* . . . . . . I. ix. 4. 9
He had not *trayned* bene in chevalree. . . . . II. iii. 46. 5
had them *traynd* in all civilitee, ... III. i. 44. 6
I have been *trained* up in warlike stowre, ... III. ii. 6. 3
So was she *trayned* up from time to time . . . . III. vi. 3. 7
yfostered to bee And *trained* up in trew feminitee: . . . . . III. vi. 51. 5
Having therein bene *trained* many a yeare, ... IV. iii. 40. 3
Traind up in feats of armes and knightlinesse; . . . . IV. vii. 45. 7
Artegall *trayn'd* in Justice lore . . . . V. i. Arg.
Thus she him *trayned,* and thus she him taught . . . . . . V. i. 8. 1
both in armes well *traind,* and throughly tride: . . . . . . V. ii. 17. 4
In which he had bene *trayned* many a day, ... V. v. 21. 2
I . . . as was convenient, Have *trayned* bene . . . . VI. ii. 31. 4
As if he long had to his heasts bene *trayned.* . . . . VI. vi. 39. 6
such fondlings whom she *trayned* Into her trap . . . . VI. vi. 42. 3
Trains. Betraying him into the *traines* of hys foe. . . . . . *S.C.* May 200
Of trecherie or *traines* nought tooke he keep, ... *Gn.* 241
There his welwoven toyles, and subtil *traines,* . . . . *As.* 97
By *traynes* into new troubles to have toste: . . . . I. iii. 24. 7
first he cast . . . by *traynes* Her to persuade . . . . I. vi. 3. 6
The subtile *traines* of Archimago old; . . . . I. vii. 26. 2
by his subtile *trains* He could escape fowle death . . . . . I. xii. 36. 4

Travelled—*Continued.*
Sir Calidore thence *travelled* not long, . . . VI. i. 11. 1
ere he thence had *traveild* many a mile, . . . VI. ii. 40. 3
So forth they *traveld,* an uneven payre . . . VI. v. 9. 1
So both together *traveld,* . . . VI. vi. 16. 6
through many a soyle Had *traveld* still on foot . . . VI. viii. 47. 2
Traveller. the *travailer,* that fares that way, . . . *Ti.* 6
wearie *traveiler,* that strayes By muddy shore . . . I. v. 18. 1
That never leads the *traveiler* astray, . . . I. x. 52. 4
Espye a *traveiler* with feet surbet, . . . II. ii. 22. 7
not like a weary *traveilere,* . . . II. ii. 23. 1
The wearie *Traveiler,* wandring that way, . . . II. v. 30. 5
Of the poore *traveiler* that went astray . . . III. i. 43. 6
A *traveiler* unwonted to such way: . . . III. vi. 4. 2
Travellers. *travailers,* which it from far behold. . . . *Col.* 115
(as *travellers* informe) . . . II. xii. 24. 8
T' allure weake *traveillers,* . . . II. xii. 31. 9
traveilers to him seemd to entize: . . . II. xii. 46. 6
many wilde woodmen which robbe and rend All *traveilers:* . . . III. x. 40. 7
All *travellers* tormented are with paine: . . . IV. iv. 47. 6
that doth to *travellers* such harmes?' . . . V. ii. 5. 2
joy to weary wandring *travailers* did lend: . . . VII. vi. 9. 9
Travellers'. he freed the *Traveilers* high-way, . . . II. x. 39. 3
Travelling. wretched people *travailing* that way, . . . *Van.* iii. 5
his shooes beaten out with *traveling.* . . . *Hub.* 214
by the wearie way were *traveiling;* . . . I. x. 36. 7
Whom bold Cymochles *traveiling* to finde, . . . II. vi. 2. 1
Latona *traveiling* that way, . . . II. xii. 13. 4
She, *traveiling* with Guyon, . . . III. ii. 4. 1
So *travelling,* he chaunst far off to heed A Damzell, . . . V. viii. 4. 1
that toylesome paine, In *travelling* on foote . . . VI. iii. 29. 4
Travels. *See* **Travails.**
render up a reckning of their *travels* . . . *Hub.* 310
'Who *travailes* by the wearie wandring way, . . . I. ix. 39. 1
Traverse. forced him his ground to *traverse* wyde, . . . II. viii. 35. 3
Traversed. long they trac'd and *traverst* to and fro, . . . IV. vi. 18. 1
Thus long they trast and *traverst* to and fro, . . . V. viii. 37. 1
Thus long they trac'd and *traverst* to and fro, . . . VI. i. 37. 1
Traversing. *traversing* the charret of the Sunne . . . *T.M.* 9
Tracing and *traversing,* now here, now there; . . . IV. vii. 28. 8
Treacher. to see this recreaunt knight, No knight, but *treachour* I. iv. 41. 5
Where may that *treachour* . . . 'be found, . . . II. i. 12. 6
the *treachour* did remove His craftie engin, . . . II. iv. 27. 3
Treacherous. hast with . . . *trecherous* train, Faire knighthood fowly shamed, . . . I. vi. 41. 2
By *treacherous* deceipt did me deprive: . . . III. x. 27. 5
void of vile and *treacherous* intent, . . . IV. viii. 30. 5
many brought to shame by treason *treacherous.* . . . V. vi. 32. 9
Like *treacherous,* like full of fraud and guile, . . . V. vi. 33. 2
Treacherously. him Allectus *treacherously* slew, . . . II. x. 57. 7
Least any should betray his Lady *treacherously.* . . . V. vi. 26. 9
Treacher's. never rest, Till I that *treachours* art have heard . I. ix. 32. 2
Treachers. those same *treachours* vile Be punished . . . *Hub.* 1255
Treachery. Had not a Goose the *treachery* bewrayde; . . . *Van.* xi. 8
never give trust to his *trecheree:* . . . *S.C.* May 222
by *trecheree* Didst underfong my lasse . . . *S.C.* Jun. 102
Of *trecherie* or traines nought tooke he keep, . . . *Gn.* 241
The Foxe, first Author of that *treacherie,* . . . *Hub.* 1379
Made it selfe famous through false *trechery,* . . . II. viii. 12. 6
To keepe a nightly watch for dread of *treachery.* . . . V. iv. 46. 9
him with *treacherie* And traynes having surpriz'd, . . . V. xii. 40. 8
to entrap him by false *treacherie:* . . . VI. vii. 23. 5
Treachetour. the king was by a *Treachetour* Disguised slaine, . II. x. 51. 3
Treachetours. 'Abide, ye caytive *treachetours* untrew, . . . VI. viii. 7. 4
Tread. the leane soules *treaden* under foote, . . . *S.C.* S. 126
teache her *tread* aloft in buskin fine, . . . *S.O.* O. 113
softly *tread* The tender grasse, . . . *D.* 311
Worthie next after Cynthia to *tread,* . . . *Col.* 514
underneath his filthy feet did *tread* The sacred thinges, . . . I. vii. 18. 6
Where never foote of living wight did *tread,* . . . I. vii. 50. 4
with his winged heeles did *tread* the wynd, . . . I. ix. 21. 8
happy earth, Whereon thy innocent feet doe ever *tread!* . . . I. x. 9. 2
their rightfull causes downe to *tread;* . . . I. x. 43. 7
Ne weene my right with strength adowne to *tread,* . . . I. xii. 28. 5
Who taught his trampling steed with equall steps to *tread.* . . II. i. 7. 9
She taught to *tread,* . . . II. iii. 28. 6
he despisd to *tread* in dew degree, . . . II. iii. 46. 7
Thinking to overthrowe and downe him *tred:* . . . II. viii. 49. 7
overronne, to *tread* them to the grownd: . . . II. ix. 15. 5
Ne scarse his feet on ground were seene to *tred:* . . . II. xi. 26. 3
The verdant gras as he thereon did *tread;* . . . III. i. 5. 6
seeking him adowne to *tread,* . . . III. iii. 39. 7
Shall *tread* adowne, and doe him fowly dye; . . . III. iii. 39. 8
tread downe the victors surquedry. . . . III. iii. 46. 9
I *tread* in dust thee and thy money both, . . . III. x. 29. 8
Unworthy wretch to *tread* upon the ground, . . . III. xi. 11. 8
kist the ground on which her sole did *tread,* . . . IV. viii. 13. 2
I count as naught, and *tread* downe under feet, . . . IV. x. 2. 7
doth their bottome *tread;* . . . IV. xi. 14. 8
gan he make him *tread* his steps anew, . . . IV. xii. 13. 8
to *tread* upon the land, . . . V. ii. 18. 4
now I begin To *tread* an endlesse trace, . . . VI. i. 6. 2
unfit to *tread* And lackey by him, . . . VI. ii. 15. 4
every foote did tremble which did *tread,* . . . VI. viii. 31. 8
under foot doth *tread* The mightie ones, . . . VI. ix. 27. 8
And *tread* my life downe in the lowly floure. . . . *Am.* xx. 4
the ground whereas her foot shall *tread,* . . . *Epith.* 48
Treadeth. *treadeth* under foote hir holie things, . . . *T.M.* 569
Treading. *treading* under foote her honest name: . . . III. i. 50. 4
as *treading* still on thorne: . . . III. x. 55. 4

Treading—*Continued.*
must, Which he was *treading* in the wine-fats see, . . . VII. vii. 39. 3
Treading downe earth as lothsome . . . *Am.* xiii. 11
Treads. The wretchedst man that *treades* this day on ground?' . *D.* 63
Or flings aloft, or *treades* downe in the flore, . . . II. viii. 42. 5
all that him withstands *Treads* down and overthrowes. . . II. xi. 33. 6
Treague. during their quiet *treague,* Into her lodging to repaire II. ii. 33. 3
Treason. For their false *treason* and vile theeverie: . . . *Hub.* 315
So would he worke the silly man by *treason* . . . *Hub.* 888
T' excuse his former *treason* and abusion, . . . *Hub.* 1363
No knight, but treachour full of . . . shameful *treason,* . . I. iv. 41. 6
him before His father fierce of *treason* false accusd, . . . I. v. 37. 8
Una, his deare dreed, Her truth had staynd with *treason* . . I. vi. 2. 4
with like *treason* now maintain Thy guilty wrong, . . . I. vi. 41. 5
By forged *treason* or by open fight, . . . II. i. 3. 3
through *treason* and deceiptfull gin, . . . II. iii. 13. 7
of him selfe to *treason* ill disposd, . . . II. iv. 22. 3
loyall truth to *treason* doest incline: . . . II. vii. 13. 3
Disloyall *Treason,* and hart-burning Hate; . . . II. vii. 22. 3
Was never wight that *treason* of him told: . . . II. viii. 13. 8
did he fall by *treason,* or by fight? . . . II. viii. 24. 4
The faithfull steele such *treason* no'uld endure, . . . II. viii. 30. 8
Nought els but *treason* from the first this land did foyle. . II. x. 48. 9
Th' eternall marks of *treason* may at Stonheng vew. . . . II. x. 66. 9
Unweeting of their wile and *treason* bad, . . . III. v. 18. 3
bad that none their joyous *treason* should reveale. . . . III. x. 5. 9
Vile *treason* and fowle falshood hidden were, . . . IV. i. 17. 8
from feare of *treason* free, . . . IV. iii. 49. 4
that same Squire of *treason* to upbraide; . . . IV. ix. 7. 7
hatred, murther, *treason,* and despight, . . . IV. x. 20. 6
least she him sought t' appeach Of *treason,* . . . V. v. 37. 4
Perceiving well the *treason* which was ment; . . . V. vi. 28. 2
all that *treason* there intended did bewray. . . . V. vi. 30. 9
many brought to shame by *treason* treacherous. . . . V. vi. 32. 9
By guilefull *treason* and by subtill slight . . . V. xi. 39. 7
shall thy *treason* understand, . . . VI. i. 25. 7
traytor, that with *treason* vile Hast slaine my men . . . VI. vi. 25. 1
To worke by wicked *treason* wayes doth find, . . . VI. vii. 1. 8
Great *treason* to him meant, his life to reave. . . . VI. vii. 12. 4
How ever they through *treason* doe trespasse. . . . VI. vii. 27. 6
have with *treason* thralled unto you These two, . . . VI. viii. 7. 5
Trust not the *treason* of those smyling lookes, . . . *Am.* xlvii. 1
Yet heresy nor *treason* didst conspire, . . . *Am.* xlviii. 7
Let no false *treason* seeke us to entrap, . . . *Epith.* 323
Treason's. his false hart, fraught with all *treasons* store, . . *Mui.* 395
thou thy *treasons* fruit . . . shalt taste Right sowre, . . . II. viii. 31. 8
Ne yet entrap in *treasons* subtill traine. . . . VI. v. 14. 4
his two knights Doe gaine their *treasons* meed: . . . VI. vii. Arg.
Which sought me to entrap in *treasons* traine. . . . *Am.* xii. 4
Treasons. The secret *treasons,* which of late I know . . . I. xii. 33. 5
treasons could bewray, and foes convince: . . . III. ii. 21. 8
full many *treasons* vile His father Dolon had deviz'd . . . V. vi. 33. 7
for vyld *treasons* and outrageous shame, . . . V. ix. 40. 8
all her traynes and all her *treasons* forth did lay. . . . V. ix. 47. 9
Treasure. And all that *treasure,* drowned in the maine: . . *Bel.*[2] xiii. 13
A trophee of his glittering spoyles and *treasure,* . . . *Gn.* 127
How he may flow in quiets matchles *treasour,* . . . *Gn.* 139
make our ease our *treasure.* . . . *Hub.* 160
his owne *treasure* he encreased more, . . . *Hub.* 1172
fild with *treasure* rackt with robberies; . . . *Hub.* 1306
Where be the sweete delights of learnings *treasure* . . . *T.M.* 175
With *treasure* passing all this worldes worth, . . . *Ti.* 286
in it did most precious *treasure* hide, . . . *Ti.* 619
my hearts eternall *threasure.* . . . *Col.* 47
seald up in the *threasure* of her hart. . . . *Col.* 571
Mamon in a delve Sunning his *threasure* hore; . . . II. vii. Arg.
spoile the *treasure* there in gard: . . . II. vii. 25. 4
T' endow her sonne with *threasure* and rich store . . . III. iv. 21. 8
forth to throw All the huge *threasure,* . . . III. iv. 22. 5
bearing with him *treasure* in close store, . . . III. x. 19. 3
forth he drew Great store of *treasure,* . . . III. x. 29. 2
the *treasure* which he did bewray, . . . III. x. 34. 5
opprest With burdein of great *treasure,* . . . III. x. 41. 5
'that ye doe leave Your *treasure* here . . . III. x. 42. 2
the place Where late his *treasure* he entombed had; . . . III. x. 54. 2
robd the world of *threasure* endlesse deare, . . . IV. ii. 33. 4
he found great store of hoorded *threasure,* . . . IV. ix. 12. 2
Paridell of love did make no *threasure,* . . . IV. ix. 21. 7
Sends forth the winds out of his hidden *threasure* . . . IV. ix. 23. 3
time to steale, the *threasure* of mans day, . . . IV. x. 14. 8
So lavishly enricht with Natures *threasure,* . . . IV. x. 23. 3
Great *threasure* sithence we did finde . . . V. iv. 13. 2
to her selfe that *threasure* appertained; . . . V. iv. 13. 5
for this *threasure* throwne upon his strand; . . . V. iv. 15. 5
Your brothers *threasure,* which from him is strayd, . . . V. iv. 18. 3
so the *threasure* yours is, Bracidas, by right.' . . . V. iv. 19. 9
on the *threasure* by that judgement seased, . . . V. iv. 20. 4
To dare not to pollute so sacred *threasure* . . . VI. viii. 43. 8
whose worth above all *threasure* They did esteeme, . . . VI. xi. 14. 5
seeke to please; that now is counted wise mens *threasure.* . . VI. xii. 41. 9
both the Indias of their *treasure* spoile; . . . *Am.* xv. 3
Fayre bosome! fraught with vertues richest *tresure,* . . . *Am.* lxxvi. 1
Treasure's. For to encrease the common *treasures* store; . . *Hub.* 1171
Ne privy bee unto your *treasures* grave.' . . . III. x. 42. 8
Treasures. With rich *treasures* this gay ship fraighted was: . . *Pet.* ii. 6
with their spoyles enlarg'd his private *treasures.* . . . *Hub.* 1130
In which all heavenly *treasures* locked are. . . . *Ti.* 630
the hid *treasures* in her sacred tombe . . . II. vii. 17. 3
all bountie naturall And *treasures* of true love . . . IV. Pr. 4. 4
the keeping have of learnings *threasures* . . . VI. Pr. 2. 3

Treasures—*Continued.*
being naked . . . The goodly *threasures* of nature appeare: . VI. viii. 41. 7
thence did all the spoyles and *threasures* take, ... VI. xi. 51. 2
*and both the Indias of their *treasures* spoile, ... *Am.* xv. 3
Had ye once seene these her celestial *threasures,* . . . . . *Epith.* 200
Treasury. her faire brest, the *threasury* of joy, ... *As.* 161
feede his eye And covetous desire with his huge *threasury.* . . II. vii. 4. 9
Where Mammon earst did sunne his *threasury;* . . . . II. viii. 4. 7
therewith fill The coffers of her wicked *threasury,* . . . . V. ii. 9. 4
For she, out of her secret *threasury* . . . . *H.H.B.* 246
Treat. Unkindnesse past, they gan of solace *treat,* . . . . . . I. vii. 4. 1
thus I heare you of your sorrowes *treat.* . . . . I. vii. 40. 4
The chearelesse man, . . . Had no delight to *treaten* of his griefe; . . . . I. viii. 43. 8
Would him disarme and *treaten* shamefully; . . . . II. viii. 25. 3
bide him batteill without further *treat.* . . . . III. viii. 16. 5
all that night they of their loves did *treat,* . . . . IV. i. 16. 1
gan to *treate* of deeds of armes abrode, ... IV. iv. 5. 4
of a truce to *treat* In milder tearmes, ... IV. ix. 35. 6
Whereof I have to *treat* here presently: . . . . V. vii. 3. 5
would no lenger *treat,* but bad them sound; . . . . V. vii. 28. 7
To *treat* with her, by way of enterdeale, ... V. viii. 21. 7
often *treat* for pardon and remission To suppliants, ... V. ix. 32. 3
this heavenly thing whereof I *treat,* . . . . V. x. 1. 2
they mote *treat* of things abrode at leasure, ... VI. iii. 22. 4
The coward Turpine, whereof now I *treat;* . . . . VI. vii. 2. 2
Treated. as they two of kindnes *treated* long, ... III. viii. 15. 1
when they long had *treated* to and fro, ... VI. ii. 36. 1
Treatise. with this present *treatise* doth agree, ... V. iii. 3. 8
Treaty. first he cast by *treatie,* . . . Her to persuade . . . . I. vi. 3. 6
Then she began a *treaty* to procure, ... II. ii. 32. 6
eke the Prince like *treaty* handeled, ... III. i. 11. 3
with faire *treaty* pacifide their yre. . . . . III. ix. 17. 2
Treble. made amends to her with *treble* praise. . . . . *Col.* 924
Fortune, . . . shall *treble* penaunce pay Of *treble* good: . . . I. viii. 43. 5, 6
sweet Zephyrus lowd whisteled His *treble,* . . . . II. xii. 33. 6
Trebling. *trebling* the dew time In which the wombes of women doe expyre, ... I. vii. 9. 6
Trebly. *Trebly* augmented was his furious mood . . . . I. xi. 22. 7
Them *trebly* breaded in a threefold lace, ... III. ii. 50. 2
that his may so be *trebly* wext. . . . . IV. ii. 52. 9
Tree. *See* **Cedar-tree, Gallows-tree, Laurel-tree, Myrtle-tree, Olive-tree, Pear-tree, Walnut-tree.**
he bare The *tree* of peace, ... *Bel.*[1] vii. 11
the faire Dodonian *tree* . . . . *Bel.* v. 1
rent this royall *tree* quite by the roote; . . . . *Pet.* iii. 12
Untill he came unto the broken *tree,* . . . . *Pet.* v. 5
the Phoenix there alas, Spying the *tree* destroid, ... *Pet.* v. 9
on a *tree* uphang'd I saw her spoyle. . . . . *Bel.*[2] vi. 14
kindling fire within the hollow *tree,* . . . . *Van.* iv. 7
There grewe an aged *Tree* on the greene, ... *S.C.* F. 102
Anger nould let him speake to the *tree,* . . . . *S.C.* F. 199
it had bene an auncient *tree,* . . . . *S.C.* F. 207
laughing lope to a *tree;* . . . . *S.C.* Mar. 81
Beating the withered leafe from the *tree,* . . . . *S.C.* S. 51
The kindelye dewe drops from the higher *tree,* . . . . *S.C.* N. 31
the rest Under the *tree* . . . . *S.C.* D. 35
Here will I hang my pype upon this *tree:* . . . . *S.C.* D. 141
tree, in which Demophoon . . . Eternall hurte left . . . . . *Gn.* 201
thou to a *tree* mayst clyme, ... *Hub.* 990
broad spreading like an aged *tree,* . . . . *Ti.* 452
Her name in every *tree* I will endosse, ... *Col.* 632
once a man, Fradubio, now a *tree;* . . . . I. ii. 33. 3
wretched *tree!* whose nature weake A cruell witch, . . . Hath thus transformd, ... I. ii. 33. 4
though a *tree* I seme, yet cold and heat me paines.' . . . . . I. ii. 33. 9
'Say on, Fradubio, then, or man or *tree,*' . . . . I. ii. 34. 1
whome ye see Now not a Lady, but a seeming *tree;* . . . . . I. ii. 35. 5
When all this speech the living *tree* had spent, ... I. ii. 44. 5
on a *tree* Sansfoy his shield is hangd . . . . I. v. 5. 7
an almond *tree* ymounted hye On top of greene Selinis . . . I. vii. 32. 5
downe he tombled; as an aged *tree,* . . . . I. viii. 22. 5
as the *tree* does fall, so lyes it ever low. . . . . I. x. 41. 9
blood, which cruelly was spilt On cursed *tree,* . . . . I. x. 57. 6
There grew a goodly *tree* him faire beside, ... I. xi. 46. 1
The *tree* of life, the crime of our first fathers fall. . . . . . I. xi. 46. 9
Another like faire *tree* eke grew thereby, ... I. xi. 47. 6
That *tree* through one mans fault hath doen us all to dy. . . I. xi. 47. 9
From that first *tree* forth flowd, ... I. xi. 48. 1
As budding braunch rent from the native *tree,* . . . . II. ii. 2. 6
him to a *tree* applyes, ... II. v. 10. 4
full of the stately *tree* . . . . II. v. 31. 2
No *tree* whose braunches did not bravely spring; . . . . . . II. vi. 13. 1
Next thereunto did grow a goodly *tree,* . . . . II. vii. 53. 6
The warlike Elfe much wondred at this *tree,* . . . . II. vii. 56. 1
His warlike Armes, . . . were hong upon a *tree;* . . . . . . II. xii. 80. 2
languish, as the leafe faln from the *tree,* . . . . III. ii. 39. 8
enrooted deepe must be that *Tree,* . . . . III. iii. 22. 2
like withered *tree* that wanteth juyce, ... IV. i. 31. 5
Like as a withered *tree,* . . . . IV. iii. 29. 6
by that he saw on every *tree,* . . . . IV. vii. 46. 1
'No *tree,* that is of count, ... IV. x. 22. 1
on a *tree* before the Tyrants dore . . . . V. viii. 45. 1
Flying from *tree* to *tree,* from wand to wand; . . . . V. ix. 17. 6
Hath pruned from the native *tree,* . . . . V. xi. 11. 9
Both hand and foote unto a *tree* was bound; . . . . VI. i. 11. 4
Till his returne unto this *tree* he bond; . . . . VI. i. 16. 8
his backe for best safegard He lent against a *tree,* . . . . VI. v. 18. 9
Had for his food late gathered from the *tree,*) . . . . . . VI. vii. 24. 5
He by the heeles him hung upon a *tree,* . . . . VI. vii. 27. 2

Tree—*Continued.*
Queene-apples, and red Cherries from the *tree,* . . . . . . VII. vi. 43. 6
a *tree* alone all comfortlesse, ... *Am.* lvi. 7
that *tree,* and that same beast, am I, ... *Am.* lvi. 13
Treen. *See* **Trees'.**
Trees. *See* **Laurel-trees, Myrtle-trees, Palm-trees.**
A twinne of forked *trees* . . . . *Bel.* v. 14
'You naked *trees,* whose shady leaves are lost, ... *S.C.* Ja. 31
his *trees* of state in compasse rownd: . . . . *S.C.* F. 146
teache the *trees* their trickling teares to shedde. . . . . . . *S.C.* Jun. 96
Others the utmost boughs of *trees* doe crop, ... *Gn.* 81
those *trees,* in whose transformed hew . . . . *Gn.* 197
There fruitfull corne, faire *trees,* fresh herbage is, ... *Col.* 298
as the *trees* do grow, her name may grow: . . . . *Col.* 633
loftie *trees,* yclad with sommers pride, ... I. i. 7. 4
Much can they praise the *trees* so straight and hy, ... I. i. 8. 5
they came at last Where grew two goodly *trees,* . . . . . . I. ii. 28. 3
earth for terror seemd to shake, And *trees* did tremble. . . . I. vii. 7. 7
Both loftie towres and highest *trees* hath rent, ... I. viii. 9. 7
all about old stockes and stubs of *trees,* . . . . I. ix. 34. 1
high *trees* overthrew, and rocks in peeces tore. . . . . . . I. xi. 37. 9
Trees, braunches, birds, and songs, were framed fitt . . . . II. vi. 13. 5
The *trees* did bud, and early blossomes bore; . . . . II. vi. 24. 7
trees of bitter Gall, and Heben sad; . . . . II. vii. 52. 2
the tall *trees* with leaves appareled . . . . II. xii. 12. 4
The painted flowres, the *trees* upshooting hye, ... II. xii. 58. 5
the heavy *trees* they clyme, ... III. vi. 42. 5
Through the tops of the high *trees* . . . . III. vii. 5. 1
mossy *trees,* which covered all with shade . . . . IV. vii. 38. 8
Against the stones and *trees* did rayle anew, ... IV. viii. 36. 8
divers *trees* enrang'd in even rankes; . . . . IV. x. 25. 2
In which all *trees* of honour stately stood, ... VI. x. 6. 4
made to growe Most dainty *trees,* . . . . VII. vii. 8. 7
from the *trees* did lop the needlesse spray: . . . . VII. vii. 42. 7
tooles to prune the *trees,* . . . . VII. vii. 43. 7
Trees'. So left her, where she now is turnd to *treen* mould. . . I. ii. 39. 9
The wretched payre transformd to *treen* mould; . . . . I. vii. 26. 5
of the *trees* owne inclination made, ... III. vi. 44. 3
Tremble. onely Rome could make great Rome to *tremble:* . . *Ro.* vi. 10
all the forrest with astonishment Thereof did *tremble,* . . . *Hub.* 1347
his own syre, . . . Did often *tremble* at his horrid vew; . . . I. vi. 25. 3
My feareful flesh did *tremble* at their strife, ... I. vi. 38. 6
earth for terror seemd to shake, And trees did *tremble.* . . . I. vii. 7. 7
tree . . . Whose tender locks do *tremble* every one . . . . . I. vii. 32. 8
his hand did quake And *tremble* like a leafe . . . . I. ix. 51. 4
his most hideous head my tongue to tell Does *tremble;* . . . I. xi. 12. 7
I quake and *tremble* over-all.' . . . . II. iii. 44. 7
inly *tremble* at the memory Of Brennus . . . . II. x. 40. 8
seemd to *tremble* evermore and quake; . . . . II. xi. 22. 5
To move and *tremble* as it were aghast, ... III. ix. 15. 6
hart Did lively seeme to *tremble,* . . . . III. xi. 30. 8
everie word did *tremble* as she spake, ... IV. i. 5. 6
Her hart did leape, and all her hart-strings *tremble,* . . . . IV. vi. 29. 2
Began to quake and *tremble* with dismay; . . . . V. xii. 41. 5
whose tempestuous rage Makes th' heavens *tremble* . . . . VI. vi. 11. 9
Began to *tremble* every limbe and vaine; . . . . VI. vii. 22. 2
every foote did *tremble* which did tread, ... VI. viii. 31. 8
made the wood to *tremble* at the noyce: . . . . VI. viii. 46. 4
That makes both heaven and earth to *tremble* at her pride. . . VII. vi. 3. 9
Trembled. a noyse alluring sleepe soft *trembled,* . . . . . . *Bel.*[2] xii. 7
The knight him selfe even *trembled* at his fall, ... I. xi. 55. 1
His hand that *trembled* as one terrifyde; . . . . II. vii. 6. 7
trembled as them passing they beheld: . . . . II. xii. 40. 7
trembled like a lambe fled from the pray; . . . . III. vii. 36. 6
trembled underneath his mighty hand, ... VI. xii. 36. 8
Trembling. joyed oft to chace the *trembling* Pricket, ... *S.C.* D. 27
walls of Carthage vow'd, *Trembling* their forces, ... *Gn.* 616
The *trembling* streames, which wont in chanels cleare . . . *T.M.* 25
doth his *trembling* Muse but lowly flie, ... *Col.* 420
their greene leaves, *trembling* with every blast, ... I. ii. 28. 5
with *trembling* cheare Her up he tooke, ... I. ii. 45. 6
seizing cruell clawes on *trembling* brest, ... I. iii. 19. 8
Trembling through hasty rage when choler in him sweld. . . I. iv. 33. 9
to the *trembling* chord Can tune their timely voices . . . . I. v. 3. 6
The *trembling* ghosts with sad amazed mood, ... I. v. 32. 5
There find the virgin, . . . *trembling* yet . . . . I. vi. 9. 5
Such fearefull fitt assaid her *trembling* hart, ... I. vi. 11. 1
His *trembling* hand he would him force to put Upon the Lyon . I. vi. 24. 3
wynd . . . through the *trembling* leaves full gently playes, . . I. vii. 3. 3
With foltring tong, and *trembling* everie vaine, ... I. vii. 24. 7
trembling feare did feel in every vaine: . . . . I. viii. 4. 2
earth, . . . *trembling* with strange feare . . . . I. viii. 8. 9
trembling horrour ran through every joynt, ... I. viii. 39. 3
trembling every joynt, did inly quake, ... I. ix. 24. 8
trembling horror did his conscience daunt, ... I. ix. 49. 3
He smote his courser in the *trembling* flanck, ... II. iii. 6. 5
Each *trembling* leafe and whistling wind they heare, ... II. iii. 20. 4
do glaunce and glide Upon the *trembling* wave, ... II. v. 2. 5
trembling Feare still to and fro did fly, ... II. vii. 22. 6
With *trembling* hand his troubled pulse gan try; . . . . . . II. viii. 9. 6
Long *trembling* still he stoode: . . . . II. viii. 46. 5
waytes for death with dread and *trembling* aw; . . . . II. viii. 50. 4
trembling terror did his hart apall; . . . . II. xi. 39. 2
So ryv'd her *trembling* hart, and wicked end did make. . . . II. xi. 47. 9
Upon the waves to spred her *trembling* light, ... II. xii. 2. 5
The *trembling* groves, the christall running by, ... II. xii. 58. 7
Th' Angelicall soft *trembling* voyces . . . . II. xii. 71. 3
hideous horror and sad *trembling* sownd, ... III. i. 14. 6
panting softe, and *trembling* every joynt, ... III. i. 60. 1
every *trembling* joynt and every vaine . . . . III. ii. 34. 3

Trembling—*Continued.*
Trembling with horror, as that did foresee III. v. 24. 3
rubd his temples and each *trembling* vaine; III. v. 31. 7
in foote doth beare A *trembling* Culver, III. vii. 39. 2
trembling yet through feare the Squire bespake: III. vii. 47. 1
trembling stood, and yielded him the pray; III. viii. 13. 2
Then tooke he him, yet *trembling* sith of late, III. viii. 36. 4
Trembling through feare least down he fallen should, III. xi. 34. 8
on every syde They *trembling* stood, III. xi. 40. 7
At that wide orifice her *trembling* hart Was drawne forth, III. xii. 21. 1
Trembling in heart, and looking pale and wan, IV. ii. 49. 4
Whilest *trembling* horrour did his sense assayle, IV. vi. 22. 8
trembling every joynt through former feare; IV. vii. 34. 2
that Squire, yet *trembling* every vaine; IV. viii. 41. 3
The *trembling* foule dismayd with dreadfull sight V. ii. 54. 3
With *trembling* joynts, as he for terrour shooke; V. xi. 28. 8
In his right hand he held a *trembling* dart, VI. ii. 6. 4
Lyke captives *trembling* at the victors sight. *Am.* i. 4
Least, *trembling*, it his workmanship should spill; *Am.* xvii. 7
I in hand her yet halfe *trembling* tooke, *Am.* lxvii. 11
The pipe, the tabor, and the *trembling* Croud, *Epith.* 131
With *trembling* steps, and humble reverence, *Epith.* 210
Rest not till they have pierst the *trembling* harts, *H.L.* 123
My *trembling* hart in her eternall chaine, *H.B.* 276
much lesse my *trembling* verse . . . can hope it to reherse. *H.H.L.* 41
Throw thy selfe downe, with *trembling* innocence, *H.H.B.* 143
through the *trembling* ayre Sweete-breathing Zephyrus did softly play *Proth.* 1

Trenchant. with his *trenchand* blade her boldly kept I. i. 17. 3
fercely tooke his *trenchand* blade in hand, I. xi. 24. 1
with his *trenchant* blade . . . he shared quite away, V. v. 9. 1

Trent. bounteous *Trent,* that in him selfe enseames IV. xi. 35. 8

Trentals. Their Diriges, their *Trentals,* and their shrifts, *Hub.* 453

Trespass. Bidding his beades all day for his *trespas,* I. i. 30. 7
The *trespass* still doth live, albee the person dye.' II. viii. 28. 9
As if no *trespas* ever had beene donne: III. x. 51. 6
Amends may for the *trespasse* soone be made, V. viii. 14. 2
whose tongue was for his *trespasse* vyle Nayld to a post, V. ix. 25. 2
How ever they through treason doe *trespasse.* VI. vii. 27. 6

Trespassed. Not unto him that never hath *trespast,* *Gn.* 365
The faults which life hath *trespassed* before. *Gn.* 448
almost had against you *trespassed* this day.' IV. vi. 3. 9

Tress. wrapt in fetters of a golden *tresse,* V. viii. 1. 7

Tressed. He, plongd in payne, his *tressed* locks dooth teare. *S.C.* Ap. 12

Tresses. The faire Medina, with her *tresses* torne II. ii. 27. 2
heare Was trimly woven and in *tresses* wrought, II. ix. 19. 7
Her golden lockes, that late in *tresses* bright Embreaded were III. vi. 18. 6
nor her golden haire Into their comely *tresses* dewly drest, VI. xii. 15. 4
her golden *tresses* She doth attyre under a net of gold; *Am.* xxxvii. 1
the fayre *tresses* of your golden hayre,) *Am.* lxxiii. 3

Trevisan. Sir *Trevisan* flies from Despeyre, I. ix. Arg.
'I, that hight *Trevisan,*' (quoth he) I. ix. 32. 5
The wofull tale that *Trevisan* had told, I. ix. 37. 2

Trial. *Triall* to make of his endevourment; *Hub.* 298
with-hold, till further *tryall* made.' I. i. 12. 6
'I wote,' (quoth he) 'whom *tryall* late did teach, I. ix. 31. 3
Which whenas trew by *tryall* he out fond, I. xii. 3. 5
wary was the knight By *tryall* of his former harmes II. i. 4. 7
after death the *tryall* is to come, II. i. 59. 3
Another her out boastes, and all for *tryall* strips. II. v. 33. 9
of his puissaunce *tryall* made extreeme: II. viii. 14. 4
To make more *triall* of his hardiment, III. i. 2. 8
by long *triall* of the inward griefe III. i. 54. 3
well can witnesse who by *tryall* it does prove. III. ii. 51. 9
through late *triall,* on that wealthy Strond III. iv. 29. 2
well I wote by *triall,* III. vi. 29. 6
Till *triall* doe more certeine truth bewray.' III. viii. 50. 5
Till time the *tryall* of her truth expyred; IV. i. 54. 5
Yet was it in due *triall* but a wandring weft. IV. ii. 4. 9
But Paridell, that had too late a *tryall* IV. ii. 6. 1
All which who list by *tryall* to assay IV. ix. 3. 1
That I too true by *triall* have approved; IV. x. 1. 6
Excludes from fairest hope withouten further *triall.* IV. x. 17. 9
due *tryall* lend Of all the rest; V. iii. 8. 1
Of both their beauties to make paragone And *triall,* V. iii. 24. 4
Whereof to make due *tryall,* V. iii. 33. 1
Which well I prove, as shall appeare by *triall,* V. iv. 15. 6
That battells utmost *triall* to adventer. V. v. 5. 5
Thereof make *tryall* in my greatest need. V. v. 29. 6
The *tryall* of a great and weightie case, V. ix. 36. 7
for *triall* of her right V. xi. 39. 4
in the *triall* of true curtesie, VI. Pr. 5. 1
they mote make *triall* of their might, VI. vii. 5. 4
For *triall* of their Titles and best Rights: VII. vi. 36. 4
Shall find by *tryall,* and confesse it then, *H.B.* 89

Triamond. Couragious Cambell, and stout *Triamond,* IV. ii. 31. 8
The second Dyamond, the youngest *Triamond.* IV. ii. 41. 9
Triamond was stout and strong alike: IV. ii. 42. 3
On horsebacke used *Triamond* to fight, IV. ii. 42. 4
Triamond to handle speare and shield, IV. ii. 42. 8
Streight entring into *Triamond* IV. iii. 22. 2
Yet nought thereof was *Triamond* adredde, IV. iii. 25. 1
Sir *Triamond* at last full faint and feeble stood. IV. iii. 28. 9
Which *Triamond* perceiving weened sure He gan to faint IV. iii. 32. 6
Triamond had Canacee to wife, IV. iii. 52. 4
Twixt Cambell and Sir *Triamond* befell, IV. iv. 2. 2
Triamond, halfe wroth to see him staid, IV. iv. 20. 5
Which doughty *Triamond* had wrought that day IV. iv. 22. 5
There where he saw the valiant *Triamond* IV. iv. 23. 6
mongst them all was not Sir *Triamond,* IV. iv. 26. 6

Triamond—*Continued.*
well knowne to be the same Which *Triamond* had worne, IV. iv. 27. 6
Whereof when newes to *Triamond* was brought IV. iv. 33. 1
did yeeld the prize To *Triamond* and Cambell IV. iv. 36. 4
But *Triamond* to Cambell it relest, IV. iv. 36. 5
Cambell it to *Triamond* transferd, IV. iv. 36. 6
Whereat full inly wroth was *Triamond,* IV. iv. 45. 1
The second was to *Triamond* behight, IV. v. 7. 6
Sir *Triamond* unto their sight The face . . . unheale; IV. v. 10. 6
Then was she judged *Triamond* his one; IV. v. 21. 8
But *Triamond* lov'd Canacee, and other none. IV. v. 21. 9

Triangular. partly circulare, And part *triangulare;* II. ix. 22. 2

Tribunal. Such as the Angels weare before Gods *tribunall!* III. v. 53. 9

Tribunals. picturals Of Magistrates, of courts, of *tribunals,* II. ix. 53. 5

Tributary. this land was *tributarie* made T' ambitious Rome, II. x. 49. 6

Tribute. of them both did foy and *tribute* raise, II. x. 41. 4
their *tribute* he refusd to let be payd. II. x. 50. 9
And *tribute* eke withall, as to his Soveraine. IV. iii. 27. 9
owe vassallage To him, . . . and *tribute* pay: IV. xi. 29. 4
tribute backe repay as to their King: VI. Pr. 7. 5

Trick. *See* **School trick.**

Trickle. honny . . . which doth softly *trickle* from the hive, *Col.* 597
the deawy humour shed Did *tricle* downe her haire, IV. xi. 46. 8

Trickled. Smal drops of gory bloud that *trickled* down the same. I. ii. 30. 9
an yvie girland . . . From under which fast *trickled* downe the sweat. I. iv. 22. 4
well, From which fast *trickled* forth a silver flood, I. xi. 29. 4
there *trickled* softly downe A gentle streame, II. v. 30. 1
Deawed with silver drops that *trickled* downe alway. IV. xi. 25. 9

Trickling. Like April shoure so stremes the *trickling* teares *S.C.* Ap. 7
the trees their *trickling* teares to shedde. *S.C.* Jun. 96
trickling stremis Adowne the dales of Kent, *S.C.* Jul. 81
Whose streames my *tricklinge* teares did ofte augment. *S.C.* Au. 156
forth powring His *trickling* streames, *Gn.* 228
trickling streame from high rock tumbling downe, I. i. 41. 2
adowne his coursers side The red bloud *trickling* I. ii. 14. 9
In which yett *trickling* blood, I. xi. 13. 3
A *trickling* streame of Balme, most soveraine I. xi. 48. 2
Few *trickling* teares she softly forth let fall, III. vii. 9. 2

Tricks. many pleasant *trickes* before her show, V. ix. 13. 6

Trie. eke her feete, those feete of silver *trye,* V. ii. 26. 7

Tried. *See* **Well-tried.**
Content who lives with *tryed* state *S.C.* S. 70
tryed time yet taught me greater thinges; *S.C.* D. 85
manie waies they sought, and manie *tryed,* *Hub.* 225
'Who hath the world not *tride,* . . . may wander wide: *Hub.* 403
thou, that hast not *tride,* *Hub.* 895
Much greater than the rude report they *tride,* *D.* 146
Whose utmost hardnesse I before had *tryde,* *Col.* 673
Till I that treachours art have heard and *tryde;* I. ix. 32. 2
Which when in vaine he *tryde* with struggeling, I. xi. 39. 5
he shortly shall againe be *tryde,* II. i. 20. 1
like herselfe, unstayned hath beene *tryde.* II. ii. 9. 9
the golden metall, ready to be *tryde.* II. vii. 35. 9
Too truely *tryde* in his extremest state. II. x. 31. 3
There she with them a cruell batteill *tryde,* II. x. 55. 1
all knights that ever batteill *tryde,* II. xii. 32. 5
Tryde all her arts and all her sleights thence out to wrest. II. xii. 81. 9
whylome full dernly *tryde.* III. i. 14. 4
Tryde often to the scath of many Deare, III. iv. 24. 2
Having him trew and faithfull ever *tride,* III. v. 12. 8
Yet *tried* did adore. III. ix. 25. 6
he so ofte had *tryde* The powre thereof, III. ix. 29. 7
goodly well advaunce that goodly well was *tryde.'* III. xii. 39. 9
she *tride* Unto his last confusion to bring, IV. i. 30. 6
then it shall be *tried,* if ye will, IV. iv. 12. 8
had in many a battell oft bene *tride,* IV. iv. 17. 8
to their *tryed* swords them selves betake; IV. iv. 29. 2
many other Ladies likewise *tride* IV. v. 17. 6
pittie is to heare the perils which she *tride.* IV. vii. 2. 9
toile which she had *tride* In salvage chase, IV. viii. 9. 3
having shortly *tride* The traines of wit, IV. viii. 31. 7
sooth is said, and *tride* in each degree, IV. ix. 27. 8
To rip up wrong that battell once hath *tried;* IV. ix. 37. 3
All twenty *tride* in warres experience long; IV. x. 7. 7
often *tride* In greater perils IV. x. 18. 1
Trew Jonathan and David trustie *tryde* IV. x. 27. 2
Can hardly but by Sacrament be *tride,* V. i. 25. 2
both in armes well traind, and throughly *tride:* V. ii. 17. 4
'Well then,' sayd Artegall, 'let it be *tride:* V. ii. 45. 4
put two wrongs together to be *tride,* V. ii. 48. 3
A noble Knight, and *tride* in hard assayes; V. iii. 5. 2
if it were not Florimell so *tride,* V. iii. 17. 7
Queene of Amazons, in armes well *tride* V. iv. 33. 5
he, that had like tempests often *tride,* V. v. 6. 6
Till thou have *tride* againe, and tempted him more neare. V. v. 48. 9
Well *tride* in all thy Ladies troubles V. xi. 38. 3
tryde all waies how each mote entrance make VI. i. 37. 2
evermore contrary hath bene *tryde,* VI. iii. 2. 1
Having oft seene it *tryde* as he did teach: VI. iv. 37. 3
Then he was *tride* unto his Lady bright; VI. viii. 33. 7
For to betray my Right before I have it *tride.* VII. vi. 34. 9
Was never in this world ought worthy *tride,* *Am.* v. 13
your powre, which I too well have *tride.* *Am.* xxv. 8
ye have theyr guylefull traynes well *tryde:* *Am.* xlvii. 2

Tries. who *tries,* shall find no lesse.' I. xii. 34. 9

Trifles. Bearing a trusse of *tryfles* *S.C.* May 239

Trilled. like pure Orient perles adowne it *trild;* II. xii. 78. 5

Trim. Gay chapelets of flowers and gyrlonds *trim.* *As.* 42
A little Gondelay, bedecked *trim* II. vi. 2. 7

Trim 895 Trophy

Trim—*Continued.*
fragrant violets, and Paunces *trim;* . . . . III. i. 36. 8
wonder was to heare their *trim* consort. . . . . III. i. 40. 6
the maskers marched forth in *trim* aray. . . . . III. xii. 6. 9
comely carriage of her count'nance *trim,* . . . . VI. ix. 9. 4
In theyr fresh garments *trim.* . . . . *Epith.* 29
all the pillours deck with girlands *trim,* . . . . *Epith.* 207
by a soveraine might Tempers so *trim,* . . . . *H.B.* 125
The which presenting all in *trim* Array, ... *Proth.* 85
Trimly. hys ditties bene so *trimly* dight, ... *S.C.* Ap. 29
trimly trodden traces, ... *S.C.* Jun. 27
How *trimly* would she trace and softly tread . . . . . . *D.* 311
others *trimly* dight Their gay attyre; . . . . I. iv. 14. 8
Her yellow golden heare Was *trimly* woven . . . . II. ix. 19. 7
Coridon could daunce, and *trimly* trace: . . . . VI. ix. 42. 4
Trinal. th' eternall majesty, In their *trinall* triplicities on hye: I. xii. 39. 5
There they in their *trinall* triplicities . . . . *H.H.L.* 64
Trip. She can *trippe* it very well. . . . . *S.C.* Au. 64
Triple. flame, Mounting like waves with *triple* point . . . . *Bel.*[1] ix. 2
flame . . . Waving aloft with *triple* point . . . . *Bel.*[2] xi. 2
He gave her . . . *triple* crowne set on her head full hye, . . I. vii. 16. 4
to darraine A *triple* warre with *triple* enmitee, ... II. ii. 26. 3
Triplicities. th' eternall majesty, In their trinall *triplicities* on hye: . . . . I. xii. 39. 5
There they in their trinall *triplicities* . . . . *H.H.L.* 64
Tripping. *Tripping* over the dale alone, ... *S.C.* Au. 63
Triptolemus. first *Triptoleme* taught how to be sowne. . . . . *Gn.* 208
Tristram. Calidore sees young *Tristram* slay . . . . VI. ii. Arg.
'And *Tristram* is my name, ... VI. ii. 28. 1
Full glad and joyous then young *Tristram* grew; . . . . . . VI. ii. 35. 6
Chyld *Tristram* prayd that he with him might goe . . . . . VI. ii. 36. 3
Tristram, . . . Long fed his greedie eyes . . . . VI. ii. 39. 1
This knight, whom *Tristram* slew, ... VI. ii. 40. 5
that discourteous knight, (Whom *Tristram* slew) . . . . . VI. ii. 43. 2
this was he whom *Tristram* earst did slay, ... VI. ii. 45. 3
by just avengement Of noble *Tristram,* . . . . VI. iii. 17. 4
Triton. *Triton,* blowing loud his wreathed horne: . . . . . . *Col.* 245
They were all taught by *Triton* to obay . . . . III. iv. 33. 3
Triton his trompet shrill before them blew, ... IV. xi. 12. 3
Tritonian. the *Tritonian* goddesse . . . Came downe . . . . *Mui.* 265
Tritons. manie *Tritons* which their hornes did sound. . . . . *Mui.* 296
Triumph. Wherewith ye *triumph* over feeble eyes, ... *Ded. Son.* xvi. 8
At last the trumpets *Triumph* sound on hie; . . . . I. v. 15. 6
thy dredd dartes in none doe *triumph* more, ... III. iii. 3. 1
gan thereat to *triumph* without victorie. . . . . IV. i. 50. 9
of your gotten spoyle their owne *triumph* to make.' . . . . IV. ii. 24. 9
For goodly *triumph* and great jollyment, ... IV. xi. 12. 4
they did addeeme the prise Of all that *Tryumph.* . . . . . V. iii. 15. 3
Thereat she gan to *triumph* with great boast, ... V. v. 10. 1
With *tryumph* entertayn'd and glorifyde, ... V. viii. 51. 3
tryumph in their blood whom she to death did dryve. . . . V. ix. 41. 9
reare My Trophee, and from all the *triumph* beare? . . . . VII. vii. 56. 5
her great *triumph,* which my skill exceeds, ... *Am.* xxix. 11
make thy *triumph* over death and sin; . . . . *Am.* lxviii. 2
Bring home the *triumph* of our victory: . . . . *Epith.* 243
For to receive the *triumph* of your glorie, ... *H.L.* 34
The whyles thou doest *triumph* in their decay; . . . . . . *H.L.* 137
Then Io, *tryumph!* . . . . *H.B.* 267
Triumphal. The double front of a *triumphall* Arke: . . . . . *Bel.* iv. 4
thighes, whose glorie did appeare Like a *triumphal* Arch, . . VI. viii. 42. 8
rich *triumphall* Arcks which they did raise, ... *Com. Son.* iii. 7
Triumphant. streame, . . . sprong from *triumphant* seat. . . . *Rev.* iv. 13
in *triumphant* chayre was set on hie, ... *Bel.*[2] iv. 7
Triumphant Arcks, spyres, neighbours to the skie, ... *Ro.* vii. 5
with you bring *triumphant* Mart, ... I. Pr. 3. 7
Then gan *triumphant* Trompets sownd on hye, ... I. xii. 4. 1
Did shew her selfe in great *triumphant* joy, ... II. iii. 31. 8
their proud girlonds of *tryumphant* bayes . . . . III. xi. 52. 7
She gan rejoyce and shew *triumphant* chere, ... V. xi. 33. 2
meriting a meere *triumphant* seate. *Com.Son.*iii.12
thy *triumphant* name then would I raise . . . . *H.L.* 303
Triumphed. th' heavens in glorie *triumpht* over all: . . . . . *Ro.* xii. 8
Triumphed oft against her enemis; . . . . II. x. 56. 7
Shee *triumphed* on death, in enemies despight. . . . . . . II. x. 56. 9
her princely gest, With which she earst *tryumphed,* . . . . III. ii. 27. 4
Thus I *triumphed* long in lovers paine, ... VI. viii. 21. 6
Triumphest. *triumphest* in the piteous spoile Of these poore folk, ... VI. vi. 25. 3
Triumpheth. that most Heroicke spirit, . . . Which now *triumpheth,* . . . . *Ded. Son.* xv. 3
Triumphing. on hie upon *triumphing* chaire, ... *Bel.*[1] iv. 7
As in their Syres new love both *triumphing:* . . . . *Mui.* 294
Triumphing in great joy and jolity, ... IV. iv. 28. 2
Triumph's. The Romane *triumphs* glorie to beholde, ... *Ro.* xiv. 12
That fillest England with thy *triumphes* fame. . . . . . . *Proth.* 151
Triumphs. By which she *triumphes* over yre and pride, ... II. ii. 31. 6
For Love his loftie *triumphes* to engrave, ... II. iii. 24. 3
triumphes of Phlegraean Jove, ... II. x. 3. 4
set his *triumphes* hye, ... III. vi. 49. 7
The wondrous *triumphs* of my great god-hed: . . . . *H.L.* 18
Troad. *See* **Trode.**
Trod. *See* **Trodden, Trode.**
is *trodde* in the durt Of cattell, ... *S.C.* F. 235
ryder . . . Would have cast downe, and *trodd* in durty myre, . I. viii. 17. 6
Trodden. *See* **Trod.**
With Heydeguyes, and trimly *trodden* traces, ... *S.C.* Jun. 27
at length she found the *troden* gras, ... I. iii. 10. 4
their . . . bayes *Troden* in dust with fury insolent, ... III. xi. 52. 8
Despisd and *troden* downe of all that over-ran. . . . . . . IV. viii. 32. 9
ever *troden* was of footings trace: . . . . IV. x. 21. 5
Trodden—*Continued.*
is behinde me *trodden* downe of Scorne, ... VI. viii. 24. 8
Trode. *See* **Trod.**
The *trode* is not so tickle: . . . . *S.C.* Jul. 14
They never sette foote in that same *troade,* . . . . *S.C.* S. 92
We have not yet the tract of anie *troad,* . . . . *Hub.* 406
The fierce Spumador, *trode* them downe like docks; . . . . II. xi. 19. 7
wholy waste and void of peoples *trode,* . . . . III. ix. 49. 7
the heard . . . *trode* downe in the durt, ... III. x. 52. 4
He . . . nycely *trode,* as thornes lay in his way, ... III. xii. 10. 6
The other backe retired and contrarie *trode.* . . . . IV. i. 28. 9
all in gore They *trode,* . . . . V. vii. 31. 8
Where foot of living creature never *trode,* . . . . VI. iv. 13. 8
Upon the ground with feeble feete he *trode,* . . . . VI. vi. 19. 5
far from all peoples *troad,* . . . . VI. x. 5. 3
Trojan. *See* **Troyan.**
erst descended from the *Trojan* bloud. . . . . *Bel.*[1] v. 8
Bett back the furie of the *Trojan* fyre. . . . . *Gn.* 496
Hector, the glorie of the *Trojan* field: . . . . *Gn.* 516
out of the auncient *Trojan* blood, ... III. iii. 22. 6
The royall seed, the antique *Trojan* blood, ... III. iii. 42. 8
made a lake Of Greekish blood so ofte in *Trojan* plaine; . . III. iv. 2. 6
Which they far off beheld from *Trojan* toures, ... III. ix. 35. 5
Gathred the *Trojan* reliques sav'd from flame, ... III. ix. 36. 8
Trojan warres and Priams citie sackt, ... III. ix. 38. 2
'The *Trojan* Brute did first that citie fownd, ... III. ix. 46. 1
of the antique *Trojan* stocke there grew Another plant, . . . III. ix. 47. 6
she saw aloft appeare The *Trojane* flames . . . . III. x. 12. 8
the *Trojane* boy so fayre . . . . III. xi. 34. 4
stout Aeneas in the *Trojane* fyre, ... *H.L.* 232
Trojans. that great warre, which *Trojanes* oft behelde? . . . *Gn.* 498
many noble Greekes and *Trojans* made to bleed. . . . . . . II. vii. 55. 9
noble Britons sprong from *Trojans* bold, ... III. ix. 38. 8
Greeks and *Trojans* which therein did die; . . . . IV. xi. 20. 7
Trojans'. With all the warlike youth of *Trojans* bloud, ... III. ix. 43. 6
Out of the *Trojans* scattered ofspring, ... III. ix. 44. 7
Trompart. *Trompart,* fitt man for Braggadochio, ... II. iii. 10. 1
coming close to *Trompart* . . . . II. iii. 12. 1
Trompart stoutly stayd . . . . II. iii. 21. 5
Such when as hartlesse *Trompart* her did vew, ... II. iii. 32. 1
Trompart forth stept . . . . II. iii. 34. 7
turning said to *Trompart;* . . . . II. iii. 43. 7
(said *Trompart*) 'lett her pas at will, ... II. iii. 44. 1
having her from *Trompart* lightly reard, ... III. viii. 19. 3
with his servant *Trompart* hoverd there, ... III. x. 23. 2
Trompart, ronning hastely, him did stay, ... III. x. 23. 6
(said *Trompart*) 'take good hart, ... III. x. 26. 1
Trompart, that his maistres humor knew . . . . III. x. 30. 1
Trompart, lowly to the grownd inclinde, ... III. x. 30. 7
'Ah! but,' (said crafty *Trompart*) 'weete ye well, ... III. x. 40. 2
Said *Trompart;* 'You, . . . stay in safetie behynd: . . . . III. x. 41. 4
after him eke fearefull *Trompart* spedd: . . . . III. x. 43. 8
Trompart bace Had it purloyned . . . . III. x. 54. 3
Whom *Trompart* had in keeping there beside, ... V. iii. 17. 2
Trompart's. On *Tromparts* steed her mounted without stay, . . III. viii. 13. 4
Troncheon, -s. *See* **Truncheon, -s.**
Tronck, Tronk. *See* **Trunk.**
Troop. a barbarous *troupe* of clownish fone . . . . *Bel.*[2] v. 10
A *troupe* of Satyres in the place did rout, ... *Bel.*[2] xii. 12
To put in preace emong the learned *troupe:* . . . . *S.C.* O. 70
that faire *troupe* of woodie Goddesses . . . . *Gn.* 182
A *troupe* of Faunes and Satyres . . . . I. vi. 7. 7
all the *troupe* of light-foot Naiades . . . . I. vi. 18. 3
The first *troupe* was a monstrous rablement . . . . II. xi. 8. 1
Gainst which the second *troupe* assignment makes; . . . . . II. xi. 10. 2
Of that third *troupe* was cruelly assayd; . . . . II. xi. 11. 2
the fift *troupe,* most horrible of hew . . . . II. xi. 13. 1
when all that *troupe* of warlike wooers Assembled were . . . IV. ii. 38. 1
There he in *troupe* found all that warlike crew, ... IV. iv. 33. 8
a *troupe* of Knights They saw . . . . IV. ix. 20. 1
he plainely then descride To be a *troupe* of women, ... V. iv. 21. 8
Dispersed all their *troupe* incontinent, ... V. iv. 24. 7
now he hath this *troupe* of villains sent . . . . V. xi. 51. 1
So forth they rode together all in *troupe* . . . . VI. v. 32. 1
There he a *troupe* of Ladies dauncing found . . . . VI. x. 10. 7
Troops. I feare I have troubled your *troupes* to longe: . . . . *S.C.* Ap. 149
murdred *troupes* upon great heapes to lay. . . . . *Gn.* 400
who shall lead Your wandring *troupes,* . . . . *D.* 317
he of them great *troups* did soone entrap. . . . . *As.* 100
Least that his toyle should of their *troups* be brust. . . . . *As.* 106
Great *troupes* of people traveild thetherward . . . . I. iv. 3. 1
the martiall *troupes* thou doest infest, ... I. xi. 6. 3
Broke their rude *troupes,* and orders did confownd, ... II. ix. 15. 7
Them in twelve *troupes* their Captein did dispart, ... II. xi. 6. 1
these twelve *troupes* with dreadfull puissaunce . . . . . . II. xi. 14. 1
The rest themselves in *troupes* did else dispose, ... IV. iv. 14. 7
did amongst the *troupes* so tyrannize, ... IV. iv. 42. 2
with their *troupes* did far asunder cast; . . . . V. iv. 43. 8
Whose presence all their *troups* so much encombred, ... V. v. 19. 5
Did set upon those *troupes* with all his powre and might. . . V. xi. 57. 9
Maugre the might of all those *troupes* in vew, ... V. xii. 5. 7
with raging brond divide Their thickest *troups,* . . . . . . VI. xi. 48. 9
Trophies. There many auncient *Trophees* were erect, ... *Bel.*[1] v. 5
clad with reliques of some *Trophees* olde, ... *Ro.* xxviii. 2
all his dayes, like dolorous *Trophees,* . . . . *T.M.* 160
famous warriors . . . Used *Trophees* to erect . . . . *Am.* lxix. 2
Trophy. She raisde a *Trophee* over all the worlde. . . . . . . *Bel.*[1] xi. 8
many an auncient *Trophee* was addrest, ... *Bel.*[2] v. 5
Over all the world did raise a *Trophee* hie; . . . . *Bel.*[2] xv. 8
A *trophee* of his glittering spoyles and treasure, ... *Gn.* 127

Trophy—*Continued.*
reare a *trophee* for devouring death, . . . *Ti.* 52
This simple *trophe* of her great conquest.'— . . . *Col.* 951
I aloft should reare My *Trophee,* . . . VII. vii. 56. 5
What *trophee* then shall I most fit devize, . . . *Am.* lxix. 5
Trot. refused To take me up . . . But forst to *trot* on foot, . . VI. ii. 22. 5
Troth. *See* **Truth.**
'None but that saw' . . . 'would weene for *troth,* . . . II. i. 11. 3
could not colour yet so well the *troth,* . . . II. ii. 34. 4
yet is my *trouth* yplight, . . . II. vii. 50. 6
Soone shalt thou see, and then beleeve for *troth,* . . . II. viii. 22. 3
Trotting. all the way from *trotting* hard to spare; . . . IV. viii. 37. 8
a *trotting* Stalion get An ambling Colt, . . . VI. iii. 1. 6
Trouble. Tydings of warre and worldly *trouble* tell? . . . I. i. 30. 8
mighty charmes to *trouble* sleepy minds. . . . I. i. 36. 9
Care . . . Who oft is wont to *trouble* gentle Sleepe. . . . I. i. 40. 6
'that should her *trouble* sore; . . . I. x. 16. 8
trouble dying soules tranquilitee; . . . II. i. 47. 8
From needlesse *trouble* of renewing fight . . . II. v. 25. 2
To *trouble* my still seate, . . . II. vii. 7. 9
great *trouble* in the kingdome grew, . . . II. x. 54. 2
endured sore Sore *trouble* of an hainous enimy, . . . III. vi. 53. 6
At last with irkesom *trouble* she abrayd; . . . III. x. 50. 1
To be most fit to *trouble* noble knights . . . IV. i. 19. 6
breedes Tumultuous *trouble,* and contentious jarre, . . . IV. i. 25. 8
Fild with false rumors and seditious *trouble,* . . . IV. i. 28. 3
heaping stormes of *trouble* on them daily more? . . . IV. vii. 1. 9
him had sought through *trouble* and long strife, . . . IV. xii. 16. 8
rather bent To peace then needlesse *trouble* to constraine, . . V. vi. 19. 7
him to *trouble* she it thought unfit, . . . VI. ii. 47. 3
Troubled. Tossing huge tempests through the *troubled* skie, . *Ro.* xvi. 6
Toward the sea turning my *troubled* eye, . . . *Van.* v. 1
I feare I have *troubled* your troupes to longe: . . . *S.C.* Ap. 149
They sought my *troubled* sense how to deceave . . . *Hub.* 23
Exceedingly they *troubled* were in thought, . . . *Hub.* 312
troubled kingdome of wilde beasts behelde, . . . *Hub.* 1231
like to *troubled* puddles have them made. . . . *T.M.* 276
Whose wordes recording in my *troubled* braine, . . . *Ti.* 481
Much was I *troubled* in my heavie spright, . . . *Ti.* 575
The stormie passion of his *troubled* brest, . . . *D.* 192
As one . . . whose dryer braine Is tost with *troubled* sights . I. i. 42. 8
with their sturre they *troubled* all the traine; . . . I. iv. 40. 4
sparkes . . . *troubled* once, into huge flames will grow; . . I. ix. 8. 2
troubled blood through his pale face was seene . . . I. ix. 51. 5
Through the dull billowes thicke as *troubled* mire, . . . II. vi. 20. 7
Troubled with terrour and unquiet jarre, . . . II. vi. 37. 8
With trembling hand his *troubled* pulse gan try; . . . II. viii. 9. 6
seemeth by your *troubled* cheare, . . . II. ix. 42. 1
to the *troubled* chamber all in armes did throng. . . . III. i. 62. 9
within her *troubled* mind . . . III. iii. 5. 1
shall spred his banner brave Over the *troubled* South, . . . III. iii. 30. 4
in thy *troubled* bowels raignes and rageth ryfe. . . . III. iv. 8. 9
To calme the tempest of his *troubled* thought: . . . IV. ii. 3. 2
Such as the *troubled* Theatres oftimes annoyes. . . . IV. iii. 37. 9
establish in the *troubled* mynd. . . . IV. iii. 43. 6
Hath *troubled* both your mindes with idle thought, . . . IV. vi. 30. 7
in his *troubled* sight Shew'd change of better cheare: . . . IV. vi. 38. 2
she in her mind Was *troubled* sore, . . . IV. xii. 21. 2
inly *troubled* was the truth to learne. . . . IV. xii. 24. 5
rather gan in *troubled* mind devize . . . IV. xii. 28. 8
He much was *troubled,* ne wist what to doo: . . . V. ii. 52. 3
she did her *troubled* mynd molest, . . . V. vi. 4. 5
Yet found no easement in her *troubled* wits, . . . V. vi. 15. 3
As being *troubled* with that stormy stowre; . . . V. vii. 15. 4
it much appald her *troubled* spright: . . . V. viii. 45. 5
gathered unto her her *troubled* wit, . . . V. viii. 45. 8
The which they *troubled* had with great turmoyle. . . . V. xi. 65. 5
tydings . . . Of their arrival: wherewith *troubled* sore . . . V. xii. 6. 6
And *troubled* had their quiet loves delight: . . . VI. iii. 21. 5
From his devotion streight he *troubled* was; . . . VI. v. 36. 3
Like *troubled* ghost, did dreadfully appeare, . . . VI. vi. 32. 8
He much was *troubled* at that straungers guize, . . . VI. ix. 38. 3
Much was the Lady *troubled* at that speach, . . . VI. xii. 18. 1
Was *troubled* much at their so strange affright, . . . VII. vi. 15. 7
Were *troubled,* and amongst themselves at ods, . . . VII. vi. 23. 3
Disguysing diversly my *troubled* wits. . . . *Am.* liv. 4
O how doth it torment His *troubled* mynd . . . *H.L.* 253
Troubler. hard necessity' . . . 'the *troubler* of my happy peace, I. xii. 19. 2
were it not that Time their *troubler* is, . . . III. vi. 41. 1
Troublers. Lovers of Lordship, and *troublers* of states. . . . *S.C.* May 123
Troubles. Free from all *troubles* and from worldly toyle, . . . *Gn.* 151
in her many *troubles* did most pleasure take. . . . I. ii. 9. 9
a faythfull mate Of her sad *troubles* and misfortunes hard: . I. iii. 9. 4
By traynes into new *troubles* to have toste: . . . I. iii. 24. 7
Blaming of Fortune, which such *troubles* threw, . . . I. vi. 31. 5
For whose deare sake so many *troubles* her did tosse. . . . I. vii. 27. 9
After long *troubles* and unmeet upbrayes . . . III. vi. 50. 3
Well tride in all thy Ladies *troubles* . . . V. xi. 38. 3
In seas of *troubles* and of toylesome paine; . . . VI. ix. 31. 6
Troublesome. her to see should be but *troublesome.'* . . . I. x. 16. 7
Such was betwixt these two the *troublesome* uprore. . . . V. ii. 15. 9
Troubling. Thinking to hide the depth by *troubling* of the flood. IV. vi. 29. 9
With many idle stoups her *troubling* still: . . . V. v. 15. 7
Troublous. mortall men tossed by *troublous* fate . . . *Pet.*[2] vii. 3
Where no such *troublous* tydes han us assayde; . . . *S.C.* O. 117
Their *troublous* strife they stinted by and by, . . . *Hub.* 1092
With *troublous* noyse did dull their daintie eares. . . . *T.M.* 30
use to paint in rimes the *troublous* state . . . *T.M.* 381
oft would dare to tempt the *troublous* winde. . . . *Mui.* 48
There came unto my minde a *troublous* thought, . . . *D.* 29

Troublous—*Continued.*
all with *troublous* feare Gathred . . . about her body . . . I. i. 25. 3
nor peoples *troublous* cryes, . . . Might there be heard; . . I. i. 41. 6
That *troublous* dreame gan freshly tosse his braine . . . I. i. 55. 6
after *troublous* sights And dreames, . . . I. ii. 4. 2
Whom broad awake she findes, in *troublous* fitt, . . . I. iv. 45. 1
Bulles, . . . fill the fieldes with *troublous* bellowing: . . . I. viii. 11. 8
As a tall ship tossed in *troublous* seas, . . . II. ii. 24. 1
his flowing toung and *troublous* spright . . . II. iii. 4. 6
Some *troublous* uprore or contentious fray, . . . II. iv. 3. 3
troublous warre proclame: . . . II. v. 1. 7
ledd with the *troublous* sowne: . . . II. vi. 47. 7
the *troublous* stormes that tosse The private state, . . . II. vii. 14. 1
That breathed strife and *troublous* enmitie. . . . II. viii. 10. 5
when they had that *troublous* rout disperst, . . . II. ix. 17. 1
This is the Port of rest from *troublous* toyle, . . . II. xii. 32. 8
with so *troublous* terror they were all dismayd. . . . III. i. 63. 9
To stirre up strife, and *troublous* contecke broch: . . . III. i. 64. 5
Instead of sleepe thou sendest *troublous* feares . . . III. iv. 57. 5
whilest all things in *troublous* uprore were, . . . III. x. 16. 1
All suddenly they heard a *troublous* noyes, . . . IV. iii. 37. 6
Which *troublous* stirre when Satyrane aviz'd, . . . IV. v. 25. 1
High Swale, unquiet Nide, and *troublous* Skell; . . . IV. xi. 37. 7
Which *troublous* stirre when Artegall perceived, . . . V. iii. 30. 6
tossed in her *troublous* minde . . . V. iv. 47. 4
The *troublous* passion of my pensive mind, . . . V. vii. 19. 2
'That Knight shall all the *troublous* stormes asswage . . . V. vii. 23. 1
She much was eased in her *troublous* thought, . . . V. vii. 24. 2
She was confused in her *troublous* thought; . . . V. vii. 25. 3
All full of people making *troublous* din . . . V. ix. 23. 3
In *troublous* wits, and mutinous uprore: . . . V. ix. 48. 6
have her drawne to all this *troublous* strife, . . . V. xi. 41. 3
To stint all strife and *troublous* enmitie, . . . V. xi. 54. 3
tost with *troublous* fit Of a proud love, . . . *Am.* xxxiii. 11
Troupe, -s. *See* **Troop,** *etc.*
Trouth. *See* **Troth.**
Trouts. The silver scaly *trouts* doe tend full well, . . . *Epith.* 57
(Those *trouts* and pikes all others doo excell;) . . . *Epith.* 59
Trow. (But now I *trowe* can better good,) . . . *S.C.* Mar. 56
I *trow,* All Kent can rightly boaste: . . . *S.C.* Jul. 43
they bene hale enough, I *trowe,* . . . *S.C.* Jul. 107
Him true in heart and trustie to you *trow.* . . . *Ti.* 203
henceforth by this daies ensample *trow,* . . . II. v. 13. 7
she is the fairest wight alive, I *trow,'* . . . III. v. 5. 9
so much is more then just to *trow.* . . . V. ii. 34. 9
Trowis. *See* **Drowes.**
Troy. as at *Troy* most dastards of the Greekes . . . *Ro.* xiv. 9
The faire Ixione captiv'd from *Troy;* . . . *Gn.* 490
He compast *Troy* thrice with his bodie dedd. . . . *Gn.* 528
To thee, O *Troy!* paid penaunce for thy fall; . . . *Gn.* 551
To succour the weake state of sad afflicted *Troy.* . . . II. iii. 31. 9
that proud towre of *Troy,* . . . II. ix. 45. 8
'*Troy,* that art now nought but an idle name, . . . III. ix. 33. 1
That warre was kindled which did *Troy* inflame, . . . III. ix. 34. 2
long before the ten yeares siege of *Troy,* . . . III. ix. 36. 2
Troy againe out of her dust was reard . . . III. ix. 44. 3
Both first and second *Troy* shall dare to equalise. . . . III. ix. 44. 9
Matchable ether to that ympe of *Troy,* . . . III. xii. 7. 3
Troyan. *See* **Trojan.**
the *Troyan* Duke with Turnus fought. . . . *Bel.*[1] vii. 8
whilome from the *Troyan* blood did flow. . . . *Bel.*[2] v. 8
the *Troyan* prince spilt Turnus blood . . . *Bel.*[2] ix. 8
to sheild Achilles life from fate of *Troyan* field. . . . *Mui.* 64
Troynovant. Ne *Troynovant,* though elder sister shee, . . . *Ti.* 102
The ruin'd wals he did reaedifye Of *Troynovant,* . . . II. x. 46. 5
Troynovant was built of old Troyes ashes cold. . . . III. ix. 38. 9
'It *Troynovant* is hight, . . . III. ix. 45. 1
'His worke great *Troynovant,* . . . III. ix. 51. 1
That was to weet the famous *Troynovant,* . . . IV. xi. 28. 8
Troy's. Troynovant was built of old *Troyes* ashes cold. . . . III. ix. 38. 9
Truce. frends to termes of gentle *truce* entize, . . . III. ii. 24. 5
To graunt unto those warriours *truce* a whyle; . . . IV. vi. 25. 7
of a *truce* to treat In milder tearmes, . . . IV. ix. 35. 6
he Talus to them sent . . . *truce* for to desire. . . . V. ii. 52. 9
signe of *truce* did make: . . . V. xii. 8. 2
with her hart-thrilling eies To make a *truce,* . . . *Am.* xii. 2
True. if that my Grandsire me sayd be *true,* . . . *S.C.* May 268
A shepheard *trewe,* yet not so *true* . . . *S.C.* Jul. 163
Adieu, good Hobbinoll, that was so *true,* . . . *S.C.* D. 155
As whome he knew to him both fast and *true.* . . . *Hub.* 1081
yet to prove more *true* he meant to see, . . . *Hub.* 1277
true wisedome to sustaine, . . . *T.M.* 80
I that in *true* Tragedies am skild, . . . *T.M.* 165
The *true* Pandora of all heavenly graces, . . . *T.M.* 578
Him *true* in heart and trustie to you trow. . . . *Ti.* 203
Deare unto all that *true* affection beare: . . . *Ti.* 243
Robd of all right and *true* nobilitie. . . . *Ti.* 294
it *true* Sea, and *true* Bull, ye would weene. . . . *Mui.* 280
seldome seene, forejudgment proveth *true.* . . . *Mui.* 320
To make the image of *true* heavinesse: . . . *D.* 329
'And ye, *true* Lovers! whom desastrous chaunce . . . *D.* 505
pittying this paire of lovers *trew,* . . . *As.* 182
like the circlet of a Turtle *true,* . . . *Col.* 340
She is the paterne of *true* womanhead, . . . *Col.* 512
She is the braunch of *true* nobilitie, . . . *Col.* 530
thy *true* love and loyaltie I deeme. . . . *Col.* 575
'*True* (answered he) . . . *Col.* 620
to *true* loves he may us evermore Preferre, . . . *Col.* 817
Ne mongst *true* lovers they shall place inherit, . . . *Col.* 893
To thee are all *true* lovers greatly bound. . . . *Col.* 899

True—*Continued.*
Succeeding them in *true* nobility: . . . . . *Ded. Son.* iii. 9
All goodly bountie and *true* honour sits. . . . . *Ded. Son.* v. 12
In which *trew* honor yee may fashioned see, ... *Ded. Son.* x. 10
to draw the semblant *trew* Of beauties Queene, ... *Ded.Son.*xvii.5
that *true* glorious type of thine, ... I. Pr. 4. 7
The Patrone of *true* Holinesse . . . . . I. i. Arg.
Right faithfull *true* he was in deede and word, ... I. i. 2. 7
with usage sly He taught to imitate that Lady *trew,* . . . I. i. 46. 8
like that virgin *true* which for her knight him took. . . . I. i. 49. 9
The *true* Saint George, was wandred far away, ... I. ii. 12. 2
The false Duessa, . . . knew well all was *true.* . . . . I. ii. 44. 3
Her up he tooke, (too simple and too *trew*) . . . . I. ii. 45. 7
Though *true* as touch, though daughter of a king, ... I. iii. 2. 5
true is, that *true* love hath no powre To looken backe; . . . I. iii. 30. 7
so misfeigning her *true* knight to bee: . . . . I. iii. 40. 4
Plaine, faithfull, *true,* and enimy of shame, ... I. vi. 20. 7
Teaching the Satyres, . . . *Trew* sacred lore, ... I. vi. 30. 9
On gentle Dame, so hurtlesse and so *trew:* . . . . I. vi. 31. 7
heard abroad of that her champion *trew,* . . . . I. vi. 36. 5
thou his errour shalt, I hope, now proven *trew.'* . . . . I. vi. 42. 9
innocents *trew,* Which there were slaine as sheepe . . . . I. viii. 35. 6
Altare, . . . On which *trew* Christians blood was often spilt, I. viii. 36. 3
O! welcome thou, that doest of death bring tydings *trew.'* . . I. viii. 38. 9
whether dreames delude, or *true* it were, ... I. ix. 14. 5
True loves are often sown, but seldom grow on grownd.' . . . I. ix. 16. 9
love establish each to other *trew,* . . . . I. ix. 18. 7
spectacle, approving *trew* The wofull tale . . . . I. ix. 37. 1
in *true* ballaunce thou wilt weigh thy state; . . . . I. ix. 45. 2
Well knowing *trew* all that he did reherse, ... I. ix. 48. 4
But simple, *trew,* and eke unfained sweet, ... I. x. 7. 8
thus recover'd by wise Patience And *trew* Repentaunce, . . . I. x. 29. 2
'Most *trew,'* then said the holy aged man; . . . . I. x. 59. 1
looked forth, to weet if *trew* indeed Those tydinges were, . . I. xii. 3. 3
Which whenas *trew* by tryall he out fond, ... I. xii. 3. 5
Or false or *trew,* or living or else dead, ... I. xii. 28. 2
The Amazon huge river, now found *trew?* . . . . II. Pr. 2. 8
A right good knight, and *trew* of word ywis: . . . . II. i. 19. 5
Braggadocchio, . . . is made the scorne Of knighthood *trew;* II. iii. Arg.
The scorne of knighthood and *trew* chevalrye, ... II. iii. 10. 5
Trew be thy words, and worthy of thy praise, ... II. iii. 38. 2
fruit, With which Acontius got his lover *trew,* . . . . II. vii. 55. 2
my *trew* liegeman yield thy selfe for ay, ... II. viii. 51. 7
when he heard, and saw the tokens *trew,* . . . . II. viii. 55. 1
the *trew* lively-head Of that most glorious visage . . . . II. ix. 3. 3
Well weeting *trew* what she had rashly told; . . . . II. ix. 39. 2
hight Phantastes by his nature *trew;* . . . . II. ix. 52. 2
true it is that, when the oyle is spent, ... II. x. 30. 1
Yet *true* it is, that long before that day . . . . II. x. 53. 6
On firme foundation of *true* bountyhed: . . . . II. xii. 1. 5
surely deeme it to bee yvie *trew:* . . . . II. xii. 61. 5
Who can it doe more lively, or more *trew,* . . . . III. Pr. 4. 3
trew love most of might, ... III. i. 29. 8
that sweete fit that doth *true* beautie love, ... III. iii. 1. 7
indew The salvage minds with skill of just and *trew:* . . . III. iii. 45. 5
Too *trew* the famous Marinell it fownd, ... III. iv. 29. 1
vew Of hunter swifte and sent of howndes *trew.* . . . . III. iv. 46. 5
honour of *trew* Ladies, ... III. v. 10. 6
Having him *trew* and faithfull ever tride, ... III. v. 12. 8
Her nourced had in *trew* Nobility: . . . . III. v. 32. 5
In all chaste vertue and *true* bounti-hed, ... III. vi. 3. 8
their *trew* loves without suspition tell abrode. . . . . III. vi. 42. 9
his *trew* love faire Psyche with him playes, ... III. vi. 50. 1
yfostered to bee And trained up in *trew* feminitee: . . . . III. vi. 51. 5
To be th' ensample of *true* love alone, ... III. vi. 52. 4
to reward my trusty *true* intent, ... III. vii. 55. 8
Hard is to teach an old horse amble *trew;* . . . . III. viii. 26. 3
To be his Leman and his Lady *trew:* . . . . III. viii. 40. 5
how may I weene it *trew,* . . . . III. viii. 48. 3
as *trew* in love as Turtle to her make. . . . . III. xi. 2. 9
Great liking unto many, but *true* love to feowe. . . . . III. xii. 13. 9
fiercely running to that Lady *trew,* . . . . III. xii. 32. 4
crowne *true* lovers with immortall blis, ... IV. Pr. 2. 8
all bountie naturall And treasures of *true* love . . . . IV. Pr. 4. 4
well she wist, as *true* it was indeed, ... IV. i. 6. 1
So could she forge all colours, save the *trew.* . . . . IV. i. 18. 5
all *true* lovers with dishonor blotten: . . . . IV. i. 51. 4
true friendships bond Doth their long strife agree. . . . . IV. iii. Arg.
Profest to her *true* friendship and affection sweet. . . . . IV. iii. 50. 9
the vertue of chast love, And wivehood *true,* . . . . IV. v. 3. 2
thought he had the *trew* And very Florimell, ... IV. v. 13. 7
then if it were *trew:* . . . . IV. v. 15. 6
ne unto whom I more *true* love did beare: . . . . IV. vi. 35. 9
True love and faithfull friendship, ... IV. vi. 46. 9
now prov'd *true* by this . . . . IV. viii. 1. 1
messengers of his *true* meaning and intent. . . . . IV. viii. 13. 9
these Squires *true* friendship more did sway . . . . IV. ix. 3. 3
'*True* he it said, what ever man it sayd, ... IV. x. 1. 1
That I too *true* by triall have approved; . . . . IV. x. 1. 6
Delightfull bowres, to solace lovers *trew;* . . . . IV. x. 24. 7
Ne ever ought but of their *true* loves talkt, ... IV. x. 25. 8
lovers lincked in *true* harts consent, ... IV. x. 26. 4
Trew Jonathan and David trustie tryde . . . . IV. x. 27. 2
Mother of blessed Peace and Friendship *trew;* . . . . IV. x. 34. 2
in them bore *true* lovers vowes entire: . . . . IV. x. 38. 5
few Could weenen whether they were false or *trew:* . . . . IV. xi. 27. 5
if old sawes prove *true* . . . . IV. xi. 35. 2
Menippe *true* in trust, ... IV. xi. 51. 8
Whether old Proteus *true* or false had sayd, ... IV. xii. 28. 4
The Champion of *true* Justice, Artegall: . . . . V. i. 3. 2

True—*Continued.*
doe it declare unto me *trew.'* . . . . V. i. 16. 2
True love despiseth shame, ... V. i. 27. 9
The right or wrong, the false or else the *trew?'* . . . . V. ii. 44. 6
First in one ballance set the *true* aside.' . . . . V. ii. 45. 5
True vertue to advance, ... V. iii. 3. 9
The more to be *true* Florimell he did surmize. . . . . V. iii. 18. 9
Like the *true* saint beside the image set, ... V. iii. 24. 2
So ought all faytours that *true* knighthood shame, ... V. iii. 38. 6
True Justice unto people to divide, ... V. iv. 1. 2
'Full *true* it is . . . . V. iv. 15. 2
'Right *true:* but faulty men use . . . To attribute their folly V. iv. 28. 1
In signe of *true* subjection to her powre, ... V. v. 18. 2
Serving proud Radigund with *true* subjection, ... V. v. 26. 2
token *true* to old Eumenias, ... V. v. 34. 3
Untill his owne *true* love his freedome gayned: . . . . V. v. 57. 8
in th' Adamantine mould Of his *true* hart . . . . V. vi. 2. 7
As if before she had not counted *trew:* . . . . V. vi. 5. 5
doth *true* justice deale To his inferiour Gods, ... V. vii. 1. 6
With fayned colours shading a *true* case; . . . . V. vii. 2. 7
Jealous suspect as *true* untruely drad: . . . . V. vii. 38. 7
did *true* Justice deale, ... V. vii. 42. 7
The *true* guide of his way and vertuous government. . . . . V. viii. 3. 9
To weete if it were *true* as she had told; . . . . V. viii. 12. 2
To prove her surname *true,* that she imposed has. . . . . V. viii. 49. 9
'*True* is that I at first was dubbed knight . . . . V. xi. 53. 1
Knights ought be *true,* and truth is one in all: . . . . V. xi. 56. 8
As their *true* Liege and Princesse naturall; . . . . V. xii. 24. 8
His studie was *true* Justice how to deale, ... V. xii. 26. 2
in the triall of *true* curtesie, ... VI. Pr. 5. 1
Good Knights and Ladies *true,* . . . . VI. i. 7. 9
swore to him *true* fealtie for aye. . . . . VI. i. 44. 4
True is, that whilome that Good Poet sayd, ... VI. iii. 1. 1
To be his Timias, his owne *true* Squire; . . . . VI. v. 23. 2
The knights beleev'd that all he sayd was *trew;* . . . . VI. vii. 5. 1
It was his owne *true* groome, the gentle Squire, ... VI. viii. 27. 6
The good Sir Calepine, her owne *true* Knight, ... VI. viii. 33. 2
Simple and *true,* from covert malice free; . . . . VI. x. 24. 5
To wend with him, and be his conduct *trew* . . . . VI. xi. 35. 3
Which too-too *true* that lands in-dwellers since have found. VII. vi. 55. 9
That well may seemen *true;* . . . . VII. vii. 7. 1
'Which to approven *true,* as I have told, ... VII. vii. 27. 1
'Right *true* it is, ... VII. vii. 48. 1
Is checkt and changed from his nature *trew,* . . . . VII. vii. 54. 8
judge then, (O thou greatest goddesse *trew*) . . . . VII. vii. 56. 6
when my pen would write her titles *true,* . . . . *Am.* iii. 11
her deep wit, that *true* harts thought can spel, ... *Am.* xliii. 13
Most lively lyke behold your semblant *trew.* . . . . *Am.* xlv. 4
true love doth tye . . . . *Am.* lxv. 5
when I hope to see theyr *trew* object, ... *Am.* lxxviii. 11
the *trew* fayre, that is the gentle wit, ... *Am.* lxxix. 3
That is *true* beautie: . . . . *Am.* lxxix. 9
from whom al *true* And perfect beauty did at first proceed: . *Am.* lxxix. 11
In my *true* love did stirre up coles of yre; . . . . *Am.* lxxxv. 8
let stil Silence *trew* night-watches keepe, ... *Epith.* 353
the type of *true* Nobility; . . . . *Com. Son.* ii. 2
gentle Love, that loiall is and *trew,* . . . . *H.B.* 176
To worke ech others joy and *true* content, ... *H.B.* 200
With pure regard and spotlesse *true* intent, ... *H.B.* 212
The heavenly prayses of *true* love to sing. . . . . *H.H.L.* 14
Eternall spring of grace and wisedome *trew,* . . . . *H.H.L.* 44
mercy . . . Unto us taught, and to approve it *trew,* . . . . *H.H.L.* 212
the Primrose *trew,* . . . . *Proth.* 32
True-love-wise. of lillyes and of roses, Bound *truelove wize,* . *Epith.* 44
True-meaning. That had such might over *true meaning* harts; I. ii. 9. 5
Truer. Yet never Turtle *truer* to his make, ... VI. viii. 33. 6
True-seeming. two . . . fittest for to forge *true-seeming* lyes: I. i. 38. 7
so *true-seeming* grace It carried, ... I. v. 27. 4
Hath writ my record in *true-seeming* sort. . . . . *Ti.* 168
Truest. she the *truest* shepheards hart made bleede, ... *S.C.* Jun. 111
he is one the *truest* knight alive, ... I. iii. 37. 6
The justest man and *trewest* in his daies, ... II. x. 42. 2
For I love one, the *truest* one on grownd, ... III. i. 24. 6
The justest man alive and *truest* did appeare. . . . . V. vii. 2. 9
'Haile, good Sir Sergis, *truest* Knight alive, ... V. xi. 38. 2
My *truest* turtle dove; . . . . *Epith.* 24
Truly. Morpheus Most *truely* doth appeare . . . . *Bel.*[1] xi. 2
Morpheus . . . *trulie* doth unto our eyes appeare, ... *Bel.*[2] xv. 2
Truly, Piers, thou art beside thy wit, ... *S.C.* May 306
those that *truely* mene; . . . . *S.C.* S. 33
Other sayne, but how *truely* I note, ... *S.C.* S. 110
Too *truely* tryde in his extremest state. . . . . II. x. 31. 3
For powre is the right hand of Justice *truely* hight. . . . V. iv. 1. 9
truly pourtray'd, as they ought to be, ... *Com. Son.* ii. 6
Jones, that *truely* it translated. . . . . *Com. Son.* ii. 14
Trump. To register, and sound in *trump* of gold, ... *T.M.* 98
So brave a *Trompe,* thy noble acts to sound! . . . . *Ti.* 434
she might immortalize In her shril *tromp,* . . . . *Ded. Son.* xiv. 4
Soone as thy dreadfull *trompe* begins to sownd, ... I. xi. 6. 6
that fame may it resound In her eternall *tromp,* . . . . II. iii. 38. 9
The hoars Night-raven, *trump* of dolefull drere; . . . . II. xii. 36. 5
That fame in *tromp* of gold eternally displayes. . . . . III. iii. 3. 9
Where I with sound of *trompe* will also rest a whyle. . . . IV. iv. 48. 9
Bold Radigund with sound of *trumpe* on hight, ... V. iv. 45. 4
I may in *trump* of fame blaze over-all. . . . . *Am.* xxix. 12
Fame in her shrill *trump* shal thunder, ... *Am.* lxxxiv. 13
Trumpet. golden *Trompet* of eternitie, ... *T.M.* 458
A shrilling *trompett* sownded from on hye, ... I. v. 6. 1
Which fame of her shrill *trompet* worthy reedes; . . . . II. vii. 2. 7
She heard a shrilling *Trompet* sound alowd, ... III. xii. 1. 5

Trumpet—*Continued.*
That ever shrilling *trumpet* did resound; . . . IV. ii. 32. 4
A *trompet* blew; they both together met . . . IV. iii. 6. 5
Triton his *trompet* shrill before them blew, . . . IV. xi. 12. 3
sounding loud a *Trumpet* from the wall, . . . V. iv. 50. 3
caused streight a *Trumpet* loud to shrill . . . V. vii. 27. 1
His *trompet* shrill hath . . . sounded, . . . *Am.* xix. 2
A gentle Bee, with his loud *trumpet* murm'ring, . . . *Epig.* iv. 3
Trumpet's. *trumpets* sound to cease did them compell: . . . IV. iv. 25. 8
trumpets sound did warne them all to rest; . . . IV. iv. 36. 2
To weeten what that *trumpets* sounding ment: . . . V. iv. 50. 7
Trumpets. For *trumpets* sterne to chaunge mine Oaten reeds, . I. Pr. 1. 4
At last the *trumpets* Triumph sound on hie; . . . I. v. 15. 6
Then gan triumphant *Trompets* sownd on hye, . . . I. xii. 4. 1
With shaumes, and *trompets,* and with Clarions sweet; . . . I. xii. 13. 2
Their murmuring small *trompetts* sownden wide, . . . II. ix. 16. 3
shrill *trompets* lowd did bray, . . . III. xii. 6. 6
shril *trompets* and loud clarions sweetly playd. . . . IV. iii. 5. 9
the *trompets* freshly blew. . . . IV. iii. 14. 9
The *trumpets* sounded, and they all arose. . . . IV. iii. 51. 2
shrilling *trompets* loudly gan to bray, . . . IV. iv. 48. 5
The *trompets* sound, then all together ronne. . . . V. iii. 6. 4
at the last the *trompets* did proclame . . . V. iii. 7. 7
Then did the *trompets* sound, . . . V. iii. 13. 6
the *trompets* shrill Don Braggadochios name resounded . . . V. iii. 15. 3
Playing on shaumes and *trumpets,* . . . V. v. 4. 5
The *Trumpets* sounded, and the field began; . . . V. v. 6. 1
The *Trumpets* sound, and they together run . . . V. vii. 29. 1
The *trompets* sound, and they together goe . . . V. xii. 17. 1
Trumpets'. no dreadfull *trompets* sound; . . . V. Pr. 9. 5
Truncheon. tother did upon his *troncheon* smyte, . . . II. viii. 38. 5
with his *troncheon* he so rudely stroke Cymochles twise, . . . II. viii. 39. 8
in his hand nought but the *troncheon* left; . . . IV. iii. 12. 2
Truncheons. in their hands their idle *troncheons* held, . . . IV. vii. 18. 8
Trunk. I heard the *tronck* (*tronke*[1]) to grone; . . . *Bel.* v. 12
on her *trunke,* all rotten and unsound, . . . *Ro.* xxviii. 7
The mightie *trunck,* halfe rent with ragged rift, . . . I. viii. 22. 8
Being diffused through the senceless *tronck,* . . . II. ii. 4. 8
The headlesse *tronke,* as heedlesse of that stower, Stood still awhile, . . . IV. iii. 20. 7
Were much amaz'd the headlesse *tronke* to see Stand up . . . IV. iii. 21. 2
That headlesse tyrants *tronke* he reard from ground, . . . IV. ix. 4. 6
Trunked. streames of blood out of the *truncked* stock Forth gushed, . . . I. viii. 10. 8
The *truncked* beast fast bleeding did him fowly dight. . . . II. v. 4. 9
Truss. Bearing a *trusse* of tryfles . . . *S.C.* May 239
To *trusse* the pray too heavy for his flight; . . . I. xi. 19. 8
up they gan their mery pypes to *trusse,* . . . III. x. 46. 1
Trussing. *trussing* me, as Eagle doth his pray, . . . IV. vii. 18. 6
Trust. By more and more she gan to *trust* hir wings, . . . *Bel.*[1] vi. 3
That did so much in his owne greatnesse *trust.* . . . *Van.* vi. 12
Little bootes all the welth and the *trust,* . . . *S.C.* May 88
never give *trust* to his trecheree: . . . *S.C.* May 222
Or care to overlooke, or *trust* to gather, . . . *Hub.* 279
Ye may me *trust* as your owne ghostly father.' . . . *Hub.* 280
Trust me, least he my Loove happely chaunce to beholde. . *Tetrasticon* 4
'O vile worlds *trust!* . . . *Ti.* 456
Nor *trust* the guile of fortunes blandishment; . . . *Col.* 671
Late learnd what harme to hasty *trust* ensu'th. . . . I. vi. 12. 4
more to mighty hands then rightfull cause doth *trust.* . . . II. ii. 29. 9
Trust me, shal find no greater enimy . . . II. v. 1. 3
trust unto his strength and manhood meare, . . . II. xi. 34. 3
unto Psyche with great *trust* and care Committed her, . . . III. vi. 51. 3
her maine strength, in which she most doth *trust,* . . . III. vii. 50. 5
if she should her *trust* in me repose. . . . III. vii. 58. 9
Defil'd the pledge committed to thy *trust?* . . . IV. i. 53. 5
Unto whose *trust* the charge thereof was lent: . . . IV. x. 12. 2
Menippe true in *trust,* . . . IV. xi. 51. 8
fayld the *trust* which she in him had plast, . . . IV. xii. 23. 3
The charge of Justice given was in *trust,* . . . V. iv. 2. 2
Her nearest handmayd, whom she most did *trust,* . . . V. v. 29. 2
'Clarinda, whom of all I *trust* alive, . . . V. v. 29. 4
turn'd the *trust* which was in her affyde, . . . V. v. 53. 6
No faith so firme, no *trust* can be so strong, . . . V. xii. 1. 8
A courteous Knight and full of faithfull *trust;* . . . VI. iii. 13. 2
Trust not the treason of those smyling lookes, . . . *Am.* xlvii. 1
His seate is Truth, to which the faithfull *trust,* . . . *H.H.B.* 159
Trusted. More in his causes truth he *trusted* then in might. . . V. viii. 30. 9
Trustily. To whom may I more *trustely* complaine . . . *Hub.* 55
Thus having her restored *trustily,* . . . VI. iii. 19. 6
Trusting. fayleth, *trusting* on his owne assurance; . . . *Am.* lviii. 10
Trustless. this tickle *trustles* state Of vaine worlds glorie, . . *Pet.*[2] vii. 1
'O! *trustlesse* state of earthly things, . . . *S.C.* N. 153
'O! *trustlesse* state of miserable men, . . . *Ti.* 197
She him condemn'd as *trustlesse* and untrew; . . . V. vi. 5. 2
Trusts. who most *trustes* in arme of fleshly might, . . . I. ix. 11. 6
Trusty. That flocks grand Captaine and most *trustie* guide . . *Gn.* 268
to me, my *trustie* friend, aread Thy councell: . . . *Hub.* 81
Him true in heart and *trustie* to you trow. . . . *Ti.* 203
to my *trustie* eare Committed . . . *D.* 69
His *trusty* sword he cald to his last aid, . . . I. xi. 42. 2
Eftsoone she said; 'Ah! gentle *trustie* Squyre, . . . II. i. 17. 1
that blacke Palmer, his most *trusty* guide, . . . II. iv. 2. 4
Guyon having lost his *trustie* guyde, . . . II. vii. 2. 1
Upon his voyage with his *trustie* guyde, . . . II. xi. 5. 2
for his *trusty* servaunts doth so strongly fight.' . . . III. i. 29. 9
to reward my *trusty* true intent, . . . III. vii. 55. 8
With her own *trusty* Squire, . . . III. xii. 44. 3
this *trustie* squire with proud disdaine . . . IV. ix. 3. 7
That *trusty* Squire he wisely well did move . . . IV. ix. 15. 3

Trusty—*Continued.*
Trew Jonathan and David *trustie* tryde . . . IV. x. 27. 2
She called forth to her a *trusty* mayd, . . . V. iv. 48. 1
The *trustie* Mayd, conceiving her intent, . . . V. v. 35. 1
snatching neare his syde His *trustie* sword, . . . VI. vii. 25. 4
The *trustie* damzell bearing it abrode . . . VI. xii. 7. 1
Whenas a storme hath dimd her *trusty* guyde, . . . *Am.* xxxiv. 3
Truth. for a *truth* great Babylon is fallen. . . . *Rev.* ii. 14
But shall I tel thee a tale of *truth,* . . . *S.C.* F. 91
To mock her selfe, and *Truth* to imitate, . . . *T.M.* 206
His love, his *truth,* his glorie, and his might, . . . *T.M.* 513
Came downe to prove the *truth,* . . . *Mui.* 267
auncient *truth* confirm'd with credence old. . . . *Col.* 103
single *Truth* and simple Honestie . . . *Col.* 727
gan himselfe advise To . . . tempt her faigned *truth.* . . . I. i. 50. 6
doubtfull words made that redoubted knight Suspect her *truth:* I. i. 53. 6
Enchaunter parts The Redcrosse Knight from *Truth:* . . . I. ii. Arg.
Forsaken *Truth* long seekes her love, . . . I. iii. Arg.
O, how can . . . simple *truth* subdue avenging wrong! . . . I. iii. 6. 5
Una, his deare dreed, Her *truth* had staynd with treason . . . I. vi. 2. 4
committ Her single person to their barbarous *truth;* . . . I. vi. 12. 2
her gentle wit she plyes To teach them *truth,* . . . I. vi. 19. 6
truth, whose shape she well can faine, . . . I. vii. 1. 5
stedfast *truth* acquite him out of all. . . . I. viii. 1. 4
time in her just term the *truth* to light should bring.' . . . I. ix. 5. 9
truth is strong her rightfull cause to plead, . . . I. xii. 28. 7
unto her *truth* Did earnestly committ, . . . II. iii. 2. 2
wisht me stay till I more *truth* should fynd. . . . II. iv. 22. 9
Till that the *truth* thereof I did out wrest; . . . II. iv. 23. 5
the *truth* to let me understand. . . . II. iv. 23. 9
loyall *truth* to treason doest incline: . . . II. vii. 13. 3
with glad thankes, and unreproved *truth,* . . . II. vii. 16. 3
Joseph of Arimathy, Who . . . preacht the *truth;* . . . II. x. 53. 9
see plaine, That *truth* is strong, . . . III. i. 29. 8
Truth is his daughter; . . . III. iv. 59. 7
in her countenaunce Dwelt simple *truth* . . . III. vii. 59. 6
Till triall doe more certeine *truth* bewray.' . . . III. viii. 50. 5
makes him alway Suspect her *truth,* . . . III. ix. 5. 4
He closely nearer crept the *truth* to weet: . . . III. x. 22. 6
Till time the tryall of her *truth* expyred; . . . IV. i. 54. 5
Gainst all that *truth* or vertue doe professe; . . . IV. viii. 24. 7
In simple *truth* and blamelesse chastitie, . . . IV. viii. 30. 3
inly troubled was the *truth* to learne. . . . IV. xii. 24. 5
the *truth* discover plaine, . . . IV. xii. 30. 7
simple *Truth* did rayne, . . . V. Pr. 3. 9
Mongst wicked men, in whom no *truth* she found, . . . V. i. 11. 3
With which he thresht out falshood, and did *truth* unfould. . V. i. 12. 9
by sleight the *truth* thereout to straine; . . . V. i. 24. 9
by no meanes the false will with the *truth* be wayd. . . . V. ii. 45. 9
judge, whether with *truth* or falshood they agree. . . . V. ii. 47. 9
set the *truth* and set the right aside, . . . V. ii. 48. 1
truth is one, and right is ever one.' . . . V. ii. 48. 6
More in his causes *truth* he trusted then in might. . . . V. viii. 30. 9
But by their *trueth* and by the causes right: . . . V. xi. 17. 5
To temporize is not from *truth* to swerve, . . . V. xi. 56. 3
Knights ought be true, and *truth* is one in all: . . . V. xi. 56. 8
loved simple *truth* and stedfast honesty. . . . VI. i. 3. 9
I will the *truth* discover . . . VI. ii. 15. 9
Faith to his knight, and *truth* to Ladies all, . . . VI. ii. 35. 2
that he the *truth* of all by him mote learne. . . . VI. x. 18. 9
Witnesse, ye Heavens, the *truth* of all that I have teld!' . . . VII. vi. 27. 9
hostages doe offer for my *truth;* . . . *Am.* xi. 2
simple *truth,* and mutuall good-will, . . . *Am.* lxv. 11
love is Lord of *truth* and loialtie, . . . *H.L.* 176
some sparkling light Of thine eternall *Truth,* . . . *H.H.B.* 11
His *truth,* his love, his wisedome, and his blis, . . . *H.H.B.* 110
His seate is *Truth,* to which the faithfull trust, . . . *H.H.B.* 159
For from th' Eternall *Truth* it doth proceed, . . . *H.H.B.* 174
Truth's. Yet in my *truthes* assurance I rest fixed fast.' . . . V. v. 38. 9
Try. *See* **Trie.**
himselfe will a daw *trie;* . . . *Hub.* 913
who so els his bounteous minde did *trie,* . . . *Ti.* 233
Which she with Neptune did for Athens *trie:* . . . *Mui.* 306
doth her tender plumes as yet but *trie* . . . *Col.* 422
as a sacred pledge His cause in combat . . . to *try:* . . . I. iv. 43. 2
O! never, Sir, desire to *try* his guilefull traine.' . . . I. ix. 31. 9
With trembling hand his troubled pulse gan *try;* . . . II. viii. 9. 6
with great honour many batteills *try;* . . . III. iii. 31. 4
knightly worth which he too late did *try,* . . . III. ix. 25. 5
Rather let *try* extremities of chaunce, . . . III. xi. 24. 8
Agreed to travell, and their fortunes *try.* . . . IV. iv. 6. 4
dread Untride is lesse then when thou shalt it *try:* . . . IV. vii. 11. 6
She staid not th' utmost end thereof to *try,* . . . IV. vii. 21. 2
weld his naked sword, and *try* the edges keene. . . . IV. vii. 45. 9
He answered that he would *try* it streight; . . . V. ii. 44. 7
rather had to lose then *trie* in armes his right. . . . V. iii. 31. 9
By law of armes there neede ones right to *trie,* . . . V. iii. 32. 2
with dint of sword . . . their rights to *try,* . . . V. iv. 6. 2
Through hard adventures deedes of armes to *try,* . . . V. iv. 29. 2
I will not rest till I her might doe *trie,* . . . V. iv. 34. 3
in single fight To *try* her Fortune, . . . V. iv. 47. 7
try in equall field whether hath greater might. . . . V. iv. 48. 9
try if thou by faire entreatie can Move Radigund? . . . V. v. 40. 3
to *trie* the right Of fayre Irenaes cause . . . V. xii. 8. 8
Thinking the utmost of their force to *trie,* . . . VI. i. 38. 3
To lend him day his better right to *trie,* . . . VI. ii. 19. 4
every way did *try,* but all in vaine; . . . VI. iv. 7. 2
To practise games and maisteries to *try,* . . . VI. ix. 43. 2
Thou mayest well *trie* if they will ever swerve, . . . *H.L.* 165
Trye. *See* **Trie.**

Tryphon. sent in haste for *Tryphon,* . . . III. iv. 43. 7
For *Tryphon* of sea gods the soveraine leach is hight. . . . III. iv. 43. 9
At last to *Tryphon* she for helpe did hie, . . . IV. xi. 6. 5
(This *Tryphon* is the seagods surgeon hight,) . . . IV. xi. 6. 6
Whyleare by *Tryphon* was not throughly healed, . . . IV. xii. 22. 6
Therefore to *Tryphon* she againe doth hast, . . . IV. xii. 23. 1
Tuck. To *tucke* about her short when she did ryde, . . . III. ix. 21. 4
Tucked. Close rownd about her *tuckt* with many a plight: . . II. ix. 40. 6
short *tucked* for light motion Up to her ham; . . . V. v. 2. 6
Tug. So did these two this Knight oft *tug* and teare. . . . VI. viii. 12. 5
snatch, and byte, and rend, and *tug,* and teare; . . . VI. xi. 17. 6
Tugged. Long while he *tug'd* and strove to get it out, . . . V. xii. 22. 1
Tumble. To *tumble* into sorrow and regreet, . . . *T.M.* 304
both rebutted *tumble* on the plaine: . . . IV. iv. 18. 5
both Squire and dwarfe did *tomble* downe . . . IV. viii. 42. 8
flud His silver waves did softly *tumble* downe, . . . VI. x. 7. 2
Tumbled. storme . . . *tumbled* (*tombled*[1]) up the sea, . . . *Pet.* ii. 8
downe he *tumbled* on the durtie field, . . . I. viii. 20. 4
downe he *tombled;* as an aged tree, . . . I. viii. 22. 5
He *tombled* on an heape, and wallowd in his gore. . . . III. iv. 16. 9
lay *tombled* in the myre, Unable to arise, . . . III. vii. 45. 8
downe *tombled* dedd From top of Hemus . . . III. ix. 22. 5
on an heape were *tumbled* horse and man: . . . IV. iv. 19. 7
downe the cliffe the wretched Gyant *tumbled;* . . . V. ii. 50. 6
All in gore bloud there *tumbled* on the ground, . . . VI. iii. 27. 4
Tumbling. *tumbling* (*tombling*[1]) through the ayre . . . *Bel.* vii. 10
with his *tumbling* streames doth beare aboord . . . *Ro.* xiv. 3
trickling streame from high rock *tumbling* downe, . . . I. i. 41. 2
He, *tumbling* downe alive, . . . his mother earth did kis, . . . I. ii. 19. 5
He, *tombling* rudely downe, to ground did rush, . . . I. iii. 35. 8
the river Dee . . . His *tombling* billowes rolls with gentle rore; I. ix. 4. 8
He, *tombling* downe on ground, . . . II. viii. 45. 6
tombling low From the high mountaines, . . . II. xi. 18. 4
tombling into mischiefe unespide: . . . II. xii. 35. 4
tombling downe apace Emongst the woody hilles . . . III. iii. 8. 5
tombling downe, . . . did bite The bitter earth, . . . III. v. 22. 1
rudely *tumbling* downe under his horse-feete fell. . . . IV. iv. 30. 9
tombling backe he downe did slyde . . . IV. iv. 44. 4
found His head before him *tombling* on the ground; . . . IV. viii. 45. 5
Strong Allo *tombling* from Slewlogher steep, . . . IV. xi. 41. 8
tumbling on the strand It bit the earth . . . V. ii. 18. 5
tombling downe upon the senselesse ground . . . V. x. 33. 4
His carkasse, *tumbling* on the threshold, . . . V. x. 36. 8
The carkasse *tumbling* downe within the dore . . . VI. i. 23. 6
through the flowry Dales she *tumbling* downe . . . VII. vi. 41. 6
Tumult. seemd some perilous *tumult* to desine, . . . IV. iii. 37. 7
Tumultuous. When that *tumultuous* rage and fearfull deene . *Ded. Son.* xi. 9
many mischiefes follow cruell Wrath: . . . *tumultuous* strife, . I. iv. 35. 2
fast beside him sat *tumultuous* Strife: . . . II. vii. 21. 6
breedes *Tumultuous* trouble, and contentious jarre, . . . IV. i. 25. 8
They gan to gather in *tumultuous* rout, . . . V. ii. 51. 3
As if that there were some *tumultuous* affray. . . . V. xi. 43. 9
Tune. *tune* hir plaint to falling rivers sound, . . . *Bel.*[1] viii. 3
in accord did *tune* their voyce To the . . . sounding . . . *Pet.* iv. 6
Well couth he *tune* his pipe and frame his stile: . . . *S.C.* Ja. 10
tune my pype Unto my plaintive pleas . . . *S.C.* Jun. 41
tune your pypes as ruthful as ye may. . . . *S.C.* Au. 150
my deadly cryes 'Most ruthfully to *tune:* . . . *S.C.* Au. 175
Bardes, that . . . Can *tune* their timely voices . . . I. v. 3. 7
Tuned. *See* **Well-tuned.**
To falling rivers sound thus *tun'd* her sobs. . . . *Bel.*[2] x. 4
tuned it unto the Waters fall. . . . *S.C.* Ap. 36
Rude ditties, *tund* to shepheards Oaten reede, . . . *S.C.* D. 14
Tuneful. *tunefull* taught to beare A Bases part . . . *T.M.* 27
make a *tunefull* Diapase of pleasures, . . . *T.M.* 549
That may thy *tunefull* eare unseason quite? . . . *Ded. Son.* viii. 4
Tuneless. in hand my *tunelesse* harp I take, . . . *Am.* xliv. 9
Tunes. To the waters fall their *tunes* attemper . . . *S.C.* Jun. 8
Chaunted their sundrie *tunes* with sweete consent; . . . *Gn.* 226
Such mournfull *tunes* were never since invented. . . . *T.M.* 12
mournfull *tunes* enough my griefe to show? . . . *Mui.* 412
here no *tunes,* save sobs and grones, shall ring. . . . *D.* 14
raise His *tunes* from laies to matter of more skill. . . . *Col.* 395
In bigger *tunes* to sound your living prayse. . . . *Ded.Son.*xiii.14
to my *tunes* thy second tenor rayse, . . . I. xi. 7. 8
Their pleasaunt *tunes* they sweetly thus applyde: . . . II. xii. 32. 2
In power of herbes, and *tunes* of beasts and burds; . . . IV. ii. 35. 6
Tuning. *Tuning* our song unto a tender Muse, . . . *Gn.* 2
to the waters fall *tuning* their accents fit. . . . VI. x. 7. 9
Tunnel. long *tonnell* thence The smoke forth threw. . . . II. ix. 29. 3
Turban. hundred turrets, like a *Turribant;* . . . IV. xi. 28. 6
Turchesca. *See* **Alla Turchesca.**
Turfs. A little mount, of greene *turffs* edifide; . . . *Gn.* 660
Of few greene *turfes* an altar soone they fayned, . . . VI. viii. 44. 8
Turks. captives to redeeme . . . From *Turkes* and Sarazins, I. x. 40. 4
The scourge of *Turkes,* and plague of infidels, . . . *Com.Son.*iii.13
Turmagant. *See* **Termagant.**
Turmoil. sudden storme did so *turmoyle* the aire, . . . *Pet.* ii. 7
fond men doe all their dayes *turmoyle.* . . . *Gn.* 152
The worldes sweet In from paine and wearisome *turmoyle.* . . II. xii. 32. 9
after your long *turmoyle,* Now cease your worke, . . . III. xii. 47. *or.* 7
The which they troubled had with great *turmoyle.* . . . V. xi. 65. 5
Might them oppresse, and painefully *turmoile,* . . . VI. viii. 23. 4
with torment and *turmoyle,* To force me live, . . . *Am.* xi. 11
Turmoiled. thus *turmoild* from one to other stowre . . . IV. ix. 39. 4
Turmoiling. destinie this huge Chaos *turmoyling,* . . . *Ro.* xix. 9
Of her long travell and *turmoyling* paine; . . . VI. viii. 32. 8
Turn. shortly *turne* unto my happie rest, . . . *Pet.*[2] vii. 6
all things *turne* to their first being. . . . *Ro.* xviii. 14
Through idlenes would *turne* to civill rage, . . . *Ro.* xxiii. 7

Turn—*Continued.*
The Axes edge did oft *turne* againe, . . . *S.C.* F. 203
Turne thee to those that weld the awful crowne, . . . *S.C.* O. 40
into weeping *turne* your wanton layes. . . . *S.C.* N. 79
Theyr sondry colours *tourne.* . . . *S.C.* N. 129
(whose *turne* shall be the next?) . . . *S.C.* N. 193
let us *turne* to our first businesse. . . . *Gn.* 64
sad Eurydice . . . no more Must *turne* to life, . . . *Gn.* 434
Ne ever did her ey-sight *turne* arere, . . . *Gn.* 468
all the Rhetaean shore to ashes *turne,* . . . *Gn.* 511
from him Laertes sonne his vewe Doth *turne* aside, . . . *Gn.* 534
when her *turne* was come her tale to tell, . . . *Hub.* 36
I meane to *turne* the next leafe of the booke: . . . *Hub.* 68
Doth *turne* the name of Souldiers to abusion, . . . *Hub.* 220
never found occasion for their *tourne,* . . . *Hub.* 579
Is not a fitter for this *turne* than yee: . . . *Hub.* 1002
Eulogies *turne* into Elegies. . . . *T.M.* 372
all her blood to poysonous rancor *turne:* . . . *Mui.* 344
As if to me had chanst some evill *tourne!* . . . *D.* 266
To *turne* aside unto my Cabinet, . . . *D.* 558
began his mournfull *tourne:* . . . *As.* Interl. 221
doth *tourn* Sweet layes of love to endlesse plaints of pittie. . *Col.* 386
rather chose back to my sheep to *tourne,* . . . *Col.* 672
She . . . sought backe to *turne* againe; . . . I. i. 16. 6
it forst him . . . from her *turne* him backe. . . . I. i. 20. 5
who can *turne* the stream of destinee, . . . I. v. 25. 4
to the wood she goes, to serve her *turne,* . . . I. vi. 22. 3
he them spying gan to *turne* aside . . . I. vi. 34. 7
everie tender part does tosse and *turne:* . . . I. vii. 21. 6
He would them gazing blind, or *turne* to other hew. . . . I. vii. 35. 9
He . . . to the beast gan *turne* his enterprise, . . . I. viii. 15. 7
to the knight . . . They *turne* themselves, . . . I. x. 15. 6
Sunne to stay, Or backward *turne* his course . . . I. x. 20. 3
'then *turne* againe Backe to the world, . . . I. x. 63. 1
pray That feared chaunce from her to *turne* away: . . . I. xi. 32. 5
His owne two hands, for such a *turne* most fitt, . . . I. xii. 37. 3
So can he *turne* his earnest unto game, . . . II. i. 31. 1
Whose freedom shall thee *turne* to greatest scath! . . . II. v. 18. 4
Both slow and swift alike do serve my *tourne;* . . . II. vi. 10. 6
Soone it must *turne* to earth; . . . II. ix. 21. 9
nathemore Would they once *turne,* . . . II. xii. 15. 5
turne thy rudder hitherward awhile . . . II. xii. 32. 6
besought The Prince of grace to let him ronne that *turne.* . . III. i. 5. 2
To weet if they would *turne* backe to that place; . . . III. i. 19. 5
her *turne* to fowle repriefe And sore reproch, . . . III. iii. 5. 7
darksom night he eke could *turne* to day: . . . III. iii. 12. 4
her Maides attyre To *turne* into a massy habergeon, . . . III. iii. 57. 8
(so time their *turne* did fitt) . . . III. iii. 58. 3
'O! when will day then *turne* to me againe, . . . III. iv. 60. 1
turne his arrowes to their exercize. . . . III. vi. 23. 5
in vaine was forst to *turne* his flight, . . . III. vii. 28. 5
turne his steede about, or sure he should be dedd. . . . III. viii. 17. 9
Turne we our steeds; that both in equall tilt May meete . III. viii. 18. 3
but God *turne* the same to good sooth-say. . . . III. viii. 50. 2
to yonder castle *turne* your gate.' . . . III. viii. 51. 9
backe agayne To *turne* your course, . . . III. ix. 40. 6
with him To *turne* she doth refuse. . . . III. x. Arg.
A fit occasion for his *turne* to finde. . . . III. x. 4. 2
Ne wist he how to *turne,* nor to what place: . . . III. x. 14. 8
His expectation to despaire did *turne,* . . . III. xii. 45. 4
Ye will me now with like good *turne* repay, . . . IV. i. 40. 5
'Last *turne* was mine, well proved to my paine; . . . IV. ii. 6. 4
forth prickt his steed . . . ere he him well could *torne;* . . IV. ii. 6. 8
turne both him and her to honour, . . . IV. ii. 37. 9
mortall foes doe *turne* to faithfull frends, . . . IV. iv. 1. 2
Albee his *turne* were next; . . . IV. iv. 20. 3
ere she backe could *turne* to taken heed, . . . IV. vii. 4. 5
They from them selves gan *turne* their furious ire, . . . IV. ix. 29. 3
They *turne* to that whereof they first were made? . . . V. ii. 40. 7
So comes it now to Florimell by *tourne,* . . . V. iii. 1. 6
turne we here to this faire furrowes end . . . V. iii. 40. 6
In hope ye will not *turne* misfortune to my blame. . . . V. iv. 28. 9
none she found so fit to serve that *turne,* . . . V. vi. 6. 3
he saw the hindmost . . . force him *turne* his face; . . . V. viii. 5. 7
turne away From her unto the miscreant him selfe; . . . V. viii. 19. 5
turne we to the noble Prince, . . . V. ix. 2. 6
To *turne* her eyes from his intent away; . . . V. ix. 13. 7
Into a Foxe himselfe he first did *tourne;* . . . V. ix. 17. 1
Alreadie seemes that fortunes headlong wheele Begins to *turne,* V. x. 20. 8
forst her *turne* againe in her despight To save her selfe, . . . V. xi. 26. 7
turne we now to noble Artegall; . . . V. xi. 36. 1
'Now *turne* againe,' (Sir Artegall then sayd) . . . V. xi. 43. 1
They *turne* afresh, and oft renew their former threat. . . . V. xi. 45. 9
turne to ill the thing that well was ment; . . . V. xii. 34. 5
turne thee soone to him of whom thou art defyde.' . . . VI. i. 18. 9
And *turne* we backe to good Sir Calidore; . . . VI. ii. 40. 2
He forced was to *turne* from him and fly: . . . VI. v. 16. 7
Small was his house, and like a little cage, For his owne *turne,* . . . VI. v. 38. 4
Bidding him *turne* againe, false traytour knight, . . . VI. vii. 7. 2
turne we now backe to that Ladie free, . . . VI. vii. 27. 7
from you *turne* the love of men to hate: . . . VI. viii. 2. 6
he which way to *turne* him scarcely wist: . . . VI. viii. 13. 5
Now *turne* againe my teme, thou jolly swayne, . . . VI. ix. 1. 1
from them for to retrate . . . or backe to *turne* againe, . . . VI. ix. 31. 8
made great mone for that unhappy *turne:* . . . VI. x. 18. 6
turne we backe to Calidore where we him found. . . . VI. xi. 24. 9
fierce assailing forst him *turne* againe: . . . VI. xii. 26. 2
could the greatest wrath soone *turne* to grace, . . . VII. vi. 31. 3
my weaker wit with skill inspire, Fit for this *turne;* . . . VII. vii. 2. 3

Turn—*Continued.*
To *turne* againe unto their earthly slime: . . . VII. vii. 18. 4
So *turne* they still about, and change in restlesse wise. . . . VII. vii. 18. 9
unlesse she *turne* to thee Ere Cuckow end, . . . *Am.* xix. 13
That greater meede at last may *turne* to mee. . . . *Am.* xxv. 14
she to stones at length all frosen *turne!* . . . *Am.* xxxii. 14
all these stormes, . . . Shall *turne* to caulmes, . . . *Am.* lxii. 12
turne to nought and loose that glorious hew; . . . *Am.* lxxix. 6
Your string could soone to sadder tenor *turne,* . . . *Epith.* 9
Shall *turne* to dust, and loose their goodly light. . . . *H.B.* 98
Thou *turne* to nought, and quite confounded be. . . . *H.H.B.* 147
Turned. I saw hir bodie *turned* all to dust, . . . *Bel.*[1] vi. 12
soone her bodie *turn'd* to ashes colde. . . . *Bel.*[2] vii. 12
faultlesse fayth is *turned* to faithlesse fere, . . . *S.C.* Jun. 110
sike happy cheere is *turnd* to heavie chaunce, . . . *S.C.* N. 103
all my hoped gaine is *turnd* to scathe: . . . *S.C.* D. 100
Turn'd to a Lapwing, fowlie them upbraydes, . . . *Gn.* 405
Was *turned* now to dismall heavinesse, . . . *T.M.* 41
Was *turned* now to dreadfull uglinesse. . . . *T.M.* 42
So all is *turned* into wildernesse, . . . *T.M.* 287
All those (O pitie!) now are *turnd* to dust, . . . *Ti.* 97
Is *turnd* to smoake, that doth to nothing fade; . . . *Ti.* 123
She *turn'd* into a winged Butterflie, . . . *Mui.* 138
Let now your blisse be *turned* into bale, . . . *D.* 320
day is *turnd* to night, . . . *D.* 482
A cruell beast . . . Upon him *turnd,* . . . *As.* 117
slyding softly forth, she *turnd* as to her ease. . . . I. i. 54. 9
So left her, where she now is *turnd* to treen mould. . . . I. ii. 39. 9
hee . . . *turned* wyde Unto an hil; . . . I. iii. 26. 4
My chearefull day is *turnd* to chearelesse night, . . . I. iii. 27. 7
There was Ixion *turned* on a wheele, . . . I. v. 35. 1
Her love she *turnd* to hate, . . . I. v. 37. 7
mightie strong was *turnd* to feeble frayle. . . . I. vii. 6. 5
The light-foot Squyre her quickly *turnd* around, . . . I. viii. 25. 7
backward still was *turnd* his wrincled face: . . . I. viii. 31. 4
is the point of death now *turnd* fro mee, . . . I. ix. 26. 3
She him obayd, and *turnd* a little wyde.— . . . I. xi. 5 .5
The wrathfull beast about him *turned* light, . . . I. xi. 16. 7
So *turned* her about, and fled away apace. . . . II. iii. 42. 9
her painted bote streightway *Turnd* to the shore, . . . II. vi. 4. 7
Onely she *turnd* a pin, . . . II. vi. 5. 5
turned all her pleasaunce to a scoffing game. . . . II. vi. 6. 9
a masse of coyne he told, And *turned* upside downe, . . . II. vii. 4. 8
blush . . . And *turnd* his face away, . . . II. ix. 44. 2
in his flight the villein *turn'd* his face . . . II. xi. 26. 6
Which now him *turnd* to disavantage deare; . . . II. xi. 34. 1
She *turnd* her bote about, . . . II. xii. 16. 9
their blisse he *turn'd* to balefulnesse. . . . II. xii. 83. 5
Now *turned* into figures hideous, . . . II. xii. 85. 4
he *turned* in his wrathfull stownd, . . . III. i. 21. 7
To get a snatch when *turned* is his face. . . . III. i. 22. 5
The fayre Adonis, *turned* to a flowre; . . . III. i. 34. 5
her rownd about she from her *turnd,* . . . III. ii. 51. 1
She *turned* her contrary to the Sunne; . . . III. ii. 51. 2
Thrise she her *turnd* contrary, and returnd . . . III. ii. 51. 3
to former hew Hee *turnd* againe, . . . III. iii. 50. 9
To sorrow huge she *turnd* her former play, . . . III. iv. 30. 3
His wicked fortune that had *turnd* aslope, . . . III. iv. 52. 8
To him he *turned,* and with rigor fell Smote him . . . III. v. 23. 4
love to frenzy *turnd,* sith love is franticke hight. . . . III. vii. 20. 9
She *turnd* her selfe backe to her wicked leares; . . . III. vii. 21. 7
She *turnd,* and semblaunce of faire fight did make, . . . III. vii. 44. 8
Once having *turnd,* no more returnd his face, . . . III. viii. 18. 8
turned hath great mirth to mourning sad, . . . III. viii. 46. 3
to her he *turnd,* And left the fire; . . . III. x. 15. 1
whenas Malbecco spyed clere, He *turned* backe, . . . III. x. 23. 5
So *turned* from him wroth . . . III. x. 29. 9
As one out of a dreame . . . She *turnd* her, . . . III. x. 49. 8
then *turnd* to the heard, . . . III. x. 52. 2
Then was he *turnd* into a snowy Swan, . . . III. xi. 32. 1
For whom he *turnd* him selfe into a Steare, . . . III. xi. 42. 3
He *turnd* him selfe into a Dolphin fayre; . . . III. xi. 42. 6
He *turnd* himselfe into a fruitfull vine, . . . III. xi. 43. 8
some, that would seeme wise, their wonder *turnd* to dout. . . IV. iii. 41. 9
eft them *turned* both againe to fight: . . . IV. iii. 47. 3
with stout courage *turnd* upon them all, . . . IV. iv. 32. 2
As fayning choler which was *turn'd* to cold: . . . IV. vi. 27. 2
Whose fire were better *turn'd* to other flame; . . . IV. vi. 32. 3
turnd her face, and fled away for evermore. . . . IV. vii. 36. 9
Unto those woods he *turned* backe againe, . . . IV. vii. 38. 3
turn'd his face away, . . . IV. x. 33. 4
all that dying to it *turned* be; . . . V. ii. 37. 7
To Artegall he *turn'd* and went with him throughout. . . . V. ii. 54. 9
turn'd aside for shame to heare what he did tell. . . . V. iii. 16. 9
Of their vaine prowesse *turned* to their proper bale. . . . V. iv. 24. 9
She *turn'd* her love to hatred manifold, . . . V. iv. 30. 7
backe againe they homeward *turnd* their feete; . . . V. iv. 51. 7
With that she *turn'd* her head, . . . V. v. 30. 1
the false mayden shortly *turn'd* againe Unto the prison, . . . V. v. 51. 8
turn'd the trust which was in her affyde, . . . V. v. 53. 6
in rage she *turn'd* from him aside, . . . V. vi. 11. 7
She *turnd* her head aside, . . . V. vii. 38. 4
backe againe upon themselves they *turned,* . . . V. viii. 38. 3
to a snake againe Have *turn'd* himselfe, . . . V. ix. 19. 2
backe she would have *turnd* for great affright: . . . V. xi. 26. 5
sure he had her slaine, had she not *turnd* her way. . . . V. xi. 26. 9
After long search and chauff he *turned* backe . . . VI. ii. 21. 2
joy, Which I expected long, now *turnd* to sad annoy? . . . VI. iii. 4. 9
did . . . Temper his griefe, and *turned* it to cheare, . . . VI. iii. 6. 2
But he, . . . *Turned* his steede about . . . VI. iii. 37. 2

Turned—*Continued.*
the beast enrag'd to loose his pray Upon him *turned,* . . . VI. iv. 20. 6
they to pitty *turnd* their former rage, . . . VI. v. 30. 8
He to him *turnd* with furious intent, . . . VI. vi. 27. 2
So likewise *turnde* the Prince upon the Knight, . . . VI. vi. 27. 8
turn'd abacke, and to retyre him hasted . . . VI. vi. 28. 3
So humbly taking leave she *turnd* aside; . . . VI. viii. 30. 6
all the stormes of fortunes former yre Were *turnd,* . . . VI. xii. 10. 5
Sternely he *turnd* againe, . . . VI. xii. 26. 3
Still tost and *turned* with continuall change, . . . VII. vii. 21. 2
all things tost and *turned* by transverse, . . . VII. vii. 56. 3
And *turned* have the tenor of my string, . . . *H.H.L.* 13
Turnest. *turnest* love divine To joylesse dread, . . . III. xi. 1. 5
Turneth. then againe he *turneth* to his play, . . . *Mui.* 185
Turney, *etc.* *See* **Tourney,** *etc.*
Turning. Toward the sea *turning* my troubled eye, . . . *Van.* v. 1
How I admire ech *turning* of thy verse! . . . *S.C.* Au. 194
To cut the ships from *turning* home againe To Argos; . . . *Gn.* 522
The chaungfull *turning* of mens slipperie state, . . . *Gn.* 554
turning all unto the Apes confusion. . . . *Hub.* 1364
turning back, he saide, with hollow sound, . . . *D.* 61
first since thy *turning* backe . . . *Col.* 19
her boldly kept From *turning* backe, . . . I. i. 17. 4
turning fierce her speckled taile advaunst, . . . I. i. 17. 6
Shee *turning* backe . . . Cride, 'Mercy, mercy, Sir, . . . I. ii. 21. 1
turning to his Lady, dead with feare her fownd. . . . I. ii. 44. 9
Thence *turning* backe in silence softe they stole, . . . I. v. 31. 1
turning wrathfull fyre to lustfull heat, . . . I. vi. 3. 3
turning backe gan fast to fly away; . . . I. vi. 28. 2
Satyrane, with strokes him *turning,* staid, . . . I. vi. 46. 6
Then *turning* to his Palmer said; . . . II. i. 57. 1
turning to that place, . . . II. ii. 11. 5
Against themselves *turning* their wrathfull spight, . . . II. ii. 23. 6
turning said to Trompart; . . . II. iii. 43. 7
Against him *turning* all his fell intent, . . . II. iv. 6. 6
turning to that woman, fast her hent . . . II. iv. 12. 2
Turning about he saw that wretched Squyre, . . . II. iv. 16. 2
He, *turning* taile, Back to the strond retyrd, . . . II. vi. 40. 5
Mammon, *turning* to that warriour, said; . . . II. vii. 32. 6
At last, him *turning* to his charge behight, . . . II. viii. 9. 5
turning to the Palmer, . . . II. viii. 23. 6
turning to those brethren, thus bespoke: . . . II. viii. 27. 1
backe againe *turning* his busie hond, . . . II. viii. 41. 6
turning soft aside, . . . II. ix. 39. 6
Tossing and *turning* them withouten end; . . . II. ix. 58. 2
turning quicke aside His light-foot beast, . . . II. xi. 25. 5
of each *turning* still kept wary heed: . . . III. iv. 48. 5
Therewith he sigh'd; and, *turning* him aside, . . . III. v. 34. 6
turning her feare to foolish wrath, . . . III. vii. 8. 1
turning backe to Scudamour, . . . III. xi. 22. 6
turning to herselfe, his fell intent, . . . III. xii. 33. 3
Then, *turning* to those Knights, he gan anew: . . . IV. ii. 24. 1
turning all to game And pleasaunt bord, . . . IV. iv. 13. 1
turning feare to faint devotion, . . . IV. vi. 24. 8
Then *turning* to the elder thus he sayd: . . . V. iv. 18. 1
to her *turning* thus began againe: . . . V. v. 30. 6
Tho *turning* all his pride to humblesse meeke, . . . V. vii. 16. 1
Then *turning* unto him; . . . V. x. 21. 1
turning backe unto that gentle boy, . . . VI. ii. 24. 1
Handling and *turning* them a thousand wayes: . . . VI. ii. 39. 5
Then *turning* to that swaine . . . VI. v. 23. 1
Then *turning* backe upon that captive thrall, . . . VI. viii. 27. 1
So many *turning* cranks these have, . . . VII. vii. 52. 9
turning to themselves at length againe, . . . VII. vii. 58. 6
Turning all loves delight to miserie, . . . *H.L.* 269
Turnings. So many pathes, so many *turnings* seene, . . . I. i. 10. 8
Turns. His sense to seeke for ease *turnes* every way: . . . *Gn.* 388
they may for their owne *turnes* be fit. . . . *Hub.* 640
By chaunge of *turnes,* each making other mery; . . . *Col.* 77
any other wight, That hither *turnes* his steps. . . . I. x. 10. 3
by even *tournes* Full measured . . . II. i. 53. 1
Good *turnes* be counted as a servile bond . . . II. viii. 56. 2
All which successively by *turnes* did rayne: . . . II. x. 44. 2
whiles wind and wether right Doe serve their *turnes:* . . . II. xi. 4. 8
painefull pleasure *turnes* to pleasing paine. . . . III. x. 60. 4
answering their wearie *turnes* around, . . . IV. v. 33. 8
Turnes him about with fell avengement: . . . VI. vi. 27. 7
he vow'd to be her debter For many moe good *turnes* . . . VII. vi. 44. 8
daily watch, and nightly wake By even *turnes,* . . . VII. vii. 45. 9
when I waile, she *turnes* hir selfe to laughter. . . . *Am.* xviii. 12
Turnus. the Troyan Duke with *Turnus* fought. . . . *Bel.*[1] vii. 8
Turnus'. the Troyan prince spilt *Turnus* blood . . . *Bel.*[2] ix. 8
Turpine. *See* **Terpin.**
'Sir *Turpine!* (*Terpine) haplesse man, what make you here? V. iv. 26. 1
whilest Calepine By *Turpine* is oppress. . . . VI. iii. Arg.
Sir *Turpine,* one of mickle might . . . VI. iii. 40. 2
Calepine . . . From *Turpine* reskewed is; . . . VI. iv. Arg.
Which *Turpine* had unto her shewed late, . . . VI. v. 33. 3
He *Turpine* doth defeate, . . . VI. vi. Arg.
Turpine is baffuld; . . . VI. vii. Arg.
The coward *Turpine,* whereof now I treat; . . . VI. vii. 2. 2
To whom false *Turpine* comming courteously, . . . VI. vii. 4. 1
'He rides' (said *Turpine*) 'there not farre afore, . . . VI. vii. 6. 1
Backe to the place where *Turpine* late he lore; . . . VI. vii. 14. 2
Thereof false *Turpin* was full glad and faine, . . . VI. vii. 17. 1
Whom when as *Turpin* saw so loosely layd, . . . VI. vii. 20. 1
The traytour *Turpin* with that other knight, . . . VI. vii. 25. 2
Turret. Sitting one day within his *turret* hye, . . . *Hub.* 1227
Up to a stately *Turret* she them brought, . . . II. ix. 44. 8
Turret's. That *Turrets* frame most admirable was, . . . II. ix. 45. 1

Turrets. In her swifte charret with high *turrets* crownde, . . . *Ro.* vi. 2
a Diademe embattild wide With hundred *turrets,* . . . IV. xi. 28. 6
Turribant. *See* **Turban.**
Turtle. The *Turtle* on the bared braunch . . . *S.C.* N. 138
followed her make like *turtle* chaste, . . . *As.* 178
like the circlet of a *Turtle* true, . . . *Col.* 340
as trew in love as *Turtle* to her make. . . . III. xi. 2. 9
Yet never *Turtle* truer to his make, . . . VI. viii. 33. 6
Turtle-dove. chose . . . the *Turtle Dove* Her deare, . . . *Col.* 865
there chaunst a *turtle Dove* To come . . . IV. viii. 3. 2
My truest *turtle dove;* . . . *Epith.* 24
Turtle-doves. there sate a gentle payre, Of *turtle doves,* . . . I. x. 31. 9
Turtle's. did bind About the *turtles* necke, . . . IV. viii. 7. 3
Turvy. *See* **Topsy-turvy.**
Tuscan. Described by that famous *Tuscane* penne: . . . IV. iii. 45. 4
Tusk. with his cruell *tuske* him deadly cloyd: . . . III. vi. 48. 4
Tusked. The spotted Panther, and the *tusked* Bore, . . . I. vi. 26. 3
huge great teeth, like to a *tusked* Bore: . . . IV. vii. 5. 6
Tusks. Where foming wrath their cruell *tuskes* they whett, . . I. vi. 44. 7
gnasht his yron *tuskes* at that displeasing sight. . . . IV. x. 33. 9
Tutor's. he had charge . . . *Tutors* nouriture to oversee. . . . I. ix. 5. 4
Pupill fitt for such a *Tutors* hand! . . . I. ix. 6. 2
Tutors. th' Infants *tutors* gathering to feare, . . . II. x. 64. 4
Twain. of the *twaine,* if choice were to me, . . . *S.C.* May 166
a sigh had nigh rent her heart in *twaine*) . . . *S.C.* May 194
His tayle he clapt betwixt his legs *twayne,* . . . *S.C.* May 280
ye jolly shepheards *twayne:* . . . *S.C.* Au. 51
the rayne Twixt them divided into even *twaine,* . . . *Hub.* 1024
wrapt his winges *twaine* In lymie snares . . . *Mui.* 428
So stood these *twaine,* unmoved as a rocke, . . . I. ii. 16. 7
the fearfull *twayne,* That blind old woman, and her daughter I. iii. 22. 1
stony hart could riven have in *twaine;* . . . I. iii. 44. 3
with his body bard the way atwixt them *twaine.* . . . I. viii. 13. 9
made such way that hewd it quite in *twaine;* . . . I. xi. 43. 7
The marriage to accomplish vowd betwixt you *twayn.* . . . I. xii. 19. 9
By breaking of the band betwixt us *twaine;* . . . I. xii. 34. 4
seemd her tender heart was rent in *twaine,* . . . II. i. 38. 4
that same froward *twaine* would accorage, . . . II. ii. 38. 7
as it would rive in *twaine.* . . . II. iii. 20. 9
Have cleft his head in *twaine,* . . . II. viii. 33. 9
So rag'd Prince Arthur twixt his foemen *twaine,* . . . II. viii. 42. 8
gnaw His hart in *twaine* with sad melancholy; . . . II. viii. 50. 8
twixt the other *twain* his kingdom whole did shayre. . . . II. x. 28. 9
his ambitious sonnes unto them *twayne* Arraught the rule, . II. x. 34. 7
her twixt her armes *twaine* Shee streightly straynd, . . . III. ii. 34. 1
it must doubled bee with death of *twaine?* . . . III. ii. 35. 4
to the chin he clefte his head in *twaine.* . . . III. v. 23. 6
a rocke of stone to rew, Or rive in *twaine:* . . . III. v. 30. 3
atweene her lilly handes *twaine* . . . III. v. 33. 3
fast her clipping twixt his armes *twayne,* . . . III. viii. 10. 1
A couple, seeming well to be his *twaine,* . . . III. x. 20. 7
gave him being, commune to them *twayne:* . . . III. xii. 9. 4
clapt on hye his coulourd winges *twaine,* . . . III. xii. 23. 7
Lightly he clipt her twixt his armes *twaine,* . . . III. xii. 45. *or.* 1
Disshivered speares, and shields ytorne in *twaine;* . . . IV. i. 21. 6
Likewise unequall were her handes *twaine;* . . . IV. i. 29. 1
With cursed knife cutting the twist in *twaine.* . . . IV. ii. 48. 8
the Prince tooke downe those Ladies *twaine* . . . IV. viii. 41. 1
her before there paced Pages *twaine,* . . . IV. xi. 47. 7
When as he saw she should be cut in *twaine,* . . . V. i. 27. 4
broke his sword in *twaine,* . . . V. iii. 37. 9
He had him surely cloven quite in *twaine:* . . . V. xi. 10. 6
'Under one hood to shadow faces *twaine:* . . . V. xi. 56. 7
pointed for the combat twixt them *twayne* The morrow next, . V. xii. 9. 7
he . . . strooke me one stroke or *twaine;* . . . VI. ii. 12. 4
So taking courteous leave they parted *twayne,* . . . VI. ii. 38. 8
And twixt them *twaine* . . . VI. iii. 12. 6
the necke thereof did cut in *twaine,* . . . VI. iii. 17. 5
up he tooke her twixt his armes *twaine,* . . . VI. iii. 28. 4
Then tooke he up betwixt his armes *twaine* . . . VI. iv. 23. 1
Have not vouchsaft to graunt unto us *twaine* . . . VI. iv. 31. 2
cryde Unto the Knight, them to dispart in *twaine;* . . . VI. v. 27. 2
yeeld some ease To these sicke *twaine,* . . . VI. v. 32. 3
his leg . . . Was crackt in *twaine,* . . . VI. viii. 25. 8
I lately left a furrow, one or *twayne,* Unplough'd, . . . VI. ix. 1. 3
sighing sore, as if her hart in *twaine* Had riven bene . . . VI. xi. 22. 7
sith they *twaine* Long since had fought in field: . . . VI. xii. 11. 3
her embracing twixt her armes *twaine,* . . . VI. xii. 19. 6
All set with yron teeth in raunges *twaine,* . . . VI. xii. 26. 7
heavenly honors yield, as to them *twaine:* . . . VII. vi. 4. 4
wrong it were that any other *twaine* . . . *H.B.* 204
the foule . . . Gan flock about these *twaine,* . . . *Proth.* 120
'Twas. That *'twas* Molanna which her so bewraid. . . . VII. vi. 51. 8
Tway. we *tway* bene men of elder witt. . . . *S.C.* May 18
Tway things doen ill agree. . . . *S.C.* Jul. 152
sorrowfull assay . . . almost rent her tender hart in *tway;* . I. vii. 27. 4
Dry-shod to passe she parts the flouds in *tway;* . . . I. x. 20. 5
quite it clove his plumed crest in *tway,* . . . II. vi. 31. 7
the sharpe steele doth rive her hart in *tway,* . . . III. xi. 11. 4
Should equally be shard betwixt us *tway.* . . . IV. ii. 13. 5
His mighty heart did almost rend in *tway,* . . . IV. iv. 22. 7
from thence not past a mile or *tway,* . . . V. iv. 35. 7
Tweed. *Twede,* the limit betwixt Logris land And Albany: . . IV. xi. 36. 6
Twelve. Square was this Citie, and *twelve* gates it had. . . . *Rev.* iv. 9
The brethren *twelve,* that kept yfere The flockes . . . *S.C.* Jul. 143
Twelve Gods doo sit around in royall state, . . . *Mui.* 307
for *twelve* huge labours high extold, . . . I. xi. 27. 3
*That have *twelve* moneths sought one, . . . II. ix. 38. 9
Them in *twelve* troupes their Captein did dispart, . . . II. xi. 6. 1
these *twelve* troupes with dreadfull puissaunce . . . II. xi. 14. 1

Twelve—*Continued.*
Mongst those *twelve* signes, which nightly we doe see . . . V. i. 11. 6
twelve of them he did by times devoure, . . . V. x. 8. 3
So past the *twelve* Months forth, . . . VII. vii. 43. 9
Twelvemonth's. at the *twelve monethes* end should bring their names . . . III. vii. 54. 8
for a *twelve moneths* day . . . V. i. 26. 7
Twelve thousand. did this knight *twelve thousand* dolours daunt, . . . I. xi. 27. 7
Twenty. his yongest sonne Shall *twentie* have, and *twentie* thou hast wonne: . . . *Hub.* 530
Of which were *twentie* sonnes, . . . II. x. 22. 5
From *twentie* Knights that did him all assay; . . . IV. i. 2. 4
'Now *twenty* daies . . . have past through heven sheene, . . . IV. vii. 13. 1
therein wonned *twenty* valiant Knights, . . . IV. x. 7. 6
All *twenty* tride in warres experience long; . . . IV. x. 7. 7
all the *twenty* I likewise entreated, . . . IV. x. 10. 5
After long travell of full *twenty* yeares, . . . V. vii. 39. 6
She had destroyed two and *twenty* more. . . . VI. vii. 38. 8
Twice. *twice* steeped in Assyrian dye; . . . *Gn.* 98
By dubble usurie doth *twise* renew it. . . . *Col.* 39
twise he reeled, readie *twise* to fall: . . . I. v. 11. 6
curse on thy cruell hond, That *twise* hath spedd; . . . II. viii. 37. 7
with his troncheon he so rudely stroke Cymochles *twise,* . . . II. viii. 39. 9
twise him forst his foot revoke. . . . II. viii. 39. 9
Eft to Cymochles *twise* so many fold; . . . II. viii. 41. 5
made him *twise* to reele, that never moov'd afore. . . . II. viii. 44. 9
on every syde *Twise* sixteene warders satt, . . . II. ix. 26. 2
twise they were repulsed backe againe, And *twise* renforst . II. x. 48. 1, 2
Thrise shall he fight with them, and *twise* shall win; . . . III. iii. 30. 6
Shall backe repulse the valiaunt Brockwell *twise,* . . . III. iii. 35. 5
twise fowre hundreth yeares shalbe supplide, . . . III. iii. 44. 5
Twise was he seene in soaring Eagles shape, . . . III. xi. 34. 1
twice hath risen . . . V. Pr. 8. 6
And wested *twice* where he ought rise aright: . . . V. Pr. 8. 7
Twifold. *twyfold* Teme, of which two blacke . . . two were browne, . . . I. v. 28. 4
Twight. *See* **Twit.**
Twigs. the woodbine *twigges* that freshly bud; . . . *Gn.* 82
enfold With her lythe *twigs,* . . . *Gn.* 221
wicker basket, Made of fine *twigs,* . . . *Proth.* 25
Twilight. with his Torche, still twinkling like *twylight,* . . . VII. vi. 9. 7
Twin. A *twinne* of forked trees . . . *Bel.* v. 14
being but halfe *twin* of that berth: . . . III. vii. 47. 9
greatest shame was to that maiden *twin,* . . . III. vii. 49. 3
Twine. *See* **Ivy-twine.**
an Harpe stroong all with silver *twyne,* . . . *Ti.* 604
In skilfull knitting of soft silken *twyne,* . . . *Mui.* 362
To draw them longer out, and better *twine,* . . . IV. ii. 51. 2
what their hands could earne by twisting linnen *twyne.* . . . V. v. 22. 9
Hemd all about with fringe of silver *twine:* . . . V. vii. 6. 5
Twined. alwaies in her hand two clewes of silke she *twynd.* . III. xii. 14. 9
twyned Were with a snake, . . . IV. x. 40. 8
Twinkle. with the onely *twinckle* of her eye . . . VI. vii. 31. 7
When suddenly, with *twincle* of her eye, . . . *Am.* xvi. 11
Twinkling. *twincling* starres the daylight hence chase. . . . *S.C.* Ap. 161
his ey-lids *twinckling* rare . . . *Gn.* 284
Distinguished with manie a *twinckling* starre; . . . *Mui.* 94
a bauldrick . . . That shind, like *twinckling* stars, . . . I. vii. 29. 9
glistred bright Like *twinckling* starres; . . . II. iii. 26. 8
It can purvay in *twinckling* of an eye; . . . II. vii. 11. 4
eyes, like *twinkling* stars in evening cleare, . . . IV. x. 50. 7
the least *twinckling* sleepe to start Into her eye, . . . V. vi. 24. 7
by the *twinkling* of their sacred fire, . . . VI. viii. 48. 2
twixt the *twinckling* of her eye-lids bright . . . VI. xi. 21. 8
with his Torche, still *twinkling* like twylight, . . . VII. vi. 9. 7
seemst to laugh atweene thy *twinkling* light, . . . *Epith.* 292
twinckling starres in frostie night; . . . *H.B.* 257
Twins. Her loved *Twinnes,* the dearlings of her joy, . . . *T.M.* 14
ye three *Twins,* to light by Venus brought, . . . *T.M.* 403
'So raisde they eke faire Ledaes warlick *twinnes,* . . . *Ti.* 386
Of her fayre *twins* was there delivered, . . . II. xii. 13. 6
Offricke and Osricke, *twinnes* unfortunate, . . . III. iii. 37. 3
These two were *twinnes,* . . . III. vi. 4. 6
So sprong these *twinnes* in womb of Chrysogone; . . . III. vi. 9. 6
These *twinnes,* men say, (a thing far passing thought) . . III. vii. 48. 5
They both her *twins,* both borne of heavenly seed, . . . IV. x. 34. 3
those two *twinnes* of Jove, . . . V. Pr. 6. 2
The *twinnes* of Leda; . . . VII. vii. 34. 5
like the *twins* of Jove they seem'd in sight, . . . *Proth.* 173
Twist. to weare garments base of wollen *twist,* . . . *Hub.* 460
With cursed knife cutting the *twist* in twaine. . . . IV. ii. 48. 8
Twisted. an horne . . . in *twisted* gold And tasselles gay. . . . I. viii. 3. 6
girded with a belt of *twisted* brake: . . . II. xi. 22. 7
Twisting. what their hands could earne by *twisting* linnen twyne. V. v. 22. 9
Twit. him sharpely *twight* For breach of faith to her, . . . V. vi. 12. 8
Twitch. she chaunst their stubborne mouths to *twitch;* . . . I. v. 28. 7
Twixt (*partial list*).
So *twixt* them both they not a lambkin left, . . . *Hub.* 321
small oddes I often see *Twixt* them . . . and them . . . *Hub.* 374
That they a Benefice *twixt* them obtained; . . . *Hub.* 555
to have the rayne *Twixt* them divided . . . *Hub.* 1024
What oddes *twixt* Irus and old Inachus, . . . *T.M.* 447
What oddes . . . *Twixt* best and worst, . . . *T.M.* 448
Distraught *twixt* feare and pitie; . . . *Ti.* 579
twixt their blessed armes it carried . . . *Ti.* 627
as befell *Twixt* him and thee, . . . *Col.* 177
twixt them both was born the bloudy bold Sans loy. . . . I. ii. 25. 9
distrest *twixt* joy and cares . . . I. vi. 1. 7
twixt feare and hope amazd does sitt, . . . I. vi. 12. 3

Twixt—*Continued.*
twixt him and his Lord did . . . stand. I. viii. 12. 9
Close creeping *twixt* the marow and the skin: I. x. 25. 5
Twixt that great faery Queene and Paynim king, I. xi. 7. 4
crowned her *twixt* earnest and *twixt* game: I. xii. 8. 7
Prince Arthur *twixt* his foemen twaine, II. viii. 42. 8
Twixt his two mighty armes engrasped fast, II. viii. 49. 6
twixt them both a quadrate was the base II. ix. 22. 6
the moore *twixt* Elversham and Dell, II. x. 24. 4
twixt the other twain his kingdom whole did shayre. II. x. 28. 9
Twixt his two mighty armes II. xi. 42. 1
caught him *twixt* his puissant hands, II. xi. 46. 1
twixt them both the narrow way doth ly.' II. xii. 18. 4
twixt them both a pleasaunt port they made, II. xii. 30. 6
her *twixt* her armes twaine Shee streightly straynd, III. ii. 34. 1
Now this, now that, *twixt* them they did devize, III. iii. 51. 8
twixt them two did share The heritage III. vi. 4. 6
left them languishing *twixt* hope and feare. III. vi. 13. 9
fast her clipping *twixt* his armes twayne, III. viii. 10. 1
Twixt inward doole and felonous despight: III. x. 17. 6
She slept; yet *twixt* her eielids closely spyde III. xi. 32. 8
Twixt both his hands few sparks he close did strayne, III. xii. 9. 7
Twixt dolour and despight halfe desperate, III. xii. 43. *or.* 3
Lightly he clipt her *twixt* his armes twaine, III. xii. 45. *or.* 1
discord breedes *Twixt* Scudamour and Blandamour: IV. i. Arg.
of their loves did treat, . . . *twixt* themselves alone, IV. i. 16. 2
stirre up strife *twixt* love and spight and ire, IV. ii. 11. 8
That *twixt* themselves did gentle purpose make, IV. ii. 30. 7
cruell battell *twixt* themselves doe make, IV. iii. 16. 6
were enterchaunged *twixt* them two; IV. iii. 17. 2
Twixt Cambell and Sir Triamond befell, IV. iv. 2. 2
Stird up *twixt* Blandamour and Paridell, IV. iv. 2. 4
whose hart *twixt* doubtfull feare And feeble hope hung IV. vi. 34. 1
thrusting boldly *twixt* him and the blow, IV. viii. 42. 1
twixt her selfe and Love did let me pas; IV. x. 36. 3
clasping *twixt* his armes, her up did reare V. xi. 64. 7
the combat *twixt* them twayne V. xii. 9. 7
And *twixt* them both with parted paines did beare, VI. ii. 48. 5
Twixt life and death, not knowing what was donne. VI. ii. 48. 6
And *twixt* them twaine VI. iii. 12. 6
up he tooke her *twixt* his armes twaine, VI. iii. 28. 4
Twixt darkenesse dread and hope VI. iii. 45. 4
twixt his pleasing tongue, and her faire hew, VI. ix. 26. 8
holding fast *twixt* both his armes extended VI. xi. 19. 7
Like a sweet Angell *twixt* two clouds uphild; VI. xi. 21. 3
twixt the twinckling of her eye-lids bright VI. xi. 21. 8
her embracing *twixt* her armes twaine, VI. xii. 19. 6
the solemne bridall cheare *Twixt* Peleus and Dame Thetis VII. vii. 12. 5
Twixt feare and hope depending doubtfully! *Am.* xxv. 4
The league *twixt* them, *Am.* lxv. 10
twixt her paps, . . . did theyr wanton winges display, *Am.* lxxvi. 9
'*Twixt* earnest and *twixt* game: *Epig.* iv. 12
lying . . . *Twixt* sleepe and wake, *Epith.* 309
see The ods *twixt* both, *Com. Son.* ii. 10
And lastly, how *twixt* robbers crucifyde, *H.H.L.* 244

Two. *Two* eager dogs did her pursue *Pet.* i. 6
suck . . . To *two* young babes: *Bel.* ix. 10
a Wolfe . . . Noursing *two* whelpes; *Bel.*[2] vi. 2
Unwisely weaves, that takes *two* webbes in hand. *S.C.* O. 102
his broad forhead like *two* hornes divide, *Gn.* 22
the *two* pearles which sight unto him lent, *Gn.* 285
'There also those *two* Pandionian maides, *Gn.* 401
the *two* brethren borne of Cadmus blood, *Gn.* 409
'There be the *two* stout sonnes of Aeacus, *Gn.* 481
Two fellowes might no where be better fitted. *Hub.* 50
(Both *two* sure bands in friendship to be tide) *Hub.* 54
two is better than one head.' *Hub.* 82
Like *two* free men, *Hub.* 160
these *two* javels Should render up a reckning *Hub.* 309
Two filthie blots in noble gentrie; *Hub.* 734
the *two* first whome he encountred *Hub.* 1067
monstrous beasts . . . Bred of *two* kindes, *Hub.* 1123
worke the avengement . . . On those *two* caytives, *Hub.* 1318
As if her eyes had beene *two* springing wells; *T.M.* 536
since these *two* eyes beheld A mightie Prince, *Ti.* 183
'Those *two* be those *two* great calamities, *Ti.* 442
I saw *two* Beares, as white as anie milke, *Ti.* 561
Two fairer beasts might not elswhere be found, *Ti.* 566
Two Angels, downe descending with swift flight, *Ti.* 625
Betwixt *two* mightie ones of great estate, *Mui.* 3
Therein *two* deadly weapons fixt he bore, *Mui.* 81
Like *two* sharpe speares his enemies to gore: *Mui.* 83
two such fannes, so silken soft *Mui.* 107
Of those he chose out *two*, the falsest *twoo*, I. i. 38. 6
Those *twoo* he tooke, and in a secrete bed, I. ii. 3. 7
As when *two* rams, . . . Fight for the rule I. ii. 16. 1
they came at last Where grew *two* goodly trees, I. ii. 28. 3
forth they ran, like *two* amazed deare, I. iii. 22. 7
Two iron coffers hong on either side, I. iv. 27. 3
two of three her Nephewes are so fowle forlorne? I. v. 23. 9
two blacke as pitch, And *two* were browne, I. v. 28. 4, 5
From surging gulf *two* Monsters streight were brought, I. v. 38. 3
'I chaunst this day, . . . To see *two* knights, I. vi. 38. 3
As when *two* Bores, with rancling malice mett, I. vi. 44. 4
The force, which wont in *two* to be disperst, I. viii. 18. 1
those *two* knights . . . Gave goodly gifts, I. ix. 18. 6
The eldest *two*, most sober, chast, and wise, I. x. 4. 5
two most goodly virgins came in place, I. x. 12. 2
when these *two* approching he aspide, I. x. 49. 1
The knight with that old Dragon fights *Two* days I. xi. Arg.

Two—*Continued.*
two sayles, in which the hollow wynd Is gathered full, I. xi. 10. 2
at the point *two* stinges in fixed arre, I. xi. 11. 8
His blazing eyes, like *two* bright shining shieldes, I. xi. 14. 1
two broad Beacons, sett in open fieldes, I. xi. 14. 3
His owne *two* hands the holy knotts did knitt, I. xii. 37. 1
His owne *two* hands, for such a turne most fitt, I. xii. 37. 3
dale that lowly lay Betwixt *two* hils, II. i. 24. 4
The face of golden Meane: Her sisters, *two* Extremities, II. ii. Arg.
from whose *two* heads . . . fresh streames do flow, II. ii. 9. 1
As from *two* weeping eyes, fresh streames do flow, II. ii. 9. 2
who did far excell The other *two:* II. ii. 14. 4
They were *two* knights of perelesse puissaunce, II. ii. 16. 6
These *two* gay knights vowd to so diverse loves, II. ii. 19. 1
two brave knightes in bloody fight II. ii. 21. 3
Meetes *two* contrarie billowes II. ii. 24. 4
two so mighty warriours he dismade. II. ii. 25. 5
her *two* other sisters, standing by, II. ii. 28. 1
those *two* froward sisters, their faire loves, II. ii. 34. 1
Which *two* . . . Had slayne Sir Mordant II. iii. 13. 7
they be *two* the prowest knights on grownd, II. iii. 15. 6
In her faire eyes *two* living lamps did flame, II. iii. 23. 1
Like *two* faire marble pillours they were seene, II. iii. 28. 1
With her *two* crooked handes she signes did make, II. iv. 13. 2
Love, that *two* harts makes one, II. iv. 19. 8
in his hand *two* dartes, II. iv. 38. 7
cause of death betweene *two* doughtie knights do breed! II. vi. 33. 9
his deepe wounded hart in *two* did rive; II. vi. 45. 7
which *two* upbeare . . . this frayle life of man, II. vii. 65. 3
two sharpe winged sheares, Decked with diverse plumes, II. viii. 5. 7
Two Paynim knights al armd as bright as skie, II. viii. 10. 2
Those were the *two* sonnes of Acrates old, II. viii. 10. 6
two foes of so exceeding might, II. viii. 34. 4
salvage Bull, whom *two* fierce mastives bayt, II. viii. 42. 1
Twixt his *two* mighty armes engrasped fast, II. viii. 49. 6
those *two* Sarazins confounded late, II. viii. 54. 8
borne of *two* faire Damsels II. ix. 19. 5
Those *two* the first and last proportions are; II. ix. 22. 3
Therein *two* gates were placed seemly well: II. ix. 23. 1
Two goodly Beacons, set in watches stead, II. ix. 46. 3
two sonnes, of pearelesse prowesse both, II. x. 40. 2
He had *two* sonnes, II. x. 46. 1
He left *two* sonnes, II. x. 46. 8
Two brethren were their Capitayns, II. x. 65. 1
Elfar, who *two* brethren gyauntes kild, II. x. 73. 5
The one of which had *two* heades, II. x. 73. 6
He left *two* sonnes, II. x. 75. 6
two then all more huge and violent, II. xi. 9. 8
those *two* brethren Gyauntes did defend The walles II. xi. 15. 6
There follow'd fast at hand *two* wicked Hags, II. xi. 23. 2
Twixt his *two* mighty armes him up he snatcht, II. xi. 42. 1
Like *two* mad dogs they ran about the lands, II. xi. 47. 2
Two dayes now in that sea he sayled has, II. xii. 2. 1
Two naked Damzelles he therein espyde, II. xii. 63. 6
her *two* lilly paps aloft displayd, II. xii. 66. 6
now there do but *two* of six remaine, III. i. 29. 5
Which *two* did yield before she did them smight. III. i. 29. 6
with her *two* crafty spyes She secretly would search III. i. 36. 5
spare to one, or *two*, or three, Rowme in their writtes; III. ii. 1. 7
Betwixt *two* shady mountaynes doth arize: III. ii. 24. 7
From whose *two* loynes thou afterwardes did rayse III. iii. 3. 6
us *two* did hither send.' III. iii. 15. 9
When the *two* fearefull wemen saw, III. iii. 50. 6
Those *two* great champions did attonce pursew III. iv. 46. 2
Did th' other *two* their cruell vengeaunce blin, III. v. 22. 7
betwixt *two* marbles plaine Shee pownded small, III. v. 33. 1
two of them the rest far overpast, III. v. 37. 8
those *two* vertues strove to fynd The higher place III. v. 55. 4
These *two* were twinnes, and twixt them *two* did share III. vi. 4. 6
two babes, as faire as springing day. III. vi. 26. 9
girt in with *two* walls on either side; III. vi. 31. 2
*teares . . . like *two* Orient pearles, III. vii. 9. 3
two burning lampes she set III. viii. 7. 1
as they *two* of kindnes treated long, III. viii. 15. 1
Two eies him needeth, for to watch and wake, III. ix. 31. 7
two rivers bownd the rest. III. ix. 46. 4
Cannot *two* fairer Cities find this day, III. ix. 51. 4
Two things he feared, but the third was death; III. x. 2. 6
those *two* sought nought but the present pray, III. x. 34. 4
Where those *two* guilers with Malbecco were. III. x. 37. 5
As for us *two*, . . . we will blyndfolded ly, III. x. 42. 6
for those *two*, and for his owne deare sonne, III. xi. 38. 1
alwaies in her hand *two* clewes of silke she twynd. III. xii. 14. 9
Led of *two* grysie Villeins, III. xii. 19. 2
those *two* villeins, which her steps upstayd, III. xii. 21. 5
like *two* senceles stocks III. xii. 45. *or.* 9
"So seemd those *two*, III. xii. 46. *or.* 5
t' accord *two* things so far in dout. IV. i. 11. 9
Two armed Knights that toward them did pace, IV. i. 17. 2
Her lying tongue was in *two* parts divided, IV. i. 27. 6
With *two* companions of like qualitie, IV. i. 32. 7
they chaunced to espie *Two* other knights, IV. i. 38. 5
As when *two* billowes . . . Do meete together, IV. i. 42. 1
So fell those *two* in spight of both their prydes; IV. i. 42. 7
As when *two* warlike Brigandines at sea, IV. ii. 16. 1
Like *two* mad mastiffes, each on other flew, IV. ii. 17. 8
Two knights that lincked rode in lovely wise, IV. ii. 30. 3
To weete, *two* Ladies of most goodly hew, IV. ii. 30. 6
Two of the prowest Knights in Faery lond, IV. ii. 31. 6
those *two* Ladies their *two* lovers deare; IV. ii. 31. 7

Two—*Continued.*
Those *two* were foes the fellonest on ground, IV. ii. 32. 2
two Tygers prickt with hungers rage IV. iii. 16. 1
The whiles were enterchaunged twixt them *two;* IV. iii. 17. 2
Of *two* grim lyons, taken from the wood, IV. iii. 39. 2
About the which *two* Serpents weren wound, IV. iii. 42. 2
having those *two* other Knights espide IV. iv. 2. 6
those *two* Ladies their *two* loves unseene; IV. iv. 3. 3
As *two* fierce Buls, that strive the rule to get IV. iv. 18. 3
So these *two* champions to the ground were feld, IV. iv. 18. 6
As *two* wild Boares together grapling go, IV. iv. 29. 8
Like captive thral *two* other Knights atweene: IV. iv. 34. 5
two greedy Wolves doe breake by force Into an heard, IV. iv. 35. 6
So did these *two* through all the field their foes enforce. IV. iv. 35. 9
made him dreame those *two* disloyall were: IV. v. 43. 8
downe both sides *two* wide long eares did glow, IV. vii. 6. 7
therewith in *two* distraught, IV. vii. 31. 7
like *two* streames procead; IV. viii. 13. 4
those *two* Ladies late, Aemylia and Amoret, abode, IV. viii. 19. 2
those *two* Ladies much asham'd did wexe: IV. viii. 35. 7
from his fearefull eyes *two* fierie beames, IV. viii. 39. 1
Shooting forth farre away *two* flaming streames, IV. viii. 39. 3
never *two* so like did living creature see. IV. viii. 55. 9
nigh at hand Those Ladies *two,* IV. viii. 62. 7
many miles they *two* together wore, IV. ix. 19. 7
those *two* other, which beside them stoode, IV. ix. 22. 1
As when *two* Barkes, . . . contrary courses sew, IV. ix. 26. 7
Against those *two* let drive, IV. ix. 29. 5
Foure charged *two,* and *two* surcharged one; IV. ix. 30. 5
did those *two* them selves so bravely beare, IV. ix. 30. 6
Had not those *two* him instantly desired IV. ix. 35. 3
Of *two* full hard to read the harder theft: IV. ix. 36. 6
Eftsoones outsprung *two* more of equall mould; IV. x. 10. 3
On either side of her *two* young men stood, IV. x. 32. 1
Begotten by *two* fathers of one mother, IV. x. 32. 4
th' oldest *two* of all the rest; IV. xi. 18. 2
all the rest of those *two* parents came, IV. xi. 18. 3
on either side she was sustained Of *two* smal grooms, IV. xi. 25. 2
The Churne and Charwell, *two* small streames, IV. xi. 25. 3
On her *two* pretty handmaides did attend, IV. xi. 47. 1
One prison fittest is to hold us *two.* IV. xii. 10. 7
those *two* twinnes of Jove, V. Pr. 6. 2
They *two* enough t' encounter an whole Regiment. V. i. 30. 9
Such was betwixt these *two* the troublesome uprore. V. ii. 15. 9
put *two* wrongs together to be tride, V. ii. 48. 3
two falses, of each equall share, V. ii. 48. 4
As when *two* sunnes appeare in the azure skye, V. iii. 19. 1
dealeth right betwixt *Two* brethren V. iv. Arg.
two comely Squires, Both brethren, V. iv. 4. 2
them beside *two* seemely damzells stood, V. iv. 4. 6
'Then weete ye, Sir, that we *two* brethren be, V. iv. 7. 2
Two Ilands, which ye there before you see V. iv. 7. 5
th' other *two* well likely to have harmed. V. iv. 36. 5
this is things compacte betwixt you *two,* V. vi. 16. 7
Two Knights all armed ready for to fight; V. vi. 29. 2
there present in her sight Those *two* false brethren V. vi. 36. 6
if *two* met, the one mote needes fall over the lidge. V. vi. 36. 9
those *two* losels scared; V. vi. 38. 5
haps to light Uppon *two* stubborne oakes, V. vi. 40. 2
So did the Championesse those *two* there strow, V. vi. 40. 8
Before *two* Knights that after her did speed V. viii. 4. 3
after those *two* former rode apace V. viii. 5. 2
he saw the hindmost overtake One of those *two,* V. viii. 5. 7
bore him . . . longer Then *two* speares length: V. viii. 7. 9
shooke And tottred, like *two* towres which through a tempest V. viii. 9. 9
asked her what were those *two* her fone, V. viii. 16. 2
soone after me she sent These *two* false Knights, V. viii. 23. 3
Like one of those *two* Knights which dead there lay; V. viii. 25. 5
Those *two* strange knights were to her presence brought; V. ix. 34. 2
Those *two* strange knights such homage to her make, V. ix. 35. 6
with more myld aspect those *two* to entertake. V. ix. 35. 9
When these *two* stranger knights arriv'd in place, V. ix. 36. 2
(Both *two* her paramours, both by her hyred, V. ix. 41. 4
Much more it praysed was of those *two* knights, V. x. 4. 1
There came *two* Springals of full tender yeares, V. x. 6. 2
these *two,* her eldest sonnes, she sent V. x. 14. 6
forth he gan to fare With those *two* gentle youthes, V. x. 17. 6
when her owne *two* sonnes she had in sight, V. x. 19. 7
Thenceforth into that Castle he her led With her *two* sonnes, V. x. 39. 7
two more of his armes did fall away, V. xi. 11. 7
Where she with her *two* sonnes did looking stand, V. xi. 15. 2
the *two* knights themselves their captains did subdew. V. xi. 59. 9
In which they *two* the combat might darraine. V. xii. 9. 4
two old ill favour'd Hags he met, V. xii. 28. 4
Two griesly creatures: V. xii. 28. 6
These *two* now had themselves combynd in one, V. xii. 37. 1
As it had bene *two* shepheards curres V. xii. 38. 5
cruell fray Betwixt them *two* VI. i. 36. 2
So long as these *two* armes were able to be wroken. VI. ii. 7. 9
wherefore Betwixt you *two* you began this strife VI. ii. 8. 9
To be *two* errant knights, VI. v. 11. 5
With which he had those *two* so ill bestad: VI. vi. 18. 5
Upon them *two* they fell with might and maine, VI. vi. 23. 3
his *two* knights Doe gaine their treasons meed: VI. vii. Arg.
At last he met *two* knights to him unknowne, VI. vii. 3. 6
when he saw those *two* so neare him stand, VI. vii. 24. 1
So now she had bene wandring *two* whole yeares VI. vii. 38. 1
in all these *two* yeares space Saved but *two;* VI. vii. 38. 5, 6
in *two* yeares before, VI. vii. 38. 6
She had destroyed *two* and twenty more. VI. vii. 38. 8

Two—*Continued.*
eies, Like *two* great Beacons, glared bright and wyde, VI. vii. 42. 2
whenas Enias Beheld *two* such, of *two* such villaines thrall, VI. viii. 5. 8
have with treason thralled unto you These *two,* VI. viii. 7. 6
Threatning to yoke them *two* and tame their corage stout. VI. viii. 11. 9
So did these *two* this Knight oft tug and teare. VI. viii. 12. 5
With these *two* lewd companions, and no more, VI. viii. 22. 7
at variaunce fell With those *two* Carles, VI. viii. 31. 4
every body *two,* and *two* she foure did read. VI. viii. 31. 9
two of them still froward seem'd to bee, VI. x. 24. 7
Like a sweet Angell twixt *two* clouds uphild; VI. xi. 21. 3
Drawne of *two* steeds, th' one black, the other white, VII. vi. 9. 2
she springs out of *two* marble Rocks, VII. vi. 41. 1
Upon *two* brethrens shoulders she did ride, VII. vii. 34. 4
Drawne of *two* fishes, VII. vii. 43. 3
did she know how ill these *two* accord *Am.* xxxi. 13
two liberties ye gayne, *Am.* lxv. 3
Twoo golden apples of unvalewd price; *Am.* lxxvii. 6
blesseth her with his *two* happy hands, *Epith.* 225
two mirrours, by opposd reflexion, *H.B.* 181
But those *two* most, which, ruling night and day, *H.H.B.* 55
I saw *two* Swannes of goodly hewe *Proth.* 37
Two fairer Birds I yet did never see; *Proth.* 39
Two of those Nymphes, meane while, *two* Garlands bound *Proth.* 83
they, enranged well, Did on those *two* attend, *Proth.* 123
Hercules *two* pillors . . . Did make to quake and feare: *Proth.* 148
Two gentle Knights of lovely face *Proth.* 169
They *two,* forth pacing to the Rivers side, *Proth.* 175
Received those *two* faire Brides, *Proth.* 176
Two-headed. With his *two-headed* dogge that Orthrus hight; V. x. 10. 6
Two hundred. ere *two hundred* yeares be full outronne, III. iii. 46. 4
Two hundred thousand. Her Host *two hundred thousand* numbred is; II. x. 56. 5
Tybris. *See* **Tiber.**
Tygre. *See* **Tiger, Tigris.**
Tyndarid. The faire *Tindarid* lasse, IV. xi. 19. 4
Tynd(e). *See* **Tined.**
Tyne. *See* **Teen.**
Next these came *Tyne,* IV. xi. 36. 1
Type. loftie *type* of honour, . . . is downe in dust *Gn.* 557
Didst to the *type* of honour earst advaunce: *T.M.* 70
that true glorious *type* of thine, I. Pr. 4. 7
Unto the *type* of kingdomes title clymes! V. ix. 42. 7
t' attaine, Unto the *type* of true Nobility; *Com. Son.* ii. 2
Typhaon. Orthrus begotten by great *Typhaon* And foule Echidna V. x. 10. 7
There did *Typhaon* with her company; VI. vi. 11. 7
Typhaon, whose tempestuous rage Makes th' heavens tremble VI. vi. 11. 8
Typhoeus. *See* **Typhon.**
Her syre *Typhoeus* was; III. vii. 47. 6
Typhoeus'. the great *Typhaeus* sister *Bel.*[1] xi. 4
Typhoeus sister comming neare; *Bel.*[2] xv. 4
Typhoeus joynts were stretched on a gin; I. v. 35. 7
Typhon. *See* **Typhoeus.**
Doubting least *Typhon* were againe uprear'd, VII. vi. 15. 8
Typhon's. *Typhons* fall, or proud Ixions paine, VII. vi. 29. 6
Tyranne. *See* **Tyrant.**
Tyranness. by law of that proud *Tyrannesse,* I. v. 46. 6
'Not by that Tyrant . . . But by a *Tyrannesse,'* V. vi. 11. 2
how the *Tyrannesse* doth joy to see *Am.* x. 5
Tyranning. In feeble Ladies *tyranning* so sore, IV. vii. 1. 6
Tyrannize. gan he rule and *tyrannize* at will, *Hub.* 1127
They in the mindes of men now *tyrannize,* *T.M.* 191
So every where they rule, and *tyrannize,* *T.M.* 337
And taught ambitious Rome to *tyrannise* *Ded. Son.* i. 3
ye . . . in subdued harts do *tyranyse;* *Ded. Son.* xvi. 9
gan Carausius *tirannize* anew, II. x. 57. 5
did amongst the troupes so *tyrannize,* IV. iv. 42. 2
he him selfe uppon the rich doth *tyrannize.* V. ii. 6. 9
Doest *tyrannize* in everie weaker part; *H.L.* 4
on thy subjects most doest *tyrannize?* *H.L.* 161
Tyrannizeth. *tyrannizeth* in the bitter smarts III. ii. 23. 3
Tyrannizing. So *tyrannizing* and oppressing all, V. x. 14. 1
Tyrannous. the East with *tyranous* despight *Gn.* 43
Subdeweth to his kingdome *tyrannous.* III. xii. 22. 5
T' obay a womans *tyrannous* direction, V. v. 26. 4
Tyrannously. They each at other *tyrannously* flew; V. ii. 13. 2
Tyranny. Unto such *tyrannie* doth aspire; *S.C.* F. 172
tyrannie is with strange ayde supported. *Hub.* 1121
did usurpe with wrong and *tyrannie* Upon the scepter I. iv. 12. 5
Thrall to that Gyaunts hatefull *tyranny:* I. viii. 2. 5
With cruell malice and strong *tyranny:* I. viii. 36. 5
raging passion with fierce *tyranny* II. i. 57. 4
exercise most bitter *tyranny* II. xi. 1. 7
comfortlesse through *tyranny* or might: III. ii. 14. 8
No guilt in you, but in the *tyranny* of love. III. ii. 40. 9
saves the Squyre of Dames From Gyaunts *tyranny.* III. vii. Arg.
'To all which cruell *tyranny,* they say, He is provokt, V. viii. 20. 1
through fell *tyranny* He slaughtred had, V. viii. 28. 7
there her selfe did hyde from his hard *tyranny.* V. x. 18. 9
That pride doe not to *tyranny* you lift; VI. viii. 1. 7
What *tyranny* is this, both my hart to thrall, *Am.* xliii. 5
Tyrans. *See* **Tyrant's.**
Tyrant. lordly love is such a *Tyranne* fell, *S.C.* O. 98
th' Assyrian *tyrant* would have made *Ti.* 496
Which when the greisly *tyrant* did espie, *Mui.* 433
Rather then of the *tyrant* to be caught: III. vii. 26. 8
he, the *tyrant,* which her hath in ward III. xi. 16. 6
The *Tyrant* selfe came forth with yelling bray, IV. viii. 62. 2
The which that *tyrant* gathered had by wrong IV. ix. 12. 3
his foe, A cruell *Tyrant,* IV. xii. 29. 8

Tyrant—*Continued.*
Whom a strong *tyrant* did unjustly thrall, ... V. i. 3. 7
Against that cruell *Tyrant,* which opprest The faire Irena . . V. i. 13. 3
is he vanquisht by his *tyrant* enemy?' . . . . V. vi. 10. 9
'Not by that *Tyrant,* his intended foe, ... V. vi. 11. 1
Like to the Thracian *Tyrant,* . . . . V. viii. 31. 1
By a strong *Tyrant,* who invaded has Her land, ... V. x. 6. 8
this fell *Tyrant,* . . . Had left her now but five . . . . V. x. 8. 1
this bold *Tyrant,* of her widowhed Taking advantage, ... V. x. 12. 1
Whereof that *Tyrant* had her now deprived, ... V. x. 18. 3
Whereof when newes was to that *Tyrant* brought, ... V. xi. 2. 1
When her that *Tyrant* did of Crowne deprive; . . . . V. xi. 38. 4
by that *Tyrant* is in wretched thraldome bound: . . . . V. xi. 38. 9
a *Tyrant,* which Grandtorto hight, ... V. xi. 50. 3
that *Tyrant* to fordoo,) . . . . V. xii. 3. 4
Willing him wend unto the *Tyrant* streight, ... V. xii. 8. 6
There wayting for the *Tyrant* till it was farre day. . . . . V. xii. 13. 9
The *Tyrant* thundred his thicke blowes so fast, ... V. xii. 17. 6
still the *tyrant* sternely at him layd, ... V. xii. 19. 6

Tyrant—*Continued.*
second Babell, *tyrant* of the West, ... *Com. Son.* iv. 3
whilst thou *tyrant* Love doest laugh and scorne . . . . . . *H.L.* 134
Tyrant's. his beheast they feared as a *tyrans* law. . . . I. vi. 26. 9
Parents deare from *tyrants* powre deliver might. . . . . . . I. vii. 46. 9
to redeeme thy woefull parents head From *tyrans* rage . . . I. x. 9. 5
from the Daniske *Tyrants* head shall rend Th' usurped crowne, III. iii. 47. 6
That headlesse *tyrants* tronke he reard from ground, ... IV. ix. 4. 6
on a tree before the *Tyrants* dore . . . . V. viii. 45. 1
For ayde against that cruell *Tyrants* theft, ... V. x. 14. 4
What else they have is all the *Tyrants* fee; . . . . V. x. 29. 8
forth to call Into the field their *Tyrants* Seneschall: . . . . V. x. 31. 5
Fallen into that *Tyrants* hand and usage bad. . . . . V. xi. 40. 9
By this came tydings to the *Tyrants* eare, ... V. xii. 6. 4
Glad to be quit from that proud *Tyrants* awe, ... V. xii. 24. 3
maintayne That *Tyrants* part with close or open ayde, . . . V. xii. 25. 6
Tyrants. monstrous *tyrants* with his club subdewed: . . . V. i. 2. 8
Tyrants, that make men subject to their law, ... V. ii. 38. 6
like *tyrants* mercilesse, the more Rejoyced . . . . V. iv. 23. 1

U

Ugliness. Was turned now to dreadfull *uglinesse.* . . . . . . *T.M.* 42
hideous monsters full of *uglinesse;* . . . . *D.* 340
A monstrous Dragon, full of fearefull *uglinesse.* . . . . . VI. vi. 10. 9
Ugly. I saw an *ugly* beast . . . . *Rev.* i. 1
him beside sits *ugly* Barbarisme, ... *T.M.* 187
he saw the *ugly* monster plaine, ... I. i. 14. 6
Such *ugly* monstrous shapes . . . . I. i. 21. 9
a dull blast, that . . . with foule *ugly* forme did her disgrace: I. ii. 38. 8
this same Monster much more *ugly* was, ... I. vii. 17. 6
More *ugly* shape yet never living creature saw. . . . . . . I. viii. 48. 9
The *ugly* vew of his deformed crimes; . . . . I. ix. 48. 6
horribly misshapes with *ugly* sightes, ... II. v. 27. 7
shame his *ugly* face did hide from living eye. . . . . . . II. vii. 22. 9
forth there lept An *ugly* feend, ... II. vii. 26. 7
And *ugly* shapes did nigh the man dismay, ... II. vii. 37. 7
So fowle and *ugly,* that exceeding feare . . . . II. xi. 5. 8
by those *ugly* formes weren pourtrayd . . . . II. xi. 11. 7
some like *ugly* Urchins thick and short: . . . . II. xi. 13. 4
Most *ugly* shapes and horrible aspects, ... II. xii. 23. 1
That *ugly* shape so sore her terrifide, ... III. vii. 24. 3
Let *ugly* shame and endlesse infamy Colour thy name . . . IV. i. 53. 6
This *ugly* creature in his armes her snatcht, ... IV. vii. 8. 1
Much more deformed fearefull, *ugly* were, ... IV. x. 20. 4
but halfe seene his *ugly* visnomie, ... V. iv. 11. 3
With *ugly* craples crawling in their way, ... V. viii. 40. 4
So *ugly* creature, she was nigh dismayd, ... V. ix. 12. 2
Whose *ugly* shape none ever saw, nor kend, ... V. xi. 20. 5
powred out of her infernall sinke Most *ugly* filth; . . . . . V. xi. 31. 7
His face was *ugly* and his countenance sterne, ... V. xii. 15. 6
made most *ugly* cases. . . . . V. xii. 28. 9
Her face was *ugly,* and her mouth distort, ... V. xii. 36. 1
Seeing the *ugly* Monster passing by, ... VI. v. 16. 2
Out of great Chaos *ugly* prison crept, ... *H.L.* 58
Ulcer. th' *ulcer* groweth daily more and more; . . . . . . III. ii. 39. 5
Ulfin. feld Great *Ulfin* thrise . . . . III. iii. 55. 6
Ulysses. also him that false *Ulysses* slewe, ... *Gn.* 531
Ulysses'. Wicked for holding guilefully away *Ulysses* men, . . *Gn.* 195
Penelope, for her *Ulisses* sake, ... *Am.* xxiii. 1
Umbrere. onely vented up her *umbriere,* . . . . III. i. 42. 8
therewith smote him on his *Umbriere* . . . . IV. iv. 44. 3
Una. a black stole, most like to seeme for *Una* fit. . . . . I. i. 45. 9
He saw . . . *Una* wandring in woods and forrests, ... I. ii. 9. 3
Dame *Una,* weary Dame, and entrance did requere: . . . . I. iii. 12. 9
Faire *Una* framed words and count'naunce fitt; . . . . . . I. iii. 14. 7
Sad *Una* downe her laies in weary plight, ... I. iii. 15. 3
Up *Una* rose, up rose the lyon eke; . . . . I. iii. 21. 2
subtill Archimag, that *Una* sought . . . . I. iii. 24. 6
Ere long he came where *Una* traveild slow, ... I. iii. 26. 1
Such joy made *Una,* when her knight she found; . . . . . . I. iii. 32. 1
Una cride, 'O! hold that heavie hand, ... I. iii. 37. 2
after that he had faire *Una* lorne, ... I. iv. 2. 1
From lawlesse lust . . . Fayre *Una* is releast: . . . . I. vi. Arg.
that *Una,* . . . Her truth had staynd with treason . . . . . I. vi. 2. 3
Where he unwares the fairest *Una* found, ... I. vi. 30. 6
Una gan to aske, if ought he knew, ... I. vi. 36. 4
Whiles *Una,* . . . Could not for sorrow follow him so fast; . I. vi. 40. 2
that earst would have suppresst Faire *Una;* . . . . I. vi. 40. 8
sad *Una* fraught with anguish sore, ... I. vi. 45. 7
Prince Arthure meets with *Una* . . . . I. vii. Arg.
on the way He wofull Lady, wofull *Una,* met, ... I. vii. 20. 2
'To doe her die,' (quoth *Una*) 'were despight, ... I. viii. 45. 7
'Such then,' (said *Una,*) . . . is the face of falshood: . . . . I. viii. 49. 3
Una faire, Did in that castle afterwards abide, ... I. viii. 50. 6
Una faire besought That straunger knight his name . . . tell; I. ix. 2. 6
gentle *Una* thus to him gan say: . . . . I. ix. 16. 5
Una earnd her traveill to renew. . . . . I. ix. 18. 5
Which whenas *Una* saw, ... I. ix. 52. 1
Her faithfull knight faire *Una* brings . . . . I. x. Arg.
Una saw That this her knight was feeble, ... I. x. 2. 1
when that fairest *Una* she beheld, ... I. x. 8. 6
They, seeing *Una,* towardes her gan wend, ... I. x. 15. 1
Then *Una* thus: 'But she, your sister deare, ... I. x. 16. 1
Fayre *Una* gan Fidelia fayre request, ... I. x. 18. 3
When him his dearest *Una* did behold . . . . I. x. 22. 7
Una, . . . tore Her guiltlesse garments . . . . I. x. 28. 4
Whom, thus recover'd by . . . trew Repentaunce, they to *Una* brought; . . . . I. x. 29. 2

Una—*Continued.*
fayre *Una* brought this unacquainted guest. . . . . I. x. 29. 9
The knight and *Una* entring fayre her greet, ... I. x. 32. 1
Una her besought, . . . to schoole her knight, ... I. x. 32. 5
To *Una* back he cast him to retyre, ... I. x. 68. 2
Una, who him joyd to see; . . . . I. x. 68. 6
High time now gan it wex for *Una* fayre . . . . I. xi. 1. 1
Una saw the second fall Of her deare knight, ... I. xi. 50. 1
when *Una* her did marke . . . . I. xi. 51. 6
Fayre *Una* to the Redcrosse Knight Betrouthed is . . . . . I. xii. Arg.
The fairest *Un',* his onely daughter deare, ... I. xii. 21. 2
he shortly did, and *Una* left to mourne. . . . . I. xii. 41. 9
Sith *Una* now he algates must forgoe, ... II. i. 2. 5
faire *Una* late fowle outraged, ... II. ii. 18. 2
Unable. he was . . . *unhable* once to stirre or go; . . . . . I. iv. 23. 2
thighes, *unable* to uphold His pined corse, ... I. viii. 40. 7
vanquish them, *unable* to withstand: . . . . I. x. 65. 5
Unhable their encounter to sustaine; . . . . II. ix. 14. 4
he was *unhable* them to fett, ... II. ix. 58. 3
unable to withstand Or helpe himselfe; . . . . III. vii. 43. 3
Unable to arise, or foote or hand to styre. . . . . III. vii. 45. 9
finding him *unable* once to weld, ... IV. i. 37. 3
He now *unable* was to wreake his old despight. . . . . . . IV. i. 39. 9
Unable he new battell to darraine, ... IV. iv. 26. 7
He may them catch *unable* to gainestrive, ... IV. vii. 12. 7
unable once to stirre or move. . . . . IV. xii. 20. 9
Me first he tooke *unhable* to withstond, ... VI. i. 16. 6
Being *unhable* else alone to ride, ... VI. iii. 46. 3
Being *unable* to digest that bone; . . . . VI. iv. 21. 7
his great force *unable* to endure, ... VI. v. 16. 6
As he *unable* were for very neede To move one foote, . . . VI. vi. 19. 6
unable to support So huge a burden . . . . VI. viii. 16. 6
unable it to ayd: . . . . VI. xii. 16. 5
That are *unable* else to see his face, ... *H.H.B.* 117
Unacquainted. She . . . th' *unacquainted* light began to feare, I. v. 21. 4
To her fayre Una brought this *unacquainted* guest. . . . . . I. x. 29. 9
Thether he brought these *unacquainted* guests, ... VI. iv. 14. 1
Unadvised. And *unadvised* oversights amend. *Ded.Son.*xii.12
Through *unadvized* rashnes woxen wood; . . . . I. iv. 34. 3
Unappeased. whose *unappeased* guilt Powr'd vengeance forth *Ro.* xxiv. 10
Unapt. to all vertue it may seeme *unapt,* . . . . VI. v. 1. 7
Unaptness. through *unaptnesse* in the substance fownd, . . *H.B.* 144
Unarmed. they might perceive his head To bee *unarmd,* . . I. ix. 22. 2
Halfe armd and halfe *unarmd,* . . . . III. i. 63. 3
his right hand *unarmed* fearefully did wield. . . . . III. xii. 12. 9
armed Knights and eke *unarmed* rout; . . . . V. vi. 30. 3
Ne surely thus *unarm'd* I likely were; . . . . VI. ii. 8. 3
'Perdie great blame . . . a wight *unarm'd* to wrong: . . . . VI. ii. 8. 7
'*Unarm'd* all was the knight, ... VI. ii. 18. 1
what cruell hand hath thus arayd This knight *unarm'd* . . . VI. ii. 42. 4
And him *unarm'd,* . . . Charg'd with his speare, ... VI. ii. 43. 4
Being *unarm'd* and set in secret shade. . . . . VI. iii. 8. 5
Unarm'd, as fearing neither foe nor frend, ... VI. iv. 17. 4
All quite *unarm'd,* as then their manner was. . . . . VII. vi. 24. 3
Love, . . . *unarmed* then and naked, ... *H.L.* 62
Una's. For fairest *Unaes* sake, of whom I sing, ... I. iii. 2. 2
Unaes foe, that all her realme did pray. . . . . I. ix. 20. 3
They turne themselves, at *Unaes* meeke request, ... I. x. 15. 6
By Arthure, when as *Unas* Knight he did maintaine. . . . . VI. vii. 41. 9
Unassailable. Both *unassaylable,* gave him great ayde: . . . V. ix. 5. 3
Unassured. The fayned friends, the *unassured* foes, ... *H.L.* 263
Unaware. least Force or Fraud should *unaware* Breake in . . II. vii. 25. 3
The Blatant Beast forth rushing *unaware* . . . . VI. iii. 24. 2
lurke In close await, to catch her *unaware:* . . . . *Am.* lxxi. 4
Unawares. *unawares* doe into daunger fall, ... *Van.* xii. 8
One of the litle yonglings *unawares:* . . . . *Mui.* 407
fort . . . *unawares* at disavantage fownd. . . . . I. ix. 11. 4
unawares upon her laying hold, ... IV. ii. 45. 6
All *unawares* he started up anon, ... IV. iii. 31. 3
all *unawares* espide An armed Knight . . . . IV. vi. 2. 4
Whiles *unawares* his saddle he forwent, ... IV. vi. 11. 8
Had *unawares* her snatched up from ground: . . . . IV. vii. 4. 6
All *unawares* the bird, ... IV. viii. 7. 5
him *unawares* there caught; . . . . IV. viii. 51. 6
Unbarred. he behight Those gates to be *unbar'd,* . . . . . II. xi. 17. 4
the gate to him *unbard;* . . . . IV. ix. 5. 8
She bad that streight the gates should be *unbard,* . . . . . V. iv. 37. 8

Unbid. with it hong him selfe, *unbid,* unblest. . . . I. ix. 54. 5
Unbind. none else from hence may us *unbynd.'* . . . I. ii. 43. 9
A Satyre . . . The loyall linkes of wedlocke did *unbinde,* . . I. vi. 22. 8
Nyne monethes I seek in vain, yet ni'll that vow *unbynd.'* . . I. ix. 15. 9
His blindfold eies he bad awhile *unbinde,* . . . III. xii. 22. 6
To know what Virgin did them thence *unbind,* . . . IV. viii. 22. 2
Therefore I cast how I may him *unbind,* . . . V. v. 32. 7
find In her false hart his bondage to *unbind,* . . . V. v. 56. 5
He first her hands beginneth to *unbind,* . . . VI. viii. 50. 5
Till Fortune would her captive bonds *unbynde:* . . . VI. xi. 8. 8
Unbinds. *And Furors chayne *unbinds:* . . . II. v. Arg.
it wilfully *unbindes.* . . . II. v. 1. 9
Unblamed. Joying together in *unblam'd* delight; . . . VI. ii. 43. 3
Unblemished. To blot your beautie, that *unblemisht* is, . . . V. xi. 62. 3
Unblest. this bold Ape, *unblest,* . . . *Hub.* 915
with it hong him selfe, unbid, *unblest.* . . . I. ix. 54. 5
To shame us all with this *Ungirt unblest!* . . . IV. v. 18. 7
streight leapt the Carle *unblest,* . . . V. ii. 12. 7
with hand *unblest* Hayling that mayden . . . VI. i. 17. 5
Unblindfold. He bad his eyes to be *unblindfold* both, . . . VI. vii. 33. 8
Unbodied. Her soule *unbodied* of the burdenous corpse. . . . *S.C.* N. 166
Unbodied, unsoul'd, unheard, unseene: . . . VII. vii. 46. 5
Unborn. thee, yet *unborne,* Thy Grandsire Nereus promist to adorne? . . . III. iv. 36. 4
Unbosomed. all the sleights *unbosomd* in his hart: . . . III. x. 7. 3
Unbound. longs to bee *unbound* From the strong shackles . . *D.* 85
His griesie lockes, long growen and *unbound,* . . . I. ix. 35. 4
like a ghost he seem'd whose grave-clothes were *unbound:* . . II. xi. 20. 9
in her snow-white smocke, with locks *unbownd,* . . . III. i. 63. 7
What bootes it him from death to be *unbownd,* . . . III. v. 42. 7
when she felt her selfe to be *unbownd* . . . III. xii. 38. 8
Eftsoones him selfe he from his hold *unbownd,* . . . V. ii. 16. 4
he softly it *unbound;* . . . VI. xii. 9. 5
Unbrace. gan soone *unbrace* His grasping hold: . . . II. iv. 9. 7
Unbraced. her lanck loynes ungirt, and brests *unbraste,* . . . III. vi. 18. 4
Unbridled. luck and loves *unbridled* lore . . . *S.C.* D. 63
Unbruised. helmes *unbruzed* wexen dayly browne. . . . *S.C.* O. 42
Unbuckling. which he *unbuckling* eft Presented to the fayrest Florimell, . . . V. iii. 27. 7
Unburied. As selfe to dyen bad, *unburied* bad to beene.' . . . II. i. 59. 9
their vile carcases now left *unburied.* . . . II. vii. 30. 9
Uncase. The Foxe . . . He did *uncase,* . . . *Hub.* 1380
Uncased. all men him *uncased* gan deride, . . . *Hub.* 930
Braggadochio is *uncas'd* In all the Ladies sights. . . . V. iii. Arg.
when these counterfeits were thus *uncased* . . . V. iii. 39. 1
Uncertain. a faint shadow of *uncertein* light: . . . II. vii. 29. 6
wandreth evermore *uncertein* and unsure. . . . II. xii. 12. 9
yet *uncertaine* by such outward sight, . . . IV. ii. 40. 7
Uncertaine whether had the better side; . . . V. ii. 17. 2
stood long staring on him mongst *uncertaine* feares. . . . V. vii. 39. 9
made him stagger with *uncertaine* sway, . . . V. xi. 11. 2
With weary travell and *uncertaine* toile, . . . VI. iv. 25. 5
by th' *uncertaine* glims of starry night, . . . VI. viii. 48. 1
Uncertainty. That ye doe tell in such *uncertaintee?* . . . III. viii. 48. 4
Unchangeable. yee make Immortall and *unchangeable* to be: . VII. vii. 54. 3
Unchaste. Seeking to match the chaste with th' *unchaste* Ladies traine.' . . . III. vii. 60. 9
Uncheerful. by the change of her *unchearefull* looke, . . . V. vii. 18. 1
Having disperst the nights *unchearefull* dampe, . . . *Epith.* 21
Uncivil. An uncouth, salvage, and *uncivile* wight, . . . II. vii. 3. 4
that vile hag, or her *uncivile* sonne; . . . III. vii. 19. 6
Whilest he reformed that *uncivill* fo, . . . V. i. 21. 4
Uncle. their *uncle* Vortigere Usurpt the crowne . . . II. x. 64. 2
Unclean. with their feete *uncleane* the water fouled, . . . *Bel.*[1] x. 13
with hands *uncleane* Dares to pollute . . . *T.M.* 567
Through vaine illusion of their lust *unclene,* . . . II. x. 8. 7
with cursed hands *uncleane* Whipping her horse, . . . VI. vii. 39. 7
all worlds glorie is but drosse *uncleane,* . . . *Am.* xxvii. 2
Uncleanness. Gods majestie, Whom no *uncleannes* may approachen nie; . . . *Hub.* 466
Uncle's. envious of *Uncles* soveraintie, . . . II. x. 48. 7
Uncombed. lockes *uncombed* cruell adders be. . . . *Gn.* 344
His carelesse locks *uncombed* and unshorne, . . . *D.* 43
curld *uncombed* heares Upstaring stiffe, . . . I. ix. 22. 2
Uncomb'd, uncurl'd, and carelesly unshed; . . . IV. vii. 40. 6
Uncomely. with *uncomely* weedes the gentle wave accloyes. . II. vii. 15. 9
Owles, with beckes *uncomely* bent; . . . II. xi. 8. 3
uncomely idlenesse . . . to build her sluggish nest, . . . III. v. 2. 1
did *uncomely* speaches crake. . . . V. iii. 16. 7
his bigge hart loth'd so *uncomely* vew: . . . V. v. 22. 5
causd him those *uncomely* weedes undight; . . . V. vii. 41. 2
with *uncomely* shame Gan him salute, . . . VI. i. 24. 8
To weet the cause of so *uncomely* fray, . . . VI. ii. 4. 4
And shrieked out, a thing *uncomely* for a knight. . . . VI. iv. 8. 9
How fortuneth this foule *uncomely* plight, . . . VI. vii. 14. 8
Throughout the world in this *uncomely* case, . . . VI. vii. 38. 2
inward shame of her *uncomely* case She did conceive, . . . VI. viii. 51. 1
Night had covered her *uncomely* face . . . VII. vii. 44. 4
Ne thought of thing *uncomely* ever may Thereto approch . *Epith.* 198
Unconquered. to the last *unconquer'd* did appeare; . . . IV. v. 8. 7
Uncontrolled. Where so us listeth, *uncontrol'd* of anie: . . *Hub.* 169
Of fortune and of envy *uncomptrold,* . . . *Col.* 662
uncontrolled freedome to obtaine. . . . V. ii. 33. 5
Uncorrupt. heavens . . . Unmoving, *uncorrupt,* and spotlesse bright, . . . *H.H.B.* 68
Uncourteous. that *uncurteous* Carle, their commune foe, . . . III. ix. 17. 8
eke thy words *uncourteous* and unkempt: . . . III. x. 29. 7
Uncouth. In hope of better that was *uncouth!* . . . *S.C.* S. 60
In some straunge habit, after *uncouth* wize; . . . *Hub.* 84
Soone as that *uncouth* light upon them shone, . . . I. i. 15. 8

Uncouth—*Continued.*
cleane dismayd to see so *uncouth* sight, . . . I. i. 50. 1
All stand amazed at so *uncouth* sight, . . . I. vi. 9. 6
The greatest Earth his *uncouth* mother was, . . . I. vii. 9. 1
very *uncouth* sight was to behold, . . . I. viii. 31. 1
dismaid with *uncouth* dread: . . . I. ix. 22. 3
with the *uncouth* smart the Monster lowdly cryde. . . . I. xi. 20. 9
He weened well to worke some *uncouth* wyle: . . . II. i. 8. 2
he Guyon guydes an *uncouth* way . . . II. i. 24. 1
Great cause, I weene, you guided, or some *uncouth* chaunce.' . II. i. 29. 9
Guyon standing by their *uncouth* strife does see. . . . II. v. 20. 9
much he wondred at that *uncouth* sight: . . . II. vi. 43. 2
An *uncouth,* salvage, and uncivile wight, . . . II. vii. 3. 4
Guyon mervayld at her *uncouth* cace; . . . II. ix. 43. 5
when his *uncouth* manner he did vew, . . . II. xi. 27. 5
what *uncouth* wind Brought her into those partes, . . . III. ii. 4. 5
What *uncouth* fit,' (sayd she) 'what evill plight . . . III. ii. 30. 7
Of much more *uncouth* thing I was affrayd, . . . III. ii. 40. 3
His *uncouth* shield and straunge armes her dismayd, . . . III. iv. 51. 1
uncouth formes, which none yet ever knew: . . . III. vi. 35. 2
Through many a wood and many an *uncouth* way, . . . III. x. 34. 2
with such *uncouth* welcome did receave Her fayned Paramour, IV. i. 36. 2
halfe affeard Of th' *uncouth* sight, . . . IV. iii. 31. 6
all men wondred at the *uncouth* sight, . . . IV. v. 17. 1
To be spectators of this *uncouth* fit, . . . IV. vi. 30. 3
his *uncouth* guise and usage quaint . . . IV. vii. 45. 1
them to view had bene an *uncouth* sight, . . . IV. viii. 34. 7
unknowen geare And *uncouth* fashion, . . . IV. xi. 45. 3
To view the building of that *uncouth* place, . . . IV. xii. 4. 6
(An *uncouth* sight) he plainely then descride . . . V. iv. 21. 7
Much did he marvell at her *uncouth* speach, . . . V. v. 37. 1
doubtfully dismayd through that so *uncouth* sight. . . . V. vii. 16. 9
when she saw that lothly *uncouth* sight . . . V. vii. 37. 6
on his backe an *uncouth* vestiment . . . V. ix. 10. 7
Which *uncouth* use when as the Prince perceived, . . . V. xi. 7. 1
That mote to all men seeme an *uncouth* sight; . . . VI. v. 9. 2
Ne skilfull of the *uncouth* jeopardy; . . . VI. v. 16. 4
What meaning mote those *uncouth* words comprize, . . . VI. viii. 18. 4
on her *uncouth* habit and sterne looke still gazed. . . . VII. vi. 13. 9
To hide the terror of her *uncouth* hew . . . VII. vii. 6. 2
With crooked crawling steps an *uncouth* pase, . . . VII. vii. 35. 6
Uncrudded. *See* **Uncurded.**
Uncurded. Her brest like to a bowle of creame *uncrudded,* . . *Epith.* 175
Uncurled. Uncomb'd, *uncurl'd,* and carelesly unshed; . . . IV. vii. 40. 6
Undefied. broken hast The law of armes to strike foe *undefide:* II. viii. 31. 7
Undefiled. With fleshly follyes *undefyled,* . . . *S.C.* Jul. 155
Dan Chaucer, well of English *undefyled,* . . . IV. ii. 32. 8
Under (*partial list*).
Let me no more see faire thing *under* sky, . . . *Bel.* iv. 12
th' earth *under* her childrens weight did grone, . . . *Ro.* xii. 7
That, in his throat him pricking softly *under,* . . . *Van.* v. 9
The blocke oft groned *under* the blow, . . . *S.C.* F. 215
summer shade, *under* the cocked hay. . . . *S.C.* N. 12
By that same River lurking *under* greene, . . . *Gn.* 649
under colour of the confidence . . . *Hub.* 1164
Truth to imitate, . . . *under* Mimick shade, . . . *T.M.* 207
All things doo change that *under* heaven abide, . . . *Ti.* 206
No braver Poeme can be *under* Sun. . . . *Col.* 411
Whose semblance she did carrie *under* feigned hew. . . . I. i. 46. 9
Monarch layd Low *under* all, yet above all in pride, . . . I. v. 48. 6
a ship, that flyes fayre *under* sayle, . . . I. vi. 1. 1
The ground eke groned *under* him . . . I. vii. 8. 6
Under the foot of Rauran mossy hore, . . . I. ix. 4. 6
borne *under* cruell starre, . . . II. ii. 2. 1
Three sonnes . . . all *under* age; . . . II. x. 64. 1
many arrowes *under* his right side, . . . II. xi. 21. 2
So held them *under* fast; . . . II. xii. 81. 6
her sexe *under* that straunge purport Did use to hide, . . . III. i. 52. 7
tell *Under* what coast of heaven the man did dwell, . . . III. iii. 6. 5
From *under* that deepe Rock most horribly rebowndes. . . . III. iii. 9. 9
He was surprisd, and buried *under* beare, . . . III. iii. 11. 2
Whose fruitlesse lives were *under* furrow sowne, . . . III. ix. 35. 8
Which hoved close *under* a forest side, . . . III. x. 20. 8
shivered speares, and swords all *under* strowen, . . . IV. iv. 38. 4
and therewith *Under* his side him nipt; . . . IV. v. 44. 4
Knight *under* a forrest side Sitting in shade . . . IV. vi. 2. 5
her away with him did beare *Under* his arme, . . . IV. vii. 24. 8
She were as faire as any *under* skie: . . . IV. viii. 49. 7
Like to a storme which hovers *under* skie, . . . IV. ix. 33. 4
Both male and female, both *under* one name: . . . IV. x. 41. 7
Venus! . . . that *under* skie Doest fayrest shine, . . . IV. x. 44. 2
Under Slewbloome in shady grove was got, . . . IV. xi. 42. 5
Under the which her feet appeared plaine, . . . IV. xi. 47. 5
Under the hanging of an hideous clieffe . . . IV. xii. 5. 1
But closely rankled *under* th' orifis: . . . IV. xii. 22. 7
There forth issewd from *under* th' Altars smooke . . . V. xi. 22. 4
he heard *under* the forrests syde A voice, . . . VI. iv. 26. 6
Under the greenewoods side . . . VI. iv. 39. 2
Seem'd *under* her protection him to shroud; . . . VI. vi. 31. 4
being bred *under* base shepheards wings, . . . VI. ix. 35. 4
When any winde doth *under* heaven blowe; . . . VII. vii. 20. 7
Ne joy of ought that *under* heaven doth hove . . . *Am.* lxxxviii. 9
Underfang. Didst *underfong* my lasse to wexe so light, . . . *S.C.* Jun. 103
looser songs of love to *underfong,* . . . *S.C.* N. 22
some by sleight he eke doth *underfong.* . . . V. ii. 7. 5
Underground. And I creepe *under ground,* . . . *Hub.* 991
under ground to goe to give them light . . . *D.* 478
Fell sodainly and faded *under ground;* . . . *D.* 481
streames . . . He *under ground* so closely did convay, . . . *Col.* 142
Lurking in rockes and caves far *under ground,* . . . II. i. 22. 3

Underground—*Continued.*
that above were added to that *under grownd*. . . . II. vii. 31. 9
It is a darksome delve farre *under ground*, . . . IV. i. 20. 4
Farre *under ground* from tract of living went, . . . IV. ii. 47. 5
Ne wist whether above she were or *under ground*. . . . IV. vii. 9. 9
what ghosts there *under ground* Lay hid . . . IV. vii. 33. 5
doth make His way still *under ground*, . . . IV. xi. 32. 9
Is wondrous strong and hewen farre *under ground*, . . . V. ix. 6. 3
Underhand. many rivers taking *under-hand* Into his waters . IV. xi. 34. 3
with her husband *under hand* so wrought, . . . VI. iv. 38. 4
Underkeep. The sectaries of my celestiall skill . . . They *underkeep*, . . . *T.M.* 77
Underkept. long bene *underkept* and down supprest, . . . II. xi. 32. 2
Rored and raged to be *underkept*; . . . III. vii. 33. 8
Underlays. golde, which *underlayes* The summer beames, . . *Gn.* 99
Undermind. *See* **Undermine.**
with slie shiftes and wiles did *underminde* All noble Knights, . V. vi. 32. 7
Undermine. *See* **Undermind.**
So striving each th' other to *undermine*, . . . II. xii. 59. 5
Undermined. as a Castle, . . . Is *undermined* from the lowest ground, . . . I. viii. 23. 3
Underneath. everie stick that *underneath* did ly, . . . *Hub.* 1008
From *underneath* his head he tooke away, . . . *Hub.* 1322
underneath her scornefull feete was layne . . . I. iv. 10. 4
gowne . . . *underneath* did hide his filthinesse; . . . I. iv. 25. 2
underneath their feet, . . . I. iv. 36. 8
Sansfoy shrinck *underneath* his speare: . . . I. v. 23. 2
Forth ryding *underneath* the castell wall, . . . I. v. 53. 7
lept from *underneath* the blow: . . . I. vii. 12. 6
underneath his filthy feet did tread . . . I. vii. 18. 6
Did grone full grievous *underneath* the blow, . . . I. viii. 8. 8
sprites, from *underneath* the stone, . . . cryde continually; . . I. viii. 36. 6
hid *underneath* the ground, . . . I. viii. 38. 7
Far *underneath* a craggy clift ypight, . . . I. ix. 33. 3
th' earth him *underneath* Did grone, . . . I. xi. 54. 3
this dead corpse, that lies here *underneath*, . . . II. i. 49. 7
His yron cote, . . . Was *underneath* enveloped with gold; . . II. vii. 4. 2
The rest hidd *underneath* him more desirous made. . . . II. xii. 66. 9
So *underneath* her feet their swords they mard, . . . III. i. 30. 6
lay *underneath* his hed, . . . III. i. 36. 3
To make his wonne, low *underneath* the ground, . . . III. iii. 7. 6
rocky Cave, . . . Hewen *underneath* that Mount, . . . III. vi. 48. 9
speare he fierce aventred . . . close *underneath* his shield, . IV. iii. 9. 2
reaching forth his sweard Close *underneath* his shield, . . . IV. iii. 33. 7
underneath, the river rolling still . . . IV. x. 15. 8
underneath, his breech was all to-torne and jagged. . . . V. ix. 10. 9
underneath her feete . . . An huge great Lyon lay, . . . V. ix. 33. 3
The Monster *underneath* the Altar lay: . . . V. xi. 21. 7
I . . . Strooke him, as seemeth, *underneath* the hart, . . . VI. ii. 12. 8
layd her *underneath* a bush to sleepe, . . . VI. iii. 44. 6
Did *underneath* them make a gloomy shade, . . . VI. iv. 13. 7
whilest many *underneath* him fell. . . . VI. vi. 23. 9
And *underneath* thy feete to place her prayse; . . . VI. x. 28. 7
underneath the ground their way was made . . . VI. x. 42. 1
Calidore Had, *underneath*, him armed privily. . . . VI. xi. 36. 4
trembled *underneath* his mighty hand, . . . VI. xii. 36. 8
the earth far *underneath* her feete Was dight . . . VII. vii. 10. 1
underneath his feet are to be found . . . *H.H.B.* 180
Undersay. by my soule, I dare *undersaye* . . . *S.C.* S. 91
Undersong. Weepe, Shepheard! weepe, to make my *undersong*. . *D.* 245
Weep, Shepheard! weep, to make mine *undersong*. . . . *D.* 294
Weepe, Shepheard! weepe, to make my *undersong*. . . . *D.* 343, 392, 441, 490
Cease, Shepheard! cease, and end thy *undersong*.' . . . *D.* 539
He cryed out, to make his *undersong*; . . . *Col.* 169
redoubled that her *undersong*, . . . *Proth.* 110
Undersongs. So weren his *under-songs* well addrest. . . . *S.C.* Au. 128
Understand. That ye may *understand* my shreiking yell. . . *Ro.* i. 8
as if they could him *understand*; . . . *Gn.* 454
'Yet doth not my dull wit well *understand* . . . *D.* 176
She could not heare, nor speake, nor *understand*; . . . I. iii. 11. 4
freends . . . Ne dare to weepe, nor seeme to *understand* . . . I. iii. 20. 7
feates of armes did wisely *understand*. . . . I. iii. 42. 5
understand The secret meaning of th' eternall might, . . . I. ix. 6. 7
trew . . . Those tydinges were, as he did *understand*: . . . I. xi. 3. 4
Suffice it heare by signes to *understand* . . . I. xii. 40. 4
their strife to *understond*; . . . II. ii. 21. 7
the truth to let me *understand*. . . . II. iv. 23. 9
Their countreys auncestry to *understond*, . . . II. ix. 60. 7
How brutish is it not to *understand* . . . II. x. 69. 7
lent her wary eare to *understand* . . . III. i. 60. 8
Which when his mother deare did *understond*, . . . III. iv. 29. 5
if ye *understand* Which way she fared hath, . . . III. v. 4. 8
he sought her . . . every where that he mote *understond* . III. x. 19. 7
to *understand* What mote they be: . . . IV. ii. 31. 3
The day was set, that all might *understand*, . . . IV. iii. 3. 3
goldsmithes cunning could not *understand* . . . IV. vi. 20. 5
made her (*him) *understand* His sorrowes cause, . . . IV. viii. 12. 3
desirous t' *understand* Tydings . . . IV. viii. 62. 8
Whose substance was uneath to *understand*: . . . IV. x. 39. 3
Whose counsels depth thou canst not *understand*; . . . V. ii. 42. 7
then you shall my sentence *understand*.' . . . V. iv. 16. 8
vertuous women wisely *understand*, . . . V. v. 25. 7
To *understand* that villeins dwelling place, . . . V. ix. 7. 2
that those knights likewise mote *understand*, . . . V. ix. 37. 4
greedy t' *understand* To whether should the victory befall, . V. xi. 15. 7
shall thy treason *understand*, . . . VI. i. 25. 7
like as she best could *understand*, . . . VI. ii. 44. 5
To *understand* what there was to be donne: . . . VI. iv. 2. 5
Or *understand* that she in safetie did remaine. . . . VI. iv. 40. 9
understand that to this grove Sir Calepine, . . . VI. viii. 46. 6

Understand—*Continued.*
ere she could thy cause wel *understand*, . . . *Am.* xlviii. 3
Understanding. Man without *understanding* doth appeare; . . *T.M.* 128
Through secret *understanding* of their feature. . . . IV. ii. 44. 5
understanding by her mightie art . . . IV. iii. 40. 6
Understands. Soone as the Redcrosse knight he *understands* To beene departed . . . II. i. 1. 4
Fayre Pastorella by great hap Her parents *understands*. . . VI. xii. Arg.
Understood. Wherein darke things were writt, hard to be *understood*. . . . I. x. 13. 9
told for secret, how he *understood* . . . II. iv. 22. 5
They wondred much; and shortly *understood* . . . III. v. 38. 3
Glaucus, that wise southsayes *understood*; . . . IV. xi. 13. 3
understood the cause of all her care . . . IV. xii. 12. 2
when he *understood* by common fame . . . V. iii. 10. 5
what of it became none *understood*: . . . V. iii. 26. 6
To hide thy state from being *understood*? . . . V. vii. 21. 5
When Calidore this ruefull storie had Well *understood*, . . . VI. ii. 44. 2
herbe . . . Whose vertue he by use well *understood*; . . . VI. iv. 12. 7
Which when her father *understood*, . . . VI. xii. 5. 5
Askt her, how mote her words be *understood*, . . . VI. xii. 17. 3
Undertake. some good course that we might *undertake*; . . . *Hub.* 411
all knights on earth, that batteill *undertake*.' . . . I. xi. 2. 9
I *undertake* Shall . . . by thy side be fond.' . . . II. iii. 18. 6
none of them durst *undertake* the fight; . . . IV. ii. 40. 4
he did *undertake* Both her and eke all others to excell: . . V. iii. 16. 5
Whose voice so soone as he did *undertake*, . . . V. iii. 34. 4
Nor *undertake* the same for cowheard feare, . . . V. x. 15. 5
for meed did *undertake* So hard a taske . . . VI. vii. 15. 2
he would *undertake* for this to get her To be his Love, . . VII. vi. 44. 5
Undertaken. the former chace Had *undertaken* after her, . . . III. v. 37. 2
his avowed quest, Which he had *undertane* to Gloriane; . . V. viii. 3. 3
Undertane. *See* **Undertaken.**
Undertime. He, comming home at *undertime*, . . . III. vii. 13. 1
Undertook. All which he *undertooke* for to repaire, . . . V. ii. 32. 7
Undeserved. Remember yet my *undeserved* paines; . . . *D.* 522
In pitie of my *undeserv'd* distresse, . . . *D.* 531
That I must rue his *undeserved* wrong: . . . I. Pr. 2. 8
hart of flint would rew The *undeserved* woes and sorrowes, . I. ii. 26. 9
she gan mone his *undeserved* smart, . . . IV. viii. 3. 8
Undid. doft his helmet, and *undid* his mayle: . . . IV. i. 43. 7
That cruell Atropos eftsoones *undid*, . . . IV. ii. 48. 7
Sir Artegall *undid* the evill fashion, . . . V. ii. 28. 7
Undight. From her fayre head her fillet she *undight*, . . . I. iii. 4. 5
she left her lockes *undight*, . . . II. xii. 15. 6
His mayled haberjeon she did *undight*, . . . III. v. 31. 8
Now loose about her shoulders hong *undight*, . . . III. vi. 18. 8
Each gan *undight* Their garments wett, . . . III. ix. 19. 6
causd him those uncomely weedes *undight*; . . . V. vii. 41. 2
For his loves sake his Lions skin *undight*; . . . V. viii. 2. 5
His warlike armes he had from him *undight*, . . . VI. iii. 20. 5
Having his armes and warlike things *undight*, . . . VI. vii. 19. 3
Undiscerned. *undiscerned* forth with him did pas. . . . IV. viii. 59. 5
Undisciplined. Like this wyld man being *undisciplynd*, . . VI. v. 1. 6
Undiscreet. 'Are mortall men so fond and *undiscreet* . . . II. vii. 14. 7
Undo. can *undoe* Dame Natures kindly course; . . . *S.C.* N. 124
since that band ye cannot . . . doen *undo*, . . . I. xii. 19. 6
So thought she to *undoe* her daughters love; . . . III. ii. 51. 6
though he could not salve, Ne done *undoe*, . . . IV. iv. 27. 2
if he should through pride your doome *undo*, . . . IV. xii. 10. 4
eke of powre her owne doome to *undo*, . . . V. v. 41. 8
But his owne doome, that none can now *undoo*.' . . . V. vi. 16. 5
His axe he could not from his shield *undoe*; . . . V. xii. 22. 5
Undone. shall backe reverse . . . and be quite *undonne*: . . . *Ro.* xxii. 12
great daunger, like to bee *undone*, . . . *Hub.* 184
To spend, to give, to want, to be *undonne*. . . . *Hub.* 906
least they should be *undone*: . . . I. x. 43. 3
ever what she did was streight *undonne*. . . . III. ii. 51. 5
To make exceeding mone, as they had been *undonne*. . . . III. vii. 19. 9
folly seem'd to leave the thing *undonne* . . . IV. x. 53. 4
In one short houre I find by her *undonne*. . . . *Am.* xxiii. 8
Undoubtedly. This doe, and live, els dye *undoubtedly*.' . . . III. xii. 35. 7
Undressed. Where groomes awayted her to have *undrest*; . . V. vi. 23. 3
she ne would *undressed* be for ought, . . . V. vi. 23. 4
Unto his bowre was brought, and there *undrest* . . . VI. iii. 9. 8
Uneasy. Deepe, darke, *uneasy*, dolefull, comfortlesse. . . . I. v. 36. 6
Uneath. *uneth* may I stand any more: . . . *S.C.* S. 48
Is it so *uneath* To leave this life, . . . *D.* 447
let him die at ease, that liveth here *uneath*? . . . I. ix. 38. 9
Whose passing price *uneath* was to be told: . . . I. x. 31. 7
seemd *uneath* to shake the stedfast ground. . . . I. xi. 4. 3
his fierce foe his steed could stay *uneath*, . . . II. i. 27. 8
the sorrowes that *uneath* My tong can tell, . . . II. i. 49. 5
Sir Guyon could *uneath* From teares abstayne; . . . II. i. 56. 5
Uneath is to assure; *uneath* to wene . . . II. x. 8. 2
whose royaltee And rich purveyance might *uneath* be red; . . III. i. 33. 3
sith it is *uneath* to finde his haunt, . . . III. ii. 16. 2
Through which it was *uneath* for wight to wade; . . . III. v. 17. 3
his faire wife, whom honest long he kept *uneath*. . . . III. x. 2. 9
who he whilome was *uneath* was to be red. . . . IV. vii. 40. 9
she *uneath* discerned whether whether weare. . . . IV. ix. 10. 9
uneath they forced were, . . . IV. ix. 25. 7
Him from his wicked will *uneath* refrayned; . . . IV. x. 36. 7
Whose substance was *uneath* to understand: . . . IV. x. 39. 3
who he was *uneath* was to descry; . . . V. iv. 22. 6
With heavie eyne, from teares *uneath* refrayning, . . . VI. ii. 41. 7
Since I him lately lost, *uneath* is to define. . . . VI. v. 28. 9
So her *uneath* at last he did revive . . . VI. xi. 50. 8
Uneaths. That now *unnethes* their feete could them uphold. . *S.C.* Ja. 6
uneathes it can refraine . . . II. vi. 1. 4

Unequal. Strove with a Spider his *unequall* peare; . . . . . *Van.* vi. 5
this was drawne of six *unequall* beasts, ... I. iv. 18. 1
daunt *unequall* armies of his foes, ... I. vii. 34. 3
Scorning the let of so *unequall* foe: . . . . I. viii. 13. 5
My selfe well wote, and mine *unequall* fate: . . . . II. vii. 50. 5
to him both far *unequall* yeares, . . . has; . . . . III. ix. 4. 6
Dissemblaunce and Suspect . . . yet an *unequall* paire; . . . . III. xii. 14. 2
Likewise *unequall* were her handes twaine; . . . . IV. i. 29. 1
With ods of so *unequall* match opprest, ... IV. ix. 32. 2
For-why, he sayd, they all *unequall* were, ... V. ii. 32. 1
Subjected hath to my *unequall* might. . . . . V. v. 32. 3
with *unequall* might doe overlay, ... V. xi. 51. 7
slaine in so *unequall* fight: . . . . VI. vi. 37. 7
Unequally. (Oppressing them with power *unequally*,) . . . VII. vii. 14. 7
Unespied. them borne aside Into a secret corner *unespide*. . . *Hub.* 1018
Passe *unespide* to meete her by the way; . . . . *Col.* 140
Shee, . . . lurkt in rocks and caves, long *unespide*. . . . . . I. viii. 50. 5
tombling into mischiefe *unespide*: . . . . II. xii. 35. 4
joyd his love in secret *unespyde*: . . . . III. i. 37. 2
Beholding all, yet of them *unespyde*. . . . . VI. x. 11. 5
Uneth. *See* **Uneath.**
Uneven. The other like a beares *uneven* paw, ... I. viii. 48. 8
gathering up himselfe . . . With his *uneven* wings, ... I. xi. 40. 8
Th' *uneven* nomber for this busines is most fitt.' . . . . III. ii. 50. 9
So forth they traveld, an *uneven* payre . . . . VI. v. 9. 1
Unexpected. Ran towards to devoure those *unexpected* guests. . II. xii. 39. 9
Unfained. *See* **Unfeigned.**
Unfaithful. him to death *unfaithfull* Paris sent; . . . . . . *Gn.* 530
Unfaulty. His humble carriage, his *unfaulty* wayes, ... *H.H.L.* 233
Unfed. playen while their flockes be *unfedde*: . . . . *S.C.* May 44
nought he car'd his carcas long *unfed*; . . . . I. x. 48. 7
Unfeigned. But simple, trew, and eke *unfained* sweet, ... I. x. 7. 8
Friendship professed with *unfained* hart. . . . . III. iii. 62. 8
For deare affection and *unfayned* zeale . . . . VI. ii. 26. 5
Unfiled. He was all armd in rugged steele *unfilde*, ... III. vii. 30. 4
Unfit. *unfitte* to thrust in skilfull thronge, ... *S.C.* N. 27
farre *unfit* it is, that person bace . . . . *Hub.* 464
With dice, with cards, with balliards farre *unfit* . . . . . . *Hub.* 803
unfit for that rude rabblement. . . . . *Hub.* 1270
In this base Poeme, for thee far *unfitt*: . . . . *Ded. Son.* ii. 5
Unfit he was for any worldly thing, ... I. iv. 23. 1
Whose fellowship seemd far *unfitt* for warlike swaine. . . . . I. iv. 37. 9
From mothers pap I taken was *unfitt*, ... I. ix. 3. 7
yet he was *unfitt* for bloody fight. . . . . I. x. 2. 6
all *unfitt* for so great purpose, ... II. ii. 43. 9
gan to ride As one *unfitt* therefore, ... II. iii. 46. 4
Unfit faire Ladies service to supply; . . . . III. ix. 5. 2
horrour of fowle death for Knight *unfit*, ... V. iv. 25. 4
unryper yeares . . . *unfit* For thing of weight . . . . VI. ii. 9. 2
Through thicke and thin, *unfit* for any Dame: . . . . VI. ii. 10. 4
unfit to tread And lackey by him, ... VI. ii. 15. 4
him to trouble she it thought *unfit*, ... VI. ii. 47. 3
fowle discourtesie, *unfit* for Knight, ... VI. iii. 33. 6
put them all about himselfe *unfit*, ... VI. v. 8. 6
She in regard hereof refusde and thought *unfit*. . . . . . . VI. x. 9. 9
Fit to keepe sheepe, *unfit* for loves content: . . . . VI. x. 37. 4
made *unfit* to serve his lawlesse mindes behest. . . . . . . VI. xi. 7. 9
This too high flight, *unfit* for her weake wing) . . . . . . VII. vii. 1. 4
Unfitly. *Unfitly* I these ydle rimes present, ... *Ded. Son.* ix. 7
Unfitly yokt together in one teeme. . . . . III. ix. 6. 2
Unfitly furnisht with thy bag and booke, ... III. x. 24. 7
Unfitter. a farre *unfitter* taske, For trumpets sterne to chaunge I. Pr. 1. 3
Unfitting. peace, Was from those Dames so farre and so *un-fitting*, ... IV. ii. 19. 3
Unfold. one, opened, mote *unfolde* many moe. . . . . *S.C.* S. 14
no tongue can well *unfold*; . . . . *D.* 74
cruell fates the carefull threds *unfould*, ... I. vii. 22. 5
you intrete, For to *unfold* the anguish of your hart: . . . . I. vii. 40. 6
Ne wist yett how his talaunts to *unfold*; . . . . I. xi. 41. 3
Let one word fall that may your grief *unfold*, ... II. i. 46. 7
In his owne kind he gan him selfe *unfold*; . . . . II. iii. 9. 4
chaunge of colour did perforce *unfold*, ... II. ix. 39. 4
Yet list them bid their businesse to *unfold*, ... III. iii. 15. 3
dared of all sinnes the secrets to *unfold*. . . . . IV. viii. 31. 9
by that meanes which fortune did *unfold*, ... IV. viii. 53. 4
could the ledden of the gods *unfold*; . . . . IV. xi. 19. 2
vaine, I see my sorrowes to *unfold*, ... IV. xii. 6. 1
With which he thresht out falshood, and did truth *unfould*. . . V. i. 12. 9
she gan *unfold* The cause of her conceived maladie, ... V. v. 31. 7
There all her subtill nets she did *unfold*, ... V. v. 52. 1
will my cares *unfolde*, in hope to find Your aide . . . . . . V. vii. 19. 4
her brode-spreading wings did wyde *unfold*; . . . . V. ix. 28. 5
And all his disadventures to *unfold*, ... VI. iii. 15. 3
like a rose her silken leaves did faire *unfold*. . . . . . . VI. xii. 7. 9
here falleth fittest to *unfold* Her antique race . . . . . . VII. vi. 2. 1
Did unto them at length these speeches wise *unfold*; . . . . . VII. vi. 19. 9
Now like great Hills, and streight like sluces them *unfold*. . . VII. vii. 20. 9
they *unfold* Ten thousand sweet belgards, ... *H.B.* 255
And those most sacred mysteries *unfold* . . . . *H.H.B.* 234
Unfolds. Whose wreathed boughtes when ever he *unfoldes*, . . I. xi. 11. 3
Unfortunate. (O sad hap, and howre *unfortunate!*) . . . . . *Mui.* 421
whether fortunate Or else *unfortunate* may I aread, ... *Col.* 565
friendlesse, *unfortunate*, Now miserable I, Fidessa, dwell, . . I. ii. 26. 1
all the nation of *unfortunate* And fatall birds . . . . II. xii. 36. 1
Offricke and Osricke, twinnes *unfortunate*, ... III. iii. 37. 3
I am th' *unfortunate* Matilde by name, ... VI. iv. 29. 3
Unfruitful. O foolish physick, and *unfruitfull* paine, ... III. v. 42. 1
Ungentle. so loose life, and so *ungentle* trade, ... III. i. 67. 5
his *ungentle* hoste n'ote him appeach . . . . III. x. 6. 8
Him of *ungentle* usage did reprove, ... VI. iii. 42. 7

Ungentleness. Ne suffereth it thought of *ungentlenesse* . . . III. v. 2. 3
appeach Of vile *ungentlenesse*, or hospitages breach. . . . . III. x. 6. 9
Ungently. But gently tooke that *ungently* came; . . . . . . *S.C.* F. 22
He so *ungently* left her, whome she loved best. . . . . . . I. ii. 8. 9
Ungirt. her lanck loynes *ungirt*, and brests unbraste, ... III. vi. 18. 4
To shame us all with this *Ungirt unblest!* . . . . IV. v. 18. 7
Ungodly. But the *ungodly* ones he doth forsake, ... *D.* 360
Such one was Wrath, the last of this *ungodly* tire. . . . . . I. iv. 35. 9
cursed usage and *ungodly* trade . . . . IV. vii. 12. 3
makes his God of his *ungodly* pelfe, ... V. viii. 19. 8
Ungracious. some *ungracious* blast, out of the gate Of Aeoles raine, ... *Mui.* 419
catching hold of her *ungratious* tonge, ... II. iv. 12. 8
thou *ungratious* Halfe of thy dayes doest lead . . . . III. iv. 55. 8
Ungratious children of one gracelesse syre, ... III. v. 15. 6
ungracious crew which faines demurest grace. . . . . VII. vii. 35. 9
Unguessed. Me hither sent for cause to me *unghest*; . . . . I. ix. 7. 2
Unguilty. ne her *unguilty* age Did weene, ... III. ii. 26. 3
Unhable. *See* **Unable.**
Unhandsome. Such were these Hags, and so *unhandsome* drest: V. xii. 38. 1
Unhappily. on his head *unhappily* he pight, ... V. viii. 8. 2
Unhappiness. doo not see their owne *unhappiness*. . . . . . . *T.M.* 150
Unhappy. thilke same *unhappye* Ewe . . . Fell headlong . . . *S.C.* Mar. 49
I, *unhappy* man! . . . . *S.C.* Jun. 14
both were craftie and *unhappie* witted; . . . . *Hub.* 49
Unhappie wight, borne to desastrous end, ... *Hub.* 907
complayning his *unhappy* stound, ... *Hub.* 940
Most *unhappie* wretches! . . . . *T.M.* 148
Unhappie Verse, the witnesse of my *unhappie* state, ... *U.V.* 1
From my *unhappie* neighborhood farre fled, ... *Ti.* 146
'But whie (*unhappie* wight!) doo I thus crie, ... *Ti.* 176
unhappie happie Flie, Whose cruell fate . . . . *Mui.* 234
'Rise, rise! *unhappy* Swaine, ... I. ii. 4. 6
whom *unhappy* howre Hath now made thrall . . . . I. ii. 22. 2
When tidings came to mee, *unhappy* maid, ... I. ii. 24. 4
gin to pittie her *unhappie* state: . . . . I. vi. 9. 7
The messenger of so *unhappie* newes Would faine have dyde: . I. vii. 21. 1
'Unhappy falls that hard necessity,' . . . . I. xii. 19. 1
we may pitty such *unhappie* bale, ... II. ii. 45. 3
Death is for wretches borne under *unhappy* starre.' . . . . . . II. vi. 44. 9
whose *unhappy* cace . . . them driven hath . . . . II. xii. 8. 7
Shall give th' enchaunter his *unhappy* hire. . . . . III. iii. 36. 6
What shall of me, *unhappy* maid, become? . . . . IV. vii. 11. 3
'Unhappy mayd' . . . 'whose dread Untride is lesse . . . . . IV. vii. 11. 5
unhappy houre me thither brought, ... IV. vii. 18. 1
Gainst wofull Niobes *unhappy* race, ... IV. vii. 30. 8
Like as it fell to this *unhappy* boy, ... IV. viii. 2. 1
Terpine, borne to' a more *unhappy* howre, ... V. v. 18. 4
'Unhappie knight! upon whose hopelesse state . . . . V. v. 36. 1
'Unhappy Squire! what hard mishap thee brought . . . . . . VI. i. 12. 1
An hard adventure with *unhappie* end, ... VI. iv. 17. 7
In th' heritage of our *unhappie* paine: . . . . VI. vi. 31. 5
made great mone for that *unhappy* turne: . . . . VI. x. 18. 6
thou *unhappy*, which them thence didst chace, ... VI. x. 20. 2
Unhasty. From her *unhastie* beast she did alight; . . . . . . I. iii. 4. 2
Unheal. suddeinly both would themselves *unhele*, ... II. xii. 64. 8
The face of his deare Canacee *unheale*; . . . . IV. v. 10. 7
Unheard. Unbodied, unsoul'd, *unheard*, unseene: . . . . . . VII. vii. 46. 5
Unhearsed. himselfe baffuld, and his armes *unherst*, ... V. iii. 37. 8
Unheedily. some lost great hope *unheedily*, ... IV. x. 13. 5
Unheedy. Threatning *unheedy* wrecke and rash decay, ... II. x. 6. 5
Unhele. *See* **Unheal.**
Unherst. *See* **Unhearsed.**
Unhorsed. many knights *unhorst*, and many wounded, ... V. iii. 6. 6
Unhurtful. Fine Counterfesaunce, and *unhurtfull* Sport, . . . *T.M.* 197
Unicorn. A prowd rebellious *Unicorn* defyes, ... II. v. 10. 2
Union. 'Thenceforth eternall *union* shall be made . . . . . . III. iii. 49. 1
United. *United* all his powres to purge him selfe from blame. . II. xi. 31. 9
Unites. The force, . . . In one alone left hand he now *unites*, . I. viii. 18. 2
Universal. an *universall* night Throughout the world he makes *Hub.* 1297
Till *universall* peace compound all civill jarre. . . . . III. iii. 23. 9
ycovered had Fayre heaven with an *universall* clowd, ... III. xii. 1. 2
Peace *universall* rayn'd . . . . V. Pr. 9. 6
Universe. the compast course of the *universe* . . . is ronne, . . *Ro.* xxii. 9
this great *Universe* seemd one confused mas. . . . . II. xii. 34. 9
within this wide great *Universe* . . . . VII. vii. 56. 1
looke on the frame Of this wyde *universe*, ... *H.H.B.* 31
Unjointed. there *unjoynted* both her bones: . . . . *S.C.* Mar. 52
Unjust. whom thou, great Jove, by doome *unjust* . . . . . . *T.M.* 69
Bereft of both by Fates *unjust* decreeing. . . . . *Ti.* 35
Is then *unjust* to each his dew to give? . . . . I. ix. 38. 7
Vaine is the vaunt, and victory *unjust*, ... II. ii. 29. 8
Ne deeme thy force by fortunes doome *unjust*, ... II. v. 12. 8
With which th' *unjust* Atheniens made to dy Wise Socrates; . II. vii. 52. 6
the falsest Judge, alas! And most *unjust*; . . . . II. vii. 62. 4
them of their *unjust* possession depriv'd. . . . . II. x. 9. 9
Untrue to God, and unto man *unjust!* . . . . IV. i. 53. 2
judgement so *unjust* against him had ordayned. . . . . V. iii. 35. 9
the heavens *unjust* . . . have agreed To thrall my looser life, V. v. 29. 7
with *unjust* detraction him did beard, ... VI. v. 12. 7
by *unjust* And guilefull meanes, ... VII. vi. 27. 3
by Dianaes doom *unjust* Slew great Orion; . . . . VII. vii. 39. 7
And slew the Just by most *unjust* decree. . . . . *H.H.L.* 154
Unjustice. As author of *unjustice*, there to let him dye. . . . II. vii. 60. 9
Unjustly. so *unjustlie* doe their judgments share . . . . . . *D.* 199
unjustly thou doest wyte them all, ... *Col.* 747
To be *unjustly* blamd, and bitterly revilde. . . . . IV. viii. 28. 9
Whom a strong tyrant did *unjustly* thrall, ... V. i. 3. 7
the gods owne principality, Which Jove usurpes *unjustly*, . . VII. vii. 16. 6
plead thy maisters cause, *unjustly* payned. . . . . *Am.* xlviii. 8

Unkempt. howe my rymes bene rugged and *unkempt;* . . . . *S.C.* N. 51
eke thy words uncourteous and *unkempt:* . . . . III. x. 29. 7
Unkenned. As child whose parent is *unkent,* . . . . *To his Booke* 2
Much more there is *unkend* then thou doest kon, ... *Col.* 294
did shame Himselfe with incest of his kin *unkend;* . . . . IV. xi. 13. 8
Unkind. Ye cruell starres, and eke ye Gods *unkinde,* . . . . *Ro.* ix. 1
Renewing in themselves that rage *unkinde,* . . . . *Ro.* x. 13
Tydings of death and massacre *unkinde:* . . . . *Gn.* 396
plaine his case with words *unkinde.* . . . . *Hub.* 52
Through envies snares, or fortunes freakes *unkind.* . . . . I. iii. 1. 4
He seemd in hart to harbour thoughts *unkind,* . . . . I. iv. 38. 8
Una, . . . Her truth had staynd with treason so *unkind:* . . . . I. vi. 2. 4
with reproch of carelesnes *unkynd* Upbrayd, ... I. vii. 3. 7
Here heaped up with termes of love *unkynd,* . . . . I. xii. 30. 4
they, how ever shamefull and *unkinde,* . . . . III. ii. 43. 6
Reproch despightfull, carelesse, and *unkinde;* . . . . III. xii. 24. 4
inly feeds it selfe with thoughts *unkind,* . . . . IV. vi. 1. 3
wound the soule it selfe with griefe *unkind;* . . . . IV. viii. 26. 7
For lending life to me, a wretch *unkind,* . . . . V. v. 32. 5
unto her mistresse most *unkind* She daily told . . . . V. v. 56. 7
with *unkind* disdaine And cruell rigour . . . . VI. xi. 24. 3
Fayre ye be sure, but cruell and *unkind,* . . . . *Am.* lvi. 1
Unkindly. My life-bloud friesing with *unkindly* cold; . . . . *S.C.* Ja. 26
A comett stird up that *unkindly* heate, ... *S.C.* D. 59
her *unkindly* foes, The fatall Sisters, ... *T.M.* 15
th' *unkindly* Impes, of heaven accurst, ... I. i. 26. 2
gan abhorre her broods *unkindly* crime, ... II. x. 9. 4
Unkindness. Of great *unkindnesse,* and of usage hard, ... *Col.* 165
Unkindnesse past, they gan of solace treat, ... I. vii. 4. 1
To see th' *unkindnes* of his Hellenore. . . . . III. x. 45. 5
Unknightly. those *unknightly* raylinges which he spoke, ... II. vi. 30. 6
t' upbrayd A gentle knight with so *unknightly* blame; . . . . III. ii. 9. 6
Yet is not this the first *unknightly* part, ... IV. vi. 7. 7
be aveng'd of their *unknightly* play. . . . . V. x. 36. 4
with so *unknightly* breach Of armes, ... VI. ii. 42. 4
'*Unknightly* Knight, the blemish of that name, ... VI. iii. 35. 1
The foule discourt'sies and *unknightly* parts, ... VI. v. 33. 2
Unknown. who will seeke for *unknowne* gayne, ... *S.C.* S. 72
Some scattred on the Hercaean shores *unknowne;* . . . . *Gn.* 588
waies *unknowne,* waies leading down to hell. . . . . *Col.* 211
Durst not adventure such *unknowen* wayes, ... *Col.* 670
They . . . wander too and fro in waies *unknowne,* . . . . I. i. 10. 5
the place *unknowne* and wilde, Breedes dreadfull doubts. . . . . I. i. 12. 3
for my sake *unknowne* such griefe unto you grew. . . . . I. i. 53. 9
pas, In waies *unknowne,* her wandring knight to seeke, ... I. iii. 21. 4
He led a wretched life, unto himselfe *unknowne.* . . . . I. iv. 28. 9
They let her goe at will, and wander waies *unknowne.* . . . . I. viii. 49. 9
Least so great good . . . Should die *unknown,* . . . . I. ix. 2. 9
what *unknowen* nation there empeopled were? . . . . I. x. 56. 9
to thee is *unknowne* the cradle of thy brood. . . . . I. x. 64. 9
thy daughter linck . . . to that new *unknowen* guest: . . . . I. xii. 26. 7
later times thinges more *unknowne* shall show. . . . . II. Pr. 3. 3
Pursew her steps through wild *unknowen* wood: . . . . II. iii. 43. 3
Making her seeke an *unknowne* Paramoure, ... III. iii. 3. 4
Were from him hidden, or *unknowne* of yore. . . . . III. iii. 15. 5
a straunger king, from *unknowne* soyle Arriving, ... III. iii. 33. 3
T' approve the *unknowen* purpose of eternall fate. . . . . III. iv. 28. 9
that Squyre *unknowne* Mote algates passe: . . . . III. v. 17. 5
hurt far off *unknowne* whom ever she envide. . . . . III. vii. 6. 9
the strife, which late befell Betwixt us both *unknowne.'* . . . . III. ix. 51. 9
they ought not thing *unknowne* reprove, ... IV. Pr. 2. 3
A new *unknowen* mischiefe did from him remove. . . . . IV. i. 2. 9
Conveyed quite away to living wight *unknowen.* . . . . IV. i. 3. 9
since he seemed valiant, though *unknowne,* . . . . IV. i. 11. 5
set it all on fire by force *unknowen,* . . . . IV. ii. 1. 4
'A stranger knight,' sayd he, '*unknowne* by name, ... IV. vi. 6. 3
from him *unknowne,* Thine honor sav'd, ... IV. vii. 19. 4
Knights and Squires to him *unknowne* afore: . . . . IV. ix. 8. 5
unknowen geare And uncouth fashion, ... IV. xi. 45. 2
grief *unknowne,* which he could not discerne: . . . . IV. xii. 24. 2
Unknowen perill of bold womens pride. . . . . V. iv. 38. 6
(that which to Britomart *Unknowen* was) . . . . V. vi. 31. 7
none is to me *unknowne* . . . . VI. ii. 31. 9
That of the like, whose linage was *unknowne,* . . . . VI. iv. 36. 2
At last he met two knights to him *unknowne,* . . . . VI. vii. 3. 6
all that night to him *unknowen* she past; . . . . VI. viii. 51. 6
enstall A new *unknowen* Colony therein, ... *H.H.L.* 104
Unlace. in haste his helmet gan *unlace,* . . . . I. iii. 37. 1
thought his armes to leave, and helmet to *unlace.* . . . . I. xi. 26. 9
th' other brother gan his helme *unlace,* . . . . II. viii. 17. 2
His shining Helmet he gan soone *unlace,* . . . . II. viii. 52. 8
Badd her old Squyre *unlace* her lofty creast: . . . . III. iv. 7. 3
refusing him to let *unlace,* . . . . V. viii. 27. 3
Unlaced. there sate a knight with helme *unlaste,* . . . . II. i. 24. 7
had *unlaste* Her silver buskins . . . . III. vi. 18. 2
her glistring helmet she *unlaced;* . . . . IV. i. 13. 1
her sunshynie helmet soone *unlaced,* . . . . V. v. 11. 8
her helmet she *unlaste,* . . . . V. vii. 8. 8
would have *unlast* His Helme, ... VI. i. 39. 5
Unlade. the huge burden of my cares *unlade.* . . . . *D.* 489
There did our ship her fruitfull wombe *unlade,* . . . . *Col.* 288
Unlast. *See* **Unlaced.**
Unlawful. Backe to be borne, though it *unlawfull* were. . . . . *Gn.* 464
rashly lusted For thing *unlawfull,* . . . . IV. i. 11. 4
Unlearned. way for one that is *unlern'd* Living to get, ... *Hub.* 535
And roughly wrought in an *unlearned* Loome: . . . . *Ded. Son.* vii. 13
Unless. *Unlesse* thou canst one conjure by device, ... *Hub.* 510
Unlesse some one perhaps of gentle kin, ... *T.M.* 345
Unles they mentiond be with infamie. . . . . *Ti.* 350
Unlesse to please it selfe it can applie; . . . . *Col.* 708

Unless—*Continued.*
Unlesse that some gay Mistresse badge he beares: . . . . *Col.* 780
Unlesse he swim in love up to the eares. . . . . *Col.* 782
Unlesse she chaunst their stubborne mouths to twitch; . . . . I. v. 28. 7
Threatning to strike *unlesse* he would withstand: . . . . IV. vi. 23. 5
Yet was he meet, *unless* mine eye did faine, ... IV. vii. 15. 8
From which, *unlesse* some heavenly powre her free . . . . IV. xi. 1. 6
Unlesse some succour had in time him overtaken. . . . . V. iii. 9. 9
Unlesse that she were continent and chast, ... V. iii. 28. 8
justice to deride, *Unlesse* it be perform'd . . . . V. iv. 1. 8
Unlesse the heavens them lift to lawful soveraintie. . . . . V. v. 25. 9
lodge with him that night, *unles* good cause empeach. . . . . V. vi. 21. 9
(*Unlesse* thou in these woods thy selfe conceale . . . . VI. ii. 26. 2
Unlesse thou dare, for thy deare Ladies sake . . . . VI. iii. 35. 7
Unlesse that with his Lord he formerly did fight. . . . . VI. iii. 38. 9
Unlesse that I were thereunto enforst: . . . . VI. iii. 39. 7
soone shall die, *Unlesse* to me thou hether bring . . . . VI. vii. 13. 4
Unlesse the kingdome of the sky yee make Immortall . . . . VII. vii. 54. 2
unlesse she turne to thee Ere Cuckow end, ... *Am.* xix. 13
wil not be staid, *Unlesse* she doe him by the forelock take; . . . . *Am.* lxx. 8
Unlike. lov'd of ladies, *unlike* faire, ... I. ii. 37. 1
yet each to each *unlich,* . . . . I. v. 28. 5
backward still was turnd his wrincled face: *Unlike* to men, ... I. viii. 31. 5
far *unlike* conditions has; . . . . III. ix. 4. 7
All three to each *unlike,* yet all made in one mould. . . . . III. xii. 24. 9
her feet were odde, And much *unlike;* . . . . IV. i. 28. 7
seem'd *unlike* unto his earthly home: . . . . IV. xii. 4. 7
though (*unlike*) they should for ever last, ... V. v. 38. 8
Unlike in forme, and chang'd by strange disguise: . . . . VII. vii. 18. 8
unlike parts amongst themselves do jarre. . . . . *H.B.* 196
Unlined. a thin silken cassock . . . That was *unlyned* all, ... VII. vii. 29. 3
Unlooked for. There him befell, *unlooked for* before, ... VI. iv. 17. 6
Unloved. let him live *unlov'd,* or love him selfe alone. . . . . IV. xii. 9. 9
Unlovely. *Unlovely* Proteus, missing to his mind . . . . IV. xi. 2. 2
Unluckily. In which his life *unluckily* was layd, ... IV. xii. 28. 2
Unlucky. *unlucky* Muse, that wontst to ease My musing mynd, ... *S.C.* Ja. 69
thrive in that *unluckie* quest; . . . . *Hub.* 916
The fearefull shepheard, . . . shund th' *unlucky* ground. . . . . I. ii. 28. 9
with this *unlucky* eye I late beheld; . . . . I. ix. 26. 7
'*Unlucky* Squire,' . . . Henceforth take heede . . . . II. iv. 36. 1
her *unlucky* lot Lay hidden in the bottome of the pot. . . . . III. ii. 26. 4
fethered with an *unlucky* quill: . . . . III. v. 20. 5
with *unluckie* glaunce Through Cambels shoulder it unwarely went, ... IV. iii. 8. 2
Unluckie Mayd, to seeke her enimie! . . . . IV. v. 29. 6
Unluckie Mayd, to seeke him farre and wide, ... IV. v. 29. 7
like *unlucky* lot Hath linckt with me . . . . IV. vii. 14. 6
The mother of *unlucky* Marinell, ... IV. xi. 3. 7
piteously complayning . . . that most *unluckie* stound, ... VI. ii. 41. 3
Too greatly grieve at any his *unlucky* case.' . . . . VI. iii. 5. 9
lamenting her *unluckie* strife, ... VI. viii. 48. 6
Unmade. sawst the secrets of the world *unmade,* . . . . I. v. 22. 6
Unmanly. many mischiefes follow cruell Wrath: . . . *Unmanly* murder, ... I. iv. 35. 3
being men they did *unmanly* looke, ... II. xii. 86. 3
As scorning his *unmanly* cowardize: . . . . IV. iv. 11. 2
hath this day so many so *unmanly* shent.' . . . . IV. v. 18. 9
Of so *unmanly* maske in misery misdight. . . . . V. vii. 37. 9
with *unmanly* guile And foule abusion, ... V. xii. 40. 3
Hast slaine my men in this *unmanly* maner, ... VI. vi. 25. 2
Unmanned. Now comest thou to rob my house *unmand,* . . . . VI. i. 25. 4
Unmanured. Unpeopled, *unmannurd,* unprovd, unpraysd; . . . . II. x. 5. 4
Unmarred. *Unmard* with ragged mosse or filthy mud; . . . . VI. x. 7. 3
Unmeet. his late chayne his Liege *unmeete* esteemeth; . . . . *Hub.* 628
that waste . . . *Unmeet* for man, ... *Col.* 185
As base, or blunt, *unmeet* for melodie. . . . . *Col.* 710
To make so bold a doome, with words *unmeet,* . . . . *Col.* 929
Upbrayd, for leaving her in place *unmeet,* . . . . I. vii. 3. 8
Duessa . . . Inveigled him to follow her desires *unmeete.* . . . . I. vii. 50. 9
Madan was young, *unmeet* the rule to sway, ... II. x. 20. 2
garments loose that seemd *unmeet* for womanhed. . . . . II. xii. 55. 9
her brought Into that wildernesse for her *unmeet,* . . . . III. vi. 20. 3
After long troubles and *unmeet* upbrayes . . . . III. vi. 50. 3
mov'd amisse with massy mucks *unmeet* regard. . . . . III. x. 31. 9
loathly mouth, *unmeete* a mouth to bee, ... IV. i. 27. 3
that Hag, *unmeet* to host such guests, ... IV. viii. 27. 1
bosting in their martyrdome *unmeet.* . . . . IV. x. 2. 5
other wing, now made *unmeete* for flight, ... V. v. 15. 3
Found nothing that he said *unmeet* nor geason, ... VI. iv. 37. 2
in this wize, and this *unmeete* array, ... VI. viii. 22. 6
Unmeetly. Upon a mangy jade *unmeetely* set, ... VI. vi. 16. 8
Unmercifully. dealt her blowes *unmercifully* sore; . . . . V. vii. 31. 2
Unmindful. Not yet *unmindfull* of her olde reproach. . . . . *Gn.* 224
Not yet *unmindfull* how not long agoe, ... *Mui.* 130
As to become *unmyndfull* of his owne. . . . . *As.* 112
Unmindfull of chiefe parts of manlinesse; . . . . *Col.* 764
Leave off their worke, *unmindfull* of their smart, ... I. v. 36. 2
Unmindfull of thy praise and prowest might, ... II. v. 36. 4
Unmindfull of his wound, of his fate ignoraunt, ... II. viii. 34. 9
Unmindfull both of that discordfull crew, ... IV. ii. 30. 8
Unmyndfull of his vow, and high beheast . . . . VI. x. 1. 3
Unmindfull of that dearest Lord of thyne; . . . . *H.H.L.* 221
Unmoved. So stood these twaine, *unmoved* as a rocke, ... I. ii. 16. 7
all the world in state *unmoved* stands, ... IV. x. 35. 2
Unmov'd with praiers or with piteous thought, ... V. ii. 23. 2
Ne once my minds *unmoved* quiet grieve; . . . . VI. ix. 22. 7
Still mooving, yet *unmoved* from her sted; . . . . VII. vii. 13. 3
That only seemes *unmov'd* and permanent, ... VII. vii. 17. 7
her *unmoved* mind Doth still persist . . . . *Am.* vi. 1

Unmoving. heavens . . . *Unmoving,* uncorrupt, and spotlesse bright, . . . *H.H.B.* 68
Unnatural. Some, of borne brethren prov'd *unnaturall;* . . . IV. i. 24. 4
She feedes on her owne maw *unnaturall,* . . . V. xii. 31. 7
Unnoble. through *unnoble* sloth, or sinfull crime, . . . *T.M.* 435
Unpared. fingers filthie with long nayles *unpared,* . . . IV. v. 35. 4
Unpeopled. *Unpeopled,* unmannurd, unprovd, unpraysd; . . . II. x. 5. 4
Unpitied. To die alone, *unpitied,* unplained; . . . *D.* 79
Unpitied, unplaynd, of foe or frend: . . . *As.* 136
waste the wearie night In . . . *unpittied* plaint, . . . I. i. 53. 3
Long languishing there in *unpittied* paine, . . . IV. x. 13. 8
did still pursew That raskall many with *unpitied* spoyle; . . . V. xi. 65. 2
Of my poore life to make *unpittied* spoile. . . . *Am.* xi. 8
Unplained. To die alone, unpitied, *unplained;* . . . *D.* 79
Unpitied, *unplaynd,* of foe or frend: . . . *As.* 136
Unpleasant. Was made the most *unpleasant* and most ill: . . VII. vi. 37. 8
th' *unpleasant* Quyre of Frogs still croking . . . *Epith.* 349
Unploughed. I lately left a furrow, one or twayne, *Unplough'd,* VI. ix. 1. 4
Unpraised. Unpeopled, unmannurd, unprovd, *unpraysd;* . . . II. x. 5. 4
Unpromised. Leave nought *unpromist* that may him perswade, V. v. 49. 2
Unproved. There for to find a fresh *unproved* knight; . . . I. vii. 47. 2
Unpeopled, unmannurd, *unprovd,* unpraysd; . . . II. x. 5. 4
Unprovided. of nought they were *unprovided;* . . . *S.C.* May 114
Unpurveyed. Of happy wights, now *unpurvaid* of light, . . . VII. vi. 14. 4
Unquenchable. To burn the same with *unquenchable* fire, . . . III. ix. 17. 7
Unquenched. wrought in Lemno with *unquenched* fire: . . . IV. v. 4. 4
Unquiet. talke, that might *unquiet* fancies reave; . . . *Hub.* 24
rash Occasion makes *unquiet* life!' . . . II. iv. 44. 7
Troubled with terrour and *unquiet* jarre, . . . II. vi. 37. 8
In restlesse anguish and *unquiet* paine; . . . III. iv. 61. 2
Unquiet Care, and fond Unthriftyhead; . . . III. xii. 25. 4
oftentimes *unquiet* strife did move Amongst her lovers, . . . IV. ii. 37. 3
Those be *unquiet* thoughts that carefull minds invade. . . . IV. v. 35. 9
High Swale, *unquiet* Nide, and troublous Skell; . . . IV. xi. 37. 7
with such *unquiet* fits Her selfe there close afflicted . . . V. vi. 15. 1
in *unquiet* brest Did closely harbour such a jealous guest) . . . V. vii. 27. 4
weary of this worlds *unquiet* waies, . . . VI. vi. 4. 7
Unquiet thought! whom at the first I bred . . . *Am.* ii. 1
forth he casts in his *unquiet* thought, . . . *H.L.* 218
Unread. Of Gods, of Nymphs, of rivers, yet *unred;* . . . IV. xii. 2. 7
Unready. Receive . . . The unripe fruit of an *unready* wit; . . . *Ded. Son.* iii. 2
his woundes wyde . . . *unready* were to ryde. . . . I. v. 45. 5
Th' Elfe . . . his *unready* weapons gan in hand to take. . . . I. vii. 7. 9
Unreave. The same at night she did againe *unreave:* . . . *Am.* xxiii. 4
Unred. *See* **Unread.**
Unredressed. unto death had doen him *unredrest,* . . . IV. viii. 41. 8
Unregarded. Since whose decease, learning lies *unregarded,* . . *Ti.* 440
ne ever . . . Had throwne to ground the *unregarded* right: . I. vii. 47. 5
Unrent. He had not left one limbe of him *unrent:* . . . VI. vi. 40. 8
Unreproved. with glad thankes, and *unreproved* truth, . . . II. vii. 16. 3
Unrest. to paint out my *unrest,* . . . *S.C.* Jun. 79
Before their rage grew to so great *unrest,* . . . I. ix. 9. 7
At last breakes forth with furious *unrest,* . . . II. xi. 32. 5
One night, when she was tost with such *unrest,* . . . III. ii. 30. 1
fairely did dissemble her sad thoughts *unrest.* . . . V. v. 44. 9
Many vaine fancies working her *unrest;* . . . V. vi. 7. 7
left his love, . . . Faire Britomart in languor and *unrest,* . V. viii. 3. 5
Wrapped in wretched cares and hearts *unrest,* . . . VI. xi. 3. 2
Attempt to work her gentle mindes *unrest:* . . . *Am.* lxxxiii. 4
Unrevealed. love it was, which in his hart lay *unrevealed.* . . IV. xii. 22. 9
these her celestial threasures, And *unrevealed* pleasures, . . . *Epith.* 201
Unrevenged. let not his restlesse spright, Be *unreveng'd,* . . . I. iv. 48. 8
Unrewarded. men of armes doo wander *unrewarded.* . . . *Ti.* 441
Unrighteous. To plague th' *unrighteous* which alive remaine; . *D.* 359
thou didst these goods bereave . . . by *unrighteous* lott, . . . II. vii. 19. 4
high degree By riches and *unrighteous* reward; . . . II. vii. 47. 2
by *unrighteous* And wicked doome, . . . II. vii. 62. 4
it usurped by *unrighteous* doome: . . . II. x. 60. 5
The wrongfull outrage of *unrighteous* men, . . . III. xi. 10. 6
Had utterly subverted his *unrighteous* state. . . . V. ix. 2. 9
With her *unrighteous* enemy to fight, . . . V. xi. 39. 5
Most shamefull, most *unrighteous,* most untrew, . . . V. xii. 42. 2
th' *unrighteous* ire . . . had given him his owne due hire? . VI. ii. 13. 8
She left th' *unrighteous* world, . . . VII. vii. 37. 9
Unrighteous Lord of Love, what law is this, . . . *Am.* x. 1
Unrighteousness. sought *unrighteousnesse,* and justice sold, . V. ii. 26. 8
Unripe. seeke for Queene-apples *unrype,* . . . *S.C.* Jun. 43
Receive . . . The *unripe* fruit of an unready wit; . . . *Ded. Son.* iii. 2
Unriper. I, whose *unryper* yeares are yet unfit . . . VI. ii. 9. 2
Unrolled. Her lockes, . . . loosely hong *unrold;* . . . II. iv. 4. 6
Unruliment. They breaking forth with rude *unruliment* . . . IV. ix. 23. 5
Unruly. her *unruly* Page With his rude clawes the wicket open rent, . . . I. iii. 13. 1
Therion, a loose *unruly* swayne, . . . I. vi. 21. 6
The most *unruly* and the boldest boy . . . II. ii. 18. 3
Whome soone as that *unruly* rablement . . . did espye, . . . II. xi. 17. 7
those *unruly* beasts to hold without; . . . II. xii. 43. 3
That fiers youngmans *unruly* maystery; . . . III. x. 2. 7
passed through th' *unruly* preace Of people, . . . IV. iii. 41. 1
ranckling inward with *unruly* stounds, . . . VI. vi. 5. 3
for th' *unruly* fiends which they did feare; . . . VII. vii. 3. 8
Unsavory. stinking Smallage, and *unsaverie* Rew; . . . *D.* 347
My rimes I know *unsavory* and sowre, . . . *Ded. Son.* viii. 8
Unseason. That may thy tunefull eare *unseason* quite? . . . *Ded. Son.* viii. 4
Unseated. by good fortune shortly him *unseated.* . . . IV. x. 10. 2
Unseemly. filthie brocage, and *unseemly* shifts, . . . *Hub.* 851
in her roome *unseemly* Sorrow sits, . . . *T.M.* 184
Unseemely man to please faire Ladies eye; . . . I. iv. 24. 6
Nether *unseemly* short, nor yet exceeding long. . . . II. ix. 24. 9
it was to Knight *unseemely* shame . . . IV. x. 54. 3
Unseen. Ne did he leave the mountaines bare *unseene,* . . . *Mui.* 155
in every other starre *unseene* . . . II. Pr. 3. 7
Himselfe he frees by secret meanes *unseene;* . . . II. i. 1. 8
Lurkt false Duessa secretly *unseene,* . . . II. i. 21. 4
not thy fault, but secret powre *unseene:* . . . III. i. 7. 8
those two Ladies their two loves *unseene;* . . . IV. iv. 3. 3
her angels face, *unseene* afore, . . . IV. vi. 19. 5
'Of things *unseene* how canst thou deeme aright,' . . . V. ii. 39. 1
Unseene of any, yet of all beheld; . . . VII. vii. 13. 4
Unbodied, unsoul'd, unheard, *unseene:* . . . VII. vii. 46. 5
Unserviceable. his late wounded wing *unserviceable* found. . . I. xi. 25. 9
Unsewed. their pillow was *unsowed:* . . . VI. iv. 14. 5
Unsheathed. shyning blade *unsheathd,* . . . II. ii. 21. 6
Unshed. Uncomb'd, uncurl'd, and carelesly *unshed;* . . . IV. vii. 40. 6
Unshod. Their feet *unshod,* their bodies wrapt in rags, . . . II. xi. 23. 4
Unshorn. His carelesse locks uncombed and *unshorne,* . . . *D.* 43
Unsoft. Great clymbers fall *unsoft.* . . . *S.C.* Jul. 12
Unsoot. *See* **Unsweet.**
Unsought. Shee comes *unsought,* and shonned followes eke. . . II. iv. 44. 3
present Unto her vew, and company *unsought;* . . . III. i. 44. 3
Had guided her, unwelcomed, *unsought?* . . . III. vii. 8. 4
of all unsuccour'd and *unsought.* . . . IV. viii. 51. 9
sorrowes of the mynd Find remedie *unsought,* . . . VI. iv. 28. 9
now no place besides *unsought* had left, . . . VI. xii. 23. 7
Unsouled. Unbodied, *unsoul'd,* unheard, unseene: . . . VII. vii. 46. 5
Unsound. on her trunke, all rotten and *unsound,* . . . *Ro.* xxviii. 7
fruitles follies and *unsound* delights. . . . *Hub.* 823
Her flitting parts, and element *unsound,* . . . I. xi. 18. 5
Devices, dreames, opinions *unsound,* . . . II. ix. 51. 7
of such subtile substance and *unsound,* . . . II. xi. 20. 8
So feeble is mans state, and life *unsound,* . . . II. xi. 30. 3
With breach of faith and loyaltie *unsound,* . . . IV. vi. 28. 4
All change is perillous, and all chaunce *unsound.* . . . V. ii. 36. 7
Yet doubting least his hold was but *unsound* . . . V. v. 42. 7
Doubting sad end of principle *unsound:* . . . V. xi. 2. 7
Made him become most faithless and *unsound:* . . . V. xii. 2. 4
that same Ladies hurt . . . was inwardly *unsound.* . . . VI. iv. 16. 9
Which may let in a little thought *unsownd.* . . . *Epith.* 237
To heale the sores of sinfull soules *unsound,* . . . *H.H.L.* 166
sight Of all that looke thereon with eyes *unsound;* . . . *H.H.B.* 179
Unsowed. *See* **Unsewed.**
Unspeakable. O huge and most *unspeakable* impression . . . *H.H.L.* 155
Unspied. With so sweet sence and secret powre *unspide,* . . . III. vii. 7. 8
Unspotted. Then hunt the steps of pure *unspotted* Maid: . . . I. vi. 46. 8
sacred lore And pure *unspotted* life: . . . I. x. 3. 3
pretious blood, . . . of that *unspotted* lam, . . . I. x. 57. 6
Pure and *unspotted* from all loathly crime . . . III. vi. 3. 4
In her *unspotted* pleasauns to delight. . . . *Am.* lxxxviii. 12
Unspotted fayth, and comely womanhood, . . . *Epith.* 192
Unstable. Nor wrath of Gods, nor spight of men *unstable,* . . *Ro.* xiii. 7
The wind *unstable,* and doth never stay. . . . II. vi. 23. 5
Unstaid. To the gay gardins his *unstaid* desire Him wholly caried, . . . *Mui.* 161
The labor of lost time, and wit *unstayd:* . . . *Ded. Son.* ix. 8
oft he made him stagger as *unstayd,* . . . VI. i. 20. 3
All flesh is frayle, and all her strength *unstayd,* . . . *Am.* lviii. 5
Unstained. In curteous usage and *unstained* hewe; . . . *Mui.* 120
like herselfe, *unstayned* hath beene tryde. . . . II. ii. 9. 9
Unsteadfast. *unstedfast* state Of all that lives . . . *Ti.* 43
still *unstedfast,* round about doth goe . . . *D.* 431
all mens states alike *unstedfast* be. . . . *D.* 518
Unsteadfastness. I knowing the worldes *unstedfastnesse,* . . *Bel.*[1] i. 12
Unsteady. On thing so tickle as th' *unsteady* ayre, . . . VII. vii. 22. 6
Unsubdued. T' afflict the other Saxons *unsubdewd;* . . . III. iii. 38. 2
Unsuccored. of all *unsuccour'd* and unsought. . . . IV. viii. 51. 9
Unsure. Shall finde his state most fickle and *unsure.* . . . *Van.* xii. 14
wandreth evermore uncertein and *unsure.* . . . II. xii. 12. 9
Unsure to whether side it would incline, . . . IV. iii. 37. 2
wast and weare away in termes *unsure,* . . . *Am.* xxv. 3
Unswear. oft *unsweare,* a Diademe to beare? . . . *Hub.* 1058
Unsweet. cast hem out as rotten and *unsoote.* . . . *S.C.* D. 118
make the life *unsweet:* . . . II. vii. 14. 2
Untamed. with so *untamed* forse Did beare them both . . . IV. ii. 15. 1
All th' East, before *untam'd,* did over-ronne, . . . V. i. 2. 2
liking in her yet *untamed* heart procure. . . . VI. x. 32. 9
Unthankful. *'Unthankfull* wretch,' (said he) 'is this the meed, III. v. 45. 1
Unthought. For thou likewise didst love, though now *unthought,* *Epith.* 378
Unthriftihead. It called was the quickesand of *Unthriftyhed.* . II. xii. 18. 9
Unquiet Care, and fond *Unthriftyhead;* . . . III. xii. 25. 4
Unthrifty. many mischiefes follow cruell Wrath: . . . *unthrifty* scath, . . . I. iv. 35. 3
Surfeat, misdiet, and *unthriftie* waste, . . . II. xi. 12. 7
Untie. he forst him to *unty* One of his grasping feete, . . . I. xi. 42. 8
sleepe his eie-strings did *untye,* . . . II. vii. 27. 4
her Gorgonian shield gins to *untye* . . . III. ix. 22. 8
Untied. Infernall furies with their chaines *untyde.* . . . I. ix. 24. 5
Soone as Occasion felt her selfe *untyde,* . . . II. v. 19. 1
Verdant (so he hight) he soone *untyde,* . . . II. xii. 82. 8
when they thought it fast, eftsoones it was *untide.* . . . IV. v. 17. 9
how from thraldome vile they were *untide,* . . . IV. viii. 21. 5
goodly greenish locks, all loose *untyde,* . . . *Proth.* 22
Unties. Pyrochles . . . Furors chayne *untyes,* . . . II. v. Arg.
Until (*partial list*).
Untill she raught the Gods owne mansions: . . . *Bel.*[2] vii. 8
Untill he came unto the broken tree, . . . *Pet.* v. 5
knewe we, fooles, what it us bringes *until,* . . . *S.C.* N. 185
Which, from their first *untill* their utmost date, . . . *Ti.* 45
Untill he quite him of this guiltie blame. . . . *Ti.* 230
untill that timelie death . . . ende my earthlie daies: . . . *Ti.* 311
untill it forth have brought Her long borne Infant, . . . *D.* 31

Until—*Continued.*
So piped we, *until* we both were weary.' *Col.* 79
Untill that we to Cynthiaes presence came: *Col.* 332
sung so long *untill* quite hoarse he grew. *Col.* 399
Untill the blustring storme is overblowne; I. i. 10. 2
Can never rest, *untill* it forth have brought I. v. 1. 3
So wept Duessa *untill* eventyde, I. v. 19. 1
Untill the witches speach she gan to heare, I. v. 21. 7
untill Dayes enemy Did him appease; I. v. 34. 6
Untill, . . . She hardly yet perswaded was I. vi. 28. 3
Untill Duessa loud to him gan crye, I. vii. 14. 4
They sadly traveild thus, *untill* they came I. viii. 2. 1
Nor leave his stand *untill* his Captaine bed.' I. ix. 41. 5
He rousd himselfe full blyth, and hastned them *untill.* I. xi. 4. 9
Untill they came where that faire virgin stood: I. xii. 7. 6
Until that Brutus, . . . Driven by fatall error II. x. 9. 6
Untill a nation straunge, with visage swart, II. x. 15. 1
Untill that Locrine for his Realmes defence, II. x. 15. 8
Untill he quite had spent his perlous store, II. xi. 27. 8
Until he came unto a standing lake; II. xi. 46. 6
Untill they nigh unto that Gulfe arryve, II. xii. 5. 2
Untill they came in vew of those wilde beasts, II. xii. 39. 6
Untill that brasen wall they up doe reare; III. iii. 11. 7
Untill the hardy Mayd . . . First entering, III. iii. 14. 5
Untill the closure of the Evening: III. iii. 27. 5
Untill a straunger king, . . . Arriving, III. iii. 33. 3
Untill that it an issew forth may finde: III. ix. 15. 7
she there wayted *untill* eventyde, III. xi. 55. 1
From the fourth howre of night *untill* the sixt; III. xii. 2. 7
Untill such time as noble Britomart Released her, IV. i. 4. 3
There they, I weene, would fight *untill* this day, IV. ii. 20. 1
Untill that they their wounds well healed had, IV. vi. 39. 8
I here will stay *Untill* another tyde IV. vi. 47. 9
I will deferre the end *untill* another tide. IV. vii. 47. 9
Untill she came where wonned his Belphebe faire. IV. viii. 8. 9
Untill the ripenesse of mans yeares he raught; V. i. 8. 3
Until that Talus had his pride represt, V. i. 29. 5
Untill that Guyon selfe unto him spake, V. iii. 34. 2
the fight did *untill* evening last. V. iv. 43. 9
Untill his owne true love his freedome gayned: V. v. 57. 8
Untill she spide the lampe of lightsome day V. vii. 17. 3
Untill they both doe heare what she to them will say. V. viii. 10. 9
Untill that state by strength was pulled downe; V. x. 26. 2
Untill he had her settled in her raine V. xi. 35. 3
untill that yron man . . . began V. xi. 47. 6
Untill late mischiefe did uppon me light, V. xi. 49. 3
Untill the love of Lordship . . . Made him become V. xii. 2. 3
Untill a Mantle she for him doe fynd VI. i. 15. 4
Untill fit time and place he mote espy, VI. vii. 3. 4
The end whereof Ile keepe *untill* another cast. VI. viii. 51. 9
untill the flying day Was farre forth spent, VI. ix. 12. 5
Untill the Damzell gan to wex more sound and strong. VI. xii. 11. 9
Untill that, . . . he broke his yron chaine, VI. xii. 38. 7
Until that Jove himselfe her selfe bespake: VII. vi. 25. 6
Untill ye have theyr guylefull traynes well tryde: *Am.* xlvii. 2
move Theyr sad protract from evening *untill* morne. *Am.* lxxxvi. 4
Untill they come to their first Movers bound, *H.H.B.* 72
Untimely. Fell to the ground, and there *untimely* dide. *Pet.* i. 12
Untimely my flowres forced to fall, *S.C.* F. 177
cutte of hys dayes with *untimely* woe, *S.C.* May 199
through *untimely* tempest fall away! *D.* 238
wandring spirits walke *untimely* howres. *D.* 336
after him did make *untimely* haste: *As.* 176
Thus fowle to hasten your *untimely* date? II. i. 44. 8
so *untimely* breach . . . halfe seemed to offend; II. x. 68. 6
The eldest brother, did *untimely* dy; II. x. 75. 7
Some for *untimely* ease, some for delight, III. i. 39. 4
leafe and fruite, both too *untimely* shed, III. ii. 31. 8
I *untimely* must Thereof make tryall V. v. 29. 5
Brought in *untimely* houre, ere it was sought: V. vi. 3. 5
whose *untimely* fate For to avenge, V. vi. 33. 6
Like fruitles seede, of which *untimely* death should grow. V. vii. 31. 9
with *untimely* drought nigh withered was, V. xii. 13. 2
he through lives despeire *Untimely* dyde, VI. ii. 28. 4
All other fayre, lyke flowres, *untymely* fade. *Am.* lxxix. 14
Untitled. false Duessa, now *untitled* Queene, V. ix. 42. 8
Unto (*partial list*). *See* **Thereunto, Whereunto.**
Unto my eyes strange showes presented were, *Van.* i. 10
Unto such tyrannie doth aspire; *S.C.* F. 172
Tuning our song *unto* a tender Muse, *Gn.* 2
yeeld (for spight) Store of firebronds . . . *Unto* her foster children, *Gn.* 510
turning all *unto* the Apes confusion. *Hub.* 1364
open shame, . . . *unto* us wrought *T.M.* 62
(so partiall *unto* none:) *As.* 110
They *unto* thee, and thou to them, most deare: *Ded. Son.* iii. 12
But forth *unto* the darksom hole he went, I. i. 14. 3
The stroke down from her head *unto* her shoulder glaunst. I. i. 17. 9
downe againe she fell *unto* the ground, I. vii. 24. 1
he came *unto* an yron doore, I. viii. 37. 3
To come *unto* his wished home in haste, I. ix. 39. 2
turne his earnest *unto* game, II. i. 31. 1
lift it selfe *unto* the highest skyes? II. x. 1. 5
gave *unto* us all what ever good we have. II. x. 69. 9
Their diverse notes t'attune *unto* his lay, II. xii. 76. 2
her ensample make *Unto* thy selfe, III. iii. 56. 9
prostrate she fell *unto* the grownd. III. xii. 38. 9
dayly more offensive *unto* each degree IV. i. 18. 9
sought to bring all things *unto* decay; IV. i. 29. 4
Did privily put coles *unto* his secret fire. IV. ii. 11. 9

Unto—*Continued.*
Which, . . . *Unto* an other Canto I will overpas. IV. xi. 53. 9
fond Dame, attempted bee *Unto* a strangers love, V. xi. 63. 2
He tooke him selfe *unto* this Hermitage, VI. vi. 4. 8
Is wont to wield the world *unto* his vow, VII. vi. 22. 3
unto Mutabilitie not thrall, VII. vii. 17. 8
this happie hower Doth leade *unto* your lovers blisfull bower, *Proth.* 93
Untold. The rest *untold* no living tongue can speake. *T.M.* 600
the old man well knew he, though *untold,* I. iii. 38. 7
Untouched. Depart to woods *untoucht,* II. iii. 43. 9
past the fire Safe and *untoucht,* III. xi. 26. 2
yet *untouched* till this present day, IV. vii. 18. 8
The Prince yet being fresh *untoucht* afore; IV. ix. 34. 2
Untoward. How he did fashion his *untoward* pace; I. viii. 31. 2
he gan to feare His toward perill, and *untoward* blame, III. i. 9. 7
Untrained. Why then doe I, *untrainde* in lovers trade, Her hardnes blame, *Am.* li. 5
Untried. Nor the ranke grassie fennes delights *untride.* *Mui.* 156
Loth . . . To taste th' *untryed* dint of deadly steele: I. iii. 34. 6
'whose dread *Untride* is lesse IV. vii. 11. 6
how to issue forth in waies *untryde,* VI. i. 6. 4
Untroubled. *Untroubled* night, . . . gives counsell best.' I. i. 33. 3
Untroubled Nature doth her selfe suffise, II. vi. 15. 4
Untroubled of vile feare or bitter fell. III. xi. 2. 5
Untrue. Albee *untrue* she wist them by assay. IV. i. 50. 5
Untrue to God, and unto man unjust! IV. i. 53. 2
Gan blame me much for being so *untrew* IV. viii. 56. 4
To his owne absent love to be *untrew:* V. v. 56. 3
She him condemn'd as trustlesse and *untrew;* V. vi. 5. 2
Against her Knight for being so *untrew;* V. vi. 12. 2
to doe unto his Idole most *untrew.* V. x. 27. 9
Most shamefull, most unrighteous, most *untrew,* V. xii. 42. 2
'Abide, ye caytive treachetours *untrew,* VI. viii. 7. 4
Untruly. Jealous suspect as true *untruely* drad: V. vii. 38. 7
Untruth. yet since no' *untruth* he knew, I. i. 53. 6
with corruptfull brybes is to *untruth* mis-trayned.' V. xi. 54. 9
Untunable. be their pipes *untunable* and craesie, *Col.* 374
Untwisting. *untwisting* his deceiptfull clew, II. i. 8. 3
Unused. The which *unused* rust did overgrow: I. viii. 30. 7
strongly wading through the waves *unused,* VI. iii. 33. 7
Unvalued. Twoo golden apples of *unvalewd* price; *Am.* lxxvii. 6
Unware. any Oedipus *unware* Shall chaunce, *Gn.* Ded. 5
Unweeting and *unware* of such mishap, II. iv. 17. 7
some wicked beast *unware* That breakes into her Dayr' house, VII. vi. 48. 3
Unwarely. Through Cambels shoulder it *unwarely* went, IV. iii. 8. 3
Unwares. Wherein while Kiddie *unwares* did looke, *S.C.* May 275
the author of her ill *unwares,* *Gn.* 631
One of his feete *unwares* from him did slide, *Ti.* 544
Upon them fell, and did *unwares* oppresse; *Ti.* 572
The foolish man, . . . is swallowed up *unwares,* I. v. 18. 8
child! whom I . . . now have seene *unwares.* I. v. 27. 9
ship . . . An hidden rocke escaped hath *unwares,* I. vi. 1. 2
her *unwares* the fiers Sansloy did overtake: I. vi. 2. 9
chaunst *unwares* to meet him I. vi. 27. 3
Where he *unwares* the fairest Una found, I. vi. 30. 6
Who him disarmed, . . . *Unwares* surprised, I. vii. 51. 4
unwares I strayd Out of my way, I. xii. 31. 7
Unwares me wrought unto her wicked will, I. xii. 32. 8
With cunning traynes him to entrap *unwares,* II. i. 4. 2
Where all the Nymphes have her *unwares* forlore, II. iii. 31. 3
oft himselfe he chaunst to hurt *unwares,* II. iv. 7. 6
overthrew him selfe *unwares,* II. iv. 8. 9
hidden lyes *unwares* him to surpryse? II. iv. 17. 3
Him to entrap *unwares* another way he wist. II. vii. 34. 9
may *unwares* bee blotted with the same: II. ix. 38. 5
them *unwares* besides the Severne did enclose. II. x. 54. 9
The faire Enchauntresse, so *unwares* opprest, II. xii. 81. 8
Mote breede him scath *unwares:* III. i. 37. 8
For feare least her *unwares* she should abrayd, III. i. 61. 2
Did weene, *unwares,* that her unlucky lot Lay hidden III. ii. 26. 4
Unwares the hidden hooke with baite I swallowed. III. ii. 38. 9
cruell Feendes should thee *unwares* devowre: III. iii. 8. 9
through thy darksom dore *Unwares* have prest; III. iii. 15. 8
Glauncing *unwares* in charmed looking glas, III. iii. 24. 2
Unwares had borne two babes, III. vi. 26. 9
Unwares she them conceivd, *unwares* she bore: III. vi. 27. 1
one, which hath gaz'd On the bright Sunne *unwares,* III. vii. 13. 7
The whiles *unwares* away III. ix. 52. 6
I *unwares* this way by fortune straid, III. x. 25. 5
unwares It shewd it selfe III. xi. 28. 6
Unwares it strooke into her snowie chest, III. xii. 33. 4
unwares to wight And to his friend unwist, IV. iv. 27. 6
all *unwares* he felt an hideous sway IV. iv. 31. 4
He her *unwares* attacht, IV. ix. 6. 9
falne *unwares* Into some pit, IV. xii. 17. 6
She chaunst *unwares* to light upon this coffer, V. iv. 10. 8
to have wrought *unwares* some villanous assay. V. iv. 23. 9
did him entrap In traytrous traine, or had *unwares* opprest; V. vi. 4. 4
Into outragious flames *unwares* did grow, V. vii. 14. 7
That from her self *unwares* he might her steale the whyle. V. ix. 12. 9
Into a Hedgehogge all *unwares* it went, V. ix. 18. 5
Least by such slight he were *unwares* deceived; V. xi. 7. 3
Unwares into the daunger of defame; VI. v. 15. 5
unwares he in the forrest heard A trampling steede, VI. v. 21. 5
Him with his fist *unwares* on th' head he strooke, VI. v. 26. 3
Wayting if he *unwares* him murther might; VI. vi. 26. 8
Unwares defrauded his intended destiny: VI. viii. 8. 9
From that *unwares* ye weetlesse doe intend; VI. viii. 17. 6
He was *unwares* surprisd in subtile bands VI. ix. 11. 6
For dread of them *unwares* to be descryde, VI. x. 11. 2

Unwares—*Continued.*
to invade Now all *unwares,* . . . VI. xi. 38. 6
Mongst whom some beast . . . *Unwares* is chaunc't, . . . VII. vi. 28. 8
her fayre eyes *unwares* doe worke in mee, . . . *Am.* xxiv. 6
Unwarily. One day as I *unwarily* did gaze . . . *Am.* xvi. 1
Unwarlike. With womanish teares, and with *unwarlike* smarts, III. xi. 44. 6
Unwary. Doest save from mischiefe the *unwary* sheepe, . . . *S.C.* D. 10
amazed stood At suddeinnesse of that *unwary* sight, . . . I. xii. 25. 2
Through an *unwary* dart, which did rebownd . . . III. v. 42. 5
T' entrap *unwary* fooles in their eternall bales. . . . VI. x. 3. 9
Unwearied. with *unwearied* wings, each part t' inquire . . . *Mui.* 39
with *unwearied* fingers drawing out The lines of life, . . . IV. ii. 48. 3
with *unwearied* powre his party still assured. . . . IV. iv. 37. 9
Unweeting, -ly. *See* **Unwitting, -ly.**
Unwelcomed. Had guided her, *unwelcomed,* unsought? . . . III. vii. 8. 4
Unwieldy. headlesse his *unweldy* bodie lay, . . . I. viii. 24. 3
At last, low stouping with *unweldy* sway, . . . I. xi. 18. 8
Some with *unweldy* clubs, some with long speares, . . . II. ix. 13. 6
Till that *unweeldy* burden she had reard, . . . III. vi. 10. 4
Whom with his weight *unweldy* downe he held, . . . VI. viii. 28. 3
Unwilling. As halfe *unwilling* to cutte the graine; . . . *S.C.* F. 204
doe *unwilling* worship to the Saint, . . . II. v. 11. 7
halfe *unwilling* from their bookes them brought, . . . II. x. 77. 8
with *unwilling* ayd, To guide the beast . . . IV. ix. 5. 3
Unwilling to behold that lovely band. . . . IV. x. 33. 5
Unwilling to be knowne or seene at all, . . . VI. viii. 27. 3
Unwillingly. unwares It shewd it selfe and shone *unwillingly;* III. xi. 28. 7
Unwise. Kidde . . . Was too very foolish and *unwise;* . . . *S.C.* May 175
'*Unwise* and wretched men, . . . *S.C.* N. 183
unwise and witlesse Colin Cloute, . . . *S.C.* D. 91
unwise, and warelesse of the evill . . . IV. ii. 3. 6
unwise Upon your selves anothers wrong to wreake? . . . V. viii. 11. 2
Unwisely. *Unwisely* weaves, that takes two webbes in hand. . *S.C.* O. 102
To lodge the warlike maide, *unwisely* loov'd; . . . III. i. 60. 4
Unwist. Of hurt *unwist* most daunger doth redound; . . . III. ii. 26. 6
a woman-wight, *unwist* to bee, . . . III. ix. 21. 8
unwares to wight And to his friend *unwist,* . . . IV. iv. 27. 7
kept in store In Joves eternall house, *unwist* of wight, . . . V. i. 9. 4
He found him selfe *unwist* so ill bestad, . . . V. i. 22. 4
her wombe, *unwist* to wight, was fraught, . . . VI. xii. 6. 4
Unwitting. Newes may perhaps some good *unweeting* beare.' . *Hub.* 606
Unweeting of the danger hee is in, . . . *T.M.* 491
Hable to melt the hearers heart *unweeting,* . . . *Col.* 598
in the witch *unweeting* joyd long time, . . . I. ii. 40. 2
As all *unweeting* of that well she knew; . . . I. ii. 45. 2
Into new woes *unweeting* I was cast . . . I. iv. 47. 3
Unweeting of the perillous wandring wayes, . . . I. v. 18. 3
Hereof this gentle knight *unweeting* was; . . . I. vii. 6. 1
all *unweeting,* an Enchaunter bad His sence abusd, . . . I. vii. 49. 3
doen thy feeble feet *unweeting* hither stray? . . . I. x. 9. 9
From thence a Faery thee *unweeting* reft, . . . I. x. 65. 6
thee a Ploughman all *unweeting* fond, . . . I. x. 66. 3
Behynd his backe, *unweeting,* where he stood, . . . I. xi. 29. 2
Unweeting and unware of such mishap, . . . II. iv. 17. 7
'Least wee *unweeting* hap to be fordonne; . . . II. xii. 11. 2
Unweeting what such horrour straunge did reare. . . . II. xii. 22. 7
unweeting to her Syre, . . . III. iii. 57. 5
Unweeting of their wile and treason bad, . . . III. v. 18. 3
stood aloofe, *unweeting* what to doe; . . . III. x. 22. 3
Unweeting of the Fates divine decree . . . IV. iii. 21. 4
Or else *unweeting* what it else might bee; . . . IV. vi. 22. 5
Unweeting of thine owne like haplesse plight: . . . IV. vii. 10. 8
unweeting unto wight, I with that Squire agreede away to flit, IV. vii. 17. 5
all *unweeting* have you wrong'd thus sore, . . . V. viii. 13. 2
Harme may arise *unweeting* unto me; . . . VI. ii. 27. 3
Unwittingly. As by the way *unweetingly* I strayd: . . . V. viii. 15. 7
Unwomanly. in so *unwomanly* a mood . . . VI. viii. 51. 4
Unwont. My shippe *unwont* in stormes to be tost. . . . *S.C.* F. 32
Unwont with heards to watch, . . . VI. xi. 40. 4
Unwonted. this great passion of *unwonted* lust, . . . I. i. 49. 1
flaming mouthes of steedes, *unwonted* wilde, . . . I. iv. 9. 3
giving warning of th' *unwonted* sound, . . . I. v. 30. 3
They, . . . Are wonne with pitty and *unwonted* ruth; . . . I. vi. 12. 7
impatient of *unwonted* payne, He loudly brayd . . . I. viii. 11. 2
eies, . . . Could not endure th' *unwonted* sunne to view; . . . I. viii. 41. 2
Her heart with joy *unwonted* inly sweld, . . . I. x. 8. 8
by force *unwonted* passage fynd, . . . I. xi. 10. 7
insolent wox through *unwonted* ease, . . . II. x. 17. 2
Gazing awhile at his *unwonted* guise; . . . II. xii. 66. 2
Full of soft passion and *unwonted* smart: . . . III. v. 30. 8
A traveiler *unwonted* to such way: . . . III. vii. 4. 2
what *unwonted* path Had guided her, . . . III. vii. 8. 3
For great despight of that *unwonted* band, . . . III. vii. 36. 4
Do greatly stand amaz'd at such *unwonted* wonder. . . . IV. ii. 16. 9
with *unwonted* terror halfe affray, . . . V. ix. 24. 4
Unworthily. Nor ever thought thing so *unworthily:* . . . VI. xii. 33. 7
Unworthy. evill hap *Unworthy* in such wretchednes doth wrap, *Hub.* 602
the world, *unworthie* such a spoyle, . . . *D.* 163
me *unworthie* willed here to stay, . . . *D.* 367
Ne for their gifts *unworthie* of his wit, . . . *As.* 51
Yet not *unworthie* of the countries store. . . . *As.* 52
Blaspheme his powre, or termes *unworthie* yield.' . . . *Col.* 822
beautie brought t' *unworthie* wretchednesse . . . I. iii. 1. 3
this false faytor, who *unworthie* ware His worthie shield, . . . I. iv. 47. 4
In their rude eyes *unworthie* of so wofull plight. . . . I. vi. 9. 9
'*Unworthy* wretch,' (quoth he) 'of so great grace, . . . I. x. 62. 1
Unworthy of faire Ladies comely governaunce. . . . II. ii. 35. 9
Unworthie of the commune breathed ayre, . . . II. iii. 7. 5
Unworthy match for such immortall mate . . . II. vii. 50. 4
Unworthie usage of redoubted knight. . . . II. viii. 25. 4

Unworthy—*Continued.*
Madan raignd, *unworthie* of his race, . . . II. x. 21. 1
Next Memprise, as *unworthy* of that place; . . . II. x. 21. 3
That may *unworthy* of it selfe be thought. . . . III. ii. 10. 5
to all th' *unworthy* world forlore . . . III. v. 50. 8
my lott (*unworthy'*) is to be one.' . . . III. viii. 46. 9
least with *unworthie* blames . . . III. ix. 1. 3
Unworthy wretch to tread upon the ground, . . . III. xi. 11. 8
this of Florimels *unworthie* paine . . . IV. i. 1. 5
'*Unworthy* life, that love with guile hast gotten; . . . IV. i. 51. 7
From wight *unworthie* of so noble meed. . . . IV. v. 28. 4
beat his breast *unworthy* of such blame, . . . IV. viii. 4. 7
Unworthy they of grace, . . . IV. x. 17. 8
deeme *unworthy* or of love or life, . . . IV. xii. 16. 6
still bemoning her *unworthy* paine. . . . IV. xii. 17. 5
He much was mov'd at so *unworthie* shame, . . . V. iii. 10. 7
lead that shamefull life, *unworthy* of a Knight.' . . . V. iv. 32. 9
'*Unworthy* sure' (quoth he) 'of better day, . . . V. v. 39. 5
Let me this crave, *unworthy* though of it, . . . VI. ii. 33. 3
With tender ruth for her *unworthy* griefe; . . . VI. iv. 34. 2
Whereof thou, caytive, so *unworthie* art, . . . VI. vi. 33. 6
where that Dame remayned With her *unworthy* knight, . . . VI. vi. 39. 9
Unworthy she to be belov'd so dere, . . . VI. vii. 29. 5
These two, *unworthy* of your wretched bands, . . . VI. viii. 7. 6
Babblers *unworthy* been of so divine a meed. . . . VII. vi. 46. 9
though she all *unworthy* were Of the Heav'ns Rule; . . . VII. viii. 1. 3
Is of the world *unworthy* most envide: . . . *Am.* v. 4
Unwound. He from those bands weend him to have *unwound;* VI. viii. 27. 4
Unwreaked. cruelty So long *unwreaked* of thine enimy? . . . III. xi. 9. 5
Up (*partial list*).
faire greene Laurel witherd *up* and dide. . . . *Bel.*[1] vii. 14
She climbed *up* to heaven in the smoke. . . . *Bel.*[1] ix. 8
in setting of hir image *up.* . . . *Rev.* i. 14
with fine perle and golde puft *up* in heart. . . . *Rev.* ii. 7
Justly proportion'd *up* unto his hight, . . . *Bel.* iii. 3
I saw raysde *up* on yvorie pillowes tall, . . . *Bel.* iv. 1
up to the throne of Gods . . . *Bel.* xi. 6
When Gods and men my honour *up* did raise? . . . *Bel.*[2] x. 8
the storme impetuous Sunke *up* these riches, . . . *Bel.*[2] xiii. 10
sudden storme . . . tumbled *up* the sea, . . . *Pet.* ii. 8
well assur'd, she mounted *up* to joy. . . . *Pet.* vi. 10
sharped steeples high shot *up* in ayre; . . . *Ro.* ii. 2
Puft *up* with pride of Romane hardiehead, . . . *Ro.* xi. 3
see huge flames . . . *up* to the heavens to spyre, . . . *Ro.* xvi. 10
Up to his eares the verdant grasse did growe, . . . *Van.* ii. 5
Burnt *up* his yong ones, . . . *Van.* iv. 8
if that fortune chaunce you *up* to call . . . *Van.* xii. 11
For youngth is a bubble blown *up* with breath, . . . *S.C.* F. 87
wandring *up* and downe the land, . . . *S.C.* Mar. 64
'Now ryse *up,* Elisa, decked as thou art . . . *S.C.* Ap. 145
Heaping *up* waves of welth and woe, . . . *S.C.* May 93
the Sonne hath reared *up* His fyerie-footed teme, . . . *S.C.* Jul. 17
I brought him *up* without the Dambe: . . . *S.C.* Au. 39
Sike question ripeth *up* cause of newe woe, . . . *S.C.* S. 13
Cuddie, for shame! hold *up* thy heavye head, . . . *S.C.* O. 1
Lyft *up* thy selfe out of the lowly dust, . . . *S.C.* O. 38
lyftes him *up* out of the loathsome myre: . . . *S.C.* O. 92
taken *up* his ynne in Fishes haske. . . . *S.C.* N. 16
Then *up,* I say, thou jolly shepeheard swayne, . . . *S.C.* N. 47
'*Up,* then, Melpomene! . . . *S.C.* N. 53
Up, grieslie ghostes! and *up* my rufull ryme! . . . *S.C.* N. 55
Whose better dayes death hath shut *up* in woe? . . . *S.C.* N. 74
Up, Colin *up!* ynough thou morned hast; . . . *S.C.* N. 207
Theyr rootes bene dryed *up* for lacke of dewe, . . . *S.C.* D. 111
My spring is spent, my sommer burnt *up* quite; . . . *S.C.* D. 128
was mounted now on hight *Up* to the heavenly towers, . . . *Gn.* 66
And high shoote *up* their heads into the skyes. . . . *Gn.* 192
whose limbs, . . . They, gathering *up,* . . . *Gn.* 200
Black stormes and fogs are blowen *up* from farre, . . . *Gn.* 572
To dig *up* sods out of the flowrie grasse, . . . *Gn.* 654
And still I hoped to be *up* advaunced, . . . *Hub.* 63
Still wayting to preferment *up* to clime, . . . *Hub.* 76
the Ape himselfe gan *up* to reare, . . . *Hub.* 237
Should render *up* a reckning of their travels . . . *Hub.* 310
The man straightway his choler *up* did move, . . . *Hub.* 364
Upon his tiptoes nicely he *up* went, . . . *Hub.* 1009
Then freely *up* those royall spoyles he tooke, . . . *Hub.* 1059
rouzing *up* himselfe, . . . *Hub.* 1335
yelling shrieks throwne *up* into the skies. . . . *T.M.* 24
puft *up* with sdeignfull insolence, . . . *T.M.* 71
learned Impes that wont to shoote *up* still, . . . *T.M.* 75
That lowly thoughts lift *up* to heavens hight. . . . *T.M.* 459
So, loathing earth, I looke *up* to the sky, . . . *T.M.* 527
And lifted *up* above the worldes gaze, . . . *T.M.* 587
Lifting the Good *up* to high Honours seat, . . . *Com. Son.* i. 11
lifting *up* her brave heroick thought Bove womens weaknes, . *Ti.* 109
Now ginnes to shoote *up* fast, . . . *Ti.* 269
With that she started *up* with cherefull sight, . . . *Ti.* 642
he dared to stie *Up* to the clowdes, . . . *Mui.* 43
that *up* she tooke Her daintie feete, . . . *Mui.* 283
And parching drougth drie *up* the christall wells; . . . *D.* 333
Ne, . . . will I take *up* my Inne. . . . *D.* 469
Whilest none is nigh, thine eylids *up* to close, . . . *As.* 137
when so ever thou it *up* doest take, . . . *As.* 197
A world of waters heaped *up* on hie, . . . *Col.* 197
wash faire Cynthiaes sheep, . . . And fold them *up,* . . . *Col.* 259
Best knowne by bearing *up* great Cynthiaes traine: . . . *Col.* 509
In rolling globes *up* to the vauted skies. . . . *Col.* 611
wander *up* and downe . . . *Col.* 728
For either they be puffed *up* with pride, . . . *Col.* 759

Up—*Continued.*
Unlesse he swim in love *up* to the eares. . . . . *Col.* 782
Therefore with me ye may take *up* your In . . . . I. i. 33. 7
Remounted *up* as light as chearefull Larke; . . . . I. i. 44. 7
All in amaze he suddenly *up* start . . . . I. ii. 5. 1
Then *up* he rose, and clad him hastily: . . . . I. ii. 6. 8
in close hart shutting *up* her payne, ... I. iii. 8. 6
the thirsty land Dronke *up* his life; . . . . I. iii. 20. 5
Up Una rose, *up* rose the lyon eke; . . . . I. iii. 21. 2
High lifted *up* were many loftie towres, ... I. iv. 4. 6
like a brutish beast, He spued *up* his gorge, ... I. iv. 21. 9
'*Up*, then! *up*, dreary Dame, . . . Go, gather *up* the reliques I. v. 24. 1, 2
Whom, . . . He nousled *up* in life and manners wilde, ... I. vi. 23. 8
Puft *up* with emptie wynd, ... I. vii. 9. 9
Then *up* he tooke the slombred sencelesse corse, ... I. vii. 15. 6
shut *up* heavens windowes . . . . I. vii. 23. 5
Mine eyes . . . seeled *up* with death . . . . I. vii. 23. 9
Then rip *up* griefe where it may not availe: . . . . I. vii. 39. 8
That three yardes deepe a furrow *up* did throw. . . . . . . I. viii. 8. 6
all my daies he traind mee *up* in vertuous lore. . . . . . . I. ix. 4. 9
High heaped *up* with huge iniquitee, ... I. ix. 46. 4
Shall he thy sins *up* in his knowledge fold, ... I. ix. 47. 3
broad-blazed fame, That *up* to heven is blowne.' . . . . . . I. x. 11. 5
His huge long tayle, wownd *up* in hundred foldes, ... I. xi. 11. 1
Forelifting *up* a-loft his speckled brest, ... I. xi. 15. 2
Like Eyas hauke *up* mounts unto the skies, ... I. xi. 34. 6
And high her burning torch set *up* in heaven bright. . . . . I. xi. 49. 9
Vere the maine shete, and beare *up* with the land, ... I. xii. 1. 3
up her eies doth seele. . . . . II. i. 38. 9
standing stoutly *up*, ... II. iii. 35. 8
He saide; '*Up, up!* thou womanish weake knight, ... II. v. 36. 2
Those that were *up* themselves kept others low; . . . . . . II. vii. 47. 6
Delivered *up* the Lord of life to dye, ... II. vii. 62. 6
Up to a stately Turret she them brought, ... II. ix. 44. 8
Stird Porrex *up* to put his brother downe; . . . . II. x. 35. 3
When suddein *up* the villeine . . . arose, ... II. xi. 35. 3
his good Squyre, him helping *up* with speed, ... II. xi. 48. 7
having swallowd *up* . . . He soone in vomit *up* againe doth lay, ... II. xii. 3. 6, 7
vented *up* her umbriere, ... III. i. 42. 8
Bene in his ashes raked *up* and hid, ... III. iii. 48. 3
At last blow *up* some gentle gale of ease, ... III. iv. 10. 3
That heales *up* one, and makes another wound! . . . . III. v. 42. 2
lapped *up* her silken leaves most chayre, ... III. v. 51. 6
Up they them tooke; . . . . III. vi. 28. 1
High *up* he cast To the wide world, ... III. x. 35. 7
Her *up* they tooke, and with them home her ledd, ... III. x. 36. 6
And fostred *up* with bitter milke of tine, ... III. xi. 1. 4
her fayre lockes were woven *up* in gold: . . . . III. xii. 13. 4
Who lookt a little *up* at that his speech, ... IV. ii. 21. 3
So all together stird *up* strifull stoure, ... IV. v. 24. 5
ye seemen much to blame To rip *up* wrong . . . . IV. ix. 37. 3
The roofe *up* high was reared from the ground, ... IV. x. 37. 5
rolles, layd *up* in heaven above, ... IV. xi. 10. 3
Still holding *up* her suppliant hands on hye, ... V. ii. 26. 4
He pulleth downe, he setteth *up* on hy; . . . . V. ii. 41. 7
She causeth them be hang'd *up* out of hand; . . . . V. iv. 32. 4
Which was short tucked . . . *Up* to her ham; . . . . V. v. 2. 7
That should their mindes *up* to devotion call, ... V. vi. 27. 4
stird *up* day and night . . . . V. viii. 20. 2
snatching her soone *up*, ere well she knew, ... V. ix. 14. 4
Up to the rocke he ran, ... V. ix. 15. 3
he then tooke it *up*, and held fast in his hand. . . . . . . V. ix. 17. 9
they passing in Went *up* the hall, ... V. ix. 23. 2
bynding *up* her locks and weeds, ... V. x. 24. 9
Shut *up* her haven, mard her marchants trade, ... V. x. 25. 6
He offred *up* for daily sacrifize My children . . . . V. xi. 19. 6
Her foe deliver *up* into her hand: . . . . VI. i. 31. 6
up and downe he wandred . . . . VI. iv. 25. 4
up to their steedes they went, ... VI. v. 24. 8
in some stable neare did set him *up* to feede. . . . . VI. vi. 19. 9
lifted *up* to honorable place, ... VI. vii. 28. 2
But being *up* he lookt againe aloft, ... VI. viii. 26. 1
started *up* like one aghast, And, catching *up* his arms, . . . VI. viii. 47. 8, 9
Blew *up* a bitter storme of foule adversity. . . . . VI. x. 38. 9
as there he romed *up* and downe, ... VI. xi. 27. 1
for great desire Rent *up* her brest, ... VI. xii. 19. 4
Therewith he mured *up* his mouth along, ... VI. xii. 34. 4
my fraile spirit, . . . Lift *up* aloft, ... VII. vii. 1. 5
dainty trees, that, shooting *up* anon, ... VII. vii. 8. 7
The whyles the boyes run *up* and downe the street, ... *Epith.* 137
Ascending *up*, with many a stately stayre, ... *Epith.* 179
Bring her *up* to th' high altar, ... *Epith.* 215
How the red roses flush *up* in her cheekes, ... *Epith.* 226
damned ghosts, cald *up* with mighty spels, ... *Epith.* 347
Up to your haughty pallaces may mount; . . . . *Epith.* 420
Lifting himselfe . . . *up* to the purest skie, ... *H.L.* 178
makes him mount . . . *up* to the heavens hight. . . . . . . *H.L.* 189
And *up* aloft above my strength doest rayse . . . . *H.B.* 6
Did puffe them *up* with greedy bold ambition, ... *H.H.L.* 79
Lift *up* to him thy heavie clouded eyne, ... *H.H.L.* 222
Lift *up* thy mind to th' Author of thy weale, ... *H.H.L.* 256

Upbare. Mercie, that his steps *upbare* And alwaies led, . . . I. x. 44. 4

Upbear. She held him fast, and firmely did *upbeare*, ... I. x. 35. 8
every weighty thing they did *upbeare*, ... II. vi. 46. 8
Many great golden pillours did *upbeare* The massy roofe, . . . II. vii. 43. 5
which two *upbeare* . . . this frayle life of man, ... II. vii. 65. 3

Upbind. To bring forth stormes, or fast them to *upbinde*, . . . IV. xi. 52. 4

Upblowing. The watry Southwinde, from the seabord coste *Upblowing*, ... III. iv. 13. 5

Upblown. His belly was *upblowne* with luxury, ... I. iv. 21. 3
Wondred to see her belly so *upblone*, ... III. vi. 9. 8
he, whose spirit was with pride *upblowne*, ... V. i. 17. 5

Upbound. which having well *upbownd*, ... III. iv. 40. 7
Her golden locks, that were in trammells gay *Upbounden*, . . III. ix. 20. 5
her golden lockes, that were *upbound* Still in a knot, ... IV. i. 13. 2

Upbraid. *See* **Upbray.**
My hurtlesse pleasaunce did me ill *upbraide;* . . . . *S.C.* D. 51
for disdaine of sinfull worlds *upbraide* . . . . *Hub.* 2
evill men, now dead, his deeds *upbraid:* . . . . *Ti.* 214
justly her *upbrayd* For loving not? . . . . *Col.* 913
name of native syre did fowle *upbrayd*, ... I. v. 48. 7
Upbrayd, for leaving her in place unmeet, ... I. vii. 3. 8
doth me *upbrayd* With breach of love . . . . I. xii. 31. 4
me behoveth rather to *upbrayd*, ... II. i. 28. 4
having not complaine, and having it *upbrayd?'* . . . . . . II. vii. 14. 9
t' *upbrayd* A gentle knight . . . . III. ii. 9. 5
ill beseemes it to *upbrayd* A dolefull heart . . . . III. vi. 21. 7
did her *upbrayd* With loosenesse of her love . . . . III. x. 50. 3
that same Squire of treason to *upbraide;* . . . . IV. ix. 7. 7
through lewd *upbraide* Of Ate and Duessa, ... IV. ix. 24. 5
They gan remember of the fowle *upbraide*, ... IV. ix. 28. 5
the proud boaster gan his doome *upbrayd*, ... V. iii. 35. 7
to *upbrayd* that chaunce which him misfell, ... V. v. 10. 2
How cleare I am from blame of this *upbraide;* . . . . V. xi. 41. 7
How to deprave or slaunderously *upbrayd*, ... V. xii. 34. 3
fowle *upbrayd* with faulty blame. . . . . VI. i. 24. 9
with sharpe words did bitterly *upbrayd:* . . . . VI. vi. 33. 3

Upbraided. they her rebuked and *upbrayded* sore. . . . . . . V. xi. 61. 9

Upbraiding. thus *upbrayding* said: . . . . V. vii. 32. 4

Upbraids. *See* **Upbrays.**
Turn'd to a Lapwing, fowlie them *upbraydes*, ... *Gn.* 405

Upbrast. The dores assayled, and the locks *upbrast:* . . . . . VI. xi. 43. 3

Upbray. knights and knighthood doest with shame *upbray*, . II. iv. 45. 3
shewing her, did Paridell *upbray;* . . . . IV. ii. 7. 4

Upbrays. After long troubles and unmeet *upbrayes* . . . . . III. vi. 50. 3
his foe for lying long *upbrayes:* . . . . IV. i. 42. 9

Upbrought. be *upbrought* in gentle thewes and martiall might. I. ix. 3. 9
three daughters, well *upbrought* In goodly thewes, ... I. x. 4. 3
Attonce I was *upbrought;* . . . . II. iv. 18. 4
To be *upbrought* in perfect Maydenhed, ... III. vi. 28. 4
To be *upbrought* in goodly womanhed; . . . . III. vi. 28. 7
Artegall in justice was *upbrought* . . . . V. i. 5. 1
Unto the battilment to be *upbrought*, ... V. ii. 23. 5
And it in goodly thewes so well *upbrought*, ... VI. iv. 38. 7
long in darksome Stygian den *upbrought*, ... VI. vi. 9. 8
with the crew of blessed Saynts *upbrought*, ... *Am.* lxi. 7

Upcaught. His booteless bow in feeble hand *upcaught*, ... III. v. 24. 6

Upcheered. Sir Calidore *upcheard*, ... VI. i. 44. 8

Upfilled. was with Nepenthe to the brim *upfild*. . . . . . . IV. iii. 42. 9

Upgathered. Himselfe he close *upgathered* more and more Into his den, ... *Mui.* 397

Upgathering. her garments loose *Upgath'ring*, ... III. vi. 19. 7

Uphanged. on a tree *uphang'd* I saw her spoyle. . . . . . . *Bel.*[2] vi. 14

Upheave. doth against the dead his hand *upheave*, ... II. viii. 29. 7

Upheld. so thy father his head *upheld*, ... *S.C.* May 205
sweet Timbrels all *upheld* on hight. . . . . I. xii. 6. 9
mightily *upheld* that royall mace . . . . II. x. 4. 3
The Palmer over them his staffe *upheld*, ... II. xii. 40. 2
scarse he him *upheld* from falling in a swound. . . . . IV. iv. 24. 9
All that long while *upheld* her wrathfull hand, ... IV. vi. 23. 2
Yet she it forst to have againe *upheld*, ... IV. vi. 27. 1
both behind *upheld* her spredding traine; . . . . IV. xi. 47. 4
Like a sweet Angell twixt two clouds *uphild;* . . . . VI. xi. 21. 3
up-held With thousand Crystall pillors . . . . VII. vi. 10. 3

Uphoarded. Heapes of huge wordes *uphoorded* hideously, . . . *T.M.* 553

Uphold. now unnethes their feete could them *uphold*. . . . . *S.C.* Ja. 6
scarse thy legs *uphold* thy feeble gate.' . . . . *Hub.* 600
to *uphold* his courtly countenaunce . . . . *Hub.* 846
ne could *upholde* His countenance . . . . *Hub.* 927
Withouten prop or pillour it t' *upholde*, ... *Ti.* 549
six wisards . . . with their counsels bad, her kingdome did *uphold*. . . . . I. iv. 12. 9
Scarse could he once *uphold* his heavie hedd, ... I. iv. 19. 5
His dronken corse he scarse *upholden* can: . . . . I. iv. 22. 8
Were not that heavenly grace doth him *uphold*, ... I. viii. 1. 3
thighes, unable to *uphold* His pined corse, ... I. viii. 40. 7
Uplifted light, and softly did *uphold:* . . . . II. i. 46. 2
to *uphold* His ydle humour with fine flattery. . . . . II. iii. 9. 7
the wals, that did the same *uphold*, ... II. ix. 55. 3
she her shield . . . Could scarse *uphold:* . . . . V. vii. 33. 5
Seemed those litle Angels did *uphold* The cloth of state, . . . V. ix. 29. 1

Upknit. When Glauce thus gan wisely all *upknit:* . . . . . . IV. vi. 30. 1

Uplaid. Save what in heavens storehouse he *uplaid:* . . . . . *Ti.* 212

Upland. They came unto a Citie farre *up land*, ... V. x. 25. 1

Upleaning. *upleaning* on his batt, ... *Gn.* 154
upleaning on her elbow weake, ... III. ii. 42. 6

Uplifted. With humble hearts to heaven *uplifted* hie, ... *Col.* 816
The gentle knight her soone with carefull paine *Uplifted* . . II. i. 46. 2
the lampe of lightsome day *Up-lifted* in the porch of heaven hie: . . . . V. vii. 17. 4
from low to high *uplifted* is your fame. . . . . VI. Pr. 6. 9

Uplifting. his hand, . . . *Uplifting* high, ... II. viii. 30. 6
Whose lofty argument, *uplifting* me, ... *Am.* lxxxii. 13

Uplook. when day gan to *uplooke*, ... VI. iii. 11. 1
He also gan *uplooke* with drery eye, ... VI. iii. 11. 2

Upmost. Deepe was he drenched to the *upmost* chin, ... II. vii. 58. 1

Upon (*partial list*). *See* **Whereupon.**
threw forth a thousand rayes *Upon* an hundred steps . . . . *Bel.*[1] ii. 8
blood, the which at first was spilt *Upon* your walls, ... *Ro.* xxiv. 13

Upon—*Continued.*
Upon the same to set foundation sure? *Ro.* xxiv. 14
Upon a sunnie banke outstretched lay, *Van.* iii. 2
he him caught *upon* a day, *S.C.* Mar. 107
In whom the heavens powrde all their gifts *upon* her. *Ti.* 280
His thoughts, his rimes, his songs were all *upon* her. *As.* 60
Sate . . . *upon* a day, Charming his oaten pipe *Col.* 4
did ride, *Uppon* a Camell loaden all with gold: I. iv. 27. 2
a Jacobs staffe, to stay His weary limbs *upon;* I. vi. 35. 8
I thinke *upon* my bitter bale. I. vii. 39. 6
mighty man of God, . . . Dwelt forty daies *upon;* I. x. 53. 6
that deare Crosse *uppon* your shield II. i. 31. 8
Purfled *upon* with many a folded plight, II. iii. 26. 5
By strife is rayld *uppon.* II. iv. Arg.
matter make for him to worke *upon,* II. iv. 42. 6
Nourish the flames which they are warmd *upon,* II. x. 26. 5
built by art *upon* the glassy See A bridge II. x. 73. 8
Soone as they bene arriv'd *upon* the brim III. iv. 34. 1
This gentle Damzell, whom I write *upon,* III. viii. 1. 4
wav'd *upon,* like water Chamelot, IV. xi. 45. 6
silke Woven *uppon* with silver, V. v. 2. 2
Withouten armes or steede to ride *upon,* VI. iv. 39. 3
Did warne his rider be *uppon* his gard; VI. v. 21. 7
laying . . . *Upon* the rest that did alive remaine; VI. vi. 38. 4
they them selves did place *Upon* the grasse, VI. viii. 39. 2
fragrant odours they *uppon* her threw; VI. x. 14. 8
He rampt *upon* him with his ravenous pawes, VI. xii. 29. 8
Upon a Bull he rode, VII. vii. 33. 3
ye fresh boyes, that tend *upon* her groome, *Epith.* 112
All which *upon* those goodly Birds they threw *Proth.* 76
Upon your Brydale day, *Proth.* 107
Upon the Brydale day, *Proth.* 161

Upper. the *upper* marge Of his sevenfolded shield II. v. 6. 2
did loosely disaray Her *upper* partes II. v. 32. 8
preaced to draw nere To th' *upper* part, II. vii. 44. 4
upper end to highest heven was knitt, II. vii. 46. 3
At th' *upper* end there sate, yclad in red II. ix. 27. 5
th' *upper* halfe their hew retayned still, II. xii. 31. 6
at the *upper* end of that faire rowme III. xi. 47. 1
she spyde at that rowmes *upper* end III. xi. 54. 6
their *upper* garment which they weare; VI. vi. 34. 7

Upraise. her upraising doest thy selfe *upraise.* *Col.* 355
Scudamour himselfe did soone *uprayse,* IV. i. 42. 8

Upraised. second Babell . . . Her ayry Towers *upraised* much more high. *Com. Son.* iv. 4

Upraising. her *upraising* doest thy selfe upraise. *Col.* 355

Uprear. it selfe *upreare* Over the world, *Ro.* xii. 10
did a stately heape of stones *upreare,* *Col.* 285
As chauffed Bore his bristles doth *upreare;* I. xi. 15. 6
doen *upreare* Their bevers bright II. i. 29. 1
*That doth against the dead his hand *upreare,* II. viii. 29. 7
They shall *upreare,* and mightily defend III. iii. 23. 7
Griffyth Conan also shall *upreare* His dreaded head, III. iii. 45. 6
ere the morrow did *upreare* His deawy head III. iv. 61. 3
thrise his hand to kill her did *upreare,* IV. i. 54. 8
he for paine himselfe n'ote right *upreare,* IV. iii. 9. 6
neither could in hast themselves againe *upreare.* IV. iv. 20. 9
scarse the Squire his hand could once *upreare,* IV. vii. 28. 6
Ne ever durst her eyes from ground *upreare,* IV. x. 50. 2
To rule his tides, and surges to *uprere,* IV. xi. 52. 3
Right so himselfe did Marinell *upreare,* IV. xii. 35. 1
him selfe he did *upreare* VI. i. 35. 1
like an Altar did itselfe *uprere* VI. viii. 42. 5

Upreared. nigh unto the Heavens in height *upreared,* *Ti.* 507
as he his hand to strike *upreard,* IV. iii. 33. 8
harkning to that voice, him selfe *upreard,* VI. i. 19. 1
Above the earth *upreard* his flaming head, VI. i. 31. 2
stouping downe . . . *Uprear'd* her from the ground VI. iii. 27. 8
Uprear'd her head to see that chearefull sight. VI. iii. 45. 5
To happie blisse he was full high *uprear'd,* VI. v. 12. 4
Doubting least Typhon were againe *uprear'd,* VII. vi. 15. 8
antique Babel . . . *Upreard* her buildings to the threatned skie: *Com. Son.* iv. 2

Uprearing. himselfe *uprearing* hy Upon his tiptoes, *Hub.* 663
I . . . lightlie him *uprearing,* Revoked life, *D.* 187
Britomart, *uprearing* her from grownd, III. xii. 40. 1

Upright. nowe *upright* he can stand no more; *S.C.* F. 234
walkes *upright* with comely stedfast pace, *Hub.* 728
His carriage was full comely and *upright;* II. i. 6. 1
Upright he rode, II. i. 18. 8
Withouten which she could not goe *upright;* II. iv. 5. 7
seemd the fountaine in that sea did sayle *upright.* II. xii. 62. 9
His double folded necke she reard *upright,* III. v. 31. 6
then which none more *upright,* IV. xi. 18. 6
lenger he note stand *upright,* IV. xii. 20. 7
ne beare him selfe *upright;* V. ii. 17. 8
Now walking soft, now sitting still *upright,* V. vi. 26. 3
With speare . . . stayd him selfe *upright,* VI. iii. 33. 8
Striving in vaine to rere him selfe *upright:* VI. xii. 31. 4

Uprightly. Areede *uprightly* who has the victorye *S.C.* Au. 130

Uprise. The Giants old should once againe *uprise,* *Ro.* iv. 6

Uprisen. *See* **Uprist.**

Upriseth. Suddein *upriseth* from her stately place The roiall Dame, I. iv. 16. 1

Uprising. *Uprising* by degrees, grewe to such height, *Ro.* xx. 10
With so fresh hew *uprysing* him to see, II. viii. 54. 3
From the *uprising* to the setting Sunne, III. i. 3. 5

Uprist. Maias bowre, That newe is *upryst* from bedde: *S.C.* Mar. 18

Uproar. Nor th' horrible *uprore* of windes high blowing, *Ro.* xiii. 9
Her nourslings did with mutinous *uprore* *Ro.* xxii. 5

Uproar—*Continued.*
that infernall feend with foule *uprore* I. i. 5. 7
all on *uprore* from her settled seat, II. ii. 20. 6
Some troublous *uprore* or contentious fray, II. iv. 3. 3
With hellish feends, or Furies mad *uprore,* II. v. 37. 7
with great *uprore* preaced to draw nere II. vii. 44. 3
whilest all things in troublous *uprore* were, III. x. 16. 1
It vaine she thought with rigorous *uprore* For to efforce, III. xii. 27. 8
all the world confound with wide *uprore,* IV. ix. 23. 8
Such was betwixt these two the troublesome *uprore.* V. ii. 15. 9
filled all the house with feare and great *uprore.* V. ii. 21. 9
Wayling, and raysing pittifull *uprore,* V. ix. 8. 8
In troublous wits, and mutinous *uprore:* V. ix. 48. 6
in that *uprore* Ye with those caytives saw, V. xi. 49. 5
wherefore Betwixt you two began this . . . sterne *uprore.* VI. ii. 8. 9
The people of the house rose forth in great *uprore.'* VI. vi. 22. 9
misdoubting least of-new Some *uprore* were VI. xi. 43. 9
with noyse of late *uprore,* VI. xi. 46. 1

Uprolled. Reeking aloft *uprolled* to the sky: III. vii. 5. 3

Uprose. after him *uprose* eke all the rest: *Col.* 953
Uprose Duessa from her resting place, I. iv. 44. 8
Uprose with hasty joy, and feeble speed, I. xii. 3. 1
Uprose from drowsie couch, II. iii. 1. 6
Sore bruzed with the fall he slow *uprose,* II. v. 5. 1
He then *uprose,* inflamd with fell despight, II. v. 37. 8
Uprose Sir Guyon, in bright armour clad, II. xi. 3. 5
Full of disdainefull wrath he fierce *uprose* III. i. 9. 1
They both *uprose* and tooke their ready way III. ii. 48. 3
that same Faery knight *Uprose,* III. x. 1. 6
They both *uprose* and to their waies them dight: IV. i. 16. 6
oft in wrath he thence againe *uprose,* IV. v. 40. 5
after her full lightly he *uprose,* IV. vii. 21. 6
Calidore *uprose* againe full light, VI. i. 34. 1

Upshooting. The painted flowres, the trees *upshooting* hye, II. xii. 58. 5

Upshot. The onely *upshot* whereto he doth ayme: *Hub.* 770

Upside down. a masse of coyne he told, And turned *upside downe,* (*upsidowne) II. vii. 4. 8

Upsprung. there is a new shepheard late *up sprong,* *Col.* 416

Upstand. die or live, for nought he would *upstand,* IV. vi. 23. 7

Upstanding. *upstanding,* gan to grind His grated teeth II. v. 14. 2
Staring with hollow eies, and stiffe *upstanding* heares. II. ix. 13. 9
with long locks *up-standing,* stifly stared Like one adawed V. vii. 20. 7

Upstared. her faire locks *up stared* stiffe on end, III. xii. 36. 6

Upstaring. they might perceive . . . curld uncombed heares *Upstaring* stiffe, I. ix. 22. 3
rearing fercely their *upstaring* crests, II. xii. 39. 8
With ragged weedes, and lockes *upstaring* hye, VI. xi. 27. 4

Upstart. Wherewith enrag'd he fiercely gan *upstart,* *Gn.* 289
Thereat enraged, soone he gan *upstart,* *Hub.* 1333
Their dam *upstart* out of her den effraide, I. i. 16. 1
All in amaze he suddenly *up start* With sword I. ii. 5. 1
lightly did *upstart,* II. iv. 9. 8
Who seeing her gan streight *upstart,* III. viii. 9. 8
With *upstart* haire and staring eyes dismay, III. x. 54. 8
then all attonce *upstart,* VI. viii. 40. 1

Upstarted. Th' Elfe, therewith astownd, *Upstarted* lightly from his looser make, I. vii. 7. 8
he *upstarted* brave Out of the well, I. xi. 34. 1
both eftsoones *upstarted* furiously, II. viii. 18. 8
Lightly *upstarted* from the dustie ground, III. vii. 7. 5
Straight he *upstarted* from the loathed layes, III. xii. 44. or. 5
At length they both *upstarted* in amaze, IV. ii. 17. 1
suddenly they both *upstarted* light, IV. iii. 35. 6

Upstarting. *rearing fiercely their *upstarting* crests, II. xii. 39. 8
upstarting from her swoune, V. v. 13. 7
Whence soone *upstarting* much he gan repine, VI. v. 26. 5

Upstayed. On Atlas mighty shoulders is *upstayd,* *Ded. Son.* ix. 6
those two villeins, which her steps *upstayd,* III. xii. 21. 5
They reared him on horsebacke and *upstayd,* IV. i. 37. 4
saw him sencelesse by the Squire *upstaide,* IV. ix. 7. 4

Upstaying. *Upstaying* still her selfe uppon her steede, VI. iii. 46. 2

Uptake. Satyran a girdle did *uptake* IV. ii. 25. 7
He sayd that he would all the earth *uptake* V. ii. 31. 1

Uptaking. the childe *Uptaking,* to the Palmer gave to beare; II. ii. 11. 2
it *uptaking* ere the fall, III. ii. 9. 3

Uptie. Her golden lockes she roundly did *uptye* II. ii. 15. 7

Uptied. The end of their sad Tragedie *uptyde,* II. ii. 1. 3
having all his bands againe *uptyde,* VI. iv. 24. 1

Upties. An hatefull Snake, the which his taile *uptyes* In many folds, I. iv. 31. 4

Uptook. Up they them tooke; each one a babe *uptooke,* III. vi. 28. 1
Artegall that golden belt *uptooke,* V. iii. 27. 1

Uptrained. well *uptraind* In all that seemed fitt for kingly seed: II. x. 27. 3

Upward. He bade me *upwarde* unto heaven looke. *Bel.*[1] i. 8
Did not once move, nor *upward* cast his eye, II. viii. 50. 6
terrify To looke adowne, or *upward* to the hight: III. x. 56. 6
Ne could it *upward* come, nor downward passe, VI. iv. 21. 8
still as every thing doth *upward* tend, *H.H.B.* 44

Upwound. taile . . . in knots and many boughtes *upwound,* I. i. 15. 3

Urania. *Urania,* sister unto Astrofell, *Col.* 487

Uranus. Both sonnes of *Uranus;* VII. vi. 27. 3

Urchins. some like ugly *Urchins* thick and short: II. xi. 13. 4

Ure. Still *Ure,* swift Werfe, and Oze the most of might, IV. xi. 37. 6

Urge. Doth *urge* her fellow Furies earnestlie *Gn.* 423
Then Zele began to *urge* her punishment, V. ix. 49. 7

Urged. *urged* sore . . . Him hasty to arise. II. v. 37. 4

Urgent. Yet others she more *urgent* did devise; II. v. 21. 8
then oppressing him with *urgent* paine, VI. iv. 22. 6

Us (*partial list*).

Us—*Continued.*
That so hath raft *us* of our meriment. . . . . *S.C.* Au. 14
Tom Piper makes *us* better melodie. . . . . *S.C.* O. 78
For-thy content *us* in thys humble shade, ... *S.C.* O. 116
They, not contented *us* themselves to scorne, ... *T.M.* 65
How much to her we owe, that all *us* gave; . . . . II. x. 69. 8
To stirre up strife, when most *us* needeth rest, ... IV. iv. 12. 3
one that hath both wronged you and *us;* . . . . IV. xii. 30. 3
Usage. Him needeth not to seeke for *usage* right Of line, . . . *Ro.* xxvi. 2
excelling all the crewe In curteous *usage* . . . . *Mui.* 120
With gentle *usage* and demeanure myld: . . . . *As.* 20
Of great unkindnesse, and of *usage* hard, ... *Col.* 165
with *usage* sly He taught to imitate that Lady trew, ... I. i. 46. 7
what that *usage* ment, ... II. vi. 9. 3
Unworthie *usage* of redoubted knight. . . . . II. viii. 25. 4
through continuall practise and *usage* . . . . II. ix. 54. 4
O! goodly *usage* of those antique tymes, ... III. i. 13. 1
far expell All civile *usage* and gentility, ... III. vi. 1. 8
to tell The diverse *usage,* and demeanure daint, ... IV. i. 5. 2
both were bent t' avenge his *usage* base, ... IV. iv. 4. 7
wearie limmes recur'd after late *usage* bad. . . . . IV. vi. 39. 9
cursed *usage* and ungodly trade The heavens abhorre, ... IV. vii. 12. 3
his uncouth guise and *usage* quaint . . . . IV. vii. 45. 1
Fallen into that Tyrants hand and *usage* bad. . . . . . . V. xi. 40. 9
those villens through their *usage* bad Them fouly rent, . . . V. xi. 60. 8
For his faire *usage* and conditions sound, ... VI. i. 3. 3
put away proud looke and *usage* sterne, ... VI. i. 40. 8
with *usage* kind He rather should have taken up . . . . . VI. ii. 11. 4
Him of ungentle *usage* did reprove, ... VI. iii. 42. 7
By gentle *usage* of that wretched Dame: . . . . VI. v. 2. 6
Seeing his royall *usage* and array . . . . VI. v. 41. 7
ywroken Of all the vile demeane and *usage* bad, ... VI. vi. 18. 4
never had acquainted beene With such queint *usage,* . . . . VI. ix. 35. 2
Usance. th' onely *usance* Of a small time, ... *D.* 503
From the worldes eye, and from her right *usaunce?'* . . . . II. vii. 7. 4
Use. as the coward beasts *use* to despise . . . . *Ro.* xiv. 5
As they which gleane, the reliques *use* to gather, ... *Ro.* xxx. 13
(As most *usen* Ambitious folke:) . . . . *S.C.* F. 161
Usen we freely our felicitie; . . . . *S.C.* May 155
With minde that ill *use* doth before deprave, ... *Gn.* 91
had the *use* of his right arme bereaved. . . . . *Hub.* 208
he is fit to *use* in all assayes, ... *Hub.* 780
Use them but well, with gracious clemencye, ... *Hub.* 1080
With which ye *use* your loves to deifie, ... *T.M.* 368
use to paint in rimes the troublous state . . . . *T.M.* 381
As men *use* most to covet forreine thing.' . . . . *Col.* 162
Had people grace it gratefully to *use:* . . . . *Col.* 325
use his ydle name to other needs, ... *Col.* 789
To *use* him so that used her so well; . . . . *Col.* 912
He hated . . . him no lesse, that any like did *use;* . . . . I. iv. 32. 2
he could not them *use,* but kept them . . . . I. viii. 30. 9
Merlin came, As was his *use,* ofttimes to visitt mee, ... I. ix. 5. 2
As miserable lovers *use* to rew, ... I. ix. 9. 8
As sparkles from the Andvile *use* to fly, ... I. xi. 42. 6
whenas *use* of speach was from her reft, ... II. iv. 13. 1
She to her *use* returnd, ... II. v. 19. 3
What bootes it al to have, and nothing *use?* . . . . II. vi. 17. 6
If then thee list my offred grace to *use,* . . . . II. vii. 18. 6
To covet more then I have cause to *use?* . . . . II. vii. 39. 4
To teach them how to *use* their present state.' . . . . . . II. vii. 60. 5
To *use* that sword so well as he it ought!' . . . . II. viii. 40. 4
use thy fortune as it doth befall; . . . . II. viii. 52. 2
others it to *use* according to his kynd. . . . . II. ix. 31. 9
Let later age that noble *use* envy, ... III. i. 13. 8
As pleased them to *use* that *use* it might; . . . . III. i. 39. 5
Did *use* to hide, and plaine apparaunce shonne) . . . . . . III. i. 52. 8
(as maydens *use* to done) . . . . III. ii. 23. 5
Ill weares he armes, that nill them *use* for Ladies sake.' . . . III. v. 11. 9
as she could well it *uze,* . . . . III. v. 33. 5
through her so kind And courteise *use,* . . . . III. vii. 15. 7
Ne how to speake, ne how to *use* his gest; . . . . III. viii. 8. 7
surpassed . . . In beastly *use,* all that I ever finde: . . . . III. xi. 4. 4
there sleights and art She cast to *use,* . . . . III. xii. 28. 2
use of awfull Majestie remove. . . . . IV. Pr. 5. 4
serving her in her malitious *use* . . . . IV. i. 31. 2
Which she by art could *use* unto her will, ... IV. ii. 44. 3
throughly skild in *use* of shield and speare; . . . . IV. iii. 7. 2
for glorie vaine, And not for vertuous *use,* . . . . IV. v. 2. 7
call ye me the Salvage Knight, as others *use.'* . . . . . . IV. vi. 4. 9
threw away, with vow to *use* no more, ... IV. vii. 39. 2
did *use* Withouten dread of perill to repaire . . . . IV. viii. 5. 1
will not *use* his gifts for thankelesse nigardise.' . . . . . . IV. viii. 15. 9
Blessed the man that well can use his blis: . . . . IV. x. 8. 8
many herbes did *use.* . . . . IV. xi. 6. 3
But to the antique *use* which was of yore, ... V. Pr. 3. 5
that *use* well knew To fight in water, ... V. ii. 13. 5
each Knight, that *use* of perill has, ... V. ii. 16. 8
use oftentimes To attribute their folly unto fate, ... V. iv. 28. 1
like a rebell stout, I will him *use;* . . . . V. v. 51. 3
He list no lenger to *use* lothfull speach, ... V. vi. 21. 6
both their skill forgot, And practicke *use* in armes; . . . . V. vii. 29. 5
as if such *use* they hated. . . . . V. vii. 29. 9
'Her name Mercilla most men *use* to call, ... V. viii. 17. 1
Which uncouth *use* when as the Prince perceived, ... V. xi. 7. 1
So also did this Monster *use* like slight . . . . V. xi. 25. 7
long since aside had set The *use* of armes, ... V. xi. 37. 4
In these strange waies where never foote did *use,* . . . . . VI. Pr. 2. 8
wisely *use,* and well apply, ... VI. i. 3. 6
'A shamefull *use* as ever I did heare,' . . . . VI. i. 14. 1
Onely the *use* of armes, . . . I have not tasted yet; . . . . VI. ii. 32. 6

Use—*Continued.*
I may beare armes, and learne to *use* them right; . . . . . VI. ii. 33. 6
Ne knew the *use* of warlike instruments, ... VI. iv. 4. 2
having now no *use* of his long speare . . . . VI. iv. 7. 6
herbe . . . Whose vertue he by *use* well understood; . . . . VI. iv. 12. 7
such as hee Did *use* his feeble body to sustaine, ... VI. v. 39. 2
Use scanted diet, and forbeare your fill; . . . . VI. vi. 14. 7
Maintaine this evil *use,* thy foes thereby to foile. . . . . . VI. vi. 34. 9
to maligne, t' envie, t' *use* shifting slight, ... VI. vii. 1. 5
to entreat The one or th' other better her to *use;* . . . . . VI. vii. 40. 2
saw those villaines her so vildely *use,* . . . . VI. vii. 45. 2
Be well aware how ye the same doe *use,* . . . . VI. viii. 1. 6
As they doe know each can most aptly *use:* . . . . VI. ix. 29. 5
So did Diana and her maydens all *Use* silly Faunus, ... VII. vi. 49. 2
'as changefull as the Moone' men *use* to say. . . . . VII. vii. 50. 9
greedy pikes which *use* therein to feed; . . . . *Epith.* 58
on the hoary mountayne *use* to towre; . . . . *Epith.* 68
as ye *use* to Venus, to her sing, ... *Epith.* 108
Used. in his small bushes *used* to shrowde . . . . *S.C.* F. 122
(as Algrind *used* to say) . . . . *S.C.* May 75
used shepheards all To feede theyr flocks . . . . *S.C.* Jul. 65
he *used* of hys keepe A sacrifice to bring, ... *S.C.* Jul. 133
I whilome *usd* to keepe, ... *S.C.* S. 63
When the good old man *used* to sleepe. . . . . *S.C.* S. 189
Long time he *used* this slippery pranck, ... *S.C.* S. 200
Unto my fathers sheepe I *usde* to looke, ... *Hub.* 292
used duly everie day Their service . . . to say, ... *Hub.* 449
he *usde* another slipprie slight, ... *Hub.* 859
he *us'd* oft to beguile Poore suters, ... *Hub.* 877
so everie one was *used,* . . . . *Hub.* 1223
to whom I *used* to applie The faithfull service . . . . . . *T.M.* 427
'Where my high steeples whilom *usde* to stand, ... *Ti.* 127
fish, which they with baits *usde* to betraie, ... *Ti.* 152
I *usde* . . . My little flocke on westerne downes to keepe, . . *D.* 99
To use him so that *used* her so well; . . . . *Col.* 912
Abessa, . . . With whom he whoredome *usd,* that few did know, I. iii. 18. 5
Repentance *used* to embay His blamefull body . . . . I. x. 27. 5
she *used* hath the practicke paine . . . . I. xii. 34. 5
To proofe of passing wonders hath full often *usd:* . . . . . II. ii. 5. 9
used in a darkesome inner bowre Her oft to meete: . . . . . II. iv. 24. 5
she often *usd* from open heat Her selfe to shroud, ... II. vii. 53. 4
Ne ever may be *used* by his fone, ... II. viii. 21. 3
Who him at first well *used* every way; . . . . II. x. 30. 7
usd to bath themselves in that deceiptfull shade. . . . . . II. xii. 30. 9
Thereof she *usd* to give to drinke to each, ... II. xii. 56. 7
Was *usd* of knightes and Ladies seeming gent: . . . . III. i. 67. 6
to their purpose *used* wicked art: . . . . III. ii. 41. 4
usd the same in batteill aye to beare; . . . . III. ii. 60. 3
complayned how that he Had *used* beene . . . . III. v. 15. 8
where most he *us'd* Whylome to haunt, ... III. vi. 13. 1
He *us'd* to slug, or sleepe in slothfull shade: . . . . III. vii. 12. 8
used her so hard To reave her honor, ... III. viii. 14. 8
Such *us'd* wise Glauce to that wrathfull knight, ... IV. ii. 3. 1
On horsebacke *used* Triamond to fight, ... IV. ii. 42. 4
With curtaxe *used* Diamond to smite, ... IV. ii. 42. 7
speare and curtaxe both *usd* Priamond in field. . . . . . . IV. ii. 42. 9
What time she *usd* to live in wively sort, ... IV. v. 3. 8
layd aside when so she *usd* her looser sport. . . . . IV. v. 3. 9
Thereto the villaine *used* craft in fight; . . . . IV. vii. 26. 1
to the present neede it wisely *usd.* . . . . IV. viii. 60. 4
vice . . . Is now hight vertue, and so *us'd* of all: . . . . V. Pr. 4. 3
Since he himselfe it *us'd* in that great fight . . . . V. i. 9. 5
Talus *usde* . . . To keepe a nightly watch . . . . V. iv. 46. 8
other beds the Priests there *used* none, ... V. vii. 9. 1
With which she *used* still to tye her fone, ... V. vii. 28. 3
usd to fish for fooles on the dry shore, ... V. ix. 11. 8
Which long he *usd* with carefull diligence, ... V. x. 12. 8
To search out those that *usd* to rob and steale, ... V. xii. 26. 7
she *used* often to resort To common haunts, ... V. xii. 34. 6
saves from Maleffort A Damzell *used* vylde: . . . . VI. i. Arg.
His hope of refuge *used* to remaine: . . . . VI. i. 22. 5
Thereto they *usde* one most accursed order, ... VI. viii. 36. 1
Which having got, he *used* without crime . . . . VI. ix. 46. 3
used to resort Unto this place, ... VI. x. 9. 2
in it She *used* most to keepe her royall court, ... VI. x. 9. 7
usde him friendly for further intent, ... VI. x. 37. 7
never *usde* to live by plough nor spade, ... VI. x. 39. 4
The gods then *us'd* . . . Oft to resort there-to, ... VII. vi. 38. 4
In her sweet streames Diana *used* oft . . . To bathe . . . . VII. vi. 42. 1
famous warriors . . . *Used* Trophees to erect . . . . *Am.* lxix. 2
Use's. of civill *uses* lore, ... V. Pr. 3. 2
Uses. make him serve to them for sordid *uses:* . . . . *Col.* 792
Which had approved bene in *uses* manifold. . . . . I. viii. 3. 9
On them she workes her will to *uses* bad: . . . . II. i. 52. 4
such vaine *uses* that him best became: . . . . III. viii. 14. 5
created . . . For other *uses* then they them translated; . . . V. vii. 29. 8
Which warlike *uses* had deviz'd of yore: . . . . V. viii. 34. 5
Useth. pastures . . . On which she *useth* for to feed her sheepe?' *Col.* 239
it there most *useth* to abound; . . . . VI. i. 1. 2
And that faire lampe, which *useth* to inflame . . . . *H.H.B.* 274
Usher. A gentle *Husher,* Vanitie by name, Made rowme, ... I. iv. 13. 3
Using. To come of him for *using* her so hard, ... IV. xii. 12. 3
Usual. The *usuall* joyes at knitting of loves band. . . . . . . I. xii. 40. 5
beare him farre from hope of succour *usuall.* . . . . II. xi. 45. 9
no *usuall* fire, nor *usuall* rage Yt is, ... III. ii. 37. 3
Upon his *usuall* beast it firmely bound, ... IV. ix. 4. 8
he him selfe through practise *usuall,* Leapes forth . . . . . V. ii. 8. 5
this with us so *usuall;* . . . . VII. vii. 26. 5
cleane without his *usuall* spheere to fare; . . . . VII. vii. 52. 4
Usurp. did *usurpe* with wrong and tyrannie Upon the scepter . I. iv. 12. 5

Usurp—*Continued.*
all the rest, which they *usurp*, be all my share. . . . . VII. vii. 26. 9
Usurped. For their *usurped* kingdomes maintenaunce, ... *T.M.* 338
it *usurped* by unrighteous doome: . . . . II. x. 60. 5
their uncle Vortigere *Usurpt* the crowne . . . . II. x. 64. 3
from the Daniske Tyrants head shall rend Th' *usurped* crowne, . III. iii. 47. 7
The liberty of women did repeale, Which they had long *usurpt*; V. vii. 42. 6
Usurping. an *usurping* Ape, with guile suborn'd, ... *Hub.* 1233
Usurps. the gods owne principality, which Jove *usurpes* unjustly, ... VII. vii. 16. 6
Usury. By dubble *usurie* doth twise renew it. . . . . *Col.* 39
Accursed *usury* was all his trade, ... I. iv. 27. 8
what I cannot quite requite with *usuree*. . . . . I. viii. 27. 9
Did life with *usury* to him restore, ... II. xi. 45. 4
repayed duely weare, And *usury* withall: . . . . IV. ix. 30. 8
taking *usurie* of time fore-past, ... V. iii. 40. 3
To have supplyde the first, and paide the *usury*. . . . . . . VI. viii. 9. 9
Pay to her *usury* of long delight: . . . . *Epith.* 33
Uther. Ambrose and *Uther*, did ripe yeares attayne, ... II. x. 67. 2
Uther, which Pendragon hight, ... II. x. 68. 1
good king *Uther* now doth make Strong warre . . . . III. iii. 52. 5
Which *Uther* with those forrein Pagans held, ... III. iii. 55. 4
Uther's. Briton kings, From Brute to *Uthers* rayne; . . . . . . II. x. Arg.
Utmost. Others the *utmost* boughs of trees doe crop, ... *Gn.* 81
the *utmost* top Of some soft Willow, ... *Gn.* 83
'There next the *utmost* brinck doth he abide, ... *Gn.* 385
from their first untill their *utmost* date, ... *Ti.* 45
Whose *utmost* hardnesse I before had tryde, ... *Col.* 673
thrilling sorrow throwne his *utmost* dart: . . . . I. vii. 25. 2
In these sad wordes she spent her *utmost* breath: . . . . . . II. i. 49. 4
ere they did their *utmost* obsequy, ... II. i. 60. 7
groneth out his *utmost* grudging spright . . . . II. v. 36. 7
by whose *utmost* brim Wayting to passe, ... II. vi. 2. 4
without the *utmost* bound Of this great gardin, ... II. vii. 56. 4
Assembling all his force and *utmost* might, ... II. viii. 47. 3
spred his empire to the *utmost* shore, ... II. x. 10. 2
Corineus had that Province *utmost* west . . . . II. x. 12. 2
feeble age Nigh to his *utmost* date . . . . II. x. 27. 7
Till they outraigned had their *utmost* date, ... II. x. 45. 2
th' *utmost* meanes of victory assay, ... II. xi. 41. 4
th' *utmost* yssew of his owne decay. . . . . II. xi. 41. 5
within the *utmost* bound Of his wide Labyrinth, ... II. xii. 20. 8
th' *utmost* sandy breach they shortly fetch, ... II. xii. 21. 3
Shall to the *utmost* mountaines fly apace. . . . . III. iii. 34. 4

Utmost—*Continued.*
Who dyes, the *utmost* dolor doth abye; . . . . III. iv. 38. 5
Into the *utmost* Angle of the world he knew. . . . . III. ix. 47. 9
resolv'd to prove her *utmost* might, ... III. xi. 25. 1
the Championesse now entred has The *utmost* rowme, ... III. xi. 27. 8
The *utmost* rowme abounding with all precious store: . . . . III. xi. 27. 9
Her love, her service, and her *utmost* wealth: . . . . IV. i. 6. 4
know the measure of their *utmost* date . . . . IV. ii. 50. 4
To draw their dayes unto the *utmost* date, ... IV. iii. 1. 2
his *utmost* prowesse there made knowen; . . . . IV. iv. 38. 2
Thinking to worke on her his *utmost* wracke, ... IV. vi. 21. 2
I me resolv'd the *utmost* end to prove; . . . . IV. vii. 16. 7
She staid not th' *utmost* end thereof to try, ... IV. vii. 21. 2
For dread of her displeasures *utmost* proofe: . . . . IV. vii. 37. 5
That battells *utmost* triall to adventer. . . . . V. v. 5. 5
the *utmost* date assynde For his returne . . . . V. vi. 3. 6
to make proofe of *utmost* shame, ... V. viii. 22. 6
From th' *utmost* brinke of the Americke shore . . . . V. x. 3. 6
Thinking the *utmost* of their force to trie, ... VI. i. 38. 3
But th' *utmost* end perforce for to aby, ... VI. iii. 44. 3
left that couple nere their *utmost* cast: . . . . VI. iv. 9. 5
Ere long enforst to breath his *utmost* blast, ... VI. iv. 22. 7
A full good pecke within the *utmost* brim, ... VI. xii. 26. 6
Let them feele the *utmost* of your crueltyes; . . . . *Am.* xlix. 9
Whose *utmost* parts so beautifull I fynd; . . . . *H.H.B.* 108
Utter. *utter* his tender head? . . . . *S.C.* Mar. 15
The inner garment frett, not th' *utter* touch: . . . . II. ii. 34. 8
unto her to *utter* his desire; . . . . III. vii. 16. 4
to the Bridges *utter* gate I came; . . . . IV. x. 11. 2
To worke his *utter* shame, and throughly him confound. . . . VI. v. 14. 9
To *utter* forth the anguish of his hart: . . . . *Am.* xlviii. 10
Utterance. with *utt'rance* grave, and count'nance sad, ... I. xii. 15. 7
Utterers. *Utterers* of secrets he from thence debard, ... II. ix. 25. 5
Uttering. wanted grace in *utt'ring* of the same, ... II. vi. 6. 8
Utterly. of their tailes are *utterlie* bereft. . . . . *Hub.* 1384
name of learning *utterly* doo scorne. . . . . *T.M.* 438
all his power was *utterly* defaste, ... II. iv. 14. 3
Till vengeaunce *utterly* the guilt bereave: . . . . II. viii. 29. 5
th' ydle breath all *utterly* exprest. . . . . II. xi. 42. 4
thy sad people, *utterly* fordonne, ... III. iii. 34. 3
vanisht *utterly* and cleane subverst . . . . III. xii. 42. 3
now it is so *utterly* decayd, ... IV. viii. 33. 1
Had *utterly* subverted his unrighteous state. . . . . V. ix. 2. 9
All other loves, . . . Thou must renounce and *utterly* displace, . *H.H.L.* 264

V

Vacant. The vaunted verse a *vacant* head demaundes, ... *S.C.* O. 100
Vade. Her power, disperst through all the world did *vade*; . . *Ro.* xx. 13
they into dust shall *vade*. . . . . V. ii. 40. 5
Vaded. Their vapour *vaded*, shewe their golden gleames, . . . III. ix. 20. 8
Vail. *Ms.* Yet would he further none but for a *vaile*. . . . . . *Hub.* 1204
Vailed. whenas *vailed* was her lofty crest, ... III. ix. 20. 3
Vain. *See* **Vein.**
trustles state Of *vaine* worlds glorie, ... *Pet.*[2] vii. 2
The ploughmans hope and shepheards labour *vaine*: . . . . . . *Ro.* xiv. 4
with *vaine* foolhardise Daring the foe . . . . *Ro.* xiv. 7
Now on these ashie tombes shew boldnesse *vaine*, ... *Ro.* xiv. 13
In *vaine* he threats his teeth, ... *Van.* x. 11
Why do *vaine* men mean things so much deface, ... *Van.* xi. 12
Ah, foolish Hobbinol! thy gyfts bene *vayne*; . . . . *S.C.* Ja. 59
The soveraigne of seas he blames in *vaine*, ... *S.C.* F. 33
Puffed up with pryde and *vaine* pleasaunce; . . . . *S.C.* F. 223
With *vayne* desire and hope to be enricht; . . . . *S.C.* S. 75
Sike words . . . wasten soone in *vayne*. . . . . *S.C.* O. 36
The praise of pitie vanisht is in *vaine*, ... *Gn.* 358
Calling in *vaine* for rest, and can have none. . . . . *Gn.* 392
let the flitting aire my *vaine* words sever.' . . . . *Gn.* 638
Ne medled with their controversies *vaine*; . . . . *Hub.* 391
whilst that other like *vaine* wits he pleased, ... *Hub.* 709
A *vaine* ensample of the Persian pride; . . . . *Hub.* 750
their *vaine* humours fed With fruitles follies . . . . *Hub.* 822
will to Court for shadowes *vaine* to seeke, ... *Hub.* 912
with *vaine* toyes the vulgare entertaine; . . . . *T.M.* 194
tell their Prince that learning is but *vaine*: . . . . *T.M.* 332
Without *vaine* art or curious complements; . . . . *T.M.* 542
'O *vaine* worlds glorie! . . . . *Ti.* 43
Hunt after honour and advauncement *vaine*, ... *Ti.* 51
'In *vaine* doo earthly Princes, then, in *vaine*, ... *Ti.* 407
All such *vaine* moniments of earthlie masse, ... *Ti.* 419
with such *vaine* illusion Hath so wise men bewitcht, ... *Ti.* 456
O *vaine* labours of terrestriall wit, ... *Ti.* 512
joy in pleasures *vaine*, ... *Ti.* 528
strugled long, . . . but all in *vaine*: . . . . *Mui.* 426
they be all but *vaine*, and quickly fade; . . . . *D.* 395
For all I see is *vaine* and transitorie, ... *D.* 495
verses *vaine*, (yet verses are not *vaine*,) . . . . *As.* 68
vaine it is to thinke, by paragone . . . . *Col.* 344
Vaine votaries of laesie Love professe, ... *Col.* 766
as a complement for courting *vaine*. . . . . *Col.* 790
with evil deed or leasing *vaine* Blaspheme . . . . *Col.* 821
Perhaps not *vaine* they may appeare to you. . . . . *Ded. Son.* ix. 12
In *vain* I thinke . . . to memorize thy name, ... *Ded. Son.* xii. 1
Against vile Zoilus backbitings *vaine*. *Ded.Son.*xii.14
hand or foot to stirr he strove in *vaine*. . . . . I. i. 18. 8
waste wordes retournd to him in *vaine*: . . . . I. i. 42. 2
Ne let *vaine* feares procure your needlesse smart, ... I. i. 54. 4
when he saw his labour all was *vaine*, ... I. i. 55. 8
when he saw his threatning was but *vaine*, ... I. ii. 2. 8

Vain—*Continued.*
Them both together laid to joy in *vaine* delight. . . . . . . I. ii. 3. 9
she rode, with so much speede . . . but all in *vaine*, ... I. ii. 8. 2
The false Duessa, . . . Heard how in *vaine* Fradubio did lament, I. ii. 44. 2
Proud of such glory and advancement *vayne*, ... I. iv. 9. 5
the stout Faery . . . Thought all their glorie *vaine* . . . . I. iv. 15. 7
a burning hart he bare, Full of *vaine* follies . . . . I. iv. 25. 4
Him selfe estraunging from their joyaunce *vaine*, ... I. iv. 37. 8
'Ah Dame,' (quoth he) 'thou temptest me in *vaine*, ... I. v. 42. 1
Proud wemen, *vaine*, forgetfull of their yoke: . . . . I. v. 50. 2
cryes, The last *vaine* helpe of wemens great distresse, . . . I. vi. 6. 3
To teach them truth, which worshipt her in *vaine*, ... I. vi. 19. 6
Then serve his Ladies love, and waste in pleasures *vayne*. . I. vi. 21. 9
with love revokt from *vaine* affright, ... I. vi. 28. 3
In *vaine* he seekes that having cannot hold. . . . . I. vi. 33. 7
Th' enchaunter *vaine* his errour should not rew: . . . . . . I. vi. 42. 8
all in *vaine* Did to him pace . . . . I. vii. 11. 4
presently was void and wholly *vaine*: . . . . I. viii. 4. 7
all in *vaine*, for he has redd his end . . . . I. viii. 21. 4
all their forces spend Them selves in *vaine*: . . . . I. viii. 21. 6
In *vaine* to mocke, or mockt in *vaine* to bee: . . . . I. viii. 33. 6
'But all in *vaine*: . . . . I. ix. 11. 1
Nyne monethes I seek in *vain*, ... I. ix. 15. 9
Ne let *vaine* words bewitch thy manly hart, ... I. ix. 53. 2
boasts of . . . *vaine* assuraunce of mortality, ... I. x. 1. 2
As for loose loves, they 'are *vaine*, ... I. x. 62. 9
th' ydle stroke yet backe recoyld in *vaine*, ... I. xi. 17. 3
His wearie pounces all in *vaine* doth spend . . . . I. xi. 19. 7
Which when in *vaine* he tryde with struggeling, ... I. xi. 39. 5
thrise in *vaine* to draw it did assay; . . . . I. xi. 41. 8
off-shaking *vaine* affright She nigher drew, ... I. xi. 55. 6
So diversly them selves in *vaine* they fray; . . . . I. xii. 11. 7
In which was nothing riotous nor *vaine*? . . . . I. xii. 14. 2
vowes may not be *vayne*) . . . . I. xii. 19. 6
suborned hath This crafty messenger with letters *vaine*, . . . I. xii. 34. 2
Which when he long awaited had in *vayne*, ... II. i. 5. 3
Witnes, ye heavens, whom she in *vaine* to help did call. . . . II. i. 10. 9
But *vaine*; for ye shall dearely do him rew, ... II. i. 25. 5
Vaine is the vaunt, and victory unjust, ... II. ii. 29. 8
Vaine Braggadocchio, . . . is made the scorne Of knighthood . II. iii. Arg.
*A pleasing *vaine* of glory *vaine* did find . . . . II. iii. 4. 5
In which *vaine* Braggadocchio was mewd, ... II. iii. 34. 3
Ne car'd he greatly for her presence *vayne*, ... II. iii. 43. 6
faine To menage steeds, . . . but in *vaine*. . . . . II. iv. 1. 9
His force was *vaine*, ... II. iv. 7. 4
threatning revenge in *vaine*: . . . . II. iv. 15. 4
Vaine others overthrowes who selfe doth overthrow. . . . . . II. v. 15. 9
Ne would with *vaine* occasions be inflam'd; . . . . II. v. 21. 7
Ne let thy stout hart melt in pitty *vayne*: . . . . II. v. 24. 6
with *vaine* delightes, And ydle pleasures . . . . II. v. 27. 2
flowes in pleasures and *vaine* pleasing toyes, ... II. v. 28. 8
Calling thy help in *vaine* . . . . II. v. 36. 9

Vain—*Continued.*
To feede her foolish humour and *vaine* jolliment. . . . . . . II. vi. 3. 9
all her wordes she drownd with laughter *vaine*, ... II. vi. 6. 7
other whiles *vaine* toyes she would devize, ... II. vi. 7. 1
'*Vaine* man,' (saide she) . . . . . . II. vi. 9. 5
fild with pleasures *vayn*, ... II. vi. 14. 2
Seeking for daunger and adventures *vaine?* . . . . . . II. vi. 17. 5
of her joy And *vaine* delight . . . . . . II. vi. 37. 3
strove in *vaine*, the one him selfe to drowne, ... II. vi. 47. 2
Sith late with him I batteill *vaine* would boste; . . . . . . II. vi. 50. 6
'Mammon,' (said he) 'thy godheads vaunt is *vaine*, ... II. vii. 9. 6
With such *vaine* shewes thy worldlinges vyle abuse; . . . . . . II. vii. 39. 5
Sterne was his looke, and full of stomacke *vayne;* . . . . . . II. vii. 41. 3
crownes, and Diademes, and titles *vaine*, ... II. vii. 43. 8
The knight, him seeing labour so in *vaine*, ... II. vii. 59. 1
So lost his labour *vaine* and ydle industry. . . . . . . II. vii. 61. 9
afford Which he had brought for Braggadochio *vaine*. . . . . II. viii. 19. 4
In *vaine* . . . should I lend The same to thee, ... II. viii. 21. 7
signes of grudge and discontentment *vaine*. . . . . . . II. viii. 23. 5
Such life ye read, and vertue in *vaine* shew; . . . . . . II. ix. 3. 2
Through *vaine* illusion of their lust unclene, ... II. x. 8. 7
fell to *vaine* voluptuous disease: . . . . . . II. x. 17. 5
Vaine feastes, and ydle superfluity: . . . . . . II. xi. 12. 8
all his vowes make *vayne;* . . . . . . II. xi. 18. 8
labor lost, and travell *vayne*, ... II. xi. 44. 2
Doth rore at them in *vaine*, ... II. xii. 5. 9
all her *vaine* allurements did forsake; . . . . . . II. xii. 17. 4
Labour'd in *vaine* to have recur'd their prize, ... II. xii. 19. 7
her lover strove, but all in *vaine;* . . . . . . II. xii. 82. 1
but all in *vaine;* . . . . . . III. i. 37. 8
with *vaine* thoughts her falsed fancy vex: . . . . . . III. i. 47. 5
Which spent in *vaine*, at last she told her briefe, ... III. i. 53. 4
Her selfe awhile therein she vewd in *vaine:* . . . . . . III. ii. 22. 6
In *vaine* seekes wonders out of Magick spell.' . . . . . . III. iii. 17. 7
To doe away *vaine* doubt and needlesse dreed: . . . . . . III. iv. 48. 7
the sights of semblants *vaine*. . . . . . . III. iv. 54. 5
labour'd long in that deepe ford with *vaine* disease. . . . . . III. v. 19. 9
in scorne Of her *vaine* playnt, ... III. vi. 21. 2
So fledd fayre Florimell from her *vaine* feare, ... III. vii. 1. 6
in *vaine* was forst to turne his flight, ... III. vii. 28. 5
in *vain* sheows, that wont yong knights bewitch, ... III. vii. 29. 6
all my dayes am like to waste in *vaine*, ... III. vii. 60. 8
Enough to hold a foole in *vaine* delight. . . . . . . III. viii. 10. 7
in vaunting *vaine* His glory did repose, ... III. viii. 11. 8
such *vaine* uses that him best became: . . . . . . III. viii. 14. 5
withstand All that she might, and him in *vaine* revild: . . . III. viii. 27. 2
A long discourse of his adventures *vayne*, ... III. viii. 44. 2
'In *vaine* he feares that which he cannot shonne; . . . . . . III. ix. 7. 1
all in *vaine*, for nought mote him relent. . . . . . . III. ix. 11. 1
lov'd so oft in *vaine*, ... III. ix. 29. 8
Bransles, Ballads, virelayes, and verses *vaine;* . . . . . . III. x. 8. 5
all in *vaine:* his woman was too wise . . . . . . III. x. 20. 1
with *vaine* hope his spirits faint supply, ... III. x. 26. 7
all that els the *vaine* world vaunten may, ... III. x. 31. 5
all the world is lost, and we in *vaine* have toyld.' . . . . . . III. x. 39. 9
He wooed her . . . But all in *vaine;* . . . . . . III. x. 52. 2
through privy griefe and horrour *vaine*, ... III. x. 60. 7
sow *vaine* sorrow in a fruitlesse eare, ... III. xi. 16. 2
daunger *vaine* it were to have assayd That cruell element, . . III. xi. 22. 3
Vaine was the watch, and bootlesse all the ward, ... III. xi. 31. 8
as those same plumes so seemd he *vaine* and light, ... III. xii. 8. 5
His garment was disguysed very *vayne*, ... III. xii. 9. 5
It *vaine* she thought with rigorous uprore For to efforce, . . III. xii. 27. 8
wisht like happinesse: In *vain* she wisht, ... III. xii. 46. *or.* 9
with *vaine* poemes weeds to have their fancies fed. . . . . . IV. Pr. 1. 9
'the fruitlesse end Of thy *vaine* boast, ... IV. i. 51. 2
Of the bad issue of his counsell *vaine*, ... IV. ii. 6. 2
With which *vaine* termes so much they did them move, ... IV. ii. 19. 8
in *vaine* yet many strive: . . . . . . IV. ii. 34. 5
strove in *vaine* him long to have withstood, ... IV. ii. 45. 7
Most wretched men, whose dayes depend on thrids so *vaine!* . IV. ii. 48. 9
Therefore this Fay I hold but fond and *vaine*, ... IV. iii. 2. 1
maketh him his wing in *vaine* to spend; . . . . . . IV. iii. 19. 7
weapon *vaine* to weld, ... IV. iii. 21. 3
life and labour both in *vaine* to spend. . . . . . . IV. iii. 32. 5
At which his *vaine* excuse they all gan smile, ... IV. iv. 11. 1
For glorie *vaine*, their fellowship to lose, ... IV. iv. 14. 5
all men threw out vowes and wishes *vaine*. . . . . . . IV. iv. 16. 6
But all in *vaine:* for what might one do more? . . . . . . IV. iv. 32. 8
In *vaine* he sought, for there he found it not; . . . . . . IV. iv. 33. 4
That many wish to win for glorie *vaine*, ... IV. v. 2. 6
with boastfull *vaine* pretense, Stept Braggadochio . . . . . . IV. v. 23. 5
enquired The cause and end thereof, but all in *vaine;* . . . . . . IV. v. 38. 4
every place seem'd painefull, and ech changing *vaine*. . . . . IV. v. 40. 9
thence forth glaunst Adowne in *vaine*, ... IV. vi. 19. 4
when in *vaine* to fight she oft assayd, ... IV. vi. 27. 6
Feared in *vaine*, sith meanes, ye see, there wants theretoo. . IV. vi. 30. 9
Vaine is the art that seekes it selfe for to deceive. . . . . . IV. vi. 40. 9
seekes to know anothers griefe in *vaine*, ... IV. vii. 10. 7
when long he follow'd had in *vaine*, ... IV. vii. 38. 1
saw that all he said and did was *vaine*, ... IV. vii. 47. 2
long he looked had in *vaine*, ... IV. viii. 8. 1
eke that age despysed nicenesse *vaine*, ... IV. viii. 27. 5
With curses *vaine* in his avengefull ire; . . . . . . IV. viii. 40. 3
To see his foe breath out his spright in *vaine:* . . . . . . IV. viii. 46. 2
she given is to *vaine* delight, ... IV. viii. 49. 8
all in *vaine:* her plaints might not prevaile, ... IV. ix. 7. 8
this shield, of many sought in *vaine*, ... IV. x. 8. 3
seeking often entraunce afterwards in *vaine*. . . . . . . IV. x. 13. 9
vaine, I see, my sorrowes to unfold, ... IV. xii. 6. 1

Vain—*Continued.*
O *vaine* judgement, and conditions *vaine*, ... IV. xii. 11. 1
long given him in *vaine:* . . . . . . IV. xii. 14. 6
But all in *vaine*, ... IV. xii. 15. 3
romed round about the rocke in *vaine*, ... IV. xii. 17. 2
To Proteus selfe to sew she thought it *vaine*, ... IV. xii. 29. 1
'To hope' (quoth he) 'him soone to overtake . . . is but *vaine;* V. i. 19. 4
In *vaine* loud crying, ... V. ii. 27. 2
cluster thicke unto his leasings *vaine*, ... V. ii. 33. 2
In *vaine* therefore doest thou now take in hand . . . . . . V. ii. 42. 5
vaine it was to thinke from him to flie; . . . . . . V. iii. 38. 2
vaine it is to deeme of things aright, ... V. iv. 1. 6
Of their *vaine* prowesse turned to their proper bale. . . . . . V. iv. 24. 9
to swell With indignation at her vaunting *vaine*, ... V. v. 10. 6
Doth beat upon the gentle bird in *vaine*, ... V. v. 15. 6
when long she struggled had in *vaine*, ... V. v. 28. 6
Scorning her offers and conditions *vaine;* . . . . . . V. v. 46. 2
Many *vaine* fancies working her unrest; . . . . . . V. vi. 7. 7
Forcing in *vaine* the rest to her to tell; . . . . . . V. vi. 11. 8
Her selfe there close afflicted long in *vaine*, ... V. vi. 15. 2
She saw it *vaine* to make there lenger stay, ... V. vi. 36. 1
her late vile reproch though vaunted *vaine*, ... V. vii. 34. 4
Which *vaine* conceipt now nourishing no more, ... V. vii. 38. 8
In *vaine* the Pagan bannes, and sweares, and rayles, ... V. viii. 39. 4
Crying to them in *vaine* that nould his crying heare. . . . . V. viii. 41. 9
Crying in *vaine* for helpe, when helpe was past: . . . . . . V. ix. 19. 6
both with hope of shadowes *vaine* inspyred) . . . . . . V. ix. 41. 5
Stryving long time in *vaine* it to withstond; . . . . . . V. x. 27. 3
It would no passage yeeld unto his purpose *vaine*. . . . . . V. xi. 10. 9
of his owne *vaine* fancies thought did frame: . . . . . . V. xi. 19. 4
who long in *vaine* their rage withstands. . . . . . . V. xi. 44. 9
But all in *vaine:* . . . . . . V. xi. 45. 6
Gainst whom my selfe I long in *vaine* have bent . . . . . . V. xi. 51. 3
In *vaine* he seeketh others to suppresse, ... VI. i. 41. 5
Would thumpe her forward . . . Weeping to him in *vaine* . VI. ii. 10. 9
a slender dart, . . . throwne not in *vaine*, ... VI. ii. 12. 7
In *vaine* complayning to be so abused; . . . . . . VI. ii. 22. 7
*Crying aloud in *vaine*, to shew her sad misfare . . . . . . VI. iii. 24. 5
prove thy manhood on the billowes *vayne*.' . . . . . . VI. iii. 32. 5
But all in *vaine;* for-why no remedy He saw . . . . . . VI. iii. 44. 1
having long eschew'd His violence in *vaine;* . . . . . . VI. iii. 50. 6
every way did try, but all in *vaine;* . . . . . . VI. iv. 7. 2
when the Salvage saw his labour *vaine* . . . . . . VI. iv. 9. 1
Stryving in *vaine* that nigh his bowels brast, ... VI. iv. 22. 2
Gnashing his cruell teeth at him in *vaine*, ... VI. iv. 22. 8
For which he long in *vaine* did sweate and swinke, ... VI. iv. 32. 4
they did employ . . . several deceipts, but all in *vaine;* . . VI. v. 14. 2
In *vaine* of me ye hope for remedie, ... VI. vi. 6. 8
in *vaine* doe salves to you applie: . . . . . . VI. vi. 6. 9
'In *vaine* therefore it were with medicine To goe about . . VI. vi. 13. 1
Crying in *vaine* to her him to bemone; . . . . . . VI. vi. 30. 5
spent my youth in *vaine*, ... VI. ix. 25. 4
Be but *vaine* shadowes to this safe retyre Of life, ... VI. ix. 27. 5
'In *vaine*' . . . The heavens of their fortunes fault accuse, . VI. ix. 29. 1
many gealous thoughts conceiv'd in *vaine*, ... VI. ix. 38. 4
hunt still after shadowes *vaine* Of courtly favour, ... VI. x. 2. 7
The woods did nought but ecchoes *vaine* rebound; . . . . . . VI. xi. 26. 6
bet abacke, threatning in *vaine* to bite, ... VI. xii. 29. 4
Striving in *vaine* to rere him selfe upright: . . . . . . VI. xii. 31. 4
After that he had labourd long in *vaine* . . . . . . VI. xii. 32. 3
Through some *vaine* errour, or inducement light, ... VII. vi. 32. 2
by proffers *vaine* Of idle hopes . . . . . . VII. vi. 34. 7
love of things so *vaine* to cast away; . . . . . . VII. viii. 1. 7
What needeth you to seeke so farre in *vaine?* . . . . . . *Am.* xv. 4
I weepe, and wayle, and pleade in *vaine*, ... *Am.* xviii. 13
In *vaine* I seeke and sew to her for grace, ... *Am.* xx. 1
lyke Narcissus *vaine*, Whose eyes him starv'd: . . . . . . *Am.* xxxv. 7
All this worlds glory seemeth *vayne* to me, ... *Am.* xxxv. 13
wishing were but *vaine*) . . . . . . *Am.* xlii. 5
Vayne man, quod I, that hast but little priefe . . . . . . *Am.* l. 5
no thought of joy, or pleasure *vaine*, ... *Am.* liii. 9
Like a *vaine* bubble . . . . . . *Am.* lviii. 6
The doubt which ye misdeeme . . . is *vaine*, ... *Am.* lxv. 1
after long pursuit and *vaine* assay, ... *Am.* lxvii. 5
Vayne man . . . that doest in *vaine* assay . . . . . . *Am.* lxxv. 5
I fynd my selfe but fed with fancies *vayne*. . . . . . . *Am.* lxxviii. 12
When others gaze upon theyr shadowes *vayne*, ... *Am.* lxxxvii. 6
not by painted shewes, and titles *vaine*, ... *Com. Son.* ii. 3
Wherefore doth *vaine* antiquitie so vaunt Her ancient monu-ments . . . . . . *Com. Son.* iii. 1
In sight whereof all other blisse seemes *vaine:* . . . . . . *H.L.* 208
Sights never seene, and thousand shadowes *vaine*, ... *H.L.* 255
The *vaine* surmizes, the distrustfull showes, ... *H.L.* 260
ye that wont with greedy *vaine* desire . . . . . . *H.H.L.* 15
The hearts of men, which . . . feed on *vaine* delight, ... *H.H.B.* 17
Hast after *vaine* deceiptfull shadowes sought, ... *H.H.B.* 291
expectation *vayne* Of idle hopes, ... *Proth.* 7

Vainglorious. in *vaine glorious* frayes he litle did delight. . I. vi. 20. 9
Vaine-glorious man . . . is lifted up to skye . . . . . . II. iii. 10. 3
'*Vaine glorious* Elfe,' (saide he) . . . . . . II. vii. 11. 1
Leasinges, backbytinges, and *vain-glorious* crakes, ... II. xi. 10. 7
Blandamour full of *vainglorious* spright, ... IV. iv. 3. 6

Vainly. So *vainely* tadvaunce thy headlesse hood; . . . . . . *S.C.* F. 86
So *vainly* shalt thou too and fro be tost, ... *Hub.* 635
vainly thinke your selves halfe happie . . . . . . *Ti.* 199
That *vainly* threatned kingdomes to displace, ... *Ded. Son.* vi. 8
Through *vainly* crossed shield he quite did perce; . . . . . . I. iii. 35. 3
made him *vainely* swincke; . . . . . . II. vii. 58. 7
vainely did expound To be hart-wownding love, ... III. iv. 28. 3
they avoyded were, and *vainely* by did slyde. . . . . . . IV. iii. 7. 9

Vainly—*Continued.*
shortly must repent that now so *vainely* bravest.' . . . V. vii. 32. 9
So all that day in wandring *vainely* he did spend. . . . VI. iv. 25. 9
How *vainely* then doe ydle wits invent, . . . *H.B.* 64
Vainness. O worlds *vainesse* (*vainenesse*[1]) ! . . . *Bel.* ii. 12
how great *vainnesse* is it then to scorne The weake, . . . *Van.* vi. 13
O *vainesse!* to be added to the rest, . . . *Ti.* 459
through meditation Of this worlds *vainnesse* . . . *D.* 34
There I beheld such *vainenesse* as I never thought. . . . VI. ix. 24. 9
Vale. *See* **Veil.**
the blacke Holme that loves the watrie *vale;* . . . *Gn.* 215
whilest I in this wretched *vale* doo stay . . . *D.* 456
gave that name unto that pleasant *vale;* . . . *Col.* 107
father Nilus gins to swell . . . above the Aegyptian *vale* . . . I. i. 21. 2
She wandred many a wood, and measurd many a *vale.* . . . I. vii. 28. 9
Phoebus gan decline . . . His weary wagon to the Westerne *vale,* . . . II. ix. 10. 2
Did seeme to overlooke the lowly *vale:* . . . VI. x. 8. 8
Valentide. As he is wont at each Saint *Valentide,* . . . VI. vii. 32. 7
Valiance. thine owne selfes *valiance,* . . . *Ti.* 324
To let him weet his doughtie *valiaunce,* . . . II. iii. 14. 5
Life will I graunt thee for thy *valiaunce,* . . . II. viii. 51. 8
'Whom gracious lott and thy great *valiaunce* . . . II. ix. 5. 2
He overthrew through his owne *valiaunce;* . . . II. x. 38. 6
proofe of thy prow *valiaunce* . . . III. iii. 28. 3
for glorie of great *valiaunce,* . . . III. iv. 3. 3
Valiant. *valiant* fortune made Dan Orpheus bolde; . . . *Gn.* 449
Ne any there doth brave or *valiant* seeme, . . . *Col.* 779
Which when the *valiant* Elfe perceiv'd, . . . I. i. 17. 1
valiant knight become a caytive thrall, . . . I. vii. 19. 3
three *valiaunt* knights to see Three combates joine in one, . . . II. ii. 26. 1
well that *valiaunt* courser did discerne; . . . II. iii. 46. 6
Shall backe repulse the *valiaunt* Brockwell twise, . . . III. iii. 35. 5
since he seemed *valiant,* though unknowne, . . . IV. i. 11. 5
There where he saw the *valiant* Triamond . . . IV. iv. 23. 6
well was knowen to be a *valiant* Knight, . . . IV. iv. 40. 4
therein wonned twenty *valiant* Knights, . . . IV. x. 7. 6
O men! which boast your strong And *valiant* hearts, . . . IV. xi. 22. 4
Sixe *valiant* Knights of one faire Nymphe yborne, . . . IV. xi. 37. 3
'if he so *valiaunt* be, . . . VI. iii. 40. 6
valiant Knights doe rashly enterprize . . . VI. vi. 35. 4
Mars, that *valiant* man, . . . VII. vii. 52. 1
Valley. His dwelling is low in a *valley* greene, . . . I. ix. 4. 5
As mountaine doth the *valley* overcaste. . . . I. xi. 8. 5
The *valley* did with coole shade overcast: . . . II. i. 24. 5
mightie woodes which did the *valley* shade . . . III. v. 39. 4
A litle *valley* subject to the same, . . . III. vii. 4. 8
every wood and every *valley* wyde . . . III. xii. 7. 8
Valleys. in the *valleies* wandring at their wills, . . . *Gn.* 76
darkesome caves in pleasaunt *vallies* pight, . . . *Gn.* 117
Out of the lowly *vallies* did arise, . . . *Gn.* 191
woods, and hills, and *valleyes* . . . *Col.* 482
Through all the fields and *vallies* did before him flie. . . . V. iv. 44. 9
Till to the Plaine she come, whose *Valleyes* she doth drowne. . VII. vi. 41. 9
Valor. not my *valour,* but his owne brave mind Subjected hath V. v. 32. 2
Yet full of *valour* the which did adorne . . . VI. iii. 7. 8
Valorous. unto things of *valorous* pretence Seemes to be borne . II. iv. 1. 4
'Ye warlike payre, whose *valorous* great might, . . . II. viii. 27. 2
gathering force and corage *valorous,* . . . II. x. 18. 3
dim'd his *valorous* And mightie deedes, . . . II. x. 43. 5
Fiercely advaunst his *valorous* right arme, . . . II. xi. 34. 7
Bards tell of many wemen *valorous,* . . . III. iii. 54. 4
he was nothing *valorous,* . . . V. vi. 32. 6
His whole exploite and *valorous* emprize, . . . VI. i. 5. 4
great deeds and *valarous* emprize. . . . *Am.* lxix. 4
Value. For prize of *value,* or for learned lore: . . . *T.M.* 466
him with equall *valew* countervayld: . . . II. vi. 29. 4
Stone more of *valew,* and more smooth and fine, . . . II. ix. 24. 2
stone Of passing *valew* and of great renowme, . . . III. xi. 47. 3
Value's. vertues might and *values* confidence: . . . III. xi. 14. 7
Vancing. *vauncing* forth from all the other band Of knights, . IV. iv. 17. 3
Vanish. Doth as a vapour *vanish,* and decaie. . . . *Ti.* 56
being prickt do *vanish* into noughts. . . . *Col.* 718
they 'are vaine, and *vanish* into nought.' . . . I. x. 62. 9
Ne into ayre did *vanish* presently, . . . IV. iii. 13. 4
Natur's selfe did *vanish,* whither no man wist. . . . VII. vii. 59. 9
Vanished. This dreadfull shape was *vanished* to nought. . . *Bel.*[2] viii. 14
The praise of pitie *vanisht* is in vaine, . . . *Gn.* 358
vanisht quite, so soone as it was sought: . . . *Ti.* 221
With dolefull shrikes shee *vanished* away, . . . *Ti.* 471
he no where doth appeare, But *vanisht* is. . . . I. v. 13. 8
That huge great body, . . . Was *vanisht* quite; . . . I. viii. 24. 8
That *vanisht* into smoke and cloudes swift; . . . I. xi. 54. 2
Was suddein *vanished* out of his sight: . . . II. iii. 19. 2
vanisht quite away. . . . II. viii. 8. 9
soone as he was *vanisht* out of sight, . . . III. v. 15. 1
they streight were *vanisht* all and some; . . . III. xii. 30. 4
vanisht utterly and cleane subverst She found, . . . III. xii. 42. 3
flame, . . . Was *vanisht* quite, as it were not the same, . . . III. xii. 43. 5
Th' enchaunted Damzell *vanisht* into nought: . . . V. iii. 24. 6
They *vanisht* all away out of his sight, . . . VI. x. 18. 2
Vanisheth. The glorious picture *vanisheth* away, . . . V. iii. 25. 6
Vanity. all is nought but flying *vanitee* (*vanitie*[1]) ! . . . *Bel.* i. 11
he himselfe through foolish *vanitie,* . . . *Van.* viii. 5
Imagery Of Baetus or of Alcons *vanity.* . . . *Gn.* 104
all that vaunts in worldly *vanitie* . . . *Gn.* 559
Through pompous pride, and foolish *vanitie:* . . . *T.M.* 92
all is *vanitie* and griefe of minde, . . . *Ti.* 583
Even such is all their vaunted *vanitie,* . . . *Col.* 719
A gentle Husher, *Vanitie* by name, Made rowme, . . . I. iv. 13. 3

Vanity—*Continued.*
Mine eyes no more on *vanitie* shall feed, . . . I. vii. 23. 8
The plumes of pride, and winges of *vanity,* . . . I. x. 39. 3
Was lightnesse seene or looser *vanitie,* . . . II. ii. 15. 4
puffed up with smoke of *vanity,* . . . II. iii. 5. 3
blow the bellowes to his swelling *vanity.* . . . II. iii. 9. 9
though he scornd his ydle *vanitee,* . . . II. iv. 39. 7
from that *vanity* With temperate advice discounselled, . . . II. xii. 34. 1
For want whereof he weighed *vanity,* . . . V. ii. 30. 7
Vanquish. wont to *vanquish* God and man, . . . IV. viii. 32. 6
To *vanquish* all the world with matchlesse might; . . . IV. xi. 16. 6
if I *vanquishe* him, he shall obay My law, . . . V. iv. 49. 2
so will I, if me he *vanquish* may, . . . V. iv. 49. 4
Calidore . . . Doth *vanquish* Crudor; . . . VI. i. Arg.
Vanquished. An hundred *vanquisht* Kings . . . *Bel.* xv. 9
Having the blood of *vanquisht* Hector shedd, . . . *Gn.* 527
Arachne, by his means was *vanquished* . . . *Mui.* 261
In every one he *vanquisht* every one, . . . *As.* 77
He *vanquisht* all, and *vanquisht* was of none. . . . *As.* 78
Who see your *vanquisht* foes before you lye, . . . I. i. 27. 4
thy foe doth *vanquisht* stand Now at thy mercy: . . . I. iii. 37. 4
But *vanquisht* thine eternall bondslave make, . . . I. viii. 14. 8
loves . . . Bought with the blood of *vanquisht* Paynim bold; . I. vii. 26. 4
vanquisht them, unable to withstand: . . . I. x. 65. 5
him *vanquisht* she to fly constraind: . . . II. x. 18. 5
left inglorious on the *vanquisht* playne, . . . II. x. 58. 2
in batteill *vanquished* Those spoylefull Picts, . . . II. x. 63. 1
yet the *vanquished* had no despight. . . . III. i. 13. 7
Then he halfe *vanquisht,* then the other seemed, . . . IV. iii. 28. 4
'Ne was he ever *vanquished* afore, . . . IV. viii. 48. 1
ever *vanquisht* all with whom he fought; . . . IV. viii. 48. 2
is he *vanquisht* by his tyrant enemy?' . . . V. vi. 10. 9
taking with him, as his *vanquisht* thrall, . . . V. viii. 26. 3
vanquished all ventrous knights in fight; . . . V. x. 30. 4
Were *vanquished,* and put to foule disgrace; . . . VI. vii. 21. 5
Yielded them by the *vanquisht* as theyr meeds, . . . *Am.* xxix. 6
Vanquishing. Cruell death *vanquishing* so noble beautie, . . *Pet.* i. 13
Vantage. needlesse feare did never *vantage* none; . . . I. iv. 49. 4
To ketch him at a *vauntage* in his snares. . . . II. i. 4. 5
making *vantage* of their civile jarre, . . . II. x. 65. 4
vauntage made of that which Merlin had ared; . . . III. iii. 20. 9
'Me, seely wretch, she so at *vauntage* caught, . . . III. vii. 51. 1
Which *vauntage* Cambell did pursue so fast, . . . IV. iv. 30. 5
Vapor. Doth as a *vapour* vanish, and decaie. . . . *Ti.* 56
fog over-spred With his dull *vapour* all that desert . . . II. xii. 34. 6
doth disperse the *vapour* lo'ste, . . . III. iv. 13. 5
A litle smoke, whose *vapour* thin and light . . . III. vii. 5. 2
Their *vapour* vaded, shewe their golden gleames, . . . III. ix. 20. 8
gan the humid *vapour* shed the grownd With perly deaw, . . III. x. 46. 5
Vapored. all his greatnes *vapoured* to nought, . . . *Ti.* 219
Vapors. earthly *vapours* gathered in the ayre, . . . *Ro.* xx. 2
In deawy *vapours* of the westerne mayne, . . . III. viii. 51. 4
Variable. Tossed with stormes of fortune *variable!* . . . *Pet.*[2] vi. 14
Ne stroke on stroke of fortune *variable,* . . . *Ro.* xiii. 5
shewes his powre in *variable* kindes: . . . III. v. 1. 3
formes are *variable,* and decay . . . III. vi. 38. 6
Was paynted all with *variable* flowers, . . . *Proth.* 13
Variance. Now one, which earst were many made through *variaunce.* . . . II. x. 38. 9
at *variaunce* fell With those two Carles, . . . VI. viii. 31. 3
Variety. flowres *varietie* With sundrie colours . . . *Gn.* 109
with most *varietie* And change of sweetnesse, . . . *Mui.* 177
This Gardin to adorne with all *variety.* . . . II. xii. 59. 9
sprinckled with such sweet *variety* . . . VI. Pr. 1. 4
Varlet. A *varlet* ronning towardes hastily, . . . II. iv. 37. 2
'*Varlet,* this place most dew to me I deeme, . . . II. iv. 40. 1
That when the *varlett* heard and saw, . . . II. iv. 45. 1
rash Pyrochles *varlett,* Atin hight, . . . II. v. 25. 4
Whylest there the *varlet* stood, . . . II. vi. 41. 1
The *varlett* saw, when to the flood he came, . . . II. vi. 42. 1
The *varlet* at his plaint was grieved so sore, . . . II. vi. 45. 6
Varlet's. After that *varlets* flight, . . . II. v. 2. 1
Vary. Sith so small thing his happines may *varie.* . . . *Van.* viii. 14
shall we *varie* our device at will, . . . *Hub.* 118
Thus did the battell *varie* to and fro, . . . IV. iii. 28. 1
Still change and *vary* thoughts, as new occasions fall. . . . VII. vii. 19. 9
flitting still doe flie, and still their places *vary.* . . . VII. vii. 21. 9
Vassal. Which I your poore *Vassall* dayly endure; . . . *S.C.* F. 153
be the *vassall* of his vassalesse; . . . *D.* 181
Vassall to one, whom all my dayes I serve; . . . *Col.* 467
made the *vassall* of his pleasures vilde. . . . I. vi. 3. 5
vassall of dread and despayre, . . . II. iii. 7. 4
be the *vassall* of her pleasures vile, . . . III. vii. 50. 8
will be made The *vassall* of the victors will bylive: . . . III. x. 10. 7
I your *vassall,* by your prowesse freed, . . . III. xii. 39. 7
vassall to the vilest wretch alive, . . . IV. vii. 12. 2
made the *vassall* of the victors might; . . . IV. viii. 32. 7
Left in the victors powre, like *vassall* bond, . . . IV. ix. 18. 7
as her *vassall* him to thraldome tooke: . . . V. v. 18. 3
his faith had plight Her *vassall* to become, . . . V. v. 23. 9
To serve the lowly *vassall* of her might, . . . V. v. 27. 7
So hast thou often done . . . To me thy *vassall,* . . . *H.L.* 142
Vassalage. I now doe live, bound yours by *vassalage;* . . . *Ded. Son.* vii. 5
shortly he renounst the *vassallage* Of Rome againe, . . . II. x. 52. 5
From their long *vassalage* gin to respire, . . . III. iii. 36. 8
All little Rivers which owe *vassallage* To him, . . . IV. xi. 29. 3
Vassaless. be the vassall of his *vassalesse;* . . . *D.* 181
Vassals. Through armes and *vassals* Rome the world subdu'd, . *Ro.* viii. 1
such vile *vassals,* borne to base vocation, . . . *Hub.* 156
all wylde beasts made *vassals* of his pleasures, . . . *Hub.* 1129

Vassals—*Continued.*
The *vassals* of Gods wrath, and slaves of sin. . . . *T.M.* 126
made all nations *vassals* of her pride, . . . *Ti.* 72
Warre against us, the *vassals* of their will. . . . *Mui.* 231
us fraile men, his wretched *vassals* here, . . . *Col.* 813
All being made the *vassalls* of his might, . . . *Col.* 885
He had subdew'd, and them his *vassals* made . . . III. iv. 21. 2
dy As thralls and *vassals* unto mens beheasts; . . . VII. vii. 19. 3
all this world, the which thy *vassals* beene, . . . *H.B.* 269
Vast. His body monstrous, horrible, and *vaste;* . . . I. xi. 8. 7
Vault. Out of deepe *vaute* threw forth a thousand rayes . . . *Bel.*[1] ii. 7
he could play, and daunce, and *vaute,* and spring, . . . *Hub.* 693
Whatso the heaven in his wide *vawte* containes, . . . *Hub.* 1229
From whose rough *vaut* the ragged breaches hong . . . II. vii. 28. 3
It was a *vaut* ybuilt for great dispence, . . . II. ix. 29. 1
Vaulted. In rolling globes up to the *vauted* skies. . . . *Col.* 611
vauted all within, like to the Skye, . . . III. iv. 43. 4
Vaults. deep digd *vawtes;* . . . *Gn.* 444
Vauncing. *See* **Vancing.**
Vaunt. with proud *vaunt* his head aloft doth holde; . . . *Gn.* 259
doest *vaunt* That good knight of the Redcrosse to have slain: . I. vi. 41. 3
prouder *vaunt* that prowd avenging boy Did soone pluck downe, I. ix. 12. 3
she is hevenly borne, and heaven may justly *vaunt.* . . . I. x. 59. 9
Champion . . . Whom famous Poetes verse so much doth *vaunt,* I. xi. 27. 2
land of Faery, Which I so much doe *vaunt,* . . . II. Pr. 1. 8
Vaine is the *vaunt,* and victory unjust, . . . II. ii. 29. 8
Th' enchaunter greatly joyed in the *vaunt,* . . . II. iii. 13. 1
He gan himselfe to *vaunt:* . . . II. iii. 37. 2
For thou to serve Acrasia thy selfe doest *vaunt.* . . . II. vi. 9. 9
'Mammon,' (said he) 'thy godheads *vaunt* is vaine, . . . II. vii. 9. 6
shamefull *vaunt* Of vile revenge. . . . II. viii. 16. 3
what so else his person most may *vaunt?*' . . . III. ii. 16. 7
all that els the vaine world *vaunten* may, . . . III. x. 31. 5
with how great *vaunt* of braverie He them abused . . . V. iii. 39. 7
he dare not returne for all his daily *vaunt.* . . . VI. iv. 29. 9
all that Venus in her selfe doth *vaunt* . . . VI. x. 15. 5
Wherefore doth vaine antiquitie so *vaunt* Her ancient monuments . . . *Com. Son.* iii. 1
Vaunted. The *vaunted* verse a vacant head demaundes, . . . *S.C.* O. 100
Even such is all their *vaunted* vanitie, . . . *Col.* 719
vaunted speare eftsoones to disadvaunce, . . . IV. iv. 7. 2
her late vile reproch though *vaunted* vaine, . . . V. vii. 34. 4
Vaunter. faine To menage steeds, as did this *vaunter,* . . . II. iv. 1. 9
Vauntest. Is this the battaile which thou *vauntst* to fight . . . I. ix. 52. 8
Vaunteth. her *vaunteth* most In skilfull knitting . . . *Mui.* 361
Vauntful. Yong Clarion, with *vauntfull* lustie-head, . . . *Mui.* 54
Vaunting. The same yet *vaunting* Greece will tell the storie . *Ro.* ii. 5
The *vaunting* Poets found nought worth a pease . . . *S.C.* O. 69
To serve at court in view of *vaunting* eye: . . . II. iii. 10. 2
in *vaunting* vaine His glory did repose, . . . III. viii. 11. 8
to swell With indignation at her *vaunting* vaine, . . . V. v. 10. 6
Vaunts. all that *vaunts* in worldly vanitie . . . *Gn.* 559
vertue *vauntes* in both her victories, . . . II. vi. 1. 8
with bold *vaunts* and ydle threatning, . . . V. xi. 3. 7
Vaute, -d. *See* **Vault, -ed.**
Veale. *See* **Veil.**
Veer. *Vere* the maine shete, and beare up with the land, . . . I. xii. 1. 3
Veereth. strikes his sayles, and *vereth* his mainsheat, . . . V. xii. 18. 8
Vehement. full of griefe and anguish *vehement,* . . . I. xi. 26. 1
Scourging and haling him more *vehement;* . . . VI. viii. 4. 8
Veil. Thrice having seene under the heavens *veale* . . . *Ro.* i. 9
his Moother with a *Veale* hath coovered his Face? . . . *Tetrasticon* 3
Yet through that darksome *vale* do glister bright; . . . *Col.* 495
Under a shady *vele* is therein writ, . . . *Ded. Son.* iii. 7
And the dim *vele* . . . aside be layd, . . . *Ded. Son.* ix. 10
Under a *vele,* that wimpled was full low; . . . I. i. 4. 4
He snatcht the *vele* that hong her face before: . . . I. vi. 4. 7
his shield, that covered was, Did loose his *vele* . . . I. viii. 19. 2
The which O! pardon me thus to enfold In covert *vele,* . . . II. Pr. 5. 2
their snowy limbes, as through a *vele,* . . . II. xii. 64. 6
All in a *vele* of silke and silver thin, . . . II. xii. 77. 4
under the blacke *vele* of guilty Night, . . . III. i. 59. 7
More hidden are then Sunne in cloudy *vele;* . . . III. iii. 19. 6
like a silken *veile* in compasse round . . . IV. i. 13. 4
His faire Cambina, covered with a *veale;* . . . IV. v. 10. 2
covered with a slender *veile* afore; . . . IV. x. 40. 7
'The cause why she was covered with a *vele* . . . IV. x. 41. 1
Covered from peoples gazement with a *vele:* . . . V. iii. 17. 3
At last from his victorious shield he drew The *vaile,* . . . V. viii. 37. 7
with a *veile,* that wimpled every where, . . . VII. vii. 5. 8
covered her uncomely face With a blacke *veile,* . . . VII. vii. 44. 5
Vein. Or pricke them forth with pleasaunce of thy *vaine,* . . . *S.C.* O. 23
honor Pan with hymnes of higher *vaine.* . . . *S.C.* N. 8
to well I wote my humble *vaine,* . . . *S.C.* N. 50
His witlesse pleasance, and ill pleasing *vaine.* . . . *Hub.* 799
Did tickle inwardly in everie *vaine;* . . . *Mui.* 394
suddein cold did ronne through every *vaine,* . . . I. vi. 37. 2
so faint in every joynt and *vayne,* . . . I. vii. 11. 7
With foltring tong, and trembling everie *vaine,* . . . I. vii. 24. 7
trembling feare did feel in every *vaine:* . . . I. viii. 4 .2
mealt'h Into the heart, and searcheth every *vaine;* . . . I. ix. 31. 6
through every *vaine* The crudled cold ran . . . I. ix. 52. 1
A pleasing *vaine* of glory he did fynd, . . . II. iii. 4. 5
every trembling joynt and every *vaine* . . . III. ii. 34. 3
rubd his temples and each trembling *vaine;* . . . III. v. 31. 7
that Squire, yet trembling every *vaine;* . . . IV. viii. 41. 3
grieve in every *vaine.* . . . IV. xii. 27. 9
scattering Contagious poyson close through every *vaine,* . . . VI. vi. 8. 8
Began to tremble every limbe and *vaine;* . . . VI. vii. 22. 2
And let thy bowels bleede in every *vaine,* . . . *H.H.L.* 248

Vein—*Continued.*
spend His plenteous *vaine* in setting forth her prayse, . . . *H.H.B.* 220
Vein-healing. *Veyne-healing* Verven, and hed-purging Dill, . . . *Mui.* 197
Veins. scorching Sunne does dry my secret *vaines;* . . . I. ii. 33. 8
drop Of living blood yet in her *veynes* did hop: . . . II. i. 43. 5
avarice gan through his *veines* inspire . . . II. vii. 17. 8
his feeble *vaines* Him faild thereto, . . . II. xi. 48. 3
ransackt all her *veines* with passion entyre. . . . III. i. 47. 9
His false venim through their *veines* inspir'd: . . . III. vi. 15. 5
Vellenage. *See* **Villeinage.**
Vellet. *See* **Velvet.**
Velvet. His *Vellet* head began to shoote out, . . . *S.C.* May 185
The *velvet* nap which on his wings doth lie, . . . *Mui.* 333
Venery. she . . . followes other game and *venery:* . . . I. vi. 22. 5
Venge. *venge* the shame that she to Knights doth show. . . . V. iv. 34. 4
Vengeable. that *vengeable* despight To punish: . . . II. iv. 30. 3
Headed with yre and *vengeable* despight. . . . II. iv. 46. 2
Vengeance. Powr'd *vengeance* forth on you eternallie? . . . *Ro.* xxiv. 11
Cruell Agave, flying *vengeance* sore . . . *Gn.* 172
Blinde through ambition, and with *vengeance* wood, . . . *Gn.* 411
Ne sorer *vengeance* wish on you to fall . . . *D.* 352
Th' importune fates, which *vengeance* on me seeke, . . . *D.* 387
nourish bloody *vengeaunce* in his bitter mind. . . . I. iv. 38. 9
greeved ghost for *vengeance* deep do grone: . . . I. iv. 49. 7
after blood and *vengeance* he did long: . . . I. v. 7. 3
quench the flame of furious despight, And bloodie *vengeance:* I. v. 14. 6
besought Some cursed *vengeaunce* on his sonne to cast. . . . I. v. 38. 2
crime with *vengeance* new Thou biddest me to eeke? . . . I. v. 42. 7
How can ye *vengeance* just so long withhold, . . . I. vi. 5. 8
Both breathing *vengeaunce,* both of wrathfull hew. . . . I. vi. 38. 5
blessed sprites, . . . To God for *vengeance* cryde continually; I. viii. 36. 7
To fly the *vengeaunce* for his outrage dew: . . . II. i. 25. 4
If I, or thou, dew *vengeaunce* doe forbeare, . . . II. i. 61. 7
mortal *vengeaunce* joyne to crime abhord? . . . II. ii. 30. 4
for feare of dew *vengeaunce* Doe lurke, . . . II. iii. 14. 7
heape more *vengeance* on that wretched wight: . . . II. iv. 5. 4
chawing *vengeaunce* all the way I went, . . . II. iv. 29. 2
Coles of contention and whot *vengeaunce* tind. . . . II. viii. 11. 5
Vile is the *vengeaunce* on the ashes cold, . . . II. viii. 13. 6
just wronges to *vengeaunce* doe provoke, . . . II. viii. 27. 3
to prolong The *vengeaunce* prest? . . . II. viii. 28. 3
vengeaunce utterly the guilt bereave: . . . II. viii. 29. 5
'Let bee therefore my *vengeaunce* to disswade, . . . III. ii. 13. 1
Nor *vengeaunce* huge relent it selfe at last? . . . III. iii. 43. 6
The mist of griefe dissolv'd did into *vengeance* powre. . . . III. iv. 13. 9
through wrath and *vengeaunce* making way, . . . III. v. 21. 1
Did th' other two their cruell *vengeaunce* blin, . . . III. v. 22. 7
To heape on him dew *vengeaunce* for his hire. . . . III. ix. 17. 5
guilty Dread Of heavenly *vengeaunce;* . . . III. xii. 25. 8
What *vengeance* due can equall thy desart, . . . IV. i. 53. 3
rather stir'd to *vengeance* and despight, . . . IV. iii. 14. 4
nought but spoyle and *vengeance* did require: . . . IV. vi. 11. 5
Throwne out by angry Jove in his *vengeance,* . . . IV. vi. 14. 2
held her wrathfull hand from *vengeance* sore: . . . IV. vi. 36. 6
flam'd with zeale of *vengeance* inwardly, . . . V. i. 14. 7
curst the hand which did that *vengeance* on him dight. . . . V. ii. 18. 9
Her wrathfull hand from greedy *vengeance* to have stayd. . . . V. v. 14. 9
Defend thee from the *vengeance* of thy fone; . . . V. vi. 37. 7
They doe his anger calme, and cruell *vengeance* stay. . . . V. ix. 31. 9
Yet would not let just *vengeance* on her light; . . . V. ix. 50. 5
Forget his patience, and yeeld *vengeaunce* dew . . . V. xii. 42. 4
to make unto his *vengeance* way: . . . VI. i. 39. 6
His heart with *vengeaunce* inwardly did swell, . . . VI. iii. 34. 8
the bitter stoure Of his sore *vengeaunce,* . . . VI. iii. 48. 5
to him leaping *vengeance* thought to take . . . VI. vii. 11. 7
To joyne with him and *vengeance* to devize, . . . VI. vii. 22. 8
taketh *vengeaunce* of his peoples spoile; . . . VI. viii. 23. 2
To serve the *vengeaunce* of his wrathfull will; . . . VI. x. 36. 2
thou of them mayst mightie *vengeance* take, . . . *Am.* x. 8
Vengeances. nought mote slake Their greedy *vengeaunces* . . VI. i. 37. 6
Vengeful. His heart with *vengefull* malice inly swelt; . . . *Mui.* 356
To save his people sad from victours *vengefull* handes. . . . III. ix. 41. 9
Through *vengeful* wrath and sdeignfull pride half mad; . . . V. iv. 43. 3
thousand deathes deviseth in her *vengefull* mind. . . . VII. vi. 48. 9
Vengement. In *vengement* of her mothers great disgrace, . . . IV. vii. 30. 6
wretched life forlorne for *vengement* of his theft. . . . VI. iii. 18. 9
Venger's. His bleeding hart is in the *vengers* hand; . . . I. iii. 20. 2
Venice. Fayre *Venice,* flower of the last worlds delight; . . . *Com. Son.* iv. 10
Venom. jawes, that with blacke *venime* swell. . . . *Van.* iii. 12
her fine corpes to a bag of *venim* grewe. . . . *Mui.* 352
the charme and *veneme* which they dronck, . . . II. ii. 4. 6
fire Did spred it selfe, and *venime* close inspire. . . . III. i. 56. 5
his false *venim* through their veines inspir'd: . . . III. vi. 15. 5
nought but gall and *venim* comprehended, . . . IV. i. 27. 4
there out sucking *venime* to her parts entyre. . . . IV. viii. 23. 9
close *venim* doth convay Into the lookers hart, . . . IV. viii. 39. 8
The other held a snake with *venime* fraught, . . . V. xii. 30. 5
He grind, hee bit, he scratcht, he *venim* threw, . . . VI. xii. 31. 8
Venomous. al good things with *venemous* tooth devowres, . . . *Mui.* 302
Envy . . . did chaw Between his cankred teeth a *venemous* tode, . . . I. iv. 30. 3
Curled with thousand adders *venemous,* . . . I. v. 34. 3
with vile tongue and *venemous* intent . . . VI. i. 8. 8
Are so exceeding *venemous* and keene, . . . VI. vi. 9. 2
Hope to escape his *venemous* despite, . . . VI. xii. 41. 2
Venemous toung, tipt with vile adders sting, . . . *Am.* lxxxv. 1
Ventail. Through whose bright *ventayle,* lifted up on hye, . . . III. i. 24. 3
Her *ventayle* shard away, . . . IV. vi. 19. 3
Ventails. *Ventailes* reare each other to behold. . . . V. viii. 12. 5
Vented. onely *vented* up her umbriere, . . . III. i. 42. 8

Venteth. See howe he *venteth* into the wynd; . . . . *S.C.* F. 75
Venture. With feeble flight *venture* to mount to heaven, . . . *Bel.*[1] vi. 2
Who will not *venture* life a King to be, ... *Hub.* 979
Ventured. So well she sped her, and so far she *ventred,* . . . . IV. vii. 31. 1
Venturing. For shewe of perill, without *venturing:* . . . . III. xi. 24. 7
Venturous. who in *venturous* vessell measured The Amazon . . II. Pr. 2. 7
the *venturous* Mariner that way Learning . . . . II. x. 6. 2
Argo, which in *venturous* peece First through the Euxine . . II. xii. 44. 8
save her honour with your *ventrous* paines: . . . . IV. ii. 27. 8
(Whylome for *ventrous* Knights the bedding best) . . . IV. v. 39. 4
upon a *ventrous* knight . . . for to prove his spere. . . . . IV. vi. 4. 2
Through his too *ventrous* prowesse proved over all. . . . . IV. xi. 7. 9
vanquished all *ventrous* knights in fight; . . . . V. x. 30. 4
Venus. where *Venus* sittes, and when. . . . . *S.C.* D. 84
ye three Twins, to light by *Venus* brought, ... *T.M.* 403
dame *Venus,* on a day In spring, ... *Mui.* 113
they in secret harts envying sore, Tolde *Venus,* . . . . *Mui.* 125
As faire as *Venus* or the fairest faire, ... *As.* 56
Venus selfe doth soly couples seeme, ... *Col.* 801
when he was requirde To pourtraict *Venus* . . . . *Ded. Son.* xvii. 2
of beautie soveraigne Queene, Fayre *Venus,* . . . . I. i. 48. 2
Sometimes dame *Venus* selfe he seemes to see; . . . . I. vi. 16. 6
Venus never had so sober mood: . . . . I. vi. 16. 7
The love of *Venus* and her Paramoure, ... III. i. 34. 4
Jove laught on *Venus* from his soverayne see, ... III. vi. 2. 7
faire *Venus* having lost Her little sonne, ... III. vi. 11. 1
Soone as she *Venus* saw behinde her backe, ... III. vi. 19. 1
Whom whenas *Venus* saw so sore displeasd, ... III. vi. 25. 1
Venus hers thence far away convayd, ... III. vi. 28. 6
their great mother *Venus* did lament . . . . III. vi. 40. 3
There wont fayre *Venus* often to enjoy . . . . III. vi. 46. 1
With which his mother *Venus* her revyld, ... III. vi. 50. 4
Hither great *Venus* brought this infant fayre, ... III. vi. 51. 1
Whom *Venus* to him gave for meed of worthinesse; . . . . III. ix. 34. 9
'Anchyses sonne, begott of *Venus* fayre,' . . . . III. ix. 41. 1
How oft for *Venus,* . . . he sore did shreek, ... III. xi. 44. 4
of great mother *Venus* bare the name, ... IV. x. 5. 4
Venus, that is hight The Queene of beautie, ... IV. x. 29. 5
' "Great *Venus!* Queene of beautie and of grace, ... IV. x. 44. 1
Venus of the fomy sea was bred, ... IV. xii. 2. 2
The sonne of *Venus,* who is myld by kynd . . . . VI. vii. 37. 1
They say that *Venus* . . . used to resort Unto this place, . . . VI. x. 9. 1
the Graces, daughters of delight, Handmaides of *Venus,* . . . VI. x. 15. 2
all that *Venus* in her selfe doth vaunt . . . . VI. x. 15. 5
So *Venus* eeke, that goodly Paragone, ... VII. vii. 51. 5
Not knowing *Venus* from the other. . . . . *Epig.* iii. 6
as ye use to *Venus,* to her sing, ... *Epith.* 108
Ye sonnes of *Venus,* play your sports at will! . . . . *Epith.* 364
When thy great mother *Venus* first thee bare, ... *H.L.* 52
Painter . . . Which pictured *Venus* with so curious quill, . . *H.H.B.* 212
let faire *Venus,* that is Queene of love, ... *Proth.* 96
Venus'. reigned (as men sayd) in *Venus* seate. . . . . *S.C.* D. 60
Through *Venus* grace, and vertues cariage. . . . . *Gn.* 488
in *Venus* silver bowre were bred, ... *T.M.* 362
Which *Venus* blood did in her leaves impresse, ... *D.* 109
mustring all his men in *Venus* vew, ... *Col.* 769
bred above in *Venus* bosome deare . . . . *Col.* 840
dreaded impe of highest Jove, Faire *Venus* sonne, ... I. Pr. 3. 2
wights Have knit themselves in *Venus* shameful chaine: . . . I. ii. 4. 8
Mars . . . is for *Venus* loves renowmed more . . . . II. vi. 35. 8
partiall Paris dempt it *Venus* dew, ... II. vii. 55. 7
hungers poynt or *Venus* sting . . . . II. xii. 39. 3
Whose image shee had seene in *Venus* looking glas. . . . . III. i. 8. 9
dred infant, *Venus* dearling dove, ... IV. Pr. 5. 2
Dame *Venus* girdle, by her steemed deare . . . . IV. v. 3. 7
Great *Venus* Temple is describ'd; . . . . IV. x. Arg.
unto *Venus* grace the gate doth open right. . . . . IV. x. 35. 9
unto *Venus* services was sold. . . . . IV. x. 54. 5
Cupids man with *Venus* mayd to hold, ... IV. x. 54. 7
Dame *Venus* sonne, ... IV. xii. 13. 3
Are *Venus* Damzels, all within her fee, ... VI. x. 21. 4
The blynd boy, *Venus* baby, ... *Epig.* i. 2
To be so bath'd in *Venus* blis? . . . . *Epig.* iv. 50
Where thou doest sit in *Venus* lap above, ... *H.L.* 24
Love, that had . . . securely slept In *Venus* lap, ... *H.L.* 62
Hercules and Hebe, and the rest Of *Venus* dearlings, . . . *H.L.* 284
you, faire *Venus* dearling, ... *H.B.* 281
through the Skie draw *Venus* silver Teeme; . . . . *Proth.* 63
Venus-star. night without a *Venus starre* is found. . . . . *D.* 483
Verdant. Up to his eares the *verdant* grasse did growe, . . . *Van.* ii. 5
streams of purple bloud new die the *verdant* fields. . . . . I. ii. 17. 9
The *verdant* gras my couch did goodly dight, ... I. ix. 13. 3
Verdant . . . he soone untyde, ... II. xii. 82. 8
whose fiery feete did burne The *verdant* gras . . . . III. i. 5. 6
Verdict. from just *verdict* will for nothing start, ... V. x. 2. 2
judge thyselfe, by *verdit* of thine eye, ... VII. vii. 27. 6
Verity. the light of simple *veritie* Buried in ruines, ... *Ti.* 171
learnd her discipline of faith and *verity.* . . . . I. vi. 31. 9
Verlame. *See* **Verulam.**
Vermeil. in her cheekes the *vermeill* red did shew . . . . II. iii. 22. 5
The greene shield dyde in dolorous *vermell?* . . . . II. x. 24. 7
otherwhere the snowy substaunce sprent With *vermell,* . . . II. xii. 45. 6
As hee that hath espide a *vermeill* Rose, ... III. i. 46. 6
did her lilly smock with staines of *vermeil* steep. . . . . III. i. 65. 9
mingled them with perfect *vermily;* . . . . III. viii. 6. 8
through the clifts the *vermeil* bloud out sponne, ... IV. ix. 27. 4
That all his garments and the grasse in *vermeill* dyde. . . . VI. ii. 40. 9
the pure snow, with goodly *vermill* stayne . . . . *Epith.* 227
With store of *vermeil* Roses, ... *Proth.* 33
Vermilion. armes . . . Into a pure *vermillion* now are dyde. . . I. v. 9. 6
Vermilion—*Continued.*
As they in pure *vermilion* had been dide, ... I. xi. 46. 3
fayre *vermilion* or pure Castory. . . . . II. ix. 41. 7
Decking her cheeke with a *vermilion* rose; . . . . V. v. 30. 4
Vermin. The subtill *vermin,* creeping closely neare, ... *Van.* vi. 7
Verolame. *See* **Verulam.**
Verse. to heare a doolefull *verse* Of Rosalend . . . . *S.C.* Au. 140
How I admire ech turning of thy *verse!* . . . . *S.C.* Au. 194
the Heavens did quake his *verse* to here. . . . . *S.C.* O. 60
The loftie *verse* of hem was loved aye. . . . . *S.C.* O. 66
The vaunted *verse* a vacant head demaundes, ... *S.C.* O. 100
O carefull *verse!* . . . *S.C.* N. 62, 72, 82, 92, 102, 112, 122, 132, 142, 152, 162
O joyfull *verse!* . . . . *S.C.* N. 172, 182, 192, 202
He shall inspire my *verse* with gentle mood . . . . *Gn.* 17
An easie running *verse* with tender feete. . . . . *Gn.* 53
Unhappie *Verse,* the witnesse of my unhappie state, ... *U.V.* 1
the whiles this *verse* Shall live, ... *Ti.* 253
with sweete Poets *verse* be glorifide. . . . . *Ti.* 427
with last duties of this broken *verse,* . . . . *Ti.* 678
To you alone I sing this mournfull *verse,* . . . . *As.* Pr. 7
The mournfulst *verse* that ever man heard tell: . . . . *As.* Pr. 8
least I marre the sweetnesse of the *vearse,* . . . . *As.* 215
verse of noblest shepheard . . . . *Col.* 534
Is in this *verse* engraven semblably, ... *Ded. Son.* vi. 13
Live, Lord, for ever in this lasting *verse,* . . . . *Ded. Son.* xi. 13
hath writ her owne record In golden *verse,* . . . . *Ded. Son.* xii. 4
the *verse* of famous Poets witt He does backebite, ... I. iv. 32. 6
Through famous Poets *verse* each where renownd, ... I. x. 54. 7
Whom famous Poetes *verse* so much doth vaunt, ... I. xi. 27. 2
"Sad *verse,* give death to him that death does give, ... II. i. 55. 4
My lowly *verse* may loftily arise, ... II. x. 1. 4
that sweete *verse,* with Nectar sprinckeled, ... III. Pr. 4. 4
that old Dame said many an idle *verse,* . . . . III. ii. 48. 8
matter made for famous Poets *verse,* . . . . III. iv. 1. 6
To whom sweet Poets *verse* hath given endlesse date. . . . . III. vi. 45. 9
measur'd many a sad *verse,* . . . . III. xii. 36. 4
in this so narrow *verse* Contayned be, ... IV. xi. 17. 3
this homely *verse,* of many meanest, ... VI. xii. 41. 1
this *verse,* that never shall expyre, ... *Am.* xxvii. 11
this *verse* . . . Shall be thereof immortall moniment; . . . *Am.* lxix. 9
My *verse* your vertues rare shall eternize, ... *Am.* lxxv. 11
whose *verse* could have enchased Your glorious name . . . . *Am.* lxxxii. 7
much lesse my trembling *verse* . . . can hope it to reherse. . . *H.H.L.* 41
Verses. *See* **Loving-verses.**
which shall never die Through your faire *verses,* . . . . *Ro.* i. 4
Hope ye, my *verses,* that posteritie . . . . *Ro.* xxxii. 1
plaintive pleas in *verses* made: . . . . *S.C.* Jun. 42
how bene thy *verses* meint . . . . *S.C.* N. 203
Ne let such *verses* Poetrie be named! . . . . *Hub.* 814
with deepe Oracles their *verses* fill: . . . . *T.M.* 562
Such grace the heavens doo to my *verses* give. . . . . *Ti.* 259
did him immortall make With *verses,* . . . . *Ti.* 431
verses vaine, (yet *verses* are not vaine,) . . . . *As.* 68
with remembraunce of your gracious name . . . adorne these *verses* . . . . *Ded. Son.* xvi. 5
thereof did *verses* frame; . . . . I. i. 37. 2
When Centaures blood and bloody *verses* charmd; . . . . I. xi. 27. 6
Bransles, Ballads, virelayes, and *verses* vaine; . . . . III. x. 8. 5
Verulam. Nigh where the goodly *Verlame* stood . . . . *Ti.* 3
Verlame I was: what bootes it that I was, ... *Ti.* 41
Beside Cayr *Verolame* in victorious fight, ... III. iii. 52. 8
Vervain. Veyne-healing *Verven,* and hed-purging Dill, ... *Mui.* 197
Very. sicker thy head *veray* tottie is, ... *S.C.* F. 55
Three thinges to beare bene *very* burdenous, ... *S.C.* May 132
Thilke same Kidde . . . Was too *very* foolish . . . . *S.C.* May 175
Sicker, I am *very* sybbe to you: . . . . *S.C.* May 269
She can trippe it *very* well. . . . . *S.C.* Au. 64
The *verie* nature of the place, ... *Gn.* 185
kept them lowe, and streigned *verie* hard. . . . . *Hub.* 1190
Sober he seemde, and *very* sagely sad, ... I. i. 29. 5
the wayne was *very* evill ledd, ... I. iv. 19. 7
But *very* uncouth sight was to behold, ... I. viii. 31. 1
as one were borne that *very* day. . . . . I. xi. 30. 5
For *very* felnesse lowd he gan to weepe, ... II. viii. 37. 5
Of which he now did *very* litle fayle, ... III. viii. 31. 7
His garment was disguysed *very* vayne, ... III. xii. 9. 5
The *very* selfe same day that she was wedded, ... IV. i. 3. 2
heart did almost rend in tway, For *very* gall, ... IV. iv. 22. 8
made a *very* griesly wound, ... IV. iv. 24. 6
thought he had the trew And *very* Florimell, ... IV. v. 13. 8
woxe nigh mad for *very* harts despight, ... IV. v. 27. 2
him afflicted to the *very* sowle. . . . . IV. v. 41. 9
He felt his hart for *very* paine to quake, ... IV. v. 44. 5
in the *very* dore him overcaught, ... IV. vii. 31. 5
seem'd to be of *very* sober mood, ... IV. x. 31. 4
very doubtfull was the warres event, ... V. ii. 17. 1
It bit the earth for *very* fell despight, ... V. ii. 18. 6
Out of his breast the *very* heart have rended: . . . . V. v. 6. 5
For *very* fell despight which she conceived, ... V. v. 47. 3
it empierced to the *very* braine, ... V. vii. 33. 8
her heart did quake For *very* ruth, ... V. vii. 36. 6
Her heart gan grudge for *very* deepe despight . . . . V. vii. 37. 8
He brayd aloud for *very* fell despight; . . . . V. xi. 8. 2
byting th' earth for *very* deaths disdaine; . . . . V. xi. 14. 7
Made kill her selfe for *very* hearts despight . . . . V. xi. 25. 4
could have frayd one with the *very* sight, ... V. xii. 15. 7
As he unable were for *very* neede To move one foote, ... VI. vi. 19. 6
Yet durst he not for *very* cowardize Effect the same, ... VI. vi. 44. 6
of her selfe in *very* deede so deemed; . . . . VI. ix. 14. 3
even his hart, for *very* fell despight, ... VI. xi. 25. 5

Very—*Continued.*
She found at last, by *very* certaine signes . . . . VI. xii. 20. 3
yet, *very* sooth to say, ... VII. viii. 1. 4
Ayming his arrow at my *very* hart: . . . . *Am.* xvi. 10
Vespasian. hither hastly sent *Vespasian,* . . . . II. x. 52. 7
Vesper. laesie *Vesper* in his timely howre . . . . *Gn.* 315
by her side there ran her Page, that hight *Vesper,* . . . . VII. vi. 9. 6
Vessel. in this golden *vessel* (*vessell*[1]) couched weare . . . . *Bel.* iii. 7
richer then that *vessell* seem'd to bee, ... *Bel.*[2] xiii. 1
Doth in the port it selfe his *vessell* rive. . . . . *Ro.* xxi. 14
Behold! an huge great *vessell* to us came, ... *Col.* 213
light this weary *vessell* of her lode: . . . . I. xii. 42. 4
who in venturous *vessell* measured The Amazon . . . . . . II. Pr. 2. 7
Bidding his winged *vessell* fairely forward fly: . . . . II. vii. 1. 9
the viaundes in the *vessell* boyld . . . . II. ix. 30. 8
in another great rownd *vessell* plaste, ... II. ix. 32. 3
mightily doth drive The hollow *vessell* . . . . II. xii. 5. 6
Here may thy storme-bett *vessell* safely ryde, ... II. xii. 32. 7
my feeble *vessell,* crazd and crackt . . . . III. iv. 9. 1
Vessels. fifty sisters water in leke *vessels* draw. . . . . . . I. v. 35. 9
On whose sharp cliftes the ribs of *vessels* broke; . . . . . . II. xii. 7. 3
His bloudy *vessels* wash, and holy fire prepare. . . . . . . VI. viii. 39. 9
Vesta. *Vesta,* of the fire aethereall; . . . . VII. vii. 26. 4
Vestment. Her covered with her sable *vestiment,* . . . . . . III. xii. 29. 4
by view of that his *vestiment,* . . . . V. vi. 19. 8
an uncouth *vestiment* Made of straunge stuffe, ... V. ix. 10. 7
Vestments. The holy Saints of their rich *vestiments* He did disrobe, ... I. iii. 17. 5
naked, without needfull *vestiments* . . . . VI. iv. 4. 4
All her array and *vestiments* to tell, ... VII. vii. 9. 2
Vesture. though his *vesture* were but meane and bace, ... *Hub.* 229
Clad in a *vesture* of unknowen geare . . . . IV. xi. 45. 2
Vetchy. There mayst thou ligge in a *vetchy* bed, ... *S.C.* S. 256
Vex. Doth *vex* my spirite with perplexitie, ... *Pet.*[2] ii. 12
ne her selfe would lenger *vex.* . . . . II. x. 20. 9
with vaine thoughts her falsed fancy *vex:* . . . . III. i. 47. 5
imperious love her hart did *vexe,* . . . . III. i. 54. 4
sad sorow . . . did *vexe* his noble brest, ... III. iv. 54. 3
all the passions . . . *vex* his caytive spright. . . . . III. x. 17. 9
that much did *vexe* His noble hart: . . . . IV. viii. 35. 4
day and night did *vexe* her carefull thought, ... VI. v. 6. 8
Vexed. my free spirite might not . . . Be *vext* with sights, . . *Pet.*[2] vii. 8
sting did threaten, And *vext* so sore, ... *Van.* ii. 12
To feele his fault, and not be further *vext.* . . . . *Gn.* Ded. 12
askt what her so *vexed.* . . . . *Ti.* 21
Them sorely *vext,* and courst, and overran, ... V. iv. 44. 3
her selfe she onely *vext,* . . . . V. xii. 35. 8
Vexeth. *vexeth* so that makes her eat her gall; . . . . V. xii. 31. 5
Vial. An angry Waspe th' one in a *viall* had, ... III. xii. 18. 7
Viands. Against the *viaundes* should be ministred . . . . . . II. ix. 27. 4
the *viaundes* in the vessell boyld . . . . II. ix. 30. 8
Vicar. some *Vicker* Content with little in condition sicker. . . *Hub.* 429
Vice. That nource of *vice,* this of insolencie, ... *S.C.* May 118
vertue to advaunce, and *vice* deride, ... *Hub.* 812
fill their bookes with discipline of *vice.* . . . . *T.M.* 336
Advancing vertue and suppressing *vice.* . . . . *Col.* 323
she that vertue loves and *vice* detests, ... IV. xi. 51. 7
vertue . . . Is now cald *vice;* . . . . V. Pr. 4. 2
that which *vice* was hight, Is now hight vertue, ... V. Pr. 4. 2
the wicked seede of *vice* Began to spring; . . . . V. i. 1. 3
Exceeding sweet, yet voyd of sinfull *vice;* . . . . *Am.* lxxvii. 9
Vicious. in a *vicious* bodie, grose disease Soone growes . . . . *Ro.* xxiii. 11
Corrupts the stomacke with gall *vitious,* . . . . III. x. 59. 7
that Argante vile and *vitious,* . . . . III. xi. 3. 7
Vicker. *See* **Vicar.**
Victor. Both those the lawrell girlonds to the *victor* dew. . . . I. v. 5. 9
clapt his yron wings as *victor* he did dwell. . . . . I. xi. 31. 9
to the mighty *victor* yields a bounteous feast. . . . . II. v. 10. 9
on his brest his *victor* foote he thrust: . . . . II. v. 12. 6
His forlorne steed from him the *victour* wan: . . . . II. vi. 41. 4
with his *victour* sword . . . . II. x. 23. 6
with fresh corage on the *victor* servd: . . . . II. x. 55. 7
he *victor* onely did remayne; . . . . II. xi. 43. 7
as a *victour* proud, gan ransack fast His inward partes, . . . III. v. 48. 4
meekely stoup unto the *victor* strong: . . . . III. vii. 35. 4
dared not his *victor* to withstand, ... III. vii. 36. 5
the *victour,* through the flood Escaped hardly, ... III. ix. 42. 8
he *victour* did survive, ... III. ix. 43. 1
Unto the Victor of the Gods this bee: . . . . III. xi. 49. 2
of them all the *victour* should his sister take. . . . . . . IV. ii. 38. 9
he sav'd the *victour* from fordonne: . . . . IV. v. 7. 7
Cambell *victour* was in all mens sight, ... IV. v. 7. 8
The Salvage Knight that *victour* was whileare, ... IV. v. 8. 5
Till like a *victor* on his backe he ride, ... IV. xii. 13. 5
Yet whether side was *victor* note be ghest: . . . . V. iii. 7. 6
her sole *victor* left. V. vii. 34. 9
the Prince, as *victour* of that day, ... VI. viii. 51. 2
Had vow'd unto the *victor* him to trace . . . . VI. vii. 21. 7
Victor of gods, subduer of mankynd, ... *H.L.* 45
My guide, my God, my *victor,* and my king: . . . . *H.L.* 305
Victoress. when the *Victoresse* arrived there . . . . III. xii. 44. 1
Victories. deckt . . . With manie garlands for his *victories,* . *Ti.* 653
woxen insolent Through many *victories,* . . . . *Ded. Son.* vi. 11
vertue vauntes in both her *victories,* . . . . II. vi. 1. 8
of his *victories* Brave moniments remaine, ... II. x. 21. 8
Victorious. that his *victorious* people should . . . not be overworne: . . . . *Ro.* xxiii. 3
Under whose conduct most *victorious,* . . . . *Gn.* 548
Bunduca, that *victorious* conqueresse, ... *Ti.* 108
Hath fild sad Belgicke with *victorious* spoile; . . . . *Ded.Son.* xiv. 10

Victorious—*Continued.*
'Faire Lady,' then said that *victorious* knight, ... I. viii. 44. 1
To see the face of that *victorious* man, ... I. xii. 9. 3
Whom his *victorious* handes did earst restore . . . . II. i. 2. 6
queld The salvage beastes in her *victorious* play, ... II. iii. 29. 4
whom your *victorious* might Hath now fast bound, ... II. iv. 32. 3
He them defeated in *victorious* fight, ... II. x. 16. 4
in that same field *victorious* . . . . II. x. 43. 7
In hope thereof to win *victorious* spoile. . . . . II. xi. 7. 5
his proud foes discomfit in *victorious* field. . . . . III. iii. 31. 9
whome hee lately brake . . . in *victorious* fight, ... III. iii. 52. 8
whose *victorious* Exployts made Rome to quake; . . . . . . III. iii. 54. 7
the spoiles of my *victorious* games. . . . . III. vii. 54. 9
raignd so many yeares *victorious,* . . . . III. ix. 39. 3
Cannot employ your most *victorious* speare . . . . III. x. 28. 3
victorious prayes Of mightie Conquerours . . . . III. xi. 52. 2
By her subdewed in *victorious* fray: . . . . V. v. 21. 5
At last from his *victorious* shield he drew The vaile, ... V. viii. 37. 6
your *victorious* arme will not yet cease, ... V. xi. 18. 5
(As their *victorious* deedes have often showen, ... VI. iv. 36. 4
fill the world with her *victorious* prayse. . . . . *Am.* xxix. 14
thy *victorious* conquests to areed, ... *H.L.* 11
Thus to ennoble thy *victorious* name, ... *H.L.* 149
through thy prowesse, and *victorious* armes, ... *Proth.* 155
Victor-like. To range the field, and *victorlike* to raine, ... IV. iv. 25. 4
Victor's. A Rosy girlond was the *victors* meede. . . . . I. ii. 37. 5
raging spoile of lawlesse *victors* will? . . . . I. iii. 43. 2
envious gage Of *victors* glory from him snacht away: . . . . I. iv. 39. 6
here thy shield is hangd for *victors* hyre? . . . . I. v. 10. 7
yields it selfe unto the *victors* might. . . . . I. viii. 23. 7
yeeldes his caytive neck to *victours* most despight. . . . . I. ix. 11. 9
Both loosers lott, and *victours* prayse alsoe; . . . . II. v. 15. 8
him reave of armes, the *victors* hire, ... II. viii. 15. 7
he, now subject to the *victours* law, ... II. viii. 50. 5
The worlds reproch; the cruell *victors* scorne; . . . . III. iii. 42. 5
To save his people sad from *victours* vengefull handes. . . . III. ix. 41. 9
will be made The vassall of the *victors* will bylive: . . . . III. x. 10. 7
To shew the *victors* might and mercilesse intent. . . . . . III. xi. 52. 9
'Lo! sluggish Knight, the *victors* happie pray! . . . . IV. ii. 7. 5
whylome wont to be the *victors* meed; . . . . IV. iv. 31. 3
both of *victors* meede And eke of honour . . . . IV. v. 9. 2
made the vassall of the *victors* might; . . . . IV. viii. 32. 7
Left in the *victors* powre, like vassall bond, ... IV. ix. 18. 7
fortune now the *victors* meed did make: . . . . VI. xi. 51. 4
Lyke captives trembling at the *victors* sight. . . . . *Am.* i. 4
Victors. delivered unto me By Romane *Victors,* . . . . *Ti.* 38
made them *victors* whome he did subdew. . . . . II. x. 57. 4
Yet *victors* both them selves alwayes esteemed: . . . . . . IV. iii. 28. 5
madest many harts to bleed Of mighty *Victors,* . . . . . . *H.L.* 13
Victors'. tread downe the *victors* surquedry. . . . . III. iii. 46. 9
Victory. On each side purtraid was a *Victorie,* . . . . *Bel.* iv. 5
onely Rome of Rome hath *victorie;* . . . . *Ro.* iii. 10
him enforst to yeeld the *victorie,* . . . . *Van.* vi. 11
Areede uprightly who has the *victorye* . . . . *S.C.* Au. 130
Did surely deeme the *victorie* his due: . . . . *Mui.* 319
The *victorie* did yeeld her as her share: . . . . *Mui.* 342
His Lady, . . . Approcht in hast to greet his *victorie;* . . . I. i. 27. 2
both stand sencelesse . . . Forgetfull of the hanging *victory:* I. ii. 16. 6
To muse on meanes of hoped *victory.* . . . . I. iv. 44. 5
victory they dare not wish to either side. . . . . I. v. 9. 9
Heralds . . . Greeting him goodly with new *victorie,* . . . . I. v. 15. 8
Came running fast to greet his *victorie,* . . . . I. viii. 26. 4
the man . . . thorough grace hath gained *victory:* . . . . . I. x. 1. 7
when thou famous *victory* hast wonne, ... I. x. 60. 5
Saint George of mery *England,* the signe of *victoree'* . . . I. x. 61. 9
The knight . . . gayns Most glorious *victory.* . . . . I. xi. Arg.
their new joy, and happie *victory* . . . . I. xii. 4. 3
Glad signe of *victory* and peace in all their land. . . . . . I. xii. 5. 9
Vaine is the vaunt, and *victory* unjust, ... II. ii. 29. 8
poursewed fast The present offer of faire *victory,* . . . . . II. v. 12. 2
whenas hee In Nemus gayned goodly *victoree:* . . . . II. v. 31. 5
Does yield unto his foe a pleasaunt *victory.* . . . . II. vi. 34. 9
Gave him great hart and hope of *victory.* . . . . II. viii. 39. 4
The king retourned proud of *victory,* . . . . II. x. 17. 1
by him Caesar got the *victory,* . . . . II. x. 49. 1
with rich spoyles and famous *victorie* . . . . II. x. 75. 4
th' utmost meanes of *victory* assay, ... II. xi. 41. 4
Then honour was the meed of *victory,* . . . . III. i. 13. 6
if he then with *victorie* can lin, ... III. iii. 30. 8
Of his successe and gladfull *victory:* . . . . III. iii. 59. 4
how to win the wished *victory,* . . . . III. vii. 33. 2
to rest in glorious *victorye.* . . . . III. ix. 22. 9
Signe of nigh battaill, or got *victory:* . . . . III. xii. 1. 6
gan thereat to triumph without *victorie.* . . . . IV. i. 50. 9
In doubt to whom she *victorie* should deeme, ... IV. ii. 17. 5
Ne desperate of glorious *victorie;* . . . . IV. iii. 25. 2
A signe which did to him the *victorie* assure. . . . . IV. iii. 32. 9
each to other seemd the *victorie* to yield. . . . . IV. iii. 34. 9
though that he first *victorie* obtayned, ... V. v. 17. 6
To whether should the *victory* befall, ... V. xi. 15. 8
gave his foe good hope of *victory:* . . . . VI. viii. 9. 6
A garland was the meed of *victory:* . . . . VI. ix. 43. 4
Ne any left that *victorie* to him envide. . . . . VI. xi. 49. 9
victory in bigger notes to sing . . . . VII. vii. 1. 7
Bring home the triumph of our *victory:* . . . . *Epith.* 243
Joy have thou of thy noble *victorie,* . . . . *Proth.* 152
View. of some heavenly wight I had the *vewe* (*vew*[1]); . . . . *Pet.* v. 4
nor marble was the wall in *view,* . . . . *Bel.*[2] ii. 5
so rare a thing to *vew;* . . . . *Bel.*[2] v. 9
ye, these rythmes doo read, and *vew* the rest, ... *Pet.*[2] vii. 11

View—*Continued.*
him behooves to *vew* in compasse round . . . *Ro.* xxvi. 5
Judge, by these ample ruines *vew*, the rest . . . *Ro.* xxvii. 5
suddenly casting aside his *vew*, . . . *Gn.* 294
from him Laertes sonne his *vewe* Doth turne aside, . . . *Gn.* 533
Th' eternall Makers majestie wee *viewe*, . . . *T.M.* 512
mercie more than mortall men can *vew*. . . . *T.M.* 514
whilst heavens with equall *vewe* Deignd to behold me . . . *Ti.* 80
none durst *vewe* the horror of his face, . . . *Ti.* 535
A fairer one . . . might no man *view*: . . . *Ti.* 593
To *view* the workmanship of heavens hight: . . . *Mui.* 45
spredding all his backe, with dreadfull *view* . . . *Mui.* 69
those hollow eyes and deadly *view*, . . . *D.* 304
Inflaming feeble eyes that her do *view*. . . . *Col.* 519
mustring all his men in Venus *vew*, . . . *Col.* 769
And the dim vele, with which from commune *vew* . . . *Ded. Son.* ix. 10
desird Of all the fairest Maides to have the *vew*. . . . *Ded. Son.* xvii. 4
To sharpe my sence with sundry beauties *vew*, . . . *Ded. Son.* xvii. 7
High on an hill, his flocke to *vewen* wide, . . . I. i. 23. 3
busying his quicke eies her face to *view*, . . . I. ii. 26. 6
A filthy foule old woman I did *vew*, . . . I. ii. 40. 8
never . . . Face of fayre Lady she before did *vew*, . . . I. iii. 11. 8
the glad marchant, that does *vew* from ground His ship . . . I. iii. 32. 3
whose glorious *vew* Their frayle amazed senses did confound: I. iv. 7. 2
the stout Faery . . . Thought all their glorie vaine in knightly *vew*, . . . I. iv. 15. 7
in all mens open *vew* Duessa placed is, . . . I. v. 5. 6
visage . . . That Phoebus chearefull face durst never *vew*, . . . I. v. 20. 2
Coverd with charmed cloud from *vew* of day, . . . I. v. 29. 4
By *vew* of her he ginneth to revive His ancient love, . . . I. vi. 17. 1
his own syre, . . . Did often tremble at his horrid *vew*; . . . I. vi. 25. 3
eye mote not the same endure to *vew*. . . . I. viii. 19. 5
the floore . . . Defiled was, that dreadfull was to *vew*; . . . I. viii. 35. 8
Since I the heavens chearefull face did *vew*. . . . I. viii. 38. 8
eies, . . . Could not endure th' unwonted sunne to *view*; . . . I. viii. 41. 2
made her . . . sad to *view* his visage pale and wan, . . . I. viii. 42. 3
Whenas the gentle Redcrosse knight did *vew*, . . . I. ix. 37. 3
The ugly *vew* of his deformed crimes; . . . I. ix. 48. 6
A little path . . . to a goodly Citty led his *vew*, . . . I. x. 55. 3
she beheld those maydens meriment With chearefull *vew*; . . . I. xii. 8. 2
fruitfullest Virginia who did ever *vew*? . . . II. Pr. 2. 9
whenas Archimago them did *view*, . . . II. i. 8. 1
we far off will here abide to *vew*.' . . . II. i. 25. 7
Pitifull spectacle, as ever eie did *vew*! . . . II. i. 40. 9
As with lamenting eyes him selfe did lately *vew*. . . . II. ii. 45. 9
To serve at court in *view* of vaunting eye; . . . II. iii. 10. 2
Such when as hartlesse Trompart her did *vew*, . . . II. iii. 32. 1
does yield to *vew* Her dainty limbes . . . II. v. 33. 7
noise of armes, or *vew* of martiall guize, . . . II. vi. 25. 8
Elfe, That darest *view* my direfull countenaunce, . . . II. vii. 7. 7
if to thy great mind, or greedy *vew*, . . . II. vii. 9. 3
'yet never eie did *vew*, . . . II. vii. 19. 6
vew of cherefull day Did never . . . it selfe display, . . . II. vii. 29. 4
most hevenly faire in deed and *vew* . . . II. vii. 45. 7
I joy thy face to *vew*: . . . II. viii. 53. 8
if the trew lively-head . . . ye did *vew*: . . . II. ix. 3. 4
Of that faire Castle to affoord them *vew*: . . . II. ix. 20. 8
Upon her fist the bird, which shonneth *vew*, . . . II. ix. 40. 7
To *vew* her Castles other wondrous frame: . . . II. ix. 44. 7
one by his *vew* Mote deeme him . . . II. ix. 52. 7
as they gan his Library to *vew*, . . . II. ix. 59. 3
Th' eternall marks of treason may at Stonheng *vew*. . . . II. x. 66. 9
vew of eye could scarse him overtake, . . . II. xi. 26. 2
when his uncouth manner he did *vew*, . . . II. xi. 27. 5
well they seeme to him, that farre doth *vew*, . . . II. xii. 12. 1
Untill they came in *vew* of those wilde beasts, . . . II. xii. 39. 6
lurking from the *vew* of covetous guest, . . . II. xii. 55. 4
wight who did not well avis'd it *vew* . . . II. xii. 61. 4
from *vew* of any which them eyd. . . . II. xii. 63. 9
From his Beauperes, and from bright heavens *vew*, . . . III. i. 35. 7
Thence they were brought to that great Ladies *vew*, . . . III. i. 41. 1
did them selves present Unto her *vew*, . . . III. i. 44. 3
A jolly person, and of comely *vew*; . . . III. i. 45. 2
Sith him whylome in Britayne she did *vew*, . . . III. ii. 17. 3
From all mens *vew*, that none might her discoure, . . . III. ii. 20. 4
Yet she might all men *vew* out of her bowre? . . . III. ii. 20. 5
The Damzell well did *vew* his Personage . . . III. ii. 26. 1
refte from men the worldes desired *vew*, . . . III. ii. 28. 3
As one with *vew* of ghastly feends affright: . . . III. ii. 29. 7
In a deepe delve, farre from the *vew* of day, . . . III. iii. 7. 7
from them fled, as light-foot hare from *vew* . . . III. iv. 46. 4
At last of her far off he gained *vew*. . . . III. iv. 48. 1
with melting eies did *vew*, . . . III. v. 30. 4
Still when her excellencies he did *vew*, . . . III. v. 44. 4
of all love taketh equall *vew*; . . . III. v. 47. 5
In a fresh fountaine, far from all mens *vew*, . . . III. vi. 6. 6
She brought her forth into the worldes *vew*, . . . III. vi. 52. 3
such whenas the wicked Hag did *vew*, . . . III. vii. 11. 4
offred kingdoms unto her in *vew*, . . . III. viii. 40. 4
With wonder of her beauty fed their hongry *vew*. . . . III. ix. 23. 9
note their hongry *vew* be satisfide, . . . III. ix. 24. 1
inly tickled with that golden *vew*. . . . III. x. 30. 3
pricked fiercely forward where she did him *vew*. . . . III. xi. 4. 9
In dolefull darkenes from the *vew* of day, . . . III. xi. 11. 2
Him selfe he chaung'd, faire Danae to *vew*; . . . III. xi. 31. 2
gan the world to hyde From mortall *vew*, . . . III. xi. 55. 4
Like knight adventurous in outward *vew*, . . . IV. i. 33. 3
Perceiv'd to be such as they seemd in *vew*, . . . IV. i. 38. 8
for this Ladie, present in your *vew*, . . . IV. ii. 24. 3
Farre from the *view* of gods and heavens bliss, . . . IV. ii. 47. 8

View—*Continued.*
To *view* and deeme the deedes of armes that day: . . . IV. iii. 4. 4
The same aloft he hung in open *vew*, . . . IV. iv. 16. 1
Leading his friend away, full sorie to his *vew*. . . . IV. iv. 33. 9
His wondrous worth declared in all mens *view*, . . . IV. iv. 37. 5
Cambello brought into their *view* His faire Cambina, . . . IV. v. 10. 1
By *view* of all the fairest to him brought, . . . IV. v. 12. 8
all, which her that time did *vew*, . . . IV. v. 13. 5
Florimell her selfe in all mens *vew* She seem'd to passe: . . . IV. v. 15. 8
Which when that scornefull Squire of Dames did *vew*, . . . IV. v. 18. 1
with the *vew* Did greatly solace . . . IV. viii. 7. 3
most was moved at the piteous *vew*, . . . IV. viii. 20. 3
them to *view* had bene an uncouth sight, . . . IV. viii. 34. 7
would have maz'd a man his dreadfull face to *vew*: . . . IV. viii. 38. 9
Him overtooke before he came in *vew*: . . . IV. viii. 40. 5
To *view* the thrals which there in bondage lay: . . . IV. viii. 52. 3
High reared mounts, the lands about to *vew*; . . . IV. x. 24. 5
Through the Agaean seas from Pirates *vew*, . . . IV. xi. 23. 7
seemed strange to common *vew*, . . . IV. xi. 27. 7
To *view* the building of that uncouth place, . . . IV. xii. 4. 6
far as they could *vew*, . . . V. ii. 29. 4
things subject to thy daily *vew* . . . V. ii. 42. 8
In warlike wise when Artegall did *vew*, . . . V. ii. 52. 2
hid themselves in holes and bushes from his *vew*. . . . V. ii. 53. 9
when as all the people such did *vew*, . . . V. iii. 23. 8
his bigge hart loth'd so uncomely *vew*: . . . V. v. 22. 5
by *view* of that his vestiment, . . . V. vi. 19. 8
when as Artegall did Arthure *vew*, . . . V. viii. 12. 6
had he not it shun'd with heedfull *vew*, . . . V. viii. 32. 7
comming full before his horses *vew*, . . . V. viii. 37. 8
th' onely feare that was before their *vew*, . . . V. viii. 38. 8
Soone as they did the monstrous Scorpion *vew* . . . V. viii. 40. 3
there did *vew* The armed knights . . . V. ix. 14. 7
had he not foreseene with heedfull *vew*, . . . V. xi. 30. 8
Maugre the might of all those troupes in *vew*, . . . V. xii. 5. 7
From *view* of men, and wicked worlds disdaine; . . . VI. Pr. 3. 4
when he saw his foe before in *vew*, . . . VI. i. 35. 6
Long shut up in the bud from heavens *vew*, . . . VI. ii. 35. 8
Which sorie sight when Calidore did *vew* . . . VI. ii. 41. 6
whenas he approched nigh in *vew*, . . . VI. iii. 47. 3
much emmoved at his perils *vew*, . . . VI. iv. 3. 4
Whom soone as his three enemies did *vew*, . . . VI. v. 22. 6
in present *vew*, Him rudely rent . . . VI. vi. 22. 5
so soone as he was out of *vew*, . . . VI. vii. 2. 8
the Gods, that mortall follies *vew*, . . . VI. vii. 32. 1
Which as they *view* with lustfull fantasyes, . . . VI. viii. 41. 8
Fly like a flocke of doves before a Faulcons *vew*. . . . VI. viii. 49. 9
downe to them descended in that earthly *vew*. . . . VI. ix. 8. 9
the object of his *vew*, . . . VI. ix. 26. 6
Another quest, another game in *vew* He hath, . . . VI. x. 2. 3
Like to one sight which Calidore did *vew*? . . . VI. x. 4. 2
soone as he appeared to their *vew*, . . . VI. x. 18. 1
shade From *view* of living wight . . . VI. x. 42. 4
One day, as he did all his prisoners *vew*, . . . VI. xi. 3. 6
like that which lately they did *vew*. . . . VI. xi. 43. 9
I with these eyes did *view* The litle purple rose . . . VI. xii. 18. 4
close might *view* That never any saw, . . . VII. vi. 45. 2
That eye of wight could not indure to *view*: . . . VII. vii. 6. 5
might delight the smell, or please the *view*, . . . VII. vii. 10. 5
By others opposition or obliquid *view*. . . . VII. vii. 54. 9
looking up with chearefull *view*, . . . VII. vii. 57. 8
Base thing I can no more endure to *view*: . . . *Am.* iii. 6
Into the object of your mighty *view*? . . . *Am.* vii. 4
in your glasse . . . Your goodly selfe for evermore to *vew*: . . . *Am.* xlv. 2
shew Thing so divine to *vew* of earthly eye, . . . *Am.* xlv. 6
Great shame it is, thing so divine in *view*, . . . *Am.* liii. 9
So let us, which this chaunge of weather *vew*, . . . *Am.* lxii. 5
She commeth in, before th' Almighties *view*; . . . *Epith.* 211
face long hidden was From heavens *view*, . . . *H.L.* 60
Worke like impression in the lookers *vew*? . . . *H.B.* 81
with th' easie *vew* Of this base world, . . . *H.H.B.* 22
By *view* whereof it plainly may appeare, . . . *H.H.B.* 43
For in the *view* of her celestiall face . . . *H.H.B.* 242

Viewed. Which when the Priest beheld, he *vew'd* it nere, . . . *Hub.* 379
Approaching nigh, his face I *vewed* nere, . . . *D.* 50
when that pitteous spectacle they *vewed*, . . . *As.* 203
Wherein her face she often *vewed* fayne, . . . I. iv. 10. 7
when they *vewed* have her heavenly grace, . . . I. vi. 18. 5
when he *vewd* Those deadly tooles . . . II. iii. 37. 2
Her selfe awhile therein she *vewd* in vaine: . . . III. ii. 22. 6
having *vewed* in a fountaine shere His face, . . . III. ii. 44. 7
So straungely *vewed* her straunge lovers shade, . . . III. iii. 6. 3
having *vewd* awhile the surges hore . . . III. iv. 7. 4
she *vewde* Her selfe freed from that foster insolent, . . . III. iv. 50. 6
So closely yet, that none but she it *vewd*, . . . III. x. 9. 4
he *vewd* Whereas his lovely wife emongst them lay, . . . III. x. 48. 1
The noble Mayd still standing all this *vewd*, . . . III. xii. 5. 1
vewed The armes he bore, . . . IV. vi. 3. 3
darkenesse dredd that never *viewed* day, . . . IV. xi. 4. 2
her gan cheare with what she there had *vewed*, . . . V. x. 38. 8
Whom Calidore awhile well having *vewed* . . . VI. ii. 7. 1
Having by chaunce a close advantage *vew'd*, . . . VI. iii. 50. 4
whereas his Lord he sleeping *vew'd*. . . . VI. vii. 23. 9
Those villeins *view'd* with loose lascivious sight, . . . VI. viii. 43. 3
Her whyles Sir Calidore there *vewed* well, . . . VI. ix. 11. 1
with firme eyes affixt the ground still *viewed*. . . . VII. vii. 57. 3
of loving eyes be *vewed* never? . . . *H.B.* 189

Viewest. As ever else in Princes Court thou *vewest*. . . . *Col.* 738

Viewing. So soone as day appeard to peoples *vewing*, . . . *Hub.* 104
Was matchable to this in equall *vewing*. . . . *Ti.* 553

Viewing—*Continued.*
Her loathly visage *viewing* with disdaine, . . . I. ii. 39. 5
The God himselfe, *vewing* that mirrhour rare, . . . I. vi. 15. 6
ofte his mother, *vewing* his wide wownd, . . . III. iv. 44. 3
viewing them more neare, Returned readie newes, . . . IV. ii. 31. 4
Descended to the Rivers open *vewing*, . . . *Proth.* 166
Views. he *vewes*, with his black-lidded eye, . . . *Hub.* 1228
Vigent. Peridure and *Vigent* him disthronized. . . . II. x. 44. 9
Vigilant. With *vigilant* regard and dew attent, . . . III. ix. 52. 3
did not them prevent with *vigilant* foresight. . . . IV. x. 20. 9
Vigor. old man, . . . Yet lively *vigour* rested in his mind, . . . II. ix. 55. 7
rings vertue, that with *vigour* new . . . him cherisht, . . . IV. iii. 29. 3
Vild. *See* **Vile.**
Truth . . . fals In hand of leachour *vylde.* . . . I. iii. Arg.
made the vassall of his pleasures *vilde.* . . . I. vi. 3. 5
sold thy selfe to serve Duessa *vild*, . . . I. ix. 46. 8
to their senses *vyld* Her gentle speach applyde, . . . III. vii. 15. 3
his fellow-servant *vild:* . . . III. vii. 17. 8
the Monster *vilde* Upon that milke-white Palfreyes carcas fedd, III. vii. 30. 7
To save her honor from that villaine *vilde*, . . . III. viii. 27. 4
Bidding her feare no more her foeman *vilde*, . . . III. viii. 34. 3
so base and *vilde* To be unjustly blamd, . . . IV. viii. 28. 8
On that *vilde* man and all his family; . . . V. vi. 35. 5
for *vyld* treasons and outrageous shame, . . . V. ix. 40. 8
Till ye have rooted all the relickes out Of that *vilde* race, . . . V. xi. 18. 7
saves from Maleffort A Damzell used *vylde:* . . . VI. i. Arg.
Vildly. gobbets raw, Which stunck so *vildly*, . . . I. i. 20. 4
With . . . disdaineful spight Her *vildly* entertaines; . . . I. iii. 43. 7
saw those villaines her so *vildely* use, . . . VI. vii. 45. 2
Vile. the *vile* blaspheming name. . . . *Rev.* i. 3
such *vile* vassals, borne to base vocation, . . . *Hub.* 156
For their false treason and *vile* theeverie: . . . *Hub.* 315
following that trade so base and *vile;* . . . *Hub.* 366
with *vile* cloaths approach Gods majestie, . . . *Hub.* 465
He hates fowle leasings, and *vile* flatterie, . . . *Hub.* 733
A servant to the *vile* affection . . . *Hub.* 817
those same treachours *vile* . . . *Hub.* 1255
'O *vile* worlds trust! . . . *Ti.* 456
it to maintaine Against *vile* Zoilus backbitings . . . *Ded.Son.* xii. 14
raise my thoughtes, too humble and too *vile*, . . . I. Pr. 4. 6
A monster *vile*, whom God and man does hate: . . . I. i. 13. 7
Most lothsom, filthie, foule, and full of *vile* disdaine. . . . I. i. 14. 9
a loose Leman to *vile* service bound: . . . I. i. 48. 6
her dew loves deryv'd to that *vile* witches shayre. . . . I. iii. 2. 9
Who had enough, yett wished ever more; A *vile* disease: . . . I. iv. 29. 6
Such one *vile* Envy was, that fifte in row did sitt. . . . I. iv. 32. 9
the faire Fidessa, loe! Is there possessed of the traytour *vile;* I. iv. 42. 3
Ne wicked envy, ne *vile* gealosy, . . . I. xii. 41. 3
lewd rybauld, with *vyle* lust advaunst, . . . II. i. 10. 3
where *vile* Acrasia does wonne; . . . II. i. 51. 2
when the *vile* Enchaunteresse perceiv'd, . . . II. i. 55. 1
'*Vile* Caytive, vassall of dread and despayre, . . . II. iii. 7. 4
In fowle reproch, and termes of *vile* despight, . . . II. iv. 5. 2
glad t' embosome his affection *vile*, . . . II. iv. 25. 3
'*Vile* knight, That knights and knighthood doest . . . upbray, II. iv. 45. 2
The *vyle* Acrasia, that with vaine delightes, . . . II. v. 27. 2
'*Vile* Miscreaunt,' (said he) wither dost thou flye . . . II. vi. 39. 6
their *vile* carcases now left unburied. . . . II. vii. 30. 9
With such vaine shewes thy worldlinges *vyle* abuse; . . . II. vii. 39. 5
That sire he fowl bespake : Thou dotard *vile*, . . . II. viii. 12. 2
Vile is the vengeaunce on the ashes cold, . . . II. viii. 13. 6
shamefull vaunt Of *vile* revenge. . . . II. viii. 16. 4
On this *vile* body from to wreak my wrong, . . . II. viii. 28. 4
For *vile* disdaine and rancour, which did gnaw . . . II. viii. 50. 7
Vile caitive wretches, ragged, rude, deformd, . . . II. ix. 13. 4
Would not endure to bee so *vile* disdaind, . . . II. x. 18. 2
Forthy this hight The Rocke of *vile* Reproch, . . . II. xii. 8. 1
he chooseth with *vile* difference To be a beast, . . . II. xii. 87. 4
Vyle rancor to avoid and cruel surquedry. . . . III. i. 13. 9
Abhorred bloodshed, and *vile* felony, . . . III. iv. 58. 3
Vile rancour their rude harts had fild with such despight. . . . III. v. 16. 9
that *vile* Hag . . . was much moved . . . III. vii. 9. 8
that *vile* hag, or her uncivile sonne; . . . III. vii. 19. 6
be the vassall of her pleasures *vile*, . . . III. vii. 50. 8
vile ungentlenesse, or hospitages breach. . . . III. x. 6. 9
that *vile* knight, who ever that he bee. . . . III. x. 32. 3
Untroubled of *vile* feare or bitter fell. . . . III. xi. 2. 5
that Argante *vile* and vitious, . . . III. xi. 3. 7
thou, *vile* man, *vile* Scudamore, art sound, . . . III. xi. 11. 6
for her sake a cowheard *vile* became . . . III. xi. 39. 3
The servant of Admetus, cowheard *vile*, . . . III. xi. 39. 4
Vile Poverty; and, lastly, Death with infamy. . . . III. xii. 25. 9
her before the *vile* Enchaunter sate, . . . III. xii. 31. 1
To give him the reward for such *vile* outrage dew. . . . III. xii. 33. 9
huge mischiefe and *vile* villany . . . III. xii. 35. 2
that same *vile* Enchauntour Busyran, . . . IV. i. 3. 1
Vile treason and fowle falshood hidden were, . . . IV. i. 17. 8
So false Duessa; but *vile* Ate thus: . . . IV. i. 47. 1
'*Vile* hag!' (sayd Scudamour) why dost thou lye, . . . IV. i. 48. 1
stop *vile* envies sting, . . . IV. ii. 26. 6
how from thraldome *vile* they were untide, . . . IV. viii. 21. 5
void of *vile* and treacherous intent, . . . IV. viii. 30. 5
vile curses and reprochfull shame . . . IV. xii. 16. 4
With bitter taunts and termes of *vile* disgrace. . . . V. v. 23. 4
apply His mightie hands the distaffe *vile* to hold . . . V. v. 24. 4
full many treasons *vile* His father Dolon had deviz'd . . . V. vi. 33. 7
These *vile* reproches gan unto her speake: . . . V. vi. 37. 3
her late *vile* reproch though vaunted vaine, . . . V. vii. 34. 4
whose tongue was for his trespasse *vyle* Nayld to a post, . . . V. ix. 25. 2
blotted with condition *vile* and base, . . . V. ix. 38. 5

Vile—*Continued.*
with the sting which in her *vile* tongue grew . . . V. xii. 42. 7
with *vile* tongue and venemous intent . . . VI. i. 8. 8
'*Vile* recreant! know that I doe much disdaine . . . VI. i. 27. 7
greedy to avenge that *vile* despight, . . . VI. iii. 45. 7
that *vile* lozell which her late offended; . . . VI. iv. 10. 2
ywroken Of all the *vile* demeane . . . VI. vi. 18. 4
with treason *vile* Hast slaine my men . . . VI. vi. 25. 1
'*Vile* cowheard dogge! now doe I much repent, . . . VI. vi. 33. 4
Be arguments of a *vile* donghill mind, . . . VI. vii. 1. 6
His foot he set on his *vile* necke, . . . VI. vii. 26. 4
how those Brigants *vyle* . . . Spoyld all our cots, . . . VI. xi. 30. 3
endammadge wight With his *vile* tongue, . . . VI. xii. 38. 4
Venemous toung, tipt with *vile* adders sting, . . . *Am.* lxxxv. 1
Therefore of clay, base, *vile*, and next to nought, . . . *H.H.L.* 106
Revyling him, that them most *vile* became, . . . *H.H.L.* 152
may Be seene of all his creatures *vile* and base, . . . *H.H.B.* 116
this *vile* world and these gay-seeming things; . . . *H.H.B.* 299
Vile-hearted. shake off this *vile harted* cowardree. . . . *Hub.* 986
Vilely. *See* **Vildly.**
Viler. Abandon, then, the base and *viler* clowne; . . . *S.C.* O. 37
Vilest. 'Thou clod of *vilest* clay, . . . III. x. 31. 2
Of all the passions in the mind thou *vilest* art! . . . III. xi. 1. 9
vassall to the *vilest* wretch alive, . . . IV. vii. 12. 2
Villain. with their *villeine* feete the streame did ray . . . *Bel.*[2] xii. 13
We met that *villen*, (God from him me blesse!) . . . I. ix. 28. 3
to the *villein* sayd; 'Thou damned wight, . . . I. ix. 37. 6
Then gan the *villein* him to overcraw, . . . I. ix. 50. 5
the *villein* sore did beate . . . his manly face; . . . II. iv. 9. 1
Where this same wicked *villein* did me light upon. . . . II. iv. 17. 9
Tho gan that *villein* wex so fiers and strong, . . . II. v. 23. 1
A sturdie *villein*, stryding stiffe and bold, . . . II. vii. 40. 4
nothing might abash the *villein* bold, . . . II. vii. 42. 8
in his flight the *villein* turn'd his face . . . II. xi. 26. 6
the *villein*, comming to their ayd, . . . II. xi. 29. 4
the *villeine* overthrowne Out of his swowne arose, . . . II. xi. 35. 3
no lesse the knight feard then that *villein* rude. . . . III. iv. 50. 9
Nathlesse the *villein* sped himselfe so well, . . . III. v. 14. 1
when that *villayn* he aviz'd, . . . III. v. 23. 1
'*Villein*,' (sayd he) 'this Lady is my deare; . . . III. viii. 12. 8
To save her honor from that *villaine* vilde, . . . III. viii. 27. 4
hayle The greedy *villein* from his hoped pray, . . . III. viii. 31. 6
the *villaine* selfe, their sorrowes sourse, . . . IV. vii. 20. 3
Thereto the *villaine* used craft in fight; . . . IV. vii. 26. 1
A *villaine* to them came with scull all raw, . . . V. ii. 11. 5
To weet, a wicked *villaine*, bold and stout, . . . V. ix. 4. 6
Eftsoones brought forth the *villaine*, . . . V. ix. 10. 2
when the *villaine* saw her so affrayd, . . . V. ix. 12. 4
So did the *villaine* to her prate and play, . . . V. ix. 13. 5
villaine, which had reft That piteous spoile . . . VI. i. 18. 4
running streight upon that *villaine* base, . . . VI. vi. 22. 3
the former *villaine*, which did lead Her tyreling jade, . . . VI. vii. 40. 6
The *villaine*, wroth for greeting him so sore, . . . VI. vii. 46. 1
The *villaine* stayd not aunswer to invent, . . . VI. viii. 8. 1
The *villaine* met him in the middle fall, . . . VI. viii. 10. 3
that other *villaine* went about Him to have bound . . . VI. viii. 11. 6
The *villaine*, leaving him unto his mate . . . VI. viii. 13. 1
Villainies. shame For his late *villanies.* . . . VI. vi. Arg.
Villainous. With so fell force, and *villeinous* despite, . . . III. v. 19. 2
with *villeinous* despight To blott her honour, . . . III. v. 45. 4
he thought, for *villeinous* despight, . . . III. xii. 32. 6
to have wrought unwares some *villanous* assay. . . . V. iv. 23. 9
him avenge of that so *villenous* despight. . . . VI. iv. 3. 9
Willing to worke his *villenous* intent . . . VI. vi. 44. 4
Villain's. so exceeding was the *villeins* powre, . . . I. vii. 12. 7
gan earne To understand that *villeins* dwelling place, . . . V. ix. 7. 2
ny Unto the rocke where was the *villains* won: . . . V. ix. 8. 2
by what traine She fell into that salvage *villaines* hand? . . . VI. v. 27. 8
when she saw him fall Under that *villaines* club, . . . VI. vii. 50. 2
in that *villaines* health her safety lies; . . . VI. viii. 18. 5
Villains. barbarous *villaines* in disordred heape, . . . *Bel.*[1] v. 10
A thousand *villeins* rownd about them swarmd . . . II. ix. 13. 2
That wicked band of *villeins* . . . II. xi. 5. 3
Led of two grysie *Villeins*, . . . III. xii. 19. 2
those two *villeins*, which her steps upstayd, . . . III. xii. 21. 5
one of those *villeins* him did rap . . . IV. v. 42. 3
what those *villaines* were, . . . V. xi. 48. 8
now he hath this troupe of *villains* sent . . . V. xi. 51. 1
those *villens* through their usage bad Them fouly rent, . . . V. xi. 60. 8
saw those *villaines* her so vildely use, . . . VI. vii. 45. 2
Beheld two such, of two such *villaines* thrall, . . . VI. viii. 5. 8
Whether I shall you leave, or from these *villaines* lose.' . . . VI. viii. 29. 9
Those *villeins* view'd with loose lascivious sight, . . . VI. viii. 43. 3
Villainy. be knowne for such thy *villanee.* . . . *S.C.* Jun. 104
Sweete Love devoyd of *villanie* or ill, . . . *T.M.* 387
To reskew her from shamefull *villany.* . . . III. i. 18. 5
huge mischiefe and vile *villany* . . . III. xii. 35. 2
That can her best defend from *villenie;* . . . IV. v. 1. 7
defiled with foule *villanie* The sacred pledge . . . IV. vi. 8. 2
evermore from *villenie* her kept: . . . IV. vi. 35. 7
For horrour of his shamefull *villany:* . . . IV. vii. 21. 5
To have revenged that his *villeny;* . . . V. iii. 36. 2
armes dishonour with base *villanie*, . . . V. iii. 38. 7
wrought all the *villany* That she could forge . . . V. iv. 29. 7
With full intent t' avenge that *villany* . . . V. vi. 35. 4
And saved from his cruell *villany.* . . . VI. iii. 51. 7
Withouten thought of shame or *villeny*, . . . VI. v. 9. 8
cowardize doth still in *villany* delight. . . . VI. vi. 26. 9
Where he mote worke him scath and *villeny.* . . . VI. vii. 3. 5
The Prince much mused at such *villenie*, . . . VI. vii. 13. 1

Villainy—*Continued.*
Would not be tempted to such *villenie*, ... VI. vii. 23. 2
afeard Of *villany* to be to her inferd: . . . . VI. viii. 31. 5
Villeinage. No wretchednesse is like to sinfull *vellenage*. . . . II. xi. 1. 9
Viminal. Mount *Viminall* and Aventine doo meete. . . . . . *Ro.* iv. 14
Vine. over them spred a goodly wild *vine*, ... *S.C.* Au. 29
His looser locks doth wrap in wreath of *vine:* . . . . *Gn.* 114
load the braunches of the fruitfull *vine;* . . . . *Col.* 601
Over the which was cast a wandring *vine*, ... II. ix. 24. 4
Archt over head with an embracing *vine*, ... II. xii. 54. 2
He turnd himselfe into a fruitfull *vine*, ... III. xi. 43. 8
forth she brought The fruitfull *vine;* . . . . V. vii. 11. 3
Hymen also crowne with wreathes of *vine;* . . . . *Epith.* 256
Vine-leaves. In greene *vine leaves* he was right fitly clad, . . I. iv. 22. 1
Vine-prop. The *vine-propp* Elme; . . . . I. i. 8. 7
Violate. Nor ordinaunce so needfull, but that hee Would *violate*, *Hub.* 1163
Their tender buds or leaves to *violate;* . . . . II. xii. 51. 4
That beautie durst presume to *violate*, ... III. viii. 36. 2
Violence. violate, though not with *violence*, ... *Hub.* 1163
Did fayre avoide the *violence* him nere: . . . . I. viii. 7. 8
almost it did haynous *violence* . . . . II. i. 28. 6
That broke the *violence* of his intent, ... II. v. 6. 6
Them to efforce by *violence* or wrong: . . . . II. vii. 30. 4
This land invaded with like *violence*, ... II. x. 15. 6
in strong bancks his *violence* enclose, ... III. vii. 34. 2
Of strong compulsion and streight *violence*, ... V. v. 33. 2
To reskue her from their rude *violence;* . . . . V. xi. 45. 2
having long eschew'd His *violence* in vaine; . . . . VI. iii. 50. 6
did from further *violence* restraine, ... VI. v. 27. 4
by some other *violence* despoyled: . . . . VI. vii. 33. 5
With cruell rage and dreadfull *violence*, ... VI. xi. 30. 4
th' outrage of his *violence* he stayd, ... VI. xii. 29. 3
Violent. harde by a *violent* streame, ... *Bel.*[1] xi. 7
With *violent* swift flight forth caried . . . . *Mui.* 422
two then all more huge and *violent*, ... II. xi. 9. 8
streame more *violent* and greedy growes: . . . . II. xii. 5. 3
Did afterwards make shipwrack *violent* . . . . II. xii. 7. 8
strooke at him with force so *violent*, ... III. v. 25. 4
with such force and furie *violent* . . . . V. xii. 17. 5
makes his way more *violent;* . . . . VI. i. 21. 5
But still his passion grew more *violent* . . . . VI. ii. 21. 9
Violently. The cup to ground did *violently* cast, ... II. xii. 57. 3
Violet. Embellish the sweete *Violet*. . . . . *S.C.* Ap. 63
She sweeter then the *Violet*. . . . . *S.C.* Au. 72
The Lilly fresh, and *Violet* belowe; . . . . *Gn.* 667
the *Violet*, pallid blew, ... *Proth.* 30
Violets. Of sweete *Violets* therein was store, ... *S.C.* Au. 71
Coole *Violets*, and Orpine growing still, ... *Mui.* 193
fragrant *violets*, and Paunces trim; . . . . III. i. 36. 8
She bath'd with roses red and *violets* blew, ... III. vi. 6. 8
Lay her in lillies and in *violets*, ... *Epith.* 302
Violins. the other Muses trace, With their *Violines*. . . . . *S.C.* Ap. 103
Viper's. In which thou lurkest lyke to *vipers* brood; . . . . . *Am.* ii. 6
Virelays. if thou algate lust light *virelayes*, ... *S.C.* N. 21
or sing your *virelayes?* . . . . *D.* 317
Bransles, Ballads, *virelayes*, and verses vaine; . . . . . . III. x. 8. 5
Virgil's. By paterne of great *Virgils* spirit divine! . . . . . *Ro.* xxv. 11
Virgin. Hard by a rivers side a *virgin* faire, ... *Bel.*[2] x. 1
(O monthly *Virgin!*) thou delay Thy nightly course, . . . *Gn.* 459
Like *virgin* Queenes, with laurell garlands cround . . . . . *T.M.* 309
Therein a goodly *Virgine* sleeping lay; . . . . *Ti.* 636
Upon a *virgin* brydes adorned head, ... *Col.* 338
O holy *virgin!* chiefe of nyne, ... I. Pr. 2. 1
like that *virgin* true which for her knight him took. . . . . I. i. 49. 9
The royall *virgin* shooke off drousy-hed; . . . . I. ii. 7. 5
I straid, A *virgin* widow, ... I. ii. 24. 8
Soone as the royall *virgin* he did spy, ... I. iii. 5. 4
Arose the *virgin*, borne of heavenly brood, ... I. iii. 8. 7
to the *virgin* comes; . . . . I. iii. 40. 1
heavens! that doe . . . heavenly *virgin* thus outraged see, . I. vi. 5. 7
the *virgin*, doolfull, desolate, With ruffled rayments, . . . I. vi. 9. 2
The gentle *virgin*, left behinde alone, ... I. vi. 33. 3
Faire *virgin*, to redeeme her deare, ... I. viii. Arg.
The roiall *Virgin* which beheld from farre, ... I. viii. 26. 1
What hath poore *Virgin* . . . Wherewith you to reward? . . . I. viii. 27. 3
'Faire *virgin*,' (said the Prince,) . . . . I. ix. 3. 1
O fayrest *virgin!* full of heavenly light, ... I. ix. 17. 3
Most vertuous *virgin*, borne of hevenly berth, ... I. x. 9. 3
To aide a *virgin* desolate, foredonne; . . . . I. x. 60. 4
Up rose the gentle *virgin* from her place, ... I. xi. 33. 5
this fayre *virgin* wearie of her way . . . . I. xii. 1. 6
they came where that faire *virgin* stood: . . . . I. xii. 7. 6
Laid first his filthie hands on *virgin* cleene, ... II. i. 10. 4
As a chaste *Virgin* that had wronged beene: . . . . II. i. 21. 5
Great and most glorious *virgin* Queene alive, ... II. ii. 40. 3
taking Conge of that *virgin* pure, ... II. iii. 2. 1
Alma she called was; a *virgin* bright, ... II. ix. 18. 1
the sad *virgin*, innocent of all, ... II. x. 19. 6
Alma, like a *virgin* Queene most bright, ... II. xi. 2. 6
The noble *Virgin*, Ladie of the Place, ... II. xi. 16. 1
forth from *virgin* bowre she comes in th' early morne. . . . II. xii. 50. 9
see the *Virgin* Rose, how sweetly shee . . . . II. xii. 74. 4
fell intent, against the *virgin* sheene: . . . . III. i. 65. 4
much cheard the feeble spright Of the sicke *virgin*, ... III. ii. 47. 2
Shee to the *virgin* sayd, thrise sayd she itt; . . . . . . III. ii. 50. 6
a sore evill, which this *virgin* bright Tormenteth . . . . . III. iii. 16. 4
'Most noble *Virgin*, that by fatall lore . . . . III. iii. 21. 6
Then shall a royall *Virgin* raine, ... III. iii. 49. 6
I saw a Saxon *Virgin*, ... III. iii. 55. 5
Thus when she had the *virgin* all arayd, ... III. iii. 61. 1

Virgin—*Continued.*
A *virgin* straunge and stout him should dismay or kill. . . III. iv. 25. 9
Most sacred *virgin* without spot of sinne. . . . . III. iv. 59. 8
The bountiest *virgin* and most debonaire . . . . III. v. 8. 2
this faire *virgin*, this Belphebe fayre; . . . . III. v. 54. 2
So was this *virgin* borne, so was she bred; . . . . III. vi. 3. 6
'Beldame, be not wroth With silly *Virgin*, ... III. vii. 8. 7
the fayre *Virgin* was so meeke and myld, ... III. vii. 15. 1
The golden ribband, which that *virgin* wore . . . . III. vii. 36. 1
a faire *virgin* that . . . above all Dames is deemd, ... III. vii. 52. 3
virgin wex that never yet was seald, ... III. viii. 6. 7
The silly *virgin* strove him to withstand . . . . III. viii. 27. 1
The *virgin* whom he had abusde so sore; . . . . III. viii. 36. 6
Most vertuous *virgin!* glory be thy meed, ... III. viii. 42. 6
Which the bold *Virgin* seeing . . . . III. xi. 13. 8
Soone as that *virgin* knight he saw in place, ... III. xii. 32. 1
Exceeding wroth therewith the *virgin* grew, ... III. xii. 33. 6
profest a *virgine* wife. . . . . IV. i. 6. 9
The warlike *virgine* . . . wexed inlie wroth; . . . . IV. i. 10. 5
chalenging the *Virgin* as his dew, ... IV. iii. 14. 8
To know what *Virgin* did them thence unbind, ... IV. viii. 22. 2
Upon a recluse *Virgin* to lay hold, ... IV. x. 54. 4
So home with her she streight the *virgin* lad, ... IV. xii. 33. 8
is the *Virgin*, sixt in her degree, ... V. i. 11. 8
'Magnificke *Virgin*, that . . . doest maske thy royall blood, . V. vii. 21. 1
the righteous *Virgin*, which of old Liv'd here . . . . . . VII. vii. 37. 6
Clad all in white, that seemes a *virgin* best. . . . . . . *Epith.* 151
A pallace fit for such a *virgin* Queene. . . . . *H.B.* 126
The *virgin* Lillie, and the Primrose trew, ... *Proth.* 32
Virginal. Of chastity and honour *virginall:* . . . . II. i. 10. 8
delight Shee to them made, with mildnesse *virginall*, ... II. ix. 20. 4
Of chastity and vertue *virginall*, ... III. v. 53. 6
Virginals. Playing alone carelesse on hir heavenlie *Virginals*. *U.V.* 6
If at hir *Virginals*, tell hir, I can heare no mirth. . . . . . *U.V.* 9
Virginia. fruitfullest *Virginia* who did ever vew? . . . . . . II. Pr. 2. 9
Virgin's. Abett that *virgins* cause disconsolate, ... I. x. 64. 2
Transformd her to a stone from stedfast *virgins* state. . . . . II. ii. 8. 9
pitty did the *Virgins* hart of patience rob. . . . . III. xi. 8. 9
That horrour gan the *virgins* hart to perse, ... III. xii. 36. 5
untide . . . by *Virgins* hond; . . . . IV. viii. 21. 6
That *Virgins* love to win by wit or wile, ... IV. xi. 2. 3
taking flesh of sacred *virgins* wombe, ... *H.H.L.* 146
Virgins. you *Virgins*, that on Parnasse dwell, ... *S.C.* Ap. 41
Elisa . . . That blessed wight, The flowre of *Virgins:* . . . . *S.C.* Ap. 48
Let none come there but that *Virgins* bene, ... *S.C.* Ap. 129
Fidelia and Speranza, *virgins* were; . . . . I. x. 4. 6
two most goodly *virgins* came in place, ... I. x. 12. 2
The comely *virgins* came, with girlands dight, ... I. xii. 6. 6
ill your goddesse services are drest By *virgins*, ... IV. x. 54. 9
A bevie of faire *Virgins* clad in white, ... V. ix. 31. 2
they were *virgins* all, and love eschewed . . . . VII. vii. 45. 4
Let all the *virgins* therefore well awayt: . . . . *Epith.* 111
Why stand ye still ye *virgins* in amaze, ... *Epith.* 181
Of her ye *virgins* learne obedience, ... *Epith.* 212
Virtue. All heavenly grace and *vertue* shrined is, ... *Pet.*[2] vii. 10
This peoples *vertue* yet so fruitfull was . . . . *Ro.* viii. 5
when the object of her *vertue* failed, ... *Ro.* xxi. 9
after *vertue* gan for age to stoope, ... *S.C.* O. 67
Horatii that in *vertue* did excell. . . . . *Gn.* 600
vertue to advaunce, and vice deride, ... *Hub.* 812
our chast bowers, in which all *vertue* rained, ... *T.M.* 269
strive in *vertue* others to excell, ... *T.M.* 452
Therefore the nurse of *vertue* I am hight, ... *T.M.* 457
yong-man, whose *vertue* found So brave a Trompe, ... *Ti.* 433
To see that *vertue* should dispised bee . . . . *Ti.* 450
whatso else of *vertue* good or ill . . . . *Mui.* 201
'No age hath bred . . . more *vertue* in a wight; . . . . . . *D.* 219
Advancing *vertue* and suppressing vice. . . . . *Col.* 323
The floure of *vertue* and pure chastitie, ... *Col.* 469
thy chaste life and *vertue* I esteeme: . . . . *Col.* 573
For love of *vertue* and of Martiall praise; . . . . *Ded. Son.* x. 6
Vertue gives her selfe light through darknesse for to wade.' . I. i. 12. 9
the sleeping spark Of native *vertue* gan eftsoones revive; . . I. ii. 19. 2
you, fresh budd of *vertue* springing fast, ... I. viii. 27. 1
liquor . . . Of wondrous worth, and *vertue* excellent, ... I. ix. 19. 4
other secret *vertue* did ensew; . . . . I. xi. 36. 5
Had *vertue* pourd into their waters bace, ... II. ii. 6. 8
Doth nourish *vertue*, and fast friendship breeds, ... II. ii. 31. 2
All *vertue* merits praise, ... II. iii. 37. 9
vertue vauntes in both her victories, ... II. vi. 1. 8
hidden *vertue* to it gave. . . . . II. viii. 20. 9
'The *vertue* is, that nether steele nor stone . . . . II. viii. 21. 1
Such life ye read, and *vertue* in vaine shew; . . . . II. ix. 3. 2
'Seldom' (said Guyon) 'yields to *vertue* aide, ... II. ix. 8. 2
this brave knight, that for this *vertue* fightes, ... II. xii. 1. 6
Such *vertue* in his staffe had eke this Palmer sage. . . . . . II. xii. 41. 9
The fayrest *vertue*, far above the rest: . . . . III. Pr. 1. 2
The secrete *vertue* of that weapon keene, ... III. i. 10. 5
It *vertue* had to shew in perfect sight . . . . III. ii. 19. 1
choseth *vertue* for his dearest Dame, ... III. iii. 1. 8
for pure chastitee and *vertue* rare, ... III. iv. 3. 4
In stedfast chastitie and *vertue* rare, ... III. v. 8. 5
Of chastity and *vertue* virginall, ... III. v. 53. 6
In all chaste *vertue* and true bounti-hed, ... III. vi. 3. 8
Your *vertue* selfe her owne reward shall breed, ... III. xii. 39. 5
it of honor and all *vertue* is The roote, ... IV. Pr. 2. 6
vertue is the band that bindeth harts most sure. . . . . . . IV. ii. 29. 9
Well was that rings great *vertue* knowen to all; . . . . . . IV. ii. 40. 1
All was through *vertue* of the ring he wore; . . . . IV. iii. 24. 1
Ne felt his blood to wast, . . . Through that rings *vertue*, . . IV. iii. 29. 3

Voice—*Continued.*
at last I heard a *voyce,* . . . *Ti.* 580
I heard a *voyce* that called farre away, . . . *Ti.* 638
when she list advance her heavenly *voyce,* . . . *D.* 313
my *voyce* is spent with crying; . . . *D.* 414
Therewith a piteous yelling *voice* was heard, . . . I. ii. 31. 1
'What *voice* of damned Ghost from Limbo lake, . . . I. ii. 32. 5
when they heard that pitteous strained *voice,* . . . I. vi. 8. 1
Nor *voice* was heard, nor wight was seene . . . I. viii. 29. 9
a little grate . . . Through which he sent his *voyce,* . . . I. viii. 37. 7
an hollow, dreary, murmuring *voyce* . . . I. viii. 38. 1
an Angels *voice* Singing before th' eternall majesty, . . . I. xii. 39. 3
They heard a ruefull *voice,* . . . II. i. 35. 7
goodly counsell, . . . tempred with sweete *voice:* . . . II. i. 44. 3
with big thundring *voice* revyld him lowd: . . . II. iii. 7. 3
Nor *voyce* sound mortall; . . . II. iii. 33. 4
Crying with pitteous *voyce,* . . . II. vi. 32. 4
a *voyce* that called lowd and cleare, . . . II. viii. 3. 7
Againe he heard a more efforced *voyce,* . . . II. viii. 4. 3
Their notes unto the *voice* attempred sweet; . . . II. xii. 71. 2
Certein sad words with hollow *voice* and bace, . . . III. ii. 50. 5
'Who would not to this vertue rather yeeld his *voice?* . . . IV. iii. 45. 9
hundred mouthes, and *voice* of brasse I had, . . . IV. xi. 9. 7
He heard the lamentable *voice* of one, . . . IV. xii. 5. 2
All creatures must obey the *voice* of the Most Hie. . . . V. ii. 40. 9
Whose *voice* so soone as he did undertake, . . . V. iii. 34. 4
of a man, they say, It has the *voice,* . . . V. xi. 20. 7
hearkning to that *voice,* . . . VI. i. 19. 1
he heard . . . A *voice,* that seemed of some woman kynd, . . . VI. iv. 26. 7
with the peoples *voyce* Confused, . . . VI. viii. 46. 2
by common *voice* esteemed The father . . . VI. ix. 14. 1
Knowing his *voice,* although not heard long sin, . . . VI. xi. 44. 3
running straight where-as she heard his *voice,* . . . VII. vi. 47. 3
'Whats this (quoth he) that gives so great a *voyce* . . . *Epig.* iv. 7
As if it were one *voyce,* . . . *Epith.* 139

Voice's. *voyces* silver sound . . . can chaunge my cherelesse cryes. . . . *S.C.* Au. 181
whose *voices* knowen sound . . . III. xii. 43. *or.* 8

Voices. frogs . . . their jarring *voyces* bent, . . . *Gn.* 230
th' hollow hills, from which their silver *voyces* . . . *T.M.* 21
Bardes, that . . . Can tune their timely *voices* . . . I. v. 3. 7
Birdes, *voices,* instruments, windes, waters, . . . II. xii. 70. 9
Th' Angelicall soft trembling *voyces* . . . II. xii. 71. 3

Void. faithlesse Rosalind and *voide* of grace, . . . *S.C.* Jun. 115
Let all, that sweete is, *voyd:* . . . *S.C.* Au. 164
anie Should of his race be *voyd* of infamie; . . . *Hub.* 1242
Simple in shew, and *voide* of malice bad; . . . I. i. 29. 7
he slept soundly *void* of evil thought, . . . I. i. 46. 3
In slombring swownd, nigh *voyd* of vitall spright, . . . I. v. 19. 5
presently was *void* and wholly vaine: . . . I. viii. 4. 7
Voide of all succour and needfull comfort; . . . II. v. 17. 5
come unto an Island waste and *voyd,* . . . II. vi. 11. 3
wholy waste and *void* of peoples trode, . . . III. ix. 49. 7
his speare he gan abase And *voide* his course: . . . IV. vi. 3. 5
void of vile and treacherous intent, . . . IV. viii. 30. 5
all *voide* of doubtfull feare, . . . IV. ix. 5. 7
Most *voide* of guile, most free from fowle despight, . . . IV. xi. 18. 8
In her faire visage *voide* of ornament, . . . V. xii. 4
Voide of malitious mind or foule offence: . . . V. v. 33. 5
All dewfull service, *voide* of thoughts impure; . . . VI. x. 32. 6
reft of sense And *voyd* of speech . . . VII. vi. 25. 5
Exceeding sweet, yet *voyd* of sinfull vice; . . . *Am.* lxxvii. 9
voide of all blemishment; . . . *H.B.* 215
sonne . . . Eternall, pure, and *voide* of sinfull blot, . . . *H.H.L.* 32

Voided. When thus the field was *voided* all away, . . . V. iv. 46. 1
Were bound about and *voyded* from before; . . . VI. vii. 43. 8

Voidness. *voydnesse* to seeke full satietie. . . . *Col.* 850

Volume. My *volume* shall renowne, . . . *Gn.* 48
it was a great And ample *volume,* . . . II. x. 70. 3
In thy great *volume* of Eternitye: . . . III. iii. 4. 5
Thy acts, O Scanderbeg, this *volume* tels. . . . *Com.Son.*iii.14

Voluntary. she gan appease Her *voluntarie* paine, . . . II. i. 16. 9
The sea unto him *voluntary* brings; . . . III. iv. 23. 7
of *voluntary* grace And soveraine favor . . . III. viii. 29. 2
looke to whom she *voluntarie* came, . . . IV. v. 25. 7
Was dight with flowers that *voluntary* grew . . . VII. vii. 10. 2

Voluptuous. Made dronke with drugs of deare *voluptuous* receipt. II. v. 34. 9
fell to vaine *voluptuous* disease: . . . II. x. 17. 5

Vomit. Her *vomit* full of bookes and papers was, . . . I. i. 20. 6
He soone in *vomit* up againe doth lay, . . . II. xii. 3. 7

Vortigern. their uncle *Vortigere* Usurpt the crowne . . . II. x. 64. 2
Vortiger have forst the kingdome to aband. . . . II. x. 65. 9
The crowne which *Vortiger* did long detayne: . . . II. x. 67. 4

Vortimer. by the helpe of *Vortimere* his sonne, . . . II. x. 66. 1

Vortipore. 'His sonne, hight *Vortipore,* shall him succeede . . . III. iii. 31. 1

Votaries. Vaine *votaries* of laesie Love professe, . . . *Col.* 766

Vouch. *vouch* antiquities, which no body can know. . . . II. Pr. 1. 9

Vouchsafe. *Vouchsafe* ye then, whom onely it concernes, . . . *T.M.* 49
Vouchsafe this moniment of his last praise . . . *Ti.* 682
The roote whereof and tragicall effect, *Vouchsafe,* . . . *Mui.* 10
when life parts *vouchsafe* to close mine eye. . . . *D.* 511
Vouchsafe to deck the same with Cyparesse; . . . *D.* 529
Them to *vouchsafe* emongst his rimes to name, . . . *As.* 38
so much grace let her *vouchsafe* to grant . . . *Col.* 939
vouchsafe thy noble countenaunce To these . . . *Ded. Son.* ii. 13
Vouchsafe in worth this small guift to receave, . . . *Ded. Son.* vii. 8
The which *vouchsafe,* dear Lord, your favorable doome. . . . *Ded.Son.*vii.14
Such as they be, *vouchsafe* them to receave, . . . *Ded. Son.* ix. 13
vouchsafe it to maintaine Against . . . backbitings . . . *Ded.Son.*xii.13
Vouchsafe from him this token in good worth to take. . . . *Ded. Son.* xv. 14

Vouchsafe—*Continued.*
The which to heare *vouchsafe,* O dearest dread, . . . I. Pr. 4. 9
'Mercy, mercy, Sir, *vouchsafe* to show On silly Dame, . . . I. ii. 21. 2
vouchsafe with patient eare The brave adventures . . . II. Pr. 5. 6
Vouchsafe to stay your steed . . . II. i. 8. 9
doe *vouchsafe* now to receive reliefe, . . . II. i. 16. 3
vouchsafe her honorable toombe.' . . . II. i. 58. 9
doth not highest God *vouchsafe* to take The love . . . III. v. 47. 6
Vouchsafe with mild regard a wretches cace to heare.' . . . III. x. 26. 9
Vouchsafe to reskue her against a Knight, . . . VI. i. 29. 6
Yet, as I well it meane, *vouchsafe* it without blame. . . . VI. iv. 34. 9
Vouchsafe, O Goddesse! to thy presence call The rest . . . VII. vii. 27. 2
Yet lowly still *vouchsafe* to looke on me; . . . *Am.* xiii. 13
That she will once *vouchsafe* my plaint to heare, . . . *Am.* xviii. 7
vouchsafe, O goddesse, to accept, . . . *Am.* xxii. 13
till she *vouchsafe* to grawnt me rest; . . . *Am.* xxxiii. 13
if thou wouldst *vouchsafe* to overspred Me . . . *H.L.* 19
vouchsafe to take of me This simple song, . . . *H.L.* 306
vouchsafe with thy love-kindling light . . . *H.B.* 19
Vouchsafe to shed into my barren spright . . . *H.H.L.* 45
Vouchsafe then, O thou most Almightie Spright! . . . *H.H.B.* 8

Vouchsafed. scarce *vouchsafte* them to requite. . . . *Hub.* 587
say, who else *vouchsafed* thee of grace?' . . . *Col.* 484
Ne other grace *vouchsafed* them to showe . . . I. iv. 14. 3
hevens just with equall brow *Vouchsafed* to behold us . . . II. i. 50. 4
vouchsafed to embace Her goodly port, . . . III. vii. 15. 2
Have not *vouchsaft* to graunt unto us twaine . . . VI. iv. 31. 2

Vouchsafes. none *vouchsafes* to answere to our call; . . . *T.M.* 352

Vouchsafeth. Or once *vouchsafeth* us to entertaine, . . . *T.M.* 344
those whom shee *Vouchsafeth* to her presence to receave, . . . *H.H.B.* 254

Vow. Ne may thee help the manie hartie *vow,* . . . *Mui.* 237
'And never *vow* to rest, till her I find, . . . I. ix. 15. 8
Nyne monethes I seek in vain, yet ni'll that *vow* unbynd.' . . . I. ix. 15. 9
Bynempt a sacred *vow,* which none should ay releace. . . . II. i. 60. 9
Sir Guyon, mindfull of his *vow* yplight, . . . II. iii. 1. 5
for my part, I *vow,* dissembled not a whitt. . . . II. iv. 18. 9
By Stygian lake I *vow,* . . . III. vi. 24. 7
the *vow* that to faire Columbell I plighted have, . . . III. vii. 51. 6
read, thou Squyre of Dames, what *vow* is this, . . . III. vii. 53. 2
The wicked weapon heard his wrathfull *vow,* . . . IV. iii. 11. 6
I *vow* you dead or living not to leave, . . . IV. vi. 38. 8
threw away, with *vow* to use no more, . . . IV. vii. 39. 2
vow by Mahoune that he should be slaine. . . . IV. viii. 44. 3
by the *vow* of their religion, . . . V. vii. 9. 6
by the holy *vow* which me doth bind, . . . V. vii. 19. 7
though revengefull *vow* she did professe, . . . V. vii. 36. 3
fatally did *vow* To wreake her on that mayden messengere, . . . V. viii. 46. 3
But I am bound by *vow,* . . . VI. ii. 37. 5
In streight observaunce of religious *vow,* . . . VI. v. 35. 6
Unmyndfull of his *vow,* and high beheast . . . VI. x. 1. 3
Is wont to wield the world unto his *vow,* . . . VII. vi. 22. 3
in her songs, sends many a wishfull *vow* . . . *Am.* lxxxviii. 3
Encline thy will t' effect our wishfull *vow,* . . . *Epith.* 385

Vowed. he has *voued* thy last confusion. . . . *S.C.* May 220
the daye in woe, I *vowed* have to wayst, . . . *S.C.* Au. 180
his *vowed* life to spill For Countreyes health, . . . *Gn.* 603
To whom the ruin'd walls of Carthage *vow'd,* . . . *Gn.* 615
To her he *vowd* the service of his daies, . . . *As.* 61
with brave deeds to her sole service *vowed,* . . . *As.* 69
One ever I all *vowed* hers to bee, . . . *Col.* 478
My . . . service, that by land and seas Have *vowd* you to defend. I. iii. 29. 9
she, all *vowd* unto the Redcrosse Knight, . . . I. vi. 32. 1
never *vowd* to rest till her I fynd: . . . I. ix. 15. 8
had *vowed* all Their life to service of high heavens King, . . . I. x. 36. 3
vowed foe of my felicity; . . . I. xii. 19. 3
The marriage to accomplish *vowd* betwixt you twayn. . . . I. xii. 19. 9
vowd to so diverse loves, . . . II. ii. 19. 1
hath *vowd* . . . never to wearen none: . . . II. iii. 12. 7
Our selves in league of *vowed* love wee knitt: . . . II. iv. 18. 6
For he has *vowd* to beene avengd that day . . . II. v. 38. 5
care of *vow'd* revenge and cruell fight, . . . II. vi. 8. 4
that in . . . honours suit my *vowed* daies do spend, . . . II. vii. 10. 2
Which to avenge on him they dearly *vowd,* . . . II. viii. 11. 1
vowd with all their power and witt . . . III. i. 12. 3
vowed never to returne againe, . . . III. v. 10. 3
vow'd that never he alive Out of that forest should escape . . . III. v. 16. 7
Whom she hath *vow'd* to dub a fayre Cucquold. . . . III. x. 11. 5
His armes, which he had *vowed* to disprofesse, . . . III. xi. 20. 4
of fayned friendship which they *vow'd* afore. . . . IV. ii. 18. 9
vow'd with speare and shield it to maintaine; . . . IV. v. 24. 8
All on her gazing wisht, and *vowd,* and prayd, . . . IV. v. 26. 3
for his sake *vow'd* to doe all the ill . . . V. iv. 30. 8
The last daies purpose of their *vowed* fight, . . . V. v. 1. 6
she *vow'd,* with many a cursed threat, . . . V. v. 47. 6
she had *vow'd* . . . not to forgo Those warlike weedes, . . . V. vi. 23. 6
her restored trustily, As he had *vow'd,* . . . VI. iii. 19. 7
each the other *vow'd* t' accompany: . . . VI. vi. 16. 1
often him besought, and prayd, and *vowd,* . . . VI. vi. 31. 7
Had *vow'd* unto the victor him to trace . . . VI. vii. 21. 7
so sacred threasure *Vow'd* to the gods: . . . VI. viii. 43. 9
the Fox, the *vowed* foe Unto my Lambes, . . . VI. ix. 23. 1
mixed threats among, and much unto her *vowed.* . . . VI. xi. 4. 9
he *vow'd* to be her debter For many moe good turnes . . . VII. vi. 44. 7
this verse, *vowd* to eternity, . . . *Am.* lxix. 9

Vowing. *vowing* great love to mee. . . . IV. viii. 59. 9
vowing not to start, But wayt on him . . . VI. ii. 36. 4
Vowing that never he in bed againe . . . VI. iv. 40. 6

Vows. Till that you come where ye your *vowes* assoyle, . . . *D.* 535
He hurles out *vowes,* and Neptune oft doth blesse . . . I. iii. 32. 5
vowes may not be vayne) . . . I. xii. 19. 6

Vows—*Continued.*
'What meane these bloody *vowes* and idle threats, . . . I. xii. 30. 1
With sacred rites and *vowes* for ever to abyde. . . . I. xii. 36. 9
soveraine moniment of mortall *vowes,* . . . II. iii. 25. 7
all his *vowes* make vayne; . . . II. xi. 18. 8
all men threw out *vowes* and wishes vaine. . . . IV. iv. 16. 6
through many *vowes* which forth he pour'd, . . . IV. vi. 41. 6
thousand *vowes* from bottome of his hart, . . . IV. vi. 43. 4
which all Asia sought with *vowes* prophane, . . . IV. x. 30. 3
The which sad lovers for their *vowes* did pay; . . . IV. x. 37. 8
in them bore true lovers *vowes* entire: . . . IV. x. 38. 5
Makes th' heavens . . . him with *vowes* asswage. . . . VI. vi. 11. 9
fooles therefore They are which fortunes doe by *vowes* devize, VI. ix. 30. 8
Playnts, prayers, *vowes,* ruth, . . . *Am.* xiv. 11
Voyage. fortunes, which to thee befell In thy late *voyage,* . *Col.* 34
'Foorth on our *voyage* we by land did passe, . . . *Col.* 330
With fresh desire his *voyage* to pursew; . . . I. ix. 18. 4
streightway on that last long *voiage* fare, . . . I. x. 63. 4
Discourst his *voyage* long, according his request. . . . I. xii. 15. 9
On the long *voiage* whereto she is bent: . . . I. xii. 42. 8
Then Guyon forward gan his *voyage* make . . . II. i. 34. 3
his *voyage* to poursew. . . . II. v. 25. 3
Upon his *voyage* with his trustie guyde, . . . II. xi. 5. 2
Which to prove, I this *voyage* have begonne. . . . III. ii. 8. 5
voyage rashly make By this forbidden way . . . III. iv. 14. 5
forth upon his former *voiage* fared, . . . IV. v. 46. 2

Voyage—*Continued.*
Upon his *voyage* forth he gan to fare . . . V. x. 17. 5
to his *voyage* gan againe proceed; . . . V. xi. 65. 8
In which her circles *voyage* is fulfild, . . . *Am.* lx. 3
Vulcan. to defend The force of *Vulcane* . . . *Gn.* 524
No lesse than that which *Vulcane* made . . . *Mui.* 63
Her husband *Vulcan* whylome for her sake, . . . IV. v. 4. 1
Vulcan, of this with us so usuall; . . . VII. vii. 26. 5
Vulcan's. fiers *Vulcans* rage to tame, . . . II. vii. 36. 5
To dry them selves by *Vulcanes* flaming light, . . . III. ix. 19. 8
Vulgar. though the *vulgar* yeeld an open eare, . . . *Hub.* 713
with vaine toyes the *vulgare* entertaine; . . . *T.M.* 194
They to the *vulgar* sort now pipe and sing, . . . *T.M.* 319
the base *vulgar,* that with hands uncleane . . . *T.M.* 567
Southsayer, seeing so sad sight, Th' amazed *vulgar* telles . I. v. 8. 9
difference Betweene the *vulgar* and the noble seed, . . . II. iv. 1. 3
heap'd together with the *vulgar* sort, . . . III. xi. 46. 2
to the *vulgare* beckning with his hand, . . . III. xii. 4. 3
Bred in assemblies of the *vulgar* sort, . . . IV. i. 28. 4
Unto the *vulgar* for good gold insted, . . . IV. v. 15. 4
Therefore the *vulgar* did about him flocke, . . . V. ii. 33. 1
So feeble skill of perfect things the *vulgar* has. . . . V. iii. 17. 9
all the *vulgar* did about them throng . . . V. xi. 34. 7
Vulture. Tityus fed a *vultur* on his maw; . . . I. v. 35. 6
a *Vulture* greedie of his pray, . . . IV. iii. 19. 1
Vultures. griesly *vultures,* make us once affeard: . . . *Epith.* 348

W

Wad. In simple cratch, wrapt in a *wad* of hay, . . . *H.H.L.* 226
Wade. light through darknesse for to *wade.'* . . . I. i. 12. 9
Thus in still waves of deepe delight to *wade,* . . . II. v. 35. 2
Through which it was uneath for wight to *wade;* . . . III. v. 17. 3
Ne durst assay to *wade* the perlous seas, . . . III. vii. 28. 3
wade in doubt what best were to be donne; . . . IV. x. 53. 2
As that in rivers swim, or brookes doe *wade;* . . . IV. xi. 9. 5
Waded. over shoes in blood he *waded* on the grownd. . . . I. viii. 16. 9
the cold liquor which he *waded* in; . . . II. vii. 58. 3
waves, through which he *waded* for his loves delight. . . . VII. vii. 33. 9
Wading. *wading* through the waves with stedfast sway, . . . V. xii. 5. 6
strongly *wading* through the waves unused, . . . VI. iii. 33. 7
Wae. *See* **Woe.**
(*wae* is me therefore!) . . . *S.C.* S. 25
Wag. They wont in the wind *wagge* their wrigle tayles, . . . *S.C.* F. 7
Which neither able were to *wag,* or once to weld. . . . IV. iv. 18. 9
That lim he could not *wag:* . . . V. i. 22. 5
Ere flitting Time could *wag* his eyas wings . . . *H.H.L.* 24
Wage. Whose witt is weakenesse, whose *wage* is death, . . . *S.C.* F. 88
th' Elfin knight, which ought that warlike *wage,* . . . I. iv. 39. 7
must *wage* Thy workes for wealth, . . . II. vii. 18. 4
battell strong to *wage* Gainst all those knights, . . . IV. ii. 28. 7
as his most worthie *wage* That could her purchase . . . IV. iii. 4. 8
Waged. there is Corydon though meanly *waged,* . . . *Col.* 382
Wager. who shall judge the *wager* wonne or lost? . . . *S.C.* Au. 44
As if her life upon the *wager* lay; . . . I. iii. 12. 2
which of those Knights . . . had the *wager* wonne: . . . IV. v. 7. 2
Is not (I *wager*) Florimell at all; . . . V. iii. 22. 6
Wag-mires. they bene like foule *wagmoires* overgrast, . . . *S.C.* S. 130
Wagon. to her yron *wagon* she betakes, . . . I. v. 28. 1
In westerne waves his weary *wagon* did recure. . . . I. v. 44. 9
Phoebus gan decline . . . His weary *wagon* to the Westerne vale, . . . II. ix. 10. 2
She to her *wagon* clombe; . . . III. iv. 31. 6
Whiles they the corse into her *wagon* reare, . . . III. iv. 42. 4
the Moones bright *wagon* still did stand, . . . VII. vi. 13. 7
sitting In an old *wagon,* . . . VII. vii. 43. 2
Wagon-beam. after all, upon the *wagon beame,* Rode Sathan . I. iv. 36. 1
Wagoner. the Northerne *wagoner* had set His sevenfold teme . I. ii. 1. 1
Waide. *See* **Weighed.**
Waif. and wander wide . . . like a forlorne *wefte;* . . . III. x. 36. 3
Yet was it in due triall but a wandring *weft.* . . . IV. ii. 4. 9
a *waift,* the which by fortune came Upon your seas, . . . IV. xii. 31. 3
yours the *waift* by high prerogative. . . . IV. xii. 31. 6
While she was flying, like a weary *weft,* . . . V. iii. 27. 5
'Leave, faytor, quickely that misgotten *weft* . . . VI. i. 18. 7
Wail. makes me *wayle* (*waile*[1]) so hard a destenie. . . . *Pet.* i. 14
Well couth he *wayle* his Woes, . . . *S.C.* Jun. 85
learne these woods to *wayle* my woe, . . . *S.C.* Jun. 95
More meete to *wayle* my woe . . . *S.C.* Au. 165
Waile ye this wofull waste of Natures warke; . . . *S.C.* N. 64
Waile we the wight . . . *S.C.* N. 65
Waile we the wight . . . *S.C.* N. 66
The beastes in forest *wayle* . . . *S.C.* N. 135
'Why *wayle* we then? . . . *S.C.* N. 173
To *waile* the wretchednes of world impure? . . . *T.M.* 120
Then gan she wofully to *waile,* . . . *T.M.* 169
Therefore I mourne and *waile* incessantly, . . . *T.M.* 293
she lowdly gan to *waile* and shrike, . . . *T.M.* 475
For whome I *waile* and weepe all that I may. . . . *T.M.* 594
Did weep and *waile,* and made exceeding mone, . . . *T.M.* 598
given like cause with thee to *waile* and weepe; . . . *D.* 66
Therewith he gan afresh to *waile* and weepe, . . . *D.* 169
Help me to *wayle* my miserable case, . . . *D.* 510
every one did weep and *waile,* and mone, . . . *As.* 207
The woods were heard to *waile* full many a sythe, . . . *Col.* 23
Then gan she *wail* and weepe to see that woeful stowre. . . . I. ii. 7. 9
The Lady, . . . Staid not to *waile* his woefull funerall, . . . I. ii. 20. 3
as shee did weepe and *waile,* A knight her mett . . . I. iii. 24. 3
To *wayle* his wofull case she would not stay, . . . I. v. 19. 8

Wail—*Continued.*
My last left comfort is my woes to weepe and *waile.'* . . . I. vii. 39. 9
all about it wandring ghostes did *wayle* and howle. . . . I. ix. 33. 9
The damned ghosts that doe in torments *waile,* . . . I. ix. 49. 7
full many soules do endlesse *wayle* and weepe. . . . II. vii. 56. 9
nought she did but *wayle,* . . . III. ii. 28. 8
shee still did waste, and still did *wayle,* . . . III. ii. 52. 3
did weepe And often *wayle* their wealth, . . . III. iv. 22. 9
who that lives is lefte to *waile* his losse: . . . III. iv. 38. 6
Where wicked ghosts doe *waile* their former sin. . . . III. v. 22. 4
As pittying to see her *waile* and weepe: . . . III. viii. 21. 8
Canacee gan *wayle* her dearest frend. . . . IV. iii. 35. 5
loudly cry, and weepe, and *waile,* . . . IV. ix. 7. 6
all the wooddy Nymphes did *wayle* and mourne; . . . V. viii. 43. 7
Gan weepe and *wayle,* as if great griefe had her affected. . V. ix. 9. 9
who did *wayle* or watch the wearie night? . . . VI. vii. 30. 6
What now is left her but to *wayle* and weepe, . . . VI. xi. 23. 6
when I *waile,* she turnes hir selfe to laughter. . . . *Am.* xviii. 12
I weepe, and *wayle,* and pleade in vaine, . . . *Am.* xviii. 13
when my joy to sorrow flits, I *waile,* . . . *Am.* liv. 8
Wailed. Shee weeped, and *wayled,* . . . *S.C.* May 301
The Sunnes sad daughters *waylde* . . . *Gn.* 198
Therewith shee *wayled* with exceeding woe, . . . *T.M.* 295
shee wept and *waild* so pityouslie, . . . *T.M.* 535
when they both had wept and *wayld* their fill, . . . I. iii. 22. 6
Nor *wayld* of friends, nor layd on groning beare, . . . I. v. 23. 4
caytive wretched thralls, that *wayled* night and day: . . . I. v. 45. 9
one that *wayld* and pittifully wept, . . . II. xii. 27. 3
He wept, and *wayld,* and false laments belyde, . . . III. x. 7. 7
He *wailed* womanlike with many a teare, . . . III. xii. 7. 7
alwaies wept and *wailed* night and day, . . . IV. viii. 2. 8
after she had wept and *wail'd* a space, . . . IV. xii. 8. 8
With that she wept and *wail'd,* . . . IV. xii. 11. 8
The whyles she *wayld,* the more they did rejoyce. . . . VI. viii. 46. 5
Wailful. Like *wailefull* widdowes hangen their crags; . . . *S.C.* F. 82
I, a *waylfull* widdowe behight, . . . *S.C.* May 201
Whose *waylefull* want debarres myne eyes from sleepe. . . . *S.C.* Au. 162
In funerall complaints and *waylfull* tyne, . . . *Mui.* 12
waste in woe and *waylfull* miserye: . . . III. iv. 38. 4
weare the weary night In *waylfull* plaints . . . V. vi. 26. 2
Wailing. Hard by a rivers side, a *wailing* Nimphe, . . . *Bel.*[1] viii. 1
My timely buds with *wayling* all are wasted; . . . *S.C.* Ja. 38
With weeping, and *wayling,* and misery. . . . *S.C.* F. 50
Wailing the wrong which he had done of late, . . . *Gn.* 327
Where wretched ghosts sit *wailing* evermore. . . . *Gn.* 384
by the *wayling* shores to waste my dayes, . . . *Gn.* 621
Was ever heard such *wayling* in this place. . . . *T.M.* 18
Like wofull Culvers, doo sit *wayling* now, . . . *T.M.* 246
A Woman sitting, sorrowfullie *wailing,* . . . *Ti.* 9
So *wailing* backe go to their wofull toomb. . . . *Ti.* 49
No *wayling* there nor wretchednesse is heard, . . . *Col.* 312
Doest thou sit *wayling* by blacke Stygian lake, . . . I. v. 10. 6
Acheron, Where many soules sit *wailing* woefully, . . . I. v. 33. 2
Yet wist not what their *wailing* ment; . . . III. iv. 32. 4
Wayling, and raysing pittifull uprore, . . . V. ix. 8. 8
Waiment. for pittie of the sad *wayment* . . . *Ti.* 390
what bootes it to weepe and to *wayment* . . . II. i. 16. 5
Shee made so piteous mone and deare *wayment,* . . . III. iv. 35. 6
Waimented. she wept and wofullie *waymented,* . . . *T.M.* 355
Wain. the welked Phoebus gan availe His weary *waine;* . . . *S.C.* Ja. 74
That did presume his fathers fyrie *wayne,* . . . I. iv. 9. 2
May seeme the *wayne* was very evill ledd, . . . I. iv. 19. 7
did alight From her nigh weary *wayne,* . . . I. v. 41. 2
O Titan! hast to reare thy joyous *waine;* . . . III. iv. 60. 3
lose the teme out of his weary *wayne,* . . . III. viii. 51. 5
the firie-mouthed steedes, which drew The Sunnes bright *wayne* V. viii. 40. 2
Phoebus with his fiery *waine* . . . VI. iii. 29. 1
Wained. The kingdome of the Night, and waters by her *wained.* VII. vi. 10. 9
Waist. *See* **Waste.**
Above the *wast* (*waste*[1]) a darke clowde shrouded her, . . . *Pet.* vi. 7

Waist—*Continued.*
gird in your *waste,* . . . *S.C.* Ap. 134
with an yvie twyne his *waste* is girt about. . . . I. vi. 14. 9
made wide shadow under his huge *waste,* . . . I. xi. 8. 4
some fashioned in the *waste* Like swine: . . . II. xi. 12. 5
wore About her sclender *waste,* . . . III. vii. 36. 2
her small *waste* girt rownd with yron bands . . . III. xii. 30. 8
round about Her tender *waste* was wound, . . . III. xii. 37. 8
Full oft about her *wast* she it enclos'd, . . . IV. v. 16. 8
it as oft was from about her *wast* disclos'd: . . . IV. v. 16. 9
raught downe to his *waste* when up he stood, . . . IV. vii. 6. 8
His *wast* was with a wreath of yvie greene Engirt about, . IV. vii. 7. 1
Unto her *waste,* with flowres bescattered, . . . IV. xi. 46. 2
Her selfe then tooke he by the sclender *wast,* . . . V. ii. 27. 1
th' emptie girdle which about her *wast* was wrought. . . . V. iii. 24. 9
round about her tender *wast* it fitted well. . . . V. iii. 27. 9
to no womans *wast* . . . it would sit, . . . V. iii. 28. 6
had three bodies in one *wast* empight, . . . V. x. 8. 8
Wait. many wyld beastes liggen in *waite* . . . *S.C.* May 217
All the cold season to wach and *waite;* . . . *S.C.* S. 237
I will but *wayte* on you, . . . *Hub.* 201
To have thy asking, yet *waite* manie yeeres; . . . *Hub.* 902
To fawne, to crowche, to *waite,* to ride, to ronne, . . . *Hub.* 905
wont to *wait* upon my traine, . . . *T.M.* 196
Would wend with me, and *waite* by me all day: . . . *D.* 128
Therin stil *wait* poore passengers to teare. . . . *Col.* 203
I my selfe was there, To *wait* on Lobbin, . . . *Col.* 736
her dwarfe, that wont to *wait* each howre: . . . I. ii. 7. 8
earely *waite* him many a gazing eye, . . . I. v. 3. 2
rocke . . . That lay in *waite* her wrack for to bewaile, . . . I. vi. 1. 3
Amendment readie still at hand did *wayt,* . . . I. x. 26. 7
watch the noyous night, and *wait* for joyous day. . . . I. xi. 50. 9
the Gard, which on his state did *wait,* . . . I. xii. 35. 4
thousand furies *wait* on wrathfull sword; . . . II. ii. 30. 7
therein did *wayt* A sturdie villein, . . . II. vii. 40. 3
That dreadfull feend, which did behinde him *wayt,* . . . II. vii. 64. 4
After she long in *waite* for me did lye, . . . III. vii. 51. 2
As if they lay in *wait,* or els them selves did hide. . . . III. x. 20. 9
Nor ward to *waite* at morne and evening late; . . . III. xi. 21. 4
On whom I *waite* to wreake that foule despight, . . . IV. vi. 5. 8
ten thousand monsters . . . Did *waite* about it, . . . IV. xi. 3. 9
did *waite* Uppon her person for her sure defence, . . . V. v. 4. 3
Upon Joves judgement-seat *wayt* day and night; . . . V. ix. 31. 7
unto the watchfull ward Which there did *wayte,* . . . V. x. 31. 4
Lying in *waite* how him he damadge might; . . . VI. i. 20. 7
But *wayt* on him in every place and part: . . . VI. ii. 36. 5
as they the time did *waite,* . . . VI. v. 15. 1
wayt advantage when they downe did light. . . . VI. viii. 14. 5
That warnes al lovers *wayt* upon their king, . . . *Am.* xix. 3
Bid her . . . ready make, To *wayt* on Love . . . *Am.* lxx. 10
many a bachelor to *waite* on him, . . . *Epith.* 28
About him *wait,* and on his will depend, . . . *H.H.L.* 65
blessed Plentie *wait* upon your bord; . . . *Proth.* 102
Waited. Shee there then *waited* upon Cynthia, . . . *Col.* 520
when she wakt, he *wayted* diligent, . . . I. iii. 9. 6
A noble crew about them *waited* rownd . . . I. xii. 5. 4
long hath *waited* by the Stygian strond. . . . III. ii. 52. 6
bold, as ever Squyre that *waited* by knights side: . . . III. v. 12. 9
before the wicket fast They *wayted,* . . . III. ix. 11. 3
Thus she there *wayted* untill eventyde, . . . III. xi. 55. 1
with meet service *waited* him about, . . . IV. xi. 30. 4
waited well To doe their dueful service, . . . IV. xi. 44. 8
on her *waited* things amisse to mend, . . . IV. xi. 47. 3
the people, which had there about Long *wayted,* . . . V. ii. 51. 2
the utmost date . . . she *waited* had for nought, . . . V. vi. 3. 7
For whom they *wayted* as his mortall fone, . . . V. xii. 37. 3
Waiting. Still *wayting* to preferment up to clime, . . . *Hub.* 76
Angels *waighting* on th' Almighties chayre. . . . *T.M.* 510
as we stood there *waiting* on the strond, . . . *Col.* 212
Full many worthie ones then *waiting* were, . . . *Col.* 737
that wilde champion *wayting* her besyde; . . . I. iii. 26. 2
Infinite sortes of people did abide There *waiting* long, . . . I. iv. 6. 8
one sate *wayting* ever them before, . . . I. x. 36. 8
The watchman *wayting* tydings glad to heare; . . . I. xi. 3. 7
by whose utmost brim *Wayting* to passe, . . . II. vi. 2. 5
still sat *wayting* on that wastfull clift . . . II. xii. 8. 6
The ruefull Strich, still *waiting* on the bere; . . . II. xii. 36. 7
Waiting advauntage on the pray to sease, . . . III. x. 30. 6
Wayting when as the Antheme should be sung on hye. . . . IV. x. 48. 9
Wayting how Fortune would resolve that daungerous dout. . . V. v. 5. 9
Like to a Spaniell *wayting* carefully . . . V. vi. 26. 8
Wayting what would ensue of that event. . . . V. vi. 28. 5
Wayting what end would be of that same daunger drad. . . . V. xi. 32. 9
With onely Talus *wayting* diligent, . . . V. xi. 36. 7
in battailous array *Wayting* his foe, . . . V. xii. 12. 8
There *wayting* for the Tyrant till it was farre day. . . . V. xii. 13. 9
Wayting if he unwares him murther might; . . . VI. vi. 26. 8
Wayting what tydings of her folke became. . . . VI. vi. 30. 3
Waits. Misfortune *waites* advantage to entrap The man . . . II. iv. 17. 4
waytes for death with dread and trembling aw; . . . II. viii. 50. 4
Wake. mery tales to keepe us *wake,* . . . *S.C.* Jun. 87
Wake, shepheards boy, at length awake for shame! . . . *Ti.* 231
I will *wake* and sorrow all the night . . . *D.* 474
Wake then, my pipe; my sleepie Muse, awake; . . . *Col.* 48
The Sprite then gan more boldly him to *wake,* . . . I. i. 43. 1
Still did he *wake,* and still did watch for dawning light. . I. v. 1. 9
praying still did *wake,* and waking did lament. . . . I. xi. 32. 9
Two eies him needeth, for to watch and *wake,* . . . III. ix. 31. 7
prayd her *wake* to heare him plaine. . . . III. x. 49. 6
forst to *wake,* He felt his hart for very paine to quake, . . . IV. v. 44. 4

Wake—*Continued.*
Looke up at last, and *wake* thy dulled spirit . . . V. v. 36. 8
Now ye have made my heart to *wake* alway, . . . V. vi. 25. 7
ah! *wake,* and rather weepe . . . V. vi. 25. 8
suffer her out of her sleepe to *wake,* . . . VI. viii. 37. 8
Which they did daily watch, and nightly *wake* . . . VII. vii. 45. 8
Wake now, my love, awake! . . . *Epith.* 74
Twixt sleepe and *wake,* after she weary was, . . . *Epith.* 309
Waked. with great noyse I *wakte* in sudden wonder. . . . *Bel.*[2] xv. 14
And *waked* againe with griefe; . . . *S.C.* Mar. 48
when I *waked,* neither most nor least I found miscaried . . . *D.* 139
when she *wakt,* he wayted diligent, . . . I. iii. 9. 6
she proov'd Whether she slept or *wakte:* . . . III. i. 60. 6
one out of a dreame not *waked* well . . . III. x. 49. 7
would have *wakt* the Satyre by her syde; . . . III. x. 50. 6
she *waked* out of dread Streight into griefe, . . . IV. vii. 9. 3
when he *wak't* out of his warelesse paine, . . . V. i. 22. 3
Like one that from his dreame is *waked* suddenlye. . . . V. v. 13. 9
she *waked* full of fearefull fright, . . . V. vii. 16. 8
Then when she *wakt* they all gave one consent . . . VI. viii. 38. 4
being *waked* with these loud alarmes, . . . VI. viii. 47. 7
Love, . . . by Clotho being *waked:* . . . *H.L.* 63
Wakeful. to comfort *wakefull* Lovers, . . . *Ti.* 132
wakeful dogges before them farre doe lye, . . . I. i. 40. 4
Which when the *wakeful* Elfe perceiv'd, . . . I. v. 2. 6
The *wakefull* dogs did never cease to bay, . . . I. v. 30. 2
wakefull watches ever to abide; . . . II. iii. 41. 6
Nor brasen walls, nor many *wakefull* spyes, . . . III. ix. 7. 5
a Beare, . . . the *wakefull* dogs espy, . . . III. x. 53. 6
Waken. For she will *waken* strayt; . . . *Epith.* 53
Wakened. Ere he had slept his fill, he *wakened* were, . . . VI. i. 35. 3
he was *wakened* with the noyse, . . . *Epig.* iv. 5
Wakens. a voyce That *wakens* men withall?' . . . *Epig.* iv. 8
Wakes. Whom suddenly he *wakes* with fearful frights, . . . I. ii. 4. 4
The Damzell *wakes;* . . . VI. viii. 40. 1
Waketh. *waketh* and if but a leafe sturre. . . . *S.C.* S. 183
Waking. then him *waking,* forced up to rize. . . . *Hub.* 1323
Waking Love suffereth no sleepe: . . . *U.V.* 10
Her, whom he, *waking,* . . . did weene To bee the chastest . I. i. 48. 3
praying still did wake, and *waking* did lament. . . . I. xi. 32. 9
For feare of *waking* him, . . . II. xii. 73. 6
To thinke of your nights want, that should yee *waking* keepe.' V. vi. 25. 9
gently *waking* them gave them the time of day. . . . VI. xi. 38. 9
Waladay. *See* **Weladay.**
Wales. *See* **South Wales.**
Walk. shepheard must *walke* another way, . . . *S.C.* May 81
let me *walke* withouten lincks of love, . . . *S.C.* Jun. 34
They *walke* not widely as they were wont, . . . *S.C.* S. 158
Walke in Elisian fieldes so free. . . . *S.C.* N. 179
we will *walke* about the world at pleasure . . . *Hub.* 159
There thou must *walke* in sober gravitee, . . . *Hub.* 496
Walk through the world of every one revilde. . . . *T.M.* 342
wandring spirits *walke* untimely howres. . . . *D.* 336
'For I will *walke* this wandring pilgrimage, . . . *D.* 372
Then with a few to *walke* the rightest way. . . . I. x. 10. 8
To *walke* this way in Pilgrims poore estate. . . . I. x. 64. 4
Her other leg was lame, that she no'te *walke,* . . . II. iv. 4. 3
her toung did *walke* In fowle reproch, . . . II. iv. 5. 1
with like labour *walke* the world arownd, . . . III. vii. 56. 2
To *walke* the woodes with that his Idole faire, . . . III. viii. 11. 2
The gentle Lady, . . . The greene-wood long did *walke,* . . . III. x. 36. 2
punish wicked men that *walke* amisse: . . . IV. i. 20. 3
walke about her gardens of delight, . . . IV. viii. 54. 3
graunt more scope to me to *walke* at large. . . . IV. viii. 61. 4
making way for death at large to *walke;* . . . VI. xi. 16. 5
Ceasse to molest the Moone to *walke* at large, . . . VII. vi. 17. 8
Walked. On hearbs and flowres she *walked* pensively, . . . *Pet.* vi. 3
walkt at will, and wandred too and fro, . . . *Mui.* 379
I *walkt* abroade to breath the freshing ayre . . . *D.* 26
whylst any beast of name *Walkt* in that forrest, . . . I. vi. 29. 4
Both plaine and pleasaunt to be *walked* in; . . . I. x. 6. 3
Seven times the Sunne . . . Hath *walkte* about the world, . . II. ix. 7. 6
there *walked* to and fro A jolly yeoman, . . . II. ix. 28. 1
eies . . . *walkte* each where for feare of hid mischaunce, . . III. xii. 15. 7
Walkt through the wood, for pleasure or for need; . . . IV. vii. 4. 2
therein thousand payres of lovers *walkt,* . . . IV. x. 25. 6
walkt abrode, and round about did rome . . . IV. xii. 4. 5
In this sad plight he *walked* here and there, . . . IV. xii. 17. 1
Whiles through the world she *walked* in this sort, . . . V. i. 6. 1
A while she *walkt,* and chauft; . . . V. vi. 13. 6
walkt about them ever and anone . . . V. x. 10. 5
When I . . . *Walkt* forth to ease my payne . . . *Proth.* 10
Walker's. To sit and rest the *walkers* wearie shankes: . . . IV. x. 25. 5
Walkest. False love! . . . Thou *walkest* free, . . . III. x. 4. 6
Walketh. she . . . *walketh* forth without suspect of crime. . I. vi. 13. 4
restlesse *walketh* all the world arownd, . . . III. ii. 14. 4
Walking. *Walking* abroad with all her Nymphes to play, . . . *Mui.* 115
When *walking* through the Gardin them she saw, . . . III. vi. 40. 6
Now *walking* soft, now sitting still upright, . . . V. vi. 26. 3
Walks. *walkes* upright with comely stedfast pace, . . . *Hub.* 728
From every coast that heaven *walks* about . . . I. vii. 45. 3
him that *walkes* in feare and sad affright. . . . II. vii. 29. 9
walkes and alleyes dight With divers trees . . . IV. x. 25. 1
Cinthia . . . *walkes* about high heaven al the night? . . . *Epith.* 375
Wall. *See* **Castle-wall.**
Of bricke, ne yet of marble was the *wall,* . . . *Bel.*[1] ii. 5
Nor brick nor marble was the *wall* . . . *Bel.*[2] ii. 5
the ground-work of an old great *wall;* . . . *Bel.*[2] viii. 2
Much wondred I to see so faire a *wall:* . . . *Bel.*[2] xiv. 9
all their wealth for painting on a *wall;* . . . *Col.* 724

Wall—*Continued.*
fast embard in mighty brasen *wall*, . . . I. vii. 44. 8
With many raunges reard along the *wall*, . . . II. ix. 29. 2
Elfiline enclosd it with a golden *wall*. . . . II. x. 72. 9
A brasen *wall* in compas to compyle . . . III. iii. 10. 3
Untill that brasen *wall* they up doe reare; . . . III. iii. 11. 7
Yar, soft washing Norwitch *wall*, . . . IV. xi. 33. 6
That Romaine Monarch built a brasen *wall*, . . . IV. xi. 36. 2
Hemd in with waters like a *wall* in sight, . . . V. ii. 35. 7
sounding loud a Trumpet from the *wall*, . . . V. iv. 50. 3
Unto the *wall* his way did fearelesse take, . . . V. iv. 50. 6
Uppon their *wall* good watch and ward did keepe. . . . V. vii. 26. 6
there stood gazing from the Citties *wall* . . . V. xi. 15. 6
from the *wall* him seeing so aghast, . . . VI. i. 23. 1
And, last, that mightie shining christall *wall*, . . . *H.H.B.* 41

Walled. *See* **Sea-walled.**
The *walled* townes doe worke my greater woe; . . . *S.C.* Au. 158
cryes, As still are wont t' annoy the *walled* towne, . . . I. i. 41. 7
blood-red billowes, like a *walled* front, . . . I. x. 53. 3
A little cottage, . . . *wald* with sods around; . . . III. vii. 6. 3
wall'd by nature gainst invaders wrong, . . . IV. x. 6. 3
wall'd it was with waves, . . . IV. xi. 3. 6

Wallet. eeke this *wallet* at your backe arreare, . . . VI. viii. 23. 8

Wallow. Did *wallow* in all other fleshly myre, . . . III. vii. 49. 6

Wallowed. he all *wallowed* in the weedes downe beaten, . . . *Van.* ii. 8
All slaine with darts, lie *wallowed* in their blood. . . . *Gn.* 432
bodie lay, All *wallowd* in his owne fowle bloody gore, . . . I. viii. 24. 4
All *wallowd* in his own yet luke-warme blood, . . . I. ix. 36. 6
He tombled on a heape, and *wallowd* in his gore. . . . III. iv. 16. 9
he lay *wallowd* all in his owne gore. . . . III. v. 26. 5
a knight all *wallowed* Upon the grassy ground, . . . III. xi. 7. 3
In her own blood all *wallow'd* wofully, . . . V. i. 14. 4

Wallowest. soyle, In which thou *wallowest* like to filthy swyne, *H.H.L.* 219

Walls. Under deep ruines, with huge *walls* oppress, . . . *Ro.* i. 2
Great Babylon her haughtie *walls* will praise, . . . *Ro.* ii. 1
These same olde *walls*, olde arches, which thou seest, . . . *Ro.* iii. 3
beating downe these *walls* with furious mood . . . *Ro.* xi. 11
these old *wals*, which ye see, . . . *Ro.* xviii. 1
blood, the which at first was spilt Upon your *walls*, . . . *Ro.* xxiv. 13
The stonie joynts of these old *walls* now rent, . . . *Ro.* xxv. 7
These *wals*, these arcks, these baths, . . . *Ro.* xxvii. 4
To whom the ruin'd *walls* of Carthage vow'd, . . . *Gn.* 615
Strong *walls*, rich porches, princelie pallaces, . . . *Ti.* 93
mountain gray That *walls* the Northside of Armulla dale) . . . *Col.* 105
all the *walls* and windows there are writ, . . . *Col.* 776
enclosd in wooden *wals* . . . our wearie daies we waste.' . . . I. ii. 42. 8
Whose *wals* were high, but nothing strong nor thick, . . . I. iv. 4. 3
The yron *walles* to ward their blowes are weak and fraile. . . . I. v. 6. 9
wals and towres were builded high and strong . . . I. x. 55. 4
from far see on the *walles* appeare, . . . I. xi. 3. 4
Deepe in their flesh, quite through the yron *walles*, . . . II. vi. 29. 8
Both roofe, and floore, and *walls*, were all of gold, . . . II. vii. 29. 1
wals Were painted faire with memorable gestes . . . II. ix. 53. 2
the *wals*, that did the same uphold, . . . II. ix. 55. 3
The ruin'd *wals* he did reaedifye Of Troynovant, . . . II. x. 46. 4
those two brethren Gyauntes did defend The *walles* . . . II. xi. 15. 7
The *wals* were round about appareiled . . . III. i. 34. 1
girt in with two *walls* on either side; . . . III. vi. 31. 2
Nor brasen *walls*, nor many wakefull spyes, . . . III. ix. 7. 5
No fort so fensible, no *wals* so strong, . . . III. x. 10. 1
round about the *walls* yclothed were . . . III. xi. 28. 1
all the *walles* did seeme to flame: . . . III. xi. 38. 6
the glistring *walles* were hong With warlike spoiles . . . III. xi. 52. 1
the riven *walls* were hung With ragged monuments . . . IV. i. 21. 1
makes the *wals* to stagger with astonishment: . . . V. x. 34. 9
through the yron *walles* their way they rent, . . . V. xii. 17. 7
sprinkle all the postes and *wals* with wine, . . . *Epith.* 253

Walnut-tree. How have I wearied . . . The stately *Walnut-tree*, *S.C.* D. 34

Wan. *See* **Won.**
pale and *wanne* he was, (alas the while!) . . . *S.C.* Ja. 8
Thou weake, I *wanne;* thou leane, I quite forlorne: . . . *S.C.* Ja. 47
So lustlesse bene they, so weake, so *wan;* . . . *S.C.* F. 78
it is all to weake and *wanne*, . . . *S.C.* O. 85
Yet I her fram'd, and *wan* so to my bent, . . . *D.* 124
made her . . . sad to view his visage pale and *wan*, . . . I. viii. 42. 3
he by many rash adventures *wan*, . . . II. ii. 17. 4
have beheld the battailes which it *wan*.' . . . II. iii. 16. 9
In their beginning they are weake and *wan*, . . . II. iv. 34. 3
Crying with pitteous voyce, and count'nance *wan*, . . . II. vi. 32. 4
His forlorne steed from him the victour *wan:* . . . II. vi. 41. 4
He seemed breathlesse, hartlesse, faint, and *wan*, . . . II. vi. 41. 5
with which th' Euboean young man *wan* Swift Atalanta, . . . II. vii. 54. 8
weake and *wan* For want of food and sleepe, . . . II. vii. 65. 2
soone by meanes thereof the Empire *wan*, . . . II. x. 61. 4
As pale and *wan* as ashes was his looke, . . . II. xi. 22. 1
Thrise shined faire, and thrise seemd dim and *wan*, . . . III. iii. 16. 3
Spoild of their rosy red were woxen pale and *wan*. . . . III. v. 29. 9
Trembling in heart, and looking pale and *wan*, . . . IV. ii. 49. 4
through long fasting woxen pale and *wan*, . . . IV. vii. 43. 3
Then did her glorious flowre wax dead and *wan*, . . . IV. viii. 32. 8
full weake and *wan*, not like him selfe to bee. . . . IV. ix. 8. 9
kissing oft his visage pale and *wan:* . . . IV. ix. 9. 5
lies in wretched thraldome, weake and *wan*, . . . V. vi. 16. 3
her hew Was *wan* and leane, . . . V. xii. 29. 5
through sicknesse now so *wan* and weake, . . . VI. xi. 12. 7
Seeing her weake and *wan* through durance long. . . . VI. xii. 11. 6

Wand. He tooke Caduceus, his snakie *wand*, . . . *Hub.* 1292
Shee smote them lightly with her powrefull *wand*. . . . IV. iii. 48. 2
She stretched forth a long white sclender *wand*. . . . V. vii. 7. 5
Her *wand* did move with amiable looke, . . . V. vii. 8. 2

Wand—*Continued.*
well perceiving how her *wand* she shooke, . . . V. vii. 8. 4
Flying from tree to tree, from *wand* to *wand;* . . . V. ix. 17. 6
like an hazell *wand* it quivered and quooke. . . . VI. vii. 24. 9
lifting up her golden *wand*, . . . VII. vi. 13. 4

Wander. Here *wander* may thy flocke, . . . *S.C.* Jun. 11
They *wander* at wil and stay at pleasure, . . . *S.C.* S. 144
so to *wander* to the worldes ende, . . . *Hub.* 87
wander free Where so us listeth, . . . *Hub.* 168
Thus wildly to *wander* in the worlds eye, . . . *Hub.* 185
Seeing them *wander* loosly, . . . *Hub.* 244
From the right way full eath may *wander* wide: . . . *Hub.* 404
So *wander* we all carefull comfortlesse, . . . *T.M.* 349
men of armes doo *wander* unrewarded. . . . *Ti.* 441
wander up and downe despys'd of all; . . . *Col.* 728
They . . . *wander* too and fro in waies unknowne, . . . I. i. 10. 5
To *wander* where wilde fortune would me lead, . . . I. vii. 50. 2
They let her goe at will, and *wander* waies unknowne. . . . I. viii. 49. 9
Where she did *wander* in waste wildernesse, . . . II. i. 22. 2
feard to *wander* in that wastefull mist, . . . II. xii. 35. 3
he by chaunce did *wander* that same way, . . . III. iv. 19. 8
To *wander* through the world abroad at will, . . . III. vii. 54. 4
wander wide At wilde adventure, . . . III. x. 36. 2
through the endlesse world did *wander* wide, . . . IV. viii. 18. 8
To *wander* in the griesly shades of night. . . . V. x. 33. 6
through this worlds wyde wildernes She *wander* should . . . VI. vii. 37. 8
Out of her course doth *wander* far astray! . . . *Am.* xxxiv. 4
wander now, in darknesse and dismay, . . . *Am.* xxxiv. 7
Till then I *wander* carefull, comfortlesse, . . . *Am.* xxxiv. 13
I *wander* as in darkenesse of the night, . . . *Am.* lxxxvii. 3

Wandered. *wandred*, I wene, about the world round, . . . *S.C.* S. 22
Like Swallow swift I *wandred* here and there; . . . *S.C.* D. 20
After which sort they *wandered* long while, . . . *Hub.* 343
in the world long time they *wandered*, . . . *Hub.* 943
walkt at will, and *wandred* too and fro, . . . *Mui.* 379
The true Saint George, was *wandred* far away, . . . I. ii. 12. 2
marinere, That long hath *wandred* in the Ocean wide, . . . I. iii. 31. 2
She *wandred* had from one to other Ynd, . . . I. vi. 2. 7
She *wandred* many a wood, and measurd many a vale. . . . I. vii. 28. 9
Hast *wandred* through the world now long a day, . . . I. x. 9. 6
long time *wandred* through the forest wyde . . . III. v. 3. 1
wandred in the world in straunge aray, . . . III. vi. 11. 8
From Stygian shores where late it *wandered:* . . . III. vii. 14. 8
To savegard her *ywandred* all alone: . . . III. viii. 46. 8
weetlesse *wandered* From shore to shore . . . III. ix. 41. 5
To seeke his wife that was far *wandered:* . . . III. x. 34. 3
Long *wandred* they, yet never met with none . . . IV. i. 16. 7
thought she *wandred* was, or gone astray: . . . IV. vi. 36. 7
the heavens revolution Is *wandred* farre . . . V. Pr. 4. 7
They all are *wandred* much; . . . V. Pr. 5. 5
The faire Serena . . . *Wandred* about the fields, . . . VI. iii. 23. 6
So up and downe he *wandred* many a mile . . . VI. iv. 25. 4
Was *wandred* in the wood another way, . . . VI. vii. 19. 6

Wanderest. further from it daily *wanderest:* . . . I. ix. 40. 3

Wandereth. Then *wandreth* he in error and in doubt, . . . *T.M.* 490
Wandreth alone with bow and arrowes keene, . . . II. iii. 31. 4
wandreth evermore uncertein and unsure. . . . II. xii. 12. 9
through this forrest *wandreth* thus alone? . . . III. v. 7. 8

Wandering. *See* **Long-wandering.**
Long *wandring* up and downe the land, . . . *S.C.* Mar. 64
hath weand my *wandring* mynde: . . . *S.C.* Jun. 2
the Wolves, that chase the *wandring* sheepe, . . . *S.C.* N. 136
choise I had to choose my *wandring* waye, . . . *S.C.* D. 62
in the valleies *wandring* at their wills, . . . *Gn.* 76
lost their time in *wandring* loose abroad; . . . *Hub.* 399
In the wide aire to make her *wandring* flight; . . . *Mui.* 139
who shall lead Your *wandring* troupes, . . . *D.* 317
wandring spirits walke untimely howres. . . . *D.* 336
'For I will walke this *wandring* pilgrimage, . . . *D.* 372
My wearie feete shall ever *wandring* be, . . . *D.* 457
Wearie your selves in *wandring* desert wayes, . . . *D.* 534
in those *wandring* stremes Seek waies unknowne, . . . *Col.* 210
to warne yong shepheards *wandring* wit, . . . *Col.* 684
This is the *wandring* wood, this *Errours* den, . . . I. i. 13. 6
al that in the wide deepe *wandring* arre; . . . I. ii. 1. 5
He saw . . . Una *wandring* in woods and forrests, . . . I. ii. 9. 3
it chaunced this proud Sarazin To meete me *wandring;* . . . I. ii. 25. 2
Or guilefull spright *wandring* in empty aire, . . . I. ii. 32. 6
By which she thought her *wandring* knight shold pas, . . . I. iii. 10. 2
pas, In waies unknowne, her *wandring* knight to seeke, . . . I. iii. 21. 4
ne ought he feares To be partaker of her *wandring* woe; . . . I. iii. 44. 8
From *wandring* Stygian shores, where it doth endlesse move.' . . . I. iv. 48. 9
Alone he, *wandring*, thee too long doth want: . . . I. v. 13. 3
Unweeting of the perillous *wandring* wayes, . . . I. v. 18. 3
A Satyre chaunst her *wandring* for to finde; . . . I. vi. 22. 6
His *wandring* perill closely did lament, . . . I. vi. 32. 2
lampe . . . First made by him mens *wandring* wayes to guyde, I. vii. 23. 2
all about it *wandring* ghostes did wayle and howle. . . . I. ix. 33. 9
'Who travailes by the wearie *wandring* way, . . . I. ix. 39. 1
his weaker *wandring* steps to guyde, . . . I. x. 34. 1
Within a *wandring* Island . . . her dwelling is. . . . II. i. 51. 5
a losell *wandring* by the way, . . . II. iii. 4. 1
suffred not his *wandring* feete to slide; . . . II. iv. 2. 5
The wearie Traveiler, *wandring* that way, . . . II. v. 30. 5
His *wandring* thought in deepe desire does steepe, . . . II. v. 34. 2
my *wandring* ship I row, . . . II. vi. 10. 2
whom *wandring* to and fro I long have lackt, . . . II. viii. 53. 7
Over the which was cast a *wandring* vine, . . . II. ix. 24. 4
Whom he at sea found *wandring* from their waies, . . . II. x. 41. 7
wandring through the world with wearie feet, . . . II. x. 71. 3

Wants—*Continued.*
So is the man that *wants* intendiment. . . . *T.M.* 144
wants she health, or busie is elswhere?' . . . I. x. 16. 3
repaired have her tackles spent, And *wants* supplide; . . . I. xii. 42. 7
Which whoso *wants, wants* so much of his rest: . . . II. i. 59. 7
Woe never *wants* where every cause is caught; . . . II. iv. 44. 6
money can thy *wantes* at will supply? . . . II. vii. 11. 2
Nought *wants* but time and place, . . . III. x. 11. 6
Feared in vaine, sith meanes, ye see, there *wants* theretoo. . . IV. vi. 30. 9
Hath not enough, but *wants* in greatest store, . . . VI. ix. 30. 4
she *wants* to temper angry Jove, . . . *Am.* xxxix. 3
dead my life that *wants* such lively blis. . . . *Am.* lxxxviii. 14

War. I saw the heavens *warre* against hir . . . *Bel.*[1] xi. 12
birdes . . . Should *warre* upon the kings, . . . *Rev.* iii. 10
I saw the heavens in *warre* against her . . . *Bel.*[2] xv. 12
for a time make *warre* Gainst time, . . . *Ro.* vii. 9
To dart abroad the thunder bolts of *warre,* . . . *Ro.* xi. 10
Beres and Tygres, that maken fiers *warre;* . . . *S.C.* Au. 28
They sayne the world is much *war* then it wont, . . . *S.C.* S. 108
that great *warre,* which Trojanes oft behelde? . . . *Gn.* 498
skies and seas doo make most dreadfull *warre;* . . . *Gn.* 574
small skill in *warre:* . . . *Hub.* 200
Their wraths at length broke into open *warre.* . . . *Mui.* 8
with importune might *Warre* against us, . . . *Mui.* 231
Tydings of *warre* and worldly trouble tell? . . . I. i. 30. 8
such is the dye of *warre.* . . . I. ii. 36. 7
of him inquerd Tidings of *warre,* . . . I. vi. 36. 2
The whole atchievement of this doubtfull *warre,* . . . I. viii. 26. 3
Ease after *warre,* death after life, . . . I. ix. 40. 9
The God of *warre* with his fiers equipage . . . I. xi. 6. 7
weening that the sad end of the *warre;* . . . I. xi. 32. 3
daily *warre* against his foeman moves, . . . II. ii. 19. 3
to darraine A triple *warre* with triple enmitee, . . . II. ii. 26. 3
love . . . maketh monstrous *warre;* . . . II. ii. 26. 6
He maketh *warre,* he maketh peace againe, . . . II. ii. 26. 7
Sad be the sights, and bitter fruites of *warre,* . . . II. ii. 30. 6
Full oft approvd in many a cruell *warre;* . . . II. iv. 41. 4
troublous *warre* proclame: . . . II. v. 1. 7
th' equall die of *warre* he well did know: . . . II. v. 13. 4
sometimes had the worse, and lost by *warre,* . . . II. v. 15. 4
'Fly, O Pyrochles! fly the dreadfull *warre* . . . II. v. 16. 1
Another *warre,* and other weapons, I Doe love, . . . II. vi. 34. 6
Delighting all in armes and cruell *warre,* . . . II. vi. 37. 6
in lucklesse *warre* His forlorne steed from him the victour wan: II. vi. 41. 3
As well in state of peace, as puissaunce in *warre.'* . . . II. ix. 4. 9
mighty kings and conquerours in *warre,* . . . II. x. 4. 5
To *war* on those which him had of his realme bereav'd. . . . II. x. 31. 9
Raisd *warre,* and him in batteill overthrew. . . . II. x. 33. 6
Made *warre* on him, . . . II. x. 35. 5
Hengist and Horsus, well approv'd in *warre,* . . . II. x. 65. 2
What *warre* so cruel, or what siege so sore, . . . II. xi. 1. 1
The feeble Britons, broken with long *warre,* . . . III. iii. 23. 6
Yet shall he long time *warre* with happy speed, . . . III. iii. 31. 3
make Strong *warre* upon the Paynim brethren, . . . III. iii. 52. 6
after all his *warre* to rest his wearie knife. . . . III. iv. 24. 9
the Titans which did make *Warre* against heven, . . . III. vii. 47. 4
That *warre* was kindled which did Troy inflame, . . . III. ix. 34. 2
he with cruell *warre* was entertaind . . . III. ix. 42. 2
most often end in bloudshed and in *warre.* . . . IV. i. 25. 9
Have rays'd this cruell *warre* and outrage fell, . . . IV. ii. 24. 4
They weened sure the *warre* was at an end; . . . IV. iii. 35. 2
when she saw that cruell *war* so ended, . . . IV. iii. 50. 4
her beloved Paramoure, The God of *warre,* . . . IV. v. 5. 3
when the world woxe old, it woxe *warre* old, . . . IV. viii. 31. 6
this *war* ye wrongfully have wielded.' . . . IV. ix. 37. 9
strife and *warre* and anger does subdew: . . . IV. x. 34. 7
No *warre* was knowne, . . . V. Pr. 9. 5
With his strange weapon, never wont in *warre,* . . . V. iv. 44. 2
though she still have worne Her dayes in *warre,* . . . V. v. 40. 5
To make new *warre* against the Gods againe. . . . V. vii. 11. 6
Ne ever was the name of *warre* there spoken, . . . V. ix. 24. 6
the weary *war* renew'th; . . . *Am.* xi. 4
All paine hath end, and every *war* hath peace; . . . *Am.* xi. 13
this continuall, cruell, civill *warre,* . . . *Am.* xliv. 5
High time it is this *warre* now ended were . . . *Am.* lvii. 2
It is no love, but a discordant *warre,* . . . *H.B.* 195

War-able. *war-hable* youth Was by Maximian lately ledd away, II. x. 62. 1

Warbles. The Ouzell shrills; the Ruddock *warbles* soft; . . . *Epith.* 82

Warbling. *See* **Gentle-warbling.**
To teach the *warbling* pipe to sound aloft, . . . *T.M.* 290
the strings, stirred with the *warbling* wind, . . . *Ti.* 613
apply Her curious skill the *warbling* notes to play, . . . I. xii. 38. 7

Ward. *See* **Out-ward.**
ever liggen in watch and *ward,* . . . *S.C.* S. 234
the flocks, which thou doest watch and *warde;* . . . *S.C.* D. 12
ward his gentle corpes from cruell wound; . . . *Mui.* 60
could both Phoebus arrowes *ward,* . . . *Mui.* 79
Him to deceive, for all his watchfull *ward,* . . . *Col.* 136
ne *ward* the daunger of the wound; . . . *Col.* 876
when she slept, he kept both watch and *ward;* . . . I. iii. 9. 5
The yron walles to *ward* their blowes are weak and fraile. . . . I. v. 6. 9
ne living wight To *warde* the same, . . . I. viii. 3. 4
his approved skill, to *ward,* Or strike, . . . II. v. 8. 6
Ne plate, ne male, could *ward* so mighty throwes, . . . II. vi. 9. 3
keeping wary watch and *ward,* . . . II. vii. 25. 2
They for us fight, they watch and dewly *ward,* . . . II. viii. 2. 6
He cast between to *ward* the bitter stownd: . . . II. viii. 32. 6
wisely watch to *ward* that deadly stowre; . . . II. viii. 35. 4
Nought could he hurt, but still at *warde* did ly: . . . II. viii. 39. 7
Forgets with wary *warde* them to awayt, . . . II. viii. 42. 3

Ward—*Continued.*
Day and night duely keeping watch and *ward;* . . . II. ix. 25. 2
th' assieged Castles *ward* Their stedfast stonds . . . II. xi. 15. 1
Kept watch and *ward* about her warily, . . . III. ii. 28. 7
he, the tyrant, which her hath in *ward* . . . III. xi. 16. 6
Nor *ward* to waite at morne and evening late; . . . III. xi. 21. 4
Vaine was the watch, and bootlesse all the *ward,* . . . III. xi. 31. 8
Since therefore she her selfe is now your *ward,* . . . IV. ii. 27. 5
From daungers dread to *ward* his naked side, . . . IV. iii. 20. 3
Ne either car'd to *ward,* or perill shonne, . . . IV. iii. 36. 4
To *ward* his bodie from the balefull stound, . . . IV. viii. 45. 2
the watch, that kept continuall *ward,* . . . IV. ix. 5. 6
day and night did watch and duely *ward* . . . IV. x. 17. 2
Uppon their wall good watch and *ward* did keepe. . . . V. vii. 26. 6
Called aloud unto the watchfull *ward* . . . V. x. 31. 3
He day and night doth *ward* both farre and wide, . . . V. xi. 42. 7
to *ward* the deadly feare; . . . V. xii. 14. 4
he it well did *ward* with wise respect, . . . V. xii. 21. 5
when he felt him shrinke, and come to *ward,* . . . VI. i. 20. 8
crie Unto the *ward* to open to him hastilie. . . . VI. i. 22. 9
That doth thus strongly *ward* the Castle . . . VI. iii. 39. 9
His first assault full warily did *ward,* . . . VI. iv. 5. 5
Yet he them all so warily did *ward,* . . . VI. v. 18. 6
weary now with carefull keeping *ward,* . . . VI. v. 21. 2
flying still did *ward,* and warding fly away. . . . VI. vi. 28. 9
Whether more wary were to give or *ward* the blow. . . . VI. viii. 13. 9
kept them with continuall watch and *ward;* . . . VI. x. 43. 2
his rage to *ward* Did cast his shield atweene; . . . VI. xii. 30. 1

Warded. I them *warded* all with wary government. . . . I. ix. 10. 9
it *warded* well Upon his shield, . . . II. xi. 24. 6
Or *warded,* or avoyded and let goe, . . . IV. iii. 17. 4
warded all which in or out did wend, . . . IV. x. 7. 3
had she not it *warded* warily, . . . V. iv. 41. 6
her selfe she *warded* From the dread daunger . . . V. v. 8. 6
Yet with her shield she *warded* it againe, . . . V. v. 10. 8
Yet *warded* well by one of mickle might . . . V. ix. 22. 5

Warders. manie *warders* round about them stood: . . . *Hub.* 1351
felly slewe Those *warders* strange, . . . *Hub.* 1371
on every syde Twise sixteene *warders* satt, . . . II. ix. 26. 2
all the *warders* it did sore amate, . . . V. ii. 21. 3

Warding. flying still did ward, and *warding* fly away. . . . VI. vi. 28. 9

Wardrobe. The third had of their *wardrobe* custody, . . . I. x. 39. 1

Wards. Enclosing you in thrice three *wards* for ever, . . . *Ro.* xv. 7
That *wardes* the Westerne coste? . . . *S.C.* Jul. 42
Who well it *wards,* and quyteth cuff with cuff: . . . I. ii. 17. 3
Attonce he *wards* and strikes; . . . II. ii. 25. 6
Strokes, wounds, *wards,* weapons, all they did despise, . . . IV. iii. 36. 3

Ware. *See* **Wore.**
shewed his *ware* . . . *S.C.* May 287
A mazer ywrought of the Maple *warre,* . . . *S.C.* Au. 26
Or corne, or cattle, or such other *ware,* . . . *Hub.* 873
thred-bare cote, and cobled shoes, hee *ware;* . . . I. iv. 28. 2
this false faytor, who unworthie *ware* His worthie shield, . . . I. iv. 47. 4
What man so wise, what earthly witt so *ware,* . . . I. vii. 1. 1
Athwart his brest a bauldrick brave he *ware,* . . . I. vii. 29. 8
to be wise, and *ware* of like agein. . . . I. viii. 44. 6
when none was *ware,* . . . III. ix. 28. 1

Wareless. unwise, and *warelesse* of the evill . . . IV. ii. 3. 6
Awayting to entrap the *warelesse* wight . . . IV. x. 20. 8
when he wak't out of his *warelesse* paine, . . . V. i. 22. 3
his owne mouth . . . spake so *warelesse* word, . . . V. v. 17. 4
In which she meant him *warelesse* to enfold, . . . V. v. 52. 3

Warely. it was *warely* watched night and day, . . . I. x. 5. 2
wrath and hatred *warely* to shonne, . . . I. x. 33. 5
they him . . . with continual watch did *warely* keepe. . . . I. xii. 36. 3

Wares. draw in Both *wares* and money, . . . *Hub.* 870
the rich *wares* to save from pitteous spoyle; . . . II. xii. 19. 8

War-hable. *See* **War-able.**

Warily. *warily* still watch which way she went, . . . *Col.* 133
cruell Sarazin, In woven maile all armed *warily;* . . . I. v. 4. 2
warily awaited day and night, . . . II. vii. 32. 3
Kept watch and ward about her *warily,* . . . III. ii. 28. 7
warily he did avoide the blow, . . . III. v. 21. 6
His mighty speare he couched *warily,* . . . III. vii. 38. 7
warily he watcheth every way, . . . III. x. 3. 4
Yet from thenceforth more *warily* he fought, . . . IV. iii. 32. 1
had she not it warded *warily,* . . . V. iv. 41. 6
He would it meete and *warily* withstand. . . . V. xi. 7. 5
His first assault full *warily* did ward, . . . VI. iv. 5. 5
Yet he them all so *warily* did ward, . . . VI. v. 18. 6

Wariment. with so good *wariment* Or warded, or avoyded . . . IV. iii. 17. 3

Warlike. the brave *warlicke* brood of Alemaine, . . . *Ro.* xxxi. 7
No deadly fight of *warlick* fleete doth feare; . . . *Gn.* 124
oft beheld the *warlike* Greekish forces, . . . *Gn.* 499
practising the proofe of *warlike* deedes, . . . *Hub.* 740
Whether for Armes and *warlike* amenaunce, . . . *Hub.* 781
a *warlike* equipage Of forreine beasts, . . . *Hub.* 1118
for *warlike* power, and peoples store, . . . *Ti.* 99
her owne people led with *warlike* rage: . . . *Ti.* 173
'So raisde they eke faire Ledaes *warlick* twinnes, . . . *Ti.* 386
Like as a *warlike* Brigandine, . . . *Mui.* 84
Whenceforth issues a *warlike* steed in sight, . . . *Mui.* 316
Such as she oft is seene in *warlicke* field: . . . *Mui.* 323
Whose *warlike* prowesse . . . Hath fild sad Belgicke . . . *Ded. Son.* xiv. 8
The *warlike* Beech; . . . I. i. 9. 7
mightie corse, As ever wielded speare in *warlike* hand, . . . I. iii. 42. 4
Whose fellowship seemd far unfitt for *warlike* swaine. . . . I. iv. 37. 9
th' Elfin knight, which ought that *warlike* wage, . . . I. iv. 39. 7
The *warlike* youthes, . . . Did chace away sweet sleepe . . . I. iv. 44. 3
The *warlike* feates of both those knights to see. . . . I. v. 5. 5

Warlike—*Continued.*
a noble *warlike* knight . . . to that forrest came I. vi. 20. 1
His *warlike* shield all closely cover'd was, I. vii. 33. 1
Old Timon, . . . In *warlike* feates th' expertest man alive, I. ix. 4. 3
never knight, that dared *warlike* deed, I. ix. 45. 3
fame, That *warlike* handes ennoblest with immortall name; I. xi. 5. 9
ne yet the *warlike* pledge to yield, I. xi. 43. 3
her to serve sixe yeares in *warlike* wize, I. xii. 18. 7
'Fayre sonne of Mars, that seeke with *warlike* spoyle, II. i. 8. 7
His *warlike* armes about him gan embrace, II. i. 26. 2
famous far abroad for *warlike* gest, II. ii. 16. 7
the boldest boy That ever *warlike* weapons menaged, II. ii. 18. 4
my liege, whose *warlike* name Is far renowmd II. iii. 35. 3
That *warlike* feats doest highest glorifie. II. iii. 38. 3
hurtle rownd in *warlike* gyre, II. v. 8. 7
Famous throughout the world for *warlike* prayse, II. v. 26. 2
Having his *warlike* weapons cast behynd, II. v. 28. 7
where that same *warlike* Lord She in receiv'd; II. vi. 4. 7
Withdraw from thought of *warlike* enterprize, II. vi. 25. 6
To chaunge love causelesse is reproch to *warlike* knight.' II. vii. 50. 9
The *warlike* Elfe much wondred at this tree, II. vii. 56. 1
thus bespoke: 'Ye *warlike* payre, II. viii. 27. 2
by your wondrous worth and *warlike* feat II. ix. 6. 3
The land which *warlike* Britons now possesse, II. x. 5. 1
warlike Caesar, tempted with the name II. x. 47. 6
Glistring in armes and *warlike* ornament, II. xi. 24. 2
His *warlike* Armes, the ydle instruments II. xii. 80. 1
sith *warlike* armes he bore III. i. 7. 2
with delightfull sport To loose her *warlike* limbs III. i. 52. 5
To lodge the *warlike* maide, unwisely loov'd; III. i. 60. 4
On thother side they saw the *warlike* Mayd III. i. 63. 6
sith they *warlike* armes have laide away, III. ii. 2. 7
Of *warlike* puissaunce in ages spent, III. ii. 3. 1
I have been trained up in *warlike* stowre, III. ii. 6. 3
affrap The *warlike* ryder to his most mishap: III. ii. 6. 5
At tilt or tourney, or like *warlike* game, III. ii. 9. 8
lov'st the shadow of a *warlike* knight; III. ii. 45. 6
The *warlike* Worthies, from antiquitye, III. iii. 4. 4
for his *warlike* feates renowmed is, III. iii. 27. 3
make The *warlike* Mertians for feare to quake: III. iii. 30. 5
till all their *warlike* puissaunce be spent. III. iii. 40. 9
persuade The *warlike* minds to learne her goodly lore, III. iii. 49. 4
that same *warlike* wize, I weene, would you misseeme; III. iii. 53. 5
great desire Of *warlike* armes III. iii. 57. 3
To heare the *warlike* feates which Homere spake III. iv. 2. 4
win him worship through his *warlike* deed, III. iv. 4. 8
Wise, *warlike*, personable, courteous, and kind. III. iv. 5. 9
did beare This *warlike* sonne unto an earthly peare, III. iv. 19. 5
The *warlike* Maide, th' ensample of that might; III. iv. 44. 7
his *warlike* courser, which was strayd III. v. 38. 6
With all the *warlike* youth of Trojans bloud, III. ix. 43. 6
Albion had conquered first by *warlike* feat.' III. ix. 46. 9
th' one was armed all in *warlike* wize, III. x. 21. 4
The *warlike* Damzell was empassiond sore, III. xi. 18. 2
the glistring walles were hong With *warlike* spoiles III. xi. 52. 2
The *warlike* Mayd, beholding earnestly III. xi. 53. 1
Scudamour and Blandamour: Their fight and *warlike* deedes. IV. i. Arg.
The *warlike* virgine . . . wexed inlie wroth; IV. i. 10. 5
Bellona in that *warlike* wise To them appear'd, IV. i. 14. 6
The *warlike* Britonesse her soone addrest, IV. i. 36. 1
As when two *warlike* Brigandines at sea, IV. ii. 16. 1
With *warlike* numbers and Heroicke sound, IV. ii. 32. 7
when all that troupe of *warlike* wooers Assembled were IV. ii. 38. 1
in *warlike* fresh aray Them found IV. ii. 53. 3
These *warlike* Champions, all in armour shine, IV. iii. 3. 8
marching thrise in *warlike* ordinance, IV. iii. 5. 7
Those *warlike* champions both together chose Homeward to march, IV. iii. 51. 4
full many a *warlike* swaine Assembled were, IV. iv. 26. 4
There he in troupe found all that *warlike* crew, IV. iv. 33. 8
So did the *warlike* Britomart restore The prize IV. iv. 48. 1
wearinesse, Both of the way and *warlike* exercise, IV. vii. 3. 4
His wonted *warlike* weapons all he broke IV. vii. 39. 1
on his *warlike* beast them both did beare, IV. viii. 22. 8
them to *warlike* discipline did trayne, IV. viii. 27. 7
The *warlike* Dame was on her part assaid IV. ix. 30. 1
father of the bold And *warlike* people IV. xi. 15. 9
doth beare his name Of *warlike* Amazons, IV. xi. 21. 9
Joy on those *warlike* women, IV. xi. 22. 1
Brutus *warlicke* sonne, Locrinus, IV. xi. 38. 1
In *warlike* wise when Artegall did vew, V. ii. 52. 2
then this *warlike* crew Together met V. iii. 8. 2
great hurly-burly moved was . . . for that same *warlike* horse V. iii. 30. 2
As was the wont of *warlike* knights of yore, V. iii. 32. 3
a troupe of women, *warlike* dight, V. iv. 21. 8
she doth them of *warlike* armes despoile, V. iv. 31. 3
How that three *warlike* persons did appeare, V. iv. 36. 3
Her *warlike* maides about her flockt so fast, V. iv. 43. 6
Unto those *warlike* Knights she warning sent. V. iv. 50. 4
she causd his *warlike* armes Be hang'd on high, V. v. 21. 6
the *warlike* Amazon . . . Gan cast a secret liking V. v. 26. 7
amongst the *warlike* rout Of errant Knights, V. vi. 6. 5
not to forgo Those *warlike* weedes, V. vi. 23. 7
much lesse honour by that *warlike* kinde Of life: V. vi. 32. 5
There did the *warlike* Maide her selfe repose, V. vii. 12. 1
The *warlike* Amazon out of her bowre did peepe. V. vii. 26. 9
when all her *warlike* traine There present saw, V. vii. 34. 7
so did *warlike* Antony neglect The worlds whole rule V. viii. 2. 6
Which *warlike* uses had deviz'd of yore: V. viii. 34. 5
Did issue forth gainst all that *warlike* rout V. viii. 50. 2

Warlike—*Continued.*
Full nobly mounted in right *warlike* wize; V. xi. 4. 3
Your honours stile, that is, your *warlike* shield. V. xi. 55. 6
His *warlike* armes he had from him undight, VI. iii. 20. 5
Ne knew the use of *warlike* instruments, VI. iv. 4. 2
Those *warlike* armes which Calepine whyleare Had left behind VI. v. 8. 4
hanging up his armes and *warlike* spoyle, VI. v. 37. 8
No wound, which *warlike* hand of enemy Inflicts VI. vi. 1. 1
Having his armes and *warlike* things undight, VI. vii. 19. 3
(as fit for *warlike* stoures) VII. vii. 28. 7
Despoyld of *warlike* armes and knowen shield. *Am.* lii. 4

Warm. *See* **Lukewarm.**
my corage cooles ere it be *warme:* *S.C.* O. 115
In the *warme* Sunne he doth himselfe embay, *Mui.* 206
downe againe her in her *warme* bed dight: III. ii. 30. 5
her downe she layd In her *warme* bed III. ii. 47. 3
As if but now the battell wexed *warme.* IV. iv. 35. 5
blowe his nayles to *warme* them if he may; VII. vii. 42. 4
To *warme* your selves at my wide sparckling fire, *H.H.L.* 17

Warmed. with the hidden fire too inly *warmd.* II. vi. 51. 5
Some rusty knifes, some staves in fier *warmd:* II. ix. 13. 7
Nourish the flames which they are *warmd* upon, II. x. 26. 5

War-monger. a *war-monger* to be basely nempt; III. x. 29. 5

Warmth. feeles the *warmth* of sunny beames reflection, IV. xii. 34. 7

Warn. he should *warne* the wronger to appeare *Hub.* 1098
to *warne* yong shepheards wandring wit, *Col.* 684
I *warne* thee now assured sitt, I. ii. 18. 5
Yet can they not *warne* death from wretched wight. II. i. 36. 5
trumpets sound did *warne* them all to rest; IV. iv. 36. 2
To *warne* her foe to battell soone be prest: V. vii. 27. 2
Did *warne* his rider be uppon his gard; VI. v. 21. 7
warne to shun the daunger of theyr wrath. *Am.* xxxi. 8

Warned. he nould *warned* be Of craft, *S.C.* May 302
Warnd him awake, from death himselfe to keep. *Gn.* 288
may *warned* be to say. *Ti.* 7
That of like ruine he may *warned* bee, *Ti.* 468
the glooming skies *Warnd* them to draw their bleating flocks *Col.* 955
chearefull Chaunticlere . . . Had *warned* once, I. ii. 1. 7
me had *warnd* old Timons wise behest, I. ix. 9. 5
Warnd him not touch, I. xii. 10. 3
warnd his other brethren joyeous III. iv. 51. 8
Well *warned* to beware with whom he dar'd to dallie. IV. i. 36. 9
She *warned* them to tend their safeties well, IV. ii. 53. 8
warned him of womens love beware, IV. xii. 27. 2
the watchman . . . all the city *warned* V. iv. 36. 2
Warn'd man and beast in quiet rest be shrowded, V. iv. 45. 3
The bird that *warned* Peter of his fall, V. vi. 27. 2
By like ensample mote for ever *warned* bee. V. viii. 44. 9
She *warn'd* the knights thereof; V. ix. 8. 4
by the like ensample *warned* bee, VI. vii. 27. 5
warn'd the shepheards to their homes to hast VI. ix. 13. 3
warn'd all men by their example to refraine. VII. vi. 29. 9

Warnest. Sicker, Willye, thou *warnest* well; *S.C.* Mar. 7

Warning. *Warning* all other to take heede. *S.C.* Ap. 90
giving *warning* of th' unwonted sound, I. v. 30. 3
Beacons . . . *warning* give that enimies conspyre I. xi. 14. 5
she gave him *warning* every day III. iv. 26. 1
weene by *warning* to avoyd his fate? III. iv. 27. 2
Unto those warlike Knights she *warning* sent. V. iv. 50. 4
Warning him hold it fast for feare of slights: V. ix. 18. 3

Warns. wisedome *warnes,* whilest foot is in the gate, I. i. 13. 4
warnes the Earth . . . To decke hir selfe, *Am.* iv. 11
That *warnes* al lovers wayt upon their king, *Am.* xix. 3

Warrant. streight his *warrant* made, IV. xii. 32. 1
durst he not the *warrant* to withstand, IV. xii. 33. 1
Loe! here this ring, which shall thy *warrant* bee, V. v. 34. 2
The *warrant* straight was made, VI. vii. 35. 6

Warranty. Withouten pasport or good *warrantye,* *Hub.* 186

Warrayed. the world with sword and fire *warrayd;* I. v. 48. 2
warreyd on Brunchild In Henault, II. x. 21. 7
Soone after this the Romanes him *warrayd,* II. x. 50. 8
puissant kinges which all the world *warrayd,* II. x. 72. 2
Thus *warreid* he long time against his will; III. v. 48. 1
my weak powres of passions *warreid* arre; *Am.* xliv. 7

Warre. *See* **War, Ware.**

Warreid. *See* **Warrayed.**

Warrior. that *warriour* gan abace His threatned speare, II. i. 26. 7
when that *warriour* heard, dismounting straict II. i. 39. 1
what mightie *warriour* that mote bee, II. iii. 12. 2
Mammon, turning to that *warriour,* said; II. vii. 32. 6
Which when that *warriour* saw, he said no more, IV. v. 39. 1
cruell *warriour,* doth herselfe addresse To battell, *Am.* xi. 3
Sweet *warriour!* when shall I have peace with you? *Am.* lvii. 1

Warrioress. that *warriouresse* with haughty crest Did forth issue V. vii. 27. 7

Warriors. An Hydra was of *warriours* glorious, *Ro.* x. 6
great *warriors,* which did overcome The world *Ti.* 61
two so mighty *warriours* he dismade. II. ii. 25. 5
those *warriours* far remove, II. v. 16. 5
Brave Captaines, and most mighty *warriours,* III. iii. 23. 3
carcases of noble *warrioures* III. ix. 35. 7
To graunt unto those *warriours* truce a whyle; IV. vi. 25. 7
many doughty *warriours,* often tride IV. x. 18. 1
These noble *warriors* . . . Them selves thereto preparde V. v. 1. 5
doth procure Great *warriours* oft their rigour to represse, V. viii. 1. 4
gazing fom the Citties wall Uppon these *warriours,* V. xi. 15. 7
famous *warriors* of anticke world Used Trophees to erect *Am.* lxix. 1

War's. All twenty tride in *warres* experience long; IV. x. 7. 7
Then very doubtfull was the *warres* event, V. ii. 17. 1
Of *warres* delight and worlds contentious toyle, VI. v. 37. 6

Wars. civill *warres* me made The whole worlds spoile, *Bel.*[2] x. 9

Wars—*Continued.*
If the blinde furie, which *warres* breedeth oft, . . . *Ro.* xxiv. 1
peace, When *wars* doe surcease: . . . *S.C.* Ap. 125
sing of bloody Mars, of *wars*, of giusts; . . . *S.C.* O. 39
did sing of *warres* and deadly drede, . . . *S.C.* O. 59
late in *warres* have spent my deerest blood, . . . *Hub.* 247
soyl . . . being through long *wars* left almost waste, . . . *Ded. Son.* v. 3
Fierce *warres* and faithful loves shall moralize my song. . . . I. Pr. 1. 9
warres for Ladies doen by many a Lord. . . . I. v. 3. 9
The wise Southsayer . . . telles of *warres* . . . I. v. 8. 9
warres, nor new adventures, none he herd. . . . I. vi. 36. 3
blood can nought but sin, and *wars* but sorrows yield. . . . I. x. 60. 9
I of *warres* and bloody Mars doe sing, . . . I. xi. 7. 2
Brave be her *warres,* and honorable deeds, . . . II. ii. 31. 5
'In woods, in waves, in *warres,* she wonts to dwell, . . . II. iii. 41. 1
Strong *warres* they make, . . . II. iv. 34. 7
more Then all his *wars* and spoiles, . . . II. vi. 35. 9
being retourned late From his fierce *warres,* . . . II. ix. 34. 8
The *warres* he well remembred of king Nine, . . . II. ix. 56. 8
taught the land from wearie *wars* to cease: . . . II. x. 25. 5
Whome Romane *warres* . . . could no whit dismay; . . . II. x. 62. 6
wemen wont in *warres* to beare most sway, . . . III. ii. 2. 2
Trojan *warres* and Priams citie sackt, . . . III. ix. 38. 2
through wearie *wars* and labours long, . . . III. ix. 50. 1
all Cupids *warres* they did repeate, . . . III. xi. 29. 5
forgetting *warres,* he onely joyed In combats of sweet love, . V. v. 24. 8
those old Gyants, which did *warres* darraine . . . VI. vii. 41. 6
warres, and wreckes, and wicked enmitie . . . VI. ix. 19. 6
doth sound on hie *Warres* and allarums . . . VII. vi. 3. 8
To sing of hilles and woods mongst *warres* and Knights, . . . VII. vi. 37. 2
Wary. O! *warie* wisedome of the man, . . . *Ro.* xxiii. 1
each thing fained ought more *warie* bee. . . . *Hub.* 495
She of my flock would take full *warie* keepe. . . . *D.* 133
his *wary* Dwarfe had spyde . . . I. v. 45. 7
he was *wary* of that deadly stowre, . . . I. vii. 12. 5
wise and *wary* was that noble Pere; . . . I. viii. 7. 6
I them warded all with *wary* government. . . . I. ix. 10. 9
so wise and *wary* was the knight . . . II. i. 4. 6
to entrap The man most *wary* . . . II. iv. 17. 5
guyde thy waies with *warie* governaunce, . . . II. iv. 36. 4
he was *wary,* and . . . advaunst his shield atweene, . . . II. iv. 46. 5
Was *wary* wise, and closely did awayt Avauntage, . . . II. v. 9. 6
he was wise, and *wary* of her will, . . . II. vi. 26. 1
keeping *wary* watch and ward, . . . II. vii. 25. 2
he was *wary* wise in all his way, . . . II. vii. 64. 6
Forgets with *wary* warde them to awayt, . . . II. viii. 42. 3
he was *warie,* and it warded well . . . II. xi. 24. 6
them the *wary* Boteman thus bespake: . . . II. xii. 17. 5
lent her *wary* eare to understand . . . III. i. 60. 8
of each turning still kept *wary* heed: . . . III. iv. 48. 5
mote to none but to the *warie* wise appeare. . . . IV. i. 17. 9
like to *warie* Centonels well stayd, . . . IV. ii. 36. 8
The *warie* fowle, that spies him toward bend . . . IV. iii. 19. 5
Like *warie* Hynd within the weedie soyle, . . . IV. x. 55. 8
with right *wary* heede, . . . V. vi. 31. 4
with *warie* heed He shund his strokes, . . . V. xii. 18. 2
And *wary* watch about her . . . keepe. . . . VI. iii. 44. 9
The *warie* foule his bill doth backward wring; . . . VI. vii. 9. 4
Whether more *wary* were to give or ward the blow. . . . VI. viii. 13. 9
Under his club with *wary* boldnesse went, . . . VI. viii. 15. 8
Was (*partial list*). *See* **'Twas, Wast.**
ne yet of marble *was* the wall, . . . *Bel.*[1] ii. 5
Whilom thou *was* peregall to the best, . . . *S.C.* Au. 8
while she *was,* (that *was,* a woful word to sayne!) . . . *S.C.* N. 93
as the thing Which never *was,* . . . *Ti.* 347
whose rugged heare, And whally eies . . . *Was* like the person I. iv. 24. 4
Such one *was* Lechery, the third of all this traine. . . . I. iv. 26. 9
Too late it *was* to Satyres to be told, . . . I. vi. 33. 5
Was never wight that heard that shrilling sownd, . . . I. viii. 4. 1
Such *was* this Gyaunts fall, . . . I. viii. 23. 8
yet he *was* unfitt for bloody fight. . . . I. x. 2. 6
There *was* an auncient house not far away, . . . I. x. 3. 1
She *was* right joyous of her just request; . . . I. x. 33. 1
thou thyselfe, that *was* both borne . . . I. x. 51. 5
this dead corpse, . . . the good Sir Mortdant *was:* . . . II. i. 49. 9
'*Was,* (ay the while, that he is not so now!) . . . II. i. 50. 1
all the wealth which is, or *was* of yore, . . . II. vii. 31. 7
So great a mistresse of her art she *was,* . . . IV. ii. 10. 1
It *was* no mortall worke, that seem'd and yet *was* not. . . . IV. xi. 45. 9
did range and raine, Whilst none *was* him to stop, . . . VI. xii. 2. 9
Wash. billowes Did *wash* the ground-work . . . *Bel.*[2] viii. 2
everie shower will *wash* and wipe away; . . . *Ti.* 205
To *wash* faire Cynthiaes sheep, when they be shorne, . . . *Col.* 258
there Tethys his wet bed Doth ever *wash,* . . . I. i. 39. 7
In wine and oyle they *wash* his woundes wide, . . . I. v. 17. 4
Gehons golden waves doe *wash* continually: . . . I. vii. 43. 9
The filthy blottes of sin to *wash* away. . . . I. x. 27. 7
wash thy hands from guilt of bloody field: . . . I. x. 60. 8
guilt of sinfull crimes cleane *wash* away; . . . I. xi. 30. 2
faynd to *wash* themselves incessantly, . . . II. vii. 61. 6
To spin, to card, to sew, to *wash,* to wring; . . . V. iv. 31. 6
with her teares his wounds did *wash* and steepe: . . . VI. iii. 10. 5
His bloudy vessels *wash,* and holy fire prepare. . . . VI. viii. 39. 9
Washed. Ne may with storming showers be *washt* away, . . . *Ti.* 404
washed all her place with watry eyen. . . . I. ix. 15. 4
clift, Whose false foundacion waves have *washt* away, . . . I. xi. 54. 6
He *washt* them oft and oft, . . . II. ii. 3. 5
washt away his guilt with guilty potion. . . . II. iv. 30. 9
all the blood and filth away was *washt;* . . . II. vi. 42. 8
my handes I *washt* in purity, . . . II. vii. 62. 8

Washed—*Continued.*
with the waves Of wealthy Thamis *washed* is along, . . . III. ix. 45. 2
Are *washt* away quite from their memorie. . . . IV. iii. 44. 7
washt the same with water . . . IV. viii. 13. 3
Her silver feet, faire *washt* against this day: . . . IV. xi. 47. 6
the streame *washt* away her guilty blood. . . . V. ii. 27. 5
The most part of my land hath *washt* away, . . . V. iv. 8. 3
never *washt* In all her life, . . . V. xii. 30. 1
So well she *washt* them, and so well she wacht . . . VI. iii. 10. 6
with thy deare blood clene *washt* from sin, . . . *Am.* lxviii. 7
But came the waves, and *washed* it away: . . . *Am.* lxxv. 2
Washeth. bright Pactolus *washeth* with his streames; . . . *Bel.*[2] xii. 4
washeth Winborne meades in season drye. . . . IV. xi. 32. 4
Washing. *Washing* his bloody wounds, . . . I. vi. 39. 9
nought they beene For all his *washing* cleaner. . . . II. ii. 3. 6
Some of them *washing* with the liquid dew . . . III. vi. 17. 5
Yar, soft *washing* Norwitch wall, . . . IV. xi. 33. 6
Wasp. I saw a *wasp,* that fiercely him defide, . . . *Van.* x. 7
An angry *Waspe* th' one in a viall had, . . . III. xii. 18. 7
Wasserman. The griesly *Wasserman,* that makes his game . . II. xii. 24. 3
Wast (*partial list*). *See* **Waist, Waste, Wasted.**
when thou *wast* in greatest hight, To greatnes growne, . . . *Ro.* xxxi. 12
thou *wast* the Empresse, . . . *Ti.* 83
Waste. *See* **Waist.**
Beholde what wreake, what ruine, and what *wast,* . . . *Ro.* iii. 5
having his wide wings spent in *wast,* . . . *Ro.* xvi. 7
As if my yeare were *wast* and woxen old; . . . *S.C.* Ja. 28
Thy *wast* bignes but combers the grownd, . . . *S.C.* F. 133
made many wounds in the *wast* Oake. . . . *S.C.* F. 202
When I them see so *waist,* . . . *S.C.* Au. 168
the daye in woe, I vowed have to *wayst,* . . . *S.C.* Au. 180
A Lambe, or a Kidde, or a weanell *wast;* . . . *S.C.* S. 198
Sike words bene wynd, and *wasten* soone in vayne. . . . *S.C.* O. 36
Waile ye this wofull *waste* of Natures warke; . . . *S.C.* N. 64
What recked I of wintrye ages *waste?*— . . . *S.C.* D. 29
My harvest, *wast,* my hope away dyd wipe. . . . *S.C.* D. 108
'I carried am into *waste* wildernesse, . . . *Gn.* 369
Waste wildernes, amongst Cymerian shades, . . . *Gn.* 370
by the wayling shores to *waste* my dayes, . . . *Gn.* 621
They cast in course to *waste* the wearie howres. . . . *Hub.* 27
To *wast* long nights in pensive discontent; . . . *Hub.* 898
Nowe doe I nightly *waste,* wanting my kindely reste: . . . *U.V.* 16
if I *waste,* who will bewaile my heavy chaunce? . . . *U.V.* 19
Nor age, nor envie, shall them ever *wast.* . . . *Ti.* 406
disdaine . . . houres in ease to *wast,* . . . *Mui.* 36
in affliction *wast* my better age: . . . *D.* 374
Into a forest wide and *waste* he came, . . . *As.* 93
So wide a forest and so *waste* as this, . . . *As.* 95
that *waste,* where I was quite forgot. . . . *Col.* 183
through long wars left almost *waste,* . . . *Ded. Son.* v. 3
waste wordes retournd to him in vaine: . . . I. i. 42. 2
waste the wearie night In secret anguish . . . I. i. 53. 2
And *wast* his inward gall with deepe despight, . . . I. ii. 6. 4
Then brought she me into this desert *waste,* . . . I. ii. 42. 6
Banisht from living wights, our wearie daies we *waste.'* . . . I. ii. 42. 9
Then serve his Ladies love, and *waste* in pleasures vayne. . . I. vi. 21. 9
Where she did wander in *waste* wildernesse, . . . II. i. 22. 2
Does *waste* his dayes in darke obscuritee, . . . II. iii. 40. 3
come unto an Island *waste* and voyd, . . . II. vi. 11. 3
waste thy joyous howres in needelesse paine, . . . II. vi. 17. 4
suffred rash Pyrochles *waste* his ydle might. . . . II. viii. 48. 9
all the liquour, which was fowle and *waste,* . . . II. ix. 32. 1
Surfeat, misdiet, and unthriftie *waste,* . . . II. xi. 12. 7
lustfull luxurie and thriftlesse *wast.* . . . II. xii. 9. 3
Through countreyes *waste,* and eke well edifyde, . . . III. i. 14. 2
Her wretched dayes in dolour she mote *waste,* . . . III. ii. 17. 8
shee still did *waste,* and still did wayle, . . . III. ii. 52. 3
Was never so great *waste* in any place, . . . III. iii. 34. 5
waste in woe and waylfull miserye: . . . III. iv. 38. 4
in lewd slouth to *wast* his carelesse day; . . . III. v. 1. 7
all his entrayles *wast,* . . . III. v. 48. 5
all my dayes am like to *waste* in vaine, . . . III. vii. 60. 8
wholy *waste* and void of peoples trode, . . . III. ix. 49. 7
Laught at his foolish labour spent in *waste,* . . . III. x. 13. 4
threatens all the world to *wast.* . . . IV. i. 45. 9
wicked Time that all good thoughts doth *waste,* . . . IV. ii. 33. 1
Ne felt his blood to *wast,* . . . IV. iii. 29. 2
wast his wretched daies in wofull plight; . . . IV. vii. 39. 8
The more his weakened body so to *wast,* . . . IV. vii. 41. 8
spoyle to make, and *wast* them unto nought, . . . IV. viii. 48. 7
I *wast* my life, and doe my daies devowre . . . IV. ix. 39. 5
let me *waste* in woe my wretched yeares, . . . IV. xii. 7. 7
his abridged dayes in dolour *wast,* . . . V. v. 46. 6
To weary him the more and *waste* his spight, . . . VI. v. 17. 4
lament . . . And *waste* her goodly beauty, . . . VI. x. 44. 5
The playnes all *waste* and emptie did appeare; . . . VI. xi. 26. 7
here to see all desolate and *wast,* . . . VI. xi. 32. 7
wast and weare away in termes unsure, . . . *Am.* xxv. 3
Through all that great wide *wast,* . . . *H.L.* 70
The daies they *waste,* the nights they grieve . . . *H.L.* 129
To breake his sleepe, and *waste* his ydle braine: . . . *H.L.* 256
a *waste* and emptie place In His wyde Pallace, . . . *H.H.L.* 101
Wasted. 'Thou barrein ground, whome winters wrath hath *wasted,* . . . *S.C.* Ja. 19
My timely buds with wayling all are *wasted;* . . . *S.C.* Ja. 38
His toppe was bald, and *wasted* with wormes, . . . *S.C.* F. 113
the day is nigh *wasted.* . . . *S.C.* F. 246
All will be soone *wasted* with misgovernaunce; . . . *S.C.* May 90
My sheepe bene *wasted;* . . . *S.C.* S. 25
my woe now *wasted* is; . . . *S.C.* N. 201

Wasted—*Continued.*
'Thus is my sommer worne away and *wasted,* . . . *S.C.* D. 97
I likewise have *wasted* much good time, . . . *Hub.* 75
The beautie of the world hath lately *wasted,* . . . *T.M.* 248
now to nought through spoyle of time is *wasted.* . . . *Ti.* 119
'*Wasted* it is, as if it never were; . . . *Ti.* 120
Since that I sawe this gardine *wasted* quite, . . . *Ti.* 529
whose brackish bitter well, I *wasted* have, . . . *D.* 251
His *wasted* life her wearie lodge forwent. . . . *As.* 174
Such, therefore, as that *wasted* soyl doth yield, . . . *Ded. Son.* v. 13
in eternall woes my weaker hart Have *wasted,* . . . I. iv. 46. 8
Through wicked pride and *wasted* welthes decay. . . . I. v. 51. 4
Their kingdome spoild, and countrey *wasted* quight: . . . I. vii. 44. 5
Where he his better dayes hath *wasted* all: . . . I. viii. 28. 8
when her well of teares she *wasted* had, . . . I. viii. 42. 5
wasted life doe lye in ashes low: . . . I. ix. 8. 5
They *wasted* had much way, and measurd many miles. . . . II. ix. 9. 9
fowr hundred yeares And more had *wasted,* . . . II. x. 62. 7
Yet still he *wasted,* as the snow congeald . . . III. v. 49. 5
He was so *wasted* and forpined quight, . . . III. x. 57. 2
Seeing his worke now *wasted,* . . . III. xii. 43. 9
Latonaes childrens wrath that all her issue *wasted.* . . . V. x. 7. 9
Which I have *wasted* in long languishment, . . . *Am.* lx. 11
now it *wasted* is with woes extreame, . . . *H.B.* 25
Wasteful. When Winters *wastful* spight was almost spent, . . . *S.C.* Ja. 2
thou were wont on *wastfull* hylls to singe, . . . *S.C.* Jun. 50
The *wastefull* hylls . . . Is a playne overture. . . . *S.C.* Jul. 27
'Ye *wastefull* Woodes! beare witnesse of my woe, . . . *S.C.* Au. 151
I went the *wastefull* woodes and forest wide, . . . *S.C.* D. 23
Sith now I am but weedes and *wastfull* gras? . . . *Ti.* 42
drownded lie in pleasures *wastefull* well, . . . *Col.* 762
'in *wastfull* wildernesse His dwelling is, . . . I. i. 32. 1
In wildernesse and *wastfull* deserts strayd, . . . I. iii. 3. 4
Through *wastfull* Pride and wanton Riotise, . . . I. v. 46. 5
Fled to the *wastfull* wildernesse apace, . . . I. viii. 50. 3
still he traveild through wide *wastfull* ground, . . . II. vii. 2. 8
still sat wayting on that *wastfull* clift . . . II. xii. 8. 6
feard to wander in that *wastefull* mist, . . . II. xii. 35. 3
in lewd loves, and *wastfull* luxuree, . . . II. xii. 80. 7
Long so they traveiled through *wastefull* wayes, . . . III. i. 3. 1
Banisht from princely bowre to *wastefull* wood! . . . III. iii. 42. 6
Shortly unto the *wastefull* woods she came, . . . III. vi. 17. 1
yonder in that *wastefull* wildernesse . . . III. x. 40. 3
wastefull emptinesse And solemne silence . . . III. xi. 53. 6
Through the wide region of the *wastfull* aire, . . . IV. viii. 8. 8
Wasteness. Through woods and *wastnes* wide him daily sought; I. iii. 3. 8
Wastes. Where she in darknes *wastes* her cursed daies and nights. . . . IV. i. 19. 9
In languor *wastes* his life: . . . IV. xii. Arg.
wounds the life, and *wastes* the inmost marrow. . . . *H.B.* 63
Wasteth. a straunge man . . . That *wasteth* all this countrie, I. i. 31. 4
Wasting. no worlds sad care nor *wasting* woe . . . *D.* 283
suckt the *wasting* breath Out of his lips . . . *As.* 165
with the *wasting* of his vitall flood, . . . IV. iii. 28. 8
Wasting the strength of her immortall age: . . . VI. vi. 11. 6
Wasting her goodly hew in heavie teares, . . . VI. vii. 38. 3
Watch. ever liggen in *watch* and ward, . . . *S.C.* S. 234
All the cold season to *wach* and waite; . . . *S.C.* S. 237
the flocks, which thou doest *watch* and warde; . . . *S.C.* D. 12
Or *watch* his mares, or take his charge of kyne? . . . *Hub.* 286
all the night that I in *watch* did spend, . . . *D.* 129
Shee would all night by mee or *watch* or sleepe . . . *D.* 131
warily still *watch* which way she went, . . . *Col.* 133
when she slept, he kept both *watch* and ward; . . . I. iii. 9. 5
at her feete the Lyon *watch* doth keepe: . . . I. iii. 15. 4
Still did he wake, and still did *watch* for dawning light. . . . I. v. 1. 9
watch the noyous night, and wait for joyous day. . . . I. xi. 50. 9
they him . . . with continual *watch* did warely keepe. . . . I. xii. 36. 3
keeping wary *watch* and ward, . . . II. vii. 25. 2
ever as he went dew *watch* upon him kept. . . . II. vii. 26. 9
They for us fight, they *watch* and dewly ward, . . . II. viii. 2. 6
watch thou, I pray; For evill is at hand . . . II. viii. 8. 6
wisely *watch* to ward that deadly stowre; . . . II. viii. 35. 4
forth looked from the highest spire The *watch,* . . . II. ix. 11. 7
Day and night duely keeping *watch* and ward; . . . II. ix. 25. 2
through long *watch,* and late daies weary toile, . . . III. i. 58. 8
Kept *watch* and ward about her warily, . . . III. ii. 28. 7
sett her by to *watch,* and sett her by to weepe. . . . III. ii. 47. 9
with *watch* and hard restraynt . . . III. ix. 6. 8
one eies *watch* escape: . . . III. ix. 31. 6
Two eies him needeth, for to *watch* and wake, . . . III. ix. 31. 7
Paridell kept better *watch* then hee, . . . III. x. 4. 1
Vaine was the *watch,* and bootlesse all the ward, . . . III. xi. 31. 8
when the second *watch* was almost past, . . . III. xii. 29. 6
the *watch,* that kept continuall ward, . . . IV. ix. 5. 6
day and night did *watch* and duely ward . . . IV. x. 17. 2
To keepe a nightly *watch* for dread of treachery. . . . V. iv. 46. 9
for which a little whyle Ye will not *watch?* . . . V. vi. 25. 4
I wote when ye did *watch* both night and day . . . V. vi. 25. 5
Thus did she *watch,* and weare the weary night . . . V. vi. 26. 1
Uppon their wall good *watch* and ward did keepe. . . . V. vii. 26. 6
He gan to *watch* the wielding of his hand, . . . V. xi. 7. 2
watch advauntage how to worke his care, . . . V. xi. 13. 4
by her wounded love did *watch* all night, . . . VI. iii. 10. 3
wary *watch* about her . . . keepe. . . . VI. iii. 44. 9
who did wayle or *watch* the wearie night? . . . VI. vii. 30. 6
to keepe them with continuall *watch* and ward; . . . VI. x. 43. 2
her all night did *watch,* and all the day molest. . . . VI. xi. 5. 9
Unwont with heards to *watch,* . . . VI. xi. 40. 4
Which they did daily *watch,* and nightly wake . . . VII. vii. 45. 8

Watched. whilest the one was *watcht,* . . . *Col.* 139
it was warely *watched* night and day, . . . I. x. 5. 2
All night shee *watcht,* . . . I. xi. 32. 7
watcht that none should enter nor issew: . . . III. xi. 31. 7
Still *watcht* on every side, of secret foes affrayd, . . . IV. ii. 36. 9
watcht continually, Lying without her dore . . . V. vi. 26. 6
Whiles Talus *watched* at the dore all night. . . . V. vii. 26. 4
With Belge, who *watcht* all this while full sad, . . . V. xi. 32. 8
well she washt them, and so well she *wacht* him, . . . VI. iii. 10. 6
He *watcht* in close awayt with weapons prest, . . . VI. vi. 44. 3
Watch's. Two goodly Beacons, set in *watches* stead, . . . II. ix. 46. 3
Watches. *See* **Night-watches.**
wakefull *watches* ever to abide; . . . II. iii. 41. 6
false *watches,* wellaway! . . . V. vi. 25. 4
Watchet. Their *watchet* mantles frindgd with silver rownd, . . . III. iv. 40. 5
All decked in a robe of *watchet* hew, . . . IV. xi. 27. 2
Watcheth. warily he *watcheth* every way, . . . III. x. 3. 4
Watchful. Him to deceive, for all his *watchfull* ward, . . . *Col.* 136
The souldier may not move from *watchfull* sted, . . . I. ix. 41. 4
they were both so *watchfull* and well eyde, . . . IV. iii. 7. 8
Called aloud unto the *watchfull* ward . . . V. x. 31. 3
Watchfulness. How, but, with heede and *watchfullnesse,* . . . *S.C.* S. 230
Thus she all night wore out in *watchfulnesse,* . . . V. vi. 34. 8
Watching. dogges . . . *Watching* to banish Care their enimy, . . . I. i. 40. 5
th' evill thinkes by *watching* to prevent: . . . III. x. 3. 6
Watching to drive the ravenous Wolfe away, . . . VI. ix. 37. 4
Watchman. The *watchman* wayting tydings glad to heare; . . . I. xi. 3. 7
the *watchman* on the castle-wall; . . . I. xii. 2. 6
by the *watchman* were Descried streight; . . . V. iv. 36. 1
Watchmen. through the *watchmen,* who him never spide: . . . *Hub.* 1302
*they arriving, by the *watchmen* were Descried . . . V. iv. 36. 1
Water. *See* **Broad-water, Blackwater, Holy water, Holy water sprinkle.**
He shed a *water,* . . . *Bel.*[1] vii. 6
with their feete uncleane the *water* fouled, . . . *Bel.*[1] x. 13
leaning on the belly of a pot, Pourd foorth a *water,* . . . *Bel.*[2] ix. 6
Strake on a rock, that under *water* lay, . . . *Pet.* ii. 9
A spring of *water,* mildly rumbling downe, . . . *Pet.* iv. 2
Spying the tree destroid, the *water* dride, . . . *Pet.* v. 9
part by land and part by *water* fed; . . . *Hub.* 1120
As if shee all to *water* would have gone; . . . *T.M.* 596
as a glasse upon the *water* shone, . . . *Ti.* 220
steeds . . . gan *water* in the west, . . . *D.* 25
water doth within his bancks appeare.' . . . *Col.* 95
Till they into the Mullaes *water* slide. . . . *Col.* 144
life to move it selfe upon the *water.* . . . *Col.* 219
the cold began to covet heat, And *water* fire; . . . *Col.* 848
'Her neather partes misshapen, monstruous, Were hidd in *water,* . . . I. ii. 41. 2
on her shoulders sad a pot of *water* bore. . . . I. iii. 10. 9
fifty sisters *water* in leke vessels draw. . . . I. v. 35. 9
a cup of gold, With wine and *water* fild . . . I. x. 13. 3
embay His blamefull body in salt *water* . . . I. x. 27. 6
in the *water* weene . . . from bloody gore to cleene. . . . II. ii. 3. 2
Might not be purgd with *water* nor with bath; . . . II. ii. 4. 2
her vertues in her *water* byde, . . . II. ii. 9. 6
clensd with *water* of this well: . . . II. ii. 10. 2
to behold the *water* worke and play . . . II. vi. 7. 8
Will die for thrist, and *water* doth refuse? . . . II. vi. 17. 8
Yet still he bet the *water,* . . . II. vi. 42. 9
Above the *water* were on high extent, . . . II. vii. 61. 5
That quicksand nigh with *water* covered; . . . II. xii. 18. 6
Ne doe they need with *water* of the ford, . . . III. vi. 34. 7
then that same *water* of Ardenne, . . . IV. iii. 45. 2
muddie *water,* that like puddle stanke, . . . IV. v. 33. 4
running *water* tempred with his teares, . . . IV. vii. 41. 7
water which did well From his moist eies, . . . IV. viii. 13. 3
water all the English soile throughout: . . . IV. xi. 30. 2
wav'd upon, like *water* Chamelot, . . . IV. xi. 45. 6
Ne ought the *water* cooled their whot bloud, . . . V. ii. 13. 3
that use well knew To fight in *water,* . . . V. ii. 13. 6
durst the depth of any *water* sownd. . . . V. ii. 16. 7
from the *water* to the land betooke his flight. . . . V. ii. 17. 9
bread and *water* or like feeble thing, . . . V. iv. 31. 8
all the *water* which doth ronne In the next brooke, . . . VI. iv. 32. 8
Yet were her words but wynd, and all her teares but *water.* . . . VI. vi. 42. 9
'Ne is the *water* in more constant case, . . . VII. vii. 20. 1
Ayre to *Water* sheere, And *Water* into Earth; yet *Water* fights With Fire, . . . VII. vii. 25. 6, 7
she sayes, Teares are but *water,* . . . *Am.* xviii. 10
Not *water;* for her love doth burne like fyre: . . . *Am.* lv. 6
The earth, the ayre, the *water,* and the fyre, . . . *H.L.* 78
Ayre hated earth, and *water* hated fyre, . . . *H.L.* 83
Ayre more then *water* . . . appeares more pure and fayre. . . . *H.H.B.* 48
Soyle their fayre plumes with *water* . . . *Proth.* 50
Water-course. The Nimph, which of that *water course* has charge, *Col.* 109
Water-courses. his *water-courses* spill. . . . *Col.* 151
Watered. han be *watered* at the Muses well; . . . *S.C.* N. 30
his faint steedes *watred* in Ocean deepe, . . . I. xi. 31. 3
Water-flood. Like a great *water flood,* . . . II. xi. 18. 4
Waterford. adornes rich *Waterford;* . . . IV. xi. 43. 2
Water-ford. he is heard back from that *water foord* Drave, . . . *Gn.* 166
Water-mill. The streame thereof would drive a *water-mill:* . . . I. xi. 22. 6
Water-nymphs. 'The *water Nymphs,* that wont with her to sing *S.C.* N. 143
Water's. the soft (gentle[1]) sounding of the *waters* fall: . . . *Pet.* iv. 7
tuned it unto the *Waters* fall. . . . *S.C.* Ap. 36
To the *waters* fall their tunes attemper . . . *S.C.* Jun. 8
The speaking woods, and murmuring *waters* fall, . . . *Col.* 636
the base murmure of the *waters* fall; . . . II. xii. 71. 6
Alebius, that know'th The *waters* depth, . . . IV. xi. 14. 8

Water's—*Continued.*
In swimming be expert, through *waters* force to pas. . . . . V. ii. 16. 9
to the *waters* fall tuning their accents fit. . . . . VI. x. 7. 9
Waters. his sweete *waters* away with him led. . . . . *Ti.* 147
a wilde wildernes of *waters* deepe: . . . . . *Mui.* 287
The running *waters* wept for thy returne, ... *Col.* 27
A world of *waters* heaped up on hie, ... *Col.* 197
Dauncing upon the *waters* back to lond, ... *Col.* 214
deep *waters* which her drownd alway: . . . . . *Col.* 858
through the world of *waters* wide and deepe, ... I. i. 39. 2
the *waters,* which from her did flow, ... I. vii. 5. 6
Thenceforth her *waters* wexed dull and slow, ... I. vii. 5. 8
Had vertue pourd into their *waters* bace, ... II. ii. 6. 8
What colour were their *waters* that same day, ... II. x. 24. 3
the hoare *waters* from his frigot ran, ... II. xii. 10. 3
to and fro doe ronne In the wide *waters:* . . . . . II. xii. 11. 6
Whose circled *waters* rapt with whirling sway, ... II. xii. 20. 5
The surging *waters* like a mountaine rise, ... II. xii. 21. 6
one would lift the other quight Above the *waters,* . . . . . II. xii. 64. 2
Birdes, voices, instruments, windes, *waters,* . . . . . II. xii. 70. 9
The *waters* fall with difference discreet, ... II. xii. 71. 7
bid His mighty *waters* to them buxome bee: . . . . . III. iv. 32. 6
the great *waters* gin apace to swell, ... III. viii. 24. 2
His borrowed *waters* forst to redisbourse, ... IV. iii. 27. 7
which Pactolus with his *waters* shere Throwes forth . . . . IV. vi. 20. 8
Else would the *waters* overflow the lands, ... IV. x. 35. 5
The *waters* play, and pleasant lands appeare, ... IV. x. 44. 8
Eurypulus, that calmes the *waters* wroth; . . . . . IV. xi. 14. 4
in whose *waters* cleane Ten thousand fishes play . . . . . IV. xi. 29. 8
let their swelling *waters* low before him fall. . . . . IV. xi. 30. 9
many rivers taking under-hand Into his *waters* . . . . . IV. xi. 34. 4
waters gray By faire Kilkenny and Rosseponte boord; . . . IV. xi. 43. 3
all mankinde do nourish with their *waters* clere. . . . . IV. xi. 52. 9
Whose *waters* with his filthy bloud it stayned; . . . . . V. ii. 19. 2
Hemd in with *waters* like a wall in sight, ... V. ii. 35. 7
In the woods shade which did the *waters* crowne, ... VI. x. 7. 7
The kingdome of the Night, and *waters* by her wained. . . . VII. vi. 10. 9
Sprinkled with wholsom *waters* more then most on ground: . . VII. vi. 38. 9
teach the woods and *waters* to lament . . . . . *Epith.* 10
in his *waters,* which your mirror make, ... *Epith.* 63
like old Peneus *Waters* they did seeme, ... *Proth.* 78
Water-sprinkle. *See* **Holy-water sprinkle.**
Water-sprinkles. As fast as *water-sprinkles* gainst a rocke are dasht. . . . . IV. iii. 25. 9
Water-stream. Forth gushed, like fresh *water streame* from riven rocke. . . . . I. viii. 10. 9
Like as a *water-streame,* . . . . . VI. i. 21. 1
Water-streams. teares, which gushed fast Like many *water streames,* . . . . . VI. viii. 19. 2
Watery. The *watrie* wette weighed downe his head, ... *S.C.* F. 232
Forsake your *watry* bowres, ... *S.C.* Ap. 39
the blacke Holme that loves the *watrie* vale; . . . . . *Gn.* 215
Though eating hipps, and drinking *watry* fome. . . . . *Hub.* 948
With fained face, and *watrie* eyne halfe weeping, ... *Hub.* 1362
His ship far come from *watrie* wildernesse; . . . . . I. iii. 32. 4
washed all her place with *watry* eyen. . . . . I. ix. 15. 4
With hart then throbbing, and with *watry* eyes, ... II. iv. 17. 1
with his oares did sweepe the *watry* wildernesse. . . . . II. xii. 29. 9
he faded to a *watry* flowre: . . . . . III. ii. 45. 4
The *watry* Southwinde, from the seabord coste Upblowing, . III. iv. 13. 4
Amongst her *watry* sisters by a pond, ... III. iv. 29. 7
to her *watry* chamber swiftly carry him. . . . . III. iv. 42. 9
His *watry* eies drizling like deawy rayne, ... III. v. 34. 3
Foolish Narcisse, that likes the *watry* shore; . . . . . III. vi. 45. 5
Do meete together on the *watry* lea, ... IV. ii. 16. 3
A *watry* cloud doth overcast the skie, ... IV. iv. 47. 7
that great banquet of the *watry* Gods, ... IV. xi. 10. 8
So went he playing on the *watery* plaine; . . . . . IV. xi. 24. 1
leaving *watry* gods, as booting nought, ... IV. xii. 25. 2
in a *watry* cloud displayed wide Her goodly bow, ... V. iii. 25. 2
Whom whylest she did with *watrie* eyne behold, ... VI. xii. 7. 6
'So likewise are all *watry* living wights Still tost . . . . VII. vii. 21. 1
Ne have the *watry* foules a certaine grange . . . . . VII. vii. 21. 7
Wave. Upon the glyttering *wave* doth playe, ... *S.C.* Au. 91
tinsell trappings, woven like a *wave,* . . . . . I. ii. 13. 8
bubbling *wave* did ever freshly well, ... I. vii. 4. 6
That makes frayle flesh to feare the bitter *wave,* . . . . . I. ix. 40. 5
In all his waies through this wide worldes *wave;* . . . . . I. x. 34. 8
As Eagle, fresh out of the ocean *wave,* . . . . . I. xi. 34. 3
with her brest breaking the fomy *wave,* . . . . . II. ii. 24. 8
do glaunce and glide Upon the trembling *wave,* . . . . . II. v. 2. 5
whose murmuring *wave* did play Emongst the pumy stones, . II. v. 30. 2
It cut away upon the yielding *wave,* . . . . . II. vi. 5. 6
The slouthfull *wave* of that great griesy lake: . . . . . II. vi. 18. 7
Whiles thus they strugled in that ydle *wave,* . . . . . II. vi. 47. 1
As Pilot well expert in perilous *wave,* . . . . . II. vii. 1. 1
with uncomely weedes the gentle *wave* accloyes. . . . . II. vii. 15. 9
dipped in the bitter *wave* Of hellish Styx, ... II. viii. 20. 8
all his sences drowned in deep sencelesse *wave:* . . . . . II. viii. 24. 9
drive The hollow vessell through the threatfull *wave;* . . . II. xii. 5. 6
by the checked *wave* they did descry It plaine, ... II. xii. 18. 7
with the angry working of the *wave* . . . . . III. viii. 37. 4
Waved. They *waved* like a penon wyde dispred, ... II. iii. 30. 4
wav'd upon, like water Chamelot, ... IV. xi. 45. 6
Waver. Perceived him to *waver,* weake and fraile, ... I. ix. 49. 2
Wavering. the heavens still *wavering* thus, ... *Bel.*[2] xv. 3
All was blowne away of the *wavering* wynd. . . . . *S.C.* D. 126
No common things may please a *wavering* wit. . . . . *Mui.* 160
into diverse doubt his *wavering* wonder clove. . . . . II. ii. 3. 9
Out of his *wavering* seat him pluckt perforse, ... III. vii. 43. 2

Wavering—*Continued.*
phantasies In *wavering* wemens witt, ... III. xii. 26. 4
flitting as the *wavering* wind After each beautie . . . . . IV. ii. 5. 2
doubtfull fortune *wavering* to and fro, ... IV. iii. 17. 7
albe he earst did wyte His *wavering* mind, ... V. xi. 57. 7
led Her *wavering* lust after her wandring sight, ... VI. iii. 23. 7
Waves. flame, Mounting like *waves* . . . . . *Bel.*[1] ix. 2
As *waves,* as winde, as fire, spred over all, ... *Ro.* xvi. 13
sweepe The fomie *waves* out of the dreadfull deep, ... *Van.* v. 5
all the *waves* were stain'd with filthie hewe. . . . . *Van.* v. 12
Heaping up *waves* of welth and woe, ... *S.C.* May 93
His brackish *waves* be meynt. . . . . *S.C.* Jul. 84
These wisards welter in welths *waves,* . . . . . *S.C.* Jul. 197
the sweete *waves* of sounding Castaly . . . . . *Gn.* 23
'Ne feard the burning *waves* of Phlegeton, ... *Gn.* 441
In liquid *waves* to cut their fomie waie, ... *Ti.* 149
feare The dashing of the *waves,* . . . . . *Mui.* 283
light fluttering Upon the *waves,* . . . . . *Mui.* 291
nor raine, Nor swelling *waves,* . . . . . *Col.* 222
His fattie *waves* doe fertile slime outwell, ... I. i. 21. 3
The Sunne . . . doth baite his steedes the Ocean *waves* emong. I. i. 32. 9
starre That was in Ocean *waves* yet never wet, ... I. ii. 1. 3
They pas the bitter *waves* of Acheron, ... I. v. 33. 1
In westerne *waves* his weary wagon did recure. . . . . I. v. 44. 9
Gehons golden *waves* doe wash continually: . . . . . I. vii. 43. 9
with innocent blood Defyld those sacred *waves,* . . . . . I. xi. 29. 8
clift, Whose false foundacion *waves* have washt away, . . I. xi. 54. 6
the cleane *waves* with purple gore did ray: . . . . . II. i. 40. 4
Ne lets her *waves* with any filth be dyde; . . . . . II. ii. 9. 8
'In woods, in *waves,* in warres, she wonts to dwell, ... II. iii. 41. 1
Thus in still *waves* of deepe delight to wade, ... II. v. 35. 2
Emongst wide *waves* sett, like a litle nest, ... II. vi. 12. 2
on the dull *waves* did lightly flote, ... II. vi. 38. 3
he rudely flasht The *waves* about, ... II. vi. 42. 7
The *waves* thereof so slow and sluggish were, ... II. vi. 46. 6
sprinckled ofte the same With liquid *waves,* . . . . . II. vii. 36. 5
many damned wightes In those sad *waves,* . . . . . II. vii. 57. 3
ne was it paysd Amid the ocean *waves,* . . . . . II. x. 5. 6
Upon the *waves* to spred her trembling light, ... II. xii. 2. 5
Over the *waves* his rugged armes doth lift, ... II. xii. 4. 4
on this rock are rent, and sunck in helples *wawes.'* . . . . II. xii. 4. 9
The *waves* come rolling, ... II. xii. 22. 1
in the fomy *waves* enrold, ... II. xii. 25. 4
on the rocke the *waves* breaking aloft . . . . . II. xii. 33. 3
seemd the *waves* were into yvory . . . sent; . . . . . II. xii. 45. 3
yvory into the *waves* were sent; . . . . . II. xii. 45. 4
through the *waves* one might the bottom see, ... II. xii. 62. 7
through the christall *waves* appeared plaine: . . . . . II. xii. 64. 7
So hidd in lockes and *waves* from lookers theft, ... II. xii. 67. 8
sparckling on the silent *waves,* . . . . . II. xii. 78. 9
his heaped *waves* he did commaund . . . . . III. iv. 22. 3
The *waves,* obedient to theyr beheast, ... III. iv. 31. 8
As swifte as swallowes on the *waves* they went, ... III. iv. 33. 5
through the brackish *waves* their passage sheare; . . . . . III. iv. 42. 7
Did heape on her new *waves* of weary wretchednesse. . . . III. viii. 20. 9
Along the fomy *waves* driving his finny drove. . . . . III. viii. 29. 9
drawne upon the *waves* that fomed him arownd. . . . . III. viii. 30. 9
drag'd him through the *waves* in scornfull state, ... III. viii. 36. 7
like to a storme Raging within the *waves:* . . . . . III. viii. 41. 4
with the *waves* Of wealthy Thamis washed is along, ... III. ix. 45. 1
Into huge *waves* of griefe and gealosye . . . emplonged was, . III. x. 17. 4
made the sparckling *waves* to smoke agayne, ... III. xi. 41. 3
wall'd it with *waves,* which rag'd and ror'd . . . . . IV. xi. 3. 6
the *waves* to tame. . . . . IV. xi. 12. 9
the *waves,* glittering like Christall glas, ... IV. xi. 27. 3
Bristow faire, which on his *waves* he builded hath. . . . . IV. xi. 31. 9
Mulla mine, whose *waves* I whilom taught to weep. . . . . IV. xi. 41. 9
with *waves* continuall Doe eate the earth, ... V. ii. 39. 4
by rage of *waves* that never rest, ... V. iv. 19. 4
wading through the *waves* with stedfast sway, ... V. xii. 5. 6
A Ladie on rough *waves* row'd in a sommer barge. . . . . VI. ii. 44. 9
strongly wading through the *waves* unused, ... VI. iii. 33. 7
flud His silver *waves* did softly tumble downe, ... VI. x. 7. 2
So now her *waves* passe through a pleasant Plaine, ... VII. vi. 53. 7
waves, through which he waded for his loves delight. . . . VII. vii. 33. 9
doth strongly part The raging *waves,* . . . . . *Am.* lix. 6
But came the *waves,* and washed it away: . . . . . *Am.* lxxv. 2
Witnesse Leander in the Euxine *waves,* . . . . . *H.L.* 231
And all the *Waves* did strew, ... *Proth.* 77
Waving. flame . . . *Waving* aloft with triple point . . . . . *Bel.*[2] xi. 2
mowes The *waving* lockes of those faire yeallow heares, . . *Ro.* xxx. 6
with his *waving* wings displayed wyde, ... I. xi. 18. 1
heares With the loose wynd ye *waving* chance to marke; . . *Am.* lxxxi. 2
Wawes. *See* **Waves.**
Wax. made this foolish Brere *wexe* so bold, ... *S.C.* F. 124
learne with Lettice to *wexe* light, ... *S.C.* Mar. 20
(As garments doen, which *wexen* old above,) . . . . . *S.C.* Jun. 39
Didst underfong my lasse to *wexe* so light, ... *S.C.* Jun. 103
Such woundes soone *wexen* wider. . . . . *S.C.* Au. 96
the cloudes *wexen* cleare. . . . . *S.C.* S. 18
helmes unbruzed *wexen* dayly browne. . . . . *S.C.* O. 42
to *wexe* olde at home in idlenesse Is disadventrous, ... *Hub.* 99
The Priest gan *wexe* halfe proud to be so praide, ... *Hub.* 413
by wrestling to *wex* strong and heedfull, ... *Hub.* 746
unhappy Swaine, That here *wex* old in sleepe, ... I. ii. 4. 7
still *wex* old in woe, whiles wo stil wexeth new. . . . . I. ix. 9. 9
High time now gan it *wex* . . . . . I. xi. 1. 1
His hart gan *wexe* as starke as marble stone, ... II. i. 42. 2
this liegeman gan to *wexe* more bold, ... II. iii. 9. 2
Now gan Pyrochles *wex* as wood as hee, ... II. v. 20. 6

Wax—*Continued.*

Tho gan that villein *wex* so fiers and strong, . . . II. v. 23. 1
vitall powres gan *wexe* both weake and wan . . . II. vii. 65. 2
when her sonne to mans estate did *wex*, . . . II. x. 20. 8
wearie *wax* of his continuall stay. . . . II. x. 30. 5
Shee greatly gan enamoured to *wex* . . . III. i. 47. 4
like a shadowe *wexe*, . . . III. ii. 44. 4
when his force gan faile his pace gan *wex* areare. . . . III. vii. 24. 9
virgin *wex* that never yet was seald, . . . III. viii. 6. 7
that other knight begonne To *wex* exceeding wroth, . . . III. viii. 17. 8
he gan to *wex* exceeding wroth, . . . III. ix. 13. 6
Then did her glorious flowre *wex* dead and wan, . . . IV. viii. 32. 8
those two Ladies much asham'd did *wexe:* . . . IV. viii. 35. 7
Calidore . . . doth make Briana *wexe* more mylde. . . . VI. i. Arg.
Did *wexe* exceeding sorrowfull and sad, . . . VI. v. 3. 3
Untill the Damzell gan to *wex* more sound and strong. . . . VI. xii. 11. 9

Waxed. *See* **Wox, Waxen, Woxen.**

His cheekes *wext* pale, . . . *D.* 542
being former foes, they *wexed* friends, . . . *Col.* 851
when he heard of harme he *wexed* wondrous glad. . . . I. iv. 30. 9
Thenceforth her waters *wexed* dull and slow, . . . I. vii. 5. 8
silver Cynthia *wexed* pale and faynt, . . . I. vii. 34. 8
that weake captive wight now *wexed* strong, . . . I. ix. 2. 3
Thus as he spake, his visage *wexed* pale, . . . I. ix. 16. 1
thrust them forth still as they *wexed* old: . . . I. x. 31. 4
the Scarcrow *wexed* wondrous prowd, . . . II. iii. 7. 1
He *wexed* wondrous wroth, . . . II. iv. 45. 2
he *wexed* wondrous woe; . . . II. viii. 53. 4
The warlike virgine . . . *wexed* inlie wroth; . . . IV. i. 10. 6
that his may so be trebly *wext*. . . . IV. ii. 52. 9
As if but now the battell *wexed* warme. . . . IV. iv. 35. 5
saw he often how he *wexed* glad . . . IV. vii. 46. 7
he *wexed* weary of his owne, . . . V. i. 17. 2
Which when the Pagan saw he *wexed* wroth, . . . V. ii. 12. 1
Wroth *wext* he then, . . . V. ii. 45. 1
onely *wexed* now the more aware . . . V. xi. 13. 2
of his wounds he *wexed* hole and strong; . . . VI. i. 47. 8
Which when as Cupid heard, he *wexed* wroth; . . . VI. vii. 33. 6
He thereat *wext* exceedingly astound, . . . VI. viii. 27. 7
he *wexed* wood And halfe enraged . . . VI. xi. 25. 3
There-at Jove *wexed* wroth, . . . VII. vi. 35. 7
In youth, before I *waxed* old, . . . *Epig.* i. 1

Waxen. *See* **Waxed, Woxen.**

Working her formall rowmes in *wexen* frame, . . . *S.C.* D. 68
so leane and meagre *waxen* late, . . . *Hub.* 599
through inward sorrowe *wexen* faint, . . . *Ti.* 472
Eftesoones long *waxen* torches weren light . . . III. i. 58. 3

Waxeth. still wex old in woe, whiles wo stil *wexeth* new. . . . I. ix. 9. 9
then *wexeth* wood and yond: . . . II. viii. 40. 9

Waxing. Mammon *wexing* wroth; . . . II. vii. 14. 6
Tho *wexing* weary of that toylesome paine, . . . VI. iii. 29. 3

Way. *See* **By-way, Everyway, Highway, Midway, Noway, Straightway, Weigh.**

A puissant armie come the selfe same *way*. . . . *Rev.* iii. 7
Ten feete each *way* in square . . . *Bel.* iii. 2
all the *way* most pleasant notes did sing, . . . *Bel.*[2] xi. 7
wretched people travailing that *way*, . . . *Van.* iii. 5
Whose *way* is wildernesse, whose ynne Penaunce, . . . *S.C.* F. 89
The Hus-bandman selfe to come that *way*, . . . *S.C.* F. 144
they play, And sing all the *way*, . . . *S.C.* Ap. 107
may depart Eche one her *way*. . . . *S.C.* Ap. 148
shepheard must walke another *way*, . . . *S.C.* May 81
does the right *way* forsake: . . . *S.C.* May 165
Making his *way* . . . *S.C.* Jul. 19
ledde of theyr sheepe what *way* they wyll, . . . *S.C.* S. 81
balk the right *way*, and strayen abroad. . . . *S.C.* S. 93
what *way* shall I wend, . . . *S.C.* S. 244
choise I had to choose my wandring *waye*, . . . *S.C.* D. 62
all things in his *way* Full stearnly rends . . . *Gn.* 271
Observ'd th' appointed *way*, as her behooved, . . . *Gn.* 467
ere that anie *way* I doo betake, . . . *Hub.* 69
put themselves (a Gods name) on their *way;* . . . *Hub.* 111
they chaunst to meet upon the *way* . . . *Hub.* 227
seeke some other *way* to gaine by giving, . . . *Hub.* 350
From the right *way* full eath may wander wide: . . . *Hub.* 404
Then must thou thee dispose another *way:* . . . *Hub.* 504
This is the *way* for one that is unlern'd . . . *Hub.* 535
So parted they, as eithers *way* them led. . . . *Hub.* 551
At last they chaunst to meete upon the *way* . . . *Hub.* 581
he tooke his *way* Into the forest, . . . *Hub.* 1064
Thus dight, into the Court he tooke his *way*, . . . *Hub.* 1300
no more endure, but came his *way*, . . . *Hub.* 1315
all the *way* he roared as he went, . . . *Hub.* 1345
the travailer, that fares that *way*, . . . *Ti.* 6
In liquid waves to cut their fomie *waie*, . . . *Ti.* 149
they see not the *way* of their confusion. . . . *Ti.* 458
all the *way* most heavenly noyse was heard . . . *Ti.* 612
still I may be readie on my *way* . . . *D.* 458
hellish hags had met upon the *way;* . . . *D.* 566
warily still watch which *way* she went, . . . *Col.* 133
Which *way* his course the wanton Bregog bent; . . . *Col.* 135
Passe unespide to meete her by the *way;* . . . *Col.* 140
which *way* he list, and whether. . . . *Col.* 251
As if the *way* she perfectly had knowne. . . . *Col.* 269
Led with delight, they thus beguile the *way*, . . . I. i. 10. 1
creeping sought *way* in the weedy gras: . . . I. i. 20. 8
forward on his *way* (with God to frend) . . . I. i. 28. 7
Long *way* he traveiled before he heard of ought. . . . I. i. 28. 9
they chaunst to meet upon the *way* An aged Sire, . . . I. i. 29. 1
all the *way* he prayed as he went, . . . I. i. 29. 8

Way—*Continued.*

'the *way* to win Is wisely to advise; . . . I. i. 33. 5
He, making speedy *way* through spersed ayre, . . . I. i. 39. 1
chaunst to meete up on the *way* A faithlesse Sarazin, . . . I. ii. 12. 5
Hee had a faire companion of his *way*, . . . I. ii. 13. 1
She intertainde her lover all the *way;* . . . I. ii. 14. 2
The red bloud trickling staind the *way*, . . . I. ii. 14. 9
weary of their *way*, they came at last . . . I. ii. 28. 2
One day, nigh wearie of the yrkesome *way*, . . . I. iii. 4. 1
Shamefully at her rayling all the *way*, . . . I. iii. 23. 3
long misery, Might fall on her, and follow all the *way*, . . . I. iii. 23. 8
And in the *way*, . . . A knight her mett . . . I. iii. 24. 3
all the *way* they spent Discoursing . . . I. iii. 32. 6
all the *way* . . . she filleth his dull eares, . . . I. iii. 44. 1
all the *way* she wetts with flowing teares; . . . I. iii. 44. 4
she is wearie of the toilsom *way*, . . . I. iv. 3. 8
He leaves the welkin *way* most beaten playne, . . . I. iv. 9. 7
when she does ride . . . through heavens bras-paved *way*, . . . I. iv. 17. 7
When such an one had guiding of the *way*, . . . I. iv. 19. 8
all the *way*, . . . He spued up his gorge, . . . I. iv. 21. 8
before their *way* A foggy mist had covered all the land; . . . I. iv. 36. 6
Through widest ayre making his ydle *way*, . . . I. v. 8. 4
to the Easterne coast of heaven makes speedy *way:* . . . I. v. 19. 9
Through mirkesome aire her ready *way* she makes: . . . I. v. 28. 3
By that same *way* the direfull dames doe drive . . . I. v. 32. 1
took her wonted *way* To ronne her timely race, . . . I. v. 44. 7
Scarse could he footing find in that fowle *way*, . . . I. v. 53. 1
Where none appeares can make her selfe a *way:* . . . I. vi. 7. 2
A wondrous *way* it for this Lady wrought, . . . I. vi. 7. 3
all the *way* their merry pipes they sound. . . . I. vi. 14. 1
chaunst unwares to meet him in the *way*, . . . I. vi. 27. 3
A weary wight forwandring by the *way;* . . . I. vi. 34. 3
soild with dust of the long dried *way;* . . . I. vi. 35. 2
To see two knights, in travell on my *way*, . . . I. vi. 38. 3
on the *way* He wofull Lady, wofull Una, met, . . . I. vii. 20. 1
the Dwarfe the *way* to her assynd; . . . I. vii. 28. 4
A goodly knight, faire marching by the *way*, . . . I. vii. 29. 2
The ydle stroke, enforcing furious *way*, . . . I. viii. 8. 2
engin, making *way*, . . . highest trees hath rent, . . . I. viii. 9. 6
That stop out of the *way* to overthroe, . . . I. viii. 13. 4
with his body bard the *way* atwixt them twaine. . . . I. viii. 13. 9
Both feet and face one *way* are wont to lead. . . . I. viii. 31. 6
Then asked he, which *way* he in might pas? . . . I. viii. 33. 1
Arthur on his *way* To seeke his love, . . . I. ix. 20. 1
As on the *way* together we did fare, . . . I. ix. 28. 2
A wyde *way* made to let forth living breath: . . . I. ix. 30. 3
'Who travailes by the wearie wandring *way*, . . . I. ix. 39. 1
he that once hath missed the right *way*, . . . I. ix. 43. 8
he is taught . . . The *way* to hevenly blesse. . . . I. x. Arg.
streight and narrow was the *way* which he did show. . . . I. x. 5. 9
What grace hath thee now hither brought this *way?* . . . I. x. 9. 8
Then with a few to walke the rightest *way*. . . . I. x. 10. 8
this good knight his *way* with me addrest, . . . I. x. 11. 3
Her stedfast eyes were bent, ne swarved other *way*. . . . I. x. 14. 9
a narrow *way*, Scattred with bushy thornes . . . I. x. 35. 2
an holy Hospitall, That was foreby the *way*, . . . I. x. 36. 2
by the wearie *way* were traveiling, . . . I. x. 36. 7
by that painfull *way* they pas . . . I. x. 46. 1
Is not from hence the *way*, . . . I. x. 50. 4
shewes the *way* his sinfull soule to save! . . . I. x. 51. 3
Who better can the *way* to heaven aread . . . I. x. 51. 4
come, thou man of earth, and see the *way*, . . . I. x. 52. 2
To walke this *way* in Pilgrims poore estate. . . . I. x. 64. 4
his toylesome teme that *way* did guyde, . . . I. x. 66. 4
the *way* that does to heaven bownd!' . . . I. x. 67. 4
Is gathered full, and worketh speedy *way:* . . . I. xi. 10. 3
he, cutting *way* With his broad sayles, . . . I. xi. 18. 6
made such *way* that hewd it quite in twaine; . . . I. xi. 43. 7
this fayre virgin wearie of her *way* Must landed bee, . . . I. xii. 1. 6
made delightfull musick all the *way*, . . . I. xii. 7. 5
all the *way* the joyous people singes, . . . I. xii. 13. 3
unwares I strayd Out of my *way*, . . . I. xii. 31. 8
privy spyals plast in all his *way*, . . . II. i. 4. 3
Upon the *way* him fortuned to meete, . . . II. i. 5. 6
Him als accompanyd upon the *way* A comely Palmer, . . . II. i. 7. 1
Least his long *way* his aged limbes should tire: . . . II. i. 7. 5
he Guyon guydes an uncouth *way* . . . II. i. 24. 1
with his steedy staffe did point his *way;* . . . II. i. 34. 6
Dan Faunus chaunst to meet her by the *way*, . . . II. ii. 7. 5
Meetes two contrarie billowes by the *way*, . . . II. ii. 24. 4
scorning both their spights, does make wide *way*, . . . II. ii. 24. 7
a losell wandring by the *way*, . . . II. iii. 4. 1
by the *way* he chaunced to espy One . . . II. iii. 6. 1
easy is the *way* and passage plaine . . . II. iii. 41. 7
from the right *way* seeke to draw him wide, . . . II. iv. 2. 7
forth faring on his *way*, . . . II. iv. 3. 1
chawing vengeaunce all the *way* I went, . . . II. iv. 29. 2
Whose flying feet so fast their *way* applyde, . . . II. iv. 37. 3
The wearie Traveiler, wandring that *way*, . . . II. v. 30. 5
lightly mounted passeth on his *way;* . . . II. v. 38. 2
Atin by no *way* She would admit, . . . II. vi. 4. 8
For it was taught the *way* which she would have, . . . II. vi. 5. 8
all the *way* the wanton Damsell found New merth . . . II. vi. 6. 1
therein making *way*. . . . II. vi. 7. 9
of his *way* he had no sovenaunce, . . . II. vi. 8. 3
Diverse discourses in their *way* they spent; . . . II. vi. 9. 1
Their *way* they forward take . . . II. vi. 11. 7
by the *way*, as was her wonted guize, . . . II. vi. 21. 1
Me litle needed from my right *way* to have straid.' . . . II. vi. 22. 9
Who fares on sea may not commaund his *way*, . . . II. vi. 23. 2

Way—*Continued.*

in the *way* he with Sir Guyon mett, II. vi. 28. 1
In his owne flesh, and make *way* to the living spright! II. vi. 32. 9
proceedes Yet on his *way*, II. vii. 2. 3
A darkesome *way*, which no man could descry, II. vii. 20. 7
with wonder all the *way* Did feed his eyes, II. vii. 24. 3
the dore To him did open and affoorded *way:* II. vii. 26. 2
Him to entrap unwares another *way* he wist. II. vii. 34. 9
They never creature saw that cam that *way:* II. vii. 37. 5
he was wary wise in all his *way*, II. vii. 64. 6
being on his *way*, approched neare II. viii. 3. 5
no *way* is lefte to wreake my spight, II. viii. 15. 6
further *way* It made, II. viii. 38. 6
To yield wide *way* to his hart-thrilling brond; II. viii. 41. 8
Forth passed on their *way* in fayre accord, II. ix. 2. 4
in her *way* throwes mischiefe and mischaunce, II. ix. 8. 3
constant keepe the *way* in which ye stand; II. ix. 8. 6
They wasted had much *way*, and measurd many miles. II. ix. 9. 9
the venturous Mariner that *way* Learning II. x. 6. 2
Through hils and dales he speedy *way* did make, II. xi. 26. 4
land-marke seemd to bee, or signe of sundry *way:* II. xi. 35. 9
led him to the Castle by the beaten *way*. II. xi. 48. 9
yonder *way* We needes must pas II. xii. 3. 2
Latona traveiling that *way*, II. xii. 13. 4
passe on forward: so their *way* does ly, II. xii. 14. 2
by the *way* there is a great Quicksand, II. xii. 18. 1
twixt them both the narrow *way* doth ly.' II. xii. 18. 4
as they passed by that *way*, II. xii. 20. 7
How to direct theyr *way* in darkenes wide, II. xii. 35. 2
Yet swarved not, but kept their forward *way* II. xii. 76. 5
The *way* they came, the same retourn'd they right, II. xii. 84. 3
Acrasia he sent . . . a nigher *way*, III. i. 2. 2
he him selfe betooke another *way*, III. i. 2. 7
every knight which doth this *way* repayre, III. i. 26. 7
To which sharp thornes and breres the *way* forstall, III. i. 46. 7
she did prepare *Way* to her love, III. i. 51. 8
She, traveiling with Guyon, by the *way* III. ii. 4. 1
ne further fastned not, But went her *way;* III. ii. 26. 3
tooke their ready *way* Unto the Church, III. ii. 48. 3
they tooke their *way:* III. iii. 7. 4
if thou ever happen that same *way* To traveill, III. iii. 8. 1
sith fates can make *Way* for themselves III. iii. 25. 5
all the *way* Grew pensive III. iv. 5. 2
voyage rashly make By this forbidden *way* III. iv. 14. 6
kept her ready *way* Along the strond; III. iv. 18. 2
he by chaunce did wander that same *way*, III. iv. 19. 8
At last they came unto a double *way;* III. iv. 46. 6
that *way* in which that Damozell Was fledd afore, III. iv. 47. 8
her *way* does cut amaine, III. iv. 49. 5
lately left the same, and tooke this *way*. III. v. 4. 7
if ye understand Which *way* she fared hath, III. v. 4. 9
Or succour her, or me direct the *way*, III. v. 10. 8
by the *way* he greatly gan complaine III. v. 12. 3
By that same *way* . . . Mote algates passe: III. v. 17. 5
The gentle Squyre came ryding that same *way*, III. v. 18. 2
through wrath and vengeaunce making *way*, III. v. 21. 1
for wretched mens reliefe make *way;* III. v. 27. 2
searched everie *way* through which his wings Had borne him, III. vi. 12. 6
A traveiler unwonted to such *way:* III. vii. 4. 2
it chaunst a knight To passe that *way*, III. vii. 29. 3
all the *way* him followd on the strand, III. vii. 36. 7
Thus as he led the Beast along the *way*, III. vii. 37. 1
crost the nearest *way*, by which he cast Her to encounter III. vii. 38. 3
she the *way* shund nathemore forthy, III. vii. 38. 5
Him needed not instruct which *way* were best III. viii. 8. 5
A knight that *way* there chaunced to repaire; III. viii. 11. 5
There them by chaunce encountred on the *way* III. viii. 15. 2
saide his boat the *way* could wisely tell; III. viii. 24. 7
retourned back againe To his first *way*. III. viii. 44. 6
will I not forsake my forward *way*, III. viii. 50. 4
they secret *way* did make Unto their wils, III. ix. 31. 5
warily he watcheth every *way*, By which III. x. 3. 4
I unwares this *way* by fortune straid, III. x. 25. 5
Through many a wood and many an uncouth *way*, III. x. 34. 2
on adventure by the *way* he past. III. x. 35. 5
Swayne would not his leasure dwell, But went his *way:* III. x. 38. 8
Before ye enterprise that *way* to wend: III. x. 40. 8
Did all the *way* him follow hard behynd; III. x. 55. 6
bad the stubborne flames to yield him *way:* III. xi. 26. 4
nycely trode, as thornes lay in his *way*, III. xii. 10. 6
hath his right *way* lost. III. xii. 17. 9
his *way* he forth did take. III. xii. 23. 9
By *way* of sport, as oft in maskes is knowen, IV. i. 3. 8
she is with her upon the *way* Marching in lovely wise, IV. i. 4. 6
on his *way* they had him forth convayd: IV. i. 37. 5
all the *way*, with wondrous griefe of mynd IV. i. 37. 6
By great adventure travelled that *way;* IV. ii. 20. 3
readie *way* did yield For bloud to gush forth IV. iii. 9. 4
making *way* unto his dearest life, IV. iii. 12. 6
Resolv'd to end it one or other *way*, IV. iii. 17. 8
so gave *way* unto his fell intent; IV. iii. 18. 7
Yet still that direfull stroke kept on his *way*, IV. iii. 34. 1
straight flew ope, and gave her *way* to ride. IV. iii. 46. 3
so weening *way* to make To Ladies love, IV. iv. 4. 3
all the *way* they rode: IV. iv. 5. 5
they past forth on their *way*. IV. iv. 13. 2
The next day, as he on his *way* did ride, IV. vi. 2. 2
When ever he this *way* shall passe IV. vi. 5. 9
yeeld unto her weapon *way* to pas: IV. vi. 15. 4

Way—*Continued.*

both wearie of the *way* We did alight, IV. vi. 36. 2
made *way* Unto the love of noble Britomart, IV. vi. 40. 1
he went Forth on his *way* IV. vi. 44. 5
Ne wight him to attend, or *way* to guide, IV. vi. 44. 6
by the *way* she sundry purpose found IV. vi. 45. 1
wearinesse, Both of the *way* and warlike exercise, IV. vii. 3. 4
till he came to th' end of all his *way*, IV. vii. 8. 7
she, deare Ladie, all the *way* was dead, IV. vii. 9. 1
hast to crosse him by the nearest *way*, IV. vii. 25. 2
His owne deare Lord Prince Arthure came that *way*, IV. vii. 42. 2
long did mark which *way* she straid, IV. viii. 7. 9
all the *way* the Prince on footpace traced, IV. viii. 34. 8
They passing forth kept on their readie *way*, IV. viii. 37. 1
all the *way* from trotting hard to spare; IV. viii. 37. 8
all the *way* full loud for aide did crie, IV. viii. 38. 4
He all the *way* did rage at that same Squire, IV. viii. 40. 1
seeking long to weet which *way* she straid, IV. ix. 24. 4
as we ride together on our *way*, IV. ix. 40. 6
by one *way* that passage did prepare. IV. x. 6. 5
by no meanes my *way* I would forslow IV. x. 15. 1
beholding all the *way* The goodly workes, IV. x. 15. 4
way unto me yield. IV. x. 19. 9
all the *way* before them, IV. xi. 12. 2
scarce her *way* could see. IV. xi. 24. 9
When to Joves pallace she doth take her *way*, IV. xi. 28. 3
The wanton Lee, that oft doth loose his *way;* IV. xi. 29. 7
doth make His *way* still under ground, IV. xi. 32. 9
making *way* By sweet Clonmell, IV. xi. 43. 1
both which prepard her *way*. IV. xi. 47. 9
By one or other *way* IV. xii. 9. 3
for-why he found no *way* To enter in, IV. xii. 15. 3
Did march amongst the many all the *way*, IV. xii. 18. 8
all the *way* did inly mourne, IV. xii. 18. 9
Did to the Faery Queene her *way* addresse, V. i. 4. 2
now together on their *way* they bin, V. i. 13. 6
'which *way* then did he make? V. i. 19. 1
as he now was uppon the *way*, V. ii. 2. 1
finding in the *way* the scattred scarfe, V. ii. 3. 3
in my *way*, a little here beyond, V. ii. 4. 5
never wight he lets to passe that *way* V. ii. 6. 2
None other *way* will I this day betake, V. ii. 10. 6
thitherward forthright his ready *way* did make. V. ii. 10. 9
He saw no *way* but close with him in hast; V. ii. 14. 2
to invent Which *way* he enter might V. ii. 20. 9
made *way* for his maister to assaile; V. ii. 24. 4
In which they measur'd mickle weary *way*, V. ii. 29. 1
Ne any of them durst come in his *way*, V. ii. 53. 7
whom he lately met Upon the *way* V. iii .10. 4
suffred cruell shipwracke by the *way:* V. iv. 13. 8
Artegall . . . Departed on his *way*, V. iv. 20. 8
So as he travelled uppon the *way*, V. iv. 21. 1
to guide the *way* Unto the dwelling of that Amazone: V. iv. 35. 5
to them *way* to make with weapons well prepard. V. iv. 37. 9
in the middle *way* they were ymet V. iv. 38. 3
what *way* She mote revenge that blot V. iv. 47. 4
Unto the wall his *way* did fearelesse take, V. iv. 50. 6
thenceforth unto daunger opened *way*. V. v. 9. 4
To which if thou canst win him any *way* V. v. 33. 6
to his fortunes helpe make readie *way?* V. v. 39. 4
Towards which coast her love his *way* addrest: V. vi. 7. 5
So forth she rode uppon her ready *way*, V. vi. 18. 1
Gan her addresse unto her former *way*. V. vi. 36. 3
Talus desir'd that he might have prepared The *way* V. vi. 38. 5
She stayd not to advise which *way* to take, V. vi. 39. 1
Thorough the midst of them she *way* did make. V. vi. 39. 3
way betwixt them none appeares in sight; V. vi. 40. 3
her noble Lord, sir Artegall, Went on his *way;* V. vii. 45. 7
The true guide of his *way* and vertuous government. V. viii. 3. 9
However loth he were his *way* to slake, V. viii. 5. 8
by the *way* Thought with his speare him quight have overwent. V. viii. 7. 3
As by the *way* unweetingly I strayd: V. viii. 15. 7
To treat with her, by *way* of enterdeale, V. viii. 21. 7
To their deseigne to make the easier *way*, V. viii. 25. 2
sent to him a Page that mote direct his *way*. V. viii. 26. 9
Gave *way* unto his horses speedie flying, V. viii. 32. 3
Seeking by every *way* to make some breach; V. viii. 37. 2
go which *way* they list, their guide they have forlore. V. viii. 39. 9
With ugly craples crawling in their *way*, V. viii. 40. 4
so would have departed on their *way;* V. ix. 3. 6
by the *way*, (As often falles) of sundry things did commen: V. ix. 4. 2
by which *way* they towards it should trace. V. ix. 7. 4
When he was readie to his steede to mount Unto his *way*, V. x. 16. 9
all his *way* before him still prepare. V. x. 17. 7
Ne to their force gave *way*, V. x. 35. 3
Thenceforth he car'd no more which *way* he strooke, V. xi. 12. 6
sure he had her slaine, had she not turnd her *way*. V. xi. 26. 9
for her entrailes made an open *way* To issue forth; V. xi. 31. 3
On which long *way* he rode, V. xi. 35. 9
So forth he fared, . . . and much *way* did pas, V. xi. 36. 8
as he traveld by the *way*, V. xi. 37. 1
as they rode together on their *way*, V. xi. 43. 6
To the sea-shore he gan his *way* apply, V. xii. 3. 8
through the yron walles their *way* they rent, V. xii. 17. 7
way did give unto their gracelesse speed: V. xii. 18. 4
Talus to revoke from the right *way* V. xii. 27. 5
all the woods and rockes nigh to that *way* Began to quake V. xii. 41. 4
still the *way* did hold To Faerie Court; V. xii. 43. 8
now he was in travell on his *way*, VI. i. 4. 1
may no Knight nor Lady passe along That *way*, VI. i. 13. 6

Way—*Continued.*
yet they needs must passe that *way*, . . . VI. i. 13. 6
as I that *way* did come . . . VI. i. 16. 1
makes his *way* more violent; . . . VI. i. 21. 5
The Dwarfe his *way* did hast, . . . VI. i. 30. 1
to make unto his vengeance *way*: . . . VI. i. 39. 6
He now againe is on his former *way* . . . VI. ii. 3. 5
as he and I together roade Upon our *way* . . . VI. ii. 16. 2
since this Ladie . . . needeth safegard now upon her *way*, . VI. ii. 38. 2
Gan freshly him addresse unto his former *way*. . . . VI. iii. 13. 9
as they past together on their *way*, . . . VI. iii. 16. 7
Ne wist which *way* he through the foord mote pas: . . . VI. iii. 30. 4
Turned his steede about another *way*, . . . VI. iii. 37. 2
He stayed not t' advize which *way* were best . . . VI. iv. 5. 1
with greedie force And furie to be crossed in his *way*, . . . VI. iv. 20. 7
To weet which *way* were best to entertaine . . . VI. iv. 24. 4
ne could tell Which *way* to take: . . . VI. iv. 25. 2
as on their *way* they went, . . . VI. v. 10. 1
She on her *way* cast forward to proceede, . . . VI. v. 31. 2
all the *way* the Prince sought to appease . . . VI. v. 32. 4
To passe the tedious travell of the *way*, . . . VI. v. 34. 6
So forth he went his *way*, . . . VI. v. 41. 5
went both on their *way*, . . . VI. vi. 15. 9
To some hid end to make more easie *way*, . . . VI. vi. 42. 2
he saw the *way* all dyde With streames of bloud; . . . VI. vii. 17. 5
Was wandred in the wood another *way*, . . . VI. vii. 19. 6
now she was uppon the weary *way*, . . . VI. vii. 39. 1
all the *way* he went, on every syde He gaz'd about . . . VI. vii. 42. 7
past through many perils by the *way*, . . . VI. vii. 50. 6
as they forward on their *way* did pas, . . . VI. viii. 4. 1
with his yron club preparing *way*, . . . VI. viii. 8. 2
So as he could not weld him any *way*: . . . VI. viii. 11. 5
he which *way* to turne him scarcely wist: . . . VI. viii. 13. 5
way to them he gave forth right to pas; . . . VI. viii. 14. 3
drawing thence his speach another *way*, . . . VI. ix. 18. 7
cleane were gone, which *way* he never knew; . . . VI. x. 18. 3
this *way* comming from feastfull glee . . . VI. x. 22. 4
no *way* Appeard for people in nor out to pas, . . . VI. x. 41. 7
their *way* was made Through hollow caves, . . . VI. x. 42. 1
making *way* for death at large to walke; . . . VI. xi. 16. 5
ymet About some carcase by the common *way*, . . . VI. xi. 17. 2
sith he well knew The readie *way* . . . VI. xi. 35. 2
To whom they both agreed to take their *way*, . . . VI. xi. 36. 8
Through the dead carcases he made his *way*, . . . VI. xi. 47. 4
Till he had strowd with bodies all the *way*; . . . VI. xi. 49. 5
Still winneth *way*, ne hath her compasse lost: . . . VI. xii. 1. 7
Right so it fares with me in this long *way*, . . . VI. xii. 1. 8
Her lightened all the *way* where she should wend, . . . VII. vi. 9. 8
What *way* is best to drive her to retire, . . . VII. vi. 21. 7
ne wist what *way* to chose: . . . VII. vi. 24. 5
No *way* he found to compasse his desire, . . . VII. vi. 43. 1
Yet is he oft eclipsed by the *way*, . . . VII. vii. 51. 8
he his *way* doth seem quite to have lost, . . . VII. vii. 52. 3
By conduct of some star, doth make her *way*; . . . *Am.* xxxiv. 2
My cruell fayre streight bids me wend my *way*: . . . *Am.* xlvi. 2
The gentle deare returnd the selfe-same *way*, . . . *Am.* lxvii. 7
her words so wise do make their *way* . . . *Am.* lxxxi. 11
all the *way* this sacred hymne do sing, . . . *H.L.* 41
Yet wanting light to guide his wandring *way*, . . . *H.L.* 71
through the world his *way* he gan to take, . . . *H.L.* 74
through heaven and hell thou makest *way* . . . *H.L.* 236
by like *way* Kindled of yours, . . . *H.B.* 179
Way, Wayd. *See* **Weigh,** *etc.*
Wayed. on a time, as they together *way'd*, . . . IV. ii. 12. 8
Wayfaring. he met An aged wight *wayfaring* all alone, . . . V. xi. 37. 2
Way's. By that *wayes* side there sate internall Payne, . . . II. vii. 21. 5
Ways. if in his *wayes* he stood? . . . *S.C.* May 86
nearer *wayes* I knowe. . . . *S.C.* Jul. 96
manie *waies* they sought, and manie tryed, . . . *Hub.* 225
wayes enough for all therein to live; . . . *Hub.* 401
These be the *wayes* by which without reward . . . *Hub.* 513
they, that are great Clerkes, have nearer *wayes*, . . . *Hub.* 537
A thousand *wayes* he them could entertaine, . . . *Hub.* 800
Were it by honest *wayes*, or otherwise, . . . *Hub.* 848
Wearie your selves in wandring desert *wayes*, . . . *D.* 534
waies unknowne, *waies* leading down to hell. . . . *Col.* 211
Durst not adventure such unknowen *wayes*, . . . *Col.* 670
wander too and fro in *waies* unknowne, . . . I. i. 10. 5
pas, In *waies* unknowne, her wandring knight to seeke, . . . I. iii. 21. 4
thousand other *waies* to bait his fleshly hookes. . . . I. iv. 25. 9
Unweeting of the perillous wandring *wayes*, . . . I. v. 18. 3
lampe . . . First made by him mens wandring *wayes* to guyde, I. vii. 23. 2
They let her goe at will, and wander *waies* unknowne. . . . I. viii. 49. 9
th' eternall might, That rules mens *waies*, . . . I. ix. 6. 9
Me hither brought by *wayes* yet never found, . . . I. ix. 7. 6
Greevd with remembrance of his wicked *wayes*, . . . I. x. 21. 6
In all his *waies* through this wide worldes wave; . . . I. x. 34. 8
The face of earth and *wayes* of living wight, . . . I. xi. 49. 8
guyde thy *waies* with warie governaunce, . . . II. iv. 36. 4
thousand *waies* invent To feede her foolish humour . . . II. vi. 3. 8
all by wrong *waies* for themselves prepard: . . . II. vii. 47. 5
fixed at his backe to cut his ayery *wayes*. . . . II. viii. 5. 9
By secret *wayes*, that none might it espy, . . . II. ix. 32. 6
Whom he at sea found wandring from their *waies*, . . . II. x. 41. 7
The other five five sondry *wayes* he sett . . . II. xi. 7. 1
Forthy he gan some other *wayes* advize, . . . II. xi. 44. 6
After long *wayes* and perilous paines endur'd, . . . III. i. 1. 2
Long so they traveiled through wastefull *wayes*, . . . III. i. 3. 1
Full many *wayes* within her troubled mind . . . III. iii. 5. 1
Full many *waies* she sought, but none could find, . . . III. iii. 5. 3

Ways—*Continued.*
Therefore submit thy *wayes* unto his will, . . . III. iii. 24. 8
What meanes shall she out seeke, or what *waies* take? . . . III. iii. 25. 2
through back *waies*, that none might them espy, . . . III. iii. 61. 7
At last their *wayes* so fell, that they mote part: . . . III. iii. 62. 6
So beene they three three sondry *wayes* ybent; . . . III. iv. 47. 5
when her *wayes* he could no more descry, . . . III. iv. 53. 1
day discovers all dishonest *wayes*, . . . III. iv. 59. 1
His late miswandred *wayes* now to remeasure right. . . . III. vii. 18. 9
All *wayes* shee sought him to restore to plight, . . . III. vii. 21. 1
Ten thousand *wayes* he cast in his confused thought. . . . III. x. 18. 9
They both uprose and to their *waies* them dight: . . . IV. i. 16. 6
Yet many *waies* to enter may be found, . . . IV. i. 20. 7
With squinted eyes contrarie *wayes* intended, . . . IV. i. 27. 2
divydes The doubtfull current into divers *wayes*. . . . IV. i. 42. 6
every secret worke of natures *wayes*; . . . IV. ii. 35. 4
By wondrous skill and many hidden *wayes* . . . she went. . IV. ii. 47. 3
through the thickest makes her nighest *waies*; . . . IV. vii. 22. 3
thenceforth reformd her *waies*, . . . IV. ix. 16. 8
through gifts, or guile, or such like *waies*, . . . IV. x. 18. 8
wooed him by all the *waies* she could: . . . V. iv. 30. 4
all the *wayes* she sought his love for to have wonne: . . . V. v. 45. 9
all within it full of wyndings is And hidden *wayes*, . . . V. ix. 6. 7
The *waies*, through which my weary steps I guyde . . . VI. Pr. 1. 1
conduct me well In these strange *waies* . . . VI. Pr. 2. 8
how to issue forth in *waies* untryde, . . . VI. i. 6. 4
tryde all *waies* how each mote entrance make . . . VI. i. 37. 2
Handling and turning them a thousand *wayes*: . . . VI. ii. 39. 5
in his measure Of so long *waies* . . . VI. iii. 22. 6
'But go thy *waies* to him, and fro me say, . . . VI. iii. 41. 1
He knew the diverse went of mortall *wayes*, . . . VI. vi. 3. 5
weary of this worlds unquiet *waies*, . . . VI. vi. 4. 7
well she knew the *wayes* to win good will . . . VI. vi. 41. 6
To worke by wicked treason *wayes* doth find, . . . VI. vii. 1. 8
Yet ceast he not to sew, and all *waies* prove, . . . VI. xi. 5. 5
sundry *wayes* and fashions as clerkes faine, . . . VII. vii. 55. 2
let my loves fayre Planet short her *wayes*, . . . *Am.* lx. 13
His humble carriage, his unfaulty *wayes*, . . . *H.H.L.* 233
Wayside. By the *way side* being together set; . . . V. xii. 28. 5
Wayward. Like as a *wayward* childe, . . . V. vi. 14. 1
We (*partial list*).
Made of the mettall that *we* honour most . . . *Bel.*[1] iii. 6
How falles it, then, *we* no merrier bene, . . . *S.C.* May 3
'Why wayle *we* then? why weary *we* the Gods . . . *S.C.* N. 173
'Least *wee* unweeting hap to be fordonne; . . . II. xii. 11. 2
Turne *we* our steeds; . . . III. viii. 18. 3
to his powre *we* all are subject borne: . . . IV. viii. 15. 2
How much, himselfe that loved us, *we* love. . . . *H.H.L.* 217
we, fraile wights! whose sight cannot sustaine . . . *H.H.B.* 120
Weak. The *weake* foundations of this citie faire. . . . *Bel.*[2] xiv. 14
The *weake*, that hath the strong so oft forlorne! . . . *Van.* vi. 14
flocke . . . Whose knees are *weake* through fast . . . *S.C.* Ja. 44
Thou *weake*, I wanne; thou leane, I quite forlorne: . . . *S.C.* Ja. 47
So lustlesse bene they, or *weake*, so wan; . . . *S.C.* F. 78
buildest strong warke upon a *weake* ground: . . . *S.C.* May 145
it is all to *weake* and wanne, . . . *S.C.* O. 85
my *weake* bodie, set on fire with griefe, . . . *Hub.* 15
weake was my remembrance it to hold, . . . *Hub.* 1387
for sustenaunce Of his *weake* infancie, . . . *T.M.* 262
raging Love dothe appall the *weake* stomacke: . . . *U.V.* 11
And noble Patrone of *weake* povertie; . . . *Ti.* 262
O, helpe thou my *weake* wit, . . . I. Pr. 2. 9
whose dryer braine Is tost with troubled sights and fancies *weake*, . . . I. i. 42. 8
whose nature *weake* A cruell witch, . . . thus transformd, . I. ii. 33. 4
mightie proud to humble *weake* does yield, . . . I. iii. 7. 3
too *weake* and feeble was the forse Of salvage beast . . . I. iii. 42. 1
so faire a mould Did on so *weake* foundation ever sitt: . . . I. iv. 5. 4
his looser life . . . joyd *weake* wemens hearts to tempt, . . . I. iv. 26. 4
The yron walles to ward their blowes are *weak* and fraile. . I. v. 6. 9
quickning faith, that earst was woxen *weake*, . . . I. v. 12. 3
his *weake* steps governing . . . on cypresse stadle stout, . . . I. vi. 14. 7
shame t' avenge so *weake* an enimy; . . . I. viii. 45. 8
that *weake* captive wight now wexed strong, . . . I. ix. 2. 3
him to be yet *weake* and wearie well she knew. . . . I. ix. 20. 9
Perceived him to waver, *weake* and fraile, . . . I. ix. 49. 2
all his sinewes woxen *weake* and raw, . . . I. x. 2. 3
she fed whiles they were *weake* and young, . . . I. x. 31. 3
the *weake* minde with double woe torment?' . . . II. i. 16. 7
Weake wretch, I wrapt myselfe in Palmers weed, . . . II. i. 52. 8
The strong through pleasure soonest falles, the *weake* through smart.' . . . II. i. 57. 9
Weake she makes strong, and strong thing does increace, . . II. ii. 31. 3
that *weake* eld hath left thee nothing wise; . . . II. iii. 16. 3
To succour the *weake* state of sad afflicted Troy. . . . II. iii. 31. 9
strong passion, or *weake* fleshlinesse, . . . II. iv. 2. 6
the *weak* to strengthen, and the strong suppresse. . . . II. iv. 2. 9
weake wretch, of many weakest one, . . . II. iv. 17. 6
In their beginning they are *weake* and wan, . . . II. iv. 34. 3
Whiles they are *weake*, betimes with them contend; . . . II. iv. 34. 5
With silly *weake* old woman that did fight! . . . II. iv. 45. 5
'Up, up! thou womanish *weake* knight, . . . II. v. 36. 2
to *weake* wench did yield his martiall might: . . . II. vi. 8. 5
his *weake* witt Was overcome . . . II. vi. 13. 7
Weake handes, but counsell is most strong in age.' . . . II. vi. 48. 5
charmes, With which *weake* men thou witchest, . . . II. vii. 10. 4
weake and wan For want of food and sleepe, . . . II. vii. 65. 2
Weake body wel is chang'd for minds redoubled forse. . . . II. ix. 55. 9
Romanes daily did the *weake* subdew: . . . II. x. 54. 5
T' allure *weake* travellers, . . . II. xii. 31. 9

Weak—*Continued.*
was the fence thereof but *weake* and thin: II. xii. 43. 4
the *weake* boughes, with so rich load opprest II. xii. 55. 5
Seeking the *weake* oppressed to relieve, III. i. 3. 8
upleaning on her elbow *weake,* III. ii. 42. 6
the Britons, late dismayd and *weake,* III. iii. 36. 7
our *weake* hands . . . teach III. iii. 53. 3
the *weake* sowle her seat did yett retaine, III. v. 31. 4
to the wound his *weake* heart opened wyde: III. ix. 29. 2
greedy eares her *weake* hart from her bore; III. ix. 52. 7
he many *weake* harts had subdewd Of yore, III. x. 9. 7
That chearful word his *weak* heart much did cheare, III. x. 26. 6
When her *weake* feete could scarcely her sustaine, III. xii. 21. 6
able was *weake* harts away to steale. IV. v. 10. 5
That needed much her *weake* age to desire, IV. v. 39. 8
full *weake* and wan, not like him selfe to bee. IV. ix. 8. 9
all those joyes that *weake* mankind entyse. IV. xi. 5. 4
Full *weake* and crooked creature seemed shee, IV. xi. 24. 8
so *weake* of limbe, and sicke of love He woxe, IV. xii. 20. 6
of *weake* Princes to be Patronesse, V. i. 4. 7
too *weake* To aunswere his defiaunce in the field, V. i. 24. 1
Beholding all that womanish *weake* fight; V. iv. 25. 8
Uppon the carkasse of some beast too *weake,* V. iv. 40. 7
all the wounded, and the *weake* in state, V. iv. 45. 8
lies in wretched thraldome, *weake* and wan, V. vi. 16. 3
Like to a *weake* faint-hearted man he fared V. vii. 20. 5
In the behalfe of wronged *weake* did fight: V. viii. 30. 8
Where still the stronger doth the *weake* devoure, V. ix. 1. 6
these *weake* impes replanted by thy might, V. xi. 16. 7
An infant, *weake* a kingdome to sustaine, VI. ii. 28. 7
But now *weake* age had dimd his candle-light: VI. iii. 3. 4
To reskue him, and his *weake* part abet, VI. v. 22. 4
Small praise to prove your powre on wight so *weake.*' VI. v. 30. 5
through sicknesse now so wan and *weake,* VI. xi. 12. 7
to prove how pale and *weake* she was. VI. xi. 12. 9
if it to revenge he were too *weake,* VI. xi. 34. 8
Seeing her *weake* and wan through durance long. VI. xii. 11. 6
This too high flight, unfit for her *weake* wing) VII. vii. 1. 4
O *weake* life! that does leane On thing so tickle VII. vii. 22. 5
he was faint with cold, and *weak* with eld, VII. vii. 31. 8
your bright beams, of my *weak* eies admyred, *Am.* vii. 11
Strong thrugh your cause, but by your vertue *weak.* *Am.* viii. 12
to amaze *weake* mens confused skil, *Am.* xvii. 2
my *weak* powres of passions warreid arre; *Am.* xliv. 7
she . . . *weake* harts doth guyde Unto her love, *Am.* xlvii. 5
So *weake* my powres, *Am.* lvii. 5
Weake is th' assurance that *weake* flesh reposeth *Am.* lviii. 1
cowardly distrust Of his *weake* wings *H.L.* 181
loves, with which the world doth blind *Weake* fancies, *H.H.L.* 263
Which in my *weake* distraughted mynd I see; *H.H.B.* 14
Ah, gentle Muse! thou art too *weake* and faint *H.H.B.* 230
Weakened. still when any Knight Is *weakned,* IV. i. 44. 8
did restore His *weakned* powers, IV. iii. 24. 4
The more his *weakened* body so to wast, IV. vii. 41. 8
Weakens. The strong it *weakens* with infirmitie, II. i. 57. 7
weakens her, and makes her party strong; V. xi. 1. 4
Weaker. dayly dooth my *weaker* wit possesse, *D.* 30
Helpe . . . Thy *weaker* Novice to performe thy will; I. Pr. 2. 2
weaker sence it could have ravisht quight: I. i. 45. 5
'My *weaker* yeares, Captiv'd to fortune I. i. 52. 4
Through highest heaven with *weaker* hand to rayne: I. iv. 9. 4
in eternall woes my *weaker* hart Have wasted, I. iv. 46. 7
strove for to amaze the *weaker* sights: I. vii. 30. 5
golden cup, . . . She lightly sprinkled on his *weaker* partes: I. viii. 14. 7
feeling wondrous comfort in her *weaker* eld: I. x. 8. 9
documents . . . That *weaker* witt of man could never reach; I. x. 19. 5
his *weaker* wandring steps to guyde, I. x. 34. 1
easy was t' inveigle *weaker* sight: I. xii. 32. 5
sweetnesse doth allure the *weaker* sence II. vi. 1. 3
Did drive the Romanes to the *weaker* syde, II. x. 51. 8
often need the helpe of *weaker* hand; II. xi. 30. 2
him selfe *weaker* through infirmity. III. vii. 33. 4
that late *weaker* band of chalengers relieved. IV. iv. 46. 9
With which my *weaker* patience fortune proves: IV. viii. 63. 8
solace in soft pleasure Those *weaker* Ladies IV. ix. 12. 8
Who ever thinkes . . . To wrong the *weaker,* oft falles VI. ii. 23. 9
all the passions heale which wound the *weaker* spright. VI. vi. 3. 9
Least they should joyne against the *weaker* side, VI. xi. 18. 2
Do thou my *weaker* wit with skill inspire, VII. vii. 2. 2
craftily enfold Theyr *weaker* harts, *Am.* xxxvii. 8
Doest tyrannize in everie *weaker* part; *H.L.* 4
Weakest. So *weakest* may anoy the most of might! *Van.* x. 14
with bold furie armes the *weakest* hart: II. i. 57. 8
weake wretch, of many *weakest* one, II. iv. 17. 6
Weakly. She *weakely* started, II. i. 45. 7
Weakely at first, but after with desyre *H.L.* 67
Weakness. Whose witt is *weakenesse,* whose wage is death, *S.C.* F. 88
lifting up her brave heroick thought Bove womens *weaknes,* *Ti.* 110
through his own foolish pride Or *weaknes,* I. viii. 1. 7
His powre is reft, and *weaknes* doth remaine. I. ix. 31. 8
Through *weaknesse* of my widowhed or woe; I. xii. 28. 6
Our faulty *weakenes,* and your matchlesse might: III. i. 30. 2
through *weaknesse* he was forst at last To yield III. v. 48. 2
his wearie sprite, opprest With fleshly *weaknesse,* V. vi. 43. 3
Whose will her *weakenesse* could no way represse, IV. ix. 18. 8
Some men, I wote, will deeme in Artegall Great *weaknesse,* V. vi. 1. 2
'Such is the *weakenesse* of all mortall hope, VI. iii. 5. 1
Weal. *See* **Common weal.**
welcome now, my Lord in *wele* or woe, I. viii. 43. 1
Which she would sure performe, betide her *wele* or wo. V. vi. 23. 9

Weal—*Continued.*
Mongst joyes mixing some tears, mongst *wele* some wo, V. xi. 16. 3
I . . . wish thee grow in worship and great *weale;* VI. ii. 26. 7
Lift up thy mind to th' Author of thy *weale,* *H.H.L.* 256
Weals. *See* **Common weals.**
Wealth. Little bootes all the *welth* and the trust, *S.C.* May 88
Heaping up waves of *welth* and woe, *S.C.* May 93
To wyten shepheards *welth:* *S.C.* Jul. 210
Or thrive in *welth,* she shalbe mine, *S.C.* Au. 111
Matching the *wealth* of th' auncient Frankincence; *Gn.* 674
thou canst not but envie My *wealth,* *Hub.* 598
Where doth she all that wondrous *welth* nowe hide? *Ti.* 75
such *wealth* might unto thee accrew; *Col.* 655
all their *wealth* for painting on a wall; *Col.* 724
Whose *welth* was want, whose plenty made him pore; I. iv. 29. 4
inwardly he chawed his owne maw At neighbours *welth,* I. iv. 30. 6
like would not for all this worldes *wealth.* I. ix. 31. 4
these rich hils of *welth* doest hide apart II. vii. 7. 3
must wage Thy workes for *wealth,* II. vii. 18. 5
all the *wealth* which is, or was of yore, II. vii. 31. 7
all the *wealth* late shewd by mee II. vii. 38. 4
to their people *wealth* they forth do well, II. x. 26. 6
their *wealth,* which he from them did keepe. III. iv. 22. 9
The *wealth* of th' East, and pompe of Persian kings: III. iv. 23. 4
his closet . . . where all his *wealth* Lay hid; III. x. 12. 3
Her love, her service, and her utmost *wealth:* IV. i. 6. 4
strength and *wealth* and happinesse she lends, IV. x. 34. 6
many Princes she in *wealth* exceedes, V. ii. 9. 6
all the *wealth* of rich men to the poore will draw.' V. ii. 38. 9
it and all the *wealth* therein V. ix. 3. 4
As either might for *wealth* have gotten bene, V. ix. 27. 7
A Ladie of great worth and *wealth* had beene, V. x. 7. 2
flourish in all *wealth* and happinesse, V. x. 11. 6
For other worldly *wealth* they cared nought. VI. ix. 5. 6
through the *wealth* wherein he did abound, VI. xii. 4. 4
From youth to eld, from *wealth* to poverty, VII. vii. 19. 5
Wealth's. These wisards welter in *welths* waves, *S.C.* Jul. 197
Through wicked pride and wasted *welthes* decay. I. v. 51. 4
Wealths. *See* **Commonwealths.**
in fame Of *wealths* and goodnesse, far above the rest VII. vi. 38. 2
Wealthy. on that *wealthy* Strond Inglorious now lies III. iv. 29. 2
with the waves Of *wealthy* Thamis washed is along, III. ix. 45. 2
Weaned. hath *weand* my wandring mynde: *S.C.* Jun. 2
Weanel. A Lambe, or a Kidde, or a *weanell* wast; *S.C.* S. 198
Weapon. with her *weapon* dredd She smote the ground, *Mui.* 324
stroke his *weapon* slie Into his heart, *Mui.* 437
He . . . soft withdrew His *weapon* huge, I. viii. 19. 8
Againe his wonted angry *weapon* proov'd, I. viii. 21. 3
In feare to lose his *weapon* in his paw, I. xi. 41. 2
The *weapon* bright . . . Ran through his mouth I. xi. 53. 5
drew his deadly *weapon* to maintaine his part. II. iv. 9. 9
well could weld That cursed *weapon,* II. vii. 40. 9
The Prince now stood, having his *weapon* broke; II. viii. 39. 6
The secrete vertue of that *weapon* keene, III. i. 10. 5
to her *weapon* ran, III. i. 62. 3
Her dreadfull *weapon* she to him addrest, III. vii. 42. 2
The wicked *weapon* rashly he did wrest, III. xii. 33. 2
The wicked *weapon* heard his wrathfull vow, IV. iii. 11. 6
weapon vaine to weld, IV. iii. 21. 3
from one a *weapon* fiercely takes. IV. iv. 34. 9
yeeld unto her *weapon* way to pas: IV. vi. 15. 4
would no longer hold The wrathfull *weapon* IV. vi. 27. 5
With dreadfull *weapon* aymed at his head, IV. viii. 41. 7
With his strange *weapon,* never wont in warre, V. iv. 44. 2
From the dread daunger of his *weapon* keene, V. v. 8. 7
Out of her fist the wicked *weapon* caught: V. viii. 48. 4
He could his *weapon* shift from side to syde, V. xi. 6. 5
One time when he his *weapon* faynd to shift, V. xi. 7. 6
ere he could his *weapon* backe repaire, V. xi. 13. 7
did against him weld His deadly *weapon* V. xii. 16. 5
armes or *weapon* had he none to fight, VI. iv. 4. 1
without *weapon* him assayling neare, VI. iv. 20. 3
Himselfe unto his *weapon* he betooke, VI. vii. 24. 6
He had no *weapon* but his shepheards hooke VI. x. 36. 1
Weaponless. Standing with emptie hands all *weaponlesse,* V. v. 14. 2
Weapon's. this *weapons* powre I well have kend II. viii. 19. 8
Weapons. The *weapons,* which Nature to him hath lent: *Gn.* 276
Flames, *weapons,* wounds, in Greeks fleete to have tynde. *Gn.* 504
th' one with fire and *weapons* did contend *Gn.* 521
Therein two deadly *weapons* fixt he bore, *Mui.* 81
Th' Elfe . . . his unready *weapons* gan in hand to take. I. vii. 7. 9
the boldest boy That ever warlike *weapons* menaged, II. ii. 18. 4
downe they lett their cruell *weapons* fall, II. ii. 32. 3
Having his warlike *weapons* cast behynd, II. v. 28. 7
Another warre, and other *weapons,* I Doe love, II. vi. 34. 6
be no whit sad For want of *weapons;* II. viii. 54. 5
his well proved *weapons* to him hent; II. xi. 17. 2
of his *weapons* did himselfe disarme. II. xi. 34. 5
they dismounting drew their *weapons* bold, III. xi. 21. 1
her wel-pointed *wepons* did about her dresse. III. xi. 55. 9
With murdrous *weapons* arm'd to cruell fight, IV. ii. 16. 2
Ne lesse his skill in *weapons* did appeare; IV. iii. 7. 4
Strokes, wounds, wards, *weapons,* all they did despise, IV. iii. 36. 3
His *weapons* which lay scattered all abrode, IV. iv. 23. 2
His wonted warlike *weapons* all he broke IV. vii. 39. 1
They gan with all their *weapons* him assay, V. ii. 53. 2
With *weapons* in their hands as ready for to fight. V. iv. 21. 9
to them way to make with *weapons* well prepard. V. iv. 37. 9
A raskall rout, with *weapons* rudely dight; V. vi. 29. 4
of all other *weapons* lesse or more, V. viii. 34. 4

Weapons—*Continued.*
His *weapons* soone from him he threw away, . . . VI. iii. 27. 6
Some of their *weapons* which thereby did lie, . . . VI. vi. 38. 8
downe his *weapons* layd, . . . VI. vi. 39. 5
He watcht in close awayt with *weapons* prest, . . . VI. vi. 44. 3
Wear. *See* **Outwear.**
All for Elisa in her hand to *weare?* . . . *S.C.* Ap. 105
that were wont greene bayes to *weare,* . . . *S.C.* N. 146
to *weare* garments base of wollen twist, . . . *Hub.* 460
should not deserve to *weare* A garment better . . . *Hub.* 473
that wicked wight his dayes doth *weare;* . . . I. i. 31. 7
fearefull freends *weare* out the wofull night, . . . I. iii. 20. 6
other clothes he could not *weare* for heate; . . . I. iv. 22. 2
with their horned feet doe *weare* the ground, . . . I. vi. 14. 3
He gave her gold and purple pall to *weare,* . . . I. vii. 16. 3
a garment she did *weare* All lilly white, . . . I. xii. 22. 6
hath vowd . . . never to *wearen* none: . . . II. iii. 12. 8
that which noblest knight on earth doth *weare.'* . . . II. iii. 17. 9
Ne other tire she on her head did *weare,* . . . II. ix. 19. 8
Such as the Angels *weare* before Gods tribunall! . . . III. v. 53. 9
Some made for beasts, some made for birds to *weare;* . . . III. vi. 35. 6
Such as false love doth oft upon him *weare;* . . . III. xi. 51. 8
That lost faire Ladies ornament should *weare,* . . . IV. ii. 26. 4
Might not the same about her middle *weare,* . . . IV. v. 3. 4
all she did was but to *weare* out day. . . . IV. vi. 45. 5
The Cle, the *Were,* the Grant, the Sture, the Rowne. . . . IV. xi. 34. 5
talk't of pleasant things the night away to *weare.* . . . V. vi. 22. 9
weare the weary night In waylfull plaints . . . V. vi. 26. 1
on his head a steele cap he did *weare* . . . V. xii. 14. 5
having long time, as his daily weed, Them wont to *weare,* . . . VI. iv. 19. 5
their upper garment which they *weare;* . . . VI. vi. 34. 7
did *weare* a crowne Of sundry flowres . . . VI. ix. 7. 7
No better doe I *weare,* no better doe I feed. . . . VI. ix. 20. 9
A guilt engraven morion he did *weare:* . . . VII. vii. 28. 8
The firmest flint doth in continuance *weare:* . . . *Am.* xviii. 4
wast and *weare* away in termes unsure, . . . *Am.* xxv. 3
The laurel-leafe, which you this day doe *weare,* . . . *Am.* xxviii. 1
Ring ye the bels, to make it *weare* away, . . . *Epith.* 274
Wearied. How have I *wearied* with many a stroke . . . *S.C.* D. 33
with toyle Himselfe hath *wearied,* . . . *Hub.* 754
'When thus our pipes we both had *wearied* well, . . . *Col.* 178
wearied with bearing of her bag . . . I. i. 6. 3
wearied his life with dull delayes. . . . III. xii. 44. *or.* 4
Weariness. To rest their limbs with *wearines* redounding. . . . *Gn.* 189
Let rest her selfe from her long *wearinesse,* . . . *D.* 338
dull *wearines* of former fight Having yrockt asleepe his . . . spright, . . . I. i. 55. 4
to bayt His tyred armes for toylesome *wearinesse,* . . . II. xii. 29. 8
faint through yrkesome *wearines,* . . . III. vi. 7. 1
Nor *wearinesse* to slack her hast, . . . III. vii. 2. 4
now for *wearinesse,* Both of the way and warlike exercise, . . . IV. vii. 3. 4
though she were with *wearinesse* nigh dead, . . . VI. vii. 40. 8
Wearing. Wretchedly *wearing* out his youthly yeares, . . . IV. vii. 41. 2
Wearing a Diademe embattild wide . . . IV. xi. 28. 5
Wearish. Who was to weet a wretched *wearish* elfe, . . . IV. v. 34. 3
Wearisome. The worldes sweet In from paine and *wearisome* turmoyle.' . . . II. xii. 32. 9
His *wearisome* pursuit perforce he stayd, . . . III. iv. 53. 5
Wears. *See* **Outwears.**
a Nimph, that wings of silver *weares,* . . . *Bel.*[2] iv. 6
time in passing *weares,* . . . *S.C.* Jun. 38
my heart-blood dropping *weares,* . . . *D.* 251
About his neck an hempen rope he *weares,* . . . I. ix. 22. 7
Ill *weares* he armes, that nill them use for Ladies sake.' . . . III. v. 11. 9
whilest other *weares* the bayes. . . . IV. i. 47. 9
hardest marble *weares:* . . . IV. xii. 7. 2
Weary. *Wearie* to see th' inconstance . . . *Bel.*[1] xi. 3
Wearie to see the heavens still wavering . . . *Bel.*[2] xv. 3
I wish I might this *wearie* life forgoe, . . . *Pet.*[2] vii. 5
To stop his *wearie* cariere suddenly: . . . *Ro.* xvi. 8
the welked Phoebus gan availe His *weary* waine; . . . *S.C.* Ja. 74
Those *weary* wanton toyes away dyd wype, . . . *S.C.* Jun. 48
weary thys long lingring Phoebus race. . . . *S.C.* O. 3
Phoebus, *weary* of his yerely taske, . . . *S.C.* N. 14
why *weary* we the Gods with playnts, . . . *S.C.* N. 173
My Muse is hoarse and *wearie* of thys stounde: . . . *S.C.* D. 140
their *wearie* limbs to rest, . . . *Gn.* 234
unto rest his *wearie* joynts prepare. . . . *Gn.* 320
They cast in course to waste the *wearie* howres. . . . *Hub.* 27
doth refresh his sprights when they be *werie.* . . . *T.M.* 138
the *wearie* Sun, After his dayes long labour . . . *D.* 22
why seeke I to prolong My *wearie* daies . . . *D.* 440
My *wearie* feete shall ever wandring be, . . . *D.* 457
sleepe (the harbenger of *wearie* wights) . . . *D.* 470
Wearie your selves in wandring desert wayes, . . . *D.* 534
His wasted life her *wearie* lodge forwent. . . . *As.* 174
So piped we, until we both were *weary.'* . . . *Col.* 79
waste the *wearie* night In secret anguish . . . I. i. 53. 2
Weary of aged Tithones saffron bed, . . . I. ii. 7. 2
she her *weary* limbes would never rest; . . . I. ii. 8. 6
weary of their way, they came at last . . . I. ii. 28. 2
rest their *weary* limbs a tide. . . . I. ii. 29. 9
Banisht from living wights, our *wearie* daies we waste.' . . . I. ii. 42. 9
One day, nigh *wearie* of the yrkesome way, . . . I. iii. 4. 1
In stead thereof he kist her *wearie* feet, . . . I. iii. 6. 1
Dame Una, *weary* Dame, . . . entrance did requere: . . . I. iii. 12. 9
Sad Una downe her laies in *weary* plight, . . . I. iii. 15. 3
she is *wearie* of the toilsom way, . . . I. iv. 3. 8
wearie traveiler, that strayes By muddy shore . . . I. v. 18. 1
alight From her nigh *weary* wayne, . . . I. v. 41. 2

Weary—*Continued.*
In westerne waves his *weary* wagon did recure. . . . I. v. 44. 9
whenas they far espide A *weary* wight . . . I. vi. 34. 3
staffe, to stay His *weary* limbs upon; . . . I. vi. 35. 8
he *wearie* sate To reste him selfe . . . I. vii. 2. 6
old man, . . . guyde his *wearie* gate both too and fro, . . . I. viii. 30. 4
To rest them selves, and *weary* powres repaire; . . . I. viii. 50. 8
him to be yet weake and *wearie* well she knew. . . . I. ix. 20. 9
'Who travailes by the *wearie* wandring way, . . . I. ix. 39. 1
ceassest not thy *weary* soles to lead; . . . I. x. 9. 7
when their *wearie* limbes with kindly rest, . . . I. x. 18. 1
by the *wearie* way were traveiling; . . . I. x. 36. 7
his fraile thighes, nigh *weary* and fordonne, . . . I. x. 47. 8
His *wearie* pounces all in vaine doth spend . . . I. xi. 19. 7
Faynt, *wearie,* sore, emboyled, grieved, brent, . . . I. xi. 28. 1
kest His *wearie* foe into that living well, . . . I. xi. 31. 6
her deare knight, who, *weary* of long fight . . . I. xi. 50. 2
To which I meane my *wearie* course to bend; . . . I. xii. 1. 2
this fayre virgin *wearie* of her way Must landed bee, . . . I. xii. 1. 6
on her *wearie* journey she did ride; . . . I. xii. 22. 5
light this *weary* vessell of her lode: . . . I. xii. 42. 4
to the wished haven bring thy *weary* barke!' . . . II. i. 32. 9
long captived soules from *weary* thraldome free. . . . II. i. 36. 9
To lett a *weary* wretch from her dew rest, . . . II. i. 47. 7
not like a *weary* traveilere, . . . II. ii. 23. 1
After their *weary* sweat and bloody toile, . . . II. ii. 33. 2
The *weary* sowle from thence it would discharge; . . . II. v. 6. 7
all breathlesse, *weary,* faint, Him spying, . . . II. v. 11. 2
The *wearie* Traveiler, wandring that way, . . . II. v. 30. 5
then by it his *wearie* limbes display, . . . II. v. 30. 7
soone leave off this toylsome *weary* stoure: . . . II. vi. 16. 4
To rest thy *weary* person in the shadow coole?' . . . II. vii. 63. 9
Phoebus gan decline . . . His *weary* wagon to the Westerne vale, . . . II. ix. 10. 2
taught the land from *wearie* wars to cease: . . . II. x. 25. 5
wearie wax of his continuall stay. . . . II. x. 30. 5
weary of that wretched life her selfe she hong. . . . II. x. 32. 9
The *weary* Britons, whose war-hable youth . . . II. x. 62. 1
wandring through the world with *wearie* feet, . . . II. x. 71. 3
Having their *weary* limbes to perfect plight Restord, . . . III. i. 1. 3
The salvage beast embost in *wearie* chace, . . . III. i. 22. 2
All were he *wearie* of his former paine; . . . III. i. 29. 4
Into the Ocean deepe to drive their *weary* drove. . . . III. i. 57. 9
through long watch, and late daies *weary* toile, . . . III. i. 58. 8
Lightly arose out of her *wearie* bed, . . . III. i. 59. 6
chaunged her *weary* side the better ease to take. . . . III. i. 61. 9
Did chaunce to still into her *weary* spright, . . . III. ii. 29. 2
mortall men their *weary* cares Do lay away, . . . III. ii. 32. 1
to rest his *wearie* knife. . . . III. iv. 24. 9
So from the *wearie* spirit thou doest drive Desired rest, . . . III. iv. 57. 8
Thus did the Prince that *wearie* night outweare . . . III. iv. 61. 1
wearie of long traveill, . . . III. vi. 10. 6
having conquered The maistring raines out of her *weary* wrest, III. vii. 2. 8
came at last in *weary* wretched plight . . . III. vii. 5. 7
rest her *wearie* syde. . . . III. vii. 5. 9
to rest her faint And *wearie* limbes awhile. . . . III. vii. 10. 5
The comfort of her age and *weary* dayes, . . . III. vii. 12. 2
Her *wearie* Palfrey, closely as she might, . . . III. vii. 18. 6
After long suit and *wearie* servicis, . . . III. vii. 53. 7
Did heape on her new waves of *weary* wretchednesse. . . . III. viii. 20. 9
Her heart nigh broken was with *weary* toyle, . . . III. viii. 32. 4
lose the teme out of his *weary* wayne, . . . III. viii. 51. 5
Each gan . . . *weary* armour free, . . . III. ix. 19. 7
Where *wearie* wandring they long time did wonne, . . . III. ix. 48. 7
through *wearie* wars and labours long, . . . III. ix. 50. 1
as hee forpassed by the plaine With *weary* pace, . . . III. x. 20. 6
wearie of their sport to sleepe they fell, . . . III. x. 49. 2
Fearing least from her cage the *wearie* soule would flit. . . . III. xi. 12. 9
nould she d'off her *weary* armes, . . . III. xi. 55. 5
All woxen *weary* of their journall toyle: . . . III. xii. 47. *or.* 4
Let forth his *wearie* ghost, . . . IV. iii. 12. 9
His *wearie* ghost assoyld from fleshly band . . . IV. iii. 13. 1
whom *wearie* winters teene Hath worne to nought, . . . IV. iii. 23. 7
So *wearie* both of fighting had their fill, . . . IV. iii. 36. 8
answering their *wearie* turnes around, . . . IV. v. 33. 8
The manner of their worke and *wearie* paine; . . . IV. v. 38. 2
thought his *wearie* limbs to have redrest. . . . IV. v. 39. 5
his *wearie* sprite, opprest With fleshly weaknesse, . . . IV. v. 43. 2
my *wearie* teeme, nigh over spent, . . . IV. v. 46. 8
having me, all *wearie* earst, downe feld, . . . IV. vi. 6. 8
Through toylesome heate and labour of her *weary* fight. . . . IV. vi. 19. 9
both *wearie* of the way We did alight, . . . IV. vi. 36. 2
wearie limmes recur'd after late usage bad. . . . IV. vi. 39. 9
rest their *wearie* limbs awhile. . . . IV. vii. 3. 6
through *weary* travel she lay sleeping sound. . . . IV. vii. 4. 9
His *weary* eie returnd to him againe, . . . IV. viii. 8. 3
After late *wearie* toile . . . IV. viii. 9. 3
Those weaker Ladies after *weary* toile; . . . IV. ix. 12. 8
To sit and rest the walkers *wearie* shankes: . . . IV. x. 25. 5
my *weary* ghost, with griefe outworne, . . . IV. xii. 8. 1
he wexed *weary* of his owne, . . . V. i. 17. 2
In which they measur'd mickle *weary* way, . . . V. ii. 29. 1
While she was flying, like a *weary* weft, . . . V. iii. 27. 5
turne we here . . . Our *wearie* yokes, . . . V. iii. 40. 7
Her *weary* barke at last uppon mine Isle did rest. . . . V. iv. 11. 9
the Elfin Knight, *Weary* of toile . . . Causd his pavilion . . . V. iv. 46. 3
weare the *weary* night In waylfull plaints . . . V. vi. 26. 1
After that long daies toile and *weary* plight: . . . V. vii. 12. 4
The waies, through which my *weary* steps I guyde . . . VI. Pr. 1. 1
none afore Through all my *weary* travell I have had; . . . VI. i. 10. 4

Weary—*Continued.*
Did sleepe all night through *weary* travell of his quest. . . . VI. iii. 9. 9
Tho wexing *weary* of that toylesome paine, . . . VI. iii. 29. 3
To which he meant his *weary* steps to guyde, . . . VI. iii. 29. 8
at length, after long *weary* chace, . . . VI. iii. 50. 3
He *wearie* woxe, and backe return'd againe . . . VI. iv. 9. 3
the *wearie* Beare Ere long he overtooke . . . VI. iv. 20. 1
With *weary* travell and uncertaine toile, . . . VI. iv. 25. 5
Would streight dislodge the wretched *wearie* life. . . . VI. v. 5. 5
To *weary* him the more and waste his spight, . . . VI. v. 17. 4
weary now with carefull keeping ward, . . . VI. v. 21. 2
trayterously did wound her *weary* Knight. . . . VI. v. 33. 9
being aged now, and *weary* to Of warres delight . . . VI. v. 37. 5
weary of this worlds unquiet waies, . . . VI. vi. 4. 7
soft dismounting, like a *weary* lode, . . . VI. vi. 19. 4
Wearie of travell in his former fight, . . . VI. vii. 19. 1
who did wayle or watch the *wearie* night? . . . VI. vii. 30. 6
now she was uppon the *weary* way, . . . VI. vii. 39. 1
when I *wearie* am, I downe doe lay My limbes . . . VI. ix. 23. 7
In sommers shade him selfe here rested *weary:* . . . VI. x. 22. 6
joy to *weary* wandring travailers did lend: . . . VII. vi. 9. 9
So they him follow'd till they *weary* were; . . . VII. vi. 53. 1
the *weary* war renew'th; . . . *Am.* xi. 4
Ye tradefull Merchants, that, with *weary* toyle, . . . *Am.* xv. 1
when shall these *wearie* woes have end, . . . *Am.* xxxvi. 1
The *weary* yeare his race now having run, . . . *Am.* lxii. 1
Lyke as a huntsman after *weary* chace, . . . *Am.* lxvii. 1
I all *weary* had the chace forsooke, . . . *Am.* lxvii. 6
Many long *weary* dayes I have outworne; . . . *Am.* lxxxvi. 2
when will this long *weary* day have end, . . . *Epith.* 278
Twixt sleepe and wake, after she *weary* was, . . . *Epith.* 309
Weasand. had his *wesand* bene a little widder, . . . *S.C.* S. 210
with the straint his *wesand* nigh he brast. . . . V. ii. 14. 5
Weasand-pipe. His *weasand-pipe* it through his gorget cleft. . IV. iii. 12. 7
Weather. as the lowring *Wether* lookes downe, . . . *S.C.*F . 29
happie winde and *weather* entertaine, . . . *Gn.* 563
To *weather* him, and his moyst wings to dry. . . . *Mui.* 184
mery wynd and *weather* call her thence away. . . . I. xii. 1. 9
Ne wind and *weather* at his pleasure call: . . . II. vi. 23. 3
whiles wind and *wether* right Doe serve their turnes: . . . II. xi. 4. 7
at last the *weather* gan to cleare, . . . II. xii. 37. 5
let us hence depart whilest *wether* serves and winde.' . . . II. xii. 87. 9
of all old dislikes they made faire *weather;* . . . IV. ii. 29. 3
one of th' ayre, without or wind or *wether:* . . . V. ii. 31. 4
To *weather* his brode sailes, . . . V. iv. 42. 3
Of which he in faire *weather* wont to take great store. . . . V. ix. 11. 9
The winde and *weather* served them so well, . . . V. xii. 4. 5
Allur'd with myldnesse of the gentle *wether* . . . VI. iii. 23. 3
As they are wont in faire sunshynie *weather,* . . . VI. ix. 41. 3
So let us, which this chaunge of *weather* vew, . . . *Am.* lxii. 5
Weatherbeaten. As *wetherbeaten* ship arryv'd on happie shore. II. i. 2. 9
Weather's. Ne ought for fayrer *weathers* false delight. . . . *Am.* lix. 8
Weave. Doo *weave* the direfull threds of destinie, . . . *D.* 17
Rude rymes, the which a rustick Muse did *weave* . . . *Ded. Son.* vii. 11
He gan to *weave* a web of wicked guyle, . . . II. i. 8. 4
With golden wyre to *weave* her curled head; . . . III. viii. 7. 6
some guilefull traine did *weave,* . . . V. v. 37. 4
faynes to *weave* false tales and leasings bad, . . . V. xii. 36. 8
oft through pride do their owne perill *weave,* . . . VI ix. 22. 3
To decke hir selfe, and her faire mantle *weave.* . . . *Am.* iv. 12
all that I in many dayes doo *weave,* . . . *Am.* xxiii. 7
Weaved. Twixt life and death long to and fro she *weaved,* . . V. iv. 10. 7
Weaver. Nor anie *weaver,* which his worke doth boast . . . *Mui.* 363
Weaves. Unwisely *weaves,* that takes two webbes in hand. . . . *S.C.* O. 102
Weaving. like a cobweb *weaving* slenderly, . . . *Gn.* 3
weaving straight a net with manie a fold . . . *Mui.* 357
Web. He gan to weave a *web* of wicked guyle, . . . II. i. 8. 4
Arachne high did lifte Her cunning *web,* . . . II. vii. 28. 8
More subtile *web* Arachne cannot spin; . . . II. xii. 77. 7
Deviz'd a *Web* her wooers to deceave; . . . *Am.* xxiii. 2
Such labour like the Spyders *web* I fynd, . . . *Am.* xxiii. 13
Webs. Unwisely weaves, that takes two *webbes* in hand. . . . *S.C.* O. 102
Wed. her good will he got her first to *wedde.* . . . *Col.* 131
Yt seemd thenchaunted flame which did Creusa *wed.* . . . II. xii. 45. 9
Where Thames doth the Medway *wedd,* . . . IV. xi. Arg.
at last relenting, she to him was *wed.* . . . IV. xi. 8. 9
closely did her *wed,* but knowne to few: . . . VI. xii. 5. 4
Till with the Fanchin she her selfe do *wed,* . . . VII. vi. 53. 8
Wedded. *wedded* th' one to Maglan king of Scottes, . . . II. x. 29. 1
Whom having *wedded,* as did him behove, . . . IV. i. 2. 8
The very selfe same day that she was *wedded,* . . . IV. i. 3. 2
to accept her to his *wedded* wife: . . . IV. ix. 15. 6
Wedding. Thetis *wedding* with Aeacidee, . . . VI. x. 22. 5
Wedding-day. Against their *wedding day,* . . . *Proth.* 125
Wedge. the tronke to grone under the *wedge.* . . . *Bel.*[1] v. 12
Under the *wedge* I heard the tronck to grone; . . . *Bel.*[2] v. 12
When heavy hammers on the *wedge* are swaid: . . . I. xi. 42. 7
Wedges. distent Into great Ingowes and to *wedges* square; . . II. vii. 5. 6
to small purpose yron *wedges* made; . . . IV. v. 35. 8
Wedlock. That was in sacred bandes of *wedlocke* tyde To
Therion, . . . I. vi. 21. 5
A Satyre . . . The loyall linkes of *wedlocke,* did unbinde, . . I. vi. 22. 8
thy daughter linck, in holy band Of *wedlocke,* . . . I. xii. 26. 7
his daughter deare He gave in *wedlocke* to Maximian, . . . II. x. 61. 2
To contract *wedlock,* . . . *Wedlocke* contract in blood, . . . III. ix. 42. 5, 6
hardly praisd his *wedlock* good. . . . III. ix. 42. 9
This daughter thought in *wedlocke* to have bound . . . VI. xii. 4. 5
The lawes of *wedlock* still dost patronize; . . . *Epith.* 391
Wedlock's. Though spousd, yet wanting *wedlocks* solemnize; . I. x. 4. 7
Enlincked fast in *wedlockes* loyall bond, . . . V. iv. 3. 2

Wedlock's—*Continued.*
should have joyned bene to her in *wedlocks* knot. . . . V. iv. 8. 9
Weed. *See* **Out-weed.**
That of a *weede* he was overcrawed. . . . *S.C.* F. 142
With painted words tho gan this proude *weede* . . . *S.C.* F. 160
whose flowre is woxe a *weede,* . . . *S.C.* Jun. 109
simple was theyr *weede:* . . . *S.C.* Jul. 168
kydst the hidden kinds of many a *wede,* . . . *S.C.* D. 92
The wicked *weed,* which there the Foxe did lay, . . . *Hub.* 1321
each mans worth is measured by his *weed,* . . . *Col.* 711
The wofull Dwarfe . . . tooke up his forlorne *weed;* . . . I. vii. 19. 4
I wrapt myselfe in Palmers *weed,* . . . II. i. 52. 8
A goodly Ladie clad in hunters *weed,* . . . II. iii. 21. 7
Below her ham her *weed* did somewhat trayne, . . . II. iii. 27. 1
Through her thin *weed* their places only signifide. . . . II. iii. 29. 9
Confest how Philemon her wrought to chaunge her *weede.* . . II. iv. 29. 9
Wrath is a fire; and gealosie a *weede;* . . . II. iv. 35. 2
The fire of sparkes, the *weede* of little seede, . . . II. iv. 35. 4
To spoile the dead of *weed* Is sacrilege, . . . II. viii. 16. 4
The soveraine *weede* . . . Shee pownded small, . . . III. v. 33. 1
ragged *weed* Made of Beares skin, . . . III. xii. 11. 1
like salvage *weed* With woody mosse bedight, . . . IV. iv. 39. 4
seemeth well to answere to your *weede,* . . . IV. vi. 5. 3
One rushing forth out of the thickest *weed,* . . . IV. vii. 4. 4
As withered *weed* through cruell winters tine, . . . IV. xii. 34. 6
they saw a Squire in squallid *weed* Lamenting sore . . . V. i. 13. 7
from you lightly throw This squalid *weede,* . . . V. iv. 34. 6
catching her fast by her ragged *weed* . . . V. xi. 61. 3
having long time, as his daily *weed,* . . . VI. iv. 19. 4
a faire Mayden clad in mourning *weed,* . . . VI. vi. 16. 7
Her *weed* she then withdrawing did him discover; . . . VI. vi. 32. 1
himselfe addrest In shepheards *weed;* . . . VI. ix. 36. 4
sweetest Season, when each Flower and *weede* . . . *Proth.* 68
Weeds. he all wallowed in the *weedes* downe beaten, . . . *Van.* ii. 8
with the *weedes* be glutted. . . . *S.C.* Jul. 112
Their *weedes* bene not so nighly wore; . . . *S.C.* Jul. 171
Sith now I am but *weedes* and wastfull gras? . . . *Ti.* 42
To feed on flowres and *weeds* of glorious feature, . . . *Mui.* 213
when your mawes are with those *weeds* corrupted, . . . *D.* 348
Muse whylome did maske . . . in lowly Shephards *weeds,* . I. Pr. 1. 2
An aged Sire, in long blacke *weedes* yclad, . . . I. i. 29. 2
In so ritch *weedes,* and seeming glorious show, . . . I. ii. 21. 5
A silly man, in simple *weeds* forworne, . . . I. vi. 35. 1
creeping close, as Snake in hidden *weedes,* . . . I. ix. 28. 8
with words, and *weedes,* of wondrous might, . . . II. i. 52. 3
like an Adder lurking in the *weedes,* . . . II. v. 34. 1
with uncomely *weedes* the gentle wave accloyes. . . . II. vii. 15. 9
Clad in fayre *weedes* but fowle disordered, . . . II. xii. 55. 8
Emongst the Roses grow some wicked *weeds:* . . . III. i. 49. 6
Of all the *weeds* that bud and blossome there; . . . III. vi. 30. 8
That he with fleshly *weeds* would them attire: . . . III. vi. 32. 5
in loathly *weedes* And wilfull want, . . . III. vii. 6. 4
with vaine poemes *weeds* to have their fancies fed. . . . IV. Pr. 1. 9
The barren ground was full of wicked *weedes,* . . . IV. i. 25. 2
Whom when she saw in wretched *weedes* disguiz'd, . . . IV. viii. 12. 5
of warlike armes despoile, And cloth in womens *weedes:* . . V. iv. 31. 4
she made him to be dight In womans *weedes,* . . . V. v. 20. 7
not to forgo Those warlike *weedes,* . . . V. vi. 23. 7
causd him those uncomely *weedes* undight; . . . V. vii. 41. 2
bynding up her locks and *weeds,* . . . V. x. 24. 9
With ragged *weedes,* and lockes upstaring hye, . . . VI. xi. 27. 4
Both clad in shepheards *weeds* agreeably, . . . VI. xi. 36. 2
wrapped well In many *weeds* . . . VII. vii. 42. 2
Weedy. Nought reaped but a *weedye* crop of care; . . . *S.C.* D. 122
creeping sought way in the *weedy* gras: . . . I. i. 20. 8
Like warie Hynd within the *weedie* soyle, . . . IV. x. 55. 8
Week. once a *weeke,* upon the Sabbath day, . . . *Hub.* 456
Thrise every *weeke* in ashes shee did sitt, . . . I. iii. 14. 2
neither day nor *weeke* He would surceasse, . . . VI. vii. 13. 8
Weeke. *See* **Wick.**
Weeks. For all so many *weekes* as the yeare has, . . . II. x. 22. 3
for *weekes* that passed were, She told but moneths, . . . V. vi. 5. 6
Ween. one would *weene* that one sole Cities strength . . . *Ro.* viii. 2
some that *weene* the contrarie in thought, . . . *Ro.* ix. 13
Willye, I *wene* thou bee assot; . . . *S.C.* Mar. 25
I *wene* the Geaunt has not such a weight, . . . *S.C.* May 142
I *weene* thou be affrayd . . . *S.C.* Jul. 71
such, I *weene,* the brethren were . . . *S.C.* Jul. 141
Never dempt more right of beautye, I *weene,* . . . *S.C.* Au. 137
wandred, I *wene,* about the world round, . . . *S.C.* S. 22
Colin Clout, I *wene,* be his selfe boye, . . . *S.C.* S. 176
The dog his maisters voice did it *wene,* . . . *S.C.* S. 219
Her like shee has not left behinde I *weene:* . . . *S.C.* N. 40
Not so much . . . I *weene,* . . . *Gn.* 181
What course ye *weene* is best for us to take, . . . *Hub.* 115
well I *weene,* . . . *Hub.* 597
it true Sea, and true Bull, ye would *weene.* . . . *Mui.* 280
(I *weene*), the wofulst man alive, . . . *D.* 5
what of him became I cannot *weene.* . . . *D.* 567
well I *weene* it worth recounting was, . . . *Col.* 85
Furthest from end then, when they neerest *weene,* . . . I. i. 10. 6
Her, whom he, . . . did *weene* To bee the chastest flowre . . . I. i. 48. 3
ramping on his shield, did *weene* the same Have reft away . I. iii. 41. 5
'Well may I *ween* your griefe is wondrous great; . . . I. vii. 40. 2
stoutest heart, I *weene,* could cause to quake: . . . I. vii. 52. 4
Old Timon . . . is the wisest now on earth I *weene:* . . . I. ix. 4. 4
now by proofe all otherwise I *weene,* . . . I. x. 58. 7
never living man, I *weene,* so sore . . . was distrest: . . . I. xii. 17. 5
Ne *weene* my right with strength adowne to tread, . . . I. xii. 28. 5
'None but that saw,' (quoth he) 'would *weene* . . . II. i. 11. 3

Ween—*Continued.*
Great cause, I *weene,* you guided, ... II. i. 29. 9
For all so great shame after death I *weene,* . . . . . II. i. 59. 8
weene . . . His guiltie handes from bloody gore to cleene. . . II. ii. 3. 2
'That am, I *weene,* most wretched man alive; . . . . . II. vi. 45. 2
I *weene,* Joves dreaded thunder light Does scorch . . . . . II. vi. 50. 7
Doth not, I *weene,* so many evils meet.' . . . . . II. vii. 14. 5
none could *weene* Them to efforce . . . . . II. vii. 30. 3
'Palmer,' (said he) 'no knight so rude, I *weene,* . . . . . II. viii. 26. 1
What mote ye *weene,* if the trew lively-head . . . . . II. ix. 3. 3
Ne ought, I *weene,* are ye therein behynd, ... II. ix. 38. 8
either me too bold ye *weene,* . . . . . II. ix. 42. 2
The wisest men, I *weene,* that lived in their ages. . . . . II. ix. 47. 9
uneath to *wene* That monstrous error, ... II. x. 8. 2
labour lost it was to *weene* approch him neare. . . . . II. xi. 25. 9
to *weene* His speares default to mend . . . . . III. i. 10. 2
To *weene* your wrong by force to justify; . . . . . III. i. 25. 2
living wit, I *weene,* cannot display . . . . . III. i. 32. 3
to *weene* by might That man to hard conditions to bind, . . . III. ii. 13. 6
Did *weene,* unwares, that her unlucky lot Lay hidden . . . III. ii. 26. 4
that same warlike wize, I *weene,* would you misseeme; . . . III. iii. 53. 6
weene by warning to avoyd his fate? . . . . . III. iv. 27. 2
'Now certes, swaine,' (saide he) 'such one, I *weene,* . . . III. v. 6. 1
That ever living eye, I *weene,* did see. . . . . . III. v. 8. 3
thou doest *weene* with villeinous despight To blott her honour, III. v. 45. 4
Well may I *weene,* faire Ladies, ... III. vi. 1. 1
well I *weene,* ye first desire to learne . . . . . III. vi. 54. 1
I *weene,* the hardest hart of stone Would hardly finde . . . III. viii. 1. 7
how may I *weene* it trew, ... III. viii. 48. 3
who would ever *weene* . . . Saturne ever weend to love? . . III. xi. 43. 1
'Gentle Dame, reward enough I *weene,* . . . . . III. xii. 40. 2
best is lov'd of all alive, I *weene,* . . . . . IV. Pr. 4. 7
There they, I *weene,* would fight untill this day, ... IV. ii. 20. 1
hard it was to *weene* which harder were. . . . . . IV. iii. 7. 5
spoyle, On which they *weene* their famine to asswage, . . . IV. iii. 16. 3
Some newborne wight ye would him surely *weene;* . . . . . IV. iii. 23. 5
some that fairest her did *weene,* . . . . . IV. v. 11. 4
Him needeth sure a golden pen, I *weene,* . . . . . IV. v. 12. 2
well I *weene,* when as these rimes be red . . . . . IV. viii. 29. 1
few Could *weenen* whether they were false or trew: . . . . . IV. xi. 27. 5
ne wist well what to *weene;* . . . . . IV. xii. 21. 2
Ne *weene* what mister maladie it is, ... IV. xii. 22. 2
Not knowing natures worke, nor what to *weene,* . . . . . V. iii. 19. 6
all on fire ye would her surely *weene;* . . . . . V. v. 8. 5
well I may this *weene* by that I fynd, ... V. v. 41. 4
How couldst thou *weene* . . . To hide thy state . . . . . V. vii. 21. 4
More happie mother would her surely *weene* . . . . . V. x. 7. 7
where he did *weene* Him selfe to save; . . . . . V. x. 37. 8
well did *weene* How each to entertaine . . . . . VI. v. 36. 8
it booteth not to *weene* . . . It ever to amend: . . . . . VI. vi. 9. 4
sure I *weene,* . . . . . VI. viii. 29. 1
wist not what to *weene;* . . . . . VI. x. 17. 4
That he by them might certaine tydings *weene* . . . . . VI. xi. 39. 3
I rather *weene,* Through some vaine errour, ... VII. vi. 32. 1
well I *weene* . . . Her garment was so bright . . . . . VII. vii. 7. 1
Ne ought to see, but like a shade to *weene,* . . . . . VII. vii. 46. 4
If Yvorie, her forehead Yvory *weene;* . . . . . *Am.* xv. 10
However now thereof ye little *weene!* . . . . . *Am.* xxvii. 4
ye would *weene* Some angell she had beene. . . . . . *Epith.* 152
thus farre happie he himselfe doth *weene,* . . . . . *H.L.* 212

Weened. She *weend* the shell-fishe to have broke, ... *S.C.* Jul. 225
I *weened* sure he was our God alone, ... *Col.* 773
furthest from her hope, when most she *weened* nye. . . . . I. iii. 21. 9
her knight by name She *weend* it was, ... I. iii. 26. 7
'At last, when perils all I *weened* past, ... I. iv. 47. 1
Whereof he *weend* possessed soone to bee, ... I. vi. 5. 4
'I *weened* well, That great Cleopolis . . . The fairest citty was I. x. 58. 1
He *weened* well to worke some uncouth wyle: . . . . . II. i. 8. 2
weened well ere long his will to win, ... II. iii. 13. 2
weend it was my love with whom he playd. . . . . . II. iv. 28. 5
well he *weened* that so glorious bayte . . . . . II. vii. 34. 3
he *weened* with Morddure . . . to cleave his head. . . . . II. viii. 30. 6
they *weened* fowle reproch Was to them doen, ... II. ix. 11. 1
Wel *weened* hee that field was then his owne, ... II. xi. 35. 1
(For shee her *weend* a fresh and lusty knight,) . . . . . III. i. 47. 3
Litle shee *weend* that love he close conceald. . . . . . III. v. 49. 4
He *ween'd* that his affection entire She should aread; . . . III. vii. 16. 7
Full litle *weened* I that chastitee Had lodging . . . . . III. vii. 59. 3
whom he had earst destroyd She *weend,* . . . . . III. viii. 2. 9
Well *weened* he, that fairest Florimell It was . . . . . III. viii. 19. 6
he *weend* Her will to win . . . . . III. viii. 41. 4
Well *weened* hee that those the same mote bee, ... III. x. 21. 1
That sullein Saturne ever *weend* to love? . . . . . III. xi. 43. 2
Whose like alive on earth he *weened* not: . . . . . IV. ii. 8. 5
Weend . . . That fayrest Florimell was present there . . . IV. ii. 22. 8
More wise they *weend* to make of love delight . . . . . IV. ii. 40. 5
weened sure He gan to faint toward the battels end, . . . IV. iii. 32. 6
They *weened* sure the warre was at an end; . . . . . IV iii. 35. 2
Whom sure he *weend,* that he some-wher tofore had eide. . . IV. iv. 7. 9
In no lesse neede of helpe then him he *weend.* . . . . . IV. iv. 45. 4
Well *weened* all, which her that time did vew, ... IV. v. 13. 5
weend no mortall creature she should bee, ... IV. v. 14. 6
weend, by secret signes of manlinesse . . . . . IV. vii. 45. 4
Well *weend* that he had beene some man of place, ... IV. viii. 14. 4
She *weened* well that then she was betraide: . . . . . IV. ix. 7. 5
sure she *weend* it was some one of those, ... IV. xii. 26. 8
death t' adward I *ween'd* did appertaine . . . . . IV. xii. 30. 4
sure they *ween'd* she was escapt away; . . . . . V. ii. 25. 2
Ne would I it have *ween'd,* . . . . . V. iv. 33. 9
Yet to awayt fit time she *weened* best, ... V. v. 44. 8

Weened—*Continued.*
Well *weend* she then . . . That it was one sent from her love V. vi. 8. 3
he *weend* that this his present guest Was Artegall, ... V. vi. 34. 1
She *weened* streight it was her Paynim Knight, ... V. viii. 26. 7
Well *weend* he streight that he should be the same . . . . . VI. i. 33. 1
shame he *weend* a sleeping wight to wound. . . . . . VI. i. 34. 4
sure he *weend* him borne of noble blood, ... VI. ii. 24. 6
He *weened* well that he in deed was dead, ... VI. vii. 20. 2
He from those bands *weend* him to have unwound; . . . . . VI. viii. 27. 4
After his rusticke wise, that well he *weend,* . . . . . VI. ix. 6. 7
she her selfe more worthy thereof *wend,* . . . . . VII. vi. 11. 3

Weenedst. or *weenedst* her thy frend . . . . . *D.* 151
weenedst thou what wight thee overthrew, ... III. i. 8. 1

Weenest. *Weenest* of love is not his mynd? . . . . . *S.C.* F. 76
Full little *weenest* thou what sorrowes are Left thee . . . II. ii. 2. 3
weenest words or charms may force withstond: . . . . . II. viii. 22. 2
knight, that *weenst* with words To steale . . . . . III. viii. 17. 1

Weeneth. The noble corage never *weeneth* ought . . . . . III. ii. 10. 4
he *weeneth* well before that tide None can have tidings . . V. xi. 42. 4

Weening. *weening* it to hit. . . . . . *S.C.* May 307
weening hys whyte head was chalke, ... *S.C.* Jul. 223
weening to returne whence they did stray, ... I. i. 10. 3
Weening their wonted entrance to have found . . . . . I. i. 25. 5
weening that the sad end of the warre; . . . . . I. xi. 32. 3
Weening it had beene thunder in the skye, ... II. iii. 45. 7
weening to have arm'd him, she did quite disarme. . . . . III. iv. 27. 9
so *weening* way to make To Ladies love, ... IV. iv. 4. 3
Him *weening,* ere he nigh approcht, to have represt. . . . IV. iv. 6. 9
Weening some heavenly goddesse he did see, ... IV. vi. 22. 4
Weening therein some holy Hermit lay, ... IV. vii. 42. 7
Well *weening* that his foe was falne withall; . . . . . V. ii. 12. 8
Weening at once her wrath on him to wreake . . . . . V. iv. 40. 4
Weening at last to win advantage new; . . . . . V. v. 7. 2
Weening her lifes last howre then neare to bee, ... V. xii. 11. 8

Weens. *weenes* with watch and hard restraynt . . . . . III. ix. 6. 8

Weep. Making his sport, that manie makes to *weep:* . . . . . *Van.* v. 7
hanging heads did seeme his carefull case to *weepe.* . . . . . *S.C.* Ja. 78
with that gan *weepe,* . . . . . *S.C.* May 189
my death shall *weepe,* . . . . . *S.C.* Au. 119
as they would learne to *weepe;* . . . . . *S.C.* N. 134
I ne wotte Whether rejoyce or *weepe* . . . . . *S.C.* N. 205
in sad tearmes gan sorrowfully *weepe,* . . . . . *Gn.* 325
could have made a stonie heart to *weep;* . . . . . *T.M.* 110
For whome I waile and *weepe* all that I may. . . . . . *T.M.* 594
Did *weep* and waile, and made exceeding mone, ... *T.M.* 598
Then gan she greatly to lament and *weepe.* . . . . . *Mui.* 288
given like cause with thee to waile and *weepe;* . . . . . *D.* 66
or any *weepe* that would, ... *D.* 76
seeke alone to *weepe,* and dye alone.' . . . . . *D.* 77
Therewith he gan afresh to waile and *weepe,* . . . . . *D.* 169
Weepe, Shepheard! *weepe,* to make my undersong. . . . . . *D.* 245
'What hart so stony hard but that would *weepe,* . . . . . *D.* 246
Ah! why does my Alcyon *weepe* and mourne, ... *D.* 264
Weep, Shepheard! *weep,* to make mine undersong. . . . . . *D.* 294
Weepe, Shepheard! *weepe,* to make my undersong. . . . . . *D.* 343
Weep, Shepheard! *weep,* to make my undersong. . . . . . *D.* 392, 441, 490
every one did *weep* and waile, and mone, ... *As.* 207
Tho can she *weepe,* to stirre up gentle ruth . . . . . I. i. 50. 8
Then gan she wail and *weepe* to see that woeful stowre. . . I. ii. 7. 9
In stead of rest she does lament and *weepe,* . . . . . I. iii. 15. 5
freends . . . Ne dare to *weepe,* nor seeme to understand . . I. iii. 20. 7
as she did *weepe* and waile, A knight her mett . . . . . I. iii. 24. 3
Crocodile . . . Doth *weepe* full sore, ... I. v. 18. 6
My last left comfort is my woes to *weepe* and waile.' . . . I. vii. 39. 9
what bootes it to *weepe* . . . . . II. i. 16. 5
Gan smyle on them, that rather ought to *weepe,* . . . . . II. ii. 1. 6
She set her downe to *weepe* . . . . . II. ii. 8. 3
full many soules do endlesse wayle and *weepe.* . . . . . II. vii. 56. 9
For very felnesse lowd he gan to *weepe,* . . . . . II. viii. 37. 5
drops of Christall seemd for wantones to *weep.* . . . . . II. xii. 61. 9
drops of purple blood thereout did *weepe,* . . . . . III. i. 65. 8
with teares which closely she did *weepe.* . . . . . III. ii. 28. 9
sett her by to watch, and sett her by to *weepe.* . . . . . III. ii. 47. 9
her great courage would not let her *weepe,* . . . . . III. iv. 11. 3
did *weepe* And often wayle their wealth, ... III. iv. 22. 8
As pittying to see her waile and *weepe:* . . . . . III. viii. 21. 8
loudly cry, and *weepe,* and waile, ... IV. ix. 7. 6
Mulla mine, whose waves I whilom taught to *weep.* . . . . . IV. xi. 41. 9
languisht, and alone did *weepe.* . . . . . IV. xii. 19. 9
With froward will doth set him selfe to *weepe,* . . . . . V. vi. 14. 3
weepe To thinke of your nights want, ... V. vi. 25. 8
Gan *weepe* and wayle, as if great griefe had her affected. . . V. ix. 9. 9
all the night for bitter anguish *weepe,* . . . . . VI. iii. 10. 4
all night did nought but *weepe,* . . . . . VI. iii. 44. 8
Thereto, when needed, she could *weepe* and pray, ... VI. vi. 42. 5
Whilest she did *weepe,* of no man mercifide: . . . . . VI. vii. 32. 5
What now is left her but to wayle and *weepe,* . . . . . VI. xi. 23. 6
Led with the infants cry that loud did *weepe,* . . . . . VI. xii. 9. 3
when I *weep,* she sayes, Teares are but water, ... *Am.* xviii. 10
So do I *weepe,* and wayle, . . . in vaine, ... *Am.* xviii. 13

Weepeth. the Firre that *weepeth* still: . . . . . I. i. 9. 2

Weeping. With *weeping,* and wayling, and misery. . . . . . *S.C.* F. 50
into *weeping* turne your wanton layes. . . . . . *S.C.* N. 79
This yron world (that same he *weeping* sayes) . . . . . *Hub.* 254
watrie eyne halfe *weeping,* . . . . . *Hub.* 1362
First comming to the world with *weeping* eye, ... *T.M.* 159
weeping said, 'Ah, my long lacked Lord, ... I. iii. 27. 1
wept, that cause of *weeping* none he had; . . . . . I. iv. 30. 8
molten starres doe drop like *weeping* eyes; . . . . . I. vi. 6. 5
As from two *weeping* eyes, fresh streames do flow, ... II. ii. 9. 2

Weeping—*Continued.*
To whom halfe *weeping* she thus answered; . . . III. vi. 20. 6
Through jealous passion *weeping* inly wroth, . . . IV. ix. 9. 8
weeping day and night did him attend, . . . IV. xii. 21. 6
Would thumpe her forward . . . *Weeping* to him in vaine . VI. ii. 10. 9
She long so held, and softly *weeping* sayd; . . . VI. xii. 19. 7
Unto his mother straight he *weeping* came, . . . *Epig.* iv. 31
Weeps. Why then *weepes* Lobbin so without remorse? . . . *S.C.* N. 167
Weet, -ing, *etc. See* **Wet, Wit,** *etc.*
Weft. *See* **Waif.**
is come to that same place where first she *wefte.* . . . II. vi. 18. 9
Ne can thy irrevocable desteny bee *wefte.* . . . III. iv. 36. 9
Where have ye all this while bin wandring, where bene *weft?'* VI. v. 23. 9
Weigh. Nought *weigh* I who my song doth prayse . . . *S.C.* Jun. 73
the Ape, beginning well to *wey* This hard adventure, . . . *Hub.* 112
in true ballaunce thou wilt *weigh* thy state; . . . I. ix. 45. 2
Whether shall *weigh* the balance downe; . . . IV. ix. 1. 4
she him taught to *weigh* both right and wrong . . . V. i. 7. 1
all the world he would *weigh* equallie, . . . V. ii. 30. 5
'Thou that presum'st to *weigh* the world anew, . . . V. ii. 34. 1
if thou now shouldst *weigh* them new in pound, . . . V. ii. 36. 5
Therefore leave off to *weigh* them all againe, . . . V. ii. 36. 8
To call to count, or *weigh* his workes anew, . . . V. ii. 42. 6
weigh the winde that under heaven doth blow; . . . V. ii. 43. 2
weigh the light that in the East doth rise; . . . V. ii. 43. 3
weigh the thought that from mans mind doth flow: . . . V. ii. 43. 4
Weigh but one word which from thy lips doth fall: . . . V. ii. 43. 6
the least word . . . he could *way* aright. . . . V. ii. 44. 4
he could justly *weigh* the wrong or right. . . . V. ii. 45. 3
Yet all the wrongs could not a litle right downe *way.* . . . V. ii. 46. 9
rather strove extremities to *way,* . . . V. ii. 49. 3
Seem'd not to *weigh* his threatfull words . . . VI. iii. 36. 2
could not *weigh* of worthinesse aright; . . . VI. vii. 29. 6
all that she so deare did *way,* . . . VII. vi. 55. 1
'Then *weigh,* O soveraigne goddesse! by what right . . . VII. vii. 16. 1
bethinke me on that speech . . . and well it *way!* . . . VII. viii. 1. 2
Weighed. The watrie wette *weighed* downe his head, . . . *S.C.* F. 232
her, whose love as lyfe I *wayd,* . . . *S.C.* Jun. 47
Yet if their deeper sence be inly *wayd,* . . . *Ded. Son.* ix. 9
right and wrong ylike in equall ballaunce *waide.* . . . I. iv. 27. 9
though they faulty were, yet well he *wayd,* . . . I. x. 40. 5
Full many things so doubtfull to be *wayd,* . . . IV. i. 7. 5
Through many perils wonne, and many fortunes *waide.* . . . IV. ix. 38. 9
if the one be with the other *wayd,* . . . IV. x. 1. 3
For want whereof he *weighed* vanity, . . . V. ii. 30. 7
weighed out in ballaunces so nere, . . . V. ii. 35. 3
by no meanes the false will with the truth be *wayd.* . . . V. ii. 45. 9
being rightly *wayd,* They are not changed . . . VII. vii. 58. 3
It down is *weighd* with thoght of earthly things, . . . *Am.* lxxii. 3
Weighing. *weighing* down his drouping drowsie hedd, . . . *Gn.* 244
weighing the decayed plight . . . of her chosen knight, . . . I. ix. 20. 4
nought *weighing* what he sayd or did, . . . VI. iii. 37. 1
thy love we *weighing* worthily, . . . *Am.* lxviii. 9
Weight. th' earth under her childrens *weight* did grone, . . . *Ro.* xii. 7
not able to beare so great *weight,* . . . *Ro.* xx. 12
His wonderous *weight* made the ground to quake, . . . *S.C.* F. 219
the Geaunt has not such a *weight,* . . . *S.C.* May 142
with the *weight* their backs nigh broken were: . . . *Hub.* 1158
With her owne *weight* down pressed now shee lies, . . . *Ti.* 76
To beare so great a *weight:* . . . I. xi. 18. 6
with the *weight* of his owne weeldlesse might He falleth . IV. iii. 19. 8
Of all whose *weight* he would not misse a fether: . . . V. ii. 31. 7
if the *weight* of these thou canst not show, . . . V. ii. 43. 5
'Which is' (sayd he) 'more heavy then in *weight,* . . . V. ii. 44. 5
by no meane could in the *weight* be stayd; . . . V. ii. 45. 8
his owne *waight* his necke asunder broke, . . . V. viii. 8. 3
unryper yeares . . . unfit For thing of *weight* . . . VI. ii. 9. 3
Whom with his *weight* unweldy downe he held, . . . VI. viii. 28. 3
with the *weight* of their own surquedry, They both are fallen, *Com. Son.* iv. 5
Weightiness. with her owne *weightinesse,* Upon them fell, . . . *Ti.* 571
Weights. A paire of *waights,* with which he did assoyle . . . VII. vii. 38. 7
Weighty. Who ever casts to compasse *weightye* prise, . . . *S.C.* O. 103
every *weighty* thing they did upbeare, . . . II. vi. 46. 8
The tryall of a great and *weightie* case, . . . V. ix. 36. 7
Weladay. 'Ah (*waladay!*) there is no end of paine, . . . *Gn.* 417
Welaway. Perdie, and *wellawaye,* ill may they thrive! . . . *S.C.* Au. 19
Wel-away the while I was so fonde . . . *S.C.* S. 58
'Ah, *well away!* most noble Lords, . . . II. vi. 32. 5
'Harrow now out, and *well away!'* he cryde, . . . II. vi. 43. 6
Harrow and *well away!* . . . II. viii. 46. 8
Now *well-away!* . . . IV. xi. 1. 3
'Ah! woe is me, and *well-away!'* . . . V. i. 15. 1
'Ah *wellaway!'* (sayd then the yron man) . . . V. vi. 16. 1
false watches, *wellaway!* . . . V. vi. 25. 4
'Ah, *well-away!'* (sayd he, then sighing sore) . . . VI. xi. 29. 1
alasse, he cryde, and *wel-away!* . . . *Epig.* iv. 27
Welcome. *welcome* now, my light, and shining lampe of blis! I. iii. 27. 9
O *welcome,* child! whom I have longd to see, . . . I. v. 27. 8
O! *welcome* thou, that doest of death bring tydings trew.' . I. viii. 38. 9
welcome now, my Lord in wele or woe, . . . I. viii. 43. 1
whose care Was guests to *welcome,* . . . I. x. 44. 3
seemely *welcome* for her did prepare: . . . I. x. 44. 7
Ne ever wight that mote so *welcome* bee . . . II. iv. 20. 5
with such uncouth *welcome* did receave Her fayned Paramour, IV. i. 36. 2
to *welcome* him well as she can . . . IV. vi. 10. 5
greatest Princes court would *welcome* fayne; . . . IV. viii. 27. 2
And make their *welcome* to them well appeare. . . . VI. iii. 6. 4
Now *welcome,* night! thou night so long expected, . . . *Epith.* 315
Welcomed. *welcomde* more for feare then charitee; . . . III. ix. 19. 4
welcomed themselves. . . . III. ix. 19. 6

Welcomed—*Continued.*
(*welcommed* with cold And chearelesse hunger) . . . IV. viii. 28. 1
There he was *welcom'd* of that honest syre . . . VI. ix. 17. 1
Weld, -s. *See* **Wield, -s.**
Welfare. thy health and thy *welfare,* . . . *S.C.* May 216
wondrous things concerning our *welfare,* . . . II. xii. 47. 5
You and your countrey both I wish *welfare,* . . . III. ii. 10. 8
(*welfare* thy heart, my deare!) . . . III. ii. 42. 1
Welk. ruddy Phebus gins to *welke* in west, . . . I. i. 23. 2
Welked. the *welked* Phoebus gan availe His weary waine; . *S.C.* Ja. 73
sadde Winter *welked* hath the day, . . . *S.C.* N. 13
Welkin. darkned was the *welkin* all about, . . . *Pet.* iii. 10
And clowdie *Welkin* cleareth. . . . *S.C.* Mar. 12
But see, the *Welkin* thicks apace, . . . *S.C.* Mar. 115
when the *Welkin* shone faire, . . . *S.C.* S. 187
He leaves the *welkin* way most beaten playne, . . . I. iv. 9. 7
the faire *welkin* fowly overcast . . . III. ix. 11. 4
dim the brightnesse of the *welkin* rownd, . . . III. x. 46. 7
Well. *See* **Outwell.**
well assur'd, she mounted up to joy. . . . *Pet.* vi. 10
He *well* foresaw . . . *Ro.* xxiii. 5
Might *well* have hop'd . . . *Ro.* xxxii. 8
Well maist thou boast, . . . *Ro.* xxxii. 12
Well worthie thou of immortalitie, . . . *Ro.* Env. 3
Well couth he tune his pipe . . . *S.C.* Ja. 10
'Thou feeble flocke, . . . Mayst witnesse *well,* . . . *S.C.* Ja. 45
Winter or Sommer they mought *well* fare. . . . *S.C.* F. 24
to replie *Well* as he couth; . . . *S.C.* F. 190
Sicker, Willye, thou warnest *well;* . . . *S.C.* Mar. 7
Whence floweth Helicon, the learned *well,* . . . *S.C.* Ap. 42
Can you *well* compare? . . . *S.C.* Ap. 67
Well is it seene theyr sheepe bene not their owne, . . . *S.C.* May 45
They sleepen in rest, *well* as other moe: . . . *S.C.* May 68
Well ywis was it with shepheards . . . *S.C.* May 109
God so *wel* them guided, . . . *S.C.* May 113
(as I can *well* devise) . . . *S.C.* May 174
Well heard Kiddie al this . . . *S.C.* May 249
that had *well* ycond his lere, . . . *S.C.* May 262
her Kidde shee knewe *well* was gone: . . . *S.C.* May 300
For *well* he meanes, but little can say. . . . *S.C.* May 311
Well couth he wayle his Woes, . . . *S.C.* Jun. 85
Shouldest *well* be knowne . . . *S.C.* Jun. 104
upon a hill, Beside a learned *well.* . . . *S.C.* Jul. 48
As *well* can prove the piercing levin, . . . *S.C.* Jul. 91
My seely sheepe like *well* belowe, . . . *S.C.* Jul. 105
The world is *well* amend, . . . *S.C.* Jul. 170
Well mought it beseme any harvest Queene. . . . *S.C.* Au. 36
Well agreed, Willie: . . . *S.C.* Au. 49
She can trippe it very *well.* . . . *S.C.* Au. 64
Well decked in a frocke of gray, . . . *S.C.* Au. 65
So weren his under-songs *well* addrest. . . . *S.C.* Au. 128
so *well* hath hym payned, . . . *S.C.* Au. 133
Perigot is *well* pleased . . . *S.C.* Au. 135
you cannot *wel* ken, . . . *S.C.* S. 42
Well is knowne that sith the Saxon king . . . *S.C.* S. 151
not but *well* mought him betight: . . . *S.C.* S. 173
mought I *well* marke, . . . *S.C.* S. 180
han be watered at the Muses *well;* . . . *S.C.* N. 30
to *well* I wote my humble vaine, . . . *S.C.* N. 50
So *well* she couth the shepherds entertayne . . . *S.C.* N. 95
well hast thow it gotte . . . *S.C.* N. 206
which *wel* could pype . . . *S.C.* D. 3
if I marked *well* the starres revolution, . . . *S.C.* Env. 3
of neither *well* withstood, . . . *Gn.* 413
having *well* before approoved . . . *Gn.* 465
'*Well* may appeare by proofe . . . *Gn.* 553
Narcisse, that, in a *well* Seeing his beautie, . . . *Gn.* 679
mirth, that seem'd her *well:* . . . *Hub.* 35
So *well* as I her words remember . . . *Hub.* 42
it likes me wondrous *well;* . . . *Hub.* 95
beginning *well* to wey This hard adventure, . . . *Hub.* 112
As *well* of worldly livelode as of life, . . . *Hub.* 147
Well seemd the Ape to like this ordinaunce; . . . *Hub.* 173
well considering of the circumstaunce, . . . *Hub.* 174
'I cannot, . . . like but *well* The purpose . . . *Hub.* 177
For *well* I wot . . . *Hub.* 179
'Right *well,* deere Gossip, ye advized have, . . . *Hub.* 193
well dispos'd him some reliefe to showe, . . . *Hub.* 261
Thereto right *well* this Curdog, . . . *Hub.* 294
Husbandman was meanly *well* content Triall to make . . . *Hub.* 297
And then ye will . . . *well* mooved bee.' . . . *Hub.* 378
All his care was, his service *well* to saine, . . . *Hub.* 392
'It seemes . . . right *well* that ye be Clerks, . . . *Hub.* 415
The Foxe was *well* induc'd to be a Parson, . . . *Hub.* 480
have I not *well* discourst . . . *Hub.* 541
him wisht good speed, and *well* to fare: . . . *Hub.* 550
th' Ape and Foxe ere long so *well* them sped, . . . *Hub.* 552
For *well* I weene, . . . *Hub.* 597
So *well* his golden Circlet him beseemeth. . . . *Hub.* 627
but that ye *well* can fashion . . . *Hub.* 651
So fare ye *well;* . . . *Hub.* 653
So *well* they shifted, that . . . *Hub.* 659
that became him *well.* . . . *Hub.* 700
he is practiz'd *well* in policie, . . . *Hub.* 783
to coosin men not *well* aware: . . . *Hub.* 874
(so *well* he him applyde) . . . *Hub.* 1014
his majestye Use them but *well,* . . . *Hub.* 1080
so *well* his message sayd, . . . *Hub.* 1101
as they were able *well* to beare, . . . *Hub.* 1157
certes, may I take it *well* in part, . . . *Hub.* 1217

Well—*Continued.*

Due praise, that is the spur of dooing *well?* . . . *T.M.* 454
one foote not fastned *well,* . . . *Ti.* 557
Well worthy he to taste of wretchednes. . . . *Mui.* 216
give unto my heavie eyes A *well* of teares, . . . *Mui.* 410
That *well* he seemd to be sum wight forlorne; . . . *D.* 45
no tongue can *well* unfold; . . . *D.* 74
Then harken *well* . . . *D.* 97
(as thou right *well* doest know) . . . *D.* 99
So *well* I wrought with mildnes and with paine, . . . *D.* 117
And *well* did hope . . . *D.* 149
doth not my dull wit *well* understand . . . *D.* 176
Well may the shepheard lasses now lament; . . . *D.* 222
whose brackish bitter *well,* I wasted have, . . . *D.* 250
'My little flocke, whom earst I lov'd so *well,* . . . *D.* 344
For *well* I wot my rymes . . . *As.* Pr. 12
Well made to strike, to throw, . . . *As.* 75
So *well* he wrought with practise . . . *As.* 99
her deare favours dearly *well* adorned; . . . *As.* 154
cald . . . Penthia, though not so *well:* . . . *As.* 194
(for *well* that skill he cond;) . . . *Col.* 74
For *well* I weene it worth recounting . . . *Col.* 85
And wrought so *well* with his continuall paine, . . . *Col.* 124
did so *well* her fancie weld, . . . *Col.* 130
'Right *well* he sure did plaine, . . . *Col.* 173
our pipes we both had wearied *well,* . . . *Col.* 178
her peerlesse skill in making *well,* . . . *Col.* 188
Appearing *well* in that well tuned song, . . . *Col.* 418
'They all . . . me graced goodly *well,* . . . *Col.* 485
She is the *well* of bountie and brave mynd, . . . *Col.* 496
Well worthie of so honourable place, . . . *Col.* 502
well worthie were those goodly favours . . . *Col.* 585
To quite them ill, that me demeand so *well:* . . . *Col.* 681
For *well* I wot, sith I . . . *Col.* 735
(Lobbin *well* thou knewest,) . . . *Col.* 736
For *well* I wot, that . . . *Col.* 751
drownded lie in pleasures wastefull *well,* . . . *Col.* 762
Well may it seeme, . . . *Col.* 831
So *well* thou wot'st the mysterie . . . *Col.* 833
To use him so that used her so *well;* . . . *Col.* 912
And *well* I wote, . . . *Col.* 919
Which so to doe may thee right *well* befit, . . . *Ded. Son.* iii. 5
As goodlie *well* ye shew'd in late assaies, . . . *Ded. Son.* x. 8
As *wel* to al that civil artes professe, . . . *Ded.Son.*xiii.10
'Be *well* aware,' quoth then that Ladie milde, . . . I. i. 12. 1
well worthy end Of such . . . I. i. 26. 6
Well worthie be you of that Armory, . . . I. i. 27. 5
And shall thee *well* rewarde . . . I. i. 31. 6
And *well* I wote, . . . I. i. 32. 5
'Right *well,* . . . ye have advised bin,' . . . I. i. 33. 4
The knight was *well* content; . . . I. i. 33. 8
And *well* could file his tongue . . . I. i. 35. 7
Thus, *well* instructed, to their worke they haste; . . . I. i. 47. 1
Full jolly knight he seemde, and *wel* addrest; . . . I. ii. 11. 7
Who *well* it wards, . . . I. ii. 17. 3
To doe none ill, if please ye not doe *well.*' . . . I. ii. 26. 4
and manhood *well* awake, . . . I. ii. 32. 2
Till we be bathed in a living *well:* . . . I. ii. 43. 4
'O! how,' sayd he, 'mote I that *well* out find, . . . I. ii. 43. 6
That may restore you to your wonted *well?*' . . . I. ii. 43. 7
And knew *well* all was true. . . . I. ii. 44. 3
As all unweeting of that *well* she knew; . . . I. ii. 45. 2
that mote ye please *Well* to accept, . . . I. iii. 29. 7
his Lady did so *well* him cheare, . . . I. iii. 34. 7
from his gored wound a *well* of bloud did gush. . . . I. iii. 35. 9
For the old man *well* knew he, . . . I. iii. 38. 7
in that court whylome her *well* they knew: . . . I. iv. 15. 5
well could daunce, and sing with ruefulnesse; . . . I. iv. 25. 7
well he could not touch, nor goe, nor stand. . . . I. iv. 29. 8
That brothers hand shall dearely *well* requight, . . . I. iv. 42. 6
So *well* they sped, . . . I. v. 29. 1
'*well* may I rew To tell . . . I. vi. 36. 7
whose shape she *well* can faine, . . . I. vii. 1. 5
bubbling wave did ever freshly *well,* . . . I. vii. 4. 6
he . . . was knowne right *well* . . . I. vii. 36. 2
'*Well* may I ween your griefe is wondrous great; . . . I. vii. 40. 2
And *well* could rule; . . . I. vii. 48. 5
your lord that could so *well* you tosse? . . . I. vii. 48. 9
'*Well* hoped I, and faire beginnings had, That . . . I. vii. 49. 1
the carefull knight gan *well* avise, . . . I. viii. 15. 5
well begonne, end all so *well,* . . . I. viii. 28. 4
The knight much honord, as beseemed *well;* . . . I. viii. 32. 2
the noble Prince had marked *well,* . . . I. viii. 34. 3
when her *well* of teares she wasted had, . . . I. viii. 42. 5
With dew repast they had recured *well,* . . . I. ix. 2. 2
'*Well* worthy impe,' . . . I. ix. 6. 1
Of that great Queene may *well* gaine worthie grace, . . . I. ix. 17. 7
For him to be yet weake and wearie *well* she knew. . . . I. ix. 20. 9
that *well* himselfe advaunst In all affayres, . . . I. ix. 27. 3
Is not short payne *well* borne, that bringes long ease, . . . I. ix. 40. 6
Well knowing trew all that he did reherse, . . . I. ix. 48. 4
The crudled cold ran to her *well* of life, . . . I. ix. 52. 2
so *well,* they say, It governd was, . . . I. x. 3. 3
The mother of three daughters, *well* upbrought . . . I. x. 4. 3
His name was Zele, that him right *well* became: . . . I. x. 6. 6
Whom *well* she knew to spring from hevenly race, . . . I. x. 8. 7
Was clad in blew, that her beseemed *well;* . . . I. x. 14. 2
*And greatly joy each other *well* to see: . . . I. x. 15. 4
Who, *well* acquainted with that commune plight, . . . I. x. 23. 2
disease of grieved conscience, And *well* could cure the same: . . . I. x. 23. 9

Well—*Continued.*

and all that noyd his heavie spright *Well* searcht, . . . I. x. 24. 4
drops of blood thence like a *well* did play: . . . I. x. 27. 4
For *well* she wist his cryme could els be never cleare. . . . I. x. 28. 9
torment *well* withstood In that sad house of Penaunce, . . . I. x. 32. 7
Of love, and righteousnes, and *well* to donne; . . . I. x. 33. 4
In which when him she *well* instructed hath, . . . I. x. 33. 8
Whose sober lookes her wisedome *well* descryde: . . . I. x. 34. 3
Mercy; *well* knowne over-all To be both gratious . . . I. x. 34. 4
And though they faulty were, yet *well* he wayd, . . . I. x. 40. 5
If not *well* ended at our dying day. . . . I. x. 41. 7
Each bone might through his body *well* be red . . . I. x. 48. 5
Who, *well* them greeting, humbly did requight, . . . I. x. 49. 8
The Citty of the greate king hight it *well,* . . . I. x. 55. 8
said then the knight, 'I weened *well,* That . . . I. x. 58. 1
And *well* beseemes all knights of noble name, . . . I. x. 59. 4
Well worthy doest thy service for her grace, . . . I. x. 60. 3
'For, *well* I wote, thou springst from ancient race . . . I. x. 65. 1
Therefore, henceforth, bee at your keeping *well,* . . . I. xi. 2. 4
But his more hardned crest was armd so *well,* . . . I. xi. 24. 5
Of auncient time there was a springing *well,* . . . I. xi. 29. 3
it rightly hot The *well* of life, . . . I. xi. 29. 9
Ne can Cephise, nor Hebrus, match this *well:* . . . I. xi. 30. 8
kest His wearie foe into that living *well,* . . . I. xi. 31. 6
the *well,* wherein he drenched lay: . . . I. xi. 34. 2
forth flowd, as from a *well,* A trickling streame . . . I. xi. 48. 1
Some feard, and fledd; some feard, and *well* it faynd; . . . I. xii. 10. 1
ye seised have the shore, And *well* arrived are, . . . I. xii. 17. 8
As that your daughter can ye *well* advize, . . . I. xii. 18. 5
And bowed low, that her right *well* became, . . . I. xii. 24. 3
So bids thee *well* to fare, Thy neither friend nor foe, . . . I. xii. 28. 9
Till *well* ye wote by grave intendiment, . . . I. xii. 31. 3
Well may she speede, . . . I. xii. 42. 9
Right *well* I wote, most mighty Soveraine, . . . II. Pr. 1. 1
for *well* he kend His credit now . . . II. i. 3. 7
Well could he tourney, and in lists debate, . . . II. i. 6. 7
He weened *well* to worke some uncouth wyle: . . . II. i. 8. 2
I present was, and can it witnesse *well,* . . . II. i. 19. 6
To be her Squire, and do her service *well* aguisd. . . . II. i. 21. 9
'Ah! deare Sir Guyon, *well* becommeth you, . . . II. i. 28. 3
'*well* mote I shame to tell The fond encheason . . . II. i. 30. 1
God guide thee, Guyon, *well* to end thy warke, . . . II. i. 32. 8
Well mote yee thee, . . . II. i. 33. 7
as *well* can wish your thought, . . . II. i. 33. 7
For *well* ye worthy bene for worth and gentle thewes.' . . . II. i. 33. 9
So *well* he did her deadly wounds repaire, . . . II. i. 43. 8
coming to this *well,* he stoupt to drincke: . . . II. i. 55. 8
himselfe inclyning on his knee Downe to that *well,* . . . II. ii. 3. 2
Whiles cause not *well* conceived ye mistake: . . . II. ii. 5. 5
'Such is this *well,* wrought by occasion straunge, . . . II. ii. 7. 1
clensd with water of this *well:* . . . II. ii. 10. 2
when the knight arriv'd, he was right *well* Receiv'd, . . . II. ii. 14. 1
In goodly garments that her *well* became, . . . II. ii. 14. 7
Him at the threshold mett, and *well* did enterprize. . . . II. ii. 14. 9
With goodly meanes to pacifie, *well* as he can. . . . II. ii. 21. 9
Where they are *well* receivd, and made to spoile . . . II. ii. 33. 7
But could not colour yet so *well* the troth, . . . II. ii. 34. 4
And weened *well* ere long his will to win, . . . II. iii. 13. 2
Yet *well* he wist that whoso would contend . . . II. iii. 17. 2
'All haile, Sir knight! and *well* may thee befall, . . . II. iii. 37. 6
Which *well* that valiaunt courser did discerne; . . . II. iii. 46. 6
Who *well* could menage and subdew his pride, . . . II. iv. 2. 2
Had he had governaunce it *well* to guyde; . . . II. iv. 7. 2
Must first begin, and *well* her amenage: . . . II. iv. 11. 2
Right *well* beseemed it To be the shield . . . II. iv. 38. 5
for *well* mote I discerne Great cause, . . . II. iv. 43. 3
That shall Pyrochles *well* requite, I wott, . . . II. iv. 45. 8
The quivering steele his aymed end *wel* knew, . . . II. iv. 46. 3
To which right *wel* the wise doe give that name, . . . II. v. 1. 5
For th' equall die of warre he *well* did know: . . . II. v. 13. 4
Before her sonne could *well* assoyled bee, . . . II. v. 19. 2
Because he had not *well* mainteind his right, . . . II. v. 20. 4
Yet seemed, nothing *well* they her became; . . . II. vi. 6. 6
And strive to passe (as she could *well* enough) . . . II. vi. 25. 3
she *well* pleased was thence to amove him farre. . . . II. vi. 37. 9
Well could he him remember, . . . II. vi. 39. 1
Him Atin spying knew right *well* of yore, . . . II. vi. 48. 1
his griefe He knew right *well,* . . . II. vi. 51. 2
As Pilot *well* expert in perilous wave, . . . II. vii. 1. 1
darkned with filthy dust, *Well* yet appeared to . . . II. vii. 4. 4
till I know it *well* be gott; . . . II. vii. 19. 2
Well hoped hee, ere long that hardy guest, . . . II. vii. 27. 1
For *well* he weened that so glorious bayte . . . II. vii. 34. 3
Avise thee *well,* and chaunge thy wilfull mood, . . . II. vii. 38. 8
Yet had both life and sence, and *well* could weld . . . II. vii. 40. 8
She held a great gold chaine ylincked *well,* . . . II. vii. 46. 2
such immortall mate My selfe *well* wote, . . . II. vii. 50. 5
And *well* perceived his deceiptfull sleight, . . . II. vii. 64. 7
Well knew they both his person, . . . II. viii. 11. 8
But *well* I wote, That of his puissaunce . . . II. viii. 14. 3
all good knights that shake *well* speare and shield. . . . II. viii. 14. 6
Well kend him so far space Th' enchaunter . . . II. viii. 17. 7
this weapons powre I *well* have kend To be contrary . . . II. viii. 19. 8
Words, *well* dispost, Have secrete powre . . . II. viii. 26. 7
For *well* of yore he learned had to ryde, . . . II. viii. 31. 4
To use that sword so *well* as he it ought!' . . . II. viii. 40. 4
Well knew The Prince, with pacience . . . II. viii. 47. 6
As *well* in state of peace, as puissaunce in warre.' . . . II. ix. 4. 9
warlike feat Ye *well* may hope, and easely attaine? . . . II. ix. 6. 4
Great guerdon, *well* I wote, should you remaine, . . . II. ix. 6. 7

Well—*Continued.*

Of Squires and Ladies equipaged *well*, ... II. ix. 17. 8
two faire Damsels which were taught That service *well*. . . . II. ix. 19. 6
two gates were placed seemly *well:* . . . . II. ix. 23. 1
set them forth, as *well* he could devise. . . . . II. ix. 31. 5
Well weeting trew what she had rashly told; . . . . II. ix. 39. 2
And counselled faire Alma how to governe *well*. . . . . . . II. ix. 48. 9
Weake body *wel* is chang'd for minds redoubled forse. . . . II. ix. 55. 9
The warres he *well* remembred . . . . II. ix. 56. 8
That *well* can witnes yet unto this day . . . . II. x. 10. 6
Encountred him in batteill *well* ordaind, ... II. x. 18. 4
Right *well* recur'd, ... II. x. 23. 4
to their people wealth they forth do *well*, ... II. x. 26. 6
three faire daughters, which were *well* uptrained . . . . . II. x. 27. 3
Who him at first *well* used every way; . . . . II. x. 30. 7
As *well* . . . Against the forreine Morands he exprest; . . . . II. x. 43. 7
And goodly *well* long time it governed; . . . . II. x. 47. 4
As *well* in curious instruments as cunning laies. . . . . . . II. x. 59. 9
Hengist and Horsus, *well* approv'd in warre, ... II. x. 65. 2
Attempred goodly *well* for health and for delight. . . . . . II. xi. 2. 9
Those could he *well* direct and streight as line, ... II. xi. 21. 6
and it warded *well* Upon his shield, ... II. xi. 24. 6
Wel weened hee that field was then his *owne*, ... II. xi. 35. 1
who was right *well* aware To shonne the engine . . . . . . II. xi. 36. 2
He then remembred *well*, that had bene sayd, ... II. xi. 45. 1
(God doe us *well* acquight!). . . . . II. xii. 3. 3
'Yet *well* they seeme to him, that farre doth vew, ... II. xii. 12. 1
'Here now behoveth us *well* to avyse, ... II. xii. 17. 6
the nimble bote so *well* her sped, ... II. xii. 38. 2
As *well* their entred guestes to keep within, ... II. xii. 43. 2
Yet each doth in him selfe it *well* perceive to bee. . . . . . II. xii. 47. 9
Gently attempred, and disposed so *well*, ... II. xii. 51. 8
Some like faire Emeraudes, not yet *well* ripened. . . . . . . II. xii. 54. 9
Infinit streames continually did *well* Out of this fountaine, . II. xii. 62. 1
And counseld *well* him forward thence did draw. . . . . . . II. xii. 69. 3
'Now, Sir, *well* avise; . . . . II. xii. 69. 6
and sory wounds right *well* recur'd, ... III. i. 1. 4
made him stagger, as he were not *well:* . . . . III. i. 6. 5
But Guyon selfe, ere *well* he was aware, ... III. i. 6. 6
Yet in his fall so *well* him selfe he bare, ... III. i. 6. 8
Through countreyes waste, and eke *well* edifyde, ... III. i. 14. 2
And downe him smot ere *well* aware he weare; . . . . III. i. 28. 8
'Too *well* we see,' (saide they) . . . . III. i. 30. 1
'and prove too *well* Our faulty weakenes, ... III. i. 30. 1
her besought, *well* as they might, To enter in . . . . III. i. 30. 7
Entyst the Boy, as *well* that art she knew, ... III. i. 35. 2
throw into the *well* sweet Rosemaryes, ... III. i. 36. 7
And cheared *well* with wine and spiceree: . . . . III. i. 42. 5
weet ye *well*, of all that ever playd . . . . III. ii. 9. 7
faire Damzell, be ye *well* aware, ... III. ii. 10. 6
The Damzell *well* did vew his Personage . . . . III. ii. 26. 1
did vew his Personage And liked *well*, ... III. ii. 26. 2
Yet wist she was not *well* at ease perdy; . . . . III. ii. 27. 8
That *well* can witnesse who by tryall it does prove. . . . . III. ii. 51. 9
Well did Antiquity a God thee deeme, ... III. iii. 2. 1
the learned Merlin, *well* could tell . . . . III. iii. 6. 4
For of their comming *well* he wist afore; . . . . III. iii. 15. 2
weeting inly *well* That she to him dissembled . . . . III. iii. 17. 2
Careticus awhile Shall *well* defend, ... III. iii. 33. 2
shall goodly *well* indew The salvage minds with skill . . . . III. iii. 45. 4
when them selves they *well* instructed had . . . . III. iii. 51. 1
her therein appareled *Well* as she might, ... III. iii. 59. 9
Then each to other, *well* affectionate, ... III. iii. 62. 7
As *well* for glorie of great valiaunce, ... III. iv. 3. 3
That all her goodly deedes doe *well* declare. . . . . III. iv. 3. 5
Bad her from womankind to keepe him *well*, ... III. iv. 25. 7
Yet he his mothers lore did *well* retaine, ... III. iv. 26. 5
yet mote they *well* Thus much afford me, ... III. iv. 39. 2
which having *well* upbownd, They pourd in . . . . III. iv. 40. 7
laide in easy couch *well* dight, ... III. iv. 43. 6
But fairely *well* shee thryvd, ... III. iv. 44. 8
and *well* did brooke Her noble deeds, ... III. iv. 44. 8
well she vewde Her selfe freed from . . . . III. iv. 50. 6
'But *well* I wote, that to an heavy hart . . . . III. iv. 57. 1
And yield her rowme to day that can it governe *well*.' . . . . III. iv. 60. 9
Her selfe, *well* as I might, I reskewd tho, ... III. v. 6. 4
Of my deare Dame is loved dearely *well:* . . . . III. v. 9. 2
the villein sped himselfe so *well*, ... III. v. 14. 1
In those same woods ye *well* remember may . . . . III. v. 27. 5
Well hoped shee the beast engor'd had beene, ... III. v. 28. 7
And round about, as she could *well* it uze, ... III. v. 33. 5
That greatest Princes liking it mote *well* delight. . . . . . III. v. 40. 9
Least that his wound were inly *well* not heald, ... III. v. 49. 2
Well may I weene, faire Ladies, all this while . . . . III. vi. 1. 1
in her bosome she compriz'd *Well* as she might, ... III. vi. 19. 8
that in short space She was *well* pleasd, ... III. vi. 25. 7
Or it in Gnidus bee, I wote not *well;* . . . . III. vi. 29. 5
But *well* I wote by triall, ... III. vi. 29. 6
And yet remember *well* the mighty word . . . . III. vi. 34. 4
But *well* I weene, ye first desire to learne . . . . III. vi. 54. 1
Now *well* recovered after long repast, ... III. vii. 18. 7
too late awaking, *well* they kent That their . . . . III. vii. 19. 7
did so *well* apply His nimble feet . . . . III. vii. 24. 5
There *well* perceivd he that it was the horse . . . . III. vii. 31. 1
His maker with her charmes had framed him so *well*. . . . . III. vii. 35. 9
well he mote perceive In that fowle plight . . . . III. vii. 46. 1
Call me the Squyre of Dames; that me beseemeth *well*. . . . III. vii. 51. 9
'Her *well* beseemes that Quest,' . . . . III. vii. 53. 1
'So *well* I to faire Ladies service did, ... III. vii. 55. 1
For onely three they were disposd so *well;* . . . . III. vii. 57. 3

Well—*Continued.*

the wyles of wemens wits knew passing *well*. . . . . III. viii. 8. 9
Much merveiled thereat, as *well* he might, ... III. viii. 12. 3
For he could *well* his glozing speaches frame . . . . III. viii. 14. 4
He it dissembled *well*, and light seemd to esteeme . . . . . III. viii. 16. 9
Well weened he, that fairest . . . . III. viii. 19. 6
and thought he yet did dreame Not *well* awakte; . . . . . . III. viii. 22. 8
But when her *well* avizing hee perceiv'd . . . . III. viii. 23. 1
Have care, I pray, to guide the cock-bote *well*, ... III. viii. 24. 4
well may she you reprove Of falsehood . . . . III. viii. 27. 8
And Panope her entertaind eke *well*, ... III. viii. 38. 3
'Faire Sir,' (quoth he) '*well* may it you succeed! . . . . . III. viii. 50. 6
'*Well* may yee speede in so praiseworthy payne! . . . . . . III. viii. 51. 2
That counsell pleased *well:* . . . . III. viii. 52. 1
Ne cares what men say of him, ill or *well;* . . . . III. ix. 3. 7
Which *well* she redd out of the learned line: . . . . III. ix. 30. 8
Him to commend to her, thus spake, of al *well* eide. . . . . III. ix. 32. 9
Sir, I greet you *well* Your countrey kin; . . . . III. ix. 51. 6
Which th' old man seeing *wel*, who too long thought . . . . III. ix. 53. 6
His halfen eye he wiled wondrous *well*, ... III. x. 5. 3
Who *well* perceived all, and all endewd. . . . . III. x. 9. 5
and to her lover told. It pleased *well:* . . . . III. x. 11. 8
So *well* they both agree: So readie rype . . . . III. x. 11. 8
A couple, seeming *well* to be his twaine, ... III. x. 20. 7
Well weened hee that those the same mote bee, ... III. x. 21. 1
Your worthy paine shall *wel* reward with guerdon rich.' . . . III. x. 28. 9
to him louted low, and greeted goodly *well;* . . . . III. x. 37. 9
(said crafty Trompart) 'weete ye *well*, That . . . . III. x. 40. 2
not for nought his wife them loved so *well*, ... III. x. 48. 8
As one out of a dreame not waked *well* . . . . III. x. 49. 7
In blessed Nectar and pure Pleasures *well*, ... III. xi. 2. 4
In th' harts of men, them governe wisely *well*, ... III. xi. 2. 7
Whose names and natures I note readen *well;* . . . . III. xii. 26. 2
And goodly *well* advaunce . . . . III. xii. 39. 9
advaunce that goodly *well* was tryde.' . . . . III. xii. 39. 9
these Stoicke censours cannot *well* deny . . . . IV. Pr. 3. 9
Yet fairely *well* he did them all dismay, ... IV. i. 2. 5
For *well* she wist, as true it was indeed, ... IV. i. 6. 1
Lord and patrone of her health Right *well* deserved, ... IV. i. 6. 3
That *well* she wist not what by them to gesse: . . . . IV. i. 7. 6
As *well* became a knight, and did to her all honor. . . . . IV. i. 8. 9
Her false Duessa, who full *well* did know . . . . IV. i. 19. 5
And now himselfe he fitted had right *well* . . . . IV. i. 32. 6
Well warned to beware with whom he dar'd to dallie. . . . IV. i. 36. 9
Nathlesse he forth did march, *well* as he might, ... IV. i. 38. 1
was shortly *well* aware Of his approch, ... IV. i. 41. 4
Well falles it thee that I am not in plight . . . . IV. i. 44. 5
whose name I wote not *well*, ... IV. i. 48. 8
(That *well* I wote) the heads of many . . . . IV. i. 48. 9
All things not rooted *well* will soone be rotten.' . . . . . . IV. i. 51. 5
Such as that prudent Romane *well* invented, ... IV. ii. 2. 7
'Last turne was mine, *well* proved to my paine; . . . . IV. ii. 6. 4
Against that Knight, ere he him *well* could torne; . . . . . IV. ii. 6. 8
And inly grudge at him that he had sped so *well*. . . . . . IV. ii. 7. 9
Well know'st thou, when we friendship first did sweare, . . IV. ii. 13. 3
And both of old *well* knowing by their names, ... IV. ii. 20. 5
and, her avizing *well*, Weend, ... IV. ii. 22. 7
This happie day I have to greete you *well*, ... IV. ii. 23. 5
Certes, me seemes, bene not advised *well;* . . . . IV. ii. 24. 5
Well knowne to appertaine to Florimell, ... IV. ii. 25. 8
for her sake he wore, as him beseemed *well*. . . . . IV. ii. 25. 9
So, *well* accorded, forth they rode together . . . . IV. ii. 29. 1
Dan Chaucer, *well* of English undefyled, ... IV. ii. 32. 8
like to warie Centonels *well* stayd, ... IV. ii. 36. 8
(The harder it to make them *well* agree) . . . . IV. ii. 38. 4
Well was that rings great vertue knowen to all; . . . . . . IV. ii. 40. 1
These three did love each other dearely *well*, ... IV. ii. 43. 1
Well worthie thou to be of Jove accurst, ... IV. ii. 49. 8
She warned them to tend their safeties *well*, ... IV. ii. 53. 8
Well mote ye wonder how that noble Knight, ... IV. iii. 23. 1
And *well* instructed by the Fay her mother, ... IV. iii. 40. 4
Which had so great dismay so *well* amended: . . . . IV. iii. 50. 7
That *well* (me seemes) appeares, by that of late . . . . IV. iv. 2. 1
Marching afore, as ye remember *well*, ... IV. iv. 2. 7
Whom he now seeing, her remembred *well*, ... IV. iv. 8. 3
A Painim knight that *well* in armes was skild, ... IV. iv. 17. 7
The shield and armes, *well* knowne to be the same . . . . . IV. iv. 27. 5
That, ere him selfe he had recovered *well*, ... IV. iv. 30. 6
and thereto *well* agreed His word, ... IV. iv. 39. 7
Who *well* was knowen to be a valiant Knight, ... IV. iv. 40. 4
After the proofe of prowesse ended *well*, ... IV. v. 2. 2
Well weened all, which her that time did vew, ... IV. v. 13. 5
That seemeth *well* to answere to your weede, ... IV. vi. 5. 3
He wist right *well* that it was Britomart, ... IV. vi. 7. 2
To dight, to welcome him *well* as she can . . . . IV. vi. 10. 5
Well weeting how their errour to assoyle, ... IV. vi. 25. 2
Therewith he rested, and *well* pleased was: . . . . IV. vi. 39. 1
Untill that they their wounds *well* healed had, ... IV. vi. 39. 8
So *well* he woo'd her, ... IV. vi. 41. 1
and so *well* he wrought her, ... IV. vi. 41. 1
My Sire, who me too dearely *well* did love, ... IV. vii. 16. 2
drawing nigh, ere he her *well* beheld, ... IV. vii. 36. 7
Well said the Wiseman, now prov'd true by this . . . . . . IV. viii. 1. 1
water which did *well* From his moist eies, ... IV. viii. 13. 3
Tho, when they both recovered were right *well*, ... IV. viii. 21. 1
So when that forrest they had passed *well*, ... IV. viii. 23. 1
Ne ever thing so *well* was doen alive, ... IV. viii. 25. 8
Here, *well* I weene, when as these rimes be red . . . . IV. viii. 29. 1
Aemylia *well* he lov'd, ... IV. viii. 57. 8
my friend . . . Did *well* accept, ... IV. viii. 60. 3

Well—*Continued.*
as *well* it did behove, IV. viii. 60. 3
And *well* perform'd; as shall appeare by his event. IV. viii. 64. 9
She weened *well* that then she was betraide: IV. ix. 7. 5
He with good thewes and speaches *well* applyde IV. ix. 14. 6
That trusty Squire he wisely *well* did move IV. ix. 15. 3
them stoutly *well* withstood; IV. ix. 29. 7
To whom the Prince thus goodly *well* replied: IV. ix. 37. 1
now so *well* accorded all anew, IV. ix. 40. 5
past perils *well* apay.' IV. ix. 40. 9
cannot in this Canto *well* Comprised be, IV. ix. 41. 9
With golden letters goodly *well* enchaced; IV. x. 8. 7
Blessed the man that well can use his blis: IV. x. 8. 8
that Dame so *well* them tempred both, IV. x. 33. 1
right *well* her workes divine did shew: IV. x. 34. 5
So *well* that Leach did hearke to her request, IV. xi. 7. 1
did so *well* employ his carefull paine, IV. xi. 7. 2
As *well* which in the mightie Ocean trade, IV. xi. 9. 4
In order as they came could I recount them *well.* IV. xi. 9. 9
They all on him this day attended *well,* IV. xi. 30. 3
and waited *well* To doe their dueful service, IV. xi. 44. 8
yet her *well* became, IV. xi. 45. 3
Eione *well* in age, IV. xi. 50. 7
Nemertea learned *well* to rule her lust. IV. xi. 51. 9
But *well* I wote that these, IV. xi. 53. 4
the antique wisards *well* invented That IV. xii. 2. 1
According their degrees disposed *well.* IV. xii. 3. 5
daunger *well* he wist IV. xii. 15. 9
ne wist *well* what to weene; IV. xii. 21. 2
her *well* assured That it was no old sore IV. xii. 23. 8
Admyr'd her beautie much, as she mote *well.* IV. xii. 33. 4
(as ye lately mote remember *well*) V. i. 3. 3
And in the rules of justice them instructed *well.* V. i. 5. 9
Well prov'd in that same day V. i. 9. 9
Expressing *well* his nature V. i. 19. 9
Well did the Squire perceive him selfe too weake V. i. 24. 1
Well pleased with that doome was Sangliere, V. i. 27. 1
Well weening that his foe was falne withall; V. ii. 12. 8
But he was *well* aware, V. ii. 12. 9
who that use *well* knew V. ii. 13. 5
in armes *well* traind, and throughly tride: V. ii. 17. 4
Ne would within his ballaunce *well* abide: V. ii. 45. 2
'*Well* then,' sayd Artegall, V. ii. 45. 4
For *well* they hoped to have got great goode V. ii. 51. 6
that had so *well* Approv'd that day V. iii. 15. 8
Stood in the preasse close covered, *well* advewed, V. iii. 20. 2
Who round about her tender wast it fitted *well.* V. iii. 27. 9
Which Artegall *well* hearing, V. iii. 32. 1
Which *well* I prove, as shall appeare V. iv. 15. 6
Being the dowry of his wife *well* knowne, V. iv. 18. 4
'Most haplesse *well* ye may Me justly terme, V. iv. 27. 5
Queene of Amazons, in armes *well* tride V. iv. 33. 5
And th' other two *well* likely to have harmed. V. iv. 36. 5
way to make with weapons *well* prepard. V. iv. 37. 9
them goodly *well* did greete, V. iv. 51. 2
Which he accepting *well,* as he could weete, V. iv. 51. 4
From that first flaw him selfe right *well* defended. V. v. 6. 7
But with her shield so *well* her selfe she warded V. v. 8. 6
With spightfull speaches, fitting with her *well;* V. v. 10. 4
well as he might, Beare off the burden of her raging yre: V. v. 16. 3
whose names right *well* he knew, V. v. 22. 2
And thereto did himselfe right *well* behave V. v. 23. 7
And eke with gratefull service me right *well* apay. V. v. 33. 9
Goe now, Clarinda; *well* thy wits advise, V. v. 34. 6
Whose hidden drift he could not *well* perceive; V. v. 37. 2
'Yet, weet ye *well,* that to a courage great V. v. 38. 1
It is no lesse beseeming *well* to beare V. v. 38. 2
For *well* I may this weene by that I fynd, V. v. 41. 4
his hold was but unsound And not *well* fastened, V. v. 42. 8
Thus he . . . there remayned, Of both beloved *well,* V. v. 57. 7
Be *well* adviz'd that he stand stedfast still; V. vi. 1. 7
For never yet was wight so *well* aware, V. vi. 1. 8
This gentle knight himselfe so *well* behaved, V. vi. 2. 2
That it was one sent *Well* weend she then, V. vi. 8. 3
Well shot in yeares he seem'd, and rather bent V. vi. 19. 6
As *well* by view of that his vestiment, V. vi. 19. 8
By outward signes (as *well* he might) did see, V. vi. 21. 5
But her besought to take it *well* in gree, V. vi. 21. 7
he, their host, them goodly *well* did cheare, V. vi. 22. 8
Thus passing th' evening *well,* till time of rest, V. vi. 23. 1
Perceiving *well* the treason which was ment; V. vi. 28. 2
Well therefore did the antique world invent V. vii. 2. 1
So *well* as could with cunning hand be wrought, V. vii. 6. 3
Who *well* perceiving how her wand she shooke, V. vii. 8. 4
They might perceive she was not *well* in plight, V. vii. 18. 2
'Certes,' (sayd she) 'sith ye so *well* have spide V. vii. 19. 1
vision . . . appeard, As *well* as to her minde it had recourse. V. vii. 20. 3
And then too *well* believ'd that which tofore V. vii. 38. 6
Who when him selfe now *well* recur'd did see, V. vii. 43. 7
'Certes I wote not *well,'* V. viii. 15. 5
'Then wote ye *well,* that I Doe serve a Queene V. viii. 16. 6
But the bold child that perill *well* espying, V. viii. 32. 1
With raynes or wonted rule, as *well* he knew: V. viii. 38. 6
a space *Well* solast in that Souldans late delight, V. ix. 3. 2
Malengin . . . *Well* knowen by his feates, V. ix. 5. 9
And snatching her soone up, ere *well* she knew, V. ix. 14. 4
Yet warded *well* by one of mickle might V. ix. 22. 5
That *well* could charme his tongue, V. ix. 39. 3
(as ye mote yet right *well* Remember) V. ix. 41. 1
This *well* I wote, that sure she is as great, V. x. 1. 5

Well—*Continued.*
For *well* she wist this knight came succour to supply. V. x. 19. 9
wield Her mind so *well,* that to his will she bends; V. x. 24. 8
(So pure the metall was and *well* refynd,) V. x. 32. 8
th' Adamantine shield . . . So *well* was tempred, V. xi. 10. 8
Well tride in all thy Ladies troubles V. xi. 38. 3
For that he weeneth *well* before that tide V. xi. 42. 4
well approv'd in many a doubt, V. xi. 47. 5
So bore her quite away, nor *well* nor ill apayd. V. xi. 64. 9
The winde and weather served them so *well,* V. xii. 4. 5
yet old Sergis did so *well* him paine, V. xii. 10. 7
as Artegall Did *well* avize, V. xii. 18. 2
But he it *well* did ward with wise respect, V. xii. 21. 5
So *well* he him pursew'd, V. xii. 23. 1
Her name was Envie, knowen *well* thereby, V. xii. 31. 1
And turne to ill the thing that *well* was ment V. xii. 34. 5
speake so ill of him that *well* deserved, V. xii. 43. 2
Into the mindes of mortall men doe *well,* VI. Pr. 2. 5
conduct me *well* In these strange waies VI. Pr. 2. 7
Right so from you all goodly vertues *well* VI. Pr. 7. 6
well beseemeth that in Princes hall VI. i. 1. 3
well approv'd in batteilous affray, VI. i. 2. 8
wisely use, and *well* apply, VI. i. 3. 6
in her guilefull traines was *well* expert. VI. i. 12. 9
Did *well* endure her womanish disdaine, VI. i. 30. 8
Well weend he streight VI. i. 33. 1
passing *well* expert in single fight, VI. i. 36. 4
court'sie doth as *well* as armes professe, VI. i. 41. 2
promist to performe his precept *well,* VI. i. 43. 3
There he remaind with them right *well* agreed, VI. i. 47. 7
That *well* in courteous Calidore appeares; VI. ii. 3. 1
A tall young man, . . . as *well* he him descryde, VI. ii. 3. 8
Whom Calidore awhile *well* having vewed VI. ii. 7. 1
his Ladie here May witnesse *well,* VI. ii. 8. 2
his speach Tempred so *well,* VI. ii. 13. 2
Which had himselfe so stoutly *well* acquit, VI. ii. 24. 2
Well may I, certes, such an one thee read, VI. ii. 25. 6
when *well* Sir Calidore had heard, VI. ii. 34. 1
Ye may doe *well,* . . . To succour her VI. ii. 38. 3
When Calidore this ruefull storie had *Well* understood, VI. ii. 44. 2
a man by nothing is so *well* bewrayd VI. iii. 1. 3
As *well* may be in Calidore descryde, VI. iii. 2. 3
So *well* and wisely did that good old Knight VI. iii. 6. 1
make their welcome to them *well* appeare. VI. iii. 6. 4
So *well* she washt them, and so *well* she wacht him, VI. iii. 10. 6
Ere they were *well* aware of living wight, VI. iii. 21. 2
So *well* he did his busie paines apply, VI. iii. 28. 1
saw his carriage past that perill *well,* VI. iii. 34. 6
Whom *well* he wist to be some enemy, VI. iii. 46. 8
as a *well* it were That . . . gushing did appere. VI. iii. 50. 8
who being *well* prepard VI. iv. 5. 4
herbe . . . Whose vertue he by use *well* understood; VI. iv. 12. 7
They tooke it *well,* and thanked God for all, VI. iv. 15. 2
he had that knightes wound Recured *well,* VI. iv. 16. 7
Well then him chaunst his heavy armes to want, VI. iv. 19. 1
So *well* he sped him, that the wearie Beare VI. iv. 20. 1
A wofull dame ye have me termed *well;* VI. iv. 28. 3
'*Well* hop't he then, when this was propheside, VI. iv. 33. 1
Yet, as I *well* it meane, vouchsafe it without blame. VI. iv. 34. 9
Agreeing *well* both with the place and season, VI. iv. 37. 5
And it in goodly thewes so *well* upbrought, VI. iv. 38. 7
The salvage serves Serena *well,* VI. v. Arg.
By which she *well* perceiving what was done, VI. v. 4. 7
Well as she could she got, VI. v. 7. 6
Yet he himselfe so *well* and wisely bore, VI. v. 12. 8
For *well* they wist that Squire to be so bold, VI. v. 15. 6
Him *well* behoved so; VI. v. 20. 1
Then turning to that swaine him *well* he knew VI. v. 23. 1
seem'd the spoile of some right *well* renownd: VI. v. 25. 5
So having all things *well* about her dight, VI. v. 31. 1
For *well* it seem'd that whilome he had beene VI. v. 36. 6
well did weene How each to entertaine with curt'sie VI. v. 36. 8
But being *well* suffiz'd them rested faine. VI. v. 39. 5
whom he did pray To tend them *well.* VI. v. 41. 5
For he right *well* in Leaches craft was seene; VI. vi. 3. 1
As he the art of words knew wondrous *well,* VI. vi. 6. 3
eke could doe as *well* as say the same; VI. vi. 6. 4
kept so *well* his wise commaundements, VI. vi. 15. 3
But the bold Prince defended him so *well,* VI. vi. 23. 6
Whereof whenas the Prince was *well* aware, VI. vi. 27. 1
He *well* remembred that the same was hee, VI. vi. 40. 3
having all things *well* in peace ordayned, VI. vi. 41. 1
For *well* she knew the wayes to win good will VI. vi. 41. 6
This *well* I wote, VI. vi. 43. 4
that she so *well* applyde Her pleasing tongue, VI. vi. 43. 4
That *well* appears in this discourteous knight, VI. vii. 2. 1
Well did he tract his steps as he did ryde, VI. vii. 3. 1
'Now sure ye *well* have earn'd your meed; VI. vii. 13. 2
the which right *well* I deeme I yearned have, VI. vii. 15. 8
He weened *well* that he in deed was dead, VI. vii. 20. 2
Be *well* aware how ye the same doe use, VI. viii. 1. 6
the Prince so *well* enured was With such huge strokes, VI. viii. 14. 1
And *well* disburdened her engrieved brest, VI. viii. 34. 2
murdrous knife *well* whet, VI. viii. 45. 5
For ill rewards him *well.* VI. ix. Arg.
After his rusticke wise, that *well* he weend, VI. ix. 6. 7
Her whyles Sir Calidore there vewed *well,* VI. ix. 11. 1
brought home and noursed *well* VI. ix. 14. 7
And of his aged Beldame homely *well;* VI. ix. 17. 2
Tho when they had their hunger slaked *well,* VI. ix. 18. 1

Well—*Continued.*
In courtesie and *well* could doe and say, VI. ix. 18. 4
for recompence hereof I shall You *well* reward, VI. ix. 32. 6
through long . . . industry, Therein *well* practisd was, VI. ix. 43. 8
Gave it to Coridon, and said he wonne it *well*. VI. ix. 44. 9
but menaged so *well*, That he, VI. ix. 46. 4
Amidst a ring most richly *well* enchaced, VI. x. 12. 8
a rosie girlond that right *well* Did her beseeme: VI. x. 14. 5
Ne lesse in vertue that beseemes her *well* VI. x. 26. 5
'Another Grace she *well* deserves to be, VI. x. 27. 1
So *well* he wood her, and VI. x. 38. 1
and so *well* he wrought her, VI. x. 38. 1
Which he so wisely *well* did prosecute, VI. x. 38. 4
A doubtfull sense of things, not so *well* seene as felt. VI. x. 42. 9
A little *well* is lent that gaineth more withall. VI. xi. 6. 9
Thereto they all attonce agreed *well;* VI. xi. 20. 7
And wrought so *well*, with labour and long VI. xi. 22. 5
Tho Coridon he prayd, sith he *well* knew VI. xi. 35. 1
Yet Calidore so *well* him wrought with meed, VI. xi. 35. 8
Right *well* knew Coridon his owne late sheepe, VI. xi. 37. 6
To hyre them *well* if they their flockes would keepe; VI. xi. 40. 2
And Bellamour againe so *well* her pleased VI. xii. 5. 1
Well she it markt, and pittied the more, VI. xii. 8. 1
Both whom they goodly *well* did entertaine; VI. xii. 11. 1
For Bellamour knew Calidore right *well*, VI. xii. 11. 2
The rosie marke, which she remembred *well* VI. xii. 15. 6
Which *well* avizing, streight she gan to cast VI. xii. 16. 1
But he, right *well* aware, his rage to ward VI. xii. 30. 1
as *well* of Gods as Men To be the Soveraine. VII. vi. Arg.
To her bold words, and marked *well* her grace, VII. vi. 28. 2
Did inly grudge, yet did it *well* conceale; VII. vi. 35. 8
To be his Love, and of him liked *well:* VII. vi. 44. 6
As *well* those that are sprung of heavenly seed, VII. vii. 3. 3
As *well* for horror of their count'naunce ill, VII. vii. 3. 7
Them *well* disposed by his busie paine, VII. vii. 4. 7
That could not any creature *well* descry; VII. vii. 5. 7
That *well* may seemen true; VII. vii. 7. 1
for *well* I weene, That this VII. vii. 7. 1
his *Plaint of kinde* describ'd it *well:* VII. vii. 9. 7
Ah, gentle Mole! such joyance hath thee *well* beseene. VII. vii. 11. 9
Deriv'd by dew descent; as is *well* knowen to thee. VII. vii. 16. 9
Yet in his time he wrought as *well* as playd, VII. vii. 35. 3
by his plough-yrons mote right *well* appeare. VII. vii. 35. 4
As fed with lard, and that right *well* might seeme; VII. vii. 40. 2
wrapped *well* In many weeds VII. vii. 42. 1
'I *well* consider all that ye have said, VII. vii. 58. 1
I behinke me on that speech . . . and *well* it way! VII. viii. 1. 2
Well is he borne, that may behold you ever, *Am.* viii. 14
your powre, which I too *well* have tride. *Am.* xxv. 8
Yet hope I *well* *Am.* xxxiv. 9
weaker harts, which are not *wel* aware? *Am.* xxxvii. 8
learne to construe *well*. *Am.* xliii. 14
Untill ye have theyr guylefull traynes *well* tryde: *Am.* xlvii. 2
And, ere she could thy cause *wel* understand, *Am.* xlviii. 3
Well worthy thou to have found better hyre, *Am.* xlviii. 5
so *well* assured Unto her selfe, *Am.* lix. 1
in her winters bowre not *well* awake; *Am.* lxx. 6
a spring Of poysoned words and spitefull speeches *well;* *Am.* lxxxv. 4
drest his wound, and it embaulmed *wel* With salve *Epig.* iv. 45
bath'd him in a dainty *well*, *Epig.* iv. 47
The *well* of deare delight. *Epig.* iv. 48
The wanton boy was shortly *wel* recured *Epig.* iv. 51
The silver scaly trouts doe tend full *well*, *Epith.* 57
Let all the virgins therefore *well* awayt: *Epith.* 111
That *well* agree withouten breach or jar. *Epith.* 132
So *well* it her beseemes, *Epith.* 152
He then them tooke, and, tempering goodly *well* *H.L.* 85
And duly *well* observed his beheast; *H.L.* 93
Which *well* perceiving, that imperious boy *H.L.* 120
Thou doest afflict as *well* the not-deserver, *H.L.* 159
Thou mayest *well* trie if they will ever swerve, *H.L.* 165
comely composition Of parts *well* measurd, *H.B.* 70
I, that have often prov'd, too *well* it know, *H.B.* 87
Tempers so trim, that it may *well* be seene *H.B.* 125
But, in your choice of Loves, this *well* advize, *H.B.* 190
at first Made of meere love, and after liked *well*, *H.H.L.* 128
O blessed *Well* of Love! O Floure of Grace! *H.H.L.* 169
So they, enranged *well*, *Proth.* 122
Whose want too *well* now feeles my freendles case; *Proth.* 140
here fits not *well* Olde woes, but joyes, to tell *Proth.* 141
Beseeming *well* the bower of anie Queene, *Proth.* 170
Well addressed. *See* **Addressed, Well.**
Well-advised. then saide the Palmer *well aviz'd*, II. xii. 26. 1
wight who did not *well avis'd* it vew II. xii. 61. 4
he the man, . . . Be *well adviz'd* that he stand stedfast V. vi. 1. 7
Welland. after him the fatall *Welland* went, IV. xi. 35. 1
Well-apaid. How can Bagpipe or joynts be *well apayd?* *S.C.* Au. 6
therewith *well apayd*, III. ii. 47. 7
Which if thou gaine, I shal be *well apayd*. III. v. 36. 5
Well-approved. *See* **Approved, Well.**
Well-attuned. song In *well attuned* notes a joyous lay, I. xii. 7. 4
Well-beseeming. him salute with *well beseeming* glee; I. x. 15. 7
Well-beseen. squaring it in compasse *well beseene*, *Gn.* 651
maske in mirth with Graces *well beseene?* *T.M.* 180
sad habiliments right *well beseene:* I. xii. 5. 3
in her self-resemblance *well beseene*, I. xii. 8. 8
All were faire knights, and goodly *well beseene;* III. i. 45. 8
fretted round with gold, and goodly *wel beseene*. III. iii. 58. 9
In glistering armes right goodly *well-beseene*, V. viii. 29. 4
How each to entertaine with curt'sie *well beseene*. VI. v. 36. 9

Well-beseen—*Continued.*
a girlond *well beseene* He wore, VII. vii. 29. 4
Al with gay girlands goodly *wel beseene*. *Epith.* 40
decke with floures thy altars *well beseene*. *H.L.* 293
Well-consorted. a *well consorted* payre, II. iii. 11. 1
Well-deemed. by slaundring his *well-deemed* name, *Col.* 695
Well-deserved. the lignage right From whence he tooke his *weldeserved* (**well deserved*) name: I. vi. 20. 4
Well dight. *See* **Dight, Well.**
Well-doing. by *well doing* sought to honour to aspyre. II. ix. 39. 9
Welled. *See* **Outwelled.**
streame . . . from a sacred fountaine *welled* forth alway. I. i. 34. 9
filthy matter from them *weld;* I. viii. 47. 7
blood . . . from his wound yet *welled* fresh, I. ix. 36. 7
as a fountaine . . . *welled* goodly forth, III. vi. 25. 6
Well-eyed. *Well-eyed*, as Argus was, *S.C.* Jul. 154
they were both so watchfull and *well eyde*, IV. iii. 7. 8
Well-favored. with her beares the fowle *welfavourd* witch. I. v. 28. 2
To make them lovely or *well-favoured* show; VI. x. 23. 3
Well-feathered. A Bird all white, *well feathered* (*fetherd*[1]) *Bel.* xi. 5
Well-guided. His goodly reason, and *well-guided* speach, I. vii. 42. 1
Well-head. At the *well-head* the purest streames arise; II. vii. 15. 7
he likened was to a *welhed* Of evill words, V. ix. 26. 8
The pure *well head* of Poesie did dwell) VII. vii. 9. 4
Well-heads. Their *welheads* spring, and are with moisture deawd; II. ii. 6. 3
Welling. *Welling* out streames of teares, II. ii. 8. 7
Well-known. *See* **Known, Well.**
The Harpe *well knowne* beside the Northern Beare. *Ti.* 616
them conjur'd by some *well knowen* token, IV. ii. 21. 7
their *well-knowen* courses they forwent; V. viii. 40. 6
Well knowne, and far renowmed heretofore, V. xi. 49. 2
That it became a famous knight *well knowne*, VI. iv. 38. 8
made her lucklesse loves *well knowne* to be: VII. vi. 40. 6
Well-learned. his *well-learned* speare Tooke surer hould, VI. vii. 11. 1
Well measured. *See* **Measured, Well.**
Well-nigh. My hart-blood is *wel nigh* frorne, I feele, *S.C.* F. 243
welnigh choked with the deadly stinke, I. i. 22. 2
wel nigh molt his hart in raging yre: II. v. 8. 5
Well-ordained. *See* **Ordained, Well.**
Well-plighted. Shee also dofte . . . her *well-plighted* frock, III. ix. 21. 3
Well-pointed. her *wel-pointed* wepons did about her dresse. III. xi. 55. 9
Well-practised. *See* **Practised, Well.**
Well-prepared. *See* **Prepared, Well.**
Well-proportioned. did appeare, . . . in his *well proportiond* face; II. xii. 79. 7
Well-proved. his *well proved* weapons to him hent; II. xi. 17. 2
Well-renowned. *See* **Renowned, Well.**
Well-rigged. The Ferriman, . . . With his *well rigged* bote: II. xi. 4. 3
Well-ruling. T' obay the heasts of mans *well-ruling* hand. V. v. 25. 4
Wells. fresh springing *wells*, as christall neate, *Gn.* 119
As if her eyes had beene two springing *wells;* *T.M.* 536
parching drough dried up the christall *wells;* *D.* 333
Both christall *wells* and shadie groves forsooke, *As.* 45
Well-savored. fruits . . . sweet and *well savored*, II. vii. 51. 7
Well-seen. *Well seene* in everie science IV. ii. 35. 3
All sixe *well-seene* in armes, and prov'd in many a fight. V. iii. 5. 9
Well-shaped. perfectly *well shapt* in every lim, VI. ix. 9. 2
Well skilled. So wise is Nereus old, And so *well skild;* IV. xi. 19. 8
Calidore, that was *well skild* in fight, VI. i. 20. 5
Well-spring. Mother of laughter, and *welspring* of blisse, IV. x. 47. 8
opened had the *welspring* of his blood; V. viii. 35. 2
Well-tempered. modest thoughts breathd from *weltempred* sprites, *Am.* lxxxiii. 6
Well-thewed. They bene so *well-thewed*, and so wise, *S.C.* F. 96
Well-timbered. the Mast of some *well-timbred* hulke V. xi. 29. 1
Well-tried. *See* **Tried, Well.**
ransackt Greece *wel tryde*, II. x. 40. 5
Well-tuned. Appearing well in that *well tuned* song, *Col.* 418
Well-wonted. the Prince, through his *well wonted* grace, IV. ix. 14. 1
Well-worthy. *See* **Well, worthy.**
Well-woven. There his *welwoven* toyles, and subtil traines, *As.* 97
Welter. These wisards *welter* in welths waves, *S.C.* Jul. 197
Wench. the rude *wench* her answerd nought at all: I. iii. 11. 3
to weake *wench* did yield his martiall might: II. vi. 8. 5
Wend. *See* **Weened.**
Must not the world *wend* in his commun course, *S.C.* F. 11
all as a poore pedler he did *wend*, *S.C.* May 238
what way shall I *wend*, *S.C.* S. 244
where-ever I did *wend*, Would *wend* with me, *D.* 127, 128
having none to let, to wood did *wend*. *As.* 126
And *wend* with him, his Cynthia to see; *Col.* 186
Wend too and fro at evening and at morne. *Col.* 247
with the Lady backward sought to *wend*. I. i. 28. 2
They, seeing Una, towardes her gan *wend*, I. x. 15. 1
with great joy into that Citty *wend*, I. x. 56. 4
The cursed land where many *wend* amis, II. i. 51. 8
whether swift I *wend*, or whether slow: II. vi. 10. 5
As Guyon hapned by the same to *wend*, II. xii. 63. 5
Ne durst adventure rashly in to *wend*, III. iii. 14. 2
He letteth in, he letteth out to *wend* III. vi. 32. 1
forth on their journey for to *wend:* III. x. 1. 6
up remounted light, and after faind to *wend*. III. x. 38. 9
Before ye enterprise that way to *wend:* III. x. 40. 8
with her *wend* to see III. xi. 20. 2
let them *wend* at will, III. xii. 45. 9
speares . . . Through shield and mayle and haberjeon did *wend*, IV. ii. 15. 4
Resolv'd with him to *wend*, gainst all her friends consent. IV. viii. 50. 9
warded all which in or out did *wend*, IV. x. 7. 3
Thus safely with my love I thence did *wend*.' IV. x. 58. 8

Wend—*Continued.*
allure with gifts and speaches milde To *wend* with her. . . . V. i. 6. 6
willed him with Artegall to *wend,* . . . . V. i. 12. 4
he her quickly stayd, and forst to *wend* withall. . . . . . V. i. 22. 9
wend with him on his adventure hard; . . . . V. i. 30. 5
wrong redresse in such as *wend* awry: . . . . V. ii. 1. 4
unto the Castle he did *wend,* . . . . V. ii. 20. 1
wend with me, that ye may see and know . . . . V. iv. 34. 7
earnestly besought to *wend* that day With her, ... V. ix. 3. 8
thence he wished her with him to *wend* . . . . V. x. 22. 6
When first to Faery court he saw her *wend,* . . . . V. xi. 37. 8
So backeward he attone with him did *wend:* . . . . V. xi. 43. 5
Willing him *wend* unto the Tyrant streight, ... V. xii. 8. 6
With him to *wend* unto his wonning neare; . . . . VI. iv. 13. 3
Upon a day he cast abrode to *wend,* . . . . VI. iv. 17. 2
wont to . . . *wend* on foot for need, ... VI. iv. 19. 5
Him oft desired home with her to *wend,* . . . . VI. iv. 39. 6
wend abrode, though feeble and forlorne, ... VI. v. 7. 3
when so she forth doth *wend* . . . . VI. x. 21. 8
freely *wend,* Or at more ease continue there . . . . VI. xi. 6. 7
To *wend* with him, and be his conduct trew . . . . VI. xi. 35. 3
Her lightened all the way where she should *wend,* . . . . VII. vi. 9. 8
My cruell fayre streight bids me *wend* my way: . . . . . . *Am.* xlvi. 2

Wends. Tho with them *wends* what they spent in cost, ... *S.C.* May 69
bynding up her locks and weeds, forth with him *wends.* . . . V. x. 24. 9

Went. *See* **Outwent, Overwent.**
Excelling all that ever *went* before. . . . . *Ro.* Env. 10
Tho *went* the pensife Damme out of dore, ... *S.C.* May 229
The fayrest May she was that ever *went,* . . . . *S.C.* N. 39
I *went* the wastefull woodes and forest wide, ... *S.C.* D. 23
To an high mountaines top he with them *went,* . . . . . . *Gn.* 73
A Gnat, unto the sleepie Shepheard *went;* . . . . *Gn.* 283
The pasport ended, both they forward *went;* . . . . *Hub.* 203
Upon his tiptoes nicely he up *went,* . . . . *Hub.* 1009
Now *went,* now stopt, now crept, ... *Hub.* 1012
So *went* the Sheepe away with heavie hart: . . . . *Hub.* 1222
all the way he roared as he *went,* . . . . *Hub.* 1345
heavily lamenting from them *went.* . . . . *T.M.* 36
ere his happie soule to heaven *went* . . . . *Ti.* 295
Scorned of everie one, which by it *went;* . . . . *Ti.* 503
ever as he *went* He sighed soft, ... *D.* 47
As the least lamb in all my flock that *went:* . . . . *D.* 126
as if to sleepe she *went,* . . . . *D.* 256
warily still watch which way she *went,* . . . . *Col.* 133
forth unto the darksom hole he *went,* . . . . I. i. 14. 3
all the way he prayed as he *went,* . . . . I. i. 29. 8
with that godly father to his home they *went.* . . . . . . I. i. 33. 9
he . . . with the old man *went;* . . . . I. ii. 5. 2
Then forth I *went* his woefull corse to find, ... I. ii. 24. 6
The Lyon . . . with her *went* along, ... I. iii. 9. 2
he . . . told her all that fell, in journey as she *went.* . . . . I. iii. 32. 9
such an one . . . knew not whether right he *went,* . . . . . I. iv. 19. 9
Scattered on every mountaine as he *went,* . . . . I. v. 38. 8
forth she *went* to seeke him far and wide. . . . . I. vii. 2. 5
forth they *went,* the Dwarfe them guiding ever right. . . . I. vii. 52. 9
lodging unto all that came and *went;* . . . . I. x. 37. 5
Still as he *went* he craftie stales did lay, ... II. i. 4. 1
foule shame him follow wher he *went!'* . . . . II. i. 30. 9
ever as she *went* her toung did walke . . . . II. iv. 5. 1
he *went,* and his owne false part playd, ... II. iv. 27. 7
chawing vengeaunce all the way I *went,* . . . . II. iv. 29. 2
I, poursewing my fell purpose, after *went.* . . . . II. iv. 31. 9
ever as he *went* dew watch upon him kept. . . . . II. vii. 26. 9
taking courteous conge . . . forth he *went.* . . . . II. xi. 17. 4
it no further *went,* But to the ground . . . . II. xi. 24. 7
as they *went* they heard a ruefull cry . . . . II. xii. 27. 2
as thorough them she *went,* . . . . II. xii. 45. 2
seek adventures as he with Prince Arthure *went.* . . . . . . III. i. 2. 9
when she saw them gone she forward *went,* . . . . III. i. 19. 6
Of the poore traveiler that *went* astray . . . . III. i. 43. 6
forth upon their journey *went.* . . . . III. i. 67. 9
ne further fastned not, But *went* her way; . . . . III. ii. 26. 3
forth together *went* with sorow fraught. . . . . III. iv. 31. 7
As swifte as swallowes on the waves they *went,* . . . . . . III. iv. 33. 5
After that wicked foster fiercely *went:* . . . . III. iv. 47. 4
So forth he *went* With heavy look . . . . III. iv. 61. 6
with him foorth into the forrest *went* . . . . III. v. 16. 3
Into the woods thenceforth in haste shee *went,* . . . . . . III. v. 32. 1
as a fountaine from her sweete lips *went.* . . . . III. vi. 25. 5
with her *went* To seeke the fugitive . . . . III. vi. 26. 3
She forth issewd, and on her journey *went:* . . . . III. vii. 19. 2
She *went* in perill, of each noyse affeard, ... III. vii. 19. 3
swifte as word that from her *went,* . . . . III. vii. 23. 6
Went forth in haste, and did her footing trace . . . . . . III. vii. 23. 7
went at will withouten card or sayle, ... III. viii. 31. 2
as they forward *went,* They spyde a knight . . . . III. viii. 44. 6
She to his closet *went,* where all his wealth Lay hid; . . . . III. x. 12. 3
Paridell . . . from her *went* to seeke another lott, ... III. x. 37. 3
Swayne would not his leasure dwell, But *went* his way: . . . III. x. 38. 8
At night, when all they *went* to sleepe, ... III. x. 48. 1
forward with bold steps into the next roome *went.* . . . . . III. xi. 50. 9
Next after him *went* Doubt, ... III. xii. 10. 1
With him *went* Daunger, cloth'd in ragged weed . . . . . . III. xii. 11. 1
With him *went* Hope in rancke, ... III. xii. 13. 1
Next him *went* Griefe and Fury, ... III. xii. 16. 1
After them *went* Displeasure and Pleasaunce, ... III. xii. 18. 1
Maid, . . . *went* unto the dore To enter in, ... III. xii. 27. 6
in *went* Bold Britomart, ... III. xii. 29. 7
So foorth they *went,* and both together giusted; . . . . . . IV. i. 11. 1
none of them once out of order *went,* . . . . IV. ii. 36. 7

Went—*Continued.*
To the three fatall sisters house she *went.* . . . . IV. ii. 47. 4
Farre under ground from tract of living *went,* . . . . IV. ii. 47. 5
Through Cambels shoulder it unwarely *went,* . . . . IV. iii. 8. 3
went away sore wounded of his haplesse hand. . . . . IV. iv. 21. 9
so *went* forth to fight. . . . . IV. iv. 27. 9
forcibly to ground they both together *went.* . . . . IV. iv. 28. 9
Since with the rest she *went* not after Florimell. . . . . . IV. v. 28. 9
Shall breath it selfe awhile after so long a *went.* . . . . . IV. v. 46. 9
to the tender flesh it *went,* . . . . IV. vi. 15. 6
he *went* Forth on his way . . . . IV. vi. 44. 4
she *went* to seeke faire Amoret, ... IV. vi. 46. 6
I thether *went;* where I did long conceale My selfe, ... IV. viii. 55. 4
on that hard adventure forth I *went,* . . . . IV. x. 5. 1
evermore his eyes about him *went,* . . . . IV. x. 12. 7
before them, as they *went,* . . . . IV. xi. 12. 2
So *went* he playing on the watery plaine; . . . . IV. xi. 24. 1
him before there *went,* as best became, ... IV. xi. 24. 4
Next him *went* Wylibourne with passage slye, ... IV. xi. 32. 5
after him the fatall Welland *went,* . . . . IV. xi. 35. 1
He now *went* with him in this new inquest, ... V. i. 13. 1
As that it seem'd above the ground he *went;* . . . . V. i. 20. 3
Ne wight with him but onely Talus *went;* . . . . V. i. 30. 8
To Artegall he turn'd and *went* with him throughout. . . . . V. ii. 54. 9
all men *went* to rest. . . . . V. iii. 7. 9
So forth he *went,* and soone them over-hent, ... V. iii. 11. 1
Ne wight with him for his assistance *went,* . . . . V. iv. 3. 8
forth to the Towne-gate *went;* . . . . V. iv. 50. 2
to her chamber *went* like solitary cell. . . . . V. vi. 11. 9
with him *went* without gaine-saying more. . . . . V. vi. 22. 3
she forward *went* To seeke her love, ... V. vii. 24. 6
her noble Lord, sir Artegall, *Went* on his way; . . . . . . V. vii. 45. 7
Ne wight but onely Talus with him *went,* . . . . V. viii. 3. 8
The Damzell straight *went,* as she was directed, ... V. ix. 9. 6
Full dreadfull wight he was as ever *went* Upon the earth, . . V. ix. 10. 4
He him pursewd where ever that he *went;* . . . . V. ix. 16. 3
Into a Hedgehogge all unwares it *went,* . . . . V. ix. 18. 5
they passing in *Went* up the hall, ... V. ix. 23. 2
streight *went* forth his gladnesse to partake With Belge, . . . V. xi. 32. 7
Of whom yet taking leave thenceforth he *went,* . . . . V. xi. 35. 7
streight way *went* On his first quest, ... V. xi. 36. 2
his way did hast, and *went* all night; . . . . VI. i. 30. 1
Streight to the carkasse of that Knight he *went,* . . . . . . VI. iii. 17. 1
ne did the other stay, But after *went* directly . . . . VI. iii. 37. 5
The groome *went* streight way in, ... VI. iii. 42. 1
now West he *went* awhile, Then North, ... VI. iv. 25. 2
Went forth streightway into the forrest wyde . . . . VI. v. 3. 6
as on their way they *went,* . . . . VI. v. 10. 1
up to their steedes they *went,* . . . . VI. v. 24. 8
So forth he *went* his way, ... VI. v. 41. 5
He knew the diverse *went* of mortall wayes, ... VI. vi. 3. 5
with sage counsell, when they *went* astray, He could enforme, VI. vi. 3. 7
went both on their way, ... VI. vi. 15. 9
Ne wight with him on that adventure *went,* . . . . VI. vi. 18. 6
him ever foot forsake Where so he *went,* . . . . VI. vi. 29. 5
a straunge knight, that neare afore him *went,* . . . . VI. vii. 4. 4
So up he rose, and forth streightway he *went* . . . . VI. vii. 14. 1
follow through the world where so he *went,* . . . . VI. vii. 21. 8
all the way he *went,* on every syde He gaz'd about . . . . VI. vii. 42. 7
that other villaine *went* about Him to have bound . . . . . VI. viii. 11. 6
Under his club with wary boldnesse *went,* . . . . VI. viii. 15. 8
Arthure with the rest *went* onward still . . . . VI. viii. 30. 7
When to the field she *went* he with her *went:* . . . . . . VI. ix. 34. 8
So being clad unto the fields he *went* . . . . VI. ix. 37. 1
as they all three together *went* To the greene wood . . . . VI. x. 34. 1
he streight *went* to the Captaines nest: . . . . VI. xi. 42. 7
he forth *went* into th' open light, ... VI. xi. 47. 6
into those theevish dens he *went,* . . . . VI. xi. 51. 1
He *went* forth on his quest, ... VI. xii. 13. 9
These, marching softly, thus in order *went;* . . . . VII. vii. 32. 1
Which on the earth he strowed as he *went,* . . . . VII. vii. 32. 8

Wept. Shee *weeped,* and wayled, ... *S.C.* May 301
she *wept* and wofullie waymented, ... *T.M.* 355
shee *wept* and waild so pityouslie, ... *T.M.* 535
The running waters *wept* for thy returne, ... *Col.* 27
when they both had *wept* and wayld their fill, ... I. iii. 22. 6
he . . . *wept,* that cause of weeping none he had; . . . . . I. iv. 30. 8
Duessa *wept* full bitterly. . . . . I. v. 17. 9
So *wept* Duessa untill eventyde, ... I. v. 19. 1
one that wayld and pittifully *wept,* . . . . II. xii. 27. 3
He *wept,* and wayld, and false laments belyde, ... III. x. 7. 7
He rav'd, he *wept,* he stampt, he lowd did cry, ... III. x. 17. 7
alwaies *wept* and wailed night and day, ... IV. viii. 2. 8
after she had *wept* and wail'd a space, ... IV. xii. 8. 8
With that she *wept* and wail'd, ... IV. xii. 11. 8
having over it a litle *wept,* . . . . VI. iv. 37. 8
seeing them for tender pittie *wept;* . . . . VI. xi. 37. 7

Were (*partial list*). *See* **All were, Wear.**
Were (= rivers) 4.11.34.5.
in this golden vessel couched *weare* The ashes . . . . . . *Bel.*[2] iii. 7
But sike fancies *weren* foolerie, ... *S.C.* F. 211
why sytten we soe, As *weren* overwent with woe, ... *S.C.* Mar. 2
were not that my sheepe would stray, ... *S.C.* Mar. 34
I am not as I wish I *were,* . . . . *S.C.* Jun. 105
Were not better to shunne the scortching heate? . . . . . *S.C.* Au. 48
ere thou die, it *were* convenient To tell . . . . *D.* 80
were he knowne to Cynthia as he ought, ... *Col.* 402
Full many worthie ones then waiting *were,* . . . . *Col.* 737
if ought higher *were* than that, did it desyre. . . . . . . I. iv. 11. 9
Were it not better I that Lady had . . . . I. vi. 47. 3
And, *were* not hevenly grace that did him blesse, ... I. vii. 12. 3

Were—*Continued.*
Were not that heavenly grace doth him uphold, . . . I. viii. 1. 3
Of that same hornes great virtues *weren* told, . . . I. viii. 3. 8
Those *were* the keyes of every inner dore; . . . I. viii. 30. 8
But whether dreames delude, or true it *were*, . . . I. ix. 14. 5
she fed whiles they *were* weake and young. . . . I. x. 31. 3
Albe Charissa *were* their chiefest founderesse. . . . I. x. 44. 9
Death better *were;* death did he oft desire, . . . I. xi. 28. 4
Whose sides with dapled circles *weren* dight; . . . II. i. 18. 7
The woods, the nymphes, my bowres, my midwives, *weare:* . II. i. 53. 7
As it some Gyeld or solemne Temple *weare.* . . . II. vii. 43. 4
A route of people there assembled *were*, . . . II. vii. 44. 1
And *were* I not, yet is my trouth yplight, . . . II. vii. 50. 6
downe him smot ere well aware he *weare;* . . . III. i. 28. 8
Till to her dew perfection she *were* (*was) ripened . . . III. vi. 3. 9
It *were* a goodly storie to declare . . . III. vi. 5. 1
So long they sought, till they arrived *were* . . . III. vi. 26. 5
children *werne* All three as one; . . . IV. ii. 41. 7
Sighes the bellows *weare.* . . . IV. v. 38. 9
she uneath discerned whether whether *weare.* . . . IV. ix. 10. 9
with their owne repayed duely *weare*, . . . IV. ix. 30. 8
wish that in his powre it *weare* Her to redresse: . . . IV. xii. 12. 7
But promist him, what ever wight she *weare*, . . . IV. xii. 27. 5
the Idoll, as it *were* inclining, . . . V. vii. 8. 1
by that Damzell *were* Directed in, . . . V. ix. 22. 1
By all the names that honorable *were.* . . . V. xi. 33. 4
'*were* not that thou wouldst fly . . . VI. i. 28. 5
Upon our way to which we *weren* bent, . . . VI. ii. 16. 2
were not that the Prince did him appeaze, . . . VI. vi. 40. 7
she entred, *were* he liefe or sory; Ne staide . . . VII. vi. 8. 7
Molanna, *were* she not so shole, *Were* no lesse faire . . . VII. vi. 40. 7, 8
in greene leaves, *as* he a Player *were;* . . . VII. vii. 35. 2
But *were* they so, . . . Yet what if I can prove, . . . VII. vii. 49. 6
that ye begotten *were* And borne . . . VII. vii. 53. 7
Ne doe I wish (for wishing *were* but vaine) . . . *Am.* xlii. 5
Were it. (*Were it* more or lesse) . . . *S.C.* May 108
Were it by honest wayes, or otherwise, . . . *Hub.* 848
Were it not. *were it not* too painfull to repeat . . . *Col.* 32
were it not for shame, he would retyre; . . . II. vii. 37. 8
were it not ill fitting . . . VII. vi. 37. 1
Werfe. *See* **Wharfe.**
West. stretch her selfe at large from East to *West;* . . . *S.C.* O. 44
steeds . . . gan water in the *west*, . . . *D.* 25
An island, which the first to *west* was showne. . . . *Col.* 271
ruddy Phebus gins to welke in *west*, . . . I. i. 23. 2
He that the wide *West* under his rule has, . . . I. ii. 22. 8
steepe His fierie face in billowes of the *west*, . . . I. xi. 31. 2
that great Emperour of all the *West;* . . . I. xii. 26. 4
Corineus had that Province utmost *west* . . . II. x. 12. 2
reeled to and fro from east to *west.* . . . III. vii. 42. 7
Hygate made the meare thereof by *West*, . . . III. ix. 46. 2
who from East to *West* will endlong seeke, . . . III. ix. 51. 3
As like can not be seene from East to *West*, . . . IV. v. 18. 4
twice hath risen where he now doth *West*, . . . V. Pr. 8. 6
all the *West* with equall conquest wonne, . . . V. i. 2. 7
She to a window came that opened *West*, . . . V. vi. 7. 4
Not farre away, but little wide by *West*, . . . V. vi. 22. 4
now *West* he went awhile, Then North, . . . VI. iv. 25. 2
second Babell, tyrant of the *West*, . . . *Com. Son.* iv. 3
Wested. *wested* twice where he ought rise aright: . . . V. Pr. 8. 7
Western. That wardes the *Westerne* coste? . . . *S.C.* Jul. 42
nowe the *Westerne* wind bloweth sore, . . . *S.C.* S. 49
My little flocke on *westerne* downes to keepe, . . . *D.* 100
had . . . Their scepters stretcht from East to *Westerne* shore, . I. i. 5. 5
In *westerne* waves his weary wagon did recure. . . . I. v. 44. 9
Phoebus gan decline . . . His weary wagon to the *Westerne* vale, II. ix. 10. 2
The *westerne* Hogh, besprincled with the gore . . . II. x. 10. 7
Camber did possesse the *Westerne* quart, . . . II. x. 14. 4
When the wroth *Western* wind does reave their locks: . . . II. xi. 19. 5
In deawy vapours of the *westerne* mayne, . . . III. viii. 51. 4
Towards the *westerne* brim begins to draw, . . . V. ix. 35. 2
to thy home, Within the *Westerne* fome: . . . *Epith.* 283
Wet. The watrie *wette* weighed downe his head, . . . *S.C.* F. 232
wett your tender Lambes . . . *S.C.* Jun. 120
there Tethys his *wet* bed Doth ever wash, . . . I. i. 39. 6
starre That was in Ocean waves yet never *wet*, . . . I. ii. 1. 3
Each gan undight Their garments *wett*, . . . III. ix. 19. 7
wiping the deawy *wet* Which softly stild, . . . IV. vii. 35. 5
from side to side till all the world it *weet.* . . . IV. ix. 33. 9
a lewd foole her leading thorough dry and *wet.* . . . VI. vi. 16. 9
wet he seem'd in sight With waves, . . . VII. vii. 33. 8
bad his billowes spare To *wet* their silken feathers, . . . *Proth.* 49
Wets. *wets* the little plants that lowly dwell. . . . *S.C.* N. 32
all the way she *wetts* with flowing teares; . . . I. iii. 44. 4
Wetting. For feare of *wetting* them before their bed. . . . VI. ix. 13. 5
Wex(e), *etc. See* **Wax,** *etc.*
Wey. *See* **Weigh.**
Whale. Like as the wounded *Whale* to shore flies from the maine. . . . VI. x. 31. 9
Whale's. through feare, as white as *whales* bone: . . . III. i. 15. 5
Whales. Spring-headed Hydres; and sea-shouldring *Whales;* II. xii. 23. 6
Whally. *whally* eies (the signe of gelosy,) . . . I. iv. 24. 3
Wharfe. swift *Werfe*, and Oze the most of might, . . . IV. xi. 37. 6
What (*partial list*). *See* **Mostwhat, Somewhat.**
beholde, *What* under this great Temple is containde, . . . *Bel.*[1] i. 1
What say I more? each thing at last we see . . . *Pet.* v. 7
What? hath some Wolfe thy tender Lambes ytorne? . . . *S.C.* Ap. 2
What shoulden shepheards other things tend, . . . *S.C.* May 63
What! should they pynen in payne and woe? . . . *S.C.* May 149
the little *what*, That Thomalin can sayne. . . . *S.C.* Jul. 31
What—*Continued.*
What neede hem caren for their flocks, . . . *S.C.* Jul. 195
What the foule evill hath thee so bestadde? . . . *S.C.* Au. 7
what I the bett for-thy? . . . *S.C.* O. 15
T' enquire of custome, *what* and whence they were? . . . *Hub.* 245
What needeth perill to be sought abroad, . . . *As.* 89
what needeth shee That is so great a shepheardesse her selfe, . *Col.* 368
(O! *what* now availeth that I was?) . . . I. ii. 22. 6
'*what* oddes can ever bee, Where both doe fight alike, . . . I. iv. 50. 3
'*What* doe I recke, . . . II. viii. 15. 2
what doth his bad death now satisfy . . . II. viii. 15. 3
What shape, *what* shield, *what* armes, *what* steed, *what* stedd, III. ii. 16. 2
but *what* thing it mote bee, Or whence . . . III. iii. 16. 6
'*What* had th' eternall Maker need of thee . . . III. iv. 56. 1
both how and *what* Her sonne had to them doen; . . . III. vi. 15. 8
But *what* doe I their names seeke to reherse, . . . IV. xi. 17. 1
What time sad tydings . . . Talus to her brought; . . . V. vi. 3. 3
What time the native Belman of the night, . . . V. vi. 27. 1
through feare *what* of his childe became . . . VI. iii. 17. 9
What and from whence she was and by *what* traine . . . VI. v. 27. 7
Such homely *what* as serves the simple clowne, . . . VI. ix. 7. 4
That *what* through wonder, and *what* through delight, . . . VI. xi. 13. 7
if Jove should do still *what* he can . . . VII. vi. 31. 9
my fraile wit cannot devize to *what* It to compare, . . . VII. vii. 7. 4
And in *what* rags, and in how base aray, . . . *H.H.L.* 228
Whatever. Who lists to see *what ever* nature, arte, . . . *Ro.* v. 1
Whatever thing seemes small in common eyes. . . . *Van.* v. 14
What ever that good old man bespake. . . . *S.C.* F. 97
Now say on, Diggon, *what ever* thou hast. . . . *S.C.* S. 55
Say it out, Diggon, *whatever* it hight, . . . *S.C.* S. 172
Whatever thing lacketh chaungeable rest, . . . *S.C.* S. 240
With shepheards swayne *what ever* fedde in field; . . . *S.C.* D. 44
But bends *what ever* power his aged yeares Him lent, . . . *Gn.* 646
'Gladly (said he) *what ever* such like paine . . . *Hub.* 287
From whom *what ever* thing is goodly thought, . . . *T.M.* 405
Therefore, *what ever* man bearst worldlie sway, . . . *Ti.* 208
To take *what ever* thing doth please the eie? . . . *Mui.* 214
What-ever man be he whose heavie minde, . . . *D.* 1
I hate *what ever* Nature made, . . . *D.* 393
Shepheard, *what ever* thou hast heard to be In this . . . *Col.* 568
What ever feeds in forest or in field, . . . *Col.* 820
Deare Sir, *what ever* that thou be in place: . . . I. iii. 37. 3
Young knight *whatever*, that dost armes professe, . . . I. iv. 1. 1
'Is not his deed, *what ever* thing is donne . . . I. ix. 42. 1
What ever thing does touch . . . I. xi. 12. 4
what ever hevenly powre, Or earthly wight thou be, . . . II. iii. 34. 8
What ever bee the cause, it sure beseemes you ill.' . . . II. ix. 37. 9
gave unto us all *what ever* good we have. . . . II. x. 69. 9
whatever in this worldly state Is sweete . . . II. xii. 42. 5
Whatever thing was in the world contaynd, . . . III. ii. 19. 2
Whatever foe had wrought, or frend had faynd, . . . III. ii. 19. 5
And love each other deare, *what ever* them befell. . . . IV. ii. 53. 9
And beating downe *what ever* nigh him came, . . . IV. iv. 41. 7
And overthrew *what ever* came her neare, . . . IV. iv. 46. 7
what ever man it sayd, . . . IV. x. 1. 1
But promist him, *what ever* wight she weare, . . . IV. xii. 27. 5
doe *what ever* thing he did intend: . . . V. i. 12. 5
'*What ever* thing is done by him is donne, . . . V. ii. 42. 1
What ever he shall like to doe or say. . . . V. iv. 49. 5
let *what ever* he desires be him denide. . . . V. v. 50. 9
tell *what ever* it be, good or bad, . . . V. vi. 10. 2
To doe *whatever* he thought good or fit: . . . V. x. 13. 3
what ever evill she conceived, Did spred abroad . . . V. xii. 33. 6
Whatever formes ye list thereto apply, . . . VI. iv. 35. 6
whatever chaunce were blowne Betwixt them to divide, . . . VI. vii. 3. 8
What ever thing he did her to aggrate, . . . VI. x. 33. 2
Ne ought he said, *what ever* he did heare, . . . VII. vi. 49. 8
all other creatures, *What-ever* life or motion do retaine, . . . VII. vii. 4. 2
wypes quite out of memory *Whatever* ill before . . . *H.L.* 242
What if. *What if* some little payne the passage have, . . . I. ix. 40. 4
What ho. *What, ho!* thou jollye shepheards swayne, . . . *S.C.* Jul. 5
What's. wretched men, to weete *whats* good or ill, . . . *S.C.* N. 183
'*Whats* this (quoth he) that gives so great a voyce . . . *Epig.* iv. 7
What so. But *what so* by my selfe may not be showen, . . . *Gn.* Ded. 13
whatso other hearb of lovely hew, . . . *Gn.* 682
over night *whatso* theretoo did neede . . . *Hub.* 106
In *whatso* please employ his personage, . . . *Hub.* 778
whatso he likte he kept. . . . *Hub.* 1146
Whatso the heaven in his wide vawte containes, . . . *Hub.* 1229
And *whatso* else of vertue good or ill . . . *Mui.* 201
And *whatso* heavens in their secret doome Ordained have, . . *Mui.* 225
And *what so* else his person most may vaunt?' . . . III. ii. 16. 7
whatso my feeble Muse can frame . . . III. viii. 43. 2
But *what so* were therein or writ or ment, . . . III. xi. 50. 6
what so good or ill . . . I hold mine owne, . . . V. iv. 14. 2
'Full true it is *what so* . . . My brother here declared . . . V. iv. 15. 2
He purposd to proceed, *what so* befall, . . . V. vii. 43. 8
Or *what so* penaunce shall by you be red.' . . . V. viii. 13. 6
To rend and teare *what so* she can oppresse; . . . V. xi. 24. 4
what so Envie good or bad did fynd . . . V. xii. 33. 4
Both horse and armes and *what so* else to lend, . . . VI. iv. 39. 8
Or *what so* else were unto him betyde: . . . VI. v. 3. 8
But *what so* sure she was, she worthy was . . . VI. x. 25. 6
Whatso is fayrest shall to earth returne. . . . *Am.* xiii. 8
Whatsoever. *whatsoever* other flowre of worth, . . . *Gn.* 681
whatsoever mother-wit or arte Could worke, . . . *Hub.* 1138
For *whatsoever* from one place doth fall . . . V. ii. 39. 7
whatsoever good by any sayd Or doen she heard, . . . V. xii. 34. 1
whatsoever else he would requere. . . . VI. i. 43. 4
'Then wote, thou shepheard, *whatsoever* thou bee, . . . VI. x. 21. 2

Whatsoever—*Continued.*
Knowing that, *whatsoere* to them we give, H.H.L. 209
What with. So *what with* hope of good, and hate of ill, *Col.* 192
Wheel. *See* **Mill-wheel.**
'And ye fond men! on fortunes *wheele* that ride, *D.* 498
There was Ixion turned on a *wheele,* I. v. 35. 1
Like to a restlesse *wheele,* still ronning round, II. xii. 20. 6
So, like a *wheele,* arownd they ronne from old to new. III. vi. 33. 9
Alreadie seemes that fortunes headlong *wheele* Begins to turne, V. x. 20. 7
What man that sees the ever-whirling *wheele,* Of Change, VII. vi. 1. 1
The rolling *wheele* that runneth often round, *Am.* xviii. 1
Wheeling. in her *wheeling* round, . . . So sorely he her strooke, IV. vi. 13. 2
Wheels. *See* **Charet-wheels.**
From fiery *wheeles* of his faire chariot Hurled his beame I. ii. 29. 4
rapt with whirling *wheeles,* inflames the skyen With fire I. iv. 9. 8
With which her yron *wheeles* did them affray, I. v. 30. 4
(With yron *wheeles* and hookes arm'd dreadfully, V. viii. 28. 5
in peeces to have torne With his sharpe *wheeles,* V. viii. 31. 7
they did draw The yron charet, and the *wheeles* did teare, V. viii. 41. 6
Whelky. Ne ought the *whelky* pearles esteemeth hee, *Gn.* 105
Whelmed. Jove . . . Her *whelm'd* with hills, *Ro.* iv. 7
many *whelmd* in deadly paine; II. ii. 43. 4
there Her *whelm'd* with stones. VII. vi. 53. 4
Whelming. entrap The man most wary in her *whelming* lap: II. iv. 17. 5
Whelps. *See* **Lion-whelps.**
a Wolfe . . . Noursing two *whelpes;* *Bel.*² vi. 2
left his *whelps* their kingdomes to devoure? *Ti.* 70
from the she Beares teats her *whelps* to teare; I. vi. 24. 5
Lyon, which hath long time saught His robbed *whelpes,* II. viii. 40. 8
with a crew Of hungry *whelpes,* III. iii. 47. 4
Whose *whelpes* are stolne away, VI. xi. 25. 9
When (*partial list*). *See* **As when.**
When ye sometimes behold the ruin'd pride *Ro.* xv. 12
But, *when* the object of her vertue failed, *Ro.* xxi. 9
When land and sea ye name, then name ye Rome; *Ro.* xxvi. 11
When shee the beames of her beauty displayes, *S.C.* Ap. 84
when all is ycladd With pleasaunce: *S.C.* May 6
When great Pan account of shepeherdes shall aske. *S.C.* May 54
For, *when* they bene dead, their good is ygoe, *S.C.* May 67
And, if he chaunce come *when* I am abroade, *S.C.* May 223
Home *when* the doubtfull Damme had her hyde, *S.C.* May 294
At the Kerke, *when* it is holliday; *S.C.* May 310
Will pype and daunce *when* Phoebe shineth bright: *S.C.* Jun. 31
When folke bene fat, and riches rancke, *S.C.* Jul. 211
when the hart is ill assayde, *S.C.* Au. 5
When holy fathers wont to shrieve; *S.C.* Au. 55
You heare all night, *when* nature craveth sleepe, *S.C.* Au. 177
When the rayne is faln, the cloudes wexen cleare. *S.C.* S. 18
Since *when* thou hast measured much grownd, *S.C.* S. 21
Which *when* they thinken agayne to quench, *S.C.* S. 88
Mought needes decay, *when* it is at best. *S.C.* S. 241
Colin, my deare, *when* shall it please thee sing, *S.C.* N. 1
Whilome in youth, *when* flowrd my joyfull spring, *S.C.* D. 19
How Phoebe fayles, where Venus sittes, and *when.* *S.C.* D. 84
When flocking Persians did the Greeks affray; *Gn.* 50
Yet *when* he saw him slaine himselfe he cheard. *Gn.* 312
Now, *when* the sloathfull fit of lifes sweete rest Had left *Gn.* 641
when all shrowded were In careles sleep, *Hub.* 333
When, weening to returne whence they did stray, I. i. 10. 3
Furthest from end then, *when* they neerest weene, I. i. 10. 6
Which *when* by tract they hunted had throughout, I. i. 11. 5
Which *when* the valiant Elfe perceiv'd, he lept I. i. 17. 1
That *when* he heard, in great perplexitie, I. i. 19. 5
But, *when* his later spring gins to avale, I. i. 21. 5
Whose corage *when* the feend perceivd to shrinke, I. i. 22. 4
When ruddy Phebus gins to welke in west, I. i. 23. 2
Where *when* all drownd in deadly sleepe he findes, I. i. 36. 6
But, *when* he saw his labour all was vaine, I. i. 55. 8
But, *when* he saw his threatning was but vaine, I. ii. 2. 8
when him he spide Spurring so hote with rage dispiteous, I. ii. 15. 1
youthly yeares, *when* corage hott The fire of love, I. ii. 35. 1
Then was she fayre alone, *when* none was faire in place. I. ii. 38. 9
Still, *when* she slept, he kept both watch and ward; I. iii. 9. 5
And, *when* she wakt, he wayted diligent, I. iii. 9. 6
When every creature shrowded is in sleepe. I. iii. 15. 2
Then furthest from her hope, *when* most she weened nye. I. iii. 21. 9
from whence *when* she him spyde, I. iii. 26. 5
They had not ridden far, *when* they might see One I. iii. 33. 1
For death it was, *when* any good he saw; I. iv. 30. 7
when lo! a darkesome clowd Upon him fell: I. v. 13. 6
Where *when* she came, she found the Faery knight I. v. 45. 3
when Phoebe fayre With all her band was following the chace, I. vii. 5. 1
So daunted *when* the Geaunt saw the knight, I. vii. 14. 1
when on the way He wofull Lady, wofull Una, met, I. vii. 20. 1
Who *when* her eyes she on the Dwarf had set, I. vii. 20. 5
At last *when* life recover'd had the raine, I. vii. 24. 5
For this young Prince, *when* first to armes he fell; I. vii. 36. 7
But, *when* he dyde, the Faery Queene it brought I. vii. 36. 8
Whose grievous fall *when* false Duessa spyde, I. viii. 25. 1
Tho, *when* her well of teares she wasted had, I. viii. 42. 5
Then, *when* they had despoyld her tire and call, I. viii. 46. 5
Ay wont to laugh *when* them I heard to cry, I. ix. 10. 5
As, *when* just time expired, should appeare. I. ix. 14. 4
When houre of death is come, let none aske whence, nor why. I. ix. 42. 9
Where, *when* that fairest Una she beheld, I. x. 8. 6
In which *when* him she well instructed hath, I. x. 33. 8
When sin, and hell, and death, doe most dismay I. x. 41. 4
There *when* the Elfin knight arrived was, I. x. 44. 1
When wintry storme his wrathful wreck does threat; I. xi. 21. 2
Whom so dismayd *when* that his foe beheld, I. xi. 28. 6

When—*Continued.*
Then, *when* with meates and drinkes of every kinde I. xii. 15. 1
Thus, *when* that Princes wrath was pacifide, I. xii. 36. 6
And ever, *when* his eie did her behold, I. xii. 40. 8
Yet all these were, *when* no man did them know, II. Pr. 3. 1
When ill is chaunst, but doth the ill increase, II. i. 16. 6
When suddeinly that warriour gan abace II. i. 26. 7
Which *when* that warriour heard, dismounting straict II. i. 39. 1
One day, *when* him high corage did emmove, II. i. 50. 5
'At last, *when* fayling breath began to faint, II. ii. 8. 1
Where *when* the knight arriv'd, he was right well II. ii. 14. 1
But still, *when* Guyon came to part their fight, II. ii. 23. 8
At last, *when* lust of meat and drinke was ceast, II. ii. 39. 3
Which was the cause, *when* earst that horne I heard, II. iii. 45. 6
Then, *when* she is withdrawne or strong withstood, II. iv. 11. 6
and eft, *when* yeares More rype us II. iv. 18. 4
when suddeinly He heard a voyce II. viii. 3. 6
Whom *when* Pyrochles saw, inflam'd with rage II. viii. 12. 1
Till that at last, *when* he advantage spyde, II. viii. 36. 2
But ever at Pyrochles *when* he smitt, II. viii. 43. 1
Tho, *when* this breathlesse woxe, that batteil gan renew, II. viii. 47. 9
As *when* a windy tempest bloweth hye, II. viii. 48. 1
As *when* a swarme of Gnats at eventide II. ix. 16. 1
That *when* it locked none might thorough pas, II. ix. 23. 7
And *when* it opened, no man might it close, II. ix. 23. 8
Expecting ever *when* some foe she might descry III. xii. 1. 9
Tho, *when* she felt her selfe to be unbownd III. xii. 38. 8
askt him where and *when* her bridale V. ii. 3. 7
not caring where nor *when.* VI. xii. 27. 9
That made you merie oft *when* ye were sorie. *H.L.* 35
Whenas (*partial list*).
when as good is meant, Evil ensueth *S.C.* May 101
Tho, *when as* Lowder was farre awaye, *S.C.* S. 196
when as season more secure Shall bring forth fruit, *Gn.* 9
when as at last he spide, Lying along *Gn.* 266
Whenas the Ape, beginning well to wey *Hub.* 112
When as they nigh approached, *Hub.* 243
Now *whenas* Time, flying with winges *Hub.* 308
Of which *whenas* they feasted had *Hub.* 337
Whither *whenas* they came they fell at words, *Hub.* 1019
Yet was she foyld, *when as* she me assaild. *Ti.* 112
When as her messenger doth come for me; *D.* 459
Ne, *when as* drouping Titan draweth neere *D.* 468
At last, *when as* he piped had his fill, *Col.* 10
And, *when as* death these vitall bands shall breake, *Col.* 630
When as ye heare her memory renewed, *Col.* 645
whenas timely meanes it purchase may, *Ded. Son.* xvi.13
At last *whenas* the dreadfull passion Was overpast, I. ii. 32. 1
But to the pray *when as* he drew more ny, I. iii. 5. 7
Now *whenas* darkesome night had all displayd I. iv. 44. 1
But *whenas* Morpheus had with leaden mace I. iv. 44. 6
Whose case *whenas* the careful Dwarfe had tould, I. v. 52. 1
They traveild had, *whenas* they far espide I. vi. 34. 2
But *whenas* monsters huge he would dismay, I. vii. 34. 2
doted ignorance, *Whenas* the noble Prince had marked I. viii. 34. 3
Whenas the gentle Redrosse knight did vew, I. ix. 37. 3
Wherto *whenas* they now approched neare, I. xi. 1. 4
With which *whenas* him list the ayre to beat, I. xi. 10. 6
Tho, *when as* still he saw him I. ii. 26. 4
whenas hee In Nemus gayned goodly victoree: II. v. 31. 4
whenas Guyon of that land had sight, II. vi. 22. 5
When as againe he armed felt his hond: II. viii. 40. 6
Whenas the Russian him in fight does chace) II. xi. 26. 8
Which stately manner *whenas* they did see, III. i. 33. 5
whenas all the world in silence deepe III. i. 59. 1
whenas none she fond, III. i. 61. 1
whenas all were put to shamefull flight, III. i. 67. 1
when as thine equall peares Their fit disports III. ii. 31. 3
Whom such *whenas* the wicked Hag did vew, III. vii. 11. 4
Tho, *whenas* vailed was her lofty crest, III. ix. 20. 3
Which *whenas* they beheld, they smitten were III. ix. 23. 1
when as the Trojane boy so fayre III. xi. 34. 4
whenas chearelesse Night ycovered had Fayre heaven III. xii. 1. 1
whenas Cambell, that was stout and wise, IV. ii. 37. 6
I weene, *when as* these rimes be red With misregard, IV. viii. 29. 1
Wayting *when as* the Antheme should be sung IV. x. 48. 9
When as mans age was in his freshest prime, V. Pr. 1. 3
When as (*who as) they to the passage gan to draw, V. ii. 11. 4
when as yet she saw him to proceede V. ii. 23. 1
when as fortune all her spight hath showne, V. iii. 1. 3
Which *when as* Marinell beheld likewise, V. iii. 18. 1
when as all the people such did vew, V. iii. 23. 8
Which *when as* all that present were beheld, V. iii. 26. 1
when as he him nam'd, V. iii. 34. 7
when as time to Artegall shall tend, V. iii. 40. 8
When as the paine of death she tasted had, V. iv. 11. 2
When as their sharpe contention he had ceased, V. iv. 20. 7
when as Artegall, arriv'd in place, V. iv. 23. 5
Which *when as* Radigund there comming heard, V. iv. 37. 6
Whom *when as* Artegall in that distresse By chaunce beheld, V. iv. 41. 1
when as daies faire shinie-beame, V. iv. 45. 1
when as he discovered had her face, V. v. 12. 1
when as yet she saw him not returne, V. vi. 6. 1
when as she long had sought for ease V. vi. 7. 1
Which *when as* hee By outward signes . . . did see, V. vi. 21. 4
when as to her owne Love she came, V. vii. 38. 1
when as she him anew had clad, V. vii. 41. 8
when as Artegall did Arthure vew, V. viii. 12. 6
when as the franticke fit Her burning tongue with rage inflamed V. viii. 49. 1
when as ny He came unto his cave, V. ix. 14. 6

Whenas—*Continued.*
when as he would to a snake againe Have turn'd himselfe, . V. ix. 19. 1
when as foes enforst, or friends sought ayde, ... V. ix. 30. 8
Which *when as* Zele perceived to abate, ... V. ix. 46. 7
All which *when as* the Prince had heard and seene, ... V. ix. 49. 1
Which uncouth use *when as* the Prince perceived, ... V. xi. 7. 1
Whereof *when as* the Gyant was aware, ... V. xi. 9. 5
when as she first beheld The armed Prince . . . . V. xi. 26. 1
When as necessitie doth it constraine.' . . . . V. xi. 56. 5
when as overblowen was that brunt, ... V. xi. 59. 1
when as nigh unto the shore they drew . . . . V. xii. 5. 2
Which cruell outrage *when as* Artegall Did well avize, . . . V. xii. 18. 1
Yet *when as* fit advantage he did spy, ... V. xii. 20. 1
When as two old ill favour'd Hags he met, ... V. xii. 28. 4
Whenas by chaunce he met uppon a day . . . . VI. i. 4. 3
whenas each of other had a sight, ... VI. i. 4. 6
When as by chaunce a comely Squire he found, ... VI. i. 11. 2
Whenas the Carle no longer could sustaine, ... VI. i. 22. 2
when as a Knight He spide come pricking on . . . . VI. i. 32. 8
when as he spyde A tall young man, ... VI. ii. 3. 6
Of all which *when as* she could nought deny, ... VI. ii. 14. 1
when as her he by no meanes could find, ... VI. ii. 21. 1
Which *when as* he perceiv'd he thus bespake: . . . . . . VI. ii. 47. 6
when as Calepine came to the brim, ... VI. iii. 34. 5
whenas he approched nigh in vew, ... VI. iii. 47. 3
when as Calepine was woxen strong, ... VI. iv. 17. 1
when as now long time he lacked had The good Sir Calepine, VI. v. 3. 1
when as no hope of his retourne She saw now left, ... VI. v. 7. 1
When as unwares he in the forrest heard . . . . VI. v. 21. 5
Whenas these Knights arriv'd, they wist not where nor how. . VI. v. 35. 9
when as with the dead He saw the ground all strow'd, . . . VI. vi. 24. 5
Whereof *whenas* the Prince was well aware, ... VI. vi. 27. 1
Whom *when as* Turpin saw so loosely layd, ... VI. vii. 20. 1
Which *when as* Cupid heard, he wexed wroth; . . . . . . VI. vii. 33. 6
When as the gentle Squire . . . Met her . . . . VI. vii. 39. 2
By Arthure, *when as* Unas Knight he did maintaine. . . . . VI. vii. 41. 9
when as he saw his Lord The witnesse of his wretchednesse . VI. viii. 5. 1
whenas Enias Beheld two such, ... VI. viii. 5. 7
Tho *when as* all her plaints she had displayd, ... VI. viii. 34. 1
when as all things readie were aright, ... VI. viii. 45. 1
One day, *when as* the shepheard swaynes together Were met VI. ix. 41. 1
when as Pastorella . . . Her flowry garlond tooke . . . . . VI. ix. 42. 5
when as they did dispose To practise games . . . . VI. ix. 43. 1
Unto this place *when as* the Elfin Knight Approcht, ... VI. x. 10. 1
when as he was dead, the fray gan ceasse; . . . . VI. xi. 20. 3
Tho, *when as* towards darksome night it drew, ... VI. xi. 41. 1
when as Calidore was comen in, ... VI. xi. 44. 1
At last, *when as* he found his force to shrincke . . . . . VI. xii. 34. 1
Whenas a storme hath dimd her trusty guyde, ... *Am.* xxxiv. 3
when as she most supposeth Her selfe assurd, ... *Am.* lviii. 3
whenas death shall all the world subdew, ... *Am.* lxxv. 13
when as day the heaven doth adorne, ... *Am.* lxxxvi. 5
when as night hath us of light forlorne, ... *Am.* lxxxvi. 7

Whence (*partial list*). *See* **From whence.**
My lookes to heaven *whence* all good gifts do come, ... *Bel.*[2] i. 8
And, mounting up againe from *whence* he came, ... *Ro.* xx. 5
Whence floweth Helicon, the learned well, ... *S.C.* Ap. 42
And also who, and *whence* that he were? . . . . *S.C.* May 261
And, *whence* thou camst, ... *S.C.* O. 84
'*Whence* is it, that the flouret of the field doth fade, ... *S.C.* N. 83
Of precious stones, *whence* no good commeth by; . . . . . *Gn.* 102
The Spartan Mirtle, *whence* sweet gumb does flowe; . . . . *Gn.* 669
T' enquire of custome, what and *whence* they were? . . . . *Hub.* 245
And doo returne from *whence* he first begun, ... *Hub.* 306
Wondring what mister wight he was, and *whence*: . . . . . *Hub.* 671
Whence, down descending, he along would flie . . . . . . *Mui.* 46
Not far from *whence* Sabrinaes streame doth flow, ... *D.* 101
Whence he them heares; . . . . *Col.* 881
When, weening to returne *whence* they did stray, ... I. i. 10. 3
let none aske *whence*, nor why. . . . . I. ix. 42. 9
Yett wist no creature *whence* that heverly sweet . . . . . I. xii. 39. 6
But *whence* should come that harme, ... II. iv. 40. 3
From *whence* it doth, as cloud from sea, aryse. . . . . . II. ix. 42. 5
But *whence* they sprong, or how they were begott, ... II. x. 8. 1
Whence as he to those woody hilles did fly, ... II. x. 33. 7
From *whence* eftsoones arrived here three hoyes Of Saxons, . II. x. 64. 8
whence that Musick seemed heard to bee, ... II. xii. 72. 1
seeking medicine *whence* she was stong, ... II. xii. 73. 3
Whence foorth it breakes in sighes and anguish ryfe, . . . III. ii. 32. 8
Whence spring all noble deedes and never dying fame: . . . III. iii. 1. 9
Or *whence* it sprong, ... III. iii. 16. 7
Chace her away, from *whence* she came, ... III. iv. 60. 6
From *whence* descend all hopelesse remedies: . . . . III. v. 34. 5
What mister wight that was, and *whence* deriv'd, ... III. vii. 14. 2
Whens dearely she with death bought her desire. . . . . . III. xi. 33. 5
Much wondred all men what or *whence* he came, ... IV. vi. 42. 1
But *whence* he was, or of what wombe ybore, ... IV. vii. 7. 7
Whence being forth produc'd, ... IV. ix. 7. 1
Now mote ye know . . . *whence* all this did proceede; . . . V. vi. 31. 7
And there arriv'd againe *whence* forth he set, ... V. xii. 28. 2
What and from *whence* she was, ... VI. v. 27. 7
For when the cause, *whence* evill doth arize, ... VI. vi. 14. 3
What mister men, and eke from *whence* they were: . . . . VI. xi. 39. 6
Whence art thou, ... VII. vi. 25. 8
heavens gate (*whence* all the gods issued) . . . . VII. vii. 45. 7
Cynthus hill, *whence* she her name did take; . . . . VII. vii. 50. 4
Of Helicon, *whence* she derived is; . . . . *Am.* i. 10
Whence they doe still behold the glorious face . . . . . . *H.H.B.* 80
From *whence* proceed her beames so pure and bright . . . *H.H.B.* 160

Whenceforth. *Whenceforth* issues a warlike steed in sight, . *Mui.* 316

Whenever. wreathed boughtes *when ever* he unfoldes, ... I. xi. 11. 3
When ever his fiers handes he free mote fynd: . . . . . . II. v. 28. 4
he did bestow Both guestes and meate, *when ever* in they came, II. ix. 28. 4
when ever he for ought did send; . . . . II. ix. 58. 5
when ever it were proov'd; . . . . II. x. 28. 4
When ever they their heavenly bowres forlore; . . . . . . II. xii. 52. 7
But she her selfe, *when ever* that she will, ... III. vi. 46. 8
When ever he this way shall passe by day or night.' . . . . IV. vi. 5. 9
Whose bodies chast, *when ever* in his powre . . . . IV. vii. 12. 6

Whenso. And *whenso* love of letters did inspire . . . . . . *Hub.* 829
When so thee list thy lofty Muse to raise: . . . . *Ded. Son.* viii. 12
he mote be found, *When so* he counseld . . . . III. iii. 7. 9
When so him list his enimies to fray; . . . . III. iii. 12. 7
When so the froward sky began to lowre; . . . . III. v. 51. 7
whenso her face She list discover, ... IV. ii. 44. 6
when so himselfe he found. . . . . IV. iv. 26. 9
But layd aside *when so* she usd her looser sport. . . . . . IV. v. 3. 9
It shall not fayle *when so* ye shall it need? . . . . IV. vi. 8. 8
When so it needs . . . . V. i. 7. 5
When so he list in wrath lift up his steely brand, ... V. i. 8. 9
When so she lagged, as she needs mote so, ... VI. ii. 10. 6
Her to adorne, *when so* she forth doth wend . . . . VI. x. 21. 8
But fayrest she, *when so* she doth display The gate . . . . *Am.* lxxxi. 9
When so ye come into those holy places, ... *Epith.* 213

Whensoever. *When* Astrophel *so ever* was away. . . . . . . *As.* 30
when so ever thou it up doest take, ... *As.* 197

Where (*partial list*). *See* **Anywhere, Eachwhere, Every-where, Nowhere, Otherwhere, Somewhere.**
'*Where* is (quoth she) this whilom honoured face? *Where* the great glorie . . . . *Bel.* x. 5, 6
Be it *where* the yerely starre doth scortch the ground, . . . *Ro.* xxvi. 7
Or *where* colde Boreas blowes his bitter stormes. . . . . . *Ro.* xxvi. 8
Spide *where* the Eagle built his towring nest, ... *Van.* iv. 6
Where have you seene the like but there? . . . . *S.C.* Ap. 72
Thou findest faulte *where* nys to be found, ... *S.C.* May 144
And from the fountaine, *where* they sat around, ... *S.C.* Jun. 60
But, when they came *where* thou thy skill didst showe, . . . *S.C.* Jun. 62
But feede his flocke in fields *where* falls hem best. . . . . *S.C.* Jun. 76
Where hast thou coverture? . . . . *S.C.* Jul. 26
The hylls *where* dwelled holy saints . . . . *S.C.* Jul. 113
O pierlesse Poesye! *where* is then thy place? . . . . *S.C.* O. 79
That *where* he rules all power he doth expell; . . . . . . *S.C.* O. 99
All musick sleepes, *where* death doth leade the daunce, . . . *S.C.* N. 105
Where bene the nosegayes that she dight for thee? . . . . . *S.C.* N. 114
How Phoebe fayles, *where* Venus sittes, and when. . . . . . *S.C.* D. 84
Springs Of Tempe! *where* the countrey Nymphs are rife, . . *Gn.* 146
Where then is now the guerdon of my paine? *Where* the reward *Gn.* 356, 357
Doo never see, *where* soules doo alwaies mourne; . . . . . *Gn.* 620
To seeke my fortune, *where* I may it mend: . . . . *Hub.* 88
Abroad, *where* change is, good may gotten bee.' . . . . . *Hub.* 101
They fled farre off, *where* none might them surprize; . . . *Hub.* 576
Lo! *where* they spide, how, in a gloomy glade, ... *Hub.* 951
Unto the forrest, *where* wilde beasts doo breed, ... *Hub.* 1248
And cast to seeke the Lion *where* he may, ... *Hub.* 1316
Where be the sweete delights of learnings treasure . . . . *T.M.* 175
Nigh *where* the goodly Verlame stood of yore, ... *Ti.* 3
Where be those learned wits and antique Sages, ... *Ti.* 59
Where those great warriors, which did overcome The world . *Ti.* 61
'And *where* is that same great seven-headded beast, ... *Ti.* 71
Where doth she all that wondrous welth nowe hide? . . . . *Ti.* 75
To highest heaven, *where* now he doth inherite All happinesse *Ti.* 383
To cast mine eye, *where* other sights I spide. . . . . . . *Ti.* 588
I beheld *where* stood A Knight . . . . *Ti.* 645
To live in heaven *where* happines is rife: . . . . *Ti.* 670
Till that you come *where* ye your vowes assoyle, ... *D.* 535
He sought, *where* salvage beasts do most abound. . . . . . *As.* 82
Ah! *where* were ye this while his shepheard peares, ... *As.* 127
Ah! *where* were ye, when he of you had need, ... *As.* 131
this same world *where* we do wone?' . . . . *Col.* 307
Ne looke for entertainement *where* none was; . . . . I. i. 35. 2
Where when all drownd in deadly sleepe he findes, ... I. i. 36. 6
low, *where* dawning day doth never peepe, His dwelling is; . I. i. 39. 5
And, comming *where* the knight in slomber lay, ... I. i. 47. 2
Come, see *where* your false Lady doth her honor staine.' . . I. ii. 4. 9
Where that false couple were full closely ment . . . . . . I. ii. 5. 4
So left her, *where* she now is turnd to treen mould. . . . . I. ii. 39. 9
Where have ye bene thus long out of my sight? . . . . . . I. iii. 27. 2
Where ever yet I be, my secret aide Shall follow you.' . . . I. iv. 51. 8
Lo! *where* the stout Sansjoy doth sleepe in deadly shade. . . I. v. 22. 9
Where many soules sit wailing woefully, ... I. v. 33. 2
Where when she came, she found the Faery knight . . . . . I. v. 45. 3
Where he unwares the fairest Una found, ... I. vi. 30. 6
'*Where* is,' (said Satyrane) 'that Paynims sonne, ... I. vi. 39. 5
Arriv'd *wher* they in erth their fruitles blood had sown. . . I. vi. 45. 9
Then rip up griefe *where* it may not availe: . . . . I. vii. 39. 8
'Despaire breeds not,' (quoth he) '*where* faith is staid.' . . . I. vii. 41. 7
Where have yee left your lord that could so well you tosse? . I. vii. 48. 9
And gently askt, *where* all the people bee, ... I. viii. 32. 3
Again he askt, *where* that same knight was layd, ... I. viii. 32. 6
Where entred in, his foot could find no flore, ... I. viii. 39. 7
Loe! *where* your foe lies strecht in monstrous length; . . . . I. viii. 45. 3
nought but pressed gras *where* she had lyen, ... I. ix. 15. 2
they come *where* that same wicked wight His dwelling has, . I. ix. 33. 1
they enter, *where* they find That cursed man, ... I. ix. 35. 1
Where justice growes, there grows eke greater grace, ... I. ix. 53. 6
Where, when that fairest Una she beheld, ... I. x. 8. 6
The deare Charissa, *where* is she become? . . . . I. x. 16. 2
In hevenly throne, *where* thousand Angels shine? . . . . . I. x. 51. 6
'What need of armes, *where* peace doth ay remaine,' . . . . I. x. 62. 7
And left not any marke *where* it did light, ... I. xi. 25. 4

Where—*Continued.*	
Behynd his backe, unweeting, *where* he stood,	I. xi. 29. 2
Where is that happy land of Faery,	II. Pr. 1. 7
Where may that treachour then,' (sayd he) 'be found,	II. i. 12. 6
he had found *Where* she did wander in waste wildernesse,	II. i. 22. 2
Where you he made the marke of his intent,	II. i. 30. 8
And now is fled: foule shame him follow *wher* he went!'	II. i. 30. 9
The cursed land *where* many wend amis,	II. i. 51. 8
He is convaide; but how, or *where,* here fits not tell.	II. ii. 11. 9
Where whenas two brave knightes in bloody fight	II. ii. 21. 3
And *where* he hits nought knowes,	II. iv. 7. 9
Woe never wants *where* every cause is caught;	II. iv. 44. 6
'Then loe! *wher* bound she sits,	II. iv. 44. 8
where he them bound did see,	II. v. 18. 8
where Titan his face never shewes.	II. v. 27. 9
where hath he hong up his mortall blade,	II. v. 35. 7
where that same warlike Lord She in receiv'd;	II. vi. 4. 7
Where soone he slumbred fearing not be harmd:	II. vi. 14. 8
is come to that same place *where* first she wefte.	II. vi. 18. 9
that wide strond *Where* she was rowing,	II. vi. 19. 3
where him she byding fond	II. vi. 19. 5
Where sleeping late she lefte her other knight.	II. vi. 22. 4
Where noise of armes . . . Might not revive desire	II. vi. 25. 8
where love does give his sweet Alarmes Without bloodshed,	II. vi. 34. 7
where the enimy Does yield unto his foe	II. vi. 34. 8
he spide *where* towards him did pace Two Paynim knights	II. viii. 10. 1
But ere the point arrived *where* it ought,	II. viii. 32. 4
Where now on earth, or how, he may be fownd;	III. ii. 14. 2
Where is the Antique glory now become,	III. iv. 1. 1
Finding the Nymph asleepe in secret *wheare,*	III. iv. 19. 7
read, Sir, how I may her finde, or *where?*'	III. v. 6. 9
askt him *where* and when	V. ii. 3. 7
these Knights arriv'd, they wist not *where* nor how.	VI. v. 35. 9
not caring *where* nor when.	VI. xii. 27. 9
Where none doo fishes take;	*Epith.* 61
Loe! *where* she comes along with portly pace,	*Epith.* 148
Where thou doest sit in Venus lap above,	*H.L.* 24
Where they doe feede on Nectar heavenly-wize,	*H.L.* 282
Whereas. when you come *whereas* shee is in place,	*S.C.* Ap. 131
In tho countryes, *whereas* I have bene,	*S.C.* S. 32
Or *whereas* mount Parnasse, the Muses brood,	*Gn.* 21
Whereas continuall shade is to be seene,	*Gn.* 118
Whereas his temples did his creast-front tyre;	*Gn.* 308
Whereas thou maist compound a better penie,	*Hub.* 523
Whereas he saw, that sorely griev'd his hart,	*Hub.* 1304
Whereas no worlds sad care nor wasting woe	*D.* 283
Where as the lucklesse boy yet bleeding lay;	*As.* 142
whereas her mother blynd Sate in eternall night:	I. iii. 12. 3
Whereas an errant knight in armes ycled,	I. iv. 38. 4
the place *whereas* the Paynim lay,	I. v. 29. 2
Phlegeton, *Whereas* the damned ghosts	I. v. 33. 4
the place had ghest, *Whereas* that Pagan proud	I. vi. 40. 5
she fownd, *whereas* he wearie sate	I. vii. 2. 6
Whereas he meant his corrosives to apply,	I. x. 25. 8
he saw *whereas* did swim Along the shore,	II. vi. 2. 5
Whereas he sitting found in secret shade	II. vii. 3. 3
Now bene they come *whereas* the Palmer sate,	II. viii. 11. 6
approched to the sted *Whereas* those Mermayds dwelt:	II. xii. 30. 2
Whereas the Bowre of Blisse was situate;	II. xii. 42. 2
Rich strond to travell, *whereas* he did wonne,	III. iv. 20. 8
whereas she playd Amongst her watry sisters	III. iv. 29. 6
Shortly she came *whereas* that wofull Squire,	III. v. 29. 1
Whereas she found the Goddesse with her crew,	III. vi. 17. 2
shady covert *whereas* lay Faire Crysogone	III. vi. 26. 6
At length he spyde *whereas* that wofull Squyre,	III. vii. 45. 6
Whereas the hungry Spaniells she does spye	III. viii. 33. 6
For lo! in heven, *whereas* all goodnes is,	III. ix. 2. 6
Whereas his lovely wife emongst them lay,	III. x. 48. 2
Whereas no living creature he mistooke,	III. xi. 13. 4
Till they arriv'd *whereas* their purpose they did plott.	III. xi. 20. 9
Whereas no gate they found them to withhold,	III. xi. 21. 3
There, *whereas* all the plagues and harmes abound	IV. i. 20. 2
where as their powre They felt,	IV. iii. 15. 4
Beheld, *whereas* he stood not farre aside,	IV. vi. 24. 2
Whereas that wofull man in languor did abide.	IV. viii. 11. 9
At length they came *whereas* a troupe of Knights	IV. ix. 20. 1
Where as my love was lodged day and night,	IV. x. 29. 4
In that same place *whereas* it now doth lie.	V. i. 18. 7
But by that Bridge *whereas* he doth abide:	V. ii. 10. 7
in the midst, *whereas* they brest to brest Should meete,	V. ii. 12. 5
At length found out *whereas* she hidden lay Under	V. ii. 25. 5
chaunst to come *whereas* two comely Squires,	V. iv. 4. 2
the lower parts . . . *Whereas* the Priestes she found	V. vii. 17. 7
the place . . . *Where as* so many knights had	V. x. 30. 9
At last they came *whereas* that Ladie bode,	V. xi. 60. 1
Whereas they readie found, them to repell, Great hostes of men	V. xii. 4. 7
To doe most dammage *where as* most they ment:	V. xii. 17. 4
a wood, *whereas* a Ladie . . . Sate with a knight	VI. ii. 16. 4
some forrein land, *where as* no need Of dreaded daunger	VI. ii. 29. 8
Came to the place *whereas* ye heard afore	VI. ii. 40. 4
to come *whereas* a jolly Knight . . . did safely rest,	VI. iii. 20. 2
the place, *whereas* he last Had left that couple	VI. iv. 9. 4
Whereas his love was sitting all alone,	VI. vi. 30. 2
whereas in evill tyde That other swayne . . . Lay	VI. vii. 17. 7
Whereas the Prince himselfe lay all alone,	VI. vii. 18. 7
whereas his Lord he sleeping vew'd.	VI. vii. 23. 9
brought Unto the barre *whereas* she was arrayned;	VI. vii. 36. 2
Whereas this Lady, like a sheepe astray, . . . lay.	VI. viii. 36. 8
Whereas the Heardes were keeping of their neat,	VI. ix. 4. 2
whereas the thiefe Lay sleeping soundly	VI. xi. 38. 3
Whereas—*Continued.*	
soone he came *where-as* the Titanesse Was striving	VII. vi. 17. 2
that *where-as* shee had out of measure Long lov'd	VII. vi. 44. 3
And, running straight *where-as* she heard his voice,	VII. vi. 47. 3
Finding *where-as* some wicked beast unware	VII. vi. 48. 3
And let the ground *whereas* her foot shall tread,	*Epith.* 48
when you come *whereas* my love doth lie,	*Epith.* 65
whereas the royall Seates . . . are set,	*H.H.B.* 89
when they came, *whereas* those bricky towres	*Proth.* 132
Whereat. *Whereat* the Foxe, deep groning in his sprite,	*Hub.* 588
and pusht with paine, *Whereat* he gan to stretch;	I. i. 42. 5
whereat he gan to quake,	I. i. 43. 3
Whereat he wondred much,	I. x. 56. 6
Whereat renfierst with wrath and sharp regret,	II. viii. 45. 1
Whereat they, burning both with fervent fire	II. ix. 60. 6
Whereat Excesse exceedingly was wroth,	II. xii. 57. 6
'*Whereat* Cadwallin wroth shall forth issew,	III. iii. 39. 1
Whereat she wondred much, but would not stay	III. iv. 18. 7
Whereat soft knocking entrance he desyrd.	III. ix. 10. 1
Whereat he gan to wex exceeding wroth,	III. ix. 13. 6
(*whereat* he raves With roring rage,	III. ix. 45. 3
Whereat she sore affrayd, yet her besought	IV. ii. 50. 1
Whereat they shewed curteous countenaunce.	IV. iv. 7. 5
Whereat full inly wroth was Triamond,	IV. iv. 45. 1
Whereat the rest gan greatly to envie,	IV. v. 19. 6
Whereat the Prince full wrath his strong right hand	IV. viii. 43. 1
Whereat her heart was fild with hope and drede,	V. vi. 8. 7
Whereat the other starting up dismayd,	VI. ii. 18. 6
Whereat Sir Calidore did much delight,	VI. ii. 36. 6
Whereat, much griev'd against that straunger knight,	VI. vii. 20. 6
Whereat the Prince awaking, when he spyde	VI. vii. 25. 1
Whereat they shouted all, and made a loud alarme.	VI. viii. 45. 9
Whereat the knight amaz'd yet did not rest,	VI. xi. 28. 7
Where-at the starres, which round about her blazed,	VII. vi. 13. 6
Where-at the Titanesse did sternly lower,	VII. vi. 18. 4
Whereby. Strange bird he was, *whereby* I thought anone,	*Pet.* v. 3
Whereby by chaunce I him knewe.	*S.C.* Mar. 36
Whereby the Ape in wondrous stomack woxe,	*Hub.* 1103
Whereby close fire into his heart does creepe:	II. v. 34. 7
Whereby her course is stopt and passage staid:	II. ix. 8. 4
whereby It was avoided quite,	II. ix. 32. 8
whereby ye may her know,	III. v. 8. 8
Whereby great riches, gathered manie a day,	IV. i. 29. 5
Whereby the name of knight-hood thou dost shend,	IV. i. 51. 3
whereby all cares forepast Are washt away	IV. iii. 44. 6
Whereby the passion grew more fierce and faine,	IV. vi. 33. 8
Which she forgot, *whereby* excuse to make;	IV. vi. 45. 8
whereby she might aread What mister wight he was,	IV. viii. 13. 5
Whereby she might apply some medicine;	IV. xii. 21. 5
Whereby to seeke some meanes it to appease.	IV. xii. 22. 3
Whereby his strengthes assay he might him teach.	V. viii. 37. 5
whereby Of all those crymes she there indited was:	VI. vii. 35. 1
enlumineth the . . . aire, *whereby* al things are red;	*H.H.B.* 165
Wherefore. 'It is not Hobbinol *wherefore* I plaine,	*S.C.* Ja. 55
'*Wherefore,* my pype, albee rude Pan thou please,	*S.C.* Ja. 67
Wherefore soone I rede thee hence remove,	*S.C.* F. 137
Wherefore with myne thou dare thy musick matche?	*S.C.* Au. 2
Wherefore ye Sisters, which the glorie bee	*Gn.* 25
wherefore, doth me upbrayd With breach of love	I. xii. 31. 4
'*Wherefore,* if me thou deigne to serve and sew,	II. vii. 9. 1
Wherefore Morddure it rightfully is hight.	II. viii. 21. 6
wherefore he now begunne To challenge her	IV. iv. 8. 5
Wherefore the Lady, which Irena hight,	V. i. 4. 1
wherefore Betwixt you two began this strife	VI. ii. 8. 8
Wherefore he stayd, till that he nearer drew,	VI. iii. 47. 1
Wherefore it now behoves us to advise	VII. vi. 21. 6
Wherefore . . . who can deny	VII. vii. 47. 8
Wherefore doth vaine antiquitie so vaunt Her ancient monuments	*Com. Son.* iii. 1
Wherein. Thy mantle mard, *wherein* thou maskedst	*S.C.* Ja. 24
trees, . . . *Wherein* the byrds	*S.C.* Ja. 32
hower *Wherein* I longd the neighbour towne to see,	*S.C.* Ja. 50
stoure *Wherein* I sawe so fayre a sight	*S.C.* Ja. 52
songs, *wherein* he all outwent.	*S.C.* Ap. 16
glasse . . . *Wherein* while Kiddie unwares did looke,	*S.C.* May 275
Medway . . . *Wherein* the Nymphes doe bathe;	*S.C.* Jul. 80
A mazer . . . *Wherein* is enchased	*S.C.* Au. 27
cloudes, . . . *Wherein* the lightsome levin shroudes,	*S.C.* Au. 87
Wherein my plaints did oftentimes resound:	*S.C.* Au. 152
Wherein old dints of deepe woundes did remaine,	I. i. 1. 3
wherin there breed Ten thousand kindes of creatures,	I. i. 21. 6
Wherein ye have great glory wonne this day,	I. i. 27. 6
Wherein the Hermite dewly wont to say	I. i. 34. 6
Wherein her face she often vewed fayne,	I. iv. 10. 7
wherein with letters red, Was writt	I. iv. 38. 5
Wherein the chearefull birds of sundry kynd	I. vii. 3. 4
Wherein captiv'd, of life or death he stood in doubt.	I. vii. 26. 9
Wherein were closd few drops of liquor pure,	I. ix. 19. 3
wherein his Saveours testament Was writt	I. ix. 19. 7
Witnes the dungeon deepe, *wherein* of late	I. ix. 45. 5
Wherein darke things were writt,	I. x. 13. 9
Wherein his weaker wandring steps to guyde,	I. x. 34. 1
Wherein an aged holy man did lie,	I. x. 46. 5
Wherein eternall peace and happinesse doth dwell.	I. x. 55. 9
Out of the well, *wherein* he drenched lay:	I. xi. 34. 2
that holy water dew *Wherein* he fell,	I. xi. 36. 3
Wherein she used hath the practicke paine	I. xii. 34. 5
Wherein were many tables fayre dispred,	II. ix. 27. 2
Wherein th' Aegyptian Phao long did lurke	III. ii. 20. 3
wherein the sicke Damosell So straungely vewed	III. iii. 6. 2

Wherein—*Continued.*
Wherein my feeble barke is tossed long Far . . . III. iv. 8. 2
thicke woods *wherein* he would have hid . . . III. v. 13. 7
how the ground he kist *Wherein* it written was, . . . IV. vii. 46. 9
Wherein the honor both of Armes ye shame, . . . IV. ix. 37. 4
wherein make abode So many learned impes, . . . IV. xi. 26. 4
the Temple, *wherein* she was plast, . . . V. xi. 28. 4
Out of the countrie *wherein* I was bred, . . . VI. ii. 30. 3
Through all the inner parts, *wherein* they dwelt; . . . VI. x. 42. 6
He, through the wealth *wherein* he did abound, . . . VI. xii. 4. 4
the watry foules a certaine grange *Wherein* to rest, . . . VII. vii. 21. 8
Whereof. *Whereof* the bases were of richest golde, . . . *Bel.*[1] iv. 2
The sight *whereof* dyd make my heart rejoyce . . . *Pet.*[1] iv. 8
(*Whereof* he wil be wroken) . . . *S.C.* Mar. 108
The floddes *whereof* shall them overflowe . . . *S.C.* May 94
The fame *whereof* doth dayly greater growe . . . *S.C.* Jun. 92
Whereof still somewhat to his share did rize: . . . *Hub.* 806
The roote *whereof* and tragicall effect, . . . *Mui.* 9
Whereof the Goddesse gathering jealous feare, . . . *Mui.* 129
The staie *whereof* shall nought these eares annoy, . . . *Col.* 98
At sound *whereof,* they all for their relief . . . *Col.* 246
Like to an horne, *whereof* the name it has, . . . *Col.* 282
With price *whereof* they buy a golden bell, . . . *Col.* 725
For want *whereof* poore people oft did pyne: . . . I. iv. 21. 7
With dread *whereof* his chacing steedes aghast . . . I. v. 38. 4
Whereof he weend possessed soone to bee, . . . I. vi. 5. 4
Of th' high descent *whereof* he was yborne, . . . I. vii. 10. 2
The light *whereof,* that hevens light did pas, . . . I. viii. 19. 3
On top *whereof* ay dwelt the ghastly Owle, . . . I. ix. 33. 6
The sight *whereof* so throughly him dismaid, . . . I. ix. 50. 1
On top *whereof* a sacred chappell was, . . . I. x. 46. 3
Whereof the keies are to thy hand behight . . . I. x. 50. 7
Whereof Georgos he thee gave to name; . . . I. x. 66. 6
The heate *whereof,* and harmefull pestilence, . . . I. xi. 45. 1
Whereof great vertues over-all were redd; . . . I. xi. 46. 4
Whereof whoso did eat, eftsoones did know . . . I. xi. 47. 7
Whereof he crav'd redresse . . . II. ii. 43. 5
With noyse *whereof* he from his loftie steed . . . II. iii. 21. 2
The joyes *whereof* and happy fruitfulnesse, . . . II. vi. 24. 3
The traine *whereof* loose far behind her strayd, . . . II. ix. 19. 3
Whereof king Nine whilome built Babell towre . . . II. ix. 21. 6
Whereof great trouble in the kingdome grew, . . . II. x. 54. 2
By meanes *whereof* their uncle Vortigere . . . II. x. 64. 2
At sight *whereof* the people stand aghast; . . . III. i. 16. 7
Whereof did grow her first engraffed payne, . . . III. ii. 17. 5
Whereof she seemes ashamed inwardly: . . . III. iii. 20. 7
With hevenly seed, *whereof* wise Paeon sprong) . . . III. iv. 41. 6
Whereof conceiving shame and foule disgrace, . . . III. vi. 10. 1
And borrow matter *whereof* they are made; . . . III. vi. 37. 2
The sight *whereof* did greatly him adaw, . . . III. vii. 13. 4
With thought *whereof* exceeding mad he grew, . . . III. viii. 4. 1
The substance, *whereof* she the body made, . . . III. viii. 6. 1
The sight *whereof* in his congealed flesh . . . III. viii. 25. 1
The privie guilt *whereof* makes him alway . . . III. ix. 5. 3
For griefe *whereof,* ye mote have lively seene . . . III. xi. 37. 6
The moniments *whereof* there byding beene, . . . IV. i. 24. 8
The hurts *whereof* me now from battell stay, . . . IV. i. 40. 4
By meanes *whereof* he hath him lightly overborne . . . IV. ii. 6. 9
Whereof full blith eftsoones his mightie hand . . . IV. iii. 33. 1
Whereof, full glad for thirst, ech drunk an harty draught; . IV. iii. 48. 9
Whereof when newes to Triamond was brought . . . IV. iv. 33. 1
The end *whereof* and daungerous event . . . IV. v. 46. 6
The feare *whereof* seem'd much her to affray; . . . IV. vi. 45. 4
The signe *whereof* yet stain'd his bloudy lips . . . IV. vii. 5. 9
(*Whereof* it hight) and, having shortly tride . . . IV. viii. 31. 7
'*Whereof* when tydings came unto mine eare, . . . IV. viii. 55. 1
Whereof I glad did not gaine say nor strive, . . . IV. viii. 56. 8
Whereof I sorie, yet myselfe did bend . . . IV. viii. 57. 3
his hindparts, *whereof* heed I tooke, . . . IV. x. 20. 3
Whereof conceiving, she in time forth brought . . . IV. xi. 42. 7
The thought *whereof* empierst his hart . . . IV. xii. 19. 6
The instrument *whereof* . . . V. Pr. 11. 9
In goodly wise, *whereof* it tooke his name, . . . V. i. 10. 4
That I mote drinke the cup *whereof* she dranke, . . . V. i. 15. 7
The sight *whereof* the Lady sore adrad, . . . V. i. 22. 7
With noise *whereof* the Lady forth appeared . . . V. ii. 22. 1
For want *whereof* he weighed vanity, . . . V. ii. 30. 7
They turne to that *whereof* they first were made? . . . V. ii. 40. 7
The sight *whereof* did all with gladnesse fill: . . . V. iii. 15. 1
For proofe *whereof* he bad them Florimell forth call . . . V. iii. 22. 9
Whereof to make due tryall, one did take . . . V. iii. 33. 1
Whereof no braver president this day . . . V. iv. 2. 6
Instead *whereof* she made him to be dight . . . V. v. 20. 6
With sight *whereof* she was dismayd right sore, . . . V. vi. 28. 1
The skill *whereof* to Princes hearts he doth reveale . . . V. vii. 1. 9
Whereof I have to treat here presently: . . . V. vii. 3. 5
'The end *whereof,* and all the long event, . . . V. vii. 22. 1
Whereof when newes to Radigund was brought, . . . V. vii. 25. 1
Whereof there was great store, and armors bright, . . . V. vii. 41. 4
The care *whereof,* and hope of his successe, . . . V. vii. 44. 6
With noyse *whereof* when as the caytive carle . . . V. ix. 9. 1
The cry *whereof* entring the hollow cave . . . V. ix. 10. 1
With the neare touch *whereof* in tender hart . . . V. ix. 46. 1
Whether this heavenly thing *whereof* I treat, . . . V. x. 1. 2
Whereof she glad, now needing strong defence, . . . V. x. 12. 6
By meanes *whereof* she did at last commit . . . V. x. 13. 1
Whereof that Tyrant had her now deprived, . . . V. x. 18. 3
Whereof when newes was to that Tyrant brought, . . . V. xi. 2. 1
Whereof when as the Gyant was aware, . . . V. xi. 9. 5
Whereof she now more glad then sory earst, . . . VI. i. 45. 1

Whereof—*Continued.*
Whereof he taking oddes, . . . VI. ii. 18. 4
Whereof befell what now is in your sight.' . . . VI. ii. 23. 4
Whereof she now bethinking, gan t' advize . . . VI. iii. 8. 6
The juyce *whereof* into his wound he wrought, . . . VI. iv. 12. 8
his young charge *whereof* he skilled nought, . . . VI. iv. 38. 2
With noise *whereof* the Squire, now nigh aghast, . . . VI. v. 21. 8
Whereof exceeding glad he to him drew, . . . VI. v. 23. 3
The meede *whereof* shall shortly be thy shame, . . . VI. vi. 25. 6
Whereof whenas the Prince was well aware, . . . VI. vi. 27. 1
Whereof thou, caytive, so unworthie art, . . . VI. vi. 33. 6
The coward Turpine, *whereof* now I treat; . . . VI. vii. 2. 2
In lieu *whereof* he would to him descrie . . . VI. vii. 12. 3
The beames *whereof* did kindle lovely fire . . . VI. vii. 28. 8
The end *whereof* Ile keepe untill another cast . . . VI. viii. 51. 9
'With sight *whereof* soone cloyd, and long deluded . . . VI. ix. 25. 1
The glaunce *whereof* their dimmed eies would daze, . . . VI. x. 4. 3
At sight *whereof* his barbarous heart was fired, . . . VI. xi. 4. 1
By meanes *whereof* she would not him permit . . . VI. xi. 8. 1
By means *whereof,* that mote not be amended, . . . VI. xi. 19. 5
Whereof right glad they seem'd, and offer made . . . VI. xi. 40. 1
Whereof they both full glad and blyth did rest, . . . VI. xi. 41. 8
With noyse *whereof* the theefe awaking light . . . VI. xi. 43. 4
Whereof she long had lackt the wishfull sight, . . . VI. xi. 50. 5
Whereof was Lord the good Sir Bellamoure; . . . VI. xii. 3. 4
Whereof her wombe, unwist to wight, was fraught, . . . VI. xii. 6. 4
Whereof her name ye then to her did give . . . VI. xii. 18. 6
a mace, On top *whereof* the moon and stars were pight; . . VII. vii. 44. 6
The light *whereof* hath kindled heavenly fyre . . . *Am.* iii. 3
With noyse *whereof* the quyre of Byrds . . . *Am.* xix. 5
At sight *whereof,* each bird . . . Comes forth . . . *Am.* xl. 9
Whereof she mote be made, that is, the skye . . . *Am.* lv. 10
The sparkes *whereof* let kindle thine own fyre, . . . *Am.* lxxxv. 9
Whereof some glance doth in mine eie remayne . . . *Am.* lxxxvii. 8
Whereof when he was wakened with the noyse, . . . *Epig.* iv. 5
In sight *whereof* all other blisse seemes vaine: . . . *H.L.* 208
The feare *whereof,* O how doth it torment . . . *H.L.* 252
In lieu *whereof* graunt, O great Soveraine! . . . *H.B.* 274
With sence *whereof,* . . . Lift up thy mind . . . *H.H.L.* 253
By view *whereof* it plainly may appeare, . . . *H.H.B.* 43
stars . . . *Whereof* each other doth in brightnesse passe, . . *H.H.B.* 54
Whereof such wondrous pleasures they conceave, . . . *H.H.B.* 256
Whereon. *Whereon* the Troyan prince spilt Turnus blood . . *Bel.*[2] ix. 8
Whereon he earst had taught his flocks to feede, . . . *S.C.* O. 57
And is there other then *whereon* we stand?' . . . *Col.* 291
Whereon nor fruit nor leafe was ever seene, . . . I. ix. 34. 2
Whereon thy innocent feet doe ever tread! . . . I. x. 9. 2
Whereon she leaned ever, as befell; . . . I. x. 14. 7
That drowned all the land *whereon* he stood; . . . I. xi. 22. 5
And kist the ground *whereon* his foot was pight; . . . I. xii. 25. 7
No braunch *whereon* a fine bird did not sitt; . . . II. vi. 13. 2
Whereon the Faery Queenes pourtract was writt,) . . . II. viii. 43. 3
Whereon the ruines of great Ossa hill, . . . II. x. 3. 3
Whereon faire Florimell was wont to ride, . . . III. vii. 31. 2
The Palfrey *whereon* she did travell slew, . . . III. viii. 49. 3
Uprear'd her from the ground *whereon* she lay, . . . VI. iii. 27. 8
I greater am in bloud (*whereon* I build) . . . VII. vi. 26. 8
Whereon he rode not easie was to deeme; . . . VII. vii. 40. 7
Where's. *wheres* no courage, theres no ruth nor mone . . . VI. vii. 18. 5
Whereso. *Where so* us listeth, uncontrol'd of anie: . . . *Hub.* 169
Where-so (**where so*) he be, . . . II. i. 18. 4
feare them followes still *where so* they beene . . . II. iii. 20. 3
Throughout the world, *wher-so* they might be found, . . . II. iii. 38. 6
To seeke Occasion, *where so* she bee: . . . II. iv. 43. 6
By sea, by land, *where so* they may be mett, . . . III. ii. 7. 3
Whereso he heares that any doth confownd . . . III. ii. 14. 7
To search her forth *where so* she might be fond, . . . III. x. 19. 2
To Ladies love, *where so* he came in place, . . . IV. iv. 4. 4
And all that while, *where so* they rode or came, . . . IV. iv. 13. 3
where so loose or happy that thou art, . . . IV. xii. 11. 6
it would pierce or cleave, *where so* it came, . . . V. i. 10. 7
every place *Where so* he fled, . . . V. ix. 16. 5
Full deadly wounds *where so* it is empight; . . . V. xi. 24. 6
Unto all errant knights, *whereso* on ground; . . . VI. i. 42. 8
through all the wood, *where so* he wist She hidden was, . . . VI. ii. 20. 8
Where so he went, but after him did make . . . VI. vi. 29. 5
him *where so* he were would seeke . . . VI. vii. 13. 9
follow through the world *where so* he went, . . . VI. vii. 21. 8
That all the people, *where so* he did go, . . . VI. xii. 37. 3
Wheresoe'er. That wondrous Paterne, *wheresoere* it bee, . . *H.B.* 36
Wheresoever. and fly forth unto my Love *whersoever* she be: . *U.V.* 3
That body, *wheresoever* that it light, . . . III. ii. 45. 8
wheresoever he did himselfe dispose, . . . IV. v. 40. 7
wheresoever it did light, it throughly shard . . . V. i. 10. 9
wheresoever they comment the same, . . . VII. vii. 53. 7
Whereto. *Wherto* approched not in anie wise . . . *Pet.* iv. 3
Whereto they dauncen, eche one with his mayd . . . *S.C.* May 24
Whereto thou list their trayned willes entice . . . *S.C.* O. 24
The onely upshot *whereto* he doth ayme: . . . *Hub.* 770
Awaite *whereto* their service he applyes, . . . I. i. 38. 4
Whereto whenas they now approched neare, . . . I. xi. 1. 4
On the long voiage *whereto* she is bent: . . . I. xii. 42. 8
Whereto he drew in hast it to agree . . . II. iv. 3. 4
Whereto that single knight did answere frame: . . . III. i. 24. 1
whereto though she did bend Her earnest minde, . . . III. xi. 54. 8
Whereto her selfe he did to witnesse call; . . . IV. v. 23. 8
Whereto great comfort in her sad misfare . . . IV. v. 30. 4
Whereto approaching nigh they heard the sound . . . IV. v. 33. 6
Whereto thus Scudamour: 'Small . . . IV. vi. 4. 1
Could that atchieve *whereto* he did aspire, . . . IV. vi. 43. 6

Whereto—*Continued.*
of the perils *whereto* he was bound, . . . IV. vi. 45. 3
Whereto full loth was he, ne would for ought Consent . . . IV. viii. 58. 5
Whereto her bashful shamefastnesse ywrought . . . V. iii. 23. 3
Whereto she ever list to make her hardy flight. . . . V. xi. 24. 9
Whereto . . . my presence he did spy To be a let, . . . VI. ii. 17. 4
tell me *whereto* can ye lyken it; . . . *Am.* xl. 2
at last arive To the most faire, *whereto* they all do strive. . *H.H.B.* 77
Whereunto. Next *whereunto* there stands a stately place, . . . *Proth.* 137
Whereupon. the courser *whereuppon* he rad Could swim . . . V. ii. 13. 8
Wherever. Flye to my love, *where ever* that she bee, . . . *S.C.* Jun. 99
To take his owne *where ever* it laye? . . . *S.C.* S. 209
'For shee in field, *where-ever* I did wend, . . . *D.* 127
where ever thou doest finde the same, . . . *As.* 195
Where ever yet I be, . . . I. iv. 51. 8
Where ever he that godly knight may fynd . . . II. i. 2. 3
Where ever that on ground they mote him find: . . . II. viii. 11. 2
Perforce her carried *where ever* he thought best. . . . III. vii. 2. 9
where ever it in field was showne. . . . III. xi. 7. 9
Be thou, *where ever* thou do go or ryde, . . . IV. i. 51. 8
Equall to this, *where ever* I have gone. . . . IV. vii. 14. 5
where ever she be straide, . . . IV. ix. 38. 8
Where ever in the darke he could them spie, . . . V. vi. 30. 5
where ever she it fond. . . . V. vii. 30. 9
He him pursewd *where ever* that he went; . . . V. ix. 16. 3
He shund his strokes, *where ever* they did fall, . . . V. xii. 18. 3
Therefore *where-ever* that thou doest behold . . . *H.B.* 134
Wherewith. *Wherewith* she languisht as the gathered floure; . *Pet.* vi. 9
Instede of bloosmes, *wherewith* your buds did flowre; . . . *S.C.* Ja. 34
Where-with my fresh flowretts bene defast: . . . *S.C.* F. 182
Wherewith they sette all the world on fire; . . . *S.C.* S. 87
Wherewith enrag'd he fiercely gan upstart, . . . *Gn.* 289
Wherewith we may our selves (if we thinke good) . . . *Hub.* 970
Of that high powre, *wherewith* thou art possest. . . . *Col.* 826
Wherewith her grypt her gorge with so great paine, . . . I. i. 19. 8
Wherewith he goeth to that soveraine Queene; . . . I. v. 16. 1
Wherewith he al enrag'd these bitter speaches said . . . I. vi. 46. 9
His mortall mace, *wherewith* his foemen he dismayde. . . . I. vii. 10. 9
Wherewith enmovd, these bleeding words she gan to say. . . I. vii. 38. 9
for such perill past *Wherewith* you to reward? . . . I. viii. 27. 4
golden chayne, *wherewith* yfere The vertues linked . . . I. ix. 1. 1
Wherewith the martiall troupes thou doest infest, . . . I. xi. 6. 3
Wherewith the stiffe beame quaked as affrayd, . . . I. xi. 20. 5
Wherewith he fiersly did his foe assaile, . . . I. xi. 42. 3
Wherewith her heavenly beautie she did hide, . . . I. xii. 22. 4
Wherewith above all knights ye goodly seeme aguizd! . . II. i. 31. 9
Wherewith she makes her lovers dronken mad; . . . II. i. 52. 2
wherewith she queld The salvage beastes . . . II. iii. 29. 3
Wherewith reviv'd, this answere forth he threw: . . . II. iii. 33. 1
Sometimes she raught him stones, *wherwith* to smite, . . . II. iv. 5. 5
Wherewith he smote his haughty crest so hye, . . . II. v. 12. 4
Wherewith astonisht, still he stood as sencelesse stone. . . II. vi. 31. 9
arrowes, *wherewith* he doth fill The world . . . II. viii. 6. 3
wherwith to ground He groveling fell, . . . II. viii. 32. 8
For all the sinnes *wherewith* his lewd life did abound. . . II. viii. 45. 9
His cruel bow, *wherewith* he thousands hath dismayd. . . . II. ix. 34. 9
Wherewith all new-come guests he gratyfide: . . . II. xii. 49. 5
Wherewith her mother Art, as halfe in scorne . . . II. xii. 50. 6
Wherewith she sighed soft, as if his case she rewd. . . . II. xii. 73. 9
Wherewith imperious love her hart did vexe, . . . III. i. 54. 4
eternal lampes, *wherewith* high Jove Doth light . . . III. i. 57. 6
Wherewith enrag'd she fiercely at them flew, . . . III. i. 66. 1
Wherewith dame Nature doth her beautify, . . . III. vi. 30. 2
Wherewith she many had of life depriv'd; . . . III. vii. 40. 2
Wherewith he was so stund that he n'ote ryde, . . . III. vii. 42. 6
Quite of all hope *wherewith* he long had fedd . . . III. viii. 3. 8
And spoiles *wherewith* he all the ground did strow, . . . III. xi. 45. 7
Wherewith the Craftesman wonts it beautify, . . . III. xii. 20. 3
Wherewith the worlds faire beautie she hath blent: . . . III. xii. 29. 5
chaine, *wherewith* not long ygoe He bound . . . III. xii. 41. 6
Wherewith the hellish fiends he doth confound: . . . IV. iii. 42. 7
Those yron fetters *wherewith* he was gyv'd, . . . V. iv. 35. 3
Wherewith though wondrous wroth, and inly burning . . . V. vi. 31. 1
Wherewith the Souldan all with furie fraught, . . . V. viii. 28. 1
Wherewith full wroth he fiercely gan assay . . . V. xi. 11. 4
wherewith troubled sore He all his forces . . . V. xii. 6. 6
Wherewith all full of wrath she thus replyde: . . . VI. i. 27. 6
Wherewith he wroth, . . . Tooke in foule scorne . . . VI. ii. 11. 6
Wherewith the beast enrag'd to loose his pray . . . VI. iv. 20. 5
Wherewith the Prince sore moved there avoud . . . VI. v. 34. 1
The same *wherewith* Dan Jove . . . was nourisht . . . VII. vii. 41. 6
Wherewith your lovers feeble eyes you feed, . . . *H.L.* 38
wall, *Wherewith* he hath encompassed this All. . . . *H.H.B.* 42
Whet. Where foming wrath their cruell tuskes they *whett*, . . I. vi. 44. 7
all the while their malice they did *whet* . . . III. v. 17. 8
therwith their keene desires were *whett*. . . . III. x. 34. 9
restore His weakned powers, and dulled spirits *whet*, . . . IV. iii. 24. 4
With cruell chaufe their courages they *whet*, . . . V. ii. 15. 3
his tongue doth *whet* Gainst all, . . . VI. vi. 12. 3
Some *whet* their knives, and strip their elboes bare: . . . VI. viii. 39. 6
murdrous knife well *whet*, . . . VI. viii. 45. 5
Whether (*partial list of conj.*). *See* **Whither.**
Whether they fare on foote, or flie aloft, . . . *Ro.* xxiv. 3
Whether on hylls, or dales, or other where, . . . *S.C.* Jun. 107
But *whether* in paynefull love I pyne, . . . *S.C.* Au. 109
Whither thou list in fayre Elisa rest, . . . *S.C.* O. 45
Whether thee list thy loved lasse advaunce, . . . *S.C.* N. 7
Whether rejoyce or weepe for great constrainte. . . . *S.C.* N. 205
(*Whether* the Muse so wrought me from my byrth, . . . *S.C.* D. 38
But *whether* luck and loves unbridled lore Woulde leade me . *S.C.* D. 63

Whether—*Continued.*
Of Poets Prince, *whether* he woon beside . . . *Gn.* 18
But *whether* God or Fortune made him bold . . . *Gn.* 302
'Suddenly, *whether* through the Gods decree, . . . *Gn.* 569
Whether shall we professe some trade or skill, . . . *Hub.* 117
Whether for Armes and warlike amenaunce, . . . *Hub.* 781
question, *whether* should assay Those royall ornaments to steale *Hub.* 997
Whether of them should be the Lord of Lords. . . . *Hub.* 1020
He then, to prove *whether* his powre would pas As currant, . *Hub.* 1094
Whether lying reastlesse in heavy bedde, . . . *U.V.* 4
Whether she were one of that Rivers Nymphes, . . . *Ti.* 15
Whether he shepheard be, or shepheards swaine, . . . *Ti.* 234
Whether should of those ashes keeper bee. . . . *Ti.* 665
whether cruell Fate Or wicked Fortune faultles him misled, . *Mui.* 417
Whether allured with my pipes delight, . . . *Col.* 61
Whether it were some hymne, or morall laie, . . . *Col.* 86
whether fortunate Or else unfortunate . . . *Col.* 564
whether rightly so, Or through our rudenesse . . . *Col.* 795
to compare *Whether* in beauties glorie did exceede: . . . I. ii. 37. 4
I, *whether* lately through her brightnes blynd, . . . I. iii. 1. 5
To looken *whether* it were night or day. . . . I. iv. 19. 6
That knew not *whether* right he went, or else astray. . . . I. iv. 19. 9
'For *whether* he, through fatal deepe foresight, . . . I. ix. 7. 1
But *whether* dreames delude, or true it were, . . . I. ix. 14. 5
whether dread did dwell Or anguish in her hart, . . . I. x. 14. 4
And doubted *whether* his late enimy It were, . . . I. xi. 35. 3
I wote not *whether* the revenging steele Were hardned . . . I. xi. 36. 1
That I note *whether* praise or pitty more; . . . I. xii. 17. 4
whether art it were or heedlesse hap, . . . II. iii. 30. 6
Or *whether* swift I wend, or *whether* slow: . . . II. vi. 10. 5
first she proov'd *Whether* she slept or wakte: . . . III. i. 60. 6
each to assay *Whether* more happy were . . . III. iv. 46. 9
That *whether* were more false full hard it is to tell. . . . IV. i. 32. 9
Whether she would them love, or in her liking brooke. . . IV. ii. 40. 9
Unsure to *whether* side it would incline, . . . IV. iii. 37. 2
Whether of them in her should have the greater share. . . IV. iii. 39. 9
Whether shall have the Hag, or hold the Lady still.' . . . IV. iv. 12. 9
Whether through foundring or through sodein feare, . . . IV. iv. 30. 3
But, *whether* willed or nilled friend or foe, . . . IV. vii. 16. 6
Whether shall weigh the balance downe; . . . IV. ix. 1. 4
she uneath discerned *whether whether* weare. . . . IV. ix. 10. 9
Or *whether* it through skill or errour were. . . . IV. ix. 11. 7
Could weenen *whether* they were false or trew: . . . IV. xi. 27. 5
Whether old Proteus true or false had sayd, . . . IV. xii. 28. 4
Or *whether* his owne hand, or *whether* other wight? . . . V. i. 14. 9
Uncertaine *whether* had the better side; . . . V. ii. 17. 2
Whether of them the greater were attone; . . . V. ii. 48. 8
Yet *whether* side was victor note be ghest: . . . V. iii. 7. 6
to make . . . triall, *whether* should the honor get. . . . V. iii. 24. 4
Whether by might extort, or else by slight deceaved? . . . V. iii. 30. 9
whether it be so or no, I can not say. . . . V. iv. 13. 9
Whether by rage of waves . . . Or else by wracke . . . V. iv. 19. 4
try in equall field *whether* hath greater might. . . . V. iv. 48. 9
whether he did woo, or *whether* he were woo'd? . . . V. vi. 15. 9
greedy t' understand To *whether* should the victory befall, . V. xi. 15. 7
That *whether* man or monster one could scarse discerne. . . V. xii. 15. 9
Ne wote I surely *whether* her he yet have fond.' . . . VI. i. 16. 9
whether they be placed high above Or low beneath, . . . VI. ii. 1. 5
whether what he spoke Were soothly so, . . . VI. ii. 13. 7
Whether high towring or accoasting low, . . . VI. ii. 32. 2
whether free with him she now were, or in band? . . . VI. v. 27. 9
whether he alive be to be found, Or . . . VI. v. 28. 7
Yet, *whether* thwart or flatly it did lyte, . . . VI. vi. 30. 8
Whether such grace were given her by kynd, . . . VI. vi. 43. 1
That, *whether* quite from them for to retrate . . . VI. ix. 31. 7
Whether it were the traine of beauties Queene, . . . VI. x. 17. 5
Whether a creature, or a goddesse graced . . . VI. x. 25. 4
(*whether* wicked fate so framed Or fault of men,) . . . VI. xii. 38. 7
Whether by open force, or counsell wise: . . . VII. vi. 21. 8
Whether those same on high, or these belowe; . . . VII. vii. 20. 2
To *whether* side should fall the soveraine place: . . . VII. vii. 57. 7
Whether in earth layd up in secret store, Or else in heaven, . *H.B.* 37
Whetting. *Whetting* their teeth, and with vaine foolhardise . . *Ro.* xiv. 7
Whey. Butter enough, honye, milke, and *whay*, . . . *S.C.* May 115
Which (*partial list*).
But not your praise, the *which* shall never die . . . *Ro.* i. 3
Hys pleasaunt Pipe, *whych* made us meriment, . . . *S.C.* Ap. 14
thee, noble swaine, The *which* art of so rich . . . *Col.* 553
high Jove, the *which* them thither sent. . . . I. v. 33. 6
Antiochus, the *which* advaunst . . . I. v. 47. 8
All *which* when Artegall . . . well advewed, . . . V. iii. 20. 1
Whose rutty Bancke, the *which* his River hemmes . . . *Proth.* 12
the gentle streame, the *which* them bare, . . . *Proth.* 47
that great Lord, *which* therein wont to dwell, . . . *Proth.* 139
While. *See* **Awhile, Long while, Meanwhile, Otherwhile, Somewhile, Whiles.**
While I was with so dreadfull sight afrayde, . . . *Bel.*[1] xi. 11
While she her neck wreath'd from them for the nones: . . *Bel.*[2] vi. 4
While on this Lawrell fixed was mine eie, . . . *Pet.* iii. 8
But, *while* herein I tooke my chiefe delight, . . . *Pet.* iv. 9
Of all the world was spoyl'd within a *while*: . . . *Ro.* xxii. 8
th' heavens looked lovely all the *while*, . . . *Van.* ix. 6
pale and wanne he was, (alas the *while*!) . . . *S.C.* Ja. 8
thus him playnd, the *while* his shepe there fedde. . . . *S.C.* Ja. 12
Both pype and Muse shall sore the *while* abye.' . . . *S.C.* Ja. 71
The *while* thilke same unhappye Ewe . . . Fell headlong . *S.C.* Mar. 49
While they, letting their sheepe runne at large, . . . *S.C.* May 40
That playen *while* their flockes be unfedde: . . . *S.C.* May 44
The *while* they here liven at ease and leasure? . . . *S.C.* May 66
While times enduren of tranquillitie, . . . *S.C.* May 154

While—*Continued.*
The *while* their foes done eache of hem scorne. . . . . S.C. May 161
Wherein *while* Kiddie unwares did looke, ... S.C. May 275
The *while* our sheepe about us safely fedde. . . . . S.C. Jun. 88
(O, seely sheepe, the *while!*) . . . . S.C. Jul. 190
The *while* my flocke did feede thereby; . . . . S.C. Au. 59
The *while* the shepheard selfe did spill. . . . . S.C. Au. 60
Her was her, *while* it was daye-light, ... S.C. S. 3
Wel-away the *while* I was so fonde . . . . S.C. S. 58
'She, *while* she was, ... S.C. N. 93
While here on earth she did abyde. . . . . S.C. N. 199
the *while* the rest . . . fell all for nuts at strife? . . . . S.C. D. 34
where were ye this *while* his shepheard peares, ... *As.* 127
all the *while*, with greedie listfull eares, ... *Col.* 7
by that which little *while* I prooved, ... *Col.* 664
all this *while*, with charmes and hidden artes, ... I. i. 45. 1
He in great passion al this *while* did dwell, ... I. ii. 26. 5
seeing all this *while* The doubtfull ballaunce equally to sway, . I. ii. 38. 1
she, . . . all this *while* Forsaken, wofull, solitarie mayd, . . I. iii. 3. 1
the virgin . . . who all this *while* Amased stands, ... I. iii. 40. 1
While flashing beames do daze his feeble eyen, ... I. iv. 9. 6
Her Lordes and Ladies all this *while* devise . . . . I. iv. 14. 5
Who all that *while* lay hid in secret shade. . . . . I. v. 15. 4
all the *while* most heavenly melody . . . musicke did divide, I. v. 17. 6
all the *while* Duessa wept full bitterly. . . . . I. v. 17. 9
pities all this *while* His mournefull plight, ... I. v. 18. 7
all the *while* she stood upon the ground, ... I. v. 30. 1
all this *while* was busy at her beades; . . . . I. x. 8. 3
all the *while* salt teares bedeawd the hearers cheaks. . . . . I. xii. 16. 9
all the *while* sweete Musicke did apply . . . . I. xii. 38. 6
(ay the *while*, that he is not so now!) . . . . II. i. 50. 1
Yet nought too dear I deemd, *while* so my deare I sought. . . II. i. 53. 9
all this *while* were at their wanton rest, ... II. ii. 16. 4
Him all that *while* Occasion did provoke . . . . II. v. 21. 1
the *while* that Guyon did abide In Mamons house, ... II. viii. 3. 1
Guyon all this *while* his booke did read, ... II. x. 70. 1
al the *while* his wounds were dressing by him stayd. . . . . II. xi. 49. 9
all that *while* right over him she hong . . . . II. xii. 73. 1
all the *while* sweet Musicke did divide . . . . III. i. 40. 1
all the *while* sweet birdes thereto applide . . . . III. i. 40. 3
all the *while* faire Malecasta bent Her crafty engins . . . . III. i. 57. 4
Which all that *while* shee felt to pant and quake, ... III. ii. 42. 8
A litle *whyle* Before that Merlin dyde, ... III. iii. 10. 1
all this *while* full hardly was assayd . . . . III. v. 13. 1
all the *while* their malice they did whet . . . . III. v. 17. 8
al this *while* lay bleding out his hart-blood neare. . . . . III. v. 32. 9
all this *while* Ye wonder . . . . III. vi. 1. 1
past a *while*, when she fit season saw To leave . . . . . . III. vii. 18. 1
all the *while* the fisher did securely sleepe. . . . . III. viii. 21. 9
all the *while* that he these speeches spent, ... III. ix. 52. 1
during the *whyle* That he there sojourned . . . . III. x. 5. 5
every where he might, and everie *while*, ... III. x. 9. 1
While teares stood in his eies, ... III. x. 25. 9
al this *while* . . . . III. xii. 27. 4
all the *while* he red, ... III. xii. 36. 8
In friendly sort that lasted but a *while*; . . . . IV. ii. 29. 2
all the *while* the disentrayled blood . . . . IV. iii. 28. 6
all that *while*, where so they rode or came, ... IV. iv. 13. 3
All that long *while* upheld her wrathfull hand, ... IV. vi. 23. 2
hung all this *while* suspence, ... IV. vi. 34. 2
all this *while* was bound Upon an hard adventure . . . . . . IV. vi. 42. 2
all the *while* he by his side her bore, ... IV. ix. 19. 5
all the *while* beheld their wrathfull moode, ... IV. ix. 22. 3
Which all the *while* I closely had conceld; . . . . IV. x. 55. 2
all that *while* . . . . IV. x. 55. 6
Unto the place he came within a *while*, ... V. ii. 11. 1
Who all this *while* behind him did remaine, ... V. iii. 13. 3
all this *while* Stood in the preasse close covered, ... V. iii. 20. 1
While she was flying, like a weary weft, ... V. iii. 27. 5
every *while* that mighty yron man . . . Them sorely vext, . . V. iv. 44. 1
all that *while* her life she safely garded; . . . . V. v. 8. 8
Yet all that *while* he would not once assay . . . . V. v. 19. 8
One *while* she blam'd her selfe; another *whyle* She . . . . . V. vi. 5. 1
he is not the *while* in state to woo; . . . . V. vi. 16. 2
for which a little *whyle* Ye will not watch? . . . . V. vi. 25. 3
That from her self unwares he might her steale the *whyle*. . . V. ix. 12. 9
With Belge, who watcht all this *while* full sad, ... V. xi. 32. 8
all this *while* did dwell In dread of death, ... VI. i. 43. 1
all the *while* that same discourteous Knight Stood . . . . . VI. iii. 34. 1
all the *while* his backe . . . He lent against a tree, ... VI. v. 18. 8
Where have ye all this *while* bin wandring, ... VI. v. 23. 9
ere that litle *while* they ridden had, ... VI. vii. 6. 6
His kingdome would continue but a *while*. . . . . VI. viii. 23. 5
all this *while* stood there beside them bound, ... VI. viii. 27. 2
all this *while* endured for her sake Great perill . . . . . . VI. viii. 33. 8
Another *while* I baytes and nets display . . . . VI. ix. 23. 5
Was by the Captaine all this *while* defended, ... VI. xi. 19. 2
all this *while* at will did range and raine, ... VI. xii. 2. 8
seeking all this *while* That monstrous Beast . . . to quell, . . VI. xii. 22. 6
all the *while* repenting That he the fly did mock. . . . . . . *Epig.* iv. 43

Whileas. But, *while as* Astrofell did live and raine, ... *Col.* 450

Whilere. That cursed wight, from whom I scapt *whyleare*, . . I. ix. 28. 4
place, in which *whyleare* He left his loftie steed . . . . . . II. ii. 11. 5
the Palmer, whom *whyleare* That wanton Mayd . . . . II. viii. 3. 2
To be avenged of that shot *whyleare*; . . . . II. xi. 25. 3
Their wofull harts he wounded had *whyleare* . . . . III. vi. 13. 8
Faire Crysogone in slombry traunce *whilere*; . . . . III. vi. 26. 7
the same which she escapt *whileare*. . . . . III. vii. 1. 9
full of guests he found *whyleare*, ... III. ix. 13. 4
Out of the flames which he had quencht *whylere*, ... III. x. 17. 3

Whilere—*Continued.*
From whom the Squyre of Dames was reft *whylere*; . . . . III. xi. 3. 8
The Salvage Knight that victour was *whileare*, ... IV. v. 8. 5
whose heart *whileare* . . . with gealous discontent Had fild, . IV. v. 30. 7
I found her not where I her left *whyleare*, ... IV. vi. 36. 6
left in his protection *whileare*, ... IV. ix. 17. 8
Whyleare by Tryphon was not throughly healed, ... IV. xii. 22. 6
(as ye have heard *whyleare*) . . . . V. ii. 3. 2
After long sorrowes suffered *whyleare*, ... V. iii. 1. 7
The which *whyleare* she was so greedily Devouring, ... V. xii. 39. 2
I will the truth discover as it chaunst *whilere*. . . . . VI. ii. 15. 9
Those warlike armes which Calepine *whyleare* Had left behind VI. v. 8. 4
the salvage (that *whyleare* . . . Was greatly growne in love . VI. v. 41. 6
whileare Wrought to Sir Calepine so foule despight; . . . . VI. vi. 17. 6
From Meliboe and from themselves *whyleare*; . . . . VI. xi. 37. 3
the which *whylere* Had from their maisters fled, ... VI. xi. 39. 8
When I bethinke me on that speech *whyleare* . . . . VII. viii. 1. 1

Whiles. *See* **Otherwhiles.**
Whiles thus I did behold, An earthquake shooke . . . . . . *Bel.*[2] ii. 12
The *whiles* that I with sacred horror sing Your glorie, . . . *Ro.* i. 13
Whiles Jove at them his thunderbolts let flie, ... *Ro.* xii. 4
One day, *whiles* that my daylie cares did sleepe, ... *Van.* i. 1
The *whiles* our flockes do graze about in sight, ... S.C. Ap. 31
The *whiles* another high doth overlooke . . . . *Gn.* 87
The *whiles* his flock their chawed cuds do eate. . . . . . . *Gn.* 144
The *whiles* the Shepheard self . . . Sate . . . . *Gn.* 237
The *whiles* their crooked keeles the surges clave. . . . . . *Gn.* 568
whiles the Lyon slepeeth sound, May we . . . . *Hub.* 967
The *whiles* the Princes pallaces fell fast . . . . *Hub.* 1175
The *whiles* we silly Maides, whom they dispize . . . . . . *T.M.* 339
the *whiles* the Foxe is crept Into the hole, ... *Ti.* 216
the *whiles* this verse Shall live, ... *Ti.* 253
Whiles thou, now in Elisian fields so free, ... *Ti.* 332
Whiles all the heavens on lower creatures smilde, ... *Mui.* 53
The *whiles* soft death away her spirit hent, ... *D.* 258
The *whiles* the captive heard his nets did rend, ... *As.* 125
The *whiles* their flocks, devoyd of dangers feare, ... *Col.* 54
Whiles single Truth and simple Honestie . . . . *Col.* 727
Whiles sad Night over him her mantle black doth spred. . . I. i. 39. 9
Whiles you in carelesse sleepe are drowned quight.' . . . . I. i. 53. 4
whiles wicked wights Have knit themselves . . . . I. ii. 4. 7
Who, *whiles* he livde, was called proud Sans foy, ... I. ii. 25. 6
Whiles none the holy things in safety kept, ... I. iii. 17. 8
He ror'd aloud, *whiles* life forsooke his stubborne brest. . . I. iii. 42. 9
Whiles old Sylvanus slept in shady arber sownd: . . . . . . I. vi. 7. 9
marched forth in hast, *Whiles* Una, ... I. vi. 40. 2
trample th' earth, the *whiles* they may respire, ... I. vi. 44. 8
the *whiles* the royall Mayd Fledd farre away, ... I. vi. 47. 8
saw his maisters fall *Whiles* he had keeping . . . . I. vii. 19. 2
groneth in my spright, *Whiles* thus I heare . . . . I. vii. 40. 4
whiles equal destinies Did ronne about, ... I. vii. 43. 4
And *whiles* he strove his combred clubbe to quight . . . . . I. viii. 10. 4
Whiles yet his feeble feet for faintnesse reeld, ... I. viii. 20. 7
Whyles he himselfe with greedie . . . . I. viii. 29. 3
Love! lay down thy bow, the *whiles* I may respyre. . . . . I. ix. 8. 9
wex old in woe, *whiles* wo stil wexeth new. . . . . I. ix. 9. 9
Whiles every sence the humour sweet embayd, ... I. ix. 13. 5
Whiles trembling horror did his conscience daunt, ... I. ix. 49. 3
Whom still she fed *whiles* they were weake and young, . . . I. x. 31. 3
whiles flashing fire about him shone: . . . . I. x. 53. 9
Whiles from their journall labours they did rest; . . . . . I. xi. 31. 4
Whiles some more bold to measure him nigh stand, ... I. xii. 11. 8
The *whiles* that hoarie king, ... I. xii. 12. 2
Whyles they his pittifull adventures heard; . . . . I. xii. 16. 3
Whiles on her wearie journey she did ride; . . . . I. xii. 22. 5
The *whiles* one sung a song of love and jollity. . . . . . . I. xii. 38. 9
Whiles cursed steele against that badge I bent, ... II. i. 27. 5
Whiles the sad pang approching shee does feele, ... II. i. 38. 8
Whiles cause not well conceived ye mistake: . . . . II. ii. 5. 5
The *whyles* a losell wandring by the way, ... II. iii. 4. 1
Whiles in the bush he lay, not yett forgott: . . . . II. iii. 43. 5
For *whiles* she spake her great words did appall . . . . . . II. iii. 44. 5
The *whiles* on foot was forced for to yeed . . . . II. iv. 2. 3
The *whiles* to me the treachour did remove . . . . II. iv. 27. 3
Whiles they are weake, betimes with them contend; . . . . II. iv. 34. 5
whiles Atin to Cymochles for ayd flyes. . . . . II. v. Arg.
the *whiles* that furious beast . . . . II. v. 10. 6
Whyles Guyon standing by their uncouth strife does see. . . II. v. 20. 9
Whiles creeping slomber made him to forget . . . . II. v. 30. 8
Whiles through their lids his wanton eies do peepe . . . . . II. v. 34. 5
Whiles sad Pyrochles lies on sencelesse ground, ... II. v. 36. 6
whiles his brother burns in furious fyre. . . . . II. vi. Arg.
Whiles thus she talked, and *whiles* thus she toyd, ... II. vi. 11. 1
The *whiles* with a love lay she thus him sweetly charmd. . . II. vi. 14. 9
Whiles nothing envious nature them forth throwes . . . . . II. vi. 15. 4
Thus to mislead mee, *whiles* I you obaid: . . . . II. vi. 22. 8
The *whiles* Cymochles with that wanton mayd . . . . II. vi. 40. 8
Whiles thus they strugled in that ydle wave, ... II. vi. 47. 1
Whiles sad Celeno, sitting on a clifte, ... II. vii. 23. 6
mortall Princes wore *whiles* they on earth did rayne. . . . . II. vii. 43. 9
The *whiles* he sterv'd with hunger, and with drouth, ... II. vii. 58. 8
The *whiles* my handes I washt in purity, ... II. vii. 62. 8
The *whiles* my soule was soyld with fowle iniquity.' . . . . II. vii. 62. 9
The *whiles* the other Ladies mind theyr mery glee. . . . . . II. viii. 6. 9
Whiles deadly fitt thy pupill doth dismay. . . . . II. viii. 7. 5
Cymochles *whiles* his shield was wyde, ... II. viii. 36. 4
The *whiles* false Archimage and Atin fled apace. . . . . . . II. viii. 56. 9
Whiles it is kept in sober government; . . . . II. ix. 1. 4
So talked they, the *whiles* They wasted had . . . . II. ix. 9. 8
Whiles in the aire their clustring army flies, ... II. ix. 16. 4

Whiles—*Continued.*
The *whyles* the viaundes in the vessell boyld . . . . II. ix. 30. 8
The *whyles* the Faery knight did entertayne . . . . II. ix. 40. 1
the *whiles* her lovely face . . . . II. ix. 43. 2
whiles the famous auncestryes . . . . II. x. 1. 7
The *whiles* with blood they all the shore did staine, ... II. x. 48. 3
whiles good fortune favoured her might, ... II. x. 56. 6
To which *whiles* absent he his mind did sett, ... II. x. 60. 3
whiles wind and wether right Doe serve their turnes: . . . . II. xi. 4. 7
Whiles his long legs nigh raught unto the ground. . . . . . II. xi. 20. 6
The *whiles* the Prince, prickt with reprochful shame, ... II. xi. 31. 6
whiles he marveild still, did still him payne; . . . . II. xi. 44. 5
whiles they fly that Gulfes devouring jawes, ... II. xii. 4. 8
Whiles the salt brine out of the billowes sprong. . . . . . . II. xii. 10. 5
Whiles the dredd daunger does behind remaine. . . . . . . II. xii. 21. 4
The *whiles* sweet Zephyrus lowd whisteled . . . . II. xii. 33. 5
Whiles th' one did row, ... II. xii. 37. 4
The *whiles* the nimble bote so well her sped, ... II. xii. 38. 2
The *whiles* their snowy limbes, ... II. xii. 64. 6
The *whiles* some one did chaunt this lovely lay: . . . . . . II. xii. 74. 1
the *whiles* the rest Fled all away . . . . II. xii. 81. 6
The *whiles* faire Britomart . . . did stay behynd, ... III. i. 19. 1
Whiles fruitfull Ceres and Lyaeus fatt . . . . III. i. 51. 3
feed on shadowes *whiles* I die for food, ... III. ii. 44. 3
whiles with entire Affection I doe languish . . . . III. ii. 44. 4
Whyles yet in infant cradle he did crall; . . . . III. iii. 26. 7
'*Whiles* thus thy Britons doe in languour pine, ... III. iii. 35. 1
The *whiles* that love it steres, and fortune rowes: . . . . . III. iv. 9. 5
I read thee soone retyre, *whiles* thou hast might, ... III. iv. 14. 8
Whiles th' altars fume with frankincense arownd, ... III. iv. 17. 4
Whiles thus he lay in deadly stonishment, ... III. iv. 19. 1
Whiles all her sisters did for her lament . . . . III. iv. 30. 7
Whiles on his broad rownd backe they softly slid, ... III. iv. 32. 2
Whiles they the corse into her wagon reare, ... III. iv. 42. 4
The *whiles* the Nymphes sitt all about him rownd, ... III. iv. 44. 1
whiles his Lord pursewd that noble Mayd, ... III. v. 13. 3
whiles that he lay in swownd, ... III. v. 38. 7
Whiles dayly playsters to his wownd she layd, ... III. v. 43. 5
The *whiles* her matchlesse beautie him dismayd. . . . . . . III. v. 43. 7
the *whiles* a gentle slombring swowne Upon her fell, ... III. vi. 7. 3
Whiles all her Nymphes did like a girlond her enclose. . . . III. vi. 19. 9
The *whiles* the joyous birdes make their pastyme . . . . . . III. vi. 42. 7
The *whiles* his nets were drying on the sand. . . . . III. vii. 27. 6
The *whiles* the pitteous Lady up did ryse, ... III. viii. 32. 1
Whiles the cold ysickles from his rough beard . . . . III. viii. 35. 3
Whiles of a wanton Lady I doe write, ... III. ix. 1. 6
Whyles thus we suffer . . . . III. ix. 8. 7
Whiles yet on Ida he a shepeheard hight, ... III. ix. 36. 3
The *whiles* unwares away . . . . III. ix. 52. 6
Hellenore, The *whiles* her husband ran . . . Laught . . . . . III. x. 13. 2
The *whiles* the Boaster from his loftie sell Faynd to alight, . III. x. 38. 5
The *whiles* their Gotes upon the brouzes fedd, ... III. x. 45. 8
whiles sleepe their sences did invade. . . . . III. x. 46. 9
The *whiles* the Championesse now entred has . . . . III. xi. 27. 7
The *whiles* her foolish garde, ... III. xi. 31. 5
Whiles the proud Bird, ruffing his fethers wyde . . . . . . III. xi. 32. 6
Whyles thus on earth great Jove these pageaunts playd, . . III. xi. 35. 5
whiles Jove to earth is gone.' . . . . III. xi. 35. 9
Whiles that from heaven he suffered exile. . . . . III. xi. 39. 5
The *whiles* the passing brightnes her fraile sences dazd. . . . III. xi. 49. 9
The *whiles* a most delitious harmony . . . . III. xii. 6. 1
The *whiles* the maskers marched forth in trim aray. . . . . III. xii. 6. 9
The *whiles* his love away the other bore, ... IV. ii. 7. 3
the *whiles* the thrid By griesly Lachesis was spun . . . . . IV. ii. 48. 5
The *whiles* shril trompets and loud clarions sweetly playd. . IV. iii. 5. 9
Whiles neither lets the other touch the soyle, ... IV. iii. 16. 7
The *whiles* were enterchaunged twixt them two; . . . . IV. iii. 17. 2
Whiles thus they communed, ... IV. vi. 9. 1
Whiles unawares his saddle he forwent, ... IV. vi. 11. 8
Whiles with long fight on foot he breathlesse was, ... IV. vi. 15. 2
The *whiles* faire Amoret, of nought affeard, ... IV. vii. 4. 1
Who lay the *whiles* in swoune, ... IV. vii. 35. 4
The *whiles* his babling tongue did yet blaspheme . . . . . . IV. viii. 45. 6
The *whiles* his life ran foorth in bloudie streame, ... IV. viii. 45. 8
The *whiles* I him condemne, ... IV. xii. 11. 3
Whiles through the world she walked in this sort, ... V. i. 6. 1
whiles he his backe bestrad. . . . . V. ii. 13. 9
whiles he did in the wood remaine, ... V. iii. 31. 4
The *whiles* his guilefull groome was fled away, ... V. iii. 38. 1
whyles heedlesse of the hooke . . . . V. v. 43. 1
Whiles Talus watched at the dore all night. . . . . V. vii. 26. 4
whiles on the greene The Briton Prince him readie did awayte, V. viii. 29. 2
That they the *whiles* may take lesse heedie keepe . . . . . . V. ix. 13. 3
The *whiles* the Prince there kept the entrance still. . . . . V. ix. 15. 2
The *whiles* the Prince hard preased in betweene, ... V. x. 37. 6
Whiles she alone is left, and thou here found? . . . . V. xi. 38. 6
whiles she no whit gainesayd: . . . . V. xi. 64. 8
The *whyles* Sir Artegall with that old knight Did forth descend, V. xii. 6. 1
The *whiles* the cursed felon high did reare His cruell hand . . V. xii. 20. 2
whiles he combred was therewith so sore, ... V. xii. 22. 8
whiles he him saw so ill bested, ... V. xii. 23. 5
whiles there with her he stayd, ... V. xii. 25. 8
And *whiles* he her pursued every where, ... VI. i. 16. 7
Thus *whiles* they spake they heard a ruefull shrieke . . . . VI. i. 17. 1
Whiles yet his foe lay fast in sencelesse swound; . . . . . . VI. i. 34. 2
Whiles he . . . did nought but weepe, ... VI. iii. 44. 8
the *whiles* he was thereof secure. . . . . VI. v. 16. 9
The *whiles* the salvage man did take his steede, ... VI. vi. 19. 8
the *whyles* the Prince did rest In carelesse couch, ... VI. vi. 44. 1
The *whyles* they strike at him with heedlesse might, ... VI. vii. 9. 3

Whiles—*Continued.*
The *whyles* his salvage page . . . Was wandred in the wood . VI. vii. 19. 5
The *whiles* his Lord in silver slomber lay, ... VI. vii. 19. 8
The *whiles* that mighty man did her demeane . . . . VI. vii. 39. 4
The *whiles* the beast doth rage and loudly rore; . . . . . . VI. vii. 47. 6
So did the Squire, the *whiles* the Carle did fret . . . . . . VI. vii. 47. 7
The *whiles* that other villaine went about . . . . VI. viii. 11. 6
The *whiles* the foole did him revile and flout, ... VI. viii. 11. 8
The *whyles* she wayld, the more they did rejoyce. . . . . . VI. viii. 46. 5
The *whyles* their beasts there . . . fed, ... VI. ix. 5. 4
Her *whyles* Sir Calidore there vewed well, ... VI. ix. 11. 1
The *whiles* their flockes in shadowes shrouded bee, ... VI. ix. 41. 4
The *whiles* his Pastorell is led Into captivity. . . . . VI. x. Arg.
whiles the candle-light Out quenched leaves no skill . . . . VI. xi. 16. 8
The *whiles* faire Pastorell . . . Was almost dead, ... VI. xi. 43. 7
The which she bore the *whiles* in prison she did dwell. . . . VI. xii. 15. 9
The *whiles* she lordeth in licentious blisse . . . . *Am.* x. 3
The *whiles* my stonisht hart stood in amaze, ... *Am.* xvi. 3
The *whiles* her foot she in my necke doth place, ... *Am.* xx. 3
Dark in my day, *whyles* her fayre light I mis, ... *Am.* lxxxviii. 13
The *whiles* doe ye this song unto her sing, ... *Epith.* 54
The *whiles* the woods shal answer, ... *Epith.* 109
The *whyles* the boyes run up and downe the street, ... *Epith.* 137
Whiles ye forget your former lay to sing, ... *Epith.* 183
The *whiles* . . . The Choristers the joyous Antheme sing, . . *Epith.* 220
whiles she before the altar stands, ... *Epith.* 223
The *whles* the maydens doe theyr carroll sing, ... *Epith.* 259
The *whiles* an hundred little winged loves, ... *Epith.* 357
The *whyles* thou doest triumph in their decay; . . . . *H.L.* 137
Whilom. 'Where is (quoth she) this *whilom* honoured face? . *Bel.* x. 5
That *whilome* from the Troyan blood did flow, ... *Bel.*[2] v. 8
Which *whilom* did those earthborn brethren blinde. . . . . . *Ro.* x. 14
Like as *whilome* the children of the earth . . . . *Ro.* xii. 1
those, which *whilome* wont with pallid cheekes . . . . *Ro.* xiv. 11
So *whilom* did this Monarchie aspyre, ... *Ro.* xvi. 12
The which this auncient Citie *whilome* made! . . . . *Ro.* xxv. 4
All that which Aegypt *whilome* did devise, ... *Ro.* xxix. 1
Whilome thy fresh spring flowrd, ... *S.C.* Ja. 21
Whilome had bene the King of the field, ... *S.C.* F. 108
Whilome on him was all my care and joye, ... *S.C.* Ap. 23
Whilome there used shepheards all To feede theyr flocks . . *S.C.* Jul. 65
That *whilome* was the first shepheard, ... *S.C.* Jul. 127
Whilome all these were lowe and lief, ... *S.C.* Jul. 165
Whilom thou was peregall to the best, ... *S.C.* Au. 8
That here by there I *whilome* usd to keepe, ... *S.C.* S. 63
(Ah, for Colin, he *whilome* my ioye!) . . . . *S.C.* S. 177
Whilome there wonned a wicked Wolfe, ... *S.C.* S. 184
Whilome thou wont the shepheards laddes to leade . . . . . *S.C.* O. 4
That *whilome* was the saynt of shepheards light, ... *S.C.* N. 176
That *whilome* was poore shepheards pryde, ... *S.C.* N. 198
Whilome in youth, when flowrd my joyfull spring, ... *S.C.* D. 19
I, that *whilome* wont to frame my pype . . . . *S.C.* D. 115
Whilome (said she) before the world was civill, ... *Hub.* 45
They *whilome* used duly everie day. . . . . *Hub.* 449
That *whilome* wont to wait upon my traine, ... *T.M.* 196
Whilom in ages past none might professe . . . . *T.M.* 559
my fatall overthrowe, That *whilom* was, ... *Ti.* 80
'Where my high steeples *whilom* usde to stand, ... *Ti.* 127
'So *whilome* raised they the puissant brood . . . . *Ti.* 379
Who *whilome* was alive the wisest wight: . . . . *Ti.* 445
that *whylome* seemed to have been The Harpe . . . . *Ti.* 606
That *whilome* wast the worldes chiefst riches, ... *Ti.* 675
'*Whilome* I usde (as thou right well doest know) . . . . . . *D.* 99
Whylom the pillours of th' earth did sustaine, ... *Ded. Son.* i. 2
I, the man whose Muse *whylome* did maske, ... I. Pr. 1. 1
whylome her well they knew: . . . . I. iv. 15. 5
That *whylome* was to me too dearely deare . . . . I. v. 23. 5
It Merlin was, which *whylome* did excell . . . . I. vii. 36. 4
day and night *Whilome* doth rancle . . . . I. ix. 7. 4
Whylome, before that cursed Dragon got . . . . I. xi. 29. 6
He nought forgott how he *whilome* had sworne, ... I. xii. 41. 6
Who dying *whilome* did divide this fort . . . . II. ii. 13. 3
Whose lives, it seemed, *whilome* there were shed, ... II. vii. 30. 8
Of whom high Jove wont *whylome* feasted bee; . . . . II. vii. 59. 6
Whereof king Nine *whilome* built Babell towre. . . . . II. ix. 21. 6
Not that, which antique Cadmus *whylome* built . . . . II. ix. 45. 6
the River that *whylome* was hight The ancient Abus, ... II. x. 16. 2
'As th' Isle of Delos *whylome*, ... II. xii. 13. 1
Of which Caduceus *whilome* was made, ... II. xii. 41. 2
are men indeed, . . . *Whylome* her lovers, ... II. xii. 85. 3
whilome in divinest wits did rayne, ... III. Pr. 3. 2
whylome full dernly tryde. . . . . III. i. 14. 4
As *whylome* was the antique worldes guize, ... III. i. 39. 3
Sith him *whylome* in Britayne she did vew, ... III. ii. 17. 3
whylome wont (they say) To make his wonne, ... III. iii. 7. 5
a faire Lady Nonne, that *whilome* hight Matilda, ... III. iii. 13. 5
whylome by false Faeries stolne away, ... III. iii. 26. 6
That *whylome* wont in wemen to appeare? . . . . III. iv. 1. 2
(This Liagore *whilome* had learned skill . . . . III. iv. 41. 2
her *whilome* upon high Pindus hill He loved, ... III. iv. 41. 4
In Paradize *whylome* did plant this flowre; . . . . III. v . 52. 3
where most he us'd *Whylome* to haunt, ... III. vi. 13. 2
her of his owne mother Earth *Whylome* begot, ... III. vii. 47. 9
Though *whilome* far much greater then thy fame, ... III. ix. 33. 3
towres of Ilion *whilome* Brought unto balefull ruine, ... III. ix. 34. 3
Who had forgot that *whylome* I heard tell . . . . III. ix. 47. 3
cruell battailes, which he *whilome* fought . . . . III. xi. 29. 6
Which were *whilome* captived . . . . III. xi. 52. 4
left him now as sad, as *whilome* jollie, ... IV. i. 36. 8
from Braggadocchio *whilome* reft The snowy Florimell, . . . IV. ii. 4. 6

Whilom—*Continued.*
Whylome, as antique stories tellen us, IV. ii. 32. 1
That *whylome* wont to be the victors meed; IV. iv. 31. 3
Whilome it was . . . Dame Venus girdle, IV. v. 3. 6
whylome for her sake, . . . did make, IV. v. 4. 1
(*Whylome* for ventrous Knights the *bedding* best) IV. v. 39. 4
whylome in your minde wont to despise them all.' IV. vi. 28. 9
For *whylome* they have conquerd sea and land, IV. vi. 31. 4
being *whylome* launcht with lovely dart, IV. vi. 40. 5
As *whylome* was the custome ancient IV. vi. 44. 7
So *whylome* didst thou to faire Florimell, IV. vii. 2. 1
who he *whilome* was uneath was to be red. IV. vii. 40. 9
he *whilome* some gentle swaine had beene, IV. vii. 45. 6
Of an huge Geauntesse *whylome* was bred, IV. viii. 47. 2
whilome were . . . Sixe valiant Knights IV. xi. 37. 2
Mulla mine, whose waves I *whilom* taught to weep. IV. xi. 41. 9
the Titans, that *whylome* rebelled Gainst highest heaven: V. i. 9. 6
Whilome those great Heroes got thereby V. ii. 1. 5
Therefore *whylome* to knights of great emprise V. iv. 2. 1
With which *whylome* he gotten had great fame: V. v. 20. 5
That *whylome* hath of Hercules bene told, V. v. 24. 2
whilome in his youth had bene a Knight, V. vi. 32. 3
th' old Aegyptian Kings that *whylome* were, V. vii. 2. 6
Was to the battell *whilome* ready dight. V. vii. 27. 6
So *whylome* learnd that mighty Jewish swaine, V. viii. 2. 1
That *whylome* wont to doe so many quake, V. ix. 35. 8
she *whylome* . . . her counsels false conspyred V. ix. 41. 1
He that *whylome* in Spaine so sore was dred V. x. 9. 3
The which *whylome* that Ladies owne had bene; V. x. 25. 2
he which *whilome* did attend On faire Irene V. xi. 37. 6
'Of Cerberus *whilome* he was begot VI. i. 8. 1
True is, that *whilome* that good Poet sayd, VI. iii. 1. 1
whilome he had beene Some goodly person, VI. v. 36. 6
For *whylome* he had bene a doughty Knight, VI. vi. 4. 1
Who *whylome* was, . . . A lustie knight VI. xii. 3. 5
That great Alcides *whilome* overthrew, VI. xii. 32. 2
Like as *whylome* that strong Tirynthian swaine VI. xii. 35. 1
I will rehearse that *whylome* I heard say, VII. vi. 1. 7
those old Titans that did *whylome* strive VII. vi. 2. 6
Whylome when IRELAND florished in fame VII. vi. 38. 1
Unto whose bed false Bregog *whylome* stole, VII. vi. 40. 4
all the gods *whylome* assembled were VII. vii. 12. 2
whylome did forray The Nemaean forrest, VII. vii. 36. 5
when the soule, . . . *whilome* did pas *H.B.* 108
There *whylome* wont the Templer Knights to byde, *Proth.* 135
Whilst. *Whilst* in the smoake she unto heaven did stie. *Bel.*[2] xi. 8
Whilst I thus mazed was with great affray, *Bel.*[2] xv. 11
Whilst systers nyne, which dwell on Parnasse hight, *S.C.* Jun. 28
And I, *whylst* youth and course of carelesse yeeres, *S.C.* Jun. 33
He, *whilst* he lived, was the soveraigne head *S.C.* Jun. 83
In such delights *whilst* thus his carelesse time *Gn.* 153
Whilest that thy life more deare and precious *Gn.* 331
Whilst each does for the Soveraignty contend, *Gn.* 410
Whilst Hector raged with outragious minde, *Gn.* 503
Whilst all the purchase of the Phrigian pray, *Gn.* 591
Whilest others alwayes have before me stept, *Hub.* 77
So *whilst* that other like vaine wits he pleased, *Hub.* 709
Whilst through the forest rechlesse they did goe, *Hub.* 950
And *whilest* the other Peeres, for povertie, *Hub.* 1177
The *whilste* thy kingdome from thy head is rent, *Hub.* 1329
Whilest favourable times did us afford Free libertie *T.M.* 243
Whilest Ignorance the Muses doth oppresse. *T.M.* 288
whilst heavens with equall vewe Deignd to behold me *Ti.* 80
And I, the *whilest* you mourne for his decease, *Ti.* 237
That *whilste* he lived was of none envyde, *Ti.* 241
'He, *whilest* he lived, happie was through thee, *Ti.* 246
So *whilst* that thou, faire flower of chastitie, *Ti.* 251
'Yet, *whilest* the fates affoord me vitall breath, *Ti.* 309
That, *whilest* thou livedst, madest the forrests ring, *Ti.* 325
Provide therefore (ye Princes) *whilst* ye live, *Ti.* 365
Whilest thus I looked, *Ti.* 603
Whilst all the way most heavenly noyse was heard *Ti.* 612
Whilest neither could the others greater might . . . endure; *Mui.* 6
Whilst heaven did favour his felicities, *Mui.* 21
(*Whilst* oft his heart did melt in tender teares) *Mui.* 30
'For *whilest* I was thus without dread or dout, *D.* 155
Whil'st yet her leafe was greene, *D.* 240
And *whilst* her braunch faire blossomes *D.* 241
'Yet, *whilest* I in this wretched vale doo stay *D.* 456
So will I travell *whilest* I tarrie heere, *D.* 466
Whilest none is nigh, thine eyelids up to close, *As.* 137
Whilest thou wast hence, all dead in dole did lie: *Col.* 22
That, *whilest* the one was watcht, *Col.* 139
He *whilest* he lived was the noblest swaine, *Col.* 440
wisedome warnes, *whilest* foot is in the gate, I. i. 13. 4
Whylst freshest Flora her with Yvie girlond crownd I. i. 48. 9
And, *whilest* him fortune favourd, fayre did thrive I. iii. 37. 8
Whylest here thy shield is hangd for victors hyre? I. v. 10. 7
whilst Phoebus pure In westerne waves . . . did recure. I. v. 44. 8
there abode, *whylst* any beast of name Walkt I. vi. 29. 3
Whilest Satyrane him from pursuit did let. I. vii. 20. 4
Whilest she her selfe thus busily did frame II. ii. 16. 1
Whilst thus they mingled were in furious armes, II. ii. 27. 1
Whilst with delight of that he wisely spake II. ii. 46. 5
Whylest reason, blent through passion, nought descryde; II. iv. 7. 7
whilest his foe did rage most rife: II. v. 9. 7
Whylest there the varlet stood, II. vi. 41. 1
Whilest each of Brutus boasted to be borne, II. x. 36. 7
Whilst they were young, Cassibalane, their Eme, II. x. 47. 1
Whilest Romanes daily did the weake subdew: II. x. 54. 5

Whilst—*Continued.*
Whylest others did them selves embay in liquid joyes. II. xii. 60. 9
Whilst round about them pleasauntly did sing Many II. xii. 72. 7
Gather therefore the Rose *whilest* yet is prime, II. xii. 75. 6
Gather the Rose of love *whilest* yet is time, II. xii. 75. 8
Whilest loving thou mayst loved be with equall crime. II. xii. 75. 9
But let us hence depart *whilest* wether serves and winde.' II. xii. 87. 9
whilst he slept she over him would spred Her mantle, III. i. 36. 1
whilst he bath'd III. i. 36. 5
That *whilest* his breath did strength to him supply, III. vii. 24. 7
Thus *whilest* all things in troublous uprore were, III. x. 16. 1
Whilest deadly torments doe her chast brest rend, III. xi. 11. 3
Where let them wend at will, *whilest* here I doe respire. III. xii. 45. 9
whilest every man, Surcharg'd with wine, IV. i. 3. 3
Whilest both you here . . . Sweare she is yours, IV. i. 47. 7
whilest other weares the bayes. IV. i. 47. 9
That none durst ever *whilest* thou wast alive, IV. ii. 34. 4
Whilest through their rifts the ruddie bloud did showre, IV. iii. 15. 7
But nathelesse, *whilst* all the lookers-on IV. iii. 31. 1
Thus *whilest* their minds were doubtfully distraught, IV. iii. 48. 6
whilst goodly grace she him did shew: IV. viii. 6. 5
Whilest I, through paines and perlous jeopardie, IV. x. 28. 7
The *whilest* their eldest brother was away, IV. x. 42. 6
Whilest thus I spake, behold! with happy eye I spyde IV. x. 48. 6
Thus *whilst* his stony heart with tender ruth Was toucht, IV. xii. 13. 1
Whilest here on earth she lived mortallie: V. i. 5. 5
Whilest he reformed that uncivill fo, V. i. 21. 4
Whilest he to gathering of the gold did fall: V. ii. 23. 8
It fortun'd, *whylest* they were thus ill beset, V. iii. 10. 1
Whilest thus they busied were bout Florimell, V. iii. 29. 1
Whilest thus, amidst the billowes V. iv. 10. 6
I will it defend *whilst* ever that I may.' V. iv. 14. 9
For that Osyris, *whilest* he lived here, V. vii. 2. 8
Where *whilest* her earthly parts with soft delight V. vii. 12. 5
Whilest Fortune favourd her successe in fight: V. vii. 41. 7
To which *whilest* she lent her intentive mind, V. ix. 14. 1
Who *whilest* in hand it gryping hard he hent, V. ix. 18. 4
Thus there he stood, *whylest* high over his head V. ix. 26. 1
Whylest kings and kesars at her feet did them prostrate. V. ix. 29. 9
Whylest underneath her feete, there as she sate, V. ix. 33. 3
Whylest he of none was stopped nor withstood: V. x. 8. 5
There, *whilest* they entring th' one did th' other stay, V. x. 36. 5
The *whilest* at him so dreadfully he drive, V. xi. 5. 8
Whilest still she stands, as stonisht and forlorne: V. xi. 29. 5
whilest Calidore Did enter in, VI. i. 23. 8
whylest an Infant from a Beare He saves, VI. iv. Arg.
Bout which *whilest* he was busied thus hard, VI. v. 11. 1
And beat them back, *whilest* many underneath him fell. VI. vi. 23. 9
Whylest every joynt for dread of death did quake, VI. vi. 29. 7
There *whilest* he thus was setling things above, VI. vi. 37. 1
Effect the same, *whylest* all the night was spent. VI. vi. 44. 7
Whylest time did offer meanes him sleeping to surprize. VI. vii. 22. 9
Thus *whylest* they were debating diverslie, VI. vii. 23. 7
Whylest she, the Ladie of her libertie, VI. vii. 31. 5
Whilest she did weepe, of no man mercifide: VI. vii. 32. 5
whilest love lackt place, She had destroyed VI. vii. 38. 7
whilest on ground he lay, Laide heavy hands on him VI. viii. 11. 2
There *whilest* in Morpheus bosome safe she lay, VI. viii. 34. 6
Whylest everie one with helping hands did strive, VI. ix. 15. 6
Whylest thus he talkt, the knight with greedy eare VI. ix. 26. 1
whilest him list remaine, Dayly beholding VI. ix. 34. 2
The *whylest* at pleasure she mote sport and play; VI. ix. 37. 5
Whilest Calidore does follow that faire Mayd, VI. x. 1. 2
Whilest his faire Pastorella was elsewhere, VI. x. 5. 2
The *whilest* the rest them round about did hemme, VI. x. 12. 4
He pypt apace, *whilest* they him daunst about. VI. x. 16. 5
Whilest Melibee is slaine: VI. xi. Arg.
Whylest thus she in these hellish dens remayned, VI. xi. 3. 1
Creepes forth of dores, *whilst* darknes him doth hide, VI. xi. 18. 7
theeves, *whilest* one sought her to hold, Fell all at ods, VI. xi. 30. 8
Whilst none was him to stop, nor none him to restraine. VI. xii. 2. 9
Whom *whylest* she did with watrie eyne behold, VI. xii. 7. 6
whylest he that monster sought Throughout the world, VI. xii. 13. 4
Whilest ye in durance dwelt, ye to me gave A little mayd, VI. xii. 17. 6
Did cast to ground, *whilest* none was them to rew; VI. xii. 25. 5
Whilest Calidore him under him downe threw; VI. xii. 32. 7
resolv'd; that *whil'st* the Gods . . . Were troubled, VII. vi. 23. 1
Whil'st she thus spake, the Gods, . . . Stood all astonied; VII. vi. 28. 1
whylst her bloody hands them slay, *Am.* xlvii. 9
To let them gaze, *whylest* he on them may pray: *Am.* liii. 4
Make hast, therefore, sweet love, *whilest* it is prime; *Am.* lxx. 13
whylest I fill my mind, I starve my body, *Am.* lxxxvii. 13
And, *whylest* she doth her dight, *Epith.* 34
Whilest they seeke onely, without further care, *H.L.* 101
That *whilst* (*the *whylst*) thou tyrant Love doest laugh *H.L.* 134
Whylest they lye languishing like thrals forlorne, *H.L.* 136
Whylest seeking to aslake thy raging fyre, *H.B.* 4
Whilest every one doth seeke and sew to have it, *H.B.* 153
whilest so thy softened spirit Is inly toucht, *H.H.L.* 253
Whil'st one did sing this Lay, *Proth.* 87
Whilstever. *See* **Ever.**
Whining. There now haunt yelling Mewes and *whining* Plovers. *Ti.* 133
Whip. Rode Sathan with a smarting *whip* in hand, I. iv. 36. 2
bitter Penaunce, with an yron *whip,* I. x. 27. 1
The one in hand an yron *whip* did strayne, II. vii. 21. 7
did with his smarting toole Oft *whip* her dainty selfe, VI. vii. 39. 9
having in his hand a *whip,* Her therewith yirks; VI. vii. 44. 6
with his *whip,* him following behynd, VI. vii. 49. 4
from him taking his owne *whip,* VI. viii. 28. 8
Whipping. with cursed hands uncleane *Whipping* her horse, VI. vii. 39. 8

Whipping—*Continued.*
He would with *whipping* him have done to dye; . . . VI. viii. 29. 3
Whips. Reproch sharpe stings, Repentaunce *whips* entwinde, . III. xii. 24. 7
Whirled. His charret wheeles about him *whirled* round, . . . V. viii. 36. 2
Whirling. *See* **Ever-whirling.**
shed his *whirling* flames on either side, . . . *Gn.* 159
rapt with *whirling* wheeles, inflames the skyen With fire . I. iv. 9. 8
Whose circled waters rapt with *whirling* sway, . . . II. xii. 20. 5
did them drive before His *whirling* charet . . . II. xii. 22. 4
Lo! where they sypde with speedie *whirling* pace, . . . IV. iii. 38. 3
Whirlpool. a *whirlepoole* of hidden jeopardy; . . . II. xii. 18. 2
called was the *Whirlepoole* of decay; . . . II. xii. 20. 2
Whirlpools. Great *whirlpooles* which all fishes make to flee; . II. xii. 23. 7
Whirlwind. a stormy *whirlwind* blew Throughout the house, . III. xii. 3. 1
Whispered. having *whispered* a space Certein sad words . . . III. ii. 50. 4
to his wife, . . . He *whispered* in her eare, . . . III. x. 49. 4
Whispering. Some litle *whispering,* and soft groning sound. . IV. vii. 33. 4
softly *whispering* him, . . . VI. vii. 22. 3
Whispers. false *whispers,* breeding hidden feares, . . . *Epith.* 336
Whist. So was the Titanesse put downe and *whist,* . . . VII. vii. 59. 6
Whistle. His chearfull *whistle* merily doth sound, . . . I. iii. 31. 8
for his paines a *whistle* him behight, . . . IV. xi. 6. 8
Whistled. sweet Zephyrus lowd *whisteled* His treble, . . . II. xii. 33. 5
Whistler. The *whistler* shrill, that whoso heares doth dy; . . II. xii. 36. 8
Whistling. Where breathe on them the *whistling* wind mote best; . . . *Gn.* 236
Each trembling leafe and *whistling* wind they heare, . . . II. iii. 20. 4
Whit. To him that hath a *whit* of Natures giving? . . . *Hub.* 418
Can no *whit* savour this celestiall food, . . . *T.M.* 591
he for none of them did care a *whit,* . . . *As.* 49
she staied not a *whit,* . . . *As.* 175
No *whit* inferiour to thy Fanchins praise, . . . *Col.* 301
Whose praise hereby no *whit* impaired is, . . . *Col.* 755
'Charmd or enchaunted,' . . . 'I no *whitt* reck; . . . I. iv. 50. 9
she no *whitt* did chaunge her constant mood: . . . I. x. 13. 6
She unto him disclosed every *whitt;* . . . I. x. 19. 3
for my part, I vow, dissembled not a *whitt.* . . . II. iv. 18. 9
'Fayre sonne, be no *whit* sad . . . II. viii. 54. 4
ne once would rest a *whit.* . . . II. ix. 49. 9
Whome Romane warres . . . could no *whit* dismay: . . . II. x. 62. 7
hid no *whit* her alablaster skin, . . . II. xii. 77. 5
'O daughter deare!' (said she) 'despeire no *whit;* . . . III. ii. 35. 6
let no *whit* thee dismay . . . III. iii. 21. 7
No *whit* lesse fayre then terrible in fight: . . . III. iii. 56. 3
She was no *whit* thereby discouraged . . . III. xi. 50. 7
The other no *whit* better was then shee, . . . IV. i. 18. 6
Ne do your selfe dislike a *whit* the more; . . . IV. i. 46. 7
Yet she no *whit* dismayd her steed forsooke, . . . IV. vi. 14. 6
to his speach he aunswered no *whit,* . . . IV. vii. 44. 1
no *whit* of them remayning one may see. . . . V. x. 29. 9
whiles she no *whit* gainesayd: . . . V. xi. 64. 8
no *whit* more appalled for the same, . . . VI. i. 32. 3
Ne from his currish will a *whit* reclame. . . . VI. iii. 43. 2
the bold knight no *whit* thereat dismayd, . . . VI. iv. 21. 1
As no *whit* dreading any living wight; . . . VI. vii. 43. 2
answere him *awhit* (*a *whit*) thereto. . . . VI. viii. 50. 9
Did care a *whit,* ne any liking lend: . . . VI. ix. 10. 8
Did litle *whit* regard his courteous guize, . . . VI. ix. 35. 6
Yet she no *whit* his presents did regard, . . . VI. ix. 40. 6
Her constant mynd could not a *whit* remove, . . . VI. xi. 5. 2
Ne Kesars spared he a *whit,* . . . VI. xii. 28. 7
Calidore, thereof no *whit* afrayd, . . . VI. xii. 29. 1
Her hart more harde then yron soft a *whit;* . . . *Am.* xxxii. 6
White. *See* **Ivory-white, Lily-white, Mark-white, Milk-white.**
upon a *white* horse set The faithfull man . . . *Rev.* iii. 1
on horses *white,* A puissant armie . . . *Rev.* iii. 6
A Bird all *white,* well feathered . . . *Bel.* xi. 5
the one was blacke, the other *white:* . . . *Pet.* i. 7
Made all of Heben and *white* Yvorie; . . . *Pet.* ii. 2
White seem'd her robes, yet woven so . . . *Pet.* vi. 5
I saw a Bull as *white* as driven snowe, . . . *Van.* ii. 2
Yclad in Scarlot . . . And ermines *white:* . . . *S.C.* Ap. 58
The Redde rose medled with the *White* yfere, . . . *S.C.* Ap. 68
weening hys *whyte* head was chalke, . . . *S.C.* Jul. 223
the *white* beare to the stake did bring. . . . *S.C.* O. 48
He cloathed them with all colours, save *white,* . . . *Hub.* 1155
I saw two Beares, as *white* as anie milke, . . . *Ti.* 561
the goodlie criew Of *white* Strimonian brood . . . *Ti.* 593
Eftsoones her *white* streight legs were altered . . . *Mui.* 349
White as the native Rose before the chaunge . . . *D.* 108
round about with mightie *white* rocks hemd, . . . *Col.* 274
a lowly Asse more *white* then snow, . . . I. i. 4. 2
Her all in *white* he clad, . . . I. i. 45. 8
And old old man, with beard as *white* as snow, . . . I. viii. 30. 2
In whose *white* alabaster brest did stick . . . II. i. 39. 5
in his hand a *white* rod menaged: . . . II. ix. 27. 7
Learning his ship from those *white* rocks to save, . . . II. x. 6. 3
deckt with blossoms dyde in *white* and red, . . . II. xii. 12. 5
rather shewd more *white,* if more might bee: . . . II. xii. 77. 6
through feare, as *white* as whales bone: . . . III. i. 15. 5
Stretch her *white* rod over the Belgicke shore, . . . III. iii. 49. 7
on a Palfrey rydes more *white* then snow, . . . III. v. 5. 6
her *white* Palfrey, having conquered The maistring raines . . III. vii. 2. 7
white seemes fayrer macht with blacke attone; . . . III. ix. 2. 4
the *white* fomy creame Did shine with silver, . . . III. xi. 41. 4
that rich Romane of *white* marble wrought, . . . III. xii. 46. *or.* 3
quilted uppon sattin *white* as milke; . . . V. v. 2. 3
put before his lap a napron *white,* . . . V. v. 20. 8
She stretched forth a long *white* sclender wand. . . . V. vii. 7. 5
A bevie of faire Virgins clad in *white,* . . . V. ix. 31. 2

White—*Continued.*
a sage old Syre, . . . with a *white* silver hed, . . . V. ix. 43. 8
Her paps, which like *white* silken pillowes were . . . VI. viii. 42. 2
Her tender sides; her bellie *white* and clere, . . . VI. viii. 42. 4
Drawne of two steeds, th' one black, the other *white,* . . . VII. vi. 9. 2
Th' one on a Palfrey blacke, the other *white;* . . . VII. vii. 44. 3
Clad all in *white,* that seemes a virgin best. . . . *Epith.* 151
Hath *white* and red in it such wondrous powre, . . . *H.B.* 71
that same goodly hew of *white* and red, . . . *H.B.* 92
Leda was (they say) as *white* as he, . . . *Proth.* 44
Yet not so *white* as these, . . . *Proth.* 45
So purely *white* they were, . . . *Proth.* 46
White-hand. *White hand* Eunica, proud Dynamene, . . . IV. xi. 49. 1
Whiter. more white then snow, Yet she much *whiter;* . . . I. i. 4. 3
Yet she her selfe is *whiter* manifold. . . . III. v. 5. 7
The snow, . . . Did never *whiter* shew, . . . *Proth.* 41
Nor Jove himselfe, . . . *whiter* did appeare; . . . *Proth.* 43
Whither. *whither* rennes this bevie of Ladies bright, . . . *S.C.* Ap. 118
Whither whenas they came they fell at words, . . . *Hub.* 1019
which way he list, and *whether.* . . . *Col.* 251
Whither the soules doe fly of men that live amis. . . . I. ii. 19. 9
And *whither* now on new adventure bownd: . . . II. ii. 39. 6
'but *whither* with such hasty flight . . . II. iv. 43. 2
'Vile Miscreaunt,' (said he) *whither* dost thou flye . . . II. vi. 39. 6
And *whither* now he traveiled so fast? . . . III. v. 3. 7
What is of her become, or *whether* reft, . . . IV. vi. 35. 2
all were fled for feare; but *whether,* nether kond. . . . V. vi. 35. 9
She forth did rome *whether* her rage her bore, . . . V. viii. 48. 6
whether shall I goe? . . . V. x. 23. 1
Ah! *whither* doost thou now, thou greater Muse, . . . VII. vii. 1. 1
whither no man wist. . . . VII. vii. 59. 9
Ah! *whither,* Love! wilt thou now carrie mee? . . . *H.B.* 1
Who (*partial list*).
Who list the Romane greatnes forth to figure, . . . *Ro.* xxvi. 1
but *who* the Godhead can define. . . . *Col.* 347
'*Who* life did limit by almightie doome,' . . . I. ix. 41. 6
That well can witnesse *who* by tryall it does prove. . . . III. ii. 51. 9
*Scudamour, *who* she had left behind, . . . IV. vi. 46. 5
'*Who* was it then,' (sayd Artegall) 'that wrought? . . . V. i. 16. 1
Who . . . Sir Calidore upcheard, and to her teld . . . VI. i. 44. 7
the Ayre; which *who* feeles not . . . VII. vii. 22. 1
Whoever. *Who ever* casts to compasse weightye prise, . . . *S.C.* O. 103
Who ever them envie: . . . *Hub.* 424
Who ever leaves sweete home, . . . *Hub.* 909
Who ever doth to temperaunce apply . . . II. v. 1. 1
defaste Of friend or foe, *who ever* it embaste; . . . III. i. 12. 5
who ever that he bee, . . . III. x. 32. 3
Who ever thinkes through confidence of might, . . . VI. ii. 23. 7
Who ever is the mother of one chylde, . . . VI. xii. 21. 1
Whole. The *whole* worlds spoile, . . . *Bel.*² x. 10
Her that did match the *whole* earths puissaunce, . . . *Ro.* vi. 13
all this *whole* shall one day come to nought. . . . *Ro.* ix. 14
Rome was th' *whole* world, . . . *Ro.* xxvi. 9
th' *whole* history Is but a jest, . . . *Gn.* 5
This all his care, this all his *whole* indevour, . . . *Gn.* 137
of the *whole* world as thou wast the Empresse, . . . *Ti.* 83
That man, who doth the *whole* worlds rule possesse, . . . *D.* 179
the *whole* assembly of those heards Moov'd at his speech, . . *Col.* 648
Who hath endur'd the *whole* can beare ech part. . . . I. vii. 25. 5
Then gan the Dwarfe the *whole* discourse declare; . . . I. vii. 26. 1
Virgin which beheld . . . The *whole* atchievement . . . I. viii. 26. 3
gan he to discourse the *whole* debate, . . . II. viii. 54. 6
My *whole* desire hath beene . . . To serve that Queene . . . II. ix. 7. 3
It might breake out and set the *whole* on fyre, . . . II. ix. 30. 2
twixt the other twain his kingdom *whole* did shayre. . . . II. x. 28. 9
the *whole* family, therewith adredd, . . . III. i. 62. 7
his wound did gather, and grow *hole,* . . . III. v. 43. 1
Madnesse to save a part, and lose the *whole!* . . . III. v. 43. 3
all her *whole* creation did her shew Pure . . . III. vi. 3. 3
all were her *whole* delight In mischiefe, . . . III. vii. 9. 8
To see his *whole* yeares labor lost so soone, . . . III. vii. 34. 8
a *whole* legione Of wicked Sprightes . . . III. ix. 2. 7
the *whole* worlds commune remedy.' . . . III. x. 26. 5
to be unbownd And perfect *hole,* . . . III. xii. 38. 9
They two enough t' encounter an *whole* Regiment. . . . V. i. 30. 9
he gan at large to her dilate The *whole* discourse . . . V. vi. 17. 2
Her minde was *whole* possessed of one thought, . . . V. vi. 21. 3
Then gan she to declare the *whole* discourse . . . V. vii. 20. 1
neglect The worlds *whole* rule for Cleopatras sight. . . . V. viii. 2. 7
Of whom we may at will the *whole* occasion know.' . . . V. viii. 15. 9
no *whole* peece of him was to be seene, . . . V. viii. 42. 8
Though nothing *whole,* but all to-brusd and broken, . . . V. viii. 44. 2
The *whole* occasion of his late misfare, . . . V. xi. 48. 7
His *whole* exploite and valorous emprize, . . . VI. i. 5. 4
of his wounds he wexed *hole* and strong; . . . VI. i. 47. 8
How to save *hole* her hazarded estate; . . . VI. iii. 12. 7
to him their cause they best esteemed *Whole* to commit, . . . VI. iii. 13. 4
Recured well, and made him *whole* againe; . . . VI. iv. 16. 7
wound Made in his tender flesh; but *whole* them all he found. VI. iv. 23. 9
So now she had bene wandring two *whole* yeares . . . VI. viii. 38. 1
challenge to themselves the *whole* worlds raign, . . . VII. vii. 15. 3
These gods do claime the worlds *whole* soverainty, . . . VII. vii. 16. 2
Then was that *whole* assembly quite dismist, . . . VII. vii. 59. 8
with one word my *whole* years work doth rend. . . . *Am.* xxiii. 12
That *whole* remaines scarse any little part; . . . *H.L.* 144
Wholesome. Through the Priests *holesome* counsell lately tought, . . . *Hub.* 553
The *wholesome* Saulge, and Lavender still gray, . . . *Mui.* 187
wholesome Statutes to her husband brought. . . . II. x. 42. 6
still it breathed forth sweet spirit and *holesom* smell: . . . II. xii. 51. 9

Wholesome—*Continued.*
More sweet and *holesome* then the pleasaunt hill Of Rhodope, II. xii. 52. 1
With *holesome* reede of sad sobriety, ... VI. vi. 5. 7
Sprinkled with *wholsom* waters more then most on ground: . VII. vi. 38. 9
Wholly. it *wholly* springeth from my wit: . . . . *Hub.* 1037
are *wholly* now defaced; . . . . *T.M.* 202
To the gay gardins . . . Him *wholly* caried, ... *Mui.* 162
To her my life I *wholly* sacrifice: . . . . *Col.* 475
presently was void and *wholly* vaine: . . . . I. viii. 4. 7
thee abandond *wholy* do possesse, ... III. ii. 46. 3
wholy waste and void of peoples trode, ... III. ix. 49. 7
she her love and hart hath *wholy* sold To him, ... III. x. 11. 2
On which their eies and harts were *wholly* sett, ... III. x. 34. 6
sweetnesse . . . The feeble sences *wholy* did confound, . . . III. xii. 6. 4
wholly dead Himselfe he wisht have beene, ... IV. iv. 22. 8
she, whose hart to love was *wholly* lent, ... IV. viii. 50. 6
her selfe she *wholy* recommended To Gods sole grace, . . . VI. iv. 10. 7
Thereon his mynd affixed *wholly* is; . . . . *H.L.* 204
Whom (*partial list*).
'Thou barrein ground, *whome* winters wrath hath wasted, . . *S.C.* Ja. 19
the ladde, *whome* long I lovd so deare, ... *S.C.* Ap. 10
Whomever. hurt far off unknowne *whom ever* she envide. . . III. vii. 6. 9
Whomso. *whom so* he overthrowes, . . . doth headlong fall; . V. ii. 8. 3
cruelly does wound *whom so* she wils: . . . . V. xii. 36. 5
Whooping. *Whooping* and hallowing on every part, ... VI. viii. 40. 3
Whore. he gave in charge unto his Squyre, That scarlot *whore* I. viii. 29. 2
Whoredom. The wine of *hooredome* in a cup . . . . *Rev.* ii. 8
Abessa, . . . With whom he *whoredome* usd, that few did know, I. iii. 18. 5
Whores. Him calling theefe, them *whores;* . . . . IV. viii. 35. 4
Whose (*partial list*).
Typhoeus sister comming neare; *Whose* head . . . Did seeme . *Bel.*[2] xv. 5
He had two sonnes, *whose* eldest, called Lud, ... II. x. 46. 1
to weet *whose* she should bee, ... IV. ii. 38. 2
to listen *whose* The honour of the prize . . . . V. iii. 13. 8
Whosever. *Whose ever be the shield, faire Amoret be his.* . . . IV. x. 8. 9
Whoso. *Who so* loathes not too much the poore estate, . . . *Gn.* 90
Praise *who so* list, ... *Ti.* 229
'And *who so* els did goodnes by him gaine, ... *Ti.* 232
And *who so* els his bounteous minde did trie, ... *Ti.* 233
Then, *who so* will with vertuous deeds assay . . . . . . *Ti.* 425
'And *who so* els that sits in highest seate . . . . *Ti.* 463
But *whoso* else in pleasure findeth sense, ... *D.* 8
And ye, *who so* ye be, that still survive, ... *Col.* 644
who so else doth otherwise esteeme, ... *Col.* 889
whoso did eat, eftsoones did know Both good and ill. . . . I. xi. 47. 7
who-so kild that monster most deforme, ... I. xii. 20. 3
Which *whoso* wants, wants so much of his rest: . . . . . . II. i. 59. 7
Yet well he wist that *whoso* would contend With either . . II. iii. 17. 2
Whoso right haunch earst my stedfast arrow strake? . . . . II. iii. 32. 8
whoso will raging Furor tame, ... II. iv. 11. 1
did disdayne To be so cald, and *who so* did him call: . . . II. vii. 41. 2
throw his ragged rift On *whoso* cometh nigh; . . . . II. xii. 4. 6
The whistler shrill, that *whoso* heares doth dy; . . . . . II. xii. 36. 8
whoso fayre thing doest faine to see, ... II. xii. 74. 2
Dy, *who so* list for him, he was loves enimy. . . . . . . III. iv. 26. 9
who so then her saw would surely say . . . . III. viii. 9. 3
That *who so* straungely had him seene bestadd, ... III. x. 54. 7
who so list looke backe to former ages, ... IV. Pr. 3. 1
Tell what thou saw'st, maulgre *who so* it heares.' . . . . IV. i. 48. 6
That *who so* winnes her may her have by right: . . . . . . IV. iv. 9. 7
When *who so* list to fight may fight his fill: . . . . . . IV. iv. 12. 6
All which *who so* dare thinke for to enchace, ... IV. v. 12. 1
For *who so* list . . . . V. Pr. 5. 1
That *who so* heares her heavinesse, would rew . . . . . . VI. xi. 2. 8
That *who so* hardie hand on her doth lay, ... VI. xi. 15. 8
Who so wil seeke, by right deserts, t' attaine, ... *Com. Son.* ii. 1
And *who so* list the like assayes to ken, ... *H.B.* 88
But *who so* may, thrise happie man him hold, ... *H.H.B.* 239
Whosoever. *whosoever* dost abide by Nyle, ... *Ro.* xxxi. 3
whosoever once hath fastened His foot thereon, ... II. xii. 12. 7
But *whosoever* contrarie doth prove, ... IV. v. 3. 3
Whot, -test. *See* **Hot, -test.**
Why (*partial list*). *See* **Forwhy.**
Why have your hands long sithence traveiled . . . . *Ro.* ix. 5
Or *why* were not these Romane palaces . . . . *Ro.* ix. 7
Why then should greatest things the least disdaine, ... *Van.* iii. 13
Why do vaine men mean things so much deface, ... *Van.* xi. 12
(alas! *why* do I love?) . . . (alas! *why* am I lorne?) . . . *S.C.* Ja. 61, 62
'*Why* standst there (quoth he) . . . . *S.C.* F. 127
Thomalin, *why* sytten we soe, ... *S.C.* Mar. 1
The sonne of his loines *why* should he regard To leave . . . *S.C.* May 83
(O! *why* should Death on hym such outrage showe?) . . . *S.C.* Jun. 90
Why done we them disease? . . . . *S.C.* Jul. 124
Why should we be bound to such miseree? . . . . *S.C.* S. 239
'*Why* doe we longer live, (ah *why* live we so long?) . . . *S.C.* N. 73
Why then weepes Lobbin so without remorse? . . . . *S.C.* N. 167
'*Why* wayle we then? *why* weary we the Gods with playnts, . *S.C.* N. 173
Why livest thou stil . . . *Why* dyest thou stil, ... *S.C.* D. 95, 96
For *why* should he that is at libertie . . . . *Hub.* 132
Why should ye doubt, ... *Hub.* 425
Whie then doo foolish men so much despize . . . . *T.M.* 145
Why doo they banish us, ... *T.M.* 147
Asked *why?* say: . . . . *U.V.* 10
Wote ye *why,* his Moother . . . hath coovered his Face? . . . *Tetrasticon* 3
'*Why* then dooth flesh, ... *Ti.* 50
'But *whie* (unhappy wight!) . . . . *Ti.* 176
Why will hereafter anie flesh delight In earthlie blis, ... *Ti.* 527
The cause *why* he this Flie so maliced Was . . . . *Mui.* 257
why did they then create The world so fayre, ... *D.* 204
Or *whie* be they themselves immaculate, ... *D.* 206

Why—*Continued.*
Ah! *why* does my Alcyon weepe and mourne, ... *D.* 264
Why should Alcyon then so sore lament . . . . *D.* 271
Why then should I desire here to remaine! Or *why* should he, . *D.* 277, 278
why seeke I to prolong My wearie daies . . . . *D.* 439
'*Why* doo I longer live in lifes despight, ... *D.* 442
Why doo I longer see this loathsome light . . . . *D.* 444
Why then do I, . . . Presume the things so sacred . . . . . *Col.* 348
'*Why?* (said Alexis then) . . . . *Col.* 368
'*Why* Colin, since thou foundst such grace . . . . *Col.* 652
Why didst thou ever leave that happie place, ... *Col.* 654
'*Why,* Dame,' (quoth he,) . . . . I. i. 52. 8
why hath he me abhord?' . . . . I. iii. 7. 9
sooth to say, *why* I lefte you so long, ... I. iii. 29. 1
And said, '*Why* Archimago, lucklesse syre, ... I. iii. 39. 1
Why they were come her roiall state to see, ... I. iv. 13. 8
'*Why,* dame,' (quoth he) . . . . I. iv. 50. 3
Why wilt not let him passe, ... I. ix. 39. 8
let none aske whence, nor *why.* . . . . I. ix. 42. 9
'*Why* then doest thou, O man of sin! desire . . . . I. ix. 46. 1
Why shouldst thou then despeire, ... I. ix. 53. 5
O foolish men! *why* hast ye to your own decay?' . . . . . I. x. 10. 9
Much more then that *why* they in bands were layd: . . . . I. x. 40. 7
why of late Didst thou behight me borne of English blood, . . I. x. 64. 5
Why then should witlesse man so much misweene, ... II. Pr. 3. 4
Or *why* should ever I henceforth desyre To see . . . . . . II. i. 17. 3
Sir Guyon, *why* with so fierce saliaunce, ... II. i. 29. 6
Why livest thou, dead dog, ... II. iii. 7. 6
'*Why* then doest thou, O man! . . . . II. vi. 17. 1
'And *why* then,' sayd, ... II. vii. 14. 6
After so wicked deede *why* liv'st thou lenger day?' . . . . II. viii. 46. 9
To weet *why* on your shield, ... II. ix. 2. 7
why beene ye thus dismayd, ... II. ix. 37. 5
'*Why* wonder yee, ... II. ix. 43. 6
yet wist she nether how, nor *why.* . . . . III. ii. 27. 6
why that same dore Was shut to all . . . . III. viii. 52. 7
why Satyrane and Paridell Mote not be entertaynd, ... III. ix. 3. 2
the cause *why* never any knight Is suffred here to enter, . . III. ix. 6. 3
why doe wee devise of others ill, ... III. ix. 8. 6
why she could not come in place; . . . . III. ix. 26. 2
why do men say thou canst not see, ... III. x. 4. 3
Why then is Amoret in caytive band, ... III. xi. 10. 2
Why then is Busirane with wicked hand Suffred, ... III. xi. 10. 7
(ah! *why* should he so?) . . . . III. xi. 45. 2
'The cause *why* she was covered with a vele . . . . IV. x. 41. 1
Why should they not likewise in love agree, ... IV. xi. 40. 4
'Who was it then,' . . . 'that wrought? And *why?* . . . . . V. i. 16. 2
Why hath thy hand . . . it selfe embrewed In blood . . . . VI. ii. 7. 3
But *why,* when I them saw, fled they away from me?' . . . VI. x. 19. 9
Why then should I accoumpt of little paine, ... *Am.* xxvi. 13
why should faire be proud, ... *Am.* xxvii. 1
why hath nature . . . Given so goodly giftes . . . . *Am.* xxxi. 1
why are ye so fierce and cruell? . . . . *Am.* xlix. 1
Why then doe ye, proud fayre, misdeeme so farre, ... *Am.* lviii. 13
Why did ye stoup . . . . *Am.* lxvi. 8
why doe ye sleepe thus long, ... *Epith.* 85
Why stand ye still ye virgins in amaze, ... *Epith.* 181
Why blush ye, love, to give to me your hand, ... *Epith.* 238
Why then do I this honor unto thee, ... *H.L.* 148
Why doe not then the blossomes of the field, ... *H.B.* 78
Or *why* doe not faire pictures like powre shew, ... *H.B.* 82
Whyleare. *See* **Whilere.**
Wick. The light goes out, and *weeke* is throwne away: . . . II. x. 30. 2
Wicked. there bred A litle *wicked* worme, ... *Van.* vii. 7
Beare witnesse all of thys so *wicked* deede: . . . . *S.C.* Jun. 108
there wonned a *wicked* Wolfe, ... *S.C.* S. 184
them amongst the *wicked* Lotos grew, ... *Gn.* 193
Wicked for holding guilefully away Ulysses men, ... *Gn.* 194
Minos righteous soules doth sever From *wicked* ones, ... *Gn.* 624
a *wicked* maladie Raign'd emongst men, ... *Hub.* 9
drew the *wicked* Shepheard to his will. . . . . *Hub.* 320
with his *wicked* charmes And strong conceipts . . . . . . *Hub.* 826
whom *wicked* fate Hath brought to Court, ... *Hub.* 892
The *wicked* weed, which there the Foxe did lay, ... *Hub.* 1321
What wrath of Gods, or *wicked* influence . . . . *T.M.* 481
a *wicked* wight, The foe of faire things, ... *Mui.* 243
to his *wicked* worke each part applie. . . . . *Mui.* 253
wicked Fortune faultles him misled, ... *Mui.* 418
Till he recanted had his *wicked* rimes, ... *Col.* 923
soone to loose her *wicked* bands did her constraine. . . . . I. i. 19. 9
that *wicked* wight his dayes doth weare; . . . . I. i. 31. 7
Bathed in wanton blis and *wicked* joy. . . . . I. i. 47. 6
messengers of hell, . . . Came to their *wicked* maister, ... I. ii. 2. 3
whiles *wicked* wights Have knit themselves . . . . I. ii. 4. 7
'The *wicked* witch, now seeing all this while . . . . I. ii. 38. 1
With *wicked* herbes and oyntments did besmeare My body . . I. ii. 42. 3
of his *wicked* pelfe his God he made, ... I. iv. 27. 6
bowing downe her aged backe, she kist The *wicked* witch, . . I. v. 27. 2
Her *wicked* daies with wretched knife did end, ... I. v. 39. 2
Through *wicked* pride and wasted welthes decay. . . . . . . I. v. 51. 4
Ne let that *wicked* woman scape away; . . . . I. viii. 28. 5
loe! that *wicked* woman in your sight, ... I. viii. 45. 4
they come where that same *wicked* wight His dwelling has, . I. ix. 33. 1
Greevd with remembrance of his *wicked* wayes, ... I. x. 21. 6
by her *wicked* arts and wylie skill, ... I. xii. 32. 6
Unwares me wrought unto her *wicked* will, ... I. xii. 32. 8
Ne *wicked* envy, ne vile gealosy, ... I. xii. 41. 3
He gan to weave a web of *wicked* guyle, ... II. i. 8. 4
mischiefes which a *wicked* Fay Had wrought, ... II. ii. 43. 3
him behynd a *wicked* Hag did stalke, ... II. iv. 4. 1

Wicked—*Continued.*
Where this same *wicked* villein did me light upon. . . . . II. iv. 17. 9
'Most wretched woman and of *wicked* race, ... II. vi. 33. 7
by unrighteous And *wicked* doome, ... II. vii. 62. 5
To serve to *wicked* man, to serve his *wicked* foe. . . . . II. viii. 1. 9
After so *wicked* deede why liv'st thou lenger day?' . . . . II. viii. 46. 9
read, what *wicked* hand hath robbed mee . . . . . II. viii. 54. 1
false Acrasia, and her *wicked* wiles; . . . . . II. ix. 9. 6
As if the rest some *wicked* hand did rend, ... II. x. 68. 4
overcame The *wicked* Gobbelines in bloody field; . . . . . II. x. 73. 2
That *wicked* band of villeins . . . . . II. xi. 5. 3
Their *wicked* engins they against it bent; . . . . . II. xi. 9. 6
their *wicked* Capitayn Provoked them . . . . . II. xi. 14. 6
There follow'd fast at hand two *wicked* Hags, ... II. xi. 23. 2
still as abroad he strew His *wicked* arrowes, ... II. xi. 28. 2
Which when those *wicked* Hags from far did spye, ... II. xi. 47. 1
ryv'd her trembling hart, and *wicked* end did make. . . . . II. xi. 47. 9
that same *wicked* witch, ... II. xii. 26. 4
with their *wicked* wings them ofte did smight, ... II. xii. 35. 8
Emongst the Roses grow some *wicked* weeds: . . . . . III. i. 49. 6
Then doth this *wicked* evill thee infest, ... III. ii. 32. 4
to their purpose used *wicked* art: . . . . . III. ii. 41. 4
So was their fortune good, though *wicked* were their minde. . III. ii. 43. 9
wicked fortune mine, though minde be good, ... III. ii. 44. 1
Ne shall availe the *wicked* sorcery . . . . . III. iii. 36. 3
The *wicked* steele through his left side did glaunce. . . . . III. iv. 16. 5
After that *wicked* foster fiercely went: . . . . . III. iv. 47. 4
he gan fowly wyte His *wicked* fortune . . . . . III. iv. 52. 8
The *wicked* steele stayd not . . . . . III. v. 20. 6
Where *wicked* ghosts doe waile their former sin. . . . . III. v. 22. 4
with that *wicked* shafte him wounded had, ... III. v. 24. 2
that the *wicked* steele empoysned were: . . . . . III. v. 49. 3
His cruell deedes and *wicked* wyles did spot: . . . . . III. vi. 13. 5
Great enimy to it . . . Is *wicked* Tyme; . . . . . III. vi. 39. 3
Nor *wicked* beastes their tender buds did crop, ... III. vi. 43. 5
Busie (as seem'd) about some *wicked* gin: . . . . . III. vii. 7. 3
such whenas the *wicked* Hag did vew, ... III. vii. 11. 4
This *wicked* woman had a *wicked* sonne, ... III. vii. 12. 1
Closely the *wicked* flame his bowels brent, ... III. vii. 16. 1
She turnd her selfe backe to her *wicked* leares; . . . . . III. vii. 21. 7
Not halfe so fast the *wicked* Myrrha fled . . . . . III. vii. 26. 1
Fiercely he flew upon that *wicked* feend, ... III. vii. 32. 2
by her *wicked* art Late foorth she sent, ... III. viii. 2. 5
By their advice, and her owne *wicked* wit, ... III. viii. 5. 1
A *wicked* Spright, yfraught with fawning guyle . . . . . III. viii. 8. 1
a whole legione Of *wicked* Sprightes . . . . . III. ix. 2. 8
The *wicked* engine through false influence . . . . . III. ix. 29. 3
saw the *wicked* fire so furiously Consume his hart, ... III. x. 14. 5
Why then is Busirane with *wicked* hand Suffred, ... III. xi. 10. 7
freely read what *wicked* felon so Hath outrag'd you, ... III. xi. 15. 2
Faire Amorett must dwell in *wicked* chaines, ... III. xi. 16. 3
His *wicked* bookes in hast he overthrew, ... III. xii. 32. 2
The *wicked* weapon rashly he did wrest, ... III. xii. 33. 2
'Thou *wicked* man, whose meed . . . Is death, ... III. xii. 35. 1
punish *wicked* men that walke amisse: . . . . . IV. i. 20. 3
The barren ground was full of *wicked* weedes, ... IV. i. 25. 2
wicked wordes that God and man offended. . . . . . IV. i. 27. 5
Firebrand of hell . . . Is *wicked* discord; . . . . . IV. ii. 1. 5
when the *wicked* feend his Lord tormented, ... IV. ii. 2. 2
wicked Time that all good thoughts doth waste, ... IV. ii. 33. 1
The *wicked* weapon heard his wrathfull vow, ... IV. iii. 11. 6
The *wicked* steele, for mischiefe first ordained, ... IV. iv. 24. 3
She through her *wicked* working did incense . . . . . IV. v. 23. 2
the *wicked* carle, the maister Smith, ... IV. v. 44. 1
The *wicked* stroke upon her helmet chaunst, ... IV. vi. 19. 1
of the *wicked* world forgotten quight, ... IV. vii. 39. 6
Of that same *wicked* Carle, ... IV. viii. 21. 6
Him from his *wicked* will uneath refrayned; . . . . . IV. x. 36. 7
By *wicked* doome condemn'd a wretched death to die. . . . . IV. xii. 29. 9
the *wicked* seede of vice Began to spring; . . . . . V. i. 1. 3
Mongst *wicked* men, in whom no truth she found, ... V. i. 11. 3
more emboldned by the *wicked* charmes, ... V. ii. 5. 5
therewith fill The coffers of her *wicked* threasury, ... V. ii. 9. 4
wicked customes of that Bridge refourmed; . . . . . V. ii. 28. 8
'Ay me,' (quoth she) 'what *wicked* destinie! . . . . . V. vi. 10. 8
A man of subtill wit and *wicked* minde, ... V. vi. 32. 2
had deviz'd of late With these his *wicked* sons, ... V. vi. 33. 9
The *wicked* shaft . . . Stayd not, ... V. viii. 34. 6
Out of her fist the *wicked* weapon caught: . . . . . V. viii. 48. 4
Fit for Adicia there to build her *wicked* bowre. . . . . . V. ix. 1. 9
To weet, a *wicked* villaine, bold and stout, ... V. ix. 4. 6
wicked sclaunders by him shed. . . . . . V. ix. 26. 9
favour not The *wicked* driftes of trayterous desynes . . . . . V. ix. 42. 2
The *wicked* stroke did wound his enemy . . . . . V. xi. 6. 8
To blot the same with blame, or wrest in *wicked* sort. . . . . V. xii. 34. 9
A *wicked* hag, and Envy selfe excelling In mischiefe; . . . . V. xii. 35. 7
From view of men, and *wicked* worlds disdaine; . . . . . VI. Pr. 3. 4
Into this *wicked* world he forth was sent . . . . . VI. i. 8. 6
he the more his *wicked* poyson forth did poure.' . . . . . VI. i. 9. 9
executes her *wicked* will with worse despight. . . . . . VI. i. 15. 9
wicked customes make, those doe defame . . . . . VI. i. 26. 7
Which had this outrage wrought with *wicked* hand. . . . . . VI. ii. 44. 4
Of former daies mishap, his sorrowes *wicked* sourse. . . . . VI. iii. 14. 9
A *wicked* Monster, that his tongue doth whet Gainst all, . . VI. vi. 12. 3
it was to thee reprochfull blame To erect this *wicked* custome, . VI. vi. 34. 4
To worke by *wicked* treason wayes doth find, ... VI. vii. 1. 8
The wretch that hyr'd you to this *wicked* deed.' . . . . . VI. vii. 13. 5
no such beast they saw, Nor any *wicked* feend . . . . . VI. ix. 6. 2
warres, and wreckes, and *wicked* enmitie . . . . . VI. ix. 19. 6
Hath wrought this *wicked* deed: . . . . . VI. xi. 29. 9

Wicked—*Continued.*
(whether *wicked* fate so framed Or fault of men,) . . . . . VI. xii. 38. 7
some *wicked* tongues did it backebite, ... VI. xii. 41. 5
some *wicked* beast unware That breakes into her Dayr' house, VII. vi. 48. 3
A *wicked* ambush which lay hidden long . . . . . *Am.* xii. 6
she to *wicked* men a scourge should bee, ... *Am.* xxiv. 11
catching hold on thine owne *wicked* hed, ... *Am.* lxxxv. 10
Wickedly. Whose wofull parents she hath *wickedly* fordonne.' II. ii. 44. 9
First ill, and after ruled *wickedly;* . . . . . III. iii. 46. 3
lewdly did miscall And *wickedly* backbite: . . . . . IV. viii. 24. 9
Wickedness. Ah, wretched world! the den of *wickednesse,* *T.M.* 121
in *wickednesse* woxe bold, ... IV. viii. 31. 8
Wicker. each one had a little *wicker* basket, ... *Proth.* 24
Wicket. her unruly Page With his rude clawes the *wicket* open rent, ... I. iii. 13. 2
before the *wicket* fast They wayted, ... III. ix. 11. 2
that yron *wicket* open flew, ... III. xii. 3. 3
Wicket's. creeping close behind the *Wickets* clink, ... *S.C.* May 251
Widder. *See* **Wider.**
Wide. *See* **Basin-wide, Greedy-wide.**
her flank *wide* rended. . . . . . *Bel.*[2] vi. 11
with *wide* pinneons To measure . . . . . *Bel.*[2] vii. 6
having his *wide* wings spent in wast, ... *Ro.* xvi. 7
The map of all the *wide* world doth containe. . . . . . *Ro.* xxvi. 14
the heaven it selfe with her *wide* wonders fill. . . . . . *Ro.* xxix. 8
That same is now nought but a champian *wide,* . . . . . *Ro.* xxxi. 1
to open *wide* The griesly gates . . . . . *Van.* iii. 9
His *wide* Abysse him forced forth to spewe, ... *Van.* v. 10
Looking far foorth into the Ocean *wide,* . . . . . *Van.* ix. 1
oft the bloud springeth from woundes *wyde;* . . . . . *S.C.* F. 176
She mought see the dore stand open *wyde.* . . . . . *S.C.* May 295
The forest *wide* is fitter to resound . . . . . *S.C.* Au. 159
wide open throte. . . . . . *S.C.* S. 195
shooting *wide,* doe misse the marked scope; . . . . . *S.C.* N. 155
I went the wastefull woodes and forest *wide,* . . . . . *S.C.* D. 23
Throgh the *wide* woods and groves, ... *Gn.* 32
Betwixt the forrest *wide* and starrie sky. . . . . . *Gn.* 34
fame now rings Through the *wide* world, ... *Gn.* 150
Birds, in their *wide* boughs embowring, ... *Gn.* 225
once assai'd to burne this world so *wide.* . . . . . *Gn.* 376
with *wide* wounds their carcases doth rend; . . . . . *Gn.* 414
wide Sigaean shores were spred with corses, ... *Gn.* 501
Wide is the world I wote, ... *Hub.* 90
as we bee sonnes of the world so *wide,* . . . . . *Hub.* 135
From the right way full eath may wander *wide:* . . . . . *Hub.* 404
with big lookes basen *wide,* . . . . . *Hub.* 670
Whatso the heaven in his *wide* vawte containes, ... *Hub.* 1229
Pierce the dull heavens and fill the ayer *wide,* . . . . . *T.M.* 118
In this *wide* world in which they, wretches, stray, ... *T.M.* 493
In that *wide* lake looking for plenteous praie . . . . . *Ti.* 151
Doo fawne on you, and your *wide* praises sing; . . . . . *Ti.* 201
like the coloured Rainbowe arched *wide:* . . . . . *Ti.* 550
Through the *wide* compas of the ayrie coast; . . . . . *Mui.* 38
the *wide* rule of his renowmed sire. . . . . . *Mui.* 40
In the *wide* aire to make her wandring flight; . . . . . *Mui.* 139
all the countrey *wide* he did possesse, ... *Mui.* 150
With his aire-cutting wings he measured *wide,* . . . . . *Mui.* 154
With fine small cords about it stretched *wide,* . . . . . *Mui.* 359
whose praises *wide* Were spred abroad; . . . . . *D.* 144
Into a forest *wide* and waste he came, ... *As.* 93
So *wide* a forest and so waste as this, ... *As.* 95
Wide wounds emongst them many one he made, ... *As.* 107
Rolling like mountaines in *wide* wildernesse, ... *Col.* 198
As the *wide* compasse of the firmament . . . . . *Ded. Son.* ix. 5
all within were pathes and alleies *wide,* . . . . . I. i. 7. 7
High on an hill, his flocke to vewen *wide,* . . . . . I. i. 23. 3
their wonted entrance . . . At her *wide* mouth; . . . . . I. i. 25. 6
a litle *wyde* There was an holy chappell edifyde, ... I. i. 34. 4
through the world of waters *wide* and deepe, ... I. i. 39. 2
al that in the *wide* deepe wandring arre; . . . . . I. ii. 1. 5
He that the *wide* West under his rule has, ... I. ii. 22. 8
Nought is there under heav'ns *wide* hollownesse, ... I. iii. 1. 1
She, . . . Through woods and wastnes *wide* him daily sought; I. iii. 3. 8
Long she thus traveiled through deserts *wyde,* . . . . . I. iii. 10. 1
too nigh at hand, but turned *wyde* Unto an hil; . . . . . I. iii. 26. 4
the . . . marinere, That long hath wandred in the Ocean *wide,* I. iii. 31. 2
to all the gates stood open *wide:* . . . . . I. iv. 6. 2
To prove the *wide* report of her great Majestee. . . . . . I. iv. 13. 9
Pecocks . . . their tayles dispredden *wide.* . . . . . I. iv. 17. 9
Seeing the gored woundes to gape so *wyde,* . . . . . I. v. 9. 8
In wine and oyle they wash his woundes *wide,* . . . . . I. v. 17. 4
staring *wide* With stony eies; . . . . . I. v. 32. 6
his woundes *wyde* Not throughly heald . . . . . I. v. 45. 4
in another corner *wide* were strowne . . . . . I. v. 49. 3
dawning light Discovered had the world to heaven *wyde,* . . I. v. 52. 6
Therion, . . . Who had more joy to raunge the forrest *wyde,* I. vi. 21. 7
made *wide* furrowes in their fleshes fraile, ... I. vi. 43. 5
forth she went to seeke him far and *wide.* . . . . . I. vii. 2. 5
shut up heavens windowes shyning *wyde;* . . . . . I. vii. 23. 5
Wyde wonders over all . . . weren told, ... I. viii. 3. 7
from the world that her discovered *wide,* Fled . . . . . I. viii. 50. 2
Raunging the forest *wide* on courser free, ... I. ix. 12. 7
staring *wyde* With stony eyes . . . . . I. ix. 24. 2
lover . . . A *wyde* way made to let forth living breath: . . . I. ix. 30. 3
In all his waies through this *wide* worldes wave; . . . . . I. x. 34. 8
all the ayre with terror filled *wyde,* . . . . . I. xi. 4. 2
She him obayd, and turnd a little *wyde.*— . . . . . I. xi. 5. 5
made *wide* devouring shadow under his huge waste, ... I. xi. 8. 4
deepe devouring jawes *Wyde* gaped, ... I. xi. 12. 8
his waving wings displayed *wyde,* . . . . . I. xi. 18. 1

Wide—*Continued.*
The percing steele there wrought a wound full *wyde,* . . . I. xi. 20. 8
All healed of his hurts and woundes *wide,* . . . I. xi. 52. 2
gaping *wyde,* . . . him to have swallowd . . . I. xi. 53. 1
He badd to open *wyde* his brasen gate, . . . I. xii. 3. 6
holy water thereon sprinckled *wide;* . . . I. xii. 37. 5
spred his glory through all countryes *wide.* . . . II. i. 35. 4
In cruell fight on Lybicke Ocean *wide,* . . . II. ii. 22. 6
scorning both their spights, does make *wide* way, . . . II. ii. 24. 7
They waved like a penon *wyde* dispred, . . . II. iii. 30. 4
her dores to all stand open *wide.* . . . II. iii. 41. 9
from the right way seeke to draw him *wide,* . . . II. iv. 2. 7
strooke more often *wyde,* . . . II. iv. 7. 4
His burning eyen . . . Stared full *wide,* . . . II. iv. 15. 6
opened *wide* a red floodgate. . . . II. v. 7. 9
'In this *wide* Inland sea, . . . II. vi. 10. 1
Emongst *wide* waves sett, like a litle nest, . . . II. vi. 12. 2
Unto the other side of that *wide* strond . . . II. vi. 19. 2
The sea is *wide,* and easy for to stray; . . . II. vi. 23. 4
still he traveild through *wide* wastfull ground, . . . II. vii. 2. 8
downe them poured through an hole full *wide* . . . II. vii. 6. 4
the gate of Hell, which gaped *wide,* . . . II. vii. 24. 6
The rowme was large and *wyde,* . . . II. vii. 43. 3
They made the further shore resounden *wide.* . . . II. vii. 57. 6
forced him his ground to traverse *wyde,* . . . II. viii. 35. 3
whiles his shield was *wyde,* . . . II. viii. 36. 4
Wyde was the wound, . . . II. viii. 39. 1
To yield *wide* way to his hart-thrilling brond; . . . II. viii. 41. 8
Their murmuring small trompetts sownden *wide,* . . . II. ix. 16. 3
His larumbell might lowd and *wyde* be hard . . . II. ix. 25. 7
There placed was a caudron *wide* and tall . . . II. ix. 29. 5
Ne under Sunne that shines so *wide* and faire, . . . II. x. 2. 1
first opened The bowels of *wide* Fraunce, . . . II. x. 23. 7
yet remaines his *wide* memoriall. . . . II. x. 76. 3
lay strong siege about it far and *wyde.* . . . II. xi. 5. 5
All were the wownd so *wide* and wonderous . . . II. xi. 38. 2
gaping *wide* to swallow them alyve . . . II. xii. 5. 7
Ne that approcheth nigh the *wyde* descent, . . . II. xii. 6. 8
to and fro doe ronne In the *wide* waters: . . . II. xii. 11. 6
Islands, which doe fleet In the *wide* sea, . . . II. xii. 14. 4
within the utmost bound Of his *wide* Labyrinth, . . . II. xii. 20. 9
How to direct theyr way in darkenes *wide,* . . . II. xii. 35. 2
At length they came into a forest *wyde,* . . . III. i. 14. 5
a spatious playne, . . . it selfe did spredden *wyde,* . . . III. i. 20. 7
To hunt the salvage beast in forrest *wyde,* . . . III. i. 37. 4
through the *wyde* worlde soone were solemniz'd. . . . III. ii. 18. 9
launched this wound *wyde.* . . . III. ii. 37. 9
With his *wide* wings upon them fiercely fly, . . . III. iii. 46. 6
vewing his *wide* wownd, . . . III. iv. 44. 3
through the raine Of the *wide* ayre . . . III. iv. 49. 5
long time wandred through the forest *wyde* . . . III. v. 3. 1
Of all good Ladies through the worlde so *wide,* . . . III. v. 11. 2
sought the salvage woods and forests *wyde,* . . . III. vi. 16. 4
double gates it had which opened *wide,* . . . III. vi. 31. 5
in the *wide* wombe of the world . . . III. vi. 36. 6
His feeble hart *wide* launched with loves cruel wownd. . . . III. vi. 52. 9
the *wide* sea importuned long space . . . III. viii. 29. 7
wide nosethrils burnd With breathed flames, . . . III. ix. 22. 3
to the wound his weake heart opened *wyde:* . . . III. ix. 29. 2
her up he cast To the *wide* world, . . . III. x. 35. 8
wander *wide* At wilde adventure, . . . III. x. 36. 2
My Lord and I will search the *wide* forest.' . . . III. x. 41. 7
the proud Bird, ruffing his fethers *wyde* . . . III. xi. 32. 6
with *wide* winges to beat the buxome ayre: . . . III. xi. 34. 2
That his swift charet might have passage *wyde* . . . III. xi. 40. 8
many *wide* woundes launched through his inner partes. . . . III. xi. 44. 9
every wood and every valley *wyde* . . . III. xii. 7. 8
a *wide* wound therein (O ruefull sight!) . . . III. xii. 20. 5
At that *wide* orifice her trembling hart Was drawne forth, . . . III. xii. 21. 1
the *wyde* wound, which lately did dispart . . . III. xii. 38. 3
Even immortal prayse and glory *wyde,* . . . III. xii. 39. 6
The God of love with wings displayed *wide* . . . IV. i. 39. 3
Like three faire branches budding farre and *wide,* . . . IV. ii. 43. 5
Unluckie Mayd, to seeke him farre and *wide,* . . . IV. v. 29. 7
In salvage forrests and in deserts *wide* . . . IV. vii. 2. 6
his *wide* mouth did gape With huge great teeth, . . . IV. vii. 5. 5
like a *wide* deepe poke, . . . IV. vii. 6. 2
downe both sides two *wide* long eares did glow, . . . IV. vii. 6. 7
Belphebe, raunging in that forrest *wide,* . . . IV. vii. 29. 2
Through the *wide* region of the wastfull aire, . . . IV. viii. 8. 8
into that forrest *wide* She drew her far, . . . IV. viii. 11. 6
through the endlesse world did wander *wide,* . . . IV. viii. 18. 8
With filthy lockes about her scattered *wide,* . . . IV. viii. 23. 7
all the world confound with *wide* uprore, . . . IV. ix. 23. 8
to me opened *wide.* . . . IV. x. 14. 3
The same to all stoode alwaies open *wide;* . . . IV. x. 16. 4
enjoyes The *wide* kingdome of love . . . IV. x. 42. 8
a Diademe embattild *wide* With hundred turrets, . . . IV. xi. 28. 5
his Adamants with which he shines And glisters *wide,* . . . IV. xi. 31. 8
In the *wide* champian of the Ocean plaine, . . . V. ii. 15. 2
The time and place was blazed farre and *wide,* . . . V. iii. 2. 5
displayed *wide* Her goodly bow, . . . V. iii. 25. 2
Yet was as great and *wide,* ere many yeares, . . . V. iv. 7. 8
To weete the cause of their assemblaunce *wide:* . . . V. iv. 21. 5
Soring through his *wide* Empire of the aire . . . V. iv. 42. 2
bedeckt Uppon the bosse with stones that shined *wide,* . . . V. v. 3. 7
Would to his hope a windowe open *wyde,* . . . V. v. 39. 3
Not farre away, but little *wide* by West, . . . V. vi. 22. 4
guyded through th' ayrie *wyde* By some bad spirit . . . V. vii. 34. 6
Then caused he the gates be opened *wyde;* . . . V. viii. 51. 1

Wide—*Continued.*
at his backe a great *wyde* net he bore, . . . V. ix. 11. 6
Stood open *wyde* to all men day and night; . . . V. ix. 22. 4
Went up the hall, that was a large *wyde* roome, . . . V. ix. 23. 2
her brode-spreading wings did *wyde* unfold; . . . V. ix. 28. 5
all his teeth *wide* bare One might have seene . . . V. xi. 9. 7
more fiercely reard Uppon her *wide* great wings, . . . V. xi. 30. 6
He day and night doth ward both farre and *wide,* . . . V. xi. 42. 7
The waies . . . Are so exceeding spacious and *wyde,* . . . VI. Pr. 1. 3
In perils strange, in labours long and *wide;* . . . VI. i. 6. 5
With many wounds full perilous and *wyde,* . . . VI. ii. 40. 8
And in his *wide* great mouth away her bare . . . VI. iii. 24. 4
Till she recured were of those her woundes *wide.* . . . VI. iii. 28. 9
the beast enrag'd . . . Gaping full *wyde,* . . . VI. iv. 20. 8
Went forth streightway into the forrest *wyde* . . . VI. v. 3. 6
He found the gate *wyde* ope, . . . VI. vi. 19. 2
Witnesse the wounds, and this *wyde* bloudie lake, . . . VI. vii. 15. 5
through this worlds *wyde* wildernes She wander should . . . VI. vii. 37. 7
eies, Like two great Beacons, glared bright and *wyde,* . . . VI. vii. 42. 2
had through the heavens *wyde* By this dispred, . . . VI. viii. 44. 5
His aged wife, with many others *wide;* . . . VI. xi. 18. 5
round about him scattreth *wide.* . . . VI. xi. 48. 9
through the Ocean *wyde* Directs her course . . . VI. xii. 1. 1
Warres and allarums unto Nations *wide,* . . . VII. vi. 3. 8
Under his belt he bore a sickle circling *wide.* . . . VII. vii. 36. 9
From whose *wide* mouth there flowed forth the Romane Flood. VII. vii. 42. 9
within this *wide* great Universe . . . VII. vii. 56. 1
rash eies which gaze on her so *wide,* . . . *Am.* v. 7
through the Ocean *wyde,* . . . *Am.* xxxiv. 1
Open them *wide* that she may enter in, . . . *Epith.* 205
many harts . . . with *wyde* wounds embrewed, . . . *H.L.* 13
open *wide* your harts . . . *H.L.* 33
Through all that great *wide* wast, . . . *H.L.* 70
a waste and emptie place In His *wyde* Pallace, . . . *H.H.L.* 102
looke on the frame Of this *wyde* universe, . . . *H.H.B.* 31
a noble Peer, . . . the Worlds *wide* wonder, . . . *Proth.* 146
al the world, fil'd with thy *wide* Alarmes, . . . *Proth.* 158
Wide-devouring. from his *wide devouring* oven sent A flake of fire, . . . I. xi. 26. 3
Wide-embayed. There also was the *wide embayed* Mayre; . . . IV. xi. 44. 1
Wide-gaping. greedy mouth *wide gaping* like hell-gate, . . . VI. x. 34. 6
Wide-glancing. with *wide-glauncing* words one day she thus him proved. . . . V. v. 35. 9
Widely. walke not *widely* . . . For feare of raungers . . . *S.C.* S. 158
Wider. Such woundes soone wexen *wider.* . . . *S.C.* Au. 96
had his wesand bene a little *widder,* . . . *S.C.* S. 210
wyder made the wound of th' hidden dart. . . . V. v. 28. 5
Wide-sparkling. To warme your selves at my *wide sparckling* fire, . . . *H.H.L.* 17
Widest. Through *widest* ayre making his ydle way, . . . I. v. 8. 4
In *widest* Ocean she her throne does reare, . . . II. ii. 40. 6
Widow. I, a waylfull *widdowe* behight, . . . *S.C.* May 201
Then forth I went . . . A virgin *widow,* . . . I. ii. 24. 8
me, sad mayd, or rather *widow* sad, . . . I. xii. 27. 1
their mother, who, a *widow,* was Wrapt in great dolours . . . V. x. 6. 6
Being then new made *widow* . . . V. x. 11. 7
The woefull *widow* had no meanes now left, . . . V. x. 14. 2
'The *widow* Queene my mother, . . . conceiving then great feare VI. ii. 29. 1
Widowhead. During the time of that her *widowhead:* . . . *T.M.* 240
mourning stole of carefull *wydowhead,* . . . *Col.* 494
Through weaknesse of my *widowhed* or woe; . . . I. xii. 28. 6
of her *widowhed* Taking advantage, . . . V. x. 12. 1
Widow-like. *widow-like* sad wimple throwne away, . . . I. xii. 22. 3
Widow's. woes the *Widdowes* daughter of the glenne; . . . *S.C.* Ap. 26
Widows. Like wailefull *widdowes* hangen their crags; . . . *S.C.* F. 82
the tender Orphans of the dead And *wydowes* ayd, . . . I. x. 43. 3
Wield. right hand did the peacefull olive *wield;* . . . *Bel.*[2] ix. 11
ye doo *weld* th' affaires of earthlie creature; . . . *Ro.* ix. 4
so his hauty hornes did he *weld.'* . . . *S.C.* May 206
those that *weld* the awful crowne, . . . *S.C.* O. 40
Whom not their kindly Sovereigne did *welde,* . . . *Hub.* 1232
rod . . . towards heaven shee seemd on high to *weld.* . . . *Ti.* 14
Bregog did so well her fancie *weld,* . . . *Col.* 130
Yet armes till that time did he never *wield.* . . . I. i. 1. 5
that high in heaven doth dwell And *wield* the world, . . . I. iv. 11. 6
none can wound the man that does them *wield.'* . . . I. iv. 50. 7
scarsely could he *weeld* his bootlesse single blade. . . . I. vii. 11. 9
gan his sturdy sterne about to *weld,* . . . I. xi. 28. 8
under him a gray steede he did (*did he) *wield,* . . . II. i. 18. 6
well could *weld* That cursed weapon, . . . II. vii. 40. 8
As all things els the which this world doth *weld;* . . . II. ix. 56. 5
peaceably the same long time did *weld,* . . . II. x. 32. 4
letteth her that ought the scepter *weeld,* . . . II. xi. 2. 3
yield it those that stouter could it *wield.* . . . III. i. 4. 6
shield . . . his right hand unarmed fearefully did *wield,* . . . III. xii. 12. 9
did those armes and that same scutchion *weld,* . . . IV. i. 34. 5
finding him unable once to *weld,* . . . IV. i. 37. 3
horse and foote knew Diamond to *wield:* . . . IV. ii. 42. 6
the headlesse tronke . . . weapon vaine to *weld,* . . . IV. iii. 21. 3
Like to the rod which Maias sonne doth *wield,* . . . IV. iii. 42. 6
An huge great speare, such as he wont to *wield,* . . . IV. iv. 17. 2
Which neither able were to wag, or once to *weld.* . . . IV. iv. 18. 9
To *weld* his naked sword, and try the edges keene. . . . IV. vii. 45. 9
the glaive which he did *wield* . . . IV. x. 19. 8
Expressing well his nature which the same did *wield.'* . . . V. i. 19. 9
Fit to catch hold of all that he could *weld,* . . . V. ix. 11. 3
With such his chearefull speaches he doth *wield* Her mind . . . V. x. 24. 7
with such nimblesse sly Could *wield* about, . . . V. xi. 6. 7
did against him *weld* His deadly weapon . . . V. xii. 16. 4
did his yron axe so nimbly *wield,* . . . V. xii. 19. 7

Wield—*Continued.*
So as he could not *weld* him any way: . . . VI. viii. 11. 5
Is wont to *wield* the world unto his vow, . . . VII. vi. 22. 3
scarse his loosed limbes he hable was to *weld*. . . . VII. vii. 31. 9
Wielded. mightie corse, As ever *wielded* speare in warlike hand, I. iii. 42. 4
the chiefe dominion By strength was *wielded* without pollicy: II. x. 39. 8
this war ye wrongfully have *wielded*.' . . . IV. ix. 37. 9
A lustie knight as ever *wielded* speare, . . . VI. xii. 3. 6
Wielding. He gan to watch the *wielding* of his hand, . . . V. xi. 7. 2
Wieldless. with the weight of his owne *weeldlesse* might He falleth . . . IV. iii. 19. 8
Wields. *welds* all things at his will, . . . *Ti.* 447
Welds kingdomes causes and affaires of state, . . . IV. Pr. 1. 2
Wife. *See* **Housewife.**
Mars sleeping with his *wife* to compasse in, . . . *Mui.* 371
From Guendolene his *wife*, . . . II. x. 17. 9
had to *wife* Dame Mertia the fayre, . . . II. x. 42. 3
Five sonnes he left, begotten of one *wife*, . . . II. x. 44. 1
to him gave for *wife* his daughter bright, . . . II. x. 59. 4
his faire *wife*, whom honest long he kept uneath. . . . III. x. 2. 9
He left his *wife*; money did love disclame: . . . III. x. 15. 4
thy *wife* shall backe be sent: . . . III. x. 32. 2
To seeke his *wife* that was far wandered: . . . III. x. 34. 3
Whereas his lovely *wife* emongst them lay, . . . III. x. 48. 2
not for nought his *wife* them loved so well, . . . III. x. 48. 8
to his *wife*, that now full soundly slept, He whispered . . . III. x. 49. 3
profest a virgine *wife*. . . . IV. i. 6. 9
Triamond had Canacee to *wife*, . . . IV. iii. 52. 4
The Squire of low degree, releast, Aemylia takes to *wife*: . . . IV. ix. Arg.
to accept her to his wedded *wife*: . . . IV. ix. 15. 6
much more aged was his *wife* then he, . . . IV. xi. 24. 6
getteth her And gives to him for *wife*. . . . IV. xii. Arg.
had refusde a God that her had sought to *wife*. . . . IV. xii. 16. 9
So faire a *wife* for her sonne Marinell. . . . IV. xii. 33. 7
many Lords have her to *wife* desired, . . . V. ii. 10. 3
Being the dowry of his *wife* well knowne, . . . V. iv. 18. 4
His *wife* was Isis; . . . V. vii. 3. 1
They . . . drive his *wife* Adicia to despaire. . . . V. viii. Arg.
stird up . . . By his bad *wife* that hight Adicia; . . . V. viii. 20. 3
With that his *wife* in friendly wise to deale, . . . V. viii. 21. 2
as his proud *wife* of her had sight, . . . V. viii. 26. 5
Matilde by name, The *wife* of bold Sir Bruin, . . . VI. iv. 29. 4
Gan greatly thanke his host and his good *wife*; . . . VI. ix. 18. 6
him beside His aged *wife*, . . . VI. xi. 18. 5
Old Meliboe and his good *wife* withall These eyes saw die, . . . VI. xi. 31. 6
So home unto his honest *wife* it bore, . . . VI. xii. 9. 8
Wifehood. the vertue of chast love, And *wivehood* true, . . . IV. v. 3. 2
Wifely. What time she usd to live in *wively* sort, . . . IV. v. 3. 8
Wight. *See* **Woman-wight.**
A worthy tombe for such a worthy *wight*. . . . *Bel.*[2] iii. 11
of some heavenly *wight* I had the vewe; . . . *Pet.* v. 4
shrilling voyce of *wight* alive . . . *Ro.* i. 5
He was so wimble and so *wight*, . . . *S.C.* Mar. 91
Elisa . . . That blessed *wight*, The flowre of Virgins: . . . *S.C.* Ap. 47
pierce her heart with poynt of worthy *wight*, . . . *S.C.* Jun. 100
now her is a most wretched *wight*: . . . *S.C.* S. 4
the *wight* whose presence was our pryde; . . . *S.C.* N. 65
the *wight* whose absence is our carke; . . . *S.C.* N. 66
griefe enough it is to grieved *wight* . . . *Gn.* Ded. 11
No lesse, I dare saie, than the prowdest *wight*; . . . *Hub.* 62
To take what paines may anie living *wight*; . . . *Hub.* 271
Unto his Church for to present a *wight*, . . . *Hub.* 526
Wondring what mister *wight* he was, . . . *Hub.* 671
Unhappie *wight*, borne to desastrous end, . . . *Hub.* 907
Ne ever stayd in place, ne spake to *wight*, . . . *Hub.* 938
an universall night . . . He makes on everie *wight*; . . . *Hub.* 1298
livelie spirits of each living *wight*, . . . *T.M.* 254
'But whie (unhappie *wight!*) doo I thus crie, . . . *Ti.* 176
whilome was alive the wisest *wight*: . . . *Ti.* 445
A fairer *wight* saw never summers day. . . . *Ti.* 637
Of all alive did seeme the fairest *wight*. . . . *Mui.* 24
how can fraile fleshly *wight* Forecast, . . . *Mui.* 226
a wicked *wight*, The foe of faire things, . . . *Mui.* 243
Where towards me a sory *wight* did cost, . . . *D.* 39
well he seemd to be sum *wight* forlorne; . . . *D.* 45
'No age hath bred . . . more vertue in a *wight*; . . . *D.* 219
May happen unto the most happiest *wight*; . . . *D.* 517
To you I sing and to none other *wight*, . . . *As.* Pr. 11
banisht had my selfe, like *wight* forlore, . . . *Col.* 182
everie living *wight* Crept forth . . . *Col.* 859
everie *wight* to shrowd it did constrain; . . . I. i. 6. 8
that wicked *wight* his dayes doth weare; . . . I. i. 31. 7
His dwelling . . . by which no living *wight* May ever passe, I. i. 32. 2
he her takes To be the fairest *wight* that lived yit; . . . I. ii. 30. 4
'Then cride she out, "Fye, fye! deformed *wight*, . . . I. ii. 39. 1
she . . . faire as ever living *wight* was fayre, . . . I. iii. 2. 6
never shew of living *wight* espyde; . . . I. iii. 10. 3
she was wondrous faire, as any living *wight*. . . . I. iv. 10. 9
Most wretched *wight*, whom nothing might suffise; . . . I. iv. 29. 1
'Pardon the error of enraged *wight*, . . . I. iv. 41. 2
erthly *wight* that with the Night durst ride. . . . I. v. 32 .9
charmes, A fordonne *wight* from dore of death mote raise, . . . I. v. 41. 8
What witt of mortal *wight* Can now devise . . . I. vi. 6. 8
To weet what *wight* so loudly did lament. . . . I. vi. 8. 4
bethinkes not what To thinke of *wight* so fayre, . . . I. vi. 16. 4
whenas they far espide A weary *wight* . . . I. vi. 34. 3
The same to *wight* he never wont disclose, . . . I. vii. 34. 1
Where never foote of living *wight* did tread, . . . I. vii. 50. 4
ne living *wight* To warde the same, . . . I. viii. 3. 3
Was never *wight* that heard that shrilling sownd, . . . I. viii. 4. 1

Wight—*Continued.*
What mortall *wight* could ever beare so monstrous blow? . . . I. viii. 18. 9
Nor voice was heard, nor *wight* was seene . . . I. viii. 29. 9
to weet if living *wight* Were housed therewithin, . . . I. viii. 37. 8
they . . . wondred at so fowle deformed *wight*. . . . I. viii. 49. 2
that weake captive *wight* now wexed strong, . . . I. ix. 2. 3
rules mens waies, and rules the thoughts of living *wight*. . . . I. ix. 6. 9
To weet what mister *wight* was so dismayd. . . . I. ix. 23. 2
That cursed *wight*, from whom I scapt whyleare, . . . I. ix. 28. 4
I, more fearefull or more lucky *wight*, . . . I. ix. 30. 4
they come where that same wicked *wight* His dwelling has, . . . I. ix. 33. 1
'Thou damned *wight*, The authour of this fact . . . I. ix. 37. 6
'Come; come away, fraile, feeble, fleshly *wight*, . . . I. ix. 53. 1
any other *wight*, That hither turnes his steps. . . . I. x. 10. 2
end, which every living *wight* Should make his marke . . . I. x. 50. 2
So wondrous force from hand of living *wight*; . . . I. xi. 17. 8
could never *wight* him harme By subtilty, . . . I. xi. 36. 8
Ne living *wight* would have him life behott: . . . I. xi. 38. 4
The face of earth and wayes of living *wight*, . . . I. xi. 49. 8
Yet can they not warne death from wretched *wight*. . . . II. i. 36. 5
'Leave, ah! leave off, whatever *wight* thou bee, . . . II. i. 47. 6
what ever hevenly powre, Or earthly *wight* thou be, . . . II. iii. 34. 9
heape more vengeance on that wretched *wight*: . . . II. iv. 5. 4
Furor, cursed cruel *wight*, . . . II. iv. 10. 6
Ne ever *wight* that mote so welcome bee . . . II. iv. 20. 5
To ridd a wretched man from handes of hellish *wight!*' . . . II. v. 23. 9
An uncouth, salvage, and uncivile *wight*, . . . II. vii. 3. 4
when an earthly *wight* they present saw . . . II. vii. 37. 1
The fairest *wight* that wonneth under skie, . . . II. vii. 49. 2
I, that am fraile flesh and earthly *wight*, . . . II. vii. 50. 3
ne living *wight* Like ever saw, . . . II. vii. 54. 3
no living *wight* Below the earth . . . II. vii. 66. 2
Was never *wight* that treason of him told: . . . II. viii. 13. 8
Nor *wight* nor word mote passe out of the gate, . . . II. ix. 25. 3
What *wight* she was that Poplar braunch did hold? . . . II. ix. 39. 7
keepes in coverts close from living *wight*, . . . II. ix. 40. 8
Fayre Helena, the fairest living *wight*; . . . II. x. 59. 5
deemd in mynd To be no earthly *wight*, . . . II. x. 71. 6
could not die, yet seemd a mortall *wight*, . . . II. xi. 40. 7
Ne ever land beheld, ne living *wight*, . . . II. xii. 2. 2
drawne many a wandring *wight* Into most deadly daunger . . . II. xii. 11. 8
wight who did not well avis'd it vew . . . II. xii. 61. 4
Right hard it was for *wight* which did it heare, . . . II. xii. 70. 5
weenedst thou what *wight* thee overthrew, . . . III. i. 8. 1
Whom when the Lady saw so faire a *wight*, . . . III. i. 47. 1
for everie *wight* Them to betake unto their kindly rest: . . . III. i. 58. 1
every mortall *wight* Was drowned . . . III. i. 59. 2
Whose prowesse paragone saw never living *wight*. . . . III. ii. 13. 9
'Nor man it is, nor other living *wight*, . . . III. ii. 38. 1
That of no living *wight* he mote be found, . . . III. iii. 7. 8
Then ever him before, or after, living *wight*: . . . III. iii. 11. 9
Of mortall Syre or other living *wight*, . . . III. iii. 13. 2
never *wight* so fast in sell could sit, . . . III. iii. 60. 6
as *wight* forlorne, Long time she fostred up, . . . III. iv. 20. 3
'What mister *wight*,' (saide he) 'and how arayd?' . . . III. v. 5. 1
A fayrer *wight* did never Sunne behold; . . . III. v. 5. 5
she is the fairest *wight* alive, I trow.' . . . III. v. 5. 9
Through which it was uneath for *wight* to wade; . . . III. v. 17. 3
hast shewed to me sinfull *wight*, . . . III. v. 35. 2
breedes the living *wight*. . . . III. vi. 9. 5
in the same did wonne some living *wight*. . . . III. vii. 5. 5
doubted her to deeme an earthly *wight*, . . . III. vii. 11. 6
What mister *wight* that was, and whence deriv'd, . . . III. vii. 14. 2
Lightly she leaped, as a *wight* forlore, . . . III. vii. 25. 7
she, that is so chaste a *wight*.' . . . III. vii. 52. 9
seeing with that Chorle so faire a *wight*, . . . III. viii. 12. 1
The fairest *wight* on ground, and most of men esteem'd. . . . III. viii. 13. 9
what *wight* Had her from so infamous fact assoyld, . . . III. viii. 32. 6
ne living *wight* was seene Save one old Nymph, . . . III. viii. 37. 8
As an immortall mote a mortall *wight*, . . . III. viii. 38. 4
Then he would make him selfe a mortall *wight*; . . . III. viii. 39. 8
To weet what *wight* he was, and what his quest, . . . III. viii. 45. 2
Ne suffreth he resort of living *wight* Approch to her, . . . III. ix. 5. 6
Redresse the wrong of miserable *wight*, . . . III. x. 28. 2
Hatefull both to him selfe and every *wight*; . . . III. x. 60. 6
she mervaild that no footings trace Nor *wight* appeard, . . . III. xi. 53. 6
every *wight* dismayd with darkenes sad . . . III. xii. 1. 3
Ne living *wight* she saw in all that roome, . . . III. xii. 30. 5
Conveyed quite away to living *wight* unknowen. . . . IV. i. 3. 9
falsly seekst a vertuous *wight* to shame?' . . . IV. i. 48. 2
it could overreach the wisest earthly *wight*. . . . IV. ii. 10. 9
the dreddest day that living *wight* Did ever see . . . IV. iii. 3. 5
Some newborne *wight* ye would him surely weene; . . . IV. iii. 23. 5
unwares to *wight* And to his friend unwist, . . . IV. iv. 27. 6
seemed fit For salvage *wight*; . . . IV. iv. 39. 7
From *wight* unworthie of so noble meed. . . . IV. v. 28. 4
dreadfull seem'd to every living *wight*, . . . IV. v. 32. 3
Ne ever was there *wight* to me more deare . . . IV. vi. 35. 8
Ne *wight* him to attend, or way to guide, . . . IV. vi. 44. 6
What mister *wight* it was that so did plaine? . . . IV. vii. 10. 5
'Ah, wretched *wight!* That seekes to know anothers griefe . . . IV. vii. 10. 6
unweeting unto *wight*, I with that Squire agreede away to flit, IV. vii. 17. 5
espies that griesly *wight* Approching nigh, . . . IV. vii. 22. 5
feare and danger of that dismall *wight*. . . . IV. vii. 33. 9
fit solitary place For wofull *wight*, . . . IV. vii. 38. 6
like strange *wight*, whom he had seene no where, . . . IV. vii. 43. 7
What mister *wight* he was, or what he ment; . . . IV. viii. 13. 6
wrath of cruell *wight* on thee ywrake, . . . IV. viii. 14. 8
If wrathfull *wight*, then fowle rebuke and shame . . . IV. viii. 15. 3
to wreake on worthlesse *wight* Your high displesure, . . . IV. viii. 17. 2

Wight—*Continued.*
rash-witted *wight,* Whose looser thought will lightly be misled, IV. viii. 29. 2
Awayting to entrap the warelesse *wight* . . . . IV. x. 20. 8
There worshipped of every living *wight;* . . . . IV. x. 29. 7
for mortall *wight* To tell the sands, ... IV. xi. 53. 1
Cares not what evils hap to wretched *wight;* . . . . IV. xii. 6. 8
In solitary silence, far from *wight,* . . . . IV. xii. 19. 2
promist him, what ever *wight* she weare, ... IV. xii. 27. 5
never *wight* so evill did or thought, ... IV. xii. 30. 8
ne fraud in *wight* was to be found: . . . . V. Pr. 9. 4
kept in store In Joves eternall house, unwist of *wight,* . . . . V. i. 9. 4
whether his owne hand, or whether other *wight?* . . . . . . V. i. 14. 9
Ne *wight* with him but onely Talus went; . . . . V. i. 30. 8
'What mister *wight*' . . . Is he, ... V. ii. 5. 1
never *wight* he lets to passe that way . . . . V. ii. 6. 2
For *wight* against his powre them selves to reare. . . . . . . V. ii. 24. 6
Ne he his mouth would open unto *wight,* . . . . V. iii. 34. 1
Ne *wight* with him for his assistance went, ... V. iv. 3. 8
Ne yet to any other *wight* on ground, ... V. v. 44. 3
never yet was *wight* so well aware, ... V. vi. 1. 8
First rings his silver Bell t' each sleepy *wight,* . . . . . . V. vi. 27. 3
To be the greatest and the gravest *wight,* . . . . V. vii. 18. 5
Ne *wight* but onely Talus with him went, ... V. viii. 3. 8
What Tygre, or what other salvage *wight,* . . . . V. ix. 1. 1
Full dreadfull *wight* he was as ever went Upon the earth, . . V. ix. 10. 4
Most sacred *wight,* most debonayre and free, ... V. ix. 20. 7
All solitarie without living *wight;* . . . . V. x. 19. 2
For wretched woman, miserable *wight,* . . . . V. x. 21. 3
me, of all most wretched *wight,* . . . . V. xi. 16. 5
he had red her Riddle, which no *wight* Could ever loose . . . V. xi. 25. 5
he met An aged *wight* wayfaring all alone, ... V. xi. 37. 2
shame he weend a sleeping *wight* to wound. . . . . VI. i. 34. 4
Rather then let my selfe of *wight* be stroken, ... VI. ii. 7. 8
'Perdie great blame' . . . a *wight* unarm'd to wrong: . . . . VI. ii. 8. 7
where no *wight* Should weet of me, ... VI. ii. 30. 6
What manner *wight* he was, and how yclad, ... VI. ii. 44. 3
Yet was he courteous still to every *wight,* . . . . VI. iii. 3. 5
Ere they were well aware of living *wight,* . . . . VI. iii. 21. 2
That he should be so sterne to stranger *wight;* . . . . . . VI. iii. 40. 7
when as she perceived A stranger *wight* in place, ... VI. iv. 27. 2
Cannot redressed be by living *wight!'* . . . . VI. iv. 28. 5
In such a salvage *wight,* of brutish kynd, ... VI. v. 29. 6
Small praise to prove your powre on *wight* so weake.' . . . . VI. v. 30. 5
infamy Infixeth in the name of noble *wight:* . . . . VI. vi. 1. 4
Ne *wight* with him on that adventure went, ... VI. vi. 18. 6
left that salvage *wight* Amongst so many foes, ... VI. vi. 37. 5
well she knew the wayes to win good will Of every *wight,* . . VI. vi. 41. 7
'Where is that *wight,* The which hath doen . . . . VI. vii. 5. 7
The more it is admir'd of many a *wight,* . . . . VI. vii. 29. 8
She was borne free, not bound to any *wight,* . . . . VI. vii. 30. 8
As no whit dreading any living *wight;* . . . . VI. vii. 43. 2
her admiring as some heavenly *wight,* . . . . VI. ix. 9. 6
though no lesse sory *wight* For that mishap, ... VI. x. 18. 7
from skill of any *wight.* . . . . VI. x. 37. 9
shade From view of living *wight* . . . . VI. x. 42. 4
Not sparing *wight,* ne leaving any balke, ... VI. xi. 16. 4
leaves no skill nor difference of *wight.* . . . . VI. xi. 16. 9
Ne *wight* he found to whom he might complaine, ... VI. xi. 26. 1
Ne *wight* he found of whom he might inquire, ... VI. xi. 26. 2
her wombe, unwist to *wight,* was fraught, ... VI. xii. 6. 4
where living *wight* Mote not bewray the secret of her lode, . . VI. xii. 7. 2
never more he mote endammadge *wight* . . . . VI. xii. 38. 3
not the worth of any living *wight* . . . . VII. vi. 33. 2
That eye of *wight* could not indure to view: . . . . VII. vii. 6. 5
So hard it is for any living *wight* . . . . VII. vii. 9. 1
in every living *wight* They mixe themselves, ... *H.L.* 90
That can restore a damned *wight* from death. . . . . *H.B.* 287
no thought of earthly *wight* Can comprehend, ... *H.H.L.* 40
Him to be Lord of every living *wight* He made . . . . *H.H.L.* 115
Presume to picture so divine a *wight,* . . . . *H.H.B.* 226
Ne ought on earth can want unto the *wight* . . . . *H.H.B.* 244
Wightly. day, that was, is *wightly* past, ... *S.C.* S. 5
Wight's. there was this *wights* abode. . . . . VI. iv. 13. 9
Wights. make all *wights* adore The beast, ... *Rev.* i. 13
Bee now become most wretched *wightes* on ground. . . . . . . *T.M.* 312
their judgments share Mongst earthlie *wightes,* . . . . *D.* 200
sleepe (the harbenger of wearie *wights*) . . . . *D.* 470
whiles wicked *wights* Have knit themselves . . . . I. ii. 4. 7
Banisht from living *wights,* our wearie daies we waste.' . . . I. ii. 42. 9
They all, beholding worldly *wights* in place, ... I. v. 36. 1
Merlin . . . did excell All living *wightes* in might of magicke spell: . . . . I. vii. 36. 5
bare wretched *wights* he dayly clad, ... I. x. 39. 6
Can call out of the bodies of fraile *wightes;* . . . . II. v. 27. 5
many damned *wightes* In those sad waves, ... II. vii. 57. 2
such dreadful *wights* As far exceeded men . . . . II. x. 8. 8
a monstrous rablement Of fowle misshapen *wightes,* . . . . . II. xi. 8. 2
What now is left of miserable *wightes,* . . . . II. xii. 9. 4
Wee mortall *wights,* whose lives and fortunes bee . . . . . . III. v. 36. 6
To succor wretched *wights* whom we captived see.' . . . . . III. v. 36. 9
Whom of all living *wightes* she loved best. . . . . III. xii. 41. 2
There was it judged, by those worthie *wights,* . . . . IV. v. 7. 3
against all manner *wights* . . . to maintaine that castels ancient rights. . . . . IV. x. 7. 8
all living *wights,* soone as they see . . . . IV. x. 45. 3
Else should afflicted *wights* oftimes despeire: . . . . V. iii. 1. 5
to infest The noblest *wights* with notable defame: . . . . . . VI. vi. 12. 6
all living *wights* have learn'd to die, ... VII. vi. 6. 5
all the heavenly crew Of happy *wights,* . . . . VII. vi. 14. 4
both heavenly Powers and earthly *wights,* . . . . VII. vi. 36. 2

Wights—*Continued.*
'So likewise are all watry living *wights* Still tost . . . . . VII. vii. 21. 1
Of all the world and of all living *wights*) . . . . VII. vii. 25. 2
the most kind preserver Of living *wights,* . . . . *H.L.* 157
how of most wretched *wights* He taken was, ... *H.H.L.* 239
But we, fraile *wights!* whose sight cannot sustaine . . . . . *H.H.B.* 120
Wilbe. *(Whereof he *wilbe* wroken) . . . . *S.C.* Mar. 108
without golde now nothing *wilbe* got, ... *Hub.* 153
Ne *wilbe* moov'd with reason, ... *Am.* xi. 5
Wild. *See* **Willed.**
many *wyld* beastes liggen in waite . . . . *S.C.* May 217
over them spred a goodly *wild* vine, ... *S.C.* Au. 29
the *wild* woodes, my sorowes to resound, ... *S.C.* Au. 166
girt in girlonds of *wild* Yvie twine, ... *S.C.* O. 111
sundrie flowers in *wilde* fieldes gathered; . . . . *Gn.* 132
made him meat for *wild* foules of the ayre. . . . . *Gn.* 380
the *wilde* beasts their furie did withhold, ... *Gn.* 451
wilde greene woods and fruitful pastures minde; . . . . . . *Gn.* 637
the *wilde* beasts, that swiftest are in chase; . . . . *Hub.* 620
So *wilde* a beast so tame ytaught to bee, ... *Hub.* 625
In the *wilde* forrest raunging fresh and free. . . . . *Hub.* 630
to sew the chace Of swift *wilde* beasts, ... *Hub.* 744
that he might be seene Of the *wilde* beasts . . . . *Hub.* 1066
no *wild* beasts should do them any torte . . . . *Hub.* 1078
all *wylde* beasts made vassals of his pleasures, ... *Hub.* 1129
the *wilde* beasts whom armes did glorifie, ... *Hub.* 1184
troubled kingdome of *wilde* beasts behelde, ... *Hub.* 1231
the forrest, where *wilde* beasts doo breed, ... *Hub.* 1248
the herds Of ravenous *wilde* beasts, ... *Hub.* 1285
Wylde beasts and forrests after him to lead, ... *Ti.* 608
An hairie hide of some *wilde* beast, ... *Mui.* 66
a *wilde* wildernes of waters deepe: . . . . *Mui.* 287
of the race that all *wild* beastes do feare, ... *D.* 123
with your carkasses *wild* beasts be glutted. . . . . *D.* 350
Thousand *wyld* beasts with deep mouthes . . . . *Col.* 202
Receive . . . a simple taste Of the *wilde* fruit . . . . . . *Ded. Son.* v. 2
the place unknowne and *wilde,* Breedes dreadfull doubts. . . . I. i. 12. 3
that *wilde* champion wayting her besyde . . . . I. iii. 26. 2
flaming mouthes of steedes, unwonted *wilde,* . . . to rayne: . I. iv. 9. 3
Led her away into a forest *wilde;* . . . . I. vi. 3. 2
The *wyld* woodgods, . . . There find the virgin, ... I. vi. 9. 1
A Satyres sonne, yborne in forrest *wyld,* . . . . I. vi. 21. 1
Whom, . . . He nousled up in life and manners *wilde,* . . . . I. vi. 23. 8
He nousled up . . . Emongst *wild* beastes and woods, ... I. vi. 23. 9
wyld roring Buls he would him make To tame, ... I. vi. 24. 6
Wyld beastes in yron yokes he would compell; . . . . I. vi. 26. 2
To wander where *wilde* fortune would me lead, ... I. vii. 50. 2
As wont ye knightes to seeke adventures *wilde,* . . . . II. i. 50. 6
Poore Orphane! in the *wild* world scattered, ... II. ii. 2. 5
Sith earst into this forrest *wild* I came. . . . . II. iii. 33. 6
doest raunge In this *wilde* forest, ... II. iii. 39. 2
Pursew her steps through *wild* unknowen wood: . . . . II. iii. 43. 3
Woven with antickes and *wyld* ymagery; . . . . II. vii. 4. 6
Sterne was their looke; like *wild* amazed steares, ... II. ix. 13. 8
wild like beastes lurking in loathsome den, ... II. x. 7. 4
wilde Bores late rouzd out of the brakes: . . . . II. xi. 10. 5
Untill they came in vew of those *wilde* beasts, ... II. xii. 39. 6
those *wild-beasts* that rag'd with furie mad; . . . . II. xii. 84. 5
Deadly engored of a great *wilde* Bore; . . . . III. i. 38. 2
all *wilde* beastes do rest, ... III. ii. 32. 2
the *wilde* beast shall dy in starved den. . . . . III. iii. 34. 9
of *wilde* beastes if she had chased beene; . . . . III. iv. 51. 4
as shee pursewd the chace Of some *wilde* beast, ... III. v. 28. 2
such *wilde* woodes should far expell All civile usage . . . . III. vi. 1. 7
In this *wilde* forrest wandring all alone, ... III. vi. 5. 4
that *wilde* Bore, the which him once annoyd, ... III. vi. 48. 5
the squirrell *wild* He brought to her in bands, ... III. vii. 17. 6
raungd abrode to seeke adventures *wilde,* . . . . III. vii. 30. 2
wander wide At *wilde* adventure, ... III. x. 36. 3
left in yonder forest *wyld;* . . . . III. x. 39. 6
many *wilde* woodmen which robbe and rend All traveilers: . . . III. xi. 40. 6
Wrought with *wilde* Antickes, ... III. xi. 51. 5
lov'd in forests *wyld* to space. . . . . IV. ii. 44. 9
As two *wild* Boares together grapling go, ... IV. iv. 29. 8
Most answerable to his *wyld* disguize . . . . IV. iv. 42. 5
as through a desert *wyld* We travelled, ... IV. vi. 36. 1
It was to weet a *wilde* and salvage man; . . . . IV. vii. 5. 1
the Beares In these *wild* woods, ... IV. vii. 23. 8
other food then that *wilde* forrest beares, ... IV. vii. 41. 5
to make experience Upon *wyld* beasts, ... V. i. 7. 8
even *wilde* beasts did feare his awfull sight, ... V. i. 8. 4
like *wyld* Goates them chaced all about, ... V. viii. 50. 7
mongst *wyld* beasts, and salvage woods, to dwell; . . . . . . V. ix. 1. 5
thereon flew Like a *wyld* Gote, ... V. ix. 15. 4
bands of nature, that *wilde* beastes restraine, ... V. xii. 1. 5
In all this forrest and *wyld* wooddie raine: . . . . VI. ii. 9. 6
like a *wilde* goate round about did chace . . . . VI. iii. 49. 3
With that the *wyld* man more enraged grew, ... VI. iv. 6. 1
after him the *wyld* man ran apace, ... VI. iv. 8. 1
the *wyld* man, . . . Came to her creeping . . . . VI. iv. 11. 1
Ne scarse *wyld* beasts durst come, ... VI. iv. 13. 9
ne ever of *wyld* beast Did taste the bloud, ... VI. iv. 14. 8
that *wyld* man did apply His best endevour . . . . VI. iv. 16. 1
Like this *wyld* man being undisciplynd, ... VI. v. 1. 6
That plainely may in this *wyld* man be red, ... VI. v. 2. 1
no one beast in forrest, *wylde* or tame, ... VI. v. 15. 7
Like a *wylde* Bull, that, being at a bay, ... VI. v. 19. 1
So now they be arrived both in sight Of this *wyld* man, . . . VI. v. 25. 2
Albe the *wyld*-man hardly would refraine. . . . . VI. v. 27. 5
Had not this *wylde* man . . . Kept and delivered me . . . . VI. v. 29. 4

Wild—*Continued.*
Amongst *wilde* beastes in desert forrests bred, VI. v. 29. 7
Ne wight with him . . . went, But that *wylde* man; VI. vi. 18. 7
With a *wyld* man soft footing by his syde; VI. vii. 6. 2
In great displeasure *wild* a Capias Should issue forth VI. vii. 35. 4
In these *wylde* deserts where she now abode, VI. viii. 35. 1
Ne mote *wylde* beastes . . . Thereto approch; VI. x. 7. 4
fared like a furious *wyld* Beare, VI. xi. 25. 8
more cruell, and more salvage *wylde*, *Am.* xx. 9
Strange thing, me seemd, to see a beast so *wyld*, *Am.* lxvii. 13
the *wylde* wolves, which seeke them to devoure, *Epith.* 69

Wild-beast. *See* **Wild.**

Wilderness. Whose way is *wildernesse*, whose ynne Penaunce, *S.C.* F. 89
'I carried am into waste *wildernesse*, *Gn.* 369
Waste *wildernes*, amongst Cymerian shades, *Gn.* 370
So all is turned into *wildernesse*, *T.M.* 287
a wilde *wildernes* of waters deepe: *Mui.* 287
Rolling like mountaines in wide *wildernesse*, *Col.* 198
'in wastfull *wildernesse* His dwelling is, I. i. 32. 1
In *wildernesse* and wastfull deserts strayd, I. iii. 3. 4
His ship far come from watrie *wildernesse*; I. iii. 32. 4
Shee, . . . Fled to the wastfull *wildernesse* apace, I. viii. 50. 3
Where she did wander in waste *wildernesse*, II. i. 22. 2
nought but desert *wildernesse* shewed all around. II. vii. 2. 9
In antique times was salvage *wildernesse*, II. x. 5. 3
with his oares did sweepe the watry *wildernesse*. II. xii. 29. 9
She fled into the *wildernesse* a space, III. vi. 10. 3
what cause her brought Into that *wildernesse* III. vi. 20. 3
in woods and wanton *wildernesse* III. vi. 22. 1
yonder in that wastefull *wildernesse* III. x. 40. 3
in that *wildernesse*, of men forlore, IV. vii. 39. 5
through this worlds wyde *wildernes* She wander should VI. vii. 37. 7

Wildest. ne fear'd the *wildest* beast, *D.* 135

Wildings. Oft from the forrest *wildings* he did bring, III. vii. 17. 1

Wildly. Thus *wildly* to wander in the worlds eye, *Hub.* 185

Wild-man. *See* **Wild, Man.**

Wild-wood. Unto the *wyld wood* ranne, her dolours to deplore. V. viii. 48. 9

Wild woods. *See* **Wild, Woods.**

Wile. For falsed letters, and suborned *wyle*, II. i. 1. 3
He weened well to worke some uncouth *wyle*: II. i. 8. 2
Unweeting of their *wile* and treason bad, III. v. 18. 3
he Malbeccoes halfen eye did *wyle*; III. x. 5. 2
That Virgins love to win by wit or *wile*, IV. xi. 2. 3
He is . . . wrought by Clarins *wile*. V. v. Arg.
through his owne guilty *wile*: V. vi. 33. 5

Wiled. His halfen eye he *wiled* wondrous well, III. x. 5. 3

Wiles. my slie *wyles* and subtill craftinesse, *Hub.* 1045
false Acrasia, and her wicked *wiles*; II. ix. 9. 6
His cruell deedes and wicked *wyles* did spot: III. vi. 13. 5
all the *wyles* of wemens wits knew passing well. III. viii. 8. 9
with slie shiftes and *wiles* did underminde All noble Knights, V. vi. 32. 7

Wilful. We be not tyde to *wilfull* chastitie, *Hub.* 477
sdeignfull pride, and *wilfull* arrogaunce: *Hub.* 1135
Yet, *wilfull* man, he never would forecast I. iv. 34. 8
Sthenoboea . . . her selfe did choke With *wilfull* chord I. v. 50. 6
For Gods deare love be not so *wilfull* bent, II. i. 16. 2
stird you up to worke your *wilfull* smarts? II. ii. 29. 4
Avise thee well, and chaunge thy *wilfull* mood, II. vii. 38. 8
Impotence with her owne *wilfull* hands II. xi. 47. 7
As one in *wilfull* bale for ever buried. III. ii. 31. 9
in loathly weedes And *wilfull* want, III. vii. 6. 5
can withhold her *wilfull* wandring feet; III. ix. 7. 6
In *wilfull* languor and consuming smart, III. xii. 16. 8
In *wilfull* anguish and dead heavinesse, III. xii. 43. *or.* 7
Through *wilfull* penury consumed quight, IV. vii. 41. 3
inward griefe or *wilfull* scorne Of life IV. viii. 15. 5
daies in *wilfull* woe are worne, IV. viii. 15. 7
He *wilfull* lost that he before attayned: V. v. 17. 8
Left to her will by his owne *wilfull* blame, V. v. 20. 2
even then ruing her *wilfull* fall V. x. 4. 7
both so *wilfull* were and obstinate VI. vii. 40. 3
The more she frieseth in her *wilfull* pryde; *Am.* xxxii. 10

Wilfully. Hys pleasaunt Pipe . . . He *wylfully* hath broke, *S.C.* Ap. 15
So will I *wilfully* increase my paine. *D.* 378
As one disposed *wilfullie* to die, *D.* 552
She *wilfully* her sorrow did augment, II. i. 15. 2
it *wilfully* unbindes. II. v. 1. 9
Wilfully make thyselfe a wretched thrall, II. vi. 17. 3
That he so *willfully* refused grace; II. viii. 52. 6
wilfully him throwing on the gras III. xi. 27. 5
He *wilfully* did cut and shape anew; IV. vii. 40. 2
Should *wilfully* be into thraldome brought, IV. viii. 58. 7

Wilfulness. his sorrow sought through *wilfulnesse*, II. v. 24. 7

Wiliness. Forstallen hem of their *wilinesse*: *S.C.* S. 231
of his *wylinesse* his name doth take, IV. xi. 32. 6

Will (*partial list of auxiliary*). *See* **Free will, Goodwill.**
Great Babylon her haughtie walls *will* praise, *Ro.* ii. 1
All that is lent to love *wyll* be lost. *S.C.* F. 70
(Whereof he *wil* be wroken) *S.C.* Mar. 108
To feede theyr flocks at *will*, *S.C.* Jul. 66
Sore against my *will* was I forst to yield. *S.C.* Au. 42
ledde of theyr sheepe what way they *wyll*, *S.C.* S. 81
They wander at *wil* and stay at pleasure, *S.C.* S. 144
hardie *will* he had To overcome, *Gn.* 303
So long as thankfull *will* may it relent. *Gn.* 368
shall we varie our device at *will*, *Hub.* 118
drew the wicked Shepheard to his *will*. *Hub.* 320
list at *will* them to revile or snib: *Hub.* 372
read he could not evidence, nor *will*, *Hub.* 382
to be a beetle-stock Of thy great Masters *will*, *Hub.* 508

Will—*Continued.*
th' evill *will* Of all their Parishners *Hub.* 560
will to Court for shadowes vaine to seeke, *Hub.* 912
gan he rule and tyrannize at *will*, *Hub.* 1127
So made by nature for to serve their *will*, *T.M.* 40
Each idle wit at *will* presumes to make, *T.M.* 215
Free libertie to chaunt our charmes at *will*, *T.M.* 244
To make men heavenly wise through humbled *will*. *T.M.* 522
welds all things at his *will*, *Ti.* 447
Of everie one he takes, and tastes at *will*, *Mui.* 203
Warre against us, the vassals of their *will*. *Mui.* 231
walkt at *will*, and wandred too and fro, *Mui.* 379
yet doth beare, and ever *will*, *Col.* 94
'Cause have I none . . . of cancred *will* *Col.* 680
at randon as he *will*, *Col.* 812
So having said, Melissa spake at *will*; *Col.* 895
Helpe . . . Thy weaker Novice to performe thy *will*; I. Pr. 2. 2
The Eugh, obedient to the benders *will*; I. i. 9. 4
Rest is their feast, and all thinges at their *will*: I. i. 35. 3
Will was his guide, and griefe led him astray. I. ii. 12. 4
On silly Dame, subject . . . to your mighty *wil!'* I. ii. 21. 4
A cruell witch, her cursed *will* to wreake, I. ii. 33. 5
With humble service to her *will* prepard: I. iii. 9. 7
Halfe mad through malice and revenging *will*, I. iii. 22. 8
Far be it from your thought, and fro my *wil*, I. iii. 28. 2
raging spoile of lawlesse victors *will?* I. iii. 43. 2
will or nill, Beares her away upon his courser light: I. iii. 43. 7
Sthenoboea, that her selfe did choke . . . wanting of her *will*; I. v. 50. 6
greater conquest . . . he gaynes, That workes it to his *will*, I. vi. 3. 9
none can breath, nor see, nor heare at *will*, I. vii. 13. 7
'great griefe *will* not be tould, I. vii. 41. 1
will to might gives greatest aid.' I. vii. 41. 4
No powre he had to stirre, nor *will* to rize. I. viii. 15. 4
They let her goe at *will*, and wander waies unknowne. I. viii. 49. 9
all the good is Gods, both power and eke *will*. I. x. 1. 9
chaste in worke and *will*: I. x. 30. 6
Unwares me wrought unto her wicked *will*, I. xii. 32. 8
In hope to win occasion to his *will*; II. i. 5. 2
with words his *will*, . . . he ofte did stay, II. i. 34. 7
On them she workes her *will* to uses bad: II. i. 52. 4
Where him that witch had thralled to her *will*, II. i. 54. 2
I him recured to a better *will*, II. i. 54. 7
'thy destinies withstand My wrathfull *will*, II. iii. 8. 4
weened well ere long his *will* to win, II. iii. 13. 2
'lett her pas at *will*, II. iii. 44. 1
Love . . . makes eke one *will*; II. iv. 19. 8
to worke her to his *will* more neare, II. iv. 25. 5
Therefore, I thee exhort To chaunge thy *will*, II. v. 17. 8
he was wise, and wary of her *will*, II. vi. 26. 1
money can thy wantes at *will* supply? II. vii. 11. 2
were your *will* her sold to entertaine, II. ix. 6. 5
doen you lack your *will?* II. ix. 37. 8
Him to succeede therein, by his last *will*: II. x. 76. 5
Brydling his *will* and maystering his might, II. xii. 53. 5
His wrathfull *will* with reason to aswage; III. i. 11. 4
Giving the bridle to her wanton *will*, III. i. 50. 3
to ease thy griefe And win thy *will*: III. ii. 33. 7
to bring his *will* to pas: III. iii. 24. 5
Therefore submit thy wayes unto his *will*, III. iii. 24. 8
Serving th' ambitious *will* of Augustine, III. iii. 35. 3
that they might him handle more at *will*, III. iv. 40. 3
Him kept from landing at his wished *will*, III. v. 20. 2
Thus warreid he long time against his *will*; III. v. 48. 1
when ever that she *will*, Possesseth him, III. vi. 46. 8
To wander through the world abroad at *will*, III. vii. 54. 4
now he strength gan adde unto his *will*, III. viii. 26. 6
went at *will* withouten card or sayle, III. viii. 31. 2
Her *will* to win unto his wished eend; III. viii. 41. 5
A womans *will*, which is disposd to go astray. III. ix. 6. 9
of his owne *will*, III. ix. 8. 8
sent close messages of love to her at *will*. III. ix. 27. 9
with thy charms . . . to thy *will* abuse? III. x. 4. 6
will be made The vassall of the victors *will* bylive: III. x. 10. 7
with fowle force unto his *will* did drive; III. x. 27. 7
by no meanes would to his *will* be wonne, III. x. 51. 8
With greedy *will* and envious desire, III. xi. 26. 3
let them wend at *will*, III. xii. 45. 9
His *will* she feard; IV. i. 8. 1
'I saw him have your Amoret at *will*; IV. i. 49. 1
Which she by art could use unto her *will*, IV. ii. 44. 3
To let them passe at *will*, for dread of shame. IV. iv. 3. 5
then it shall be tried, if ye *will*, IV. iv. 12. 8
had no *will* To hasten greatly to his parties ayd, IV. iv. 20. 1
wreake on him her *will* for so great injurie. IV. vi. 23. 9
Nathlesse her tongue not to her *will* obayd, IV. vi. 27. 8
Relent the rigour of your wrathfull *will*, IV. vi. 32. 2
wonne her *will* to suffer him depart; IV. vi. 43. 2
to worke Time to my *will*, IV. vii. 17. 2
at his *will* may whom he list restore, IV. viii. 54. 8
thereto did with readie *will* consent, IV. viii. 64. 8
Whose *will* her weakenesse could no way represse, IV. ix. 18. 8
your *will* be donne. IV. x. 3. 5
seem'd to serve the workmans *will*. IV. x. 15. 9
Him from his wicked *will* uneath refrayned; IV. x. 36. 7
sore against his *will* did him retaine, IV. xi. 7. 7
though unto his *will* she given were, IV. xii. 15. 6
'Then doth he take the spoile of them at *will*, V. ii. 9. 1
Ne any may his mighty *will* withstand; V. ii. 42. 2
Not wronging any other by my *will*, V. iv. 14. 4
I hold mine owne, and so *will* hold it still. V. iv. 14. 5

Will—*Continued.*
The worke of heavens *will* surpasseth humaine thought.' . . . V. iv. 27. 9
For ought or nought be wonne unto her *will*, . . . V. iv. 30. 6
to morrow I with him *wil* fight, . . . V. iv. 48. 8
he that helpe from her against her *will* discarded. . . . V. v. 8. 9
The foolish Kyte, led with licentious *will*, . . . V. v. 15. 5
Left to her *will* by his owne wilfull blame, . . . V. v. 20. 2
not of cancred *will*' . . . I have forbore this duetie to fulfill; . V. v. 41. 1
Till I the conquest of my *will* recover.' . . . V. v. 51. 5
To th' insolent commaund of womens *will;* . . . V. vi. 1. 4
she in her wrathfull *will* did cast How to revenge . . . V. vi. 13. 1
With froward *will* doth set him selfe to weepe, . . . V. vi. 14. 3
Of whom we may at *will* the whole occasion know.' . . . V. viii. 15. 9
neither *will* one foot, till we that carle have hent.' . . . V. ix. 7. 9
dauncing on the craggy cliffes at *will;* . . . V. ix. 15. 5
to his *will* she bends; . . . V. x. 24. 8
deeme it doen of *will*, that through inforcement came. . . . V. xi. 52. 9
Agreeing in bad *will* and cancred kynd; . . . V. xii. 33. 2
executes her wicked *will* with worse despight. . . . VI. i. 15. 9
as if against his *will*, . . . VI. i. 35. 2
Ne from his currish *will* a whit reclame. . . . VI. iii. 43. 2
Flying the fury of his bloudy *will:* . . . VI. iii. 49. 4
From your owne *will* to cure your maladie. . . . VI. vi. 7. 3
Abstaine from pleasure, and restraine your *will;* . . . VI. vi. 14. 5
layd at him amaine with all his *will* and might. . . . VI. vi. 27. 9
Fortune did not with his *will* conspire; . . . VI. viii. 15. 5
Ne any *will* had thence to move away, . . . VI. ix. 12. 2
some, that hath abundance at his *will*, . . . VI. ix. 30. 3
thence he had no *will* away to fare, . . . VI. x. 30. 8
To serve the vengeaunce of his wrathfull *will;* . . . VI. x. 36. 2
at the last unto his *will* he brought her; . . . VI. x. 38. 3
Unto his lust, and make his *will* his law, . . . VI. xi. 6. 3
rise against the remnant at their *will:* . . . VI. xi. 18. 3
all this while at *will* did range and raine, . . . VI. xii. 2. 8
Against his *will* fast bound in yron chaine, . . . VI. xii. 35. 3
rule both sea and land unto their *will:* . . . VII. vii. 3. 5
For though he colours could devize at *will*, . . . *Am.* xvii. 5
easie things, that may be got at *will*, . . . *Am.* xxvi. 11
move the Dolphin from her stubborn *will*, . . . *Am.* xxxviii. 8
Is it her nature, or is it her *will*, . . . *Am.* xli. 1
If *will;* then she at *will* may *will* forgoe. . . . *Am.* xli. 4
if her nature and her *wil* be so, . . . *Am.* xli. 5
willing me against her *will* to stay. . . . *Am.* xlvi. 4
But as she *will*, whose *will* my life doth sway, . . . *Am.* xlvi. 7
Yet live for ever, though against her *will*, . . . *Am.* xlviii. 13
But if it be your pleasure, and proud *will*, . . . *Am.* xlix. 5
Mote soften it and to his *will* allure: . . . *Am.* li. 10
So goodly wonne, with her owne *will* beguyld. . . . *Am.* lxvii. 14
yeeld theyr services unto her *will;* . . . *Epith.* 197
Poure out to all that *wull*, . . . *Epith.* 252
Ye sonnes of Venus, play your sports at *will!* . . . *Epith.* 364
Encline thy *will* t' effect our wishfull vow, . . . *Epith.* 385
when he hath found favour to his *will*, . . . *H.L.* 245
corrupt, and wrested unto *will:* . . . *H.B.* 158
An heavenly beautie to his fancies *will;* . . . *H.B.* 222
About him wait, and on his *will* depend, . . . *H.H.L.* 65
Both heaven and earth obey unto her *will*, . . . *H.H.B.* 197
Angels, which her goodly face behold And see at *will*, . . . *H.H.B.* 233

Willed. *See* **Self-willed.**
me unworthie *willed* here to stay, . . . *D.* 367
Tho (as he *wild*) unto his loved lasse, . . . *As.* 147
after *wild* it should to her remaine, . . . II. x. 32. 3
whether *willed* or nilled friend or foe, . . . IV. vii. 16. 6
And *willed* him with Artegall to wend, . . . V. i. 12. 4
she his fury *willed* him to slake: . . . V. vii. 36. 7
him seeing so to rage *Wild* him to stay, . . . V. xii. 8. 2
willed him for to reclayme with speed His scattred people, . . V. xii. 9. 1
he *wild* her doe away all dread; . . . VI. i. 31. 7
wild the damzell rise; . . . VI. ix. 13. 9
willed streight the slaves should forth be called, . . . VI. xi. 10. 8

Willing. asked him, if he could *willing* bee . . . *Hub.* 284
thereby *willing* to affoord them aide; . . . *Hub.* 414
The knights were *willing* all things to excuse, . . . III. ix. 18. 8
Did yield him selfe right *willing* to prolong his date: . . . III. xii. 35. 9
Whom when so *willing* Artegall perceaved; . . . V. i. 28. 1
willing them forth to call Into the field . . . V. x. 31. 4
Willing him wend unto the Tyrant streight, . . . V. xii. 8. 6
Willing to worke his villenous intent . . . VI. vi. 44. 4
willing eke to wreake The guilt on him . . . VI. vii. 13. 6
further then she *willing* was he prest, . . . VI. xi. 7. 6
As *willing* me against her will to stay. . . . *Am.* xlvi. 4

Willingly. So *willingly* she came into his armes, . . . I. vii. 15. 3
Who her as *willingly* to grace did take, . . . I. vii. 15. 4
Is it not better to doe *willinglie*, . . . I. ix. 47. 7

Willingness. Sweete is the love that comes alone with *willingnesse*. . . . IV. v. 25. 9

Willow. some soft *Willow*, or new growen stud; . . . *Gn.* 84
The *Willow*, worne of forlorne Paramours; . . . I. i. 9. 3
To win a *willow* bough, . . . IV. i. 47. 9

Wills. Whereto thou list their trayned *willes* entice. . . . *S.C.* O. 24
in the valleies wandring at their *wills*, . . . *Gn.* 76
diff'ring both in *willes* agreed in fine: . . . II. xii. 59. 7
to your *willes* both royalties and Reames Subdew, . . . III. v. 53. 3
they secret way did make Unto their *wils*, . . . III. ix. 31. 6
none That to their *willes* could them direct aright, . . . IV. i. 16. 8
from revenge their *willes* they scarce asswag'd: . . . IV. v. 27. 3
cruelly does wound whom so she *wils:* . . . V. xii. 36. 5
For nought against their *wils* might countervaile: . . . VII. vi. 49. 7
Love, that long hath slept . . . *Wils* him awake, . . . *Am.* iv. 7

Willy. Sicker, *Willye*, thou warnest well; . . . *S.C.* Mar. 7

Willy—*Continued.*
Willye, I wene thou bee assot; . . . *S.C.* Mar. 25
Ah! *Willye*, when the hart is ill assayde, . . . *S.C.* Au. 5
Ah! *Willye*, now I have learnd a newe daunce; . . . *S.C.* Au. 11
Well agreed, *Willie:* . . . *S.C.* Au. 49
Willye is not greatly overgone, . . . *S.C.* Au. 127
let the Lambe be *Willye* his owne: . . . *S.C.* Au. 132
Ne can *Willye* wite the witelesse herdgroome. . . . *S.C.* Au. 136
Our pleasant *Willy*, ah! is dead of late: . . . *T.M.* 208

Wilt (*partial list*).
till that thou thy Poeme *wilt* make knowne, . . . *Ded.Son.*viii.13
Why *wilt* not let him passe, . . . I. ix. 39. 8
Wilt give thy beard, though it but little bee? . . . VI. i. 19. 8

Wily. Like as a *wily* Foxe, . . . *Mui.* 401
The *wily* lover did devise this slight: . . . *Col.* 137
by her wicked arts and *wylie* skill, . . . I. xii. 32. 6
by his false allurements *wylie* draft . . . IV. ii. 10. 4
his owne *wylie* wit, . . . V. ix. 5. 1

Wily-witted. For he was *wylie witted*, . . . II. iii. 9. 5

Wimble. He was so *wimble* and so wight, . . . *S.C.* Mar. 91

Wimborne. washeth *Winborne* meades in season drye. . . . IV. xi. 32. 4

Wimple. widow-like sad *wimple* throwne away, . . . I. xii. 22. 3

Wimpled. a vele, that *wimpled* was full low; . . . I. i. 4. 4
with a veile, that *wimpled* every where, . . . VII. vii. 5. 8

Win. *See* **Out-win.**
Forcing with gyfts to *winne* his wanton heart. . . . *S.C.* Ap. 24
Ne strive to *winne* renowne, . . . *S.C.* Jun. 74
after we may favour seeke to *win?*' . . . *Hub.* 644
in his liking to *winne* worthie place, . . . *Hub.* 776
Both wares and money, by exchange to *win:* . . . *Hub.* 870
When the Naemean Conquest he did *win*. . . . *Mui.* 72
by no meanes I could him *win* thereto, . . . *D.* 561
wrought to *win* delight. . . . *Col.* 119
To *winne* him worshippe, and her grace to have, . . . I. i. 3. 4
Resolvd in minde all suddenly to *win*, . . . I. i. 24. 4
'the way to *win* Is wisely to advise; . . . I. i. 33. 5
For hoped love to *winne* me certaine hate? . . . I. i. 51. 5
prickte with pride And hope to *winne* his Ladies hearte . I. ii. 14. 7
but yet could never *win* The Fort, . . . I. ii. 25. 3
Both seemde to *win*, and both seemde won to bee, . . . I. ii. 37. 6
What not by right she cast to *win* by guile; . . . I. ii. 38. 3
waiting long, to *win* the wished sight Of her, . . . I. iv. 6. 8
Where both doe fight alike, to *win* or yield?' . . . I. iv. 50. 4
And *win* rich spoile of ransackt chastitee. . . . I. vi. 5. 5
both chose to *win*, or die. . . . I. vi. 43. 9
hardly he the flitted life does *win* . . . I. vii. 21. 7
never any could that girlond *win*, . . . I. vii. 45. 6
battels, which thou boasts to *win* Through strife, . . . I. ix. 43. 3
In hope to *win* occasion to his will; . . . II. i. 5. 2
thy sight could *win* thee grace. . . . II. i. 9. 9
In hope to *win* more favour with his mate, . . . II. ii. 19. 4
weened well ere long his will to *win*, . . . II. iii. 13. 2
mote him honour *win* to wreak so foule despight. . . . II. iii. 13. 9
swore him fealty to *win* or loose. . . . II. x. 37. 9
In hope thereof to *win* victorious spoile. . . . II. xi. 7. 5
Nought feard theyr force that fortilage to *win*, . . . II. xii. 43. 5
in hope to *win* thereby Most goodly meede, . . . III. i. 18. 7
Till she mote *winne* fit time for her desire; . . . III. i. 56. 2
Achilles armes, which Arthegall did *win:* . . . III. ii. 25. 6
to ease thy griefe And *win* thy will: . . . III. ii. 33. 7
Thrise shall he fight with them, and twise shall *win;* . . . III. iii. 30. 6
win him worship through his warlike deed, . . . III. iv. 4. 8
more happy were to *win* so goodly pray. . . . III. iv. 46. 9
Which darknesse shall subdue and heaven *win:* . . . III. iv. 59. 6
how to *win* the wished victory, . . . III. vii. 33. 2
To *winne* her liking unto his delight: . . . III. viii. 38. 5
Her will to *win* unto his wished eend; . . . III. viii. 41. 5
we will by force it *win*, . . . III. ix. 9. 5
To *win* faire Leda to his lovely trade: . . . III. xi. 32. 2
to *win* Deucalions daughter bright, . . . III. xi. 42. 5
Should either *winne* him one, or lye without the dore. . . . IV. i. 9. 9
as to a Knight That did her *win* . . . IV. i. 12. 4
To *win* a willow bough, whilest other weares the bayes. . IV. i. 47. 9
her love prepare, and liking *win* theretoo. . . . IV. ii. 8. 9
That shall you *win* more glory than ye here find gaines.' . . IV. ii. 27. 9
Ne which of them did *winne*, ne which were wonne. . . . IV. iii. 36. 7
Yee shall her *winne*, as I have done, in fight: . . . IV. iv. 9. 4
Where beauties prize shold *win* that pretious spoyle: . . . IV. iv. 48. 8
That many wish to *win* for glorie vaine, . . . IV. v. 2. 6
to *winne* the same So many Ladies sought, . . . IV. v. 6. 3
for to *winne* the saddle lost the steed. . . . IV. v. 22. 5
To *win* her grace his libertie to get: . . . IV. viii. 53. 6
To *winne* me honour by some noble gest, . . . IV. x. 4. 4
That Virgins love to *win* by wit or wile, . . . IV. xi. 2. 3
By timely death shall *winne* her wished rest, . . . IV. xii. 8. 2
That she might *win* some time, . . . V. ii. 23. 7
all strove with perill to *winne* fame; . . . V. iii. 7. 5
though my land he first did *winne* away, . . . V. iv. 14. 6
Threw many threats, if they the towne did *win*, . . . V. iv. 37. 4
Weening at last to *win* advantage new; . . . V. v. 7. 2
To which if thou canst *win* him any way . . . V. v. 33. 6
Make meanes to *win* thy libertie forlorne, . . . V. v. 40. 2
swift Talus did the formost *win;* . . . V. vii. 35. 2
Did *win* the shore; . . . V. xii. 5. 8
sought to *win* his love by all the meanes she might. . . . VI. i. 14. 9
even in the Porch he him did *win*, . . . VI. i. 23. 4
well she knew the wayes to *win* good will . . . VI. vi. 41. 6
To *winne* the love of the faire Pastorell, . . . VI. ix. 46. 2
didst bring away Captivity thence captive, us to *win:* . . . *Am.* lxviii. 4
Certes small glory doest thou *winne* hereby, . . . *H.L.* 153

Win—*Continued.*
though he do not *win* his wish to end, ... *H.L.* 211
To *win* them worship which to thee obay. . . . . *H.L.* 237
wight Who of her selfe can *win* the wishfull sight. . . . . *H.H.B.* 245

Winborne. *See* **Wimborne.**

Wind. *See* **Outwind, South wind.**
wrathfull *winde,* Which blows cold storms, ... *Bel.*[2] viii. 11
Milde was the *winde,* calme seem'd the sea . . . . *Pet.* ii. 4
As waves, as *winde,* as fire, spred over all, ... *Ro.* xvi. 13
If too great *winde* against the port him drive, ... *Ro.* xxi. 13
though she owe her fall to the first *winde,* . . . . *Ro.* xxviii. 9
Faire blew the *winde* into her bosome right; . . . . *Van.* ix. 5
winde nor tide could move her thence away. . . . . *Van.* ix. 12
They wont in the *wind* wagge their wrigle tayles, ... *S.C.* F. 7
See howe he venteth into the *wynd;* . . . . *S.C.* F. 75
The simple ayre, the gentle warbling *wynde,* . . . . *S.C.* Jun. 4
nowe the Westerne *wind* bloweth sore, ... *S.C.* S. 49
The more to *wind* it out thou doest swinck, ... *S.C.* S. 132
Sike words bene *wynd,* and wasten soone . . . . *S.C.* O. 36
All was blowne away of the wavering *wynd.* . . . . *S.C.* D. 126
Where breathe on them the whistling *wind* mote best; . . . *Gn.* 236
happie *winde* and weather entertaine, ... *Gn.* 563
'Them therefore as bequeathing to the *winde,* . . . . *Gn.* 633
meane for better *winde* about to throwe. . . . . *Hub.* 80
the common *winde* Of Courts inconstant mutabilitie, ... *Hub.* 722
the strings, stirred with the warbling *wind,* . . . . *Ti.* 613
oft would dare to tempt the troublous *winde.* . . . . *Mui.* 48
She fel away like fruit blowne downe with *winde.* . . . . . . *D.* 244
So soone as on them blowes the Northern *winde,* . . . . . . *D.* 396
neither car'd for *wynd,* nor haile, nor raine, ... *Col.* 221
like bladders blowen up with *wynd,* . . . . *Col.* 717
raine . . . Mixt with a murmuring *winde,* . . . . I. i. 41. 4
bayes His sweatie forehead in the breathing *wynd,* . . . . . I. vii. 3. 2
masse of earthly slyme, Puft up with emptie *wynd,* . . . . I. vii. 9. 9
with the *winde* it did him overthrow, ... I. vii. 12. 8
Long tost with stormes, and bet with bitter *wind,* . . . . . I. vii. 28. 7
Her dried dugs, lyke bladders lacking *wind,* Hong downe, . . I. viii. 47. 6
with his winged heeles did tread the *wynd,* . . . . I. ix. 21. 8
sayles, in which the hollow *wynd* Is gathered full, ... I. xi. 10. 2
mery *wynd* and weather call her thence away. . . . . I. xii. 1. 9
when fluttring *wind* does blow . . . . II. iii. 10. 3
The Northerne *winde* his wings did broad display . . . . II. iii. 19. 3
Each trembling leafe and whistling *wind* they heare, ... II. iii. 20. 4
when the *winde* emongst them did inspyre, ... II. iii. 30. 3
winged canvas with the *wind* to fly: . . . . II. vi. 5. 4
t' appease the stormy *winde* Of malice . . . . II. vi. 8. 8
Ne care, ne feare I how the *wind* do blow, ... II. vi. 10. 4
Whom nether *wind* out of their seat could forse . . . . . . II. vi. 20. 8
Ne *wind* and weather at his pleasure call: . . . . II. vi. 23. 3
The *wind* unstable, and doth never stay. . . . . II. vi. 23. 5
with forst *wind* the fewell did inflame; . . . . II. vii. 36. 2
wind his horne under the castle wall, ... II. ix. 11. 4
the fierce Northerne *wind* with blustring blast . . . . . . II. ix. 16. 8
whiles *wind* and wether right Doe serve their turnes: . . . II. xi. 4. 7
When the wroth Western *wind* does reave their locks: . . . II. xi. 19. 5
as the *winde* ran underneath his lode, ... II. xi. 20. 5
as the winged *wind* his Tigre fled, ... II. xi. 26. 1
not one puffe of *winde* there did appeare, ... II. xii. 22. 5
Now soft, now loud, unto the *wind* did call; . . . . II. xii. 71. 8
The gentle warbling *wind* low answered to all. . . . . . . II. xii. 71. 9
let us hence depart whilest wether serves and *winde.'* . . . II. xii. 87. 9
what uncouth *wind* Brought her into those partes, ... III. ii. 4. 5
saile withouten starres gainst tyde and *winde:* . . . . . . III. iv. 9. 8
Ne the sharp Northerne *wind* thereon to showre; . . . . . III. v. 51. 5
shaketh with the least Murmure of *winde,* . . . . III. vii. 1. 5
He forth issew'd: like as a boystrous *winde,* . . . . III. ix. 15. 2
lay still in the *winde,* . . . . III. x. 30. 5
As if the *wind* him on his winges had borne; . . . . III. x. 55. 2
an hideous storme of *winde* arose, ... III. xii. 2. 1
flitting as the wavering *wind* After each beautie . . . . . IV. ii. 5. 2
he their words as *wind* esteemed light. . . . . IV. v. 27. 7
Like to the Northren *winde,* that none could heare: . . . . IV. v. 38. 8
Me hether brought with him as swift as *wind,* . . . . . . IV. vii. 18. 7
winged feete as nimble as the *winde,* . . . . IV. vii. 30. 2
flew away as lightly as the *wind:* . . . . IV. viii. 7. 7
breathed forth with blast of bitter *wind;* . . . . IV. viii. 26. 5
this caried with the tide, That with the *wind,* . . . . . . IV. ix. 26. 8
If *wind* and tide doe change, ... IV. ix. 26. 9
sailers save from wreckes of wrathfull *winde.* . . . . . . IV. xi. 52. 5
Talus, that could like a lime-hound *winde* her, ... V. ii. 25. 3
one of th' ayre, without or *wind* or wether: . . . . V. ii. 31. 4
weigh the *winde* that under heaven doth blow; . . . . . . V. ii. 43. 2
her winged thoughts, more swift then *wind,* . . . . V. vi. 7. 8
oversprad her like a puffe of *wind;* . . . . V. ix. 14. 3
shivered all about, and scattered in the *wynd:* . . . . . . V. x. 32. 9
Like scattred chaffe the which the *wind* away doth fan. . . . V. xi. 47. 9
The *winde* and weather served them so well, ... V. xii. 4. 5
Did spred abroad and throw in th' open *wynd:* . . . . . . V. xii. 33. 7
Him selfe out of the forest he did *wynd,* . . . . VI. iv. 26. 2
Yet were her words but *wynd,* . . . . VI. vi. 42. 9
Were brought by errour or by wreckfull *wynde;* . . . . . . VI. viii. 36. 4
Is met of many a counter *winde* and tyde, ... VI. xii. 1. 3
When any *winde* doth under heaven blowe; . . . . VII. vii. 20. 7
fruitlesse worke is broken with least *wynd.* . . . . *Am.* xxiii. 14
heares With the loose *wynd* ye waving chance to marke; . . *Am.* lxxxi. 2

Winding. *See* **Ivy-winding.**
nor brere, nor *winding* witche: . . . . *S.C.* Jun. 20
to entrappe the fish in *winding* sale . . . . *S.C.* D. 81

Windings. all within it full of *wyndings* is . . . . V. ix. 6. 6

Window. Being one day at my *window* all alone, ... *Pet.* i. 1

Window—*Continued.*
he by conning sleights in at the *window* crept. . . . . I. iii. 17. 9
So soone as heavens *window* shewed light, ... IV. iii. 3. 7
Would to his hope a *windowe* open wyde, ... V. v. 39. 3
She to a *window* came that opened West, ... V. vi. 7. 4
Forth of her *window* as she looking lay, ... V. viii. 26. 6
Ne lightned was with *window,* nor with lover, ... VI. x. 42. 7
Who is the same, which at my *window* peepes? . . . . . . *Epith.* 372

Windows. Light out of heavens *windowes* forth to looke, . . . *Hub.* 109
Forth looking through the *windowes* of the East, ... *Col.* 605
all the walls and *windows* there are writ, ... *Col.* 776
goodly galleries . . . Full of faire *windowes* . . . . I. iv. 4. 8
shut up heavens *windowes* shyning wyde; . . . . I. vii. 23. 5
The *windowes* of bright heaven opened had, ... II. xi. 3. 2

Winds. Nor th' horrible uprore of *windes* high blowing, . . . *Ro.* xiii. 9
bitter-breathing *windes* with harmfull blast, ... *Ti.* 405
Whom raging *windes* . . . doe diversly disease, ... II. ii. 24. 2
Birdes, voices, instruments, *windes,* waters, ... II. xii. 70. 9
'Thou God of *windes,* that raignest in the seas, ... III. iv. 10. 1
all his *windes* Dan Aeolus did keepe . . . . III. viii. 21. 6
Sends forth the *winds* out of his hidden threasure . . . . . IV. ix. 23. 3
thee the *winds,* the clouds doe feare, ... IV. x. 44. 6

Windy. tost in th' ayre with everie *windie* blast: . . . . . . *Gn.* 334
With *windy* Nitre and quick Sulphur fraught, ... I. vii. 13. 3
As when a *windy* tempest bloweth hye, ... II. viii. 48. 1
in his hand a *windy* fan did beare, ... III. xii. 8. 3

Wine. The *wine* of hooredome in a cup . . . . *Rev.* ii. 8
Bring Coronations, with Sops in *wine,* . . . . *S.C.* Ap. 138
girlonds of roses, and Sopps in *wine.* . . . . *S.C.* May 14
when with *Wine* the braine begins to sweate, ... *S.C.* O. 107
if my temples were distaind with *wine,* . . . . *S.C.* O. 110
fill the same with store of timely *wine.* . . . . *Col.* 603
in the *wine* a solemne oth they bynd . . . . I. v. 4. 8
In *wine* and oyle they wash his woundes wide, ... I. v. 17. 4
a cup of gold, With *wine* and water fild . . . . I. x. 13. 3
Then gan they sprinckle all the posts with *wine,* . . . . . I. xii. 38. 1
In *wine* and meats she flowd above the banck, ... II. ii. 36. 6
With balme, and *wine,* and costly spicery, ... II. xi. 49. 4
A mighty Mazer bowle of *wine* was sett, ... II. xii. 49. 3
to taste their lushious *wine,* . . . . II. xii. 54. 4
so faire winepresse made the *wine* more sweet: . . . . . . II. xii. 56. 6
cheared well with *wine* and spiceree: . . . . III. i. 42. 5
A sacrament prophane in mistery of *wine.* . . . . III. ix. 30. 9
So proov'd it eke that gratious God of *wine,* . . . . III. xi. 43. 6
Surcharg'd with *wine,* were heedlesse and ill-hedded, ... IV. i. 3. 4
beare with you both *wine* and juncates fit, ... V. iv. 49. 8
Ne drinke of *wine;* for *wine,* they say, is blood, ... V. vii. 10. 3
Poure out the *wine* without restraint or stay, ... *Epith.* 250
sprinkle all the postes and wals with *wine,* . . . . *Epith.* 253

Wine-fat's. must, Which he was treading in the *wine-fats* see, VII. vii. 39. 3

Winepress. so faire *winepresse* made the wine more sweet: . . II. xii. 56. 6

Wines. They bring them *wines* of Greece and Araby, ... I. v. 4. 5

Wing. A Bird all white, well feathered on each *wing,* . . . *Bel.*[2] xi. 5
for succoure flee Under the shadow of his *wing;* . . . . . *To his Booke* 7
There may thy Muse display her fluttryng *wing,* . . . . . . *S.C.* O. 43
Under the left *wing* stroke his weapon . . . . *Mui.* 437
my Muse . . . With bolder *wing* shall dare alofte to sty, . . *Ded. Son.* ii. 9
did glyde Close under his left *wing,* . . . . I. xi. 20. 7
his late wounded *wing* unserviceable found. . . . . I. xi. 25. 9
maketh him his *wing* in vaine to spend; . . . . IV. iii. 19. 7
Whose other *wing* . . . Was lately broken . . . . V. v. 15. 3
At an Herneshaw, that lyes aloft on *wing,* . . . . VI. vii. 9. 2
This too high flight, unfit for her weake *wing*) . . . . . . VII. vii. 1. 4
to overspred Me with the shadow of thy gentle *wing,* . . . . *H.L.* 20
Spread thy broad *wing* over my love and me, ... *Epith.* 319

Winged. *See* **Leather-winged, Winged-heeled.**
sayd, he was a *winged* lad, ... *S.C.* Mar. 112
thy gay Sonne, that *winged* God of Love, ... *T.M.* 401
With which I wont the *winged* words to tie, ... *T.M.* 548
where the *winged* ships were seene . . . . *Ti.* 148
A Knight all arm'd, upon a *winged* steed; . . . . *Ti.* 646
She turn'd into a *winged* Butterflie, ... *Mui.* 138
Before the Bull she pictur'd *winged* Love, ... *Mui.* 289
that false *winged* boy Her chaste hart had subdewd . . . . I. i. 47. 8
with his *winged* heeles did tread the wynd, ... I. ix. 21. 8
winged canvas with the wind to fly: . . . . II. vi. 5. 4
Bidding his *winged* vessell fairely forward fly: . . . . . . II. vii. 1. 9
two sharpe *winged* sheares, Decked with diverse plumes, . . II. viii. 5. 7
as the *winged* wind his Tigre fled, ... II. xi. 26. 1
Her little sonne, the *winged* god of love, ... III. vi. 11. 2
thither haunt, and with the *winged* boy, ... III. vi. 49. 3
On which the *winged* boy in colours cleare Depeincted was, . III. xi. 7. 7
The *winged* boy did thrust into his throne, ... III. xi. 35. 6
like a *winged* horse he tooke his flight . . . . III. xi. 42. 7
the *winged* God him selfe Came riding . . . . III. xii. 22. 1
winged feete as nimble as the winde, ... IV. vii. 30. 2
streight the *winged* words out of his ballaunce flew. . . . . V. ii. 44. 9
her *winged* thoughts, more swift then wind, ... V. vi. 7. 8
the *winged* God that woundeth harts . . . . VI. viii. 22. 1
the *winged* God . . . A thousand sowres hath tempred . . . VI. xi. 1. 6
With which her *winged* speed is let and crost, ... VI. xii. 1. 4
the *winged* god . . . Began in me to move, ... *Am.* lx. 5
an hundred little *winged* loves, ... *Epith.* 357

Winged-foot. The *wingd-foot* God so fast his plumes did beat, VII. vi. 17. 1

Winged-heeled. he fast away did fly, . . . *winged heeld,* . . . III. xii. 12. 6

Wing-footed. At last me seem'd *wing-footed* Mercurie, ... *Ti.* 666
his *wingfooted* coursers him did beare So fast away . . . . V. viii. 33. 4

Wings. With golden *wings* in habite of a Nymph. . . . . . *Bel.*[1] iv. 6
more she gan to trust hir *wings,* . . . . *Bel.*[1] vi. 3
with hir *wings* to reache The place . . . . *Bel.*[1] vi. 7

Wings—*Continued.*
A bird all white, well fetherd on hir *winges* . . . *Bel.*[1] ix. 5
like a Nimph, that *wings* of silver weares, . . . *Bel.*[2] iv. 6
With feeble *wings* assay to mount . . . *Bel.*[2] vii. 2
more she gan her *wings* t' assure . . . *Bel.*[2] vii. 3
With purple *wings,* and crest of golden hewe; . . . *Pet.* v. 2
having his wide *wings* spent in wast, . . . *Ro.* xvi. 7
scortching Sunne had brent His *wings* . . . *Ro.* xvii. 6
With *winges* of purple and blewe; . . . *S.C.* Mar. 33
sprong forth a naked swayne With spotted *winges,* . . . *S.C.* Mar. 80
make thee *winges* of thine aspyring wit, . . . *S.C.* O. 83
The soothe of byrdes by beating of their *winges,* . . . *S.C.* D. 87
Time, flying with *winges* swift, . . . *Hub.* 308
with his azure *wings* he cleav'd The liquid clowdes, . . . *Hub.* 1258
Make thy selfe fluttring *wings* . . . *U.V.* 2
Fame with golden *wings* aloft doth flie, . . . *Ti.* 421
with unwearied *wings,* each part t' inquire . . . *Mui.* 39
Lastly his shinie *wings* as silver bright, . . . *Mui.* 89
Beares in his *wings* so manie a changefull token. . . . *Mui.* 101
sure those *wings* were fairer manifolde. . . . *Mui.* 104
She placed in her *wings,* . . . *Mui.* 142
that flie them in her *wings* doth beare. . . . *Mui.* 144
With his aire-cutting *wings* he measured wide, . . . *Mui.* 154
his moyst *wings* to dry. . . . *Mui.* 184
The velvet nap which on his *wings* doth lie, . . . *Mui.* 333
wrapt his *winges* twaine In lymie snares . . . *Mui.* 428
had it armes and *wings,* . . . *Col.* 218
their tender *wings* He brusheth oft, . . . I. i. 23. 8
on his litle *winges* the dreame he bore . . . I. i. 44. 8
a Dragon . . . over all did spredd His golden *winges:* . . . I. vii. 31. 5
The plumes of pride, and *winges* of vanity, . . . I. x. 39. 3
His flaggy *winges* . . . Were like two sayles, . . . I. xi. 10. 1
with his waving *wings* displayed wyde, . . . I. xi. 18. 1
with his *winges* to stye above the ground; . . . I. xi. 25. 8
clapt his yron *wings* as victor he did dwell. . . . I. xi. 31. 9
gathering up himselfe . . . With his uneven *wings,* . . . I. xi. 40. 8
when fluttring wind does blow In his light *winges,* . . . II. iii. 10. 4
The Northerne winde his *wings* did broad display . . . II. iii. 19. 3
'Feare gave her *winges,* . . . II. iv. 32. 1
Did alwaies sore, beating his yron *wings;* . . . II. vii. 23. 2
he gan display His painted nimble *wings,* . . . II. viii. 8. 9
who shall lend me *wings,* . . . II. x. 1. 3
some had *wings,* and some had clawes to teare: . . . II. xi. 8. 5
with their wicked *wings* them ofte did smight, . . . II. xii. 35. 8
Taketh his nimble *winges,* and soone away is gone.' . . . III. i. 25. 9
With his wide *wings* upon them fiercely fly, . . . III. iii. 46. 6
after her his nimble *winges* doth straine, . . . III. iv. 49. 7
Fancies bett his ydle brayne With their light *wings,* . . . III. iv. 54. 5
Carried away with *wings* of speedy feare.' . . . III. v. 6. 6
way through which his *wings* Had borne him, . . . III. vi. 12. 6
Ile clip his wanton *wings,* that he no more shall flye.' . . . III. vi. 24. 9
with his flaggy *winges* Beates downe both leaves and buds . . . III. vi. 39. 7
from Prince Arthure fled with *wings* of idle feare. . . . III. vi. 54. 9
fear gave her *wings,* and need her corage taught. . . . III. vii. 26. 9
with plumy *wings* doth sheare The subtile ayre . . . III. vii. 39. 3
As if the wind him on his *winges* had borne; . . . III. x. 55. 2
that doth his golden *wings* embay In blessed Nectar . . . III. xi. 2. 3
with wide *winges* to beat the buxome ayre: . . . III. xi. 34. 2
winges it had with sondry colours dight, . . . III. xi. 47. 6
clapt on hye his coulourd *winges* twaine, . . . III. xii. 23. 7
The God of love with *wings* displayed wide . . . IV. i. 39. 3
her nimble *wings* displaid, And flew away . . . IV. viii. 7. 6
With nimble *wings* of gold and purple hew; . . . IV. x. 42. 3
Under the *wings* of Isis all that night; . . . V. vii. 12. 2
Carried with *wings* of feare, like fowle aghast, . . . V. viii. 4. 7
her brode-spreading *wings* did wyde unfold; . . . V. ix. 28. 5
on their purpled *wings* Did beare the pendants . . . V. ix. 29. 2
And Eagles *wings,* for scope and speedinesse, . . . V. xi. 24. 7
more fiercely reard Uppon her wide great *wings,* . . . V. xi. 30. 6
His brode black *wings* had . . . dispred, . . . VI. viii. 44. 5
being bred under base shepheards *wings,* . . . VI. ix. 35. 4
wings of gold fit to employ. . . . VII. vii. 46. 9
His wanton *wings* and darts of deadly power. . . . *Am.* iv. 8
Legions of loves with little *wings* did fly; . . . *Am.* xvi. 6
when my spirit doth spred her bolder *winges,* . . . *Am.* lxxii. 1
They loosely did theyr wanton *winges* display, . . . *Am.* lxxvi. 11
He tooke his *wings* and away did fly. . . . *Epig.* i. 6
Bathing thy *wings* in her ambrosiall kisse, . . . *H.L.* 25
taking to him *wings* of his owne heate, . . . *H.L.* 64
cowardly distrust Of his weake *wings* . . . *H.L.* 181
Love, lift me up upon thy golden *wings,* . . . *H.H.L.* 1
Ere flitting Time could wag his eyas *wings* . . . *H.H.L.* 24
Either with nimble *wings* to cut the skies, . . . *H.H.L.* 66
faulcon . . . That flags awhile her fluttering *wings* beneath, . . . *H.H.B.* 27
Cherubins, Which all with golden *wings* are overdight, . . . *H.H.B.* 93
To impe the *wings* of thy high flying mynd, . . . *H.H.B.* 135

Wingyheeled. *As ashes pale of hew, and *wingyheeld;* . . . III. xii. 12. 6

Wink. evermore, when he began to *winke,* . . . IV. v. 41. 3

Winneth. Still *winneth* way, ne hath her compasse lost: . . . VI. xii. 1. 7

Wins. *winnes* an Olive girlond for her meeds. . . . II. ii. 31. 7
Blandamour *winnes* false Florimell; . . . IV. ii. Arg.
Britomart *winnes* the prize from all, . . . IV. iv. Arg.
who so *winnes* her may her have by right: . . . IV. iv. 9. 7

Winter. is in *Winter* lord of all the plaine, . . . *Ro.* xiv. 2
Winter or Sommer they mought well fare. . . . *S.C.* F. 24
Age and *Winter* accord full nie, . . . *S.C.* F. 27
Comes the breme *Winter* with chamfred browes, . . . *S.C.* F. 43
eftsones *Winter* gan to approche; . . . *S.C.* F. 225
when *Winter* doth her straine. . . . *S.C.* O. 12
sadde *Winter* welked hath the day, . . . *S.C.* N. 13

Winter—*Continued.*
My harveste hasts to stirre up *Winter* sterne, . . . *S.C.* D. 129
Winter is come that blowes the bitter blaste, . . . *S.C.* D. 143
after *Winter* dreerie death does hast. . . . *S.C.* D. 144
Ere the breme *Winter* breede you greater griefe. . . . *S.C.* D. 148
Winter is come, that blowes the balefull breath, . . . *S.C.* D. 149
after *Winter* commeth timely death. . . . *S.C.* D. 150
did all *winter* as in sommer bud, . . . VI. x. 6. 5
of their *Winter* spring another Prime, . . . VII. vii. 18. 7
Lastly, came *Winter* cloathed all in frize, . . . VII. vii. 31. 1

Winter's. When *Winters* wastful spight was almost spent, . . . *S.C.* Ja. 2
'Thou barrein ground, whome *winters* wrath hath wasted, . . . *S.C.* Ja. 19
now is come thy *wynters* stormy state, . . . *S.C.* Ja. 23
'Such rage as *winters* reigneth in my heart, . . . *S.C.* Ja. 25
wil rancke *Winters* rage . . . never ginne tasswage? . . . *S.C.* F. 1
Lewdly complainest thou . . . Of *Winters* wracke . . . *S.C.* F. 10
Of Sommers flame, nor of *Winters* threat, . . . *S.C.* F. 20
beare Cherefully the *Winters* wrathful cheare; . . . *S.C.* F. 26
slake the *winters* sorowe. . . . *S.C.* Mar. 6
Winters wrath beginnes to quell, . . . *S.C.* Mar. 8
sadde *winters* wrathe, and season chill, . . . *S.C.* N. 33
lyeth buryed long in *Winters* bale; . . . *S.C.* N. 84
winters stormie wrath . . . *T.M.* 236
far more bitter storme than *winters* stowre . . . *T.M.* 247
whom wearie *winters* teene Hath worne to nought, . . . IV. iii. 23. 7
As withered weed through cruell *winters* tine, . . . IV. xii. 34. 6
Like as the Moone in foggie *winters* night . . . V. v. 12. 8
where shepherds lie In *winters* wrathfull time, . . . VI. ix. 4. 9
calling forth out of sad *Winters* night . . . *Am.* iv. 5
in her *winters* bowre not well awake; . . . *Am.* lxx. 6

Winters'. With hardned frosts of former *winters* ire, . . . VII. vii. 11. 4

Wintry. What recked I of *wintrye* ages waste?— . . . *S.C.* D. 29
wintry storme his wrathful wreck does threat; . . . I. xi. 21. 2

Wipe. all their teares he shall *wipe* cleane away. . . . *Rev.* iv. 7
Those weary wanton toyes away dyd *wype,* . . . *S.C.* Jun. 48
my hope away dyd *wipe.* . . . *S.C.* D. 108
everie shower will wash and *wipe* away; . . . *Ti.* 205
And *wipe* their faults out of your censure grave. . . . *Ded. Son.* ix. 14
filth *wipe* cleane away: . . . II. iv. 35. 8
all thy wronges will *wipe* out of my sovenaunce.' . . . II. viii. 51. 9
Her Lions clawes he from her feete away did *wipe.* . . . V. xi. 27. 9
her sad selfe . . . constrayning To *wype* his wounds, . . . VI. ii. 41. 5

Wiped. as things *wipt* out with a sponge . . . *Ti.* 361
wypt away his toilsom sweat. . . . II. v. 30. 9
They softly *wipt* away the gelly blood . . . III. iv. 40. 6
have the sterne remembrance *wypt* away . . . IV. viii. 1. 8
so soone As she her face had *wypt* . . . V. v. 45. 7
From his soft eyes the teares he *wypt* away, . . . VI. iv. 23. 4
eek my name bee *wyped* out lykewize. . . . *Am.* lxxv. 8

Wipes. With her soft garment *wipes* away the gore . . . III. i. 38. 5
Eftsoones he *wypes* quite out of memory . . . *H.L.* 241

Wiping. *Wiping* the teares from her suffused eyes, . . . III. vii. 10. 3
wiping out remembrance of all ill, . . . IV. vi. 32. 4
From her faire eyes *wiping* the deawy wet . . . IV. vii. 35. 5

Wire. *See* **Copper-wire.**
Her yellow lockes, crisped like golden *wyre,* . . . II. iii. 30. 1
Fast bounden hand and foote with cords of *wire,* . . . III. vii. 37. 8
With golden *wyre* to weave her curled head; . . . III. viii. 7. 6
golden *wyre* was not so yellow . . . III. viii. 7. 7
To frame such subtile *wire,* so shinie cleare; . . . IV. vi. 20. 6
Her long loose yellow locks lyke yellow *wyre,* . . . *Epith.* 154
That golden *wyre,* those sparckling stars so bright, . . . *H.B.* 97

Wiry. her yeolow locks, like *wyrie* gold . . . *Ti.* 10

Wisdom. O! warie *wisedome* of the man, . . . *Ro.* xxiii. 1
government of state Will without *wisedome* soone be ruinate. . . . *Hub.* 1040
His *wisdome* he above their learning deemed. . . . *Hub.* 1192
true *wisedome* to sustaine, . . . *T.M.* 80
God himselfe for *wisedome* most is praised, . . . *T.M.* 89
wants the staffe of *wisedome* him to stay, . . . *T.M.* 140
th' ornaments of *wisdome* are bereft? . . . *T.M.* 489
want the blis that *wisedom* would them breed, . . . *T.M.* 530
of all *wisedome* knew the perfect somme? . . . *Ti.* 60
count of *wisedome* more than of thy Countie. . . . *Ti.* 273
now his *wisedome* is disprooved quite; . . . *Ti.* 446
Adorn'd with *wisedome* and with chastitie, . . . *D.* 215
Her power, her mercy, and her *wisdome,* (*and her *wisedome*) *Col.* 346
wisedome warnes, whilest foot is in the gate, . . . I. i. 13. 4
He wondred at her *wisedome* hevenly rare, . . . I. vi. 31. 1
I hope . . . your *wisedome* will direct my thought, . . . I. vii. 42. 7
It governd was, . . . Through *wisedome* of a matrone grave . . . I. x. 3. 5
heare the *wisedom* of her wordes divine. . . . I. x. 18. 6
sober lookes her *wisedome* well descryde: . . . I. x. 34. 3
with great *wisedome* and grave eloquence . . . I. xii. 24. 5
Who, with his *wisedom* won, him streight did choose . . . II. x. 37. 8
of all *wisedom* bee thou precedent, . . . III. ii. 3. 3
deare *wisedom* bought too late! . . . III. iv. 37. 9
Her *wisedome* did admire, and hearkned to her loring. . . . V. vii. 42. 9
wisedome is most riches: . . . VI. ix. 30. 7
Eternall spring of grace and *wisedome* trew, . . . *H.H.L.* 44
His truth, his love, his *wisedome,* and his blis, . . . *H.H.B.* 110

Wisdom's. th' heavenly gift of *wisdomes* influence, . . . *T.M.* 86
wisedomes powre, and temperaunces might, . . . II. xii. 43. 6
Endewd with *wisedomes* riches, heavenly, rare. . . . *H.H.L.* 112

Wise. *See* **Albanese-wise, Heavenly-wise, Thiswise, Thuswise, True-love-wise.**
fashiond were they all in Dorike *wise.* . . . *Bel.*[1] ii. 4
Their armes in shamefull *wise* bounde . . . *Bel.*[1] xi. 10
wrought with Diamond after Dorick *wize:* . . . *Bel.*[2] ii. 4
armes bound at their backs in shamefull *wize.* . . . *Bel.*[2] xv. 10
Whereto approched not in anie *wise* . . . *Pet.* iv. 3

Wise—*Continued.*
All that which Athens ever brought forth *wise;* . . . *Ro.* xxix. 9
They bene so well-thewed, and so *wise,* . . . *S.C.* F. 96
To be *wise,* and eke to love, . . . *S.C.* Mar.Emb.1
they gang in more secrete *wise,* . . . *S.C.* S. 156
He is so meeke, *wise,* and merciable, . . . *S.C.* S. 174
Roffy is *wise,* and as Argus eyed,) . . . *S.C.* S. 203
Bacchus fruite is frend to Phoebus *wise;* . . . *S.C.* O. 106
wise Curius, companion Of noble vertues, . . . *Gn.* 609
Began to comfort me in chearefull *wise,* . . . *Hub.* 19
In some straunge habit, after uncouth *wize;* . . . *Hub.* 84
'Now read, Sir Reynold, as ye be right *wise,* . . . *Hub.* 114
devise A pasport for us both in fittest *wize,* . . . *Hub.* 196
in handsome *wise* Your selfe attyred, . . . *Hub.* 487
cope with thee in reasonable *wise;* . . . *Hub.* 527
Lowly they him saluted in meeke *wise;* . . . *Hub.* 585
With whom he close confers with *wise* discourse, . . . *Hub.* 763
for *wise* and civill governaunce . . . *Hub.* 782
through *wise* speaches and grave conference . . . *Hub.* 791
kindle *wise* desire, . . . *Hub.* 830
He gan enquire of some in secret *wize,* . . . *Hub.* 1272
wring Her wretched hands in lamentable *wise;* . . . *T.M.* 170
To make men heavenly *wise* through humbled will. . . . *T.M.* 522
wise wordes, taught in numbers for to runne, . . . *Ti.* 402
He lookt aside as in disdainefull *wise,* . . . *D.* 59
Calling to me (ay me!) this *wise* bespake; . . . *D.* 262
Both *wise* and hardie, (too hardie, alas!) . . . *As.* 72
Those prudent heads, that with theire counsels *wise* . . . *Ded. Son.* i. 1
In ampler *wise* it selfe will forth display. . . . *Ded. Son.* xvi.14
hastie heat tempring with sufferance *wise,* . . . I. i. 50. 4
Wringing her hands, in wemens pitteous *wise,* . . . I. i. 50. 7
As many formes and shapes in seeming *wise,* . . . I. ii. 10. 3
open breakes the dore in furious *wize,* . . . I. iii. 19. 5
She thancked them in her disdainefull *wise;* . . . I. iv. 14. 2
The *wise* Southsayer . . . telles of warres . . . I. v. 8. 8
he learned had in secret *wise* The hidden cause . . . I. v. 46. 2
salvage nation . . . learnes her *wise* beheast. . . . I. vi. Arg.
he would learne The Lyon stoup to him in lowly *wise,* . . . I. vi. 25. 7
At last in privy *wise* . . . I. vi. 32. 6
What man so *wise,* what earthly witt so ware, . . . I. vii. 1. 1
wise and wary was that noble Pere; . . . I. viii. 7. 6
Aread in graver *wise* what I demaund of thee.' . . . I. viii. 33. 9
th' only good that growes of passed feare Is to be *wise,* . . . I. viii. 44. 6
yfere The vertues linked are in lovely *wize;* . . . I. ix. 1. 2
me had warnd old Timons *wise* behest, . . . I. ix. 9. 5
The eldest two, most sober, chast, and *wise,* . . . I. x. 4. 5
Ne wanted ought to shew her bounteous or *wise.* . . . I. x. 11. 9
Ylinked arme in arme in lovely *wise:* . . . I. x. 12. 3
wise Speranza gave him comfort sweet, . . . I. x. 22. 1
thus recover'd by *wise* Patience . . . I. x. 29. 1
to thy hand behight By *wise* Fidelia? . . . I. x. 50. 8
sayd that royall Pere in sober *wise;* . . . I. xii. 17. 1
her to serve sixe yeares in warlike *wize,* . . . I. xii. 18. 7
so *wise* and wary was the knight . . . II. i. 4. 6
when she heard, as in despightfull *wise* . . . II. i. 15. 1
Through goodly handling and *wise* temperaunce. . . . II. i. 31. 2
In this faire *wize* they traveild long yfere, . . . II. i. 35. 1
through *wise* handling and faire governaunce, . . . II. i. 54. 6
Fayre marching forth in honorable *wize,* . . . II. ii. 14. 8
More huge in strength then *wise* in workes he was, . . . II. ii. 17. 6
that waeke eld hath left thee nothing *wise;* . . . II. iii. 16. 3
To which right wel the *wise* doe give that name, . . . II. v. 1. 5
Was wary *wise,* and closely did awayt Avauntage, . . . II. v. 9. 6
But he was *wise,* . . . II. v. 21. 6
he was *wise,* and wary of her will, . . . II. vi. 26. 1
more happy he then *wise,* . . . II. vi. 46. 4
th' unjust Atheniens made to dy *Wise* Socrates; . . . II. vii. 52. 7
he was wary *wise* in all his way, . . . II. vii. 64. 6
Seven yeares this *wize* they us besieged have, . . . II. ix. 12. 8
Shewing her selfe both *wise* and liberall. . . . II. ix. 20. 5
Did order all th' Achates in seemely *wise,* . . . II. ix. 31. 4
The which them did in modest *wise* amate, . . . II. ix. 34. 4
halfe in disdaineful *wise,* . . . II. ix. 38. 1
He now was growne right *wise* and wondrous sage: . . . II. ix. 54. 5
the *wise* Cordelia Was sent to Aggannip of Celtica. . . . II. x. 29. 4
The *wise* Elficleos, in great Majestie, . . . II. x. 75. 2
flew about his heeles in wanton *wize,* . . . II. xii. 46. 8
Long they thus traveiled in friendly *wise,* . . . III. i. 14. 1
So was that chamber clad in goodly *wize:* . . . III. i. 39. 1
be led in courteous *wize* Into a bowre, . . . III. i. 42. 3
In playner *wise* to tell her grievaunce she begonne. . . . III. i. 52. 9
in discourteise *wise* Scorne the faire offer . . . III. i. 55. 1
A comely knight, all arm'd in complete *wize,* . . . III. ii. 24. 2
There the *wise* Merlin whylome wont . . . To make his wonne, III. iii. 7. 5
that same warlike *wize,* I weene, would you misseeme; . . . III. iii. 53. 5
Wise, warlike, personable, courteous, and kind. . . . III. iv. 5. 9
whereof *wise* Paeon sprong) . . . III. iv. 41. 6
To lurke emongst your Nimphes in secret *wize,* . . . III. vi. 23. 2
built of stickes and reedes In homely *wize,* . . . III. vii. 6. 3
gan recomfort her in her rude *wyse,* . . . III. vii. 10. 1
In secret *wize* herselfe thence to withdraw, . . . III. vii. 18. 3
In loathly *wise* like to a carrion corse, . . . III. vii. 43. 5
in that monstrous *wise* did to the world appere. . . . III. vii. 48. 9
to the Castle gate approcht in quiet *wise.* . . . III. ix. 9. 9
all in vaine: his woman was too *wise* . . . III. x. 20. 1
th' one was armed all in warlike *wize,* . . . III. x. 21. 4
All which disguized marcht in masking *wise* . . . III. xii. 26. 6
all the workes of those *wise* sages, . . . IV. Pr. 3. 3
Marching in lovely *wise,* . . . IV. i. 4. 7
Bellona in that warlike *wise* To them appear'd, . . . IV. i. 14. 6

Wise—*Continued.*
mote to none but to the warie *wise* appeare. . . . IV. i. 17. 9
'Sir, him *wise* I never held, . . . IV. i. 34. 7
with whom now she goth In lovely *wise,* . . . IV. i. 47. 6
Such Musicke is *wise* words, . . . IV. ii. 2. 5
Such us'd *wise* Glauce to that wrathfull knight, . . . IV. ii. 3. 1
Sometimes estranging him in sterner *wise;* . . . IV. ii. 9. 6
prov'd himselfe most foole in what he seem'd most *wise.* . . . IV. ii. 9. 9
Two knights that lincked rode in lovely *wise,* . . . IV. ii. 30. 3
In wittie riddles, and in *wise* soothsayes; . . . IV. ii. 35. 5
Cambell, that was stout and *wise,* . . . IV. ii. 37. 6
turne both him and her to honour, in this *wise.* . . . IV. ii. 37. 9
More *wise* they weend to make of love delight . . . IV. ii. 40. 5
Long while they then continued in that *wize,* . . . IV. iii. 36. 1
The charet decked was in wondrous *wize* . . . IV. iii. 38. 6
some, that would seeme *wise,* their wonder turnd to dout. . . IV. iii. 41. 9
In lovely *wise* she gan that Lady greet, . . . IV. iii. 50. 6
wise Cambina, taking by her side Faire Canacee, . . . IV. iii. 51. 6
The battell, offred in so knightly *wize:* . . . IV. iv. 11. 5
when they could not learne it by no *wize,* . . . IV. iv. 42. 4
entertaind him in so rude a *wise,* . . . IV. vi. 10. 6
as in his wonted *wise* His doole he made, . . . IV. viii. 3. 1
It was a bridge ybuilt in goodly *wize* . . . IV. x. 6. 6
that which that *wise* King of Jurie framed . . . IV. x. 30. 6
she in gentle *wise* me entertayned, . . . IV. x. 36. 2
her sad semblant and demeanure *wyse:* . . . IV. x. 49. 6
Glaucus, that *wise* southsayes understood; . . . IV. xi. 13. 3
So *wise* is Nereus old, . . . IV. xi. 19. 7
Panopae and *wise* Protomedaea, . . . IV. xi. 49. 8
Liagore much praisd for *wise* behests; . . . IV. xi. 51. 4
by faire and humble *wise* . . . IV. xii. 14. 3
garnisht all with gold upon the blade In goodly *wise,* . . . V. i. 10. 4
pols and pils the poore in piteous *wize;* . . . V. ii. 6. 8
In sdeignfull *wize* he drew unto him neare, . . . V. ii. 33. 8
take thy ballaunce, if thou be so *wise,* . . . V. ii. 43. 1
In warlike *wise* when Artegall did vew, . . . V. ii. 52. 2
That they might execute her judgements *wise,* . . . V. iv. 2. 3
With which *wise* Nature did them strongly bynd . . . V. v. 25. 3
Armies of lovely lookes, and speeches *wise,* . . . V. v. 34. 8
more my gratious mercie by this *wize,* . . . V. v. 48. 7
gan gently her salute . . . in the most comely *wize;* . . . V. vi. 20. 2
they received were In seemely *wise,* . . . V. vi. 22. 7
There she received was in goodly *wize* . . . V. vii. 4. 1
With that his wife in friendly *wise* to deale, . . . V. viii. 21. 2
upon the soyle Having her selfe in wretched *wize* abjected, . V. ix. 9. 8
Just Dice, *wise* Eunomie, myld Eirene; . . . V. ix. 32. 6
powring forth their bloud in brutishe *wize,* . . . V. x. 28. 8
Full nobly mounted in right warlike *wize;* . . . V. xi. 4. 3
he it well did ward with *wise* respect, . . . V. xii. 21. 5
he did upreare In lustlesse *wise;* . . . VI. i. 35. 2
To whose *wise* read she hearkning sent me streight . . . VI. ii. 30. 7
by no *wize* He could him force to loose, . . . VI. iv. 6. 8
Which though I be not *wise* enough to frame, . . . VI. iv. 34. 8
in his homely *wize* began to assay T' amend what was amisse, . VI. v. 10. 8
The second, not so strong but *wise,* Decetto; . . . VI. v. 13. 8
The third, nor strong nor *wise,* but spightfullest, Defetto. . . VI. v. 13. 9
This *wize* did they each other entertaine . . . VI. v. 34. 5
needes *wise* read and discipline, . . . VI. vi. 13. 3
kept so well his *wise* commaundements, . . . VI. vi. 15. 3
in rude *wise* him asked, what he was . . . VI. vi. 20. 2
rising up at last in ghastly *wize,* . . . VI. vi. 32. 7
in this *wize,* and this unmeete array, . . . VI. viii. 22. 6
wondred much at Cupids judg'ment *wise,* . . . VI. viii. 25. 2
After his rusticke *wise,* that well he weend, . . . VI. ix. 6. 7
in that litle is both rich and *wise;* . . . VI. ix. 30. 6
the Captaine in full angry *wize* Made answere, . . . VI. xi. 12. 1
Did unto them at length these speeches *wise* unfold; . . . VII. vi. 19. 9
Whether by open force, or counsell *wise:* . . . VII. vi. 21. 8
straight gan cast their counsell grave and *wise.* . . . VII. vi. 22. 6
He thus againe in milder *wise* began: . . . VII. vi. 31. 6
those three sacred Saints, though else most *wise,* . . . VII. vii. 7. 6
So turne they still about, and change in restlesse *wise.* . . . VII. vii. 18. 9
none so rich or *wise,* so strong or fayre, . . . *Am.* lviii. 9
Trophees to erect in stately *wize;* . . . *Am.* lxix. 2
her words so *wise* do make their way . . . *Am.* lxxxi. 11
In angry *wize* he flyes about, . . . *Epig.* iv. 9
Most *wise,* most holy, most almightie Spright! . . . *H.H.L.* 39
Which He had fashiond in his *wise* foresight, . . . *H.H.L.* 109
All which are made with wondrous *wise* respect, . . . *H.H.B.* 34

Wisely. throgh their owne faire handling *wisely* wroght, . . . *Hub.* 554
credit . . . he *wisely* did maintaine . . . *Hub.* 690
In case the good . . . they would *wisely* take. . . . *Hub.* 963
Fortunes freakes, is *wisely* taught to beare: . . . *T.M.* 130
'the way to win Is *wisely* to advise; . . . I. i. 33. 6
He that the stubborne Sprites can *wisely* tame, . . . I. i. 43. 7
feates of armes did *wisely* understand. . . . I. iii. 42. 5
They binden up so *wisely* as they may, . . . I. v. 29. 7
Faire feeling words he *wisely* gan display, . . . I. vii. 38. 6
wisely comforted all that she might, . . . I. x. 23. 4
all with patience *wisely* she did beare, . . . I. x. 28. 8
with delight of that he *wisely* spake . . . II. ii. 46. 5
I *wisely* you advise to doon, . . . II. iii. 15. 3
both from rocks and flats it selfe could *wisely* save. . . . II. vi. 5. 9
wisely watch to ward that deadly stowre; . . . II. viii. 35. 4
*To use that sword so *wisely* as it ought. . . . II. viii. 40. 4
so *wisely* as I may.' . . . II. ix. 42. 9
a God him sage Antiquity Did *wisely* make, . . . II. xii. 48. 2
all that I ever fownd so *wisely* stayd, . . . III. vii. 57. 2
saide his boat the way could *wisely* tell; . . . III. viii. 24. 7
in his eye his meaning *wisely* redd, . . . III. ix. 28. 6

Wisely—*Continued.*
them governe *wisely* well, ... III. xi. 2. 7
When Glauce thus gan *wisely* all upknit: . . . . IV. vi. 30. 1
to the present neede it *wisely* usd. . . . . IV. viii. 60. 4
That trusty Squire he *wisely* well did move . . . . . . IV. ix. 15. 3
all things secrete *wisely* could bewray, ... V. ii. 25. 4
vertuous women *wisely* understand, ... V. v. 25. 7
Yet *wisely* moderated her owne smart, ... V. vii. 44. 3
wisely use, and well apply, ... VI. i. 3. 6
he, that could his wrath full *wisely* guyde, ... VI. i. 30. 7
So well and *wisely* did that good old Knight . . . . . VI. iii. 6. 1
Ne she lesse glad; for she so *wisely* did, ... VI. iv. 38. 3
Yet he himselfe so well and *wisely* bore, ... VI. v. 12. 8
The Infant hearkned *wisely* to her tale, ... VI. viii. 25. 1
Which he so *wisely* well did prosecute, ... VI. x. 38. 4
Wise man. Well said the *Wiseman,* now prov'd true by this . IV. viii. 1. 1
taking counsell of a *wise man* red, ... VI. ii. 30. 1
Wise men. Hath so *wise men* bewitcht, ... *Ti.* 457
Wise men's. seeke to please; that now is counted *wise mens* threasure. . . . . VI. xii. 41. 9
Wiser. The *wiser* Muses after Colin ranne. . . . . *S.C.* D. 48
One, that would *wiser* seeme then all the rest, ... I. xii. 10. 2
Wisest. whilome was alive the *wisest* wight: . . . . *Ti.* 445
Old Timon . . . is the *wisest* now on earth I weene: . . . . . I. ix. 4. 4
have from *wisest* ages hidden beene; . . . . II. Pr. 3. 2
The *wisest* men, I weene, that lived in their ages. . . . . II. ix. 47. 9
By Phoebus doome the *wisest* thought alive, ... II. ix. 48. 2
it could overreach the *wisest* earthly wight. . . . . . IV. ii. 10. 9
it can blynd The *wisest* sight . . . . VI. Pr. 5. 7
Wish. I *wish* I might this wearie life forgoe, ... *Pet.*[2] vii. 5
I am not as I *wish* I were, ... *S.C.* Jun. 105
and *wish* him to chuse His Master, ... *Hub.* 884
Ne sorer vengeance *wish* on you to fall . . . . *D.* 352
To *wish* you backe returne with foule disgrace, ... I. i. 13. 3
henceforth ever *wish* that like succeed it may!' . . . . I. i. 27. 9
victory they dare not *wish* to either side. . . . . I. v. 9. 9
Well mote yee thee, as well can *wish* your thought, . . II. i. 33. 7
Least thou perhaps hereafter *wish,* . . . . II. vii. 38. 9
wishing it far off his ydle *wish* doth lose. . . . . III. i. 46. 9
You and your countrey both I *wish* welfare, ... III. ii. 10. 8
wish that Lady faire mote bee His Faery Queene, ... III. iv. 54. 6
oftentimes doe *wish* it never had bene writ. . . . . . . IV. i. 1. 9
doe not rather *wish* them soone expire, ... IV. iii. 1. 3
That many *wish* to win for glorie vaine, ... IV. v. 2. 6
nor hart could *wish* for any queint device, ... IV. x. 22. 8
wish to life return'd againe to bee, ... IV. x. 23. 8
inly *wish* that in his powre it weare . . . . IV. xii. 12. 7
art mov'd to *wish* me better, ... V. v. 37. 8
And *wish* that he part of his spoyle might share: . . . . VI. ii. 17. 3
I . . . *wish* thee grow in worship . . . . VI. ii. 26. 7
I rather *wish* that some more noble hire . . . . VI. ii. 34. 7
(Being his harts owne *wish,*) . . . . VI. ix. 16. 9
wish my lot were plast in such felicitie.' . . . . VI. ix. 19. 9
ne *wish* for more it to augment, ... VI. ix. 20. 4
wish th' heavens so much had graced mee, ... VI. ix. 28. 6
wish that more and greater they might be, ... *Am.* xxv. 13
Ne doe I *wish* (for wishing were but vaine) . . . . . . *Am.* xlii. 5
Hart need not *wish* none other happinesse, ... *Am.* lxxii. 13
I *wish* that night the noyous day would end: . . . . . . *Am.* lxxxvi. 6
I *wish* that day would shortly reascend. . . . . *Am.* lxxxvi. 8
Make us to *wish* theyr choking. . . . . *Epith.* 350
though he do not win his *wish* to end, ... *H.L.* 211
Wished. *See* **Long-wished.**
The Priest him *wisht* good speed, ... *Hub.* 550
wisht that two such fannes, so silken soft . . . . *Mui.* 107
I goe with gladnesse to my *wished* rest, ... *D.* 282
wished tydinges none of him unto her brought. . . . . . I. iii. 3. 9
waiting long, to win the *wished* sight Of her, ... I. iv. 6. 8
Who had enough, yett *wished* ever more; . . . . I. iv. 29. 5
To come unto his *wished* home in haste, ... I. ix. 39. 2
to the *wished* haven bring thy weary barke!' . . . . . . II. i. 32. 9
ear that *wished* day his beame disclosd, ... II. iv. 22. 1
wisht me stay till I more truth should fynd. . . . . . . II. iv. 22. 9
Him kept from landing at his *wished* will. . . . . III. v. 20. 2
how to win the *wished* victory, ... III. vii. 33. 2
Her will to win unto his *wished* eend; . . . . III. viii. 41. 5
to her selfe oft *wisht* like happinesse: . . . . III. xii. 46. *or.* 8
wisht like happinesse: In vain she *wisht,* . . . . III. xii. 46. *or.* 9
wisht them without blot or blame To let them passe . . IV. iv. 3. 4
wholly dead Himselfe he *wisht* have beene, ... IV. iv. 22. 9
All on her gazing *wisht,* and vowd, and prayd, ... IV. v. 26. 3
As though she *wished* to have pleasd them all, ... IV. v. 26. 7
He by no meanes could *wished* ease obtaine: . . . . . . IV. v. 40. 8
wisht it were in her to doe him any grace. . . . . IV. viii. 12. 9
Could she her *wished* freedome fro me wooe: . . . . . . IV. x. 57. 5
By timely death shall winne her *wished* rest, ... IV. xii. 8. 2
thence he *wished* her with him to wend . . . . V. x. 22. 6
wisht that with that shepheard he mote dwelling share. . VI. x. 30. 9
Which oft I *wisht,* yet never was so blest. . . . . *Am.* lxxvi. 14
For lo! the *wished* day is come at last, ... *Epith.* 31
the *wished* scope Of my desire, ... *H.L.* 296
Wishes. all men threw out vowes and *wishes* vaine. . . . . IV. iv. 16. 6
Wisheth. dead himselfe he *wisheth* for despight. . . . . . *Van.* x. 13
Each *wisheth* to him selfe, and to the rest envyes:— . . . VI. viii. 41. 9
Wishful. *wishfull* thing this sad life to forgoe: . . . . . . *D.* 452
With hope of her some *wishfull* boot to have. . . . . . V. ix. 10. 3
Whereof she long had lackt the *wishfull* sight, ... VI. xi. 50. 5
in her songs, sends many a *wishfull* vow . . . . *Am.* lxxxviii. 3
Encline thy will t' effect our *wishfull* vow, ... *Epith.* 385
wight Who of her selfe can win the *wishfull* sight. . . . . *H.H.B.* 245

Wishing. *wishing* it far off his ydle wish doth lose. . . . . III. i. 46. 9
lives a loathed life, and *wishing* cannot die. . . . . . . IV. vii. 11. 9
wishing oft that he were present there . . . . VI. xi. 33. 8
Ne doe I wish (for *wishing* were but vaine) . . . . *Am.* xlii. 5
Wist. Never I *wist* thee in so poore a plight. . . . . *S.C.* S. 8
Ne *wist* what answere unto him to frame, ... *Hub.* 313
Litle *wisht* he his fatall future woe, ... *Mui.* 381
never *wist* I till this present day, ... *Col.* 827
Ne ever *wist* but that she was the same; . . . . I. ii. 40. 3
Approaching nigh she *wist* it was the same; . . . . . . I. iii. 26. 8
resemblaunce of Deceipt, I *wist,* Did closely lurke; . . . . I. v. 27. 3
well she *wist* his cryme could els be never cleare. . . . I. x. 28. 9
Ne *wist* yett how his talaunts to unfold; . . . . I. xi. 41. 3
wist no creature whence that hevenly sweet Proceeded, . I. xii. 39. 6
He *wist* not whether blott of fowle offence . . . . II. ii. 4. 1
They *wist* their houre was spent; . . . . II. ii. 46. 9
well he *wist* that whoso would contend . . . . II. iii. 17. 2
did he *wist* not what in his avengement. . . . . II. iv. 6. 9
He *wist* him selfe amisse, and angry said; . . . . II. vi. 22. 6
Him to entrap unwares another way he *wist.* . . . . . . II. vii. 34. 9
Ne *wist* he what to thinke of that same sight, ... II. xi. 39. 3
ne *wist* How to direct theyr way . . . . II. xii. 35. 1
wist her life at last must lincke in that same knot. . . . III. ii. 23. 9
yet *wist* she nether how, nor why. . . . . III. ii. 27. 6
She *wist* not, silly Mayd, what she did aile, ... III. ii. 27. 7
Yet *wist* she was not well at ease perdy; . . . . III. ii. 27. 8
She *wist* not how t' amend, nor how it to withstond. . . . III. ii. 52. 9
of their comming well he *wist* afore; . . . . III. iii. 15. 2
Yet *wist* not what their wailing ment; . . . . III. iv. 32. 4
Yet *wist* she nought thereof, ... III. vi. 9. 7
He *wist* not how him to despoile of life, ... III. vii. 33. 1
Ne *wist* he how to turne, nor to what place: . . . . . . III. x. 14. 8
Ne in that stownd *wist* how her selfe to beare; . . . . . III. xi. 22. 2
wist not what it might intend. . . . . III. xi. 54. 9
well she *wist,* as true it was indeed, ... IV. i. 6. 1
well she *wist* not what by them to gesse: . . . . IV. i. 7. 6
Albee untrue she *wist* them by assay. . . . . IV. i. 50. 5
As if the conquest his he surely *wist.* . . . . IV. iii. 5. 3
He *wist* right well that it was Britomart, ... IV. vi. 7. 2
Ne *wist* whether above she were or under ground. . . . . IV. vii. 9. 9
who was that Belphebe he ne *wist;* . . . . IV. vii. 46. 6
ere he *wist,* he found His head before him tombling . . . IV. viii. 45. 4
well she *wist* now in a mighty hond Her person, ... IV. ix. 18. 2
He *wist* not how her thence away to bere, ... IV. xii. 15. 8
daunger well he *wist* long to continue there. . . . . . . IV. xii. 15. 9
As he had lost him selfe he *wist* not where; . . . . . . IV. xii. 17. 3
ne *wist* well what to weene; . . . . IV. xii. 21. 2
He much was troubled, ne *wist* what to doo: . . . . . . V. ii. 52. 3
Ne *wist* he what to thinke, or to devise; . . . . V. iii. 18. 3
well she *wist* this knight came succour to supply. . . . . V. x. 19. 9
the wood, where so he *wist* She hidden was, ... VI. ii. 20. 8
Ne *wist* which way he through the foord mote pas: . . . VI. iii. 30. 4
Whom well he *wist* to be some enemy, ... VI. iii. 46. 8
well they *wist* that Squire to be so bold, ... VI. v. 15. 6
Whenas these Knights arriv'd, they *wist* not where nor how. VI. v. 35. 9
He *wist* not to which side him to addresse: . . . . . . VI. vi. 26. 5
he which way to turne him scarcely *wist:* . . . . VI. viii. 13. 5
wist not what to weene; . . . . VI. x. 17. 4
ne *wist* what way to chose: . . . . VII. vi. 24. 5
Natur's selfe did vanish, whither no man *wist.* . . . . . VII. vii. 59. 9
Wit. *See* **Mother-wit.**
No worke it seem'd of earthly craftsmans *wit,* . . . . . . *Bel.*[2] iv. 9
Some greater learned *wit* will magnifie: . . . . *Ro.* ii. 12
Apelles *wit,* or Phidias his skill, ... *Ro.* xxix. 6
Whose *witt* is weakenesse, whose wage is death, ... *S.C.* F. 88
we tway bene men of elder *witt.* . . . . *S.C.* May 18
wit to beware, ... *S.C.* May 181
Piers, thou art beside thy *wit,* . . . . *S.C.* May 306
make thee winges of thine aspyring *wit,* . . . . *S.C.* O. 83
to *weete* whats good or ill, ... *S.C.* N. 183
have no *wit* to live withouten toyle; . . . . *Hub.* 158
T' enrich the the storehouse of his powerfull *wit,* . . . . *Hub.* 790
With shuttelcocks, misseeming manlie *wit,* . . . . *Hub.* 804
Be with the worke of losels *wit* defamed, ... *Hub.* 813
it wholly springeth from my *wit:* . . . . *Hub.* 1037
In his chiefe parts, that is, in *wit* and spirite; . . . . *Hub.* 1043
The golden brood of great Apolloes *wit,* . . . . *T.M.* 2
The flowre of *wit,* finde nought to busie me: . . . . . . *T.M.* 166
With seasoned *wit* and goodly pleasance graced, ... *T.M.* 200
Each idle *wit* at will presumes to make, ... *T.M.* 215
For vertues meed and ornament of *wit,* . . . . *T.M.* 310
O vaine labours of terrestriall *wit,* . . . . *Ti.* 512
No common things may please a wavering *wit.* . . . . . *Mui.* 160
dayly dooth my weaker *wit* possesse, ... *D.* 30
'Yet doth not my dull *wit* well understand . . . . *D.* 176
if any nycer *wit* Shall hap to heare, ... *As.* Pr. 13
Ne for their gifts unworthie of his *wit,* . . . . *As.* 51
On her he spent the riches of his *wit:* . . . . *As.* 62
another swaine Of gentle *wit* . . . . *As.* Interl. 218
all the ornaments of wondrous *wit,* . . . . *Col.* 189
hablest *wit* of most I know this day. . . . . *Col.* 383
spends his *wit* in loves consuming smart: . . . . *Col.* 429
to warne yong shepheards wandring *wit,* . . . . *Col.* 684
handle his deceitfull *wit* In subtil shifts, ... *Col.* 693
Ne is there place for any gentle *wit,* . . . . *Col.* 707
any gentle *wit* of name Nor honest mynd . . . . *Col.* 733
ye ne *weet* How great a guilt . . . . *Col.* 927
praise her worth, though far my *wit* above. . . . . *Col.* 942
whose vertues . . . merit a most famous Poets *witt* . . . . *Ded. Son.* ii. 2
Receive . . . The unripe fruit of an unready *wit;* . . . . . *Ded. Son.* iii. 2

Wit—*Continued.*
The labor of lost time, and *wit* unstayd: *Ded. Son.* ix. 8
give leave a while To baser *wit* *Ded. Son.* xii.10
O, helpe thou my weake *wit,* I. Pr. 2. 9
The maker selfe, for all his wondrous *witt,* I. i. 45. 6
Which to expresse he bends his gentle *wit:* I. ii. 30. 5
he her wronged innocence did *weet.* I. iii. 6. 3
To *weet* if dwelling place were nigh at hand; I. iii. 11. 2
He was, to *weete,* a stout and sturdy thiefe, I. iii. 17. 1
It . . . spake the praises of the workmans *witt;* I. iv. 5. 2
the verse of famous Poets *witt* He does backebite, I. iv. 32. 6
To *weet* what end to straunger knights may fall. I. v. 3. 3
Such wondrous science in mans *witt* to rain I. v. 40. 1
What *witt* of mortal wight Can now devise I. vi. 6. 8
To *weet* what wight so loudly did lament. I. vi. 8. 4
commeth out To *weet* the cause, I. vi. 14. 7
During which time her gentle *wit* she plyes, I. vi. 19. 5
Whose like in womens *witt* he never knew; I. vi. 31. 2
all her *witt* in secret counsels spent, I. vi. 32. 5
to ride, To *weete* of newes I. vi. 34. 5
What man so wise, what earthly *witt* so ware, I. vii. 1. 1
to *weet* what suddein stowre Had wrought that horror strange, I. viii. 5. 8
to *weet* if living wight Were housed therewithin, I. viii. 37. 8
A thing without the compas of my *witt;* I. ix. 3. 2
To *weet* what mister wight was so dismayd. I. ix. 23. 2
The knight much wondred at his suddeine *wit,* I. ix. 41. 1
documents . . . That weaker *witt* of man could never reach; I. x. 19. 5
nor *wit* of man can tell; I. x. 55. 6
to *weet* if trew indeed Those tydinges were, I. xii. 3. 3
His practick *witt* and his fayre fyled tonge, II. i. 3. 6
To *weete* what course he takes, II. i. 4. 4
said the Redcrosse knight; 'Now mote I *weet,* II. i. 29. 5
To *weet* what dreadfull thing was there in hond; II. ii. 21. 2
did *weet* To been with Guyon knitt in one consent, II. iii. 11. 7
To let him *weet* his doughtie valiaunce, II. iii. 14. 5
To *weete* which of the gods I shall thee name, II. iii. 33. 8
As her fantasticke *wit* did most delight: II. vi. 7. 2
his weake *witt* Was overcome II. vi. 13. 7
Atin drew nigh to *weet* what it mote bee, II. vi. 43. 1
'doest not thou *weet,* II. vii. 11. 1
To *weet* whence all the wealth . . . Proceeded, II. vii. 38. 4
To *weet* who called so importunely: II. viii. 4. 2
To *weet* why . . . Beare ye the picture II. ix. 2. 7
mote I *weete* What straunge adventure II. ix. 9. 1
To *weete* what they so rudely did require? II. ix. 11. 8
working *wit* That never idle was, II. ix. 49. 8
Ne can devized be of mortall *wit;* II. ix. 50. 5
wondrous *wit* to menage high affayres, II. x. 37. 2
he called Elfe, to *weet* Quick, II. x. 71. 1
in haste he yode The cause to *weet,* II. xi. 20. 3
seemd a worke of admirable *witt;* II. xii. 44. 2
Poets *witt,* that passeth Painter farre III. Pr. 2. 6
choicest *witt* Cannot your glorious pourtraict figure playne, III. Pr. 3. 6
vowd with all their power and *witt* III. i. 12. 3
To *weet* if they would turne backe to that place; III. i. 19. 5
living *wit,* I weene, cannot display III. i. 32. 3
A worke of rare device and wondrous *wit.* III. i. 34. 6
'Faire Sir, I let you *weete,* III. ii. 6. 1
mote I *weet* of you, right courteous knight, Tydings III. ii. 8. 6
weet ye well, of all that ever playd At tilt III. ii. 9. 7
To *weet,* the learned Merlin, III. iii. 6. 4
in her foolhardy *wit* Conceiv'd a bold devise, III. iii. 52. 1
The baser *wit* . . . It stirreth up to sensuall desire, III. v. 1. 4
'Perdy, me lever were to *weeten* that,' III. v. 7. 1
to *weete* if life Yett . . . did remaine; III. v. 31. 1
That was, to *weet,* the goodly Florimell; III. vi. 54. 5
It was to *weete* the good Sir Satyrane, III. vii. 30. 1
To *weet,* the mightie Ollyphant, III. vii. 48. 2
'To *weet,* that I my traveill should resume, III. vii. 56. 1
By their advice, and her owne wicked *wit,* III. viii. 5. 1
if that thou, Sir Satyran, didst *weete,* III. viii. 28. 1
to *weet* what wight Had her from so infamous fact assoyld, III. viii. 32. 6
To *weet* what wight he was, III. viii. 45. 2
The which to let you *weet* will further time requyre. III. viii. 52. 9
if ye list to *weet* The cause III. ix. 3. 1
Fashioning . . . fancies evermore In her fraile *witt,* III. ix. 52. 5
did smyle To *weet* how he her love away did steale, III. x. 5. 8
He closely nearer crept the truth to *weet:* III. x. 22. 6
weete henceforth, that all that golden pray, III. x. 31. 4
To *weete,* the treasure which he did bewray, III. x. 34. 5
'*weete* ye well, That yonder . . . dangers dwell; III. x. 40. 2
neither may This fire be quencht by any *witt* or might, III. xi. 23. 7
sweet *wit* of the man, III. xi. 32. 3
By any ridling skill, or commune *wit.* III. xi. 54. 5
phantasies In wavering wemens *witt,* III. xii. 26. 4
to *weet* what end would come of all. III. xii. 37. 6
gan grow in secret dout . . . according to each *wit:* IV. i. 14. 4
what of them became themselves did scarsly *weete.* IV. i. 41. 9
Ran hastily, to *weete* what did him ayle. IV. i. 43. 4
It was to *weete* the bold Sir Ferraugh hight, IV. ii. 4. 5
Drew nigh, to *weete* the cause of their debate: IV. ii. 20. 6
To *weete,* two Ladies of most goodly hew, IV. ii. 30. 6
wooers Assembled were to *weet* whose she should bee, IV. ii. 38. 2
To *weeten* what that sudden clamour ment: IV. iii. 38. 2
To *weet* what sudden tidings was befeld: IV. iii. 50. 3
It was to *weete* that snowy Florimell, IV. iv. 8. 1
Salvagesse sans finesse, shewing secret *wit.* IV. iv. 39. 9
That was to *weet* the stout Sir Sangliere, IV. iv. 40. 3
Who was to *weet* a wretched wearish elfe, IV. v. 34. 3

Wit—*Continued.*
by *wit* or art Could that atchieve IV. vi. 43. 5
It was to *weet* a wilde and salvage man; IV. vii. 5. 1
read to me, by what devise or *wit* IV. vii. 19. 3
to *weet* who there did wonne; IV. vii. 42. 6
Ne signe of sence did shew, ne common *wit,* IV. vii. 44. 3
thinking to let her *weet* The great tormenting griefe IV. viii. 9. 7
having shortly tride The traines of *wit,* IV. viii. 31. 8
to *weet,* The deare affection unto kindred sweet, IV. ix. 1. 4
To *weet,* sterne Druon, and lewd Claribell, IV. ix. 20. 8
seeking long to *weet* which way she straid, IV. ix. 24. 4
To *weet* faire Britomart, IV. ix. 36. 2
'That was to *weet* the Porter of the place, IV. x. 12. 1
That Virgins love to win by *wit* or wile, IV. xi. 2. 3
To which no *wit* of man may comen neare; IV. xi. 10. 5
That was to *weet* the famous Troynovant, IV. xi. 28. 8
many a gentle Muse and many a learned *wit.* IV. xi. 34. 9
with magnificke might and wondrous *wit* V. Pr. 11. 3
Another, that would seeme to have more *wit,* V. iii. 33. 6
'Then *weete* ye, Sir, that we two brethren be, V. iv. 7. 2
To *weete* the cause of their assemblaunce wide: V. iv. 21. 5
To *weeten* what that trumpets sounding ment: V. iv. 50. 7
Which he accepting well, as he could *weete,* V. iv. 51. 4
'Yet, *weet* ye well . . . It is no lesse beseeming V. v. 38. 1
(*weet* thou) was not borne Of Beares and Tygres, V. v. 40. 5
all the engins of her *wit* display; V. v. 52. 2
A man of subtill *wit* and wicked minde, V. vi. 32. 2
To *weete* if it were true as she had told; V. viii. 12. 2
gathered unto her her troubled *wit,* V. viii. 45. 8
To *weet,* a wicked villaine, bold and stout, V. ix. 4. 6
his owne wylie *wit,* V. ix. 5. 1
this heavenly thing whereof I treat, To *weeten* Mercie, V. x. 1. 3
To *weet,* to worke Irenaes franchisement, V. xi. 36. 4
To *weete* if shipping readie he mote there descry. V. xii. 3. 9
To *weet* the cause of so uncomely fray, VI. ii. 4. 4
bend my carelesse *wit* To salvage chace, VI. ii. 9. 4
hearing th' answeres of his pregnant *wit,* VI. ii. 24. 4
where no wight Should *weet* of me, VI. ii. 30. 6
Yet could she not devise by any *wit,* VI. ii. 47. 1
He was to *weete* a man of full ripe yeares, VI. iii. 3. 1
his gentle words and goodly *wit* VI. iii. 22. 1
he stayd . . . To *weet* what issue would VI. iii. 47. 2
To *weet* which way were best to entertaine VI. iv. 24. 4
Those were to *weet* . . . Prince Arthur and young Timias, VI. v. 11. 7
(To *weet,* great store of forrest frute VI. vii. 24. 4
He was, to *weet,* by common voice esteemed VI. ix. 14. 1
He nigher drew to *weete* what mote it be: VI. x. 10. 6
She was, to *weete,* that jolly Shepheards lasse, VI. x. 16. 1
to let men *weet* That here on earth is no sure happinesse, VI. xi. 1. 6
To *weet* what mortall hand or heavens grace VI. xii. 8. 7
She was, to *weet,* a daughter by descent Of those old Titans VII. vi. 2. 5
To *weet,* the God of Nature, VII. vi. 35. 6
was, to *weet,* upon the highest hights VII. vi. 36. 5
To *weet,* that where-as shee had . . . Long lov'd the Fanchin, VII. vi. 44. 3
To *weet,* that Wolves . . . Should harbour'd be VII. vi. 55. 4
Do thou my weaker *wit* with skill inspire, VII. vii. 2. 2
my fraile *wit* cannot devize to what It to compare, VII. vii. 7. 4
The wonder that my *wit* cannot endite. *Am.* iii. 14
beat on th' andvile of her stubberne *wit* *Am.* xxxii. 8
How then should I, without another *wit,* *Am.* xxxiii. 9
it seemeth, in my simple *wit,* *Am.* xl. 5
her deep *wit,* that true harts thought can spel, *Am.* xliii. 13
the trew fayre, that is the gentle *wit,* *Am.* lxxix. 3
ye mote invent Som hevenly *wit,* *Am.* lxxxii. 7
Whose image printing in his deepest *wit,* *H.L.* 197
From whom all guifts of *wit* and knowledge flow, *H.H.B.* 9
Two gentle Knights . . . With gifts of *wit,* *Proth.* 171

Witch. nor brere, nor winding *witche:* *S.C.* Jun. 20
A cruell *witch,* her cursed will to wreake, I. ii. 33. 5
'The wicked *witch,* cast to win by guile; I. ii. 38. 1
The false *witch* did my wrathfull hand withhold: I. ii. 39. 8
in the *witch* unweeting joyd long time, I. ii. 40. 2
bowing downe her aged backe, she kist The wicked *witch,* I. v. 27. 2
with her beares the fowle welfavourd *witch.* I. v. 28. 2
The *witch* approching gan him fayrely greet, I. vii. 3. 6
Then tooke the angrie *witch* her golden cup, I. viii. 14. 1
So, as she bad, that *witch* they disaraid, I. viii. 46. 1
when they had the *witch* disrobed quight, I. viii. 49. 7
Where him that *witch* had thralled to her will, II. i. 54. 2
that same wicked *witch,* II. xii. 26. 4
the faire *Witch* her selfe now solacing II. xii. 72. 2
In which a *witch* did dwell, III. vii. 6. 4
by the *witch* or by her sonne compast. III. vii. 18. 5
The *Witch* creates a snowy Lady III. viii. Arg.
Through that false *witch,* and that foule aged drevill; IV. ii. 3. 8
Which that same *witch* had in this forme engraft, IV. ii. 10. 7

Witchcraft. with her *witchcraft,* and misseeming sweete, I. vii. 50. 8
through sorceree And *witchcraft,* II. xii. 72. 4

Witches. When *Witches* wont do penance for their crime,) I. ii. 40. 5
mischivous *witches* with theyr charmes, *Epith.* 342

Witchest. charmes, With which weake men thou *witchest,* II. vii. 10. 4

Witching. Sometime with *witching* smyles; IV. x. 57. 3

Witch's. her dew loves deryv'd to that vile *witches* shayre. I. iii. 2. 9
the *witches* speach she gan to heare, I. v. 21. 7
seemes some cursed *witches* deed, III. iii. 18. 8
The *witches* sonne loves Florimell: III. vii. Arg.
having reft her from the *witches* sonne, IV. iv. 8. 4

Wite. That shepheardes so *witen* ech others life, *S.C.* May 159
To *wyten* shepheards welth: *S.C.* Jul. 210
Ne can Willye *wite* the witelesse herdgroome. *S.C.* Au. 136

Wite—*Continued.*
all men would them *wyte:* . . . *Hub.* 348
unjustly thou dost *wyte* them all, . . . *Col.* 747
Rashly to *wyten* creatures so divine; . . . *Col.* 916
Scoffing at him that did her justly *wite,* . . . II. xii. 16. 8
he gan fowly *wyte* His wicked fortune . . . III. iv. 52. 7
doth sharply *wite* For praising love . . . IV. Pr. 1. 3
albe he earst did *wyte* His wavering mind, . . . V. xi. 57. 6
his own thought he knew most cleare from *wite:* . . . VI. iii. 16. 6
free from all that *wite* . . . VI. xii. 41. 4
Witeless. Ne can Willye wite the *witelesse* herdgroome. . . . *S.C.* Au. 136
With (*partial list*). *See* **Forthwith, Wherewith.**
So hie as mought an Archer reache *with* sight. . . . *Bel.*[1] iii. 4
Clothed *with* cold, and hoary *wyth* frost, . . . *S.C.* F. 79
With that Alexis broke his tale asunder, . . . *Col.* 352
With sword in hand, and *with* the old man went; . . . I. ii. 5. 2
Which when he saw, he burnt *with* gealous fire; . . . I. ii. 5. 6
The eie of reason was *with* rage yblent, . . . I. ii. 5. 7
with letters red, Was writt *Sansjoy,* . . . I. iv. 38. 5
he *with* Sir Guyon mett, . . . II. vi. 28. 1
Accompanyde *with* Phaedria the faire: . . . II. vi. 28. 2
With that, her mortall speare She mightily aventred . . . III. i. 28. 6
With that I saw two Swannes . . . *Proth.* 37
Withal. manie Muses, and the Nymphes *withall,* . . . *Pet.* iv. 5
laesie Vesper . . . gan proceede *withall;* . . . *Gn.* 316
Base is the style, and matter meane *withall.* . . . *Hub.* 44
this I wot *withall,* . . . *Hub.* 183
key found not . . . to open it *withall;* . . . I. viii. 37. 5
grypt it fast *withall.* . . . I. xi. 40. 9
Long maist thou live, and better thrive *withall* . . . II. i. 37. 4
she sought for helps to cloke her crime *withall.* . . . II. vii. 45. 9
he strooke, and thother strooke *withall,* . . . II. viii. 38. 1
Wroth was the Prince, and sory yet *withall,* . . . II. viii. 52. 5
all so faire and fensible *withall;* . . . II. ix. 21. 3
To decke my song *withall,* . . . II. x. 3. 8
she had cause to busie them *withall;* . . . II. xii. 15. 3
bugs to fearen babes *withall,* . . . II. xii. 25. 8
Withall she laughed, and she blusht *withall,* . . . II. xii. 68. 1
the great Castle smite so sore *withall,* . . . III. iii. 49. 8
Conge tooke *withall;* . . . III. iv. 4. 5
to stay and comfort her *withall.* . . . III. iv. 48. 9
Besought them humbly him to beare *withall,* . . . III. ix. 18. 5
glad to rest *withall.* . . . IV. ii. 21. 9
And tribute eke *withall,* as to his Soveraine. . . . IV. iii. 27. 9
For sudden joy and secret feare *withall;* . . . IV. vi. 29. 3
repayed duely weare, And usury *withall:* . . . IV. ix. 30. 9
there mote find to please it selfe *withall;* . . . IV. x. 22. 7
Plenty of pearles to decke his dames *withall;* . . . IV. xi. 39. 6
he her quickly stayd, and forst to wend *withall.* . . . V. i. 22. 9
That is both swift and dangerous deepe *withall;* . . . V. ii. 8. 2
Well weening that his foe was falne *withall;* . . . V. ii. 12. 8
both her Ladie, and her selfe *withall,* . . . V. v. 52. 6
To whom she eke inclyning her *withall,* . . . V. ix. 34. 6
Would have the passion hid, and up arose *withall.* . . . V. ix. 50. 9
arming him *withall* Eftsoones forth pricked proudly . . . V. x. 31. 7
comely guize *withall* And gracious speach, . . . VI. i. 2. 5
ye have much adoe to deale *withall.'* . . . VI. i. 10. 8
And courteous *withall,* becomming her degree. . . . VI. iii. 20. 9
tell *with all* the lamentable plight . . . VI. iii. 41. 7
As if he would have daunted him *withall:* . . . VI. viii. 26. 4
may perhaps you better much *withall,* . . . VI. ix. 32. 7
A little well is lent that gaineth more *withall.* . . . VI. xi. 6. 9
Old Meliboe and his good wife *withall* These eyes saw die, . . . VI. xi. 31. 6
a voyce That wakens men *withall?'* . . . *Epig.* iv. 8
That they may sweat, and drunken be *withall.* . . . *Epith.* 254
Withdraw. I will *withdraw* me to some darksome place, . . . *D.* 486
badd the knight his Lady . . . to an hill herselfe *withdraw* . I. xi. 5. 2
drive me to *withdraw* my blind abused love. . . . II. iv. 24. 9
Withdraw from thought of warlike enterprize, . . . II. vi. 25. 6
they did themselves *withdraw* To wonder at the sight; . . . II. vii. 37. 3
doth soone *withdraw* His feeble eyne, . . . III. vii. 13. 7
In secret wize herselfe thence to *withdraw,* . . . III. vii. 18. 3
like a Bull, Europa to *withdraw:* . . . III. xi. 30. 6
her enhaunced hand she downe can soft *withdraw.* . . . IV. vi. 26. 9
looser thoughts to lawfull bounds *withdraw;* . . . IV. vi. 33. 7
From all forbidden things his liking to *withdraw.* . . . IV. viii. 30. 9
he was forced to *withdraw* aside, . . . V. ii. 20. 7
'Some of his diet doe from him *withdraw,* . . . V. v. 50. 1
his Ladie, . . . did her selfe *withdraw,* . . . VI. ii. 20. 3
Hoping unto some refuge to *withdraw:* . . . VI. vi. 29. 3
Withdrawing. Her weed she then *withdrawing* did him discover; VI. vi. 32. 1
Withdrawn. when she is *withdrawne* or strong withstood, . . II. iv. 11. 6
a veale; Which, being once *withdrawne,* . . . IV. v. 10. 3
Withdraws. His minde unto the Muses he *withdrawes:* . . . *Hub.* 760
Withdrew. from himselfe to them *withdrew* his eies. . . . *As.* 114
He . . . soft *withdrew* His weapon huge, . . . I. viii. 19. 7
himselfe he soft *withdrew* Out of the field, . . . IV. iv. 25. 1
though some while Fortune from him *withdrew,* . . . IV. iv. 37. 7
day . . . Nights humid curtaine from the heavens *withdrew,* V. v. 1. 2
Wither. it *wither* must agayne: . . . *S.C.* O. 77
Where they do *wither,* and are fowly mard: . . . III. vi. 39. 6
Withered. faire greene Laurel *witherd* up and dide. . . . *Bel.*[1] vii. 14
Beating the *withered* leafe from the tree, . . . *S.C.* S. 51
Bene *withered,* as they had bene gathered long; . . . *S.C.* D. 110
al his flesh shronk up like *withered* flowres. . . . I. viii. 41. 9
braunch . . . throwen forth, till it be *withered.* . . . II. ii. 2. 7
As *withered* leaves drop from their dryed stockes, . . . II. xi. 19. 4
skin all *withered* like a dryed rooke; . . . II. xi. 22. 3
the drie *withered* stocke it gan refresh, . . . III. viii. 25. 3
he is old, and *withered* like hay, . . . III. ix. 5. 1

Withered—*Continued.*
like *withered* tree that wanteth juyce, . . . IV. i. 31. 5
Like as a *withered* tree, . . . IV. iii. 29. 6
As *withered* weed through cruell winters tine, . . . IV. xii. 34. 6
with untimely drought nigh *withered* was, . . . V. xii. 13. 2
Some deaw of grace into my *withered* hart, . . . *H.B.* 27
Withhault. *See* **Withheld.**
soone againe as he his light *withhault,* . . . II. xi. 9. 5
Withheld. *See* **Withhault.**
them perforce *withheld* with threatned blade, . . . II. xi. 31. 4
Carados her hand *withheld* From rash revenge, . . . III. iii. 55. 7
the stout Damzell, . . . His cursed hand *withheld,* . . . III. xii. 32. 9
The fayrest Ladie reft, and ever since *withheld.'* . . . IV. vi. 6. 9
withheld from me by wrongfull might, . . . V. xi. 49. 8
Withhold. the wilde beasts their furie did *withhold,* . . . *Gn.* 451
Could not from teares my melting eyes *withholde.* . . . *Ti.* 532
because it doth *withhold* Me from my love, . . . *D.* 400
your stroke, Sir Knight, *with-hold,* till . . . I. i. 12. 6
The false witch did my wrathfull hand *withhold:* . . . I. ii. 39. 8
How can ye vengeance just so long *withhold,* . . . I. vi. 5. 8
bands, Nor noyous smell, his purpose could *withhold,* . . . I. viii. 40. 2
Withhold, O soverayne Prince! your hasty hond . . . I. xii. 28. 3
withhold this deadly howre. . . . II. iii. 34. 9
Withhold your bloody handes from battaill fierce; . . . II. vi. 33. 3
Mammon did his hasty hand *withhold,* . . . II. vii. 42. 6
can *withhold* her wilfull wandring feet; . . . III. ix. 7. 6
Whereas no gate they found them to *withhold,* . . . III. xi. 21. 3
Might not my steps *withhold,* . . . IV. x. 29. 2
Did with strong hand *withhold;* . . . V. i. 3. 9
By what good right doe you *withhold* this day?' . . . V. iv. 17. 5
'Can dread of ought your dreadlesse hart *withhold,* . . . V. v. 31. 2
Withholds. I hate to tast, for food *withholds* my dying; . . *D.* 416
Withholdes it to her selfe, . . . V. v. 53. 3
Within (*partial list*).
Being *within,* the Kidde made him good glee, . . . *S.C.* May 282
all *within* were dead and hartles left: . . . *Hub.* 1355
all *within* were pathes and alleies wide, . . . I. i. 7. 7
dead was his hart *within,* Yet outwardly . . . I. vii. 21. 2
all *within* full rich arayd he found, . . . I. viii. 35. 1
festring sore did ranckle yett *within,* . . . I. x. 25. 4
within his reach . . . I. xi. 12. 5
far *within,* as in a hollow glade, . . . I. xi. 14. 8
all *within* with flowres was garnished, . . . II. v. 29. 7
That houses forme *within* was rude and strong, . . . II. vii. 28. 1
dispainted all *within* With sondry colours, . . . II. ix. 50. 1
their entred guestes to keep *within,* . . . II. xii. 43. 2
housed is *within* her hollow brest, . . . III. iii. 18. 7
vauted all *within,* like to the Skye, . . . III. iv. 43. 4
was al *within* most richly dight, . . . III. v. 40. 8
within, the riven walls were hung With ragged monuments . IV. i. 21. 1
Such was her house *within;* . . . IV. i. 25. 1
doe you here *within* this forrest wonne, . . . IV. vi. 5. 2
an Hynd *within* some covet glade, . . . IV. vi. 12. 4
all that came *within* his might. . . . IV. viii. 47. 9
I spide *within* the same Where one stood . . . IV. x. 11. 7
Within the compasse of that Islands space; . . . IV. x. 21. 2
Like warie Hynd *within* the weedie soyle, . . . IV. x. 55. 8
A broken sword *within* a bloodie field; . . . V. i. 19. 8
Unto the place he came *within* a while, . . . V. ii. 11. 1
Ne *within* reasons rule her madding mood containe. . . . V. vii. 11. 9
the Prince arrived *Within* the land . . . V. x. 18. 2
what she had not seene *within* unto her shewed: . . . V. x. 38. 9
Soone as he did *within* the listes appeare, . . . V. xii. 16. 1
tumbling downe *within* the dore . . . VI. i. 23. 6
a covert glade *Within* a wood, . . . VI. ii. 16. 4
his Ladie, . . . hid her selfe *within* the grove. . . . VI. ii. 20. 4
silly Faunus, now *within* their baile: . . . VII. vi. 49. 2
within this wide great Universe . . . VII. vii. 56. 1
May kindle living fire *within* my brest. . . . *Am.* vii. 12
You frame my thoughts, and fashion me *within;* . . . *Am.* viii. 9
thy home, *Within* the Westerne fome: . . . *Epith.* 283
Be heard all night *within,* nor yet without: . . . *Epith.* 335
Within the closet of her chastest bowre, . . . *H.H.B.* 249
Without. Thou raylest on, right *withouten* reason, . . . *S.C.* May 146
Withouten dreade of Wolves to bene ytost: . . . *S.C.* Jun. 12
From Plutoes balefull bowre *withouten* leave, . . . *S.C.* O. 29
Which have no wit to live *withouten* toyle; . . . *Hub.* 158
withouten (*without) pasport or good warrantye, . . . *Hub.* 186
Withouten helme or Pilot her to sway: . . . *T.M.* 142
Withouten prop or pillour it t' upholde, . . . *Ti.* 549
Ne (may it be *withouten* perill spoken?) . . . *Mui.* 97
whilest I was thus *without* dread or dout, . . . *D.* 155
On hills and downes, *withouten* dread or daunger: . . . *Col.* 317
And in thy person, *without* paragone, . . . *Ded. Son.* v. 11
require A thing *without* the compas of my witt; . . . I. ix. 3. 2
All lilly white, *withoutten* spot or pride, . . . I. xii. 22. 7
He left his steed *without,* . . . II. iii. 3. 8
stretch themselves *without* the utmost bound . . . II. vii. 56. 4
those unruly beasts to hold *without;* . . . II. xii. 43. 3
They, here arriving, staid awhile *without,* . . . III. iii. 14. 1
Of all those persons which she saw *without:* . . . III. xii. 30. 3
all *without,* The barren ground was full of wicked weedes, . IV. i. 25. 1
Withouten comfort and *withouten* guide, . . . IV. vii. 2. 8
forth *without* impediment I past, . . . IV. x. 11. 1
Excludes from fairest hope *withouten* further triall. . . . IV. x. 17. 9
all *without* were walkes and alleyes . . . IV. x. 25. 1
So left he her *withouten* remedie. . . . IV. xii. 24. 3
all the people there *without* it heard, . . . V. xi. 30. 2
And, as he past afore *withouten* dread, . . . V. xii. 39. 8
Withouten dowre or composition; . . . VI. i. 43. 8

Without—*Continued.*
That ye will make me Squire *without* delay, VI. ii. 33. 4
I may not, certes, *without* blame denie, VI. ii. 34. 6
And him . . . mortally did wound, *Withouten* cause, VI. ii. 43. 6
Without suspect of ill or daungers VI. iii. 23. 9
naked, *without* needfull vestiments VI. iv. 4. 4
And *without* sword his person to defend: VI. iv. 17. 5
And *without* weapon him assayling neare, VI. iv. 20. 3
did thinke *without* remorse To be aveng'd VI. iv. 20. 8
Yet, as I well it meane, vouchsafe it *without* blame. VI. iv. 34. 9
Withouten armes or steede to ride upon, VI. iv. 39. 3
he of malice, *without* her desarts, . . . her excluded VI. v. 33. 7
That durst so boldly, *without* let or shame, VI. vi. 20. 3
All they *without* were raunged in a ring, VI. x. 12. 1
cleane *without* his usuall spheere to fare; VII. vii. 52. 4
let me aske you this *withouten* blame; VII. vii. 53. 4
Without some spark of such self-pleasing pride. *Am.* v. 14
Without hope of aswagement or release? *Am.* xxxvi. 4
Be heard all night within, nor yet *without*: *Epith.* 335
And sit in Gods owne seat *without* commission; *H.H.L.* 82
borne *Without* all blemish or reprochfull blame, *H.H.L.* 149
attend On Gods owne person, *without* rest or end. *H.H.B.* 98

Withstand. Dragon, or may him *withstande?* *Rev.* i. 10
grove . . . That promist ayde the tempest to *withstand*; I. i. 7. 3
Mercy not *withstand*; I. iii. 37. 5
too weake . . . his puissance to *withstand*; I. iii. 42. 2
vanquisht them, unable to *withstand*: I. x. 65. 5
nothing seemd the puissaunce could *withstand*: I. xi. 24. 3
With ydle force did faine them to *withstand*, I. xii. 35. 8
strive you it to *withstand*, II. ii. 10. 3
'thy destinies *withstand* My wrathfull will, II. iii. 8. 3
mortall hands may not *withstand* his might, II. iv. 42. 2
more hardly he mote him *withstond*. II. v. 22. 9
weenest words or charms may force *withstond*: II. viii. 22. 2
though they both stood stiffe, yet could not both *withstond*. II. viii. 41. 9
nothing may *withstand* his stormy stowre, II. viii. 48. 2
withstond Oppressours powre by armes and puissant hond? II. viii. 56. 4
left none heire them to *withstand*, II. x. 61. 8
Yet no'te the same amend, ne yet *withstand*, II. xii. 57. 7
That mortall puissaunce mote not *withstond*. III. i. 10. 6
how t' amend, nor how it to *withstond*. III. ii. 52. 9
to *withstand* The powre of forreine Paynims III. iii. 27. 8
dared not his victor to *withstand*, III. vii. 36. 5
unable to *withstand* Or helpe himselfe; III. vii. 43. 3
she with angry scorne did him (*him did) *withstond*, III. viii. 25. 8
The silly virgin strove him to *withstand* III. viii. 27. 1
withstand The wrongfull outrage III. xi. 10. 5
To make an end of all that did *withstand*: IV. iii. 33. 3
none his force were able to *withstond*, IV. iv. 23. 8
Yet mote he not *withstand* what was decreede, IV. v. 9. 4
Threatning to strike unlesse he would *withstand*: IV. vi. 23. 5
that nought may them *withstand*. IV. vi. 31. 5
had it bene right hard him to *withstand*, IV. vii. 25. 8
able was all daungers to *withstond*: IV. ix. 18. 4
her commaundment he could not *withstand*, IV. x. 33. 7
durst he not the warrant to *withstand*, IV. xii. 33. 1
durst *withstand* His dreadfull heast, V. i. 8. 6
Ne any may his mighty will *withstand*; V. ii. 42. 2
her proud observaunce will *withstand*, V. iv. 32. 2
then all rule and reason they *withstand* V. v. 25. 5
Maugre so many foes which did *withstand*: V. ix. 30. 5
Stryving long time in vaine it to *withstond*; V. x. 27. 3
He would it meete and warily *withstand*. V. xi. 7. 5
Ne any able was him to *withstand*, V. xii. 7. 6
Me first he tooke unhable to *withstond*, VI. i. 16. 6
spoile my selfe that can not thee *withstand?* VI. i. 25. 5
Ne powre had to *withstand*, ne hope of any ayd. VI. vii. 48. 9
nor once *withstand* The proved powre of noble Calidore, VI. xii. 36. 6
Threatned to strike her if she did *with-stand*: VII. vi. 13. 5
Ne ought so strong that may his force *withstand*, *H.L.* 229

Withstands. Despeyre, Whom Redcros knight *withstands*. I. ix. Arg.
all that him *withstands* Treads down II. xi. 33. 5
who long in vaine their rage *withstands*. V. xi. 44. 9

Withstood. of neither well *withstood*, *Gn.* 413
being there *withstood*, They flocked all about I. i. 25. 6
all his torment well *withstood* I. x. 32. 7
when she is withdrawne or strong *withstood*, II. iv. 11. 6
Least thou perhaps hereafter wish, and be *withstood*.' II. vii. 38. 9
stoutly he *withstood* their strong assay; II. viii. 36. 1
strove in vaine him long to have *withstood*, IV. ii. 45. 7
them stoutly well *withstood*; IV. ix. 29. 7
Tygris fierce, whose streames of none may be *withstood*; IV. xi. 20. 9
Which Britomart *withstood* with courage stout, V. vii. 31. 3
Whylest he of none was stopped nor *withstood*: V. x. 8. 5
Yet he them all *withstood*, and often made relent. VI. v. 20. 9
their assault *withstood* so mightily, VI. vi. 23. 7
Their Captaine long *withstood*, and did her death forstall. VI. xi. 31. 9

Witless. with fond termes, and *witlesse* (*weetlesse) words, *S.C.* Jul. 35
unwise and *witlesse* Colin Cloute, *S.C.* D. 91
His *witlesse* pleasance, and ill pleasing vaine. *Hub.* 799
Why then should *witlesse* man so much misweene, II. Pr. 3. 4
weetlesse eke of lately wrought despight, II. v. 36. 5
Did smyle full smoothly at her *weetlesse* wofull stound. III. ii. 26. 9
weetlesse wandered From shore to shore III. ix. 41. 5
From that unwares ye *weetlesse* doe intend; VI. viii. 17. 6
all *weetlesse* of the wretched stormes, VI. viii. 47. 5
Begin his *witlesse* note apace to clatter. *Am.* lxxxiv. 4

Witness. *See* **Eyewitness.**
'Thou feeble flocke . . . Mayst *witnesse* well, *S.C.* Ja. 45
Beare *witnesse* all of thys so wicked deede: *S.C.* Jun. 108

Witness—*Continued.*
Witnesse shee slewe me with her eye, *S.C.* Au. 115
beare *witnesse* of my woe, *S.C.* Au. 151
The Woodes can *witnesse* many a wofull stowre. *S.C.* D. 66
Adieu, ye Woodes, that oft my *witnesse* were: *S.C.* D. 154
The famous *witnesse* of our wonted praise, *T.M.* 274
Unhappie Verse, the *witnesse* of my unhappie state, *U.V.* 1
Be *witnesse* of her bountie here alive, *Col.* 646
Unto the world for ever *witnesse* bee, *Col.* 949
proofe he since hath made (I *witnes* am) I. vii. 47. 7
Witnes the dungeon deepe, wherein I. ix. 45. 5
Witnesse the burning Altars, which he swore, I. xii. 27. 5
High God be *witnesse* that I guiltlesse ame; I. xii. 30. 6
Witnes, ye heavens, whom she in vaine to help did call. II. i. 10. 9
I present was, and can it *witnesse* well, II. i. 19. 6
Hath made sad *witnesse* of thy fathers fall, II. i. 37. 2
Of whose fowle deedes . . . I *witnesse* am, II. ii. 44. 8
Witnesse the guiltlesse blood pourd oft on ground, II. vii. 13. 4
well can *witnes* yet unto this day II. x. 10. 6
for *witnes* of his hard assay III. i. 2. 5
well can *witnesse* who by tryall it does prove. III. ii. 51. 9
Witnesse the father of Philosophie, IV. Pr. 3. 6
Witnesse their broken bandes there to be seene, IV. i. 24. 6
Whereto her selfe he did to *witnesse* call; IV. v. 23. 8
Witnesse th' exceeding fry which there are fed, IV. xii. 2. 4
To *witnesse* to the world that she by him is dead.' V. i. 26. 9
take with thee to *witnesse* it Sixe of thy fellowes V. iv. 49. 6
Witnesse the Paynims both, V. viii. 11. 6
witnesse forth aright in forrain land, V. ix. 37. 5
witnesse unto me, ye heavens! V. xi. 41. 6
Witnesse may Burbon be; V. xii. 2. 1
witnesse be Gerioneo found, V. xii. 2. 5
his Ladie here May *witnesse* well, VI. ii. 8. 2
Witnesse thereof he shew'd his head there left, VI. iii. 18. 8
Witnesse the wounds, and this wyde bloudie lake, VI. vii. 15. 5
The *witnesse* of his wretchednesse in place, VI. viii. 5. 2
Witnesse, ye Heavens, the truth of all that I have teld!' VII. vi. 27. 9
Witnesse the world how worthy to be prayzed! *Am.* iii. 2
Witnesse Leander in the Euxine waves, *H.L.* 231

Wits. France . . . though fruitfull of brave *wits*, *Ro.* Env. 2
Tho gan the streames of flowing *wittes* to cease, *S.C.* O. 71
To learned *wits* givest courage worthily, *Gn.* 36
Deeply doo your sad words my *wits* awhape, *Hub.* 72
doo not doubt but duly to encline My *wits* theretoo, *Hub.* 549
Then was high time their *wits* about to geather. *Hub.* 570
whilst that other like vaine *wits* he pleased, *Hub.* 709
To such delights the noble *wits* he led *Hub.* 821
love of letters did inspire Their gentle *wits*, *Hub.* 830
as one whose *wits* were reft, Fled here and there, *Hub.* 1356
wont to be the glorie of gay *wits*, *T.M.* 182
those sweete *wits*, which wont the like to frame, *T.M.* 203
Be fild with praises of divinest *wits*, *T.M.* 581
Where be those learned *wits* and antique Sages, *Ti.* 59
cared not to cherishe No gentle *wits*, *Ti.* 363
Poets *wits* are had in peerlesse price: *Col.* 321
dwel . . . gentle Nymphes, delights of learned *wits*; *Ded. Son.* v. 10
makes them doubt their *wits* be not their owne: I. i. 10. 7
through many yeares thy *wits* thee faile, II. iii. 16. 2
skill That whilome in divinest *wits* did rayne, III. Pr. 3. 2
As diverse *witts* to diverse things apply; III. i. 57. 3
as one nigh of her *wits* depriv'd, III. vii. 14. 5
all the wyles of wemens *wits* knew passing well. III. viii. 8. 9
her *wits* nigh fayld, III. viii. 34. 8
'Pardon, I pray, . . . for my *wits* beene light. III. ix. 47. 4
workes of noblest *wits* to nought outweare, IV. ii. 33. 2
sith workes of heavenly *wits* Are quite devourd, IV. ii. 33. 8
all the artes, that subtill *wits* discover, IV. iii. 40. 2
As diverse *wits* affected divers beene. IV. v. 11. 5
like a ghastly Gelt whose *wits* are reaved, IV. vii. 21. 3
well thy *wits* advise, V. v. 34. 6
Yet found no easement in her troubled *wits*, V. vi. 15. 3
In troublous *wits*, and mutinous uprore: V. ix. 48. 6
As women wont their guilefull *wits* to guyde, VI. vi. 43. 2
all his *wits* with doole were nigh distraught, VI. xi. 33. 3
Ne spareth he most learned *wits* to rate, VI. xii. 40. 7
Yet on mount Thabor quite their *wits* forgat, VII. vii. 7. 7
Disguysing diversly my troubled *wits*. *Am.* liv. 4
Onely I feare my *wits* enfeebled late, *H.L.* 15
How vainely then doe ydle *wits* invent, *H.B.* 64
That in light *wits* did loose affection move; *H.H.L.* 11
But feele my *wits* to faile, and tongue to fold. *H.H.B.* 7
Whose nature yet so much is marvelled Of mortall *wits*, *H.H.B.* 167
And were as faire as fabling *wits* do fayne, *H.H.B.* 216
those *wits*, the wonders of their dayes, *H.H.B.* 218

Wits'. Nigh his *wits* end then woxe th' amazed knight, II. xi. 44. 1

Witted. *See* **Rash-witted, Wily-witted.**
both were craftie and unhappie *witted*; *Hub.* 49

Wittily. all that in the world was ay thought *wittily*. II. ix. 53. 9

Witting. Well *weeting* trew what she had rashly told; II. ix. 39. 2
weeting inly well That she to him dissembled womanish guyle, III. iii. 17. 2
Well *weeting* how their errour to assoyle, IV. vi. 25. 2
Much greater then was ever in her *weeting*, V. x. 39. 3
the whyles the Prince did rest . . . not *weeting* what was ment, VI. vi. 44. 2

Wittingly. He stole away, and *weetingly* beguyld. *As.* 22
for his sake had *weetingly* Now brought her selfe, VI. iii. 11. 7

Witty. Both by your *wittie* words, and by your werks. *Hub.* 416
In *wittie* riddles, and in wise soothsayes; IV. ii. 35. 5
Thereto adde art, even womens *witty* trade, V. v. 49. 5

Wizard. the sage *wisard* telles, as he has redd, III. i. 16. 8
The *wisard* could no lenger beare her bord, III. iii. 19. 1

Wizards. These *wisards* welter in welths waves, *S.C.* Jul. 197
strong advizement of six *wisards* old, I. iv. 12. 8
memorable gestes Of famous *Wisards,* II. ix. 53. 4
the antique *wisards* well invented IV. xii. 2. 1
Aegyptian *wisards* old, Which in Star-read . . . have best insight, V. Pr. 8. 1
even itselfe is mov'd, as *wizards* saine: VII. vii. 55. 7
amaze The greatest *wisards* which thereon do gaze. *H.H.B.* 168
Wode. *See* **Wood.**
Woe. *See* **Wae.**
restles seas of wretchednes and *woe;* *Pet.*[2] vii. 4
As weren overwent with *woe,* *S.C.* Mar. 2
Heaping up waves of welth and *woe,* *S.C.* May 93
should they pynen in payne and *woe?* *S.C.* May 149
cutte of hys dayes with untimely *woe,* *S.C.* May 199
learne these woods to wayle my *woe,* *S.C.* Jun. 95
That art the roote of all this ruthfull *woe!* *S.C.* Jun. 116
beare witnesse of my *woe,* *S.C.* Au. 151
The walled townes doe worke my greater *woe;* *S.C.* Au. 158
More meete to wayle my *woe* *S.C.* Au. 165
With sight of such as chaunge my restlesse *woe.* *S.C.* Au. 172
of my *woe* cannot bewray least part) *S.C.* Au. 176
the daye in *woe,* I vowed have to wayst, *S.C.* Au. 179
The memory of hys misdeede that bred her *woe.* *S.C.* Au. 186
you that feele no *woe,* *S.C.* Au. 187
Sike question ripeth up cause of newe *woe,* *S.C.* S. 13
better dayes death hath shut up in *woe?* *S.C.* N. 74
my *woe* now wasted is; *S.C.* N. 201
To be partaker of their common *woe;* *Hub.* 14
Therewith shee wayled with exceeding *woe,* *T.M.* 295
till mickle *woe* Thereof arose, *Mui.* 132
Litle wist he his fatall future *woe,* *Mui.* 381
My Lyonesse (ah, *woe* is mee!) is gon! *D.* 161
no worlds sad care nor wasting *woe* *D.* 283
Driven with streames of wretchednesse and *woe,* *D.* 433
life drawes care, and care continuall *woe;* *D.* 450
t' expresse their inward *woe,* *As.* Interl. 225
ne ought he feares To be partaker of her wandring *woe;* I. iii. 44. 8
Sowen in bloodie field, and bought with *woe:* I. iv. 42. 5
soone redeeme from his long-wandring *woe:* I. v. 11. 2
they should live in *wo,* and dye in wretchednesse. I. v. 46. 9
welcome now, my Lord in wele or *woe,* I. viii. 43. 1
still wex old in *woe,* whiles *wo* stil wexeth new. I. ix. 9. 9
fond, that joyest in the *woe* thou hast! I. ix. 39. 7
Great *woe* and sorrow did her soule assay, I. xi. 32. 2
Through weaknesse of my widowhed or *woe;* I. xii. 28. 6
To worke new *woe* and improvided scath, I. xii. 34. 3
To worken mischiefe, and avenging *woe,* II. i. 2. 2
the weake minde with double *woe* torment?' II. i. 16. 7
ended all her *woe* in quiet death. II. i. 56. 4
As carelesse of his *woe,* or innocent II. ii. 1. 7
Thus enter we Into this life with *woe,* II. ii. 2. 9
both against the middest meant to worken *woe.* II. ii. 13. 9
unto knighthood workes much shame and *woe;* II. iv. 10. 7
Woe never wants where every cause is caught; II. iv. 44. 6
Wo worth the man, II. vi. 32. 7
he wexed wondrous *woe;* II. viii. 53. 4
'Then *woe,* and *woe,* and everlasting *woe,* III. iii. 42. 1
If they be dead, then *woe* is me therefore; III. iv. 2. 1
waste in *woe* and waylfull miserye; III. iv. 38. 4
Sister of heavie death, and nourse of *woe,* III. iv. 55. 2
'Ah, dearest God!' (quoth he) 'that is great *woe,* III. v. 6. 7
the ground of all our *woe.* III. v. 9. 9
uncurteous Carle, . . . wrap in grievous *woe.* III. ix. 17. 9
Perhaps this hand may helpe to ease your *woe,* III. xi. 15. 4
That he might taste the sweet consuming *woe,* III. xi. 45. 4
captive with her led to wretchednesse and *wo.* III. xii. 41. 9
He was full *wo,* and gan his former griefe renew. IV. i. 38. 9
of all his *woe* and wrong Companion she became, IV. viii. 5. 8
daies in wilfull *woe* are worne, IV. viii. 15. 7
'by all the *woe* I pas, IV. viii. 63. 7
In wretched anguishe and incessant *woe,* IV. ix. 39. 6
let me waste in *woe* my wretched yeares, IV. xii. 7. 7
Who was the root and worker of her *woe,* IV. xii. 29. 2
'Ah! *woe* is me, and well-away!' V. i. 15. 1
him captived hath in haplesse *woe.'* V. vi. 11. 3
Which she would sure performe, betide her wele or *wo.* V. vi. 23. 9
through his want her *woe* did more increase: V. vii. 45. 2
Working to all that love her deadly *woe,* V. viii. 20. 8
gave beginning to her *woe* and wretchednesse. V. x. 11. 9
Mongst joyes mixing some tears, mongst wele some *wo,* V. xi. 16. 3
Weeping to him in vaine and making piteous *woe.* VI. ii. 10. 9
to question of her present *woe,* VI. viii. 50. 6
(*woe* is me!) VI. xi. 31. 1
take delight t' encrease a wretches *woe;* *Am.* xli. 7
Many lewd layes (ah! *woe* is me the more!) *H.H.L.* 8
Woebegone. Was greatly *woe begon,* and gan to feare III. vii. 20. 7
what was she her selfe so *woe-begone,* V. viii. 16. 4
Woeful. if thou wilt bewayle my *wofull* tene, *S.C.* N. 41
Waile ye this *wofull* waste of Natures warke; *S.C.* N. 64
(that was, a *woful* word to sayne!) *S.C.* N. 93
The Woodes can witnesse many a *wofull* stowre. *S.C.* D. 66
Like *wofull* Culvers, doo sit wayling now, *T.M.* 246
So wailing backe go to their *wofull* toomb. *Ti.* 49
'Who is it that dooth name me, *wofull* thrall, *D.* 62
with *wofull* heavie thought; *D.* 465
When passing by ye read these *wofull* layes, *D.* 536
falshood . . . workes him *woefull* ruth. I. ii. Arg.
Then gan she wail and weepe to see that *woeful* stowre. I. ii. 7. 9
The Lady, . . . Staid not to waile his *woefull* funerall, I. ii. 20. 3

Woeful—*Continued.*
Then forth I went his *woefull* corse to find, I. ii. 24. 6
all this while Forsaken, *wofull,* solitarie mayd, I. iii. 3. 2
fearefull freends weare out the *wofull* night, I. iii. 20. 6
how many a *woeful* stowre For him she late endurd; I. iii. 30. 5
'Ah! wretched sonne of *wofull* syre, I. v. 10. 5
To wayle his *wofull* case she would not stay, I. v. 19. 8
after their *wofull* falles, I. v. 51. 3
In their rude eyes unworthie of so *wofull* plight. I. vi. 9. 9
The *wofull* Dwarfe, which saw his maisters fall I. vii. 19. 1
on the way He *wofull* Lady, *wofull* Una, met, I. vii. 20. 2
'Tell on,' (quoth she) 'the *wofull* Tragedy, I. vii. 24. 8
woefull Lady, let me you intrete, I. vii. 40. 5
no where could he find that *wofull* thrall: I. viii. 37. 2
That *wofull* lover, loathing lenger light, I. ix. 30. 2
The *wofull* tale that Trevisan had told, I. ix. 37. 2
to redeeme thy *woefull* parents head From tyrans rage I. x. 9. 4
The *wofull* daughter and forsaken heyre I. xii. 26. 3
What comfort can I, *wofull* wretch, conceave? II. i. 17. 2
Whose *wofull* parents she hath wickedly fordonne.' II. ii. 44. 9
he would not endure that *wofull* theame II. v. 37. 3
with wretched miseryes and *woefull* ruth, II. x. 62. 3
the Prince, seeing her *wofull* plight, II. xi. 16. 4
Did smyle full smoothly at her weetlesse *wofull* stound. III. ii. 26. 9
that *wofull* Squire, With blood deformed, III. v. 29. 1
Their *wofull* harts he wounded had III. vi. 13. 8
in the *wofull* harts Of many wretches III. vi. 49. 6
The *wofull* husbandman doth lowd complaine III. vii. 34. 7
that *wofull* Squyre, Whom he had reskewed III. vii. 45. 6
Yt yrkes me leave thee in this *wofull* state, III. viii. 43. 8
He was not in the cities *wofull* fyre Consum'd, III. ix. 40. 8
Was never wretched man in such a *wofull* cace. III. x. 14. 9
Save that same *woefull* Lady, III. xii. 30. 6
wretched Lady, quitt from *wofull* state, III. xii. 39. 3
A *wofull* wretched maid, of God and man forgot! IV. vii. 14. 9
Led with that *wofull* Ladies piteous crying, IV. vii. 25. 3
Gainst *wofull* Niobes unhappy race, IV. vii. 30. 8
fit solitary place For *wofull* wight, IV. vii. 38. 6
wast his wretched daies in *wofull* plight; IV. vii. 39. 8
Whereas that *wofull* man in languor did abide. IV. viii. 11. 9
wofull man, what heavens hard disgrace, IV. viii. 14. 7
me, *woefull* thrall, Deliver hence IV. xii 9. 3
About that *wofull* couple which were slaine, V. iii. 31. 2
The *woefull* widow had no meanes now left, V. x. 14. 2
all that wrong unto that *wofull* Dame So long had done, V. xi. 4. 5
beside him sate . . . His *wofull* Ladie, VI. ii. 41. 2
'What be you, *wofull* Dame, which thus lament, VI. iv. 27. 8
A *wofull* dame ye have me termed well; VI. iv. 28. 3
So much more *wofull,* as my *wofull* plight VI. iv. 28. 4
in that *wofull* stead Kept and delivered me VI. v. 29. 4
As th' onely author of her *wofull* tine; VI. viii. 33. 3
Pastorella, *wofull* wretched Elfe, VI. xi. 19. 1
'Where shall I then commence This *wofull* tale? VI. xi. 30. 3
Woefulest. (I weene), the *wofulst* man alive, *D.* 5
Woefully. gan she *wofully* to waile, *T.M.* 169
wept and *wofullie* waymented, *T.M.* 355
Acheron, Where many soules sit wailing *woefully,* I. v. 33. 2
In her owne blood all wallow'd *wofully,* V. i. 14. 4
doth lie In wretched bondage, *wofully* bestad.' V. vi. 10. 7
Woefulness. 'One, whome like *wofulnesse,* impressed deepe, *D.* 64
Woe's. His owne *woes* author, who so bound it findes, II. v. 1. 8
Woes. *See* **Woos.**
Their heavenly vertues from these *woes* assoyling, *Ro.* xix. 11
Well couth he wayle his *Woes,* *S.C.* Jun. 85
hart of flint would rew The undeserved *woes* and sorrowes, I. ii. 26. 9
in eternall *woes* my weaker hart Have wasted, I. iv. 46. 7
Into new *woes* unweeting I was cast I. iv. 47. 3
My last left comfort is my *woes* to weepe and waile.' I. vii. 39. 9
Death is the end of *woes:* I. ix. 47. 9
in my *woes* beginner it to end: II. iv. 31. 4
Whose future *woes* so plaine he fashioned; III. iii. 43. 3
Where she, captived long, great *woes* did prove; IV. vi. 34. 8
of her widowhed Taking advantage, and her yet fresh *woes,* V. x. 12. 2
Fell into wretched *woes,* which she repented late. VI. viii. 2. 9
all the *woes* and wrecks which I abide, *Am.* xxv. 11
when shall these wearie *woes* have end, *Am.* xxxvi. 1
I waile, and make my *woes* a Tragedy. *Am.* liv. 8
The doubts, the daungers, the delayes, the *woes,* *H.L.* 262
all the paines and *woes* that I endure, *H.L.* 295
all my *woes* to be but penance small. *H.L.* 300
now it wasted is with *woes* extreame, *H.B.* 25
here fits not well Olde *woes,* but joyes, to tell *Proth.* 142
Woe-working. Outrageous anger, and *woe-working* jarre, II. v. 16. 3
Woke. when droncke with drowsinesse he *woke,* III. viii. 22. 1
Wolf. at his feete a bitch *Wolfe* did give sucke *Bel.*[1] vii. 9
I saw a *Wolfe* under a rockie cave *Bel.*[2] vi. 1
at his feete a bitch *wolfe* suck did yeeld *Bel.*[2] ix. 9
hath some *Wolfe* thy tender Lambes ytorne? *S.C.* Ap. 2
sith the Saxon king Never was *Woolfe* seene, *S.C.* S. 152
there wonned a wicked *Wolfe,* *S.C.* S. 184
As if a *Woolfe* were emong the sheepe: *S.C.* S. 192
tooke out the *Woolfe* in his counterfect cote, *S.C.* S. 206
by the hyde the *Wolfe* Lowder caught; *S.C.* S. 223
the *Wolfe,* her mortall enemie, *Hub.* 1209
ye my cousin *Wolfe* so fowly thwart, *Hub.* 1218
Ne fear'd the *Wolfe,* ne fear'd the wildest beast, *D.* 135
next to him malicious Envy rode Upon a ravenous *wolfe,* I. iv. 30. 2
a greedy *Wolfe,* through honger fell, I. vi. 10. 3
The Antelope, and *Wolfe* both fiers and fell; I. vi. 26. 5
A ravenous *Wolfe* amongst the scattered flockes: V. xii. 38. 6

Wolf—*Continued.*
Watching to drive the ravenous *Wolfe* away, ... VI. ix. 37. 4
Wolfish. This *Wolvish* sheepe woulde catchen his pray, ... *S.C.* S. 197
Wolf's. Thereby is a Lambe in the *Wolves* jawes: . . . . *S.C.* Au. 31
Wolves. There crept in *Wolves*, ... *S.C.* May 127
Withouten dreade of *Wolves* to bene ytost: . . . . *S.C.* Jun. 12
Wolves that would them teare. . . . . *S.C.* Jul. 56
bene of ravenous *Wolves* yrent, ... *S.C.* S. 148
the fewer *Woolves* . . . The more bene the Foxes . . . . *S.C.* S. 154
If sike bene *Wolves*, as thou hast told, ... *S.C.* S. 228
the *Wolves*, that chase the wandring sheepe, ... *S.C.* N. 136
Withouten dreade of *Wolves* to bene espyed. . . . . *S.C.* D. 24
Be ye the pray of *Wolves;* . . . . *D.* 349
No ravenous *wolves* the good mans hope destroy . . . . *Col.* 318
hungry *wolves* continually did howle . . . . I. v. 30. 8
greedy *Wolves* doe breake by force Into an heard, ... IV. iv. 35. 6
certes was with milke of *Wolves* and Tygres fed. . . . . IV. vii. 7. 9
that *Wolves* . . . Should harbour'd be . . . . VII. vi. 55. 4
Doth to this day with *Wolves* and Thieves abound: . . . . VII. vi. 55. 8
the wylde *wolves*, which seeke them to devoure, ... *Epith.* 69
Wolvish. *See* **Wolfish.**
Woman. *See* **Old woman.**
a *Woman* sitting on a beast . . . . *Rev.* ii. 1
Most fierce and fell this *woman* seemde to me. . . . . *Rev.* ii. 11
A *Woman* sitting, sorrowfullie wailing, ... *Ti.* 9
'The wretched *woman*, whom unhappy howre . . . . I. ii. 22. 2
bestow Upon the daughter of this *woman* blind, ... I. iii. 18. 3
Ne let that wicked *woman* scape away; . . . . I. viii. 28. 5
loe! that wicked *woman* in your sight, ... I. viii. 45. 4
She was a *woman* in her freshest age, ... I. x. 30. 1
what *woman* . . . doth me upbrayd With breach of love . . . . I. xii. 31. 4
this false *woman* that Fidessa hight, ... I. xii. 32. 2
this wretched *woman* overcome Of anguish, ... II. i. 58. 6
seemd to be a *woman* of great worth, ... II. iii. 21. 8
turning to that *woman*, fast her hent . . . . II. iv. 12. 2
Unto an aged *woman*, poore and bare, ... II. v. 17. 3
'Most wretched *woman* and of wicked race, ... II. vi. 33. 7
thereon satt a *woman*, gorgeous gay . . . . II. vii. 44. 6
first taught men a *woman* to obay: . . . . II. x. 20. 7
A *woman* worthy of immortall praise, ... II. x. 42. 4
She seemd a *woman* of great bountihed, ... III. i. 41. 5
of a *woman* he should have much ill; . . . . III. iv. 25. 8
This was that *woman*, this that deadly wownd, ... III. iv. 28. 1
This wicked *woman* had a wicked sonne, ... III. vii. 12. 1
'Safe her, I never any *woman* found . . . . III. vii. 60. 1
all in vaine: his *woman* was too wise . . . . III. x. 20. 1
Ne ever word to speake to *woman* more; . . . . IV. vii. 39. 4
Ne *woman* yet so faire, but he her brought . . . . IV. viii. 48. 4
Nor all the Moenades so furious were, As this bold *woman* . . V. viii. 47. 9
taken have this toylesome paine For wretched *woman*, ... V. x. 21. 3
pitty craves, as he of *woman* was yborne.' . . . . VI. iii. 41. 9
a *woman* spoyld of all attire . . . . VI. viii. 48. 5
'Of that bad seed is this bold *woman* bred, ... VII. vi. 21. 1
'Speake, thou fraile *woman*, speake with confidence; . . . . VII. vi. 25. 7
Whether she man or *woman* inly were, ... VII. vii. 5. 6
She is no *woman*, but a senceless stone. . . . . *Am.* liv. 14
Womanhead. from the shape of *womanhed*, ... *Mui.* 345
She is the paterne of true *womanhead*, ... *Col.* 512
garments loose that seemd unmeet for *womanhed*. . . . . II. xii. 55. 9
Her wanton eyes, ill signes of *womanhed*, ... III. i. 41. 7
th' honorable stage of *womanhead*, ... III. v. 54. 8
To be upbrought in goodly *womanhed;* . . . . III. vi. 28. 7
In all the lore of love, and goodly *womanhead*. . . . . III. vi. 51. 9
with her joyn'd Regard of *womanhead;* . . . . V. ix. 45. 4
To drive you . . . gainst all *womanhead*.' . . . . VI. ii. 15. 5
Womanhood. gratious *womanhood*, and gravitie, ... II. ii. 15. 5
in her semblant shew'd great *womanhood:* . . . . IV. x. 31. 5
Her name was *Womanhood;* . . . . IV. x. 49. 5
Even in the lap of *Womanhood* there sate, ... IV. x. 52. 3
inward shame . . . through care of *womanhood*, ... VI. viii. 51. 2
Unspotted fayth, and comely *womanhood*, ... *Epith.* 192
Womanish. then to him these *womanish* words gan say: . . . I. vi. 28. 5
Throwne out from *womanish* impatient mynd? . . . . I. xii. 30. 2
'Up, up! thou *womanish* weake knight, ... II. v. 36. 2
onely *womanish* fine forgery, ... II. xii. 28. 8
she to him dissembled *womanish* guyle, ... III. iii. 17. 3
With *womanish* compassion of her plaint, ... III. vii. 10. 2
Discolourd like to *womanish* disguise, ... III. x. 21. 7
With *womanish* teares, and with unwarlike smarts, ... III. xi. 44. 6
with *womanish* art To hide her wound, ... IV. vi. 40. 7
sooth it was not sure for *womanish* shame, ... IV. x. 41. 4
Beholding all that *womanish* weake fight; . . . . V. iv. 25. 8
Of men disguiz'd in *womanishe* attire, ... V. vii. 37. 7
womanish complaints she did represse, ... V. vii. 44. 8
Did well endure her *womanish* disdaine, ... VI. i. 30. 8
Womankind. the immortall praise Of *womankinde*, ... *Gn.* 429
That men admire in goodlie *womankinde*, ... *D.* 212
'I hate all men, and shun all *womankinde;* . . . . *D.* 421
Such as all *womankynd* did far excell; . . . . *Col.* 190
She is the ornament of *womankind*, ... *Col.* 498
fast fealty, Which I do owe unto all *womankynd*, ... I. iii. 1. 7
So scabby was that would have loathd all *womankind*. . . . I. viii. 47. 9
in the calme of pleasaunt *womankind*. . . . . II. vi. 8. 9
th' authour of all *woman kynd;* . . . . II. x. 71. 7
Ne blott the bounty of all *womankind;* . . . . III. i. 49. 4
not indifferent to *woman kind*, ... III. ii. 1. 3
Bad her from *womankind* to keepe him well, ... III. iv. 25. 7
In gentle Ladies breste and bounteous race Of *woman kind* . III. v. 52. 8
both encreast the prayse of *woman kynde*, ... III. v. 55. 7
So shamefully forlorne of *womankynd*, ... III. x. 55. 8

Womankind—*Continued.*
sister did in feminine And filthy lust exceede all *womankinde*, III. xi. 4. 2
The shame of men, and plague of *womankind:* . . . . IV. vii. 18. 5
raging fire of love to *womankind*, ... IV. ix. 1. 6
on *womankinde* His mighty hand to shend, ... V. iv. 24. 3
Such is the crueltie of *womenkynd*, ... V. v. 25. 1
Towards all *womenkind* them kindly to behave. . . . . VI. ii. 14. 9
A voice, that seemed of some *woman kynd*, ... VI. iv. 26. 7
Woman-like. He wailed *womanlike* with many a teare, . . . III. xii. 7. 7
Woman's. For ruth of that same *womans* piteous paine; . . . *Ti.* 480
th' other halfe did *womans* shape retaine, ... I. i. 14. 8
more foule . . . Then *womans* shape man would beleeve to bee. I. ii. 41. 4
she of *womans* force did feare no harme; . . . . III. iv. 27. 8
Not this the worke of *womans* hand ywis, ... III. iv. 37. 3
A *womans* will, which is disposd to go astray. . . . . III. ix. 6. 9
womans subtiltyes Can guylen Argus, ... III. ix. 7. 2
perfectly practiz'd in *womans* craft, ... IV. ii. 10. 2
womans hand Hath conquered you . . . . IV. vi. 31. 2
of a *womans* hand it was ywroke, ... IV. xi. 5. 6
to no *womans* wast . . . it would sit, ... V. iii. 28. 6
she made him to be dight In *womans* weedes, ... V. v. 20. 7
So hard it is to be a *womans* slave. . . . . V. v. 23. 5
T' obay a *womans* tyrannous direction, ... V. v. 26. 4
his balefull smart In *womans* bondage . . . . V. vi. 3. 4
To fierce avengement of that *womans* pride, ... V. vi. 18. 7
Woman-wight. a *woman-wight*, unwist to bee, ... III. ix. 21. 8
The fairest *woman-wight* that ever eie did see. . . . . III. ix. 21. 9
Woman-wronger. Bidding him turne againe, . . . Foule *woman-wronger*, ... VI. vii. 7. 3
Womb. Out of her *womb* a thousand rayons threw . . . . *Bel.*[2] ii. 7
out of her massie *wombe* forth sent That antique horror, . . *Ro.* xvii. 7
Shall in great Chaos *wombe* againe be hid. . . . . *Ro.* xxii. 14
They crying creep out of their mothers *woomb*, ... *Ti.* 48
out of her happie *womb* did bring The sacred brood . . . . *Ti.* 278
There did our ship her fruitfull *wombe* unlade, ... *Col.* 288
out of the fruitfull *wombe* of their great mother. . . . . *Col.* 854
with his breath . . . Her hollow *womb* did secretly inspyre, . I. vii. 9. 4
she of late is lightned of her *wombe*, ... I. x. 16. 5
in his *wombe* might lurke some hidden nest . . . . I. xii. 10. 5
my *wombe* her burdein would forbeare, ... II. i. 53. 4
The great earthes *wombe* they open to the sky, ... II. i. 60. 2
Besought them by the *womb* which them had born, ... II. ii. 27. 5
from my mothers *wombe* this grace I have . . . . II. iii. 45. 1
the quiet *wombe* Of his great Grandmother . . . . II. vii. 17. 1
earth out of her fruitfull *woomb* Throwes forth . . . . II. vii. 51. 6
from her *womb* new spirits to reprize. . . . . II. xi. 44. 9
So soone as he unto her *wombe* did fall: . . . . II. xi. 45. 6
from thy *wombe* a famous Progenee Shall spring . . . . III. iii. 22. 5
from the sacred mould Of her immortall *womb*, ... III. iv. 11. 9
her *wombe* did fill With hevenly seed, ... III. iv. 41. 5
Her berth was of the *wombe* of Morning dew, ... III. vi. 3. 1
pierst into her *wombe*, ... III. vi. 7. 7
So sprong these twinnes in *womb* of Chrysogone; . . . . III. vi. 9. 6
in the wide *wombe* of the world . . . . III. vi. 36. 6
While in their mothers *wombe* enclosd they were, ... III. vii. 48. 6
whence he was, or of what *wombe* ybore, ... IV. vii. 7. 7
Of mortall sire, though of immortall *wombe*, ... IV. xii. 4. 2
Both brethren, whom one *wombe* together bore, ... V. iv. 4. 3
Under her *wombe* his fatall sword he thrust, ... V. xi. 31. 2
from his mothers *wombe* . . . He was invulnerable . . . . VI. iv. 4. 8
her *wombe*, unwist to wight, was fraught, ... VI. xii. 6. 4
fild her *wombe* with fruitfull hope of nourishment. . . . . VII. vii. 32. 9
Till greater then my *wombe* thou woxen art: . . . . *Am.* ii. 4
From mothers *womb* deriv'd by dew descent: . . . . *Am.* lxxiv. 6
the chast *wombe* informe with timely seed, ... *Epith.* 386
taking flesh of sacred virgins *wombe*, ... *H.H.L.* 146
Womb's. Till thy *wombes* burden thee from them do call, . . . III. iii. 28. 6
Wombs. the dew time In which the *wombes* of wemen doe expyre, I. vii. 9. 7
Bove all the sonnes that were of earthly *wombes* ybore. . . III. iv. 21. 9
Women. *Wemen*, that of Loves longing once lust, ... *S.C.* May 134
all *wemen* are thy debtors found, ... *Col.* 901
of those fearfull *women* none durst rize. . . . . I. iii. 19. 2
Amongst these mightie men were *wemen* mixt, ... I. v. 50. 1
Proud *wemen*, vaine, forgetfull of their yoke: . . . . I. v. 50. 2
the dew time In which the wombes of *wemen* doe expyre, . I. vii. 9. 7
Most mercilesse of *women*, Wyden hight, ... II. x. 35. 7
wemen wont in warres to beare most sway, ... III. ii. 2. 2
When the two fearefull *wemen* saw, ... III. iii. 50. 6
Bards tell of many *wemen* valorous, ... III. iii. 54. 4
That whylome wont in *wemen* to appeare? . . . . III. iv. 1. 2
The love of *women* not to entertaine; . . . . III. iv. 26. 2
What wonder then if one, of *women* all, did mis? . . . . III. ix. 2. 9
Had thousand *women* of their love beraft, ... IV. ii. 10. 5
on the spoile of *women* he doth live, ... IV. vii. 12. 5
Seaven *women* by him slaine, and eaten clene: . . . . IV. vii. 13. 5
Great God of men and *women*, ... IV. x. 47. 7
Joy on those warlike *women*, ... IV. xi. 22. 1
Yet was admired much of fooles, *women*, and boys. . . . . V. ii. 30. 9
he plainely then descride To be a troupe of *women*, ... V. iv. 21. 8
vertuous *women* wisely understand, ... V. v. 25. 7
Yet did she not lament with loude alew, As *women* wont, . . V. vi. 13. 9
Not with amaze, as *women* wonted bee, ... V. vii. 25. 2
The liberty of *women* did repeale, ... V. vii. 42. 5
not, as *women* wont, in dolefull fit She was dismayd, ... V. viii. 45. 6
Ay me, that ever guyle in *women* was invented! . . . . V. xi. 50. 9
As *women* wont their guilefull wits to guyde, ... VI. vi. 43. 2
often called art Of *women* in their smart; . . . . *Epith.* 395
Womenkind. *See* **Womankind.**
Women's. lifting up her brave heroick thought Bove *womens* weaknes, ... *Ti.* 110

Women's—*Continued.*
Wringing her hands, in *wemens* pitteous wise, . . . I. i. 50. 7
O! who does know the bent of *womens* fantasy? . . . I. iv. 24. 9
his looser life . . . joyd weake *wemens* hearts to tempt, . . . I. iv. 26. 4
cryes, The last vaine helpe of *wemens* great distresse, . . . I. vi. 6. 3
Whose like in *womens* witt he never knew; . . . I. vi. 31. 2
O famous moniment of *womens* prayse! . . . II. x. 56. 1
His mother bad him *wemens* love to hate, . . . III. iv. 27. 7
not as other *wemens* commune brood . . . III. vi. 5. 6
nor with commune food, As other *wemens* babes, . . . III. vi. 5. 9
feeds on *wemens* flesh as others feede on gras. . . . III. vii. 22. 9
that faire Maide, the flowre of *wemens* pride; . . . III. vii. 31. 5
To stirre and roll them like to *womens* eyes: . . . III. viii. 7. 4
all the wyles of *wemens* wits knew passing well. . . . III. viii. 8. 9
So readie rype to ill ill *wemens* counsels bee! . . . III. x. 11. 9
phantasies In wavering *wemens* witt, . . . III. xii. 26. 4
Confusd with *wemens* cries and shouts of boyes, . . . IV. iii. 37. 8
wemens love did from his hart expell, . . . IV. xi. 5. 3
his mothers former charge Gainst *womens* love, . . . IV. xii. 14. 6
warned him of *womens* love beware, . . . IV. xii. 27. 2
That he of *womens* hands so base a death should dy. . . . V. iv. 22. 9
to proude oppression Of *womens* powre, . . . V. iv. 26. 5
of warlike armes despoile, And cloth in *womens* weedes: . . . V. iv. 31. 4
Unknowen perill of bold *womens* pride. . . . V. iv. 38. 6
Thereto adde art, even *womens* witty trade, . . . V. v. 49. 5
To th' insolent commaund of *womens* will; . . . V. vi. 1. 4
he, at first or last, was trapt in *womens* snare. . . . V. vi. 1. 9
They doe thy love forlorne in *womens* thraldome see. . . . V. vii. 21. 9
Such wondrous powre hath *wemens* faire aspect . . . V. viii. 2. 8
sith of *wemens* labours thou hast charge, . . . *Epith.* 383
For she the daughters of all *wemens* race, . . . doth excell, . . . *H.H.B.* 205

Won. *See* **Wan.**
spoile, Which she had *wonne* from all the world . . . *Ro.* xxii. 7
I *wonne* her with a gyrdle of gelt, . . . *S.C.* F. 65
whether he *woon* beside Faire Xanthus . . . *Gn.* 18
who shall judge the wager *wonne* or lost? . . . *S.C.* Au. 44
twentie thou hast *wonne:* . . . *Hub.* 530
Thou hast it *wonne,* for it is of franke gift, . . . *Hub.* 531
after he had *wonne* th' Assyrian foe, . . . *Hub.* 751
Romane Victors, which it *wonne* of yore; . . . *Ti.* 38
he that river for his daughter *wonne:* . . . *Col.* 125
this same world where we do *wone?'* . . . *Col.* 307
there is not her *won;* . . . *Col.* 521
Armory, Wherein ye have great glory *wonne* this day, . . . I. i. 27. 6
Both seemde to win, and both seemde *won* to bee, . . . I. ii. 37. 6
Disdaind to loose the meed he *wonne* in fray; . . . I. iv. 39. 8
hath to thee *wonne* Great pains, . . . I. v. 43. 8
They, . . . Are *wonne* with pitty and unwonted ruth; . . . I. vi. 12. 7
He had in armes abroad *wonne* muchell fame, . . . I. vi. 20. 5
Her children deare, whom he away had *wonne:* . . . I. vi. 27. 7
wonne from death, she bad him tellen plaine . . . I. vi. 37. 7
he the stoutest knight that ever *wonne?'* . . . I. vi. 39. 2
'Not far away,' (quoth he) 'he hence doth *wonne,* . . . I. vi. 39. 7
fort . . . will at last be *wonne* with battrie long, . . . I. ix. 11. 3
'How may a man,' . . . 'with idle speach Be *wonne* . . . I. ix. 31. 2
nor would for gold or fee Be *wonne* . . . I. x. 43. 7
by her helpe the top at last he *wonne.* . . . I. x. 47. 9
when thou famous victory hast *wonne,* . . . I. x. 60. 5
he hath great glory *wonne,* . . . II. i. 19. 9
you a Saint with Saints your seat have *wonne:* . . . II. i. 32. 5
where vile Acrasia does *wonne;* . . . II. i. 51. 2
Till I that false Acrasia have *wonne;* . . . II. ii. 44. 6
I that Lady to my spouse had *wonne;* . . . II. iv. 21. 2
th' one (said shee) Bycause he *wonne;* . . . II. v. 19. 5
the other, because hee Was *wonne.* . . . II. v. 19. 6
That hath so many haughty conquests *wonne?* . . . II. v. 35. 8
where hast thou thy *wonne,* . . . II. vii. 20. 3
Who, with his wisedom *won,* him streight did choose . . . II. x. 37. 8
He Easterland subdewd, and Denmarke *wonne,* . . . II. x. 41. 3
not firme land, nor any certein *wonne,* . . . II. xii. 11. 4
Where daungers dwelt, and perils most did *wonne,* . . . III. i. 3. 2
they honour ever *wonne,* . . . III. i. 3. 7
when shee mote not thereunto be *wonne,* . . . III. i. 52. 6
Doe many famous knightes and Ladies *wonne,* . . . III. ii. 8. 2
great worth and worship may be *wonne;* . . . III. ii. 8. 4
To make his *wonne,* low underneath the ground, . . . III. iii. 7. 6
the crowne, which they from Britons *wonne* . . . III. iii. 46. 2
whereas he did *wonne,* . . . III. iv. 20. 8
How that a noble hunteresse did *wonne,* . . . III. v. 27. 6
in the same did *wonne* some living wight. . . . III. vii. 5. 5
In hope unto my pleasure to have *won;* . . . III. vii. 59. 8
To steale away that I with blowes have *wonne,* . . . III. viii. 17. 2
There was his *wonne;* . . . III. viii. 37. 8
frock, which she did *won* To tucke about her short . . . III. ix. 21. 3
was soone *wonne* his malice to relent, . . . III. ix. 25. 3
Where wearie wandring they long time did *wonne,* . . . III. ix. 48. 7
had from death to life him newly *wonne.* . . . III. x. 33. 4
by no meanes would to his will be *wonne,* . . . III. x. 51. 8
chose emongst the jolly Satyres still to *wonne.* . . . III. x. 51. 9
brave exploits which great Heroes *wonne,* . . . IV. Pr. 3. 4
he hated . . . because his love he *wonne* by right: . . . IV. i. 39. 6
So hast thou to thy selfe false honour often *wonne.'* . . . IV. i. 44. 9
This hand her *wonne,* this hand shall her defend.' . . . IV. ii. 14. 6
Ne which of them did winne, ne which were *wonne.* . . . IV. iii. 36. 7
Which Ferrau late from Braggadochio *wonne:* . . . IV. iv. 8. 2
Whom formerly he had in battell *wonne,* . . . IV. iv. 8. 7
still the Knights of Maidenhead the better *wonne;* . . . IV. iv. 38. 9
which of those Knights . . . had the wager *wonne:* . . . IV. v. 7. 2
That bore the Hebene speare, as *wonne* in fight. . . . IV. v. 20. 5
by him in battell *wonne* long sens: . . . IV. v. 23. 7

Won—*Continued.*
doe you here within this forrest *wonne,* . . . IV. vi. 5. 2
wonne her will to suffer him depart; . . . IV. vi. 43. 2
to weet who there did *wonne;* . . . IV. vii. 42. 6
to repaire Unto his *wonne,* . . . IV. viii. 5. 3
Where was her *won,* and how he mote her find. . . . IV. viii. 22. 4
eke the famous prize of beauty from them *wonne.* . . . IV. ix. 28. 9
Through many perils *wonne,* and many fortunes waide. . . . IV. ix. 38. 9
this shield of love I late have *wonne,* . . . IV. x. 3. 2
had never *wonne* Mongst men of worth, . . . IV. x. 53. 7
By whom those old Heroes *wonne* such fame; . . . IV. xi. 13. 2
also those which *wonne* in th' azure sky: . . . IV. xii. 1. 4
all the West with equall conquest *wonne,* . . . V. i. 2. 7
A cursed cruell Sarazin doth *wonne,* . . . V. ii. 4. 6
yet little lost or *wonne:* . . . V. iii. 6. 7
For ought or nought be *wonne* unto her will, . . . V. iv. 30. 6
if she him *wonne* in fight. . . . V. v. 23. 9
all the wayes she sought his love for to have *wonne:* . . . V. v. 45. 9
hath he lost or *wun?'* . . . V. vi. 9. 3
I Doe serve a Queene that not far hence doth *wone,* . . . V. viii. 16. 7
There let her *wonne,* . . . V. ix. 2. 1
ny Unto the rocke where was the villains *won:* . . . V. ix. 8. 2
th' actours *won* the meede meet for their crymes. . . . V. ix. 42. 5
After that them in battell he had *wonne:* . . . V. x. 30. 6
hard preased in betweene, And entraunce *wonne:* . . . V. x. 37. 7
Where curteous Knights and Ladies most did *won* . . . VI. i. 1. 8
That in these woods . . . dost *wonne,* . . . VI. ii. 25. 2
As by thy worth thou worthily hast *wonne,* . . . VI. ii. 25. 7
These goodly gilden armes which I have *won* . . . VI. ii. 33. 9
In which a worthy auncient Knight did *wonne:* . . . VI. ii. 48. 8
to the Castle rid, Where was his *won:* . . . VI. iii. 37. 4
A salvage man, which in those woods did *wonne,* . . . VI. iv. 2. 2
And by good fortune the plaine champion *wonne:* . . . VI. iv. 26. 3
he grace and glory *wonne* alwaies, . . . VI. vi. 4. 4
The spoiles of Princes hang'd which were in battel *won.* . . . VI. viii. 42. 9
The glorie of the great mongst whom I *won,* . . . VI. ix. 28. 2
Gave it to Coridon, and said he *wonne* it well. . . . VI. ix. 44. 9
He backe returned to his rusticke *wonne,* . . . VI. x. 32. 2
what befell her in that theevish *wonne,* . . . VI. x. 44. 8
The readie way unto that theevish *wonne,* . . . VI. xi. 35. 2
So led this Knight his captyve with like conquest *wonne.* . . . VI. xii. 35. 9
Have *wonne* the Empire of the Heavens bright; . . . VII. vi. 33. 7
The harder *wonne,* the firmer will abide. . . . *Am.* vi. 4
to see a beast so wyld, So goodly *wonne,* . . . *Am.* lxvii. 14

Wond. *See* **Wonned.**

Wonder. I start in sodaine *wonder.* . . . *Bel.*[1] xi. 14
I wakte in sudden *wonder.* . . . *Bel.*[2] xv. 14
Makes the world *wonder* what they from thee reft. . . . *Ro.* xiii. 14
The huge Leviathan, dame Natures *wonder,* . . . *Van.* v. 6
wondren at bright Argus blazing eye; . . . *S.C.* O. 32
For *wonder* of the world, long in me lasted, . . . *Ti.* 118
The worlds late *wonder,* and the heavens new joy; . . . *Ti.* 303
'Such one Mausolus made, the worlds great *wonder,* . . . *Ti.* 414
To be a *wonder* to all age ensuing, . . . *Ti.* 552
thy selfe thou mak'st us more to *wonder,* . . . *Col.* 354
They, in . . . *wonder* of her beautie soverayne, . . . I. vi. 12. 6
wonder was to heare her goodly speach: . . . I. x. 19. 7
No *wonder* if he wondred at the sight, . . . I. xi. 35. 2
Ne *wonder;* for her own deare loved knight . . . Did *wonder* I. xii. 23. 6, 8
He *wonder* would much more; . . . II. Pr. 3. 9
into diverse doubt his wavering *wonder* clove. . . . II. ii. 3. 9
with *wonder* all the way Did feed his eyes, . . . II. vii. 24. 3
themselves withdraw To *wonder* at the sight; . . . II. vii. 37. 4
abasht he was Through fear and *wonder* . . . II. viii. 7. 2
how great *wonder* would your thoughts devoure, . . . II. ix. 3. 8
with rare delight And gazing *wonder* . . . II. ix. 33. 3
Great *wonder* had the knight . . . II. ix. 41. 8
'Why *wonder* yee, . . . II. ix. 43. 6
Ne *wonder* then, if that he were depriv'd . . . II. ix. 57. 4
all the world with *wonder* overspred; . . . II. x. 2. 6
wonder of antiquity long stopt his speach. . . . II. x. 68. 9
His *wonder* far exceeded reasons reach, . . . II. xi. 40. 1
Ne *wonder,* if these did the knight appall; . . . II. xii. 25. 6
the *wonder* of her beames bright, . . . III. Pr. 4. 8
wonder was to heare their trim consort. . . . III. i. 40. 6
'Forthy great *wonder* were it, . . . III. ii. 10. 1
who does *wonder,* that has red the Towre . . . III. ii. 20. 2
Wonder it is to see in diverse mindes . . . III. v. 1. 1
Ye *wonder* how this noble Damozell . . . III. vi. 1. 2
They were through *wonder* nigh of sence berev'd, . . . III. vi. 27. 5
What *wonder* then if one, of women all, did mis? . . . III. ix. 2. 9
With *wonder* of her beauty fed their hongry vew. . . . III. ix. 23. 9
it a *wonder* of the world is song In forreine landes; . . . III. ix. 45. 7
What *wonder* then, if she were likewise carried? . . . III. x. 9. 9
Ne seeing could her *wonder* satisfie, . . . III. xi. 49. 7
The warlike Mayd . . . Did greatly *wonder;* . . . III. xi. 53. 3
Do greatly stand amaz'd at such unwonted *wonder.* . . . IV. ii. 16. 9
fild the lookers on attonce with ruth and *wonder.* . . . IV. iii. 15. 9
Well mote ye *wonder* how that noble Knight, . . . IV. iii. 23. 1
(that *wonder* is to tell) . . . IV. iii. 39. 1
Some laught for sport, some did for *wonder* shout, . . . IV. iii. 41. 8
some, that would seeme wise, their *wonder* turnd to dout. . . . IV. iii. 41. 9
Wonder it is that sudden change to see: . . . IV. iii. 49. 2
Ne certes *wonder,* for no powre of man Could bide . . . IV. iv. 46. 3
No *wonder* then . . . So many Ladies sought, . . . IV. v. 6. 3
All that her saw with *wonder* ravisht weare, . . . IV. v. 14. 5
of his *wonder* made religion, . . . IV. vi. 22. 3
The Prince did *wonder* much, yet could not ghesse . . . IV. vii. 45. 2
Such mortall malice *wonder* was to see . . . IV. ix. 27. 6
Ne *wonder;* . . . V. Pr. 4. 6

Wonder—*Continued.*
all men stood amaz'd, and at his might did *wonder*. . . . . . V. iii. 8. 9
Are rapt with *wonder* and with rare affright. . . . . V. iii. 19. 7
all men *wonder* at her colours pride; . . . . V. iii. 25. 4
Not so great *wonder* and astonishment . . . . V. vii. 39. 1
Ne to their force gave way, that was great *wonder;* . . . . V. x. 35. 3
his hart was inly child . . . and his thought with *wonder* fild. . VI. ii. 4. 9
oft rejoyce, and oft for *wonder* shout, ... VI. ix. 8. 7
what through *wonder,* and what through delight, ... VI. xi. 13. 7
who them sees would *wonder* at their fray, ... VI. xi. 17. 7
The *wonder* that my wit cannot endite. . . . . *Am.* iii. 14
That *wonder* is how I should live a jot, ... *Am.* lvii. 6
Rather then envy, let them *wonder* at her, ... *Am.* lxxxiv. 7
Let the world chose to envy or to *wonder*. . . . . *Am.* lxxxiv. 14
Much more then would ye *wonder* at that sight, ... *Epith.* 188
Then would ye *wonder,* . . . . *Epith.* 202
rapt with *wonder* of their famous praise, ... *Com. Son.* iii. 5
What *wonder* then, if with such rage extreme . . . . *H.L.* 117
In th' only *wonder* of her selfe to rest, ... *H.H.B.* 238
a noble Peer, . . . the Worlds wide *wonder,* . . . . *Proth.* 146
Wondered. Much *wondred* I to see so faire a wall: . . . . . . *Bel.*^{2} xiv. 9
Thereat I *wondred* much, till wondring more . . . . *Col.* 264
halfe ashamed *wondred* at the sight: . . . . I. iii. 38. 6
He *wondred* at her wisedome hevenly rare, ... I. vi. 31. 1
they . . . *wondred* at so fowle deformed wight. . . . . I. viii. 49. 2
The knight much *wondred* at his suddeine wit, ... I. ix. 41. 1
Whereat he *wondred* much, and gan enquere, ... I. x. 56. 6
No wonder if he *wondred* at the sight, ... I. xi. 35. 2
wondred at his breathlesse hasty mood: . . . . I. xii. 25. 3
wondred in his minde what mote that Monster make. . . . . II. iii. 18. 9
The knight at his great boldnesse *wondered;* . . . . II. iv. 39. 6
Whose bounty more then might, yet both, he *wondered*. . . . II. v. 14. 9
much he *wondred* at that uncouth sight: . . . . II. vi. 43. 2
he *wondred* sore To see Pyrochles there . . . . II. vi. 48. 6
The warlike Elfe much *wondred* at this tree, ... II. vii. 56. 1
wondred at his endlesse exercise: . . . . II. ix. 59. 2
The *wondred* Argo, which . . . through the Euxine . . . . . II. xii. 44. 8
Much *wondred* Guyon at the fayre aspect . . . . II. xii. 53. 1
wondred whence so sumptuous guize Might be maintaynd, . . III. i. 33. 8
Whereat she *wondred* much, ... III. iv. 18. 7
Stood gaping at their gate, and *wondred* them to see. . . . . III. iv. 32. 9
They *wondred* much; and shortly understood . . . . III. v. 38. 3
Wondred to see her belly so upblone, ... III. vi. 9. 8
both at her, and each at other *wondered*. . . . . III. vii. 14. 9
Much *wondred* all men what or whence he came, ... IV. iv. 42. 1
all men *wondred* at the uncouth sight, ... IV. v. 17. 1
at which so suddain case He *wondred* much. . . . . IV. vi. 3. 6
wondred much at his so selcouth case; . . . . IV. viii. 14. 2
At which he *wondred* much when all those signes he fond. . . IV. viii. 21. 9
Thus gazing long at them much *wondred* he: . . . . IV. ix. 11. 8
wondred at their impacable stoure, ... IV. ix. 22. 4
Wondred Agave, Poris, and Nesaea, ... IV. xi. 49. 6
She *wondred* at the workemans passing skill, ... V. vii. 5. 6
even she her selfe much *wondered* At such a chaunge, ... V. vii. 13. 7
wondred much at Cupids judg'ment wise, ... VI. viii. 25. 2
Much *wondred* Calidore at this straunge sight, ... VI. x. 17. 1
seeing it much *wondred* at the sight: . . . . VI. xii. 37. 6
Were much afraid, and *wondred* at that sight; . . . . VII. vi. 14. 5
He *wondred* much, and feared her no lesse: . . . . VII. vi. 17. 5
Wonderful. in her sex more *wonderfull* and rare. . . . . . . *Col.* 491
It is most straunge and *wonderfull* . . . . VI. v. 29. 8
kindle fyre by *wonderfull* devyse! . . . . *Am.* xxx. 12
Wondering. *Wondring* what mister wight he was, ... *Hub.* 671
wondring more And more, ... *Col.* 264
'By *wondring* at thy Cynthiaes praise, ... *Col.* 353
her *wondring* eye And greedy eares . . . . III. ix. 52. 6
Who *wondring* much at that so sodaine fit, ... IV. ix. 29. 6
wondring long at those so straunge events, ... VI. xii. 20. 7
To reade my fault, and, *wondring* at my flame, ... *H.H.L.* 16
Their *wondring* eyes to fill; . . . . *Proth.* 59
Wonderment. Of beauties Queene, the worlds sole *wonder-ment,* *Ded.Son.*xvii.6
gazd upon with gaping *wonderment;* . . . . I. xii. 9. 5
whose beauties *wonderment* She lesse esteem'd . . . . IV. v. 20. 8
So stolen from their fancies *wonderment* . . . . V. iii. 26. 5
It ravisht is with fancies *wonderment:* . . . . *Am.* iii. 12
When I behold that beauties *wonderment,* . . . . *Am.* xxiv. 1
admire such worlds rare *wonderment;* . . . . *Am.* lxix. 12
The rest be works of natures *wonderment:* . . . . *Am.* lxxxi. 13
Wonderments. Seven Romane Hils, the worlds Seven *Wonder-ments.* . . . . *Ro.* ii. 14
Wonders. the heaven it selfe with her wide *wonders* fill. . . . *Ro.* xxix. 8
Far off he *wonders* what them makes so glad; . . . . I. vi. 15. 1
Wyde *wonders* over all . . . weren told, ... I. viii. 3. 7
To proofe of passing *wonders* hath full often usd: . . . . . II. ii. 5. 9
Who *wonders* not, that reades so wonderous worke? . . . . . III. ii. 20. 1
oft hath *wonders* donne.' . . . . III. ii. 36. 6
In vaine seekes *wonders* out of Magick spell.' . . . . III. iii. 17. 7
One of the worlds seven *wonders* sayd to bee, ... IV. x. 30. 4
That workes such *wonders* in the minds of men; . . . . . . *H.B.* 86
many *wonders* doe they reede To their conceipt, ... *H.B.* 246
those wits, the *wonders* of their dayes, ... *H.H.B.* 218
Wondren. *See* **Wonder.**
Wondrous. With *wondrous* signes . . . . *Rev.* i. 13
Of *wondrous* length, and streight proportion, ... *Van.* vii. 2
Throughly rooted, and of *wonderous* hight; . . . . *S.C.* F. 107
His *wonderous* weight made the ground to quake, ... *S.C.* F. 219
wondrous cares . . . full sore opprest; . . . . *Gn.* 642
'it likes me *wondrous* well; . . . . *Hub.* 95
(said the Ape, as sighing *wondrous* sad) . . . . *Hub.* 368

Wondrous—*Continued.*
the charge is *wondrous* great, ... *Hub.* 431
the Ape in *wondrous* stomack woxe, ... *Hub.* 1103
Where doth she all that *wondrous* welth nowe hide? . . . . . *Ti.* 75
Of *wondrous* powre, and of exceeding stature, ... *Ti.* 534
wrought by *wonderous* device . . . . *Mui.* 74
all the Gods, which saw his *wondrous* might, ... *Mui.* 318
With excellent device and *wondrous* slight, ... *Mui.* 330
wondrous wroth, for that so foule despight, ... *Col.* 148
all the ornaments of *wondrous* wit, ... *Col.* 189
her owne great mynd, And *wondrous* worth, ... *Col.* 365
all that therein *wondrous* doth appeare. . . . . *Col.* 842
with *wondrous* skill, Hast Cupid selfe depainted . . . . . . *Col.* 897
The maker selfe, for all his *wondrous* witt, ... I. i. 45. 6
Who, thereat *wondrous* wroth, ... I. ii. 19. 1
In charmes and magick to have *wondrous* might, ... I. iii. 38. 8
she was *wondrous* faire, ... I. iv. 10. 9
he wexed *wondrous* glad. . . . . I. iv. 30. 9
The Sarazin was stout and *wondrous* strong, ... I. v. 7. 1
a Cave ywrought by *wondrous* art, ... I. v. 36. 5
Such *wondrous* science in mans witt to rain . . . . I. v. 40. 1
From lawlesse lust by *wondrous* grace . . . . I. vi. Arg.
A *wondrous* way it for this Lady wrought, ... I. vi. 7. 3
His tayle was stretched out in *wondrous* length, ... I. vii. 18. 1
stone Of *wondrous* worth, and eke of *wondrous* mights, ... I. vii. 30. 2
your griefe is *wondrous* great; . . . . I. vii. 40. 2
wondrous great griefe groneth in my spright, ... I. vii. 40. 3
wondrous anguish in his hart it wrought, ... I. viii. 15. 8
gore, Which flowed from his wounds in *wondrous* store. . . . I. viii. 24. 5
wondrous faith . . . Was firmest fixt in myne extremest case. . I. ix. 17. 4
liquor . . . Of *wondrous* worth, and vertue excellent, ... I. ix. 19. 4
A worke of *wondrous* grace, and hable soules to save. . . . . I. ix. 19. 9
feeling *wondrous* comfort in her weaker eld: . . . . I. x. 8. 9
added wordes of *wondrous* might. . . . . I. x. 24. 6
Of *wondrous* beauty, and of bounty rare, ... I. x. 30. 2
Adornd with gemmes and owches *wondrous* fayre, ... I. x. 31. 6
The *wondrous* workmanship of Gods owne mould, ... I. x. 42. 6
wondrous quick and persaunt was his spright, ... I. x. 47. 5
to increase his *wondrous* greatnes more, ... I. xi. 8. 8
more *wondrous* . . . in either jaw Three ranckes of yron teeth I. xi. 13. 1
So *wondrous* force from hand of living wight; . . . . I. xi. 17. 8
The griefe thereof him *wondrous* sore diseasd, ... I. xi. 38. 8
nought so *wondrous* puissaunce might sustaine: . . . . I. xi. 43. 5
with words, and weedes, of *wondrous* might, ... II. i. 52. 3
wondrous strong by nature, ... II. ii. 12. 9
Wondrous great prowesse . . . He shewd that day, ... II. ii. 25. 3
all were they *wondrous* loth, ... II. ii. 34. 2
the Scarcrow wexed *wondrous* prowd, ... II. iii. 7. 1
So passing persant, and so *wondrous* bright, ... II. iii. 23. 4
with her *wondrous* beauty ravisht quight, ... II. iii. 42. 4
A knight of *wondrous* powre and great assay, ... II. iv. 40. 6
He wexed *wondrous* wroth, ... II. iv. 45. 2
wondrous glad, out of the path Did lightly leape, ... II. v. 18. 7
Gave *wondrous* great contentment to the knight, ... II. vi. 8. 2
Her face right *wondrous* faire did seeme to bee, ... II. vii. 45. 1
man, Of *wondrous* beauty and of freshest yeares, ... II. viii. 5. 2
he wexed *wondrous* woe; . . . . II. viii. 53. 4
by your *wondrous* worth and warlike feat . . . . II. ix. 6. 3
To vew her Castles other *wondrous* frame: . . . . II. ix. 44. 7
This parts great workemanship and *wondrous* powre, ... II. ix. 47. 2
He now was growne right wise and *wondrous* sage: . . . . . II. ix. 54. 5
Ensample of his *wondrous* faculty, ... II. x. 26. 1
wondrous wit to menage high affayres, ... II. x. 37. 2
All were the wownd so wide and *wonderous* . . . . II. xi. 38. 2
Such *wondrous* powre did in that staffe appeare, ... II. xii. 40. 8
wondrous things concerning our welfare, ... II. xii. 47. 5
A worke of rare device and *wondrous* wit. . . . . III. i. 34. 6
wondrous myrrhour, by which she In love with him did fall. . III. ii. Arg.
The royall Maid woxe inly *wondrous* glad, ... III. ii. 11. 1
Who wonders not, that reades so *wonderous* worke? . . . . . III. ii. 20. 1
wondrous massy and assured sownd, ... III. ii. 25. 3
I in my fathers *wondrous* mirrhour saw, ... III. ii. 38. 7
Which the late world admyres for *wondrous* moniments. . . . III. iii. 2. 9
Deepe busied bout worke of *wondrous* end, ... III. iii. 14. 7
wondrous ruth to all that shall it heare: . . . . III. v. 6. 8
he *wondrous* pensive grew in minde, ... III. v. 12. 5
through conquest of your *wondrous* might, ... III. v. 53. 4
(a *wondrous* thing to say) . . . . III. vi. 26. 8
wondrous gladnes to her hart applyde. . . . . III. viii. 2. 9
She there deviz'd a *wondrous* worke to frame, ... III. viii. 5. 2
wondrous sore Thereat displeasd they were, ... III. viii. 52. 5
great amazement of so *wondrous* sight; . . . . III. ix. 23. 2
Another plant, that raught to *wondrous* hight, ... III. ix. 47. 7
His halfen eye he wiled *wondrous* well, ... III. x. 5. 3
The foolish man thereat woxe *wondrous* blith, ... III. x. 33. 1
he them both outran a *wondrous* space, ... III. xi. 5. 7
O *wondrous* skill! and sweet wit of the man, ... III. xi. 32. 3
Wondrous delight it was . . . . III. xi. 34. 6
In his divine resemblance *wondrous* lyke: . . . . III. xi. 40. 2
That *wondrous* sight faire Britomart amazd, ... III. xi. 49. 6
everie looke was coy and *wondrous* quaint, ... IV. i. 5. 7
with *wondrous* griefe of mynd And shame, ... IV. i. 37. 6
wondrous chast of life, yet lov'd of Knights and Lords. . . . IV. ii. 35. 9
By *wondrous* skill and many hidden wayes . . . . IV. ii. 47. 3
wondrous paine, that did the more enhaunce His haughtie courage . . . . IV. iii. 8. 7
smote the other with so *wondrous* might, ... IV. iii. 30. 2
The charet decked was in *wondrous* wize . . . . IV. iii. 38. 6
With which they wrought such *wondrous* marvels there, . . . IV. iv. 29. 3
His *wondrous* worth declared in all mens view, ... IV. iv. 37. 5

Wondrous—*Continued.*
she *wondrous* deeds of arms atchieved, . . . IV. iv. 46. 6
as seeming *wondrous* glad, . . . IV. vii. 24. 8
Cast into sundry shapes by *wondrous* skill, . . . IV. x. 15. 6
as als' of *wondrous* Bath, . . . IV. xi. 31. 8
wondrous sholes which may of none be red. . . . IV. xii. 2. 5
with magnificke might and *wondrous* wit . . . V. Pr. 11. 3
they hoped to have got great good, And *wondrous* riches . . . V. ii. 51. 7
She heard a *wondrous* noise below the hall: . . . V. vi. 27. 5
though *wondrous* wroth, and inly burning . . . V. vi. 31. 1
There did appeare unto her heavenly spright A *wondrous* vision, V. vii. 12. 8
Could ought on earth so *wondrous* change have wrought, . . . V. vii. 40. 6
Such *wondrous* powre hath wemens faire aspect . . . V. viii. 2. 8
So faire a creature and so *wondrous* bold, . . . V. viii. 12. 7
Is *wondrous* strong and hewen farre under ground, . . . V. ix. 6. 3
making troublous din And *wondrous* noyse, . . . V. ix. 23. 4
She humbly thankt him for that *wondrous* grace, . . . V. xi. 18. 1
Yet *wondrous* faire she was, . . . V. xi. 60. 6
both were *wondrous* practicke in that play, . . . VI. i. 36. 3
a *wondrous* chaunce his reskue wrought, . . . VI. iii. 51. 6
As he the art of words knew *wondrous* well, . . . VI. vi. 6. 3
Through tempering of her words and lookes by *wondrous* skill. VI. vi. 41. 9
deckt with *wondrous* giftes of natures grace, . . . VI. vii. 28. 5
wondrous joy felt in her spirits thrall: . . . VI. xi. 44. 5
Thinks of her Dairy to make *wondrous* gaine, . . . VII. vi. 48. 2
Her garment was so bright and *wondrous* sheene, . . . VII. vii. 7. 3
delight Of his celestiall song, and Musicks *wondrous* might. . VII. vii. 12. 9
Yet are they chang'd (by other *wondrous* slights) . . . VII. vii. 25. 4
wondrous beauty fit to kindle love; . . . VII. vii. 45. 3
At *wondrous* sight of so celestiall hew. . . . *Am.* iii. 8
What *wondrous* vertue is contaynd in you, . . . *Am.* vii. 2
Yet many *wondrous* things there are beside: . . . *Am.* xvii. 8
The *wondrous* triumphs of my great god-hed: . . . *H.L.* 18
The *wondrous* cradle of thine infancie, . . . *H.L.* 51
The *wondrous* matter of my fyre to prayse. . . . *H.B.* 7
That *wondrous* Paterne, wheresoere it bee, . . . *H.B.* 36
Hath white and red in it such *wondrous* powre, . . . *H.B.* 71
shew what *wondrous* powre your beauty hath, . . . *H.B.* 286
Yet form'd by *wondrous* skill, and by His might, . . . *H.H.L.* 107
images . . . Whose *wondrous* beauty, breathing sweet delights . *H.H.B.* 4
All which are made with *wondrous* wise respect, . . . *H.H.B.* 34
With the great glorie of that *wondrous* light . . . *H.H.B.* 176
Whereof such *wondrous* pleasures they conceave, . . . *H.H.B.* 256

Wondrously. his wound that *wondrously* did bleed! . . . *As.* 132
A looking glasse, right *wondrously* aguiz'd, . . . III. ii. 18. 8
wondrously begotten, and begonne . . . III. iii. 13. 3
wondrously they were begot and bred . . . III. vi. 6. 1
He was therewith right *wondrously* dismayd; . . . IV. vi. 24. 3
So *wondrously* now chaung'd from that she was afore. . . . VI. i. 46. 9
How *wondrously* would he her face commend, . . . *H.H.B.* 222

Wone. *See* **Won.**

Woning. With him to wend unto his *wonning* neare; . . . VI. iv. 13. 3

Wonned. *See* **Wont.**
thereto aye *wonned* to repayre . . . *S.C.* F. 119
wonned not the great God Pan Upon mount Olivet, . . . *S.C.* Jul. 49
there *wonned* a wicked Wolfe, . . . *S.C.* S. 184
only *woond* in fields and forests here:' . . . *Col.* 774
he which *wonned* there, . . . II. ix. 52. 1
she came where *wonned* his Belphebe faire. . . . IV. viii. 8. 9
therein *wonned* twenty valiant Knights, . . . IV. x. 7. 6
wonned there where now Yorke people dwell; . . . IV. xi. 37. 5
comming down to seeke them where they *wond,* . . . V. vi. 35. 6
wonned in a rocke not farre away, . . . V. ix. 4. 7
this land, where I have *wond* thus long . . . VI. ii. 30. 8

Wonneth. The fairest wight that *wonneth* under skie, . . . II. vii. 49. 2
he ne *wonneth* in one certeine stead, . . . III. ii. 14. 3
He *wonneth* in the land of Fayeree, . . . III. iii. 26. 3
'She *wonneth* in the forrest there before.' . . . III. x. 38. 3

Wonning. *See* **Woning.**

Wons. *wonnes* in Faerie lond: . . . II. iii. 18. 4
Here *wonnes* Acrasia, whom we must surprise, . . . II. xii. 69. 8
Wher most she *wonnes* when she on earth does dwell; . . . III. vi. 29. 2
Of all that on this earthly compasse *wonnes;* . . . V. vi. 33. 3
There is a mighty man, which *wonnes* hereby, . . . V. viii. 18. 2

Wont. *See* **Wonned.**
wont . . . The Romane triumphs glorie to behold, . . . *Ro.* xiv. 11
His wings which *wont* the earth to overspredd, . . . *Ro.* xvii. 6
Was *wont* this auncient Citie to adorne, . . . *Ro.* xxix. 7
Wherein the byrds were *wont* to build their bowre, . . . *S.C.* Ja. 32
They *wont* in the wind wagge their wrigle tayles, . . . *S.C.* F. 7
Thy Ewes, that *wont* to have blowen bags, . . . *S.C.* F. 81
to continue their *wont* countenaunce: . . . *S.C.* May 80
thou were *wont* on wastfull hylls to singe, . . . *S.C.* Jun. 50
they dwell (As goteheards *wont*) upon a hill, . . . *S.C.* Jul. 47
wont to make the jolly shepeheards gladde, . . . *S.C.* Au. 9
When holy fathers *wont* to shrieve; . . . *S.C.* Au. 55
in your songs were *wont* to make a part: . . . *S.C.* Au. 154
the fayre flocke thou was *wont* to leade? . . . *S.C.* S. 9
They sayne the world is much war then it *wont,* . . . *S.C.* S. 108
The fatte Oxe, that *wont* ligge in the stal, . . . *S.C.* S. 118
They walke not widely as they were *wont,* . . . *S.C.* S. 158
wont to repayre Unto the flocke, . . . *S.C.* S. 186
ranne out as he was *wont* of yore. . . . *S.C.* S. 221
thou *wont* the shepheards laddes to leade . . . *S.C.* O. 4
The dapper ditties, that I *wont* devise . . . *S.C.* O. 13
Ne *wont* with crabbed care the Muses dwell: . . . *S.C.* O. 101
As thou were *wont,* . . . *S.C.* N. 2
As shee was *wont* in youngth and sommer dayes; . . . *S.C.* N. 20
wont with her to sing and daunce, . . . *S.C.* N. 143
that were *wont* greene bayes to weare, . . . *S.C.* N. 146

Wont—*Continued.*
'I *wont* to raunge amydde the mazie thickette, . . . *S.C.* D. 25
not as I *wont* afore, . . . *S.C.* D. 61
I was *wont* to seeke the honey Bee, . . . *S.C.* D. 67
'To make fine cages . . . was my *wont:* . . . *S.C.* D. 80
which be *wont* t' enrage the restlesse sheepe, . . . *S.C.* D. 89
which be *wont* to worke eternall sleepe. . . . *S.C.* D. 90
that whilome *wont* to frame my pype . . . *S.C.* D. 115
wont to macerate And rend . . . *Gn.* 94
make them seeke for that they *wont* to scorne, . . . *Hub.* 257
not so great, as it was *wont* of yore, . . . *Hub.* 447
(As it was *wont*) . . . *Hub.* 650
As that same Apish crue is *wont* to doo: . . . *Hub.* 731
huckster man, That *wont* provide his necessaries, . . . *Hub.* 926
Of their sweete instruments were *wont* to sound, . . . *T.M.* 20
Were *wont* redoubled Echoes to rebound, . . . *T.M.* 22
wont in chanels cleare To romble gently downe . . . *T.M.* 25
all that els was *wont* to worke delight . . . *T.M.* 37
That *wont* to be the worlds chiefe ornament, . . . *T.M.* 74
learned Impes that *wont* to shoote up still, . . . *T.M.* 75
wont with Comick sock to beautefie The painted Theaters, . . *T.M.* 176
I late was *wont* to raine as Queene, . . . *T.M.* 179
wont to be the glorie of gay wits, . . . *T.M.* 182
wont to wait upon my traine, . . . *T.M.* 196
those sweete wits, which *wont* the like to frame, . . . *T.M.* 203
we, that earst were *wont* in sweet accord . . . *T.M.* 241
those fresh buds, which *wont* so faire to flowre, . . . *T.M.* 249
yong plants, which *wont* with fruit t' abound, . . . *T.M.* 251
with our musick *wont* so oft to ring, . . . *T.M.* 278
Were *wont* so oft their Pastoralls to sing, . . . *T.M.* 280
Such as ye *wont,* . . . *T.M.* 373
Love *wont* to be schoolmaster of my skill, . . . *T.M.* 385
wont the world with famous acts to fill; . . . *T.M.* 430
noble Peeres, whom I was *wont* to raise, . . . *T.M.* 467
the rich fee, which Poets *wont* divide, . . . *T.M.* 471
With which I *wont* the winged words to tie, . . . *T.M.* 548
The sacred lawes therein they *wont* expresse, . . . *T.M.* 561
hir pleasures were *wonte* to lull me asleepe: . . . *U.V.* 13
hir beautie was *wonte* to feede mine eyes: . . . *U.V.* 14
hir sweete Tongue was *wonte* to make me mirth. . . . *U.V.* 15
On which the lordly Faulcon *wont* to towre . . . *Ti.* 128
wont forth to powre Her restles plaints, . . . *Ti.* 131
where the christall Thamis *wont* to slide . . . *Ti.* 134
Were *wont* to play, from all annoyance free, . . . *Ti.* 138
wont his songs to praise: . . . *Ti.* 228
where yong Clarion Was *wont* to solace him, . . . *Mui.* 243
wont full merrilie to pipe and daunce, . . . *D.* 55
wont to feede with finest grasse that grew, . . . *D.* 345
My love . . . that *wont* to be their Starre: . . . *D.* 424
wont, on pipes of oaten reed, Oft times to plaine . . . *As.* Pr. 1
as he was *wont* to doo For her . . . *As.* 39
wont to be with flowers and gyrlonds dight, . . . *As.* 153
heard to sound as she was *wont* on hye, . . . *Col.* 20
still are *wont* most happie states t' annoy: . . . *Col.* 663
Oft from those grave affaires were *wont* abstaine, . . . *Ded. Son.* i. 5
whose famous ofspring The antique Poets *wont* . . . to sing; *Ded. Son.* vi. 5
Ay *wont* in desert darknes to remaine, . . . I. i. 16. 8
the Hermite dewly *wont* to say His holy thinges . . . I. i. 34. 6
Care . . . Who oft is *wont* to trouble gentle Sleepe. . . . I. i. 40. 6
cryes, As still are *wont* t' annoy the walled towne, . . . I. i. 41. 7
What frayes ye, that were *wont* to comfort me affrayd?' . . . I. i. 52. 9
her dwarfe, that *wont* to wait each howre: . . . I. ii. 7. 8
ne *wont* there sound His mery oaten pipe, . . . I. ii. 28. 8
When Witches *wont* to penance for their crime,) . . . I. ii. 40. 5
thrise nine hundred *Aves* she was *wont* to say. . . . I. iii. 13. 9
Wont to robbe churches of their ornaments, . . . I. iii. 17. 2
Ne ever *wont* in field, ne in round lists, to fight: . . . I. iii. 38. 9
wont in charett chace the foming bore: . . . I. v. 37. 2
The sacred Nymph, which therein *wont* to dwell, . . . I. vii. 4. 8
The same to wight he never *wont* disclose, . . . I. vii. 34. 1
The force, which *wont* in two to be disperst, . . . I. viii. 18. 1
men, . . . Both feet and face one way are *wont* to lead. . . . I. viii. 31. 6
people . . . Which in that stately building *wont* to dwell: . . . I. viii. 32. 4
mighty brawned bowrs Were *wont* to rive steele plates, . . . I. viii. 41. 7
Ay *wont* to laugh when them I heard to cry, . . . I. ix. 10. 5
Wont on a staffe his feeble steps to stay, . . . I. x. 5. 7
bitter Penaunce, . . . Was *wont* him once to disple every day: I. x. 27. 2
He cryde, as raging seas are *wont* to rore . . . I. xi. 21. 1
As *wont* ye knightes to seeke adventures wilde, . . . II. i. 50. 6
In fayre defence . . . was *wont* to fight; . . . II. iv. 8. 4
Of whom high Jove *wont* whylome feasted bee; . . . II. vii. 59. 6
More ample spirit then hitherto was *wount* . . . II. x. 1. 6
wemen *wont* in warres to beare most sway, . . . III. ii. 2. 2
I loathed have my life to lead, As Ladies *wont,* . . . III. ii. 6. 7
whylome *wont* (they say) To make his wonne, . . . III. iii. 7. 5
That whylome *wont* in wemen to appeare? . . . III. iv. 1. 2
Are *wont* to cleave unto the lowly clay, . . . III. v. 1. 5
There *wont* fayre Venus often to enjoy . . . III. vi. 46. 1
in vain sheows, that *wont* yong knights bewitch, . . . III. vii. 29. 6
As was his *wont,* in forest and in plaine; . . . III. vii. 30. 3
horse Whereon faire Florimell was *wont* to ride, . . . III. vii. 31. 2
Where she was *wont* her Sprightes to entertaine, . . . III. viii. 4. 4
Ne ever is he *wont* on ought to feed But todes and frogs, . . III. x. 59. 1
erst all entrers *wont* so cruelly to scorch. . . . III. xii. 42. 9
to her bed, which she was *wont* forbeare, . . . IV. i. 15. 8
Such is thy *wont,* that still when any Knight Is weakned, . . IV. i. 44. 7
she, as Fayes are *wont,* in privie place Did spend her dayes, . IV. ii. 44. 8
ghost . . . Did not, as others *wont,* directly fly Unto her rest . IV. iii. 13. 2
Are *wont* . . . To drincke hereof, . . . IV. iii. 44. 5
him selfe thereby to grace, As was his *wont:* . . . IV. iv. 4. 3

Wont—*Continued.*
An huge great speare, such as he *wont* to wield, ... IV. iv. 17. 2
whylome *wont* to be the victors meed; . . . . IV. iv. 31. 3
(as Faeries *wont* report) . . . . IV. v. 3. 6
She with the pleasant Graces *wont* to play. . . . . IV. v. 5. 6
The which he never *wont* to combe, or comely sheare. . . . IV. v. 34. 9
whylome in your minde *wont* to despise them all.' . . . . . IV. vi. 28. 9
In which he *wont* the relickes of his feast . . . to stow: . . . IV. vii. 6. 3
wont to stop the mouth thereof, ... IV. vii. 20. 5
wont with ointment sweet To be embaulm'd, ... IV. vii. 40. 3
mournfull plaint to make, As was her *wont*, ... IV. viii. 9. 7
wont to vanquish God and man, ... IV. viii. 32. 6
in Star-read were *wont* have best insight, ... V. Pr. 8. 2
old Saturne, that was *wont* be best. . . . . V. Pr. 8. 9
To tast of joy, and to *wont* pleasures to retourne. . . . . . V. iii. 1. 9
As was the *wont* of warlike knights of yore, ... V. iii. 32. 3
(as all Knights are *woont*) . . . . V. iv. 29. 1
With his strange weapon, never *wont* in warre, ... V. iv. 44. 2
With which he *wont* to stirre up battailous alarmes. . . . . . V. v. 21. 9
Yet did she not lament with loude alew, As women *wont*, . . V. vi. 13. 9
Which still was *wont* with Artegall remaine; . . . . V. vi. 34. 4
palmes, the which ye *wont* t' embrew In bloud of Kings, . . V. vii. 40. 4
'All times have *wont* safe passage to afford . . . . V. viii. 22. 1
not, as women *wont*, in dolefull fit She was dismayd, ... V. viii. 45. 6
Of which he in faire weather *wont* to take great store. . . . . V. ix. 11. 9
Are *wont* in Princes courts to worke great scath and hindrance: V. ix. 22. 9
whylome *wont* to doe so many quake, ... V. ix. 35. 8
In which she *wont* to harbour happily: . . . . V. x. 18. 6
sunne to shine more bright Then it was *wont*, ... V. x. 20. 9
To whom he *wont* shew all the shame he might, ... V. x. 30. 5
when he his weapon faynd to shift, As he was *wont*, ... V. xi. 7. 7
With which he *wont* to fight to justifie his wrong: . . . . . V. xii. 14. 9
With which he *wont* to launch the salvage hart . . . . VI. ii. 6. 7
the Nymphs . . . to thy sweete lookes repayre, As they are *wont* VI. ii. 25. 4
Whose gealous dread . . . Is *wont* to cut off all . . . . . . VI. ii. 29. 6
Not *wont* on foote with heavy armes to trace, ... VI. iii. 29. 5
having long time, as his daily weed, Them *wont* to weare, . . VI. iv. 19. 5
Was *wont* his howres and holy things to bed; . . . . VI. v. 35. 7
As women *wont* their guilefull wits to guyde, ... VI. vi. 43. 2
his salvage page, that *wont* be prest, ... VI. vii. 19. 5
As he is *wont* at each Saint Valentide, ... VI. vii. 32. 7
wont doe suit and service to his might, ... VI. vii. 34. 2
As they are *wont* in faire sunshynie weather, ... VI. ix. 41. 3
are *wont* to haunt Uppon this hill, ... VI. x. 15. 2
the Graces, that here *wont* to dwell, ... VI. x. 26. 7
were *wount* To skim those coastes . . . . VI. xi. 9. 2
Where *wont* the shepheards oft their pypes resound, ... VI. xi. 26. 8
Which with those gentle shepherds here I *wont* to lead.' . . . VI. xi. 32. 9
Is *wont* to wield the world unto his vow, ... VII. vi. 22. 3
where she was *wont* to space, ... VII. vi. 55. 4
Are *wont* for Princes states to fashion; . . . . VII. vii. 8. 4
backward yode, as Bargemen *wont* to fare . . . . VII. vii. 35. 7
those small forts which ye were *wont* belay: . . . . *Am.* xiv. 6
wont with her bright ray Me to direct, ... *Am.* xxxiv. 5
wont to please Some dainty eares, ... *Am.* xxxviii. 5
hart, that *wont* on your fayre eye To feed his fill, ... *Am.* lxxiii. 7
was *wont* to lead my thoughts astray; . . . . *Am.* lxxxvii. 2
ye that *wont* . . . To reade my fault, ... *H.H.L.* 15
There whylome *wont* the Templer Knights to byde, ... *Proth.* 135
that great Lord, which therein *wont* to dwell, ... *Proth.* 139

Wonted. *See* **Well-wonted.**
doth forbeare His *wonted* songs, ... *S.C.* Ap. 16
My sheepe did leave theyr *wonted* food, ... *S.C.* Au. 73
The earth now lacks her *wonted* light, ... *S.C.* N. 68
shepherds *wonted* solace is extinct. . . . . *S.C.* N. 106
at his *wonted* time in that same place . . . . *Gn.* 249
my late maymed limbs lack *wonted* might . . . . *Hub.* 272
The famous witnesse of our *wonted* praise, ... *T.M.* 274
Doth scorne the pride of *wonted* ornaments: . . . . *T.M.* 544
want the *wonted* sweetnes of thy voice, ... *Ti.* 331
Lift up thy notes unto their *wonted* height, ... *Col.* 390
Weening their *wonted* entrance to have found . . . . I. i. 25. 5
wonted feare of doing ought amis, ... I. i. 49. 2
That may restore you to your *wonted* well?' . . . . I. ii. 43. 7
took her *wonted* way To ronne her timely race, ... I. v. 44. 7
Againe his *wonted* angry weapon proov'd, ... I. viii. 21. 3
'Henceforth, Sir knight, take to you *wonted* strength, ... I. viii. 45. 1
advaunce his broad discoloured brest Above his *wonted* pitch, I. xi. 31. 8
with *wonted* rage he him advaunced neare. . . . . I. xi. 52. 9
If *wonted* force and fortune doe me not much fayl.' . . . . . II. v. 5. 9
nimbly ran her *wonted* course . . . . II. vi. 20. 6
as was her *wonted* guize, ... II. vi. 21. 1
their sweet skill in *wonted* melody; . . . . II. xii. 31. 7
Forceth it swell above his *wonted* mood, ... III. vii. 34. 3
courtly blis and *wonted* happinesse, ... III. viii. 20. 8
now had chang'd her former *wonted* hew; . . . . IV. i. 18. 2
Having through stirring loosd their *wonted* band, ... IV. vi. 20. 2
Gan dight him selfe unto his *wonted* sinne; . . . . IV. vii. 20. 8
as was her *wonted* joy, ... IV. vii. 23. 8
His *wonted* warlike weapons all he broke . . . . IV. vii. 39. 1
Ne ought mote make him change his *wonted* tenor, ... IV. vii. 47. 3
as in his *wonted* wise His doole he made, ... IV. viii. 3. 1
The Prince on foot, not *wonted* so to fare; . . . . IV. viii. 37. 6
about the *wonted* howre, ... IV. viii. 59. 1
All mindlesse of her *wonted* modestie . . . . IV. viii. 63. 3
loath their *wonted* food: . . . . IV. x. 46. 2
in short space his *wonted* chearefull hew Gan fade, ... IV. xii. 20. 1
Not with amaze, as women *wonted* bee, ... V. vii. 25. 2
from flying stay With raynes or *wonted* rule, ... V. viii. 38. 6
with fresh *wonted* grace Dispreds the glorie . . . . V. xii. 13. 5

Wonted—*Continued.*
why she did her *wonted* course forslowe; . . . . VII. vi. 16. 4
leave your *wonted* labors for this day: . . . . *Epith.* 262

Wontest. unlucky Muse, that *wontst* to ease My musing mynd, *S.C.* Ja. 69
wontst the tragick stage for to direct, ... *Mui.* 11

Wontless. What *wontlesse* fury dost thou now inspire . . . *H.B.* 2

Wonts. *Wonts* not t' enrage the hearts of equall beasts, . . . *Ro.* xxiv. 2
wonts to decke the Gods immortall crew . . . . *Hub.* 1268
his cunning theeveries He *wonts* to worke, ... *Hub.* 1288
An yearely solemne feast she *wontes* to hold, ... II. ii. 42. 6
'In woods, in waves, in warres, she *wonts* to dwell, ... II. iii. 41. 1
(As *wonts* the Tartar by the Caspian lake, ... II. xi. 26. 7
he *wonts* the Stygian realmes invade . . . . II. xii. 41. 4
Wherewith the Craftesman *wonts* it beautify, ... III. xii. 20. 3
In her great iron charet *wonts* to ride, ... IV. xi. 28. 2
the rocke, in which he *wonts* to dwell, ... V. ix. 6. 2
*With which she *wonts* to temper angry Jove, ... *Am.* xxxix. 3

Woo. Full many Maydens often did him *woo*, ... *As.* 37
to *wooe* a wandring guest, ... III. i. 55. 7
finding litle leasure her to *wooe* . . . . III. viii. 13. 3
Therefore he her did court, did serve, did *wooe*, ... IV. ii. 8. 6
Fearing least she your loves away should *woo*: . . . . IV. vi. 30. 8
Could she her wished freedome fro me *wooe*: . . . . IV. x. 57. 5
wooe with fair intreatie, ... IV. xii. 26. 6
whether he did *woo*, or whether he were woo'd? . . . . V. vi. 15. 9
he is not the while in state to *woo*; . . . . V. vi. 16. 2

Wood. *See* **Coltwood, Greenwood, Wild wood.**
Within this *wood*, out of a (the[1]) rocke . . . . *Pet.* iv. 1
I saw a Phoenix in the *wood* alone, ... *Pet.* v. 1
A mighty Lyon, Lord of all the *wood*; . . . . *Van.* x. 1
Thelf was so wanton and so *wood*, ... *S.C.* Mar. 55
Tho to the greene *Wood* they speeden hem all, ... *S.C.* May 27
gazd on her as they were *wood*, ... *S.C.* Au. 75
Woode as he that did them keepe. . . . . *S.C.* Au. 76
to the *wood* would he speede him fast. . . . . *S.C.* S. 199
The beastes in forest wayle as they were *woode*, ... *S.C.* N. 135
thy sacred *wood* (O Delian Goddesse!) . . . . *Gn.* 169
Blinde through ambition, and with vengeance *wood*, ... *Gn.* 411
his skinne, the terror of the *wood*, ... *Hub.* 969
he roar'd alowd, as he were *wood*, ... *Hub.* 1352
the Oetaean *wood* Had him consum'd, ... *Ti.* 381
A curious Coffer made of Heben *wood*, ... *Ti.* 618
fill with pleasance every *wood* and plaine. . . . . *D.* 56
miscaried or in plaine or *wood*. . . . . *D.* 140
many a Nymph both of the *wood* and brooke, ... *As.* 43
having none to let, to *wood* did wend. . . . . *As.* 126
This is the wandring *wood*, this *Errours* den, ... I. i. 13. 6
The which at last out of the *wood* them brought. . . . . . . I. i. 28. 6
she . . . each *wood* and plaine, Did search, ... I. ii. 8. 7
out of the thickest *wood* A ramping Lyon rushed . . . . . . I. iii. 5. 1
her plaint, Which softly ecchoed from the neighbour *wood*; I. iii. 8. 2
Through unadvized rashnes woxen *wood*; . . . . I. iv. 34. 3
on their rusty bits did champ as they were *wood*. . . . . . . I. v. 20. 9
Faunes . . . Within the *wood* were dauncing . . . . I. vi. 7. 8
worship her as Goddesse of the *wood*; . . . . I. vi. 16. 2
to the *wood* she goes, to serve her turne, ... I. vi. 22. 3
sownd, Which through the *wood* loud bellowing did rebownd, I. vii. 7. 5
She wandred many a *wood*, and measurd many a vale. . . . . I. vii. 28. 9
youth . . . His speare of heben *wood* behind him bare, . . . I. vii. 37. 2
with his cruell clawes he snatcht the *wood*, ... I. xi. 22. 2
Beholdes her nymphes enraung'd in shady *wood*, ... I. xii. 7. 8
through the *wood* re-echoed againe; . . . . II. i. 38. 2
Throughout the *wood* that ecchoed againe, ... II. iii. 20. 8
The *wood* is fit for beasts, ... II. iii. 39. 9
Pursew her steps through wild unknowen *wood*: . . . . II. iii. 43. 3
calme the tempest of his passion *wood*: . . . . II. iv. 11. 8
Now gan Pyrochles wex as *wood* as hee, ... II. v. 20. 6
in frayle *wood* on Adrian gulf doth fleet, ... II. vii. 14. 4
Clothed with leaves, that none the *wood* mote see, ... II. vii. 53. 8
then wexeth *wood* and yond: . . . . II. viii. 40. 9
not of *wood*, nor of enduring bras, ... II. ix. 23. 4
Of that same *wood* it fram'd was cunningly, ... II. xii. 41. 1
as nigh out of the *wood* she came, ... III. i. 20. 1
Banisht from princely bowre to wastefull *wood*! . . . . III. iii. 42. 6
a Lion from the sea-bord *wood* Of Neustria . . . . III. iii. 47. 2
as if that he were *wood*, ... III. iii. 47. 7
Within that *wood* there was a covert glade, ... III. v. 17. 1
he would have fled into the *wood*; . . . . III. v. 25. 1
The driest *wood* is soonest burnt to dust. . . . . III. viii. 25. 5
Through many a *wood* and many an uncouth way, ... III. x. 34. 2
The *wood* they enter, and search . . . . III. xi. 6. 8
every *wood* and every valley wyde . . . . III. xii. 7. 8
Seeking adventures in the salvage *wood*, ... IV. ii. 45. 2
Which she with her long fostred in that *wood*, ... IV. ii. 46. 1
rived were like rotten *wood* asunder; . . . . IV. iii. 15. 6
Of two grim lyons, taken from the *wood*, ... IV. iii. 39. 2
Walkt through the *wood*, for pleasure or for need; . . . . . IV. vii. 4. 2
as he through the wandring *wood* did stray, ... IV. vii. 42. 4
as through that *wood* he rode, ... IV. viii. 19. 1
Against those two let drive, as they were *wood*: . . . . . . IV. ix. 29. 5
The raging Buls rebellow through the *wood*, ... IV. x. 46. 4
The pleasaunt Bandon crownd with many a *wood*; . . . . IV. xi. 44. 2
whiles he did in the *wood* remaine, ... V. iii. 31. 4
made him rave, like to a Lyon *wood*, ... V. viii. 35. 5
Cannot come neare him in the covert *wood*, ... V. viii. 35. 7
like a Lion *wood* amongst them fares, ... V. xi. 45. 3
a covert glade Within a *wood*, ... VI. ii. 16. 4
gan rove And range through all the *wood*, ... VI. ii. 20. 8
Into the *wood* was bearing her apace . . . . VI. iii. 25. 2
running streight into the thickest *wood*, ... VI. iv. 12. 5

Wood—*Continued.*
though he were still in this desert *wood*, ... VI. v. 2. 2
When he did raunge the *wood* for salvage game, ... VI. v. 15. 2
They fled, and fast into the *wood* did get. . . . . . VI. v. 22. 7
Was wandred in the *wood* another way, ... VI. vii. 19. 6
The Salvage forth out of the *wood* issew'd . . . . . VI. vii. 23. 8
made the *wood* to tremble at the noyce: . . . . . VI. viii. 46. 4
round about was bordered with a *wood* . . . . . VI. x. 6. 2
in the covert of the *wood* did byde, ... VI. x. 11. 4
Out of the *wood* he rose, ... VI. x. 17. 9
A Tigre forth out of the *wood* did rise, ... VI. x. 34. 4
when he backe returned from the *wood*, ... VI. xi. 25. 1
he wexed *wood* And halfe enraged . . . . . VI. xi. 25. 3
An hatchet keene, with which he felled *wood* . . . . . VII. vii. 42. 6
Woodbine. the *woodbine* twigges that freshly bud; . . . . . *Gn.* 82
woodbynd flowers and fragrant Eglantine; . . . . . *Am.* lxxi. 10
Wood-born. The *woodborne* people fall before her flat, ... I. vi. 16. 1
Wooden. Yet was it but a *wooden* frame and fraile, ... *Col.* 216
enclosd in *wooden* wals . . . our wearie daies we waste.' . . . . . I. ii. 42. 8
knight, . . . with fresh clay did close the *wooden* wound: . . . . . I. ii. 44. 8
Their *wooden* ribs are shaken nigh asonder. . . . . . IV. ii. 16. 6
Wood-god. decked all with woods Like a *wood god*, ... IV. xi. 33. 2
Wood-god's. that same would spill The *Wood-gods* breed, ... VII. vi. 50. 4
Wood-gods. *Woodgods*, and Satyres, and swift Dryades, ... *Gn.* 178
woodgods for them often sighed sore: . . . . . *As.* 50
The wyld *woodgods*, . . . There find the virgin, ... I. vi. 9. 1
Woodman. else some *woodman* shrowded there from scorching sunne. . . . . . IV. vii. 42. 9
Woodman's. All in a *woodmans* jacket he was clad . . . . . VI. ii. 5. 6
Woodmen. many wilde *woodmen* which robbe and rend All traveilers: . . . . . III. x. 40. 6
Woodness. with fell *woodnes* he effierced was, ... III. xi. 27. 4
Wood's. *See* **Greenwood's.**
In the *woods* shade which did the waters crowne, ... VI. x. 7. 7
Woods. *See* **Greenwood.**
the *Woods* With greene leaves, ... *S.C.* May 7
learne these *woods* to wayle my woe, ... *S.C.* Jun. 95
'Ye wastefull *Woodes!* beare witnesse of my woe, ... *S.C.* Au. 151
the wild *woodes*, (*woddes) my sorowes to resound, ... *S.C.* Au. 166
I went the wastefull *woodes* and forest wide, ... *S.C.* D. 23
The *Woodes* can witnesse many a wofull stowre. . . . . . *S.C.* D. 66
Adieu, ye *Woodes*, that oft my witnesse were: . . . . . *S.C.* D. 154
in the *woods* of Astery abide; . . . . . *Gn.* 20
Throgh the wide *woods* and groves, ... *Gn.* 32
They now amongst the *woods* and thickets ment, ... *Gn.* 75
the shrill *woods*, which were of sense bereav'd, ... *Gn.* 455
a Farmer, that would sell Bargaines of *woods*, ... *Hub.* 872
The *woods*, the rivers, and the medowes green, ... *Mui.* 153
shady *woods* resound with dreadfull yells; . . . . . *D.* 331
The *woods* were heard to waile full many a sythe, ... *Col.* 23
both *woods* and fields and floods revive, ... *Col.* 29
woods, and hills, and valleyes . . . . . *Col.* 482
The speaking *woods*, and murmuring waters fall, ... *Col.* 636
a hollowe cave Amid the thickest *woods*. . . . . . I. i. 11. 7
He saw . . . Una wandring in *woods* and forrests, ... I. ii. 9. 3
She, . . . Through *woods* and wastnes wide him daily sought; I. iii. 3. 8
all the *woodes* and forestes did resownd: . . . . . I. vi. 7. 6
all the *woods* with doubled Eccho ring; . . . . . I. vi. 14. 2
He nousled up . . . Emongst wild beastes and *woods*, ... I. vi. 23. 9
mother came . . . Unto the *woodes*, to see her little sonne; . . . . . I. vi. 27. 2
Unto those native *woods* for to repaire, ... I. vi. 30. 3
they the *woods* are past, and come now to the plaine. . . . . . I. vi. 33. 9
The neighbor *woods* arownd with hollow murmur ring. . . . . . I. viii. 11. 9
Through *woods* and mountaines, till they came at last . . . . . II. i. 24. 2
The *woods*, the nymphes, my bowres, my midwives, weare: . . . . . II. i. 53. 7
she the *woodes* with bow and shaftes did raunge, ... II. ii. 7. 3
'In *woods*, in waves, in warres, she wonts to dwell, ... II. iii. 41. 1
Depart to *woods* untoucht, ... II. iii. 43. 9
Through *woods* and plaines so long I did her chace, ... II. iv. 32. 2
Through the thicke *woods* wherein he would have hid . . . . . III. v. 13. 7
knowledge of those *woods* where he did dwell, ... III. v. 14. 3
There in await with thicke *woods* overgrowne, ... III. v. 17. 7
In those same *woods* ye well remember may . . . . . III. v. 27. 5
Into the *woods* thenceforth in haste shee went, ... III. v. 32. 1
strayd Farre in the *woodes* . . . . . III. v. 38. 7
mightie *woodes* which did the valley shade . . . . . III. v. 39. 4
such wilde *woodes* should far expell All civile usage . . . . . III. vi. 1. 7
sought the salvage *woods* and forests wyde, ... III. vi. 16. 4
Shortly unto the wastefull *woods* she came, ... III. vi. 17. 1
in *woods* and wanton wildernesse . . . . . III. vi. 22. 1
forth her damzells sent Through all the *woods*, ... III. vi. 25. 8
All coverd with thick *woodes* that quite it overcame. . . . . . III. vii. 4. 9
To walke the *woodes* with that his Idole faire, ... III. viii. 11. 2
when amid the thickest *woodes* they were, ... III. x. 43. 1
the Beares In these wild *woods*, ... IV. vii. 23. 8
Unto those *woods* he turned backe againe, ... IV. vii. 38. 3
the Rother, decked all with *woods* . . . . . IV. xi. 33. 1
Upon wyld beasts, which she in *woods* did find . . . . . V. i. 7. 8
Through *woods*, and rocks, and mountaines . . . . . V. viii. 41. 5
his faire limbs left in the *woods* forlorne; . . . . . V. viii. 43. 5
mongst wyld beasts, and salvage *woods*, to dwell; . . . . . V. ix. 1. 5
all the *woods* and rockes nigh to that way Began to quake . . . . . V. xii. 41. 4
That in these *woods* . . . dost wonne, ... VI. ii. 25. 2
(Unlesse thou in these *woods* thy selfe conceale . . . . . VI. ii. 26. 2
Through *woods* and hils he follow'd him so fast, ... VI. iii. 26. 6
A salvage man, which in those *woods* did wonne, ... VI. iv. 2. 2
In seeking all the *woods* both farre and nye . . . . . VI. iv. 16. 3
all the *woods* with piteous plaints did fill, ... VI. iv. 18. 2
For nought but *woods* and forrests farre and nye, ... VI. iv. 24. 8
through thicke *woods* and brakes and briers him drew, ... VI. v. 17. 3

Woods—*Continued.*
he to seeke Serena through the *woods* did rove. . . . . . VI. viii. 46. 9
wanton squirrels in the *woods* farre sought, ... VI. ix. 40. 3
in hils, in *woods*, in dales, ... VI. x. 3. 6
through the *woods* their Eccho did rebound. . . . . . VI. x. 10. 5
one day, when Calidore Was hunting in the *woods*, ... VI. x. 39. 2
Island . . . Covered with shrubby *woods*, ... VI. x. 41. 7
He sought the *woods*, but no man could see there; . . . . . VI. xi. 26. 4
The *woods* did nought but ecchoes vaine rebound; . . . . . VI. xi. 26. 6
To sing of hilles and *woods* mongst warres and Knights, . . . VII. vi. 37. 2
soveraine Queene profest Of *woods* and forrests . . . . . VII. vi. 38. 8
Through many *woods* and shady coverts flowes, ... VII. vi. 41. 7
all the *woods* and dales . . . Did ring againe, ... VII. vi. 52. 8
Should harbour'd be and all those *Woods* deface, ... VII. vi. 55. 5
those *Woods*, and all that goodly Chase . . . . . VII. vi. 55. 7
Me from these *woods* and pleasing forrests bring, ... VII. vii. 1. 2
the *woods* theyr ecchoes back rebounded, ... *Am.* xix. 7
teach the *woods* and waters to lament . . . . . *Epith.* 10
The *woods* shall to me answer, ... *Epith.* 18
That all the *woods* may answer, ... *Epith.* 36
The *woods* shall to you answer, ... *Epith.* 55
That all the *woods* may answer, ... *Epith.* 73
That all the *woods* them answer, ... *Epith.* 91
The whiles the *woods* shal answer, ... *Epith.* 109
all the *woods* shal answer, ... *Epith.* 128
al the *woods* them answer, ... *Epith.* 147
To which the *woods* did answer, ... *Epith.* 184
al the *woods* should answer, ... *Epith.* 203
That al the *woods* may answere, ... *Epith.* 222
That all the *woods* may answere, ... *Epith.* 241
To which the *woods* shall answer, ... *Epith.* 260
That all the *woods* may answer, ... *Epith.* 277
all the *woods* them answer, ... *Epith.* 295
The *woods* no more shall answere, ... *Epith.* 314
Ne let the *woods* them answer . . . . . *Epith.* 333, 352
Ne will the *woods* now answer, ... *Epith.* 371
Ne let the *woods* us answere, ... *Epith.* 389
Ne any *woods* shall answer, ... *Epith.* 408
The *woods* no more us answer, ... *Epith.* 426
Woody. that faire troupe of *woodie* Goddesses . . . . . *Gn.* 182
The *wooddy* nymphes, . . . Her to behold do thither runne . I. vi. 18. 1
all the Satyres scorne their *woody* kind, ... I. vi. 18. 8
with the *woody* Nymphes when she did play, ... II. iii. 28. 7
as he to those *woody* hilles did fly, ... II. x. 33. 7
Emongst the *woody* hilles of Dynevowre: . . . . . III. iii. 8. 6
the Mayd And daughter of a *woody* Nymphe, ... III. v. 36. 3
like salvage weed With *woody* mosse bedight, ... IV. iv. 39. 5
Belphebe with her peares, The *woody* Nimphs, ... IV. vii. 23. 6
all the *wooddy* Nymphes did wayle and mourne; . . . . . V. viii. 43. 7
In all this forrest and wyld *wooddie* raine: . . . . . VI. ii. 9. 6
Latonaes sonne After his chace on *woodie* Cynthus . . . . . VI. ii. 25. 5
For love amongst the *woodie* Gods to dwell) . . . . . VI. ii. 26. 3
at length unto a *woody* glade He came, ... VI. v. 17. 6
With whom the *woody* Gods did oft consort, ... VII. vi. 39. 8
Wooed. A rulesse rout of yongmen which her *woo'd*, ... *Gn.* 431
Ne her with ydle words alone he *wowed*, ... *As.* 67
He *woo'd* her thus: . . . . . II. iv. 25. 6
was shee *woo'd* of many a gentle knight, ... II. ix. 18. 3
wooed him her Paramoure to bee, ... III. i. 35. 3
I *woo'd* her with due observaunce, ... III. vii. 59. 7
With flattering wordes he sweetly *wooed* her, ... III. viii. 38. 6
He *wooed* her till day-spring he espyde, ... III. x. 52. 1
So well he *woo'd* her, and so well he wrought her, ... IV. vi. 41. 1
wooed him her paramour to bee: . . . . . IV. viii. 52. 7
she *woo'd* and prayd him fast, ... IV. viii. 52. 8
Before that day her *wooed* to his bed, ... IV. xi. 8. 6
And, *wooed* him by all the waies she could: . . . . . V. iv. 30. 4
whether he did woo, or whether he were *woo'd?* . . . . . V. vi. 15. 9
she them *woo'd*, by all the meanes she might, ... V. ix. 3. 7
So well he *wood* her, ... VI. x. 38. 1
With looks, with words, with gifts he oft her *wowed*, ... VI. xi. 4. 8
Wooers. when all that troupe of warlike *wooers* Assembled were IV. ii. 38. 1
Deviz'd a Web her *wooers* to deceave; . . . . . *Am.* xxiii. 2
Wool. A garment better than of *wooll* or heare. . . . . . *Hub.* 474
a fleece of *wooll*, (*woll) which privily The Latmian shepherd . . . brought, ... *Epith.* 379
Woolen. to weare garments base of *wollen* twist, ... *Hub.* 460
Woolly. of their lambes, and of their *woolly* fleece. . . . . . *Hub.* 302
Woon. *See* **Won.**
Woos. *woes* the Widdowes daughter of the glenne; . . . . . *S.C.* Ap. 26
Word. The *worde* of God made him a noble name. . . . . . *Rev.* iii. 4
(that *word* she spake with payne, ... *S.C.* May 193
with his *word* his worke is convenable. . . . . . *S.C.* S. 175
(that was, a woful *word* to sayne!) . . . . . *S.C.* N. 93
I would be readie, both in deed and *word*, ... *Hub.* 252
Ne tell a written *word*, ne write a letter, ... *Hub.* 383
this good Sir did follow the plaine *word*, ... *Hub.* 390
soone as he receiv'd That *word*, ... *Hub.* 1258
Right and loyall did his *word* maintaine. . . . . . *Ti.* 189
Of whome no *word* we heare, ... *Ti.* 360
For her departure, had no *word* to say; . . . . . *Ti.* 474
Right faithfull true he was in deede and *word*, ... I. i. 2. 7
she . . . nor in *word* nor deede ill meriting, ... I. iii. 2. 7
Ne *word* to speake, ne joynt to move, she had; . . . . . I. vi. 11. 2
That cruell *word* her tender hart so thrild, ... I. vi. 37. 1
In *word* and deede that shewd great modestee, ... I. x. 7. 4
'That *word* shall I,' (said he) 'avouchen good, ... I. x. 64. 8
ne *word* to creature spake. . . . . . I. xii. 29. 4
threatned death with many a bloodie *word:* . . . . . II. i. 11. 8
A right good knight, and trew of *word* ywis: . . . . . II. i. 19. 5

Word—*Continued.*
Let one *word* fall that may your grief unfold, II. i. 46. 7
Not one *word* more she sayd, II. i. 56. 1
to observe in *word* of knights they did assure. II. ii. 32. 9
At which bold *word* that boaster gan to quake, II. iii. 18. 8
round about the wreath this *word* was writ, II. iv. 38. 4
The merry mariner unto his *word* Soone hearkned, II. vi. 4. 5
They forward passe; ne Guyon yet spoke *word*, II. vii. 31. 1
word so deepe did in their harts impresse, II. viii. 18. 7
Nor wight nor *word* mote passe out of the gate, II. ix. 25. 3
Through his faire daughters face and flattring *word*. II. x. 66. 5
Ne any noise she made, ne *word* she spake, III. i. 61. 6
The *worde* gone out she backe againe would call, III. ii. 9. 1
'Glauce, what needes this colourable *word* III. iii. 19. 3
Ne *word* did speake, but lay as in a swowne, III. iv. 30. 6
remember well the mighty *word* III. vi. 34. 4
Ne had one *word* to speake for great amaze, III. vii. 7. 8
swifte as *word* that from her went, III. vii. 23. 6
'tell at one *word*, How many fownd'st thou III. vii. 56. 8
'one *word* may tell All that I ever fownd III. vii. 57. 1
bayted every *word*, III. x. 6. 7
That chearful *word* his weak heart much did cheare, III. x. 26. 6
As if the *word* so spoken were halfe donne, III. x. 33. 2
Ne *word* he had to speake his griefe to tell, III. x. 37. 8
she it all refused at one *word*, III. x. 51. 7
No *word* they spake, III. xii. 45. *or.* 8
everie *word* did tremble as she spake, IV. i. 5. 6
Ne *word* had he to speake for great dismay, IV. i. 50. 2
thereto well agreed His *word*, IV. iv. 39. 8
Ne ever *word* to speake to woman more; IV. vii. 39. 4
Yet spake no *word*, whereby she might aread IV. viii. 13. 5
never heard one *word* Of tydings IV. viii. 18. 5
Ne more sincere in *word* and deed profest; IV. xi. 18. 7
with her least *word* can asswage The surging seas, IV. xi. 50. 4
with that *word* him strooke, V. ii. 11. 9
Weigh but one *word* which from thy lips doth fall: V. ii. 43. 6
the least *word* that ever could be layd Within his ballaunce V. ii. 44. 3
never *word* from that day forth he spoke. V. iii. 33. 5
Much was the knight incenst with his lewd *word* V. iii. 36. 1
'Unto yourselfe,' said they, 'we give our *word*, V. iv. 16. 4
Till they had told their message *word* by *word*: V. iv. 51. 3
his owne mouth . . . spake so warelesse *word*, V. v. 17. 4
Sadly she rode, and never *word* did say V. vi. 18. 3
With golden giftes and many a guilefull *word* V. xi. 50. 4
Much was the Knight abashed at that *word* VI. i. 26. 1
'To take defiaunce at a Ladies *word* VI. i. 28. 1
Whose every deed and *word*, . . . Was like enchantment, VI. ii. 3. 2
Fell flat to ground, ne *word* unto him sayd, VI. vii. 25. 8
she, for nought . . . One *word* durst speake, VI. viii. 50. 9
was so opprest, That he no *word* could speake, VI. xi. 28. 5
No *word* was heard of her that most it ought; *Am.* xix. 10
with one *word* my whole years work doth rend. *Am.* xxiii. 12
with one *word* she can it save or spill. *Am.* xxxviii. 11
speake no *word* to her of these sad plights, *Am.* lxxxiii. 11
Even for his sake, and for his sacred *word*, *H.H.L.* 206

Words. With painted *words* tho gan this proude weede *S.C.* F. 160
with fond termes, and witlesse *words*, *S.C.* Jul. 35
Sike *words* bene wynd, and wasten soone *S.C.* O. 36
throwe out thondring *words* of threate, *S.C.* O. 104
let the flitting aire my vaine *words* sever.' *Gn.* 638
So well as I her *words* remember may. *Hub.* 42
plaine his case with *words* unkinde. *Hub.* 52
Deeply doo your sad *words* my wits awhape, *Hub.* 72
Both by your wittie *words*, and by your werks. *Hub.* 416
with big *words*, and with a stately pace, *Hub.* 646
him the Foxe with hardy *words* did stay, *Hub.* 957
whenas they came they fell at *words*, *Hub.* 1019
raged sore In bitter *words*, *Hub.* 1089
With which I wont the winged *words* to tie, *T.M.* 548
Heapes of huge *wordes* uphoorded hideously, *T.M.* 553
wise *wordes*, taught in numbers for to runne, *Ti.* 402
Whose *wordes* recording in my troubled braine, *Ti.* 481
So of as I record those piercing *words*, *D.* 295
Ne her with ydle *words* alone he wowed, *As.* 67
both in deeds and *words* he nourtred was, *As.* 71
Her *words* were like a streame of honny fleeting, *Col.* 596
want I *words* to speake it fitly forth: *Col.* 625
stood awhile astonisht at his *words*, *Col.* 650
haughtie *words* most full of highest thoughts: *Col.* 716
To make so bold a doome, with *words* unmeet, *Col.* 929
that olde man of pleasing *wordes* had store, I. i. 35. 6
choosing out few *words* most horrible, I. i. 37. 1
waste *wordes* returnd to him in vaine: I. i. 42. 2
doubtfull *words* made that redoubted knight Suspect her truth: I. i. 53. 5
fed with *words* that could not chose but please: I. i. 54. 8
'Nor guileful sprite to thee these *words* doth speake; I. ii. 33. 2
Faire Una framed *words* and count'naunce fitt; I. iii. 14. 7
His lovely *words* her seemd due recompence I. iii. 30. 1
Her piteous *wordes* might not abate his rage, I. iii. 38. 1
He never meant with *words*, but swords, to plead his right: I. iv. 42. 9
With gentle *wordes* he can her fayrely greet, I. iv. 46. 1
Her *words* prevaild: I. v. 44. 1
With fawning *wordes* he courted her a while; I. vi. 4. 1
wordes, and lookes, and sighes she did abhore; I. vi. 4. 4
then to him these womanish *words* gan say: I. vi. 28. 5
With foule reprochfull *words* he boldly him defide. I. vi. 40. 9
With fowle *words* tempring faire, I. vii. 3. 9
bloody *wordes* of bold Enchaunters call; I. vii. 35. 2
Faire feeling *words* he wisely gan display, I. vii. 38. 6
Wherewith enmovd, these bleeding *words* she gan to say. I. vii. 38. 9

Words—*Continued.*
His chearefull *words* reviv'd her chearelesse spright, I. vii. 52. 8
Ne living man like *wordes* did ever heare, I. ix. 14. 7
Till he these *wordes* to him deliver might: I. ix. 23. 6
foltring tongue, at last, these *words* seemd forth to shake; I. ix. 24. 9
wounding *words*, and termes of foule repriefe, I. ix. 29. 4
Ne let vaine *words* bewitch thy manly hart, I. ix. 53. 2
heare the wisedom of her *wordes* divine. I. x. 18. 6
she was hable with her *wordes* to kill, . . . the hart I. x. 19. 8
added *wordes* of wondrous might. I. x. 24. 6
With hartie *wordes* her knight she gan to cheare, I. xi. 1. 5
When he these bitter byting *wordes* had red, I. xii. 29. 1
with *words* his will, . . . he ofte did stay, II. i. 34. 7
These *words* she breathed forth from riven chest: II. i. 47. 5
In these sad *wordes* she spent her utmost breath: II. i. 49. 4
with *words*, and weedes, of wondrous might, II. i. 52. 3
wordes with bitter teares did steepe: II. ii. 1. 9
with pitthy *words*, and counsell sad, II. ii. 28. 5
Her gracious *words* their rancour did appall, II. ii. 32. 1
began these *words* aloud to sownd. II. ii. 39. 9
Sweete *wordes* like dropping honny she did shed; II. iii. 24. 7
ere her *words* ensewd, II. iii. 34. 1
Trew be thy *words*, and worthy of thy praise, II. iii. 38. 2
fild with delight Of her sweete *words* II. iii. 42. 3
her great *words* did appall My feeble corage, II. iii. 44. 5
Ne chaffar *words*, prowd corage to provoke, II. v. 3. 2
sweet *wordes*, dropping like honny dew; II. v. 33. 4
With percing *wordes* and pittifull implore, II. v. 37. 5
all her *wordes* she drownd with laughter vaine, II. vi. 6. 7
Such powre have pleasing *wordes*: II. vi. 36. 5
weenest *words* or charms may force withstond: II. viii. 22. 2
Words, well dispost, Have secrete powre II. viii. 26. 7
Who now shall give unto me *words* and sound II. x. 1. 1
Now throwing forth lewd *wordes* immodestly; II. xii. 16. 4
As in approvaunce of his pleasing *wordes*. II. xii. 76. 3
through want of *words*, her excellence to marre. III. Pr. 2. 9
His feeling *wordes* her feeble sence much pleased, III. ii. 15. 1
pleasing *wordes* are like to Magick art, III. ii. 15. 5
'These idle *wordes*' (said she) 'doe nought aswage III. ii. 37. 1
'Beldame, your *words* doe worke me litle ease; III. ii. 43. 1
Her chearefull *words* much cheard the feeble spright III. ii. 47. 1
Certein sad *words* with hollow voice and bace, III. ii. 50. 5
by *wordes* could call out of the sky Both Sunne and Moone, III. iii. 12. 1
Th' old woman wox half blanck those *wordes* to heare, III. iii. 17. 8
Her harty *wordes* so deepe into the mynd . . . sunke, III. iii. 57. 1
Wordes fearen babes. III. iv. 15. 3
Many meeke *wordes* to stay and comfort her withall. III. iv. 48. 9
So them with bitter *words* he stird to bloodie yre. III. v. 15. 9
With sugred *words* and gentle blandishment, III. vi. 25. 4
with bold *words* and bitter threat III. viii. 16. 2
knight, that weenst with *words* To steale III. viii. 17. 1
At those prowd *words* that other knight begonne III. viii. 17. 7
With flattering *wordes* he sweetly wooed her, III. viii. 38. 6
Which *wordes* when Paridell had heard, III. viii. 48. 1
skill his *words* to frame III. ix. 32. 7
eke thy *words* uncourteous and unkempt: III. x. 29. 7
Those feeling *words* so neare the quicke did goe, III. xi. 15. 7
these few *words* lett fly. III. xi. 15. 9
her *words* false coynd, III. xii. 14. 8
The seedes of evill *wordes* and factious deedes; IV. i. 25. 5
wicked *wordes* that God and man offended. IV. i. 27. 5
for the *words* which she heard say, IV. i. 50. 4
With sober *words*, that sufferance desired, IV. i. 54. 4
Such Musicke is wise *words*, IV. ii. 2. 5
to Sir Paridell these *words* he sent: IV. ii. 5. 6
Whose scoffed *words* he taking halfe in scorne, IV. ii. 6. 6
With golden *words* and goodly countenance, IV. ii. 9. 2
When they the reason of his *words* had hard, IV. ii. 28. 1
She modest was in all her deedes and *words*, IV. ii. 35. 8
For evill deedes may better then bad *words* be bore. IV. iv. 4. 9
For he their *words* as wind esteemed light. IV. v. 27. 7
Which sory *words* her mightie hart did mate IV. viii. 17. 6
Her *words* were not, as common *words* are ment, IV. viii. 26. 1
Her spightfull *words* did pricke and wound the inner part. IV. viii. 26. 9
there were none her hatefull *words* to heare. IV. viii. 36. 4
with kind *words* accoyd, vowing great love to mee. IV. viii. 59. 9
No *words* may rate, nor rigour him remove IV. ix. 31. 7
With gentle *words* perswading them to friendly peace. IV. ix. 32. 9
So he the *words* into his ballaunce threw, V. ii. 44. 8
streight the winged *words* out of his ballaunce flew. V. ii. 44. 9
sayd that *words* were light, V. ii. 45. 1
of *words* . . . The eare must be the ballance, V. ii. 47. 7
Much did his *words* the gentle Ladie quell, V. iii. 16. 8
of those *words*, the which that boaster threw, V. iii. 23. 6
Now with faire *words*, but *words* did little good, V. iv. 4. 8
with wide-glauncing *words* one day she thus him proved. V. v. 35. 9
The art of mightie *words* that men can charme; V. v. 49. 6
with faire *words*, fit for the time and place, V. v. 55. 6
gan gently her salute With curteous *words*, V. vi. 20. 2
Strange were the *words* in Britomartis eare, V. vi. 38. 1
Which spitefull *words* she . . . Thus answer'd: V. vii. 32. 7
all obedience both to *words* and deeds They quite forgot, V. viii. 41. 3
with guilefull *words* her to perswade To banish feare; V. ix. 12. 5
he likened was to a welhed Of evill *words*, V. ix. 26. 9
speaches forth doth send, Even blasphemous *words*, V. xi. 20. 8
O! who may not with gifts and *words* be tempted? V. xi. 50. 6
Yet this in all her *words* might be perceived, V. xii. 33. 8
among most bitter *wordes* they spake, V. xii. 42. 1
some hope your *words* unto me add.' VI. i. 10. 5
He burst into these *wordes*, VI. ii. 24. 9

Words—*Continued.*
And from her sory hart few heavie *words* forth sight: . . . . VI. ii. 42. 9
so dolefull dreare, That he these *words* burst forth: . . . . VI. iii. 4. 6
With which his gentle *words* and goodly wit . . . . VI. iii. 22. 1
Seem'd not to weigh his threatfull *words* at all, ... VI. iii. 36. 2
to make avoure Of the lewd *words* and deedes . . . . VI. iii. 48. 6
confused sound Of senselesse *words,* . . . . VI. iv. 11 .8
With such faire *words* she did their heat asswage, ... VI. v. 30. 6
As he the art of *words* knew wondrous well, ... VI. vi. 6. 3
Not sparing him with bitter *words* to taunt, ... VI. vi. 21. 7
with reprochfull *words* him thus bespake on hight. . . . . . VI. vi. 24. 9
with sharpe *words* did bitterly upbrayd: . . . . VI. vi. 33. 3
Through tempering of her *words* and lookes by wondrous skill. VI. vi. 41. 9
Yet were her *words* and lookes but false and fayned, ... VI. vi. 42. 1
Yet were her *words* but wynd, ... VI. vi. 42. 9
Words sharpely wound, but greatest griefe of scorning growes. VI. vii. 49. 9
What meaning mote those uncouth *words* comprize, ... VI. viii. 18. 4
Whose sensefull *words* empierst his hart so neare, ... VI. ix. 26. 3
his *words,* which he with reason red, ... VI. x. 30. 5
With looks, with *words,* with gifts he oft her wowed, ... VI. xi. 4. 8
as they *words* amongst them multiply, ... VI. xi. 16. 1
faire bespoke with *words,* . . . . VI. xi. 35. 9
Askt her, how mote her *words* be understood, ... VI. xii. 17. 3
spake licentious *words* and hatefull things . . . . VI. xii. 28. 5
the Gods, that gave good eare To her bold *words,* . . . . . . VII. vi. 28. 2
So her with flattering *words* he first assaid; . . . . VII. vi. 43. 4
Thus gan her plaintif Plea with *words* to amplifie: . . . . . VII. vii. 13. 9
her *words* so wise do make their way . . . . *Am.* lxxxi. 11
poysoned *words* and spitefull speeches . . . . *Am.* lxxxv. 4
words should faile me to relate . . . . *H.L.* 17
verse With equall *words* can hope it to reherse. . . . . *H.H.L.* 42
And give me *words* equall unto my thought, ... *H.H.L.* 48
Words'. rather more enrag'd for those *words* sake; . . . . . . VI. i. 19. 4
when her *words* embassade forth she sends, ... *H.B.* 251
Wore. *See* **Outwore, Ware, Worn.**
Their weedes bene not so nighly *wore;* . . . . *S.C.* Jul. 171
A chapelet on her head she *wore,* . . . . *S.C.* Au. 69
all mine Oten reedes bene rent and *wore,* . . . . *S.C.* O. 8
Upon his head an old Scotch cap he *wore,* . . . . *Hub.* 209
That on his head he *wore,* and in his hand . . . . *Hub.* 1291
that Citie, which the garland *wore* Of Britaines pride, ... *Ti.* 36
For whose sweete sake that glorious badge he *wore,* . . . . . I. i. 2. 3
like a Persian mitre on her hed Shee *wore,* . . . . I. ii. 13. 5
next her wrinkled skin rough sackecloth *wore,* . . . . I. iii. 14. 3
on her head she *wore* a tyre of gold, ... I. x. 31. 5
titles vaine, Which mortall Princes *wore* . . . . II. vii. 43. 9
he first *wore* crowne of gold for dignity. . . . . II. x. 39. 9
Upon his head he *wore* an Helmet light, ... II. xi. 22. 8
The golden ribband, which that virgin *wore* . . . . III. vii. 36. 1
with their horned feet the greene gras *wore,* . . . . III. x. 45. 7
Which for her sake he *wore,* . . . . IV. ii. 25. 9
All was through vertue of the ring he *wore;* . . . . IV. iii. 24. 1
ne other garment *wore,* For all his haire was like a garment . IV. vii. 7. 2
pind and *wore* away, Ne ever laught, ... IV. viii. 2. 6
many miles they two together *wore,* . . . . IV. ix. 19. 7
on her head a crowne She *wore,* . . . . IV. x. 31. 7
on his head like to a Coronet He *wore,* . . . . IV. xi. 27. 7
A Chapelet of sundry flowers she *wore,* . . . . IV. xi. 46. 6
She *wore* for her defence a mayled habergeon. . . . . V. v. 2. 9
on her legs she painted buskins *wore,* . . . . V. v. 3. 1
Thus she all night *wore* out in watchfulnesse, ... V. vi. 34. 8
They *wore* rich Mitres shaped like the Moone, ... V. vii. 4. 6
Uppon her head she *wore* a Crowne of gold; . . . . V. vii. 6. 6
Buskins he *wore* of costliest cordwayne, ... VI. ii. 6. 1
He *wore* no armour, ne for none did care, ... VI. vii. 43. 1
on his head a roll of linnen plight . . . he *wore,* . . . . . . VI. vii. 43. 6
the crowne, which Ariadne *wore* . . . . VI. x. 13. 1
on his head a girlond . . . He *wore,* . . . . VII. vii. 29. 5
Work. *See* **Groundwork.**
The *worke* did shew it selfe not wrought by man, ... *Bel.*[1] iv. 9
bases were of richest mettalls *warke,* . . . . *Bel.*[2] iv. 2
No *worke* it seem'd of earthly craftsmans wit, ... *Bel.*[2] iv. 9
Mausolus *worke* will be the Carians glorie; . . . . *Ro.* ii. 7
So meane Harpes *worke* may chalenge for her meed? . . . . *Ro.* xxxii. 4
to *worke* me more spight; . . . . *S.C.* F. 180
buildest strong *warke* upon a weake ground: . . . . *S.C.* May 145
what wants me here to *worke* delyte? . . . . *S.C.* Jun. 3
The walled townes doe *worke* my greater woe; . . . . *S.C.* Au. 158
with his word his *worke* is convenable. . . . . *S.C.* S. 175
Waile ye this wofull waste of Natures *warke;* . . . . *S.C.* N. 64
which be wont to *worke* eternall sleepe. . . . . *S.C.* D. 90
to *worke* more ghastly feares. . . . . *Gn.* 584
His *worke* he shortly to good purpose brought, ... *Gn.* 655
it may no painfull *worke* endure, ... *Hub.* 275
Be with the *worke* of losels wit defamed, ... *Hub.* 813
So would he *worke* the silly man by treason To buy . . . . *Hub.* 888
faintly gan into his *worke* to enter, ... *Hub.* 1006
the *worke* of your nimble hand, ... *Hub.* 1035
whatsoever mother-wit or arte Could *worke,* . . . . *Hub.* 1139
his cunning theeveries He wonts to *worke,* . . . . *Hub.* 1288
That he might *worke* the avengement . . . . *Hub.* 1317
all that els was wont to *worke* delight . . . . *T.M.* 37
that great Towre, . . . King Ninus *worke,* . . . . *Ti.* 511
to *worke* our decay; . . . . *Mui.* 222
to *worke* thy miserie. *Mui.* 236
to his wicked *worke* each part applie. . . . . *Mui.* 253
So to their *worke* they sit, ... *Mui.* 275
round about her *worke* she did empale . . . . *Mui.* 297
A goodly *worke,* full fit for kingly bowres; . . . . *Mui.* 300
Her selfe likewise unto her *worke* to dight. . . . . *Mui.* 304

Work—*Continued.*
Nor anie weaver, which his *worke* doth boast . . . . *Mui.* 363
So to his *worke* Aragnoll him prepares. . . . . *Mui.* 408
To slaughter them, and *worke* their finall bale, ... *As.* 105
hast not seene least part of natures *worke:* . . . . *Col.* 293
for want of other *worke,* . . . . *Col.* 765
To make his *worke* more absolute, desird . . . the vew. . . . *Ded.Son.*xvii.3
with new day new *worke* at once begin: . . . . I. i. 33. 2
he gave . . . other *worke* to doo. . . . . I. i. 38. 9
well instructed, to their *worke* they haste; . . . . I. i. 47. 1
How he may *worke* unto her further smarts; . . . . I. ii. 9. 7
a felon strong To many knights did daily *worke* disgrace; . . I. iii. 29. 4
From everie *worke* he chalenged essoyne, ... I. iv. 20. 3
They all . . . Leave off their *worke,* . . . . I. v. 36. 2
A *worke* of wondrous grace, and hable soules to save. . . . . I. ix. 19. 9
resolv'd to *work* his finall smart, ... I. ix. 51. 8
death he could not *worke* himselfe thereby; . . . . I. ix. 54. 6
chaste in *worke* and will: . . . . I. x. 30. 6
thristy give to drinke; a *worke* of grace. . . . . I. x. 38. 3
godly *worke* of Almes and charitee, ... I. x. 45. 4
A *worke* of labour long, and endlesse prayse: . . . . I. xi. 7. 6
To *worke* new woe and improvided scath, ... I. xii. 34. 3
full of malicious mynd, To *worken* mischiefe, ... II. i. 2. 2
He weened well to *worke* some uncouth wyle: . . . . II. i. 8. 2
God guide thee, Guyon, well to end thy *warke,* . . . . II. i. 32. 8
It was an auncient *worke* of antique fame, ... II. ii. 12. 8
both against the middest meant to *worken* woe. . . . . II. ii. 13. 9
stird you up to *worke* your wilfull smarts? . . . . II. ii. 29. 4
to *worke* her to his will more neare . . . . II. iv. 25. 5
matter make for him to *worke* upon, ... II. iv. 42. 6
Least thy foolhardize *worke* thy sad confusion.' . . . . II. iv. 42. 9
To *worke* such shame. II. v. 17. 7
to behold the water *worke* and play About her little frigot, . II. vi. 7. 8
A *worke* of rich entayle and curious mould, ... II. vii. 4. 5
From their whot *work* they did themselves withdraw . . . . II. vii. 37. 3
contrary to the *worke* which ye intend: . . . . II. viii. 19. 9
O *worke* divine! . . . . II. ix. 22. 2
all this other worldes *worke* doth excell, ... II. ix. 47. 3
stole fire from heven to animate His *worke,* . . . . II. x. 70. 8
to *worke* us dreed, ... II. xii. 26. 4
best alyve, That natures *worke* by art can imitate: . . . . . . II. xii. 42. 4
seemd a *worke* of admirable witt; . . . . II. xii. 44. 2
Each did the others *worke* more beautify; . . . . II. xii. 59. 6
A *worke* of rare device and wondrous wit. . . . . III. i. 34. 6
Long *worke* it were, and needlesse, ... III. i. 42. 1
worke so hainous tort, In shame of knighthood, ... III. ii. 12. 8
Who wonders not, that reades so wonderous *worke?* . . . . III. ii. 20. 1
worthy *worke* of infinite reward, ... III. ii. 21. 7
'Beldame, your words doe *worke* me litle ease; . . . . III. ii. 43. 1
During which *worke* the Lady of the Lake, ... III. iii. 10. 6
Ne ever to his *worke* returnd againe: . . . . III. iii. 11. 3
those feends may not their *work* forbeare, ... III. iii. 11. 4
Deepe busied bout *worke* of wondrous end, ... III. iii. 14. 7
Not this the *worke* of womans hand ywis, ... III. iv. 37. 3
ne lettest see The beautie of his *worke?* . . . . III. iv. 56. 4
Long *worke* it were Here to account the endlesse progeny . . III. vi. 30. 6
Nor Aeolus sharp blast could *worke* them any wrong. . . . . III. vi. 44. 9
To bringe her backe againe, or *worke* her finall bale. . . . . III. vii. 21. 9
She there deviz'd a wondrous *worke* to frame, ... III. viii. 5. 2
'His *worke* great Troynovant, his *worke* is eke Faire Lincolne, III. ix. 51. 1
a wide wound . . . (The *worke* of cruell hand) . . . . III. xii. 20. 8
Seeing his *worke* now wasted, ... III. xii. 43. 9
Now cease your *worke,* and . . . play: . . . . III. xii. 47. *or.* 8
Now cease your *work;* to morrow is an holy day. . . . . . . III. xii. 47. *or.* 9
That were too long a *worke* to count them all; . . . . IV. i. 24. 2
out throwen Into this world to *worke* confusion, ... IV. ii. 1. 3
every secret *worke* of natures wayes . . . . IV. ii. 35. 4
Full busily unto his *worke* ybent; . . . . IV. v. 34. 2
In which his *worke* he had sixe servants prest, ... IV. v. 36. 1
The manner of their *worke* and wearie paine; . . . . IV. v. 38. 2
for nought would from their *worke* refraine, ... IV. v. 38. 5
To *worke* such outrage on so faire a creature; . . . . IV. vi. 17. 2
Thinking to *worke* on her his utmost wracke, ... IV. vi. 21. 2
to *worke* Time to my will, ... IV. vii. 17. 1
nature had so well disguized Her *worke,* . . . . IV. ix. 11. 4
on his foes did *worke* full cruell wracke: . . . . IV. ix. 25. 4
any blemish which the *worke* mote blame; . . . . IV. x. 41. 5
It was no mortall *worke,* . . . . IV. xi. 45. 9
what an endlesse *worke* have I in hand, ... IV. xii. 1. 1
Were *worke* fit for an Herauld, not for me: . . . . V. iii. 3. 6
Not knowing natures *worke,* . . . . V. iii. 19. 6
The *worke* of heavens will surpasseth humaine thought.' . . . V. iv. 27. 9
Doth them compell to *worke,* to earne their meat, ... V. iv. 31. 5
That he with *worke* may be forwearied: . . . . V. v. 50. 4
his *worke* lessened, that his love mote grow: . . . . V. v. 57. 3
he no *worke* at all left for the leach: . . . . V. vii. 35. 8
With all their force to *worke* avengement strong . . . . . . V. viii. 24. 6
in Princes courts to *worke* great scath and hindrance: . . . . V. ix. 22. 9
watch advauntage how to *worke* his care, ... V. xi. 13. 4
to *worke* Irenaes franchisement, ... V. xi. 36. 4
unfit For . . . *worke* of greater care, ... VI. ii. 9. 3
where no wight Should . . . *worke* me any wrong: . . . . . . VI. ii. 30. 6
To *worke* his utter shame, and throughly him confound. . . . VI. v. 14. 9
Willing to *worke* his villenous intent . . . . VI. vi. 44. 4
To *worke* by wicked treason wayes doth find, ... VI. vii. 1. 8
Where he mote *worke* him scath and villeny. . . . . VI. vii. 3. 5
discoursing diversly . . . to *worke* delay; . . . . VI. ix. 12. 7
to occasion meanes to *worke* his mind, ... VI. ix. 27. 1
worke his foe great shame. . . . . VI. ix. 43. 9
by natures skill Devized to *worke* delight . . . . VI. x. 5. 7

Work—*Continued.*
O pittious *worke* of Mutability, . . . VII. vi. 6. 7
that power and vertue . . . That ye here *worke,* . . . VII. vii. 54. 5
Do *worke* their owne perfection so by fate: . . . VII. vii. 58. 7
the *worke* of Nature or of Art, . . . *Am.* xxi. 1
the *worke* that she all day did make, . . . *Am.* xxiii. 3
with one word my whole years *work* doth rend. . . . *Am.* xxiii. 12
fruitlesse *worke* is broken with least wynd. . . . *Am.* xxiii. 14
her fayre eyes unwares doe *worke* in mee, . . . *Am.* xxiv. 6
my proud one doth *worke* the greater scath, . . . *Am.* xxxi. 9
Sufficient *worke* for one mans simple head, . . . *Am.* xxxiii. 7
I joy to see how, in your drawen *work,* . . . *Am.* lxxi. 1
as your *worke* is woven all above . . . *Am.* lxxi. 9
stoutly will that second *worke* assoyle, . . . *Am.* lxxx. 7
this the *worke* of harts astonishment. . . . *Am.* lxxxi. 14
Attempt to *work* her gentle mindes unrest: . . . *Am.* lxxxiii. 4
Their prety stealthes shal *worke,* . . . *Epith.* 361
To Nenna first, that first this *worke* created, . . . *Com. Son.* ii. 13
Worke like impression in the lookers vew? . . . *H.B.* 81
To *worke* ech others joy and true content, . . . *H.B.* 200

Worker. who can love the *worker* of her smart? . . . III. xii. 31. 7
Who was the root and *worker* of her woe, . . . IV. xii. 29. 2
to returne againe To his wounds *worker,* . . . VI. x. 31. 7
The cruell *worker* of your kindly smarts, . . . *H.L.* 32

Workest. *workst* such wreck, on her to whom thou dearest art! IV. vi. 16. 9
Which there thou *workest* by thy soveraine might, . . . *H.H.L.* 4

Worketh. Is gathered full, and *worketh* speedy way: . . . I. xi. 10. 3

Working. *See* **Woe-working.**
each to other *working* cruell wrongs, . . . *Ro.* xxiv. 7
Working her formall rowmes in wexen frame, . . . *S.C.* D. 68
In *working* of Strymonian Rhaesus fall, . . . *Gn.* 535
Adventure which might them a *working* set; . . . *Hub.* 224
Working belgardes and amorous retrate; . . . II. iii. 25. 3
working wit That never idle was, . . . II. ix. 49. 8
with the angry *working* of the wave . . . III. viii. 37. 4
All that is by the *working* of thy Deitee. . . . III. x. 4. 9
Through *working* of the stone therein yset. . . . IV. iii. 24. 5
She through her wicked *working* did incense . . . IV. v. 23. 2
neither day nor night from *working* spared, . . . IV. v. 35. 7
Many vaine fancies *working* her unrest; . . . V. vi. 7. 7
Working to all that love her deadly woe, . . . V. viii. 20. 8

Workman. Like as the *workeman* had their courses taught; . . . V. v. 2. 5

Workman's. It . . . spake the praises of the *workmans* witt; I. iv. 5. 2
goodly order and great *workmans* skill . . . II. ix. 33. 1
seem'd to serve the *workmans* will. . . . IV. x. 15. 9
She wondred at the *workemans* passing skill, . . . V. vii. 5. 6
could be fram'd by *workmans* rare device; . . . V. ix. 27. 8

Workmanship. To view the *workmanship* of heavens hight: . . *Mui.* 45
due reward For her prais-worthie *workmanship* . . . *Mui.* 268
mastered with *workmanship* so rare, . . . *Mui.* 338
Nor anie skil'd in *workmanship* embost, . . . *Mui.* 365
in her *workmanship* no pleasure finde, . . . *D.* 394
The wondrous *workmanship* of Gods owne mould, . . . I. x. 42. 6
So goodly *workemanship* should not endure: . . . II. ix. 21. 8
Did th' other far in *workmanship* excell; . . . II. ix. 23. 3
This parts great *workemanship* and wondrous powre, . . . II. ix. 47. 2
Ne ought their goodly *workmanship* might save Them . . . II. xii. 83. 3
So hard a *workemanship* adventure darre, . . . III. Pr. 2. 8
With which high God his *workmanship* hath deckt; . . . III. vi. 12. 5
all this worlds faire *workmanship* she tride Unto his last confusion to bring, . . . IV. i. 30. 6
Yet did the *workmanship* farre passe the cost: . . . IV. iv. 15. 8
To spoyle so goodly *workmanship* of nature, . . . IV. vi. 17. 4
goodly *workmanship* farre past all other . . . IV. x. 29. 8
Least, trembling, it his *workmanship* should spill; . . . *Am.* xvii. 7

Workmaster. What time this worlds great *Workmaister* did cast *H.B.* 29

Workmen. Since of all *workmen* helde in reckning best; . . . *Ro.* xxvii. 7
thereby forst his *workemen* to forsake, . . . III. iii. 10. 8

Works. shall ruinate Your *workes* and names, . . . *Ro.* vii. 11
the ruin'd pride Of these old Romane *works,* . . . *Ro.* xv. 13
Corinth skil'd in curious *workes* to grave; . . . *Ro.* xxix. 4
Both by your wittie words, and by your *werks.* . . . *Hub.* 416
all those needlesse *works* are laid away; . . . *Hub.* 455
Of Natures *workes,* of heavens continuall course, . . . *Hub.* 764
to be Lord of all the *workes* of Nature, . . . *Mui.* 211
workes with loome, with needle, and with quill. . . . *Mui.* 272
falshood . . . *workes* him woefull ruth. . . . I. ii. Arg.
He hated all good *workes* and vertuous deeds, . . . I. iv. 32. 1
greater conquest . . . he gaynes, That *workes* it to his will, I. vi. 3. 9
plight, Which sinfull horror *workes* in wounded hart, . . . I. x. 23. 3
that proud Paynim king that *works* her teene: . . . I. xii. 18. 8
On them she *workes* her will to uses bad: . . . II. i. 52. 4
More huge in strength then wise in *workes* he was, . . . II. ii. 17. 6
unto knighthood *workes* much shame and woe; . . . II. iv. 10. 7
must wage Thy *workes* for wealth, . . . II. vii. 18. 5
she may thee advance for *works* and merits just.' . . . II. vii. 49. 9
all his *workes* with mercy doth embrace, . . . II. viii. 1. 7
Of all Gods *workes* which doe this worlde adorne, . . . II. ix. 1. 1
that which all faire *workes* doth most aggrace, . . . II. xii. 58. 8
all the *workes* of those wise sages, . . . IV. Pr. 3. 3
workes of noblest wits to nought outweare, . . . IV. ii. 33. 2
sith *workes* of heavenly wits Are quite devourd, . . . IV. ii. 33. 8
daies, by which the sonnes of men Divide their *works,* . . . IV. vii. 13. 2
beholding all the way The goodly *workes,* . . . IV. x. 15. 5
The which right well her *workes* divine did shew: . . . IV. x. 34. 5
all his *workes* with Justice hath bedight. . . . V. Pr. 10. 5
To call to count, or weigh his *workes* anew, . . . V. ii. 42. 6
Comaunded them their daily *workes* renew, . . . V. v. 1. 4
To doe those *workes* to them appointed dew; . . . V. v. 22. 7
The rest be *works* of natures wonderment: . . . *Am.* lxxxi. 13

Works—*Continued.*
That *workes* such wonders in the minds of men; . . . *H.B.* 86
Him to behold, is on his *workes* to looke, . . . *H.H.B.* 128

Workwoman. The most fine-fingred *workwoman* on ground, . . *Mui.* 260

World. nought in this *worlde* but griefe endures. . . . *Bel.*[1] iii. 12
me the spoile and bootie of the *world,* . . . *Bel.*[1] viii. 10
raisde a Trophee over all the *worlde.* . . . *Bel.*[1] xi. 8
this *world* doth nought but grievance hold! . . . *Bel.*[2] iii. 12
Over all the *world* did raise a Trophee . . . *Bel.*[2] xv. 8
Loath this base *world,* . . . *Pet.*[2] vii. 12
what els in the *world* is of like worth, . . . *Ro.* ii. 11
Tam'd all the *world,* . . . *Ro.* iii. 7
Doo make her Idole through the *world* appeare. . . . *Ro.* v. 14
Through armes and vassals Rome the *world* subdu'd, . . . *Ro.* viii. 1
To frame this *world* that doth endure so long? . . . *Ro.* ix. 6
it selfe upreare Over the *world,* . . . *Ro.* xii. 11
Makes the *world* wonder what they from thee reft. . . . *Ro.* xiii. 14
With his great bellie spreds the dimmed *world,* . . . *Ro.* xx. 6
Her power, disperst through all the *world* did vade; . . . *Ro.* xx. 13
Had all the *world* in armes against her bent, . . . *Ro.* xxi. 6
spoile, Which she had wonne from all the *world* . . . *Ro.* xxii. 7
Of all the *world* was spoyl'd within a while: . . . *Ro.* xxii. 8
Rome was th' whole *world,* and al the *world* was Rome; . . *Ro.* xxvi. 9
The map of all the wide *world* doth containe. . . . *Ro.* xxvi. 14
fill the *world* with never dying fame! . . . *Ro.* Env. 14
the Romaine Empire bore the raine Of all the *world* . . . *Van.* xi. 2
Must not the *world* wend in his commun course, . . . *S.C.* F. 11
layen her faults the *world* beforne, . . . *S.C.* May 160
The *world* is well amend, . . . *S.C.* Jul. 170
wandred, I wene, about the *world* round, . . . *S.C.* S. 22
Wherewith they sette all the *world* on fire; . . . *S.C.* S. 87
They sayne the *world* is much war then it wont, . . . *S.C.* S. 108
The sonne of all the *world* is dimme and darke: . . . *S.C.* N. 67
fame now rings Through the wide *world,* . . . *Gn.* 150
the *world* parting by an equall lott, . . . *Gn.* 158
once assai'd to burne this *world* so wide. . . . *Gn.* 376
Rome, that holds the *world* in sovereigntie, . . . *Gn.* 597
before the *world* was civill, . . . *Hub.* 45
Wide is the *world* I wote, . . . *Hub.* 90
as we bee sonnes of the *world* so wide, . . . *Hub.* 135
this might better be the *world* of gold; . . . *Hub.* 152
Drudge in the *world,* and for their living droyle, . . . *Hub.* 157
we will walke about the *world* at pleasure . . . *Hub.* 159
fashion both our selves to bee, Lords of the *world;* . . . *Hub.* 168
This yron *world* (that same he weeping sayes) . . . *Hub.* 254
Seeing the *world,* in which they bootles boad, . . . *Hub.* 400
'Who hath the *world* not tride, . . . may wander wide: . . . *Hub.* 403
you, which the *world* have proved, . . . *Hub.* 409
not by that which is, the *world* now deemeth, . . . *Hub.* 649
through the *world* had with long travel far'd, . . . *Hub.* 686
in the *world* long time they wandered, . . . *Hub.* 943
blot his brutish name Unto the *world,* . . . *Hub.* 1241
an universall night Throughout the *world* . . . *Hub.* 1298
Doo seeke to make us of the *world* forlorne, . . . *T.M.* 66
all that in this *world* is worthie hight . . . *T.M.* 105
To waile the wretchednes of *world* impure? . . . *T.M.* 120
Ah, wretched *world!* the den of wickednesse, . . . *T.M.* 121
Ah, wretched *world!* the house of heavinesse, . . . *T.M.* 123
Ah, wretched *world!* and all that is therein, . . . *T.M.* 125
First comming to the *world* with weeping eye, . . . *T.M.* 159
The beautie of the *world* hath lately wasted, . . . *T.M.* 248
Walk through the *world* of every one revilde. . . . *T.M.* 342
wont the *world* with famous acts to fill; . . . *T.M.* 430
In this wide *world* in which they, wretches, stray, . . . *T.M.* 493
all that in this *world* is great or gaie . . . *Ti.* 55
did overcome The *world* with conquest of their might . . . *Ti.* 62
in the necke of all the *world* did ride? . . . *Ti.* 74
of the whole *world* as thou wast the Empresse, . . . *Ti.* 83
So I of this small Northerne *world* was Princesse. . . . *Ti.* 84
For wonder of the *world,* long in me lasted, . . . *Ti.* 118
of the *world* admired ev'rie where, . . . *Ti.* 122
Too soone for all this wretched *world,* . . . *Ti.* 293
Although the compast *world* were sought around. . . . *Ti.* 567
Ne other comfort in this *world* can be, . . . *Ti.* 584
him, whom all the *world* did glorifie: . . . *Ti.* 663
glorie of the *world* your high thoughts scorne, . . . *Ti.* 681
With gentle calme the *world* had quieted, . . . *Mui.* 50
Her blazed fame which all the *world* had fil'd, . . . *Mui.* 266
Least that the *world* thee dead accuse of guilt, . . . *D.* 82
'Out of the *world* thus was she reft awaie, . . . *D.* 162
Out of the *world,* unworthie such a spoyle, . . . *D.* 163
why did they then create The *world* so fayre, . . . *D.* 205
(since fayre Astraea left The sinfull *world*) . . . *D.* 219
all the *world* subdued unto it, . . . *D.* 307
Throughout the *world* from one to other end, . . . *D.* 373
'So all the *world,* and all in it I hate, . . . *D.* 428
sought For faire Eurydice . . . Throughout the *world,* . . . *D.* 465
Such as the *world* admyr'd, . . . *Col.* 191
A *world* of waters heaped up on hie, . . . *Col.* 197
Under what skie, or in what *world* we were, . . . *Col.* 230
From thence another *world* of land we kend, . . . *Col.* 272
this same *world* where we do wone?' . . . *Col.* 307
shootes his arrowes every where Into the *world,* . . . *Col.* 812
long before the *world* he was ybore, . . . *Col.* 839
by his powre the *world* was made of yore, . . . *Col.* 841
love is Lord of all the *world* by right, . . . *Col.* 883
Unto the *world* for ever witnesse bee, . . . *Col.* 949
nought to the *world* denying, . . . *Col.* 950
And in the neck of all the *world* to rayne; . . . *Ded. Son.* i. 4
ye grace And deck the *world,* . . . *Ded. Son.* xvi. 5

World—*Continued.*

If all the *world* to seeke I overwent, . . . *Ded. Son.* xvii. 9
Whom that most noble Briton Prince . . . Sought through the *world,* . . . I. Pr. 2. 7
Like Phoebus lampe throughout the *world* doth shine, . . . I. Pr. 4. 4
all the *world* in their subjection held; . . . I. i. 5. 6
through the *world* of waters wide and deepe, . . . I. i. 39. 2
many yeares throughout the *world* I straid, . . . I. ii. 24. 7
when broad day the *world* discovered has, . . . I. iii. 21. 1
that high in heaven doth dwell And wield the *world,* . . . I. iv. 11. 6
sawst the secrets of the *world* unmade, . . . I. v. 22. 6
the *world* with sword and fire warrayd; . . . I. v. 48. 2
old Ninus . . . of all the *world* obayd. . . . I. v. 48. 4
thither were assembled day by day From all the *world,* . . . I. v. 51. 3
dawning light Discovered had the *world* to heaven wyde, . . . I. v. 52. 6
with his breath, which through the *world* doth pas, . . . I. vii. 9. 3
praise, Which flying fame throughout the *world* had spred, . I. vii. 46. 2
chevalrie, That with your worth the *world* amazed make, . . . I. viii. 26. 8
from the *world* that her discovered wide, Fled . . . I. viii. 50. 2
so soone as life did me admitt Into this *world,* . . . I. ix. 3. 6
necessitie, That holds the *world* . . . I. ix. 42. 7
Renowmd throughout the *world* for sacred lore . . . I. x. 3. 2
Hast wandred through the *world* now long a day, . . . I. x. 9. 6
hath encreast the *world* with one sonne more, . . . I. x. 16. 6
wretched *world* he gan for to abhore, . . . I. x. 21. 4
for the sinnes of al the *world* was kilt: . . . I. x. 57. 7
Backe to the *world,* whose joyes so fruitlesse are; . . . I. x. 63. 2
To move the *world* from off his stedfast henge, . . . I. xi. 21. 8
that great Champion of the antique *world,* . . . I. xi. 27. 1
In all the *world* like was not to be fownd, . . . I. xi. 47. 1
th' antique *world* excesse and pryde did hate: . . . I. xii. 14. 8
as through the *world* I did proclame, . . . I. xii. 20. 2
to the *world* does bring long-wished light: . . . I. xii. 21. 8
of the *world* least part to us is red; . . . II. Pr. 2. 2
Poore Orphane! in the wild *world* scattered, . . . II. ii. 2. 5
That may this day in all the *world* be found. . . . II. ii. 42. 5
Throughout the *world* her mercy to maintaine, . . . II. ii. 43. 7
Thrise seene the shadowes of the neather *world,* . . . II. ii. 44. 2
Throughout the *world,* wher-so they might be found, . . . II. iii. 38. 6
Famous throughout the *world* for warlike prayse, . . . II. v. 26. 2
decke the *world* with their rich pompous showes; . . . II. vi. 15. 7
'God of the *world* and worldlings I me call, . . . II. vii. 8. 1
'The antique *world* . . . Fownd no defect . . . II. vii. 16. 1
Could gathered be through all the *world* arownd, . . . II. vii. 31. 8
this darksom neather *world* her light Doth dim . . . II. vii. 49. 3
Into the *world* to guyde him backe, . . . II. vii. 65. 9
he doth fill The *world* with murdrous spoiles . . . II. viii. 6. 4
Of all Gods workes which doe this *worlde* adorne, . . . II. ix. 1. 1
Throughout the *world,* renowmed far and neare, . . . II. ix. 4. 4
Seven times the Sunne . . . Hath walkte about the *world,* . . II. ix. 7. 6
Some such as in the *world* were never yit, . . . II. ix. 50. 4
all that in the *world* was ay thought wittily. . . . II. ix. 53. 9
As all things els the which this *world* doth weld; . . . II. ix. 56. 5
all the *world* with wonder overspred; . . . II. x. 2. 6
through the *world* then swarmd in every part, . . . II. x. 15. 3
Regan greater love to him profest Then all the *world,* . . . II. x. 28. 4
With which the *world* did in those dayes abound: . . . II. x. 63. 6
wandring through the *world* with wearie feet, . . . II. x. 71. 3
puissant kinges which all the *world* warrayd, . . . II. x. 72. 2
into the *world* the dawning day Might looke, . . . II. xi. 3. 3
ghosts doen often creepe Backe to the *world,* . . . II. xii. 6. 6
her bright hed Discovers to the *world* discomfited: . . . III. i. 43. 5
high Jove Doth light the lower *world,* . . . III. i. 57. 7
the *world* in silence deepe Yshrowded was, . . . III. i. 59. 1
restlesse walketh all the *world* arownd, . . . III. ii. 14. 4
through the wyde *worlde* soone were solemniz'd. . . . III. ii. 18. 9
Whatever thing was in the *world* contaynd, . . . III. ii. 19. 2
Like to the *world* itselfe, and seemd a *world* of glas. . . . III. ii. 19. 9
His joyous face did to the *world* revele, . . . III. ii. 48. 2
Which the late *world* admyres for wondrous moniments. . . . III. iii. 2. 9
As if ought in this *world* . . . Were from him hidden, . . . III. iii. 15. 4
though all the *world* do shake; . . . III. iii. 25. 7
The *world* in darkenes dwels; . . . III. iv. 13. 3
The spoyle of all the *world;* . . . III. iv. 23. 3
The *world* in his continuall course to keepe, . . . III. iv. 56. 2
Of all good Ladies through the *worlde* so wide, . . . III. v. 11. 2
to all th' unworthy *world* forlore . . . III. v. 50. 8
Adorne the *world* with like to heavenly light, . . . III. v. 53. 2
wandred in the *world* in straunge aray, . . . III. vi. 11. 8
Whence all the *world* derives the glorious Features of beautie, III. vi. 12. 3
All that to come into the *world* desire: . . . III. vi. 32. 2
sent into the chaungefull *world* agayne, . . . III. vi. 33. 7
daily forth are sent Into the *world,* . . . III. vi. 36. 2
in the wide wombe of the *world* . . . III. vi. 36. 6
By her hid from the *world,* . . . III. vi. 46. 6
with spoiles and cruelty Ransackt the *world,* . . . III. vi. 49. 6
Ere they into the lightsom *world* were brought, . . . III. vii. 48. 7
in that monstrous wise did to the *world* appere. . . . III. vii. 48. 9
To wander through the *world* abroad at will, . . . III. vii. 54. 4
with like labour walke the *world* arownd, . . . III. vii. 56. 2
'Most famous Worthy of the *world,* . . . III. ix. 34. 1
The glory of the later *world* to spring, . . . III. ix. 44. 2
soveraine king Of all the *world,* . . . III. ix. 44. 5
it a wonder of the *world* is song In forreine landes; . . . III. ix. 45. 7
Into the utmost Angle of the *world* he knew. . . . III. ix. 47. 9
Bewrayed had the *world* with early light, . . . III. x. 1. 2
all that els the vaine *world* vaunten may, . . . III. x. 31. 5
all the *world* confound with cruelty; . . . III. x. 33. 8
her up he cast To the wide *world,* . . . III. x. 35. 8
Then all the *world* is lost, . . . III. x. 39. 9

World—*Continued.*

all the sorrow in the *world* . . . III. xi. 14. 6
all the *world* with flashing fire brent; . . . III. xi. 38. 5
sad shadowes gan the *world* to hyde . . . III. xi. 55. 3
through the *world* make to be notifyde, . . . III. xii. 39. 8
threatens all the *world* to wast. . . . IV. i. 45. 9
from thence out throwen Into this *world* . . . IV. ii. 1. 3
robd the *world* of threasure endlesse deare, . . . IV. ii. 33. 4
Did ever see upon this *world* to shine, . . . IV. iii. 3. 6
all the wretched *world* recomforteth againe. . . . IV. iv. 47. 9
of the wicked *world* forgotten quight, . . . IV. vii. 39. 6
through the endlesse *world* did wander wide, . . . IV. viii. 18. 8
when the *world* woxe old, it woxe warre old, . . . IV. viii. 31. 6
all the *world* confound with wide uprore, . . . IV. ix. 23. 8
from side to side till all the *world* it weet. . . . IV. ix. 33. 9
To whom the *world* this franchise ever yeelded, . . . IV. ix. 37. 6
all, that else through all the *world* is named . . . IV. x. 30. 8
all the *world* in state unmoved stands, . . . IV. x. 35. 2
al the *world* shews joyous cheare. . . . IV. x. 44. 9
all the *world* by thee at first was made, . . . IV. x. 47. 1
to the gloomy *world* itselfe bewray'd: . . . IV. x. 52. 7
Of puissant Nations which the *world* possest, . . . IV. xi. 15. 2
To vanquish all the *world* with matchlesse might; . . . IV. xi. 16. 6
all the *world* have with their issue fild? . . . IV. xi. 17. 2
present time The image of the antique *world* compare, . . . V. Pr. 1. 2
Me seemes the *world* is runne quite out of square . . . V. Pr. 1. 7
Of all this lower *world,* . . . V. Pr. 4. 9
this *world* with them amisse doe move. . . . V. Pr. 6. 7
all the *world* with goodnesse did abound: . . . V. Pr. 9. 2
till the *world* from his perfection fell . . . V. i. 5. 6
Whiles through the *world* she walked in this sort, . . . V. i. 6. 1
when the *world* with sinne gan to abound, . . . V. i. 11. 1
To witnesse to the *world* that she by him is dead.' . . . V. i. 26. 9
all the *world* he would weigh equallie, . . . V. ii. 30. 5
'Thou that presum'st to weigh the *world* anew, . . . V. ii. 34. 1
So many monsters which the *world* annoyed, . . . V. v. 24. 6
Well therefore did the antique *world* invent . . . V. vii. 2. 1
To captive men, and make them all the *world* reject. . . . V. viii. 2. 9
Famous through all the *world,* and honor'd far and nie. . . V. viii. 16. 9
This lower *world* nigh all to ashes brent, . . . V. viii. 40. 8
She could it sternely draw, that all the *world* dismayde. . . V. ix. 30. 9
all the *world* spake shame. . . . V. xi. 4. 7
So soone as it did to the *world* display His chearefull face, . V. xii. 11. 3
through the *world* incessantly doe chase, . . . VI. i. 7. 2
Into this wicked *world* he forth was sent . . . VI. i. 8. 6
follow through the *world* where so he went, . . . VI. vii. 21. 8
Throughout the *world* in this uncomely case, . . . VI. vii. 38. 2
I through the *world* should stray, . . . VI. viii. 22. 8
in all that *world* of beauties rare, . . . VI. x. 4. 6
'Sunne of the *world,* great glory of the sky, . . . VI. x. 28. 1
through the *world* thereby should glorifie his name. . . . VI. xii. 12. 9
whylest he that monster sought Throughout the *world,* . . . VI. xii. 13. 5
got into the *world* at liberty againe. . . . VI. xii. 38. 9
So now he raungeth through the *world* againe, . . . VI. xii. 40. 1
all this *world* is woxen daily worse. . . . VII. vi. 6. 6
Mean-while the lower *World* . . . was darkned quite; . . . VII. vi. 14. 1
Is wont to wield the *world* unto his vow, . . . VII. vi. 22. 3
all the *world* beneath for terror quooke, . . . VII. vi. 30. 8
those that all the other *world* do fill, . . . VII. vii. 3. 4
the ground-work bee Of all the *world* . . . VII. vii. 25. 2
The rest which doe the *world* in being hold; . . . VII. vii. 27. 3
She left th' unrighteous *world,* . . . VII. vii. 37. 9
this lower *world* who can deny But to be subject . . . VII. vii. 47. 8
fills the darkned *world* with terror and dismay. . . . VII. vii. 51. 9
borne here in this *world;* . . . VII. vii. 53. 9
Witnesse the *world* how worthy to be prayzed! . . . *Am.* iii. 2
Is of the *world* unworthy most envide: . . . *Am.* v. 4
Was never in this *world* ought worthy tride, . . . *Am.* v. 13
That to the *world* naught else be counted deare; . . . *Am.* viii. 4
Dark is the *world,* where your light shined never; . . . *Am.* viii. 13
Into this sinfull *world* from heaven to send; . . . *Am.* xxiv. 10
fill the *world* with her victorious prayse. . . . *Am.* xxix. 14
Thrugh the broad *world* doth spred . . . *Am.* xl. 8
the new yeares . . . send, Into the glooming *world,* . . . *Am.* lxii. 10
famous warriors of anticke *world* . . . *Am.* lxix. 1
whenas death shall all the *world* subdew, . . . *Am.* lxxv. 13
The *world* that cannot deeme of worthy things, . . . *Am.* lxxxiv. 1
Let the *world* chose to envy or to wonder. . . . *Am.* lxxxiv. 14
al, that ever in this *world* is fayre, . . . *Epith.* 101
old Heroes, which their *world* did daunt . . . *Com. Son.* iii. 3
through the *world* his way he gan to take, . . . *H.L.* 74
The *world,* that was not till he did it make, . . . *H.L.* 75
lights the *world* forth from his firie carre. . . . *H.B.* 112
doth the *world* with her delight adorne, . . . *H.B.* 151
all this *world,* the which thy vassals beene, . . . *H.B.* 269
From this base *world* unto thy heavens hight, . . . *H.H.L.* 2
loves, with which the *world* doth blind Weake fancies, . . . *H.H.L.* 262
this base *world,* subject to fleshly eye, . . . *H.H.B.* 23
this darke *world,* whose damps the soule do blynd, . . . *H.H.B.* 137
For of her fulnesse which the *world* doth fill They all partake, *H.H.B.* 199
That all the *world* shold with his rimes be fraught! . . . *H.H.B.* 224
this vile *world* and these gay-seeming things; . . . *H.H.B.* 299
name may ring Through al the *world,* . . . *Proth.* 158

Worldlings. 'God of the world and *worldlings* I me call, . . . II. vii. 8. 1
With such vaine shewes thy *worldlinges* vyle abuse; . . . II. vii. 39. 5

Worldly. Sike *worldly* sovenance he must forsay. . . . *S.C.* May 82
Free from all troubles and from *worldly* toyle, . . . *Gn.* 151
all that vaunts in *worldly* vanitie . . . *Gn.* 559
As well of *worldly* livelode as of life, . . . *Hub.* 147
in midst of *worldlie* smarts: . . . *T.M.* 136

Worldly—*Continued.*
what ever man bearst *worldlie* sway, *Ti.* 208
Nought carde I then for *worldly* change or chaunce, *D.* 103
Tydings of warre and *worldly* trouble tell? I. i. 30. 8
'My weaker yeares, Captiv'd to . . . frayle *worldly* feares, I. i. 52. 5
From *worldly* cares himselfe he did esloyne, I. iv. 20. 1
Unfit he was for any *worldly* thing, I. iv. 23. 1
They all, beholding *worldly* wights in place, I. v. 36. 1
Did love . . . above all *worldly* blisse; I. vi. 17. 7
Ne other *worldly* busines did apply: I. x. 46. 7
of no *worldly* thing he care did take: II. vi. 18. 2
Regard of *worldly* mucke doth fowly blend, II. vii. 10. 5
whatever in this *worldly* state Is sweete II. xii. 42. 5
Ne *worldly* price, cannot redeeme my deare III. xi. 16. 4
for no *worldly* meed, Nor no entreatie, IV. xi. 8. 7
of no *worldly* thing he tooke delight; IV. xii. 19. 7
For guiftes of gold or any *worldly* glee, V. xi. 63. 3
doe all *worldly* riches farre excell, VI. Pr. 2. 4
For other *worldly* wealth they cared nought. VI. ix. 5. 6
From all the tempests of these *worldly* seas, VI. ix. 19. 4
That *worldly* chaunces doe amongst them cast, VI. xi. 1. 3
That maketh them all *worldly* cares forget, *H.H.B.* 265

World's. I knowing the *worldes* unstedfastnesse, *Bel.*[1] i. 12
all *worldes* hap [and honour] *Bel.*[1] viii. 7
O *worlds* (*worldes*[1]) vainesse! *Bel.* ii. 12
I, that know this *worlds* inconstancies, *Bel.*[2] i. 12
all *worlds* felicitie *Bel.*[2] x. 7
The whole *worlds* spoile, *Bel.*[2] x. 10
trustles state Of vaine *worlds* glorie, *Pet.*[2] vii. 2
Seven Romane Hils, the *worlds* Seven Wonderments. *Ro.* ii. 14
O *worlds* inconstancie! *Ro.* iii. 12
Rome, living, was the *worlds* sole ornament, *Ro.* xxix. 13
Rome, . . . dead, is now the *worlds* sole moniment. *Ro.* xxix. 14
Where all this *worlds* pride once was situate. *Ro.* xxxi. 2
Palinodie, thou art a *worldes* childe: *S.C.* May 73
they casten too much of *worlds* care, *S.C.* S. 114
It shall continewe till the *worlds* dissolution, *S.C.* Env. 4
Through the *worlds* endles ages to survive. *Gn.* 56
for disdaine of sinfull *worlds* upbraide *Hub.* 2
so to wander to the *worldes* (**worlds*) ende, *Hub.* 87
Thus wildly to wander in the *worlds* eye, *Hub.* 185
other great one in the *worldes* eye, *Hub.* 490
simple men, which never came in place Of *worlds* affaires, *Hub.* 835
That wont to be the *worlds* chiefe ornament, *T.M.* 74
all this *worlds* affliction *T.M.* 129
Through knowledge we behold the *worlds* creation, *T.M.* 499
lifted up above the *worldes* gaze, *T.M.* 587
like a Looker-on Of this *worldes* Stage, *Com. Son.* i. 3
The *worlds* sad spectacle, and fortunes scorne.' *Ti.* 28
'O vaine *worlds* glorie! *Ti.* 43
With treasure passing all this *worldes* worth, *Ti.* 286
The *worlds* late wonder, and the heavens new joy; *Ti.* 303
With mortall cares and cumbrous *worlds* anoy! *Ti.* 305
'Such one Mausolus made, the *worlds* great wonder, *Ti.* 414
'O vile *worlds* trust! *Ti.* 456
sits in highest seate Of this *worlds* glorie, *Ti.* 464
Henceforth all *worlds* felicitie I hate. *Ti.* 574
Exceeding all this baser *worldes* good: *Ti.* 620
whilome wast the *worldes* chiefst riches, *Ti.* 675
loath this drosse of sinfull *worlds* desire! *Ti.* 686
through meditation Of this *worlds* vainnesse *D.* 34
in *worlds* ficklenesse Reposedst hope, *D.* 150
That man, who doth the whole *worlds* rule possesse, *D.* 179
no *worlds* sad care nor wasting woe *D.* 283
Her *worlds* bright sun, her heavens fairest light, *Col.* 41
that Emperesse, The *worlds* sole glory *Ded. Son.* xi. 4
Of beauties Queene, the *worlds* sole wonderment, *Ded.Son.*xvii.6
That the *worlds* pride seemes gathered there to bee. *Ded.Son.* xvii.12
'What *worlds* delight, or joy of living speach, Can hart . . . reach? I. vii. 39. 1
like would not for all this *worldes* wealth. I. ix. 31. 4
In all his waies through this wide *worldes* wave; I. x. 34. 8
all, that els this *worlds* enclosure bace Hath great II. ii. 41. 3
doest hide apart From the *worldes* eye, II. vii. 7. 4
Honour, estate, and all this *worldes* good, II. vii. 8. 6
'Loe! here the *worldes* blis: loe! here the end, II. vii. 32. 7
Here is the fountaine of the *worldes* good: II. vii. 38. 6
this *worldes* blis, For which ye men doe strive; II. vii. 48. 8
all this other *worldes* worke doth excell, II. ix. 47. 3
deepe engorgeth all this *worldes* pray; II. xii. 3. 5
The *worldes* sweet In from paine and wearisome turmoyle.' II. xii. 32. 9
As whylome was the antique *worldes* guize, III. i. 39. 3
refte from men the *worldes* desired vew, III. ii. 28. 3
From the *worlds* end, through many a bitter stowre: III. iii. 3. 5
The *worlds* reproch; the cruell victors scorne; III. iii. 42. 5
She brought her forth into the *worldes* vew, III. vi. 52. 3
the whole *worlds* commune remedy.' III. x. 26. 5
The *worlds* foundations from his centre fixt: III. xii. 2. 4
Wherewith the *worlds* faire beautie she hath blent: III. xii. 29. 5
all this *worlds* faire workmanship IV. i. 30. 6
One of the *worlds* seven wonders sayd to bee, IV. x. 30. 4
neglect The *worlds* whole rule for Cleopatras sight. V. viii. 2. 7
when in wrath he threats the *worlds* decay, V. ix. 31. 8
change of love for any *worlds* delight! V. xi. 62. 5
From view of men, and wicked *worlds* disdaine; VI. Pr. 3. 4
Tell me what *worlds* despight, or heavens yre, VI. v. 23. 7
Of warres delight and *worlds* contentious toyle, VI. v. 37. 6
From all this *worlds* incombraunce did himselfe assoyle. VI. v. 37. 9
weary of this *worlds* unquiet waies, VI. vi. 4. 7
Gotten great worship in this *worldes* sight: VI. vi. 35. 8

World's—*Continued.*
through this *worlds* wyde wildernes She wander should VI. vii. 37. 7
'To them that list the *worlds* gay showes I leave, VI. ix. 22. 1
all this *worlds* gay showes, which we admire, VI. ix. 27. 4
all the *worlds* faire frame . . . She alter'd quite; VII. vi. 5. 5
challenge to themselves the whole *worlds* raign, VII. vii. 15. 3
These gods do claime the *worlds* whole soverainty, VII. vii. 16. 2
I do possesse the *worlds* most regiment; VII. vii. 17. 2
she doth comptroll All this *worlds* pride, *Am.* x. 11
All this *worlds* riches that may farre be found: *Am.* xv. 6
this *worlds* worthlesse glory to embase, *Am.* xvii. 3
all *worlds* glorie is but drosse uncleane, *Am.* xxvii. 2
All this *worlds* glory seemeth vayne to me, *Am.* xxxv. 13
disdayne Of all *worlds* gladnesse, *Am.* lii. 12
Made for to be the *worlds* most ornament, *Am.* liii. 10
Of this *worlds* Theatre in which we stay, *Am.* liv. 1
admire such *worlds* rare wonderment; *Am.* lxix. 12
the *worlds* light-giving lampe *Epith.* 19
Fayre Venice, flower of the last *worlds* delight; *Com. Son.* iv.10
ere this *worlds* still moving mightie masse *H.L.* 57
The *worlds* great Parent, *H.L.* 156
Mother of love, and of all *worlds* delight, *H.B.* 16
this *worlds* great Workmaister *H.B.* 29
faire Dames! the *worlds* deare ornaments *H.B.* 162
Before this *worlds* great frame, . . . found any being-place, *H.H.L.* 22
Thenceforth all *worlds* desire will in thee dye, *H.H.L.* 274
'Ye gentle Birdes! the *worlds* faire ornament, *Proth.* 91
a noble Peer, . . . the *Worlds* wide wonder, *Proth.* 146

Worlds. Of other *worldes* he happily should heare, II. Pr. 3. 8
Fashioning *worldes* of fancies evermore III. ix. 52. 4
Meeke Lambe of God, before all *worlds* behight, *H.H.L.* 173

Worm. *See* **Canker-worm.**
Out of hir ashes as a *worme* arise. *Bel.*[1] vi. 14
Out of her dust like to a *worm* arise. *Bel.*[2] vii. 14
there bred A litle wicked *worme,* *Van.* vii. 7
a little Ant, a silly *worme,* *Van.* viii. 9
Then wounde of gealous *worme,* II. iv. 28. 9

Worm-eaten. all *worm-eaten* and full of canker holes. II. ix. 57. 9

Worms. Onely supports herselfe for meate of *wormes;* *Ro.* xxviii. 8
His toppe was bald, and wasted with *wormes,* *S.C.* F. 113
like *wormes* out of her slimie nature. *Col.* 860

Worn. *See* **Outworn, Overworn, To-worn, Wore.**
Selfe have I *worne* out thrise threttie yeares, *S.C.* F. 17
Coronations and Sops in wine, *Worne* of Paramoures: *S.C.* Ap. 139
'Thus is my sommer *worne* away and wasted, *S.C.* D. 97
yeares . . . spent and *worne* In meane regard, *Hub.* 59
Whose memorie is quite *worne* out with yeares, *Ti.* 67
His name is *worne* alreadie out of thought, *Ti.* 222
is *worne* with raine: *Ti.* 417
With showres of heaven and tempests *worne* away; *Ti.* 501
alleies wide, With footing *worne,* and leading inward farr. I. i. 7. 8
The Willow, *worne* of forlorne Paramours; I. i. 9. 3
his Portesse still he bare, That much was *worne,* I. iv. 19. 2
all behinde was bald, and *worne* away, II. iv. 4. 7
a Snake, whom wearie winters teene Hath *worne* to nought, IV. iii. 23. 8
well knowne to be the same Which Triamond had *worne,* IV. iv. 27. 6
out of all mens knowledge he was *worne* at last. IV. vii. 41. 9
daies in wilfull woe are *worne,* IV. viii. 15. 7
Like as the sea . . . Had *worne* the earth; V. ii. 32. 4
though she still have *worne* Her dayes in warre, V. v. 40. 4

Worse. From good to badd, and from badde to *worse,* *S.C.* F. 12
From *worse* unto that is worst of all, *S.C.* F. 13
though mochell *worse* I fared: *S.C.* Au. 23
Too good for him had bene a great deale *worse;* *S.C.* S. 213
The better please, the *worse* despise; *S.C.* Env. 12
worse than that I have I cannot meete. *Hub.* 89
Ne make one title *worse,* ne make one better: *Hub.* 384
'Ne *worse* to you, my sillie sheepe! I pray, *D.* 351
worse and *worse,* young Orphane, be thy payne, II. i. 61. 6
for feare of *worse* that may betide, II. iii. 46. 1
Least *worse* betide thee by some later chaunce. II. iv. 36. 5
sometimes had the *worse,* and lost by warre, II. v. 15. 4
Worse is the daunger hidden then descride. II. xii. 35. 5
Sad life *worse* then glad death; III. iv. 38. 8
Least *worse* on sea then us on land befell.' III. viii. 24. 5
as bad as she, and *worse,* if *worse* ought were. III. xi. 3. 9
Yet otherwise much *worse,* if *worse* might bee, IV. i. 18. 8
such an Hag, that seemed *worse* then nought, IV. iv. 10. 5
Shall death be th' end, or ought else *worse,* aread?' IV. vii. 11. 4
once amisse growes daily *wourse* and *wourse:* V. Pr. 1. 9
And if then those may any *worse* be red, V. Pr. 2. 8
make much *worse* by telling, V. xii. 35. 2
every matter *worse* was for her melling: V. xii. 35. 4
executes her wicked will with *worse* despight. VI. i. 15. 9
Ne durst abide behind, for dread of *worse* effort. VI. xi. 42. 9
all this world is woxen daily *worse.* VII. vi. 6. 6
for better be allured, Ne feard with *worse* *Am.* lix. 4

Worship. now thee *worship* mongst that blessed throng *Ti.* 340
Might *worship* it, and fall on lowest staire. *Ti.* 494
So we him *worship,* so we him adore *Col.* 815
To winne him *worshippe,* and her grace to have, I. i. 3. 4
Do *worship* her as Queene with olive girlond cround. I. vi. 13. 9
The woodborne people . . . *worship* her I. vi. 16. 2
bootlesse zeale she did restrayne From her own *worship,* I. vi. 19. 9
they her Asse would *worship* fayn. I. vi. 19. 9
an Elfin borne of noble state And mickle *worship* II. i. 6. 6
unto thee dew *worship* I may rightly frame' II. iii. 33. 9
doe unwilling *worship* to the Saint, II. v. 11. 7
great worth and *worship* may be wonne; III. ii. 8. 4
win him *worship* through his warlike deed, III. iv. 4. 8

Worship—*Continued.*
worship her as some celestiall vision. . . . IV. vi. 24. 9
I . . . wish thee grow in *worship* . . . VI. ii. 26. 7
Gotten great *worship* in this worldes sight: . . . VI. vi. 35. 8
many now much *worship* and admire! . . . *Am.* xxvii. 8
To win them *worship* which to thee obay. . . . *H.L.* 237
Worshiped. of Gods and man I *worshipt* was? . . . *Bel.*[1] viii. 8
Of him his God is *worshipt* with his sythe, . . . *Gn.* 129
worshipped of all, . . . *Ti.* 464
To teach them truth, which *worshipt* her in vaine, . . . I. vi. 19. 6
There *worshipped* of every living wight; . . . IV. x. 29. 7
Such heavenly formes ought rather *worshipt* be, . . . *Am.* lxi. 13
Worst. From worse unto that is *worst* of all, . . . *S.C.* F. 13
Ne for all his *worst* . . . Open the dore . . . *S.C.* May 225
have I not well discourst . . . (though plaine, not *wourst?*) . . . *Hub.* 542
Twixt best and *worst,* when both alike are dedd; . . . *T.M.* 448
best or fayrest, more Than *worst* or fowlest, . . . *D.* 203
Its best to hope the best, though of the *worst* affrayd.' . . . IV. vi. 37. 9
To thrust him out of dore doing his *worst* assay. . . . VI. vi. 21. 9
Nor that thing *worst* which men do most refuse; . . . VI. ix. 29. 7
in charge of one, the best Of many *worst,* . . . VI. xi. 24. 3
From good to bad, from bad to *worst* of all: . . . VII. vii. 19. 6
Worth. what els in the world is of like *worth,* . . . *Ro.* ii. 11
Such as they were (faire Ladie!) take in *worth,* . . . *Van.* i. 13
Here is a long tale, and little *worth.* . . . *S.C.* F. 240
nought *worth* a pease To put in preace . . . *S.C.* O. 69
for thy *worth* frame some fit Poesie: . . . *Gn.* 12
whatsoever other flowre of *worth,* . . . *Gn.* 681
With treasure passing all this worldes *worth,* . . . *Ti.* 286
well I weene it *worth* recounting was, . . . *Col.* 85
her owne great mynd, And wondrous *worth,* . . . *Col.* 365
ought could fynd *Worth* harkening to, . . . *Col.* 367
For her great *worth* and noble governance; . . . *Col.* 503
I cannot thinke according to her *worth:* . . . *Col.* 627
each mans *worth* is measured by his weed, . . . *Col.* 711
praise her *worth,* though far my wit above. . . . *Col.* 942
Nought is thy *worth* disparaged thereby; . . . *Ded. Son.* ii. 6
Which them succeed in fame and *worth,* . . . *Ded. Son.* iv. 6
Receive dear Lord, in *worth,* the fruit of barren field. . . . *Ded. Son.* v. 14
Vouchsafe in *worth* this small guift to receave, . . . *Ded. Son.* vii. 8
Vouchsafe from him this token in good *worth* to take. . . . *Ded. Son.* xv. 14
A dram of sweete is *worth* a pound of sowre. . . . I. iii. 30. 4
Yet did she thinke her pearelesse *worth* to pas That parentage, I. iv. 11. 3
through al Faery lond his famous *worth* was blown. . . . I. vi. 29. 9
stone Of wondrous *worth,* and eke of wondrous mights, . . . I. vii. 30. 2
chevalrie, That with your *worth* the world amazed make, . . . I. viii. 26. 8
liquor . . . Of wondrous *worth,* and vertue excellent, . . . I. ix. 19. 4
well ye worthy bene for *worth* and gentle thewes.' . . . II. i. 33. 9
as knight of so much *worth* became, . . . II. ii. 14. 2
Wondrous great prowesse and heroick *worth* He shewd . . . II. ii. 25. 3
all knights of *worth* and courage bold . . . II. ii. 42. 8
without desert of gentle deed And noble *worth,* . . . II. iii. 10. 7
seemd to be a woman of great *worth,* . . . II. iii. 21. 8
Wo *worth* the man, . . . II. vi. 32. 7
The *worth* of all men by their end esteeme, . . . II. viii. 14. 7
by your wondrous *worth* and warlike feat . . . II. ix. 6. 3
great *worth* and worship may be wonne; . . . III. ii. 8. 4
esteemd For her great *worth:* . . . III. vii. 52. 6
knightly *worth* which he too late did try, . . . III. ix. 25. 5
he hated . . . for his *worth,* that all men did adore, . . . IV. i. 39. 5
Now with opinion of his owne more *worth,* . . . IV. ii. 12. 3
Sir Priamond, with equall *worth* And equall armes, . . . IV. iii. 6. 3
With pearle and precious stone, *worth* many a marke; . . . IV. iv. 15. 7
His wondrous *worth* declared in all mens view, . . . IV. iv. 37. 5
thousand pretious gifts *worth* many a pound, . . . IV. x. 37. 7
had never wonne Mongst men of *worth,* . . . IV. x. 53. 8
The pride of Ladies, and the *worth* of knights, . . . V. iii. 3. 4
others *worth* with leasings doest deface, . . . V. iii. 20. 8
A Ladie of great *worth* and wealth had beene, . . . V. x. 7. 2
Lauding and praysing his renowmed *worth* . . . V. xi. 33. 3
As by thy *worth* thou worthily hast wonne, . . . VI. ii. 25. 7
Old love is litle *worth* when new is more prefard. . . . VI. ix. 40. 9
whose *worth* above all threasure They did esteeme, . . . VI. xi. 14. 5
sure thy *worth* no lesse then hers doth seem to showe. . . . VII. vi. 32. 9
not the *worth* of any living wight . . . VII. vi. 33. 2
your thrall, in whom is little *worth;* . . . *Am.* lxxxii. 10
Her *worth* is written with a golden quill, . . . *Am.* lxxxiv. 10
Worthies. all the *worthies* liggen wrapt in leade, . . . *S.C.* O. 63
ennoble with immortall name The warlike *Worthies,* . . . III. iii. 4. 4
Such famous men, such *worthies* of the earth, . . . IV. iii. 44. 1
Worthies'. all the antique *Worthies* merits far did passe. . . . III. ix. 50. 9
Worthiest. when her as the *worthiest* She praisd', . . . *Mui.* 125
to the highest and the *worthiest* . . . III. v. 2. 5
Worthily. *See* **Praiseworthily.**
To learned wits givest courage *worthily,* . . . *Gn.* 36
having *worthily* him punished, . . . *Hub.* 923
they cannot her honour *worthylie?'* . . . *Col.* 375
How *worthily* . . . Justice that day of wrong her selfe had wroken; . . . V. viii. 44. 6
As by thy worth thou *worthily* hast wonne, . . . VI. ii. 25. 7
Did *worthily* revenge this maydens pride; . . . VI. vii. 32. 2
thy love we weighing *worthily,* . . . *Am.* lxviii. 9
Worthiness. her *worthinesse* Much greater than the rude report *D.* 145
Renowmed Lord, that, for your *worthinesse* . . . *Ded. Son.* xi. 1
Whom Venus to him gave for meed of *worthinesse;* . . . III. ix. 34. 9
could not weigh of *worthinesse* aright; . . . VI. vii. 29. 6
Worthless. to wreake on *worthlesse* wight Your high displesure, IV. viii. 17. 2
this worlds *worthlesse* glory to embase, . . . *Am.* xvii. 3
Worth's. high *worths* surpassing paragon . . . *Am.* lxvi. 5
Worthy. *See* **Praiseworthy.**

Worthy—*Continued.*
worthy (*worthie*[1]) tombe for such a *worthy* (*worthie*[1]) wight (corps[1]). . . . *Bel.* iii. 11
worthie sure (If ought here *worthie*) of immortall dayes, . . . *Bel.*[2] xiv. 6, 7
Well *worthie* thou of immortalitie, . . . *Ro.* Env. 3
Helpe me to blaze Her *worthy* praise, . . . *S.C.* Ap. 44
pierce her heart with poynt of *worthy* wight, . . . *S.C.* Jun. 100
Advaunce the *worthy* whome shee loveth best, . . . *S.C.* O. 47
Bold sure he was, and *worthie* spirite bore, . . . *Gn.* 437
sweete love of pardon *worthie* is, . . . *Gn.* 473
All jolly Prelates, *worthie* rule to beare, . . . *Hub.* 423
in his liking to winne *worthie* place, . . . *Hub.* 776
'I am most *worthie,* (said the Ape) . . . *Hub.* 1027
Finde nothing *worthie* to be writ, . . . *T.M.* 100
all that in this world is *worthie* hight . . . *T.M.* 105
Have both desire of *worthie* deeds forlorne, . . . *T.M.* 437
worthie to commend For prize of value, . . . *T.M.* 465
shall rehearse His *worthie* praise, . . . *Ti.* 256
Worthie of heaven it selfe, . . . *Ti.* 287
As should be *worthie* of his fathers throne. . . . *Mui.* 32
Well *worthy* he to taste of wretchednes. . . . *Mui.* 216
worthie of a better place was she: . . . *D.* 366
Her, and but her, of love he *worthie* deemed; . . . *As.* 65
Worthie of Colin selfe, that did it make. . . . *Col.* 158
There eke is Palin *worthie* of great praise, . . . *Col.* 392
Well *worthie* of so honourable place, . . . *Col.* 502
Worthie next after Cynthia to tread, . . . *Col.* 514
Ne thee lesse *worthie,* gentle Flavia, . . . *Col.* 572
Ne thee lesse *worthie,* curteous Candida, . . . *Col.* 574
'Colin, well *worthie* were those goodly favours . . . *Col.* 585
Full many *worthie* ones then waiting were, . . . *Col.* 737
Full many persons of right *worthie* parts, . . . *Col.* 752
In this same Pageaunt have a *worthy* place, . . . *Ded. Son.* vi. 6
Doth promise fruite *worthy* the noble kind . . . *Ded. Son.* x. 3
Here eke of right have you a *worthie* place, . . . *Ded. Son.* xi. 5
In golden verse, *worthy* immortal fame: . . . *Ded. Son.* xii. 4
Had not Mecaenas, for his *worthy* merit, . . . *Ded. Son.* xiii. 3
well *worthy* end Of such as drunke her life . . . I. i. 26. 6
Well *worthie* be you of that Armory, . . . I. i. 27. 5
the *worthie* meed Of him that slew Sansfoy . . . I. iii. 36. 3
Ne other grace vouchsafed them to showe Of Princesse *worthy;* I. iv. 14. 4
this false faytor, who unworthie ware His *worthie* shield, . . . I. iv. 47. 5
me, thy *worthy* meed, unto thy Leman take.' . . . I. vii. 14. 9
'Well *worthy* impe,' said then the Lady gent, . . . I. ix. 6. 1
Of that great Queene may well gaine *worthie* grace, . . . I. ix. 17. 7
onely *worthie* you through prowes priefe, . . . I. ix. 17. 8
living man mote *worthie* be to be her liefe.' . . . I. ix. 17. 9
Well *worthy* doest thy service for her grace, . . . I. x. 60. 3
well ye *worthy* bene for worth and gentle thewes.' . . . II. i. 33. 9
Trew be thy words, and *worthy* of thy praise, . . . II. iii. 38. 2
By this time was the *worthy* Guyon brought . . . II. vi. 19. 1
Which fame of her shrill trompet *worthy* reedes; . . . II. vii. 2. 7
Worthie of heven and hye felicitie, . . . II. vii. 49. 5
And of that shield, more *worthy* of good knight; . . . II. viii. 15. 8
of more *worthy* substance fram'd it was: . . . II. ix. 23. 5
Argument *worthy* of Maeonian quill; . . . II. x. 3. 1
worthy of great Phoebus rote, . . . II. x. 3. 2
assigned for his *worthy* lott, . . . II. x. 12. 3
A woman *worthy* of immortall praise, . . . II. x. 42. 4
for each of other *worthy* are.' . . . III. ii. 10. 9
worthy worke of infinite reward, . . . III. ii. 21. 7
Be it *worthy* of thy race and royall sead, . . . III. ii. 33. 4
one that *worthy* may perhaps appeare; . . . III. ii. 42. 3
Well *worthie* stock, from which the branches sprong . . . III. iv. 3. 6
As may be *worthy* of his haynous sin.' . . . III. ix. 9. 7
all thy *worthie* prayses being blent . . . III. ix. 33. 8
'Most famous *Worthy* of the world, . . . III. ix. 34. 1
Your *worthy* paine shall wel reward with guerdon rich.' . . . III. x. 28. 9
what *worthy* meede Can wretched Lady . . . Yield you . . . III. xii. 39. 2
Himselfe she bound, more *worthy* to be so, . . . III. xii. 41. 8
On Fames eternall beadroll *worthie* to be fyled. . . . IV. ii. 32. 9
Well *worthie* thou to be of Jove accurst, . . . IV. ii. 49. 8
as his most *worthie* wage . . . IV. iii. 4. 8
So *worthie* of the perill, *worthy* of the paine. . . . IV. iv. 16. 9
There was it judged, by those *worthie* wights, . . . IV. v. 7. 3
For *worthy* thou of her doest rightly seeme. . . . V. i. 28. 4
worthie is for to be sewd unto, . . . V. v. 41. 6
had receiv'd their follies *worthy* hire, . . . V. viii. 15. 3
worthie paterns of her clemencies; . . . V. x. 5. 7
Grantortoes *worthy* punishment. . . . V. xi. 36. 5
In which a *worthy* auncient Knight did wonne: . . . VI. ii. 48. 8
none she *worthie* thought to be her fere, . . . VI. vii. 29. 2
Yet was she lov'd of many a *worthy* pere: . . . VI. vii. 29. 4
Slay not that Carle, though *worthy* to be slaine, . . . VI. viii. 17. 7
her *worthy* deemed To be a Princes Paragone esteemed, . . . VI. ix. 11. 4
so sure she was, she *worthy* was . . . VI. x. 25. 6
Albe they *worthy* blame, or cleare of crime: . . . VI. xii. 40. 6
she her selfe more *worthy* thereof wend, . . . VII. vi. 11. 3
worthy deeme partakers of our blisse to bee. . . . VII. vi. 33. 9
Witnesse the world how *worthy* to be prayzed! . . . *Am.* iii. 2
Was never in this world ought *worthy* tride, . . . *Am.* v. 13
Well *worthy* thou to have found better hyre, . . . *Am.* xlviii. 5
Of all alive most *worthy* to be praysed. . . . *Am.* lxxiv. 12
cannot deeme of *worthy* things, . . . *Am.* lxxxiv. 1
Whom ye thought *worthy* of your gracefull rymes, . . . *Epith.* 3
all those which thereof *worthy* bee. . . . *H.H.B.* 252
None thereof *worthy* be, but those . . . *H.H.B.* 253
Wot. Cuddie, I *wote* thou kenst little good, . . . *S.C.* F. 85
Ne *wote* I how to cease it. . . . *S.C.* Mar. 102
God *wote,* such cause hath she none) . . . *S.C.* May 98

Wot—*Continued.*
I *wote* my rymes bene rough, *S.C.* Jun. 77
I *wote* ne, Hobbin, how I was bewitcht *S.C.* S. 74
nowe I *wote* it is nothing sich; *S.C.* S. 79
to well I *wote* my humble vaine, *S.C.* N. 50
I ne *wotte* Whether rejoyce or weepe *S.C.* N. 204
Wide is the world I *wote,* *Hub.* 90
well I *wot* . . . that Beggers life is best; *Hub.* 179
this I *wot* withall, that we shall ronne *Hub.* 183
And yet (God *wote*) small oddes I often see *Hub.* 373
little els (God *wote*) could thereof skill; *Hub.* 381
manie eke of them (God *wote*) are driven *Hub.* 539
little *wote* what doth thereto behove. *T.M.* 396
Wote ye why, his Moother . . . hath coovered his Face? *Tetrasticon* 3
well I *wot* my rymes bene rudely dight. *As.* Pr. 12
well I *wot,* sith I my selfe was there, *Col.* 735
well I *wot,* that there amongst them bee *Col.* 751
well I *wote,* that oft I heard it spoken, *Col.* 919
'the perill of this place I better *wot* then you: I. i. 13. 2
I *wote,* that of your later fight Ye . . . forwearied be; I. i. 32. 5
Dead long ygoe, I *wote,* thou haddest bin, I. ii. 18. 3
Them to renew, I *wote,* breeds no delight, I. viii. 44. 3
'I *wote,*' (quoth he) 'whom tryall late did teach, I. ix. 31. 3
'The lenger life, I *wote,* the greater sin; I. ix. 43. 1
I *wote* that of youre toyle . . . ye both forwearied be: I. x. 17. 2
I *wote,* thou springst from ancient race I. x. 65. 1
I *wote* not whether the revenging steele Were hardned I. xi. 36. 1
well ye *wote* . . . What woman, I. xii. 31. 3
Right well I *wote,* most mighty Soveraine, II. Pr. 1. 1
'I *wote* not how he hight, II. i. 18. 5
That shall Pyrochles well requite, I *wott,* II. iv. 45. 8
Ne *wote* I but thou didst these goods bereave II. vii. 19. 3
My selfe well *wote,* and mine unequall fate: II. vii. 50. 5
But well I *wote,* II. viii. 14. 3
Great guerdon, well I *wote,* should you remaine, II. ix. 6. 7
well I *wote* . . . Thou art the roote and nourse of bitter cares, III. vi. 57. 1
All these, I *wote,* in thy protection bee, III. iv. 58. 6
Or it in Gnidus bee, I *wote* not well; III. vi. 29. 5
well I *wote* by triall, III. vi. 29. 6
My looser rimes (I *wote*) doth sharply wite IV. Pr. 1. 3
whose name I *wote* not well, IV. i. 48. 8
(That well I *wote*) IV. i. 48. 9
to let men plainely *wot* It was no mortall worke, IV. xi. 45. 8
well I *wote* that these, which I descry, IV. xi. 53. 4
Some men, I *wote,* will deeme in Artegall Great weaknesse, V. vi. 1. 1
I *wote* when ye did watch both night and day V. vi. 25. 5
'Certes I *wote* not well,' V. viii. 15. 5
'Then *wote* ye well, that I Doe serve a Queene V. viii. 16. 6
This well I *wote,* that sure she is as great, V. x. 1. 5
'Then *wote* you, Sir, that in this Church hereby V. xi. 19. 1
Ne *wote* I surely whether her he yet have fond.' VI. i. 16. 9
Then *wote* ye that I am a Briton borne, VI. ii. 27. 6
This well I *wote,* VI. vi. 43. 4
'Then *wote,* thou shepheard, whatsoever thou bee, VI. x. 21. 2
wote thou this, thou hardy Titanesse, VII. vi. 33. 1

Wots. who *wotes* not, that womans subtiltyes Can guylen Argus, III. ix. 7. 2

Wottest. So well thou *wot'st* the mysterie of his might, *Col.* 833
Thou litle *wotest* what this right-hand can: II. iii. 16. 8

Would (*partial list*).
would That Carthage towres from spoile should be forborne, *Ro.* xxiii. 1
Through idlenes *would* turne to civill rage, *Ro.* xxiii. 7
thou pleasest not where most I *would:* *S.C.* Ja. 68
The previe marks I *would* bewray, *S.C.* Mar. 35
That some good body *woulde* once pitie mee!' *S.C.* May 248
For-thy *woulden* drawe with hem many moe. *S.C.* S. 99
of them slew at pleasure what they *wolde.* *Hub.* 336
Then *would* he seeme a Farmer, that *would* sell *Hub.* 871
Ne *would* his looser life be tide to law, I. iv. 26. 3
Ne dint of direfull sword divide the substance *would.* I. vii. 33. 9
he that never *would* Could never: I. vii. 41. 3
That like *would* not for all this worldes wealth. I. ix. 31. 4
to health restore The man that *would* not live, I. x. 27. 9
yet some he *would* give to the pore. I. x. 38. 9
ne *would* thereout be gott: I. xi. 38. 7
Would God! thy selfe now present were in place II. i. 9. 8
would, O! *would* it so had chaunst, II. i. 10. 1
ever of their loves they *would* be glad: II. ii. 28. 4
Here may ye not have entraunce, though we *would:* II. ix. 12. 4
We *would,* and *would* againe, if that we could; II. ix. 12. 5
never idle was, ne once *would* (*could) rest a whit. II. ix. 49. 9
Full many did affray, that else faine enter *would.* IV. x. 16. 9
He *wold,* by all good means he might, deserve such grace. V. v. 55. 9
Compelling her, wher she *would* not, by force, VI. vii. 44. 3

Wouldst (*partial list*).
wouldest me my springing youngth to spil: *S.C.* F. 52
(As now thou *wouldest* me: *S.C.* Jul. 218
'Vaine man,' . . . 'that *wouldest* be reckoned A II. vi. 9. 5
Wouldst gather faine, and yet no paines *wouldst* take: IV. ii. 14. 4
But *wouldest* needs thine owne conceit areed! VII. vi. 46. 8

Wound. freshly bleeding of a grievous *wounde.* *Rev.* i. 8
Laments the *wound* that death did launch. *S.C.* N. 139
ranckling *wound* as yet does rifelye bleede. *S.C.* D. 94
hast thy deathes *wound?* *S.C.* D. 95
I felt such anguish *wound* my feeble heart, *Ti.* 482
ward his gentle corpes from cruell *wound;* *Mui.* 60
Gave her the fatall *wound* of deadlie smart, *D.* 158
accents, which like swords Did *wound* my heart, *D.* 298
So deadly was the dint and deep the *wound,* *As.* 121
To stop his *wound* that wondrously did bleed! *As.* 132
They stopt his *wound,* *As.* 145

Wound—*Continued.*
ne ward the daunger of the *wound;* *Col.* 876
The Mirrhe sweete-bleeding in the bitter *wound;* I. i. 9. 6
her huge traine All suddenly about his body *wound,* I. i. 18. 7
They flocked all about her bleeding *wound,* I. i. 25. 7
with fresh clay did close the wooden *wound:* I. ii. 44. 8
from his gored *wound* a well of bloud did gush. I. iii. 35. 9
In stead of foe to *wound* my friend amis?' I. iii. 39. 5
none can *wound* the man that does them wield.' I. iv. 50. 7
the first *wound* That launched hath my brest I. vii. 25. 6
She fedd her *wound* with fresh renewed bale. I. vii. 28. 6
Dismayed with so desperate deadly *wound,* I. viii. 11. 1
A sea of blood gusht from the gaping *wownd,* I. viii. 16. 6
Such percing griefe her stubborne hart did *wound,* I. viii. 25. 4
that fresh bleeding *wound,* which . . . doth rancle I. ix. 7. 3
'what secret *wound* Could ever find to grieve the gentlest hart I. ix. 7. 8
That any *wownd* could heale incontinent. I. ix. 19. 5
blood . . . from his *wound* yet welled fresh, I. ix. 36. 7
His huge long tayle, *wownd* up in hundred foldes, I. xi. 11. 1
The percing steele there wrought a *wound* full wyde, I. xi. 20. 8
The beast, impatient of his smarting *wound* I. xi. 25. 6
to the scull a yawning *wound* it made: I. xi. 35. 8
The cruell *wound* enraged him so sore, I. xi. 37. 1
The stricken Deare doth chalenge by the bleeding *wound.'* II. i. 12. 9
A cruell knife that made a griesly *wownd,* II. i. 39. 6
Out of her gored *wound* the cruell steel II. i. 43. 1
gor'd with many a *wownd,* II. iv. 3. 8
As steele can *wound,* or strength can overthroe. II. iv. 10. 5
Then *wounde* of gealous worme, II. iv. 28. 9
Through many a stroke and many a streaming *wound,* II. v. 36. 8
purple robe gored with many a *wound,* II. vii. 13. 7
gan a cursed hand the quiet wombe . . . to *wound,* II. vii. 17. 2
He groveling fell, all gored in his gushing *wound.* II. viii. 32. 9
Unmindfull of his *wound,* of his fate ignoraunt. II. viii. 34. 9
Out of the *wound* the red blood flowed fresh, II. viii. 36. 8
Wyde was the *wound,* II. viii. 39. 1
All were the *wownd* so wide and wonderous II. xi. 38. 2
that same net so cunningly was *wound,* II. xii. 82. 2
lost much blood through many a *wownd,* III. i. 21. 5
tasted many a bloody *wownd.'* III. i. 24. 9
her *wound* still inward freshly bledd, III. i. 56. 3
yet was the *wound* not deepe, III. i. 65. 6
she did not feele the *wound,* III. ii. 26. 8
mine is not' (quoth she) 'like other *wownd;* III. ii. 36. 1
launched this *wound* wyde. III. ii. 37. 9
With such selfe-pleasing thoughts her *wound* she fedd, III. iv. 6. 1
the deepe *wound* more deep engord her hart, III. iv. 6. 4
This was that woman, this that deadly *wownd,* III. iv. 28. 1
so deepe *wound* through these deare members drive. III. iv. 37. 4
They softly gan to search his griesly *wownd:* III. iv. 40. 2
ofte his mother, vewing his wide *wownd,* III. iv. 44. 3
Three fosters Timias *wound;* III. v. Arg.
Exceeding griefe that *wound* in him empight, III. v. 20. 8
a large streame of blood out of the *wound* did flow. III. v. 21. 9
of that cruell *wound* he bled so sore, III. v. 26. 2
Into his *wound* the juice thereof did scruze; III. v. 33. 4
She with her scarf did bind the *wound* III. v. 33. 9
their Lady dresse his *wownd,* III. v. 38. 2
His readie *wound* with better salves new drest: III. v. 41. 4
heales up one, and makes another *wound!* III. v. 42. 2
his *wound* did gather, and grow hole, III. v. 43. 1
Whiles dayly playsters to his *wownd* she layd, III. v. 43. 5
Least that his *wound* were inly well not heald, III. v. 49. 2
His feeble hart wide launched with loves cruel *wownd.* III. vi. 52. 9
to the *wound* his weake heart opened wyde: III. ix. 29. 2
For whom so faire a Lady feeles so sore a *wound!'* III. xi. 11. 9
a wide *wound* therein . . . Entrenched deep with knyfe III. xii. 20. 5
Albe the *wound* were nothing deepe imprest, III. xii. 33. 7
round about Her tender waste was *wound,* III. xii. 37. 8
the wyde *wound,* which lately did dispart III. xii. 38. 3
golden lockes, . . . About her backe and all her bodie *wound:* IV. i. 13. 5
Yet from the *wound* no drop of bloud there fell, IV. iii. 8. 6
through both sides the *wound* appeard. IV. iii. 33. 9
in his head an hideous *wound* imprest: IV. iii. 34. 4
About the which two Serpents weren *wound,* IV. iii. 42. 2
therein made a very griesly *wound,* IV. iv. 24. 6
Through grievaunce of his late received *wound,* IV. iv. 26. 8
his *wound* he soone forgot, IV. iv. 33. 2
Such was the *wound* that Scudamour did gride, IV. vi. 1. 8
long time his grieved hart did *wound,* IV. vi. 28. 5
To hide her *wound,* that none might it perceive: IV. vi. 40. 8
adding anguish to the bitter *wound* IV. vii. 1. 7
of his owne rash hand one *wound* was to be seene. IV. vii. 35. 9
Shap'd like a heart yet bleeding of the *wound,* IV. viii. 6. 8
Through her late hurts, and through that haplesse *wound* IV. viii. 19. 8
wound the soule it selfe with griefe unkind; IV. viii. 26. 7
Her spightfull words did pricke and *wound* the inner part. IV. viii. 26. 9
with deadly *wound* My heart was launcht, IV. x. 1. 7
to my *wound* her gratious help impart. IV. x. 48. 5
Marinells former *wound* is heald, IV. xi. Arg.
of the *wound* he yet in languor lyes, IV. xi. 5. 7
that same former fatall *wound* of his IV. xii. 22. 5
th' heapes of those which he did *wound* and slay, V. v. 19. 6
wyder made the *wound* of th' hidden dart. V. v. 28. 5
'This griefes deepe *wound* I would to thee disclose, V. v. 30. 7
Yet durst she not disclose her fancies *wound,* V. v. 44. 1
it bit Unto the bone, and made a griesly *wound,* V. vii. 33. 3
of her *wound* which sore did paine, V. vii. 34. 5
made a griesly *wound* in his enriven side. V. viii. 34. 9
Torne all to rags, and rent with many a *wound;* V. viii. 42. 7

Wound—*Continued.*
The wicked stroke did *wound* his enemy . . . . V. xi. 6. 8
Fought many battels without *wound* or losse; . . . . V. xi. 53. 7
cruelly does *wound* whom so she wils: . . . . V. xii. 36. 5
to make them pierce and *wound* more deepe, ... V. xii. 42. 6
He sore doth *wound*, and bite, and cruelly torment.' . . . . VI. i. 8. 9
shame he weend a sleeping wight to *wound*. . . . . VI. i. 34. 4
through the *wound* his spirit shortly did depart.' . . . . . VI. ii. 12. 9
And him unarm'd, . . . mortally did *wound*, ... VI. ii. 43. 5
Having both sides through grypt with griesly *wound*. . . . VI. iii. 27. 5
Yet ceast he not for all that cruell *wound*, ... VI. iii. 51. 1
Ne sparing him the more for all his grievous *wound*. . . . VI. iv. 2. 9
Yet in his bodie made no *wound* nor bloud appeare. . . . . VI. iv. 5. 9
the sharpnesse of her rankling *wound*: . . . . VI. iv. 9. 9
The juyce whereof into his *wound* he wrought, ... VI. iv. 12. 8
ere long he had that knightes *wound* Recured well, ... VI. iv. 16. 6
Least that the beasts sharpe teeth had any *wound* Made . . VI. iv. 23. 8
staunch the bleeding of her dreary *wound*: . . . . VI. v. 6. 5
both in minde, . . . And body have receiv'd a mortall *wound*, VI. v. 28. 4
trayterously did *wound* her weary Knight. . . . . VI. v. 33. 9
No *wound*, which warlike hand of enemy Inflicts . . . . . . VI. vi. 1. 1
all the passions heale which *wound* the weaker spright. . . VI. vi. 3. 9
with many a *wound* Did slay againe, ... VI. vii. 16. 8
Words sharpely *wound*, but greatest griefe of scorning growes. VI. vii. 49. 9
with the selfe same *wound* Launcht through the arme, . . . VI. xi. 19. 8
Ne cared she her *wound* in teares to steepe, ... VI. xi. 23. 8
scarsely suffring her infestred *wound* . . . to be drest. . . VI. xi. 24. 6
with secret *wound* . . . empierced were, ... VI. xii. 4. 7
He tooke it up and in his mantle *wound*; . . . . VI. xii. 9. 7
Deepe is the *wound*, that dints the parts . . . . *Am.* vi. 11
Shoot out his darts to base affections *wound*; . . . . *Am.* viii. 6
Of my harts *wound*, and of my bodies griefe; . . . . *Am.* l. 2
Seekes . . . to salve each others *wound*: . . . . *Am.* lxv. 12
how great the smart Of those whom thou dost *wound*: . . . *Epig.* iv. 36
She drest his *wound*, ... *Epig.* iv. 45
loves deepe *wound*, that pierst the piteous hart . . . . . . *H.H.L.* 156
What . . thought can think the depth of so deare *wound*? . *H.H.L.* 163

Wounded. *See* **Deep-wounded, Late-wounded.**
Him Love hath *wounded* with a deadly darte: . . . . *S.C.* Ap. 22
Full mortally this Knight *ywounded* was, ... *Ti.* 650
A virgin widow, whose deepe *wounded* mind . . . did languish, I. ii. 24. 8
With flashing thunderbolt *ywounded* sore: . . . . I. v. 40. 6
To Aesculapius brought the *wounded* knight: . . . . I. v. 41. 3
The sad earth, *wounded* with so sore assay, ... I. viii. 8. 7
Th' eternall bale of heavie *wounded* harts: . . . . I. viii. 14. 5
sinfull horror workes in *wounded* hart, ... I. x. 23. 3
goodly counsell, that for *wounded* hart Is meetest med'cine, . II. i. 44. 2
Shee sight from bottome of her *wounded* brest; . . . . II. i. 47. 2
Such *wounded* beast as that I did not see, ... II. iii. 33. 5
he his foe has hurt and *wounded* sore, ... II. v. 22. 3
with that wicked shafte him *wounded* had, ... III. v. 24. 2
which with her arrowes keene She *wounded* had, ... III. v. 28. 3
Thither they brought that *wounded* Squyre, ... III. v. 41. 1
Their wofull harts he *wounded* had whyleare . . . . III. vi. 13. 8
as a Snake, still lurked in his *wounded* mynd. . . . . . . III. x. 55. 9
A *wounded* Dragon under him did ly, ... III. xi. 48. 6
maske her *wounded* mind, ... IV. i. 7. 4
noble Knight, After he had so often *wounded* beene, ... IV. iii. 23. 2
went away sore *wounded* of his haplesse hand. . . . . IV. iv. 21. 9
many knights unhorst, and many *wounded*, ... V. iii. 6. 6
all the *wounded*, . . . To be convayed in, ... V. iv. 45. 8
Being fast fixed in her *wounded* spright, ... V. v. 27. 4
She *wounded* was with her deceipts owne dart, ... V. v. 43. 6
being *wounded* of the huntsmans hand . . . . V. viii. 35. 6
to daunger drove, And left sore *wounded*: . . . . VI. ii. 20. 6
This knight, . . . had *wounded* sore Another knight . . . . VI. ii. 40. 5
that courteous deed Done to that *wounded* Knight . . . . . VI. iii. 2. 5
And was the Father of that *wounded* Knight, ... VI. iii. 3. 7
But by her *wounded* love did watch all night, ... VI. iii. 10. 3
him seemed fit that *wounded* Knight To visite, ... VI. iii. 14. 1
By reason that her knight was *wounded* sore: . . . . VI. iv. 10. 6
comming likewise to the *wounded* knight, ... VI. iv. 12. 1
this Squire, who likewise *wounded* was . . . . VI. v. 31. 6
that beastes teeth, which *wounded* you tofore, ... VI. vi. 9. 1
Like as the *wounded* Whale to shore flies from the maine. . . VI. x. 31. 9
The inward languor of my *wounded* hart, ... *Am.* l. 10
Love *wounded* my Loves hart, ... *Epig.* ii. 7
I *wounded* am full sore: . . . . *Epig.* iv. 28
he *wounded* hath my selfe With his sharpe dart of love: . . *Epig.* iv. 55
Whom having *wounded*, backe againe they go, ... *H.B.* 242

Woundeth. the winged God that *woundeth* harts . . . . . . VI. viii. 22. 1

Wounding. *See* **Heart-wounding.**
wounding words, and termes of foule repriefe, ... I. ix. 29. 4

Woundless. doubted Knights, whose *woundlesse* armour rusts, *S.C.* O. 41

Wound's. to returne againe To his *wounds* worker, ... VI. x. 31. 7

Wounds. *wounds* my soule with rufull memorie, ... *Pet.*[2] iv. 13
Nor the deep *wounds* of victours raging blade, ... *Ro.* xiii. 2
oft the bloud springeth from *woundes* wyde; . . . . *S.C.* F. 176
made many *wounds* in the wast Oake. . . . . *S.C.* F. 202
Such *woundes* soone wexen wider. . . . . *S.C.* Au. 96
With bitter *woundes* her owne deere babes to slay, ... *Gn.* 399
with wide *wounds* their carcases doth rend; . . . . *Gn.* 414
Flames, weapons, *wounds*, in Greeks fleete to have tynde. . . *Gn.* 504
blood throgh many *wounds* therein receaved, ... *Hub.* 207
launch your hearts with lamentable *wounds* . . . . *T.M.* 375
Wide *wounds* emongst them many one he made, ... *As.* 107
Wherein old dints of deepe *woundes* did remaine, ... I. i. 1. 3
Seeing the gored *woundes* to gape so wyde, ... I. v. 9. 8
In wine and oyle they wash his *woundes* wide, ... I. v. 17. 4
His cruell *wounds*, with cruddy bloud congeald, ... I. v. 29. 6

Wounds—*Continued.*
His cunning hand gan to his *wounds* to lay, ... I. v. 44. 2
his *woundes* wyde Not throughly heald . . . . I. v. 45. 4
Washing his bloody *wounds*, ... I. vi. 39. 9
with their drery *wounds*, and bloody gore, ... I. vi. 45. 5
Arthure . . . *wounds* the beast, ... I. viii. Arg.
bloody gore, Which flowed from his *wounds* . . . . I. viii. 24. 5
The swelling of his *woundes* to mitigate; . . . . I. x. 26. 4
With heat, toyle, *wounds*, armes, smart, and inward fire, . . I. xi. 28. 2
deadly *wounds* could heale, ... I. xi. 48. 7
Did heale his *woundes*, and scorching heat alay; . . . . . . I. xi. 50. 6
All healed of his hurts and *woundes* wide, ... I. xi. 52. 2
Sharpe be thy *wounds*, but sweete the medicines be, ... II. i. 36. 8
he did her deadly *wounds* repaire, ... II. i. 43. 8
He gan to comfort, and his *woundes* to dresse. . . . . II. iv. 16. 6
Through *wounds*, and strokes, and stubborne handeling, . . . II. iv. 33. 2
Furors chayne untyes, Who him sore *wounds*: . . . . II. v. Arg.
His deadly *woundes* within my liver swell, ... II. vi. 50. 3
Then searcht his secret *woundes*, ... II. vi. 51. 3
their sharpe *wounds* and noyous injuries, ... II. ix. 16. 7
medicine, That mote recure their *wounds*; . . . . II. xi. 21. 9
Wounds without hurt, a body without might, ... II. xi. 40. 5
Through losse of blood which from his *wounds* did bleed, . . . II. xi. 48. 5
al the while his *wounds* were dressing by him stayd. . . . . II. xi. 49. 9
sory *wounds* right well recur'd, ... III. i. 1. 4
Salves to his *wounds*, and medicines of might; . . . . III. iv. 43. 8
Hast drest my sinfull *wounds*? . . . . III. v. 35. 9
Full many *wounds* in his corrupted flesh . . . . III. vii. 32. 6
he there sojourned his *woundes* to heale; . . . . III. x. 5. 6
many wide *woundes* launched through his inner partes. . . . III. xi. 44. 9
Dying . . . with inward *wounds* of dolours dart. . . . . . . III. xii. 16. 9
Had power to staunch al *wounds* that mortally did bleed. . . IV. iii. 39. 9
all his *wounds*, and all his bruses guarisht; . . . . IV. iii. 29. 5
Strokes, *wounds*, wards, weapons, all they did despise, . . . IV. iii. 36. 3
by their many *wounds* and carelesse harmes, ... IV. iv. 38. 3
Untill that they their *wounds* well healed had, ... IV. vi. 39. 8
did softly dew, Her *wounds*, ... IV. viii. 20. 8
shew the *wounds* which unto thee befell; . . . . V. iii. 21. 7
(so shewed forth his *wounds*) . . . . V. iii. 22. 3
Him to refresh, and her late *wounds* to heale: . . . . V. vii. 42. 2
Full deadly *wounds* where so it is empight; . . . . V. xi. 24. 6
many *wounds* into his flesh it made, ... V. xii. 19. 8
of his *wounds* he wexed hole and strong; . . . . VI. i. 47. 8
With many *wounds* full perilous and wyde, ... VI. ii. 40. 8
her sad selfe . . . constrayning, To wype his *wounds*, ... VI. ii. 41. 5
And powring balme, . . . Into his *wounds*, ... VI. ii. 48. 4
so ill bedight With bleeding *wounds*, ... VI. iii. 4. 2
And with her teares his *wounds* did wash . . . . VI. iii. 10. 5
Till she recured were of those her *woundes* wide. . . . . . . VI. iii. 28. 9
both whose sides are pearst With *wounds*, ... VI. iii. 39. 4
so much her *wounds* did bleede; . . . . VI. iii. 46. 4
having there their *wounds* awhile redrest, ... VI. iv. 15. 8
In seeking . . . For herbes to dresse their *wounds*; . . . . . VI. iv. 16. 4
Regardlesse of her *wounds* yet bleeding rife, ... VI. v. 5. 2
now her *wounds* corruption gan to breed: . . . . VI. v. 31. 5
for grievous paine Of their late *woundes*, ... VI. v. 39. 8
Such were the *wounds* the which that Blatant Beast Made . . VI. vi. 2. 1
humour which did most infest Their rancKling *wounds*, . . . VI. vi. 2. 9
as he was searching of their *wounds*, ... VI. vi. 5. 1
when they did perceave Their *wounds* recur'd, ... VI. vi. 15. 7
was fall'n into this feeble case Through many *wounds*, . . . VI. vi. 20. 8
griesly *wounds* that him appalled sore; . . . . VI. vii. 14. 5
Witnesse the *wounds*, and this wyde bloudie lake, ... VI. vii. 15. 5
So weake my powres, so sore my *wounds*, ... *Am.* lvii. 5
al my *wounds* wil heale in little space. . . . . *Am.* lvii. 14
many harts . . . with wyde *wounds* embrewed, ... *H.L.* 13
yet bleeding hart With thousand *wounds* . . . . *H.L.* 143
wounds the life, and wastes the inmost marrow. . . . . . . *H.B.* 63
With bitter *wounds* through hands, through feet, and syde! . *H.H.L.* 245

Wounds'. Sharpe Isope, good for greene *wounds* remedies, . . . *Mui.* 190

Wount. *See* **Wont.**

Woven. *See* **Well-woven.**
woven so they were, As snowe and golde together . . . . . *Pet.* vi. 5
Whose cruell fate is *woven* even now . . . . *Mui.* 235
tinsell trappings, *woven* like a wave, ... I. ii. 13. 8
cruell Sarazin, In *woven* maile all armed warily; . . . . . . I. v. 4. 2
That seemd like silke and silver *woven* neare; . . . . I. xii. 22. 8
With boughes and arbours *woven* cunningly, ... II. vi. 2. 8
Woven with antickes and wyld ymagery; . . . . II. vii. 4. 6
heare Was trimly *woven* and in tresses wrought, ... II. ix. 19. 7
nets, which oft we *woven* see Of scorched deaw, ... II. xii. 77. 8
goodly arras . . . *Woven* with gold and silke, ... III. xi. 28. 3
her fayre lockes were *woven* up in gold: . . . . III. xii. 13. 4
Woven uppon with silver, subtly wrought, ... V. v. 2. 2
as your worke is *woven* all above . . . . *Am.* lxxi. 9

Wox. *See* **Waxed.**
So faynt they *woxe*, and feeble in the folde, ... *S.C.* Ja. 5
whose flowre is *woxe* a weede, ... *S.C.* Jun. 109
the Ape in wondrous stomack *woxe*, ... *Hub.* 1103
doubly faire *wox* both in mynd and face. . . . . *As.* 18
He *woxe* dismaid, and gan his fate to feare: . . . . I. xi. 52. 8
Carelesse the man soone *woxe*, ... II. vi. 13. 7
The Palmer . . . *Woxe* sore affraid, ... II. viii. 9. 3
when this breathlesse *woxe*, that batteil gan renew. . . . . II. viii. 47. 9
insolent *wox* through unwonted ease, ... II. x. 17. 2
Nigh his wits end then *woxe* th' amazed knight, ... II. xi. 44. 1
all the three thereat *woxe* much afrayd, ... II. xii. 22. 6
The royall Maid *woxe* inly wondrous glad, ... III. ii. 11. 1
full of fancies fraile, She *woxe*; . . . . III. ii. 27. 6
Th' old woman *wox* half blanck those wordes to heare, . . . III. iii. 17. 8

Wox—*Continued.*
All suddeinly dim *wox* the dampish ayre, . . . III. iv. 52. 1
his hart *woxe* sore, and health decayd: . . . III. v. 43. 2
woxe halfe wroth against her damzels slacke, . . . III. vi. 19. 3
The foolish man thereat *woxe* wondrous blith, . . . III. x. 33. 1
woxe afeard Of outrage for the words . . . IV. i. 50. 3
He *woxe* full blithe, as he had got thereby, . . . IV. i. 50. 8
he *woxe* therewith displeased sore, . . . IV. iv. 45. 6
woxe nigh mad for very harts despight, . . . IV. v. 27. 2
when the world *woxe* old, it *woxe* warre old, . . . IV. viii. 31. 6
in wickednesse *woxe* bold, . . . IV. viii. 31. 8
he *woxe* full glad To see his foe . . . IV. viii. 46. 1
so weake of limbe, and sicke of love He *woxe*, . . . IV. xii. 20. 7
woxe inclined much unto her part, . . . V. ix. 46. 3
He *wox* right blyth, as he had got thereby, . . . V. xi. 9. 6
when her he mist, He *woxe* halfe mad; . . . VI. ii. 20. 7
He wearie *woxe*, and backe return'd againe . . . VI. iv. 9. 3
He *woxe* nigh mad with wrath and fell despight, . . . VI. vi. 24. 8
Then Coridon *woxe* frollicke, that earst seemed dead. . . . VI. ix. 42. 9
Woxen. *See* **Waxed, Waxen, Wox.**
As if my yeare were wast and *woxen* old; . . . *S.C.* Ja. 28
good Harpalus, now *woxen* aged . . . *Col.* 380
that proud people, *woxen* insolent Through many victories, . *Ded. Son.* vi. 10
Through unadvized rashnes *woxen* wood; . . . I. iv. 34. 3
quickning faith, that earst was *woxen* weake, . . . I. v. 12. 3
all his sinewes *woxen* weake and raw, . . . I. x. 2. 3
By this Charissa, . . . Was *woxen* strong, . . . I. x. 29. 8
her sisters children, *woxen* strong, . . . II. x. 32. 6
Spoild of their rosy red were *woxen* pale and wan. . . . III. v. 29. 9
he, through privy griefe . . . Is *woxen* so deform'd . . . III. x. 60. 8
All *woxen* weary of their journall toyle: . . . III. xii. 47. *or.* 4
Scudamour, now *woxen* inly glad . . . IV. vi. 28. 1
through long fasting *woxen* pale and wan, . . . IV. vii. 43. 3
when as Calepine was *woxen* strong, . . . VI. iv. 17. 1
all this world is *woxen* daily worse. . . . VII. vi. 6. 6
Till greater then my wombe thou *woxen* art: . . . *Am.* ii. 4
Wrack. Lewdly complainest thou . . . Of Winters *wracke* . . . *S.C.* F. 10
Thy scepter rent, and power put to *wrack;* . . . *T.M.* 400
rocke . . . That lay in waite her *wrack* for to bewaile, . . . I. vi. 1. 3
Thinking to worke on her his utmost *wracke,* . . . IV. vi. 21. 2
on his foes did worke full cruell *wracke:* . . . IV. ix. 25. 4
by *wracke* that wretches hath distrest, . . . V. iv. 19. 5
with bitter *wracke* To wreake on me the guilt . . . VI. ii. 21. 5
at her perill bide the wrathfull Thunders *wrack.* . . . VII. vi. 12. 9
through tempests cruel *wracke,* . . . *Am.* xxxviii. 1
Will both together me too sorely *wracke.* . . . *Am.* xlvi. 12
Wracked. it must be *wrackt* On the rough rocks, . . . III. iv. 9. 3
Wrackful. Fearelesse of foes, and fortunes *wrackfull* yre . . . VI. ix. 27. 7
Wrake. *See* **Wroke, Wroken.**
wrath of cruell wight on thee *ywrake,* . . . IV. viii. 14. 8
Wrap. His looser locks doth *wrap* in wreath of vine: . . . *Gn.* 114
evill hap Unworthy in such wretchednes doth *wrap,* . . . *Hub.* 602
enfold In covert vele, and *wrap* in shadowes light, . . . II. Pr. 5. 2
uncurteous Carle, . . . *wrap* in grievous woe. . . . III. ix. 17. 9
shadowes gan . . . *wrap* in darkenes dreare; . . . III. xi. 55. 4
Wrapped. His hinder heele was *wrapt* in a clout, . . . *S.C.* May 243
lyeth *wrapt* in lead, . . . *S.C.* Jun. 89
all the worthies liggen *wrapt* in leade, . . . *S.C.* O. 63
Dead, and lyeth *wrapt* in lead. . . . *S.C.* N. 59
wrapt his scalie boughts with fell despight, . . . *Gn.* 255
wrapt his winges twaine In lymie snares . . . *Mui.* 428
the man so *wrapt* in Errours endlesse traine! . . . I. i. 18. 9
carelesse Quiet lyes *Wrapt* in eternall silence . . . I. i. 41. 9
His garment . . . his naked sides he *wrapt* abouts; . . . I. ix. 36. 3
wrapped be in loves of former Dame, . . . I. xii. 30. 8
I *wrapt* myselfe in Palmers weed, . . . II. i. 52. 8
Their feet unshod, their bodies *wrapt* in rags, . . . II. xi. 23. 4
wrapt in fetters of a golden tresse, . . . V. viii. 1. 7
Wrapt in great dolours and in deadly feares . . . V. x. 6. 7
Cover'd with cold, and *wrapt* in wretchednesse; . . . VI. iii. 44. 7
wrapt In sad misfortunes foule deformity . . . VI. v. 1. 2
Wrapped in wretched cares and hearts unrest, . . . VI. xi. 3. 2
when he *wrapped* found Th' abandond spoyle, . . . VI. xii. 9. 4
wrapped well In many weeds . . . VII. vii. 42. 1
She tooke him streight . . . And *wrapt* him in her smock: . . . *Epig.* iv. 42
She *wrapt* him softly, . . . *Epig.* iv. 43
In simple cratch, *wrapt* in a wad of hay, . . . *H.H.L.* 226
Wrapping. *wrapping* up her wrethed sterne arownd, . . . I. i. 18. 5
Wrast. *See* **Wrest.**
Wrate. *See* **Writ, Wrote.**
With living blood he those characters *wrate,* . . . III. xii. 31. 3
Wrath. Nor *wrath* of Gods, nor spight of men unstable, . . . *Ro.* xiii. 7
'Thou barrein ground, whome winters *wrath* hath wasted, . . . *S.C.* Ja. 19
Encreasing his *wrath* with many a threate: . . . *S.C.* F. 194
Winters *wrath* beginnes to quell, . . . *S.C.* Mar. 8
They heapen hylles of *wrath;* . . . *S.C.* Jul. 202
sadde winters *wrathe,* and season chill, . . . *S.C.* N. 33
through Joves avengefull *wrath,* . . . *T.M.* 8
The vassals of Gods *wrath,* and slaves of sin. . . . *T.M.* 126
winters stormie *wrath* . . . *T.M.* 236
What *wrath* of Gods, or wicked influence . . . *T.M.* 481
in their *wrath* breake off the vitall bands, . . . *D.* 18
gan threaten hellish paine, And sad Proserpines *wrath,* . . . I. ii. 2. 7
his light-foot steede, Pricked with *wrath* . . . I. ii. 8. 4
Paynim forward came so . . . full of *wrath,* . . . I. iii. 35. 2
him beside rides fierce revenging *Wrath,* Upon a Lion, . . . I. iv. 33. 1
Full many mischiefes follow cruell *Wrath:* . . . I. iv. 35. 1
Such one was *Wrath,* the last of this ungodly tire. . . . I. iv. 35. 9
burning blades . . . The instruments of *wrath* and heavinesse. I. v. 6. 5
mov'd with *wrath,* and shame, and Ladies sake, . . . I. v. 12. 5

Wrath—*Continued.*
Can Night defray The *wrath* of thundring Jove, . . . I. v. 42. 9
Provokt with *Wrath* and Envyes false surmise, . . . I. v. 46. 7
Where foming *wrath* their cruell tuskes they whett, . . . I. vi. 44. 7
Inflamd with scornefull *wrath* and high disdaine, . . . I. viii. 7. 2
calmd his *wrath* with goodly temperance. . . . I. viii. 34. 5
Against the day of *wrath* to burden thee? . . . I. ix. 46. 5
ever burning *wrath* before him laid, . . . I. ix. 50. 3
wrath and hatred warely to shonne, . . . I. x. 33. 5
That drew on men Gods hatred and his *wrath,* . . . I. x. 33. 6
his avenging *wrath* to clemency incline. . . . I. x. 51. 9
Was swoln with *wrath* and poyson, . . . I. xi. 8. 9
Did burne with *wrath,* and sparkled living fyre: . . . I. xi. 14. 2
*The knight was *wrath* to see his stroke beguyld, . . . I. xi. 25. 1
Inflam'd with *wrath,* his raging blade he hefte, . . . I. xi. 39. 6
when that Princes *wrath* was pacifide, . . . I. xii. 36. 6
suffred not in *wrath* his hasty steps to stray. . . . II. i. 34. 9
Imprinted had that token of his *wrath,* . . . II. ii. 4. 4
O! fly from *wrath;* . . . II. ii. 30. 5
he feard her *wrath,* and threatned shott, . . . II. iii. 43. 4
him move to *wrath,* and indignation reare. . . . II. iv. 5. 9
Occasion; the roote of all *wrath* and despight. . . . II. iv. 10. 9
To wreake my *wrath* on him that first it wrought: . . . II. iv. 30. 5
Wrath, gelosy, griefe, love, this Squyre have laide thus low. . . . II. iv. 34. 9
'*Wrath,* gealosie, griefe, love, do thus expell: . . . II. iv. 35. 1
Wrath is a fire; and gealosie a weede; . . . II. iv. 35. 2
So shall *wrath,* gealosy, griefe, love, die and decay.' . . . II. iv. 35. 9
breathes out *wrath* and hainous crueltee: . . . II. iv. 43. 8
'that does seek Occasion to *wrath,* and cause of strife: . . . II. iv. 44. 2
now quench thy whott emboyling *wrath:* . . . II. v. 18. 5
griefe and *wrath,* that be her enemies . . . II. vi. 1. 6
The *wrath* which Atin kindled in his mind, . . . II. vi. 2. 3
Mammon emmoved was with inward *wrath;* . . . II. vii. 51. 1
To wreake your *wrath* on this dead seeming knight, . . . II. viii. 27. 4
fraught with great griefe And *wrath,* . . . II. viii. 33. 2
Breathing out *wrath,* and bellowing disdaine, . . . II. viii. 42. 6
Whereat renfierst with *wrath* and sharp regret, . . . II. viii. 45. 1
with *wrath* outrageous And cruell rancour . . . II. x. 43. 4
Flying from Junoes *wrath* and hard assay, . . . II. xii. 13. 5
some for *wrath* to see their captive Dame: . . . II. xii. 86. 5
Full of disdainefull *wrath* he fierce uprose . . . III. i. 9. 1
To slake your *wrath,* and mollify your mind' . . . III. ii. 13. 4
'Ne shall he yet his *wrath* so mitigate, . . . III. iii. 37. 1
thy cruell *wrath* and spightfull wrong . . . III. iv. 8. 7
Her former sorrow into suddein *wrath,* . . . III. iv. 12. 6
To wreake the *wrath,* which he did earst revive . . . III. v. 16. 4
through *wrath* and vengeaunce making way, . . . III. v. 21. 1
turning her feare to foolish *wrath,* . . . III. vii. 8. 1
with countenance sterne All full of *wrath,* . . . IV. ii. 25. 2
his sword he drew, The instrument of *wrath,* . . . IV. iv. 41. 4
touched was with secret *wrath* and shame . . . IV. v. 17. 4
oft in *wrath* he thence againe uprose, . . . IV. v. 40. 5
oft in *wrath* he layd him downe againe. . . . IV. v. 40. 6
full of *wrath* for that late stroke, . . . IV. vi. 23. 1
in her *wrath* she thought them both have thrild . . . IV. vii. 36. 4
wrath of cruell wight on thee ywrake, . . . IV. viii. 14. 8
her inburning *wrath* she gan abate, . . . IV. viii. 17. 8
Whereat the Prince full *wrath* . . . IV. viii. 43. 1
instantly desired T' asswage his *wrath,* . . . IV. ix. 35. 4
When so he list in *wrath* lift up his steely brand, . . . V. i. 8. 9
To wreake your *wrath* on such a carle as hee: . . . V. iii. 36. 8
Weening at once her *wrath* on him to wreake . . . V. iv. 40. 4
Through vengeful *wrath* and sdeignfull pride half mad; . . . V. iv. 43. 3
shun the dred despight Of her fierce *wrath,* . . . V. v. 16. 2
With sodaine stounds of *wrath* and griefe attone; . . . V. vi. 17. 6
The one of them, which most her *wrath* increast, . . . V. vi. 39. 4
doth wreake her *wrath* On man and beast . . . V. viii. 49. 4
when in *wrath* he threats the worlds decay, . . . V. ix. 31. 8
Latonaes childrens *wrath* that all her issue wasted. . . . V. x. 7. 9
all full of *wrath* she thus replyde: . . . VI. i. 27. 6
he, that could his *wrath* full wisely guyde, . . . VI. i. 30. 7
the stroke That . . . had so sternely wroke His *wrath* . . . VI. ii. 13. 5
as it were t' avenge his *wrath* on mee, . . . VI. ii. 22. 1
That ye will not your *wrath* upon him wreake, . . . VI. v. 30. 2
He woxe nigh mad with *wrath* and fell despight, . . . VI. vi. 24. 8
Fled from his *wrath,* . . . VI. xi. 49. 7
could the greatest *wrath* soone turne to grace, . . . VII. vi. 31. 3
I would her yield, her *wrath* to pacify: . . . *Am.* xi. 10
warne to shun the daunger of theyr *wrath.* . . . *Am.* xxxi. 8
The dreadfull tempest of her *wrath* appease, . . . *Am.* xxxviii. 7
if I speake, her *wrath* renew I shall; . . . *Am.* xliii. 2
From the just *wrath* of his avengefull threate . . . *H.H.B.* 150
Wrathful. *wrathfull* winde, Which blows cold storms, . . . *Bel.*[2] viii. 11
Like as ye see the *wrathfull* Sea from farre . . . *Ro.* xvi. 1
beare Cherefully the Winters *wrathful* cheare; . . . *S.C.* F. 26
Stir'd up through *wrathfull* Nemesis despight, . . . *Mui.* 2
The false witch did my *wrathfull* hand withhold: . . . I. ii. 39. 8
His suddein eye flaming with *wrathfull* fyre, . . . I. v. 10. 2
turning *wrathfull* fyre to lustfull heat, . . . I. vi. 3. 3
Both breathing vengeaunce, both of *wrathfull* hew. . . . I. vi. 38. 5
Jove, in *wrathfull* mood, . . . Hurles forth his thundring dart I. viii. 9. 1
Fortune, mine avowed foe, Whose *wrathful* wreakes . . . I. viii. 43. 4
The *wrathfull* beast about him turned light, . . . I. xi. 16. 7
wintry storme his *wrathful* wreck does threat; . . . I. xi. 21. 2
fate That heapd on him so many *wrathfull* wreakes; . . . I. xii. 16. 6
Against themselves turning their *wrathfull* spight, . . . II. ii. 23. 6
thousand furies wait on *wrathfull* sword; . . . II. ii. 30. 7
'thy destinies withstand My *wrathfull* will, . . . II. iii. 8. 4
With *wrathfull* hand I slew her innocent, . . . II. iv. 29. 4

Wrathful—*Continued.*
the rash assault and *wrathful* stowre Of his fiers foe, II. v. 10. 3
So pleased did his *wrathfull* purpose faire appease. II. vi. 13. 9
With *wrathfull* fire his corage kindled bright, II. vi. 30. 7
wrathfull hand wrought not her owne desire? II. viii. 15. 5
wrathfull Neptune did them drive before His whirling charet II. xii. 22. 3
His *wrathfull* will with reason to aswage; III. i. 11. 4
he turned in his *wrathfull* stownd, III. i. 21. 7
about her swayd Her *wrathfull* steele, III. i. 66. 6
disclo'ste Her clowdy care into a *wrathfull* stowre, III. iv. 13. 8
Such us'd wise Glauce to that *wrathfull* knight, IV. ii. 3. 1
The wicked weapon heard his *wrathfull* vow, IV. iii. 11. 6
Their *wrathfull* blades downe fell out of their hand, IV. iii. 48. 4
All that long while upheld her *wrathfull* hand, IV. vi. 23. 2
Therewith her *wrathfull* courage gan appall, IV. vi. 26. 7
would no longer hold The *wrathfull* weapon IV. vi. 27. 5
Relent the rigour of your *wrathfull* will, IV. vi. 32. 2
from his *wrathfull* sight To hide th' intent IV. vii. 17. 2
held her *wrathfull* hand from vengeance sore: IV. vii. 36. 6
If *wrathfull* wight, then fowle rebuke and shame IV. viii. 15. 3
all the while beheld their *wrathfull* moode, IV. ix. 22. 3
soone as they with *wrathfull* eie bewraide, IV. ix. 28. 4
sailers save from wreckes of *wrathfull* winde. IV. xi. 52. 5
Together strove, and kindled *wrathfull* fires: V. iv. 4. 5
Her *wrathful* hand from greedy vengeance to have stayd. V. v. 14. 9
she in her *wrathfull* will did cast How to revenge V. vi. 13. 1
He mote not come to wreake his *wrathfull* mood: V. viii. 35. 4
As when the *wrathfull* Boreas doth bluster, V. xi. 58. 7
having somewhat calm'd his *wrathfull* heat VI. i. 40. 2
his heart did inly flame With *wrathfull* fury VI. iii. 43. 5
laying hand upon his *wrathfull* blade VI. v. 26. 6
soone she pacifyde The *wrathfull* Prince, VI. vi. 43. 6
Then to the rest his *wrathfull* hand he bends; VI. viii. 49. 5
where shepherds lie In winters *wrathfull* time, VI. ix. 4. 9
To serve the vengeaunce of his *wrathfull* will; VI. x. 36. 2
at her perill bide the *wrathfull* Thunders wrack. VII. vi. 12. 9

Wrathfully. his sword he drew all *wrathfully,* V. i. 18. 5

Wrathfulness. So they him left inflam'd with *wrathfulnesse,* II. i. 25. 8
save Them from the tempest of his *wrathfulnesse,* II. xii. 83. 4

Wraths. Their *wraths* at length broke into open warre. *Mui.* 8
So both to wreake their *wrathes* on Britomart agreed. IV. vi. 8. 9

Wrawling. some of cats, that *wrawling* still did cry; VI. xii. 27. 4

Wreak. *See* **Wrake, Wroke.**
Beholde what *wreake,* what ruine, and what wast, *Ro.* iii. 5
to *wreake* their rash contempt, *Gn.* 579
A cruell witch, her cursed will to *wreake,* I. ii. 33. 5
brothers death to *wreak,* Sansjoy Doth chaleng I. iv. Arg.
Anothers wrongs to *wreak* upon thy selfe: I. vi. 42. 3
Jove, . . . To *wreake* the guilt of mortall sins is bent, I. viii. 9. 2
wanted sword to *wreake* his enmitee? II. iii. 12. 4
mote him honour win to *wreak* so foule despight. II. iii. 13. 9
wreake on them their hainous hatefull deed.' II. iii. 14. 9
provokt her sonne to *wreake* her wrong; II. iv. 12. 6
To *wreake* my wrath on him that first it wrought: II. iv. 30. 5
To *wreake* it selfe on beast all innocent, II. v. 5. 4
bent to *wreake* on him The wrath II. vi. 2. 2
no way is lefte to *wreake* my spight, II. viii. 15. 6
To *wreake* your wrath on this dead seeming knight, II. viii. 27. 4
On this vile body from to *wreak* my wrong, II. viii. 28. 4
wreake your wronges wrought to this knight alone, III. i. 28. 5
The which I seeke to *wreake,* and Arthegall he hight.' III. ii. 8. 9
On his sonne Edwin all those wrongs shall *wreake;* III. iii. 36. 2
To *wreake* the wrath, which he did earst revive III. v. 16. 4
Great *wreake* to many errant knights of yore, III. vii. 48. 3
wreake your sorrow on your cruell foe; III. xi. 15. 5
He now unable was to *wreake* his old despight. IV. i. 39. 9
to *wreake* the dammage by thee donne. IV. i. 44. 6
Why do I not it *wreake* on thee, now in my might? IV. i. 52. 9
On whom I waite to *wreake* that foule despight, IV. vi. 5. 8
So both to *wreake* their wrathes on Britomart agreed. IV. vi. 8. 9
wreake on him her will for so great injurie. IV. vi. 23. 9
wreake on him that did her reave.' IV. vi. 38. 9
on him selfe to *wreake* his follies owne despight. IV. vii. 39. 9
to *wreake* on worthlesse wight Your high displesure, IV. viii. 17. 2
Upon the sea to *wreake* his fell intent; IV. ix. 23. 4
To *wreake* your wrath on such a carle as hee: V. iii. 36. 8
Weening at once her wrath on him to *wreake* V. iv. 40. 4
There they did thinke them selves on her to *wreake;* V. vi. 37. 1
Upon your selves anothers wrong to *wreake?* V. viii. 11. 3
He mote not come to *wreake* his wrathfull mood: V. viii. 35. 4
To *wreake* her on that mayden messengere, V. viii. 46. 4
doth *wreake* her wrath On man and beast V. viii. 49. 4
To *wreake* on me the guilt of his owne wrong: VI. ii. 21. 6
That ye will not your wrath upon him *wreake,* VI. v. 30. 2
To this attempt to *wreake* his hid despight, VI. vii. 12. 8
willing eke to *wreake* The guilt on him VI. vii. 13. 6
wreake him selfe on them that him despise. VI. viii. 25. 4
how he her death might *wreake,* VI. xi. 34. 6

Wreaked. *See* **Recked, Wrake, Wroke, Wroken.**

Wreakful. bide the horror of his *wreakfull* hand, V. i. 8. 8

Wreaks. anie fortunes *wreakes* Could breake her course *Ro.* xxi. 7
Fild with the *wreaks* of mortall miserie; *T.M.* 124
Where mortall *wreakes* their blis may not remove; *Ti.* 397
Fortune, mine avowed foe, Whose wrathful *wreakes* I. viii. 43. 4
fate That heapd on him so many wrathfull *wreakes;* I. xii. 16. 6

Wreath. *See* **Wreathe.**
His looser locks doth wrap in *wreath* of vine: *Gn.* 114
She compast with a *wreathe* of Olyves hoarie. *Mui.* 328
round about the *wreath* this word was writ, II. iv. 38. 4
With golden *wreath* and gorgeous ornament; III. vii. 11. 3

Wreath—*Continued.*
His wast was with a *wreath* of yvie greene Engirt about, IV. vii. 7. 1
a *wreath,* that was enrold With ears of corne VII. vii. 30. 6

Wreathe. from so heavie sight his head did *wreath,* II. i. 56. 7

Wreathed. *See* **Snaky-wreathed.**
she her neck *wreath'd* from them *Bel.*[2] vi. 4
Shewing her *wreathed* rootes, and naked armes, *Ro.* xxviii. 6
his *wreathed* hornes gan newly sprout: *S.C.* May 186
passing by with rolling *wreathed* pace, *Gn.* 253
Triton, blowing loud his *wreathed* horne: *Col.* 245
wrapping up her *wrethed* sterne around, I. i. 18. 5
Whose *wreathed* boughtes when ever he unfoldes, I. xi. 11. 3
with her *wreathed* taile her middle did enfold. V. vii. 6. 9

Wreathings. dilate Their clasping armes in wanton *wreathings* intricate: II. xii. 53. 9

Wreaths. Hymen also crowne with *wreathes* of vine; *Epith.* 256

Wreck. *See* **Wreak.**
wintry storme his wrathful *wreck* does threat; I. xi. 21. 2
Threatning unheedy *wrecke* and rash decay, II. x. 6. 5
workst such *wrecke* on her to whom thou dearest art! IV. vi. 16. 9
To *wrecke* on them their follies hardyment: V. iv. 24. 5
Which death, or love, or fortunes *wreck* did rayse, *Epith.* 8
ship, . . . Doth suffer *wreck* both of her selfe and goods. *Am.* lvi. 12
Whom ye doe *wreck,* doe ruine, and destroy. *Am.* lvi. 14

Wrecked. shivered ships, which had beene *wrecked* late, II. xii. 7. 4
Either by being *wreckt* uppon the sands, V. iv. 5. 4

Wreckful. Were brought by errour or by *wreckfull* wynde; VI. viii. 36. 4

Wrecks. through the overthrow And *wreckes* of many wretches, III. iv. 22. 8
he others wrongs, and *wreckes* himselfe: III. ix. 4. 3
sailers save from *wreckes* of wrathfull winde. IV. xi. 52. 5
warres, and *wreckes,* and wicked enmitie VI. ix. 19. 6
all the woes and *wrecks* which I abide, *Am.* xxv. 11

Wrenock. A good old shepheardè, *Wrenock* was his name, *S.C.* D. 41

Wrest. *See* **Outwrest, Wrist.**
Whose meaning much I labored foorth to *wreste,* *Ti.* 486
Tryde all her arts and all her sleights thence out to *wrest.* II. xii. 81. 9
From her, . . . The wicked weapon rashly he did *wrest,* III. xii. 33. 2
he sought by slight It forth to *wrest,* IV. iii. 10. 6
by no meanes it backe againe he forth could *wrast.* V. xii. 21. 9
To blot the same with blame, or *wrest* in wicked sort. V. xii. 34. 9
Long did he *wrest* and wring it to and fro, VI. iv. 7. 1

Wrested. So unto wrong to yield my *wrested* right: III. i. 24. 5
corrupt, and *wrested* unto will: *H.B.* 158

Wrestle. Some *wrestle,* some do run, some bathe in christall flood. I. xii. 7. 9
seemed to contend And *wrestle* wantonly, II. xii. 63. 8

Wrestled. *See* **Over-wrestled.**

Wrestling. by much *wrestling* to leese the grosse. *S.C.* S. 135
by *wrestling* to wex strong and heedfull, *Hub.* 746
In *wrestling* nimble, and in renning swift, *As.* 73
Did chalenge Calidore to *wrestling* game; VI. ix. 43. 6

Wretch. 'What have I, *wretch,* deserv'd, *Gn.* 329
I, poore *wretch,* am forced to retourne *Gn.* 618
who is so bold a *wretch,* *Hub.* 973
The which, I, *wretch,* endured have thus long. *D.* 532
'Unworthy *wretch,*' (quoth he) 'of so great grace, I. x. 62. 1
What comfort can I, wofull *wretch,* conceave? II. i. 17. 2
To lett a weary *wretch* from her dew rest, II. i. 47. 7
Weake *wretch,* I wrapt myselfe in Palmers weed, II. i. 52. 8
'Which when I, *wretch*'—Not one word more she sayd, II. i. 56. 1
'Ay *wretch,*' (quoth he) II. iii. 8. 3
weake *wretch,* of many weakest one, II. iv. 17. 6
Then gan the cursed *wretch* alowd to cry, II. vii. 60. 6
espyde Another *wretch,* II. vii. 61. 2
'Unthankfull *wretch,*' (said he) 'is this the meed, III. v. 45. 1
'Me, seely *wretch,* she so at vauntage caught, III. vii. 51. 1
when she is nigh defild Of filthy *wretch?* III. viii. 27. 8
reward the *wretch* for his mesprise, III. ix. 9. 6
Unworthy *wretch* to tread upon the ground, III. xi. 11. 8
vassall to the vilest *wretch* alive, IV. vii. 12. 2
living thus a *wretch,* IV. ix. 39. 8
For lending life to me, a *wretch* unkind, V. v. 32. 5
The *wretch* that hyr'd you to this wicked deed.' VI. vii. 13. 5
Many a *wretch* for want of remedie Did languish VI. vii. 31. 2
maketh *wretch* or happie, rich or poore; VI. ix. 30. 2
Him, *wretch,* in doole would let no lenger dwell, *H.H.L.* 131

Wretched. Which make this life *wretched* and miserable, *Pet.*[2] vi. 13
wretched people travailing that way, *Van.* iii. 5
now her is a most *wretched* wight: *S.C.* S. 4
'Unwise and *wretched* men, *S.C.* N. 183
my poore *wretched* ghost Is forst to ferrie *Gn.* 337
Where *wretched* ghosts sit wailing evermore. *Gn.* 384
wretched boy, they slew with guiltie blades; *Gn.* 403
thy *wretched* need Praiseth the thing *Hub.* 595
Ah, *wretched* world! the den of wickednesse, *T.M.* 121
Ah, *wretched* world! the house of heavinesse, *T.M.* 123
Ah, *wretched* world! and all that is therein, *T.M.* 125
Of *wretched* life the onely joy shee is, *T.M.* 131
wretched persons to misfortune borne; *T.M.* 154
wring Her *wretched* hands *T.M.* 170
Bee now become most *wretched* wightes on ground. *T.M.* 312
Starres conspiring *wretched* men t' afflict, *T.M.* 482
comfort can I, *wretched* creature, have? *Ti.* 23
Too soone for all this *wretched* world, *Ti.* 293
now, more happie thou, and *wretched* wee *Ti.* 330
joyes on *wretched* lovers to be wroken, *Mui.* 99
in this *wretched* life dooth take delight, *D.* 9
Hath made fit mate thy *wretched* case to heare, *D.* 65
freed from *wretched* long imprisonment! *D.* 273
How happie was I then, and *wretched* now! *D.* 308

Wretched—*Continued.*
The one, because as I they *wretched* are; *D.* 422
whilest I in this *wretched* vale doo stay *D.* 456
I sore griev'd to see his *wretched* case. *D.* 553
Ah! *wretched* boy, the shape of dreryhead, *As.* 133
Most *wretched* he, that is and cannot tell.' *Col.* 659
us fraile men, his *wretched* vassals here, *Col.* 813
Die is my dew; yet rew my *wretched* state, I. i. 51. 7
'The *wretched* woman, whom unhappy howre I. ii. 22. 2
that happened to me heare, And to this *wretched* Lady, I. ii. 31. 6
Wretched man, *wretched* tree! I. ii. 33. 4
by my *wretched* lovers side me pight; I. ii. 42. 7
Which ever after in most *wretched* case, . . . by the hedges lay. I. iv. 3. 5
He led a *wretched* life, unto himselfe unknowne. I. iv. 28. 9
Most *wretched* wight, whom nothing might suffise; I. iv. 29. 1
'Ah! *wretched* sonne of wofull syre, I. v. 10. 5
Her wicked daies with *wretched* knife did end, I. v. 39. 2
caytive *wretched* thralls, that wayled night and day: I. v. 45. 9
the endlesse routes of *wretched* thralles, I. v. 51. 1
The *wretched* payre transformd to treen mould; I. vii. 26. 5
now in darkesome dungeon, *wretched* thrall, I. vii. 51. 7
woman . . . The roote of all your care and *wretched* plight, I. viii. 45. 5
'Thou, *wretched* man, of death hast greatest need, I. ix. 45. 1
to relieve the needes Of *wretched* soules, I. x. 3. 7
wretched world he gan for to abhore, I. x. 21. 4
he desirde to end his *wretched* dayes: I. x. 21. 8
bare *wretched* wights he dayly clad, I. x. 39. 6
wretched men, and lived in like paine.' I. x. 62. 4
wretched we, . . . Must now anew begin II. i. 32. 6
Yet can they not warne death from *wretched* wight. II. i. 36. 5
Which plonged had faire Lady in so *wretched* state. II. i. 56. 9
this *wretched* woman overcome Of anguish, II. i. 58. 6
this their *wretched* sonne, II. ii. 44. 8
heape more vengeance on that *wretched* wight: II. iv. 5. 4
he saw that *wretched* Squyre, II. iv. 16. 2
O *wretched* man, that would abuse so gentle Dame! II. iv. 20. 9
'Most *wretched* man, That to affections does the bridle lend! II. iv. 34. 1
To ridd a *wretched* man from handes of hellish wight!' II. v. 23. 9
Wilfully make thyselfe a *wretched* thrall, II. vi. 17. 3
'Most *wretched* woman and of wicked race, II. vi. 33. 7
'That am, I weene, most *wretched* man alive; II. vi. 45. 2
To save my Lord in *wretched* plight forlore; II. vi. 48. 3
much more *wretched* were the cace II. viii. 1. 4
The *wretched* man gan then avise too late, II. x. 31. 1
weary of that *wretched* life her selfe she hong. II. x. 32. 9
In *wretched* prison long he did remaine, II. x. 45. 1
from *wretched* Adams line To purge away II. x. 50. 3
With *wretched* miseryes and woefull ruth, II. x. 62. 3
Her *wretched* dayes in dolour she mote waste, III. ii. 17. 8
that same *wretched* boy Was of him selfe the ydle Paramoure, III. ii. 45. 1
where long in *wretched* cace He liv'd, III. iii. 41. 4
The *wretched* sonne of *wretched* mother borne, III. iv. 36. 2
for *wretched* mens reliefe make way; III. v. 27. 2
To succor *wretched* wights whom we captived see.' III. v. 36. 9
Me seemes I see Amintas *wretched* fate, III. vi. 45. 8
came at last in weary *wretched* plight III. vii. 5. 7
makes ensample of mans *wretched* state, III. ix. 39. 8
The *wretched* man hearing her call for ayd, III. x. 14. 1
Was never *wretched* man in such a wofull cace. III. x. 14. 9
The *wretched* man at his imperious speach III. x. 25. 1
from thenceforth a *wretched* life they ladd, III. xii. 16. 7
wretched Lady, quitt from wofull state, III. xii. 39. 3
Most *wretched* men, whose dayes depend on thrids so vaine! IV. ii. 48. 9
O! why doe *wretched* men so much desire IV. iii. 1. 1
all the *wretched* world recomforteth againe. IV. iv. 47. 9
Who was to weet a *wretched* wearish elfe, IV. v. 34. 3
'Ah, *wretched* wight! IV. vii. 10. 6
Death is to him, that *wretched* life doth lead, IV. vii. 11. 7
A wofull *wretched* maid, of God and man forgot! IV. vii. 14. 9
I rest his *wretched* thrall, the sad Aemylia.' IV. vii. 18. 9
wast his *wretched* daies in wofull plight; IV. vii. 39. 8
he found this *wretched* man IV. vii. 43. 1
Whom when she saw in *wretched* weedes disguiz'd, IV. viii. 12. 5
doth thee thus *wretched* make? IV. viii. 14. 9
Him *wretched* thrall unto his dongeon brought, IV. viii. 51. 8
rive Out of their *wretched* corses, IV. ix. 22. 9
In *wretched* anguishe and incessant woe, IV. ix. 39. 6
that *wretched* Greeke, that life forlore, IV. x. 40. 5
nam'd the river of his *wretched* fate IV. xi. 38. 7
Cares not what evils hap to *wretched* wight; IV. xii. 6. 8
let me waste in woe my *wretched* yeares, IV. xii. 7. 7
She gan afresh thus to renew her *wretched* case. IV. xii. 8. 9
In which his *wretched* love lay IV. xii. 19. 4
By wicked doome condemn'd a *wretched* death to die. IV. xii. 29. 9
downe the cliffe the *wretched* Gyant tumbled; V. ii. 50. 6
'The *wretched* mayd, that earst desir'd to die, V. iv. 11. 1
that same *wretched* man, ordayned to die, V. iv. 25. 1
That ever in this *wretched* case ye were? V. iv. 26. 3
she might his *wretched* life bereave. V. v. 37. 5
For yeelding so himselfe a *wretched* thrall V. vi. 1. 3
by hard mishap doth lie In *wretched* bondage, V. vi. 10. 7
lies in *wretched* thraldome, weake and wan, V. vi. 16. 3
In which her *wretched* love was captive layd: V. vii. 37. 3
upon the soyle Having her selfe in *wretched* wize abjected, V. ix. 9. 8
in that *wretched* semblant V. ix. 38. 8
wretched ruine of so high estate; V. ix. 46. 5
With piteous ruth of her so *wretched* plight, V. ix. 50. 2
yeelding the last honour to her *wretched* corse. V. x. 4. 9
taken have this toylesome paine For *wretched* woman, V. x. 21. 3
And that so *wretched* one, as ye do see, V. x. 21. 8

Wretched—*Continued.*
powred forth his *wretched* life in deadly dreare. V. x. 35. 9
me, of all most *wretched* wight, V. xi. 16. 5
by that Tyrant is in *wretched* thraldome bound: V. xi. 38. 9
holding up her *wretched* hands To him for aide, V. xi. 44. 8
To be the plague and scourge of *wretched* men, VI. i. 8. 7
What cruell hand thy *wretched* thraldome wrought, VI. i. 12. 3
The *wretched* man, that all this while VI. i. 43. 1
For he, . . . Is now him selfe in much more *wretched* plight: VI. ii. 45. 6
That was a straunger to her *wretched* case; VI. ii. 47. 4
And *wretched* life forlorne for vengement VI. iii. 18. 9
In sad misfortunes foule deformity And *wretched* sorrowes, VI. v. 1. 4
By gentle usage of that *wretched* Dame: VI. v. 2. 6
Now wringing both his *wretched* hands in one, VI. v. 4. 4
Would streight dislodge the *wretched* wearie life. VI. v. 5. 5
remained in most *wretched* state, VI. v. 29. 3
wretched end which still attendeth on her.' VI. vi. 25. 7
with the ruth of her so *wretched* case, VI. vi. 31. 8
onely suffred him this *wretched* life to live. VI. vi. 36. 9
Lay in the lap of death, rewing his *wretched* bale. VI. vii. 17. 9
The more would *wretched* lovers her adore. VI. vii. 30. 4
slaine he was, or made a *wretched* thrall, VI. vii. 50. 3
Fell into *wretched* woes, which she repented late. VI. viii. 2. 9
These two, unworthy of your *wretched* bands, VI. viii. 7. 6
can me, most *wretched* mayd, Deliver VI. viii. 19. 5
all weetlesse of the *wretched* stormes, VI. viii. 47. 5
she nought did but lament Her *wretched* life VI. x. 44. 4
Wrapped in *wretched* cares and hearts unrest, VI. xi. 3. 2
Pastorella, wofull *wretched* Elfe, VI. xi. 19. 1
So leave we her in *wretched* thraldome bound, VI. xi. 24. 8
The sad remembrance of her *wretched* plight: VI. xi. 50. 7
Yet could not remedie her *wretched* case; VI. xii. 8. 2
Would for the *wretched* infants helpe provyde; VI. xii. 8. 8
Mongst *wretched* men (dismaide with her affright) VII. vi. 32. 7
feeds at pleasure on the *wretched* pray: *Am.* xlvii. 8
to us *wretched* earthly clods . . . lend desired light; *Epith.* 411
how of most *wretched* wights He taken was, *H.H.L.* 239

Wretchedest. The *wretchedst* man that treades this day on ground? *D.* 63
The *wretchedst* Dame that lives this day on ground; VI. v. 28. 2

Wretchedly. *Wretchedly* wearing out his youthly yeares, IV. vii. 41. 2

Wretchedness. restles seas of *wretchednes* and woe; *Pet.*[2] vii. 4
evill hap Unworthy in such *wretchednes* doth wrap, *Hub.* 602
shortly brought to hopelesse *wretchednesse.* *Hub.* 934
I chose before a life of *wretchednes.* *Hub.* 984
To waile the *wretchednes* of world impure? *T.M.* 120
lie drowned in deep *wretchednes,* *T.M.* 149
to be so reliev'd is *wretchednesse.* *T.M.* 348
did at last decline To lowest *wretchednes:* *Mui.* 15
Well worthy he to taste of *wretchednes.* *Mui.* 216
this worlds vainnesse and lifes *wretchednesse,* *D.* 34
Driven with streames of *wretchednesse* and woe, *D.* 433
No wayling there nor *wretchednesse* is heard, *Col.* 312
That many errant knights hath broght to *wretchednesse.* I. ii. 34. 9
beautie brought t' unworthie *wretchednesse* I. iii. 1. 3
they should live in wo, and dye in *wretchednesse.* I. v. 46. 9
death him did awaite in daily *wretchednesse.* I. xii. 33. 9
that caytives thrall, the thrall of *wretchednesse.* II. iv. 16. 9
No *wretchednesse* is like to sinfull vellenage. II. xi. 1. 9
Did heape on her new waves of weary *wretchednesse.* III. viii. 20. 9
life is *wretchednesse.* III. xi. 14. 9
captive with her led to *wretchednesse* and wo. III. xii. 41. 9
Come home to her in piteous *wretchednesse,* V. vii. 39. 5
gave beginning to her woe and *wretchednesse.* V. x. 11. 9
Cover'd with cold, and wrapt in *wretchednesse;* VI. iii. 44. 7
The witnesse of his *wretchednesse* in place, VI. viii. 5. 2
Liker to heaven then mortall *wretchednesse:* VI. xi. 1. 5

Wretches. Most unhappie *wretches!* *T.M.* 148
In this wide world in which they, *wretches,* stray, *T.M.* 493
those *wretches* which I there descryde.' *Col.* 675
stubs of trees . . . On which had many *wretches* hanged beene, I. ix. 34. 4
Death is for *wretches* borne under unhappy starre.' II. vi. 44. 9
Vile caitive *wretches,* ragged, rude, deformd, II. ix. 13. 4
sat wayting . . . For spoile of *wretches,* II. xii. 8. 7
through the overthrow And wreckes of many *wretches,* III. iv. 22. 8
in the wofull harts Of many *wretches* III. vi. 49. 7
by wracke that *wretches* hath distrest, V. iv. 19. 5
Is but a bayt such *wretches* to beguile, *Am.* xli. 10
drinketh up the lyfe, Of carefull *wretches* *H.L.* 126
Us *wretches* from the second death did save; *H.H.L.* 193
That we the like should to the *wretches* shew, *H.H.L.* 215

Wretch's. heavens refuse to heare a *wretches* cry; *D.* 355
Vouchsafe with mild regard a *wretches* cace to heare.' III. x. 26. 9
ruth of *wretches* wrong, IV. xii. 9. 2
take delight t' encrease a *wretches* woe; *Am.* xli. 7
make a lovers life a *wretches* hell. *H.L.* 265

Wriggle. They wont in the wind wagge their *wrigle* tayles, *S.C.* F. 7

Wring. Should able be so great an one to *wring.* *Van.* ix. 14
he the same did to his purpose *wring.* *Hub.* 1142
wring Her wretched hands *T.M.* 169
the grievous smart which him did *wring,* I. xi. 39. 2
To spin, to card, to sew, to wash, to *wring;* V. iv. 31. 6
Long did he wrest and *wring* it to and fro, VI. iv. 7. 1
The warie foule his bill did backward *wring;* VI. vii. 9. 4

Wringing. *Wringing* her hands, in wemens pitteous wise, I. i. 50. 7
Wringing her handes, and making piteous mone: II. i. 13. 7
Now *wringing* both his wretched hands in one, VI. v. 4. 4
Wringing her hands, and ruefully loud crying? VI. xi. 23. 7

Wrinkled. next her *wrinkled* skin rough sackecloth wore, I. iii. 14. 3
backward still was turnd his *wrincled* face: I. viii. 31. 4

Wrinkled—*Continued.*
A loathly, *wrinckled* hag, ill favoured, old, . . . I. viii. 46. 8
Wrinkles. browes, Full of *wrinckles* and frostie furrowes, . . . *S.C.* F. 44
her face ill-favourd, full of *wrinckles* old. . . . II. iv. 4. 9
Wrist. His sunbroad shield about his *wrest* he bond, . . . II. ii. 21. 5
many-folded shield he bound about his *wrest*. . . . II. iii. 1. 9
Guyons shield about his *wrest* he bond: . . . II. viii. 22. 7
Adowne he kest it with so puissant *wrest*, . . . II. xi. 42. 7
having conquered The maistring raines out of her weary *wrest*, III. vii. 2. 8
Wrists. Their shining shieldes about their *wrestes* they tye, . . I. v. 6. 3
Hyponeo with salt-bedewed *wrests;* . . . IV. xi. 51. 2
Writ. *See* **Holy Writ, Wrate, Written, Wrote.**
The name of Mysterie *writ* in hir face; . . . *Rev.* ii. 9
These moniments, which not in paper *writ*, . . . *Ro.* xxxii. 6
In whose high front was *writ* as doth ensue. . . . *Gn.* 686
Finde nothing worthie to be *writ*, . . . *T.M.* 100
Hath *writ* my record in true-seeming sort. . . . *Ti.* 168
In which sad Death his pourtraicture had *writ*, . . . *D.* 303
Of onely her he sung, he thought, he *writ*. . . . *As.* 64
all the walls and windows there are *writ*, . . . *Col.* 776
Yet doe not sdeigne to let thy name be *writt* . . . *Ded. Son.* ii. 4
Under a shady vele is therein *writ*, . . . *Ded. Son.* iii. 7
Whose learned Muse hath *writ* her owne record . . . *Ded. Son.* xii. 3
In whose great shield was *writ* with letters gay . . . I. ii. 12. 7
spightfull poison spues . . . on all that ever *writt*. . . . I. iv. 32. 8
heathnish shield, wherein with letters red, Was *writt Sansjoy*, I. iv. 38. 6
writt with golden letters rich and brave: . . . I. ix. 19. 8
Wherein darke things were *writt*, hard to be understood. . . . I. x. 13. 9
her sacred Booke, with blood *ywritt*, . . . I. x. 19. 1
writt in stone With bloody letters . . . I. x. 53. 6
to his handes that *writt* he did betake, . . . I. xii. 25. 8
round about the wreath this word was *writ*, . . . II. iv. 38. 4
Whereon the Faery Queenes pourtract was *writt*,) . . . II. viii. 43. 3
in the which were *writ* Infinite shapes . . . II. ix. 50. 2
therein all the famous history Of Jason and Medaea was *ywritt;* II. xii. 44. 4
Therein was *writt* how . . . Jove Had felt the point . . . III. xi. 30. 1
All which in that faire arras was most lively *writ*. . . . III. xi. 39. 9
what so were therein or *writ* or ment, . . . III. xi. 50. 6
over that same dore was likewise *writ*, . . . III. xi. 54. 2
Another yron dore, on which was *writ*, . . . III. xi. 54. 7
oftentimes doe wish it never had bene *writ*. . . . IV. i. 1. 9
His word, which on his ragged shield was *writ*, . . . IV. iv. 39. 8
All were it, as the rest, but rudely *writ?* . . . *Am.* xxxiii. 8
Write. *See* **Wrate.**
by myne eie the Crow his clawe dooth *wright:* . . . *S.C.* D. 136
Ile *write* in termes as she the same did say, . . . *Hub.* 41
Ne tell a written word, ne *write* a letter, . . . *Hub.* 383
Thou onely fit this Argument to *write*, . . . *Ded. Son.* viii. 5
My chaster Muse for shame doth blush to *write;* . . . I. viii. 48. 2
write the battailes of his great godhed: . . . II. iii. 24. 4
It falls me here to *write* of Chastity, . . . III. Pr. 1. 1
faire Britomart, whose prayse I *wryte;* . . . III. ii. 3. 2
This gentle Damzell, whom I *write* upon, . . . III. viii. 1. 4
Whiles of a wanton Lady I doe *write*, . . . III. ix. 1. 6
therein *write* to lett his love be showne; . . . III. ix. 30. 7
when my pen would *write* her titles true, . . . *Am.* iii. 11
I then both speake and *write* The wonder . . . *Am.* iii. 13
in the hevens *wryte* your glorious name. . . . *Am.* lxxv. 12
doe ye *write* it downe, . . . *Epith.* 263
Writing. *See* **Handwriting.**
Life, and Death, is in thy doomefull *writing!* . . . *Com. Son.* i. 13
the same *writing* small Does all their deedes deface, . . . III. ii. 1. 8
writing straunge characters in the grownd, . . . III. iii. 14. 8
Writings. her brave *writings*, which her famous merite . . . *Ro.* v. 12
Writs. long hast traveld, by thy learned *writs*, . . . *Ro.* Env. 4
her eternize with their heavenlie *writs!* . . . *T.M.* 582
spare to one, or two, or three, Rowme in their *writtes;* . . . III. ii. 1. 8
O cursed Eld! the cankerworme of *writs*, . . . IV. ii. 33. 6
More then my former *writs*, . . . VI. xii. 41. 3
Written. *See* **Writ.**
Ne tell a *written* word, ne write a letter, . . . *Hub.* 383
(as in stories it is *written* found) . . . *Mui.* 258
these wofull layes, On my grave *written*, . . . *D.* 537
ensample hath this lesson deare Deepe *written* in my heart . . I. viii. 44. 8
times in his eternall booke of fate Are *written* sure, . . . I. ix. 42. 5
As it in bookes hath *written* beene of old. . . . III. ii. 18. 3
In which there *written* was, with cyphres old, . . . III. ii. 25. 5
thinke of that fayre visage *written* in her hart. . . . III. ii. 29. 9
underneath his feet was *written* thus, . . . III. xi. 49. 1
Over the dore thus *written* she did spye, . . . III. xi. 50. 3
the ground he kist Wherein it *written* was, . . . IV. vii. 46. 9
in the marble stone was *written* this, . . . IV. x. 8. 6
There *written* was the purport of his sin, . . . V. ix. 26. 2
but *Bon*, that once had *written* bin, Was raced out, . . . V. ix. 26. 4
the sorrowes . . . *Written* with teares . . . *Am.* i. 8
Her worth is *written* with a golden quill, . . . *Am.* lxxxiv. 10
Which they have *written* in their inward ey; . . . *H.H.B.* 285
Wrizzled. Her *wrizled* skin, as rough as maple rind, . . . I. viii. 47. 8
Wroke. *See* **Wrake, Wroken.**
him stirring to bee *wroke* Of his late wronges, . . . II. v. 21. 3
Thereof devising shortly to be *wroke*, . . . II. vi. 30. 8
With fell intent on him to bene *ywroke;* . . . IV. vi. 23. 3
Whilest he on him was greedy to be *wroke*, . . . IV. vii. 26. 7
of a womans hand it was *ywroke*, . . . IV. xi. 5. 6
the stroke That . . . had so sternely *wroke* His wrath . . . VI. ii. 13. 4
Wroken. *See* **Wrake, Wroke.**
(Whereof he wil be *wroken*) . . . *S.C.* Mar. 108
joyes on wretched lovers to be *wroken*, . . . *Mui.* 99
Through judgement of the gods to been *ywroken*, . . . *Col.* 921
Both greedie fiers on other to be *wroken:* . . . IV. ii. 21. 5

Wroken—*Continued.*
'Be not upon thy balance *wroken*, . . . V. ii. 47. 4
Justice that day of wrong her selfe had *wroken;* . . . V. viii. 44. 7
threates of any to be *wroken*. . . . V. ix. 24. 9
So long as these two armes were able to be *wroken*. . . . VI. ii. 7. 9
in mynd to bene *ywroken* Of all the vile demeane . . . VI. vi. 18. 3
Wrong. Caused of *wrong* and cruell constraint, . . . *S.C.* F. 152
to *wrong* holy eld did forbeare; . . . *S.C.* F. 206
They maken many a *wrong* chevisaunce, . . . *S.C.* May 92
Evil ensueth of *wrong* entent. . . . *S.C.* May 102
casten to compasse many *wrong* emprise: . . . *S.C.* S. 83
Wailing the *wrong* which he had done of late, . . . *Gn.* 327
they all eternally complaine Of others *wrong*, . . . *Gn.* 408
if that *wrong* on eyther side there were, . . . *Hub.* 1097
hold by *wrong* that wee should have by right. . . . *T.M.* 318
For age to dye is right, but youth is *wrong;* . . . *D.* 243
For she it is that hath me done this *wrong*, . . . *D.* 341
rue my Daphnes *wrong*, And mourne for me . . . *D.* 537
with outragious *wrong* . . . the roses rent away; . . . *As.* 159
when thou doest me *wrong?*' . . . *Col.* 171
do not thy selfe that *wrong*, . . . *Col.* 406
That I must rue his undeserved *wrong:* . . . I. Pr. 2. 8
O, how can . . . simple truth subdue avenging *wrong!* . . . I. iii. 6. 5
all that he by right or *wrong* could find, . . . I. iii. 18. 1
did usurpe with *wrong* and tyrannie Upon the scepter . . . I. iv. 12. 5
riht and *wrong* ylike in equall ballaunce waide. . . . I. iv. 27. 9
So th' one for *wrong*, the other strives for right. . . . I. v. 8. 1
So th' one for *wrong*, the other strives for right, . . . I. v. 9. 1
with like treason now maintain Thy guilty *wrong*, . . . I. vi. 41. 6
his *wrong* with greater puissance maintaine.' . . . II. i. 14. 9
deceave A gentle Lady, or her *wrong* through might: . . . II. i. 17. 8
whom he endamaged By tortious *wrong*, . . . II. ii. 18. 8
provokt her sonne to wreake her *wrong;* . . . II. iv. 12. 6
His am I Atin, his in *wrong* and right, . . . II. iv. 42. 5
him pricks with spurs of shame and *wrong*. . . . II. v. 38. 9
Outrageous *wrong*, and hellish covetize, . . . II. vii. 12. 8
Thou canst preserve from *wrong* and robbery?' . . . II. vii. 20. 4
Them to efforce by violence or *wrong:* . . . II. vii. 30. 4
all by *wrong* waies for themselves prepard: . . . II. vii. 47. 5
On this vile body from to wreak my *wrong*, . . . II. viii. 28. 4
to recover right for such as *wrong* did grieve. . . . III. i. 3. 9
So unto *wrong* to yield my wrested right: . . . III. i. 24. 5
To weene your *wrong* by force to justify; . . . III. i. 25. 2
by *wrong* or right To compas thy desire, . . . III. ii. 46. 8
thy cruell wrath and spightfull *wrong* . . . III. iv. 8. 7
To reskew her from shame, and to revenge her *wrong*. . . . III. iv. 45. 9
threatned death for his outrageous *wrong*. . . . III. v. 13. 9
Nor Aeolus sharp blast could worke them any *wrong*. . . . III. vi. 44. 9
to avenge the implacable *wrong* . . . III. vii. 35. 5
Redresse the *wrong* of miserable wight, . . . III. x. 28. 2
The golden Apple, cause of all their *wrong*, . . . IV. i. 22. 5
answere for thy *wrong* as shall fall out in fight.' . . . IV. ii. 13. 9
ye doe *wrong* To stirre up strife, . . . IV. iv. 12. 2
first I may that *wrong* to him requite; . . . IV. vi. 9. 8
But—if the heavens helpe to redresse her *wrong*, . . . IV. vii. 23. 3
of all his woe and *wrong* Companion she became, . . . IV. viii. 5. 8
Hath done this *wrong*, to wreake on worthlesse wight . . . IV. viii. 17. 2
gathered had by *wrong* And tortious powre, . . . IV. ix. 12. 3
To rip up *wrong* that battell once hath tried; . . . IV. ix. 37. 3
'a greater *wrong* remaines: . . . IV. ix. 38. 1
wall'd by nature gainst invaders *wrong*, . . . IV. x. 6. 3
Gainst all that would it faine to force or *wrong:* . . . IV. x. 7. 5
that I have doen such *wrong*, . . . IV. xi. 1. 3
ruth of wretches *wrong*, . . . IV. xii. 9. 2
me seemes of double *wrong* ye plaine, . . . IV. xii. 30. 2
Right now is *wrong*, and *wrong* that was is right; . . . V. Pr. 4. 4
wrong repressed, and establisht right, . . . V. i. 2. 3
she him taught to weigh both right and *wrong* . . . V. i. 7. 1
In all the skill of deeming *wrong* and right, . . . V. i. 8. 2
wrong redresse in such as wend awry: . . . V. ii. 1. 4
makes them subject to his mighty *wrong;* . . . V. ii. 7. 4
Instead of right me seemes great *wrong* dost shew, . . . V. ii. 34. 3
Were it not good that *wrong* were then surceast, . . . V. ii. 37. 8
What *wrong* then is it, . . . V. ii. 40. 6
The right or *wrong*, the false or else the trew?' . . . V. ii. 44. 6
he could justly weigh the *wrong* or right. . . . V. ii. 45. 3
counterpeise the same with so much *wrong*.' . . . V. ii. 46. 2
To fill the other scale with so much *wrong;* . . . V. ii. 46. 5
they doe nought but right or *wrong* betoken; . . . V. ii. 47. 5
they with *wrong* or falshood will not fare, . . . V. ii. 48. 2
for to maister *wrong* and puissant pride: . . . V. iv. 1. 5
seeming to have suffred mickle *wrong*, . . . V. iv. 5. 3
till she revenge had wrought Of a late *wrong* . . . V. vi. 23. 8
Upon your selves anothers *wrong* to wreake? . . . V. viii. 11. 3
'Ne him sufficeth all the *wrong* and ill, . . . V. viii. 19. 1
on his Lady, th' author of that *wrong*, . . . V. viii. 24. 8
Justice that day of *wrong* her selfe had wroken; . . . V. viii. 44. 7
Purchast through lawlesse powre and tortious *wrong* . . . V. viii. 51. 6
furious and fell As *wrong*, when it hath arm'd it selfe . . . V. ix. 1. 3
right long time is overborne of *wrong* . . . V. xi. 1. 2
all that *wrong* unto that wofull Dame So long had done, . . . V. xi. 4. 5
Can keepe from outrage and from doing *wrong*, . . . V. xii. 1. 6
right and *wrong* most cruelly confound: . . . V. xii. 2. 7
With which he wont to fight to justifie his *wrong:* . . . V. xii. 14. 9
That thorough some more mighty enemies *wrong* . . . VI. i. 11. 3
it hath long mayntaind with mighty *wrong:* . . . VI. i. 13. 4
recompence of all their former *wrong*. . . . VI. i. 47. 6
'For not I him, . . . did offer first to *wrong*, . . . VI. ii. 8. 2
'Perdie great blame' . . . a wight unarm'd to *wrong:* . . . VI. ii. 8. 7
To wreake on me the guilt of his owne *wrong:* . . . VI. ii. 21. 6

Wrong—*Continued.*
Who ever thinkes . . . To *wrong* the weaker, oft falles . . . . VI. ii. 23. 9
where no wight Should . . . worke me any *wrong:* . . . . VI. ii. 30. 6
in approvance of thy *wrong,* . . . . VI. vi. 35. 1
greater force there needs to maintaine *wrong* then right. . . . VI. vi. 35. 9
Sith he likewise did *wrong* by him sustaine, ... VI. vii. 22. 7
Fortune, not with all this *wrong* Contented, ... VI. xi. 2. 5
unto lovely Lady doing *wrong;* . . . . VI. xii. 34. 7
all such persons as he earst did *wrong* . . . . VI. xii. 37. 7
wrong of right, and bad of good did make . . . . VII. vi. 6. 3
Damning all *Wrong* and tortious Injurie, ... VII. vii. 14. 5
after *Wrong* was lov'd, and Justice solde, ... VII. vii. 37. 8
me captiving streight with rigorous *wrong,* . . . . *Am.* xii. 11
Great *wrong* I doe, ... *Am.* xxxiii. 1
For feare the stones her tender foot should *wrong,* . . . . *Epith.* 49
wrong it were that any other twaine . . . . *H.B.* 204
Had it beene *wrong* to aske his owne with gaine? . . . . *H.H.L.* 180
Wrong-doers. makes *wrong doers* justice to deride, ... V. iv. 1. 7
Wronged. *Wrong'd* yet not daring to expresse my paine, . . . *Gn.* Ded. 1
he her *wronged* innocence did weet. . . . . I. iii. 6. 3
As a chaste virgin that had *wronged* beene: . . . . II. i. 21. 5
wrong'd by Carle, by Proteus sav'd, ... III. viii. Arg.
Gainst one that hath both *wronged* you and us; . . . . IV. xii. 30. 3
I am the *wrong'd,* whom ye did enterprise Both to redresse, . V. viii. 11. 4
all unweeting have you *wrong'd* thus sore, ... V. viii. 13. 2
In the behalfe of *wronged* weake did fight: . . . . V. viii. 30. 8
doubting to be *wronged* or beguyled, ... VI. vii. 33. 7
Wronger. *See* **Woman-wronger.**
he should warne the *wronger* to appeare . . . . *Hub.* 1098
So mischiefe overmatcht the *wronger.* . . . . V. vii. 7. 9
Wrongest. Rudely thou *wrongest* my deare harts desire, . . *Am.* v. 1
Wrongful. So mak'st thou kings, and gaynest *wrongfull* government. . . . . II. vii. 13. 9
The *wrongfull* outrage of unrighteous men, ... III. xi. 10. 6
had foyled . . . by *wrongfull* fight . . . . IV. ix. 36. 3
she that *wrongfull* challenge soone assoyled, ... IV. ix. 36. 7
With *wrongfull* powre oppressing others of their kind. . . . V. i. 7. 9
requere That Damsell whom he held as *wrongfull* prisonere. . V. viii. 27. 9
To which they had no right, nor any *wrongfull* state. . . . . V. xi. 3. 9
withheld from me by *wrongfull* might, ... V. xi. 49. 8
A *wrongfull* quarrell to maintaine by fight; . . . . VI. vi. 35. 6
hath doen to thee this *wrongfull* deed, ... VI. vii. 5. 8
for revengement of those *wrongfull* smarts, ... VI. viii. 22. 3
Wrongfully. this war ye *wrongfully* have wielded.' . . . . IV. ix. 37. 9
though *wrongfully* from heaven exil'd. . . . . VII. vi. 26. 9
Wronging. Not *wronging* any other by my will, ... V. iv. 14. 4
Wrongs. each to other working cruell *wrongs,* . . . . *Ro.* xxiv. 7
all those plaints unto him brought Of *wronges,* . . . . *Hub.* 1253
Anothers *wrongs* to wreak upon thy selfe: . . . . I. vi. 42. 3
Fortune, . . . for these *wronges* shall treble penaunce pay . I. viii. 43. 5
All *wrongs* have mendes, ... II. i. 20. 5
did begin To plaine of *wronges,* . . . . II. iii. 13. 5
to bee wroke Of his late *wronges,* . . . . II. v. 21. 4
just *wronges* to vengeaunce doe provoke, ... II. viii. 27. 3
casting *wronges* and all revenge behind, ... II. viii. 51. 3
all thy *wronges* will wipe out of my sovenaunce.' . . . . II. viii. 51. 9
wreake your *wronges* wrought to this knight alone, ... III. i. 28. 5
On his sonne Edwin all those *wrongs* shall wreake; . . . . III. iii. 36. 2
he others *wrongs,* and wreckes himselfe: . . . . III. ix. 4. 3
The open *wrongs* thou doest me day by day: . . . . IV. ii. 13. 2
dayly he his *wrongs* encreaseth more; . . . . V. ii. 6. 1
Which she with *wrongs* hath heaped up so hy . . . . V. ii. 9. 5
all the *wrongs* that he therein could lay . . . . V. ii. 46. 6
Yet all the *wrongs* could not a litle right downe way. . . . V. ii. 46. 9
put two *wrongs* together to be tride, ... V. ii. 48. 3
whence mortal men implore Right in their *wrongs,* . . . . V. vii. 1. 5
having throughly heard and seene Al those great *wrongs,* . . V. viii. 24. 2
whose *wrongs* though long She suffred, ... V. xi. 1. 7
Wrote. *See* **Wrate, Writ.**
triumphes of Phlegraean Jove, he *wrote,* . . . . II. x. 3. 4
One day I *wrote* her name upon the strand; . . . . *Am.* lxxv. 1
Agayne, I *wrote* it with a second hand; . . . . *Am.* lxxv. 3
Wroth. when as the Foule was *wroth,* . . . . *Van.* iv. 13
wondrous *wroth,* for that so foule despight, ... *Col.* 148
Who, thereat wondrous *wroth,* . . . gan eftsoones revive; . . I. ii. 19. 1
The goddesse *wroth* gan fowly her disgrace, ... I. vii. 5. 5
The knight was *wroth* to see his stroke beguyld, ... I. xi. 25. 1
sayd then the knight halfe *wroth,* . . . . II. i. 11. 1
when Sir Guyon saw, all were he *wroth,* . . . . II. ii. 12. 1
He wexed wondrous *wroth,* . . . . II. iv. 45. 2
Exceeding *wroth* was Guyon at that blow, ... II. v. 7. 1
hasty *wroth,* and heedlesse hazardry, ... II. v. 13. 8
Mammon wexing *wroth;* . . . . II. vii. 14. 6
'Foolish old man,' said then the Pagan *wroth,* . . . . II. viii. 22. 1
Wroth was the Prince, and sory yet withall, ... II. viii. 52. 5
when they were *wroth;* . . . . II. x. 40. 5
When the *wroth* Western wind does reave their locks: . . . II. xi. 19. 5
Whereat Excesse exceedingly was *wroth,* . . . . II. xii. 57. 6
'Whereat Cadwallin *wroth* shall forth issew, ... III. iii. 39. 1
woxe halfe *wroth* against her damzels slacke, ... III. vi. 19. 3
'Beldame, be not *wroth* With silly Virgin, ... III. vii. 8. 6
that other knight begonne To wex exceeding *wroth,* . . . . III. viii. 17. 8
he gan to wex exceeding *wroth,* . . . . III. ix. 13. 6
So turned from him *wroth.* . . . . III. x. 29. 9
Exceeding *wroth* therewith the virgin grew, ... III. xii. 33. 6
The warlike virgine . . . wexed inlie *wroth;* . . . . IV. i. 10. 6
Ne be ye *wroth,* Sir Scudamour, ... IV. i. 46. 5
Exceeding *wroth* thereat was Blandamour, ... IV. ii. 14. 1
Triamond, halfe *wroth* to see him staid, ... IV. iv. 20. 5
Whereat full inly *wroth* was Triamond, ... IV. iv. 45. 1

Wroth—*Continued.*
Thereat exceeding *wroth* was Satyran; . . . . IV. v. 24. 1
wroth with Satyran was Blandamour; . . . . IV. v. 24. 2
wroth with Blandamour was Erivan; . . . . IV. v. 24. 3
Through jealous passion weeping inly *wroth,* . . . . IV. ix. 9. 8
Eurypulus, that calmes the waters *wroth;* . . . . IV. xi. 14. 4
he aunswerd *wroth,* 'Loe! there thy hire;' . . . . V. ii. 11. 8
Which when the Pagan saw he wexed *wroth,* . . . . V. ii. 12. 1
'Thou foolishe Elfe,' (said then the Gyant *wroth*) . . . . V. ii. 37. 1
Wroth wext he then, ... V. ii. 45. 1
though wondrous *wroth,* and inly burning . . . . V. vi. 31. 1
she thereat was *wroth,* . . . . V. vi. 38. 6
the earth . . . *Wroth* with the Gods, ... V. vii. 10. 7
Wherewith full *wroth* he fiercely gan assay . . . . V. xi. 11. 4
Wherewith he *wroth,* . . . Tooke in foule scorne . . . . VI. ii. 11. 6
inly *wroth* Against her Knight, ... VI. iii. 33. 1
Calepine, however inly *wroth,* . . . . VI. iii. 45. 6
Which when as Cupid heard, he wexed *wroth;* . . . . VI. vii. 33. 6
The villaine, *wroth* for greeting him so sore, ... VI. vii. 46. 1
There-at Jove wexed *wroth,* . . . . VII. vi. 35. 7
Wrothful. The knight, yet *wrothfull* for his late disgrace, . . II. xi. 34. 6
they at last their *wrothfull* hands let fall, ... IV. ii. 21. 8
the *wrothfull* Britonesse Stayd not . . . . V. vii. 34. 1
Eftsoones they gan their *wrothfull* hands to hold, ... V. viii. 12. 4
Wrothfully. 'Cease, foolish man!' (saide he, halfe *wrothfully*) *D.* 71
(quoth he halfe *wrothfully*) . . . . VI. vii. 16. 1
Wrought. *See* **Lately-wrought, Outwrought.**
The worke did shew it selfe not *wrought* by man, ... *Bel.*[1] iv. 9
pillours . . . All *wrought* with Diamond . . . . *Bel.*[2] ii. 4
rather *wrought* by his owne industry, ... *Bel.*[2] iv. 10
As snowe and golde together had been *wrought:* . . . . *Pet.* vi. 6
that *wrought* so deadly spight. . . . . *S.C.* Jun. 101
A mazer *ywrought* of the Maple warre, ... *S.C.* Au. 26
To him be the *wroughten* mazer alone. . . . . *S.C.* Au. 134
The coloured chaplets *wrought* with a chiefe, ... *S.C.* N. 115
the Muse so *wrought* me from my byrth, ... *S.C.* D. 38
who has *wrought* my Rosalind this spight, ... *S.C.* D. 113
throgh their owne faire handling wisely *wroght,* . . . . *Hub.* 554
is day by day unto us *wrought* . . . . *T.M.* 62
In contemplation of things heavenlie *wrought:* . . . . *T.M.* 526
Wrought with faire pillours and fine imageries; . . . . *Ti.* 96
wrought both joy and sorrow in my mind: . . . . *Ti.* 614
Burganet . . . *wrought* by wonderous device . . . . *Mui.* 74
wrought her shame, and sorrow never ended. . . . . *Mui.* 264
a faire border *wrought* of sundrie flowres, ... *Mui.* 298
So well I *wrought* with mildnes and with paine, ... *D.* 117
So well he *wrought* with practise and with paines, ... *As.* 99
traine, Which he with Mulla *wrought* . . . . *Col.* 119
wrought so well with his continuall paine, ... *Col.* 124
Emongst the seats of Angels heavenly *wrought,* . . . . *Col.* 614
growing he his owne perfection *wrought,* . . . . *Col.* 805
And roughly *wrought* in an unlearned Loome: *Ded.Son.*vii.13
Shall I accuse . . . mightie causes *wrought* in heaven above, I. i. 51. 3
that late vision which th' Enchaunter *wrought,* . . . . I. iii. 3. 6
a Cave *ywrought* by wondrous art, ... I. v. 36. 5
A wondrous way it for this Lady *wrought,* . . . . I. vi. 7. 3
that divelish yron Engin, *wrought* In deepest Hell, ... I. vii. 13. 1
all he *wrought* For this young Prince, ... I. vii. 36. 6
the breach Which love and fortune in her heart had *wrought;* I. vii. 42. 4
what suddein stowre Had *wrought* that horror strange, ... I. viii. 5. 9
wondrous anguish in his hart it *wrought,* . . . . I. viii. 15. 8
so great good, as he for her had *wrought,* . . . . I. ix. 2. 8
The percing steele there *wrought* a wound full wyde, ... I. xi. 20. 8
Unwares me *wrought* unto her wicked will, ... I. xii. 32. 8
treasons . . . *wrought* by that false sorceresse: . . . . I. xii. 33. 6
'And lives he yet' . . . 'that *wrought* this act? . . . . II. i. 12. 2
read who hath ye *wrought* this shamefull plight, ... II. i. 18. 2
yonder he,' . . . 'That *wrought* the shamefull fact . . . . II. i. 25. 2
grievous outrage, which he red A knight had *wrought* . . . II. i. 30. 6
'His be the praise that this atchiev'ment *wrought,* . . . . II. i. 33. 2
'Such is this well, *wrought* by occasion straunge, ... II. ii. 7. 1
mischiefes which a wicked Fay Had *wrought,* . . . . II. ii. 43. 4
T' avenge his Parents death on them that had it *wrought.* . . II. iii. 2. 9
So fortune *wrought,* . . . . II. iii. 3. 6
such grace I found, and meanes I *wrought,* . . . . II. iv. 21. 1
Confest how Philemon her *wrought* to chaunge her weede. . . II. iv. 29. 9
To wreake my wrath on him that first it *wrought:* . . . . II. iv. 30. 5
thousand causes *wrought.* . . . . II. v. 19. 9
wrought by art and counterfetted shew, ... II. vii. 45. 5
wrathfull hand *wrought* not her owne desire? . . . . II. viii. 15. 5
hath to Paynim knights *wrought* gret distresse, ... II. viii. 18. 5
it in flames of Aetna *wrought* apart, ... II. viii. 20. 7
Through all those foldes the steelehead passage *wrought,* . . II. viii. 32. 7
with gold and perle most richly *wrought,* . . . . II. ix. 19. 4
heare Was trimly woven and in tresses *wrought,* . . . . II. ix. 19. 7
Of hewen stone the porch was fayrely *wrought,* . . . . II. ix. 24. 1
nothing pourtrahed nor *wrought;* Not *wrought* nor pourtrahed, II. ix. 33. 8, 9
Ascending by ten steps of Alablaster *wrought.* . . . . II. ix. 44. 9
many hard Atchievement *wrought,* . . . . II. xi. 15. 4
the gate was *wrought* of substaunce light, ... II. xii. 43. 8
The art which all that *wrought* appeared in no place. . . . II. xii. 58. 9
Her garments all were *wrought* of beaten gold, ... III. i. 15. 6
wreake your wronges *wrought* to this knight alone, ... III. i. 28. 5
in that cloth was *wrought* as if it lively grew. . . . . III. i. 38. 9
Whatever foe had *wrought,* or frend had faynd, ... III. ii. 19. 5
by what means his love might best be *wrought:* . . . . III. iii. 6. 6
wrought Great wreake to many errant knights . . . . III. vii. 48. 2
her out of astonishment he *wrought;* . . . . III. viii. 35. 6
massacres, which he *wrought* On mighty kings . . . . III. xi. 29. 8
Which he had *wrought* to many others moe. . . . . III. xi. 45. 5

Wrought—*Continued.*

pure gold . . . *Wrought* with wilde Antickes, ... III. xi. 51. 5
mightie Conquerours . . . *wrought* their owne decayes. . . . III. xi. 52. 5
none but hee Which *wrought* it could the same recure againe. III. xii. 34. 7
that rich Romane of white marble *wrought*, ... III. xii. 46. *or*. 3
much the more by that he lately *wrought*, ... IV. i. 8. 3
How she might overthrow the things that Concord *wrought*. . IV. i. 29. 9
the evill That by themselves unto themselves is *wrought* . . . IV. ii. 3. 7
unquiet strife . . . great quarrels *wrought*, ... IV. ii. 37. 4
Which doughty Triamond had *wrought* that day . . . . . IV. iv. 22. 5
With which they *wrought* such wondrous marvels there, . . . IV. iv. 29. 3
wrought in Lemno with unquenched fire: . . . . IV. v. 4. 4
Which secret fate hath in this Ladie *wrought* . . . . IV. vi. 30. 4
So well he woo'd her, and so well he *wrought* her, ... IV. vi. 41. 1
his exchange or freedom might be *wrought*. . . . . IV. viii. 58. 4
of a fishes shell was *wrought* with rare delight. . . . . . . IV. xi. 6. 9
Florimell it was which *wrought* his paine, ... IV. xi. 27. 8
Read therefore who it is which this hath *wrought*, ... IV. xii. 30. 6
'Who was it then,' (sayd Artegall) 'that *wrought*? . . . . . V. i. 16. 1
powr of charms, which she against him *wrought*, ... V. ii. 22. 8
this the sword which *wrought* those cruell stounds, ... V. iii. 22. 1
Whereto her bashful shamefastnesse *ywrought* A great increase V. iii. 23. 3
th' emptie girdle which about her wast was *wrought*. . . . . V. iii. 24. 9
to have *wrought* unwares some villanous assay. . . . . . . V. iv. 23. 9
who can scape what his owne fate hath *wrought*? . . . . . V. iv. 27. 8
unto them *wrought* all the villany . . . . V. iv. 29. 7
He is . . . *wrought* by Clarins wile. . . . . V. v. Arg.
silke Woven uppon with silver, subtly *wrought*, ... V. v. 2. 2
So cunningly she *wrought* her crafts assay, ... V. v. 52. 5
till she revenge had *wrought* Of a late wrong . . . . V. vi. 23. 7
So well as could with cunning hand be *wrought*, ... V. vii. 6. 3
royall gifts of gold and silver *wrought* . . . . V. vii. 24. 4
Could ought on earth so wondrous change have *wrought*, . . . V. vii. 40. 6
That false Duessa, which had *wrought* great care . . . . . . V. ix. 40. 3
What cruell hand thy wretched thraldome *wrought*, ... VI. i. 12. 3

Wrought—*Continued.*

that knight *wrought* knightlesse shame; . . . . VI. ii. 14. 7
Which had this outrage *wrought* with wicked hand. . . . . VI. ii. 44. 4
for that despight, Which to your selfe he *wrought* . . . . . VI. ii. 45. 9
Because of one that *wrought* him fowle despight.' . . . . . VI. iii. 40. 5
a wondrous chaunce his reskue *wrought*, ... VI. iii. 51. 6
The juyce whereof into his wound he *wrought*, ... VI. iv. 12. 8
with her husband under hand so *wrought*, ... VI. iv. 38. 4
ever more and more her owne affliction *wrought*. . . . . . VI. v. 6. 9
It never rests till it have *wrought* his finall bane. . . . . . VI. vi. 8. 9
Wrought to Sir Calepine so foule despight; . . . . VI. vi. 17. 7
wrought her husbands peace. . . . . VI. vi. 43. 6
in the Princes gardin daily *wrought*: . . . . VI. ix. 24. 8
his speach, that *wrought* him great content, ... VI. ix. 26. 5
So it surely *wrought* With this faire Mayd, ... VI. ix. 45. 6
So well he wood her, and so well he *wrought* her, ... VI. x. 38. 1
wrought so well, with labour and long paine, ... VI. xi. 22. 5
Hath *wrought* this wicked deed: . . . . VI. xi. 29. 9
Yet Calidore so well him *wrought* with meed, ... VI. xi. 35. 8
so with his keepers *wrought*, ... VI. xii. 6. 2
Whom to recomfort all the meanes he *wrought*, ... VI. xii. 13. 7
such spoile, such havocke, and such theft He *wrought*, . . . VI. xii. 23. 5
Thenceforth more mischiefe and more scath he *wrought* . . . VI. xii. 39. 1
Yet in his time he *wrought* as well as playd, ... VII. vii. 35. 3
For being, as she is, divinely *wrought*, ... Am. lxi. 5
His pleasures with thee *wrought*. . . . . Epith. 381
What brave exploit, what perill hardly *wrought* . . . . . H.L. 220
To tell the marveiles by thy mercie *wrought*. . . . . . . H.H.L. 49
According to an heavenly patterne *wrought*, ... H.H.L. 108
to love . . . our brethren, to his image *wrought*. . . . . . H.H.L. 189
And let thy soule, whose sins his sorrows *wrought*, ... H.H.L. 251
And glorious images in heaven *wrought*, ... H.H.B. 3

Wry. This chill, that cold; this crooked, that *wrye*; . . . . . S.C. F. 28
Wyden. Most mercilesse of women, *Wyden* hight, ... II. x. 35. 7
Wylyebourne. Next him went *Wylibourne* with passage slye, . IV. xi. 32. 5

X

Xanthus. Faire *Xanthus* sprincled with Chimaeras blood, . . . Gn. 19
Simois and *Xanthus* blood outwelde ; . . . . Gn. 502

Xanthus'. *Xanthus* sandy bankes with blood all overflowne. . . III. ix. 35. 9
Xiphias. Huge *Ziffius,* whom Mariners eschew No lesse then rockes, II. xii. 24. 7

Y

Yar. *See* Yare.
Yard. *See* Tilt-yard.
Yards. *See* Main-yards.
three *yardes* deepe a furrow up did throw. . . . . I. viii. 8. 6
Yare. Him follow'd *Yar*, soft washing Norwitch wall, ... IV. xi. 33. 6
Yate. *See* Gate.
Yawning. begot amisse By *yawning* Sloth . . . . T.M. 263
yawning gulfe of deepe Avernus hole. . . . . I. v. 31. 3
to the scull a *yawning* wound it made: . . . . I. xi. 35. 8
Ybent. *See* Bent.
Ybet. *See* Bet.
Yblent. *See* Blent.
Ybore. *See* Bore.
Yborn(e). *See* Born.
Ybownd. *See* Bound.
Ybred(d). *See* Bred.
Ybrent. *See* Brent.
Ybrought. *See* Brought.
Ybuilded. Great Ptolomaee it . . . *Ybuilded* all of glasse, . . III. ii. 20. 7
Ybuilt. *See* Built.
Ycarved. *See* Carved.
Yclad. *See* Clad.
Ycled. *See* Clad.
Yclepe. *See* Clepe.
himselfe he did *ycleepe* The Shepheard of the Ocean . . . . . Col. 65
Ycleped. *See* Cleped.
Yclothed. *See* Clothed.
Yclowded. *See* Clouded.
Ycond. *See* Conned.
Ycovered. *See* Covered.
Ycrouned. *See* Crowned.
Ydlesse. *See* Idlesse.
Ydrad. *See* Adrad, Dread.
Ydreaded. *See* Dreaded.
Who more then losse of life *ydreaded* it; . . . . V. iv. 25. 5
Ydred. *See* Adrad, Dread.
Ye (partial list).
And *ye*, faire Ladie, in whose bounteous brest . . . . . . Pet.² vii. 9
The purpose of the complot which *ye* tell; . . . . Hub. 178
Yee shall our pasport at your pleasure see, ... Hub. 377
Where have *yee* (*you) left your lord . . . . I. vii. 48. 9
gay sonne, that gives *ye* so good ayd . . . . III. vi. 21. 4
Sir Knight, sith *ye* this Lady clame, . . . *Yee* shall her winne, IV. iv. 9. 1, 4
'*Ye* dolefull Dame, let not your griefe . . . . VI. ii. 42. 2
Whom if *ye* please . . . . Am. i. 14
'*Ye* gentle Birdes! . . . . Proth. 91
Yea (partial list).
'*Yea* but' . . . I better wot then you: . . . . I. i. 13. 1
'*Yea*, but,' (quoth she) 'he beares a charmed shield, ... I. iv. 50. 5
Year. *See* New-year.
As if my *yeare* were wast and woxen old; . . . . S.C. Ja. 28
You thinken to be Lords of the *yeare*; . . . . S.C. F. 41
bene thine eyes attempred to the *yeare*, ... S.C. Ap. 5
my *yeare* drawes to his latter terme, ... S.C. D. 127
I have made a Calender for every *yeare*, ... S.C. Env. 1

Year—*Continued.*

ere the *yeare* have halfe his course out-run, ... Hub. 305
Demaunds a *yeare* it duly to display. . . . . Col. 595
Full measured three quarters of her *yeare*, ... II. i. 53. 2
The day that first doth lead the *yeare* around, ... II. ii. 42. 7
For all so many weekes as the *yeare* has, ... II. x. 22. 3
ere the *yeare* his course had compassild, ... III. vii. 55. 3
Having therein bene trained many a *yeare*, ... IV. iii. 40. 3
Which hath in charge the ingate of the *yeare*: . . . . . IV. x. 12. 6
Each hour did seeme a moneth, and every moneth a *yeare*. . V. vi. 5. 9
My lambes doe every *yeare* increase their score, ... VI. ix. 21. 7
times and seasons of the *yeare* that fall: . . . . VII. vii. 27. 4
forth issew'd the Seasons of the *yeare*. . . . . VII. vii. 28. 1
he his course doth alter every *yeare*, ... VII. vii. 51. 3
To every planet point his sundry *yeare*: . . . . Am. lx. 2
one *yeare* is spent; . . . . Am. lx. 6
short her wayes, This *yeare* ensuing, ... Am. lx. 14
The weary *yeare* his race now having run, ... Am. lxii. 1
doe the seasons of the *yeare* allot, ... Epith. 100
To chose the longest day in all the *yeare*, ... Epith. 271
Yearly. their rule of *yearely* Presidents Grew great, ... Ro. xviii. 7
Be it where the *yerely* starre doth scorch the ground, . . . Ro. xxvi. 7
Phoebus, weary of his *yerely* taske, ... S.C. N. 14
if the living *yerely* doo arise To fortie pound, ... Hub. 528
An *yearely* solemne feast she wontes to hold, ... II. ii. 42. 6
Where I did sell my selfe for *yearely* hire, ... VI. ix. 24. 7
Yearn, -ed. *See* Earn, -ed.
Year's. *See* New-year's.
To see his whole *yeares* labor lost so soone, ... III. vii. 34. 8
wth one word my whole *years* work doth rend. . . . . . Am. xxiii. 12
The old *yeares* sinnes forepast let us eschew . . . . Am. lxii. 7
chaunge old *yeares* annoy to new delight. . . . . Am. lxii. 14
Years. In six and thirty thousand *yeares* is ronne, ... Ro. xxii. 10
Selfe have I worne out thrise threttie *yeares*, ... S.C. F. 17
were thy *yeares* greene, as now bene myne, ... S.C. F. 59
youth and course of carelesse *yeeres*, ... S.C. Jun. 33
yeeres more rype . . . toyes away dyd wype, ... S.C. Jun. 46
in thilke same looser *yeares*, ... S.C. D. 37
Hereafter many *yeares* remembred be . . . . Gn. 61
bends what ever power his aged *yeares* Him lent, ... Gn. 646
Thus manie *yeares* I now have spent, ... Hub. 59
shall we tie our selves for certaine *yeares* . . . . Hub. 120
To have thy asking, yet waite manie *yeeres*; . . . . . . Hub. 902
Whose memorie is quite worne out with *yeares*, ... Ti. 67
in a siege seaven *yeres* about me dwelt. . . . . Ti. 105
which his yong toward *yeares* . . . Did largely promise, . Mui. 26
ye fayre Mayds, the matches of his *yeares*, ... As. 129
Resembling Stella in her freshest *yeares*, ... As. 189
'My weaker *yeares*, Captiv'd to fortune . . . . I. i. 52. 4
many *yeares* throughout the world I straid; . . . . . . I. ii. 24. 7
'In prime of youthly *yeares*, when corage hott . . . . . I. ii. 35. 1
one loving howre For many *yeares* of sorrow can dispence ; . I. iii. 30. 3
till riper *yeares* he gan aspyre, ... I. iii. 27. 7
till ryper *years* he raught, ... I. vi. 29. 2
He has them now fowr *years* besiegd to make them thrall. . I. vii. 44. 9

Years—*Continued.*
Old Timon, who in youthly *yeares* hath beene . . . I. ix. 4. 2
'It was in freshest flowre of youthly *yeares,* . . . I. ix. 9. 1
her to serve sixe *yeares* in warlike wize, . . . I. xii. 18. 7
Soone as the terme of those six *yeares* shall cease, . . . I. xii. 19. 7
Of rypest *yeares,* and heares all hoarie gray, . . . II. i. 7. 3
Above the reason of her youthly *yeares.* . . . II. ii. 15. 6
so soone as ryper *yeares* he raught, . . . II. iii. 2. 6
through many *yeares* thy wits thee faile, . . . II. iii. 16. 2
when *yeares* More rype us reason lent . . . II. iv. 18. 4
man, Of wondrous beauty and of freshest *yeares,* . . . II. viii. 5. 2
Seven *yeares* this wize they us besieged have, . . . II. ix. 12. 8
have three *years* (*twelve moneths) sought one, yet no where can her find.' . . . II. ix. 38. 9
A man of *yeares* yet fresh, as mote appere, . . . II. ix. 52. 3
The *yeares* of Nestor nothing were to his, . . . II. ix. 57. 1
Till ryper *years* he raught . . . II. x. 20. 4
Gorbogud, till far in *years* he grew: . . . II. x. 34. 6
had seven hundred *yeares* this scepter borne . . . II. x. 36. 2
fowr hundred *yeares* And more had wasted, . . . II. x. 62. 6
Ambrose and Uther, did ripe *yeares* attayne, . . . II. x. 67. 2
twise fowre hundreth *yeares* shalbe supplide, . . . III. iii. 44. 5
ere two hundred *yeares* be full outronne, . . . III. iii. 46. 4
in late *yeares* so faire a blossome bare, . . . III. iv. 3. 7
Some thousand *yeares* so doen they there remayne, . . . III. vi. 33. 5
yet three *yeares* I now abrode have strayd, . . . III. vii. 57. 4
to him both far unequall *yeares,* . . . has; . . . III. ix. 4. 6
there he many *yeares* did raine, . . . III. ix. 37. 2
raignd so many *yeares* victorious, . . . III. ix. 39. 3
long was led Full many *yeares,* . . . III. ix. 41. 5
seemd of ryper *yeares* then th' other Swayne, . . . III. xii. 9. 2
Wretchedly wearing out his youthly *yeares,* . . . IV. vii. 41. 2
'The first of them did seeme of ryper *yeares* . . . IV. x. 49. 1
let me waste in woe my wretched *yeares,* . . . IV. xii. 7. 7
in these few thousand *yeares* They all are wandred much; . V. Pr. 5. 4
fourteene hundred *yeres,* . . . V. Pr. 7. 5
In which she noursled him till *yeares* he raught, . . . V. i. 6. 8
Untill the ripenesse of mans *yeares* he raught; . . . V. i. 8. 3
Where many *years* it afterwards remayned, . . . V. ii. 19. 5
In which they doe these many *yeares* remaine, . . . V. ii. 36. 3
Yet was as great and wide, ere many *yeares,* . . . V. iv. 7. 8
Well shot in *yeares* he seem'd, . . . V. vi. 19. 6
After long travell of full twenty *yeares,* . . . V. vii. 39. 6
There came two Springals of full tender *yeares,* . . . V. x. 6. 2
through his *yeares* long since aside had set The use of armes, . V. xi. 37. 3
seventeene *yeares,* but tall and faire of face, . . . VI. ii. 5. 4
I, whose unryper *yeares* are yet unfit . . . VI. ii. 9. 2
before I did attaine Ripe *yeares* of reason . . . VI. ii. 28. 5
where I have wond . . . Since I was ten *yeares* old, . . . VI. ii. 30. 9
Nor spilt the blossome of my tender *yeares* . . . VI. ii. 31. 2
For the rare hope which in his *yeares* appear'd, . . . VI. ii. 34. 3
He was to weete a man of full ripe *yeares,* . . . VI. iii. 3. 1
The good Sir Bruin growing farre in *yeares,* . . . VI. iv. 33. 6
So now she had bene wandring two whole *yeares* . . . VI. vii. 38. 1
in two *yeares* before, . . . She had destroyed two and twenty . VI. vii. 38. 6
'In prime of youthly *yeares,* . . . VI. viii. 20. 1
in my first prime of *yeares,* . . . VI. ix. 24. 1
ten *yeares* my selfe excluded From native home, . . . VI. ix. 25. 3
Matched with equall *years,* . . . VI. xii. 18. 8
wherewith Dan Jove in tender *yeares* . . . was nourisht . . . VII. vii. 41. 6
some in longer *yeares,* . . . VII. vii. 55. 3
Mars in three-score *yeares* doth run his spheare. . . . *Am.* lx. 4
spheare of Cupid fourty *yeares* containes: . . . *Am.* lx. 10
a chyld, renewing still thy *yeares,* . . . *H.L.* 55
Years'. during eight *yeares* space, . . . III. iii. 41. 2
long before the ten *yeares* siege of Troy, . . . III. ix. 36. 2
in all these two *yeares* space Saved but two; . . . VI. vii. 38. 5
Yede. if they with thy Gotes should *yede,* . . . *S.C.* Jul. 109
to theyr foldes *yeed* (*yead) at their owne leasure. . . . *S.C.* S. 145
Then badd the knight his Lady *yede* aloof, . . . I. xi. 5. 1
on foot was forced for to *yeed* . . . II. iv. 2. 3
Yeelded. *See* **Yielded.**
Yell. That ye may understand my shreiking *yell.* . . . *Ro.* i. 8
With that aloude she gan to bray and *yell,* . . . V. xi. 28. 1
Yelled. loud he *yelled* (*yelded) for exceeding paine; . . . I. xi. 37. 2
Thereat he brayed loud, and *yelled* dreadfully. . . . V. xii. 20. 9
Yelling. *yelling* shrieks throwne up into the skies. . . . *T.M.* 24
There now haunt *yelling* Mewes . . . *Ti.* 133
Therewith a piteous *yelling* voice was heard, . . . I. ii. 31. 1
He loudly brayd with beastly *yelling* sownd, . . . I. viii. 11. 3
with their piteous cryes, and *yelling* shrightes, . . . II. vii. 57. 5
They reard a most outrageous dreadfull *yelling* cry: . . . II. xi. 17. 9
th' one of them with dreadfull *yelling* crye, . . . II. xi. 47. 3
yelling Meawes, with Seagulles hoars and bace, . . . II. xii. 8. 4
With *yelling* outcries, and with shrieking sowne; . . . III. iv. 30. 8
The Tyrant selfe came forth with *yelling* bray, . . . IV. viii. 62. 2
Yellow. The bottome *yellow* like the shining land, . . . *Bel.*[1] x. 3
The bottome *yeallow,* like the golden grayle . . . *Bel.*[2] xii. 3
mowes The waving lockes of those faire *yeallow* heares, . . . *Ro.* xxx. 6
Rending her *yeolow* locks, like wyrie gold . . . *Ti.* 10
Her *yellow* locks that shone so bright and long, . . . *As.* 157
all in *yellow* robes arayed still. . . . I. x. 30. 9
Her *yellow* lockes, crisped like golden wyre, . . . II. iii. 30. 1
Her *yellow* golden heare Was trimly woven . . . II. ix. 19. 6
their *yellow* heare Christalline humor dropped downe apace. II. xii. 65. 5
her faire *yellow* locks behind her flew, . . . III. i. 16. 3
Instead of *yellow* lockes . . . III. viii. 7. 5
golden wyre was not so *yellow* . . . III. viii. 7. 7
round about the same her *yellow* heare, . . . IV. vi. 20. 1
Hayling that mayden by the *yellow* heare, . . . VI. i. 17. 6

Yellow—*Continued.*
Then came the Autumne all in *yellow* clad, . . . VII. vii. 30. 1
Her long loose *yellow* locks lyke golden wyre, . . . *Epith.* 154
Yells. so let your yrksome *yells* augment. . . . *S.C.* Au. 178
shrieks and cries and dreery *yells.* . . . *T.M.* 538
shady woods resound with dreadfull *yells;* . . . *D.* 331
the night Raven, that still deadly *yels;* . . . *Epith.* 346
Yeoman. A good *yeoman* he was of honest place, . . . *Hub.* 230
A jolly *yoeman,* Marshall of the same, . . . II. ix. 28. 2
Yeomen. Tall *yeomen* seemed they and of great might, . . . II. ix. 26. 4
So did his forty *yoemen,* which there with him came. . . . VI. vi. 25. 9
Yerks. who having in his hand a whip, Her therewith *yirks;* . VI. vii. 44. 7
Yes (*partial list*).
Yes, but they gang in more secrete wise, . . . *S.C.* S. 156
Yesterday. Who *yeester day* (*yesterday) drove us to such distresse: . . . V. iv. 48. 7
Had him abusde and shamed *yesterday;* . . . VI. iii. 47. 6
Yet (*partial list*). *See* **As yet.**
The same *yet* vaunting . . . *Ro.* ii. 5
Under these antique ruines *yet* remaine. . . . *Ro.* xix. 14
That *yet* those sights empassion me full nere . . . *Van.* i. 12
And *yet,* alas! but now my spring begonne, . . . *S.C.* Ja. 29
And *yet,* alas! yt is already donne. . . . *S.C.* Ja. 30
Yet for thou pleasest not where most I would: . . . *S.C.* Ja. 68
Yet not so previlie but the Foxe him spyed; . . . *S.C.* May 253
Yet little good hath got, . . . *S.C.* O. 10
tryed time *yet* taught me greater thinges; . . . *S.C.* D. 85
Whose ranckling wound as *yet* does rifelye bleede. . . . *S.C.* D. 94
Why livest thou stil, and *yet* hast thy deathes wound? . . . *S.C.* D. 95
Yet dewed with teares they han be . . . *S.C.* D. 112
Wrong'd *yet* not daring to expresse my paine, . . . *Gn.* Ded. 1
Ne *yet* his cup embost with Imagery . . . *Gn.* 103
Not *yet* unmindfull of her olde reproach. . . . *Gn.* 224
Tityus, mindefull *yet* Of thy displeasure, . . . *Gn.* 377
Yet manie waies they sought, . . . *Hub.* 225
Yet for their purposes none fit espyed. . . . *Hub.* 226
Yet though his vesture were but meane . . . *Hub.* 229
That *yet* the skill thereof I have not loste: . . . *Hub.* 293
Ne *yet* of Latine, ne of Greeke, . . . *Hub.* 386
yet spite bites neare. . . . *Hub.* 424
To have thy Princes grace, *yet* want her Peeres; . . . *Hub.* 901
To have thy asking, *yet* waite manie yeeres; . . . *Hub.* 902
Scarse could the Ape *yet* speake, . . . *Hub.* 964
yet is not death the next, . . . *Hub.* 987
Which *yet* to prove more true he meant to see, . . . *Hub.* 1277
Roaring *yet* lowder that all harts it daunted, . . . *Hub.* 1368
How ever *yet* they mee despise . . . *T.M.* 523
Praise who so list, *yet* I will him dispraise, . . . *Ti.* 229
the deaw which *yet* on them does lie, . . . *Mui.* 181
And bring to hand that *yet* had never beene; . . . *D.* 116
Whil'st *yet* her leafe was greene, . . . *D.* 240
Which *yet* are deepe engraven in my brest, . . . *D.* 296
verses vaine, (*yet* verses are not vaine,) . . . *As.* 68
as the lucklesse boy *yet* bleeding lay; . . . *As.* 142
Yet bleeding lay, and *yet* would still have bled, . . . *As.* 143
he did beare, And *yet* doth beare, . . . *Col.* 94
though knowen *yet* to few; *Yet,* were he knowne . . . *Col.* 401, 402
doth her tender plumes as *yet* but trie . . . *Col.* 422
Admyr'd of all, *yet* envied of none, . . . *Col.* 550
I ever *yet* did see, A fairer Nymph *yet* never saw mine eie: *Col.* 558, 559
Besides *yet* many mo . . . *Col.* 576
Yet will I think of her, *yet* will I speake, . . . *Col.* 628
many *yet* remaine, Whose names . . . *Col.* 739
Ne is there shepheard, ne *yet* shepheards swaine, . . . *Col.* 819
her sence was dazd; *Yet* kindling rage . . . I. i. 18. 2
starre That was in Ocean waves *yet* never wet, . . . I. ii. 1. 3
the fairest wight that lived *yit;* . . . I. ii. 30. 4
though a tree I seme, *yet* cold and heat me paines.' . . . I. ii. 33. 9
Who had enough, *yett* wished ever more; . . . I. iv. 29. 5
Ne *yet* of present perill be affraid, . . . I. iv. 49. 3
Where ever *yet* I be, my secret aide Shall follow you.' . . . I. iv. 51. 8
To salve his hurts, that *yet* still freshly bled. . . . I. v. 17. 3
'*Yet,* O thou dreaded Dame! I crave . . . I. v. 21. 8
the thing, which daily *yet* I rew, . . . I. v. 42. 2
Low under all, *yet* above all in pride, . . . I. v. 48. 6
How fayre he was, and *yet* not fayre to this; . . . I. vi. 17. 4
She hardly *yet* perswaded was to stay, . . . I. vi. 28. 4
The thing that might not be, and *yet* was donne?' . . . I. vi. 39. 4
More ugly shape *yet* never living creature saw. . . . I. viii. 48. 9
from mee are hidden *yitt;* . . . I. ix. 3. 4
So fayre a creature *yet* saw never sunny day. . . . I. ix. 13. 9
I seek in vain, *yet* ni'll that vow unbynd.' . . . I. ix. 15. 9
Yett still he strove . . . I. ix. 16. 3
Him *yett* againe, and *yett* againe, bespake . . . I. ix. 24. 6
halfe dead with dying feare; Ne *yet* assur'd of life . . . I. ix. 30. 7
own *yet* luke-warme blood, That from his wound *yet* welled . I. ix. 36. 6, 7
Yet nathelesse it could not doe him die, . . . I. ix. 54. 8
Though spousd, *yet* wanting wedlocks solemnize; . . . I. x. 4. 7
festring sore did ranckle *yett* within, . . . I. x. 25. 4
though they faulty were, *yet* well he wayd, . . . I. x. 40. 5
never *yet* was seene of Faeries sonne; . . . I. x. 52. 3
'ne maist thou *yitt* Forgoe . . . I. x. 63. 6
constraine To loose, ne *yet* the warlike pledge to yield, . I. xi. 43. 3
Scarsely had Phoebus . . . *Yett* harnessed . . . I. xii. 2. 2
'And lives he *yet,*' (said he) 'that wrought this act? . . . II. i. 12. 2
Ne would she speake, ne see, ne *yet* be seene, . . . II. i. 15. 6
Full loth she seemd thereto, but *yet* did faine, . . . II. i. 20. 8
red Did paint his chearefull cheekes, *yett* being ded; . . . II. i. 41. 5
in the bush he lay, not *yett* forgott: . . . II. iii. 43. 5
in me *yet* stickes the mortall sting, . . . II. iv. 33. 5

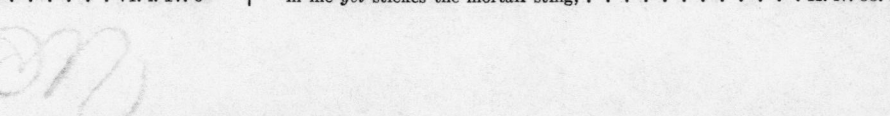

Yet—*Continued.*
That never *yet* encountred enemy . . . . II. iv. 40. 7
Yet nathemore did it his fury stint, ... II. v. 8. 3
all, though pleasaunt, *yet* she made much more: . . . . . II. vi. 24. 5
dying dayly, dayly *yet* revive. . . . . II. vi. 45. 4
long he yode, *yet* no adventure found, ... II. vii. 2. 6
'*yet* never eie did vew, Ne tong did tell, ... II. vii. 19. 6
And were I not, *yet* is my trouth yplight, ... II. vii. 50. 6
He daily dyde, *yet* never throughly dyen couth. . . . . . II. vii. 58. 9
Yet will I not forgoe, ne *yet* forgett . . . . II. viii. 8. 3
Their strokes did raine: *yet* did he never quaile, ... II. viii. 35. 6
As one that loathed life, and *yet* despysd to dye. . . . . II. viii. 50. 9
Wroth was the Prince, and sory *yet* withall, ... II. viii. 52. 5
My whole desire hath beene, and *yet* is now, ... II. ix. 7. 3
For though they bodies seem, *yet* substaunce from them fades. II. ix. 15. 9
had not *yet* felt Cupides wanton rage; *Yet* was shee woo'd . . II. ix. 18. 2, 3
Not built of bricke, ne *yet* of stone . . . . II. ix. 21. 4
Nether unseemly short, nor *yet* exceeding long. . . . . . II. ix. 24. 9
the bird, . . . Did sitt, as *yet* ashamd . . . . II. ix. 40. 9
Some such as in the world were never *yit*, ... II. ix. 50. 4
A man of yeares *yet* fresh, ... II. ix. 52. 3
That well can witnes *yet* unto this day . . . . II. x. 10. 6
Yet lives his memorie, though carcas sleepe . . . . II. x. 43. 9
Nennius, whom he *yet* did slay, But lost his sword, *yet* to be seene this day. . . . . II. x. 49. 4, 5
That could doe harme, *yet* could not harmed bee, ... II. xi. 40. 6
That could not die, *yet* seemd a mortall wight, ... II. xi. 40. 7
like faire Emeraudes not *yet* well ripened. . . . . II. xii. 54. 9
Gather therefore the Rose whilest *yet* is prime, ... II. xii. 75. 6
Gather the Rose of love whilest *yet* is time, ... II. xii. 75. 8
never *yet*, with warlike armes he bore . . . . III. i. 7. 2
Whose root and stalke so bitter *yet* did taste, ... III. ii. 17. 6
Whose shape or person *yet* I never saw, ... III. ii. 38. 4
'But *yet* the end is not.' . . . . III. iii. 50. 1
Yet wist not what their wailing ment; *yet* did, . . . bid . . . III. iv. 32. 4
thee, *yet* unborne, . . . promist to adorne? . . . . III. iv. 36. 4
Or all the good that ever *yet* I gat: . . . . III. v. 7. 3
yet no paines did spare To doe him ease, ... III. v. 50. 1
Whose like on earth was never framed *yit;* . . . . III. viii. 5. 3
Whiles *yet* on Ida he a shepeheard hight, ... III. ix. 36. 3
'And *yet*' (quoth she) 'a greater wrong remaines: . . . . . IV. ix. 38. 1
Divine Scamander, purpled *yet* with blood . . . . IV. xi. 20. 6
Whose bad condition *yet* it doth retaine, ... IV. xi. 38. 8
But, when as *yet* she saw him to proceede . . . . V. ii. 23. 1
Yet loth she was, . . . *yet* could she not forbeare. . . . . . V. vi. 4, 8, 9
yet neither has forgon His horses backe, ... V. viii. 9. 7, 8
yet to and fro long shooke And tottred, ...
of her widowhed Taking advantage, and her *yet* fresh woes, . V. x. 12. 2
Deliver him his owne, ere *yet* too late, ... V. xi. 3. 8
their garments *yet*, Being all rag'd and tatter'd, ... V. xii. 28. 7
Yet brancheth forth in brave nobilitie, ... VI. Pr. 4. 4
Yet know I not . . . in what place To find him out, ... VI. i. 7. 4
yet still I forward trace.' . . . . VI. i. 7. 5
And laying *yet* afresh, . . . Upon the rest . . . . VI. vi. 38. 3
Yet rather counseld him contrarywize, ... VI. vii. 22. 6
The greatest shame that ever eye *yet* saw, ... VI. viii. 6. 2
That having small *yet* doe I not complaine . . . . VI. ix. 20. 3
Which that to all may better *yet* appeare, ... VII. vi. 1. 6
Yet not so quite, but that there did succeed . . . . VII. vi. 20. 7
Still mooving, *yet* unmoved from her sted; . . . . VII. vii. 13. 3
Unseene of any, *yet* of all beheld; . . . . VII. vii. 13. 4
Be heard all night within, nor *yet* without: . . . . *Epith.* 335
And *yet* a chyld, renewing still thy yeares, ... *H.L.* 55
And *yet* the eldest of the heavenly Peares? . . . . *H.L.* 56
Yet (*yeat) did by signes his glad affection show, ... *Proth.* 117
Yeven. *See* **Given.**
Yew. The *Eugh*, obedient to the benders will; . . . . . . I. i. 9. 4
Yewen. his stiffe armes to stretch with *Eughen* bowe, . . . *Hub.* 747
So far as *Ewghen* bow a shaft may send, ... I. xi. 19. 2
Yfed. *See* **Fed.**
Yfere. The Redde rose medled with the White *yfere*, ... *S.C.* Ap. 68
kept *yfere* The flockes of mighty Pan. . . . . *S.C.* Jul. 143
yfere The vertues linked are . . . . I. ix. 1. 1
In this faire wize they traveild long *yfere*, ... II. i. 35. 1
they both *yfere* Forth passed on their way . . . . II. ix. 2. 3
So goodly all agreed they forth *yfere* did ryde. . . . . . . III. i. 12. 9
In fleshly lust were mingled both *yfere*, ... III. vii. 48. 8
all *yfere* Forth marched to a Castle . . . . III. viii. 52. 1
swore that he would lodge with them *yfere*, ... III. ix. 13. 7
So beene they gone *yfere*, ... III. x. 16. 8
forth they both *yfere* make their progresse, ... III. xi. 20. 7
Griefe and Fury, matcht *yfere;* . . . . III. xii. 16. 1
if Gods should strive with flesh *yfere*, ... VII. vi. 31. 7
Yfostered. *See* **Fostered.**
Yfraught. *See* **Fraught.**
Yfretted. *See* **Fretted.**
Yglanced. Cymochles sword on Guyons shield *yglaunst*, . . . II. vi. 31. 3
Ygo, Ygoe, Ygone. *See* **Ago, Agone, Go.**
their good is *ygoe*, ... *S.C.* May 67
Ygot. *See* **Got.**
Ygyrt. *See* **Girt.**
Yield. *See* **Yold.**
so pleasant sent did *yeld* (*yelde*[1]), ... *Bel.* xi. 13
wolfe suck did *yeeld* To two young babes: . . . . *Bel.*[2] ix. 9
Do *yelde* unto thy lorde a sweete request, ... *Pet.*[1] vii. 3
May of the bodie *yeeld* a seeming sight, ... *Ro.* v. 6
him enforst to *yeeld* the victorie, ... *Van.* vi. 11
mochell mast to the husband did *yielde*, ... *S.C.* F. 109
Sore against my will was I forst to *yield*. . . . . *S.C.* Au. 42
to *yield* the timely eare, ... *S.C.* O. 58

Yield—*Continued.*
To Pan his owne selfe pype I neede not *yield:* . . . . *S.C.* D. 46
To *yeeld* Eurydice unto her fere . . . . *Gn.* 463
did *yeeld* (for spight) Store of firebronds . . . . *Gn.* 507
yeeld them timely profite for their paine. . . . . *Hub.* 236
Great thankes I *yeeld* you for your discipline, ... *Hub.* 547
though the vulgar *yeeld* an open eare, ... *Hub.* 713
unto all doth *yeeld* due curtesie; . . . . *Hub.* 729
yeeld us some reliefe in this distresse; . . . . *T.M.* 347
If none should *yeeld* him his deserved meed, ... *T.M.* 453
due reward For her prais-worthie workmanship to *yeild;* . . *Mui.* 268
did *yield* A fruitfull Olyve tree, ... *Mui.* 325
The victorie did *yeeld* her as her share: . . . . *Mui.* 342
Blaspheme his powre, or termes unworthie *yield*.' . . . . . . *Col.* 822
Such, therefore, as that wasted soyl doth *yield*, ... *Ded. Son.* v. 13
Which if ye *yield*, perhaps ye may her rayse *Ded.Son.*xiii.13
As much disdayning to the curbe to *yield:* . . . . I. i. 1. 7
His Lady, . . . Did *yield* her comely person to be at my call. I. ii. 36. 9
mightie proud to humble weake does *yield*, ... I. iii. 7. 3
I would not *yeeld* that to Sansfoy I gave. . . . . I. iv. 47. 9
Where both doe fight alike, to win or *yield?*' . . . . I. iv. 50. 4
Her to persuade that stubborne fort to *yilde:* . . . . I. vi. 3. 7
maintain Thy guilty wrong, or els thee guilty *yield*.' . . . . I. vi. 41. 6
I hope . . . your prowesse can me *yield* reliefe: . . . . . . I. vii. 42. 8
nathemore would that corageous swayne To her *yeeld* passage I. viii. 13. 7
seemd himselfe as conquered to *yield*. . . . . I. viii. 20. 5
blood can nought but sin, and wars but sorrows *yield*. . . . I. x. 60. 9
to his force to *yielden* it was faine; . . . . I. xi. 37. 7
ne yet the warlike pledge to *yield*, ... I. xi. 43. 3
day-light gan to . . . *yield* his rowme to sad succeeding night, I. xi. 49. 6
Both daughter and eke kingdome lo! I *yield* to thee.' . . . . I. xii. 20. 9
yield his sence to bee too blunt and bace, ... II. Pr. 4. 4
Now forst to *yield*, now forcing to invade; . . . . II. ii. 25. 7
thyselfe my captive *yield* for ay. . . . . II. iii. 7. 8
yield he would not, ... II. iv. 14. 6
to her captive sonne *yield* his first libertee. . . . . II. v. 17. 9
to thee I *yield* them free.' . . . . II. v. 18. 6
does *yield* to vew Her dainty limbes . . . . II. v. 33. 7
to weake wench did *yield* his martiall might: . . . . II. vi. 8. 5
Bid thee to them thy fruitlesse labors *yield*, ... II. vi. 16. 3
to me this grace Both *yield*, ... II. vi. 33. 5
Does *yield* unto his foe a pleasaunt victory. . . . . II. vi. 34. 9
yield him ready passage to that other part. . . . . II. vi. 36. 9
dew praise or dew reproch them *yield;* . . . . II. viii. 14. 8
To *yield* wide way to his hart-thrilling brond; . . . . . . II. viii. 41. 8
my trew liegeman *yield* thy selfe for ay, ... II. viii. 51. 7
Pensive I *yeeld* I am, ... II. ix. 38. 6
yeeld His partes to reasons rule obedient, ... II. xi. 2. 1
Ne once did *yield* it respitt day nor night; . . . . II. xi. 9. 3
yield it those that stouter could it wield. . . . . III. i. 4. 6
So unto wrong to *yield* my wrested right: . . . . III. i. 24. 5
Which two did *yield* before she did them smight. . . . . . III. i. 29. 6
yield the pray of love to lothsome death at last. . . . . . III. ii. 17. 9
yield your heart whence ye cannot remove? . . . . III. ii. 40. 8
Against it strongly strive, and *yield* thee nott . . . . . . III. ii. 46. 4
Pitty our playnt, and *yield* us meet reliefe.' . . . . III. iii. 21. 3
shall be forst to *yield:* . . . . III. iii. 31. 6
Shall *yield* him selfe his liegeman, and sweare fealty. . . . III. iii. 37. 9
yield her rowme to day that can it governe well.' . . . . . III. iv. 60. 9
To *yield* himselfe unto the mightie ill, ... III. v. 48. 3
yield herselfe to spoile of greedinesse: . . . . III. vii. 25. 6
Peece, . . . Will shortly *yield* it selfe, ... III. x. 10. 6
I pardon *yield*, and with thy rudenes beare; . . . . III. x. 31. 3
to *yield* him love she doth deny, ... III. xi. 17. 3
bad the stubborne flames to *yield* him way: . . . . III. xi. 26. 4
Did *yield* him selfe right willing to prolong his date: . . . III. xii. 35. 9
Yield you in lieu of this your gracious deed? . . . . III. xii. 39. 4
dread . . . Made her not *yeeld* so much as due she deemed. IV. i. 8. 7
Ten thousand thankes did *yeeld* her for her meed, ... IV. i. 15. 3
cursed seedes . . . *yeeld* her living food: . . . . IV. i. 26. 2
readie way did *yield* For bloud to gush forth . . . . IV. iii. 9. 4
Yet leave unto his sorrow did not *yeeld*, ... IV. iii. 14. 3
each to other seemd the victorie to *yield*. . . . . IV. iii. 34. 9
Who would not to this vertue rather *yeeld* his voice? . . . IV. iii. 45. 9
did *yeeld* the prize To Triamond and Cambell . . . . IV. iv. 36. 3
yeeld the fayrest her due fee. . . . . IV. v. 9. 9
What medicine can any Leaches art *Yeeld* such a sore, . . IV. vi. 1. 6
yeeld unto her weapon way to pas: . . . . IV. vi. 15. 4
To *yeeld* strong succour to that gentle swayne, ... IV. ix. 4. 2
way unto me *yield*. IV. x. 19. 9
his hard rocky hart for no entreating Will *yeeld*, ... IV. xii. 7. 4
rather guilty chose himselfe to *yield:* . . . . V. i. 24. 5
Did *yield* she rather should with him remaine Alive, ... V. i. 27. 5
To whom that day they should the girlond *yield*, ... V. iii. 14. 6
to greet his brave emprise, And thousand thankes him *yeeld*, V. iii. 15. 8
he himselfe would *yield;* . . . . V. v. 16. 6
Yet would she not thereto *yeeld* free accord . . . . V. v. 27. 6
Can *yeeld* great thankes for such her curtesie; . . . . . . V. v. 55. 5
Was glad to *yeeld* unto his good request, ... V. vi. 22. 2
Yeeld for amends my selfe yours evermore, ... V. viii. 13. 5
Yeeld me an hostry mongst the croking frogs, ... V. x. 23. 8
Some place shall us receive and harbour *yield;* . . . . . . V. x. 24. 2
yeeld to his despight; . . . . V. xi. 5. 7
It would no passage *yeeld* unto his purpose vaine. . . . . . V. xi. 10. 9
yeeld great thankes for their so goodly deed, ... V. xi. 48. 3
Dye, rather then doe ought that mote dishonour *yield*.' . . . V. xi. 55. 9
much to gaine, a litle for to *yield:* . . . . V. xii. 19. 4
Forget his patience, and *yield* vengeaunce dew . . . . V. xii. 42. 4
Refused hath to *yeeld* her love againe, ... VI. i. 15. 3
bids him . . . to *yeeld* his Love, or else to fight: . . . . . VI. ii. 18. 5

Yield—*Continued.*
thousand thankes to Calidore . . . Did *yeeld:* . . . VI. iii. 19. 5
To seeke some place the which mote *yeeld* some ease . . . VI. v. 32. 2
Therefore now *yeeld* . . . My due reward, . . . VI. vii. 15. 7
men might her admire, And heavenly honors *yield,* . . . VII. vi. 4. 4
The simple mayd did *yield* to him anone; . . . VII. vi. 45. 1
Nature did *yeeld* thereto; . . . VII. vii. 27. 8
Yet my poore life, . . . I would her *yield,* . . . *Am.* xi. 10
Was forst to *yeeld* my selfe . . . *Am.* xii. 10
Disdayne to *yield* unto the first assay. . . . *Am.* xiv. 8
The silly lambe that to his might doth *yield.* . . . *Am.* xx. 8
yield for pledge my poore captyved hart; . . . *Am.* xlii. 8
yeeld To sorrow and to solitary paine; . . . *Am.* lii. 5
yeeld theyr services unto her will; . . . *Epith.* 197
to the sense most daintie odours *yield,* . . . *H.B.* 80
will not *yield* unto her formes direction, . . . *H.B.* 146
did fragrant odours *yeild,* . . . *Proth.* 75

Yielded. *See* **Yold.**
But *yeelded,* with shame and greefe adawed, . . . *S.C.* F. 141
yielded pryde and proud submission, Still dreading death, . . . I. iii. 6. 6
Which when none *yielded,* her unruly Page . . . the wicket open rent, . . . I. iii. 13. 1
Her selfe a *yielded* pray to save or spill: . . . I. iii. 43. 4
Yielded by him that held it forcibly: . . . II. iv. 40. 2
yeilded passage to his cruell knife. . . . II. v. 9. 4
yielded had to that same straunger knight. . . . II. v. 20. 5
Ne ever to them *yielded* foot of grownd, . . . III. i. 21. 4
Them *yielded* ready passage, and their rage surceast. . . . III. iv. 31. 9
trembling stood, and *yielded* him the pray; . . . III. viii. 13. 2
Which straight to her was *yeelded* without let. . . . IV. i. 12. 5
It *yielded* was by them that judged it: . . . IV. v. 20. 3
Which being *yeelded,* he his threatfull speare Gan fewter, . . . IV. vi. 10. 1
Which *yeelded,* they their bevers up did reare, . . . IV. vi. 25. 8
she *yeelded* her consent To be his love, . . . IV. vi. 41. 7
she for the present was appeased, And *yeelded* leave, . . . IV. vi. 44. 2
He *yeelded,* and her tooke; . . . IV. ix. 15. 9
Ne *yeelded* foote, ne once abacke did flit, . . . IV. ix. 29. 8
To whom the world this franchise ever *yeelded,* . . . IV. ix. 37. 6
have ye *yeelded* you to proude oppression . . . V. iv. 26. 4
to her *yeelded* of his owne accord; . . . V. v. 17. 2
Ne *yielded* ought for favour or for feare; . . . VII. vi. 12. 4
That ye were blooded in a *yeelded* pray. . . . *Am.* xx. 14
Yielded them by the vanquisht as theyr meeds, . . . *Am.* xxix. 6

Yieldeth. and ech to other *yealdeth* land. . . . I. ii. 15. 9
that which *yeeldeth* vertues meed alway? . . . V. xi. 17. 8

Yielding. *yeelding* soft, in that she nought gainsaid, . . . I. ii. 27. 7
with strong flight did forcibly divyde The *yielding* ayre, . . . I. xi. 18. 4
Him stayd from *yielding* pitifull redresse, . . . II. v. 24. 4
It cut away upon the *yielding* wave, . . . II. vi. 5. 6
From *yielding* succour to that cursed Swaine, . . . II. xi. 28. 5
not *yielding* to his ills, . . . III. iii. 41. 3
as a thonder bolt Perceth the *yielding* ayre, . . . III. xi. 25. 7
Praysing their god, and *yeelding* him great thankes, . . . IV. x. 25. 7
For *yeelding* so himselfe a wretched thrall . . . V. vi. 1. 3
For *yeelding* to a straungers love so light, . . . V. vi. 12. 6
yeelding the last honour to her wretched corse. . . . V. x. 4. 9
rudenesse for not *yeelding* what they owe: . . . VI. ii. 1. 8
Scarse *yeelding* her due food or timely rest, . . . VI. xi. 24. 5

Yields. Armulla *yields* None fairer, . . . *Col.* 278
repining courage *yields* No foote to foe: . . . I. ii. 17. 6
she . . . *yieldes* her to extremitie of time: . . . I. vi. 13. 2
yields it selfe unto the victours might. . . . I. viii. 23. 7
yeeldes his caytive neck to victours most despight. . . . I. ix. 11. 9
yields by and by, . . . I. x. 1. 4
thousand thankes him *yeeldes* for all his paine. . . . I. xii. 12. 7
to the mighty victor *yields* a bounteous feast. . . . II. v. 10. 9
'Seldom' (said Guyon) '*yields* to vertue aide, . . . II. ix. 8. 2

Yirks. *See* **Yerks.**
Ykindled. *See* **Kindled.**
Yled. *See* **Led.**
Yleft. *See* **Left.**
Ylike. *See* **Alike.**
Ylinked. *See* **Linked.**
Ylke. *See* **Ilk.**
Ymet(t). *See* **Met.**
Ymixt. *See* **Mixed.**
Ymner. *Ymner* slew of Logris miscreate; . . . II. x. 38. 2
Ymolt. *See* **Molt.**
Ymounted. *See* **Mounted.**
Ymp, -t, -es. *See* **Imp, -ed, -s.**
Ynd. *See* **Ind.**
Ynne. *See* **Inn.**
Ynough. *See* **Enough.**

Yode. Before them *yode* a lusty Tabrere, . . . *S.C.* May 22
The Gate . . . *Yode* forth abroade . . . *S.C.* May 178
Yet forth shee *yode,* . . . *S.C.* May 233
Yode late on Pilgrimage To Rome, . . . *S.C.* Jul. 182
his army dry-foot through them *yod,* . . . I. x. 53. 5
long he *yode,* yet no adventure found, . . . II. vii. 2. 6
in haste he *yode* The cause to weet, . . . II. xi. 20. 2
They courteous conge tooke, and forth together *yode.* . . . III. i. 1. 9
as through an open plaine they *yode,* . . . III. i. 4. 1
Florimell It was with whom in company he *yode,* . . . III. viii. 19. 7
Tho to him *yode,* And him saluting . . . III. viii. 45. 6
when th' one forward *yode,* The other backe retired . . . IV. i. 28. 8
forth they *yode,* and forward softly paced, . . . IV. viii. 34. 6
backward *yode,* as Bargemen wont to fare . . . VII. vii. 35. 7

Yoke. freed is from Cupids *yoke* by fate, . . . *Col.* 566
Proud wemen, vaine, forgetfull of their *yoke:* . . . I. v. 50. 2
made it beare the *yoke* of Inquisition, . . . V. x. 27. 2

Yoke—*Continued.*
His foot he set on his vile necke, in signe Of servile *yoke,* . . . VI. vii. 26. 5
Threatning to *yoke* them two and tame their corage stout. . . . VI. viii. 11. 9
Till they him force the buxome *yoke* to beare: . . . VI. viii. 12. 4

Yoked. Unfitly *yokt* together in one teeme. . . . III. ix. 6. 2
Yokes. Wyld beastes in yron *yokes* he would compell; . . . I. vi. 26. 2
I will their sweatie *yokes* assoyle . . . III. xii. 47. *or.* 5
turne we here . . . Our wearie *yokes,* . . . V. iii. 40. 7

Yold. *See* **Yielded.**
Once to me *yold,* not to be *yolde* againe: . . . III. xi. 17. 4
So to her *yold* the flames, . . . III. xi. 25. 9
ripened fruits the which the earth had *yold.* . . . VII. vii. 30. 9

Yond. Seest howe brag *yond* Bullocke beares, . . . *S.C.* F. 71
I shall thee give *yond* Cosset . . . *S.C.* N. 42
then wexeth wood and *yond:* . . . II. viii. 40. 9
Florimell fled from that Monster *yond,* . . . III. vii. 26. 5
Good lucke presents you with *yond* lovely mayd, . . . IV. i. 33. 8
Will chalenge *yond* same other for my fee.' . . . IV. i. 35. 8
'thou seest *yond* Fayry Knight, . . . V. v. 32. 1
uppon *yond* rocky hill, . . . VI. i. 13. 1
Yond Lady and her Squire with foule despight Abusde, . . . VI. viii. 6. 3
do surely prieve That *yond* same is your daughter sure, . . . VI. xii. 18. 9

Yonder. sittes on *yonder* bancke, . . . *S.C.* Jul. 2
Thereto will I pawne *yonder* spotted Lambe, . . . *S.C.* Au. 37
That shall *yonder* heardgrome, . . . *S.C.* Au. 45
'Lo! *yonder* is the same, . . . I. viii. 2. 3
pilgrimage To *yonder* same Hierusalem doe bend, . . . I. x. 61. 4
yonder is,' (said she) 'The brasen towre, . . . I. xi. 3. 1
'Lo! *yonder* he,' cryde Archimage . . . II. i. 25. 1
yonder is no game . . . II. iii. 35. 1
now in shade he shrowded *yonder* lies.' . . . II. iii. 35. 5
yonder comes the prowest knight alive, . . . II. viii. 18. 3
yonder way We needes must pas . . . II. xii. 3. 2
to *yonder* castle turne your gate.' . . . III. viii. 51. 9
left in *yonder* forest wyld; . . . III. x. 39. 6
yonder in that wastefull wildernesse . . . III. x. 40. 3
justifie my cause on *yonder* knight.' . . . IV. i. 40. 6
yet he pricked over *yonder* plaine, . . . V. i. 19. 5
Whom he did overthrow by *yonder* foord; . . . VI. iv. 29. 7
The same is *yonder* Lady, whom high God did save.' . . . VI. xii. 17. 9

Yore. such this Cities honour was of *yore,* . . . *Ro.* xxviii. 13
the saynets Which han be dead of *yore.* . . . *S.C.* Jul. 116
The jolly shepheard that was of *yore* . . . *S.C.* S. 26
ranne out as he was wont of *yore.* . . . *S.C.* S. 221
dead shee is, that myrth thee made of *yore.* . . . *S.C.* N. 57
of *yore* Came the bad daughter of old Cadmus brood, . . . *Gn.* 170
of *yore* Through fatall charmes transformd . . . *Gn.* 204
not so great, as it was wont of *yore,* . . . *Hub.* 447
to whom of *yore* The Foxe had promised . . . *Hub.* 1205
Nigh where the goodly Verlame stood of *yore,* . . . *Ti.* 3
Romane Victors, which it wonne of *yore;* . . . *Ti.* 38
by his powre the world was made of *yore,* . . . *Col.* 841
that had of *yore* Their scepters stretcht . . . I. i. 5. 4
Into an Oxe he was transformd of *yore.* . . . I. v. 47. 5
noble mindes of *yore* allyed were, . . . I. ix. 1. 3
he hath polluted oft of *yore,* . . . I. xii. 27. 7
wars and spoiles, the which he did of *yore.'* . . . II. vi. 35. 9
Him Atin spying knew right well of *yore,* . . . II. vi. 48. 1
all the wealth which is, or was of *yore,* . . . II. vii. 31. 7
of *yore* Which Merlin made . . . II. viii. 20. 1
well of *yore* he learned had to ryde, . . . II. viii. 31. 4
of *yore* Fayre Daphne Phoebus hart with love did gore; . . . II. xii. 52. 4
in this royall Maid of *yore,* . . . III. iii. 3. 3
Were from him hidden, or unknowne of *yore.* . . . III. iii. 15. 5
Which Bladud made by Magick art of *yore,* . . . III. iii. 60. 2
As it at first created was of *yore:* . . . III. vi. 36. 5
To which sad lovers were transformde of *yore;* . . . III. vi. 45. 2
Great wreake to many errant knights of *yore,* . . . III. vii. 48. 3
Proteus is Shepheard of the seas of *yore,* . . . III. viii. 30. 1
For all that art he learned had of *yore;* . . . III. ix. 28. 4
he many weake harts had subdewd Of *yore,* . . . III. x. 9. 8
goodly learned had of *yore* . . . IV. ix. 19. 2
Phidias did make in Paphos Isle of *yore,* . . . IV. x. 40. 4
But to the antique use which was of *yore,* . . . V. Pr. 3. 5
Ram . . . Hath now forgot where he was plast of *yore,* . . . V. Pr. 5. 8
What was the poyse of every part of *yore:* . . . V. ii. 34. 7
of the earth they formed were of *yore:* . . . V. ii. 40. 3
As was the wont of warlike knights of *yore,* . . . V. iii. 32. 3
Which warlike uses had deviz'd of *yore:* . . . V. viii. 34. 5
of *yore* His poysnous point deepe fixed in his hart . . . VI. x. 31. 1
A lawlesse people, Brigants hight of *yore,* . . . VI. x. 39. 3
after him Sir Lamoracke of *yore,* . . . VI. xii. 39. 7

York. wonned there where now *Yorke* people dwell; . . . IV. xi. 37. 5

You (*partial list*).
(for perhaps some one of *you* . . . *Ro.* xv. 9
Let dame Elisa thanke *you* for her song: . . . *S.C.* Ap. 150
your tender Lambes that by *you* trace. . . . *S.C.* Jun. 120
blowe your pypes, shepheards, til *you* be at home; . . . *S.C.* Au. 197
She *you* from death, *you* me from dread, redeemd; . . . III. vii. 52. 7
'That shall I *you* recount,' . . . III. vii. 53. 4
'Now tell, if please *you,* . . . VI. i. 5. 1
That is, the rule of all, all being rul'd by *you.'* . . . VII. vii. 56. 9
Whome if *you* please I care for others none . . . *Am.*[1] i. 14
The laurel-leafe, which *you* this day doe weare, . . . *Am.* xxviii. 1
It *you* behoves to love, . . . *H.B.* 184

Young. *See* **Young man.**
suck . . . To two *young* (*yong*[1]) babes: . . . *Bel.* ix. 10
Lawrell tree, Amidst (*Amidde*[1]) the *yong* greene wood; . . . *Pet.* iii. 3
manie *yong* plants spring out of her rinde: . . . *Ro.* xxviii. 11
Burnt up his *yong* ones, . . . *Van.* iv. 8

Young—*Continued.*
Such an one would make thee *younge* againe. . . . *S.C.* F. 68
so enamoured of her *young* one, . . . *S.C.* May 97
a motherly care Of her *young* sonne, . . . *S.C.* May 181
'Ah, good *young* maister!' . . . *S.C.* May 255
a *yong* alder hard beside him pight, . . . *Gn.* 299
the *yong* lustie gallants he did chose To follow, . . . *Hub.* 797
yong plants, which wont with fruit t' abound, . . . *T.M.* 251
which his *yong* toward yeares . . . Did largely promise, . . . *Mui.* 26
The fresh *yong* flie, in whom the kindly fire . . . *Mui.* 33
Yong Clarion, with vauntfull lustie-head, . . . *Mui.* 54
where *yong* Clarion Was wont to solace him, . . . *Mui.* 242
With his *yong* brother Sport, . . . *Mui.* 290
a faire *young* Lionesse, White as the native Rose . . . *D.* 107
a pledge I leave with thee . . . My *yong* Ambrosia; . . . *D.* 290
Young Astrophel, the pride of shepheards praise, . . . *As.* 7
Young Astrophel, the rusticke lasses love: . . . *As.* 8
to warne *yong* shepheards wandring wit, . . . *Col.* 684
Of her there bred A thousand *yong* ones, . . . I. i. 15. 5
he spred A seeming body . . . Like a *young* Squire, . . . I. ii. 3. 4
Young knight whatever, that dost armes professe, . . . I. iv. 1. 1
all he wrought For this *young* Prince, . . . I. vii. 36. 7
she fed whiles they were weake and *young,* . . . I. x. 31. 3
them before the fry of children *yong* . . . I. xii. 7. 1
Great joy was made that day of *young* and old, . . . I. xii. 40. 1
worse and worse, *young* Orphane, be thy payne, . . . II. i. 61. 6
young Perissa was of other mynd, . . . II. ii. 36. 1
like *young* fruit in May, . . . II. iii. 29. 7
From which *young* Hectors blood by cruell Greekes was spilt. II. ix. 45. 9
Madam was *young,* unmeet the rule to sway, . . . II. x. 20. 2
sonnes, too *young* to rule aright, . . . II. x. 46. 8
Whilst they were *young,* . . . II. x. 47. 1
Emongst his *young* ones shall divide . . . III. iii. 47. 9
into the mynd Of the *yong* Damzell sunke, . . . III. iii. 57. 2
the *yong* Mayd She might in equall armes accompany, . . . III. iii. 61. 3
young birds, which he had taught to sing, . . . III. vii. 17. 3
in vain sheows, that wont *yong* knights bewitch, . . . III. vii. 29. 6
that *young* Squyre Gan them informe the cause, . . . III. viii. 52. 6
that *young* Squyre him reared from below; . . . III. ix. 16. 8
that *young* Knight . . . Ten thousand thankes did yeeld her IV. i. 15. 1
in his hand a tall *young* oake he bore, . . . IV. vii. 7. 4
Her captive lovers friend, *young* Placidas, . . . IV. viii. 63. 2
About that wofull couple . . . And their *young* bloodie babe V. iii. 31. 3
abase Unto this shame, and my *young* hope subvert, . . . VI. i. 12. 8
Calidore sees *young* Tristram slay . . . VI. ii. Arg.
Full glad and joyous then *young* Tristram grew; . . . VI. ii. 35. 6
But lov'd this fresh *young* Knight . . . VI. iii. 7. 5
his *young* charge whereof he skilled nought, . . . VI. iv. 38. 2
Prince Arthur and *young* Timias, . . . VI. v. 11. 8
A faire *young* Mayden, full of comely glee; . . . VI. vi. 10. 7
this *young* Mayd, whom chance to her presents, . . . VI. xii. 20. 5
Great Nature, ever *young,* yet full of eld; . . . VII. vii. 13. 2
Life was like a faire *young* lusty boy, . . . VII. vii. 46. 6
yong blossomed Jessemynes: . . . *Am.* lxiv. 12
a *young* fawne, that late hath lost the hynd; . . . *Am.* lxxviii. 2

Younger. Her *younger* sister, that Speranza hight, . . . I. x. 14. 1
The *yonger* daughter of Chrysogonee, . . . III. vi. 51. 2
Hate was the elder, Love the *younger* brother; . . . IV. x. 32. 7
was the *younger* stronger in his state . . . IV. x. 32. 8
my *younger* brother, Amidas, . . . V. iv. 9. 1
So having sayd, the *younger* did ensew: . . . V. iv. 15. 1
Then Artegall thus to the *younger* sayd: . . . V. iv. 17. 1
The *younger* thrust the elder from his right: . . . VII. vi. 27. 5

Youngest. then his *yongest* sonne Shall twentie have, . . . *Hub.* 529
th' *youngest* is the highest in degree. . . . *Col.* 543
bred Of one bad sire, whose *youngest* is Sans joy; . . . I. ii. 25. 8
The eldest did against the *youngest* goe, . . . II. ii. 13. 8
he that lov'd the *youngest* was Sansloy; . . . II. ii. 18. 1
The second Dyamond, the *youngest* Triamond. . . . IV. ii. 41. 9

Youngling. She stoppeth the breath of her *youngling.* . . . *S.C.* May 100
Shee set her *youngling* before her knee, . . . *S.C.* May 182
an enraged cow That is berobbed of her *youngling* dere, . . . V. viii. 46. 2

Youngling's. shee sawe in the *younglings* face . . . *S.C.* May 211

Younglings. Soone as my *younglings* cryen for the dam . . . *S.C.* Ap. 95
bene thy *younglings* miswent? . . . *S.C.* Au. 16
Love hath misled both my *younglings* and mee: . . . *S.C.* Au. 17
snatcheth quite away One of the litle *yonglings* . . . *Mui.* 407
More dear unto their God then *younglings* to their dam.' . . . I. x. 57. 9

Young man. On this side them there is a *yongman* layd, . . . *Gn.* 493
O fortunate *yong-man,* . . . *Ti.* 433
with which th' Euboean *young man* wan Swift Atalanta, . . . II. vii. 54. 8
Beside his head there satt a faire *young man,* . . . II. viii. 5. 1
The *young man,* sleeping by her, seemd to be . . . II. xii. 79. 1
Far off aspyde a *young man,* . . . III. xi. 3. 3
he spyde A tall *young man,* . . . VI. ii. 3. 7
(as this *young man* did see) . . . VI. ii. 22. 3
'So passed we till this *young man* us met; . . . VI. ii. 23. 1

Young man's. That fiers *youngmans* unruly maystery; . . . III. x. 2. 7

Young men. A rulesse rout of *yongmen* which her woo'd, . . . *Gn.* 431
tall *young men,* all hable armes to sownd; . . . I. xii. 5. 7
To seeke *young men* to quench her flaming thrust, . . . III. vii. 50. 2
On either side of her two *young men* stood, . . . IV. x. 32. 1
Ring ye the bels, ye *yong men* of the towne, . . . *Epith.* 261
let the mayds and *yongmen* cease to sing; . . . *Epith.* 332

Young men's. (so *young mens* thoughts are bold) . . . IV. x. 4. 6

Youngth. wouldest me my springing *youngth* to spil: . . . *S.C.* F. 52
youngth is a bubble blown up with breath, . . . *S.C.* F. 87
As shee was wont in *youngth* and sommer dayes; . . . *S.C.* N. 20
the kindly fire Of lustfull *yongth* . . . *Mui.* 34

Youngthly. now passed *youngthly* pryme, . . . *S.C.* D. 75

Youngthly—*Continued.*
all his *yongthly* forces idly spent, . . . *Mui.* 431

Younker. that same *younker* soone was overthrowne, . . . IV. i. 11. 2

Younkers. For *Younkers,* Palinode, such follies fitte, . . . *S.C.* May 17

Your (*partial list*).
joying in the brightnes of *your* day, . . . *Ro.* xv. 2
Both yield, to stay *your* deadly stryfe a space.' . . . II. vi. 33. 5
'Sir knight, *your* bounteous proffer . . . VI. ix. 33. 3
Kindled of yours, *your* likenesse doth display; . . . *H.B.* 180

Yours (*partial list*).
Her losse is *yours,* your losse Amyntas is, . . . *Col.* 438
I now doe live, bound *yours* by vassalage; . . . *Ded. Son.* vii. 5
The conquest *yours;* I *yours;* the shield, and glory *yours.'* . . . I. v. 14. 9
Forthy, faire Sir, *yours* be the Damozell, . . . III. i. 30. 3
the land was *yours* . . . And so the threasure *yours* is, . . . V. iv. 19. 8, 9
he cannot expresse his simple minde Ne *yours* conceive, . . . VI. v. 30. 4
In slaying him that would live gladly *yours!* . . . *Am.* lvii. 12
With my reflex *yours* shall encreased be. . . . *Am.* lxvi. 14
Enough it is that all the day was *youres:* . . . *Epith.* 297

Yourself (*partial list*).
Assure *your selfe* I will you not forsake.' . . . I. vii. 52. 7
That of *your selfe* ye thus berobbed arre, . . . I. viii. 42. 8
doe purvay *Your selfe* of sword . . . II. iii. 15. 5
Do arme *your self* against that day, . . . II. iii. 15. 9
Your self his prowesse prov'd, . . . II. viii. 13. 9
**Your selfe* (*M.* Thy selfe) you covet to see pictured, . . . III. Pr. 4. 2
to *your selfe* . . . and to your loved knight. . . . VI. ii. 45. 9
in *your selfe* your onely helpe doth lie To heale your selves, VI. vi. 7. 1

Yourselves (*partial list*).
unto batteil doe *your selves* addresse; . . . II. viii. 18. 2
save *your selves* from neare decay; . . . II. ix. 12. 3
in your selfe your onely helpe doth lie To heale *your selves,* VI. vi. 7. 2
even yee *Your selves* are likewise chang'd, . . . VII. vii. 49. 9

Youth. *See* **Youngth.**
The blossome which my braunch of *youth* did beare . . . *S.C.* Ja. 39
my flowring *youth* is foe to frost, . . . *S.C.* F. 31
Which I cond of Tityrus in my *youth,* . . . *S.C.* F. 92
Many meete tales of *youth* did he make, . . . *S.C.* F. 98
youth and course of carelesse yeeres, . . . *S.C.* Jun. 33
to restraine The lust of lawlesse *youth* . . . *S.C.* O. 22
in *youth,* when flowrd my joyfull spring, . . . *S.C.* D. 19
the seede that in my *youth* was sowne . . . *S.C.* D. 101
Ladies gentle sports, The joy of *youth,* . . . *Hub.* 758
For age to dye is right, but *youth* is wrong; . . . *D.* 243
ruth . . . for her noble blood, and for her tender *youth.* . . . I. i. 50. 9
They, in compassion of her tender *youth,* . . . I. vi. 12. 5
A gentle *youth,* his dearely loved Squire, . . . I. vii. 37. 1
him . . . Who earst in flowres of freshest *youth* was clad. . . . I. viii. 42. 4
In vertuous lore to traine his tender *youth,* . . . II. iii. 2. 4
'The antique world, in his first flowring *youth,* . . . II. vii. 16. 1
war-hable *youth* Was by Maximian lately ledd away, . . . II. x. 62. 1
The bud of *youth* to blossome faire began, . . . III. v. 29. 8
With all the warlike *youth* of Trojans bloud, . . . III. ix. 43. 6
By which fraile *youth* is oft to follie led, . . . IV. Pr. 1. 6
The hot spurre *youth* so scorning to be crost, . . . IV. i. 35. 5
tameth stubborne *youth* With iron bit, . . . IV. xii. 13. 3
whilome in his *youth* had bene a Knight, . . . V. vi. 32. 3
that *youth* had kild That armed knight, . . . VI. ii. 4. 6
and saw to bee A goodly *youth* . . . VI. ii. 5. 2
To whom then thus the noble *Youth:* . . . VI. ii. 27. 1
That in his *youth* had beene of mickle might, . . . VI. iii. 3. 2
When pride of *youth* forth pricked my desire, . . . VI. ix. 24. 2
spent my *youth* in vaine, . . . VI. ix. 25. 4
From *youth* to eld, from wealth to poverty, . . . VII. vii. 19. 5
faire flowre! in whom fresh *youth* doth raine, . . . *Am.* iv. 13
In *youth,* before I waxed old, . . . *Epig.* i. 1
I have in th' heat of *youth* made heretofore, . . . *H.H.L.* 10

Youthful. Her *youthfull* sports and kindlie wantonnesse, . . . *D.* 111
The *youthfull* Knight could not . . . be staide; . . . I. i. 14. 2
Her mate, he was a jollie *youthfull* knight . . . IV. i. 32. 1
heat of *youthfull* spright . . . IV. viii. 29. 7
Had in him kindled *youthfull* fresh desire, . . . VII. vii. 11. 7

Youthly. in her *youthlie* daies An Hydra was . . . *Ro.* x. 5
'In prime of *youthly* yeares, when corage hott . . . I. ii. 35. 1
The knight was fiers, and full of *youthly* heat, . . . I. v. 7. 4
Old Timon, who in *youthly* yeares hath beene . . . I. ix. 4. 2
'It was in freshest flowre of *youthly* yeares, . . . I. ix. 9. 1
deckt himselfe with fethers *youthly* gay, . . . I. xi. 34. 5
Above the reason of her *youthly* yeares. . . . II. ii. 15. 6
Therein I have spent all my *youthly* daies, . . . II. iii. 38. 4
the brave *youthly* Champions to assay . . . III. vii. 41. 6
with him ledd to sea an *youthly* trayne; . . . III. ix. 48. 6
Did all that *youthly* rout so much appall, . . . IV. ii. 40. 3
a noble *youthly* knight, Seeking adventures . . . IV. ii. 45. 1
Wretchedly wearing out his *youthly* yeares, . . . IV. vii. 41. 2
being fresh and full of *youthly* spright, . . . VI. vii. 5. 2
'In prime of *youthly* yeares, . . . VI. viii. 20. 1

Youth's. *Yougthes* folke now flocken in every where, . . . *S.C.* May 9
dapper ditties, . . . To feede *youthes* fancie, . . . *S.C.* O. 14
spred Abroad thy fresh *youths* fayrest flowre, . . . III. ii. 31. 7
Layes of sweete love and *youthes* delightfull heat: . . . VI. ix. 4. 4
in his *youthes* freshest flowre, . . . VI. xii. 3. 5
faire blossomes of *youths* wanton breed, . . . *H.L.* 36

Youths. The warlike *youthes,* . . . Did chace away sweet sleepe I. iv. 44. 3
forth he gan to fare With those two gentle *youthes,* . . . V. x. 17. 6

Ypaid. *See* **Ill-apaid.**
Ypaynted. *See* **Painted.**
Ypent. *See* **Pent.**
Ypight. *See* **Pight.**
Yplaste. *See* **Placed.**

Yplight. *See* Plight.
Yrapt. *See* Rapt.
Yre. *See* Ire.
Yrent. *See* Rent.
  away Shee flong, and her faire deawy lockes *yrent;* . . . . . III. iv. 30. 2
Yrived. *See* Rived.
Yrketh, Yrkes. *See* Irketh, Irks.
Yrockt. *See* Rocked.
Yron. *See* Iron.
Ysame. *See* I-same.
Y scuith gogh. *y scuith gogh,* signe of sad crueltee. . . . . . II. x. 24. 9
Yse. *See* Ice.
Yset. *See* Set.
Yshend. should it not *yshend* Your roundels fresh, ... *S.C.* Au. 139
Yshrilled. my pipes delight, Whose pleasing sound *yshrilled* far
    about, ... *Col.* 62
Yshrowded. *See* Shrouded.
Ysicles. *See* Icicles.
Yslain. *See* Slain.

Yslaked. *See* Slaked.
Yspent. *See* Spent.
Yssew, d. *See* Issue, -d.
Ystabled. *See* Stabled.
Ytake. *See* Take.
Ytaught. *See* Taught.
Ythrild. *See* Thrilled.
Ythundered. *See* Thundered.
Ytold. *See* Told.
Ytorn. *See* Torn.
Ytost. *See* Tossed.
Ywandered. *See* Wandered.
Ywis. *See* Iwis.
Ywist. *See* Had-I-wist.
Ywounded. *See* Wounded.
Ywrake. *See* Wrake.
Ywrit. *See* Writ.
Ywroke, -n. *See* Wroke, -n.
Ywrought. *See* Wrought.

Z

Zeal. There must thou fashion eke a godly *zeale,* . . . . . . *Hub.* 493
  when their bootlesse *zeale* she did restrayne . . . . I. vi. 19. 8
  with constant *zele* and corage bold, ... I. viii. 40. 4
  With firie *zeale* he burnt in courage bold, ... I. ix. 37. 4
  His name was *Zele,* that him right well became: . . . . . I. x. 6. 6
  since thy faithful *zele* lets me not hyde My crime, ... III. ii. 37. 6
  With great devotion, and with little *zele:* . . . . III. ii. 48. 5
  full of firy *zele,* him followed long, ... III. iv. 45. 8
  Caried with fervent *zeale:* . . . . IV. iv. 34. 3
  fervent *zeale* Which I to him . . . did beare, ... IV. viii. 55. 2
  zeale of friends combynd with vertues meet: . . . . IV. ix. 1. 7
  flam'd with *zeale* of vengeance inwardly, ... V. i. 14. 7
  his name was called *Zele.* . . . . V. ix. 39. 4
  Strongly did *Zele* her haynous fact enforce, ... V. ix. 43. 1
  Which when as *Zele* perceived to abate, ... V. ix. 46. 7
  with constant firme intent For *zeale* of Justice, ... V. ix. 49. 5
  Then *Zele* began to urge her punishment, ... V. ix. 49. 7
  For deare affection and unfayned *zeale* . . . . VI. ii. 26. 5

Zeal—_Continued._
  to intimate Each others griefe with *zeale* affectionate, ... VI. iii. 12. 5
  spirit Is inly toucht, and humbled with meeke *zeale* . . . . *H.H.L.* 254
  and set thee all on fire With burning *zeale,* . . . . *H.H.L.* 271
Zealous. hath a *zealous* disposition To God, ... *Hub.* 491
  with fierce yre And *zealous* haste . . . . II. i. 13. 2
  Mote not mislike you also to abate Your *zealous* hast, . . . III. viii. 51. 7
  With *zelous* envy of Greekes cruell fact . . . . III. ix. 38. 5
  in their spirits kindling *zealous* fire, ... IV. x. 26. 8
  after him he ran with *zealous* haste . . . . VI. iv. 18. 6
  And learne to love, with *zealous* humble dewty, ... *H.H.B.* 20
Zephyrus. when myld *Zephyrus* emongst them blew, ... II. v. 29. 8
  sweet *Zephyrus* lowd whisteled His treble, ... II. xii. 33. 5
  Sweete-breathing *Zephyrus* did softly play . . . . *Proth.* 2
Zeuxis. All were it *Zeuxis* or Praxiteles, ... III. Pr. 2. 3
Ziffius. *See* Xiphias.
Zoilus'. Against vile *Zoilus* backbitings vaine. *Ded.Son.*xii.14